Who's Who in the West®

Published by Marquis Who's Who®

Titles in Print

Who's Who in America®
Who Was Who in America®
  Historical Volume (1607–1896)
  Volume I (1897–1942)
  Volume II (1943–1950)
  Volume III (1951–1960)
  Volume IV (1961–1968)
  Volume V (1969–1973)
  Volume VI (1974–1976)
  Volume VII (1977–1981)
  Volume VIII (1982–1985)
  Volume IX (1985–1989)
  Volume X (1989–1993)
  Volume XI (1993–1996)
  Index Volume (1607–1996)
Who's Who in the World®
Who's Who in the East®
Who's Who in the Midwest®
Who's Who in the South and Southwest®
Who's Who in the West®
Who's Who in American Art™
Who's Who in American Education®
Who's Who in American Law®
Who's Who in American Nursing®
Who's Who in American Politics™
Who's Who in Entertainment®
Who's Who in Finance and Industry®
Who's Who in Medicine and Healthcare™
Who's Who in Religion™
Who's Who in Science and Engineering®
Who's Who in the Media and Communications™
Who's Who of American Women®
Who's Who of Emerging Leaders in America®
Index to Marquis Who's Who® Publications
The *Official* ABMS Directory of Board Certified Medical Specialists®

Available on CD-ROM

The Complete Marquis Who's Who® on CD-ROM
ABMS Medical Specialists *PLUS*™

Who's Who in the West®

1998~1999

26th Edition

Including Alaska, Arizona, California, Colorado,
Hawaii, Idaho, Montana, Nevada, New Mexico,
Oregon, Utah, Washington, and Wyoming;
and in Canada, the provinces of Alberta, British
Columbia, and Saskatchewan, and the Northwest
and Yukon Territories.

MARQUIS Who's Who®   121 Chanlon Road
New Providence, NJ 07974 U.S.A.

Who's Who in the West ®

Marquis Who's Who®

Vice President & Co-publisher Sandra S. Barnes   **Vice President, Database Production & Co-publisher** Dean Hollister

Editorial & Marketing Director Paul Canning   **Research Director** Judy Redel   **Senior Managing Editor** Fred Marks

Editorial

Senior Editor	Kathleen Litzenberg
Associate Editor	Hazel Conner
Assistant Editors	Maurice Brooks
	Launa Heron
	Aries Mateo
	Francine Richardson
	Josh Samber

Editorial Services

Manager	Nadine Hovan
Supervisors	Mary Lyn Koval
	Debra Krom
Coordinator	Anne Marie Caldarola

Editorial Support

Manager	Sharon L. Gonzalez
Coordinators	J. Hector Gonzalez
	Christine Zeppi

Mail Processing

Supervisor	Kara A. Seitz
Staff	Tyrone Hines
	Cheryl A. Rodriguez
	Jill S. Terbell

Database Operations

Production Manager	Mark Van Orman
Production Editor	Matthew O'Connell

Research

Senior Managing Research Editor	Lisa Weissbard
Senior Research Editor	Robert Docherty
Associate Research Editors	Christian Loeffler
	Oscar Maldonado

Support Services

Assistant	Jeanne Danzig

Published by Marquis Who's Who, a division of Reed Elsevier Inc.

Library of Congress Catalog Card Number 49-48186

International Standard Book Number   0-8379-0928-7 (Classic Edition)
                                     0-8379-0929-5 (Deluxe Edition)

International Standard Serial Number   0083-9817

Manufactured in the United States of America

Table of Contents

Preface

The 26th Edition of *Who's Who in the West* is a compilation of biographical information on men and women of distinction whose influence is concentrated in the western region of North America. Such individuals are of reference interest locally and, to a degree, nationally.

The volume contains approximately 19,500 names from the western region of the United States including Alaska, Arizona, California, Colorado, Hawaii, Idaho, Montana, Nevada, New Mexico, Oregon, Utah, Washington, and Wyoming. Also included are the Canadian provinces of Alberta, British Columbia, and Saskatchewan, and the Northwest and Yukon Territories. In some instances, persons who do not reside in the western region of the United States or Canada have also been included as Biographees. They appear in this edition because they have made significant professional or civic contributions to this region. Reviewed, revised, and amended, the 26th Edition offers current coverage of a broad range of Westerners based on position or individual achievement.

The persons sketched in this volume represent virtually every important field of endeavor. Included are executives and officials in government, business, education, medicine, religion, the press, law, and other fields. This edition also includes significant contributors in such areas as contemporary art, music, and science.

In most cases, Biographees have furnished their own data, thus assuring a high degree of accuracy. In some cases where individuals failed to supply information, Marquis staff members compiled the data through careful, independent research. Sketches compiled in this manner are denoted by an asterisk. As in previous editions, Biographees were given the opportunity to review prepublication proofs of their sketches to make sure they were correct.

The question is often asked, "How do people get into a Marquis Who's Who volume?" Name selection is based on one fundamental principle: reference value.

Biographees of *Who's Who in the West* can be classified in two basic categories: (1) Persons who are of regional reference importance to colleagues, librarians, researchers, scholars, the media, historians, biographers, participants in business and civic affairs, and others with specific or general inquiry needs; (2) Individuals of national reference interest who are also of such regional or local importance that their inclusion in the book is essential.

In the editorial evaluation that resulted in the ultimate selection of the names appearing in this directory, an individual's desire to be listed was not sufficient reason for inclusion; rather it was the person's achievement that ruled. Similarly, neither wealth nor social position was a criterion; only occupational stature or achievement in a field within the western region of North America influenced selection.

A Professional Index is again included in *Who's Who in the West.* Within the index, each Biographee is listed by occupation, and under each occupational category, names are listed alphabetically by country, state, and city. This reference tool will make it easier than ever for interested readers to find Biographees in any given profession or location.

Marquis Who's Who editors exercise the utmost care in preparing each biographical sketch for publication. Occasionally, however, errors occur. Users of this directory are requested to draw the attention of the publisher to any errors found so that corrections can be made in a subsequent edition.

The 26th Edition of *Who's Who in the West* carries on the tradition of excellence established in 1899 with the publication of the first edition of *Who's Who in America*. The essence of that tradition is reflected in our continuing effort to produce reference works that are responsive to the needs of their users throughout the world.

Board of Advisors

Marquis Who's Who gratefully acknowledges the following distinguished individuals who have made themselves available for review, evaluation, and general comment with regard to the publication of the 26th Edition of *Who's Who in the West*. The advisors have enhanced the reference value of this edition by the nomination of outstanding individuals for inclusion. However, the Board of Advisors, either collectively or individually, is in no way responsible for the final selection of names, or for the accuracy or comprehensiveness of the biographical information or other material contained herein.

Standards of Admission

The foremost consideration in selecting Biographees for *Who's Who in the West* is the extent of an individual's reference interest. Such reference interest is judged on either of two factors: (1) the position of responsibility held, or (2) the level of achievement attained by the individual.

Admissions based on the factor of position include:

Members of the U.S. Congress

Federal judges

Governors of states covered by this volume

Premiers of Canadian provinces covered by this volume

State attorneys general

Judges of state and territorial courts of highest appellate jurisdiction

Mayors of major cities

Heads of major universities and colleges

Heads of leading philanthropic, educational, cultural, and scientific institutions and associations

Chief ecclesiastics of the principal religious denominations

Principal officers of national and international business

Admission for individual achievement is based on objective qualitative criteria. To be selected, a person must have attained conspicuous achievement.

Key to Information

[1] **ASHTON, HARDY AMES,** [2] lawyer; [3] b. Topeka, Aug. 3, 1934; [4] s. Samuel Taylor and Barbara (Hanson) A.; [5] m. Nancy Richardson, June 20, 1955; [6] children: Marilyn Ashton Heim, Barbara Anne, William Marc. [7] BA, Pa. State U., 1955; JD, Syracuse U.,1960. [8] Bar: Calif.1960, U.S. Supreme Ct. 1968. [9] Assoc. Prine, Belden and Coates, Sacramento, 1960-67; mem. Johnson, Randolph, Sikes and Bord, Sacramento, 1967—, ptnr., 1969-74, sr. ptnr., 1974—; [10] legal cons. Sacramento Urban League. [11] Author: Urban Renewal and the Law, 1975, Changes in California Zoning Laws: A Perspective, 1987. [12] Commr. Sutter County Park Dist., 1971-78; mem. planning com. Arroyo Seco Redevel. Project, Sacramento, 1980—; bd. dirs. Hargrave Inst. [13] Served with U.S. Army, 1956-57. [14] Named Man of the Yr., Sacramento C. of C., 1996. [15] Mem. ABA, Calif. Bar Assn., Sacramento Bar Assn., Am. Judicature Soc., Order of Coif. Clubs: Twelve Trees Country, Tuesday Luncheon. Lodge: Lions (Sacramento). [16] Democrat. [17] Episcopalian. [18] Home: 3080 Grant St Sacramento CA 95814 [19] Office: Johnson Randolph Sikes & Bord 10 Saint Paul St Sacramento CA 95822

KEY

[1]	Name
[2]	Occupation
[3]	Vital statistics
[4]	Parents
[5]	Marriage
[6]	Children
[7]	Education
[8]	Professional certifications
[9]	Career
[10]	Career-related
[11]	Writings and creative works
[12]	Civic and political activities
[13]	Military
[14]	Awards and fellowships
[15]	Professional and association memberships, clubs and lodges
[16]	Political affiliation
[17]	Religion
[18]	Home address
[19]	Office address

Table of Abbreviations

The following abbreviations and symbols are frequently used in this book.

*An asterisk following a sketch indicates that it was researched by the Marquis Who's Who editorial staff and has not been verified by the Biographee.

A Associate (used with academic degrees only)

AA, A.A. Associate in Arts, Associate of Arts

AAAL American Academy of Arts and Letters

AAAS American Association for the Advancement of Science

AACD American Association for Counseling and Development

AACN American Association of Critical Care Nurses

AAHA American Academy of Health Administrators

AAHP American Association of Hospital Planners

AAHPERD American Alliance for Health, Physical Education, Recreation, and Dance

AAS Associate of Applied Science

AASL American Association of School Librarians

AASPA American Association of School Personnel Administrators

AAU Amateur Athletic Union

AAUP American Association of University Professors

AAUW American Association of University Women

AB, A.B. Arts, Bachelor of

AB Alberta

ABA American Bar Association

ABC American Broadcasting Company

AC Air Corps

acad. academy, academic

acct. accountant

acctg. accounting

ACDA Arms Control and Disarmament Agency

ACHA American College of Hospital Administrators

ACLS Advanced Cardiac Life Support

ACLU American Civil Liberties Union

ACOG American College of Ob-Gyn

ACP American College of Physicians

ACS American College of Surgeons

ADA American Dental Association

a.d.c. aide-de-camp

adj. adjunct, adjutant

adj. gen. adjutant general

adm. admiral

adminstr. administrator

adminstrn. administration

adminstrv. administrative

ADN Associate's Degree in Nursing

ADP Automatic Data Processing

adv. advocate, advisory

advt. advertising

AE, A.E. Agricultural Engineer

A.E. and P. Ambassador Extraordinary and Plenipotentiary

AEC Atomic Energy Commission

aero. aeronautical, aeronautic

aerodyn. aerodynamic

AFB Air Force Base

AFL-CIO American Federation of Labor and Congress of Industrial Organizations

AFTRA American Federation of TV and Radio Artists

AFSCME American Federation of State, County and Municipal Employees

agr. agriculture

agrl. agricultural

agt. agent

AGVA American Guild of Variety Artists

agy. agency

A&I Agricultural and Industrial

AIA American Institute of Architects

AIAA American Institute of Aeronautics and Astronautics

AIChE American Institute of Chemical Engineers

AICPA American Institute of Certified Public Accountants

AID Agency for International Development

AIDS Acquired Immune Deficiency Syndrome

AIEE American Institute of Electrical Engineers

AIM American Institute of Management

AIME American Institute of Mining, Metallurgy, and Petroleum Engineers

AK Alaska

AL Alabama

ALA American Library Association

Ala. Alabama

alt. alternate

Alta. Alberta

A&M Agricultural and Mechanical

AM, A.M. Arts, Master of

Am. American, America

AMA American Medical Association

amb. ambassador

A.M.E. African Methodist Episcopal

Amtrak National Railroad Passenger Corporation

AMVETS American Veterans of World War II, Korea, Vietnam

ANA American Nurses Association

anat. anatomical

ANCC American Nurses Credentialing Center

ann. annual

ANTA American National Theatre and Academy

anthrop. anthropological

AP Associated Press

APA American Psychological Association

APGA American Personnel Guidance Association

APHA American Public Health Association

APO Army Post Office

apptd. appointed

Apr. April

apt. apartment

AR Arkansas

ARC American Red Cross

arch. architect

archeol. archeological

archtl. architectural

Ariz. Arizona

Ark. Arkansas

ArtsD, ArtsD. Arts, Doctor of

arty. artillery

AS American Samoa

AS Associate in Science

ASCAP American Society of Composers, Authors and Publishers

ASCD Association for Supervision and Curriculum Development

ASCE American Society of Civil Engineers

ASHRAE American Society of Heating, Refrigeration, and Air Conditioning Engineers

ASME American Society of Mechanical Engineers

ASNSA American Society for Nursing Service Administrators

ASPA American Society for Public Administration

ASPCA American Society for the Prevention of Cruelty to Animals

assn. association

assoc. associate

asst. assistant

ASTD American Society for Training and Development

ASTM American Society for Testing and Materials

astron. astronomical

astrophys. astrophysical

ATLA Association of Trial Lawyers of America

ATSC Air Technical Service Command

AT&T American Telephone & Telegraph Company

atty. attorney

Aug. August

AUS Army of the United States

aux. auxiliary

Ave. Avenue

AVMA American Veterinary Medical Association

AZ Arizona

AWHONN Association of Women's Health Obstetric and Neonatal Nurses

B. Bachelor

b. born

BA, B.A. Bachelor of Arts

BAgr, B.Agr. Bachelor of Agriculture

Balt. Baltimore

Bapt. Baptist

BArch, B.Arch. Bachelor of Architecture

BAS, B.A.S. Bachelor of Agricultural Science

BBA, B.B.A. Bachelor of Business Administration

BBB Better Business Bureau

BBC British Broadcasting Corporation

BC, B.C. British Columbia
BCE, B.C.E. Bachelor of Civil Engineering
BChir, B.Chir. Bachelor of Surgery
BCL, B.C.L. Bachelor of Civil Law
BCLS Basic Cardiac Life Support
BCS, B.C.S. Bachelor of Commercial Science
BD, B.D. Bachelor of Divinity
bd. board
BE, B.E. Bachelor of Education
BEE, B.E.E. Bachelor of Electrical
  Engineering
BFA, B.F.A. Bachelor of Fine Arts
bibl. biblical
bibliog. bibliographical
biog. biographical
biol. biological
BJ, B.J. Bachelor of Journalism
Bklyn. Brooklyn
BL, B.L. Bachelor of Letters
bldg. building
BLS, B.L.S. Bachelor of Library Science
BLS Basic Life Support
Blvd. Boulevard
BMI Broadcast Music, Inc.
BMW Bavarian Motor Works (Bayerische
  Motoren Werke)
bn. battalion
B.&O.R.R. Baltimore & Ohio Railroad
bot. botanical
BPE, B.P.E. Bachelor of Physical Education
BPhil, B.Phil. Bachelor of Philosophy
br. branch
BRE, B.R.E. Bachelor of Religious
  Education
brig. gen. brigadier general
Brit. British, Brittanica
Bros. Brothers
BS, B.S. Bachelor of Science
BSA, B.S.A. Bachelor of Agricultural Science
BSBA Bachelor of Science in Business
  Administration
BSChemE Bachelor of Science in Chemical
  Engineering
BSD, B.S.D. Bachelor of Didactic Science
BSEE Bachelor of Science in Electrical
  Engineering
BSN Bachelor of Science in Nursing
BST, B.S.T. Bachelor of Sacred Theology
BTh, B.Th. Bachelor of Theology
bull. bulletin
bur. bureau
bus. business
B.W.I. British West Indies

CA California
CAA Civil Aeronautics Administration
CAB Civil Aeronautics Board
CAD-CAM Computer Aided Design–
  Computer Aided Model
Calif. California
C.Am. Central America
Can. Canada, Canadian
CAP Civil Air Patrol
capt. captain
cardiol. cardiological
cardiovasc. cardiovascular
CARE Cooperative American Relief
  Everywhere
Cath. Catholic
cav. cavalry
CBC Canadian Broadcasting Company
CBI China, Burma, India Theatre of
  Operations
CBS Columbia Broadcasting Company
C.C. Community College
CCC Commodity Credit Corporation
CCNY City College of New York

CCRN Critical Care Registered Nurse
CCU Cardiac Care Unit
CD Civil Defense
CE, C.E. Corps of Engineers, Civil Engineer
CEN Certified Emergency Nurse
CENTO Central Treaty Organization
CEO chief executive officer
CERN European Organization of Nuclear
  Research
cert. certificate, certification, certified
CETA Comprehensive Employment Training
  Act
CFA Chartered Financial Analyst
CFL Canadian Football League
CFO chief financial officer
CFP Certified Financial Planner
ch. church
ChD, Ch.D. Doctor of Chemistry
chem. chemical
ChemE, Chem.E. Chemical Engineer
ChFC Chartered Financial Consultant
Chgo. Chicago
chirurg. chirurgical
chmn. chairman
chpt. chapter
CIA Central Intelligence Agency
Cin. Cincinnati
cir. circle, circuit
CLE Continuing Legal Education
Cleve. Cleveland
climatol. climatological
clin. clinical
clk. clerk
C.L.U. Chartered Life Underwriter
CM, C.M. Master in Surgery
CM Northern Mariana Islands
CMA Certified Medical Assistant
cmty. community
CNA Certified Nurse's Aide
CNOR Certified Nurse (Operating Room)
C.&N.W.Ry. Chicago & North Western
  Railway
CO Colorado
Co. Company
COF Catholic Order of Foresters
C. of C. Chamber of Commerce
col. colonel
coll. college
Colo. Colorado
com. committee
comd. commanded
comdg. commanding
comdr. commander
comdt. commandant
comm. communications
commd. commissioned
comml. commercial
commn. commission
commr. commissioner
compt. comptroller
condr. conductor
Conf. Conference
Congl. Congregational, Congressional
Conglist. Congregationalist
Conn. Connecticut
cons. consultant, consulting
consol. consolidated
constl. constitutional
constn. constitution
constrn. construction
contbd. contributed
contbg. contributing
contbn. contribution
contbr. contributor
contr. controller
Conv. Convention
COO chief operating officer

coop. cooperative
coord. coordinator
CORDS Civil Operations and Revolutionary
  Development Support
CORE Congress of Racial Equality
corp. corporation, corporate
corr. correspondent, corresponding,
  correspondence
C.&O.Ry. Chesapeake & Ohio Railway
coun. council
CPA Certified Public Accountant
CPCU Chartered Property and Casualty
  Underwriter
CPH, C.P.H. Certificate of Public Health
cpl. corporal
CPR Cardio-Pulmonary Resuscitation
C.P.Ry. Canadian Pacific Railway
CRT Cathode Ray Terminal
C.S. Christian Science
CSB, C.S.B. Bachelor of Christian Science
C.S.C. Civil Service Commission
CT Connecticut
ct. court
ctr. center
ctrl. central
CWS Chemical Warfare Service
C.Z. Canal Zone

D. Doctor
d. daughter
DAgr, D.Agr. Doctor of Agriculture
DAR Daughters of the American Revolution
dau. daughter
DAV Disabled American Veterans
DC, D.C. District of Columbia
DCL, D.C.L. Doctor of Civil Law
DCS, D.C.S. Doctor of Commercial Science
DD, D.D. Doctor of Divinity
DDS, D.D.S. Doctor of Dental Surgery
DE Delaware
Dec. December
dec. deceased
def. defense
Del. Delaware
del. delegate, delegation
Dem. Democrat, Democratic
DEng, D.Eng. Doctor of Engineering
denom. denomination, denominational
dep. deputy
dept. department
dermatol. dermatological
desc. descendant
devel. development, developmental
DFA, D.F.A. Doctor of Fine Arts
D.F.C. Distinguished Flying Cross
DHL, D.H.L. Doctor of Hebrew Literature
dir. director
dist. district
distbg. distributing
distbn. distribution
distbr. distributor
disting. distinguished
div. division, divinity, divorce
divsn. division
DLitt, D.Litt. Doctor of Literature
DMD, D.M.D. Doctor of Dental Medicine
DMS, D.M.S. Doctor of Medical Science
DO, D.O. Doctor of Osteopathy
docs. documents
DON Director of Nursing
DPH, D.P.H. Diploma in Public Health
DPhil, D.Phil. Doctor of Philosophy
D.R. Daughters of the Revolution
Dr. Drive, Doctor
DRE, D.R.E. Doctor of Religious Education
DrPH, Dr.P.H. Doctor of Public Health,
  Doctor of Public Hygiene
D.S.C. Distinguished Service Cross

DSc, D.Sc. Doctor of Science
DSChemE Doctor of Science in Chemical Engineering
D.S.M. Distinguished Service Medal
DST, D.S.T. Doctor of Sacred Theology
DTM, D.T.M. Doctor of Tropical Medicine
DVM, D.V.M. Doctor of Veterinary Medicine
DVS, D.V.S. Doctor of Veterinary Surgery

E, E. East
ea. eastern
E. and P. Extraordinary and Plenipotentiary
Eccles. Ecclesiastical
ecol. ecological
econ. economic
ECOSOC Economic and Social Council (of the UN)
ED, E.D. Doctor of Engineering
ed. educated
EdB, Ed.B. Bachelor of Education
EdD, Ed.D. Doctor of Education
edit. edition
editl. editorial
EdM, Ed.M. Master of Education
edn. education
ednl. educational
EDP Electronic Data Processing
EdS, Ed.S. Specialist in Education
EE, E.E. Electrical Engineer
E.E. and M.P. Envoy Extraordinary and Minister Plenipotentiary
EEC European Economic Community
EEG Electroencephalogram
EEO Equal Employment Opportunity
EEOC Equal Employment Opportunity Commission
E.Ger. German Democratic Republic
EKG Electrocardiogram
elec. electrical
electrochem. electrochemical
electrophys. electrophysical
elem. elementary
EM, E.M. Engineer of Mines
EMT Emergency Medical Technician
ency. encyclopedia
Eng. England
engr. engineer
engring. engineering
entomol. entomological
environ. environmental
EPA Environmental Protection Agency
epidemiol. epidemiological
Episc. Episcopalian
ERA Equal Rights Amendment
ERDA Energy Research and Development Administration
ESEA Elementary and Secondary Education Act
ESL English as Second Language
ESPN Entertainment and Sports Programming Network
ESSA Environmental Science Services Administration
ethnol. ethnological
ETO European Theatre of Operations
Evang. Evangelical
exam. examination, examining
Exch. Exchange
exec. executive
exhbn. exhibition
expdn. expedition
expn. exposition
expt. experiment
exptl. experimental
Expy. Expressway
Ext. Extension

F.A. Field Artillery
FAA Federal Aviation Administration
FAO Food and Agriculture Organization (of the UN)
FBA Federal Bar Association
FBI Federal Bureau of Investigation
FCA Farm Credit Administration
FCC Federal Communications Commission
FCDA Federal Civil Defense Administration
FDA Food and Drug Administration
FDIA Federal Deposit Insurance Administration
FDIC Federal Deposit Insurance Corporation
FE, F.E. Forest Engineer
FEA Federal Energy Administration
Feb. February
fed. federal
fedn. federation
FERC Federal Energy Regulatory Commission
fgn. foreign
FHA Federal Housing Administration
fin. financial, finance
FL Florida
Fl. Floor
Fla. Florida
FMC Federal Maritime Commission
FNP Family Nurse Practitioner
FOA Foreign Operations Administration
found. foundation
FPC Federal Power Commission
FPO Fleet Post Office
frat. fraternity
FRS Federal Reserve System
FSA Federal Security Agency
Ft. Fort
FTC Federal Trade Commission
Fwy. Freeway

G-1 (or other number) Division of General Staff
GA, Ga. Georgia
GAO General Accounting Office
gastroent. gastroenterological
GATE Gifted and Talented Educators
GATT General Agreement on Tariffs and Trade
GE General Electric Company
gen. general
geneal. genealogical
geod. geodetic
geog. geographic, geographical
geol. geological
geophys. geophysical
geriat. geriatrics
gerontol. gerontological
G.H.Q. General Headquarters
GM General Motors Corporation
GMAC General Motors Acceptance Corporation
G.N.Ry. Great Northern Railway
gov. governor
govt. government
govtl. governmental
GPO Government Printing Office
grad. graduate, graduated
GSA General Services Administration
Gt. Great
GTE General Telephone and ElectricCompany
GU Guam
gynecol. gynecological

HBO Home Box Office
hdqs. headquarters

HEW Department of Health, Education and Welfare
HHD, H.H.D. Doctor of Humanities
HHFA Housing and Home Finance Agency
HHS Department of Health and Human Services
HI Hawaii
hist. historical, historic
HM, H.M. Master of Humanities
HMO Health Maintenance Organization
homeo. homeopathic
hon. honorary, honorable
Ho. of Dels. House of Delegates
Ho. of Reps. House of Representatives
hort. horticultural
hosp. hospital
H.S. High School
HUD Department of Housing and Urban Development
Hwy. Highway
hydrog. hydrographic

IA Iowa
IAEA International Atomic Energy Agency
IATSE International Alliance of Theatrical and Stage Employees and Moving Picture Operators of the United States and Canada
IBM International Business Machines Corporation
IBRD International Bank for Reconstruction and Development
ICA International Cooperation Administration
ICC Interstate Commerce Commission
ICCE International Council for Computers in Education
ICU Intensive Care Unit
ID Idaho
IEEE Institute of Electrical and Electronics Engineers
IFC International Finance Corporation
IGY International Geophysical Year
IL Illinois
Ill. Illinois
illus. illustrated
ILO International Labor Organization
IMF International Monetary Fund
IN Indiana
Inc. Incorporated
Ind. Indiana
ind. independent
Indpls. Indianapolis
indsl. industrial
inf. infantry
info. information
ins. insurance
insp. inspector
insp. gen. inspector general
inst. institute
instl. institutional
instn. institution
instr. instructor
instrn. instruction
instrnl. instructional
internat. international
intro. introduction
IRE Institute of Radio Engineers
IRS Internal Revenue Service
ITT International Telephone & Telegraph Corporation

JAG Judge Advocate General
JAGC Judge Advocate General Corps
Jan. January
Jaycees Junior Chamber of Commerce
JB, J.B. Jurum Baccalaureus

JCB, J.C.B. Juris Canoni Baccalaureus
JCD, J.C.D. Juris Canonici Doctor, Juris
   Civilis Doctor
JCL, J.C.L. Juris Canonici Licentiatus
JD, J.D. Juris Doctor
jg. junior grade
jour. journal
jr. junior
JSD, J.S.D. Juris Scientiae Doctor
JUD, J.U.D. Juris Utriusque Doctor
jud. judicial

Kans. Kansas
K.C. Knights of Columbus
K.P. Knights of Pythias
KS Kansas
K.T. Knight Templar
KY, Ky. Kentucky

LA, La. Louisiana
L.A. Los Angeles
lab. laboratory
L.Am. Latin America
lang. language
laryngol. laryngological
LB Labrador
LDS Latter Day Saints
LDS Church Church of Jesus Christ of Latter
   Day Saints
lectr. lecturer
legis. legislation, legislative
LHD, L.H.D. Doctor of Humane Letters
L.I. Long Island
libr. librarian, library
lic. licensed, license
L.I.R.R. Long Island Railroad
lit. literature
litig. litigation
LittB, Litt.B. Bachelor of Letters
LittD, Litt.D. Doctor of Letters
LLB, LL.B. Bachelor of Laws
LLD, L.L.D. Doctor of Laws
LLM, L.L.M. Master of Laws
Ln. Lane
L.&N.R.R. Louisville & Nashville Railroad
LPGA Ladies Professional Golf Association
LPN Licensed Practical Nurse
LS, L.S. Library Science (in degree)
lt. lieutenant
Ltd. Limited
Luth. Lutheran
LWV League of Women Voters

M. Master
m. married
MA, M.A. Master of Arts
MA Massachusetts
MADD Mothers Against Drunk Driving
mag. magazine
MAgr, M.Agr. Master of Agriculture
maj. major
Man. Manitoba
Mar. March
MArch, M.Arch. Master in Architecture
Mass. Massachusetts
math. mathematics, mathematical
MATS Military Air Transport Service
MB, M.B. Bachelor of Medicine
MB Manitoba
MBA, M.B.A. Master of Business
   Administration
MBS Mutual Broadcasting System
M.C. Medical Corps
MCE, M.C.E. Master of Civil Engineering
mcht. merchant
mcpl. municipal
MCS, M.C.S. Master of Commercial Science

MD, M.D. Doctor of Medicine
MD, Md. Maryland
MDiv Master of Divinity
MDip, M.Dip. Master in Diplomacy
mdse. merchandise
MDV, M.D.V. Doctor of Veterinary
   Medicine
ME, M.E. Mechanical Engineer
ME Maine
M.E.Ch. Methodist Episcopal Church
mech. mechanical
MEd., M.Ed. Master of Education
med. medical
MEE, M.E.E. Master of Electrical
   Engineering
mem. member
meml. memorial
merc. mercantile
met. metropolitan
metall. metallurgical
MetE, Met.E. Metallurgical Engineer
meteorol. meteorological
Meth. Methodist
Mex. Mexico
MF, M.F. Master of Forestry
MFA, M.F.A. Master of Fine Arts
mfg. manufacturing
mfr. manufacturer
mgmt. management
mgr. manager
MHA, M.H.A. Master of Hospital
   Administration
M.I. Military Intelligence
MI Michigan
Mich. Michigan
micros. microscopic, microscopical
mid. middle
mil. military
Milw. Milwaukee
Min. Minister
mineral. mineralogical
Minn. Minnesota
MIS Management Information Systems
Miss. Mississippi
MIT Massachusetts Institute of Technology
mktg. marketing
ML, M.L. Master of Laws
MLA Modern Language Association
M.L.D. Magister Legnum Diplomatic
MLitt, M.Litt. Master of Literature, Master
   of Letters
MLS, M.L.S. Master of Library Science
MME, M.M.E. Master of Mechanical
   Engineering
MN Minnesota
mng. managing
MO, Mo. Missouri
moblzn. mobilization
Mont. Montana
MP Northern Mariana Islands
M.P. Member of Parliament
MPA Master of Public Administration
MPE, M.P.E. Master of Physical Education
MPH, M.P.H. Master of Public Health
MPhil, M.Phil. Master of Philosophy
MPL, M.P.L. Master of Patent Law
Mpls. Minneapolis
MRE, M.R.E. Master of Religious Education
MRI Magnetic Resonance Imaging
MS, M.S. Master of Science
MS, Ms. Mississippi
MSc, M.Sc. Master of Science
MSChemE Master of Science in Chemical
   Engineering
MSEE Master of Science in Electrical
   Engineering

MSF, M.S.F. Master of Science of Forestry
MSN Master of Science in Nursing
MST, M.S.T. Master of Sacred Theology
MSW, M.S.W. Master of Social Work
MT Montana
Mt. Mount
MTO Mediterranean Theatre of Operation
MTV Music Television
mus. museum, musical
MusB, Mus.B. Bachelor of Music
MusD, Mus.D. Doctor of Music
MusM, Mus.M. Master of Music
mut. mutual
MVP Most Valuable Player
mycol. mycological

N. North
NAACOG Nurses Association of the
   American College of Obstetricians and
   Gynecologists
NAACP National Association for the
   Advancement of Colored People
NACA National Advisory Committee for
   Aeronautics
NACDL National Association of Criminal
   Defense Lawyers
NACU National Association of Colleges and
   Universities
NAD National Academy of Design
NAE National Academy of Engineering,
   National Association of Educators
NAESP National Association of Elementary
   School Principals
NAFE National Association of Female
   Executives
N.Am. North America
NAM National Association of Manufacturers
NAMH National Association for Mental
   Health
NAPA National Association of Performing
   Artists
NARAS National Academy of Recording
   Arts and Sciences
NAREB National Association of Real Estate
   Boards
NARS National Archives and Record Service
NAS National Academy of Sciences
NASA National Aeronautics and Space
   Administration
NASP National Association of School
   Psychologists
NASW National Association of Social
   Workers
nat. national
NATAS National Academy of Television
   Arts and Sciences
NATO North Atlantic Treaty Organization
NATOUSA North African Theatre of
   Operations, United States Army
nav. navigation
NB, N.B. New Brunswick
NBA National Basketball Association
NBC National Broadcasting Company
NC, N.C. North Carolina
NCAA National College Athletic Association
NCCJ National Conference of Christians and
   Jews
ND, N.D. North Dakota
NDEA National Defense Education Act
NE Nebraska
NE, N.E. Northeast
NEA National Education Association
Nebr. Nebraska
NEH National Endowment for Humanities
neurol. neurological
Nev. Nevada
NF Newfoundland

NFL National Football League
Nfld. Newfoundland
NG National Guard
NH, N.H. New Hampshire
NHL National Hockey League
NIH National Institutes of Health
NIMH National Institute of Mental Health
NJ, N.J. New Jersey
NLRB National Labor Relations Board
NM New Mexico
N.Mex. New Mexico
No. Northern
NOAA National Oceanographic and
    Atmospheric Administration
NORAD North America Air Defense
Nov. November
NOW National Organization for Women
N.P.Ry. Northern Pacific Railway
nr. near
NRA National Rifle Association
NRC National Research Council
NS, N.S. Nova Scotia
NSC National Security Council
NSF National Science Foundation
NSTA National Science Teachers Association
NSW New South Wales
N.T. New Testament
NT Northwest Territories
nuc. nuclear
numis. numismatic
NV Nevada
NW, N.W. Northwest
N.W.T. Northwest Territories
NY, N.Y. New York
N.Y.C. New York City
NYU New York University
N.Z. New Zealand

OAS Organization of American States
ob-gyn obstetrics-gynecology
obs. observatory
obstet. obstetrical
occupl. occupational
oceanog. oceanographic
Oct. October
OD, O.D. Doctor of Optometry
OECD Organization for Economic
    Cooperation and Development
OEEC Organization of European Economic
    Cooperation
OEO Office of Economic Opportunity
ofcl. official
OH Ohio
OK Oklahoma
Okla. Oklahoma
ON Ontario
Ont. Ontario
oper. operating
ophthal. ophthalmological
ops. operations
OR Oregon
orch. orchestra
Oreg. Oregon
orgn. organization
orgnl. organizational
ornithol. ornithological
orthop. orthopedic
OSHA Occupational Safety and Health
    Administration
OSRD Office of Scientific Research and
    Development
OSS Office of Strategic Services
osteo. osteopathic
otol. otological
otolaryn. otolaryngological

PA, Pa. Pennsylvania

P.A. Professional Association
paleontol. paleontological
path. pathological
PBS Public Broadcasting System
P.C. Professional Corporation
PE Prince Edward Island
pediat. pediatrics
P.E.I. Prince Edward Island
PEN Poets, Playwrights, Editors, Essayists
    and Novelists (international association)
penol. penological
P.E.O. women's organization (full name not
    disclosed)
pers. personnel
pfc. private first class
PGA Professional Golfers' Association of
    America
PHA Public Housing Administration
pharm. pharmaceutical
PharmD, Pharm.D. Doctor of Pharmacy
PharmM, Pharm.M. Master of Pharmacy
PhB, Ph.B. Bachelor of Philosophy
PhD, Ph.D. Doctor of Philosophy
PhDChemE Doctor of Science in Chemical
    Engineering
PhM, Ph.M. Master of Philosophy
Phila. Philadelphia
philharm. philharmonic
philol. philological
philos. philosophical
photog. photographic
phys. physical
physiol. physiological
Pitts. Pittsburgh
Pk. Park
Pky. Parkway
Pl. Place
P.&L.E.R.R. Pittsburgh & Lake Erie
    Railroad
Plz. Plaza
PNP Pediatric Nurse Practitioner
P.O. Post Office
PO Box Post Office Box
polit. political
poly. polytechnic, polytechnical
PQ Province of Quebec
PR, P.R. Puerto Rico
prep. preparatory
pres. president
Presbyn. Presbyterian
presdl. presidential
prin. principal
procs. proceedings
prod. produced (play production)
prodn. production
prodr. producer
prof. professor
profl. professional
prog. progressive
propr. proprietor
pros. atty. prosecuting attorney
pro tem. pro tempore
PSRO Professional Services Review
    Organization
psychiat. psychiatric
psychol. psychological
PTA Parent-Teachers Association
ptnr. partner
PTO Pacific Theatre of Operations, Parent
    Teacher Organization
pub. publisher, publishing, published
pub. public
publ. publication
pvt. private

quar. quarterly
qm. quartermaster

Q.M.C. Quartermaster Corps
Que. Quebec

radiol. radiological
RAF Royal Air Force
RCA Radio Corporation of America
RCAF Royal Canadian Air Force
RD Rural Delivery
Rd. Road
R&D Research & Development
REA Rural Electrification Administration
rec. recording
ref. reformed
regt. regiment
regtl. regimental
rehab. rehabilitation
rels. relations
Rep. Republican
rep. representative
Res. Reserve
ret. retired
Rev. Reverend
rev. review, revised
RFC Reconstruction Finance Corporation
RFD Rural Free Delivery
rhinol. rhinological
RI, R.I. Rhode Island
RISD Rhode Island School of Design
Rlwy. Railway
Rm. Room
RN, R.N. Registered Nurse
roentgenol. roentgenological
ROTC Reserve Officers Training Corps
RR Rural Route
R.R. Railroad
rsch. research
rschr. researcher
Rt. Route

S. South
s. son
SAC Strategic Air Command
SAG Screen Actors Guild
SALT Strategic Arms Limitation Talks
S.Am. South America
san. sanitary
SAR Sons of the American Revolution
Sask. Saskatchewan
savs. savings
SB, S.B. Bachelor of Science
SBA Small Business Administration
SC, S.C. South Carolina
SCAP Supreme Command Allies Pacific
ScB, Sc.B. Bachelor of Science
SCD, S.C.D. Doctor of Commercial Science
ScD, Sc.D. Doctor of Science
sch. school
sci. science, scientific
SCLC Southern Christian Leadership
Conference
SCV Sons of Confederate Veterans
SD, S.D. South Dakota
SE, S.E. Southeast
SEATO Southeast Asia Treaty Organization
SEC Securities and Exchange Commission
sec. secretary
sect. section
seismol. seismological
sem. seminary
Sept. September
s.g. senior grade
sgt. sergeant
SHAEF Supreme Headquarters Allied
    Expeditionary Forces
SHAPE Supreme Headquarters Allied Powers
    in Europe
S.I. Staten Island

S.J. Society of Jesus (Jesuit)
SJD Scientiae Juridicae Doctor
SK Saskatchewan
SM, S.M. Master of Science
SNP Society of Nursing Professionals
So. Southern
soc. society
sociol. sociological
S.P.Co. Southern Pacific Company
spkr. speaker
spl. special
splty. specialty
Sq. Square
S.R. Sons of the Revolution
sr. senior
SS Steamship
SSS Selective Service System
St. Saint, Street
sta. station
stats. statistics
statis. statistical
STB, S.T.B. Bachelor of Sacred Theology
stblzn. stabilization
STD, S.T.D. Doctor of Sacred Theology
std. standard
Ste. Suite
subs. subsidiary
SUNY State University of New York
supr. supervisor
supt. superintendent
surg. surgical
svc. service
SW, S.W. Southwest
sys. system

TAPPI Technical Association of the Pulp and Paper Industry
tb. tuberculosis
tchg. teaching
tchr. teacher
tech. technical, technology
technol. technological
tel. telephone
Tel. & Tel. Telephone & Telegraph
telecom. telecommunications
temp. temporary
Tenn. Tennessee
Ter. Territory
Ter. Terrace
TESOL Teachers of English to Speakers of Other Languages
Tex. Texas
ThD, Th.D. Doctor of Theology
theol. theological

ThM, Th.M. Master of Theology
TN Tennessee
tng. training
topog. topographical
trans. transaction, transferred
transl. translation, translated
transp. transportation
treas. treasurer
TT Trust Territory
TV television
TVA Tennessee Valley Authority
TWA Trans World Airlines
twp. township
TX Texas
typog. typographical

U. University
UAW United Auto Workers
UCLA University of California at Los Angeles
UDC United Daughters of the Confederacy
U.K. United Kingdom
UN United Nations
UNESCO United Nations Educational, Scientific and Cultural Organization
UNICEF United Nations International Children's Emergency Fund
univ. university
UNRRA United Nations Relief and Rehabilitation Administration
UPI United Press International
U.P.R.R. United Pacific Railroad
urol. urological
U.S. United States
U.S.A. United States of America
USAAF United States Army Air Force
USAF United States Air Force
USAFR United States Air Force Reserve
USAR United States Army Reserve
USCG United States Coast Guard
USCGR United States Coast Guard Reserve
USES United States Employment Service
USIA United States Information Agency
USMC United States Marine Corps
USMCR United States Marine Corps Reserve
USN United States Navy
USNG United States National Guard
USNR United States Naval Reserve
USO United Service Organizations
USPHS United States Public Health Service
USS United States Ship
USSR Union of the Soviet Socialist Republics
USTA United States Tennis Association

USV United States Volunteers
UT Utah

VA Veterans Administration
VA, Va. Virginia
vet. veteran, veterinary
VFW Veterans of Foreign Wars
VI, V.I. Virgin Islands
vice pres. vice president
vis. visiting
VISTA Volunteers in Service to America
VITA Volunteers in Technical Assistance
vocat. vocational
vol. volunteer, volume
v.p. vice president
vs. versus
VT, Vt. Vermont

W, W. West
WA Washington (state)
WAC Women's Army Corps
Wash. Washington (state)
WATS Wide Area Telecommunications Service
WAVES Women's Reserve, US Naval Reserve
WCTU Women's Christian Temperance Union
we. western
W. Ger. Germany, Federal Republic of
WHO World Health Organization
WI Wisconsin
W.I. West Indies
Wis. Wisconsin
WSB Wage Stabilization Board
WV West Virginia
W.Va. West Virginia
WWI World War I
WWII World War II
WY Wyoming
Wyo. Wyoming

YK Yukon Territory
YMCA Young Men's Christian Association
YMHA Young Men's Hebrew Association
YM & YWHA Young Men's and Young Women's Hebrew Association
yr. year
YT, Y.T. Yukon Territory
YWCA Young Women's Christian Association

zool. zoological

Alphabetical Practices

Names are arranged alphabetically according to the surnames, and under identical surnames according to the first given name. If both surname and first given name are identical, names are arranged alphabetically according to the second given name.

Surnames beginning with De, Des, Du, however capitalized or spaced, are recorded with the prefix preceding the surname and arranged alphabetically under the letter D.

Surnames beginning with Mac and Mc are arranged alphabetically under M.

Surnames beginning with Saint or St. appear after names that begin Sains, and are arranged according to the second part of the name, e.g. St. Clair before Saint Dennis.

Surnames beginning with Van, Von, or von are arranged alphabetically under the letter V.

Compound surnames are arranged according to the first member of the compound.

Many hyphenated Arabic names begin Al-, El-, or al-. These names are alphabetized according to each Biographee's designation of last name. Thus Al-Bahar, Neta may be listed either under Al- or under Bahar, depending on the preference of the listee.

Also, Arabic names have a variety of possible spellings when transposed to English. Spelling of these names is always based on the practice of the Biographee. Some Biographees use a Western form of word order, while others prefer the Arabic word sequence.

Similarly, Asian names may have no comma between family and given names, but some Biographees have chosen to add the comma. In each case, punctuation follows the preference of the Biographee.

Parentheses used in connection with a name indicate which part of the full name is usually deleted in common usage. Hence Chambers, E(lizabeth) Anne indicates that the usual form of the given name is E. Anne. In such a case, the parentheses are ignored in alphabetizing and the name would be arranged as Chambers, Elizabeth Anne. However, if the name is recorded Chambers, (Elizabeth) Anne, signifying that the entire name Elizabeth is not commonly used, the alphabetizing would be arranged as though the name were Chambers, Anne. If an entire middle or last name is enclosed in parentheses, that portion of the name is used in the alphabetical arrangement. Hence Chambers, Elizabeth (Anne) would be arranged as Chambers, Elizabeth Anne.

Where more than one spelling, word order, or name of an individual is frequently encountered, the sketch has been entered under the form preferred by the Biographee, with cross-references under alternate forms.

Who'sWho in the West®

Biographies

AADAHL, JORG, business executive; b. Trondheim, Norway, June 16, 1937; came to U.S., 1966; s. Ottar P. and Gurli (Lockra) A.; MS in Mech. Engring., Tech. U. Norway, 1961; MBA, U. San Francisco, 1973; m. Inger R. Holst, July 13, 1973; children: Erik, Nina. Rsch. fellow Tech. U. Norway, Trondheim, 1961-62; mgr. arc welding devel. NAG, Oslo, 1964-66; mfg. engr. Varian Assocs., Palo Alto, Calif., 1966-67; sr. tech. writerLynch Comm. Sys., 1967-69; indsl. engr., project mgr., 1969-74, bus. mgr. United Airlines, San Francisco, 1974-75, sr. systems analyst, 1976-81; strategic planning specialist Magnex Corp., San Jose, 1981-82; cons. in mgmt., 1982-84; founder, pres. Safeware, Inc., San Mateo, Calif., 1984—; founder, prin. CampuSafe Sys., 1996—; dir. Safeware Sys.Ltd., U.K., 1990—. Developer Safechem Hazardous Chem. Mgmt. Sys. Recipient Cert. of Honor, San Francisco Bd. Suprs., 1973. Mem. Leif Erikson League (pres. 1973), Norwegian Soc. Profl. Engrs. Club: Young Scandinavians (v.p. 1971), Environment and Safety Data Exch. (founding mem., dir.). Author: Strength Analysis, Welded Structures, 1967; contbr. articles in various fields to profl. jours.; editor Nordic Highlights, 1972. Office: Safeware Inc PO Box 6745 2575 Flores St San Mateo CA 94403

AAGAARD, EARLA GARDNER, retired psychiatrist; b. Java, Dec. 5, 1922; came to U.S., 1937; d. J. Earl and Ethel (Swing) Gardner; m. Carl M.J. Aagaard, Mar. 13, 1943; children: Carla, Earl, Victor, Lola. BA, Pacific Union Coll., 1941; MD, Loma Linda U., 1945. Intern L.A. County Gen. Hosp., 1945-46; resident Childrens Hosp., San Francisco, 1947-48, Mendocino State Hosp., Talmage, Calif., 1949-52, Langley-Porder Clinic, San Francisco, 1952-54; pvt. practice psychiatry Ukiah, Calif., 1955-96; ret., 1996. Mem. Am. Psychiat. Assn. (life).

AALTO, MADELEINE, library director. BA, Wellesley Coll., 1964; BLS, U. Toronto, 1967. Clerical asst. Toronto Pub. Libr., 1964-66, children's libr. Parkdale br., 1968-69, collection libr. Spaced Out libr., 1969-73, br. head Annette St. br., 1973-74, coord. adult svcs., 1974-75; chief libr. East York Pub. Libr., 1975-84, Greater Victoria Pub. Libr., 1984-88; dir. Vancouver (B.C.) Pub. Libr., Can., 1988—. Contbr. intro. to A Geography for Children (Philippe du Fresnoy), 1968. Recipient Commerative medal 125th Anniversary Confederation Can., 1993. Mem. B.C. Libr. Assn. Office: Vancouver Pub Libr, 350 W Georgia St, Vancouver, BC Canada V6B 6B1

AARESTAD, NORMAN O., radiologist; b. Minot, N.D., Nov. 19, 1933; s. Gerhard and Gustava (Lee) A.; m. Margaret Anne Helling, Aug. 21, 1966; children: David, Tor. BA, Concordia Coll., Moorhead, Minn., 1955; BS in Medicine, U. N.D., 1957; MD, Harvard U., Boston, 1959; MS in Radiologic Biology, U. Rochester, 1966. Diplomate Am. Bd. Radiology. Intern U. Oreg. Med. Sch. Hosp. and Clinics, Portland, 1959-60, resident, 1960-63; asst. chief radiation oncology Walter Reed Med. Ctr., Washington, 1968-69; chief radiation oncology Letterman Gen. Hosp., San Francisco, 1969-71, St. Luke's Hosp., Denver, 1971-89; med. dir. M.R. Hart Regional Radiation Ctr., Boulder, Colo., 1988-93; med. dir. radiation oncology Swedish Med. Ctr., Englewood, Colo., 1992—; med. dir. radiation oncology Columbia (Colo. divsn.), Denver, 1994—, chmn. oncology adv. bd., 1995—; chmn. cancer com. Swedish Med. Ctr., 1993—; med. advisor radiation oncology therapy tng. program Cmty. Coll. Denver, 1985—. Mem. exec. com., pres. Colo. divsn. Am. Cancer Soc., Denver, 1973—; bd. dirs. Marie Droste Svcs., Denver, 1992—, Ebenezer Luth. Health, brush, Colo., 1990—, also v.p.; pres. Augustana Found., Denver, 1992—. Lt. col. U.S. Army, 1963-71. Fellow Am. Coll. Radiology; mem. AMA, Am. Soc. Therapeutic Radiation Oncology, Am. Coll. Radiation Oncology, Internat. Soc. Stereotactic Radiosurgery, Arapahoe Med. Soc., Colo. Med. Soc. (del. 1994-96). Lutheran. Office: 799 E Hampden Ave Ste 100 Englewood CO 80110

AARON, BUD, systems analyst; b. White Sulphur Springs, Mont., Apr. 27, 1927; m. Dina Aaron, Jan. 10, 1960; children: Alex, Roy, Erica, Bill. Owner Microkits, 1963-67; prodn. mgr. Ednl. Computer Products, 1967-68, mfg. rep., 1968-69; instr. Control Data Inst., 1969-70; supr. ICL, Kidsgrove, England, 1970-73; tech. writer Philips Small Computers, Fontenay aux Rose, France, 1973-74; designer, developer computer programs Hughes, JPL. Lawrence Livermore Labs. and others, 1974-76; programmer, mgr., sales BusinessMaster, Carlsbad, Calif., 1976-86; mgr., writer, programmer CheckMaster Corp., Oceanside, Calif., 1986—.

AARON, ROY HENRY, lawyer, arbitrator, business consultant; b. Los Angeles, Apr. 8, 1929; s. Samuel Arthur and Natalie (Krakauer) A.; m. Theresa Gesas, Dec. 20, 1953; 1 child, Jill. BA, U. Calif.-Berkeley, 1951; LLB, U. So. Calif., 1956. Bar: Calif. 1957. Mem. Pacht, Ross, Warne, Bernhard & Sears, Inc., L.A., 1957-79, of counsel, 1979-83; sr. v.p., gen. counsel Plitt Theatres, Inc. and Plitt Theatre Holdings, Inc., L.A., 1978-80, pres., COO, 1980-85; pres. Plitt Entertainment Group, Inc., L.A., 1985—; pres., chief exec. officer Showscan Corp., L.A., 1985-93; lectr. Calif. Continuing Edn. of Bar; lectr. continuing legal edn. Loyola U. Law Sch., Los Angeles. Mem. editorial bd. U. So. Calif. Law Rev., 1954-56. Trustee, mem. exec. com. Vista Del Mar Child-Care Svc., 1968-80, Reiss-Davis Child Study Ctr., 1977-80, Plitt So. Theaters Inc., Employees Trust; bd. dirs. Rape Found.; mem. adv. bd. dirs. Rape Treatment Ctr. of Santa Monica, UCLA Med. Ctr.; pres. UCLA Royce Two Seventy, 1986-88; mem. UCLA Bd. Visitors, UCLA Found., pres. 1996—, bd. dirs., trustee. Fellow Am. Bar Found. (life), L.A. County Bar Found. (life); mem. ABA, State Bar Calif., L.A. County Bar Assn. (trustee 1977-83, v.p. 1979-80, sr. v.p. 1980-81, pres.-elect 1982-83, pres. 1982-83, Shattuck-Price Meml. award 1996), U. Calif.-Berkeley Alumni Assn., UCLA Alumni Assn., Found. Motion Pictures Pioneers (bd. dirs.), So. Calif. Tennis Assn. (bd. dirs.).

ABANES, RICHARD JAMES, freelance journalist, religion writer; b. Portsmouth, Va., Oct. 13, 1961; s. Albert F. and Delores Abanes; m. Evangeline B. Kim, Dec. 7, 1985. Religion rschr. Christian Rsch. Inst., Irvine, Calif., 1989-94; freelance journalist, Rancho Santa Margarita, Calif., 1994—; mem. editl. adv. bd. Skeptic Soc., Altadana, Calif., 1996—. Co-author: Prophets of the Apocalypse: David Koresh and Other American Messiahs, 1994; author: Embraced by the Light and the Bible, 1994, The Less Traveled Road and the Bible, 1995, Journey into the Light: Exploring Near Death Experiences, 1996, American Militias: Rebellion, Racism and Religion, 1996; contbr. articles to religious jours. and mags. Mem. Evang. Press Assn., Investigative Reports and Editors, Soc. Profl. Journalists. Evangelical. Office: Religious Info Ctr PO Box 80961 Rancho Santa Margarita CA 92688

ABARBANELL, GAYOLA HAVENS, financial planner; b. Chgo., Oct. 21, 1939; d. Leonard Milton and Lillian Love (Leviten) Havens; m. Burton J. Abarbanell, June 1, 1965 (div. 1972); children: Jeffrey J. Reddick, Dena Reddick Lamb. Student, UCLA, 1975; student, San Joaquin Coll. Law, 1976-77. Cert. fin. planner; lic. real estate rep. Calif.; lic. life ins. broker, Calif., Wash., Nev., N.Y., Ill., S.C.; lic. securities broker. Postal clk. Van Nuys, Calif., 1966-69; regional mgr. Niagara Cyclo Massage, Fresno, Calif., 1969-72; owner, mgr. AD Enterprises, Fresno, 1970-72; agt., field supr. Equitable of Iowa, Fresno, 1972-73; rep. Ciba Pharms., Fresno, 1973-75; owner, operator Creativity Unltd., Fresno, 1975-76; registered fin. advisor Univ. Securities Corp., L.A., 1976-83, Financial Network Investment Corp., L.A., 1983—; lectr. seminars for civic orgns.; mem. adv. bd. Financial Network, Torrance, Calif., 1985-88. Co-author: Guidelines to Feminist Consciousness Raising, 1985. Mem. bus. adv. bd. of 2d careers. Recipient award Women in Ins., 1972. Mem. Bus. and Profl. Assn., L.A. Internat. Assn. Fin. Planners (bd. dirs. 1993-94), Inst. Cert. Fin. Planners, So. Calif. Socially Responsible Investment Profls., ACLU, NOW (nat. consciousness raising coord. 1975-76), Gay Acad. Union, Nat. Gay Task Force, Culver City C. of C., Internat. Assn. Fin. Planners, Social Investment Forum, Rotary (founding mem. L.A. Westside Sunrise Club sgt. at arms 1990-91, community svc. chair 1991-94, v.p. 1992-93, found. chair 1993-94). Democrat. Jewish. Home: 57124 Mono Wind Way North Fork CA 93643-9797 Office: Fin Network Investment Corp 5625 Green Valley Cir Apt 103 Culver City CA 90230-7120

ABBOTT, ANTON DWIGHT, aerospace engineer; b. Indpls., Aug. 28, 1936; s. Horace Emerson and Evelyn (Goff) A.; m. Janet Mavis Kyseth, June 27, 1964; children: Steven, Douglas. BS in Aero. Engring., Purdue U., 1958, MS in Indsl. Adminstrn., 1965. Mgr. systems definition Aerospace Corp., San Bernardino, Calif., 1965-68; dir. advanced projects Aerospace Corp., Los Angeles, 1968-75; prin. dir. Eastern tech. div. Aerospace Corp., Washington, 1975-82; prin. dir. Space Transp. Plans and Architecture Aerospace Corp., Los Angeles, 1982-90; prin. dir. Design Engring. Aerospace Corp., L.A., 1990-92; gen. mgr. Bus. Mgmt. Aerospace Corp., L.A., 1992-97; gen. mgr. sys. engring. Aerospace Corp., L.A., 1997—. Patentee in field. Fellow AIAA (assoc.); mem. AAAS, Purdue U. Gimlet Club. Home: 1825 Via Estudillo Palos Verdes Estates CA 90274-1907

ABBOTT, CHARLES FAVOUR, JR., lawyer; b. Sedro-Woolley, Wash., Oct. 12, 1937; s. Charles Favour and Violette Doris (Boulter) A.; m. Oranee Harward Sept. 19, 1958; children: Patricia, Stephen, Nelson, Cynthia, Lisa, Alyson. BA in Econs., U. Wash., 1959, JD, 1962. Bar: Calif. 1962, Utah 1981. Law clk. Judge M. Oliver Koelsch, U.S. Ct. Appeals (9th cir.), San Francisco, 1963; assoc. Jones, Hatfield & Abbott, Escondido, Calif., 1964; pvt. practice, Escondido, 1964-77, Provo, Utah, 1983-93; of counsel Meuller & Abbott, Escondido, 1977—; ptnr. Abbott, Thorn & Hill, Provo, 1981-83, Abbott & Abbott, Provo, 1993—. Mem. Utah Bar Assn., Calif. Bar Assn., U.S. Supreme Ct. Bar Assn., Assn. Trial Lawyers Am. Mem. Ch. of Jesus Christ of Latter Day Saints. Editorial bd. Wash. Law Rev. and State Bar Assn. Jour., 1961-62; author: How to Do Your Own Legal Work, 1976, 2d edit., 1981, How to Win in Small Claims Court, 1981, How to be Free of Debt in 24 Hours, 1981, How to Hire the Best Lawyer at the Lowest Fee, 1981, The Lawyers' Inside Method of Making Money, 1979, The Millionaire Mindset, 1987, How to Make Big Money in the Next 30 Days, 1989, Business Legal Manual and Forms, 1990, How To Make Millions in Marketing, 1990, Telemarketing Training Course, 1990, How To Form A Corporation In Any State, 1990, The Complete Asset Protection Plan, 1990, Your Injury and the Law, 1997; weekly columnist The Daily Herald; contbr. articles to profl. jours. Home and Office: 1325 S 100 East Ste 315 Orem UT 84058

ABBOTT, JOHN RODGER, electrical engineer; b. L.A., Aug. 2, 1933; s. Carl Raymond and Helen Catherine (Roche) A.; m. Theresa Andrea McQuaide, Apr. 20, 1968. BS with honors, UCLA, 1955; MSEE, U. So. Calif., 1957. Registered profl. engr., Calif.; cert. tchr. Calif. Advanced study engr. Lockheed Missile Systems, L.A., 1955-56; B-58 aircraft doppler radar systems engr. Hughes Aircraft Co., L.A., 1956-59; devel. engr. F-104 aircraft air data computer Garrett Airesearch Co., L.A., 1959-63, instr. in-plant tng. program, 1962-63; asst. project engr. Litton Industries, L.A., 1963; space power systems engr. Pioneer 6, world's oldest functioning satellite TRW Systems, L.A., 1963-65; engr. specialist L.A. Dept. Water and Power, 1965-92; engr. specialist Abtronix, 1992—; frequency coordination chmn. Region X, Utilities Telecommunications Coun., 1977-79, sec.-treas. Utilities Telecommunication Coun., 1979-80; instr. amateur radio course L.A. City Schs., Birmingham High Sch., Van Nuys, Calif., 1965-66, Los Feliz Elem. Sch., Hollywood, Calif., 1990—. Author, pub.: Ride The Airwaves with Alfa & Zulu; contbr. articles to profl. jours. Mem. IEEE, Am. Radio Relay League (Pub. Svc. award 1971), Tau Beta Pi. Office: Abtronix PO Box 220066 Santa Clarita CA 91322-0066

ABBOTT, PATTI MARIE, middle school educator; b. Lewistown, Mont., Mar. 15, 1942; d. Vernal Hall and Marquerite (Cowen) A. BS, Ea. Mont. Coll., 1963, MS, 1968; postgrad. in adminstrn., Mont. State U., 1980. Tchr. Sch. Dist. No. 1, Glendive, Mont., 1964; tchr. Billings (Mont.) Pub. Schs., 1964—, pub. rels. rep., 1983-87. Contbr. articles to profl. jours. Resource person Girl Scouts U.S., Billings, 1973—, cadet leader, 1976-79; resource person Campfire Girls, Billings, 1978—; vol. Heart Fund, Am. Cancer Soc., Birth Defects Found., 1976—; v.p. Sweet Adelines, Billings, 1981-83. Named Tchr. of Yr., Masonic Order, Billings, 1985, 86. Mem. NEA, ASCD, AAUW (sec. Billings chpt. 1985-87, scholar 1987, essay chairperson 1992-93), Am. Bus. Women's Assn. (pres. Billings chpt. 1980-82, Woman of Yr. award 1980), Harmony Club (pres. 1986-87), Rebeccas, Eagles, Alpha Delta Kappa (mem. internat. exec. bd., grand historian, grand v.p. 1983-87, grand pres. 1993-95, exec. bd. 1995—). Home: 701 Torch Dr Billings MT 59102-5925 Office: Lewis and Clark Jr High 1315 Lewis Ave Billings MT 59102-4237

ABBOTT, ROBERT CARL, management company executive; b. Riverside, Calif., Oct. 20, 1955; s. Orville Hancock and Erna Adella (Sparber) Whitney; m. Diane Alicia Sallstrom, Aug. 5, 1978; children: Ryan Christian, Aaron Matthew, Kalen James. MBA, Century U., 1993. Ordained to ministry Calvary Grace Christian, 1976; firefighter, Wash., Emergency Med. Tech., first aid instr. and survival instr.; reg. hypnotherapist. Affirmative action officer State of Wash., Spokane, Wash., 1976-77; personnel supr. Key Tronic Corp., Spokane, 1977-80; personnel mgr. ISC Systems Corp., Spokane, 1980-84; fire chief Millwood Fire Dept., Millwood, Wash., 1982-88; pres. and CEO Total Mgmt. Systems, Inc., Millwood, 1984-88; gen. mgr. Ptarmigan Village, Whitefish, Mont., 1988-91, Unitech Composites, Inc., Hayden Lake, Idaho, 1991-93; CEO Total Mgmt Sys., Rathdrum, Idaho, 1993-94; dir. staffing and employee devel. N.W. Natural Gas Co., 1994-97; human resources mgr. Great Western Chem., 1997—; dir. Northwest Psychic Rsch., Oregon City, Oreg. Mem. Gov.'s Com. of Vet. Bus., Washington, 1983-84; chmn. Whitefish Fire Svcs. Area Commn., 1989-91; mem. CAP. Named Most Influential for the Year, Millwood Fire Dept., 1984. Mem. Millwood Fire Assn. Christian. Home and Office: 17957 S Greenfield Dr Oregon City OR 97045-7848

ABBOTT, TRUMAN CLEVELAND, school administrator; b. Jacksonville, Tex., Aug. 12, 1940; s. Truman Clifton and Marita Belle (McCauley) A.; m. Loretta L. Abbott, July 11, 1965; children: Jennifer Lynn Abbott Smith, Jonathan Paul. BS, Colo. U., 1969; MEd, U. No. Colo., 1980. Tchg. cert. type A, Colo. Tchr. Jeffco Pub. Schs., Lakewood, Colo., 1970-85; adminstr. Riverview Christian Acad., Denver, 1985-88; pres. Marilyn Hickey Bible Coll., Denver, 1986-88; adminstr. Harvest Christian Acad./Front Range Christian Acad., Englewood, Franktown, Colo., 1988-89; sales rep. Computer Networking Specialists, Walla Walla, Wash., 1990-91; min. adminstrn. Christian Fellowship, Lakewood, 1990—; athletic chmn. ORUEF, Tulsa, Okla., 1995—; sec.-treas. Ft. Range Christian Athletic Conf., Denver, 1996—, pres. 1992-93, 94-96, v.p. 1991-92. Mem. Internat. Fellowship Christian Sch. Adminstrs., Internat. Christian Accrediting Assn. (bd. commrs. 1996—). Republican. Home: 5675 S Routt St Littleton CO 80127 Office: Christian Fellowship Sch 7350 W Eastman Pl Lakewood CO 80227-5006

ABBRESCIA, JOSEPH LEONARD, artist, educator; b. Bronx, N.Y., Oct. 1, 1936; s. John and Elizabeth (Mollicone) A.; m. Suzanne Carole Berkheiser, Apr. 20, 1963; children: Joseph Antonio, Anthony John. Artist, lectr., demonstrator, workshop facilitator. Exhibited in one-man shows at Ace Powell Art Gallery, Kalispell, Mont., 1975, Tex. Art Gallery, Dallas, 1982, 84, Driscol Gallery, Beaver Creek, Colo., 1988, Newman Gallery, Boston, 1988, others; group shows include Finley Point Gallery, Polson, Mont., Hockaday Ctr. for the Arts, Kalispell, Mus. of Native Am. Cultures, Spokane, Holter Mus., Helena, Miller Gallery, Cin., also shows in Whitefish, Mont., Scottsdale, Ariz., Catalina Island, Calif., Tucson, Kansas City, Mo., Casper, Wyo., others; works featured in numerous publs. including Freshen Your Paintings with New Ideas, Energize Your Paintings with Color, S.W. Art, Art of the West, Western Art Digest, Western Horseman mags. Named Artist of Yr., Am. Royal Western Art Assn., 1984; recipient Artists' Choice award CM Russell Mus. Show, 1994, Best Painting award CM Russell Mus. Show, 1997. Home and Studio: 12 1st Ave W Kalispell MT 59901-4440

ABDALJABBAR, ABDALHAMEED A., educational administrator; b. Falluja, Iraq, July 1, 1941; came to U.S., 1982; s. Abdullah A. Abdaljabbar and Baseirra (Saleh) Mustafah; m. Amal Abdalrazak, Feb. 1, 1971; children: Bushra, Nagam, Azaheer. BA, Almustansyriah U., Baghdad, Iraq, 1967; MA, Baghdad U., 1977; EdD, U. No. Colo., 1989. Tchr. Ramadi (Iraq) Sch. Dist., 1968-73, Baghdad-Risafa Sch. Dist., 1973-77; lectr. Mosel (Iraq) U., 1977-82; prin. Granada Sch., Santa Clara, Calif., 1991-93, 1993-94, dir. curriculum and staff devel., 1994-95. Postdoctoral fellow U. No. Colo., 1990-91. Home: 1000 Kiely Blvd Apt 116 Santa Clara CA 95051-4819

ABDUL, CORINNA GAY, software engineer, consultant; b. Honolulu, Aug. 10, 1961; d. Daniel Lawrence and Katherine Yoshie (Kanada) A. BS in Computer Sci., U. Hawaii, 1984. Programmer, analyst, adminstrv. and fiscal svcs. U. Hawaii, Honolulu, 1982-84, software engr. libr. of divsn. of planetary geoscis., 1984; sys. software engr. II, test systems and software engr. dept space and tech. TRW Inc., Redondo Beach, Calif., 1985-89; systems software engr. II, Sierra On-Line, Inc., Oakhurst, Calif., 1989-90; sr. programmer, analyst Decision Rsch. Corp., Honolulu, 1990-92; ind. computer cons. Honolulu, 1992-94; computer cons. Wailuku, Hawaii, 1994—. Recipient The 20th Century award for achievement, 1994. Home: 856 W Kaena Pl Wailuku HI 96793-9620

ABDUL-JABBAR, KAREEM (LEWIS FERDINAND ALCINDOR), retired professional basketball player, sports commentator; b. N.Y.C., Apr. 16, 1947; s. Ferdinand Lewis and Cora Alcindor; m. Habiba (Janice Brown), 1971 (div. 1973); children: Habiba, Kareem, Sultana, Amir. B.A., UCLA, 1969. Basketball player with Milw. Bucks, 1969-75, Los Angeles Lakers, 1975-89; owner Kareem Productions; now commentator ESPN, Bristol, Ct. Became NBA all-time leading scorer, 1984; appeared on TV in episodes of Mannix, The Man from Atlantis, Diff'rent Strokes, Tales from the Darkside, Pryor's Place, The ABC Afterschool Spl.; appeared in movies: The Fish that Saved Pittsburgh, 1979, Airplane, 1980, Fletch, 1985; author: (with Peter Knobler) Giant Steps: An Autobiography of Kareem Abdul-Jabbar, 1983, (with Mignon McCarthy) Kareem, 1990. Named Rookie of Year NBA, 1970; recipient Maurice Podoloff Cup; named Most Valuable Player NBA, 1971, 72, 74, 76, 77, 80; player NBA All-Star game, 1970-87, 89; named to NBA 35th Anniversary All-Time Team, 1980; NBA Playoff Most Valuable Player, 1971, 85; mem. NBA Championship Team, 1971, 80, 82, 85, 87, 88, NCAA Championship Team, 1967, 68, 69; named NCAA Tournament Most Outstanding Player, 1967, 68, 69. Muslim. Office: ESPN ESPN Plaza Bristol CT 06010-7454 also: Kareem Productions 10100 Santa Monica Blvd Ste 460 Los Angeles CA 90067

ABEL, MARK JEFFREY, electrical engineer, communications researcher; b. Cleve., May 30, 1957; married; 2 children. BSEE summa cum laude, U. Mich., 1979; MSEE, Stanford U., 1980. Mem. tech. staff AT&T Bell Labs., Naperville, Ill., 1979-83; staff engr. Siemens AG, Munich, Germany, 1983-85; mem. rsch. staff Xerox PARC-NW, Portland, Oreg., 1985-87; MTS, rsch. sci., mgr. U.S. West Advanced Technologies, Portland, Englewood and Boulder, Colo, 1987-91; mgr., prin. engr. Intel Corp., Hillsboro, Oreg., 1991—; bd. dirs. Multimedia Commn. Forum; chair, founder MMCF Transport Svcs. Interface Working Group, 1993-95; mem. tech. adv. bd. Oreg. Advanced Computing Inst., 1991-92; vis. rschr. NW Regional Ednl. Lab., Portland, 1990-91; invited del. comm. People's Republic China, 1987. Co-holder several patents. Co-founder, mem. Lake Oswego Citizen Traffic Adv. Com., 1990-92; spkr. engring. career K-12 students, 1980—; bd. dirs. Forest Highlands Neighborhood Assn., 1991-92. Mem. IEEE, ACM. Office: Intel Corp MS JF3-206 2111 NE 25th Ave Hillsboro OR 97124-6463

ABEL, RICHARD EUGENE, book publishing consultant; b. Great Falls, Mont., July 7, 1925; s. Ernest E. and Anna (Rempel) A.; m. Katherine F. Ferguson, Dec. 14, 1947; children: Katherine A. Hawkins, Corinne A. Bacher. BA, Reed Coll., 1948. Founder, pres. Richard Abel & Co., Inc., Portland, Oreg., 1960-74, Internat. Book Svcs., Portland, Oreg., 1967-79; co-founder, pres. Rsch. Studies Press, Portland, Oreg., 1976-78, Dilithiam Press Inc., Portland, Oreg., 1977-79; founder, pres. Timber Press Inc., Portland, Oreg., 1978-89, Dioscorides Press, Inc., Portland, Oreg., 1980-89, Amadeus Press, Inc., Portland, Oreg., 1983-89; book trade cons. Richard Abel Consultant, Portland, Oreg., 1989—. Contbr. articles to Publishers Rsch. Quar., Logos and others. Bd. dirs. Oreg. Mus. Sci. and Industry, Portland, 1971-74, Oreg. Sch. of Arts and Crafts, Portland, 1978-80, Oreg. State Bd. Forestry, Salem, 1976-80; chmn. Gov.'s Task Force on Small Woodlands, Salem, 1978-79. Mem. AAAS. Home: 1730 SW 90th Ave Portland OR 97225-6509

ABEL, WILLIAM EDWARD, applied physicist, consultant; b. Great Falls, Mont., May 23, 1928; s. Ernest Edward and Anna Lucille (Rempel) A.; m. Theodora Louise Hartho, Mar. 24, 1964; children: Stephen Edward, Jeffrey William. BA, Whitman Coll., 1952; MFA, Cranbrook Acad. Art, 1954. Owner William Abel Design, Portland, Oreg., 1955-76, Lake Oswego, Oreg., 1976—; dir. Audiotrainer, Inc., Mountain View, Calif., 1967-85; cons. in field, 1965—. Dir. Riverdale RFPD, Portland, 1983—; chmn. bldg. and bonding com. Riverdale Sch. Dist., 1988. Served to sgt. USAF, 1946-48. Home: 12203 SW Tryon Hill Rd Portland OR 97219-8314

ABELS, MICHAEL ALAN, university administrator; b. Newark, Dec. 16, 1957. BS, U. Alaska, Fairbanks, 1980. EMT; cert. tchr. Alaska. Field ops. Inst. Arctic Biology, Fairbanks, Alaska, 1976-90; program mgr. Inst. Artic Biology, Fairbanks, Alaska, 1990—; sta. mgr. Toolik Field Sta., Toolik Lake, Alaska, 1990—; dir. ops. Wilderness Search & Rescue, Fairbanks, 1986-92 (Outstanding mem. 1990); head instr. Sei Shin Kai Aikido (2d degree black belt 1993, 3d degree 1995), Fairbanks, 1984—; Hakko Ryu Jujitsu (1st degree black belt 1995, 2nd degree 1996); leader 4-H, Fairbanks, 1988-91. CPR instr. Am. Heart Assn., Fairbanks, 1991. Named Eagle Scout, 1976, Woodbadge Beads Boy Scouts Am., 1977, Outstanding Young Men of Am., 1988, Rifle Disting. Expert Nat. Rifle Assn., 1976; recipient U. Alaska Merit award, 1989, Support award Interior Fire Chief's Assn., 1992, State of N.J. Gen. Assembly commentation, Am. Legion Good Citizen citation, 1976, Dist. Award of Merit Midnight Sun Coun. Boy Scouts Am., 1980, U. Alaska Army ROTC Charles J. Keim award, 1976, Chancellor's medal, 1977. Mem. Am. Soc. Safety Engrs., Nat. Assn. Search and Rescue, Internat. Shooting Coaching Assn. (founder, bd. dirs.), Nat. Eagle Scout Assn. (chpt. pres. 1978), Internat. Design Extreme Environ. Assembly, Interior Fire Chiefs Assn. (bd. dirs.), Soc. Rsch. Admisntrs., No. Region Critical Incident Stress Debriefing Team, Order of Arrow (vigal mem.), NRA (cert. rifle, pistol, shotgun instr.), Kappa Alpha Mu (chpt. pres. 1978-80), Sigma Delta Chi. Home: PO Box 80981 Fairbanks AK 99708-0981 Office: U Alaska Inst Artic Biology PO Box 757000 Fairbanks AK 99775-7000

ABELS, ROBERT FREDERICK, tax consultant; b. West Palm Beach, Fla., Nov. 18, 1926; s. John Frederick and Nelly (Bulfin) A.; m. Shirley Mae Larsen, May 31, 1953; children: Robert Frederick, Steven John, Richard Alan. Student, U. S.C., 1946-47; ed. flight tng. program, Naval Air Sta., Pensacola, Fla., 1947-49; BS, Naval Postgrad. Sch., Monterey, Calif., 1965; MBA in Finance, U. West Fla., 1971. Enlisted USN, 1944, commd. ensign, 1949, advanced through grades to comdr., 1963, radar operator PT boats, 1945-46, radar and radio operator PT Boats World War II; aviator USN, Republic of Korea, 1950, 51, 53, Pensacola, Fla., Vietnam, 1962-63, 65-66; ret. USN, 1969; tchr. math. and bus. Skyline H.S., Lemon Grove, Calif., 1971-83; ind. tax cons. Sun City West, Ariz., 1971—; past ptnr., salesman area real estate co.; enrolled agent IRS, Washington, 1984. Decorated Bronze Star, Air medal, Commendation medal; Vietnamese Cross Gallantry. Mem. Nat. Assn. Enrolled Agts., Inland Soc. Tax. Cons., Nat. Assn. Tax Consultors. Republican. Lutheran. Office: 20411 N Wintergreen Dr Sun City West AZ 85375-5458

ABENDROTH, KATHI JUDKINS, archivist; b. Seattle, Aug. 20, 1937; d. John Ronald and Eleanor Louise (Geary) Judkins; m. Raymond Orie Abendroth, Mar. 19, 1955; children: Ron, Don, Scott, Susan. Pres., archivist, rschr. Judkins Family Assn., Seattle, 1985—, editor, publisher, 1985-87, 89—; editor, publisher Holy Angels Acad. Alumnae Assn., Seattle, 1994-96. Pres. Adams Grade Sch. PTA, Seattle, 1970-71; pack leader, den mother Boy Scouts Am., Seattle. Mem. N.H. Soc. Genealogists, Maine Genealogy Soc., New Eng. Hist. Geneal. Soc. Roman Catholic. Home and Office: 1538 NW 60th St Seattle WA 98107-2328

ABERBACH, JOEL DAVID, political science educator, author; b. New York City, June 19, 1940; s. Isidore and Miriam (Meltzer) A.; m. Joan F. Gross, June 17, 1962; Children: Ian Mark, Amy Joyce, Matthew Daniel, Rachel Ann. AB, Cornell U., 1961; MA, Ohio State U., 1963, Yale U., 1965; PhD, Yale U., 1967. Asst. prof. U. Mich., Ann Arbor, 1967-72; research scientist U. Mich., 1967-88, assoc. prof., 1972-78, prof., 1978-88; sr. fellow Brookings Inst., Washington, 1977-80; dir. Ctr. for Am. Politics and Pub. Policy, UCLA, 1988—; prof. UCLA, 1986—; cons. Commn. on the Op. of the Senate, Washington, 1976, U.S. Office of Pers. Mgmt., Washington, 1983, Nat. Pub. Radio, Washington, 1983-84, U.S. Gen. Acctg. Office, 1990—. Author: Keeping a Watchful Eye, 1990; co-author: Race in the City, 1973, Bureaucrats and Politicians in Western Democracies, 1981; co-editor: The Role of the State in Taiwan's Development, 1994. Del. Mich. Dem. Conv., Detroit, 1972; editorial bd. Congress and the Presidency, Washington, 1981—, Governance, Oxford, Eng., 1987—. Research grantee Nat. Sci. Found., Washington, 1969-73, 1978-81, 1986-89, 1993-98. Fellow Brookings Inst., Ctr. for Advanced Study in Behavioral Scis., Swedish Collegium for Advanced Study in the Social Scis.; mem. Am. Polit. Sci. Assn., Am. Sociol. Assn. (com. on viable constitutionalism, exec. bd., 1993—), Rsch. Com. on Structure and Orgn. Govt. of Internat. Polit. Sci. Assn. (exec. bd. 1985-89, co-chmn. 1989—), Phi Beta Kappa. Jewish. Home: 10453 Colina Way Los Angeles CA 90077-2041 Office: UCLA 4289 Bunche Hall Los Angeles CA 90095

ABERCROMBIE, NEIL, congressman; s. G. Don and Vera June (Giersdorf) A.; m. Nancie Ellen Caraway, July 18, 1981; BA Union Coll., 1959, MA U. Hawaii, 1964, PhD in Am. Studies, 1974; Mem. Hawaii state legislature, 1974-86; elected to U.S. Congress, 1986, 91—, mem. armed svcs., ranking minority mem. Resources subcom. on Energy & Mineral Resources; mem. Nat. Security Coun., Honolulu City Coun., 1988-90. Democrat. Address: US Ho of Reps 1233 Longworth Washington DC 20515-1101

ABERLE, DAVID FRIEND, anthropologist, educator; b. St. Paul, Nov. 23, 1918; s. David Winfield and Lisette (Friend) A.; m. Eleanor Kathleen Gough, Sept. 5, 1955 (dec. Sept. 1990); 1 son. A.B. summa cum laude, Harvard U., 1940; Ph.D. in Anthropology, Columbia U., 1950; postgrad., U. N.Mex., summers 1938-40, No. Ariz. U., summers 1971, 73, Harvard U., 1946-47. Instr. dept. social rels. Harvard U., Cambridge, Mass., 1947-50, rsch. assoc. Sch. Pub. Health, 1948-50; vis. assoc. prof. Page Sch., Johns Hopkins U., Balt., 1950-52; assoc. prof., then prof. dept. sociology and dept. anthropology U. Mich., Ann Arbor, 1952-60; fellow Ctr. Advanced Study in Behavioral Scis., Stanford, Calif., 1955-56; Simon vis. prof. and hon. research assoc. dept. social anthropology Manchester U., Eng., 1960-61; prof., chmn. dept. anthropology Brandeis U., Waltham, Mass., 1961-63; prof. dept. anthropology U. Oreg., Eugene, 1963-67; prof. dept. anthropology and sociology U. B.C., Vancouver, Can., 1967-83, prof. emeritus, 1983—; cons. Inst. Devel. Anthropology, Inc., Binghamton, N.Y., 1978-79; cons. to attys. Navajo Tribe, 1976-77; disting. lectr. at ann. meeting Am. Anthrop. Assn., 1986. Author: The Peyote Religion Among the Navaho, 1966, (with Isidore Dyen) Lexical Reconstruction, the Case of the Proto-Athapaskan Kinship System, 1974; contbr. articles on anthropological theory and Navajo Indians to scholarly jours.; rev. editor: Am. Anthropologist, 1952-55. Served with U.S. Army, 1942-46. Recipient Social Sci. Research Council Demobilization award, 1946; Harvard U. Nat. scholar; NIMH grantee; USPHS grantee; Wenner-Gren Found. grantee, 1954-63; NSF grantee, 1965-72; Can. Council grantee, 1969-77; Social Scis. and Humanities Research Council Can., 1978-80, 84-86. Fellow Royal Soc. Can., Royal Anthropol. Inst. of Gt. Britain and Ireland; mem. Am. Anthropol. Assn. (mem. panel on Navajo-Hopi land dispute 1973-95), Am. Sociol. Assn., Soc. Applied Anthropology, Am. Ethnol. Assn., Can. Anthropology Soc., Soc. Lesbian and Gay Anthropologists, Phi Beta Kappa. Jewish. Office: U BC Dept Anthropology, 6303 NW Marine Dr, Vancouver, BC Canada V6T 2B2

ABERNATHY, SHIELDS B., allergist, immunologist, internist; b. Bronxville, N.Y., Mar. 14, 1951; m. Leslie Abernathy; children: Amelia, Camille, Lant. BA, Ohio Wesleyan U., 1973; MS, Harvard U., 1975; MD, Med. Coll. Pa., 1979. Diplomate Am. Bd. Internal Medicine, Am. Bd. Allergy and Immunology, eligible Am. Preventive Medicine, Nat. Bd. Med. Examiners; Qualified Med. Examiner Calif.; Fed. Aviation Med. Examiner; ACLS Am. Heart Assn. Intern in internal medicine L.A. County/U. So. Calif. Med. Ctr., L.A., 1979-80; resident in internal medicine Hosp. of Good Samaritan, L.A., 1980-81; resident UCLA Wadsworth VA Med. Ctr., 1981-82, fellow allergy and immunology, 1982-84; instr. pub. edn. programs; rschr. in field. Fellow Am. Coll. Allergy and Immunology, Am. Acad. Allergy and Immunology; mem. Am. Med. Health Assn., Am. Pub. Health Assn. (internat. health sect.). Office: 1050 Las Tablas Rd Ste 3 Templeton CA 93465-9792

ABERNETHY, ROBERT JOHN, real estate developer; b. Indpls., Feb. 28, 1940; s. George Lawrence and Helen Sarah (McLandress) A. BA, Johns Hopkins U., 1962; MBA, Harvard U., 1968; cert. in real estate fin. and constrn., UCLA, 1974. Asst. to chief scientist Phoenix missile program Hughes Aircraft Co., L.A., 1968-69, asst. program mgr. Iroquois night fighter and night tracker program, 1969-71, asst. to contr. space and comm. group, 1971-72, contr. tech. divsn., 1972-74; pres. Am. Std. Devel. Co., L.A., 1974—; bd. dirs., chmn. audit com. Pub. Storage, Inc., Glendale, Calif., Marathon Nat. Bank, L.A., L.A. Bancorp, Met. Water Dist., L.A., Met. Transp. Authority, L.A. County, Pub. Storage, Inc.; pres. Self Svc. Storage Assn., San Francisco, 1978-83. Asst. to dep. campaign mgr. Humphrey for Pres., Washington, 1968; commr. L.A. Planning Commn., 1984-88, L.A. Telecom. Commn., 1992-93; vice chmn. L.A. Econ. Devel. Coun., 1988-93; chmn. Ctr. for Study Dem. Inst., Santa Barbara, Calif., 1986—; bd. dirs. Met. Transp. Authority L.A. County, World Children's Transplant Fund, French Found. for Alzheimers Rsch., Pacific Coun. on Internat. Policy; adv. bd. mem. Peabody Conservatory, 1992—, Nitse Sch. Advanced Internat. Studies, 1993— Harvard Ptnrs., 1996—; bd. vis. Davidson Coll.; bd. dirs. L.A. Theatre Ctr., 1986-92, YMCA; trustee Johns Hopkins U., 1991—; mem. Coun. on Fgn. Rels., L.A. Com. on Fgn. Rels. Lt. USNR, 1962-66. Mem. So. Calif. Planning Congress (bd. dirs.), Parker Found. (bd. dirs.), Californian Club, St. Francis Yacht Club, Jonathan Club, Calif. Yacht Club, Alpha Lambda. Home: 5800 W Century Blvd Los Angeles CA 90009-5600 Office: Am Standard Devel Co 5221 W 102nd St Los Angeles CA 90045-6001

ABNER, EDDIE LEE, lawyer; b. Oran, Mo., Nov. 10, 1950; s. Edgar and Ruby Ellen (Wood) A.; m. Margaret Abner, July 2, 1980; children: Eric, Damian, Rebecca; stepchildren: Nicole, Desiree, Arlene Miranda. BA, Southeast Mo. State U., 1975; JD, Whitter Coll. Sch. Law, 1982. Real estate salesman Los Altos Realty, Hacienda Heights, Calif., 1976-80; pvt. practice law San Dimas, Calif., 1982—. Author: The Coming of the Crowned and Conquering Child, 1993, The Defense Rests, 1995. Served with USMC, 1968-72, Vietnam. Office: 163A Bonita Ave Ste B San Dimas CA 91773

ABRAHAM, CAROL JEANNE, artist, photography educator; b. Phila., Jan. 14, 1949; d. Hans Alfred and Lillian Elizabeth (Fredericks) A. BS in Edn., Tufts U., 1971; MFA, Rochester Inst. Tech., 1973; diploma, Brooks Inst. Photography, 1988. Cert. tchr. Calif. Tchr. Framingham (Mass.) Pub. Sch., 1970, Boston Pilot Sch. (Harvard Project), 1970, Boston State Coll., 1971; tchr. Rochester (N.Y.) Inst. Tech., 1972-73; asst. prof. Southern Utah State U., Cedar City, 1975-77; tchr. El Camino Coll., Torrance, Calif., 1980-81, Ventura (Calif.) Community Coll., 1982-84, Brooks Inst. Photography, Santa Barbara, Calif., 1989—; curator Western States Mus. of Photography, Santa Barbara, 1985-88; colections Mus. Ceramics, Italy, Internat. Acad. Ceramics, Can., Nova Inst. Ceramics, Italy, Smithsonian Inst., Washington. Artist (book) Ceramics: A Potters Handbook, 1978, 84, Contempory International Ceramics, 1980, Porcelain: Traditions and New Visions, 1981; author: (photography) Egypt, Images and Adventures, 1988. Bd. trustees United Boys & Girls Club, Santa Barbara, 1991—. Nat. Park Assn. grantee, 1974.

ABRAHAM, CLAUDE KURT, language educator; b. 1931. Prof. French U. Fla., 1964-75; mem. faculty U. Ill., 1959-64; prof. French U. Calif., Davis, 1975—. Author: Gaston d'Orleans et sa Cour, 1963, 64, Strangers: The Tragic World of Tristan L'Hermite, 1966, Enfin Malherbe, 1971 (SAMLA Studies award), Corneille, 1972, J. Racine, 1977, Tristan L'Hermite, 1980, Norman Satirists of the Age of Louis XIII, 1983, Moliere's Comedies-Ballets, 1984, 85; editor, translator various others.

ABRAHAM, WILLARD, special education educator; b. 1919. Assoc. prof. edn. Roosevelt U., Chgo., 1946-53; newspaper columnist various; syndicated columnist, 1972—; cons. Grolier Ednl. Svcs., 1973—; prof. dept. spl. edn. Ariz. State U., 1953—. Author: Your Post-War Career, 1945, Common Sense About Gifted Children, 1958, A Study of the Devereux Found., 1970, Living With Preschoolers, 1976, others; co-author: A Dictionary of Special Education Terms, 1980, You Always Lag One Child Behind, 1980, Education of the Gifted, 1982; conbtr. numerous articles to profl. jours.

ABRAHAMS, SIDNEY CYRIL, physicist, crystallographer; b. London, May 28, 1924; arrived in U.S., 1948; s. Aaron Harry and Freda (Cohen) A.; m. Rhoda Banks, May 1, 1950; children: David Mark, Peter Brian, Jennifer Anne. BSc, U. Glasgow, Scotland, 1946; PhD, U. Glasgow, 1949, DSc, 1957; Fil. Dr. (hon.), U. Uppsala, Sweden, 1981. Rsch. fellow U. Minn., Mpls., 1949-50; mem. staff MIT, Cambridge, 1950-54; rsch. fellow U. Glasgow, 1954-57; mem. tech. staff Bell Labs., Murray Hill, N.J., 1957-82; disting. mem. tech. staff AT&T Bell Labs., Murray Hill, 1982-88; Humboldt sr. scientist Inst. Crystallography, U. Tübingen, Fed. Republic Germany, 1989-90; guest scientist Brookhaven Nat. Lab., Upton, N.Y., 1957—; vis. prof. U. Bordeaux, France, 1979, 90; Humboldt sr. scientist U. Tübingen, Germany, 1995; adj. prof. physics So. Oreg. U., 1990—. Mem. editorial bd., Rev. Sci. Instruments, 1963-65; co-editor, Anomalous Scattering, 1975; editor, World Directory of Crystallographers, 1977; editor-in-chief Acta Crystallographica, 1978-87; book rev. editor, Ferroelectrics, 1975—. Recipient Sr. U.S. Scientist award, Alexander von Humboldt Found., 1989-90. Fellow AAAS, Am. Phys. Soc.; mem. Am. Crystallographic Assn. (pres. 1968, mng. editor 1965-90), Royal Soc. Chemistry, Am. Inst. Physics (chmn. pub. policy com. 1981-91), Internat. Union Crystallography (chmn. commn. on crystallographic apparatus 1972-75, commn. on jours. 1978-87, commn. on crystallographic nomenclature 1978—), Internat. Union Pure and Applied Chemistry (rep. interdivsnl. com. on nomenclature and symbols 1984—), Sigma Xi (founding pres. So. Oreg. State Coll. 1993-95). Home: 89 Mallard St Ashland OR 97520-7316 Office: So Oreg State Coll Physics Dept Ashland OR 97520

ABRAM, JOHN CHARLES, energy consultant, retired; b. Des Moines, Sept. 1, 1920; s. John C. and Mary (Jones) A.; m. Dorothy Jean Buettner, Dec. 28, 1946; children: James Morgan, Susan Diane. AA, Glendale Coll., 1940; BS in Engring., UCLA, 1949; postgrad., U. Calif., Berkeley, 1949. With Pacific Lighting Service Co., 1959-69, v.p., 1969-71; with So. Calif. Gas Co., Los Angeles, 1951-57, 71-85, v.p., 1972-74, sr. v.p., 1974-81, vice chmn., 1980-81, chmn. bd., chief exec. officer, 1981-85; chief exec. officer AEA Internat. Ltd., Los Angeles, 1985—. Vice chmn. Calif. Mus. Sci. and Industry Found., Los Angeles, 1985-86; vice chmn. Econ. Devel. Corp. Los Angeles County, 1984-85, Cen. City Assn., 1983-85. Mem. Internat. Gas Union, Internat. Energy Economists, The Atlantic Council, U.S.-Japan Energy Conf., Pacific Coast Gas Assn. (bd. dirs. 1973-82, chmn. 1980-81), Am. Gas Assn. (bd. dirs. 1981-85, Disting. Service award 1984), Gas Research Inst. (bd. dirs. 1980-87, chmn. 1981-83), UCLA Alumni Assn., U. Calif. at Berkeley Alumni Assn., Australian Gas Assn., Japan Am. Soc., Asia Soc., Japanese Am. Cultural and Community Ctr. Republican. Congregationalist. Clubs: The Los Angeles, Calif.; Oakmont Country (Glendale, Calif.).

ABRAMOVITZ, MICHAEL JOHN, lawyer; b. N.Y.C., Feb. 7, 1939; s. Max and Anne (Causey) A.; m. Patricia Carson, 1959 (div. 1968); 1 child, Deborah Woodbury; m. Frances Koncilja, Nov. 12, 1972 (div. 1983); 1 child, Nicholas; m. Carol Lay, May 24, 1988; 1 child, Alexandra. AB, Harvard U., 1961; MA in Maths., U. Calif., 1967; postgrad., U. Calif., Berkeley; JD, U. Colo., 1972. Bar: Colo. 1972, U.S. Dist. Ct. Colo. 1972, U.S. Ct. Appeals (10th cir.) 1973, U.S. Tax Ct. 1973, U.S. Supreme Ct. 1975, U.S. Ct. Claims 1977. Law clk. to presiding justice Colo. Supreme Ct., Denver, 1972-73; ptnr. Drexler, Wald & Abramovitz, Denver, 1973-84, Berenbaum & Weinshienk, Denver, 1984-86, Abramovitz, Merriam & Shaw, Denver, 1987-94, Abramovitz & Merriam, Denver, 1994—. Mem. ABA (taxation sect., civil and criminal tax penalties com., litigation sect.), Colo. Bar Assn. Office: Abramovitz & Merriam 1625 Broadway Ste 770 Denver CO 80202-4707

ABRAMOVITZ, MOSES, economist, educator; b. Bklyn., Jan. 1, 1912; s. Nathan and Betty (Goldenberg) A.; m. Carrie Glasser, June 23, 1937; 1 son, Joel Nathan. A.B., Harvard U., 1932; Ph.D., Columbia U., 1939; Ph.D. (hon.), Uppsala U., Sweden, 1985, U. Ancona, Italy, 1992. Instr. Harvard U., 1936-38; mem. research staff Nat. Bur. Econ. Research, 1938-69; lectr. Columbia U., 1940-42, 46-48; prof. econs. Stanford U., 1948—, Coe prof. Am. econ. history, exec. head dept. econs., 1963-65, 71-74; vis. prof. U. Pa., 1955; prin. economist WPB, 1942, OSS, 1943-44; econ. adviser to U.S. rep. on Allied Commn. on Reparations, 1945-46; econ. adviser to sec.-gen. Orgn. for Econ. Coop. and Devel., 1962-63; vis. fellow All Souls Coll., Oxford, Eng., 1968. Author: Price Theory for a Changing Economy, 1939, Inventories and Business Cycles, 1950, The Growth of Public Employment in Great Britain, 1957, (with Vera Eliasberg) Thinking About Growth, 1989; also articles.; editor: Capital Formation and Economic Growth, 1955; mng. editor Jour. Econ. Lit., 1981-85. Served as lt. AUS, 1944-45. Recipient Nitti prize Accademia Nazionale Dei Lincei, Rome, 1990. Fellow Am. Acad. Arts and Scis., Am. Econ. Assn. (disting., pres. 1980), Am. Statis. Assn.; mem. Am. Econ. History Assn. (pres. 1991-92), Western Econ. Assn. (pres. 1988), Accademia Nazionale dei Lincei (fgn.), Phi Beta Kappa. Home: 762 Dolores St Stanford CA 94305-8428 Office: Stanford U Dept Econs Stanford CA 94305

ABRAMOWITZ, MARGARET FITCH, accountant, tax specialist; b. Warrenton, Va., June 17, 1928; d. Thomas Lindsey and Edna Marie (Rhodes) F.; m. Charles Abramowitz, Dec. 3, 1968; children: Thomas Lindsey Huey, Hazel Preston Morrighan, Patricia Huey. Student, Warrenton (Va.) Country Sch., 1947, Wells Coll., Aurora, N.Y., 1948-49. Enrolled to practice IRS. Office mgr. Bookkeeper Bus. Svc., Beaumont, Tex., 1965-68; acct. Wolf & Strobel, San Mateo, Calif., 1982-85; tax preparer Coastal Tax Svc., Half Moon Bay, Calif., 1985-86; acct., tax preparer S/E, 1987-96; v.p., treas., Sonoma Valley Democratic Club, Calif., 1989-96. Mem. Calif. Assn. of Ind. Tax Prep., Sonoma Valley Democratic Club. Democrat. Office: Doublecheck Business Svc 740 Donner Ave Sonoma CA 95476

ABRAMS, GARY MITCHELL, neurologist, educator; b. N.Y.C., June 9, 1949; s. Abraham and Harriet (Vogel) A.; m. Joan Roth, July 4, 1971; children: Bryan Curtis, Lindsey June, Elizabeth Sara. BA, SUNY, Buffalo, 1970; MD, U. Pitts., 1974. Diplomate in neurology Am. Bd. Psychiatry and Neurology. Med. intern Presbyn.-U. Hosp., Pitts., 1974-75; neurology resident Columbia-Presbyn., N.Y.C., 1975-77, chief resident in neurology, 1977-78; fellow in neuroendocrinology Columbia U., N.Y.C., 1978-79, asst. prof. neurology, 1980-87, assoc. prof., 1987-95; asst. attending neurologist Presbyn. Hosp., N.Y.C., 1980-87; attending neurologist Helen Hayes Hosp., West Haverstraw, N.Y., 1982-95, chief of neurology, 1985-93, med. dir., 1986-93; dir. rehab. U. Calif. San Francisco/Mt. Zion Med. Ctr., 1995—; assoc. prof. neurology U. Calif., San Francisco, 1995—; interim dir. neurology U. Calif. San Francisco/Mt. Zion Med. Ctr., 1997—. Pres. Leonia (N.J.) Bd. Health, 1989-95. Recipient Tchr.-Investigator Devel. award NIH, 1980-85; Nat. Inst. for Med. Rsch. fellow in peptide chemistry, London, 1979-80. Fellow Am. Acad. Neurology; mem. Am. Soc. Neurorehab. (cert.), Am. Congress Rehab. Medicine. Office: U Calif San Francisco Mt Zion Med Ctr 1600 Divisadero St San Francisco CA 94115-3010

ABRAMS, HERBERT KERMAN, physician, educator; b. Chgo., 1913. BS, Northwestern U.; MD, MS, U. Ill., 1940; MPH, Johns Hopkins U., 1947. Intern Cook County Hosp., Chgo., 1940-41; chief Bur. of Adult Health, Calif. Health Dept., 1947-52; dir. Chgo. Union Health Service, 1952-66; prof., chair dept. community medicine Chgo. Med. Sch.-Mt. Sinai Hosp., Chgo., 1966-68; prof., head dept. family community medicine U. Ariz., Tucson, 1968-78, prof. emeritus, 1990—; dir. Ariz. Center for Occupational Safety and Health, 1978-83. Surgeon USPHS, 1942-46. Mem. AMA, APHA (v.p. 1981-82), Ariz. Med. Assn., Assn. Tchrs. Preventive Medicine, Am. Coll. Occupational Environ. Medicine, Physicians for Social Responsibility, Internat. Physicians Prevention Nuclear War. Office: U Ariz Dept Family and Community Medicine Ariz Health Scis Center Tucson AZ 85724

ABRAMS, NORMAN, law educator, university administrator; b. Chgo., July 7, 1933; s. Harry A. and Gertrude (Dick) A.; m. Toshka Alster, 1977; children: Marshall David, Julie, Hanna, Naomi. AB, U. Chgo., 1952, JD, 1955. Bar: Ill. 1956, U.S. Supreme Ct. 1967. Assoc. in law Columbia U., 1955-57; rsch. assoc. Harvard U., 1957-59; sec. Harvard-Brandeis Coop. Rsch. for Israel's Legal Devel., 1957-58, dir., 1959; mem. faculty law sch. UCLA, 1959—, prof. law, 1964—, assoc. dean law, 1989-91, vice chancellor acad. pers., 1991—, co-dir. Ctr. for internat. and strategic studies, 1982-83, chmn. steering com., 1985-87, 88-89; vis. prof. Hebrew U., 1969-70, Forchheimer vis. prof., 1986; vis. prof. Bar Ilan U., 1970-71, 78, U. So. Calif., 1972, 73, Stanford U., fall 1977, U. Calif. at Berkeley, fall 1977, Loyola U., Los Angeles, summers 1974, 75, 76, 79; spl. asst. to U.S. atty. gen., also prof.-in-residence criminal div. Dept. Justice, 1966-67; reporter for So. Calif. indigent accused persons study Am. Bar Found., 1963; cons. Gov. Calif. Commn. L.A. Riots, 1965, Pres.'s Commn. Law Enforcement and Adminstrn. Justice, 1966-67, Nat. Commn. on Reform of Fed. Criminal Laws, 1967-69, Rand Corp., 1968-74, Ctr. for Adminstrv. Justice, ABA, 1973-77, Nat. Adv. Commn. on Criminal Justice Stds., Organized Crime Task Force, 1976; spl. hearing officer conscientious objector cases Dept. Justice, 1967-68; vis. scholar Inst. for Advanced Studies, Hebrew U., summer, 1994. Author: (with others) Evidence, Cases and Materials, 7th edit., 1983, 8th edit., 1988, 9th edit., 1997, Federal Criminal Law and Its Enforcement, 1986, 2d edit. (with S. Beale), 1993; mem. editorial bd. Criminal Law Forum, 1990—. Chmn. Jewish Conciliation Bd., L.A., 1975-81; bd. dirs. Bet Tzedek, 1975-85, L.A. Hillel Coun., 1979-82; chmn. So. Calif. region Am. Profs. for Peace in Middle East, 1981-83; bd. dirs. met. region Jewish Fedn., 1982-88, v.p. 1982-83; pres. Westwood Kehillah Congregation, 1985. Mem. Soc. for Reform of Criminal Law (mem. exec. com. 1994—), Phi Beta Kappa. Office: UCLA 405 Hilgard Ave Los Angeles CA 90024-1301

ABRAMS, ROBERT EDWARD, English educator; b. N.Y.C., May 9, 1943; s. George Justice and Pearl (Bilsky) A.; m. Ellen Prashner Azose, July 14, 1973 (div. Nov. 1979). BA, Dartmouth Coll., 1965; PhD, Ind. U., 1973. English prof. U. Wash., Seattle, 1973—; sec. Am. Lit., Philological Assn. Pacific Coast, 1983, presiding officer, 1984; adv. bd. Ind. Study, U. Wash., Seattle, 1991-96. Contbr. articles to profl. jours. Bd. dirs. Taylor-Lee Homeowners Assn., Seattle, 1991-92, pres., 1992-93; bd. dirs. Honest Ballot Assn., N.Y.C., 1979-85. Capt. U.S. Army, 1969-71. Grad. Study Rsch. Fund grantee U. Wash., 1984; John H. Edwards fellow, Ind. U., 1967-68, Univ. fellow, 1966-67. Mem. MLA. Home: 1250 Taylor Ave N Apt 401 Seattle WA 98109-3347 Office: Univ Washington Dept English Box 354330 Seattle WA 98195

ABRAMSON, ALBERT, television historian, consultant; b. Chgo., June 9, 1922; s. Joseph David and Minnie Lillian Abramson; m. Arlene Betty Corin, Jan. 8, 1950; children: Jay Allen, Susan Marie. BA, U. So. Calif., 1950. Tchr. L.A. City Schs., 1950-52; TV engr. CBS-TV, Hollywood, Calif., 1952-87; hist. cons. RCA, Princeton, N.J., Ampex Mus., Redwood City, Calif., UCLA/ATAS TV Archives, L.A. Author: Electronic Motion Pictures, 1955, The History of Television, 1880-1941, 1987, Zworykin: Pioneer of Television, 1995—; contbr. articles to profl. jours. With U.S. Army Air Forces. Recipient J.T. Taylor award for preserving history of television, Antique Wireless Assn., 1996. Mem. IEEE, Royal TV Soc. London, Brit. Kinematagraph, Sound and TV Soc., LeComité d'histoire de la Télévision, Acad. TV Arts and Scis., Soc. Motion Picture and TV Engrs. Democrat. Jewish. Home: 2224 Beacon Ridge Dr Las Vegas NV 89134

ABRAMSON, PAUL RICHARD, psychologist, educator; b. Norwalk, Conn., Dec. 24, 1949; s. Leonard and Ethel (Sakowitz) A.; Children: Annaka Bland, Sienna Bland. BA, U. Miami, 1971; MA, Conn. Coll., 1974; PhD, U. Conn., 1976. Prof. psychology UCLA, 1976—; tech. advisor World Health Orgn. Global Programme on AIDS, Geneva, 1989-91. Author: With Pleasure, 1995, Sexual Nature/Sexual Culture, 1995, A Case for Case Studies, 1991, Sarah: A Sexual Biography, 1984, Bias in Psychotherapy, 1983, Personality, 1980; editor: Jour. Sex Rsch., 1988—. NIMH fellow, 1975-76. Fellow Soc. for Scientific Study Sex; mem. AAAS. Office: UCLA Dept Psychology Los Angeles CA 90024-1563

ABRAVANEL, ALLAN RAY, lawyer; b. N.Y.C., Mar. 11, 1947; s. Leon and Sydelle (Berenson) A.; m. Susan Ava Paikin, Dec. 28, 1971; children: Karen, David. BA magna cum laude, Yale U., 1968; JD cum laude, Harvard U., 1971. Bar: N.Y. 1972, Oreg. 1976. Assoc. Paul, Weiss, Rifkind, Wharton & Garrison, N.Y.C., 1971-72, 74-76; fellow Internat. Legal Ctr., Lima, Peru, 1972-74; from assoc. to ptnr. Stoel, Rives, Boley, Fraser & Wyse, Portland, Oreg., 1976-83; ptnr. Perkins Coie, Portland, 1983—. Editor, pub. Abravanel Family Newsletter; bd. dirs. Portland Met. C. of C. Mem. Oreg. Internat. Trade Adv. Com., Oreg. Dist. Export Coun. Mem. ABA, Portland Met. C. of C. (bd. dirs.). Office: Perkins Coie 1211 SW 5th Ave Portland OR 97204-3713

ABRUMS, JOHN DENISE, internist; b. Trinidad, Colo., Sept. 20, 1923; s. Horatio Ely and Clara (Apfel) A.; m. Annie Louise Manning, June 15, 1947; children: Louanne C. Abrums Sargent, John Ely. BA, U. Colo., 1944; MD, U. Colo., Denver, 1947. Diplomate Am. Bd. Internal Medicine. Intern Wisc. Gen. Hosp., Madison, 1947-48; resident in internal medicine VA Hosp., Albuquerque, 1949-52, attending physician, 1956-80; mem. staff Presbyn. Hosp. Ctr., Albuquerque; cons. staff physician St. Joseph Hosp., Albuquerque, 1957-85; attending physician U. N.Mex. Hosp., Albuquerque, 1954-95; med. dir. Turquoise Lodge, Albuquerque; cons. physician A.T. & S.F. Meml. Hosp., Albuquerque, 1957-83; clin. assoc. in medicine U. N.Mex.; mem. N.Mex. Bd. of Med. Examiners. Bd. dirs. Blue Cross/Blue Shield, 1962-76. Brig. gen. M.C., U.S. Army, ret., N.Mex. Nat. Guard. Fellow ACP (life), AMA, Am. Soc. Internal Medicine (trustee 1976-82, pres. 1983-84), N.Mex. Soc. Internal Medicine (pres. 1962-64), N.Mex. Med. Soc. (pres. 1980-81), Nat. Acads. Practice (disting. practitioner), Albuquerque and Bernalillo County Med. Assn. (bd. govs. 1959-61, chmn. pub. rels. com. 1959-61), Am. Geriatric Soc., 1992—. Brig. gen. M.C., U.S. Army, ret. Republican. Episcopalian. Office: Turquoise Lodge N Mex Dept Health 600 Isleta Blvd SW Albuquerque NM 87105-3828

ABUL-HAJ, SULEIMAN KAHIL, pathologist; b. Palestine, Apr. 20, 1925; s. Sheik Khalil and S. Buteina (Oda) Abul-H.; BS, U. Calif. at Berkeley,

1949; M.S., U. Calif. at San Francisco, 1951, MD, 1955; m. Elizabeth Abood, Feb. 11, 1948; children: Charles, Alan, Cary; came to U.S., 1946, naturalized, 1955. Intern, Cook County Hosp., Chgo., 1955-56; resident U. Calif. Hosp., San Francisco, 1949, Brooke Gen. Hosp., 1957-59; chief clin. and anatomic pathology Walter Reed Army Hosp., Washington, 1959-62; assoc. prof. U. So. Calif. Sch. Medicine, Los Angeles, 1963-96; sr. surg. pathologist L.A. County Gen. Hosp., 1963; dir. dept. pathology Cmty. Meml. Hosp., Ventura, Calif., 1964-80, Gen. Hosp. Ventura County, 1966-74; dir. Pathology Service Med. Group, 1970—; cons. Calif. Tumor Tissue Registry, 1962-96, Camarillo State Hosp., 1964-70, Tripler Gen. Hosp., Hawaii, 1963-67, Armed Forces Inst. Pathology, 1960—. Bd. dirs. Tri-Counties Blood Bank, Am. Cancer Soc. Served to maj., M.C., U.S. Army, 1956-62. Recipient Borden award Calif. Honor Soc., 1949; Achievement cert. Surgeon Gen. Army, 1962. Fellow Am. Soc. Clin. Pathologists, Coll. Am. Pathologists; mem. Internat. Coll. Surgeons, World Affairs Coun. Contbr. articles to profl. jours. Research in cardiovascular disease, endocrine, renal, skin diseases, also cancer. Home and Office: 105 Encinal Way Ventura CA 93001-3317

ABU-MOSTAFA, AYMAN SAID, computer consultant; b. Giza, Egypt, June 1, 1953; came to U.S., 1978; s. Said S. Abu-Mostafa and Faiza A. Ibrahim. BME, Cairo U., 1976; MS in Mech. and Aerospace Engring., Okla. State U., 1980, PhD, 1984. Tchg. asst. Cairo U., Giza, Egypt, 1978; tchg. asst. Okla. State U., Stillwater, 1978-79, rsch. assoc., 1979-81; software engr. SEAM Internat. Corp., Palos Verdes, Calif., 1984-87; computing and networking cons. Calif. State U., Los Alamitos, 1987-92; sr. sys. analyst Allied Signal Aerospace, Torrance, Calif., 1992-93; pres., CEO NeuroDollars, Inc., Huntington Beach, Calif., 1993—. Author papers, articles in field. Undergrad. fellow Ministry of Higher Edn., Cairo, 1971, 72, 76; NASA/Ames grantee, 1979-81. Mem. AIAA, IEEE, Assn. for Computing Machinery.

ABU-SAMRAH, SAMEER ABDALLAH, internist; b. Jerusalem, Mar. 13, 1953; came to U.S., 1973; s. Abdallah Tawfiq and Neamati Abdul-Jabbar (Salaymeh) A.; m. Cynthia Marie Trahms, Nov. 1, 1975. BS in Chemistry, So. Ill. U., 1979, MD, 1983. Intern in internal medicine L.A. County Hosp., 1983-84; resident in internal medicine Kaiser-Permanente Hosp., Santa Clara, Calif., 1984-86; internist FHP Sr. Ctr., Huntington Beach, Calif., 1986-87; vice chmn. dept. internal medicine FHP Hosp., Fountain Valley, Calif., 1987-88; chmn. dept. internal medicine FHP Hosp., 1988-90, assoc. med. dir., 1990-91, med. dir., 1991-92; internist FHP Garden Grove Med. Clinic, Fountain Valley, 1992—;, 1992-94; med. dir. Sierra Health Svcs., Las Vegas, Nev., 1994-96; v.p. med. affairs Sierra Health Svcs., Las Vegas, 1997—; asst. clin. prof. Sch. Medicine U. Nev., Las Vegas, 1994—. Mem. Am. Coll. Physician Execs. Home: 8980 W El Campo Grande Ave Las Vegas NV 89129-3347 Office: Sierra Health Svcs PO Box 15645 Las Vegas NV 89114-5645

ACE, KATHERINE, artist; b. Chgo., Jan. 31, 1953; d. Karl Peak and Evelyn (Schmitt) Zerfoss; m. Brian Corbett, Apr. 25, 1987 (div. 1980); m. Mark Ace, Dec. 10, 1983; 1 child, Corinna. BA cum laude, Knox Coll., 1975. Artist various galleries including Woodside/Braseth (Seattle); illustrator, 1979-92; illustrator Women of the American West, Native American series, 1983-92, Silver Burdette Composer series; numerous other illustrations for publs.; recipient comms. in field; collections held by Ambac Corp., N.Y.C., Children's Hosp., Oakland, Calif., Corestates Fin. of Phila. Bank, Dieber, Lazar, Paccar/Seattle, Stroup, MDPA, Fla., DuPont Pvt. Collection, Fla., Temple Sinai, Oakland; fine arts pub. Pomegranate Pub.-Cards Calendars. One-woman shows include So. Oreg. State Coll./The OtherArt Gallery, Ashland, 1992, U. Portland, 1993, Stanford U., Palo Alto, Calif., 1993, Shoreline Coll., Seattle, 1993, Paccar Corp., Seattle, 1994, Pacific U., Oreg., 1995, Grants Pass Mus. Art, 1994, Oreg. Sch. Arts and Crafts, 1994, Cultural Forum U. Oreg., Eugene, 1995, Maude Kerns Art Ctr., 1995, Acanthus Gallery, 1995, 97, Phinney Art Ctr., 1996, Portland State U., Auburn, Wash., 1997, Woodside/Braseth, Seattle, 1997, The Cliff Dwellers, Chgo., 1997, Oreg. Health Sci. U., Portland, 1997; group exhibns. include Parliament fo World's Religions, Chgo., 1993, Belleview Art Mus., 1995, Hoyt Nat., 1994, Bumbershoot Seattle, 1995, 96, Whatcom Mus., 1996. Recipient numerous awards in field including Portland Symphony Program Cover, 1997, Student Choice award Seattle U., 1995, Northwest Poets and Artists Calendar runner-up, Bainbridge Island, Wash., 1994, 95, Spirit Echoes Gallery, Austin, Tex., 1992, 1st pla. Invitational Christmas competition, Sacramento Mag., 1987, Grumbacher Gold Medallion award Batavia Soc. Artists 3rd Ann. Nat. Exhbn., Calif., 1985, numerous others. Home and Office: 4017 SW 41st Pl Portland OR 97221-3704

ACHEN, MARK KENNEDY, city manager; b. Vancouver, Wash., Apr. 13, 1943; s. George Ben and Marjorie Beth (Pierson) A.; m. Mary Ann Uzzell, Aug. 14, 1971; children: Wyndi Marie, Kara Lynn. BA, U. Wash., 1967; MA, U. Mo., 1981. Asst. to city mgr. City of Ferguson, Mo., 1972-74; city adminstr. City of Mounds View, Minn., 1974-79; city mgr. City of Gladstone, Mo., 1979-84, City of Grand Junction, Colo., 1984—; cons. U.S. Nat. Fire Acad., Emmitsburg, Md., 1990-91, adj. faculty, 1991-92. Gates Found. fellow Harvard U. Sr. Govt. Exec. Program, 1987. Mem. ASPA (Kansas City chpt. Adminstr. of Yr. 1983), Colo. City Mgmt. Assn. (pres. 1988-89, bd. dirs. 1985-91), Internat. City Mgmt. Assn. (chmn. 1988, internat. conf. planning com., co-chmn. 1995, internat. conf. host com.), Rotary (pres. 1983-84, bd. dirs. 1989-90, 92-93, Paul Harris fellow 1991). Home: 3344 Northridge Dr Grand Junction CO 81506-1926 Office: City Grand Junction 250 N 5th St Grand Junction CO 81501-2628

ACHESON, ALICE BREWEN, publicist; b. Indiana, Pa., July 26, 1936; d. Stewart F. and Anna M.J. (Mohr) Brewen; m. Donald H. Acheson, Dec. 12, 1970 (dec.); m. Edward B. Greub, Sept. 8, 1990. AB, Bucknell U., 1958; MA, CUNY, 1963. Tchr. English and Spanish, Mt. Vernon (N.Y.) High Sch., 1958-69; exec. sec., then exec. asst. Media Medica, Inc., N.Y.C., 1969-71; with McGraw Hill Book Co., N.Y.C., 1971-78, assoc. editor, 1971-76, publicity assoc., 1977-78; assoc. publicity dir. Simon & Schuster, N.Y.C., 1979-80, Crown Pubs., Inc., N.Y.C., 1980-81; ind. publicist, prin. Alice B. Acheson, N.Y.C., 1981-88, San Francisco, 1988-96, Friday Harbor, 1996—; mem. faculty Willamette Writers' Conf., 1981, Folio Pub. Week, 1983, 84, Face to Face Pub. Conf. and Expn., 1977, 79, 81, Howard U. Press Book Pub. Inst., 1984, NYU Pub. Inst., 1985, Nat. Writers Union seminar, 1985, Small Press Expo, 1987, 88, Pubs. Mktg. Assn., 1990-96, Tucson Book Pubs. Assn., 1991-92, Book Passage, 1990—, Skagit Valley Coll., 1996—, Pacific Northwest Booksellers Assn., 1997; mem. publishing bd. Aperture Found., 1987-89. Recipient Ptnr.-in-Edn. award N.Y.C. Bd. Edn., 1977, 78, award for outside svcs. advertising, promotion, publicity, Literary Market Place, 1993. Mem. Pubs. Publicity Assn. (program com. 1979-83), No. Calif. Book Publicists Assn. (bd. dirs. 1989-92), Pubs. Mktg. Assn. (bd. dirs. 1991-92). Office: PO Box 735 Friday Harbor WA 98250-0735

ACHESON, BARBARA, real estate broker, small business owner; b. Mpls., Dec. 13, 1946; d. Wallace Chandler Fisher and Barbara Jane Zaiser; m. Richard Barclay, June 13, 1976 (div. 1987); m. Edward Paul Acheson, Jan. 15, 1989 (dec. 1992). BA in English, U. Calif., Santa Barbara, 1976. Lic. real estate broker, Calif. Owner, broker Del Sol Properties, Idyllwild, Calif., 1989—. Mem. DAR, Nat. Assn. Realtors, Calif. Assn. Realtors, Hemet-San Jacinto Bd. Realtors, Soc. Mayflower Descendants in State of Calif. Office: Del Sol Properties PO Box 70 54585A N Circle Dr Idyllwild CA 92549

ACHTEL, ROBERT ANDREW, pediatric cardiologist; b. Bklyn., May 5, 1941; s. Murray and Amelia (Ellian) A.; m. Erica Noel Woods, Mar. 10, 1963; children: Bergen Alison, Roland Hugh. BA, Adelphi U., 1963; MD, U. Cin., 1967. Diplomate Am. Bd. Pediatric Cardiology. Intern, Cin. Children's Hosp., 1967-68; resident in pediatrics Yale U., 1968-69, fellow in pediatric cardiology, 1969-71; clin. instr. pediatrics U. Calif.-Davis, 1972-73, clin. asst. prof., 1977-83; asst. prof. pediatrics, U. Ky., 1973-76; dir. pediatric ICU, Sutter Meml. Hosp., Sacramento, 1977-85, dir. pediatric Cardiology, 1982—, chmn. instl. rev. com., 1981-85; chmn. dept. pediatrics Mercy Hosp., Sacramento, 1981-83, vice chmn. pediatrics, 1983-85, 95—; dir. pediatric ICU, 1982-83; dir. Laurel Hills Devel. Ctr., 1985-89.; chmn. rsch com. Sutter Inst. for Med. Rsch., 1989—; trustee, mem. exec. com. Sutler Hosps. Found., vice chmn., 1992-93, CEO Access Care, 1994-95, med. dir. FastServe Med. Group, 1995; vice chmn. dept. pediatrics Mercy Hosp., 1995-97, chmn., 1997—. mem. tech. adv. com. pediat. cardiology State of Calif.; CEO AccessCare; chmn. regional instnl. rev. bd. Sutter/CHS Ctrl., 1996; lectr. Mooney Aircraft Pilots Assn., FAA; bd. dir. Mooney Aircraft Pilots Assn. Safety Found. Contbr. articles in cardiovascular rsch. Bd. dirs. Sutter Meml. Hosp. Found., 1986—; bd. dirs. Sutter Found., 1989, trustee, 1989—. Maj. M.C., USAF, 1971-73. Recipient grants from Heart Assn., U. Ky. Tobacco and Health Rsch. Found. Mem. Am. Heart Assn. (dir. Sacramento chpt., mem. councils congenital heart disease and atherosclerosis and cardiovascular surgery), Am. Coll. Chest Physicians, Am. Acad Pediatrics, S.W. Pediatric Cardiology Soc., So. Soc. Pediatric Rsch. Office: Pediatric Cardiology Assocs 5609 J St Ste A Sacramento CA 95819-3948

ACHTERMAN, GAIL LOUISE, lawyer; b. Portland, Oreg., Aug. 1, 1949. AB in Econs. with distinction, Stanford U., 1971; MS in Natural Resource Policy and Mgmt., U. Mich., 1975, JD cum laude, 1974. Bar: Oreg. 1974, U.S. Dist. Ct. Oreg. 1978, U.S. Supreme Ct. 1978, U.S. Ct. Appeals (fed. and 10th cirs.). Atty.-advisor U.S. Dept. Interior, 1975-78; asst. for natural resources Gov. Neil Goldschmidt, 1987-91; mem. Stoel Rives LLP, Portland; adj. prof. Lewis & Clark Law Sch., 1978-83; adj. prof. forest policy, Coll. Forestry, Oreg. State U., 1991—. Mem. Oreg. Water Resources Commn., 1981-85; chair Strategic Water Mgmt. Group, 1987-91, Interagency Hazard Comm. Coun., 1987-91. Mem. ABA (natural resources sect., adminstrv. law sect.), Am. Leadership Forum, Rocky Mountain Mineral Law Found. (trustee), Oreg. Women's Forum, Portland C. of C. (bd. dirs. 1996—). Office: Stoel Rives LLP 900 SW 5th Ave Ste 2300 Portland OR 97204-1232

ACKER, LOREN CALVIN, medical instrument company executive; b. Lamar, Colo., Mar. 3, 1934; s. John C. and Ada M. (Ecton) A.; m. Judy N. Willms, Sept. 17, 1955 (dec. Oct. 1968); children: Cheryl Acker Hoge, Keith B., Karen Acker Kime; m. Darla C. Copeland, July 24, 1976. BS in Mech. Engring., Fresno State Coll., 1956; Bus. and Mgmt. cert., U. Calif., Berkeley, 1961; MBA, U. Santa Clara, 1966. Flight test technician NASA, Edwards, Calif., 1954-56; engring. mgr. Westinghouse, Sunnyvale, Calif., 1956-69; assoc. dir. Kitt Peak Nat. Obs., Tucson, Ariz., 1969-73; chmn., CEO founder Engr. & Rsch. Assocs., Inc. (SEBRA), Tucson, 1973—; gen. ptnr. Winged Foot Assocs., Tucson, 1974—; dir., founder NYPA Inc., Tucson, 1988—. Patentee in field. Chmn. park and recreation City of Cupertino, Calif., 1968. Mem. Am. Assn. Blood Banks, Am. Soc. Apherises, Internat. Soc. for Hematotherapy and Graft Engring. Republican. Home: 4831 Winged Food Pl Tucson AZ 85718 Office: 500 N Tucson Blvd Tucson AZ 85716-4412

ACKERLEY, BARRY, professional basketball team executive, communications company executive. Student, U. Iowa, 1956. Exec. v.p. Advan, Inc.; owner Golden West Outdoor Advt., 1968-75; chmn., CEO Ackerley Comm., Inc., 1975—; owner, chmn. bd. dirs. Seattle SuperSonics, 1984—. Office: Seattle SuperSonics PO Box C-900911 190 Queen Anne Ave N Ste 200 Seattle WA 98109-9711 also: Ackerley Group 1301 5th Ave Ste 400 Seattle WA 98101-3122*

ACKERMAN, BETTYE LOUISE (MRS. SAM JAFFE), actress; b. Cottageville, S.C., Feb. 28, 1924; d. Clarence Kilgo and Mary Mildred (Baker) A.; m. Sam Jaffe, June 7, 1956 (dec.). Student, Columbia Coll., 1945; B.A., Columbia U., 1946-50; student, Otis Art Inst., 1964-68, Theatre Wing, N.Y.C., 1954-56, Stella Adler Sch., 1956-58; L.H.D. (hon.), Drew U., 1983; D.F.A. (hon.), Columbia Coll., 1986. Stage appearances include Pheelie in No 'count Boy, 1954, Elmire in Tartuffe, 1955, 56, Antigone In Sophocles Trilogy, N.Y.C., 1956, tour of The Lark, 1956-57, Portia in Merchant of Venice, Dickinson (N.D.) State Coll., 1971, An Evening with Edna St. Vincent Millay, Wesleyan Coll., Macon, Ga., 1986, A Pure Desire, Georgia O'Keeffe Centennial Celebration, Columbia (S.C.) Coll., 1987; (films) Face of Fire, 1958, Rascal, 1969, Love and Venice, 1989, Pre-Hysteria II, 1994; (TV movies) Companions in Nightmare, 1968, Heat of Anger, 1971, Murder or Mercy, 1974, The Feather and Father Gang, 1977, The Yeagers, 1979, Confessions of a Married Man, 1982, A Day of Thanks on Walton's Mountain, 1982, others; appeared as Maggie Graham on Ben Casey TV series, 1961-66; as Anne Frazier in TV series Bracken's World; appeared in over 400 television shows, numerous guest appearances Good Morning America; numerous others; tchr. body movement, Lucy Feagin Sch. Drama, N.Y.C., 1953, recorded Salome and School for Scandal; lectr., demonstrator ethnic dances, Louise Gifford Pantomime classes Columbia U., 1954-56; one-woman art shows, Erskine Coll., Due West, S.C., 1970, 76, 82, 96, Lambert Gallery, Los Angeles, 1970, Columbia Coll., 1971, 86, Monterey Peninsula Mus. of Art, 1980, Drew U., 1982, U.S. Internat. U., 1982, Wesleyan Coll., 1986; retrospective show Atrium Gallery, Augusta, Ga, 1992, one woman Art Show, Heritage Gallery Los Angeles, Calif., 1996,; group shows, Gallery 8, Claremont, Calif., 1976, Galleria Beretich, Claremont, Calif., 1981, Ambassador Galleries, Inc., N.Y.C., 1996, Heritage Gallery, Los Angeles Calif., 1996, United States Internat. U., San Diego Calif., 1985, Two Person Art Shows Include; Harvey Mudd Coll., Claremont, Calif., 1993, Galleria Beretich, Claremont, Calif., 1993, 87, 81. West Coast campaign chmn. Muscular Dystrophy Assn., 1963-69; sec., bd. dirs. Hollywood Motion Picture and TV Mus.

ACKERMAN, GERALD MARTIN, art historian, consultant; b. Alameda, Calif., Aug. 21, 1928; s. Alois M. and Eva L. (Sadler) A. B.A., U. Calif.-Berkeley, 1952; postgrad., U. Munich, W.Ger., 1955-58; Ph.D., Princeton U., 1964. Instr. Bryn Mawr Coll., Pa., 1960-64; asst. prof. Stanford U., Calif., 1964-70; assoc. prof. dept. art Pomona Coll., Claremont, Calif., 1970-75, prof., 1975-89, chmn. dept. art, 1972-82; prof. emeritus, 1989—; Fulbright prof. U. Leningrad, 1980; prof. Florence (Italy) Acad. Art, 1996—. Author: (plays) Family and Friends, 1979, The Surfer, 1981, The Life and Work of J.L. Gerome, 1986, American Orientalists, 1994, British Orientalists, 1997; contbr. articles to profl. jours. Appleton eminent scholar Fla. State U., 1994. Democrat. Home: 360 S Mills Ave Claremont CA 91711-5331

ACKERMAN, RICHARD CHARLES, lawyer, state legislator; b. Long Beach, Calif., Dec. 5, 1942; s. Jay Fuller and Marge Mae (Lyon) A.; m. Linda Irene Vranesic, May 4, 1968; children: Lauren, Marc, Brett. AB in Math., U. Calif., Berkeley, 1964; JD, Hastings Sch. Law, 1967. Ptnr. Ackerman, Mordock & Bowen, Fullerton, Calif., 1982—; mem. Calif. State Assembly. Mem. city coun. City of Fullerton, 1980-92; pres. Orange County Waste Mgmt., Santa Ana, Calif., 1982-95; v.p. So. Calif. Hazardous Waste Mgmt., L.A., 1982-95. Named Ofcl. of Yr., O.C. Com. Persons with Disabilities, 1996. Mem. Orange County Bar Assn., Fullerton C. of C. (pres., Man of Yr. 1983, Educator of Yr. 1996), Fullerton Rotary Club (pres.), Elks, Fullerton Yacht Club (commodore 1976—). Republican. Presbyterian. Home: 808 Panorama Rd Fullerton CA 92831 Office: 305 N Habor Blvd # 303 Fullerton CA 92832

ACKERMAN, ROBERT EDWIN, anthropology educator. BA, U. Mich., 1950, MA, 1951; PhD, U. Pa., 1961. Rsch. asst. U. Mus., U. Pa., 1957-59; fellow in anthropology Ea. Pa. Psychiat. Inst., Phila., 1959-61; instr. anthropology U. Del., Wilmington, 1960-61; from instr. to prof. anthropology Wash. State U., Pullman, 1961—, acting chmn. dept. anthropology, 1971-72, editor report of investigations dept. anthropology, 1987-88; dir. Mus. Anthropology Wash. State U., 1987—; rschr. and lectr. in field. Contbr. articles to profl. jours. Fellow AAAS, Am. Anthropol. Assn., Arctic Inst. N.Am., Explorers Club; mem. Internat. Arctic Social Scis. Assn., Alaska Anthropol. Assn., Am. Quaternary Assn., Can. Archaeol. Assn., Pacific Sci. Assn., Soc. for Am. Archaeology, Sigma Xi. Office: Mus Anthropology Dept Anthropology Wash State Univ Pullman WA 99164-4910

ACKERMAN, SUSAN MOON, editor; b. Pasadena, Calif., Mar. 30, 1969; d. Donald V. and Margaret (Miklas) A. Editor Nocturnal Lyric, Pasadena, San Pedro, Calif., San Francisco, 1987—; tchr. Civic Ctr. Childcare, San Francisco, 1992-94; pre-sch. tchr. Worldtots L.A., San Pedro, 1994—. Author: Solitude, 1989, Time Wanderer, 1990. Libertarian. Home: PO Box 115 San Pedro CA 90733-0115 Office: Nocturnal Lyric 3330 Peck San Pedro CA 90731 also: 1919 Mariposa San Francisco CA 94107

ACKERSON, BRADLEY KENT, physician; b. Fort Wayne, Ind., Apr. 30, 1956; s. Benjamin Ralph and Beverly Ann (Preston) A. BA in Biology, UCLA, 1978, MD, 1982. Intern in pediatrics Harbor-UCLA, 1982-83, residency in Pediatrics, 1983-85, felllowin infectious disease, 1985-86; pediatrician Kaiser Permanente, Harbor City, Calif, 1986—; asst. chief pediatrician Kaiser Permanente, Harbor City, Calif., 1987-93. conbtr. articles to profl. jours. Excellence in Rsch., U Calif. San Diego, 1982—, UCLA fellow, 1994-97. Mem. Los Angeles Pediatrics Soc., 1994—, Hamtat for Humanity , 1990—, mem. Sierra Club, 1994—, mem. Nature Conservancy, 1988—. Office: Kaiser Permanente 25825 S Vermont Dr Harbor City CA 90710

ACKERSON, DUANE WRIGHT, JR., economist; b. N.Y.C., Oct. 17, 1942; s. Duane Wright and Virginia Gale (Rabe) A.; m. Catherine Eleanor McFarland, Aug. 19, 1967; 1 child, Elizabeth. Student, George Washington Univ., 1960-63; BA, Univ. Oreg., 1964, MFA, 1967. Instr. English Salem Coll., Winston-Salem, N.C., 1967-68; asst. prof. English Idaho State Univ., Pocatello, 1968-74; writer-in-residence Willamette Univ., Salem, Oreg., 1976-78; rsch. analyst Oreg. Vocat. Rehab. Divsn., Salem, 1978-80; employment economist Oreg. Employment Dept., Salem, 1980—; part-time instr. Chemeketa C.C., Salem, 1976-92; union officer, shop steward, activist Oreg. Pub. Employees Union, 1978-93. Author: Weathering, 1973, The Eggplant and Other Absurdities, 1978; co-editor: 54 Prose Poems, 1974; vis. writer State Arts Orgn., various states, 1970-78. Creative Writing fellow NEA, 1974-75, Arts Adminstrn. fellow, 1975; recipient Rhysling award Sci. Fiction Poetry Assn., 1978, 79. Home: 1850 Corina Dr SE Salem OR 97302-1624 Office: Oreg Employment Dept 875 Union NE Salem OR 97311

ACKLEY, MARJORIE ROSE, health educator; b. Shanghai, China, Nov. 15, 1922; came to U.S., 1926; d. Millard Charles Ackley and Luella Alice (Williams) Scharffenberg; m. Donald Wilton Oswald, Sept. 24, 1942 (dec. 1955); children: Donald Theodore Oswald, Jacklyn Rae Hoiland; m. J. Paul Vaughn. AS, Grossmont Coll., 1977; BS in Allied Health Professions, Loma Linda U., 1987, MPH, 1988. RN, registered dietitian, fitness instr.; lic. M/V operator. Adminstrv. grant sec. Palo Alto (Calif.) Med. Research Found., 1962-67; devel. dir. San Francisco Eye and Ear Hosp., 1967-70; fin. planner Robert W. P. Holstrom Co., San Francisco, 1971-74; health educator San Francisco, 1972-74; registered nurse Groves Registry, San Francisco, 1977-88, Humana Hosp., Anchorage, 1983-85; owner, dir. Profl. Health Svcs., 1984-95; nurse Providence Hosp., Anchorage, 1983-85, 90-95; registered nurse MedPro Nurses Registry, San Diego, 1984-89; cardiac rehab. Providence Hosp., Anchorage, 1990-95; health educator Anchorage, 1983-95; mgr. Kodiak Island Hosp., Kodiak, Alaska, 1995—; nurse mgr. home care and wellness; med. coord. Canvasback Mission, Inc., Benecia, Calif., 1988-93; health educator, Sch. of Pub. Health, Loma Linda, Calif., 1988, Seventh-Day Adventist Ch., San Francisco, 1973, Health Expo, Yucaipa, Calif., 1988; health edn. lectr. 1990-93. Author of numerous articles in field. Vol. Health Expo, Alaska, 1988. Mem. Am. Dietetic Assn. (Eleanor Mitchell Meml. award 1986), Alaska Dietetic Assn., Seventh-Day Adventist Dietetic Assn., Am. Pub. Health Assn. Seventh-Day Adventist. Home: 1612 Mission Rd Kodiak AK 99615-6508

ACOSTA, CRISTINA PILAR, artist; b. L.A., Sept. 23, 1959; d. Joaquin Enrique and Sandra Diane (Wisner) A.; m. Randall Scott Barna, May 25, 1991; 1 child, Isabella Pilar Acosta Barna. AA, Ctrl. Oreg. C.C., 1984; BFA, U. Oreg., 1988. Freelance comml. sign painter, window graphics Bend and Eugene, Oreg., 1985-92; sign maker Safeway Corp., Bend and Eugene, Oreg., 1987-88; billboard, mural & lettering artist Carlson Sign, Bend, Oreg., 1989-91; instr. Ctrl. Oreg. C.C., Bend, 1990-96; comml. artist, fine artist Bend, 1990—. One-woman shows include Pinkney Gallery, Bend, 1987, Upper Gallery, Sunriver, Oreg., 1992, The Welcome Ctr., Bend, 1992, North Gallery, Grants Pass, Oreg., 1995; group shows include Sunriver Juried Art Show, 1987, Gallery 141, Eugene, Oreg., 1989, Sunbird Gallery, Bend, 1992, Ramskull Gallery, Hood River, Oreg., 1991-92, Columbia Art Gallery, Hood River, 1991-93, City Hall, Bend, 1992-93, Beaverton (Oreg.) Arts Commn. Juried Show, 1992-93, Wickman Gallery, Redmond, Oreg., 1992, Linn Benton C,C,m 1992, Blue Sky Gallery, Bend, 1993, Ctrl. Oreg. C.C., Bend, 1995, Works of Faith, Portland, 1995, others; contbr. art to mags. and books. Mem. Ctrl. Oreg. Arts Assn. (bd. dirs. 1992-93), Tile Heritage Found. Studio: Cristina Acosta Design PO Box 923 Bend OR 97709

ACTON, WILLIAM JOHN, real estate appraiser and consultant; b. Jackson, Mich., Apr. 17, 1958; s. Richard David and Patricia Jean (Rifenberg) A. BA in Econs./Mgmt. and Polit. Sci., Albion (Mich.) Coll., 1980. Cert. gen. real estate appraiser, Ariz. Sr. appraiser cons. Greenberg Chin Cons., Tucson, 1984-87; chief appraiser Pima County Govt., Tucson, 1987-92; pres. Acton Valuation Group, Inc., Tucson, 1992—; Pima County rep. Govt. Chief Appraisers Inter-Agy. Coalition, Phoenix, 1988-93. Benefactor Boys and Girls Club, Tucson, 1993—, bd. dirs., 1996; benefactor Jacobs YMCA, Tucson, 1994—; precinct committeeman Pima County Rep. Party, 1995—. Paul Harris fellow Rotary Internat. Mem. Internat. Right of Way Assn., MAI Appraisal Inst., Rotary Club of Tucson, Encanto Canyon Homeowners Assn. (bd. dirs). Home: 7864 E Castle Valley Way Tucson AZ 85750-7042 Office: Acton Valuation Group Inc 6890 E Sunrise Dr # 120-344 Tucson AZ 85750-0829

ADAM, CORNEL See LENGYEL, CORNEL ADAM

ADAMS, ANN ELIZABETH, corporate communications executive, lawyer; b. Guthrie, Okla., Jan. 29, 1948; d. Jack P. and Billie E. (May) A. BA in Journalism, U. Okla., 1970, MA, 1971; JD, Oklahoma City U., 1984. Lic. atty. Supr. teleshopper advt. KOCO-TV, Oklahoma City, 1971-72; pub. info. officer Met. Libr. System, Oklahoma City, 1972-78; editor/writer Kerr-McGee Corp., Oklahoma City, 1978-79, assoc. editor, 1979-81, mgr. publs., 1981-84, mgr. corp. communications, 1984-88; asst. to chancellor Okla. State Regents for Higher Edn., Oklahoma City, 1988-90; dir. pub. rels. div. Jordan Assocs. Advt./Communications, Oklahoma City, 1990-93; dir. pub. rels. and advtg. The Dial Corp, Phoenix, 1993-96; dir. pub. rels. The Dial Corp., Phoenix, 1996—. Mem. Myriad Gardens Conservatory, Oklahoma City, 1986-92, bd. dirs., 1986-88; bd. dirs. Friends of Met. Libr. System, Oklahoma City, 1986-92, pres., 1990-92; divsn. chmn. United Way Greater Oklahoma City, 1989; women's adv. bd. Bapt. Med. Ctr., 1990-93; trustee Met. Library System Endowment Trust, 1992-93; mem. mktg. com. Phoenix Zoo, 1993—; bd. dirs. Scottsdale Prevention Inst., 1995—, v.p. cmty. rels., 1996—; bd. dirs. Ariz. Found. for Women, 1996—; mem. mktg. com. Scottsdale Ctr. for the Arts, 1996—; mem. Desert Botanical Gardens, Phoenix Art Mus., Valley Leadership Class XVIII, 1996. Recipient Paragon award Leadership Oklahoma City, 1986, 92, Outstanding Alumni award U. Okla. Sch. of Journalism and Mass Communication, 1993, Addy award Am. Advt. Fedn., 1984, Pub. Rels. award N.Am. Advtg. Agy. Network, 1992. Mem. Women in Communications, Inc. (pres. Oklahoma City chpt. 1987-88, chmn. nat. progress of women in communication com. 1989-90, chmn. nat. pub. rels. com. 1990-91), Publ. Rels. Soc. Am., Okla. Bar Assn., Friends and Alumni of U. Okla. Sch. Journalism and Mass Communication (pres. 1989-90), Leadership Oklahoma City Alumni Assn., Soap and Detergent Assn. (pub. rels. com.), Nat. Investor Rels. Inst. (assoc.), Cosmetics Toiletry & Fragrance Assn. (pub. affairs. com.). Episcopalian. Home: 8012 E Via Campo Scottsdale AZ 85258-2833 Office: The Dial Corporation 1850 N Central Ave Phoenix AZ 85004-4527

ADAMS, BYRON, composer, conductor; b. Mar. 9, 1955. BM, Jacksonville U., 1977; MM, U. So. Calif., 1979; DMA, Cornell U., 1984. Composer-in-residence Music Ctr. U. of the South, 1979-84; lectr. Cornell U., N.Y.C., 1985-87; from asst. lectr. to assoc. prof. U. Calif., Riverside; guest composer 26th Warsaw Autumn Festival, 1983, San Francisco Conservatory, 1966. Composer: Quintet for piano and strings, 1979, Concerto for trumpet and string orch., 1983, Sonata for trumpet and piano, 1983, Concerto for violin and orch., 1984, Go Lovely Rose for male chorus, 1984, Missa Brevis, 1988, Three Epitaph, 1988; recordings include Nightingales, 1979, Serenata Aestiva, 1986; contbr. articles to music jours. Vaughan Williams Rsch. fellow Carthusian Trust, 1985; recipient Grand prize Delius Festval Composition Competition, 1977 Am. Soc. Composers, Medly P. Ray Composition award, 1985. Office: U Calif Dept Music Riverside CA 92521

ADAMS, CHARLES FRANCIS, advertising and real estate executive; b. Detroit, Sept. 26, 1927; s. James R. and Bertha C. (DeChant) A.; m. Helen R. Harrell, Nov. 12, 1949; children: Charles Francis, Amy Ann, James Randolph, Patricia Duncan. BA, U. Mich., 1948; postgrad., U. Calif., Berkeley, 1949. With D'Arcy-MacManus & Masius, Inc., 1947-80, exec. v.p., dir., 1970-76, pres., chief operating officer, 1976-80; pres. Adams Enterprises, 1971—; exec. v.p., dir. Washington Office, Am. Assn. Advt. Agys., 1980-84; chmn., chief exec. officer Wajim Corp., Detroit; past mem. steering com. Nat. Advt. Rev. Bd.; mem. mktg. com. U.S. Info. Agy.; pres. Internat.

Visitors Ctr. of the Bay Area, 1988-89. Author: Common Sense in Advertising, 1965, Heroes of the Golden Gate, 1987, California of the Year 2000, 1992, The Magnificent Rogues, 1996. Past chmn. exec. com. Oakland U. Mem. Am. Assn. Advt. Agys. (dir., mem. govt. relations com.), Advt. Fedn. Am. (past dir.), Nat. Outdoor Advt. Bur. (past chmn.), Theta Chi, Alpha Delta Sigma (hon.). Republican. Roman Catholic. Clubs: Bloomfield Hills Country; Carmel Valley Ranch (Calif.); Nat. Golf Links Am. (Southampton, L.I.); Olympic, The Family (San Francisco). Home: 2240 Hyde St San Francisco CA 94109-1509 also: 25450 Loma Robles Dr Carmel CA 93923-8409 Office: 10 W Long Lake Rd Bloomfield Hills MI 48304-2765

ADAMS, CLINTON, artist, historian; b. Glendale, Calif., Dec. 11, 1918; s. Merritt Cooley and Effie (Mackenzie) A.; m. Mary Elizabeth Atchison, Jan. 9, 1943; 1 child, Michael Gerald. Ed.B., UCLA, 1940, M.A., 1942. Instr. art UCLA, 1946-48, asst. prof., 1948-54; prof. art, head dept. U. Ky.; also dir. Art Gallery, 1954-57; prof. art, head dept. U. Fla., 1957-61; dean Coll. Fine Arts U. N.Mex., Albuquerque, 1961-76, asso. provost, dean faculties, 1976-77; dir. Tamarind Inst., 1970-85; asso. dir. Tamarind Lithography Workshop, Los Angeles, 1960-61, program cons., 1961-70. Represented in permanent collections Bklyn. Mus., Art. Inst. Chgo., Australian Nat. Gallery, Grunwald Center Graphic Arts, Mus. Modern Art, Los Angeles County Art Mus., and others; author: (with Garo Antreasian) The Tamarind Book of Lithography: Art and Techniques, 1970, Fritz Scholder: Lithographs, 1975, American Lithographers, 1900-1960: The Artists and Their Printers, 1983, (with others) Lasting Impressions: Lithography As Art, 1988, Printmaking in New Mexico, 1880-1990, 1991, Crayonstone: The Life and Work of Bolton Brown, 1993; editor The Tamarind Papers, 1974-90, Second Impressions: Modern Prints and Printmakers Reconsidered, 1996; subject: bibliography Clinton Adams: Paintings and Watercolors 1945-87; exhbn. catalogue Albuquerque: University of New Mexico Art Mus., 1987; biography A Spectrum of Innovation: Color in American Printmaking, 1890-1990, 1990. Recipient Gov.'s award for outstanding contbns. to arts of N.Mex., 1985. Mem. NAD (academician), Coll. Art Assn. (program chmn. 1963), Nat. Coun. Fine Arts Deans (chmn. 1965-67), Mid-Am. Coll. Art Assn. (pres. 1973). Home: 1917 Morningside Dr NE Albuquerque NM 87110-4927

ADAMS, DEBORAH ROWLAND, lawyer; b. Princeton, N.J., July 28, 1952; d. Bernard S. and Natalie S. Adams; m. Charles L. Campbell, June 16, 1990. BA, Colo. Coll., Colorado Springs, 1974; JD, U. Colo., 1978. Bar: Ind. 1978, Colo. 1978, U.S. Dist. Ct. Colo. 1978. Atty. Legal Svcs. Orgn. Ind., Indpls., 1978-79, Pikes Peak Legal Svcs., Colorado Springs, 1979-80, Pub. Defender's Office, Colorado Springs, 1980-81; assoc. Ranson, Thomas, Cook and Livingston, Colorado Springs, 1982-84, Ranson, Thomas, Adams, Petinga and Yukawa, Colorado Springs, 1984; pvt. practice Colorado Springs, 1985—; mem. state Jud. Nominating Commn. for 4th Jud. Dist., 1994—. Bd. dirs. Domestic Violence Prevention Ctr., 1980-86, pres., 1982-84; bd. dirs. Pikes Peak Legal Svcs., 1983-88, pres., 1986-87, pro bono advocacy sch. faculty, 1990-92; co-chairperson Colo. Springs Devel. Com., Colo. Women's Found., 1987, mem. grant selection com., 1988, 90; bd. dirs. Vis. Nurses Assn., 1989-91; bd. dirs. Chins Up, 1991-97, pres., 1997—; co-chairperson El Paso County sect. COLTAF Fundraising Com. for benefit of Colo. Legal Aid Found., 1991-97, chairperson, 1994-95. Recipient Pro Bono award Pikes Peak Legal Svcs., 1988; named Atty of Yr. El Paso County Legal Secs. Assn., 1990. Mem. Colo. Bar Assn. (family law sect. 1991-95, conciliation panel subcom. of profls. com. 1992, bd. govs. 1994-97, exec. com. 1995-97, nominating com. 1996), Colo. Bar Found., Colo. Women's Bar Assn., El Paso County Bar Assn. (pres.-elect 1994-95, pres. 1995-96, Trial Advocacy Sch. faculty 1990, 94, Moot Ct. judge 1992, 95, fee arbitration dispute com. 1990-95), Women Lawyer's Assn. Fourth Jud. Dist.(chairperson jud. nominating com. 1991-93, Portia award 1992), Zonta Club Colorado Springs (pres. 1989-90, co-chairperson dist. 12 regional conf. 1991-92, Zontian of Yr. 1990-91). Democrat. Office: 324 S Cascade Ave Colorado Springs CO 80903-3804

ADAMS, DONALD ELWIN, cultural and organization development consultant; b. Sioux Falls, S.D., July 13, 1953; s. James Robert and Louise (Lewis) A.; m. Arlene Frances Goldbard, Dec. 1, 1978. Student, U. S.D., 1971-74; MA in Arts Adminstrn., Sangamon State U., 1976. Cmty. devel. dir. Arts and Humanities Coun., Baton Rouge, 1975-76; dep. dir. Calif. Arts Coun., Sacramento, 1976-77; ptnr. Adams & Goldbard, Ukiah, Calif., 1978—; dir. Inst. for Cultural Democracy, Talmage, Calif., 1987—; writer-in-residence Blue Mountain Ctr., Blue Mountain Lake, N.Y., 1982, Rockefeller Found., Bellagio, Italy, 1994. Author: Crossroads: Reflections on the Politics of Culture, 1990. Dir. Webster's World of Cultural Democracy, Talmage, 1995—. Fellow Nat. Endowment for the Arts, Washington, 1976. Office: PO Box 404 Talmage CA 95481-0404

ADAMS, ELAINE, art agent, publicist; b. L.A., Sept. 15, 1960; d. Mikhael Nikitovich Perieva-Shelby and Emma (Davidian) Shelby; m. Peter Seitz Adams, Mar. 12, 1990. BA in Econs. and Math., U. So. Calif., 1982. Stock broker Crowell, Weedon & Co., L.A., 1983-89; art agt., artist rep. Peter Adams Studio, Pasadena, Calif., 1990—; publicity chmn. Calif. Art Club, Pasadena, 1993. Editor Calif. Art Club newsletter, 1994—. Assoc. trustee Pacific Asia Mus., Pasadena, 1993, chmn. Festival of the Autumn Moon, 1994; bd. dirs. Pasadena Symphony, 1994. Mem. Am. Art Coun. (steering com.), Art Ctr. One-Hundred (bd. mem.). Republican. Russian Orthodox. Office: Calif Art Club PO Box 92555 Pasadena CA 91109-2555

ADAMS, ELINOR RUTH, retired laboratory technician; b. Irby, Wash., May 26, 1921; m. Curtis Edward Adams, Sept. 14, 1940 (dec. Oct. 1987); children: Curtis Joseph, Anna May, Neal Edward, Janice Helen. Grad. h.s., Spokane, Wash. Apprentice lab. technician Hollister-Stier Labs., Spokane, 1962-63, mgr. animal rm., 1962-73, raised animals, 1972-79. Contbr. poetry to anthologies. Active People Pet Program, Coeur d'Alene, Idaho, 1989—; vol. Kootenai Med. Ctr., Coeur d'Alene, 1990—. Recipient Golden Poet award World of Poetry, 1987-92, other awards. Mem. Phi Sigma Alpha (program chmn., Woman of Yr. 1987). Republican. Roman Catholic. Home: 2115 N 8th St Coeur D Alene ID 83814

ADAMS, FRANK, education specialist; b. Cleve., Sept. 11, 1948; s. Frank Albin and Helen (Coleman) Kovacevic. BS in Bus. Adminstrn., Bowling Green (Ohio) State U., 1970, MEd in Phys. Edn., 1978. Tech. writer Soldier Phys. Fitness Sch., Ft. Ben Harrison, Ind., 1983-85; edn. specialist Directorate of Tng. and Doctrine, Ft. Huachuca, Ariz., 1985-90, Dept. Tactics Intelligence Mil. Sci., Ft. Huachuca, 1990-93, 111th Mil. Intelligence Brigade, Ft. Huachuca, 1993—; mem. steering com. tng. and doctrine command, staff and faculty devel. divsn., El Paso, Tex., 1987. Co-author: (field manual) Physical Fitness Training, 1984, (Internet site) Total Fitness; contbr. articles to profl. jours. and local newspapers. Recipient Civilian Achievement medal Dept. Army, Ft. Huachuca 1993, Comdr.'s award, 1995. Mem. AAHPERD (life), Mil. Intelligence Corp., Self-Realization Fellowship. Home: 4838 Corte Vista Sierra Vista AZ 85635 Office: 304th MI BN 111th MI BDE Fort Huachuca AZ 85613-6000

ADAMS, FRANK STEWART, family service agency director, bishop/pastor; b. Ludlow, Mass., Mar. 16, 1944; s. Leon S. and Alice G. (Bell) A.; m. Suzan Y. Blocker, Apr. 17, 1993; children: Rochelle, Matthew, Ashlee. BS in Nuclear Engring., U. Mo., Rolla, 1962; MDiv, Weston Sch. Theology, Cambridge, Mass., 1980; M in Devel. Psychology, Jesuit Sch. Theology, Berkeley, Calif., 1982; PhD, Ohio State U., 1985. Consecrated bishop of Am. Ind. Cath. Ch., 1996. Quality assurance inspection engr. U.S. Indsl. Chem. Co., Tuscola, Ill., 1966-69; project quality assurance engr. Gilbert Assocs., Reading, Pa., 1969-71; quality control supt. Monsanto, Joliet, Ill., 1971; pastor, tchr. Mo. Prov. Edn. Inst., St. Louis, 1972-81, 85-90; grad. asst. Ohio State U., Columbus, 1982-85; supt. schs., pastor St. Francis X, Corozal, Belize, 1990-91; pvt. practice counselor Aurora, Colo., 1992; instr. Met. State Coll., Denver, 1992; area dir. Luth. Family Svcs., Ft. Collins/Colo. Springs, Colo., 1992—; engring. cons., Reading, 1969-72; domestic violence counselor, 1991-92; chaplain Hospice of Larimer County, Ft. Collins, 1993-95. Author: Technical-Ethical Aspects of Nuclear Power Debate, 1979; monthly columnist Belize Diocesan Paper, 1991-92. Home: 3225 Killdeer Dr Fort Collins CO 80526-2831 Office: Lutheran Family Svcs 503 Remington St Fort Collins CO 80524-3022

ADAMS, FREDERICK MARSHALL, mathematical educator; b. Durham, N.C., Nov. 25, 1943; s. E. Clark and Frances Marshall A.; m. Sheila Anne Wloff, June 14, 1975 (div. Sept. 1982). Student, U. Fla., 1962-64; BSBA, U. Ariz., 1967; postgrad., San Jose State U., 1970. Labor negotiator Kaiser Inds., Lucerne Valley, Calif., 1967-70; educator math. East Side Union High Sch. Dist., San Jose, Calif., 1970—; travel agt. Ind. Travel Cons., San Jose, Calif., 1994—; mentor East Side Union High Sch., 1986, 90-93. Author: Math A, 1992. Mem. NEA (rep., del. 1991-92), Calif. Tchrs. Assn. (state rep. 1982-92), East Side Tchrs. Assn. (exec. bd. dirs. 1978-92, labor negotiator 1982-87). Home: 6944 Avenida Rotella San Jose CA 95139-1109 Office: Ind Travel Cons 1361 S Winchester Blvd Ste 109 San Jose CA 95128-4328

ADAMS, H. RICHARD, physiatrist; b. Springfield, Mo., Oct. 5, 1945; s. Roy J. and Carmen A. (Coteron) A.; m. Cheryl A. Bachman, June 6, 1970; 1 child, Eric R. MD, U. Calif., Irvine, 1980. Diplomate Am. Bd. Phys. Medicine and Rehab. Assoc. med. dir. Meml. Med. Ctr., Long Beach, Calif., 1985—. Mem. AMA, Nat. Brain Injury Found., Rotary. Office: Rehab Assocs Med Group 701 E 28th St Ste 416 Long Beach CA 90806-2767

ADAMS, HARLENE CAROLYN, speech communications educator; b. Chico, Calif., Oct. 18, 1939; d. Harlen Martin and Lois Vivian (Carman) A.; m. George Byron Beattie, Dec. 22, 1961 (div. June 1987); children: Dresden Elizabeth Beattie, Denver Michelle Beattie, Ryan Amery Beattie. BA, Stanford U., 1960; MA, San Francisco State U., 1965; postgrad., McGeorge Sch. Law, 1972. Legis. asst. Calif. State Senate, Sacramento, 1961-63; asst. dir. internat. programs Calif. State U., San Francisco, Calif., 1963-68; instr. Calif. State U., Sacramento, 1982-96, Yuba Coll., Marysville, Calif., 1988-89, Sierra Coll., Rocklin, Calif., 1989—; instr. European divsn. U. Md., Germany, Iceland, England, 1994-95; instr. Cosumnes River Coll. El Dorado Ctr., Placerville, Sacramento City Coll., Am. River Coll., Sacramento, 1981—; keynote spkr. Calif. Employment Devel. Dept., Sacramento, 1991; workshop dir., presenter Calif. Jour. Inst. for Pub. Policy Rev., Sacramento, 1991. Pres., v.p., clk. San Juan Unified Sch. Dist. Bd. Edn., Sacramento, 1975-79; mem. scholarship com. AAUW, Sacramento, 1970-72; mem. program planning com., actor Sacramento Civic Theater and Eleanor McClatchy Performing Arts Ctr., 1975—. Recipient Outstanding Professor award Delta Gamma Sorority, 1992.

ADAMS, HOWARD, state agency administrator; married; 3 children. BSBA, Duquesne U., 1960; grad. degree, Am. Grad. Sch. Internat. Mgmt., 1961. Employee Western Mgmt. Consulting, Inc., 1960-61; export mgr. Crane Co., 1961-64; co-owner Cafe Corner Book Store, Phoenix, Ariz., 1978—; pres. Ariz. Emergency Med. Sys.; dir. Ariz. Dept. Liquor Licenses and Control, 1993—. Ariz. state rep., 1971-74; vice-chmn. Health and Welfare Com., Environ. Future Com. and Natural Resources and Econ. Affairs Com.; mem. Citizens Charter Rev. Com., chmn. Mayor's Fin. Adv. Com.; city councilman, Phoenix; chmn. Comty. Devel. Block Grant Subcom. and Pub. Safety Subcom.; dir. Econ. Devel. Growth Corp.; chmn. Urban Infill Subcom.; coord. Gov.'s Office of Hwy. Safety, 1991-93; mem. Paraplegia Found. of Am. (past pres.), Gov.'s Alliance Against Drugs, Pvt. Enterprise Rev. Bd., Ariz. Assn. Chiefs of Police. With USAF, 1953-56. Recipient The Samaritan award, Salisbury award. Mem. Ariz. Acad.

ADAMS, JACK, film company executive, screenwriter, producer, educator; b. Lakehurst, N.J., Sept. 15, 1952; s. John Carey and Dorothy Jeanne (Conover) A.; m. Shirley Janulewicz, June 28, 1975; children: Carey Miller, Chanine Angelina, Mikael Walter, Jozef Conover. MusB in Music Edn., U. Del., 1974. Pres. Koala Studio, Valencia, Calif., 1977—; v.p. devel. Unifilms, Inc., North Hollywood, Calif., 1984—; instr. film, TV writing and script analysis Coll. of Canyons, Valencia, 1988—, L.A. City Coll., 1989—, EveryWoman's Village, Van Nuys, Calif., 1990—, Info. Exch., L.A., 1990—, Learning Tree U., Chatsworth, Calif., 1990—, U. Wis., Madison, 1991—, U. Hawaii, 1992—, USIA, Washington, 1991—, Info. Network, South Pasadena, Calif., 1990—, Moorpark Coll., 1991—, Oxnard Coll., 1991—, Northwestern U., Evanston, Ill., 1991—, Glendale (Calif.) Community Coll., 1991—; co-founder ScripTip, 1990, Classes Unlimited, 1992—, Johnson County Community Coll., Kansas City, 1993, Univ. Wis., Milwaukee, 1993, Irvine (Calif.) Valley Coll., 1992—, Shenandoah Valley Writer's Guild, Front Royal, Va., 1993—, Rancho Santiago Coll., Santa Ana, Calif., 1993—, Orange Coast Coll., Costa Mesa, Calif., 1993—; script cons. Wis. Screenwriters Forum; mem. KNX Speakers Bur., CBS Radio, 1989—, Story Bd. Devel. Group, Paramount Studios, 1989—; pres. NBC Writers Workshop; mem. Larry Wilson Devel. Workshop, Paramount Studios, Le Group, Paramount Studios; founding mem., officer, bd. dirs. L.A. Filmmakers Workshop, 1989-91; founder Santa Clarita Scriptwriters Workshop, Writers Anonymous, 1988; pres. Entertainment Writers' Workshop, 1990, Adams Entertainment, 1993; ptnr. Flying Cow, 1994; mem. Ind. Feature Project West; presenter numerous seminars and workshops. Composer (film) Eat, 1980 (Filmex award 1981, best short film award Cinemagic mag. 1981); writer, co-creator sitcom pilot Lola, Universal Studios, 1991; writer, developer sitcom pilot Fat Farm; writer, producer, dir. sitcom pilot Box # 22; line producer sitcom pilots Zebra, It's Not My Fault; creator: Screenwriting Warriors: Basic Training, 1988; columnist: Creative Screenwriting Mag., 1994—; TV editor Freelance Screenwriters' Forum Newsletter; columnist ScreenWrite Now mag.; creator (audiotapes) Top 50 Script Marketing Tips, Get An Agent to Sell Your Script, Write To Get Past the Script Reader, Pitch Your Film and Television Projects. Mem. Indian Guides/Princesses Program, chief Apache tribe YMCA, 1990—, produced annual haunted house fundraiser for Santa Clarita Family YMCA, 1991-94, participate in annual fundraising campaign, 1990, Am. Youth Soccer Orgn. AYSO, 1988. Mem. Am. Film Inst. (alumni assn. writers workshop), Scriptwriters Network (bd. advisors), Film Artists Network, Ind. Writers So. Calif. Scriptwriters Caucus, Assn. Info. Systems Profls. (bd. dirs. 1983), Freelance Screenwriter's Forum (founding), Comedy Writers Co-op (founding ABC), Wis. Screenwriters Forum (advisor 1989—). Home and Office: 22931 Sycamore Creek Dr Santa Clarita CA 91354-2050

ADAMS, JAMES FREDERICK, psychologist, educational administrator; b. Andong, Korea, Dec. 27, 1927; s. Benjamin Nyce and Phyllis Irene (Taylor) A.; m. Carol Ann Wagner, Jan. 17, 1980; children—James Edward, Dorothy Lee Adams Vanderhorst, Robert Benjamin. B.A. In Psychology, U. Calif.-Berkeley, 1950; Ed.M. in Counseling and Psychology, Temple U., 1951; Ph.D. in Exptl. Psychology, Wash. State U., 1959. Cert. psychologist, Wash., Pa.; lic. psychologist, Pa. Psychometrician Measurement and Research Ctr., Temple U., Phila., 1951-52; asst. prof. psychology Whitworth Coll., Spokane, Wash., 1952-55; teaching and research asst. State U. Wash., 1955-57; research assoc. Miami U., Oxford, Ohio, 1957-59; asst. prof. psychology Coll. Liberal Arts, Temple U., 1959-62, assoc. prof., 1962-66, prof., 1966-80, chmn. dept. counseling psychology, 1969-72; vis. prof. psychology Coll. Soc. Scis., U. P.R., Rio Piedras, 1963-64, Coll. Scis., Cath. U., Ponce, P.R., 1971-72; chmn. dept. counseling psychology Coll. Edn., Temple U., 1973-77, coordinator div. ednl. psychology, 1974-76; grad. dean, prof. psychology Grad. Coll., U. Nev., Las Vegas, 1980-85; acad. (sr.) v.p. Longwood Coll., Farmville, Va., 1985-86. Author: Problems in Counseling: A Case Study Approach, 1962, Instructors Manual for Understanding Adolescence, 1969; (exhbn. catalogue with J. D. Selig) Colonial Spanish Art of the Americas, 1976; (comml. pamphlet with C. L. Davis) The Use of the Vu-graph as an Instructional Aid, 1960; editor: Counseling and Guidance: A Summary View, 1965, Understanding Adolescence: Current Developments in Adolescent Psychology, 1968, 4th edit., 1980, Human Behavior in a Changing Society, 1973, Songs that had to be Sung (by B. N. Adams), 1979; contbr. chpts., articles, tests and book revs. to profl. publs. Served to cpl. USMC, 1945-46. Recipient Alexander Meiklejohn award AAUP, 1984; James McKean Cattell research fund grantee Miami U., Oxford, Ohio, 1958, Bolton fund research grantee Temple U., 1960, 62, faculty research grantee Temple U., 1961, 63, Commonwealth of Pa. research grantee Temple U., 1969, 70, 71, 72, summer research fellow Temple U., 1979; recipient scholarship U. Munich, 1955. Fellow Am. Psychol. Assn. (divs. 26, 17); mem. Eastern Psychol. Assn., Western Psychol. Assn., Interam. Soc. Psychology, Sigma Xi, Psi Chi. Home: 130 Palacio Rd Corrales NM 87048-9648

ADAMS, JEANNE CLARE, computer scientist; b. Utica, N.Y., June 15, 1921; d. Charles W. and Rose C. (Struve) Clare; children: Clare, Douglas, Samuel. BA, U. Mich., 1943; MA, U. Colo., 1979. With Nat. Ctr. for Atmospher Rsch., Boulder, Colo., 1960-82, various mgnt. positions, 1960-75; mgr. user svcs. and planning Nat. Ctr. for Atmospher Rsch., Boulder, 1975-82, mem. computational support group, 1985—; CYBER 205 project coord., mgr. sys. Inst. for Computational Studies, Colo. State U., 1982-84; chair and convenor Internat. Fortran Experts under ISO, 1977-85; chair fortran stds. com. X3J3 Am. NAt. Stds. Orgn., 1977-92. Author: Programmers Guide to Fortran 90, 1990, Fortran 90 Handbook, 1992, Fortran Top 90, 1994; mem. editorial bd. Computer Standards and Interfaces; contbr. numerous articles to profl. jours. Mem. Assn. for Computing Machinery, Am. Nat. Stds. Orgn., Internat. Stds. Orgn. Office: Nat Ctr Atmospheric Rsch PO Box 3000 Boulder CO 80309

ADAMS, JO-ANN MARIE, lawyer; b. L.A., May 27, 1949; d. Joseph John and Georgia S. (Wein) A.; AA, Pasadena City Coll., 1968; BA, Pomona Coll., 1970; MA, Calif. State U., L.A., 1971; MBA, Pacific Luth. U., 1983; cert. in Telecomm. and Info. Resource Mgmt., U. Hawaii, 1993; JD, Santa Clara U., 1996. Secondary tchr. South Pasadena (Calif.) Unified Schs., 1970-71; appraiser Riverside County (Calif.) Assessor's Office, 1972-74; systems and procedures analyst Riverside County Data Processing Dept., 1974-76, supervising systems analyst, 1976-79; systems analyst computer Boeing Computer Svcs. Co., Seattle, 1979-81; sr. systems analyst Thurston County Central Svcs., Olympia, Wash., 1981-83, data processing systems mgr., 1983-84; data processing systems engr. IBM Corp., 1984-87; realtor-assoc., Dower Realty, 1987-92; corp. sales rep. UniGlobe Met. Travel, 1988-89; project mgr. Servco Pacific, 1989-90, Scott Software Systems, 1990-91; systems analyst Dept. Atty. Gen., 1991-93; cons. in field, 1993—; pvt. practice, 1996—; law clerk HiTech Law, 1995-96, Law Offices Thomas R. Hogan, 1995; instr. Riverside City Coll., 1977-79; vis. lectr. Santa Clara U., 1997. Chairperson legis. task force Riverside/San Bernardino chpt. NOW, 1975-76, chpt. co-chairperson, 1978; mem. ethics com. Calif. NOW Inc., 1978; alt. del. Calif Dem. Caucus, 1978. Mem. ABA, SCCBA, NAFE, Pomona Coll. Alumni Assn., Santa Clara U. Alumni Assn. Home: 18415 Purdue Dr Saratoga CA 95070-4712

ADAMS, JOHN M., library director; b. Chicago, Ill., June 10, 1950; s. Merlin J. and Esther (Bohn) A.; m. Nancy Ileen Coultas, June 12, 1970; 1 child, Arwen Lee. B.A. in English, U. Ill., 1972, M.L.S., 1973. Grad. asst. U. Ill. Libr., Urbana, 1972-73; libr.-reference Sherman Oaks Libr., L.A., 1973-75; libr. philosophy dept. L.A. Pub. Libr., 1975-77, head gen. reading svc., 1977-78; dir. Moline Pub. Libr., Ill., 1978-83, Tampa (Fla.)-Hillsborough County Pub. Libr. System, 1983-91; dir., county librarian Orange County (Calif.) Public Library System, 1991—; dir. Tampa Bay Libr. Consortium, Fla., 1983-91, Santiago Libr. System, 1991—; mem. adv. com. on pub. librs. OCLC, 1992-95. Contbr. articles to profl. jours. Bd. dirs. Planned Parenthood of Tampa, 1984. Recipient Frontier award ALA Mag., 1981; named Outstanding Young Man, Moline Jaycees, 1983. Mem. ALA (J.C. Dana award 1982, 93), Calif. Libr. Assn., Calif. County Librs. Assn., Orange County C. of C. Office: Orange County Pub Libr 1501 E Saint Andrew Pl Santa Ana CA 92705-4930

ADAMS, JULIAN, writer, retired educator; b. Pasadena, Calif., Jan. 29, 1919; s. Julian Leland and May Adams (Latham) A.; m. Ruth Metz, Apr. 1, 1950 (dec. Apr. 1983); children: Gregory M. Thomas, Shirley M. McDonald. AB, U. Calif., Berkeley, 1939; MA, San Francisco State U., 1960. Adminstr. Mare Island Navy Yard, Vallejo, Calif., 1940-48; tchr. Richmond (Calif.) Schs., 1950-74, counselor, 1958-65; Author: Press Time, 1963, 85, Mass Communication, 1981, Freedom and Ethics, 1983, Journalism Bibliography, 1994; contbr. to jour. Communications, 1982-89. Scoutmaster Boy Scouts Am., Berkeley, 1940-89 (Silver Beaver award 1963); mem. Berkeley Breakfast Club, 1980-89; elder Presbyn. Ch., 1980—. With USN, 1944-46. Recipient Pioneer award Nat. Scholastic Press Assn., 1985. Mem. Journalism Edn. Assn. (bd. mem. 1984-86, Carl Towley award 1978), Calif. Writers Club (bd. dirs. 1992—), City Commons Club (sec.-treas. 1984—). Presbyterian. Home: 52 El Camino Real Berkeley CA 94705-2424

ADAMS, JULIE KAREN, clinical psychologist; b. Portland, Oreg., Dec. 12, 1955; d. Allen Hays and Susanna Angelina (Meyers) A. B degree, Willamette U., 1977; M degree, Ctrl. Wash. U., 1982; cert. in bus. adminstrn., U. Wash., 1986; D degree, Pacific U., 1992. Lic. clin. psychologist; cert. counselor, sch. psychologist, Wash. Sch. psychologist Highline Sch. Dist., Seattle, 1987-90; psychology intern Elmcrest Psychiat. Hosp., Portland, Conn., 1990, clinician, 1991; rsch. asst. Yale U., New Haven, Conn., 1991; clinician Advanced Clin. Svcs., Seattle, 1991-93; postdoctoral fellow U. Wash., Seattle, 1991-93; acad. counselor Johns Hopkins U., Balt., 1993; behavior intervention specialist Edmonds (Wash.) Sch. Dist., 1993-94, Marysville Sch. Dist., Marysville, Wash., 1994—; instr. Seattle U., 1995—; guest spkr. in field to profl. assns., also Pacific U., U. Wash., U. Oreg., 1989—. Contbr. articles to profl. jours. Mem. tng. com., kids week com., nursing home com., pub. policy com. Jr. League of Seattle, 1988—; health care researcher Wash. State Legis., Olympia, 1993; campaigner Bush for Pres., Seattle, 1988, 92; rsch. asst. to state senator Oreg. State Legis., Salem, 1985; press page nat. conv. Rep. Nat. Com., Detroit, 1980; student grad. v.p., faculty rep. com. Pacific U. Sch. of Profl. Psychology, 1989-90. Mem. APA (health psychology com. student rep. 1992-93), Wash. Psychol. Assn., Willamette U. Alumni Assn. (bd. dirs. 1983-88), Vols. for Outdoor Wash. (bd. dirs. 1986-87), City Club of Seattle (membership com. 1986-88), Jr. League Seattle, Psi Chi, Beta Alpha Gamma. Home: 1038 NE 125th St Seattle WA 98125-4044

ADAMS, KEN R., gaming analyst, consultant, historian; b. Carson City, Nev., Sept. 8, 1942; s. Maurice Adams and Gertrude Aloha (Wilson) Burke; m. Maria C. Saldavia, Mar. 15, 1971; 1 child, John Anthony. Prin. Ken Adams and Assoc., Sparks, Nev., 1990—; coord. gaming history series of the oral history program U. Nev., continuing edns. gaming mgmt. program adv. com., 1988-97, chmn., 1988. Co-author: Playing the Cards That Are Dealt, 1992, Always Bet on the Butcher, 1994, War Stories, 1995; publ., assoc. editor: Nev. Gaming Almanac, 1991-97, Nev. Gaming Directory, 1993-97, Adams' Report. Chmn. mktg. com. Downtown Improvement Assn., 1994—; steering com., chmn. gaming com. Festival Reno, 1984-86; mem. adv. bd. Leadership Reno Alumni Assn., 1995-97. Mem. Internat. Platform Assn. Home and Office: Ken Adams and Assoc 5370 Point View Way Sparks NV 89431-1019

ADAMS, LILIANA OSSES, music performer, harpist; b. Poznan, Poland, May 16, 1939; came to U.S., 1978, naturalized, 1990; d. Sylwester and Helena (Koswenda) O.; m. Edmund Pietryk, Sept. 4, 1965 (div. Aug. 1970); m. Bruce Meredith Adams, Feb. 3, 1978. MA, Music Acad. Poznan, Poland, 1971. Prin. harpist Philharm. Orch. of Szczecin, Poland, 1964-72, Imperial Opera and Ballet Orch., Tehran, Iran, 1972-78; pvt. music tchr. Riyadh, Saudi Arabia, 1979-81; soloist Austrian Radio, 1981-86; solo harpist, pvt. tchr. harp and piano Antioch, Calif., 1986—; music cons. Schs. and Librs., Calif., 1991—. Contbr. articles to profl. jours. Mem. Am. Fedn. of Musicians, Am. Harp Soc., Music Tchrs. Assn. Calif., Internat. Soc. of Harpers, U.K. Harp Assn., Internat. Harp Ctr. (Switzerland). Home: PO Box 233 Antioch CA 94509-0023

ADAMS, LINDA ALCORN, telecommunications policy professional; b. L.A., Feb. 28, 1943; d. William Fort and Marilynne (Dalton) Alcorn; m. Judd Noah Adams, Sept. 26, 1964; 1 child, Julisa Danae. BA, UCLA, 1966; MA, Sangamon State U., Springfield, Ill., 1975. Adminstrv. asst. U. Calif. Santa Barbara Alumni Office, 1967-70; grad. student advisor UCLA Sch. Architecture and Urban Planning, 1970-72; program analyst Econ. and Fiscal Commn., Springfield, 1972-75; dir. program rev. and investigation Conn. Gen. Assembly, Hartford, 1975-79; dir. adminstrn. and fin. Nat. Conf. State Legislatures, Denver, 1979-83; govt. affairs dir. AT&T, Denver, 1983—; mem. exe. com. Nat. Conf. State Legislatures, Denver, 1977-79; bd. dirs. Wyo. Taxpayers Assn., Cheyenne, 1990—, Found. for State Legislatures, Denver, 1986—; pres. State Govt. Affairs Coun., Washington, 1992-93. Named to Outstanding young Women of Am., 1978. Mem. N.Am. Trail Ride Conf. (nat. championship 1988), Boulder County Horsemen's Assn. (bd. dirs.). Democrat. Home and Office: 179 Cordova Ct Boulder CO 80303-4906

ADAMS, LISA KAY, artist; b. Bristol, Pa., Aug. 3, 1955; d. Charles Joseph Jr. and Liese-Lotte (Leiss) Adams. Student, U. Heidelberg, West Germany, 1976; BA, Scripps Coll., Claremont, Calif., 1977; MFA, Claremont Grad. Sch., 1980. Exhibited in one-person shows at Newspace, L.A., 1989, 90, 92, 93, Daniel Maher Gallery, L.A., 1991, Century Gallery, Sylmar, Calif., 1992,

William Turner Gallery, Venice, Calif., 1994, Coll. So. Nev., North Las Vegas, 1995; group shows include U. Calif., Irvine, Soho Ctr. for Visual Arts, N.Y.C., East Hawaii Cultural Ctr., Hilo, Santa Monica (Calif.) Art Complex, L.A. Mcpl. Art Gallery, Lanning Gallery, Houston, Dorothy Goldeen Gallery, Santa Monica, Calif., William Turner Gallery, Venice, Calif.; represented in permanent collections at Aratex, Burbank, Calif., Laguna Mus. of Art, Laguna Beach, Calif., Nippon Steel USA Inc., L.A., Sun Am., L.A.; also pvt. collections. Bd. dirs. Side St. Projects, 1994-95. Brody Arts Fund fellow, 1992; recipient Fulbright Sr. award, 1996. Mem. L.A. Contemporary Exhbns. Home and Office: PO Box 2456 Venice CA 90294

ADAMS, LORETTA, marketing executive. BS in Internat. Mktg., Am. U., 1962; postgrad. in Econs., U. Panama, Panama City, 1963-64. Mgmt. trainee Sears Roebuck & Co., Panama City, Panama, 1962-63, mgmt. pers., 1963-65; supr. internat. advertising projects Kenyon & Eckhardt Advertising, Inc., N.Y.C., 1965-68; asst. rsch. dir. divsn. L.Am. and Far E. Richardson-Vicks Internat., Mexico City and Wilton, Conn., 1968-69, rsch. dir. divsn. Mex. and L.Am., 1969-75, mem. top mgmt. strategic planning team, 1975-78; founder, pres. Mkt. Devel., Inc., San Diego, 1978—. Contbr. articles to profl. jours. Mem. Am. Mktg. Assn., European Soc. for Opinion & Market Rsch., Advt. Rsch. Found., Coun. Am. Survey Rsch. Orgns., Market Rsch. Assn. Office: Market Devel Inc Transcultural Rsch 1643 16th Ave San Diego CA 92101-5628*

ADAMS, MARK, artist; b. Ft. Plain, N.Y., Oct. 27, 1925; s. Earl D. and Edith (Wohlgemuth) A.; m. Beth Van Hoesen, Sept. 12, 1953. Student, Syracuse U., 1943-46, Hans Hofmann Sch. Fine Arts, 1946, 48, Jean Lurcat, 1955. Instr. San Francisco Art Inst., 1961; panelist Internat. Symposium on Tapestry, San Francisco, 1976; disting. vis. prof. U. Calif. at Davis, 1978; painter in residence Am. Acad. in Rome, 1963. Book: Mark Adams, 1985; one-man shows include deYoung Mus., San Francisco, 1959, Portland (Oreg.) Mus., 1961, Calif. Palace of Legion of Honor, San Francisco, 1961, retrospective, 1970, San Francisco Mus. Modern Art, 1962, French & Co., N.Y.C., 1964, John Berggruen Gallery, San Francisco, 1978, 80, 82, 83, 85, 87, 90, 94, Graham Modern, N.Y.C., 1981, 84, Jane Haslem Salon, Washington, 1989, Palo Alto (Calif.) Cultural Ctr., 1990; exhibited in numerous group shows including Mus. Contemporary Crafts, N.Y.C., 1957, 58, 62, 65, Dallas Mus., 1958, Internat. Biennial of Tapestry, Lausanne, Switzerland, 1962, 65, St. Louis Art Mus., 1964, Norfolk Mus., 1966; represented in permanent collections San Francisco Mus. Modern Art, Dallas Mus. Fine Arts, Chase Manhattan Bank, N.Y.C., San Francisco Pub. Library, Legion of Honor Mus., San Francisco; maj. archtl. commns. include tapestries, Bank of Calif., San Francisco, Weyerhauser Co., Tacoma, Wash., Fairmont Hotel, Dallas, San Francisco Internat. Airport, Luth. Brotherhood, Mpls., stained glass, Temple Emanu-el, San Francisco, St. Thomas More Cath. Ch., San Francisco, St. Andrews Episcopal Ch., Saratoga, Calif. Office: care John Berggruen Gallery 228 Grant Ave San Francisco CA 94108-4612*

ADAMS, MARY ELIZABETH, counselor, psychotherapist, writer; b. Washington, Iowa, Oct. 22, 1920; d. Arthur Ernest and Annabelle (Marshall) Atchison; m. Clinton Adams, Jan. 9, 1943; 1 child, Michael Gerald. BA, UCLA, 1943; MA, U. N.Mex., 1978. Cert. counselor, Nat. Bd. Cert. Counselors; lic. profl. clin. counselor N.Mex. Counseling and Therapy Practice Bd. Sec., adminstrv. asst. USAF, Colorado, N.Y., 1943-46; tchr. L.A. Pub. Schs., 1946-50; sec., bur. bus. econ. rsch. UCLA, 1951-53; asst. to dir. J. Paul Getty Mus., Malibu, Calif., 1954; news reporter Radio WLAP/UPress, Lexington, Ky., 1955-57; adminstrv. asst. mgmt. sci. rsch. UCLA, 1960-62; editor U. N.Mex. Press, Albuquerque, 1962-68, mng. editor N.Mex. Quarterly, 1965-68, acting dir., 1967; resource developer HELP, N.Mex., 1969-78; counselor/therapist med. sch. U. N.Mex., Albuquerque, 1978-88; pvt. practice Albuquerque, 1981—; cons. The Ford Found., Colo., N.Mex., Tex., 1977-82. Freelance editor, 1978—; contbr. articles to profl. jours., periodicals, books. Active Friends of Art, Albuquerque, 1962—; vol. counselor Cmty. Mental Health Ctrs., Albuquerque, 1978—; bd. dirs. Albuquerque Symphony, 1962-63, Friends of Dance, Albuquerque, 1990-95. Mem. Am. Counseling Assn., Nat. Cert. Clin. Mental Health Counselors Assn., N.Mex. Counseling Assn., N.Mex. Clin. Mental Health Counselors Assn., N.Mex. Psychoanalytic Soc. Democrat. Home: 1917 Morningside Dr NE Albuquerque NM 87110-4927

ADAMS, PHILIP, lawyer; b. Los Angeles, July 18, 1905; s. Thaddeus Lafayette and Lena (Kelly) A.; m. Alice Rahman, 1933 (div.); children: Stephen, Judith, Deborah, Kate; m. Elaine Margaret Anderson, 1968 (wid. 1996). Student, Pomona Coll., 1924-27; JD, Hastings Coll. Law, U. Calif., 1938; LLD (hon.), Ch. Div. Sch. of Pacific, Berkeley, Calif., 1965. Bar: Calif. 1938. Purser Panama Mail S.S. Line, 1928-29; profl. investigator, 1930-38; individual practice law San Francisco, 1938-95; ptnr. Adams & Romer, 1996—; atty. U.S. Govt., 1942-46. Author: Adoption Practice in California, 1956. Dir. ACLU of No. Calif., 1933-54, Children's Protective Soc., 1939-44, United Cerebral Palsy Assn., San Francisco, 1952-72, Assn. Mental Health, 1952-70, Unitee Bay Area Crusade, 1955-61, United Community Fund, San Francisco, 1957-62, San Francisco State Coll., 1964-69; trustee Ch. Divinity Sch. of Pacific, 1951-76; chancellor Episcopal Diocese Calif., 1960-67; dep. Episcopal Gen. Conv., 1946-70; trustee Grad. Theol. Union, Berkeley, 1959-66, pres. bd., 1963-66. Fellow Am. Acad. Matrimonial Lawyers (dir. No. Calif. chpt. 1968-80), Acad. Calif. Adoption Lawyers (dir. 1988—); mem. ABA (chmn. com. on adoption, family law sect. 1959-60), Calif., San Francisco Bar Assn., Lawyers Club San Francisco (gov. 1956), San Francisco Symphony Assn., Chamber Soloists San Francisco (dir. 1985—), Soc. Genealogists (London). Clubs: Villa Taverna, Commonwealth. Home: 2170 Jackson St San Francisco CA 94115-1550 Office: 220 Montgomery St San Francisco CA 94104-3402

ADAMS, ROBERT GRANVILLE, marketing professional; b. Indpls., July 2, 1927; s. Jack and Iris (Trippeer) A.; m. Marilyn Howe (div.); m. Ilona Molnar (div.); children: Lynn, Victoria, Amy. BS, Ind. U., 1953. Capt. USAF, 1945-65; various assignments as pilot Adams Mktg., Inc.; horse rancher Am. Quarter Horse Assn., Scottsdale, Ariz., 1965-88; wholesaler Nat. Home Furnishings Assn., Scottsdale, 1988—; pres. Adams Mktg., Inc., Scottsdale, 1980—. Bd. dirs. Desert Caballeros, Wickenburg, Ariz., Rancheros Visitadores, Santa Barbara, Calif. Mem. Desert Caballeros (Wickenburg, Ariz., bd. dirs.), Rancheros Visitadores (Santa Barbara, Calif.), Sigma Chi (life Loyal Sig). Office: PO Box 14350 Scottsdale AZ 85267-4350

ADAMS, ROBERT MONROE, retired dermatologist, educator; b. Pasadena, Calif., May 4, 1926; s. Oscar D. and Mamie (Butler) A.; m. Lorene Tassi, Mar. 21, 1948; children: Cynthia, Gregory. AB with distinction, Stanford U., 1946, MD, 1950. Diplomate Am. Bd. Dermatology. Rotating intern San Francisco City and County Hosp., 1949-50; resident in internal medicine Tripler Army Hosp., Honolulu, 1950-52; pvt. practice in family medicine Stockton, Calif., 1952-64; dermatologist Palo Alto (Calif.) Med. Clinic, 1967-75; resident in dermatology Stanford (Calif.) U. Med. Ctr., 1964-67, fellow in dermatology, 1966-67, dir. Contact Dermatitis and Occupational Skin Disease Clinic, 1967-96; from instr. to clin. prof. dermatology Stanford U., 1966-82, clin. prof. dermatology, 1982-96; mem. staff Stanford U. Hosp., 1967-96; pvt. practice in dermatology Menlo Park, Calif., 1975—; ret., 1996; dir. or co-dir. various profl. courses and symposia; guest lectr. many sci. confs. and ednl. instns., most recently Skin and Cancer Found. Seminar, Sidney, Australia, 1992, Cypress Found., Carmel, Calif., 1994, U. Calif., San Francisco, L.A. and Davis, numerous occasions. Author: (textbooks) Occupational Contact Dermatitis, 1969, Occupational Skin Disease, 1983, 2nd edit., 1990; co-author: Color Text of Contact Dermatitis, 1992; editor: Occupational Medicine, State of the Art Reviews, 1986; contbr. 13 chpts. to books; founding editor Am. Jour. Contact Dermatitis, editor-in-chief, 1989-92, mem. editl. bd., 1992—; mem. editl. bd. Jour. Am. Acad. Dermatology, 1986—, Health Hazards of the Workplace Report, 1989; contbr. numerous articles and revs. to sci. jours. Recipient Jean Spencer Felton award for Excellence in Sci. Writing, 1983. Mem. AMA (mem. adv. panel on med. standards 1979-83), Am. Acad. Dermatology (mem. task force on contact dermatitis 1976-91, Gold award for Teaching 1981, bd. dirs. 1989-93), Calif. Med. Assn. (mem. adv. panel on occupational medicine 1975-83), We. Occupational Med. Assn. (pres. 1983-84), Am. Soc. for Contact Dermatitis (pres., founder 1989-91), Am. Conf. Govtl. Indsl. Hygienists, San Francisco Dermatology Soc. (pres. 1985-86), Soc. for Investigative Dermatology, Pacific Dermatol. Assn., Internat. Soc. for Tropical Dermatology, Santa Clara Med. Soc., Brit. Assn. Dermatologist (hon.), Mex. Acad. Dermatology (hon.), Chilean Soc. Dermatology (hon.), Venezuelan Soc. Dermatology (hon.), Chinese Contact Dermatitis Rsch. Group (hon.). Home: 555 Laurel Ave Apt 108 San Mateo CA 94401-4157

ADAMS, SARAH VIRGINIA, family counselor; b. San Francisco, Oct. 23, 1955; d. Marco Tulio and Helen (Jorge) Zea; m. Glenn Richard Adams, Mar 22, 1980; children: Mark Vincent, Elena Giselle, Johnathan Richard. BA, Calif. State U., Long Beach, 1978, MS, 1980; MACL, Fuller Sem., Pasadena, 1996. Lic. marriage, family, child counseling. Tutor math. and sci. Montebello, Calif., 1979-82; behavioral specialist Cross Cultural Psychol. Corp., L.A., 1979-80; psychol. asst. Legal Psychology, L.A., 1980-82, Eisner Psychol. Assocs., L.A., 1982-83; assoc. dir. Legal Psychodiagnosis and Forensic Psychology, L.A., 1982-83; adminstrv. dir. Diagnostic Clinic, Calif., 1983-85; dir. Diagnostic Clinic of West Covina, Calif., 1985-87; owner Adams Family Counseling Inc., Calif., 1987—; tchr. piano, Montebello, 1973-84; ins. agent Am. Mut. Life Ins., Des Moines, 1982-84. Fellow Am. Assn. Marriage and Family Therapists, Am. Psychol. Assn.; mem. NAFE, Calif. Assn. Marriage and Family Therapists, Calif. State Psychol. Assn., Calif. Soc. Indsl. Medicine and Surgery, Western Psychol. Assn., Psi Chi, Pi Delta Phi. Republican. Roman Catholic. Office: Adams Family Counseling Inc 260 S Glendora Ave # 101 West Covina CA 91790-3041

ADAMS, TUCKER HART, economic research company executive; b. Prescott, Ark., Jan. 11, 1938; d. Hugh Ross and Mildred (Dunn) Hart; m. Daniel Williams Adams, Sept. 6, 1957; children: Virginia Schoenthaler, Carolyn, Catherine Adams-Gravley, Anne Green. BA in Math., Wellesley Coll., 1959; MA in Econs., U. Colo., 1977, PhD in Econs., 1979. V.p., chief economist United Banks of Colo., Denver, 1978-88; pres., chief exec. officer The Adams Group, Inc., Colorado Springs, Colo., 1988—; pres. Am. Russian Collaborative Enterprises, LLC, 1994—; bd. dirs. Mortgage Analysis Corp., Mont. Power Co., Guaranty Nat. Corp., Ag Am., Tax Free Fund Colo., Rocky Mountain Equity Fund, ROC Cmtys. Author: (newsletter) Today's Economy: A Colorado Viewpoint, 1989—. Bd. dirs. Colo. Health Facilities Authority, Denver, Denver Found., Colo. Sch. Mines Found., Univ. Hosp., Denver, U. Colo. Found., Boulder. Pendleton scholar Wellesley Coll., 1955; grad. fellowship U. Colo., 1977. Mem. Colo. Womens Forum (pres. 1988), Internat. Womens Forum. Republican. Presbyterian. Office: The Adams Group Inc 4822 Alteza Dr Ste 300 Colorado Springs CO 80917-4002

ADAMS, WILLIAM WESLEY, III, architect; b. Lexington, Ky., Dec. 18, 1961; s. William Wesley II and Cathryn (Inman) A.; m. Lesli Rachelle Lewis, July 15, 1989; 1 child, William Wesley IV. BArch, Howard U., 1986. Lic. architect, Calif. Architect Clas, Riggs, Owens & Ramos, Silver Spring, Md., 1986-88; prin. Kennard Design Group Architecture & Planning, L.A., 1988-95; owner InVision Architecture, L.A., 1995—; draftsman Washington pub. schs., 1984, NSF, Washington, 1985. Mem. AIA, Nat. Orgn. Minority Architects (nat. treas. 1992-95, nat. 2d v.p. 1995—, Svc. award 1993). Home: 3823 Sutro Ave Los Angeles CA 90008-1924 Office: InVision Architecture 3660 Wilshire Blvd # 842 Los Angeles CA 90010-2756

ADAMSON, GEOFFREY DAVID, reproductive endocrinologist, surgeon; b. Ottawa, Ont., Can., Sept. 16, 1946; came to U.S., 1978, naturalized, 1986; s. Geoffrey Peter Adamson and Anne Marian Allan; m. Rosemary C. Oddie, Apr. 28, 1973; children: Stephanie, Rebecca, Eric. BSc with honors, Trinity Coll., Toronto, Can., 1969; MD, U. Toronto, 1973. Diplomate Am. Bd. Ob-Gyn., Am. Bd. Laser Surgery; cert. Bd. Reproductive Endocrinology. Resident in ob-gyn. Toronto Gen. Hosp., 1973-77, fellow in ob-gyn., 1977-78; fellow reproductive endocrinology Stanford (Calif.) U. Med. Ctr., 1978-80; practice medicine specializing in infertility Los Gatos, Calif., 1980-84; instr. Stanford U. Sch. Medicine, 1980-84; clin. asst. prof. Stanford U. Sch. Medicine, Calif., 1984-92; clin. assoc. prof. Stanford U. Sch. Medicine, 1992-95, clin. prof., 1995—; assoc. clin. prof. Sch. Medicine U. Calif., San Francisco, 1992—. Mem. editl. adv. bd. Can. Doctor mag., 1977-83, numerous others; contbr. numerous articles to sci. jours., mags.; editor: (textbook) Endoscopic Management of Gynecologic Disease, 1996. Ontario Ministry of Health fellow, 1977-78. Fellow ACS, Royal Coll. Surgeons Can., Am. Coll. Ob-Gyns.; mem. AAAS, AMA, Am. Assn. Gynecol. Laparoscopists (adv. bd.), Am. Soc. Reproductive Medicine (numerous coms.), Soc. Reproductive Endocrinologists (charter), Soc. Reproductive Surgeons (charter, bd. dirs., sec., treas., v.p.), Soc. Assisted Reproductive Tech. (treas., dir., v.p. elect), Pacific Coast Fertility Soc. (dir., sec., pres.-elect), Pacific Coast Ob-Gyn. Soc., Soc. Gynecologic Surgeons, San Francisco Ob-Gyn. Soc., Bay Area Reproductive Endocrinologists Soc. (founding pres.), Gynecol. Laser Soc., N.Y. Acad. Scis., Shufelt Gynecol. Soc., Peninsula Gynecol. Soc. (past pres.), Calif. Med. Assn., San Mateo County Med. Assn., Santa Clara County Med. Assn., Am. Fedn. Clin. Rsch., Nat. Resolve (sec., dir.), Can. Assn. Interns and Residents (hon. life, pres. 1977-79, bd. dirs. 1974-79, rep. AMA resident physician sect. 1978-79, rep. Can. Med. Protective Assn. 1975-78, rep. Can. Med. Assn. 1975-78, Disting. Svc. award 1980), Profl. Assn. Interns and Residents Ont. (bd. dirs. 1973-76, v.p. 1974-75, pres. 1975-76), Royal Coll. Physicians and Surgeons Can. (com. exams. 1977-80), Ont. Med. Assn. (sec. interns and residents sect. 1973-74). Home: 20140 Rancho Bella Vista Saratoga CA 95070 Office: 540 University Ave # 200 Palo Alto CA 94301-1912

ADAMSON, H. DOUGLAS, English language educator; b. Salt Lake City, Sept. 30, 1944; s. Jack Hale and Margaret (Boyle) A.; m. Alice Leeth, Dec. 29, 1969; children: Marie Donnell, Katherine Boyle. AB in English, U. Calif., Berkeley, 1967; cert., UCLA, 1970; MA in Linguistics, San Jose State U., 1972; PhD in Linguistics, Georgetown U., 1980. Asst. prof. George Mason U., Fairfax, Va., 1979-88; assoc. prof. U. Ariz., Tucson, 1988—, dir. grad. studies English dept., 1992-94, advisor PhD program in second lang. acquisition, 1994-97, chair PhD program in second lang. acquistion, 1997—. Author: Variation Theory and Second Language Acquisition, 1988, Academic Competence: Theory and Classroom Practice, 1993. Mid-career fellowship Mellon Found., 1988. Mem. Linguistics Soc. of Am., TESOL, Ariz. TESOL. Office: U Ariz English Dept Tucson AZ 85721

ADAMSON, ROBERT MICHAEL KNAGGS, spiritual teacher, whole body wellness and health restoration specialist; b. Elkins, W.Va., Sept. 14, 1945; s. Howard Robert and Elizabeth Jane (Adamson) Knaggs; 1 child, Galen Dougal. BS, W.Va. U., 1967, MEd in Wellness Promotion, 1973, MEd in Counseling, 1974; Doctoral Studies, Internat. U. Profl. Studies. Dir. Adamson Leadership and Personal Devel. Seminars, San Diego, 1982—; therapist Palomar/Pomerado Hosps., Escondido, Calif., 1991-93, therapist, counselor, 1988-90; counselor Palomar Coll., San Marcos, Calif., 1990—; dir. health edn. meml. Gen. Hosp., Elkins, W.Va., 1982-84. Author: Serenity Principle, 1993, Secret of Transformation, 1994, How to Solve Your Problems by Not Facing Them, 1995. Office: Adamson Leadershp & Pers Devel Seminars 12194 Waverly Downs San Diego CA 92128

ADAPA, RAMBABU, electrical engineer; b. Adapavaripalem, Andhra Pradesh, India, Sept. 2, 1956; s. Kanakayya and Vanavalamma (Annisetti) A.; m. Indira Devi Samba, Oct. 30, 1983; 1 child, Priyanka Sai. BTech in Elec. Engring, Jawaharlal Nehru Tech. U., Andhra Pradesh, India, 1979; MTech in Elec. Engring., Indian Inst. Tech., Kanpur, India, 1981; PhD in Elec. Engring., U. Waterloo, Ont., Can., 1986. Registered profl. engr., Wis. Power sys. staff engr. Thomas A. Edison Tech. Ctr., McGraw-Edison Power Sys., Franksville, Wis., 1986-89; mgr. power sys. planning, power delivery group Electric Power Rsch. Inst., Palo Alto, Calif., 1989—. Mem. IEEE (sr., vice chmn. local Santa Clara Valley PES chpt. 1983-84, chmn. chpt. 1994-95, awards chmn. Pitts. sect., chmn. edn. com. Pitts. chpt., mem. numerous other coms.). Home: 3242 Alder Ave Fremont CA 94536-3502 Office: Electric Power Rsch Inst 3412 Hillview Ave Palo Alto CA 94304-1395

ADDAMS, ROBERT JEAN, finance executive; b. Salt Lake City, Sept. 24, 1942; s. Harvey J. and Virginia (Dutson) A.; children: Ryan, Kelley, Amy, Michael. BS, U. Utah, 1968, MBA, 1969. Dir. budgets & cost control Western Airlines, Inc., L.A., 1976-80; v.p., gen. mgr. Ball Bros., Inc., Everette, Wash., and Anchorage, 1980-82; pres., cons. Addams & Assocs., Woodinville, Wash., 1982-89; contr. Lafayette F. Sharies, Seattle, 1990-93; CFO Internat. Inetegrators, Seattle; CFO Mountain High Knitting, Seattle and San Diego, 1995—. Author: Care and Handling of Wetsalted Cod Fish, 1984; also articles on budgeting and business plans to nat. monthly newsletter. Scoutmaster, Explorer advisor Gt. Salt Lake and L.A. councils Boy Scouts Am., 1973-75; served 2-yr. mission for Ch. Jesus Christ Latter-day Saints, 1962-64. Served with U.S. Army, 1961-62. Named Outstanding Grad., Coll. Bus., 1968, Beehive Honor Soc., 1969. Mem. U. Utah Alumni Assn. (pres. So. Calif. chpt. 1976-80), U. Utah Coll. of Bus. Alumni (pres. So. Calif. group 1978-79), Alpha Kappa Psi. Republican. Home: 12920 177th Pl NE Redmond WA 98052

ADDIS, RICHARD BARTON, lawyer; b. Columbus, Ohio, April 9, 1929; s. Wilbur Jennings and Leila Olive (Grant) A.; m. Marguerite C. Christjohn, Feb. 9, 1957; children: Jacqueline Carol, Barton David. BA, Ohio State U., 1954, JD, 1955. Bar: Ohio 1956, U.S. Dist. Ct. (no. dist.) Ohio 1957, N.Mex. 1963, U.S. Dist. Ct. N.Mex. 1963, Laguna Pueblo (N.Mex.) Tribal Ct. 1986. Pvt. practice, Canton, Ohio, 1956-63, Albuquerque, 1963—, Laguna Pueblo, Navajo Nation, 1986—. With USMC, 1946-48, 50-52. Mem. Ohio Bar Assn., N.Mex. Bar Assn., Am. Arbitration Assn. (arbitrator 1968—). Office: PO Box 25923 Albuquerque NM 87125-5923

ADDIS, THOMAS HOMER, III, professional golfer; b. San Diego, Nov. 30, 1945; s. Thomas H. and Martha J. (Edwards) A.; student Foothill Jr. Coll., 1963, Grossmont Jr. Coll., 1965; degree in profl. golf mgmt. (hon.) Ferris State U.; m. Susan Tera Buckley, June 13, 1966; children: Thomas Homer IV, Bryan Michael. Head golf profl., mgr. Sun Valley Golf Course, La Mesa, Calif., 1966-67; head golf profl., dir. golf Singing Hills Country Club and Lodge, 1969—; pres. PGA of Am., 1994-96; gen. chmn. Nat. Jr. Golf championship U.S. Golf Assn., 1973, 89; lectr.; owner Golf Cons. & Design, Rocky Mountain Chocolate Factory, Mammoth. Pres. Calif. State Open, 1980-84; chmn. Nat. Com. Liaison for Physically Challenged, 1984-88; dir. Cuyamaca Coll. Found. Recipient Retailer award Golf Industry mag., 1985; named to Lady Aztec San Diego State U. Hall of Fame. Mem. PGA (pres. San Diego chpt. 1978-79; pres. sect. 1980-82, bd. dirs. sect. 1974-90, speaker, chmn. mem. svc. com. 1986-87, bd. dirs. San Diego sect. 1974-90, assn. coord. bus. schs. and seminars, named Profl. of Yr. So. Calif. sect. 1979, 89, Horton Smith award So. Calif. sect. 1980-81, 89, PGA Golf Profl. of Yr. 1989, Nat. Horton Smith award 1981, Resort Merchandiser of Yr., So. Calif. sect. 1978, 83, mem. nat. bd. control 1978-85, chmn. nat. bd. control 1991-92, membership com. 1978, 89-90, nat. edn. com. 1980-85, 89-90, nat. bd. dirs., 1986-88, rules com. 1986-90, championship com. 1986—, hon. life mem. So. Calif. sect. and San Diego PGA, sec. PGA Am. 1991, 92, v.p. PGA Am. 1993, 94, pres. 1994-96), Nat. Golf Found. (Joe Graffis award, 1988) Nat. Amputee Golf Assn. (hon. mem.), San Diego Jr. Golf Assn. (dir.), Assn. Golf Educators, Golf Collector's Soc., Singing Hills Tennis Club, Rotary. Author articles. Office: Singing Hills Golf Course 3007 Dehesa Rd El Cajon CA 92019-2806

ADDISON, ALONZO CHURCH, multimedia communications executive, educator, consultant; b. Berkeley, Calif., 1965; s. John West Jr. and Mary Ann A. BS in Engring., Princeton U., 1988; MArch, U. Calif., Berkeley, 1992, postgrad., 1994. Computer graphics programmer ALK Assocs., Princeton, N.J., 1988-89; strategic tech. cons. ACA Group, El Cerrito, Calif., 1989—; project dir. U. Calif., Berkeley, 1992; v.p. CYRA Technologies, Inc., Orinda, Calif., 1993—; mem. corp. found. rels. com. U. Calif., Berkeley, 1985—; mng. dir., co-founder Mus. of Future Consortium, Berkeley, Milan, 1994—; panel chair, author ACM Siggraph Internat. Conf., 1994, 95; chmn., founder, Asterix Tech. and Design, Inc., Berkeley, 1996; cons., web strategist Bus. Internat. Networks, Inc., Virginia Beach, 1996—; conf. chair Internat. Workshop on Cities, Design and Internet, 1996, 97. Adv. bd. Berkeley Contemporary Opera, 1984—; asst. scoutmaster Mt. Diablo coun. Boy Scouts Am., 1984—. Recipient AIA award, 1992; fellow U. Calif., 1994; rsch. grantee Taisei Am. Corp, 1992-94, Dai Nippon Printing Corp., 1996. Mem. Assn. Computing Machinery Siggraph, Assn. Computer Aided Design in Architecture. Home: 7927 Terrace Dr El Cerrito CA 94530

ADDISON, JOHN ROBERT, counselor; b. Northfield, Mass., Aug. 4, 1927; s. Warren Grant and Mildred Elizabeth (Vorce) A.; m. Emily Loveland Kirk, Jan. 3, 1953; children: Karen Louise, David Martin. BA, U. Mass., 1950; MA, U. Colo., 1963, postgrad., 1964-87. Tchr. Jeffco Pub. Schs., Arvada, Colo., 1956-64; counselor Jeffco Pub. Schs., Arvada Sr. High Sch., Arvada, Colo., 1964-91; admissions counselor Red Rocks C.C., Golden, Colo., 1991-96; mem. Jeffco Area Vocat. Sch. Adv. Coun., 1990-91; mem. Cooperative Occupational Adv. Bd., 1976-91; mem. various adv. coms. Warren Occupational Tng. Ctr., 1970-91. Coach Arvada Soccer Assn., 1971-76; chmn., trustee Arvada Pub. Libr.; active charter rev. com. City of Arvada. With U.S. Army, 1945-47; lst lt. USAF, 1950-55. Decorated Air medal. Mem. NEA, Jefferson County Edn. Assn. (pres. salary com.), Jeffco Counselors Assn. (pres.), Colo. Edn. Assn., Colo. Guidance Counselors Assn. Home: 6066 Lewis Ct Arvada CO 80004-4928 Office: Red Rocks Cmty Coll 13300 W 6th Ave Lakewood CO 80401-5398

ADDY, JOHN KELLY, lawyer; b. Shelby, Mont., May 9, 1949; s. Vearle Delford and Meri Jane (Hyer) A.; m. Marylynn McIntosh, Apr. 16, 1977 (div. 1979); m. Lynne Turner-Fitzgerald, Dec. 31, 1987 (div. 1997); children: Amanda, Caleb, 1 stepchild, Taylor. BA in Govt. with honors, Mont. State U., 1971; JD, Georgetown U., 1974. Bar: D.C. 1975, U.S. Ct. Mil. Appeals 1975, Mont. 1979, U.S. Dist. Ct. Mont. 1979, U.S. Ct. Appeals (9th cir.) 1988, U.S. Supreme Ct. 1991. Asst. to majority U.S. Senate, Washington, 1974; asst. judge advocate BMD Command, U.S. Army, Huntsville, Ala., 1975-77; command judge adv. U.S. Army, Camp Humphreys, Republic of Korea, 1977-78; assoc. Anderson, Brown, Billings, Mont., 1979-81; pvt. practice Billings, 1981-84; gen. ptnr. Matovich & Addy, Billings, 1984-86; sec. Matovich, Addy & Keller, P.C., Billings, 1986—; speaker pro tempore Mont. Ho. Reps., 1989-90. Co-author: Construction Law in Montana, 1981, Employment Law in Montana, 1987. Lay leader Hope United Meth. Ch., Billings, 1984-87, vice chair adminstrv. coun., 1997—; pres. Yellowstone Meth. Found., Billings, 1986-89, Yellowstone Dem. Club, Billings, 1981, Mont. Arthritis Found., Billings, 1981-83; bd. dirs. Deering Clinic, Billings, 1986-92, Alpha Halfway House, Billings, 1984-92; mem. Mont. Ho. of Reps., Helena, 1983-90; vice chair Mont. Dem. Party, 1991-93, chair 1993-97; gen. counsel Alternatives, Inc. Halfway House, 1992—, Regional Mental Health Ctr., 1988—; exec. com. Assn. of State Dem. Chairs, 1997—. Capt. U.S. Army, 1975-78. Named Outstanding Legislator AARP Mont. Chpt., 1987. Mem. ABA, Assn. Trial Lawyers Am., D.C. Bar Assn., State Bar of Mont. (chair pub. rels. com. 1989-94, Disting. Svc. award 1994), Yellowstone Bar Assn., Mont. Trial Lawyers Assn. Democrat. Methodist. Office: Matovich Addy & Keller PC 2812 1st Ave N Billings MT 59101-2312

ADELMAN, IRMA GLICMAN, economics educator; b. Cernowitz, Rumania, Mar. 14, 1930; came to U.S., 1949, naturalized, 1955; d. Jacob Max and Raissa (Ettinger) Glicman; m. Frank L. Adelman, Aug. 16, 1950 (div. 1979); 1 son, Alexander. BS, U. Calif., Berkeley, 1950, MA, 1951, PhD, 1955. Teaching assoc. U. Calif., Berkeley, 1955-56; instr. U. Calif., 1956-57, lectr. with rank asst. prof., 1957-58; vis. asst. prof. Mills Coll., 1958-59; acting asst. prof. Stanford, 1959-61, asst. prof., 1961-62; assoc. prof. Johns Hopkins, Balt., 1962-65; prof. econs. Northwestern U., Evanston, Ill., 1966-72, U. Md., 1972-78; prof. econs. and agrl. econs. U. Calif. at Berkeley, 1979-94; prof. emeritus, 1994—; cons. divsn. indsl. devel. UN, 1962-63, AID U.S. Dept. State, Washington, 1963-72, World Bank, 1968—, ILD, Geneva, 1973—. Author: Theories of Economic Growth and Development, 1961, Institutions and Development Strategies: Selected Essays of Irma Adelman Volume I, 1994, Dynamics and Income Distribution: Selected Essays of Irma Adelman Volume II, 1994, Selected Essays (in Spanish), 1994, (with A. Pepelasis and L. Mears), Economic Development: Analysis and Case Studies, 1961, (with Eric Thorbecke) The Theory and Design of Economic Development, 1966, (with C.T. Morris) Society, Politics and Economic Development—A Quantitative Approach, 1967, Practical Approaches to Development Planning-Korea's Second Five Year Plan, 1969, (with C.T. Morris) Economic Development and Social Equity in Developing Countries, 1973, (with Sherman Robinson) Planning for Income Distribution, 1977-78, (with C. T. Morris) Comparative Patterns of Economic Growth, 1850-1914, 1987, (with Irma and J. Edward Taylor) Village Economies: Design, Estimation and Application of Village Wide Economic Models, 1996, (with Irma and Song Byong Nak) The South Korean Miracle: How Replicable Is It?, 1997. Fellow Center Advanced Study Behavioral Scis., 1970-71; named Women's Hall Fame U. Calif., Berkeley, 1994. Fellow Am. Acad. Arts and Scis., Econometric Soc., Royal Soc. Encouragement Arts, Mfgs. & Commerce

(Berkeley citation 1996); mem. Am. Econ. Assn. (mem. exec. com., v.p. 1969-71). Office: Univ Calif Dept Agr & Natural Resources 207 Giannini Hall Spc 3310 Berkeley CA 94720-3310

ADELMAN, JANET ANN, English literature educator; b. Mt. Kisco, Jan. 28, 1941; d. Emanuel and Ceil (Greenfeld) A.; m. Robert Osserman, July 21, 1976; children: Brian, Stephen. BA, Smith Coll., 1962; postgrad., Oxford (Eng.) U., 1962-63; MA, Yale U., 1968, PhD, 1968. Prof. English lit. U. Calif., Berkeley, 1968—. Author: The Common Liar: An Essay on Antony and Cleopatra, 1973, Suffocating Mothers: Fantasies of Maternal Origin in Shakespeare, Hamlet to The Tempest, 1992; editor: Twentieth Century Interpretations of King Lear, 1978. Fellow Am. Coun. Learned Socs., 1976-77, Guggenheim Found., 1981-82. Mem. MLA, Shakespeare Assn. Am., San Francisco Psychoanalytic Inst. Office: U Calif Dept English Berkeley CA 94720

ADELSMAN, (HARRIETTE) JEAN, newspaper editor; b. Indpls., Oct. 21, 1944; d. Joe and Beatrice Irene (Samuel) A. BS in Journalism, Northwestern U., 1966, MS in Journalism, 1967. Copy editor Chgo. Sun-Times, 1967-75, fin. news editor, 1975-77, entertainment editor, 1977-80, asst. mng. editor features, 1980-84; now mng. editor Daily Breeze, Torrance, Calif. Office: Daily Breeze 5215 Torrance Blvd Torrance CA 90503-4009*

ADELSON, LEONARD JOSEPH, physician; b. N.Y.C., June 3, 1950; s. Arthur and Alice (Schorr) A.; m. Rose Ann Vasta, 1974 (div. 1982); m. Lorin Ann Schiff, Sept. 7, 1985; children: Aaron S., Matthew S. BA in Math. and Psychology, U. Pa., 1972; MD, Jefferson Med. Sch., 1977. Diplomate Am. Bd. Internal Medicine, Am. Bd. Critical Care, Am. Bd. Pulmonary Diseases. Intern internal medicine Med. Ctr. U. So. Calif., 1977-78, resident internal medicine Med. Ctr., 1978-80, pulmonary disease fellow Med. Ctr., 1981-83; pvt. practice Mid. Valley Pulmonary Med. Group, North Hollywood, Calif., 1983—; pulmonary cons., med. dir. respiratory therapy Sherman Oaks (Calif.) Hosp. and Health Ctr., 1983—, chief of staff, 1994-95. Fellow Am. Coll. Chest Physicians; mem. AMA, Calif. Med. Assn., L.A. County Med. Assn. Home: 4811 Andasol Ave Encino CA 91316-3802 Office: 12626 Riverside Dr Ste 404 North Hollywood CA 91607-3420

ADELSON, MERV LEE, entertainment and communication industry executive; b. Los Angeles, Oct. 23, 1929; s. Nathan and Pearl (Schwarzman) A.; m. Thea Nesis, May 25, 1993; 1 child, Lexi Rose; children from previous marriage: Ellen, Gary, Andrew. Student, Menlo Park Jr. Coll. Pres. Markettown Supermarket and Builders Emporium, Las Vegas, 1953-63; mng. ptnr. Paradise Devel., Las Vegas, 1958—; pres. Realty Holdings, 1962—, La Costa, Inc., 1963-87; chmn. bd. dirs. Lorimar Inc., Culver City, Calif., 1969-86; chmn. bd. dirs., chief exec. officer Lorimar Telepictures Corp., Culver City, 1986-89; vice chmn. Warner Communications, 1989—; chmn. East-West Capital Assocs., Inc., 1989—; bd. dirs. Time-Warner Inc. Co-founder Nathan Adelson Hospice Found. Recipient Sherill Corwin Human Relations award Am. Jewish Com., 1987. Mem. Am. Film Inst. (trustee), Am. Mus. of Moving Images (trustee), Entertainment Industries Council (trustee), Acad. Motion Pictures Arts and Scis., Acad. TV Arts and Sciences, Nat. Acad. Cable Programming, Alliance for Capital Access (bd. dirs.), Com. Publicly Owned Cos. (bd. dirs.).

ADENIRAN, DIXIE DARLENE, library administrator; b. L.A., May 26, 1943; d. Alfred and Madge (Clare) Harvey. BA, U. Calif., Santa Barbara, 1965; MA, Mich. State U., 1968; MLS, U. Mich., 1970. Libr. Free Libr. of Phila., 1970-72, Coll. Sci. and Tech., Port Harcourt, Nigeria, 1972-73; libr. Ventura (Calif.) County Libr. Svcs. Agy., 1974-79, libr. dir., 1979—; chair Black Gold Coop. Libr. Sys., 1995—. Pres. Ventura County Master Chorale and Opera Assn., 1985. Mem. ALA, Calif. Libr. Assn. (assembly 1994—), Calif. County Librs. Assn. (pres. 1988), Soroptimists (pres. Ventura club 1984). Home: 5548 Rainier St Ventura CA 93003-1135 Office: Ventura County Libr Svcs 4274 Telegraph Rd Ventura CA 93003-3706

ADEY, WILLIAM ROSS, physician; b. Adelaide, Australia, Jan. 31, 1922; s. William James and Constance Margaret (Weston) A.; m. Alwynne Sidney Morris (div. 1970); children: John, Susan, Geoffrey. MB and BS, U. Adelaide, Australia, 1943, MD, 1949. Sr. lectr. and reader, Dept. Anatomy U. Adelaide, Australia, 1947-53; sr. lectr., Dept. Anatomy U. Melbourne, Australia, 1955-56; prof. anatomy and physiology UCLA, 1957-77; dir. rsch. VA Med. Ctr., Loma Linda, Calif., 1977—; dir. UCLA Space Biology Lab., 1965-77; cons. Office of Sci. and Tech. Policy, Washington,. 1964—, NIH, 1961—, NAS, 1965—. Author: Nonlinear Electrodynamics in Biological Systems, 1984, Magnetic Resonance Imaging of the Brain, Head and Neck, 1984. Surgeon lt. Australian Navy, 1944-46, South Pacific. Fellow IEEE, Royal Soc. and Nuffield Found. (London), AAAS, Am. Electroencephalographic Soc., Royal Soc. Medicine (London), Am. Assn. Neurolog. Surgeons. Home: Rte 1 Box 615 31866 3rd Ave Redlands CA 92374 Office: VA Med Ctr 11201 Benton St Loma Linda CA 92357-1000

ADKINS, BEN FRANK, management and engineering consultant; b. West Liberty, Ky., Mar. 6, 1938; s. Stuart Kendall Adkins and Dorothy Elizabeth (Shaver) Indes; m. Judith Ann Williams, Mar. 14, 1959; children: Michelle Rene, Lori Lee. BS in Indsl. Engring., Ariz. State U., 1964; MBA, Western New Eng. Coll., Springfield, Mass., 1971; MS in Systems Mgmt., U. So. Calif., 1983. Registered profl. engr. Enlisted USAF, 1955, commd. 2d lt., 1964, advanced through grades to maj., 1975, ret., 1979; internal cons., mgr. State of Wash., Olympia, 1979-87; mgmt. and engring. cons. Olympia, 1987-88; sr. rsch. sci. Battelle Pacific N.W. Labs., Richland, Wash., 1988-89; mng. prin. Ben Adkins & Assocs., Olympia, 1989—. Decorated Bronze star USAF. Mem. Inst. Indsl. Engrs. (sr. mem., bd. dirs. Puget Sound chpt. 1984-86, asst. dir. and dir. govt. div. 1979-83, v.p. Washington chpt. 1969-76). Home: 6606 Miner Dr SW Olympia WA 98512-7257 Office: Ben Adkins & Assocs PO Box 7613 Olympia WA 98507-7613

ADLER, CHARLES HOWARD, neurologist; b. N.Y.C., Mar. 6, 1958. BA summa cum laude, Temple U., 1980; MS, N.Y.U., 1984, PhD, 1986, MD, 1986. Intern NYU Manhattan VA Hosp., N.Y.C., 1986-87; resident Hosp. U. Pa., Phila., 1987-90; sr. assoc. cons. neurology Mayo Clinic, Scottsdale, Ariz., 1991-94, cons. neurology, 1994—; asst. prof. neurology Mayo Med. Sch., Scottsdale, Ariz., 1992-97, assoc. prof., 1997—. Contbr. articles to profl. jours. Movement Disorders fellow, Phila., 1990-91; Pres.'s scholar, Temple U., 1980. Mem. AMA, Am. Acad. Neurology, Movement Disorders Soc., Phi Beta Kappa. Office: Mayo Clinic 13400 E Shea Blvd Scottsdale AZ 85259-5499

ADLER, CHARLES SPENCER, psychiatrist; b. N.Y.C., Nov. 27, 1941; s. Benjamin H. and Anne (Greenfield) A.; m. Sheila Noel Morrissey, Oct. 8, 1966 (dec.); m. Peggy Dolan Bean, Feb. 23, 1991. BA, Cornell U., 1962; MD, Duke U., 1966. Diplomate Nat. Bd. Med. Examiners, Am. Bd. Psychiatry and Neurology. Intern Tucson Hosps. Med. Edn. Program, 1966-67; psychiat. resident U. Colo. Med. Sch., Denver, 1967-70; pvt. practice medicine specializing in psychiatry and psychosomatic medicine Denver, 1970—; chief divsn. psychiatry Rose Med. Ctr, 1982-87; co-founder Applied Biofeedback Inst., Denver, 1972-75; prof. pro tempore Cleve. Clinic, 1977; asst. clin. prof. psychiatry U. Colo. Med. Ctr., 1986—, chief psychiatry and psychophysiology Colo. Neurology and Headache Ctr., 1988-95; med. dir. Colo. Ctr. for Biobehavioral Health, Boulder, 1994—; bd. dirs. Acad. Cert. Neurotherapists. Author: (with Gene Stanford and Sheila M. Adler) We Are But a Moment's Sunlight, 1976, (with Sheila M. Adler and Russell Packard) Psychiatric Aspects of Headache, 1987; contbr. (with S. Adler) sect. biofeedback med. and health ann. Ency. Britannica, 1986; chpts. to books, articles to profl. jours.; mem. editorial bd. Cephalalgia: an Internat. Jour. of Headache, Headache Quar. Emeritus mem. Citizen's Adv Bd. Duke U. Ctr. Aging and Human Devel. Recipient Award of Recognition, Nat. Migraine Found., 1981; N.Y. State regents scholar, 1958-62. Fellow Am. Psychiat. Assn.; mem. AAAS (rep. of AAPB to med. sect. com.), Am. Assn. Study Headache, Internat. Headache Soc. (chmn. subcom. on classifying psychiat. headaches), Am. Acad. Psychoanalysis (sci. assoc.), Colo. Psychiat. Soc., Biofeedback Soc. Colo. (pres. 1977-78), Assn. for Applied Psychophysiology and Biofeedback (rep. to AAAS, chmn. ethics com. 1983-87, bd. dirs. 1990-93, Sheila M. Adler cert. honor 1988). Jewish. Office: 955 Eudora St Apt 1605 Denver CO 80220-4341

ADLER, ERWIN ELLERY, lawyer; b. Flint, Mich., July 22, 1941; s. Ben and Helen M. (Schwartz) A.; m. Stephanie Ruskin, June 8, 1967; children: Lauren, Michael, Jonathan. B.A., U. Mich., 1963, LL.M., 1967; J.D., Harvard U., 1966. Bar: Mich. 1966, Calif. 1967. Assoc. Pillsbury, Madison & Sutro, San Francisco, 1967-73; assoc. Lawler, Felix & Hall, L.A., 1973-76, ptnr., 1977-80; ptnr. Rogers & Wells, L.A., 1981-83, Richards, Watson & Gershon, L.A., 1983—. Bd. dirs. Hollywood Civic Opera Assn., 1975-76, Children's Scholarships Inc., 1979-80. Mem. ABA (vice chmn. appellate advocacy com. 1982-87), Calif. Bar Assn., Phi Beta Kappa, Phi Kappa Phi. Jewish. Office: Richards Watson & Gershon 333 S Hope St Bldg 38 Los Angeles CA 90071-1406

ADLER, LOUISE DECARL, bankruptcy judge; b. 1945. BA, Chatham Coll., Pitts.; JD, Loyola U., Chgo. Bar: Ill., 1970, Calif., 1972. Practicing atty. San Diego, 1972-84; standing trustee Bankruptcy Ct. So. Dist. Calif., San Diego, 1974-79, chief judge bankruptcy, 1996—. Mem. editorial bd. Calif. Bankruptcy Jour., 1991-92. Fellow Am. Coll. Bankruptcy; mem. San Diego County Bar Assn. (chair bus. law study sect. 1979, fed. ct. com. 1983-84), Lawyers Club of San Diego (bd. dirs. 1972-73, treas. 1972-75, sec. 1972-74, v.p. 1974-75), San Diego Bankruptcy Forum (bd. dirs. 1989-92), Nat. Conf. Bankruptcy Judges (bd. dirs. 1989-91, sec. 1992-93, v.p. 1993-94, pres. 1994-95). Office: US Bankruptcy Ct Rm 2 325 W F St San Diego CA 92101-6017

ADLER, MICHAEL I., lawyer; b. San Francisco, May 10, 1949. BA in Polit. Sci. summa cum laude, UCLA, 1971, JD, 1976; MA, Columbia U., 1973. Bar: Calif. 1977. Extern to Hon. Matthew O. Tobriner Calif. Supreme Ct., 1975; law clerk to Hon. William B. Enright U.S. Dist. Ct. (so. dist.) Calif., 1976-77; mem. Lichter, Grossman, Nichols & Adler, Inc., L.A., 1977—; mem. entertainment law symposium com. UCLA, 1979—; instr. UCLA Extension, 1980. Woodrow Wilson fellow, 1972; Columbia U. Presdl. fellow, 1973. Mem. ABA, State Bar Calif., L.A. County Bar Assn., Beverly Hills Bar Assn., Phi Beta Kappa, Phi Eta Sigma. Office: Lichter Grossman Nichols & Adler Inc 9200 Sunset Blvd Ste 530 Los Angeles CA 90019

ADLER, PETER, sociologist, educator; b. N.Y.C., Feb. 3, 1952; s. Jacob and Beatrice (Kaplan) A.; m. Patricia Ann Heller, Aug. 20, 1972; children: Jori, Brye. AB, Washington U., St. Louis, 1973; MA, U. Chgo., 1974; PhD, U. Calif., San Diego, 1980. Asst. prof. U. Tulsa, 1980-86; assoc. prof. Washington U., 1986-87; assoc. prof., chair sociology dept. U. Denver, 1987-93, prof. sociology, 1993—. Author: Momentum, 1981, Membership Roles in Field Research, 1987, Backboards and Blackboards, 1991, Peer Power, 1998; editor: (book) Constructions of Deviance, 1994, The Social Dynamics of Financial Markets, 1984, Jour. of Contemporary Ethnography, 1986-94, Sociol. Studies of Child Devel., 1985-92. Mem. Am. Sociol. Assn. (chair sect. on childre), Soc. for Study of Social Problems, Soc. for Study of Symbolic Interaction (v.p.), Midwest Sociol. Soc. Office: U Denver Dept Sociology Denver CO 80208

ADLER, RICHARD PAUL, technology consultant, writer; b. N.Y.C., Nov. 8, 1942; s. Alan and Pauline (Bloomgarden) A.; m. Elizabeth Walcott Fouratt Adler, Aug. 11, 1968; 1 child, Hilary Elizabeth Walcott Adler. AB, Harvard Coll., 1964; MA, U. Calif., Berkeley, 1968; MBA, McLaren Sch. Bus., 1992. Asst. dir. Aspen Inst., Palo Alto, Calif., 1972-76; sr. rsch. fellow Inst. for the Future, Menlo Park, Calif., 1979-90; sr. v.p. SeniorNet, San Francisco, 1990-96; pres. People and Tech., Palo Alto, 1996—; asst. prof. Oberlin (Ohio) Coll., 1969-72; bd. dirs. Interactive Svcs. Assn., Arlington, Va. (chair rsch. com. 1986-88). Co-author: The Electronic Box Office, 1974, The Effects of Television Advertising on Children, 1979, Teletext and Videotex in the United States, 1984, Electronic Banking-A Decision Makers Guide, 1988. Home: 425 Seale Ave Palo Alto CA 94301-3828 Office: People and Tech 425 Seale Ave Palo Alto CA 94301

ADLER, SARA, arbitrator; b. Chgo., Jan. 26, 1942; d. Matthew Michael and Mildred Paula (Eckhaus) Lewison; m. James N. Adler, Aug. 19, 1967; children: Michael, Philip, Matthew. AB, U. Chgo., 1961; JD, UCLA, 1969. Bar: Calif. Cons. Inst. Criminal Justice Adminstrn. U. Calif. Davis, 1969-71; assoc. Law Office of Sarah Radin, L.A., 1971-72; assoc. dir. Paralegal Tng. Inst. U. So. Calif., L.A., 1972-74; assoc. Wyman, Bautzer, et al, L.A., 1974-78; arbitrator, mediator L.A., 1978—. Mem. ABA (neutral co-chair ADR in Labor/employment Law 1995—), Am. Arbitration Assn. (bd. dirs.), Nat. Acad. Arbitrators (regional chair 1994-96), Indsl. Rels. Rsch. Assn. (pres. so. Calif. 1991-92), L.A. County Bar Assn. (chmn. labor and employment sect.). Office: Dispute Resolution Svcs 1034 Selby Ave Los Angeles CA 90024-3106

ADLER, SHELLEY, barber, poet; b. Detroit, Sept. 28, 1945; d. Calvin Jerome and Florence Jeanne (Cohen) Goodman; m. Norman T. Adler, 1968 (div. 1986); children: Shira Tamar, Tanya Aviv, Ari Chaim, Kiva Tal, Tahg Khorin; life ptnr. Susan B. Weinstein; co-parent of Keshet Tari Weinstein. BA in English, UCLA, 1966, MA in English, 1968; MS in Edn., U. Pa., 1972; MS in Counseling, Villanova U., 1983. Cert. tchr., Calif.; lic. barber, Calif. Barber. Poet: 4 Lyric Poets, 1968, Voices of Two Women, 1974, Poems of a Pervert, 1975, Seasons, 1980, Little Rages, 1985. Committeeman Narberth (Pa.) City, 1973-75; mem. task force Phila., 1984, 85. Sgt. U.S. Women's Army Res., 1973-75. Democrat. Jewish.

ADNET, JACQUES JIM PIERRE, astronautical and electrical engineer, consultant; b. Sermaize-les-Bains, Marne, France, Dec. 12, 1929; came to U.S., 1947; s. Julien Charles and Aline Georgette (Klein) A.; m. Mildred Ann Pruet, June 8, 1952 (div. Apr. 1982); children: Denise E., Lisa A., Paul A.; m. Helen Ilene Milam, Nov. 3, 1990. BA with honors, U. Fla., 1951, BEE with honors, 1960; MS in Astronautics, AF Inst. Tech., 1965; student, Indsl. Coll. of Armed Forces, 1972. Enlisted USAF, 1951, commd. 2d lt., 1952, advanced through grades to lt. col., 1968; elec. warfare officer USAF, Wiesbaden, Germany, 1954-57; with Radar Evaluation Flt./Air Def. Command, Griffiss AFB, N.Y., 1957-58; flight test engr. USAF Systems Command, Hanscom Field, Mass., 1960-61, subsystem devel. engr., 1961-63; site implementation engr. USAF Systems Command, France, Belgium, Italy, 1968; chief space systems divsn. USAF Fgn. Tech. Divsn., Dayton, 1968-71; R&D dir. aero. sys. divsn. USAF Systems Command, Dayton, Ohio, 1971-73; ret., 1973; instr., course dir. Air Force Acad., Colorado Springs, Colo., 1974-81; tech. cons. and tech. translator Adnetech, Colorado Springs, 1973—; dir. Dept. Def. Protocol Office Paris Internat. Air and Space Show, 1969, 71, 73, 75, 77. Contbr. articles to profl. jours. Dir. of Protocol, 1986 World Cycling Championships, Colo. Springs, 1985-86; mem. Tri-Lakes (Colo.) Comprehensive Plan Com. Recipient Ordre National Du Mérite French Govt., Paris, 1982. Mem. AIAA, VFW, Am. Legion, Air Force Assn., The Ret. Officers' Assn., USAF Acad. École de l'Air Exch. Assn. (hon., exec. sec.). Roman Catholic. Home and Office: Adnetech 4360 Diamondback Dr Colorado Springs CO 80921-2364

ADOLPH, MARY ROSENQUIST, financial executive; b. Springfield, Mass., Oct. 7, 1949; d. Jesse Woodson and Doris May (Marquette) Rosenquist; m. Earl Anthony Soares, Mar. 18, 1972 (div. 1982); m. Joseph Edward Adolph, Oct. 3, 1986. Student San Domenico Sch., 1966-68, Dominican Coll., San Rafael, 1967-69, Calif., San Francisco Conservatory of Music, 1968-70; A.A., Coll. of Marin, 1969. Asst. v.p. Western Travelers Life Ins. Co./Putnam Fin. Services, San Rafael, 1970-80; v.p. Unimarc, Ltd., Novato, Calif., 1980-83; v.p. mktg. Western States Monetary Planning Services, Inc., Newhall, Calif., 1983-88; asst. to pres. Fed. Inventory Wholesale, Inc., 1988-90; v.p. E.W. Richardson & Assocs. Inc., Newhall, Calif., 1991-94; v.p. ops. Tri Telic Inc., Santa Rosa, Calif., 1994—. Prodr. Radio Talk Show Financial Information, 1994—. Mem. exec. com. San Marin Valley Homeowners Assn., 1979-81. Mem. Internat. Assn. Fin. Planners, Life Underwriters Assn. Democrat. Roman Catholic. Home: 1676 Guerneville Rd Santa Rosa CA 95403-4110 Office: Tri Telic Inc 555 5th St Ste 320 Santa Rosa CA 95401-6342

AFFLECK, JULIE KARLEEN, accountant; b. Upland, Calif., Dec. 23, 1944; d. Karl W. and Juliette O. (Oppegaard) Hall; m. William J. Affleck, Aug. 29, 1964; children: Stephen, Tamara. BS in Bus., U. Colo., 1967; MBA, U. Denver, 1972. CPA, Colo. Cost acct. IBM, Boulder, Colo., 1967-71; audit supr. Ernst & Young, Denver, 1972-79, Rosemary E. Weiss & Co., Denver, 1979-80; ptnr. Affleck, Melaragno, Gilman & Co., Denver, 1980—; tchr. Colo. Soc. CPA's., U. Denver; dir., corp. sec. Better-Way Electric, Inc. Treas., bd. dirs. Bal Swan Children's Ctr. for Handicapped, Broomfield, Colo. Mem. Am. Inst. CPA's., Colo. Soc. CPA's., Am. Soc. Women Accts. (pres. chpt. 1980-81), Nat. Assn. Women Bus. Owners (treas., dir., pres. 1988-89). Republican. Lutheran. Home: 1270 Elmwood Ct Broomfield CO 80020-7609

AFSARY, CYRUS, artist; b. Oct. 18, 1940; s. Jacqui and Bonnie Mitra. BA in Art, U. Mid. East, 1962, BA in Interior Design, 1971. Resident artist Grand Gallery, Las Vegas, Nev., 1975-80; freelance artist Las Vegas, 1980-88, Scottsdale, Ariz., 1988—; art tchr., Mid. East, 1967-68; participant Artists of Am., 1988, 92. Works featured in Southwest Art, 1987, Midwest Art, 1988, Arts of the West, 1988. Recipient Exceptional award Pastel Soc. Am., 1986; named Best of Show, C.M. Russell Show, 1985, Best Oil, Amarillo Rotary Club Art Show, 1991, chosen Ofcl. Poster Artist, 1991. Mem. Nat. Acad. Western Art (gold medal 1987, Robert Lougheed gold medal 198, silver medal 1989), N.W. Renedzvous Art (merit award 1987). Studio: PO Box 3217 Scottsdale AZ 85271-3217

AGCAOILI, LAWRENCE E., systems analyst, programmer; b. Honolulu, June 1, 1964; s. Pacifico Malasig and Loraine (Balanay) A.; m. Lorna Gayle Chang, May 25, 1987; children: Leanna, Andrew. BS in Computer Sci., Chaminade U., Honlulu, 1987. Sys. nalyst Regulated Industries and Complaint Office, Hwawii Dept. Commerce and Consumer Affairs, Honolulu, 1987-94; pres. Advanced Computer Cons., Inc., Honolulu, 1980—; gen. mgr. Hawaii Mushrooms, Inc. Mem. Data Processing Mgmt. Assn. (edn. spl. interest group), Hawaii PC Users Group, Hawaii Macintosh and Apple Users Soc., Chaminade U. Alumni Assn. (pres.), Rotary. Office: Advanced Computer Cons Inc PO Box 17040 Honolulu HI 96817

AGERBEK, SVEN, mechanical engineer; b. Soerabaya, Dutch Indies, Aug. 2, 1926; came to U.S., 1958, naturalized, 1964; s. Niels Magnus and Else Heidam (Nielsen) Agerbek-Poulsen; m. Helen Hadsbjerg Gerup, May 30, 1963; 1 child, Jesper. MSME, Tech. U., Denmark, 1952; LLB, LaSalle Ext. U., 1967; postgrad., UCLA, 1969. Registered profl. engr., Calif., Ohio, Fla. With Danish Refrigeration Rsch. Inst., Copenhagen, 1952; engr. B.P. Oil Co., Copenhagen, 1952-54; refrigeration insp. J. Lauritzen, Copenhagen, 1954-56; engr. Danish-Am. Gulf Oil Co., Copenhagen, 1956-58; instr. Ohio U., Athens, 1958-60; asst. prof. Calif. State Poly. U., San Luis Obispo, 1960-62; prin. engr. dept. environ. Ralph M. Parsons Co., L.A., 1962-73; engring. supr. Bechtel Power Co., Norwalk, Calif., 1973-85; pres., owner Woodcraft Cabinets, Inc., Rancho Cordova, Calif., 1985-90; owner Acrebrook Cons., Fair Oaks, Calif., 1990—; exec. v.p. U.S.E., Inc., Incline Village, Nev., 1994—. Past mem. Luth. Ch. coun., pres. Luth. Sch. bd. With Danish underground movement, WWII. Mem. ASHRAE (mem. tech. com., author Guide on Air Conditioning of Nuclear Power Plants), Danish Engring. Soc. Home and Office: Acrebrook Consulting 5201 Vista Del Oro Way Fair Oaks CA 95628-4148 also: USE Inc Engring Office 9244 Old State Hwy Newcastle CA 95658-9998

AGRESTI, JACK JOSEPH, construction company executive; b. San Francisco, 1937. Grad., San Jose State U., 1959. Pres., CEO Guy F. Atkinson Co., South San Francisco. Mem. Constrn. Industry Inst., Soc. Am. Mil. Engrs., Am. Arbitration Assn. Office: Guy F Atkinson Co 1001 Bayhill Dr Fl 2 San Bruno CA 94066-3061*

AGUIAR, WILLIAM, JR., music and dance critic; b. San Francisco, Feb. 8, 1933; s. William and Maria Theresa (von Heyden) A. Pvt. mus. studies, Igor Stravinsky, Wilhelm Kempff, Igor Markevitch. Music and dance critic Hokubei Mainichi, San Francisco, 1968—. Mem. Music Critic Assn., Press Club of San Francisco. Democrat. Roman Catholic.

AGUILAR, JULIA ELIZABETH, real estate associate, writer; b. Organal, Mex., Feb. 16, 1943; came to U.S., 1965; d. Felix and Leticia (Rodriguez) Vergara; m. Aaron Aguilar, Feb. 1, 1964; children: Juan Antonio, Elizabeth, Alex. Grad., San Fernando (Calif.) Adult Sch., 1980; Real Estate Assoc., Anthony Real Estate Sch., Sepulveda, Calif., 1985. Real estate assoc. ERA Rocking Horse Realty, San Fernando, 1986—. Author poetry, cooking recipes, song lyrics. Democrat. Roman Catholic. Home: 626 Newton St San Fernando CA 91340-2107 Office: ERA Rocking Horse Realty 832 N Maclay Ave San Fernando CA 91340-1467

AGUILAR, ROBERT P., federal judge; b. Madera, Calif., Apr. 15, 1931. B.A., U. Calif., Berkeley, 1954; J.D., Hastings Coll. Law, San Francisco, 1958. Bar: Calif. 1960, U.S. Supreme Ct. 1966. Ptnr. Mezzetti and Aguilar, 1960-70, Aguilar and Aguilar, 1970-76, Aguilar & Edwards, San Jose, Calif., 1976-79; superior ct. judge Santa Clara County, 1979-80; judge U.S. Dist. Ct., No. Dist. Calif., San Francisco, 1980—; Mem. Regional Criminal Justice Planning Bd., from 1974; chmn. Santa Clara County (Calif.) Juvenile Justice Commn., 1975; mem. Santa Clara County Drug Abuse Task Force, 1974. Mem. Calif. Trial Lawyers Assn., Santa Clara County Criminal Trial Lawyers Assn., Am. Bar Assn., Calif. Bar Assn., Santa Clara County Bar Assn. (pres. 1972). Office: US Dist Ct 280 S 1st St San Jose CA 95113-3002*

AGUILERA, DONNA CONANT, psychologist, researcher; b. Kinmundy, Ill.; d. Charles E. and Daisy L. (Frost) Conant; m. George Limon Aguilera; children: Bruce Allen, Craig Steven. B.S., UCLA, 1963, M.S., 1965; Ph.D., U. So. Calif., 1974. Teaching asst. UCLA, 1965, grad. rsch. asst., 1965-66; prof. Calif. State U., L.A., 1966-81; cons. crisis intervention Didi Hirsch Community Mental Health Ctr., L.A., 1967-82; mem. Def. Adv. Com. Women in the Services, 1978-82; originator, project dir. Project Link Lab. U. Author: Crisis Intervention: Theory and Methodology, 1974, 8th edit., 1997 (pub. in 14 langs., braille and tapes), Review of Psychiatric Nursing, 1977, 7th edit., 1978, Crisis Intervention: Therapy for Psychological Emergencies, 1983; contbr. articles to profl. jours. Docent Huntington Libr. San Marino, Calif. 1991—; mem. disaster mental health svcs. ARC. NIH fellow, 1972-75. Fellow Am. Acad. Nursing (sec. 1976-77, pres. 1977-78), Acad. Psychiat. Nurse Specialists, Internat. Acad. Eclectic Psychotherapists (pres. 1987-89); mem. Am. Nurses Assn., Faculty Women's Assn., Am. Psychol. Assn., Calif. Psychol. Assn., AAUP, Alpha Tau Delta, Sigma Theta Tau. Home: 3924 Dixie Canyon Ave Sherman Oaks CA 91423-4830 Office: 450 N Bedford Dr Ste 210 Beverly Hills CA 90210-4306

AGUINSKY, RICHARD DANIEL, software and electronics engineer; b. Buenos Aires, Dec. 26, 1958; s. Elias Lorenzo and Rosa Isabel (Grille) A.; m. Adriana Faiman. Electronics Engr., Univ. Tech. Nacional, Avellaneda, 1984; MS in Elec. Engring. San Jose State U., 1991. Serial prodn. technician Norman S.A., Buenos Aires, 1978-80; electronics lab. technician Univ. Technologica Nacional, Avellaneda, 1980-84; engring. sub mgr. Northern Telecom, Buenos Aires, 1983-86; project engr. No. Telecom, Santa Clara, Calif., 1986—; instr. digital technics Univ. Tech. Nacional, Avellaneda, 1985; mentor adelante program San Jose City Coll. Contbr. articles to Revista Telegrafica Electronica, No. Telecom, Am. Nat. Standard Telecommunications. Avocations: travel, camping, windsurfing, skiing, sky diving. Office: No Telecom/BNR 2305 Mission College Blvd Santa Clara CA 95054-1521

AGUIRRE, LINDA G., state legislator; b. Flagstaff, Ariz., July 12, 1951; m. John Aguirre; children: Eric, Stephanie. BA, Ariz. State U., 1978. Educator; mem. Ariz. Ho. of Reps., mem. banking and ins., human svcs. and transp. coms., mem. banking and ins., environmental, transp., & economic dev coms. Active Ariz. Sch. Bd., Nat. Sch. Bd., Nat. Hispanic Sch. Bd., Ariz. Citizens Edn. Mem. South Mountain C. of C. Democrat. Office: Ariz House of Reps 1700 W Washington Phoenix AZ 85007*

AGUIRRE-BATTY, MERCEDES, Spanish and English language and literature educator; b. Cd Juarez, Mex., Dec. 20, 1952; came to U.S., 1957.; d. Alejandro M. and Mercedes (Péon) Aguirre; m. Hugh K. Batty, Mar. 17, 1979; 1 child, Henry B. BA, U. Tex., El Paso, 1974, MA, 1977. Instr. ESL Paso del Norte- Prep Sch., Cd Juarez, 1973-74; tchg. asst. ESL and English U. Tex., El Paso, 1974-77; instr. ESL English Lang. Svcs., Bridgeport, Conn., 1977-80; instr. Spanish and English, coord. modern lang. Sheridan (Wyo.) Coll., 1980—, pres. faculty senate, 1989-90; pres. faculty senate, chair dist. coun. No. Wyo. C.C. Dist., 1995-96; mem. planning com. No. Wyo. C.C. Dist., 1996-97; mem. advanced placement faculty Spanish cons. Coll.

Bd. Ednl. Testing Svc.; adj. prof. Spanish, U. Autonoma Cd Juarez, 1975; adj. prof. Spanish and English, Sacred Heart U., Fairfield, Conn., 1977-80; spkr. in field. Bd. dirs. Wyo. Coun. for the Humanities, 1988-92; translator county and dist. cts., Sheridan; vol. Wmen's Ctr.; translator Sheridan County Meml. Hosp.; del. Citizen Ambassador Program, People to People-India, 1996. NEH fellow, 1991, 92; Wyo. State Dept. Edn. grantee, 1991. Mem. Wyo. Fgn. Lang. Tchrs. Assn. (pres. 1990-92), Am. Assn. Tchrs. Spanish and Portuguese (founder, 1st pres. Wyo. chpt. 1987-90), TESOL, Sigma Delta Mu (v.p. 1992—), Sigma Delta Pi (pres. 1974-75). Office: Sheridan Coll NWCCD 3059 Coffeen Ave Sheridan WY 82801-9133

AHART, ALAN M., judge. AB, U. Calif., Berkeley, 1970; JD, SUNY, 1975; LLM, U. Pa., 1979. Judge U.S. Bankrupty Ct. Cen. Dist. Calif., L.A., 1988—. Contbr. articles to profl. jours. Office: US Bankruptcy Ct Calif Edward R Roybal Bldg 255 E Temple St Rm 1382 Los Angeles CA 90012

AHERN, ARLEEN FLEMING, retired librarian; b. Mt. Harris, Colo., Oct. 15, 1922; d. John R. and Josephine (Vidmar) Fleming; m. George Irving Ahern, June 14, 1944; 1 child, George Irving Jr. BA, U. Utah, 1943; MA, U. Denver, 1962; postgrad. U. Colo., 1967. Library asst. Army Air Force Library, Salt Lake City, 1943-44; library asst. Colo. Women's Coll. Library (now U. Denver/CWC Campus), 1952-60, acquisitions librarian, 1960—, rep. Adult Edn. Council Denver, 1960-90, reference librarian Penrose Library, WEC librarian, assoc. prof. librarianship through 1987, U. Denver Penrose Libr.; prof. emeritus, U. Denver; retired. Committeewoman, Republican Com., Denver, 1958-59; vol., Opera Colo. Guild; treas., bd. dirs. Denver Lyric Opera; bd. dirs., treas. Denver Lyric Opera Guild; bd. dirs. U. Denver Women's Libr. Assn., 1992-93, Samaritan House Guild, Jeanne Jugan (Little Sisters Poor) Aux., Colo. Symphony Guild, Cinema Study Club Colo., Carson Brierly Dance Libr., bd. dirs.; mem. exec. bd., treas. Denver Lyric Opera Guild. Mem. AAUP, ALA, Mountain Plains Library Assn., Colo. (1st v.p., pres. 1969-70, dir. 1971—), Library Assn., Altrusa Club of Denver (2d v.p. 1968-69, dir. 1971-74, 76, 78), Soc. Am. Archivists, Mountain Plains Adult Edn. Assn., Denver Botanic Gardens. Home: 746 Monaco Pky Denver CO 80220-6041

AHERN, GEOFFREY LAWRENCE, behavioral neurologist; b. N.Y.C., Feb. 20, 1954. BA, SUNY, Purchase, 1976; MS, Yale U., 1978, PhD in Psychology, 1981, MD, 1984. Med. intern Waterbury (Conn.) Hosp., 1984-85; resident in neurology Boston U., 1985-88; fellow in behavioral neurology Beth Israel Hosp., Boston, 1988-90; instr. neurology Harvard Med. Sch., Boston, 1988-90; asst. prof. neurology and psychology U. Ariz., Tucson, 1990-96, assoc. prof., 1996—. Contbr. articles to profl. jours., chpts. to books. Mem. Am. Acad. Neurology. Office: Univ Med Ctr Dept Neurology 1501 N Campbell Ave Tucson AZ 85724-0001

AHLEM, DIANA GRACE, systems analyst; b. Turlock, Calif., Sept. 12, 1952; d. Ralph Nathaniel Ahlem and Grace Diana (Labes) Torbonn; m. Charles James Schwartz, Jan. 28, 1984; 1 child. BA, Stanford U., 1974; MPH, U. Hawaii, 1977. Sys. analyst UCLA Extension, L.A., 1987. Mem. Stanford Assn. Democrat. Office: Intelligent Analytical Svcs 11610 Regent St Los Angeles CA 90066

AHLGREN, ALEDA JOAN, nursing administrator, career officer; b. Devils Lake, N.D., Sept. 25, 1941; d. Lucas Valentine and Hazel Mary (Vanderlin) Kirchoffner; m. Robert M. Gibbs, Sept. 5, 1965 (dec. Feb. 1966); m. Robert C. Ahlgren, May 7, 1987. Cert., Sisters of St. Joseph Sch. Nursing, Grand Forks, N.D., 1962; BSN, Loretto Heights Coll., 1978; MEd, U. Okla., 1982; attended, Air Command and Staff Coll., 1980; student, Air War Coll., 1984. cert. advanced nursing adminstrn. Commd. 2d lt. USAF, 1964, advanced through grades to col., 1988; staff nurse multiservice unit USAF, Webb AFB, Tex., 1964-66; staff nurse surg./pediatric unit USAF, Eglin AFB, Fla., 1966; staff nurse casualty staging flight USAF, Scott AFB, Ill., 1966-68; flight nurse 56th AES USAF, Yokota AB, Japan, 1968-69; staff nurse med./surg. USAF, Luke AFB, Ariz., 1970-72; staff nurse, nurse mgr. med./surg./OB USAF, Lajes Field, Azores, Portugal, 1972-74; nurse mgr. med. unit USAF, Eglin AFB, 1974-77; edn. coord. USAF, Sheppard AFB, Tex., 1978-82; chief nurse 1st aeromedical staging unit USAF, Scott AFB, 1982-84; chief nursing svcs. USAF, Hahn AB, Germany, 1984-87; chief nursing svc. USAF, Kirtland AFB, N.Mex., 1987-89; chairperson dept. nursing USAF, Scott AFB, 1989-92; command nurse, chief nurse exec. USAF Acad., Colo., 1992-96; ret., 1996; cons. nursing adminstrn. Mil. Airlift Command, Scott AFB, 1991-92, cons. aeromedical staging facilities, 1991-92; presenter in field. Decorated Legion of Merit, Commendation medal with one oak leaf cluster, Meritorious Svc. medal with five oak leaf clusters, Outstanding Merit award with five oak leaf clusters, Vietnam Svc. medal with staff, RVN Gallantry Cross with palm, Republic of Vietnam Campaign medal, Humanitarian Svc. medal with two oak leaf clusters. Mem. Nat. League Nursing, Am. Orgn. Nurse Execs., Air Force Assn., Sigma Theta Tau. Home: 18040 Forest View Rd Monument CO 80132

AHN, SAMUEL SEUNGHAE, vascular surgeon, researcher, consultant; b. Pusan, Korea, Feb. 9, 1954; came to U.S., 1959; s. Chai Ho and Sun Duk A.; m. Mi Ryu, Aug. 20, 1983; children: Justin, Alexander. BA in Biology, U. Tex., 1972-74; MD, U. Tex. Southwestern, 1974-78. Dimplomate Am. Bd. Surgery, Am. Bd. Med. Examiners; lic. Tex., Calif. Gen. surgery intern UCLA Med. Ctr., 1978-79, jr. resident gen. surgery, 1979-80, NIH rsch. fellow in surg. oncology, 1980-82, sr. resident gen. surgery, 1982-83, chief resident gen. surgery, 1983-84, clin. fellwo vascular surgery, 1984-85, rsch. fellow vascular surgery, 1985-86, attending surgeon, 1984—; asst. prof. surgery UCLA Med. Sch., 1986-93, assoc. clin. prof., 1994—; attending surgeon Sepulveda (Calif.) VA Med. Ctr., 1985-94; cons. surgeon UCLA Student Health Svcs., 1986—; surg. cons. Endovascular Equipment Cos., 1986-94; organizer facilities and programs in field; task force mem.; numerous com. appointments UCLA, 1985; guest lectr. and rsch. in field. Editor: (with W.S. Moore) Endovascular Surgery, 1989, 2d edit., 1992, (with J. Seeger) Endovascular Surgery for Peripheral Vascular Disease: Surgical Clinics of North America, 1992, (with D. Eton, K. Hodgson) Current Concepts in Endovascular Surgery, 1994; mem. editorial bd. Vascular Forum, 1993-94, Jour. Endovascular Surgery, 1994, Vascular Surgery, 1994; guest reviewer Jour. of Vascular Surgery, 1991-94, Postgraduate Vascular Surgery Jour., 1992-93, Surgery, 1992, Atherosclerosis and Thrombosis, 1992, Jour. of Am. Geriatrics Soc., 1992-93; abstractor Jour. of Vascular Surgery, 1994; contbr. chpts. books, articles to profl. jours. Mem. stroke coun. Am. Heart Assn., 1991—; vol. Korean Med. Missionary, 1969-88, Pub. Edn. of Cancer, 1980-83. East Tex. Chest Found. fellow East Tex. Chest Hosp., Tyler, 1976, Sigvaris award 1986; preceptee Am. Soc. Anestehsiologists, 1976; grantee E.R. Squibb and Sons. 1985-87, 85-86, Olympus Corp., 1985-86, UCLA Med. Aux., 1986, BioQuantum Tech., 1986-87, W.L. Gore and Assocs., 1986-87, 94, UCLA Sch. Medicine, 1986-87, NIH, 1987, 88, 93, Boston Scientific/Diasonics, 1989, Quadralogic Tech., Inc., 1990, Endo Vascular Instruments, Inc., 1993-94, Echocath and Acuson, 1993-94. Fellow Am. Coll. Surgeons; mem. AMA, Assn. Academic Surgery , Interant. Soc. Cardiovascular Surgery (N.Am. Chapter, rsch. fellow 1992, 93), So. Calif. Vascular Surg. Soc., Western Vascular Soc., Pacific Coast Surg. Assn., L.A. Surg. Soc., Acad. Surg. Rsch., Peripheral Vascular Surgery soc., Soc. Clin. Vascular Surgery, The Soc. for Vascular Surgery, Longmire Surg. Soc. Office: UCLA Med Ctr 100 Ucla Medical Plz Ste 510 Los Angeles CA 90024-6970

AHN, TINA MARIE, development executive; b. San Francisco, Sept. 8, 1959; d. Wilson and Hei Kyung (Hong) A. BA, San Francisco State U., 1982; MBA, U. San Francisco, 1994. Admissions supr. Calif. Acad. Scis., San Francisco, 1982-85, membership coord., 1985-87; mktg. assoc. Coun. on Edn., Walnut Creek, Calif., 1987-88; asst. dir. Western Network for Edn. in Health Adminstrn., Berkeley, Calif., 1989-91; dir. membership Neighbor to Neighbor, San Francisco, 1993-94; dir. devel. On Lok Inc., San Francisco, 1994—; bd. mem., treas. Neighbor to Neighbor Action Fund, San Francisco, 1993-95. Vol. Tenderloin Neighborhood Devel., San Francisco, 1993-94, Bridge for Kids, San Francisco, 1992-93; mem. World Affairs Coun., San Francisco, 1994; treas., bd. dirs. Lyon-Martin; bd. dirs. St. Anthony's Found. Office: On Lok Inc 1333 Bush St San Francisco CA 94109

AHNA, ALICE ALMEDA See NEVILLE-HARRIS, ALICE ALMEDA

AHRENS, PAMELA, state legislator; b. Portland, Oreg., Nov. 15, 1945; m. Steve Ahrens; children: Melissa Ann, Elaine, Annette, Shanna. Grad., Ea. Wash. State U. Mem. Idaho Ho. of Reps., 1983-95; dir. Dept. Adminstrn. State of Idaho, Boise; owner equipment rental bus. Chmn. Satewide Safety and Less Control Com.; bd. dirs. Warm Springs Counseling Ctr., Boise City Club. Named to Hall of Fame, Idaho Rep. Party. Mem. Idaho Hosp. Assn. (dir. polit. activities), Idaho Rep. Women's Fedn. (nat. fedn. rep. v.p.), Idaho Info. Tech. Resource Mgmt. Coun. (chair); mem. Lincoln Day Banquet Assn. (pres.), Rotary. Republican. Presbyterian. Home: 5186 S Farmhouse Pl Boise ID 83716 Office: Dept of Adminstrn State of Idaho PO Box 83720 Boise ID 83720-0003

AHSAN, OMAR FARUK, computer engineer, manager, consultant; b. Suri, India, Feb. 20, 1964; came to U.S., 1981; s. Mohammad and Masuda (Gowas) A.; m. Angela Rahim, August 4, 1991. BS, Rensselaer Poly. Inst., 1986, MS in Computer Systems Engrng., 1987. Coop. student IBM, Atlanta, 1984-85; coop. student Factron, Latham, N.Y., 1985-87, design engr., 1987-88; lead design engr. Schlumberger, Simi Valley, Calif., 1988-90, new product introduction project mgr., 1990-92, product mgr. diagnostic systems, 1992-93, product mgr. diagnostic systems and well svcs., 1993-94, product mgr. diagnostic systems, well svcs., front end mfg., 1994-95, product mgr. test systems, 1995—; con. Omega Rsch. & Applications, Valencia, Calif., 1989—; instr. Calif. Luth. U., 1991—. Recipient scholarship Rensselaer Poly. Inst., 1981-85, Nat. Honor Soc., 1981. Mem. Am. Prodn. and Inventory Control Soc., World Affairs Coun., Eta Kappa Nu. Office: Schlumberger Techs 85 Moreland Rd Simi Valley CA 93065-1662

AH-TYE, KIRK THOMAS, lawyer; b. L.A., Mar. 31, 1951; s. Thomas and Ruth Elizabeth (Liu) Ah-T.; m. Deborah Ann Wells, Jan. 31, 1981; 1 child, Torrey Ann. BA, U. Calif., Santa Barbara, 1973; JD, Boston Coll., 1976. Bar: Calif. 1977, U.S. Dist. Ct. (cen. dist.) Calif. 1978, U.S. Dist. Ct. (ea. dist.) Calif. 1994, U.S. Ct. Appeals (9th cir.) 1978, U.S. Supreme Ct. 1981. Mng. atty. Channel Counties Legal Svcs. Assn., Santa Barbara, 1977—; expert witness Assembly Com. on Edn., Calif. Legis., Sacramento; panelist Ctr. for the Study of Dem. Instns., Santa Barbara; panelist, instr. CLE approved classes; past legal cons. Santa Barbara chpt. calif. Assn. Bilingual Educators; inaugural prodr., moderator Santa Barbara Law, Sta. KTMS-AM, 1994—. Editor (bar newsletter) The Quibbler, 1992-93; contbr. articles to profl. jours. Trustee Montessori Ctr. Sch., Santa Barbara, 1991-93; bd. dirs., v.p. Santa Barbara Internat. Film Festival, 1991-93; chair adv. bd. Santa Barbara Regional Health Authority, 1985; mem. blue-ribbon com. County Bd. Suprs., Santa Barbara, 1988; chair Santa Barbara County Affirmative Action Commn., 1987-88; mem. grant-making com. Fund for Santa Barbara, 1988-92. Recipient Local Hero award Santa Barbara Ind., 1988. Mem. State Bar of Calif. (state resolutions com. to state bar conf. of dels. 1994-96), Santa Barbara County Bar Assn. (jud. svc. award com. 1992, chair pro bono com. 1993, bd. dirs., sec., cfo 1992—, pres. 1996-97), Lawyer Referral Svc. Santa Barbara (bd. dirs., pres. 1992). Office: Channel Counties Legal Svcs Assn 324 E Carrillo St Ste B Santa Barbara CA 93101

AHUMADA, MARTIN MIGUEL, education association administrator; b. San Luis, Sonora, Mex., Nov. 22, 1954; came to U.S., 1958; s. Miguel Ruiz Ahumada; m. Iveliz Valle, Dec. 28, 1980; children: Litzaya Ayde, Melibea Pilar. BA, Carleton Coll., 1977; MS, U. Ariz., 1979, PhD, 1983. Edn. specialist IBM, Tucson, 1983; analyst higher edn. policy Edn. Commn. of States, Denver, 1984-85; analyst sr. policy Calif. Postsecondary Edn. Commn., Sacramento, 1985-88; faculty mem., pres.'s liaison U. Ariz., Tucson, 1989-90; faculty assoc. Harvard U., Cambridge, Mass., 1991-94; pres. Internat. Ctr. Higher Edn. and Philanthropy, Tucson, 1995—; cons. U. Ariz., Tucson, 1994-95, Navajo Cmty. Coll., 1989, U. Autonoma de la Laguna, 1993, U. Autonoma de Nuevo Leon, 1983, U. Monterrey, 1983, 80; advisor Mass. Commn. on Future of State Coll. and Cmty. Coll. Sys., 1991. Presenter in field; contbr. articles to profl. jours. Office: Internat Ctr Higher Edn PO Box 503 Tucson AZ 85702-0503

AHURUONYE, HYACINTH CHIDI, accountant, consultant; b. Aba, Imo, Nigeria, Sept. 20, 1961; came to U.S., 1983; s. Silas A. and Evelyn Ahuruonye); m. Terri Anita Sharp, May 28, 1988; children: Derrick Chidi, Amara Jenay. BS in Acctg. with honors, Ala. A&M U., 1987. enrolled agt. Mng. prin. HCA Acctg. & Tax Svcs., San Francisco, 1987—; acct. R.H. Macys, Inc., San Francisco, 1990, staff acct. Den-Herder & Co., CPA's, San Francisco, 1989-91; tax preparer H&R Block, San Francisco, 1988; cons. in field, 1987—; mem Accreditation Coun. for Accountancy and Taxation, Inc. Co-prodr. Designer of the Yr. Awards, 1991—. Mem. Rep. Nat. Com., Washington, 1990—, San Francisco Refugee Com., Mayor's Employment 1000 Task Force, Ala. A&M Univ. Youth Motivation Task Force; bd. mgrs. Buchanan YMCA, San Francisco; sec. African Internat. Univ. Found. Recipient Mayoral Proclamation, Disting. Alumni Citation of Yr. award, 1994. Mem. Nat. Soc. Pub. Accts., Nat. Assn. Enrolled Agts., Nat. Assn. Tax Practitioners, Nat. Assn. Black Accts., Am. Soc. Accts., Calif. Soc. Enrolled Agts. (Golden Gate chpt.), Calif. Soc. Ind. Accts., Nat. Assn. Equal Opportunity Higher Edn., Ala. A&M U. Alumni Assn. (pres. San Francisco Bay Area chpt. 1991—), Alpha Phi Alpha (rec. sec.). Office: HCA Acctg & Tax Svcs 988 Market St Ste 603 San Francisco CA 94102-4007

AI, EVERETT, ophthalmologist; b. N.Y.C., July 15, 1950. Student, SUNY, Stonybrook, 1967-69; BA, U. Iowa, 1971; MD, SUNY, Syracuse, 1975. Diplomate Am. Bd. Ophthalmology. Intern Northwestern U., Chgo., 1975-76, resident ophthalmology, 1976-79; fellowship disease of retina and vitreous Pacific Med. Ctr., 1979-80; fellow vitreoretinal surgery St. Lukes Hosp., Western Res. U., Cleve., 1981; asst. prof. dept. ophthalmology Northwestern U., Chgo., 1980-81, dir. ophthalmology residency program, 1980-81, dir. divsn. clin. echography, 1980-81; asst. clin. prof. U. Calif., Berkeley, 1983—; dir. retina unit CPMC, San Francisco, 1983—; ophthalmic examiner early treatment diabetic retinopathy study Pacific Presbyn. Med. Ctr., San Francisco, 1979-80, prin. investigator, 1983-89; retinal cons. Lakeside VA Hosp., Chgo., 1980-81, The Permanente Med. Group, Oakland, Calif., 1982-83, Fort Ord (Calif.) Army Med. Ctr., 1983—; assoc. examiner Am. Bd. Ophthalmology, San Francisco, 1985—; pres. Western Assn. for Vitreoretinal Edn., 1990-91; bd. dirs. Am. Diabetes Assn., San Francisco, pres., 1991-92; sci. reviewer Ophthalmology, 1990—; med. adv. bd. MID Labs., 1993—, Diabetes Interview, 1993—; active Diabetes 2000 Nat. Ops. Com., 1993—; presenter and lectr. in field. Contbr. articles to profl. jours. N.Y. State Regents Coll. scholar, 1967; Heed Ophthalmic fellow, 1979. Mem. Am. Acad. Ophthalmology (continuing ophthalmic video edn. com. 1993—, nat. coord. for edn. courses 1993—), Am. Assn. Ophthalmology, Internat. Soc. for Ophthalmic Ultrasound, Assn. for Rsch. in Vision and Ophthalmology, Vitreous Soc., Calif. Assn. Ophthalmology (bd. dirs. 1991—), Calif. Med. Assn. (sect. asst. sec. sci. adv. panel on ophthalmology 1988-89, sci. program planner for ophthalmology 1988-89, ophthalmology sect. sec. sci. adv. panel on ophthalmology 1989-90, sect. chmn. 1990-91), Pacific Coast Oto-Ophthalmologic Soc. (sci. program com. 1991—, councillor 1991—), San Francisco Med. Soc., Soc. Heed Fellows., Ophthalmic Photographers' Soc. (med. adv. com. 1989—), Phi Beta Kappa. Office: Schatz McDonald Johnson Ai 1 Daniel Burnham Ct #210C San Francisco CA 94109-5455

AIDELLS, BRUCE, food products executive; b. 1944. Founder, chef Poulet Deli, Berkeley, Calif., 1979-83; owner, chef Aidells Sausage Co., San Leandro, Calif., 1983—. Co-author: Great Meals in Minutes: Salads, 1985, Regional American Classics, 1987, Barbecuing, Grilling, and Smoking, 1988, Hot Links and Country Flavors, 1990, Real Beer and Good Eats, 1992; columnist "Budget Gourmet" San Jose Mercury News; contbr. articles to mags. including Gourmet, Bon Appetit, others. Rsch. fellow Imperial Cancer Rsch. Fund, London, 1974-77, NIH, Bethesda, 1977-78. Office: Aidells Sausage Co 1625 Alvarado St San Leandro CA 94577

AIJIAN, HAIG SCHUYLER, pathologist, educator; b. Detroit, Apr. 2, 1919; s. Misak Michael and Mabel Maude (Schuyler) A.; m. Ethel Louise Johnson, May 14, 1948; children: Paul S., Mark M., Peter C., Lane Louise, Maria V. (adopted). BS, UCLA, 1940; MD, USC, 1945. Diplomate Am. Bd. Pathology, anatomical and clin. Mem. faculty USC Sch. of Medicine, L.A., 1945—; asst. pathologist St. Luke Hosp., Pasadena, Calif., 1952-57; pathologist St. Francis Hosp., Lynwood, Calif., 1957-68, Meth. Hosp. So. Calif., Arcadia, Calif., 1968-83, Goleta Valley Hosp., Santa Barbara, 1983-87, St. Francis Hosp., Santa Barbara, 1983-87; insp. blood bank Am. Assn. Blood Banks, Chgo., Med. Technician Schs., Am. Soc. Clin. Pathologists Bd. of Schs., Chgo.; mem. joint generalist com. ASCP Bd. of Schs., Chgo. Mem. Santa Barbara County Reps. Home: 956 Via Fruteria Santa Barbara CA 93110-2322

AIKAWA, JERRY KAZUO, physician, educator; b. Stockton, Calif., Aug. 24, 1921; s. Genmatsu and Shizuko (Yamamoto) A.; m. Chitose Aihara, Sept. 20, 1944; 1 son, Ronald K. AB, U. Calif., 1942; MD, Wake Forest Coll., 1945. Intern, asst. resident N.C. Baptist Hosp., 1945-47; NRC fellow in med. scis. U. Calif. Med. Sch., 1947-48; NRC, AEC postdoctoral fellow in med. scis. Bowman Gray Sch. Medicine, 1948-50, instr. internal medicine, 1950-53, asst. prof., 1953; established investigator Am. Heart Assn., 1952-58; exec. officer lab. service Univ. Hosps., 1958-61, dir. lab. services, 1961-83, dir. allied health program, 1969—, assoc. dean allied health program, 1983—, pres. med. bd.; assoc. dean clin. affairs asst. prof. U. Colo. Sch. Medicine, 1953- 60, asso. prof. medicine, 1960-67, prof., 1967—, prof. biometrics, 1974—, assoc. dean clin. affairs, 1974—; Pres. Med. bd. Univ. Hosps. Fellow ACP, Am. Coll. Nutrition; mem. Western Soc. Clin. Research, So. Soc. Clin. Research, Soc. Exptl. Biology and Medicine, Am. Fedn. Clin. Research, AAAS, Central Soc. Clin. Research, AMA, Assn. Am. Med. Colls., Phi Beta Kappa, Sigma Xi, Alpha Omega Alpha. Home: 3233 Lake Albano Cir San Jose CA 95135-1467 Office: U Colo Sch Medicine 4200 E 9th Ave Denver CO 80220-3706

AIKEN, SUSAN HARDY, English language educator; b. Bklyn., Nov. 4, 1943; d. Sutton Labon and Mae (Eppinger) Hardy; m. Christopher Franklin Carroll, Jan. 1, 1978; children: James Buchanan Aiken, Alden Hardy Carroll. BA, Furman U., 1964; MA, Duke U., 1966, PhD, 1971. Instr. English U. Ga., Athens, 1966-69; asst. prof. SUNY, Stony Brook, 1971-72, Suffolk Coll., Selden, N.Y., 1972-73; asst. prof. U. Ariz., Tucson, 1973-77, assoc. prof., 1977-90; prof., 1990—, acting head dept. French and Italian, 1992-93; cons. U. Ariz. Press, 1984—, U. Ariz. Women's Studies Program, 1981—; Ariz. Humanities Coun., 1978-83, Ford Found. Western States Curriculum Project, 1984, Hobart and William Smith Coll., 1988, Am. U., 1988, Rice U., 1995, referee John Simon Guggenheim Meml. Found., 1985, 86, 87, 88, 90, 91, 92, 96, Newberry Libr. Rsch. Ctr., 1989, ACLS, 1989, NEH, 1988, 89, 90, 91. 92; judge Margaret Church award Modern Fiction Studies, 1995-96. Author: Isak Dinesen and the Engendering of Narrative, 1990; co-author: Dialogues/Dialogi: Literary and Cultural Exchanges Between (Ex)Soviet and American Women, 1992; editor: (with others) Changing Our Minds: Feminist Transformations of Knowledge, 1988; mem. editorial bd. U. Ariz. Press; contbr. Signs: Jour. Women in Culture and Soc., Scandinavian Studies, PMLA (publications MLA), 1985-88, Papers in Lang and Lit., 1988, Modern Fiction Studies, 1996, articles to profl. jours., chpts. to books. Fellow Ford Found., 1964-65, Woodrow Wilson II, 1965-66, Duke U., 1969-70; grantee U. Ariz., 1984, WOSAC, 1987; recipient U. Ariz. Creative Teaching award, 1985, Women's Studies Adv. Coun. award, 1987, Mortar Bd. citation for acad. excellence, Provost's Teaching award, 1988, Faculty Achievement award Burlington No. Found., NEH fellowships, 1988, 89, 91, 92, NEH interpretive rsch. grant, 1991-93. Mem. MLA (adv. com. publs. 1985-89), Nat. Women's Studies Assn., Soc. for the Advancement of Scandinavian Studies, Browning Inst. Office: U Ariz Dept English Tucson AZ 85721

AIKENS, C(LYDE) MELVIN, anthropology educator, archaeologist; b. Ogden, Utah, July 13, 1938; s. Clyde Walter and Claudia Elena (Brown) A.; m. Alice Hiroko Endo, Mar. 23, 1963; children: Barton Hiroyuki, Quinn Yoshihisa. A.S., Weber Coll., 1958; B.A., U. Utah, 1960; M.A., U. Chgo., 1962, Ph.D., 1966. Curator U. Utah Mus. Anthropology, Salt Lake City, 1963-66; asst. prof. U. Nev., Reno, 1966-68; asst. prof. anthropology U. Oreg., Eugene, 1968-72, assoc. prof., 1972-78, prof., 1978—, dir. U. Oreg. Mus. Natural History, 1996—. Author: Fremont Relationships, 1966, Hogup Cave, 1970, Great Basin Archaeology, 1978, The Last 10,000 Years in Japan and Eastern North America, 1981, From Asia to America: The First Peopling of the New World, 1990, Archaeology of Oregon, 1993; co-author: Prehistory of Japan, 1982, Great Basin Numic Prehistory, 1986, Early Human Occupation in Far Western North America, 1988; editor: Archaeological Studies Willamette Valley, 1975; co-editor: Prehistoric Hunter-Gatherers in Japan, 1986, Pacific Northeast Asia in Prehistory, 1992, Archaeological Researches in the Northern Great Basin, 1994. NSF research grantee, 1970, 73, 78-80, 84; NSF Sci. Faculty fellow Kyoto U., Japan, 1971-72; Japan Found. research fellow Kyoto U., 1977-78, Tokyo U., 1986. Fellow Am. Anthrop. Assn., AAAS; mem. Soc. for Am. Archaeology. Home: 3470 Mcmillan St Eugene OR 97405-3317 Office: U Oreg Dept Anthropology Eugene OR 97403-1218

AIKENS, DONALD THOMAS, educational administrator, consultant; b. L.A., June 17, 1931; s. Clarence Beatty and Edith Grace (Crippin) A.; m. Marjorie Jane Conley, Aug. 6, 1960. AA, Glendale Coll., 1951; BS, U. So. Calif., 1953, MS, 1959. Cert. tchr., pupil pers., adminstr., Calif. Indsl. rels. mgr. Gen. Petroleum Corp., L.A., 1953-55; elem. tchr. Gallatin Elem. Dist., Downey, Calif., 1955-57; jr. high tchr. Burbank (Calif.) Unified Sch. Dist., 1957-59; jr. high tchr. Palm Springs (Calif.) Unified Sch. Dist., 1959-65, counselor, 1965-70, asst. prin., 1970-77, adminstr. The Ind. Study Program, 1977-94; trustee, pres. Palm Springs Unified Sch. Dist. Bd. Edn., 1995—; creator The Ind. Study Program, Palm Springs Unified Sch. Dist., 1977. Chairperson United Way of the Desert, Palm Springs, 1987—. Mem. Nat. Assn. Secondary Sch. Prins. (cons., presentor 1980—), Calif. Consortium for Ind. Study (pres. 1983-85), Rotary Club (pres. 1987-88), Trojan Club of the Desert (pres. 1983-88). Methodist. Office: Palm Springs Unified Sch Dist 333 S Farrell Dr Palm Springs CA 92262-7905

AILOR, KAREN TANA, marketing writer, proposal consultant; b. Seattle, June 1, 1943; d. Dale Ingram and Neva Gail (Houck) A. Student, U. Calif., Berkeley, 1961-63; BA in Journalism, U. Oreg., 1992. Copy editor Physical Review Letters, Brookhaven, N.Y., 1963-65; proposal writer TRW Def. Systems, L.A., 1965-73; mktg. support mgr. TRW Electronics, L.A., 1973-79; proposal cons. TRW, Hughes, Northrop, Logicon, and others, L.A., 1980—; contbg. writer Old Oreg. Mag., Eugene, 1991-94. Mem. Phi Beta Kappa (award 1992), Kappa Tau Alpha (award 1991). Democrat. Home and Office: 125 Rosetta Ave Eugene OR 97404-2849

AINGE, DANNY RAY, professional basketball coach; b. Eugene, Oreg., Mar. 17, 1959; m. Michele Ainge; children: Ashlee, Austin, Tanner, Taylor, Cooper, Crew. Grad., Brigham Young U., 1981. Basketball player Boston Celtics, 1981-89, Sacramento, 1989-90, Portland Trailblazers, 1990-92; basketball player Phoenix Suns, 1992-95, head coach, 1996—; player Celebrity Golf Assn. Tour. Active Children's Miracle Network, Spl. Olympics. Holder of record for most 3-pointers mde and attempted in playoffs; one of 4 players in NBA history to make 1,000 or more career 3-pointers. Office: Phoenix Suns 201 E Jefferson Phoenix AZ 85004

AINSWORTH, HARRIET CRAWFORD, journalist, public relations consultant; b. Columbus, Ohio, Nov. 27, 1914; d. Harry Hoskins and Pansy Lucy (Graham) Crawford; m. J. Gordon Ainsworth, Oct. 6, 1945; children: J. Gordon Jr., Adeline Ainsworth Forrest. BA, Ohio Wesleyan U., 1934; postgrad., Columbia U. Sch. Journalism, 1934-35, Gonzaga U., 1940, Calif. Coll. Arts and Crafts, 1968; life adult edn.-C.C. tchg. credential, U. Calif., Berkeley, 1967. Reporter Portland Oregonian, 1936-37; ind. pub. rels. writer, 1937-42; fgn. corr. Oakland Tribune, Indpls. Star, Japan, China, The Philippines, 1946; pub. info. dir. Am. Cancer Soc., Contra Costa County, Calif., 1958-89; cons. Calif. divsn. Am. Cancer Soc., 1965-77; pres. Ainsworth-Powell Pub. Rels., 1965-77; v.p. Corp. Identity Assocs., Orinda, Calif., 1968-94, pres., 1994—; columnist (Sunbeams), feature writer Contra Costa Sun, Contra Costa Times, 1990—. Co-author: The Road Back, 1968; contbr. articles to profl. jours., newspaper columns. Mem. Citizen's Recreation Commn., dist. 6, Orinda, 1974-79; founder, pres. Orinda Found., 1975; chmn. spl. events Calif. Shakespeare Festival Amphitheater campaign, 1988-92. Lt. comdr. USNR, 1942-58. Named Orinda Citizen of Yr., 1976; recipient Plaque and Resolution Commendation Recreation Dist. 6, Orinda, 1979, Recognition award Plaque Pres. U.S. People-to-People Sports Com. Mem. San Francisco Pub. Rels. Round Table, Contra Costa Press Club, East Bay Women's Press Club (pres.), Orinda Country Club, Orindawoods Tennis Club, Orinda Tennis Club, Kappa Alpha Theta (co-founder Diablo Valley chpt.).

AITCHISON, STEWART WAYNE, photojournalist; b. Chgo., Sept. 27, 1947; s. Lawrence Foster and Leona Rachel (Bogdansky) A.; m. Margaret Ann Kramer, Aug. 14, 1981; 1 child, Kate Lynne Kramer Aitchison. BS, No. Ariz. U., 1969. Rsch. biologist Mus. of No. Ariz., Flagstaff, 1967-78; freelance writer/photographer Flagstaff, 1968—; naturalist Lindblad Spl. Expdns., others, 1976—. Author/photographer: A Traveler's Guide to Monument Valley, 1993, Red Rock-Sacred Mountain, 1992, A Wilderness Called Grand Canyon, 1991, others; contbr. articles, photographs to numerous publs. Bd. dirs. Kokopeli Adventures in Learning, 1979-82. Mem. No. Ariz. Natural History Assn., The Author's Guild, Inc. Home and Office: 995 Tolani Trl Flagstaff AZ 86001-9613

AITKEN, ROBERT CAMPBELL, engineer; b. Vancouver, B.C., Can., Apr. 21, 1963; came to U.S., 1990; s. Robert and Mary Elizabeth A.; m. Denise Kathleen Maloney, Aug. 2, 1986; children: Robert James, Colin Campbell. BS with hons., U. Victoria, B.C., Can., 1985, MS, 1986; PhD, McGill U., Montreal, Que., Can., 1990. Rsch. assoc. Alberta Rsch. Coun., Calgary, Alberta, Can., 1986-87; mem. tech. staff Hewlett-Packard Co., Palo Alto, Calif., 1990—; tech. program com. mem. Internat. Conf. on Computer-Aided Design, Santa Clara, 1993-94, local arrangements chmn., 1995, tutorials chmn., 1996-97; tech. program com. Custom Integrated Cirs. Conf., Santa Clara, 1995-97; panel and poster chmn. Test Synthesis Workshop, Santa Barbara, Calif., 1995, fin. chmn., 1996-97; mem. program com. Internat. Test Conf., 1996-97. local arrangements chmn. Internat. Conf. on Computer-Aided Design, Santa Clara, 1995, tech. program com. mem., 1993-95; tech. program com. Custom Integrated Cirs. Conf., Santa Clara, 1995; panel and poster chmn. Test Synthesis Workshop, Santa Barbara, Calif., 1995. Recipient award for Best paper, Internat. Test Conf., Balt., 1992, hon. mention, 1991. Mem. IEEE. Office: Hewlett-Packard Co 1501 Page Mill Rd # Ms 6uk Palo Alto CA 94304-1126

AITKEN, STUART CAMPBELL, geography educator; b. Glasgow, Scotland, July 20, 1958; came to U.S., 1980; s. William Scott and Margaret Brodie (Fleming) A.; m. Peggy Ann Beninger, July 6. 1987; children: Ross, Catherine. BSc, Glasgow U., 1980; MA, Miami U., Oxford, Ohio, 1981; PhD, U. West Ont., London, Can., 1985. Prof. geography U. Ariz., Tucson, 1985-86; asst. prof. San Diego State U., 1986-89, assoc. prof., 1990-92, prof., 1993—; vis. faculty fellow U. Edinburgh, Scotland, 1993. Author, editor: Place, Power, Situation and Spectacle, 1994; author: Putting Children in Their Place, 1994. Creator/organizer Children's Geographies of San Diego Program, 1988-91. NSF grantee, 1990-96. Office: San Diego State Univ Dept Geography San Diego CA 92182-4493

AJER, RANDOLF E., airport terminal executive; b. 1953. With Union Home Loans, L.A., 1974-80, Maytag Aircraft Corp., Colorado Springs, Colo., 1981—; CFO Mercury Airgroup, Inc., L.A. Office: Mercury Airgroup Inc 5456 McConnell Ave Los Angeles CA 90066*

AKAKA, DANIEL KAHIKINA, senator; b. Honolulu, Sept. 11, 1924; s. Kahikina and Annie (Kahoa) A.; m. Mary Mildred Chong, May 22, 1948; children: Millannie, Daniel, Gerard, Alan, Nicholas. BEdn, U. Hawaii, 1952, MEdn, 1966. Tchr. Hawaii, 1953-60; vice prin., then prin. Ewa Beach Elem. Sch., Honolulu, 1960-64; prin. Pohakea Elem. Sch., 1964-65, Kaneohe Elem. Sch., 1965-68; program specialist Hawaii Compensatory Edn., 1978-79, from 1985; dir. Hawaii OEO, 1971-74; spl. asst. human resources Office Gov. Hawaii, 1975-76; mem. 95th-101st Congresses from 2d Dist., Hawaii, 1977-90; U.S. senator from Hawaii, 1990—; chmn. Hawaii Principals' Conf. Bd. dirs. Hanahauoli Sch.; mem. Act 4 Ednl. Adv. Council, Library Adv. Council.; Trustee Kawaiahao Congl. Ch. Served with U.S. Army, 1945-47. Mem. NEA, Musicians Assn. Hawaii. Democrat. Office: US Senate 720 Senate Hart Bldg Washington DC 20510

AKANA, KEITH KALANI, elementary education educator, consultant; b. Honolulu, June 8, 1957; s. Arthur Kaheakulani and Iola Shinae (Hangai) A. BE, U. Hawaii, 1980; MEd, 1994. Resource tchr. Leeward Dist. Office, Manoa, 1984-89; lectr. Leeward Cmty. Coll., Pearl City, 1985-87; tchr. Waiau Elem. Sch., Pearl City, Hawaii, 1989—; lectr. U. Hawaii, Manoa, 1994; cons. Ike Pono Cons., Honolulu, 1979—; dir. Ka Pa Hooheno Hawaii, Pearl City, 1984—, prodr., "Manaleo" TV series. Author: Pleiades, 1985; contbr. articles to profl. jours. V.p., 1980—, dir., 1992-94, pres. Ahahui Olelo Hawaii, Honolulu, 1996; pres. Ahahui Kapiolani, Honolulu, 1990-94. Recipient Chant Competition King Kamehameha Commn., 1975, 80, 85, Ke Kukui Malamalama, Office of Hawaiian Affairs, 1991; grantee Bishop Mus., 1990; named Tchr. of Yr. Leeward Dist. Office, 1994. Mem. ASCD, NAESP.

AKBARIAN, SHAH-ROKH, management consultant; b. Abadan, Khuzestan, Iran, May 20, 1953; came to U.S., 1969; s. Ramezan and Mahin A.; m. Joni Louise Stump, Nov. 1, 1980; 1 child, Katayun Alexandra. BA, Westminster Coll., 1976, BS, 1977; M of Internat. Mgmt., Am. Grad. Sch. Internat. Mgmt., Glendale, Ariz., 1980; postgrad., U. Utah, 1993; Cert. in Advanced Mgmt., The Grad. Sch. of Am., Mpls., 1997; Cert. Program on Negotiation, Harvard Law Sch., 1997. Account exec. Bonneville Rsch., Salt Lake City, 1980-84; prin. Pendar Internat., Salt Lake City, 1984—; bd. dirs. Sports Am, Salt Lake City, 1980—. Pub., editor Commerce Internat. News; contbr. articles to profl. jours. Mem. adv. bd. U. Utah Internat. Ctr., 1992—, mem. chmn. bus. and industry com.; mem. adv. bd. Salt Lake County Cmty. and Econs. Devel., 1994-95; exec. coun. Westminster Coll. Alumni Assn., 1993-96, pres., 1995-96, trustee, 1995, mem. instnl. advancement com., 1994-95; alumni ednl. counselor Am. Grad. Sch. Internat. Mgmt., 1994—; adv. bd. Salvation Army, 1982-84. Mem. Inst. Indsl. Engrs., Assn. MBA Execs., Salt Lake Area C. of C. (mem. export devel. com., mem. editl. bd. chamber newsletter, pub. rels. coord.).

AKELEY, KURT BARTON, computer graphics company executive, engineer; b. Wilmington, Del., June 8, 1958; s. David Francis and Marcy Claire (McCullough) A. BSEE, U. Del., 1980; MSEE, Stanford U., 1982. Mem. tech. staff, co-founder Silicon Graphics, Inc., Mountain View, Calif., 1982-87, prin. engr., 1987-89, chief engr., 1989-90, v.p., chief engr., 1990—; mem. Coll. Engring. Adv. Coun., U. Del., 1993—. Patentee, inventor in field; contbr. articles to profl. publs. Named Disting. Alumnus, Dept. Elec. Engring., Coll. Engring., U. Del., 1993. Mem. Assn. Computing Machinery. Home: 3360 Milton Ct Mountain View CA 94040-4500 Office: Silicon Graphics Inc 2011 N Shoreline Blvd Mountain View CA 94043-1321

AKINS, GEORGE CHARLES, accountant; b. Willits, Calif., Feb. 22, 1917; s. Guy Brookins and Eugenie (Swan) A.; A.A., Sacramento City Coll., 1941; m. Jane Babcock, Mar. 27, 1945. Accountant, auditor Calif. Bd. Equalization, Dept. Finance, Sacramento, 1940-44; controller-treas. DeVons Jewelers, Sacramento, 1944-73, v.p., controller, 1973-80, v.p., chief fin. officer, dir., 1980-84; individual accounting and tax practice, Sacramento, 1944—. Accountant, cons. Mercy Children's Hosp. Guild, Sacramento, 1957-77. Served with USAAF, 1942. Mem. Soc. Calif. Pioneers, Nat. Soc. Accts., U.S. Navy League, Calif. Hist. Soc., Drake Navigators Guild, Internat. Platform Assn., Mendocino County Hist. Soc. (life), Sacramento County Hist. Soc. (life), Northwestern Pacific Railroad Hist. Soc., Crocker Art Mus. (life). Republican. Roman Catholic. Clubs: Commonwealth of Calif., Comstock. Contbg. author: Portfolio of Accounting Systems for Small and Medium-Sized Business, 1968, rev., 1977. Home and Office: 96 S Humboldt St Willits CA 95490-3539

AKIYAMA, CAROL LYNN, motion picture industry executive; b. Chgo.; d. Makio M. Akiyama and Mary (Uyeda) Maruyama. BA magna cum laude, U. So. Calif., 1968, JD, 1971. Bar: Calif. Atty. NLRB, Los Angeles, 1971-75, ABC-TV, Hollywood, Calif., 1975-79, So. Calif. Edison, Rosemead, 1980-81; asst. gen. atty. CBS Inc., Los Angeles, 1981-82; sr. v.p. Alliance of Motion Picture and TV Producers, Sherman Oaks, Calif., 1982-88; ind. producer and writer TV, motion pictures and multimedia/new techs., Rancho Palos Verdes, 1988—. Mem. Los Angeles County Bar Assn. (chmn. labor law sect. 1981-82, exec. com. 1975-85), Phi Kappa Phi, Phi Beta Kappa. Office: 1761 Cochran St Ste G Simi Valley CA 93065

AKUTAGAWA, DONALD, psychologist, educator; b. Grace, Idaho, June 7, 1923; s. Fred T. and Shizue (Oyama) A.; children: Trina Bortko, Murray, Doran. MA, U. Chgo., 1951; PhD, U. Pitts., 1956. Group counselor Orthogenic Sch., U. Chgo., 1951-52; clin. psychologist Inst. Pa. Hosp., Phila., 1959-67; pvt. practice Phila., 1957—, Bellevue, Wash., 1968—; chief community services Eastside Community Mental Health Center, Bellevue, 1968-72; clin. prof. psychology U. Wash., Seattle, 1974-90. Served with AUS, 1944-46. Fellow Am. Orthopsychiat. Assn. Office: Family Treatment Ctr 10845 Main St Bellevue WA 98004-6323 *Ideal: To so live my life that the world is better for my having been a part of it.*

ALADEEN, LARY JOE, secondary school educator; b. St. Joseph, Mo., Oct. 17, 1946; s. Joseph Harold and Hilda Marie (Bowman) A.; m. Donna Marlene Hill, July 1, 1972; 1 child, Juliana Hill. BA, Calif. Bapt. Coll., Riverside, 1971; MA, Calif. State U., Hayward, 1989. Cert. secondary tchr., cmty. coll. tchr., Calif. Tchr. Norbridge H.S., Castro Valley, Calif., 1974-75, Foothill H.S., Pleasanton, Calif., 1975—; cons. George Lucas Edn. Found., Mill Valley, Calif., 1992; reader Golden State exam. Calif. Dept. Edn., Sacramento, 1994-96; mem. social studies curriculum rev. com. Pleasanton (Calif.) Unified Sch. Dist., 1989-90; presenter seminar workshop Calif. Coun. for Social Studies Conv., 1993. Editor: Supplemental Readings for A.P. U.S. History, 1994. Media rep. Dem. Campaign Com., Riverside, 1972; vol. Dem. Election campaigns, Pleasanton, 1976-94, Love, Inc., San Mateo, Calif., 1992—. With USMC, 1967-70. Recipient Outstanding Svc. award Amador Valley Secondary Edn. Assn., Pleasanton, 1982-83; Mentor Tchr., Pleasanton Unified Sch. Dist., 1985-86, Master Tchr., 1988-91. Mem. Orgn. Am. Historians, Nat. Coun. for the Social Studies, Calif. Coun. for the Social Studies. Democrat. Presbyterian. Home: 4179 Silver St Pleasanton CA 94566-6223 Office: Foothill High Sch 4375 Foothill Rd Pleasanton CA 94588-9720

ALAMEDA, RUSSELL RAYMOND, JR., radiologic technologist; b. San Jose, Calif., Oct. 13, 1945; s. Russell Raymond and Rose Margaret (Manzone) A.; m. Gayle Evileen Allison, Feb. 16, 1969 (div. 1975); children: Lynda Rae, Anthony David. Student San Jose City Coll., 1963-65. Served with U.S. Navy, 1966-75; x-ray technician VA Hosp., Palo Alto, Calif., 1975-78; office mgr., radiologic technologist, responsible safety officer, orthopedic surgery Mountain View (Calif.), 1978—; owner, operator Ren-Tech, San Jose, 1982-87; radiologic technologist San Jose (Calif.) Med. Clinic, 1982-93. Mem. DeFrank Community Ctr. Recipient Mallinckrodt Outstanding Achievement award Mallinckrodt Corp., 1971. Mem. DAV (life), ACLU, NOW, Am. Registry of Radiologic Technologists, United We Stand Am., BAYMEC, Lamda Legal Def., Calif. Soc. Radiologic Technologists, Am. Soc. Radiologic Technologist. Democrat. Lutheran. Home: 165 Blossom Hill Rd # Sp76 San Jose CA 95123 Office: Orthopedic Surgery 2500 Hospital Dr Bldg 7 Mountain View CA 94040-4115

ALANIZ, MIGUEL JOSÉ CASTAÑEDA, library director; b. L.A., Oct. 21, 1944; s. Francisco and Amalia (Castañeda) A.; m. Mercedes P., June 7, 1980. AA, Chabot C.C., 1972; BS in Child/Human Devel., Calif. State U., Hayward, 1974; MS in LS, Calif. State U., Fullerton, 1975; MS Pub. Admnstrn., Calif. State U., San Bernardino, 1988. Spanish svcs. libr. Alameda County Libr., Hayward, 1975-77; branch mgr. San Jose Pub. Libr., 1977-78, Santa Ana (Calif.) Pub. Libr., 1978-79; divsn. chief, tech. process San Bernardino (Calif.) County Libr., 1979-84; city libr. Azusa City (Calif.) Libr., 1984-92; libr. dir. Inglewood Pub. (Calif.) Libr., 1992—. With U.S. Army, 1965-71. Recipient Grad. Rsch. Fellow Clif. State U., 1974. Mem. ALA, Calif. Libr. Assn., Reforma, Am. Heart Assn., Nat. Exch Club. Office: City of Inglewood Public Library 101 W Manchester Blvd Inglewood CA 90301-1753

ALARCON, ARTHUR LAWRENCE, federal judge; b. L.A., Aug. 14, 1925; s. Lorenzo Marques and Margaret (Sais) A.; m. Sandra D. Paterson, Sept. 1, 1979; children—Jan Marie, Gregory, Lance. B.A. in Polit. Sci, U. So. Calif., 1949, J.D., 1951. Bar: Calif. 1952. Dep. dist. atty. L.A. County, 1952-61; exec. asst. to Gov. Pat Brown State of Calif., Sacramento, 1962-64, legal adv. to gov., 1961-62; judge L.A. Superior Ct., 1964-78; assoc. justice Calif. Ct. Appeals, L.A., 1978-79; judge U.S. Ct. Appeals for 9th Circuit, L.A., 1979—. Served with U.S. Army, 1943-46, ETO. Office: US Ct Appeals 9th Cir 1607 US Courthouse 312 N Spring St Los Angeles CA 90012-4701*

ALARCÓN, FRANCISCO XAVIER, poet, educator; b. L.A., Feb. 21, 1954; s. Jesús Pastor and Consuelo (Vargas) A. Student, East L.A. Coll., 1973-74; BA, Calif. State U., Long Beach, 1977; MA, Stanford U., 1979. Rsch. asst. Mex.-Am. Studies, Calif. State U., Long Beach, 1976-77; summer youth counselor Horizons Unltd., San Francisco, 1981; program dir. Milagro Books, Oakland, Calif., 1981-82; translator Computer Curriculum Corp., Palo Alto, Calif., 1984; Spanish tchr. San Francisco U. High Sch., 1984; lectr. U. Calif., Santa Cruz, 1985-92, Davis, 1992—; pres. Aztlán Cultural/Centro Chicano de Escritores, Oakland, 1985—. Author: (poetry) Tattoos, 1985, Quake Poems, 1989, Body in Flames, 1990, Loma Prieta, 1990, Of Dark Love, 1992, Poemas Zurdos, 1992, Snake Poems, 1992, No Golden Gate for Us, 1993, (with others) Ya vas, carnal, 1985, Mundo 21, 1995, Pasaporte al Mundo 21, 1995, Tu mundo, 1996, Nuestro mundo, 1996, La enseñanza de español a hispanohablantes, 1996, Laughing Tomatoes and Other Spring Poems, 1997; co-editor Chicanas y Chicanos en diálogo, 1989. Bd. dirs. La Raza/Galería Posada, Sacramento, 1993—, Familia Ctr., Santa Cruz, 1990-92, Mission Cultural Ctr., San Francisco, 1986—, San Francisco Poetry Ctr., 1988—. Recipient Am. Book award, 1993, PEN Oakland Josephine Miles Lit. award, 1993, Writer's fellowship Calif. Arts Coun., 1989-90, Fulbright fellowship, 1982-83, Dorothy Danforth Compton Dissertation fellowship Stanford U., 1983; recipient First Prize 10th Ann. Chicano Lit. prize U. Calif., 1984, Palabra Nueva 2d prize U. Calif., 1983. Mem. Nat. Poetry Assn. (bd. dirs.). Home: 1712 Albion Pl Davis CA 95616-1446 Office: U Calif Dept Spanish Davis CA 95616

ALBA, BENNY, artist; b. Columbus, Ohio, May 7, 1949; d. Louis Peter and Marjorie Helen (Post) Benua. Student, Kent State U., 1968-70; BA in Psychology, U. Mich., 1982. artist-in-residence St. Charles Boy's Pres. Sch., Columbus, 1982-85; represented by numerous cons., Calif., Fla., Ill., Tex., Md., N.J., N.Y., Va., Mass.; lectr. Columbus Cultural Arts Ctr., 1983, 84, 93; presenter workshops in field; panelist Calif. Inst. for Intergral Studies, San Francisco, 1995. Solo shows include Columbus Cultural Arts Ctr., 1993, Apprentice Alliance, San Francisco, 1994, Las Vegas (Nev.) Mus., 1994, Artist TV Access, San Francisco, 1994, Western Wyo. Coll., Rock Springs, 1994, A Gallery in the Clock Tower, San Francisco, 1994, Ctr. for Psychol. Studies, Albany, Calif., 1994, Idyllwild (Calif.) Sch. Music and Art, 1995, Merced (Calif.) Coll. Art G., 1997, N. Country Mus. of Art, Plain Rapids, Minn., 1997 ; exhibited in group shows at Informative Edge, San Francisco, 1992, YWCA Youngstown, Ohio, 1992, Mus. Without Walls, Bemis Pt., N.Y., 1993, Davis (Calif.) Art Ctr., 1993, Kunst für Begegnungen, Munich, 1993, Ednl. Testing Svc., Emeryville, Calif., 1993-94, Diablo (Calif.) Valley Coll. Gallery, 1994, N. Mex. Art League, Albuquerque, 1995, Nat. Congress Art & Design, Salt Lake City, 1995, Danville (Calif.) Fine Arts, 1995, Lillian Paley Ctr. Visual Arts, Oakland, 1995, Lamar U., Beaumont, Tex., 1996, John Jay Coll. of Criminal Justice, N.Y., 1996, Serra House, Stanford U., 1996, Fed. Bldgs. Window Project, Oakland, 1996, Civic & Cultural Ctr., Brea, Calif., 1997, Palm Springs (Calif.) Desert Mus., 1997; represented in private and public collections Nat. Mus. Women in Arts, Ark. A Ctr., Little Rock, U. Mich. Mus. Art, Kalamazoo (Mich.) Inst. Arts, Greenpeace, Ulli Wachter (Germany), Las Vegas (N. Mex.) Art Mus., Ctr. for Psychol. Studies, Albany, Calif., Birmingham (Ala.) Mus. Art, Portland (Oreg.) Art Mus., others. Bd. dirs. No. Calif. Women's Caucus for Art, 1991, sec. 1991-92, phone liaison, 1991-93. Recipient Lenore Miles award North Platte Valley Art Gallery, 1991, Body of Work award Women Artists, A Celebration, 1990, Merit award San Francisco Women Artist Gallery, 1986, Dr. S. Mackoff award Palm Springs Desert Mus., 1997. Mem. Women's Caucus for Art (bd. dirs. No. Calif. 1991-94, sec. 1991, 92). Studio: 4400 Market St Oakland CA 94608-3424

ALBA, FELIX, industrial computer systems company executive; b. Burgos, Spain, May 14, 1948; came to the U.S., 1983; s. Francisco Paula and Maria Salome (Juez) A.; m. Susana Agüero, Dec. 30, 1976; children: Araceli, Nicholas. MA in Elec. Engring., U. Nacional del Sur, Argentina, 1974. Adj. prof. U. Nacional San Juan, Argentina, 1974-77, assoc. prof., 1977-78, prof., 1978-83; postdoctoral fellow U. Utah, 1983, rsch. assoc., 1984-87; pres. Felix Alba Cons., Murray, Utah, 1987—. Patentee in field. Mem. AAAS, Instrument Soc. Am., Assn. for Computer Machinery, Soc. Mining Engrs., Indsl. Computer Soc., The Planetary Soc. Home and Office: 5760 Ridge Creek Rd Murray UT 84107-6617

ALBANO, ANDRES, JR., real estate developer, real estate broker; b. Honolulu, Apr. 16, 1941; s. Andres Pacis and Florence (Paglinawan) A.; m. Sandra Kam Mee Ymas, Nov. 29, 1961; children: Cheryl Ann, Denise Lynn. BEE, U. Hawaii, 1965, MBA, 1972. Engr. nuclear power USN, 1965-67; elec. engr. U.S. Aviation Adminstrn., Honolulu, 1967-69, Honolulu Bd. Water Supply, 1969-79; exec. v.p. MidPac Devel. Ltd., Honolulu, 1979-84; pres. Albano & Assocs., Honolulu, 1984—; prin. broker Gen. Growth Mgmt. of Hawaii, Inc., 1993-96. Mem. NSPE, Hawaii Soc. Profl. Engrs. (pres. 1979-80), Devel. Assn. Hawaii (pres. 1992-93), Nat. Assn. Realtors, Hawaii Developers Coun. (pres. 1995-96), Rotary, Beta Gamma Sigma. Roman Catholic. Home: 748 Kokomo Pl Honolulu HI 96825-1603 Office: Albano & Assocs Inc 3322 Campbell Ave Honolulu HI 96815-3856

ALBERT, SIDNEY PAUL, philosophy educator; b. Syracuse, N.Y., Apr. 11, 1914; s. Simon and Gertrude Dora (Siskin) A.; m. Lucy Ann Schroeder, Oct. 30, 1955 (div.); children: Vivian Risa Albert Shemesh, Alan Edward, Laurence David. AB, Syracuse U., 1934; PhD in Philosophy, Yale U., 1939; postgrad., Carnegie Inst. Tech., Northwestern U., Stanford U., U. Ill., 1950-53, U. Ill., 1953-54, Columbia U., 1954-56. Instr. philosophy U. Conn., Storrs, 1946, Syracuse (N.Y.) U., 1946; asst. prof., philosophy Triple Cities Coll./Syracuse U., 1946-50, Harpur Coll., 1950-53; part time instr. speech dept. U. Ill., 1953-54; asst. prof., philosophy L.A. State Coll., 1956-60, assoc. prof., philosophy, 1960-64; prof., philosophy Calif. State U., L.A., 1964-79, prof. emeritus, 1979—; chair dept. philos., Calif. State U., L.A., 1960-63, assoc. chair 1967-68, acad. senate, 1962-64; first chair assembly sch. letters and sci., 1966-67, mem.-at-large, 1966-68. Dir. (coll. prodn.) Claudia, 1947; directed coll. and cmty. theatre prodns.; contbr. numerous articles about George Bernard Shaw and reviews to profl. jours. Pres. West San Gabriel (Calif.) Dem. Club, 1960-64; mem. Calif. Dem. State Ctrl. Com., 1960-62; mem. L.A. County Dem. Ctrl. Com., 1962-64; mem. com. recommend appointment Postmaster of Alhambra, 1961; mem. state human rels. com. Calif. Dem. Coun., 1963-64. Warrant officer (j.g.) U.S. Army, 1941-46. Fellow Syracuse U., 1934-35; scholar Yale U., 1935-36; Hon. Rsch. fellow Yale U., 1940-41; Rsch. grantee, 1964-65, 66-67, 69, 73-74; Sidney P. Albert/George Bernard Shaw Collection named in his honor at Brown Univ., 1991. Mem. MLA, AAUP (sec. and treas. Triple Cities Coll. chpt 1947-48, pres. Harpur Coll. chpt. 1950-51, treas. L.A. Coll. chpt. 1959-61, mem. exec. com. 1960-61, 63-64, pres. 1962-63, del. 1963; state coll. rep. exec. com. So. Calif. Conf. 1963-64, chair com. Emeriti and retirement issues, ex-officio mem. exec. com. Calif. Conf., 1980—, ret. com. 1996—, awarded cert. 50 years of distinguished membership), Emeriti Assn. (founder, 1978, v.p., 1983-84, pres. 1984-85), Am. Philos. Soc., Am. Soc. Aesthetics (v.p. Pacific div. 1962-63, pres. 1963-64), Modern Lang. Assn., Am. Soc. Theatre Rsch. (mem. nominating com. 1971), Theatre Libr. Assn., Assn. Calif. State Univ. Profs. (v.p. L.A. state coll. chpt. 1959-60), Shaw Soc. (London), Bernard Shaw Soc. (N.Y.C.), Shaw Soc. Calif. (bd. dirs. 1959-65, mem. editorial bd. Shaw Review, 1968-80, Shaw: The Annual of Bernard Shaw Studies, 1981-85), Shaw Soc. (Japan, lect. 1980), Phi Beta Kappa, Phi Kappa Phi, Pi Gamma Mu. Home: 847 Eaton Dr Pasadena CA 91107-1837 Office: Calif State U Dept Philosophy 5151 State University Dr Los Angeles CA 90032

ALBERT-GALTIER, ALEXANDRE, language educator; b. Graveson, France, June 3, 1960; came to U.S., 1989; BA, U. Lyon II, 1981, MA with honors, 1982, PhD with honors, 1988. Tech. dir. Festival D'Avignon, France, 1983-90; Dia Art Found., N.Y.C., 1989-90; chargé de cours U. Lyon II, 1986-88; vis. instr. U. Oreg., Eugene, 1990-91; vis. asst. prof. U. Oreg., 1991-93, assoc. prof., 1996—; asst. prof. Mt. Holyoke Coll., 1993-94. Author: (poetry book) La Connaissance des Corps, 1995; contbr. articles to profl. jours.; invited spkr. Le Festival d'Avignon, U. Mass., 1994, others. Mem. MLA, Soc. d'Etudes du XVIIème Siè, Coll. de France, N.Am. Assn. for 17th Century French Lit., S.E. Am. Soc. for French 17th Century Studies, Centre Méridional de Rencontres sur le XVIIème Siècle, Soc. Internat. d' Etu des Yourcenariennes, Assn. des Amis d'Andre Gide, Assn. des Amis de Lancelot Desquais (pres.). Office: U Oreg Romance Langs 2450 Spring Blvd Eugene OR 97403

ALBERTI, DEL JOSEPH, school system administrator; b. Sacramento, July 28, 1939; s. Delmo J. and Bena M. (Bertoni) A.; m. Sharon Lynn Gregory, Feb. 3, 1962; children: Heidi, Martin, Matthew. BA, U. of the Pacific, 1963, MA, Calif. State U., Sacramento, 1969; PhD, Pacific Western U., 1989. Cert. tchr., adminstr., Calif. Tchr. Sacramento City Schs., 1963-69; sci. specialist Nueva Learning Ctr., Hillsborough, Calif., 1969-75, dir., 1976-79; prin. Merced (Calif.) City Schs., 1979-80; supt. Portola Valley (Calif.) Schs., 1980-83, Auburn (Calif.) Union Schs., 1983-89, Washington Unified Sch. Dist., West Sacramento, Calif., 1989-94; assoc. supt. Lodi (Calif.) Unified Sch. Dist., 1994—, supt., 1995—; curriculum devel. and supplemental materials commr. State of Calif., 1991-95; instr. Calif. State U., San Francisco, San Jose, 1972-80; lectr. Oreg. State U., 1979-83, Fresno (Calif.) Pacific Coll., 1986—; edn. cons. Learning Inst., Springfield, Pa., 1978—; mem. dean's adv. com. Sch. Edn., U. of the Pacific. Co-author: Correlation of Activity-Centered Science-Mathematics, 1972, Laboratory Laughter, 1976, McGraw-Hill: Elementary Science Study, 1975-76. Bd. dirs., treas. Placer United Soccer Club, Roseville, Calif., 1984-85; v.p., pres. Cen. Homeowners Asns., Belmont, Calif., 1976-79; bd. dirs. Belmont Bobby Sox Softball, 1976-77; bd. dirs. Lodi Boys and Girls Club; active various polit. campaigns, Belmont, Roseville, 1972-90. Mem. Assn. Calif. Sch. Adminstrs. (pres. Yolo County 1991-92), Am. Assn. Sch. Adminstrs., West Sacramento C. of C., Lodi C. of C., Rotary. Roman Catholic. Office: Lodi Unified Sch Dist 1305 E Vine St Lodi CA 95240-3148

ALBERTS, DAVID, artistic director, mime; b. Akron, Ohio, Nov. 14, 1946; married (div. 1972); 1 child, Morgan Elizabeth; married (div. 1992); children: Sarah Aimee, Samantha Kaitlin Wynne. BA in Music, Kent State U., 1972; MA in Theatre, West Va. U., 1978; PhD in Theatre, Bowling Green State U., 1989. Instr. Akron (Ohio) U., 1970-71, W.Va. U., 1978, Va. Commonwealth U., Richmond, 1979-81, Calif. State U., Turlock, Calif., 1981-83, Kent (Ohio) State U., 1986-87, Bowling Green (Ohio) State U., 1987-89; artistic dir. Theatre of the One Actor, San Diego, 1995—; mime artist in field. Author: Pantomime: Exercises and Elements, 1971, Talking About Mime, 1994 (San Diego Book award 1994), Rehearsal Management for Directors, 1995, (play) Death by Arrangement, 1981; contbr. articles to profl. jours. Recipient Founders award Internat. Thespian Soc., 1972, Directing award Am. Coll. Theatre Festival, 1982. Mem. Internat. Mimes and Pantomimes, Assn. for Theatre in Higher Edn., Speech Comms. Assn.

ALBERTS, DAVID SAMUEL, physician, pharmacologist, educator; b. Milw., Dec. 30, 1939; m. Heather Alberts; children: Tim, Sabrina. BS, Trinity Coll., Hartford, Conn., 1962; MD, U. Va., 1966. Cert. physician, Ariz. Dir. clin. pharmacology Ariz. Cancer Ctr., Tucson, 1975—, prof. medicine and pharmacology, 1982—, dir. cancer prevention and control, 1988—, dep. dir., 1989-96, assoc. dean rsch. Coll. Medicine, 1996—; external adv. U. Chgo. Cancer Ctr., 1993—, Tulane U. Cancer Ctr., New Orleans, 1993—, divsn. cancer prevention M.D. Anderson Cancer Ctr., Houston, 1994—, Norris Cotton Cancer Ctr., Hanover, 1995—; mem. bd. sci. counselors divsn. Cancer PRevention and Control, NCI-NIH, 1990-94; chmn. gynecologic cancer com. S.W. Oncology Group, 1977—; mem. monitoring and adv. panel Nat. Prostate Lung-Colon-OVary Cancer Study, NCI-NIH, 1994—; chmn. cancer prevention com. Gynecologic Oncology Group, 1995—; chmn. oncologic adv. com. U.S. FDA, 1982-84, spl. cons., 1984-86. Assoc. editor Cancer Rsch., 1989—, Cancer Chemother and Pharmacol., 1992—, Clin. Cancer Rsch., 1994-96; contbr. articles to profl. jours.; inventor azamitosene and anthracene anticancer agts., tumorimeter, hypodermic needle with automatic retracting point. NIH grantee, 1975—. Mem. Am. Soc. for Clin. Pharmacology and Therapeutics, Am. Soc. Clin. Oncology, Am. Soc. Preventive Oncology, Am. Assn. for Cancer Rsch., Soc. Gynecologic Oncologists. Office: Ariz Cancer Ctr 1501 N Campbell Ave Tucson AZ 85724

ALBERT-SHERIDAN, LENORE LUANN, legal research fellow, business owner; b. Coldwater, Mich.; d. Samuel George and Carol Louise (Huttenen) Albert; m. James Christopher Sheridan, Feb. 23, 1991. AA in Liberal Arts, Long Beach City Coll.; BA in Econs., Calif. State U., Long Beach, 1992; JD in Law, U. of the Pacific, 1997. Asst. purchasing agt., supr. warehouse assembly, head inventory control Neill Aircraft Co., Long Beach, 1987-89; head inventory control/regional purchasing & receiving supr. Internat. Paper, Inc., L.A., 1989-91; fin./gen. ledger acct. Port of Long Beach, 1991-92; corp. acct. Weber Aircraft Inc., Fullerton, Calif., 1993; fin. analyst Sizzler Internat., L.A., 1993; rsch. fellow McGeorge Sch. Law, Sacramento, Calif., 1994-97; pres. LeJam, Sacramento, 1997—; participant Nat. Inst. Judicial Hearsay Study, McGeorge/U. Calif.-Davis, Sacramento, 1994, pres. Lejam, Sacramento, Calif., 1997—; tutor minority bus. program Calif. State U., Long Beach, 1992. Back stage mgr. San Pedro (Calif.) Theatre Performing Arts, 1987. Mem. ABA (internat. law and antitrust sects., export control and econ. sects. com. mem., internat. intellectual property rights com.), Inst. Managerial Accts., Internat. Platform Assn., Phi Alpha Delta (Clair Engle chpt. alumni com. 1994-95). Lutheran. Office: LeJam PO Box 214412 Sacramento CA 95821

ALBERTSON, DAVID, food products executive. V.p., treas. Ballantine Produce Co. Inc., Sanger, Calif., 1971—. Office: Ballatine Produce Co Inc 325 L St Sanger CA 93657-2122*

ALBERTSON, JACK AARON PAUL, prosecutor; b. Rantoul, Ill., Apr. 28, 1962; s. Jack Collier and Sandra Lou (Cole) A. BA, U. Redlands, 1984; JD, Willamette U., 1987. Bar: Calif. 1989. Law libr. Riverside County Law Libr., Indio, Calif., 1989-90; dep. Imperial County Dist. Atty., El Centro, Calif., 1990—. Mem. ABA, Phi Alpha Delta. Republican. Mem. Ch. of Christ. Office: Imperial County Dist Atty 939 W Main St El Centro CA 92243-2843

ALBERTSON OWENS, SHIRLEY A., psychology educator, researcher; d. James Blaine and Majorie Ruth (Lyle) Albertson; m. Max Owens, May 22, 1988. children: James Robert, Jennifer Christine. BA in Experimental Rsch. Psychology, Calif. State Univ., Long Beach, 1980, MA in General Psychology, 1983; PhD in Cognitive Developmental Psychology, Claremont Grad. Sch., Calif., 1990. Rsch. asst. Calif. State Univ., 1980-83, asst. instr., 1982; rsh. asst. Scripps Coll., Claremont, Calif., 1983; rsch. asst. Pitzer Coll., Claremont, Calif., 1983-90; bus. cons., statistician Lindair Inc., Calif., 1985-86; instr. Calif. State, Long Beach, 1986-89; clin. rschr. House Ear Inst., L.A., 1986-87; instr. Golden West Coll., Huntington Beach, Calif., 1987—; assoc. prof. psychology Southern Calif. Coll., Costa Mesa, Calif., 1988—; peer counselor Calif. State Univ., Long Beach, 1980-81; support group facilitator Leisure World Retirement Cmty., Seal Beach, Calif., 1981-83; chair dept. psychology, 1988—, chair divsn. soc. svc. Southern Calif. Coll. Costa Mesa, 1988—; dir. tchng. effectiveness; speaker in the field. Author: (with others) Aging and Technological Advances, 1985, Language, Memory and Aging, 1988, Psychology and Aging, 1989, Adult Information Processing: Limits on Loss, 1993; author: (with A. Gibson) A Survey of Social Science: Psychology, 1993. Full Tuition Fellowship grant Claremont Grad. Sch., 1984, Rupley Fellowship grant House Eat Inst., 1986, Rsch. grant Coun. Grad. Students Claremont Grad. Sch., 1987, Haynes Dissertation Fellowship grant Claremont Grad. Sch., 1988; recipient Outstanding Rsch. award Christian Assn. Psychology, 1993. Mem. Am. Pub. Health Assn., Am. Inst. Hypnotherapy, Am. Psychol. Assn., Am. Psychol. Soc., Christian Assn. Psychol. Studies, Am. Soc. on Aging, Gerontological Soc. Am., Sigma Xi, Soc. Personality and Social Psychology Inc., Soc. Scientific Study Religion, Western Psychol. Assn. Office: Southern Calif Coll 55 Fair Dr Costa Mesa CA 92626

ALBIN, RANDY CLARK, record company executive; b. Pasadena, Calif., Sept. 25, 1957; s. Clark Eugene and Aileen Mary (Vrooman) A. AA, Foothill Coll., Los Altos Hills, Calif., 1983; student, Stanford U., 1984; BA, Menlo Coll., 1985. With Recreation Tennis, Inc., Stanford, Calif., 1986, Roberta's Personnel Agy., Palo Alto, Calif., 1988, Wollborg-Michelson Personnel, Palo Alto, Calif., 1988; pres., chief exec. officer Randall Record Co., Los Altos, Calif., 1988—. Mem. Foothill Coll. Alumni Assn. (bd. dirs. 1986—), Menlo Coll. Alumni Assn. (treas. 1988). Home and Office: PO Box 920 Los Altos CA 94023-0920

ALBINO, JUDITH E.N., university president; b. Jackson, Tenn.; m. Salvatore Albino; children: Austin, Adrian. BJ, U. Tex., 1967, PhD, 1973. Mem. faculty sch. dental medicine SUNY, Buffalo, 1972-90, assoc. provost, 1984-87, dean sch. arch. and planning, 1987-89, dean grad. sch., 1989-90; v.p. acad. affairs and rsch, dean system grad. sch. U. Colo., Boulder, 1990-91, pres., 1991-95, pres. emerita, prof. psychiatry, 1995-97; pres. Calif. Sch. Profl. Psychology, San Francisco, 1997—; bd. dirs. Storage Tek, Colo. Nat. Bank. Contbr. articles to profl. jours. Acad. Adminstrn. fellow Am. Coun. on Edn., 1983; grantee NIH. Fellow APA (treas., bd. dirs.); mem. Behavioral Scientists in Dental Rsch. (past pres.), Am. Assn. Dental Rsch. (bd. dirs.). Office: Calif Sch Profl Psychology 2749 Hyde St San Francisco CA 94109

ALBRECHT, ALBERT PEARSON, electronics engineer, consultant; b. Bakersfield, Calif., Aug. 23, 1920; s. Albert Waldo and Elva (Shuck) A.; m. Muriel Elizabeth Grenell, June 15, 1942 (dec. Apr. 1943); m. Edith J. Dorner, July 18, 1944. BSEE, Calif. Inst. Tech., 1942; MSEE, U. So. Calif., L.A., 1947. Registered profl. engr., Calif. Rsch. assoc. radiation lab. MIT, Cambridge, Mass., 1942-43; chief engr. Gilfillan Bros., L.A., 1943-58; v.p. Space Gen. Corp., El Monte, Calif., 1958-68; exec. v.p. Telluran Cons., Santa Monica, Calif., 1968-72; dir. systems evaluation Office of Asst. Sec. of Def. for Intelligence, Washington, 1972-76; assoc. adminstr. FAA, Washington, 1976-86; cons., prin. AP Albrecht-Cons., Bellingham, Wash., 1986—; bd. dirs. Air Traffic Control Assn.; mem. exec. bd. RADIO Tech. Commn. for Aeronautics, Washington, 1980-86; mem. aeronautics adv. com. NASA, Washington, 1980-90. Co-author: Electronic Designers Handbook-Design Compendium, 1957, 2d edit., 1974. Fellow AIAA (adv. com. Aerospace Am. 1984—), IEEE (Engr. Mgr. of the Yr. 1989). Home and Office: 3224 Eagleridge Way Bellingham WA 98226-7821

ALBRECHT, DONNA G., author; b. Bridgeton, N.J., Feb. 26, 1949; d. Walter S. and Helen Louise (McCabe) Garrison; m. Michael C. Albrecht, Aug. 16, 1970; children: Katherine (dec.), Abigail. BA, Antioch U., San Francisco, 1983. Tchr. U. Calif. Ext.; lectr. in field; cons. in field. Author Deals and Discounts: If You're 50 or Older, 1990, Buying a Home When You're Single, 1994, Raising A Child Who Has A Physical Disability, 1995, Overcoming the Four Deceptions: In Career Relationships (with Dwaine L. Canova), 1995, Promoting Your Business with Free (or Almost Free) Publicity, 1997; contbr. over 400 articles to mags., including Entrepreneur Mag. (columnist), Ms., Modern Maturity, Real Estate Today, Calif. Bus., San Francisco Bus. Times, San Francisco Examiner, Contra Costa Times, Writer's Digest, Sharing Ideas, Exceptional Parent, Accent on Living, others. Pres. exec. com. No. Calif. chpt. Muscular Dystrophy Assn., 1992. Mem. Am. Soc. Journalists and Authors (founding co-chmn. for regional symposium 1992, chmn. 1994, chpt. pres. 1991-93, nat. bd. dirs. 1994—), Author Guild, Assn. for Care of Children's Health, Am. Med. Writers Assn. Lutheran. Home: 4603 Lincoln Dr Concord CA 94521-1334 Office: PO Box 21423 Concord CA 94521-0423

ALBRECHT, JOIE, television and film producer, director, writer; b. Denver; d. Alfred Emil and Virginia Lee Albrecht; m. Scott N. Garen, Sept. 17, 1979 (div. Aug. 1989). Student, U. Colo., 1976-78, U. Calif., Bakersfield, 1979. V.p. Garen/Albrecht Prodns. Inc., Santa Monica, Calif., 1980-88; owner, pres. Albrecht & Assocs., Inc., Topanga, Calif., 1989—; guest lectr. Am. Film Inst., L.A., 1981, Women's Image Network, L.A., 1994; judge Emmy awards, L.A., 1985—; producer, writer, dir. Scandals, pilot for ABC/Stephen J. Cannelll Prodns.; producer, writer CBS Comedy Bloopers; author Adam's Guide to Eve. Prodr. (HBO spl.) The Cliffwood Avenue Kids—, Up Close HBO, co-creator, developer, prodr.: (TV spl.) Sixty Years of Seduction--ABC spl., cable spl. Carole King: One to One, TV's Bloopers and Practical Jokes--NBC; developer, prodr., writer: (TV spls.) Television's Greatest Commercials; creator, prodr., writer, dir.: Down and Out with Donald Duck, 1987; prodr., writer, co-dir.: Mickey's 60th Birthday, Totally Minnie--Disney/NBC; prodr., writer, dir.: (TV spl.) Comedy Bloopers. Recipient Belding bowl for outstanding contbn. to advt. Belding Awards, 1984, gold award for Smart Investing, N.Y. Film Festival, 1986, bronze award for outstanding achievement in film and TV music video category Cindy Awards,; talent scholar U. Colo., 1976-78. Mem. AFTRA, ASCAP, SAG, Dirs. Guild Am. (women's com. 1991—), Writers Guild Am., Women in Film, Topanga Assn. for Scenic Cmty., Old Topanga Homeowners Assn. Democrat. Office: PO Box 8533 Calabasas CA 91372-8533

ALCANTARA, THEO, conductor; b. Cuenca, Castile, Spain, 1941; student Real Conservatorio de Musica, Madrid; grad. Akademie Mozarteum, Salzburg, Austria, 1964; m. Susan Alcantara; children: Rafael, Carlos. Conducting debut with Teatro de la Zarzuela, Madrid; condr. Frankfurt Opera Theatre Orch., 1964-66; dir. orchs. U. Mich., Ann Arbor, 1968-73; music dir., condr. Grand Rapids Symphony, 1973-78; music dir., prin. condr. Phoenix Symphony Orch., from 1978; music dir., condr. Music Acad. of West Summer Festival, Santa Barbara, Calif., 1981-85, prin. condr. Pitts. Opera, 1987—; artistic dir., prin. condr. Bilbao Symphony, Spain, 1993—; prin. guest condr. Nat. Orch. Spain, 1994—; guest condr. numerous orchs. including: world premier Christopher Columbus, Teatro Colon, Buenos Aires, Met. Opera, Pitts. Opera, Washington Opera, Am. Symphony, orchs. of Paris, Berlin, Madrid, Barcelona, Mexico City, Montevideo, New Orleans, Detroit, Pitts., Rochester (N.Y.) Philharm., Oreg. Symphony, Utah Symphony. Recipient Lili Lehman medal; silver medal Dimitri Mitropoulos Internat. Conducting Competition, 1966; Disting. Service award Mich. Found. for the Arts, 1977. Office: ICM Artists Ltd 40 W 57th St New York NY 10019*

ALCINDOR, LEWIS FERDINAND See ABDUL-JABBAR, KAREEM

ALCORN, JAMES M., state insurance administrator. BS in Bus., Eastern Ill. U., 1967, postgrad. in econs. Owner various ind. property and casualty ins. agys., Idaho, 1970—; investigator, various other positions to dep. dir. Idaho Dept. Ins., Boise, 1989—, acting dir., 1994-96, dir., 1996—; Cert. Ins. Counselor, 1981. Mem. Gooding County (Idaho) Fair bd.; chmn. hosp. adv. bd. Walker Ctr. of Gooding; founding bd. dirs. Payette (Idaho) Recreation Dist.; mem. CIC Edn. Com. Idaho. With USMC Inf., Vietnam. Recipient Outstanding Cmty. Achievement award, 1979. Mem. Ind. Agts. Assn., Profl. Ins. Agts. Assn., Gooding (Idaho) C. of C., Gooding Rotary Club. Office: Idaho Dept Insurance 700 W State St 3d Fl PO Box 83720 Boise ID 83720-0043

ALCORN, KAREN ZEFTING HOGAN, artist, art educator, analyst; b. Hartford, Conn., Sept. 29, 1949; d. Edward C. and Doris V. (Anderson) Zefting; m. Wendell R. Alcorn, Apr. 12, 1985. BS, Skidmore Coll., 1971; MFA, Boston U., 1976. Secondary art tchr. Scituate (Mass.) High Sch., 1971-73, Milton (Mass.) High Sch., 1973-79; engr. VEDA, Inc., Arlington, Va., 1979-80; analyst Info. Spectrum, Inc., Arlington, Va., 1980-82, Pacer Systems, Inc., Arlington, Va., 1982-84; dir. ops., mgr. tng. program Starmark Corp., Arlington, Va., 1984; sr. systems analyst VSE Corp., Arlington, Va., 1984-85; analyst, tech. writer Allen Corp., Las Vegas and Fallon, Nev., 1987-88; mem. faculty Western Nev. C.C., 1989; instr. Newport (R.I.) Art Mus., 1990-92; dir. North Tahoe (Calif.) Art Ctr.; dir. Artward Bound, 1994; instr. Sierra Nevada Coll., 1995—. Exhbns. include Am. Artists Profl. League Grand. Nat., N.Y.C., 1995, Nev. Artists Assn., 1996, Nev. Biennial, 1996, Catharine Lorillard Wolfe Art Club, N.Y.C., 1996, Nat. Oil and Acrylic Painters Soc., 1996. Recipient silver medal Calif. Discovery Awards, 1994, finalist Artists' Mag., 1994, Coun. Am. Artist Socs. award Graphic Am. Artists Profl. League, 1995; grantee Sierra Arts Found., 1996. Mem. AAUW, Nev. Artists Assn., Allied Artists Am. (assoc.), Catharine Wolfe Art Club (assoc.), Am. Artists Profl. League, Nat. Art Edn. Assn., Nat. Oil and Acrylic Painters Soc. Home: 2221 Manhattan Dr Carson City NV 89703-5417

ALCOSSER, SANDRA, English language educator; b. 1944. Assoc. editor Mademoiselle, N.Y.C., 1966-69; dir. Poets-in-the-Park, N.Y.C., 1975-77; instr. La. State U., 1982-85, asst. prof. English,, 1985-87; dir. creative writing program San Diego State U., 1988-91, assoc. prof. English,, 1986-89, prof., 1990—; writer-in-residence, workshop dir. various locations, 1973-85; vis. prof. creative writing U. Mich., 1994; guest spkr. Nat. Pub. Radio and Pub. TV programs. Author: (poetry) Each Bone a Prayerpoetry, 1982, A Fish to Feed All Hunger, 1986, Sleeping Inside the Glacier, 1997; contbr. to books and jours.

ALDAG, RICHARD JEFFREY, composer, educator; b. N.Y.C., Aug. 8, 1955; s. Russell Thomas and Emily (Carro) A.; m. Maria Celi, July 2, 1977 (div.); m. Astrid Juárez, Dec. 30, 1989. B.A., Queens Coll., 1977, M.A., 1979; Ph.D., CUNY, 1990. Music events coordinator CUNY Grad. Ctr., N.Y.C., 1981-84; chmn. dept. theory Bklyn. Conservatory Music, Flushing, N.Y., 1981-92; exec. dir. Musica Poetica Publs., 1992—; adj. asst. prof. Fordham U., Bronx, 1984-92; bd. dirs. Am. New Music Consortium, N.Y.C., 1985-86, Access Chamber Ensemble, N.Y.C., 1987—; dir. Silicon Valley Youth Conservatory, 1994—; lectr. music San Jose (Calif.) State U., 1993—; vis. prof. composition Shanghai Conservatory of Music, 1993-94; artistic dir. Shanghai Global Arts Festival, 1996—. Composer numerous vocal and instrumental works. CUNY fellow, 1980, 84. Mem. League of Composers/Internat. Soc. for Contemporary Music (bd. dirs. 1988-91), Internat. Alban Berg Soc. (sec.-treas. 1982-86), Roger Sessions Soc. (v.p. 1988—). Avocation: Mexican cooking.

ALDEN, MEREDITH, state agency administrator. Dir. State of Utah Divsn. Mental Health, Salt Lake City; mem. faculty U. Utah, Salt Lake City; psychiatric staff, adult residential treatment unit Valley Mental Health, Salt Lake City, Valley Storefront; former mem. state bd. mental health. Contbr. devel. mental health policy State of Utah through work with Utah Alliance for Mentally Ill, Mental Health Assn. Utah, mental health tech. adv. group Gov.'s Health Policy Commn. Office: Utah Divsn Mental Health 120 N 200 West #415 Salt Lake City UT 84101

ALDEN, SUSAN JANE, technical writing/multimedia agency executive; b. Cleve., Mar. 17, 1952; d. Walter Everett and Irvina Mary (Knight) Watson; m. John Hansen Alden, Sept. 11, 1982; children: Jonathan Starbuck, Darcy Priscilla. BFA, Miami U., Oxford, Ohio, 1974. Textile designer Von Hamm Textiles, Inc., Honolulu, 1974-75; artist/designer Capricorn Graphics, Inc., Honolulu, 1975-80; tech. writer/cons. CFC, Inc., Dayton, Ohio, 1980-82; freelance writer/producer Northlight Comm., L.A., 1982-87; sr. mgr. tech. publ. dept. Fujitsu GTE Bus. Systems, Phoenix, 1987-89; owner, pres. Alden Creative Enterprises, Ventura, Calif., 1990—. Author software manuals. Recipient purchase award City of Honolulu, 1977. Mem. NAFE, Soc. Tech. Comm., Phoenix Art Mus. Republican. Methodist.

ALDERMAN, MINNIS AMELIA, psychologist, educator, small business owner; b. Douglas, Ga., Oct. 14, 1928; d. Louis Cleveland Sr. and Minnis Amelia (Wooten) A. AB in Music, Speech and Drama, Ga. State Coll., Milledgeville, 1949; MA in Supervision and Counseling Psychology, Murray State U., 1960; postgrad. Columbia Pacific U., 1987—. Tchr. music Lake County Sch. Dist., Umatilla, Fla., 1949-50; instr. vocal and instrumental music, dir. band, orch. and choral Fulton County Sch. Dist., Atlanta, 1950-54; instr. English, speech, debate, vocal and instrumental music, dir. drama, band, choral and orch. Elko County Sch. Dist., Wells, Nev., 1954-59; tchr. English and social studies Christian County Sch. Dist., Hopkinsville, Ky., 1960; instr. psychology, counselor critic prof. Murray (Ky.) State U., 1961-63, U. Nev., Reno, 1963-67; owner Minimizer Exercising Salon, Ely, Nev., 1969-71, Knit Knook, Ely, 1969—, Minimimeo, Ely, 1969—, Gift Gamut, Ely, 1977—; prof. dept. fine arts Wassuk Coll., Ely, 1986-91, assoc. dean, 1986-87, dean, 1987-90; counselor White Pine County Sch. Dist., Ely, 1960-68; dir. Child and Family Ctr., Ely Indian Tribe, 1988-93, Family and Cmty. Ctr., Ely Shoshone Indian Tribe, 1988-93, Family Resource Ctr., Great Basin Rural Nev. Youth Cabinet, 1996—; adv. Ely Shoshone Tribal Youth Coun., 1990-93, Budge Stanton Meml. Scholarship, 1991-93, Budge Stanton Meml. Living Mus. and Cultural Ctr., 1991-93; fin. aid contracting officer Ely Shoshone Tribe, 1990-93; instr. No. Nev. C.C., 1995—; supr. testing Ednl. Testing Svc., Princeton, N.J., 1960-68, Am. Coll. Testing Program, Iowa, 1960-68, U. Nev., Reno, 1960-68; chmn. bd. White Pine Sch. Dist. Employees Fed. Credit Union, Ely, 1961-69; psychologist mental hygiene div. Nev. Pers., Ely, 1969-75, dept. employment security, 1975-80; sec.-treas. bd. dirs. Gt. Basin Enterprises, Ely, 1969-71; speaker at confs. Author various news articles, feature stories, pamphlets, handbooks and grants in field. Pvt. instr. piano, violin, voice and organ, Ely, 1981—; dir. Family Resource Ctr. (Great Basin Rural Nev. Youth Cabinet), 1996—; bd. dirs. band Sacred Heart Sch., Ely, 1982—; mem. Gov.'s Mental Health State Commn., 1963-65, Ely Shoshone Tribal Youth Camp, 1991-92, Elys Shoshone Tribal Unity Conf., 1991-92, Tribal Parenting Skills Coord., 1991; bd. dirs. White Pine County Sch. Employees Fed. Credit Union, 1961-68, pres., 1963-68; 2d v.p. White Pine Community Concert Assn., 1965-67, pres., 1967, 85—, treas., 1975-79, dr. chmn., 1981-85; chmn. of bd., 1984; bd. dirs. White Pine chpt. ARC, 1978-82; mem. Nev. Hwy. Safety Leaders Bd., 1979-82; mem. Gov.'s Commn. on Status Women, 1968-74, Gov.'s Nevada State Juvenile Justice Adv. Commn., 1992-94, White Pine Overall Econ. Devel. Plan Coun., 1992-94; sec.-treas. White Pine Rehab. Tng. Ctr. for Retarded Persons, 1973-75; mem. Gov.'s Commn. on Hwy. Safety, 1979-81, Gov's. Juvenile Justice Program; sec.-treas. White Pine County Juvenile Problems Cabinet, 1994—; dir. Ret. Sr. Vol. Program, 1973-74; vice chmn. Gt. Basin Health Coun., 1973-75, Home Extension Adv. Bd., 1977-80; sec.-treas. Great Basin chpt. Nev. Employees Assn.; bd. dirs. United Way, 1970-76; vice chmn. White Pine Coun. on Alcoholism and Drug Abuse, 1975-76, chmn., 1976-77; grants author 3 yrs. Indian Child Welfare Act; originator Community Tng. Ctr. for Retarded People, 1972, Ret. Sr. Vol. Program, 1974, Nutrition Program for Sr. Citizens, 1974, Sr. Citizens Ctr., 1974, Home Repairs for Sr. Citizens, 1974, Sr. Citizens Home Assistance Program, 1977, Creative Crafters Assns., 1976, Inst. Current World Affairs, 1989, Victims of Crime, 1990-92, grants author Family Resource Ctr., 1995; bd. dirs. Family coalition, 1990-92, Sacred Heart Parochial Sch., 1982—, dir. band, 1982—; candidate for diaconal ministry, 1982-93; dir. White Pine Community Choir, 1962—, Ely Meth. Ch. Choir, 1960-84; choir dir., organist Sacred Heart Ch., 1984—. Precinct reporter ABC News 1966; speaker U.S. Atty. Gen. Conf. Bringing Nev. Together; bd. dirs. White Pine Juvenile Cabinet, 1993—. Recipient Recognition rose Alpha Chi State Delta Kappa Gamma, 1994; mem. adv. com. William Bee Ririe Hosp., 1996—, Ea. Nev. Child and Family Svcs., 1996—. Fellow Am. Coll. Musicians, Nat. Guild Piano Tchrs.; mem. NEA (life), UDC, DAR, Nat. Fedn. Ind. Bus. (dist. chair 1971-85, nat. guardian coun. 1985—, state guardian coun. 1987—), AAUW (pres. Wells br. 1957-58, pres. White Pine br. 1965-66, 86-87, 89-91, 93—, bd. dirs. 1965-87, rep. edn. 1965-67, implementation chair 1967-69, area advisor 1969-73, 89-91), Nat. Fedn. Bus. and Profl. Women (1st v.p. Ely chpt. 1965-66, pres. Ely chpt. 1966-68, 74-76, 85—, bd. dirs. Nev. chpt. 1966—, 1st v.p. Nev. Fedn. 1970-71, pres. Nev. chpt. 1972-73, nat. bd. dirs. 1972-73), White Pine County Mental Health Assn. (pres. 1960-63, 78—), Mensa (supr. testing 1965—), Delta Kappa Gamma (br. pres. 1968-72, 94—, state bd. 1967—, chpt. parliamentarian 1974-78, state 1st v.p. 1967-69, state pres. 1969-71, nat. bd. 1969-71, state parliamentarian 1971-73, 97—, chmn. state nominating com. 1995-97, workshop presenter S.W. Regional Conf. 1995), White Pine Knife and Fork Club (1st v.p. 1969-70, pres. 1970-71, bd. dirs. 1979—), Soc. Descendants of Knights of Most Noble Order of Garter, Nat. Soc. Magna Charta Dames, Delta Kappa Gamma, Myths and Misconceptions of Asing as Related to learning and Intelligence. Office: Box 150457 East Ely NV 89315-0457 *My mission in this life: To use to the fullest good, the talents and abilities that have been given me in order to productively help whenever and wherever the opportunity arises.*

ALDERMAN, WILLIAM FIELDS, lawyer; b. Hamilton, Ohio, 1945. AB summa cum laude, Miami U., 1967; JD, Yale U., 1970. Bar: Calif. 1971. Ptnr. Orrick, Herrington & Sutcliffe, San Francisco; ct. apptd. arbitrator, mediator and evaluator, 1988—. Dir. Lawyers Com. for Civil Rights of the San Francisco Bay Area, 1985—, St. Thomas More Soc. San Francisco, 1987-94, pres. 1993; dir. San Francisco Neighborhood Legal Assistance Found., 1995—. Mem. Phi Beta Kappa. Office: Orrick Herrington & Sutcliffe Old Federal Reserve Bank Bldg 400 Sansome St San Francisco CA 94111-3308

ALDOUS, RICHARD ALLEN, ophthalmologist; b. Salt Lake City, Jan. 8, 1930; s. Heber F. and June (Orrock) A.; m. LaRee Baird, Sept. 10, 1954; children: Kathleen, Julie, Michael, Annette, Sharon, John. BS, U. Utah, 1953, MD, 1956. Diplomate Am. Bd. Ophthalmology. Resident U. Calif., San Francisco, 1960; med. officer USAF, 1960-64; pvt. practice ophthalmologist Salt Lake City, 1964—. Capt. USAF, 1960-64. Fellow Am. Acad. Ophthalmology; mem. AMA, Utah Ophthalmol. Soc. (sec. 1969-72, pres. 1972-73). Mem. LDS Ch. Office: 857 E 2nd S Salt Lake City UT 84102-2334

ALDRICH, DANIEL EUGENE, small business owner; b. Colony, Kans., May 26, 1954; s. Harold Eugene and Dorothy May (Connor) A.; m. Sandra May Lindsay, Aug. 16, 1972 (div. 1976); children: Latisha Ilean, Blain Dean, Paula L.; m. Donna L. Audet, Mar. 15, 1977 (div. Apr. 1979); m. Wanda Hamm (div. 1989); 1 child: Amber Dove. AA, Big Bend C.C., 1979; student, Ea. Wash. U., 1981-83. With Bunker Hill Mines, Kellogg, Idaho, 1972-74; prin. Aldrich Inc., South Beach, Oreg., 1988—. Vol. Lincoln County Food Share, Newport, Oreg., 1988-90. With U.S. Army, 1974-76. Mem. ABATE of Oreg. Republican. Methodist. Home and Office: 11628 SE Birch St South Beach OR 97366-9766

ALDRICH, DAVID LAWRENCE, public relations executive; b. Lakehurst Naval Air Sta., N.J., Feb. 21, 1948; s. Clarence Edward and Sarah Stiles (Andrews) A.; m. Benita Susan Massler, Mar. 17, 1974. BA in Communications, Calif. State U.-Dominguez Hills, 1976. Pub. info. technician City of Carson (Calif.), 1973-77; pub. rels. dir./adminstrv. asst. Calif. Fed. Savs., L.A., 1977-78; v.p., group supr. Hill & Knowlton, L.A., 1978-81; v.p., mgr. Ayer Pub. Rels. western div. N.W. Ayer, L.A., 1981-84; pres. Aldrich and Assocs. Inc., L.A., 1984—; bd. dirs., exec. com. Drum Corps Internat. With USAF, 1968-72. Home: 25 15th Pl Unit 704 Long Beach CA 90802-6061 Office: Aldrich & Assocs 110 Pine Ave Ste 620 Long Beach CA 90802-4423

ALDRICH, MICHAEL RAY, library curator, health educator; b. Vermillion, S.D., Feb. 7, 1942; s. Ray J. and Lucile W. (Hamm) A.; AB, Princeton, 1964; MA, U. S.D., 1965; PhD, SUNY, 1970; m. Michelle Cauble, Dec. 26, 1977. Fulbright tutor Govt. Arts and Commerce Coll., Indore, Madhya Pradesh, India, 1965-66; founder Lemar Internat., 1966-71; mem. faculty Sch. Critical Studies, Calif. Inst. Arts, Valencia, 1970-72; workshop leader Esalen Inst., San Francisco, 1972; co-founder AMORPHIA, Inc., The Cannabis Coop., Mill Valley, Calif., 1969-74; curator Fitz Hugh Ludlow Meml. Libr., San Francisco, 1974—. Freelance writer, photographer, lectr., cons. on drug rsch., and sociolegal reform specializing in drug laws and history to various colls., drug confs., publishers, svc. groups; cons. Commn. of Inquiry into Non-Med. Use of Drugs, Ottawa, Ont., 1973; rsch. aide, select com. on control marijuana Calif. Senate, 1974. Bd. dirs. Ethno-Pharmacology Soc., 1976-83. Calif. Marijuana Initiative, 1971-74; mem. nat. adv. bd. Nat. Orgn. for Reform of Marijuana Laws, 1976—; mem. Princeton working group Future of Drug Policy, 1990-93; asst. dir. Nat. Inst. on Drug Abuse AIDS Project Menu Youth Environment Study, San Francisco, 1987-88; project adminstr. YES Tng. Ctr., 1989, program coord. Calif. AIDS Intervention Tng. Ctr. Inst. for Cmty. Health Outreach, 1990—. Author: The Dope Chronicles 1850-1950, 1979, Coricancha, The Golden Enclosure, 1983; co-author: High Times Ency. of Recreational Drugs, 1978, Fiscal Costs of California Marijuana Law Enforcement, 1986, YES Tng. Manual, 1989, Methods of Estimating Needle Users at Risk for AIDS, 1990; editor: Marijuana Review, 1968-74, Ludlow Library Newsletter, 1974-81; contbg. author Cocaine Handbook, 1981, 2d edit., 1987; mem. editorial rev. bd. Jour. Psychoactive Drugs, 1981—, marijuana theme issue editor, 1988; research photographer Life mag., 1984; contbg. editor High Times, 1979-85; contbr. articles to profl. pubis. Office: PO Box 640346 San Francisco CA 94164-0346

ALDRICH, WILLARD MAXWELL, retired college president and educator; b. Tacoma, Jan. 4, 1909; s. Porter Chauncey and Ida May (Metcalfe) A.; m. Doris Virginia Coffin (dec. May 1958); children: Jane, Jonathan, Joseph, Rebecca, Timothy, Virginia, Annette, Willard, Barbara; m. Mildred Georgine Bouckaert, June 20, 1959. BA, Wheaton (Ill.) Coll., 1931; MTh, Dallas Sem., 1934, DTh, 1936. Ordained to ministry Evangelical Protestant Ch. Mem.faculty Multnomah Bible Coll., Portland, Oreg., 1936-91, pres., 1943-78; mem. coun. First Bible Conf., Bellingham, Wash.; pres. Am. Assn. Bible Colls., Fayetteville, Ark. Author: The Battle for Your Faith, 1975, When God was Taken Captive, 1989, also numerous mag. articles; editor leaflet Doorstep Evangel. Trustee Multnomah Bible Coll., 1936-97. Recipinet Disting. Svc. to Society award Wheaton Coll., 1979. Mem. Twin Rivers Writers Assn. Republican. Home: 7535 NE Livingston Rd Camas WA 98607

ALENIKOV, VLADIMIR, motion picture director and writer; b. Leningard, Russia, Aug. 7, 1948; came to U.S., 1990; s. Michael and Stella

(Alenikova) Volkenshtein; 1 child, Philip; m. Tamara Karpovitch; 1 child, Anastassia. Student, Leningrad State U., 1965-67, Leningrad Inst. Theatre, 1967-69, Moscow State U., 1969-72. Tchr. Russian lit. and french, dep. prin. Secondary Sch. 2, Moscow, 1969-72; dir. Gorky Film Studios, Moscow, 1974-78, 88-89, Odessa Film Studio, 1982-84; dir. music Ekran TV Studio, Moscow, 1979-81, dir., 1985-87; dir., pres. Aquilon Co., Moscow, 1989—; dir., owner Destiny Films, L.A., 1992—; lectr. at film showing; mem. 1st Soviet del. of cinematographers, Cyprus, Greece. Author: The White Page, 1972, The Mysteries of a Women's Heart, 1975, also articles, poems and short stories; Dir. and writer of feature films: The Garden, 1973, The Composer Comitas, 1974, The Room of Laughter, 1975, What a Mess, 1976, There Lived a Piano-Tuner, 1979, The Adventures of Petrov and Vasechkin, Ordinary and Extraordinary, 1982, The Hooligan, 1983, The Knight, 1983, Unique, 1986, Valuable Friends, 1987, The Drayman and the King, 1989, The Time of Darkness, 1991, The Awakening, 1991, Monique, 1993; Dir. and writer of stage plays: The Locals, 1976, The Adventures of d'Artagnan, 1986, (with David Wolcomb), Peace Child, 1985, The Hooligan is Coming, 1986, The Tale of the Warrior, 1987, The Tower, 1988, White Mercedes, 1992; Screen plays include: August Weather Forecast, 1984, A Night Story, 1985, To Kill and be Alive, 1990, The Incredible Adventures of Ricky Plim, 1992, Without Past, 1993, War of Princess, 1993. Pres. Russian-Am. Art Ctr., L.A., 1992—. Recipient 1st prize for best TV film 22d Internat. Festival Children and Youth Films Gijon Spain 1984, award for best film dir.'s debut Internat. Festival TV Films Montreux Switzerland 1979, Danube prize 8th Internat. Festival Childrens' TV Films Bratislava Czechoslovakia 1985, Grand Prix Soviet Nat. Festival Youth-83 1983, Grand Prix First Moscow Film Festival of Children's Scetches 1987, prize for funniest movie 10th Internat. Festival Children's Films Moscow 1987, AFI Film Internat. Festival award L.A. 1990, Jerusalem Film Festival award 1990, Toronto Festival of Festivals diploma 1990, Moscow Internat. Film Festival award 1991; also others. Mem. Russian Film Makers, Russian Guild Scriptwriters, Russian Guild Dir., Moscow Guild Diirs., L.A. Press Club. Jewish. Home and Office: 1274 N Crescent Heights # 122 West Hollywood CA 90046

ALEXANDER, ANDREW DALLAS, JR., archaeologist, petroglyph researcher; b. Las Cruces, N.Mex., Aug. 23, 1947; s. A.D. and Mary Theresa (Veitch) A.; m. Suzanna Julia Apodaca, Mar. 24, 1971 (div. Nov. 1980); 1 child, Dawn Selena. AS in Computer Sci., N.Mex. State U., 1990, BA in Cultural Anthropology, 1992, postgrad., 1993—. Cert. real estate broker N.Mex.; cert. archaeologist N.Mex. USDA, N.Mex. U.S. Dept. Interior. Property mgr. Sunbelt Mgmt. Inc./Davco Corp., Santa Fe, 1982-85; owner The Alexander Agy., Santa Fe and Las Cruces, 1982-89, Petroglyph Rschrs., Santa Fe and Las Cruces, 1983—; computer operator, programmer N.Mex. State U. Found., Las Cruces, 1989-90; archaeol. technician USDA Forest Svc., Silver City, N.Mex., 1992, Magdalena, N.Mex., 1993; archaeologist U.S. Dept. Interior/Bur. Land Mgmt., Las Cruces, 1992, 93-94; archaeologist, author Alexander Enterprises, Las Cruces, 1994-96. Contbr. articles to profl. jours. With USMC, 1965-69, Vietnam. Recipient Martin and Mary Gemoets Rsch. award Dona Ana Hist. Rev.. Republican. Avocations: artist, writer, computer programmer, photographer, fishing. Home: PO Box 147 Mesilla NM 88046 Office: Petroglyph Rschrs PO Box 147 Mesilla NM 88046

ALEXANDER, CHRISTOPHER, architecture educator; b. Eng., 1936. Asst. prof. architecture U. Calif., Berkeley, 1963-66, assoc. prof., 1966-70, prof., 1970—; with Village Devel. Planning Dept., Govt. Gujarat, India, 1962; cons. urban housing, Arthur D. Little Co., San Francisco, 1963; cons. architec Bay Area Rapid Transit Sys., San Francisco, 1963-64; cons. user needs Ministry of Pub. Bldgs. and Works, London, 1965-66. Author: Notes on the Synthesis of Form, 1964, Systems Generating Systems, 1967, Forshadowing of Twenty-First Century Art: The Color and Geometry of Very Early Turkish Carpets, 1990, others; co-author: The Production of Houses, 1985, A New Theory of Urban Design, 1987, others.

ALEXANDER, DEAN, museum director. Supt. Kalaupapa (Hawaii) Nat. Hist. Park. Office: Kalaupapa Nat Hist Park 7 Puahi St Kalaupapa HI 96742

ALEXANDER, DEBORAH SIMS, public administration educator; b. Terre Haute, Ind., Sept. 21, 1958; d. Bishop William Samuel and Sallie (Brown) Sims; m. Lawrence D. LeBlanc, Dec. 9, 1978 (div. Apr. 1993); children: Marcellus Y., Loren A.; m. Michael D. Alexander, Nov. 22, 1994. BA in Polit. Sci., Calif. Poly. U., 1977; MPA, U. So. Calif., 1981; MS in Mgmt. and Orgnl. Behavior, U. La Verne, 1986, D in Pub. Adminstrn., 1986. Adminstrv. dep. L.A. City Coun., 1979-83; program mgr. L.A. County Cmty. Devel. Commn., L.A., 1983-85; dep. dir. Upland (Calif.) Housing Authority, 1985; pres. DLB Assocs., Beverly Hills, Calif., 1985-95; prof. pub. adminstrn. Nat. U., San Diego, 1987—; regional faculty coord. Nat. U., L.A., 1990-92, dept. chair, San Diego, 1991-93; presenter, speaker Internat. Women in Higher Edn., 1992-96; corp. liaison YWCA/T.W.I.N. Program, San Diego, 1993-95 (Woman of Yr. 1993). Author: Like A Rose, 1988; (with others) Crack in the Wall, 1993. Mem. exec. staff Internat. Pentecostal Young People Orgn. of Pentecostal Assemblies of the World, 1977-92; founding mem. Black Women's Forum, L.A., 1979—; cmty. activist La Jolla (Calif.) Dem. Club, 1992-96; cmty. fundraiser, La Jolla YMCA, 1995. Mem. NAACP, Am. Soc. Pub. Adminstrs., Urban League, Alpha Kappa Alpha (pres. 1982). Home: 4165 Camino Islay San Diego CA 92122-1810

ALEXANDER, GERRY L., justice; b. Aberdeen, Wash., Apr. 28, 1936. BA, U. Wash., 1958, JD, 1964. Bar: Wash. 1964. Pvt. practice Olympia, Wash., 1964-73; judge Wash. Superior Ct., Olympia, 1973-85, Wash. Ct. Appeals Divsn. II, Olympia, 1985-95; justice Wash. Supreme Ct., Olympia, 1995—. Lt. U.S. Army, 1958-61. Mem. ABA, Wash. State Bar Assn., Thurston-Mason County Assn. (pres. 1963). Office: Temple of Justice PO Box 40929 Olympia WA 98504-0929

ALEXANDER, JACK DUDLEY, III, natural resources consultant; b. Nashville, Apr. 8, 1962; s. Jack Dudley II and Linda Lee (Shackleford) A. BS, Texas A&M U., 1984; MS, Mont. State U., 1989. Ranch mgr. Caldwell Estate, McKinney, Tex., 1986-89; extension mgr. U. Nebr., Scottsbluff, 1989-90; natural resources cons. Resource Concepts, Inc., Carson City, Nev., 1990—. Editor: Drought Mgmt. Handbook, 1990; contbr. articles to jours. Mem. Soc. Range Mgmt. Home: PO Box 2408 Carson City NV 89702-2408 Office: Resource Concepts, Inc. 340 N Minnesota St Carson City NV 89703-4152

ALEXANDER, J.D., publishing executive; m.; 1 child. Degree in English and history, Wake Forest U. Reporter Winston-Salem (N.C.) Jour., 1958-59; dir. info. Bowman Gray Sch. Medicine, Winston-Salem, 1960; from copy editor to asst. nat. editor Washington Post, 1967-74; exec. asst. to publ. N.Y.C., 1975-76; mng. editor San Diego Union, 1977-86; exec. editor Seattle Post-Intelligencer, 1986-93, editor, publ., 1993—; lectr. in field. Founding dir. Calif. Soc. Newspaper Editors; past chmn. journalism edn. com. Pacific N.W. Newspaper Assn.; trustee Seattle Alliance for Edn., Corp. Coun. for the Arts. With USAF. Mem. Am. Soc. Newspaper Editors, Allied Daily Newspapers (bd. dirs.), Greater Seattle C. of C. (trustee). Office: Seattle Post Intelligencer 101 Elliott Ave W Seattle WA 98119

ALEXANDER, JEFFREY CHARLES, sociology educator; b. Milw., May 30, 1947; s. Frederick Charles and Esther Lea (Schlossman) A.; m. Ruth Heidi Bloch (div. Feb. 1997); children: Aaron, Benjamin; m. Maria Pia Lara, Apr., 1997. BA, Harvard Coll., 1969; PhD, U. Calif., Berkeley, 1978. Lectr. U. Calif., Berkeley, 1974-76; asst. prof. UCLA, 1976-81, prof., 1981—; chair dept. sociology UCLA, 1989-92, dir. social sci. collegium, 1992-97; prof. U. Bordeaux, France, 1994; vis. prof. Inst. Advanced Studies, Vienna, Austria, 1995. Author: Theoretical Logic in Sociology, vols. I-IV, 1982-83, Twenty Lectures: Sociological Theory Since World War Two, 1987, Action and Its Environments: Towards a New Synthesis, 1988, Structure and Meaning: Relinking Classical Sociology, 1989, Teoria Sociologia E Mutamento Sociales, Un Analisi Multidemensionale della Modernita, 1990, Soziale Differenzierung und Kultureller Wandel Studien zur Neofunktionalistischen Gesellschaftstheorie, 1993, Fin-de-Siecle Social Theory: Relativism, Reduction and the Problem of Reason, 1995, Neofunctionalism and After, 1997, (Japanese trans.) Neofunctionalism and Civil Society, 1996; editor: Neofunctionalism, 1985, Durkheimian Sociology: Cultural Studies, 1988, Real Civil Societies, 1997; co-editor: The Micro-Macro Link, 1987, Differentiation Theory and Social Change: Historical and Comparative Perspectives, 1990, Rethinking Progress: Movements, Forces and Ideas at the End of the Twentieth Century, 1990, Culture and Society: Contemporary Debates, 1990. Guggenheim fellow, 1979-80; Travel and Study fellow Ford Found., 1980; Princeton Inst. for Advanced Studies fellow, 1985-86; Swedish Colloquium for Advanced Study in the Social Scis., 1992, 96. Mem. Am. Sociol. Assn., Internat. Sociol. Assn. (founder, co-chair rsch. com. sociol. theory 1990-94), Sociol. Rsch. Assn. Democrat. Jewish. Home: 36 26th Ave Venice CA 90291 Office: U Calif Dept Sociology Los Angeles CA 90024

ALEXANDER, JOHN CHARLES, editor, writer; b. Lincoln, Nebr., Jan. 25, 1915; s. John Merriam Alexander and Helen (Abbott) Boggs; m. Ruth Edna McLane, Aug. 20, 1955. Student, U. Nebr., 1933-37, Chouinard Art Inst./Ben Bard Playhouse Sch., L.A., 1937-38, Pasadena Playhouse, 1939-42, UCLA, 1945-47. Aircraft assembler N. Am. aviation, Inglewood, Calif., 1941-42; engrng. writer Lockheed-Vega Aircraft, Burbank, Calif., 1942-45; prodn. mgr/actor Gryphon Playhouse, Laguna Beach, Calif., 1947-49; asst. producer/writer Young & Rubicam/ABC, Hollywood, Calif., 1949-51; editor-in-chief Grand Cen. Aircraft, Tucson, 1952-53; sr. writer/editor various cos., Calif., 1953-60; sr. editor/writer, sec. Sci. Guidance Rsch. Coun. Stanford Rsch. Inst., U.S. Army Combat Devel. Command, Menlo Park, Calif., 1962-66; editor-in-chief Litton Sci. Support Lab. USACDC, Fort Ord, Calif., 1966-70; editorial dir./sec. The Nelson Co., Film and Video Prodn., Tarzana, Calif., 1971—; editorial cons., dir. Human Resources Rsch. Office, George Washington U., The Presidio, Monterey, Calif., 1960-62; book editor The Dryden Press, Hinsdale, Ill., 1971-72; book editor/adaptor Gen. Learning Press, Silver Burdette Co., Morristown, N.J., 1972-74; contbg. editor West Coast Writers Conspiracy mag., Hollywood, Calif., 1975-77; contbg. editor/book reviewer Santa Ynez Valley Times, Solvang, Calif., 1976-77; participant Santa Barbara Writers Conf., Montecito, Calif., 1974, 75. Author: (TV plays) Michael Has Company for Coffee, 1948, House on the Hill, 1958, (radio drama) The Couple Next Door, 1951; co-author nine films for U.S. Dept. Justice: Under the Law, Parts I and II, 1973; co-author 10 films for Walt Disney Ednl. Media Co.: Lessons in Learning, Parts I and II, 1978-81; author: (with others) The American West Anthology, 1971; editorial cons. Strangers in Their Land: CBI Bombardier, 1939-45, 1990-92. Recipient award for short story, Writer's Digest, 1960, 61, Gold award, The Festival of the Americas, Houston Internat. Film Festival, 1977. Mem. Nat. Cowboy Hall of Fam, Nat. Geog. Soc., Nat. Soc. Lit. and Arts, Western Hist. Soc., Calif. Acad. Sci., Nat. Air and Space Mus., Smithsonian Instn., Woodrow Wilson Internat. Ctr. for Scholars, Aircraft Owners and Pilots Assn., Air Force Assn., U. Nebr.-Lincoln Alumni Assn., Stanford Rsch. Inst. Alumni Assn., Sigma Nu, Alpha Phi Omega. Home: 23123 Village 23 Camarillo CA 93012-7602

ALEXANDER, JOHN DAVID, JR., college administrator; b. Springfield, Tenn., Oct. 18, 1932; s. John David and Mary Agnes (McKinnon) A.; m. Catharine Coleman, Aug. 26, 1956; children: Catharine McKinnon, John David III, Julia Mary. BA, Southwestern at Memphis, 1953; student, Louisville Presbyn. Theol. Sem., 1953-54; DPhil (Rhodes Scholar), Oxford (Eng.) U., 1957; LLD, U. So. Calif., Occidental Coll., 1970, Centre Coll. of Ky., 1971, Pepperdine U., 1991, Albertson Coll. Idaho, 1992; LHD, Loyola Marymount U., 1983; LittD, Rhodes Coll., 1986, Pomona Coll., 1996. Assoc. prof. San Francisco Theol. Sem., 1957-65; pres. Southwestern at Memphis, 1965-69; pres. Pomona Coll., Claremont, Calif., 1969-91, trustees prof., 1991; Am. sec. Rhodes Scholarship Trust, 1981—; mem. commn. liberal learning Assn. Am. Colls., 1966-69, mem. commn. instl. affairs, 1971-74; mem. commn. colls. So. Assn. Colls. and Schs., 1966-69; mem. Nat. Commn. Acad. Tenure, 1971-72; dir. Am. Coun. on Edn., 1981-84, Nat. Assn. Ind. Colls. and Univs.; bd. dirs. Gt. Western Fin. Corp., Children's Hosp. L.A.; trustee Tchrs. Inst. and Annuity Assn., 1970—, Woodrow Wilson Nat. Fellowship Found., 1978—, Seaver Inst., 1992—, Phi Beta Kappa Assocs., 1993—, Wenner-Gren Found. for Anthrop. Rsch., 1995—, Webb Schs. Calif., 1995—; bd. overseers Huntington Libr., 1991—. Mem. Soc. Bib. Lit., Soc. Religion in Higher Edn., Phi Beta Kappa Alumni in So. Calif. (pres. 1974-76), Century Club, Calif. Club, Bohemian Club, Phi Beta Kappa, Omicron Delta Kappa, Sigma Nu. Office: Pomona Coll Office Am Sec Rhodes Scholarship Trust 333 N College Way Claremont CA 91711-4429

ALEXANDER, JOHN M., physician; b. Montreal, Que., Mar. 4, 1940; m. Ella Y. Oh, June 24, 1979; children: Laura, John, Mike, Laura, Lisa. BA, Harvard U., 1962; MD, Columbia U., 1966. Diplomate Am. Bd. Internal Medicine, Am. Bd. Pulmonary Medicine. Asst. prof. medicine UCLA, 1974-91; pvt. practice Northridge, Calif., 1985—; med. dir. hyperbaric medicine Northridge Hosp., 1985—. Served with USN, 1968-71. Office: Dept Hyperbaric Medicine 18350 Roscoe Blvd Northridge CA 91325-4109

ALEXANDER, KATHARINE VIOLET, lawyer; b. N.Y.C., Nov. 19, 1934; d. George Clifford and Violet (Jambor) Sziklai; m. George Jonathon Alexander, Sept. 6, 1958; children: Susan Katina, George J. II. Student, Smith Coll., Geneva, 1954-55; BA, Goucher Coll., 1956; JD, U. Pa., 1959; student specialized courses, U. Santa Clara, 1974-76. Bar: Calif. 1974, U.S. Dist. Ct. (no. dist.) Calif. 1974, U.S. Ct. Appeals (9th cir.) 1974; cert. criminal lawyer Calif. State Bar Bd. Legal Specialization. Research dir., adminstr. Am. Bar Found., Chgo., 1959-60; lectr. law San Jose (Calif.) State U., 1972-74; sr. atty. Santa Clara County, San Jose, 1974—. Editor: Mentally Disabled and the Law, 1961; contbg. author: The Aged and the Need for Surrogate Management, 1969-70, Jury Instructions on Medical Issues, 1965-67. Community rep. Office Econ. Opportunity Com., Syracuse, N.Y., 1969-70. Mem. AAUW, Food and Wine Inst., Calif. Bar Assn., Santa Clara County Bar Assn. (trustee 1981-82), Calif. Attys. for Criminal Justice (bd. govs. 1988-92), Calif. Pub. Def. Assn., Jr. League. Presbyterian. Home: 11600 Summit Wood Ct Los Altos CA 94022 Office: 120 W Mission San Jose CA 95110-1705

ALEXANDER, RICHARD, lawyer; b. Cleve., Sept. 26, 1944; m. Nancy L. Biebel, Mar. 16, 1968; children: Marshall, Meredith. BA, Ohio Wesleyan U., 1966; JD (Nat. Honor scholar), U. Chgo., 1969. Bar: Mich. 1969, U.S. Dist. Ct. (ea. and we. dists.) Mich. 1970, U.S. Dist. Ct. (so. dist.) Ind. 1970, Calif. 1971, U.S. Dist. Ct. (no. dist.) Calif. 1971, U.S. Ct. Appeals (9th cir.) 1971, U.S. Dist. Ct. (cen. dist.) Calif. 1972, U.S. Dist. Ct. (ea. dist.) Calif. 1973, U.S. Dist. Ct. D.C. 1980. Diplomate Nat. Bd. Trial Advocacy. Asst. prof. Grad. Sch. Bus., Mich. State U., 1969-71; assoc. Belli, Ashe, Ellison, Choulos & Lieff, San Francisco, 1971-72, Lieff, Alexander, Wilcox & Hill, San Francisco, 1972-74, Boccardo, Lull, Niland & Bell, San Francisco and San Jose, Calif., 1974-80; ptnr. Boccardo Law Firm, San Jose, 1980-87; Alexander & Bohn, San Jose, 1987-91; The Alexander Law Firm, San Jose, 1992—; v.p. State Bar Calif., 1987-88, bd. govs. 1985-88; mem. Santa Clara County Criminal Justice Adv. Bd., 1978-82, chmn., 1978-80; mem. Santa Clara County Jail Over-crowding Task Force, 1978-81; mem. Santa Clara County Pub. Defender Charter Amendment Task Force, 1980; judge pro tem Santa Clara County Superior Ct., 1976-83, 85-90, arbitrator, 1976-96; co-chmn. Superior Ct. Arbitration Adminstrn. Com., 1979—; spl. master State Bar Calif., 1980—, lectr. continuing edn., 1975, 78, 81-89, bd. govs. 1985—, mem. com. profl. ethics, 1977-80; speaker legal seminars. Pub. The Consumer Law Page; contbr. articles to profl. jours. Mem. Palo Alto (Calif.) Unified Sch. Dist. Task Force on Spl. Edn., 1975-79; vice chmn. sch. improvement program Palo Alto Unified Sch. Dist., 1977-78, mem. found. exploration com., 1984; mem. Santa Clara County Data Confidentiality Commn., 1976-78, chmn., 1977-78; mem. Santa Clara County Democratic Central Com., 1978-80; bd. dirs. Japanese Am. Environ. Conf., 1979-81. Recipient Santa Clara County Youth Commn. medal, 1980, Man of Yr. Women's Fund.; commendation for disting. service Mayor San Jose, 1982; Roscoe Pound fellow; named one of Outstanding Young Men of Am., Man of Yr. The Women's Found., 1989; recipient Pro Bono award Ctr. Occupl. Safety Health, 1993. Mem. San Francisco Bar Assn., Nat. Bd. Trial Advocacy (cert. civil adv. 1980, 85, 90, 95), Nat. Bar Register of Preeminent Lawyers, Santa Clara County Bar Assn. (pres. 1984), Calif. Attys. for Criminal Justice (founding; treas. 1972-74, gov. 1972-75), Calif. Trial Lawyers Assn. (recognized trial lawyer 1980-89, bd. govs. 1989-94, v.p. 1994-96), Nat. Assn. Consumer Advocates (founding), Consumer Attys. Calif. (v.p. 1995), State Bar Calif. (bd. govs., 1985—, v.p. 1987—), Assn. Trial Lawyers Am., NAACP, Stanford Alumni Assn., Alexander Graham Bell Assn. for Deaf, Nat. Trust Hist. Preservation, San Jose Mus. San Jose Symphony. Clubs: U. Chgo. Alumni, Silicon Valley Capital. Office: The Alexander Law Firm 55 S Market St Ste 1080 San Jose CA 95113-2326

ALEXANDER, ROBB SMITH, JR., academic program director; b. Salt Lake City, Mar. 13, 1955; s. Robb Smith and Jane (Felt) A.; m. Cami Blau, Apr. 26, 1985; children: Nathan Spencer, Parker Thomas. BA, Weber State U., 1978. Ter. mgr. Burroughs Corp., Salt Lake City, 1978-81; dir. advt. and pub. rels. A&K Railroad Materials, Inc., Salt Lake City, 1981-84; asst. dir. devel. Weber State U., Ogden, Utah, 1984-92, dir. devel., 1992—. Chmn., ptnrs. in edn. com. Mission 2002, 1997—; mem. Utah exec. com. CASE, 1997. Recipient Outstanding Alumni award Weber State U., 1983. Mem. Utah Soc. Fund Raisers (bd. dirs. 1986-87), Coun. for Support and Advancement Edn., Ogden/Weber C. of C. (pub. rels. adv. com. 1990-92, Spikers com., events com. chair 1993-94), Ogden Breakfast Exch. Club, Mt. Ogden Rotary Club. Office: Weber State U Devel Office Ogden UT 84408-1008

ALEXANDER, ROBERT C., lawyer; b. Clarksville, Tenn., Aug. 7, 1947; s. Donald C. and Margaret S. Alexander; m. Rosalie Bailey, June 14, 1969. BA cum laude, Yale Coll., 1969; JD magna cum laude, Harvard U., 1972. Bar: Calif. 1972, D.C. 1973. Law clk. to Hon. Alfred T. Goodwin U.S. Ct. Appeals, 9th cir., San Francisco, 1972-73; assoc., ptnr. Heller, Ehrman, White & McAuliffe, San Francisco, 1973-86, 88—; prin. Babcock & Brown, San Francisco, 1986-87; writer in field. Mem. ABA, State Bar Calif., D.C. Bar, Internat. Fiscal Assn., Equipment Leasing Assn. Office: Heller Ehrman White & McAuliffe 333 Bush St Ste 3100 San Francisco CA 94104-2806

ALEXANDER, STEPHEN J., mayor. Mayor City of Azusa, Calif. Office: City of Azusa 213 E Foothill Blvd Azusa CA 91702

ALEXANDER, SUE, writer; b. 1933. Writer. Author: Small Plays for You and a Friend, 1973, Nadir of the Streets, 1975, Peacocks Are Very Special, 1976, Witch, Goblin and Sometimes Ghost, 1976, Small Plays for Special Days, 1977, Marc the Magnificent, 1978, More Witch, Goblin and Ghost Stories, 1978, Seymour the Prince, 1979, Finding Your First Job, 1980, Whatever Happened to Uncle Albert? and Other Puzzling Plays, 1980, Witch, Goblin and Ghost in the Haunted Woods, 1981, Witch, Goblin and Ghost's Book of Things to Do, 1982, Nadua the Willful, 1983, Dear Phoebe, 1984, World Famous Muriel, 1984, Witch, Goblin and Ghost Are Back, 1985, World Famous Muriel and the Scary Dragon, 1985, Lila on the Landing, 1987, There's More-Much More, Said Squirrel, 1987, America's Own Holidays, 1988, World Famous Muriel and the Magic Mystery, 1990, Who Goes Out on Halloween?, 1990. Home or Office: 6846 McLaren Canoga Park CA 91307

ALEXANDER, WILLIAM, mayor. Mayor City of Rancho Cucamanga, Calif. Office: City of Rancho Cucamanga 10500 Civic Center Dr Rancho Cucamonga CA 91730

ALEXANDER-KING, PEARL COQUEECE, nurse; b. Drumright, Okla., Dec. 21, 1936; d. Alonzo Cottrol and Marjorie Opal (Price) Alexander; degree Long Beach City Coll., 1961; R.N., Assoc. Sci., 1971; B.S.N., Calif. State U.-Long Beach, 1983; cert. psychiat./mental health nurse, chem. dependency nurse specialist; m. Carl Dee King, Dec. 8, 1951; children: Carl Dee, Crystal, Michael (dec.), Marcus. Office nurse for gen. practitioner, Long Beach, Calif., 1961-66; nurse VA Hosp., Long Beach, 1966-69; nursing supr. outpatient alcoholism treatment and rehab. center Long Beach Gen. Hosp., 1971-78; dir. nursing Viewpark Community Hosp., Los Angeles, 1978-79; asst. nursing dir. Augustus F. Hawkins Psychiat. Facility, Los Angeles, 1981-84; mental health counselor Long Beach Mental Health Clinic, 1984—; dept. adminstr. chem. dependency svcs. addiction medicine dept. Kaiser Permanente Med. Ctr., Orange, Calif., 1984-96; dept. adminstr. addiction medicine svcs. inpatient and outpatient Kaiser Permanente Med. Ctr., Harbor City, 1996—; tchr. Long Beach City Coll., 1975. Rotary Club scholar, 1970-71; Cert. of Honor, Long Beach City Coll., 1971. Mem. Nat. Consortium Chem. Dependency Nurses Inc., Consolidated Assn. Nurses in Substance Abuse, Calif., Sigma Theta Tau (Iota Eta chpt.). Democrat. Baptist. Office: 23621 S Main St Carson CA 90745

ALFARO, FELIX BENJAMIN, physician; b. Managua, Nicaragua, Oct. 22, 1939; came to U.S., 1945, naturalized, 1962; s. Agustin Jose and Amanda Julieta (Barillas) A.; student (State scholar) U. San Francisco, 1958-59, 61-62; M.D., Creighton U., 1967; m. Carmen Heide Meyer, Aug. 14, 1965; children—Felix Benjamin, Mark. Clk., Pacific Gas & Electric Co., San Francisco, 1960-61; intern St. Mary's Hosp., San Francisco, 1967; resident Scenic Gen. Hosp., Modesto, Calif., 1970; practice family medicine, Watsonville, Calif., 1971—; active staff Watsonville Community Hosp., 1971—. Served to capt., M.C., U.S. Army, 1968-69. Lic. physician, Nebr., La., Calif. Diplomate Am. Bd. Family Practice. Fellow Am. Acad. Family Practice; mem. AMA, Calif. Med. Assn., Santa Cruz County Med. Soc., 38th Parrallel Med. Soc. of Korea, Nat Rifle Assn., VFW. Republican. Roman Catholic. Office: 30 Brennan St Watsonville CA 95076-4303

ALFORD, JOAN FRANZ, entrepreneur; b. St. Louis, Sept. 16, 1940; d. Henry Reisch and Florence Mary (Shaughnessy) Franz; m. Charles Hebert Alford, Dec. 28, 1978; stepchildren: Terry, David, Paul. BS, St. Louis U., 1962; postgrad. Consortium of State U., Calif., 1975-77; MBA, Pepperdine U., 1987, postgrad., Fielding Inst., 1988-90. Head user svcs. Lawrence Berkeley Lab., Calif., 1977-78, head software support and devel. Computer Ctr., 1978-82, dep. head, 1980-81; regional site analyst mgr. Cray Rsch., Inc., Pleasanton, Calif., 1982-83; owner, pres. Innovative Leadership, Oakland, Calif., 1983-91; realtor, assoc. Mason-McDuffie Real Estate, Inc., 1991-96, Coldwell Banker, 1996—; bd. dirs. Oakland Multiple Listing Svc., 1994, 96—, treas., 1994, pres., 1997—; co-chair computer user com. OAR, 1992-93, chair, 1993-94; bd. dirs. Oakland Assn. Realtors, 1995—, chair of bus. and tech., 1996—. Contbr. articles to profl. jours. Bd. dirs., sec. Vol. Ctrs. of Alameda County, 1985, chair nominating com., 1990-91, pres. bd. dirs., 1991—; campaign mem. Marge Gibson for County Supr., Oakland, 1984; pres. bd. dirs. Vol. Ctrs. Alameda City, 1991-92; mem. Oakland Piedmont Rep. Orgn., Alameda County Apt. Owners Assn., 1982. Mem. Assn. Computing Machinery, Spl. Interest Group on Computer Pers. Rsch. (past chmn.), Nat. Assn. Realtors, Calif. Assn. Realtors (bus. and tech. com. 1997), Oakland Assn. Realtors, Internat. Platform Assn., Small Owners for Fair Treatment. Republican. Clubs: Claremont Pool and Tennis, Lakeview, San Francisco Opera Guild. Avocations: swimming, skiing, opera, horseback riding, gardening. Home: 2605 Beaconsfield Pl Piedmont CA 94611-2501 Office: Coldwell Banker 6137 La Salle Oakland CA 94611

ALHADEFF, DAVID ALBERT, economics educator; b. Seattle, Mar. 22, 1923; s. Albert David and Pearl (Taranto) A.; m. Charlotte Pechman, Aug. 1, 1948. B.A., U. Wash., 1944; M.A., Harvard U., 1948, Ph.D., 1950. Faculty U. Calif.-Berkeley, 1949-87, prof. bus. adminstrn., 1959-87, prof. emeritus, 1987—, assoc. dean Sch. Bus. Adminstrn.,, 1980-82, 85-86. Author: Monopoly and Competition in Banking, 1954, Competition and Controls in Banking, 1968, Microeconomics and Human Behavior, 1982; Contbr. articles to profl. jours., chpts. to books. Served with AUS, 1943-46. Recipient The Berkeley Citation U. Calif.-Berkeley, 1987. Mem. Am. Econ. Assn., Western Econ. Assn., Am. Fin. Assn. Home: 2101 Shoreline Dr Apt 456 Alameda CA 94501-6209 Office: Haas Sch Bus Berkeley CA 94720

ALINDER, MARY STREET, writer, lecturer; b. Bowling Green, Ohio, Sept. 23, 1946; d. Scott Winfield and McDonna Matlock (Sitterle) Street; m. James Gilbert Alinder, Dec. 17, 1965; children: Jasmine, Jesse, Zachary. Student, U. Mich., 1964-65, U. N.Mex., 1966-68; BA, U. Nebr., 1976. Mgr. The Weston Gallery, Carmel, Calif., 1978-79; chief asst. Ansel Adams, Carmel, 1979-84; exec. editor, bus. mgr. The Ansel Adams Pub. Rights Trust, Carmel, 1984-87; freelance writer, lectr., curator, Gualala, Calif., 1989—; ptnr. The Alinder Gallery, Gualala, 1990—; selector and writer biographies Focal Press Ency., 3d edit., 1993; curator Ansel Adams: 80th Birthday Retrospective, Friends of Photography, Carmel, Acad. Sci., San Francisco, Denver Mus. Natural History; co-curator One With Beauty, M.H. deYoung Meml. Mus., 1987, Ansel Adams: American Artist, The Ansel Adams Ctr., San Francisco; lectr. Nat. Gallery Art, Barbican Ctr., M.H. deYoung Meml. Mus., Stanford U., L.A. County Mus., U. Mich.; vis. artist and lectr. Nebr. Art Assn., 1997. Author: Picturing Yosemite (Places), 1990, The Limits of Reality: Ansel Adams and Group f/64 (Seeing Straight), 1992, Ansel Adams, A Biography (Henry Holt), 1996, Mabel Dodge Luhan, 1997 (ViewCamera); co-author: Answel Adams: An Autobiography, 1985;

co-editor: Ansel Adams: Letters and Images, 1988; columnist Coast Mag., 1993—; columnist (Internet site) biz travel.com, 1996—; contbr. articles to jours. and popular mags. Office: Alinder Gallery PO Box 1146 Gualala CA 95445-1146

ALISKY, MARVIN HOWARD, political science educator; b. Kansas City, Mo., Mar. 12, 1923; s. Joseph and Bess June (Capp) A.; m. Beverly Kay, June 10, 1955; children: Sander Michael, Joseph. BA, U. Tex., 1946, MA, 1947, PhD, 1953; cert., Instituto Tecnologico, Monterey, Mex., 1951. News corr. S.W. and Latin Am. NBC, 1947-49, news corr. Midwest, 1954-56; news corr. NBC and Christian Sci. Monitor, Latin Am., 1957-72; asst. prof. Ind. U., 1953-57; assoc. prof. journalism and polit. sci. Ariz. State U., Tempe, 1957-60; prof. polit. sci. Ariz. State U., 1960—, founding chmn. dept. mass communication (now Sch. Journalism and Telecommunications), 1957-65, founding dir. Ctr. Latin Am. Studies, 1965-72; vis. fellow Princeton U., 1963-64, Hoover Inst., Stanford, 1978; Fulbright prof. Cath. U., Lima, Peru, 1958, U. Nicaragua, 1960; researcher U.S.-Mex. Interparliamentary Conf., Baja, Calif., 1965, Latin Am. Inst., Chinese Acad. Social Scis., Beijing, 1986, European Inst. Def. and Strategic Studies, London, 1985, Politics Inst., Copenhagen, Denmark, 1987, U. So. Calif., 1982—; U.S. del. UNESCO Conf., Quito, Ecuador, 1960; dir. Gov.'s Ariz.-Mex. Commn., 1975—; U.S. State Dept. lectr., Costa Rica, Peru, Argentina, Chile, 1983, 88; bd. dirs. Goldwater Inst. Pub. Policy Rsch., 1989—. Author: Governors of Mexico, 1965, Uruguay: Contemporary Survey, 1969, The Foreign Press, 1964, 70, Who's Who in Mexican Government, 1969, Political Forces in Latin America, 1970, Government in Nuevo Leon, 1971, Government in Sonora, 1971, Peruvian Political Perspective, 1975, Historical Dictionary of Peru, 1979, Historical Dictionary of Mexico, 1981, Latin American Media: Guidance and Censorship, 1981, Global Journalism, 1983; co-author: Political Systems of Latin America, 1970, Political Parties of the Americas, 1982, Yucatan: A World Apart, 1980, (with J.E. Katz) Arms Production in Developing Nations, 1984, Mexico: Country in Crisis, 1986, (with Phil Rosen) International Handbook of Broadcasting Systems, 1988, Dictionary Latin American Political Leaders, 1988, (with W.C. Soderlund) Mass Media and the Caribbean, 1990; contbr. numerous articles to profl. jours. and mags. Bd. dirs. Phoenix Com. on Fgn. Res., 1975—, Ariz. Acad. Town Hall, 1981, Tempe Pub. Libr., 1974-80; mem. U.S. Bd. Fgn. Scholarships Fulbright Commn. Bd., 1984—, Acad. Coun. Goldwater Inst. of Pub. Policy, 1989—. Ensign USNR, 1944-45. NSF grantee, 1984, Ariz. State U. rsch. grantee, 1962, 65, 70, Southwestern Studies Ctr. rsch. grantee, 1983, Latin Am. Rsch. in China grantee, 1986, World Media Rsch. in Soviet Union grantee, 1989, rsch. grantee, London, 1992, 94, Edinburgh, 1994. Fellow Hispahic Soc. Am.; mem. Am. Polit. Sci. Assn., Western Polit. Sci. Assn., Latin Am. Studies Assn., Pacific Coast Coun. Latin Am. Studies (bd. dirs.), Inter-Am. Press Assn., Inter-Am. Broadcasters Assn. (rsch. assoc.), Assocs. Liga de Municipios de Sonora, Friends of Mex. Art, Southwestern Polit. Sci. Assn. (chmn. 1976-77), Nat. Assn. Scholars, Soc. Profl. Journalists (life), Tempe Rep. Men's Club, Knights of Sq. Roundtable, Sigma Delta Chi. Home: 44 W Palmdale Dr Tempe AZ 85282-2139 Office: Ariz State U Dept Polit Sci Tempe AZ 85287-2001 *My life as an educator, writer, and journalist-broadcaster has enable me to share and exchange important and vital thought with friends, associates, and fellow Americans.*

ALKANA, LINDA KELLY, history educator; b. Calgary, Alta., Can., Nov. 9, 1946; came to U.S., 1963; d. Bernard Joseph and Lorna Lucille (Sutherland) Kelly; m. Ronald Lee Alkana, Sept. 12, 1970; children: Alexander Philippe, Lorna Jane. BA, UCLA, 1969; MA, U. Calif., Irvine, 1975, PhD, 1985. Lectr. humanities U. Calif., Irvine, 1985-93; lectr. history Calif. State U., Long Beach, 1981—; affiliate scholar Ctr. for the Study of Women, L.A., 1987-89; lectr. in women, popular culture and peace, critical thinking. Assoc. editor The History Teacher, 1987—; contbr. articles to profl. jours. Mem. Am. Hist. Assn., Western Assn. of Women Historians. Office: Calif State U Long Beach Dept History 1250 N Bellflower Blvd Long Beach CA 90840-0006

ALKANA, LOUIS DAVID, writer, editor; b. Bklyn., Aug. 29, 1955; s. Samuel and Mildred Carol (Matorin) A.; m. Lisa Ann Haggard, Mar. 28, 1992. AA, West Los Angeles Coll., 1975; BA, Calif. State U., Northridge, 1979. Freelance sportswriter Seattle, 1980-82; asst. mng. editor Frames Publs., Newport Beach, Calif., 1982-84; assoc. editor Lets Live Mag., L.A., 1984-85; mgr. employee comm. Nat. Med. Enterprises, L.A., 1985-88; dir. editl. svcs. Russell Comm. Group, L.A., 1988-92; cons. corp. comm. Culver City, Calif., 1992-94; sr. assoc. Silverman Heller Assocs., L.A., 1994-97. Author: (short stories) A Spy Alone, 1994, The Fifth Down, 1995. Recipient Citizen's award Seattle Police Dept., 1981, Award of Excellence, Greater L.A. Press Club, 1986, Bronze Quill award Internat. Assn. Bus. Communicators (L.A. chpt.), 1987, Maggie award Western Publs. Assn., 1988.

ALKANA, RONALD LEE, neuropsychopharmacologist, psychobiologist; b. L.A., Oct. 17, 1945; s. Sam Alkana and Madelyn Jane Davis; m. Linda Anne Kelly, Sept. 12, 1970; children; Alexander Philippe Kelly, Lorna Jane Kelly. Student, UCLA, 1963-66; PharmD, U. So. Calif., 1970; PhD, U. Calif., Irvine, 1975. Postdoctoral fellow Nat. Inst. Alcohol Abuse and Alcoholism, U. Calif., Irvine, 1974-76; resident asst. dir. div. neurochemistry, dept. psychiatry and human behavior U. Calif., Irvine, 1976; asst. prof. pharmacy (pharmacology) U. So. Calif., L.A., 1976-82, assoc. prof. pharmacy (pharmacology and toxicology), 1982-89, prof. molecular pharmacology and toxicology, 1989—, asst. dean grad. affairs Sch. Pharmacy U. So. Calif., 1995—. Editl. bd. Alcoholism: Clinical and Experimental Research, 1989-94, assoc. editor, 1994—; contbr. chpts. to books, articles to profl. jours. Recipient various scholarships and grants. Mem. AAAS, Soc. Neurosci., Am. Soc. Pharmacology and Exptl. Therapeutics, Internat. Soc. Biomed. Research on Alcoholism, Research Soc. Alcoholism, Internat. Brain Rsch. Organizational World Fedn. Neuroscientists, Western Pharmacology Soc., Sigma Xi, Phi Delta Chi (Omicron chpt., Outstanding Alumnus of Yr. 1996). Office: U So Calif Sch Pharmacy Dept Molecular Pharmacolgy Toxicology 1985 Zonal Ave Los Angeles CA 90033

ALKIRE, JOHN D., lawyer; b. Seattle, Nov. 15, 1948; s. Durwood Lee and Dorys (Maryon) A.; m. Karen A. Heerensperger, May 6, 1994; children: Lauren M., Kevin G. Student, U. Calif., Berkeley, 1967-68; BA, Principia Coll., Elsah, Ill., 1970; JD, U. Wash., 1975. Bar: Wash. 1975, Washington 1977, U.S. Dist. Ct. (we. dist.) Wash., U.S. Ct. Appeals (4th, 9th and D.C. cirs.), U.S. Supreme Ct. Budget analyst Office Mgmt. and Budget, Seattle, 1970-72; law clk 9th cir. Honorable Eugene A. Wright, Seattle, 1975-76; assoc. Jones, Grey & Bayley, Seattle, 1976-77, Steptoe & Johnson, Washington, 1977-80; assoc. Perkins Coie, Seattle, 1980-85, ptnr., 1985—; lectr. U. Wash. Sch. Environ. Studies, Seattle, 1976-77. Bd. mem. Hospice of Seattle, 1982-85. Mem. ABA, Wash. State Bar Assn., Internat. Bar Assn. Office: Perkins Coie 1201 3rd Ave Fl 40 Seattle WA 98101-3099

ALL, WILLIAM HAMILTON, IV, military officer; b. Honolulu, Aug. 7, 1958; s. William Hamilton III and Mary Eleanor (Swain) A.; m. Teresa Ann Ysseldyke, Dec. 10, 1983; children: Maile Ann, Ryland Makena. BA in Econ., Emory U., 1982; MA in Strategic Planning, Naval Postgrad. Sch., 1992. Commd. ensign USN, 1983, advanced through grades to lt. comdr., 1993; naval aviator Patrol Squadron Four, USN, Honolulu, 1984-88; flight instr. Patrol Squadron Thirty One, USN, Mt. View, Calif., 1989-90; asst. air officer USS Nimitz, USN, Bremerton, Wash., 1992-95; ops. officer Patrol Squadron Forty NAS, Whidbey Island, Wash., 1995—; mem.-at-large VP Internat., Halifax, Nova Scotia, 1990—. Mem. Chi Phi. Episcopalian. Home: 1970 W Buckthorn Rd Oak Harbor WA 98277-8801 Office: Patrol Squadron Forty NAS Whidbey Island Naval Air WA 98278

ALLAN, DAVID R., safety engineer; b. Port Angeles, May 14, 1944; s. Kenneth Vincint and Jane (Alstrum) A.; m. Linda Lee Cope, Sept. 29, 1983; children: Jennifer Lynn, Jeffery Brian. BA, UCLA, 1966. Dir. safety/health Thomason Mech. Corp., Rancho Dominguez, Calif., 1992—; mgr. safety/health Schultz Mech. Corp., Long Beach, Calif., 1990-93, E.O.S. Constrn., Torrance, Calif., 1990; field safety supr. Veco Constrn., Long Beach, Calif., 1987-90, Brown & Root Co., Houston, 1984-87. Contbr. articles to profl. jours. Recipeint John C. Cayman award. Home: 11401 Rancho Del Oro Dr Riverside CA 92505-3582

ALLAN, ROBERT MOFFAT, JR., corporate executive, educator; b. Detroit, Dec. 8, 1920; s. Robert M. and Jane (Christman) A.; m. Harriet Spicer, Nov. 28, 1942; children: Robert M. III, Scott, David, Marilee. BS, Stanford U., 1941; postgrad. Stanford Grad. Sch. Bus., 1941-42; MS, UCLA, 1943; postgrad. Loyola Law Sch., 1947-50. Economist research dept. Security First Nat. Bank, 1942; exec. Marine Ins., 1946-53; asst. to pres., work mgr. Zinsco Elec. Products, 1953-55, v.p., dir., 1956-59; asst. to pres. The Times-Mirror Corp., 1959-60, corp. v.p., 1961-64; pres., dir. Cyprus Mines Corp., 1964-67; pres. Litton Internat., 1967-69; pres. U.S. Naval Postgrad. Sch. Found., prof. internat. mgmt. 1969-85. Bd. dirs., advisor U.S. Naval Acad.; trustee Boys Republic, Pomona Grad. Sch., Claremont Grad. Sch., Del Monte Forest Homeowners; vis. prof. of internat. mgmt. grad. schs. of bus. MBA Stanford, Harvard, U. of Chgo., UCLA, USA and Internat. Inst. Fgn. Studies, Monterey; adv. trustee Monterey County Sheriff, 1982—. Capt. USAF, 1942-45. Recipient award Helms Athletic Found., 1947, 49, Navy Cross of Merit, 1976, Plaque of Merit USCG, 1990, Medal for Heroism, 1990; named Outstanding Businessman of Yr., L.A., Nat. Assn. Accts., 1966; elected to Sailing Hall of Fame, 1969; named Monterey Inst. Fgn. Studies trustee and sr. fellow, 1976. Mem. Mchts. and Mfrs. Assn. (dir.), Intercollegiate Yachting Assn. (regional dir. 1940-55), Phi Gamma Delta, Phi Delta Phi. Clubs: Newport Harbor Yacht (commodore 1962), Trans-Pacific Yacht, Carmel Valley Country. Home: 165 Del Mesa Carmel CA 93923

ALLARD, A. WAYNE, congressman, veterinarian; b. Ft. Collins, Colo., Dec. 12, 1943; m. Joan Malcolm, Mar. 23, 1967; children: Cheryl, Christie. D.V.M., Colo. State U., 1968. Veterinarian, Allard Animal Hosp.; mem. Colo. State Senate, 1982-91, chmn. health, environment and instn. com., chmn. senate majority caucus; mem. 102nd-104th Congresses from 4th dist., Colo., 1991-96; mem. agrl. com., 1991-92, 93-94, 95-96, mem. small bus. com., 1991-92, mem. interior and insular affairs com., 1991-92, mem. com. on coms., 1991-92, 93-94, mem. budget com., 1993-94, 95-96, mem. natural resources com., 1993-94, 95-96, mem. joint com. on reorganization of Congress, 1993-94, 95-96, chmn. subcom. of agr. conservation, forest and water, 1995-96; senator 105th Congress, 1997—, mem. banking, urban affairs com., 1997—, environment and pub. works com., 1997—, intelligence select com., 1997—; health officer Loveland, Colo.; mem. regional adv. council on vet. medicine Western Interstate Commn. Higher Edn.; mem. Colo. Low-level Radioactive Waste Adv. Com. Chmn. United Way; active 4-H Found. Mem. Loveland C. of C., AVMA, Colo. Vet. Medicine Assn., Latimer County Vet. Medicine Assn. (past pres.), Bd. Vet. Practitioners (charter mem.), Am. Animal Hosp. Assn., Nat. Conf. State Legislatures (vice chmn. human resources com. 1987—, healthcare cost containment com.). Republican. Methodist. Home: 1203 Jennifer Dr Loveland CO 80537-8054 Office: US Senate 716 Hart Bldg Washington DC 20510

ALLARD, JAMES WILLARD, JR., philosophy educator; b. Lincoln, Nebr., Dec. 8, 1945; s. James Willard Sr. and Mary Irene (Dieterich) A.; m. Celia Anne Ahrens, Jan. 2, 1968 (div. May 1990); 1 child, Mary Dorinda; m. Mary Catherine Bushing, Sept. 22, 1994. BA, U. Mont., 1969, MA, 1970; PhD, Princeton U., 1976. Instr. philosophy Mont. State U., Bozeman, 1973-76, asst. prof., 1976-84, assoc. prof., 1984—. Co-editor F.H. Bradley: Writings on Logic and Metaphysics, 1994; contbr. chpt. to book and articles to profl. jours. Mem. Am. Philos. Assn., Bradley Soc. Office: Mont State U Dept History and Philosophy Bozeman MT 59717

ALLARD, THURMAN J., electrical engineer; b. U.S. Canal Zone, Nov. 15, 1959; s. George W. and Martha Cynthia (Rapp) A.; m. Heather Lorelei Ingham, Aug. 12, 1983; children: Chase Kehr, Duncan G. BSEE, U. N.Mex., 1981; MSEE, Purdue U., 1982. With Sandia Nat. Labs., Albuquerque, 1977-80, mem. tech. staff, 1980-90, dept. mgr., 1990-96, dep. dir., 1996—. Mem. IEEE (sr.). Republican. Home: 13617 Crested Butte Dr NE Albuquerque NM 87112-6623 Office: Sandia Nat Labs PO Box 5800 Albuquerque NM 87185

ALLARDICE, LINDA MARIE, controller, financial executive; b. Pitts., Mar. 12, 1953; d. Martin Joseph and Marian Ruth (Altenhof) Stickley; m. Dwight W. Buben, Sept. 12, 1975 (div. Mar. 1982); children: Eric Michael, Andrew Brian, David J.; m. Jeremiah Daniel Allardice, Apr. 26, 1989. BSBA, U. Ariz., 1975. Various retail positions Globe Discount, 1971-76; auditor Bd. of Regents Audit Staff, Tucson, 1976-77; asst. to comptroller, bus. agt. Pima C.C., Tucson, 1981-82; comptroller La Frontera Ctr., Inc., Tucson, 1983—. Mem. Healthcare Fin. Mgrs. Assn. Democrat. Lutheran. Office: La Frontera Ctr Inc 502 W 29th St Tucson AZ 85713-3353

ALLAWAY, WILLIAM HARRIS, retired university official; b. Oak Park, Ill., Mar. 31, 1924; s. William Horsford and Helen Margaret (Harris) A.; m. Olivia Woodhull Foster, June 28, 1952; children: William Harris Jr., Ben Foster, Eve Olivia. BS, U. Ill., 1949; postgrad., U. Grenoble, France, 1950-51; MA, U. Ill., 1951; EdD, U. Denver, 1957. Traveling sec. World Student Svc. Fund, 1947-48; spl. asst. to chmn. U.S. Nat. Commn. for UNESCO, 1949; asst. to field dir. World U. Svc. attached to Internat. Refugee Orgn., Salzburg, Austria, 1951; field rep. Inst.of Internat. Edn., Chgo. and Denver, 1952-54; gen. sec. U. Kans. YMCA, 1954-57; asst. dean of men and dir. Wilbur Hall Stanford (Calif.) U., 1957-61; dir. edn. abroad program U. Calif., Santa Barbara, 1961-89, spl. asst. to chancellor, 1990-93; cons. and lectr. in field; mem. ednl. assoc. adv. com. Inst. Internat. Edn., 1984-87; mem. Pres.'s Coun. for Internat. Youth Exch., 1982-85; mem. U.S. Del. to conf. on ednl. exch. between U.S. and U.K., 1970, 1974. Co-chair Peace and Justice Com., Goleta Presbyn. Ch., chair steering com. PAX 2100; mem. Nuclear Age Peace Found., Santa Barbara, Internat. Peace Rsch. Assn., Yellow Springs, Ohio; mem. Coun. on Internat. Ednl. Exch., 1961—, chmn. bd. dirs. 1978-83; past bd. dirs., hon. trustee Am. Ctr. for Students and Artists, Paris; bd. advisors Hariri Found., 1987—; exec. sec. Internat. Com. for Study of Edn. Exch., 1970-95, exec. com. Inter-Univ. Ctr. Postgrad. Studies, Dubrovnik, 1988-96, bd. dirs., 1996—. With USAAF, 1943-46. Hon. DHC, U. Sussex, Eng., 1992; PhD h.c. U. Bergen, Norway, 1990; DHC, U. Bordeaux, France, 1988; Hon. Dr. of U. of Stirling, Scotland, 1981; recipient Scroll of Appreciation Leningrad State U., 1989, Award for Svc. to Internat. Ednl. Exch. Council on Internat. Ednl. Exch., 1989, Silver medal U. Lund, Sweden, 1990, Alumni Achievement award Coll. Liberal Arts and Sci. Alumni Assn. U. Ill., 1990, Gold Medal of Honor of the Complutense U. of Madrid, Spain, 1991. Mem. NAFSA Assn. Internat. Educators (hon. life mem.), Comparative and Internat. Edn. Soc., European Assn. for Internat. Edn., Internat. Assn. Univs. (dep. mem., adminstrv. bd. 1995—), La Cumbre Golf and Country Club. Democrat. Presbyterian. Home: 724 Calle De Los Amigos Santa Barbara CA 93105-4439

ALLBAUGH, MARY ELLEN, reading educator; b. Gt. Falls, Mont., June 20, 1939; d. Herman G. and Jeanette (Spoelder) Bouma; m. Allen LeRoy Allbaugh, Dec. 21, 1963; children: Dianna Lynn, Juileen Ruth, Dan'Neile Jean. BS, Western Mont. Coll. Edn., 1962; postgrad., Chapman U., Tucson, 1988—. Cert. tchr., Ariz.; community coll. spl. teaching cert. Elem. tchr. Gt. Falls Sch. Dist., 1962-64, Salem (Oreg.) Sch. Dist., 1967-68; substitute tchr. Sultan (Wash.) Sch. Dist., 1972-76; laundry worker VA Hosp., Knoxville, Iowa, 1978-80; mgr. Colonial Mobile Home Park, Tucson, 1984—; elem. instrnl. aide Elvira Sch., Tucson, 1986-88; mem. assoc. faculty reading and math. Pima Community Coll., Tucson, 1988—, instrnl. asst. for computer and reading, 1988-89; elem. substitute tchr. Sunnyside Sch. Dist., Tucson, 1985-89, mem. planning com. all-day kindergarten, Tucson, 1987-88; instr. reading and math. series State Prison for Pima C.C., 1990—, Tucson Ednl. Svcs., 1993—; substitute tchr. Pima C.C., 1992—. Mem. dist. parent coun. Chaparral Jr. High Sch., Tucson, 1987-89; mem. SEPAC, Sunnyside Sch. Dist., 1993—. Recipient hon. award Sunnyside Sch. Dist., 1989. Home: 6410 S Fontana Ave Unit 37 Tucson AZ 85706-5453 Office: Pima County C C Community Campus 1901 N Stone Ave Tucson AZ 85709-5001 also: Desert Vista Campus 5901 S Calle Santa Cruz Tucson AZ 85709-6000

ALLBEE, SANDRA MOLL, real estate broker; b. Reading, Pa., July 15, 1947; d. Charles Lewars and Isabel May (Ackerman) Frederici; m. Thomas J. Allbee, Oct. 18, 1975 (div. 1987). Exec. sec. Hamburg (Pa.) State Sch. and Hosp., 1965-73; regional mgr. Am. Bus. Service Corp., Newport Beach, Calif., 1973-78; v.p. T.A.S.A., Inc., Long Beach, Calif., 1978-86; realtor Very Important Properties, Inc., Rolling Hills Estates, Calif., 1986-90, Re/Max Palos Verdes Realty, Rolling Hills Estates, Calif., 1990—. Bd. dirs., v.p. Nat. Coun. on Alcoholism, Torrance, Calif., 1987-96; pres. Rollingwood Homeowners Assn., Rolling Hills Estates, Calif., 1985-92. Mem. Palos Verdes Rep. Women's Club (bd. dirs. 1989-94). Office: Re/Max Palos Verdes Realty 4030 Palos Verdes Dr N Ste 104 Rolling Hills CA 90274

ALLEN, BONNIE LYNN, pension actuary; b. L.A., Oct. 2, 1957; d. David and Lucille M. (Scott) A. B.A. summa cum laude, UCLA, 1979. Math. tutor, L.A., 1971—; reader math. dept. UCLA, 1977-79; pension actuary Martin E. Segal Co., L.A., 1980-92. Author short stories and poetry. Active mentor program UCLA Alumni Assn., 1978-79, bd. dirs. Westside Bruins. Mem. Math. Assn. Am., Am. Math. Soc., L.A. Film Tchrs'. Assn., Acad. Sci. Fiction, Fantasy and Horror Films, UCLA Alumni Assn. (life), Westside Bruin Club (bd. dirs.), L.A. Actuarial Club, Phi Beta Kappa.

ALLEN, BRUCE JOHN, writer, activist; b. Buffalo, Apr. 16, 1960; s. John Edgar and Isabel Sarah (Nicholson) A.; m. Sarah Bragg Lindsley, Mar. 31, 1992. BA in English Lit. magna cum laude, U. Colo., 1985. Columnist Colo. Daily, Boulder, 1985; field mgr. Colo. Pub. Interest Rsch. Group, Boulder, 1985-86; editor Nat. Student News Svc., Boston, 1986-88; writer The New Paper, Providence, 1988-91; comm. dir. Save the Bay, Providence, 1990-92, Ctr. for Econ. Conversion, Mountain View, Calif., 1993-96; publs. cons. Calif. Abortion Rights Action League, San Francisco, 1993. Mem. Save El Dorado Mountain Campaign, Boulder, 1985; advisor People Against the CIA, Providence, 1989; co-founder Preserve the Presidio Campaign, San Francisco, 1994; bd. dirs. Calif. Peace Action, 1996—. Home: 995 Guerrero St # 2 San Francisco CA 94110-2225

ALLEN, DAVID CHARLES, computer science educator; b. Syracuse, N.Y., Jan. 15, 1944; s. Charles Robert and Jane Loretta (Doolittle) A.; m. Mary Ann Stanke, June 15, 1968 (div. Mar. 1994); children: Meredith Rae, Amelia Kathrine, Carl James; m. Barbara Ann Riis, Mar. 14, 1994. B.Tech. Edn., Nat. U., San Diego, 1983, MA in Human Behavior, 1984. Dir. retail sales Nat. U. Alumni Assn., 1981-83; audiovisual technician Grossmont Union H.S. Dist., La Mesa, Calif., 1983-84; spl. project instr. San Diego C.C., 1985-91; instr. computer tech. Coleman Coll., 1991—. Mem. Presdl. Task Force; mem. Congl. Adv. Com. on Vets. Benefits for congressmen 44th. With USN, 1961-81. Mem. DAV, VFW, Am. Legion, Vietnam Vets. Am., Fleet Reservation Assn., Nat. U. Student and Alumni Assn., Am. Tech. Edn. Assn., Beta Sigma Phi (hon.). Republican. Roman Catholic. Home: 9860 Dale Ave Apt E3 Spring Valley CA 91977-2436 Office: Coleman Coll Computer Applications & Networking 7380 Parkway Dr La Mesa CA 91942-1532

ALLEN, DAVID HARLOW, business educator, consultant; b. Lynn, Mass., May 26, 1930; s. Donald H. and Miriam Ellsworth (Harlow) A.; m. Roberta Arlene Miller, July 15, 1952; children: Donald Bruce, Richard Leroy, William David. BS in Gen. Edn., U. Nebr., Omaha, 1967; MBA, N.Mex. Highlands U., 1978. Cert. profl. logistician, cert. cost analyst. Commd. 2d lt. USAF, 1955, advanced through grades to lt. col., 1970; instr., planner, aircraft maintenance, staff, prodn. control officer, squadron comdr., wing asst. dep. comdr. maintenance SAC, 1948-74; dir. aircraft maintenance, dir. material Air Force Inspection and Safety Ctr., San Bernardino, Calif., 1969-72; dep. dir. logistics Air Force Test and Evaluation Ctr., Albuquerque, 1974-78; ret., 1978; sr. systems analyst, space systems project leader Arinc Rsch. Corp., 1978-84; airborne missile system dep. program mgr. for logistics, logistics project mgr. Ventura div. Northrop Corp., 1984-91; assoc. prof. Coll. Bus. and Mgmt. West Coast U., L.A., 1988—, asst. dean, 1988-90; mem. com. chmn. So. Calif. Logistics Conf. and Workshop, 1989, 91, 92, 93; v.p., mem. bd. govs. and bd. trustees Logistics Edn. Found., 1993-96; program chmn. 29th Internat. Logistics Conf. and Tech. Expn., 1994. Contbr. articles to profl. publs. Mem. state and nat. Rep. orgns., 1978—; mem. Ventura County-Santa Barbara County Planning Com. for Nat. Engring. Week, 1990—. Decorated Bronze Star; recipient Pres.'s award for merit Logistics Edn. Found., 1996. Mem. Nat. Contract Mgmt. Assn., Soc. Logistics Engrs. (chmn. chpt. 1988-90, Pres.'s Merit award 1994), Inst. Cost Analysis, Configuration and Data Mgmt. Assn. (chmn. fin. com. 1989), Logistics Edn. Found. (pres. merit award 1996), Am. Mgmt. Assn., Air Force Assn., Phi Kappa Phi. Home and Office: 428 Moondance St Thousand Oaks CA 91360-1209

ALLEN, DEBORAH COLLEEN, state legislator; b. Denver, Jan. 25, 1950; d. Anton Jr. and Esther Ochs; m. Bob Allen; 1 child, Dallas. Student, Aurora C.C. Jr. acct. Am. TV & Comm.; bus mgr. Deer Trail Pub. Schs., sch. bus driver; data entry clk. United Banking Svcs.; caretaker Evergreen Cemetery; owner, mgr. Custom Data Sys. Specialists, Aurora, 1979—; mem. Colo. Ho. of Reps., 1992—, mem. various coms., 1993—. Former sec., vice chmn., chmn. Arapahoe County Rep. Party; past pres. Aurora Rep. Forum; active Arapahoe County Chmn.'s Cir.; block capt. Am. Cancer Soc., Am. Arthritis Found. Recipient 5 Yr. Award as Leathercraft Instr., 4-H. Mem. Nat. Fedn. Rep. Women, Colo. Fedn. Rep. Women, South Metro C. of C., Colo. Rep. 250 Club, Arapahoe Rep. Men's Club. Republican. Home: 923 S Ouray St Aurora CO 80017-3152 Office: Colo House of Reps 200 E Colfax State Capitol Denver CO 80203

ALLEN, DONALD MERRIAM, editor, publisher; b. Muscatine, Iowa, Mar. 26, 1912; s. Paul Edward and Mildred Gertrude (Quinn) A. BA, U. Iowa, 1934, MA, 1935; postgrad., U. Wis., 1941-42, U. Calif., Berkeley, 1947-49. Editor Grove Press, N.Y.C., 1951-53, adv. editor, 1956-63; editor, pub. New Directions, N.Y.C., 1954, Criterion Books, N.Y.C., 1955; pres. Four Seasons Found., San Francisco, 1964—, Grey Fox Press, San Francisco, 1971—. Co-editor Evergreen Rev., 1956-60; editor: (anthology) The New American Poetry, 1960, (book) Frank O'Hara Collected Poems, 1971 (Nat. Bank award 1971); translator (drama): Ionesco - 4 Plays, 1958. Lt. USN, 1942-47. Decorated Purple Heart, Bronze Star medal.

ALLEN, DONALD VAIL, investment executive, author, concert pianist; b. South Bend, Ind., Aug. 1, 1928; s. Frank Eugene and Vera Irene (Vail) A.; m. Betty Dunn, Nov. 17, 1956. BA magna cum laude, UCLA, 1972, MA, 1973, D (hon.), 1973. Pres., chmn. bd. dirs. Cambridge Investment Corp.; music editor and critic Times-Herald, Washington; music critic L.A. Times; lectr. George Washington U., Am. U., Washington, Pasadena City Coll. Transl. works of Ezra Pound from Italian into English; author of papers on the musical motifs in the writings of James Joyce; mem. Steinway Roster of Concert Artists; specialist in works of Beethoven, Chopin, Debussy and Liszt; premiere performances of works of Paul Creston, Norman dello Joio, Ross Lee Finney, appearances in N.Y., L.A., Washington; represented by William Matthews Concert Agy., N.Y.C. Pres. Funds for Needy Children, 1974-76. Mem. Ctr. for Study of Presidency, Am. Mgmt. Assn., Internat. Platform Assn., Nat. Assn. Securities Dealers, Am. Guild Organists, Chamber Music Soc., Am. Mus. Natural History. Home: QueensGate 2503 Russett Glen Escondido CA 92029-6650

ALLEN, DONALD WAYNE, accountant, educator; b. Billings, Mont., Apr. 9, 1936; s. D. Wayne and Olga Carmen (Ferguson) A.; m. Judith Marie Johnson, Dec. 28, 1959; children: Brian Kieth, Brendan Kirk. BS in Bus. Adminstrn., U. Denver, 1958. CPA, Mont., Wyo. Staff acct. Pan Am. Petroleum Corp., Casper, Wyo., 1958-61, Raab, Roush & Gaymon CPAs, Casper, 1961-64; office mgr. Sumatra Oil Corp., Billings, 1964-68; treas., dir. Oil Resources, Inc., Billings, 1968-73; ptnr. Smith, Birkeland, Mangis, Allen & Deming, Billings, 1973-78; pres. Allen & Nelson CPAs P.C., Billings, 1978-88, Donald W. Allen, CPA, P.C., Billings, 1988—; instr. Ea. Mont. Coll., Billings, 1983-85. Treas. Billings Jaycees, 1965; pres. Yellowstone Kiwanis, Billings, 1971; bd. dirs. J.K. Ralston Found., Billings, 1988-91, Billings Symphony Orch,. 1990-92, treas., 1991-92; mem. resource adv. coun. Miles City Bur. Land Mgmt., 1995—; bd. dirs., treas. Parmly Billings Libr. Found., 1995—, treas., 1995-97, pres., 1997—. Mem. AICPA, Mon. Soc. CPAs (dir. 1968-71, instr., 1982-85, Outstanding Com. Chmn. 1984), Wyo. Soc. CPAs, Billings Rotary. Home: 3221 Country Club Cir Billings MT 59102-0609 Office: 490 N 31st Ste 206 Billings MT 59101-1256

ALLEN, EDGAR BURNS, records management professional; b. L.A., Sept. 1, 1929; s. Harry James and Hela Ruth (Graham) A.; m. Eleanor Angela Gregory, July 24, 1960; children: Linda Marie, Lisa Ann. AA, L.A. City Coll., 1958; student, Calif. State U., L.A., 1958, 81; BS, UCLA, 1985. Supr. records ctr. L.A. Dept. Water and Power, 1958-67, records mgr., 1967-76; records mgmt. officer City of L.A., 1976-85; records mgmt. cons. L.A., 1985—; profl. creator records mgmt. systems, tax preparer, L.A., 1990—. Chmn. Leimert Pk. Community Assn., L.A., 1972-75. Mem. Assn. Records Mgrs. and Adminstrs. (bd. dirs. 1975-76), Soc. Calif. Archivists, All Yr. Figure Skating Club (bd. dirs. 1970-79). Democrat. Roman Catholic.

ALLEN, EDWARD RAYMOND, retired business educator, accountant; b. Indpls., Sept. 30, 1913; s. Edward L. and Emmeline (Rice) A.; BS in Commerce, Drake U., 1950, MA in Accounting, 1951; m. Norma D. M. Brennan, May 10, 1941. CPA, Idaho. Asst. prof. bus. adminstrn. Parsons Coll., Fairfield, Iowa, 1952-56; faculty Coll. of Idaho, Caldwell, 1956-93, prof. bus. adminstrn., 1956-73, head dept., 1962-70, chmn. social sci. divsn., 1972-73, emeritus, 1973—, vis. lectr., 1973-74; practicing CPA, Caldwell, 1958-92; ret., 1992. Contbr. articles to profl. jours. Served to capt. AUS, 1942-46; lt. col. Res. ret. Decorated Bronze Star with 1 palm, Med. Badge. Mem. AICPA, Idaho Soc. CPAs (dir., regional v.p. 1958-61, mem. standards of practice com. 1974-83, chmn. com. 1980-83, chmn. relations with ednl. instns. com. 1984-86, mem. 1993—), AAUP (past pres. Coll. of Idaho chpt.), Elks, Pi Kappa Phi. Home: PO Box 336 Caldwell ID 83606-0336

ALLEN, GARY KING, aerospace advance development engineer; b. Buffalo, June 27, 1944; s. Howard W. and Ethel M. (King) A.; m. Catherine Reardon, July 12, 1969; children: Matthew W., Sarah A. BSCE, Clarkson U., 1966; MBA with distinction, Nat. U., San Diego, 1977. Lead prin. engr. Boeing Co., Seattle, 1966-73, 90—; lead preliminary design engr. Rohr Industries, Chula Vista, Calif., 1974-78; advanced devel. specialist Rho Co., Bellevue, Wash., 1978-82; sr. specialist on assignment to Lockheed Corp., Burbank, Calif., 1982-83, on assignment to Boeing, Seattle, 1978-82, 84-89. Mem. nat. adv. bd. Am. Security Council, 1970-76. Recipient Pride in Excellence award Boeing Co., 1980, 86, 95. Mem. AIAA. Home: 702 Kirkland Way 17 Kirkland WA 98033-3957 Office: The Boeing Co PO Box 3707 Seattle WA 98124-2207

ALLEN, GLORIA LINDSAY, interpreter, translator, publisher; b. Boston, July 19, 1949; d. Stanley Ernest and Marjorie Phyllis (Haydon) A. BA in Psychology, L.I. U., 1971. Translator, Hilti Tools Conv., Caracas, Venezuela, summer 1967; substitute interpreter for Dist. Atty. Morganthau's office for N.Y.C. Grand Jury, 1977-78; free-lance Spanish/English interpreter various agys., N.Y.C., 1978—; pvt. practice astrology and numerology, Woodstock, N.Y.; Spanish tutor C.W. Post Coll., Brookville, N.Y., 1967-71; translator Select Com. on Correctional Inst. and Programs, Attica proposal for prison rights, N.Y., 1971; examining Spanish-English interpreter on panel for hiring N.Y. State Interpreters, N.Y.C., 1981. lectr. numerology People Resource Club, N.Y.C., Three of Cups, Woodstock, 1987. Author: All English-Spanish translation of Most Commonly Asked Questions in Depositions for Motor-Vehicle and Slip-and-Fall Accidents, 1986, All English-Spanish Translation of Most Commonly Asked Questions in Depositions for: Medical Malpractice, Machine Guard Cases, Construction Accidents, A Widow's Compensation in a Wrongful Death, Housing and Elevator Accidents, 1987. Playwright: (skits) Cabaret Theater, 1977, Running Numbers, 1980. Fundraiser Tandem Skydive against teenage suicide for Family House, Woodstock, 1987. Mem. Am. Translators Assn., ACLU, Amnesty Internat. (active Urgent Action Network & Freedom Writers Colo. 1986-87), Nat. Mus. Women in the Arts (charter), Nat. Writers Union, Dramatist Guild. Avocations: martial arts, gardening, swimming, weight-lifting, tandem sky diving. Address: 556 W 12th Ave Eugene OR 97401-3447

ALLEN, GORDON KELLEY, communications company executive; b. Oklahoma City, July 4, 1957; s. Vincent H. Jr. and Carole Ann (Koch) A.; m. Kimberly Ann Hulse, July 15, 1995; children: Gordon Luke, Haley Lynne, Jacob Michael. BS in Econs. and Bus. Adminstrn., Westminster Coll., 1980. V.p. Vince Allen & Assoc., Denver, 1980-94, pres., 1994-95; v.p. CTG Telecom., Denver, 1987-93; pres. CTG Telecom., 5, 1993-95; mng. ptnr. Data Choice Network Svcs., LLC, Littleton, Colo., 1996—. Republican. Office: Data Choice Network Svcs LLC 9200 W Cross Dr Ste 313 Littleton CO 80123-2238

ALLEN, HAROLD JIM, secondary school English educator; b. Cleve., Apr. 15, 1938; s. Harold and Hazel May (Zacasky) A.; m. Elaine Frances Riechenstein, Jan. 30, 1965 (div. July 1992); 1 child, Jill Ann; m. Martha Ellen Gioia, July 10, 1993; stepchildren: Deborah Burke, Patrick Burke. AA, Coll. of San Mateo, 1960; AB, San Francisco State U., 1968; MA, U. Redlands, 1982. Cert. secondary tchr., Calif. Reading, lang. arts tchr. San Benito H.S., Hollister, Calif., 1969-71, English and drama dir., 1971-84; English tchr. San Benito H.S., Hollister, 1985—, U.S. history tchr., 1992-95; mentor tchr. San Benito H.S., 1983, 84, 94, 96. Mem. San Benito County Dem. Ctrl. Com., 1980-91. Lance cpl. USMCR, 1956-65. Recipient 5 Superior Play awards Amador Drama Festival, Best Play award Stanislaus Drama Festival, 1975. Mem. Calif. Tchrs. Assn. (pres. San Benito H.S. chpt. 1978-91, We Honor Ours award 1985), Phi Delta Kappa. Home: 522 Humes Ave Aptos CA 95003-5241 Office: San Benito HS Dist 1220 Monterey St Hollister CA 95023

ALLEN, JACQUELYN MAY, school psychologist, consultant; b. L.A., Nov. 6, 1943; d. John Richard and Ida May (Townsend) Hinson; m. James William Allen, Dec. 19, 1970; children: Julene May, Jason William. BA, U. Redlands, 1965; MA, Berkeley Bapt. Div. Sch., 1969; MS, Calif. State U., Hayward, 1972; DEd, U. San Francisco, 1990. Lic. marriage and family counselor, Calif; nat. cert. counselor, nat. cert. sch. counselor. ESL tchr. U. Mexico, Mexico City, 1967; missionary Am. Bapt. Conv., El Salvador, Ctrl. Am., 1966-67; tchr. Foothill Intermediate Sch., Walnut Creek, Calif., 1968-72; marriage, family, child counselor Fremont Inst. Transactional Analysis, Fremont, Calif., 1977-78; career cons. Pvt. Sch. & Chronicle Guidance Project, Fremont, 1989-91; CEO, pres. Am. Sch. Counselor Assn., Alexandria, Va., 1993-94; cons. Allen Cons. Assocs., Fremont, 1985—; sch. psychologist, sch. counselor Fremont Unified Sch. Dist., 1972—; liaison Counseling for High Skills, De Witt Wallace Reader's Digest, Manhattan, Kans., 1994-95; liaison for Am. Sch. Counseling Assn., Nat. Bus. Adv. Bd., Alexandria, Va., 1993-95; project coord. Ednl. Devel. Ctr. Grant on Comprehensive Health and HIV, AIDS Prevention, Boston, 1994-95; pres., negotiator Fremont Counseling and Psychologists Assn., 1972-73, 75-77, 90-91; mem. retirement and bilingual spl. edn. coms. Fremont Unified Sch. Dist., 1994-95; adj. faculty Chapman U., 1995—. Editor: (compendium) Action-Oriented Desk Guide for Professional School Counselors, 1992. Treas. Antelope Hills Home Owners Assn., Fremont, 1984-85; leader troop 1382 Girl Scouts Am., Fremont, 1990-94. Named Outstanding Young Educator Fremont Jaycees, 1974. Mem. ACA (governing coun. 1991-94, exec. com. 1993-94, pub. policy and legis. com. 1994-97), Am. Sch. Counselor Assn. (pres., CEO 1993-94, exec. and fin. com. 1992-95, grant 1990), Calif. Assn. Counseling and Devel. Edn. Found. (bd. dirs., v.p.), Calif. Assn. Counseling and Devel. (pres. 1991-92, editl. bd. jour. 1995-97), Calif. Alliance for Pupil Pers. Svc. Orgns., Calif. Career Devel. Assn. (conf. com., grant 1990), Delta Kappa Gamma (rsch. chair 1988-92, scholarships 1988-89, profl. devel. 1995-96). Home: 705 Montana Vista Ct Fremont CA 94539-6242

ALLEN, JANICE FAYE CLEMENT, nursing administrator; b. Norfolk, Nebr., Aug. 19, 1946; d. Allen Edward and Hilda Bernice (Stange) Reeves; m. Roger Allen Clement, Oct. 6, 1968 (dec. July 1974).; m. August H. Allen, Sept. 17, 1988. RN, Meth. Sch. Nursing, Omaha, 1967; BS in Nursing, magna cum laude, Creighton U., 1978; MS in Nursing, U. Nebr., 1981; cert. in nursing adminstrn., cert. in infection control. With Meth. Hosp., 1967-68, 72-83, asst. head nurse, 1974-77, staff devel. nurse, 1977-81, dir. staff adminstrv. services, 1981-83; pub. health nurse Wichita-Sedgwick County Health Dept., Wichita, Kans., 1970-72; dir. nursing Meth. Med. Ctr., St. Joseph, Mo., 1983-84, Broadlawns Med. Ctr., Des Moines, 1984-93; dir. staff mgmt./infection control Ea. N.Mex. Med. Ctr., Roswell, 1993—; adj. clin. faculty nursing Drake U. Nursing, Des Moines, 1986-93, mem. adv. bd., 1984-93, Cen. Campus Practical Nursing, 1984-93; mem. adv. bd. Des Moines Area Community Coll. Dist., 1987—, Des Moines Area C.C. Nursing Bd., 1987-93, Grandview Coll., 1988-93; bd. dirs. Vis. Nurse Svcs., 1988-93; assoc. Am. Coll. Healthcare Execs. Mem. Am. Nurses Assn., Am. Orgn. Nurse Execs., N.Mex. Nurses Assn. (bd. dirs. 1995), Cen. Iowa Nursing Leadership Conf. (pres. 1985), Colloquium Nursing Leaders Cen. Iowa, Iowa League for Nursing (treas. 1987-89, pres. 1989), Iowa Orgn. Nurse Execs. (treas. 1987, sec. 1989, pres.-elect 1993), Assn. Infection Control and Epidemiology, Sigma Theta Tau (pres. Zeta Chi chpt. 1990-92). Democrat. Presbyterian. Avocations: flying, sewing, golf, walking, reading. Home: 3201 Allison Dr Roswell NM 88201-1011 Office: Ea NMex Med Ctr 405 W Country Club Rd Roswell NM 88201-5209

ALLEN, JEFFREY DOUGLAS, engineering manager; b. San Francisco, Nov. 17, 1954; s. Douglas D. and Marilyn Klea (Miles) A.; m. Leann Bair, May 7, 1977; children: Jacob, Louis, Anneliese, Miriam, Mark. BSME, Brigham Young U., 1979; MSME, Stanford U., 1984. R&D engr. Hewlett Packard Co., Boise, Idaho, 1979-84; R&D project mgr. Hewlett Packard Co., Greeley, Colo., 1984-86; R&D project mgr. Hewlett Packard Co., Boise, 1986-92, mfg. engring. mgr., 1992-93, R&D sect. mgr., 1993—. Patroller Nat. Ski Patrol, Boise, 1991-95. Office: Hewlett Packard Co Disk Memory Divsn PO Box 39 Boise ID 83707

ALLEN, JEFFREY MICHAEL, lawyer; b. Chgo., Dec. 13, 1948; s. Albert A. and Miriam (Feldman) A.; m. Anne Marie Guaraglia, Aug. 9, 1975; children: Jason M., Sara M. BA in Polit. Sci. with great distinction, U. Calif., Berkeley, 1970, JD, 1973. Bar: Calif. 1973, U.S. Dist. Ct. (no. and so. dists.) Calif. 1973, U.S. Ct. Appeals (9th cir.) 1973, U.S. Dist. Ct. (ea. dist.) Calif. 1974, U.S. Dist. Ct. (cen. dist.) Calif. 1977, U.S. Dist. Ct. (so. dist.) Calif., U.S. Supreme Ct.; lic. real estate broker. Ptnr. Graves, Allen, Cornelius & Celestre and predecessor firms, Oakland, Calif., 1973—; teaching asst. dept. polit. sci. U. Calif., Berkeley, 1970-73; lectr. St. Mary's Coll., Moraga, Calif., 1976—; mem. faculty Oakland Coll. of Law, 1996—; bd. dirs. Family Svcs. of the East Bay, 1987-92, 1st v.p., 1988, pres., 1988-91; mem. panel arbitrators Ala. County Superior Ct.; arbitrator comml. arbitration panel Am. Arbitration Assn. Mem. editorial bd. U. Calif. Law Rev., 1971-73, project editor, 1972-73; mem. Ecology Law Quar., 1971-72; contbr. articles to profl. jours. Treas. Hillcrest Elem. Sch. PTA, 1984-86, pres., 1986-88; past mem. GATE adv. com., strategic planning com. on fin. and budget, dist. budget adv. com., instructional strategy counsel Oakland Unified Sch. Dist., 1986-91; mem. Oakland Met. Forum, 1987-91, Oakland Strategic Planning Com., 1988-90; mem. adv. com. St. Mary's Coll. Paralegal Prog.; bd. dirs. Montera Sports Complex, 1988-89; bd. dirs. Jack London Youth Soccer League, 1988-94; commr. Bay Oaks Youth Soccer, 1988-94; asst. dist. commr. dist. 4 Calif. Youth Soccer Assn., 1990-92, also bd. dirs., pres. dist. 4 competitive league, 1990-93; sec., bd. dirs. Calif. Youth Soccer Assn., 1993-96, chmn. bd. dirs., 1996—; bd. dirs. Calif. Soccer Assn. North, 1996—. Mem. ABA (chmn. real property com. gen. practice sect. 1987-91, mem. programs com. 1991-93, chmn. subcom. on use of computers in real estate trans. 1985-86, adv. coord. 1993-96, sect. coun. 1994—, mktg. bd. 1996—), Alameda County Bar Assn. (past vice chmn. com. continuing edn., exec. com. alternative dispute resolution programs), U.S. Soccer Assn. (database mktg. com.), Calif. Bar Assn., Calif. Scholarship Fedn., U.S. Soccer Fedn. (nat. C lic. coach and state referee, referee instr. and state referee assessor), Calif. North Referee Assn. (referee adminstr. dist. 4 1992-96, state bd. dirs. 1996—), Soc. for Profls. in Dispute Resolution, Oakland C. of C., Rotary (bd. dirs. Oakland 1992-94). Office: Graves & Allen 2101 Webster St Ste 1746 Oakland CA 94612-3037

ALLEN, JOHN JEFFREY BECK, psychology educator; b. Northampton, Mass., Aug. 10, 1961; s. Ronald Royce and JoAnne Elizabeth (Kuehl) A; m. Connie J.A. Beck; 1 child, Gabrielle JoAnne Allenbeck. BS, U. Wis., 1986; MA, U. Minn., 1991, PhD, 1992. Lic. psychologist, Ariz. Instr. psychology U. Minn., Mpls., 1988-92; intern psychology VA Med. Ctr., Mpls., 1991-92; asst. prof. psychology U. Ariz., Tucson, 1992—. Contbr. articles to profl. jours. Acupuncture as a treatment for depression grantee NIH, 1993-95. Mem. APA, Am. Psychol. Soc., Soc. for Psychophysiol. Rsch., Internat. Neuropsychol. Soc., Cognitive Neurosci. Soc., Sigma Xi, Phi Beta Kappa, Phi Kappa Phi. Office: U Ariz Dept Psychology Tucson AZ 85721-0068

ALLEN, JOSE R., lawyer; b. Panama, Sept. 8, 1951; arrived in U.S., 1956; s. Joseph R. and Grace A. (Osborne) A.; m. Irvenia E. Waters, July 20, 1986; children: Jeffrey, Richard Allen. BA, Yale U., 1973; JD, Boston Coll., 1976. Bar: Mass. 1977, Calif. 1986. Asst. atty. gen. Mass. Atty. Gen. Office, Boston, 1976-79; trial atty. U.S. Dept. Justice, Washington, 1979-80, asst. sect. chief, 1980-82, sect. chief, 1982-85; of counsel Orrick, Herrington & Sutcliffe, San Francisco, 1985-88; ptnr. Skadden, Arps, Slate, Meagher & Flom, San Francisco, 1988—; mem. adv. com. Practicing Law Inst., N.Y.C., 1992—. Bd. dirs. San Francisco Bay Area Lawyers' Com. Urban Affairs, 1990, Legal Aid Soc. San Francisco, 1993, San Francisco Food Bank, 1992. Mem. ABA, Bar Assn. San Francisco, Charles Houston Bar Assn., State Bar Calif. (mem. environ. law sect.). Office: Skadden Arps Slate Meagher & Flom Four Embarcadero Ctr San Francisco CA 94111

ALLEN, JUDITH SYMA, art educator, artist; b. N.Y.C., Jan. 21, 1956. BA, Oberlin Coll., 1977; postgrad., Columbia U., 1978; MFA, Mills Coll., 1990. Lectr. photography Cornish Coll. of the Arts, Seattle, 1992—; lectr. photography San Francisco State U., 1991, 92, Acad. Art Coll., San Francisco, 1991, 92, Calif. State Summer Sch. for Arts, Oakland, 1990, 91. One-woman shows include Lloyd Gallery, Spokane, Wash., 1982, New Performance Gallery, San Francisco, 1982; exhibited in group shows at Ctr. on Contemporary Art, Seattle, 1994, 95, Fisher Gallery, Seattle, 1993, 94, 95, 96, San Francisco Arts Commn. Gallery, 1991, Berkeley (Calif.) Art Ctr., 1991, Richmond (Calif.) Art Ctr., 1991, 86, San Francisco State U. Art Gallery, 1991, Intersection for Arts, San Francisco, 1990, 88, Bellevue (Wash.) Art Mus., 1994. Fellow Nat. Endowment for Arts, 1990-91; recipient Trefethen award Mills Coll., 1989, Betty Bowen Meml. Spl. Recognition award Seattle Art Mus., 1994. Mem. Soc. for Photographic Edn., Coll. Art Assn. Office: Cornish Coll of Arts 1501 10th Ave E Seattle WA 98102-4210

ALLEN, LEW, JR., laboratory executive, former air force officer; b. Miami, Fla., Sept. 30, 1925; s. Lew and Zella (Holman) A.; m. Barbara Frink Hatch, Aug. 19, 1949; children: Barbara Allen Miller, Lew III, Marjorie Allen Dauster, Christie Allen Jameson, James Allen. BS, U.S. Mil. Acad., 1946; MS, U. Ill., 1952, PhD in Physics, 1954. Commd. 2d lt. USAAF, 1946; advanced through grades to gen. USAF, 1977, ret., 1982; physicist test div. AEC, Los Alamos, N.Mex., 1954-57; sci. advisor Air Force Spl. Weapons Lab., Kirtland, N.Mex., 1957-61; with office of spl. tech. Sec. of Def., Washington, 1961-65; from dir. spl. projects to dep. dir. adv. plans Air Force Space Program, 1965-72; dir. Nat. Security Agy., Ft. Meade, Md., 1973-77; comdr. Air Force Systems Command, 1977-78; vice chief of staff USAF, Washington, 1978, chief of staff, 1978-82; dir. Jet Propulsion Lab., Calif. Inst. Tech., Pasadena, Calif., 1982-90; chmn. bd. Draper Lab, Boston, 1991-95. Decorated Def. D.S.M. with two clusters, Air Force D.S.M. with one cluster, Nat. Intelligence D.S.M., NASA D.S.M., Legion of Merit with two oak leaf clusters; recipient Robert H. Goddard Astronautics award Am. Inst. Aeronautics and Astronautics, 1995. Fellow AIAA (hon.), Am. Phys. Soc.; mem. Am. Geophys. Union, Nat. Acad. Engring., Coun. on Fgn. Rels., Sigma Xi, Sunset Club (L.A.), Alfalfa Club (Washington). Republican. Episcopalian.

ALLEN, LOUIS ALEXANDER, management consultant; b. Glace Bay, N.S., Oct. 8, 1917; s. Israel Nathan and Emma (Greenberg) A.; m. Ruth Graham, Aug. 24, 1946; children: Michael, Steven, Ace, Terry Allen Beck, Deborah Allen. BS cum laude, Washington State U., 1941. Cert. mgmt. cons. Asst. to dean of men Washington State U., Pullman, Wash., 1940-42; tng. supr. Aluminum Co. of Am., Pitts., 1946-49; mgr. personnel adminstrn. Koppers Co. Inc., Pitts., 1949-53; dir., rsch. projects The Conference Bd., N.Y.C., 1953-56; dir. orgnl. planning Booz, Allen & Hamilton, Chgo., 1956-58; pres., chmn. emeritus Louis Allen Assocs., Los Altos, Calif., 1958—; lectr. on bus. mgmt. Stanford U., U. Chgo., NYU, Japan, China, Australia, Africa and Europe. Author: Improving Staff and Line Relationships, 1956, Preparing the Company Organization Manual, 1957, Organization of Staff Functions, 1958, Management and Organization, 1958, The Management Profession, 1964, Professional Management: New Concepts and Proven Practices, 1973, Time before Morning: Art and Myth of the Australian Aborigines, 1975, Making Managerial Planning More Effective, 1982, The Allen Guide for Management Leaders, 1989, Common Vocabulary for Management Leaders, 1989, The Louis Allen Leader's Handbook, 1995, The New Leadership, 1996; (mus. catalog) Australian Aboriginal Art, 1972; translated into Japanese, German, French, Finnish, Swedish, Dutch, Spanish, Portuguese, Bahasa; contbr. numerous articles and monographs to profl. jours. on mgmt., primitive art; exhibitor primitive art major mus. worldwide, 1969—. Maj. USAF, 1942-55, PTO. Decorated Legion of Merit; recipient McKinsey award Acad. Mgmt. Mem. Inst. Mgmt. Cons. (sr. assoc., regional pres. 1985). Office: Louis Allen Rsch PO Box 11 Palo Alto CA 94302

ALLEN, MIRIAM MARX, writer; b. 1927. Writer Charlotte Gusay Lit. Agyt. Editor: Love, Groucho:Letters from Groucho Marx to his Daughter Miriam, Faber & Faber, 1992. Office: care Charlotte Gusay Literary Agency 10532 Blythe Ave Los Angeles CA 90064

ALLEN, PAGE RANDOLPH, artist; b. St. Charles, Ill., Sept. 6, 1951; d. Thomas Eliot and Ann Page (Platt) A.; m. W. Scott Morris, June 19, 1970 (div. May 1977); m. Nathaniel Otis, July 26, 1981; 1 child, Maya Jehan. Student, Prineton U., 1969-70; BA, Hampshire Coll., 1974; MA, No. Ill. U., 1980; postgrad., Santa Fe Inst. Fine Arts. One woman shows include ARC Gallery, Chgo., 1980, Raw Space/ARC Gallery, Chgo., 1981, Fine Arts Gallery, U. Mont., Missoula, 1983, U. Club Gallery, Chgo., 1984, Northcutt Gallery, Ea. Mont. Coll., Billings, 1986, Owings-Dewey Fine Art, Santa Fe, 1987, 88, 90, 91, 94, CAFE Gallery, Albuquerque, 1992, DeWeese Gallery of Contemporary Arts, Bozeman, Mont., 1994, Danforth Gallery, Livingston, Mont., 1994, Meredith Long & Co., Houston, 1996; exhibited in group shows at Arvada (Colo.) Ctr. Arts and Humanities, 1992, Meredith Long & Co., 1993, Albuquerque Mus., 1994, Nora Eccles Harrison Mus. Art, Logan, Utah, 1994; represented in permanent collections Albuquerque Mus. Art, Arvada Ctr. Arts and Humanities, Eiteljorg Mus. Am. Indian and Western Art, Indpls., Missoula Mus. Arts, Mus. Fine Arts, Mus. N.Mex., Santa Fe, Pepsi Cola/Frito Lay Corp., Dallas, Telecomm. France Corp., N.Y.C., Temple (Tex.) Ctr. Contemporary Art. NEA grantee, 1981, Ill. State Arts Coun. grantee, 1981; named Artist in Edn., Mont. Arts Coun., NEA, 1982-84. Democrat. Office: Page Allen Studio 1229 Bishops Lodge Rd Santa Fe NM 87501

ALLEN, PAUL, computer executive, professional sports team owner. Student, Wash. State U. Co-founder Microsoft Corp., Redmond, Wash., 1975, exec. v.p., 1975-83; founder Asymetrix Corp., Bellevue, Wash., 1985—, Starwave Corp., Bellevue, Intervas Rsch., Palo Alto, Calif.; owner, chmn. bd. Portland (Oreg.) Trail Blazers, 1988—; bd. dirs. Egghead Discount Software, Microsoft Corp., Darwin Molecular, Inc.; owner, chmn., bd. dirs. Ticketmaster Holdings Group, L.A. Office: The Paul Allen Group Ste 530 110-110th Ave NE Bellevue WA 98004*

ALLEN, PAULA GUNN, English educator; b. 1939. Lectr. U. N.Mex., Fort Lewis Coll., Durango, Calif.; lectr., dept. chair San Francisco State U.; with native Am. studies U. Calif., Berkeley; prof. English, UCLA. Author: (poetry) The Blind Lion, 1974, Coyote's Daylight Trip, 1978, A Cannon Between My Knees, 1981, Skin and Bones, 1988; editor: Grandmother of the Light, Medicine Woman's Sourcebook, 1990, The Voice of the Turtle: American Indian Literature, 1994, others. Office: UCLA Dept English 405 Hilgard Ave Los Angeles CA 90024

ALLEN, RICK (FREDERICK ALLEN KLYCINSKI), magician, advertising and publicity consultant; b. Detroit, Nov. 4, 1941; s. Chester Bruno and Johana Jean (Guzdzial) Klycinski; m. Marie DeLeon, Nov. 2, 1965 (div. Mar. 1985); children: John Paul, Marie Louise, Diane Lynn, Mark Frederick. AA, Pasadena Coll., 1961. Account exec. Knight Ridder Newspapers, Long Beach, Calif., 1966-68, advt. mgr., 1969-71; advt. mgr. Copley Newspapers, Torrance, Calif., 1972-73; cons. Scripps Newspapers, Napa, Calif., 1974-75; founder, owner, mgr. Creative Advt. Svc., Vallejo, Calif., 1976—; dir. mail advt. cons. Vallejo, 1980—; profl. magician for fund-raising orgns., 1976—. Author: Public Relations and Publicity for Entertainers, 1978; editor: Stick to the Cash Register, 1970; contbr. articles to various publs. Founder Anti-Grafitti Task Force. Named top fund raiser United Way, L.A., Long Beach, 1971; recipient awards for creative advt. Calif. Advt. Assn., Calif. Pubs. Assn., Am. Assn. Advt. Agys. Mem. Soc. Am. Magicians, Internat. Brotherhood Magicians, Pacfic Coast Assn. Magicians, Lions Club Internat. Home and Office: 917 Bradford Ct Benicia CA 94510

ALLEN, ROBERT EUGENE BARTON, lawyer; b. Bloomington, Ind., Mar. 16, 1940; s. Robert Eugene Barton and Berth R. A.; m. Cecelia Ward Dooley, Sept. 23, 1960 (div. 1971); children: Victoria, Elizabeth, Robert, Charles, Suzanne, William; m. Judith Elaine Hecht, May 27, 1979 (div. 1984); m. Suzanne Nickolson, Nov. 18, 1995. BS, Columbia U., 1962; LLB, Harvard U., 1965. Bar: Ariz. 1965, U.S. Dist. Ct. Ariz. 1965, U.S. Tax Ct., 1965, U.S. Supreme Ct. 1970, U.S. Ct. Customs and Patent Appeals 1971, U.S. Dist. Ct. D.C. 1972, U.S. Ct. Appeals (9th cir.) 1974, U.S. Ct. Appeals (10th, and D.C. cirs.) 1984, U.S. Dist. Ct. N.Mex., U.S. Dist. Ct. (no. dist.) Calif., U.S. Dist. Ct. (no. dist.) Tex. 1991, U.S. Ct. Appeals (fed. cir.) 1992, U.S. Dist. Ct. (ea. dist.) Wis. 1995. Ptnr., dir. Allen & Price, Phoenix; spl. asst. atty. gen. 1978, Ariz. Ct. Appeals, judge pro-tem, 84, 92. Nat. pres. Young Dems. Clubs Am., 1971-73; mem. exec. com. Dem. Nat. Com., 1972-73; mem. Ariz. Gov.'s Kitchen Cabinet working on wide range of state projects; bd. dirs. Phoenix Bapt. Hosp., 1981-83, Phoenix and Valley of the Sun Conv. and Visitors Bur., United Cerebral Palsy Ariz., 1984-89, Planned Parenthood of Cen. and No. Ariz., 1984-90; mem. Ariz. Aviation Futures Task Force; chmn. Ariz. Airport Devel. Criteria. Subcom.; mem. Apache Junction Airport Rev. Com.; Am. rep. exec. bd. Atlantic Alliance of Young Polit. Leaders, 1973-77, 1977-80; trustee Am. Counsel of Young Polit. Leaders, 1971-76, 1981-85, mem. Am. delegations to Germany, 1971, 72, 76, 79, USSR, 1971, 76, 88, France, 1974, 79, Belgium, 1974, 77, Can., 1974, Eng., 1975, 79, Norway, 1975, Denmark, 1976, Yugoslavia and Hungary, 1985; Am. observer European Parliamentary elections, Eng., France, Germany, Belgium, 1979, Moscow Congressional, Journalist delegation, 1989, NAFTA Trade Conf., Mexico City, 1993, Atlantic Assembly, Copenhagen, 1993; trustee Environ. Health Found., 1994, Friends of Walnut Canyon, 1994, Cordell Hull Found., 1996. Spkr. seminars and profl. assns.; contbr. articles on comml. litigation to profl. jours. Mem. ABA, Ariz. Bar Assn., Maricopa County Bar Assn., N. Mex. State Bar, D.C. Bar Assn., Am. Judicature Soc., Fed. Bar Assn., Am. Arbitration Assn., Phi Beta Kappa. Democrat. Episcopalian (lay reader). Club: Harvard (Phoenix). Office: Allen & Price 2850 E Camelback Rd Phoenix AZ 85016-4304 *Founder of the law firm Allen & Price, Allen practices in the areas of intellectual property and technology, health care, patent and trade secret litigation, antitrust and securities litigation, and general business and personal counseling. The firm of Allen & Price has been the subject of newspaper and magazine articles emphasizing the firm's use of technology to provide prompt and timely business representation at lower cost than the traditional large law firms.*

ALLEN, ROBERT MARK, lawyer; b. Seattle, Dec. 7, 1947; s. Robert Matthew and Dorothy Lee (DePue) A.; m. Carole Ann Klinich, June 19, 1970 (div. Mar. 1986); 1 child, Christopher R.; m. Nancy Louise Zussy, Dec. 20, 1986. BA, U. Wash., 1970; JD cum laude, Southwestern U., L.A., 1980. Bar: Wash. 1980, D.C. 1995, U.S. Dist. Ct. (we. dist.) Wash. 1981. Disc jockey KREM-AM/FM Radio, Spokane, Wash., 1970-74, KSJO-FM Radio, San Jose, 1974-75, KJR Radio, Seattle, 1976; assoc. Ogden Murphy Wallace, Seattle, 1980-87; owner/proprietor Mark Allen Govt. Rels., Olympia, Wash., 1987-90; exec. dir., legal counsel Wash. State Assn. Broadcasters, Olympia, 1990-96; pres., CEO Wash. STate Assn. Broadcasters, 1996—; seminar lectr. Wash. State U., Pullman, 1992—. Co-author: EEO Rules in Broadcasting, 5th edit., 1981, 1984 License Renewals, 5th edit., 1984, Political Broadcasts, 3d edit., 1986. Event mgr. Seattle Seafair Unltd. Hydroplane Race, 1990-91, 97—. Recipient Pres.'s award Wash. Libr. Assn., 1987, Race Mgmt. Team of the Yr. Unltd. Racing Commn. of Am. Power Boat Assn., 1990. Mem. ABA (forum on comms. law), Fed. Comms. Bar Assn., Am. Soc. Assn. Execs. (govt. rels. sect. coun. 1994-96). Office: Wash State Assn Broadcaster 924 Capitol Way S # 104 Olympia WA 98501-1210

ALLEN, ROY VERL, life insurance company executive; b. Hyrum, Utah, Aug. 3, 1933; s. Winfrd A. and Sarah Ann (Nielsen) A.; m. Judith Green, Aug. 11, 1961; children: Ann Marie Allen Webb, Michael R., Blair J. BS, Utah State U., 1958. CLU, Chartered Fin. Cons. Mgr. employee benefits Thiokol Chem. Corp., Brigham City, Utah, 1959-61; employment interviewer Hercules, Salt Lake City, 1962-63; agy. mgr. Standard Ins. Co., Salt Lake City, 1963—. Maj. U.S. Army Res., 1962-79. Mem. CLUs (bd. mem. 1973-75), Estate Planning Coun. (bd. mem. 1979-81), Utah Gen. Agts. and Mgrs. (sec., v.p., pres. 1979-83), Utah Assn. Life Underwrtiers (pres. 1988-89), Exchange Club. Republican. Mormon. Home: 2526 Olympus Dr Salt Lake City UT 84124-2916 Office: Standard Ins Co 525 3rd Ave Salt Lake City UT 84103-2973

ALLEN, RUSSELL PLOWMAN, opera company executive; b. Washington, Dec. 30, 1951; s. Gale Wilson and Anne (Plowman) A. BA, Macalester Coll., 1974. Gen. mgr. Shreveport (La.) Symphony Orchestra, 1979-80; mgr. Houston Symphony Orchestra, 1980-84, San Antonio Symphony

Orchestra, 1984-86; gen. mgr. Phoenix Symphony Orchestra, 1986-94, Va. Opera, Norfolk, 1994—; cons. N.Mex. Symphony Orchestra, Albuquerque, 1986, Chattanooga (Tenn.) Symphony Orchestra, 1986. Mem. grants rev. panel Ariz. commn. on Arts, Phoenix, 1987-90, Phoenix Arts Commn., 1987; program chmn. Phoenix Symphony Coun., 1986-94; mem. mktg. com. Downtown Phoenix Parternship Class XIII, Valley Leadership; mem. Heritage Sq. Adv. Bd., 1991-94. Mem. Am. Symphony Orchestra League, Phoenix City Club. Home: 696 Mowbray Arch Apt 940 Norfolk VA 23507-1836 Office: Va Opera PO Box 2580 Norfolk VA 23501-2580*

ALLEN, SAM RAYMOND, organization development specialist; b. Cody, Wyo., Oct. 6, 1953; s. Robert Sam and Jerrine (Cross) A.; m. Melinda Jo Daniels, Oct. 23, 1979; children: Eric Samuel, Andrew William. BS, U. Wyo., 1976, MBA, 1986; postgrad., George Washington U., 1977-79, Hastings Coll., Nebr., 1972-74. Accredited pub. rels. cert. Teller Bank of Va., Rosslyn, Va., 1978-79; legis. asst. U.S. Senate/Alan K. Simpson, Washington, 1979-81; bus. mgr. Coors Brewing Co., Golden, Colo., 1986-87; vol. prog. mgr. Coors Brewing Co., 1987-90, tng. mgr., 1990-96; exec. dir. tng. svcs. Red Rocks Inst., Lakewood, Colo., 1996—. Editor V.I.C.E. Activity Guide newsletter, 1987-90. Bus. advisor Jr. Achievement, Denver, 1988-90; corp. mem. Assn. for Vol. Adminstrn., Boulder, 1987-90; elder Shepherd of the Hills Presbyn. Ch., 1986-89. Named Outstanding Corp. Coord., Adopt-A-School, Denver, 1987. Mem. ASTD, U. Wyo. Alumni Assn., Pub. Rels. Soc. Am., Rotary (community svc. dir. 1989), Alpha Kappa Psi. Republican. Presbyterian. Home: 11636 W 74th Way Arvada CO 80005-3274 Office: Red Rocks Institute c/o Red Rocks Cmty College 13300 W 6th Ave Lakewood CO 80401

ALLEN, STEPHANIE WEST, mediator, workplace entertainment company owner; b. Modesto, Calif., Feb. 6, 1948; d. Charles Douglas Allen and Patricia Ann (West) King; m. Richard J. Bartlett, Aug. 13, 1977 (div. 1986). BS, U. Calif., Davis, 1970; JD, Santa Clara U., 1979. Bar: Calif. Dir. program integration vision resource ctr. SunRise Springs Resort, Santa Fe, 1987-88, dir. living ctr., 1987-89; mgr. profl. svcs. Davis, Graham & Stubbs, Denver, 1989-93; owner Court Jesters; adj. prof. Regis Coll., Denver, 1991, U. Colo., Denver, 1993, 94, 96, 97; lectr., writer and speaker in field. Author: Triversity Fantasy: Seven Keys to Unlock Prejudice, 1994, Manual for Becoming A Jester, 1997; writer (tng. forum) Lawyer Hiring and Training Report, 1991-95. Mem. Scribes. Republican. Episcopalian. Office: Court Jesters PO Box 9311 Denver CO 80209-0311

ALLEN, STEPHEN VALENTINE PATRICK WILLIAM, television comedian, author, pianist, songwriter; b. N.Y.C., Dec. 26, 1921; s. Carroll and Isabelle (Donohue) A.; m. Dorothy Goodman, Aug. 23, 1943; children: Stephen, Brian, David; m. Jayne Meadows, July 31, 1954; 1 child, William Christopher. Student journalism, Drake U., 1941, State Tchrs. Coll., Ariz., 1942. Radio announcer Sta. KOY, Phoenix, 1942, Stas. KFAC and KMTR, Los Angeles, 1944; comedian MBS, 1945; entertainer CBS, 1948-50; wrote narration and appeared in movie: Down Memory Lane; also appeared in motion pictures Warning Shot, The Benny Goodman Story, Amazon Women on the Moon, Great Balls of Fire, The Player, after 1950; appeared in Broadway play The Pink Elephant, 1953; creator, host Tonight Show, NBC, 1953-57; host TV shows Steve Allen Show, NBC, 1956-60, WBC syndicate, 1961-64, I've Got A Secret, 1964-67, Laughback, 1976-77, Meeting of Minds, 1977-81; composer over 5,000 songs including Picnic, Impossible, This Could Be The Start; author 43 books including Fourteen for Tonight, 1955, Bop Fables, 1955, The Funny Men, 1956, Wry on the Rocks, 1956, The Girls on the Tenth Floor, 1958, The Question Man, 1959, Mark It and Strike It; autobiography, 1960, Not All of Your Laughter, Not All of Your Tears, 1962; Letter to a Conservative, 1965, The Ground is Our Table, 1966, Bigger Than A Breadbox, 1967, A Flash of Swallows, 1969, The Wake, 1972, Princess Snip-Snip, 1973, Curses!, 1973, Schmock-Schmock!, 1975, What To Say When It Rains, 1974, Meeting of Minds, 1978, Chopped Up Chinese, 1978, Ripoff, 1979, Explaining China, 1980, Funny People, 1981, The Talk Show Murders, 1982, More Funny People, 1982 Beloved Son: A Story of the Jesus Cults, 1982, More Funny People, 1982, How To Make a Speech, 1986, How To Be Funny, 1987, Murder on the Glitter Box, 1989, (with Bill Adler Jr.) The Passionate Nonsmoker's Bill of the Rights, 1989, Dumbth: And 81 Ways to Make Americans Smarter, 1989, The Public Hating, 1990, Murder in Manhattan, 1990, Steve Allen and The Bible: Religion and Morality, 1990, Murder in Vegas, 1991, Hi-Ho, Steverino! My Adventures in the Wonderful Wacky World of TV, 1992, How to be Funny, 1992, The Murder Game, 1993, More Steve Allen on the Bible, Religion & Morality, Book Two, 1993, Make 'Em Laugh, 1993, Reflections, 1994, Murder on the Atlantic, 1995, The Man Who Turned Back the Clock and Other Short Stories, 1995. Recipient Grammy award for Gravy Waltz, 1964; named to TV Acad. Hall of Fame, 1986. Address: 15201 Burbank Blvd Van Nuys CA 91411-3532*

ALLEN, WILLIAM MERLE, university administrator, museum director; b. San Luis Obispo, Calif., Oct. 9, 1939; s. Lloyd Marion and Berwyn Rose (Palmer) A.; m. Janet Laurentine Clayton, June 11, 1963; children: Barbara, Gregory. BA in Chemistry, La Sierra Coll., 1961; PhD in Organic Chemistry, U. Md., 1967. From instr. to asst. prof. chemistry Andrews U., Berrien Springs, Mich., 1966-68; from asst. prof. to prof. chemistry Loma Linda U., Riverside, Calif., 1968-84; sr. v.p. acad. adminstrn. So. Coll. Seventh Day Aventists, Collegedale, Tenn., 1984-87; dean grad. sch. Loma Linda U., 1987-88; dir. ctr. lifelong learning, world mus. natural history La Sierra U., Riverside, 1988—; chair chemistry dept. Loma Linda U., 1971-79, dir. divsn. natural sci., 1977-81; sec., trustee So. Coll. Seventh Day Adventists, 1984-87. Trustee Smyrna Hosp., Atlanta, 1986-87. Republican. Office: La Sierra U World Museum Natural History 4700 Pierce St Riverside CA 92515-8247

ALLERY, KENNETH EDWARD, air force officer; b. Holyoke, Mass., Mar. 3, 1925; s. Alfred Edward and Anne (Millen) A.; m. Constance DuFresne, June 22, 1946; children—Katherine Ann, Kenneth Scott, Bryan Keith, David Edward. B.A., Park Coll., 1965; M.S., George Washington U., 1969; grad., Air Command and Staff Coll., 1961, Nat. War Coll., 1969. Commd. 2d lt. U.S. Army Air Force, 1944; advanced through grades to brig. gen. U.S. Air Force, 1972; insp. with Insp. Gen. Team 17th Air Force; exec. officer, ops. officer 526th Fighter Interceptor Squadron, Ramstein Air Base, Germany, 1961; sr. Air Force adviser Oreg. Air N.G., Portland Internat. Airport, 1965-67; dir. ops. and tng. 1st Air Force, Stewart AFB, N.Y., 1967-68; mem. N.Am. br. Directorate Plans and Programs, Orgn. Joint Chiefs of Staff, 1969-71; asst. dep. chief of staff for plans Aerospace Def. Command, Ent AFB, Colo., 1971-72; asst. dep. chief of staff for plans N.Am. Air Def. Command/Continental Air Def. Command, 1972-73, asst. dep. chief of staff for ops., 1973-74; also dep. chief of staff for ops. Aerospace Def. Command; command insp. gen. NORAD/CONAD/ADC, 1974-76; ret.; asst. to v.p. Syscon Corp., Colorado Springs, 1976-85; bus. devel. mgr. Litton Computer Services, Colorado Springs, 1985-96; founder Allery Enterprises, Inc., Colorado Springs, 1996—; bd. govs. Nat. Coll., Colorado Springs, 1993-94. Decorated D.S.M., D.F.C., Air medal with 4 oak leaf clusters, Meritorious Service medal with oak leaf cluster, Air Force Commendation medal. Office: Allery Enterprises Inc 1320 Rangeley Dr Colorado Springs CO 80921

ALLING, ABIGAIL KINGSLEY, scientist, expedition director; b. N.Y.C., Oct. 12, 1959; 1 child, Christopher. Student sea semester, Boston U., 1977; grad. in organic chemistry with honors, Harvard U., 1979; grad. in zoology lab. with honors, Cambridge (Eng.) U., 1981; BA in Biology with honors, Middlebury Coll., 1982; MS in Environ. Studies with honors, Yale U., 1985; postgrad., George Mason U., 1991—. Project coord. Cetacean Seas Rsch., Lincoln, Mass., 1985, Oceanic Rsch. and Comm. Alliance, 1987; project dir., RV heraclitus, expedition chief Expedition to Circumnavigate S.Am., 1987-89; dir. marine sys. Space Biospheres Ventures, 1985-94, assoc. dir. R&D, 1991-94, dir. devel., 1992-94, asst. v.p. biospheric devel., 1993-94; pres., dir. Planetary Coral Reef Found., Belize, 1991—; exec. v.p., dir. Biospheres, LLC, 1994—; dir. expdn. to Indian Ocean and S.E. Asia archipelagos R.V. Heracllitus, 1996—; pres. Ocean Expeditions Inc., 1985-93; sci. chief, marine sys. mgr. Biosphere 2, 1991-93; dir. Indian Ocean and Southeast Asia Archipelagos Coral Reef Expedition, 1995—. Author: Life Under Glass, 1994; contbr. articles to sci. jours. Recipient Internat. Cetacean Soc. award, 1982; Thomas J. Watson fellow, 1981, N.Y. Explorers Club fellow, 1993-97. Home: 32038 Caminito Quieto Bonsall CA 92003-4305

ALLISON, HENRY EDWARD, philosophy educator; b. 1937. Asst. prof. philosophy SUNY, Potsdam, 1964-65, Pa. State U., 1965-68; assoc. prof. U. Fla., 1968-72, prof., 1972-73; prof. U. Calif., San Diego, 1973—, chmn. dept., 1978-82. Author: Lessing and the Enlightenment: His Philosophy of Religion and Its Relation to Eighteenth Century Thought, 1966, Benedict de Spinoza, 1975, revised edit., 1987, Kant's Transcendental Idealism: An Interpretation and Defense, 1983, Kant's Theory of Freedom, 1990; editor: The Kant-Eberhard Controversy: An English Translation Together With Supplementary Materials, 1973. Office: U Calif Dept Philosophy B-002 Revelle Coll La Jolla CA 92093

ALLISON, LAIRD BURL, business educator; b. St. Marys, W.Va., Nov. 7, 1917; s. Joseph Alexander and Opal Marie (Robinson) A.; m. Katherine Louise Hunt, Nov. 25, 1943 (div. 1947); 1 child: William Lee; m. Genevieve Nora Elmore, Feb. 1, 1957 (dec. July 1994). BS in Personnel and Indsl. Relations magna cum laude, U. So. Calif., 1956; MBA, UCLA, 1958. Chief petty officer USN, 1936-51, PTO; asst. prof. to prof. mgmt. Calif. State U., L.A., 1956-83; asst. dean Calif. State U. Sch. Bus. and Econs., L.A., 1971-72, assoc. dean, 1973-83, emeritus prof. mgmt., 1983—; vis. asst. prof. mgmt. Calif. State U., Fullerton, 1970. Co-authored the Bachelors degree program in mgmt. sci. at Calif. State U., 1963. Mem. U.S. Naval Inst., Navy League U.S. Ford Found. fellow, 1960. Mem. Acad. Mgmt., Inst. Mgmt. Sci., Western Econs. Assn. Internat., World Future Soc., Am. Acad. Polit. Social Sci., Calif. State U. Assn. Emeriti Profs., Calif. State U. L.A. Emeriti Assn. (program v.p. 1986-87, v.p. adminstrn. 1987-88, pres. 1988-89, exec. com. 1990-91, treas. 1991—), Am. Assn. Individual Investors, Am. Assn. Ret. Persons, Ret. Pub. Employees Assn. Calif. (chpt. sec. 1984-88, v.p. 1989, pres. 1990-92), Am. Legion, Phi Kappa Phi, Beta Gamma Sigma, Alpha Kappa Psi. Home: 2176 E Bellbrook St Covina CA 91724-2346 Office: Calif State U Dept Mgmt 5151 State University Dr Los Angeles CA 90032-4221

ALLISON, RALPH BREWSTER, psychiatrist; b. Manila, May 13, 1931; s. W. Theodore and Metta L. (Brewster) A.; m. Mary Burden, Jan. 1, 1957 (div. 1997); children: Ann Allison-Marsh, Amy Allison Maiman, Jill Allison, John Allison. BA, Occidental Coll., L.A., 1952; MD, UCLA, 1956. Diplomate Am. Coll. Forensic Examiners. Staff psychiatrist Santa Clara County Mental Health Svcs., Palo Alto, Calif., 1962-63; program chief Santa Cruz County Mental Health Svcs., Santa Cruz, Calif., 1964-67; pvt. practice Palo Alto & Santa Cruz, 1962-78; staff psychiatrist Yolo County Mental Health Svcs., Broderick, Calif., 1978-81; forensic psychiatrist Davis, Calif., 1978-81; sr. psychiatrist Calif. Men's Colony, San Luis Obispo, Calif., 1981-93, ret. annuitant psychiatrist, 1994-95; sec. UAPD, Oakland, Calif., 1988-93; pres. SEPA, Oakland, 1990-93; mem. Mental Health adv. bd., Santa Cruz, 1964-67. Co-author: Minds in Many Pieces, 1980; contbr. articles to profl. jours. Founder Suicide Prevention Svcs., Santa Cruz, 1968-74. Capt. USAF, 1957-59. Recipient Cornelia B. Wilbur award ISSD, Skokie, Ill., 1995. Fellow Am. Psychiatric Assn. (life); mem. Am. Anthropological Assn., Internat. Soc. for Study Dissociation (charter), Rotary. Home: 2162 Mountain View Dr Los Osos CA 93402-3312

ALLISON, ROBERT CLYDE, business and computers consultant; b. Portland, Oreg., May 14, 1953; s. Harry Updike and Charlene Ann (Hare) A. BS, Portland State U., 1993. Owner Bob Allison Enterprises, Beaverton, Oreg., 1990—. Republican. Roman Catholic.

ALLISON, TERRY LANE, librarian; b. Ft. Worth, Oct. 2, 1955; s. Franklin D. and Betty (Burnett) A. AB, U. Calif., Berkeley, 1977, M Libr. and Info. Sci., 1983; MA in Comparative Lit., U. Calif., San Diego, 1992, 1997. Libr. asst. Gen. Libr. U. Calif., Berkeley, 1977-83; libr. I-II N.Y. Pub. Librs., Rsch. Librs., N.Y.C., 1983-86; asst. then assoc. libr. Ctrl. Libr. U. Calif.-San Diego, La Jolla, 1986-91; collections libr. Calif. State U., San Marcos, 1991—; statewide senator Acad. Senate-Calif. State U., Long Beach, 1994-96. Contbr. to books: Gay and Lesbian Literature, 1994, Recruiting, Educating and Training Librarians for Collection Development, 1994; editor, contbr.: States of Rage, 1996. Mem. ALA (chair program planning com., gay and lesbian task force 1992-94), MLA, Popular Culture Assn. Democrat. Office: Calif State U Libr Svcs San Marcos CA 92096-0001

ALLISON, WILLIAM ROBERT, company executive; b. Newport, Vt., Feb. 4, 1941; s. William Hugh and Eva Marie (Herbert) A.; m. Linda Kay Jarrett, Aug. 13, 1962 (div. Nov. 1974); children: Cherie Louise Allison Coughlin, William Robert Jr.; m. Joan Marie Lisowski, Aug. 4, 1979; 1 child, Donna Marie. BS in Bus. and Psychology, La Roche Coll., 1981. Foreman RCA Computer Systems, Palm Beach Gardens, Fla., 1965-67; mgr. tng. and adminstrn. RCA Computer Systems, Marlboro, Mass., 1967-72; dir. tng. Fruehauf Corp., Detroit, 1972-73; mgr. tng. and edn.automotive ops. Rockwell Internat., Troy, Mich., 1973-76, mgr. personnel adminstrn., 1977-79; mgr. mgmt. succession planning corp. Rockwell Internat., Pitts., 1979-81, dir. exec. resources, 1981-82, dir. orgn. planning, 1982-85; dir. mgmt. and orgn. planning Rockwell Internat., El Segundo, Calif., 1985-88, v.p. orgn. and human resources planning, 1988-91; mgmt. cons. William Allison & Assocs., Rancho Palos Verdes, Calif., 1991-96, Blue Marble Ptnrs., Torrance, Calif., 1994-96; chief adminstrv. officer Blue-Line/On-Line, Inc., Gardena, Calif., 1996—; corp. bd. advisors Nat. Coun. of La Raza, Washington, 1988-91; bd. advisors MESA, Berkeley, Calif., 1989-91; bd. dirs. Couns. Roundtable So. Calif., 1992-97, chmn., 1995-97. Served with USAF, 1961-65. Mem. N.Am. Coun. on Mgmt. and Orgn. (conf. bd.), Am. Soc. Human Resources Mgmt., Human Resources Planning Soc., Va. Country Club of Long Beach, Calif. (bd. dirs. 1991-93, 96—). Republican. Roman Catholic. Office: Blue-Line/On-Line Inc 1515 W 190th St Ste 417 Gardena CA 90248

ALLMAN, JAMES KIRK, physician's assistant; b. Arlington, Tex., Mar. 9, 1961; s. James Nathan Allman and Gloria (Kirk) Glass; m. Susan Lynn Garrity, Sept. 27, 1986; children: James Eric, Matthew Tyler. BS as Physician Asst., U. Okla., 1985. Bd. cert. physician asst. in primary care and surgery; lic. physician asst., Okla., N.Mex. Physician asst. Dennis E. Ester MD, Orthopedic Surgeon, Oklahoma City, 1985-95, Richard E. White, MD, N.Mex. Orthopedic Assoc., Albuquerque, 1995—; instr., assoc. prof. dept. family medicine U. Okla., Health Sci. Ctr., Coll. Medicine. Fellow Orthopedic Surgery-Am. Bd. Physician Asst. Practice; mem. Am. Acad. Physician Assts., Okla. Acad. Physician Assts., N.Mex. Acad. Physician Assts. Home: 5806 Broken Arrow Ln NW Albuquerque NM 87120-3046

ALLRED, GARY DANE, secondary education educator; b. Salt Lake City, Jan. 17, 1958; s. Gary Parley Allred and Shirley Louise Hale Wosak; m. Debra Jean Dunn, Oct. 14, 1977; children: Aleesa Anne, Tia Marie. BFA in Theatre Edn., U. Utah, 1979, BS in Speech Edn., 1979. Tchr. Camarillo (Calif.) H.S., 1979-81, Provo (Utah) H.S., 1981-86; mktg. dir. Jefferson Inst., Springville, Utah, 1986-88; tchr. Provo Canyon Sch., Provo, 1988-90; tchr. debate and theatre Payson (Utah) H.S., 1990—. Author: (poetry) Utah Signs, 1984. State del. Utah Dem. Party, Salt Lake City, 1992. Mem. Nat. Forensic League (nat. qualifying coach 1996), Internat. Thespian Soc., Nebo Edn. Assn. (v.p. 1992, pres. 1993). Office: Payson HS 1050 S Main St Payson UT 84651-3319

ALLRED, RUEL ACORD, education educator; b. Spring City, Utah, Mar. 30, 1929; s. Reid Henderson and Anna Elizabeth (Acord) A.; m. Betty Brown Best, Sept. 3, 1954; children: Anita, Chad R., Lynette, Eileen, Brent B., Marie, Reid R. AA, Snow Jr. Coll., Ephraim, Utah, 1949; BS in Elem. Edn. with honors, Brigham Young U., 1954, MS in Pers. and Guidance with honors, 1958; EdD in Elem. Edn., U. Oreg., 1965. Elem. sch. tchr. Provo City (Utah) Sch. Dist., 1958-61; elem. tchr. lab. sch. Brigham Young U., Provo, 1961-62, writer curriculum materials lab. sch., 1962-63, prin. elem. lab. sch., 1963-64, clin. instr. elem. edn., 1965-66, asst. prof., 1966-68; assoc. prof., 1968-73; prof. Brigham Young U., Provo, Utah, 1963-94, prof. emeritus, 1994—; grad. coord. elem. edn., 1971-78; assoc. dean coll. edn. Brigham Young U., Provo, 1988-89, 1991-92; prof. emeritus, 1994; test adminstr. Provo City Sch. Dist., 1958; vis. asst. prof. U. Mo., St. Louis, 1966; vis. lectr. U. Alaska, Anchorage, 1974, 76; cons. in field, 1967—. Author: Spelling: The Application of Research Findings, 1977, Spelling Trends, Content, and Methods, 1984, 2nd edit., 1987; co-author: The Sucher-Allred Reading Placement Inventory, 1972, 2nd edit., 1981, Continuous Progress in Spelling: An Individualized Spelling Program, 1972, 2nd edit., 1977, 3rd edit., 1982, Keys to Spelling Mastery: A Basal Spelling Program for Schools: Grades 1-8, 1984, Microspell: A Comprehensive Computer Spelling Program for Schools: Grades 2-8, 1984, AEC Spelling: A Spelling Program for the Home: Grades 2-8, 1984, The Computer and Education, 1984, 2nd edit., 1991, McGraw Hill Spelling Grades 1-8, 1990. Missionary Netherlands Mission LDS Ch., 1949-52; mission pres. Belgium Antwerp Mission LDS Ch., 1978-81; bd. dirs. Provo City Libr., 1984-89. Lt. USAF, 1955-57, Japan. Recipient Disting. Svc. award Brigham Young U. Alumni Assn., 1976, Karl G. Maeser Disting. Teaching award, 1977; Outstanding Alumnus award Snow Coll., 1988. Mem. Phi Kappa Phi, Phi Delta Kappa. Mem. LDS Ch. Home: 1067 Grand Ave Provo UT 84604-3009

ALLSHOUSE, MICHAEL JAMES, pediatric surgeon; b. U.S. Canal Zone, Panama, Feb. 24, 1954; s. Thomas James and Elsie Dale (Hamilton) A.; m. Denise Lynn Glass, Aug. 18, 1979; children: Anthony James, Victoria Lynn, Charles Michael. BS, Allegheny Coll., 1976; DO, Phila. Coll. Osteopathy, 1982. Diplomate Am. Bd. Surgery with subspecialty in critical care and pediatric surgery. Staff gen. surgeon Naval Hosp., Guam, 1988-90, Oakland, Calif., 1990-91; fellow in pediatric trauma Children's Nat. Med. Ctr., Washington, 1991-92; chief resident pediatric surgery The Children's Hosp., Denver, 1992-94; head div. pediatric surgery Naval Med. Ctr., San Diego, 1994—. Cmdr. USN, 1982-94. Recipient order of ancient chamorri Govt. Guam, 1990. Fellow Am. Coll. Surgeons. Home: 7685 Bromeliad Ct San Diego CA 92119-1535 Office: Naval Med Ctr 34800 Bob Wilson Dr San Diego CA 92134-5002

ALLUMBAUGH, BYRON, retired grocery company executive. Student, Long Beach, Calif., City Coll. Dir. meat ops. Ralph's Grocery Co., Compton, Calif., from 1958, v.p. store ops., 1967-69, exec. v.p., then pres., 1969-1976; chmn., CEO Ralph's Grocery Co., 1976-97, ret., 1997. Office: 620 Newport Centr Dr Newport Beach CA 92660*

ALLUMS, HENRIENE, elementary education educator; b. Jackson, Miss., July 30, 1945; d. Henry and Annie (Johnson) A. BA, Calif. State U., Long Beach, 1967; MA, U. San Francisco, 1978. Cert. elem., secondary tchr., Calif., ESL tchr., cross cultural, language and acad. devel. tchr. Tchr., grades 1-3 L.A. Unified Sch. Dist. Mem. Calif. Assn. bilingual Edn., Calig. Tchrs. English to Speakers of Other Langs., Internat. Reading Assn., Tchrs. English to Speakers of Other Langs. Home: 1522 E 123rd St Los Angeles CA 90059-2920

ALM, STEVE, prosecutor; m. Haunani Ho; 1 child. MEd, U. Oreg., 1979; JD, U. Pacific, 1983. Editor West Pub. Co., 1983-85; dep. prosecuting atty. City and County of Honolulu, 1985-87, line-dep., then felony team supr., 1987-90, dir. dist. and family ct. divsn., 1990-94; U.S. atty. for Hawaii U.S. Dept. Justice, Honolulu, 1994—; adj. prof. Richardson Sch. Law U. Hawaii. Mem. ABA (mem. gov. com. on crime), Hawaii State Bar Assn. (ex-officio mem. domestic violence coordinating coun., v.p. criminal justice and corrections sect.). Office: US Dept Justice Box 50183 300 Ala Moana Blvd Honolulu HI 96850*

ALMOND, JOAN HARWOOD ELKINS, photographer; b. L.A., June 3, 1935; d. Benjamin and Jeanne (Yourell) Harwood; m. George W. Elkins Jr., June 12, 1954 (dec. 1969); children: George W. III, Tracy Ann Elkins Stoker, Timothy J., Chris H. Solo exhbns. include Saiyde Bronfman Ctr., Montreal, 1987, Tekeyan Cultural Ctr., Montreal, 1988, Manougian Cultural Ctr., Detroit, 1989, Soc. Contemporary Photography, Kansas City, 1992, Nile Gallery, Cairo, 1992, Schatten Gallery, Atlanta, 1993, Brooks Inst. Photography, Santa Barbara, Calif., 1994, U. Calif., Berkeley, 1996, Gallery Contemporary Photography, Santa Monica, Calif., 1997; group exhbns. include Internat. Design Ctr., Montreal, 1988, U. Judaism, L.A., 1990, Jacob Javits Conv. Ctr., N.Y., 1991; permanent pub. collections include Bernaissance Mus., Montreal, and other pvt. collections; photographer: (films) Killing of a Chinese Bookie, The Disappearence, Opening Night, Every Person is Guilty, The Burning Book, Ups and Downs, Captive Heart, The Dance Goes On; (theatre) Knives, Lovestreams; also featured in numerous articles. Studio: PO Box 954 Malibu CA 90265-0954

ALMORE-RANDLE, ALLIE LOUISE, special education educator; b. Jackson, Miss., Apr. 20; d. Thomas Carl and Theressa Ruth (Garrett) Almore; m. Olton Charles Randle, Sr., Aug. 3, 1974. BA, Tougaloo (Miss.) Coll., 1951; MS in Edn., U. So. Calif., L.A., 1971. Recreation leader Pasadena (Calif.) Dept. Recreation, 1954-56; demonstration tchr. Pasadena Unified Schs., 1956-63; cons. spl. edn. Temple City (Calif.) Sch. Dist., 1967; supr. tchr. edn. U. Calif., Riverside, 1971; tchr. spl. edn. Pasadena Unified Sch. Dist., 1955-70, dept. chair spl. edn. Pasadena H.S., 1972—, also adminstrv. asst. Pasadena H.S., 1993—; supr. Evelyn Frieden Ctr., U. So. Calif., L.A., 1970; mem. Coun. Exceptional Children, 1993—. Organizer Northwest Project, Camp Fire Girls, Pasadena, 1963; leader Big Sister Program, YWCA, Pasadena, 1966; organizer, dir. March on The Boys' Club, the Portrait of a Boy, 1966; pub. souvenir jours. Women's Missionary Soc., AME Ch., State of Wash. to Mo.; mem. NAACP, Ch. Women United, Afro-Am. Quilters L.A. Recipient Cert. of Merit, Pasadena City Coll., 1963, Outstanding Achievement award Nat. Coun. Negro Women, Pasadena, 1965, Earnest Thompson Seton award Campfire Girls, Pasadena, 1968, Spl. Recognition, Outstanding Community Svc. award The Tuesday Morning Club, 1967, Dedicated Svc. award AME Ch., 1983, Educator of Excellence award Rotary Club of Pasadena, 1993, Edn. award Altadena NAACP, 1994; named Tchr. of Yr., Pasadena Masonic Bodies, 1967, Woman of the Yr. for Community Svc. and Edn., Zeta Phi Beta, 1992; grad. fellow U. So. Calif., L.A., 1970. Mem. NAACP (bd. mem., chmn. ch. workers com. 1955-63, Fight for Freedom award West Coast region 1957, NAACP Edn. award Altadena, Calif. chpt. 1994), ASCD, Calif. Tchrs. Assn., Nat. Coun. Negro Women, Phi Delta Gamma (hospitality chair 1971—), Alpha Kappa Alpha (membership com.), Phi Delta Phi (founder, organizer 1961), Phi Delta Kappa. Democrat. Mem. AME Ch. Home: 1710 La Cresta Dr Pasadena CA 91103-1261

ALOIA, ROLAND CRAIG, scientist, administrator, educator; b. Newark, Dec. 21, 1943; s. Roland S. and Edna M. (Mahan) A. BS, St. Mary's Coll., 1965; PhD, U. Calif., Riverside, 1970. Postdoctoral fellow City of Hope, Duarte, Calif., 1971-75; research biologist U. Calif., Riverside, 1975-76; asst. prof. Sch. of Medicine Loma Linda (Calif.) U., 1976-79; assoc. prof. Loma Linda (Calif.) U., 1979-89, prof. anesthesiology and biochemistry, 1989—; chemist VA, Loma Linda, 1979-94, chief rsch. ops., 1994—; pres., chmn. Loma Linda VA for Rsch. and Edn., 1988-94, pres., CEO, 1994—. Editor: Membrane Fluidity in Biology, Vols. 1-4, 1983, 85; sr. editor: (series) Advanced in Membrane Fluidity vols. 1-3, 1988, vol. 4, 1989, vol. 5, 1991, vol. 6, 1992. Pres. Riverside chpt. Calif. Heart Assn., 1979-80, 1984-86, bd. dirs., exec. com. mem., 1973-86. Calif. Heart Assn. fellow, 1971-73. Mem. Am. Chem. Soc., N.Y. Acad. Scis., Soc. Cell Biology, Sigma Xi (pres. Loma Linda chpt. 1991-92, pres.-elect 1990-91). Office: VA Med Ctr Rsch Svc 151 JL Pettis Loma Linda CA 92357

ALPERS, EDWARD ALTER, history educator; b. Phila., Apr. 23, 1941; s. Bernard Jacob and Lillian (Sher) A.; m. Ann Adele Dixon, June 14, 1963; children: Joel Dixon, Leila Sher. AB magna cum laude, Harvard U., 1963; PhD, U. London, 1966. Lectr. history Univ. Coll., Dar es Salaam, Tanzania, 1966-68; from asst. prof. to prof. history UCLA, 1968—, dean div. honors Coll. Letters and Sci., 1985-87, dean honors and undergrad. programs, 1987-96. Author: Ivory and Slaves in East Central Africa, 1975; editor: Walter Rodney: Revolutionary and Scholar, 1982, (newsletter) Assn. Concerned Africa Scholars, 1983-85; contbg. editor: Comparative Studies of South Asia, Africa and the Middle East, 1997; contbr. articles to scholarly jours. Fellow Ford Found., 1972-73, NEH, 1978-79, Fulbright Found., 1980; Fundacao Calouste Gulbenkian grantee, Lisbon, Portugal, 1975. Mem. Africa Studies Assn. (bd. dirs. 1985-88, v.p. 1992-93, pres. 1993-94), Assn. Concerned Africa Scholars (bd. dirs. 1983-93), Alliance for Undergrad. Edn. (UCLA rep. 1987-95, co-chair 1989-92), Hist. Abstracts (adv. bd. 1994—). Office: UCLA Dept History Los Angeles CA 90095-1473

ALPERS, JOHN HARDESTY, JR., financial planning executive, retired military officer; b. Richmond, Va., Sept. 7, 1939; s. John Hardesty and Laura Elizabeth (Gaylor) A.; m. Sharon Kay Kurrle, May 1, 1971; 1 child, John Hardesty III. BS, U. Colo., 1963; MBA, InterAm. U., 1969; postgrad. USAF Squadron Officers Sch., 1968-69, USAF Command and Staff Coll., 1976-78, USAF Air War Coll., 1978-79, CFP, Nat. Endowment for Fin. Edn., 1989; CFS, Inst. Cert. Fund Specialists, 1994; registered investment adv. svc. exec. Commd. 2d lt. U.S. Air Force, 1964, advanced through grades to lt. col.,

1979; SAC B-52 navigator, select radar bombardier, P.R., 1967-70; squadron weapon systems officer Ubon RTAFB, Thailand, 1970-71, radar strike officer Linebacker II strike plans officer, 1972; prisoner of war, Hanoi, N. Vietnam, 1972-73; asst. wing weapons officer Seymour-Johnson AFB, N.C., 1971-72, wing command post controller, 1973-74; asst. prof. aerospace studies AFROTC, U. Ariz., Tucson, 1974-78; asst. div. chief aviation sci. USAF Acad., Colorado Springs, 1978-79, spl. asst. to commandant, 1979-80, div. chief plans, policy and standardization/evaluation, 1980-83; ret., 1983; reg. rep. Waddell & Reed, Inc., 1986-90, Fin. Network Investment Corp.; v.p. Fin. Planning & Mgmt., Inc. Boulder, Colo., 1990-97; mng. dir. Gateway Fin. Strategies LLC; registered rep. Royal Alliance Assocs, Inc, 1997—; lectr., speaker in field. POW/MIA Activist. With USCG, 1961-63. Decorated Legion of Merit, D.F.C. (2), Bronze Star, Air Medal (9), Air Force Commendation medal (2), Purple Heart (2), Vietnamese Cross of Gallantry; recipient ceremonial sabre U.S. Air Force Acad. Cadet Corps, 1983. Mem. Air Force Assn., Ret. Officers Assn., U.S. Strategic Inst., Am. Def. Inst., Red River Valley Fighter Pilots Assn., Inst. Cert. Fund Specialists (cert.), Arnold Air Soc., Nam-POWS, Inc., Inst. CFPs, CFP Bd. Standards, Registry Fin. Planning Practitioners, Internat. Assn. Fin. Planning, Internat. Platform Assn., Pi Kappa Alpha. Republican. Home: JSR Boulder Heights 189 Overlook Ln Boulder CO 80302-9444 Office: Gateway Fin Strategies Inc 189 Overlook Ln Boulder CO 80302

ALPERT, DEIRDRE WHITTLETON, state legislator; b. N.Y.C., Oct. 6, 1945; d. Harry Mark and Dorothy (Lehn) Whittleton; m. Michael Edward Alpert, Jan. 1, 1964; children: Lehn, Kristin, Alison. Student, Pomona Coll., 1963-65; LLD (hon.), Western Am. U., 1994. Mem. from 78th dist. Calif. State Assembly, Sacramento, 1990—; chairwoman Women's Legislators Caucus, Sacramento, 1993; active Calif. Tourism Commn., Sacramento, 1990—, Calif. Libr. Allocations Bd., Sacramento, 1993—. dist. rep., troop leader Girl Scouts Am., San Diego, 1977-83; spl. advocate Voices for Children, San Diego, 1982-90; mem. bd. Solana Beach (Calif.) Sch. Bd., 1983-90, also pres.; pres. beach and county guild United Cerebral Palsy, San Diego, 1986. Recipient Legis. award Calif. Regional Occupation Program, 1991-92, Am. Acad. Pediats., 1991-92, San Diego Psychol. Assn., 1993-94, Commitment to Children award Calif. Assn. for Edn. of Young Children, 1991-92, Legis. Commendation award Nat. Assn. for Yr.-Round Edn., 1991-92, State Commn. on Status of Women, 1993-94; named Friend of Yr., Children's PKU Network, 1991-92, Woman of Yr., Nat. Women's Polit. Caucus San Diego, 1991-92, Orgn. for Rehab. through Tng., 1993-94, Legislator of Yr., Am. Electronics Assn., 1991-92, 1993-94, Calif. Sch.-Age Consortium, 1993-94, Women of Distinction, Soropimists Internat. of La Jolla, 1993-94, Assemblymember of Yr., Calif. Assn. Edn. Young Children, 1993-94. Mem. Charter 100 of San Diego, Calif. Elected Women's Assn. for Edn. and Rsch. (v.p. 1994—). Democrat. Mem. Congregation Ch. Office: State Capitol District 39 Sacramento CA 95814 also: 1557 Columbia St San Diego CA 92101-3607*

ALPERT, DOLORES ESTHER, secondary education educator; b. Chgo., Feb. 25, 1944; d. Harry and Hannah (Lewis) Karp; m. Ronald H. Alpert, Dec. 22, 1968; children: Lauren, Craig, Jonathan. BA in English, U. Ill., 1965; BS in Edn., Azusa (Calif.) Pacific U., 1965. Cert. tchr. English (K-12), math. (K-9), Calif. Tchr. English, Ida Crown Acad., Chgo., 1965-69, Hollenbeck Jr. H.S., L.A., 1969-70, Woodbridge H.S., Irvine, Calif., 1983-86; tchr. English and math. Lyle S. Briggs Sch., Chino, Calif., 1986—; tng. cons. Anti-Defamation League "A World of Difference", L.A., 1991—, facilitator E. Pluribus Unum Diversity trainer, 1996—; cultural diversity mentor Chino Unified Sch. Dist., 1993—; newmast tchr. NASA, 1996. V.p. Bat Yahm Temple, Newport Beach, Calif., 1978, 79, pres. Sisterhood, 1980. Fellow Calif. Writing Project, 1991, Calif. Math. Project, 1994. Mem. Nat. Coun. Tchrs. Math., Calif. Math. Coun. Office: Lyle S Briggs Sch 11880 Roswell Ave Chino CA 91710-1515

ALSAKER, ROBERT JOHN, information systems specialist; b. Los Angeles, June 15, 1945; s. Lauris Ronald and Hazel Mildred (Danz) A.; m. Cynthia Ann Gillesvog, Feb. 25, 1984; children: Troy R., Erik G., Karlee A. AA, Fullerton (Calif.) Jr. Coll., 1966; BS, Moorhead (Minn.) State Coll., 1970. Project mgr. Jet Propulsion Lab., Pasadena, Calif., 1970-80; mgr. mgmt. info. systems Kroy Inc., Scottsdale, Ariz., 1980-85; adminstr. City of Pasadena, 1985-86; mgr. tech. cons. U.S. West Info. Systems, Phoenix, 1986-88; v.p. MIS ACB Cos., Phoenix, 1988-95; dir. MIS Midwest Pub., Inc., Phoenix, 1995—. Served in U.S. Army, 1968-69, Vietnam. Republican. Lutheran. Office: 10844 N 23rd Ave Phoenix AZ 85029-4924

ALSTROM, SVEN ERIK, architect; b. Emporia, Kans., July 27, 1951; s. William E. and Willa M. (Russell) A.; m. Lynn M. Mathews, June 22, 1974 (div. June 1983). B. Gen. Studies, U. Kans., 1975; student evening div. U. Denver Coll. Law, 1984. Registered architect, Calif., Colo., Kans., Mo., N.Mex.; cert. Nat. Council Archtl. Registration Bds. Architect, PGAV Architects, Kansas City, Mo., 1972-74, Horner Blessing, Kansas City, 1977-79, MSFS Architects, Kansas City, 1979-80, Marshall & Brown, Kansas City, 1980-81, Urban Design, Denver, 1981-82, Dominick Assocs., Denver, 1983-84; with C. Welton Anderson & Assocs., Aspen, Colo., 1989-90; pvt. practice Alstrom Group, Aspen, 1990—. Mem. AIA, Colo. AIA, Denver AIA, Zen-Presbyterian. Home: PO Box 551 Aspen CO 81612-0551 Office: Alstrom Group PC 121 S Galena Ste B Aspen CO 81611

ALTER, EDWARD T., state treasurer; b. Glen Ridge, N.J., July 26, 1941; s. E. Irving and Norma (Fisher) A.; m. Patricia R. Olsen, 1975; children: Christina Lyn, Ashly Ann, Darci Lee. B.A., U. Utah, 1966; M.B.A., U. Utah, 1967. C.P.A., Calif., Utah. Sr. acct. Touche Ross & Co., Los Angeles, 1967-72; asst. treas. U. Utah, Salt Lake City, 1972-80; treas. State of Utah, Salt Lake City, 1981—; pres. Nat. Assn. State Treas., 1987-88. Bd. dirs. Utah Housing Fin. Agy., Utah State Retirement Bd., pres., 1984-93; mem. Utah State Rep. Cen. Com., 1981—, Anthony Com. on Pub. Fin., 1988—. Sgt. USAR, 1958-66. Named to All-pro Govt. Team, City and State Mag., 1988; recipient Jesse M. Uhruh Award for Svc. to State Treas.', 1989. Mem. Am. Inst. CPAs, Nat. Assn. State Treas. (past sr. v.p., pres. 1987), Delta Sigma Pi, Delta Phi Kappa. Club: Utah Bond (pres. 1981-82). Office: State Capitol 215 State Capitol Building Salt Lake City UT 84114-1202*

ALTER, GERALD L., real estate executive; b. Rensselaer, Ind., Aug. 24, 1910; s. Leslie and Lettie (Willis) A.; m. Margaret A. Davis, Sept. 15, 1939 (dec. Nov. 13, 1996); children: Judith Ann (dec.), John Edward. Student Bus. Coll., 1927-28. Clk. and office mgr., 1929-35; bldg. contractor, 1936-45; real estate broker, 1946—; officer Torrance Police Res., 1948-63; pres. Alter Realty & Ins., Leads, Inc., investments, Alter Ins. Agy., Inc., REMCO Real Estate Mgmt. Co., Alter Devel. Co.; pres. Developers & Builders. Planning commr. City of Torrance, 1966-83, chmn. Torrance Planning Commn. 1982-83; water commr. City of Torrance, 1982-91, chmn. 1987-88; former bd. dirs. Harbor Area United Way. With Calif. State Guard, 1942-43; U.S. Army, 1945-46. Mem. Torrance-Lomita-Carson Bd. Realtors (pres. 1978, v.p. 1980-81), Calif. Assn. Realtors (dir. 1978-81), Nat. Assn. Realtors, Torrance C. of C. (past dir.), Am. Legion, Rotary (recipient Torrance Rotary 38 yr. perfect attendance pin 1996). Republican. Clubs: OX-5 (pioneer airman). Home: 1337 Engracia Ave Torrance CA 90501-2603 Office: 2305 Torrance Blvd Torrance CA 90501-2520

ALTHEIMER, BRIAN P. See TUTASHINDA, ABD KARIM KWELI

ALTMAN, ADELE ROSENHAIN, radiologist; b. Tel Aviv, Israel, June 4, 1924; came to U.S., 1933, naturalized, 1939; d. Bruno and Salla (Silberzweig) Rosenhain; m. Emmett Altman, Sept. 3, 1944; children: Brian R., Alan L., Karen D. Diplomate Am. Bd. Radiology. Intern Queens Gen. Hosp., N.Y.C., 1949-51; resident Hosp. for Joint Diseases, N.Y.C., 1951-52, Roosevelt Hosp., N.Y.C., 1955-57; clin. instr. radiology Downstate Med. Ctr., SUNY, Bklyn., 1957-61; asst. prof. radiology N.Y. Med. Coll., N.Y.C., 1961-65, assoc. prof., 1965-68; assoc. prof. radiology U. Okla. Health Sci. Ctr., Oklahoma City, 1968-78; assoc. prof. dept. radiology U. N.Mex. Sch. Medicine, Albuquerque, 1978-85. Author: Radiology of the Respiratory System: A Basic Review, 1978; contbr. articles to profl. jours. Fellow Am. Coll. Angiology, N.Y. Acad. Medicine; mem. Am. Coll. Radiologist, Am. Roentgen Ray Soc., Assn. Univ. Radiologists, Radiol. Soc. N.Am., B'nai B'rith Anti-Defamation League (bd. dirs. N.Mex. state bd.), Hadassah Club.

ALTMAN, LEONARD CHARLES, physician; b. Fresno, Calif., Sept. 1, 1944; s. Martin and Ida (Sharnoff) A.; m. Gaylene M. Bouska, Dec. 26, 1970; children: Jonathan David, Matthew Charles, Katherine Ann. BA, U. Pa., 1965; MD, Harvard U., 1969. Diplomate Am. Bd. Internal Medicine, Am. Bd. Allergy and Immunology, Nat. Bd. Med. Examiners. Intern, resident U. Wash. Affiliated Hosps., Seattle, 1969-71; sr. rsch. assoc. NIDR/NIH, Bethesda, Md., 1971-74; chief med. resident Harborview Med. Ctr., Seattle, 1974-75, chief allergy divsn., 1979—; asst. prof. medicine U. Wash., Seattle, 1975-79, assoc. prof. medicine, 1979-85, clin. assoc. prof. medicine, 1985-88, clin. prof. medicine, affiliate prof. environ. health, 1988—; ptnr. N.W. Asthma and Allergy Ctr., Seattle, 1985—; reviewer Alaska Soc. Tech. Found. Editor: Clinical Allergy and Immunology, 1984, Autoimmune Diseases, 1993; mem. editl. bd. Infection and Immunity; contbr. articles to profl. jours. Lt. col. USPHS. Mem. ACP, Am. Acad. Allergy and Clin. Immunology, Am. Assn. Immunologists, Am. Fedn. for Clin. Rsch., Am. Soc. for Microbiology, Clin. Immunology Soc., Infectious Disease Soc. Am., King County Med. Soc. (environ. health com. chmn. 1987—), Western Soc. for Clin. Rsch., Wash. State Med. Assn., Wash. State Soc. of Allergy and Immunology (sci. program com. chmn., v.p., pres.), Reticuloendothelial Soc., Puget Sound Allergy Soc. (pres. 1977), N.W. Allergy Forum (sci. program com. chmn.), Physicians Bur. King County (adv. com., rep. on allergy), Seattle Acad. Internal Medicine, Alpha Epsilon Delta, Alpha Omega Alpha. Office: NW Asthma & Allergy Ctr 4540 Sand Point Way NE Ste 200 Seattle WA 98105-3941

ALTSCHUL, DAVID EDWIN, record company executive, lawyer; b. N.Y.C., Apr. 8, 1947; s. Norbert and Grace (Aderer) A.; m. Margaret Berne, July 4, 1969; children: Jonathan, Jared, Eric, Emily. BA summa cum laude, Amherst Coll., 1969; JD, Yale U., 1974. Bar: Calif. 1974. Law clerk U.S. Dist. Ct. Conn., Hartford, 1974-75; assoc. Tuttle & Taylor, Los Angeles, 1975-76, Pryor, Cashman, Sherman & Flynn, Beverly Hills, Calif., 1976-77, Hardee, Barovick, Konecky & Braun, Beverly Hills, 1977-79; prin. Rosenfeld, Kassoy & Kraus, Beverly Hills, 1979-80; dir. bus. affairs Warner Bros. Records, Inc., Burbank, Calif., 1980-83, v.p. bus. and legal affairs, 1983-88, sr. v.p. bus. and legal affairs, 1988-93, gen. counsel and sr. v.p. bus. affairs, 1993-95, vice chmn., gen. counsel, 1995—; bd. dirs. Rec. Industry Assn. Am. Bd. dirs. Los Encinos Sch., Encinos, Calif., 1986-93, treas., 1986-87, pres., 1987-92; bd. dirs. People for the Am. Way, 1991—, bd. dirs. exec. com., 1993—, vice chmn., 1996—; bd. dirs. San Fernando Valley Neighborhood Legal Svcs., Inc., 1989-90, Rock the Vote, 1997—. Mem. Phi Beta Kappa. Democrat. Jewish. Office: Warner Bros Records Inc 3300 Warner Blvd Burbank CA 91505-4632

ALTSHILLER, ARTHUR LEONARD, secondary education educator; b. N.Y.C., Aug. 12, 1942; s. Samuel Martin and Betty Rose (Lepson) A.; m. Gloria Silvern, Nov. 23, 1970 (div. 1975); m. Carol Heiser, Aug. 16, 1980. BS in Physics, U. Okla., 1963; MS in Physics, Calif. State U., Northridge, 1971. Elec. engr. Garrett Corp., Torrance, Calif., 1963-64, Volt Tech. Corp., Phoenix, 1965; engr., physicist Aerojet Gen. Corp., Azusa, Calif., 1966-68; elec. engr. Magnavox Rsch. Labs., Torrance, 1968-69; sr. engr. Litton Guidance & Control, Canoga Park, Calif., 1969; physics tchr. L.A. Unified Sch. Dist./Van Nuys Math/Sci. Magnet High Sch., 1971—; math. instr. Valley Coll., Van Nuys, Calif., 1986—; part-time physics and chemistry tchr. West Coast Talmudical Sem., L.A., 1978-88; foster tchr. Seti Inst. and NASA Ames Rsch. Ctr., 1994; coach Van Nuys (Calif.) H.S. Nat. Championship Sci. Bowl Team, 1995; tchr. mem. U.S. Olympic Physics Team, 1996. Mesa Club sponsor Math.-Engrng. Sci. Achievement L.A. High Sch. and U. So. Calif., 1984-87. Recipient Cert. of Honor Westinghouse Sci. Talent Search, 1990. Mem. AAAS, Am. Assn. Physics Tchrs., Nat. Coun. Tchrs. Math., N.Y. Acad. Scis., Am. Meteorol. Soc., So. Calif. Striders, Santa Monica Astron. Soc., United Tchrs. L.A. Home: 6776 Vickview Dr Canoga Park CA 91307-2751 Office: Van Nuys High Sch 6535 Cedros Ave Van Nuys CA 91411-1506

ALTSTOCK, MARSHA MARIE, pediatrics nurse; b. Toledo, Feb. 8, 1955; d. Jack Stanley and Cecelia Jean Kirkland; m. Robert Randolph Altstock, May 13, 1978; c..ildren: matthew, Danielle. BS in Nursing, U. Portland, Oreg., 1978. Cert. pediatric nurse. Pediatric and obstectic charge nurse Cary Med. Ctr., Caribou, Maine, 1978-80; pediatric charge nurse Sutter Meml. Med. Ctr., Sacramento, 1980-83; charge nurse pediatrics Hendrick Med. Ctr., Abilene, Tex., 1986-90, pediatric and PICU nurse mgr., 1990-94, ednl. cons., 1994—; pediatric nurse provider Tex. Dept. Human Svcs., Austin, Tex., 1992—; Tex. medicare provider Nat. Heritage Ins. Co., Austin, Tex., 1993—; pediatric ednl. cons. Gamma Assocs., Carlsbad, Calif., 1994—; bd. dirs. The House That Kerry Built, Abilene; pediatric cons. Hendrick Med. Ctr., Abilene, 1994-95, Pediatric Svcs. Am., 1995—; v.p. Gamma Assocs., Carlsbad, Calif., 1994—. Reviewer:(book) Pediatric Critical Care, 1993. Dist. recorder Boy Scouts of Am., Abilene, 1993; svc. mgr. Girl Scouts Am., 1994-. Fellow Nat. Assn. Pediatric Nurses and Practioners; mem. Soc. Pediatric Nurses.

ALVARES, JOEL G., songwriter, recording artist; b. San Francisco, June 28, 1963. BA in Comm., San Diego State U., 1986. Owner, ptnr. Vision Import/distbn., San Carlos, Calif., 1991-94. Band leader bygone dogs; contbr. music to 2 CD Rom games; writer, performer (TV comml.) Ice Monkey, 1992. Vol. San Francisco Homeless Soc., 1981—, Calif. State Boys & Girls Club, Redwood City, 1988; fundraiser United Way, Menlo Park, Calif., 1988-90. Mem. Tau Kappa Epsilon (asst. dir. 1982-86). Home: 527 Elm St # 5 San Carlos CA 94070

ALVAREZ, ROBERT SMYTH, editor, publisher; b. San Francisco, June 7, 1912; s. Walter Clement and Harriet (Smyth) A.; m. Janet Crosby, Nov. 4, 1935; children: David Crosby, Robert Smyth, Nancy (Mrs. Eric Wallace). AB, U. Chgo., 1934, PhD, 1939; BSLS, U. Ill., 1935. Dir. Brockton (Mass.) Public Library, 1941-43, Nashville Public Library, 1946-59, Berkeley (Calif.) Public Library, 1959-61, South San Francisco Public Library, 1966-80; editor, pub. Libr. Adminstrs. Digest (formerly Adminstrs. Digest), 1965-96; Editor, pub. Bus. Info., 1969—, Supt.'s Digest, 1977-88; pres. Adminstrs. Digest Press, Foster City, Calif., 1987—; tchr. public library adminstrn. George Peabody Coll., Nashville, 1946-59; library cons., surveyor. Author: Qualifications of Public Library Directors in North Central States, 1943, Library Boss, 1987, Library Log, 1991; pub. Business Books Buying Guide, 1990—; contbr. articles to profl. jours. Chmn. Boy Scouts Am., North San Mateo County, 1973. Named Boss of Year Nashville Secs. Assn., 1958, Citizen of Year, South San Francisco, 1976. Mem. Sequoia Swimming and Tennis Club (organizer), Glendale Club (Nashville) (organizer), Reliez Valley Country Club (Pleasant Hill, Calif.) (organizer), Calif. Golf Club (South San Francisco), Rotary (pres. South San Francisco 1979-80), Phi Gamma Delta. Episcopalian. Home and Office: 719 San Miguel Ln Foster City CA 94404-3722

ALVES, CAROL ANN, office assistant; b. Salem, Oreg., July 10, 1947; d. Elver John and Virginia Alexina (French) Owings; m. James William Alves, July 21, 1989. Student, Inst. Applied Sci., 1972, Chemeketa C.C., 1982. Clk. typist Oreg. State Police Criminal Divsn., Salem, 1966-68; data entry operator Oreg. State Police Data Processing Divsn., Salem, 1968-70; fingerprint technician Oreg. State Police Bur. Criminal Identification, Salem, 1970-85, clerical specialist, 1985-89; recs. clk. San Bernardino (Calif.) County Sheriff, 1989; office asst. Hesperia (Calif.) City Clks. Office, 1989-93, Hesperia Animal Control, 1993-95; planning commn. sec., 1995—. Columnist: Yesterday's Tomorrows, 1992—, Lightsabre, 1992—. Vol. San Bernardino County Mus., Redlands, Calif., 1994; dir., southwest regional rep. Sci. Fiction Mus., 1991—. Mem. Coun. British Socs., Costumers Guild West, Jedi Knights (v.p. 1990-92, 96-97). Office: Sci Fiction Mus PO Box 18091 Salem OR 97305

ALVI, KHISAL AHMED, chemist; b. Karachi, Pakistan, Mar. 15, 1958; came to U.S., 1989; s. Wisal Ahmed Alvi and Abida Begum; m. Tanvir Sultana, July 4, 1989; children: Rida, Rohail. BS with honors, U. Karachi, 1981, MS, 1983, PhD, 1987. Rsch. asst. U. Southhampton, Eng., 1988-89; postdoctoral rsch. fellow U. Calif., Santa Cruz, 1989-91, sr. rsch. fellow, 1991-92; sr. scientist PANLABS, Inc., Bothell, Wash., 1993—; presenter in field. Contbr. articles to profl. jours. Spl. predoctoral scholar U. Grant Commn. Pakistan, 1986, postdoctoral scholar U. Calif. Cancer Rsch. Coordinating Com., 1989. Mem. AAAS, Am. Chem. Soc., Am. Soc. Pharmacognosy, Soc. Indsl. Microbiology, N.Y. Acad. Scis. Office: PANLABS Inc 11804 N Creek Pky Bothell WA 98011

ALVORD, DAVID MICHAEL, marketing and sales executive; b. National City, Calif., June 17, 1945; s. Donald Lee and Eleanor Alvord; m. Marie-Christine Lanryd, Aug. 10, 1979; children: Cecilia, Charlotte. BS in Aeronautics, San Jose State U., 1969; MBA in Mktg., So. Ill. U., 1973. V.p., co-founder Seattle Tech., Kirkland, Wash., 1973-78; dir. Europe Intel, Brussels, 1979-83; area mgr. Measurex Inc., Cupertino, Calif., 1983-84; sales mgr. Androx Inc., Boston, 1984-89; gen. mgr. N.Am. DuPont Pixel Sys., Wilmington, Del., 1989-92; corp. v.p., divsn. mgr. BTG, Saeffle, Sweden, 1992-95; pres. Accord Groupe, Mercer Island, Wash., 1995—. Mem. Comty. Coun., Seattle, 1988-89. Capt. USAF, 1969-73. Mem. TAPPI, Wash. Athletic Club. Office: Accord Groupe 7683 SE 27th St Ste 342 Mercer Island WA 98040

ALWAN, AMEEN, writing educator; b. Damascus, Syria, July 6, 1930; came to U.S., 1930; s. Muneer and Fausya (Zimberkji) A.; m. Georgia Joy Hueber (div. 1992); 1 child, Yasmine. Student, NYU, 1948-50, U. So. Calif., 1950-52, 56; BA, Mexico City Coll., Mexico, 1957, postgrad. Writing tchr. through workshops, 1974—; poet-in-residence L.A. Ctr. Enriched Studies, 1980—. Contbr. poetry and transls. to numerous jours. With U.S. Army, 1952-54. Grantee Columbia U., 1975, L.A. Cultural Affairs Dept., 1993-96; recipient Artist in Schs. award Calif. Arts Coun., 1980-81, 82-93, 96—. Home and Office: 992 N Madison Ave Pasadena CA 91104-3625

AMALFITANO, ANDREW MICHAEL, advisory reliability manager; b. Bridgeport, Conn., 1954; s. Andrew L. and Florence Amalfitano; m. Melinda Louise Amalfitano, Nov. 5, 1988; children: Owen, Bryn. BS in Physics, Fairfield U., 1976, MA in Edn., 1981. Tchr. secondary math. and physics St. Joseph H.S., Trumbull, Conn., 1976-79; data processer, sys. analyst Plastic Tooling Aids Labs., Boulder, Colo., 1979-81; from staff sys. analyst to adv. reliability engr. StorageTek Corp., Louisville, Colo., 1981-94; adv. devel. mgr. StorageTek Corp., Louisville, 1994—. Author, pub.: First Aid in Schools, 1989, (mag.) Emergency Services Stand-by, 1985-88. Vol., mem. Boulder Emergency Squad (chief, pres. 1985-95, EMT, rescuer, William R. Hughes Founder award, 1995; med. rescuer Cherryvale Fire Dept., Monroe Vol. Emergency Squad, pres. 1976-79. Roman Catholic. Home: PO Box 2311 Boulder CO 80306 Office: StorageTek Corp 2270 S 88th St Stop 2220 Louisville CO 80028

AMATO, CAROL JOY, writer, anthropologist; b. Portland, Oreg., Apr. 9, 1944; d. Sam Lawrence and Lena Dorothy (Dindia) A.; m. Neville Stanley Motts, Aug. 26, 1967 (div. 1978); children: Tracy, Damon. BA, U. Portland, 1966; MA, Calif. State U., 1986. Freelance writer, Westminster, Calif., 1969—; human factor cons. Design Sci. Corp., L.A., 1979-90; dir. software documentation Trans-Ed Communications, Westminster, 1980-84, pres. Advanced Profl. Software, Inc., Westminster, 1984-86, Systems Rsch. Analysis, Inc., Westminster, 1986-95, pres. Stargazer Pub. Co., Westminster, 1995—. Author: The Earth, 1992, Astronomy, 1992, The Human Body, 1992, Inventions, 1992, Inside Out: The Wonders of Modern Technologies Explained, 1992, 50 Nifty Science Fair Projects, 1993, The Super Science Project Book, 1994, The World's Easiest Guide to Using the APA, 1995, The Earth, 1995, Creepy Crawlies, 1995; editor, Cultural Futuristics, 1975-80, numerous articles and short stories; participant in numerous radio and TV interviews. Sec. bd. dirs. Am. Space Meml. Found., L.A., 1986-87; bd. dirs. Orange County Acad. Decathalon, 1986-94. Mem. Ind. Writers of So. Calif. (bd. dirs. Orange County sect. 1986-93), Profl. Writers Orange County (bd. dirs. 1993—, pres. 1994—), Writers' Club of Whittier, Inc., Internat. Pen. Office: Stargazer Pub Co PO Box 2178 Westminster CA 92683

AMAYA, PATRICIA MOJARRO, elementary education educator; b. Orange, Calif., Feb. 25, 1965; d. Guillermo Jimenez and Maria Angelina (Avalos) Mojarro; m. Elias Amaya, Oct. 22, 1988 (dec. Oct. 1993); 1 child, Eliana Ashley. BA in Spanish, U. Calif., Irvine, 1987; postgrad. in writing, Inst. Children's Lit., West Redding, Conn., 1996. Cert. elem. tchr., bilingual, cert. bilingual competence, Calif., 1989. Biliterate instrnl. asst. Franklin Elem. Sch., Santa Ana, Calif., 1986-89, bilingual tchr., 1989-91; bilingual tchr. Alcott Elem. Sch., Pomona, Calif., 1991—. Mem. ASCD, NEA, Calif. Tchrs. Assn., U. Calif.-Irvine Alumnae Assn. Home: 12836 Tehama Cir Riverside CA 92503-4501 Office: Alcott Elem Sch 1600 S Towne Ave Pomona CA 91766-5367

AMBROSE, JANINE LEE, primary school educator; b. Casper, Wyo., Dec. 29, 1964; d. Jerry Lee and Noeleen Judith (Edgeington) Jones; m. Mark Lee Ambrose, July 9, 1994. AS, Casper Coll., 1987; BA, Univ. Wyo., 1988; MEd, No. Ariz. Univ., 1995. Cert. tchr., Ariz. Tchr. Parker (Ariz.) Schs., 1988-91; pre-sch. tchr. Natrona County Headstart, Casper, 1991-92; tchr. Casa Grande (Ariz.) Schs., 1992-94, Pendergast Schs., Phoenix, 1994—; assessment writer Pendergast Schs., Phoenix, 1995-96. Mem. steering com. Pendergast Career Ladder, Phoenix, 1994—; mem. consortium Goals 2000 Com., Phoenix, 1995-96. Mem. ASCD, Assn. Ariz. Tchrs. Para-Profls., Chi Omega (social chmn. 1985—, Order of Owl 1987-88). Democrat. Lutheran. Home: 110 W Mohawk Dr Phoenix AZ 85027 Office: Pendergast Elem Schs 3802 N 91st Ave Phoenix AZ 85037-2368

AMBROSE, JAYASEELAN, cardiovascular physician; b. Peermade, Kerala, India, Nov. 29, 1962; came to U.S., 1971; s. Jebamoni and Victoria Ambrose; m. Reena Henrietta Morris, 1987; 1 child, Jonathan Morris. B Medicine and Surgery, Christian Med. Coll., 1985. Diplomate Am. Bd. Internal Medicine. Rotating resident intern Christian Med. Coll. Hosp., Vellore, India, 1985-86; asst. surgeon Kanyakumari Med. Mission Ch. of South India, Neyoor, India, 1986-89; resident in internal medicine SUNY, Stony Brook, 1989-92, chief resident in internal medicine, 1992-93; fellow in cardiovascular medicine Oreg. Health Scis. U., Portland, 1993-95, U. Calif., San Diego, 1995—; chief med. officer Palmayra Workers Devel. Soc., Marthandam, India, 1986-89. Mem. AMA, ACP, Royal Coll. Physicians London, Am. Coll. Cardiology. Office: U Calif San Diego Med Ctr Divsn Cardiovascular Medicine 200 W Arbor Dr San Diego CA 92103-8411

AMBROSE, THOMAS CLEARY, communications executive; b. Kalispell, Mont., Mar. 6, 1932; s. William Patrick and Anne Marie (Cleary) A.; m. Joyce Leona Demco, Aug. 13, 1960; children: Thomas Neal, John Alan, Bridget Sharon. BA in Journalism, U. Mont., 1952. Editor Choteau (Mont.) Acantha, 1952; reporter Daily Chronicle, Spokane, Wash., 1954-57, bus. editor, 1957-64; rep., mgr. media rels. Weyerhaeuser Co., Tacoma, 1964-74, dir. external communications, 1974-91; prin. Ambrose & Assocs., Seattle and Sun Valley, 1991—. Author, editor: Where The Future Grows, 1989. Pres. Spokane Editorial Soc., 1963-64, Spokane Press Club, 1959-60; dir. Federal Way C. of C., 1968-71, Ketchum/Sun Valley Hist. Soc., 1995-96. 1st lt. U.S. Army, 1952-54, Korea.

AMBROSE, WILLIAM WRIGHT, JR., college dean, accounting educator, tax researcher; b. Norfolk, Va., Oct. 13, 1947; s. William Wright and Charlotte Gertrude (Williamson) A.; m. Marcelia A. Conerly, Aug. 7, 1971 (div. Dec. 1986); children: William Wright III, Xandrea M., Mark S. BSBA, Norfolk State U., 1974; MBA, Pepperdine U., 1982; postgrad., Walden U. Enrolled agt. IRS; lic. ins. broker, notary pub., community coll. teaching credential, Calif. Quality assurance mgr. mfg. Corning (N.Y.) Glass Co., 1974-78; contr., plant mgr. Phillips Auburn, N.Y., 1978-79; sr. exec. mgr. Kerr Glass Corp., L.A., 1979-84; instr. Nat. Edn. Corp., Anaheim, Calif., 1985-87; assoc. prof., chmn. dept. acctg. and bus. DeVry Inst. Tech., Univ. Ctr., Pomona, Calif., 1987—; entrepreneur dba The Tax Inst., 1990; cons. Internat. Transls., Santa Ana, Calif., 1985—, Castillo Electronics, Los Alamitos, Calif., 1986, Heriberto Constrn., Santa Ana, 1985—. Co-patentee polarized contaminate viewer. Sgt. Army Security Agy., U.S. Army, 1967-71, Vietnam. Mem. AAUP, Nat. Assn. Accts., Nat. Bus. Edn. Assn., Am. Acctg. Assn., Am. Mgmt. Assn., Am. Prodn. and Inventory Control Soc., Nat. Soc. Tax Profls., Nat. Soc. Pub. Accts., Phi Beta Lambda, Sigma Beta Delta. Home: 795 S Pampas Ave Rialto CA 92376-2102 Office: DeVry Inst Tech 901 Corporate Center Dr Pomona CA 91768-2642

AMBROSIA, VINCENT GERARD, geographer and researcher; b. Chgo., July 19, 1956; s. Vincent Walter and June Marjorie (Morrissey) A.; m. Mary Ann Murray, Apr. 10, 1982; children: Rachael Louise, Caitlin Marjorie. BS,

Carroll Coll., Waukesha, Wis., 1978; MS, U. Tenn., 1980. Rsch. scientist T.G.S. Tech., Moffett Field, Calif., 1980-89; remote sensing lab. scientist ATAC Inc., Moffett Field, 1989-92; rsch. scientist J.C.W.S., Inc., Moffett Field, 1992—; cons. VGA Cons., San Jose, 1989—. Mem. Assn. Am. Geographers (chmn. remote sensing com.), Nat. Coun. for Geog. Edn. (bd. dirs., mem. remote sensing com.), Gamma Theta Upsilon. Republican. Roman Catholic. Office: JCWS Inc MS 242-4 NASA Ames Rsch Ctr Moffett Field CA 94035

AMDUR, JUDITH DEVORAH, artist, cook; b. Mpls., Sept. 18, 1948; d. Elias Joshua Amdur and Rosalyn Bassis Baker; m. Gary Dennis Jackson, May 26, 1985. BFA, Mpls. Coll. Art and Design, 1974; student, Sch. Painting and Sculpture, Skowhegan, Maine, 1973; MFA, Boston U., 1976. Exhibited in shows at Downey (Calif.) Mus. Art, 1996, LA. Mcpl. Art Gallery, 1996, San Bernardino (Calif.) County Mus., 1997, Armory Ctr. for the Arts, Pasadena, Calif., 1997. Home: 2107 Camorilla Dr Los Angeles CA 90065

AMELIO, GILBERT FRANK, electronics company executive; b. N.Y.C., Mar. 1, 1943; s. Anthony and Elizabeth (DeAngelis) A.; m. Glenda Charlene Amelio; children: Anthony Todd, Tracy Elizabeth, Andrew Ryan; stepchildren: Brent Paul Chappell, Tina LaRae Chappell. B.S. in Physics, Ga. Inst. Tech., 1965, M.S. in Physics, 1967, Ph.D. in Physics, 1968. Tech. dir., cofounder Info. Sci., Atlanta, 1962-65; mem. tech. staff Bell Telephone Labs., Murray Hill, N.J., 1968-71; div. v.p., gen. mgr. Fairchild, Mountain View, Calif., 1971-83; pres. semiconductor products div. Rockwell Internat., Newport Beach, Calif., 1983-88; pres. communication systems Rockwell Internat., Dallas, 1988-91; pres., chief exec. officer Nat. Semicondr. Corp., Santa Clara, Calif., 1991—, chmn., 1995-96; CEO Apple Computer, Inc., Cupertino, Calif., 1996—; mem. nat. adv. bd. Ga. Inst. Tech., Atlanta, 1981-87, Ga. Inst. tech. Rsch. Inst., 1982-89; bd. dirs. SEMATECH Chiron Corp., Emeryville, Calif., Apple Computer; bd. dirs., chmn. Recticon, Pottstown, Pa., 1983-87. Patentee in field. Mem. chief exec. roundtable Univ. Calif., Irvine, 1985-89. Fellow IEEE (chmn. subcom. 1974-81, Masaru Ibuka consumer electronics award 1991); mem. Semiconductor Industry Assn. (bd. dirs. 1983—, vice chmn. 1992, chmn. 1994), Electronic Industries Assn. (bd. govs.), Nat. Assn. Mfrs. (bd. govs.), Bus. Higher Edn. Forum. Republican. Roman Catholic. Home: 1090 Kifer Rd Stop 16-300 Sunnyvale CA 94086-5301 Office: Apple Computer Inc 1 Infinite Loop Cupertino CA 95014*

AMENT, JONATHAN JAY, governmental affairs specialist; b. Sterling, Colo., Dec. 12, 1971; s. Don and Patricia (Gessley) A. BS in Fin., Colo. U., 1994. Nat. cons. PDC Multimedia Prodns., Norman, Okla., 1990-94; pres. J.J. Ament Internat., Denver, 1992—; legis. asst. Congressman Scott McInnis, Washington, 1993; exec. dir. Colo. Assn. Wheat Growers, Englewood, Colo., 1995-96; mem. selection com. Pres. Leadership Class-U. Colo., Boulder, 1995-96; mem. 50 for Colo. Bus. Leaders' Network. Chmn. Young Reps., Arapahoe County, 1996; dir. ops. Don Ament for Congress, Inc., Greeley, Colo., 1995-96; bd. dirs. South Suburban Christian Ch., 1997—; mem. State Bus. and Mktg. Edn. Tech. Com. Mem. Am. Soc. Assn. Execs., Colo. Soc. Assn. Execs. Republican. Mem. Christian Ch. Office: Colo Assn Wheat Growers 5500 S Quebec St Ste 111 Englewood CO 80111-1914

AMERMAN, JOHN W., toy company executive; b. 1932; married. BA, Dartmouth Coll., 1953, MBA, 1954. With Colgate-Palmolive Co., 1958-64, Warner-Lambert Co., 1965-80; v.p. Du Barry Cosmetics, 1971-72, v.p. internat. group, 1972-77, from v.p. to pres. Am. Chicle divsn., 1977-80; pres. Mattel Internat., from 1980; chmn. Mattel Inc., El Segundo, Calif., 1987—; also bd. dirs. Mattel Inc., Hawthorne, Calif.; bd. dirs. Unocal Corp., Vanstar, Phoenix House Calif., Amos Tuck Sch. Dartmouth Coll. Bd. govs. Hugh O'Brian Youth Found. Served with U.S. Army, 1954-57. Office: Mattel Inc 333 Continental Blvd El Segundo CA 90245-5032

AMES, A. GARY, communications company executive; b. 1944. BA, Portland State U., 1967. Acct. supr. Pacific N.W. Bell, 1967-72, with, 1974-83, treas., 1981; dist. mgr. fin. AT&T, N.Y., 1972-74; v.p., treas. U.S. West, Englewood, Colo., from 1983, group v.p., from 1984; chief operating officer, exec. v.p. Mountain State Tel. & Tel. Co., 1986-87; pres. Mountain Bell, Denver, from 1987, also former chief exec. officer; now pres., chief exec. officer U.S. West Comm., Denver. Office: U S West Inc 9785 Maroon Circle Ste 140 Englewood CO 80112*

AMES, RICHARD GALYON, epidemiologist; b. Boston, June 2, 1935; s. Lawrence Marion and Willa Love (Galyon) A.; m. Sue Ann Roedell, June 19, 1971; 1 child, Andrea Elizabeth. BA, George Washington U., 1958; MA, Am. U., 1962; PhD, U. N.C., 1970; MPH, U. Calif., Berkeley, 1980. Instr. sociology U. So. Calif., L.A., 1965-67; asst. prof. sociology Syracuse (N.Y.) U., 1967-69; asst. prof. sociology Calif. State U., Hayward, 1969-71, assoc. prof., 1971-86, prof., 1986-87; epidemiologist, demographer NIOSH, Morgantown, W.Va., 1980-84; epidemiologist Calif. EPA, Berkeley, 1985—. Co-author: The Handicapped Children of Alamance County, 1965, Elementary Statistical Theory in Sociology, 1976; contbr. numerous articles to profl. jours. USPHS fed. trainee, Berkeley, 1979-80; So. Pacific Co., L.A., 1967, U.S. Forest Svc., Hayward, 1978-80. Mem. APHA. Home: 16872 Columbia Dr Castro Valley CA 94552-1614 Office: Calif EPA OEHHA 2151 Berkeley Way # 11 Berkeley CA 94704-1011

AMICO, CHARLES WILLIAM, management consultant; b. Boston, May 6, 1942; s. William Charles and Marie Josephine (Nicholas) A. Assoc. in Engring., Franklin Inst., 1962; BS, Suffolk U., 1968. Jr. chem. technician Avco Corp., Lowell, Mass., 1963-64; advanced vacuum tech. technician Nat. Rsch. Corp., Newton, Mass., 1964-68; semicondr. engr. IBM, Essex Junction, Vt., 1968-72, semicondr. mfg. engring. mgr., 1972-76, mgmt. devel. cons., 1976-86; founder, pres., CEO Creative Directions, Inc., San Francisco, Burlington, Vt., 1982—; bd. dirs. Holiday Project, 1987-88. State chmn. Vt. Hugh O'Brian Youth Leadership Seminar; bd. dirs. Vt. Hugh O'Brian Youth Seminars, Inc., CEO, 1984-85; corp. pres. Hugh O'Brian Youth Found., No. Calif., 1994-95. Recipient Hugh O'Brian Outstanding State Chmn. in Nation award, 1984, 85. Office: Creative Directions Inc PO Box 10101 Zephyr Cove NV 89448

AMINOFF, MICHAEL JEFFREY, medical educator; b. Little Paxton, Eng., May 24, 1941; came to U.S., 1974; s. A.S. and Helena (Cate) A.; m. Janette Dawn Williamson, July 22, 1976; children: Alexandra, Jonathan, Anthony. BSc with honors, U. London, 1962, MB, BS, 1965, MD, 1973. Diplomate Am. Bd. Clin. Neurophysiology. Diplomate Am. Bd. Psychiatry and Neurology. Jr. staff mem. various London teaching hosps., 1965-69; registrar in applied electrophysiology Nat. Hosp., London, 1969-70, registrar and sr. registrar in neurology, 1971-76; registrar in neurology Middlesex Hosp., London, 1970-71; vis. asst. prof. neurology U. Calif., San Francisco, 1974-75, assoc. prof. neurology, 1976-82, prof. neurology, 1982—; dir. clin. neurophysiol. labs., movement disorders clinic, attending physician U. Calif., San Francisco, 1976—. Contbr. some 150 sci. articles to profl. jours., author or editor of 14 med. books. Recipient Queen Square prize for rsch. Inst. of Neurology, London, 1973, Royer award U. Calif. San Francisco, 1991. Fellow Royal Coll. Physicians, Am. Acad. Neurology; mem. Am. Neurol. Assn., Am. EEG Soc. (pres. 1994-95), Am. Acad. Clin. Neurophysiology (pres. 1991-93). Office: U Calif San Francisco 505 Parnassus Ave San Francisco CA 94122-2722

AMIOKA, WALLACE SHUZO, retired petroleum company executive; b. Honolulu, June 28, 1914; s. Tsurumatsu and Reye (Yoshimura) A.; BA, U. Hawaii, 1966, MBA, 1968; m. Ellen Misao Honda, Aug. 9, 1942; children: Carol L. Amioka Price, Joanne M. Amioka Chikuma. With Shell Oil Co., 1931-77, fin. svcs. mgr., Honolulu, 1962-77; pub. affairs cons., Honolulu, 1977-87; gen. ptnr. Pub. Affairs Cons. Hawaii, 1988-94; ret., 1994; lectr. econs. U. Hawaii, 1969-79. Mem. Honolulu Police Commn., 1965-73, vice chmn., 1966, 68, chmn., 1971; U.S. civil adm. Ryuku Islands, 1950-52. Mem. City and County of Honolulu Charter Commn., 1981-82; bd. dirs. Honolulu Symphony Soc., 1968. With M.I., AUS, 1944-48. Mem. M.I. Svc. Vets. (pres. 1981-82), Hawaii C. of C. (chmn. edn. com. 1963-64, chmn. pub. health com. 1966-67), Hui 31 Club, Hui Aikane Club, Honolulu Police Old Timers Club, Phi Beta Kappa, Phi Kappa Phi. Home: 4844 Matsonia Dr Honolulu HI 96816-4014

AMIRKHANIAN, JOHN DAVID, geneticist, researcher, educator; b. Iran, Nov. 10, 1927; came to U.S., 1979; s. Gregor D. and Astghik (Alexandrian) A.; m. Romelia Grigorian, Jan. 30, 1957; children: Varouj, Areg, Aspet. BSc in Biology, Tehran U., 1973; PhD in Genetics, King's Coll., U. London, 1977. Researcher on genetics of insect vectors of diseases Tehran U. Sch. Pub. Health, 1967-70; asst. prof. Sch. of Pub. Health Tehran U., 1977-79; rsch. scientist and assoc. Natural History Mus., L.A., 1980—; vis. prof. U. So. Calif., L.A., 1979-81; mem. faculty, sr. rsch. assoc. UCLA Sch. Medicine-King-Drew Med. Ctr., 1981-92; neonatal lung researcher, surfactant replacement models, mechanisms of lung surfactant damage by oxygen-derived species and glutathione levels and longevity in rats, U. Calif., Davis, 1992—. Fellow Royal Micros. Soc. London, Linnean Soc. London; mem. AAAS, Inst. Biology, Genetics Soc. Eng., N.Y. Acad. Scis., Oxygen Soc. Office: U Calif Sch of Medicine Divsn Neonatology TB 193 Davis CA 95616

AMMIRATO, VINCENT ANTHONY, lawyer; b. Somerville, N.J., Dec. 6, 1942; s. Vincent Salvatore and Elizabeth L. (Masiello) A.; m. Anna Maria Cook, June 19, 1965 (div. Apr. 1994); children: Lisa Maria, Vincent Salvatore II. BA, Long Beach (Calif.) State U., 1968; JD, U. San Diego, 1971. Bar: Calif. 1971, U.S. Supreme Ct. Atty. Buck, Ammirato, and Rutter, Long Beach, 1972-73, 73-88; dep. prosecutor Long Beach Prosecutor, 1973; atty. Burns, Ammirato, Palumbo, Milam & Baronian, Pasadena, Calif., 1989—. V.p. Shadow Park Home Owners Assn., Cerritos, Calif., 1978-83; mem. adv. coun. John Crowley for City Coun., Cerritos, 1988; advisor YMCA, Sacramento, 1993—; bd. dirs., pres. Cerritos-Artesia Little League, 1986-89. With U.S. Army, 1966-68, Germany. Mem. Am. Bd. Trial Advocates, Long Beach Bar Assn., Long Beach C. of C., Los Angeles County Bar Assn., Italian/Am. Lawyers of L.A., Forty-Niner Athletic Assn. Home: 115 Belmont Long Beach CA 90803 Office: Burns Ammirato Palumbo Milam & Baronian 65 N Raymond Ave Pasadena CA 91103

AMNÉUS, JOHN SIGFRID, retired research mechanical engineer; b. Dedham, Mass., Jan. 16, 1917; s. Nils August and Harriet Sofia (Anchersen) A.; m. Carolyn Ann Weaver, July 7, 1946; children: Payton, Mary, John III Richard. BSME, U. Calif., Berkeley, 1940. Registered profl. engr., Calif. Mech. engr. Johnson Drake & Piper Cons., Alameda, Calif., 1941-42; test engr. U. Calif., 1942; design engr. Grove Regulator Co., Emeryville, Calif., 1943; head rsch. design sect. Jet Propulsion Lab., Calif. Inst. Tech., Pasadena, 1944-48; head mech. sect. Rocket Propulsion Lab., U. Mich., Ann Arbor, 1949-51; head mech. sect. rsch. div. Am. Standard, Redwood City, Calif., 1952-55; chief engr. controls div. Am. Standard, Detroit, 1955-59; rsch. engr. Procter and Gamble Co., Cin., 1960-82. Contbr. articles to Parenteral Drug Assn. mag., Jour. TAPPI. Councilman Village of Woodlawn, Ohio, 1963-65, chmn. Planning Commn., 1966-82; chmn. Ohio chpt. Sierra Club, San Francisco, 1965-66. Fellow ASTM (chmn. flexible barrier com. 1976-79), TAPPI (chmn. fluid mechanics com. 1966-68), Watercolor Soc. Oreg. (local chmn. 1987—), Audubon Soc., Nature Conservancy, Masons. Home: 42 N River Dr Roseburg OR 97470-9473

AMOAKO, JAMES KWAKU, transportation services executive, financial analyst; b. Nkwatia, Ghana, Dec. 4, 1951; came to U.S., 1970; s. Kwame and Amma (Nyame) A.; m. Rose Tiokor; children: James Jr., Nicole, Jennifer. AS, Cosumnes River Coll., 1977; BS, Calif. State U., Sacramento, 1978; MBA, Golden Gate U., 1979; PhD, LaSalle U., 1997. Bank examiner Calif. State Banking Dept., San Francisco, 1979-80; fin. analyst Artec Internat. Corp., Mountain View, Calif., 1980-83; cost acct. Sun Microsystems, Mountain View, Calif., 1983-88; pres., CEO Alpha Transp. Corp., Phoenix, Ariz., 1988—. Recipient Svc. award Am. Field Svc., 1970. Home: 8826 W Encanto Blvd Phoenix AZ 85037-3619 Office: Alpha Transp Corp 4024 S 16th St Phoenix AZ 85040-1315

AMOR, SIMEON, JR., photographer; b. Lahaina, Hawaii, Apr. 24, 1924; s. Simeon and Victoria Amor. Grad. high sch., Hilo, Hawaii. Post commdr. Engrs. Post #22, Am. Legion, Honolulu, 1952-53; approp. acct. Hawaii Air Nat. Guard, Honolulu, 1953-64; prodn. control supr. Svc. Bur. Corp., Honolulu, 1964-73; prodn. control computer ops. Bank of Hawaii, Honolulu, 1973-86; owner, propreitor Image Engring., Honolulu, 1986—; historian VFW Dept. Hawaii, Honolulu, 1987-90, 96—, First Filipino Infantry Regiment Hawaii Connection; treas. DAV Dept. Hawaii, Honolulu. Tech. advisor: (film documentary) Untold Triumph, Saga of the American Filipino Soldier. Cpl. U.S. Infantry, 1943-46, master sgt. USNG, 1952-64. Recipient Disting. Svc. award Nat. Disabled Am. Vet., 1992-94, Oahu chpt. Disabled Am. Vet., 1992-94. Mem. Am. Photographer's Internat., VFW. Home: 1634 Kino St Honolulu HI 96819-2651

AMORY, THOMAS CARHART, management consultant; b. N.Y.C., Oct. 29, 1933; s. George Sullivan and Marion Renee (Carhart) A.; m. Elisabeth Andrews Jackson, June, 1956 (div. Mar. 1969); children: Renee Elizabeth, Caroline Carhart, Gillian Brookman; m. Carolyn Marie Pesnell, May 10, 1969 (div. Nov. 1987) ; m. Doris Ruth Mack, Mar. 18, 1989. A.B., Harvard U., 1956. Comml. mgr. N.Y. Telephone Co., N.Y.C., 1957-60; sales mgr. Royce Chem. Co., East Rutherford, N.J., 1960-62; asst. to chmn. Seatrain Lines, Inc., Edgewater, N.J., 1963-65; mgmt. cons. Booz Allen & Hamilton, N.Y.C., 1966-67; ptnr. William H. Clark Assocs., Inc., N.Y.C., 1967-75, pres., 1975-79, chmn., 1979-88; mgmt. cons. Montecito, Calif., 1989—. Trustee Mus. City, N.Y., 1971-92, Santa Barbara Mus. Art, 1990-95, Santa Barbara Chamber Orch., 1991-96, United Boys' and Girls' Clubs of Santa Barbara County, 1995-96. Mem. Santa Barbara Club, Birnam Wood Golf Club, Coral Beach Club (Bermuda). Republican. Roman Catholic. Office: 1187 Coast Village Rd Ste 1-386 Santa Barbara CA 93108-2737

AMOS, WALLY, entrepreneur; b. Tallahassee, Fla., July 1, 1936; s. Wallace Sr. and Ruby Amos; m. Maria LaForey (div.); children: Michael, Gregory; m. Shirlee Ellis (div.); 1 child, Shawn; m. Christine Amos, 1979; 1 child, Sarah. Stockroom clk. Saks Fifth Ave., N.Y.C., 1957-58, stockroom supr., 1958-61; mail room clk. William Morris Agy., N.Y.C., 1961, sec., 1961-62, asst. agt., 1962; talent agt., 1962-67; ind personal mgr. L.A., 1967-75; founder Famous Amos Chocolate Chip Cookie Corp., Hollywood, Calif., 1975-89, Wally Amos Presents: Chip and Cookie, 1991-92, UNCLE Nonamé Cookie Co., 1992—. Author: The Famous Amos Story: The Face That Launched a Thousand Chips, 1983, The Power In You: Ten Secret Ingredients for Inner Strength, 1988, Mau with No Name: Turn Lemons Into Lemonade, 1994. Nat. spokesman Literacy Vols. of Am., 1979. With USAF, 1953-57. Recipient Pres.' award for Entrepreneurial Excellence, 1986, Horatio Alger award 1987, Nat. Literacy Honors award 1990. Office & Home: PO Box 897 Kailua HI 96734-0897*

AMSTUTZ, HARLAN CABOT, orthopaedic surgeon; b. Santa Monica, Calif., July 17, 1931; m. Patricia Price, 1957; children: Julie, Mark, Catherine. BA, UCLA, 1953, MD, 1956. Cert. Calif., N.Y., Am. Bd. Orthopaedic Surgeons. Intern L.A. County Hosp., 1956-57; resident gen. surgery UCLA, 1957-58, resident hosp. spl. surgery-orthopaedics, 1958-61; fellow Royal Nat. Orthopaedic Hosp., London, 1963-64; assoc. scientist Hosp. for Spl. Surgery, N.Y.C., 1964-70, chief prosthetics, 1965-70, dir. bioengring., 1968-70; prof., chief orthopaedics UCLA Med. Ctr., L.A., 1970-89, prof., chief joint replacement, 1970-91, prof. emeritus, 1991—; med. dir. Joint Replacement Inst., L.A., 1991—; lectr. in bioengring. Poly. Inst. Bklyn., N.Y., 1967-70; chief orthopaedic surgery V.A. Wadsworth Med. Ctr., L.A., 1975-89; sci. advisor, mem. Orthomet, Mpls., 1993—. Author: Hip Arthroplasty, 1991; editl. bd. mem. Gaucher's Clin. Perspectives, 1993—, Hip Internat., 1993—, The Knee, 1993—; inventor in field. Capt. USAF, 1961-63. Fellow ACS; mem. Am. Acad. Orthopaedic Surgeons (chmn. com. on biomed. engring. 1978-81), Am. Orthopaedic Assn. (pres. 1992-93), Assn. Bone and Joint Surgeons (pres. 1984-85, Nicolas Andry award 1987), Orthopaedic Rsch. Soc. (pres. 1973), Internat. Hip Soc., The Hip Soc. (pres., exec. com. 1979-80, John Charnley award 1977, 84, 90, 94, Otto Aufranc award 1979), Phi Beta Kappa. Office: Joint Replacement Inst 2400 S Flower St Fl 3 Los Angeles CA 90007-2629

AMUNDSON, EVA DONALDA, civic worker; b. Langdon, N.D., Apr. 23, 1911; d. Elmer Fritjof and Alma Julia (Nelson) Hultin; m. Leif Amundson, Mar. 1, 1929 (dec. 1974); children: Constance, Eleanor, Ardis, Priscilla. Bd. dirs. Opportunity Workshop, Missoula, Mont., 1950—, Rockmont Group Homes, Missoula, 1976—, Bethany L'Arche (group home for girls), 1976—; sec. bd. dirs. Opportunity Industries, 1990-91, pres. 1991—; mem. Missoula Sr. Citizen's Ctr., 1980-82, 88—, pres., 1982-85, bd. dirs., 1988—; tchr. Norwegian cooking and baking, 1954-56, Norweigan Rosemaling, 1975-79; treas. Sacakawea Homemakers Club, 1979-81; mem. Am. Luth. Ch. Women St. Pauls' Lutheran Ch., 1951—; active Easter Seal Program, Heart Fund, March of Dimes, United Way, Campfire Girls; mem. adv. council Area Agy. on Aging, Missoula, 1984—. Recipient Outstanding Sr. award Missoula Jr. C. of C., 1984. Mem. Sons. of Norway (sec. 1989—), Orchard Homes Country Club (mem. art judging com.), Order of Eastern Star, Elks. Avocations: rosemaling, oil painting, poetry. Home: 324 Kensington Ave Missoula MT 59801-5726

AN, HAEJUNG, food technology educator; b. Seoul, Republic of Korea, May 13, 1958; came to U.S., 1981; d. Sung-Ho Ahn and Seung-Ah Park; m. Thomas A. Seymour, June 18, 1986; 1 child, Jillian A. BS, Seoul Nat. U., 1981; MS, La. State U., 1984; PhD, U. Fla., 1989. Postdoctoral U. Fla., Gainesville, 1989-90; asst. prof. Oreg. State U., Astoria, 1991—. Contbr. articles to profl. jours. Grantee Oreg. State U., 1991-93, Sea, 1993-97, USDA, 1993-98. Mem. Am. Inst. Fihsery Rsch. Biologists, Isnt. Food Technologists. Home: 2272 Manion Dr Warrenton OR 97146-9784 Office: Oreg State U Seafood Lab 250 36th St Astoria OR 97103-2403

ANACKER, EDWARD WILLIAM, retired chemistry educator; b. Chgo., June 2, 1921; s. Edward Frederick and Nellie Adelaide (Adolfs) A.; m. Stella Evelyn Lillo, Jan. 16, 1945; children: Steven Edward, David Carlyle, Eric Roland, John William. BS, Mont. State Coll., 1943; PhD, Cornell U., 1949. Instr. Mont. State Coll., Bozeman, 1949-52, asst. prof., 1952-58, assoc. prof., 1958-63, prof. chemistry, 1963-91, prof. emeritus, 1991—, head chemistry dept., 1972-77; summer participant Oak Ridge (Tenn.) Inst. Nuclear Studies, summer 1957; vis. prof. NSF Sci. Faculty Fellowship, U. Oreg., Eugene, 1964-65. Contbr. articles to profl. jours. Ensign USN, 1944-46, PTO. Named one of 100 Soc. Centennial Alumni, Mont. State U., Bozeman, 1993; grantee Rsch. Corp., 1950-56, Petroleum Rsch. Fund, 1957-60, Bur. of Reclamation, 1961-66, NSF, 1960-72, Mont. State U., 1981. Mem. Am. Chem. Soc. (chmn. Mont. sect. 1952-53, 67-68), Mont. Acad. Scis. (pres. 1959-60), Sigma Xi (pres. Mont. chpt. 1973-74, faculty rsch. award 1967), Phi Kappa Phi, Alpha Chi Sigma. Lutheran. Office: Montana State U Bozeman MT 59717

ANAND, SURESH CHANDRA, physician; b. Mathura, India, Sept. 13, 1931; came to U.S., 1957, naturalized, 1971; s. Satchit and Sumaran (Bai) A. m. Wiltrud, Jan. 29, 1966; children: Miriam, Michael. MB, BS, King George's Coll., U. Lucknow (India), 1954; MS in Medicine, U. Colo., 1962. Diplomate Am. Bd. Allergy and Immunology. Fellow pulmonary diseases Nat. Jewish Hosp., Denver, 1957-58, resident in chest medicine, 1958-59, chief resident allergy-asthma, 1960-62; intern Mt. Sinai Hosp., Toronto, Ont., Can., 1962-63, resident in medicine, 1963-64, chief resident, 1964-65, demonstrator clin. technique, 1963-64, U. Toronto fellow in medicine, 1964-65; rsch. assoc. asthma-allergy Nat. Jewish Hosp., Denver, 1967-69; clin. instr. medicine U. Colo., Denver, 1967-69; internist Ft. Logan Mental Health Ctr., Denver, 1968-69; pres. Allergy Assocs. & Lab., Ltd., Phoenix, 1974—; mem. staff Phoenix Bapt. Hosp., chmn. med. records com., 1987; mem. staff St. Joseph's Hosp., St. Luke's Hosp., Human Hosp., John C. Lincoln Hosp., Good Samaritan Hosp., Phoenix Children's Hosp., Tempe St. Luke Hosp., Desert Samaritan Hosp., Mesa Luth. Hosp., Scottsdale Meml. Hosp., Phoenix Meml. Hosp., Chandler (Ariz.) Regional Hosp., Valley Luth. Hosp., Mesa, Ariz.; pres. NJH Fed. Credit Union, 1967-68. Contbr. articles to profl. jours. Mem. Camelback Hosp. Mental Health Ctr. Citizens Adv. Bd., Scottsdale, Ariz., 1974-80; mem. Phoenix Symphony Coun., 1973-90; mem. Ariz. Opera Co., Boyce Thmpson Southwestern Arboretum; mem. Ariz. Hist. Soc., Phoenix Arts. Mus., Smithsonian Inst. Fellow ACP, Am. Coll. Chest Physicians (crit. care com.), Am. Acad. Allergy, Am. Assn. Cert. Allergists, Am. Coll. Allergy and Immunology (aerobiology com., internat. com., pub. edn. com. 1991-94); mem. AAAS, AMA, Internat. Assn. Allergy and Clin. Immunology, Ariz. Med. Assn., Ariz. Allergy Soc. (v.p. 1988-90, pres. 1990-91), Maricopa County Med. Soc. (del. ariz. Med. Assn., bd. dirs. 1996-98, exec. com. 1996-98), West Coast Soc. Allergy and Immunology, Greater Phoenix Allergy Soc. (v.p. 1984-86, pres. 1986-88, med. adv. team sports medicine Ariz. State U.), Phoenix Zoo, N.Y. Acad. Scis., World Med. Assn., Internat. Assn. Asthmology, Assn. Care of Asthma, Ariz. Thoracic Soc., Nat. Geog. Soc., Ariz. Wild Life Assn., Village Tennis Club. Office: 1006 E Guadalupe Rd Tempe AZ 85283-3044 also: 6550 East Broadway Ste 206 Mesa AZ 85206-1752 also: 7331 E Osborn Dr Ste 340 Scottsdale AZ 85251-6422

ANANG, KOFI, artistic director, educator, dancer; b. Pakro, Ghana. Degree, U. Ghana, 1971. Lead dancer Profl. OBOADE African Music and Dance Co., 1972-77; instr. African dance and music U. Washington, 1973-74; instr. African games and music Everybody's Creative Arts Ctr., Oakland, Calif., 1978; instr. W. African dance and drumming Madrona Dance Studio, 1978; instr. W. African games and drumming Langston Hughes Cultural Arts Ctr., Seattle, 1978-80; artistic dir., master drummer, dancer Ocheami-Afrikan Dance Co., Seattle, 1978—; rschr. devels. in music and dance, Ghana and Nigeria; founder Internat. Directory Black and African Choreographers; African music instr. Prescott (Ariz.) Coll., 1993, 94; dance accompanist Cornish Coll. Arts, Seattle, 1993—. Creative designer, musician (play) Sigi- Three W. African Stories, 1994; numerous appearances worldwide. Inst. African Studies scholar. Office: Ocheami Afrikan Dance Co PO Box 31635 Seattle WA 98103*

ANASTASI, MICHAEL ANTON, journalist; b. Kitzbuhel, Tirol, Austria, Sept. 15, 1965; s. Antone Frank and Waltraud (Salinger) A; m. Julie Hibbs Anastasi, Nov. 18, 1995; 1 child, Grace Antonia. BA in Internat. Rels., U. Calif., Davis, 1988; Journalism, Calif. State U., Long Beach. Reporter The Daily Democrat, Woodland, Calif., 1984-85, dep. sports editor, 1985-87; sports editor The Davis (Calif.) Ent., 1987-93; asst. sports editor L.A. Dailey News, 1993-95, sports editor, 1995—. Recipient 1st prize best sports sect. Calif. Newspaper Pubrs. Assn., 1990, APSE award, (Best Dailey News section, 1995, honorable mention, Best spl. section under 175,000, 1993, 1st place and honorable mention, Best interprise reporting, under 50,000, 1993, 4th place columnist under 50,000, honorable mention, 1989);Best sports columns award (Nat. Newspaper Assn., 2nd, 1992, hon. mention, 1993),Best sports pages, (3rd 1993, N.M., 1992). Mem. Soc. Profl. Journalists (1st place best columnist, 1991, 93, 94,), AP Sports Editors. Roman Catholic. Office: LA Daily News 21221 Oxnard St Woodland Hills CA 91367

ANASTASIA, PAULA JEAN, oncological nurse; b. Lawrenceburg, Ind., Nov. 16, 1960; d. Peter Francis and Ruth Evelyn (Gill) A.; m. Martin James Davis, Dec. 31, 1988. BS, Hanover (Ind.) Coll., 1983; BSN, Rush U., 1983; M in Nursing, UCLA, 1993. RN, Calif., La. Gynecology/oncology clin. nurse specialist UCLA, 1993—, clin. instr., 1993—, assoc. prof. Sch. Nursing, 1995—. Contbr. articles to profl. jours. Vol. Am. Cancer Soc., Culver City, Calif. Mem. Oncology Nursing Soc., Soc. Gynecologic Nurse Oncologists, Calif. Nurses Assn., Nat. League for Nursing, Sigma Theta Tau. Democrat. Roman Catholic. Office: UCLA Med Ctr 10833 Le Conte Ave Los Angeles CA 90024-1602

ANASTASIOU, MARY M., pediatrician; b. Leicester, U.K., June 11, 1954; came to U.S., 1980; d. Thalis and Elli Michaelides; m. Stephen Anastasiou, Jan. 4, 1980; children: Alex, Christine. MD, U. Athens, Greece, 1979. Intern, resident Kaiser Hosp., Oakland, Calif., 1982-85; pvt. practice Pleasanton, Calif., 1985—. Mem. Am. Acad. Pediatrics (Chpt. 1), Calif. Med. Assn., Alameda Contra Costa Med. Assn. Home: 3501 Kamp Dr Pleasanton CA 94588-2632 Office: 5565 W Las Positas Blvd Ste 240 Pleasanton CA 94588-4001

ANAWALT, PATRICIA RIEFF, anthropologist; b. Ripon, Calif., Mar. 10, 1924; d. Edmund Lee and Anita Esto (Capps) Rieff; m. Richard Lee Anawalt, June 8, 1945; children: David, Katherine Anawalt Arnoldi, Harmon Fred. BA in Anthropology, UCLA, 1957, MA in Anthropology, 1971, PhD in Anthropology, 1975. Cons. curator costumes and textiles Mus. Cultural History UCLA, 1975-90, dir. Ctr. for Study Regional Dress, Fowler Mus. Cultural History, 1990—; trustee S.W. Mus., L.A., 1978-92; rsch. assoc. The San Diego Mus. Man, 1980—, UCLA Inst. Archaeology, 1994—; trustee Archaeol. Inst. Am., U.S., Can., 1983-95, traveling lectr., 1975-86, 94-96, Pres.'s Lectureship, 1993-94, Charles E. Norton lectureship, 1996-97; cons. Nat. Geog. Soc., 1980-82, Denver Mus. Natural History,

1992-93; apptd. by U.S. Pres. to Cultural Property Adv. Com., Washington, 1984-93; fieldwork Guatemala, 1961, 70, 72, Spain, 1975, Sierra Norte de Puebla, Mex., 1983, 85, 88, 89, 91. Author: Indian Clothing Before Cortés: Mesoamerican Costumes from the Codices, 1981, paperback edit., 1990; co-author: The Codex Mendoza, 4 vols., 1992 (winner Archaeol. Inst. Am. 1994 James Wiseman Book award), The Essential Codex Mendoza, 1996; contbr. articles to profl. jours. Adv. com Textile Mus., Washington, 1983-87. grantee NEH, 1990, 96, J. Paul Getty Found. 1990, Nat. Geog. Soc., 1983, 85, 88, 89, 91, Ahmanson Found., 1996; Guggenheim fellow, 1988. Fellow Am. Anthrop. Assn.; mem. Centre Internat. D'Etude Des Textiles Anciens, Am. Ethnol. Soc., Soc. Am. Archaeology, Soc. Women Geographers (Outstanding Achievement award 1993), Textile Soc. Am. (bd. dirs. 1992-96, co-coord. 1994 biennial symposium). Office: Fowler Mus Cultural History Ctr Study of Regional Dress Los Angeles CA 90095-1549

ANCHES, JERRY, investment company executive; b. Seattle, June 15, 1939; s. Irving and Reyna (Cohn) A.; (div.); children: Jennifer, Eric, Aaron. BA, U. Calif., Berkeley, 1961. Mng. ptnr. Shelby Co., Seattle, 1963—, Seattle Union St. Assoc., 1978-83; pres. Martin Warehousing and Distbn., Honolulu, 1983—. Dir. Big Bros. of Seattle, 1965-73, Pacific New Ballet, Seattle, 1979-83, Seattle Opera, 1991-93; pres. Jewish Family Svc., Seattle, 1974-77; chmn. Anti Defamation League, Seattle, 1980-83. Lt. U.S. Army, 1965-68. Mem. Washington Athletic Club, Seattle Yacht Club. Home: 8762 Sand Point Way NE Seattle WA 98115-3951 Office: 801 Pine St Seattle WA 98101

ANCOLI-ISRAEL, SONIA, psychologist, researcher; b. Tel Aviv, Israel, Dec. 25, 1951; came to U.S., 1955.; m. Andrew G. Israel; 2 children. BA, SUNY, Stony Brook, 1972; MA, Calif. State U., Long Beach, 1974; PhD, U. Calif., San Francisco, 1979. Lic. psychologist, Calif. Staff psychologist U. Calif. San Diego, La Jolla, 1979-84, asst. adj. prof., 1984-88, assoc. prof., 1988-94; prof., 1994—; assoc. dir. Sleep Disorders Ctr., VA Med. Ctr., San Diego, 1981-92, dir., 1992—. Author: All I Want Is A Good Night's Sleep, 1996; contbr. over 200 articles to profl. jours. Mem. bd. mgrs. Jewish Cmty. Ctr., La Jolla, 1985-91; mem. exec. bd. Nat. Sleep Found., 1990-95. Recipient Robert E. Harris Meml. award, U. Calif., San Franicsco, 1978. Mem. AAAS, Sleep Rsch. Soc. (bd. dirs. 1993-96), Am. Sleep Disorders Assn., Soc. for Light Treatment and Biol. Rhythms (bd. dirs. 1994-97), Gerontol. Soc. Am., Soc. Psychophysiol. Rsch., N.Y. Acad. Scis.

ANCONA, GEORGE E., photographer, film producer, author; b. N.Y.C., Dec. 4, 1929; s. Ephraim Jose and Emma Graziana (Diaz) A.; m. Helga Von Sydow, July 20, 1968; children: Lisa, Gina, Tomas, Isabel, Marina, Pablo. Student, Academia de San Carlos, Mexico, 1949, Art Students League, 1950, Cooper Union Sch. Design, 1950. Art dir. Esquire Inc., N.Y.C., 1951-53, Seventeen mag., N.Y.C., 1953-54, Grey Advt. Agy., N.Y.C., 1954-58, Daniel & Charles Advt. Agy., N.Y.C., 1958-60; free lance photographer, film producer N.Y.C., 1960—; lectr. graphic design, photography Rockland Community Coll., 1973—, Parsons Sch. Design, 1974—, Sch. Visual Arts, 1978—. Author: Handtalk, 1974, Monsters on Wheels, 1974, What Do You Do?, 1976, I Feel, 1977, Growing Older, 1978, It's A Baby!, 1979, Dancing Is, 1981, Bananas, from Maolo to Margie, Team Work, 1983, Monster Movers, Sheepdog, Helping Out, Freighters, 1985, Handtalk Birthday, 1986 (N.Y. Times 10 Best Illustrated Children's Books of Yr.), Turtle Watch, 1987, The American Family Famr, 1989, Handtalk Zoo, 1989, Riverkeeper, 1990, Harry's Helicopter, 1990, Handtalk School, 1991, The Aquarium Book, 1991, Man and Mustang, 1992, Pow Wow, 1992, My Camera, 1992, Pablo Remembers, 1993, The Pinatamaker, 1994, The Golden Lion Tamarin Comes Home, 1994, Fiesta U.S.A., 1995, Cutters, Carvers & the Catherdral, 1995, Sally's Submarine, 1995, Earth Daughter, 1995, Mayeros, 1997. *Curiosity is the biggest element in my work. Watching people and making contact through my photographs have given me a sense of myself. My work keeps me in touch with the world around me. Whether a person bakes, builds, sings or drives, people reach one another in their own way. Mine is taking pictures. Reaching out to others ... I think that's what living is all about.*

ANDARY, THOMAS JOSEPH, biochemist; b. Sault Sainte Marie, Mich., Oct. 8, 1942; s. Joseph Boula and Marion (Schwifetti) A. BS, No. Mich. U., 1966, MA, 1968; PhD, Wayne State U., 1974. Instr. biology No. Mich. U., Marquette, 1967-69; rsch. assoc. physiology Wayne State U., Detroit, 1973-76; sr. rsch. scientist, mgr. coagulation research Hyland Labs., Costa Mesa, Calif., 1976-83; dir. quality control Hyland Therapeutics, Glendale, Calif., 1983-90; dir. quality assurance and regulatory affairs Baxter/Hyland Div., Glendale, 1990-91; v.p. quality assurance and regulatory affairs, 1991—, responsible head, 1993-96; cons. in regulatory affairs/quality assurance to biopharmaceutical industry, 1996—; lectr. in field. Mem. Parenteral Drug Assn. NDEA fellow, 1969-72. Mem. Am. Chem. Soc., N.Y. Acad. Sci., Internat. Assn. Biol. Standardization, Drug Info. Assn., Sigma Xi (Rsch. award 1973). Roman Catholic. Contbr. over 25 articles to profl. publs. Home and Office: 531 N Canyon Blvd Monrovia CA 91016-1707

ANDERBERG, ROY ANTHONY, journalist; b. Camden, N.J., Mar. 30, 1921; s. Arthur R. and Mary V. (McHugh) A.; m. Louise M. Brooks, Feb. 5, 1953; children: Roy, Mary. AA, Diablo Valley Coll., 1975. Enlisted USN, 1942, commd. officer, 1960, ret., 1970; waterfront columnist Pacific Daily News, Agana, Guam, 1966-67; pub. rels. officer Naval Forces, Marianas Islands, 1967; travel editor Contra Costa (Calif.) Times, 1968-69; entertainment and restaurant editor Concord (Calif.) Transcript, 1971-75; entertainment editor Contra Costa Advertiser, 1975-76; dining editor Rossmoor News, Walnut Creek, Calif., 1977-78; free-lance non-fiction journalist, 1976—. Recipient Best Feature Story award Guam Press Assoc., 1966. Mem. VFW, DAV, U.S. Power Squadron, Ret. Officers Assn., Am. Legion, U.S. Submarine Vets. WWII (state comdr., regional dir., nat. 2d v.p.), Naval Submarine League (XO), Martinez Yacht Club (charter), Rossmoor Yacht Club (commodore 1995), Toastmasters. Democrat. Home: 1840 Tice Creek Dr Apt 2228 Walnut Creek CA 94595-2460 Office: PO Box 52 Concord CA 94522-0052

ANDEREGG, RONALD HENRY, artist; b. Portland, Oreg., Mar. 22, 1939; s. Henry Herman and Isabel (Dimbat) A. Designer, artist Walt Disney Entertainment, Burbank, Calif., 1962; soldier, artist U.S. Army, Washington, 1963-64; comml. artist Richter/Mracky Advt. Agy., L.A., 1965-72, Anderegg/Thornton Design Studio, L.A., 1972-85; fine artist, painter, sculptor L.A., 1986—; creative art dir., graphic designer Max Factor Point of Purchase Displays and Catalogs, Hollywood, Calif., 1965-85. designer display for John F. Kennedy, 1963, Max Factor Mus., 1985. Home and Office: 8101 Laurelmont Dr Los Angeles CA 90046-1511

ANDERS, WILLIAM ALISON, aerospace and defense manufacturing executive; b. Hong Kong, Oct. 17, 1933; s. Arthur Ferdinand and Muriel Florence (Adams) A.; m. Valerie Elizabeth Hoard, June 26, 1955; children: Alan Frank, Glen Thomas, Gayle Alison, Gregory Michael, Eric William, Diana Elizabeth. BS, U.S. Naval Acad., Annapolis, 1955; MS in Nuclear Engring., U.S. Inst. Tech., Wright-Patterson AFB, 1962. Commnd. 2d lt. U.S. Air Force, 1955, pilot, engr., 1955-69; astronaut NASA-Johnson Space Ctr., Houston, 1963-69, Apollo 8, 1st lunar flight, 1968; exec. sec. Nat. Aero. and Space Council, Washington, 1969-73; commr. AEC, Washington, 1973-74; chmn. Nuclear Regulatory Commn., Washington, 1975-76; U.S. Ambassador to Norway, 1976-77; v.p., gen. mgr. nuclear energy products div. Gen. Electric Co., 1977-80; v.p., gen. mgr. aircraft equipment div. Gen. Electric Co., DeWitt, N.Y., 1980-84; sr. exec., v.p. ops. Textron Inc., Providence, R.I., 1984-89; vice chmn. Gen. Dynamics, St. Louis, 1990-91; chmn., CEO Gen. Dynamics, 1991—; chmn. bd. dirs. N000, 1993—; pres. Apogee Group. Trustee Battell Meml. Inst. Maj. gen. USAFR, 1983-88. Decorated various mil. awards; recipient Wright, Collier, Goddard and Arnold flight awards; co-holder several world flight records. Mem. Soc. Exptl. Test Pilots, Nat. Acad. Engring., Tau Beta Pi. Office: Apogee Group PO Box 1630 Eastsound WA 98245

ANDERSEN, DALE GORDON, academic administrator; b. Gopher, S.D., Oct. 4, 1933; s. Andrew and Mildred Andersen; m. Sharon Lee Hippler, Dec. 28, 1958; children: David Scott, Julie Kay, Brian Douglas. BS, Mont. State U., 1955, MEd, 1958; MEd, U. So. Calif., 1961; EdD, Ariz. State U., 1964. Asst. prof. edn. U. Mont., Missoula, 1964-66; from asst. prof. to prof., chmn. dept., acting dean Coll. Edn. Wash. State U., Pullman, 1966-84; dean Coll. of Edn. U. Nev., Las Vegas, 1984-96, provost's spl. advisor, 1996—; cons. Heuristic Systems, Inc., Tempe, Ariz., 1970-75; invited speaker, lectr. various orgns. Contbr. articles to profl. jours. Served with U.S. Army, 1955-57. Mem. APA, Assn. Colls. and Schs. of Edn. in State Univs. and Land Grant Colls. and Affiliated Pvt. Univs. (nat. sec. 1987-90, pres. elect 1991-92, pres. 1992-94, past pres. 1994-95), Am. Assn. Colls. for Tchr. Edn. (exec. bd. 1992-94, pres.-elect 1996-97, pres. 1997-98), Phi Delta Kappa (chpt. pres. 1990-91). Methodist. Home: 5504 Indian Hills Ave Las Vegas NV 89130 Office: U Nev Coll of Edn 4505 S Maryland Pky Las Vegas NV 89154-3001

ANDERSEN, FRANCES ELIZABETH GOLD, religious leadership educator; b. Hot Springs, Ark., Feb. 11, 1916; d. Benjamin Knox and Pearl Scott (Smith) Gold; m. Robert Thomas Andersen, June 27, 1942; children: Nancy Ruth (Mrs. Bernd Neumann), Robert Thomas. BA, UCLA, 1936, sec. teaching credential, 1937. Tchr. math. L.A. City Schs., 1937-42, 46-48; faculty Ariz. State Coll., Tempe, 1943-45; mem. nat. bd. missions United Meth. Ch., 1940-44; dir. Christian edn. 1st Presbyn. Ch., Phoenix, 1943-45, Trinity Meth. ch., L.A., 1953-55, 1st Bapt. Ch., Lakewood, Calif., 1955-57; dir. Christian edn. Grace Bapt. Ch., Riverside, 1958-83, chmn. nursery sch. bd., 1969-83; mem. nat. bd. Bible sch. and youth Bapt. Gen. Conf., 1966-71; coord. leadership tng. insts. Greater L.A. Sunday Sch. Assn., 1956-80; exec. dir. San Bernardino-Riverside Sunday Sch. Assn., 1959—; prin. Riverside Christian Sch., 1985-87, bd. dirs., 1985—; mem. Christian edn. bd. S.W. Bapt. Conf., 1956-59, 63-66, 72-75, 80-83; bd. dirs. GLASS, 1956—; dir. Women's guild, Calif. Bapt. Coll., Riverside, 1983-96. Author: How to Organize Area Leadership Training Institutes, 1964. Pres. Univ. Jr. H.S., PTA, Riverside, 1963-64, Poly. H.S., PTA, 1965-67; life mem. PTA; judge Nat. Sunday Sch. Tchrs. Awards, 1993-95. Named Grace Bapt. Mother of Yr., 1981, People Who Make a Difference Press-Enterprise, 1984, One of Outstanding Women of Riverside, Calif. Bapt. Coll., 1985. Mem. Sons of Norway, Alpha Delta Chi (nat. pres. 1950-51, exec. sec. 1952-54), Pi Mu Epsilon. Home: 1787 Prince Albert Dr Riverside CA 92507-5852 *Serving the Lord brings joy and fulfillment—working together with God's dedicated servants; witnesssing lives transformed by the power of the Holy Spirit; seeing children, youth and adults grow in grace and in the knowledge of God as they are taught God's Word.*

ANDERSEN, LUBA, electrologist, electropigmentologist; b. Germany, Mar. 29, 1945; came to U.S., 1955; d. Osyp and Justyna (Drozd) Nahorniak; m. Roger A. Andersen, Dec. 9, 1989. A in Bus. and Acctg., DePaul U., 1977; BS in Commerce and Social Studies, LaSalle U., 1978; postgrad., U. Mich., 1984; cert., Ariz. Inst. Electrolysis, 1993. Cert. profl. electrologist, clin. electropigmentologist. From analyst to contr. Fed. Home Loan Bank, Chgo., 1965-83, v.p., contr., 1985-92; owner electrolysis and permanent cosmetic enhancement clinic The Electrolysis Connection, Tucson, 1993—. Mem. NAFE, Am. Soc. Women Accts. (chairperson bylaws com. 1981), Am. Electrology Assn., Electrologists Assn. Ill., Internat. Guild Profl. Electrologists, Inc., Fin. Mgrs. Soc., Soc. Cosmetic Profls., Assn. Clin. Electropigmentologists. Republican. Roman Catholic. Office: Electrolysis Connection 3131 N Country Club Rd Ste 110 Tucson AZ 85716-1637

ANDERSEN, ROBERT, health products business executive; b. Bklyn., Oct. 9, 1937; s. Ingulf Bertel Andersen and Helen Jane Akin (McDowell) Miller; m. Elaine Marie Wood, June 13, 1958; children: Susan Marie, Robert Alan, Dori Ann. Grad. h.s., La Mesa, Calif. Area sales mgr. Golden Arrow Dairy, San Diego, 1958-66; retail sales mgr. Hollandia Dairy, San Marcos, Calif., 1966-69; pres. Health Best Inc., San Marcos, 1969—; founding ptnr. Escondido Mills, San Marcos, 1980—; owner, operator Andersen Trading Co., Valley Center, Calif., 1984—; ptnr. Earth Products, Valley Center, 1989—; founding ptnr. Elaina's Snacks, San Marcos, 1991—; owner, operator Andersen Gallery, Valley Center, 1992—. Bd. dirs. Russian Art Guild, San Diego, 1992—; exec. v.p. Kamut Assn. N.Am., San Marcos, 1990-97, pres., 1997—. Republican. Home: 30126 Castlecrest Dr Valley Center CA 92082-4923 Office: Health Best 295 Distribution St San Marcos CA 92069-4359

ANDERSEN, TORBEN BRENDER, optical researcher, astronomer, software engineer; b. Naestved, Denmark, May 17, 1954; came to U.S., 1983; U.S. citizen, 1994; s. Bjarne and Anna Margrethe (Brender) A.; m. Alice Louise Palmer, Nov. 3, 1990; children: Iris, Erik. PhD, Copenhagen U., Denmark, 1979. Rsch. fellow Copenhagen U., 1980-82, sr. rsch. fellow, 1982-85; optical cons. Nordic Optical Telescope Assn., Roskilde, Denmark, 1985; optical systems analyst Telos Corp., Santa Clara, Calif., 1985-88; rsch. scientist Lockheed Martin Missiles and Space, Palo Alto, Calif., 1988—, staff scientist, 1993-95, sr. staff scientist, 1995-96; staff software engr. Lockheed Martin Missiles and Space, 1996—; vis. scholar Optical Scis. Ctr., U. Ariz., Tucson, 1983-85. Editor: Astronomical Papers Dedicated to Bengt Strömgren, 1978; contbr. articles to Jour. Quantitative Spectroscopy Radiation Transfer, Applied Optics, Astronomische Nachrichten. Mem. Optical Soc. Am., Internat. Astron. Union, Soc. Photo-Optical Instrumentation Engrs. Office: Lockheed Martin Advanced Tech Ctr O/H1-52 3251 Hanover St # 254G Palo Alto CA 94304-1191

ANDERSON, ARTHUR GEORGE, laboratory director, former computer company executive, consultant; b. Evanston, Ill., Nov. 22, 1926; s. Arthur G. and Margaret (Bree) A.; m. Eliza Chavez Heninger, 1975; children: Joseph S., Robin R., Jennifer M. B.S., U. San Francisco, 1947-49; M.S., Northwestern U., 1951; Ph.D., NYU, 1958. With IBM Corp., 1951-84, head numerous engring. and managerial positions, 1951-65; staff dir. corporate tech. com. IBM Corp., Armonk, N.Y., 1965-67; dir. research IBM Corp., Yorktown, N.Y., 1967-69; v.p., dir. research IBM Corp., Yorktown, 1969-70; dir. tech. assessment IBM Corp., 1971-72; pres. Gen. Products div. IBM Corp., San Jose, Calif., 1972-79, 82-83; v.p., group exec. Data Products group IBM Corp., White Plains, N.Y., 1979-81; ret., 1984—; dir. Compression Labs. Inc., 1984—; chmn. bd. dirs. Compression Labs., 1996—. Served with USNR, 1944-46. Fellow Am. Phys. Soc. (Pake award 1984), IEEE; mem. AAAS, Nat. Acad. Engring. Home: PO Box 1032 Prescott AZ 86302-1032

ANDERSON, ARTHUR LEE, sculptor, writer; b. Washington, Nov. 28, 1952; s. Kenneth Arthur and Marjorie Ruth (Anderson) A.; m. Marion Mann, Oct. 18, 1981 (div. Nov. 1987); 1 child, Tanya Leah. Grad., Gemological Inst. Am., Santa Monica, Calif., 1986. Importer Washington, 1971-75; contractor New Orleans, 1976-80; deckhand Chotin Shipping Co., New Orleans, 1980-81; gem cutter, sculptor Speira Gems, Ashland, Oreg., 1984—; vol. spkr. on gemstone-related topics, pub. schs., Ashland, 1990—; bd. mem. Gemartists N.Am., 1996; judge Am. Gem Trading Assn. cutting edge competition, 1996. Editor Gemartists N.Am. Newsletter, 1995, 96; contbr. tech. articles to Gems and Gemology, Lapidary Jour. Recipient 1st pl. for creative gem cut Am. Gem Trade Assn., 1992, 1st pl. for objet d'art, 1993, 2d pl. fancy gem cut, 1994, 3d pl. pairs and suites, 1994, 1st pl. pairs and suites, 1995, others. Libertarian. Office: Speira Gems PO Box 849 Ashland OR 97526

ANDERSON, ARTHUR SALZNER, publishing company executive, marketing executive; b. Boise, Idaho, Jan. 17, 1923; s. Howard Ballantyne and Mildred Ina (Salzner) A.; m. Janice Virginia Jacobsen, June 21, 1948; children: Roger Bruce, Gregory Bryan, Julie Janice Olsen, Lane Jacobsen, Margaret Virginia Ence, Heidi Gail Eldredge, Steven Jacobsen. B.A., U. Utah, 1947. Sales promotion asst. Internat. Harvester Co., 1947-48, zone mgr., 1948-51; sr. v.p., dir., chmn. exec. com. Evans Communications, Inc., Salt Lake City, 1977-84, dir., chmn. exec. com., 1984-87, pres., 1984-87; chmn. bd. Panoram Prodns., 1977-82; pres. Deseret Book Co., 1975-80, dir., 1975-92; pres., chief exec. officer Anderson Mktg. Inc., Salt Lake City, 1987—. Author: By Example, 1961. Vice-pres. Salt Lake Area United Fund, 1977-80; mem. governing bd. Primary Children's Med. Ctr., 1975—, vice chmn., 1981-83, chmn., 1983-92; bd. dirs. Osmond Found., 1982-83. Served with AUS, 1943-46. Mem. Utah Advt. Fedn. (pres. 1967-68), Sales and Mktg. Execs. Utah (pres. 1965-66). Mem. LDS Ch. Home: 2242 Kensington Ave Salt Lake City UT 84108 Office: Anderson Mktg Inc 514 Pickett Cir Ste C Salt Lake City UT 84115

ANDERSON, AUSTIN GILMAN, economics research company consultant; b. Mpls.; s. Clifford Hawkins and Katharine (Irving) A.; m. Marilyn Wheeler, Mar. 17, 1968; children: Guy, Alisa, Michael, Emily. BS, Stanford U., 1964, MBA, 1966. Systems analyst Jet Propulsion Lab., Pasadena, Calif., 1966-68; assoc. Econs. Rsch. Assoc., L.A., 1968-72, sr. v.p., 1977-88, pres., chief exec. officer, 1988—; dir. rsch. Property Rsch. Corp., L.A., 1972-73; prin. Levander, Partridge & Anderson, Beverly Hills, Calif., 1973-77; instr. Grad. Sch. Mgmt. UCLA, 1989, extension, 1987; bd. dirs. Crown Iron Works Co., Mpls., 1983—; mem. bd. counselors Sch. Urban and Regional Planning U. So. Calif., L.A., 1984-95; mem. bd. trustees Real Estate Investment Trust of Calif., 1994—. Mem. Urban Land Inst. Home: 328 17th St Manhattan Beach CA 90266-4636 Office: Econs Rsch Assocs 10990 Wilshire Blvd Ste 1600 Los Angeles CA 90024-3913

ANDERSON, BARBARA ELAINE, information specialist, librarian; b. L.A., Sept. 10, 1934; d. William and Louise Anderson. BA, UCLA, 1956; MLS, U. Calif., Berkeley, 1957, post-MLS cert., 1978. Libr. Free Library, Phila., 1957-59; edn. libr. San Francisco State U., 1959-75; instr., rsch. asst. U. Calif., Berkeley, 1975-78; mgr. publs. Dialog Info. Svcs., Palo Alto, Calif., 1978-84, mgr. customer svcs., 1984-90; market analyst, competetive intelligence specialist Knight-Ridder Info. Inc., Mountain View, Calif., 1991—; Fulbright lectr. Pahlavi U. Library, Shiraz, Iran, 1966-67; library advisor U. Isfahan, Iran, 1971-73. Mem. Spl. Libraries Assn., Soc. of Competitive Intelligence Profls. Home: 1943 Mt Vernon Ct Apt 302 Mountain View CA 94040 Office: Knight-Ridder Info Inc 2440 W El Camino Real Mountain View CA 94040-1400

ANDERSON, BARBARA LOUISE, retired library director; b. San Diego, Jan. 5, 1933; d. Lorenzo and Louise (Morgan) A.; 1 child, Sean Allen. BS, San Diego State U., 1954; MLS, Kans. State Teachers Coll., 1955. Br. librarian L.A. Pub. Library, 1956-59; br. librarian, reference, young adult librarian San Diego Pub. Library, 1959-64; librarian U.S. Army, Europe, 1964-69; coordinator Serra Reference Project, Serra Regional Library System, San Diego, 1969-71; head readers services Riverside (Calif.) City and County Pub. Library, 1972-74; county librarian San Bernardino County (Calif.) Library, 1974-94; ret. 1994; del. White House Conf. on Libraries and Info. Services, 1979. Bd. dirs. Inland Empire Symphony, 1982-84, Riverside Mental Health Assn., 1975-79; mem. citizens adv. bd. San Bernardino YWCA, 1988-89. Mem. ALA, Calif. Library Assn., Black Caucus of Calif. Library Assn., Congress of Pub. Library Systems (pres. 1984), Calif. County Librarians Assn., Calif. Soc. Librarians (pres. 1974-75, mem. OCLC Users Council 1984-88), AAUW (pres. Riverside Br. 1976-77), NAACP, Bus. and Profl. Women San Bernardino. Democrat. Baptist. Contbr. articles to publs. in field.

ANDERSON, BERNARD JOSEPH, social studies educator; b. Reno, May 15, 1942; s. Bernard and Bridget T. Anderson; m. Clyda J. Hooper, Aug. 5, 1967; children: Cairn L., Natha Clyde. BS in Edn., U. Nev., 1970. Tchr. social studies Washoe County Sch. Dist., Reno, 1972—. Co-chair Sparks (Nev.) Charter Com., 1980-90; mem. Nev. State Legis. Com., Carson City, 1990—. Mem. NEA (bd. dirs.), KC (Grand Knight), Nev. State Edn. Assn. (bd. dirs.), Washoe County Tchr. Assn. (bd. dirs.). Democrat. Roman Catholic. Address: State Capitol Members of the Assembly District 31 Carson City NV 89710

ANDERSON, BRUCE E., association executive; b. Portland, Oreg., Oct. 29, 1962; s. John Wesley and Selma (Shupp) A.; m. Lois C. Dunham, Feb. 24, 1990; 1 child, Elizabeth C. BA in Polit. Sci., Oreg. State U., 1986. Bus. reporter Dun & Bradstreet, Portland, Oreg., 1987-88; legis. aide State Rep. Bob Repine, Salem, Oreg., 1989; dir. govtl. affairs Oreg. State Home Builders Assn., Salem, Oreg., 1989-93; exec. dir. Oreg. Life Underwriters Assn., Portland, 1994—. Precinct com. Marion County Rep. Ctrl. Com., Salem, 1990—; mem. devel. coun. Oreg. State U. Coll. Liberal Arts, Corvallis, 1995—; active in local polit. campaigns. Eagle Scout, Boy Scouts Am., 1980. Mem. Am. Soc. Assn. Execs., Oreg. Soc. Assn. Execs. Republican. Baptist. Office: Oreg Life Underwriters Assn 2701 NW Vaughn St Ste 448 Portland OR 97210

ANDERSON, BRUCE MORGAN, computer scientist; b. Battle Creek, Mich., Oct. 8, 1941; s. James Albert and Beverly Jane (Morgan) A.; m. Jeannie Marie Hignight, May 24, 1975; children: Ronald, Michael, Valerie, John, Carolyn. BEE, Northwestern U., 1964; MEE, Purdue U., 1966; PhD in Elec. Engring., Northwestern U., 1973. Rsch. engr. Zenith Radio Corp., Chgo., 1965-66; assoc. engr. Ill. Inst. Tech. Rsch. Inst., Chgo., 1966-68; sr. electronics engr. Rockwell Internat., Downers Grove, Ill., 1973-75; computer scientist Argonne (Ill.) Nat. Lab., 1975-77; mem. group tech. staff Tex. Instruments, Dallas, 1977-88; sr. scientist BBN Systems and Techs., Cambridge, Mass., 1988-90; systems engr. Lockheed Martin, Denver, 1990-94; sr. scientist CTA Inc., Englewood, Colo., Colo., 1994—; lectr. computer sci. U. Tex.-Arlington and Dallas; adj. prof. computer sci. N. Tex. State U.; vis. indsl. prof. So. Meth. U.; computer systems cons. Info. Internat., Culver City, Calif., HCM Graphic Systems, Gt. Neck, N.Y.; computer cons. depts. geography, transp., econs., sociology and computer sci. Northwestern U., also instr. computer sci.; expert witness for firm Burleson, Pate and Gibson. Contbr. articles to tech. jours. NASA fellow Northwestern U., 1973. Mem. IEEE Computer Soc. (chmn. Dallas 1984-85), Am. Assn. Artificial Intelligence, Assn. Computing Machinery (publs. chmn. 1986 fall joint computer conf. IEEE and Assn. Computing Machinery), Toastmasters Internat., Sigma Xi, Eta Kappa Nu, Theta Delta Chi. Home: 3473 E Euclid Ave Littleton CO 80121-3663 Office: 41 Inverness Dr E Englewood CO 80112-5412

ANDERSON, CAROL RUTH, secondary school educator; b. Conewango, N.Y., Aug. 24, 1926; d. Maynard William and Hila Martha (Kent) Phillips; m. George Boyer, Mar. 27, 1948 (div. July 1967); children: Gregory, Gail, Martha; m. Donald Anderson, Jan. 13, 1978 (div. Jan. 1981). Assoc. BS, Jamestown (N.Y.) Community Coll., 1962; BEd, U. Buffalo, 1966; MS in Edn., SUNY, Fredonia, 1971; postgrad., Ariz. State U., 1980-81. Cert. secondary tchr., N.Y., Ariz. Sec. Jamestown Metal Corp., 1957-61; sec. to judge Cattaraugus County, Little Valley, N.Y., 1961-66; bus. educator Jamestown High Sch., 1966-82, Phoenix Union High Sch. Dist., 1982-88; ret., 1988. Rep. committeewoman Cattaraugus County, 1960-62. Mem. N.Y. State Ret. Tchr.'s Assn., U. of Buffalo Alumni Assn., NEA, Jamestown High Sch. Tchrs. Club (sec., treas. 1967-82), Ariz. State Ret. Tchrs. Assn., Am. Legion, VFW, Women of Moose. Republican. Methodist.

ANDERSON, CHARLES MICHAEL, accountant; b. Londonderry, N. Ireland, England, July 15, 1944; came to U.S., 1946; s. Albert and Elizabeth (McDaid) A.; m. Terri Lynn Good, Oct. 6, 1981; children: Sean Michael, Kevin Patrick, Kelli Marie. BS, Northern Ill. U., 1966; MBA, U. Southern Calif., 1970. CPA. Staff acct. Price Waterhouse Co., Chgo., 1966-69; mgmt. cons. Price Waterhouse Co., L.A., 1970-72, pvt practice, Manahttan Beach, Calif., 1972-73; mgr. corp. budgets Great Southwest Corp., L.A., 1973-76; dir. internal audit Standard Brands Paint, Torrance, Calif., 1976-86; dir. control systems Standard Brands Paint, 1986-87; chief fin. officer One-Day Paint & Body, Torrance, 1988-89; ptnr. Anderson & Assocs., Manhattan Beach, 1989—. Contbr. articles to profl. jours. Chmn. city budget rev. com. Torrance Area C. of C., 1990-93; pres. Joie De Vive Homeowners Assn., Manhattan Beach, 1979-82, treas., 1985—; pres., chmn. Calif. Mus. Sci. & Industry, L.A., 1975-78; mem. Cath. Big Bros., Torrance, 1973-84 (Ten Yr. award 1984). Fellow AICPA, Calif. Soc. CPAs, Am. Inst. Profl. Bookkeepers; mem. Irish Network So. Calif., Le Tip Internat. (treas./sec. 1991—), Rotary (bd. dirs. 1989—). Democrat. Roman Catholic. Home: 1220 9th St Manhattan Beach CA 90266-6018

ANDERSON, CHARLES ROSS, civil engineer; b. N.Y.C., Oct. 4, 1937; s. Biard Eclare and Melva (Smith) A.; m. Susan Breinholt, Aug. 29, 1961; children: Loralee, Brian, Craig, Thomas, David. BSCE, U. Utah, 1961; MBA, Harvard U., 1963. Registered profl. engr.; cert. land surveyor. Owner, operator AAA Engring. and Drafting, Inc., Salt Lake City, 1960—; mem. acad. adv. com. U. Utah, 1990-91, chmn. civil engring. adv. bd., 1995—. Mayoral appointee Housing Devel. Com., Salt Lake City, 1981-86; bd. dirs., vice chmn., cons. Met. Water Dist., Salt Lake City, 1985—; bd. dirs., pres., v.p., sec. bd. Utah Mus. Natural History, Salt Lake City, 1980-92; asst. dist. commr. Sunrise Dist. Boy Scouts Am., Salt Lake City, 1985-86; fundraising coord. architects and engrs. United Fund; mem. Sunstone Nat. Adv. Bd., 1980-88; bd. dirs. Provo River Water Users Assn., 1986—. Fellow Am. Gen. Contractors, Salt Lake City, 1960; recipient Hamilton Watch award, 1961. Mem. ASCE, Am. Congress on Surveying and Mapping, U. Utah Alumni Assn. (bd. dirs. 1989-92), Harvard U. Bus. Sch. Club (pres. 1970-72), The Country Club, Rotary (v.p. Club 24 1990-91, chmn. election com. 1980-81, vice chmn. and chmn. membership com. 1988-90, 1st. v.p. 1996-97, pres. elect 1996-97), U. Utah Crimson Club (bd. dirs. 1996—), Pi Kappa Alpha (internat. pres. 1972-74, trustee endowment fund 1974-80, Outstanding Alumnus 1967, 72, mem. Hall of Fame 1995), Phi Eta Sigma, Chi Epsilon, Tau Beta Pi. Home: 2689 Comanche Dr Salt Lake City UT 84108-2846 Office: AAA Engring & Drafting Inc 1865 S Main St Salt Lake City UT 84115-2045

ANDERSON, CLIFFTON, science educator; b. French Camp, Calif., Sept. 5, 1961; s. Horace and Mamie Anderson; m. Melody R.M. Creer. BS in Biology, Pacific Union Coll., Angwin, Calif., 1991. Sci. tchr. Bakersfield (Calif) Adventist Acad., 1991—. Facilitator Boys to Men, Bakersfield, 1992—. With U.S. Army, 1979-82. Home: 813 Greenwood Dr Bakersfield CA 93306-5927 Office: Bakersfield Adventist Acad 3333 Bernard St Bakersfield CA 93306-3005

ANDERSON, CLIFTON EINAR, writer, communications consultant; b. Frederic, Wis., Dec. 17, 1923; s. Andrew John and Ida Louise (Johnson) A.; m. Phyllis Mary Nolan, Oct. 5, 1943; children: Kristine, Craig. BS, U. Wis., 1947; MA, U. Calif., Berkeley, 1954. News editor Chgo. Daily Drover's Jour., 1943-45; asst. editor The Progressive, Madison, Wis., 1946-47; dir. publs. Am. Press, Beirut, 1948-53; mgr. rural programs Houston C. of C., 1957-62; faculty Tex. A&M U., College Station, 1962-65; rsch. fellow U. Tex., Austin, 1965-68; faculty Southwestern Okla. U., Weatherford, 1968-72; extension editor U. Idaho, Moscow, 1972—; speaker John Macmurray Centennial Conf. Marquette U., 1991; speaker Nat. Conf. on Peacemaking and Conflict Resolution, 1993, moderator the UN at 50 seminar, 1995; moderator Korea Today and Tomorrow Symposium Wash. State U., 1995. Editor: The Horse Interlude, 1976; author: (with others) Ways Out: The Book of Changes for Peace, 1988, The Future: Opportunity Not Destiny, 1989, The Years Ahead: Perils, Problems and Promises, 1993, Eating Agendas: Food and Nutrition as Social Problems, 1995, Futurevision: Ideas, Insights, and Strategies, 1996; contbr. articles to profl. jours. and mags. Treas. Moscow Sister City Assn., 1986—; founding mem. Coalition for C.Am., Moscow, 1986; chmn. U. Idaho Affirmative Action Com., 1990; mem. coun. on home and cmty. care Area Agy. on Aging, 1995; writer campaign staff Senator R.M. La Follette, Jr., Madison, Wis., 1946; on senatorial campaign staff of Hubert H. Humphrey, Mpls., 1948; chmn. Borah Found. for Outlawry of War, U. Idaho, 1986-87, chmn. Borah Symposium, 1986-87. Recipient Rsch. award Fund for Adult Edn., 1954-55, U.S. Office Edn., 1965-68, 1st prize in newswriting competition Assn. Am. Agrl. Coll. Editors, 1976, merit award Agrl. Rels. Coun., 1995, Nat. Svc. award Washington Times Found., 1996. Fellow Martin Inst. Peace Studies and Conflict Resolution; mem. World Future Soc. (speaker 6th gen. assembly 1989, 7th gen. assembly 1993), Agr., Food and Social Values Soc., Agrl. Communicators in Edn., Am. Acad. Religion, Profs. World Peace Acad., World Constn. and Parliament Assn. Democrat. Home: 234 N Washington St Moscow ID 83843-2757 Office: U Idaho Agrl Communications Ctr Moscow ID 83844-2332

ANDERSON, DAN, state agency administrator. BA in Psychology, Macalester Coll.; MS in Psychology, U. S.D.; postgrad. in psychology, U. R.I. Various positions State of Mont. Dept. Instns. and Dept. Corrections, Helena; appt. adminstr. State of Mont. Addictive and Mental Disorders Divsn., Helena, 1995—. Office: Montana Dept Instns Addictive Divsn PO Box 202951 Helena MT 59620

ANDERSON, DANIEL DAVID, health care executive; b. Butte, Mont., Sept. 19, 1964; s. Neil Robert and Joan Marie (Potland) A.; m. Susan Ann Nicholson, Oct. 1, 1988; 1 child, Lauren Ashleigh. BS, Mont. Tech. Coll., 1986. Fin. specialist NCAT, Butte, 1985-87; controller Beta Factor Home Care, Butte, 1987-89; fin. dir. MHS, Inc., Helena, Mont., 1989—; bd. dirs. Beta Factor Home Care, Inc. Bd. dirs. Jr. Achievement, Helena, Mont., 1989—, Camelot Homeowners Assn., Helena, 1991—. Republican. Roman Catholic. Home: 625 Stadler Rd Helena MT 59602-6945 Office: MHS Inc 512 Logan St Helena MT 59601-4003

ANDERSON, DAVID E., zoological park administrator. Student, Pfeiffer Coll., 1964-65; BS in Zoology/Psychology, Duke U., 1972, postgrad., 1973. Colony supervisor Primate Ctr. Duke U., Durham, N.C., 1972-77, asst. dir. Primate Ctr., 1977-78; curator of mammals San Francisco Zool. Gardens, 1978-81, gen. curator, 1981-87, assoc. dir., gen. curator, 1987-90, dir., 1990—; tech. advisor Nature Conservancy La., 1987-90; animal tech. cons., mem. advisement com. La. State U.; mem. animal care com. Tulane U.; chmn. steering com. Madagascar Fauna Captive Propagation Group. Revs. editor Zoo Biology, 1982-88; contbr. articles to profl. publs. With USMC, 1965-69, Vietnam. Mem. Am. Assn. Zool. Parks and Aquariums (grad. mgmt. sch. 1982, ethics com., long range planning com., accreditation com., program chmn. Nat. Conf. 1981, others), Internat. Union Dirs. Zool. Gardens (captive breeding specialist group). Office: San Francisco Zool Gardens 1 Zoo Rd San Francisco CA 94132-1027

ANDERSON, DAVID MATTHEW, computer programmer; b. Kennewick, Wash., Jan. 25, 1955; s. Samuel Kingdon Anderson and Beverly Jean Clarke. BA, Columbia Coll., 1977; MA, Columbia U., 1980, MPhil, 1981. Project analyst Integral Rsch. Inc., N.Y.C., 1981-84; instr. econs. Iowa State U., Ames, 1984-87; data analyst Cutter Labs Miles Inc, Berkeley, Calif., 1987-89; programmer The Learning Co., Fremont, Calif., 1990-93, Know Ware, Fremont, 1993—. Mem. steering com. Islanders, Lafayette, Calif., 1991—. Mem. Tri-ValleyStargazers, Livermore, Calif., 1995. Democrat. Home: 39663 Leslie St Apt 388 Fremont CA 94538-2240 Office: Know Ware 2450 Peralta Blvd Ste 201 Fremont CA 94536-3826

ANDERSON, DEE, government relations and management consultant; b. Fresno, Calif., Dec. 23, 1953; d. Calvin Carroll Coolidge and Gonvella (Parrish) A.; 1 child, Shakibria Shauntae. BA, U. Wash., 1978, MPA, 1987. Cert. secondary tchr., 1978. Bus. tchr. Seattle and Renton, Wash., 1983-84; bus. edn. instr. Seattle Cen. Community Coll., 1984-86; grad. teaching asst. U. Wash., Seattle, 1985-87; program specialist Wash. State Office of Minority and Women's Bus. Enterprises, Olympia, 1987-89; exec. dir. Operational Emergency Ctr., Seattle, 1989-93; dir. Ctrl. Area Youth Assn., Seattle, 1993-94; bus. advisor/cons. U.S. Peace Corps/Ukraine, 1996—; legis. asst. Seattle City Coun., 1984. Dep. dir. Mondale-Ferraro Presdl. campaign, Seattle, 1984; mem. World Affairs Coun., Seattle; Seattle King County Pvt. Industry Coun., 1990-96—; U.S. del. Seattle Goodwill Games Women's Conf., 1990; USSR/U.S./G.B./Ireland/Japan Internat. Women's Forum in Soviet Union; mem. Dem. Nat. Com., 1992-96; U.S. del., White House Conf. on Small Bus., 1995. Mem. Nat. Women's Politic Caucus (honored as Wash. state woman leader 1989), Alpha Kappa Alpha. Democrat. Baptist.

ANDERSON, DONALD NORTON, JR., retired electrical engineer; b. Chgo., Aug. 15, 1928; s. Donald Norton and Helen Dorothy (Lehmann) A. BS, Purdue U., 1950, MS, 1952. With Hughes Aircraft Co., Culver City and El Segundo, Calif., 1952-84, sect. head, sr. project engr., 1960-65, tech. mgr. Apollo program, 1965-66, mgr. visible systems dept., 1966-69, 70-73, project mgr., 1969-70, mgr. space sensors lab., 1973-79, mgr. space electro-optical systems labs., 1979-80, mgr. space electro-optical systems labs., 1980-84, ret., 1984. Recipient Apollo Achievement award, 1970; Robert J. Collier Landsat award, 1974. Mem. Research Soc. Am., Nat. Speleological Soc., Am. Theatre Organ Soc., Sigma Xi (sec. Hughes Labs. br. 1974-75), Eta Kappa Nu, Sierra Club. Home: 1885 Craigs Store Rd Afton VA 22920-9634

ANDERSON, DOROTHY FISHER, social worker, psychotherapist; b. Funchal, Madeira, May 31, 1924; d. Lewis Mann Anker and Edna (Gilbert) Fisher (adoptive father David Henry Fisher); m. Theodore W. Anderson, July 8, 1950; children: Robert Lewis, Janet Anderson Yang, Jeanne Elizabeth. BA, Queens Coll., 1945; AM, U. Chgo., 1947. Diplomate Am. Bd. Examiners in Clin. Social Work; lic. clin. social worker, Calif.; registered cert. social worker, N.Y. Intern Cook County (Ill.) Bur. Pub. Welfare, Chgo., 1945-46, Ill. Neuropsychiat. Inst., Chgo., 1946; clin. caseworker, Neurol. Inst. Presbyn. Hosp., N.Y.C., 1947; therapist, Mental Hygiene Clinic VA, N.Y.C., 1947-50; therapist, Child Guidance Clinic Pub. Elem. Sch. 42, N.Y.C., 1950-53; social worker, counselor Cedarhurst (N.Y.) Family Service Agy., 1954-55; psychotherapist, counselor Family Service of the Midpeninsula, Palo Alto, Calif., 1971-73, 79-86, George Hexter, M.D., Inc., 1972-83; clin. social worker Tavistock Clinic, London, 1974-75, El Camino Hosp., Mountain View, Calif., 1979; pvt. practice clin. social work, 1978-92, ret., 1992; cons. Human Resource Services, Sunnyvale, Calif., 1981-86. Hannah G. Solomon scholar U. Chgo., 1945-46; Commonwealth fellow U. Chgo., 1946-47. Fellow Soc. Clin. Social Work (Continuing Edn. Recognition award 1980-83); mem. Nat. Assn. Social Workers (diplomate in clin. social work).

ANDERSON, EDWARD VIRGIL, lawyer; b. San Francisco, Oct. 17, 1953; s. Virgil P and Edna Pauline (Pedersen) A.; m. Kathleen Helen Dunbar, Sept. 3, 1983; children: Elizabeth D., Hilary J. AB in Econs., Stanford U., 1975, JD, 1978. Bar: Calif. 1978. Assoc. Pillsbury Madison & Sutro, San Francisco, 1978—, ptnr., 1987-94; ptnr. Skjerven Morrill MacPherson Franklin and Friel, San Jose, Calif., 1994—. Editor IP Litigator, 1995—; mem. bd. editors Antitrust Law Devel., 1983-86. Trustee Lick-Wilmerding H.S., San Francisco, 1980—, pres.; trustee Santa Clara Law Found., 1995—. Mem. ABA, Calif. Bar Assn., San Francisco Bar Assn., Santa Clara Bar Assn. (counsel), City Club San Francisco, Stanford Golf Club, Phi Beta Kappa. Republican. Episcopal. Home: 45 Dorantes Ave San Francisco CA 94116-1430 Office: Skjerven Morrill MacPherson Franklin and Friel 25 Metro Dr Ste 700 San Jose CA 95110-1339

ANDERSON, ELIZABETH ANN, real estate, property manager; b. Sioux Falls, S.D., July 1, 1967; d. James Wilbur and Gloria Ann (Nelson) Johnson; m. Thomas Glen Froseth, July 8, 1989 (div. Aug. 10, 1993); m. Dwight Dean Anderson, June 18, 1994. Student modern office syss., Dakota State U., 1987. Real estate broker Colo. Dept. Regulatory Agys.; Cert. Edn. Completion Life Office Mgmt. Assn. Customer svc. rep. Citibank, Sioux Falls, S.D., 1986; with employee change dept. Midland Nat. Life Ins. Co., Sioux Falls, S.D., 1987-90; sr. clk. policy svc. Woodmen of the World Life Ins. Co., Littleton, Colo., 1990-95; co-owner, operator Anderson Rental Properties, Highlands Ranch, Colo., 1994—. Office counselor Alternative Pregnancy Ctr., Denver, Colo., 1996—. Mem. Mothers of Pre-Schoolers (discussion group leader). Republican. Office: Anderson Rental Properties PO Box 260191 Highlands Ranch CO 80126

ANDERSON, ELIZABETH ANNE, psychologist; b. Edmonton, Alta., Can., Nov. 5, 1952; came to the U.S., 1986; d. Clarence Carl and Esther Eleanor (Knebel) Kuhnke; m. Orland Leonard Anderson, Feb. 15, 1986; 45 foster children. BSc in Hydrology, U. Alta., Edmonton, 1972, MSc in Hydrology, 1974, PhD in Hydrology, 1977; MBA, U. B.C., Vancouver, 1985; MEd in Counseling, Heritage Coll., 1990, BA in Social Work, 1992, MEd in Tchg., 1993; EdD in Child and Youth Studies, Nova Southeastern U., 1996. Cert. sch. counselor; cert. psychologist; cert. spl. edn. tchr. grades K-12; lic. clin. profl. counselor; lic. master addiction counselor; cert. criminal justice counselor. Cons. hydrologist Norecol Environ./BC Rsch., Vancouver, 1977-86; prof. environ. sci. Trinity Western U., Vancouver, 1984-86; prof. social work and psychology Heritage Coll., Toppenish, Wash., 1989-93; child and adolescent therapist Cath. Family & Child Svc., Yakima, Wash., 1992-93; sch. counselor grades K-6 Auburn (Wash.) Sch. Dist., 1993-95; prof. spl. edn. Salish Kootenai Coll., Pablo, Mont., 1994-95; sch. psychologist Plains (Mont.) and Arlee (Mont.) Sch. Dists., 1995-96, West Valley Schs., Yakima, 1996—; spl. edn. specialist Nat. Indian Sch. Bd. Assn., Utah, Ariz., S.D., 1995—; in-svc. specialist Western Navajo Agy., Tuba City, Ariz., 1996—. Contbr. articles to profl. jours. Founder Healthy Kids Clubs, 1993—. Mem. NEA, Nat. Assn. Forensic Counselors, Nat. Assn. Sch. Psychologist.

ANDERSON, FORD A., II (DREW ANDERSON), foundation executive; b. June 8, 1968; m. Ann Arthur, June 8, 1968; 1 child, Megan Elizabeth. BA in History magna cum laude, Butler U., 1968; MA in Am. History, U. Wis., 1973, MA in Bus., 1976. Adminstrv. asst. The Kresge Found., Troy, Mich., 1976-80; program officer M.J. Murdock Charitable Trust, 1980-84, sr. program officer, 1985-88, exec. dir., 1988-96; cons., 1996—. Former pres., mem. adv. bd. Ctr. Arts Adminstrn., U. Wis.-Madison; past pres., treas. Pacific N.W. Grantmakers Forum. Officer Engr. and Mil. Intelligence Specialists, U.S. Army, 1968-71, lt. col. res. Mem. Res. Officer Assn. (former v.p. Army Oreg. dept., former sec., pres. 1993-94). Home: 12706 SE 24th St Vancouver WA 98683*

ANDERSON, GARRY MICHAEL, diagnostic radiologist; b. Houston, May 17, 1955; s. Dan Luther and Marcella Marie (Hanel) A. BS in Biology, Tarleton State U., Stephenville, Tex., 1977; BS in Medicine, Tex. A&M U., 1979, MD, 1981. Diplomate Nat. Bd. Med. Examiners, Am. Bd. Radiology. Intern in pathology Scott & White Hosp., Temple, Tex., 1981-82, resident in diagnostic radiology, 1982-86; fellow in imaging UCLA Ctr. of the Health Scis., 1986-87, asst. attending clin. prof., 1987-88; diagnostic radiologist Long Beach (Calif.) Cmty. Hosp., 1987—. Mem. Second Decade Coun., Am. Film Inst., L.A., 1993—. Named Outstanding Young Alumnus, Tarleton State U., 1991. Mem. Am. Coll. Radiology, Radiol. Soc. N.Am. Roman Catholic. Home: 1811 Termino Ave Apt 7108 Long Beach CA 90815-2672 Office: Cmty Radiology Med Group 1703 Termino Ave Ste 107A Long Beach CA 90804-2126

ANDERSON, GERALD VERNE, retired aerospace company executive; b. Long Beach, Calif., Oct. 25, 1931; s. Gordon Valentine and Aletha Marian (Parkins) A.; m. Judith B. Marx, May 14, 1992; children by previous marriage: Lori Jean Anderson Fronk, Gregory Verne, David Harman, Lynn Elaine Anderson Lee, Brian Earl, Michael Gordon. AA, Long Beach City Coll., 1952; BS, U. Calif., Berkeley, 1958. Registered profl. engr., Calif. Tech. specialist N. Am. Aviation Co., L.A., 1958-65; tech. specialist McDonnell Douglas Astronautics, Huntington Beach, Calif., 1965-84; mgr. McDonnell Douglas Astronautics, Huntington Beach, 1984-87; sr. mgr. McDonnell Douglas Aerospace, Huntington Beach, 1987-94; cons. Mitsubishi Heavy Industries, Nagoya, Japan, 1972-73, Aeritalia, Turin, Italy, 1975-76. Patentee, portable vacuum chamber, electron beam welding device. Mem. Westminster (Calif.) Planning Com., 1974, Huntington Beach Citizens Adv. Com., 1975, Westminster Bicentennial Com., 1976, L.A. Classical Ballet Guild, 1992—. Mem. Soc. Mfg. Engrs., Soc. Automotive Engrs., Aerospace Industries Assn., AIAA. Republican. Home: 3452 Falcon Ave Long Beach CA 90807-4814

ANDERSON, GUNNAR DONALD, artist; b. Berkeley, Calif., Mar. 3, 1927; s. Sven Gunnar and Margaret (Hultien) A.; m. Virginia Fletcher Bullock, Jan. 31, 1953; children: Greta, Karin, Paul. BFA, Art Ctr. Coll. of Design, Pasadena, Calif., 1951. Art dir. McCann ERickson, N.Y.C., 1951-53, Cunningham & Walsh, N.Y.C., 1953-55, Batten, Barton, Durstine & Osborne, San Francisco, 1955-63; artist Sonoma, Calif., 1963—. Artist: (children's book) Oscar Lincoln Busby Stokes, 1970; one man shows include U. Nebr., Lincoln, Frye Mus., Seattle, Conacher Galleries, San Francisco, Guildhall Galleries, Chgo., Meredith Long Galleries, Houston, Dalzell Hatfield Galleries, L.A., Lord and Taylor Art Galleries, N.Y.C., Rosicrution Mus., San Jose, Calif., Phillips Galleries, Dallas; exhibited in group shows at Ft. Worth Art Ctr., Palace of Fine Arts, San Francisco, De Saisset Gallery, Santa Clara, Calif. With USCG, 1945-46. Recipient Best in Fine Art award Soc. Art Ctr. Alumni, 1972. Mem. Soc. Western Artists (trustee 1993—, Best Figure or Portrait award 1971, 1st place award 1985, 90, 91, Grumbacher gold medallion 1986), Soaring Soc. Am., Bohemian Club. Home: 4583 Belmont Ct Sonoma CA 95476-6001

ANDERSON, HAROLD STERLING, elementary school educator; b. Bethel, Conn., Sept. 24, 1928; s. Harold Julius and Mabelle Harriet (Nelson) A.; m. Margaretha Gall, Dec. 23, 1950; children: Steve (dec.), Dave Robert. BS, Mayville State Coll., 1951; MEd, Colo. State Coll., 1954, EdD, 1957. Instr. Ctrl. Wash. Coll., Ellensburg, 1954-55; assoc. prof. to prof. So. State Coll., Springfield, S.D., 1957-65; prof. Tchrs. Coll. Columbia U., N.Y.C., 1965-69; prof. Coll. Gt. Falls, Mont., 1969-94, dir. grad. studies, 1972-94, prof. emeritus, 1994—. Author: Primer of Planned Change, 1982, rev. edit., 1993; co-author: Thinking Skills Instruction, 1987. With U.S. Army, 1951-53. Recipient award Mont. Probation Officers Assn., 1980. Mem. NEA, AAUP, Phi Delta Kappa. Republican. Home: 44 US Hwy 87 Belt MT 59412

ANDERSON, HERSCHEL VINCENT, librarian; b. Charlotte, N.C., Mar. 14, 1932; s. Paul Kemper and Lillian (Johnson) A. B.A., Duke U., 1954; M.S., Columbia U., 1959. Library asst. Bklyn. Public Library, 1954-59; asst. bookmobile librarian King County Public Library, Seattle, 1959-62; asst. librarian Longview (Wash.) Public Library, 1962-63; librarian N.C. Mus. Art, Raleigh, 1963-64; audio-visual cons. N.C. State Library, Raleigh, 1964-68; dir. Sandhill Regional Library, Rockingham, N.C., 1968-70; asso. state librarian Tenn. State Library and Archives, Nashville, 1970-72; unit dir. Colo. State Library, Denver, 1972-73; state librarian S.D. State Library, Pierre, 1973-80; dir. Mesa (Ariz.) Public Library, 1980—; dir. Bibliographical Ctr. for Rsch., Denver, 1974-80, v.p. 1977; mem. Western Coun. St. Librs., 1975-80, v.p., 1978, pres., 1979; mem. Ariz. St. Libr., LSCA Adv. Coun., 1981-84, pres., 1982-83; Ariz. Libr. Devel. Coun., 1991-93; mem. libr. technician tng. adv. com. Mesa C.C., 1982-85, mem. commn. for excellence, 1993—; chmn. Serials On-Line in Ariz. Consortia, 1985-86. Jr. warden St. Mark's Episcopal Ch., Mesa, 1985-87, vestryman, 1987-90, 95—, sr. warden, 1996—; del. ann. conv. Episcopal Diocese of Ariz., 1989-92, 94—, mem. archives com., 1990—, mem. Diocesan Coun. Episcopal, Diocese of Anzma, 1996-98; mem., treas. Maricopa County Libr. Coun., 1991—, pres., 1983, 93; mem. Valley Citizens League, 1991—. With U.S. Army, 1955-57. Recipient Emeritus Honors Ariz. Library Friends, 1987. Mem. ALA, S.D. Libr. Assn. (hon. life, Libr. of Yr. award 1977), Mountain Plains Libr. Assn. (pres. 1974, bd. dirs. 1974-77, 86-87, Intellectual Freedom award 1979, Ariz. Libr. Assn. (exe. com. 1986-87), Chief Officers of State Libr. Agys. (bd. dirs. 1974-76), Kiwanis (bd. dirs. Mesa 1981-86, v.p. 1983, pres. 1985-86), Phi Kappa Psi. Office: Mesa Pub Libr 64 E 1st St Mesa AZ 85201-6768

ANDERSON, HOLLY GEIS, women's health facility administrator, commentator, educator; b. Waukesha, Wis., Oct. 23, 1946; d. Henry H. and Hulda (Sebroff) Geis; m. Richard Kent Anderson, June 6, 1969. BA, Azusa Pacific U., 1970. CEO Oak Tree Antiques, San Gabriel, Calif., 1975-82; pres., founder, CEO Premenstrual Syndrome Treatment Clinic, Arcadia, Calif., 1982—, Breast Healthcare Ctr., 1986-89, Hormonal Treatment Ctrs., Inc., Arcadia, 1992-94; lectr. radio and TV shows, L.A.; on-air radio personality Women's Clinic with Holly Anderson, 1990—. Author: What Every Woman Needs to Know About PMS (audio cassette), 1987, The PMS Treatment Program (video cassette), 1989, PMS Talk (audio cassette), 1989. Mem. NAFE, The Dalton Soc. Republican. Office: PMS Treatment Clinic 150 N Santa Anita Ave Ste 755 Arcadia CA 91006-3113

ANDERSON, IRIS ANITA, retired secondary education educator; b. Forks, Wash., Aug. 18, 1930; d. James Adolphus and Alma Elizabeth (Haase) Gilbreath; m. Donald Rene Anderson, 1951; children: Karen Christine, Susan Adele, Gayle Lynne, Brian Dale. BA in Teaching, U. Wash., 1969; MA in English, Seattle U., 1972. Cert. English tchr., adminstr., Calif. Tchr. Issaquah (Wash.) Sr. High Sch., 1969-77, L.A. Sr. High Sch., 1977-79. Contbr. article to Skeptic mag. Nutrition vol. Santa Monica (Calif.) Hosp. Aux., Jules Stein Eye Inst., L.A.; mem. Desert Beautiful, Palm Springs Panhellenic; mem. Rancho Mirage Reps. W-Key activities scholar U. Wash. Mem. NEA, DAR (vice regent Palm Springs, 1st vice regent Cahuilla chpt.), AAUW, LEV, Wash. Speech Assn., Nat. Thespians, Bob Hope Cultural Ctr., Palm Springs Press Women, Desert Music Guild, Coachella Valley Hist. Soc., Palm Desert Womens Club, Calif. Ret. Tchrs. Assn., CPA Wives Club, Desert Celebrities, Rancho Mirage Womens Club, Round Table West, World Affairs Coun., Living Desert Wildlife and Bot. Preserve. Republican.

ANDERSON, ISABEL, artist, educator; b. N.Y.C., Apr. 10, 1931; d. William and Mary Elizabeth (Doerr) Smith; m. Hugh Riddell Anderson, Feb. 4, 1955 (div. Jan. 1968); m. William Anthony Dietz, Apr. 29, 1978. Student, Art Students' League, 1951-52; BA, Antioch Coll., 1954; postgrad., UCLA, 1956; MFA, State U. of Iowa, 1956. Cert. h.s. tchr., Calif. C.C. standard teaching credential, instr. credential. Stained glass artist Paul L. Phillips Studio, Altadena, Calif., 1960-64, Roger Daricarrerre Studio, L.A., 1965-66; h.s. art tchr. L.A. Unified Sch. Dist., 1967-76; instr. art Glendale (Calif.) C.C., 1979-80; asst. prof. screen printing Pasadena (Calif.) City Coll., 1980-90; artist, writer, 1990—; invited spkr., panelist in field. Exhbns., prints, drawings, paintings, 1965—; represented in permanent collections Boston Coll. Art, Home Savs. and Loan, Antioch Coll., Pasadena City Coll., Kerala State U., India, Hanover Bank, L.A.; contbr. articles and art revs. to profl. jours. Recipient Award of Merit 11th All-City Art Exhbn., 1963, Purchase award State Coll. Art, 1963, Spl. award Inland XII Art Exhbn., 1981, James Jones Purchae award Ink & Clay Exhbn. Calif. Poly., 1982; grantee Screen Printing Assn. Internat., 1985-88. Mem. L.A. Printmaking Soc. (sec. 1978-79, newsletter editor 1978-79), Women's Caucus for Art, SITE (mem. exhbn. com.), Beyond Baroque Found. Office: 1564 Talmadge St Los Angeles CA 90027-1543

ANDERSON, JACK JOE, communications and multi-media training consultant; b. Lipan, Tex., Oct. 22, 1928; s. William Amon and Tommie Lucille (Roberts) A.; B.A., San Jose State U., 1965, M.A., 1967; postgrad. in bus. adminstrn. Pepperdine U., Los Angeles; m. Maria I. Kamantauskas, Mar. 13, 1976; children: Mark, Douglas, Craig. Asst. mgr. edn. systems Lockheed Missiles & Space Co., Sunnyvale, Calif., 1966-69; v.p. Learning Achievement Corp., San Jose, Calif., 1969-74; mgr. instrnl. systems Ford Aerospace & Communications Corp., Pasadena, Calif., 1974-83; pres. Anderson & Assocs., Alta Loma, Calif., 1983—; cons. tng. programs and systems, 1969—. Served with USAF, 1946-66. Recipient Nat. award for tng. program design Indsl. TV Assn., 1974. Mem. Am. Mgmt. Assn., Am. Soc. Tng. and Devel. Contbr. tech. and gen. instrnl. materials in field. Office: Anderson & Assocs 9155 Carrari Ct Alta Loma CA 91737-1557

ANDERSON, JAMES ARTHUR, research laboratory administrator; b. Montgomery, Ala., July 18, 1948; s. John Arthur and Jessie Jean (Smith) A. BA in Secondary Edn., Carroll Coll., Helena, Mont., 1970; JD, Gonzaga U., 1975. Cert. secondary sch. tchr., Mont.; registered stockbroker, registered investment advisor; lic. health ins. agt., Wash., lic. life ins. agt., Wash. Legal intern U.S. Atty., Spokane, Wash., 1973-75; atty./contracts specialist Spokane County, 1975-80; contracts mgr./exec. dir. Wash. Energy, Spokane, 1980-82; sr. contracts assoc./atty. Battelle Pacific N.W. Nat. Lab., Richland, Wash., 1982-90, contracting officer, 1994—; fin. planner Am. Express Co., Kennewick, Wash., 1990-91; registered investment advisor James A. Anderson, Kennewick, Wash., 1992-93. Case law editor Gonzaga Law Rev., 1974-75; contbr. articles to profl. jours. Bd. trustees Richland Players Theater, 1984, treas., 1985, chmn. bd. trustees, 1986; mem. Vanderpoole Trust Com., Richland, 1985-89. With U.S. Army, 1970-71. David Sullivan Meml. scholar Carroll Coll., 1969-70, Gonzaga U. Law Coun. scholar, 1973-74, Law Rev. scholar, 1973-74, 74-75. Fellow Nat. Contract Mgmt. Assn. (cert. assoc. contract mgr., Columbia Basin chpt. awards chmn., ednl. v.p., N.W. Region Golden Nugget award 1991); mem. Wash. Bar Assn., Delta Epsilon Sigma. Office: Battelle Pacific Northwest Nat Lab Battelle Blvd Richland WA 99352

ANDERSON, JANET ALM, librarian; b. Lafayette, Ind., Dec. 20, 1952; d. Charles Henry and Lenore Elaine Alm; m. Jay Allan Anderson, May 21, 1983. BS, Bemidji State U., 1975; MA in Folklore, Western Ky. U., 1981, MSLS in Libr. Sci., 1982; PhD in Recreation Resources Mgmt., Utah State U., 1994. Cert. elem. tchr., sch. libr. and media specialist. Storyteller, puppeteer North Country Arts Coun., Bemidji, Minn., 1975-76; head children's libr. Bemidji State U., 1976-77; mid. sch. libr. Custer County Sch. Dist., Miles City, Mont., 1977-79; tchr. of gifted and talented Custer County Sch. Dist., Miles City, 1979-80; folklore archivist Western Ky. U., Bowling Green, 1981-83; head children's and young adults' svcs. Bowling Green Pub. Libr., 1983-85; head of serials Utah State U., Logan, 1986-91, campus svcs. libr., 1991—, adj. asst. prof. forestry, 1995—, chmn. adv. bd. Women's Ctr., 1988-92; adj. instr. Miles Community Coll., 1978-80; cons. to various Am. outdoor museums; speaker Utah Endowment for the Humanities Speakers Bur., Salt Lake City, 1987-90; mem. acad. freedom and tenure com. Utah State U., 1995—, chair, 1997—. Author: Old Fred, 1972, A Taste of Kentucky, 1986 (Ky. State Book Fair award), Bounty, 1990, (with others) Advances in Serials Management, Vol. 3, 1989, Vendors and Library Acquisitions, 1991; contbr. to Ency. of Am. Popular Beliefs and Superstitions, articles on folklore, librarianship, museology, and natural resource mgmt. to mags. and periodicals; assoc. editor: (jour.) InterpEdge; delivered radio and TV presentations on folklore and librarianship. Co-founder, past pres. Rosebud chpt. Nat. Audubon Soc., Miles City, Mont., 1978-80; mem. Providence/River Hts. Libr. Bd.; trustee Cache County Libr. Bd.; bd. dirs. Denzil Stewart Nature Park; invited author Ky. State Book Fair, 1986, Utah Arts Festival, 1991; life mem. Women and Gender Rsch. Inst., Friends of Brooks Free Libr. Recipient Exhibit and Program Grant Nat. Endowment for the Arts, Bowling Green, Ky., 1984-85. Mem. ALA, Nat. Audubon Soc.

(trustee Bridgerland chpt. 1994-97), Nat. Assn. Interpretation, John Muir Assn. (founding mem. environ. ctr.), Utah Libr. Assn., Consortium of Utah Women in Higher Edn. (campus coord. 1989-91), Am. Folklore Soc., Utah Folklore Soc., Assn. Living Hist. Farms and Agrl. Mus., Visitor Studies Assn., Am. Assn. Mus., Assn. Coll. and Rsch. Librs., Old Main Soc., Xi Sigma Pi. Democrat. Lutheran. Home: 1090 S 400 E Providence UT 84332-9461 Office: Utah State U Merrill Libr Logan UT 84322-3000

ANDERSON, JOHN DAVID, architect; b. New Haven, Dec. 24, 1926; s. William Edward and Norma Vere (Carson) A.; m. Florence A. Van Dyke, Aug. 26, 1950; children—Robert Stewart, David Carson. A.B. cum laude, Harvard U., 1949, M.Arch., 1952. Draftsman John K. Monroe, Architect, Denver, 1952-54; draftsman, designer, assoc. Wheeler & Lewis, Architects, Denver, 1954-60; prin. John D. Anderson, Denver, 1960-64; ptnr. Anderson, Barker Rinker, Architects, Denver, 1965-69, A-B-R Partnership, Architects, Denver, 1970-75; prin., CEO Anderson Mason Dale P.C., Denver, 1975-96, sr. v.p., 1997—; vis. lectr. U. Colo., U. N.Mex., U. Nebr., U. Cape Town, Colo. State U., Plymouth Polytech., Eng.; chmn. Denver Bldg. Dept. Bd. Appeals, 1974-75; chmn. Colo. Gov.'s Task Force on Removal of Archtl. Barriers, 1972-74; vice chmn. Colo. Bd. Non-Residential Energy Conservation Stds., 1978-80. Prin. works include: Community Coll. Denver, North campus, Westminster, 1977, Solar Energy Rsch. Inst., Golden, 1980 (award winning solar heated structures). Served with USNR, 1944-46. Fellow AIA (pres. Colo. chpt. 1967, Western Mountain region dir. 1995-97, Silver medal, 1984, Firm of Yr. award 1986 Western Mountain region); mem. Colo. Soc. Architects (Architect of Yr. award 1987, pres. 1971), Internat. Solar Energy Soc., Council Ednl. Facility Planners (internat. chmn. energy com. 1980). Republican. Congregationalist. Home: 57 S Rainbow Trail Golden CO 80401-8301 Office: Anderson Mason Dale PC 1615 17th St Denver CO 80202-1203

ANDERSON, JOHN DAVID, astronomer, researcher; b. Moscow, Idaho, Mar. 5, 1934; s. Elmer Fridolph and Jean Fife (Little) A.; m. Betty Williamson, July 7, 1956 (div. Sept. 1972); children: David W., Norman C., Marilyn L. Anderson Benoit; m. Lillian Yuriko Takemoto, Jan. 8, 1977; 1 child, Michelle Miki. BA, UCLA, 1956, MA, 1962, PhD, 1967. Mem. tech. staff Sys. Lab. Corp., L.A., 1956-60; mem. tech. staff Jet Propulsion Lab., Pasadena, Calif., 1960-67, group supr., 1967-77, staff scientist, 1977-80, sr. rsch. scientist, 1980—; vis. prof. Stanford (Calif.) U., 1971, Monash U., Australia, 1985-90. Contbr. articles to Astrophys. Jour., Planetary Report, Space Sci. Revs., Icarus, Jour. Geophys. Rsch., Astron. Jour., Sci., Nature. With USAFR, 1957-65. Recipient Exceptional Sci. Achievement award NASA, 1974. Mem. Am. Astron. Soc., Am. Geophys. Union, Japanese Am. Nat. Mus. Republican. Episcopalian. Office: Jet Propulsion Lab Mail Stop 301-230 4800 Oak Grove Dr Pasadena CA 91109-8001

ANDERSON, JOHN THOMAS, librarian, historian; b. Burlington, Iowa, Feb. 7, 1955; s. Alvin Jay and Margaret Ann (Thomas) A. BA, U. No. Iowa, 1976; MA, Coll. William and Mary, 1979; PhD, U. Va., 1982; M in Info. and Libr. Studies, U. Mich., 1987. Cert. postsecondary educator; cert. substitute tchr. Temp. asst. prof. history Chadron (Nebr.) State Coll., 1984; asst. libr. pub. svcs. Mid. Ga. Coll., Cochran, 1989-91; temp. reference libr. U. No. Iowa, Cedar Falls, 1991; reference libr. Palm Beach County Libr. Sys., Boca Raton, Fla., 1992; reference libr. Salve Regina U., Newport, R.I., 1992-93, catalog libr., 1993-94; libr. tech. asst. II Tucson-Pima Pub. Libr., Ajo, Ariz., 1997—. Exhibits judge Nat. History Day Competition, Chadron, 1984. Philip Francis du Pont fellow Coll. William and Mary, 1976; Philip Francis du Pont fellow U. Va., 1977; Va. Mason Davidge fellow U. Va., 1978, 79. Mem. ALA, Soc. Historians Am. Fgn. Rels., Phi Alpha Theta. Republican. Unitarian. Home: 201 La Mina Ave Ajo AZ 85321-2724 Office: Tucson Pima Pub Libr Ajo Br Libr 33 Plaza St Ajo AZ 85321

ANDERSON, KARL RICHARD, aerospace engineer, consultant; b. Vinita, Okla., Sept. 27, 1917; s. Axel Richard and Hildred Audrey (Marshall) A.; B.S., Calif. Western U., 1964, M.A., 1966; Ph.D., U.S. Internat. U., 1970; m. Jane Shigeko Hiratsuka, June 20, 1953; 1 son, Karl Richard. Engr. personnel subsystems Atlas Missile Program, Gen. Dynamics, San Diego, 1960-63; design engr. Solar divsn. Internat. Harvester, San Diego, 1964-66, sr. design engr., 1967-69, project engr., 1970-74, product safety specialist, 1975-78; aerospace engring. cons., 1979-86; cons. engring., 1979—; lectr. Am. Indian Sci. and Engring. Soc. Served to maj. USAF, 1936-60. Recipient Spl. Commendation award San Diego County Bd. Supervisors, 1985, Spl. Commendation award San Diego City Council, 1985, Spl. Commendation award City of San Diego, 1994, Grace "Peter" Sargent award San Diego City Natural Park, 1994. Registered profl. engr., Calif. Republican. Episcopalian. Home: 5886 Scripps St San Diego CA 92122-3212

ANDERSON, KATHLEEN GAY, mediator, hearing officer, arbitrator, educator; b. Cin., July 27, 1950; d. Harold B. and Trudi L. (Chambers) Briggs; m. J.R. Carr, July 4, 1988; 1 child, Jesse J. Anderson. Student, U. Cin., 1971-72, Antioch Coll., 1973-74; cert., Nat. Jud. Coll., U. Nev., Reno, 1987, Inst. Applied Law, 1987, Acad. Family Mediators, 1991. Cert. Am. Arbitration Assn. Comml. Arbitration Panel, Nat. Assn. Securities Dealers Arbitration and Mediation Panels, Lemmon Mediation Inst., Acad. Family Mediators. Paralegal Lauer & Lauer, Santa Fe, 1976-79, Wilkinson, Cragun & Barker, Anchorage, 1981-82; employment law paralegal specialist Hughes, Thorsness, Gantz, Powell & Brundin, Anchorage, 1983-91; investigator, mediator Alaska State Commn. Human Rights, 1991; mediator, arbitrator, trainer The Arbitration and Mediation Group, Anchorage, 1987—; hearing officer Municipality of Anchorage, 1993—; State of Alaska, 1994—; mem. faculty nat. Jud. Coll., U. Nev., Reno, 1988-89; adj. prof. U. Alaska, Anchorage, 1985—, Alaska Pacific U., 1990-96, Chapman U., 1990; mem. Alaska Supreme Ct. Mediation Task Force, 1991-96; adv. com. Am. Arbitration Assn. for Alaska, 1995—, panel comml. arbitrators; trainer mediation svcs. pvt. profit and nonprofit groups, pub. groups, U.S. mil., state and fed. govt. Author, editor: Professional Responsibility Handbook for Legal Assistants and Paralegals, 1986; contbr. articles to profl. jours. Lectr. Alaska Bar Assn., 1989—, NLRB, Anchorage, 1986, Alaska Assn. Bus. and Profl. Women, 1988—, Coun. on Edn. and Mgmt., 1993—, Small Bus. Devel. Coun., various employers and bus. groups. Mem. ABA (ethics com., alt. dispute resolution sect.), Am. Arbitration Assn. (mem. cert. comml. arbitration panel 1996—), Soc. Profls. in Dispute Resolution, Nat. Assn. Mediation in Edn., Nat. Inst. Dispute Resolution, Nat. Fedn. Paralegal Assn. (edn. task force coord. 1988-89, adminstrv. v.p. 1988-91), Acad. Family Mediators (practitioner mem.), Alaska Bar Assn. (employment, alt. dispute resolution, family law sect.), Bus. and Profl. Women, Alaska Dispute Settlement Assn. (v.p. 1992-93, chair com. on credentialing and stds. of practice, pres. 1996—). Home: PO Box 100098 Anchorage AK 99510-0098 Office: PO Box 240783 Anchorage AK 99524-0783

ANDERSON, KATHRYN CORINN, counselor, educator; b. Oakland, Calif., Sept. 19, 1959; d. Paul Edward and Joyce Marie (Hemma) Anderson; m. L. Jesse Rivera, Apr. 30, 1989. BA in Internat. Rels., U. of the Pacific, 1981; MA in Counseling, San Jose State U., 1985. Nat. cert. career counselor; nat. cert. counselor; lic. profl. counselor, Idaho; cert. HIV counselor. Student advisor, tutor U. Pacific, Stockton, Calif., 1980-81; refugee resettlement worker Internat. Rescue Com., San Jose, Calif., 1981-83; juvenile probation officer Ada County Juvenile Ct. Svcs., Boise, Idaho, 1986-88; counselor Health Psychology, Inc., Boise, 1988-91; psychometrician Shoreline Psychol. Assn., Boise, 1989-91; dir. programs Idaho Elks Rehab. Hosp., Boise, 1990-91; health educator, counselor San Ysidro (Calif.) Health Ctr., 1991-92; psychometrician San Diego State U., 1991-93; vocational evaluator Grossmont Hosp., 1992—; adj. instr. Coll. of Idaho, Caldwell, 1989-91; instr. Nat. Traffic Safety Inst., Boise, 1988-91; founder, bd. pres. Luth. Social Svcs. of Idaho, Boise, 1987-90; bd. dirs. Luth. Social Svcs. of Wash. and Idaho, Seattle, 1989-90, Ctr. for Employment Tng., San Jose, 1985-86; mem. adv. bd. Stanford U. Employment Experience Program, Palo Alto, 1982-84. State coord., trainer Amnesty Internat. USA, Idaho and Calif., 1987—; mem. fund distbn. panel United Way of Ada County, Idaho, 1990-91. Mem. AAUW, ASTD, ACA, Career Planning and Adult Devel. Network, Assn. for Psych ol. Type, Calif. Assn. for Counseling and Devel., Amnesty Internat. (bd. dirs.). Lutheran. Home: PO Box 23641 San Diego CA 92193-3641 Office: PO Box 158 La Mesa CA 91944-0158

ANDERSON, KATHRYN DUNCAN, surgeon; b. Ashton-Under-Lyne, Lancashire, Eng., Mar. 14, 1939; came to U.S., 1961; m. French Anderson, June 24, 1961. BA, Cambridge (Eng.) U., 1961, MA, 1964; MD, Harvard U., 1964. Diplomate Am. Bd. Surgery. Intern in pediat. Children's Hosp., Boston, 1964-65; resident in surgery Georgetown U. Hosp., Washington, 1965-69, chief resident in surgery, 1969-70, attending surgeon, 1972-74, vice chmn. surgery, 1984-92; chief resident in pediat. surgery Children's Hosp., Washington, 1970-72, sr. attending surgeon, 1974-84; surgeon-in-chief Children's Hosp., L.A., 1992—; prof. surgery U. So. Calif. Fellow ACS (sec. 1992—), Am. Acad. Pediatrics (sec. surg. sect. 1982-85, chmn. 1985-86), Am. Pediatric Surg. Assn. (sec. 1988-91); Am. Surg. Assn., Soc. Univ. Surgeons. Office: Childrens Hosp 4650 W Sunset Blvd Los Angeles CA 90027-6016

ANDERSON, KENNETH JEFFERY, family financial planner, accountant, lawyer; b. Daytona Beach, Fla., May 7, 1954; s. Kenneth E. and Petronella G. (Jeffer) A.; m. Susan Wagner, Aug. 19, 1978; children: Melissa, Kiersten. BSBA, Valparaiso U., 1976, JD, 1979. CPA, Ill. Prof. staff, mgr. Arthur Andersen & Co., Chgo., 1979-84; mgr. Arthur Andersen & Co., L.A., 1984-90, ptnr., 1990—, dir. individual tax fin. svcs., western region. Bd. govs., treas. Idyllwild (Calif.) Arts, 1990—; mem. L.A. Philanthropic Found., 1995; profl. adv. bd. Children's Bur., 1995; adv. bd. L.A. Philharmonic, 1996—; mem. assocs. bd. Chgo. Lung Assn., 1980-84; vol. Hospice of North Shore, Winnetka, Ill., 1981. Mem. AICPA, Fla. Bar Assn., Ill. Bar Assn., Ill. CPA Soc., Calif. CPA Soc. (apptd. to state com. on personal fin. planning), Soc. CPA-Fin. Planners (bd. dirs. 1987-89), Sports Lawyers Assn., Calif. Club. Republican. Home: 28 Cinch Rd Bell Canyon CA 91307-1003 Office: Arthur Andersen & Co 633 W 5th St 26th Flr Los Angeles CA 90071-2005

ANDERSON, LORRAINE PEARL, writer, editor; b. San Jose, Calif., July 3, 1952; d. Edward Eltwood Jr. and Audrey Beatrice (Haug) A. BA, U. Utah, 1975. Editorial asst. Lifetime Learning Publs., Belmont, Calif., 1979-80, prodn. editor, 1980-81; freelance writer and editor Palo Alto, Calif., 1981-90, Davis, Calif., 1990—. Author: (with Rick Palkovic): Cooking With Sunshine: The Lazy Cook's Guide to Solar Cuisine, 1994; editor: Sisters of the Earth: Women's Prose and Poetry about Nature, 1991, (with Scott Slovic and John P. O'Grady) Literature and the Environment, 1997. Mem. Assn. for Study of Lit. and Environment, Sierra Club (life). Mem. Green Party. Home and Office: 2657 Portage Bay E Apt 202 Davis CA 95616-2900

ANDERSON, LOUISE STOUT, crime analyst; b. Wellsville, N.Y., Aug. 11, 1952; d. Carlton C. and Mary (Gasdik) Stout; m. Leonard M. Anderson, June 2, 1973. BA in German Lit., Polit. Sci., Mt. Holyoke Coll., 1974; MA in Polit. Sci., San Diego State U., 1977; MS Human Resources and Organizational Devel., 1994. Cert. C.C. tchr., Calif. Statistician Grossmont Coll., El Cajon, Calif., 1976-78; crime analyst San Diego Police Dept., 1978-80; crime analyst Career Criminal Apprehension Program, Marin County Sheriff's Office, San Rafael, Calif., 1980-83; crime analyst CCAP Unit, Sonoma County Sheriff's Office, Santa Rosa, Calif., 1983-85; mgr. mktg. svcs. Command Data Systems, Dublin, Calif., 1985-87, client svcs. mgr., 1988-92; contracts mgr. Tiburon Inc., 1992; mgr. field svcs. OCS Techs., 1992-95, v.p. nat. customers support, 1994-95; project mgr. Integrated Systems Solution Corp., 1995—; cons. Search Group Inc. for Automated Crime Analysis. Contbr. articles in field. Owner Acacia Assocs., public safety cons. and training orgn.; project mgmt. profl. Project Mgmt. Inst., 1994; bd. dirs. Mltc. Club So. Calif., 1996—. Mem. Antioch Police Commn.; alumna recruiter Mt. Holyoke Club No. Calif., 1981-86.

ANDERSON, MARILYN NELLE, elementary education educator, librarian, counselor; b. Las Animas, Colo., May 5, 1942; d. Mason Hadley Moore and Alice Carrie (Dwyer) Coates; m. George Robert Anderson, Sept. 4, 1974; children: Lisa Lynn, Edward Alan, Justin Patrick. BEd magna cum laude, Adams State Coll., 1962, postgrad., 1965; MEd, Ariz. State U., 1967; postgrad., Idaho State U., 1971, 86, Columbia Pacific U., 1991—. Cert. elem. tchr., K-12 sch. counselor. Tchr. Wendell (Idaho) Sch. Dist. 232, 1962-66, Union-Endicott (N.Y.) Sch. Dist., 1967-68; counselor, librarian West Yuma (Colo.) Sch. Dist., 1968-69; elem. sch. counselor Am. Falls (Idaho) Sch. Dist. 381, 1969-73; project dir. Gooding County (Idaho) Sr. Citizens Orgn., 1974-75; tchr. Castleford (Idaho) Sch. Dist. 417, 1982-92; placement specialist, referral counselor Idaho Child Care Program South Ctrl. Idaho Community Action Agy., Twin Falls, 1992—; mem. Castleford Schs. Merit Pay Devel. program, 1983-84, Accreditation Evaluation com., 1984-85, Math. Curriculum Devel. com., 1985-86. Leader Brownie Scouts, Endicott, 1967-68; chmn. fundraising com. Am. Falls Kindergarten, 1971-73. Recipient Leader's award Nat. 4-H Conservation Natural Resources Program, 1984. Mem. NEA, ASCD, Nat. Assn. Edn. Young Children, Assn. Childhood Edn. Internat., Idaho Edn. Assn., So. Idaho Assn. for Childhood Edn. Internat. (pres.), Idaho Coun. Internat. Reading Assn., Magic Valley Reading Assn., Support Unltd. Providers and Parents. Republican. Baptist. Home: 1675 BBH Wendell ID 83355-9801 Office: South Ctrl Idaho Community Action Agency Twin Falls ID 83301

ANDERSON, MARK ALEXANDER, lawyer; b. Santa Monica, Calif., Nov. 15, 1953; s. William Alexander and Christina (Murray) A.; m. Rosalie Louise Movius, Nov. 28, 1986; 1 child, Morgan Anderson Movius. AB, U. So. Calif., 1974; JD, Yale U., 1978. Bar: Calif. 1979, U.S. Dist. Ct. (no. dist.) Calif. 1979, U.S. Ct. Appeals (9th cir.) 1979, Oreg. 1982, U.S. Dist. Ct. Oreg. 1982, Wash. 1985, U.S. Dist. Ct. (we. dist.) Wash. 1986, U.S. Supreme Ct. 1989. Law clk. U.S. Ct. Appeals (9th cir.), San Francisco, 1978-79, U.S. Dist. Ct. Oreg., Portland, 1980-82; atty. Miller, Nash, Wiener, Hager & Carlsen, Portland, 1983-92; gen. counsel, asst. sec. Dark Horse Comics, Inc., Milwaukie, Oreg., 1992—. Chair Raleigh Hills-Garden Home Citizen Participation Orgn., 1992-93. Mem. ABA, N.W. Lawyers and Artists (pres. 1988-90), State Bar Calif., Wash. State Bar Assn., Oreg. State Bar (chair antitrust, trade regulation and unfair bus. practices sect. 1991-92), U.S. Dist. Ct. Oreg. Hist. Soc., City Club of Portland (chair arts and culture standing com. 1990-92). Home: PO Box 8154 Portland OR 97207-8154 Office: Dark Horse Comics Inc 10956 SE Main St Milwaukie OR 97222-7644

ANDERSON, MARK EUGENE, specialized truck driver, safety inspector; b. Richland Center, Wis., Oct. 9, 1952; s. Harold Eugene and Laila Marie (Jacobson) A.; m. Marilyn Jones, June 22, 1972 (div. 1984); children: Michael, Kenneth, Thomas; m. Georgina Therese Scinta, Sept. 29, 1984. Grad., Mich. Ctr. for Design Driving, 1993, Mich. Ctr. Decision Driving. Enlisted U.S. Army, 1970, ret., 1977; mgr. Taco Bell, Farmington, N.Mex., 1977-78; truck driver Farmington Meat Processors, 1978-80, Nobel/Sysco, Albuquerque, 1980-89; specialized truck driver transuranic nuclear waste Dawn Enterprises Inc., Farmington, 1989-95, Steere Tank Lines, 1995, ABF Freight Sys. Inc., 1995—; truck driver, cert. safety inspector Comml. Vehicle Safety Alliance, Oreg., 1991; truck driver transp. safeguards div. U.S. Dept. Energy, Albuquerque, 1989. Mem. Mich. Truck Safety Commn., 1993. Named N.Mex. State Truck Driving Champion N.Mex. Motor Carriers, 1988, Grand Champion Truck Driving Championship, N.Mex. Motor Carriers, 1994. Home: 5201 Chuckwagon Trl NW Albuquerque NM 87120-2889 Office: Dawn Enterprises Inc PO Box 204 Farmington NM 87499-0204

ANDERSON, MARK ROBERT, data processing executive, biochemist; b. Oak Park, Ill., Aug. 11, 1951; s. Robert Hugo and Marilyn Pettee (Johnson) A.; m. Mary Jane Helsell, June 6, 1980; children: Berit Bracken, Evan Robert. BS, Stanford U., 1972; MS, Stanford U., Hopkins Marine Sta., 1973; postgrad., U. Brit. Columbia, Vancouver, 1973. Publisher Potlatch Press, Friday Harbor, Wash., 1974-77; assoc. prof. Western Wash. U., Bellingham, 1977, Harvard U., Boston, 1978; chief scientist Ocean Research & Ed. Soc., Boston, 1978; v.p. Moclips Cetological Soc., Friday Harbor, 1979-81; founder, dir. The Whale Mus., Friday Harbor, 1979-81; pres. The Oikos Co., Friday Harbor, 1980—, San Juan Software, Friday Harbor, 1983-84; pres., bd. dirs. Island Tech. Inc., Friday Harbor, 1984—; founder, pres. Tech. Alliance Ptnrs., 1989—; bd. dirs. Worldesign, PreText, Inc., Wa. Software Assn., PreText; bd. advisors HIT Lab., U. Wash., 1991—; founder Strategic News Svc., 1995—, WSA Investment Fourm; CEO, bd. dirs. Carrier Wave, Inc., 1996—; program chair Online Advantage 96. . Author: Nineteen Fathers, 1971, (software) The Agent's Advantage, 1983; producer TV film Survivors, 1980; editor, founder Jour. Cetus, 1981; discoverer Resonance Theory, 1981. Founder San Juan Musicians Guild, 1974-78, Anti-Spray Coalition, 1977. Mem. Wash. Software Assn. (bd. dirs. 1988-90, chair pres.'s group 1989—), Database Standards Com., Am. Electronics Assn.

ANDERSON, MARSHA KOBRE, educational administrator; b. Passaic, N.J., Mar. 18, 1948; d. Irving Jack and Sylvia (Slatkin) Kobre; m. Peter Joe Anderson, Jan. 4, 1970 (div. Nov. 1982); children: Brian Jacob, Emily Jane. BA, Douglass Coll., 1969; M of Arts in Tchg., Trenton State Coll., 1972; PhD, U. Denver, 1988. Cert. tchr. English, N.J. Onsite coord., instr. basic skills Loretto Heights Coll., Denver, 1979-84; asst. to pres. Consortium of State Colls., Denver, 1985; coord. program in bus. Felician Coll., Lodi, N.J., 1986; asst. dir. spl. projects N.J. Com. for Humanities, New Brunswick, 1987; asst. dean Grad. Sch. Edn. Rutgers U., New Brunswick, 1987-92; adminstrv. specialist, writer Clark County Sc. Dist., Las Vegas, Nev., 1992—; cons. The Document Dr., 1989—; state coord. N.J. ACE/NIP, Washington, 1990-92, Am. Coun. on Edn./Nat. Indentification Program. Author: Douglass Coll. Alumnae Bull., 1989, (newsletter) Grants for School Districts, 1994, mem. editl. bd., 1993-96; editor: (newsletter) Jewish Community Center of Southern Nevada, 1993-95. Mem. adv. com. Denver Pub. Schs. Spl. Edn. Adv. Com., 1983-85; bd. dirs. Desertview Svcs., Inc., Las Vegas, 1993—, Jewish Comty. Ctr. So. Nev., Las Vegas, 1993-96, mem., 1993—; chair adv. coun. Nev. Parent Connection, Las Vegas, 1994-95. Mem. AAUW, Nev. Fed. Program Adminstrs. Assn., Nev. Ednl. Equity Task Force, Clark County Assn. Sch. Adminstrs., Soc. for Values in Higher Edn., Kappa Delta Pi, Alpha Psi Omega. Democrat. Jewish. Home: 1694 Clear Look Ct Henderson NV 89014 Office: Clark County Sch Dist 2832 E Flamingo Rd Las Vegas NV 89121-5205

ANDERSON, MATTHEW L., lawyer; b. L.A., June 30, 1960; s. James and Linda (Peters) A.; m. Patricia Donovan, June 20, 1988; children: Charles, Debbie. BA, U. Calif., Berkeley, 1982, JD, 1984. Bar: Calif. 1984. Pvt. practice San Francisco, 1985-90; ptnr. Werik & Anderson, Palo Alto, 1990—. Author: The Average Person's Guide to Law, 1993; contbr. articles to profl. jours. Bd. dirs. United Way, Palo Alto, 1995—. Mem. ABA, Calif. Bar Assn. Democrat. Office: Werik & Anderson 260 Sheridan Ave Ste 216 Palo Alto CA 94306-2009

ANDERSON, MICHAEL GEORGE, marketing and advertising executive; b. Boulder, Colo., Aug. 3, 1951; s. George Martin and Annette Elizabeth (Girmann) A.; m. Susan Elliott, Mar. 19, 1977; children: Gregory Michael, Richard Charles. BS in Aero. Engring., U. Colo., 1973, MBA in Fin., 1978. Design engr. Beech Aircraft, Boulder, 1976-78, liaison engr., 1978-79; mech. engr. Dieterich Standard, Boulder, 1979-80, mgr. engring. design, 1980-84, quality assurance mgr., 1984-87, mgr. advt., mktg. strategic planning and quality assurance, 1987-90, mgr. regional mktg., advt. mgr., 1990-96; product group mgr. Advanced Forming Tech., Longmont, Colo., 1996—. Author (computer software) Tektronix Header Program, 1982. V.p. Luth. Ch. Coun.,1 988-91; asst. scoutmaster Troop 161 Boy Scouts Am.; football and basketball coach Niwot Youth Sports. Recipient NPT Stamp and Cert., ASME, Boulder, 1986. Mem. Instrument Soc. Am., Boulder Flycasters Club, U. Colo. Alumni Assn. (bd. dirs. 1985-87, v.p. bd. dirs. Boulder chpt. 1985-86), Buff Club (v.p., bd. dirs. 1985-87, pres. 1988-90), Moose. Republican. Home: 7400 Mount Meeker Rd Longmont CO 80503-7143 Office: PCC/Advanced Forming Technology 2150 Miller Dr Longmont CO 80501-9000

ANDERSON, MICHAEL KENNETH, marketing professional; b. Des Moines, Feb. 4, 1953; s. Gerald Vernon and Marianne (Blachley) A.; m. Elizabeth S. Cunningham, May 8, 1976; children: Sarah Elizabeth, Jennifer Suzanne. BSBA, Calif. State U., Sacramento, 1981. Mgr. mktg. and pub. rels. western divsn. Pargas Inc., Waldorf, Md., 1981-84; nat. mgr. advt./sales Amerigas Inc., Sacramento, 1984-87; pres. Anderson Solone Inc., Sacramento, 1987—. Office: Anderson Solone Inc 3100 Fite Cir Ste 101 Sacramento CA 95827-1805

ANDERSON, MICHAEL ROBERT, marketing representative; b. Mpls., Nov. 3, 1953; s. Arthur Robert Anderson and Patricia Roberta Carlson; divorced; children: Jenna Courtney, Evan Brendan. BSEE, U. Minn., 1976; MS in Sys. Mgmt., U. So. Calif., 1981. Microelectronics engr. Hughes Aircraft Co., Fullerton, Calif., 1977; mktg. rep. Hewlett Packard, Orange County, Calif., 1977-81; regional mgr. Group III Elec., Orange County, 1981-85; mktg. rep. Lisp Machines Inc., L.A., 1985-87, Sun Microsys., Inc., Orange, Calif., 1987-91; mktg.rep. Auspex Sys., Inc., Santa Clara, Calif., 1992-95, Raptor Systems, Waltham, Mass., 1995—. Big Brother, Big Bros. Inc., Orange, Calif., 1979-81. Fellow AAAS, Am. Assn. Artificial Intelligence, Planetary Soc. Home: PO Box 5199 San Clemente CA 92674-5199 Office: Raptor Systems Inc 302 N El Camino Real Ste 200 San Clemente CA 92672-4778

ANDERSON, MITCHELL, chiropractor; b. L.A., Aug. 9, 1963; s. Charles Terry and Anita Louise (Rose) A.; m. Patricia Elaine Evora, June 10, 1989. AA, Cerritos Coll., 1983; BS, Cleveland Chiropractic Coll., L.A., 1985; D of Chiropractic, Cleveland Chiropractic Coll., 1987; sports cert., L.A. Chiropractic Coll., 1988. Cert. chiropractor Nat. Bd. Chiropractic Examiners; diplomate Am. Bd. Chiropractic Sports Physicians; lic. chiropractor, Calif., Hawaii. Massage therapist/owner Body Work by Mitch, Downey, Calif., 1983-87; chiropractor Anderson Chiropractic Ctr., Los Alamitos, Calif., 1987—; referal doctor/owner Anderson Worker's Referal Svc., Orange, Calif., 1991—; physician Bretheren Christian High Sch., Cypress, Calif., 1988—; team chiropractor Anaheim Bullfrogs, 1993—; pres. Calif. Chiropractic Coun. on Sports Injuries and Phys. Fitness; physician 1992 Olympic Games, Barcelona, Spain, Profl. Rodeo, 1992—, 1996 Olympic Games, Atlanta. Mem. Am. Chiropractic Assn. (sports cert. 1989, coun. sports injuries 1988—), Fed. Internat. Chiropractic Sportive, Calif. Chiropractic Assn., Rotary, Masons (3 degree), Scottish Rite (32 degree). Republican. Baptist. Home: PO Box 5116 Los Alamitos CA 90721-5116 Office: Anderson Chiropractic Ctr 10671 Los Alamitos Blvd Los Alamitos CA 90720-2137

ANDERSON, NED, SR., Apache tribal chairman; b. Bylas, Ariz., Jan. 18, 1943; s. Paul and Maggie (Rope) A.; m. Delphina Hinton; children—Therese Kay, Linette Mae, Magdalene Gail, Ned, Sean. AA, Ea. Ariz. Coll., 1964, AAS in computer sci., 1989; BS, U. Ariz., 1967, JD, 1973. Field dir. Nat. Study Indian Edn., dept. anthropology U. Ariz., Tucson, 1968-70; tech. asst. Project Head Start, Ariz. State U., Tempe, 1970; ethnographer Smithsonian Instn., Washington, 1970-73; dir. Jojoba Project, Office of Arid Land Studies, U. Ariz. Tucson, 1973-76; with Jojoba devel. project San Carlos Apache Tribe, Ariz., 1976-78, tribal councilman, 1976-78, 93—, tribal chmn., 1978-86, gen. mgr. spl. housing projects, 1991—. Contbr. articles to profl.jours. Bd. dirs. Southwestern Indian Devel., Inc., 1971; mem. affirmative action com. City of Tucson, 1975-76; bd. dirs. Indian Enterprise Devel. Corp., 1976-78; mem. study panel NAS, 1975-77; pres. Inter-Tribal Coun. Ariz., 1979—; mem. supervisory bd. Ariz. Justice Planning Commn., 1978—, Indian adv. bd. Intergovtl. Personnel Program, 1978—; pres. bd. Ft. Thomas High Sch. Unified Dist., 1987—, clk. bd., 1989—; trustee Bacone Coll., 1986—; mem. adv. bd. Am. Indian Registry for Performing Arts, 1985—, San Carlos Fish and Game Commn., 1975—, chmn., 1976—; mem. exec. com. San Carlos Apache Tribal Coun., 1976-78, budget, fin. com., 1976—, constn. and ordinance com. 1976-78, investment com. 1997—, chmn. law and order com., 1976-78; adv. bd. Gila Pueblo Community Coll. extension Ea. Ariz. Coll., 1979—; mem. sch. bd. Ft. Thomas High Sch. Unified Dist., 1977—, clk., 1987—, pres. sch. bd., 1992—; mem. County Govt. Study Commn. State Ariz., 1981-84; adv. bd. Indian Edn., Ariz. State U., Tempe, 1978—, U. Ariz., Tucson, 1978—; bd. dirs. San Carlos Lake Devel., 1994—, Western Apache Constrn. Co., 1994—; mem. reinvention mgmt. lab. workgroup Nat. Housing Improvement Program, 1995-96. Recipient Outstanding Community Coll. Alumni award Ariz. Community Coll. Bd./Ea. Ariz. Coll., 1982, Outstanding Cooperation award U.S. Secret Svc., 1984, A.T. Anderson Meml. scholarship, 1989, Univ. Rels. award AT&T, 1989. Mem. Nat. Tribal Chmn.'s Assn. (bd. dir. 1978—, adv. bd. 1978—), Ariz. Acad., Globe C. of C., Phi Theta Kappa.

ANDERSON, NORMAN HENRY, psychology educator, researcher; b. Mpls., July 23, 1925. BS in Physics, U. Chgo., 1946, MS in Math., 1949; MS in Psychology, U. Wis., 1955, PhD in Psychology, 1956. Mathematician ERA/Sperry Rand, Arlington, Va., 1951-53; asst. prof. psychology UCLA, 1958-62, assoc. prof., 1962-65; prof. U. Calif.-San Diego, La Jolla, 1965—; vis. asst. prof. Yale U., New Haven, Conn., 1957-58, Ind. U., Bloomington, 1962-63; mem psychobiology panel NSF, 1963-65, mem. social psychology panel, 1973-75. Author: Foundations of Information Integration Theory,

1981, Methods of Information Integration Theory, 1982, A Functional Theory of Cognition, 1996; editor, contbr.: Information Integration Theory, Vols. I-III, 1991; mem. editorial bd. Jour. Math. Psychology, 1964-73, Behavior Research Methods and Instrumentation, 1968-80; contbr. numerous articles to profl. jours. Served with U.S. Army, 1946-47. Recipient Socio-Psychol. prize AAAS, 1972; fellow Ctr. Advanced Study in Behavioral Scis., Stanford U., 1968-69. Mem. Soc. Exptl. Psychologists. Office: U Calif Dept Psychology La Jolla CA 92093-0109

ANDERSON, PARKER LYNN, editorial columnist, playwright; b. Wickenburg, Ariz., Apr. 19, 1964; s. Harry Milton and Darla Raejean (Hangartner) A. Mem. prodn. com. Prescott (Ariz.) Fine Arts Assn., 1993-95; columnist The Prescott News, 1995-96; adv. mem. The Blue Rose Theatre Co., Prescott, 1994—. Author: (plays) The Startled Cowboys, 1991, Voices From the Past, 1995, The Sleeping Toad, 1997. Home: PO Box 1285 Prescott AZ 86302

ANDERSON, PATRICK LEE, electrical/electronics engineer; b. Clarinda, Iowa, Mar. 17, 1956; s. Richard Lee and Gene Ann Anderson; m. Divina Guytingco, May 30, 1987; children: Christopher, Colin. BS in Psychology, Iowa State U., 1978, BS in Speech, 1978, MS in Elec./Computer Engring., 1988; MS in Speech Pathology and Audiology, U. Iowa, 1980. Speech pathologist Laconia (N.H.) State Sch., 1980-81, Southbury (Conn.) Tng. Sch., 1981-84; pvt. practice Woodbury, Conn., 1981-84; rsch. and tchg. asst. Iowa State U., Ames, 1985-88; rsch. engr. Boeing Comml. Airplane, Seattle, 1988—. Inventor in field. Block coord. Am. Cancer Soc., Redmond, Wash., 1994; sponsor Child Reach, Providence, R.I., 1994. Mem. IEEE Computer Soc., Iowa State Alumni Assn., Am. Speech and Hearing Assn., Phi Beta Kappa. Democrat. Roman Catholic. Home: 21602 NE 29th St Redmond WA 98053-6361

ANDERSON, PAUL NATHANIEL, oncologist, educator; b. Omaha, May 30, 1937; s. Nels Paul E. and Doris Marie (Chesnut) A.; BA, U. Colo., 1959, MD, 1963; m. Dee Ann Hipps, June 27, 1965; children: Mary Kathleen, Anne Christen; Diplomate Am. Bd. internal Medicine, Am. Bd. Med. Mgmt. Intern Johns Hopkins Hosp., 1963-64, resident in internal medicine, 1964-65; rsch. asso., staff assoc. NIH, Bethesda, Md., 1965-70; fellow in oncology Johns Hopkins Hosp., 1970-72, asst. prof. medicine, oncology Johns Hopkins U. Sch. Medicine, 1972-76; attending physician Balt. City Hosps., Johns Hopkins Hosp., 1972-76; dir. dept. med. oncology Penrose Cancer Hosp., Colorado Springs, Colo., 1976-86; clin. asst. prof. dept. medicine U. Colo. Sch. Medicine, 1976-90, clin. assoc. prof., 1990—; dir. Penrose Cancer Hosp., 1979-86, chief dept. medicine, 1985-86; founding dir. Cancer Ctr. of Colorado Springs, 1986-95, founding dir., Pikes Peak Forum for Health Care Ethnics, 1996—; dir. Rocky Mountain Cancer Ctr., Colorado Springs, 1995—; med. dir. So. Colo. Cancer Program, 1979-86; pres., chmn. bd. dirs. Preferred Physicians, Inc., 1986-92; mem. Colo. Found. for Med. Care Health Standards Com., 1985, sec., exec. com., 1990, bd. dirs., pres. 1992-93; mem., chmn. treatment com. Colo. Cancer Control and Rsch. Panel, 1980-83; prin. investigator Cancer Info. Svc. of Colo., 1981-87. Editor Advances in Cancer Control; editorial bd. Journal of Cancer Progam Management, 1987-92, Health Care Management Review, 1988—. Mem. Colo. Gov.'s Rocky Flats Employee Health Assessment Group, 1983-84; mem. Gov.'s Breast Cancer Control Commn. Colo., 1984-89; pres., founder Oncology Mgmt. Network, Inc., 1985-95; founder, bd. dirs. Timberline Med. Assocs., 1986-87; founder, dir. So. Colo. AIDS project 1986-91; mem. adv. bd. Colo. State Bd. Health Tumor Registry, 1984-87; chmn., bd. dirs. Preferred Physicians, Inc., 1986-92; bd. dirs. Share Devel. Co. of Colo. Share Health Plan of Colo., 1986-90, vice chmn., 1989-91; bd. dirs., chmn. Preferred Health Care, Inc., 1991-92; founding dir. Pikes Peak Forum for Health Care Ethics, 1996—; mem. health care standards com., trustee Colo. Found. for Med. Care (PRO); mem. nat. bd. med. dirs. Fox Chase Cancer Ctr. Network, Phila., 1987-89; mem. tech. expert panel Harvard Resource-Based Relative Value Scale Study for Hematology/Oncology, 1991-92; founding dir. Colo. Healthcare Improvement Found., 1994-95, Pike's Peak Forum Health Care Ethics, 1996—. Served with USPHS, 1965-70. Diplomate Am. Bd. Internal Medicine, Am. Bd. Med. Oncology. Mem. Am. Soc. Clin. Oncology (chmn. subcom. on oncology clin. practice standards, mem. clin. practice com., rep. to AMA 1991—, mem. healthcare svcs. rsch. com., chmn. clin. guidelines subcom. 1993—), Am. Assn. Cancer Rsch., Am. Assn. Cancer Insts. (liaison mem. bd. trustees 1980-92), Am. Coll. Physician Execs., Am. Hospice Assn., Am. Soc. Internal Medicine, Nat. Cancer Inst. (com. for community hosp. oncology program evaluation 1982-83), Colo. Soc. Internal Medicine, Assn. Community Cancer Ctrs. (chmn. membership com. 1980, chmn. clin. rsch. com. 1983-85, sec. 1983-84, pres.-elect 1984-85, pres. 1986-87, trustee 1981-88), AAAS, N.Y. Acad. Scis., Johns Hopkins Med. Soc., AMA (mem. practice parameters forum 1989—, adv. com. to HCFA on uniform clin. data set), Colo. Med. Soc., Am. Mgmt. Assn., Am. Assn. Profl. Cons., Am. Soc. for Quality Control, Am. Acad. Med. Dirs., Am. Coll. Physician Execs., El Paso County Med. Soc., Rocky Mountain Oncology Soc. (chmn. clin. practice com. 1989-94, pres.-elect 1990, pres. 1993-95), Acad. Hospice Physicians, Coalition for Cancer, Colo. Springs Clin. Club, Alpha Omega Alpha. Contbr. articles to med. jours. Office: Rocky Mountain Cancer Ctr 110 East Monroe St Ste 200 PO Box 7148 Colorado Springs CO 80933-7148 also: 32 Sanford Rd Colorado Springs CO 80906-4233

ANDERSON, PEGGY REES, accountant; b. Casper, Wyo., Sept. 8, 1958; d. John William and Pauline Marie (Harris) Rees; m. Steven R. Anderson, May 26, 1984 (div. Sept. 1990). BS in Acctg. with honors, U. Wyo., 1980. CPA. Audit staff to sr. Price Waterhouse, Denver, 1980-84; asst. contr. to contr. Am. Investments, Denver, 1984-88; cons. ADI Residential, Denver, 1988-89; contr., treas. Plante Properties, Inc., Denver, 1989-92; acctg. mgr. Woodward-Clyde Group, Inc., Denver, 1992-96; internat. acctg. mgr. US-West, Inc., Denver, 1996—. Recipient diving scholarship U. Wyo., 1976-77, 77-78. Mem. Colo. Soc. CPAs. Roman Catholic. Office: US West Inc 9785 Maroon Ctr Ste 210 Englewood CO 80155-6515

ANDERSON, RACHAEL KELLER, library administrator; b. N.Y.C., Jan. 15, 1938; d. Harry and Sarah Keller; 1 child, Rebecca. A.B., Barnard Coll., 1959; M.S., Columbia U., 1960. Librarian CCNY, 1960-62; librarian Mt. Sinai Med. Ctr., N.Y.C., 1964-73, dir. library, 1973-79; dir. Health Scis Libr. Columbia U., N.Y.C., 1979-91, acting v.p., univ. libr., 1982; dir. Ariz. Health Scis. Libr., U. Ariz., Tucson, 1991—; bd. dirs. Med. Libr. Ctr. of N.Y., N.Y.C., 1983-91; mem. biomed. libr. rev. com. Nat. Libr. Medicine, Bethesda, Md., 1984-88, chmn., 1987-88; mem. bd. regents Nat. Libr. Medicine, 1990-94, chmn., 1993-94; pres. Ariz. Health Info. Network, 1995. Contbr. articles to profl. jours. Mem. Med. Libr. Assn. (pres. elect 1996-97, pres. 1997-98, bd. dirs. 1983-86), Assn. Acad. Health Scis. Libr. Dirs. (bd. dirs. 1983-86, pres. 1991-92). Office: Ariz Health Scis Libr 1501 N Campbell Ave Tucson AZ 85724-5079

ANDERSON, RAYMOND EUGENE, land revegetation specialist; b. Joliet, Ill., Aug. 22, 1927; s. Albert Robert and Ebba Evelyn (Nelson) A.; m. Nilene Washburn, 1955 (div.); children: Leslie Lynne, Terry Evelyn, Allison Rae. BS in Agr., Utah State U., 1951; BS in Fgn. Trade, Am. Inst. Fgn. Trade, 1957. Cowboy, ranch hand, 1948-54; range conservationist Bur. Land Mgmt., Phoenix, Ariz., 1954-56; Ariz. fieldman Western Livestock Jour., L.A. and Denver, 1957-61; ranch mgr. Sonora, Mex., 1962-64; livestock cons. Inter-Am. Devel. Bank, Caracas, Venezuela, 1965-66; livestock advisor fgn. aid program U. Ariz., Ceará, Brazil, 1967-71; livestock cons. Niger, Iran, Botswana, Kenya, Turkey, 1971-84; pres. Land Revegetation Internat., Tucson, 1982-86; developer specialization in dry land revegetation without irrigation, reversing desertification and climate change. Contbr. articles on desertification to profl. jours. including UN publs. Desertivication Control Bull. and CERES, also Agroforestry Today, World Farming, Rangelands Western Livestock Jour., Ariz. Daily Star. Served with USAAC, 1945-47. Mem. Am. Soc. for Range Mgmt. (author Rangelands). Home and Office: Land Revegetation Internat PO Box 12594 Tucson AZ 85732-2594

ANDERSON, RICHARD ERNEST, agribusiness development executive, rancher; b. North Little Rock, Ark., Mar. 8, 1926; s. Victor Ernest and Lillian Josephine (Griffin) A.; m. Mary Ann Fitch, July 18, 1953; children: Vicki Lynn, Lucia Anita. BSCE, U. Ark., 1949; MSE, U. Mich., 1959. Registered profl. engr., Mich., Va., Tex., Mont. Commd. ensign USN, 1952, advanced through grades to capt., 1968, ret., 1974; v.p. Ocean Resources, Inc., Houston, 1974-77; mgr. maintenance and ops. Holmes & Narver, Inc., Orange, Calif., 1977-78; pres. No. Resources, Inc., Billings, Mont., 1978-81; v.p. Holmes & Narver, Inc., Orange, Calif., 1981-82; owner, operator Anderson Ranches, registered Arabian horses and comml. Murray Grey cows, Pony, Mont., 1982—; pres., dir. Carbon Resources Inc., Butte, Mont., 1983-88, Agri Resources, Inc., Butte, Mont., 1988-95, Anderson Holdings, Inc., Pony, Mont., 1995—. Trustee Lake Barcroft-Virginia Watershed Improvement Dist., 1973-74; pres. Lake Barcroft-Virginia Recreation Center, Inc., 1972-73. With USAAF, 1944-45. Decorated Silver Star, Legion of Merit with Combat V (2), Navy Marine Corps medal, Bronze Star with Combat V, Meritorious Service medal, Purple Heart; Anderson Peninsula in Antarctica named in his honor. Mem. ASCE, Soc. Am. Mil. Engrs. (Morrell medal 1965). Republican. Methodist. Office: Anderson Holdings Inc PO Box 266 Pony MT 59747

ANDERSON, RICHARD LEE, ophthalmologist, educator; b. Grinnell, Iowa, Feb. 24, 1945; s. James Lee and Priscilla Jane (McKibbin) A.; m. Karen Nettie Altemeier, Aug. 21, 1965 (div. 1990); m. Susan Annette Aho, July 31, 1992; children: Mark, Erin, Sadie. BA, Grinnell Coll., 1967; MD, U. Iowa, 1971. Diplomate Am. Bd. Ophthalmology. Resident in ophthalmology U. Iowa, Iowa City, 1971-74; resident in plastic surgery U. Calif., San Francisco, 1974-76; from asst. prof. to prof. ophthalmology U. Iowa, Iowa City, 1976-84; prof. ophthalmology U. Utah, Salt Lake City, 1984—, chief div. ophthalmic plastic surgery, 1986—. Author: Clinical Orbital Anatomy, 1983; assoc. editor Archives Ophthalmology, 1984-94, Ophthalmic Surgery, 1984—, Ophthalmic Plastic and Reconstructive Surgery, 1984—; contbr. more than 300 articles to profl. jours. Served to maj. U.S. Army N.G., 1971-76. Named to Best Drs. in Am., 1991,-94; named to Best 400 Drs. in Am., Good Housekeeping mag., 1991. Fellow ACS; mem. Am. Acad. Ophthalmology (Sr. Honor award 1994, Heed award 1990), Am. Soc. Ophthalmic Plastic and Reconstructive Surgery (v.p. 1984-85), Am. Acad. Facial Plastic and Reconstructive Surgery, Alpha Omega Alpha. Republican. Christian. Office: U Utah Dept Ophthalmology Moran Eye Ctr 50 N Medical Dr Salt Lake City UT 84132-0001

ANDERSON, ROBERT ERNEST, safety engineer, consultant; b. Heavener, Okla., July 30, 1926; s. Ernest L. and Dewey M. (Vaught) A., m. Eleanor Jeanne Mauzy, Sept. 15, 1948; children: Robert, Sarah, David, Hans. BS, Okla. State U., 1949, MS, 1950. Registered profl. engr., Calif.; cert. safety profl. Instr. Okla. State U. Agr. and Applied Sci., Stillwater, 1950-51, asst. prof., 1951-52; with Mine Safety Appliances Co., Beaumont, Tex., Gary, Ind., and Little Rock, 1952-63; mgr. safety products MSA Internat., Pitts., 1963-67; mgr. intermountain dist. MSA, Salt Lake City, 1967-87; pvt. practice safety engring. cons. Salt Lake City, 1987—; adj. asst. prof. safety engring. U. Utah., 1988—; cons. Indsl. Health Inc. With USNR, 1944-46. Mem. AIME, Am. Indsl. Hygiene Assn., Am. Soc. Safety Engrs. (v.p. region II 1986-87, Safety Profl. of Yr. Utah chpt. 1993), Masons. Democrat. Methodist. Home and Office: 3372 Pioneer St Salt Lake City UT 84109-3048

ANDERSON, ROBERT MONTE, lawyer; b. Logan, Utah, Feb. 19, 1938; s. E. LeRoy and Grace (Rasmussen) A.; m. Kathleen Hansen, Aug. 12, 1966; children: Jennifer, Katrina, Alexander. AB, Columbia Coll., 1960; LLB, U. Utah, 1963. Bar: Utah 1963, U.S. Cir. Ct. Appeals (10th cir.) 1967, U.S. Supreme Ct. 1976. Assoc., shareholder, v.p. Van Cott, Bagley, Cornwall & McCarthy, Salt Lake Cit, 1963-82; pres., shareholder Berman & Anderson, Salt Lake Cit, 1982-86; v.p., shareholder Hansen & Anderson, Salt Lake Cit, 1986-90; pres., shareholder Anderson & Watkins, Salt Lake Cit, 1990-95; pres. Anderson & Smith, Salt Lake Cit, 1995—; bd. dirs. Anderson Lumber Co., Ogden, Utah. Trustee The Children's Ctr., Salt Lake City, 1973-77; pres. Utah Legal Svcs., Salt Lake City, 1978. Mem. ABA, Utah State Bar Assn. (cts. and judges com. 1991——), Alta Club, Cottonwood Club, Bonneville Knife and Fork Club, Rotary. Office: Anderson & Smith 136 S Main St # 900 Salt Lake City UT 84101-1601

ANDERSON, ROBERT T., anthropologist, researcher, physician; b. Oakland, Calif., Dec. 27, 1926; s. Victor T. and Stella Irene (Hansen) A.; m. Barbara Gallatin Anderson, Aug. 20, 1956 (div. Aug. 20, 1972); children: Andrea, Robin, Scott; m. Edna May Steiner Mitchell, Oct. 10, 1973; children: Debby, Tom, Kris. BA in Anthropology with hons., U. Calif., 1949, MA in Anthropology, 1953, PhD in Anthropology, 1956; MD, U. Autonoma Ciudad Juarez, Mex., 1986; D in Chiropractics, Life Chiropractic Coll. West, 1982. Cert. physician, surgeon Mex.; cert. physician, surgeon Ednl. Commn. Fgn. Med. Grads., U.S.; cert. radiology x-ray supr., oper., Calif.; lic. chiropractor, Calif. Asst. prof. anthropology U. Wash., Seattle, 1959-60; Asst. prof. anthropology U. Calif., Berkeley, 1960, assoc. prof., 1966-67, prof. anthropology, 1967; asst. prof. anthropology Mills Coll., Oakland, 1960-63, assoc. prof. anthropology, 1963-66, prof. anthropology, 1967—; dir. rsch. Life Chriropractic Coll. W., 1978-83, Am. Coll. Traditional Chinese Medicine, 1989-92; dir. manual medicine San Francisco Spine Inst. at Seton Med. Ctr., 1988-91; researcher in field; med. anthropologist, Mex., Nepal, Brazil. Author: Magic Science and Health: The Aims and Achievements of Medical Anthropology, 1996; co-editor: Conservative Care of Low Back Pain, 1991; assoc. editor: Newsletter of the Am. Back Soc., 1988-92; mem. editl. bd. Med. Anthropology, 1990-96, Yearbook of Transcultural Medicne Psychotherapy, 1991—; contbr. 8 chpts. to books, 44 articles to profl. jours. Served with USN, 1946-48. Decorated WWII Victory medal. Home: 2007 Manzanita Dr Oakland CA 94611 Office: Mills Coll 5000 MacArthur Blvd Oakland CA 94613

ANDERSON, ROGER BANKS, retired surgeon; b. Albert Lea, Minn., June 13, 1918; s. Joseph Leonard and Exine Pearl (Robertson) A.; m. June Beverly Green, Sept. 1, 1939 (dec. 1986); 1 child, David Roger; m. Emily Agnes Sheldorf, Feb. 5, 1988. Student, Macalester Coll., 1936-38; D of Osteopathy, Des Moines Still Coll. Osteopathy, 1951. Diplomate Am. Osteopathic Bd. of Surgery, 1962. Intern Des Moines Gen. Hosp., 1943-44, resident, 1944-45; founder Manning (Iowa) Gen. Hosp., 1945, chmn. dept. surgery, 1951-64; staff mem. Gordon Meml. Hosp., Sioux City, Iowa, 1956-57, chmn. dept. surgery, 1957-64; staff mem. Davenport (Iowa) Gen. Hosp., 1964-69; chmn. dept. surgery Davenport (Iowa) Osteo. Hosp., 1969-74; staff mem. St. Luke Hospital, Davenport, 1974-81; staff mem. dept. surgery Mercy Hosp., Davenport, 1974-81, ret., 1981; fellow in surgery Coll. Osteo. Physicians and Surgeons, L.A., 1954-55; cons. Dickinson County Meml. Hosp., Spitit Lake, Iowa, 1958-64; clin. assoc. prof. surgery Kirksville Coll. Osteopathy, 1969-77; with Iowa State Bd. Osteopathic Examiners, 1953-56, chmn., 1956-62; Iowa State Bd. Med. Examiners, 1963-75; mem. founding and adv. com. Illowa Health Planning Coun., 1967. Contbr. articles to profl. jours. Recipient Boss of the Yr. award Am. Bus. Women's Assn., 1969; recipient Disting. Svc. award West Ctrl. Iowa Healthcare Found., 1992. Fellow Am. Coll. Osteopathic Medicine and Surgery (surg.); mem. AMA, Am. Osteop. Assn. (life, del., mem. profl. affairs com. 1968-69, mem. hosp. inspection team), Nat. Alumnae Assn. (pres. 1965-66), Iowa Soc. Osteopathic Physicians and Surgeons (dist. V chmn. 1950, mem. legal and legislative com. 1952-75, chmn. legal and legislative com. 1960-75, mem. M.D.-D.O. com. 1958-75, chmn. M.D.-D.O. liaison com. 1960-75, ann. conclave chmn. 1964, pres. 1965-66), Iowa Osteopathic Med. Assn. (life), Iowa Med. Soc. (life), Scott County Med. Soc. (life, exec. com. 1979-80), Masons (32 degrees), Psi Sigma Alpha (scholar 1942) . Address: 12442 Marble Dr PO Box 5048 Sun City West AZ 85375

ANDERSON, ROSS, columnist. Editorial writer, columnist The Seattle Times. Recipient Pulitzer Prize for nat. reporting, 1990. Office: The Seattle Times 1120 John St PO Box 70 Seattle WA 98111

ANDERSON, ROY A., aerospace company executive; b. Ripon, Calif., Dec. 15, 1920; s. Carl Gustav and Esther Marie (Johnson) A.; m. Betty Leona Boehme, 1948; 4 children. Grad. Humphrey's Sch. Bus., Stanford U. Mgr. factory acctg. Westinghouse Electric Corp., 1952-56; mgr. acctg. and fin., dir. mgmt. controls Lockheed Missiles and Space Co., 1956-65; dir. finance Lockheed Ga. Co., 1965-68; asst. treas. Lockheed Aircraft Corp. (now Lockheed Corp.), 1968-69, v.p., controller, 1969-71, sr. v.p. finance, 1971-75, vice chmn. bd. dirs., chief fin. adminstrv. officer, 1975-77, chair, CEO, 1977-85, dir., chair exec. com., 1985-88, chair emeritus, 1989—; chair Weingart Found., 1994—. Office: Lockheed Corp 606 S Olive St Fl 23 Los Angeles CA 90014-1501

ANDERSON, STANLEY EDWARD, JR., lawyer; b. Chgo., Oct. 11, 1940; s. Stanley Edward and Margaret Mary (Turner) A.; m. Louise Ann Perko, July 12, 1968; 1 child, Stephanie Elizabeth. BA, Northwestern U., 1962, MBA, 1964; MS, U. Del., 1966; postgrad., U. Minn., 1967-68; JD, Am. U., 1972. Bar: Va. 1973, D.C. 1974, Ill. 1973, Calif. 1976; registered patent atty. 1973. Chemist E.I. duPont de Nemours & Co., Inc., Wilmington, Del., 1966-67; patent assoc. Hooker Chem. Corp., 1969-70; patent advisor Office of Naval Rsch., Arlington, Va., 73-74; patent atty. Merck & Co., Inc., Rahway, N.J., 1974-76, Harris, Kern, Wallin & Tinsley, L.A., 1977-78; pvt. practice law Thousand Oaks, Calif., 1978—; prof. law So. Calif. Inst. Law, Ventura. With USN, 1958-64. USPHS rsch. fellow, 1965; recipient Book Awards in Agy. and Creditors Rights, Am. U., 1972. Mem. Ill. Bar Assn., D.C. Bar Assn., Va. Bar Assn., State Bar of Calif. Republican. Roman Catholic. Home and Office: 1529 Lynnmere Dr Thousand Oaks CA 91360-1948

ANDERSON, STEPHEN HALE, federal judge; b. 1932; m. Shirlee G. Anderson. Student, Eastern Oreg. Coll. Edn., Brigham Young U.; LLB, U. Utah, 1960. Bar: Utah 1960, U.S. Claims Ct. 1963, U.S. Tax Ct. 1967, U.S. Ct. Appeals (10th cir.) 1970, U.S. Supreme Ct. 1971, U.S. Ct. Appeals (9th cir.) 1972, various U.S. Dist. Cts. Tchr. South High Sch., Salt Lake City, 1956-57; trial atty. tax div. U.S. Dept. Justice, 1960-64; ptnr. Ray, Quinney & Nebeker, 1964-85; judge U.S. Ct. Appeals (10th cir.), Salt Lake City, 1985—; spl. counsel Salt Lake County Grand Jury, 1975. Editor in chief Utah Law Rev. Cpl. U.S. Army, 1953-55. Mem. Utah State Bar (pres. 1983-84, various offices), Salt Lake County Bar Assn. (pres. 1977-78), Am. Bar Found., Salt Lake Area C. of C. (bd. govs. 1984), U. Utah Coll. Law Alumni Assn. (trustee 1979-83, pres. 1982-83), Order of Coif. Office: US Ct Appeals 4201 Fed Bldg 125 S State St Salt Lake City UT 84138-1102

ANDERSON, STUART ANTON, education consultant, educator; b. Mpls., May 17, 1913; s. Alvin Leo and Estelle (Newell) A.; m. Helen Robinson, June 7, 1935 (dec. Feb. 1994); children: Judith, David; m. Mary Virginia Metcalf, Sept. 17, 1994. BS, U. Wis., Stout, 1935; MEd, Marquette U., 1938; PhD, U. Wis., 1948. Cert. prin., supt. Ill.; all-grade supervisory, K-14 tchg. cert. Tchr. Milw. Pub. Schs., 1935-45; assoc. prof. edn. U. Wis., Stout, 1946-52; tech. dir. vocat. edn. USA/T.A. Mission, Lima, Peru, 1952-54; dir. student tchg. Ea. Ill. U., Charleston, 1954-56; head of project UNESCO, Manila, 1956-57; assoc. prof. dept. edn. U. Chgo., 1957-58; asst. supt. Niles H.S., Skokie, Ill., 1958-62; supt. Riverside-(Ill.) Brookfield H.S., 1963-69; prof. adminstrn. Sangamon State U., Springfield, Ill., 1970-94, prof. emeritus, 1984—. Author: Successful School Board Meetings, 1989 (Best Seller); contbr. articles to profl. jours. Mem. ASCD, Nat. Coun. Profs. of Ednl. Adminstrn., Nat. Assn. Secondary Prins., Nat. Soc. Study of Edn., Nat. Sch. Pub. Rels. Assn., Ill. Assn. Sch. Adminstrs. (hon. life mem., cons. 1975-85), Ill. Congress Parents/Tchrs. (hon. life mem.), C. of C. (pres. 1965). Democrat. Home and Office: 26645 S Brentwood Dr Sun Lakes AZ 85248

ANDERSON, TERRY DREW, small business owner; b. Spokane, Wash., May 21, 1955; s. Ernest Wendle Jr. and Leona Emily (Drewes) A. AS, North Idaho Coll., 1977; BA, Ea. Wash. U., 1983; postgrad., U. Alaska, Juneau, 1985-89. Tchg. asst. Ea. Wash. U., Cheney, 1980-84; fish broker Anderson's Fish, Auke Bay, Alaska, 1984—, chartered fisherman, 1995—; tchr. guitar cmty. schs., Juneau, 1986—. Author: (song poems) Fifty Fifty, 1985. Vol. fireman Juneau Fire Dist., Auke Bay, 1992—. Sgt. Alaska Army N.G. Mem. ASCAP (assoc.), KC (3d degree). Office: Co A 3d Bn Sct 297th Inf 355 Whittier St Juneau AK 99801

ANDERSON, TERRY MARLENE, civil engineer; b. Honolulu, Sept. 26, 1954; d. Stanley Dale and Anna Clara (Heigert) A.; m. Jack Willard Steinberg, Feb. 29, 1980 (div. May 1983). Student, U. San Diego, 1971-72, U. Calif., San Diego, 1972-74; BS in Biol. Scis., U. Calif., Davis, 1974, BS in Aquacultural Engrs., 1979. Registered civil engr., Calif., Colo. Project mgr. John Carollo Engrs., Walnut Creek, Calif., 1979-85; assoc. civil engr. Grice Engring. Inc., Salinas, Calif., 1985; self-employed Durango, Colo., 1985-86; project engr. CWC-HDR, Inc., Cameron Park, Calif., 1987; sr. civil engr. El Dorado County Dept. Transp., Placerville, Calif., 1987-90; dep. dir. pub. works Medocino County Dept. Pub. Works, Ukiah, Calif., 1990-94; enging. div. mgr. pub. works Sonoma County, 1994—, dist. engr., Lake County Spl. Dist. Recipient Resolution of Appreciaiton, City Coun., City of Gonzales, 1983. Mem. Woman's Transp. Seminar, ASCE, WateReuse. Republican. Office: County of Lake Spl Dists Dept Pub Works Dept 230 A North Main St Lakeport CA 95453

ANDERSON, THEODORE WILBUR, statistics educator; b. Mpls., June 5, 1918; s. Theodore Wilbur and Evelynn (Johnson) A.; m. Dorothy Fisher, July 8, 1950; children: Robert Lewis, Janet Lynn, Jeanne Elizabeth. BS with highest distinction, Northwestern U., 1939, DSc, 1989; MA, Princeton U., 1942, PhD, 1945; LittD, North Park Coll. and Theol. Sem., 1988. Asst. dept. math. Northwestern U., 1939-40; instr. math. Princeton U., 1941-43, rsch. assoc., 1943-45; rsch. assoc. Cowles Commn., U. Chgo., 1945-46; staff Columbia U., 1946-67, successively instr. math. stats., asst. prof., assoc. prof., 1946-56, prof., 1956-67, chmn. math. stats. dept., 1956-60, 64-65, acting chmn., 1950-51, 63; prof. stats. and econs. Stanford U., 1967-88, prof. stats. and econs. emeritus, 1988—; dir. project Office Naval Rsch., 1950-82; prin. investigator NSF project, 1969-92, Army Rsch. Office project, 1982-92; vis. prof. math. U. Moscow, 1968; vis. prof. stats. U. Paris, 1968; vis. prof. econs. NYU, 1983-84; acad. visitor math. Imperial Coll. Sci. and Tech., U. London, 1967-68, London Sch. Econs. and Polit. Sci., 1974-75, U. So. Calif., 1989; C.G. Khatri Meml. lectr. Pa. State U., 1992; rsch. visitor Tokyo Inst. Tech., 1977; sabbaticant IBM Systems Rsch. Inst., 1984; rsch. assoc. Naval Postgrad. Sch., 1986-87; cons. RAND Corp., 1949-66; mem. com. on basic rsch. adv. Office Ordnance Rsch., Nat. Acad. Scis.-NRC, 1955-58; mem. panel on applied math. adv. Nat. Bur. Standards, 1964-65; chmn. com. on stats. NRC, 1961-63; mem. exec. com. Conf. Bd. Math. Scis., 1963-64; mem. com. on support rsch. in math. scis. Nat Acad. Scis., 1965-68; mem. com. Pres.'s Statis. Socs., 1962-64; sci. dir. NATO Advanced Study Inst. on Discriminant Analysis and Its Applications, 1972. Author: An Introduction to Multivariate Statistical Analysis, 1958, 2nd edit., 1984, The Statistical Analysis of Time Series, 1971, (with Somesh Das Gupta and George P.H. Styan) A Bibliography of Multivariate Statistical Analysis, 1972, (with Stanley Sclove) Introductory Statistical Analysis, 1974, An Introduction to the Statistical Analysis of Data, 1986, (with Jeremy D. Finn) The New Statistical Analysis of Data, 1996; editor: (with Krishna B. Athreya and Donald L. Iglehart) Probability, Statistics and Mathematics: Papers in Honor of Samuel Karlin, 1989, (with Kai Tai Fang) Statistical Inference in Elliptically Contoured and Related Distributions, 1990, (with K.T. Fang and I. Olkin) Multivariate Analysis and Its Applications, 1994; editor Anns. of Math. Stats., 1950-52; assoc. editor jour. Time Series Analysis, 1980-88; mem. adv. bd. Econometric Theory, 1985—, Jour. Multivariate Analysis, 1988—; mem. editl. bd. Psychometrika, 1954-72. Recipient R.A. Fisher award Pres.'s Statis. Socs., 1985, Disting. Alumnus award North Park Coll. and Theol. Sem., 1987, Minnehaha Acad., 1992, Award of Merit Northwestern U. Alumni Assn., 1989; named Wesley C. Mitchell Vis. Prof. Columbia U., 1983-84; Guggenheim fellow, 1947-48, fellow Ctr. for Advanced Study in Behavioral Scis., 1957-58; vis. scholar, 1972-73, 80; Sherman Fairchild disting. scholar Calif. Inst. Tech., 1980; vis. disting. prof. Norwegian Coun. Sci. and Indsl. Rsch. U. Oslo; Abraham Wald Meml. lectr., 1982; S.S. Wilks lectr. Princeton U., 1983, P.C. Mahalanobis Meml. lectr., 1985, S.N. Roy Meml. lectr. Calcutta U., 1985, Allen T. Craig lectr. U. Iowa, 1991, C.G. Khatri Meml. lectr. Pa. State U., 1992, George Zyskind Meml. lectr. Iowa State U., 1995. Fellow AAAS (chmn. sect. 1990-91), Am. Statis. Assn. (v.p. 1971-73, Samuel S. Wilks Meml. medal 1988, R.A. Fisher lectr. 1985), Econometric Soc., Royal Statis. Soc., Inst. Math. Stats. (pres. 1963), Am. Acad. Arts and Scis.; mem. NAS, Am. Math. Soc., Internat. Statis. Insts., Internat. Chinese Stats. Assn., Psychometric Soc. (coun. dirs.), Bernouilli Soc. for Math. Stats. and Probability, Norwegian Acad. Sci. and Letters (fgn.), Phi Beta Kappa. Home: 746 Santa Ynez St Stanford CA 94305-8441 Office: Stanford U Dept Stats Stanford CA 94305-4065

ANDERSON, THOMAS E., computer scientist, educator; b. Orlando, Fla., Aug. 28, 1961; s. John L. Anderson and Elizabeth D. Bond; m. Robin Briggs; 1 child, Alexandra. AB in Philosophy cum laude, Harvard U., 1983; MS in Computer Sci., U. Wash., 1989, PhD, 1991. Devel. engr., sr. devel. engr. GenRad Inc., 1983-87; rsch. asst. dept. computer sci. U. Wash., Seattle, 1987-91; asst. prof. computer sci. divsn. U. Calif., Berkeley, 1991-96, assoc.

prof. computer sci. divsn., 1996—; cons. Digital Equipment Corp. Systems Rsch. Ctr., Palo Alto, Calif., 1991—, Xerox Corp. Palo Alto Rsch. Ctr., 1993—. Contbr. articles to profl. jours. IBM grad. fellow, 1989-91; NSF nat. young investigator, 1992; Alfred P. Sloan rsch. fellow, 1994; NSF Presdl. Faculty fellow, 1994. Office: U Calif Berkeley Computer Sci Divsn Berkeley CA 94720

ANDERSON, THOMAS LEIF, physician, researcher; b. New Orleans; s. Maurice John and Kitty Thordis (Thomstad) A.; m. Charlotte Ann Hull, Oct. 11, 1980; children: Laurel Emelia, Timothy Leif. BA, Denison U., 1971; MD, Yale U., 1975. Diplomate Am. Bd. Pschiatry and Neurology. Intern in medicine U. Fla. Hosps., Gainesville, 1975-76; resident Harbor-UCLA Med. Ctr., Torrance, 1976-79; fellow Barnes Hosp., St. Louis, 1979-80, staff physician, 1980—; mem. med. adv. com. L.A. County Muscular Dystrophy Assn., 1982—. Mem. Am. Acad. Neurology. Office: Harbor-UCLA Med Ctr 1000 W Carson St Torrance CA 90502-2004

ANDERSON, WALTER TRUETT, author; b. Oakland, Calif., Feb. 27, 1933; s. Elbert William and Susan Alice (Martin) A.; m. Maurica Griffith Osborne, Feb. 10, 1968; 1 child, Daniel Griffith. BA in Polit. Sci., U. Calif., Berkeley, 1955; MA in Polit. Sci., Calif. State U., Northridge, 1967; PhD in Polit. Sci., U. So. Calif., L.A., 1972. Pvt. practice writer and lectr., 1965—; vis. lectr. Sch. Pub. Policy, U. Calif., Berkeley, 1988-89; fellow, faculty mem. Western Behavioral Scis. Inst., La Jolla, Calif., 1988-92; cons. Values and Lifestyles Program, SRI Internat., Menlo Park, Calif., 1991-92; v.p. Meridian Internat. Inst., San Francisco, 1992—. Author: Evaluating Democracy (with Joseph Allman), 1973, A Place of Power, 1976, Therapy and the Arts, 1977, Open Secrets, 1979, 80, 89, The Upstart Spring, 1983, 84, Rethinking Liberalism, 1983, To Govern Evolution, 1987, Reality Isn't What It Used To Be, 1990, 92, The Truth About the Truth, 1995, Evolution Isn't What it Used to Be, 1996, others; assoc. editor, columnist Pacific News Svc., San Francisco, 1982—; bd. editors: Jour. Humanistic Psychology, 1976—; editorial cons. Calif. Tomorrow, 1976-81; contbg. editor Human Behavior Mag., 1971-80. mem. adv. bd. Rollo May Ctr. for Humanistic Studies, San Francisco, 1987—, U. Calif. Biotech. Rsch. and Edn. Program, 1988—; mem. coun. Biofocus Found., Stockholm, 1988—; chair biotech. task force Sierra Club, San Francisco, 1988-92; bd. dirs. Bay Area Biosci. Ctr., Oakland, 1990—; bd. trustees Inst. for Sci. in Soc., Washington, 1991-95; chair bd. trustees Saybrook Inst. and Grad. Sch., San Francisco, 1992-94. With U.S. Army, 1954-56. Mem. Assn. for Politics and the Life Scis., Internat. Soc. Polit. Psychology, World Future Soc., World Future Studies Fedn., Am. Inst. Biol. Scis., World Acad. Art and Sci. (pres. Am. divsn. 1993—). Office: Meridian Internat Inst One Sansome St Ste 2100 San Francisco CA 94104

ANDERSON, WILLIAM, retail company executive, business education educator; b. L.A., May 21, 1923; s. William Bert and Marie (Novotney) A.; m. Margaret Lillian Phillips, Aug. 16, 1951; children: Margaret Gwen, Deborah Kay, William Keven, Denise Marie. BA in Econs., UCLA, 1948, MEd, 1957. Cert. secondary tchr. (life), Calif. Tchr. bus. edn. Big Bear Lake (Calif.) High Sch., 1949-52, Ventura (Calif.) Unified Sch. Dist. Buena High Sch., 1952-89; chief exec. officer Day's Aircraft Inc., Santa Paula, Calif., 1967—; cons. micro computers Calif. State Dept. Edn., 1983-85; pres. "Dollars for Schollars", Ventura. Crew chief Olympic Games basketball stats., 1984, basketball stats. World Games for the Deaf, 1985, U.S. Olympic Festival, 1991; vol. Calif. Police Olympics, 1989. With USAAF, 1943-45, PTO. Mem. NEA (life), Calif. Bus. Edn. Assn. (pres. So. sect. 1959-60, state sec. 1960-61, hon. life 1991), Internat. Soc. Bus. Edn. (voting del. to Soc. Internat. pour l'Enseignement Comml., Western rep. 1988-89, apptd. historian 1991), Am. Aviation Hist. Soc., Calif. Assn. Work Experience Educators (life), Air Force Assn. (life), So. Calif. Badminton Assn. (past bd. dirs.), Phi Delta Kappa, Delta Pi Epsilon (hon. life). Democrat. Lutheran. Home: 334 Manzanita Ave Ventura CA 93001-2227 Office: Day's Aircraft Co Inc PO Box 511 Santa Paula CA 93061-0511

ANDERSON, WILLIAM J., lawyer; b. Winnipeg, Can., Nov. 28, 1949. BA, Claremont Men's Coll., 1971; JD, Southwestern U., 1975. Bar: Calif. 1975. Lawyer Stockwell, Harris, Anderson & Widom, Pomona, Calif. Mem. ABA, State Bar Calif., L.A. County Bar Assn. Office: Stockwell Harris 363 S Park Ave Pomona CA 91766-1560

ANDERSON, WILLIAM SCOVIL, classics educator; b. Brookline, Mass., Sept. 16, 1927; s. Edgar Weston and Katrina (Brewster) A.; m. Lorna Candee Bassette, June 12, 1954 (dec. Dec. 1977); children: Judith, Blythe, Heather, Meredith, Keith; m. Deirdre Burt, May 28, 1983. B.A., Yale U., 1950, Ph.D., 1954; A.B., Cambridge U., (Eng.), 1952; M.A., Cambridge U., 1955. Prix de Rome fellow Am. Acad. in Rome, 1954-55; instr. classics Yale U., 1955-59; resident in Rome, Morse fellow, 1959-60; mem. faculty U. Calif., Berkeley, 1960—, prof. Latin and comparative lit., 1966—, prof. charge Intercollegiate Ctr. Classical Studies, 1967-68, chmn. classics, 1970-73; rsch. prof. U. Melbourne, 1984; Robson lectr. Victoria Coll., Toronto, 1987; Blegen rsch. prof. Vassar Coll., 1989-90, vice chair comparative lit., 1990-93; vis. disting. prof. Fla. State U., spring 1995. Author: The Art of the Aeneid, 1969, Ovid, Metamorphoses, Critical Text, 1977, Essays on Roman Satire, 1982, Barbarian Play: Plautus' Roman Comedy, 1993. Served with AUS, 1946-48, Korea. NEH sr. fellow, 1973-74. Mem. Am. Philol. Assn. (pres. 1977), Danforth Assocs., Soc. Religion. Episcopalian. Office: Univ Calif Dept Classics Berkeley CA 94720

ANDERSON, WILLIAM THOMAS, art educator, artist; b. Mpls., Dec. 13, 1939; s. Bob and Evelyn Louise (Marsh) A.; m. Mary Kratzenstein, May 26, 1988; children: Susy, Chris, Brighton, Brandon. AA, El Camino Coll., Hawthorne, Calif., 1964; BA, Calif. State U., L.A., 1966, MA, 1967. Prof. art Humbolt State U., Arcata, Calif., 1967—, chmn. dept. art, 1985-90; chief reader advanced placement program studio art Ednl. Testing Svcs., Princeton, N.J., 1985-89. Search and rescue, disaster relief pilot Eureka (Calif.) Squadron 34, Calif. Wing CAP, 1990—. Office: Humbolt State U Art Dept Arcata CA 95521

ANDRADE, JOSEPH J., III, counselor, educator; b. Salem, N.J., Apr. 17, 1957; s. Joseph T. Jr. and Clara B. (Stanton) A.; m. Katrina P. Andrade, May 21, 1957. BA, U. N.Mex., 1981; MS, Calif. State U., Sacramento, 1986. Lic. profl. clin. counselor, N.Mex.; nat. cert. counselor. Testing svcs. asst. Brookdale C.C., Lincroft, N.J., 1982-83; counseling intern Calif. State U., Sacramento, 1983-86; counselor Salisbury (Md.) State U., 1987-89, asst. dir., 1989-91; sr. counselor U. N.Mex., Albuquerque, 1992—; mem. steering com. Human Svcs. Collaborative, Albuquerque, 1994-96, chmn. suspension task force, 1995-96; mem. adv. bd. Highland H.S., Albuquerque, 1994-96, Van Buren Mid. Sch., Albuquerque, 1994-96; mem. faculty depts. comm., psychology, gen. studies, sociology and health sci. U. Phoenix, 1994—. Mem. ACA, Am. Coll. Counselors Assn., N.Mex. Counseling Assn., N.Mex. Mental Health Counselors Assn. Office: U NMex Programs for Children 2600 Marble NE Albuquerque NM 87131

ANDRAIN, CHARLES FRANKLIN, political science educator; b. Fortuna, Calif., Feb. 22, 1937; s. Milton D. and Alberta W. (Gatton) A. A.B., Whittier Coll., 1959; M.A., U. Calif.-Berkeley, 1961, Ph.D., 1964. Asst. prof. dept. polit. sci. San Diego State U., 1964-67, assoc. prof., 1967-70, prof., 1970—, chmn. dept., 1972-74; research assoc. Inst. Internat. Studies, U. Calif.-Berkeley, 1975-76, 78-79, 80-81, 82, 86. Author: Children and Civic Awareness, 1971; Political Life and Social Change, 2d edit., 1975; Politics and Economic Policy in Western Democracies, 1980; Foundations of Comparative Politics: A Policy Perspective, 1983, Social Policies in Western Industrial Societies, 1985, Political Change in the Third World, 1988, Comparative Political Systems, 1994, (with David E. Apter) Political Protest and Social Change, 1995. Woodrow Wilson Found. fellow, 1959-60; Nat. Def. Edn. Act fellow, 1960-63; Ford Found. fellow, 1968-69; NIMH fellow, 1971-72. Mem. Am. Polit. Sci. Assn., Am. Sociol. Assn., Internat. Soc. Polit. Psychology. Office: San Diego State U Dept Polit Sci San Diego CA 92182

ANDRASICK, JAMES STEPHEN, agribusiness company executive; b. Passaic, N.J., Mar. 27, 1944; s. Stephen Adam and Emily (Spolnik) A.; children: Christopher J., Gregory O.; m. Ginger Michael Simon, Feb. 22, 1997. BS, USCG Acad., 1965; MS, MIT, 1971. Commd. ensign USCG, 1965, advanced through grades to lt., 1968; assigned to Vietnam, 1967-68; resigned, 1969; sys. analyst Jamesbury Corp., 1970; corp. fin. and product devel. staffs Ford Motor Co., 1971-74; mgr. corp. devel. IU Internat. Corp., Phila., 1974-78; from v.p. planning, contr. to exec. v.p. C. Brewer & Co., Ltd., Honolulu, 1978-92, pres., 1992—, also bd. dirs.; chmn. bd., mng. gen. ptnr. Mauna Loa Macadamia Ptnrs., 1986-88; chmn. bd. HCPC, Olokele Sugar Co., Hawaiian Sugar and Transp. Coop., 1993-96; chmn. Hawaiian Sugar Planters Assn., 1992-93; bd. dirs. Wailuku Agribus. Co.; adv. bd. Hawaii Coun. on Econ. Edn., 1997. Bd. dirs. Aloha United Way, Honolulu, 1983-89; treas., bd. dirs. ARC, Hawaii, 1983-94, 96—, chmn., 1989-90; bd. dirs. Hawaii Employers Coun., 1992—, chmn., 1995—; trustee UH Found., 1988-94, vice chmn., 1992-93, chmn., 1993-94; trustee Hawaii Maritime Ctr., 1993—; bd. dirs. Coast Guard Found., chmn., 1994; founding mem. adv. bd. Hawaii Coun. on Econ. Edn., 1997. Office: C Brewer & Co Ltd 827 Fort Street Mall Honolulu HI 96813-4317

ANDRE, JAMES P., nuclear engineer; b. Kenmore, N.Y., May 7, 1959; s. Ambrose J. Jr. and Erma C. (Ellis) A.; m. Teresa A. McGarry, Nov. 10, 1984; children; Kristen L., Brian J. BS in Physics, Rensselaer Polytechnic Inst., 1981, MBA, 1988. Physicist U.S. Dept. Energy/Schenectady (N.Y.) Naval Reactors Office, 1981-92; sr. devel. engr. Battelle, Pacific Northwest Nat. Lab., Richland, Wash., 1992—; adj. faculty U.S. Dept. Energy Ctrl. Tng. Acad., Albuquerque, 1992—; mem. USDOE Material Control and Accountability Tng. Working Group, Albuquerque, 1992-94; material control and accountability rep. U.S. Dept. Energy/Material Control and Accountability Rep. Com., Washington, 1985-92. Bd. dirs. Three Rivers Children's Mus., Kennewick, Wash., 1993—, pres., 1994-95; tech. adv. Adult Literacy Program, Columbia Basin Coll., Pasco, Wash., 1993-96. Mem. Inst. Nucl. Materials Mgmt. (exec. bd. Pacific N.W. chpt. 1995—), IEEE, Nat. Trust Hist. Preservation. Home: 8109 W Hood Ave Kennewick WA 99336-1618 Office: Batelle Pacific NW Nat Lab PO Box 999 Richland WA 99352

ANDREASEN, STEVEN W., lawyer; b. Salt Lake City, Sept. 17, 1948. BA, U. Utah, 1970, JD, 1974. Bar: Washington 1974. Mem. Davis Wright Tremaine, Seattle. Comment Editor: Utah Law Review 1973-74. Mem. Seattle Estate Planning Coun., Order of Coif, Phi Kappa Phi. Office: Davis Wright Tremaine 2600 Century Sq 1501 4th Ave Seattle WA 98101-1662

ANDREASSIAN, ELLIE E., private school educator, educational administrator; b. Beirut, Lebanon, Jan. 3, 1939; came to U.S., 1974; d. Shahe Galstian and Azad Galstian Dovletian; m. Ara Andreassian, Dec. 26, 1959; children: Arus, Anahid. MA in Fgn. Lang., Erevan (Armenia) State U., 1966; MA in French, R.I. Coll., 1978; PhD in Edn., Boston U., 1990. Prof. fgn. langs. Brussof Inst., Erevan; fgn. students advisor Johnson and Wales U., Providence, from 1975; elem. sch. prin. Armenian Gen. Benevolent Union Sch., Watertown, Mass.; vice prin. Armenian Gen. Benevolent Union Manoogian-Demirdjian H.S., L.A., 1991—; chmn. faculty coun. Mashdots Coll., Glendale, Calif. Author: Enhancement of Identity, 1990; contbr. articles to profl. jours. Mem. ASCD, Nat. Assn. Armenian Studies and Rsch., Am. Internat. Women's Assn., Armenian Gen. Benevolent Union. Armenian Women's Assn. L.A. Home: 512A N Isabel Glendale CA 91206 Office: AGBU Manoogian-Demirdjian Sch 6844 Oakdale Ave Canoga Park CA 91306-3913

ANDREOPOULOS, SPYROS GEORGE, writer; b. Athens, Greece, Feb. 12, 1929; came to U.S., 1953, naturalized, 1962; s. George S. and Anne (Levas) A.; m. Christiane Loesch Loriaux, June 6, 1958; 1 child, Sophie. AB, Wichita State U., 1957. Pub. info. specialist USIA, Salonica, Greece, 1951-53; asst. editorial page editor Wichita (Kans.) Beacon, 1955-59; asst. dir. info. svcs., editor The Menninger Quar., The Menninger Found., Topeka, 1959-63;; info. officer Stanford U. Med. Ctr., 1963-83; dir. comm., editor Stanford Medicine, 1983-93, dir. emeritus comm., editor emeritus, 1993—; editor Sun Valley Forum on Nat. Health, Inc. (Idaho), 1972-83, 85-95. Co-author, editor: Medical Cure and Medical Care, 1972, Primary Care: Where Medicine Fails, 1974, National Health Insurance: Can We Learn from Canada? 1975, Heart Beat, 1978, Health Care for an Aging Society, 1989; contbr. articles to newspapers and profl. jours. With Royal Hellenic Air Force, 1949-50. Mem. AAAS, Assn. Am. Med. Colls., Nat. Assn. Sci. Writers, Am. Med. Writers Assn., Am. Hosp. Assn., Am. Soc. Hosp. Mktg. and Pub. Rels., Coun. for Advancement and Support of Edn. Home: 1012 Vernier Pl Stanford CA 94305

ANDRES, EUGEN CHARLES, lawyer; b. Boston, July 15, 1939. B.S. in Econs., UCLA, 1961; LL.B., Hastings Coll. Law, 1968. Bar: Calif. 1969. Dep. dist. atty. Orange County (Calif.), 1969-71; sole practice, Santa Ana, Calif., 1971-72; ptnr. Aitken, Bradshaw & Andres, Santa Ana, 1972-78, Bradshaw & Andres, Orange, Calif., 1978-81, Andres & Andres, Santa Ana, Calif., 1981—. Pres. Bowers Mus. Found., Santa Ana, 1979. Mem. ABA, Calif. Trial Lawyers Assn., Orange County Trial Lawyers Assn. (pres. 1978), Calif. State Bar, Orange County Bar Assn. pres. 1982). Office: 322 W 3rd St Santa Ana CA 92701-5226

ANDRESS, CATHY, psychologist, educator; b. Akron, Ohio, June 17, 1960; d. Samuel Coe and Joan (Ferguson) A. BA, Randolph-Macon Woman's Coll., 1982; MA, So. Ill. U., Edwardsville, 1985; PsyD, Chgo. Sch. Profl. Psychology, 1991. Child and family therapist No. Wyo. Mental Health Ctr., Newcastle, 1988-89; sr. therapist Tri-City Community Mental Health Ctr., East Chicago, Ind., 1990; part-time instr. Oakton C.C., Des Plaines, Ill., 1989-91, adj. counselor, 1991; part-time instr. Northeastern Ill. Univ., Chgo., 1990-91; instr. psychology Big Bend C.C., Moses Lake, Wash., 1991-97. Mem. NEA, Assn. for Humanistic Psychology, Assn. for Transpersonal Psychology, Wash. Edn. Assn. (mem. minority affairs commn. 1992-96, mem. woman's caucus steering com. 1995-97), Wash. State Psychol. Assn.

ANDREW, JANE HAYES, non-profit organization executive; b. Phila., Jan. 1, 1947; d. David Powell and Vivian Muriel (Saeger) Hayes; m. Brian David Andrew, June 14, 1977; 1 child, Kevin Hayes. AB, Barnard Coll., 1968, grad., Harvard Arts Administrn. Instit., 1972; MBA, U. Wash., 1994. Mgr. theater Minor Latham Playhouse, Barnard Coll., N.Y.C., 1970-74; co. mgr. Houston Ballet, 1974-77, Ballet West, Salt Lake City, 1978-83; gen. mgr. Pacific N.W. Ballet, Seattle, 1983-87; organizer non-profit consortium nat. ballet cos. and nat. presenting orgns., 1987; pres., exec. dir. Ballet/America, 1988-91; ind. cons. arts mgmt., 1991-94; dir. Found. for Internat. Understanding Through Students, 1995—. panelist NEA Dance Program Presentors, 1987-88, 88-89, 89-90, Seattle Arts Commn. dance grants, 1989, 90; cons. Ariz. Arts Commn., Phoenix, 1985-86; com. mem. 25th Anniversary of World's Fair, Seattle, 1986-87; panelist NEA Local Programs, 1987. Editor (directory) Philadelphia Cultural Orgns., 1977. Bd. dirs. Good Shepherd Adv. Bd., Seattle, 1985-87. Recipient Dorothy D. Spivack award Barnard Coll., N.Y.C., 1972. Mem. Dance/USA (chmn. Mgrs. Coun. 1986). Home and Office: 7706 146th Ave NE Redmond WA 98052-4105

ANDREWS, DONALD L., performing arts company executive. Pres., CEO Utah Symphony, Salt Lake City. Office: Utah Symphony Maurice Abravanel Hall 123 W South Temple Salt Lake City UT 84101

ANDREWS, RALPH HERRICK, television producer; b. Chgo., Dec. 17, 1927; s. Henry Karl and Sylvia Angelica (Lorenzen Barth; m. Margaret Ann Belt, Feb. 5, 1951 (div. 1977); m. Aleksandra Vaz vel Wezykowska, June 1, 1986; children: William, Herrick, Phyllis, Patrice, Peter, James, Jakub, Matthew. Announcer, disc jockey, salesman radio stas. WSAM and WKNX, Saginaw, Mich.; page NBC, Hollywood; with Don Fedderson Prodns., Ralph Edwards Prodns.; dir. live programming Desilu; prin. Ralph Andrews Prodns.; co-founder, bd. dirs. Entertainment Industries Coun. Producer: Divorce Hearing, By the Numbers, Zoom, Show Me, You Don't Say, I'll Bet, Wedding Party, The Family Game, It Takes Two, It's Your Bet, Liars Club, The Mickie Finn Show, Celebrity Sweepstakes, 50 Grand Slam, Lingo, (movies) Silent Treatment, Skyjacked; producer, host: Lie Detector. Cand. for Congress, 1972; nat. dir. edn. and tng. Rep. Nat. Com., Washington, 1972 (Presidential commendation). Republican. Roman Catholic. Home and Office: 5449 Paradise Valley Rd Hidden Hills CA 91302-2435

ANDRIANO-MOORE, RICHARD GRAF, naval officer; b. Petaluma, Calif., May 25, 1932; s. Norvel Moore and Thelma Elizabeth (Cook) Koch-Andriano Atkins; m. Janice Lynn Hironaka, Jan. 10, 1976 (div. Feb. 1990); children: Erika Lynn, Stephen Albert. BS, San Jose State U., 1956; MBA, Pepperdine U., 1977; B in Metaphysical Sci., U. Metaphysics, 1993. Commd. ens. USN, 1957, advanced through grades to comdr.; 1st lt., and gunnery officer U.S.S. Jefferson Count LST1068, 1957-60; 7th grade tchr. Oasis Sch., Riverside County, Calif., 1960-63; pers. and legal officer U.S.S. Maury AGS-16, 1963-65; commdg. officer Naval & Marine Corps reserve Training Cen, Port Arthur, Tex., 1965-68; ops. officer U.S.S. Muliphen LKA 64, 1968-69; ASW & surface program officer 11th Naval Dist., San Diego, 1970-74; commdg. officer Naval Reserve Cen., Hunters Point, Calif., 1974-75; comdr. officer Army, Navy & Marine Corps Reserve Ctr, San Bruno, Calif., 1975-79; dir. of adminstrn. Nat. Com. for Employer, Washington, 1979-82; comdr., regional recruiting coord. for 10 western states, Alameda, Calif., 1982-84; chief of staff N.R. Readiness comdr., Treasure Island, Calif., 1984-85; tchr. Shoreline Unified Sch. Dist., Tomales, Calif., 1985-92, 94-97. Editor-in-chief: California Compatriot, 1976-80. Insp. Precinct Bd., Petaluma, Calif., 1987-90; scoutmaster Boy Scouts Am., 1989-92, dist. exec., 1992-94. Decorated Defense Meritorious Svc. medal Sec. of Def., Washington, 1982; recipient Ancestral Coat of Arms of the Counts of Andriano, Wappenrolle, Austria, 1985, Rome, Italy, 1994, Disting. Alumni award San Jose State U., 1991; knighted Order St. John of Jerusalem, 1991. Mem. The Augustan Soc. Inc. (v.p. 1990-93, 95-97), Calif. Socs. Sons of the Am. Revolution (state pres. 1986-87, Patriot medal 1985, San Francisco chpt. pres. 1976-77, Silver Good Citizenship medal 1978, Meritorious Svc. medal 1987, oak leaf cluster 1996), Mil. Order of Loyal Legion of U.S. (calif. comdr. 1982-88), Naval Order U.S. Office: 1253 Bertha Ln Santa Rosa CA 95405-7003

ANDRING, RONALD PAUL, protective services official; b. Yakima, Wash., Apr. 17, 1953; s. Richard Joseph and JeRene Estelle (Krienke) A.; m. Margaret Anne Yount, Jan. 13, 1978; children: Margaret Ann, Ronald Paul Jr. BA in Criminal Justice, Ea. Wash. U., 1990, MPA, 1995. Enforcement officer Wash. State Patrol, Kennewick, 1975-78, Walla Walla (Wash.) Police Dept., 1978-79; correctional officer Wash. State Penitentiary, Walla Walla, 1979-89, adminstrv. asst., 1990-91, correctional sgt., 1991—; mem. regional adv. com. Dept. Corrections, Olympia, Wash., 1991-93, trainer, 1988-97; adj. faculty Ea. Wash. U., Cheney, 1997—. Contbr. articles to profl. jours. and mags. Organizer Jr. Achievement awards, Walla Walla, 1991-93, Kid's Classic Fun Run, Walla Walla, 1991-93; candidate 14th legis. dist. Dem. Cen. Com., Wash., 1972; vol. Friends and Families of Violent Crime Victims, 1989-92; chair publs. com. Blue Ridge PTA, 1989-91. Recipient Pub. Adminstrn. Honors Student award Ea. Wash. U., 1995. Mem. Am. Correctional Assn. (adv. com. 1991—, del. assembly 1994—, coord. mid-winter conf., 1995, 96, 125th congress of corrections, vice chair mem. com. 1996-97, com. mem. coun. congress programs 1996-97), Wash. Correctional Assn. (exec. bd. 1989—, treas. 1994-95, Spl. Svc. award 1993, pres. 1996—), Western Correctional Assn., Am. Criminological Soc., Am. Platform Assn., Masons (master 1992-93), Scottish Rite. Congregationalist. Home: 502 W Chestnut St Walla Walla WA 99362-3963 Office: Washington State Penitentiary PO Box 520 Walla Walla WA 99362-0520

ANDRIST, CHRIS G., crime lab supervisor/forensic scientist; b. St. Francis, Kans., Oct. 20, 1955; s. Bill and Gerre (Ingamells) A.; m. Kimberly Anne Habegger, May 13, 1988. Grad., N.W. Inst. Med. Lab. Tech., 1976; BS, U. Kans., 1980; cert. in Scrology Tng., FBI Acad., 1992, cert. in Hair and Fiber Tng., 1996. cert. med. technologist. Lab. supr. N.W. Kans. Med. Ctr., Goodland, 1980-82; med. technologist Providence Hosp., Waco, Tex., 1982-84, Medicenter I and II, Waco, Tex., 1984-88; asst. mgr., tech. supr. Waco Clin. Pathology Lab., 1986-89; mgr. forensic toxicology Metwest Labs., Denver, 1989-91; criminalist, forensic serologist Jefferson County Sheriff's Dept., Golden, Colo., 1991-96, crime lab supr./forensic scientist, 1996—; criminalist, forensic serologist Necrosearch Internat., Denver, 1993—; crime lab. supervisor/forensic scientist, 1996—; criminalistics adv. bd. Metro State Coll., Denver, 1994—. Mem. Am. Acad. Forensic Sci., Internat. Assn. Identification (bd. dirs. Rocky Mountain divsn., sec., 1996), Internat. Assn. Bloodstain Pattern Analysts, Rocky Mountain Assn. Bloodstain Pattern Analysts, Nat. Tech. Investigators Assn., Colo. Law Enforcement Officers Assn, Colo. Assn. Computer Crime Investigators, Internat. Homicide Investigators Assn., Jefferson County Critical Incident Response Team. Office: Jefferson County Sheriff's Dept 200 Jefferson County Pkwy Golden CO 80401-6008

ANDRUS, CECIL DALE, academic administrator; b. Hood River, Oreg., Aug. 25, 1931; s. Hal Stephen and Dorothy (Johnson) A.; m. Carol Mae May, Aug. 27, 1933; children: Tana Lee, Tracy Sue, Kelly Kay. Student, Oreg. State U., 1948-49; LLD (hon.), Gonzaga U., U. Idaho, U. N.Mex., Coll. Idaho, Idaho State U., Whitman Coll. State gen. mgr. Paul Revere Life Ins. Co., 1969-70; gov. State of Idaho, 1971-77, 87-95; sec. of interior, 1977-81; dir. Albertson's, Inc., 1985-87, 95—, Coeur d'Alene Mines, 1995—; chmn. Andrus Ctr. for Pub. Policy, Boise (Idaho) State U., 1995—; bd. dirs. KeyCorp.; mem. Idaho Senate, 1961-66, 69-70; mem. exec. com. Nat. Gov.'s Conf., 1971-72, chmn., 1976; chmn. Fedn. Rocky Mountain States, 1971-72. Chmn. bd. trustees Coll. of Idaho, 1985-89; bd. dirs. Sch. Forestry, Duke U. With USN, 1951-55. Recipient Disting. Citizen award Oreg. State U., 1980, Collier County Conservancy medal, 1979, Ansel Adams award Wilderness Soc., 1985, Audubon medal, 1985, Statesman of the Yr. award Idaho State U., 1990, Torch of Liberty award B'nai B'rith, 1991; named Conservationist of Yr. Nat. Wildlife Fedn., 1980, Idaho Wildlife Fedn., 1972, Man of Yr., VFW, 1959. Mem. VFW, Idaho Taxpayers Assn. (bd. dirs. 1964-66). Democrat. Office: Boise State U Andrus Ctr Pub Policy 1910 University Dr Boise ID 83725-0001

ANG, PAUL THIENCHAI, entrepreneur, international business consultant; b. Bangkok, July 4, 1937; came to U.S., 1982; s. Jer Tang and Noi Poh (Eah) A.; m. Agnes Lovett; children: Paul L., Paulette A. BCommerce, Melbourne Inst. Tech., Australia, 1959; student Advanced Mgmt. Program, Harvard U., 1980. Mktg. exec. Exxon, Thailand, 1960-63; comml. mgr. Thai Dairy Industry, 1963-65; div./dept. mgr. East Asiatic Co., Thailand, 1965-70; comml. mgr., regional chief exec. Imperial Chem. Industies, Thailand, 1971-72; pres., CEO Chem. Thailand Co. and Multi-Thai Co., 1973-81, PTA Internat. Inc. and C.A., N.J., 1982—. Roman Catholic.

ANGEL, ARMANDO CARLOS, rheumatologist, internist; b. Las Vegas, N.Mex., Mar. 25, 1940; s. Edmundo Clemente and Pauline Teresa (Flores) Sanchez A.; m. Judith Lee Weedin, Aug. 5, 1961; children: Stephanie, Renee. BA, San Jose State U., 1963; MS, U. Ariz., 1970, PhD, 1971, M.D., 1977. Chemist Tracerlab, Inc., Richmond, Calif., 1963-67; prof. chemistry Pima Coll., Tucson, Ariz., 1971-74; intern U. N.Mex., Albuquerque, 1977-78, resident, 1978-80; resident VA Hosp., Lovelace Med. Ctr., Albuquerque, 1978-80; practice medicine specializing in internal medicine, Las Cruces, N.Mex., 1980-88; pvt. practice, El Paso, Tex., 1990—; dir. pain program Rio Vista Rehab. Hosp., 1992; med. dir. Ctr. for Rehab. and Evaluation, 1992—; chief of staff Rio Vista Rehab. Hosp., 1997—; cons. minority biomed. sci. project NIH, Washington, 1970-74, Ednl. Assocs., Tucson, 1971-74. Author: Llevve Tlaloc No. 2, 1973. Treas. Nat. Chicano Health Orgn., Los Angeles, 1974-75; v.p. Mexican-Am. Educators, Tucson, 1973-74; pres. N.Mex. affiliate Am. Diabetes Assn., Albuquerque, 1983-85. Fellow U. Ariz., 1988-90. Fellow Am. Coll. Rheumatology; mem. AMA, Tex. Med. Soc., El Paso County Medical Soc., Am. Diabetes Assn., ACP, Dona Ana County Med. Soc. (pres. 1983), Am. Coll. Rheumatology, Am. Assn. Internal Medicine, Alpha Chi Sigma.

ANGEL, STEVEN, musician; b. Bklyn., Aug. 2, 1953; s. Morris and Rosalyn (Sobiloff) A. Grad. H.S., L.I. Pres. Daystar Records, Santa Monica, Calif., 1991—; profl. drummer, 1960—; lectr. The Whole Life Expo, Pasadena, 1992-95, Inst. for the Advanced Studies of Human Sexuality, San Francisco. Author (music and book) Angels Rejoice, 1976-80; wrote music for tv show Another World, 1987-91; wrote, recorded, produced three songs for Playboy album Music for Lovers, 1993; wrote, recorded, produced album The Erotic God, 1993; editor Unity and Difference Jour., 1994—. Home and Office: Daystar Records 2132 Montana Ave Apt B Santa Monica CA 90403-2017

ANGELE, ALFRED ROBERT, police labor union executive; b. N.Y.C., Dec. 9, 1940; s. Alfred Otto and Alma Margaret (Branda) A.; m. Barbara Ann Chavez, Sept. 30, 1961; children: Cynthia Lynn, Lynda Renee. AA, L.A. Valley Coll., 1968. Cert. tchr. community coll. police adminstrn. Patrolman Burbank (Calif.) Police Dept., 1963-67, detective, 1967-74, sgt., dept. self def. instr., 1974-78; gen. mgr. Calif. Orgn. Police and Sheriffs, Sacramento, 1978-89, exec. dir., 1989—; internat. sec./treas. Internat. Union Police Assns. AFL-CIO, Alexandria, Va., 1985-90; internat. sec./treas. emeritus Internat. Union Police Assns. AFL-CIO, Alexandria, 1990-92; Govt. appt. commr. on Peace Officer Standards/Tng., Sacramento, 1979-84; mem. AFL-CIO observer team sent to Nicaragua to monitor presdl. election, 1990, Police Adv. Coun. on Car Clubs, 1967-70; mem. exch. progrm with German Police Union, 1987. Contbr. articles to profl. jours. including USA Today. Mem. L.A. Host committee for nat. tour Bill of Rights, 1991. Recipient Mike Maggiora Meml. Humanitarian award Maggiora family, 1980, Commendations, Letters of Appreciation Burbank Bar Assn., Elks, Calif. Hwy. Patrol, Mayor's Drug and Alcohol Abuse Com., L.A. County Dist. Atty.'s Office, Houston Police Patrolmans Union, Calif. Dept. Corrections, Mayor of L.A., numerous others; named 1st Officer of the Month Jaycees, 1977. Mem. Burbank Police Officers Assn. (pres. 1976-81, named dir. of yr. 1972, commendation award), Internat. Union Police Assns. AFL-CIO (sec.-treas. 1985—, dir. 1981-85, named law enforcement editor of the yr. 1987), Calif. Narcotics Officers Assn., Calif. Orgn. Police/Sheriffs (gen. mgr. 1978—, sec. 1976-78, commendation award), Calif. Narcotics Info. Network. Democrat. Roman Catholic. Office: 301 E Olive Ave Ste 224 Burbank CA 91502-1216

ANGELO, SANDRA MCFALL, television and video producer, writer; b. St. Louis, Apr. 24, 1950; d. Ernest Allison and Virginia Rose (Vickrey) McFall. BA in Art, Seattle Pacific U., 1972; MBA in Mktg., Nat. U., San Diego, 1985. Cert. K-12 and cmty. coll. tchr., Calif. Tchr. art Downers Grove (Ill.) H.S., 1974-79, La Jolla (Ill.) Country Day Sch., 1981-86; prof. Palomar Coll., San Marcos, Calif., 1986—; video/TV prodr., exec. dir. Discover Art, San Diego, 1994—; nat. dir. Internat. Ann. Colored Pencil Symposium, San Diego, 1989—; columnist Michael's Arts and Crafts Mag., Decorative Painter. Author: So You Thought You Couldn't Draw, 1994, Colored Pencil Basics, 1994, Creating With Colored Pencils on Wood, 1996; author, developer Colored Pencil Art Kit, 1994, Madonna & Child needlepoint kit, 1995; contbg. editor Art Materials Today, 1994; writer. prodr., dir. (video series) The Easy Way to Draw Faces, 1994, The Easy Way to Draw Flowers, Landscapes and Wter, 1994, The Easy Way to Draw Animals, 1994 (nominated for Emmy), Drawing Basics, 1994, (videos) Special Effects with Colored Pencils, 1994, Getting Started with Colored Pencils, 1994, Seven Common Drawing Mistakes and How to Correct Them, 1994, Color Theory Made Really Easy, 1995, Paint Like Monet in a Day with Oil Pastels, 1994, Easy Pen and Ink Techniques for Artists and Crafters, 1996, Realistic Colored Pencil Textures: A Mixed Media Approach, 1996, Time Saving Colored Pencil Techniques, 1996, Drawing Your Loved Ones: People, Building a Nature Sketchbook, 1997, Drawing Your Loved Ones: Pets, Creating with Colored Pencils on Wood, 1997. Recipient fellowship R.I. Sch. of Design, 1986, award Western Access Video Excellence, 1995; articles written about her in Creative Living Mag., 1995, Michael's Mag., 1996. Republican. Home and Office: Discover Art PO Box 262424 San Diego CA 92196

ANGELOV, GEORGE ANGEL, pediatrician, anatomist, teratologist; b. Bulgaria, May 12, 1925; came to U.S., 1978; s. Angel Christov and Maria Angelov; m. Olga Valerie Minkova, Dec. 21, 1952; 1 child, Angel. MD, Sch. of Medicine, Sofia, Bulgaria, 1952. Pediatrician Distric Hosp., Bulgaria, 1952-53; asst. prof. Sch. of Medicine, Sofia, Bulgaria, 1953-64; prof. anatomy and anthropology Sch. of Biology, Sofia, Bulgaria, 1964-77; mgr. reproductive toxicology Lederle Labs., Pearl River, N.Y., 1979-89; cons. reproductive toxicology pvt. practice, Laguna Niguel, Calif., 1989—; assoc. dean Sch. of Biology, Sofia, 1970-72; vis. scientist Sch. of Medicine, Geneva, 1971, 74. Author: (textbook) Anatomy, 1970; mem. glossary com. Teratology Glossary, 1987-89; reviewer several sci. jours.; contbr. numerous sci. publs. on anatomy, teratology, and growth and devel. of adolescents to profl. jours. Mem. Teratology Soc. USA, European Teratology Soc., Human Biology Coun. USA, Free Union of Univ. Profs. of Anatomy. East Orthodox.

ANGIER, JOSEPH, television producer, writer; b. L.A., Sept. 10, 1953; s. Keith and Adele (Rosenthal) A. BA, SUNY, Binghamton, 1974. Prodr. HBO Am. Undercover, 1986-87, PBS-KCET, 1988-93, ABC News Turning Point, L.A., 1994-97. Recipient Cine Golden Eagle award, 1994. Mem. Writers Guild Am. (Best Documentary Script 1989, 91), Acad. TV Arts and Scis. (Emmy for best documentary script 1984). Home: 2268 28th St # 6 Santa Monica CA 90405 Office: PO Box 377 Santa Monica CA 90406

ANGLESIO, FRANCO J., hotel executive; b. Turin, Italy, Sept. 14, 1943; s. Cesare and Alma (Cattaneo) A.; m. Mary C. Bartlett, Aug. 22, 1970; children: Marco P., Michael S. Gen. mgr. Chateau Laurier, Ottawa, Can., 1980-83, Hotel Vancouver, Can., 1983-86; v.p. ops. Coast Hotels & Resorts, Vancouver, 1986-91, exec. v.p., 1991-92, pres., 1992—; bd. dirs. Coast Hotels & Resorts Ltd., Vancouver, Okabe N.Am. Inc., Vancouver. Mem. Skal Club, Chaine des Rotisseurs. Roman Catholic. Home: 1278 Bracknell Pl, North Vancouver, BC Canada V7R1V5 Office: Coast Hotels & Resorts, 900-1090 W Georgia St, Vancouver, BC Canada V6E 3V7

ANGSTADT, PETER J., mayor; m. Denise Angstadt; children: Peter Jr., Adam, Alexander, Jonathan. BS in Biol. Sci., Colo. State U., 1976, M in Edn., 1978; MBA, Idaho State U., 1988. Adminstrv. staff Fort Lewis Coll., Durango, Colo., U. Wis., LaCrosse, Calif. State U., Chico, U. Calif., Davis; housing dir. Idaho State U., Pocatello; elected mayor City of Pocatello, 1990-93, re-elected, 1993—. Office: Office of Mayor 911 N 7th PO Box 4189 Pocatello ID 83205

ANNERINO, JOHN JOSEPH, photojournalist, author; b. Chgo.; s. John Samuel and Ida Barbra (Schwan) A.;m. Alejandrina Delgado, Jan. 30, 1993. BA, Prescott Coll., 1975. Freelance photographer Gamma-Liaison, N.Y.C., 1983—. Photojournalist, author: High Risk Photography: The Adventure Behind the Image, 1991, Canyons of the Southwest, 1993, Wild Country of Mexico/La tierra salvaje de Mexico, 1994, People of Legend: Native Americans of the Southwest, 1996; author: Adventuring in Arizona, 1991, rev. edit., 1996, Running Wild: Through the Grand Canyon, 1992, new edit., 1997, Hiking the Grand Canyon, 1993. Home and Office: 2325 W Wagon Wheels Dr Tucson AZ 85745-1379

ANNON, JACK DORCEY STAFFORD, forensic and criminal psychologist, detective; b. Chgo., Nov. 26, 1929; s. Stafford Dorcey and Marjorie Louise (Sites) A.; m. Leilehua Becker, 1955 (div. 1961); 1 child, Jeffrey; m. Arvillie Ann Reed, Sept. 16, 1962; children: Jason Kaipokea, Tyron Makua, Marselene Uanoe. BA in Psychology summa cum laude, U. Hawaii, 1966, MA in Counseling Psychology, 1968, PhD in Clin. Psychology, 1971. Diplomate Am. Bd. Forensic Psychology. Am. Bd. Med. Psychotherapists, Am. Bd. Sexology, Am. Bd. Forensic Examiners. In TV ops. and prodn., 1952-63; tng. and rsch. in psychology and counseling, 1966-68; counseling psychologist U. Hawaii, 1968-69; psychologist Merry-Go-Round Child Care Ctrs., Inc., Honolulu, 1968-81; clin. and forensic psychologist in pvt. practice Honolulu, 1971—; assoc. prof. clin. faculty dept. psychiatry John A Burns Sch. Medicine, U. Hawaii, Honolulu, 1979—; pvt. investigator Honolulu, 1983—. Contbr. numerous articles to profl. jours. Fellow APA, Am. Acad. Clin. Sexologists, Am. Assn. Marriage and Family Therapy, Am. Assn. State Psychology Bds., Am. Coll. Forensic Psychology, Internat. Coun. Sex Edn. and Parenthood, Behavior Therapy and Rsch. Soc.; mem. Acad. Forensic Psychology, Am. Fedn. Police, Am. Law Enforcement Officers Assn., Am. Police Acad., Am. Soc. Law and Medicine, Am. Soc. Trial Cons., Assn. for Applied Psychophysiology and Biofeedback, Assn. of Sexologists, Soc. Sci. Study Sex, World Assn. Detectives, Phi Beta Kappa, Sigma Xi, Phi Eta Sigma, Psi Chi, Phi Kappa Phi, Omicron Delta Kappa. Office: 680 Ainapo St Honolulu HI 96825-1042

ANSCHUTZ, PHILIP F., transportation executive; b. 1939. BS, Univ. Kansas, 1961. Former pres. Anschutz Corp., now chmn. bd., also dir.; chmn. bd. So. Pacific Rail Corp., San Francisco. Office: Southern Pacific Rail Corp 1 Market Plz San Francisco CA 94105-1019 also: Anschutz Corp 555 17th St Ste 2400 Denver CO 80202-3941

ANSEL, LEE, surgeon; b. Chgo., Jan. 9, 1947; s. Harvey and Dorothy Ansel. BS, No. Ill. U., 1968; MD, Loyola U., 1972. Intern St. Joseph's Hosp., Phoenix, 1972-73; resident in surgery Michael Reese Hosp., Chgo., 1973-74; resident in surgery Maricopa County Hosp., Phoenix, 1974-77, fellow, 1977-78; pvt. practice Phoenix, 1979—; mem. exec. com. St. Joseph's Hosp. Grad. Valley Leadership, Phoenix, 1982. Mem. ACS (past pres. Ariz. chpt. 1989), AMA, F.A.C.S., S.W. Surg. Congress, Soc. Clin. Vascular Surgeons,. Office: Ariz Vascular Surgeons 1144 E Mcdowell Rd Phoenix AZ 85006-2664

ANSELL, GEORGE STEPHEN, metallurgical engineering educator, academic administrator; b. Akron, Ohio, Apr. 1, 1934; s. Frederick Jesse and Fanny (Soletsky) A.; m. Marjorie Boris, Dec. 18, 1960; children: Frederick Stuart, Laura Ruth, Benjamin Jesse. B. in Metall. Engring., Rensselaer Poly. Inst., 1954, M. in Metall. Engring., 1955, PhD, 1960. Physical metallurgist USN Research Lab., Washington, 1957-58; mem. faculty Rensselaer Poly. Inst., Troy, N.Y., 1960-84, Robert W. Hunt prof., 1965-84, chmn. materials div., 1969-74, dean engring., 1974-84; pres. Colo. Sch. Mines, Golden, 1984—; bd. dirs. Norwest Bank, Cyprus Minerals Co., Norwest Colo., Cyprus Amax Minerals Co., OEA, Inc. Editor books; patentee in field; contbr. over 100 articles to profl. jours. Served with USN, 1955-58. Recipient Hardy Gold Medal AIME, 1961, Curtis W. McGraw award Am. Soc. Engring. Edn., 1971, Souzandrade Gold Medal of Univ. Merit Fed. U. Maranhao, 1986. Fellow Metall. Soc. (pres. 1986-87), Am. Soc. Metals (Alfred H. Geisler award 1964, Bradley Stoughton award 1968); mem. NSPE, Am. Soc. Engring. Edn. (Curtis W. McGraw award 1971), Sigma Xi, Tau Beta Pi, Phi Lambda Upsilon. Club: Denver. Office: Colo Sch of Mines Pres Office 1500 Illinois St Golden CO 80401-1887*

ANSHEL, JEFFREY ROBERT, optometrist; b. Chgo., Nov. 8, 1949; s. Bernard and Rochelle (Berger) A.; m. Elaine Denise Bussinger, June 3, 1990; children: Trisha, David, Casey. BS, Ill. Coll. Optometry, 1974, OD, 1975. Pvt. practice Mission Vision Ctr., Oceanside, Calif., 1990-95, Poinsettia Vision Ctr., Carlsbad, Calif., 1995—; pres. Corporate Vision Consulting, La Costa, Calif., 1990—; vis. lectr. Santa Fe Coll. Natural Medicine, 1979-83. Author: Healthy Eyes, Better Vision, 1990. Lt. USN, 1975-77. Mem. Am. Optometry Assn., Am. Acad. Optometry, Coll. Optometrists in Vision Devel., Calif. Optometric Assn., Quid Pro Quo Bus. Club. Home: 2404 Sacada Cir # A Carlsbad CA 92009-8030 Office: Poinsettia Vision Ctr 7130 Avenida Encinas Ste 103 Carlsbad CA 92009-4657

ANSLEY, JULIA ETTE, elementary school educator, consultant, poet, writer; b. Malvern, Ark., Nov. 10, 1940; d. William Harold and Dorothy Mae (Hamm) Smith; m. Miles Ansley, Nov. 8, 1964 (div. June 1976); children: Felicia Dianne, Mark Damon. BA in Edn., Calif. State U., Long Beach, 1962; postgrad., UCLA Ext. Early childhood edn., life, Miller-Unruh reading specialist credentials, Calif. Elem. tchr. L.A. Unified Sch. Dist., 1962—; coord. Proficiency in English Program, L.A., 1991-93; mem., advisor P.E.P. instrnl. tchrs. network, 1993—, workshop presenter and classroom demonstration tchr. in field; also poetry presentations, L.A., 1989—; owner Poetry Expressions, L.A.; self-markets own poetry posters; creator, presenter KidChess integrated lang. arts program, 1987—. Author: (poetry vols.) Out of Heat Comes Light, From Dreams to Reality. Bd. dirs. New Frontier Dem. Club, L.A., 1990-93; mem. exec. bd. L.A. Panhellenic Coun., rec. sec., 1993-95; vol., cmty. orgns. Greater South L.A. Affirmative Action Project, 1995-96. Honored by Teacher mag., 1990; recipient Spirit of Edn. award Sta. KNBC-TV, L.A., 1990; grantee L.A. Ednl. Partnership, 1985, 87, 89, 93. Mem. L.A. Alliance African-Am. Educators (exec. bd. 1991-94, parliamentarian 1992-94), Black Women's Forum, Black Am. Polit. Assn. (edn. co-chair 1993-95), Sigma Gamma Rho. Mem. FAME Ch. Home: 3828 Sutro Ave Los Angeles CA 90008 Office: Hillcrest Dr Sch 4041 Hillcrest Dr Los Angeles CA 90008-2902

ANSORGE, IONA MARIE, retired real estate agent, musician, high school and college instructor; b. Nov. 3, 1927; d. Edgar B. and Marie Louise (Bleeke) Bohn; m. Edwin James Ansorge, Sept. 13, 1949; children: Richard, Michelle. BA, Valparaiso U., 1949; cert. teaching, Drake U., 1964; MA, U. Iowa, 1976. Min. of music Our Savior Luth. Ch., Des Moines, 1949-63; tchr. Johnston (Iowa) High Sch., 1964-75; instr. Iowa Meth. Sch. Nursing, Des Moines, 1978-87; owner, pres. Bed and Breakfast in Iowa, Ltd., 1982-86; realtor Better Homes and Gardens First Realty, Des Moines, 1986-92. Pres. Des Moines Jaycee-ettes; spearheaded drive Des Moines Zoo; founder Messiah Luth. Ch., Des Moines, 1978; started Iowa Bed and Breakfast Industry, 1982; owner, pres. Bed and Breakfast in Iowa, Ltd.; mem. First Luth. Ch. Mem. LWV, AAUW, Des Moines Bd. Realtors, Women's Coun. Realtors, Realtor's Million Dollar Club, Jaycee-ettes (pres. Des Moines chpt. 1957-58), Valparaiso U. Guild (charter mem. Des Moines chpt.). Lutheran. Home: 8345 Twinberry Point Colorado Springs CO 80920

ANTHONY, ELAINE MARGARET, real estate executive, interior designer; b. Mpls., Apr. 23, 1932; d. Jerome Pius and Adeline (Shea) Clarkin; m. Ronald Carl Anthony, Aug 28, 1954 (div. 1977); children: Richard, Lisa, Laura. Student, U. Minn., 1950-51; AA, Diablo Valley Coll., 1978; postgrad., San Jose (Calif.) State U., 1979, U. Calif., Berkeley, 1983-91. Agt., broker Sycamore Realty, Danville, Calif., 1972-75; broker, project sales mgr. Crocker Homes, Dublin, Calif., 1975-80; exec. v.p. BlackHawk Properties, Danville, 1980-82; broker, project sales mgr. Harold W. Smith Co., Walnut Creek, Calif., 1982-86; pres. Elaine Anthony & Assocs., Inc., San Francisco, 1986—. Mem. vol. coun. San Francisco Symphony, 1986. Mem. Bldg. Industry Assn. (Outstanding Sales Person of Yr. No. Calif. chtp. 1983), Inst. Residential Mktg., Calif. Assn. Realtors, Contra Costa Assn. of Realtors, Bellevue Club Alameda County. Republican. Roman Catholic. Home and Office: 1875 Grand View Dr Oakland CA 94618-2339

ANTHONY, JAMES, protective services official. Chief of police Glendale, Calif. Office: 140 N Isabel St Glendale CA 91206

ANTHONY, JAMES PETER, plastic surgeon, educator; b. Queens, N.Y., Dec. 19, 1957; s. James Francis and Wilma Helen (Stadelman) A.; m. Christine Anita Evers, Aug. 12, 1979. BS, Stony Brook U., 1979, MD, 1983. Intern in gen. surgery The N.Y. Hosp. Cornell Med. Ctr., N.Y.C., 1983-84, resident in gen. surgery, 1984-88; resident in plastic surgery U. Calif., San Francisco, 1988-90, asst. prof. surgery, 1990—. Contbr. articles to profl. jours. Office: U Calif San Francisco Divsn Plastic Surgery 1635 Divisadero Ste 530 San Francisco CA 94115

ANTHONY, KAY CARROLL, librarian; b. Taft, Calif., Mar. 9, 1937; d. Henry Martin and Kathryn Grace (Hall) Carroll; m. David B. Anthony, Oct. 12, 1958; children: Jonathan David, Andrew James. Student, West-Hills Coll., 1955-56. Ref. libr. Coalinga (Calif.) Libr. Dist., 1965-79, adult svcs. libr., 1979-89, dist. libr., 1989—. Bd. dirs., sec. Coalinga Youth Baseball, 1982-86; treas. Ctrl. Valley Rabbit and Cavy Breeders Assn., Hanford, Calif., 1992—. Mem. ALA, Calif. Libr. Assn., Pub. Libr. Assn., Am. Rabbit Breeders Assn. Office: Coalinga Libr Dist 305 N 4th St Coalinga CA 93210-2817

ANTIN, MICHAEL, lawyer; b. Milw., Nov. 30, 1938; s. David Boris and Pauline (Mayer) A.; m. Evelyne Judith Hirsch, June 19, 1960; children: Stephanie, Bryan, Randall. BS, Univ. Calif., 1960; JD, U. Calif., 1963. Bar: Calif. 1963; cert. tax specialist. Tax atty. Cruikshank, Antin & Grebow, Beverly Hills, Calif., 1963-81, Antin, Litz & Grebow, Beverly Hills, 1981-91, Antin & Taylor, L.A., 1993—; bd. dirs. Small Bus. Counsel Am., Washington, The Group, Inc.; speaker in field; instr. Solomon S. Heubner Sch. CLU Studies, 1977-86. Author: How to Operate Your Trust or Probate, 1983; contbr. articles to profl. jours. With U.S. Air Force, 1959-67. Fellow Am. Coll. Tax Counsel, Am. Coll. of Trust & Estate Counsel, L.A. County Bowlers Assn. (bd. dirs. 1996). Office: Antin & Taylor 1875 Century Park E Ste 700 Los Angeles CA 90067-2508

ANTIOCO, JOHN F., convenience store chain executive. Pres., CEO The Circle K Corp., Phoenix, 1991—; COO Pearle Vision, Dallas, 1990; pres., COO Circle K Corp, Phoenix, Ariz., 1991-96. Office: The Circle K Corporation Box 52084 Phoenix AZ 85072-2084

ANTOCH, ZDENEK VINCENT, electrical engineering educator; b. Prague, Czechoslovakia, Oct. 16, 1943; came to U.S., 1950; s. Zdenek Antoch and Marta (Smidova) Frank; m. Maureen O. Shaw, June 24, 1968 (div.); 1 child, Anna Marie. BS, Portland State U., 1971, postgrad. in Engring., 1971-73, postgrad. in Physics, 1973-75, MS, 1989, postgrad., 1989—. Research asst. Portland (Oreg.) State U., 1972-75; electronics instr. Portland (Oreg.) Community Coll., 1975-80, 81—. Mem. IEEE, Am. Soc. Engring. Edn. Democrat. Office: Portland Community Coll 12000 SW 49th Ave Portland OR 97219-7132

ANTREASIAN, GARO ZAREH, artist, lithographer, art educator; b. Indpls., Feb. 16, 1922; s. Zareh Minas and Takouhie (Daniell) A.; m. Jeanne Glascock, May 2, 1947; children: David Garo, Thomas Berj. BFA, Herron Sch. Art, 1948; DFA (hon.), Ind. U.-Purdue U. at Indpls., 1972. Instr. Herron Sch. Art, 1948-64; tech. dir. Tamarind Lithography Workshop, Los Angeles, 1960-61; prof. art U. N.Mex., 1964-87, chmn. dept. art, 1981-84; tech. dir. Tamarind Inst., U. N.Mex., 1970-72; vis. lectr., artist numerous univs.; Bd. dirs. Albuquerque Mus., 1980-90; printmaker emeritus Southern Graphics Coun., 1994. Prin. author: The Tamarind Book of Lithography: Art and Techniques, 1970; one-man shows include Malvina Miller Gallery, San Francisco, 1971, Marjorie Kauffman Gallery, Houston, 1975-79, 84, 86, U. Colo., Boulder, 1972, Calif. Coll. Arts & Crafts, Oakland, 1973, Miami U., Oxford, Ohio, 1973, Kans. State U., 1973, Atlanta Coll. Art, 1974, U. Ga., Athens, 1974, Alice Simsar Gallery, Ann Arbor, 1977-79, Elaine Horwich Gallery, Santa Fe, 1977-79, Mus. of N.Mex., Santa Fe, 1979, Robischon Gallery, Denver, 1984, 86, 90, Moss-Chumley Gallery, Dallas, 1987, Rettig-Martinez Gallery, Santa Fe, 1988, 91, 92, U. N.Mex. Art Mus., 1988, Albuquerque Mus., 1988, Louis Newman Gallery, L.A., 1989, Expositum Gallery, Mexico City, 1989, State U. Coll., Cortland, N.Y., 1991, Mus. Art, U. Ariz., Tucson, 1991, Indpls. Mus. Art, 1994, Ruschmon Gallery, Indpls., 1994, Mitchell Mus. Art, Vernon, Ill., 1995; exhibited group shows Phila. Print Club, 1960-63, Ind. Artists, 1947-63, White House, 1966, Nat. Lithographic Exhbn. Fla. State U., 1965, Library Congress, 1961-66, Bklyn. Mus., 1958-68, 76, U.S. Pavilion Venice Biennale, 1970, Internat. Biennial, Bradford, Eng., 1972-74, Internat. Biennial, Tokyo, 1972, City Mus. Hong Kong, 1972, Tamarind UCLA, 1985, Roswell Mus., 1989, Pace Gallery, 1990, Worcester (Mass.) Art Mus., 1990, Amon Carter Mus., Ft. Worth, 1990, Albuquerque Mus., 1991, 92, Art Mus. U. N.Mex., 1991, 92; represented in permanent collections: Bklyn. Mus., Guggenheim Mus., N.Y.C., Cin. Mus., Chgo. Art Inst., Ind. State Mus., Mus. Modern Art, N.Y.C., Library of Congress, Met. Mus., N.Y.C., also, Albuquerque, Boston, Indpls., Seattle, Phila., San Diego, Dallas, N.Mex., Worcester Art Museums, Los Angeles County Mus., Roswell Mus. and Art Ctr., murals, Ind. U., Butler U., Ind. State Office Bldg. Fulbright vis. lectr. U. São Paulo and Found. Armando Alvares Penteado, Brazil, 1985. Combat artist with USCGR, World War II, PTO. Recipient Distinguished Alumni award Herron Sch. Art, 1972, N.Mex. Annual Gov.'s award, 1987; Grantee Nat. Endowment for Arts, 1983. Fellow NAD; mem. World Print Coun. (bd. dirs. 1980-87), Nat. Print Coun. Am. (co-pres. 1980-82), Coll. Art Assn. Am. (bd. dirs. 1977-80). Home: 6004 Torreon Dr NE Albuquerque NM 87109

ANTWEILER, DENNIS FRANCIS, mechanical engineer; b. Cleve., June 16, 1949; s. Ralph Joseph and Marie Leola (Freeman) A.; m. Karen Lisa Porter, Feb. 27, 1971; children: Christopher J., Brandon D., Jamie A. BSME, U. Calif. Berkeley, 1972. Mech. engr. Altare Sys., Inc., Oakland, Calif., 1973; controls and instrumentation engr. Exxon, USA Corp., Benicia, Calif., 1973-78, Hess Oil Virgin Islands Corp., St. Croix, V.I., 1978-79, Union Camp Corp., Savannah, Ga., 1979-81; mgr. ops. Stanford (Calif.) U., 1981-86; v.p. Cascade Controls, Inc., Sunnyvale, Calif., 1986—. Mem. ASME, Instrument Soc. Am. Office: Cascade Controls Inc 712 E Evelyn Ave Sunnyvale CA 94086-6526

APLON, ROGER LAURENCE, writer, poet; b. Chgo., July 28, 1937; s. Carl Bernard and Mildred (Schneider) A.; m. Judith Rubinstein, July 5, 1962 (div. Nov. 1967); 1 child, Jason Alexander; m. Ellen Virginia Perkins/Flippen, Mar. 26, 1992. BA, Roosevelt U., 1995. Author: (books of poetry) Stiletto, 1976, By Dawn's Early Light at 120 mph, 1983, It's Mother's Day, 1996. Mem. PEN West, Acad. Am. Poets. Home: 2238 Oak Hill Dr Escondido CA 92027-3808

APODACA, RUDY SAMUEL, judge; b. Las Cruces, N.Mex., Aug. 8, 1939; s. Raymond and Elisa (Alvarez) A.; m. Bunny N. Gray, Nov. 1958 (div. 1963); m. Nancy R. Apodaca, Jan. 16, 1967; children: Cheryl Ann, Carla Renee, Cynthia Lynn, Rudy Samuel. BS, N.Mex. State U., 1961; JD, Georgetown U., 1964. Bar: N.Mex. 1964, U.S. Dist. Ct. N. Mex. 1965, U.S. Ct. Appeals (10th cir.) 1965, U.S. Supreme Ct. 1971. Pvt. practice Las Cruces, 1964-86; judge N.Mex. Ct. Appeals, Santa Fe, 1987-94, chief judge, 1994—; real estate broker, Las Cruces, 1984-86; gen. counsel Citizens Bank Las Cruces, 1976-86. Author: The Waxen Image, 1977; author screenplay: A Rare Thing, 1987. Bd. regents N.Mex. State U., 1975-83; mem. Coord. Coun. for Higher Edn., Santa Fe, 1975-78; pres. Assocs. N.Mex. State U., Las Cruces, 1982-84; bd. dirs. Am. S.W. Theatre Co., Las Cruces, 1984-86. Capt. U.S. Army, 1964-66. Mem. Inst. Jud. Adminstrn., N.Mex. Bar Assn., Poets and Writers, Phi Kappa Phi, Am. Mensa, Intertel, Pen Ctr. USA West, Pen N.Mex. Democrat. Home: 829 Canterbury Arc Las Cruces NM 88005-3715 Office: NMex Ct Appeals 201 W Picacho Ave Ste C Las Cruces NM 88005-1833

APPELBAUM, BRUCE DAVID, physician; b. Lincroft, N.J., Apr. 24, 1957; s. John S. and Shirley B. (Wolfson) A. BS in pharmacy, Rutgers Coll., 1980; MS in pharmacology, Emory U., 1983, PhD in pharmacology, 1985; MD, Medical Coll. Ga., 1989. Diplomate Nat. Bd. Med. Examiners, Am. Bd. Psychiatry and Neurology. Rsch. assoc. Emory U. Dept. Pharmacology, Atlanta, 1985; resident physician U. Calif. Dept. Psychiatry, Irvine, Calif., 1989-93; pvt. practice Pacifica Therapists, Huntington Beach, Calif., 1993—; cons. Avalon Med. Group, Garden Grove, Calif., 1990—. Contbr. articles to profl. jours. Recipient Nat. Rsch. Svc. award Nat. Inst. Health, 1982-83, Ea. Student Rsch. Forum U. Miami Medical Sch., 1984, Nat. Student Rsch. Forum, 1987. Mem. AMA, Am. Psychiat. Assn., Orange County Psychiat. Soc., N.Y. Acad. Scis., Sigma Xi. Home: 18602 Creek Ln Huntington Beach CA 92648-1629 Office: 18811 Huntington St Ste 200 Huntington Beach CA 92648-6003

APPLE, DANIEL BRYCE, finance company executive, financial planner; b. Nevada City, Calif., June 30, 1951; s. Stanley Bryce and Bonnie Ruth (Kelley) A. BA, Chico (Calif.) State U., 1973; MS in Fin. Planning, Coll. for Fin. Planning, 1997. CFP. Engring. technician Clendenen & Assoc., Auburn, Calif., 1976-77; field engr. Pacific Gas & Electric Co., Sacramento, 1974-76, United Engrs. & Contractors, Richland, Wash., 1977-81; civil and structural engr. Bechtel Corp., Richland, 1981-84; rep. Fin. Network Investment Corp., Grass Valley, Calif., 1984-89, br. mgr., 1989-95, prin., 1989-95; prin. Associated Securities Corp., Grass Valley, 1995—. Past. pres. Nevada County Arts Coun., 1993-94. Mem. Inst. Cert. Fin. Planners, Gold Country Estate Planning Coun. (chrter, past treas. Grass Valley chpt. 1989—), Rotary Internat. (treas.). Republican. Office: Associated Securities Corp 10565 Brunswick Rd Ste 8 Grass Valley CA 95945

APPLE, JACQUELINE B. (JACKI APPLE), artist, writer, educator; b. N.Y.C.. Student, Syracuse U.; BFA, Parsons Sch. Design. Curator exhbns. and performance Franklin Furnace, N.Y.C., 1977-80; prodr., host Sta. KPFK-FM, North Hollywood, Calif., 1982-95; mem. faculty Art Ctr. Coll. Design, Pasadena, Calif., 1983—; mem. faculty adv. com. Art Ctr. Coll. Design, Pasadena, 1993; vis. faculty UCSD, LaJolla. Contb. writer: L.A. Weekly, 1983-89; contbg. editor: Artweek, 1983-90, High Performance Mag., 1984-95; writer, performer, dir., prodr.: (record) The Mexican Tapes, 1979-80, (performance/radio work) Voices in the Dark, 1989-90, (radio art work) Swan Lake, 1989; artist, prodr.: (installations and audio work) The Culture of Disappearance, 1991-95; author, designer: (book, installation) Trunk Pieces, 1975-78, (cd) Thank You for Flying American, 1995; radio art series Redefining Democracy in America Parts 1-6, Zeitghosts: Angeles in the Architecture, 1995; (photowork) ghost.dance series 1995—); author: Doing it Right in L.A., 1990. Recipient Vesta award Media Arts Women's Bldg., 1990; NEA visual artists fellow, 1979, 81; InterArts program grantee NEA, 1984-85, 91-92; Calif. Arts Coun. Visual Arts/New Genres fellowship, 1996. Mem. Internat. Art Critics Assn., Nat. Writers Union, Coll. Art Assn. Home: 3827 Mentone Ave Culver City CA 90232-3108

APPLEBERRY, WALTER THOMAS, aerospace engineering project executive; b. Wilmington, N.C., Mar. 8, 1926; s. William Pembroke and Carroll Ernesteen (Shingleton) A.; m. Mae Magdalene Bozeman, Feb. 21, 1953; children: Thomas Kent, Robert William, Rebecca Jean. BS in Mech. Engring., Calif. State U., Long Beach, 1974. Facilities engr. Douglas Aircraft, Long Beach, 1942-50; missionary Mormon Ch., Salt Lake City, 1950-53; supr. engring. test McDonnell Douglas, Huntington Beach, Calif., 1953-74; adv. engring. project mgr. Rockwell Internat., Downey, Calif., 1974-94. Patentee in field. Mem. Pi Tau Sigma. Republican. Mormon. Home: 3440 Val Verde Ave Long Beach CA 90808-3148

APPLEGATE, ARTHUR DAVID, computer software developer, consultant; b. Glendale, Calif., May 23, 1965; s. Howard Cornell Applegate and Mary Alice Keenan. BS in Computer Sci. with distinction, U. Sydney, Australia, 1985. Pres. Crystal Script, Sydney, 1983-85; sr. computer scientist Inference Corp., L.A., 1986-90; software engr. Wall Data Inc., Redmond, Wash., 1990-91; pres. Applegate Software, Redmond, Wash., 1991—. Author computer software FastData, 1991, OptiMem for Windows, 1991, SmartHeap, 1992, HeapAgent, 1994. Mem. Wash. Software Assn. (speaker 1992). Office: Applegate Software 4317 264th Ave NE Redmond WA 98053-8730

APPLEOFF, SANDRA S., artist, educator; b. Falls City, Nebr., Dec. 3, 1956; d. Robert Gustavius and Mildred Vivian (Hinton) A. Student, U. Sorbonne, Paris; BFA, Iowa State U.; postgrad., Kans. State U., U. Mo., Kansas City. Artist Hallmark Cards, Kansas City, Mo., 1980-82; studio artist Triad Prodns., 1982-84; freelance illustration and artist Kansas City, Aspen, Colo., 1984—; assoc. prof. Kansas City Art Inst., U. Kans., Lawrence; spl. instr. Colo. Mountain Coll., Aspen. Exhibited in various faculty exhbns. and gallery shows Kansas City area. Artist Spl. Olympics, Kansas City, 1989-90. Home: 490 S Riverside Ave Aspen CO 81611

APPLETON, JAMES ROBERT, university president, educator; b. North Tonawanda, N.Y., Jan. 20, 1937; s. Robert Martin and Emma (Mollnow) A.; m. Carol Koelsch, Aug. 8, 1959; children: Steven, Jon, Jennifer. AB in Social Sci., Wheaton Coll., 1958; MA, PhD, Mich. State U., 1965. Lectr. Mich. State U., East Lansing, 1969-72; assoc. dean students Oakland U., Rochester, Mich., 1965-68, dean student life, 1968-72, assoc. prof. behavioral scis., 1969-72, v.p., 1969-72; v.p. student affairs U. So. Calif., L.A., 1972-82, v.p. devel., 1982-87; pres., Univ. prof. U. Redlands, Calif., 1987—; bd. dirs. Tuition Exch.; mem. steering com. Calif. Compact. Author: Pieces of Eight: Rights, Roles & Styles of the Dean; guest editor Nat. Assn. Student Pers. Adminstrs. Jour., 1971; contbr. articles to profl. jours. Bd. dirs. So. Calif. Ind. Colls., Assn. Ind. Calif. Colls. and Univs., Inland Action; trustee San Francisco Presbyn. Sem. 1st lt. U.S. Army, 1958-60. Named One of 100 Emerging Young Leaders in Higher Edn., Am. Council Edn./Change, 1978; recipient Fred Turner award Nat. Assn. Student Personnel Adminstrs., 1980. Mem. AAUP, NCAA (mem. pres.'s commn.), Assn. Ind. Calif. Colls. & Univs. (govtl. rels. com., natural exec. com. tuition exch.), Am. Assn. Higher Edn., Western Coll. Assn. (past pres.). Home: 808 Carmel Ave Los Altos CA 94022-1101 Office: U of Redlands 1200 E Colton Ave PO Box 3080 Redlands CA 92373-0999*

APPLETON, STEVEN R., electronics executive. BBA, Boise State U., 1982. Fab supr., prodn. mgr., dir. mfg., v.p. mfg. Micron Tech., Inc., Boise, Idaho, 1983-91, pres., COO, 1991, now chmn., CEO, pres.; chmn., CEO Micron Semiconductor, 1992. bd. dirs. Semiconductor Industry Asssn., St. Luke's Hosp.; trustee Boise State U.; mem. Coll. Bus. Adv. Coun., Semiconductor Tech. Coun. Office: Micron Semiconductor Inc 8000 Federal Way Boise ID 83716-9632

APPLIN, GEORGE STEWART, journalist; b. Phila., May 13, 1949; s. Harold Albert and Elizabeth Patricia (McCafferty) A. Student, Bowdoin Coll., Brunswick, Maine, 1967-70. Editor Franklinton (La.) Era-Leader, 1975; sports editor The Daily Star, Hammond, La., 1976-78, St. Tammany Farmer, Covington, La., 1978-81, The Burleson (Tex.) Star, 1981-84; editor The Keller (Tex.) Citizen, 1984-86; news editor/mng. editor The Arlington (Tex.) News, 1986-90; editl. page editor The Times-Herald, Vallejo, Calif., 1990—. Office: Times-Herald 440 Curtola Pkwy Vallejo CA 94590-6923

APT, CHARLES, artist; b. N.Y.C., Dec. 10, 1933; s. Gustav Lee and Tami (Vera Salzman) A.; m. Ursula Edith Betz, July 24, 1959; children—Gregory, Sam. B.F.A., Pratt Inst., 1956. Exhibited in group shows Mus. Fine Art, Springfield, Mass., 1966, Expn. Intercontinentale, Monaco, France, 1966, 68, NAD, 1965, 68, 77, 78, 79, 80, 81, 83, 85, 87, Am. Watercolor Soc., 1965, 66, 68, 69, Allied Artists Am., 1964, 65, 67, 69, 70, 72, Nat. Mus. Racing, Saratoga, N.Y., 1967, Atlantic City Race Track, 1967, Nat. Arts Club, 1967; one-man shows Ground Floor Art Gallery, N.Y.C., 1967, 68, 69, Aqueduct Race Track Art Gallery, N.Y.C., 1967, Grand Central Art Galleries, 1969, Far Gallery, N.Y.C., 1972, 78, Talisman Gallery, Bartlesville, Okla., 1976, Gallery 52, South Orange, N.J., 1976, 77, Lorings Gallery, Cedarhurst, N.Y., 1985, 87, Huntsman Gallery, Aspen Colo., Dassin Gallery, Los Angeles, Calif., Loring North Gallery, Sheffield, Mass.; two-man show Palm Beach (Fla.) Galleries, 1973. Served with AUS, 1956-58. Recipient Gold medal Am. Vets. Soc. Artists, 1965; Best in Show award Saratoga Mus. Racing Ann., 1967; 2d Benjamin Altman award for figure painting NAD, 1968; Le Prix Prince Souverain Monaco, 1968; hon. mention Allied Artists Am., 1970; Bronze medal Annual Open Watercolor Exhbn. Nat. Arts Club, 1971; Sutherland prize Annual Open Oil Exhbn., 1972; Ject-key prize Salmagundi Club, 1972, 1st prize Product Design award for Aquarelle fabric collection Resource Council, 1984. Mem. NAD (academician), Artists Equity Assn. N.Y. Home and Studio: 9 Saint Raphael Laguna Niguel CA 92677-2761

APURON, ANTHONY SABLAN, archbishop; b. Agana, Guam, Nov. 1, 1945; s. Manuel Taijito and Ana Santos (Sablan) P. BA, St. Anthony Coll., 1969; MDiv, Maryknoll Sem., 1972, M Theology, 1973; MA in Liturgy, Notre Dame U., 1974. Ordained priest Roman Catholic ch., 1972, ordained bishop, 1984, installed archbishop, 1986. Chmn. Diocesan Liturgical Commn., Agana, 1974-86; vice chmn. Chamorro Lang. Commn., Agana, 1984-86; aux. bishop Archdiocese of Agana, 1984-85, archbishop, 1986—; chmn. Interfaith Vols. Caregivers, Agana, 1984—; mem. Civilian Adv. com., Agana, 1986—; pres. Cath. Bishops' Conf. of Pacific, 1990—; v.p. Cath. Bishops' Conf. of Aceania, 1990—. Author: A Structural Analysis of the Content of Myth in the Thought of Mircea Eliade, 1973. Chmn. Cath. Ednl. Radio. Named Most Outstanding Young Man, Jaycees of Guam, 1984. Office: Archbishop's Office Cuesta San Ramon Agana GU 96910*

ARABIAN, ARMAND, arbitrator, mediator, lawyer; b. N.Y.C., Dec. 12, 1934; s. John and Aghavnie (Yalian) A.; m. Nancy Arabian, Aug. 26, 1962; children: Allison Ann, Robert Armand. BSBA, Boston U., 1956, JD, 1961; LLM, U. So. Calif., L.A., 1970; LLD (hon.), Southwestern Sch. Law, 1990, Pepperdine U., 1990, U. West L.A., 1994. Bar: Calif. 1962, U.S. Supreme Ct. 1966. Dep. dist. atty. L.A. County, 1962-63; pvt. practice law Van Nuys, Calif., 1963-72; judge Mcpl. Ct., L.A., 1972-73, Superior Ct., L.A., 1973-83; assoc. justice U.S. Ct. Appeal, L.A., 1983-90, U.S. Supreme Ct. Calif., San Francisco, 1990-96; ret., 1996. 1st lt. U.S. Army, 1956-58. Recipient Stanley Litz Meml. award San Fernando Valley Bar Assn., 1986, Lifetime Achievement award San Fernando Valley Bar Assn., 1993/. Republican. Office: 6259 Van Nuys Blvd Van Nuys CA 91401

ARAKI, TAKAHARU, editor, mineralogist, crystallographer, consultant; b. Kyoto, Japan, Dec. 22, 1929; came to U.S., 1965; s. Shiro and Kiyo (Ohmori) A.; m. Motoko Yoshizawa, Nov. 23, 1958 (dec. Apr. 1993). MS, Kyoto U., Japan, 1957, DSc, 1961. Rsch. assoc. Kyoto U., Japan, 1960-62; sr. chemist Tekkosha Corp., Mitaka, Tokyo, Japan, 1962-65, 68-70; rsch. fellow U. Minn., Mpls., 1965-67, 70-71; sr. rsch. scientist U. Chgo., 1971-82; sr. rsch. assoc. McGill U., Montreal, Can., 1983-85; sr. assoc. editor Chem. Abstracts Svc., Columbus, Ohio, 1985-94; pvt. contractor Chem. Abstracts Svc., 1995—. Contbr. articles to profl. jours. Fellow Mineralogical Soc Am.; mem. Am. Ceramic Soc., Am. Chem. Soc., Am. Crystallographic Assn. Home and Office: 4612 182nd Pl SW Lynnwood WA 98037-4625

ARAUZ, CARLOS GASPAR, city official; b. Havana, Cuba, Jan. 6, 1949; came to U.S., 1960, naturalized, 1974; s. Agnelio Alejandro and Mariana (Rodriguez) A.; BS, Loyola U., Los Angeles, 1970; MS, Ga. Inst. Tech., 1975, postgrad., 1975—. Bacteriologist, Emory U. Hosp., Atlanta, 1970-72; rsch. psychologist Atlanta Regional Commn., 1973-74; dir. personnel City of College Park (Ga.), 1974-75; indsl. psychology cons. Lockheed Ga. Co., Marietta, 1976; asst. dir. human resources City of Miami, 1976-81, spl. asst. to city mgr., 1981-82; bur. chief labor rels./personnel adminstrn. City of Orlando, Fla., 1982-85; dir. personnel and labor relations City of Corpus Christi, Tex., 1985-86; dir. personnel City of Phoenix, 1986—; cons. govt. and industry. Bd. dirs. Valle del Sol, Inc., Ariz. Govt. Tng. Svc. Mem. Internat. Personnel Mgmt. Assn. (young personnel profl. award N. Ga. 1975; pres. N. Ga. chpt. 1976, S. Fla. chpt. 1978, pres. So. region 1980-81, exec. coun. 1990-92, pres.-elect 1993, pres. 1994), Soc. Human Resource Mgmt., Metro Phoenix Human Resource Mgmt. Assn., Internat. City Mgmt. Assn., Nat. Pub. Employer Labor Rels. Assn., Rocky Mountain Pub. Employer Labor Rels. Assn. (pres. 1989-91), Sigma Xi. Roman Catholic. Club: Lake Arrowhead Yacht and Country. Office: City of Phoenix 135 N 2nd Ave Phoenix AZ 85003-2018

ARAZI, LORRI ROSENBERG, realtor; b. Bowling Green, Ohio, Apr. 5, 1958; d. Benjamin George and Peggy Lee (Hull) Rosenberg; m. Yaacov Kobi Arazi, June 22, 1986 (div. Dec. 1993). BA, U. Calif. Berkeley, 1979; postgrad., Antioch U., San Francisco, 1981-82; MA, San Francisco State U., 1994. Dist. mgr. ClothesFreak, Berkeley, 1977-79; asst. buyer Emporium Dept. Stores, San Francisco, 1980-82, asst. store mgr., 1983-84; dist. mgr. Maquette Leather Fashions, Tel Aviv, Israel, 1985-86; pers. mgr. Ross Stores, Walnut Creek, Calif., 1986-88; residential realtor Mason-McDuffie Real Estate, Berkeley, 1993—. Democrat. Jewish. Office: Mason-McDuffie Real Estate 1539 Shattuck Ave Berkeley CA 94709-1516

ARBEIT, WENDY SUE, writer; b. Jersey City, May 14, 1941; d. Carl and Ethel Arbeit. BA, Temple U., 1963; MA, Columbia U., 1968. Author: What Are Fronds For?, 1985, Baskets in Polynesia, 1990, Tapa in Tonga, 1994; assoc. editor Pacific Arts, 1992—; prodr./dir. (video): From Mortal to Ancestor: The Funeral in Tonga, 1994, Pacific Passengers, 1997. Mem. Pacific Arts Assn., Tongan History Assn., Cmty. TV Prodrs. Assn. (dir. 1995—). Office: PO Box 23296 Honolulu HI 96823

ARBIB, MICHAEL ANTHONY, computer scientist, educator, neuroscientist, cybernetician; b. Eastbourne, U.K., May 28, 1940; came to U.S., 1961; s. John R. and Helen (Arbib) A.; m. Prue Hassell, Dec. 29, 1965; children: Phillipa Jane, Benjamin Giles. BSc with honors, U. Sydney, 1960; PhD in Math., MIT, 1963. Mem. faculty Stanford (Calif.) U., 1965-70, assoc. prof. elec. engring., 1969-70; adj. prof. psychology, prof. computer and info. sci. U. Mass., Amherst, 1970-86, chmn. dept. computer and info. sci., 1970-75; dir. Ctr. for Systems Neurosci., 1974-86, dir. Cognitive Sci. Program, 1980-82, dir. Lab. Perceptual Robotics, 1982-86; prof. biomed. engring., computer sci., elec. engring., neurobiology, physiology and psychology U. So. Calif., L.A., 1986-94, dir. physiology Ctr. for Neural Engring., 1987-94; dir. human brain project Ctr. for Neural Engring., Univ. So. Calif., 1994-95; dir. brain project Univ. So. Calif., 1994—; vis. prof. U. Western Australia, Perth, 1974, 96, Technion, Israel, 1975, Washington U., St. Louis, 1976, U. Edinburgh, 1976-77, U. Calif., Irvine, 1980; vis. scientist Inst. Cybernetics, Barcelona, spring 1985, Cognitive Scis. Inst., U. Calif., San Diego, 1985-86; vis. lectr. U. New South Wales, Australia, 1962, 65, 68, Mont. State U., summers, 1963, 65, Imperial Coll. London, 1964; Gifford lectr. in natural theology U. Edinburgh, Scotland, 1983; John Douglas French lectr. Brain Rsch. Inst., UCLA, 1993; lectr. tours to U.S., USSR, Japan, Australia and China. Author: Brains, Machines and Mathematics, 1964, 2d. edit., 1987, Theories of Abstract Automata, 1969, The Metaphorical Brain, 1972, Computers and the Cybernetic Society, 1977, 2d edit., 1984, In Search of the Person, 1985, The Metaphorical Brain 2, 1989; (with others) Topics in Mathematical System Theory, 1969, System Theory, 1974, Discrete Mathematics, 1974, Conceptual Models of Neural Organization, 1974, Arrows, Structures and Functors, 1975, Design of Well-Structured and Correct Programs, 1978, A Basis for Theoretical Computer Science, 1981, A Programming Approach to Computability, 1982, Algebraic Approaches to Program Semantics, 1986, The Construction of Reality, 1986, From Schema Theory to Language, 1987, An Introduction to Formal Language Theory, 1988, Neural Organization: Structure, Function, Dynamics, 1997; editor: The Handbook of Brain Theory and Neural Networks, 1995, (with others) Algebraic Theory of Machines, Languages and Semigroups, 1968, Neural Models of Language Processes, 1982, Competition and Cooperation in Neural Nets, 1982, Adaptive Control of Ill-Defined Systems, 1983, Vision, Brain and Cooperative Computation, 1987, Dynamic Interactions in Neural Networks: Models and Data, 1988, Visuomotor Coordination: Amphibia, Comparisons, Models, and Robots, 1989, Natural and Artificial Parallel Computation, 1990, Visual Structures and Integrated Functions, 1991, Neuroscience: From Neural Networks to Artificial Intelligence; contbr. articles to profl. jours. Mem. IEEE, AAAS, Soc. Neurosci. Office: U So Calif Ctr Neural Engring Los Angeles CA 90089-2520

ARBOGAST, GENEVIEVE L., interior designer; b. Belington, W.Va., Jan. 19, 1936; m. Norman R. Arbogast, June 11, 1955. AS in Interior Design with honors, Miami-Dade C.C., 1975. Facilities space planner-interior designer Bank Western, Denver, 1978-89; owner Ambience N.W., Everett, Wash. Prin. works include interior design for numerous bank brs., office bldg. for Shelter-Am., Inc. Mem. Am. Soc. Interior Designers (Seattle chpt.). Office: 12424 36th Ave SE Everett WA 98208-5671

ARBUTHNOT, ROBERT MURRAY, lawyer; b. Montreal, Quebec, Can., Oct. 23, 1936; s. Leland Claude and Winnifred Laura (Hodges) A.; m. Janet Marie O'Keefe, Oct. 6, 1968; children: Douglas, Michael, Mary Kathleen, Allison Anne. BA, Calif. State U., San Francisco, 1959; JD, U. Calif., San Francisco, 1966. Bar: Calif. 1967, U.S. Dist. Ct. (no. and cen. dists.) Calif. 1967, U.S. Ct. Appeals (9th cir.) 1967, U.S. Supreme Ct. 1975. Assoc. trial lawyer Rankin & Craddick, Oakland, Calif., 1967-69; assoc. atty. Ericksen, Arbuthnot, Brown, Kilduff & Day, Inc., San Francisco, 1970-73, ptnr., 1973-80, chmn. bd., mng. dir., 1980—; gen. counsel CFS Ins. Svcs., San Francisco, 1990—; pro tem judge, arbitrator San Francisco Superior Ct., 1990—; lectr. in field. Bd. regents St. Mary's Coll. High Sch., Berkeley, Calif., 1988-91. With U.S. Army, 1959-62. Recipient Honors plaque St. Mary's Coll. High Sch., 1989. Mem. Internat. Assn. of Ins. Counsel, No. Calif. Assn. of Def. Counsel, Def. Rsch. Inst., Assn. Trial Lawyers Am., San Francisco Lawyers Club. Office: Ericksen Arbuthnot Brown Kilduff & Day Inc 260 California St Ste 1100 San Francisco CA 94111-4803

ARCADI, JOHN ALBERT, urologist; b. Whittier, Calif., Oct. 23, 1924; s. Antonio and Josephine (Ramirez) A; m. Doris M. Bohanan, Apr. 11, 1951; children: Patrick, Michael, Judith, Timothy, Margaret, William, Catherine. BS cum laude, U. Notre Dame, 1947; MD, Johns Hopkins U., 1950. Diplomate Am. Bd. Urology. Intern Johns Hopkins Hosp., Balt., 1950-51, resident, 1951-52, 53-55; instr. urology Johns Hopkins U., Balt., 1953-55, U. So. Calif., L.A., 1955-60; research assoc. Whittier (Calif.) Coll., 1957-70, research prof., 1970—; coord. prostate cancer rsch. Huntington Med. Rsch. Inst., Pasadena, Calif., 1993—; staff mem. urology sect. Presbyn. Hosp., Whittier, 1960—. Fellow AAAS, ACS; mem. Endocrine Soc., Am. Urology Assn., Am. Micros. Soc., Internat. Urol. Soc., Am. Assn. Clin. Anatomy, Am. Assn. Anatomists, Soc. for Basic Urologic Rsch., Soc. for Invertebrate Pathology. Republican. Roman Catholic. Home: 6202 Washington Ave Whittier CA 90601-3640 Address: PO Box 9220 Whittier CA 90608-9220

ARCHBOLD, RICHARD, newspaper editor; m. Pat Archbold; children: Kelly, Katie. Degree in polit. sci., U. Ill., 1960. Statehouse reporter UPI, Lincoln, Nebr.; govt. reporter Omaha World-Herald; pub. affairs reporter, city editor, mng. editor Broward County Bur.-Miami Herald, Ft. Lauderdale, Fla.; mng. editor Press-Telegram, 1978—. Co-chmn. Long Beach (Calif.) Pub. Safety Summit I, 1995, II, 1996, III, 1997; active Leadership Long Beach. Mem. AP Mng. Editors Assn. (past pres. 1994). Office: 604 Pine St Long Beach CA 90844

ARCHER, BARBARA LOUISE, hospital administrator, nursing consultant; b. Cottage Grove, Oreg., Feb. 5, 1944; d. Robert John Jones and Wilberta O. (Wilson) Price; m. Prasanna K. Pati, Aug. 15, 1966 (div. 1970); children: Jeffrey A., Michael M.; m. Henry T. Lum, Jr., May 15, 1981 (div. 1992); m. Stephen G. Archer, June 4, 1994. Diploma, Sacred Heart Sch. Nursing, Eugene, Oreg., 1965; BA in Psychology, Willamette U., 1970; MBA, U. Portland, 1980. RN, Oreg., Wash., Mont. Clin. nurse Willamette U., Salem, Oreg., 1965-66; staff nurse Salem Meml. Hosp., 1966; instr. nursing Oreg. State Hosp., Salem, 1970; DON Columbia View Hosp., Vancouver, Wash., 1971-76; nursing cons. Brim & Assocs., Portland, Oreg., 1976-80, dir. profl. services, 1980-88; cons. Virginia Mason Health Services Consortium, Seattle, 1988; pres. B. L. Cons., Vancouver, 1988—; v.p. rsch. and devel. Oreg. Assn. Hosps., Portland, 1990-93; v.p. ops. Oreg. Healthcare Enterprises, Lake Oswego, 1990-93; v.p. Oreg. Assn. of Hosps., Lake Oswego, 1990-93; assoc. adminstr. Hood River (Oreg.) Meml. Hosp., 1993—; mem. adj. faculty Concordia Coll., Portland, exec. dir., La Clinical del Carino, 1996—. Contbr. articles to nursing publs. Mem. Nat. League Nursing, Am. Coll. Health Care Execs., Healthcare Info. & Mgmt. Systems Soc.,. Republican. Roman Catholic. Office: BL Cons 1110 NE 125th Ave Vancouver WA 98684-5864 also: La Clinical del Carino Hood River Meml Hosp Hood River OR 97031

ARCHER, DOUGLAS ROBERT, mayor, insurance services executive; b. Winnipeg, Man., Can., Mar. 23, 1948; s. Robert Clive and Annette Diane (Brabant) A.; m. Gloria Jean Knight, Feb. 28, 1976; children: James, Lindsey, Tracy. BA in Econs., U. Sask., Saskatoon, Can., 1970. Civil servant Govt. Sask., Regina, 1971-83; ptnr. Knight Archer Ins. Svcs., Regina, 1983—; mayor City of Regina, 1988—; chair City Coun., Regina Bd. Police Commrs., Wascana Centre Authority, Mayor's Bd. of Inquiry into Hunger in Regina. Mem. Regina Econ. Devel. Authority, Mayor's Task Force on Women, Sherwood-Regina Dist. Planning Commn.; chair Mayor's Task Force on Accessibility; past pres. Regina Open Door Soc., Sask. Fedn. Community Clinics. Mem. Fedn. Can. Municipalities (bd. dirs.), Regina Exhbn. Assn. Office: Office of Mayor, Queen Elizabeth II Ct PO Box 1790, Regina, SK Canada S4P 3C8*

ARCHER, MARY JANE, state agency administrator; b. Oakland, Calif., Aug. 23, 1949; d. Doris Marlene (Howard) Wood; m. Bradley Eugene Archer; Nov. 10, 1984. BS in Acctg., Calif. State U., Hayward, 1971, MBA in Acctg., 1977. Cert. govtl. fin. mgr. Auditor Calif. State Controller's Office, Sacramento, 1972-81, supr., 1981-84, asst. div. chief, divsn. tax adminstrn., 1984-90, acting div. chief, 1990-95; bur. chief div. acctg. and reporting Calif. State Controller;s Office, Sacramento, 1995; chief acctg. Dept. Justice, Sacramento, 1996—. Tutor Sacramento Literacy Ctr. Mem. Calif. Assn. Mgmt., Assn. Govtl. Accountants. Republican. Office: Dept Justice Acctg Office 1300 I St 12th Fl Sacramento CA 95814

ARCHER, STEPHEN HUNT, economist, educator; b. Fargo, N.D., Nov. 30, 1928; s. Clifford Paul and Myrtle Mona (Blair) A.; m. Carol Rosa Mohr, Dec. 29, 1951 (div. Feb. 1971); children—Stephen Paul, Timothy William, David Conrad; m. Lana Jo Urban, Sept. 23, 1972. B.A., U. Minn., 1949, M.S., 1953, Ph.D., 1958; postdoctoral student (Ford Found. grantee), U. Calif. at Los Angeles, 1959-60. Mgr. trader J.M. Dain Co., Mpls., 1950; account exec. J.M. Dain Co., 1952-53; instr. econs. U. Minn., Mpls., 1954-56; asst. prof. fin. U. Wash., Seattle, 1956-60; assoc. prof. U. Wash., 1960-65, prof., 1965-73, chmn. dept. fin., bus. econs. and quantitative methods, 1966-70; dean Grad. Sch. Adminstrn. Willamette U., Salem, Oreg., 1973-76, 83-85; prof. Willamette U., 1976-79, Guy F. Atkinson prof., 1979-96; Fulbright sr. lectr. Bocconi U., Milan, Italy, 1982; v.p. Hinton, Jones & Co., Inc. (investment brokers), Seattle, 1969-70; cons. Wash. Bankers Assn., 1971-72, Weyerhaeuser Co., 1971, Bus.-Econs. Adv. & Research Inc., 1969-77, State of Oreg., 1984, 86, 88, 91; vis. prof. Manchester Bus. Sch., Manchester, Eng., 1990-91. Author: Introduction to Mathematics for Business Analysis, 1960, Business Finance: Theory and Mgmt, 1966, revised edit., 1972, The Theory of Business Finance, 1967, 2d revised edit., 1983, Portfolio Analysis, 1971, revised edit., 1979, Introduction to Financial Management, 1979, revised edit., 1983, Cases and Readings in Corporate Finance, 1988; editor Jour. Fin. and Quantitative Analysis, 1966-70, Economic Perspectives, Economica Aziendale, Jour. Bus. and Entrepreneurship. Served with USNR, 1950-52. Mem. Fin. Mgmt. Assn. (pres. 1973-74), Western Fin. Assn., Am. Fin. Assn., Phi Beta Kappa, Beta Gamma Sigma. Home: PO Box 249 Neotsu OR 97364-0249

ARCHER, VIOLET BALESTRERI, music educator, composer, pianist, organist, percussionist, adjudicator; b. Montreal, Apr. 24, 1913; d. Cesar B. and Beatrice (Azzi) A. Licentiate in piano, McGill U., 1934, B.Mus., 1936, D.Mus. (hon.), 1971; B.Mus., Yale, 1948, M.Mus., 1949; MusD (hon.), U. Windsor, Ont., Can., 1986; LLD (hon.), U. Calgary, 1989; MusD (hon.), Mount Allison U., Sackville, N.B., Can., 1992, U. Alta., 1993. Instr. music McGill U., 1943-47; performer concerts Eng., 1950; resident composer North Tex. State Coll., Denton, 1950-53; asst. prof. music U. Okla., Norman, 1953-61; assoc. prof. U. Alta., Edmonton, Can., 1962-70, prof. music, 1970-78, prof. emeritus, 1978—; also chmn. divsn. music theory and composition; vis. prof. music Cornell U., Ithaca, N.Y., summer 1952; mem. theory com. Can. Univ. Music Soc.; voting mem. coun. Can. Music Ctr., Toronto; artistic advisor N.Y. Music Soc.; mem. bd. Can. Music Competition, Montreal; speaker Yale U. Conf. on Paul Hindemith in the U.S.A., 1995. Composer works including Sonatina for Organ, operas Sganarelle and The Meal, sonatas for oboe and piano, clarinet and piano, alto saxophone and piano, for organ, anthems for SATB and organ Psalmody, for orch., chorus and baritone voice, Sonata No. 2 for piano, song cycles Divertimento for Saxophone Quartet, Divertimento for piano and strings; commd. Piano Sonata No. 2, 1979, 4 Duets for Violin and Cello, 1979, Song Cycle, 1979, (film score) Whatsoever Things Are True, 1980, Sonata for Bassoon and Piano, 1980, Psalm 145 a cappella, 1981, Sonata for Solo Cello, 1981, Soliloquies in B Flat and A for Clarinets, 1982, 2 Fanfares for a Festive Day, for Brass Quintet, 1989, The Owl Queen for High Voice and Piano, 1990, Variations for Violin and Piano, Improvisation for Solo Snare Drum, 1990; more than 300 compositions performed extensively in Can., U.S., Europe. Mem. adv. bd. Celebration of Women in the Arts. Recipient citation Yale Sch. Music Alumni Assn., 1968, Merit award Govt. Alta., 1970, Creative and Performance award City of Edmonton, 1972, Queen's Jubilee Silver medal, 1977, Order of Can. award, 1983, cert. of recognition for contbns. to musical heritage of Alta., 1980, Conf. of Women in Arts award, 1983, Women in the Arts award Edmonton YWCA, 1987, Sir Frederick Haultain prize Govt. of Alta., 1987, Great Can. award, 1992, Woman of the Yr., Alta., 1993, The Twentieth Achievement award, Alta., 1994, Gold Record of Achievement, Alta., 1994; park and festival named in her honor, City of Edmonton, 1985; named to Edmonton's Cultural Hall of Fame, 1987; fellow MacDowell Colony, 1956, Can. Coun. sr. fellow, 1958-59; fellow named in honor of musical achievements, Arts U., Alta., 1993; music scholarship named in her honor Music at Milford, 1994—. Fellow Royal Can. Coll. Organists (hon.); mem. Can. Music Council (exec. bd., Composer of Yr. 1984), Am., Can. music centres, PRO Can., Am. Fedn. Musicians, Can. League Composers, Can. Assn. Univ. Profs., Alta. Registered Music Tchrs. Assn., Canadian Fedn. Music Tchrs., Internat. Folk Music Council, Canadian Folk Music Soc., Canadian Music Educators Assn., Canadian U. Music Soc. (citation for distinguished svc. 1992, hon. life 1993), Music Educators Nat. Conf., Am. Women Composers (asso.), Soc. Artists (hon. life, dir.), Edmonton Composers' Concert Soc. (v.p. 1986—), Accademia Tiberina of Rome (hon. life acad. mem.), Frau und Musik, Internationaler Arbeitskreis, Assn. Can. Women Composers, Sigma Alpha Iota (hon.), Pi Kappa Lambda. Home: 10805 85th Ave, Edmonton, AB Canada T6E 2L2*

ARCHIBOLD, JOHN EWING, lawyer, consultant; b. Denver, Mar. 15, 1933; s. Robert French and Eleanor Eileen (Ewing) A.; m. Mary Ellen Ogelsby, Sept. 12, 1964; children: John Christopher, Stephen Ewing, Mary Elizabeth Eileen, Sarah Ellen Dean. A.B., Princeton U., 1955; LL.B., U. Denver, 1959; LL.M., Georgetown U., 1965. Bar: Colo. 1960, D.C. 1964, U.S. Supreme Ct. 1965. Spl. liaison asst. U.S. Dept. State, Washington, 1960; trial atty. U.S. Dept. Justice, Washington, 1960-66; assoc. Grant, Shafroth, Toll & McHendrie, Denver, 1966-68; ptnr. Casey, Klene, Horan & Archibold, Denver, 1968-69; asst. atty. gen. Colo. Dept. Law, Denver, 1970-72; assoc. counsel Colo. Pub. Utilities Commn., Denver, 1972-74, chief counsel, 1974-90; of counsel Kelly, Stanfield & O'Donnell, Denver, 1991-1993; v.p. Info-Media, Inc., Denver, 1990—. Contbr. articles to legal pubs. Precinct committeeman Denver Rep. Party, 1958-59; chmn. Citizenship Day Com., Denver, 1967; dir. Rude Park Nursery, 1957-59; chancellor Anglican Cath. Ch. 1979-80, Diocese of Holy Trinity, 1977-90. Col. U.S. Army, 1955-86. Mem. Denver Bar Assn., Colo. Bar Assn. Avocations: reading, traveling. Home: 700 Lafayette St Denver CO 80218

ARCHIE, CAROL LOUISE, obstetrician and gynecologist, educator; b. Detroit, May 18, 1957; d. Frank and Mildred (Barmore) A.; m. Edward Louis Keenan III, Mar. 7, 1993. BA in History, U. Mich., 1979, postgrad. in Pub. Health Adminstrn., 1979-83; MD, Wayne State U., 1983. Diplomate Am. Bd. Ob-Gyn., Am. Bd. Maternal-Fetal Medicine. Resident ob-gyn.

Wayne State U., Detroit, 1983-87; fellow in maternal fetal medicine UCLA, 1987-89, asst. prof. ob-gyn., 1989-97, assoc. prof., 1997—; cons. Office Substance Abuse Prevention, Washignton, 1989—, NIH, Bethesda, Md., 1990—, RAND, 1995—. Peer reviewer jours. Obstetrics and Gynecology, 1989—, Am. Jour. Pub. Health, 1994—, Am. Jour. Obstetrics and Gynecology, 1993—; contbr. chpts. to books. Mem. internal rev. bd. Friends Med. Rsch., 1991—; bd. dirs. Matrix Inst. on Addictions, L.A., 1993—; bd. dirs., vice chair Calif. Advocates for Pregnant Women, 1993—; bd. dirs., asst. v.p. med. svcs. Venice (Calif.) Free Clinic, 1994—. Clin. Tng. grantee UCLA, 1993—; recipient Faculty Devel. award Berlex Found., 1992. Fellow ACOG; mem. AMA, APHA, Soc. Perinatal Obstetricians, Royal Soc. of Medicine (Eng.), Assn. Profs. of Gynecology and Obstetrics. Office: UCLA Sch Medicine Rm 22-132 Dept Ob-gyn 10833 Le Conte Ave Los Angeles CA 90024-1602

ARCHULETA, KEITH ANTHONY, arts administrator, consultant, educational administrator; b. Denver, Mar. 13, 1955; s. Willie M. and Judith Ruth (Archuleta) Suggs; m. Iris Curtis, May 27, 1995; 1 child, Dorian. BA in African and African Am. Studies, Stanford U., 1978, BA in Comm., 1978; MA, U. San Francisco, 1992. Founder, bus. mgr. Stanford Black Media Inst., 1976; dir. So. Africa Media Ctr., San Francisco, 1979-80; program coord. Student Arts at Stanford (Calif.), 1982-84; asst. dir. Stanford Residential Edn., 1984-88; founder/dir. Black Cmty. Svcs. Ctr., Stanford, 1987-92; exec. dir. Oakland (Calif.) Youth Chorus, 1993; project adminstr. Arts Edn. Funders Collaborative, San Francisco, 1994—; site adminstr. Young African Am. Achievers Program, San Francisco, 1995—; interim exec. dir. LEAP...Imagination in Learning, San Francisco, 1996; founder/pres. Emerald Consulting, Hayward, Calif., 1992—; mem. adv. bd. CIIS MBA Program, San Francisco, 1994—; mem. bd. devel./mktg. chair LEAP...Imagination in Learning, San Francisco, 1995—; rev. panelist Arts Coun. Santa Clara County, San Jose, Calif., 1996-97. Author: (play) Their Spirits are Free, 1982; prodr., editor (ednl. video) Song for Melvin Truss, 1986. Fellow Calif. State Legislature, Sacramento, 1978-79; vol. Crossroads Africa, Liberia, West Africa, 1979, San Francisco Sch. Vols., 1995—; founder Kuumba Arts Ensemble, 1979, East Palo Alto Youth Theatre Project, 1985; congrl. dist. coord./del. Jesse Jackson for Pres., Santa Clara County, Calif., 1984, 88; bd. emeritus Theatre Works, Palo Alto, Calif., 1991—. Mem. ASCD, Calif. Alliance Arts Edn., Calif. Assn. Non-Profits, Commonwealth Club Calif., Co-Op Am. Bus. Network, Fellowship Cos. Christ Internat., Bus. Social Responsibility (founder), San Francisco Christian Ctr., Youth for Christ (mem. nat. adv. bd. 1997—). Office: Emerald Consulting 665 Dartmoor Ln Ste 154 Hayward CA 94544 *Keith Archuleta has provided over 20 years of service to schools, businesses, agencies, and nonprofits throughout the U.S. as consultant, executive director, and board member. Wife Iris Archuleta, a recognized expert in community reinvestment, often called upon to advise on the economic condition of inner city communities, has contributed to youth development in the Bay Area for over 15 years. Son Dorian Archuleta, a college student planning to become a teacher, interns with the family business, Emerald Consulting, which combines their skills and training with a love and faith in God to develop whole people, healthy organizations, and sustainable communities.*

ARCHULETA, WALTER R., educational consultant, language educator; b. Embudo, N.Mex., Apr. 7, 1951; s. Luis M. and Josefina (Romero) A.; m. Carmel Bustos, Oct. 19, 1994. BS in Spanish and Social Sci., N.Mex. State U., 1974; MA in Spanish Linguistics, U. N.Mex., 1981, postgrad., 1991-93. Tchr. Spanish John F. Kennedy Jr. H.S., San Juan, N.Mex., 1974-76; oral history collector VISTA, Dixon, N.Mex., 1976-77; tchr. Spanish Santa Fe H.S., N.Mex., 1981-82, 85-88, Los Alamos (N.Mex.) H.S., 1982-85, Capital H.S., Santa Fe, 1988-91; edn. cons. N.Mex. State Dept. Edn., Santa Fe, 1995—; cons. Hispanic Culture Found., Albuquerque, 1991-93. U. N.Mex. Opportunity fellow, 1991-93, travel grantee, 1996. Mem. Am. Assn. Tchrs. Spanish and Portuguese, Am. Coun. on Tchg. of Fgn. Lang., Nat. Assn. Bilingual Edn. Democrat. Roman Catholic.

ARCINIEGA, TOMAS ABEL, university president; b. El Paso, Tex., Aug. 5, 1937; s. Tomas Hilario and Judith G. (Zozaya) A.; m. M. Concha Ochotorena, Aug. 10, 1957; children: Wendy M. Heredia, Lisa, Judy, Laura. BS in Tchr. Edn., N. Mex. State U., 1960; MA, U. N. Mex., 1966, PhD, 1970; postdoc., Inst. for Ednl. Mgmt., Harvard U., 1989. Asst. dean Grad. Sch. U. Tex.-El Paso, 1972-73; co-dir. Southwestern Schs. Study, U. Tex.-El Paso, 1970-73; dean Coll. Edn. San Diego State U., 1973-80; v.p. acad. affairs. Calif. State U., Fresno, 1980-83; pres. Calif. State U., Bakersfield, 1983—; prof. ednl. adminstrn. and supervision U. N.Mex., U. Tex.-El Paso, San Diego State U., Calif. State U., Fresno, Calif. State U., Bakersfield; cons. in edn. to state and fed. agys., instns.; USAID advisor to Dominican Republic U.S. Dept. State., 1967-68; dir. applied rsch. project U. N.Mex., 1968-69, dep. chief party AID Project, Colombia, 1969-70; cons. in field. Author: Public Education's Response to the Mexican-American, 1971, Preparing Teachers of Mexican Americans: A Sociocultural and Political Issue, 1977; co-author: Chicanos and Native Americans: The Territorial Minorities, 1973; guest editor: Calif. Jour. Tchr. Edn., 1981; editor Commn. on Hispanic Underrepresentation Reports, Hispanic Underrepresentation: A Call for Reinvestment and Innovation, 1985, 88; contbr. articles to profl. jours. Trustee emeritus Carnegie Corp. N.Y.; trustee Ednl. Testing Svc., Princeton, N.J., The Aspen Inst.; bd. dirs. Math., Engring., Sci. Achievement, Berkeley, Calif.; mem. bd. dirs. Air U., Nat. Hispanic Scholarship Fund; mem. Am. Coun. on Edn.; founding mem., trustee Tomas Rivera Policy Studies Ctr.; dir. Civic Kern Citizens Effective Local Govt.; mem. adv. bd. Beautiful Bakersfield; advisor Jr. League Bakersfield. Vis. scholar Leadership Enrichment Program, 1982; recipient Legis. commendation for higher edn. Calif. Legislature, 1975-78, Meritorious Svc. award Am. Assn. Colls. Tchr. Edn., 1977-78, Meritorious Svc. award League United L.Am. Citizens, 1983, Pioneer award Nat. Assn. Bilingual Edn., 1994; named to Top 100 Acad. Leaders in Higher Edn. Change Mag., 1978. Mem. Am. Ednl. Rsch. Assn. (editl. com. 1979-82), Assn. Mexican Am. Educators (various commendations), Am. Assn. Higher Edn. (instl. rep.), Western Coll. Assn. (past pres.), Rotary, Stockdale Country Club, Bakersfield Petroleum Club. Democrat. Roman Catholic. Home: 2213 Sully Ct Bakersfield CA 93311-1560 Office: Calif State U 9001 Stockdale Hwy Bakersfield CA 93311-1022 *Ensuring the right of every American youngster to a first-rate public education has been a driving interest in my life. I consider myself extremely fortunate in having had numerous opportunities to become involved in meaningful efforts to ensure that basic right in our country.*

ARD, JAMES GEORGE, family physician; b. St. Anthony, Idaho, Mar. 22, 1951; s. George Francis and Belva Jeanne (Spillman) A.; m. Amanda Middleton, Apr. 6, 1985 (div. Oct. 1992); 1 child, Hayley Elizabeth. AA, Ricks Coll., 1971; BS, Brigham Young U., 1979; DO, Mich. State U., 1984. Diplomate Am. Bd. Family Practice. Comdr., gen. med. officer 545th Gen. Dispensary, Pusan, Korea, 1985-87; family practice resident Silas B. Hayes Army Cmty. Hosp., Fort Ord, Calif., 1987-89; family practice physician 67th Evac Hosp. U.S. Army, Wurzburg, Germany, 1989-92; locum tenens family practice Alaska, Ariz., Calif., Colo., Hawaii, Mich., Minn., Tex., Guam, and Saipan, 1992-96; family physician Kaiser Permanente, Lahaina, Hawaii, 1996—. Served with M.C., U.S. Army, 1985-96. Mem. AMA, Am. Acad. Family Practice, Am. Med. Informatics Assn. Office: Kaiser Permanente 910 Wainee St Lahaina HI 96761-1622

ARDANTZ, HENRI, agricultural products executive; b. 1936. Student, Fresno State Coll. With Ferini & Ardantz, Santa Maria, Calif., 1958-63; ptnr. Betteravia Farms, Santa Maria, Calif., 1963—. Office: Betteravia Farms PO Box 5845 Santa Maria CA 93456-5845 Office: Betteravia packing 1850 W Stowell Santa Maria CA 93454*

ARDOLF, DEBORAH ANN, speech pathologist; b. Mpls., Apr. 12, 1960; d. Bernard Joseph and Mary Ann (Snyder) A. BS cum laude, Moorhead State U., 1982; MA, U. Northern Colo., 1986. Cert. speech lang. pathologist, Minn., Hawaii. Speech pathologist Pelican Rapids (Minn.) Pub. Schs., 1982-84; speech pathologist intern Vet. Adminstrn. Medical Ctr., Seattle, Washington, 1985-86; speech pathologist Rehabilitation Hosp. Pacific, Honolulu, 1986-87, Dept. Edn., Honolulu, 1987-89, Queen's Med. Ctr., Honolulu, 1989-95; pvt. practice speech pathologist Honolulu, 1987—; instr. U. Hawaii, 1993-94. Recipient Search for Excellence award U. Northern Colo., 1984-85. Mem. Hawaii Speech, Lang. Hearing Assn. (spkr. at conf. 1993, com. mem., pres.-elect 1995-96), Am. Hearing and Speech Assn., Autistic Soc. Hawaii, Hawaii Bicycle League, Mid-Pacific Road Runners Club (vol. 1991—), Hawaii Small Bus. Assn. Office: Ohana Speech Lang Conss 350 Ward Ave Ste 106-87 Honolulu HI 96814-4004

ARENBERG, IRVING KAUFMAN, ear surgeon, educator; b. East Chicago, Ind., Jan. 10, 1941; s. Harry and Gertrude (Field) Kaufman; divorced; children: Daniel Kaufman, Michael Harrison, Julie Gayle. BA in Zoology, U. Mich., Ann Arbor, 1963; MD, U. Mich., 1967. Diplomate Am. Bd. Otolaryngology. Intern Chgo. Wesley Meml. Hosp., 1967-68; resident Barnes and Allied Hosps., St. Louis, 1969-74; asst. prof. surgery U. Wis., Madison, 1976-80, chief otolaryngology, 1976-80; clin. assoc. prof. otolaryngology U. Colo., Denver, 1980—; pres., CEO Ear Ctr. PC, Englewood, Colo., 1989-96; pres., CEO Neurobiometrix Inc., IEMDS, Inc., 1994—; dir., founder Internat. Meniere's Disease Rsch. Inst., Denver, 1971—; guest of honor 39th Chinese Nat. ENT Congress, Taipei, 1985, U. Antwerp, 1995, West German ENT Soc., 1996; vis. scientist Swedish Med. Rsch. Coun., 1975-76, vis. surgeon, 1987; vis. prof. U. Mich., Ann Arbor, 1988, 94, St. Mary's Hosp. and Med. Sch., London, 1988, U. Verona (Italy) Med. Sch., 1989, U. N.C., Chapel Hill, 1989, U. Wurzburg (Germany) Med. Sch., 1989, 90, 92, U. Ark., Little Rock, 1990, 95, U. Innsbruck, Austria, 1991, U. Sydney, Australia, 1992, U. Tex., Dallas, 1993. Editor: Meniere's Disease, 1983, Inner Ear Surgery, 1991, Dizziness and Balance Disorders, 1993; assoc. editor AMA Archives of Otolaryngology, 1968-81; mem. editorial bd. Am. Jour. Otology, 1978-91, Head and Neck Surgery Jour., 1992—, Jour. Club Jour., 1993; guest editor Otolaryngologic Clinics N.Am., 1980, 83, Neurologic Clinics N.Am., 1990; editor Inner Ear Surgery, 1991; mem. editl. rev. bd. Rev. de Laryngologie et Otology (France), 1984—; contbr. articles to profl. jours. Recipient Pietro Caliceti prize and Gold Medal Honor award U. Bologna, Italy, 1983, Spl. Tchr. Investigation Tng. award NIH; fellow Barnes and Allied Hosps., 1968-69, 75, NIH, 1971-76, U. Uppsala-Royal Acad. Hosp., Sweden, 1975-76; grantee NIH, 1971-77, Deafness Rsch. Found., 1971-73. Fellow ACS, Am. Acad. Otolaryngology, Am. Soc. Neurophysiologic Monitoring; mem. AMA, Am. Neurotology Soc., Am. Soc. Laser Medicine and Surgery, Am. Acad. Otolaryngic Allergy, N.Y. Acad. Scis., Colo. Orologic Rsch. Ctr. (pres., bd. dirs. 1980-88), Internat. Meniere's Disease Rsch. Inst. (founder, dir. 1971—), Internat. ECoG Monitoring Correspondence Group (founder), Internat. Electric Response Audiometry Study Group, Assn. Rsch. in Otolaryngology, Barany Soc., Triological Soc., Politzer Soc., Prosper Meniere Soc. (founder, exec. dir. 1981—), Children's Deafness Found. (pres., bd. dirs. 1983-88), Acoustical Soc. Am., Von Bekesy Soc., N.Am. Skull Base Soc. (founder), Ogura Soc., Sigma Xi. Office: Neuro Biometrix Inc Quorum E Ste 110 7995 E Prentice Ave Englewood CO 80111

ARENDS, JACK, journalist; b. Olympia, Wash., Nov. 30, 1956; s. John Henry and Carol Louise (Ellingson) A. BA, Wash. State U., 1979. Reporter intern St. Maries (Idaho) Gazette-Record, spring 1978; copyeditor intern Medford (Oreg.) Mail-Tribune, summer 1978; copyeditor Memphis Press-Scimitar, 1979-81, zone sect. editor, 1981-83; copyeditor Tacoma (Wash.) News-Tribune, 1984, The Jour. Am., Bellevue, Wash., 1984-89; editor The Ind., Port Orchard, Wash., 1991-93, Queen Anne/Magnolia News, Seattle, 1993—. Mem. Soc. Profl. Journalists (bd. dirs. we. Wash. chpt.). Office: Queen Anne/Magnolia News 225 W Galer St Seattle WA 98119-3331

ARENOWITZ, ALBERT HAROLD, psychiatrist; b. N.Y.C., Jan. 12, 1925; s. Louis Isaac and Lena Helen (Skovron) A.; m. Betty Jane Wiener, Oct. 11, 1953; children: Frederick Stuart, Diane Helen. BA with honors, U. Wis., 1948; MD, U. Va., 1951. Diplomate Am. Bd. Psychiatry, Am. Bd. Child Psychiatry. Intern Kings County Gen. Hosp., Bklyn., 1951-52; resident in psychiatry Bronx (N.Y.) VA Hosp., 1952-55; postdoctoral fellow Youth Guidance Ctr., Worcester, Mass., 1955-57; dir. Ctr. for Child Guidance, Phila., 1962-65, Hahnemann Med. Service Eastern State Sch. and Hosp., Trevose, Pa., 1965-68; dir., tng. dir. Child and Adolescent Psychiat. Clinic, Phila. Gen. Hosp., 1965-67; asst. clin. prof. psychiatry Jefferson Med. Coll., Phila., 1974-76; exec. dir. Child Guidance and Mental Health Clinics, Media, Pa., 1967-74; med. dir. Intercommunity Child Guidance Ctr., Whittier, Calif., 1976—; cons. Madison Pub. Schs., 1957-60, Dane County Child Guidance Ctr., Madison, 1957-62, Juvenile Ct., Madison, 1957-62; clin. asst. prof. child psychiatry Hahnemann Med. Coll., Phila., 1966-74; asst. clin. prof. psychiatry U. Wis., Madison, 1960-62, clin. asst. prof. psychiatry, behavioral scis. and family medicine U. So. Calif., L.A., 1976—; mem. med. staff Presbyn. Intercommunity Hosp., Whittier, 1976—. Pres. Whittier Area Coordinating Coun., 1978-80; chmn. ethics com. Presbyn. Intercommunity Hosp. Flight officer, navigator USAF, 1943-45. Decorated Air medal, POW medal. Fellow Am. Psychiat. Assn., Am. Acad. Child Psychiatry; mem. AAAS, Los Angeles County Med. Assn., So. Calif. Psychiat. Soc., So. Calif. Soc. Child Psychiatry, Phila. Soc. Adolescent Psychiatry (pres. 1967-68), Peace Sci. Soc. Office: Intercommunity Child Guidance Ctr 8106 Broadway Ave Whittier CA 90606-3118

ARENT, DOUGLAS JAY, electrical engineer; b. Denver, Aug. 22, 1960; s. Jacob and Ruth (Phillips) A.; m. Joan M. Whalen; 1 child, Etienne Jacob. BSc, Harvey Mudd Coll., Claremont, Calif., 1982; PhD, Princeton Univ., 1987; MBA, Regis Univ., 1995. Postdoctoral fellow NATO, IMEC, Leuven, Belgium, 1987-89; rsch. fellow IBM, Zurich, Switzerland, 1989-91; sr. rsch. assoc. Nat. Renewable Energy Lab., Golden, Colo., 1991-95; sr. project coord. Nat. Renewable Energy Lab., Golden, 1995—; cons. Prudential Relocation Svcs., Boulder, Colo., 1992-95, AT&T, Baskin Ridge, N.J., 1994-95. Author numerous book chpts.; reviewer Recording for the Blind, 1984-87. Mem. IEEE, Am. Inst. Physics. Office: Nat Renewable Energy Lab 1617 Cole Blvd Golden CO 80401-3305

ARGENT, PHILIP, artist, educator; b. Southend-on-Sea, Essex, Eng., Sept. 6, 1962; came to U.S., 1988; s. Anthony Louis and Sheila Pamela (Grove) A.; m. Jane Callister, Mar. 10, 1995. BFA, Cheltenham Sch. Art, 1985; MA, U. Idaho, 1990; MFA, U. Nev., 1994. Instr./tchg. asst., dept. art U. Idaho, Moscow, 1988-90; instr./grad. asst., dept. art U. Nev., Las Vegas, 1991-94; asst. curator visual resource facility, dept. art U. Nev., 1992-93, adj. faculty, dept. art, 1994-96. Solo exhibit Donna Beam Fine Art Gallery, Las Vegas, 1996; co-collaborator commn. Nevada Inst. for Contemporary Art and Rio Ste. Hotel and Casino, Las Vegas, 1996. Recipient Nev. State Coun. on the Arts Artists' fellowship, 1996, Liquitex Excellence in Art, Internat. Student Grant Program Purchase award Binney & Smith Inc., Easton, Pa., 1993, Elizabeth Greenshields Found. Internat. Painting award, Que., Can., 1991. Mem. Nev. Inst. for Contemporary Art, Contemporary Arts Collective (Las Vegas). Home: 6900 Whittier Dr #125 Goleta CA 93117

ARGUE, JOHN CLIFFORD, lawyer; b. Glendale, Calif., Jan. 25, 1932; s. J. Clifford and Catherine Emily (Clements) A.; m. Leah Elizabeth Moore, June 29, 1963; children: Elizabeth Anne, John Michael. AB in Commerce and Fin., Occidental Coll., 1953, LLD (hon.), 1987; LLB, U. So. Calif., 1956. Bar: Calif. 1957. Since practiced in Los Angeles; mem. firm Argue & Argue, 1958-59, Flint & MacKay, 1960-72; mem. firm Argue, Pearson, Harbison & Myers, 1972-94, of counsel, 1995—; bd. dirs. Avery Dennison, CalMat Inc., Coast Fed. Savs. and Loan, Compensation Resource Group; mem. adv. bd. LAACO, Ltd., TCW/DW Mut. Funds, TCW Galileo Funds; chmn. The Rose Hills Found., Amateur Athletic Found., L.A. Sports Coun., Criminal Justice Legal Found. Pres. So. Calif. Com. Olympic Games, 1972—; founding chmn. L.A. Olympic Organizing Com., 1978-79; trustee, vice chmn. Pomona Coll., U. So. Calif., Occidental Coll., Mus. Sci. and Industry; mem. nat. adv. coun. Autry Mus. Western Heritage; chmn. bd. Greater L.A. affiliate Am. Heart Assn., 1982, chmn. adv. bd., 1985—; chmn. Verdugo Hills Hosp., 1979, chmn. adv. bd., 1983—; pres. Town Hall of Calif., 1985, U. So. Calif. Assocs., 1988-93; chmn. PGA Championship, 1983, chmn. adv. bd., 1995; vice chmn., sec. L.A. 2000 Com., 1991 Olympic Sports Festival, 1993 Superbowl, 1994 World Cup. Mem. L.A. Bar Assn., Calif. Bar Assn., Southern Calif. Golf Assn. (pres. 1979), Calif. Golf Assn. (v.p. 1979), Calif. State Srs. Golf Assn. (treas.), L.A. Area C. of C. (chmn. 1989), Chancery Club (pres. 1985-86), Calif. Club (pres. 1983-84), L.A. Athletic Club, Riviera Country Club, Oakmont Country Club (pres. 1972), L.A. Country Club, Rotary, Phi Delta Phi, Alpha Tau Omega. Home: 1314 Descanso Dr La Canada Flintridge CA 91011-3149 Office: 801 S Flower St Ste 5000 Los Angeles CA 90017-4607

ARIAS, JOE, agricultural products company executive. With subsidiaries of Valley Fresh Foods, Inc., 1966—; pres., chmn. bd. Valley Fresh Foods, Inc., Turlock, Calif., 1991—. Office: Valley Fresh Foods Inc 3600 E Linwood Ave Turlock CA 95380-9108*

ARIEFF, ALLEN IVES, physician; b. Chgo., Sept. 30, 1938. BS in Math. and Chemistry, U. Ill., 1960; MS in Physiology, Northwestern U., 1964, MD, 1964. Intern Phila. Gen. Hosp., 1964-65; resident SUNY, Bklyn., 1967-68; renal fellow U. Colo., Denver, 1968-69; rsch. and edn. assoc., clin. investigator Wadsworth VA Med. Ctr., L.A., 1970-74; asst. prof. medicine, rsch. scientist UCLA Med. Ctr., 1971-74; asst. prof. medicine, dir. hemodialysis U. Calif. VA Med. Ctr., San Francisco, 1975-76, assoc. prof. medicine, dir. nephrology sect., 1976-83, prof. medicine, chief clin. nephrology, 1983-86, prof. medicine, dir. rsch. & edn. geriatrics, 1986—; cons. and speaker in field. Author 6 books; contbr. 54 chpts. med. textbooks, over 300 articles to profl. jours. Fellow ACP; mem. Am. Soc. Nephrology, Am. Fedn. Clin. Rsch., Am. Diabetes Assn., Am. Physiol. Soc., Am. Soc. Neurochemistry, Am. Soc. Clin. Investigation, Am. Soc. Bone and Mineral Rsch., Assn. Am. Physicians, Western Assn. Physicians, Western Soc. Clin. Rsch., Internat. Soc. Nephrology, Soc. Neurosci. Office: U Calif San Francisco 299 South St Sausalito CA 94965

ARISS, DAVID WILLIAM, SR., real estate developer, consultant; b. Toronto, Ont., Can., Nov. 29, 1939; s. William H. and Joyce Ethel (Oddy) A.; m. Lillie Ariss, Jan. 26, 1962 (div. 1989); m. Debra Ann Nocciolo, Nov. 17, 1990 (div. 1996); children: Katherine Joyce, David William Jr., Dylan William. BA, Claremont Men's Coll., 1961. Lic. real estate broker. Real estate broker Coldwell Banker, Torrance, Calif., 1971-75; v.p. The Lusk Co., Irvine, Calif., 1975-77; pres. DAL Devel. Co., Corona, Calif., 1977-84; mng. dir. Calif. Commerce Ctr. at Ontario, Ontario, Calif., 1984—. Chmn. Inland Empire Econ. Coun., Ontario, Calif., 1991-92; pres., adv. com. Chaffey Coll., Ontario, 1989; apptd. Calif. World Trade Commn., 1993, 95. Maj. USMC, 1961-70, Vietnam. Decorated Silver Star, Disting. Flying Cross, two Purple Hearts, numerous Air medals. Mem. Urban Land Inst., Nat. Assn. Fgn. Trade Zone, Nat. Assn. Indsl. and Office Parks. Republican. Office: Pib Realty Advisors 3200 Inland Empire Blvd Ste 235 Ontario CA 91764-5513

ARITA, GEORGE SHIRO, biology educator; b. Honolulu, Oct. 9, 1940; s. Ichimatsu and Natsu (Kimoto) A.; m. Harriet Yooko Ide, Dec. 26, 1964; children: Laurie Reiko, Daren Shizuo. BA, U. Hawaii, 1962, MS, 1964; MS, U. B.C., Vancouver, 1967; postgrad., U. Calif., Santa Barbara, 1967-71. Cert. community coll. tchr., Calif. Prof. biology Ventura (Calif.) Coll., 1971—, curator fish collection, 1976—, head dept. biology, 1989—. Author: (with others, lab. manual) Basic Concepts in Biology, 1981, Study Guide to Accompany Biology: Today and Tomorrow, 2d edit., 1984; contbr. articles on ichthyology to profl. jours. Fushiminomiya Meml. scholar U. Hawaii, 1961-62, Fisheries Assn. B.C. scholar U. B.C., 1964-65; NSF grad. trainee U. Calif. Santa Barbara, 1969-71. Mem. AAAS, Am. Soc. Ichthyologists and Herpetologists, Western Soc. Naturalists, Sigma Xi. Home: 94 Howard Ave Oak View CA 93022-9524 Office: Ventura Coll Dept Biology Ventura CA 93003

ARKENBERG, JEROME STEPHEN, law and history researcher; b. Oak Park, Ill., June 20, 1958; s. Raymond John and Genevieve Catherine (Sejud) A. BA, Loyola U. Chgo., 1980, MA, 1988; JD, U. Ill., 1983; PhD, UCLA, 1990. Bar: Ill. 1983, U.S. Dist. Ct. (no. dist.) Ill. 1984, U.S. Ct. Appeals (7th cir.) 1984, U.S. Supreme Ct. 1985. Prin. Law Offices Jerome S. Arkenberg, Esq., Oak Park, 1983-86; rschr. Loyola U. Chgo., 1986-87; lectr. Calif. State U., L.A., 1992-93; rschr. Ctr. Medieval and Renaissance Studies, L.A., 1993-94, Huntington Libr., San Marino, Calif., 1992—; lectr. Calif. State U., Fullerton, 1996—. Contbr. articles to profl. jours. Fellow faculty Loyola U., Chgo., 1986, UCLA, 1987-91, Andrew Mellon Found., 1992, Ball Bros. Found., 1993, Lilly Found., 1996; recipient Brit. Acad. Neil Ker award, 1994. Mem. ABA, Am. Soc. Legal History, Am. Hist. Assn., Medieval Acad. Am., Assn. Ancient Historians, Selden Soc. Office: Huntington Libr 1151 Oxford Rd San Marino CA 91108-1218

ARMENTROUT, PETER BRUCE, chemistry educator; b. Dayton, Ohio, Mar. 13, 1953; s. Harry Martin and Lorraine (Johnson) A.; m. Mary Ann White, Aug. 6, 1983; children: Matthew Martin, Patricia Christine, Erin Irene. BS, Case Western Res. U., 1975; PhD, Calif. Inst. Tech., 1980. Postdoctoral fellow Bell Telephone Labs., Murray Hill, N.J., 1980-81; asst. prof. chemistry U. Calif., Berkeley, 1981-87; assoc. prof. chemistry U. Utah, Salt Lake City, 1987-89, prof. chemistry, 1989—. Mem. editorial bd. Internat. Jour. Mass Spectrometry and Ion Processes, 1987—, Jour. Cluster Sci., 1989—, Advances in Ion Chemistry and Physics, 1991—. Named Presdl. Young Investigator, NSF, 1984; Dreyfus Found. grantee, 1981, tchr.-scholar, 1988; A.P. Sloan fellow, 1986. Fellow AAAS, Am. Phys. Soc.; mem. Am. Chem. Soc. (mem. editl. bd. Jour.), Am. Phys. Soc., Am. Soc. Mass. Spectrometry. Office: U Utah Dept Chemistry Salt Lake City UT 84112

ARMENTROUT, STEVEN ALEXANDER, oncologist; b. Morgantown, W.Va., Aug. 22, 1933; s. Walter W. and Dorothy (Gasch) A.; m. Johanna Ruszkay; children—Marc, Susan, Sandra, Nancy. A.B., U. Chgo., 1953, M.D., 1959. Intern U. Hosp., Cleve., 1959-60; resident in medicine, fellow Am. Cancer Soc. Western Res. U. Hosp., 1960-63; project dir. USPHS, 1963-65; asst. prof. Case Western Res. U. Med. Sch., 1965-71; mem. faculty U. Calif. Med. Sch., Irvine, 1971—; prof. medicine, chief divsn. hematology-oncology U. Calif. Med. Sch., 1978—, also dir. program in oncology.; pres. med. staff U. Calif.-Irvine Med. Ctr., 1983-85; researcher in multiple sclerosis. Mem. Am. Assn. Cancer Research, AAUP, ACP, Am. Cancer Soc. (chmn. bd. 1973, pres. Orange County chpt. 1985-86), AMA, Am. Soc. Clin. Oncology, Am. Soc. Hematology, Orange County Med. Assn., Am. Soc. Internal Medicine, Calif. Med. Assn., Cen. Soc. Clin. Research, Leukemia Soc. Am., Orange County Chief of Staff Council. Office: 101 The City Dr S Orange CA 92868-3201

ARMEY, DOUGLAS RICHARD, minister; b. Fresno, Calif., Oct. 23, 1948; s. Wilbur Rutter and Mildred (Broadbent) A.; m. Jennifer Louise Armey, Sept. 23, 1972; children: Laura Elizabeth, Andrew Douglas. AA, Fresno (Calif.) City Coll., 1969; BS summa cum laude, Calif. State U., Fresno, 1971; MA, Mennonite Brethren Sem., Fresno, 1976. Ordained to ministry, Ch. of Brethren, 1973. Intern pastor The Peoples Ch. of Fresno, 1972-73; founding chaplain Fresno County Juvenile Hall, 1973; pres. Precision Parts Distbrs., Inc., Fresno, 1973-80, Rutter Armey Engine Co., Inc., Bakersfield, Calif., 1980-88; sr. pastor Fresno Ch. of the Brethren, 1988—; radio broadcaster Fresno Fellowship of Christian Athletes/KIRV Radio, 1987-96. Contbr. articles to profl. jours. and mags. Bd. dirs. Fresno Youth for Christ, 1985-87. With Calif. Air N.G., 1968-74. Mem. Nat. Assn. Evangelicals, Sigma Alpha Epsilon. Republican. Ch. of the Brethren. Office: 3901 E Clinton Ave Fresno CA 93703-2517

ARMINANA, RUBEN, academic administrator, educator; b. Santa Clara, Cuba, May 15, 1947; came to U.S., 1961; s. Aurelio Ruben and Olga Petrona (Nart) A.; m. Marne Olson, June 6, 1954; children: Cesar A. Martino, Maria G. Arminana. AA, Hill Jr. Coll., 1966; BA, U. Tex., 1968, MA, 1970; PhD, U. New Orleans, 1983; postgrad. Inst. of Applied Behavioral Scis., Nat. Tng. Labs., 1971. Nat. assoc. dir. Phi Theta Kappa, Canton, Miss., 1968-69; dir. ops. and tng. Inter-Am. Ctr., Loyola U., New Orleans, 1969-71; adminstrv. analyst City of New Orleans, 1972, adminstrv. analyst and organizational devel. and tng. cons., 1972-78; anchor and reporter part time STA. WWL-TV, New Orleans, 1973-81; v.p. Commerce Internat. Corp., New Orleans, 1978-83; exec. asst. to sr. v.p. Tulane U., New Orleans, 1983-85, assoc. exec. v.p., 1985-87, v.p., asst. to pres., 1987-88; v.p. fin. and devel. Calif. State Poly U., Pomona, 1988-92; pres, Sonoma State U., 1992—; TV news cons., New Orleans, 1981-88; lectr. Internat. Trade Mart, New Orleans, 1983-89, U.S. Dept. Commerce, New Orleans. Co-author: Hemisphere West-El Futuro, 1968; co-editor: Colloquium on Central America-A Time for Understanding, Background Readings, 1985. Bd. dirs. Com. on Alcoholism and Substance Abuse, 1978-79, SER, Jobs for Progress, Inc., 1974-82, Citizens United for Responsive Broadcasting, Latin Am. Festival Com.; dir., bd. advisors Sta. WDSU-TV, 1974-77; mem. Bus. Govt. Rsch., 1987-88, Coun. Advancment of Support to Edn.; mem. League of United Latin Am. Citizens, Mayor's Latin Am. Adv. Com., Citizens to Preserve the Charter, Met. Area Com., Mayor's Com. on Crime. Kiwanis scholar, 1966, Books scholar, 1966. Mem. Assn. U. Related Rsch. Prks., L.A. Higher Edn. Roundtable, Soc. Coll. and U. Planning, Nat. Assn. Coll. and U. Bus. Officers Cou., Am.

Econ. Assn., Assn. of Evolutionary Econs., Am. Polit. Sci. Assn., AAUP, Western Coll. Assn. (pres. 1994-95), Latin Am. C. of C. (founding dir. New Orleans and River Region 1976-83), Cuban Profl. Club, Phi Theta Kappa, Omicron Delta Epsilon, Sigma Delta Pi, Delta Sigma Pi. Democrat. Roman Catholic. Avocation: mask collecting. Office: Sonoma State U 1801 E Cotati Ave Rohnert Park CA 94928-3613

ARMINTROUT, EDWARD GILBERT, human resources executive; b. Englewood, Colo., June 25, 1940; s. Gilbert Edgar and Lucy Henrietta (Grotz) A.; m. Jeanne Kathleen Vuich, Feb. 28, 1986; children: Julie Elizabeth, Lori Anne. BS, U. Colo., 1967. Mng. human resources Litton Industries Corp., Beverly Hills, Calif., 1967-69, Syntex Corp., Palo Alto, Calif., 1969-73; dir. human resources SYVA Co., Palo Alto, 1973-75; cons. human resources Denver, 1975-80; v.p. human resources Wells Fargo Bank, San Francisco, 1980-82, John Muir Med. Ctr., Walnut Creek, Calif., 1982-90; v.p. Drake Beam Morin, San Jose, Calif., 1990-93; cons. Drake Beam Morin, Denver, 1993-95; human resources instr. Wyo.-Tech. Inst., Laramie, 1995—. Author: Guide to Effective Hiring, 1990. Cons. to sch. bd. Albany County Schs., Laramie, Wyo., 1994. Republican. Home and Office: 1661 Inca Dr Laramie WY 82070-5072

ARMOUR, GEORGE PORTER, lawyer; b. Bryn Mawr, Pa., June 10, 1921; s. Charles Joseph and Florence (Eagle) A.; m. Isabel Blondet, Nov. 22, 1958; children: Luis O., Carlos O. B.A., Temple U., 1943, J.D., 1949. Bar: Pa. 1949, N.Y. 1969, Calif. 1975. Assoc. Bennett & Bricklin, Phila., 1949-59; atty. Atlantic Richfield Co., 1959-83, gen. atty., Phila., 1965-68, assoc. gen. counsel, Phila., N.Y.C., L.A., 1968-78, dep. gen. counsel, L.A., 1978-83; pvt. practice law, 1983—; chmn. Internat. and Comparative Law Ctr., Southwestern Legal Found., Dallas, 1980-82. Mem. Assocs. Calif. Inst. Tech., 1981—; mem. Soc. of Fellows Huntington Library and Art Gallery, San Marino, Calif., 1982—. Served with USAAF, 1943-46. Mem. ABA, Calif. Bar Assn., Calif. Club (L.A.), Valley Hunt Club (Pasadena). Republican. Episcopalian. Home and Office: 1621 Orlando Rd Pasadena CA 91106-4130

ARMSTRONG, BILLIE BERT, retired highway contractor; b. Roswell, N.Mex., Apr. 18, 1920; s. Gayle G. and Murphy (Shannon) A.; m. Betty-Ellen Wilcox, Aug. 16, 1941; children: Billie B. Jr., Judith C., Robert G., Riley A. Student, N.Mex. Mil. Inst., 1935-39, Washington & Lee U., 1939-41. Mng. ptnr. Armstrong & Armstrong Ltd., Roswell, 1950—, G.G. Armstrong & Son, Ltd., Roswell, 1950—; chmn. bd. dirs. Sunwest Nat. Bank of Roswell, 1967-84; pres. Assoc. Gen. Contractors Am., Washington, 1966-67, Assoc. Contractors N.Mex., Santa Fe, 1952-53, 63; bd. dirs. Southwestern Pub. Svc. Co., Sunwest Fin. Svcs., Inc. Pres. Conquistador Coun. Boy Scouts Am., Roswell, 1981-82, bd. regents N.Mex. Mil. Inst., Roswell, 1960-62. Major U.S. Army, 1942-45. Named Citizen of Yr. Realtors N.Mex., 1969, Roswell, 1968, Jaycees, 1964; recognized for svc. to mankind Sertoma, 1966. Mem. Masons, Shriners, Jesters. Methodist. Home: 2619 Coronado Dr Roswell NM 88201-3404 Office: Armstrong & Armstrong Ltd PO Box 1873 Roswell NM 88202-1873

ARMSTRONG, BRUCE IRVING, mechanical engineer; b. Montebello, Calif., July 28, 1957; s. John William and Kathryn Winifred (Stevenson) A. AA in Engring., Mt. San Antonio Coll., Walnut, Calif., 1979; BSME, Calif. State U., Fresno, 1985. Mech. engr. Naval Warfare Assessment divsn. USN, Corona, Calif., 1985—; participant in fastener hearings Gen. Acctg. Office, Washington, 1991; advisor thread tech. U.S. Dept. Commerce, Washington, 1992; advisor USN Gen. Coun., Washington, 1993. Mem. ASME (mem. B1.2 screw thread std. com. 1992—, B1.15 screw thread std. com. 1992—), Lambda Chi Alpha. Republican. Presbyterian. Home: 3157 Florinda St Pomona CA 91767-1013

ARMSTRONG, C. MICHAEL, computer business executive; b. Detroit, Oct. 18, 1938; s. Charles H. and Zora Jean (Brooks) A.; m. Anne Gossett, June 17, 1961; children: Linda, Julie, Kristy. B.S. in Bus. Econs, Miami U., Oxford, Ohio, 1961; grad., Dartmouth Inst., 1976. With IBM Corp., 1961-92, dir. systems mgmt. mktg. div., White Plains, N.Y., 1975-76, v.p. market ops. East, 1976-78, pres. data processing div., 1978-80, v.p., asst. group exec. plans and controls, data processing product group, 1980-83, v.p., group exec., 1983-84, sr. v.p., group exec., 1984-92; also pres. IBM Corp., Europe, Paris, until 1988; pres., dir. gen. World Trade Europe/Middle East/Africa IBM Corp., 1987-89, chmn. World Trade Corp., 1989-92; chmn., CEO Hughes Aircraft Co., L.A., 1992-93, GM Hughes Electronics (now Hughes Electronics Corp.), 1993—; Mem. GM Pres. Coun.; bd. dirs. Travelers Corp., Hartford, Conn., The Times-Mirror-Co., L.A.; mem. supervisory bd. Thyssen-Bornemisza Group; chmn. Pres.'s Export Coun., The White House, 1994—. Trustee Johns Hopkins U., chmn. adv. bd. Johns Hopkins Med. Sch.; mem., CEO bd. of adv. U. So. Calif. Bus. Sch.; mem. bus. adv. coun. Miami U.; mem. Coun. on Fgn. Rels., Nat. Security Telecomm. Adv. Com., Def. Policy Adv. Com. on Trade (DPACT); mem. adv. bd. Yale Sch. Mgmt.; vice chmn. World Affairs Coun., L.A.; chmn. Sabriya's Castle of Fun Found. Mem. Calif. Bus. Roundtable. Office: Hughes Electronics Corp PO Box 80028 Los Angeles CA 90080-0028

ARMSTRONG, DALE P., plastic surgeon; b. Detroit, July 25, 1933; s. Clifford Earl and Lauretta Marie (Wilson) A.; m. Margaret Charlotte Goebel, June 16, 1956; children: Karen, Clifford, Douglas. BS, U. Mich., 1958, MD, 1958. Diplomate Am. Bd. Plastic Surgery. Intern U. Mich., Ann Arbor, 1958-59, resident gen. surgery, 1959-62; resident plastic surgery Duke U., 1962-65; pvt. practice plastic and reconstructive surgery Denver, 1965-66, Ventura, Calif., 1966—; presenter in field. contbr. articles to books and med. jours. chmn. United Way Ventura County Physician's Campaign, 1981-83, bd. trustees 1981-83; chief of staff Cmty. Meml. Hosp., 1984, bd. trustees 1984-85; clin. faculty mem. UCLA, 1985—; bd. dirs. Ventura Meml. Healthcare Found., chmn. svcs. assessment com., 1984—. Fellow ACS; mem. Am. Soc. Plastic and Reconstructive Surgeons, Am. Soc. Aesthetic Plastic Surgery, Calif. Med. Assn., Ventura County Med. Soc. (sec. 1972-73), L.A. Soc. Plastic Surgeons (pres. 1980-81), Soc. Clin. Aesthetic Surgery. Republican. Home: 1051 Rancho Vista Ln Santa Paula CA 93060 Office: 168 N Brent St Ste 403 Ventura CA 93003-2824

ARMSTRONG, DAVID MICHAEL, biology educator; b. Louisville, July 31, 1944; s. John D. and Elizabeth Ann (Horine) A.; children: John D., Laura C. BS, Colo. State U., 1966; MA in Teaching, Harvard U., 1967; PhD, U. Kans., 1971. From asst. prof. natural sci. to full prof. U. Colo., Boulder, 1971-93, prof. environ., population, and organismic biology, 1993—; sr. scientist Rocky Mountain Biol. Lab., Gothic, Colo., 1977, 79; resident naturalist Sylvan Dale Ranch, Loveland, Colo., 1984—; acting dir. Univ. Mus., 1987-88, dir., 1989-93; cons. ecologist. Author: Distribution of Mammals in Colorado, 1972, Rocky Mountain Mammals, 1975, 87, Mammals of the Canyon Country, 1982; co-author: Mammals of the Northern Great Plains, Mammals of the Plains States, Mammals of Colorado. Mem. non-game adv. council Colo. Div. Wildlife, 1972-76, Colo. Natural Areas Council, 1975-80. Mem. Am. Soc. Mammalogists (editor 1981-87), Southwestern Assn. Naturalists (editor 1976-80), Rocky Mountain Biol. Lab. (trustee 1979-83), The Nature Conservancy (Colo. chpt. trustee 1989—). Office: U Colo EPO Biology Box 334 Boulder CO 80309-0334

ARMSTRONG, GENE LEE, systems engineering consultant, retired aerospace company executive; b. Clinton, Ill., Mar. 9, 1922; s. George Dewey and Ruby Imald (Dickerson) A. m. Lael Jeanne Baker, Apr. 3, 1946; children: Susan Lael, Roberta Lynn, Gene Lee. BS with high honors, U. Ill., 1948, MS, 1951. Registered profl. engr., Calif. With Boeing Aircraft, 1948-50, 51-52; chief engr. astronautics divsn., corp. dir. Gen. Dynamics, 1954-65; chief engr. Def. Sys. Group TRW, Redondo Beach, Calif., 1956-86; pvt. cons. sys. engring. Def. Sys. Group TRW, 1986—; Mem. NASA Rsch. Adv. Com. on Control, Guidance & Navigation, 1959-62. Contbr. chpts. to books, articles to profl. publs. 1st lt. USAAF, 1942-45. Decorated Air medal; recipient alumni awards U. Ill., 1965, 77;. Mem. Am. Math. Soc., AIAA, Nat. Mgmt. Assn., Am. Def. Preparedness Assn., Masons. Home: 5242 Bryant Cir Westminster CA 92683-1713 Office: Armstrong Sys Engring Co PO Box 86 Westminster CA 92684-0086

ARMSTRONG, HARRY, mayor. Mayor City of Clovis, Calif., 1982-84, 90-92, 1994—. 1st v.p. League of Calif. Cities, 1982, pres. 1983, numerous other offices; pres. South San Joaquin Divsn. of League of Calif. Cities Coms., 1972-73, other coms.; chmn. Fresno County Transp. Authority, 1994—; bd. dirs. Fresno County Coun. of Govts., 1994—, DARE; chmn. Fresno County Dem. Cen. Com., 1997. Office: 655 W Stuart Clovis CA 93612

ARMSTRONG, JOANNA, education educator; b. Vienna, Austria, Feb. 3, 1915; came to U.S., 1946; m. David B. Armstrong, Mar. 12, 1946 (dec. Feb. 1992). Diploma, Kindergarten Tchr. State Coll., Vienna, 1933; diploma French Lit., Sorbonne, Paris, 1935; MA, U. Utah, 1951; EdD, U. Houston, 1959. Caseworker, interpreter Czech Refugee Trust Fund, London, 1939-41; tchr. French Gt. Missenden, Bucks, Eng., 1941-43; sec., translator-interpreter U.S. Army, England and France, 1943-46; instr. Coll. William and Mary, Williamsburg, Va., 1951-55, U. St. Thomas, Houston, 1957-59; chmn. langs. sect. South Tex. Coll., Houston, 1961-62; assoc. prof. fgn. langs. Tex. So. U., Houston, 1962-68; dir. NDEA Inst. U. Tex. at Houston, Houston, summer 1964, 65; assoc. prof. sch. edn. tng. Headstart tchrs. U. Tex., El Paso, 1968-71; cons. office Child Devel. HEW, Kansas City, Mo., 1973-75; ret., 1975; cons. Tex. Edn. Agy., Austin, 1965; sec. U.S. Forest Svc., Ely, Nev., 1948; dir. summer programs U. Bordeaux at Pau, U. Zaragoza at Jaca. Author: (book) A European Excursion-From the Mediterranean to the Alps, 1967, Surprising Encounters, 1994; contbr. articles to profl. publs. Vol. Long Beach (Calif.) Symphony, 1978-81, Long Beach Opera, 1982-88, Long Beach Cambodian Scs., 1983-85; mem. Normandy Found. (participant 50th D-Day anniversary 1994). Decorated chevalier Ordre des Palmes Academiques, 1969; recipient award Heart Start, 1971, Pres. plaque Alliance Francaise El Paso, 1971, Commemorative Medal of Freedom, Coun. of Normandy, France, 1994. Mem. Long Beach Women's Music Club (program chmn. 1986-88, mem. choral sect. 1989-96, 1st v.p. 1990-92, rec. sec., chmn. opera sect. 1993-94), U.S.-China Peoples Friendship Assn. (rec. sec. 1987—), W.A.C. (Queen City chpt. 57). Home: 120 Alamitos Ave Apt 34 Long Beach CA 90802-5330

ARMSTRONG, JOHN, newspaper editor. Exec. editor Contra Costa (Calif.) Times. Office: 2640 Shadelands Dr Walnut Creek CA 94596

ARMSTRONG, LLOYD, JR., university official, physics educator; b. Austin, Tex., May 19, 1940; s. Lloyd and Beatrice (Jackson) A.; m. Judith Glantz, July 9, 1965; 1 son, Wade Matthew. BS in Physics, MIT, 1962; PhD in Physics, U. Calif., Berkeley, 1966. Postdoctoral physicist Lawrence Berkeley (Calif.) Lab., 1965-66, cons., 1976; sr. physicist Westinghouse Research Labs., Pitts., 1967-68, cons., 1968-70; research asso. Johns Hopkins U., 1968-69, asst. prof. physics, 1969-73, assoc. prof., 1973-77, prof., 1977-93, chmn. dept. physics and astronomy, 1985-87, dean Sch. Arts and Scis., 1987-93; provost, sr. v.p. for acad. affairs U. So. Calif., L.A., 1993—, prof. physics, 1993—; assoc. rsch. scientist Nat. Ctr. Sci. Rsch. (CNRS), Orsay, France, 1972-73; vis. fellow Joint Inst. Lab. Astrophysics, Boulder, Colo., 1978-89; program officer NSF, 1981-83, mem. adv. com. for physics, 1985-87, mem. visitors com. physics divsn., 1991; chmn. com. atomic and molecular scis. NAS/NRC, 1985-88, mem. bd. physics and astronomy, 1989-96; mem. adv. bd. Inst. for Theoretical Physics, Santa Barbara, 1992-96, chmn., 1994-95, Inst. Theoretical Atomic and Molecular Physics, Cambridge, Mass., 1994-97, Rochester Theory Ctr. for Optical Sci. and Enging.; bd. dirs. So. Calif. Econ. Partnership, 1994—, Calif. Coun. on Sci. and Tech., 1994—, Pacific Coun. on Internat. Policy, 1996—. Author: Theory of Hyperfine Structure of Free Atoms, 1971; contbr. articles to profl. jours. NSF grantee, 1972-90; Dept. Energy grantee, 1975-82. Fellow Am. Phys. Soc.

ARMSTRONG, ORVILLE, judge; b. Austin, Tex., Jan. 21, 1929; s. Orville Alexander and Velma Lucille (Reed) A.; m. Mary Dean Macfarlane; children: Anna Louise Glenn, John M., Paul Jefferson. BBA, U. Tex., Austin, 1953; LLB, U. So. Calif., 1956. Bar: Calif., 1957, U.S. Ct. Appeals (9th cir.) 1958, U.S. Supreme Ct. 1980. Ptnr., Gray, Binkley & Pfaelzer, 1956-61, Pfaelzer, Robertson, Armstrong & Woodard, L.A., 1961-66, Armstrong & Lloyd, L.A., 1966-74, Macdonald, Halsted & Laybourne, L.A., 1975-88, Baker & McKenzie, 1988-90; judge Superior Ct. State of Calif., 1991-92, assoc. justice ct. appeal State of Calif., 1993—; lectr. Calif. Continuing Edn. of Bar. Served with USAF, 1946-49. Fellow ABA, Am. Coll. Trial Lawyers; mem. State Bar Calif. (gov. 1983-87, pres. 1986-87), L.A. County Bar Assn. (trustee 1971-72), Chancery Club (pres. 1988), Calif. Club. Baptist. Home: 2385 Coniston Pl San Marino CA 91108-2102 Office: 300 S Spring St Los Angeles CA 90013-1230

ARMSTRONG, PETER BROWNELL, biologist; b. Syracuse, N.Y., Apr. 27, 1939; s. Philip Brownell and Marian Louise (Schmuck) A.; m. Margaret Tryon, Sept. 22, 1962; children: Katharine, Elisabeth, Philip. BS, U. Rochester, 1961; PhD, Johns Hopkins U., 1966. Asst. prof. Biology U. Calif., Davis, 1966-72, assoc. prof. Biology, 1972-80, prof. Biology, 1980—; sci. trustee Marine Biol. Lab., Woods Hole, Maine, 1986-90. Contbr. articles to profl. jours. Office: U Calif Dept Molecular & Cell Biology Davis CA 95616-8535

ARMSTRONG, R(OBERT) DEAN, entertainer; b. Serena, Ill., July 2, 1923; s. Francis Robert and Viola D. (Thompson) A.; m. Ardith Roberta Taylor, Jan. 10, 1943; 1 child, Larry Dean. Grad. high sch., Serena, Ill.; student, Joliet (Ill.) Conservatory of Music, 1942. Host Dean Armstrong Show Sta. KOLD-TV, Tucson, 1953-75; leader, owner Ariz. Dance Hands, Tucson, 1946—. Served with U.S. Mil., 1943-45, ETO, PTO. Recipient Jefferson award Am. Inst. for Pub. Svc., 1992; inducted into Tucson Area Music Assn. Hall of Fame, 1994. Mem. Tucson Musicians Assn. (meritorious svc. award 1981), VFW, Western Music Assn. (charter mem.), Profl. Western Music Assn. Democrat. Methodist. Lodges: Elks, Eagles. Home and Office: 4265 N Avenida Del Cazador Tucson AZ 85718-7005

ARMSTRONG, SARA JO, elementary school educator; b. Raleigh, N.C., Nov. 26, 1947; d. James Burgin and Mary Lou (Morrow) Soesbee; m. Kevin Vaughan Armstrong, July 30, 1988; 1 child, Elizabeth Pualani. BA, Erskine Coll, Due West, S.C., 1969; MEd, Miami U., Oxford, Ohio, 1971, U. Hawaii. Tchr. English and French, Eaton (Ohio) High Sch., 1970-73; elem. tchr. Le Jardin Acad., Kailua, Hawaii, 1974-81, Cathedral Sch. for Boys, San Francisco, 1982-85, Hanahauoli Sch., Honolulu, 1985—; team mem. Consortium for Teaching Asia and Pacific in Schs., 1990-91. Mem. music and worship com., choir and handbell group Calvary Luth. Ch., Honolulu, 1980-81, 85-91; bd. dirs. Waikiki Skyliner, Honolulu, 1990-92. Mem. Hawaii Assn. Ind. Schs., Elem. Sch. Ctr. Democrat. Office: Hanahauoli Sch 1922 Makiki St Honolulu HI 96822-2032

ARMSTRONG, SAUNDRA BROWN, federal judge; b. Oakland, Calif., Mar. 23, 1947; d. Coolidge Logan and Pauline Marquette (Bearden) Brown; m. George Walter Armstrong, Apr. 18, 1982. B.A., Calif. State U.-Fresno, 1969; J.D., U. San Francisco, 1977. Bar: Calif. 1977, U.S. Supreme Ct. 1984. Policewoman Oakland Police Dept., 1970-77; prosecutor, dep. dist. atty. Alameda County Dist. Atty., Oakland, 1978-79, 80-82; staff atty. Calif. Legis. Assembly Com. on Criminal Justice, Sacramento, 1979-80; trial atty. Dept. Justice, Washington, 1982-83; vice chmn. U.S. Consumer Product Safety Commn., Washington, 1984-86; commr. U.S. Parole Commn., Washington, 1986-89; judge Alameda Superior Ct., 1989-91, U.S. Dist. Ct. (no. dist.) Calif., San Francisco, 1991—. Recipient commendation Calif. Assembly, 1980. Mem. Nat. Bar Assn., ABA, Calif. Bar Assn., Charles Houston Bar Assn., Black C. of C., Phi Alpha Delta. Democrat. Baptist. Office: US Dist Ct Ste 400 S Tower 1301 Clay St Oakland CA 94612-5212*

ARMSTRONG, WALLACE DOWAN, JR., data processor; b. Los Angeles, Feb. 9, 1926; s. Wallace Dowan and Vina Edith (Kreinbring) A.; BS cum laude, U. So. Calif., 1951; postgrad. U. Oslo (Norway), 1955; 1 son, Erik Bentung. Supr. accounting Ramo Wooldridge Corp., 1955-60; mgr. programmers, systems analyst Aerospace Corp., El Segundo, Calif., 1960-80, mgr. bus. systems, 1980—. Mem. Common Cause, Handgun Control, Inc. With USMCR, 1944-46, 51. Mem. Data Processing Mgmt. Assn., Marine Corp. Assn. Home: 25713 Crest Rd Torrance CA 90505-7022 Office: Aerospace Corp 2350 E El Segundo Blvd El Segundo CA 90245-4609

ARNBERGER, ROBERT, museum administrator. Supr. Grand Canyon Nat. Park, Ariz. Office: Grand Canyon Nat Park Mus Collections PO Box 129 Grand Canyon AZ 86023*

ARNELL, WALTER JAMES WILLIAM, mechanical engineering educator, consultant; b. Farnborough, Eng., Jan. 9, 1924; came to U.S., 1953, naturalized, 1960; s. James Albert and Daisy (Payne) A.; m. Patricia Catherine Cannon, Nov. 12, 1955; children—Sean Paul, Victoria Clare, Sarah Michele Arnell. Aero. Engr., Royal Aircraft Establishment, 1946; BSc, U. London, 1953, PhD, 1967; MA, Occidental Coll., L.A., 1956; MS, U. So. Calif., 1958. Lectr. Poly. and Northampton Coll. Advance Tech., London, 1948-53; instr. U. So. Calif., L.A., 1954-59; asst. prof. mech. engring. Calif. State U., Long Beach, 1959-62, assoc. prof., 1962-66, prof., 1966-71, chmn. dept. mech. engring., 1964-65, acting chmn. divsn. engring., 1964-66, dean engring., 1967-69; rschr. Calif. State U. Ctr. Engring. Rsch., Long Beach; affiliate faculty dept. ocean engring. U. Hawaii, 1970-74; adj. prof. systems and insdl. engring. U. Ariz., 1981—; pres. Lenra Assocs. Ltd., 1973—; chmn., project mgr. Hawaii Environ. Simulation Lab., 1971-72. Contbr. articles to profl. jours. Trustee Rehab. Hosp. of the Pacific, 1975-78. Mem. Royal Aero. Soc., AIAA, IEEE Systems Man and Cybernetics Soc., AAUP, Am. Psychol. Assn., Soc. Engring., Psychology, Human Factors Soc., Ergonomics Soc., Psi Chi, Alpha Pi Mu, Tau Beta Pi, Phi Kappa Phi, Pi Tau Sigma. Home: 4491 E Ft Lowell Rd Tucson AZ 85712-1106

ARNESON, PATRICIA ANN, speech communication educator; b. Glencoe, Minn., Mar. 22, 1961; d. Richard Norman and Darlene Marie (Hanke) A. AA, St. Cloud State U., 1981, BA, 1983; MS, So. Ill. U., 1984; PhD, Ohio U., 1987. Teaching asst. So. Ill. U., Carbondale, 1983-84, Ohio U., Athens, 1984-87; asst. prof. speech comm. Bowling Green (Ohio) State U., 1987-90; asst. prof. speech comm. U. No. Colo., Greeley, 1990-93, assoc. prof., 1993—; cons. Colo. Air N.G., Greeley, 1994; speaker and trainer in field; manuscript reviewer for profl. jours. Author book chpts.; contbr. articles to profl. jours. Vol. A Woman's Place, Greeley, 1991-93, Eldergarden, Greeley, 1994—, Poudre Wilderness Vols, 1996—. Named 1 of Outstanding Young Women of Am., 1989. Mem. Speech Comm. Assn. (nat. com. on assessment and testing 1995—), We. States Comm. Assn. (sec., vice chair, chair comm. theory and rsch. div.), Colo. Speech Comm. Assn. (co-chair interpersonal, small group and orgnl. comm. interest group). Office: U No Colo Dept Speech Comm Greeley CO 80639

ARNEY, JAMES DOUGLAS, forestry biometrics consultant; b. Hoquiam, Wash., Dec. 9, 1941; s. James Dennis and Martha (Wylam) A.; m. Jo Ann Joyce Loehrke, Febr. 14, 1991; children: Michael, BettiJean. BS in Forest Mgmt., U. Mont., 1965; MS in Forest Mensuration, Oreg. State U., 1968, PhD in Forest Biometrics, 1971. Forest mensurationist U.S. Forest Svc. Expt. Sta., Portland, 1965-66; rsch. scientist Canadian Forestry Svc., Victoria, B.C., 1970-72; rsch. mgr. Weyerhaeuser Co., Centralia, Wash., 1973-80; mgr. forest dept. Reid, Collins & Assocs., Vancouver, B.C., 1980-81; rsch. forester Potlatch Corp., Lewiston, Idaho, 1982-84; forestry cons. Applied Biometrics, Spokane, Wash., 1985-88, Mason, Bruce & Girard, Inc., Portland, 1989-94, Forest Biometrics, Gresham, Oreg., 1995—. Mem. Soc. Am. Foresters, We. Forestry Assn. Home: 3486 SW Tegart Ave Gresham OR 97080-5433 Office: Forest Biometrics 655 W Burnside Rd Gresham OR 97030

ARNOLD, DAVID, film company executive; b. L.A., 1963; s. Danny and Donna (Cook) A. AA, L.A. City Coll., 1983. Assoc. dir. ABC/Tetragram Ltd., L.A., 1984-86; post prodn. supr. Tetragram Ltd., L.A., 1986-87, v.p., exec. prodr., 1992—; dir. spl. events for Jumbotron broadcast L.A. Meml. Coliseum, 1987-88; dir., prodr. VTE Mobile Prodns., L.A., 1987-89; v.p. prodn. Comar Inc., Rancho Dominguez, Calif., 1989-91. Mem. Dirs. Guild Am. Office: Tetragram Ltd 9200 Sunset Blvd # 1215 Los Angeles CA 90069

ARNOLD, JAMES RICHARD, chemist, educator; b. New Brunswick, N.J., May 5, 1923; s. Abraham Samuel and Julia (Jacobs) A.; m. Louise Clark, Oct. 11, 1952; children: Robert C., Theodore J., Kenneth C. A.B., Princeton U., 1943, M.A., 1945, Ph.D., 1946. Postdoctoral fellow Inst. Nuclear Studies, U. Chgo., 1946-47, mem. faculty, 1948-55; NRC fellow Harvard U., 1947-48; mem. faculty chemistry Princeton U., 1955-58; assoc. prof. chemistry U. Calif., San Diego, 1958-60; prof. U. Calif., 1960-92, Harold C. Urey prof., 1983-92, chmn. dept. chemistry, 1960-63; assoc. Manhattan Project, 1943-46; dir. Calif. Space Inst., 1980-89, interim dir., 1996-97; prin. investigator Calif. Space Grant Consortium, 1989—; mem. various bds. NASA, 1959—; mem. space sci. bd. NAS, 1970-74, mem. com. on sci. and pub. policy, 1970-77. Mem. editorial bd.: Ann. Rev. Nuclear Chemistry, 1972; asso. editor: Revs. Geophysics and Space Physics, 1972-75, Moon, 1972—; contbr. articles to profl. jours. Pres. Torrey Pines Elem. Sch. PTA, 1964-65; pres. La Jolla Democratic Club, 1965-66; mem. nat. council World Federalists-U.S.A., 1970-72. Recipient E.O. Lawrence medal AEC, 1968, Leonard medal Meteoritical Soc., 1976, Kuiper award Am. Astron. Soc., 1993; asteroid 2143 named Jimarnold in his honor, 1980; Guggenheim fellow, India, 1972-73. Mem. Nat. Acad. Sci., Am. Acad. Arts and Scis., Internat. Acad. Astronautics, Am. Chem. Soc., AAAS, Fedn. Am. Scientists, World Federalist Assn. Office: U Calif San Diego Dept Chemistry Code 0524 La Jolla CA 92093

ARNOLD, MICHAEL NEAL, real property appraiser, consultant; b. Madera, Calif., June 6, 1947; s. John Patrick and Patricia (Neal) A.; m. Suzanne Elizabeth Badal, Aug. 31, 1968; children: C. Matthew Neal Arnold, Nathaniel T. Badal Arnold, Andrew T. White Arnold, Thomas A. Badal Arnold. BA in Geography, U. Calif., Santa Barbara, 1974. Cert. appraiser. Assoc. R.W. Raymond & Co., Santa Barbara, 1974; appraiser Madera County Assessor Office, 1975; assoc. Pickthorne & Assocs., San Bruno, Calif., 1975-76; ptnr. Hammock, Arnold, Smith, Santa Barbara, 1976—; instr. Santa Barbara City Coll., 1980-85. Contbr. articles to profl. jours. Coach AYSO, Santa Barbara, 1978—; cub master Boy Scouts Am., Santa Barbara, 1985. Mem. Vieja Valley Site Coun., Santa Barbara Coun. Real Estate Appraisers (sec., speaker bur.), Appraisal Inst. (instr. 1990—, grader, com. chair, officer, chpt. pres.), Amateurs Club, Santa Barbara City Coll. (adv. coun. mem.). Episcopalian. Home: 2325 Santa Barbara St Santa Barbara CA 93105-3547 Office: Hammock Arnold Smith & Co 215 W Figueroa St 2nd Fl Santa Barbara CA 93101-3627

ARNOLD, ROBERT LLOYD, investment broker; b. Seattle, June 18, 1952; s. Vern Lloyd and Ruth Francis (Bruty) A. Student, Bellevue Coll., Wash., 1971-72; BS magna cum laude, U. Wash., 1975; MS, Yale U., 1977. Lic. fed. securities agt. Group leader U.S. Govt., Miramonte, Calif., 1977-78; economist U.S. Govt., Walla Walla, Wash., 1978-79; gen. mgr. Full Value Roofing, Bellevue, 1979-81; transp. mgr. N.W. Hydra-Line, Inc., Seattle, 1981-83; owner Fairfields, Seattle, 1982—; sr. fin. advisor Waddell & Reed, Inc., Bellevue, 1983—; coord. Charles Givens Found., Seattle, 1984-85, 88-90; lectr. Cmty. Sch., Seattle, 1984-91; guest spkr. Kiwanis, Puyallup, Wash., 1985; seminar leader Chgo. Title Ins. Co., Seattle, 1985-90. Fund raiser ARC, Seattle, 1984-85; chmn. fin. com. Unity Ch. of Seattle, 1988-90. Grantee Bloedel Found., 1973-74, Bishop Soc. grantee, 1974-75; fellow Yale U., 1975-77. Mem. Rainier Club (reciprocity com. 1994—, young Rainiers com. 1994-95, arts and libr. com. 1996—), Yale Alumni Assn., Seattle Delta Group (life, chmn. 1985—), Letip Internat. Eastside (v.p. 1996, pres. 1996), U. Wash. Alumni Assn., Inglewood Beach Club (trustee 1996—, v.p. 1996—), Bellevue Master Mind (pres. 1996-97), Xi Sigma Pi (treas. 1974-75). Republican. Office: 12340 NE 8th St Ste 100 Bellevue WA 98005-3189

ARNOLD, RONALD HENRI, nonprofit organization executive, consultant; b. Houston, Aug. 8, 1937; s. John Andrew and Carrie Virginia (Henri) A.; m. Phoebe Anne Trogdon, Oct. 12, 1963 (dec. Feb. 1974); 1 child, Andrea; m. Janet Ann Parkhurst, Aug. 8, 1974; stepchildren: Andrea Wright, Rosalyn Wright. Tech. publ. Boeing Co., Seattle, 1961-71; cons. Northwoods Studio, Bellevue, Wash., 1971—; exec. v.p. Ctr. for Def. of Free Enterprise, Bellevue, 1984—; advisor Nat. Fed. Lands Conf., 1988-92. Author: James Watt and the Environment, 1981, Ecology Wars, 1987, The Grand Prairie Years, 1987, (with Alan Gottlieb) Trashing the Economy, 1993, Politically Correct Environment, 1996, Ecoterror, 1997; editor: Stealing the National Parks, 1987; contbg. editor Logging Mgmt. mag., 1978-81, Western Conservation Jour., 1974-81. Recipient Editorial Achievement award Am. Bus. Press, 1981. Mem. AFTRA, Forest History Soc. Republican. Home: 12605 NE 2nd St Bellevue WA 98005-3206

ARNOLD, SHEILA, former state legislator; b. N.Y.C., Jan. 15, 1929; d. Michael and Eileen (Lynch) Keddy; coll. courses; m. George Longan

Arnold, Nov. 12, 1960; 1 child, Peter; 1 child by previous marriage, Michael C. Young (dec.); stepchildren: Drew, George Longan, Joe. Mem. Wyo. Ho. of Reps., 1978-93, vice chmn. Laramie Regional Airport Bd. Former mem., sec. Wyo. Land Use Adv. Coms.; past pres. Dem. Women's Club, Laramie; past chmn. Albany County Dem. Party; past mem. Dem. State Com.; mem. adv. bd. Wyo. Home Health Care; former mem. Nat. Conf. State Legislatures Com. on Fiscal Affairs and Oversight Com. Recipient Spl. Recognition award from Developmentally Disabled Citizens of Wyo., 1985. Mem. Laramie Area C. of C. (pres. 1982; Top Hand award 1977), LWV (Laramie bd. dirs. 1993-94), Internat. Platform Assn., Faculty Women's Club (past pres.), VFW Ladies Aux. (past pres. Post 2221), Zonta (Laramie bd. dirs.), Laramie Women's Club.

ARNOLD, TALITHA JANE, minister; b. Phoenix, Sept. 25, 1953; d. Lee Weight and Elizabeth (Standring) A. BA cum laude, Pomona Coll., 1975; MDiv, Yale U., 1980. Ordained minister, United Ch. of Christ, 1980. Interim assoc. univ. chaplain Yale U., New Haven, 1980-81; assoc. minister First Ch. of Christ, Middletown, Conn., 1981-87; sr. minister United Ch. of Santa Fe, N.Mex., 1987—; chmn., mem. Office for Ch. Life and Leadership, United Ch. of Christ, N.Y.C., 1981-87; mem. United Ch. Bd. for Homeland Ministries, N.Y.C., Cleve., 1988-93. Bd. dirs., pres. Habitat for Humanity, Santa Fe, 1991-93, 93-95; pres. Santa Fe Ministerial Alliance, 1991-93; mem. Children and Youth Commn., Santa Fe, 1988-93. Named Disting. Recent Alumni Yale Div. Sch., 1996. Mem. Phi Beta Kappa. Office: United Church Santa Fe 1804 Arroyo Chanuso Santa Fe NM 87505

ARNOLDSON, EARL RANDON, educator; b. Mt. Pleasant, Utah, Oct. 13, 1962; s. Elliot J. and R. LaRane (Bjerregaard) A. AS, Snow Coll., Ephraim, Utah, 1984; BS, Utah State Univ., 1986; MEd, Univ. So. Miss., 1992. Cert. elem. sch. tchr., adminstr. Tchr. Millard Sch. Dist., Delta, Utah, 1987—, contract negotiator, 1990-93, head tchr., 1996-97. Dist. chmn. Delta Dem. Com., 1992-94; coord. drug prevention Delta North Elem. Sch., 1994-96; referee Delta Youth Football, 1995-96. mem. ASCD, NEA, Utah Edn. Assn., Millard Edn. Assn. Office: 50 North 100 East Delta UT 84624

ARNOTT, ROBERT DOUGLAS, investment company executive; b. Chgo., June 29, 1954; s. Robert James Arnott and Catherine (Bonnell) Cameron; children: Robert Lindsay, Sydney Allison. BA, U. Calif., Santa Barbara, 1977. V.p. Boston Co., 1977-84; pres., chief exec. officer TSA Capital Mgmt., L.A., 1984-87; v.p., strategist Salomon Bros. Inc., N.Y.C., 1987-88; pres., CEO First Quadrant Corp., Morristown, N.J., Pasadena, Calif., and London, 1988-96; mng. ptnr. First Quadrant, L.P., Pasadena, London, Boston, 1996—; mem. chmn.'s adv. coun. Chgo. Bd. Options Exch., 1989—; bd. dirs. Internat. Faculty in Fin.; mem. product adv. bd. Chgo. Mercantile Exch., 1990. Editor: Asset Allocation, 1988, Active Asset Allocation, 1992; mem. editorial bd. Jour. of Investing, 1990—, Jour. Portfolio Mgmt., 1984—; contbr. articles to profl. jours. and chpts. to books. Mem. Inst. Internat. Rsch. (adv. bd. 1990—), Assn. for Investment Mgmt. and Rsch., Inst. Quantitative Rsch. in Fin., Toronto Stock and Futures Exch. (adv. coun. 1992—). Office: 1st Quadrant Corp PO Box 7183 Pasadena CA 91109-7183

ARNQUIST, JEANETTE GREEN, charitable foundation administrator, activist; b. Muskogee, Okla., June 11, 1944; d. Jess Edwin and Violet (Bisoni) Green; m. Clifford Warren Arnquist, Sept. 26, 1970; children: Catherine Ann, Paula Jeanette, Steven Clifford. BA, La. Poly. U., 1966; MA, Ariz. State U., 1968; MPS, Loyola U., New Orleans, 1995. Asst. mgr. Fashion Fabrics, L.A., 1972-73; substitute tchr. Hemet (Calif.) Unified Sch. Dist., 1980-84; tchr. Aquinas H.S., San Bernardino, Calif., 1984; instr. Mt. San Jacinto C.C., San Jacinto, Calif., 1984-89; coord. children and family coun. Cath. Charities, San Bernardino, Calif., 1991—; bd. dirs. Valley Restart Shelter, Calif. Homeless and Housing Coalition, Sacramento. Mem. Cath. Social Action Dirs. of Calif., Roundtable. Office: Cath Charities 1450 North D San Bernardino CA 92405

ARNSBERGER, BRADLEY KIRK, family nurse practitioner, physician assistant; b. Santa Cruz, Calif., Dec. 11, 1954; s. Frederick Wayne and Lillian Miranda (Kornmann) A.; m. Lorice Jene Weidman, Nov. 5, 1983; children: Amy Michelle, Ryan Bradley. AS, ASN with high honors, Cabrillo Coll., 1982; degree in Family Nurse Practitioner, U. Calif., Davis, 1984. RN, Calif. family nurse practitioner; cert. physician asst. Nurse practitioner, physician asst. family practice, Susanville, Calif., 1982-88, Robert T. Petty D.O., Selma, Calif., 1988—; ptnr. A.W. Assocs., Santa Cruz, 1983-86; guest lectr. local hosp. and civic groups, 1988—; guest lectr. gynecology issues U. Calif., Davis. Provider of sideline med. care for football team Orosi H.S., Calif.; mem. sch. bd. Cathedral Christian Sch., 1995-96, 96-97. Fellow Am. Acad. Physician Asst., Calif. Acad. Physician Assts. Home: 2507 Magnolia Ct Kingsburg CA 93631-1453 Office: Robert T Petty DO 2511 Logan Selma CA 93662

ARO, GLENN SCOTT, environmental and safety executive; b. Balt., Jan. 18, 1948; s. Raymond Charles Sr. and Elizabeth Virginia (Coppage) A.; m. Marlene Rose Lefler, Jan. 8, 1972 (div. June 1987); children: Vincent Wade, Marlena Irene; m. Rosie Ann Lucero, Nov. 22, 1994. BS in Mech. Engring., Gen. Motors Inst., Flint, Mich., 1972; MBA in Fin., Wayne State U., 1980. Registered environmental assessor, Calif. From engr. to supr. GM, Detroit, Balt., L.A., 1966-84; environ. specialist New United Motor, Fremont, Calif., 1984-86; environ. engring. mgr. Def. Systems FMC Corp., San Jose, Calif., 1986-89; cons./exec. sales rep. Gaia Systems, Menlo Park, Calif., 1990; corp. environ. & safety mgr. Ampex Corp., Redwood City, Calif., 1990-92; gen. ops. mgr. Hughes Environ. Systems, El Segundo, Calif., 1992—; lectr. colls. and seminars Environ. Regulatory Issues, 1988—. Author: Developing a National Environmental Policy in a Global Market, 1989; contbd. articles to profl. jours. Panel mem. Toxics Awareness Project, San Francisco, 1989—; com. mem. Environ. Working Group, Sacramento, 1986-88. Mem. Peninsula Indsl. & Bus. Assn. (bd. dirs., v.p. 1988-91). Republican. Roman Catholic. Home: 241 Palos Verdes Dr W Apt 203 Palos Verdes Estates CA 90274-1327

ARONOWITZ, JOEL ALAN, plastic and reconstructive surgeon; b. Memphis, Dec. 5, 1956. MD, Baylor Coll. Medicine, 1982. Intern in gen. surgery Cedars Sinai Med. Ctr., 1983-85, resident in plastic surgery, 1985-87, attending plastic surgeon, 1987—, vice chmn. plastic surgery divsn., 1996—. Office: 8635 W 3rd St Ste 1170W Los Angeles CA 90048-6101

ARONSON, BRADLEY ALAN, construction management company executive; b. Napa, Calif., Nov. 30, 1965; s. Stanley and Beverly Jean (Oberg) A. BS in Constrn. Mgmt., Calif. State U., Sacramento, 1988; MS in Civil Engring., Stanford U., 1990. Cert. constrn. mgr. Constrn. mgr. Vanir CM, Sacramento, 1987-95; owner Pacific Program Mgmt., Walnut Creek, Calif., 1995—. Song writer. Elected dir. So. County ConservationDsit., Gilroy, Calif., 1994. Recipient Saul Horowitz Meml. award Assoc. Gen. Contractors Am., 1989. Mem. Constrn. Mgmt. Assn. Am. Republican. Office: Pacific Program Mgmt Inc 2945 Santos # 1731 Walnut Creek CA 94596

ARORA, SANJEEV, gastroenterology educator; b. India, Sept. 26, 1956; came to U.S., 1980; s. Ramrakha and Sudarshan (Chopra) A.; m. Madhu Ahuja, July 21, 1956; children: Anita, Sarah. Grad., Maharajah's Coll., Jaipur, India, 1974; MB, BS, Armed Forces Med. Coll., Pune, India, 1978; M Med. Mgmt., Tulane U., New Orleans, 1997. Diplomate Am. Bd. Internal Medicine, Am. Bd. Gastroenterology, Am. Bd. Med. Mgmt. Intern Army Hosp., Delhi, India, 1978-80; resident in medicine Safdurjung Hosp., New Delhi, 1980-81, Sisters of Charity Hosp., SUNY, Buffalo, 1982-85; resident in surgery Maimonides Med. Ctr., Bklyn., 1981-82; fellow in gastroenterology New Eng. Med. Ctr., Boston, 1985-87, staff physician, 1987-93; asst. prof. medicine Tufts U. Sch. Medicine, Boston, 1987-93, assoc. prof., 1993; assoc. prof. medicine, sect. chief U. N.Mex., Albuquerque, 1993—; staff gastroenterologist U. N.Mex. Hosp., 1993—; numerous lectures in field. Contbr. articles and abstracts to med. jours., chpts. to books. Fellow Am. Coll. Gastroenterology (gov. State of N.Mex. 1997-98); mem. ACP, AAAS, Am. Gastroenterology Assn. Office: U NMex Dept Medicine 2211 Lomas Blvd NE # 5 Albuquerque NM 87106-2745

ARREOLA, DANIEL DAVID, geography educator; b. Santa Monica, Calif., May 20, 1950; s. Salvador Arreola and Beatrice (Diaz) Chamberlain; m. Patricia Marie Becerra, Aug. 1, 1980. BA, UCLA, 1972; MA, Calif. State U., 1975; PhD, UCLA, 1980. Vis. asst. prof. Tex. A&M U., College Station, 1980; asst. prof. U. Ariz., Tucson, 1980-83; from asst. to assoc. prof. Tex. A&M U., College Station, 1983-90; assoc. prof. Ariz. State U., Tempe, 1990-94, prof., 1994—. Author: The Mexican Border Cities, 1993; mem. editl. bd. The Profl. Geographer, 1986-90; editl. adv. bd. Geog. Rev., 1993—; contbr. articles to profl. jours. Fellow Am. Geog. Soc.; mem. Assn. Borderland Scholars, Conf. Latin Am. Geographers, Assn. Am. Geographers, Assn. Pacific Coast Geographers. Office: Ariz State Univ Dept Geography Box 870104 Tempe AZ 85287

ARRIETA, MARCIA, poet, editor, publishing executive, educator; b. Santa Monica, Calif., Aug. 24, 1952; d. Cecil and Dora Teresa (Ramos) A.; m. Kevin Timothy Joy, June 10, 1978; children: Matthew Kevin, Brendan Yeats, Dylan James. BA, UCLA, 1975. Profl. clear tchg. credential, Calif. Tchr. English L.A. Unified Sch. Dist., 1985—; editor, publ. Indefinite Space, Pasadena, Calif., 1992—; participant The Frost Place, Franconia, N.H., 1993; leader poetry workshop, tchr. Pasadena (Calif.) Citywide Arts Program, 1991-92. Contbr. poems to The Midwest Quarterly, Wind, Bitterroot, Minotaur, Small Pond, Abbey, Perceptions, Pacific Rev., The? WHY? Project, Blue Unicorn, Sierra Nevada Coll. Rev., Psychopoetica, Riverrun, Amaranth Rev., Atticus Rev., Tight, Camellia, West/Word, Bogg, Elf, Big Scream, Generator, So To Speak, Yefief, Juxta, Lost and Found Times, Atelier, Plainsongs, Hyphen, Tin Wreath, Pacific Coast Journal, NRG. Grantee Literary Arts Pasadena City Arts Commn., 1991; recipient Literary Arts award Pasadena Arts Coun., 1993. Mem. Am. Fedn. Tchrs., Assoc. Writing Program, Pasadena Poets. Office: Indefinite Space PO Box 40101 Pasadena CA 91114

ARRIETA, OLIVIA, humanities educator; b. Morenci, Ariz., Oct. 4, 1948; d. Gilberto B. and Aurora (Lopez) A. BA, U. Ariz., 1970, MA, 1972, PhD, 1984. Staff anthropologist U.S.-Mex. Environ. Control Project, Tucson, 1971-73; rsch. asst. Bur. Ethnic Rsch. U. Ariz., Tucson, 1973-74; rsch. evaluator Tucson Unified Sch. Dist., 1983-89; asst. rsch. social scientist Mex. Am. studies U. Ariz., 1988-89; vis. rsch. scholar S.W. Hispanic Rsch. Inst. U. N.Mex., Albuquerque, 1989-90; vis. faculty Mex. Am. studies U. Ariz., Tucson, 1990-91; rsch. assoc. Family and Consumer Resource Family and Consumer Resources, Tucson, 1991-92; adj. faculty U. Ariz., Tucson, 1991-92; asst. prof. Ctr for Studies of Ethnicity and Race U. Colo., Boulder, 1992-94; coord. curriculum project Pascua Yaqui Tribe, Tucson, 1995-96. Author: (monograph) Tribal Management Procedures-Ak Chin Reservation, 1975. Precinct rep. Dem. Party, Tucson, 1983; mem. Mujeres Activas en Letras y Cambio Social, Davis, Calif., 1988-94; ofcl. historian Sociedad Nuevo Mexican ada Mutua Proteccion, Albuquerque, 1990-96. Postdoctoral fellow Ford Found., 1991, Rockefeller Found., 1989. Mem. Soc. for Applied Anthropology, Nat. Assn. for Chicano Studies. Home: 1248 N 4th Ave Tucson AZ 85705 Office: Pascua Yaqui Tribe 4747 W Calle Vicam Tucson AZ 85746

ARRINGTON, HARRIET ANN, historian, women's biographer, writer; b. Salt Lake City, June 22, 1924; d. Lyman Merrill and Myrtle (Swainston) Horne; m. Frederick C. Sorensen, Dec. 22, 1943 (div. Dec. 1954); children: Annette S. Rogers, Frederick Christian, Heidi S. Swinton; m. Gordon B. Moody, July 26, 1958 (div. Aug. 1963); 1 child, Stephen Horne; m. Leonard James Arrington, Nov. 19, 1983. BS in Edn., U. Utah, 1957. Cert. tchr., Utah, Ga. Supr. surg. secs. Latter-day Sts. Hosp., Salt Lake City, 1954-58; tchr. Salt Lake City Schs., 1954-57, Glynn County Schs., Brunswick, Ga., 1957-59, 60—; from med. sec. to office mgr. Dr. Horne, Salt Lake City, 1962-83; tchr. Carden Sch., Salt Lake City, 1973-74, women's history rschr., tchr.; mem. Utah Women's Legis. Coun.; co-establisher Arrington Archives, Utah State U. Author: Heritage of Faith, 1988; contbr. articles to profl. jours. and confs. Dist. chmn. Utah Rep. Com., 1972-76; mem. art com. Salt Lake City Bd. Edn.; chmn. art exhibit Senator Orrin Hatch's ann. Utah Women's Conf., 1987; past pres., cultural revinement and/or spiritual living tchr. LDS Women's Relief Soc.; chmn. Utah Women Artists' Exhbn., AAUW, Utah divsn., 1986-87. Recipient Vol. Action award Utah Women Artists' Exhbn., 1987, resolution of appreciation Utah Arts Coun., 1989. Mem. AAUW (Utah state cultural refinement chmn., cert. of appreciation 1988), DAR (Utah Am. history chmn., editor state paper Utah State U., Friends of Humanities, Arts, Scis. & Social Sci. award 1995), Old Main Soc. Utah State U., Chi Omega (past pres. alumni chpt.). Home and Office: 2236 S 2200 E Salt Lake City UT 84109-1135

ARROW, KENNETH JOSEPH, economist, educator; b. N.Y.C., Aug. 23, 1921; s. Harry I. and Lillian (Greenberg) A.; m. Selma Schweitzer, Aug. 31, 1947; children: David Michael, Andrew. BS in Social Sci., CCNY, 1940; MA, Columbia U., 1941, PhD, 1951, DSc (hon.), 1973; LLD (hon.), U. Chgo., 1967, CUNY, 1972, Hebrew U. Jerusalem, 1975, U. Pa., 1976, Washington U., St. Louis, 1989; D. Social and Econ. Scis. (hon.), U. Vienna, Austria, 1971; LLD (hon.), Ben-Gurion U. of the Negev, 1992; D. Social Scis. (hon.), Yale, 1974; D (hon.), Université René Descartes, Paris, 1974, U. Aix-Marseille III, 1985, U. Cattolica del Sacro Cuore, Milan, Italy, 1994, U. Uppsala, 1995; Dr.Pol., U. Helsinki, 1976; MA (hon.), Harvard U., 1968; DLitt, Cambridge U., Eng., 1985. Research assoc. Cowles Commn. for Research in Econs., 1947-49; asst. prof. econs. U. Chgo., 1948-49; acting asst. prof. econs. and stats. Stanford, 1949-50, assoc. prof., 1950-53, prof. econs., statistics and ops. research, 1953-68; prof. econs. Harvard, 1968-74, James Bryant Conant univ. prof., 1974-79; exec. head dept. econs. Stanford U., 1954-56, acting exec. head dept., 1962-63, Joan Kenney prof. econs. and prof. ops. research, 1979-91, prof. emeritus, 1991—; economist Coun. Econ. Advisers, U.S. Govt., 1962; cons. RAND Corp. Author: Social Choice and Individual Values, 1951, Essays in the Theory of Risk Bearing, 1971, The Limits of Organization, 1974, Collected Papers, Vols. I-VI, 1983-85; co-author: Mathematical Studies in Inventory and Production, 1958, Studies in Linear and Nonlinear Programming, 1958, Time Series Analysis of Inter-industry Demands, 1959, Public Investment, The Rate of Return and Optimal Fiscal Policy, 1971, General Competitive Analysis, 1971, Studies in Resource Allocation Processes, 1977, Social Choice and Multicriterion Decision Making, 1985. Served as capt. AUS, 1942-46. Social Sci. Research fellow, 1952; fellow Center for Advanced Study in the Behavioral Scis., 1956-57; fellow Churchill Coll., Cambridge, Eng., 1963-64, 70, 73, 86; Guggenheim fellow, 1972-73; Recipient John Bates Clark medal Am. Econ. Assn., 1957; Alfred Nobel Meml. prize in econ. scis., 1972, von Neumann prize, 1986. Fellow AAAS (chmn. sect. K. 1983), Am. Acad. Arts and Scis. (v.p. 1979-81, 91-93), Econometric Soc. (v.p. 1955, pres. 1956), Am. Statis. Assn., Inst. Math. Stats., Am. Econ. Assn. (exec. com. 1967-69, pres. 1973), Internat. Soc. Inventory Rsch. (pres. 1983-90); mem. NAS (mem. coun. 1990-93), Internat. Econs. Assn. (pres. 1983-86), Am. Philos. Soc., Inst. Mgmt. Scis. (pres. 1963, chmn. coun. 1964), Finnish Acad. Scis. (fgn. hon.), Brit. Acad. (corr.), Western Econ. Assn. (pres. 1980-81), Soc. Social Choice and Welfare (pres. 1991-93), Pontifical Acad. Social Scis. Office: Stanford U Dept Econs Stanford CA 94305-6072

ARSHAM, GARY, medical educator; b. Cleve., 1941; s. Sanford Ronald and Florence A.; m. Diana Silver, 1971. AB cum laude, Harvard U., 1963; MD, Case-Western Res. U., 1967; PhD, U. Ill., 1971. Fellow in med. edn. U. Ill., Chgo., 1968-71; asst. then assoc. dean curriculum devel., asst. prof. medicine and health scis. communication SUNY, 1971-72; assoc. prof., prof. health professions edn. U. of Pacific, San Francisco, 1972-79; chmn. Council on Edn. Pacific Med. Ctr., San Francisco, 1976-81; v.p. Arsham Cons., Inc., San Francisco, 1981—; adminstr. Pacific Vision Found., 1977-84, dir. edn., 1983—; mem. nat. adv. bd. John Muir Hosp. Med. Film Festival, 1981—; mem. task force on interdisciplinary edn. Nat. Joint Practice Commn., 1973-74; bd. dirs. U.S.-China Ednl. Inst., 1980—, sec., 1986-88, treas., 1993—; chair, CEO Nat. Accreditation Commn. for Schs. and Colls. of Acupuncture and Oriental Medicine, 1993—. Co-author: Diabetes: A Guide To Living Well, 1989, 2d edit. 1992, 3d edit., 1997; chief editor Family Medicine Reports, San Francisco, 1983. Fellow ACP; mem. Am. Assn. Individual Investors (chpt. bd. dirs. 1984-88), Am. Ednl. Rsch. Assn., Assn. Am. Med. Colls., Assn. Study Med. Edn., Assn. Hosp. Med. Edn. (past exec. com., sec.-treas.), Am. Diabetes Assn. (chpt. bd. dirs. 1984—, pres. 1990-91, v.p. Calif. 1992-93, pres.-elect 1993-94, pres. 1994-95, nat. bd. dirs. 1995—), Am. Assn. Diabetes Educators (assoc. editor 1985-92, bd. dirs. 1994—), Calif. Med. Assn., San Francisco Med. Soc., Harvard Club San Francisco (bd. dirs., past pres.), Harvard Alumni Assn. (bd. dirs. 1993-96), Lane Med. Soc., Tech. Security Analysts Assn. Office: Arsham Cons Inc PO Box 15608 San Francisco CA 94115-0608

ARTERBURN, JAMES DAVID, health care executive; b. Plano, Ill., Aug. 18, 1942; s. James Brown and Norma Lee (Nelson) A.; m. Doris Yvonne Klein, July 13, 1968; children: James Eric, Matthew Christopher. BS in Edn., U. Nebr., Lincoln, 1964; MPA, San Diego State U., 1972; MPH, UCLA, 1975. Diplomate Am. Coll. Health Care Execs. Asst. adminstr. Rancho Los Amigos Hosp., Downey, Calif., 1971-74; asst. adminstr. Orthopaedic Hosp., L.A., 1974-80, COO, 1980-85, CEO, 1985-87; COO Washington Hosp., Fremont, Calif., 1987-92; med. group adminstr. Permanente Med. Group, Martinez, Calif., 1992-94, Oakland, Calif., 1994—; treas. UCLA Program in Health Alumni, 1985, v.p., 1986. Lt. USN, 1964-69, Vietnam. Mem. Calif. Healthcare Assn., Hosp. Coun. No. Calif. Episcopalian. Home: 5910 Via Del Cielo Pleasanton CA 94566

ARTHUR, PAUL KEITH, electronic engineer; b. Kansas City, Mo., Jan. 14, 1931; s. Walter B. and Frieda J. (Burckhardt) A.; m. Joy N. Lim, Apr. 26, 1958; children: Gregory V., Lia F. Student Ohio No. U., 1947, Taylor U., Upland, Ind., 1948-49; BSEE, Purdue U., 1956; postgrad. N.Mex. State U., 1957-78. Registered profl. engr., N.Mex.; cert. army acquisition profl.; cert. Naval engring. duty officer, Navy material profl. With White Sands Missile Range, N.Mex., 1956—, electronic engr. field engring. group missile flight surveillance office, 1956-60, chief field engring. group, 1960-62, project engr. Pershing weapon system Army Missile Test and Evaluation Directorate, 1962-74, chief high altitude air def. projects br., 1974-82, chief air def. materiel test div., 1982-91, dep. dir. Materiel Test Directorate, 1991-95, dir., 1995—, spl. asst. to WSMR comdr. for Space Programs, 1994—; mem. N.Mex. Spaceport Commn., Southwest Regional Space Task Force, Metro Planning Orgn.; past pres. missile range pioneer group; bd. dirs. Dagupan Electric Corp. of the Philippines. Chmn. adminstrv. bd. Meth. Ch., 1992-95. Served with USN, 1949-53, USNR, 1954-87, rear adm. and, sr. engring. duty officer, 1984-87. Decorated Legion of Merit, Meritorious Svc. medal, Navy Achievement medal, Mil. Order St. Barbara, others. Mem. Am. Def. Preparedness Assn. (past pres.), AIAA (past vice chmn.), Assn. Old Crows, Naval Res. Assn., Res. Officers Assn. (pres. 1983-85), United Vets. Council (chmn. 1984-85), Am. Soc. Naval Engrs., Naval Inst., Navy League, Surface Navy Assn., Assn. U.S. Army, U.S. Field Arty. Assn., Purdue Alumni Assn. (past pres.), N.Mex. State U. Alumni Assn., Mesilla Valley Track Club, Bujutsukan Acad. Martial Arts. Author numerous plans and reports on weapon systems test and evaluation and topics in naval engring. Home: 2050 San Acacio St Las Cruces NM 88001-1570 Office: STEWS-MTD White Sands Missile Range NM 88002

ARTHUR, WILLIAM LYNN, environmental foundation administrator; b. Spokane, Wash., May 22, 1954; s. Robert Cyril and Mabel Mildred (Collison) A.; m. Debora Lee Donovan, Feb. 2, 1975; children: Kathleen, Jonathan. BA in Econs., Wash. State U., 1976, postgrad., 1982-83. Rsch. asst. Wash. State U., 1976-77; project mgr. Ctr. Environ. Understanding, Cheney, Wash., 1977-78; program dir. Wash. Energy Extension Svc., Spokane, 1978-79; econs. instr. Spokane Falls Community Coll., 1977-81; economist, cons. Biosystems Analysis Inc., Spokane, 1983; assoc. N.W. rep. Sierra Club, Seattle, 1983-87, N.W. rep., 1987-91, N.W. regional dir., 1992—; chmn. bd. N.W. Conservation Act Coalition, Seattle, 1982-83, bd. dirs., 1988-96; adv. com. N.W. Renewable Resources Ctr., Seattle, 1987-91, bd. dirs., 1992—; cons. energy workshops N.W. Regional Found., Spokane, 1982; mem. exec. com. Save Our Wild Salmon Coalition, 1991-95; mem. adv. com. Inland Empire Pub. Lands Coun., 1990—. Chmn., mem. city commn. Environ. Quality Commn., Pullman, Wash., 1976-77; bd. dirs. Ryegrass Sch., Spokane, 1978-81; conservation rep. Internat. Mountain Caribou Tech. Com., 1978-81; bd. dirs. Wash. Citizens for Recycling, Seattle, 1980-82; chair Wash. State Environmentalists for Clinton/Gore Com., 1992, 96; environ. rep. Northwest Forest Conf. convened and chaired by Pres. Clinton, Apr. 2, 1993; mem. steering com. on the No Initiative 164 Coalition, 1995; mem. Wash. State Steering Com. to Re-elect Clinton/Gore, 1996. Office: Sierra Club NW Office 180 Nickerson St Ste 103 Seattle WA 98109-3608

ARTINGSTALL, THOMAS, electrical and mechanical engineer; b. Chgo., Oct. 28, 1920; s. William Thomas and Louise Mary (Hanson) A.; m. Laura Ann Swanson, June 23, 1946 (div. June 1955); m. Arloah Darlene Norelius, June 26, 1965. BSME, Ill. Inst. Tech., 1944; postgrad., U. So. Calif., 1956. Registered profl. engr., Calif., Ill. Designer Solar Capacitator Co., L.A., 1945-48; chief designer, developer Kollsman Instrument, L.A., 1948-55; mem. radar/antenna/transmitter devel. staff Autonetics, Anaheim, Calif., 1956-70; tech. rsch. staff L.A. Aircraft, 1970-71; chief engr. Space Div. So. Calif., Yorba Linda, 1980-86; engring. specialist Rockwell Internat., Downey, Calif., 1977-90; cons. engr. Pace-Arrow, Pomona, Calif., 1970-78; engring. developer and rschr. Swanson Electronics, Arcadia, Calif., 1965-70; cons. forensic engr. Orange county Superior courts, 1990—; retirement fin. planning specialist. Patentee in field. Mem. Archtl. com. City of Yorba Linda, 1968; mem. com. Ad Hoc City Incorp., 1966; mem. bd. parks and recreation City of Yorba Linda, 1975. Mem. ASME, Nat. Mgmt. Assn., Profl. Engrs., Langlauflers Ski Club. Democrat. Roman Catholic.

ARTOF, SUSAN DALE, publisher, writer, psychology educator; b. L.A., Feb. 17, 1949; d. Ben Greenspan and Geraldine Pessin; m. Paul Edward Artof, Mar. 25, 1972; children: Jason, Lindsay. BA, Calif. State U., Northridge, 1970, MA, 1972; ABD, UCLA, 1987. Instr. psychology Santa Monica Coll., Calif., 1972-94; pub. Center-Parent Enrichment, L.A., 1990-92, The Center Press, Westlake Village, Calif., 1992—; cons. KCS, Orange County, Calif., 1973-75; real estate sales agt. 20th Century, L.A., 1977-79. Author: Don't Smoke the Joists, 1990, Writing for Pleasure, 1990, Boat Naming, 1991, Sailing: A Parents Handbook, 1992, Little Book of No, 1996; editor: US Sabot Assn., 1995—, Market Watch fin. newsletter. Event chmn. fund raise Westlake Yacht Club, 1994-96; pres. Conejo Scholastic Sailing Assn., Westlake, 1995—; mem. fund devel. bd. Casa Pacifica, Camarillo, Calif. 1996; v.p. DRAAA Del Rey Amature Athletics, Marina Del Rey, 1996—. Recipient Burgee of Merit award Del Rey Yacht Club, 1992. Mem. Am. Book Assn., Pubs. Mktg. Assn., Southern Calif. Youth Yacht Racing Assn. (del. 1994—). Office: The Center Press 30961 W Agoura Rd # 223B Westlake Village CA 91361

ARTRU, ALAN ARTHUR, anesthesiologist, educator; b. Oakland, Calif., Apr. 30, 1949; s. Frank George and Evelyn Dolores (Markstrom) A.; m. Linda Marie Mason, Aug. 18, 1973; children: Rebecca, Naomi, Aaron, Alana. BA in Psychology and Biology, U. Calif., Santa Cruz, 1971; MD, Med. Coll. Wis., 1975. Resident U. Calif., San Francisco, 1975-78; assoc. cons. in anesthesiology Mayo Cliic, Rochester, Minn., 1978-80; asst. prof. U. Wash., Seattle, 1980-84, assoc. prof., 1984-89, prof., 1989—; head rsch. dept. anesthesiology U. Wash., 1992—; cons. in field; reviewer Collaboration in Basic Sci. and Engring. Nat. Rsch. Coun. NIH, Bethesda, Md., 1993. Contbr. chpts. to books; mem. editorial bd. Jour. Neurosurg. Anesthesiology, 1987—. Del. Wash. State Rep. Conv., Bellingham, 1994; head adult edn. com., mem. outreach com. St. Madeline Sophie Ch., Bellevue, Wash., 1986. Mem. Soc. Neurosurg. Anesthesiology and Critical Care (past pres. 1993-94), Am. Soc. Anesthesiologists, Internat. Soc. Cerebral Blood Flow and Metabolism, Internat. Anesthesia Rsch. Soc., Am. Heart Assn., Am. Assn. Lab. Animal Sci. Roman Catholic. Home: 6308 129th Pl SE Bellevue WA 98006-4045 Office: U Wash Sch Dept Anesthesiology Box 356540 1959 NE Pacific St Seattle WA 98195-0004

ARUNDEL, JAMES D., lawyer; b. Omaha, July 30, 1947. BA, U. Nebr., 1969; JD, U. Chgo., 1972. Bar: Nebr. 1972, Colo. 1981. Vice chmn. Kutak Rock, Denver. Mem. Nebr. State Bar Assn., Colo. State Bar Assn., Omaha Bar Assn., Denver Bar Assn., Phi Beta Kappa. Office: Kutak Rock 717 17th St Ste 2900 Denver CO 80202

ARZUBE, JUAN ALFREDO, bishop; b. Guayaquil, Ecuador, June 1, 1918; came to U.S., 1944, naturalized, 1961; s. Juan Bautista and Maria (Jaramillo) A. B.S. in Civil Engring, Rensselaer Poly. Inst., 1942; B.A., St. John's Sem., 1954. Ordained priest Roman Catholic Ch., 1954; asso. pastor St. Agnes Ch., Los Angeles, Resurrection Ch., Los Angeles, Ascension Ch., Los Angeles, Our Lady of Guadalupe Ch., El Monte, Calif.; aux. bishop, vicar gen. Diocese L.A., Los Angeles, 1971-93; episcopal vicar for Spanish speaking Los Angeles, 1973—; mem. nat. bishops coms. Ad Hoc Com. for Spanish Speaking; chmn. Com. for Latin Am. Recipient Humanitarian award Mexican Am. Opportunity Found., 1978, John Anson Ford award Los Angeles County Commn. Human Relations, 1979. Home: Sacred Heart Ch 2889 N Lincoln Ave Altadena CA 91001-4530*

ASADI, ROBERT SAMIR, high school principal; b. Salt Lake City, Dec. 21, 1953; s. Abdul-Aziz and Wilma (Craig) A.; m. Karen Lee Schenk, June 16, 1990; children: Scott, Ryan. BS, U. Wyo., 1986; MEd, No. Ariz. U., 1994. Cert. tchr. and adminstr. Tchr., coach Cactus H.S., Glendale, Ariz., 1986-89, Holbrook (Ariz.) H.S., 1989-91; tchr., adminstrv. asst., coach Agua Fria Union H.S. South, Avondale, Ariz., 1991-94; prin. Agua Fria Union H.S.-North, Goodyear, Ariz., 1994—. mem. West Valley Fine Arts Coun., Avondale, 1995-96, Leadership West II, Avondale, 1995-96. Mem. ASCD, Tri City West C. of C., Ariz. Sch. Adminstrs., Nat. Assn. of Secondary Sch. Prins. Republican. Episcopalian. Home: 9139 W Evans Dr Peoria AZ 85381 Office: Agua Fria Union HS North PO Box 459 Litchfield Park AZ 85340

ASANO, HISAKO, fine arts educator; b. Osaka City, Japan, Jan. 5, 1944; came to the U.S., 1960; d. Denzo and Matsuko Asano; m. Michael B. Gould, Feb. 12, 1972 (div. 1981). BFA, U. So. Calif., 1966, MFA, 1971. Educator U. So. Calif., L.A., 1970—; instr. Loyola Marymount U., L.A., 1971-72, L.A. County High Sch., 1986, South Bay Adult Sch., Manhattan Beach, Calif., 1977-88, L.A. County Mus. Art, 1989, Palos Verdes (Calif.) Art Ctr., 1989-90, Torrance (Calif.) Art Ctr., 1990—, So. Coast Botanic Garden, Rolling Hills, Calif., 1987—, L.A. Harbor Coll., 1976—, L.A. County Mus. Art, 1997; Japanese brush painting instr. L.A. County Mus. Art, 1996. Exhibited works in numerous shows including U. So. Calif., 1971, Malone Gallery, L.A., 1975, L.A. Mus., 1974-75, So. Coast Botanic Garden, 1989. Mem. Printmaking Soc., Women Archtl. League, L.A. Jr. Chamber Com., Friends of Fine Arts. Home: 27838 Palos Verdes Dr E Rancho Palos CA 90275-5151 Office: U So Calif University Park Los Angeles CA 90089-0292

ASBURY, TIMOTHY EDWARD, editor; b. Bloomington, Ill., July 12, 1949; s. Earl E. and Sally (Carstens) A.; m. Nancy Lynne Coleman, Aug. 26, 1972; children: Jill, Katie, John. BS, U. Colo., 1972. Reporter Estes Park (Colo.) Trail-Gazette, 1972-79, editor, 1979—. Recipient Bausch & Lomb Sci. award Las Animas High Sch., 1967. Mem. Internat. Soc. Weekly Newspaper Editors, Colo. Press Assn. (open recs. com. 1989—). Home: PO Box 83 Estes Park CO 80517-0083 Office: Estes Park Trail-Gazette PO Box 1707 Estes Park CO 80517-1707

ASCENSÃO, JOÃO LUIS AFONSO, physician, researcher; b. Maputo, Mozambique, July 6, 1948; came to U.S., 1974; s. João F. A. and Maria (Almeida) A.; m. Vivian Pereyra, June 27, 1993; children: João Andre, Vitor Luís. MD, U. Lisbon Sch. Medicine, 1972, PhD, 1989. Resident U. Hosp. St. Mary, Lisbon, Portugal, 1972-74; immunology fellow Meml. Sloan-Kettering Cancer Ctr., N.Y.C., 1974-76; internal medicine resident U. Minn. Hosps., Mpls., 1977-78, hematology oncology fellow, 1979-81, instr., 1981-82, asst. prof., 1982-84; assoc. prof., assoc. dir. BMT program N.Y. Med. Coll., Valhalla, 1984-89; assoc. prof., dir. BMT program U. Conn. Health Sci. Ctr., Farmington, 1989-92; prof. medicine, pathology, microbiology and immunology U. Nev. Sch. Medicine, Reno, 1992—; adv. bd. mem. Calif. Cancer Ctr., Modesto, 1992—; bd. mem. Nev. Am. Cancer Soc., Reno, 1992—. Editor: Regulation of Erythropoiesis, 1987, Molecular Biology of Hemopoiesis, 1988, Molecular Biology of Erythropoiesis, 1989. Portugal Sci. Found. fellow Ministry of Edn., 1974-75, Charles H. Revson Found. fellow, 1984-86; recipient Young Investigator award NIH, 1991-94. Fellow ACP; mem. Am. Soc. Hematology, Am. Soc. Clin. Oncology, Am. Assn. Cancer Rsch., Internat. Soc. Experimental Hematology (councillor), European Soc. Med. Oncology, Clin. Immunology Soc. Office: Univ Nev Sch Medicine 1000 Locust St Reno NV 89520-0102

ASCHAFFENBURG, WALTER EUGENE, composer, music educator; b. Essen, Germany, May 20, 1927; came to U.S., 1938, naturalized, 1944; s. William Arthur and Margarete (Herz) A.; m. Nancy Dandridge Cooper, Aug. 14, 1951 (div.); children: Ruth Margareta, Katherine Elizabeth; m. Rayna Klatzkin Barroll, Aug. 5, 1987. Diploma, Hartford Sch. Music, 1945; BA, Oberlin Coll., 1951; MA, Eastman Sch. Music, 1952. Prof. composition and music theory, former chmn. composition dept. Oberlin (Ohio) Coll. Conservatory of Music, prof. emeritus, 1987—, also former chmn. dept. music theory., 1952-87. Composer: Divertimento for Trumpet, Horn Trombone 1951-52, Chaconne for Brass Ensemble, 1952, Ozymandias-Symphonic Reflections for Orch., 1952, cello Sonata, 1953, Sonata for Solo Violin, 1954, Piano Sonatina, 1954, String Quartet, 1955, Bartleby-opera, 1962, Elegy for Strings, 1961, The 23d Psalm for chorus, tenor solo, and oboe, 1963, Three Dances for Orch., 1966, Three Shakespeare Sonnets, 1967, Quintet for Winds, 1967, Proem for Brass and Percussion, 1969, Duo for Violin and Cello, 1971, Conversations-Six Pieces for Piano, 1973, Summit Records, 1994, Libertatem Appellant for Tenor, Baritone and Orch., 1976, Carrousel—24 Pieces for Piano, 1980, Concertino for Violin, Ten Winds and Contrabass, 1982, Laughing Time for Mixed Chorus, 1983, Concerto for Oboe and Orch., 1985, New World Records, 1997. From South Mountain for Brass Quintet, 1988, Coalescence for Oboe and Cello, 1989, Sonata for the Fortepiano or Pianoforte, 1990, Parings for Clarinet and Piano, 1993. Served with AUS, 1945-47. Recipient award Fromm Music Found., 1953; Nat. Inst. Arts and Letters award, 1966; Cleve. arts prize, 1980; Guggenheim fellow, 1955-56, 73-74. Mem. ASCAP, Soc. Composers, Am. Music Ctr., Soc. Music Theory. Home: 4639 E Monte Way Phoenix AZ 85044-7517

ASCHE, ELIZABETH HILL, retired public health nurse; b. Victorville, Calif., Oct. 24, 1902; d. Sherman Sperry and Grace Mabel (Barnes) Hill; m. Sherman Asche, Dec. 15, 1974 (dec. Apr. 6, 1984). BS, U. Calif., 1928, postgrad. in pub. health nursing, 1929; MA, Columbia U., 1934. RN, Calif., 1927; cert. pub. health nurse Calif. State Dept. Pub. Health, 1928. Pub. health nurse Red Cross, Santa Rosa, Calif., 1928-33, E. Harlem Nursing Svc., N.Y.C., 1934-36; public health nurse, field supr. Nat. Red Cross, Pa., Md., Del., 1936-40; first exec. dir. L.A. Vis. Nurse Assn., 1940-44; region supr. relief, rehab China mission UN, Shanghai, Beijing, 1946-48; pub. health nurse City Health Dept., Oakland, Calif., 1949-50; first regional nurse adv. We. Pacific region WHO H.Q., Manila, Philippines, 1950-55; asst. chief nurse WHO H.Q., Geneva, 1955-64; coord. fgn. students, visitors U. Calif., San Francisco, 1965-74, ret., 1974; organizer two regional nurse seminars. Vol. United Way Santa Barbara County, Calif., 1984-86;, home visitor Hospice, Santa Barbara, Calif., 1985-88. 2nd lt., nurse U.S. Army, 1944-46. Mem. USPHS (maj.), Montecito Retirement Assn. (bd. dirs. med. com. 1994—, rsch., leadership gerntol. nurse practitioner alzheimer's/dementia program special care unit 1997). Democrat. Episcopalian. Home: 300 Hot Springs Rd # 86 Santa Barbara CA 93108

ASCHENBRENNER, FRANK ALOYSIOUS, former diversified manufacturing company executive; b. Ellis, Kans., June 26, 1924; s. Philip A. and Rose E. Aschenbrenner; m. Gertrude Wilhelmina DeBie, Nov. 15, 1946; children: Richard David, Robert Wayne, Mary Lynne. BS with high honors, Kans. State U., 1950; PhD in Physics, M.I.T., 1954. Mgr. physics and math. Gen. Electric, Cin., 1958-61; asst. dir. space div. Rockwell Internat., Downey, Calif., 1961-69; corp. dir. tech. Rockwell Internat., Pitts., 1969-71; v.p., gen. mgr. div. yarn machinery Rockwell Internat., Charlotte, N.C., 1971-75; pres. COR, Inc., Charlotte, 1975-77; v.p. research and devel. and engring. Ball Corp., Muncie, Ind., 1977-86; pvt. bus. cons. Poway, Calif., 1986—; chmn. bd. RAMZ Corp., Dunkirk, Ind., 1985—; nat. bd. advisors Rose-Hulman Inst., Terre Haute, Ind., 1984—, U. Tenn. Space Inst., Tullahoma, 1982—. Served with USN, 1943-47. Mem. AIAA, Am. Phys. Soc., Naval Res. Assn., San Diego Venture Group. Home and Office: 14258 Palisades Dr Poway CA 92064-6443

ASCIAN, KYTHE See MEADER, JONATHAN GRANT

ASH, LAWRENCE ROBERT, public health educator, administrator; b. Holyoke, Mass., Mar. 5, 1933; s. Lawrence Clifton and Alice (Sartini) A.; m. Luana Lee Smith, Aug. 4 1960; 1 child, Leigh I. BS in Zoology, U. Mass., 1954, MA in Zoology, 1956; PhD in Parasitology, Tulane U., 1960. Asst. parasitologist U. Hawaii, Honolulu, 1960-61; instr. Tulane U., New Orleans, 1961-65; med. parasitologist South Pacific Commn., Noumea, New Caledonia, 1965-67; asst. prof. pub. health UCLA Sch. Pub. Health, 1967-71, assoc. prof., 1971-75, prof., 1975-94, chmn. dept., assoc. dean, 1979-84, prof. emeritus, 1994—; panelist U.S. Panel on Parasitic Diseases, U.S.-Japan Program, Washington, 1972-78, chmn., 1978-84; cons. Naval Med. Rsch. Unit # 2 Taipei, China, Manila, 1970-80. Sr. author: Atlas of Human Parasitology, 1980, 4th rev. edit., 1997, Parasites: A Guide to Laboratory Procedures and Identification, 1987; co-author: Parasites in Human Tissues, 1995. NIH grantee, 1970-84. Fellow Royal Soc. Tropical Medicine and Hygiene; mem. Am. Soc. Tropical Medicine and Hygiene (councilor 1974-77), Am. Soc. Parasitologists (councilor 1972-75, 88-92, v.p. 1982-83). Home: 10400 Northvale Rd Los Angeles CA 90064-4332 Office: UCLA Sch Pub Health Los Angeles CA 90095-1772

ASH, WALTER BRINKER, lawyer; b. Wichita, Kans., June 8, 1932; s. Walter Bonsall and Gladys Elvira (Brinker) A.; m. Fern Ostrom, Sept. 16, 1986; children: Paul B., Allison L., Carolyn A. BA, U. Kans., 1955, BL, 1957. Bar: Kans. 1957, Colo. 1959. Personal asst. to Solicitor Gen. U.S. Dept. Justice, Washington, 1957-58, trial atty., 1958-59; assoc. Davis, Graham & Stubbs, Denver, 1959-63, ptnr., 1964-82; ptnr. Wade Ash Woods Hill & Guthery P.C., Denver, 1982-91, Wade Ash Woods & Hill P.C., Denver, 1991-93, Wade Ash Woods Hill & Farley, P.C., Denver, 1993—. Fellow Am. Coll. Trust and Estate Counsel; mem. ABA, Colo. Bar Assn., Denver Bar Assn., Internat. Acad. Estate and Trust Law. Home: 6814 N Trailway Cir Parker CO 80134-6200 Office: Wade Ash Woods Hill & Farley 360 S Monroe St Ste 400 Denver CO 80209-3709

ASHBY, DARREL LEROY, history educator; b. Grand Junction, Colo., Nov. 19, 1938; s. Samuel Franklin and Mildred May (Hooker) A.; m. Mary Elizabeth Gross, July 3, 1958; children: Steven Eugene, Eric Lee (dec.). AA, Mesa Jr. Coll., Grand Junction, Colo., 1958; BA, Adams State Coll., 1960; MA, U. Wyoming, 1961; PhD, U. Md., 1966. Asst. prof. history U. Bridgeport, Conn., 1966-70, Ill. State U., Normal, 1970-72; assoc. prof. history Wash. State U., Pullman, 1972-76, prof. history, 1976-94, Claudius and Mary Johnson prof. history, 1994—. Author: The Spearless Leader, 1972, Saving the Waifs, 1984, William Jennings Bryan, 1987, Endangered Children, 1997; co-author (with Rod Gramer) Fighting the Odds, 1994. Named Prof. of Yr., State of Wash., Coun. for Advancement & Support of Edn., 1990, 93. Mem. Orgn. of Am. Historians, Am. Studies Assn., Western History Assn. Home: NE 1280 Hillside Cir Pullman WA 99163 Office: Wash State Univ Dept History Pullman WA 99164

ASHBY, RANDALL FAWCETT, engineering company executive, lodge operator; b. Valdez, Alaska, Dec. 16, 1947; s. George Ingram and Katherine Elizabeth (Horton) A.; m. Marianne Rolland, June 1982 (div. Nov. 1990); children: Carly Elizabeth, Christina Rose; m. Lisa Gay Brunner, July 24, 1992; children: Shawnna Marie Brunner, Ryan Autumn Brunner. BSCE, U. Santa Clara, 1970; JD, U. Puget Sound, 1986; JD (hon.), Seattle U., 1994. Profl. land surveyor, Alaska. Constrn. engr. State of Alaska Dept. Transp., Valdea, Alaska, 1970-74, Tonsina Engring., Copper Center, Alaska, 1974-77, Northwestern Constrn., Anchorage, 1977-78, Aleution Constructors, Anchorage, 1979; constrn. engr. Miner & Miner Engrs., Glennallen, Alaska, 1980-82, Greeley, Colo., 1984-86; divsn. mgr. Miner & Miner Engrs., Greeley, 1986-87; design engr. Aurora Engrs., Anchorage, 1982-83; divsn. mgr. ASCG, Inc., Anchorage, 1988-93; operator, mgr. Copper Center Lodge, 1992—; pres. GEODE Engring. Inc., Big Lake, Alaska, 1994—. Home: PO Box 521117 Big Lake AK 99652 Office: Copper Center Lodge Drawer J Copper Center AK 99573

ASHDOWN, FRANKLIN DONALD, physician, composer; b. Logan, Utah, May 2, 1942; s. Donald and Theresa Marie (Hill) A. BA, Tex. Tech. U., 1963; MD, U. Tex., 1967. Chief of med. Holloman Air Force Base, New Mexico, 1971-73; chief of staff Gerald Champion Mem. Hosp., Alamogordo, N.M., 1976, 91, 92; pres. Otero County Concerts Assn., Alamogordo, 1985-94, Otero County Med. Soc., Alamogordo, 1986; cons. New Mexico Sch. for Visually Handicapped, Alamogordo, 1973-76. Composer of more than 30 published and recorded works. Bd. dirs. Otero County Mental Health Assn., Alamogordo, 1973-77, Flickinger Found. for Performing Arts, 1995; bd. trustees Gerald Champion Meml. Hosp., 1992. Mem. Gerald Champion Mem. Hosp., N.M. Med. Soc., Am. Soc. Internal Med., ASCAP. Republican. Home: 1435 Rockwood Alamogordo NM 88310-3920 Office: 1301 Cuba Ave Alamogordo NM 88310-5727

ASHER, JAMES EDWARD, forestry consultant, engineer, arborist, forensic expert; b. L.A., July 22, 1931; s. John Edward and Dorothy (Ingraham) A.; m. Marilyn Lee Struebing, Dec. 28, 1953; children: Lynne Marie, Laure Ann. Student Pasadena City Coll., 1949-50; BS, Oreg. State U., 1954. Certs. continuing forestry edn. Soc. of Am. Foresters. With U.S. Forest Svc., San Bernardino (Calif.) Nat. Forest, summers 1950-53, forester, 1956-57; prin. James E. Asher, ACF, Cons. Forester, 1957—; capt., bn. chief, asst. chief, fire prevention officer Crest Forest Fire Protection Dist., Crestline, Calif., 1960-69, chief, 1969-71; forester Big Bear div. Golden State Bldg. Products, Redlands, 1972, timber mgr., 1972-74; mem. profl. foresters exam. com. Calif. Bd. Forestry, 1978-90, vice chmn., 1982-90; mem. Calif. Bd. Forestry Resolution of Gratitude, 1990—; mem. Calif. Forest Pest Control Coun.; mem. Forest Adv. Com., 1982—; chmn. Profl. Foresters Ad Hoc Task Force, 1983-90. Vol. firewarden State of Calif., 1967—; mem. adv. com. Range Mgmt. Program, 1986-90; chmn. Tree Conservation Subcom., First Dist. Suprs. Ad Hoc Com. on Soil Erosion and Sediment Control, County of San Bernardino, 1984—; forensic expert witness. With AUS, 1954-56. Recipient Certificate of Merit Nat. Fire Protection Assn., San Bernardino Mountains Assn.; Resolution of Commendation, County Bd. Suprs.; Forester of Year award So. Calif. sect. Soc. Am. Foresters, 1977, Superior Continuing Forestry Edn. accomplishment Soc. Am. Foresters, 1996; others. Registered profl. forester, registered profl. engr., Calif.; lic. pest control advisor, pest control applicator, Calif. Mem. Internat. Soc. Arboriculture (cert. arborist 1988—), So. Calif. Assn. Foresters and Fire Wardens, Soc. Am. Foresters (cert., chmn. licensing and ethics com. So. Calif. sect., chmn. So. Calif. 1983), Assn. Cons. Foresters, Internat. Soc. Arboriculture, Calif. Urban Forests Coun., Calif. Agrl. Prodn. Cons. Assn., Pesticide Applicators Profl. Assn., Masons, Tau Kappa Epsilon. Presbyterian. Author: (with others) A Technical Guide for Community and Urban Forestry in Washington, Oregon and California. Contbr. 72 articles to profl. jours.; presenter in field. Office: PO Box 2326 Lake Arrowhead CA 92352-2326

ASHER, JAMES JOHN, psychology educator; b. Detroit, Aug. 10, 1929; s. James Joseph and Antoinette Marie (Abdo) Asher; m. Virginia Lee Gardner, Apr. 20, 1954; children: Jeffrey John Asher, Melissa Marie Smith. BA, U. N.Mex., 1951; MA, U. Houston, 1955, PhD, 1957; postdoctoral, various univs. Instr. dept. psychology U. Houston, 1956-57; asst. prof. dept. psychology San Jose (Calif.) State U., 1957-60, assoc. prof., 1961-65, prof., 1965—, assoc. dean sch. of social scis., 1976-78; lectr. in psychology U. Calif., Berkeley, 1960-61, U. Santa Clara, Calif., 1964, Monterey Peninsula Coll., 1964; vis. lectr. NYU, 1966, 67 summer, UCLA, 1971, U. Calif., Santa Barbara, 1971. Author: Learning Another Language Through Actions, 5th edit., Brainswitching, 1988, The Super School of the 21st Century, 1995; contbr. numerous articles to profl. jours. With U.S. Army, 1951-54. Rsch. grantee U.S. Office of Edn., Office of Naval Rsch., Office of Postal Rsch. and Engring., Dept. of Def., Def. Lang. Inst., State of Calif. Mem. Am. Psychol. Assn., Western Psychol. Assn., Am. Speech-Lang. Hearing Assn. (editl. bd. 1994). Home: PO Box 1102 Los Gatos CA 95031-1102

ASHFORD, ROBERT LOUIS, computer professional; b. Meridian, Miss., Sept. 8, 1938; s. Walter and Bertha (Edmonds) A.; m. Ruth L. Sypert, May 16, 1992. Student, Tougaloo Coll., 1956-58. Programmer, analyst State of Calif., San Francisco, 1964-68; programming mgr. Control Data Corp., Palo Alto, Calif., 1968-73; office tech. cons. Hewlett-Packard Co., Palo Alto, 1973-95. Mem. Legal Def. Fund: Com. of 100, N.Y.C. With U.S. Army, 1961-64. Mem. NAACP (life), Space Studies Inst., Search for Extraterrestrial Intelligence, Union Concerned Scientists, Astron. Soc. Pacific (advisor, cons. 1989—, Vol. of Yr. award 1992), Group 70 (bd. dirs. pub. rels. large amateur telescope project), Project Astro (adv. bd.). Democrat. Home: 3005 Breen Ct San Jose CA 95121-2412

ASHLEY, SHARON ANITA, pediatric anesthesiologist; b. Goulds, Fla., Dec. 28, 1948; d. John H. Ashley and Johnnie Mae (Everett) Ashley-Mitchell; m. Clifford K. Sessions, Sept. 1977 (div. 1985); children: Cecili, Nicole, Erika. BA, Lincoln U., 1970; postgrad., Pomona Coll., 1971; MD, Hahnemann Med. Sch., Phila., 1976. Diplomate Am. Bd. Pain Mgmt., Am. Bd. Anesthesiologists. Intern pediatrics Martin Luther King Hosp., L.A., 1976-77, resident pediatrics, 1977-78, resident anesthesiology, 1978-81, mem. staff, 1981—. Named Outstanding Tchr. of Yr., King Drew Med. Ctr., Dept. Anesthesia, 1989, Outstanding Faculty of Yr., 1991. Mem. Am. Soc. Anesthesiologists, Calif. Med. Assn., L.A. County Med. Soc., Soc. Regional Anesthesia, Soc. Pediatric Anesthesia. Democrat. Baptist. Office: Martin Luther King Hosp 12021 Wilmington Ave Los Angeles CA 90059-3019

ASHMAN, STUART, museum director; b. N.Y.C., Apr. 10, 1948. BA, CUNY, 1972. Mus. intern in mus. studies and cinematography Staten Island (N.Y.) Inst. Arts and Scis., 1970-72; with Apeiron Workshops in Photography, Rochester Inst. Tech., 1972-78; gallery dir., visual arts coord. Armory for the Arts, Santa Fe, 1978-80; art instr. Santa Fe Preparatory Sch., 1980-82; artist in residence N.Mex. rural pub. schs., 1982-84; art instr. Penitentiary of N.Mex., 1984-86; studio artist Santa Fe, 1986-90; founder, coord. Mus. on Wheels program Santa Fe Children's Mus., 1990-92; Art with Elders coord. Open Hands Inc., 1990-92; artist in residence N.Mex. Arts Divsn., Santa Fe, 1990-92; curator/dir. The Gov.'s Gallery Mus. Fine Arts, Mus. N.Mex., Santa Fe, 1992-95, dir., 1995—; chmn. acquisitions com. Mus. N.Mex.; adv. bd. Georgia O'Keeffe Mus., SITE Santa Fe; bd. dirs. N.Mex. Counseling and Therapy Bd., Art Therapy Standards Com., Capitol Arts Found. Mem. Am. Assn. Muss., Am. Fedn. Arts, Mus. N.Mex. Found., Friends of Contemporary Art, Folk Art Soc. Am. Home: Rt 4 Box 16K Santa Fe NM 87501 Office: Mus Fine Arts PO Box 2087/107 W Palace Ave Santa Fe NM 87504-2087

ASHMEAD, ALLEZ MORRILL, speech, hearing, and language pathologist, orofacial myologist, consultant; b. Provo, Utah, Dec. 18, 1916; d. Laban Rupert and Zella May (Miller) M.; m. Harvey H. Ashmead, 1940; children: Harve DeWayne, Sheryl Mae Harames, Zeltha Janeel Henderson, Emma Allez Broadfoot. BS, Utah State U., 1938; MS summa cum laude, U. Utah, 1952, PhD summa cum laude, 1970; postgrad., Idaho State U., Oreg. State Coll., U. Denver, U. Utah, Brigham Young U., Utah State U., U. Washington, U. No. Colo. Cert. secondary edn., remedial reading, spl. edn., learning disabilities; cert. ASHA clin. competence speech pathology and audiology; profl. cert. in orofacial myology. Tchr. pub. schs. Utah, Idaho, 1938-43; speech and hearing pathologist Bushnell Hosp., Brigham City, Utah, 1943-45; sr. speech correctionist Utah State Dept. Health, Salt Lake City, 1945-52; dir. speech and hearing dept. Davis County Sch. Dist., Farmington, Utah, 1952-65; clin., field supr. U. Utah, Salt Lake City, 1965-70, 75-78; speech pathologist Box Elder Sch. Dist., Brigham City, 1970-75, 78-84; teaching specialist Brigham Young U., Provo, 1970-73; speech pathologist Primary Children's Med. Ctr., Salt Lake City, 1975-77; pvt. practice speech pathology and orofacial myology, 1970-88; del. USSR Profl. Speech Pathology seminar, 1984, 86; participant numerous internat. seminars. Author: Physical Facilities for Handicapped Children, 1957, A Guide for Training Public School Speech and Hearing Clinicians, 1965, A Guide for Public School Speech Hearing Programs, 1959, Impact of Orofacial Myofunctional Treatment on Orthodontic Correction, 1982, Meeting Needs of Handicapped Children, 1975, Relationship of Trace Minerals to Disease, 1972, Macro and Trace Minerals in Human Metabolism, 1971, Electromotive Potential Differences Between Stutterers and Non-stutterers, 1970, Learning Disability, An Educational Adventure, 1969, New Horizons in Special Education, 1969, Developing Speech and Language in the Exceptional Child, 1961, Parent Teacher Guidance in Primary Stuttering, 1951, numerous others; contbr. research articles to profl. jours. Student Placement chair Am. Field Service, Kaysville, Utah, 1962-66; ednl. del. Women's State Legis. Council, Salt Lake City, 1958-70; chairwoman fund raising Utah Symphony Orch., Salt Lake City, 1970-71; sec., treas. Utah chpt. U.S. Council for Exceptional Children, 1958-62, membership com. chair, 1962-66, program com. chair, 1966-68. Recipient Scholarship award for Higher Edn. U. Utah, Salt Lake City, 1969; Delta Kappa Gamma scholar, 1968; rsch. grantee Utah Dept. Edn., 1962. Mem. NEA, Utah Ednl. Assn., Am. Speech, Lang. Hearing Assn. (life, continuing edn. com. 1985, Ace award for Continuing Edn. 1984), Western Speech Assn., Internat. Assn. Orofacial Myology (life, bd. examiners, Sci. Contribution award 1982), Utah Speech, Hearing and Lang. Assn. (life, sec., treas. 1956-60), AAUW (Utah state bd. chair status of women 1959-62, Kaysville br. 1957-60, bd. dirs. Kaysville-Davis br. 1987-92, chair internat. rels. 1987-91, chair cultural interests Kaysville-Davis br. 1991-92), Delta Kappa Gamma (state scholarship award 1968, del. Woman's State Legis. Coun. 1958-70, profl. affairs chair 1963-67, tchr. of yr. award 1978), AAUW (bd. dirs. internat. rels. Kaysvile-Davis br., 1988-91), Sigma Alpha Eta, Theta Alpha Phi, Psi Chi, Zeta Phi Eta, Phi Kappa Phi. Republican. Mem. LDS Ch. Lodges: Daus. Utah Pioneers (parliamentarian Kaysville 1980-92, historian 1974-80, lesson leader 1992-95, capt. 1996—), Soroptimists (charter, bd. dirs. 1954-56, pres. Davis County chpt. 1965-69, Rocky Mountain regional bd. dirs. 1965-70, cmty. svc. award 1968, pub. svc. award 1970). Home: 719 E Center St Kaysville UT 84037-2138

ASHMEAD, HARVE DEWAYNE, nutritionist, executive, educator; b. Brigham City, Utah, June 6, 1944; s. Harvey Harold and Allez (Morrill) A.; m. Eugele Baird, June 24, 1966; children: Stephen, Jilane, Brett, Angelique, Heidi. BS, Weber State U., 1969; PhD, Pacific Inst., 1970; PhD magna cum laude, Donsbach U., 1981. Cert. nutritional cons. With Ch. Jesus Christ of Latter Day Saints, Paris, 1963-66; v.p. Albion Labs., Ogden, Utah, 1966-71, exec. v.p., Clearfield, Utah, 1971-82, pres., 1982—, also bd. dirs.; pres. Albion Internat.; adj. prof. Weber State Coll., also adv. coun. U. Utah; former advisor Weber County Sch. Dist.; bd. dirs. Albion Internat., Zions Bank, Albion Labs., Inc., Unilabco, Inc., Albion Middle East, Albion Europe; guest lectr. Adv. Fruit Heights City (Utah); pres. PTA. Fellow Am. Coll. Nutrition; mem. Am. Soc. Animal Sci., Am. Assn. Nutrition and Dietary Cons., Internat. Acad. Nutritional Cons., Am. Assn. Nutritional Cons., Am. Acad. Applied Health Sci., AAAS, Am. Biographical Inst. (bd. govs.), Clearfield C. of C. (bd. dirs.), Delta Sigma Pi. Mormon. Author: Chelated Mineral Nutrition, 1981, Mineral Absorption Mechanisms, 1981, Chelated Mineral Nutrition in Plants, Animals and Man, 1982, A New Era in Plant Nutrition, 1982, Intestinal Absorption of Metal Ions and Chelates, 1985, Foliar Feeding of Plants with Amino Acid Chelates, 1986, In Search of a Rainbow, 1988, Amino Acids in Animal Nutrition, 1991; Conversations on Chelation and Mineral Nutrition, 1989, The Roles of Amino Acid Creates in Animal Nutrition, 1993; contbr. numerous articles to profl. jours. Office: Albion Labs 101 N Main St Clearfield UT 84015-2243

ASHTON, RICK JAMES, librarian; b. Middletown, Ohio, Sept. 18, 1945; s. Ralph James and Lydia Marie (Thornbery) A.; m. Marcia K. Zuroweste, Dec. 23, 1966; children: Jonathan Paul, David Andrew. AB, Harvard U., 1967; MA, Northwestern U., 1969, PhD, 1973; MA, U. Chgo., 1976. Instr., asst. prof. history Northwestern U., Evanston, Ill., 1972-74; curator local and family history Newberry Library, Chgo., 1974-77; asst. dir. Allen County Pub. Library, Ft. Wayne, Ind., 1977-80, dir., 1980-85; city librarian Denver Pub. Library, 1985—; mem. Ind. Coop Libr. Svcs. Authority, 1980-85, pres., 1984-85; cons. Nat. Endowment Humanities, Nat. Ctr. Edn. Stats., Northwestern U. Office Estate Planning, Snowbird Leadership Inst. Author: The Life of Henry Ruiter, 1742-1819, 1974, The Genealogy Beginner's Manual: A New Edition, 1977, Stuntz, Fuller, Kennard and Cheadle Ancestors, 1987 (with others) Trends in Urban Library Management, 1989. Bd. dirs. Cmty. Coordinated Child Care, Evanston, 1972-74, Three Rivers Montessori Sch., Ft. Wayne, 1977-80; bd. dirs., sec. Allen County-Ft. Wayne Hist. Soc., 1977-83; conscientious objector. Recipient Nat. Merit scholar, 1963-67, Old City Hall Hist. Service award, 1985; NDEA fellow, 1967-69, Downtown Denver award, 1996; Woodrow Wilson fellow, 1971-72. Mem. ALA, Colo. Libr. Assn., Colo. Alliance Rsch. Librs. (pres. 1987-88, sec. 1993-95, chmn. 1995—), Rotary. Home: 2974 S Verbena Way Denver CO 80231-4219 Office: Denver Pub Libr 10 W 14th Ave Pky Denver CO 80204-2749

ASKELID, BERTIL RUNE, computer scientist; b. Bromölla, Sweden, June 11, 1952; came to U.S., 1988; s. Rune G. and Suzanne (Sterner) A.; m. Anja Ruben, May 21, 1982; children: Andreas, Rebecca, Nicolas. MS in Engring. Physics, Lund (Sweden) Inst. Tech., 1979. Mem. tech. staff Ericsson Telecom, Stockholm, 1980-88, U.S. West Advanced Techs., Denver, 1988-90, Ericsson Bus. Systems, Cypress, Calif., 1991-95, Quintus, Freemont, Calif., 1995-96, Telops Mgmt., L.A., 1996—. Office: Telops Mgmt 11845 W Olympic Blvd Los Angeles CA 90064

ASKEW, DENNIS LEE, poet; b. Las Vegas, Apr. 19, 1953; s. John Vernon and Dorothy Grace (Rogers) A. Grad. high sch., Las Vegas. Columnist Las Vegas Sun Newspaper, 1980-85; customer svc. Charles Schwab, Inc., Newport Beach, Calif.; credit specialist Dean Witter, Inc., Santa Ana, Calif.; trade adminstrn. mgr. Bankers Pension Svcs., Tustin, Calif.; writer Quest Capital Mgmt., Laguna Hills, Calif. Author: (novel) A Handful of Dreams,

1990, (stageplay) The Paint Box, 1992, (poetry) Big World of Love Vol. I, 1993, Vol. II, 1995, Vol. III, 1996. Vol. Street Svcs., Santa Ana, 1992—. Democrat.

ASKEW, ELDON WAYNE, army officer, biochemist, researcher; b. Pontiac, Ill., Aug. 23, 1942; s. Robert Eldon and Dora (Carter) A.; m. Sharon Lee Bess, Feb. 13, 1982; children: Rebecca C., Jennifer J. BS, U. Ill., 1964, MS, 1966; PhD, Mich. State U., 1970. Commd. 2d lt. U.S. Army, 1964, advanced through grades to col., 1990; chief lipid nutrition br. Med. Rsch. and Nutrition Lab., Denver, 1969-74; chief energy metabolism br. Letterman Army Inst. Rsch., San Francisco, 1974-78, chief radioisotope svcs., 1978-82; asst chief dept. clin. investment Tripler Army Med. Ctr., Honolulu, 1982-85; dir. Mil. Nutrition Rsch., U.S. Army Rsch.Inst. Environ. Medicine, Natick, Mass., 1985-94; dir. divsn. foods and nutrition U. Utah, Salt Lake City, 1994—; mem. food safety adv. com. FDA. Contbr. chpts. to books, articles to profl. jours. Decorated Meritorious Svc. medal with one oak leaf cluster, Legion of Merit; Danforth Found. fellow, 1961; NIH fellow, 1969. Mem. Am. Soc. Nutrition Scis., Am. Soc. Clin. Nutrition, Am. Coll. Sports Medicine, Wilderness Medicine Soc., Am. Dietetic Assn., Sigma Xi, Alpha Zeta (pres. 1963-64), Gamma Sigma Delta. Office: Divsn Foods & Nutrition 239 N-HPR U Utah Salt Lake City UT 84121

ASKIN, JERALD MARK, podiatrist; b. Detroit, Feb. 16, 1949; s. David and Sarah Askin; m. Bonni R. Fish, Feb. 10, 1980; children: Josh, Amy, Jeff. BS, U. Mich., 1971; DPM, Calif. Coll. Podiatric Medicin, 1975. Diplomate Am. Bd. Podiatric Surgery. Preceptor Earl Kaplan DPM Kern Hosp., Warren, Mich., 1975-76; pvt. practice Paramount, Calif., 1977—. Fellow Am. Coll. Foot Surgeons. Home: 25701 Dillon Rd Laguna Hills CA 92653-5871

ASKIN, RICHARD HENRY, JR., entertainment company executive; b. Flushing, N.Y., Feb. 11, 1947; s. Richard H. and Anne Margaret A.; children: Jennifer Leigh, Michael Richard. BA in Econs., Rutgers Coll., 1969; MA in Comm., U. Tex., 1971; MBA in Fin., Fordham U., 1976. Sales rep. Proctor & Gamble Distbg. Co., Jericho, N.Y., 1969; account exec. CableRep, Inc., N.Y.C., 1973-74, WNBC-TV Nat. Broadcasting Co., N.Y.C., 1974-75, NBC-TV, NBC, N.Y.C., 1975-76, sales mgr. KNBC-TV, Los Angeles, 1976-79, dir. sales, 1979-85; v.p. domestic sales Fries Distbn. Co., Los Angeles, 1985-86, sr. v.p. distbn., 1986-87; pres. TV, The Samuel Goldwyn Co., L.A., 1987-96, pres., CEO Tribune Entertainment Co., 1996—; pres. The Breckford Group, Inc. Served to 1st lt. Adj. Gen. Corps, U.S. Army, 1971-73. Decorated Army Commendation medal; Alcoa fellow, 1969-70. Mem. Hollywood Radio and TV Soc., Advt. Industry Emergency Fund (pres., bd. dirs.), Acad. of TV, Arts and Scis., Sierra Club, Alpha Rho Alumni Assn., Chi Psi. Home: 1520 Aldercreek Pl Westlake Village CA 91362-4211 Office: Tribune Entertainment 5800 Sunset Blvd Los Angeles CA 90028

ASKREN, CARL COLWELL, plastic surgeon; b. Atlanta, Nov. 10, 1956; s. Edward Leroy and Anne Colwell Askren; m. Karen Ashe, June 4, 1983; children: Annette Nicole, Charles Colin. BS, Ga. Tech., Atlanta, 1978, MS, 1980; MD, Emory U., 1984. Diplomate Am. Bd. Plastic Surgery. Asst. clin. prof. U. Calif./San Francisco and Fresno Affiliated Hosps., Fresno, 1995—; med. dir. Cranio Facial Anomalies Panel, Valley Children's Hosp., Fresno, 1994—. Contbg. author: (book) Reoperative Aesthetic and Reconstructive Plastic Surgery, 1995; illustrator: (book) Cardiovascular Pathophysiology, 1987. Fellow ACS; mem. Am. Soc. Plastic and Reconstructive Surgeons. Office: Sierra Plastic Surgery 6153 N Thesta St Fresno CA 93710-5266

ASKREN, MISHA, physician; b. Holton, Kans., Jan. 27, 1952; s. Melvin Earl Askren and Bonita Marie (Cornelssen) Askren Anderson; m. Ruth Ellen Moskovitz, Sept. 9, 1979; children: Hana Leora, Ariella, Shoshana Clara. BA in Chemistry and Zoology, Pomona Coll., Clarement, Calif., 1974; MD, U. Calif., Davis, 1978. Diplmomate Am. Bd. Family Physicians. Intern in family practice Kaiser Found., L.A., 1978-79, resident in family practice, 1979-81; pvt. practice L.A., 1981-93; physician FHP, Inc., Cerritos, Calif., 1993—. Fellow Am. Acad. Family Practice. Office: Talbert Med Group 29050 S Western Ave Rancho Palos Verdes CA 90275

ASMUNDSON, MARK, mayor. Mayor City of Bellingham, Wash. Office: Mayor of Bellingham 210 Lottie St Bellingham WA 98225

ASTAIRE, CAROL ANNE TAYLOR, artist, educator; b. Long Beach, Calif., Aug. 26, 1947; d. John Clinton and Carolyn Sophie (Wright) Taylor; m. Frederic Astaire, Jr., Feb. 14, 1971; children: John Carroll, Johanna Carolyn. BFA, UCLA, 1969; grad. summer studies, Salzburg Summer Sch., Klessheim, Austria, 1969; cert. secondary sch. tchr., Calif. State U., Long Beach, 1971; postgrad., Calif. Polytechnic State U., San Luis Obispo, 1986-87. Cert. secondary sch. tchr. life, Calif. Tchr., tutor, cons. art edn. San Luis Coastal Unified Sch. Dist., San Luis Obispo, 1980-89. Author: (book) Left Handed Poetry from the Heart, 1993; artist: work in permanent collections. Yergeau Musée Internat. Art, Montreal, Can., 1991, Travis (Calif.) AFB Mus., 1990. Founder, trustee, San Luis Coastal Unified Sch. Dist./Found. Arts Art Core, 1988-92; mem. adv. coun. Coastal Comty. Edn. and Svcs., San Luis Obsipo, 1989-92, screening com. UCLA Alumni scholarship, 1993-95. Nat. finalist Kodak Internat. Newspaper Snapshot award, 1993. Mem. Nat. Mus. of Women in Arts (charter), Fine Arts Coun., San Luis Obispo Art Ctr., San Luis Obispo Art Coun., Oil Pastel Acrylic Group Brushstrokes (hon. mention 1994), Ctrl. Coast Watercolor Soc., Ctrl. Coast Photo. Soc. Republican. Episcopalian.

ASTLE, RICHARD SHARP, computer programmer, poet; b. Lexington, Ky., May 19, 1943; s. Melvin Jensen and Alice (Sharp) A.; m. Ruth Sallein, May 18, 1966; divorced; 1 child, Jennifer; m. Leslie Brooke Neilson, July 19, 1981 (dec. Mar. 1986); m. Sarai Austin, Apr. 30, 1995. BS in Math., Stanford U., 1964; MA in Creative Writing, San Francisco State U., 1968; PhD in English Lit., U. Calif., San Diego, 1977. English lectr. UCLA, 1976-77, San Diego State U., 1977-82; lit. lectr. U. Calif., San Diego, 1977-82; programmer Centaurus, Inc., San Diego, 1982-83; sr. engr. Practor Care, Inc., San Diego, 1984—. Contbr. articles and fiction to profl. jours. Mem. Assn. of Computing Machinery, Forth Interest Group. Home: 20120 Date Ln Escondido CA 92029-6442 Office: 4115 Sorrento Valley Blvd San Diego CA 92121-1406

ATAIE, ATA JENNATI, oil products marketing executive; b. Mashad, Iran, Mar. 15, 1934; s. Hamid Jennati and Mohtaram (Momeni) A.; came to U.S., 1957, naturalized, 1969; B.S. in Agr., Fresno (Calif.) State U., 1964; B.A. in Econs., San Francisco State U., 1966; m. Judith Garrett Bush, Oct. 7, 1961; children—Ata Jennati, Andrew J. Mktg. exec. Shell Oil Co., Oakland, Calif., 1966-75; pres. A.J. Ataie & Cos., Danville, Calif., 1975—; Am. Value Inc., 1976—. Served as 2d lt. Iranian Army, 1953. Mem. Nat. Petroleum Retailers Assn. Democrat.

ATAIE, JUDITH GARRETT, middle school educator; b. San Francisco, July 24, 1941; m. Ata Jennati Ataie Sr., Oct. 7, 1961; children: A.J. Jr., Andrew Jennati. BA, U. Calif., Berkeley, 1980; postgrad., U. Hawaii, Manoa, 1982—. Art instr., dean faculty The Athenian Sch., Danville, Calif., 1980—.

ATCHESON, SUE HART, business educator; b. Dubuque, Iowa, Apr. 12; d. Oscar Raymond and Anna (Cook) Hart; m. Walter Clark Atcheson (div.); children: Christine A. Hischar, Moffet Zoe, Claye Williams. BBA, Mich. State U.; MBA, Calif. State Poly. U., Pomona, 1973. Cert. tchr. and adminstr. Instr. Mt. San Antonio Coll., Walnut, Calif., 1968-90; bd. dirs. faculty assn. Mt. San Antonio Coll.; mem. acad. senate Mt. San Antonio Coll.; originator vol. income tax assistance Mt. San Antonio Coll.; speaker in field. Author: Fractions and Equations on Your Own, 1975. Speaker Howard Ruff Nat. Conv., San Diego, 1983, Mike DeFalco Numismatics Seminar, Claremont, Calif., 1986; charter mem. Internat. Commn. on Monetary and Econ. Reform; panelist infrastructure funding reform, Freeport, Ill., 1989. Mem. Cmty. Concert Assn. Inland Empire (bd. dirs.), Scripps Coll. Fine Arts Found., Recyclers Club (pres. 1996).

ATCHISON, RODNEY RAYMOND, lawyer, arbitrator; b. Hanford, Calif., Nov. 14, 1926; s. Clyde Raymond and Velma May (Watts) A.; m. Evaleen Mary McFadden, June 27, 1948; children: Cathlin Feldman, Susan Barisone, Kerry Dexter, Brian. Student, San Jose State Coll., 1946-49; JD, U. Santa Clara, 1952. Bar: Calif. 1953, U.S. Dist. Ct. (all dists.) Calif. 1953, U.S. Ct. Appeals (9th cir.) 1953, U.S. Supreme Ct. 1971. Assoc. Mullen & Phillipi, Attys., San Francisco, 1953-55; dep. county counsel Santa Clara Calif. County Counsel, San Jose, 1955-57; city atty. City of Mountain View, Calif., 1957-62, City of Santa Cruz, Calif., 1962-90; pres. Atchison, Anderson, Hurley & Barisone, Profl. Law Corp., Santa Cruz, 1980-96; of counsel Atchison & Barisone, Profl. Law Corp., Santa Cruz, 1996—, Law Offices of Rodney R. Atchison, 1996—; arbitrator Am. Arbitration Assn., San Francisco, 1970—. Pres. Rotary Club Mountain View, Calif., 1961-62, Santa Cruz (Calif.) County Bar Assn., 1973. With USNR, 1944-46. Mem. ABA, Santa Cruz Rotary Club, Elks Lodge (life). Roman Catholic. Office: Atchison & Barisone 333 Church St Santa Cruz CA 95060-3811

ATENCIO, J(OSEPH) ANDREW, computer systems official, computer designer; b. Canon City, Colo., May 26, 1965; s. Joseph Andrew Atencio and Carol Lynn (Gordon) Pross; m. Kimberly Ann Maritz, Aug. 8, 1992. AS in Applied Techs., Phoenix Inst. Tech., 1988; BS in Bus. Info. Sys., U. Phoenix, 1996. Cert. AUTOCAD technician; Microsoft cert. sys. engr. Designer, drafter Fine Line Designs, Tempe, Ariz., 1987-89; tchr. Phoenix Inst. Tech., 1989-90; computer aided designer, computer system mgr. PRC Environ. Mgmt., Inc., Denver, 1990-91; mgr. computer systems RUST Environ. and Infrastructure (formerly SEC Donohue), Englewood, Colo., 1991-92, regional info. sys. mgr., 1992-95, applications and sys. devel. engr., 1995—; computer aided drafter Greeley & Hansen Engrs., Phoenix, 1988-90; owner, designer, cons. Midnight Wind Design Svcs., Phoenix and Denver, 1990—. Mem. Am. Design Drafting Assn. Democrat. Office: RUST Environ-Infrastructure 5575 DTC Pkwy Ste 200 Englewood CO 80111-3016

ATKINS, WILLIAM THEODORE, community volunteer, retired insurance executive; b. Lebanon, Pa., May 14, 1918; s. William Theodore and Edna Marie (Phillips) A.; m. Katherine Melinda Shank, Apr. 25, 1942 (dec. June 1973); children: Karen J. Birdsall, Judith Ann Karman, William T., Sarah J. Ramsey; m. Elena Garcia Ramsey, Sept. 29, 1974. BS in Commerce, Ctrl. YMCA Coll., 1945; JD, DePaul U., 1949. Bar: Ill. 1950, Calif. 1960. Surety claim adjuster Continental Casualty Co., Chgo., 1940-52; mgr. surety claims Mfrs. Casualty/Pacific Nat. Fire Ins. Cos., Phila. and San Francisco, 1952-59; with United Pacific/Reliance Ins. Cos./United Pacific Life Ins., Tacoma, Wash., 1959-81, v.p., assoc. counsel, 1981; v.p. Reliance Ins. Co., Tacoma, 1975-81; ret., 1981. Pres. Pacific Claim Execs. Assn., 1966-67; chmn. N.W. adv. coun. Nat. Assn. Ins. Adjusters, 1965-67; trustee, 1st pres. United Meth. Found. of N.W., 1966-69; chmn. fin. com. Lihue United Ch., 1982-86, 89-95, 97—, moderator, 1987-88, vice chmn. bd. trustees, 1996—; bd. dirs. Kauai (Hawaii) Concert Assn., 1982—, pres., 1983-85, treas., 1986—; bd. dirs. Hawaii Assn. Music Socs., Honolulu, 1983-90, treas., 1985-87, pres., 1987-89; sec. Na Lima Kokua, The Vols. of Nat. Tropical Bot. Garden, Kauai, 1987-91, treas., 1991-95; bd. dirs. Hawaii United Meth. Union, Honolulu, 1993—, fin. com., 1994—; treas. Interfaith Com., 1994—; trustee Waioli Corp.-Grove Farm Homestead Mus., Hanalei Mission House Mus., Lihue, 1985—, mem. fin. com., 1985-90, mem. pers. com., 1986-90, mem. exec. com., 1987-90, pres., 1990-95; pres. NuHou Corp., 1995—; treas. Kauai Interfaith Iniki Recovery Effort, Lihue, 1992-94. Mem. ABA (vice chn. fidelity and surety com. 1969-81), State Bar Calif., Kauai Orchid Soc. (treas. 1994—). Republican. Methodist. Home: 5867 Haaheo Pl Kapaa HI 96746-9646

ATKINSON, JOHN CHRISTOPHER, magazine editor, critic, writer; b. Hitchin, Eng., June 12, 1948; came to U.S., 1987; s. Harry Archer and Jacqueline Ellen (Elliott) A.; m. Maree Froy, Dec. 12, 1970 (div. 1981); m. Pamela Margaret Edwards, June 19, 1982 (div. 1987); 1 child, Heather Louise; m. Laura Jean LoVecchio, Nov. 28, 1987; children; Henry Joseph, Emily Claire. BSc in Chemistry and Physics, U. London, 1972; grad. cert. in edn., 1974. Sci. officer Warren Spring Lab., Stevenage, Eng., 1969-72; freelance bass guitarist, London, 1972-76; news editor Hi-Fi News and Record Rev. mag., Croydon, Surrey, Eng., 1976-78, dep. editor, 1978-82, editor, 1982-86; internat. editor Stereophile UK Ltd., London, 1986-87; editor Stereophile mag., Santa Fe, 1987—. Prodn. compact discs Hi-Fi News Test Disc, 1985, Poem (flute/piano music), 1989, Stereophile Test Disc, 1990, Intermezzo (Brahms piano music), 1991, Stereophile Test CD 2, 1992, Concert (piano recital), 1994, Stereophile Test CD 3, 1995, Festival (orchestral works by Copland, Kohjiba, Milhaud), 1995, Sonata (Liszt piano music), 1996, Serenade (chamber works by Mozart, Brahms, Dvorak), 1996, Rhapsody (works by Gershwin), 1997; contbr. numerous articles and revs. of hi-fidelity components to music mags. Office: 208 Delgado St Santa Fe NM 87501-2728

ATKINSON, RICHARD CHATHAM, university president; b. Oak Park, Ill., Mar. 19, 1929; s. Herbert and Margaret (Feuerbach) A.; m. Rita Loyd, Aug. 20, 1952; 1 dau., Lynn Loyd. Ph.B., U. Chgo., 1948; Ph.D., Ind. U., 1955. Lectr. applied math. and stats. Stanford (Calif.) U., 1956-57, assoc. prof. psychology, 1961-64, prof. psychology, 1964-80; asst. prof. psychology UCLA, 1957-61; dep. dir. NSF, 1975-76, acting dir., 1976, dir., 1976-80; chancellor, prof. cognitive sci. U. Calif., San Diego, 1980-95; pres. U. Calif., 1995—. Author: (with Atkinson, Smith and Bem) Introduction to Psychology, 12th edit., 1996, Computer Assisted Instruction, 1969, An Introduction to Mathematical Learning Theory, 1965, Contemporary Developments in Mathematical Psychology, 1974, Mind and Behavior, 1980, Stevens' Handbook of Experimental Psychology, 1988. Served with AUS, 1954-56. Guggenheim fellow, 1967; fellow Ctr. for Advanced Study in Behavioral Scis., 1963; recipient Distinguished Research award Social Sci. Research Council, 1962. Fellow APA (Disting. Sci. Contbn. award 1977, Thorndike award 1980), AAAS (pres. 1989-90), Am. Psychol. Soc. (William James fellow 1985), Am. Acad. Arts and Scis.; mem. NAS, Soc. Exptl. Psychologists, Am. Philos. Soc., Nat. Acad. Edn., Inst. of Medicine, Cosmos Club (Washington), Explorer's Club (N.Y.C.). Home: 70 Rincon Rd Kensington CA 94707-1047 Office: U Calif Office of Pres 300 Lakeside Dr Oakland CA 94612-3550

ATKINSON, ROLAND MOORE, psychiatrist; b. San Jose, Calif., Feb. 19, 1936; s. Roland Moore and Mayme June (Scales) A.; (div. 1996); children: Barry David, Julia Lynn, Michael Ian, Daniel Paul. BA in Biology, Stanford U., 1957, MD, 1961; postgrad. in Geriatric Psychiatry, U. London, Eng., 1987. Intern UCLA, 1961-62; resident UCLA Neuropsychiatric Inst., L.A., 1962-65; asst. chief Psychiatry U.S.P.H.S. Hosp., S.I., N.Y., 1965-67; mem. faculty in Psychiatry UCLA, 1967-70, U. Calif., Irvine, 1970-76; assoc. prof. Psychiatry Oreg. Health Scis. U., Portland, 1976-84, prof. Psychiatry, 1984—, acting chmn. psychiatry dept., 1994-96; staff mem. VA Med. Ctr., Portland, 1976-96, chief of svc., 1980-94; rschr. Clin. Studies of Alcoholism and Aging, 1982—; dir. Geriatric Psychiatry Fellowship, 1990-95. Editor (book) Alcohol and Drug Abuse in Old Age, 1984; contbr. articles to profl. jours. Mem. Oreg. Gov.'s Adv. Com. on Alcohol and Drug Problems, 1978-85; cons. Samaritan Pastoral Counseling Ctr., Portland, 1985-92. Fellow Am. Psychiat. Assn.; mem. Am. Assn. for Geriatric Psychiatry, Internat. Psychogeriatric Assn., Oreg. Psychiat. Assn. Democrat.

ATKINSON, SHERIDAN EARLE, lawyer; b. Oakland, Calif., Feb. 14, 1945; s. Arthur Sheridan and Esther Louise (Johnson) A.; m. Margie Ann Lehtin, Aug. 13, 1966. 1 son, Ian Sheridan. BS, U. Calif.-Berkeley, 1966, MBA, 1971; JD, U. San Francisco, 1969. Bar: Calif. 1970. Prin. Atkinson & Assocs., fin. and mgmt. cons., corp. and bus. valuations, San Francisco, 1968—; assoc. Charles O. Morgan, Jr., San Francisco, 1972-76; pvt. practice, San Francisco Bay Area,1976—. With USAR, 1970-76. Mem. Calif. Bar Assn. Republican.

ATLASS, THEODORE BRUCE, lawyer, educator; b. Chgo., June 2, 1951; s. Ralph Louis Atlass and Opal Jeanne Collins. BSBA, U. Denver, 1972; JD, DePaul U., 1975; LLM, U. Miami, Coral Gables, Fla., 1976. Bar: Colo. 1975, U.S. Tax Ct. 1976, U.S. Supreme Ct. 1982. Shareholder Theodore B. Atlass, P.C., Denver, 1976-83, Atlass Profl. Corp., Denver, 1986—; ptnr. Welborn, Dufford, Brown & Tooley, Denver, 1983-85; lectr. Colo. Soc. CPAs, 1977—, Coll. Law U. Denver, 1976—. Chmn. Advanced Estate Planning Symposium U. Denver, 1982-97; bd. dirs. St. Joseph Hosp. Found., Denver, 1982-97, Colo. Ballet, Denver, 1985-92. Fellow Am. Coll. Tax Counsel, Am. Coll. Trust & Estate Counsel (Colo. state chair 1996—; fiduciary income tax com. chair 1997—); mem. Denver Estate Planning Coun. (pres. 1991-92), Denver Tax Assn. (pres. 1985), Centennial Estate Planning Coun. (pres. 1993-94). Republican. Presbyterian. Office: Atlass Profl Corp Ste 100 3665 Cherry Creek North Dr Denver CO 80209-3712

ATTIG, JOHN CLARE, secondary education educator, consultant; b. Chgo., Apr. 2, 1936; s. Clare McKinley and Elsie Bertha (Nagel) A.; m. Harriet Jane Rinehart, June 13, 1959; children: Laura, Victoria. BA, DePauw U., 1958; MA, U. Chgo., 1961. Cert. tchr., Calif. Social studies tchr. Lyons Twp. H.S., LaGrange, Ill., 1961-65, Henry Gunn H.S., Palo Alto, Calif., 1965-72, 78—; univ. faculty assoc. Simon Fraser U., Burnaby, Canada, 1972-73; social studies tchr. Jordan Jr. H.S., Palo Alto, 1973-75, Cubberley Sr. H.S., Palo Alto, 1975-78; lectr., demonstrator, pub. simulation games for classes in history and govt. various univs. and sch. dists. in U.S. and Can. Contbr. numerous articles to profl. jours.; author numerous simulation games; dir. simulation games pub. History Alive. With USAR, 1958-64. NEH fellow, 1983, 87, 89, Tchr. fellow St. Andrews U., Scotland, 1993. Mem. NEH (project dir. Masterworks Seminar 1991), Western History Assn. Methodist. Office: Henry Gunn Sr HS 780 Arastradero Rd Palo Alto CA 94306-3827

ATWOOD, KELLY PALMER, insurance agency executive; b. Portland, Oreg., Jan. 7, 1946; s. Baird Ewing and Lelia Claire (Donham) McNeese A.; m. Regina Louise Hamilton, July 30, 1983; children: Derek, Lynn, Jason, Beri, Courtney. Student, U. Oreg., 1964-66, Chemeketa Community Coll., 1976-78. Pres., chief exec. officer Group Ins. Mktg., Inc., Salem, Oreg., 1970-85, Contractors Ins. Svcs. Inc., Lake Oswego, Oreg., 1985—; also bd. dirs. Metro Ins. Agy., Inc., Lake Oswego, Oreg. Contbr. articles on ins. to profl. jours. Former mem. Reagan Task Force, Washington, 1985-86, Denny Smith Task Force on Crime, Salem, 1988. Served with USN, 1967-69. Named Sr. Agt. of Yr. Salem Life Underwriters Assn., 1980, 81. Mem. Nat. Assn. Life Underwriters, Nat. Assn. Home Builders, Oreg. State Home Builders Assn., Home Builders Assn. Met. Portland (bd. dirs. 1985—). Republican. Home: 3300 River Woods Pl Lake Oswego OR 97034-5115 Office: Contractors Ins Svcs Inc PO Box 2267 Lake Oswego OR 97035-0071

ATWOOD, MARY SANFORD, writer; b. Mt. Pleasant, Mich., Jan. 27, 1935; d. Burton Jay and Lillian Belle (Sampson) Sanford; B.S., U. Miami, 1957; m. John C. Atwood, III, Mar. 23, 1957. Author: A Taste of India, 1969. Mem. San Francisco/N. Peninsula Opera Action, Hillsborough-Burlingame Newcomers, Suicide Prevention and Crisis Center, DeYoung Art Mus., Internat. Hospitality Center, Peninsula Symphony, San Francisco Art Mus., World Affairs Council, Mills Hosp. Assos. Mem. AAUW, Suicide Prevention Aux. Republican. Club: St. Francis Yacht. Office: 40 Knightwood Ln Hillsborough CA 94010-6132

ATWOOD, ROBERT BRUCE, publisher; b. Chgo., Mar. 31, 1907; s. Burton H. and Mary Beach (Stevenson) A.; m. Evangeline Rasmuson, Apr. 2, 1932(dec. Nov. 1987); children: Marilyn A. Odom (dec.), Sara Elaine. A.B., Clark U., 1929; Litt.D. (hon.), Alaska Meth. U., 1967; D.Journalism (hon.), U. Alaska, 1979; LLD (hon.), Alaska Pacific U., 1996. Reporter Worcester (Mass.) Telegram, 1926-29, 34-35, Ill. State Jour., Springfield, 1929-34; pres. and pub. Anchorage Times, 1935-89, pub. emeritus, 1989-92; dir. Alaska Sales and Svc., Inc., Anchorage, 1991—. Author pamphlets, articles, editorials pub. in various jours. Chmn. Alaska Statehood Com., 1949-59; hon. Norwegian consul at Anchorage, 1960-86; mem. civilian affairs bd. Alaskan Air Command, 1962—, now chmn.; bd. dirs. Commonwealth North; founder Atwood Found.; elder Presbyn. Ch.; sponsor Internat. Airline Ski Races, Alyeska; elder Presbyn. ch. Decorated knight of first rank Order of St. Olaf, 1976; Alaska commr. to Expo '88, Australia; named Alaskan of Yr., 1967, Outstanding Civilian of Yr. Alaskan Command, 1996, Outstanding Civilian of Yr., Alaskan Command, 1996; recipient award for 25 yrs. outstanding svc. to cmty. and state, 1984, award for lifetime achievement Alaska Press Club, 1995. Mem. Am. Soc. Newspaper Editors, Am. Polar Soc. (bd. govs.), C. of C. (pres. 1944, 48), Soc. Profl. Journalists, Anchorage C. of C., Explorers Club, Nat. Press Club, Sons of Norway, Anchorage Rotary (founder), Elks, Masons, Pioneers of Alaska, Anchorage Ski Club (founder, 1st pres.), Anchorage Rotary Club (founder). Republican. Home and Office: 2000 Atwood Dr Anchorage AK 99517-1333

ATWOOD, ROY ALDEN, academic administrator, communications educator; b. Glendale, Calif., Sept. 11, 1952; s. John Alden and Frances Elizabeth (McCreight) A.; m. Beverlee Joyce Kvale, Apr. 13, 1973; children: Hannah Kvale Atwood, Ethan Kvale Atwood. AB in Philosophy, Dordt Coll., 1975; MA in Religion, Westminster Theol. Sem., 1977; PhD in Mass Comm., U. Iowa, 1984. Instr. comm. Gonzaga U., Spokane, Wash., 1981-84; asst. prof. U. Idaho, Moscow, 1984-87, assoc. prof., 1987—, dir. Sch. Comm., 1995—; rsch. chair Pacific N.W. Assn. Journalism Educators Ann. Conf., Lake Wilderness, Wash., 1985, Corbett, Oreg., 1986; mem. rsch. com. Assn. Edn. Journalism and Mass Comm., 1985-86, chair tchg. stds. com. History Divsn., 1987-88, sec., 1988-89, rsch. chair, 1989-90, head, 1990-91, mem. coun. divsns., 1990-91; organizer and coord. West Coast Journalism Historians Conf., San Francisco, 1986; moderator and convener N.W. Comm. Educators Meeting, Spokane, 1987; bd. dirs. Am. Journalism Historians Assn., 1987-91, nat. conv. host and organizer, Coeur d'Alene, Idaho, 1990; U. Idaho rep. Pacific N.W. Can. Studies Consortium, 1989-95; coord. U. Idaho and Wash. State U.'s Can.-Am. Studies Summer Inst., Moscow, Idaho, Pullman, Wash., 1990, 91; vice chair Faculty Coun., U. Idaho, 1990-91; sr. Fulbright lectr. Inst. Journalism, Warsaw (Poland) U., 1991-92, vis. prof., 1995; vis. prof. Egerton U., Njoro, Kenya, 1992; mem. bd. govs. and sr. fellow New St. Andrews Coll., Moscow, Idaho, 1994—. Author: Mass Communication Law in Idaho, 1992; (with D.J. Wilson) The Quest for Authentic Higher Education, 1995; editor and graphic designer: Introduction to Educational Research, 1993; editor The Jour. Communication Inquiry, 1979-80, Clio Among Media, 1988-89; book rev. editor Am. Journalism, 1983-86; contbg. editor Credenda/Agenda, 1994—; mem. editl. bd. Am. Communication Jour., 1996—; contbr. articles and revs. to profl. jours.; Videos include (prodr.) Stars, Stripes, and Maple Leaves, 1991; (prodr. and scriptwriter) U.S. Fulbright Scholars: A Video Proposal, 1993. Recipient Warren C. Price Grad. Rsch. prize Assn. Edn. Journalism and Mass Comm., 1980, Disting. Svc. award, 1992, Faculty Rsch. award, 1993; NEH fellow Summer Inst. Quantitative Hist. Analysis and Hist. Demography, 1980; Can. Faculty Enrichment grantee, 1988; Can. Studies Programme Devel. grantee Can. and Am. Studies Summer Inst., 1990, 91; Small Travel grantee U. Idaho, 1994, 95; Kosciuszko Found. N.Y. grantee, 1995. Office: U Idaho Sch Comm Moscow ID 83844-1072

AU, MELINDA L., osteopathic family practice physician; b. Westminster, Calif., Sept. 23, 1962; d. William C.F. and Lola C. Au; m. James O. Mann, Dec. 8, 1990; 1 child, Makai M. BS in Zoology, Calif. State Poly. U., Pomona, 1985; DO, Kirksville Coll. Osteo. Medicine, 1989. Diplomate Am. Bd. Family Practice. Intern Hillside Hosp., San Diego, 1989-90; resident in family practice Riverside (Calif.) Gen. Hosp., 1990-92; pvt. practice, San Diego, 1992-93, Encinitas, Calif., 1993-95; physician U. Calif.-San Diego Healthcare, Encinitas, 1995—. Mem. Am. Acad. Family Practice, Am. Osteo. Assn., San Diego Osteo. Med. Assn. Office: UCSD Healthcare 477 N El Camino Real Ste A204 Encinitas CA 92024-1329

AUBREY, JAMES REYNOLDS, English educator; b. Kittanning, Pa., Dec. 3, 1945; s. Samuel Moss and Alice (Reynolds) A.; m. Marilyn Sue Awbrey, June 8, 1968; children: Sarah Elizabeth, Meredith Anne. BS, USAF Acad., 1968; MA, Northwestern U., 1973; PhD, U. Wash., 1979. Commd. 2d lt. USAF, 1968, advanced through grades to lt. col.; ret., 1989; prof. English Met. State Coll., Denver. Author: John Fowles, 1991.

AUERBACK, SANDRA JEAN, social worker; b. San Francisco, Feb. 21, 1946; d. Alfred and Molly Loy (Friedman) A. BA, U. Calif., Berkeley, 1967; MSW, Hunter Sch. Social Work, 1972. Diplomate clin. social work. Clin. social worker Jewish Family Services, Bklyn., 1972-73; clin. social worker Jewish Family Services, Hackensack, N.J., 1973-78; pvt. practice psychotherapy San Francisco, 1978—; dir. intake adult day care Jewish Home for the Aged, San Francisco, 1979-91. Mem. NASW (cert., bd. dirs. Bay Area Referral Svc. 1983-87, chmn. referral svc. 1984-87, state practice com. 1987-91, regional treas. 1989-91, rep. to Calif. Coun. Psychiatry, Psychology, Social Work and Nursing, 1987—, chmn. 1989, 93, v.p. cmty. svcs. 1991-93, chair Calif. polit. action com. 1993-95), Am. Group Psychotherapy Assn., Mental Health Assn. San Francisco (trustee 1987—).

Home: 1100 Gough St Apt 8C San Francisco CA 94109-6638 Office: 450 Sutter St San Francisco CA 94108

AUGERBRIGHT, PAMELA JEAN, entrepreneur; b. San Pedro, Calif., Oct. 24, 1944; d. Thurman and Ernestine (Smith) Thomas; m. Theodore Alfred Augerbright, Feb. 3, 1963; 1 child, Theodore Alfred II. Student, Long Beach City Coll., 1978—. Owner Cake Decorating by PJ, Long Beach, Calif., 1964-78; statis. clk./sec. Douglas Aircraft Co., Long Beach, 1977-80; owner Pam's Bridal Experience, Long Beach, 1978—; buyer/sec. Hughes Aircraft Co., El Segundo, Calif., 1981-85. Author: I Remember Mom Bet, 1992. Adminstrv. asst. to pastor St. John Bapt. Ch., Long Beach, 1990—. Home and Office: 866 W 33rd Way Long Beach CA 90806-1257

AUGUSTYN, DAMIAN HENRY, gastroenterologist; b. Seattle, Jan. 11, 1952; m. Caroline Craig; 2 children. BS in Biol. Scis. with honors, Stanford U., 1974; MD, Harvard Med. Sch., 1978. Diplomate Am. Bd. Internal Medicine, Am. Bd. Gastroenterology. Intern U. Colo. Med. Ctr., Denver, 1978-79, resident in internal medicine, 1979-80; sr. resident in internal medicine U. Calif. Med. Ctr., San Francisco, 1980-81, gasteroenterology fellow, 1981-83, from clin. instr. to asst. clin. prof. medicine, 1983-91, assoc. clin. prof. medicine, 1991—; pvt. practice San Francisco, 1983—; staff Calif. Pacific Med. Ctr., San Francisco, 1983—, chmn., divsn. gastroenterology and hepatology, 1994—; bd. dirs., pres. Patient Assistance Found. Office Patient Svcs., Calif. Pacific Med. Ctr., 1986-93, pres., 1994—; mem. bd. med. advisors Blue Cross Calif., Woodland Hills; mng. ptnr. Pacific Internal Medicine Assoc., San Francisco, 1985—. Bd. dirs. Calif. Pacific Med Ctr., 1997—. Mem. ACP, Am. Gastroenterological Assn., Am. Soc. Gastrointestinal Endoscopy (No. Calif. rep. to coun. regional endoscopic soc.), San Francisco Med. Soc. (bd. dirs. 1996—), No. Calif. Soc. for Clinical Gastroenterology (bd. dirs. 1987-94, pres. 1992-93), Calif. Fedn. Digestive Disease Soc. (bd. dirs. 1989—, pres. 1991-93). Office: Calif Pacific Profl Bldg 2100 Webster St Ste 423 San Francisco CA 94115-2380

AULT, PHILLIP HALLIDAY, author, editor; b. Maywood, Ill., Apr. 26, 1914; s. Frank W. and Bernda (Halliday) A.; m. Karoline Byberg, June 5, 1943 (dec. Jan. 1990); children: Frank, Ingrid, Bruce; m. Jane Born, May 1, 1993. AB, DePauw U., 1935. Reporter LaGrange (Ill.) Citizen, 1935-37; corr. editor UPI, Chgo., N.Y.C., Iceland, North Africa, London, 1938-48; bur. chief UPI, London, 1944-45; asst. mng. editor, dir. editorial page Times-Mirror Co., L.A., 1948; editorial page editor L.A. Mirror-News, 1948-57; exec. editor Associated Desert Newspapers, 1958-68; assoc. editor South Bend (Ind.) Tribune, 1968-79, cons. editor, 1979—. Author: This Is the Desert, 1959, News Around the Clock, 1960, How to Live in California, 1961, Home Book of Western Humor, 1967, Wonders of the Mosquito World, 1970, These Are The Great Lakes, 1972, Wires West, 1974, All Aboard, 1976, By the Seat of Their Pants, 1978, Whistles Round the Bend, 1982; co-author: Springboard to Berlin, 1943, Reporting and Writing the News, 1983, Introduction to Mass Communications, 1960, Public Relations: Strategies and Tactics, 1986; editor: Santa Maria Historical Photo Album, 1987. Mem. Am. Soc. Newspaper Editors, Assn. Edn. in Journalism, Western Writers Am. (Spur award 1977), Sigma Nu. Home: 21408 157th Dr Sun City West AZ 85375-6626

AUNG-THWIN, MICHAEL ARTHUR, history educator; b. Rangoon, Burma, 1946. BA, Doane Coll., 1969; MA, U. Ill., Urbana, 1971; PhD, U. Mich., 1976. Asst. prof. Asian history Elmira (N.Y.) Coll., 1980-87; assoc. prof. history No. Ill. U., DeKalb, 1987-95; dir. Ctr. S.E. Asian Studies No. Ill. U., DeKalb, Ill., 1987-95; assoc. prof. Asian Studies U. Hawaii, Honolulu, 1995—; vis. prof. Cornell U., 1981; vis. scholar Ctr. for S.E. Asian Studies, Kyoto, Japan. Contbr. articles to profl. jours. NEH fellow, 1977-80. Mem. Assn. for Asian Studies (bd. dirs. 1980-83, mem. S.E. Asia Coun.), Burma Studies Found. (sec.-treas.). Office: U Hawaii Sch Hawaiian Asian Studies 413 Moore Hall Honolulu HI 96822

AURAND, CHARLES HENRY, JR., music educator; b. Battle Creek, Mich., Sept. 6, 1932; s. Charles Henry and Elisabeth Dirk (Hoekstra) A.; m. Donna Mae Erb, June 19, 1954; children: Janice, Cheryl, Sandra, Charles III, William. MusB, Mich. State U., 1954, MusM, 1958; PhD, U. Mich., 1971. Cert. tchr., Mich., Ohio. Asst. prof. music Hiram Coll., Ohio, 1958-60; dean, prof. music Youngstown State U., 1960-73; dean No. Ariz. U., Flagstaff, 1973-88, prof. music, 1988-94, prof. emeritus, 1994—; chmn. Ariz. Alliance for Arts Edn., 1974-77; solo clarinetist Flagstaff Symphony; solo, chamber music and orch. musician, 1973-86; fine arts cons. Miami U. of Ohio, 1982. Author: Selected Solos, Methods, 1963. Elder Presbyterian Ch., 1965; chmn. Boy Scouts Am., Coconino dist., 1974-78; bd. dirs. Ariz. Com. Arts for the Handicapped, 1982-88, Flagstaff Symphony Orch., 1973-85, Flagstaff Festival of Arts, 1973-89; bd. dirs. Sedona Chamber Mus. Soc., 1989—; conf. dir. Internat. Clarinet Soc., 1991. Served to 1st lt. USAF, 1955-57. Recipient award of merit Boy Scouts Am., 1977; cert. appreciation John F. Kennedy Ctr. Performing Arts, 1985. Mem. Am. Assn. Higher Edn., Ariz. Humanities Assn., Music Educators Nat. Conf., State Adminstrs. of Music Schs. (chmn. 1971-73), Internat. Clarinet Soc./ClariNetwork Internat. (conf. dir. 1991). Republican. Presbyterian. Lodge: Kiwanis (pres. 1984-85). Home: 140 Fairway Oaks Ln Sedona AZ 86351-8835 Office: No Ariz U Box 6040 Flagstaff AZ 86011

AURBACH, ROBERT MICHAEL, lawyer, consultant, photographer; b. Chgo., Mar. 12, 1952; s. Arthur B. and Helen T. Aurbach; m. Elizabeth Cervantes, Aug. 7, 1994; children: Elyse Louise, Rebecca Michelle. BA summa cum laude, Boston U., 1974; JD, Cornell U., 1979; postgrad., U. N.Mex., 1992. Bar: N.Mex. 1979, U.S. Dist. Ct. N.Mex. 1979, U.S. Ct. Appeals (10th cir.) 1979, U.S. Supreme Ct. 1984. Assoc. Montgomery & Andrews, P.A., Santa Fe, 1979-80; asst. dist. atty. 1st Jud. Dist. Atty.'s Office, Santa Fe, 1980-84; exec. dir. N.Mex. Adminstrv. Office of Dist. Attys., Santa Fe, 1984-89; sr. assoc. U. N.Mex. Inst. Criminal Justice, Albuquerque, 1989-90; pvt. practice law Santa Fe, 1989-90; gen. counsel N.Mex. Workers' Compensation Adminstrn., Albuquerque, 1990—; cons. Navajo Nation Workers' Compensation Task Force, Windowrock, Ariz., 1993—, U.S. V.I. Workers Compensation Adminstrn., Charlotte Amalie, 1992-93; chmn. Children's Justice Act Adv. Group, Albuquerque, 1989; instr. N.Mex. Law Enforcement Acad., Santa Fe, 1985-90. Author: (handbook) Peace Officer Prosecutions, 1985. Mem. bar coun. Disciplinary Bd. of N.Mex. Supreme Ct., 1979—; em. com. Unauthorized Practice of Law Com., 1991-97; bd. dirs. Albuquerque Met. Crimestoppers, 1994-95. Mem. Internat. Assn. Indsl. Accident Bds., So. Assn. WCA, Phi Beta Kappa. Home: 2845 Quincy NE Albuquerque NM 87110 Office: NMex Workers Compensation 1820 Randolph SE Albuquerque NM 87125

AURNER, ROBERT RAY, author, corporate executive; b. Adel, Iowa, Aug. 20, 1898; s. Clarence Ray and Nellie (Slayton) A.; m. Kathryn Dayton, June 16, 1921; 1 son, Robert Ray II. B.A. summa cum laude, U. Iowa, 1919, M.A., 1920, Ph.D., 1922. Dir. customer relations, new bus. The State Bank, Madison, Wis., 1925-28; research dir. Walker Co., 1925-30; established Aurner and Assocs., Cons. to Mgmt., bus. adminstrn., market distbn. and human relations, pres., chmn., chief exec. officer, 1938—, pres., 1988—; v.p., dir. Pacific Futures, Inc., 1962—; dir., chmn. bus adv. com. VNA Corp., 1959-62; fin. cons., dir. Carmel Savs. & Loan Assn., Calif., 1960-71; lectr. NBC Station WTMJ, 1929-30; state commr. Wis. Library Certification Bd., 1931-38; pres. Am. Bus. Communication Assn., 1939-40; mem. faculty, adminstrv. staff U. Wis., 1925-48, ranking research prof. bus. adminstrn., chmn. adminstrn. and mgmt. div., mem. univ. lectr. bur., 1930-48; vis. prof. bus. mgmt. U. Pitts., 1934, 36, 39; vis. research prof. Rare Book Rm., Huntington Library, San Marino, Calif., 1941; adminstrv. cons. Internat. Cellucotton Products Co., Chgo., 1947-52; cons., dir. Communications Div., Fox River Paper Corp., Appleton, Wis., 1947-60; v.p., gen. cons., dir. Scott, Inc., Milw. and Carmel, 1949—; cons. U.S. Naval Postgrad. Sch., Mgmt. Sch. Div., Dept. Navy, Dept. Def., 1957—, Jahn & Ollier Corp., Morris, Schenker, Roth, Inc., First Nat. Bank, Chgo., Library Research Service, New Haven, Nat. Assn. Real Estate Bds., N.Y.C., Allis-Chalmers Corp., Milw.; ltd. partner Salinas-Peninsula Investment Co., 1963-72; cons. Wis. Div. Vital Statistics, 1930-48; Dean Coll. of Commerce, Biarritz Am. U., France, U.S. Army Univ. Center No. 2, ETO, 1945-46; attached U.S. Army, USFET, I. and E. Div., Field Grade, rank of col., 1945-46; spl. lectr. Netherlands Sch. Econs., Rotterdam, 1945; U.S. State Dept. rep. Dutch-Am. Conf., The Hague, Holland, 1945; mem. nat. adv. com. Conf. Am. Small Business Orgns., 1947—; Dir. SAE Corp., Evanston, Ill., 1943-53, pres., chmn. bd., chief exec. officer, 1951-53, Eminent Supreme Archon; mem. nat. adv. counsel Atlantic Union, Inc., 1949—. Author: Specialized Field Approach, 1963, Language Control for Business, 1965, Success Factors in Executive Development, 1967, Effective English for Colleges, 6th edit., 1980, Effective English for Business Communication, 8th edit., 1982, Effective Communication in Business with Management Emphasis, 8th edit., 1988; contbg. editor: Am. Ency. Social Scis.; co-author, contbg. editor, American Business Practice (4 vols.). Trustee Levere Meml. Found., Chgo., 1943-53, pres., chmn. bd., chief exec. officer, 1951-53; chmn. bd., pres., chief exec. officer Carmel Found., Calif., 1981-85, v.p., 1977-81, dir., past chmn. fin. com., past chmn. meml. policy com. mem. internal trusteeship com., exec. com., 1954-83; mem. bd. investment mgmt. Hazeltine Fund Calif., 1963-83; adv. gov., bd. dirs. Monterey Fund Edn., 1965—; dir., chmn. com. endowments York Sch., 1966-69; bd. dirs. Wis. div. AAA, 1936-47. Recipient Disting. Service award with gold medal Sigma Alpha Epsilon, 1967; Championship Gold Medal award N.O.L. Big Ten Univ. Debate Competition, 1919. Fellow Assn. Bus. Communication (hon.); mem. Am. Mktg. Assn., Nat. Assn. Mktg. (v.p. 1931), Smithsonian Instn. Nat. Assos., Wis. Acad. Scis., Arts and Letters, State Hist. Soc. Iowa, Phi Beta Kappa, Delta Sigma Rho, Alpha Kappa Psi (vice chmn. com. profl. programs, exec. group 1955—), Sigma Alpha Epsilon (supreme council 1943-53, nat. pres. 1951-53). Clubs: Continental (Chgo.); Highlands (Monterey Peninsula), Decemvir (Monterey Peninsula), Convivium (Monterey Peninsula); Statesman's (Los Angeles); The Group (Pebble Beach, Calif.). also: Bristlecone Trading and Devel Corp Executive Campus Ste D3 703 Mill Creek Rd Manahawkin NJ 08050 *Hold forever in trust the advantages you have enjoyed; and to the peak of your powers, let it be your mandated obligation to pass these advantages on to all who come within your sphere of influence.**

AUSLANDER, STEVEN LAWRENCE, advertising executive, newspaper editor; b. Passaic, N.J., Oct. 30, 1959; s. Tibor and Myrna Natalie (Sorkin) A.; m. Nancy Mosow, June 20, 1982. BA, U. Ariz., 1983. Pub., editor Tucson Thymes, 1982-83; copywriter Advantage Publs., Tucson, 1982-83; mgr. Am. Multi-Cinema, Tucson, 1984-85; advt. agy. owner Ad Infinitum, Tucson, from 1985; advertising exec., editor Arizona Daily Star; producer pub. service announcements Pima County Atty's Office, Tucson, 1982. Republican. Jewish. Office: The Arizona Daily Star 4850 S Park Ave PO Box 26807 Tucson AZ 85726-6807

AUST, CAROL PETERSON, artist, educator; b. Fresno, Calif., June 8, 1958; d. Clarence Calvin and Esther Elaine (Hanson) P.; m. Edward Ernest Aust, June 18, 1983; children: Noah benjamin, Sophia Peterson. BA, Calif. State U., Chico, 1981. Elem. tchr. Pleasant Valley Sch., Penn Valley, Calif., 1983-85; tchr. English as a fgn. lang. Henan Agrl. U., China, 1986-87; tchr. English as a 2d lang. Asian Multi Svcs., Oakland, Calif., 1987-88, Richmond (Calif.) Adult Sch., 1988-91. Solo exhibits include: Torsiello Gallery, Oakland, Calif., 1990, 92, Biola Univ., La Mirada, Calif., 1992, Gallery W, Sacramento, Calif., 1993, Women's Art Project, San Francisco, 1993, Artistic Impressions Gallery, Greensboro, N.C., 1996, Taylor Univ., Upland, Indiana, 1997; Group exhibits include: Santa Cruz Art League, Calif., 1991, Works/San Jose, Calif., 1992, Peconic Gallery, Riverhead, N.Y., 1993, Bade Gallery, Berkeley, Calif., 1993, 92, Opts Art Gallery, San Francisco, 1993, San Mateo Arts Council, 1994, Sun Gallery, Hayward, Calif., 1994, Weir Gallery, Berkeley, 1995, Gallery One, Mendocino, Calif., 1995, Berkeley Art Ctr., 1990, 95, Coll. of Marin, Kentfield, Calif., 1995, Bedford Gallery, Walnut Creek, Calif., 1996. Mem. ProArts.

AUSTEN, HALLIE IGLEHART, author; b. N.Y.C., Nov. 4, 1947; d. Francis Nash and Harriet Austen (Stokes) Iglehart. AB, Brown U., 1969; student, Union Grad. Sch., Columbus, Ohio, 1983-86. Mem. Museum of Modern Art, San Francisco, 1978, Glyptotek Museum, Copenhagen, 1980, Damon Studio, N.Y.C., 1980, Cerridwen Salon, N.Y.C., 1980, Esalen Inst., Big Sur, Calif., 1981, U. Calif., L.A., 1985; dir., instr. Women In Spiritual Edn., Berkeley, Point Reyes, Calif., 1975—; instr. Nat. Women's Studies Assn. Rutgers U., Camden, N.J., 1984; lectr. Jung Inst. of San Francisco, 1991, Inst. of Transpersonal Psychology, Coll. of Marin, 1992—, U. Calif., Berkeley, 1975-76, 86, 88, Santa Cruz, 1978, Feminist Therapy Ctr. Conf., Malibu, Calif., 1980, UN Non-Govtl. Orgns. Women's Conf., Copenhagen, 1980, San Jose State U., 1980, Heartwood Coll., Santa Cruz, 1981, Interface Ctr., Boston, 1984, San Francisco State U., 1985, Women's Alliance, Nevada City, Calif., 1985-86, Long Beach Womanspirit, 1988, U. Calif., 1988, John F. Kennedy U., Orinda, Calif., 1988, Calif. Sch. of Herbal Studies, Guerneville, Calif., 1978-80, 83-84, 87-88, Oasis Ctr., Chgo., 1992, Coll. of Marin, 1992—. Appeared in Take Back the Night, 1978, Presence of the Goddess (Balcorman Films), 1985; author: Womanspirit: A Guide to Women's Wisdom, 1983, The Heart of the Goddess: Art, Myth and Meditations of the World's Sacred Feminine, 1990, Quest: A Feminist Quarterly, 1977; contbr. numerous articles to books, newspapers and mags. Counselor San Francisco Women's Switchboard, 1973-74; instr. Am. Friends Svcs. Com., San Francisco, 1974; workshop leader Nat. Conf. on Violence Against Women, San Francisco, 1977; mem. Nat. Caucus of Women and the Arts, San Francisco, 1982, San Francisco Art Inst., 1982, Nat. Film Bd. of Can., 1985, 97; active West Marin Cmty. Sustainability Project, 1995—. Mem. San Francisco Women's Found. (assoc. 1983—), Point Reyes Dzog Chen, San Francisco Sonar, Druid Heights Artists Retreat (v.p. 1988-93). Democrat. Office: Women In Spiritual Edn PO Box 697 Point Reyes Station CA 94956-0697

AUSTEN, SHELLI, radio news anchor, consultant; b. Tulsa, Sept. 8, 1954; m. Fred Chris Sorenson, Dec. 31, 1984 (div. Oct. 1988); 1 child, Kristen Amara. BA, U. Calif., Santa Barbara, 1974. Actress Starlight Theatre, Pasadena Playhouse, 1974; with various improvisational acting troupes, 1974-80; news dir. Sta. KMVI, Maui, Hawaii, 1980-83; v.p. Bill Baker Advt., Honolulu, 1983-85; advt. dir. Ground Swell Mag., Haleiwa, 1985-87; prodr., reporter, anchor Sta. KHVH, Honolulu, 1987-92; dir. adv. Beachcomber Mag., 1992-93; disc jockey Sta. KGY, Olympia, Wash., 1994—; reporter Alameda (Calif.) Times Star, 1994-96; morning news anchor KSRO AM Radio, Santa Rosa, Calif., 1996—; pres. In House Prodns. Media Consulting Firm, 1997—; media cons. Rep. Party of Hawaii, Honolulu, 1987—; actress Altarina Playhouse, 1994-95. Contbr. articles to profl. jours. Media coord. Merimed found., Honolulu, 1988; del. Rep. Party, Honolulu, 1989, mem. presdl. task force, Honolulu, 1989-90. Christian. Home: 58-032 Kapuai Pl Haleiwa HI 96712

AUSTERER-WILLIAMS, ELEONORE, art gallery owner, director; b. Vienna, Austria, Nov. 19, 1944; came to U.S., 1982.; d. Maximilian Julius and Maria Magdalena (Mitsche) Austerer; m. Mark R. Williams. BA in Liberal Arts, Hochschule, 1962; postgrad., U. Geneva, 1962-66. Translator in German, French, Spanish, and English, UN, Geneva, 1968-71; real estate agent Edificio Marino S.A., Marbella, Spain, 1971-73; dir., owner Chelsea Market, Art & Antiques, Marbella, 1973-81; owner . Eleonore Austerer Fine Art, San Mateo, Calif., 1982-87; dir., owner Eleonore Austerer Gallery, San Francisco, 1987—. Co-author/editor: Catalogue Raisonnee "A Retrospective" of the works by artist Roberto Lauro, 1992. Mem. Mus. Modern Art and the Legion of Honor Fine Art Museums, San Francisco, 1981, San Francisco Visitors and Conv. Bur., 1988. Office: Eleonore Austerer Gallery 540 Sutter St San Francisco CA 94102-1102

AUSTIN, JAMES ALBERT, healthcare executive, obstetrician-gynecologist; b. Phoenix, Sept. 23, 1931; s. Albert Morris and Martha Lupkin (mercer) A.; m. Margaret Jeanne Arnold, July 26, 1952 (div. 1978); children: Cynthia Milee Ludgin, Lauri Jeanne Fuller, Wendy Patrice Rhea; m. Sandra Lee Marsh, Jan. 3, 1979 (div. 1992); m. Sharon Marie Reichle, Sept. 9, 1993. BA, U. So. Calif., 1952; MD, George Wash. U., 1956; MBA, Pepperdine U., 1991. Diplomate Am. Bd. Ob-Gyn., Am. Bd. Med. Mgmt. Intern U.S. Naval Hosp., Bethesda, Md., 1956-57, resident in ob-gyn, 1957-60; ob-gyn. Washington Gynecologists, Washington, 1966-69; pres. Ariz. Obstetrics and Gynecology Ltd., Phoenix, 1969-79; chmn. dept. ob-gyn. USN, Agana Hgts., Guam, 1979-81; ob-gyn. Sanger Med. Group, Coronado, Calif., 1981-83; chmn. ob-gyn. FHP Corp., Salt Lake City, 1983-84, assoc. med. dir., 1984-85; hosp. med. dir. FHP Corp., Fountain Valley, Calif., 1985-86; assoc. v.p. med. affairs FHP Corp., Fountain Valley, 1987-90; chief exec. officer Ultra Link Nationwide HMO Network, Costa Mesa, Calif., 1990-93; chief med. officer Downey (Calif.) Community Hosp., 1993-94; sr. advisor FHP Internat. Cons. Group, Costa Mesa, Calif., 1995—; med. dir. So. Calif. Prudential HealthCare Plan of Calif., 1995—; clin. prof. ob-gyn. George Wash. U., Georgetown, Washington, 1966-69; asst. clin. prof. U. Calif. San Diego, 1981-83, U. Utah, Salt Lake City, 1983-85. Rear adm. USNR, 1956-88. Fellow Am. Coll. Ob-Gyn.; mem. AMA, Am. Acad. Med. Dir., Ariz. Med. Assn. (bd. dirs. 1978), Am. coll. Physician Execs. Republican. Presbyterian. Home: PO Box 1450 16811 S Pacific Ave Sunset Beach CA 90742-1450

AUSTIN, JOHN NORMAN, classics educator; b. Anshun, Kweichow, China, May 20, 1937; s. John Alfred and Lillian Maud (Reeks) A. B.A., U. Toronto, Ont. Can., 1958; M.A., U. Calif.-Berkeley, 1959, Ph.D., 1965. Vis. lectr. Yale U., New Haven, 1971; asst. prof., then assoc. prof. UCLA, 1966-76; Aurelio prof. Greek Boston U., 1976-78; prof., chmn. dept. classics U. Mass., Amherst, 1978-80; prof. classics U. Ariz., Tucson, 1980—, acting dean humanities, 1987-88, head, dept. classics, 1995—. Author: Archery at the Dark of the Moon, 1975, Meaning and Being in Myth, 1990, Helen of Troy and Her Shameless Phantom, 1994; editor: (with others) The Works of John Dryden, vol. III; sr. editor Calif. Studies Classical Antiquity, vols. VI and VII. Jr. fellow Ctr. for Hellenic Studies, 1968-69, J.S. Guggenheim Found. fellow, 1974-75. Mem. Am. Philol. Assn. (bd. dirs. 1983-86). Episcopalian. Home: 2939 E 3rd St Tucson AZ 85716-4122 Office: U Ariz Dept Classics PO Box 210067 Tucson AZ 85721-0067

AUTH, ROBERT RALPH, art educator; b. Bloomington, Ill., Oct. 27, 1926; s. Phillip C. and Frances E. A. BFA, Ill. Wesleyan U., 1953; MFA, Wash. State U., 1963. Art tchr. Burley, Idaho, 1959, Boise (Idaho) Ind. Sch. Dist., 1960-81; art supr. Boise Ind. Sch. Dist., Boise, ID, 1981-87. Author: ID State Humanities Curriculum Guide, 1985; creator historic prints, paintings, sculptures. Cmty. svc. adv. Boise's Jr. League; mem. Allied Arts Coun.; bd. dirs., Boise Gallery of Art, Boise Edn. Assn., Alliance for Arts in Edn. Recipient Allied Arts Coun. Artist of the Year award, 1972, Nat. Art Edn. award, 1979, Idaho Hist. Soc. Hon. Curator of Military Hist. award, 1983, Gov. of Idaho medal for Excellence in the Arts, 1988, The Idaho Statesman's Distinguished Citizen award, 1988, Phi Delta Kappa Friend of Edn. award, 1989. Roman Catholic. Home: PO Box 91 Yellow Pine ID 83677-0091

AUTOLITANO, ASTRID, consumer products executive; b. Havana, Cuba, Aug. 25, 1938; came to U.S., 1966; d. Manuel and Efigenia (Giquel) Rodriguez; m. Dominick Autolitano, July 23, 1977; children: Astrid Martinez, Manuel Martinez. Student, U. Havana, 1962-64, El Camino Coll., Torrance, Calif., 1968-71, UCLA, Westwood, 1973-75, Columbia U., 1983. Multi-lingual sec. Mattel Toys, Hawthorne, Calif., 1966-69, coord. internat. sales, 1969-73, mgr. Pan Am. sales, 1973-78, dir. export sales and licensees, 1978-83, v.p. Latin Am., 1983-89; sr. v.p. Latin Am. Mattel Toys, El Segundo, Calif., 1989-95, exec. v.p. Latin Am., 1995-96, exec. v.p. Ams., 1996; pres. internat. Mattel Toys, 1996—. Office: Mattel Toys 333 Continental Blvd El Segundo CA 90245-5032*

AUTRY, GENE (ORVON GENE AUTRY), actor, entertainer, broadcasting executive, baseball team executive; b. Tioga, Tex., Sept. 29, 1907; s. Delbert and Elnora (Ozmont) A.; m. Ina Mae Spivey, Apr. 1, 1932; m. Jacqueline Ellam, 1981. Grad., Tioga (Tex.) High Sch., 1925. R.R. telegraph operator Sapulpa, Okla., 1925; owner, chmn. bd. Calif. Angels; pres. Flying A Prodns.; owner Golden West Broadcasters; chmn. bd. Autry Mus. of Western Heritage, L.A.; pres. several music and publ. cos. Made first phonograph record of cowboy songs, 1929; radio artist Sta. WLS, Chgo., 1930-34; motion picture actor, 1934-53, including In Old Santa Fe; starred in 88 musical Western feature pictures, 91 half-hour TV pictures 1950-55; has written or co-written over 200 songs including That Silver-Haired Daddy of Mine, 1931 (1st gold record given to anyone), You're the Only Star in My Blue Heaven, 1938, Dust, 1938, Tears On My Pillow, 1941, Be Honest With Me, 1941, Tweedle O'Twill, 1942, Here Comes Santa Claus, 1948; host Melody Ranch Theater Nashville Network, 1987, 88. With USAAF, 1942-45. Recipient: D.W. Griffith award, 1991. Mem. Internat. Footprinters, Masons (33 degree), Shriners, Elks. Office: Autry Museum of Western Heritage 4700 Western Heritage Wy Los Angeles CA 90027-1462

AVAKIAN, JAMES LAWRENCE, engineering executive; b. L.A., Feb. 14, 1957; s. James Haig and Alice Louise Avakian; m. Alice Arzoumanian. Degree in electronics engring., Calif. Poly., 1986. Pres. Computer Tech., Inc., San Luis Obispo, Calif., 1985-86; devel. engr. Hughes Aircraft Co., El Segundo, Calif., 1986-87; pres. Optical Automation, Inc., Tarzana, Calif., 1987—, owner, 1987-96, corp. pres., CEO, 1996—. Inventor in field. Mem. IEEE, Internat. Solid State Circuits Conf., Digital Signal Processing Exposition, Visual Hardware Descriptive Lang. Internat., Optical Lab. Assn., Optical Mfr. Assn. Democrat.

AVAKOFF, JOSEPH CARNEGIE, medical and legal consultant; b. Fairbanks, Alaska, July 15, 1936; s. Harry B. and Margaret (Adams) A.; m. Teddy I. Law, May 7, 1966; children: Caroline, Joey, John. AA, U. Calif., Berkeley, 1956, AB, 1957; MD, U. Calif., San Francisco, 1961; JD, Santa Clara U., 1985. Bar: Calif. 1987; diplomate Am. Bd. Surgery, Am. Bd. Plastic Surgery. Physicist U.S. Naval Radiol. Def. Lab., San Francisco, 1957, 59; intern So. Pacific Gen. Hosp., San Francisco, 1961-62; resident in surgery Kaiser Found. Hosp., San Francisco, 1962-66; resident in plastic surgery U. Tex. Sch. Medicine, San Antonio, 1970-72; pvt. practice specializing in surgery Sacramento, 1966-70; pvt. practice specializing in plastic surgery Los Gatos and San Jose, Calif., 1972-94; cons. to med. and legal professions, 1994—; clin. instr. surgery U. Calif. Sch. Medicine, Davis, 1967-70; chief dept. surgery Mission Oaks Hosp., Los Gatos, 1988-90; chief divsn. plastic surgery Good Samaritan Hosp., San Jose, 1989-91; expert med. reviewer Med. Bd. Calif., 1995—; spl. cons. Calif. Dept. Corps., 1997—; presenter numerous med. orgns. Contbr. numerous articles to med. jours. Mem. San Jose Adv. Commn. on Health, 1975-82; bd. govs. San Jose YMCA, 1977-80. Mem. AMA, Calif. Med. Assn., Santa Clara County Bar Assn., Santa Clara County Med. Assn., Union Am. Physicians and Dentists, Phi Beta Kappa, Phi Eta Sigma. Republican. Presbyterian. Home: 6832 Rockview Ct San Jose CA 95120-5607

AVERETT, ROBERT LEE, educator, information system professional; b. Richfield, Utah, Dec. 4, 1952; s. Robert Elmo and Patsy (Meyer) A.; m. Alice Greenhalgh, Mar. 23, 1972; children: Nathan Christopher, Rachel Leah, Christian Alexander, Jeduthan William. BA, Brigham Young U., 1975, MLS, 1976; MA, Ball State U., 1979; D of Pub. Adminstrn., George Mason U., 1991. Cert. computer profl.; cert. secondary tchr., counselor, Utah. Commd. 2d lt. U.S. Army, 1976, advanced through grades to lt. col., 1993, ret., 1996; chief personnel info. system dept. Mil. Personnel Ctr., Alexandria, Va., 1982-84; info. systems project mgr. Orgn. of Joint Chiefs of Staff, The Pentagon, 1984-85; mgmt. info. systems officer Hqrs. Dept. of Army, The Pentagon, 1985-87; comdr. 201st Signal Co., Seoul, Republic of Korea, 1987-89, Mil. Entrance Process Sta., Amarillo, Tex., 1989-92; asst. prof. mil. sci. Brigham Young U., Provo, Utah, 1992-93; chair, prof. mil. sci. U. Utah, Salt Lake City, 1993—, 1993-96; counselor Granite Sch. Dist., Salt Lake City, 1995; Cons., adj. Amarillo Coll., 1989-92, Limestone Coll., 1979-82; treas. Utah Sch. Counselor Assn., 1995. Leader Boy Scouts Am., Nat. Capitol Coun., Alexandria, 1982-87, Golden Spread Coun., Amarillo, 1987-89. Recipient Meritorious Svc. award N.G. Bur., 1987, Armed Forces Comm-Elec Assn., 1989. Mem. ASPA. Home: 484 Rocky Mouth Ln Draper UT 84020

AVERILL, RONALD HENRY, political science educator, retired military officer; b. L.A., Jan. 9, 1938; s. Alexander Anthony Averill and Anita Marie (Moser) Mitchell; m. Janice Louise Vaughan, Apr. 4, 1961; 1 child, Ella Louise Averill Morales. BA in Fgn. Svc., U. So. Calif., 1959; MA, Am. U., 1974. Lt. U.S. Army, Darmstadt, Germany, 1959-62; asst. prof. Mil. Sci. Okla. St. U., Stillwater, 1963-66; staff officer U.S. Army, 1968-73, comdr., 1974-89; instr. Hawaii Pacific U., Honolulu, 1989-91, South Puget Sound C.C., Olympia, Wash., 1992—. Chmn. St. Mary's Parish Coun., Centralia, 1993-96, Lewis County Nat. Resources Com., Chehalis, 1994—, Lewis County Solid Waste Adv. Com., Chehalis, 1994—, Lewis County Rep. Cen. Com., 1997—. Mem. Nat. Intersch. Coaches Assn. (soccer coach 1969—), Assn. U.S. Army, The Retired Officers Assn., Lewis County Farm Bur. (legis. liaison 1994), Knights of Columbus (past grand knight, recorder, 1995—). Republican. Roman Catholic. Home: 2523 Graf Rd Centralia WA 98531 Office: S Puget Sound C C 2011 Mottman Rd S W Olympia WA 98512

AVERY, KEITH WILLETTE, artist, educator; b. Lansing, Mich., Dec. 3, 1921; s. Norton Louis and Ruby Mae (Willette) A.; m. Carol Joyce Haddan, Oct. 10, 1946; children: Carleton Louis, David Keith, Jane Ellen Avery Gray. BS, N.Mex. State U., 1955, LittD, 1986. Cert. secondary edn. tchr., N.Mex., Ariz., Mich. Horse trainer and exhibitor A.B. Johnson Chevrolet Co., Grand Rapids, Mich., 1946-47; ranch foreman and horse trainer Lazy U Ranch, Bartlesville, Okla., 1949-50, Mill Iron Lazy 3 Ranch, Carrizozo, N.Mex., 1950-51; artist N.Mex. State U., Las Cruces, 1951-55; instr. and calf roping coach Judson Sch., Scottsdale, Ariz., 1955-59; instr. Lowell (Mich.) High Sch., 1961-74; artist horseman Springer, Roswell, N.Mex., 1974—; dir. alumni rels. N.Mex. State U., Las Cruces, 1959-60. Author: Ridden Hard and Put Up Wet, 1990, Campfire Echoes, 1994, (biography) Trails of a Wanderer, 1995. With U.S. Air Force, 1942-46. Recipient Champion Working Stock Horse Nat. Horse Show Assn., Chgo., 1946, Gold, Silver and Bronze medals Phippen Invitational Art Show, Prescott, Ariz., 1978, Stetson Hat award Tex. Cowboy Artists Gold Medal Exhibit, San Angelo, Tex., 1983, Best of Show Painting award S.W. Regional Art Show Roswell, 1982, Gov.'s award of Excellence and Achievement in the Arts as the dean of N.Mex. cowboy poets and premier painter of the working cowboy, 1994; rep. N.Mex. Cowboy Poetry gathering Nat. Endowment fot the Arts, Elko, Nev., 1986. Republican. Methodist. Home: 2809 S Graves Rd Roswell NM 88201-9024

AVOLIO, WENDY FREEDMAN, speech and language pathologist; b. Phila., Feb. 24, 1953; d. Harold Stanley and Phyllis Maxine (Broodno) Freedman; m. Michael Howard Strauss, Aug. 31, 1975 (div. 1981); children: Nicole Erin, Mallary Blair; m. Mark Richard Avolio, Mar. 24, 1985. BS, Bradley U., 1973; MA, No. Ill. U., 1975. Speech-lang. pathologist Bartlett (Ill.) Sch. Dist., 1975-76, Proviso Area for Exceptional Children, Maywood, Ill., 1976-77, Cen. Reading and Speech Clinic, Mt. Prospect, Ill., 1977-78, Tucson Unified Sch. Dist., 1978-79, Handmaker Jewish Geriatric Ctr., Tucson, 1981; mgr. speech-lang. therapy program Dept. Econ. Security/Div. Devel. Disabilities, Tucson, 1981-86, So. Ariz. Spl. Edn. Coop., Vail, 1986-92, Amphitheater Sch. Dist., 1992-95; therapeak Life Care Ctr.-Tucson, 1993-95; speech-lang. pathologist Sundance Rehab. Corp., Tucson, 1995-97; pvt. practice Tuscon, 1997—; cons. speech-lang. Parent Support Group, Tucson, 1981-87, Ariz. Adv. Com. For Deaf-Blind, Tucson, 1983-87; lang. cons. Community Outreach Program for Deaf, Tucson, 1983. Active youth and children com. Jewish Comty. Ctr., Tucson, 1986-88, Tucson Classics, 1989-94; bd. dirs. Tucson Residence Found., 1993—. Mem. Am. Speech Lang. and Hearing Assn. (cert.), Ariz. Speech and Lang. Assn. Home and Office: 3532 N Fiesta Del Sol Tucson AZ 85750

AVRIN, DAVID LAWRENCE, public relations executive, legislative liason, vocalist; b. San Gabriel, Calif., Oct. 9, 1963; s. Philip Avrin and Barbara (Tell) A. BA in Journalism and Mass Comms., U. No. Colo., 1987; post grad. study in pub. rels. mgmt., Colo. State U., 1991—. Copywriter, producer KYOU Radio, Greeley, Colo., 1987; account exec., copywriter Up the Creek Newspaper, Greeley, 1987-89, copywriter , conceptmedia advt., pub. rels., 1989; spokesman Denver City Health Dept. and Denver Gen. Hosp., 1989-92; spokesman, media rels. dir. The Children's Hosp., Denver, 1992-93, legis. liaison, 1993-95; pres. The Capitol Group, Denver, 1995—; mgr., performer The Diners, male a cappella siinging group; part time profl. announcer, spokesman. Recipient Eugenia Rawls scholarship, Univ. departmental music scholarship. Mem. Pub. Rels. Soc. Am. (accredited pub. rels. profl., mem. health acad.), Colo. Healthcare Comms. (bd. dirs.), Am. Soc. for Healthcare Pub. Rels. and Mktg., Colo. Child Advocacy and Safety Coalition, Mortar Board. Office: The Capitol Group 515 E 2nd Ave Denver CO 80203-4106

AVSHALOMOV, DAVID, conductor, composer; b. N.Y.C., May 6, 1946; s. Jacob David and Doris (Felde) A.; m. Cheryl Lee Stray, 1968 (div. 1975); m. Carrie Kourkoumelis, 1976 (div. 1980); m. Randi Lynn Grafman, June 18, 1982; children: Jesse Alexander, Zachary Aaron. BA magna cum laude, Harvard U., 1967; Dr. Musical Arts, U. Wash., 1976; conducting studies with Leo Mueller, Peabody Conservatory, 1969-72; studies with Leonard Bernstein, Seiji Ozawa and Gunther Schuller, Tanglewood, 1979; studies with Jean Morel, Werner Torkanowsky and Herbert Blomstedt, Aspen Sch. Music, 1972. Staff condr. Tacoma Opera, 1975-76; music dir. Bremerton (Wash.) Symphony Orch., 1973-75; condr., music dir. Missoula (Mont.) Symphony Orch. and Chorale, 1976-78, Los Angeles Drs. Symphony Orch., 1981-85; founding condr., music dir. Santa Monica (Calif.) Chamber Orch., 1981-90; resident guest condr. Portland (Oreg.) Philharm., 1979, 80, 89; guest condr. more than 30 ensembles; tours in U.S,. Europe, Soviet bloc, Japan, China, Russia; vocalist, timpanist and percussionist various orgns.; asst. prof. music U. Mont., Missoula, 1976-78; adj. prof. humanities Pacific Western U., L.A., 1989—. Composer works for orch., string quartet, band, chorus, chamber ensembles; recs. Served with USAF Band, 1968-72. NDEA fellow, 1967, 72-74; recipient 1st prize Aspen Student Composition Contest, 1972. Mem. Phi Beta Kappa. Democrat. Jewish. Home and Office: 2402 4th St Apt 5 Santa Monica CA 90405-3637*

AXELSON, CHARLES FREDERIC, retired accounting educator; b. Chgo., Apr. 24, 1917; s. Charles Frederic and Katherine (Strong) A.; m. Dorothy L. Jepson, July 23, 1940 (dec. Oct. 1994); children: Linda Axelson Masters, Fred, Lorraine Axelson Gresty; m. Marion I. Murray, Mar. 11, 1995. A.B., M.B.A., U. Chgo., 1937. Staff acct. Lybrand, Ross Bros. & Montgomery, Chgo., 1938-41; with U.S. Gypsum Co., Chgo., 1941-70; asst. controller U.S. Gypsum Co., 1946-52, controller, 1952-60, controller, asst. treas., 1960-70; v.p. controller Libby, McNeill & Libby, Chgo., 1970-78; v.p., chief fin. officer Lawry's Foods, Inc., Los Angeles, 1978-82; prof. acctg. U. So. Calif., Los Angeles, 1982-85; vis. lectr. Darling Downs Inst. Advanced Edn., Toowoomba, Queensland, Australia, 1985; lectr. acctg. Calif. State Poly. U., Pomona, 1985-92; lectr. emeritus, 1992; lectr. acctg. Northwestern U., 1946-53; bd. dirs. Air Conditioning Co., 1982-96, Goodwill Industries So. Calif., treas., 1994—. Trustee emeritus Nat. Louis U.; former chmn. Crippled Children's Soc. So. Calif., vice chmn., 1990—, also bd. dirs. Named to Calif. Poly. Acctg. Hall of Fame, 1996. Mem. AICPA, Fin. Execs. Inst. (past dir. L.A. chpt., past pres. Chgo. chpt., past nat. dir., past v.p. Midwestern area), Phi Delta Theta. Presbyterian. Club: Town Hall (Los Angeles). Home: 888 S Orange Grove Blvd # 2-w Pasadena CA 91105-1790 *Whatever successes I've had - business and personal - can be traced to self-discipline, a good education, a reputation for integrity, much reading, good health, outside interests to offset business pressures and lots of advance planning.*

AXELSON, JOSEPH ALLEN, professional athletics executive, publisher; b. Peoria, Dec. 25, 1927; s. Joseph Victor Axelson and Florence (Ealen) Massey; m. Malcolm Rae Smith, Oct. 7, 1950 (dec.); children: David Allen, Mark Stephen, Linda Rae. B.S., Northwestern U., 1949. Sports info. dir. Ga. So. U., Statesboro, 1957-60, Nat. Assn. Intercollegiate Athletics, Kansas City, Mo., 1961-62; tournament dir. Bowling Proprs. Assn. Am., Park Ridge, Ill., 1963-64; asst. exec. sec. Nat. Assn. Intercollegiate Athletics, Kansas City, Mo., 1964-68; exec. v.p., gen. mgr. Cin. Royals Profl. Basketball Team, Cin., 1969-72; mgr. Cin. Gardens, 1970-72; pres., gen. mgr. Kansas City Kings Profl. Basketball Team, Kansas City, Mo., 1972-79, 82-85; pres., gen. mgr. Sacramento Kings Profl. Basketball Team, 1985-88, exec. v.p., 1988-90; pres. Arco Arena, Sacramento, 1985-88; exec. v.p. Sacramento Sports Assn., Arco Sports Complex, 1988-90, Profl. Team Publs., Inc., Stamford, Conn., 1991-92; pub. Between The Vines Newsletter, 1993—; exec. v.p. ops. NBA, N.Y.C., 1979-82, chmn. competition and rules com., 1975-79; trustee Naismith Basketball Hall of Fame; co-host The Sports Page, Sta. KFMB-AM, San Diego, 1994—. Author: Basketball Basics, 1987. Mem. Emil Verban Meml. Soc., Washington. Capt. Signal Corps. AUS, 1949-54. Named Nat. Basketball Exec. of Yr. The Sporting News, St. Louis, 1973, Sportsman of Yr., Rockne Club, Kansas City, 1975; recipient Annual Dirs. award Downtown, Inc., Kansas City, Mo., 1979, Nat. Assn. Intercollegiate Athletics Frank Cramer Nat. Svc. award, 1983, Man of Yr. award Sacramento (Calif.) C. of C., 1986; named to Ga. So. U. Sports Hall of Fame, 1990. Mem. Am. Philatelic Soc., Phi Kappa Psi. Republican. Presbyterian. Office: 1112 1st St Ste 410 Coronado CA 92118-1407

AXLEY, HARTMAN, underwriter; b. Madison, Wis., Apr. 17, 1931; s. Ralph Emerson and Katharine Nella (Hartman) A.; m. Marguerite Ann Thessin, Sept. 4, 1954; children: Colleen Lynn Axley Patrick, Timothy Hartman Axley. BA, U. Wis., 1952, JD, 1956; MSFS, Am. Coll., Bryn Mawr, Pa., 1983. CLU, cert. fin. planner, accedited estate planner; chartered fin. cons.; registered health underwriter. Assoc. atty. Holland & Hart, Denver, 1956-58; life underwriter Colo. Assocs. of Allmerica Fin. (formerly State Mut. Cos.), Denver, 1958—; mem. bd. editl. advisors Life and Health Insurance Sales, Lexington, Ky.; mem. Colo. Ethics in Bus. Award Bd., 1995—; mem. Denver Estate Planning Coun., pres., 1968-69. Author: National Ski Patrol Ski Lift Evacuation Manual, 1975, National Ski Patrol Awards Manual, 1980. Bd. dir. Met. Denver YMCA, 1978-81; bd. dirs. S.W. Denver Family YMCA, 1973—, chmn. bd. dir., 1978-81; mem. First Aider Mile High chpt. ARC, Denver, 1956-86; bd. dir., officer Community Concert Assn. Denver, 1962-65; bd. dir. Colo. Ski Mus., 1994—; chair Colo. Ski Hall of Fame, 1996—; mem. Nat. Ski Patrol System, 1948-90, asst. nat. dir., 1969-76, Rocky Mountain div. dir., 1963-69 (Minnie Dole award 1988, Schobinger Outstanding Adminstr. award 1973); mem. Olympic Ski Patrol, Squaw Valley, Calif., 1960; mem., patroller Arapahoe Basin Ski Patrol, 1956-85, front range dir., 1961-63; coord. badminton Rocky Mountain Sr. Games, 1987—. Capt. USAF, 1958-60. Named to Roll of Honor, Mile High ARC, 1974, to Denver YMCA Hall of Fame, Met. Denver YMCA, 1987, to Colo. Ski Hall of Fame, 1993; recipient Award of Merit (Lifesaving) ARC, 1959, J. Stanley Edwards award Colo. and Denver Assn. Life Underwriters, 1980, Badminton medal Rocky Mountain Sr. Games, 1987—, U.S. Badminton Assn. Sr. Championship, 1988, 92, U.S. Nat. Sr. Games, 1991, 93, 95. Mem. ABA (real property, probate and trust sect.), Nat. Assn. Estate Planning Cons. (bd. dirs. 1970-76, pres. 1974-75, patron chair 1975—, accreditation com. 1991—), Nat. Assn. Estate Planners (founding mem. bd. dirs. 1987), Am. Soc. CLU and ChFC (bd. dirs. 1992-95, western region v.p. 1994-95, nat. pub. rels. com. 1990-94, vice chair 1992, chair baby boomer rsch. project 1990, Colo.-Wyo. liaison 1992—), Am. Soc. CLU and ChFC (Rocky Mountain chpt. bd. dirs. 1985-91, pres. 1989-90), Assn. for Advanced Life Underwriters (Colo. liaison, 1996—), Denver Assn. Life Underwriters (Wesley Whitney award 1995, qualifying and life mem., Million Dollar Round Table 1970-85), Colo. Ins. Commr.'s Adv. Coun. (chmn. 1990—), Colo. Assn. Commerce and Industry (Health Care Task Force 1990-94), Colo. Assn. Life Underwriters, Nat. Assn. Life Underwriters (Nat. Quality award, Nat. Sales Achievement award), Life Underwriter Charities, Inc. (founding mem. bd. dirs. 1989-92), Wis. Bar Assn., Metro Denver Assn. Health Underwriters (founding mem. bd. dirs. 1990-92, legis. chair 1990-92), Colo. State Assn. Health Underwriters (charter 1986—, founding mem. bd. dirs. 1986-92, legis. chair 1986-92), Nat. Assn. Health Underwriters (leading producers roundtable 1981-89), U.S. Badminton Assn. (staff vol. Olympic Games 1996), U. Wis. Alumni Assn. (bd. dirs. 1970-89, Spark Plug award 1977), Wis. Bar Assn. Congregationalist. Office: State Mutual Cos 44 Cook St Ste 500 Denver CO 80206-5815

AXON, DONALD CARLTON, architect; b. Haddonfield, N.J., Feb. 27, 1931; s. William Russell Sr. and Gertrude L. (Ellis) A.; m. Rosemary Smith, Sept. 1952 (div. Oct. 1967); children: Donald R., James K., Marianne Axon Flannery, Darren H., William R. II; m. Janice Jacobs, Mar. 16, 1968; stepchildren: Jonathan Lee, Elise Marie. BArch, Pratt Inst., 1954; MS in Arch., Columbia U., 1966. Registered architect, N.Y., Pa., Calif. Designer, drafter Keith Hibner, Assoc., Hicksville, N.Y., 1954-56; designer Charles Wood, Riverhead, N.Y., 1956-59; architect, prin Donald C. Axon, Assoc., Wantaugh, N.Y., 1959; ptnr. Bailey-Axon & Assoc., Long Beach, N.Y., 1960-66; project mgr. Caudill Rowlett Scott, Houston, 1966-69; in-house architect Kaiser Permanente Hosp., L.A., 1969-75; dir. med. facilities Daniel Mann Johnson Mendenhall, L.A., 1975-78, Lyon Assocs., L.A., 1979-80; pres. Donald C. Axon, FAIA, Inc., L.A., 1980—; tchr. bldg. sci. program U. So. Calif., 1978-82; lectr. in field; profl. advisor dept. architecture U. Tex., 1968-69; advisor to chmn. Sch. Architecture Rice U., Houston, 1968-69; profl. dir. Future Architect Am., 1965-66. Mem. Crestwood Hills Assn., bd. dirs. 1971-75, pres., 1973-75, archtl. rev. com., 1987—; bd. dirs. Brentwood Community Fedn., 1973-75, v.p., 1974-75. Recipient L.A. Beautiful award KPH Norwalk Hosp. Fellow AIA (Calif. regional bd. dirs. 1987-89, mem. various subcoms., chair steering com. 1980, liaison 1991—, bd. dirs. L.A. chpt. 1983-84, pres. 1986, chair com. on architecture for health 1974, chair health facilities com. Calif. coun. 1975, Disting. Svc. citation 1992), Royal Soc. Health, Health Facilities Inst.; mem. Archtl. Found. L.A. (founding, v.p. 1985-89, pres. 1989-90), Internat. Conf. Bldg. Ofcls., Am. Hosp. Assn., Forum for Health Care Planning (bd. dirs. 1982—, pres. 1993-94). Office: 823 Hanley Ave Los Angeles CA 90049-1913

AXTELL, KEITH ELTON, federal agency administrator; b. San Bernardino, Calif., Mar. 10, 1942; s. John Dewey and Nelta (George) A.; m. Patricia Boster, Dec. 1964 (div. Oct. 1980); children: Andrea Miriam, Jonathan Patrick; m. Holly Berna Handler, Nov. 30, 1980. BA, U. Calif., Berkeley, 1965, MA in Pub. Adminstrn., 1966. Dir. housing programs br. U.S. Dept. Housing and Urban Devel., San Francisco, 1971-74, asst. regional adminstr. for adminstrn. Regional Office, 1974-78, dir. Office of Indian Programs, 1978-79, exec. asst. to regional adminstr., 1979-83, dir. Regional Office of Housing, 1983-94, dir. Office of Housing FHA, 1995-97; mem. adv. bd. pub. adminstrn. dept. Calif. State U., Hayward, 1988—; cons. Calif. State Legis., Sacramento. Commr. Met. Transp. Commn., San Francisco Bay Area, 1996—. Recipient Pres.'s Spl. award Pres. Richard Nixon, Washington, 1970. Mem. ASPA (exec. com. Bay area 1981-93, pres. Bay area 1990-91, nat. coun. mem., regional rep. 1994-95, Achievement award 1993, Chpt. Contbr. award 1993), Rotary Internat. Office: US Dept HUD Box 36003 450 Golden Gate Ave San Francisco CA 94925

AYBAR, CHARLES ANTON, aviation executive; b. N.Y.C., Sept. 27, 1956; s. Louis Adolf and Elisabeth A. (Schwarz) A.; m. Deborah Ann Benson, May 1, 1988; 1 child, Heidi Brita. AS in Aeronautics, Embry-Riddle Aero. U., 1987; BS in Aviation Mgmt., Pacific-Western U., 1988, MBA in Mktg., 1988, PhD in Mgmt., 1993. Lic. airline transport pilot; cert. FAA flight instr. and aircraft dispatcher. V.p. mktg. Commuter Air Tech., Inc., Scottsdale, Ariz., 1996—; written test examiner FAA, Orlando, Fla., 1989-91, accident prevention counselor, 1991—; cons. CBS TV Network, 1979-80; prodr., host TV show series Flightline, Aviation Today in Ariz., 1994-96. Recipient Silver medal award FAA, 1995, A.C.E. award FAA, Flight Instr. of Yr. award FAA, 1994. Home: 3922 E Kimberly Way Phoenix AZ 85024

AYCOCK, DALE, minister; b. Moffatt, Tex., Feb. 3, 1930; s. Bobbie Hugh and Elsie (Norman) A.; m. Patricia Ann Brandes, Mar. 2, 1951; children: Norman Scott, Patricia Yvonne Shumaker, Timothy Dale, Benjamin Glen. Student, Hardin-Simmons U., 1949-50, Baylor U., 1950-52, Long Beach State U., 1959-60, San Jose State U., 1962-63; BA, Calif. Bapt. Coll., 1965; postgrad., Golden Gate Sem., 1974-75, U. Calif., Riverside, 1976. Ordained min. Bapt. Ch. Pastor Harriett (Tex.) Bapt. Ch., 1950-52; pastor, organizer First So. Bapt. Ch. of Santa Monica, Calif., 1952-53; pastor Trinity Bapt. Ch., Santa Maria, Calif., 1953-55, First Bapt. Ch., Granda Hills, Calif., 1955-57, First So. Bapt. Ch., Huntington Beach, Calif., 1957-60, First Bapt. Ch., Belmont, Calif., 1960-63, Olive St. Bapt. Ch., Colton, Calif., 1963-67, First So. Bapt. Ch., Long Beach, Calif., 1967-80, First Bapt. Ch. of Rosedale, Bakersfield, Calif., 1980—. Pres. Calif. Bapt. Found., 1980-81; active Jordan H.S. Human Rels. Com., Long Beach, 1975-76. Republican. Home: 6604 Edgemont Dr Bakersfield CA 93309-5520 Office: First Bapt Ch Rosedale 18210 Rosedale Hwy Bakersfield CA 93312-9488

AYER, CAROL ANNE, librarian; b. Olympia, Wash., Sept. 6, 1953; d. Harold Stevens and Leoni (Bleston) A. BS, Portland State U., 1975; M of Librarianship, U. Wash., 1977. Libr. USDA Forest Svc., Juneau, Alaska, 1980-87, Washington, 1987; tech. info. officer USDA Forest Svc., Ogden, Utah, 1987—, Collins, Colo., 1997—. Mem, bd. dirs. Pinto Horse Assn. Am., Ft. Worth, Tex., 1990—. Mem. Am. Libr. Assn., Spl. Librs. Assn., Utah Libr. Assn. (sec. spl. libr. sect. 1990-94, bd. dirs. 1997—). Democrat. Unitarian-Universalist. Office: USDA Forest Svc Intermountain Rsch Sta 324 25th St Ogden UT 84401-2303

AYER, DAVID CLAY, architect; b. Salt Lake City, Dec. 26, 1952; s. John Lowell and Ethel (Schumann) A.; m. Colleen J. Dorsey, May 8, 1982; children: Kaitlin Ashley, Austin Michael. BS with honors, U. Utah, 1976, MArch, 1979. Registered architect, Utah, Hawaii. Project architect EDA, Salt Lake City, 1978-80, project mgr., assoc., 1981-83; project mgr. IMH Architects, Salt Lake City, 1980-81; dir. architecture DMJM-Utah, Salt Lake City, 1983-88; prin. STA Ltd., Honolulu, 1988-92; divsn. mgr. DMJM-Hawaii, Honolulu, 1992—; bd. dirs. Assist, Inc., Salt Lake City, 1986. Recipient 1st place award City and County of Honolulu, 1991. Mem. AIA (chair com. 1981-94, bd. dirs. 1986, Merit award 1991), Nat. Assn. Indsl. and Office Parks, Urban Land Inst., Rotary. Office: DMJM Hawaii 1100 Alakea St Ste 200 Honolulu HI 96813-2833*

AYERS, RENDALL PAUL, public relations consultant; b. Wichita Falls, Tex., Aug. 25, 1937; s. Richard Kelly and Gertrude Christine (Paul) A.; m. Sara Lee Hoffman, Aug. 27, 1960; children: Sydney Lynn, Reed A. BA in Journalism, U. Colo., 1961. Asst. bur. chief AP, Helena, Mont., 1960-61; asst. city editor Denver Post, 1962-67; dist. mgr. Ins. Info. Inst., Denver, 1968-69; pub. relations mgr. Denver div. Safeway Stores, Inc., 1970-74; pres. William Kostka & Assocs., Denver, 1975-80; prin. Rendall Ayers Pub. Relations, Denver, 1980-87; ptnr. Ayers, Grimm, Starzel & Assocs., Denver, 1985-87; chmn., Darcy Communications, Inc., Denver, 1988—; lectr. in field. Bd. dirs. Men's Assistance Ctr., 1970-82, pres., 1974-76; bd. dirs. Colo. Heart Assn., 1970—, pres., 1977-78, chmn. Colo. Heart Fund campaign, 1971-73; v.p. Hope for the Children, 1987-88; bd. dirs. Goodwill Industries Denver, 1970-84, v.p. 1981-84; bd. dirs. Colo. Retail Council, 1972-74, Kempe Nat. Ctr. for Prevention and Treatment Child Abuse, 1984-87, Colo. Endowment for Humanities, 1996—; dir. Colo. chpt. Am. Parkinson Disease Assn., 1993-96. Recipient award Outstanding Reporting, Denver Newspaper Guild, 1966; Outstanding Vol. award Colo. Heart Assn., 1973. Fellow Pub. Rels. Soc. Am. (accredited, pres. Colo. chpt. 1978, mem. Counselors Acad.), Sigma Delta Chi, Alpha Delta Sigma. Democrat. Unitarian. Clubs: Press, Lakewood Country, Meadow Creek Racquet (Denver). Office: 12265 W Bayaud Ave Ste 210 Denver CO 80228-2116

AYLER, MAYNARD FRANKLIN, mining engineer; b. Tacoma, Wash., Oct. 15, 1922; s. Thomas Frank and Edith Agusta (Sivear) A.; m. Marjory Annabelle Loyd, Aug. 25, 1945; children: Corliss Ann, David Franklin. Engr. of Mining, Colo. Sch. Mines, Golden, 1945; MS, Colo. Sch. Mines, 1963. Registered profl. engr., Colo. Geologist U.S. Bur. Reclamation, Denver, 1945-47; petroleum geologist Calif. Co., Denver, 1947-52; mining engr. Bur. of Mines, Denver, 1961-64, 66-77; faculty Colo. Sch. Mines, Golden, 1958-63; chief Libyan Geol. Survey, Tripoli, 1964-66; faculty U. Md. Overseas, Tripoli, 1965-66; mining cons. Golden, 1952—; pres. Oil Mining Corp., Golden, 1986—, Oil Mining Group Ltd., Seattle, 1993-94. Patentee in field. Playing mem. Jefferson Symphony, Golden, 1956-75, Denver Concert Band, 1975—, Rocky Mountain Symphony, Denver, 1988-95; playing mem., bd. dirs. Brico Symphony, Denver, 1958-85; founder, playing mem. Mostly Strauss Orch., Denver, 1980—. Mem. Am. Def. preparedness Assn. (dir. 1982—). Home and Office: 1315 Normandy Rd Golden CO 80401-4124

AYLOUSH, CYNTHIA MARIE, financial executive; b. Jackson, Mich., July 2, 1950; d. Leonard Edward and Violet Caroline (Kroeger) Ullrich; m. Abbott Selim Ayloush, June 21, 1980; children: Sasha Christine, Nadia Marie, Ramsey Abbott. AA, Fullerton Coll., 1970; diploma in fashion mdse., Brooks Coll., 1975; BS, Pepperdine U., 1980. Receptionist, Hydraflow, Commerce, Calif., 1968-74, pers. mgr., Cerritos, Calif., 1979—, treas., 1979—, corp. sec., 1985—, exec. v.p., CFO, 1995—; with sales dept. Robinson's, Cerritos, Calif., 1974-75, dept. mgr., 1975-79. Mem. Am. Soc. Pers. Adminstrs., Pers. Indsl. Rels. Assn., Mchts. and Mfrs. Assn., Cerritos C. of C. (bd. dir. 1983-89). Republican. Roman Catholic. Clubs: Soroptimist (sec. 1979—, pres. 1993-94), Damas de Caridad (sec. 1992-93), Century, Pepperdine U. Office: Hydraflow 13259 166th St Cerritos CA 90703-2203

AYRES, JANICE RUTH, social service executive; b. Idaho Falls, Idaho, Jan. 23, 1930; d. Low Ray and Frances Mae (Salem) Mason; m. Thomas Woodrow Ayres, Nov. 27, 1953 (dec. 1966); 1 child, Thomas Woodrow Jr. (dec.). MBA, U. So. Calif., 1952, M in Mass Comms., 1953. Asst. mktg. dir. Disneyland, Inc., Anaheim, Calif., 1954-59; gen. mgr. Tamasha Town & Country Club, Anaheim, Calif., 1959-65; dir. mktg. Am. Heart Assn., Santa Ana, Calif., 1966-69; state exec. dir. Nev. Assn. Mental Health, Las Vegas, 1969-71; exec. dir. Clark Co. Easter Seal Treatment Ctr., Las Vegas, 1971-73; mktg. dir., fin devel. officer So. Nev. Drug Abuse Coun., Las Vegas, 1973-74; exec. dir. Nev. Assn. Retarded Citizens, Las Vegas, 1974-75; assoc., cons. Don Luke & Assocs., Phoenix, 1976-77; program dir. Inter-Tribal Coun. Nev., Reno, 1977-79; exec. dir. Ret. Sr. Vol. Program, Carson City, Nev., 1979—; chair sr. citizen summit State of Nev., 1996; conductor workshops in field. Bd. suprs. Carson City, Nev., 1992—; commr. Carson City Parks and Recreation, 1993—; obligation bond com., legis. chair Carson City; bd. dirs. Nev. Dept. Transp., 1993; active No. Corp. for Nat. and Cmty. Svc. by Gov., 1994, V&TRR Commn., 1993, chair, 1995, vice-chmn., chmn. pub. rels. com., bd. dirs. Hist. V&TRR Bd., chair PR Cmty./V&RR Commn., vice-chair Carson City Gen. Obligation Bond Commn., Nev. Home Health Assn.; appointed liaison Carson City Sr. Citizens Bd., 1995; chmn. 1st ann. summit Rural Nev. Sr. Citizens, Carson City; pres. No. Nev. R.R. Found., 1996—; chair Tri-Co-R.R. Commn., 1995; chair Gov.'s Nev. Commn. for Corp. in Nat. and Cmty. Svc., 1997—. Named Woman of Distinction, Soroptimist Club, 1988, Outstanding Dir. of Excellence, Gov. State of Nev., 1989, Outstanding Dir., Vol. Action Ctr., J.C. Penney Co.; named to Western Fairs Assn. Hall of Fame for outstanding contbns. to the fair industry, 1995. Mem. AAUW, Am. Mgmt. Assn. (bd. dirs.), Am. Mktg. Assn., Internat. Platform Assn., Pub. Rels. Soc. Am. (chpt. pres., Silver Spike award 1996), Women Radio and TV, Nat. Soc. Fund Raising Execs., Nev. Fair and Rodeo Assn. (pres.), Nev. Assn. Transit Svcs. (bd. dirs., legis. chmn.), Nev. Women's Polit. Caucus, Nat. Women's Polit. Caucus, Am. Soc. Assn. Execs. Home: 1624 Karin Dr Carson City NV 89706-2626 Office: Ret Sr Vol Program 501 E Caroline St Carson City NV 89701

AZARI, ANN, mayor; b. June 20, 1930; d. Spencer Doran and Grace (Donaghu) Coates; m. Paul Azari, July 21, 1955; children: Aaron, Nina, Katherine, Doran, Victoria. BA, U. Calif., Berkeley, 1961; postgrad., U. Colo., Boulder, Colo. State U. Owner Caspian Ltd., 1978-81; dir. Larimer County Employment and Tng. Svcs., 1981-83; assoc. dir. Gov.'s Job Tng. Office, 1983-84; dir. info. resources/dir. field ops. Colo. Dept. Labor and Employment, Ft. Collins, 1984-87; pres., owner Ann Azari Cons., Ft. Collins, 1988—; mayor City of Ft. Collins, 1993—; chair Census 2000 adv. com. U.S. Dept. Commerce. Mem. LWV, Am. Soc. Pub. Adminstrs., Soc. Human Resource Mgmt., Am. Vocat. Assn., Rotary. Democrat. Home: 1825 Essex Dr Fort Collins CO 80525 Office: PO Box 580 Fort Collins CO 80522

AZARNOFF, DANIEL LESTER, pharmaceutical company consultant; b. Bklyn., Aug. 4, 1926; s. Samuel J. and Kate (Asarnow) A.; m. Joanne Stokes, Dec. 26, 1951; children: Rachel, Richard, Martin. BS, Rutgers U., 1947, MS, 1948; MD, U. Kans., 1955. Asst. instr. anatomy U. Kans. Med. Sch., 1949-50, research fellow, 1950-52, intern, 1955-56, resident, Nat. Heart Inst. research fellow, 1956-58, asst. prof. medicine, 1962-64, assoc. prof., 1964-68, dir. clin. pharmacology study unit, 1964-68, assoc. prof. pharmacology, 1965-68, prof. medicine and pharmacology, 1968, dir. Clin. Pharmacology-Toxicology Ctr., 1967-78, Disting. prof., 1973-78, also prof. medicine, 1965-67, pres. Sigma Xi Club, 1968-69, clin. prof. medicine, 1982—; Nat. Inst. Neurol. Diseases and Blindness spl. trainee Washington U. Sch. Medicine, St. Louis, 1958-60; asst. prof. medicine St. Louis U. Sch. Medicine, 1960-62; vis. scientist, Fulbright scholar Karolinska Inst., Stockholm, Sweden, 1968; sr. v.p. worldwide research and devel. G.D. Searle & Co., Skokie, 1978; pres. Searle Research and Devel., Skokie, 1979-85, Azarnoff Assocs., Inc., Evanston, Ill., 1987—, D.L. Azarnoff Assocs., Burlingame, Calif., 1986—; prof. pathology, clin. prof. pharmacology Northwestern U. Med. Sch., 1978-85; commr. Nat. Commn. on Orphan Diseases, 1985-87; chmn. bd. dirs. Alpha RX Corp., South San Francisco, Calif., 1992-94; professorial lectr. U. Chgo., 1978-86; dir. Second Workshop on Prins. Drug Evaluation in Man, 1970; chmn. com. on problems of drug safety NRC-NAS, 1972-76; bd. dirs. Oread, Inc., Lawrence, Kans., De Novo, Inc., Memlo Park, Calif.; chmn. Cibus Pharms., Burlingame, Calif.; cons. numerous govt. agys.; chmn. bd. dirs. Cibus Pharm., Inc., 1996—. Editor: Devel. of Drug Interactions, 1974-77, Yearbook of Drug Therapy, 1977-79; series editor: Monographs in Clin. Pharmacology, 1977-84; mem. editorial bd. Drug Investigation, 1989—, others. Served with U.S. Army, 1945-46. Recipient Ginsburg award in phys. diagnosis U. Kanas. Med. Ctr., 1953, Outstanding Intern award, 1956, Ciba award for gerontol. rsch., 1958, Rectors medal U. Helsinki, 1968; named Disting. Med. Alumnus, U. Kans. Coll. Health Sci., 1995; John and Mary R. Markle scholar, 1964, William N. Creasy vis. prof. clin. pharmacology Med. Coll. Va., 1975; Bruce Hall Meml. lectr. St. Vincents Hosp., Sydney, 1976, 7th Sir Henry Hallett Dale lectr. Johns Hopkins U. Med. Sch., 1978. Fellow ACP, N.Y. Acad. Scis., Am. Assn. Pharm. Scientists (Rsch. Achievement award in clin. scis. 1995); mem.

Am. Soc. Clin. Nutrition, Am. Nutrition Instn., Am. Soc. Pharmacology and Exptl. Therapeutics (chmn. clin. pharmacology divsn. 1969-71, mem. exec. com. 1966-73, 78-81, del. 1975-78, bd. publ. trustees), Am. Soc. Clin. Pharmacology and Therapeutics (Oscar B. Hunter Meml. award 1995), Am. Fedn. Clin. Rsch., Brit. Pharmacol. Soc., AMA (vice chmn. coun. on drugs 1971-72, editl. bd. jour.), Ctrl. Soc. Clin. Rsch., Royal Soc. for Promotion Health, Inst. Medicine of Nat. Acad. Scis., Soc. Exptl. Biology and Medicine (councillor 1976-80), Internat. Union Pharmacologists (sec. clin. pharmacology sect. 1975-81, internat. adv. com. Paris Congress 1978), GPIA (blue ribbon com. on generic medicine 1990), Sigma Xi.

BAAB, CARLTON, advertising executive. COO, CFO CKS Ptnr., Cupertino, Calif. Office: CKS Partners 10443 Bandley Dr Cupertino CA 95014*

BAACK, BRET ROLYN, plastic surgeon; b. Albuquerque, July 27, 1958; s. Rolyn Ernest and Karen Lee (Engelbert) B.; m. Elena Lisa Sandoval, Feb. 14, 1987; children: Amy, David. BS in Chemistry, U. N.Mex., 1979, BA in Biology, 1979, MD, 1983. Diplomate Am. Bd. Plastic Surgery. Asst. prof. U. N.Mex., 1990—. Fellow ACS; mem. Am Soc. Plastic and Reconstructive Surgeons (socioecon. com. 1993—), Alpha Omega Alpha, Phi Beta Kappa. Luth. Office: Univ Hosp Dept Surg 2211 Lomas Blvd NE Albuquerque NM 87106-2745

BAAS, JACQUELYNN, art historian, museum administrator; b. Grand Rapids, Mich., Feb. 14, 1948. BA in History of Art, Mich. State U.; Ph.D. in History of Art, U. Mich. Registrar U. Mich. Mus. Art, Ann Arbor, 1974-78, asst. dir., 1978-82; editor Bull. Museums of Art and Archaeology, U. Mich., 1976-82; chief curator Hood Mus. Art, Dartmouth Coll., Hanover, N.H., 1982-84, dir., 1985-89; dir. U. Calif. Berkeley Art Mus. and Pacific Film Archive, Calif., 1989—; organizer exhbns. Contbr. articles to jours. and catalogues. NEH fellow, 1972-73; Nat. Endowment Arts fellow, 1973-74, 87-88. Mem. Coll. Art Assn. Am., Print Council Am., Am. Assn. Museums, Assn. Art Mus. Dirs.. Office: U Calif Berkeley Art Mus and Pacific Film Archive 2625 Durant Ave Berkeley CA 94720-2251

BABAO, DONNA MARIE, community health, psychiatric nurse, educator; b. St. Louis, May 6, 1945; d. Wilbert C. and Cecelia (Hogan) Bremer; widowed; 1 child, Tonya J. Diploma, Henry Ford Hosp. Sch. Nursing, Detroit, 1966; BSN, Calif. State U., Sacramento, 1978, MS in Nursing, 1989; MA in Edn., Calif. State U., Chico, 1985. Cert. pub. health nurse; master tchr. cert.; cert. clin. use of interactive guided imagery. Staff nurse U. Calif. Med. Ctr., San Franicsco, 1968-72; staff and charge CCU nurse Children's Hosp. of San Francisco, 1972-78; pub. health nurse Sutter-Yuba Health Dept., Yuba City, Calif., 1979-81; instr. nursing Yuba Coll., Marysville, Calif., 1981—; psychiat. charge nurse Sunridge Hosp., Yuba City, 1994-96. Writer health column, 1986-90; chpt. to textbooks; reviewer nursing textbooks. 1st lt. Nurse Corps, U.S. Army, 1966-68. Mem. Nat. League Nursing, Calif. Tchrs. Assn., Vietnam Vets. Am., Am. Holistic Nurses Assn.

BABAYANS, EMIL, financial planner; b. Tehran, Iran, Nov. 9, 1951; came to U.S., 1969; s. Hacob and Jenik (Khatchatourian) B.; m. Annie Ashjian. B.S., U. So. Calif., 1974, M.S., 1976; Cert. fin. planner; chartered life underwriter, fin. cons. Pres. Babtech Internat., Inc., Sherman Oaks, Calif., 1975-85; sr. ptnr. Emil Babayans & Assocs., Woodland Hills, Calif., 1985—. Mem. Am. Mgmt. Assn., Nat. Assn. Life Underwriters, Inst. Cert. Fin. Planners, Internat. Assn. Fin. Planners, Am. Soc. CLU and Chartered Fin. Cons., Million Dollar Round Table. Armenian Orthodox. Office: 21700 Oxnard St Ste 1100 Woodland Hills CA 91367-3668

BABCOCK, CATHERINE MARLY, public relations executive; b. Mpls., Mar. 23, 1954; d. Edmund Page and Madolyn Evelyn (Youse) B.; m. Jeffrey C. Beyer, Jan. 20, 1979; children: Marly Elizabeth, James Conrad. BA in Polit. Sci., Macalester Coll., St. Paul, 1976; MA in Pub. Adminstrn., Univ. Wash., 1981. Welfare specialist Minn. Dept. Pub. Welfare, St. Paul, 1976-79; cmty. affairs officer First Interstate Bank, Seattle, 1981-85; asst. v.p. cmty. rels. Seattle First Nat. Bank, 1985; comm. coord. Huntington Libr., San Marino, Calif., 1988-92; comm. dir. Huntington Libr., San Marino, 1992—. Editor Huntington Calendar. Mem. Am. Assn. Mus., Pub. Rels. Soc. Am. Office: Huntington Libr Art Collection Botanical Gardens 1151 Oxford Rd San Marino CA 91108-1218

BABCOCK, DALE ARLAN, school psychologist, counselor; b. Albert Lea, Minn., Oct. 6, 1940; s. Terrance Babcock and Lorraine (Stieler) B.; m. Karen D. Wholrabe, Mar. 28, 1968; children: Jacqueline, Juliet. BS, Mankato State Coll., 1964; MS, Bemidji State Coll., 1968. Cert. sch. psychologist, Idaho; lic. profl. counselor, Idaho. Tchr. McIntosh (Minn.) Pub. Schs., 1964-65; tchr. Menahga (Minn.) Pub. Schs., 1965-68, sch. counselor, 1968-75; sch. psychologist Meridian (Idaho) Pub. Schs., 1975—; pvt. practice Meridian, 1984—; presenter workshops on depression, self-esteem, parenting, marriage, Boise, 1989—; hotline cons. Reachout, Boise, 1989—. Co-author: I Don't Know Who You Are Anymore, 1992. Mem. ACA, Nat. Bd. Cert. Counselors, Am. Mental Health Counselors Assn., Nat. Assn. Sch. Psychologists, Idaho Soc. Individual Psychology. Office: Inst for Counseling 1450 E Fairview Ave Meridian ID 83642

BABCOCK, JO, artist, educator; b. St. Louis, Feb. 24, 1954; s. Boyd Leon and Shirley Lynn (Hamm) B.; m. Diane DeVoto, Aug. 20, 1973 (div. June 1975); domestic ptnr. Kitty Costello, Oct. 1991—. Student, UCLA, 1975; BFA, San Francisco Art Inst., 1976, MFA, 1979. Color printer Rolling Stone mag., San Francisco, 1976, Outside mag., San Francisco, 1977; cameraman 1st Calif. Press, San Francisco, 1977-80; electrician Bros. Electric, San Francisco, 1984-89; assoc. prof. San Francisco Art Inst., 1989—; exhibit designer Levi Strauss & Co., 1989—. One-man shows include Zwinger Gallery, Berlin, 1987, Marcuse Pfeiffer Gallery, N.Y.C., 1988, Artspace, San Francisco, 1989, Visual Studies Workshop, Rochester, N.Y., 1990, Ctr. for the Arts, San Francisco, 1995, Terrain Gallery, San Francisco, 1997, others; exhibited in group shows at Friends of Photography Gallery, Carmel, 1976, Sao Paulo (Brazil) Bienal, San Francisco Mus. of Modern Art, 1989, Rena Bransten Gallery, San Francisco, 1991, Oliver Art Ctr., CCAC, 1991, Lieberman & Saul, N.Y., 1991, Tampa Mus. Art, 1992, San Jose Mus. Art, 1992, Palm Springs Desert Mus., 1993, 100 Years of Landscape Art in the Bay Area, M.H. de Young Mus., San Francisco, 1995, Bay Area Landscapes, 1995, Addison Gallery of Am. Art, Andover, Mass., 1997, others; represented in permanent collections at San Francisco Mus. Modern Art, Bklyn. Mus., Newport Harbor Art Mus., Lightwork, Syracuse, N.Y., La Biblioteque, Avignon, France, San Francisco Pub. Libr., San Francisco Arts Commn., George Eastman House, Rochester, N.Y., Nat. Collection, Smithsonian Instn., others. Grantee City of Oakland, 1985, N.Y. State Coun. on Arts, 1988, Nat. Endowment for Arts, 1990. Mem. Primitive Hunting Soc. Studio: 378 San Jose Ave Apt B San Francisco CA 94110-3700

BABCOCK, LEWIS THORNTON, federal judge; b. 1943. BA cum laude, U. Denver, 1965, JD, 1968; LLM, U. Va., 1968. Ptnr. Mitchell and Babcock, Rocky Ford, Colo., 1968-76; atty. City Las Animas, Colo., 1969-74, City Rocky Ford, 1970-76; asst. dist. atty. 11th Jud. Cir., La Junta, Colo., 1973-76, dist. judge, 1978-83; judge Colo. Ct. Appeals, 1983-88, U.S. Dist. Ct. Colo., Denver, 1988—; escrow and loan closing agt. FHA, Rocky Ford, 1973-76. Bd. dirs. Colo. Rural Legal Svcs. Inc., 1974-76. With Colo. N.G., 1968-74. Named to Order St. Ives. Mem. ABA, Colo. Bar Assn., Denver Bar Assn., Colo. Bar Found., North Ind. Dist. Bar Assn. Office: US Dist Ct 1929 Stout St Rm 550C Denver CO 80294-0001*

BABCOCK, ROSEMARY ANN DOUGLAS, animal behavior researcher, naturalist, biomedical librarian, multimedia writer, editor, producer; b. Wenatchee, Wash., Mar. 12, 1940; d. Donald Stephens and Myrle Alice (Miller) Douglas; m. Michael Jamieson Babcock, Aug. 18, 1963. BA magna cum laude, Lewis and Clark Coll., 1962; postgrad., Ind. U., 1965-71, San Francisco State U., 1985-92. Rsch. asst. Agrl. Rsch. Svc., USDA, Aberdeen, Idaho; tchr. music various pub. schs., Cleve., Ohio, 1966-67, Coos Bay and Parkrose, Oreg., 1962-66; teaching asst., assoc. instr. Ind. U., Bloomington, 1968-71; vis. faculty Chgo. Mus. Coll. of Roosevelt U., 1974; lectr. fine arts (music) Loyola U. Chgo., 1972-77; reader, rsch. asst., editor disability rsch. ctrs. San Francisco State U., U. Calif.-Davis, 1985-92; info. pers. Stanford (Calif.) U. Data Ctr., 1986-90; naturalist City of Palo Alto (Calif.), 1989—; libr., info. specialist Linus Pauling Inst. Sci. and Medicine, Palo Alto, 1990-96, contractor, multimedia svcs., 1996—; animal behavior researcher Chelonian Connection, Mountain View, Calif., 1979—; copy editor The Vivarium, 1991-92; pvt. cons., editor, music tchr. Contbr. articles to profl. jours. NEH fellow Summer Seminar for Coll. Tchrs., 1977. Mem. Animal Behavior Soc., Soc. for Study Amphibians and Reptiles, Bay Area Amphibian and Reptile Soc. (bd. dirs.-at-large, corr. sec.), Nature Sounds Soc., Authorware Users' Forum, Pi Kappa Lambda (hon., sec. pro tem, chmn. scholarship benefit). Home and Office: 2511 Alvin St Mountain View CA 94043-2707

BABCOCK, WALTER CHRISTIAN, JR., membrane company executive; b. Oakland, Calif., Oct. 20, 1947; s. Walter Christian and Beatrice Alice (Sommerfield) B.; m. Jacqueline Ann Mills, Dec. 30, 1971; children: Jennifer Suzanne, Rebecca Christine. BS, U. Calif., San Diego, 1969; MS, U. Oreg., 1970, PhD, 1976. V.p. Rsch. Cons. and Design, La Jolla, Calif., 1970-71; rsch. chemist Bend (Oreg.) Rsch. Inc., 1976-81, dir. separations div., 1981-86, v.p., 1983-87, pres., 1987—, chief oper. officer, 1987-89, chief exec. officer, 1989—, pres.; bd. dirs. Consep Membranes, Bend. Contbr. articles to profl. jours. Bd. dirs. St. Charles med. Ctr., Bend, 1986. Mem. Am. Chem. Soc., N.Am. Membrane Soc., Oreg. Biotech. Assn. (bd. dirs. 1990-91). Republican. Office: Bend Rsch Inc 64550 Research Rd Bend OR 97701-8583*

BACA, HILDA SUE, primary education educator; b. L.A., Aug. 25, 1963; d. Alberto and Betty (Jaramillo) B.; children: Lawrence, Luis. AA, East L.A. Coll., 1983; BA, Calif. State U., L.A., 1987; MEd, Calif. State U., Dominguez Hills, 1997. Cert. tchr., Calif., 1996. Sch. design team rep. Global Studies for Multicultural Understanding, Norwalk, Calif., 1992—; bilingual tchr. Calif. State Dept. Cultural Diversity Focus Group, Sacramento, 1996—; tchr. on spl. assignment Norwalk-La Mirada Unified Sch. Dist., 1996-97; ednl. cons. Xerox Corp./NLM Sch. Dist., Atlanta, 1995, GTE, Long Beach, Calif.; presenter Calif. Assn. Bilingual Educators, 1993, 94, 95, Computer Users in Edn., 1994, South Bay Area Reading Conf., Carson, Calif., 1994, Magnet Schs. Conf., San Jose, Asian-Pacific Conf., Carson, Norwalk-La Mirada Unified Sch. Dist. Symposium on Tech. in Schs., GTE. Mem. Assn. Mex.-Am. Educators (sec. 1992-93), Calif. Assn. Bilingual Educators (v.p. 1991-96). Democrat. Home: 3101 E 1st St Long Beach CA 90803

BACA, JOSEPH FRANCIS, state supreme court justice; b. Albuquerque, Oct. 1, 1936; s. Amado and Inez (Pino) B.; m. Dorothy Lee Burrow, June 28, 1969; children: Jolynn, Andrea, Anna Marie. BA in Edn., U. N.Mex., 1960; JD, George Washington U., 1964; LLM, U. Va., 1992. Asst. dist. atty. 1st Jud. Dist., Santa Fe, 1965-66; pvt. practice Albuquerque, 1966-72; dist. judge 2d Jud. Dist., Albuquerque, 1972-88; justice N.Mex. Supreme Ct., Santa Fe, 1989—; spl. asst. to atty. gen. Office of N.Mex. Atty. Gen., Albuquerque, 1966-71. Dem. precinct chmn., albuquerque, 1968; del. N.Mex. Constl. Conv., Santa Fe, 1969; bd. dirs. State Justice Inst., 1994—. Recipient Judge of Yr. award Peoples Commn. for Criminal Justice, 1989, Quincentennial Commemoration Achievement award La Hispanidad Com., 1992, Luchando por la Justicia award Mex. Am. Law Students Assn. U. N.Mex. Law Sch., 1993; J. William Fulbright Disting. Pub. Svc. award George Washington U. Alumni Assn., 1994, Recognition and Achievement award Commn. on Opportunities for Minorities in the Profession, 1992, others. Mem. ABA, Hispanic Nat. Bar Assn., N.Mex. Bar Assn., Albuquerque Bar Assn., Santa Fe Bar Assn., Alumni Assn. (pres. 1980-81), Kiwanis (pres. Albuquerque chpt. 1984-85), KC (dep. grand knight 1968). Roman Catholic. Office: Supreme Ct NMex PO Box 848 Santa Fe NM 87504-0848

BACA, SHERRY ANN, secondary school educator; b. Huron, S.D., Jan. 11, 1950; d. Myron Marion Moberg and Emily Ann (Matkovich) Baxter; m. Ed R. Baca, Oct. 14, 1972; children: Jamie Marie, Jennifer Lea. BS in Edn., No. Az. U., 1971, M.A. T. in Math., 1972, cert. secondary sch. principle, 1982. Cert. secondary sch. math. tchr., secondary sch. prin., supr. Math. tchr. Prescott (Ariz.) Jr. High, 1972-75; adj. math. tchr. Yavapai Coll., Prescott, 1975-84; math. tchr. grades 7-9 and dept. chmn. Granite Mt. Jr. High, Prescott, 1976-88; math. coord. Prescott Unified Schs., 1979—; math. tchr. grades 9-12 Prescott High Sch., 1988—; adj. math. instr. Prescott Coll., 1980—, No. Ariz. U., 1988—; dir. math. sci. N. Ctrl. Ariz. Consortium, 1992—; presenter and lectr. at many ednl. workshops and confs. Editor (monthly sci./ math. newsletter) Prescott Unified Schs., 1979—; contbr. articles to profl. pubs. Recipient Quality Edn. Program award, Ariz. Dept. Edn., 1981, Gov.'s citation for excellene in math. teaching, 1984, Presidential award for excellence in math. teaching, 1984,, Disting. Alumni award No. Ariz. U., 1989, State Farm Good Neighbor award, 1992, Outstanding Women in Edn. award, Delta Kappa Gamma, 1992, 93; featured in mags. and on TV; named U.S. West Tchr. of Yr. for Ariz., 1993; recipient Tandy Tech. Scholar award for excellence in math. teaching, 1995. Mem. Nat. Coun. Tchrs. of Math., Nat. Coun. Suprs. of Math., Coun. Presidential Awardees in Math. (co-historian 1989—), Ariz. Assn. Tchrs. of Math. (sec. 1984-87, v.p. 1989-91, newsletter editor 1991-95, pres. 1995—), Ariz. Sci. Tchrs. Assn., Ariz. Alliance for Math. Sci. and Tech. Edn. (bd. dirs. 1986-88, adv. bd. 1988—, continued svc. award 1991), Ariz. Math. Coalition (adv. bd. 1990—), Ariz. Math. Network (regional dir. 1989-91), Sch. Sci. and Math. Assn., Phi Delta Kappa (many offices), Alpha Delta Kappa. Office: Prescott High Sch 1050 Ruth St Prescott AZ 86301-1730

BACH, MARTIN WAYNE, stockbroker, owner antique clock stores; b. Milw., Mar. 30, 1940; s. Jack Baer and Rose (Weiss) B.; m. Roberta Sklar, Aug. 19, 1962; children: David Louis, Emily Elizabeth. BA, U. Wis., 1963. Stockbroker J. Barth & Co., Oakland, Calif., 1966-72, v.p., 1970-72; sr. v.p., stockbroker Dean Witter & Co., Oakland, 1972—; founder The TimePeace, Carmel, Calif., 1972-83, San Francisco, 1975-83, La Jolla, 1977-83; instr. fin. San Leandro, Lafayette and Hayward (Calif.) Adult Sch., 1970—. Chmn. bd. dirs. Diablo Light Opera Co., 1985-87; bd. dirs. East Bay Hosp., 1985-90. 1st lt. U.S. Army, 1963-65. Mem. Calif. Thoroughbred Breeders Assn., Calif. Thoroughbred Assn., Nat. Assn. Clock and Watch Collectors, Am. Horse Coun., East Bay Brokers Club, Blackhawk Country Club, Dean Witter Chairmen's Club, B'nai B'rith. Home: 4431 Deer Ridge Rd Danville CA 94506-6019 Office: #2 Theatre Sq Ste 322 Orinda CA 94563

BACHAR, GREGORY PAUL, English educator, editor; b. Cheektowaga, N.Y., Dec. 3, 1964; s. Paul and Jacqueline Lois (Miller) B. BA in English, UCLA, 1987; MFA in Creative Writing, U. Mass., 1994. Creative writing instr. U. Mass., Amherst, 1991-92; composition instr. Seattle Ctrl. C.C., 1994-95; editor Jack Mackerel mag./Rowhouse Press, Seattle, 1996—. Author: 47 Poems, 1994, The Shaman, 1995, Fragments, 1995, Steuben's 47, 1996, Work Stories, 1997, Party Stories, 1997, Green Clown on a Black Cross, 1997, Permeke's Constant, 1997. Program evaluator seattle Arts Commn., 1995—. Office: Jack Mackerel Magazine/Rowhouse Press PO Box 23134 Seattle WA 98102-0434

BACHARACH, JERE L., history educator, academic administrator; b. N.Y.C., Nov. 18, 1938; divorced; children: Deborah, Julia. BA, Trinity Coll., 1960; MA, Harvard U., 1962; PhD, U. Mich., 1967. Prof. history U. Wash., Seattle, 1967—, dir. Jackson Sch. Internat. Studies, 1995—. Office: U Wash Jackson Sch Internat Study PO Box 353650 Seattle WA 98195

BACHENHEIMER, BETH ADAIR, artist, educator; b. L.A., Aug. 20, 1948; d. Kur Joseph and Barbara May (Mirkin) B. Student, Chouinard Art Inst., 1967, U. Guadalajara, Mex., 1969; BA, Calif. Inst. Arts, 1972; grad., Vt. Coll., 1996. Tchr. L.A. Unified Sch. Dist., 1987—; with Met. H.S., 1993-94; chair art and spl. edn. dept. Duke Ellington H.S., 1995-96; artist in residence Irvine Art Ctr., 1993; presenter, lectr. workshops and seminars in field. One women shows include 11 E. Ashland Gallery, Phoenix, 1988, L.A. Arts Festival, 1990, El Camino Coll., Torrance, Calif., 1990, Centro Colombo Americano, Bogota Colombia, Medellin Colombia, 1991, Musco de Arte Moderno/Cámara de Comercio, Bucaramanga, Colombia, 1991, Museo Arqueológico La Merced, Cali, Colombia, 1991, Brand Art Libr., Glendale, Calif., 1991, Art Store, West Los Angeles, Calif., 1991, Museo de Moderne Arte, CartegeÑa, Colombia, 1992, Museo Bolivariano de Arte Contempo, Santa Marta, Colombia, 1992, El Area Cultural del Banco de la República, Cucuta, Colombia, 1993, Midnight Spl., Santa Monica, Calif., 1993, Post-Columbian Antiques, Venice, Calif., 1994; group shows include Calif. State U., L.A., 1971, Otis Parsons Sch. Design, L.A., 1980, L.A.C.E. Gallery, L.A., 1981, 84, Long Beach (Calif.) Mus. Art, 1983, 88, 89, 90, Mesa Coll., San Diego, 1986, 4 Zero 9 Gallery, Venice, 1987, Irvine (Calif.) Art Ctr., 1987, 93, L.A. Art Coun., 1988, Artworks, L.A., 1988, Downey (Calif.) Mus. Art, 1989, City Hall, L.A., 1990, Sumner Sch., Washington, 1991, Space Gallery, Hollywood, Calif., 1992, Da Vinci Gallery, L.A., 1993, Megaboom Gallery, Hollywood, 1993, Orange County Ctr. for Contemporary Arts, Santa Ana, Calif., 1994, Barnsdall Mcpl. Art Gallery, L.A., 1994, Bronx Mus. Art, N.Y.C., 1995, Divsn of Labor Show Museum of Contemporary Arts, 1995-96; represented in permanent collections Art Resource Ctr., Laguna Beach, Calif., Mitsui Corp., L.A., Museo de Arte Moderna de Medellin, Colombia, numerous pvt. collections; author: Power of Feminist Art, Other Vision; Other Chapter 6 on Beth Bachenheim voices. Grantee Calif. Art Coun./Nat. Endowment Arts, 1992, L.A. Cultural Affairs Dept., J.P. Getty Found., 1992, Irvine Art Ctr., 1993, L.A. Cultural Affairs Dept., 1993-94, L.A. Arts Recovery Program, 1992. Home: 1419 S Bentley Ave Apt 103 Los Angeles CA 90025-3437

BACHICHA, JOSEPH ALFRED, obstetrician, gynecologist, educator; b. Rock Springs, Wyo.; s. Alfred and Helen B. BA, Stanford U., 1977; MD, Boston U., 1982. Diplomate Am. Board of Obstetrics and Gynecology. Intern St. Luke's-Roosevelt Hosp., N.Y.C., 1982-83; resident in ob-gyn Stanford U. Hosp., Palo Alto, Calif., 1983-86; pvt. practice ob-gyn. Chgo., 1986-95; asst. prof. U. Calif., San Francisco, 1996—; cons. WHO, UN Family Planning Assn.; asst. prof. Northwestern U., Chgo., 1986-95; asst. prof. dept. ob-gyn. San Francisco Gen. Hosp., 1996—, dir. student health edn. dept. ob-gyn., 1995—; dir. Excelsior Group Health Care for Women and Children, San Francisco, 1995—; dir. low-risk obstetrics, coord. undergrad. med. edn. Prentice Women's Hosp., Chgo.; mem. Liaison Com. on Med. Edn. Contbr. articles to med. jours. Mem. Chgo. Coun. Fgn. Rels. Rotary Found. grad. fellow, 1980; mem. Harvard Macy Scholars Inst., 1995. Fellow Am. Coll. Ob-Gyn., Assn. Profs. Gynecology and Obstetrics, Internat. Coll. Surgeons, Royal Soc. Medicine; mem. AMA, APHA, Am. Assn. Maternal and Neonatal Health, Am. Fertility Soc., Chgo. Gynecol. Soc., San Francisco Med. Soc., Stanford U. Alumni Assn., Boston U. Sch. Medicine Alumni Assn., Commonwealth Club Calif. Roman Catholic.

BACHRACH, CHARLES LEWIS, advertising agency executive; b. N.Y.C., Feb. 22, 1946; s. Herbert and Lilla Clare (Blumberg) B.; m. Lois Susan Davis, Sept. 12, 1968; 1 dau., Jennifer Leigh. B.S., Ithaca (N.Y.) Coll., 1968. Assoc. producer MPO Sports Co., N.Y.C., 1968-69; unit mgr. NBC, N.Y.C., 1969; with Ogilvy & Mather, Inc., N.Y.C., 1969—; sr. v.p. broadcast Ogilvy & Mather, Inc., 1978-83, dir. Network and Programming Dept; sr. v.p. network and programming Western Internat. Media, 1983-89, exec. v.p., 1989—; pres. Western Internat. Syndication, 1983—; sr. v.p., dir. network and program purchasing Rubin Postaer & Assocs., L.A., 1990-92, exec. v.p., dir. media and resources and programming, 1992—; vis. prof. Ithaca Coll. Sch. Communications; vis. lectr. New Sch.; guest lectr. UCLA, Calif. State, L.A., Marymount Coll.; guest commentator NPR, CNN, NBC. Contbr. articles to profl. publs. Judge Internat. Emmy Awards.; Lobbyist N.Y. State pvt. colls.; bd. dirs. Caption Ctr., 1992. Recipient Disting. Alumni award Ithaca Coll., 1980, Aid to Advt. Edn. award Am. Advt. Fedn., 1986, Mavin award Advt. Age Media, 1996; named One of Top 100 Young People in Advt., 1985. Mem. AAAA (com. broadcast network and programming), TV Acad. Arts and Scis., L.A. Advt. Club (bd. dirs. 1989). Home: 3121 Dona Marta Dr Studio City CA 91604-4327 Office: Rubin Postaer & Assocs 1333 2nd St Santa Monica CA 90401-1100

BACHTEL, ANN ELIZABETH, educational consultant, researcher, educator; b. Winnipeg, Man., Can., Dec. 12, 1928; d. John Wills and Margaret Agnes (Gray) Macleod; m. Richard Earl Bachtel, Dec. 19, 1947 (dec.); children: Margaret Ann, John Macleod, Bradley Wills; m. Louis Philip Nash, June 30, 1978 (div. 1987). AB, Occidental Coll., 1947; MA, Calif. State U.-L.A., 1976; PhD, U. So. Calif., 1988. Cert. life tchr., adminstr., Calif. Elem. tchr. pub. and pvt. schs. in Calif., 1947-50, 64-77; dir. Emergency Sch. Aid Act program, spl. projects, spl. arts State of Calif., 1977-80; leader, mem. program rev. team Calif. State Dept. Edn., 1981-85; cons. Pasadena Unified Sch. Dist., 1981-86; teaching asst., adj. prof. U. So. Calif.; cons. sch. dists., state depts. internat. edn.; presenter workshops/seminars; mem. legis. task forces. Chair resource allocation com. City of Pasadena, 1982-90, Pasadena-Mishima (Japan) Sister Cities Internat. Com., 1983-87; asst. chair Pasadena-Jarvenpaa, Finland, 1990-92, chair, 1992-95; asst. chair Pasadena-Mishima, 1996—; mem. L.A. World Affairs Coun., Bonita Unified Sch. Dist. Curriculum Coun., 1990-93, Dist. Task Force Fine Arts, 1990-93, Dist. Task Force Tech., 1990-93, Dist. Handwriting Task Force, 1993; active Pasadena Hist. Soc., Pasadena Philharm. Com., Women's Com. Pasadena Symphony Assn.; deacon Pasadena Presbyn. Ch., 1989-92, elder 1997—. Emergency Sch. Aid Act grantee, 1977-81. Named to Hall of Fame Bonita Unified Sch. Dist., 1990-91. Mem. World Coun. Gifted and Talented Children, Internat. Soc. Edn. Through Art, Nat. Art Educators Assn. (dels. assembly 1988-92), Clan MacLeod Soc. (bd. dirs. So. Calif. chpt.), Phi Delta Kappa, Kappa Delta Pi, Pi Lambda Theta (Ella Victoria Dobbs Nat. Rsch. award 1989, pres. L.A chpt. 1991-95, nat. rsch. awards com. 1989-91, chair 1991-95, co-pres. region V 1993-95, 95—, Outstanding Pi Lambda Thetan in region V 1993-95), Assistance League of Pasadena. Contbr. articles to publs.; writer/editor: Arts for the Gifted and Talented, 1981; author Nat. Directory of Programs for Artistically Gifted and Talented Students, K-12.

BACHUS, BENSON FLOYD, mechanical engineer, consultant; b. LeRoy, Kans., Aug. 10, 1917; s. Perry Claude and Eva Pearl (Benson) B.; m. Ruth Elizabeth Beck, May 31, 1942; children: Carol Jean Schueler, Bruce Floyd, Linda Ruth Gadway. Degree, Hemphill Diesel Sch., Chgo., 1937; student, Sterling Coll., 1937-39; BSME, Kans. State U., 1942; postgrad., Ohio State U., 1961, Stevens Inst., 1964; MBA, Creighton U., 1967. Registered profl. engr., Ariz., Ill., Nebr. Researcher, mech. engr. Naval Ordnance Rsch. Lab., Washington, 1942-43; jr. product engr. Western Electric Co., Inc., Chgo. and Eau Claire, Wis., 1944-46; sr. devel. engr. Western Electric Co., Inc., Chgo., 1946-56; devel. engr. Western Electric Co., Inc., Omaha, 1960-66; product engr. mgr. Century Electronics and Instruments, Inc., Tulsa, Okla., 1956-60; sr. staff engr. Western Electric Co. div. AT&T Techs., Phoenix, 1966-85; cons. in field, Phoenix, 1985—; chmn. energy conservation AT&T Techs., Inc., 1973-85; advisor to student engrs. Ariz. State U., 1967-87. Patentee in field (9). Trustee Village of Westchester (Ill.), 1949-53; sec.-treas. Westchester Broadview Water Commn., 1949-53; Sunday Sch. supr. Westchester Cmty. Ch., 1949-56; vol. campaign worker, precinct committeeman, capt. Phoenix Rep. Party, 1986—. Named Westchester Family of Yr., Westchester Cmty. Ch., 1952; recipient Centennial medal Am. Soc. Engrs., 1979, Recognition and Appreciation award Sterling Coll., 1996; inducted Kans. State U. Coll. Engring. Hall of Fame, 1995. Fellow ASME (state legis. coord. 1985-86, 88-93, treas. Ariz. sect. 1971-72, sec. 1972-73, vice chmn. 1973-74, chmn. 1974-75, 50-Yr. Membership award, President's Dedicated Svc., Devotion, Leadership, Performance award 1992, Dedicated Svc. award 1993); mem. TAPPI, NSPE (Engr. of Yr. award 1979), Soc. Profl. Engrs. (editor mag. 1972-86), Ariz. Coun. Engring. and Sci. Assn., Am. Security Coun., Soc. Plastics Engrs., Weoma Sci. Club (pres. 1963-66), Tel. Pioneers Am., Order of Engrs., Elks, Airstream Wally Byam Caravan Club Internat. Trailer Club. Home and Office: 5229 N 43d St Phoenix AZ 85018

BACIGALUPA, ANDREA, art gallery owner, writer, artist; b. Balt., May 26, 1923; s. Andrew Leo and Maria Laura (Merolla) B.; m. Ellen Wilcox Williams, Oct. 9, 1952; children: Gian Andrea, Pier Francesca, Ruan Saire, Chiara Domenica, Daria Concessa. BFA, Md. Inst. of Fine Arts, 1950; postgrad., Accademia di Belli Arti, Florence, Italy, 1950-51. Owner The Studio of Gian Andrea, Santa Fe, 1954—; cons. on interior sacred art and ch. design Diocese of Amarillo, Tex., 1974—, St. Thomas More Ch., Manhattan, Kans., 1987-90, Our Lady of the Rosary Ch., Albuquerque, 1990-92, Shrine of St. Therese, Pueblo, colo. Author: Journal of Itinerant Artist, 1977, Good and Perfect Gift, 1978, Song of Guadalupana, 1979, Franco and Pirata, 1985 (column) The Santa Fe Reporter, 1989-92; feature reporting, contbr. The Santa Fe New Mexican, 1993-94; bronze sculptures in permanent installations Santa Fe City Hall, 1980, Santa Maria del Lauro, Meta di Sorrento, Italy, 1993. Sgt. U.S. Army, 1943-46, ETO. Recipient 1st Prize City of Santa Fe, 1980. Mem. AIA (1st Prize 1975). Roman Catholic.

BACINO, BIRGER GREG, lawyer; b. Loves Park, Ill., Apr. 1, 1959; s. Birger and Fonda Bacino. BS, Western Ill. U., Macomb, 1983; JD, Calif. Western Sch. Law, San Diego, 1990. Bar: Calif. 1990. Owner, atty. Law Offices of Birger Greg Bacino, San Diego, 1990—. Mem. ABA, San Diego

County Bar Assn., Consumer Attys. of San Diego, Consumer Attys. of Calif. Office: 3033 5th Ave Ste 301 San Diego CA 92103

BACIU, MICHAEL, photographer; b. Bucharest, Romania, Mar. 17, 1955; came to U.S., 1983; s. Clement Baciu and Sultanica (Chirulescu) Niculescu-Baciu; m. Doina Sherban, Aug. 18, 1980. Student, U. Bucharest, 1974-79, UCLA, Santa Cruz, 1984-90. One-man shows including Bella Gallery, Santa Monica, Calif., 1993; exhibited in groups shows at Miami Internat. Show, 1991, ArtFest, Corona del Mar, Calif., 1991; portfolios include: Art of California Mag., Color Foto Mag. (Germany), Amateur Photographer Mag. (Eng.), Photographers' Forum Mag. (Santa Barbara, Calif.). Recipient N.Y. Festivals Gold World medal 1995, Black Book 100AR awards for the 1994 Starbucks Ann. Report, Mo. Arrow award, 1996. Home and Office: 5271 Newcastle Ave # 3 Encino CA 91316-3005

BACKLUND, MICHAEL ANDERS, clinical psychologist, priest; b. San Bernardino, Calif., Mar. 13, 1951; s. James William and Dorothy Mae (Anderson) B. BA, U. San Diego, 1973, MS, 1975; MDiv, St. Patrick's Sem., Menlo Park, Calif., 1979; PhD, Pacific Grad. Sch. Psychology, Palo Alto, Calif., 1990. Lic. psychologist, Calif.; ordained Episcopal priest. Vicar Christ Ch., Calumet, Mich., 1980-82; asst. rector All Saint's Ch., Palo Alto, Calif., 1982-84; assoc. priest Grace Cathedral, San Francisco, 1984-89; psychotherapist Seattle, 1989-91; clin. psychologist San Francisco, 1990—; assoc. priest Trinity Ch., San Francisco, 1991—; clin. psychologist Calif. Dept. of Corrections, Vacaville and San Quentin, Calif., 1991-93, San Francisco, 1993—. Author: Faith and AIDS, 1990. Episcopal Ch. Found. fellow, 1985. Mem. APA, Calif. Psychol. Assn. Democrat. Office: 2041 15th St San Francisco CA 94114

BACKUS, JOHN, computer scientist; b. Phila., Dec. 3, 1924; m. Una Stannard, 1968; children: Karen, Paula. BS, Columbia U., 1949, AM, 1950; D.Univ. (hon.), U. York, Eng., 1985; ScD (hon.), U. Ariz., 1988; Docteur honoris causa, Université de Nancy 1, France, 1989; ScD (hon.), Ind. U., 1992. Programmer IBM, N.Y.C., 1950-53, mgr. programming rsch., 1954-59; staff mem. IBM T.J. Watson Rsch. Ctr., Yorktown Heights, N.Y., 1959-63; IBM fellow IBM Rsch., Yorktown Heights and San Jose, Calif., 1963-91; mgr. functional programming IBM Almaden Rsch. Ctr., San Jose, 1980-91; cons., 1991—. Mgr. Incest Info. Bay Area, 1992—. With AUS, 1943-46. Recipient W. Wallace McDowell award IEEE, 1967; Nat. medal of Sci., 1975; Harold Pender award Moore Sch. Elec. Engring., U. Pa., 1983; Achievement award Indsl. Research Inst., Inc., 1983. Fellow Am. Acad. Arts and Scis.; mem. NAS, NAE (Charles Stark Draper prize 1993), Assn. Computing Machinery (Turing award 1977). Home: 91 St Germain Ave San Francisco CA 94114-2129

BACKUS, VARDA PELLER, psychiatrist; b. Tel Aviv, Aug. 5, 1931; came to U.S., 1950; d. Moshe Peller; m. Leo Ganz, June 18, 1953 (div. Dec. 1976); children: Eric David, Karen Jennifer; m. George Edward, Jan. 18, 1977. Intern, Michael Reese Hosp., Chgo., 1957-58; resident in psychiatry, Mass. Mental Health Ctr., Boston, 1958-60; psychoanalytic tng., Boston Psychoanalytic Soc., 1960-62; BS cum laude, CCNY, 1953; MD, U. Chgo., 1957. Bd. cert. psychiatry and neurology. Pvt. practice psychiatrist Riverside, Calif., 1963-65, N.W. Clinic of Psychiatry and Neurology, Seattle, 1966; psychiatrist ct. and corrections unit Psychiat. Mental Health Cons. Svc., San Mateo County, San Mateo, Calif., 1967-69; psychiatrist for med. students Stanford (Calif.) U., 1968-69, psychiatrist Cowell Student Health Svc., 1969-77, clin. coord. Student Health Svc., 1974-77; psychiatrist Scripps Clinic Med. Group, La Jolla, Calif., 1977—. Mem. editl. bd. Jour. Hosp. and Cmty. Psychiatry, 1977-89, Am. Psychiat. Press, Inc., 1985-88. Bd. mem. La Jolla (Calif.) Chamber Musics Soc., chair program com. Recipient Appreciation for Excellent Tchg. award U. Calif., San Diego, 1985-86, Am. Coll. Psychiatrists, 1993—. Fellow APA (life constl. membership com. 1984-87); mem. San Diego Psychiat. Soc. (chair membership com. 1978-79, chair peer rev. com. 1980-82, chair com. on women 1982-84, chair ethics com. 1993-95), San Diego Soc. for Adolescent Psychiatry (pres. 1985), Sigma Alpha. Office: Scripps Clinic Med Group 10666 N Torrey Pines Rd La Jolla CA 92037-1027

BACON, LEONARD ANTHONY, accounting educator; b. Santa Fe, June 10, 1931; s. Manuel R. and Maria (Chavez) Baca; m. Patricia Balzaretti; children—Bernadine M., Jerry A., Tiffany A. B.E., U. Nebr.-Omaha, 1965; M.B.A., U. of the Americas, Mexico City, 1969; Ph.D., U. Miss., 1971. CPA; cert. mgmt. acct., internal auditor. Commd. 2d lt. U.S. Army, 1951, advanced through grades to maj., 1964, served fin. and acctg. officer mainly Korea, Vietnam; ret., 1966; asst. prof. Delta State U., Cleveland, Miss., 1971-76; assoc. prof. West Tex. State U., Canyon, 1976-79; prof. acctg. Calif. State U., Bakersfield, 1979—; cons. Kershen Co. (now Atlantic Richfield Oil Co.), Canyon, 1979-80. Contbr. articles to profl. jours. U.S., Mex., Can., papers to profl. confs. Leader Delta area Boy Scouts Am., Cleveland, 1971-76; dir. United Campus Ministry, Canyon, 1976-79; min. Kern Youth Facility, Bakersfield, 1983—, Christians in Commerce, 1990—. Paratrooper Brazilian Army, 1955. Mem. Am. Acctg. Assn., Am. Inst. CPA's, Am. Assn. Spanish Speaking CPA's, Inst. Mgmt. Accts. (pres. Bakersfield chpt. 1981-82, Most Valuable Mem. award 1981), Am. Mgmt. Assn., Inst. Mgmt. Acctg., Calif. Faculty Assn., Acad. Internat. Bus., Inst. Internal Auditors, Inst. Cost Estimators and Analysts, Alpha Kappa Psi (Dedicated Service award 1979), Omicron Delta Epsilon, Beta Gamma Sigma. Clubs: Jockey (Rio de Janeiro). Lodges: Lions (v.p. Cleveland 1971-73), Kiwanis (v.p. 1974-79, A Whale of a Guy award, Cleveland 1975, Plaque of Appreciation, 1992-93). Office: Calif State U 9001 Stockdale Hwy Bakersfield CA 93311-1022

BACON, VICKY LEE, lighting services executive; b. Oregon City, Oreg., Mar. 25, 1950; d. Herbert Kenneth and Lorean Betty (Boltz) Rushford; m. Dennis M. Bacon, Aug. 7, 1971; 1 child, Randene Tess. Student, Portland Community Coll., 1974-75, Mt. Hood Community Coll., 1976, Portland State Coll., 1979. With All Electric Constrn., Milwaukie, Oreg., 1968-70, Lighting Maintenance Co., Portland, Oreg., 1970-78; svc. mgr. GTE Sylvania Lighting Svcs., Portland, 1978-80, br. mgr., 1980-83; div. mgr. Christenson Electric Co. Inc., Portland, 1983-90, v.p. mktg. and lighting svcs., 1990-91, v.p. svc. ops. and mktg., 1991—; chmn. Oreg. Ltd. Energy Com., 1993—; vice chmn. to labor commr. Oreg. State Appenticeship Coun., 1996—. Mem. Energy Contractors Assn., Illuminating Engring. Soc., Nat. Elec. Contractors Assn. (bd. dirs. 1997—), Nat. Assn. Lighting Maintenance Contractors. Office: Christenson Electric Co Inc 111 SW Columbia St Ste 480 Portland OR 97201-5838

BACZUK, ROBERT JOSEPH, analytical chemist, consultant; b. Joliet, Ill., Feb. 7, 1937; s. Joseph Robert and Mary Agnes (Pucel) B.; m. Peggy Geraldine Johnson, Apr. 25, 1959; children: Michael John, Rebecca Lynn, Jennifer Ann, Paul Robert. AS, Weber State Coll., 1957; BS in Chemistry, U. Utah, 1962, postgrad., 1973. Clin. chemist VA Hosp., Salt Lake City, 1957-61; propulsion chemist Hercules Powder Co., Magna, Utah, 1961-67; rsch. chemist Hercules Aerospace Co., Magna, 1967-75, tech. supt., 1975-92, resident scientist, 1992-94; cons. Baczuk Enterprises, Salt Lake City, 1994—; cons., expert panel mem. SAIC, U.S. Army, Nat. Rsch. Coun., Edgewood, Md., 1994—. Contbr. articles to profl. jours. Mem. Am. Chem. Soc. (Salt Lake City sect.), U. Utah Crimson Club, Salt Lake Wood Carving Assn., Ducks Unltd. Democrat. Roman Catholic. Home: 3690 Golden Hills Ave Salt Lake City UT 84121

BADER, GERALD LOUIS, JR., lawyer; b. St. Louis, Mar. 15, 1934; s. Gerald L. and Mabel A. (Stephens) B.; (div.); children: Gerald L. III, Stephanie, Cynthia, Carlie, Deborah; m. Barbara Anne Lien, June 2, 1979; children: Matthew Stephen, Mary Rachel. BA, Washington U., 1956; LLB, U. Mich., 1959. Bar: Colo. 1960, Mo. 1960, N.Y. 1961, U.S. Supreme Ct. 1972. Assoc. White & Case, N.Y.C., 1960-62, 64-65, Hodges, Silverstein & Harrington, Denver, 1965-68; pres. Bader, Vilanueva and Feder, P.C. and predecessors, Denver, 1969—. Sec. Denver City Rep. Ctrl. Com., 1969-73; pres. Rocky Mountain Child Devel. Fedn., Denver, 1982—; dir. Ctrl. City Opera House Assocs., Denver, 1984—, The Legal Ctr., Denver, 1992—. 1st lt. U.S. Army, 1960-62. Republican. Roman Catholic. Office: Bader & Villanueva PC 1660 Wynkoop St Denver CO 80202-1115

BADERTSCHER, VERA MARIE, political consultant and freelance writer; b. Millersburg, Ohio, Mar. 4, 1939; d. Paul and Harriette V. (Anderson) Kaser; m. Kenneth Ross Badertscher, June 11, 1960; children: Kenneth Paul, Michael Alan, Brent William. BA with high distinction, BSc in Edn., Ohio State U., 1960; MA in Fine Arts, Ariz. State U., 1976. Actor, dir. Invisible Theatre, Tucson, 1979-81; campaign mgr. Lew Murphy for Mayor, Tucson, 1979, 83, Jim Kolbe for Congress, Tucson, 1982, 84; dir. dist. office Office of Congressman Jim Kolbe, Tucson, 1985-90; campaign mgr. Fife Symington for Gov., Phoenix, 1990-91; chief of staff Office of the Ariz. Gov., Phoenix, 1991; cons. Connect Consulting, Tucson, 1992—; trainer Women's Campaign Rsch. Fund, Washington, 1993-96; commentator Sta. KUAT-TV, Tucson, 1994—. Publ., editor Baja Ariz. Polit. News, Tucson, 1992-96. Bd. dirs. Invisible Theatre, Tucson, 1984-90; mem. chair so. Ariz. chpt. Ariz. Coalition for Tomorrow, Phoenix, 1991-93; bd. dirs. spl. events Tucson Ctr. for Women & Children, Tucson, 1992-96, Women's Studies Adv. Coun., 1994-96. Named one of Tucson Women on the Move YWCA, 1994. Mem. Rotary Club of Tucson (sec. 1996-97), Pima County Rep. Women (2d v.p. 1996). Office: Connect Consulting PO Box 35981 Tucson AZ 85740

BADGER, SANDRA RAE, health and physical education educator; b. Pueblo, Colo., Nov. 2, 1946; d. William Harvey and Iva Alberta (Belveal) Allenbach; m. Graeme B. Badger, Oct. 9, 1972; 1 child, Jack Edward. BA in Phys. Edn., U. So. Colo., Pueblo, 1969; MA in Arts and Humanities, Colo. Coll., 1979; postgrad., Adams State U., Alamosa, Colo., 1980-91. Cert. tchr., secondary endorsement in health and phys. edn., Colo. Head women's swimming coach Mitchell High Sch., Doherty High Sch., Colorado Springs, Colo., 1969-90; head dept. Health Edn. Doherty High Sch., 1979—; trainer student asst. program CARE, Colorado Springs, 1983—; trainer drug edn. U.S. Swim Olympic Tng. Ctr., Colorado Springs, 1988-89; trainer in track and field, Colorado Springs, 1989, 91; cons. Assocs. in Recovery Therapy, 1989—; speaker in field. Author, editor: Student Assistant Training Manual, 1983-95. Bd. dirs. ARC, Colo. Springs, 1990-96, sec., 1991-92, mem. health and safety com., 1990-95; reviewer ARC/Olympic Com. Sports Safety Tng. Manual Handbook Textbooks; mem. comprehensive health adv. com. Dept. Edn., State of Colo., Denver, 1991. Recipient Svc. award ARC, 1985, Coach of Yr. award Gazette Telegraph, 1979, 84, CARE award State of Colo., 1988, others; Gamesfield grantee, 1985; Nat. Coun. on Alcoholism grantee, 1990. Mem. NEA, Colorado Springs Edn. Assn. Office: Doherty High Sch 4515 Barnes Rd Colorado Springs CO 80917-1519

BADGLEY, JOHN ROY, architect; b. Huntington, W. Va., July 10, 1922; s. Roy Joseph and Fannie Myrtle (Limbaugh) B.; m. Janice Atwell, July 10, 1975; 1 son, Adam; children by previous marriage: Dan, Lisa, Holly, Marcus, Michael. AB, Occidental Coll., 1943; MArch, Harvard, 1949; postgrad., Centro Internazionale, Vincenza, Italy, 1959. Pvt. practice, San Luis Obispo, Calif., 1952-65; chief architect, planner Crocker Land Co., San Francisco, 1965-80; v.p. Cushman & Wakefield Inc., San Francisco, 1980-84; pvt. practice, San Rafael, Calif., 1984—; tchr. Calif. State U. at San Luis Obispo, 1952-65; bd. dirs. Ft. Mason Ctr., Angel Island Assn. Served with USCGR, 1942-54. Mem. AIA, Am. Arbitration Assn., Golden Gate Wine Soc. Home and Office: 1356 Idylberry Rd San Rafael CA 94903-1074

BADHAM, ROBERT E., former congressman; b. Los Angeles, June 9, 1929; s. Byron J. and Bess (Kissinger) B.; m. Anne Carroll; children: Sharron, Robert, William, Phyllis Badham Alzamora, Jennifer Badham Stewart. A.B., Stanford U., 1951. V.p., dir. Hoffman Hardware Co., L.A., 1955-69; mem. Calif. Assembly from 71st Dist., 1962-76, 95th-100th Congresses from 40th Calif. Dist., 1977-89; pres. The Badham Group, Polit. Cons., Sacramento, 1989—, Robert E. Badham Assocs., Govt. Rels., Newport Beach, Calif., 1989—. Author articles. Del. So. Pacific Dist. conv. Am. Luth. Ch., 1967, Nat. conv., 1968, bd. dirs. ch. com., Newport Harbor area; alt. del. Rep. Nat. Conv., 1964-68, del., 1980, 84, 88; mem. Calif. Rep. Central Com., 1962-88, Orange County Rep. Cen. Com., 1962-88. Lt. (j.g.) USNR, 1951-54. Mem. Am. Soc. Archtl. Hardware Cons., Orange Coast Assn., Am. Legion, NRA, Phi Gamma Delta. Office: 204 Emerald Ave Newport Beach CA 92662-1007

BADZEY, PETER GYULA GUSZTAV, aerospace engineer; b. L.A., Apr. 9, 1966; s. Eugene Sandor Jr. and Dora Amalia (Szabo) B.; m. Siobhan Artesani, Nov. 4, 1995. BS in Aerospace Engring., Calif. State Polytechnic U., 1989. Assoc. engr. scientist McDonnell Douglas Aerospace, Huntington Beach, Calif., 1989-90, engr. scientist, 1990-95, engrring. scientist specialist, 1995-96, sr. engring. scientist, 1996—. Comm. dir. Corpus Christi Fellowship, 1993-94, meeting planning dir., 1994-95. Mem. AIAA (sr., Nat. Student Design Competition 1st pl. award 1989), Sigma Gamma Tau. Republican. Roman Catholic. Office: McDonnell Douglas Aerospace 5301 Bolsa Ave Huntington Beach CA 92647-2048

BAEHR, ROBERT E., electrical contractor; b. Deer Lodge, Mont., Jan. 19, 1919; s. Alexander Ernest and Bertha (McKy) B.; m. Kathryn E. Kendig, Mar. 14, 1953 (dec. Apr. 1994). Student, Mont. Sch. Mines, 1937-38, Mont. State U., 1938-40. V.p. Baehr Elec. Shop Inc., Deer Lodge, 1953-78, pres., 1978—. Active Mont. Radio Amateur Civil Emergency Svc., Deer Lodge, 1975-85, Navy-Marine Corps Mil. Affiliate Radio System, 1962—; emergency coord. Powell County, Deer Lodge, 1968-88. Capt. U.S. Army, 1940-47, ETO, PTO. Mem. Vets. of Office of Strategic Svcs., Am. Radio Relay League, Masons, Blue Lodge, Royal Arch Lodge, Commandry Lodge, Shriners. Republican. Presbyterian. Home: 803 Mill St Deer Lodge MT 59722-1814

BAENA, JULIO, Spanish language and literature educator; b. Madrid, Sept. 15, 1955; came to U.S., 1980; s. Domingo and Albina (Martinez) B.; m. Obdulia Castro, Aug. 2, 1980; 1 child, Diego. Licenciado en Letras summa cum laude, U. Catolica Andres Bello, Caracas, Venezuela, 1980; MS in Spanish, Georgetown U., 1982, PhD in Spanish Lit., 1986. Lectr. Georgetown U., Washington, 1983-86; vis. asst. prof. St. Lawrence U., Canton, N.Y., 1986-87; asst. prof. Spanish U. Wyo., Laramie, 1987-89; assoc. prof. Spanish U. Colo., Boulder, 1989—. Author: El Poemario de Fray Luis de Leon, 1989, El circulo y la flecha, 1996; contbr. articles to profl. jours. Mem. MLA, Am. Assn. Tchrs. Spanish and Portuguese, Cervantes Soc. Am., Assn. Comediantes. Home: 450 S Michigan Ave Lafayette CO 80026-2242 Office: U Colo Dept Spanish & Portuguese Campus Box 278 Boulder CO 80309-0278

BAENZIGER, MARSHA SIMS, archaeologist; b. Connersville, Ind., Nov. 13, 1950; d. Theodore Edward and Marjorie Anna (Martin) Sims; m. Peter Stephen Baenziger, Mar. 13, 1976; children: Peter Émil, Aubrie Anna. BA in Anthropology and Design, Purdue U., 1974; MA in Anthropology, U. Nebr., 1990; postgrad., U. Mo., 1990—. Clk.-typist anthropology dept. Smithsonian Instn., Washington, 1976-77; editl. asst. Soil Conservation Svc., USDA, Hyattsville, Md., 1977-78; editor Soil Conservation Svc., USDA, Lanham, Md., 1978-80, Nat. Resources Conservation Svc., USDA, Lincoln, Nebr., 1989-95; vis. rsch. technician dept. agronomy U. Nebr., 1992-95, cons. State Mus., U. Nebr., 1994-95. Hispanic Emphasis Program Mgr., 1996—, Sociology Coord., 1996—. Mem. Soc. Am. Archaeology, Plains Anthropologists, Colo. Coun. Profl. Archaeologists. Home: 11768 Wonder Dr Conifer CO 80433-7206 Office: Nat Resources Conservation Svc USDA 655 Parfet St Lakewood CO 80215-5505

BAER, CYNTHIA LYNN, adult education educator; b. Elwood, Ind., July 3, 1953; d. Theodore Glen and Ednamae (Russell-Parsons) Beach; m. Mark Dean Baer (dec. June 1994); 1 child, Jonathan Chase. BA in Elem. Edn., Adams State Coll., 1975, MA in Elem. Edn., 1976. Reading tchr. grades K-6 Zuni (N.Mex.) Elem. Sch., 1976-78; secondary lang. devel. tchr. Zuni (N.Mex.) H.S., 1978-79; K-2 reading/oral lang. devel. tchr. Washington Primary, Rocky Ford, Colo., 1979-82; reading and English tchr. Ft. Wingate (N.Mex.) H.S., 1982-83; reading instr. grades 7-12 Manzanola (Colo.) H.S., 1984; reading instr. grades K-6 Cheraw (Colo.) Schs., 1985; basic skills instr., program dir. Lamar (Colo.) C.C., 1985—; judges coord. S.E. Colo. Sci. Fair, Lamar, 1988—; tchr. aid curriculum cons. Lamar C.C., 1990-91, com. mem. Kids Kollege, 1995—; adv. bd. mem. Acad. Advancement Program, Lamar, 1993—. Reader S.E. Colo. Knowledge Bowl, Lamar, 1992—; mem. S.E. Colo. Transition Governing Bd., Lamar, 1994—; chairperson Children's Ch., Lamar, 1996—; mem. Hispanic Coun., Lamar, 1996—. Mem. ASCD, Nat. Assn. for Developmental Educators, Colo. Assn. for Developmental Educators, Phi Delta Kappa, Delta Kappa Gamma (rec. sec. 1994—). Methodist. Office: Lamar Cmty Coll 2401 S Main St Lamar CO 81052-3912

BAER, D(AVID) RICHARD, film archive administrator; b. Oakland, Calif., Jan. 18, 1946; s. Oliver Albrecht and Beatrice Faye (Shrager) B. BS in Bus. Adminstrn., UCLA, 1967. Founder, pres. Hollywood Film Archive, 1972—. Author: The Film Buff's Bible of Motion Pictures, 1915-72, 1972, The Film Buff's Checklist of Motion Pictures, 1912-1979, 1979; editor Film Superlist series; reprint editor Harrison's Reports and Film Reviews, 1919-1962. Mem. Am. Political Item Collectors. Office: Hollywood Film Archive 8391 Beverly Blvd Hollywood CA 90048

BAERWALD, HANS H., political science educator; b. 1927. Asst. prof. govt. Miami U., Oxford, Ohio, 1956-61, assoc. prof., 1961-62; lectr. polit. sci. UCLA, 1962-65, assoc. prof., 1965-69, prof., 1969-91, prof. emeritus, 1992—.

BAERWALD, SUSAN GRAD, television broadcasting company executive producer; b. Long Branch, N.J., June 18, 1944; d. Bernard John and Marian (Newfield) Grad; m. Paul Baerwald, July 1, 1969; children: Joshua, Samuel. Degre des Arts and Lettres, Sorbonne, Paris, 1965; BA, Sarah Lawrence Coll., 1966. Script analyst United Artists, L.A., 1978-80; v.p. devel. Gordon/Eisner Prodns., L.A., 1980-81; mgr. mini-series and novels for TV, NBC, Burbank, Calif., 1981-82, dir. mini-series and novels for TV, 1982, v.p. mini-series and novels for TV, 1982-89; exec. producer NBC Prodns., 1989-95, Savoy Pictures TV, 1995-96, Citadel Entertainment, 1996—. Producer TV mini-series: Blind Faith, 1990, Lucky Chances (Jackie Collins), 1990, One Spl. Victory, 1991, Cruel Doubt, 1993, A Time to Heal, 1994, Inflammable, 1995. Bd. dirs. The Paper Bag Players, N.Y.C., 1974—; vol. L.A. Children's Mus., 1978-80; mem. awards com. Scott Newman Found., 1982-84; bd. dirs. L.A. Goal, 1996—. Recipient Vol. Incentive award NBC, 1983. Mem. ATAS (bd. govs. 1993—), Am. Film Inst., Hollywood Radio and TV Soc.

BAEZ, JOAN CHANDOS, folk singer; b. S.I., N.Y., Jan. 9, 1941; d. Albert V. and Joan (Bridge) B.; m. David Victor Harris, Mar. 1968 (div. 1973); 1 son, Gabriel Earl. Appeared in coffeehouses, Gate of Horn, Chgo., 1958, Ballad Room, Club 47, 1958-68, Newport (R.I.) Folk Festival, 1959-69, 85, 87, 90, 92, 93, 95, extended tours to colls. and concert halls, 1960s, appeared Town Hall and Carnegie Hall, 1962, 67, 68, U.S. tours, 1970—, concert tours in Japan, 1966, 82, Europe, 1970-73, 80, 83-84, 87-90, 93—, Australia, 1985; rec. artist for Vanguard Records, 1960-72, A&M, 1973-76, Portrait Records, 1977-80, Gold Castle Records, 1986-89, Virgin Records, 1990-93, Grapevine Label Records (UK), 1995—, Guardian Records, 1995—, European record albums, 1981, 83, award 8 gold albums, 1 gold single; albums include Ring Them Bells, 1995, Rare, Live & Classic (box set), 1993; author: Joan Baez Songbook, 1964, (biography) Daybreak, 1968, (with David Harris) Coming Out, 1971, And a Voice to Sing With, 1987, (songbook) An Then I Wrote, 1979. Extensive TV appearances and speaking tours U.S. and Can. for anti-militarism, 1967-68; visit to Dem. Republic of Vietnam, 1972, visit to war torn Bosnia-Herzegovina, 1993; founder, v.p. Inst. for Study Nonviolence (now Resource Ctr. for Nonviolence, Santa Cruz, Calif.), Palo Alto, Calif., 1965; mem. nat. adv. coun. Amnesty Internat., 1974-92; founder, pres. Humanitas/Internat. Human Rights Com., 1979-92; condr. fact-finding mission to refugee camps, S.E. Asia, Oct. 1979; began refusing payment of war taxes, 1964; arrested for civil disobedience opposing draft, Oct., Dec., 1967. Office: Diamonds & Rust Productions PO Box 1026 Menlo Park CA 94026-1026

BAGDIKIAN, BEN HAIG, journalist, emeritus university educator; b. Marash, Turkey, Jan. 30, 1920; came to U.S., 1920, naturalized, 1926; s. Aram Theodore and Daisy (Uvezian) B.; m. Elizabeth Ogasapian, Oct. 2, 1942 (div. 1972); children: Christopher Ben, Frederick Haig; m. Betty L. Medsger, 1973 (div.); m. Marlene Griffith, 1983. A.B., Clark U., 1941, LittD, 1963; LHD, Brown U., 1961, U. R.I., 1992. Reporter Springfield (Mass.) Morning Union, 1941-42; assoc. editor Periodical House, Inc., N.Y.C., 1946; successively reporter, fgn. corr., chief Washington corr. Providence Jour., 1947-62; contbg. editor Sat. Eve. Post, 1963-67; project dir. study of future U.S. news media Rand Corp., 1967-69; asst. mng. editor for nat. news Washington Post, 1970-71, asst. mng. editor, ombudsman, 1971-72; nat. corr. Columbia Journalism Review, 1972-74; prof. Grad. Sch. Journalism, U. Calif., Berkeley, 1976-90, prof. emeritus, 1990—, dean, 1985-88. Author: In the Midst of Plenty: The poor in America, 1964, The Information Machines: Their Impact on Men and the Media, 1971, The Shame of the Prisons, 1972, The Effete Conspiracy, 1972, Caged: Eight Prisoners and Their Keepers, 1976, The Media Monopoly, 1983, 5th edit., 1997, Double Vision: Reflections on My Heritage, Life and Profession, 1995; also pamphlets; contbr.: The Kennedy Circle, 1961; editor: Man's Contracting World in an Expanding Universe, 1959; bd. editors Jour. Investigative Reporters and Editors, 1980-88. Mem. steering com. Nat. Prison Project, 1974-82; trustee Clark U., 1964-76; bd. dirs. Nat. Capital Area Civil Liberties Union, 1964-66, Com. to Protect Journalists, 1981-88, Data Ctr., Oakland, Calif., 1990—; pres. Lowell Mellett Fund for Free an Responsible Press, 1965-76; acad. adv. bd. Nat. Citizens Com. for Broadcasting, 1978—; judge Ten Most Censored Stories, 1976—. Recipient George Foster Peabody award, 1951, Sidney Hillman Found. award, 1956, Most Perceptive Critic citation Am. Soc. Journalism Adminstrs., 1978, Career Achievement award Soc. Profl. Journalists, John and Catherine Zeuger award, 1996; named to R.I. Journalism Hall of Fame, 1992; fellow Ogden Reid Found., 1956, Guggenheim fellow, 1961-62. Mem. ACLU. Home: 25 Stonewall Rd Berkeley CA 94705-1414 *Personal philosophy: The most compelling principles in my life have been, in private life the pervasive need of love and trust in human relations, in public life dignity of the individual combined with devotion to the common good, in intellectual life a distrust of detachment from the human condition, and in journalism honesty and clarity.*

BAGGENSTOS, PIUS A., neurosurgeon; b. Gersau, Switzerland, May 29, 1939; came to U.S., 1972; s. Martin and Cecilia (Camenzind) B.; m. Jennifer O. Folkes, June 4, 1976; children: Martin, Peter. MD, U. Zurich, 1968. Diplomate Am. Bd. Neurol. Surgeons, Am. Bd. Pain Medicine. Resident neurology U. Hamburg, Germany, 1969-71, resident in neurosurgery, 1971-72; rotating intern Summerset Hosp., N.J., 1972; resident gen. surgery St. Peter's hosp., New Brunswick, N.J., 1972-73; resident neurosurgery Downstate Med. Ctr./ Kings County Hosp., Bklyn., 1973-78; asst. clin. prof. U. N.D. Med. Sch., Grand Forks, 1978-81; attending neurosurgeon St. James Cmty. Hosp., Butte, Mont., 1981—; attending neurosurgeon United Hosp., Grand Forks, 1978-81. Mem. Lions (pres. 1994-95). Office: Neurol/ Neurosurg Clinic 400 W Porphyry St Butte MT 59701-2312

BAGLEY, CONSTANCE ELIZABETH, lawyer, educator; b. Tucson, Dec. 18, 1952; d. Robert Porter Smith and Joanne Snow-Smith. AB in Polit. Sci. with distinction, with honors, Stanford U., 1974; JD magna cum laude, Harvard U., 1977. Bar: Calif. 1978, N.Y. 1978. Tchg. fellow Harvard U., 1975-77; assoc. Webster & Sheffield, N.Y.C., 1977-78, Heller, Ehrman, White & McAuliffe, San Francisco, 1978-79; assoc. McCutchen, Doyle, Brown & Enersen, San Francisco, 1979-84, ptnr., 1984-90; lectr. bus. law Stanford (Calif.) U., 1988-90, lectr. mgmt., 1990-91, lectr. law and mgmt., 1991-95, sr. lectr. law and mgmt., 1995—; also lectr. Stanford Exec. Program; lectr. exec. program for growing cos. Stanford U.; lectr. Stanford Mktg. Mgmt. Exec. Program; bd. dirs. Alegre Enterprises, Inc., Latina Publ. LLC; corp. practice series adv. bd. Bur. Nat. Affairs, 1984—; faculty adv. bd. Stanford Jour. Law, Bus. and Fin., 1994—, adv. bd. The Internet Lawyer, 1997—; lectr., planning com. Calif. Continuing Edn. Bar, L.A., San Francisco, 1983, 85-87; lectr. So. Area Conf., Silverado, 1988, Young Pres. Orgn. Internat. U. for Pres., Hong Kong, 1988. Author: Mergers, Acquisitions and Tender Offers, 1983, Managers and the Legal Environment: Strategies for the 21st Century, 1991, 2d edit., 1995; co-author: Negotiated Acquisitions, 1992, Cutting Edge Cases in the Legal Environment of Business, 1993, Proxy Contests and Corporate Control: Strategic Considerations, 1997, Proxy Contests and Corporate Control: Conducting the Proxy Campaign, 1997, The Entrepreneur's Guide to Business Law, 1997; mem. adv. bd. The Internet Lawyer, 1997—; contbg. editor: Calif. Bus. Law Reporter, 1984-95. Vestry mem. Trinity Episcopal Ch., San Francisco, 1984-85; vol. Moffit Hosp. U. Calif., San Francisco, 1983-84; bd. dirs. Youth and Family Assistance, Redwood City, Calif., 1996—. Mem. ABA, Acad. Legal Studies in Bus., Stanford Faculty Club, Phi Beta Kappa. Republican. Office: Stanford U Grad Sch Bus Stanford CA 94305-5015

BAGLEY, FENTON LLOYD, mechanical engineer; b. Van Wert, Ohio, Sept. 29, 1934; s. Fenton Lloyd and Mildred Ida (Ries) B.; m. Jessie Marie Barnett, June 2, 1956; children: Fenton Dean, Enora Marie, Joan Lea Bagley

McClellan. BSME, Purdue U., 1956; MSME, MIT, 1960; postgrad., Carnegie Mellon U., 1965-68. Teaching asst. MIT, Cambridge, 1957-58; project engr. Rodman Lab., Watertown, Mass., 1958-60; rsch. engr. PPG Glass Rsch. Ctr., Pitts., 1960-65; tchr. Steel Valley Tech. Sch., West Mifflin, Pa., 1965-66; assoc. prof. Allegheny C.C., Pitts., 1966-73; project engr. Snap-Tite, Inc., Union City, Pa., 1973-78; design cons. Am. Sterilizer, Erie, Pa., 1978; design engr. Reed Mfg. Co., Erie, 1979-81; ptnr. Fenton Bagley, Holman, N.Mex., 1981—. Co-author: (with Tse Woo) 4th Internat. Congress on Reology; contbr. articles to profl. jours. Capt. USAR, 1956-70. Mem. ASME (profl. practice and ethics com. 1972-78, past chmn., past vice chmn.). Home and Office: Rural Box 1 Holman NM 87723-9801

BAGLEY, JAMES R., real estate company executive; b. L.A., Mar. 13, 1956. AA in Polit. Sci., Coll. of Desert, 1977; BA in Polit. Sci., UCLA, 1979. Grad. Realtor Inst., Calif. Assn. Realtors. Broker assoc. Coldwell Banker, Twentynine Palms, Calif., 1981-90; owner, agt. Desert Locations, Twentynine Palms, 1985—; owner, broker S.W. Real Estate, Twentynine Palms, 1990—; v.p. Bd. Realtors. Planning commr. San Bernardino (Calif.) County, 1985-88; pres. Desert Mountain Divsn.-Calif. League Cities, 1992—; bd. mem. San Bernardino County Assn. Govt., 1992—; mayor Twentynine Palms City Coun., 1995. Mem. Rotary Club (pres. 1990-91, Paul Harris fellow 1991). Republican. Home: PO Box 219 Twentynine Palms CA 92277-0219

BAGNULL, GARY LYNN, accountant; b. Jefferson City, Mo., June 24, 1956; s. Paul Edward and Irma Marie (Mueller) B.; m. Julie Anne Brown, May 12, 1990. Student, Mesa C.C., San Diego, 1974-76; BS in Bus. Adminstrn. and Mgmt., U. Phoenix, San Diego, 1995. Warehouseman Navy Exch., San Diego, 1974-76; drafting aide Archtl. div. County of San Diego, 1976-77; account clk. Probation Dept., County of San Diego, 1978-80; night auditor Best Western Inn, Jefferson City, 1981-82; night auditor Sheraton Harbor Island Hotel, San Diego, 1983-85, income auditor, 1986-87, project contr., 1990-91; chief acct. Sheraton San Diego Hotel & Marina, 1988—.

BAGWELL, STEVEN KENT, newspaper editor; b. Kokomo, Ind., Mar. 22, 1948; s. Chester A. and Lois Alberta (Gordon) B.; m. Dolly Jean Demase, June 10, 1974; children: Stephanie, Bryan. BA in History, Stanford U., 1970; MA in Journalism, U. Oreg., 1973. Sportswriter Coos Bay (Oreg.) World, 1971-72; reporter, photographer Springfield (Oreg.) News, 1972-73, The Daily Astorian, Astoria, Oreg., 1973-76; reporter, copy editor, asst. city editor, assoc. city editor, mem. editl. bd. The Oreg. Statesman and Salem (Oreg.) Statesman-Jour., 1976-86; city editor, editl. page editor The Idaho Statesman, Boise, 1986-91; mng. editor The Bull., Bend, Oreg., 1991—. Mem. Atty. Gen.'s Victim's Rights Task Force, Boise, 1989-90. Recipient over 30 state, regional, and national awards for photography, newswriting, investigative reporting, pub. svc., editl. writing, among others. Mem. Soc. Profl. Journalists, Pacific N.W. Newspaper Assn., Oreg. Newspaper Assn., State Bar/Press/Broadcasters Coun., AP Mng. Editors, Oreg. Assoc. Press Editors (pres. 1994-95). Office: The Bulletin 1526 NW Hill St Bend OR 97701-1919

BAHN, GILBERT SCHUYLER, retired mechanical engineer, researcher; b. Syracuse, N.Y., Apr. 25, 1922; s. Chester Bert and Irene Eliza (Schuyler) B.; m. Iris Cummings Birch, Sept. 14, 1957 (dec.); 1 child, Gilbert Kennedy. BS, Columbia U., 1943; MS in Mech. Engring., Rensselaer Poly. Inst., 1965; PhD in Engring., Columbia Pacific U., 1979. Chem. engr. GE Co., Pittsfield, Mass., 1946-48, devel. engr., Schenectady, 1948-53; sr. thermodynamics engr. Marquardt Co., Van Nuys, Calif., 1953-54, rsch. scientist, 1954-64, rsch. cons., 1964-70; engring. specialist LTV Aerospace Corp., Hampton, Va., 1970-88; ret.; freelance rsch. FDR at Nadir, 1988—. Mem. JANNAF performance standardization working group, 1966-83, Thermochemistry Working Group, 1967-72; propr. Schuyler Tech. Libr., 1952—. Air raid warden, 1941-43; active Boy Scouts Am., 1958-78. Served to capt. USAAF, 1943-46. Recipient Silver Beaver award Boy Scouts Am., 1970. Registered profl. engr., N.Y., Calif. Mem. ASME, Combustion Inst. (sec. western states sect. 1957-71), Soc. for Preservation Book of Common Prayer. Episcopalian (vestryman 1968-70). Author: Reaction Rate Compilation for the H-O-N System, 1968, Blue and White and Evergreen: William Byron Mowery and His Novels, 1981, Oliver Norton Worden's Family, 1982, Studies in American Historical Demography to 1850, Vol. 1, 1987, Overall Population Trends, Age Profiles, and Settlement, Vol. 2, 1987, The Wordens, Representative of the Native Northern Population, Vol. 3, 1994, Computerized Treatment and Statistical Evaluation of the 1790 Federal Census for the Northern Half of the State of New York, The Ancient Worden Family in America: A Story of Growth and Migration, 1988, FDR at Nadir: 1937 & 1938, 1993, Senator Alva B. Adams of Colorado, 1993, Senator Bennett Champ Clark of Missouri, 1993, Senator Walter F. George of Georgia, 1993, Senator Guy Mark Gillette of Iowa, 1993, Senator Augustine Lonergan of Connecticut, 1993, Senator Frederick Van Nuys of Indiana, 1993, Senator Patrick Anthony Mc Carran of Nevada, 1994, Senator Ellison D. Smith of South Carolina, 1995, Senator Millard E. Tydings of Maryland, 1996, Franklin D. Roosevelt's Appointments and Itineraries for the New Deal Years in Alphabetical Fashion, 1996; founding editor Pyrodynamics, 1963-69; proceedings editor Kinetics, Equilibria and Performance of High Temperature Systems, 1960, 63, 67; contbr. articles to profl. jours.; discoverer free radical chem. species diboron monoxide, 1966. Home: 4519 N Ashtree St Moorpark CA 93021-2156

BAHR, DIANA MEYERS, humanities educator; b. Long Beach, Calif., Sept. 14, 1930; d. Omar Nelson Wood and Ruth Lulu (Harscher) Crossman; m. Ian Henry Meyers, June 25, 1950 (dec. Mar. 1973); children: Gary, Timothy, Christopher; m. Ehrhard Carl Bahr, Nov. 21, 1973. PhD in Am. Indian Studies, UCLA, 1990. Founder, dir. Northrop U. Lang. Inst., Inglewood, Calif., 1976-84; lectr. S.W. Mus., L.A., 1990—, UCLA, 1990—; cons. A&E TV Series Mysteries of the Bible, L.A., 1994, TV Series Am. Indian Issues, L.A., 1991—. Author: From Mission to Metropolis: Cupeno Indian Women in Los Angeles, 1993. Vol. lectr. Fowler Mus. Cultural History, UCLA, 1986—, Calif. Coast Walk, Sebastopal, Calif., 1994. Mem. Oral History Assn., Calif. Hist. Soc., Ethnic Arts Coun. L.A. Home: 2364 Nalin Dr Los Angeles CA 90077-1806 Office: UCLA Ctr for the Study of Women 80 Powell Los Angeles CA 90024

BAHR, EHRHARD, German language educator; b. 1932. MEd, U. Kans., 1958; PhD, U. Calif., 1968. From acting asst. prof. to prof. German, UCLA, 1968—, chmn. dept. Germanic langs., 1981-84, 93—. Co-translator: Nelly Sachs: Beryll Sees in the Night (play), 1969, Die Ironie in Goethes Spatwerk, 1972, Georg Lukacs, 1972, Ernst Bloch, 1974; editor: Kant: What is Enlightenment, 1974, Nelly Sachs, 1980, History of German Literature (3 vols.), 1987-88, others. Office: U Calif Dept Germanic Langs Los Angeles CA 90024-1539

BAHR, HOWARD MINER, sociologist, educator; b. Provo, Utah, Feb. 21, 1938; s. A. Francis and Louie Jean (Miner) B.; m. Rosemary Frances Smith, Aug. 28, 1961 (div. 1985); children: Bonnie Louise, Howard McKay, Rowena Ruth, Tanya Lavonne, Christopher J., Laura L., Stephen S., Rachel M.; m. Kathleen Slaugh, May 1, 1986; children: Alden Keith, Jonathan Andrew. B.A. with honors, Brigham Young U., 1962; M.A. in Sociology, U. Tex., 1964, Ph.D., 1965. Research asso. Columbia U., N.Y.C., 1965-68; vis. lectr., summer 1968; lectr. in sociology N.Y. U., 1967-68, Bklyn. Coll., City U. N.Y., 1967; asso. prof. sociology Wash. State U., Pullman, 1968-73; prof. Wash. State U., 1972-73, chmn. dept. rural sociology, 1971-73; prof. sociology Brigham Young U., Provo, Utah, 1973—; dir. Family Research Inst., 1977-83; fellow David M. Kennedy, 1992; vis. prof. sociology U. Va., 1976-77, 84-85. Author: Skid Row: An Introduction to Disaffiliation, 1973, Old Men Drunk and Sober, 1974, Women Alone: The Disaffiliation of Urban Females, 1976, American Ethnicity, 1979, Sunshine Widows: Adapting to Sudden Bereavement, 1980, Middletown Families, 1982, All Faithful People: Change and Continuity in Middletown's Religion, 1983, Life in Large Families, 1983, Divorce and Remarriage: Problems, Adaptations and Adjustments, 1983, Social Science Research Methods, 1984, Recent Social Trends in the United States 1960-90, 1991; contbr. articles to profl. jours.; asso. editor: Rural Sociology, 1978-83, Jour. Marriage and the Family, 1978-83. NIMH grantee, 1968-70, 71-73; NSF grantee, 1971-72, 76-80. Mem. Soc. Applied Anthropology, Rural Sociol. Assn., Nat. Coun. Family Rels. Mem. LDS Ch. Office: Brigham Young U Dept Sociology 842 SWKT Provo UT 84602

BAHR, MARY See FRITTS, MARY MADELYN

BAILEY, BRENDA MARIE, accountant; b. Chgo., June 21, 1940; d. Walter E. and Dorothy Virginia (Seyl) B.; m. Norman R. Hill, Nov. 30, 1985 (dec. Nov. 1993); 1 stepchild, Andrea M. Hill. BS, So. Ill. U., 1966. CPA, Calif. U.S. govt. gen. svcs. adminstrn. auditor U.S. Navy, Barstow, Calif., 1966-69; staff acct. Stanford Bruns & Co., San Diego, 1969-74; pvt. practice La Mesa, Calif., 1974-91; ptnr. Bailey & Dana CPAs, La Mesa, 1991—; cons. to dirs. Santa Fe Rlwy. Hist. Soc., L.A., 1988-95; treas. Pacific S.W. Rlwy. Mus., San Diego, 1979-86, San Diego Rlwy. Mus. of Balboa Park, 1981—. Mem. AICPAs, Calif. Soc. CPAs, La Mesa C. of C., Am. Soc. Women Accts. (bd. dirs. 1975-77, pub. editor 1976-77), Nat. Model R.R. assn. (mem. planning and asminstrv. com. Pacific S.W. divsn. conv. 1994), Santa Fe Rlwy. Hist. Soc. (mem. planning com., treas. ann. conv. 1986, 94, 97, asst. treas. 1995—). Republican. Presbyterian. Home: 1931 Aspen Ln El Cajon CA 92019-4178 Office: 4817 Palm Ave # 3 La Mesa CA 91941-3840

BAILEY, CHARLES RICHARD, political consultant; b. Logan, Utah, Nov. 16, 1929; s. Charles Bradshaw and Laura (Merrill) B.; m. Janice Johnson, Jan. 12, 1949; children: Steven, Kenneth, Rodger. Student, Utah State Coll., 1947-50. Salesman Am. Greetings Co., Cleve., 1955-60; wage and salary analyst The Boeing Co., Seattle, 1960-69; dep. chmn. Rep. Nat. Com., Washington, 1969-80, dir. U.S. senate campaigns, 1980-81, dep. chmn., 1981-82; chmn. Bailey Polit. Consultants, Washington and Ogden, Utah, 1982—; mem. Nat. Policy Forum Rep. Nat. Com., Washington, 1994-96; cons. Vietnam Meml. Fund, Washington, 1982; creator coll. degree program Am. Inst. Applied Politics, 1980, Utah State U., lecture series Politics=Power, 1996. Developer Sunset (Utah) city recreation programs, 1954-64; v.p. Jaycees, Sunset, 1955; mem. City Coun. Sunset, 1959, mayor, 1965. Recipient Leadership award Sunset Recreation Programs, 1961. Mem. LDS Ch. Office: Bailey Consulting 1104 Country Hills Dr Ste 304 Ogden UT 84403-2400

BAILEY, CHARLES-JAMES NICE, Linguistics educator; b. Middlesborough, Ky., May 2, 1926; s. Charles Wise and Mary Elizabeth (Nice) B. AB in Classical Philology with highest honors, Harvard U., 1950, MTh, 1955; DMin, Vanderbilt U., 1963; AM, U. Chgo., 1966, PhD, 1969. Mem. faculty dept. linguistics U. Hawaii, Manoa, 1968-71, Georgetown U., 1971-73; prof. Technische U. Berlin, 1974-91, univ.-prof. emeritus, 1991—; vis. prof. U. Mich., Ann Arbor, 1973, U. Witwatersrand, Johannesburg, 1976, U. Brunei, Darussalam, 1990; Forcheimer prof. U. Jerusalem, 1986; proprietor Orchid Land Publs.; hon. col. Staff Gov. of Ky. Fellow Netherlands Inst. Advanced Study (life), Internat. Soc. Phonetic Scis.; mem. European Acad. Scis., Arts and Letters (corr.), Linguistic Soc. Am., Soc. Linguistica Europaea, Am. Dialect Soc., Internat. Palm Soc., N.Y. Acad. Scis. Home: 16-650 Orchid Land Dr PO Box 1416 Keaau HI 96749-1416

BAILEY, DAVID H., computer scientist; married; 4 children. BS in Math., Brigham Young U., 1972; PhD in Math., Stanford U., 1976. Computer scientist U.S. Govt., Fort Meade, Md., 1976-80, TRW/ESL, Inc., Sunnyvale, Calif., 1980-82, SRI Internat., Menlo Park, Calif., 1982-84, NASA Ames Rsch. Ctr., Moffett Field, Calif., 1984—; mem. editl. bd , referee numerous profl. jours.; presenter in field; contbr. articles to profl. jours. Recipient Chauvenet prize Math. Assn. Am., 1993, Merten Hasse prize, 1993. Mem. IEEE (Sidney Fernbach award 1993), SIAM, Assn. for Computing Machinery. Office: NASA Ames Research Ctr Mail Stop T27A-1 Moffett Field CA 94035-1000

BAILEY, EXINE MARGARET ANDERSON, soprano, educator; b. Cottonwood, Minn., Jan. 4, 1922; d. Joseph Leonard and Exine Pearl (Robertson) Anderson; m. Arthur Albert Bailey, May 5, 1956. B.S., U. Minn., 1944; M.A., Columbia U., 1945; profl. diploma, 1951. Instr. Columbia U., 1947-51; faculty U. Oreg., Eugene, 1951—, prof. voice, 1966-87, coordinator voice instrn., 1969-87, prof. emeritus, 1987—; faculty dir. Salzburg, Austria, summer 1968, Europe, summer 1976; vis. prof., head vocal instrn. Columbia U., summers 1952, 59; condr. master classes for singers, developer summer program study for h.s. solo singers, U. Oreg. Sch. Music, 1988—, mem. planning com. 1998-99 MTNA Nat. Convention. Profl. singer, N.Y.C.; appearances with NBC, ABC symphonies; solo artist appearing with Portland and Eugene (Oreg.) Symphonies, other groups in Wash., Calif., Mont., Idaho, also in concert; contbr. articles, book revs. to various mags. Del. fine arts program to Ea. Europe, People to People Internat. Mission to Russia for 1990. Recipient Young Artist award N.Y.C. Singing Tchrs., 1945, Music Fedn. Club (N.Y.C.) hon. award, 1951; Kathryn Long scholar Met. Opera, 1945. Mem. Nat. Assn. Tchrs. Singing (lt. gov. 1968-72), Oreg. Music Tchrs. Assn (pres. 1974-76), Music Tchrs. Nat. Assn. (nat. voice chmn. high sch. activities 1970-74, nat. chmn. voice 1973-75, 81-85, NW chmn. collegiate activities and artists competition 1978-80, editorial com. Am. Music Tchr. jour. 1987-89), AAUP, Internat. Platform Assn., Kappa Delta Pi, Sigma Alpha Iota, Pi Kappa Lambda. Home: 17 Westbrook Way Eugene OR 97405-2074 Office: U Oreg Sch Music Eugene OR 97403 *My chief goal in life is to realize my innate talents through perfecting my innate talents and capabilities.*

BAILEY, JOHN ARTHUR, management consultant; b. Bryan, Tex., July 6, 1918; s. Arthur Chester and Laura Elizabeth (Brogdon) B.; m. Barbara Jane Elliott, Jan. 6, 1946; children: Louise B. Duback, John Elliott. BS in Mech. Engring., Tex. A & M U., 1939; M in Govt. Adminstrn. cum laude, U. Pa., 1949, PhD in Polit. Sci., 1966. Registered profl. engr., Pa. Engr. Pepsi-Cola Co., L.I., N.Y., 1946-48; mgr. Edgeworth (Pa.) Borough, 1949-53; dep. mng. dir. City of Phila., Pa., 1953-61; exec. dir. Passenger Svc. Improvement Corp., Phila., 1961-64; dep. gen. mgr. S.E. Pa. Transp. Authority, Phila., 1964-67; dir., prof. Transp. Ctr., Northwestern U., Evanston, Ill., 1967-75; v.p. Murphy Engring., Chgo., 1975-76; ptnr. L. T. Klauder & Assoc., Phila., 1976-81; pres. Transp. Sys. Assocs., Inc., Santa Fe, 1983—; pres., chmn. Soc. for Advancement of Mgmt., Phila., 1953-55, Met. Planning Coun., Chgo., 1969-73; mem. rapid transit com. Transp. Rsch. Bd., Washington, 1984-90. Mem., chmn. Santa Fe County Transp. Devel. Dist., 1993—; mem., pres. Park Plazas Cmty. Svcs. Assn., Santa Fe, 1995—; mem. N.Mex. First; mem. com. on rail transit sys. Transp. Rsch. Bd., Washington, 1992—. Fels scholar, Phila., 1948-49. Mem. Am. Pub. Works Assn. (life), Am. Soc. for Polit. & Social Scis., Santa Fe Coun. on Internat. Rels. (treas. 1995—), Cosmos Club (Washington), Tau Beta Pi. Democrat. Unitarian.

BAILEY, JULIA NANCY, epidemiologist; b. Van Nuys, Calif., Aug. 13, 1965; d. David Bertram and Elizabeth Mary (Kiss) B. BSc with honors, Concordia U., Montreal, Que., 1988; PhD, Yale U., 1996. Rsch. asst. Yale U., New Haven, 1989-96; rsch. assoc. U. Miami, Fla., 1990-94; postdoctoral fellow UCLA, 1996—. Contbr. articles to profl. jours. Yale U. fellow, 1989-96, NIMH fellow, 1996. Mem. Am. Soc. Human Genetics, Internat. Soc. Genetic Epidemiology, Soc. for Creative Anacronism. Office: UCLA 760 Westwood 47421 Los Angeles CA 90024

BAILEY, KATHERINE CHRISTINE, artist, writer; b. Glendale, Calif., Dec. 1, 1952; d. Carl Leonard and Anna Alice (Dzamka) Abrahamson; m. David Francis Bailey, Sept. 27, 1975. BA, Calif. State U., L.A., 1974, MA, 1975; PhD, U. N.Mex., 1982. Exhbns. include Miniature Painters Sculptors & Gravers Soc., Washington, Oil Pastel Assn., N.Y.C., Mont. Miniature Art Soc. Internat., many others; author: (novel) Brush With Death; also numerous short stories; participant in Cyberspace Exhbn. on internet. Recipient hon. mention in mixed media category Nat. Western Small Painting Show, Bosque Art Gallery, N.Mex., 1985, 2d pl. award in pastels, 1986, Cert. of Merit award 4th Ann. Holiday Exhbn. of Oil Pastel Assn., 1994; tuition fellow U. N.Mex., 1977; Alpha Gamma Sigma scholar, 1972. Mem. Oil Pastel Assn., Nat. Mus. Women in Arts, Mont. Miniature Art Soc., Laramie Art Guild, N.W. Pastel Soc., Phi Kappa Phi, Alpha Gamma Sigma. Home and Studio: PO Box 301 Daggett CA 92327-0301

BAILEY, MARSHA ANN, association executive; b. Muskegon, Mich., Oct. 26, 1950; d. Howard Charles and Shirley Eileen (Wiersma) B.; m. Francis Joseph Borden III, Sept. 8, 1973 (div. 1978); m. William Lawton Rader Anderson, May 3, 1986; children: (twins) Samuel Lawton Bailey Anderson, Maxwell Channing Bailey Anderson. BA (with honors), Mich. State U., 1972; MA, U. Calif., Santa Barbara, 1984. Regional advt. dir. MacElhenny, Levy & Co., Santa Barbara, 1978-80; publicist Berkus Group Archs., Santa Barbara, 1980-81; cmty. edn. dir. Rape Crisis Ctr., Santa Barbara, 1983-88; exec. dir., founder Women's Econ. Ventures, 1988—; founder Small Bus. Loan Fund of Santa Barbara, 1995; faculty mem. Santa Barbara (Calif.) City Coll., 1989-90; bd. dirs. Fund for Santa Barbara, Calif., 1990-95, Pvt. Industry Coun., Santa Barbara, 1993-96; adv. bd. Santa Barbara (Calif.) City Coll. Small Bus. Assistance Ctr., 1992-95. Named Woman of Distinction, Soroptimists Internat., Goleta, Calif., 1994, Santa Barbara County Woman of Yr., 1996. Democrat. Office: Womens Econ Ventures 1136 E Montecito St Santa Barbara CA 93103-2635

BAILEY, PAUL LEROY, career officer; b. Miami, Fla., Nov. 17, 1952; s. Edward Legare and Paula Marie (Foster) B.; m. Deborah Land Denison, Dec. 27, 1974; children: Scott Denison, Jillian Marie. BS, Fla. State Univ., 1974; MA, Webster Univ., 1977; MS, Def. Intelligence Coll., Washington, 1991. Commd. USAF, 1974, advanced through ranks to lt. col., 1995; missile crew commdr. USAF, Little Rock, 1974-79; intelligence officer USAF, various, 1979-86; intelligence specialist pentagon USAF, Washington, 1989-93; intelligence specialist U.S. Army, Washington, 1986-89; intelligence officer USAFR, Peterson AFB, Colo., 1986—; intelligence plans specialist U.S. Space Command, Peterson AFB, 1993—. Leader, Boy Scouts Am., Va., 1989-92, 4-H, Va., 1991-93. Decorated Meritorious Svc. medal, 1986, Performance awards, 1993, 94, 95, 96, Joint Svc. Commendation medal Def. Intelligence Agy., 1993; recipient Mil. Outstanding Vol. Svc. medal USAF, 1996. Mem. Res. Officer Assn. (dept. pres. 1995-96), Nat. Mil. Intelligence Assn. (chpt. v.p. 1991-93), Masonic Knights Templar (jr. warden 1996—), Masonic Royal Arch Chpt. (prin. 1995-96), Masonic Tejon 104 Lodge, Grand Chpt. Colo. (grand ambassador, rep.), Assn. Old Crows. Presbyterian. Home: 3640 Windjammer Dr Colorado Springs CO 80920-4435 Office: HQ USSpacecom/J5I 250 S Peterson Blvd Ste 116 Cheyenne Mountain AFB CO 80914-3110

BAILEY, STEPHEN FAIRCHILD, museum director and curator, ornithologist; b. Stamford, Conn., Feb. 7, 1948; s. Edwin Montgomery and Frances (Sherman) B.; m. Karen Lynn Burtness Bailey, Aug. 18, 1971 (div. July 1987); divorced. BA in Biology magna cum laude, Beloit Coll., 1971; PhD in Zoology, U. Calif., Berkeley, 1978. Museum dir. and curator Pacific Grove Mus. of Natural Hist., Calif., 1992—; collections mgr. for ornithology and mammalogy Calif. Acad. Scis., San Francisco, 1984-92; biological cons., 1979-92; adj. prof. biology San Francisco State U., 1986—; teaching Albany Adult Sch., Calif., 1979-85. Co-author Atlas of the Breeding Birds of Monterey County, 1993; co-author, photographer Audubon Society Master Guide to Birding 3 vols., 1983; regional editor American Birds jour.; contrb. articles to profl. jours. Rsch. fellowship Christensen Rsch. Inst., Papua New Guinea, 1989. Mem. Am. Birding Assn. (elected), Ecological Soc. Am. (life), Am. Ornithologists Union, Cooper Ornithological Soc. (life), Pacific Seabird Group, Soc. Preservation of Natural Hist. Collections, Phi Eta Sigma, Phi Beta Kappa. Home: 830 Sunset Dr Apt J Pacific Grove CA 93950-4729 Office: Pacific Grove Museum Natural History 165 Forest Ave Pacific Grove CA 93950-2612

BAILEY, THOMAS EVERETT, engineering company executive; b. Atlantic, Iowa, Mar. 30, 1936; s. Merritt E. and Clara May (Richardson) B.; m. Elizabeth Jane Taylor, Sept. 9, 1956; children: Thomas E., Douglas L., Steven W. BS, U. Iowa, 1959. Registered profl. engr., environ. assessor, expert witness. Engr. Calif. Dept. Water Resources, Sacramento, 1960-67; sr. engr. Calif. Water Quality Control Bd., San Luis Obispo, 1967-72; asst. div. chief, dir. water quality planning State Water Resources Control Bd., Sacramento, 1972-75, chief div. planning rsch., 1975-77, chief tech. support br., 1977-79; sr. tech. advisor Yemen Arab Republic, Sana'a, 1979-81; chief Calif. superfund program Calif. Dept. Health Svcs., Sacramento, 1982-86; prin., v.p. Kleinfelder Inc., Walnut Creek, Calif., 1986-92; also bd. dirs. Kleinfelder Inc., Walnut Creek; pres. Bailey Environ., Sacramento, 1992—; cons. engr. Contbr. articles to profl. jours. Mem. San Luis County Obispo Rep. Ctrl. Com., 1969-72, vice-chmn., 1970-71, chmn., 1971-72; vice-chmn. bd. trustees Meth. Ch., San Luis Obispo, 1970-72; mem. Contra Costa County Hazardous Materials Com., 1988-89; chmn. bus. practices com. Hazardous Waste Action Coalition, 1991-93, bd. dirs., 1992-93; mem. Calif. Remedial Action Group, co-chmn., 1991-92. With U.S. Army, 1959-60. Mem. ASCE. Office: Bailey Environ Engring 7064 Riverside Blvd Sacramento CA 95831-2956

BAILLY, JULIE ANN, manufacturing engineer; b. Pittsfield, Mass., Sept. 3, 1969; d. Richard August and Barbara Louise (Gillett) B. BS in Mfg. Engring., Worcester Polytech. Inst., 1992. Quality assurance trainee Pratt & Whitney Aircraft, East Hartford, Conn., 1992; mfg. engr. Ragsdale Machinery Ops. Alcoa Packaging Machinery, Englewood, Colo., 1993-96; indsl. engr. Mark VII Equipment, Arvada, Colo., 1996—. Mem. Am. Soc. Quality Control, Am. Welding Soc., Soc. Mfg. Engrs., Soc. Women Engrs. Office: Mark VII Equipment Inc 5981 Tennyson St Arvada CO 80003

BAIRD, ALAN C., screenwriter; b. Waterville, Maine, Jan. 5, 1951; s. Chester A. and Beverly E. (Gilbert) B. BA, Mich. State U., 1973. Pres. Souterrain Teeshirts, Nice, France, 1977-78; page NBC, N.Y.C., 1979-80; producer, dir. Random Prodns., Hollywood, Calif., 1981; writer, producer Preview STV, N.Y.C., 1982-83, Sta. KCOP-TV, Hollywood, 1983-84; writer Vidiom Prodns., Hollywood, 1985—. Author: ATS Operations, 1976, Writes of Passage, 1992; prodr. TV script Live at the Palomino, 1981; writer TV scripts Night Court, 1986, 20/60, 1986, Golden Girls, 1986, Family Ties, 1986, Max Headroom, 1987, Dave's World, 1993, movie scripts Trading Up, 1988, Merlinsky, 1989, Eleven Thousand Virgins, 1994, The Fall in Budapest, 1997. Crisis counselor San Francisco Suicide Prevention, 1975; prodn. asst. March of Dimes Telethon, Hollywood, 1985; escort, host, vol. Verdugo Hills Hosp., 1994—. Recipient Harvard Book prize Harvard U., Cambridge, Mass., 1969.

BAIRD, ALBERT WASHINGTON, III, minister; b. Beaumont, Tex., June 21, 1940; s. Albert W. and Daisy (West) B.; m. Gloria Elaine Treat, Sept. 11, 1961; children—Staci, Kristi, Keri. B.A., Abilene Christian U., 1962; B.S. in Elec. Engring., U. Tex., 1963, Ph.D., 1968. Ordained to ministry Ch. of Christ, 1984; research scientist Sperry Research Ctr., Sudbury, Mass., 1968-83; elder Boston Ch. of Christ, 1983—. Contbr. articles to sci. jours. Patentee in field. Mem. IEEE (sr.), Tau Beta Pi, Eta Kappa Nu. Fellow Tex. Atomic Energy Research Found., 1964, NASA, 1965-68. Home: 758 Maryland St El Segundo CA 90245-3117

BAIRD, DONALD ROBERT, secondary school educator; b. Boise, Idaho, June 26, 1941; s. Donald Whitney and Pauline June (Cox) B.; m. Donna Colleen Karnes, Sept. 18, 1970; children: Patricia Colleen Baird Duffey, Diane Marie. BS, Coll. Idaho, 1963; MS, Boise State U., 1980. Advanced secondary teaching cert. Instr. NESEP USN, San Diego, summers 1969-75; tchr. South Jr. H.S., Boise, 1969-80, Capital H.S., Boise, 1980—; instr. BOOST USN, San Diego, summers 1984-89; tchr. Boise State U., 1981-82; computer cons. Capital H.S., Boise, 1990—; dept. chmn. South Jr. H.S., Boise, student body advisor, 1975-76. Info. officer U.S. Naval Acad., Annapolis, Md., 1991—. Comdr. USN, 1963-66, res., 1967-89. Recipient Outstanding Educator award Acad. of Am. Educators, 1973. Mem. Nat. Coun. Tchrs. Math., Idaho Coun. Tchrs. of Math. (sec.-treas. 1983-85), Naval Res. Assn. (chpt. pres. 1985-89), Boise Edn. Assn. (rep.), Order of Demolay (chevalier 1959), Masons (Master # 39). Republican. Presbyterian. Office: Capital H S 8055 Goddard Rd Boise ID 83704-3127

BAIRD, LOURDES G., federal judge; b. 1935. BA with highest honors, UCLA, 1973, JD with honors, 1976. Asst. U.S. atty. U.S. Dist. Ct. (ctrl. dist.) Calif., L.A., 1977-83, U.S. atty., 1990-92; ptnr. Baird & Quadros, 1983-84, Baird, Munger & Myers, 1984-86; judge East L.A. Mcpl. Ct., 1986-87; adj. prof. law Loyola U., L.A., 1986-90; judge L.A. Mcpl. Ct., 1987-88, L.A. Superior Ct., 1988-90; U.S. atty. ctrl. dist. Calif., 1990-92; judge U.S. Dist. Ct. (ctrl. dist.) Calif., L.A., 1992—; faculty civil RICO program Practicing Law Inst., San Francisco, 1984-85, western regional program Nat. Inst. Trial Advocacy, Berkeley, Calif., 1987-88; adj. prof. trial advocacy Loyola U., L.A., 1987-90. Recipient Silver Achievement award for the professions YWCA, 1994; named Woman of Promise, Hispanic Womens' Coun., 1991, Alumnus of Yr., UCLA Sch. Law, 1991. Mem. Mexican-Am. Bar Assn., Calif. Women Lawyers, Hispanic Nat. Bar Assn., UCLA Sch. Law alumni Assn. (pres. 1984). Office: US Dist Ct Ctrl Dist Calif Edward R Roybal Bldg 255 E Temple St Ste 770 Los Angeles CA 90012-3334*

BAIRD, MELLON CAMPBELL, JR., electronics industry executive; b. Corsicana, Tex., Feb. 24, 1931; s. Mellon Campbell and Katherine (Wasson) B.; m. Mary Beth Norman, Dec. 27, 1956. BBA, North Tex. State U., 1957, MBA, 1961. Adminstrv. asst. VARO Inc., Garland, Tex., 1957-59; western region mgr. VARO Inc., Los Angeles, 1959-61; dir. mktg. VARO Inc., Santa Barbara, Calif., 1961-63; exec. v.p., pres. F&M Systems Co., Dallas, 1963-74; pres., bd. dirs. fed. systems group Sanders Assocs. Inc., Nashua, N.H., 1974-81; pres. def. and electronics group Eaton Corp., Cleve., 1981-86; pres., chief oper. officer, bd. dirs. Tracor Inc., Austin, 1986-87, pres., chief exec. officer, 1988-89; pres., chief exec. officer, chmn. bd. dirs. Delfin Systems, Sunnyvale, Calif., 1990—; bd. dirs. Software Spectrum Inc., Dallas, EDO Corp., College Point, N.Y. Served with USN, 1951-55. Mem. Nat. Security Indsl. Assn. (trustee 1974—), Navy League U.S. (life), Armed Forces Communications & Electronics Assn., Assn. Old Crows (life, tech. symposium chmn. 1987), Security Affairs Support Assn. (bd. dirs. 1988-91), Tex. Assn. Taxpayers (bd. dirs. 1988-91). Home: 4204 Green Cliffs Rd Austin TX 78746-1241 Office: Delfin Systems 3000 Patrick Henry Dr Santa Clara CA 95054-1814

BAKEMAN, CAROL ANN, administrative services manager, singer; b. San Francisco, Oct. 27, 1934; d. Lars Hartvig and Gwendolyne Beatrice (Zimmer) Bergh; student UCLA, 1954-62; m. Delbert Clifton Bakeman, May 16, 1959; children: Laurie Ann, Deborah Ann. Singer, Roger Wagner Chorale, 1954-92, L.A. Master Chorale, 1964-86, The Wagner Ensemble, 1991—; libr. Hughes Aircraft Co., Culver City, Calif., 1954-61; head econs. libr. Planning Rsch. Corp., L.A., 1961-63; corporate libr. Econ. Cons., Inc., L.A., 1963-68; head econs. libr. Daniel, Mann, Johnson & Mendenhall, archs. and engrs., L.A., 1969-71, corporate libr., 1971-77, mgr. info. svcs., 1978-81, mgr. info. and office svcs., 1981-83, mgr. adminstrv. svcs., 1983—, sr. assoc., 1996—; travel mgr. AECOM Tech. Corp., 1996—; pres., Creative Libr. Sys., L.A., 1974-83; libr. cons. ArchiSystems, divsn. SUMMA Corp., L.A., 1972-81, Property Rehab. Corp., Bell Gardens, Calif., 1974-75, VTN Corp., Irvine, Calif., 1974, William Pereira & Assos., 1975; mem. office sys. and bus. edn. adv. bd. Calif. State U. Northridge, 1992—. Mem. Assistance League, So. Calif., 1956-86, mem. nat. auxilaries com. 1968-72, 75-78, mem. nat. by laws com. 1970-75, mem. assoc. bd. dirs., 1966-76. Mem. AFTRA, SAG, Am. Guild Musical Artists, Adminstrv. Mgmt. Soc. (v.p. L.A. chpt. 1984-86, pres. 1986-88, internat. conf. chmn. 1988-89, internat. bd. dirs. 1988-90, internat. v.p. mgmt. edn. 1990-92), L.A. Master Chorale Assn. (bd. dirs. 1978-83), L.A. Bus. Travel Assn. (bd. dirs. 1995, 97), Nat. Bus. Travel Assn. (nat. conv. seminar com. 1994-95). Office: DMJM 3250 Wilshire Blvd Los Angeles CA 90010-1502

BAKEN, TERRY LEE, mental health services professional; b. Battle Creek, Mich., Aug. 10, 1957; s. Charles Leroy Baken and Carolyn Jean (Rose) Yuille; m. Jeannette May Yazzie, May 29, 1994; 1 child, Sarah Marie. B of Arts and Scis. in Law and Justice, Ctrl. Wash. U., Ellensberg, 1986, B of Arts and Scis. in Sociology, 1986; MEd, Heritage Coll., 1993. Surveyor Gray & Osborne Cons. Engrs., Yakima, Wash., 1980-86; correctional officer Yakima County Juvenile Ct., 1980-86; environ. engr. Wash. State Dept. of Ecology, Yakima, 1983-90; mental health profl. Ctrl. Wash. Comprehensive Mental Health, Yakima, 1990—; mem. risk mgmt. com., safety com. Ctrl. Wash. Comprehensive Mental Health, Yakima, 1993—. Vol. crisis program YWCA, Yakima, 1988, Sons of Norway, Yakima, 1996, Union Gospel Mission, Yakima, 1996. Mem. DAV, Am. Counseling Assn., Am. Mental Health Counselors Assn., Assn. for Multicultural Counseling & Devel., Loyal Order of Moose. Democrat. Mem. Ch. of Nazarene. Home: 405 W Kiowa Dr PO Box 2349 Whiteriver AZ 85941 Office: Gateway Coun Svc 405 W Kiowa Dr Whiteriver AZ 85941

BAKER, ALLISON PAIGE, photographer, musician, educator; b. Bend, Oreg., Aug. 21, 1950; s. Franklyn Lyle and Juanita Ellen (Martin) B.; m. Brenda Sue Anderson, Sept. 20, 1996. BA in Edn. and Music, Ctrl. Wash. U., 1978; postgrad., U. Portland, 1978-82. Cert. tchr., Wash. Comml. fisherman, Oreg., Wash., and Alaska, 1968-83, profl. musician and sound engr., Wash. and Oreg., 1971-84; part-time tchr., grad. asst. U. Portland, 1978-84; prof. music Mt. Hood C.C., Gresham, Oreg., 1978-84; membership and mktg. mgr. Costco Wholesale, Alaska, 1984-86; mgr. membership and adminstrn. Costco Wholesale, Clackamas, Oreg., 1986-88, supervising field engr. computer sys. N.W. region, 1988-93; receiving and front end mgr. Costco Wholesale, Tualatin, Oreg., 1993-95; computer sys. mgr. Citizens Graphic Arts, Portland, Oreg., 1995—; profl. photographer, 1995—. Bd. dirs. Oreg. Repertory Singers, Portland, 1994-96, singer, 1st tenor, 1980-83, 93—; mem. Mazamas, 1993—. Named Outstanding Musician Nat. Assn. Jazz Educators, 1974. Democrat. Office: Citizens Graphic Arts 709 SE 7th Ave Portland OR 97214-2235

BAKER, BRIDGET DOWNEY, newspaper executive; b. Eugene, Oreg., Sept. 14, 1955; d. Edwin Moody and Patricia B.; m. Guy Dominique Wood, June 30, 1977 (div. Oct. 1981); m. Rayburn Keith Kincaid, June 27, 1987; stepchildren: Benjamin, Jacob. BA in English, French and Theatre, Lewis and Clark Coll., 1977; MA in Journalism, U. Oreg., 1985. Circulation dist. supr. The Register-Guard, Eugene, 1978-80, pub. relations coordinator, 1980-83, promotion dir., 1983-86, mktg. dir., 1986-88; corp. pub. rels. dir., 1989—; bd. dirs. Guard Pub. Co., Eugene. Bd. dirs. Wilani Coun. Camp Fire, 1982-88, pres. bd. dirs., 1986-88; bd. dirs. Lane County United Way, 1982-88, community info. com. chairperson, 1982-84; chair planning com., 1987-88; bd. dirs. Eugene Opera, 1988-91, pres. bd. dirs., 1990-91. Recipient 1st pl. advt. award Editor and Pub. Mag., N.Y.C., 1984, also 1st pl. TV promotion, 1st pl. newspaper rsch. award, 1988, Best Mktg. Idea/Campaign award Oreg. Newspaper Pub. Assn., 1984, 85; named Woman of Yr., Lane County Coun. of Orgns., 1994. Mem. Internat. Mktg. Assn. (bd. dirs. Western region 1986-88, internat. bd. dirs. 1995—, 8 1st pl. Best in the West awards 1983-91), Pub. Rels. Soc. Am. (pres. Greater Oreg. chpt. 1995-96, Spotlight award 1986), Eugene C. of C. (bd. dirs. 1989-92), U. Oreg. Alumni Assn. (bd. dirs. 1990-93), Lane C.C. Found. (bd. dirs. 1995—), Town Club (bd. dirs. 1995—), Downtown Athletic Club, Eugene Yacht Club, Zonta Internat. (pres. Eugene Club 1994-96, area dir. 1997—). Republican. Office: Guard Pub Co PO Box 10188 Eugene OR 97440

BAKER, C. B., retired day care director, organizer, communicator; b. Ft. Wayne, Ind.; d. James Edwin Doelling Sr. and Susie Mae Nutter; m. Gerald R. Baker, June, 1962 (div. 1966); 1 child, Erin Lee; m. Jeffrey E. Baker, June, 1967 (div. 1972); 1 child, Shannon Rae. Student, Internat. Bus. Coll., Ft. Wayne, 1961. Expeditor Wayne Fabricating, Ft. Wayne, 1971; county adminstr. Champaign (Ill.) County Bd., 1974-76; sec. WICD-TV, Champaign, 1976-77; ops. chmn. 40 Plus of Colo., Inc., Denver, 1983, v.p., 1984-85, pres., 1985-86; co-dir. St. Anne's Extended Day Program, Denver, 1986-88; self-employed organizer Denver, 1988—. Editor The Village Voice newsletter, Savoy, Ill., 1974. Chmn. Winfield Village Swimming Pool Com., Savoy, 1975; dir. Mich. Sugar Festival, Sebewaing, 1991. Mem. Am. Bus. Women's Assn., Colo. Women's C. of C.

BAKER, CHARLES DEWITT, research and development company executive; b. Dayton, Ohio, Jan. 5, 1932; s. Donald James and Lillian Mae (Pund) B.; m. June Thordis Tandberg, June 25, 1954; children: Charles, Robert, Thomas, Michael. AA in Elec. Engring., Long Beach City Coll., 1953; ed., Boston U., 1954, Pacific Coast U., 1963, U. Utah, 1980. Registered profl. mfg. engr., Calif. Chemist Shell Oil, Torrance, Calif., 1957-60; materials and process engr. Northrop Corp., Hawthorne, Calif., 1960-63; packaging engr. Jet Propulsion Lab., Pasadena, Calif., 1963-71; med. design engr. Utah Biomed. Test Lab., Salt Lake City, 1971-78, sect. mgr., 1978-83; v.p. Tech. Rsch. Assocs., Salt Lake City, 1983-88, pres., 1988—; pres. Thordis Corp., 1980—. Contbr. articles to profl jours.; 20 patents in field. Chmn. bd. dirs. Care Holder Group, 1996—; mem. cmty. adv. com. Heart and Lung Inst., spl. study sect rev. NIH, Tech. Transfer Forum, U. Utah, 1984. Recipient Cost Reduction award NASA, 1969, New Tech. award, 1969, 71, 75. Mem. ASME, Soc. Mfg. Engrs., Utah Mfg. Assn., Acad. of Tech., Entrepreneurs and Innovators. Republican.

BAKER, CHARLES LYNN, management consultant; b. Dallas, Mar. 17, 1934; s. Leonard Allan and Nellie (Boals) B.; m. Joan Heverly, June 1, 1968; 1 child, Annette Lynn. BS in Internat. Rels. summa cum laude, Syracuse U., 1967; MA in Polit. Sci. cum laude, Auburn U., 1975. Commd. USAF, advanced through grades to col.; dep. inspector gen. USAF, Washington, 1975-80; retired USAF, 1980; mng. ptnr. T.Z. Assocs., Balt., 1980-83; pres. McDermott Internat. Trading A.G., Zurich, 1983-88; mng. dir. McDermott Internat. Gen. Svcs., Hong Kong, 1983-88; pres. Baker Assocs., Redlands, Calif., 1988—; bd. dirs. T.Z. Assocs., Balt., Environ. Scis., San Diego, Broadleaf Industries, San Diego; adj. prof. U. Redlands Grad. Bus. Sch. Author: Strategic Planning, 1987. Pres. Redlands Ballet Co., 1987-89; chmn. Redlands Cultural Art Commn., 1988—. Mem. Am. C. of C. (v.p. Hong Kong br. 1984-86), Rotary (pres. Redlands chpt. 1989-90, bd. dirs. internat. chpt. in Hong Kong 1983-85), Pres.'s Assn. (chmn. 1988—), Calif. Cultural Arts Commn. Republican. Episcopalian. Office: Baker Assocs 16047 Via Galan Rancho Santa Fe CA 92091-4014

BAKER, DANIAL EDWIN, director, consultant, pharmacy educator; b. Whitefish, Mont., May 25, 1955; s. Arby E. and Cathy Lee (Yarroll) B.; m. Patricia Samuelson, Aug. 28, 1976; 1 child, Kristin Nicole. B in Pharmacy, Wash. State U., 1978; PharmD, U. Minn., 1980. Lic. pharmacist, Wash. Instr. in pharmacology for respiratory therapist St. Paul Tech. Vocat. Inst., 1980; asst. prof. U. Okla., 1980-83; asst. prof. Wash. State U., Spokane, 1983-88, dir. Drug Info. Ctr., 1983—, assoc. prof., 1988-95; prof. Wash. State U., 1995—; dir. clin. pharmacy programs, interim chmn. pharmacy dept., 1994-95, 96—; mem. drug formulary adv. com. divsn. med. assistance Wash. Dept. Social and Health Svcs., Olympia, 1990, chmn., 1990-92; mem. cons. panel The Upjohn Co., Kalamazoo, 1990-93; mem. adv. panel on drug info. sci. U.S. Pharmacopeial Conv., Inc., Rockville, Md., 1990-95; mem. Inst. for Safe Medication Practices, Inc., Huntington Valley, Pa., 1990—, Inst. Rev. Bd., Spokane, 1992—, Wash. State U., 1993—; mem. adv. bd. Syntex Area Adv. Bd., Denver, 1994—; cons., mem. pharmacy and therapeutics com. Merck Medco Managed Care, Montvale, N.J., 1995—; mem. pharmacy and therapeutics com. Whatcom Med. Bur., Bellingham, Wash., 1996—. Mem. Nat. Ski Patrol, 49 degree North Chewelah, Wash., 1994—. Recipient Pharmacist Achievement award Merck Sharpe and Dohme, 1993. Fellow Am. Soc. Cons. Pharmacists, Am. Soc. Hosp. Pharmacists; mem. Am. Assn. Colls. Pharmacy, Am. Coll. Clin. Pharmacy, Am. Diabetes Assn., Am. Pharm. Assn., Wash. Pharmacists Assn. (senator 1991-95, continuing edn. com. 1988—, award com. 1989-95, co-chmn. undergrad. affairs com. 1990-92, del. quinquinnel conv. 1987—, Pharmacist of Yr. award 1992), Wash. Soc. Hosp. Pharmacists (coun. edn. and manpower 1989-92, chmn. 1990-92, bd. dirs. 1989-93, pres. Spokane chpt. 1992-93), Wash. Pharmacy Coun., Drug Info. Assn. Republican. Office: Wash State U 601 W 1st Ave Spokane WA 99204-0317

BAKER, DANIEL NEIL, physicist; b. Postville, Iowa, Nov. 10, 1948; s. Joseph N. and Alvira H. (Amundson) B.; m. A. Victoria Vaughan, Aug. 14, 1971. BA, U. Iowa, 1969, MS, 1973, PhD, 1974. Research aide dept. physics U. Iowa, Iowa City, 1967-69, grad. research asst., 1970-74, postdoctoral research assoc., 1974-75; research fellow Calif. Inst. Tech., Pasadena, 1975-78; mem. staff Los Alamos (N.Mex.) Nat. Lab., 1978-81, group leader, 1981-87; chief Lab. for Extraterrestrial Physics NASA, Goddard Space Flight Ctr., Greenbelt, Md., 1987-94; dir. Lab. for Atmospheric and Space Physics U. Colo., Boulder, 1994—; chmn. data sys. users group NASA, Washington, 1982-90, tech. cons., 1985—, mem. space physics mgmt. and ops. com., adv. coun. Space Sci. and Applications, 1988-92, grand tour cluster mission study scientist, 1991-95; mem. com. solar and space physics NAS, Washington, 1983-86, com. data mgmt. and computation, 1986-88, space studies bd., 1995—; mem. panel on long-term observations NRC, Washington, 1985-88, commn. D Sci. Com. on Solar-Terrestrial Physics, 1986-90, U.S. coordinating com. Solar Terrestrial Energy Program, 1988—, U.S. STEP project scientist, 1990—, Geospace Environ. Modeling com. NSF, 1988-91; project sci. NASA small explorer program, prin. investigator NASA rocket program, numerous NASA ESA satellite missions in field; project sci. Internat. Solar-Terrestrial Physics POLAR Space craft Mission, 1992-94; U.S. rep. Internat. Assn. Geomagnetism and Aeronomy, 1996—. Assoc. editor Geophys. Research Letters, Washington, 1986-88; mem. space tech. rev. bd. Los Alamos Nat. Lab.; contbr. numerous articles to profl. jours. Mem. external adv. com. Boston U. Ctr. for Space Rsch., 1989-94; mem. sci. vis. com. U. Md. Inst. Phys. Sci. and Tech., 1990-94; mem. external adv. com. Solar-Terrestrial Environ. Lab., Nagoya (Japan) U., 1995—. NSF research fellow U. Iowa, 1970-74; grantee Inst. Geophys. and Planetary Physics U. Calif., 1980-89. Fellow Am. Geophys. Union (mem. natural hazards panel 1996—); mem. AAAS, Am. Geophys. Union (geomagnetism assessment panel 1987-88, sec. magnetospheric sect. 1988-90), Internat. Acad. Astronautics, Sigma Xi. Office: U Colo Lab Atmospheric & Space Physics Campus Box 590 Boulder CO 80309

BAKER, DAVID L., university administrator; b. Louisville, Nov. 23, 1940; s. David L. Baker and Evelyn Diana (Beville) Woods; m. Mary Anne King, Sept. 7, 1961 (div. Aug. 1984); m. Sara Marie Martin, May 25, 1985; children: David III, Margaret Anne, Simon. BA, U. Louisville, 1963, JD, 1969. Bar: Wyo., Ky., U.S. Supreme Ct. Dir. pub. rels. U. Louisville, 1968-76, univ. counsel, 1976-86; spl. asst. to pres. U. Wyo., Laramie, 1986—. Home: 1910 Sheridan Ave Laramie WY 82070 Office: University of Wyoming University Sta Laramie WY 82071

BAKER, DENNIS MICHAEL, counselor, retired law enforcement officer; b. Houston, July 9, 1952; s. Percy M. Jr. and Marguite (Montgomery) B. BA, U. North Tex., Denton, 1991; MA, U. Colo., Colorado Springs, 1996. Cert. probation officer, Tex.; specialized tng. in child abuse, sexual assault, family violence and crisis intervention. Asst. dir. Help House Inc., Denton, 1974-77; juvenile detective Lewisville (Tex.) Police Dept., 1978-81; detective Denton Police Dept., 1981-86, sr. detective in charge child abuse investigations, 1987-91; crime victims coord. Denton Count, Sheriff's Dept., Denton, 1991-92; probation officer Denton County Adult Probation Dept., Denton, 1992-93; counselor in pvt. practice Colorado Springs, 1993—. Recipient Appreciation award Southwestern Tex. State U., 1980, Loyalty award VFW, 1984, Appreciation award Denton County Task Force on Family Violence, 1986, others. Mem. ACA, Nat. Assn. Forensic Counselors. Home: 720 Duclo Manitou Springs CO 80829 Office: 2211 W Colorado Ave Ste A Colorado Springs CO 80904-3324

BAKER, DON ROBERT, chemist, inventor; b. Salt Lake City, Apr. 6, 1933; s. Ralph H. and Ruth Eve (Thalmann) B.; m. Shirley May Nelson, Nov. 20, 1954 (dec. 1993); children: Robert, David, George, Barbara; m. Shirlee Ann Call, Sept. 17, 1994. AA, Sacramento City Coll., 1953; AB, Calif. State U., Sacramento, 1955; PhD, U. Calif., Berkeley, 1959. Sr. rsch. chemist Stauffer Chem. Co., Richmond, Calif., 1958-72, rsch. assoc., 1970-74, supr., 1974-85; sr. rsch. assoc. ICI Ams. Inc. Zeneca Ag Products, Richmond, 1985—. Editor Calif. Chemists Alert, 1986—, Synthesis and Chemistry of Agrochems., 1987, 90, 92, 95; contbr. articles to profl. jours.; over 200 patents. Recipient Zeneca Patent award, 1996. Mem. Am. Chem. Soc. (chmn. Calif. sect. 1973, councilor 1971—, chmn. nat. divsn. profl. rels. 1980, coordinating com. Calif. sects. 1970—, vice-chmn. agrochem. divsn. 1993, chmn. agrochems. divsn. 1995, Fellow award 1992, Walter Petersen award 1991), Plant Growth Regulator Soc., Orchid Soc. Calif. (pres. 1979-80), Oakland Family History Ctr. (libr. 1967—). Republican. Mormon. Home: 15 Muth Dr Orinda CA 94563-2805 Office: Zeneca Ag Products 1200 S 47th St Richmond CA 94804-4610

BAKER, EDWIN MOODY, retired newspaper publisher; b. Cleve., Dec. 20, 1923; s. Alton Fletcher and Mildred Elizabeth (Moody) B.; m. Patricia Petersen, 1954 (dec. 1983); children: Bridget Baker Kincaid, Amanda Baker Barber, Jonathan; m. Marie Kottkamp Randall, 1984; children: Steven, Mark, Bruce Randall. B.S. in Bus. Adminstrn., U. Oreg., 1948. With Eugene (Oreg.) Register-Guard, 1948-88, successively advt. mgr., bus. mgr., gen. mgr., pub., pres., chmn. bd. Guard Pub. Co.; pres. Community Newspapers, Inc., Beaverton, Oreg., v.p. N.W. Web. Mem. exec. bd. Oreg. Trail Council, Boy Scouts Am., 1953—, pres. 1960-61, chmn. Region XI Area I (Northwest) 1971, pres., 1972, mem. nat. exec. bd., 1971-72, nat. adv. council, 1972-82; trustee U. Oreg. Found., 1975-90, Lane Community Coll.; bd. dirs. Oreg. Community Found., 1982-90; Oreg. Hist. Soc., 1988-92; trustee Eugene Arts Found., 1980-85; pres. Oreg. Pacific Econ. Devel. Corp., 1984-85; 2d v.p. Eugene Springfield Met. Ptnrship.; mem., chmn. Sister City com., 1986-88. Served with AUS, World War II. Decorated Bronze Star, Purple Heart; recipient Silver Beaver award, Boy Scouts Am., 1962, Silver Antelope, 1965, Pioneer award U. Oreg., 1982, Disting. Eagle Scout, 1982, Awbrey Watzig award Lewis and Clark Coll., 1988; named Eugene First Citizen, 1983. Mem. Am. Newspaper Pubs. Assn. (research inst. lab. com. 1978-79), Oreg. Newspaper Pubs. Assn. (dir. 1982-90, pres. 1988-89), U. Oreg. Pres. Assocs., Nat. Assn. Fund Raising Execs. (vol. 1994 Oreg. chpt., Fund Raiser of Yr. 1993), Rotary, Eugene Country Club. Home: 2121 Kimberly Cir Eugene OR 97405-5821 Office: PO Box 10188-2188 975 High St Eugene OR 97401-3204

BAKER, EDWIN STUART, retired computer consultant; b. Ottumwa, Iowa, Feb. 14, 1944; s. Edwin Moore and Geraldine Vivian (Irby) B; m. Wilma Jeanne Parker, 1968 (div. 1970). Student, Whitman Coll., 1962-64; BS, Oreg. State U., 1978. Programmer agrl. engring. dept. Oreg. State U., Corvallis, 1977-78, rsch. asst., 1979-83, sr. rsch. asst., 1984-89; measurement standards specialist Oreg. Dept. Agr., Salem, 1990-93; cons. in field. Mem. IEEE, Assn for Computing Machinery, Am. Legion, DAV, NRA, Nat. Intercollegiate Rodeo Assn., 59ers Svc. Club. Home: PO Box 68 Fairview OR 97024-0068 Office: Oreg Dept Agr Measurements Standards Divsn Salem OR 97310

BAKER, GINGER LEE, oncological and cardiac nurse; b. East Chicago, Ind., June 6, 1944; d. William Lester and Edith (Craig) Savitz; m. Ray Baker, Aug. 5, 1988; children: Darcey, Eric, Ronald, Donald, Scott, Angela, Cody, Casey. Assocs., Purdue U., 1983; BSN, U. Phoenix, 1994. Cert. oncology nurse. Staff nurse St. Catherine Hosp., East Chicago; staff coord. Riverside (Calif.) Community Hosp., now shift coord. Recipient Women of Achievement award YWCA, 1987, ACE award, 1994. Mem. Oncology Nursing Soc., ACLS.

BAKER, GRANT CODY, civil engineering educator; b. Eugene, Oreg., May 16, 1956; s. Irwin Gerald and Louise (Powell) B.; m. Tina Louise Denton, Apr. 9, 1988; children: Jessica, Calvin, Benjamin. BSChemE, U. Wash., 1978; MS in Mining Engring., U. Alaska, 1983, PhD in Geophysics, 1987. Chem. engr. UOP, Chgo., 1978-79; comml. fisherman F/V Patricia Sue, Anchorage, 1979-80; asst. prof. mech. engring. U. Alaska, Fairbanks, 1988-94; asst. prof. civil engring. U. Alaska, Anchorage, 1994—; author, pub. Edutech, Anchorage, 1992—. Author: Bridge to Engineering, 1993, FORTRAN Reference Programs, 1995, ANSI C Reference Programs, 1996. Named Mech. Engring. Prof. of Yr., 1996, U. Alaska student chpt. ASME, ASCE, 1993, 94. Republican. Baptist. Home: PO Box 240986 Anchorage AK 99524 Office: U Alaska 3211 Providence Dr Anchorage AK 99508

BAKER, ISRAEL, musician, music educator; b. Chgo., Feb. 11, 1921. Studied with Adolf pick, Chgo. Conservatory; studied with Louis Persinger, Juilliard Sch. Music; Jacques Gordon, Bronislaw Huberman. Soloist Various orchs.; concertmaster; mem. Pacific Art Trio; prof. music Scripps Coll., Claremont, Calif. Numerous chamber music appearances; 2nd violinist Heifetz-Platigorsky Chamber Concerts; featured in Schoenberg's Concerto, Berg's Chamber Concerto; recordings as soloist include works by Ives, Antheil, Kubik, Stravinsky. Office: Scripps Coll 1030 Columbia Claremont CA 91711

BAKER, JAMES RUPERT, English educator; b. 1925. Co-founder, mem. editl. bd. Twentieth Century Lit., 1955—; asst. prof. English, San Diego State U., 1956-61, assoc. prof., 1962-67, prof., 1967—. adv. editor James Joyce Quarterly, 1966-85; author: William Golding: A Critical Study, 1965, Critical Essays on William Golding, 1988; editor: Poems of Bishop Henry King, 1960, Casebook Edition of William Golding's Lord of the Flies, 1964, James Joyce's Dubliners: A Critical Handbook, 1968. Office: San Diego State U Dept English San Diego CA 92182

BAKER, JOSEPH RODERICK, III, aviculturist; b. Middletown, Ohio, Sept. 26, 1947; s. Joseph Roderick and Lois Patricia (Barnhart) B. BS in Math., Rensselaer Poly. Tech., 1969. Systems rep. Burroughs Corp., Honolulu, 1973-80; mgr. data processing Kenault Inc., Honolulu, 1980-81; v.p. Software Solutions Inc., Honolulu, 1982-83; br. mgr. DataPhase Corp., Honolulu, 1983-88; pres. Birds of Paradise, Kurtistown, Hawaii, 1987—. Lt. (j.g.) USN, 1969-73. Mem. Am. Fedn. Aviculture, Nat. Cockatoo Soc., Macaw Soc. Am., Eclectus Soc., Am. Contract Bridge League, Pionus Breeders Assn., Amazona Soc.

BAKER, KAREN, newspaper editor. Mng. editor Idaho Statesman, Boisie. Office: Idaho Statesman 1200 N Curtis Rd Boise ID 83707

BAKER, KATHLEEN ANN, student services counselor; b. Seattle, Oct. 6, 1935; d. Clifford A. and Inez E. (Clark) Duncan; m. David G. Baker, June 11, 1955; children: Mark Allen, Susan Baker Abyad. BS in Home Econs., UCLA, 1958, postgrad., 1959; MA in Human Devel., Pacific Oaks Coll., 1976. Calif. Community Coll. Teaching Credentials; cert. nursery sch. and presch. educator, community coll. supr. Teaching asst. UCLA, 1958-59; coll. instr. Fullerton (Calif.) Coll., 1959-61, 73-83; dir. Placentia (Calif.) Coop Nursery Sch., 1970-72; coll. counselor Fullerton Coll., 1983-85, dir. sch. and coll. rels., 1985-92, counselor, articulations officer, 1992—; pres. Pacific Oaks Coll. Alumni Assn., Pasadena, Calif., 1987-88, Faculty Senate, Fullerton Coll., 1981-82; del. Calif. C.C. Gt. Tchrs. Conf., Santa Barbara, 1982, Asilomar (Calif.) Leadership Skills Seminar, 1986. Editor: Fullerton College Guide to Majors, 1985—. Charter pres. AAUW, Placentia, Yorba Linda, Calif., 1967; trustee Yorba Linda Elem. Sch. Dist., 1973-76; mem. Orange County Child Care Task Force, Santa Ana, Calif., 1983; mem. curriculum com. Calif. State Acad. Senate; mem. Intergenerational Articulation Coun., U.S.C. Articulation Officer's Coun. Named one of Outstanding Young Woman of Am., 1968, Outstanding Home Econs. for Rsch. and Leadership, 1977; recipient Cert. of Achievement, No. Orange County YWCA, 1986, Cert. of Appreciation, Calif. Articulation Number System, 1989. Mem. Nat. Assn. Women Deans, Adminstrs. & Counselors, Assn. of Psychol. Type, South Counties Women in Edn., UCLA and Pacific Oaks Coll. Alumni Assns., Calif. Tchrs. Assn., Calif. Community Coll. Counselors Assn. Presbyterian. Office: Fullerton Coll 321 E Chapman Ave Fullerton CA 92832-2011

BAKER, KENT ALFRED, broadcasting company executive; b. Sioux City, Iowa, Mar. 22, 1948; s. Carl Edmund Baker and Miriam M. (Hawthorn) Baker Nye. Student, Iowa State U., 1966-70. Editor Iowa State Daily, 1969-70; mem. U.S. Peace Corps., 1971-72; editor The Glidden (Iowa) Graphic, 1973-75; bureau chief The Waterloo (Iowa) Courier, Iowa, 1975; state editor The Des Moines Register, 1976-77; news dir. Sta. WQAD-TV, Moline, Ill., 1978; Sunday editor The Des Moines Sunday Register, 1979; news dir. Sta. KHON-TV, Honolulu, 1980-95, v.p., gen. mgr., 1996—; chmn. Hawaii Freedom of Info. Coun., 1992-94. Recipient news writing awards Iowa Press Assn., 1973-74. Mem. Radio and TV News Dirs. Assn., Bishop Mus. Assn., Hoover Libr. Assn., Iowa State U. Alumni Assn. Office: Sta KHON-TV 1170 Auahi St Honolulu HI 96814-4917

BAKER, LUCINDA, novelist, short story writer; b. Atlanta, Ill., July 10, 1916; m. Willard Alan Greiner, June 27, 1946. Author: The Place of Devils, 1976, Walk the Night Unseen, 1977, The Memoirs of the First Baroness, 1978; contbr. hundreds of short stories to women's mags. and articles to Christian Sci. Monitor, Christian Sci. Jour., Christian Sci. Sentinel.

BAKER, LYNN DALE, lawyer, educator; b. Miles City, Mont., Jan. 11, 1946; s. Robert Franklin and June D. (Babcock) B.; m. Imogene D. Baker, Oct. 8, 1967 (div. 1987); children: Channing Treavor, Chanelle Tete, Cory Justin. BA, U. Mont., 1968, JD, 1986; MA, U. of the Ams., 1970. Bar: Mont. 1986, U.S. Dist. Ct. (fed. dist) 1986, U.S. Ct. Appeals (9th cir.) 1987. H.s. tchr. The Glenham (S.D.) Sch., 1970-71; linguist, title VII Rocky Boy (Mont.) Schs., 1971-74; prof. edn. U. Alberta, Edmonton, 1974-78; paralegal Hartelius & Ferguson, Great Falls, Mont., 1979-83; atty. Hartelius & Ferguson, Great Falls, 1986-87; ptnr. Hartelius, Ferguson & Baker, Great Falls, 1987-95, Hartelius, Howard, Crosswhite & Baker, LLP, Lakeside, Mont., 1995—; adj. prof. Coll. of Great Falls, 1991—; cons. bilingual edn. N.W. Regional Ednl. Lab., Portland, Oreg., 1972-74; dir. Far North Ednl. Lab., Edmonton, 1974-79. Nat. Indian Bilingual Edn. Conf., Billings, Mont., 1974; mem. Province of Alberta Cross Cultural Edn. Com., 1974-78; paralegal program adv. com. May Coll., Great Falls, Mont., 1994—. State bd. mem. MS Soc. of Great Falls, 1993—; com. mem. Am. Cancer Soc. Jail-A-Thon, Great Falls, 1987-92; vol. atty. Am. Radio Relay League, Newington, Conn., 1990—; mem. Cascade County Dem. Com., 1992—. mem. ABA (com. on women and minorities 1992—), Mont. Bar Assn., Am. Trial Lawyers Assn., Mont. Trial Lawyers Assn., Cascade County Bar Assn.

Democrat. Office: Hartelius Ferguson Baker & Kazda 600 Central Ave Great Falls MT 59401-3124

BAKER, MALCOLM, marketing executive. Pres. BRS Group Inc., Calif. Office: BRS Group Inc 100 Shoreline Hwy Mill Valley CA 94941*

BAKER, MARIA, zoological park administrator. CEO, city dir. Sacramento Zoo, Calif. Office: Sacramento Zoo 3930 W Land Park Sacramento CA 95822*

BAKER, MARJORIE NEUMAN, information broker; b. Bakersfield, Calif., Nov. 28, 1939; d. Herbert Henry and Margaret Emma (Woodham) Neuman; children from previous marriage: Brian E. Nelson, Bradley R. Nelson; m. James Lawrence Baker, Nov. 28, 1986. BA, UCLA, 1961, MLS, 1962. Reference libr. L.A. Pub. Libr., 1972-86; dep. dir. rsch. Rsch. on Demand, Berkeley, Calif., 1987-92; pres. Info. First, Alameda, Calif., 1992—. Mem. Spl. Librs. Assn., Assn. Ind. Info. Profls.

BAKER, MARSHALL MANFRED, health facility administrator; b. Wichita, Kans., Aug. 26, 1943; s. Robert Winfred Baker; m. Kathleen Mary Nagel, June 7, 1969; children: Wendy Colleen, Robert Marshall, Brandon Matthew. AA in Gen. Bus., Wenatchee Valley Coll., 1966; BS in Bus. Mgmt., U. Idaho, 1968, MS in Bus. Adminstrn., 1970. Adminstrv. asst. Gritman Meml. Hosp., Moscow, Idaho, 1966-68; adminstrv. intern Fronk Clinic, Honolulu, 1968; adminstr. Walla Walla (Wash.) Clinic, 1969-77; exec. dir. Ctrl. Ohio Med. Group, Columbus, 1977-84; exec. v.p. Anesthesia Med. Cons., Albuquerque, 1984-92; sr. v.p. Tulsa Regional Med. Ctr., 1992-94; exec. dir. St. Luke's Regional Med. Ctr., Boise, Idaho, 1994-97; pres. Phys. Advisory Svcs., Boise, 1997—. Pres. Idaho Theater Youth, 1996—. Fellow Am. Coll. Med. Practice Execs. (pres. 1990); mem. Med. Group Mgmt. Assn. (pres. Ohio chpt. 1984, N.Mex. chpt. 1987), Soc. Ambulatory Care Profls., Rotary Internat., Southwest Boise chpt. Office: St Luke's Regional Med Ctr Ste 209 1770 West State Boise ID 83702

BAKER, MICHAEL J., lawyer; b. Lexington, Ky., Apr. 14, 1947. AB cum laude, Harvard U., 1969; JD, U. Calif., Berkeley, 1973. Bar: Calif. 1973. Ptnr. Jackson, Tufts, Cole & Black, San Francisco; chief legal divsn., litigation dir. Calif. Fair Political Practices Com., 1976-78. Contbr. articles to profl. jours. Mem. ABA. Office: Jackson Tufts Cole & Black 650 California St Fl 32 San Francisco CA 94108-2702

BAKER, PATRICIA (JEAN), lawyer, mediator; b. June 28, 1948. BS summa cum laude, Wright State U., Dayton, Ohio, 1973; MBA, Northeastern U., Boston, 1989; JD, Calif. Western U., San Diego, 1993. Bar: Calif. 1993; cert. mediator. With GenRad Inc., Boston, 1974-82; mktg./sales staff GE Co., Boston, 1982-84; major accounts mgr. Fluke Mfg. Co., Boston, 1984-89; pub. rels. mgr. Racal Dana, Irvine, Calif., 1989-90; legal intern Pub. Defenders Dependancy, San Diego, 1992; law clk. Civil divsn. U.S. Atty., San Diego, 1992; personal injury atty. L.H. Parker, Long Beach, Calif., 1993; mediator/atty. Baker & Assocs., San Diego, 1993-94; dir. Orange County region Am. Arbitration Assn., Irvine, 1994-97; v.p. govt. programs Am. Arbitration Assn., Washington, 1997—; mediator San Diego Mediation Ctr., 1993—; trainer mediation skills Am. Arbitration Assn., 1994—; adj. prof. Western State U., Irvine, 1995—; MCLE presenter San Diego County Bar, 1994, State Bar of Calif., 1996, ABA, 1997; mediator Superior Ct., San Diego, 1994—, U.S. Bankruptcy Ct. (cen. dist.) Calif., 1995—. Bd. dirs. Legal Aid Soc., San Diego, 1994, T. Homann Law Assn., San Diego, 1994. Recipient Am. Jurisprudence awards, 1992/. Mem. State Bar of Calif., San Diego County Bar Assn. (ADR sect.), Orange County Bar Assn. (chair ADR com.), So. Calif. Mediation Assn.

BAKER, RICHARD W., structural and architectural engineer; b. Glendale, Calif., Aug. 16, 1945; s. Elwood V. and Eleanor J. (Vickers) B.; m. Judith K. Fields, July 5, 1969; children: Carrie A., Brian R. AA, Pasadena City Coll., 1965; BS in Archtl. Engring., Calif. State Poly. Coll., San Luis Obispo, 1968. Naval architect Long Beach (Calif.) Naval Shipyard, 1968-69; stress engr. Lockheed Aero. Systems Co., Burbank, Calif., 1969-73, 75-87, Rockwell Internat., Downey, Calif., 1974; group engr. Lockheed Advanced Devel. Co., Burbank, Calif., 1987-89, project structures engr., 1989-90; dep. chief engr. Lockheed Advanced Devel. Co., Burbank, 1991-93; dir. engring. Lockheed Martin Skunk Works, Palmdale, Calif., 1994-96; program mgr. Lockheed Martin Skunk Works, Palmdale, 1996—; archtl. cons., Cerritos, Calif., 1972-- . Editor: Aircraft Stress Analysis, 1987. Mgr. Frontier Little League, Cerritos, 1985-92; coach City of Cerritos Parks & Recreation Dept., 1982-87. Mem. AIAA. Republican. Methodist. Office: Lockheed Martin Skunk Works Dept 72-34 Bl 611 Plant 10 1011 Lockheed Way Palmdale CA 93599-7234

BAKER, ROBERT KERRY, college administrator, author, editor; b. Glendale, Calif., Nov. 24, 1948; s. Robert Klein and Louise Eleanor (Winters) B.; m. Linda Jean Voorhees, Jan. 14, 1972 (div. 1978). B.A. in French, Calif. State U.-Northridge, 1971; MA in French, UCLA, 1973, MLS, 1976; postgrad. U. Paris, 1971-72; EdD in Ednl. Leadership, No. Ariz. U., 1996. Cert. life librarian, Wash., Community Coll. instr., Calif. Asst. catalog librarian, Gonzaga U., Spokane, Wash., 1976-77; pub. services librarian Spokane C.C. Coll., 1977-80, tech. services librarian, 1980-83; library dir. Lower Columbia Coll., Longview, Wash., 1983-90; coll. adminstr. Pima C.C., 1990—. Author: Introduction to Library Research in French Literature, 1978; Doing Library Research, 1981; editor Westview Guides to Library Research, Boulder, Colo., 1979—; contbr. articles to publs. in field. Marjorie Sether Mardellis fellow, UCLA, 1975. Mem. ALA, Am. Assn. Higher Edn., Ariz. State Libr. Assn., Assn. Coll. and Rsch. Librs., Phi Kappa Phi. Democrat. Roman Catholic. Home: 10401 E Boundary Dr Tucson AZ 85748-3819 Office: Pima CC 4905C E Broadway Blvd Tucson AZ 85709-1130

BAKER, ROBERT N., neurologist; b. Inglewood, Calif., Mar. 25, 1923; s. Glyn Maynard and Ruth Elizabeth (Norton) B.; m. Noreen Jacquelyne Isaak, June 19, 1971; children: Mark, Kent, Melanie. BA, Park Coll., 1944; MD, U. So. Calif., 1950. Diplomate Am. Bd. Psychiatry & Neurology. From instr. to assoc. prof. neurology UCLA Med. Sch., L.A., 1950-70; prof. U. Nebr. Med. Sch., Omaha, 1970—. Capt. USAF, 1994-96. Grantee NIH, 1956-76. Fellow Am. Acad. Neurology (sec./treas. 1962-64), Am. Neurol. Assn.; mem. AMA, Colo. Med. Soc. Democrat. Unitarian. Home: 690 Summerset Ct Estes Park CO 80517 Office: Estes Park Specialty Clinic 555 Prospect Ave Estes Park CO 80517-6318

BAKER, ROSALYN HESTER, state legislator; b. El Campo, Tex., Sept. 20, 1946. BA, Southwest Tex. State U., 1968; student, U. Southwestern La., 1969. Lobbyist, asst. dir. Govt. Rels. Nat. Edn. Assn., Washington, 1969-80; owner, retail sporting goods store Maui, Hawaii, 1980-87; legis. aide to Hon. Karen Honita Hawaii Ho. of Reps., Honolulu, 1987, mem., 1989-93; house majority leader, 1993, state senator Hawaii, 1993—, majority leader, 1995-96; co-chair commerce, consumer protection and info. tech. com.; mem. human resources com., water, land and Hawaiian affairs com.; co-chair rules com. Hawaii State Dem. Conv., 1990, resolutions com. 1994. Del.-at-large Dem. Nat. Conv., 1984, 92, 96; mem. exec. com. Maui County Dem. Com., 1986-88; vice chmn. Maui Svc. Area Bd. on Mental Health and Substance Abuse; active Am. Cancer Soc., Work Day Vol., Soroptimist Internat. Democrat. Home: PO Box 10394 Lahaina HI 96761-0394 Office: Hawaii State Senate State Capitol Honolulu HI 96813

BAKER, THERESE LOUISE, sociology educator; b. Mpls., June 20, 1939; d. Lloyd L. and Gussie G. (Miller) Elzas; m. Keith Michael Baker, Oct. 25, 1961; children—Julian Charles, Felix James. B.A., Cornell U., 1961; Ph.D., U. Chgo., 1973. Secondary sch. tchr. Rosa Bassett Sch., London, 1962-64, Gresham High Sch., Portland, Oreg., 1964-65; instr. sociology U. Ill., Chgo., 1969-71; asst. prof. DePaul U., Chgo., 1971-81, assoc. prof., 1981-87, prof., 1988-89, chmn. dept. sociology, 1981-87; dir. Chgo. Area Studies Ctr., DePaul U., 1983-89, dir. Urban Studies Program, 1987-89; asst. to vice provost Stanford (Calif.) U., 1989; founding prof. Calif. State U., San Marcos, 1989—, chmn. sociology program, 1990—, acad. senator, 1989-93, dir. social scis. major, 1990—, evening studies program, 1994-96; vis. scholar Inst. for Research on Women and Gender, Stanford (Calif.) U., 1987. Author: Doing Social Research, 1988, 2d edit., 1994, 3d edit., 1997; contbr. articles to profl. jours. Research grantee NIMH, 1977-78; research contractee Nat. Inst. Child Health and Devel., 1979-81. Mem. Am. Sociol. Assn., Midwest Sociol. Soc. (state dir. 1982-84), Sociologists for Women in Soc., Pacific Sociol. Soc. Avocations: swimming, collecting plates. Home: 914 Mears Ct Stanford CA 94305-1029 Office: Calif State U San Marcos CA 92096

BAKER, TIMOTHY ALAN, healthcare administrator, educator, consultant; b. Myrtle Point, Oreg., July 30, 1954; s. Farris D. and Billie G. (Bradford) B.; 1 child, Amanda Susann. BS in Mgmt. with honors, Linfield Coll., McMinnville, Oreg., 1988; MPA in Health Adminstrn. with distinction, Portland State U., 1989, PhD in Pub. Adminstrn. and Policy, 1992. Registered emergency med. technician. Gen. mgr. Pennington's, Inc., Coos Bay, Oreg., 1974-83; dep. dir. Internat. Airport Projects Med. Svcs., Riyadh, Saudi Arabia, 1983-87; adminstrv. intern Kaiser Sunnyside Hosp., Portland, Oreg., 1988-89; grant mgr. Oreg. Health Sci. U., Portland, 1989-90; dir. health sci. program Linfield Coll., Portland, Oreg., 1992—, asst. prof. health scis.; rsch. assoc. Portland State U., 1990—; instr. S.W. Oreg. C. C., Coos Bay, 1980-83; pres. Intermed. Inc., Portland, 1987—; sr. researcher small area analysis Oreg. Health Sci. U., 1990, The Oreg. Health Plan Project, 1990-91; developer, planner, prin. author trauma system devel. S.W. Wash. EMS and Trauma System, 1991-93, Vancouver, adminstr.; cons. ednl. def. Min. Civil Def., Riyadh, Saudi Arabia, 1992. Author: TQ: EMS: Total Quality Emergency Medical Services, 1995; pub. Jour. Family Practice, Internat. Jour. Emergency Med. Svcs., 1997. Planner mass disaster plan King Khaled Internat. Airport, 1983; EMS planner Emergency Med. Plan, Province of Cholburi, Thailand, 1985; bd. dirs. Coos County Kidney Assn., 1982, Coos Bay Kiwanis Club, 1979; regional adv. com. EMS and Trauma, State Wash. Dept. Health, 1990—. Recipient Pub. Svc. award Am. Radio and Relay League, 1969, Med. Excellence award KKIA Hosp., 1985; named Fireman of Yr. Eastside Fire Dept., 1982, Adminstr. of Yr., Wash. Dept. Health, 1993. Mem. Am. Soc. Pub. Adminstrn. (doctoral rep. to faculty senate Portland State U. 1990), Am. Pub. Health Assn., Am. Coll. Healthcare Execs. Home: 608 N Hayden Bay Dr Portland OR 97217-7964 Office: Linfield Coll Portland Campus 2255 NW Northrup St Portland OR 97210-2952

BAKER, VICTOR RICHARD, geology and hydrology researcher, educator, planetary sciences researcher; b. Waterbury, Conn., Feb. 19, 1945; s. Victor A. Baker and Doris Elizabeth (Day) MacGregor; m. Pauline Marie Heaton, June 10, 1967; children: Trent Heaton, Theodore William. BS, Rensselaer Poly. Inst., 1967; PhD, U. Colo., 1971. Geophysicist U.S. Geol. Survey, Denver, 1967-71; asst. prof. geology U. Tex., Austin, 1971-76, assoc. prof., 1976-81; prof. U. Ariz., Tucson, 1981—, Regents' prof., 1988—, head dept. hydrology and water resources; cons. Lunar and Planetary Inst., Houston, 1983-86, Salt River Project, Phoenix, 1984-87, Argonne (Ill.) Nat. Lab., 1983-93, Sandia (N.Mex.) Nat. Labs., 1991-92, U.S. Bur. of Reclamation, 1994—; com. mem. NRC, Washington, 1978—, NASA, 1978—; vis. fellow Nat. Inst. Hydrology, Roorkee, India, 1987-88, Deccan Coll., Pune, India, 1987-88, U. Adelaide, Australia, 1988, Udall Ctr. for Studies in Pub. Policy, Tucson, 1994-95. Author: The Channels of Mars, 1982, co-author: Surficial Geology, 1981; editor: Catastrophic Flooding, 1981, co-editor: The Channeled Scabland, 1978, Flood Geomorphology, 1988, Global Continental Paleohydrology, 1995. Capt. U.S. Army, 1971-72. Recipient David Linton award Brit. Geomorphological Rsch. Group, 1995; Fulbright sr. research fellow, 1979-80, vis. fellow Australian Nat. U., Canberra, 1979-80; research grantee NASA, 1975—, NSF, 1977—. Fellow AAAS (chmn. geol., geography sect. 1992-93, councilor 1992-93), Geol. Soc. Am. (chmn. planetary geology divsn. 1986, Quatenary geology and geomorphology divsn. 1987, councilor 1990-93, v.p. 1996-97); mem. Internat. Assn. of Geomorphologists (treas. 1993-97), Am. Geophys. Union, Am. Quaternary Assn., Internat. Union Quaternary Rsch. (pres. commn. on global paleohydrology 1995—), Nat. Assn. Geology Tchrs., Soc. Sedimentary Geologists, Polish Acad. Scis. (fgn. mem.), Sigma Xi. Office: U Ariz Dept Geoscis Tucson AZ 85721

BAKER, WARREN J(OSEPH), university president; b. Fitchburg, Mass., Sept. 5, 1938; s. Preston A. and Grace F. (Jarvis) B.; m. Carol Ann Fitzsimons, Apr. 28, 1962; children: Carrie Ann, Kristin Robin, Christopher, Brian. B.S., U. Notre Dame, 1960, M.S., 1962; Ph.D., U. N.Mex., 1966. Research assoc., lectr. E. H. Wang Civil Engring. Research Facility, U. N.Mex., 1962-66; assoc. prof. civil engring. U. Detroit, 1966-71, prof., 1972-79, Chrysler prof., dean engring., 1973-78, acad. v.p., 1976-79; NSF faculty fellow M.I.T., 1971-72; pres. Calif. Poly. State U., San Luis Obispo, 1979—; mem. bd. Internat. Food and Agrl. Devel., 1983-85; mem. Nat. Sci. Bd., 1985-94, Calif. Bus. Higher Edn. Forum, 1993—; founding mem. Calif. Coun. on Sci. and Tech., 1989—; trustee Amigos of E.A.R.T.H. Coll., 1991—; bd. dirs. John Wiley & Sons, Inc., 1993—; bd. regents The Am. Archtl. Found., 1995—; co-chair Joint Policy Coun. on Agr. and Higher Edn., 1995—. Contbr. articles to profl. jours. Mem. Detroit Mayor's Mgmt. Adv. Com., 1975-76; mem. engring. adv. bd. U. Calif., Berkeley, 1984—; bd. dirs. Calif. Coun. for Environ. and Econ. Balance, 1980-85; trustee Nat. Coop. Edn. Assn.; chmn. bd. dirs. Civil Engring. Rsch. Found., 1989-91, bd. dirs., 1991-94. Fellow Engring. Soc. Detroit; mem. ASCE (chmn. geotech. div. com. on reliability 1976-78, civil engring. edn. and rsch. policy com. 1985-89), NSPE (pres. Detroit chpt. 1976-77), Am. Soc. Engring. Edn., Am. Assn. State Colls. and Univs. (bd. dirs. 1982-84). Office: Calif Polytech State U Office of Pres San Luis Obispo CA 93407

BAKER, WILLIAM P. (BILL BAKER), former congressman; b. Oakland, Calif., June 14, 1940; m. Joanne Atack; children: Todd, Mary, Billy, Robby. Grad. in Bus. and Indsl. Mgmt., San Jose State Coll. Budget analyst State Dept. Fin., Calif.; assemblyman 15th dist. State of Calif., 1980-92; mem. of Congress from 10th Calif. dist., 1993—; vice chmn. budget writing Ways and Means Com., 1984-91. Exec. v.p. Contra Costa Taxpayers Assn.; active Contra Costa County Farm Bur. With USCG Res., 1958-65. Republican. address: 10935 Ricefield Pl Fairfax Station VA 22039*

BAKER-LIEVANOS, NINA GILLSON, jewelry store executive; b. Boston, Dec. 19, 1950; d. Rev. John Robert and Patricia (Gillson) Baker; m. Jorge Alberto Lievanos, June 6, 1981; children: Jeremy John Baker, Wendy Mara Baker, Raoul Salvador Baker-Lievanos. Student, Mills Coll., 1969-70; grad. course in diamond grading, Gemology Inst. Am., 1983; student in diamondtology designation, Diamond Coun. Am., 1986—. Cert. store mgr., Jewelers Cert. Coun., Jewelers Am. Artist, tchr. Claremont, Calif., 1973-78; escrow officer Bank of Am., Claremont, 1978-81; retail salesman William Pitt Jewelers, Puente Hills, Montclair, Calif., 1981-83, asst. mgr., 1983; mgr. William Pitt Jewelers, Puente Hills, Santa Maria, Calif., 1983-91, corp. sales trainer, 1988-89; sales and design specialist Merksamer Jewelers, Santa Maria, 1991; mgr. Merksamer Jewelers, San Luis Obispo, Calif., 1991-92, Santa Maria, Calif., 1992-94; diamond specialist cons. Merksamer Jewelers, Santa Maria, 1994-96; pres., ops. mgr. Dancer House Designs, Santa Maria, Calif., 1996—. Artist tapestry hanging Laguna Beach Mus. Art, 1974. Mem. Cen. Coast Pla. Adv. Bd., 1992. Recipient Cert. Merit Art Bank Am., 1968. Mem. NAFE, Internat. Platform Assn., Speaker's Bur., Santa Maria C. of C., Compassion Internat. Republican. Roman Catholic. Office: Dancer House Designs 323-B Town Center West Santa Maria CA 93454

BAKKEN, GORDON MORRIS, law educator; b. Madison, Wis., Jan. 10, 1943; s. Elwood S. and Evelyn A. H. (Anderson) B.; m. Erika Reinhardt, Mar. 24, 1943; children: Angela E., Jeffrey E. B.S., U. Wis., 1966, M.S., 1967, Ph.D., 1970, J.D., 1973. Asst., then assoc. prof. history Calif. State U.-Fullerton, 1969-74, dir. faculty affairs, 1974-86, prof. history, 1974—; cons. Calif. Sch. Employees Assn., 1976-78; cons. Calif. Bar Commn. Hist. Law., 1985—; mem. mgmt. task force on acad. grievance procedures Calif. State Univ. and Colls. Systems, 1975; mem. Calif. Jud. Coun. Com. Trial Ct. Records Mgmt., 1992—. Placentia Jusa referee coordinator, 1983. Russell Sage resident fellow law, 1971-72; Am. Council Learned Socs. grantee-in-aid, 1979-80; Am. Bar Found. fellow in legal history, 1979-80, 84-85. Mem. Orgn. Am. Historians, Am. Soc. Legal History, Law and Soc. Assn., Western History Assn., Calif. Supreme Ct. Hist. Soc. (v.p.), Phi Alpha Theta (v.p. 1994-95, pres. 1996—). Democrat. Lutheran. Author 5 books on Am. legal history; contbr. articles to profl. jours. Office: Calif State U 800 N State College Blvd Fullerton CA 92834-6846

BAKKENSEN, JOHN RESER, lawyer; b. Pendleton, Oreg., Oct. 4, 1943; s. Manley John and Helen (Reser) B.; m. Ann Marie Dahlen, Sept. 30, 1978; children: Michael, Dana, Laura. AB magna cum laude, Harvard U., 1965; JD, Stanford U., 1968. Bar: Oreg. 1969, Calif. 1969, U.S. Dist. Ct. Oreg. 1969. Ptnr. Miller, Nash, Wiener, Hager & Carlsen, Portland, Oreg., 1968—; lawyer del. 9th Cir. Jud. Conf., San Francisco, 1980-82. Author: (with others) Advising Oregon Businesses, 1979. Past bd. dirs. Assn. for Retarded Citizens, Portland; advisor Portland Youth Shelter House; mem. and counsel to bd. dirs. Friends of Pine Mountain Observatory, Portland. Mem. ABA (forum on constrn. industry and sect. pub. contract law and sci. and tech.), Oreg. State Bar, Oreg. Assoc. Gen. Contractors (legal com. 1991, counsel to bd. dirs. 1992), Multnomah Athletic Club. Office: Miller Nash Wiener Hager & Carlsen 111 SW 5th Ave Portland OR 97204-3604

BAKUS, GERALD JOSEPH, biology educator; b. Thorp, Wis., Dec. 5, 1934; s. Joseph John and Marie Loretta (Kalkstein) B.; m. Grace Elaine Munsey, Dec. 26, 1953; children: Melanie Ann, Paul Gerald. BA in Biology, Calif. State U., L.A., 1955; MA in Zoology, U. Mont., 1957; PhD, U. Wash., 1962. Asst. prof. biology Calif. State U., Northridge, 1961-62; asst. prof. U. So. Calif., L.A., 1962-67, assoc. prof., 1967-85, prof., 1986—; staff officer Nat. Acad. Sci., Washington, 1969-70; chief biologist Tetra Tech Inc., Pasadena, 1976-79. Author: The Spanish Guitar, 1977, Computers and Programs for Beginners, 1984, Quantitative Ecology and Marine Biology, 1990, Coral Reef Ecosystems, 1994, Ecology (CD-ROM), 1996, Sponges (CD-ROM), 1996, Natural History of Southern California (CD-ROM), 1997. Fulbright fellow, 1987, Disting. Fulbright fellow, 1996. Fellow Great Barrier Reef Com. Australia, AAAS; mem. Internat. Soc. Chem. Ecology, Pacific Sci. Assn., Western Soc. Naturalists. Office: U So Calif Dept Biological Sciences Los Angeles CA 90089-0371

BALCOM, ORVILLE, engineer; b. Inglewood, Calif., Apr. 20, 1937; s. Orville R. and Rose Mae (Argo) B.; B.S. in Math., Calif. State U., Long Beach, 1958, postgrad., 1958-59; postgrad. UCLA, 1959-62; m. Gloria Stadtmiller, July 23, 1971; children—Cynthia, Steven. Engr., AiResearch Mfg. Co., 1959-62, 64-65; chief engr. Meditron, El Monte, Calif., 1962-64; chief engr. Astro Metrics, Burbank, Calif., 1965-67; chief engr., gen. mgr. Varadyne Power Systems, Van Nuys, Calif., 1968-71; owner, chief engr. Brown Dog Engring., Lomita, Calif., 1971—. Mem. IEEE Computer Group, Independent Computer Cons. Assn. Patentee in field. Club: Torrance Athletic. Home: 24521 Walnut St Lomita CA 90717-1260 Office: PO Box 427 Lomita CA 90717-0427

BALDASSIN, MICHAEL ROBERT, secondary school educator; b. Tacoma, Wash., July 26, 1955; s. Robert Allen and Mary Lee (Hager) B.; Mary Katherine Hartman, Oct. 10, 1981; children: Jessica, Corrine, Beau, Kaylee. BS in Sociology, U. Wash., 1980. Profl. football player San Francisco 49ers, 1977-80; police officer Seattle Police dept., 1980-83, Oakland (Calif.) Police Dept., 1983-91; Wash. state dir. drug and alcohol Fellowship of Christian Athletes, Kansas City, Mo., 1991-92; tchr., head football coach Bellarmine Prep, Tacoma, 1992—. Sec. Sparrow Found., Seattle, 1995—. Decorated Medal of Valor, Oakland Police Dept., 1985; named Coach of Yr. Nat. Football Found., 1996. Office: Bellarmine Preparatory High Sch 2300 S Washington St Tacoma WA 98405-1304

BALDERSTON, FREDERICK EMERY, business administration educator, university dean; b. 1923. Rsch. assoc. MIT, 1950-53; from asst. prof. to prof. bus. adminstrn. U. Calif., Berkeley, 1953-78; assoc. dean Grad. Sch. Bus. Adminstrn., U. Calif., 1979—; exec. v.p. Bernard Osher Found., 1994—; bd. trustees Am. Field Svc. Internat. Scholarships, Inc. Author: Thrifts in Crisis: The Structural Transformation of the Savings and Loan Industry, 1985, Managing Today's University, 2d edit., 1995; editor: Public Policy for Marketing, 1980, numerous others. Office: Univ Calif Haas Sch Bus Dept Bus Adminstrn Berkeley CA 94720-1900

BALDO, TRACY DEE BOSTWICK, counselor, educator; b. Marion, Ind., Oct. 21, 1964; d. John Dee and Peggy Jean (Wooldridge) Pormen; m. David Robert Bostwick, Aug. 9, 1986 (div. Apr. 1993); m. Anthony John Baldo, Oct. 17, 1994. BS in Supervision, Purdue U., 1986, MS in Counseling and Pers., 1989, PhD in Profl. Counseling, 1990. Nat. cert. counselor; lic. profl. counselor. Staff supr. Baskin Robbins Ice Cream, Marion, 1981-83, West Lafayette, Ind., 1984-86; line supr. GM, Muncie, Ind., 1985; mgr. TCBY Yogurt, Lafayette, Ind., 1986-87; counselor dean of students office Purdue U., West Lafayette, 1987-88, instr., 1987-90; counselor, educator Auburn (Ala.) U., 1990-91, U. No. Colo., Greeley, 1991—; pvt. practice Counseling Clinic, Greeley, 1994—. Mem. ACA, Assn. Counselor Edn. and Supervision, Colo. Counseling Assn., Rocky Mountain Counselor Edn. and Supervision, Colo. Coll. Counseling Assn. (pres., mem. exec. bd. 1993-94). Home: 200 S Quentine Ave Milliken CO 80543 Office: Univ No Colo McKee 248 PPSY Greeley CO 80639

BALDOCK, BOBBY RAY, federal judge; b. Rocky, Okla., Jan. 24, 1936; s. W. Jay and S. Golden (Farrell) B.; m. Mary Jane (Spunky) Holt, June 2, 1956; children: Robert Jennings, Christopher Guy. Grad., N.Mex. Mil. Inst., 1956; JD, U. Ariz., 1960. Bar: Ariz. 1960, N.Mex. 1961, U.S. Dist. Ct. N.Mex., 1965. Ptnr. Sanders, Bruin & Baldock, Roswell, N.Mex., 1960-83; adj. prof. Eastern N.Mex. U., 1962-81; judge U.S. Dist. Ct. N.Mex., Albuquerque, 1983-86, U.S. Ct. Appeals (10th cir.), 1986—. Mem. N.Mex. Bar Assn., Chaves County Bar Assn., Ariz. Bar Assn., Phi Alpha Delta. Office: US Ct Appeals PO Box 2388 Roswell NM 88202-2388*

BALDON, CLEO, interior designer; b. Leavenworth, Wash., June 1, 1927; d. Ernest Elsworth and Esther Jane (Hannan) Chute; m. Lewis Smith Baldon, Nov. 20, 1948 (div. July 1961); 1 child, Dirk; m. Ib Jørgen Melchior, Jan. 18, 1964; 1 stepson, Leif Melchior. BS, Woodbury Coll., 1948. Ptnr. Interior Designs Ltd., Los Angeles, 1948-50; freelance illustrator Los Angeles, 1952-54; prin. Cleo Baldon & Assocs., Los Angeles and Venice, Calif., 1954—; ptnr. Galper/Baldon Assocs., Landscape Archs., Venice, 1970—. Co-author: Steps and Stairways, 1989, Reflections on the Pool, 1997; contbr. articles to profl. jours.: patentee in field. Recipient City Beautification awards L.A., 1974-77, 80, 83, 85-90, 92, Beverly Hills, 1982, Calif. Landscape Contbr., 1975, 79, Pacifica award Resources Coun., CAlif., 1979, Honor awards Landscape Archs. Fund, 1988, 89, Award of Excellence, Landscape Archs. Fund, 1990. Home: 8228 Marmont Ln West Hollywood CA 90069-1624 Office: Galper/Baldon Assocs 723 Ocean Front Walk Venice CA 90291-3270

BALDRIDGE, THAD CLIFTON WALKER, psychotherapist, consultant; b. Oklahoma City, Okla., Oct. 8, 1939; s. Thad Spires and Winifred Ernestine (Glass) B.; m. Jeanne Ellen Gallagher, Aug. 15, 1958 (div. 1962); children: Dorothy Joyce, Thad Matthew; m. Patricia Ann Baker, June 1964 (dec. 1977); children: Deborah Jeanne, Kenneth Michael; m. Ruth Marie Mendus, May 15, 1978 (div.); children: Summer Earthsong, Fletcher. BS summa cum laude, Mo. Valley Coll., 1991; M of Counseling, U. Phoenix, Tucson, 1993. Nat. bd. cert. clin. hypnotherapist; nat. cert. counselor NBCC; master addictions counselor; cert. chem. dependency counselor, Mont. Resident house dir. Mo. Valley Coll., Marshall, Mo., 1989-91; chemical dependency counselor La Frontera Ctr., Inc, Tucson, 1991-93, Gateway, Inc., Tucson, 1991-93; human svcs. specialist Ariz. Dept Econ. Security, Tucson, 1993-94; psychotherapist Ariz. Dept. Health Svcs., Tucson, 1994-95; cons. Pathways of Casa Grande, Tucson, 1994-95; psychotherapist Coronado Behavioral Healthcare, Inc., Sierra Vista, Ariz., 1994-95, Eastern Mont. Mental Health Ctr., Glasgow, 1995; allied staff (cons.), Francis Mahon Deaconess Hosp., Glasgow. Mem. nat. disaster mental health svcs. team ARC; bd. dirs. Hi-Line chpt. ARC; mem. governing bd. Valley County Coalition. Mem. ACA, Nat. Assn. Alcoholism and Drug Abuse Counselors, Mont. Assn. Alcoholism and Drug Abuse Counselors, Mont. Counseling Assn. Mem. Unitarian Ch.

BALDWIN, BETTY JO, computer specialist; b. Fresno, Calif., May 28, 1925; d. Charles Monroe and Irma Blanche (Law) Inks; m. Barrett Stone Baldwin Jr.; two daughters. AB, U. Calif., Berkeley, 1945. With NASA Ames Rsch. Ctr., Moffett Field, Calif., 1951-53, math tech. 14' Wind Tunnel, 1954-55, math analyst 14' Wind Tunnel, 1956-63, supr. math analyst Structural Dynamics, 1963-68, supervisory computer programmer Structural Dynamics, 1968-71, computer programmer Theoretical Studies, 1971-82, adminstrv. specialist Astrophys. Experiments, 1982-85, computer specialist, resource mgr. Astrophysics br., 1985—; v.p. B&B Baldwin Farms, Bakersfield, Calif., 1978—. Mem. IEEE, Assn. for Computing Machinery, Am.

Geophys. Union, Am. Bus. Womens Assn. (pres., v.p. 1967, one of Top 10 Women of Yr. 1971). Presbyterian. Office: NASA Ames Rsch Ctr Mail Stop 245-6 Moffett Field CA 94035-1000

BALDWIN, BRIAN EUGENE, medical devices manufacturing company executive; b. Schuyler, Nebr., Jan. 24, 1931; s. George Willard and Edna Marie (Carlson) B.; m. Elizabeth Ann Voris, Dec. 18, 1954 (div. Mar. 1979); children: Laura, Gregory, Jeffery; m. Elizabeth Ann Stone, Dec. 22, 1979. BSME, Northwestern U., 1954, MS in Indsl. Engring., 1955. Mfg. engr. Shure Bros., Evanston, Ill., 1955-56; product devel. engr. Am. Hosp. Supply, Evanston, 1956-58; founder, pres. MPL, Inc., Chgo., 1958-74, HypoMed Corp., Skokie, Ill., 1974-86; chmn. ASIK A/S, Rødby, Denmark, 1978-81; chmn., CEO, Pharm. Basics, Inc., Denver, 1981-86; founder, chmn., CEO, Baxa Corp., Englewood, Colo., 1983—. Patentee over 20 med. and related devices. Counsel to pres. Eleanor Roosevelt Inst., Denver, 1993-94. Mem. Med. Device Mfrs. Assn. (bd. dirs. 1994—), Colo. Med. Device Assn. (founder, pres. 1995), Econ. Club Colo., Valley Country Club, Sigma Xi. Office: Baxa Corp 13760 E Arapahoe Rd Englewood CO 80112-3903

BALDWIN, C. ANDREW, JR., retired science educator; b. Chgo., May 18, 1927; s. C. Andrew Sr. and Lillian (Evans) B.; m. Claire Awkerman, July 10, 1954; children: Debbie, Judi. BA in Zoology, U. Tex., 1951; MA in Theology, Berkeley Bapt. Sem. of West, 1956, MDiv, 1961; postgrad., numerous colls., univs. Cert. elem. tchr., Calif., secondary tchr., Calif., Tex., Ill.; edn. adminstr., Calif., K-12 substitute and biology, Oreg. Sci. tchr. Brazosport Ind. Sch. Dist., Freeport, Tex., 1951-53; sustitute tchr. Chgo. Pub. Sch., 1953-54; child care and substitute tchr. Berkeley (Calif.) Pub. Sch., 1954-56; tchr. 7th and 8th grades Redwood City (Calif.) Elem. Sch., 1956-60; swimpool mgr. San Mateo County Parks/Recreation, 1957-64; 6th grade/jr. high biology/geology tchr., coord. field biology Palo Alto (Calif.) Unified Sch. Dist., 1960-93; vice prin. Franklin-McKinley Sch. Dist., San Jose, Calif., 1970-71; Biology, 1-12th grade substitute Salem and Woodburn, Oreg. schs., Salem and Woodburn, Oreg., 1993—; founder, dir. pvt. summer ecology and field biology camp program-Summer Sci. Safaris, 1972-76; coord. sci. fairs Wilbur Jr. H.S. & Stanford Middle Sch. Contbr. articles to publs. Unit dir., counselor, mem. water safety staff YMCA, Chgo., Denver, Berkeley and Oakland, Calif.; active Chgo. Boys Club and Oakland (Calif.) Cath. Youth Orgn., 1945-56; elected trustee Redwood City Sch. Dist. Bd. Edn., 1961-69, pres., 1968-69; active com. against racism, various others Sequoia Union H.S. Dist.; candidate for U.S. Congress, 1967; pres. Sequoia YMCA's Men's Club, Redwood City, 1967-69, Lorelei Homeowners Assn., Menlo Park, Calif., 1959-60; elder Trinity Presbyn. Ch., San Carlos, Calif., mem. choir, various coms., 1st Presbyn. Ch., San Mateo, rep. to No. Calif. Presbyn. United Mission Advance; staff assoc. Carlmont Meth. Ch.; vol. asst. min. Woodside Rd. Cmty. United Meth. Ch., Redwood City, Calif.; v.p. Hoover Elem. Sch. PTA, 1959-60; elected Sequoia Unifed Sch. Dist. Bd.; pres. Freeport Jr. H.S. PTA, 1952-53; pres. Senn H.S. Crusaders Club, Chgo.; mem. Men's Bible Fellowship, Internat.; vol. YMCA, Chgo. Boys' Clubs, Boy Scouts Am., ARC. Sgt. U.S. Army Air Force, 1945-47. Decorated Brevet 2nd Lt. Commn. U.S. Army, 1945; named Outstanding Citizen, Redwood City YMCA, 1968, Realtors, South San Mateo County, 1967; recipient Oak Leaf and Life Membership award Calif. PTA, 1959, 5 and 10 yr. Vol. pin ARC, Vol. pin Chgo. Boys' Club; nominated for Presdl. award for excellence in tchg., 1992; Chevron Corp. grantee, 1985. Mem. AAAS, NEA, Calif. Tchrs. Assn., Palo Alto Edn. Assn. (sch. rep., salary com.), Christian Educators Assn. Internat., Astron. Soc. Pacific, Earth Sci. Tchrs. Assn., Calif. Sci. Tchrs. Assn., Nat. Sci. Tchrs. Assn. (12th dist. dir. 1984-86, local leader 1993—), Oreg. Sci. Tchrs. Assn., Nat. Assn. Biology Tchrs.

BALDWIN, EWART MERLIN, geologist, educator; b. Pomeroy, Wash., May 17, 1915; s. Charles Milton and Augusta Elizabeth (Sears) B.; m. Margaret Ethel Maxwell, Oct. 2, 1942; children—Donald Maxwell, Neil Alan. B.S., Wash. State U., 1938, M.S., 1939; Ph.D., Cornell U., 1943. Cert. profl. geologist. Geologist, Oreg. Dept. Geology and Mining Industry, Portland, 1943-47; asst. prof. geology U. Oreg., Eugene, 1947-50, assoc. prof., 1950-59, prof., 1959-80; Arnold vis. prof. Whitman Coll., Walla Walla, Wash., 1981; Fulbright prof. U. Dacca, East Pakistan, 1959-60; prof. emeritus U. Oreg., Eugene, 1980—. Author: Geology of Oregon, 1959, 64, 76, 81. Contbr. articles to profl. jours. Mem. Geol. Soc. Am. (v.p. cordilleran sect. 1961), Am. Assn. Petroleum Geologists, Paleontol. Soc. (cordilleran sect. chmn.), Am. Inst. Profl. Geologists, N.W. Sci. Soc. (life). Club: Civitan (pres.) (Eugene). Home: 1020 E 18th Ave Apt 3 Eugene OR 97403-1313

BALDWIN, HUGH JOHN, dean; b. Ashern, Man., Can., Feb. 24, 1940; came to the U.S., 1964; s. George Herbert and Margaret Edith (Mackey) B.; m. Marilyn Jean Halloran, Nov. 17, 1973 (dec. Nov. 1991). BSc in Pharmacy, U. Man., 1962; MS, Purdue U., 1967, PhD, 1969. Pharmacist Gurvey's Pharmacies, Winnipeg, Man., 1962-64; tchg. asst., instr. Purdue U., West Lafayette, Ind., 1964-68; asst. prof. pharmacy U. Mo., Kansas City, 1968-72, Ohio State U., Columbus, 1973-74; from assoc. prof. to prof., dept. chair W.Va. U., Morgantown, 1974-85; dean Sch. Pharmacy U. Wyo., Laramie, 1985—; bd. dirs. Pharmat, Lawrence, Kans. Co-editor: Pharmacy Ethics, 1991; contbr. articles to profl. jours. Amb. Laramie C. of C. Recipient Appreciation award Wyo. State Bd. Pharmacists, Jackson, 1993. Mem. Am. Assn. Colls. Pharmacy (sect. chair, sec.-treas. 1975-77), Am. Inst. History Pharmacy, Am. Soc. Health-Sys. Pharmacy, Am. Pharm. Assn., Wyo. Pharmacists Assn., Laramie Country Club (bd. dirs.). Office: Univ Wyo Sch Pharmacy Box 3375 Laramie WY 82071

BALDWIN, PETER, history educator; b. Ann Arbor, Mich., Dec. 22, 1956; s. John W. and Jenny (Jochens) B.; m. Dagmar Richter, 1985; children: Lukas, Elias. BA, Yale U., 1978; MA, Harvard U., 1980, PhD, 1986. Asst. prof. Harvard U., Cambridge, Mass., 1986-90; assoc. prof. history UCLA, 1992—. Author: The Politics of social Solidarity, 1990. Office: UCLA Dept of History 405 Hilgard Ave Los Angeles CA 90095-1473

BALDWIN, RHONDA, state health services administrator. BSW, U. South Dakota, 1978; MSW, Ariz. State U., 1982. Cert. Ind. Social Worker. Spl. asst. to dep. dir. Ariz. Dept. Econ. Security, Phoenix, 1982-83; exec. asst. to dir. Ariz. Dept. Health Svcs., Phoenix, 1983-86; dep. asst. dir. divsn. behavioral health Ariz. Dept. Health Svcs., Phoenix, 1993-95, asst. dir., 1996—; exec. v.p., CEO Cmty. Care Network, Phoenix, 1986-92. Office: Ariz Dept Health Svcs Behavioral Health Svcs 2122 E Highland Ste 200 Phoenix AZ 85016

BALDWIN-HALVORSEN, LISA ROGENE, community health and critical care nurse; b. Silverton, Oreg., Aug. 17, 1960; d. Roger W. Baldwin and Udene L. Allen. BSN, Walla Walla Coll., 1982; MS in Nursing, Oreg. Health Scis. U., 1991, post Masters cert. Cmty. Health Nursing, 1993, postgrad., 1993—. RN, Oreg. Staff nurse Providence Med. Ctr., Portland, Oreg., 1982-96; asst. clin. mgr. ICU VA Med. Ctr., Portland, 1991-93, nurse educator critical care, 1994—; nurse mgr. Providence Med. Ctr., 1996—; tchg. asst. Oreg. Health Scis. U., Portland, 1992-94, 95-96, rsch. asst., 1994-96; mem. logical job analysis panel Nat. Coun. State Bds., Chgo., 1993, item writer, Princeton, N.J., 1993. U. Club Found. fellow, Portland, 1994. Mem. ACCN, Oreg. Health Decisions. Office: Cardiac Intensive Care Unit 4805 NE Glisan Portland OR 97213

BALENTINE, JOHN L., county official; b. Hollywood, Calif., Apr. 14, 1948; s. John L. and Roberta Ella (Wyatt) B.; m. Eva A. Grimm, Sept. 20, 1975 (div. Feb. 8, 1992); m. Jennie L. LaBranch, July 16, 1995. AA, L.A. Valley Coll., Van Nuys, Calif., 1968; BA, San Fernando Valley State Coll, Northridge, Calif., 1970. Cert. purchasing mgr. Nat. Assn. Purchasing Mgmt. Spl. asst. to Mayor City of L.A., 1967-75; CEO, ptnr. Total Travel Internat., Nashville, 1975-78; program evaluator II Comptroller Office, State of Tenn., Nashville, 1978-80; asst. chief security Onslow Hotel/Casino, Reno, Nev., 1980-85; sr. buyer State of Nev., Carson City, 1986-92; purchasing and contract adminstr. Washoe County, Reno, 1992—. Contbr. articles to profl. jours. Dir. No. Nev. Consortium of Coop. Purchasing, Reno, 1986—, Washoe County Detention Facility Industries, Reno, 1992—, Nat. Purchasing Inst., 1996—; res. dep. sheriff Washoe County Sheriff's Office, Reno, 1982-85. Recipient Meritorious Citation, Gov. of Nev., 1991, Cert. of Merit, Human Rels. Commn., City of L.A., 1971, Cert. of Appreciation, Mayor of L.A., 1971, Youth Adv. Coun. of L.A., 1969. Mem. Nat. Assn. Purchasing Mgmt. (cert., No. Nev. chpt. pres. 1989-94, dir. nat. affairs 1994—), Nat. Purchasing Inst., Nat. Inst. Govt. Purchasing, Nat. Corvette Owners Assn. Jehovah's Witnesses. Home: PO Box 143 Sparks NV 89432-0143 Office: Washoe County Purchasing PO Box 11130 Reno NV 89520-0027

BALET, JAN, artist; b. Bremen, Germany, 1913. Student, Sch. Arts and Crafts, Munich, Sch. Arts and Crafts, Berlin. Former art dir. Mademoiselle mag., Seventeen. One-man shows Galeriei Niebuhr, Berlin, Galerie Niggli, Zurich, Switzerland, Paula Modersohn Becker Haus, Bremen, Galerie Charlotte, Munich, Stadtmuseum, Munich; represented in permanent collections Stadtische Galerie, Stadtmuseum, Bayerische Staatsgemaldesammlungen, Munich, Kunsthalle, Bremen, also pvt. collections in U.S., Mex., Austria, Israel, Sweden, The Netherlands, Germany, France, Switzerland. Recipient 25 gold, silver and awards of merit Art Dirs. Club. *

BALINT, JOSEPH PHILIP, medical products executive; b. Passaic, N.J., Mar. 24, 1948; s. Joseph and Margaret (Birish) B. BA, Rutgers U., 1970, PhD, 1977. Cert. med. technologist, Am. Soc. Clin. Pathology. Med. technologist N.J. Coll. Medicine and Dentistry, Newark, 1970-72; grad. student Rutgers U., New Brunswick, N.J., 1972-77; rsch. fellow Rsch. Inst. of Scripps Clinic, La Jolla, Calif., 1977-80; rsch. assoc. Baylor Coll. Medicine, Houston, 1980-82, rsch. instr., 1982; cons. Imré Corp., Seattle, 1982-83, rsch. dir., 1983-89, v.p. product devel., 1989-92, dir. device devel., 1993, v.p. R&D, 1994-96. Contbr. articles profl. jours., patentee in field. Recipient N.J. State scholarship, 1966-70, NIH rsch. grants, 1983, 84, Nat. Cancer Inst. grant, 1984. Home: 520 2nd Ave W Apt 311 Seattle WA 98119-3979

BALK, DAVID MICHAEL, career officer, marine engineer, aquanaut; b. Tucson, Apr. 16, 1957; s. Sheldon and Melvina Lee (Bellman) B.; m. Juanita Paula Ammerman, Sept. 27, 1980; children: Alexander Sean, Meghan Anne. BS in Arch. Engring., Calif. Poly Tech. U., 1980; ME in Ocean Engring., Tex. A&M, 1985. Registered profl. engr. Commd. ensign USN, 1980—; commanding officer Underwater Constrn. Team Two, Port Hueneme, Calif., 1993-95. Adult leader Boy Scouts Am., 1990—. Recipient HMNI award of excellence Naval Med. Rsch. Inst., 1986, Naval Sea award of merit Naval Sea System Command, Washington, 1992. Mem. ASCE, Soc. Am. Mil. Engrs. (bd. dirs.), Marine Tech. Soc., Surfrider, Alpha Epsilon Pi (pres. 1975—). Office: Naval Facilities Engring Svc Ctr 1100 23rd Ave Port Hueneme CA 93043-4333

BALL, DONALD EDMON, architect; b. Evansville, Ind., July 18, 1942; s. Harvey and Myrl (Norris) B. BA in Design, So. Ill. U., 1967. Registered architect Ariz., Calif., Colo., Nev.; cert. Nat. Coun. Archtl. Registration Bd. With design dept. Leo A. Daly Co., Architects and Engrs., Omaha, 1968; project mgr. Buetow & Assocs., St. Paul, 1969-70; ptnr. Comprehensive Design, Mpls., 1971-73; with Caudill Assocs., Aspen, Colo., 1973-76, Hagman Yaw, Ltd., Aspen, 1977; project mgr. Hauter Assocs., Aspen, 1978; pres. Jacobs, Ball & Assocs., Architects, Aspen and Denver, 1978-85; project mgr. Moshe Safdie & Assocs., Boston, 1985-87; dir. design Dwayne Lewis Architects, Inc., Phoenix, 1987-88; prin. Donald Ball and Assocs., Scottsdale, Ariz., 1988—. Mem. Aspen Bldg. Insp. Selection Com., 1982, Pitkin County Housing Authority Bd., Aspen, 1984. Mem. AIA (chmn. Colo. West chpt., documents com.), Ariz. Soc. Architects (profl. practice com.). Home and Office: 7702 E Sutton Dr Scottsdale AZ 85260

BALL, JACQUELINE, park administrator. Park supt. Gov.'s Mansion State Historic Park, Sacramento, 1993—. Office: Governors Mansion State Historic Park Sacramento CA 95814

BALL, JAMES HERINGTON, lawyer; b. Kansas City, Mo., Sept. 20, 1942; s. James T. Jr. and Betty Sue (Herington) B.; m. Wendy Anne Wolfe, Dec. 28, 1964; children: James H. Jr., Steven Scott. AB, U. Mo., 1964; JD cum laude, St. Louis U., 1973. Bar: Mo. 1973. Asst. gen. counsel Anheuser-Busch, Inc., St. Louis, 1973-76; v.p., gen. counsel, sec. Stouffer Corp., Solon, Ohio, 1976-83; sr. v.p., gen. counsel Nestle Enterprises, Inc., Solon, 1983-91; gen. counsel, sr. v.p. Nestle USA, Inc., Glendale, Calif., 1991—. Editor-in-chief St. Louis U. Law Jour., 1972-73. Bd. dirs. Alliance for Children's Rights, L.A., 1992—, Am. Swiss Found., N.Y.C., 1996—. Lt. comdr. USN, 1964-70, Vietnam. Mem. Mo. Bar Assn. Office: Nestle USA Inc 800 N Brand Blvd Glendale CA 91203-1244

BALL, JENNIFER LEIGH, writer, editor; b. South Charleston, W.Va., Aug. 6, 1961; d. Robert Lee Ball and Lois Jean (Sovine) White. BA, Marshall U., Huntington, W.Va., 1983; MA, U. Colo., Colorado Springs, 1997. Copy writer Klausner Cooperage, Louisville, 1986; staff writer Ky. Power Co., Ashland, 1987-91; print buyer Focus on the Family, Colorado Springs, 1992-94; publs. mgr. Compassion Internat., Colorado Springs, 1994-96; internat. comms. assoc. Internat. Bible Soc., Colorado Springs, 1996—. Mem. Internat. Assn. Bus. Communicators, Evangelical Press Assn. Home: 231 Elmwood Dr Colorado Springs CO 80907

BALL, LAWRENCE, retired physical scientist; b. Albion, N.Y., Aug. 10, 1933; s. Harold Witheral and Gladys (Gibbs) B.; m. Caroline Moran, June 21, 1957; children: Daniel Lawrence, Logan Edward, Stacey Laura Ball Lucero, Ryan Laird (dec.). Diploma, Williston Acad., 1952; BSME, Antioch Coll., 1957; MSc in Elec. Engring., Ohio State U., 1962. Engring. aid Wright Air Devel. Ctr., Dayton, Ohio, 1957-60; engr. Deco Electronics Inc., Boulder, Colo., 1962-66; sr. engr. Westinghouse Rsch. Labs., Boulder, 1966-73, Westinghouse Ocean Rsch. Lab., Annapolis, Md., 1973-74; program mgr. div. geothermal energy U.S. Dept. Energy, Washington, 1974-79; lab. dir. U.S. Dept. Energy, Grand Junction, Colo., 1979-93; ret., 1993; pres. Liberty Cons. Co., Grand Junction, 1984—; emergency coord. dist. 3 Amateur Radio Emergency Svcs., 1995—. Co-inventor coal mine communications; contbr. articles to profl. jours. Mem. various vol. fire depts., 1954-79; mem., sr. patroller Nat. Ski Patrol Sys., Md., Colo., 1973-92; coord. Amateur Radio Emergency Svcs., 1995—; bd. dirs. Colo. Head Injury Found., chpt. pres., 1989-91. Named Profl. Govt. Employee of Yr., Western Colo. Fed. Exec. Assn., 1991. Mem. Soc. Exploration Geophysicists, Toastmasters Internat. (area gov. 1991-92, divsn. gov. 1992-93, Toastmaster of Yr. Western Colo. 1990, DTM & ATM-S 1994), West Slope Wheelman (charter bd. dirs. 1992-93), Western Colo. Amateur Radio Club, Inc. (pres. 1994-96, bd. dirs. 1996—, emergency coord. Amateur Radio Emergency Svcs. 1995—).

BALL, ROBERT EDWIN, engineering educator; b. Indpls., Aug. 2, 1935; s. Robert Raymond and Marjory May (McComb) B.; m. Rana Niola Applegate, Sept. 2, 1956; children: Robert Edwin Jr., Susan Marie Ball Culcasi. BSCE, Northwestern U., 1958, MSCE, 1959, PhD, 1962. Mem. tech. staff NESCO, 1962-65; dir. solid mechanics Dynamic Sci., 1965-67; disting. prof. dept. aeronautics and astronautics Naval Postgrad. Sch., Monterey, Calif., 1967—. Author: The Fundamentals of Aircraft Combat Survivability Analysis and Design, 1985. Fellow AIAA (chmn. survivability tech. com. 1989-92, Survivability award 1996, chmn. com. on weapons effects on airborne sys. Nat. Rsch. Coun., 1991-93). Home: 642 Toyon Dr Monterey CA 93940-4225

BALL, ROBERT JEROME, classics educator; b. N.Y.C., Nov. 4, 1941; s. William and Pauline Ball. BA, Queens Coll., 1962; MA, Tufts U., 1963; PhD, Columbia U., 1971. Asst. prof. classics U. Hawaii, Honolulu, 1971-76, assoc. prof., 1976-83, prof., 1983—. Author: Tibullus The Elegist: A Critical Survey, 1983, Reading Classical Latin: A Resonable Approach, 1987, Reading Classical Latin: The Second Year, 1990; editor: The Classical Papers of Gilbert Highet, 1983; co-editor: Alfred Burns' Biography, From Austria to Hawaii: Odyssey of a Classicist, 1994. Recipient Excellence in Teaching award U. Hawaii, 1979; Presdl. scholar U. Hawaii, 1985. Mem. Am. Philol. Assn. (Excellence in Teaching award 1981). Office: U Hawaii at Manoa Dept European Langs Honolulu HI 96822

BALL, WILLIAM PAUL, physicist, engineer; b. San Diego, Nov. 16, 1913; s. John and Mary (Kajla) B.; m. Edith Lucile March, June 28, 1941 (dec. 1976); children: Lura Irene Ball Raplee, Roy Ernest. AB, UCLA, 1940; PhD, U. Calif., Berkeley, 1952. Registered profl. engr. Calif. Projectionist, sound technician studios and theatres in Los Angeles, 1932-41; tchr. high sch. Montebello, Calif., 1941-42; instr. math. and physics Santa Ana (Calif.) Army Air Base, 1942-43; physicist U. Calif. Radiation Lab., Berkeley and Livermore, 1943-58; mem. tech. staff Ramo-Wooldridge Corp., Los Angeles, 1958-59; sr. scientist Hughes Aircraft Co., Culver City, Calif., 1959-64; sr. staff engr. TRW-Def. Systems Group, Redondo Beach, Calif., 1964-83, Hughes Aircraft Co., 1983-86; cons. Redondo Beach, 1986—. Contbr. articles to profl. jours.; patentee in field. Bd. dirs. So. Dist. Los Angeles chpt. ARC, 1979-86. Recipient Manhattan Project award for contbn. to 1st atomic bomb, 1945. Mem. AAAS, Am. Phys. Soc., Am. Nuclear Soc., N.Y. Acad. Scis., Torrance (Calif.) Area C. of C. (bd. dirs. 1978-84), Sigma Xi. Home and Office: 209 Via El Toro Redondo Beach CA 90277-6561

BALLANTINE, MORLEY COWLES (MRS. ARTHUR ATWOOD BALLANTINE), newspaper editor; b. Des Moines, May 21, 1925; d. John and Elizabeth (Bates) Cowles; m. Arthur Atwood Ballantine, July 26, 1947 (dec. 1975); children—Richard, Elizabeth Ballantine Leavitt, William, Helen Ballantine Healy. A.B., Ft. Lewis Coll., 1975; L.H.D. (hon.), Simpson Coll., Indianola, Iowa, 1980. Pub. Durango (Colo.) Herald, 1952-83, editor, pub., 1975-83, editor, chmn. bd., 1983—; dir. 1st Nat. Bank, Durango, 1976—, Des Moines Register & Tribune, 1977-85, Cowles Media Co., 1982-86. Mem. Colo. Land Use Commn., 1975-81, Supreme Ct. Nominating Commn., 1984-90; mem. Colo. Forum, 1985—, Blueprint for Colo., 1985-92; pres. S.W. Colo. Mental Health Ctr., 1964-65, Four Corners Opera Assn., 1983-86; bd. dirs. Colo. Nat. Hist. Preservation Act, 1968-78; trustee Choate/Rosemary Hall, Wallingford, Conn., 1973-81, Simpson Coll., Indianola, Iowa, 1981—, U. Denver, 1984—, Fountain Valley Sch., Colorado Springs, 1976-89, trustee emerita, 1993—; mem. exec. com. Ft. Lewis Coll. Found., 1991—. Recipient 1st place award for editorial writing Nat. Fedn. Press Women, 1955, Outstanding Alumna award Rosemary Hall, Greenwich, Conn., 1969, Outstanding Journalism award U. Colo. Sch. Journalism, 1967, Distinguished Service award Ft. Lewis Coll., Durango, 1970; named to Colo. Community Journalism Hall of Fame, 1987; named Citizen of Yr. Durango Area Chamber Resort Assn., 1990. Mem. Nat. Soc. Colonial Dames, Colo. Press Assn. (bd. dirs. 1978-79), Colo. AP Assn. (chmn. 1966-67), Federated Women's Club Durango, Mill Reef Club (Antigua, W.I.) (bd. govs. 1985-91). Episcopalian. Address: care Durango Herald PO Drawer A Durango CO 81302

BALLANTYNE, JAMES HENRY, IV, investor, developer; b. Boise, Idaho, Jan. 8, 1932; s. James Henry III and Meta Christina (Houmann) B.; m. Mary Rand, June 12, 1954; children: Janet Marie, John Irving, Helen Kristina, Michael Joseph, Mary Elizabeth. BS, U. Idaho, 1954; student, Gonzaga Coll. at Boise, 1977-78, Boise State U., 1967—. Lic. real estate broker, Idaho. Owner farms and ranch, Idaho and Oreg., 1956—; owner, broker Ballantyne Land Co., Boise, 1963-89; ptnr. Succor Creek Oil Co., Boise, 1975-80; owner Ice Rink, Inc., Boise, 1975-87, investment/devel. co., Boise, 1963—; mem. adv. bd. dept. geology Boise State U., 1988—; mem. fin. bd. Diocese of Boise, Cath. Ch., 1985-89. Artist, working in India ink; author: (poetry) Cold Drill, 1984. Bd. dirs. Head Start, Ada County, Idaho, 1991—, Ada County 4-H Endowment, 1989—; mem. adv. bd. Nazareth Retreat Ctr., Boise, 1978—; pres. Ecumenical Chs. in Idaho, 1980-85. Lt. USNR, 1954-56, Korea. Named Citizen of Yr., Grange, Maple Grove, Boise, 1988; recipient various awards. Mem. Agrarian Club (pres.), Wranglers, Friday Fried Poets, Kiwanis Internat. (gov. 1994-95, Disting. lt. gov. 1991), Alpha Zeta, Sigma Chi. Home: 10250 Whispering Cliffs Dr Boise ID 83704-1907

BALLARD, CLYDE, state legislator; b. Batesville, Ark., June 8, 1936; s. Jeffery C. and Monnie F. Ballard; m. Ruth L. Guthrie, Feb. 6, 1955; children: Jeff, Shawn, Scott. Store mgr., gen. mgr. Peter Rabbit Stores, Wenachee, Wash., 1955-66; owner Ballard Svcs., Wenachee, 1967-87; caucus chmn., minority leader Wash. Ho. Rep., Olympia, 1985-94, spkr. house, 1995—. Republican. Methodist. Home: 1790 N Baker East Wenatchee WA 98802 Office: Wash Ho of Reps Dist 12 Olympia WA 98504

BALLARD, JACK STOKES, engineering educator; b. Gravette, Ark., July 23, 1928; s. Freeman Stokes and Chloe Katherine (Clarry) B.; m. Arleda Anne Greenwood, Feb. 21, 1954; children: Kenneth Stokes, Donald Steven, Cheryl Anne. BSE, U. Ark., 1950; MA, U. So. Calif., 1953; PhD, UCLA, 1974. Cert. secondary tchr. Commd. 2d lt. USAF, 1954, advanced through grades to lt. col., 1974, ret., 1980; tchr. Coalinga & Whittier (Calif.) High Schs., 1951-54; tng. and pers. officer USAF, Travis AFB, Calif., Alaska, 1954-59; asso. prof. air sci. Occidental Coll., L.A., 1959-64; asst. prof. history USAF Acad., Colorado Springs, Colo., 1964-69; sr. tng advisor Korean Air Force Tng. Wing, Taejon, 1969-70; air force historian Office of Air Force History, Washington, 1970-74; chief plans and requirement div. Lowry Tech. Tng. Ctr., Denver, 1974-80; chief strategic systems tng. Martin Marietta Corp., Denver, 1980-92; instr. history, U. Alaska, Anchorage, 1958-59, U. Md., Taejon, 1969-70; adj. instr. history U. Colo., Colorado Springs, 1977-83, U. Colo., Denver, 1983-87. Author: Development and Employment of Fixed Wing Gunships, 1982, Shock of Peace, 1983; contbg. author USAF in S.E. Asia, 1977; contbr. articles to profl. jours. Pres. Occidental Coll. Faculty Club, 1962-63; chmn. Adv. Coun. Sch. Improvement, Littleton, Colo., 1984-89; sec. Large Sch. Dist. Accountability Coun., Denver, 1988-89; elected sch. bd. dirs. Littleton Pub. Schs., 1991; pres. Littleton Sch. Bd., 1995; recognized as Colo. All-State Sch. Bd. mem., 1996; sec. Mile High chpt. Air Force Assn., 1988; pres. Littleton Lions Club, 1996—. Recipient Commendation medal USAF, Washington, 1970, Meritorious Svc. medal, Lowry AFB, 1974. Mem. Orgn. Am. Historians, Western History Assn., Air Force Hist. Found., Am. Def. Preparedness Assn., Colo. Hist. Soc. Republican. Methodist. Home: 7820 S Franklin Way Littleton CO 80122-3116

BALLARD, LORREN LEE, fire protection official; b. Denver, May 8, 1939; s. David Crockett and Dorothy (Canter) B.; m. Barbara Ballard, Feb. 15, 1961 (div. 1967); children: Lorren Jr., Christopher; m. Donna Mae Veenstra, Dec. 30, 1988; 1 child, Erika Rasmussen. BS, Regis Coll., 1987. From firefighter to divsn. chief City of Denver, 1963-89; fire chief City of Billings, Mont., 1989—; active Comm. Ctr. Adv. Bd., Billings, 1989—. Chmn. Local Emergency Planning Com., Billings, 1989—; v.p. adv. bd. Salvation Army, 1989—; chmn. adv. bd. Critical Incident Stress Debriefing Team, 1989—. Office: Billings Fire Dept 2305 8th Ave N Billings MT 59101-1018*

BALLARD, REX KEVIN, science administrator; b. Okinawa, Japan, Dec. 19, 1956; s. James Kenneth and Daisy G.N. (Tom) B.; m. Elisa Marie Ballard, Jan. 7, 1978; children: Brandon Kent, Krista Marie. BS, Calif. State U., Hayward, 1980. Dep. dir. contracts Cubic Corp., Cubic Western Data, San Diego; cubic adminstr. Def. Contract Adminstrn. Svc., San Diego; contract negotiator USN, San Diego; v.p., group bus. ops. mgr. tech. devel. group Sci. Applications Internat. Corp., San Diego. Mem. Nat. Contracts Mgmt. Assn., Armed Forces Communications and Electronics Assn. Republican. Office: 4161 Campus Point Ct San Diego CA 92121

BALLENTINE, LEE KENNEY, writer, publishing company executive; b. Teaneck, N.J., Sept. 4, 1954; s. George Kenney and Veda Avis Maxine (Havens) B.; m. Jennifer Ursula Marie Moore, Aug. 20, 1983; 1 child, Philip Alden Emerson. Student, Harvey Mudd Coll., 1972-73; BS in Computer Sci., SUNY, Albany, 1976; postgrad., U. Colo., 1976-77, U. Calif., Berkeley, 1977-78. Software engr. Osborne & Assocs. Pubs., Berkeley, 1978-80, Triad Systems Corp., Sunnyvale, Calif., 1981-84; group leader, operating systems and communications Daisy Systems Corp., Sunnyvale, 1984-85; software applications engr. mgr. Fairchild Clipper Div., Palo Alto, Calif., 1985-87; cons. numerous electronic and pub. industry clients, 1987-88; pres. Ocean View Tech. Publs., Mountain View, Calif., 1989-91, Profl. Book Ctr., Denver, 1991—; pub. Ocean View Books, Denver, 1986—; seminar presenter Willamette Writer's Conf., Portland, Oreg., 1990, Rocky Mountain Book Festival, 1993, Rocky Mountain Book Publishers, 1993, Denver Book Mall, 1994, Tattered Cover Book Store, 1993, 94, Boulder Pub. Libr., 1995; cons. Prentice-Hall Pub. Co., Englewood Cliffs, N.J., 1989-90, Amdahl Corp., Sunnyvale, 1988-90; mem. New Eng. Book Show, 1991. Author: Directional Information, 1981, Basements in the Music Box, 1986, Dream Protocols, 1992, Phase Language, 1995; editor: Poly: New Speculative Writing, 1989, An Anatomy of wonder, 1995; pub. Phi Beta Kappa newsletter, San Francisco, 1987-89; art editor High Fantastic: Colorado's Fantasy, Dark Fantasy and Science Fiction, 1996. Presenter Mount View Pub. Libr., 1990. Recipient Ednl. Explorations award Reader's Digest, 1975, Outstanding Scholarly Book award Am. Pub. Assn., 1995; Nat. Merit scholar, 1972. Mem. Am. Book Producers Assn., Sci. Fiction Writers of Am., Sci. Fiction Poetry Assn., USR Group Unix Profl. Assn., Book Builder's West (cert. of merit), The Am. Booksellers Assn., Small Press Book Ctr., Poeisis (adv. bd.

1993), PEN West. Office: Profl Book Ctr PO Box 102650 Denver CO 80250-2650

BALLING, ROBERT C., JR., geography educator; b. 1952. Asst. prof. geography U. Nebr., 1979-84; mem. faculty Ariz. State U., 1985—, assoc. prof.; dir. Office of Climatology; lectr. greenhouse effect debate, Australia, New Zealand, Can., Kuwait, U.S. Author: The Heated Debate: Greenhouse Predictions Versus Climate Reality, 1992; contbr. articles to sci. jours. Office: Ariz State U Box 871508 Tempe AZ 85287-1508

BALLINGER, CHARLES KENNETH, information specialist; b. Johnstown, Pa., July 28, 1950; s. Delores Jean (Cool) B.; m. Deb C. Delger, Sept. 14, 1985. Programmer analyst Cowles Pub. Co., Spokane, Wash., 1975-78; systems analyst Old Nat. Bank, Spokane, 1978-82; software engr. ISC System, Spokane, 1982; micro computer analyst Acme Bus. Computers, Spokane, 1982-85; info. ctr. analyst Wash. Water Power Co., Spokane, 1985-92; office automation analyst EDS Corp., Spokane, 1992-96, software engr.-mini/micro, 1996—; cons. IDP Co., Spokane, 1978—. Contbr. articles to profl. jours. Served with Signal Corps, U.S. Army, 1968-71. Mem. IEEE (assoc.), Spokane Health Users Group (pres. 1979-83). Home: 3810 S Havana St Spokane WA 99223-6006 Office: EDS-I/S Wash Water Power Co 1411 E Mission Ave Spokane WA 99202-2617

BALLINGER, JAMES K., art museum executive; b. Kansas City, Mo., July 7, 1949; s. Robert Eugene and Yvonne (Davidson) B.; m. Nina Lundgaard, Aug. 21, 1971; children—Erin, Cameron. B.A., U. Kans., 1972, M.A., 1974. Gallery coordinator Tucson Art Ctr., 1973; registrar U. Kans., Lawrence, 1973-74; curator collections Phoenix Art Mus., 1974-81, asst. dir., 1981, dir., 1982—. Author: (exhbn. catalogues) Beyond the Endless River, 1980, Visitors to Arizona 1846 to 1980, 1981, Peter Hurd, 1983, The Popular West, 1982, Thomas Moran, 1986, Frederick Remington, 1989. Bd. dirs. Balboa Art Conservation Ctr. Fellow Am. Assn. Mus. Dirs. (bd. dirs.), Western Assn. Art Museums; mem. Central Ariz. Mus. Assn. (v.p. 1983). Home: 5002 E Calle Tuberia Phoenix AZ 85018-4425 Office: Phoenix Art Mus 1625 N Central Ave Phoenix AZ 85004-1624*

BALLOT, MICHAEL HARVEY, business administration educator, consultant; b. N.Y.C., Jan. 8, 1940; s. Max and Claire (Bayer) B.; m. Nancy Diann Christiansen, Feb. 23, 1963; children: Michele Ann Dodge, David Andrew, Edward Carter. BME, Cornell U., 1962; MBA, U. Santa Clara, 1964; MA in Econs., Stanford U., 1968, PhD in Bus. and Econs., 1973. Mfg. engr. Lockheed Missiles & Space Co., Sunnyvale, Calif., 1962-64, Beckman Instruments, Palo Alto, Calif., 1964-65; asst. prof. econs. Chico (Calif.) State Coll., 1968-71; asst. prof. bus. adminstrn. Univ. of Pacific, Stockton, Calif., 1971-74, assoc. prof., 1974-79, prof., 1979—; cons., spkr. in field; arbitrator, Stockton, Calif., 1975—. Author: Decision-Making Models in P/OM, 1986, Labor Management-Relations in a Changing Environment, 1996 (2nd edit.). Cons. U.S. Dept. Transp., 1973, Stockton State Hosp., 1974, Stockton Econ. Devel. Agy., 1971, 85-86. Mem. Decision Scis. Inst., Am. Econs. Assn., Soc. for Computer Simulation, Am. Acad. Polit. and Social Sci., Prodn. and Ops. Mgmt. Assn., Indsl. Rels. Rsch. Assn., Beta Gamma Sigma. Home: 5149 Gadwall Cir Stockton CA 95207-5331 Office: U of the Pacific Eberhardt Sch Bus Stockton CA 95211

BALLOU, NATHAN ELMER, chemist; b. Rochester, Minn., Sept. 28, 1919; s. Sidney Vaughan and Josephine (Elmer) B.; m. Elaine Louise Chapman, Dec. 28, 1973; children: Robert K., Douglas P. BS, Duluth State Tchrs. Coll., 1941; MS, U. Ill., 1942; PhD, U. Chgo., 1947. Rsch. scientist Manhattan Project, Oak Ridge, Tenn., 1942-46; rsch. assoc. U. Calif., Berkeley, 1947-48; head nuclear chemistry br. Naval Radiol. Def. Lab., San Francisco, 1948-69; chief chemistry dept. Belgian Nuclear Energie Ctr., Mol, 1959-61; mgr. analytical and nuclear rsch. sect. Battelle-Northwest, Richland, Wash., 1969-87; scientist Battelle-Northwest, Richland, 1987—. Contbr. numerous articles to profl. jours. Fellow Nat. Rsch. Coun., 1946-47; recipient Superior Svc. award USN, 1966. Mem. NAS (nuclear sci. com. 1959-66, chmn. radiochem. subcom. 1962-66), Am. Chem. Soc. (treas. nuclear chemistry and tech. divsn. 1969-77). Office: Battelle-Northwest PO Box 999 Richland WA 99352-0999

BALLSUN, KATHRYN ANN, lawyer; b. Calif., May 8, 1946; d. Zan and Doris (Pratt) B.; m. Paul L. Stanton, June 1, 1981; 1 child, Brian Paul. BA, U. So. Calif., 1969, MA, 1971; JD, Loyola U., L.A., 1976. Bar: Calif. 1976, U.S. Dist. Ct. (cen. dist.) Calif. 1977. Ptnr. Stanton & Ballsun, L.A.; vis. prof. UCLA Law Sch., Loyola U. Law Sch., L.A.; adj. prof. U. So. Calif. Law Sch.; mem. planning com. U. So. Calif. Progate and Trust Conf., 1985-87; lectr. various schs. Author: (with others) Estate Planning for the General Practitioner; editor: How to Live and Die with California Probate; contbr. articles to profl. jours. Mem. graphic arts coun. L.A. County Mus. Art, Children's Coun., Westwood Meth. Ch.; co-chmn. for Class of 1976 Greater Loyola Law Sch. Devel. Program, 1983; advisor Am. Cancer Soc. Program; radio vol. sta. KUSC; bd. dirs. Planned Protective Svcs. Inc.; bd. dirs. L.A. Philharm. Orch., com. profl. women, treas. 1985-86. Fellow Am. Coll. Probate Counsel; mem. ABA (real property, probate and trust law, taxation sects., pre-death planning com.), State Bar Calif. (resolutions com., exec. com., co-vice chair estate planning techniques, post death, pre-death com., trust and probate, bus. law, taxation sects., law revision study team 1983-85), L.A. County Bar Assn. (trustee, exec. com., trust and probate, taxation sects.), Beverly Hills Bar Assn. (treas. 1985-86, bd. govs. 1982-84, 84-86, probate and trust com., taxation com., sr. vice chair resolutions com., del. State Bar Conv. 1981-85, v.p. 1987-89, pres.-elect, pres. 1989—, panelist), Nat. Acad. Elder Law Attys., Inc., Calif. Women Lawyers, L.A. Women Lawyers, Women in Business (sec., polit. action com.), Beverly Hills Estate Planning Com., Estate Counselor's Forum (past pres., v.p., bd. dirs.), Los Angeles County Mus. Art, L.A. C. of C., ACLU (L.A. chpt.), UCLA Ctr. for Study of Women, ACLU (L.A. chpt.), Kappa Alpha Theta. Office: Tuttle & Taylor 355 S Grand Ave 40th Fl Los Angeles CA 90071

BALMER, THOMAS ANCIL, lawyer; b. Longview, Wash., Jan. 31, 1952; s. Donald Gordon and Elisabeth Clare (Hill) B.; m. Mary Louise McClintock, Aug. 25, 1984; children: Rebecca Louise, Paul McClintock. AB, Oberlin Coll., 1974; JD, U. Chgo., 1977. Bar: Mass. 1977, D.C. 1981, U.S. Dist. Ct. Mass. 1977, Oreg. 1982, U.S. Dist. Ct. Oreg. 1982, U.S. Ct. Appeals (9th cir.) 1982, U.S. Ct. Appeals (D.C. cir.) 1983, U.S. Supreme Ct. 1987. Assoc. Choate, Hall & Stewart, Boston, 1977-79, Wald, Harkrader & Ross, Washington, 1980-82; trial atty. antitrust div. U.S. Dept. Justice, Washington, 1979-80; assoc. Lindsay, Hart, Neil & Weigler, Portland, Oreg., 1982-84; ptnr. Lindsay, Hart, Neil & Weigler, Portland, 1985-90, Ater Wynne Hewitt Dodson & Skerritt, Portland, 1990-93, 97—; dep. atty. gen. State of Oregon, Salem, 1993-97; adj. prof. of law Northwestern Sch. Law Lewis and Clark Coll., 1983-84, 90-92. Contbr. articles to law jours. Active mission and outreach com. United Ch. of Christ, Portland, 1984-87, Met. Svc. Dist. Budget Com., Portland, 1988-90; bd. dirs. Multnomah County Legal Aid Svc., Inc., 1989-93 (chair 1992-93). Mem. ABA, Oreg. Bar Assn. (chmn. antitrust sect. 1986-87). Democrat. Home: 2521 NE 24th Ave Portland OR 97212-4831 Office: 222 SW Columbia Ste 1800 Portland OR 97201

BALMUTH, BERNARD ALLEN, retired film editor; b. Youngstown, Ohio, May 19, 1918; s. Joseph and Sadie (Stein) B.; m. Rosa June Bergman, Mar. 2, 1952; children: Mary Susan, Sharon Nancy. BA in English, UCLA, 1942. Postal clk. U.S. Postal Svc., L.A., 1946-55; asst. and apprentice film editor, film editor L.A., 1955-90; ret., 1990; instr. film editing dept. of the arts UCLA Extension, 1979—; film editing cons. Am. Film Inst., L.A., 1982-92. Author: (manual) The Language of the Cutting Room, 1979, (text) Introduction to Film Editing, 1989. Initiator petition STOP Save TV Original Programming and Stop Excessive Reruns, 1972. Sgt. U.S. Army, 1942-46. Recipient Honor Cert. for Contribution Acad. TV Arts and Scis., 1974, Emmy nomination Best Film Editing, 1982. Mem. Am. Cinema Editors (bd. dirs. 1982-85, sec. 1978-90, v.p. 1987-91, chmn., mem. spl. awards com. 1988—, hon. historian 1993—), Hollywood Film and Labor Coun. (rep. for Editors Guild 1972—), Stage Soc. (bd. dirs., sec. 1949-54). Democrat. Jewish. Address: care Rosallen Prodns PO Box 927 North Hollywood CA 91603

BALOIAN, EDWARD, food products executive; b. 1921. With Charles Baloian Co., Fresno, Calif., 1946-86; v.p. Balo Packing Co., Inc., Fresno, 1978—; chmn. bd. dirs. Baloian Packing Co., Fresno, 1985—. Office: Baloian Packing Co 324 N Fruit Ave Fresno CA 93706-1420*

BALOIAN, TIMOTHY, food products executive; b. 1952; s. Edward Baloian. Pres. Balo Packing Co., Fresno, 1978—, Baloian Packing Co., Fresno, 1985—. Office: Baloian Packing Co Inc 324 N Fruit Ave Fresno CA 93706-1420*

BALSWICK, JACK ORVILLE, social science educator. Asst. prof. sociology Wis. State U., 1967; asst. prof. sociology U. Ga., 1968-71, assoc. prof., 1972-78, prof., 1978-82; prof. sociology and family devel. Fuller Theol. Sem., Pasadena, Calif., dir. rsch. marriage and family ministries. Author (with wife, Judith K. Balswick): The Family, 1989, Social Problems, 1990. Office: Fuller Theol Sem 135 North Oakland Pasadena CA 91101

BALTAKE, JOE, film critic; b. Camden, N.J., Sept. 16; s. Joseph John and Rose Clara (Bearint) B.; m. Susan Shapiro Hale. BA, Rutgers U., 1967. Film critic Gannett Newspapers (suburban), 1969, Phila. Daily News, 1970-85; movie editor Inside Phila., 1986—; film critic The Sacramento Bee, 1987—; leader criticism workshop Phila. Writer's Conf., 1977-79; film critic. Contbg. editor: Screen World, 1973-87 ; author: The Films of Jack Lemmon, 1977, updated, 1986; contbr. articles to Films in Rev., 1969—, broadcast criticism for Prism Cable TV, 1985; cons. Jack Lemmon: American Film Institute Life Achievement Award, 1987, Jack Lemmon: A Life in the Movies, 1990. Recipient Motion Picture Preview Group award for criticism, 1986, citation Phila. Mag., 1985, First Pl. commentary award Soc. of Profl. Journalists, 1995. Mem. Nat. Soc. Film Critics. Office: Sacramento Bee 2100 Q St Sacramento CA 95816-6816 *Life's philosophy: "Living well is the best revenge."*

BALTHASER, ANITA YOUNG, legal assistant; b. Ft. Benning, Ga., Aug. 24, 1951; d. Burnham James and Mary Kenyon (Brown) Young; m. James Lee Balthaser, July 14, 1979. BA, Hofstra U., 1973; MSLS, Case Western Reserve U., 1977. Libr. Ohio Legis. Ref. Bur., Columbus, 1977-79, Parsons Behle & Latimer, Salt Lake City, 1979-82; legal asst. Kimball Parr Waddoups & Gee, Salt Lake City, 1982-84, Watkiss & Saperstein, Salt Lake City, 1984-92, Ballard, Spahr Andrews & Ingersoll, Salt Lake City, 1992—. Mem. Nat. Assn. Bond Lawyers. Lutheran. Office: 201 S Main St Ste 1200 Salt Lake City UT 84111-2210

BALTZ, ANTONE EDWARD, III, journalist, writer; b. Memphis, Aug. 23, 1965; s. Antone Edward Jr. and Mary (Tobin) B.; m. Kristine Lynn Harrison, Mar. 16, 1996. BA, U. Notre Dame, 1987. News editor The Observer, Notre Dame, Ind., 1986-87; intern Notre Dame Mag., 1987; reporter City News Bur., Chgo., 1987-88; legal writer DuPage Press Svc., Wheaton, Ill., 1988-90; staff writer Chgo. Daily Law Bull., 1990-92; staff corr. Bur. Nat. Affairs, Washington, 1992—; instr. Coll. DuPage, Glen Ellyn, Ill., 1990-92; freelance writer Chgo. Sun-Times, 1990-92, DuPage Press, Elmhurst, Ill., 1990-91. Contbr. articles to legal jours. Mem. student adv. bd. U. Denver, 1994-96; pres. St. Vincent's Single Adults, Denver, 1994. Recipient Media award for sensitivity to Asian Americans, Asian-Am. Bar Assn., 1991, Achievement award Chgo. Bar Assn., 1992. Mem. Soc. Profl. Journalists. Roman Catholic.

BALZ, JAMES B., surgeon; b. Fargo, N.D., Apr. 1, 1946; s. Fredric and Betty Ann (Beal) B.; m. Lynn Margaret Owen, Aug. 25, 1969 (dec. Sept. 1979); children: Ryan, Sara, Reika; m. Jeanine Marie Greb, July 11, 1981. BA in Biology, U. Puget Sound, 1968; MD, St. Louis U., 1972. Intern, resident, fellow Ohio State U. Hosps.; chief of staff Eugene (Oreg.) Hosp., 1982-84; dept. chief of surgery Sacred Heart Hosp., Eugene, 1990-92, divsn. chief of surgery, 1994—; pvt. practice Eugene, 1977—. Contbr. articles to profl. publs. Fellow ACS, Am. Soc. Colon and Rectal Surgeons, N.W. Soc. Colon and Rectal Surgeons; mem. AMA, Oreg. Med. Assn. Home: 1948 Olive St Eugene OR 97405-2834 Office: 3203 Willamette St Eugene OR 97405-3348

BANAS, EMIL MIKE, physicist, educator; b. East Chicago, Ind., Dec. 5, 1921; s. John J. and Rose M. (Valcicak) B.; m. Margaret Fagyas, Oct. 9, 1948; children: Mary K., Barbara A. BA, Benedictine Univ., 1943; student (U.S. Rubber fellow), U. Notre Dame, 19 Home: SE 1426 Fancy-Free Dr Pullman WA 99163

BANCEL, MARILYN, fund raising management consultant; b. Glen Ridge, N.J., June 15, 1947; d. Paul and Joan Marie (Spangler) B.; m. Rik Myslewski, Nov. 20, 1983; children: Carolyn, Roxanne. BA in English with distinction, Ind. U., 1969. Cert. fund raising exec. Ptnr. The Sultan's Shirt Tail, Gemlik, Turkey, 1969-72; prodn. mgr. High Country Co., San Francisco, 1973-74; pub. Bay Arts Rev., Berkeley, Calif., 1976-79; dir. devel. Oakland (Calif.) Symphony Orch., 1979-81; assoc. dir. devel. Exploratorium, San Francisco, 1981-86, dir. devel., 1986-91; prin. Fund Devel. Counsel, San Francisco, 1991-93; v.p. The Oram Group, Inc., San Francisco, 1993—; co-chmn. capital campaign com. Synergy Sch., San Francisco, 1993-95, adj. prof. U. San Francisco, 1993—. Fellow U. Strasberg, France, 1968. Mem. Nat. Soc. Fund Raising Execs. (bd. mem. Golden Gate chpt.), Am. Assn. Fund Raising Counsel, Devel. Execs. Roundtable, Phi Beta Kappa. Democrat. Office: The Oram Group 44 Page St Ste 604C San Francisco CA 94102-5986

BANDT, PAUL DOUGLAS, physician; b. Milbank, S.D., June 22, 1938; s. Lester Herman and Edna Louella (Sogn) B.; m. Mary King, Aug. 26, 1962 (div. Feb. 1974); children: Douglas, Peggy; m. Inara Irene Von Rostas, Apr. 1, 1974; 1 child, Jennifer. BS in Edn. with distinction, U. Minn., 1960, BS in Medicine, 1966, D in Medicine, 1966. Diplomate Am. Bd. Diagnostic Radiology, Am. Bd. Nuclear Medicine. Intern U.S. Pub. Health Svc., San Francisco, 1966-68; physician U.S. Pub. Health Svc., Las Vegas, 1968-69; resident Stanford U., Palo Alto, Calif., 1969-72; physician Desert Radiologists, Las Vegas, 1972—; vice chief med. staff Desert Springs Hosp., Las Vegas, chmn. dept. radiology; immediate past chief of staff U. Med. Ctr. So. Nev., Las Vegas. Contbr. articles on diagnostic radiology to profl. jours. With USPHS, 1966-69. Mem. AMA, Am. Coll. Radiology, Am. Coll. Nuclear Medicine, Clark Med. Soc. Office: Desert Radiologists 2020 Palomino Ln Las Vegas NV 89106-4812

BANGS, JOHN WESLEY, III, law enforcement administrator; b. Phila., Dec. 26, 1941; s. John Wesley Jr. and Sarah Emily (Morcom) B.; m. Donna Louise McClanahan, June 1, 1963; children: Louis M., Terry M., John W. IV. AA summa cum laude, E. Los Angeles Coll., 1976. Calif. Commn. on Peace Officer Standards and Training: Basic, Intermediate, Advanced, Supervisory, Mgmt. Police officer Los Angeles Police Dept., 1964-70, sgt., 1970-74, lt., 1974-84; chief spl. officer I L.A. Dept. Airports Police, 1988—; lectr. U. So. Calif., 1978-79. Author: Narcotics Overview, 1983, Psychological Evaluation for Police Candidates, 1969. Cub master Cub Scouts Am., Ontario, Calif., 1968; scout master Boy Scouts Am., Ontario, 1971; explorer leader Explorer Scouts Am., Los Angeles, 1976; mem. Greater Los Angeles Scouting Council, 1976. Sgt. U.S. Army, 1959-62. Mem. Internat. Assn. Chiefs of Police, Calif. Peace Officers Assn., Calif. Narcotics Officers, Los Angeles Police Protective League, Los Angeles Police Relief Assn. Republican. Episcopalian. Office: Los Angeles Airport Police 1 World Way Los Angeles CA 90045-5803

BANISTER, JAMES HENRY, JR., manufacturing company executive, consultant; b. Springfield, Mo., June 18, 1930; s. James Henry and Frances Kellond (Williams) B.; m. Sara Lee Cinegran, Mar. 27, 1933; children: Jeffrey, James, Mark, Robert, Douglas. SB in Mgmt., MIT, 1951. Mgr. contract adminstrn. SRI Internat., Menlo Park, Calif., 1953-64; contracts mgr. Physics Internat., San Leandro, Calif., 1964-67, v.p. adminstrn., 1967-70; pres. Cintra, Inc., Sunnyvale, Calif., 1970-71; sr. v.p. fin. and adminstrn. Physics Internat., San Leandro, 1972-87; pres. MSI, Chantilly, Va., 1987-89; cons. in mgmt. Alamo, Calif., 1989-93; pres. Kinetic Ceramics Inc., Hayward, Calif., 1993—; bd. dirs. JMAR Industries, San Diego, Pacific Precision Labs., Chatsworth, Calif., Benchmark Industries, Goffstown, N.H., Teralite, Inc., Warwick, R.I. 1st lt. USAF, 1951-53. Republican. Home: 721 Fair Oaks Dr Alamo CA 94507-1457 Office: Kinetic Ceramics 26240 Industrial Blvd Hayward CA 94545-2922

BANKOFF, PETER ROSNER, anesthesiologist; b. Michigan City, Ind., Apr. 18, 1951; s. Milton Lewis and Sylvia (Rosner) B.; m. Mary Patrice Norman, Aug. 18, 1974; children: Amy Elizabeth, Michael Jacob, Benjamin Eric. MusB cum laude, Ind. U., 1974, BA in Chemistry, 1977, MD, 1981. Diplomate Am. Bd. Anesthesiology. Intern Good Samaritan Hosp., Phoenix, 1981-82; resident Maricopa Med. Ctr., Phoenix, 1982-84; anesthesiologist Cigna Healthplan of Ariz., Phoenix, 1984-85, Med. Ctr. Anesthsiologists, Phoenix, 1985-92, Park Ctrl. Anesthesiologists, Phoenix, 1992—; mem. anesthesia com. Good Samaritan Regional Med. Ctr., Phoenix, 1988-92, Phoenix Children's Hosp., Phoenix, 1990, 92, 94. Founding mem. Physicians for Phoenix Symphony, 1988—; com. precinctman Reps., Phoenix, 1994; bd. dirs. Interlochen (Mich.) Ctr. for Arts Alumni Orgn. Mem. AMA, Am. Soc. Anesthesiologists, Internat. Anesthesia Rsch. Soc., Soc. for Ambulatory Anesthesia. Home: 14217 N 68th St Scottsdale AZ 85254 Office: Park Ctrl Anesthesiologists 222 W Thomas Rd Ste 102 Phoenix AZ 85013-4420

BANKOWSKY, RICHARD JAMES, English educator; b. Wallington, N.J., Nov. 25, 1928. BA, Yale U., 1952; MA, Columbia U., 1954. Prof. English Calif. State U., Sacramento, 1959—. Author: A Glass Rose, 1958, After Penetcost, 1961, On a Dark Night, 1964, The Pale Criminals, 1967, The Barbarians at the Gates, 1972. Grantee Nat. Inst. Arts and Letters, 1964, Rockefeller Found., 1967. Office: Calif State U English Dept 6000 J St Sacramento CA 95819

BANKS, CHERRY ANN MCGEE, education educator; b. Benton Harbor, Mich., Oct. 11, 1945; d. Kelly and Geneva (Smith) McGee; m. James A. Banks, Feb. 15, 1969; children: Angela Marie, Patricia Ann. BS, Mich. State U., 1968; MA, Seattle U., 1977, EdD, 1991. Tchr. Benton Harbor Pub. Sch., 1968; staff assoc. Citizens Edn. Ctr. N.W., Seattle, 1984-85; edn. specialist Seattle Pub. Schs., Seattle, 1985-87; pres. Edn. Material and Svcs. Ctr., Edmonds, Wash., 1987—; asst. prof. edn. U. Wash., Bothell, 1992-96, assoc. prof. edn., 1996—; cons. Jackson (Miss.) Pub. Schs., 1988, Seattle Pub. Schs., 1988-90, Little Rock Pub. Schs., 1989, Scott Foreman Pub. Co., Glenview, Ill., 1992—; vis. asst. prof. Seattle U., 1991-92. Co-author: March Toward Freedom, 1978; co-editor: Multicultural Education: Issues and Perspectives, 1989, rev. edit., 1993; assoc. editor Handbook of Rsch. on Multicultural Edn.; contbr. chpts. to books. Mem. Jack and Jill Am., Seattle, 1978-94, First AME Headstart Bd., Seattle, 1981-83; trustee Shoreline C.C., Seattle, 1983-95; bd. dirs. King County Campfire, Seattle, 1985-88. Recipient Outstanding Commitment and Leadership of C.C. award Western Region Nat. Coun. on Black Am. Affairs, 1989. Mem. ASCD, Nat. Coun. for Social Studies Programs Com. (vice chairperson Carter G. Woodson Book award com. 1991-92, chair person 1992-93, mem. nominating com.), Am. Rsch. Assn., The Links, Inc., Phi Delta Kappa (founding, Seattle U. chpt.), Alpha Kappa Alpha. Office: U Wash Edn Program 22011 26th Ave SE Bothell WA 98021-4900

BANKS, ERNEST (ERNIE BANKS), retired professional baseball player; b. Dallas, Jan. 31, 1931; s. Eddie B. Student, Northwestern U. Baseball player Kansas City Monarchs (Negro Am. League), 1950-51, 53; baseball player Chgo. Cubs, 1953-71, mgr. group sales, to 1982; with New World Van Lines, 1984—; formerly co-owner, v.p. Bob Nelson-Ernie Banks Ford, Inc., Chgo.; with Associated Films Promotions, L.A., 1982-84. Author: (with Jim Enright) Mr. Cub. Past mem. bd. Chgo. Transit Authority; active Boy Scouts Am., YMCA. Served with AUS, 1951-53, Europe. Named most valuable player Nat. League, 1958, 59; recipient awards from Fans, 1969, awards from Press Club, 1969, awards from Jr. C. of C., 1971; inducted into Tex. Sports Hall Fame, 1971, Baseball Hall of Fame, 1977; mem. Nat. League All-Star Team, 1957-70; hold major league record for most career grand slam home runs.

BANKS, JAMES ALBERT, educational research director, educator; b. Marianna, Ark., Sept. 24, 1941; s. Matthew and Lula (Holt) B.; m. Cherry Ann McGee, Feb. 15, 1969; children: Angela Marie, Patricia Ann. A.A., Chgo. City Coll., 1963; B.E., Chgo. State U., 1964; M.A. (NDEA fellow 1966-69), Mich. State U., 1967, Ph.D., 1969; LHD, Bank St. Coll. Edn., 1993. Tchr. elementary sch. Joliet, Ill., 1965, Francis W. Parker Sch., Chgo., 1965-66; asst. prof. edn. U. Wash., Seattle, 1969-71; assoc. prof. U. Wash., 1971-73, prof., 1973—, chmn. curriculum and instrn., 1982-87; dir. Ctr. for Multicultural Edn., 1991—; vis. prof. edn. U. Mich., 1975, Monash U., Australia, 1985, U. Warwick, Eng., 1988, U. Minn., 1991; vis. lectr. U. Southampton, Eng., 1989, Harry F. and Alva K. Ganders disting. lectr. Syracuse U., 1989; disting. scholar lectr. Kent State U., 1978, U. Ariz., 1979, Ind. U., 1983; vis. scholar Brit. Acad., 1983; Sachs lectr. Tchrs. Coll. Columbia U., 1996; com. examiners Ednl. Testing Svc., 1974-77; nat. adv. coun. on ethnic heritage studies, U.S. Office Edn., 1975-78; com. on fed. role in ednl. rsch. NAS, 1991-92, mem. com. on developing a rsch. agenda on edn. of ltd. proficient and bilingual students, 1995—. Author: Teaching Strategies for Ethnic Studies, 1975, 6th edit., 1997, Teaching Strategies for the Social Studies, 1973, 4th edit., 1990, Teaching the Black Experience, 1970, Multiethnic Education: Practices and Promises, 1977, An Introduction to Multicultural Education, 1994, Educating Citizens in A Multicultural Soc., 1997, (with Cherry Ann Banks) March Toward Freedom: A History of Black Americans, 1970, 2d edit., 1974, rev. 2nd edit., 1978, Multiethnic Education: Theory and Practice, 1981, 3rd edit., 1994, (with others) Curriculum Guidlines for Multicultural Education, 1976, rev. edit., 1992, We Americans: Our History and People, 2 vols., 1982; contbg. author Internat. Ency. of Edn., 1985, Handbook of Research on Teacher Education, 1990, Handbook of Research on Social Studies Teaching and Learning, 1991, Encyclopedia of Ednl. Rsch., 1992, Handbook of Research on the Education of Young Children, 1993, Review of Research in Education, vol. 19, 1993; editor: Black Self Concept, 1972, Teaching Ethnic Studies: Concepts and Strategies, 1973, Educating Citizens in a Multicultural Society, 1997, (with William W. Joyce) Teaching Social Studies to Culturally Different Children, 1971, Teaching the Language Arts to Culturally Different Children, 1971, Education in the 80's: Multiethnic Education, 1981, (with James Lynch) Multicultural Education in Western Societies, 1986, (with C. Banks) Multicultural Education: Issues and Perspectives, 1989, 3d edit., 1997, Handbook of Research on Multicultural Education, 1995, Multicultural Education, Transformative Knowledge, and Action, 1996; editorial bd. Jour. of Tch. Edn., 1985-89, Coun. Interracial Books for Children Bull., 1982-92, Urban Edn., 1991-96; contbr. articles to profl. jours. Recipient Outstanding Young Man award Wash. State Jaycees, 1975, Outstanding Service in Edn. award Seattle U. Black Student Union, 1985; Spencer fellow Nat. Acad. Edn., 1973-76; Kellogg fellow, 1980-83; Rockefeller Found. fellow, 1980. Mem. ASCD (bd dirs. 1976-79, Disting. lectr. 1986, Disting. scholar, lectr. 1994), Nat. Coun. Social Studies (bd. dirs. 1973-74, 80-85, pres. 1982), Internat. Assn. Intercultural Edn. (editl. bd.), Social Sci. Edn. Consortium (bd. dirs. 1976-79), Am. Ednl. Rsch. Assn. (Disting. scholar/rschr. on minority edn. 1986, Rsch. Review award 1994, com. on role and status of minorities in edn. rsch. 1992-94, mem. publs. com. 1995-96; Disting. Career Contbn. award, 1996; pres.-elect 1996-97, pres. 1997—), Phi Delta Kappa, Phi Kappa Phi, Golden Key Nat. Honor Soc. Office: U Wash 110 Miller Hall Box 353600 Seattle WA 98195-3600 *One of the greatest strengths of our nation is its tremendous ethnic, racial, and cultural diversity. A major goal of my career is to increase understanding and communication across different ethnic, cultural and racial groups and to make it possible for each ethnic, cultural and racial group to make its greatest contribution to the nation. My belief that educational institutions can play a major role in improving race relations in our nation has greatly influenced my life and career.*

BANKS, MELISSA RICHARDSON, fund raising professional; b. Corpus Christi, Tex., June 5, 1962; d. Henry Gary and Patricia Lou (Kurth) Richardson; m. Steven Matisons Banks, Nov. 25, 1987. BA, Southwest Tex. State U., 1986; MS, Tex. A&M U., 1992. Devel. coord. Tex. A&M U., College Station, 1990-93; dir. devel. Autry Mus. Western Heritage, L.A., 1993—. Mem. Am. Assn. Mus., Am. Prospect Rsch. Assn., Nat. Soc. Fund Raising Execs., Planned Giving Roundtable, Phi Beta Delta. Home: 800 Traction Ave Ste 5 Los Angeles CA 90013-1854 Office: Autry Mus Western Heritage 4700 Western Heritage Way Los Angeles CA 90027-1462

BANKS, RONALD TED, information technologist, consultant; b. Big Spring, Tex., Mar. 3, 1954; s. William Russell Jr. and Doris Elizabeth (Ruehlow) B.; m. Jackie Lynn Condron, July 7, 1973; children: Kristal, Nathan, Timothy, Kayla. AD, LeTourneau Coll., Longview, Tex., Moody

Aviation, Elizabethton, Tenn. Cert. in aviation. Med. tech., ambulance driver LeTourneau Coll., 1973-75; helicopter mechanic Campbell Air Svc., Vivian, La., 1975-79; flight instr. Tex. Regional, Big Spring, 1983; missionary pilot Mission Aviation Fellowship, Tamatama, Venezuela, 1985-91; missions program mgr. Mission Aviation fellowship, Pto. Ayacucho, Venezuela, 1992-95; missions-info. tech. cons. Mission Aviation fellowship, Redlands, Calif., 1995—; missionary jungle pilot Mission Aviation Fellowship, Venezuela, 1985-95. Home: 2021 Anzio Ave Mentone CA 92359 Office: Mission Aviation Fellowship 1849 Wabash Ave Redlands CA 92373

BANNATYNE, MARK WILLIAM MCKENZIE, technical graphics educator; b. West Chester, Pa., May 22, 1952; s. Isobel Steel B.; m. Tatiana Yurievna Shcherbakova, Sept. 2, 1990; children: Yuri Markovich, Kirill Markovich. AAS, B.C. Inst. Tech., Burnaby, Can., 1982; BS, Utah State U., 1988, MS, 1991; PhD, Purdue U., 1994. Staff tchr. indsl. tech. and edn. dept. Utah State U., Logan, 1986-89, lectr. indsl. tech. and edn. dept., 1990, grad. prof. indsl. tech. and edn. dept., 1990-92; grad. instr. Purdue U., West Lafayette, Ind., 1992-94; asst. prof. dept. instnl. and curricular studies Coll. Edn. U. Nev., Las Vegas, 1995-97; asst. prof. tech. graphics dept. Purdue U., West Lafayette, 1997—; instr. Bridgerland Applied Tech. Ctr., Logan, 1988-92; mem. Engring. State Com., Logan, 1990-92, Gov.'s Coun. on Fgn. Exch., Salt Lake City, 1991-92; presenter Far West Popular Am. Culture Conf., 1996, 97, Rocky Mountain States Conf., Moscow, 1992, Tech. Edn. Assn., Kansas City, Mo., 1994, Jistec '96, Jerusalem, 1996, Far West Popular and Am. Culture Conf., 1996, 97; dir. Focus 1996, Moscow, 1996. Author: (book review) Tech. Tchr., 1989, ERIC Documents, 1996, Popular Culture Rev., 1997; contbr. articles to profl. publs. Leader Boy Scouts of Am., Logan, 1984-86. Mem. Internat. Tech. Edn. Assn. (conf. chair fgn. and internat. programs 1991), Am. Vocat. Assn. (presenter conf. 1991), Phi Kappa Phi. Mem. LDS Ch. Office: Purdue Univ Tech Graphics Dept 1419 Knoy Hall # 363 Purdue University IN 47907-1419

BANNER, BOB, television producer, director; b. Ennis, Tex., Aug. 15, 1921; s. Robert James and Viola (Culbertson) B.; m. Alice Jane Baird, Jan. 14, 1946; children—Baird Allen, Robert James, Charles Moore. B.B.A., So. Meth. U., 1943; M.A., Northwestern U., 1948. Pres. Bob Banner Assocs.; vis. prof. So. Meth. U. Dir. Garroway-at-Large, NBC-TV; producer, dir. Fred Waring Show, CBS-TV; dir. Omnibus; TV producer, pres., Bob Banner Assos.; TV shows include (series) The Uptown Comedy Club, It's Showtime at the Apollo, Garroway At Large, Fred Waring Show, Don Ho, Omnibus, Jr. Almost Anything Goes, Almost Anything Goes, Candid Camera, Carol Burnett Show, Garry Moore Show, Dinah Shore Chevy Show, Kraft Summer Music Hall, Solid Gold, Star Search, It's Showtime at the Apollo, The Uptown Comedy Club; (spls.) Perry Como Holiday Spls., Carnegie Hall Salutes Jack Benny, Julie & Carol at Carnegie Hall, Ford Motor Co.'s 75th Ann., Am. West of John Ford, A Spl. Sesame St. Christmas; spls. starring Bob Hope, Julie Andrews, Andy Williams; (movies) My Sweet Charlie, My Husband is Missing, Warning Shot, Journey from Darkness, The Darker Side of Terror, If Things were Different, Yes Virginia There Is A Santa Claus, 1991, Crash Landing, 1992, With Murder In Mind, 1992, The Sea Wolf, 1993. Recipient 15 Emmy awards, 11 Christopher awards, 3 Peabody awards. Mem. Acad. of TV Arts and Scis. Presbyn. Office: 10350 Santa Monica Blvd Ste 290 Los Angeles CA 90025*

BANTJES, ADRIAN ALEXANDER, history educator; b. Kingston, Ont., Can., Sept. 19, 1959; s. Adrian and Aida Mercedes (Aróstegui) B.; m. Mary Margaret Henning, May 14, 1994. MA in History, Rijksuniversiteit Leiden, The Netherlands; PhD in L.Am. History, U. Tex., 1991. Asst. prof. L.Am. history U. Wyo., Laramie, 1991-97, assoc. prof. L.Am. history, 1997—. Author: Cardenismo and the Political Culture of the Mexican Revolution in Sonora, 1929-1940, 1997; contbr. articles to profl. jours. NEH grantee, 1991. Office: U Wyo Dept History Laramie WY 82071-3198

BANUELOS, BETTY LOU, rehabilitation nurse; b. Vandergrift, Pa., Nov. 28, 1930; d. Archibald and Bella Irene (George) McKinney; m. Raul, Nov. 1, 1986; children: Patrice, Michael. Diploma, U. Pitts., 1951; cert., Loma Linda U., 1960. RN, Calif.; cert. chem. dependency nurse. Cons. occupational health svcs. Bd. Registered Nurses, 1984—; lectr., cons. in field. Recipient Scholarship U. Pitts. Mem. Dirs. of Nursing, Calif. Assn. Nurses in Substance Abuse. Home and Office: 15 Oak Spring Ln Laguna Beach CA 92656-2980

BANUK, RONALD EDWARD, mechanical engineer; b. Brockton, Mass., Oct. 22, 1944; s. Joseph John and Leocadia Marilyn (Gusciora) B.; m. Patricia Audrey Ryan, July 4, 1969; children: Kim, Lance. BSME, Northea. U., 1967; MSME, San Diego State U., 1971. Design and stress engr. in advanced systems Ryan Aero. Co., San Diego, 1967-76; sr. tech. specialist Northrop Corp., Pico Rivera, Calif., 1976-94, program mgr., 1987-89, structures tech. area mgr., 1991, prin. investigator in advanced structure and foam devel., 1986-93; prin. engr. structures Advt. Tech. Transit Bus, 1993—. Author: Papers on Foam and Composites: SAMPE, 1993, 97, DOE & ASME, 1996, Mary: Past, Present and Future, 1997. Mem. Soc. Adv. Material and Process Engring. Home: 6441 Ringo Cir Huntington Beach CA 92647-3323 Office: Adv Structural Design/Devel 9B73/GK 8900 E Washington Blvd Pico Rivera CA 90660-3765

BAO, JOSEPH YUE-SE, orthopaedist, microsurgeon, educator; b. Shanghai, Feb. 20, 1937; s. George Zheng-En and Margaret Zhi-De (Wang) B.; m. Delia Way, Mar. 30, 1963; children: Alice, Angela. MD, Shanghai First Med. Coll., 1958. Intern affiliated hosps. Shanghai First. Med. Coll.; resident Shanghai Sixth People's Hosp., orthopaedist, 1958-78, orthopaedist-in-charge, 1978-79, vice chief orthopaedist, 1979-84; rsch. assoc. orthop. hosp. U. So. Calif., L.A., 1985-90, 94—, vis. clin. assoc. prof. dept. orthops., 1986-89; coord. microvascular svcs. Orthopaedic Hosp., L.A., 1989-91; clin. assoc. prof. dept. orthops. U. So. Calif., L.A., 1989—; attending physician Los Angeles County and U. So. Calif. Med. Ctr., L.A., 1986, 90—; cons. Rancho Los Amigos Med. Ctr., Downey, Calif., 1986. Contbr. articles to profl. jours., chpts. to books. Mem. Internat. Microsurg. Soc., Am. Soc. for Reconstructive Microsurgery, Am. Soc. for Peripheral Nerve, Orthop. Rsch. Soc. Home: 17436 Terry Lyn Ln Cerritos CA 90703-8522 Office: LA County Med Ctr Dept Orthopaedics 1200 N State St Ste 3900 Los Angeles CA 90033-4525

BARAB, MARVIN, financial consultant; b. Wilmington, Del., July 16, 1927; s. Jacob and Minnie (Press) B.; m. Gertrude Klein, June 13, 1951; children: Jordan, Neal, Caryn. BS with distinction, Ind. U., 1947, MBA, 1951. Dir. mktg. Edward Weiss & Co., Chgo., 1951-56; dir. bus. rsch. Parker Pen Co., Janesville, Wis., 1956-59; dir. mktg. rsch. packaging and graphics Mattel Inc., Hawthorne, Calif., 1959-65; pres. Barcam Pub. Co., Rolling Hills Estates, Calif., 1959-70, Rajo Publs., Rolling Hills Estates, 1967-70, So. Calif. Coll. Med. & Dental Careers, Anaheim, 1970-81, Barbrook, Inc., Rolling Hills Estates, 1981-86; cons. Marvin Barab & Assocs., Rolling Hills Estates, Calif., 1981—. Editor: Rand McNally Camping Guide, 1967-70; contbr. articles to various publs., 1982-87. Treas. Harbor Free Clinic, 1990-92; bd. dirs. So. Bay Contemporary Art Mus., 1993-94, sec., 1994. Mem. Nat. Assn. Trade and Tech. Schs. (hon. life, sec. 1977-79, pres. 1979-81, bd. dirs.), Calif. Assn. Paramed. Schs. (pres. 1973-77). Office: 904 Silver Spur Rd Ste 110 Palos Verdes Peninsula CA 90274-3800

BARABINO, WILLIAM ALBERT, science and technology researcher, inventor; b. Bay Shore, N.Y., Feb. 11, 1932; s. John Joseph and Anna Marie (Gates) B.; children: Susan Beth, Diane Marie, William John. Student, Fordham U., 1951; AS, SUNY, Farmingdale, 1952; student, St. Louis U., 1957; diploma, Alexander Hamilton Inst., N.Y.C., 1963. Dist. mgr. Piper Aircraft Corp., Ctrl. Am., Mex., 1960-62; application engr. Lab. for Electronics, Boston, 1962-63; mktg. mgr. spl. equipment divsn. Itek Corp., Waltham, Mass., 1963-65; bus. cons. North Reading, Mass., 1965-68; dir. Andover (Mass.) Inst. Bus., 1968-70; sci. and tech. rschr. North Reading, 1970—; founder, mng. gen. ptnr. Mass Light Internat. Group, Agoura Hills, Calif., 1992—; founder, CEO Brief Necessities, Agoura Hills, Calif., 1990; cons. CTS Corp., Proctor and Gamble, Scovill Corp., Am. Environ. Products, Inc., Plessey Co., Ltd., GM, Goodyear Aerospace, Ford Motor Co. Patentee tire pressure alarm and warning systems (6), brake wear warning system, fluid level and condition detection systems, personal feminine and infant hygiene systems (7), treatment for causes of scalp diseases, based on theory then electron-microscopy capture of mitochondria with dual set of double-walled membranes, liquid dispensing swab applicator, others; contbr. articles to profl. jours. Mem. 1996 Rep. Presdl. Task Force; sponsor Children's Internat. Capt., rated pilot/rated navigator USAF, 1952-59. Mem. VFW, DAV, Am. Legion. Republican.

BARAD, JILL ELIKANN, toy company executive; b. N.Y.C., May 23, 1951; d. Lawrence Stanley and Corinne (Schuman) Elikann; m. Thomas Kenneth Barad, Jan., 28, 1979; children: Alexander David, Justin Harris. BA English and Psychology, Queens Coll., 1973. Asst. prod. mgr. mktg. Coty Cosmetics, N.Y.C., 1976-77, prod. mgr. mktg., 1977; account exec. Wells Rich Greene Advt. Agy., L.A., 1978-79; product mgr. mktg. Mattel Toys, Inc., L.A., 1981-82, dir. mktg., 1982-83, v.p. mktg., 1983-85, sr. v.p. mktg., 1985-86, sr. v.p. product devel., from 1986, exec. v.p. product design and devel., exec. v.p. mktg. and worldwide product devel., 1988-89; pres. girls and activity toys div. Mattel Toys, Inc. (name now Mattel Inc.), L.A., 1989—; pres., bd. dirs. Mattel USA, El Segundo, Calif., 1990—; pres., CEO Mattel, Inc., El Segundo, Calif., 1992—; bd. dirs. Bank of Am., Microsoft Corp., Claremont U. Ctr. Bd. dirs. Town Hall of Calif.; trustee Queens Coll.; chair exec. adv. bd. Children Affected by AIDS Found.; bd. govs. Childrens Miracle Network. Mem. Am. Film Inst. (charter). Office: Mattel Inc 333 Continental Blvd El Segundo CA 90245-5032

BARBAKOW, JEFFREY, health facility administrator; b. 1944. BS, San Jose U.; MBA, U. So. Calif. With Merrill Lynch Capital Mkts. and several additional affiliates, 1972-88, MGM/UA Communications Inc., 1988-91, Donaldson, Lufkin & Jenrette Securities Corp., 1991; dir. Nat. Med. Enterprises, 1990—, chmn. bd., CEO, 1993—. Office: Nat Med Enterprises Inc 3820 State St Santa Barbara CA 93105*

BARBAS, JEFFREY LAWRENCE, finance company executive; b. Detroit, Oct. 22, 1947; s. Sidney and Betty (Rosenberg) B.; m. Lynne Goodstein, Feb. 15, 1974 (div. Mar. 1990); children: Sean, Christopher. BA in Journalism, Calif. State U., Northridge, 1973. Dist. mgr. CIT Group, L.A., 1974-79; v.p., mgr. Cmty. Bank, L.A., 1979-85; v.p., gen. mgr. Mazak Corp., Gardena, Calif., 1985-91; pres. C D Financing, Inc., Anaheim, Calif., 1991—; cons. Fine CNC Sys., Anaheim. Author: (poem) Poem for the Living, 1991; author Fin. Forum, 1984—. Comdr. Club L.A. Rescue Mission; medallion mem. Orange (Calif.) County Rescue Mission; pacesetter CFIDS Assn. Am. With mil. intelligence U.S. Army, 1965-69, Vietnam. Home: 5752 Anthony Ave Garden Grove CA 92845-2612 Office: C D Financing Inc 1125 E Stanford Ct Anaheim CA 92805

BARBEE, JOE ED, lawyer; b. Pharr, Tex., Feb. 27, 1934; s. Archie Allen and Concha (Leal) B.; m. Yolanda Margaret Atonna, Feb. 17, 1962; children—Cynthia M., Adam A., Walter J. BSEE, U. Ariz., 1961; JD, Western New Eng. Coll., 1973. Bar: Mass. 1973, U.S. Patent Office 1973, U.S. Ct. Appeals (fed. cir.) 1982. Engr. Gen. Electric Co., Pittsfield, Mass., 1961-73; patent atty. Fort Wayne, Ind., 1973-75, Magnavox, Fort Wayne, 1975-76, Motorola, Inc., Phoenix, 1976—. Sgt. U.S. Army, 1953-56. Recipient Outstanding Performance award U.S. Civil Svc., 1960. Mem. ABA, Am. Patent Law Assn., Am. Intellectual Property Law Assn. Republican. Methodist. Home: 7611 N Mockingbird Ln Paradise Valley AZ 85253-3126 Office: Motorola Inc 8220 E Roosevelt St # B3 Scottsdale AZ 85257-3804

BARBER, CLARENCE LYLE, economics educator; b. Wolseley, Sask., Can., May 5, 1917; s. Richard Edward and Lulu Pearl (Lyons) B.; m. Barbara Anne Patchet, May 10, 1947; children—Paul Edward, Richard Stephen, David Stuart, Alan Gordon. BA, U. Sask., 1939; MA, Clark U., 1941; postgrad., U. Minn., 1941-43, PhD, 1952; LLD (hon.), U. Guelph, 1988. With Stats. Can., 1945-48; mem. faculty McMaster U., 1948-49, U. Man., Winnipeg, Can., 1949-85; prof. econs. U. Man., 1956-85, disting. prof., 1982-85, emeritus, 1985—, head dept., 1963-72; vis. prof. Queen's U., 1954-55, McGill U., 1964-65; Commr. Royal Commn. on Farm Machinery, 1966-71; spl. adviser on nat. income Phillipines Govt., 1959-60; commr. for study welfare policy in Man., 1972; mem. Nat. Commn. on Inflation, 1979, Royal Commn. Econ. Union and Devel. Prospects for Can., 1982-85. Author: Inventories and the Business Cycle, 1958, The Theory of Fiscal Policy as Applied to a Province, 1966, (with others) Inflation and Unemployment: The Canadian Experience, 1980, Controlling Inflation: Learning from Experience in Canada, Europe and Japan, 1982, False Promises: The Failure of Conservative Economics, 1993. Served with RCAF, 1943-45. Named Officer in Order of Can., 1987; Can. Coun. Profl. Leave fellow, 1970-71. Fellow Royal Soc. Can.; mem. Canadian Assn. U. Tchrs. (pres. 1958-59), Canadian Econ. Assn. (pres. 1971-72), Am. Econ. Assn., Royal Econ. Soc., Social Sci. Research Council Can. (mem. exec. 1972-73), U. Victoria Faculty Club. Home: 766 Richmond Ave, Victoria, BC Canada V8S 3Z1

BARBER, ELIZABETH JANE WAYLAND, archeology and linguistics educator, researcher; b. Pasadena, Calif., Dec. 2, 1940; d. James Harold and Virginia Jane Wayland; m. Paul Thomas Barber, June 14, 1965. BA, Bryn Mawr (Pa.) Coll., 1962; PhD, Yale U., 1968. Rsch. assoc. Princeton (N.J.) U., 1968-69; asst. to assoc. to full prof. Occidental Coll., L.A., 1970—. Author: Archaeological Decipherment, 1974, Prehistoric Textiles, 1991, Women's Work- The First 20,000 Years, 1994. Grantee Am. Coun. Learned Soc., 1977, Edn. grant NEH, 1972-74, 1993; fellow John Simon Guggenheim Meml. Found., 1979-80. Mem. Linguistic Soc. Am., Archeol. Inst. Am., Textile Soc. Am. Office: Occidental Coll 1600 Campus Rd Los Angeles CA 90041-3384

BARBER, JAMES P., lawyer; b. Berkeley, Calif., Nov. 11, 1944. BA, U. Calif., Santa Barbara, 1967; JD, U. Calif., 1973. Bar: Calif. 1973. Ptnr. Hancock, Rothert & Bunshoft, San Francisco. Articles editor Hastings Law Jour., 1972-73. Mem. ABA, State Bar Calif., Bar Assn. San Francisco, Def. Rsch. Inst., Thurston Soc., Order of the Coif. Office: Hancock Rothert & Bunshoft 4 Embarcadero Ctr Fl 10 San Francisco CA 94111-4106

BARBER, LARRY EUGENE, financial planner; b. Sabetha, Kans., Aug. 4, 1931; s. Paul W. and Nellie C. (Nicholas) B.; m. Norma J. Schroeder, Sept. 9, 1951; children: Mark E., Gary P., Jay D., Craig A., Kirk N. BSBA, U. Nebr.-Omaha, 1952; M. of Fin. Svcs., Am. Coll., 1981. CLU; CFP; chartered fin. cons.; accredited estate planner, accredited tax preparer. Ins. Agt. Conn. Gen., Omaha, 1970-77; tax and fin. planning, cons. Colo. Agy. State Mut. Life (now Allmerica Fin. Svcs.), Denver, 1977—; v.p. Bus. and Personal Fin. Planning Ltd., Denver, 1985—; pres. Barco Enterprises, Inc., 1996—. Lt. col. USAFR, 1951-52, USAF Ret. Res. Mem. Nat. Assn. Life Underwriting, Am. Soc. CLUs, Internat. Assn. Fin. Planners, Optimists. Home: 1030 S Garrison St Lakewood CO 80226-4129 Office: 44 Cook St Denver CO 80206-5822

BARBER, MARK EDWARD, lawyer; b. Enumclaw, Wash., Dec. 30, 1952; s. Earl Marion Barber and Delila Mae Willis Lontz; m. Pamela Johnson, Aug. 30, 1974; 1 child, Matthew Edward. BA, U. Wash., 1975; JD, Pepperdine U., 1978. Bar: Wash. 1978, U.S. Dist. Ct. Wash. 1978, U.S. Ct. Appeals (9th cir.) 1980, U.S. Supreme Ct. 1985. Atty. Heavey & Woody, Inc. P.S., Seattle, 1978-79; sole practitioner Seattle, 1979-81; atty., prin. shareholder Warren, Kellogg, Barber Dean & Fontes, P.S., Renton, Wash., 1981—. Bd. dirs. Justice Polit. Action Com., Tacoma, 1993-95, Sunset Valley Farms Homeowners Assn., Issaquah, Wash., 1991-92, 95-96. Mem. ATLA, Wash. State Bar Assn., King County Bar Assn., Wash. State Trial Lawyers Assn. (pres. 1995-96). Office: Warren Kellogg et al 100 S 2nd St Renton WA 98055-2013

BARBER, PATRICIA LOUISE, clinical specialist; b. St. Paul, Jan. 11, 1953; d. James Bernard and Margaret Mary (Neagle) B. BSN, U. Minn., 1975; cert. nurse practitioner, U. Ill., 1978. RN, Colo., Ill., Minn. Staff nurse U. Minn., Mpls., 1974-75; transplant coord. U. Ill., Chgo., 1978-90; nurse practitioner emergency rm. Denver Presbyn., 1990-93; nurse practitioner in-patient svc. cardiovascular Denver Presbyn. St. Luke's Med. Ctr., 1993-95, nurse practitioner nephrology, 1995-96, nurse practitioner in-patient svc., 1996—; cons. in field, Chgo., 1983—. Editor: Resource Manual for Transplant Coordinators, 1982. Co-chmn. S/A Patient Svcs. Com., 1983-90. Mem. N.Am. Transplant Coords. Orgn. (co-chmn. 1979-90, Honors 1983), Am. Diabetes Assn. (speakers bur. 1982—), Nat. Kidney Found. (bd. dirs. 1983-90). Office: Denver Presbyn Saint Lukes Med Ctr 1719 E 19th Ave Denver CO 80218-1235

BARBERA, HENRY RAYMOND, sociology educator; b. N.Y.C., Dec. 21, 1929. PhD, Columbia U., 1971. Prof. City Coll., N.Y.C., 1971-82, U. Calif., Irvine, 1983-96. Author: Rich Nations and Poor in Peace and War, 1973, The First Absolute State, 1994, Hope and Discontent, 1995, The State as Revolution, 1997; co-editor newsletter Sicilia Parra, 1980—. Mem. Am. Socio. Assn., Am. Polit. Sci. Assn., Patrons of Italian Culture (pres. 1992—). Home: 24975 Acacia Ln Laguna Hills CA 92653-4909

BARBERS, RICHARD GEORGE, physician, educator; b. Calasiao, The Philippines, Jan. 12, 1949; came to U.S., 1960; s. Jess Victor and Mary (Fernandez) B.; m. Stephanie Gertrude Weck, June 4, 1994. BS, Loyola Coll., Balt., 1971; MD, Georgetown U., 1975. Bd. cert. in internal medicine, pulmonary disease, allergy and immunology, critical care medicine. Intern internal medicine Med. Ctr. U. So. Calif., L.A., 1975-76; resident internal medicine Cedars-Sinai Med. Ctr., L.A., 1976-78; postdoctoral fellow clin. immunology and allergy Med. Ctr. UCLA, 1979-81, postdoctoral fellow pulmonary disease Med. Ctr., 1981-82, adj. asst. prof. Sch. Medicine, 1982-87; asst. prof. Med. Sch. U. Mass., Worcester, 1987-90; assoc. prof. clin. medicine U. So. Calif. Sch. Medicine, L.A., 1990—; dir. UCLA Asthma & Immunology Lung Disease Ctr., 1982-87, U. So. Calif. Bronchoscopy Svcs., 1990—, Asthma and Allergy Ctr., 1994—; co-dir. U. So. Calif. Lung Transplant Program, 1992—. Contbr. articles to med. jours. and books. Fellow ACP, Am. Coll. Chest Physicians, Am. Acad. Allergy and Immunology; mem. Am. Thoracic Soc., Am. Fedn. Clin. Rsch., Internat. Heart and Lung Transplant Soc., Nat. Tri-Beta Hon. Soc. Roman Catholic. Office: USC Sch Med GD 11-900 2025 Zonal Ave Los Angeles CA 90033

BARBORKA, CLIFFORD JOSEPH, III, broadcaster, marketing consultant; b. Chgo., Aug. 31, 1950; s. Clifford Joseph Jr. and Melva (Niles) B.; m. Karen Diane Judd, Aug. 8, 1996; children: Jason, Tara, Brett, Christopher. A, Ricks Coll., Rexburg, Idaho, 1973; student, Brigham Young U., 1973-74. Dir. student devel. assn. Ricks Coll., 1974-75; account exec. WHO-TV, Des Moines, 1976-80, KSL-TV and Radio, Salt Lake City, 1980-87; v.p. Advt. Mgmt. Svcs., Salt Lake City, 1987-89; sales mgr. KBCK Radio, Salt Lake City, 1989-90; broadcaster KBBK Radio, Rupert, Idaho, 1990-93; broadcaster, cons. Tri-Market Broadcasting, Rupert, 1993—; mktg. cons. Minidoka Meml. Hosp., Rupert, 1992—. Mem. Iowa Advt. Fedn., Utah Advt. Fedn., Utah Sales and Mktg. Assn., Kiwanis, Rupert C. of C. Home: PO Box 612 Burley ID 83318 Office: Tri-Market Broadcasting Inc 120 S 300 W Rupert ID 83350

BARBOUR, ALTON BRADFORD, human communication studies educator; b. San Diego, Oct. 13, 1933; s. Ancel Baxter and Mary Jane (Fay) B.; m. Betty Sue Burch, Aug. 19, 1961 (div. 1991); children: Elizabeth, Christopher, Damon, Meagan; m. Jacqueline Moorhead, Feb. 29, 1996. BA, U. No. Colo., 1956; MA, U. Denver, 1961, PhD, 1968; postdoctoral, Moreno Inst., 1976. Diplomate Am. Bd. Psychotherapy. Lectr. Colo. Sch. Mines, Golden, 1964-65; instr. U. Denver, 1965-68; asst. prof. human comm. studies U. Denver, Denver, 1968-71, assoc. prof., 1971-77, prof., 1977—, chairperson dept. human comm. studies, 1980—; vis. lectr. Swiss Inst. for Group Psychotherapy, Switzerland, 1992, Chinese U. of Hong Kong. Co-author (books) Interpersonal Communication: Teaching Resources, 1972, Louder Than Words: Nonverbal Communication, 1974, Assessing Functional Communication, 1978; contbr. articles to profl. jours. With USN, 1956-58. Fellow Am. Soc. for Group Psychotherapy and Psychodrama, Am. Bd. of Med. Psychotherapists, Internat. Acad. of Behavioral Medicine, Counselling and Psychotherapy; mem. Am. Bd. Examiners in Group Psychotherapy (sec. 1983-93). Home: 1195 S Vine St Denver CO 80210-1830 Office: Univ Denver Human Comm Studies Denver CO 80208

BARCA, GEORGE GINO, winery executive, financial investor; b. Sacramento, Jan. 28, 1937; s. Joseph and Annie (Muschetto) B.; m. Maria Sclafani, Nov. 19, 1960; children—Anna, Joseph, Gina and Nina (twins). A.A., Grant Jr. Coll.; student LaSalle U., 1963. With United Vintners, U.S.A., St. Helena, Napa Valley, Calif., 1960—; pres., gen. mgr. Barcamerica U.S.A., Barca Wine Cellars, Calif. Wine Cellars, U.S.A., Calif. Grape Growers, U.S.A., Calif. Vintage Wines, U.S.A., Am. Vintners, U.S.A.; cons. in field. Gen. trustee Barca Investment Trust, U.S.A. Named Best Producer of Sales and Fin. Investments, United Vintners, U.S.A. Roman Catholic. Club: KC. Developer wine trademarks and brands.

BARCA, KATHLEEN, marketing executive; b. Burbank, Calif., July 26, 1946; d. Frank Allan and Blanch Irene (Griffith) Barnes; m. Gerald Albino Barca, Dec. 8, 1967 (dec. May 1993); children: Patrick Gerald, Stacia Kathleen. Student, Pierce Coll., 1964; B in Bus., Hancock Coll., 1984. Teller Security Pacific Bank, Pasadena, Calif., 1968-69, Bank Am., Santa Maria, Calif., 1972-74; operator Gen. Telephone Co., Santa Maria, Calif., 1974-83, supr. operator, 1983-84; account exec. Sta. KRQK/KLLB Radio, Lompoc, Calif., 1984-85; owner Advt. Unltd., Orcutt, Calif., 1986-88; regional mgr. A.L. Williams Mktg. Co., Los Alamos, Calif., 1988-89; supr. Matol Botanical Internat., 1989-91; account exec. Santa Maria Times, 1989—. Author: numerous local TV and radio commercials, print advt. Activist Citizens Against Dumps in Residential Environments, Polit. Action Com., Orcutt and Santa Maria; chmn. Community Action Com., Santa Maria, Workshop EPA, Calif. Div., Dept. Health Svcs. State of Calif.; vice coord. Toughlove, Santa Maria, 1988-89; parent coord., mem. steering com. ASAP and Friends, 1988-89. Mem. NAFE, Womens Network-Santa Maria, Ctrl. Coast Ad (recipient numerous awards), Santa Maria C. of C. (amb. representing Santa Maria Times 1990-94, asst. chief amb. 1993-94). Democrat. Home: 2509 Solano Rd Shell Beach CA 93449

BARCHI, BARBARA ANN, education educator; b. Detroit, Feb. 11, 1940; d. John and Ann (Kovachevich) B.; m. Alan L. McBroom, Oct. 1, 1960 (div. Nov. 1976). BS, Wayne State U., 1961, MEd, 1967; PhD, U. Mich., 1975. Permanent cert. in teaching, Mich. Tchr. Detroit Pub. Schs., 1961-62, Garden City (Mich.) Sch. Dist., 1962-65, Livonia (Mich.) Pub. Schs., 1965-73; asst. prof. elem. edn. Ill. State U., Normal, 1975-78; nat. coord., dir. Nat. Diffusion Network Project U.S. Dept. Edn., Ill., 1978-82; coord. edn. project U.S. Dept. Edn., Ill., 1985-86; 1st edn. specialist Nat. PTA, Chgo., 1984-85; pres., dir. Ednl. Renewal Assocs. Inc., Chgo., 1982-86; assoc. prof. sci., tech. and soc. Pa. State U., University Park, 1986-90, dir., prin. co-investigator nationwide STS project for NSF, 1987-90; pres. Barchi & Assocs., Edn.and Tng. Svcs., Fullerton, Calif., 1991—; cons., program evaluator Future Scientists and Engrs. Am., NSF, Anaheim, Calif., 1993-95; presenter in field. Author: (support manual) Looking in on Your School: To Improve Public Education, 1985; creator curriculum materials; contbr. articles to profl. jours. Grantee NSF, 1987-90, U.S. Dept. Edn., 1979-81. Mem. Nat. Coun. Social Studies (adv. coms. tchr. edn. and cert. 1977-80, sci. and soc. 1981-84, citizenship edn. 1985-88), Nat. Diffusion Network (elec. adv. com. 1982-84), Am. Ednl. Rsch. Assn., Phi Delta Kappa. Home and Office: Barchi and Assocs 2851 E Rolling Hills Dr Spc 222 Fullerton CA 92835

BARCHILON, JACQUES, foreign language educator, researcher, writer; b. Casablanca, Morocco, Apr. 8, 1923; came to U.S., 1947; s. Jaime and Perla (Bendavid) B.; (div.); children: Nicole Andrée, Paul Émile. BA in History, U. Rochester, 1950; MA in Comparative Lit., Harvard U., 1951, PhD in Romance Langs., 1956. Tchg. fellow Harvard U., Cambridge, Mass., 1953-55; instr. Smith Coll., Northampton, Mass., 1955-56, Brown U., Providence, 1956-59; asst. prof. U. Colo., Boulder, 1959-65; assoc. prof. U. Colo., 1965-71, prof., 1971-91, prof. emeritus, 1991—; dir. study abroad program, U. Bordeaux, France, 1966-67; exch. prof. French and comparative lit. Ctr. Univ. de Savoie, Chambéry, France, 1978-79; dir. internat. colloquium on Conte merveilleux Ctr. Culturel Internat., Cerisy-La-Salle, France, 1983; lectr. in field. Author: Perrault's Tales of Mother Goose, The Dedication Manuscript of 1695, 1956, The Authentic Mother Goose Fairy Tales and Nursery Rhymes, 1960, Le Conte merveilleux français de 1690 à 1790, cent ans de féerie et de poésie ignorées de l'histoire littéraire, 1975, Le Nouveau Cabinet des Fées, 18 vols., 1978, Contes de Perrault, 1980, Charles Perrault, 1981; co-editor: (with E.E. Flinders and J. Anne Foreman) A Concordance to Charles Perrault's Tales, Vol I Contes de Ma mère l'Oye, 1977, Vol. II, The Verse Tales, Griselidis, Peau d'Ane and Les Souhaits ridicules, Charles Perrault, a Critical Biography, 1979, (with Catherine Velay-Vallantin and J. Anne Foreman) Pensées chrétiennes, 1987; editor Cermeil, 1984-86, Marvels and Tales, 1987—; contbr. numerous articles to profl. jours. With Free French Forces, 1943-45. Grantee Am. Philos. Soc., 1962, 63, 71, 79, 93;

travel Am. Coun. Learned Socs., 1983, Coun. Internat. Exch. Scholars, 1978-79, Fulbright Found., 1978-79. Mem. MLA, Am. Assn. Tchrs. of French, Soc. d'Études du 17ème Siècle, N.Am. Soc. 17th Century French Lit., Soc. Amis de Jean de La Fontaine. Democrat. Mem. Soc. of Friends. Office: U Colo Dept French & Italian Campus Box 238 Boulder CO 80309-0238

BARCLAY, JOHN ALLEN, lawyer; b. L.A., Feb. 14, 1951; s. George H. and Shirley Iris (Handler) B. AA, L.A. Valley Coll., 1970; BA, U. Southern Calif., 1972, JD, 1975. Bar: Calif. 1975, U.S. Dist. Ct. (cen., ea., and no. dists.) Calif. 1976, U.S. Ct. Appeals (9th cir.) 1976, U.S. Tax Ct. 1976, U.S. Ct. Claims, 1995. Assoc. Karno & Fisher, Encino, Calif., 1975-78; prin. Barclay & Brestoff, Encino, 1978-80, Barclay & Moskatel, Beverly Hills, Calif., 1980-82, Barclay Law Corp., Newport Beach, Calif., 1982—; instr. U. Calif.-Irvine, 1985-87, UCLA, 1982-85, L.A. Valley Coll., Van Nuys, 1980-82. Author: Exchanging in the '80's, 1986, Accumulating Wealth, 1987, Insurance for Environmental Claims Against Bankruptcy Estates, 1992, (with others) Deducting Your Down Payment, 1984; contbr. articles to profl. jours. Mem. adv. bd. Calif. State U.; dir. Orange County Nat. Conf. Christians and Jews; dir. Parent Help USA. Mem. ABA, Legion Lex (bd. dirs. Orange County chpt. 1987-95, pres. 1992), Masons (master Hollywood chpt. 1982). Jewish. Office: Barclay Law Corp 5000 Birch St Ste 2900 Newport Beach CA 92660-2139 *Notable cases include: Palmdale redevel. agy. vs. Germano, eminent domain case, represented property owner.*

BARCLAY, STEVEN CALDER, lawyer; b. Phoenix, Ariz., Jan. 17, 1956; s. Leslie Calder and Ruth (Lindke) B.; m. Janice Marie Reno, Sept. 25, 1982; 1 child, Jordan Nicole. BA magna cum laude, Oral Roberts U., 1977; JD cum laude, Notre Dame U., 1980. Bar: Ariz. 1980, U.S. Dist. Ct. Ariz. 1980, U.S. Ct. Appeals (9th cir.) 1980. Assoc. Snell & Wilmer, Phoenix, 1980-83; corp. counsel S.W. divsn. CIGNA Healthplans, Inc., Phoenix, 1983-85; ptnr. Barclay & Reece, Phoenix, 1985-87; sole practice Phoenix, 1987-90; shareholder, pres. Barclay & Goering, P.C., Phoenix, 1990—. Mem. editl. bd. Today's Health Care Mag., 1994—. Mem. State Bar Ariz., Ariz. Assn. HMOs (counsel, lobbyist 1987-96), Ariz. Assn. Health Care Lawyers, Pub. Affairs Profls. Ariz. (dir.), Maricopa County Bar Assn. Republican. Office: Barclay & Goering PC 1001 N Central Ave Ste 600 Phoenix AZ 85004-1947

BARCUS, BENJAMIN FRANKLIN, lawyer; b. Tacoma, June 24, 1960; s. George Eldon Barcus and Gwendolyn (Evans) Johnson. BBA, U. Wash., 1982; JD, U. Puget Sound, 1985. Bar: Wash. 1986, U.S. Dist. Ct. (we. dist.) Wash. 1986, U.S. Ct. Appeals (9th cir.) 1986, U.S. Supreme Ct. 1991. Customer svc. rep. Tacoma News Tribune, 1979-80; claims rep., investigator Office Atty. Gen. State of Wash., Seattle, 1980-81; ind. svc. contractor Am. Express Co. Inc., Seattle, 1981-85; assoc. Talbot, Orlandini, Waldron & Hemmen, Tacoma, 1986-88; pvt. practice, Tacoma, 1989—. Precinct committeeman Wash. Dem. Com., Tacoma, 1982-88. Mem. ABA, ATLA, Wash. State Bar Assn., Wash. State Trial Lawyers Assn., Wash. Assn. Criminal Def. Lawyers, Tacoma-Pierce County Bar Assn., Mopars Unltd. (treas. Tacoma chpt. 1982-88), Ferrari Owner's Club, Ferrari Club Am., Mercedes Benz Club Am., Rolls Royce Owners Club, Fircrest Golf Club, Tacoma Yacht Club. Congregational. Home: 2223 E Day Island Blvd W Tacoma WA 98466-1816 Office: 4303 Ruston Way Tacoma WA 98402-5378

BARDACH, SHELDON GILBERT, lawyer; b. Holyoke, Mass., Sept. 4, 1937; s. Arthur Everett and Ruth (Goodstein) B.; m. Martha Robson, June 7, 1970; 1 child, Noah Arthur. AB, Bklyn. Coll., 1958; JD, UCLA, 1961. Bar: Calif. 1962. Pvt. practice Beverly Hills, Calif., 1962-67, Century City, Calif., 1967-85; sr. mem. Law Offices Sheldon G. Bardach, L.A.; bd. dirs. Mambo Films, Inc.; arbitrator L.A. Superior Ct., 1979—; gen. counsel Century Artists, Ltd.; mem. nat. and internat. panels arbitrators Am. Arbitration Assn. Bd. editors Law in Transition Quar., 1967; contbr. articles to profl. jours. Bd. govs. Studio Watts Workshop, 1963-71; founder, bd. dirs. UCLA Sch. Law, 1968. Recipient Lubin award Sch. Law UCLA, 1961, Bancroft-Whitney award UCLA Sch. Law, , 1961. Mem. ABA, Calif. Bar Assn., Beverly Hills Bar Assn. (bd. govs. varristers 1964-69), Am. Arbitration Assn., UCLA Law Sch. Alumni Assn. (bd. dirs. 1991-94), L.A. County Bar Assn., Assn. Trial Lawyers Am., Comml. Law League Am., Vikings of Scandia, Zeta Beta Tau, Phi Alpha Delta. Democrat. Jewish. Office: 11755 Wilshire Blvd Los Angeles CA 90025-1506 *The most difficult problems we face require emotional decisions. It is when factors on both sides are intellectually disparate that solutions are easy. It is only when the intellect cannot distinguish between the advantages and disadvantages of making a choice that one deals with truly difficult problems. Then, the only solutions available are emotional. Trust in your feelings.*

BARDAS, SANDRA LEIGH, pharmacist. BA magna cum laude, Wheaton Coll., Norton, Mass., 1972; BS in Pharmacy, Mass. Coll. Pharmacy, Boston, 1975. Pharmacy resident Mass. Gen. Hosp., Boston, 1976-77, staff pharmacist, 1977-78; clin. pharmacist Stanford (Calif.) U. Hosp., 1979—. Office: Stanford Univ Hosp Dept Of Pharmacy Ho # 301 Stanford CA 94305

BARDHAN, PRANAB, economics educator; b. India, 1939. From asst. to assoc. prof. econ. MIT, 1966-69; prof. Indian Stats. Inst., New Delhi, 1969-73, Delhi Sch. Econ., 1973-76; prof. econ. U. Calif., Berkeley, 1976—. Author: Economic Growth, Development and Foriegn Trade, 1970, Land, Labor and Rural Poverty, 1984, The Political Economy of Development in India, 1984; co-editor: Rural Poverty in South Asia, 1988, Market Socialism: The Current Debate, 1993; editor: The Econmic Theory of Agrarian Institutions, 1989, Conversations between Economists and Anthropologists, 1989.

BARELA, BERTHA CICCI, elementary education educator, artist; b. McKeesport, Pa., June 13, 1913; d. James and Julia (Kolesar) Faix; m. John Slebodnik, June 23, 1934 (dec. 1967); children: Dolores S. Garvis, James, John, Judith Greene, Jane Minda, William, Cyrilla Lombardi, Rosemary Lewis, Martha Williams; m. Amerigo Cicci, May 25, 1974 (dec. 1975); m. Abran Barela, Dec. 8, 1984 (div. Nov. 1992). BA, Seton Hill Coll., 1970. Elem. tchr. Blessed Sacrament Sch., Greensburg, Pa., 1967-74; ind. artist, clown Phoenix, 1985—; asst. pre-sch. tchr. Sunnyslope Ctr.; guest art tchr. various schs., 1980—; Westmoreland (Pa.) County Girl Scout Leader; internat. del. St. Louis. Formerly news and mag. writer; numerous commissioned art works. Dep. registrar Maricopa County, Phoenix, 1983-86, election bd. worker, 1980—; Dem. committeewoman, election worker, Pa., 1960-73, Phoenix, 1980—. Mem. Sunnyslope Recreation Ctr. Home: 841 E Cinnabar Ave Phoenix AZ 85020-1732

BARGER, JAMES DANIEL, physician; b. Bismarck, N.C., May 17, 1917; s. Michael Thomas and Mayte (Donohue) B.; m. Susie Belle Helm, 1945 (dec. 1951); m. Josephine Steiner, 1952 (dec. 1971); m. Jane Ray Regan, Apr. 21, 1980 (dec. Feb. 1991); children: James Daniel, Mary Susan, Michael Thomas, Mary Elizabeth. Student, St. Mary's Coll., Winona, Minn., 1934-35; A.B., U. N.D., 1939, B.S., 1939; M.D., U. Pa., 1941; M.S. in Pathology, U. Minn., 1949. Diplomate Am. Bd. Pathology; registered quality engr., Calif. Intern. Milw. County Hosp., Wauwatosa, Wis., 1941-42; fellow in pathology Mayo Found., Rochester, Minn., 1941-49; pathologist Pima County Hosp., Tucson, 1949-50, Maricopa County Hosp., Phoenix, 1950-51; chmn. dept. pathology Good Samaritan Hosp., 1951-63; assoc. pathologist Sunrise Hosp., Las Vegas, Nev., 1964-69, chief pathology dept., 1969-81, sr. pathologist, 1981—; former med. dir. S.W. Blood Bank, Blood Services, Ariz., Blood Services Nev.; treas. Commn. for Lab. Assessment, 1988; emeritus clin. prof. pathology U. Nev. Sch. Medicine, 1988. Served to maj. AUS, 1942-46. Recipient Sioux award U. N.D. Alumni Assn., 1975; recipient disting. physician award NSMA, 1983; ASCP-CAP Disting. Service award, 1985. Mem. AAAS, AMA, Am. Assn. Pathologists, Am. Assn. Clin. Chemists, Am. Assn. History Medicine, Coll. Am. Pathologists (gov. 1966-72, sec.-treas. 1971-79, v.p. 1979-81, pres. 1980-81, historian 1988—, Pathologist of Yr. 1977), Nev. Soc. Pathologists (AMA del. 1990), Am. Assn. Blood Banks, Am. Soc. Quality Control (sr. mem.), Am. Mgmt. Assn., Soc. Advancement Mgmt., Am. Soc. Clin. Pathologists, Am. Cancer Soc. (nat. dir. 1974-80), Nat. Acad. Practice Medicine (dist. practitioner 1984—, del. AMA Ho. Dels. 1989—), others. Lodge: Knights of St. Lazarus (comdr. 1983). Home: 1307 Canosa Ave Las Vegas NV 89104-3132 Office: 3196 S Maryland Pkwy Ste 405 Las Vegas NV 89109-2315

BARISH, JONAS A., English educator; b. 1922. From asst. prof. to prof. emeritus English, U. Calif., Berkeley, 1954—. Author: The Antitheatrical Prejudice, 1981, Ben Johnson and the Language of Prose Comedy, 1960; editor: Volpone, 1958, Ben Johnson: A Collection of Critical Essays, 1963, All's Well That Ends Well, 1964, Sejanus, 1965, Volpone: A Casebook, 1972. Office: U Calif Dept English Berkeley CA 94720

BARKER, ALAN FREUND, internist; b. St. Louis, Aug. 27, 1944; s. Irven M. and Gladys (Freund) B.; m. Julieann Brixner; children: Sara, David. BA, Carleton Coll., 1966; MD, U. Mo., 1970. Internship internal medicine U. Wash. Affiliated Hosps., Seattle, 1970-71, residency internal medicine, 1971-73; chief med. resident internal medicine U. Wash. Affiliated Hosps., USPH Hosp., Seattle, 1973-74; fellow pulmonary medicine U. Calif., San Diego, 1974-76; asst. prof. medicine Oreg. Health Scis. U., Portland, 1976-82, assoc. prof. medicine Divsn. Pulmonary & Critical Care, 1982-95; prof., 1995—; med. dir., cons Respiratory Therapy Program, Mt. Hood C.C., 1978—, chair adv. com., 1992—; cons. Multnomah County Tuberculosis Clinic, 1981—. Contbr. articles to profl. jours. and chpts. to books. Mem. Gov.'s Commn. for Pub. Health Policy, 1984-85; bd. dirs. Univ. Med. Assocs., 1980-85, pres., 1983-85; mem. Med. Bd. Univ. Hosp., 1984-87, exec. coun., 1984-85. Grantee NIH, 1989-94, Genentech, 1993-94, Miles, 1993-94. Fellow Am. Coll. Chest Physicians; mem. Am. Thoracic Soc., Oreg. Thoracic Soc. (pres. 1982-83). Office: Oreg Health Scis U Pulmonary/Critical Care Portland OR 97201

BARKER, DOUGLAS P., food products executive; b. 1935. With Sunkist Growers, Van Nuys, Calif., 1961-78, Sun World Internat. Inc., Bakersfield, Calif., 1978-81, 84—, Blue Anchor, Sacramento, Calif., 1981-84. Office: Sun World Internat Inc 16350 Driver Rd Bakersfield CA 93308*

BARKER, FRED, research geologist, scientific editor; b. Seekonk, Mass., Nov. 4, 1928; s. Reuben and Eleanor Regina (Mead) B.; m. Margaret Walsh, May 7, 1961; children: Matthew F., Thomas A., Aileen M. BS, MIT, 1950; MS, Calif. Inst. Tech., 1952, PhD, 1954; postgrad., Harvard U., 1956-57. Rsch. geologist U.S. Geol. Survey, Juneau, Alaska, 1954-55, Menlo Park, Calif., 1955-56, Washington, 1957-62; rsch. geologist U.S. Geol. Survey, Denver, 1962-93, geologist emeritus, 1993—; editl. adviser Elsevier Pub. Co., Amsterdam, The Netherlands, 1974-93. Author: Trondhjemites, Dacites, and Related Rocks, 1979; contbr. articles to profl. publs. Vis. rsch. fellow U. Witwatersrand, Johannesburg, South Africa, 1974; rsch. grantee Nat. Geog. Soc., Swaziland, 1972, Mariana Islands, 1976. Fellow Geol. Soc. Am. (editl. advisor, 1974-78), Mineral Soc. Am.; mem. Am. Geophys. Union (guest editor 1981). Home: 14155 W 21st Pl Golden CO 80401 Office: US Geol Survey Box 25046 Stop 973 Denver CO 80025

BARKER, GORDON, consumer products company executive. BS in Pharmacy, Wash. State U. Pharmacist and supr. PayLess Drug Stores, Lewiston, Ohio, 1968-77, store mgr., 1977-80, dist. mgr., 1980-87; gen. mgr. store ops. PayLess Drug Stores, 1987-89, v.p. of pharmacy, 1989-91, sr. v.p. of pharmacy, 1991-92, exec. v.p., 1992-94; sr. exec. v.p. Thrift PayLess, Inc., 1994, pres. and COO, pres. and CEO, 1996—. Mem. bd. dirs. Waverly Children's Home, Salvation Army Cascade Divsn., Cascade Pacific Coun. Boy Scouts of Am. Office: Thrifty PayLess Holdings Inc 9275 SW Peyton Ln Wilsonville OR 97070-9200

BARKER, MITCHELL FREDERICK, government public relations official; b. Tulsa, June 29, 1948; s. Albert B. and Dorothy L. (Bashe) B. B. Univ. Studies, U. N.Mex., 1976; MA, U. Okla., 1985. News dir. Sta. KBRR-AM, Leadville, Colo., 1976-77, Sta. KAFE-AM-FM, Santa Fe, 1977; pub. affairs asst. U.S. Army Engr. Dist., Albuquerque, 1978-79; seminar asst. VA InterWest Regional Med. Edn. Ctr., Salt Lake City, 1979-80; tech. writer Robins AFB, Ga., 1980-81; pub. affairs specialist U.S. Army Engr. Dist., Walla Walla, Wash., 1981-82; pub. affairs officer Fitzsimons Army Med. Ctr., Aurora, Colo., 1982-84. Served with U.S. Army, 1969-73. Recipient Keith L. Ware award for radio prodn. Dept. of Army, 1972. Unitarian. Office: FAA Pub Affairs ANM-5 1601 Lind Ave SW Renton WA 98055

BARKER, NANCIE LYNNE, engineer; b. Berkeley, Calif., Apr. 25, 1942; d. Paul Thomas Marsh and Roberta Mildred (Wiggins) Brubaker; m. Loy Lee Barker, July 27, 1963; 1 child, Cindy Elizabeth. AS in Tool Design magna cum laude, De Anza Coll., 1979. Quality mgr. KRAS-West Corp., San Jose, Calif., 1979-82; quality engring. mgr. Siliconix, Santa Clara, Calif., 1982-87, package devel. engr., 1987-89, sr. engr. purchasing dept., 1989-91, mgr. supplier quality programs, 1991—; leader task force Semicondr. Equipment Materials Inst., Mountain View, Calif., 1989-91, chairperson packaging com., 1993—. Leader Camp Fire Girls, Cupertino, Calif., 1970-80; instr. in first aid ARC, San Jose and Los Gatos, Calif., 1970-84. Mem. Am. Soc. Metals, Internat. Soc. Hybrid Mfg., Am. Soc. for Quality Control. Office: Siliconix 2201 Laurelwood Rd Santa Clara CA 95054-1516

BARKER, ROBERT WILLIAM, television personality; b. Darrington, Wash., Dec. 12, 1923; s. Byron John and Matilda Kent (Tarleton) B.; m. Dorothy Jo Gideon, Jan. 12, 1945 (dec. Oct. 1981). BA in Econs. summa cum laude, Drury Coll., 1947. Master of ceremonies: Truth or Consequences, Hollywood, Calif., 1957-75, Price is Right, 1972—, Miss Universe Beauty Pageant, 1966-87, Miss U.S.A. Beauty Pageant, 1966-87, Pillsbury Bake-Off, 1969-85, Bob Barker Fun and Games Show, 1978—; host: Rose Parade, CBS, 1969-88; appeared in (feature film) Happy Gilmore, 1996. Served to lt. (j.g.) USNR, 1943-45. Recipient Emmy award for Best Audience Participation Host, 1981-82, 82-83, 86-87, 87-88, 89-90, 90-91, 91-92, 93-94, 94-95. Mem. AGVA, AFTRA, Screen Actors Guild. Office: The Price is Right care CBS TV 7800 Beverly Blvd Los Angeles CA 90036*

BARKER, RONALD C., lawyer; b. Newton, Utah, Sept. 28, 1927; s. Stephen Waldo and Hazel Vilate (Larsen) B.; married Apr. 2, 1952; children: Stephen, Bart, LuAnn, Mitchell, Beth, Sterling, Heather, Dawn, Marshall. BS in Acctg., Utah State U., 1949; JD in Law, U. Utah, 1955. Bar: Utah, U.S. Ct. Appeals (10th cir.), U.S. Supreme Ct. Acct. Jones and Atwood, Ogden, Utah, 1949-50; CPA Burnett & Humphries, Idaho Falls, Idaho, 1950-52; CPA Salt Lake City, 1952-60, atty. self employed, 1956—. Lt. U.S. Army Corps Engrs., 1946. LDS. Home: 5655 W 3500 S Salt Lake City UT 84120-2601 Office: Barker Law Office 2870 S State St Salt Lake City UT 84115-3624

BARKER, WILEY FRANKLIN, surgeon, educator; b. Santa Fe, Oct. 16, 1919; s. Charles Burton and Bertha (Steed) B.; m. Nancy Ann Kerber, June 8, 1943; children: Robert Lawrence, Jonathan Steed, Christina Lee. B.S., Harvard, 1941, M.D., 1944. Intern, then resident Peter Bent Brigham Hosp., Boston, 1944-46; Arthur Tracy Cabot fellow Harvard Med. Sch., 1948-49; asst. chief surg. service, then chief surg. sect. Wadsworth VA Hosp., Los Angeles, 1951-54; attending physician Wadsworth VA Hosp., 1951—; mem. faculty U. Calif. at Los Angeles Med. Sch., 1954—, prof. surgery, 1964-86, prof. emeritus, 1986—, chief div. gen. surgery, 1955-77; cons. Sepulveda VA Hosp., 1966-78, chief of staff, 1978-83; Mem. com. trauma NRC, 1964-68. Author: Surgical Treatment of Peripheral Vascular Disease, 1962, Peripheral Arterial Disease, 1966, 2d edit., 1976, Clio Chirugica: The Arteries, vols. I and II, 1992, , also papers, chpts. in books. Served as lt. (j.g.) M.C. USNR, 1946-47. Harvard Nat. scholar, 1937-44. Fellow ACS (2d v.p. 1986-87); mem. Am. Surg. Assn., Am. Bd. Surgery (diplomate, bd. dirs. 1964-70), Soc. Clin. Surgery (pres. 1972-74), Soc. Univ. Surgeons, Soc. Vascular Surgery (pres. 1972-73), Internat. Cardiovascular Soc. (v.p. N.Am. chpt. 1964-65, pres. 1979-80), So. Surg. Assn., Pacific Coast Surg. Assn. (pres. 1982-83), Pan Pacific Surg. Assn. (pres. 1986-88), Am., Calif., Los Angeles County med. assns., Phi Beta Kappa, Sigma Xi, Alpha Omega Alpha. Republican. Episcopalian. Address: 13216 Dobbins Pl Los Angeles CA 90049-3623 Office: Univ Calif Sch Medicine Dept Surgery Los Angeles CA 90024

BARKEY, BRENDA, technical writer, publications manager; b. Hawthorne, Calif., Dec. 22, 1959; d. Greta E. Barkey; 1 child, Vladimir. BS in Civil Engring./Comm., U. Washington, 1983. Cert. aerobics instr., Am. Coun. on Exercise. Tech. writer, editor Care Computer Systems, Bellevue, Wash., 1983-87, tech. writing supr., 1987-88; tech. writer Municipality of Met. Seattle, 1988-91; project mgr. West Point Treatment Plant Ops. Documentation, King County, Seattle, 1991—. Co-author, conf. presenter, A Team Approach to Training and Documentation in a Changing Organization, 1993, Putting Operations and Maintenance Manuals to Work for You, 1991; author West Point Treatment Plant Operations and Maintenance Manual. Bd. mem., sec., Edmonds (Wash.) Greenery Assn., 1996. Recipient Merit awards, Soc. Tech. Communication, Seattle, 1989, 91. Office: King County 821 2d Ave MS-138 Seattle WA 98104

BARKIN, ELAINE RADOFF, composer, music educator; b. N.Y.C., Dec. 15, 1932; m. George J. Barkin, Nov. 28, 1957; 3 children. BA in Music, Queens Coll., 1954, MFA in Composition, 1956; PhD in Composition and Theory, Brandeis U., 1971; Cert. in Composition and Piano, Berlin Hochschule Musik, 1957; studied with Karol Rathaus, Irving Fine, Boris Blacher, Arthur Berger. Lectr. in music Queens Coll., 1964-70, Sarah Lawrence, 1969-70; from asst. to assoc. prof. music theory U. Mich., 1970-74; from asst. prof. to prof. composition and theory U. Calif., L.A., 1974-97; vis. asst. prof. Princeton (N.J.) U., 1974; lectr. in field. Asst. to co-editor: Perspectives of New Music, 1963-85; composer String Quartet, 1969, Sound Play for violin, 1974, String Trio, 1976, Plein Clhant, alto flute, 1977, Ebb Tide, 2 vibraphones, 1977, ...the Supple Suitor...for soprano and five players, 1978, (chamber mini opera) De Amore, 1980, Impromptu for violin, cello, piano, 1981, (theatre piece) Media Speak, 1981, At the Piano, piano and piano, 1982, For String Quartet, 1982, Quilt Piece graphic score for 7 instruments, 1984, On The Way To Becoming for 4-track Tape Collage, 1985, Demeter and Persephone for violin, tape, chamber ensemble, dancers, 1986, 3 Rhapsodies, flutes and clarinet, 1986, Encore for Javanese Gamelan Ensemble, 1986, Out of the Air for Basset Horn and Tape, 188, To Whom It May Concern 4 track tape collage, reader and 4 players, 1989, Legong Dreams, oboe, 1990, Gamélange harp and mixed gamelan band, 1992, Five Tape Collages, Open Space CD #3, 1993, "for my friends' pleasure," soprano and harp, 1994, numerous improvised group and duo sessions on tape; produced cassette and video: New Music in Bali, 1994; "touching all bases" for electronic bass, electronic percussion, and Balinese gamelan, 1996. Recipient Fulbright award, 1957, awards NEA, 1975, 79, awards Rockefeller Found., 1980, Meet the Composer award, 1994. Office: U Calif Dept Music 405 Hilgard Ave Los Angeles CA 90075

BARKLEY, CHARLES WADE, professional basketball player; b. Leeds, Ala., Feb. 20, 1963. Student, Auburn U., 1981-84. mem. U.S. Olympic Basketball Team, 1992. With Phila. 76ers, 1984-92, Phoenix Suns, 1992—; mem. U.S. Olympic team, 1992, 1996. Author: (with Roy S. Johnson) Outrageous! The Fine Life and Flagrant Good Times of Basketball's Irresistible Force, 1992; film appearances include: Forget Paris, 1995. Recipient NBA All-Star Game Most Valuable Player award, 1991, Schick Pivotal Player award, 1986-88, NBA Most Valuable Player Award, 1993, IMB award, 1986-88; named to NBA All-Star team, 1988-93. Office: Phoenix Suns 201 E Jefferson St Phoenix AZ 85004-2412

BARKLEY, THIERRY VINCENT, lawyer; b. Paris, Mar. 21, 1955; s. Jacques and Michéline Marié (Rossi) B.; came to U.S., 1967, naturalized, 1974; m. Mary Ellen Gamble, June 18, 1983; children: Richard A., Robert V., Marriah E., Christopher R. BA in Polit. Sci., UCLA, 1976; JD, Calif. Western Sch. Law, San Diego, 1979. Bar: Nev. 1980, U.S. Dist. Ct. Nev. 1982, U.S. Supreme Ct. 1986. Intern, Calif. Ct. Appeals 4th Circuit, San Diego, 1978-79; law clk. Nev. Dist. Ct., 7th Jud. Dist., Ely, 1979-81; assoc. firm C.E. Horton, Ely, 1982-83; asst. city atty. Ely, 1982-83; assoc. firm Barker, Gillock & Perry, Reno, 1983-87, Perry & Spann, 1987-89, ptnr., 1990—. Editor Internat. Law Jour., 1979. Mem. Internat. Moot Ct. Team, 1978; recipient Dean's award Calif. Western Sch. Law, 1979. Mem. Rep. Presdl. Task Force, 1990. Mem. Nev. Bar Assn., Washoe Bar Assn., U.S. Jaycees (past pres. White Pine, Nev.). Republican. Roman Catholic. Lodge: Elks (past treas. Ely club). Office: Perry & Spann 6130 Plumas St Reno NV 89509-6060

BARKLEY, WILLIAM DONALD, museum executive director; b. New Westminster, B.C., Can., Apr. 4, 1941; s. Donald MacMillan and Ethel Margaret (Mines) B.; m. Helen Gayle Alanson, Aug. 29, 1964; children: Warren Vincent, Colleen Michelle. BS, U. B.C., 1964, MA, 1971. Cert. tchr. Can. Tchr. Salmon Arm (B.C.) Sr. Secondary Sch., 1965-68; wildlife biologist Wye Marsh Wildlife Ctr., Midland, Ont., Can., 1968-72; chief interpretation Can. Wildlife Svc., Ottawa, Ont., 1972-77; asst. dir. B.C. Provincial Mus., Victoria, 1977-84; dir. Royal B.C. Mus., Victoria, 1984—; advisor cultural resource mgmt. program U. Victoria, 1985—; lectr. univs. Contbr. articles to Nat. History Interpretation mag., 1965—. Bd. dirs. Tourism Victoria, 1985—. Recipient Disting. Svc. award Interpretation Can., Ottawa, 1983, Can. 125 award for svc. to mus. cmty. Fellow Can. Mus. Assn.; mem. Can. Mus. Assn. (pres. 1987-89), B.C. Mus. Assn., Internat. Coun. of Mus.-Can., Can. Pks. and Wilderness Soc., Can. Nature Fedn., Victoria A.M. Tourism Svcs. Assn. (treas.). Mem. United Ch. Can. Office: Royal BC Museum, PO Box 9815 Stn Prov Govt, Victoria, BC Canada V8W 9W2

BARLEY, LEONARD VAUGHN, physician; b. San Antonio, Mar. 21, 1946; s. Leonard V. Sr. and Peggy B.; m. Linda M. Malo, Dec. 23, 1967; 1 child, Isaac E. BS, U. Houston, 1969; MD, U. Tex., San Antonio, 1973. Resident in psychiatry Letterman Army Med. Ctr., San Francisco, 1973-76; chief outpatient svcs. Brooke Army Med. Ctr., San Antonio, 1976-78; med. dir. West Ctrl. Mental Health, Carson City, Colo., 1979-82; pvt. practice Colorado Springs, Colo., 1978—; med. dir. Eating Disorders, Colorado Springs, Colo., 1992-94; chmn. MedLogic Global Corp., Colorado Springs, Colo., 1992—; med. dir. Cedar Springs Hosp., Colorado Springs, Colo., 1994—. Patentee in field. Chmn. Victim Compensation Bd., Colorado Springs, 1986-88. Maj. U.S. Army, 1973-88. Fellow Am. Psychiat. Assn.; mem. Colo. Psychiat. Assn. (trustee 1986-88), Colorado Springs Psychiat. Soc. (pres. 1986). Office: 2135 Southgate Rd Colorado Springs CO 80906-2605

BARLOW, DEBORAH LYNN, librarian; b. Cooperstown, N.Y., Dec. 14, 1958; d. John Ford and Anne Eldora (Woodbury) B. BA in Art and History, U. San Diego, 1981; MA in Art History, mus. studies diploma, Boston U., 1985; MS in Libr. Sci., Simmons Coll., 1984. Visual resources libr. Cooper Union, N.Y.C., 1985-87; art libr., curator Queens Coll., CUNY, N.Y.C., 1987-90; reference libr. art libr. U. So. Calif., L.A., 1990-94; head libr. L.A. County Mus. Art, L.A., 1995—. Compiler: (bibliographies) Hendrick Goltzius and the Classical Tradition, 1992, Richard Diebenkorn: Prints From the Harry W. and Mary Margaret Anderson Collection, 1993. Mem. Art Librs. Soc. N.Am. (western regional rep., exec. bd. 1996—, chair Gerd Muehsam award com. 1995-96, chair publs. com. 1993-95), Art Librs. Soc. S.C. (sec. 1992-94). Office: L A County Mus Art Rsch Libr 5905 Wilshire Blvd Los Angeles CA 90036

BARLOW, HAVEN J., state legislator, realtor; b. Clearfield, Utah, Jan. 4, 1922; s. Jesse and Asdora (Beck) B.; m. Bonnie Rae Ellison, Nov. 23, 1944; children: Jesselie Anderson, Heidi Harris, Rachel, Haven J., Stewart E., Duncan. BS, Utah State U., 1944, postgrad. U. Utah Law Sch., Harvard U. Sch. Bus. Mem. Utah Ho. of Reps., 1953-57, senator Utah State Senate, 1957-94; pres. Barlow Ins., Inc. 1950—; bd. dirs. 1st Nat. Bank of Layton. Past pres. Lake Bonniville council Boy Scouts Am.; bd. dirs., former trustee Utah State Symphony; mem. Davis County Pvt. Industry council. Served to lt. (j.g.) USN, 1942-44; PTO, ETO. Recipient Disting. Service award Utah State U., 1986, Humanitarian award Utah Vocat. Assn., Light of Learning award State Bd. Edn., Silver Beaver award Boy Scouts Am., Disting. Svc. award Weber State U., 1988, Profl. Achievement award Utah State U., Disting. Svc. award Utah Symphony Orch. Republican. Mormon. Home: 552 Elm St Layton UT 84041-4308*

BARLOW, WILLIAM PUSEY, JR., accountant; b. Oakland, Calif., Feb. 11, 1934; s. William P. and Muriel (Block) B.; student Calif. Inst. Tech., 1952-54. AB in Econs., U. Calif.-Berkeley, 1956. CPA, Calif. Acct. Barlow, Davis & Wood, San Francisco, 1960-72, ptnr., 1964-72; ptnr., J.K. Lasser & Co., 1972-77, Touche Ross & Co., San Francisco, 1977-78; self employed acct., 1978-89; ptnr. Barlow & Hughan, 1990—. Co-author: Collectible Books: Some New Paths, 1979, The Grolier Club, 1884-1984, 1984; editor: Book Catalogues: Their Varieties and Uses, 2d edit., 1986, Officially Sealed Notes, 1996—; contbr. articles to profl. jours. Fellow Gleeson Libr. Assocs., 1969, pres., 1971-74; mem. Coun. Friends Bancroft Libr., 1971—, chmn., 1974-79; bd. dirs. Oakland Ballet, 1982—, pres. 1986-89, chmn. 1995—. Recipient Sir Thomas More medal Gleeson Libr. Assocs., 1989;

named to Water Ski Hall of Fame, 1993. Mem. Am. Water Ski Assn. (bd. dirs., regional chmn. 1959-63, pres. 1963-66, chmn. bd. 1966-69, 77-79, hon. v.p. 1969—), Internat. Water Ski Fedn. (exec. bd. 1961-71, 75-78), Bibliog. Soc. Am. (coun. 1986-92, pres. 1992-96), Grolier Club (N.Y.C.), Roxburghe Club (San Francisco), Book of Calif. Club (bd. dirs. 1963-76, pres. 1968-69, treas. 1971-83). Home: 1474 Hampel St Oakland CA 94602-1346 Office: 449 15th St Oakland CA 94612-2821

BARMAN, ROBERT JOHN, home electronics company executive; b. Glendale, Calif.; s. Robert Grant and Geraldine (Howe) B.; m. Jean Ann Crane, June 19, 1965; children: John Robert, Jeffrey Wynn. BS in Mktg., Calif. State U., L.A., 1965. Sales coord. Teledyne Packard Bell, L.A., 1965-67; dist. mgr. Teledyne Packard Bell, Fresno, L.A., 1968-71; regional sales mgr. Teledyne Packard Bell, Boston, 1971-73; major accounts sales mgr. Quasar Co., L.A., 1973-75, regional sales mgr., 1975-76, sales mgr., 1976-77, zone mgr., 1985—; v.p., br. mgr. Quasar Co., Seattle, 1977-84; gen. mgr. Matsushita, L.A., 1985-95; mem. mgmt. com. Matsushita Elec. Corp. of Am. West; mem. distbg. coun. Quasar Co., Chgo.; mgr. spl. markets, region mgr., gen. mgr. Panasonic Co. West, 1995—. Bd. dirs. Irvine (Calif.) Aquatics Swim Team, Bellevue (Wash.) Athletic Club Swim Team. Office: Panasonic Co West 6550 Katella Ave Cypress CA 90630-5102

BARNA, ARPAD ALEX, electrical engineering consultant; b. Budapest, Hungary, Apr. 3, 1933; came to U.S., 1957; s. Sandor and Erzsebet (Markus) B. Diploma of Elec. Engring., Tech. U. Budapest, 1956; Degree of Engr., Stanford U., 1966, PhD in Elec. Engring., 1968; BA in Lit., U. Calif., Santa Cruz, 1986. Part-time grad. asst. Poly. U. Budapest, 1954-56; with Ctrl. Rsch. Inst. for Physics, Hungarian Acad. Scis., Budapest, 1956, Calif. Inst. Tech., Pasadena, 1957-61, Ransom Systems, San Pedro, Calif., 1961, U. Chgo., 1961-63, Stanford Linear Accelerator Ctr., 1963-69; assoc. prof. elec. engring. U. Hawaii, Honolulu, 1969-72; with Hewlett-Packard Labs., Palo Alto, Calif., 1972-83; pvt. elec. engring. cons. Capitola, Calif., 1966—; cons. Harshaw Chem. Co., Cleve., 1966-69, Cintra, Inc., Mountain View, Calif., 1969, Avantek, Inc., Santa Clara, 1969-72, W.W. Hansen Labs. of Physics, Stanford U., 1972-83, Audio Devel., Inc., Palo Alto, 1977, Monolithic Microsystems, Inc., Santa Cruz, Calif., 1982-84, SiScan Corp., Campbell, Calif., 1982-86, IMEC, Berkeley, Calif., 1990—; mem. faculty Calif. State U., Sacramento, 1972, UCLA, 1977, 81, Stanford U., 1981, U. Calif., Santa Cruz, 1984, 87. Reviewer IEEE Jour. Solid State Circuits, IEEE Transactions on Info. Theory, Jour. Optical Soc. Am., IEEE Electron Devices Letters, IEEE Proceedings, Jour. Applied Physics; contbr. articles to profl. jours.; author: High Speed Pulse Circuits, 1970, Operational Amplifiers, 1971, 2d edit. 1989, High Speed Pulse and Digital Techniques, 1980, VHSIC Technologies and Tradeoffs, 1981; co-author: Integrated Circuits in Digital Electronics, 1973, 2d edit. 1987, others. Mem. IEEE (sr.). Jewish. Home and Office: 750 Bay Ave Apt 305 Capitola CA 95010-2741

BARNARD, ANNETTE WILLIAMSON, elementary school educator; b. Phoenix, Nov. 29, 1948; d. Water Albert and Geraldine Williamson; m. Richard W. Heinrich, Sept. 1969 (div.); 1 child, Jennifer Anne; m. Charles Jay Barnard, June 6, 1981. AA, Mesa C.C., 1979; BA in Spl. Edn., Elem. Edn., Ariz. State U., 1981, postgrad., 1989; M in Edn. Leadership, 1996, No. Ariz. U., 1996. Cert. tchr., Ariz. Tchr. spl. edn. Tempe (Ariz.) Sch. Dist., 1981-83, tchr. Indian community, 1983-84; tchr. elem. sch. Kyrene Sch. Dist., Tempe, 1984-86, 90—; sch. dist. mentor coord., 1994-96; tchr. Chandler (Ariz.) Sch. Dist., 1986-89; chair profl. stds. and cert. com. Ariz. Bd. Edn., Phoenix, 1990-94; chair facilitator Kyrene Legis. Action Community, 1991-94; mentor Kyrene Sch. dist., 1990—; commencement spkr. Ariz. State U., 1981; design. team. mem. Quality Cert. Employee Appraisal System; speaker in field. Contbg. author: Environmental Education Compendium for Energy Resources, 1991, System of Personnel Development, 1989; contbr. articles to profl. jours. Bd. dirs. Ariz. State Rep. Caucus, Phoenix, 1990-93, precinct committeewoman, Tempe, 1990-92. Recipient Profl. Leadership award Kiwanis Club Am., Tempe, 1984; nominee to talent bank Coun. on Women's Edn. Programs U.S. Dept. Edn., 1982; named Tchr. of Yr., local newspaper, 1993. Mem. ASCD, Kyrene Edn. Assn. (chair legis. com. 1990-94), Kappa Delta Pi, Phi Kappa Phi, Phi Theta Kappa, Pi Lambda Theta. Home: 3221 W Jasper Dr Chandler AZ 85226-1421

BARNARD, ARLENE, retired secondary education educator; b. Red Lion, Pa., Apr. 7, 1922; d. W. Collins and Nettie Ellen (Curran) Workinger; 1 child, Tiffany West. BS, Indiana U. of Pa., 1942; MA, San Diego State U., 1979; postgrad., Stanford U., 1983. Cert. secondary tchr., computer ctr. dir., Calif. Tchr. S.W. Jr. H.S., Sweetwater H.S. Dist., San Diego, 1968-76, tchr. 12th grade English and English lit., 1976-94; chair English dept.; gifted/talented edn. coord., 1979-83; microcomputer instr., summer 1983; Stanford U. intern, summer 1984. Recipient scholarship Stanford U. Mem. NEA, Calif. Tchrs. Assn., Sweetwater Edn. Assn., Calif. Scholarship Fedn. (advisor), Phi Delta Kappa. Home: 3334 Rio Vista Dr Bonita CA 91902-1039

BARNARD, DALE LYNN, microbiologist; b. Ogden, Utah, July 13, 1951; s. Wayne Taylor and Lottie Elaine (Child) B.; m. Vickie Lynn Wilde, Aug. 14, 1974; children: Nikolas, Joseph, Melissa, David, Thomas. BS in Microbiology, Chemistry, Weber State Coll., 1977; MS in Microbiology, Idaho State U., 1979; PhD in Microbiology, Biochemistry, Brigham Young U., 1987; postgrad., Utah State U., 1988. Teaching asst. dept. microbiology & chemistry Idaho State U., Pocatello, 1979; instr., rsch. asst. dept. microbiology Brigham Young U., Provo, Utah, 1979-87; lab. tech. Utah state health dept. Brigham Young U., Utah County Mosquito Abatement Dist., Provo, 1983; instr. Snow Coll., 1983; rsch. asst. prof. dept. animal, dairy & vet. scis. Utah State U., Logan, 1988—; chmn. Associated Students Brigham Youn gU. Rsch. Fund, 1983-81; presenter in field. Contbr. articles to profl. jours. Asst. scoutmaster Boy Scouts Am., Nibley, Utah, 1989-90, 90-92, chartered orgn. rep., 1992-93, explorer post leader, 1993-94; mem. Up with Down's Syndrome Soc. Postdoctoral fellow Dept. Animal, Dairy & Vet. Scis., Utah State U., 1987-88. Mem. Internat. Soc. Antiviral Rsch., Am. Soc. Microbiology (sec. Intermountain br. 1990-91), Am. Soc. Virology, Sigma Xi. Mem. LDS Ch. Office: Utah State U Dept ADVS Inst Antiviral Rsch 5600 University Blvd Logan UT 84322-5600

BARNARD, ROLLIN DWIGHT, retired financial executive; b. Denver, Apr. 14, 1922; s. George Cooper and Emma (Riggs) B.; m. Patricia Reynolds Bierkamp, Sept. 15, 1943; children: Michael Dana, Rebecca Susan (Mrs. Paul C. Wulfestieg), Laurie Beth (Mrs. Kenneth J. Kostelecky). B.A., Pomona Coll., 1943. Clk. Morey Merc. Co., Denver, 1937-40; ptnr George C. Barnard & Co. (gen. real estate and ins.), Denver, 1946-47; v.p. Foster & Barnard, Inc., 1947-53; instr. Denver U., 1949-53; dir. real estate U.S. P.O. Dept., Washington, 1953-55, dep. asst. postmaster gen., bur. facilities, 1955-59, asst. postmaster gen., 1959-61; pres., dir. Midland Fed. Savs. & Loan Assn., Denver, 1962-84; vice chmn. Bank Western Fed. Savs. Bank, 1984-87; vice chmn., pres. Western Capital Investment Corp., 1985-87. Mayor City of Greenwood Village, Colo., 1989-93, chmn. Planning and Zoning Commn., 1969-73, mem. coun., 1975-77; pres. Denver Area coun. Boy Scouts Am., 1970-71, mem. exec. bd., 1962-73; mem. adv. bd. Denver Area coun. Boy Scouts Am., 1973—; bd. dirs. Downtown Denver Improvement Assn., pres., 1965; bd. dirs. Bethesda Found., Inc., 1973-82, Children's Hosp., 1979-84, treas., 1983-84; bd. dirs. Children's Health Corp., Inc., 1982-93; trustee Mile High United Fund, 1969-72, Denver Symphony Assn., 1973-74; bd. dirs. Colo. Coun. Econ. Edn., 1971-80, chmn. 1971-76; trustee, v.p., treas. Morris Animal Found., 1969-81, pres., chmn. 1974-78, trustee emeritus, 1981—; trustee Denver Zool. Found., 1994—, exec. v.p. 1996—; mem. acquisitions com. Friends Found. Denver Pub. Libr., 1994—; bd. dirs. Wings Over the Rockies Mus., 1996—. Nominated One of Ten Outstanding Young Men in Am., U.S. Jaycees, 1955, 57; recipient Disting. Svc. award Postmaster Gen. U.S., 1960; Silver Beaver award Boy Scouts Am., 1969; named Outstanding Citizen of Yr., Sertoma, 1982, Colo. Citizen of Yr., Colo. Assn. Realtors, 1982, Citizen of West, Nat. Western Stockshow, 1994. Mem. Greater Denver C. of C. (pres. 1966-67), U.S. League Savs. Instns. (bd. dirs. 1972-77, vice chmn. 1979-80, chmn. 1980-81, mem. nat. legis. com., exec. com. 1974-77), Savs. League Colo. (exec. com. 1969-73, pres. 1971-72), Colo. Assn. Commerce and Industry (dir. 1971-76), Fellowship Christian Athletes (Denver area dir. 1963-76), Western Stock Show Assn. (dir. 1971—, exec. com. 1982-94, 1st v.p. 1985-94), Mountain and Plains Appaloosa Horse Club (pres. 1970-71), Roundup Riders of the Rockies (bd. dirs. 1979—, treas. 1980-87, v.p. 1987-89, pres.-elect 1989-91, pres. 1991-93). Republican. Presbyterian. Home: 3151 E Long Rd Greenwood Village CO 80121-1716

BARNARD, WILLIAM CALVERT, retired news service executive; b. Corpus Christi, Tex., Feb. 25, 1914; s. W.C. and Eleanor (Erb) B.; m. Julia Lacy Salter, Mar. 25, 1961; children: William Cornell, Diana Eugenia. Student, Tex. Coll. Arts and Industries, Kingsville, 1933-35. Reporter-columnist Corpus Christi Caller-Times, 1935-40; feature editor San Antonio Express-News, 1941-42; writer, state editor AP, Dallas Bur., 1942-50; AP war corr. Korean War, Far East news editor, 1953-54; bur. chief AP, Dallas, 1954-62; gen. exec. AP, N.Y.C., 1962-71; gen. exec. for ten Western states AP, San Francisco, 1971-81; gen. exec. for 24 Western states AP, 1981-85. Recipient Journalism Forum award for coverage Korean War So. Meth. U., 1954. Presbyterian. Home: 551 Walnut St Apt 8 San Carlos CA 94070-2337*

BARNARD, WILLIAM MARION, psychiatrist; b. Mt. Pleasant, Tex., Dec. 17, 1949; s. Marion Jaggers and Med (Cody) B. BA, Yale U., 1972; MD, Baylor U., 1976. Diplomate Am. Bd. Psychiatry and Neurology. Resident NYU/Bellevue Med. Ctr., 1976-79; liaison, consultation fellow L.I. Jewish/Hillside Med. Ctr., 1979-80; chief, liaison, consultation psychiatrist Queens (N.Y.) Med. Ctr., 1980-83; liaison, consultation psychiatrist Mt. Sinai Med. Ctr., N.Y.C., 1983-84; clin. asst. prof. NYU Med. Sch., N.Y.C., 1984-87; emergency psychiatrist VA Med. Ctr., N.Y.C., 1984-87; pvt. practice Pasadena, Calif., 1987—; chief psychiat. svc. Las Encinas Hosp., Pasadena, 1989, chief staff, 1990, med. dir. gen. adult. psychiat. svc., 1990-92, asst. med. dir., 1992; med. dir. CPC Alhambra Hosp., Rosemead, Calif., 1992—. Chmn. mental health com. All Saints AIDS Svc. Ctr., Pasadena, 1990-94, bd. dirs., 1991-94, v.p., 1996—; bd. dirs. Pasadena Symphony, 1989—, Whiffenpoof Alumni, New Haven, 1991—; bd. dirs. Whiffenpoof Alumni, New Haven, 1991—, haberdasher, 1995—. Wilson scholar Yale U., 1973. Mem. APA, NYU-Bellevue Psychiat. Assn., Am. Soc. Addiction Medicine, Calif. Med. Assn., So. Calif. Psychiat. Soc., Acad. Psychosomatic Medicine, L.A. County Med. Assn., Amateur Comedy Club N.Y.C., Met. Opera Club, Yale Club N.Y.C., Univ. Glee Club of N.Y.C., Order of St. John (comdr.). Republican. Episcopalian. Office: 2810 E Del Mar Blvd Pasadena CA 91107-4321

BARNES, A. KEITH, management educator; b. Peterborough, Eng., July 5, 1934; came to U.S., 1975; s. Archibald and Constance Louise (Snart) B.; m. Judith Anne Lamplugh, Dec. 26, 1955; children: Warren, Douglas, Lisa. BSc in Engring., Nene Univ., 1955; MBA in Mgmt., Pepperdine U., 1980, EdD in Adminstrn., 1984. Engr., designer Perkins Diesel, Eng. and Can., 1954-57; various positions Blackwood Hodge, Toronto, Can., 1957-70; various mgmt. positions J.I. Case Co. (Tenneco), Toronto, Can., 1970-81; from asst. to assoc. prof. U. La Verne, Calif., 1981-84; from assoc. prof. to Hunsaker prof. mgmt. U. Redlands, Calif., 1984—; spkr. numerous orgns., 1974—. Author: Management Maturity: Prerequisite to Total Quality, 1994; editor Jour. Applied Bus. Rsch., 1988-93; mem. editl. bd. Jour. Mgmt. Sys., 1986—. Bd. dirs. San Gorgonio Meml. Hosp., 1993-94. Republican. Home: 40903 Lincoln Pl Cherry Valley CA 92223-6004 Office: U Redlands Box 3080 1200 E Colton Redlands CA 92373-0999

BARNES, CAROL PARDON, education educator; b. Ann Arbor, Mich., Jan. 21, 1941; d. Reinhold Walter and Ruth Ardillis (McKillen) Pardon; m. Mitchell Russakow, July 20, 1991; children: Katherine, Erik. BA in Edn., U. Mich., 1962; MEd, Wright State U., 1970; PhD, Claremont Grad. Sch., 1975. Cert. elem. tchr., Mich., Ohio. Tchr. Plymouth, Mich., 1962-63, Mad River Twp. Schs., Dayton, Ohio, 1963-64, Mad River-Greene Twp. Schs., Enon, Ohio, 1965-67; coll. instr. Wright State U., Dayton, Ohio, 1970-72, Claremont (Calif.) Grad. Sch., 1973-74; prof. Calif. State U., Fullerton, 1975—; chair dept. elem. and bilingual edn. Calif. State U., 1990-95; exec. dir. DELTA L.A. Annenberg Met. Project; cons. to various sch. dists., Calif., Ohio, Peoples Rep. of China, Orange County Grand Jury, Santa Ana, Calif., 1986, various law firms, Calif., 1984—; pres. Programetrics Ltd., Huntington Beach., Calif., 1980-89; co-chair Calif. Com. on Accreditation. Co-author: Studies of College Teaching, 1984; contbr. articles to profl. jours. exec. com. mem.-at-large Acad. Senate of Calif. State U., Long Beach, 1984-87. Recipient Meritorious Performance award Calif. State U., Fullerton, 1984-89, Outstanding Prof. award Sch. Human Devel. and Community Svc., 1985, Disting. Faculty Mem. award, 1992. Mem. ASCD, Am. Ednl. Rsch. Assn., Calif. Assn. for Supervision and Curriculum Devel. (bd. dirs. 1982-84), Orange County Reading Assn., Calif. Reading Assn. Republican. Presbyterian. Home: 6543 E Via Estrada Anaheim CA 92807-4226 Office: Calif State U 800 N State College Blvd Fullerton CA 92831-3547

BARNES, CLOYD RAY, sculptor, retired engineer; b. Hartford, Ark., July 18, 1934; s. Cloyd Hiram and Esta Elizabeth (McCafferty) B.; m. Wanda Jean Carlton, Oct. 17, 1954; children: Mark E., Stephanie Barnes Veasman. BS in Physics, Tulsa U., 1968. Mem. tech. staff N.Am. Rockwell, Tulsa, 1964-68; sr. aerosystems engr. Gen. Dynamics, Alamogordo, N.Mex., 1968-72; mgr. project engring. Dynalectron Corp., Alamogordo, 1972-77; mgr. ops. dept. Dynalectron Corp., Alamagordo, 1977-80, tech. dir. radar backscatter divsn., 1980-84, tech. dir., site mgr., 1984-86; mgr. radio frequency test ops. Martin Marietta Denver Aerospace, 1986-89, dept. staff engr., 1989-91; represented by numerous galleries, including Fenn Galleries, Santa Fe, Knox Galleries, Vail and Beaver Creek, Colo., Paint Horse Gallery, Breckenridge, Colo.; interim instr. Denver Art Students League, 1994. Exhibited in group shows at Southeastern Wildlife Expo, Charleston, S.C., Nat. Acad. Design, N.Y.C., Audubon Show, N.Y.C., Am. Artists Profl. League, N.Y.C., (Helen G. Oehler award), 1991, Nat. Wildlife Show, Kansas City, 1993 (Best of Show), Cantigny Park, Chgo., BCCFA Show, Clifton, Tex. (Best of Show award), Western Regional Show, Cheyenne, Wyo., N.Am. Sculpture Exhibit, Golden, Colo., Rough Rider Art Show, Williston, N.D., 1993 (Grand Prize 1993), Ho. Reps. Office Bldg.-Rotunda, Washington, 1994, Am. Artists Profl. League, 1994 (Leila G. Sawyer award), Visual Individualists United, Bklyn., 1995 (Grumbacher Gold Medallion award), Pacific Rim Wildlife Art Show, Tacoma, Wash.; commissioned works include life-size bronze portrait figure of C.L. Tutt, Colo. Coll., Colorado Springs, 1992, monumental bronze running buffalo Buffalo Run Golf Course, Adams County, Colo., 1996. Mem. IEEE, Rocky Mountain Elk Found. (assoc.), Allied Artists Am. (assoc.), Knickerbocker Artists (assoc.). Home and Studio: 7425 S Milwaukee Way Littleton CO 80122-1951

BARNES, GERALD R., bishop; b. Phoenix, Ariz., June 22, 1945. Grad., St. Leonard Sem., Dayton, Ohio; student, Assumption-St. John's Sem., San Antonio. Ordained priest Roman Cath. Ch., 1975, titular bishop of Monte Fiascone. Bishop San Bernardino, Calif., 1996—. Office: 1201 E Highland Ave San Bernardino CA 92404-4607

BARNES, (BENJAMIN WARREN) GRANT, lawyer, poet; b. Kansas City, Mo., May 30, 1948; s. Benjamin Franklin and Cena Rosalie Barnes. BA, U. Tex., 1972; AM, Harvard U., 1981, JD, 1982. Bar: Calif., 1986, D.C., 1984, Hawaii, 1996, Mass., 1983, N.Mex., 1986, N.Y., 1983. Atty. advisor Sec. of USAF, Washington, 1983-85; assoc. McKenna, Conner and Cuneo, L.A., 1985-90; pvt. practice L.A., 1990—. Bd. dirs. Program for Torture Victims, L.A., 1990—; legal counsel U.S. Servas, N.Y.C., 1985—. Fulbright scholar, 1972. Mem. State Bar Calif. (exec. com. internat. law sect. 1995—), Phi Beta Kappa. Home: PO Box 70280 Harvard Sta Los Angeles CA 90070 Office: 507 S Catalina Ste 8 Los Angeles CA 90020

BARNES, H. LEE, English and creative writing educator, writer; b. Moscow, Idaho, Mar. 15, 1944; s. Vernon Hughs Barnes and Evelyn Alberta (Olmstead) Harris; m. Georgia Standish, Dec. 4, 1984 (div. Aug. 1987). BA with high distinction, U. Nev., Las Vegas, 1989; MFA, Ariz. State U., 1992. Dep. sheriff Clark County Sheriff's Office, Las Vegas, 1966-72; agt. Nev. Divsn. Narcotics, Reno, 1973-76; with Maxim Hotel & Casino, Las Vegas, 1977-84, Sands Casino, Las Vegas, 1984-89; instr. English, C.C. So. Nev., North Las Vegas, 1992—, U. Nev., 1994—. Asst. editor Red Rock Rev., 1996; contbr. short stories to lit. publs. Fiction writing mentor Writers at Work, YMCA, Phoenix, 1992, Clark County Parks and Recreation, Las Vegas, 1995. Recipient hon. mention for fiction Soc. Southwestern Authors, 1991. Mem. Assoc. Writing Programs, Phi Kappa Phi. Home: 6717 Wenatchee Dr Las Vegas NV 89107-3354

BARNES, JOANNA, author, actress; b. Boston, Nov. 15, 1934; d. John Pindar and Alice Weston (Mutch) B. BA, Smith Coll., 1956. Actress appearing in motion pictures: Auntie Mame, 1958, B.S. I Love You, 1971, Spartacus, 1963, The Parent Trap, 1966, The War Wagon, 1971; TV appearances include What's My Line, The Tonight Show with Johnny Carson, Merv Griffin Show, Trials of O'Brien, Dateline: Hollywood, Murder She Wrote; book reviewer L. A. Times, syndicated columnist Chgo. Tribune, N.Y. News Syndicate, 1963-65; author: Starting from Scratch, 1968, The Deceivers, 1970, Who Is Carla Hart, 1973, Pastora, 1980, Silverwood, 1985. Mem. Phi Beta Kappa.

BARNES, PETER FRANCIS, physician, researcher, medical educator; b. Kowloon, Hong Kong, Apr. 22, 1956; came to U.S., 1974; s. Robert Joseph and Sylvia Maria (Remedios) B.; m. Susan Alison Barrows, July 12, 1980; children: Jason, Amanda. BS in Biology, Stanford U., 1977; MD, U. So. Calif., 1981. Diplomate Am. Bd. Internal Medicine, Am. Bd. Infectious Diseases. Intern U. So. Calif. Med. Ctr., L.A., 1981-82, resident, 1982-84, chief resident, 1984-85; asst. prof. clin. medicine U. So. Calif., L.A., 1985-88, asst. prof. medicine, 1989-92, assoc. prof. medicine, 1992—. Contbr. articles to profl. jours. Infectious Diseases fellowship U. So. Calif. Med. Ctr., 1992-94. Mem. Am. Thoracic Soc. (program com. 1993—, long-range planning com. 1993-96), Am .Soc. for Microbiology, Western Soc. for Clin. Investigation, Am. Assn. Immunologists, Internat. Union Against Tuberculosis, Infectious Diseases Soc. Am., Alpha Omega Alpha. Office: U So Calif Sch Medicine HMR 904 2025 Zonal Ave Los Angeles CA 90033

BARNES, RAYMOND EDWARD, fire department official; b. Denver, Colo., May 1, 1950; s. Carroll E. and Margaret A. (Minckler) B.; m. Katherine Michele Sanchez, Jan. 3, 1970; 1 child, Tamara Adrienne. BS in Aerospace Tech., Bus., Edn., Met. State Coll., 1971; postgrad., Red Rocks C.C., 1974-75, U. No. Colo., 1976; grad. exec. fire officer program, Nat. Fire Acad., 1990; MPA, U. Colo., 1991. With City of Aurora (Colo.) Fire Dept., 1971—, paramedic and rescue technician, 1976-79, lt., 1979-82, capt., 1982-85, battalion chief, suppression, 1985-87, dir. tng., 1987-91, fire chief, 1991—; adj. instr. Nat. Fire Acad., Md., 1987—; co-dir. Rocky Mountain Fire Acad.; metro co-chair Region VIII Tng. Resources and Data Exch. Active Aurora Gang Task Force; past committeeman, del. to county, state polit. assemblies;. Mem. Internat. Assn. Fire Chiefs, Internat. Assn. Metro Fire Chiefs, Internat. Soc. Fire Svc. Instrs., Internat. Assn. Firefighters (occupational safety and health com.), Soc. Nat. Fire Acad. Instrs., Soc. Exec. Fire Officers, Fire Dept. Safety Officers Orgn., State Fire Chiefs, Denver Metro Fire Chiefs, Aurora C. of C. (bd. dirs. leadership forum), Homeowners Assn. (past pres. bd. dirs.). Home: 3966 S Sable Cir Aurora CO 80014-5176 Office: City of Aurora Fire Dept 1470 S Havana St Aurora CO 80012-4014*

BARNES, ROBERT JAMES, cosmetologist; b. Washburn, Ill., Jan. 10, 1934; s. John William and Margaret Gladys (Imhoff) B.; m. Norene Davis, Sept. 4, 1955 (div. Jan. 1975); 1 child, Annette. Student, Ill. State U., 1952-53, Bradley U., 1953-56, Denver U., 1973, Purdue U., 1973. Registered cosmetologist, Ill., Tex., Colo.; cert. ins. agt. and broker, Colo. Operator attendant Std. Oil Svc., Washburn, summer 1948; carpenter Barnes Constrn. Co., Washburn, summers 1949-52; with coll. tng. program Caterpillar Tractor Co., Peoria, Ill., 1953-57; pvt. practice registered cosmetologist various locations, 1958-71, pvt. practice profl. model, 1958-73; ins. broker Barnes Ins. Agy., Denver and Salido, Colo., 1973-79; owner Log Cabin Ct. Motel, Salida, 1973—; treas. Colo. Cosmetologist Assn., 1967-72; pres. Denver Cosmetologist Assn., 1968-71; mem. trade and indsl. edn. adv. com. Denver Pub. Schs., 1971-73; Gov. apptd. mem. State Bd. Cosmetology, State of Colo., 1971-73. Sr. ptnr. Ptnrs. Inc., Denver, 1972-73; precinct com. man Rep. Party, Salida, Colo., 1974-80; mem. Chaffee County Ctrl. Com. Rep. Party, 1974-80; pres., adv. Alliance Against Domestic Abuse, Chaffee County, 1993-95. Sgt. U.S. Army, 1953-61. Recipient Cmty. Leadership awards Nat. Hairdressers and Cosmetologist Assn., 1971, Colo. Cosmetologist Assn., 1971, Denver Cosmetologist Assn., 1971, Cert. for Outstanding Advocacy, Alliance Against Domestic Abuse, Chaffee County, 1993, 93, 94, 95, Cert. for Exemplary Svc. and Dedication, Alliance Against Domestic Abuse, 1995. Mem. Nat., State and Local Parents Families and Friends of Lesbians and Gays, Chaffee County Lodgeing Assn., Columbine Gem and Mineral Soc., So. Colo. Consistory (32nd degree), Washburn Lodge #421 AF and AM (3rd degree), Al Kaly Temple (Shrine of N.Am.), SAR (Fla. Soc. SAR ctrl. Fla. chpt.). Home: 237 E St Salida CO 81201 Office: 536 E First St Salida CO 81201 also: 6109 Jibway Ct Orlando FL 32807

BARNES, STEPHEN PAUL, financial planner; b. Corsicana, Tex., July 30, 1957; s. Paul Gordon and Barbara Jewell (Hawkins) B.; m. Tina Marie Dacus, Dec. 20, 1980 (div. 1985); m. Kathie Jo Beck, Feb. 20, 1988; 1 child, Stephanie Kathryn. BS, Grand Canyon U., 1982. CFA, CFP. Sales rep. Phil Bramsen Distbrs., Mesa, Ariz., 1978-81, credit mgr., 1981-82; registered rep. John Hancock Fin. Svcs., Phoenix, 1983-86; mktg. mgmt. assoc. John Hancock Fin. Svcs., Boston, 1986-87; sales mgr. John Hancock Fin. Svcs., Phoenix, 1987-90; portfolio mgr. Barnes Investment Adv., Phoenix, 1990—; bd. dirs. Desert Schs. Fed. Credit Union, 1990—, vice chmn. bd. dirs., 1995, chmn. bd. dirs., 1995-97. Editor Ariz. Stock Analysis Newsletter, 1996—. Pub. address announcer home basketball games Grand Canyon Coll., 1977-96; dir. United Way capital dr. Western region John Hancock Fin. Svcs., 1988, 89; com. chair capital dr. John C. Lincoln Day Care Ctr., Phoenix, 1987. Named one of 200 Best Fin. Advisors, Worth Mag., 1996. Mem. Inst. CFPs (nat. dir., past pres., dir. Phoenix soc.), Assn. for Investment Mmgt. and Rsch., Phoenix Soc. of Fin. Analysts, Ariz. Assn. of Inst. CFPs (chmn. 1993-96). Republican. Methodist. Home: 7516 N 22nd St Phoenix AZ 85020-4705 Office: Ste 208 5225 North Central Ave Phoenix AZ 85012

BARNES, STEVE JAMES, elementary education educator; b. Spokane, Wash., Feb. 17, 1960; s. Roy Martin and Janette Marta (Schlicting) B.; m. Peggy Louis Stretch, June 23, 1984; children: Brandon James, Brittney Nicole. BA in Edn., Ea. Wash. U., 1982, M in Curriculum, 1989, adminstrv. cert., 1991. Profl. edn. cert. in tchg. and adminstrn. Wash. Tchr. 7th and 9th grade math and social studies Ctrl. Valley Sch. Dist. #356, Spokane, 1983; tchr. 6th grade Nine Mile Falls (Wash.) Sch. Dist., 1983-86; tchr. 6th grade Spokane Pub. Schs., 1986-95, title 1 facilitator, 1995-96; large sch. facilitator/instrnl. facilitator Holmes Elem. Sch., Spokane Pub. Schs., 1996—. Soccer, baseball, basketball coach YMCA and Spokane Youth Sports, 1991—. Mem. ASCD, NEA, Wash. Edn. Assn., Wash. Sci. Tchrs. Assn. Home: 3921 S Sunderland Spokane WA 99206 Office: Spokane Pub Schs Dist #81 N 200 Bernard Spokane WA 99201

BARNES, WILLIAM ANDERSON, real estate investment manager; b. Cin., Mar. 11, 1944; s. Frederick Walter and Catherine Gardner (Bowden) B.; m. Sara Winkler, Dec. 13, 1980; children: Tucker, Charlie, Hanne. BA, Yale U., 1966; MBA, Harvard U., 1970; postgrad. in Internat. Econs., Inst. D'Etudes Politiques, Paris, 1993. Adminstrv. asst. to pres. Boise Cascade Corp., Palo Alto, Calif., 1970-71; project gen. mgr. Boise Cascade Corp., Incline Village, Nev., 1971-73; sr. devel. dir. The Rouse Co., Columbia, Md., 1973-76; exec. dir. Pa. Ave. Devel. Corp., Washington, 1977-82; mng. dir. Edward Plant Co., San Francisco, 1982-87; pres. Broadacre Pacific Corp., San Francisco, 1987-92, Barnes and Co., San Francisco, 1992-96; CEO Stapleton Devel. Corp., Denver, 1996—; guest lectr. Harvard Bus. Sch., Cambridge, Mass.; faculty mem. Profl. Devel. Sem.; dist. coun. exec. com. Urban Land Inst.; lectr. Smithsonian Instn., U. San Francisco, mem. adv. coun.; chair Am. Russian Tech. Assn. Trustee Navy Meml. Found., Brichard Properties Trust, S.H. Children's Svcs., Inc., Columbia Interfaith Housing Corp., 1974-76; mem. U.S./USSR Trade Mission, 1975, Bay Area Coun. Housing Action Task Force, 1983-85, Mill Valley City Gen. Plan Com.; treas. Yale U. Class of 1966. U.S. White House fellow, Washington, 1976, German Marshall Fund fellow, 1979; recipient Presdl. Design award, 1988. Home: 1450 Wynkoop Ave Denver CO 80202 Office: Stapleton Devel Corp 1125 17th St # 2000 Denver CO 80202

BARNES-ROBERTS, PHILIP IRWIN, engineer; b. L.A., Jan. 19, 1945; s. Charles Herman and Romania Vera (Pratt) Roberts; m. Kathy Ashby, June 2, 1966 (div. 1974); children: Romania Valerie Roberts Fowler, Kristi Ann Roberts; m. Donna Lynn Barnes, June 30, 1984. Student, Palomar Coll., 1962-63, U. Utah, 1966-68; AA, Orange Coast Coll., 1976; student, Calif. State U., L.A., 1986—. Lic. FCC Gen. Radiotelephone. Gyro-optic mechanic Philco-Ford Aeronutronics, Newport Beach, Calif., 1972-74; rsch.

assoc. Hughes Aircraft, Newport Beach, 1974-80; systems engr. Anderson Jacobson I.O.S., Anaheim, Calif., 1980-83; sr. hardware engr. Honeywell Ericsson Devel. Co., Anaheim, 1983-85; engring. assoc. Jet Propulsion Lab., Pasadena, Calif., 1985-93, engring. asst., 1995—; devel. engr. Loral E.O.S., Pasadena, 1993-95. Sgt. USMC, 1964-72. Mem. Assn. Computing Machinery, Forth Interest Group, Nat. Space Soc. Libertarian.

BARNETT, BARON GALE, prosthodontist; b. St. Cloud, Minn., Dec. 17, 1946; s. Edgar Clinton Barnett and Delores (Robertson) Kelly; m. Jean Drabbe, June 9, 1968 (div. 1982); children: Dirk, Kiva, Alex; m. Barbara Jean Masters, May 9, 1984. BA, U. Calif., Riverside, 1969; DDS, UCLA, 1973. Diplomate Am. Bd. Prosthodontics. Rotating intern Long Beach (Calif.) VA Hosp., 1973-74; resident in fixed prosthodontics Wadsworth VA Health Ctr., L.A., 1974-76; pvt. practice, Tualatin, Oreg., 1976—; coord. for Multnomah County, Oreg. Peer Rev., 1984-92; vis. lectr. dept. fixed prosthodontics Oreg. Health Scis. U., Portland, 1976—; lectr. in field to profl. meetings. Contbr. articles to dental jours. Recipient Alumnus award UCLA, 1973. Fellow Am. Coll. Prosthodontics, Internat. Coll. Prosthodontics; mem. ADA, Acad. Osseointegration, Am. Acad. Restorative Dentistry, Pacific Coast Soc. Prosthodontics, Oreg. Dental Assn., Wash. Co. Dental Soc., Osseointegration Study Club So. Calif., Clackamas County DentL Soc. (editor 1978, treas. 1979, v.p. 1980), Omicron Kappa Upsilon. Home: PO Box 595 Lake Oswego OR 97034-0065 Office: 7965 SW Mohawk St Tualatin OR 97062-9193

BARNETT, DAVID HUGHES, software engineer, information technology architect; b. Rockville Centre, N.Y., Oct. 9, 1947; s. Paul Wilson Jr. and Patricia (Hughes) B.; m. Rosemary Friday, July 9, 1979 (div. 1983); m. Demery Culum, Apr. 10, 1996. BA, Drew U., 1970. Cert. software quality engineer, cert. quality engr. Program analyst So. Nev. Drug Abuse Coun., Las Vegas, 1974-75; project supr. Treatment Alternatives to Street Crime, Las Vegas, 1975-78; sr. project assoc. Helix Group, Berkeley, Calif., 1978-81; cons. Pacific Inst. for Rsch. and Evaluation, Berkeley, 1979-80; rsch. tech. Sonoma State U., Rohnert Park, Calif., 1981-82; system mgr. Database Minicomputers, San Francisco, 1982-84; cons. sys. programmer Wells Fargo Bank, San Francisco, 1984-89; messaging architect Kaiser Permanente, Walnut Creek, Calif., 1989-06; info. tech. architect IBM, San Ramone, Calif., 1996; info. tech. cons. Digital Equipment Corp., Walnut Creek, 1996—. Contbr. articles to profl. jours. Mem. Am. Soc. for Quality Control (cert. software quality engr.). Office: 230 Northcreek Cir Walnut Creek CA 94598

BARNETT, KERRY EVAN, state business administrator. BA, U. Rochester, N.Y., 1978; JD, Yale U., 1987. Attorney Lindsey, Hart, Neil and Weigler, Oreg., 1987-89; asst. to Gov., Office of the Gov., Oreg., of counsel, sr. policy advisor, 1991-93; dir., ins. commr., supt. banks Oreg. Dept. Consumer and Business Svcs., Salem, 1993—; mem. Oreg. Med. Ins. Pool Bd., 1993—, Small Employer Reins. Pool, 1993—; mem. Oreg. Health Coun., 1993-96, Oreg. Health Reform Implementation Group, 1993-95. Office: Dept Consumer & Bus Svcs 350 Winter St NE Salem OR 97310

BARNETT, LESTER A., advertising executive. Exec. v.p., exec. creative dir. FCB Healthcare, San Francisco, Calif. Office: One Lombard St San Francisco CA 94111*

BARNETT, MARY LOUISE, elementary education educator; b. Exeter, Calif., May 1, 1941; d. Raymond Edgar Noble and Nena Lavere (Huckaby) Hope; m. Gary Allen Barnett, Aug. 9, 1969; children: Alice Marie, Virginia Lynn. BA, U. of Pacific, 1963; postgrad., U. Mont., 1979-82, U. Idaho, 1984—. Cert. life elem. tchr., Calif.; standard elem. credential, Idaho; elem. tchr., Mont. Tchr. Colegio Americano de Torrean, Torreon, Coahuila, Mexico, 1962-63, Summer Sch. Primary Grades South San Francisco, 1963-66, Visalia (Calif.) Unified Sch. Dist., 1966-69, Sch. Dist. # 1, Missoula, Mont., 1969-73, Fort Shaw-Simms Sch. Dist., Fort Shaw, Mont., 1976-83, Sch. Dist. #25, Pocatello, Idaho, 1983-93, Greenacres Elem., Pocatello, 1993-94; tchr. 2d grade Bonneville Elem., Pocatello, 1994-95; tchr. Windsong Presch., Missoula, Mont., 1995—. Foster mom Ednl. Found. Fgn. Students, Pocatello, Idaho, 1986-89; vol. Am. Heart Assn., Am. Cancer Soc., Pocatello, 1986-88, Bannock March of Dimes, Pocatello, 1988, Pocatello Laubach Lit. Tutoring, 1989; state v.p. membership, del. to P.W. Australian Mission Study; vice moderator Kendall Presbyn. Women, moderator, 1991—; moderator Kendall P.W. 1990-92. Recipient scholarship Mont. Delta Kappa Gamma Edn. Soc., Great Falls, Mont., 1976, Great Falls AAUW, 1980, Great Falls Scottish Rite, 1981, Five Valleys Reading Assn., Missoula, Mont., 1982. Mem. AAUW (v.p., mem. com. Idaho divsn. 1990-92, book chair 1995—), ASCD, NEA, Nat. Coun. Tchrs. English, Internat. Reading Assn., Assn. Childhood Edn. Internat., Laubach Literacy Tutors (sec. 1993—), Bus. and Profl. Women Pocatello (sec. 1993—), Mortar Bd., Alpha Lambda Delta, Delta Kappa Gamma (state fellowship chmn., corr. sec. Pocatello chpt. 1986-88, 2d v.p. 1994-96), Moose (musician 1981-82), Order Eastern Star (musician 1984-85), Gamma Phi Beta (sec. Laubach Tutors 1993-95), Delta Kappa Gamma (2d v.p. Phi chpt. 1996—). Democrat. Presbyterian. Home: 103 E Crestline Dr Missoula MT 59803-2412 Office: Windsong Presch 303 Pattee Canyon Dr Missoula MT 59803-1624

BARNETT, MICHAEL, sports agent, business manager; b. Olds, Alta., Can., Oct. 9, 1948; came to U.S., 1988; s. Terence R. and Mary M. Barnett; m. Dalyce M. Giordano, Apr. 2, 1988; children: Jesse, Joey, Justin, Janie. Student, St. Lawrence U., 1968-70; BS in Health and Phys. Edn., U. Calgary, 1973. Registered agent Nat. Hockey League Players Assn. Profl. hockey player, 1973-75; founder, CEO Corpsport Internat.; agent, bus. mgr. Wayne Gretzky, 1981—; internat. v.p. Internat. Mgmt. Group; gen. mgr. Ninety-Nine All Stars; pres. Internat. Mgmt. Group Hockey, 1990. Active H.E.L.P., L.A. Named one of Top 100 Most Powerful in Sports, The Sporting News, 1994, 95, 96, Oe of Twelve Most Powerful in Hockey, Hockey News, 1995. Mem. U.S.A. Hockey, U.S. Golf Assn., Edmonton Klondike Days Assn. (dir.). Home: PO Box 50 Lake Arrowhead CA 92352 Office: Ste 850 11755 Wilshire Blvd Los Angeles CA 90025-1415

BARNETT, SUZANNE WILSON, history educator; b. Columbus, Ohio, June 1, 1940; d. George Leedom and Dorothy May (Macklin) Wilson; m. Redmond James Barnett, June 7, 1969. BA, Muskingum Coll., New Concord, Ohio, 1961; AM, Harvard U., 1963, PhD, 1973. Lectr. Suffolk U., Boston, 1970-72, Boston U., 1971-72; instr. Wellesley (Mass.) Coll., 1972-73; asst. prof. U. Puget Sound, Tacoma, 1973-79; assoc. prof. U. Puget Sound, 1979-85, prof., 1985—; vis. asst. prof. U. Va., Charlottesville, 1973. Author, co-editor: Christianity in China: Early Protestant Missionary Writings, 1985; contbr. articles to profl. jours. Bd. dirs. Chinese Reconciliation Project Found., Tacoma, 1994—. Fulbright-Hays Grad. fellow U.S. Office Edn., Taiwan, Japan, 1967-68, Lang. and Rsch. fellow Inter-Univ. Program and Academia Sinica, Taipei, Taiwan, 1986-87, Postdoctoral fellow History of Christianity in China Project, 1990. Mem. Am. Hist. Assn. (coun., tchg. divsn. 1992-95), Assn. Asian Studies (bd. dirs., China and Inner Asia coun. 1979-82), ASIANetwork (bd. dirs. 1996—), Soc. History Edn. (nat. adv. coun. 1996—). Democrat. Home: 3401 N 29th St Tacoma WA 98407-6250 Office: U Puget Sound Dept History 1500 N Warner Tacoma WA 98416-0040

BARNEY, SUSAN LESLIE, academic administrator; b. Quantico, Va., Oct. 7, 1945; d. Duane Edwin and Joan Clarice (Long) B. BA, Ohio State U., 1972; JD, Capital U., 1977. Bar: Ohio 1979. With acctg. dept. Golden Gate U., San Francisco, 1977-80, dir. acctg., 1980-83, v.p. adminstrn., 1983-94, emerita v.p. adminstrn., 1994—; asst. sec. bd. trustees Golden Gate U., 1983-94. Mem. ABA. Methodist. Home: 436 Lombard St San Francisco CA 94133

BARNHURST, CHRISTINE LOUISE, broadcast executive; b. Salt Lake City, Sept. 3, 1949; d. Joseph Samuel and Luana Jean (Jackson) B. BS, U. Utah, 1971. From account exec. to mktg. specialist Bonneville Internat. Corp. KSL TV, Salt Lake City, 1972-84; mgr. corp. media funding U. Utah, Salt Lake City, 1985-86; dir. advt. Larry H. Miller Group, Salt Lake City, 1986-89; dir. mktg. and promotion Sta. KXIV TV Am. TV of Utah, Salt Lake City, 1989-92; gen. sales, mktg. and promotion mgr. Sta. KJZZ TV Larry H. Miller Comms., Salt Lake City, 1993-96; freelance producer of corp. sales and tng. videos. Bd. dirs., telethon producer March of Dimes; bd. dirs. YWCA, Relief Soc. LDS Ch. Gen. Bd. Recipient Nat. Print Ad award Athena, 1990, Walt Disney Top Mktg. and Promotion award, 1992, INTV Indy award, 1991, BPME Gold/Silver/Bronze awards, 1989-93, Telly awards, 1992, 93, 94, 95, 96, Gold/Silver/Bronze Addy award Utah Advt. Fedn., Emmy award, 1992, 94, March of Dimes Recognition Svc. award, 1982. Mem. Am. Mktg. Assn. (exec. mem.), Promax.

BARNUM, ALEXANDER STONE, journalist; b. N.Y.C., May 15, 1960; s. John Wallace and Nancy (Grinnell) B. BA, Antioch Coll., Yellow Springs, Ohio, 1983; MS, Columbia U., 1987. Editl. asst. Washington Post, 1983-86; staff writer San Jose Mercury News, 1987-91, San Francisco Chronicle, 1991—; mentor, San Francisco State U., 1992-94, freelance writer. Vol. Project Open Hand, San Francisco, 1992-94, Tsongas for Pres., San Francisco, 1992. Knight Sci. Journalism fellow MIT, Cambridge, 1994-95. Mem. Soc. for Profl. Journalists, Soc. for Environ. Journalists. Office: San Francisco Chronicle 901 Mission St San Francisco CA 94103-2905

BARNWELL, DAVID R., financial and computer systems analyst, computer programmer; b. Amarillo, Tex., Sept. 9, 1953; s. Jasper Clarence and Mary Evelyn (King) B.; m. Maria Milagrosa Bellido, July 7, 1975; 1 child, Miriam Louise. Student Army and Navy Acad., Carlsbad, Calif., 1971; AA in Bus. Adminstrn., Cerritos Coll., Norwalk, Calif., 1979, AA in Econs., 1986; BSBA, U. Redlands, 1981; MBA, 1990. tutor Cerritos Coll., 1977-79; adjuster Western Thrift and Loan Assn., Long Beach, Calif., 1978-80; prodn. cost analyst, space shuttle orbiter div. Rockwell Internat., Downey, Calif., 1980-85; mem. space shuttle speaker's bur., 1981-88, sr. cost analyst space shuttle orbiter div., 1985-86, sr. computer systems analyst, 1986-88, computer systems devel. specialist, 1988-92; sr. ops. bus. analyst of appraisal ops., Home Savings Am., Irwindale, Calif., 1993—; founder, pres. Bus. Electronics, 1985; adj. faculty mem. Park Coll., USMC Logistics Facility, Barstow, Calif., 1993—, Marine Corp Base, Camp Pendleton. With USMC, 1970-76. Recipient First Shuttle Flight Achievement award, NASA, 1981; Alfred North Whitehead Leadership Soc. fellow U. Redlands (pres. 1992-93). Mem. AIAA, 1st Marine Div. Assn., Assn. for Computing Machinery, IEEE Computer Soc., Am. Legion, Mensa. Home: 8031 De Vries Ln La Palma CA 90623-2031 Office: Home Savings Am 100 S Vincent Ave West Covina CA 91790

BARON, CHARLOTTE FOEHNER, publishing executive; b. Hugoton, Kans., Aug. 7, 1941; d. John Garland and Marjorie Corinne (Parsons) Persinger; m. Olin Harold Foehner, Jr., Sept. 9, 1962 (dec. May 1983); children: Brett Olin, Kristen Kathleen; m. Robert Charles Baron, Nov. 29, 1986. BS in Med. Tech., U. Colo., Boulder, 1965; MPA, U. Colo., Denver, 1980. Registered med. technologist. Rsch. asst. virology U. Colo., Denver, 1965-66; med. technologist So. Nev. Meml. Hosp., Las Vegas, 1966, AMC Cancer Rsch. Ctr., Denver, 1975-78; computer systems analyst Fitzsimons Army Med. Ctr., Denver, 1981-82, Pentagon, Army Chief of Staff, Washington, 1982-83; computer specialist Bur. Reclamation, Denver, 1983-85; chief fin. and adminstrn. Fulcrum Pub., Inc., Golden, Colo., 1985—; treas., dir. Oxion, Inc., Hugoton, Kans., 1990—, Yale Heights Homeowners, Denver, 1992—; presdl. mgmt. intern Office Pers. Mgmt., Washington, 1980. Author: The Widows Handbook, A Guide for Living, 1988; writer, presenter articles, speeches women's groups, fin., banks, fin. seminars, 1988-92. Mem. Denver Pub. Libr. Friends, 1991-96, Denver Natural History Mus., Denver, 1992-96. Mem. Am. Soc. Pub. Adminstrn., Pi Alpha Alpha. Republican. Methodist. Home: 6969 W Yale Ave Apt 62 Denver CO 80227-3585 Office: Fulcrum Pub Inc 350 Indiana St Ste 350 Golden CO 80401-5093

BARON, MELVIN FARRELL, pharmacy educator; b. L.A., July 29, 1932; s. Leo Ben and Sadie (Bauchman) B.; m. Lorraine Ross, Dec. 20, 1953; children: Lynn Baron Friedman, Ross David. PharmD, U. So. Calif., 1957, MPA, 1973. Lic. pharmacist, Calif. Pres. Shield Health Care Ctrs., Van Nuys, Calif., 1957-83; v.p. Shield Health Care Ctrs., Inc. (C.R. Bard, Inc. subsidiary), 1983-86; pres. Merit Coll., 1988-92, PharmCom., L.A., 1990—; asst. prof. clin. pharmacy U. So. Calif., L.A., 1991—, asst. dean pharm. care programs, 1995—; adj. asst. prof. U. Without Walls, Shaw U., Raleigh, N.C., 1973; project dir. Hayne Found. Drug Rsch. Ctr. U. So. Calif., L.A., 1973; assoc. dir. Calif. Alcoholism Found., 1973-75; adj. asst. prof. clin. pharmacy Sch. of Pharmacy U. So. Calif., L.A., 1981-91; cons. Topanga Terr. Convalescent Hosp., 1970-80, Calif. Labor Mgmt. Plan for alcoholism programs and coords., 1974, Office of Alcoholism, State of Calif., Nat. In-Home Health Svc., 1975, Continuity of Life Team, 1975, others; vis. prof. Tokyo Coll. Pharmacy, 1994, Sandoz Pharm Co., 1995; lectr. Meijo U., Nagoya U., Japan, 1994. Adv. bd. Pharmacist Newsletter, 1980—. Chmn. Friends of Operation Bootstrap, 1967-77; svc. chmn. tng. coord. Am. Cancer Soc., San Fernando Valley, Calif., 1980; mem. adv. bd. L.A. VNA, 1982; bd. dirs. pres. QSAD, 1987-88; pres. bd. Everywoman's Village, 1988-89; bd. dirs. Life Svcs., 1988—; pres. bd. counselors, U. So. Calif., 1988-92, mem. Calif. State Bd. Pharmacy Com. on Student/Preceptor Manual, 1991-93. Named Disting. Alumnus of Yr., U. So. Calif., Sch. of Pharmacy Alumni Assn., 1979, U. So. Calif. Torchbearer, 1990-91, hon. mem. Phi Lambda Sigma, L.A., 1994. Fellow Am. Coll. Apothecaries; mem. Am. Pharm. Assn., Am. Soc. Health Sys. Pharmacists, Calif. Pharmacist Assn. (chair edn. com.), Am. Soc. Pub. Adminstrn., Am. Assn. Colls. of Pharmacy, Phi Kappa Phi, Rho Chi. Home: 323 San Vicente Santa Monica CA 90402-1629 Office: U So Calif 1985 Zonal Ave Los Angeles CA 90033-1058

BARON, ROBERT CHARLES, publishing executive; b. L.A., Jan. 26, 1934; s. Leo Francis and Marietta (Schulze) B.; m. Faye Helen Rogers, Jan. 28, 1961 (div. 1984); m. Charlotte Rose Persinger, Nov. 29, 1986; stepchildren: Brett, Kristen. BS in Physics, St. Joseph's Coll., 1956. Registered profl. engr., Mass. Engr. RCA, Camden, N.J., 1955-57, Computer Control Co., Framingham, Mass., 1959-61; program mgr. Mariner II and IV space computers Computer Control Co., Framingham, 1961-65, engring. mgr., 1965-69; worldwide systems mgr. Honeywell Minicomputer, Framingham, 1970-71; founder, pres., CEO Prime Computer, Framingham, 1971-75; pvt. practice Boston, 1976-83; founder and pres. Fulcrum Pub., Golden, Colo., 1984—; bd. dirs. Prime Computer, Framingham, Mass., Alling-Lander, Cheshire, Conn., Oxion, Hugoton, Kans., Fulcrum Pub., Golden Colo. Author: Digital Logic and Computer Operations, 1966, Micropower Electronics, 1970, America in the Twentieth Century, 1995; editor: The Garden and Farm Books of Thomas Jefferson, 1987, Soul of America: Documenting Our Past, 1492-1974, 1989, Colorado Rockies: The Inaugural Season, 1993, Thomas Hornsby Ferril and the American West, 1996. Trustee Lincoln Filene Ctr., Tufts U., Medford, Mass., 1982-84; vice chmn. bd. dirs. Mass. Audubon Soc., Lincoln, 1980-85; bd. dirs. Rocky Mountain Women's Inst., Denver, 1987-90; bd. dirs. Denver Pub. Libr. Friends Found., 1989-96, pres., 1994-96. Mem. Am. Antiquarian Soc. (bd. dirs., chmn. 1993—), Internat. Wilderness Leadership Found. (bd. dirs. 1990—, chmn. 1994—), Thoreau Soc., Mass. Hist. Soc., Western History Assn., Grolier Club. Office: Fulcrum Pub 350 Indiana St Ste 350 Golden CO 80401-5093

BARONE, ANGELA MARIA, artist, researcher; b. Concesio, Brescia, Italy, June 29, 1957; came to U.S., 1983; d. Giuseppe and Adelmina (D'Ercole) B. Laurea cum laude in geol. scis., U. Bologna, Italy, 1981; PhD in Marine Geology, Columbia U., 1989. Cert. in profl. photography, N.Y. Inst. Photography, N.Y.C., 1992; cert. in the fine art of painting and drawing North Light Art Sch., Cin., 1993. Collaborative asst. Marine Geology Inst., Bologna, 1981-83, Inst. Geology and Paleontology, Florence, Italy, 1982-83, Sta. de Geodynamique, Villefranche, France, 1982; grad. rsch. asst. Lamont-Doherty Geol. Obs., Palisades, N.Y., 1983-89; postdoctoral rsch. asst. Lamont-Doherty Geol. Obs., Palisades, 1989; postgrad. rschr. Scripps Instn. of Oceanography, La Jolla, Calif., 1990-92; artist San Diego, 1993—. Contbr. articles to profl. jours. Mem. Am. Geophysical Union (co-pres. meeting session 1990), Nat. Assn. Fine Artists, Nat. Mus. Women in Arts (assoc.). Mem. Christian Ch. Home: 7540 Charmant Dr Apt 1222 San Diego CA 92122-5044

BARONE, JANINE MASON, foundation administrator; b. Fullerton, Calif., Apr. 18, 1964; d. Guy T. and Helen M. Mason; m. John J. Barone, Aug. 15, 1992; 1 child, Alexander Mason Barone. BA, U. San Diego, 1986. Sales assoc. Mutual of Omaha, San Diego, 1986-87; regional mgr. Fieldstone Found., San Diego, 1988—; mem. steering panel Union Inst., Washington, 1995—. Mem. adv. bd. Ptnrs. in Edn., San Diego, 1988-94, Eureka Cmtys., San Diego, 1995—; bd. dirs. San Diego Children's Initiative, 1992—, San Diego Blood Bank Found., 1994—; mem. com. United Way, San Diego, 1993—; chair, capt. Neighborhood Watch, Del Mar, Calif., 1993—. Mem. San Diego Grantmakers (chair), LEAD San Diego (Alumni of Yr. 1995), Univ. San Diego Class of '86 Alumni Group.

BARR, CARLOS HARVEY, lawyer; b. Greeley, Colo., Oct. 12, 1936; s. Charles Allen B. and Zelma Arvilla (Sechler) Turner; m. Martha Lucia Sánchez-Morales, May 10, 1985. BA in Polit. Sci., U. Wash., 1959, MA in Polit. Sci., 1967; JD, George Wash. U., 1971. Bar: Wash. 1971, U.S. Dist. Ct. (ea. dist.) Wash. 1972, U.S. Dist. Ct. (we. dist.) Wash. 1979, U.S. Ct. Appeals (9th cir.) 1973, U.S. Supreme Ct. 1981, U.S. Tax Ct. 1985; cert. Spanish-English interpreter, Wash. Mgmt. intern U.S. Dept of Army, Ft. Lewis, Wash., 1960; joined Fgn. Svc., Dept. State, 1960, officer, 1960-61; vice consul U.S. Consulate Gen., Monterrey, Mex., 1961-64; consular officer, third sec. Am. Embassy, Khartoum, Sudan, 1964-66; analyst Latin Am. Bur., Washington, 1967-68; personnel officer Washington, 1968-70, consular affairs officer, 1970-71, resigned; dir. legal svcs. Community Action Com. OEO, Pasco, Wash., 1971-72; lawyer Spokane (Wash.) County Legal Svc., 1972-73; pvt. practice Kennewick, Wash., 1973-75, Richland, Wash., 1975—. Mem. ABA, ATLA, Wash. Bar Assn., Wash. Trial Lawyers Assn., Fed. Bar Assn., Hispanic Bar Assn. Wash., Inter-Am. Bar Assn., Nat. Hispanic Bar Assn., Acad. Polit. Sci. Office: 1207 George Washington Way Richland WA 99352-3411

BARR, CHERYL B., curator. Head curator Essig Mus. Entomology U. Calif., Berkeley, 1994—. Office: U Calif Berkeley 211 and 311 Wellman Hall Berkeley CA 94720

BARR, JAMES NORMAN, federal judge; b. Kewanee, Ill, Oct. 21, 1940; s. James Cecil and Dorothy Evelyn (Dorsey) B.; m. Trilla Anne Reeves, Oct. 31, 1964 (div. 1977); 1 child, James N. Jr.; m. Phyllis L. DeMent, May 30, 1986. BS, Ill. Wesleyan U., 1962; JD, Ill. Inst. Tech., 1971. Bar: Ill. 1972, Calif. 1977. Assoc. Pretzel, Stouffer, Nolan & Rooney, Chgo., 1974-76; claims counsel Safeco Title Ins. Co., L.A., 1977-78; assoc. Kamph & Jackman, Santa Ana, Calif., 1978-80; lawyer pvt. practice Law Offices of James N. Barr, Santa Ana, 1980-86; judge U.S Bankruptcy Ct. Ctrl. Dist. Calif., Santa Anna, 1987—. Lt. (s.g.) USN, 1962-67, Vietnam. Mem. Orange County Bankruptcy Forum (bd. dirs. 1989—), Peter M. Elliott Inn Ct. (pres. 1990-91). Office: US Bankruptcy Ct 34 Civic Center Plz Rm 522 Santa Ana CA 92701-4025

BARR, MAURICE ALAN, elementary education educator; b. Hazelhurst, Miss., Dec. 31, 1951; s. Robert Guiton and Mavis (Mitchem) B.; m. Marcella Isabel Palma, Dec. 19, 1981; 1 child, Alan Maurice. AS, Modesto (Calif.) Jr. Coll., 1978; BS, Calif. Christian Coll., 1981; MDiv, Mennonite Brethren Bibl. Sem., 1988. Middle sch. tchr. Reef-Sunset Unified Sch. Dist., Avenal, Calif., 1992—; coach Reef-Sunset Middle Sch., Reef-Sunset Unified Sch. Dist., Avenal, 1993-95, mem. curriculum and instrn. coun., 1994-96, dist. math chair, 1994-96. Mem. West Kings County Tchrs. Assn. (pres. 1995-96, negotiator 1995-96), Mariners (chaplain 1995-96). Presbyterian. Office: Reef-Sunset Middle Sch 608 N 1st Ave Avenal CA 93204-1071

BARR, ROBERT EDWARD, computer company executive; b. Neosho, Mo., July 29, 1956; s. Donald A. and Cecilia K.; m. Aileen Conlon, Nov. 10, 1978; children: Stephanie E., Dacia K., Marysia S. BS, U. S.C., 1978; MBA, U. Pa., 1984. Cert. systems profl., cert. in prodn. and inventory mgmt. Analyst Hanes Hosiery, Winston-Salem, N.C., 1978-80; project leader Cryovac div. WR Grace, Duncan, S.C., 1980-82; mktg. dir. Cullinet Software, Westwood, Mass., 1984-86, Online/Database Software, Pearl River, N.Y., 1986-88; info. resource mgmt. mgr. S.C. Tax Commn., Columbia, 1988-92; v.p. govt. programs Intuit Inc., San Diego, 1995-96; mem. adj. faculty Midlands Tech. Coll., Columbia, 1989-92; instr. APICS, Westwood, Mass., 1985; mem. IRS Commr.'s Adv. Group, 1994-96, IRS Info. Returns Program Adv. Com., 1995—. Co-author: Employee Relations..., 1987; contbr. articles to profl. jours. Capt. March of Dimes, Columbia, 1989, 90, 91; steering com. Mainstreet Celebrates Edn., Columbia, 1990; mem. PTO, Columbia, 1989, 90, 91; pres. Hotspurs Soccer Club, 1996—, pres., 1996—; v.p. PTA, 1996—; mem. Cmty. Planning Group, San Diego, 1996—. Mem. Am. Prodn. and Inventory Control Soc. (sec. 1981-82, Svc. award 1982, 85), Am. Payroll Assn. (svc. award 1993, 96), Am. Nat. Stds. Inst. (accredited stds. com. x12, subcom. chair 1991-92), Cert. Electronic Trade Profls. Assn. (chmn. 1991-92), Coun. for Electronic Revenue Comm. Advancement (pres. 1994-96), Columbia Forum, U. S.C. Alumni Assn., Wharton Alumni Assn. Home: 3110 Sunflower Glen Ct Jamul CA 91935-1502 Office: Intuit Inc 6220 Greenwich Dr San Diego CA 92122

BARR, SUE, secondary education educator. Tchr. S. Eugene High Sch., Oreg. Named Spl. Recogniton adviserJournalism, 1990, Disting. adviser Journalism Dow Jones Newspaper Fund, 1992. Office: South Eugene High Sch 400 E 19th Eugene OR 97401

BARRATT, BRUCE RICHARD, physics educator; b. Kansas City, Kans., Aug. 19, 1939; s. Buford Russell and Miriam Aileen (Adams) B.; m. Gail Louise Geiger, Sept. 3, 1961 (div. Aug. 1969); m. Joan Frances Livermore, May 21, 1979. BS, U. Kans., 1961; postgrad., Swiss Poly., Zurich, 1961-62; MS, Stanford U., 1964, PhD, 1967. Research fellow Weizmann Inst. Sci., Rehovot, Israel, 1967-68; postdoctoral research fellow, research assoc. U. Pitts., 1968-70; asst. prof. physics U. Ariz., Tucson, 1970-72, assoc. prof., 1972-76, prof., 1976—, assoc. chmn. dept., 1977-83, mem. faculty senate, 1979-83, 88-90, 91-97, program dir. theoretical physics NSF, 1985-87, mem. tech. transfer com., 1996-97; chmn. adv. com. Internat. Scholars, Tucson, 1985-96; chmn. rsch. policy com. U. Ariz. Faculty Senate, 1993-94, 95-96. Woodrow Wilson fellow, 1961-62; NSF fellow, 1962-66; Weizmann Inst. fellow, 1967-68; Andrew Mellon fellow, 1968-69; Alfred P. Sloan Found. research fellow, 1972-74; Alexander von Humboldt fellow, 1976-77; NSF grantee, 1971-85, 87—; Netherlands F.O.M. research fellow Groningen, 1980; recipient sr. U.S. scientist award (Humboldt prize) Alexander von Humboldt Found., 1983-85. Fellow Am. Phys. Soc. (mem. publs. com. 1983-86, mem. program com. 1993-94, divsn. nuclear physics), Phi Beta Kappa (pres. Alpha Ariz. chpt. 1992), Sigma Xi, Sigma Pi Sigma, Omicron Delta Kappa, Beta Theta Pi. Office: U Ariz Dept Physics Bldg 81 Tucson AZ 85721

BARRETT, CHRISTINE KHAN, engineering project management coordinator; b. Tewksbury, Mass., Oct. 17, 1955; d. Jeanne (Rousseau) Khan; m. William E. Barrett, Jr., Oct. 11, 1986; children: Antonia, James, Winora. BA in Sociology magna cum laude, Boston Coll., 1977; MS in Pub. Mgmt. and Policy, Carnegie-Mellon U., 1979. Park aide Minuteman Nat. Hist. Park, Concord, Mass., 1976-77; rsch. policy analyst U.S. Dept. Labor, Washington, 1978; sr. bus. sys. analyst, analyst/task mgr. Am. Mgmt. Sys., Inc., Arlington, Va., 1979-86; comm. support mgr. Las Vegas Valley Water Dist., 1986-94, sr. projects analyst, 1994—; liason Nev./Calif. region underground svc. alert Las Vegas Valley Water Dist., 1989-91, mem. strategic planning team, corp. culture task force, pilot empowerment tng. and amb., field and office coordination com., 1991-95. Crisis phone vol. Temporary Asst. Domestic Crisis, 1988-90; parent vol., CCD instr. Our Lady Las Vegas Sch., 1989—; career day speaker Clark County High Schs., 1996—. Recipient Certs. Appreciation, Temporary Asst. Domestic Crisis, 1990-95. Mem. ASPA (Nev. chpt.), Project Mgmt. Inst., Am. Pub. Works Assn., Am. Water Works Assn.,.

BARRETT, CRAIG R., computer company executive; b. 1939. Assoc. prof. Stanford U., 1965-74; with Intel Corp., 1974—, v.p. components tech. and mfg. group, sr. v.p., gen. mgr. components tech. and mfg. group, exec. v.p., mgr. components tech., now exec. v.p., COO, dir. Office: Intel Corp 5000 W Chandler Blvd Chandler AZ 85226-3691*

BARRETT, DARRELL GENE, secondary education educator; b. Phoenix, May 2, 1956; s. Bobby Joe and Jane Maxine (Dettenheim) B.; m. Lori Sue Hungerford, June 12, 1982; children: Traci Nicole, Jesse Micah. BS in Edn., No. Ariz. U., 1979. Tchr. English Greenway H.S., Phoenix, 1979—. Mem. Ariz. English Tchrs. Assn. (standards task force chmn. 1995-96, pres.-elect 1996-97). Democrat. Methodist. Home: 19423 N 73d Ave Glendale AZ 85308

BARRETT, DOROTHY, performing arts administrator; b. L.A., Feb. 28, 1917; d. Lester Arnold and Kathryn (Halverson) Silvera; m. Robert A.H.

Cochrane, May 20, 1949 (div. Feb. 1965); 1 stepchild, Michele Cochrane Shaw. Student, LA C.C., 1937-38. Adminstrv. dir. Am. Nat. Acad. of Performing Arts, 1964—; founder, dir. Acad. Children's Workshop, 1964—; produced, choreographed 30 Christmas shows, 1964—; tchr. of dance Barrett Sch. of the Arts, North Hollywood, 1948, Am. Nat. Acad., Studio City, 1964—, tchr. of acting, 1964—; tchr. of speech UCLA Extension, West Hollywood, 1972. Actress, dancer: (motion pictures) A Damsel in Distress, 1937, The Great Waltz, 1938, Gone with the Wind, 1939, Frisco Sal, Wizard of Oz, 1939, Juke Box Soundies, 1942, Hot Money, 1944, Monsieur Beaucaire, 1945, The Imperfect Lady, 1947, Perils of Pauline, 1945, The Stork Club, 1945, Mildred Pierce, 1945, A Bell for Adano, 1945, Weekend at the Waldorf, 1945, Blue Skies, 1946, Connecticut Yankee in King Arthur's Court, 1947, California, 1947, Samson and Deliliah, 1948, The Babe Ruth Story, 1948; (Broadway stage productions) Earl Carroll's Vanities, 1939, Buddy De Sylva's Louisiana Purchase, 1940, Billy Rose's Diamond Horseshoe, 1943, George Abbott's Beat the Band, 1942, others; (TV) co-star KTLA's Secrets of Gourmet, 1946; prodr., dir.: A Touch of Broadway, 1996, 97; author: (poetry) Between the Bookends, 1942, The Tolucan, The Legal Journal, 1959, Valley Green Sheet & Van Nuys News; contbr. articles to jours. Active Am. Women's Vol. Svc., 1942. Named Miss Culver City, 1937; recipient award ARC, 1943, Humanitarian award for work with children City of L.A., 1994. Office: Am Nat Acad Performing Arts 10944 Ventura Blvd Studio City CA 91604-3340

BARRETT, ETHEL, juvenile fiction writer. Author: Joseph, 1979, Fanny Crosby, Puff the Uppity Ant, 1989, Smarty the Adventurous Fly, 1989, Sunny the Greedy Goat Learns the Value of Self-Control, 1989; author 30 albums; inspirational spkr. Office: care Regal Books 2300 Knoll Dr Ventura CA 93003

BARRETT, JOHN CHARLES, accountant, financial advisor; b. Kalispelll, Mont., Mar. 12, 1965; s. Jack Francis and Shirley Barrett. BS in Bus. Acctg., Mont. State U., 1988. CPA, Mont. Staff acct. Sorenson & Hanson, CPAs, Kalispell, 1988-92; investment mgr. Invent Fin. at Glacier Bank, Kalispell, 1993-94; owner, mgr. John C. Barrett CPA, Kalispell, 1994—. Coach, umpire Evergreen (Mont.) Pee Wee Baseball, 1994-96; instr. dream ski program Big Mountain Ski Resort, 1994-96. Capt. USAR; with Desert Storm/Desert Shield, 1990-91. Mem. Lions (pres. Evergreen 1996—, Lion of Yr. award 1996). Home: 1742 Bison Dr Kalispell MT 59901-5104 Office: 2302 Hwy 2 E Kalispell MT 59901

BARRETT, LARRY LEON, housing and dining services administrator; b. Taft, Calif., July 5, 1940; m. Jean Orrison, Nov. 17, 1989. BS in Phys. Sci., Calif. State Poly., San Luis Obispo, 1964. Supr. trainee U. Calif., Santa Barbara, 1964-65, unit mgr., 1965-69, food svc. dir., 1969-72; dir. housing and dining svc. U. Calif., San Diego, 1972—. Contbr. articles to profl. jours. Recipient Food Svc. Operator of Yr. Silver Plate award Internat. Food Mfrs. Assn., 1981. Mem. Nat. Assn. of Coll. and Univ. Food Svc. (treas. 1979, pres. 1979-81, Theodore Minah Disting. Svc. 1990). Office: U Calif # 0090 La Jolla CA 92093

BARRETT, REGINALD HAUGHTON, biology educator, wildlife management educator; b. San Francisco, June 11, 1942; s. Paul Hutchison and Mary Lambert (Hodgkin) B.; m. Katharine Lawrence Ditmars, July 15, 1967; children: Wade Lawrence, Heather Elizabeth. BS in Game Mgmt., Humboldt State U., 1965; MS in Wildlife Mgmt., U. Mich., 1966; PhD in Zoology, U. Calif., Berkeley, 1971. Rsch. biologist U. Calif., Berkeley, 1970-71, acting asst. prof., 1971-72; rsch. scientist div. wildlife rsch. Commonwealth Scientific and Indsl. Rsch. Orgn., Darwin, Australia, 1972-75; from asst. prof. to prof. U. Calif., Berkeley, 1975—; assoc. dir. Ctr. for Assessment and Monitoring of Forest and Environ. Resources, Berkeley, 1996—. Author: (with others) Report on the Use of Fire in National Parks and Reserves, 1977, Research and Management of Wild Hog Populations, Proceedings of a Symposium, 1977, Sitka Deer Symposium, 1979, Symposium on Ecology and Management of Barbary Sheep, 1980, Handbook of Census Methods for Birds and Mammals, 1981, Wildlife 2000: Modeling Habitat Relationships of Terrestrial Vertebrates, 1986, Translocation of Wild Animals, 1988, Wildlife 2001: Populations, 1992; contbr. articles, abstracts, reports to profl. jours. Recipient Outstanding Profl. Achievement award Humboldt State U. Alumni Assn., 1986, Bruce R. Dodd award, 1965, Howard M. Wight award, 1966; Undergrad. scholar Nat. Wildlife Fedn., 1964, NSF grad. fellow, 1965-70; Union found. Wildlife Rsch. grantee, 1968-70. Mem. The Wildlife Soc. (pres. Bay Area chpt. 1978-79, cert. wildlife biologist, R.F. Dasmann Profl. of Yr. award western sect. 1989), Am. Soc. Mammalogists (life), Soc. for Range Mgmt. (life), Ecol. Soc. Am. (cert. sr. ecologist), Soc. Am. Foresters, Australian Mammal Soc., Am. Inst. Biol. Scis., AAAS, Calif. Acad. Scis., Internat. Union for the Conservation of Nature (life), Calif. Bot. Soc., Orgn. Wildlife Planners, Sigma Xi, Xi Sigma Pi. Episcopalian. Office: U Calif 145 Mulford Hall Berkeley CA 94720

BARRETT, ROBERT MITCHELL, electrical engineer; b. San Diego, Dec. 7, 1943; s. William Francis and Dorothy Lillian (Noll) B.; m. Darleene Frances Fuller, Aug. 8, 1971; children: Katherine Louise, Michelle Frances. BSEE, N.Mex. State U., 1967; MBA, U. So. Calif., L.A., 1973. Commd. 2d lt. USAF, 1967, advanced through grades to maj., 1981, ret., 1987; sys. engr. Air Force Ballistics Missile Office, Norton AFB, Calif., 1978-82, chief launch control sys., 1982-83; sys. engr. GPS user equipment Air Force Space Divsn., L.A., 1983-85, chief, IONS sys. engring., 1985-87; self-employed engr. Mentone, Calif., 1987-89; mem. tech. staff Jet Propulsion Lab., Pasadena, Calif., 1989-93, stds. engr., 1993—. Decorated Air Force Commendation medal, Meritorious Svc. medal. Mem. IEEE, Soc. Automotive Engrs. Office: Jet Propulsion Lab 4800 Oak Grove Dr Pasadena CA 91109

BARRETT, STEPHEN DEYOE, marketing executive; b. Hartford, Conn., Sept. 1, 1945; s. Fredric D. and Elsie (Owen) B.; m. Margaret Mary Lynch, Nov. 23, 1974; children: Owen J., S. Benedict. BA/BS, Syracuse U., 1968. Ops. rep. Pan Am. World Airways, Boston, 1970-71; assoc. editor Electric Light & Power Mag., Boston, 1971-72; mgr. public and tech. info. Combustion Engring., Inc., Windsor, Conn., 1972-77; v.p., group mgr. Creamer Dickson Basford, Providence, 1977-82; pres. LMS/Barrett Pub. Rels. Inc., Providence, 1982-90; asst. v.p. corp. comms. Aetna Life and Casualty, Hartford, Conn., 1990-91; dir. mktg. Choate, Hall & Stewart, Boston, 1992-94; dir. practice devel. Paul, Hastings, Jauofsky & Walker, L.A., 1994—. Mem., chmn. Conservation Com., Barrington, R.I., 1979-83; corporator Pub. Libr., Providence, 1988-90, St. Andrews Sch., Barrington, 1988-90; cofounder Community Boating Ctr., Providence, 1989-91. Recipient Roalman award Nat. Investor Rels. Inst., 1981-82. Mem. Pub. Rels. Soc. Am. (treas. 1974-77, v.p. 1978-80, dir. 1983-85), Nat. Law Firm Marketers Assn., Am. Mktg. Assn. Episcopalian. Home: 30404 Camino Porvenir Palos Verdes Peninsula CA 90275-4535 Office: 555 S Flower St Los Angeles CA 90071-2300

BARRETT, TOM, state agency administrator. Dir. mental health divsn. Denver. Office: 3520 W Oxford Ave Denver CO 80236

BARRETTA-KEYSER, JOLIE, professional athletics coach, author; b. Phila., Aug. 17, 1954; d. Philip Francis and Norma Roberta (Podoszek) Barretta; m. Joel D. Keyser; children: Evan Barrett, Kyra Lani. Student, U. Calif., Long Beach, 1972-76, U. Florence, Italy, 1974-75. Tchr. gymnastics Los Angeles City Sch. Dist., 1973-77, judge, 1976-82; coach, choregrapher Kips Gymnastic Club, Long Beach, Calif., 1976-78, So. Calif. Acrobatics Team, Huntington Beach, Calif., 1979-81, UCLA, 1980-82; pres. West Coast Waves Rhythmic Gymnastics, Rolling Hills Estates, Calif., 1980—; mem. coaching staff U.S. Nat. Rhythmic Gymnastics Team, 1983—; exec. Cell Tech Health Corp., 1996—; coach Centro Olimpico Nazionale Italia, Rome, 1974-76; lectr. dance, phys. edn. Calif. State U., Dominguez Hills, Carson, 1981-92; French lang. mistress of ceremonies rhythmic gymnastics event U.S. Olympic Games, L.A., 1984; invited observer Inst. Phys. Culture, Bejing, 1985, Bulgarian Gymnastics Fedn., Sophia, 1982-90; meet dir. state and regional championships, L.A. County, 1984, '86; internat. lectr. body alignment; pres. Rhythymic Gymnasts Devel. Program, 1984—; developer RIGOR (Rhythmic Gymnastics Outreach) for U.S.A. recreation programs; mem. rhythmic gymnastics adv. com. & bd. Internat. Spl. Olympics, 1990—. Author: Body Alignment, 1985; columnist Internat. Gymnast Mag., 1987-90; contbg. columnist The Crayon Report, 1996—. Tour leader Acad. Tours Inc. U.S./Bulgaria Friendship Through Sports Ann. Tour, N.Y. and Bulgaria, 1987. Recipient recognition plaque U.S. Womens Sports Awards Banquet, 1984-89. Mem. U.S. Rhythmic Gymnastics Coaches Assn. (pres. 1984—), U.S. Gymnastics Fedn. (bd. dirs. 1985—, nat. team coach 1984-93, appointed to ethics com., mem. del., coach internat. competitions U.S., Mex., Hungary, Bulgaria, Belgium, Can. 1984—, choreographer age group devel. compulsory div. 1987, staff Olympic Tng. Ctr. 1984—, charter mem. ethics com. 1991-94), Inst. Noetic Scis., Internat. Spl. Olympics (adv. bd. rhythmic gymnastics), Womans Sports Found. Republican. Office: West Coast Waves 11661 San Vicente Blvd Ste 609 Los Angeles CA 90049-5114

BARRIE, JOAN PARKER, elementary school educator; b. L.A., Aug. 25, 1932; d. Joseph Alexander and Madeline Agnes (Smith) Parker. EdB, Seattle U., 1959; MEd, Loyola Marymount, 1973. Cert. elem., secondary tchr., Calif.; cert. reading specialist, lang. devel. specialist. 6th grade tchr. Sisters of Immaculate Heart, Hollywood, Calif., 1953-56; reading specialist Lakewood (Wash.) Schs., 1959-60, Beverly Hills (Calif.) Sch. Dist., 1960-62; 2nd grade tchr., 6th grade reading specialist Inglewood (Calif.) Unified Sch. Dist., 1962-76; owner Everest Cultural Enrichments, L.A., 1975—; various positions Torrance and Redondo, Calif., 1979-82; office mgr. Starbecca Records, Redondo Beach, Calif., 1982-83; 5th and 6th grades tchr. St. Anthonys, El Segundo, Calif., 1984-85; 2nd grade bilingual tchr. Hawthorne (Calif.) Sch. Dist., 1985—. Author, illustrator: Did You See It, Too?, 1982, Tiggy, Primary Academies, 1989, Reading English, 1994, Reading Spanish, 1995; composer, lyricist Valentine, 1986, (screenplay) Castles of Dreams, 1995. Active United We Stand, 1994, Concern America, Redondo Beach, 1994. Mem. NEA, Calif. Tchrs. Assn., Nat. Coun. Social Studies, S.W. Manuscripters, Dramatist Guild, Smithsonian, Ednl. Dealer. Roman Catholic. Office: Everest Cultural Enrichments PO Box 7000-445 Redondo Beach CA 90277

BARRITT, CLAY FRANKLIN, psychiatrist, educator; b. Marion, Kans., May 31, 1925; s. Clay Franklin and Temple Nadine (White) B.; children: Theresa Jean Ferguson, Christopher Franklin Barritt, Timothy Paul Barritt. Student, Stanford U.; grad., Washington U., 1944, MD, 1948. Diplomat Am. Bd. Psychiatry and Neurology; lic. Calif., Mo., Md., D.C., Pa. Jr. resident psychiatry Henry Phipps Psychiatric Clinic Johns Hopkins Hosp., Balt., 1949-50, sr. resident, 1951-52; sr. resident Letterman Army Hosp., San Francisco, 1952-53, Chestnut Lodge Sanitarium, Rockville, Md., 1954-56; psychoanalytic tng. Psychoanalytic Inst., Washington, 1954-65; pvt. practice Rockville, Md., 1955-62, Kensington, Md., 1962-64, Washington, 1964-67, Bethesda, Md., 1967-70, Chevy Chase, Md., 1970-74, Santa Monica, Calif., 1978-86, Calabasas, Calif., 1986-87, Woodland Hills, Calif., 1987-90, Pacific Palisades, Calif., 1990-93; ret., 1993; chief acute psychotic adolescent inpatient unit, med. program cons. adolsescent treatment ctr. Camarillo (Calif.) State Hosp., 1974-77, chief acute psychotic adult inpaitent unit, med. program cons., 1977-81, chief male geriatric psychotic admission unit, 1981-83; psychiatric cons. Brentwood VA Hosp., 1983-85, chief crisis-oriented psychiatric evaluation svc., 1985-86, staff psychiatrist evaluations and admissions svcs, 1986-88; asst. clin. prof. UCLA, 1983—, instr., 1983-88; rsch. prof. psychiatry, cons. counseling svcs. Gallaudet Coll. for Deaf, Washington, 1963-66; mem. teaching faculty Camarillo State Hosp., 1977-83, chief of staff, pres. med. staff, 1978-79, mem. various coms.; cons. Parkwood Cmty. Hosp. and Valley Park Med. Ctr., Canoga Park, Calif., 1981-85, Humana Hosp., West Hills, Calif., 1985-89, Pathways Valley Presbyn. Hosp., Van Nuys, Calif., 1985-86; active med. staff A Touch of Care, L.A., 1989-90; mem. med. exec. com. Life Plus CCH and TCA Hosps., 1989-90; chmn. med. records com. Life Plus Treatment Ctr., 1989-90, mem. active staff, 1988-91; mem. pharmacy and therapeutics com. Coldwater Canyon Hosp., 1988-89; vice-chief of staff Ingleside Hosp., 1993, chmn. quality assurance med. records and risk mgmt. com., 1993, med. dir. John Bradshaw Ctr., 1990-93, hon. mem. med. staff, 1993. Writer and presenter in field. With AUS, 1943-46; capt. Regular Army Med. Corps, 1950-54; psychiatrist third inf. divsn., 1950-51, Korea. Mem. Am. Psychiatric Assn. (life), So. Calif. Psychiatric Soc. Republican. Home: 1539 Michael Ln Pacific Palisades CA 90272-2022

BARRON, MARYANN, public relations executive; b. Seattle, Nov. 13, 1957; d. Mark McAfee and Jane (Piper) B.; m. Todd Blake Wagner, Feb. 12, 1994. BA in Journalism, Univ. Wash., 1981, cert. tech. writing, 1996; student, Harvard Univ., 1988. Pub. rels. asst. Meaney Theatre Discover Dance Series, Seattle, 1981-84; mktg. mgr. Seattle Symphony, 1984-88; mktg. dir. Empty Space Theatre, Seattle, 1989-90; pub. rels. dir. Mus. History, Seattle, 1990-96; cmty. rels. dir. Frye Art Mus., Seattle, 1996—; mem. adv. bd. Pub. Rels. for Non-Profits, Seattle, 1984-88, Pocock Rowing Found., Seattle, 1984-88; pub. rels. adv., dancer Radost Folk Ensemble, Seattle, 1988-96. Art dir., docent Jr. League Seattle, 1984-95. Mem. Pub. Rels. Soc. Am., Lake Washington Rowing Club (instr. 1985-92), Seattle Tennis Club. Office: Frye Art Mus 704 Terry Ave Seattle WA 98104

BARRON, TIANA LUISA, foundation developer, fundraiser, educator; b. Omaha, Mar. 26, 1952; d. James Patrick Barron and Maria Isabel (Pasos) McAdoo; m. Jerry Peter Mastora (div.); children: Peter Uriah Mastora, Travis Burnell Thom, Taylor Morgan Lewis. Pres., founder S.A.V.E., Sherman Oaks, Calif., 1987—; producer, writer, dir. S.A.V.E., L.A., 1992—. Author: Mommy Was I Adopted, 1992. Adv. bd. The Family Hispanic Ins., L.A., 1990; vol., counselor San Fernando Valley Juvenile Hall, Slymar, Calif., 1990, Sojourn. Recipient Honor for S.A.V.E. Day George Bush, George Deukmejian, Mayor Bradley, Bd. Suprs., L.A., 1989. Home and Office: 4375 Ventura Canyon Ave Apt 1 Sherman Oaks CA 91423-3736

BARROW, THOMAS FRANCIS, artist, educator; b. Kansas City, Mo., Sept. 24, 1938; s. Luther Hopkins and Cleo Naomi (Francis) B.; m. Laurie Anderson, Nov. 30, 1974; children—Melissa, Timothy, Andrew. B.F.A., Kansas City Art Inst., 1963; M.S., Ill. Inst. Tech., 1965. With George Eastman House, Rochester, N.Y., 1966-72; asst. dir. George Eastman House, 1971-72; assoc. dir. Art Mus., U. N. Mex., Albuquerque, 1973-76; assoc. prof. U. N.Mex., 1976-81, prof., 1981—, Presdl. prof., 1985-90. Author: The Art of Photography, 1971; sr. editor: Reading into Photography, 1982; contbr. to Brit. Ency. Am. Art, 1973, A Hundred Years of Photographic History: Essays in Honor of Beaumont Newhall, 1975, Experimental Vision, 1994; forward The Valiant Knights of Daguerre, 1978; contbr. articles to profl. jours.; one-man shows include Light Gallery, N.Y.C., 1974-76, 79, 82, Amarillo Art Ctr., 1990, Andrew Smith Gallery, Santa Fe, 1992, Laurence Miller Gallery, N.Y.C., 1996; exhibited in group shows including Nat. Gallery Can., 1970, Pace Gallery, N.Y.C., 1973, Hudson River Mus., Yonkers, N.Y., 1973, Internat. Mus. Photography, Rochester, 1975, Seattle Art Mus., 1976, Mus. Fine Arts, Houston, 1977, Retrospective exhbn. L.A. County Mus. Art, 1987—; represented in permanent collections Nat. Gallery Can., Mus. Modern Art, Getty Ctr. for Arts and Humanities. Nat. Endowment for Arts fellow, 1971, 78. Office: U NMex Dept Art Albuquerque NM 87131

BARRY, BRENT ROBERT, professional basketball player; b. Dec. 31, 1971; s. Rick Barry. Diploma, Oreg. State U., 1995. Guard L.A. Clippers, 1995—. Ranked 1st among rookies in 3-point field goal percentage, 1995-96; winner Nestle Slam-Dunk competition, 1996. Office: LA Clippers 3939 Figueroa St Los Angeles CA 90037

BARRY, RICK (RICHARD FRANCIS DENNIS BARRY, III), sportscaster, retired professional basketball player, marketing professional; b. Elizabeth, N.J., Mar. 28, 1944; s. Richard Francis and Alpha Monique (Stephanovich) B.; m. Pamela Hale, June 1965 (div.); children: Richard Francis IV, Jon Alan, Brent Robert, Drew William, Shannon Leigh; m. Pamela Stenesen, Sept. 1981 (div.); m. Lynn Norenberg, Aug. 1991; 1 child, Canyon Shane. Student, U. Miami, 1961-65. Basketball player San Francisco Warriors, NBA, 1965-67, Oakland Oaks, Am. Basketball Assn., 1967-69, Washington, Am. Basketball Assn., 1969-70, Virginia Squires, 1970, N.Y. Nets, Am. Basketball Assn., 1970-72, Golden State Warriors, NBA, 1972-78, Houston Rockets, NBA, 1978-80; sports broadcaster, basketball analyst CBS Sports, 1974-81; NBA color analyst Turner Sports, 1984-91; dir. mktg. Profl. Logistics Mgmt. Inc., Lafayette, Calif., 1994—. Mem. Am. Basketball Assn. All-Star Team, 1968-72, NBA All-Star Team, 1966-67, 73-78, NBA Championship Team, 1975; named Rookie of Yr., NBA, 1966, Most Valuable Player All Star Game, 1966, Most Valuable Player Championship Series, 1975; inducted into Basketball Hall of Fame, 1986. *

BARRY, STEVE, sculptor, educator; b. Jersey City, June 22, 1956; s. Thomas Daniel and Lorraine (Lowery) B. BFA, Sch. Visual Arts, N.Y.C., 1980; MFA, Hunter Coll., N.Y.C., 1984. Adj. lectr. Hunter Coll., 1984-89; assoc. prof. U. N.Mex., Albuquerque, 1989—; Kohler Arts and Industry Residency, 1996. Exhbns. include Bklyn. Army Terminal, N.Y.C., 1983, City Gallery, N.Y.C., 1986, 90, Storefront for Art and Architecture, 1988, Artists Space, N.Y.C., 1989, Santa Barbara Art Mus., 1990, Kohler Arts Ctr., Sheboygan, Wis., 1991, Hirshhorn Mus., Washington, 1990, Fla. State U., 1992, Contemporary Art Mus., Houston, 1992, CAFE Gallery, Albuquerque, 1993, Charolette Jackson, Santa Fe, 1993, Ctr. for Contemporary Arts, Santa Fe, 1994, U. Wyo. Art Mus., 1995, Site Santa Fe, 1996. Grantee Clocktower Nat. Studio, 1985, NEA, 1986, 88, 90, N.Y. State Coun. for the Arts, 1987, N.Y. Found. for the Arts, 1988; recipient AVA award, 1990. Home: PO Box 1046 Corrales NM 87048 Office: U NMex Dept Art & Art History Albuquerque NM 87131-1401

BARS, ITZHAK, physics educator, researcher, consultant; b. Izmir, Turkey, Aug. 31, 1943; came to U.S., 1967; s. Albert Shemoel and Claire (Benshoam) Barsimantov; m. Paulette P. Navaro, Aug. 22, 1967 (div. 1993); m. Annie S. Rosenschein, Oct. 1993; children: Julie, Jamie. BS in Physics, Robert Coll., 1967; MPhil in Physics, Yale U., 1969, PhD in Physics, 1971. Asst. rsch. physicist U. Calif., Berkeley, 1971-73; asst. prof. Stanford (Calif.) U., 1973-75; asst. prof. Yale U., New Haven, 1975-79, assoc. prof., 1979-83; prof. U. So. Calif., L.A., 1983—; vis. asst. prof. Harvard U., Cambridge, Mass., 1978; mem. Inst. for Advanced Study, Princeton, N.J., 1979, 90; sci. assoc. CERN, Geneva, Switzerland, 1996-97. Editor: (book) Symmetries in Particle Physics, 1984, Future Directions in String Theory; contbr. some 160 articles to profl. jours. Fulbright scholar Robert Coll., 1964-67; Gibbs fellow Yale U., 1967-69, grad. fellow IBM, 1969-71; A.P. Sloan Found. fellow, 1976-80; recipient 1st award Gravity Rsch. Found., 1988; named Outstanding Jr. Investigator U.S. Dept. Energy, 1983. Fellow Am. Phys. Soc., N.Y. Acad. Scis. Democrat. Jewish. Home: 1827 El Vista Cir Arcadia CA 91006-1662

BARSAN, RICHARD EMIL, oral and maxillofacial surgeon; b. Selma, Ala., Dec. 18, 1945; s. Emil and Letitia Barsan; m. Sandra Sherrick, June 22, 1974; children: Kelly Lynn, Robert Scott. BS in Chem. Engring., U. Cin., 1968; DDS, Ohio State U., 1979. Diplomate Am. Bd. Oral and Maxillofacial Surgeons. Chem. engr. various cos., 1968-76; resident VA Hosp., Sepulveda, Calif., 1979-80; resident in oral and maxillofacial surgery La. State U., New Orleans, 1980-84; pvt. practice, La Jolla and El Centro, Calif., 1985—. Chrysler scholar U. Cin., 1964. Fellow Am. Assn. Oral and Maxillofacial Surgeons; mem. ADA, Calif. Dental Assn., San Diego County Dental Soc. (bd. dirs. 1988-92), San Diego County Oral Surgeons (pres. 1990), So. Calif. Soc. Oral and Maxillofacial Surgeons, Imperial Valley Dental Soc. (pres. 1993), Paul Revere Study Club (pres. 1988), Toastmasters (pres. La Jolla chpt. 1988), Omicron Kappa Upsilon. Republican. Home: 3211 Via Marin La Jolla CA 92037-2937 Office: 4320 Genesee Ave Ste 101 San Diego CA 92117-4900 also: 1745 S Imperial Ave Ste 107 El Centro CA 92243-4243 also: 1073 Ross Ave # A El Centro CA 92243

BARSCH, WULF ERICH, artist, educator; b. Reudnitz, Bohemia, Aug. 27, 1943; came to U.S., 1967; s. Erich and Maria Klaubert; m. Sandra Porter; children: Kelee, Garn, James, Aram, Joseph. Studied drawing, Studienatelier K. Kaschak, Hamburg, Fed. Republic of Germany, 1961-62; studied design, Staatliche Hochschule fur Bildende Kunste, Hamburg, Germany, 1962-63; BFA, Werkkunstschule, Hannover, Germany, 1968; MA in Printmaking, Brigham Young U., 1971, MFA in Painting, 1972. Tchr. German Lang. Tng. Mission, 1970-71; tchr. D.L.I. Inst., Monterey, Calif., 1971, Utah Tech. Coll., Provo, Utah, 1972; prof. dept. art Brigham Young U., Provo, Utah, 1972—; adminstr. asst. Brigham Young U. One-man shows include Galerie des Volksheims, Hamburg, 1966, Galerie Werkkunstschule, Hannover, 1969, Salt Lake City Ctr., 1971, 80, Am. Acad., Rome, 1976, Harris Fine Arts Ctr., Provo, 1976, 84, Kimball Art Ctr., Park City, Utah, 1979, Utah Mus. Art, Salt Lake City, 1984, Scottsdale (Ariz.) Ctr. for Arts, 1985, Oklahoma Ctr. for Arts, Oklahoma City, 1985, Mus. Ch. History and Art, Salt Lake City, 1985-86, Gremillion Fine Art, Houston, 1986, Mack Gilman Galleries, Chgo., 1986, Amarillo (Tex.) Ctr. for Arts., 1986, Gremillion & Co. Fine Arts, Atlanta, 1987, 88, 91, Dolores Chase Fine Arts, Salt Lake City, 1987, 89, 91, River Ctr. Gallery, Memphis, 1988, NO HO Gallery, Stamfort, Conn., 1988, Van der Voort Fine Art, Houston, 1988, Ricks Coll., Rexburg, Idaho, 1988, Art Space, Atlanta, 1989, Liza Kurtz Gallery, Memphis, 1989, Trinity Gallery, Atlanta, 1989, 91, 93, Strecker Gallery, Manhattan, Kans., 1991, Elaine Horwitcz Galleries, Scottsdale, 1991, Sylvia Schmidt Gallery, New Orleans, 1991, 1 Tego Arcaner Dei Gremillion & Co. Fine Arts, Houston, 1993; exhibited in group shows at Mus. Art, Monterey, Calif., 1973, Bringham Young U, Provo, Utah, 1973, 74, 75, 76, 77, 78, 79, 80, 81, 82, 84, 86, 87, Mus. Modern Art, San Francisco, 1974, 76, 83, Am. Acad. Rome, 1975, Am. Acad. Rome, N.Y.C., 1975, Springville Mus. Art, 1977, 78, 80, Centennial Arts Ctr., Surrey, B.C., Can., 1977, Fine Arts Mus., Anchorage, 1977, Smithsonian Inst. traveling show, Washington, 1977-78, 80-82, U. Art Gallery SUNY, Albany, 1978, Salt Lake Art Ctr., Salt Lake City, 1979, 80, 92, Brusberg Gallerie, Hanover, 1979, Mus. Art, Salt Lake City, 1980, Madras (Oreg.) Art Gallery, 1980, Siskiyous Art Gallery, Weed, Calif., 1980, Utah Mus. Art, Salt Lake City, 1981, 83, 86, Mus. Art, Denver, 1982, Mus. Art, Long Beach, Calif., 1983, Bklyn. Mus., 1983, Mus. Art, Albuquerque, 1983, Mus. Ch. History and Art, Salt Lake City, 1984, 86, 91, Dolores Chase Fine Arts, 1985, 86, Marilyn Butler Fine Arts, Scottsdale, Ariz., 1985, Colorado Springs Fine Art Ctr., 1986, Gremillion & Co. Fine Arts, Inc., Houston, 1987, Nora Eccles Harrison Mus. Art, Logan, Utah, 1988, Prairie Lee Gallery, Chgo., 1988, Utah Arts Festival, 1989, Zoe Machs Gallery, Salt Lake City, 1990, MacGillman-Gruen Galleries, Chgo., 1991, Frederic Weissman Collection, Japan, 1991, Dixie Coll., St. George, Utah, 1991, Bharan Internat. Biennial Prints, India, 1991, and more. Recipient CCAC Spl. Edition Purchase award alternate San Francisco Mus. Modern Art, 1973, Rome prize in painting, Am. Acad. Rome, 1975-76, award Springville Mus. Art, 1980, Snowbird Inst. award in art, 1980, Printmaking award Western States Art Found., 1980, Merit award Sch. Art, Terme, Italy, 1981, Visual Arts Nomination award, 1982, World Culture award Centro Studie Ricerecke Belle Nazioni, Italy, 1983, Western States Painting award, 1983, Gold medal nomination Accademia Italia, Parma, Italy, 1980, 85, Karl G. Maeser Rsch. and Creative Arts award Karl G. Maeser Found., 1985, Purchase award Springville Mus. Arts, 1986, Purchase award Cliff Lodge Inaugural Exhbn., 1987, Utah Works on Paper award, 1989. Home: PO Box 1359 Boulder UT 84716-1359 Office: Brigham Young Univ C502 Hfac Provo UT 84602-1026

BARSIS, EDWIN HOWARD, physicist; b. N.Y.C., June 28, 1940; s. Morris J. and Rose Barsis; children: James, Benjamin. BEP, Cornell U., 1963, MS, 1965, PhD, 1967. Mem. tech. staff Sandia Nat. Labs., Livermore, Calif., 1967-69; supr. applied physics Sandia Nat. Labs., Livermore, 1969-75, supr. advanced weapons div., 1975-77; mgr. electronic subsystems dept. Sandia Nat. Labs., Albuquerque, 1977-86, dir. computer scis. and math., 1986-95, dir. engring. scis., 1989-92; chmn. bd. dirs. Urologics, Inc., Albuquerque, 1984-95; ptnr. BMV Assocs., Albuquerque, N.Mex., 1995—. Contbr. articles to profl. jours. Capt. C.E., U.S. Army, 1967-69. Mem. Am. Phys. Soc. Home: 1538 Catron Ave SE Albuquerque NM 87123-4259 Office: BMV Assocs 1538 Catron Ave SE Albuquerque NM 87123-4259

BARSKY, MARTIN, editor, publisher; b. Phila., Jan. 26, 1927; s. Philip and Mollie (Cohen) B.; children: Larry, Steve, Laura. Grad. high sch., Phila. Advt. mgr. Kiddie City Stores, Phila., 1954; mgr., prodr. various radio and TV stas., Pa., Mont., Calif., 1955-70; founder, editor, pub. So. Calif. Retailer, L.A., 1971-81; owner, editor, pub. Retailer News, Anaheim, Calif., 1981-88; pres., pub. Video Software Dealer News, L.A., 1984-86, Rental Dealer News, Orange, Calif., 1987-90; founder, editor, pub. Buying Group News mag. and Retailing News mag., Anaheim, 1990—. Prodr. Folk Music Theatre, 1967; contbr. articles to profl. jours. Bd. dirs. City of Hope Consumer Electronics, L.A., 1987-88, pres., 1985-86. Sgt. USAAF, 1943-45. Recipient Cert. of Appreciation, Am. Legion, 1968, Outstanding Contbns. award Associated Vol. Buyers, 1977, United Stores Inc., 1980. Mem. Soc. Profl. Journalists, Electronics Reps. Republican. Jewish. Home: 13490 Prospector Ct Victorville CA 92392-8849 Office: Retailing News 14962 Bear Valley Rd Ste 288 Victorville CA 92392-9236

BART, PETER BENTON, newspaper editor, film producer, novelist; b. N.Y.C., July 24, 1932; m. Leslie Cox; children: Colby, Dilys. BA, Swarthmore Coll., 1954; MA, London Sch. Econs., 1956. Staff reporter The Wall Street Jour., N.Y.C., 1956-57, The N.Y. Times, N.Y.C., 1957-67; v.p. Paramount Pictures, Los Angeles, 1967-74; pres. Bart Palevsky Prodn., L.A., 1974-77, Lorimar Film Co., Los Angeles, 1977-82; sr. v.p., film producer Metro Goldwyn Mayer/United Artists, L.A., 1982-85; v.p., editorial dir. Variety and Daily Variety, L.A., 1989—. Author: Destinies, 1980, Thy Kingdom Come, 1983, Fade Out: The Calamitous Final Days of MGM, 1990; prodr.: (films) Fun with Dick and Jane, Islands in the Stream, Youngblood. Office: Variety 5700 Wilshire Blvd Ste 120 Los Angeles CA 90036-3659

BARTEL, ARTHUR GABRIEL, educational administrator, city official; b. San Francisco, Oct. 20, 1934; s. Irving Peter and Elian Leah (Barker) B.; m. Dottie Lu Smith, Dec. 14, 1963 (dec. Apr. 1972); children: Brian Blake, Scott Michael; m. Suzane M. Loftis, Feb. 14, 1989. Student, San Jose State Coll., 1952-54; BS, U. Calif., Berkeley, 1957; postgrad., U. So. Calif., 1968-70; MA, Pepperdine U., 1973, Calif. State U., Fresno, 1995. Cert. FAA air traffic controller, 1957-77, naval flight officer, 1965; lic. standard tchr., life standard svc., life cmty. coll. life chief coll. adminstrv. officer, life cmty. coll. supr., life comty. coll. instr., spl. edn. svcs. credential, Calif. Enlisted USMC, 1954, commd. 2d lt., 1957, advanced through grades to maj., 1967; comdg. officer VMFA-314 Fighter-Attack Squadron USMC, El Toro, Calif., 1970-72; ret. USMC, 1977; gen. mgr. Nieuport 17 Restaurant, Santa Ana, Calif., 1977-78; pres., chief exec. officer High Flight Inc., Hanford, San Diego, Calif., 1978-81; teaching vice prin. Armona (Calif.) Union Elem. Sch., 1982-84, tchr. sci. and lang. arts., 1981-84; curriculum cons. Kings County Office Edn., Hanford, 1984-86; program specialist Kings County Supt. Schs., Hanford, 1986-91; prin. Kings County Cmty. Sch., Hanford, 1994—; councilman City of Hanford, 1986-90, mayor, 1988-90; mem. adv. bd. San Joaquin Valley Writing Project, 1984-86, 92—. Vice chmn. Hanford Planning Commn., 1982-86; vice chmn. bd. trustees Sacred Heart Hosp., 1987-93; bd. dirs. Navy League, 1992—. Decorated Air medal, Vietnam Cross of Gallantry; fellow internat. writing project U. Calif., Irvine, 1985. Mem. Assn. Calif. Sch. Adminstrs., Calif. Soc. Program Specialists, Hanford C. of C., DAV (life), Ret. Officers Assn., Navy League (v.p. 1993-95), Delta Upsilon (life). Office: Kings County Office Edn Kings Govt Ctr Hanford CA 93230

BARTELINK, DIRK JAN, physicist, engineer; b. Heumen, The Netherlands, Oct. 28, 1933; came to U.S., 1958; s. Dirk Leonard and Johanna Judith (Jannink) B.; m. Donna Maurie Merifield, Mar. 2, 1957; children: Debbie Bartelink Jones, John Dirk. BSc, U. Western Ont., London, 1956; MS, Stanford U., 1959, PhD, 1962. Mem. tech. staff AT&T Labs., Murray Hill, N.J., 1961-66, supr., 1966-73; prin. scientist, area mgr. Xerox, Palo Alto, Calif., 1973-82; dept. mgr. Hewlett-Packard Labs., Palo Alto, Calif., 1982—; with Semiconductor Rsch. Corp., Research Triangle Park, N.C., 1995—; vis. scientist Stanford U., 1981-82; mem. strategic adv. bd. SEMATECH, Austin, Tex., 1989—; mem. nat. tech. roadmap Semiconductor Industry Assn., San Jose, 1992, 94; chmn. symposium on Ultra Large Scale Integration Tech., 1990-91. Mem. IEEE (sr.). Office: Hewlett-Packard Labs 3500 Deer Creek Rd Palo Alto CA 94304-1317

BARTELS, ALOYSIA DE BESSIERÉS, mariculturist, seafood producer; b. Victoria, B.C., Can., Aug. 11, 1923; d. Jean Marie de Hedouville and Aloysia Theresa van Goidtsoven (Sant Anna); m. Jay Murray Bartels; m. George P. Meade III; m. Karl L. Agricola; children: Joseph W., William L. II; m. Jay Bartels. Owner shrimp fishing boats Fla., Tex., 1972-86; pres., dir. W.I. Sea Farms Ltd., Carriacore, Grenada, 1986-92. Author: (poem) Navaho, 1993 (Best of 1993 award); co-author: Pageant of Eight Flags, 1993. Mem. Fernandina Beach Fla. Hist. Soc. (past pres., head restoration commn.). Republican. Home: 3917 Saint Andrews Dr Rio Rancho NM 87120

BARTER BOWLUS, NADINE CHRISTENA, biology educator; b. Seattle, May 25, 1948. BS in Liberal Arts, Regents Coll., U. State N.Y., Albany, 1989; MA in Biology, San Jose (Calif.) State U., 1992. Grad. asst. San Jose State U., 1989-93, lectr. biology, 1993—; instr. biology West Valley C.C., Saratoga, Calif., 1993—. Author: Using the Macintosh, Tools for Biologists, 2d edit., 1994, 3d edit., 1995. Mem. AAAS, Ecol. Soc. Am. (sec. We. chpt. 1990-94), Nat. Assn. Biology Tchrs., Am. Inst. Biol. Scis., The Wildlife Soc.

BARTH, DAVID VICTOR, computer systems designer, consultant; b. Tulsa, Sept. 23, 1942; s. Vincent David and Norma (Bell) B. BS summa cum laude, Met. State Coll., Denver, 1977; MS, U. No. Colo., 1982; PhD, Kennedy-Western U., Boise, Idaho, 1995. Programming mgr. Am. Nat. Bank, Denver, 1967-72; cons. Colo. Farm Bur. Ins. Corp., Denver, 1972; systems analyst Mid-Continent Computer Services, Denver, 1972-73; programming mgr. Bayly Corp., Denver, 1973-75; project leader Cobe Labs. Inc., Denver, 1976-84; part-time tchr. Met. State Coll., 1982-83; systems analyst Affiliated Banks Service Co., Denver, 1985-87; real estate broker Van Schaack & Co., Denver, 1985; tech. supr. Affiliated Banks Svc. Co., Denver, 1987-89; software engr. Computer Data Systems, Inc., Aurora, Colo., 1990-91, 1994—; sr. computer systems designer Martin Marietta Corp., Golden, Colo., 1991-92; owner, operator Computer Shop, Lakewood, Colo., 1992-93; cons. Ross Co., Denver, 1993-95; sr. software engr. Computer Data Systems, Inc., Aurora, Colo., 1994—; freelance flight instr., 1977—. Vol. Am. Red Cross, 1987—; Served with USN, 1961-66. Mem. Soc. for Info. Mgmt. (editor newsletter 1983), Exptl. Aircraft Assn. (editor newsletter chpt. 660, 1989-91), Aircraft Owners and Pilots Assn., Flying Circus Skating Club. Republican. Home: 509 S Cody St Lakewood CO 80226-3047 Office: Computer Data Sys Inc 3025 S Parker Rd Ste 1100 Aurora CO 80014-2933

BARTH, ERNEST A.T., sociologist, educator; b. N.Y.C., June 30, 1924; s. Ernest Albert and Jeanette Elvira (Thomson) B.; m. Grace Leone Williams (div. 1972); children: William Thomson, Georgia Jean, Donna, Joseph; m. Dorloes Schretz, 1993. BS in Psychology, U. Rochester, 1950; MA in Sociology, U. N.C., 1949, PhD in Sociology, 1950. From instr. to prof. sociology U. Wash., Seattle, 1950-88, prof. emeritus, 1988—. Author: Sandy's Gist, 1996, Grandpa Tom Tells Stories of Robin, 1996. Democrat. Home: 2500 Canterbury Ln E #203 Seattle WA 98112

BARTH, SHARON LYNN, nurse; b. Stamford, Conn., Oct. 27, 1948; d. Donald Eric and Jane Dolores (Fabrizio) Walker; m. James Leander Barth Jr., June 8, 1967; children: Kristen Lynne, Jennifer Leigh, Shannon Lynlee. AA summa cum laude, Coll. of Albermarle, Elizabeth City, N.C., 1974; BSN cum laude, Calif. State U., Sacramento, 1991; postgrad., U. Phoenix, Sacramento. RN, Calif.; Neonatal Advanced Life Support, Calif.; cert. lactation educator. Staff nurse Kaiser Permanente, Sacramento, 1991-93, charge nurse, 1993-97, leadership team facilitator, 1997—; guest lectr. Teen Parenting classes, Maternal-Child classes CSUS. Mem. Assn. Women's Health, Assn. Obstetric and Neonatal Nurses, Phi Kappa Phi, Sigma Theta Tau, Golden Key. Home: 8142 Bonnie Oak Way Citrus Heights CA 95610

BARTH, UTA, artist, educator; b. Berlin, Jan. 29, 1958. BA, U. Calif., Davis, 1982; MFA, UCLA, 1985. From asst. prof. to assoc. prof. art dept. U. Calif., Riverside, 1990—. One-woman shows include Howard Yezersky Gallery, Boston, 1990, Rochester (N.Y.) Inst. Tech., 1993, Calif. Mus. Photography, Riverside, 1993, Wooster Gardens, N.Y.C., 1994, Mus. Contemporary Art, L.A., 1995, ACME, Santa Monica, Calif., 1995, Tanya Bonakdar Gallery, N.Y.C., 1996, London Projects, London, 1996, S.L. Simpson Gallery, Toronto, Ont., Can., 1996, Mus. Contemporary Art, Chgo., 1997; group shows include Tom Solomon's Garage, L.A., 1994, Long Beach (Calif.) Mus. Art, 1994, Mus. De Beyerd, Netherlands, 1994, Los Angeles County Mus. Art, 1994, San Bernardino County Mus., 1994, The New Mus., N.Y.C., 1995, Mus. Modern Art, N.Y.C., 1995, Rooseum-Ctr. for Contemporary Art, Malmo, Sweden, 1996, Magasin 3 Stockholm Konsthall, 1996, Wexner Ctr. for Art, Columbus, Ohio, 1997, Mus. Contemporary Art, Miami, 1997. NEA grantee, 1990-91, 94-95; Art Matters Inc. grantee, 1992-93, 95. Home and Office: 2900 Airport Ave Ste G Santa Monica CA 90405-6102

BARTLETT, ALBERT ALLEN, retired physics educator; b. Shanghai, China, Mar. 21, 1923; s. Willard William and Marguerite (Allen) B.; m. Eleanor Frances Roberts, Aug. 24, 1946; children—Carol Louise, Jane Elizabeth, Lois Jeanne, Nancy Marie. Student, Otterbein Coll., 1940-42; B.A., Colgate U., 1944; M.A., Harvard U., 1948, Ph.D., 1951. Research asst. Los Alamos Sci. Lab., 1944-46; faculty U. Colo., Boulder, 1950—; prof. physics U. Colo., 1962-88, chmn. faculty council, 1969-71, prof. emeritus, 1988—; faculty Harvard U. Summer Sch., 1952, 53, 55, 56; vis. research worker Nobel Inst. Physics, Stockholm, Sweden, 1963-64; lectr. on arithmetic, population and energy. Contbr. articles to profl. jours. Mem. Boulder City Parks and Recreation Adv. Bd., 1967-72, vice chmn., 1969, 70, chmn., 1971. Recipient Thomas Jefferson award U. Colo., 1972, Robert L. Stearns award, 1974, service award Girl Scouts Am., 1974, Univ. Gold medal, 1978, Plan Boulder County Ann. award, 1990. Fellow AAAS, Am. Phys. Soc.; mem. Am. Assn. Physics Tchrs. (recipient Disting. Service citation 1970, Robert A. Millikan award 1981, pres. 1978, Melba Newell Phillips award 1990), Phi Beta Kappa, Sigma Xi, Alpha Tau Omega. Clubs: Colo. Mountain, Rocky Mountain Railroad. Home: 2935 19th St Boulder CO 80304-2719

BARTLETT, SUE, state legislator; b. Billings, Mont., July 4, 1947; m. Gene Fenderson. BA, Wash. U. Clk., recorder Lewis and Clark County, 1983-91; asst. sec. Mont. Senate, 1991-92, mem.; tech. writer. Democrat. Home: 416 N Beattie St Helena MT 59601-3701*

BARTLETT, THOMAS ALVA, educational administrator; b. Salem, Oreg., Aug. 20, 1930; s. Cleave Wines and Alma (Hanson) B.; m. Mary Louise Bixby, Mar. 20, 1954; children: Thomas Glenn, Richard A., Paul H. Student, Willamette U., 1947-49, DCL (hon.), 1986; A.B., Stanford U., 1951, Ph.D., 1959; M.A. (Rhodes scholar), Oxford U., 1953; L.H.D. (hon.), Colgate U., 1977, Mich. State U., 1978, Union Coll., 1979; D.C.L. (hon.), Pusan Nat. U., Korea, 1985, U. Ala., 1983. Mem. U.S. Permanent Mission to UN, 1956-63; advisor Gen. Assembly Dels., 1956-63; pres. Am. U., Cairo, 1963-69, Colgate U., Hamilton, N.Y., 1969-77, Assn. Am. Univs., Washington, 1977-82; chancellor U. Ala. System, 1982-89, Oreg. State System of Higher Edn. Office, Eugene, 1989-94; ret.; mem. UAR-U.S. Ednl. Exch. Commn., 1966-69; mem. Task Force on Financing Higher Edn. in N.Y. State (Keppel Commn.), 1972-73; chmn. Commn. Ind. Colls. and Univs. N.Y., 1974-76; bd. dirs. Nat. Assn. Ind. Colls. and Univs., 1975-76; trustee Univs. Field Staff Internat., 1985-87; mem. NASA Comml. Space Adv. Com., 1988-90. Mem. nat. bd. examining Chaplains Episcopal Ch., 1978-91; trustee Gen. Theol. Sem., 1977-82, Am. U. in Cairo, 1978—, U.S.-Japan Found., 1988—. Mem. Coun. Fgn. Rels., Cosmos Club (Washington), Phi Beta Kappa. Home: 2550 Fairmont Eugene OR 97403*

BARTLETT ABOOD, KATHLEEN GENE, artist, educator; b. Detroit, Jan. 31, 1949; d. William Jacob and Anne Myrtle Bartlett; m. George Thomas Abood, Aug. 21, 1981; children: Thomas Michael Bartlett, Jessica Cody, Lily Brook. Student, Wayne State U., Detroit, 1967-69; cert. in graphic arts, U. Calif., Santa Cruz, 1986, BFA in Studio Art, 1988. Multimedia artist Primal Visions Studio, Santa Cruz, 1980—; project coord. Santa Cruz Lifeyard Project, 1982-84; artist in residence William James Assn., Santa Cruz, 1984—; program dir. West Hawaii Arts Guild, Kailua-Kona, 1990-91; program designer Art Mus. Santa Cruz County, 1992-93; project dir., artist in residence 1st Night Santa Cruz, 1994-96; lead artist in residence Cmty. Youth Arts Project, Santa Cruz, 1994—; dir. vis. artists West Hawaii Arts Guild, 1990-91; Youth Arts Project, 1994-96; artist in the cmty. Cultural Coun. Santa Cruz Cou; cons. edn. program Mus. Santa Cruz County, 1991-92. One-woman shows include The Poet and Patriot, Santa Cruz, 1983, Cafe Riva at Santa Cruz Mcpl. Wharf, 1985, 320 Gallery, Santa Cruz, 1986, Santa Cruz Art Ctr., 1986, Pearl Alley Bistro, Santa Cruz, 1987, U. Calif. Santa Cruz Women's Ctr., 1988; exhibited in group shows at Lifeyards Cmty. Arts Project at San Lorenzo Pk., Santa Cruz, 1982, Cooper House Gallery, Santa Cruz, 1983, Mt. St. Mary's Coll., L.A., 1986, L.A. Printmaking Soc. Invitational, 1987, William James Gallery, Santa Cruz, 1988, Eloise Pickard Smith Gallery, 1988, 89, 94, West Hawaii Gallery, Kailua-Kona, 1991, Wailoa Art Ctr., Hilo, Hawaii, 1991, Kona Village Resort, Kaupulehu, Hawaii, 1991, Santa Cruz Art League, 1991, Nordstrom, San Francisco and San Jose, Calif., 1991, L.A. Printmaking Soc./Honolulu Printmakers Traveling Exhbn., 1991, Stevenson Libr. U. Calif. Santa Cruz, 1992, Galeria Museo, San Francisco, 1992, Many Hands Gallery at Santa Cruz Art Ctr., 1993, New Women's Art Gallery, Santa Cruz, 1993, Pajaro Valley Gallery, Watsonville and Gavilan Coll., Gilroy, Calif., 1993, Art Mus. of Santa Cruz Palomar Annex and Rental Gallery, 1993, Galeria Tonantzin, San Juan Batista, Calif., 1994, 95, Fresno (Calif.) Arts Coun., 1994, Primal Visions Art Gallery, 1994, Chaminade Artists Series 22, Santa Cruz, 1995, 4th World Conf. of Women, Beijing, 1995, Nat. Mus. Women in the Arts, Washington, 1996, Made in Santa Cruz Gallery, 1997. Bd. dirs. 1st Night Santa Cruz, 1996—, coord. cmty. outreach, 1994-96; mem. arts edn. com. Art Mus. Santa Cruz County, 1991-93; mem. open studios steering com. Cultural Coun. Santa Cruz County, 1993-95; mem. adv. bd. William James Found., 1994-96; mem. adv. coms. social environment and children's issues, cmty. needs assessment United Way of Santa Cruz County, 1994-95; mem. Bay St. Art Wall rev. com. City of Santa Cruz Arts Commn., 1994-95. Artist in residence grantee Calif. Arts Coun., Sacramento, 1982—, Santa Cruz County Cmty. Found., 1994-96, City of Santa Cruz Arts Commn., 1982-84, 94, Cultural Coun. Santa Cruz County, 1995-96. Mem. Nat. Mus. Women in Arts, Calif. Wellness Found., L.A. Printmaking Soc., Art Mus. of Santa Cruz County. Home: 300 Plateau Ave Santa Cruz CA 95060

BARTLING, JUDD QUENTON, research corporation executive; b. Muncie, Ind., July 24, 1936; s. Hubert George and Hildagarde (Good) B.; m. Madeline Levesque, June 9, 1973 (div. 1989); stepchildren—Mary Johnson, Michael Johnson. BA, U. Calif., 1960, PhD, 1969; MS, Purdue U., 1964. Research asst. U. Calif., Riverside, 1965-69; cons. Dept. Def. Rsch., Azak Corp., Chatsworth, Calif., 1969-71, pres., 1971—. Served with U.S. Army, 1960-62. NSF grantee U. Fla., 1969. Research in bus., solid state physics, signal processing, quantum electronics, electromagnetics and radar. Office: 21032 Devonshire St Ste 113 Chatsworth CA 91311-2368

BARTON, ANN ELIZABETH, retired financial executive; b. Long Lake, Mich., Sept. 8, 1923; d. John and Inez Mabel (Morse) Seaton; m. H. Kenneth Barton, Apr. 3, 1948; children: Michael, John, Nancy. Student Mt. San Antonio Coll., 1969-71, Adrian Coll., 1943, Citrus Coll., 1967, Golden Gate U., 1976, Coll. Fin. Planning, 1980-82. CFP. Tax cons., real estate broker, Claremont, Calif., 1967-72, Newport Beach, Calif., 1972-74; v.p., officer Putney, Barton, Assocs., Inc., Walnut Creek, Calif., 1975-94, ret., 1997; bd. dir. Fin. Svc. Corp. Cert. fin. planner. Mem. Internat. Assn. Fin. Planners (registered investment advisor), Calif. Soc. Enrolled Agts., Nat. Assn. Enrolled Agts., Inst. CFP.

BARTON, BILLIE JO, artist, educator; b. Childress, Tex., June 23, 1926; d. Robert Douglas and Erma Ada (Collier) Perry; m. Hudson James Barton, June 28, 1947; 1 child, David Douglas. Student, Frank Wiggins Sch., 1944-45, ABC Sch. Dist., 1956-86; studied with Ken Decker, Mary Bugher. Art instr. Smithys Art Gallery, Orange, Calif., 1976-77, Internat. Studio, Cerritos, Calif., 1978-79, Lakewood, Calif., 1980—; juror Fine Art Commn., Buena Park, Calif., 1993-96. Author: The Guidebook for Oil Painters, 1993; work pub. in books: Artists of California, 1993, Encyclopedia of Living Artist, 1997; editor Buena Park Art Guild newsletter, 1993; group exhibits and juried shows include The La Mirada (Calif.) Art Gallery, 1993-94, Art Assocs. Gallery, Huntington Beach, Calif., 1994, Calif. Coun. Art League, 1992, 93, 94, Knott's Berry Farm Artist Round-Up, Buena Park, 1992, 93, 94, Fine Art Inst. San Bernadino County Mus., Redlands, Calif., 1992, 93, 94, Santa Barbara 6th Ann. Festival Art, 1994, Festival Whales Dana Point Harbor, Dana Point, Calif., 1995, Newport Beach Festival Art, Newport, Calif., 1995, Tall Ships Show, Dana Point, 1995, 21st Ann. Juried Art Exhibit, Cypress, Calif., 1996, Sunday Arts Delight, Cypress, 1996, Ann. Father's Day Celebration, Dana Point, 1996. Parent aide PTA, Lakewood, 1959-64; den mother Cub Scouts Am., Lakewood, 1961; precinct worker Los Angeles County Elections, Norwalk, Calif., 1949, Lakewood, 1965-86. Fellow Nat. Mus. Women in Arts, Niguel Art Assn., Nat. Assn. Fine Art, Buena Art Guild (recording sec. 1992-96, Best of Show award 1992), Ea. Star Lodge (hostess 1966-67); mem. La Palma Art Assn. (news editor, v.p. 1975-76, Artist of Yr. award 1976). Republican. Home and Studio: 11720 207th St Lakewood CA 90715-1331

BARTON, LARRY LUMIR, mircobiology educator, consultant; b. West Point, Nebr., May 13, 1940; s. Lumir and Sophia Tresa (Ahrndt) B.; m. Sandra L. Reiners, Aug. 21, 1968; children: Brian, Gregory. BS in biology and chem., U. Nebr., 1962, MS in microbiology, 1966, PhD in microbiology, 1969. Rsch. assoc. dept. biochemistry U. Ga., Athens, 1969-71; asst. prof. dept. pathobiology Johns Hopkins U., Balt., 1971-72; asst. prof. dept. biology U. N.Mex., Albuquerque, 1972-77, assoc. prof., 1978-93, prof., 1993—; vis. scientist life sci. div. Los Alamos Nat. Lab., Los Alamos, 1988; dir. microbiology div. Northwestern N.Mex. Sci. and Engring. Sci. Fair; editorial bd. Biology of Metals, 1988-91, Biometals, 1991—; editor-in-chief Anaerobes: Academic Press Jour. 1994—. Author numerous book chpts.; editor numerous books; contbr. articles to profl. jours. Jt. appointment Am. Leprosy Assn., Washington, 1971-72. Mem. Am. Soc. Microbiology (pres. 1987-89), Sigma Xi (treas. 1991-93, v.p. 1993-94). Office: U N Mex Dept Biology Albuquerque NM 87131

BARTON, PHOEBE LINDSEY, healthcare educator; b. Franklin, Pa., May 22, 1947; d. Harold Leslie Jr. and Elsie L. (Pryer) Lindsey; m. Dennis Raymond Barton, Sept. 3, 1991. BA, Boise State U., 1969, MPA, 1977; PhD, UCLA, 1987. Dir. Mountain States Regional Med. Program, Boise, Idaho, 1970-75, Health Policy Network, Boise, 1975-78; adminstr. Idaho Dept. Health and Welfare, Boise, 1978-80, Alaska Dept. Health and Social Svcs., Juneau, 1980-83; asst. prof. UCLA, 1987-90; assoc. prof. U. Colo. Health Scis. Ctr., Denver, 1990—; cons. RAND Corp., Santa Monica, Calif., 1986—. Author: Understanding the U.S. Health Care System, 1997; contbr. articles to Helath Care Fin. Rev., Jour. Health Policy, Health Svcs. Rsch. Bd. dirs. Assn. Tchrs. Preventive Medicine Found., Washington, 1990—. Office: U Colo Health Scis Ctr 4500 E 9th Ave Box C-245 Denver CO 80262

BARTOSIK, NORBERT JOHN, state fair association executive; b. Chgo., Oct. 16, 1949; s. John Edward and MaryJane (Murphy) B.; m. Darlene M. Drop (div. 1979); m. Joan P. Weil, Nov. 14, 1992. AA, Chgo. City Coll., 1969; BS, So. Ill. U., 1972. CFE, cert. fair mgr. Adminstrn. asst. Duquoin (Ill.) State Fair Assoc., 1972-74; concessions mgr. Duquoin State Fair Assoc., 1974-76, controller, 1976-77, v.p., bus. mgr., 1977-79, pres., gen. mgr., 1979-81; gen. mgr. Antelope Valley Fair, Lancaster, Calif., 1981-83; gen. mgr., chief exec. officer Orange County Fair Exposition Ctr., Costa Mesa, Calif., 1983-93; gen. mgr., CEO Calif. State Fair, Sacramento, 1994—; bd. dirs. Calif. Authority Racing (pres. 1989). Bd. dirs. Duquoin Boys Club Am., 1976, past pres.; bd. dirs. Perry County United Way, Duqoin, 1979. Named to Hall of Fame, So. Ill. U. Coll. of Bus., 1990. Mem. Western Fairs Assn. (pres. 1985, 86), Duquoin Bus. Assn. (v.p. 1980), Internat. Assn. Fair Expositions (2d v.p. 1997), Mid-West Fairs Assn. (pres. 1989), Pi Sigma Epsilon (pres. 1970-71). Republican. Home: 9217 Los Puentes Rd Newcastle CA 95658-9706 Office: Calif State Fair PO Box 15649 Sacramento CA 95852

BARUCH, RUTH-MARION EVELYN, photographer, writer; b. Berlin, Ger., June 15, 1922; d. Max and Bertha (Zweigenhaft) Baruch; m. Pirkle Jones, 1949. BA in Creative Writing, U. Mo., 1944, BJ, 1944; MFA in Photography, Ohio U., 1946; postgrad., Calif. Sch. Fine Arts, San Francisco, 1946-48. Grad. asst. Ohio U., 1944-46; tchr. workshops Home Studio, Mill Valley, Calif., 1969-71; guest artist San Francisco Art Inst., 1970, 75. Works in permanent collections at Art Inst. Chgo., San Francisco Mus. Art, Oakland Mus. Art, Polaroid Corp., Cambridge, Mass., George Eastman House, Rochester, N.Y., Ctr. for Creative Photography (Ansel Adams Collection), U. Ariz., Tucson, Ariz. State U., Temple; author: The Vanguard: A Photographic Essay on the Black Panthers, 1970; included in Photography in the Twentieth Century, 1967, Photographers Ency. Internat., book and exhbn.: Family of Man, 1954; one person shows at San Francisco Mus. Modern Art, 1966, Carmel Photography Ctr., 1967, M.H. DeYoung Meml. Mus., San Francisco, 1968, Amon Carter Mus. Western Art, Ft. Worth, 1968, Focus Gallery, San Francisco, 1976, San Francisco Mus. Modern Art Rental Gallery, 1980; group shows include Mus. Modern Art, N.Y.C., 1954, Kongresshalla, Berlin, 1957, George Eastman House, 1960, DeCordova Mus., Lincoln, Mass., 1967, Focus Gallery, San Francisco, 1976, 80, Friends of Photography, Carmel, 1984, Monterey Peninsula Mus. Art, 1986, Ariz. State U., 1987, San Francisco Art Inst., Trans Am. Pyramid Gallery, San Francisco, 1996. Home and Office: 663 Lovell Ave Mill Valley CA 94941-1086

BARVILLE, REBECCA PENELOPE, elementary school educator; b. Tulare, Calif., Nov. 7, 1936; m. David Leopold Barville, June 8, 1958; children: Mark, Becky, Curtis. BA, Simpson Coll., San Francisco, 1958; MA summa cum laude, Fresno State U., 1974. Cert. reading specialist, edn. adminstr., elem. tchr., Calif. Social worker Tulare County Welfare Dept., Porterville, Calif., 1961-63, San Bernadino Welfare, Ontario, Calif., 1963-65; tchr., reading specialist Pleasant View Sch., Porterville, 1969—; instr. Porterville Coll., 1993—. Pres. PTA, Lindsay, Calif., 1966-67. Fellow Delta Kappa Gamma; mem. AAUW (bd. dirs. 1974-83), Calif. Reading Assn. (sec. 1974), Pleasant View Educators Assn. (past pres., sec. 1985—). Republican. Presbyterian. Club: P.E.O. (v.p. 1986-87).

BASCH, REVA, information services company executive; b. Chgo., Aug. 1, 1947; d. Victor Hugo and Hertha (Levi) B.; m. Jerrald C. Shifman, Apr. 17, 1982. BA in English Lit. summa cum laude, U. Pa., 1969; MLS, U. Calif., Berkeley, 1971. Head libr. Cogswell Coll., San Francisco, 1971-72; tech. info. specialist Gilbert Assocs. Inc., Reading, Pa., 1973-79; tech. libr. NuTech, San Jose, Calif., 1980-81; rsch. assoc. Info. on Demand, Berkeley, Calif., 1981-82, asst. dir. rsch., 1982-83, dir. rsch., 1983-86, v.p., dir. rsch., 1985-86; software designer Mead Data Ctrl., Personal Computer Sys. Group, Menlo Park, Calif., 1986-88; pres. Aubergine Info. Svcs., The Sea Ranch, Calif., 1986—. Author: Secrets of the Super Searchers, 1993, Electronic Information Delivery: Ensuring Quality and Value, 1995, Secrets of the Super Net Searchers, 1996; mem. editorial bd. The Info. Advisor; contbr. articles to profl. jours. Recipient award for best paper UMI/Data Courier, 1990, Online Champion award Dun & Bradstreet. Mem. Assn. of Ind. Info. Profl.(pres.1991-92), Spl. Librs. Assn. , Assn. Info. and Dissemination Ctrs., Info. Bay Area, So. Calif. Online Users Group.

BASCOM, RUTH F., former mayor; b. Ames, Iowa, Feb. 4, 1926; d. Frederick Charles and Doris Hays Fenton; m. John U. Bascom, June 14, 1950; children: Lucinda, Rebecca, Ellen, Thomas, Paul, Mary. BS, Kans. State U., Manhattan, 1946; MA, Cornell U., 1949. Tchr. Dickinson County Cmty. H.S., Kans., 1946-48, Nat. Coll. Edn., Chgo., 1949-51; co-chair Cascadia High Speed Rail, 1995—. Former chair City and State Bicycle Com., 1971-83; mem., former chair Met. Park Bd., Eugene, 1972-82; former bd. pres. Youth Symphony; city councilor City of Eugene, Oreg., 1984-92, coun. v.p., pres., 1988-90, mayor, 1993-97; v.p., pres. Eugene LWV, 1967-69. Recipient Gold Leaf award Internat. Soc. Arboriculture, 1993. Democrat. Congregational. Home: 2114 University St Eugene OR 97403 Office: City of Eugene 777 Pearl St Ste 105 Eugene OR 97401-2720

BASCONCILLO, LINDY, insurance and financial services company executive; b. Honolulu, Dec. 11, 1943; s. Catalino M. and Primitiva (Barientos) B.; children: Lisa M., Rod Alan. BA, Pacific Union Coll., 1965; MA, Azusa Pacific U., 1979. Chartered life underwriter. Tchr., vice prin. Santa Monica (Calif.) Jr. Acad., 1965-68; tchr., coach Temple City (Calif.) Unified Sch. Dist., 1968-79; sales agent N.Y. Life Ins. Co., Eugene, Oreg., 1980-81, tng. mgr., 1981-87; sales mgr. MONY Fin. Svcs., Eugene, 1987-88; sr. mktg. cons. Prudential Ins. and Fin. Svcs., Woodland Hills, Calif., 1988-89; sales mgr. Prudential Ins. and Fin. Svcs., Sacramento, 1989-91; bus., estate, retirement specialist John Deere Life Ins. Co., Calif. and Nev., 1991-94; dist. sales mgr. Mut. of Omaha, 1994-95; mng. dir. Elite Consulting, Lincoln, Calif., 1994—; brokerage dir. Nat. Life of Vt., 1995-96; reg. rep. Mass-Mutual, 1996—; bus. cons. Jr. Achievement, Eugene, 1986; pres.-elect Eugene Life Underwriters Assn., 1988, v.p., 1987; chairperson Life Underwriter Tng. Coun., 1987, moderator, 1984-86. Mem. coun. for minority edn. U. Oreg., Eugene, 1986-88; mem. Lane County Tng. and Devel. Com., Eugene, 1985-87. Mem. Sacramento Chpt. CLU's, Sacramento Life Underwriters Assn. Home: 1812 5th St Lincoln CA 95648-2328 Office: Ste 375 2180 Harvard St Sacramento CA 95815

BASHORE, IRENE SARAS, research institute administrator; b. San Jose, Calif.; d. John and Eva (Lionudakis) Saras; m. Vincent Bashore (div.); 1 child, Juliet Ann. BA, Pepperdine U., 1950; MA in Theatre Arts, Calif. State U., Fullerton, 1977. Founder, exec. dir. Inst. for Dramatic Rsch., Fullerton, Calif., 1967—.

BASICHIS, GORDON ALLEN, author, screenwriter; b. Phila., Aug. 23, 1947; s. Martin and Ruth (Gordon) B.; m. Marcia Hammond; 1 child, Casey James. BS, Temple U., 1969. Reporter Phila. Bull., 1969; writer, reporter Santa Fe News, 1971-72; with advt., pub. relations Jay Bernstein Pub. Relations, Los Angeles, 1978-80; screenwriter Metro Goldwyn Mayer Feature Films, Culver City, Calif., 1982-83; ind. writer, 1983—; pres. Moonlight, Inc., L.a., 1982—; exec. v.p. Antigua Rd. Prodns., 1996. Author: Beautiful Bad Girl: The Vicki Morgan Story, 1985, (novel) Constant Travelers, 1978; producer, dir. (video documentary) Jerry: One Man's Triumph, 1980; co-prodr. (TV series) Frank and Jesse; screenwriter (feature film) Return of the Jersey Devil, 1988, Breach of Trust, 1994; co-writer Shysters, 1996; exec. prodr. Land of Dreams, 1996-97. Mem. Dem. Nat. Com. Mem. Writers Guild Am. West, Am. Film Inst., Simon Wiesenthal Inst., Statue of Liberty/Ellis Island Found. Office: PO Box 1511 Beverly Hills CA 90213-1511

BASILE, PAUL LOUIS, JR., lawyer; b. Oakland, Calif., Dec. 27, 1945; s. Paul Louis and Roma Florence (Paris) B.; m. Linda Lou Paige, June 20, 1970; m. 2d Diane Chierichetti, Sept. 2, 1977. BA, Occidental Coll., 1968; postgrad., U. Wash., 1969; JD, UCLA, 1971. Bar: Calif. 1972, U.S. Dist. Ct. (cen. dist.) Calif. 1972, U.S. Dist. Ct. (no. dist.) Calif. 1985, U.S. Ct. Appeals (9th cir.) 1972, U.S. Tax Ct. 1977, U.S. Ct. Claims. 1978, U.S. Customs Ct. 1979, U.S. Ct. Customs and Patent Appeals 1979, U.S. Ct. Internat. Trade 1981, U.S. Supreme Ct. 1977; cert. specialist in taxation law Bd. of Legal Specialization, State Bar of Calif. Assoc. Parker, Milliken, Kohlmeier, Clark & O'Hara, L.A., 1971-72; corp. counsel TFI Cos., Inc., Irvine, Calif., 1972-73; pvt. practice L.A., 1973-80, 90-96; mem. Basile & Siener, L.A., 1980-86, Clark & Trevithick, L.A., 1986-90; ptnr. Wolf, Rifkin & Shapiro, L.A., 1990, of counsel, 1990-92; ptnr. Basile & Lane, LLP, L.A., 1996—; of counsel Shaffer, Gold & Rubaum, L.A., 1996—; gen. counsel J.W. Brown, Inc., L.A., 1980—, asst. sec., 1984-92; sec., gen. counsel Souriau, Inc., Valencia, Calif., 1981-90; v.p., sec., dir., gen. counsel Pvt. Fin. Assocs., L.A., 1983-94; gen. counsel Quest Relocation Group, Toluca Lake, Calif., 1994—, v.p. fin., 1996—. Trustee, sec. Nat. Repertory Theatre Found., 1975-94, mem. exec. com., 1976-94, chmn. bd. dirs., 1991-94; mem. fin. com., bd. dirs. Calif. Music Theatre, 1988-92; bd. dirs. March of Dimes Birth Defects Found., Los Angeles County, 1982-87, mem. exec. com., 1983-86, sec., 1985-86; dist. fin. chmn. L.A. Area coun. Boy Scouts Am., 1982-83; trustee Occidental Coll., L.A., 1989-94; active L.A. Olympic Organizing Com., Ketchum Downtown YMCA, Vols. Am. L.A., others. Mem. ABA (taxation sect., corp. tax com., vice chmn. closely held bus. com. 1992-94, chair, 1994-96, chmn. subcom. on continuing legal edn. 1990-94, chmn. subcom. on estate planning 1992, sec. 1996-97, small firm lawyers com., bus. law sect., real property sect., probate and trust law sect., spl. problems of bus. owners com., estate planning and drafting, pre-death planning issues com.), State Bar Calif. (bus. law sect., nonprofit and unicorporated orgns. com. 1989-92, taxation sect., estate planning, trust and probate sect., taxation law adv. commn. 1994—, vice chmn. 1995-96, chair 1996—), L.A. County Bar Assn. (taxation sect., com. on closely-held and pass-through entities, bus. and corps. law sect., sole practitioner section exec. com. 1995—), Beverly Hills Bar Assn. (probate, trust & estate planning section, taxation section, law practice mgmt. section), Can. Calif. C. of C. (dir. 1980-89, 2d v.p. 1983-84, 1st v.p. 1984-85, pres. 1985-87), L.A.-Vancouver Sister City Assn. (dir., exec. com. 1987-92, treas. 1987-89, pres. 1989-92), French-Am. C. of C. (councilor 1979-84, v.p. 1980, 82-84), L.A. Area C. of C. (dir. 1980-81), Occidental Coll. Alumni Assn. (pres. 1979-80, v.p. 1978-79, alumni bd. govs. 1977-81, chmn. annual fund campaign 1990-91), Grand People (bd. dirs. 1985-92, chmn. bd. 1986-92), Rotary Club of L.A. (dir. 1994-96, sergeant-at-arms 1986-87, chmn. gateway com. 1993-94, chmn. world cmty. svc. com. 1991-93, chmn. vols. Am. of L.A. com. 1988-90, chmn. golf com. 1986-87, vice-chmn. pres. com. 1985-86), Rotary Internat. (chmn. club extension com. 1995-96, cmty. svc. dir. 1993-95, chmn. gift of life com. 1992-93), Small Bus. Coun. of Am., Inc. (legal adv. bd. 1989—), The Group, Inc., Attorneys for Family Held Enterprises. Democrat. Baptist. Home: 3937 Beverly Glen Blvd Sherman Oaks CA 91423-4404 Office: Basile & Lane LLP 11400 W Olympic Blvd 9th Fl Los Angeles CA 90064-1565

BASINGER, RICHARD LEE, lawyer; b. Canton, Ohio, Nov. 24, 1941; s. Eldon R. and Alice M. (Bartholomew) B.; m. Rita Evelyn Gover, May 14, 1965; children: David A., Darron M. BA in Edn., Ariz. State U., 1963; postgrad. Macalester Coll., 1968-69; JD, U. Ariz., 1973. Bar: Ariz. 1973, U.S. Dist. Ct. Ariz. 1973, U.S. Tax Ct. 1977, U.S. Ct. Appeals (6th cir.) 1975, U.S. Ct. Appeals (9th cir.) 1976, U.S. Supreme Ct. 1977; cert. arbitrator. Assoc. law offices, Phoenix, 1973-74; sole practice, Scottsdale, Ariz. 1974-75; pres. Basinger & Assocs., P.C., Scottsdale, 1975—, also bd. dirs. Contbr. articles to profl. jours. Bd. dirs. Masters Trail Ventures, Scottsdale, 1984-85, Here's Life, Ariz., Scottsdale, 1976—; precinct committeeman Republican Party, Phoenix, 1983—; bd. dir. Ariz. Coll. of the Bible, 1992-93. NSF grantee, 1968-69. Mem. ABA, Ariz. Bar Assn., Maricopa County Bar Assn., Ariz. State Horseman's Assn. (bd. dirs. 1984-86, 1st v.p. 1986), Scottsdale Bar Assn., Western Saddle Club (bd. dirs. 1983-86, pres. 1985-86), Scottsdale Saddle Club, Saguaro Saddle Club. Baptist. Office: Basinger & Assocs PC 5010 E Shea Blvd Ste A-208 Scottsdale AZ 85254-4681

BASLER, RICHARD ALAN, biomedical instruments manufacturer; b. San Francisco, Sept. 12, 1939; s. Henry Edwin and Margaret Henrietta (Cooper) B.; m. Carol Audrey Foster, Aug. 4, 1962; children: Rodney Giles, Eric Richard. BA, U. Calif., Berkeley, 1960; MBA, U. Phoenix, Irvine, Calif., 1983. Indsl. engr., prodn. supt. Standard Register, Oakland and Corcoran, Calif., 1967-72; knitting supt. Duplan Knits West, Carson, Calif., 1972-75; prodn. supr. Am. Edwards Labs., Irvine, 1976-78, chief indsl. engr., 1978-80, supr. mfg. engring., 1980-86, with engring. systems devel., 1986-87; mgr. quality assurance/quality control Cardiovascular Devices Inc., 1987-88; dir. quality assurance/quality control Applied Vascular Devices Inc., 1988-90, dir. compliance, 1990-94; dir. compliance Micro Therapeutics, Inc., 1994-96; v.p. ops. Laurus Med. Corp., Irvine, Calif., 1996—; owner Internat. Numismatics, Irvine, 1974—. Editor Calif. Engr. mag., 1959; contbr. articles to mags. Bd. dirs. UNCAP, Inc., L.A., 1980-82; pres. Colonnade of History, 1990—. Recipient Kenneth Brainard Meml. Literary award, George Bennett Meml. Literary award. Mem. Am. Soc. Quality Control, U.S. Kerry Blue Terrier Club (gov. 1983-85), Gt. Western Terrier (bd. dirs. 1979-92). Republican. Office: Laurus Med Corp 10 Chrysler Ste B Irving CA 92618

BASS, AUDREY, commodities trader; b. 1946. With Berger & Plate Co., San Francisco, 1966-74, Berger & Co., San Francisco, 1974-88; asst. sec., treas. Berdex Internat. Inc., San Francisco, 1988—. Office: Berdex International Inc 1050 Sansome St Ste 300 San Francisco CA 94111-1325*

BASS, CHARLES MORRIS, financial and systems consultant; b. Miami, Fla., Sept. 21, 1949; s. Benjamin and Ellen Lucille (Williams) B; children: Cheryl Ellen, Benjamin Charles. BA, U. Md., 1972; MS, Am. Coll., 1982. CLU; chartered fin. cons. Group rep. Monumental Life Ins. Co., 1972-73; agt. Equitable Life Ins. Co., N.Y., 1973-76; ptnr. Bass, Bridge and Assocs., Columbia, Md., 1976-81; pres. Multi-Fin Svc., Inc., Balt., 1981-83; gen. mgr. Mfrs. Fin. Group, Denver, 1983-85; ptnr. Regency Econometrics Group, Denver, 1985—; speaker in field. Chmn. United Way Howard County, 1977-78; mem. Econ. Devel. Adv. Coun. Howard County, 1979-83. Served with USAF, 1968-71. Mem. Million Dollar Round Table, Nat. Assn. Life Underwriters, Am. Soc. C.L.U.s, Gen. Agts. and Mgrs. Assn., Columbia Life Underwriters Assn. (pres. 1982), Estate Planning Coun., Howard County C. of C., Howard County Bus. Club, Columbia Bus. Exchange. Methodist. Home and Office: 5690 W Coal Mine Ave Littleton CO 80123

BASS, DAVID LOREN, artist; b. Conway, Ark., July 19, 1943; s. Deward Clark Bass and Gillian Henrietta (Oliver) Bass Carter. BS in Edn., Ark. State Tchrs., Coll., 1965; student Aspen Sch. Contemporary Art, summer 1964; MFA, U. N.C.-Greensboro, 1975; postgrad. U. N.C., Chapel Hill, summer 1974. Tchr. 7th-8th grades Met. Schs. Nashville and Davidson County, Tenn., 1965-67; tchr. 7th-12th grades U.S. Def. Dept., Kenitra, Morocco, 1967-73; artist, Greensboro, N.C., 1975-92, Santa Fe, 1992—; artist-in-residence Washington and Lee U., Lexington, Va., 1976; curator Peter Agostini sculpture exhbn. DuPont Art Gallery, Lexington, 1976; cons. Waterworks Gallery, Salisbury, N.C., 1983; dir. United Arts Council, Greensboro, 1978-80, Ctr. for Creative Arts, Greensboro, 1978-80, Green Hill Ctr. for N.C. Art, Greensboro, 1977-80, 83—. One-man shows include: Theater Art Gallery, High Point, N.C., 1977, 82, 90, Asheville Art Mus., 1980, Recent Works, 1985, St. John's Mus. Art, Wilmington, N.C., 1989; group shows include: Miss. Mus. Art, Jackson, 1980, Biennial Exhbn. Piedmont Painting, Mint Mus., Charlotte, N.C., 1983, Equitable Gallery, N.Y.C., 1994, Springfield (Mo.) Mus. Art, 1993, Hickory (N.C.) Mus. Art, 1994. Bd. dirs. O. Henry Festival, Greensboro, 1985. Fellow Corp. Yaddo, Saratoga Springs, N.Y., 1978, 81, 84. Ossabaw Island Project, Ga., 1979, Va. Ctr. for Creative Arts, Sweetbriar, 1978. Mem. Am. Inst. Archaeology, Santa Fe Contemporary Art, Ctr. for Contemporary Art/Santa Fe. Home: 319 Villeros St Santa Fe NM 87501-1424 Studio: 821 Canyon Rd Santa Fe NM 87501

BASS, HAROLD NEAL, pediatrician, medical geneticist; b. Chgo., Apr. 14, 1939; s. Louis A. and Minnie (Schachter) B.; m. Phyllis Appell, June 25, 1961; children: Laura Renee, Alana Suzanne. Student, U. Ill., 1956-59; MS in Pharmacology, U. Chgo., 1963, MD, 1963. Diplomate Am. Bd. Pediatrics, Am. Bd. Med. Genetics, Nat. Bd. Med. Examiners. Intern Children's Meml. Hosp., Chgo., 1963-64; resident Children's Meml. Hosp., 1964-65, chief resident, 1965-66, fellow in med. genetics, 1965-66; chief pediatrics and profl. svcs. Norton AFB Hosp., Calif., 1966-68; attending pediatrician/med. geneticist Kaiser Permanente Med. Ctr., Panorama City, Calif., 1968—; dir. med. genetics prog. Kaiser Permanente Med. Care Program So. Calif., 1987—; clin. prof. pediatrics UCLA Med. Sch., 1970—; pres. med. staff Kaiser Permanente Med. Ctr., 1989; adj. prof. biology Calif. State U., Northridge, 1995—. Contbr. articles to profl. jours. Mem. transp. commn. San Fernando Valley, City of L.A., 1973-78. Capt. M.C., USAF, 1966-68. Fellow Am. Coll. Human Genetics, Western Soc. Pediat. Rsch., L.A. Pediats. Soc., San Fernando Valley Interfaith Coun., Pacific S.W. Regional Genetics Network, Handgun Control, ACLU, Am. Soc. Human Genetics, Amnesty Internat. Democrat. Jewish. Home: 11922 Dunnicliffe Ct Northridge CA 91326-1324 Office: Kaiser Permanente Med Ctr 13652 Cantara St Panorama City CA 91402-5423

BASS, MARTHA POSTLETHWAITE, high school principal; b. Wichita, Kans., Dec. 6, 1942; d. John Emmett and Norma Louise (Lanning) Postlethwaite; m. Elmer Lee Bass, July 22, 1981; step children: Sheryl, Terry. BA in Edn., U. N.Mex., 1964, MA, 1966. Endl. lic. adminstr., supt., English tchr., drama speech tchr., counselor. Asst. dean women, instr. Hanover (Ind.) Coll., 1966-68; asst. dean women U. N.Mex., Alburquerque, 1968-69; elem. counselor Alburquerque Pub. Schs., 1969-74, guidance coord., 1974-77, high sch. asst. prin., 1977-87; high sch. prin. Del Norte High Sch. Alburquerque Pub. Schs., 1987-97; ret., 1997; bd. dirs. Albuquerque Child Guidance Ctr.; pres., cons. Acad. Ednl. Leadership, Alburquerque, 1986-90. Title VII Fed. grantee Child Encouragement Project, Alburquerque, 1977; named Woman on the Move YWCA, Alburquerque, 1990. Mem. Nat. Assn. Secondary Sch. Prins., Albuquerque Assn. Secondary Sch. Prins. (past bd. dirs., treas. 1986-87), Rotary Club of Albuquerque (RYLA chair 1990-93). Office: Del Norte High Sch 5323 Montgomery Blvd NE Albuquerque NM 87109-1302

BASSETT, CAROL ANN, journalism educator, freelance writer, producer; b. Langley AFB, Va., Mar. 2, 1953; d. William Brainard and Genevieve (Rivaldo) B. BA summa cum laude in Humanities, Ariz. State U., 1977; MA in Journalism, U. Ariz., 1982. Ptnr. Desert West News, Tucson, 1985-90; freelance writer Tucson, 1980-95; freelance writer for mags. Missoula, Mont., 1995—; mem. faculty Sch. Journalism U. Mont., Missoula, 1996—. Editor Tucson Weekly, 1989-90; contbr. numerous articles to nat. and internat. mags. including N.Y. Times. Recipient 2d Place Gen. Reporting award Ariz. Press Club, 1987, Gold medal for best environ. documentary Houston Internat. Film Festival, 1990, 1st Place Gen. Reporting award Ariz. Press Club, 1992, Silver Medal for Energy Issues documentary, Houston Internat. Film Festival, 1992; co-recipient Alfred I. duPont Columbia award, 1984-85, First Place award Investigative Reporting, 1986, 1st Place Polit. Reporting, 1989, First Amendment Journalism award, 1986; grantee Fund for Investigative Journalism, 1985, 87, Corp. for Pub. Broadcasting, 1988, Oxfam Am., 1991.

BASSETT, EDWARD POWERS, university official; b. Boston, Feb. 27, 1929; s. Fraser W. and Fanny (Powers) B.; m. Karen Elizabeth Jack, Dec. 21, 1954; children: Sarah Jack Bassett Williams, Laura Powers, Lisa Wightman. AB, Washington and Lee U., 1951, LLD, 1984; MA, U. Mich., 1955; PhD, U. Iowa, 1967. Ct. reporter Louisville Courier-Jour., 1955-56; asst. editor Falmouth (Mass.) Enterprise, 1956-57; city editor Anderson (Ind.) Herald, 1957-58; editorial writer Longview (Wash.) Daily News, 1958-60; instr., pub. U. Iowa, 1960-67; asst. prof. journalism U. Mich., 1967-70, acting chmn. dept. journalism, 1969-70; dean Sch. Journalism U. Kans., 1970-74, assoc. vice chancellor acad. affairs, 1974-75; dir. Sch. Journalism U. So. Calif., 1975-80; editor Statesman-Jour., Salem, Oreg., 1980-84; dean Medill Sch. Journalism Northwestern U., Evanston, Ill., 1984-89; McKenzie scholar, dir. Sch. Communications U. Wash., Seattle, 1989-96, dir. grad. sch. libr. and info. sci., 1996—; adj. prof. Can. studies U. Wash., 1992—. Recipient citation for reporting Am. Polit. Sci. Assn., 1960. Mem. Assn. Edn. in Journalism and Mass Comm. (pres. 1975-76), Am. Assn. Schs. and Depts. Journalism (pres. 1974-75, Freedom Forum Adminstr. medal 1993), Soc. Profl. Journalists. Office: Univ of Washington Sch of Communications Box 353740 Seattle WA 98195-3740

BASSMAN, THEDA RITA, writer; b. Jan. 1, 1920; d. Morris and Lena (Rothbart) Rothblatt; m. Alexander Newman, Dec. 29, 1940 (div. Dec. 1959); children: Leslie Claudia, Gary Charles; m. Michael Melvin Bassman, Aug. 31, 1969. Author: Southwestern Indian Art: Hopi Kachina Dolls and Their Carvers, 1991, Zuni Jewelry, 1992, The Beauty of Hopi Jewelry, 1993, The Kachina Dolls of Cecil Calnimptewa, 1994, The Beauty of Navajo Jewelry, 1997, Treasures of the Hopi, 1997, Treasures of the Navajo, 1997, Treasures of the Zuni, 1997. Del. Dem. Nat. Conv., Fresno, 1950s.

BASU, ASOKE ARIEL, sociologist, educator; b. Calcutta, India, Apr. 28, 1938; came to U.S., 1958; s. Sri Sudhir and Srimati Ila (Dutta) B.; m. Mollie Saine Pope, Nov. 13, 1944; 1 child, Melissa. BA in Sociology, W.Va. U., 1961; MA in Sociology, Okla. U., 1963, PhD in Polit. Sci., 1966. Asst. prof.sociology U. So. Calif., Los Angeles, 1966-68; prof. Calif. State U., Hayward, 1968—; research assoc., Ctr. for S. Asian Studies U. Calif., Berkeley, 1978-79; spl. asst. to the dean Sch. of Arts, Letters and Social Scis. Calif. State U., Hayward; rsch. assoc. dept. sociology U. Calif., Berkeley, 1992-96; chair dept. sociology Calif. State U., Hayward, 1992-95; vis. scholar Harvard U., Boston, 1973, Hoover Inst., Stanford, Calif., 1981-83. Author: Elementary Statistical Theory in Society, 1976, Culture, Politics and Critical Academics, 1981; co-author: Poverty in America: The Welfare Dilemma, 1981; contbr. articles to profl. jours. Named Outstanding Immigrant Internat. Inst. of the East Bay, 1972; recipient Scholarly Pub. award, Calif. State U., Northridge, 1981; Sr. Fulbright lectureship Council Internat. Exchange of Scholars, 1984-85; Sr. Smithsonian Research fellow Am. Inst. Indian Studies, 1985, Adminstrv. fellow Calif. State U. Chancellor's Office, 1987-88; Fulbright grantee U.S. Dept. Edn., 1988-89. Fellow AAAS; nen. Indian Sociol. Assn. (life), Internat. Soc. Assn. (pres. research com. sociology edn.), Pacific Soc. Assn. (chmn. com. status of minorities inthe profession). Home: 2378 Woolsey St Berkeley CA 94705-1931 Office: Calif State U Dept Sociology Hayward CA 94542

BATABYAL, AMITRAJEET AMARNATH, economics educator; b. Chittaranjan, India, Sept. 6, 1965; came to U.S. 1983; s. Amar Nath and Sutapa (Bhattasali) B.; m. Swapna Bhattacharya, Mar. 8, 1995; 1 child, Sanjana S. BS with honors and distinction, Cornell U., 1987; MS, U. Minn., 1990; PhD, U. Calif., Berkeley, 1994. Asst. prof. econs. Utah State U., Logan, 1995—; vis. asst. prof. econs. Coll. William & Mary, Williamsburg, Va., 1994-95; legal asst. Spiegel & McDiarmid, Washington, 1987-88; Smith lectr. Brigham Young U., 1997. Contbr. articles to profl. jours. Rsch. grantee USDA, Berkeley, 1992-94; Dorab Tata scholar, India, 1983. Mem. Am. Econs. Assn., Assn. Environ. and Resource Economists, Am. Agrl. Econs. Assn., Internat. Soc. for Ecol. Econs. Home: 278 W 1140 N Logan UT 84341 Office: Utah State U Dept Econs Logan UT 84322-3530

BATCHELOR, KAREN LEE, English language educator; b. Oregon City, Oreg., June 17, 1948; d. Jewel Elaine Durham; m. Luis Armando, Mar. 17, 1978 (div. Aug. 1988); children: Virginia, Travis. BA in English, San Francisco State U., 1971, MA in English, 1980. Vol. U.S. Peace Corps, Andong, South Korea, 1972-74; tchr. English as second lang. City Coll. San Francisco, 1975—; tchr. trainer U. Calif., Berkeley, 1986—; acad. specialist USIA, 1991—; speaker in field. Co-author: (textbooks) Discovering English, 1981, In Plain English, 1985, More Plain English, 1986, The Writing Challenge, 1990; contbr. articles to profl. jorus. Mem. Tchrs. English to Speakers of Other Langs., Calif. Tchrs. English to Speakers of Other Langs. Office: City Coll San Francisco 50 Phelan Box L 168 San Francisco CA 94112

BATEMAN, DAVID ALFRED, lawyer; b. Pitts., Jan. 28, 1946; s. Alfred V. and Ruth G. (Howe) B.; m. Trudy A. Heath, Mar. 13, 1948; children: Devin C., Mark C. A.B. in Geology, U. Calif.-Riverside, 1966; J.D., U. San Diego, 1969; LL.M., Georgetown U., 1978. Bar: Calif. 1970, U.S. Dist. Ct. (so. dist.) Calif. 1970, U.S. Ct. Mil. Appeals 1972, Wash. 1973, U.S. Dist. Ct. (we. dist.) Wash. 1973, U.S. Supreme Ct. 1974, D.C. 1976, U.S. Dist. Ct. D.C. 1977, U.S. Ct. Claims 1979, U.S. Ct. Appeals (9th cir.) 1981. Assoc. Daubney, Banche, Patterson and Nares, Oceanside, Calif., 1969-72; asst. atty. gen. State of Wash., Olympia, 1977-81; ptnr. Bateman & Woodring, Olympia, 1981-85, Woodring, Bateman & Westbrook, 1985-89, Hanemann & Bateman, 1989-92, Hanemann, Bateman & Jones, 1992—; instr. Am. Inst. Banking, San Diego, 1972, U. Puget Sound, Olympia campus, spring, 1979. Served to capt. JAGC, USAF, 1972-77; col. JAGC, USAFR, 1977—. Mem. Wash. State Bar Assn. Roman Catholic. Club: Rotary (past chmn. internat. services com.).

BATEMAN, JANE BRONWYN, ophthalmology educator; b. Rochester, Minn., Aug. 17, 1948; d. Gordon and Olive Bateman; m. Douglas Hershey. BA in Biochemistry, U. Calif., Berkeley, 1970; MD, Columbia U., 1974. Cert. mem. Am. Bd. Human Genetics, diplomate Nat. Bd. Med. Examiners, Am. Bd. Ophthalmology. Intern in internal medicine UCLA Ctr. For Health Scis., L.A., 1974-75; resident in ophthalmology Jules Stein Eye Inst. - UCLA, 1975-78, fellow in pediat. ophthalmology and strabismus, 1978; fellow in pediat. ophthalmology and strabismus Nat. Childrens' Med. Ctr., Washington, 1979; fellow in ophthalmic genetics Johns Hopkins U., Balt., 1979-80; asst. prof. in residence dept. ophthalmology UCLA Sch. Medicine, 1980-84, assoc. prof. in residence, 1984-90, prof. in residence, 1990-95; chair dept. ophthalmology U. Colo., Denver, 1995—; mem. staff UCLA Med. Ctr., 1980-95, Santa Monica (Calif.) Hosp. Med. Ctr., 1990-95, U. Colo. Ctr. Health Scis., Denver, 1995—; vis. prof. Pacific Presbyn. Med. Ctr., 1990, Georgetown U., 1993; lectr. Duke U., 1993, numerous others; rsch. presenter in field; assoc. examiner Am. Bd. Ophthalmology, 1984, 86, 88, 90; tech. expert panel Harvard Resource-based Value Scale study, 1988-93; rsch. award selection com. Am. Assn. Med. Colls., 1991, nominating com., coun. acad. socs., 1994; spl. study sect. Visual Scis. B Study Sect. NIH, 1993; bd. dirs. Women in Ophthalmology, 1993-94, Glaucoma Rsch. Found., 1994—, Pan-Am. Ophthal. Found., 1995—, sec.-treas 1995—. Author: Basic Ophthalmology for Medical Students and Practitioners of Medicine, 1993; contbr. over 70 articles and book revs. to profl. jours.; mem. editl. bd. Am. Jour. Ophthalmology, 1991—, Revista "Sociedad Ecuatoriana de Oftalmologia", 1991—, Investigative Ophthalmology & Visual Sci., 1992—, Molecular Vision, 1996—; co-editor Noticiero Oftalmologico Panamericano, 1995—; reviewer Am. Jour. Mental Deficiency, 1982, Graefe's Archive for Clin. and Exptl. Ophthalmology, 1984, 88, 89, Am. Jour. Ophthalmology, 1984-86, 88-96, Archives of Ophthalmology, 1985, 87-90, 93, 96, Ophthalmology, 1986, 88, 90-93, 95, (book) Ophthalmic Paediatrics and Genetics Survey of Ophthalmology, 1986, Jour. Pediat. Ophthalmology and Strabismus, 1987, 89-91, 96, Survey of Ophthalmology, 1987, 90, Math. Bioscis., 1988, Am. Jour. Human Genetics, 1988-94, Investigative Ophthalmology, 1989, Exptl. Eye Rsch., 1989-90, 94, Clin. Genetics, 1990, Genomics, 1991-93, 96, Am. Jour. Diseases in Children, 1992, Ophthalmic Pediat. and Genetics, 1993-94, Investigative Ophthalmology and Visual Sci., 1993-96, Dysmorphology & Clin. Genetics, 1994, Current Eye Rsch., 1994, Devel. Brain Dysfunction, 1995, Ophthalmic Genetics, 1995, German Jour. Ophthalmology, 1995. Participant Little People of Am. ann. meeting, 1980, Teamwork, Do It Together program spl. edn. divsn. Calif. State U., 1986, Retinitis Pigmentosa Found. program Jules Stein Inst., 1990; lectr. for Spanish speaking parents Frances Blend Sch., 1981; lectr. Blind childrens' Ctr., L.A., 1992; cons. Family Circle Mag., 1995. Heed Ophthalmic fellow 1979, Mary and William Greve Internat. Rsch. scholar 1987, grantee Vision Rsch. Ctr. Nat. Eye Inst., 1980-81, grantee Nat. Eye Inst. NIH, 1986-87, 90-94, 95—, grantee Charles Ruggles Found., 1987—, grantee Nat. Retinitis Pigmentosa Found., 1987—, grantee Kirschgessner Ophthalmology Endowment Fund, 1994-95; recipient Rsch. to Prevent Blindness Manpower award 1981. Fellow Am. Coll. Med. Genetics (founding); mem. ACS, AAUP, Internat. Strabismological Assn., Am. Acad. Ophthalmology (rep. to coun. on acad. socs. Am. Assn. Med. Colls., 1988—, alt. councillor 1989-90, councillor 1990—, med. student edn. com. 1989-95, assoc. sec. 1993—, ins. com. 1989-94, pediat. ophthalmology panel of quality of care, 1990—, chair hearing com. on quality of care/ outcomes, 1993, mem. nominating com., 1993, com. state orgnl. devel. 1993-96, selection com. Disting. Tchr. Award, 1994, mem. hearing com. on future of eye care, 1994, chair pediat. PPP panel, 1995—, Honor award 1986), Am. Assn. Pediat. Ophthalmology and Strabismus (rsch. com. 1985-86, bd. dirs. 1987-89, 3d party payors com. 1989-92, socioecon. com. 1991-95, chair 1992-95, sec.-treas. 1995—, chair fin. com. 1995—, Honor award 1991), Am. Med. Women's Assn., Am. Ophthal. Soc., Am. Soc. Human Genetics, Assn. Women Surgeons, Calif. Assn. Ophthalmology (asst. v.p. edn. and meetings 1989-90, v.p. edn. and meetings 1990-92, rep. dist. 4B, bd. dirs. 1990-95, chair ann. ednl. confs. 1990, 91), Calif. Med. Assn., Children's Eye Care Found., Colombian Assn. Ophthalmology (hon.), Costenbader Alumni Assn. (nominating com. 1986, bd. dirs., mem. at large, 1990-93), Ecuadorian Soc. Ophthalmology (hon.), L.A. County Med. Assn., L.A. County Med. Women's Assn., L.A. Soc. Ophthalmology (program chair 1993-94, treas. 1994-95), Pan Am. Assn. Ophthalmology (bd. dirs. 1991—, chair vis. prof. program 1991-95, sec.-treas. English sect., 1995—), UCLA Dept. Ophthalmology Assn., Wilmer Residents Assn., Mortar Bd., Prytanean Soc., Phi Beta Kappa, Alpha Omega Alpha. Office: U Colo Box B204 4200 E 9th Ave Denver CO 80262

BATEMAN, MERRILL JOSEPH, university president; b. Lehi, Utah, June 19, 1936; s. Joseph Fredric and Belva (Smith) B.; m. Marilyn Scholes, Mar. 23, 1959; children: Michael, Mark, Michele, Melisa, Merilee, Matthew, McKay. BA, U. Utah, 1960; PhD, MIT, 1965. Exec. Mars, Inc., 1971-75; dean Sch. Mgmt. Brigham Young U., Provo, Utah, 1975-79; pres. Brigham Young U., 1996—; mgmt. cons. Provo, 1979-92; mem. 2d Quorum of 70 LDS Ch., Salt Lake City, 1992-94, presiding bishop, 1994-95, mem. 1st Quorum of 70, 1996—; pres. Deseret Mgmt. Corp., Salt Lake City, 1993-95. 1st lt. USAF, 1964-67. Danforth fellow, 1960-64, Woodrow Wilson fellow, 1960-61. Mem. Am. Assn. Presidents of Colls. and Univs., Western Athletic Conf. Coun. of Presidents, Phi Kappa Phi, Phi Beta Kappa. Office: Brigham Young U PO Box 21346 Provo UT 84602

BATES, CHARLES EMERSON, library administrator; b. Los Angeles, Dec. 1, 1946; s. Willard Emerson Bates and Erica (Schmidt) Bates Beckwith; m. Mary Joan Genz, Aug. 7, 1971; children—Christopher, Noah, Colin. BA, Valparaiso U., 1968; MEd, Loyola U., Chgo., 1970; MLS, Rosary Coll., 1973. Head of reference Decatur Pub. Libr., Ill., 1973-74; cons. Rolling Prairie Libr. System, Decatur, 1974-76; asst. dir. Fond du Lac Pub. Libr., Wis., 1976-81; dir. Pueblo Libr. Dist., Colo., 1981—. Bd. dirs. Pueblo United Way, 1982-86; pres., bd. dirs. Sangre de Cristo Arts and Conf. Ctr., Pueblo, 1990-96; pres. bd. dirs. Rosemount Victorian House Mus., Pueblo, 1984-90 . Mem. ALA, Colo. Libr. Assn., Ark. Valley Libr. System (pres. 1984-85, 89-90, 96-97), Rotary (pres. bd. dirs. 1981—). Lutheran. Office: Pueblo Libr Dist McClelland Libr 100 E Abriendo Ave Pueblo CO 81004-4232

BATES, CHARLES WALTER, human resources executive, lawyer, internal auditor; b. Detroit, June 28, 1953; s. E. Frederick and Virginia Marion (Nunneley) B. BA in Psychology and Econs. cum laude, Mich. State U., 1975, M in Labor and Indsl. Rels., 1977; postgrad. DePaul U., 1979-80; JD William Mitchell Coll. Law, 1984. Bar: Wash. 1990, U.S. Dist. Ct. (we. dist.) Washington, 1992; cert. sr. profl. in human resources. Vista vol., paralegal, Ventura County Legal Aid Assn. (now Channel Counties Legal Aid Assn.), Calif., 1975-76; job analyst Gen. Mills, Inc., Mpls., 1977-78, plant pers. asst. II, Chgo., 1978-80, asst. plant pers. mgr., Chgo., 1980-81, pers. mgr. consumer foods mktg., Mpls., 1981-82; pers. mgr. consumer foods mktg. divs. Saluto Pizza, Mpls., 1982-84; human resources mgr. Western div., Godfather's Pizza, Inc., Costa Mesa, Calif., 1984-85, human resources mgr. Western U.S., Can., Bellevue, Washington, 1985-91; dir. human resources. Royal Seafoods, Inc., Seattle, 1991-92, dir. human resources and employee rels. counsel, 1992-94, dir. human resources and coun., 1994-95; sr. internal auditor PACCAR, Inc, Bellevue, Wash., 1995—; instr. employee and labor rels., Lake Wash. Tech. Coll., 1992-94. mem. editorial adv. bd. Recruitment Today mag., 1990-91. Candidate for lt. gov., 1982, Minn.; asst. scoutmaster Boy Scouts Am., 1971—, asst. advisor-activities Order of Arrow, 1989-92, 96— (recipient Vigil Honor 1990); elected Sammamish Community Coun., Bellevue, 1989, councilman, 1990-93; mem. E. Bellevue Transp. Study Adv. Group, 1989-92. Rep. precinct com. officer, 1990-94; del. state conv. Wash. State Rep. Party, 1992, 94. Recipient Scouter's Tng. award Boy Scouts Am., 1979, Dist. award of merit, 1991, Nat. Vantage Recruiting award, 1990. Mem. ABA (labor and employment law), Nat. Eagle Scout Assn., N.W. Human Resources Mgmt. Assn. (Lake Washington chpt.), Soc. for Human Resources Mgmt, Wash. State Bar Assn., King County Bar Assn. (labor law), Mich. State U. Alumni Assn. Home: 232 168th Ave NE Bellevue WA 98008-4522 Office: PACCAR Inc 777 106th Ave NE Bellevue WA 98004-5001

BATES, CRAIG DANA, curator, ethnographer, government official; b. Oakland, Calif., Aug. 2, 1952; s. Dana Raymond and June (Robinson) B.; m. Jennifer Dawn Bernido, May 12, 1973 (div. 1987); 1 child, Carson Dana. Park technician Nat. Park Svc., Yosemite National Park, Calif., 1973-76, Indian cultural specialist, 1976-80, asst. curator, 1980-82, curator ethnography, 1982—; rsch. assoc. Santa Barbara (Calif.) Mus. Natural History, 1983—; cons. Calif. Indian exhbn. SW Mus., L.A., 1985, Culin exhbn. Bklyn. Mus., 1988-89, Lowie Mus. Anthropology, U. Calif., Berkeley, 1990. Co-author: (with Martha Lee) Tradition and Innovation: A Basket History of the Indians of the Yosemite Mono Lake Area, 1990; contbr. more than 90 articles on Am. Indian culture to profl. jours. Office: Nat Park Svc Yosemite Mus PO Box 577 Yosemite National Park CA 95389-0577*

BATES, DEBORAH FILBECK, career counselor; b. Stockton, Calif., Dec. 27, 1963; d. William Frederick Filbeck and Bettegene (Steinbrecher) Holley; m. Russell Allan Bates, Jan. 3, 1993; children: Laura, Tess. AA in Performing Arts and English, San Joaquin Delta Coll., 1986; BA in Psychology, Calif. State U., Chico, 1993; postgrad., John F. Kennedy U., Orinda, Calif. Greater Avenues to Independence assessment cert. Summer youth employment program coord. Job Tng. Ctr. of Tehama County, Red Bluff, Calif., 1993; job developer Job Tng. Ctr. of Tehama County, Red Bluff, 1994, case mgr., 1995—; mem. recruiting bd. Head Start, Los Molinos, Calif., 1994. Mem. ACA., 1995—. Office: Job Tng Ctr of Tehama County 333 Main St Red Bluff CA 96080-3413

BATES, DWIGHT LEE, mechanical engineer; b. Miles City, Mont., Aug. 19, 1943; s. Edmond Russell and Verna Elizabeth (Johnson) B.; m. Diane Marie Seppi, Aug. 19, 1967. BSME, U. Wyo., 1966; MBA in Mktg., Seattle U., 1971. Registered profl. engr., Wash. Rsch. engr. comml. airplane div. Boeing Co., Seattle, 1966-70; product devel. engr. internat. mktg. div. Warn Industries, Seattle, 1972-73, 1972-73; prin. engr. Heath Tecna, Kent, Wash., 1973-74; mech. design engr. Puget sound naval shipyard U.S. Dept. Def., Bremerton, Wash., 1974-78; supervisory indsl. engr. Supship Seattle, 1978-85; sr. specialist engr. Comml. Airplane div. Boeing Co., Seattle, 1985—; cons. in field. Contbr. publs. in field. Pres. Melrose E. Condo Assn., Seattle, 1978-81; bus. adv. coun. Resource Ctr. for Handicapped. With USCG Aux. Recipient 2 letters of appreciation and 2 letters of commendation U.S. Dept. Def., award Am. Mktg. Assn., 1973; honored as grad. with successful career U. Wyo. Coll. Engring., 1993. Mem. Resource Ctr. for Handicapped Bus. Adv. Coun. (7 letters of commendation, Mus. Flight award, Seattle Block Capt. award), AIAA (pres. Laramie, Wyo. chpt. 1966), NSPE, Wash. State Profl. Engrs. Soc., Wash. State Power Squadron, Am. Inst. Indsl. Engrs., Seattle U. MBA Assn.. Democrat. Lutheran. Home: 1912 E Mcgraw St Seattle WA 98112-2629 Office: Boeing Co PO Box 707 Seattle WA 98111-0707

BATES, GEORGE E., oil industry executive; b. 1943. BS, U. Hawaii, 1967, MBA, 1981. With Gasco, Inc., Honolulu, 1967-91. Office: B H P Hawaii Inc 733 Bishop St Ste 2700 Honolulu HI 96813-4022*

BATES, JAMES ROBERT, newspaper editor; b. Great Bend, Kans., Dec. 12, 1954; s. Robert Lane and Phyllis Fern (Koltermann) B.; m. Jennifer Petkus, Nov. 7, 1986. BS, U. Kans., 1977; postgrad., U. Colo., 1979-80. Copy editor Springfield (Mo.) Daily News, 1977-78; reporter Colo. Springs (Colo.) Sun, 1978-79, news editor, 1980-86; copy editor, asst. news editor Denver Post, 1986-87, news editor, 1987-89, exec. news editor, 1989—. Recipient design and editing awards Colo. Press Assn., Colo. AP, 1986—. Mem. Soc. Newspaper Design. Office: The Denver Post 1560 Broadway Denver CO 80202-6000

BATES, KENNETH NORRIS, scientist; b. Dallas, June 15, 1949; s. Kenneth L. Bates and Lesta J. (Norris) Johnson; m. Carmen Lorz, June 14, 1981; children: Kevin, Cassandra. BS, U. Tex., 1972; MS, Stanford (Calif.) U., 1975, PhD, 1982. Project mgr. Hewlett Packard, Palo Alto, Calif., 1979-82; prin. engr. Advanced Tech. Labs., Bothell, Wash., 1982-85; founder, v.p. engring. Ariel Electronics, Sunnyvale, Calif., 1985-89; sr. scientist KLA Instruments Corp., Springfield, Oreg., 1989-91; pres. Applied Concepts, Eugene, Oreg., 1991—. Contbr. articles on materials, signal processing, acoustics and ednl. aids to profl. jours.; inventor solar collector device. Mem. AAAS, IEEE. Office: Applied Concepts 9210 SW Cutter Pl Beaverton OR 97008

BATINA, KIMBERLY JEANNE, elementary education educator; b. Trenton, N.J., Apr. 7, 1964; d. John William and Sandra Jeanne (White) Marquette; m. John Robert Batina, June 24, 1995; 1 child, Kori Eileen. BA in Lang. Arts, U. Tex., 1986; MA in Tchg., Trenton State Coll., 1991. Paralegal Schrader, Harrison, Segal and Lewis, Phila., 1987-90; tchr. Santa Cruz Valley Union H.S., Eloy, Ariz., 1992-94, Picacho (Ariz.) Elem. Sch., 1994—. Mem. NEA, Ariz. Edn. Assn. Republican. Roman Catholic. Home: 1669 E Kielly Ln Casa Grande AZ 85222 Office: PO Box 8 Picacho AZ 85241

BATIZ, ENRIQUE, pianist, conductor; b. Mexico City, May 4, 1942; divorced; children: Enrique Batiz Zuk, Martha Batiz Zuk. BMus, Mexico Univ. Ctr., 1959; student, So. Meth. U., Dallas, 1960-62, Juilliard Sch. of Music, N.Y.C., 1963-66; postgrad., Warsaw (Poland) Conservatory; studied piano with Adele Marcus, 1963-66, studied conducting with Jorge Mester, 1963-66, studied piano with Zbignieg Drzewieckie, 1966-70, studied conducting with Stanislaw Wislocki, 1970. Founder, condr. Symphony Orch. of State of Mexico, 1971-83, 90—; artistic dir. Philharm. Orch. of Mexico City, 1983-89; guest condr. Royal Philharm. Orch., London, 1984—, condr. tour in Mexico, 1988, and with over 180 orchs. worldwide. Recs. include complete works of Bizet, Revueltas, Villa-Lobos: Bachianas Brazileiras 1-9, Rodrigo, Ponce; albums include The Afternoon of a Faun (Debussy), 1984 (Records award Music Trades Assn. 1984), Symphony No. 3 in C minor Op. 78 for organ (Saint-Saëns), 1985 (Best Recorded Version, Penguin Stereo Rec. Guide 1985), Petroushka (Stravinsky), 1986 (Best Record of Yr., The Sunday Times, London 1986), Rachmaninoff Symphonic Dances, Op. 45, The Isle of the Dead, Op. 29, 1992 (Best Record of Yr., CD Rev., 1992); recs. with famous soloists including Henryk Szeryng, Francisco Araiza, Aldo Ciccolini, Barbara Hendricks, Alfonso Moreno, Jorge Federico Osorio, Jorge Luis Prats and Eva Maria Zuk. Decorated officer grade Order of Rio Branco (Brazil); Van Cliburn scholar Juilliard Sch. Music, 1963-65, Carlos Trouyet scholar, 1963-69, Pan-Am. Union scholar, 1965; recipient La Lira de Oro award Sindicato Unico de Trabajadores de la Musica, 1974; named Best Condr. of Yr., Mexican Union of Theatre and Music Critics, 1971, 81, 83. Mem. Internat. Airline Passengers Assn., Club de Clubes, Cambridge Club (Mexico City). Home: Cerrada Rancho Los Colorines 11, Col Huipulco Tabla del Llano, 14380-22 Mexico City Mexico also: State of Mexico Symphony Orch, Plaza Fray Andres de Castro, Edif C 1er Piso Toluca Mexico City Mexico

BATSON, DARRELL LYNN, librarian, consultant; b. Las Vegas, Nev., Nov. 24, 1951; s. George Burnell and Olive Emily (Lang) B.; m. Laurel Jean Bushman, May 21, 1974; children—Gary Burnell, Eric Louis, Jeremy Lynn, Lacey Jean, Katrina Lauren, Genevieve Lee. A.S., Dixie Jr. Coll., 1971; B.A., Brigham Young U., 1975, M.L.S., 1976. Reference librarian Elko Library, Nev., 1977-78; outreach librarian Clark County Library, Las Vegas, 1978-80, adminstr., 1980-94, dir., 1994—; cons., 1982. Mem. ALA, Mountain Plain Library Assn., Nev. Library Assn. Republican. Mem. Ch. of Jesus Christ of Latter-day Saints. Office: Las Vegas Clark County Libr Dist 833 Las Vegas Blvd N Las Vegas NV 89101-2030*

BATSON, RAYMOND MILNER, retired cartographer; b. Lincoln, Nebr., July 8, 1931; s. Avery A. and Margaret Elizabeth (Milner) B.; m. Rhoda May Meier, Aug. 31, 1955; children: Beverly Ann Batson White, Frederick Avery, Thomas Raymond. Student, U. Colo., 1953-57, BA, 1962. Field engr., photogrammetrist U.S. Geol. Survey, Denver, 1957-63; rsch. cartographer U.S. Geol. Survey, Flagstaff, Ariz., 1963-94, chief planetary cartography, 1963-92; ret., 1994; mem. planetary cartography working group NASA, Washington, 1978-94, mem. planetary geol. and geophys. working group, 1982-92, expert mem. U.S./USSR joint working group for planetary data exch., 1988-92. Author, editor: Planetary Mapping, 1990, NASA Atlas of the Solar System, 1997. Staff sgt. USAF, 1951-52. Fellow Am. Soc. for Photogrammetry; mem. Am. Soc. Photogrammetry (chmn. extraterrestrial sci. com. 1981-88), Astron. Soc. of the Pacific (hon.), Internat. Soc. PHotogrammetry (chmn. working group 3 com. IV 1982-85), Internat. Astron. Union (working group for planetary system nomenclature com. 16, 1991-94).

BATT, PHILIP E., governor; b. Wilder, Idaho, Mar. 4, 1927; m. Jacque Fallis, 1948; children: Bill, Rebecca, Leslie. Attended, U. Idaho, 1944-48. Elected mem. Idaho State Legislature, 1965-77; lt. gov. State of Idaho, 1978-82, gov., 1995—. First pres. Idaho Food Producers; co-chmn. Wilder United Charity Auction; mem. Idaho Potato Growers Commn.; mem. bd. dirs. Wilder Farm Labor Com.; mem. bd. trustees Coll. Idaho; past pres. Idaho Hop Growers Assn., Hop Growers of Am., Homedale PTA. Office: Office of the Gov PO Box 83720 Boise ID 83720-0034

BATTISTI, DAVID STEPHEN, atmospheric sciences educator; b. Ithaca, N.Y., May 19, 1956; s. Frank Leon and Charlotte B.; m. Lynn Alison McMurdie, Sept. 14, 1985; children: Eric Michael, Adrian Thomas, Nathaniel Peter. BS in Physics, U. Mass., 1978; MS in Oceanography, U. Washington, Seattle, 1981; PhD in Atmospheric Scis., 1988. Rsch. assoc. JISAO, Seattle, 1988; asst. prof. meteorology U. Wis., Madison, 1989-90; asst. prof. atomspheric scis. U. Wash., Seattle, 1990-94, assoc. prof. atmospheric scis., 1995—, dir. JISAO, 1997—. Contbr. numerous articles to profl. jours. Mem. Am. Meteorol. Soc., Am. Geophys. Union Panels of Nat. Rsch. Coun. for NAS. Office: U Wash 351640 Dept Atmospheric Scis Seattle WA 98195

BATTISTI, PAUL ORESTE, county supervisor; b. Herkimer, N.Y., Mar. 16, 1922; s. Oreste and Ida (Fiore) B.; m. Constance Muth Drais, May 18, 1985; children—Paul J., Cathy (Mrs. D. Capage), Deborah, Thomas, Daniel, Melora, Stephen. Student, Cornell U., Ithaca, N.Y., 1947-48, U. Neb., 1951-52. With VA, 1946-75; dir. VA Hosp., Martinez, Calif., 1969-73; western region dir. San Francisco, 1973-75; adminstr. State Vets. Home Calif., 1976-86; supr. County of Napa, 1989—; chmn., CEO Medam., Inc.; dir. Med. Am. Corp.; health care cons. 1975-88; chmn. Bay Area Air Quality Mgmt. Dist.; mem. exec. bd. Assoc. Bay Area Govts.; chmn. Bay Area Regional Planning Com.; mem. exec. bd. Bay Area Econ. Forum; chmn. Napa River Flood Control Dist. Fellow Am. Coll. Hosp. Adminstrs.; mem. Hosp. Conf. No. Calif. (pres.), Nat. Assn. State Vets. Homes (pres.). Home: Silverado Country Club 117 Milliken Creek Dr Napa CA 94558-1240 Office: County Bd of Suprs County of Napa 1195 3rd St Napa CA 94559-3035

BATTS, MICHAEL STANLEY, German language educator; b. Mitcham, Eng., Aug. 2, 1929; s. Stanley George and Alixe Kathleen (Watson) B.; m. Misao Yoshida, Mar. 19, 1959; 1 dau., Anna. BA, U. London, 1952, BA with honors, 1953, LittD, 1973; PhD, U. Freiburg, Germany, 1957; M.L.S., U. Toronto, 1974. Mem. faculty U. Mainz, Germany, 1953-54, U. Basel, Switzerland, 1954-56, U. Wurzburg, Germany, 1956-58; instr. German U. Calif., Berkeley, 1958-60; mem. faculty dept. German U. B.C., Can., 1960-91; prof. U. B.C., 1967-91, head dept., 1968-80. Author: Die Form der Aventiuren im Nibelungenlied, 1961, Bruder Hansens Marienlieder, 1964, Studien zu Bruder Hansens Marienliedern, 1964, Das Hohe Mittelalter, 1969, Das Nibelungenlied-Synoptische Ausgabe, 1971, Gottfried von Strasburg, 1971, A Checklist of German Literature, 1945-75, 1977, The Bibliography of German Literature: An Historical and Critical Survey, 1978, A History of Histories of German Literature, 1835-1914, 1993; editor: Seminar, 1970-80. Served with Brit. Army, 1947-49. Alexander von Humboldt fellow, 1964-65, 83; Can. Council sr. fellow, 1964-65, 71-72; Killam fellow, 1981-82. Fellow Royal Soc. Can.; mem. Canadian Assn. Univ. Tchrs. German (pres. 1982-84), Modern Humanities Rsch. Assn., Alcuin Soc. (exec. v.p. 1972-79, pres. 1979-80), Internat. Assn. for Germanic Studies (pres. 1990-95). Office: U Brit Columbia, German Dept, Vancouver, BC Canada V6T 1Z1

BATTY, HUGH KENWORTHY, physician; b. Kansas City, Kans.; s. James Jacob and Genevieve Adeline (Johnston) B.; m. Mercedes Aguirre, Mar. 17, 1979; 1 child, Henry Briton. BS in Zoology, U. Wash., 1970; PhD in Anatomy, U. Utah, 1974; MD, Ciudad Juárez, Mex., 1977. Intern, asst. resident St. Vincent's Med. Ctr., Bridgeport, Conn., 1977-78, resident, 1978-79, chief resident, 1979-80; pvt. practice Sheridan, Wyo., 1980—; chmn. dept. medicine Meml. Hosp. Sheridan, 1989, 91, 95, 96, 97, chmn. ICU, 1995. Contbr. articles to profl. jours. Del. Citizen Ambassador Program, India. Eleanor Roosevelt Cancer Rsch. Found. grantee, 1972. Mem. ACP, Wyo. Med. Soc., Sheridan County Med. Soc. Office: 1260 W 5th St Sheridan WY 82801-2702

BATY, ROGER MENDENHALL, anthropology educator; b. Helena, Mont., Oct. 2, 1937; s. Harvey Franklin and Emma Lou (Neffner) B.; m. Phebe Nelson, June 14, 1966; children: Iliniza Mary, Jonathan Harvey, Marquerite Louise. BA cum laude, U. Mont., 1958; BA, MA, U. Oxford, 1964; PhD, Stanford U., 1970. Dir. intercultural dimension U. Redlands, Calif., 1969-79; dir. Armacost Libr. U. Redlands, 1979-83, prof. anthropology, 1983—; Farquhar prof. Am. Southwest, 1989—. Author: Re-educating Teachers for Cultural Awareness, 1972, Faustino Pena - Potter of Tzintzuntzan, 1978. Commr., dist. chmn. Boy Scouts Am., Redlands, 1979-89. Rhodes scholar, 1958. Fellow Am. Anthropology Assn., Royal Geog. Soc.; mem. Am. Geol. Soc., Archaeol. Survey Assn. So. Calif. (pres. 1991-94). Episcopal. Office: U Redlands Dept Sociology Anthropology 1200 E Colton Ave Redlands CA 92373

BATZDORF, ULRICH, neurosurgeon, educator; b. Breslau, Germany, July 22, 1928; came to U.S., 1940; s. Erwin Erich and Lotte Marie (Ollendorff) B.; m. Ellen Kirstein Batzdorf, Dec. 17, 1962; children: Nicholas, Mark, Caroline. BS cum laude in Chemistry, CCNY, 1948; MS in Biochemistry and Physiology, Rutgers U., 1950; MD, N.Y. Med. Coll., 1955. Diplomate Am. Bd. Neurosurgery. Intern U.S. Naval Hosp., Newport, R.I., 1955-56; asst. resident in Surgery U. Md. Hosp., Balt., 1958-60; trainee in neuropathology Nat. Inst. for Neurol. Diseases and Blindness, San Francisco, 1961-62; asst. resident Wasdworth VA Hosp., L.A., 1962-63; resident in neurol. surgery UCLA Ctr. for Health Scis., L.A., 1963-65, sr. resident in neurosurgery, 1965, from asst. to assoc. attending physician, 1968-79, attending physician, 1979—; attending physician Wadsworth VA Hosp., L.A., 1967—; asst. instr. Biochemistry N.Y. Med. Coll., N.Y.C., 1950-53; asst. prof. in residence dept. surgery/neurosurgery UCLA Ctr. for Health Scis., L.A., 1966-68, asst. prof., 1968-71, assoc. prof., 1971-79, prof., 1979—; cons. physician St. John's Hosp. and Health Ctr., Santa Monica, Calif., 1993—; lectr. in field; med. staff Olive View-UCLA Med. Ctr, 1993—. Ad hoc reviewer Clin. Orthopaedics and Related Rsch., 1968—; mem. editl. bd.: Neurosurgery, 1992—; contbr. articles to profl. jours., chpts. to books. Rsch. grantee 1967-78. Mem. ACS, AAAS, AMA, Am. Assn. for Neurol. Surgeons (chmn. Bylaws com. 1976-77), Am. Assn. Cancer Rsch., Assn. Acad. Surgery, Bay Surg. Soc. (bd. dirs. 1987), Brain Rsch. Inst., Calif. Assn. Neurol. Surgeons (bd. dirs. 1982—, 2d v.p. 1987, 1st v.p. 1989, pres. 1991), Calif. Med. Assn., Congress of Neurol. Surgeons, Jonsson Comprehensive Cancer Ctr., L.A. Soc. Neurol. Sci., So. Calif. Neurosurg. Soc. (pres. 1979-80), Tissue Culture Assn., Internat. Assn. Study of Pain, Sigma Xi, Alpha Omega Alpha. Office: UCLA Med Ctr Box 956901 Los Angeles CA 90095-6901

BATZER, GABRIELLE BEMIS, physician, psychiatrist; b. Arlington, Va., July 24, 1953; d. Lawrence Ralph and Grace Southall (Cock) Bemis; m. Wayne Batzer, Nov. 29, 1980; children: Darien Bemis Batzer, Eliot Bemis Batzer. BA, Lewis and Clark Coll., 1974; MD, Georgetown U., 1981. Diplomate in psychiatry and addiction psychiatry Am. Bd. Psychiatry and Neurology; diplomate Nat. Bd. Med. Examiners. Intern, resident Georgetown U. Hosp., Washington, 1981-86, fellow alcohol and drug svc., 1986-87; clin. instr. dept. pschiatry Georgetown U., 1986-87; cons. assoc. dept. psychiatry Duke U., Durham, N.C., 1987-91; psychiatrist (USPHS) Lee-Harnett Mental Health Ctr., Buies Creek, N.C., 1987-91; asst. clin. prof. U. Hawaii Sch. Medicine, Honolulu, 1991—; dir. addiction psychiatry Hawaii State Hosp., Kaneohe, 1991-94; dir. substance abuse program VA, Honolulu, 1994—; bd. dirs. Pacific Inst. Chem. Dependency, Honolulu, 1993—; mem. Hawaii Adv. Commn. Drug Abuse and Controlled Substances, Honolulu, 1993—; mem. Hawaii State Coun. on Mental Health, Honolulu, 1993—; examiner Am. Bd. Psychiatry and Neurology, 1993—. Contbr. chpts. to books. Fellow Am. Soc. Addiction Medicine (cert.); mem. Am. Psychiat. Assn., Am. Acad. Addiction Psychiatry (charter mem.), Hawaii Psychiat. Med. Assn., Hawaii Med. Assn. Episcopalian. Office: VA 116E Substance Abuse Treatment 300 Ala Moana Blvd Honolulu HI 96850-0001

BAUCUS, MAX S., senator; b. Helena, Mont., Dec. 11, 1941; s. John and Jean (Sheriff) B.; m. Wanda Minge, Apr. 23, 1983. BA, Stanford U., 1964, LLB, 1967. Bar: D.C. 1969, Mont. 1972. Staff atty. CAB, Washington, 1967-68; lawyer SEC, Washington, 1968-71; legal asst. to chmn. SEC, 1970-71; sole practice Missoula, Mont., 1971-74; mem. Mont. Ho. of Reps., 1973-74; mem. 94th-95th congresses from 1st Dist. Mont., 1975-79, mem. com. appropriations; U.S. senator from Mont., 1979—, ranking minority mem., mem. environ. and pub. works com., mem. fin. subcom. on internat. trade, mem. health com., taxation and IRS oversight com., mem. agrl./nutrition and forestry coms., mem. intelligence/joint com. on taxation, mem. Senate Dem. steering and coordination com. Office: US Senate 511 Hart Senate Bldg Washington DC 20510-2602

BAUDOIN, JAMES, museum director. Mng. dir. Chandler (Ariz.) Ctr. for Arts, 1994—. Office: Chandler Ctr for Arts 25 S Arizona Pl Ste 301 Chandler AZ 85225

BAUER, A(UGUST) ROBERT, JR., surgeon, educator; b. Phila., Dec. 23, 1928; s. A(ugust) Robert and Jessie Martha-Maynard (Monie) B.; BS, U. Mich., 1949, MS, 1950, MD, 1954; M Med. Sci.-Surgery, Ohio State U., 1960; m. Charmaine Louise Studer, June 28, 1957; children: Robert, John, William, Anne, Charles, James. Intern Walter Reed Army Med. Ctr., 1954-55; resident in surgery Univ. Hosp., Ohio State U., Columbus, also instr., 1957-61; pvt. practice medicine, specializing in surgery, Mt. Pleasant, Mich., 1962-74; chief surgery Ctrl. Mich. Community Hosp., Mt. Pleasant, 1964-65, vice chief of staff, 1967, chief of staff, 1968; clin. faculty Mich. State Med. Sch., East Lansing, 1974; mem. staff St. Mark's Hosp., Salt Lake City, 1974-91; pvt. practice surgery, Salt Lake City, 1974-91; clin. instr. surgery U. Utah, 1975-91. Trustee Rowland Hall, St. Mark's Sch., Salt Lake City, 1978-84; mem. Utah Health Planning Coun., 1979-81. Served with M.C., U.S. Army, 1954-57. Diplomate Am. Bd. Surgery. Fellow ACS, Southwestern Surg. Congress; mem. AMA, Salt Lake County Med. Soc., Utah Med. Assn. (various coms.), Utah Soc. Certified Surgeons, Salt Lake Surg. Soc., Pan Am. Med. Assn. (affiliate), AAAS (affiliate), Sigma Phi Epsilon, Phi Rho Sigma. Episcopalian. Club: Zollinger. Contbr. articles to profl. publs., researcher surg. immunology. Office: PO Box 17533 Salt Lake City UT 84117-0533

BAUER, BETSY (BAUER ELIZABETH), artist; b. Mt. Holly, N.J., Jan. 18, 1959; d. Richard Bryam and Melvina Barnett (Miller) B. Student, MIT, 1979; BFA, Phila. Coll. Art, 1980; postgrad., Santa Fe Art Inst., 1995, Sch. Visual Arts, Parsons Sch. Design. One-woman shows at Hahn Ross Gallery, Santa Fe, 1996, NAS, Washington, 1997; works exhibited in group shows at Visual Arts Mus., N.Y.C., 1984 , N.Y. Feminist Art Inst., N.Y.C., 1987, Hunter Mus., Chattanooga, 1996, Site Santa Fe, 1997, Bridgewater/Lustberg Gallery, N.Y.C., 1997; represented in permanent collections at Hallmark Fine Art Collection, Kansas City, Mo., Rohm and Haas Corp., Phila. (award); animator for advt. Fox-TV, 1993; contbr. articles to profl. jours. Mem. Santa Fe Coun. for Arts. Home: Rt 19 Box 110-R Santa Fe NM 87505 Office: Hahn Ross Gallery 409 Canyon Rd Santa Fe NM 87501

BAUER, CHARLES EDWARD, microelectronics consultant; b. Astoria, Oreg., May 11, 1950; s. Leo Leu and Evelyn Marie (Fordyce) B.; m. Katherine Blanche Harrison, July 31, 1976; children: Scott Charles, Christopher Harrison. BS in Materials Sci. Engring., Stanford U., 1972; MS in Metallurgical Engring., Ohio State U., 1975; PhD in Materials Sci. Engring., Oreg. Grad. Inst., 1980; MBA in Mktg. and Internat. Bus., Portland U., 1988. Materials scientist, engr. III Tektronix Inc., Beaverton, Oreg., 1978-80, engring. mgr. I, 1980-84, engring. mgr. II, 1984-86, IC packaging ops. mgr., 1986-89; dir. rsch. & tech. MicroLithics Corp., Golden, Colo., 1989-90; mng. dir. Tech Lead Corp., Evergreen, Colo., 1990—; judge Milton S. Kivor Awards, Anaheim, Calif., 1993—; advisor Elec. Packaging and Prodn. Mag., Des Plaines, Ill., 1993—. Contbr. articles to profl. jours.; patentee/inventor in field. Pres. Nat. Plains Youth Soccer Assn., North Plaine, Oreg., 1986-87; founder Evergreen Enterprises Exch., 1994—; asst. chair, chair Washington (Oreg.) City Citizens Adv. Bd., 1982-84. Ohio State Student fellow, 1973-75. Fellow ISHM Microelectronic Soc. (nat. tech. v.p. 1988-90, dir. ednl. found. 1988-90); mem. IEEE, ASM Internat. (fellow 1972), Colo. Advanced Tech. Inst. (adv. bd. 1991—), Surface Mount Tech. Assn. (pres. Rocky Mountain chpt. 1994), Semicondr. Equipment and Materials Internat. (advisor 1993—), Hiwan Golf Club. Roman Catholic.

BAUER, JAY S., architect. AB, Washington U., 1970, MArch, 1972. Fellow AIA. Office: Bauer and Wiley 2507 W Coast Hwy Ste 202 Newport Beach CA 92663-4722*

BAUER, JEROME LEO, JR., chemical engineer; b. Pitts., Oct. 12, 1938; s. Jerome L. and Anna Mae (Tucker) B.; children from previous marriage: children: Lori, Trish, Jeff. BSChemE, U. Dayton, 1960; MSChemE, Pa. State U., 1963; postgrad., Ohio State U., 1969. Registered profl. engr., Ohio. Asst. prof. chem. engring. U. Dayton, Ohio, 1963-67; mgr. advanced composites dept. Ferro Corp., Cleve., 1967-72; engring. material and process specifications mgr. Lockheed Missiles & Space Co., Inc., Sunnyvale, Calif., 1972-74; gen. dynamics design specialist Convair Div., San Diego, 1974-76, project devel. engr., 1976-77; dir. research Furane div. M&T Chems. Inc., Glendale, Calif., 1980-82; mem. tech. staff Jet Propulsion Lab., Calif. Inst. Tech., Pasadena, Calif., 1977-80, 82-90; mem. tech. staff mfg. engring. The Aerospace Corp., El Segundo, Calif., 1990—. Editor: Materials Sciences for Future, 1986, Moving Foreward With 50 Years of Leadership in Advanced Materials, 1994; contbr. articles to profl. jours. Jr. warden St. Luke Episcopal Ch., La Crescenta, Calif., 1980, sr. warden 1981. Mem. Am. Inst. Chem. Engrs. (founder, chmn. Dayton sect. 1964-66, spl. projects chmn. Cleve. sect. 1968-69), Soc. Advancement of Material Process Engring. (membership chmn. no. Calif. sect. 1973-74, sec. San Diego sect. 1974-75, vice chmn. 1975-76, chmn. 1976, chmn. Los Angeles sect. 1977, nat. treas. 1978-82, gen. chmn. 31st internat. symposium exhibition, Las Vegas, Nev., 1986, Meritorious Achievement award 1983, internat. v.p. 1987-89, internat. pres. 1989-90), Internat. Electronics Packaging Soc. (pres. Los Angeles chpt. 1982), Phi Lambda Upsilon, Delta Sigma Epsilon. Republican. Home: PO Box 3298 El Segundo CA 90245-8398 Office: The Aerospace Corp 2350 E El Segundo Blvd El Segundo CA 90245-4609

BAUER, JUDY MARIE, minister; b. South Bend, Ind., Aug. 24, 1947; d. Ernest Camiel and Marjorie Ann (Williams) Derho; m. Gary Dwane Bauer, Apr. 28, 1966; children: Christine Ann, Steven Dwane. Ordained to ministry Christian Ch., 1979. Sec. adminstrv. asst. Bethel Christian Ctr., Riverside, Calif., 1975-79; founder, pres. Kingdom Advancement Ministry, San Diego, 1979—, trainer, mgr. cons., Tex., Ariz., Calif., Oreg., Washington, Ala., Okla., Idaho and Republic of South Africa, Guam, Egypt, The Philippines, Australia, Can., Mozambique, Malarwie, Mex., Zimbabwe, Poland, Guatemala, Israel, Scotland, Ireland, Japan, Eng., Zambia, Botheswana, Holland, 1979—; pres. Witty Outerwear Distbrs. Internat., Inc., 1993-96 ; founder, co-pastor Bernardo Christian Ctr., San Diego, 1981-91; evangelism dir. Bethel Christian Ctr., 1978-81, undershepherd minister, 1975-79, adult tchr., 1973-81; pres., founder Bethel Christian Ctr. of Rancho Bernardo, Calif., 1991—; condr. leadership tng. clinics, internat. speaker, lectr. in field. Author syllabus, booklet, tng. material packets. Pres., Bernardo Christian Ctr., San Diego, 1981-91. Mem. Internat. Conv. Faith Ministries, Inc. (area bd. dirs. 1983-88). *It's only in selling out to a cause worth dying for that we truly come alive and experience life to the fullest.*

BAUER, LYNTON G., insurance company executive; b. Denver, Aug. 11, 1928; s. Marvin G. Bauer; children: Grant C., Joan Biggs, Sharon Lisack. BS, U. Mo., 1951. CLU. Field asst. Travelers Ins. Co., Denver, 1953-59; owner R-H Life Co., Phoenix, 1959-66; pres. Bauer & Assocs., Albuquerque, 1966—. Mem. Albuquerque Conv. and Visitor Bur., Albuquerque Indsl. Devel. Commn.; mem. Gov.'s Prionser Release Bd. Capt. USNR, 1946-82. Mem. Nat. Assn. Life Underwriters, N.Mex. Life Leaders assn., C. of C., Res. Officers Assn. (past pres., disting. svc. award), Naval Res. Assn. (past pres., disting. svc. award), Navy League of N.Mex. (past pres.), Lions (past pres.). Home and Office: 7540 Lantern NE Albuquerque NM 87109

BAUER, MARVIN AGATHER, lawyer; b. Milw., June 28, 1940; m. Gray Bauer; children: Laura, Andrew. BS, U. Wis., 1962; JD, U. Chgo., 1965. Bar: Calif. 1966. Dep. atty. gen. State of Calif., Los Angeles, 1965-69; ptnr. Archbald & Spray, Santa Barbara, Calif., 1969-82, Bauer, Harris & McEvoy, Santa Barbara, 1982—; lectr. U. Calif., 1975-77. Bd. dirs. Carpinteria Valley Assn., Calif., 1980-83, Carpinteria Boys Club, 1983-84. Mem. Am. Coll. Trial Lawyers, Santa Barbara Bar Assn. (pres. 1978-79, bd. dirs. 1974-80), Calif. Med.-Legal Com., Santa Barbara Med. Legal Com. Home: PO Box 1307 Summerland CA 93067-1307 Office: Bauer Harris & McEvoy 925 De La Vina St Santa Barbara CA 93101

BAUER, RALPH H., mayor; b. 1930. BS, UCLA, 1952, PhD, 1958. Mayor Huntington Beach, Calif., 1997—. Address: 2000 Main St Huntington Beach CA 92648

BAUER, RALPH LEROY, business executive; b. Evansville, Ind., Dec. 19, 1925; s. John George and Elfrieda Louise (Gresser) Huber; m. Margaret Ellen Masters, Sept. 11, 1948 (div. 1975); children: Clinton L., Warren L., Brian E., Scott A.; m. Anna Mae Cooke, Nov. 9, 1984. BSEE, U. Evansville, 1950; postgrad., U. Calif., Riverside, 1956-58, UCLA, 1960, 65, U. Mich., 1969. Ordnance engr. Internat. Harvester Co., Evansville, Ind., 1950-54; test & product design Naval Ordnance Lab., Silver Springs, Md., 1954-55; test engr. Naval Ordnance Lab., Carona, Calif., 1955-57, br. head, 1957-61, div. head, 1961-70; div. head Naval Weapons Ctr., China Lake, Calif., 1970-82, assoc. dept. head, 1982-83; pres. RB Assocs. Inc., Lake Arrowhead, Calif., 1983-95; retired, 1996; cons. to major aerospace firms in missile guidance/fuzing and electronic counter-countermeasures. Inventor in field. Elder, local sec. Presbyn. Ch., U.S.A., 1994-96; elected alumni bd. dirs. U. Evansville, 1996—. With U.S. Army Air Corps, 1944-46, radar operator-VH Bomb Group. Mem. IEEE (life mem., sect. chmn. 1968, sect. vice chmn. 1967, sect. sec.-treas. 1966), Am. Def. Preparedness Assn., Assn. Old Crows. Home: PO Box 2172 987 LeMont Way Lake Arrowhead CA 92352

BAUER, RANDY MARK, management training firm executive; b. Cleve., Sept. 2, 1946; s. Ralph I. and Gloria P. Bauer; B.S. summa cum laude, Ohio State U., 1968; M.B.A., Kent State U., 1971; m. Sue Dellva, July 4, 1975; children—Sherri, Kevin. Mgmt. auditor Peat Marwick Mitchell & Co., Cleve., 1971-72; mgmt. devel. specialist GAO, Denver, 1972-80; adj. prof. mgmt. Columbia Coll., Denver, 1979—; pres. Leadership Tng. Assos., Denver, 1979—; condr. exec. devel. workshops U. Colo., Denver, 1979—. Recipient Best in 1976 award GAO. Mem. Am. Soc. for Tng. and Devel., Beta Gamma Sigma. Address: 10462 E Prentice Ave Englewood CO 80111-6200

BAUER, STEVEN MICHAEL, cost containment engineer; b. Hemet, Calif., Nov. 8, 1949; s. Donald Richard and Jeanne Patricia (Lamont) B.; m. Myung-Hee Min, Sept. 10, 1983; children: Claudia Margaret, Monica Anne. BA in Physics, Calif. State U., San Bernardino, 1971, BS in Physics, 1984, cert. in acctg., 1980, cert. in computer programming, 1986; postgrad., U. Calif., 1974, Calif. State U., 1982-87; cert. in counseling skills, U. Calif. extension, 1991., cert. in alcohol and other drug studies, 1992; Cert. in Micro Computer Applications, U. Calif. Ext., 1996. Registered engr. in tng., Calif., 1976. Asst. nuclear engr. So. Calif. Edison Co., Rosemead, 1973-76, assoc. nuclear engr., 1976-88, cost containment engr., 1988—; cons. rsch. dept. Jerry L. Pettis Meml. Vets. Hosp., 1978-79, Calif. State U., San Bernardino, 1983-84; cons. planning San Bernardino County, 1975-76; cons. alumni rels. Calif. State U., San. Bernardino, 1989-90. Supporter St. Labre Indian Sch., 1984, Asian Relief Fund, 1985—, So. Poverty Law Ctr., Amnesty Internat., Freedom Writer, 1988; mem. Greenpeace, Wilderness Soc., Internat. Platform Assn.; supporter United Negro Coll. Fund, 1985, vol., 1988; vol. counselor San Bernardino Girls' Juvenile Hall, ARC, 1990—; fellow Casa Colina Hosp.; mem. Robert V. Fullerton Art Mus.; campaign vol. Congressman George E. Brown, 1986; block capt. Neighborhood Watch Assn., sec., 1991-92, v.p., 1992-93, pres., 1994-96; chpt. sec. Sierra Club, 1992. Mem. Am. Nuclear Soc. (assoc.)., Calif. State U. San Bernardino Alumni Assn. (sec. bd. 1979-80, rep. food com. 1980-82), Nat. Assn. Accts., Astron. Soc. Pacific, Assn. Computing Machinery (assoc.), Ams. for Energy Independence (bd. dirs. 1990—), KC (sec., recorder 1989, cmty. dir. Outstanding Svcs. award 1989), Toastmasters, UCLA Alumni (life), Calif. State U. Fullerton Computer Club, Sierra Club (sec. San Gorgonio chpt. 1992). Home and Office: 131 Monroe Ct San Bernardino CA 92408-4137

BAUGH, BRADFORD HAMILTON, occupational and environmental health advisor; b. Seattle, Jan. 18, 1943; s. Sheppard McReynolds and Naomi Emma (Hugel) B.; m. Karyl Eileen Onstad, June 8, 1974; children: Taggart, Darin, Robyn, Patrick, Tracy. BS in Zoology, BS in Psychology, Wash. State U., 1972; MS in Biology, Ea. Wash. State U., 1976, BSN, 1983, MS in devel. psychology, 1992; postgrad., Kennedy-Western U., 1986—. Cert. med. lab. tech., Community Health Nurse. Environ. chemist, research and devel. USCG, Groton, Conn., 1975-76; occupational health advisor USCG, Alameda, Calif., 1983—; adj. prof. Whitworth Coll., Spokane, Wash., 1973-82; counselor Morning Star Ranch, Spokane, 1982-83; instr. Chapman Coll., Alameda, 1983—; indsl. hygienist, fire chief VA, American Lake, Wash., 1986-87; child mental health specialist Tamarack Ctr., Spokane, Wash., 1987-92; occupational and environ. health cons., Nine Mile Falls, Wash., 1987—; indsl. hygienist Wash. State U., Pullman, 1990-93; environ. protection specialist no. cluster USDA Agr. Rsch. Svc., Pullman, 1993—. With USCGR, 1961-93. Mem. APHA, Am. Med. Techs., Am. Indsl. Hygiene Assn., Nat. Environ. Health Assn. (registered environ. health specialist and sanitarian), Am. Conf. Govt. Indsl. Hygienists World Safety Orgn. Mormon. Home: PO Box 209 Nine Mile Falls WA 99026-0209 Office: USDA Agr Rsch Svc Pullman WA 99164-6216

BAUGHN, ALFRED FAIRHURST, lawyer; b. Florence, Ariz., May 1, 1912; s. Otis James and Mary Holman (Fairhurst) B.; m. Barbara Hobbs, June 17, 1935; children: Brent F., Barbara E. AB, U. So. Calif., 1935, JD, 1938. Bar: Calif. 1938, U.S. Dist. Ct. (so. dist.) Calif. 1939, U.S. Ct. Appeals (9th cir.) 1945, U.S. Dist. Ct. Ariz. 1948, Ariz. 1959, U.S. Supreme Ct. 1967. With Title Guarantee & Trust, L.A., 1937-41; corp. counsel Pacific Western Oil Co., 1942-43; pvt. practice law, L.A. and Hollywood, Calif., 1943-56; head Ariz. atty. Signal/Garrett Co., 1956-77, ret., 1977; pvt. practice law, Ariz. and Calif., 1977-94; Ariz. Assn. Industries spl. atty. utility rate hearings Ariz. Corp. Commn., 1977-80; bd. dirs. EPI-HAB, Inc., 1974-90. Adopted by Hopi Indian Chief Seletstewa and Squaw (2d Mesa), 1967; Pres. scholar U. So. Calif., 1931-35. Mem. L.A. Philanthropic Found. (life), Skull and Scales (U. So. Calif.), Phi Alpha Delta (chpt. pres. 1938), Kappa Sigma (pres. L.A. alumni 1945, pres. Phoenix Alumni 1960). Republican. Mem. Christian Ch. Clubs: Hollywood Exch. (pres. 1947); Kiwanis (Phoenix pres. club 1965); Hopi Kachina Klub (organizer, charter v.p. 1974), Hon. Order Ky. Cols. (pres. Phoenix chpt. 1980—), Phoenix Teocali of Order Quetzalcoatl (pres. 1984), Ariz. Bola Tie Soc., Masons (Master 1953), Shriners (Potentate 1971), Jesters (head Phoenix Ct. 1969), Internat. Gorillas (chief 1971—).

BAULE, JOHN ALVIN, museum director, consultant; b. Dubuque, Iowa, July 20, 1948; s. Kenneth Edward and Edith (Stiles) B. BA in Math. and Physics summa cum laude, U. Dubuque, 1970; postgrad., Loras Coll., Dubuque, 1972-75, Coll. of St. Thomas, St. Paul, 1990; MA in History of Mus. Studies, SUNY, Oneonta, 1979. Dir. St. Lawrence County Hist. Assn., Canton, N.Y., 1976-86, Hennepin County Hist. Soc., Mpls., 1986-90; assoc. dir. Hist. Soc. Western Pa., Pitts., 1990-92; dir. Yakima (Wash.) Valley Mus., 1992—; interpretive cons. Minn. Hist. Soc., Hennepin History Mus. and City of Mpls., 1992; mus. aid panelist N.Y. State Coun. on Arts, N.Y.C., 1983-86; grant reviewer Inst. Mus. Svcs., Washington, 1988-91; mem. long-range planning com. Am. Swedish Inst., Mpls., 1988-90; mem. St. Anthony Falls Heritage Bd., Mpls., 1988-90; founding chmn. Preservation Adv. Bd., Canton, 1978-82; trustee, mem. exec. com., workshop leader, speaker, sec. corp. Regional Conf. Hist. Agys., Manlius, N.Y., 1978-84; also others. Contbr. articles to profl. publs. Coord. 50th Anniversary Exhbn., Mpls. Aquatennial Assn., 1989; performer, treas. Grasse River Cmty. Theater, Canton, 1977-86; mem. citizens adv. group West River Parkway Task Force, Mpls., 1988-89; pres. Rivermill Townhomes Assn., 1987-90; chmn. entertainment div. 4th of July Cmty. Celebration Com., 1993—. Recipient North Country citation St. Lawrence U., Canton, 1986, pub. commendation Hennepin County Bd. Commrs., 1990; fellow Bush Found., 1990. Mem. Am. Assn. for State and Local History, Am. Assn. Mus., Mid-Atlantic Mus. Conf., Midwest Mus. Conf., Wash. Assn. Mus., Rotary. Home: 1800 River Rd Apt 18 Yakima WA 98902-6209 Office: Yakima Valley Mus 2105 Tieton Dr Yakima WA 98902-3766

BAUM, CARL EDWARD, electromagnetic theorist; b. Binghamton, N.Y., Feb. 6, 1940; s. George Theodore and Evelyn Monica (Bliven) B. BS with honors, Calif. Inst. Tech., 1962, MS, 1963, PhD, 1969. Commd. 2d lt. USAF, 1962; advanced through grades to capt., 1967, resigned, 1971; project officer Phillips Lab. (formerly Air Force Weapons Lab.), Kirtland AFB, N.Mex., 1963-71, sr. scientist for electromagnetics, 1971—; pres. SUMMA Found.; U.S. del. to gen. assembly Internat. Union Radio Sci., Lima, Peru, 1975, Helsinki, Finland, 1978, Washington, 1981, Florence, Italy, 1984, Tel Aviv, 1987, Prague, Czechoslovakia, 1990, Kyoto, Japan, 1993, Lille, France, 1996; mem. Commn. B U.S. Nat. Com., 1975—, Commn. E, 1982—, Commn. A, 1990—. Author: (with others) Transient Electromagnetic Fields, 1976, Electromagnetic Scattering, 1978, Acoustic, Electromagnetic and Elastic Wave Scattering, 1980, Fast Electrical and Optical Measurements, 1986, EMP Interaction: Principles, Techniques and Reference Data, 1986, Lightning Electromagnetics, 1990, Modern Radio Science, 1990, Recent Advances in Electromagnetic Theory, 1990, Direct and Inverse Methods in Radar Polarimetry, 1992, (with A.P. Stone) Transient Lens Synthesis: Differential Geometry in Electromagnetic Theory, 1991; editor: (with H.N. Kritikos) Electromagnetic Symmetry, 1995; contbr. articles to profl. jours. Recipient award Honeywell Corp., 1962, R&D award USAF, 1970, Harold Brown award Air Force Systems Command, 1990; Phillips Lab. fellow, 1996; Electromagnetic pulse fellow. Fellow IEEE (Harry Diamond Meml. award, 1987, Richard R. Stoddart award, 1984); mem. Electromagnetics Soc. (pres. 1983-85), Electromagnetics Acad., Sigma Xi, Tau Beta Pi. Roman Catholic. Home: 5116 Eastern Ave SE Apt D Albuquerque NM 87108-5618 Office: Phillips Lab WSQW Kirtland AFB NM 87117

BAUM, KENNETH FRANCIS, medical educator, physician; b. Dyersville, Iowa, July 25, 1950; s. F. Gerald and Clarabelle (Loes) B.; m. Patti Jo Thureen, June 17, 1978; children: Alexander, Christina. BS, St. John's U., Collegeville, Minn., 1972; MS, U. N.D., 1975, MB, 1977; MD, U. Pa., 1979. Diplomate Nat. Bd. Med. Examiners, Am. Bd. Internal Medicine (infectious diseases). Intern U. Wis. Hosps., Madison, 1979-80, resident in internal medicine, 1980-82; fellow in infectious diseases U. Colo. Health Scis. Ctr., Denver, 1984-87, instr. divsn. infectious diseases, dept. medicine, 1987-89, asst. prof. divsn. infectious diseases, dept. medicine, 1989—, dir. Sexually Transmitted Diseases Clinic, 1991-92; med. dir. Antero Healthplans, 1995—; clin. investigator MRC Sickle Cell Unit, U. W.I., Kingston, Jamaica, 1982-83; staff Riverside Hosp., Wisconsin Rapids, Wis., 1984, Univ. Hosp., Denver, 1987—, Denver VA Med. Ctr., 1989—; med. dir. Antero Healthplans, 1995—; prin. investigator Ctr. for Disease Control Hantavirus Treatment Task Force, State of Colo. Contbr. articles to profl. jours. Nat. Found. for Infectious Diseases and Eli Lilly Corp. fellowship, 1986-87. Mem. Infectious Disease Soc. Am., Soc. Protozoology, Am. Soc. Microbiology. Office: Univ of Colo HSC Divsn Infectious Diseases 4200 E 9th Ave # B168 Denver CO 80220-3706

BAUM, KERRY ROBERT, retired military officer; b. LaGrande, Oreg., May 25, 1939; s. Guy Hiatt B. and Niola (Anderson) Jones; m. Lynda Sue Christian, Dec. 18, 1964; children: Kerry Jr., Tatia D., Christian H., Buffy Jo, Patrick H., Britta Sue, Natalie A. BA in History, Brigham Young U., 1967; MBA in Mktg., Murray State U., 1978; postgrad., Webster Coll., St. Louis, 1979-80. Commd. 2d lt. U.S. Army, 1957, advanced through grades to col., 1990, ret., 1991; mgr. emergency preparedness Brigham Young U., 1993—; U.S. rep. to Major NATO Comdrs. Alert Conf., 1987-90; joint staff rep LIVE OAK, 1986-90. Author, editor: NATO Alert Procedures for Joint Staff, 1988, Transfer of U.S. Forces to NATO Command, 1990, Focal Point Procedures Manual, 1989. Bishop Mormon Ch., Hopkinsville, Ky., 1974-78, councilor, bishopric, Newport, R.I., 1985-86; bishop Mormon Ch. BYU 185th Ward, 1996—. Decorated Bronze Star, Army Commendation medal, Air Force Commendation medal, Defense Superior Service Medal. Mem. Res. Officers Assn., Assn. Contingency Planners. Home: 10938 N 5870 W American Fork UT 84003-9487

BAUM, PHYLLIS GARDNER, travel management consultant; b. Ashtabula, Ohio, Dec. 13, 1930; d. Charles Edward Schneider and Stella Elizabeth (Schaefer) Gardner; m. Kenneth Walter Baum, Oct. 21, 1948 (div. July 1971); children: Deidre Adair, Cynthia Gail; m. Dennis Carl Marquardt, Sept. 22, 1979 (dec. 1991). Grad. high sch., Cleve. Am. Soc. Travel Agents. Travel cons. Fredo Travel Svc., Ashland, Ohio, 1960-66; sales mgr. Travelmart, Willoughby, Ohio, 1966-68; br. mgr. Travelmart, Mentor, Ohio, 1966-68, Diners Fugazy Travel, Sun City, Ariz., 1968-69; travel cons. Jarrett's Travel Svc., Phoenix, 1969-72; sr. cons. Loyal Travel, Phoenix, 1972-74; co-mgr. Phil Carr Travel, Sun City, 1974-77; tour ops. mgr. ASL Travel, Phoenix, 1978-79; owner, mgr. Travel Temporaries, Glendale, Ariz., 1979—; cons. and lectr. in field. Adv. bd. mem. Small Bus. Devel. Ctr., Phoenix, 1986—. Mem. Pacific Asia Travel Assn. Ariz. (bd. dirs. 1986—), Ariz. Women in Travel, NAFE, Altrusa. Republican. Home and Office: Travel Temporaries 10249 N 45th Ave Glendale AZ 85302-1901

BAUM, RALPH WERNER, primary education educator; b. Chgo., Mar. 21, 1955; s. Walter and Hilde (Gruenebaum) B.; m. Eileen Ann Magrath, Feb. 6, 1983 (div.); 1 child, Molly. BS, Ill. State U., Normal, 1977. Multiple subjects credential, San Francisco State U., 1988. Lead computer operator Roosevelt Hosp., Chgo., 1977-81; computer supr. Anesthesiologists Svcs., San Francisco, 1981-83, Peninsula Hosp., Burlingame, Calif., 1983-84; lead computer operator Electronic Data Systems, Walnut Creek, Calif., 1984-85; tchr. West Contra Costa Unified Sch. Dist., Richmond, Calif., 1988—; head tchr. Pinole (Calif.) Day Care, 1990-96; phys. edn. instr. Shannon Shines Program, Pinole, 1994-95; faculty advisor Shannon Sch. Student Coun., Pinole, 1994-95. Umpire, Pinole Hercules (Calif.) Little League, 1994-96. Calif. Tchrs. Assn., United Tchrs. Richmond. Democrat. Office: Margaret Collins Elem Sch 1224 Pinole Valley Rd Pinole CA 94564

BAUMAN, FREDERICK CARL, lawyer; b. Harrisburg, Pa., July 31, 1952; s. Carl Frederick Jr. and June Edna (Roeder) B. BA, U. Dela., 1974; JD, Harvard U., 1977. Bar: N.Y. 1978, Pa. 1985, Tex. 1988, N.J. 1989, Ariz. 1996. Assoc. Davis Polk & Wardwell, N.Y.C., 1977-81, Hawkins Delafield & Wood, N.Y.C., 1981-83; atty. Bell Atlantic Corp., Phila., 1983-86; v.p., counsel Bell Atlantic Compushop, Dallas, 1986-88; v.p., spl. counsel Bell Atlantic Capital Corp., Paramus, N.J., 1988; v.p., counsel, sec. Bell Atlantic TriCon Leasing Corp., Paramus, 1989, sr. v.p., gen. counsel, sec., 1990-94; sr. v.p., gen. counsel, sec. TriCon Capital Corp., Paramus, 1993-94; v.p., assoc. gen. counsel Finova Capital Corp. (f/k/a Greyhound Fin. Corp.), Phoenix, 1994—. C. Rodney Sharp scholar, 1970, Harvard Club of Del. scholar, 1976. Mem. ABA, Am. Corp. Counsel Assn., Tex. Bar Assn., Ariz. Bar Assn., Phi Beta Kappa. Presbyterian. Office: Finova Capital Corp 1850 N Central Ave Phoenix AZ 85004

BAUMAN, JOSEPH MATTHEW, journalist, author; b. Phila., Apr. 10, 1946; s. Joseph Matthew and Mary Elberta (Stone) B.; m. Cory Jeanne Wilcox, Jan. 7, 1971; 1 child, Sky Joseph Cornelius Bauman. Student, U. Utah, 1965-68, U. Md., 1969-70. Tchr. Trust Territory of Pacific, Ebeye, Marshall Islands, 1966; tchr. Head Start U.S. Cmty. Action Project, Snow Hill, Md., 1967; reporter WBOC-TV, Salisbury, Md., 1968-69; reporter/photographer Beachcomber, Ocean City, Md., 1969, Delmarva News, Selbyville, Del., 1970; editor Beachcomber, Ocean City, 1971; gen. reporter Deseret News, Salt Lake City, 1971-73, environ. specialist, 1973-93, sci./med. reporter, 1993—. Author: Stone House Lands, 1987; editor: The Iron House, 1990. Recipient numerous journalism awards including 1st place personal cols. Utah-Idaho-Spokane AP Assn., 1982, 2d place spot news, 1986, 1st place spot news, 1989, 2d place in ongoing coverage, 1991, 1st place cols. Soc. Profl. Journalists, Utah Headliners chpt., 1984, 2d place, 1988, 1st place series/spl. projects, 1994, 1st place news writing Rocky Mountain Collegiate Press Assn., 1968, 2d place cols., 1968. Mem. Mensa. Office: Deseret News 30 E 100 S Salt Lake City UT 84111-1902

BAUMAN, MARTIN HAROLD, psychiatrist, therapist; b. N.Y.C., Oct. 14, 1936. Pre-med. student, U. Fla., 1952-54, Tulane U., 1955-56, U. Tenn., 1956-67; MD, Northwestern U., 1957-59. Diplomate Am. Bd. Psychiatry and Neurology; lic. Calif., Wis., Vt., N.H. Rotating gen. intern L.A. County Hosp., 1959-60; psychiatric resident U. Wis. Med. Sch., Madison, 1964-67; clin. asst. prof. Dartmouth Coll. Med. Sch., Hanover, N.H., 1967-70; psychiatrist, outpatient, family and couple therapy Sonoma County Mental Health Svcs., Santa Rosa, Calif., 1970-72; pvt. practice Santa Rosa, 1972—; psychiatrist Sonoma State U. Student Health Ctr. and Counseling Svc., Rohnert Park, Calif., 1970—; asst. clin. prof. family and community medicine U. Calif., San Francisco, 1976-82, assoc. clin. prof. family and cmty. medicine, 1982—, assoc. clin. prof. psychiatry, 1982—; co-dir. family therapy program Langley Porter Neuropsychiat. Inst., San Francisco, 1982—; supr. of residents Mendocino State Hosp., Talmage, Claif., 1970-71; psychiatric dir. Social Advocates for Youth, Santa Rosa, 1971-96; med. dir. Cherry St. House, Santa Rosa, 1974-81; cons. Dept. Vocat. Rehab, Calif., 1974—, Sonoma County Mental Health Assn., 1976—, Occidental (Calif.) County Health Ctr., 1982—; bd. dirs. Santa Rosa R. House, Family Svc. Agy. Sonoma County; psychiatric supr. U. Calif., San Francisco, 1972—; family practice residency supr. Community Hosp., Santa Rosa, 1972—, lectr. in field. Lectr. in field; contbr. articles to profl. jours. Bd. dirs. Sonoma County Big Brothers, 1977-78; psychiatric work group North Bay Health Systems Agy., 1980-81. Mem. Am. Psychiat. Assn., Am. Acad. Psychotherapists, Am. Assn. Tchrs. of Family Medicine, Am. Family Therapist Acad. (charter), Am. Orthopsychiat. Assn., No. Calif. Psychiat. Assn., Redwood Empire Psychiat. Soc. (sec.-treas. 1976-77, pres. 1978-79, acting pres. 1982—). Office: Waterfall Towers 2455 Bennett Valley Rd # 300 B Santa Rosa CA 95404-5663

BAUMAN, STEPHEN ADRIAN, lawyer; b. L.A., Jan. 25, 1935. BS in Bus. Adminstrn., UCLA, 1956; JD, Stanford U., 1959; LLM, Harvard U., 1960. Bar: Calif. 1960; cert. taxation specialist Calif. State Bar Bd. Legal Specialization. Ptnr. Seyfarth, Shaw, Fairweather & Geraldson, L.A.; lectr. tax law and estate planning U. So. Calif. Law Ctr. Advanced Profl. Program; U. So. Calif. Tax Inst., Calif. Continuing Edn. of Bar, Practising Law Inst. Mem. State Bar Calif. Office: Seyfarth Shaw Fairweather & Geraldson 2029 Century Park E # 3300 Los Angeles CA 90067-2901

BAUMAN, WALTER JOSEPH, telecommunication company executive; b. Berlin, Nov. 1, 1946; s. William Louis and Lois Lanora (Sickels) B.; m. Sharon Sue Hatfield, July 1965 (div. Mar. 1977); children: Leslie Lynn, Julie Ann, Christopher Michael, Brian Anthony. BS in Edn., Mo. Western U., 1970. Tchr. H.S. history Bishop LeBland H.S., St. Joseph, Mo., 1970-76, Sch. Dist. Kansas City, Mo., 1978-81, Metro State Coll., Denver, 1983-84; project coord., field engr. Coaxial Analysts, Denver, 1986-92; pres., owner Infotechs, Colorado Springs, Colo., 1992—. Roman Catholic. Home: 2878 Maverick Dr Colorado Springs CO 80918-1636

BAUMANN, ERNST FREDERICK, college president; b. N.Y.C., Oct. 4, 1943; s. Ernst and Grace (Crowley) B.; m. Kathleen Ann Brennan, June 17, 1967; children: Lori Ann, Macushla, Katrinka, Victoria, Greta. BA, Harvard U., 1967; postgrad., Colo. U. Observer, rsch. asst. High Altitude Obs., Nat. Ctr. for Atsmospheric Rsch., Boulder, Colo., 1967-69; uranium geologist, grade control engr. Kerr-McGee Corp., Casper, Wyo., 1969-71; mine geologist engr. Am. Smelting and Refining Co., Leadville, Colo., 1975; chief geologist, engr. Leadville (Colo.) Lead Corp., 1977-86; dir. adult basic edn. and gen. ednl. devel., counselor Upper Ark. Area Coun. Govts., Cañon City, Colo., 1980-87; corr. officer, supr. C.T.C.F./D.O.C., Cañon City, 1987-96; pres., chmn. Coll. of the Cañons, Cañon City, 1996—; officer Colo. Territorial Correctional Facility, Dept. Corrections, Cañon City; recruiter Harvard U., Cañon City; pres., chmn. bd. Working in SETI Search for Extra-Terrestrial Intelligence. Co-author: Toward a New World: Powerful Proof of the Existence of God, 1995; patentee collapsible ski. Mayoral candidate City of Cañon City, 1983, 85. Maj. CAP, USAF Aux., 1980-97. Mem. K. of C. (scribe). Republican. Roman Catholic. Home: 1101 Phay Ave Canon City CO 81215 Office: Coll of the Cañons Forge Rd/Indsl Park Canon City CO 81212

BAUMANN, FREDERICK, management consultant; b. Los Angeles, Nov. 26, 1930; s. Christian Frederick and Marie (Tiemann) B.; m. Flora Jane Sick, May 5, 1962; children: David, Chris, Hilary. B.S., UCLA, 1952; Ph.D., U. Wis., 1956. Rsch. chemist Chevron Rsch. Corp., Richmond, Calif., 1956-65; tech. group leader Varian Instrument Group, Walnut Creek, Calif., 1965-70, rsch. and engring. mgr., 1970-80, mng. dir., Melbourne, Australia, 1980-81, tech. dir., Palo Alto, Calif., 1981-82, mgr. lab. data systems, Walnut Creek, 1983-89, mgr. tech. and strategic planning, 1989-91; cons., 1991—; mem. adv. bd. Analytical Chemistry, Washington, 1972-75; instr. U. Calif.-Berkeley, 1968-74. Contbr. articles to profl. jours. Mem. Am. Chem. Soc., Sigma Xi, Alpha Chi Sigma. Home: 166 Rudgear Dr Walnut Creek CA 94596-6316

BAUMANN, MICHELLE RENAE, editor, writer; b. Walnut Creek, Calif., Aug. 17, 1970; d. Garry Benton and Beverly Ann (Harper) Miller; m. Brad Christopher Baumann, Oct. 19, 1996. BA, Calif. State U., Long Beach, 1992. Intern L.A. Mag., 1991-92; asst. editor Builder and Developer Mag., Newport Beach, Calif., 1992-93; mng. editor Indoor Comfort News, L.A., 1993-94; exec. editor Bobit Pub. Co., Redondo Beach, Calif., 1994—. Mem. emergency response team, Huntington Beach, Calif., 1996; vol. PAWS, Irvine, Calif., 1995, In Def. of Animals, Calif., 1996. Mem. Soc. Profl. Journalists (treas. Long Beach State chpt. 1992). Democrat. Methodist.

BAUMANN, THEODORE ROBERT, aerospace engineer, consultant, army officer; b. Bklyn., May 13, 1932; s. Emil Joseph and Sophie (Reiblein) B.; m. Patricia Louise Drake, Dec. 16, 1967; children: Veronica Ann, Robert Theodore, Joseph Edmund. B in Aerospace Engring., Poly. U., Bklyn., 1954; MS in Aerospace Engring., U. So. Calif., L.A., 1962; grad., US Army C&GS Coll., 1970, Indsl. Coll. of Armed Forces, 1970, US Army War Coll., 1979, Air War Coll., 1982. Structures engr. Glenn L. Martin Co., Balt., 1954-55; structural loads engr. N.Am. Rockwell, L.A., 1958-67; dynamics engr. TRW Systems Group, Redondo Beach, Calif., 1967-71, systems engr., 1971-75, project engr., 1975-84, sr. project engr., 1984-92; cons. SAAB-Scania Aerospace Div., Linkoping, Sweden, 1981-82; asst. dir. Dir. Weapons Systems, U.S. Army, Washington, 1981-85, staff officer Missile & Air Def. System div., 1975-81. Contbr. articles to Machine Design, tech. publs., tech. symposia. Asst. scoutmaster Boy Scouts Am., Downey, Calif., 1985-93; instr. Venice Judo Boys Club, 1966-86. Served from 2d lt. U.S. Army to col. USAR, 1954-88. Decorated Legion of Merit. Mem. AIAA; mem. Soc. Am. Mil. Engrs (life), Am. Legion, Res. Officers Assn. (life), U.S. Judo Fedn., Nat. Rifle Assn. Republican. Roman Catholic. Office: Theodore R Baumann & Assoc 7732 Brunache St Downey CA 90242-2206

BAUMGARTNER, ANTON EDWARD, automotive sales professional; b. N.Y.C., May 18, 1948; s. Hans and Carmen Maria (Figueroa) B.; m. Brenda Lee Lemmon, May 24, 1969 (div. 1990); 1 child, Anton Nicholaus; m. Virginia Thiele, 1992; 1 child, Bree Alexandra. BS, Woodbury U., 1970. Sales mgr. Maywood Bell Ford, Bell, Calif., 1966-69, O.R. Haan, Inc., Santa Ana, Calif., 1969-72; pres. Parkinson Volkswagen, Placentia, Calif., 1972-77; exec. v.p. United Moped, Fountain Valley, Calif., 1975-82; pres. Automobili Intermeccanica, Fountain Valley, 1975-82; gen. mgr. Bishop (Calif.) Volkswagen-Bishop Motors, 1982-85, Beach Imports-Irvine Imports, Newport Beach, Calif., 1985-88; chmn. bd. Stan and Ollie Ins. Co., Santa Ana, Calif., 1989—; exec. v.p. Asterism, Inc., 1992-96; chmn. Marich Acceptance Inland Empire, 1996—; mem. faculty, Automotive World Congress, Detroit, 1980. Contbr. articles to weekly serial publs. Mem. Coachbuilders Assn. N.Am. (sec. 1975-78). Office: Marich Acceptance 6 Satinbush Aliso Viejo CA 92656-1827

BAUMRIND, DIANA, research psychologist; b. N.Y.C., Aug. 23, 1927. A.B., Hunter Coll., 1948; M.A., U. Calif., Berkeley, 1951, Ph.D., 1955. Cert. and lic. psychologist, Calif. Project dir. psychology dept. U. Calif., Berkeley, 1955-58; project dir. Inst. of Human Devel., 1960—, also rsch. psychologist and prin. investigator family socialization and devel. competence project; lectr. and cons. in field; referee for rsch. proposals Grant Found., NIH, 1970—, NSF, 1970—. Contbr. numerous articles to profl. jours. and books; author 2 monographs; mem. editorial bd. Devel. Psychology, 1986-90. Recipient Rsch. Scientist award, NIMH; grantee NIMH, 1955-58, 60-66, Nat. Inst. Child Health and Human Devel., 1967-74, MacArthur Found., Grant Found., 1967-92. Fellow Am. Psychol. Assn., Am. Psychol. Soc. (G. Stanley Hall award 1988); mem. Soc. Research in Child Devel. Office: U Calif Inst of Human Devel 1203 Tolman Hall Berkeley CA 94720-1691*

BAUSTIAN, ROBERT FREDERICK, conductor; b. Storm Lake, Iowa, June 4, 1921; s. Alfred A. and Grace E. (Martin) B. MusB, Eastman Sch. Music, 1942, MusM, 1948; postgrad., Zurich (Switzerland) Conservatory., 1948-49. Coach, condr. Zurich Opera, 1949-53; 2d condr. Hessian State Opera, Wiesbaden, Fed. Republic of Germany, 1953-57; prof. orch. U. Kans., Lawrence, 1957-66; prof. conducting Oberlin (Ohio) Coll. Conservatory, 1966-83; condr., coach Merola Program, San Francisco, 1983-87; condr., mus. adminstr. Santa Fe Opera, 1957-78; adj. Met. Opera auditions, Tex., 1975—; bd. dirs. Santa Fe Opera, 1984-90, Santa Fe Symphony, 1985-93. Guest condr. Ariz. Opera, N.Y.C. Opera, orchs. of Atlanta, Kansas City, Akron, also Spain, France, Yugoslavia. Mem. Santa Fe Arts Commn., 1992-96. With AUS, 1942-46, ETO. Decorated Bronze Star. Mem. Am. Symphony Orch. League, Nat. Opera Assn., Pi Kappa Lambda. Republican. Home and Office: 424 Abeyta St Santa Fe NM 87501-2806

BAUTISTA, ANTHONY HERNANDEZ, biomedical company executive; b. Palo Alto, Calif., Sept. 19, 1955; s. Anthony Hernandez and Velma Rose (Morinan) B.; m. Jill Davis, June 17, 1978; children: Evan Thomas, Laura Anne. AA in Electronic Tech., Coll. of San Mateo, 1976; BSEE, San Jose (Calif.) State U., 1994. Elec. engr. Hewlett Packard, Palo Alto, Calif., 1976-86; mfg. engrng. mgr. Molecular Devices Corp., Menlo Park, Calif., 1986-91; ops. v.p. LJL Biosystems, Inc., Sunnyvale, Calif., 1991—. Mem. Toastmasters (adminstrv. v.p. 1990), Tau Beta Pi.

BAUTISTA, JOHN, mayor, lawyer; m. Marilyn Bautista. BA in Econs. and Internat. Studies, UCLA; JD, Harvard U. Lawyer Venture Law Group, Menlo Park, Calif.; elected Cupertino (Calif.) City Coun., 1993; elected mayor City of Cupertino, 1993—. Office: City Hall Office of the Mayor 10300 Torre Ave Cupertino CA 95014

BAUZA, CHRISTINE DIANE, special education educator; b. Santa Monica, Calif., Sept. 16, 1961; d. William Gene and Dorothy Louise (Evans) Lough; m. Joseph Henry Bauza, July 26, 1986; 1 child, Crystal Marie. AA in Liberal Arts, Crafton Hills Coll., Yucaipa, Calif., 1981; BA in Liberal Studies, Calif. State U., Northridge, 1983, MA in Deaf Edn., 1986, mu tiple subjects-spl. edn. credentials, 1986. Tchr. communication handicapped edn. San Bernardino County Supt. Schs., Rialto, Calif., 1986—; tchr., cons. Community Adv. Com., San Bernardino, Calif., 1990-91. Mem. Conv. Am. Instrs. of Deaf. Home: 1031 Cimarron Dr Redlands CA 92374-6335 Office: Bemis Elem Sch 774 E Etiwanda Ave Rialto CA 92376-4508

BAVARDO, PATRICIA CAROL, marketing executive, author; b. Freeport, Ill., Sept. 14, 1941; d. John Patrick and Hazel Irene (Bott) Murphy; m. Corman Wilkins, Mar. 29, 1959 (div. 1964); m. Michael Bavardo, Dec. 11, 1965; children: Michael Allen, Jeffrey Lee, Steven Charles. Grad., Freeport H.S., 1958. Owner, operator beauty salon Downey, Calif., 1965-68; sec. med. office Hemet, Calif., 1982-85; mktg. dir. Spotlight West, Canyon Lake, Calif., 1985-96; founder, co-chair Tale Spinners Writer's Workshop, Canyon Lake, 1994—. Author: (poems) Heart's Love, 1991 (Golden Poet award 1991), (autobiography) Naked Goes My Heart, 1994 (award 1995). Democrat. Roman Catholic. Home: 26760 Oakmont Dr Sun City CA 92586

BAWDEN, GARTH LAWRY, museum director; b. Truro, Eng., Dec. 31, 1939; s. Richard Thomas and Susan Elizabeth Olga (Lawry) B.; m. Margaret Ruth Greet, Dec. 21, 1963 (div. Mar. 1978); children: Michael Greet, Teona Mary, Kerenza Elizabeth; m. Elaine Louise Comack, Oct. 26, 1978; children: Jonathan Richard, Rebecca Lawry. Diploma in phys. medicine, West Middlesex Sch. Phys. Medicine, Isleworth, Eng., 1961; BA in Art History, U. Oreg., 1970; PhD in Anthropology, Harvard U., 1977. Assoc. in archaeology Harvard U., Cambridge, Mass., 1977-81, instr., 1980-85, asst., acting dir. Peabody Mus., 1980-85; assoc. prof. U. N.Mex., Albuquerque, 1985-91; prof. U. Mex., Albuquerque, 1991—; dir. Maxwell Mus. U. N.Mex., Albuquerque, 1985—; dir. field research project Harvard U., Galindo, Peru, 1971-74, dir. field survey Peabody Mus., Saudi Arabian Archaeol. Survey, 1978-80; field supr. Cuntisuyu Project, Moquegua, Peru, 1983-86; dir. U. N.Mex. Acheol. Project, So. Peru, 1985—. Author: (with G. Conrad) The Andean Heritage, 1982; contbr. articles on archaeology to profl. jours. Fellow Woodrow Wilson, U. Oreg., 1970, Tinker, Harvard U., 1983. Mem. Soc. Am. Archaeology, Assn. Field Archaeology, Assn. Sci. Mus. Dirs., Current Anthropology (assoc.), Phi Beta Kappa, Sigma Xi. Home: 6 Applewood Ln NW Albuquerque NM 87107-6404 Office: Univ New Mexico Maxwell Mus Anthropology Albuquerque NM 87131-1201*

BAWMANN, BRAD CRAIG, health facility administrator; b. St. Louis, June 25, 1962; s. Ronald George and Janet Anne (Griffin) B.; m. Wendy Jeanne Borchart, June 5, 1986; 1 child, Oliver Marcus. BA, Augustana Coll., 1985. Assoc. dir. pub. rels. U. Colo., Denver, 1987-91; dir. pub. rels. Healthone, Denver, 1991-95; dir. pub. affairs Columbia/HCA Healthcare Corp., Denver, 1995-96; pres. The Bawmann Group, Denver, 1996—, Englewood, 1996—. Pres. The Uptown Partnership, Denver, 1992-96; pres. Justice Info. Ctr., Denver, 1991-97. Mem. Colo. Healthcare Communicators (pres., v.p. 1991-96). Home: 478 Ogden St Denver CO 80218

BAXTER, BETTY CARPENTER, educational administrator; b. Sherman, Tex., 1937; d. Granville E. and Elizabeth (Caston) Carpenter; m. Cash Baxter; children: Stephen Barrington, Catherine Elaine. AA in Music, Christian Coll., Columbia, Mo., 1957; MusB in Voice and Piano, So. Meth. U., Dallas, 1959; MA in Early Childhood Edn., Tchrs. Coll., Columbia, 1972, MEd, 1979, EdD, 1988. Tchr. Riverside Ch. Day Sch., N.Y.C., 1966-71; headmistress Episcopal Sch., N.Y.C., 1972-87, headmistress emeritus, 1987—; founding head Presbyn. Sch., Houston, 1988-94; dir. Chadwick Village Sch., Palos Verdes Peninsula, Calif. Author: The Relationship of Early Tested Intelligence on the WPPSI to Later Tested Aptitude on the SAT. Mem. ASCD, Nat. Assn. Episcopal Schs. (former gov. bd., editor Network publ.), Nat. Assn. Elem. Sch. Prins., Ind. Schs. Assn. Admissions Greater N.Y. (former exec. bd.), Nat. Assn. for Edn. of Young Children, L.A. Assn. Sch. Heads, Nat. Assn. Elem. Sch. Prins., Assn. Supervision and Curriculum Devel., Kappa Delta Pi, Delta Kappa Gamma. Republican. Presbyterian. Home and Office: 26800 Academy Dr Palos Verdes Peninsula CA 90274-3980

BAXTER, CAROL CAIRNS, fiber artist; b. Oakland, Calif., Dec. 24, 1940; d. Walter V. and Helen Cairns; m. William F. Baxter, Mar. 27, 1987; 1 child, Bernard Treanor. AB, Stanford U., 1962; MA, U. Calif., Berkeley, 1966, EdD, 1969. Systems engr. Internat. Bus. Machines, Oakland, Calif., 1962-64; rsch. specialist U. Calif., Berkeley, 1969-71; rsch. dir. Ctr. for Advanced Study, Stanford, Calif., 1972-81; dir. computer rsch. Am. Enterprise Inst., Washington, 1981-83; rsch. dir. Ctr. for Advanced Study, Stanford, Calif., 1983-93; pvt. practice fiber artist Los Altos, Calif., 1993—.

BAXTER, DAN, manufacturing executive; b. Odessa, Tex., June 23, 1953; s. Ray and Juanita (Luttrell) B.; m. Suzanne Baxter, Aug. 6, 1983; 1 child, Amber Rose. BS, C.C. of USAF, Kelly and Randolf AFB, Tex., 1976; BSBA, Newport U., 1992. Devel. engr. TRW/IRC, Corpus Christi, Tex., 1976-80, regional sales mgr., 1980-83; area mgr. TRW/ECG, Elsegundo, Calif., 1983-86; mgr. Western area Litton/Clifton, Clifton Heights, Pa., 1986-92; v.p., gen. mgr. Renco Encoders, Inc., Goleta, Calif., 1992—. Active Santa Barbara Bus. Roundtable, 1994—; sponsor, mem. Santa Barbara Exec. Roundtable, 1993—. With USAF, 1971-76. Republican. Office: Renco Encoders Inc 26 Coromar Dr Goleta CA 93117

BAXTER, MARVIN RAY, state supreme court judge; b. Fowler, Calif., Jan. 9, 1940; m. Jane Pippert, June 22, 1963; children: Laura, Brent. BA in Econs., Calif. State U., 1962; JD, U. Calif.-Hasting Coll. Law, 1966. Bar: Calif. 1966. Dep. dist. atty. Fresno County, Calif., 1967-68; assoc. Andrews, Andrews, Thaxter & Jones, 1968-70, ptnr., 1971-82; prin. advisor to gov. Office of Gov., 1983-88; assoc. justice Calif. Ct. Appeal (5th dist.), 1988—, Calif. Supreme Ct. Mem. Fresno County Bar Assn. (bd. dirs. 1977-82, pres. 1981), Calif. Young Lawyers Assn. (bd. gov. 1973-76, sec.-treas. 1974-75), Fresno County Young Lawyers Assn. (pres. 1973-74), Fresno County Legal Svcs., Inc. (bd. dirs. 1973-74), U. Calif. Alumni Assn. (pres. 1970-71), Alumni Trust Coun. (pres. 1970-75). Office: Calif Supreme Ct S Tower 8th Flr 303 2nd St 8th Flr S Tower San Francisco CA 94107-1366*

BAXTER, RALPH H., JR., lawyer; b. San Francisco, 1946. AB, Stanford U., 1968; MA, Cath. U. Am., 1970; JD, U. Va., 1974. Chmn. Orrick, Herrington & Sutcliffe, San Francisco; mem. adv. bd. nat. Employment Law Inst. Author: Sexual Harassment in the Workplace: A Guide to the Law, 1981, 2nd. rev. edit., 1989, 94, Manager's Guide to Lawful Terminations, 1983, rev. edit., 1991; mem. editorial bd. Va. Law Rev., 1973-74; mem. editorial adv. bd. Employee Rels. Law Jour. Mem. ABA (mgmt. co-chair com. on employment rights and responsibilities in workplace labor and employment law sect. 1987=90). Office: Orrick Herrington & Sutcliffe Old Federal Reserve Bank Bldg 400 Sansome St San Francisco CA 94111-3308

BAYDA, EDWARD DMYTRO, judge; b. Alvena, Sask, Can., Sept. 9, 1931; s. Dmytro Andrew and Mary (Bilinski) B.; m. Marie-Thérèse Yvonne Gagné, May 28, 1953; children: Paula, Christopher, Margot, Marie-Therèsé, Sheila, Kathryn. BA, U. Sask., 1951, LLB cum laude, 1953; LLD (hon.), 1989. Bar: Sask. 1954; created Queen's Counsel, Exec. Br. of Govt., 1966. Barrister, solicitor Regina, Sask., 1953-72; sr. ptnr. Bayda, Halvorson, Scheibel & Thompson, 1966-72; justice Ct. Queen's Bench for Sask., Regina, 1972-74, Ct. Appeal for Sask., Regina, 1974-81; chief justice Sask., Regina, 1981—. Roman Catholic. Home: 3000 Albert St, Regina, SK Canada S4S 3N7 Office: Ct Appeal Sask Courthouse, 2425 Victoria Ave, Regina, SK Canada S4P 3V7

BAYLESS, RAYMOND, writer, artist, parapsychologist; b. Oakland, Calif., 1920. Author: The Enigma of the Poltergeist, 1967, Animal Ghosts, 1970, The Other Side of Death, 1971, Experiences of a Psychical Researcher, 1972, Apparitions and Survival of Death, 1973, Voices from Beyond?, 1976; co-author: Phone Calls from the Dead, 1979, The Case of Life After Death, 1981; contbr. articles to profl. jours., publs.; artist represented in permanent collections, including U.S. Dept. Air Force, U.S. Dept. Navy, U.S. Dept. State, Art in Embassies Program, Nat. Air and Space Mus., Internat. Aerospace Hall of Fame, San Diego, Kern Oil and Refining Co., Long Beach, Calif., Bank of Am., L.A., Weingart Found., L.A., Permanent Civil War Exhibit; various paintings displayed in The Pentagon, Washington, 1974-76, 75-88, 91-96; exhibited in group shows Air Force Art Collection, Pentagon, Washington, Washington Navy Mus., Naval Hist. Ctr., Washington Navy Yard; illustrator 6 book jackets. Mem. Parapsychol. Assn., Brentwood (Calif.) Area C. of C. Address: 11348 Cashmere St Los Angeles CA 90049-3426

BAYLOR, DON EDWARD, professional baseball manager; b. Austin, Tex., June 28, 1949; s. George Edward and Lillian Joyce B.; m. Rebecca Giles, Dec. 12, 1987; 1 child by previous marriage, Don Edward. Student, Miami-Dade Jr. Coll., Miami, Fla., Blinn Jr. Coll., Brenham, Tex. With Balt. Orioles, 1970-76, Oakland Athletics, 1976, 88, California Angels, 1976-82, N.Y. Yankees, 1983-86, Boston Red Sox, 1986-87, Minnesota Twins, 1987; mem. World Series Championship Team, 1987; mgr. Colorado Rockies, Denver, CO, 1992—; Set new career record for hit by pitches; hit safely in 12 consecutive Am. League Championship Series games. Author: (with Claire Smith) Don Baylor, Nothing But the Truth: A Baseball Life, 1989. Chmn. nat. sports Cystic Fibrosis Found. Recipient Designated Hitter of Yr. award, 1985, 86, Roberto Clemente award, 1985; named Am. League's Most Valuable Player, 1979, Sporting News Player of Yr., 1979; player All-Star Game, 1979; named Nat. League Mgr. of Yr. Sporting News, 1995, Baseball Writers Assn. Am., 1995. Office: Colorado Rockies 2001 Blake St Denver CO 80205-2008 Office: Major League Baseball Players Assn 805 3rd Ave New York NY 10022-7513

BAYLOR, ELGIN GAY, professional basketball team executive; b. Washington, Sept. 16, 1934; m. Elaine; 1 dau., Krystle. Ed., Coll. Idaho, Seattle U. Profl. basketball player Los Angeles (formerly Minneapolis) Lakers, 1958-72; asst. coach New Orleans Jazz, NBA, 1974-76, coach, 1976-79; exec. v.p., gen. mgr. Los Angeles Clippers, 1986—, v.p. basketaballops. Most Valuable Player, NCAA Tournament, 1958; mem. NBA All-Star Team, 1959-65, 67-70; Rookie of the Yr., NBA, 1959; co-Most Valuable Player, NBA All-Star Game, 1959; named to NBA 35th Anniversary All-Time Team, 1980. Office: Los Angeles Clippers 3939 S Figueroa St Los Angeles CA 90037-1200*

BAYNE, KIM MIKLOFSKY, marketing communications and public relations professional, consultant, author. BA in Music, Colo. Coll.; MA in Computer Resources Mgmt., Webster U. Mktg. comms. mgr., mktg. and sales rep. Info. Storage Inc., Colorado Springs, 1985; various positions Laser Magnetic Storage Internat. Co., Colorado Springs, 1986-91; mktg. comms./pub. rels. assoc. Origin Systems, Inc., Colorado Springs, 1991; mktg. comms. mgr. Array Microsystems, Inc., Colorado Springs, 1991-93; mktg. comm./pub. rels. specialist, freelance writer Colorado Springs, 1981-93; pres. wolfBayne Comms., Colorado Springs, 1993—; bd. dirs. Colorado Springs Software Roundtable; founder, owner HTMARCOM Internet Forum, 1994—. Author: The Internet Marketing Plan, 1997; editor, pub. Marketing Lists on the Internet, 1994—; contbr. articles to profl. jours.; speaker in field. Bd. dirs. Keep Colo. Springs Beautiful, Inc., 1993-94. Recipient Excellence award for print ad campaign Bus. Communicators and Mktg. Assn. L.A., 1991, Award of Excellence, Award of Achievement Soc. for Tech. Communication, 1991, numerous awards Toastmasters Internat. Mem. Colo. MARCOM Network (pres. 1993, chairperson Silcon Mountain symposium 1992). Office: wolfBayne Communications PO Box 50287 Colorado Springs CO 80949-0287

BAYS, ERIC, retired bishop; b. Portage La Prairie, Man., Can., Aug. 10, 1932; s. Percy Clarence and Hilda (Harper) B.; m. Patricia Ann Earle, Dec. 28, 1967; children: Jonathan Edmund, Rebecca Jane. BS, U. Man., Winnipeg, Can., 1955; BA, U. Sask., Saskatoon, Can., 1959; L in Theology, U. Emmanuel Coll., Saskatoon, 1959, DD (hon.), 1987; M in Ministry, Christian Theol. Sem., Indpls., 1974. Ordained to ministry Anglican Ch., 1959. Asst. curate All Saints' Anglican Ch., Winnipeg, 1959-61; lectr. Emmanuel Coll., Saskatoon, 1961-62; mission priest Diocese Caledonia, B.C., 1962-64; novice in religion Community of the Resurrection, Mirfield, Eng., 1964-65; vicar St. Saviour's with St. Catherine Parish, Winnipeg, 1965-67; rector All Saints' Parish, Winnipeg, 1968-76; prof. Coll. Emmanuel/St. Chad, Saskatoon, 1976-81; vice-prin. Coll. of Emmanuel/St. Chad, Saskatoon, 1981-86; bishop Diocese Qu'Appelle, Regina, Sask., 1986-97; ret., 1997. With RCAF, 1955-59. Office: Diocese of Qu'Appelle, 1501 College Ave, Regina, SK Canada S4P 1B8

BEACH, ARTHUR O'NEAL, lawyer; b. Albuquerque, Feb. 8, 1945; s. William Pearce and Vivian Lucille (Kronig) B.; BBA, U. N.Mex., 1967, JD, 1970; m. Alex Clark Doyle, Sept. 12, 1970; 1 son, Eric Kronig. Bar: N.Mex. 1970. Assoc. Smith & Ransom, Albuquerque, 1970-74; assoc. Keleher & McLeod, Albuquerque, 1974-75, ptnr., 1976-78, shareholder Keleher & McLeod, P.A., Albuquerque, 1978—; teaching asst. U. N. Mex., 1970. Bd. editors Natural Resources Jour., 1968-70. Mem. ABA, State Bar N.Mex. (unauthorized practice of law com., adv. opinions com., med.-legal panel, legal-dental-osteo.-podiatry com., jud. selection com., specialization bd.), Albuquerque Bar Assn. (dir. 1978-82). Democrat. Mem. Christian Sci. Ch. Home: 2015 Dietz Pl NW Albuquerque NM 87107-3240 Office: Keleher & McLeod PA PO Drawer AA Albuquerque NM 87103

BEACH, CHRISTOPHER JOHN, American literary arts educator; b. Mpls., Nov. 12, 1959; s. Northrop and Myrtle Mary (Webb-Johnson) B.; m. Carrie Jaurès Noland, Aug. 18, 1958; 1 child, Julian. BA, Pomona Coll., 1981; AM, Harvard U., 1985, PhD, 1988. Asst. prof. Bates Coll., Lewiston, Maine, 1989-90, Columbia U., N.Y.C., 1990-92, Claremont (Calif.) Grad. Sch., 1992-93, U. Mont., Missoula, 1993-95, U. Calif., Irvine, 1995—. Author: ABC of Influence, 1992, Politics of Distinction, 1996, From Artifice to Indeterminacy, 1997-1998. Office: U Calif Irvine CA 92697

BEACH, GEO, journalist, poet; b. Boston, Feb. 14, 1957; s. George Richard Plagenz and Faith Hanna-Williams; m. Sydney Liane Webb, March 16, 1991; 1 child, Miranda Rose. Lit., Phillips Exeter Acad., N.H., 1975; Theatre, Yale U., 1979. Dir. commn. Yale U. Tutoring Agency, New Haven, 1979-82; public info. officer Dept. Pub. Safety, Homer, Alaska, 1983-87; columnist, editor Tempest Media Prodn., Arcata, Calif., 1988—; Essayist, Monitor Radio News, Boston, 1994—. Featured Essayist (Pub. Radio Series) Tales of The Great North, 1995. Trustee, Homer Fire Dept. Inc., 1983-87. Recipient Atlantic Monthly mag. Poetry prize, Boston, 1975, Rescuer of Yr. award Homer Fire Dept., 1987, Mencken award Free Press Assn., Port Hadlock, Wash., 1994, Davidoff Journalist award, Wesleyan Writers Confr., Middletown Ct., 1996, Sigma Delta Chi award for Radio Commentaries, Greencastle, Ind., 1997. Mem. Nat. Soc. of Newspaper Columnists, Soc. of Profl. Journalists (sports reporting, 1995), Nat. Press Club, Alaska Press Club (columnist sports analysis, radio essayist, 1994-97). Home: Lookout Dr Homer AK 99603-9121 Office: Tempest Media Prodn PO Box 3600 Homer AK 99603-3600

BEACH, LEE ROY, psychologist, educator; b. Gallup, N.Mex., Feb. 29, 1936; s. Dearl and Lucile Ruth (Krumtum) B.; m. Barbara Ann Heinrich, Nov. 13, 1971. B.A., Ind. U., 1957; M.A., U. Colo., 1959, Ph.D., 1961. Aviation psychologist U.S. Sch. Aviation Medicine, Pensacola, Fla., 1961-63; human factors officer Office of Naval Research, Washington, 1963-64; postdoctoral research U. Mich., Ann Arbor, 1964-66; faculty dept. psychology U. Wash., Seattle, 1966-89; faculty mgmt. & policy, psychology U. Ariz., Tucson, 1990—, McClelland chair mgmt. & policy, 1989—. Contbr. articles to profl. jours. Recipient Feldman rsch. award, 1981, Disting. Tchr. award U. Wash., 1986, Prof. of Yr. award State of Wash., 1989, nat. teaching award Coun. for Advancement and Support Edn., 1989; fellow NIMH, 1964-66. Fellow Am. Psychol. Soc.; mem. Soc. for Orgnl. Behavior. Office: Univ Arizona Coll Bus & Pub Adminstrn Tucson AZ 85721

BEACH, ROGER C., oil company executive; b. Lincoln, Nebr., Dec. 5, 1936; s. Melvin C. and L. Mayme (Hoham) B.; m. Elaine M. Wilson, Oct. 1954 (div. 1972); children: Kristi, Mark, Anne; m. Karen Lynn Ogden, July 27, 1974. BS, Colo. Sch. Mines, 1961. Profl. petroleum refining engr., Calif. With Unocal Corp., L.A., 1961—; mgr. spl. projects Unocal Corp., Los Angeles, 1976-77, dir. planning, 1977-80, v.p. crude supply, 1980-86, pres. refining and mktg., 1986-92, corp. sr. v.p., 1987-1992, pres., 1992-94, CEO, 1994—, now chmn. and COO. Chmn. bd. trustees Nat. 4-H Coun. Mem. Pres.'s Interchange Exec. Alumni Assn. Office: Unocal Corp 2141 RoseCrans Ave El Segundo CA 90245

BEACH, WILLIAM BROWN, psychiatrist, educator; b. Scranton, Pa., Mar. 22, 1921; s. William Brown and Florence Mae (Sluman) B.; m. J. Mona Boyden. BS in Pharmacy, Wash. State U., 1943; MD, U. Chgo., 1947. Diplomate Am. Bd. Psychiatry and Neurology. Intern Highland Alameda County Hosp., Oakland, Calif., 1947-48; psychiatric resident Ea. State Hops., Medical Lake, Wash., 1949-50, Inst. of Living, Hartford, Conn., 1950-51, 52-53; fellow in child psychiatry Langley Porter Neuropsychiat. U. Calif. Sch. Medicine, San Francisco, 1953-55; asst. dir. outpatient dept. Calif. Dept. Mental Hygiene, San Francisco, 1955-57, chief of child psychiatry Berkeley State Mental Hygiene, 1957, regional chief No. Calif. Cmty. Svcs. Divsn., 1957-61, chief bur. mental retardation and children's svcs., 1961-65, dep. dir. cmty. mental health, 1965-71; dep. sec. for mental health and med. programs Pa. Dept. Pub. Welfare, 1971-74; group leader White House Conf. on Children and Youth, Washington, 1960; chmn. Calif. Statewide Conf. on Children and Youth; surveyor, cons. NIMH, HCFA on medicare reimbursement program, 1974-86; intermittent physician surveyor Hosp. Accreditation Svcs., Joint Commn. on Accreditation of Healthcare Orgns., 1987—; participant, cons. Child Psychiatry Residency Tng. Program, Children's Hosp. and Med. Ctr., U. Wash., Dept. Psychiatry and Behavioral Scis., 1989—; vice chmn., chmn. Atlantic States Conf. Contbr. articles to profl. jours. Trustee Vt. Hosp. Assn., 1974-88, Windham Coll., Putney, Vt.; mem. Vt. State Bd. of Health, 1975-88; mem., bd. dirs. Vt. Profl. Rev. Orgn., 1986-88; chmn. Vt. State Mental Health Adv. Coun., 1976-79. Capt. USAF, 1951-52. Fellow Am. Acad. Child Psychiatry (life), Am. Psychiat. Assn. (life, program com. Inst. on Hosp. and Cmty. Psychiatry 1981-86, chmn. 1986), Am. Coll. Mental Health Adminstrs. (founding), Am. Coll. Psychiatrists (long-range planning and policy com. 1986-89, task force on psychiat. edn.); mem. King County Med. Soc., Wash. State Med. Assn.

BEACHLEY, DEANNA EILEEN, history educator; b. Somerset, Pa., Aug. 22, 1963; d. Ronald D. and Linda E. (Brougher) B.; m. John M. Ziebell, Jan. 13, 1993. BA, Youngstown State U., 1985, MA, 1988; postgrad., No. Ariz. U., 1988—. Prof. history C.C. of So. Nev., North Las Vegas, 1992—. Active Nev. Women's History Project. Mem. Orgn. Am. Historians, Western Women's History Assn. Office: CC of So Nev 3200 E Cheyenne Ave S2C North Las Vegas NV 89030

BEAGLE, JOHN GORDON, real estate broker; b. Spokane, Wash., Dec. 31, 1943; s. Gordon Avril and Sylvia Alberta (Dobbs) B.; m. Shihoko Ledo, Nov. 14, 1964; children: James, Steven, Kevin, Melanie. BS, Mont. State U., 1970; GRI, Realtors Inst., Helena, Mont. Cert. real estate broker. Instr. Kalispell (Mont.) High Sch., 1970-71; gen. mgr. Equity Coop. Assn., Harlem, Mont., 1971-76; owner, operator Howards Pizza, Livingston, Mont., 1976-79; broker, owner Beagle Properties, Sidney, Mont., 1979—. Appointed to Mont. Bd. Realty Regulation, 1995. With USN, 1963-67. Mem. Mont. Assn. Realtors (v.p. ea. dist. 1982-84, 90-94), Gateway Bd. Realtors (pres. 1987-88), Kiwanis, Masons (past master). Republican. Mem. Ch. of Christ. Home: Holly & North Dr Sidney MT 59270 Office: ERA Beagle Properties 120 2nd Ave SW Sidney MT 59270-4018

BEAIRD, STEVEN EDWARD, fundraising professional; b. Rockford, Ill., June 1, 1955; s. Edward Louis and Jeanette Josephine (Renk) B.; m. Linda Teresa Moreno, May 6, 1988. BA in Comms., U. Wash., 1977; MBA in Mgmt., Marylhurst Coll., Portland, Oreg., 1993. Asst. dir. pub. rels. St. Peter Hosp., Olympia, Wash., 1978-80; devel. dir. Cath. Diocese of Spokane, 1980-84, Cath. Diocese of Tucson, 1984-89; v.p. devel. and pub. rels. Jesuit High Sch., Portland, 1989—. Past bd. dirs. Nat. Cath. Stewardship Coun.; mem. St. Cecilia Parish, Beaverton, Oreg.; bd. dirs. Giving in Oreg. Coun. Mem. Nat. Soc. Fundraising Execs. (cert.), N.W. Planned Giving Roundtable, Jesuit Secondary Edn. Assn. Advancement and Alumni Dirs. (past nat. chair), Willamette Valley Devel. Officers (bd. dirs.), City Club of Portland, Alpha Delta Phi. Roman Catholic. Office: Jesuit High Sch 9000 SW Beaverton Hwy Portland OR 97225

BEAL, GRAHAM WILLIAM JOHN, museum director; b. Stratford-on-Avon, Eng., Apr. 22, 1947; came to U.S., 1973; s. Cecil John Beal and Annie Gladys (Barton) Tunbridge; m. Nancy Jane Andrews, Apr. 21, 1973: children: Priscilla Jane, Julian William John. BA, Manchester U., Eng., 1969; MA, U. London, 1972. Acad. asst. to dir. Sheffield City (Eng.) Art Galleries, 1972-73; gallery dir. U. S.D., Vermillion, 1973-74, Washington U., St. Louis, 1974-77; chief curator Walker Art Ctr., Mpls., 1977-83; dir. Sainsbury Ctr. for Visual Arts, Norwich, Eng., 1983-84; chief curator San Francisco Mus. Modern Art, 1984-89; dir. Joslyn Art Mus., Omaha, 1989-96, Los Angeles County Mus. Art, 1996—; mem. Fed. Adv. Com. on Internat. Exhbns., 1991-94. Author: (book, exhbn. catalog) Jime Dine: Five Themes, 1984; co-author: (book, exhbn. catalog) A Quiet Revolution, 1987, David Nash: Voyages and Vessels, 1994, Joslyn Air Museum: Fifty Favorities; contbr. to Apollo Mag., London, 1989—. Trustee Djerassi Found., Woodside, Calif., 1987-89; mem. Capitol Murals Commn., Lincoln, Nebr. Mem. Assn. Art Mus. Dirs. Office: Los Angeles County Mus Art 5905 Wilshire Blvd Los Angeles CA 90036-4523*

BEALL, BURTCH W., JR., architect; b. Columbus, Ohio, Sept. 27, 1925; s. Burtch W. and Etta (Beheler) B.; m. Susan Jane Hunter, June 6, 1949;

children: Brent Hunter, Brook Waite. Student, John Carroll U., 1943; BArch, Ohio State U., 1949. Draftsman Brooks & Coddington, Architects, Columbus, 1949-51, William J. Monroe, Architects, Salt Lake City, 1951-53, Lorenzo Young, Architect, Salt Lake City, 1953-54; prin. Burtch W. Beall, Jr., Architect, Salt Lake City, 1954—; vis. lectr. Westminster Coll., 1955; adj. prof. U. Utah, 1955-85, 92-97; treas. Nat. Coun. Archtl. Registration Bds., 1982-84. Restoration architect Salt Lake City and County Bldg; contbr. projects to: A Pictorial History of Architecture in America, America Restored, This Before Architecture. Trustee Utah Found. for Arch., 1985, pres., 1987-91; mem. Utah State Bd. Fine Arts, 1987-95, chmn., 1991-93; chmn. Utah State Capitol Adv. Com., 1986-90, Western States Art Fedn., Bd. trustees, 1991-94; mem. exec. residence com. State of Utah, 1991-97; mem. Utah: A Guide to the State Found. With USN, 1943-45. Recipient several merit and honor awards; Found. fellow Utah Heritage Found., 1985. Fellow AIA; mem. Masons, Sigma Alpha Epsilon. Methodist. Home: 4644 Brookwood Cir Salt Lake City UT 84117-4908 Office: Burtch W Beall Jr Architect 2188 Highland Dr Salt Lake City UT 84106-2837

BEALL, DENNIS RAY, artist, educator; b. Chickasha, Okla., Mar. 13, 1929; s. Roy A. and Lois O. (Phillips) B.; 1 son, Garm. Musician,, Okla. City U., 1950-52; B.A., San Francisco State U., 1953, M.A., 1958. Registrar Oakland (Calif.) Art Mus., 1958; curator Achenbach Found. for Graphic Arts, Calif. Palace of the Legion of Honor, San Francisco, 1958-1965; asst. prof. art San Francisco State U., 1965-69, assoc. prof., 1969-76, prof. art, 1976-92; prof. emeritus, 1992—. Numerous one-man shows of prints, 1957—, including: Award Exhbn. of San Francisco Art Commn., Calif. Coll. Arts and Crafts, 1978, San Francisco U. Art Gallery, 1978, Los Robles Galleries, Palo Alto, Calif.; numerous group shows 1960— including Mills Coll. Art Gallery, Oakland, Calif., Univ. Gallery of Calif. State U., Hayward, 1979, Marshall-Meyers Gallery, 1979, 80, Marin Civic Ctr. Art Galleries, San Rafael, Calif., 1980, San Francisco Mus. Modern Art, 1985; touring exhibit U. Mont., 1987-91; represented in numerous permanent collections including Libr. of Congress, Washington, Mus. Modern Art, N.Y.C., Nat. Libr. of Medicine, Washington, Cleve. Mus., Whitney Mus., Phila. Mus., U.S. embassy collections, Tokyo, London and other major cities, Victoria and Albert Mus., London, Achenbach Found. for graphic Arts, Calif. Palace of Legion of Honor, San Francisco, Oakland Art Mus., Phila. Free Libr., Roanoke (Va.) Art Ctr., various colls. and univs. in U.S. Served with USN, 1947-50, PTO. Office: San Francisco State Univ Art Dept 1600 Holloway Ave San Francisco CA 94132-1722

BEALL, DONALD RAY, multi-industry high-technology company executive; b. Beaumont, Calif., Nov. 29, 1938; s. Ray C. and Margaret (Murray) B. BS, San Jose State Coll., 1960; MBA, U. Pitts., 1961; postgrad., UCLA; D of Engring. (hon.), GMI Engring. and Mgmt. Inst., 1994, Milw. Sch. Engring., 1994. With Ford Motor Co., 1961-68; fin. mgmt. positions Newport Beach, Calif., 1961-66; mgr. corp. fin. planning and contracts Phila., 1966-67; controller Palo Alto, Calif., 1967-68; exec. dir. corp. fin. planning N.Am. Rockwell, El Segundo, Calif., 1968-69, exec. v.p. electronics group, 1969-71; exec. v.p. Collins Radio Co., Dallas, 1971-74; pres. Collins Radio Group, Rockwell Internat. Corp., Dallas, 1974-76; corp. v.p., pres. Electronic Ops., Dallas, 1976-77; exec. v.p. Rockwell Internat. Corp., Dallas, 1977-79; pres., chief operating officer Rockwell Internat. Corp., Pitts., 1979-88; chmn. bd., chief exec. officer Rockwell Internat. Corp., Seal Beach, Calif., 1988—; mem. bd. overseers and Grad. Sch. of Mgmt.; bd. visitors U. Calif., Irvine, 1988—; trustee Calif. Inst. Tech.; bd. dirs. Procter & Gamble Co., Amoco Corp., Times-Mirror Corp., L.A. World Affairs Coun.; mem. Bus. Higher Edn. Forum, Bus. Coun., Bus. Roundtable, SRI Adv. Coun., Coun. on Competitiveness. Recipient Exemplary Leadership in Mgmt. award John E. Anderson Sch. Mgmt., UCLA, 1991, Excellence in Tech. award Gartner Group, 1991, Spirit of Achievement award Jr. Achievement of So. Calif., 1993, Adm. Chester W. Nimitz award Navy League's Fleet, 1995, Inaugural Front and Ctr. award Calif. State U., Fullerton, 1996, Human Rels. award Am. Jewish Com., Orange County, 1996; named hon. chmn. Nat. Engrs. Week, 1994. Fellow AIAA, Soc. Mfg. Engrs.; mem. Navy League U.S., Young Pres.'s Orgn., Sigma Alpha Epsilon, Beta Gamma Sigma. Office: Rockwell Internat Corp PO Box 4250 2201 Seal Beach Rd Seal Beach CA 90740-8250

BEAMON, RUBY T., elementary education educator; m. Andrew Beamon, 1958. BA, Oakwood Coll., 1957; MA, Calif. State U., Dominguez Hills, 1989. Cert. tchr. (lifetime), Calif. Tchr. L.A. Unified Sch. Dist., 1966—, mentor tchr., 1989—; coord. gifted program Wadsworth Ave. Elem. Sch., L.A., 1975—, libr. chmn., 1985—. Recipient Fulfillment award, 1996. Mem. Assn. Supervision and Curriculum Devel., Alexes Club L.A. (1st v.p. 1992—). Adventist.

BEAR, GREGORY DALE, writer, illustrator; b. San Diego, Aug. 20, 1951; s. Dale Franklin and Wilma (Merriman) B.; m. Astrid May Anderson, June 18, 1983; children: Erik William, Alexandra. AB in English, San Diego State U., 1973. Tech. writer, host Reuben H. Fleet Space Theater, 1973; freelance writer, 1975—. Author: Hegira, 1979, Psychlone, 1979, Beyond Heaven's River, 1980, Strength of Stones, 1981, The Wind From a Burning Woman, 1983, The Infinity Concerto, 1984, Blood Music, 1985, Eon, 1985, The Serpent Mage, 1986, The Forge of God, 1987, Eternity, 1988, Tangents, 1989, Heads, 1990, Queen of Angels, 1990, Anvil of Stars, 1992, Moving Mars, 1993 (Nebula award 1994), Songs of Earth and Power, 1993, Legacy, 1995, Slant, 1997; short stories: Blood Music (Hugo and Nebula awards), 1983, Hardfought (Nebula award), 1993, Tangents (Hugo and Nebula awards), 1987; editor: New Legends, 1995. Cons. Citizen's Adv. Council on Nat. Space Policy, Tarzana, Calif., 1983-84. Mem. Sci. Fiction Writers of Am. (editor Forum 1983-84, chmn. grievance com. 1985-86, v.p. 1987, pres. 1988-90). Home: 506 Lakeview Rd Lynnwood WA 98037-2141

BEARMAN, SCOTT IRVIN, internist, educator; b. Coral Gables, Fla., Nov. 16, 1954; s. Julius Edwin and Martha (Ebstein) B.; m. Theresa Ann Skalabrin, Mar. 17, 1990; children: Samuel Asher, Anna Gabriel. BS, Tufts U., 1976, MD, 1981. Diplomate Am. Bd. Internal Medicine. Intern in Medicine U. Wash., Seattle, 1981-82, resident in Medicine, 1982-84, fellow in Med. Oncology Fred Hutchinson Cancer Rsch. Ctr., 1984-87, assoc. clin. rsch. Fred Hutchinson Cancer Rsch. Ctr., 1987-91; clin. dir. Bone Marrow Transplant program Health Scis. Ctr. U. Colo., Denver, 1991—, assoc. prof. Medicine, 1991—, co-dir. Clin. Investigations Core Cancer Ctr., 1992—, prin. investigator S.W. Oncology Group, 1992—. Reviewer: (jours.) Blood, Bone Marrow Transplantation, Am. Jour. Hematology, Clin. Cancer Rsch., Jour. AMA, Experimental Hematology, Annals of Internal Medicine. Mem. ACP, Am. Fedn. Clin. Rsch., Am. Soc. Hematology, Am. Soc. Clin. Oncology, Am. Soc. Blood and Marrow Transplantation, Phi Beta Kappa. Office: U Colo Health Sci Ctr PO Box B 190 4200 E 9th Ave Denver CO 80220-3706

BEART, ROBERT W., JR., surgeon, educator; b. Kansas City, Mo., Mar. 3, 1945; s. Robert Woodward and Helen Elizabeth (Wamsley) B.; m. Cynthia Anne, Jan. 23, 1971; children: Jennifer, Kristina, Amy. AB, Princeton U., 1967; MD, Harvard U., 1971. Diplomate Am. Bd. Surgery, Am. Bd. Colorectal Surgery. Intern, resident U. Colo.; prof. surgery Mayo Clinic, Rochester, Minn., 1976-87, Scottsdale, Ariz., 1987-92; prof. surgery U. So. Calif., L.A., 1992—. Maj. USMC, 1972-83. Fellow Am. Soc. Colon and Rectal Surgery (pres. 1994); mem. Commn. on Cancer (chmn.). Office: U So Calif Dept Surgery 1510 San Pablo St Ste 514 Los Angeles CA 90033-4586

BEARWALD, JEAN HAYNES, company executive; b. San Francisco, Aug. 31, 1924; d. Joseph Robert and Edna Haynes (Goudey) Bearwald; m. William Henry Sherburn, Apr. 12, 1969 (dec. 1970); 1 child by previous marriage, David Richard Cross. BA, Stephens Coll., Columbia, Mo., 1945. Adminstrv. asst. Bearwald & Assocs., Sacramento, 1966-78; acct. Truck Parts Co., Sand City, Calif., 1979-80; pres., chief exec. officer Bearwald and Assocs., Fresno, Calif., 1980-89, Las Vegas, N.Mex., 1989-91; owner Traditions D'Elegance, Santa Fe, 1991—; program dir. hosp. and institution State of Calif. Ann. Conf., Carmel, 1980-82. Chmn. Sunset Serenade Gala, Santa Fe Opera Guild, 1993-94. Republican. Episcopalian. Home and Office: 941 Calle Mejia Apt 1604 Santa Fe NM 87501-1470

BEASLEY, BRUCE MILLER, sculptor; b. L.A., May 20, 1939; s. Robert Seth and Bernice (Palmer) B.; m. Laurence Leaute, May 21, 1973; children: Julian Bernard, Celia Beranice. Student, Dartmouth Coll., 1957-59; B.A., U. Calif. at Berkeley, 1962. One-man shows include Everett Ellin Gallery, L.A., 1963, Kornblee Gallery, N.Y.C., 1964, Hansen Gallery, San Francisco, 1965, David Stuart Gallery, L.A., 1966, Andre Emmerich Gallery, N.Y.C., 1971, DeYoung Mus., San Francisco, 1972, Santa Barbara Mus. Art, 1973, San Diego Mus. Art, 1973, Fuller-Goldeen Gallery, San Francisco, 1981, Hooks-Epstein Gallery, Houston, 1990, 93, 95, Pepperdine U., L.A., 1990, So. Oreg. State U., 1991, Sonoma State U., Rhonert Park, Calif., 1991, Fresno Art Mus., 1992, Oakland Mus., 1992, Utermann Gallery, Dortmund, Germany, 1993, Scheffel Gallery, Bad Homberg, Germany, 1993, Galerie Rudolfinum, Prague, 1994, Kunsthalle Mannheim, Germany, 1994, Harcourts Gallery, San Francisco, 1994, Galerie Wirth, Zurich, Switzerland, 1995, Yorkshire Sculpture Park, Eng., 1995; exhibited in group shows at San Francisco Mus. of Modern Art, 1961, Mus. of Modern Art, N.Y.C., 1961,62, Dallas Mus. Contemporary Art, 1962, Musee d'Art Moderne, Paris, 1963, U. Art Mus., Berkeley, 1964, Fine Arts Museums, San Francisco, 1965, Guggenheim Mus., 1966, Krannert Art Mus., Ill., 1969, Jewish Mus., N.Y.C., 1970, Milw. Art Ctr., 1970, Expo '70, Osaka, Japan, Stanford Art Mus., 1972, Musee d'Art Moderne, Paris, 1973, Nat. Mus. Am. Art, 1980, Musee d'Art Contemporain Bordeaux, France, 1984, Kunsthalle Mannheim, 1984, Palace of Exhbns., Budapest, Hungary, 1987, Middleheim Sculpture Park, Belgium, 1987, Yorkshire Sculpture Park, Eng., 1989, 87, Hakone Open-Air Mus., Japan, 1993, 95, Landesgartenschau, Germany, 1994; represented in permanent collections Mus. Modern Art, N.Y.C., Guggenheim Mus., N.Y.C., Musee d'Art, Paris, Nat. Mus. Am. Art, Washington, Kunsthalle Mannheim, Germany, San Franciso Mus. Modern Art, L.A. County Mus. Art, Sheldon Mem. Art Gallery, Lincoln, Nebr., Hood Mus. Art, Spencer Mus. Art, Lawrence, Kans., Laguna Art Mus., Franklin D. Murphy Sculpture Garden, UCLA, Crocker Art Mus., Sacramento, Bellevue Art Mus., Fresno Art Mus., Xantus Janos Mus., Hungary, Fine Art Muss., San Francisco, Oakland Mus. Calif., Santa Barbara Mus. Art, San Jose (Calif.) Mus. Art, Dartmouth Coll., N.H.; commissions include State of Calif., Oakland Mus., City San Francisco, Miami Internat. Airport, San Francisco Internat. Airport, Fed. Home Loan Bank, San Francisco, Stanford U., City Anchorage, City Salinas, Calif., Fresno Art Mus. Bd. dirs. Internat. Sculpture Ctr., Washington. Home: 322 Lewis St Oakland CA 94607-1236

BEATTIE, GEORGE CHAPIN, orthopedic surgeon; b. Bowling Green, Ohio, Sept. 24, 1919; s. George Wilson and Mary Turner (Chapin) B.; m. Nancy U. Fant, Mar. 1, 1947; children: Michael, Suzanne, Eric. BA, Bowling Green U., 1939; MD, U. Chgo., 1943. Diplomate Am. Bd. Orthopaedic Surgery. Commd. lt. (j.g.) MC USN, 1943, advanced through grades to lt. comdr., 1951; med. officer, intern U.S. Naval Hosp., Great Lakes, Ill., 1943-44; resident, fellow in orthopaedic surgery Lahey Clinic, Boston, 1944; ward med. officer orthopaedic services Naval Hosp., Guam, 1944-46; sr. med. officer USN, Manus Island, Papua New Guinea, 1946; resident tng. in orthopaedic surgery U.S. Naval Hosp. St. Albans, N.Y.C., 1947-48; resident in orthopaedic surgery Children's Hosp., Boston, 1949; asst. chief orthopaedic surgery U.S. Naval Hosp. Oak Knoll, Oakland, Calif., 1950-52; comdg. officer med. co. 1st Marine Div. Med. Bn., Republic of Korea, 1952-53; chief orthopaedic service Dept. Phys. Medicine and Navy Amputee Ctr. U.S. Naval Hosp., Phila., 1954; resigned USN, 1954; practice medicine specializing in orthopaedic surgery San Francisco, 1954—; co-chmn. handicapping conditions com. Health Action Study San Mateo County, 1965; 1st chmn. orthopaedic sect. surg. dept. Peninsula Hosp. and Med. Ctr., Burlingame, Calif., 1967, chmn. rehab. service, 1967-71, chmn. phys. therapy and rehab. com., 1956—, vice chmn. orthopaedic dept., 1973-76, chmn., 1977-79; med. dir. research and rehab. ctr. San Mateo (Calif.) County Soc. Crippled Children and Adults, 1958-63; mem. exec. com. Harold D. Chope Community Hosp., San Mateo, 1971-76, chief, co-chmn. orthopaedic sect., 1971-76; chief orthopaedic surg. sect. Mills Meml. Hosp., San Mateo, 1976-78; others. Contbr. articles to profl. jours. Active Indian Guides, 1972-77; pres. Calif. Easter Seal Soc., 1969-71. Decorated Bronze Star. Fellow Am. Acad. Orthopaedic Surgeons (exhibit com. 1979-86); mem. AMA (Billings Bronze medal 1954), Western Orthopaedic Assn. (pres., bd. dirs. 1986), Leroy Abbott Orthopaedic Soc. U. Calif. San Francisco (assoc. clin. prof.), Alpha Omega Alpha. Office: 1828 El Camino Real Ste 606 Burlingame CA 94010-3120

BEATTIE, GERALDINE ALICE (GERI BEATTIE), advocate; b. Harrisburg, Pa., Jan. 8, 1943; d. John Martin and Marian Pauline (Coulson) Ramsey; m. Robert Bruce Beattie, Nov. 22, 1969; children: Michelle Nichols, Bryan Scott, Todd Alan. Student, U. Pa., 1960-62, Germantown (Pa.) Med. Ctr., 1960-63. Staff nurse Germantown (Pa.) Med. Ctr., 1963; head nurse Shore Meml. Hosp., Somers Point, N.J., 1964; head nurse Children's Hosp., San Diego, 1965-73, nursing supr., 1977-81, founder, supr. child abuse evidentiary program, 1981-93, asst. dir., mgr. Ctr. Child Protection, 1993—; bd. suprs. Multi-Victim Protocol Task Force, San Diego, 1987-88, Victim Witness Protocol Task Force, San Diego, 1989—; mem. Strategic Plan Task Force, Dept. Social Svcs., San Diego, 1996—. Author/editor: (protocol manual) Victim Witness Protocol, 1991. Mem. Am. Humane Soc., Am. Profl. Soc. Abuse of Children, Calif. Profl. Soc. Abuse of Children, Calif. Sexual Assault Investigators Assn., Calif. Network Sexual Offending, San Diego Cmty. Child Abuse Coord. Coun. (chair sexual abuse rev. com. 1984-86, Outstanding Svc. to Cmty. award). Republican. Presbyterian. Home: 2298 Windmill View Rd El Cajon CA 92020 Office: Ctr Child Protection-Childrens Hosp 3020 Childrens Way San Diego CA 92123

BEATTIE, LANE, state senator; b. Sept. 29, 1951; m. Joy Hadlow; 3 children. Student, U. Utah. Mem. Utah State Senate, 1988—, majority leader, 1993-94, pres., 1995-96; co-chair state strategic planning com.; mem. various coms. including retirement, transportation and pub. safety. Toll fellow Coun. of State Govt., 1991; recipient Colleen M. Bangerter award, 1992. Mem. Utah Assn. Realtors, Nat. Assn. Realtors, Bountiful Area C. of C. Republican. Office: 1313 North 1100 West West Bountiful UT 84087

BEAUMONT, MONA, artist; b. Paris; d. Jacques Hippolyte and Elsie M. (Didisheim) Marx. m. William G. Beaumont; children: Garrett, Kevin. Postgrad., Harvard U., Fogg Mus., Cambridge, Mass. One-woman shows include Galeria Proteo, Mexico City, Gumps Gallery, San Francisco, Palace of Legion of Honor, San Francisco, L'Armitiere Gallery, Rouen, France, Hoover Gallery, San Francisco, San Francisco Mus. Modern Art, Galeria Van der Voort, San Francisco, William Sawyer Gallery, San Francisco, Palo Alto (Calif.) Cultural Ctr., Galerie Alexandre Monnet, Brussels, Honolulu Acad. Arts; group shows include San Francisco Mus. Modern Art, San Francisco Art Inst., DeYoung Meml. Mus., San Francisco, Grey Found. Tour of Asia, Bell Telephone Invitational, Chgo., Richmond Art Ctr., L.A. County Mus. Art, Galerie Zodiaque, Geneva, Galerie Le Manoir, La Chaux de Fonds, Switzerland, William Sawyer Meml. Exhibit, San Francisco, others; represented in permanent collections Oakland (Calif.) Mus. Art, City and County of San Francisco, Hoover Found., San Francisco, Grey Found., Washington, Bulart Found., San Francisco; also numerous pvt. collections. Mem. Soc. for Encouragement of Contemporary Art, Bay Area Graphic Art Coun., San Francisco Art Inst., San Francisco Mus. Modern Art, Capp Street Project, San Diego Mus. Contemporary Art, L.A. Mus. Contemporary Art. Recipient ann. painting award Jack London Square, 2 ann. awards San Francisco Women Artists, One-man Show award San Francisco Art Festival; purchase award Grey Found., San Francisco Women Artists (2), San Francisco Art Festival; included in Printworld Internat., Internat. Art Diary, Am. Artists, N.Y. Art Rev., Calif. Art Rev., Art in San Francisco Bay Area. Address: 1087 Upper Happy Valley Rd Lafayette CA 94549-2805

BEAUMONT, RODERICK FRASER, education consultant; b. Gourock, Scotland, Dec. 3, 1955; came to U.S., 1984; s. Robert Charles and Cathrine (Kendall) B.; m. Mary Elizabeth Beaumon; children: Timothy Michael, Allyn Joseph, Kathryn Nicol. BS in Edn., U. Ctrl. Eng., Birmingham, 1977; MA in Comm. Arts, U. Birmingham, 1979; AAS in Aerospace Sci., Emery Sch. Aviation, 1985. Tchr. various schs., Eng., 1977-82; photojournalist UPI, Europe and Am., 1982-90; instr. U. N.D., Grand Forks, 1990-92; program cons. Paradigm Group, Prescott, Ariz., 1990—; tech. prep coord. Amite County, Liberty, Miss., 1992-94; sch.-to-work dir. Yavapai Coll., Prescott, 1994-96; editor-in-chief Sch.-To-Work News, Prescott, 1995—; cons., Kans., Miss., N.D., Ariz., Colo., 1990—. Contbr. articles to profl. jours. Fellow Royal Geog. Soc., London, 1978, Inst. of Journalists, London, 1980. Democrat. Home and Office: 450A Overland Tr Prescott AZ 86303

BEAVER, WILLIAM LAWRENCE, retired scientist, consultant; b. Yuciapa, Calif., Oct. 9, 1920; s. Ivon Rosco and Velma (White) B.; m. May Merit, Oct. 21, 1944 (dec. Mar. 1991); children: Judith Elizabeth, Robert Alan. BS, U. Calif., Berkeley, 1944, PhD, 1951. Rsch. engr. U. Calif., Berkeley, 1946-51; rsch. scientist Varian Assocs., Palo Alto, Calif., 1951-57, mgr. microwave tube rsch., 1957-61, sr. scientist, 1961-64, 67-74, mgr. applied math., 1964-66; rsch. fellow physiology Sch. Medicine Stanford (Calif.) U., 1966-67, adj. prof., 1974-78; cons. in ultrasonic imaging Varian Assocs., 1974-78; cons. in med. computers Med. Graphics Corp., St. Paul, 1982-85; cons. in physiology and biomed. UCLA Sch. Medicine, Torrance, 1968—. Author numerous papers in field. Mem. IEEE (sr.), Am. Physiol. Soc., Sigma Xi. Home: PO Box 390157 Mountain View CA 94039-0157

BECAR, MICHAEL NOEL, protective services official; b. Logan, Utah, Aug. 12, 1946; s. Loyal E. and Margene Pumphrey; m. Rene Beecham, July 2, 1978; children: Tammy, Kevin, Stuart, Yvonne. BS in Edn., U. Idaho, 1994. Cert. advance peace officer, 1982, mgmt., 1990. Patrol sgt. Caldwell (Idaho) Police Dept., 1967-79; tng. coord., dep. dir. Peace Officer Stds. and Tng., Meridian, Idaho, 1979-95; exec. dir. Peace Officer Stds. and Tng., Meridian, 1995—; chmn. foster parent planning com. Casey Family Program, Boise, Idaho, 1992, 93; pres. Idaho Peace Officer meml. Fund, Meridian, 1995—. Mem. Phi Kappa Phi. Office: Peace Officer Stds & Tng 700 S Stratford Meridian ID 83642

BECERRA, XAVIER, congressman, lawyer; b. Sacramento, Jan. 26, 1958; s. Manuel and Maria Teresa B.; m. Carolina Reyes, 1987. AB, Stanford U., 1980, JD, 1984. Atty., 1984—; dir. dist. office State Senator Art Torres, L.A.; dep. atty. gen. dept. justice, Calif., 1987-90; assemblyman, 59th dist. State of Calif., 1990-93; mem. 105th Congress from 30th Calif. dist., 1993—; mem. ways and means com.; chmn. Congl. Hispanic Caucus. Mem. Mexican-Am. Bar Assn., Calif. Bar Assn., Assn. Calif. State Attys. and Adminstrv. Law Judges. Democrat. Office: House of Representatives 1119 Longworth Bldg Washington DC 20515-0530

BECHELIAN, LISA, interior designer; b. Beirut, Lebanon, Oct. 14, 1956; came to U.S., 1984; d. Antranig and Nelly (Ajemian) B. Student, Academie Des Beaux Arts, Beirut, 1977-81; Cert. in Interior Design, UCLA, 1990. Cons. Lisa Beshlian DEcoration, Beirut, 1982-87; asst. designer E.L.K. Assocs., L.A., 1991-93; prin., owner L.A.B. Interiors, L.A., 1993—; cons. Calif. State Univs. ADA Program, L.A., 1992; mem. design bd. Ronald McDonald Expansion Project, L.A., 1992-94; mem. programming com. ECO-EXPO Seminars, L.A., 1991. Mem. Young Women's Cir./United Armenian Congl. Ch., 1987—. Mem. Am. Soc. Interior Designers. Home and Office: 5801 Hickory Dr Agoura CA 91301-3944

BECHER, STUART LORENZ, writer, planetarium show producer; b. Harvey, Ill., May 16, 1949; s. Raymond Edwin and Margurite Elsie (Lorenzen) B.; m. Debra Balbach. BS, U. Ill., Chgo., 1980. Engring. technician Grayhill Electronics, La Grange, Ill., 1977-81; in quality control Knowles Electronics, Franklin park, Ill., 1981-85; R&D technician Sorensen Rsch., Salt Lake City, 1986-87; designer technician Hansen Planetraium, Salt Lake City, 1987—; lectr. in field. Author: (children's show scripts) A Perfect Place for Penguins, 1989, SCIPPI, The Magic Telescope, 1991, (show script) The Endless Horizon, 1992, (book) The Endless Horizon, 1993; writer, dir., prodr. Riders in the Sky and The Doorway to Doom, 1995, From Out of the Darkness, 1997. Vol. Pioneer Trails State Park, Salt Lake City, 1991—; served to sgt. USAF, 1967-72, Viet Nam. Office: Hansen Planetraium 15 S State St Salt Lake City UT 84111-1518

BECHTEL, RILEY PEART, engineering company executive; s. Stephen Davison Bechtel, Jr. BA in Polit. Sci., Psychology, U. Calif., Davis, 1974; JD, MBA, Stanford U., 1979. Bar: Calif. 1979. With Bechtel Group, Inc., San Francisco, 1966-79, 81—, Thelen, Marrin, Johnson & Bridges, San Francisco, 1979-81; bd. dirs. Bechtel Group Inc., 1987—, pres., coo, 1989-1990, chmn. exec. com., ceo, 1990—; CEO, 1993—; mem. Bus. Coun., Bus. Roundtable policy com., Calif. Bus. Roundtable, J.P. Morgan Internat. Adv. Coun.; adv. coun. Stanford U. Grad. Sch. of Bus.; dean's adv. coun. Stanford Law Sch. Trustee Thacher Sch., Ojai, Calif. Mem. ABA. Office: Bechtel Group Inc 50 Beale St San Francisco CA 94105-1813

BECHTEL, STEPHEN DAVISON, JR., engineering company executive; b. Oakland, Calif., May 10, 1925; s. Stephen Davison and Laura (Peart) B.; m. Elizabeth Mead Hogan, June 5, 1946; 5 children. Student, U. Colo., 1943-44; BS, Purdue U., 1946, D. in Engring. (hon.), 1972; MBA, Stanford U., 1948; DSc (hon.), U. Colo., 1981. Registered profl. engr., N.Y., Mich., Alaska, Calif., Md., Hawaii, Ohio, D.C., Va., Ill. Engring. and mgmt. positions Bechtel Corp., San Francisco, 1941-60, pres., 1960-73, chmn. of cos. in Bechtel group, 1973-80; chmn. Bechtel Group, Inc., 1980-90, chmn. emeritus, 1990—; bd. dirs. Remington Arms, former chmn., mem. bus. coun., emeritus life councillor, past chmn. conf. bd.; chmn. emeritus Fremont Group, Inc., Sequoia Ventures, Inc., 1995—. Trustee, mem., past chmn. bldg. and grounds com. Calif. Inst. Tech.; mem. pres.'s coun. Purdue U.; adv. coun. Inst. Internat. Studies, bd. visitors, former charter mem., adv. coun. Stanford U. Grad. Sch. Bus. With USMC, 1943-46. Decorated officer French Legion of Honor; recipient Disting. Alumnus award Purdue U., 1964, U. Colo., 1978, Ernest C. Arbuckle Disting. Alumnus award Stanford Grad. Sch. Bus., 1974, Disting. Engring. Alumnus award 1979; named Man of Yr. Engring. News-Record, 1974, Outstanding Achievement in Constrn. award Moles, 1977, Chmn.'s award Am. Assn. Engring. Soc., 1982, Washington award Western Soc. Engrs., 1985, Nat. Medal Tech. from Pres. Bush, 1991, Golden Beaver award 1992, Herbert Hoover medal 1980. Fellow ASCE (engirng. mgmt. award 1979, pres. award 1985), AAAS, Inst. Chem. Engrs. (U.K., hon.); mem. AIME, NSPE (hon. chmn. Nat. Engrs. Week 1990), Nat. Acad. Engring. (past chmn.), Calif. Acad. Scis. (hon. trustee), Am. Soc. French Legion Honor (bd. dirs., disting. achievement medal 1994), Royal Acad. Engring. (U.K., fgn. mem.), Pacific Union Club, Bohemian Club, San Francisco Golf Club, Claremont Country Club, Cypress Point Club, St. Francis Yacht Club, Bear River Club (Utah), Wild Goose Club (Calif.), Chi Epsilon, Tau Beta Pi. Office: Bechtel Group Inc PO Box 193965 San Francisco CA 94119

BECHTLE, ROBERT ALAN, artist, educator; b. San Francisco, May 14, 1932; m. Nancy Elizabeth Dalton, 1963 (div. 1982); children: Max Robert, Anne Elizabeth; m. Whitney Chadwick, 1982. B.A., Calif. Coll. Arts and Crafts, Oakland, 1954, M.F.A., 1958; postgrad., U. Calif.-Berkeley, 1960-61. Graphic designer Kaiser Industries, Oakland, 1956-59; instr. Calif. Coll. Arts and Crafts, 1957-61, assoc. prof. to prof.; lectr. U. Calif.-Berkeley, 1965-66; vis. artist U. Calif.-Davis, 1966-68; assoc. prof. San Francisco State U., 1968-76, prof., 1976—. One-man shows Mus. of Art, San Francisco, 1959, 64, Berkeley Gallery, 1965, Richmond Art Ctr. (Calif.), 1965, U. Calif.-Davis, 1967, O.K. Harris Gallery, N.Y.C., 1971, 74, 76, 81, 84, 87, 92, Berggruen Gallery, San Francisco, 1972, E.B. Crocker Art Gallery, Sacramento, 1972, Univ. Art Mus., U. Calif.-Berkeley, 1979, Daniel Weinberg Gallery, Santa Monica, 1991, Gallery Paul Anglim, San Francisco, 1991, San Francisco Mus. Modern Art, 1991; exhibited in group shows San Francisco Art Inst., 1966, Whitney Mus. N.Y.C., 1967, Milw. Art Ctr., 1969, Mus. Contemporary Art, Chgo., 1971, Serpentine Gallery, London, 1973, Toledo Mus. Art, 1975, San Francisco Mus. Modern Art, 1976, Pushkin Fine Arts Mus., Moscow, 1978, Pa. Acad. Fine Arts, Phila., 1981, San Antonio Mus. Art, 1981, Pa. Acad. Fine Arts, Phila, 1981, Calif. Palace of Legion of Honor, San Francisco, 1983, Mus. Contemporary Art, L.A., 1984, San Francisco Mus. Modern Art, 1985, Univ. Art Mus., U. Calif., Berkeley, 1987; represented in permanent collections Achenbach Found. for Graphic Arts, San Francisco, Chase Manhattan Bank, N.Y.C., E.B. Crocker Art Gallery, Sacramento, Gibbes Art Gallery, S.C., High Mus. Art, Atlanta, Hunter Art Mus., Chattanooga, Library of Congress, Washington, Lowe Art Mus.-U. Miami, Coral Gables, Fla., Mills Coll., Oakland, Mus. Modern Art, N.Y.C., Met. Mus., N.Y.C., Neue Gal der Stadt Aachen, West Germany, Oakland Mus., San Francisco Mus. Modern Art, Univ. Art Mus.-U. Calif-Berkeley, Fine Arts Mus. of San Diego, Rose Art Mus., Brandeis U., Waltham, Mass., U. Nebr.-Lincoln, Whitney Mus., N.Y.C., Guggenheim Mus., N.Y.C., Nat. Academician, Nat. Acad. Design, 1993. Served with U.S. Army, 1954-56. Recipient James D. Phelan award, 1965; named Nat. Academician, Nat. Acad. Design, 1993; Nat. Endowment for Arts grantee, 1977, 83, 89, Guggenheim grantee, 1986. Office: San Francisco State U Dept Art 1600 Holloway Ave San Francisco CA 94132*

BECK, COLLEEN MARGUERITE, archaeologist; b. San Jose, Calif., Feb. 21, 1951; d. William Robert and Willa Rose (Moore) Beck; m. William Keith Kolb; children: William Logan Kolb, Alexa Rose Kolb. BA, U. Calif., Berkeley, 1973, MA, 1974, PhD, 1979. Dir. Agy. for Conservation Archaeology, Eastern N.Mex. U., Portales, 1980-83, asst. prof., 1983-84; rsch. assoc. Lowie Mus. Anthropology, Berkeley, 1985-89; asst. rsch. prof. Desert Rsch. Inst., Las Vegas, 1990-92, dep. dir. quaternary scis. ctr., 1992—; postdoctoral fellow Carnegie Mus. Natural History, Pitts., 1979-80; mem. N.Mex. Hist. Preservatio Adv. Bd., Santa Fe, 1981-86; mem. San Joaquin County Historic Records Commn., Stockton, Calif., 1986-89. Author: Ancient Roads on the North Coast of Peru, 1979; editor: Views of the Jornada Mogollon, 1984; author articles. Mem. tech. adv. bd. Las Vegas Sch. Dist., 1994-96; mem. tech. adv. bd. Bur. Land Mgmt., 1995-97, Las Vegas Historic Preservation Commn., 1996—. NSF fellow, 197-76; Tinker Found. grantee, 1974-77. Fellow Am. Anthropology Assn. (life); mem. Soc. for Am. Archaeology, Nev. Archaeology Assn. (bd. dirs. 1993—, pres. 1995—), Archaeo-Nev. Soc., Nat. Trust for Hist. Preservation, Inst. Andean Studies (life), Nev. State Mus. Hist. Soc. Office: Desert Rsch Inst 755 E Flamingo Rd Las Vegas NV 89119-7363

BECK, DORIS OLSON, library media director; b. Kingsville, Tex., June 4, 1930; d. Thomas Leon and Estelle (Fosselman) Olson; m. John Roland Beck, Feb. 9, 1951; children: Elizabeth Joan, Thomas Roland, Patricia Lind, John William. BS in Chemistry, Tex. A & I Coll., 1949, BSChemE, 1950; MLS, Wayne State U., 1975. Cert. secondary educator with libr. endorsement, Ariz. Chemist Patterson's Lab., Harlingen, Tex., 1950-51; asst. libr. Tex. A & I Coll., Kingsville, Tex., 1951; chemist U.S. Geol. Svc., Stillwater, Okla., 1951-53; bookkeeper, nurse's aide McKenzie Co. Hosp., Watford City, N.D., 1953-54; math. tchr. Prescott Jr. High, Corpus Christi, Tex., 1954; chemist U.S. Geol. Svc., Columbus, Ohio, 1957-58; math. tchr. Christiansberg (Va.) High Sch., 1967-69; sci. tchr. East Jr. High Sch., Farmington, Mich., 1969-70; sci./math. tchr. Jane Addams Jr. High Sch., Royal Oak, Mich., 1970-78; math support Oakland Vocat. Sch., Royal Oak, 1978-79; head libr. S.W. Bapt. Coll., Pontiac, Mich., 1977-79; libr. media dir. Humboldt (Ariz.) Jr. High, 1979-87, Bradshaw Mt. Jr. High, Dewey, Ariz., 1987—; site based com. Bradshaw Mt. Jr. High Sch., Dewey, Ariz., 1992—. Ch. libr., cons., 1993—. Mem. Ariz. Libr. Assn., Ariz. Ednl. Media Assn., Alpha Delta Kappa. Republican. Baptist. Home: PO Box 25824 3829 Valorie Prescott Valley AZ 86312 Office: Bradshaw Mt Jr High Sch Humboldt Unified Sch Dist Dewey AZ 86327

BECK, GORDON EUGENE, art history educator, consultant; b. Goshen, Ind., Mar. 23, 1929; s. Ralph Lea and Lydia Elizabeth (Greenlee) B.; m. Elizabeth Alice Arnholt, Mar. 22, 1951; children: Anne Elizabeth, Susan Elizabeth, Stephen Lea, John Lyons. BA, Bowling Green State U., 1951; MA, Western Res. U., 1952; PhD, U. Ill., 1964; postdoctoral student, Cini Found., Venice, Italy, 1979. Asst. instr. U. Ill., Urbana, 1954-56; instr. Bowling Green (Ohio) State U., 1956-57; instr., dir. univ. theatre U. Kans., Lawrence, 1957-65; asst. prof., dir. univ. theatre Cornell U., Ithaca, N.Y., 1965-71; prof. art history Evergreen State Coll., Olympia, Wash., 1971-94, prof. emeritus art history and archaeology, 1994—; cons. European travel, Euro-Files, Olympia; dir. U. Kans. Theatre, 1957-65, Cornell U. Cinema, 1965-70, Mus. and Monuments Program, Olympia, 1975—; del. Cannes Internat. Film Festival, 1996, 97. Editor, Players Mag., 1961-67; contbr. articles to Theatre Ann., 1964-69, Ency. World Drama, 1969; producer feature film, Branches, 1970. Cpl. M.C., U.S. Army, 1952-54. Mem. Coll. Art Assn., Mediaeval Acad. Am., Am. Soc. Aesthetics. Democrat. Home: 2406 18th Ave NW Olympia WA 98502-4119 Office: Evergreen State Coll 1605 Library Bldg Olympia WA 98505

BECK, JEROME JOSEPH, health care administrator, biomedical technologist; b. Mesa, Ariz., Nov. 7, 1957; s. Robert Leon and Marie Margaret (Curry) B.; m. Catherine Elizabeth Williams, June 27, 1981; 1 child, John Robert. BSBA, U. Phoenix, 1989. Cert. hemodialysis technologist Bd. of Nephrology Examiners Nursing & Tech. Dialysis unit housekeeper Good Samaritan Hosp., Phoenix, 1976-78, dialysis equipment technician, 1978-81, dialysis sr. equipment technician, 1981-83, coord. tech. staff devel., 1983-88, mgr. dialysis tech. svcs., 1988-89; dir. tech. svcs. East Valley Dialysis Svcs., Mesa, 1989-91, program dir., 1991-93; ops. mgr. Renalwest L.C. (formerly East Valley Dialysis Svcs.), Mesa, 1993—; dir. ops.; bd. dirs. Bd. Nephrology Examiners, Madison, Wis., 1990-92; mem. renal disease and detoxification com. Assn. for the Advancement of Med. Instrumentation, 1989-93; mem. technicians com. ESRD Network VI, Albuquerque, 1984-85; nephrology conf. lectr. nationwide. Mem. editl. adv. bd. Nephrology News and Issues, 1996—; contbr. articles to profl. jours. Mem. Nat. Assn. Nephrology Technologists (bd. dirs., western v.p. 1989-91, Torchbearer award 1994). Republican. Office: Renalwest LC 1750 S Mesa Dr Ste 110 Mesa AZ 85210-6213

BECK, JOHN ROLAND, environmental consultant; b. Las Vegas, N.Mex., Feb. 26, 1929; s. Roland L. and Betty L. (Shrock) B.; m. Doris A. Olson, Feb. 9, 1951; children: Elizabeth J., Thomas R., Patricia L., John William. BS, Okla. A&M U., 1950; MS, Okla. State U., 1957; postgrad., U. Tex., 1954, George Washington U., 1965. Registered sanitarian, Ohio, Ariz.; cert. wildlife biologist. Wildlife researcher King Ranch, Kingsville, Tex., 1950-51; faculty Inst. Human Physiology U. Tenn., Martin, 1954-55; rsch. biologist FWS, USDI, Grangeville, Idaho, 1955-57; ctr. dir. Job Corps, OEO, Indiahoma, Okla., 1965-67; supr. animal control biology FWS, USDI, 1953-69; operating v.p. Bio-Svc. Corp., Troy, Mich., 1969-78; pres. BECS Ltd., Prescott, Ariz., 1981-85; spl. asst. USDA - APHIS, Washington, 1986-87; prin. cons. Biol. Environ. Cons. Svc. Inc., Phoenix, 1978-93; faculty assoc. Ariz. State U., Tempe, 1980-89; expert witness in bus. evaluations, 1979-96; expert witness in pesticide litigations, 1989-94; participant fin. seminars, 1980-85. Sr. author: Managing Service for Success, 1987, 2d edit., 1991; columnist mo. column on pest control in 2 mags., 1980-88; contbr. articles to profl. jours. Life mem. Rep. Nat. Com., 1993—; mem. Rep. Senatorial Inner Cir., 1994—, Rep. Presdl. Roundtable, 1995-97. Capt. USAR, 1950-62. Fellow Royal Soc. Health, N.Y. Explorers Soc.; mem. ASTM (chmn. pesticide com. 1979-81, chmn. vertebrate pesticides 1994-), Wildlife Soc., Sigma Xi. Republican. Baptist.

BECK, JONATHAN P., French language educator; b. Mpls., Aug. 28, 1947; s. Joseph H. and Sophia Belle (Shapero) B.; m. Sharon McInerney, June 20, 1970 (div. Mar. 1980); 1 child, Jonathan Matthew; m. Ann K. Farmer, Jan. 9, 1992; children: Nicholas William, Galen Joseph. BA, Columbia U., 1970; MA, Harvard U., 1971, PhD, 1974. Asst. prof. Emory U., Atlanta, 1974-80; assoc. prof. U. Ariz., Tucson, 1983-86, prof. French, 1987—, dept. head French and Italian, 1985-90; vis. assoc. prof. Stanford (Calif.) U., 1980. Author: Le Concil de Basle, 1979, Theatre et propagande, 1986; mem. editl. bd. Romance Philology, 1989—; contbr. articles to profl. jours. Grantee Am. Coun. Learned Socs., 1977, 86; Guggenheim fellow John Simon Guggenheim Meml. Found., 1982. Home: 1138 High Ct Berkeley CA 94708-1625 Office: U Ariz Dept French Tucson AZ 85721

BECK, KAREN PORTSCHE, elementary education educator; b. Salt Lake City, June 30, 1950; d. Vernon Willis and Gretchen Ann (Roeser) Portsche; m. James Kenneth Vogler, Aug. 2, 1968 (div. May 1991); children: Philip Justin Vogler, Shaun Wade Vogler; m. Harvey William Beck, Mar. 18, 1995. BA, Boise (Idaho) State U., 1979, MA, 1994. Cert. tchr., Idaho. Tchr. Boise Sch. Dist., 1979—, Hillcrest Elem. Sch., 1979-84; tchr. grades 1-3 Hawthorne Elem., 1984—; mem. com., prin. asst. Ptnrs. in Edn., Boise, 1990—; computer coord. Hawthorne Elem. Sch., Boise, 1994—. Author: (tchrs. manual) Education Strategies FAS and FAE Students, 1994.

BECK, MARTIN, journalist; b. Kaslo, B.C., Can., Dec. 21, 1964; came to U.S., 1965; s. Bruce and Freda (Rush) B.; m. Stephanie Robinson, May 6, 1990; children: Jillian, Benjamin. BA, U. Calif., Irvine, 1987; MA, U. Mo., 1989. Sports writer, editor L.A. Times, Costa Mesa, Calif., 1989—. Office: LA Times 1375 Sunflower Ave Costa Mesa CA 92626

BECK, RODNEY ROY, professional baseball player; b. Burbank, Calif., Aug. 3, 1968. With Oakland (Calif.) Atheletics, 1986-88; pitcher San Francisco Giants, 1988—; mem. Nat. League All-Star Team, 1993, 94. Office: San Francisco Giants 3 Com Park Candlestick Point San Francisco CA 94124*

BECK, TIMOTHY DANIEL, human resources specialist, consultant; b. Santa Monica, Calif., Mar. 21, 1953; s. James Daniel and Bettye June (Cisler) B.; m. Marcia Ann Smith, Jan. 16, 1977; children: Tracy Beth and Erica Brandy (twins), Jenna Michelle. AA, El Camino Community Coll., 1974; BA, Calif. State U., Northridge, 1979. Registered health underwriter, registered employee benefits cons. Candidate cert. employee benefit specialist, group claims supr. Prudential Ins. Co. Am., L.A., 1973-79; employee benefits cons. Olanie, Hurst & Hemrich, L.A., 1979-81; v.p. policyholder svc. dept. Health Maintenance Life Ins. Co., Fountain Valley, Calif., 1981; v.p. Robert E. French Ins. Svcs., Inc., Huntington Beach, Calif., 1981-85; v.p., mng. cons. employee benefits Warren, McVeigh & Griffin, Inc., Newport Beach, Calif., 1985-91; mng. cons. employee benefits A. Foster Higgins and Co., Inc., 1991-96; prin. Buck Cons., Inc., L.A., 1996—; mem. Kaiser Permanente Orange County Consumer Coun., 1987—; mem. pub. edn. com. Calif. Health Decision, 1988—; mem. bus. and health adv. panel Am. Health Pub.; speaker to confs. and profl. socs.; cons. Healthnet Adv. Coun., 1996—, Orange County Bus. Coun., Town Hall, 1996—; mem. Healthnet Cons. Adv. Coun., 1997—. Creator, contbg. editor Employee Benefits Mgmt. Letter, 1985-91; contbr. articles to profl. publs. Mem. Internat. Found. Employee Benefits, Nat. Assn. Health Underwriters, Calif. Assn. Health Underwriters, Employee Benefit Planning Assn. So. Calif. (bd. dirs. 1992-93), So. Calif. Assn. Benefit Plan Adminstrs., Orange County Assn. Health Underwriters (founder, 1st v.p. 1987-88), Orange County Bus. Coun., Orange County Employee Benefit Coun., Calif. State U. Northridge Alumni Assn.

BECKER, ANNE MARGARET, neonatal nurse; b. San Rafael, Calif., Sept. 4, 1953; d. Robert E. and Helen (Grondorf) Spitzer; m. Michael Becker, Nov. 21, 1973; children: Miriam, Davina. Diploma, St. Luke's Sch. Nursing, San Francisco, 1974; AS, San Francisco Community Coll., 1974; BS, U. Calif., San Francisco, 1984, MS, 1986. RN, Calif.; cert. high-risk perinatal nurse ANCC. Staff nurse II Children's Hosp. Med. Ctr., Oakland, Calif., 1974-86; outreach educator Children's Hosp., San Francisco, 1986; staff nurse Med. Personnel Pool, San Francisco, 1986-87; staff nurse II-IV Stanford (Calif.) U. Hosp., 1987-91; staff nurse IV Lucile Salter Packard Children's Hosp. at Stanford, Palo Alto, Calif., 1991—, acting clin. nurse specialist, 1993—. Mem. editorial bd. Neonatal Network jour., Petaluma, Calif., 1987—; peer reviewer Jour. Am. Acad. Nurse Practitioners, Pitts., 1990-92; author (poetry) Waiting, 1989; contbr. chpt. to book, 1997. Mem. ANA Calif. (exec com. coun. on maternal-child nursing 1993-94, exec. com. mem. coun. for acute care nursing practice 1994—, chair, 1996—), ANCC (perinatal nurse test devel. com. 1989-92, bd. on cert. for maternal-child nursing 1989-91, mem. founding bylaws com. 1995-96, chair nursing practice commn. 1991-93, commr. 1991-94, co-founder, vice chair coun. on children and families 1991-94), Calif. Nurses Assn., Nat. Assn. Neonatal Nurses, U. Calif. San Francisco Nursing Alumni Assn. (editl. cons. grad. nursing students 1991-92). Republican. Episcopalian. Home: 612 Stonegate Dr South San Francisco CA 94080-1564

BECKER, BRUCE DOUGLAS, mechanical engineer; b. Tacoma, Mar. 19, 1959; s. Walter A. and Mary Jane (Barr) B.; m. Jamie M. Russell, Sept. 10, 1988; 1 child, Catherine Anne. BSME, Wash. State U., 1981. Registered profl. engr., Oreg. Design engr. Hyster Corp., Portland, Oreg., 1981-85; devel. engr. Precision Castparts Corp., Portland, 1985-95; design engr. Autostack Corp., Portland, 1995-96, Gunderson, Inc., Portland, Oreg., 1996—. Eagle scout Boy Scouts Am., Pullman, Wash., 1975; citizen amb. People to People Internat., People's Republic of China, 1985; mem. Milw. Lutheran Ch., 1996—. Mem. ASME (assoc.), NSPE. Home: 811 NW Drake St Camas WA 98605 Office: Gunderson Inc 4350 NW Front Ave Portland OR 97210-1422

BECKER, DONALD PAUL, surgeon, neurosurgeon; b. Cleve., 1935. MD, Case Western Res. U., 1961. Diplomate Am. Bd. Neurol. Surgery. Intern U. (Cleve.) Hosps., 1961-62, resident in surgery, 1962-63, resident in neurol. surgery, 1963-67; fellow in neurosurgery NIH, Bethesda, Md., 1966; prof., chief neurosurgery UCLA Med. Ctr., 1967-85. Mem. ACS, AMA. Office: UCLA Medical Center Div Neurosurgery Box 957039 Rm 18-228NPI Los Angeles CA 90095-7039

BECKER, JOHN DAVID, career officer, philosophy educator; b. Worthington, Minn., May 22, 1958; s. Donald R. and Anna M. (Garrow) B.; m. Joanne T. Schaeder, July 21, 1979; children: Justin, Matthew, Scott, Robin, Steven. BA in Polit. Sci., Calif. State U., Turlock, 1978; MA in Internat. Rels., Boston U., 1983; MA in Philosophy, Emory U., 1989. Commd. 2nd lt. U.S. Army, 1978; advanced through grades to lt. col., 1995; battery officer 1/79 FA Bn., Ft. Ord, Calif., 1979-80; team leader 559th USAAG, Vicenza, Italy, 1980-83; battery comdr. 3/18 FA Bn., Ft. Sill, Okla., 1984-87; asst. prof. English U.S. Mil. Acad., West Point, N.Y., 1989-92; bn. S-3 and XO 3/41 FA Bn., Ft. Stewart, Ga., 1993-95; asst. prof. philosophy USAF Acad., Colo., 1995—. Co-Author: Moral Dimensions of the Military Profession, 1997; contbr. articles to profl. jour. Mem. West Point bd. edn., U.S. Mil. Acad., 1989-92; mem. sch. bd. Holy Trinity Ch., Colorado Springs, Colo., 1995—. Mem. Army U.S. Assn., Assn. U.S. Inst., Joint Conf. Profl. Ethics. Office: USAF Acad Dept Philosophy and Fine Arts U S A F Academy CO 80840

BECKER, MICHAEL KELLEHER, university administrator, consultant; b. L.A., June 27, 1941; s. George Joseph and Marion Julia (Kelleher) B.; m. Eugenia Margosian, June 11, 1963; children: Gwendolyn Becker O'Keefe, Sean Michael Becker, Katherine Becker. BA, Swarthmore Coll., 1963; MA, U. Calif., Berkeley, 1965; PhD, U. Calif., 1970. Contract negotiator Oakland Naval Supply Ctr., 1966-67; instr., asst., assoc. prof. Ctrl. Conn. State U., New Britain, 1967-77; dean pers. adminstrn. Ctrl. Conn. State U., 1978-89; dir. employee rels. So. Ill. U. Sys., Carbondale, 1989-92; asst. v.p. acad. affairs-faculty rels. U. Toledo, 1992-96; dir. human resources Western Washington U., Bellingham, 1996—. Mem. New Britain Sch. Bd., 1983-89 (pres. 1988-89). Woodrow Wilson fellow Woodrow Wilson Found., 1963. Mem. Acad. for Acad. Pers. Adminstrn., Coll. and Univ. Pers. Assn. Unitarian. Home: 3014 Windtree Ct Bellingham WA 98226 Office: Western Wash Univ Human Resources Mail Stop 9021 Bellingham WA 98225

BECKER, STEPHEN ARNOLD, museum executive; b. Redwood City, Calif., Aug. 24, 1951; s. Leo H. and May B. (Goldberg) B.; m. Beverly Nichols-Fredotovich, July 31, 1977; 1 child, Joseph Nikola. Asst. curator mus. Ind. U., Bloomington, 1973-77, lectr. folklore dept., 1975-77; historian Sacramento History Ctr., 1977-78; dir. history divsn. County Pks. Dept., Riverside, Calif., 1979-85; asst. dir. Mus. Internat. Folk Art, Santa Fe, 1985-89; dir. Mus. Indian Arts and Culture/Lab. Anthropology, Santa Fe, 1989-95; pres., CEO Museums of Turtle Bay, Redding, Calif., 1995—. Mem. Am. Assn. Museums, Am. Folklore Soc. Office: Museums of Turtle Bay 800 Auditorium Dr Redding CA 96001

BECKHAM, STEPHEN DOW, history educator; b. Marshfield, Oreg., Aug. 31, 1941; s. Ernest Dow and Anna Marie (Adamson) B.; m. Patricia Joan Cox, Aug. 26, 1967; children: Andrew Dow, Ann-Marie Catherine. BA, U. Oreg., 1964; MA, UCLA, 1966, PhD, 1969. Lectr. Long Beach (Calif.) State U., 1968-69; from asst. to assoc. prof. Linfield Coll., McMinnville, Oreg., 1969-77; from assoc. prof. to prof. Lewis and Clark Coll., Portland, Oreg., 1977-93, Pamplin prof. history, 1993—, named endowed chair in history, 1993—; assoc. Heritage Rsch. Assoc., Eugene, Oreg., 1979—, USA Rsch. Author: Requiem for a People: The Rogue Indians and the Frontiersmen, 1971, 2nd edit., 1996, The Simpsons of Shore Acres, 1971, Coos Bay: The Pioneer Period, 1973, The Indians of Western Oregon: This Land Was Theirs, 1977, Land of the Umpqua: A History of Douglas County, Oregon, 1986; editor: Tall Tales from Rogue River, 1974, 2d edit., 1990, Lewis & Clark Coll., 1991, Many Faces: An Anthology of Oregon Autobiography, 1993, Seventy-Five Years of Buildings: Hoffman Construction Company, 1995; contbr. numerous to profl. publs. Mem. bd. advisers Nat. Trust for Hist. Preservation, Washington, 1978-85; mem. State Adv. Com. on Hist. Preservation, Salem, Oreg., 1977-85; mem. Oreg. Geog. Names Bd., Portland, 1990-93; pres., bd. dirs. John and LeRee Caughey Found., L.A., 1985—. Can. Govt. faculty enrichment fellow, 1985; recipient Ruth McBride Powers Preservation of Yr. award, 1986, Oreg. Prof. of Yr. award, 1992. Mem. Am. Hist. Assn. (Asher Disting. Teaching award 1995), Am. Anthropol. Assn., Oreg. Hist. Soc. (bd. dirs., exec. com. 1994—), Native Am. Arts Coun. Democrat. Baptist. Home: 1389 Hood View Ln Lake Oswego OR 97034-1505 Office: Lewis and Clark Coll Portland OR 97219

BECKMAN, JAMES WALLACE BIM, economist, marketing executive; b. Mpls., May 2, 1936; s. Wallace Gerald and Mary Louise (Frissell) B. BA, Princeton U., 1958; PhD, U. Calif., 1973. Pvt. practice econ. cons., Berkeley, Calif. 1962-67; cons. Calif. State Assembly, Sacramento, 1967-68; pvt. practice market rsch. and econs. cons., Laguna Beach, Calif., 1969-77; cons. Calif. State Gov.'s Office, Sacramento 1977-80; pvt. practice real estate cons., L.A. 1980-83; v.p. mktg. Gold-Well Investments, Inc., L.A. 1982-83; pres. Beckman Analytics Internat., econ. cons. to bus. and govt., L.A. and Lake Arrowhead, Calif., 1983—, East European/Middle East Bus. and Govt., 1992—; adj. prof. Calif. State U. Sch. Bus., San Bernardino, 1989—, U. Redlands, 1992—; cons. E European, environmental issues. Contbr. articles on regional & internat. econ. devel. & social change to profl. jours. Maj. USMC 1958-67. NIMH fellow 1971-72. Fellow Soc. Applied Anthropology; mem. Am. Econs. Assn., Am. Statis. Assn., Am. Mktg. Assn. (officer), Nat. Assn. Bus. Economists (officer). Democrat. Presbyterian.

BECKMAN, PATTY ZOE, special education educator, consultant; b. L.A., Mar. 2, 1941; d. Alson Collins Peckham and Doris Lee (Baker) White; m. Bruce William Beckman, Aug. 18, 1962; children: Brenda, Robert, Jeffrey, Janine. BA, Whittier Coll., 1963; MEd, U. Utah, 1988. Cert. gen. edn., spl. edn. tchr., Utah. Tchr. East Whittier (Calif.) Sch. Dist., 1967-69, Santee (Calif.) Sch. Dist., 1969-77, Jordan Sch. Dist., Sandy, Utah, 1982—; cons. Jordan Sch. Dist., 1995—; instr. U. Utah, Salt Lake City, 1996—. Contbr. articles to profl. jours. Mem. ASCD, NEA, Coun. for Exceptional Children (Snowbird chpt. pres. 1995-96), Utah Divsn. Learning Disabilities (pres. 1997—), Utah Edn. Assn. (Utah Disting. Educator 1997), Jordan Edn. Assn. (Tchr. of Month 1993, 95). Home: 8706 Alta Canyon Dr Sandy UT 84093 *Pat Beckman has taught for 25 years in both general and special education classrooms. Her area of focus is on teaching children to be the best learners they can be by using strategies and developing independent learning skills. She has developed methods and materials that help teachers promote strategic, independent learning in their classrooms. The strategies and skills she teaches increase learning in all areas of the curriculum. She consults, instructs teachers, holds parent/student workshops, and teaches at the university level.*

BECKMANN, ROBERT OWEN, artist; b. Phila., Mar. 20, 1942; s. John Harry and Hazel (Bowers) B.; m. Pauline Kay Hahn, Sept. 29, 1984. BA, Coll. of Wooster, Ohio, 1964; MA, U. Iowa, 1966, MFA, 1967. Instr. art U. South Ala., Mobile, 1967-68, No. Ill. U., Dekalb, 1968-71; artist Beckmann Studio, Denver, 1971-77; project dir. cmty. murals project City of Las Vegas, Nev., 1977-79; pres. Wallternatives, Inc., Las Vegas, 1979-92; artist Beckmann Studio, Las Vegas, 1992—; artist-in-residence Artrain, NEA, Mich. Arts Coun., Fedn. Rocky Mountain States, 1973, NEA, Idaho State U., Pocatello, 1974-75, Nev. State Coun. on Arts, Carson City, 1976, Las Vegas, 1977. One man shows include Ferrari Gallery, Las Vegas, 1989, Nev. Mus. Art, Reno, 1993, U. Nev., Las Vegas, 1993, HERE Art, N.Y.C., 1994, Coll. Charleston, S.C., 1995, pARTs Gallery, Mpls., 1995, Va. Commonwealth Univ., Richmond, 1995, Univ. Ariz., Tuscon, 1996, Univ. Idaho, Moscow, 1996, Univ. Md., College Pk., 1996, State Mus. Pub. Sculpture, St. Petersberg, Russia, 1996; group shows include Monumental Propaganda World Fin. Ctr., N.Y.C., 1993, Inst. Contemporary Art, Moscow, 1993, Internat. Gallery at Smithsonian, Washington, 1995, Dunlop Gallery Regina Pub. Libr., Saskatchewan, Can., 1995, Contemporary Art Mus., Tallinn, Estonia, 1995, Lubiljana, Slovenia, 1995, Terrain Gallery, San Francisco, 1996. Vice commr. Las Vegas Arts Commn., 1994-97. Recipient Laura Slobe Meml. prize Chgo. Art Inst., 1971, Gov.'s award State of Nev., 1996; Western States Arts Found. fellow, 1976, Nev. State Coun. on the Arts fellow, 1990.

BECKNER, ARDIS STERN, nutrition specialist, educator; b. Gillett, Wis., Jan. 15, 1935; d. Herman G. and Marie Adam (Kopitzke) Stern; m. William G. Beckner, Dec. 24, 1961 (div.); children: Robert M., Cheryl S.; m. Lloyd M. Eggebrecht, Jan. 1992. AA in Elem. Edn., Andrews U., 1955, BS in Nutrition, 1959; MS in Nutrition, Loma Linda U., 1963. Registered dietition, Calif.; cert. diabetes educator, lactation educator, Calif; cert. adaptive and Alpine ski instr. Profl. Ski Instrs. Am. Elem. sch. tchr. Am. Tchrs. Assn., Gobles, Mich., 1956-58; jr. h.s. home econ. tchr. Am. Tchrs. Assn., Berrien Springs, Mich., 1958-59; home econ. fellow Andrews U., Berrien Springs, 1959-60; clin. dietition White Meml. Hosp., L.A., 1961-64; metabolic genetic dietition L.A. Children's Hosp., 1964-67, Loma Linda (Calif.) U. Hosp., 1969-76; clin. dietetics and metabolic nutritionist Kaiser Permanente Med. Group, Fontana, Calif., 1976—; part-time asst. prof. nutrition Sch. Pub. Health, Loma Linda (Calif.) U., 1996—; part-time instr. Mt. San Jacinto Coll., Gillman Hot Springs, Calif., 1967-69; cons. in field. Editor: SDA Diet Manual, 1964, Diabetes Manual, 1989; author chpt. to book. Investigator, leader, counselor pathfinder clubs Seventh Day Adventist Ch., Loma Linda, 1974-84; instr. Calif. Handicapped Sports and Recreation Assn., Big Bear, 1989—, vol. instr. Bear Mountain Adaptive Ski Sch.; vol., mem. news and info. com. Nat. Forest Svc., 1992—. Recipient Spkrs. award Foster Parents Assn. Inland Execs., 1990, Everyday Heros award San Bernardino (Calif.) Sun, 1993, Vol. Svc. award Nat. Forest Svc., 1994, 95, 96; named Outstanding Program Dir., Pathfinder Clubs So. Calif., 1977, 78, 79. Mem. Am. Dietetic Assn., Am. Assn. Diabetes Educators. Home: 1465 Padua Ave Redlands CA 92374-3866 Office: Kaiser Permanente Med Group 9985 Sierra Ave Fontana CA 92335-6720

BECKS, RONALD ARTHUR, film producer; b. N.Y.C., July 9, 1953; s. Wellington and Vivian (Newkirk) B. Student, York Coll., 1969-71; cert. for prodrs., Cintel Corp., 1974-75; cert., Ch. Religious Sc., 1975-77; D of Religious Communication (hon.), Temple Faith, 1974. Owner, pres., chmn. Ronald A. Becks Internat. Theatre Soc., N.Y.C., 1978-90; v.p. Miracle Prodns., N.Y.C., 1978-90; pres. Magic Circle Players, Australia and Hong Kong, Sodeko Films, Australia and Hong Kong; mktg. dir. V.R.B. Enterprises, Australia and Hong Kong, Multi-Media Svcs., Australia and Hong Kong; pres. Noduki Films, Australia and Hong Kong, 1990, Face Affair, Beverly Hills, Calif., 1991, Film Gods Prodns., Beverly Hills, 1991—; founder, pres. STN TV Network, 1994; prodr. Blues TV, Century Cable, 1996, Inside Press TV, 1997, MASC TV, 1997; v.p. BBH Cosmetics Labs., Beverly Hills, 1994; mem. adv. coun. Internat. Biog. Ctr., Cambridge, Eng., 1995, Inside Press TV Show, Blues TV; pres. Sir Ronald Blues Band, 1996; bd. dir. Beverly Hills Cmty. Theatre Co., 1997; exec. dir. United Citizens Com. Am., 1997. Author: The 3rd Testament, 1990, Legend of Billy Blue, 1988, Black Diamond, 1989, Come and Get It, 1991, Say a Little Prayer, 1991, Stagecoach Mary, 1993, Gigi and the Bogey-Man, 1993; prodr.: You Bring Out the Best in Me, 1984 (top 40 song); inventor phone device; songwriter Perfume in My Coffee; prodn. coord. Asian Belle, 1995. Dep. chmn. UN Assn., 1979, dep. amb., 1979, chmn. Song Quest, 1979; entertainment coord. Keep Australia Beautiful, 1980; prodr. children's show Consulate of Peru, 1979; prodr. and host I Love New York, N.Y.C., 1978; mem. notary pub. commn., 1996. Recipient Internat. Order of Merit, Cambridge. Fellow Highlander Club (life); mem. Prodrs. and Dirs. Guild, Prodrs. Assn., PEN Internat., Am. Soc. Notaries, NAACP, Internat. Platform Assn., Rainbow Coalition, Writers Guild, Journalists Club, Hollywood Press Club, Noetic Scis. Home and Office: 505 S Beverly Dr Ste 364 Beverly Hills CA 90212-4542

BECK-VON-PECCOZ, STEPHEN GEORGE WOLFGANG, artist; b. Munich, Oct. 18, 1933; came to U.S., 1937; s. Wolfgang Anna Marie and Martha Jeanette (Morse) Beck-von-P.; m. Dorothy Ann Freytag, June 16, 1956 (div. 1971); m. Michele Marie Perry, Feb. 8, 1972; children: Stephen Jr., David, Kenneth, Lisa. BEE, Cornell U., 1956; MA in Art, Calif. State U., San Diego, 1974. Electronic engr. Stromberg Carlson Co., San Diego, 1958-60; project mgr. Control Data Corp., San Diego, 1960-65, Digital Devel. Corp., San Diego, 1965-66; project engr. Stromberg Datagraphix, Inc., San Diego, 1966-69; project mgr. Digital Sci. Corp., San Diego, 1969-71; artist San Diego, 1974—; cons. elec. engring., San Diego, 1974-78. Served to 2d lt. USAF, 1956-58. Mem. Internat. Sculpture Ctr., Kappa Alpha Soc. Home and Studio: 636 Nardito Ln Solana Beach CA 92075-2306

BECKWITH, JOHN, musician, composer, educator; b. Victoria, B.C., Can., Mar. 9, 1927. BMus, U. Toronto, 1947, MMus, 1961; DMus (hon.), Mt. Allison U., Sackville, N.B., 1974, McGill U., Montreal, 1978, U. Guelph, Ont., 1995. Pvt. piano studies Alberto Guerrero, Royal Conservatory of Music, Toronto, 1945-50; pvt. composition studies Nadia Boulanger, Paris, 1950-51; pub. relations dir. Royal Conservatory of Music, Toronto, 1948-50;

staff writer for radio music continuity Can. Broadcasting Corp., Toronto, 1953-55; freelance radio programmer and writer, 1955-70; spl. lectr. U. Toronto, 1952-53, lectr., 1954-60, asst. prof. music, 1960-66, assoc. prof., 1966-70, dean, 1970-77, prof., 1977-90, 1st holder Jean A. Chalmers chair in Can. music, 1984-90. Debut: Toronto, 1950; over 100 compositions including 4 operas, works for orch., chorus, etc.; 30 works published including: 4 songs to poems by E.E. Cummings, 1950; Fall Scene and Fair Dance, 1956; Music for Dancing, 1959; Jonah, 1963; Sharon Fragments, 1966; Circle, with Tangents, 1967; Gas, 1969; Taking a Stand, 1972; Musical Chairs, 1973; 3 Motets on Swan's China, 1981; Sonatina in 2 Movements, 1982; Harp of David, 1985; recorded compositions include: Music for Dancing; The Trumpets of Summer; Sharon Fragments; Circle, with Tangents; Quartet; Keyboard Practice; 3 Motets on Swan's China; Upper Can. Hymn Preludes; Etudes, Arctic Dances, Harp of David; recordings: Music at Sharon, 1982; Musical Toronto, 1984; arranger, dir. of instrumental ensemble; editor: The Modern Composer and His World, 1961; Contemporary Canadian Composers, 1975; Canadian Composer series, 1975-90, Musical Canada, 1988; Canadian Consultant, The New Grove, London, 1980; author: Music Papers, 1997; contbr. articles to profl. jours. Recipient Can. Music Coun. ann. medal, 1972, Arts Found. of Greater Toronto ann. music award, 1994; named to Order of Can., 1987. Mem. Can. League of Composers (former sec.), Ency. of Music in Can. (bd. dirs. 1972-94), Can. Musical Heritage Soc. (editl. bd. 1981—). Office: 121 Howland Ave, Toronto, ON Canada M5R 3B4

BEDERKA, STEPHEN EDWARD, management consultant; b. N.Y.C., July 6, 1930; s. Stephen and Emilia Rose (Toth) B.; m. Ann Sabina Canor, Nov. 29, 1952; children: Celeste Ann, Valerie Ann Bederka Collins. BS in Physics, St. Bernadine of Siena, 1952; postgrad., Stanford U., 1968. Radar design engr. GE, Utica, N.Y., 1952-55; communications system engr. Lockheed Martin, Sunnyvale, Calif., 1955-66, system engring. mgr., 1966-74, program mgr., 1974-91; founder, mgmt. and bus. cons. Toth Rsch. Inst., Los Gatos, Calif., 1991—; counselor Svc. Corps Ret. Execs., 1992—. Contbr. articles to profl. jours. and mags. Mem. IEEE (past officer San Francisco chpt.). Home and Office: 15286 Via Palomino Los Gatos CA 95030-2238

BEDFORD, AMY ALDRICH, public relations executive, corporation secretary; b. Pendleton, Oreg., July 13, 1912; d. Edwin Burton and Elsie (Conklin) Aldrich; m. J.M. Bedford (wid.); 1 child, Jacqueline Bedford Brown. BS, Oreg. State U., 1933. Mgr. comml. dept. East Oregonian, Pendleton, 1950-75, mgr. pub. rels., 1975—; corp. sec. East Oregonian Pub. Co., Pendleton, 1950—. Bd. dirs. Oreg. Status of Women Com., 1972-75, Oreg. Law Enforcement Commn., 1975-82, Arts Coun. Pendleton. Recipient Pendleton First Citizen award C. of C., 1962, Gov.'s award for the Arts, 1988. Mem. Women in Communications, Oreg. Press Women, AAUW (pres. 1956-58, grantee 1965), LWV, Pendleton River Parkway Found., World Affairs Coun. Oreg., Altrusa. Home: PO Box 1456 Pendleton OR 97801-0360 Office: East Oregonian Pub Co PO Box 1089 Pendleton OR 97801-1089

BEDROSIAN, JAMES KENNETH, food products executive; b. 1944. V.p., sec., co-owner Sunshine Raisin Corp., Fowler, Calif. Office: Sunshine Raisin Corp PO Box 219 Fowler CA 93625-9745*

BEEBE, JOHN HOWARD (JACK BEEBE), economist, banker; b. Hackensack, N.J., May 11, 1942. BA, Williams Coll., 1964; MS in Indsl. Engring., U. Tex., 1966; MA in Econs., Stanford U., 1970, PhD in Econs., 1972. Asst. prof. bus. Calif. Polytech. State U., San Luis Obispo, Calif., 1966-68; economist FRS Assocs., Menlo Park, Calif., 1972-76; vis. lectr. Stanford (Calif.) Grad. Sch. Bus., 1979-82, 86; from economist to v.p. Fed. Reserve Bank San Francisco, 1976-86, sr. v.p., dir. rsch., 1987—; Bd. dirs. 1990 Inst., Burlingame, Calif. 1993—. Co-author: (book) Television Economics, 1974; contbr. numerous articles to profl. jours. Mem. Am. Econs. Assn. Office: Fed Res Bank San Francisco 101 Market St San Francisco CA 94105-1530

BEEBE, MARY LIVINGSTONE, curator; b. Portland, Oreg., Nov. 5, 1940; d. Robert and Alice Beebe. B.A., Bryn Mawr Coll., 1962; postgrad. Sorbonne, U. Paris, 1962-63. Curatorial asst. Fogg Art Mus., Harvard U., Cambridge, Mass., 1966-68; Apprentice Portland Art Mus., 1963-64, Boston Mus. Art, 1964-65; exec. dir. Portland Ctr. for Visual Arts, 1973-81; dir. Stuart Collection U. Calif.-San Diego, La Jolla, 1981—; cons. in field. Mem. art steering com. Portland Devel. Commn., 1977-80; bd. dirs. Henry Gallery, U. Wash., Seattle, 1977-80; project cons. Nat. Rsch. Ctr. for Arts, N.Y.C., 1978-79; bd. dirs. Art Mus. Assn. San Francisco, 1978-84; bd. dirs., trustee Art Matters Inc., 1985-96; trustee Russell Found., 1982-94; hon. mem. bd. dirs. Portland Ctr. for Visual Arts, 1984-91; mem. arts adv. bd. Centre City Devel. Corp., San Diego, 1982-94; arts adv. bd. Port of San Diego; panel mem., cons. Nat. Endowment Arts; juror numerous art shows and exhbns. Nat. Endowment Arts fellow, 1979. Recipient Allied Professions award AIA, 1992. Contbr. articles to profl. jours. Office: U Calif San Diego The Stuart Collection 9500 Gilman Dr La Jolla CA 92093-5003

BEEBE, NAOMI MARIE, financial consultant, accountant; b. Schenectady, N.Y.; m. William Lloyd Beebe, Nov. 5, 1983. AA in Bus. Adminstrn., Schenectady C.C., 1979; postgrad., Union Coll., 1983, U. Phoenix, San Jose, Calif., 1989-90. Lic. tax preparer, Calif. Sr. cost acctg. clk., cost specialist, labor analyst GE, Schenectady, N.Y., 1973-83; acct. Accts. Inc., 1986-89; owner, fin. cons. Real-Time Consulting, Bookkeeping & Tax Svc., Santa Clara, Calif., 1989—; named del. to Fin. Mgmt. and Auditing Delegation to Russia People to People Internat.; authorized reseller, software cons. State of the Art (Mas90) Accounting Software, 1994—. Creator: (software enhancement) Financial Analysis, 1983 (Merit award 1983). Ch. youth advisor Fisher United Meth. Ch., Schenectady, 1983; treas. Sunnyvale (Calif.) Homeowners Assn., 1990. Mem. Nat. Soc. Pub. Accts., Inst. Mgmt. Accts., Calif. Assn. Ind. Accts. (chpt. pres. 1991-92), Inland Soc. Tax Cons. (chpt. sec. 1993-94). Office: Real-Time Consulting 1556 Halford Ave # 103 Santa Clara CA 95051-2661

BEEBE, SANDRA E., retired English language educator, artist, writer; b. March AFB, Calif., Nov. 10, 1934; d. Eugene H. and Margaret (Fox) B.; m. Donald C. Thompson. AB in English and Speech, UCLA, 1956; MA in Secondary Edn., Calif. State U., Long Beach, 1957. Tchr. English, Garden Grove (Calif.) High Sch., 1957-93, attendance supr., 1976-83, ret., 1993; tchr. watercolor courses, Asilomar, Calif., 1997—; jury chmn. N.W.S., 1997. Contbr. articles to English Jour., chpts. to books; watercolor artist; exhbns. include AWS, NWS, Okla. Watercolor Soc., Watercolor West, La. Watercolor Soc., Knickerbocker Artists N.Y., Montana WCS, Midwest Watercolor Soc., Butler Inst. Am. Art, Youngstown, Ohio, Kings Art Ctr., Audubon Artists N.Y.; cover artist Exploring Painting, 1990, title page Understanding Watercolor, American Artist, 1991. mem. faculty Asilomar, 1997; chmn. of jurors N.W.S. Open, 1997. Named one of the Top Ten Watercolorists The Artists Mag., 1994; recipient Best Watercolors award Rockport Press, 1995; chosen for Design Poster selection, 1995, 97. Mem. Am. Watercolor Soc., Nat. Watercolor Soc., Midwest Watercolor Soc., Watercolor West, Allied Artists N.Y., Knickerbocker Artists N.Y., Audubon Artists N.Y., West Coast Watercolor Soc., Rocky Mountain Nat. Watermedia Honor Soc., Jr. League Long Beach, Kappa Kappa Gamma. Republican. Home: 7241 Marina Pacifica Dr S Long Beach CA 90803-3899 Studio: B-Q Gallery 3920 E 4th St Long Beach CA 90814-1656 also: 239 Mira Mar Ave Long Beach CA 90803-6153

BEECHER, EARL WILLIAM, marketing professional; b. Chgo., June 18, 1942; s. Adolph Bernard and Dorothy M. (McEwen) B.; m. Karen Lillian Hegner, Dec. 1, 1962; children: Katherine, Ann. BS in Bus., St. Matthews U., 1964; A in Fin., Loyola U., 1967; LHD (hon.), Mt. Sinai Theol. Sem., 1971. Sales rep. Burroughs Corp., Detroit, 1964-67; br. mgr. Friden Co., Chgo., 1967-71; dir. mktg. Friden Co., San Leandro, Calif., 1971-75; pres. Standard Bus. Machine Co., Los Angeles, 1975-81; nat. sales mgr. Xerox Corp., Dallas, 1981-83; pres. EBS Data, Denver, 1983-86; v.p. Hedman Co., Chgo., 1986-89; advisor Pacific Bell, 1989—; advisor Pacific Bell, 1989—, Impact Solutions Corp., 1990—, R.M. Dudley Corp., 1990—; prs. Comml. Resources, Denver, 1981—, also bd. dirs.; chmn. bd. dirs. Pacific Telecommunication and Automation, San Francisco, 1990—; bd. dirs. Roma Corp., 1984-86, Credifi, Paris; mem. nat. adv. bd. Joint House Com. on Internat. Affairs, 1993—; pres., ind. distbn. cons. Internet Developers Consortium; corp. dir. Fine Art Galerie Adrienne San Francisco, 1995-96; dir. Fine Art Galerie de La Monde, 1996; cons. Weinstein Gallery, San Francisco; artist agt. Rep. precint cpt., Shaumburg, Ill., 1969; rep. fund raiser, Dallas, 1982. Mem. Duke of Manchester Hunt Club, Hyannis Yacht Club, San Francisoc Yacht Club (assoc.), Elks Club #3 San Francisco, Alpha Psi Omega (bd. dirs. 1971). Office: Comml Resources Inc 3817 S Carson St # 265 Carson City NV 89701-5538

BEEGLE, EARL DENNIS, family physician; b. Ashland, Ohio, July 24, 1944; s. Ray Benjamin and Alice Mae (Imhoff) B.; m. Isabel Sloan-Kerr Adamson, Sept. 3, 1964; children: Ryan Benjamin, Kevin Ian. BA, Manchester Coll., 1967; MS, Purdue U., 1970; MB BChir, MD, BAO, Queen's U., Belfast, No. Ireland, 1978. Diplomate Am. Bd. Family Practice. Life scis. tchr. Elkhart (Ind.) Schs., 1967-72; house officer Nat. Health Svc. of U.K., 1978-79; resident in family practice Riverside Hosp. Med. Coll. Ohio, Toledo, 1979-81, chief resident, 1981-82; pvt. practice Everett, Wash., 1982-93; med. dir. Providence Primary Care Network, Everett, 1993-96; v.p., med. dir. Medalia Healthcare, Seattle, 1997—; credentials com. Providence Gen. Med. Ctr., 1996—, physician well-bring com., 1997—; med. dir. Planned Parenthood, Everett, 1983-86; chmn. utilization Providence Hosp., Everett, 1987-90, chmn. quality assurance, 1991-92; chmn. dept. family practice Providence-Gen. Med. Ctr., Everett, 1993-94; dir. Sisters of Providence Health Plans, Seattle, 1993—. Active Friends of the Somme, No. Ireland, 1991—. NSF fellow, 1967-70. Fellow Am. Acad. Family Practice; mem. Irish and Am. Pediatric Soc., Snohomish County Med. Soc., Associated Physicians of Snohomish County (bd. dirs.), Internat. Soc. Travel Medicine. Office: Providence Claremont Clinic 5007 Claremont Way Everett WA 98203-3321

BEEMAN, MALINDA MARY, artist, program administrator; b. Pomona, Calif., Jan. 23, 1949; d. Earl Wilson and Mary (Alvey) B. BA, San Diego State U., 1971; MFA, San Francisco Art Inst., 1973. Area coord. printmaking U. Houston, 1985-92; program dir. Anderson Ranch Art Ctr., Snowmass Village, Colo., 1992—. Recipient Visual Artists award Nat. Endowment for Arts, 1988, Covision Recognition award Colo. State Arts Coun., 1992. Office: Anderson Ranch Arts Ctr 5263 Owl Creek Rd Snowmass Village CO 81615*

BEENE, M. MELANIE, arts management consultant; b. Athens, Tenn., Mar. 13, 1948; d. Jones C. and Margaret F. (Nankivell) B. BA, Vanderbilt U., 1970, MA in Asian Art History, 1976; JD, U. Tenn., Knoxville, 1977. Bar: Calif. Pub. info. specialist Brevard (N.C.) Music Ctr., summer 1977; assoc. devel. dir. San Francisco Symphony, 1977-78; assoc. dir. Calif. Assn. for the Am. Conservatory Theater, San Francisco, 1978-79; dir. mgmt. assistance program Nat. Alliance of Media Arts Orgns., 1984-88; cons. to nonprofit orgns., 1979—; cons. to the advancement program Nat. Endowment for the Arts, Washington, 1983-90, 94-96, mng. cons. for the advancement program, 1990-95; program officer The Wm. and Flora Hewlett Found., Menlo Park, Calif., 1996; workshop facilitator, panel mem.; mem. faculty, arts adminstrn. program U. Calif., San Francisco Extension, 1981; also tchr. law and art history courses. Author: (with F. Johnson and P. Mitchell) Autopsy of an Orchestra, (with J.Grenzeback) Arts Manager/s Toolbox-Financial Management, 1991. Bd. dirs. Paul Dresher Ensemble, Spirit Rock Meditation Ctr., 1997; mem. bd. advisors Inst. Non-Profit Mgmt., U. San Francisco; mem. nat. adv. com. Asian CineVision; bd. dirs. Headlands Ctr. for Arts, 1984, Legal Svcs. for Children, 1984; vol. counselor Planned Parenthood, 1982-83; treas. San Francisco Arts Advocates, 1978-79. Mem. State Bar Calif. Office: Melanie Beene & Assocs 1339 Diamond St San Francisco CA 94131-1823

BEENE, RICHARD STUART, editor; b. Knoxville, Tenn., June 11, 1951; s. William Wolbach and Julia (Swysgood) B.; m. Dianne Elise Klein, May 29, 1983; children: Lauren Elizabeth, Hannah Julia. BA in History, Ga. So. U., 1973. Reporter Fort Lauderdale (Fla.) Sentinel, 1978-80; state mgr. UPI, N.Y.C., Miami & Atlanta, 1980-84; bur. chief UPI, Cairo, 1983; L.Am. corr. Dallas Times Herald, 1984-87; city editor L.A. Times, 1987-94; exec. editor Bakersfield (Calif.) Californian, 1994—. Recipient Pulitizer, L.A. Times, 1995. Mem. Am. Soc. Newspaper Editors, Calif. Soc. Newspaper Editors, Sigma Delta Chi. Office: Bakersfield Californian 1707 Eye St Bakersfield CA 93301-5208

BEER, FRANCIS ANTHONY, political science educator; b. N.Y.C., Feb. 5, 1939; s. William Joseph and Anne (Benedikt) B.; m. Diana Darnall, June 12, 1965; children: Omar, Marie, Jeremy. AB cum laude, Harvard U., 1960; MA, U. Calif., Berkeley, 1963, PhD, 1967. Asst. prof. dept. govt. U. Tex., Austin, 1967-70, assoc. prof. dept. govt., 1970-75; prof. dept. polit. sci. U. Colo., Boulder, 1975—. Author: Integration and Disintegration in NATO: Processes of Alliance Cohesion and Prospects for Atlantic Community, 1969, Peace Against War: The Ecology of International Violence, 1981; editor Alliances: Latent War Communities in the Contemporary World, 1970; coeditor: (with Ted. R. Gurr) Conflict, Violence, Peace: An International Series of Books, 1990-93, (with R. Hariman) Post-Realism: The Rhetorical Turn in International Relations, 1996; asst. editor Jour. Politics, 1968-71; contbr. articles to profl. jours. Lt. USNR, 1960-62. Fulbright fellow, 1965-66, 71, Mershon fellow, 1966-67, NEH fellow, 1990; grantee Earhart Found., 1972, Inst. World Order, 1974-77. Mem. Internat. Polit. Sci. Assn., Internat. Soc. Polit. Psychology, Am. Polit. Sci. Assn., Internat. Studies. Assn. Office: U Colo Polit Sci Dept Campus Box 333 Boulder CO 80309

BEER, JOSEPH ERNEST, telecommunications manager; b. Pasadena, Calif., June 5, 1959; s. Joseph Andrew and Pauline Sylvia (Micciche) B.; m. Amy Shun-Fong Wu, Oct. 13, 1984. BS in Internat. Bus., Calif. State U., L.A., 1982; MBA in Info. Tech. Mgmt., U. So. Calif., 1987. Asst. engr. ARCO-Electronics & Telecommunications, L.A., 1979-83, sr. coord., 1983-84, project engr., 1984-85, sr. project engr., 1985-87; sr. mgr. Ernst & Young, L.A., 1987-91; dir. telecommunications and network svcs. South Coast Air Quality Mgmt. Dist., L.A., 1991-94; mgr. info. tech. svcs. Tosco Northwest Co., Seattle, 1994-96; dir. profl. svcs. Mosaix Inc., Seattle, 1996—. Recipient scholarship, Ebell Found., L.A., 1981, Bank Am. scholarship, Bank Am. Found., 1981. Mem. Soc. Telecommunications Consultants, Project Mgmt. Inst. Republican. Home: 24012 SE 37th Pl Issaquah WA 98029-6320 Office: Mosaix Inc 6464 185th Ave NW Redmond WA 98052

BEESON, MONTEL EILEEN, human services administrator, gerontologist; b. El Dorado, Ark., Dec. 22, 1939; d. Waymon Willett and Myrtle May (Roach) B. BS in Recreation, Calif. State U., Hayward, 1963; MA in Edn. and Human Devel., Holy Names Coll., Oakland, Calif., 1979. Lic. nursing home adminstr.; cert. community coll. instr.; cert. gerontology. Dist. exec. Ariz. Cactus-Pine Girl Scouts Coun., Phoenix, 1963-66, dist. exec. San Francisco Bay coun., Oakland, Calif., 1966-68, bus. mgr., 1968-71, exec. dir. Shabonee coun., Moline, Ill., 1971-73, Tongass-Alaska coun., Ketchikan, 1973-74, Muir Trail coun., Modesto, Calif., 1974-78; asst. adminstr. Beulah Home, Inc., Oakland, 1980-86; elder care cons., 1986—; exec. dir. Community Adult Day Health Svcs., Oakland, 1987-88; adminstr. Greenhills Retirement Ctr. Millbrae, Calif., 1988—. Mem. Am. Coll. Health Care Adminstrs., Am. Soc. on Aging. Avocations: cross-country skiing, history, travel, reading, music. Home: 3393 Kiwanis St Oakland CA 94602-4005

BEESTON, JOSEPH MACK, metallurgist; b. Fillmore, Utah, Aug. 12, 1918; s. Joseph W. and Florence (Swallow) B.; m. Blanche Weight, Dec. 20, 1946; children: Miriam, Jolynn. BChEng, U. Utah, 1949; postgrad., Oreg. State U., 1949-50; PhD in Metall. Engring., U. Utah, 1953. Asst. prof. Wash. State U., Pullman, 1953-58; sr. metallurgist Phillips Pet Atomic Energy Div., Idaho Falls, Idaho, 1958-61, leader irr. material group, 1961-64; chief materials rsch. sect. Idaho Nuclear, Idaho Falls, 1964-71; chief irradiation material engring. Aerojet Gen., Idaho Falls, 1971-78; sci. specialist EG&G Idaho Inc., Idaho Falls, 1978-85; cons. metallurgist Garrison, Utah, 1985—. Contbr. over 100 articles to profl. jours. With USAF, 1941-45. Mem. ASTM (com. nuclear tech. and applications), Am. Soc. Metals. Home and Office: 625 Circle Dr Garrison UT 84728

BEETHAM, STANLEY WILLIAMS, international management consultant; b. Montpelier, Idaho, Nov. 2, 1933; s. Harry Stanley and Mary (Williams) B.; m. Barbara Burnham, June 20, 1987; 1 child, Lara Mary. BA, Wesleyan U., 1956; MA, U. Amsterdam, The Netherlands, 1957; postgrad., Harvard U., 1958-59, U. Wash., 1959-60. Internat. market mgr. U.S. Rubber/Uniroyal, N.Y.C., 1960-63; corp. mktg. cons. GE, N.Y.C., 1963-65; assoc. dir. Benton & Bowles, Inc., N.Y.C., 1965-67; dir. corp. planning Esmark, Chgo., 1967-72, Consol. Packaging Co., Chgo., 1972-74; sr. cons. Booz Allen Hamilton/Hay Assocs., N.Y.C. and Phila., 1975-80; sr. v.p. U.S. Tobacco Co., Greenwich, Conn., 1981-87; pres. S.W. Beetham & Co., Seattle, 1987—. Contbr. articles in field. Candidate for U.S. Congress from 13th Ill. Dist., 1972, 74; chmn. roundtable Westchester (Conn.) Planning Forum; bd. dirs. Am. Heritage Assn. Fulbright scholar, 1956, Marshall scholar, 1957; Woodrow Wilson fellow, 1958. Mem. N.Am. Soc. Corp. Planning, Nat. Assn. Bus. Economists, Coun. for Urban Econ. Devel., Internat. Soc. for Planing and Strategic Mgmt., Rainier Club, Phi Beta Kappa. Office: 1223 Spring St Ste 501 Seattle WA 98104

BEEZER, ROBERT RENAUT, federal judge; b. Seattle, July 21, 1928; s. Arnold Roswell and Josephine (May) B.; m. Hazlehurst Plant Smith, June 15, 1957; children: Robert Arnold, John Leighton, Mary Allison. Student, U. Wash., 1946-48, 51; BA, U. Va., 1951, LLB, 1956. Bar: Wash. 1956, U.S. Supreme Ct. 1968. Ptnr. Schweppe, Krug, Tausend & Beezer, P.S., Seattle, 1956-84; judge U.S. Ct. Appeals (9th cir.), Seattle, 1984—; alt. mem. Wash. Jud. Qualifications Commn., Olympia, 1981-84. 1st lt. USMCR, 1951-53. Fellow Am. Coll. Trust and Estate Counsel, Am. Bar Found.; mem. ABA, Seattle-King County Bar Assn. (pres. 1975-76), Wash. Bar Assn. (bd. govs. 1980-83). Clubs: Rainier, Tennis (Seattle). Office: US Ct Appeals 802 US Courthouse 1010 5th Ave Seattle WA 98104-1130

BEGERT, MATTHEW, engineering company official; b. Topeka, July 19, 1950; s. John Frederick and Betty Lykel (Prosser) B.; m. Pamela Helen Weidman, Nov. 12, 1982; 1 child, Eric Matthew. BS in Journalism and Mass Comm., U. Kans., 1972, BA in Anthropology, 1973; grad. with honors, Naval War Coll., 1994. Commd. officer USMC, 1973, advanced through grades to lt. col., 1991; exec. officer 1st Air and Naval Gunfire Liaison Co., Oceanside, Calif., 1984-87; ops. action officer 3d Marine Aircraft Wing, El Toro, Calif., 1987-88; adminstr., exec. officer Marine Strike Fighter Squadron 121, El Toro, 1988-89; ops. officer Marine Aircraft Group 11, El Toro, 1989-91; exec. officer Marine Aviation Tng. Support Group, Oak Harbor, Wash., 1991-94; dep. dir. Precision Guided Weapons Countermeasures, White Sands Range, N.Mex., 1994—; mem. integrated process team J.F. Begert and Sons, Lawrence, Kans., 1985—; mktg. cons. Bakhtar Assocs., Newport Beach, Calif., 1994-96; contbr. Nat. Security Studies Program, Calif. State U., San Bernardino, 1995-96; assoc. Aardvark Tactical Sys., Arcadia, Calif., 1995-96. Screenwriter Beck Prodns., La Canada, Calif., 1994-96; dir., playwright White Sands Missile Range Cmty. Theatre, 1995-97. Decorated Navy Commendation medal with gold star Sec. of the Navy, 1987, Air medal with combat V, Sec. of the Navy, 1993, Meritorious Svc. medal Sec. of the Navy, 1994. Mem. Am. Def. Preparedness Assn., Assn. Naval Aviation, Airplane Owerns and Pilots Assn., Mesilla Valley Track Club, Nat. Geog. Soc. Office: PGWCM T&E Directorate E1407 M L King Ave White Sands Missile NM 88002

BEGGS, HARRY MARK, lawyer; b. Los Angeles, Nov. 15, 1941; s. John Edgar and Agnes (Kentro) B.; m. Sandra Lynne Mikal, May 25, 1963; children: Brendan, Sean, Corey, Michael. Student, Ariz. State U., 1959-61, Phoenix Coll., 1961; LL.B., U. Ariz., 1964. Bar: Ariz. 1964, U.S. Dist. Ct. Ariz. 1964, U.S. Ct. Appeals (9th cir.) 1973, U.S. Ct. Appeals (fed. cir.) 1995, U.S. Supreme Ct. 1991. Assoc. Carson Messinger Elliott Laughlin & Ragan, Phoenix, 1964-69, ptnr., 1969-93; mem. and mng. lawyer Carson Messinger Elliott Laughlin & Ragan, P.L.L.C., Phoenix, 1994—. Mem. editorial bd. Ariz. Law Rev. 1963-64; contbr. articles to profl. jours. Recipient award for highest grade on state bar exam. Atty. Gen. Ariz., 1964; Fegtly Moot Ct. award, 1963, 64; Abner S. Lipscomb scholar U. Ariz. Law Sch., 1963. Fellow Ariz. Bar Found. (founder); mem. State Bar Ariz., Ariz. Acad., Maricopa County Bar Assn. Office: PO Box 33907 Phoenix AZ 85067-3907

BEGGS, VINCENT, museum director. Exec. dir. L.A. Children's Mus. Office: LA Childrens Mus 310 N Main St Los Angeles CA 90012

BEGLINGER, SUSAN MARIE, marriage and family therapist, rehabilitation counselor; b. Huntington Park, Calif., Nov. 21, 1948; m. William Christian Beglinger, Jan. 29, 1969; children: Bryen, Erin. BS in Med. Microbiology, No. Ariz. U., 1976; MS in Counseling, U. Nev., Las Vegas, 1992. Lic. marriage and family therapist, Nev.; cert. rehab. counselor, family therapist, disability analyst, drug and alcohol abuse counselor, Nev. Rehab. counselor D.G. Morrow & Assocs., Las Vegas, 1991-92, Crawford & Co. Health and Rehab., Las Vegas, 1992; rehab. counselor, supr. Cooley Assocs., Las Vegas, 1992-93; rehab. cons. Lynn Maguire Phys. Therapy, Las Vegas, 1992—, Green Valley Spine and Sports, Henderson, Nev., 1995—; marriage and family therapist, program dir. Cmty. Counseling Ctr., Las Vegas, 1993-96; patient and family therapist Columbia Sunrise Health Strategies, Las Vegas, 1996—; co-chairperson Bringing Everyone's Strength Together, Coalition, Las Vegas, 1994-96. Recipient award Disting. Women of So. Nev., 1995, 97. Fellow Am. Bd. Disability Analysts; mem. ACA, Am. Soc. Clin. Hypnosis, Am. Assn. Marriage and Family Therapists (clin. mem.), Am. Soc. Clin. Pathologists (assoc.). Office: Columbia Sunrise Health Strategies 3131 La Canada St Ste 107 Las Vegas NV 89109-2579

BEHLMER, RUDY H., JR., director, writer, film educator; b. San Francisco, Oct. 13, 1926; s. Rudy H. and Helen Mae (McDonough) B.; 1 child by previous marriage, Curt; m. Stacey Endres, Oct. 1992. Student, Pasadena Playhouse Coll., 1946-49, Los Angeles City Coll., 1949-50. Dir. Sta. KLAC-TV, Hollywood, Calif., 1952-56; network TV dir. ABC-TV, Hollywood, 1956-57; TV comml. producer-dir., exec. Grant Advt., Hollywood, 1957-60; exec. producer-dir. Sta. KCOP-TV, Hollywood, 1960-63; v.p., TV comml. producer-dir. Hollywood office Leo Burnett USA, 1963-84; lectr. film Art Ctr. Coll. of Design, Pasadena, Calif., 1967-92, Calif. State U., Northridge, 1984-92, UCLA, 1988. Author: Memo from David O. Selznick, 1972, (with Tony Thomas) Hollywood's Hollywood, 1975, America's Favorite Movies-Behind the Scenes, 1982, Inside Warner Bros., 1985, Behind the Scenes: The Making of..., 1990, Memo From Darryl F. Zanuck, 1993, W.S. Van Dyke's Journal-White Shadows in the South Seas, 1996; co-author: The Films of Errol Flynn, 1969; text on Warner Bros. Fifty Years of Film Music, 1973; editor: The Adventures of Robin Hood, 1979, The Sea Hawk, 1982 (Wis./Warner Bros. screenplay series); contbr. articles on film history; writer and narrator for laserdiscs and video documentaries. Served with AC, USNR, 1944-46. Mem. Dirs. Guild Am.

BEHNEY, CHARLES AUGUSTUS, JR., veterinarian; b. Bryn Mawr, Pa., Nov. 30, 1929; s. Charles Augustus and Victoria Parks (Wythe) B.; B.S., U. Wyo., D.V.M., Colo. State U., 1961; m. Judith Ann Boggs, May 26, 1979; children—Charles Augustus III, Keenan F. Owner, Cochise Animal Hosp., Bisbee, Ariz., 1961—; veterinarian, dir. S.W. Traildust Zoo, Bisbee, 1966—; owner Kazam Arabians, Bisbee, 1969—; asso. prof. Cochise Coll. Chmn., Comprehensive Health Planning, Cochise County, Ariz., 1968. Mem. Am. Vet. Med. Assn., Soc. for Breeding Soundness, Internat. Platform Assn. Republican. Episcopalian. Rotarian, Elk. Patentee ultrasound device and eye cover for treating infections, apparatus to alter equine leg conformation, external vein clamp, equine sanitation instrument; developer ear implant instrumentation system. Home and Office: PO Box 4337 Bisbee AZ 85603-4337

BEHNKE, DONNA BETH, counselor; b. Burbank, Calif., May 19, 1957; d. Frank Michael and Dorothy Eva (Dubis) Behnke; m. Sherman Voorhies, Mar. 22, 1980 (div. Dec. 1985); children: Paul, Daniel; m. Neil Art Jones, Apr. 7, 1990; children: Neil, Jr., Jimmy. BA in English, Calif. State Univ., L.A., 1980, MA in Ednl. Adminstrn., 1990; student, Calif. Luth. Univ., Thousand Oaks, 1996. Cert. counselor, English, speech, drama instr. Tchr. L.A. Unified Sch. Dist., 1985-88, tchr., forensics dir., 1988-94, counselor, 1994—; table leader, scorer Calif. Assessment Program Ednl. Testing Svcs., Berkeley, 1986-94. Roman Catholic. Home: 4343 Ocean View Blvd Apt 266 Montrose CA 91020-1238 Office: LA Unified Sch Dist Sylmar HS 13050 Borden Ave San Fernando CA 91340

BEHNKE, RICHARD FREDERICK, investment banking executive; b. N.Y.C., June 17, 1939; s. William Robert and Herta Adeleheid Hedwig (Reimers) B.; m. Gayle Pualani Kufferath, Aug. 28, 1971; 1 child, Christopher Arnold Keola. BA, Centre Coll. of Ky., 1961; MBA, U. Hawaii,

1969, profl. teaching cert., 1970; postgrad., Fed. Bur. Narcotics Tng. Sch., 1965. Criminal investigator, agt. U.S. Treasury Dept., N.Y.C., 1963-68; pres., prin. Abel-Behnke Corp., Honolulu, 1968—; ptnr., appraiser Abel-Appraisers & Bus. Valuation, Inc., Honolulu, 1990—; realtor assoc. Sand Dollar Realty, Honolulu, 1989-96. Patentee automated pub. transport system. Rsch. assoc. Ctr. for Psychosocial Rsch., Inc., Honolulu, 1991. With USN, 1962-64. Mem. Pacific and Asian Affairs Coun., Pacific Club, Hawaii Econ. Assn., Investment Soc. Hawaii, Honolulu Bd. Realtors. Home: 46-091 Ipuka St Kaneohe HI 96744-4038 Office: Abel-Appraisers & Bus Valuation Inc 1188 Bishop St Ste 911 Honolulu HI 96813-3304

BEHREND, DONALD FRASER, university administrator; b. Manchester, Conn., Aug. 30, 1931; s. Sherwood Martin and Margaret (Fraser) B.; m. Joan Belcher, Nov. 9, 1957; children: Andrew Fraser, Eric Hemingway, David William. BS with honors and distinction, U. Conn., 1958, MS, 1960; PhD in Forest Zoology, SUNY, Syracuse, 1966. Forest game mgmt. specialist Ohio Dept. Natural Resources, Athens, 1960; res. asst. Coll. Forestry, SUNY, Newcomb, 1960-63, res. assoc., 1963-67; dir. Adirondack ecol. ctr. Coll. Environ. Science and Forestry, SUNY, Newcomb, 1968-73; acting dean grad. studies Syracuse, 1973-74; asst. v.p. research programs, exec. dir. Inst. Environ. Program Affairs, 1974-79, v.p. acad. affairs, prof., 1979-85, prof. emeritus, 1987—; asst. prof. wildlife mgmt. U. Maine, Orono, 1967-68; provost, v.p. acad. affairs U. Alaska Statewide System, Fairbanks, 1985-87, exec. v.p., provost, 1988; chancellor U. Alaska, Anchorage, 1988-94, chancellor emeritus, 1994—; mem. patent policy bd. SUNY, 1983-85, chmn. Res. Found. com. acad. res. devel., 1984-85; chmn. 6-Yr. planning com. U. Alaska, 1985-86; bd. dirs. Commonwealth North, 1991-92; mem. selection com. Harry S. Truman Scholarship Found.; mem. Pres.'s Commn., NCAA, 1992-95; chmn. spl. com. on student athlete welfare access and equity, 1993-95; chmn. 20th Great Alaska Shootout, 1997. Contbr. numerous articles and papers to profl. jours. Mem. Newcomb Planning Bd., 1967-69; mem., pres. Bd. Edn. Newcomb Cent. Sch., 1967-73; chmn. governing bd. N.Y. Sea Grant Inst., 1984-85; trustee U. Ala. Found., 1990-94. Served with USN, 1950-54. Mem. Wildlife Soc., Soc. Am. Foresters, AAAS, Phi Kappa Phi (hon.), Sigma Xi, Gamma Sigma Delta, Sigma Lambda Alpha (hon.). Lodges: Rotary (bd. dirs. Fairbanks club 1985-86), Lions (bd. dirs. Newcomb club 1966-67). Home: 333 M St Apt #403 Anchorage AK 99501-1902

BEHRENS, BEREL LYN, physician, academic administrator; b. New South Wales, Australia, 1940. MB, BS, Sydney (Australia) U., 1964. Cert. pediatrics, allergy and immunology. Intern Royal Prince Alfred Hosp., Australia, 1964; resident Loma Linda (Calif.) U. Med. Ctr., 1966-68; with Henrietta Egleston Hosp. for Children, Atlanta, 1968-69, T.C. Thompson Children's Hosp., Chattanooga, 1969-70; instr. pediatrics Loma Linda U., 1970-72, with dept. pediatrics, 1972—, dean Sch. Medicine, 1986-91, pres., 1990—. Office: Loma Linda U Office of the President Loma Linda CA 92350

BEHRING, KENNETH E., professional sports team owner; b. Freeport, Ill., June 13, 1928; s. Elmer and Mae (Priewe) B.; m. Patricia Riffle, Oct. 16, 1949; children: Michael, Thomas, David, Jeffrey, Scott. Student, U. Wis., 1947. Owner Behring Motors, Monroe, Wis., 1953-56, Behring Corp., Ft. Lauderdale, Fla., 1956-72; owner Blackhawk Corp., Danville, Calif., 1972—, also chmn. bd. dirs.; owner Seattle Seahawks, NFL, 1988—; Calif. land developer; mem. policy adv. bd. real estate and urban econs. U. Calif., Berkeley.; chmn. bd. dirs. Behring-Hofmann Ednl. Inst., Inc. U. Calif. Trustee U. Calif., Berkeley; regent St. Mary's Coll., Moraga, Calif., Holy Name Coll., Oakland, Calif.; hon. trustee Mt. Diablo Hosp. Found., Concord, Calif.; hon. chmn. Seattle Art Mus., Am. Cancer Soc., Muscular Dystrophy, Silverado Concours. Named Man of Yr. Boys Town Italy, Entrepreneur of Yr. INC mag. Mem. Am. Acad. Achievement (honoree 1989), Assn. Wash. Bus., Seattle Master Builders Assn., Blackhawk Club, Vintage Club, Seattle Yacht Club, Wash. Athletic Club. Office: Blackhawk Corp PO Box 807 Danville CA 94526-0807 also: Seattle Seahawks 11220 NE 53rd St Kirkland WA 98033-7505*

BEILENSON, ANTHONY CHARLES, former congressman; b. New Rochelle, N.Y., Oct. 26, 1932; s. Peter and Edna (Rudolph) B.; m. Dolores Martin, June 20, 1959; children: Peter, Dayna, Adam. B.A., Harvard Coll., 1954; LL.B., Harvard U., 1957. Bar: Calif. 1957. Mem. Calif. Assembly from 59th Dist., 1963-66, Calif. Senate from 22d Dist., 1967-76, 95th-103rd Congresses from 23rd (now 24th) Calif. Dist., 1977-96; ranking minority mem. subcom. on Rules & Orgn. of Ho. Democrat. Home: 8109 Kerry Ln Chevy Chase MD 20815*

BEIRNE, DANIELLE ULULANI, former state legislator; m. David Haili Keawe; 4 children. AA, Windward C.C., 1988; BA, U. Hawaii, 1988, poestgrad., 1988-92. Rep. dist. 46 State of Hawaii; with Outrigger Hotels; mem. bd. dirs. Hui Na'auao; v.p. Kahana 'Ohana Unity Coun. Mem. Ko'olauloa Hawaiian Civic Club (v.p.), Ka'a'awa, Kahana, Punaiu'u, Hauula, Laie, Kahalu'u & Ko'olauloa Cmty. Assns. Democrat. Home: PO Box 653 Kaneohe HI 96744-0653*

BEITZ, RICHARD THEODORE, JR., family physician, acute care physician; b. Greeley, Colo., Aug. 30, 1953; s. Richard Theodore and Geraldine Ann (Weiss) B.; m. Valerie Robin Finch, Dec. 27, 1974; children: Ryan Richard, Kevin Matthew, Eric Jonathan, Evan Nicholas. AS, C.C. Denver, 1980; BS in Biology, BA in Chemistry, Metropolitan State Coll., Denver, 1981; DO, U. Health Scis. Coll Osteo., Kansas City, Mo., 1986. Diplomate Am. Bd. Family Practice. Intern in family practice Womack Army Cmty. Hosp., Ft. Bragg, N.C., 1986-87; brigade surgeon HHC 2d Brigade 4th ID, Ft. Carson, Colo., 1987-89; resident in family practice D.D. Eisenhower Med. Ctr., Ft. Gordon, Ga., 1989-90; chief resident D.D. Eisenhower Med. Ctr., 1990-91; resident in family practice Eisenhower Army Med. Ctr., Ft. Gordon, Ga., 1991-92; staff physician 547th med. clearing co. U.S. Army, Saudi Arabia, Iraq, 1990-91; comdr. 547th gen. dispensary U.S. Army, Grafenwoehr, Germany, 1992-93; chief AMIC/PAC Evans Army Cmty. Hosp., Ft. Carson, Colo., 1994—; chmn. family advocacy com., Grafenwoehr, 1992-93; flight surgeon 547th Gen. Dispensary, Grafenwoehr, 1992-93, med. rev. officer, 1992-93; mem. hosp. pharmacy & therapeutics com. Evans Army Cmty. Hosp., 1994—, competency chmn., 1995—. Instr. ACLS Am. Heart Assn., Ft. Carson, 1995. Maj. U.S. Army, 1986—. Decorated Meritorious Svc. medal U.S. Army, 1988, 93, Army Commendation medal, 1989, 91. Mem. AMA (Physician Recognition award 1995), Am. Osteo. Assn., Am. Acad. Family Physicians, Uniformed Svcs. Acad. Family Practice. Lutheran. Office: Evans Army Cmty Hosp Fort Carson CO 80913

BEJAR, EZRA, pharmacologist, biology educator; b. Mexico City, Sept. 2, 1958; came to the U.S., 1987; s. Ezra and Marisabel (Ocampo) B.; m. M. Veronica Angeles, Dec. 29, 1982; children: Ezra A., Paula C. BS, Autonomous Met. U., Mexico City, 1981, MSc, 1985; PHD, U. of the Pacific, 1991. Assoc. scientist Mexican Inst. Social Security, Mexico City, 1985-87; rsch. scientist Rsch. Inst. Pharm. Scis., U. Miss., Oxford, 1991-92; lab. dir. Rees-Stealy Rsch. Found., San Diego, 1993—; adj. prof. San Diego (Calif.) State U., 1993—; rsch. assoc. Mus. of Man, 1995—; peer reviewer Jour. Nat. Products, 1993—. Contbr. articles to profl. jours. Rsch. grantee Sharp Found., San Diego, 1994, Calif. Metabolic Rsch. Found., San Diego, 1994; rsch. scholar Mexican Inst. Social Security, 1982-85; scholar Nat. Coun. for Sci. and Tech. Mex., 1983-85, 87-90. Mem. Am. Soc. for Pharmacology and Exptl. Therapeutics, Am. Soc. Pharmacognosy (Travel award 1989), Soc. for the Advancement Chicanos and Native Ams. in Sci. Home: 5702 Baltimore Dr Apt 265 La Mesa CA 91942-1667 Office: 2001 4th Ave San Diego CA 92101-2303

BEKAVAC, NANCY YAVOR, academic administrator, lawyer; b. Pitts., Aug. 28, 1947; d. Anthony Joseph and Elvira (Yavor) B. BA, Swarthmore Coll., 1969; JD, Yale U., 1973. Bar: Calif. 1974, U.S. Dist. Ct. (cen. dist.) 1974, (no. dist.) Calif. 1975, (so. dist.) Calif. 1976, U.S. Ct. Appeals (9th cir.) 1975, (8th cir.) 1981, U.S. Supreme Ct. 1979. Law clk. at large U.S. Ct. Appeals (D.C. cir.), Washington, 1973-74; assoc. Munger, Tolles & Rickershauser, L.A., 1974-79, ptnr., 1980-85; exec. dir. Thomas J. Watson Found., Providence, 1985-87, cons., 1987-88; counselor to pres. Dartmouth Coll., Hanover, N.H., 1988-90; pres. Scripps Coll., Claremont, Calif., 1990—; adj. prof. law UCLA Law Sch., 1982-83; mem. Calif. Higher Edn. Roundtable, 1996—. Bd. mgrs. Swarthmore Coll., 1984—; trustee Wenner-Gren Found. for Anthr. Rsch. 1987-94. Recipient Human Rights award L.A. County Commn. on Civil Rights, 1984; Woodrow Wilson fellow, Thomas J. Watson fellow, 1969. Mem. Assn. Ind. Calif. Colls. and Univs. (chair 1996), Sierra Club. Office: Scripps Coll Office of President 1030 Columbus Claremont CA 91711-3948

BEKEY, SHIRLEY WHITE, psychotherapist; b. L.A.; d. Lawrence Francis and Alice (King) White; m. George Albert Bekey, June 10, 1951; children: Ronald S., Michelle E. BA in Psychology, Occidental Coll., L.A., 1949; MSW in Psychiat. Social Work, UCLA, 1954; PhD in Edn. Psychology, U. So. Calif., 1980. Lic. clin. social worker, Calif.; cert. in pupil pers., parent-child edn. Caseworker outpatient svcs. Calif. State Dept. Mental Health, Montebello; caseworker Lowman Sch. for Handicapped, L.A. Unified Sch. Dist., North Hollywood, Calif., 1971-72; psychotherapist Hofmann Psychiat. Clinic, Glendale (Calif.) Adventist Hosp., 1973-75; pvt. practice psychotherapy Encino, Calif., 1980—; speaker nat. radio, TV expert on children's emotional problems. 1st hosp volunteer Candystriper in U.S., Hollywood Hosp, Los Angeles, 1942; mem. World Affairs Coun., L.A., 1960—. Fellow Soc. for Clin. Social Work; mem. NASW, APA, Am. Ednl. Rsch. Assn., Nat. Assn. Gifted Children, Assn. Transpersonal Psychology, Inst. Noetic Sci., Assn. Ednl. Therapists, Calif. Soc. Clin. Hypnosis, Analytical Psychology Club L.A., Nat. Assn. Poetry Therapy, Calif. Assn. Gifted. Office: 4924 Balboa Blvd # 199 Encino CA 91316-3402

BEKIR, NAGWA ESMAT, electrical engineer, educator, consultant; b. Cairo, Dec. 31, 1944; came to U.S., 1972; s. Mohammed Ragab Shalaby and Kamla (Abdel Megued) Mahmood; m. Esmat Chibl, Sept. 23, 1971; children: Ahmad C., Badr E. BSEE, Cairo U., Egypt, 1966; MSEE, U. So. Calif., 1975, PhD in EE, 1978. Rsch. and hardware engr. Egyptian Indsl. Rsch. Inst., Cairo, 1966-69; quality control engr. Nat. Egyptian Co. for TV and Electronics, Cairo, 1969-72; mem. tech. staff Axiomatics, L.A., 1978; sr. staff engr. Hughes Aircraft Co., Canoga Park, Calif., 1985, mem. tech. staff, 1978-80; assoc. prof. elec. and computer engrng. dept. Calif. State U., Northridge, 1980-83, prof., 1984—; mem. tech. staff ITT Gilfillan, Van Nuys, Calif., 1984; cons. aircraft divsn. Northrop Co., El Segundo, Calif., 1987; cons. Budlong & Assocs., Inc., Agoura Hills, Calif., 1992-93; rschr. Northrop Grumman Co., El Segundo, 1994-95. Contbr. articles to profl. jours. Recipient Meritorious Performance and Profl. Promise award Calif. State U., Northridge, 1989, Outstanding Faculty awards Sch. of Engrng. and Computer Sci., 1990. Mem. IEEE (sr.), Health and Tennis Corp. Am., Eta Kappa Nu, Tau Beta Pi. Office: Calif State U 18111 Nordhoff St Northridge CA 91330-0001

BELEC, MARGUERITE ELIZABETH, naval officer; b. Newark, Aug. 24, 1952; d. Marvin Benson and Betty Mae (Job) Emmons; m. James Medric Belec, Nov. 10, 1984; children: Renee Medric, Aaron Amadeus Fiqiri, AnnaLisa Danielle Fiquirete. BS in Consumer Scis., U. Wis., 1974; MA in Ednl. Adminstrn., San Diego State U., 1989; MA in Nat. Security/Strategic Studies, Naval War Coll., Newport, R.I., 1993. Commd. ensign U.S. Navy, 1982, advanced through grades to lt. comdr., 1992; comdr. Seattle Mil. Entrance Processing Sta., 1994-96; tng. officer USSS Nimitz (CVN-68), 1996—. Decorated Navy Commendation medal, Navy Achievement medal. Office: Mil Entrance Processing Sta 2801 3rd Ave Seattle WA 98121-1242

BELILLE, RONALD, safety and security coordinator; b. Portland, Nov. 22, 1947; s. Frank and Geraldine (Kron) B. AA in Law Enforcement, Portland Community Coll., 1970; student, Fed. Law Enforcement Tng. Ctr., Glynco, Ga., 1978; BS in Adminstrn. Justice, Portland State U., 1979; AA in Occupational Safety and Health, Mt. Hood Community Coll., 1985; grad., Police Reserve Acad., Oregon City, Oreg., 1985; grad. Intermediate Security Acad., Clackamas Community Coll., 1987; AA in Mgmt. and Supervisory Devel., Portland Community Coll., 1988; postgrad., Portland State U., 1985. Cert. emergency med. technician 1. Correctional officer State Penitentiary, Salem, Oreg., 1972; fed. protective officer Fed. Protective Svcs., Portland, 1978; safety/security officer Precision Castparts, Portland, 1979-83, security coordinator, 1983-93; security coordinator Portland Gen. Elec., 1995—; CPR instr., first aid instr., portable fire extinguishers instr. Precision Castparts, 1983-85; chmn. steering com. Intermediate Security Acad. Clackamas Community Coll., 1987; project coord.City of Portland Office of the City Auditor, 1993, project asst. City of Portland Office of the Mayor, 1994. Vol. asst. counselor Multiple County Adult Probation/Parole, Portland, Oreg., 1975; vol. asst. recognizance Officer Multiple County Ct., Oreg., 1982; mem. police and law enforcement task force Citizen's Crime Commn., 1989-93); vice chair Citizens Bur. Adv. Coordinating Com. City of Portland; mem. Portland bur. adv. com. Portland Police Bureau; bd. dirs. Ryles Med. Ctr. Evaluation and Treatment. With USAF, 1966-68. Mem. Am. Soc. for Indsl. Security (chmn. legis. com. 1989-90, treas. 1990-91), Am. Soc. Safety Engrs., Nat. Assn. Chiefs Police, Portland Police Athletic Assn., Masons, Elks, Phi Theta Kappa. Home: 1238 SE 47th Ave Portland OR 97215-2512

BELK, JOHN BLANTON, educational and cultural organization executive; b. Orlando, Fla., Feb. 4, 1925; s. John Blanton and Jennie (Wannamaker) B.; m. Elizabeth Jane Wilkes, Dec. 11, 1954; children: Virginia Elizabeth, Katherine Wilkes. Student, Davidson Coll., 1943, U. N.C., 1943-45. With Moral Re-Armament (numerous locations), 1950-68, exec. dir., 1966-68; founder, chmn. bd., pres. Up With People, Tucson, 1968-91, chmn. exec. com., 1991—. Bd. dirs. Internat. Fund Sports Disabled, Arnhem, Netherlands; mem. Gov.'s Ariz.-Mexico Commn. Lt. (j.g.) USNR, 1943-45. Decorated officer Order Vasco Nunez de Balboa (Panama); officer Order of Leopold (Belgium). Mem. Zeta Psi. Clubs: Mountain Oyster; Guaymas Yacht (Mexico). Home: 3090 Binghampton Pl Tucson AZ 85712 Office: Up With People One International Ct Broomfield CO 80021

BELKNAP, MARIA ANN, writer; b. Portland, Oreg., Mar. 28, 1958; d. Russell Lee B. Student, U. Calif. Santa Barbara, 1976-78; BS in Resource Mgmt., U. Oreg., 1980. Buyer Splendiferous Inc., L.A., 1982-83; v.p. Am. Croissant, L.A., 1983-90; contract adminstr. Southcoast Air Quality Mgmt. Dist., Diamond Bar, Calif., 1990—; writer L.A., 1989—, Party Planner, Beverly Hills, Calif., 1994—. Author: The Horseman's Spanish-English Dictionary, 1991, The Horseman's German-English Dictionary, 1994, The Horseman's English-Spanish Dictionary, 2d edit., 1996, The Equine Dictionary, 1997. Fund raiser AIDS Project L.A., 1991-96, Outward Bound., L.A., 1991-96, Pet Adoption Fund, L.A., 1990-93. Democrat. Home and Office: PO Box 15452 Beverly Hills CA 90209

BELL, DANIEL CARROLL, realtor, community association, ranch and land manager; b. Chgo., July 17, 1940; s. Daniel Gregory and Inez Margarite (Carroll) B.; m. Elaine Paula Rhody, Feb. 1, 1960; children: Tana Lou, Daniel Arden, Andrea Jane. Student, Colo. State U., 1958-62, Reisch Coll. Auctioneering, Mason City, Iowa, 1983. Mgr. ptnr. Three Bell Ranch, Ft. Collins, Colo., 1958-69; sales rep. Pacific Vegetable Oil Co., San Francisco, 1969-70; mng. dir. Paveocor A.G. subs. PVO Internat., Rotterdam, Netherlands, 1970-71; nat. sales mgr. PVO Internat., San Francisco, 1971-72; v.p. commodity trading San Pablo Mfg. Co. subs. PVO Internat., Manila, Philippines, 1972-74; v.p. Rothschild Brokerage Co., San Francisco, 1975-76; owner, prin. Feed, Etc., Harbor, Oreg., 1976-79; commodity specialist Shearson Loeb Rhodes, Medford, Oreg., 1979-80; exec. v.p., gen. mgr. Superior Credit Assocs., Inc., Medford, 1981-86; mng. ptnr. Three Bell Land Co., Pierce, Colo., 1986—; ptnr. Legacy Transp. Co., 1986-93; co-owner Bell & Assocs. Ltd., 1993—; gen. mgr. Greenfield Village RV Resort Assn., 1994—; ptnr. Bell & Assocs., Ltd., 1993—. Mem. Medford (Oreg.) Planning Commn., 1981-84, Medford Sister Cities Commn., 1984; treas. Jackson County Rep. Ctrl. Com., Medford, 1982-84; arbitrator Better Bus. Bur., Medford and Ft. Collins, Colo., 1984-89; candidate Oreg. Ho. Reps., 1984; mem. Mesa (Ariz.) Human Svcs. Adv. Bd.; grad. Mesa Citizens Police Acad., 1995, v.p., 1996. With USAR, 1958-63, Colo. Air N.G., 1963-65. Mem. Nat. Assn. Realtors, Ariz. Assn. Realtors, Mesa, Chandler, Tempe Assn. Realtors, Am. Legion, Elks, NRA. Republican. Presbyterian. Office: 111 S Greenfield Rd Mesa AZ 85206-1252

BELL, DENISE LOUISE, newspaper reporter, photographer, librarian; b. Washington, Nov. 27, 1967; d. Richard Keith Bell and Kay Lorraine (Sutherland) Reynolds. Student, Inst. Adventiste du Saleve, Collonges, France, 1988; BA in French, Loma Linda U., 1990. Yearbook editor Loma Linda U., La Sierra, Calif., 1989-90; desk technician Loma Linda U., Loma Linda, Calif., 1990-92; staff writer Inland Empire Cmty. Newspapers, Colton, Calif., 1990-91; city editor Inland Empire Cmty. Newspapers, San Bernardino, Calif., 1991-94; asst. circ. supr. Del Webb Meml. Libr. Loma Linda (Calif.) U., 1994—; reporter City Newspaper Group, Calton, Calif., 1995—. Asst. leader Girl Scouts U.S., Walla Walla, Wash., 1986; co-leader Girl Scouts Switzerland, Geneva, 1987, Girl Scouts U.S., Loma Linda, 1988-93. Mem. Toastmasters. Home: 10944 Evans St Loma Linda CA 92354-2760

BELL, DONALD WILLIAM, experimental psychologist; b. L.A., Apr. 28, 1936; s. Samuel Chamblis and Betty M. (Welz) B. BA, U. So. Calif., 1959, MA, 1963, PhD, 1966. Rsch. assoc. Subcom. on Noise Rschr. Ctr., L.A., 1962-66; postdoctoral fellow Stanford (Calif.) U., 1966-68; rsch. psychologist SRI Internat., Menlo Park, Calif., 1968-76, sr. rsch. psychologist, 1976-82, program mgr., 1982-83, dir. speech rsch. program, 1983-89, dir., sensory sci. and tech. ctr., 1989-93; pres. Digital Voice Corp., 1982—; prin., dir. Security Group Inc., 1996—; pres. Digital Voice Corp., 1982—; prin., dir. Security Group, Inc., 1996—. Contbr. articles to profl. jours. Mem. planning commn. Town of Portola Valley, Calif., 1980-92. Mem. IEEE, Acoustical Soc. Am., Psychonomic Soc., Am. Voice I/O Soc. (dir.). Republican. Home and Office: 909 Buena Vista Montecito CA 93108

BELL, DOUGLAS SCOTT, internist; b. Toledo, May 20, 1963; s. Kenneth Charles and Barbara Jean (Freed) B. BA in Biochemistry, Case Western Res. U., 1985; MD with honors, Harvard U., 1990. Intern Mt. Auburn Hosp., Cambridge, Mass., 1990-91; rsch. fellow in med. informatics Harvard Med. Sch., Boston, 1991-94; resident in internal medicine Stanford (Calif.) U. Hosp., 1994-96; rsch. fellow UCLA Sch. Medicine, 1996—. Contbr. articles to profl. jours. Rsch. scholar Howard Hughes Med. Inst., 1988-89. Mem. ACP (assoc.), NAAS, Am. Med. Informatics Assn., Soc. for Med. Decision Making, Assn. for Computing Machinery, N.Y. Acad. Scis.

BELL, HELEN LAVIN, artist; b. Allentown, Pa.; d. Thomas Joseph and Anna Helen (Miko) Lavin; m. Paul Edward Bell, June 10, 1950; children: Celine Butler, Sharon Neiman, Paul Jr., Christine Schlacter. Student, Western Md. Coll., 1945-47, Md. Inst. Art, 1947-48, Telfair Acad. Arts, 1958-59, U. Calif., Riverside, 1970-71, 80-81. Asst. art dir. Davison's, Atlanta, 1950-51. One-woman shows include Riverside (Calif.) Art Mus., 1980, Mind's Eye Gallery, Riverside, 1983, Rizzoli Internat., Costa Mesa, Calif., 1987, Zola Fine Art, Beverly Hills, Calif., 1990, others; group shows include City of Riverside, Calif., 1975, Riverside County Mus., Beaumont, Calif., 1976, 90, Nat. Orange Show, San Bernardino, Calif., 1976, 89, Calif. Poly. U., Pomona, 1987, Calif. Small Works, Santa Rosa, 1992, 93, others. Event chair Nat. Charity League, Riverside, Calif., 1979-83; trustee Riverside Art Mus., 1979-82. Merit scholar Telfair Acad. Arts and Scis., Savannah, Ga., 1958. Mem. Redlands Art Assn. (trustee 1985-87, 91-95, sec.), Art Alliance (pres. 1979-80, com. chairs 1978, 81, 82), Nat. Assn. Women Artists, Inc. Republican. Roman Catholic. Office: Valerie Miller Fine Arts 41801 Corporate Dr Palm Desert CA 92260

BELL, KIMBERLY JEANNE, secondary school and adult education educator; b. San Diego, Aug. 17, 1960; d. Lewis Barclay and Vivian Elsie (Jacobsen) B. BS in Phys. Edn., Biola U., 1982; MA in Human Behavior, Nat. U., 1988. Cert. tchr., Calif., profl. teacher. Assn. Christian Schs. Internat. Tchr., coach Christian Unified Schs. of San Diego, El Cajon, Calif., 1983—, phys. edn. dept. chmn., 1990—; instr. Christian Heritage Coll., El Cajon, 1989—. Mem. Am. Alliance Health Phys. Edn. Recreation Dance, Am. Volleyball Coach's Assn. (100 Victory Club award 1990, 200 Victory Club award 1993). Republican. Office: Christian High Sch 2100 Greenfield Dr El Cajon CA 92019-1161

BELL, LARRY STUART, artist; b. Chgo., Dec. 6, 1939; s. Hyman David and Rebecca Ann (Kriegmont) B.; three children. Student, Chouinard Art Inst., L.A., 1957-59. One man exhbns. include Stedelijk Mus., Amsterdam, 1967, Pasadena (Calif.) Art Mus., 1972, Oakland (Calif.) Mus., 1973, Ft. Worth Art Mus., 1975, Santa Barbara (Calif.) Mus. Art, 1976, Washington U., St. Louis, 1976, Art Mus. So. Tex., Corpus Christi, 1976, Erica Williams, Anne Johnson Gallery, Seattle, 1978, Hayden Gallery, MIT, Cambridge, Mass., 1977, Hudson River Mus., Yonkers, N.Y., 1981, Newport Harbor Art Mus., 1982, Marian Goodman Gallery, N.Y.C., 1982, Ruth S. Schaffner Gallery, Santa Barbara, Calif., Arco Ctr. Visual Arts, L.A., 1983, Unicorn Gallery, Aspen, Colo., 1983, Butler Inst. Am. Art, Youngstown, Ohio, 1984, Leigh Yawkey Woodson Art Mus., Wausau, Wis., 1984, Colorado Springs, Colo. Fine Arts Ctr., 1987, Cleve. Ctr. for Contemporary Art, Ohio, 1987, Mus. Contemporary Art, L.A., 1987, Am. Acad. and Inst. Arts and Letters, N.Y.C., 1987, Boise (Idaho) Gallery Art, 1987, Gilbert Brownstone Gallery, Paris, 1987, Braunstein/Quay Gallery, San Francisco, 1987, 89, Fine Arts Gallery, N.Mex. State Fairgrounds, 1987, Laguna Art Mus., Laguna Beach, Calif., 1987, High Mus. Art, Atlanta, 1988, Sena Galleries West, Santa Fe, 1989, Kiyo Higashi Gallery, L.A., 1989, 90, 94, Musee D'Art Contemporain, Lyon, France, 1989, Contemporary Art Ctr., Kansas City, Mo., 1989, San Antonio Art Inst., 1990, New Gallery, Houston, 1990, Braunstein/Quay Gallery, San Francisco, 1990, Galerie Rolf Ricke, Koln, Fed. Republic Germany, 1990, Galerie Montenay, Paris, 1990, 95, The Works Gallery, L.A., 1990, Galerie Kammer, Hamburg, Germany, 1990, Tony Shafrazi Gallery, N.Y.C., 1991, Tucson Mus. Art, 1991, New Gallery, Houston, 1991, Janus Gallery, Santa Fe, 1992, Kiyo Higashi Gallery, L.A., 1992, 93, New Gallery, Houston, 1992, Tampa Mus. Art, 1992, Kiyo Higashi Gallery, L.A., 1993, 94, New Directions Gallery, Taos, N.M., 1993, Dartmouth St. Gallery, Albuquerque, 1994, Braunstein/Quay Gallery, San Francisco, 1994, Leedy/Voulkos Gallery, Kansas City, 1994, Kiyo Higashi Gallery, L.A., 1994, U. Wyo. Art Mus., Laramie, 1995, Denver Art Mus., 1995, Indigo Gallery, Boca Raton, Fla., 1995, Harwood Mus. U. N. Mex., Taos, 1995, Galerie Montenay, Paris, 1995, Joy Tash Gallery, Scottsdale, Ariz., 1996, Kiyo Higashi Gallery, L.A., 1996, Boulder Mus. Contemporary Art, 1996, Braunstein/Quay Gallery, San Francisco, 1996, Art et Industrie Gallery, N.Y.C., 1996, The Albuquerque Mus., 1997, The Reykjavik Mcpl. Art Mus., Iceland, 1997; group exhbns. include Mus. Modern Art, N.Y.C., 1965, 79, Jewish Mus., N.Y.C., 1966, Whitney Mus. Am. Art, 1966, Guggenheim Mus., N.Y.C., 1967, Tate Gallery, London, 1970, Hayward Gallery, London, 1971, Detroit Inst. Arts, 1973, Nat. Collections Fine Arts, 1975, San Francisco Mus. Modern Art, 1976, Museo de Arte Contemporaneo de Caracas, Venezuela, 1978, Aspen Ctr. for Visual Arts, 1980, Fruit Market Gallery, Edinburgh, Scotland, 1980, Albuquerque Mus., 1980, Art Inst. Chgo., 1982, Santa Barbara Art Mus., 1984, The Rufino Tamayo Mus., Mexico City, 1985, Colorado Springs Fine Art Ctr., 1986, Mus. Contemporary Art, 1986, AAAL, 1986, Ariz. State U., Tempe, 1987, Phoenix Art Mus., 1987, Braunstein/Quay Gallery, 1987, The Works Gallery, Long Beach, 1987, Davis/McClain Gallery, Houston, 1987, Basel (Switzerland) Art Fair, 1989, Galerie Joan Prats, Barcelona, Spain, 1989, Musee d'Art Contemporain, Lyon, 1989, Harcus Gallery, Boston, 1989, Colorado Springs Gallery Contemporary Art, 1990, Mus. Contemporary Art, L.A., 1990, Musee de Grenoble, France, 1990, L.A. County Mus. Art, 1991, U. So. Calif. Fisher Gallery, L.A., 1991, Espace Lyonnais d'Art Contemporain, France, 1991, Galerie Montenay, Paris, 1991, Galerie Rolf Ricke, Köln, Germany, 1991, Arolsen, Germany, 1992, Leedy/Voulkos Gallery, Kansas City, Mo., 1993, Musee du Palais du Luxembourg, Paris, 1993, Denver Art Mus., 1993, New Gallery, Houston, 1993, Whitney Mus. Am. Art, N.Y.C., 1993, Conn., 1994, Parrish Art Mus., Southampton, N.Y., 1994, Kiyo Higashi Gallery, L.A., 1994, Madison (Wis.) Art Ctr., 1994, Whitney Mus. Am. Art, 1995, Galerie Ncht St. Stephen, Vienna, 1995, Galerie Rolf Ricke, Cologne, 1996, Colorado Springs Fine Art Ctr., 1996, Mus. N.Mex., Santa Fe, 1996; represented in permanent collections including Nat. Collection Fine Arts, Musee de Art Contemporaine, Lyon, France, Mus. of Fine Arts, Santa Fe, N.Mex., Whitney Mus. Am. Art, N.Y.C., 1994, Laguna Gloria Mus., Austen, 1994, H & W Bechtler Gallery, Charlotte, 1994, Calif. Crafts Mus., San Francisco, 1994, Parrish Art Mus., Southampton, 1994, Tate Gallery, London, Gallery New South Wales, Australia, Albright-Knox Gallery, Buffalo, Art Inst. Chgo., Denver Art Mus., Dallas Mus. Fine Arts, Guggenheim Mus., Houston, L.A. County Mus., Victoria and Albert Mus., London, San Antonio Mus. Art, The Menil Collection, Houston, Mpls. Inst. Arts, Mus. Ludwig, Koln, Albuquerque Mus., Mpls. Inst. Arts, others; instr. sculpture, U. South Fla., Tampa, U. Calif., Berkeley, Irvine, 1970-73, So. Calif. Inst. of Architecture, 1988, Taos (N.Mex.) Inst. of Art, 1989-94. Copley Found. grantee, 1962; Guggenheim Found. fellow, 1970; Nat. Endowment Arts grantee, 1975; recipient Gov.'s award for excellence in visual arts, N.Mex., 1990. Office: PO Box 4101 Taos NM 87571-9998

BELL, LEE PHILLIP, television personality, television producer; b. Chgo.; d. James A. and Helen (Novak) P.; m. William Joseph Bell, Oct. 23, 1954; children: William J., Bradley, Lauralee. B.S. in Microbiology, Northwestern U., 1950. With CBS-TV, Chgo., 1952-86; pres. Bell-Phillip TV Prodns., 1985—; bd. dirs. William Wrigley, Jr. Co., Chgo. Bank Commerce, Phillips Flowers Inc. TV and radio shows include Lee Phillip Show, Chgo., from 1952, Lady and Tiger Show WBBM Radio, from 1962, WBBM TV from 1964; hostess Noon Break, numerous TV Spls. including Forgotten Children, The Rape of Paulette (nat. Emmy award, duPont Columbia award); Children and Divorce (Chgo. Emmmy award) co-creator: (with William Bell) The Young and the Restless CBS-TV daytime drama, 1973 (Emmy award); co-creator, exec. producer The Bold and the Beautiful, 1987—. Bd. dirs. United Cerebral Palsy, Chgo. Unlimited, Northwestern U. Hosp., Chgo. Heart Assn., Nat. Com. Prevention of Child Abuse, Mental Health Assn., Children's Home and Aid Soc., Salvation Army (L.A. bd. dirs.), Family Focus; mem. Chgo. Maternity Ctr.; life mem. Northwestern U. Bd. Trustees. Recipient 16 Chgo. Emmys; Top Favorite Female award TV Guide mag., 1956, Outstanding Woman of Radio and TV award McCall's mag., 1957-58, 65, bd. govs. award Chgo. chpt. Nat. Acad. TV Arts and Scis., 1977, William Booth award for community svc. Salvation Army, 1990; named Person of Yr. Broadcast Advt. Club, Chgo., 1980. Mem. Am. Women Radio and TV (Golden Mike award 1968, Broadcaster of Yr. 1993), Acad. TV Arts and Scis. (bd. dirs.), Chgo. chpt. Acad. TV Arts and Scis., Women's Athletic Club of Chgo., Comml. Club, Delta Delta Delta. Office: CBS-TV City 7800 Beverly Blvd Los Angeles CA 90036-2165*

BELL, LEO S., retired physician; b. Newark, Nov. 7, 1913; s. Alexander M. and Marie (Saxon) B.; AB, Syracuse U., 1934; MD, 1938; m. Edith Lewis, July 3, 1938; children: Jewyl Linn, David Alden. Intern, N.Y.C. Hosp., 1938, Bklyn. Hosp., 1939-40; resident in pediatrics Sea View Hosp., N.Y.C., 1940-41, N.Y.C. Hosp., 1941-42; practice medicine specializing in pediatrics, San Mateo, Calif., 1946-86; mem. staff Mills Meml. Hosp., San Mateo, Peninsula Hosp. & Med. Ctr., Burlingame, Children's Hosp., San Francisco; assoc. clin. prof. pediatrics U. Calif. Med Sch., San Francisco, prof. clin. emeritus Stanford Med. Sch., Palo Alto; mem. curriculum & ednl. affairs comm. U. San Francisco Med. Sch., adminstv. coun.; med. columnist San Mateo Times. Bd. dirs. Mills Hosp. Found., San Mateo, U. Calif. San Francisco Hosp., San Mateo County Heart Assn., Hillsborough Schs. Found. (Calif.), 1980-83. Capt. as flight surgeon USAAF, 1942-46. Recipient bronze and silver medals Am. Heart Assn. Diplomate Am. Bd. Pediatrics. Fellow Am. Acad. Pediatrics, Am. Pub. Health Assn.; mem. Clin. Faculty Assn. (pres.), Calif. Fedn. Pediatric Socs. (pres.), Am. Fedn. Pediatric Socs. (pres.), Calif. Med. Assn., Am. Pub. Health Assn., Air Force Assn., AMA (alt. del. to ho. of dels.), Calif. Med. Assn. (ho. of dels.), San Mateo County Med. Assn., Internat. Snuff Bottle Soc., Hong Kong Snuff Bottle Soc., San Francisco Gem and Mineral Soc., World Affairs Coun. San Francisco, U. San Francisco Med. Sch. Clin. Faculty Assn. (coun., pres.), Peninsula Golf and Country Club, Commonwealth Club. Contbr. articles to profl. jours. Home: 220 Roblar Ave Burlingame CA 94010-6846 Office: PO Box 1877 San Mateo CA 94401-0946

BELL, M. JOY MILLER, financial planner, real estate broker; b. Enid, Okla., Dec. 29, 1934; d. H. Lee and M.E. Madge (Hatfield) Miller; m. Richard L.D. Berlemann, July 21, 1957 (div. Nov. 1974); children: Richard Louis, Randolph Lee; m. Donald R. Bell, Aug. 17, 1996; children: Jeri Lynn, Johnna Kay, Nolan Ray, Charles, Mary. BSBA, N.Mex. State U., 1956. CFP; grad. Realtors Inst.; fellow Life Underwriting Tng. Coun. Tchr. of bus. and mathematics Alamogordo (N.Mex.), Las Cruces (N. Mex.) and Omaha Pub. Schs., 1956-63; tchr., dir. Evelyn Wood Reading Dynamics Southern N.Mex. Inst., 1967-68; registered rep. Westamerica Fin. Corp., Denver, 1968-76; gen. agt. Security Benefit Life, Topeka, 1969—, Delta Life & Annuity, Memphis, 1969—; registered rep. Am. Growth Fund Sponsors, Inc., Denver, 1976—; pres., broker Fin. Design Corp. R.E. (name changed to Bell, Inc. 1997), Las Cruces, 1977—; ofcl. goodwill amb. U.S. Treasury, U.S. Savs. Bond Divsn., Washington, 1968-70. Contbr. articles to profl. jours. Vice pres. Dona Ana County Fedn. Rep. Women. Recipient Top Sales Person award Investment Trust and Assurance, 1976-77. Mem. Nat. Assn. Realtors, Nat. Assn. Life Underwriters, Internat. Assn. Registered Fin. Planners, S.W. N.Mex. Assn. Life Underwriters (treas. 1990-91, pres.-elect 1991-92, pres. 1992-93), Las Cruces City Alumnae Panhellenic, Altrusa, Order Ea. Star, Delta Zeta. Methodist. Home: 4633 Lamar Rd Las Cruces NM 88005 Office: Bell Inc PO Box 577 Las Cruces NM 88004-0577

BELL, MELODIE ELIZABETH, artist, massage therapist; b. Long Beach, Calif., Apr. 21, 1958; d. Robert I. and Bettymay (Shelley) Bell; m. Timothy Monroe Roach, Feb. 4, 1993; children: Chelsea Ann Bell, Rory Michael Bell. Student, Calif. State U., Long Beach, 1976-78, Humboldt State U., 1978-79; BA in Art (Photography), Calif. State U., Fullerton, 1984. Cert. massage therapist, L.A. Coll. Massage and Phys. Therapy, 1978. Owner Mel's Place, Cypress, Calif., 1982-91; mgr. George Galanoudes Apts., Garden Grove, Calif., 1991-93; massage therapist Office of Stephen Waldman, MD, Fullerton, Calif., 1992-93; freelance portrait artist, photographer, 1984—. Solo exhbns. include Calif. State U., Fullerton, 1979, 84, Rossmoor Pub. Libr., Seal Beach, Calif., 1992, Six Flags Magic Mountain, Saugus, Calif., 1983-85; commd. portraits and paintings in pvt. collections. Leader Webelos Boy Scouts Am., Garden Grove, 1994-95; vol. Thanksgiving for the Homeless, Santa Ana, Calif., 1996, Fryberger Elem. Sch., Westminster, Calif., 1995-96, Choc Walk, 1995, AIDS Dance-a-Thon, 1997—. Democrat. Jewish. Home: 8642 Gloria Apt C Garden Grove CA 92844

BELL, RANDALL, real estate analyst, consultant; b. Cleve., Jan. 4, 1959; s. Preston Bernhisal and Frances Caroline B.; m. Melanie Marie Davis, Feb. 3, 1990; children: Michael Preston, Steven Randall, Britten Ashby. BS, Brigham Young U., 1988; MBA, UCLA, 1991. Broker lic., Calif., 1991; appraisal lic., Calif., 1991. Pres. Bell & Assocs., Santa Monica, Laguna Niguel, Calif., 1986—; instr. Appraisal Inst., L.A., 1994, mem. ethics panel, 1995, mem. adv. bd., Orange County, 1996. Author: Bell's Guide to Real Estate, 1991, Home Owners Manual, 1996, Real Estate Professionals Handbook, 1996. Mem. Internat. Right of Way Assn. Office: Bell & Assocs 30100 Town Ctr Dr Ste 330 Laguna Niguel CA 92677

BELL, WAYNE STEVEN, lawyer; b. L.A., June 24, 1954; s. Joseph and Jane Barbara (Barsook) B.; m. M. Susan Modzelewski, Apr. 1, 1989. BA magna cum laude, UCLA, 1976; JD, Loyola U., L.A., 1979; Advanced Mgmt. Program, Rutgers U., 1992. Bar: Calif. 1980, U.S. Dist. Ct. (cen. dist.) 1981, U.S. Tax Ct. 1981, U.S. Ct. Appeals (9th cir.) 1981, U.S. Dist. Ct. (so. and no. dists.) Calif. 1983, U.S. Supreme Ct. 1984, D.C. 1986, Tex. 1995; lic. real estate broker, Calif. Intern office of gov. State of Calif., Sacramento, summer 1976; assoc. Levinson, Rowen, Miller, Jacobs & Kabrins, L.A., 1980-82; sr. assoc. Montgomery, Gascou, Gemmill & Thornton, L.A., 1982-84; counsel, project developer Thomas Safran & Assocs., L.A., 1984-85; of counsel Greenspan, Glasser & Medina, Santa Monica, Calif., 1984-86; assoc. gen. counsel Am. Diversified Cos., Costa Mesa, Calif., 1985-88; legal cons. Project Atty., L.A., 1988-89; sr. counsel, asst. sec. Ralphs Grocery Co., L.A., 1989—; judge pro tem Mcpl. Ct. South Bay Jud. Dist., 1987, L.A. Superior Ct., 1991, 94, 97; settlement officer L.A. Mcpl. Ct., Settlement Officer Program, 1990-92; spl. master State Bar Calif., 1991-92. Chief note and comment editor Loyola U. Law Rev., 1978-79; contbr. articles to profl. jours. and gen. pubs. Vol. atty. Westside Legal Svcs., Santa Monica, 1982-87; legal ombudsman Olympics Ombudsman Program L.A. County Bar Assn., 1984; gov. apptd. mem. Calif. adv. coun. Legal Svcs. Corp., 1982-88, Autism Soc. Am., Amnesty Internat.; contbg. mem. Dem. Nat. Com.; mem. leadership coun. So. Poverty Law Ctr.; charter mem. presdl. task force Ams. for Change; bd. dirs. Am. Theatre Arts, Hollywood, Calif., 1983-84; pres., exec. com., bd. dirs. Programs for the Developmentally Handicapped, Inc., L.A., 1987-92; chmn. bd. appeals handicapped accommodations City of Manhattan Beach, 1986-88; bd. dirs. The Foodbank of So. Calif., 1991-94, sec., 1993; legal oversight com. Legal Corps L.A., 1995—; sec. bd. trustees The Ralphs/Food 4 Less Found., 1995—; vol. L.A. County Bar Assn., Barristers Homeless Shelter Advocacy Project, 1996—. Mem. Calif. Bar Assn. (legal svcs. sect. standing com. legal problems of aging 1983-86, chmn. legis. subcom. 1984-86, conf. dels. alternate 1987), D.C. Bar Assn. (real estate sect. com. on comml. real estate), Legal Assistance Assn. Calif. (bd. dirs., mem. exec. com., legis. strategy com. 1984-86), Loyola Law Sch. (advocate). Democrat. Office: Ralphs Grocery Co PO Box 54143 Los Angeles CA 90054-0143

BELLAH, ROBERT NEELLY, sociologist, educator; b. Altus, Okla., Feb. 23, 1927; s. Luther Hutton and Lillian Lucille (Neelly); m. Melanie Hyman, Aug. 17, 1949; children: Jennifer, Harriet. BA, Harvard U., 1950, PhD, 1955. Rsch. assoc. Inst. Islamic Studies, McGill U., Montreal, Can., 1955-57; with Harvard U., Cambridge, Mass., 1957-67, prof., 1966-67; mem. faculty dept. sociology U. Calif., Berkeley, 1967-97, Elliott prof. emeritus, 1997—. Author: Tokugawa Religion, 1957, Beyond Belief, 1970, The Broken Covenant, 1975 (Sorokin award Am. Sociol. Assn. 1976), (with Charles Y. Glock) The New Religious Consciousness, 1976, (with Phillip E. Hammond) Varieties of Civil Religion, 1980, (with others) Habits of the Heart, 1985, (with others) The Good Society, 1991. With U.S. Army, 1945-46. Fulbright fellow, 1960-61; recipient Harbison award Danforth Found., 1971. Mem. Am. Acad. Arts and Scis., Am. Sociol. Assn., Am. Acad. Religion, Am. Philos. Soc. Episcopalian. Office: U Calif Dept Sociology Berkeley CA 94720-1980

BELLER, GERALD STEPHEN, professional magician, former insurance company executive; b. Phila., Aug. 6, 1935; s. Nathan and Adelaide B. (Goldfarb) B.; m. Nancy R. Nelson, June 8, 1968; children: Fay A., Mark S., Royce W., Merrilee A., Marie A., Frank A. CLU, Am. Coll., Bryn Mawr, Pa., 1972. Spl. agt. Prudential Ins. Co., San Bernardino, Calif., 1959-62, div. mgr., 1962-66; agy. supr. Aetna Life & Casualty, L.A., 1966-69, gen. agt., 1969-77; rsch. analyst Investigative Svcs. Bur. San Bernardino County Sheriff's Dept., 1991-95; capt. specialized svcs. bur. San Bernardino County (Calif.) Sheriff's Dept.; profl. magician, 1982—; mem. Magician Magic Castle, Hollywood, Calif. mem. sheriff's coun. San Bernardino County Sheriff's Dept., Apple Valley sheriff's adv. bd. Served with USAF, 1953-57. Recipient Man of Year award, 1961; Manpower Builders award, 1966-69; Agy. Builders award, 1970-72; Pres.'s Trophy award, 1973-74. Mem. Am. Soc. CLUs, Golden Key Soc., Internat. Exec. Svc. Corps. (vol.), Acad. Magical Arts, Internat. Brotherhood of Magicians (Outstanding Magic Lectr. of Yr. 1989-90, Aldini Meml. award 1990), Soc. Am. Magicians. Home: 20625 Tonawanda Rd Apple Valley CA 92307-5736

BELLES, DONALD ARNOLD, pastoral therapist, mental health counselor; b. Sayre, Pa., Mar. 7, 1948; s. William and Alice (Arnold) B.; m. Linda Scheel, July 9, 1981. BA, St. Martin's U., 1973; MDiv, Fuller Theol. Sem., 1977; PhD, Calif. Grad. Sch. Theology, 1981; MBA, City U. Bellevue, 1994. Lic. amateur radio operator; ordained to ministry Worldwide Congl. Fellowship, 1989; cert. c.c. tchr., Calif., mental health counselor, Wash., profl. stage hypnotist. Chaplain Vols. of Am., L.A., 1976-78; therapist Greater life Found., Seattle, 1979-81; industrial engr. commercial airplane divsn. Boeing, 1979-80, program planner aerospace divsn., 1980-86, sr., lead program planner electronics divsn., 1986-97, systems analyst, contract tech. mgr., 1989-92, analyst software engring. practices, mgr. total quality improvement project, 1992-95, lead, mgr. computing infrastructure archtl. design team, 1995—, mgr. computing infrastructure design, 1996-97; therapist, dir. clinic Creative Therapies, Seattle, 1982-83; clin. dir. Applied Hypnosis, Tacoma, 1984-87; dir. Active Therapy Assoc., Tacoma, 1988-89; dean of students Coll. Therapeutic Hypnosis, Puyallup, Wash., 1989-93; cons. theological issues, abduction rsch., psychic phenomena, paranormal events; adult edn. instr. Tacoma Community Coll., 1987-88, Pierce Coll., 1990-92; mem. U.S. Acad. Team to CIS, U. St. Petersburg, Russia, 1994; presenter, lectr. in field; instr. Olympia Diocese Sch. of Theology, 1995. Contbr. articles to profl. jours., prodr. hypnosis, mental health vi deos in field. Exec. dir. Nat. Assn. to Prevent and Eliminate Child Abuse, Tacoma, 1987-89. Maj. U.S. Army, 1969-75, USAR, 1975—. Fellow Am. Assn. Profl. Hypnotherapists; mem. Nat. Assn. Clergy Hypnotherapists (bd. dirs. 1987-88, editor jour. 1987), Internat. Med. Dental Hypnotherapy Assn., Wash. State Head Injury Found.

BELLEVILLE, PHILIP FREDERICK, lawyer; b. Flint, Mich., Apr. 24, 1934; s. Frederick Charles and Sarah (Adelaine) B.; m. Geraldean Bickford, Sept. 2, 1953; children—Stacy L., Philip Frederick II, Jeffrey A. BA in Econs. with high distinction and honors, U. Mich., 1956, J.D., 1960. Bar: Calif. 1961. Assoc. Latham & Watkins, LA., 1960-68; ptnr. Latham & Watkins, L.A. and Newport Beach, Calif., 1968-73; ptnr., chmn. litigation dept. Latham & Watkins, L.A. and Newport Beach, 1973-80; ptnr. Latham & Watkins, L.A., Newport Beach, San Diego, Washington, 1980—, Chgo., 1983—, N.Y.C., 1985—, London, 1990—, Moscow, 1992—, Hong Kong, 1995—, Tokyo, 1995. Asst. editor Mich. Law Rev., Ann Arbor, 1959-60. Past mem. So. Calif. steering com. NAACP Legal Def. Fund, Inc., L.A.; mem. cmty. adv. bd. San Pedro Peninsula Hosp., Calif., 1980-88. James B. Angell scholar U. Mich., 1955-56. Mem. ABA (antitrust and trade regulation and bus. law sects.), L.A. County Bar Assn. (bus. trial lawyers sect.), Assn. Bus. Trial Lawyers, Order of Coif, Portuguese Bend (Calif.) Club, Palos Verdes (Calif.) Golf Club, Caballeros, Phi Beta Kappa, Phi Kappa Phi, Alpha Kappa Psi. Republican. Office: Latham & Watkins 633 W 5th St Ste 4000 Los Angeles CA 90071-2005

BELLIS, CARROLL JOSEPH, surgeon; b. Shreveport, La.; s. Joseph and Rose (Bloome) B.; m. Mildred Darmody, Dec. 26, 1939; children: Joseph, David. BS, U. Minn., 1930, MS in Physiology, 1932, PhD in Physiology, 1934, MD, 1936, PhD in Surgery, 1941. Diplomate Am. Bd. Surgery. Resident surgery U. Minn. Hosps., 1937-41; pvt. practice surgery Long Beach, Calif., 1945—; mem. staff St. Mary's Med. Ctr., Long Beach; cons. surgery Long Beach Gen. Hosp.; prof., chmn. dept. surgery Calif. Coll. Medicine, 1962—; surgical cons. to Surgeon-Gen., U.S. Army; adj. prof. surgery U. Calif. Author: Fundamentals of Human Physiology, 1935, A Critique of Reason, 1938, Lectures in Medical Physiology; contbr. numerous articles in field of surgery, physiology to profl. jours. Served to col. M.C. AUS, 1941-46. Recipient Charles Lyman Green prize in physiology, 1934, prize Mpls. Surg. Soc., 1938, ann. award Mississippi Valley Med. Soc., 1955; Alice Shevlin fellow U. Minn., 1932. Fellow ACS, Royal Soc. Medicine, Internat. Coll. Surgeons, Am. Coll. Gastroenterology, Am. Med. Writers Assn., Internat. Coll. Angiology (sci. council), Gerontol. Soc., Am. Soc. Abdominal Surgeons, Nat. Cancer Inst., Phlebology Soc. Am., Internat. Acad. Proctology, Peripheral Vascular Soc. Am. (founding); mem. AAAS, Am. Assn. Study Neoplastic Diseases, Mississippi Valley Med. Soc., N.Y. Acad. Scis., Hollywood Acad. Medicine, Am. Geriatrics Soc., Irish Med. Assn., Am. Assn. History Medicine, Pan Pacific Surgical Assn., Indsl. Med. Assn., L.A. Musicians Union (hon.), Pan Am. Med. Assn. (diplomate), Internat. Bd. Surgery (cert.), Internat. Bd. Proctology (cert.), Wisdom Soc. (wisdom award of honor), Sigma Xi, Phi Beta Kappa, Alpha Omega Alpha. Home: 904 Silver Spur Rd Ste 804 Rolling Hills Estates CA 90274-3800

BELLMAN, MICHAEL STANLEY, forester, freelance writer; b. Wadena, Minn., Apr. 8, 1947; s. Stanley and Margaret (Hoffman) B.; m. Virginia Ann Arnold, June 21, 1969; children: William Michael, Matthew James. BS, U. Mont., 1969. Forester Bur. Land Mgmt., Salem, Oreg., 1969-74, Boise Cascade Corp., Monmouth, Oreg., 1974-79, Avison Lumber Co., Molalla, Oreg., 1979—; bd. dirs. Columbia River Scaling Bur., Eugene, Oreg., 1994—; editl. advisor Oreg. Fish and Wildlife Jour., 1988—. Columnist Molalla Pioneer, 1992—, Itemizer Observer, 1994—. Mem. Oreg. Writers Colony, Salem Writers and Pubs. (treas. 1995-96). Republican. Roman Catholic. Home: 5840 Basil St NE Salem OR 97301

BELLON-FISHER, LINDA SUE, cultural organization administrator; b. Gary, Ind., Dec. 28, 1948; d. James Michael and Mary Ellen Flynn; children from a previous marriage: Brigette Ann, Cheri Evette; m. Ronald Max Fisher, Dec. 28, 1984; 1 stepdaughter, Dana Marin. BA in Art, Calif. State U., 1980, MA in Art, 1982. Lifetime cmty. coll. tchg. credential, Calif. Adj. prof. Calif. Poly. Pomona, Mt. Sac Coll., Coastline C.C., 1982-85; program adminstr. The Friends of Photography, Carmel, Calif., 1985-87; exec. dir. Monterey County Cultural Coun., Salinas, Calif., 1987-90; mgr. arts in edn. programs Wash. State Art Commn., Olympia, 1990—; tutor English pvt., Calif. State U., Fullerton, 1977-82; organizaer, curator 1989 Internat. Women in Photography Exhbn., 1989-91; juror Flashback: A Photographic Reflection of Monterey (Calif.), 1990; bd. dirs. ex-officio Wash. Alliance forArts Edn., 1993-96; founder, mem. Cultural Arts Network, Monterey County, Calif., 1988-90. Art critic ARTWEEK, other publs., 1982—; work featured in textbook Photography, 6th edit., 1990, catalogue Printmaking, 1982. Bd. dirs. City of Shelton (Wash.) Historic Preservation Bd., 1994-96; mem. Shelton City Hall Resource Com., Wash., 1995; mem. arts day planning com. Leadership Monterey, 1988, 89, participant 1989 Peninsula Class. Fellow Exhbn. Devel. Kellogg Fellowship, Field Mus., 1986, Leadership Inst., Humphry Inst. U. Minn., 1989. Office: Wash State Arts Commn 234 E 8th Ave Olympia WA 98504

BELLOWS, ROBERT ALVIN, research physiologist; b. Bozeman, Mont., Aug. 22, 1934; s. Alvin O. and Lucy E. (Norman) B.; m. Laura Mae Pasha, Dec. 27, 1957; children: Donna Kay, William, Norman, David. BS, Mont. State U., 1956, MS, 1958; PhD, U. Wis., 1962. Registered profl. animal scientist. Rsch. physiologist USDA-Agrl. Rsch. Svc., Miles City, Mont., 1962-67, rsch. physiologist, investigations leader, 1967-71, rsch. physiology supr., 1971-79, rsch. leader, 1979-84, rsch. physiologist, 1984—; reviewer, cons. State Expt. Stas., USDA-Agrl. Rsch. Svc., Can., Mex., Egypt, Soviet Union, Kazakhstan, Kyrgyzstan, Nat. Cattleman's Assn., Angus, Hereford, Charolais and Simmental Breed Assn., 1971—; adj. prof. Mont. State U. Reviewer Agriculture Can., 1996. Recipient internat. honor award Office of Internat. Cooperation and Devel., 1993. Mem. Am. Soc. Animal Sci. (western dir. 1967, sec., pres. elect, pres. western sect. 1989-91, disting. svc. award 1983, animal mgmt. award 1993, sr. scientist of yr. North Gt. Plains area 1994, sect. editor Jour. Animal Sci. 1979-81, 94-96), Soc. for Study of Reproduction, Coun. Agrl. Sci. and Tech., Alpha Zeta. Office: US Dept Agr Agrl Rsch Svc Livestock & Range Rsch Lab Rte 1 Box 2021 Miles City MT 59301

BELLUOMINI, FRANK STEPHEN, accountant; b. Healdsburg, Calif., May 19, 1934; s. Francesco and Rose (Giorgi) B.; m. Alta Anita Gifford, Sept. 16, 1967; 1 child, Wendy Ann. AA, Santa Rosa Jr. Coll., 1954; BA with honors, San Jose State U., 1956. CPA, Calif. Staff acct. Hood, Gire & Co., CPA's, San Jose, Calif., 1955-60, ptnr., 1960-66; ptnr. Touche Ross & Co., CPA's, San Jose, 1967-89, ptnr.-in-charge San Jose office, 1971-85, sr. ptnr. San Jose office, 1985-89; ptnr. Deloitte & Touche, San Jose, 1989-95. Bd. dirs. Santa Clara Valley chpt. ARC, 1993—, chmn. bd. dirs. 1995-97; mem. adv. bd. Salvation Army, San Jose, 1979-85, San Jose Children's Coun., 1982-89; mem. citizens adv. coun. Via Rehabilitation Svcs., Inc., 1989-94, bd. dirs., 1995—, sec./treas., 1975-95; trustee Santa Clara County (Calif.) United Way, 1979-95, v.p. planning and allocations, 1981-83, vice chmn., 1985-87, chmn. 1987-89; bd. dirs. San Jose Mus. Art, 1984-86; mem. Presentation High Sch. Devel. Bd., 1989-92; mem. dean's adv. coun. San Jose State U. Bus. Sch., 1990-95, mem. adv. bd. The Acad. of Fin., 1992-94. Named Disting. Alumnus, San Jose State U. Sch. Bus., 1978. Mem. Santa Clara County Estate Planning Council (pres. 1979-80), Calif. Soc. CPA's (pres. chpt. 1968-69, state v.p. 1976-77), Am. Inst. CPA's (chmn. state and local govt. com. 1976-79), San Jose State Alumni Assn. (treas. 1960-61, dir. 1961-62, exec. com. 1961-62), San Jose State Acctg. Round Table (bd. dirs., treas. 1982-87, 92—, pres. 1994-95), Beta Alpha Psi (San Jose State U. Outstanding Alumnus award 1986). Clubs: San Jose Rotary (dir. 1979-81, trustee and treas. San Jose Rotary Endowment 1976-83).

BELLUS, RONALD JOSEPH, marketing and communications executive; b. Travis AFB, Calif., Feb. 25, 1951; s. Vincent Joseph and Katherine Veronica (Giudice) B.; m. Beth Ann Johnson, June 26, 1976 (div.); children: Veronica Lee, Joseph Vincent, Kenneth James; m. Gina Jean Prom, Aug. 9, 1990; children: Anthony Taylor, Andrew Tyler. BA in Communications, Brigham Young U., 1977. Lic. FCC radio telephone operator, 1979. Sports dir. Sta. KGUY-AM, Palm Desert, Calif., 1979; news, sports dir. Sta. KBLQ-AM/FM, Logan, Utah, 1979-80; gen. sales mgr. Sta. KSTM-FM/KVVA-AM, Phoenix, 1980-84, Sta. KLFF-AM/KMZK-FM, Phoenix, 1984-85; media cons. Mediacorp Planning & Buying, Phoenix, 1985-86; press sec. Gov. of Ariz., Phoenix, 1986-87; asst. dir. Ariz. Office of Tourism, Phoenix, 1987-88; media cons. Bellus Media, Phoenix, 1988-93; pres. Taska Ltd. (formerly Bellus Media), Phoenix, 1993—; ptnr. Desertwest Media Group, Inc., Phoenix, 1988-96; v.p. Nat. Restaurant Group, Inc., Phoenix, 1990-91; media cons. Mecham for Gov. com., Glendale, Ariz., 1986; host cable TV show Arizona-Now and Then, Cox Cable, 1990—; v.p. Infosystems, Tempe, 1991-94, Green Valley Health Group, Phoenix, 1992—; co-founder Cinema Concepts Found., Scottsdale, 1994—; co-founder, CEO Bronze Memories Ltd., Phoenix, 1994—. Author: Mecham: Silence Cannot Be Misquoted, 1988, Ariz. Tourism Travel Planner, 1988. Comm. mem. Phoenix Boys Choir, 1988; precinct committeeman Rep. State Com., Phoenix, 1987-89, del., 1988; candidate for state senate, Phoenix, 1988; bd. dirs. Cinema Concepts Found., 1994—; mem. Gilbert Anti-Gang Task Force, 1994—, Gilbert Action Inter-Faith Network, 1994—; chmn. adv. bd. Original Kids TV, Inc. Named one of Outstanding Young Men Am., 1987. Mem. Phoenix Press Box Assn. (treas. 1984-85, exec. dir. 1985-86). Ch. of Latter Day Saints. Office: 15812 N 32nd St Ste 9 Phoenix AZ 85032

BELLVER, CATHERINE GULLO, foreign language educator; b. Chgo., July 31, 1941; d. Samuel A. and Jean V. (Galva) Gullo; m. Josè A. Bellver, Dec. 30, 1967 (div. Aug. 1984). BA, Northwestern U., Evanston, Ill., 1963; MA, U. Calif., Berkeley, 1965, PhD, 1972. Instr. U. Calif., Davis, 1970-72; asst. prof. U. Nev., Las Vegas, 1972-77, assoc. prof., 1977-83, prof., 1983—; interim dir. women's studies U. Nev., Las Vegas, 1991-93, dept. chair, 1991-93. Author: Rafael Alberti en sus horas de destierro, 1984, El mundo poètico de Juan Jose Domenchina, 1979; contbr. articles to profl. jours. Mem. MLA (exec. bd. West Coast Women's Caucus 1981-85), Am. Assn. Tchrs. of Spanish and Portuguese (Best Essay on Pedagogy 1988), Assn. y Seminario de Lit. Femenina Contempóranea (editl. bd. Letras Femininas), Pacific Ancient and Modern Lang. Assn. (exec. bd. 1995—), Rocky Mountain Modern Lang. Assn., Soroptimist Internat. (Greater Las Vegas chpt., Women Helping Women award 1991). Office: U Nev Las Vegas Dept Fgn Langs Las Vegas NV 89154-5047

BELMARES, HECTOR, chemist; b. Monclova, Coahuila, Mex., Feb. 21, 1938; s. Armando and Guadalupe (Sarabia) B.; B.Sc., Instituto Tecnológico de Monterrey (Mex.), 1960; Ph.D. (Todd fellow 1961-63), Cornell U., 1963; postdoctoral student Calif. Inst. Tech., 1965; m. Eleanor Johanna Wold, Aug. 28, 1965; children: Michelle Anne, Michael Paul, Elizabeth Myrna, Mary Eleanor. Sr. research chemist Rohm and Haas Co., Phila., 1965-71; gen. mgr. tech. and quality control Fibras Quìmicas, S.A., Monterrey, Mex., 1972-75; sr. research chemist Centro de Investigación en Química Aplicada, Saltillo Coahuila, Mex., 1976-83, Sola Optical USA Inc., 1984—; mem. adv. panel Modern Plastics Mgmt., 1986-87; cons. on polymers for industry; cons. UN Indsl. Devel. Orgn. Community rep. Against Indsl. Air Pollution, Moorestown, N.J., 1968-70. Mem. Am. Chem. Soc., N.Y. Acad. Scis., AAAS, Sigma Xi. Mem. Christian Evangelical Ch. Patentee in field. Contbr. articles to profl. jours. Home: 1100 Shadyslope Dr Santa Rosa CA 95404 Office: Sola Optical USA Inc 1500 Cader Ln Petaluma CA 94954-6905

BELMONT, LARRY MILLER, health association executive; b. Reno, Apr. 13, 1936; s. Miller Lawrence and Madeline (Echante) B.; m. Laureen Metzger, Aug. 14, 1966; children: Miller Lawrence, Rebecca Madeline, Amie Echante, Bradley August. BA in Psychology, U. Nev., 1962; MPH, U. Mich., 1968; cert. in environ. mgmt., U. So. Calif., 1978; M in Pub. Adminstrn., U. Idaho, 1979. Rep. on loan to city health depts. USPHS, Los Angeles and Long Beach, 1962-63; advisor pub. health on loan to Alaska dept. health and welfare USPHS, Anchorage, 1963-64, Juneau and Anchorage, 1964-67; dep. dir. Wash./Alaska Regional Med. Program, Spokane, Wash., 1968-71; dir., sec.-treas. bd. of health Panhandle Health Dist., Coeur d'Alene, Idaho, 1971—; past mem. adj. faculty Whitworth Coll., Spokane; presenter papers internat., nat., region, state confs., testifier congl. coms., Washington, state legis. com., Idaho. Chmn. nominating com. Kootenai Econ. Devel. Council, Idaho, 1985, bd. dirs. 1981-86; mem. adv. com. Kootenai County Council Alcoholism, 1979-80; regional coordinator Gov.'s Com. Vol. Services, Idaho, 1979-80; chmn. Montessori Adv. Bd., Idaho, 1975-79; chmn. personnel com. North Idaho Hospice, 1985-88, bd. dirs. 1985-88; bd. dirs. North Idaho Spl. Services Agy., 1972-76; bd. dirs., vice chmn. Pub. Employees Credit Union, 1990-95; bd. dirs. United Way of Kootenai County, Inc., 1990-91; mem. nat. steering com. APEX/PH, 1987-91; active numerous other organizations. USPHS trainee U. Mich., 1967-68, EPA trainee U. So. Calif., 1978. Mem. Am. Pub. Health Assn., Nat. Assn. Home Health Agys. (chmn. legis. com. 1979-82, bd. dirs. 1978-81), Nat. Assn. County Health Ofcls. (bd. dirs. 1986-88, registry com. 1990), Idaho Pub. Health Assn. (bd. dirs., treas. 1973-77), Idaho Conf. Dist. Health Dirs. (vice-chmn. and chmn. 1993-95), Idaho Forest Owners Assn., Kootenai County Environ. Alliance, Idaho Conservation League, Kootenai County Quality of Life Coalition, Kootenai County Perspective, Idaho Rural Health Coalition, Ducks Unltd. Democrat.

BELNAP, NORMA LEE MADSEN, musician; b. Tremonton, Utah, Dec. 2, 1927; d. Doyle Franklin and Cleo (Crawforth) Madsen; m. H. Austin Belnap, Jan. 19, 1980; 7 stepchildren. Student, Brigham Young U., summer 1947, San Francisco Conservatory of Music, summer 1949; B.S., U. Utah, 1951; postgrad., Aspen Inst. Music, 1953, Music Acad. of West, Santa Barbara, Calif., 1962. Sec.-treas., dir., mem. faculty Treasure Mountain Festival of Arts, 1965, 66; mem. nat. adv. com. Nat. Black Music Colloquium and Competition, 1951-93; instr., 1965, adj. asst. prof. music, 1969-73, adj. assoc. prof., 1973-77, adj. prof., 1977-93; exec. v.p. LOZO Pub. Co., 1991-94. Violinist, Utah Symphony, 1944-93, ret. 1993; asst. concert master Utah Symphony, 1977-93, mem., Utah Opera Theatre Orch., 1951-54, Utah Ballet Theatre Orch., 1953-93; assoc. concertmaster Southwest Symphony St. George, Utah, 1994—, Melody Maids, 4 violins and piano, 1943-49; active in chamber music circles, 1946-81, concert mistress, U. Utah Symphony, 1947-58, prin. violist, 1958-62, soloist, Utah Artist Series, 1964, mem., Treasure Mountain String Quartet, Park City, Utah, 1964, 65, 66; appeared as violin soloist, U. Utah Symphony and Ballet Theatre Orch., 1954, 56, 57, 82; 2d violinist (affiliated with Young Audiences, Inc.) Utah String Quartet, 1958-68; Quartet-in-residence U. Utah, 1968-81, Idaho State U., 1967; with Bach Festival Orch., Carmel, Calif., 1963, 69, Sunriver Festival Orch., summer 1988, Utah-ASTA Faculty Quartet, 1970-79, tour of Europe with Utah Symphony, 1966, 77, 81, 86, S. and Cen. Am., 1971, Brit. Isles, 1975, Hawaii, 1979, concertizing throughout Western states, frequent festival adjudicator; numerous solo recitals. Recipient Tchr. Recognition award Music Tchrs. Nat. Assn., 1971, 72, 73. Mem. Music Educators Nat. Conf., Utah String Tchrs. Assn. (state membership chmn. 1969-73), Utah Music Tchrs. Assn. (state cert. bd. 1968-94), Utah Fedn. Music Clubs (1st v.p.), Am. String Tchrs. Assn. (dir. Utah nat. string conf. ann. 1970-79), Mortar Bd., Mu Phi Epsilon (founder, 1st pres. U. Utah chpt. 1950, compiler Mu Phi Epsilon Composers and Their Works 1956, nat. v.p., music adv., province gov. 1954-58, chpt. honoree for 30 yrs. of dedicated svc. 1981, chpt. honoree for 50 yrs. as mem. with Utah Symphony, honoree for 43 yrs of svc. 1994), Alpha Lambda Delta, Phi Kappa Phi, Alpha Xi. Delta, Lambda Delta Sigma. Mem. LDS Ch. Home: 2702 Aquarias Circle Saint George UT 84790

BELOVANOFF, OLGA, retired health care facility administrator; b. Buchanan, Sask., Can., July 1, 1932; d. Frederick Alexander and Dora (Konkin) B. Grad. high sch., Kamsack, Sask., Can. From clk. to adminstrv. officer Sask. Health Dept. Cancer Clinic, Saskatoon, 1951-78; bus. mgr. Sask. Cancer Found. Saskatoon Clinic, Saskatoon, 1979-90, ret., 1990. Dir. Sask. Br. Can. Tenpin Fedn., Inc. Home: 420 3d Ave N, Saskatoon, SK Canada S7K 2J3

BELPORT, STANLEY CURTIS, computer professional; b. Tucson, Ariz., June 7, 1949; s. Samuel Abraham and Dortha Jean (Luttrell) B.; m. Mary Sue Huddle, Aug. 10, 1991. BA in Radio and TV, U. Ariz., 1974, postgrad., 1975-79. Applications architect & developer, project leader Data Systems Ariz., Tucson, 1980-84; cons. CER Corp., Las Vegas, 1984-87, SAI Corp., Las Vegas, 1987-89, Computer Task Group, Las Vegas, 1989-94, Belport Consulting Inc., Las Vegas, 1994—. Producer, writer local PBS TV shows, 1973-74. Active Cato Inst., Washington, 1993—. Cpl. USMC, 1969-71. Mem. Assn. for Computing Machinery, MicroSoft Developer Network, Sisity Raidus. Office: 6740 Coley Ave Las Vegas NV 89102-6514

BELTRAMI, ALBERT PETER, state commissioner; b. Sacramento, Feb. 26, 1934; s. Battista and Anastasia Beltrami; m. Patricia Jean Kearns, July 28, 1957; children: Katharine Clare, Robert Richard. AA in English, Modesto (Calif.) Jr. Coll., 1953; AB in Polit. Sci., U. Calif., Berkeley, 1955, MA in Pub. Adminstrn., 1957. Dep. marshal Modesto (Calif.) Mcpl. Ct., 1954-55; adminstrv. asst. County San Luis Obispo, Calif., 1960-61; asst. adminstrv. officer County San Luis Obispo, 1961-65; county adminstrv. officer County of Mendocino, Ukiah, Calif., 1965-90; pub. svc. cons. Pub. Svc. Skills, Inc., Sacramento, 1990-91; county exec. officer County of Stanislaus, Modesto, 1991-93; dep. dir. intergovt. affairs Office of Gov. Peter Wilson, Sacramento, 1993-95; exec. dir. Mendocino County Employers Coun., Ukiah, 1996—; mem. adv. com. Grad. Sch. Pub. Adminstrn., Golden Gate U., San Francisco, 1975-80; Gov. apptd. pub. mem. Calif. Commn. on State Mandates, Sacramento, 1996—. Gov. apptd. mem. North Coast Regional Water Quality Control Bd., Santa Rosa, 1972-93; atty. gen. apptd. mem. telecom. adv. com. Calif. Law Enforcment, Sacramento, 1974-90; bd. dirs. Mendocino County Devel. Corp., 1987-89. Comdr. USNR, 1957-84. Fellow Order of the Golden Bear; mem. ASPA, Inter City Mgmt. Assn., Calif. Assn. County Adminstrv. Officers (sec. 1979-80, v.p. 1980-81, pres. 1981-82), Navy League, Naval Res. Assn. (life), Commonwealth Club Calif. (life), U.S. Naval Inst. (life), U. Calif. Alumni (life),. Republican. Roman Catholic. Home: 145 Mendocino Pl Ukiah CA 95482-5612 Office: Mendocino County Employers Ukiah CA 95482

BELTRÁN, ANTHONY NATALICIO, military non-commissioned officer, deacon; b. Flagstaff, Ariz., Aug. 17, 1938; s. Natalicio Torres and Mary Mercedes (Sandoval) B.; m. Patricia Emily Cañez, Nov. 18, 1962; children: Geralyn P., Bernadette M., Albert A., Catherine M., Elizabeth R., Michael J., Theresa R., Christopher M. AA, Phoenix Jr. Coll., 1971, C.C. of Air Force, 1992; grad., Def. Equal Oppty. Mgmt. Inst., 1991. Gen. clk. Blue Cross Blue Shield, Phoenix, 1958-61; enlisted Air N.G., advanced through ranks to chief master sgt.; unit clk. Ariz. Air N.G., Phoenix, 1961, personnel technician, 1962-65, adminstrv. supr., 1965-81, support services supr., 1981-88, equal employment specialist, 1988-95, state sr. enlisted advisor, 1995—; with St. Matthew Cath. Ch., Phoenix. Bd. dirs. Friendly House, Phoenix, 1982-86, mem. aux. bd., 1989—; mem. Alma de la Gente, Phoenix, 1982-92, Chiefs Police Community Adv. Group, Phoenix, 1984-85, Mayor's Task Force on Juvenile Crime, Phoenix, 1979-81; pres. IMAGE de Phoenix, 1985-87. Staff sgt. USAF, 1961-62. Recipient Community Service award Phoenix C. of C., 1982. Mem. Fed. Exec. Assn. (sec., treas. Phoenix chpt. 1985-86, 1st v.p. 1987, pres. 1987-88, Community Svc. award 1986), Am. GI Forum (sec. Sylvestre Herrera chpt. 1995-96, chmn. 1996—), Ariz. Hispanic Employment Program Mgrs. (treas. 1980-81, v.p. 1981-82, pres. 1982-84, named Outstanding Mem. of Yr. 1981, 83), Enlisted Assn. N.G. Ariz. (pres. Copperhead chpt. 1987-90), Non-Commd. Officers Acad. Grad. Assn. (chpt. 46 v.p. 1992-94). Democrat. Home: 4109 W Monte Vista Rd Phoenix AZ 85009-2005 Office: Hdqs Ariz Air NG 5636 E Mcdowell Rd Phoenix AZ 85008-3455 also: Saint Matthew Cath Ch 320 N 20th Dr Phoenix AZ 85009

BELZBERG, HOWARD, critical care physician, educator; b. Bronx, N.Y., Apr. 11, 1951. BA in Psychology, U. Calif., L.A., 1974; MD, Autonomous U., Guadalajara, Mex., 1978, Albert Einstein Coll. Medicine, SUNY, Bronx, N.Y., 1979. Diplomate Am. Bd. Internal Medicine, Am. Bd. Critical Care Medicine; cert. instr. advanced cardiac life support, advanced trauma life support. Residency in internal medicine Kern Med. Ctr., UCLA, Bakersfield, Calif., 1979-82; fellowship in critical care medicine U. Md. Shock Trauma Ctr., MIEMSS, Balt., 1982-83; attending intensivist Shock Trauma Ctr., Md. Inst. for Emergency Med. Svcs. Sys., Balt., 1982-92; sr. intensivist Neuro Trauma Ctr., Balt., 1986-92; asst. prof. medicine U. Md., Balt., 1987-92; asst. prof. surgery U. So. Calif., L.A., 1993—; assoc. dir. surgical intensive care unit L.A. County and Univ. So. Calif. Med. Ctr., L.A., 1993—; chair UMMS Pharmacy and Therapeutics Com., 1985-92, Monitoring and Data Transmission Com., 1990-92; med. dir. Md. Inst. for Emergency Med. Svcs. Sys. Computer Ctr., 1990-92; mem. L.A. County and U. So. Calif. Pharmacy and Therapeutics Com., 1993—, L.A. County Violence Prevention Coalition, 1993—; mem. adv. com. L.A. County Trauma Hosp., 1993—; rep. for L.A. County and U. So. Calif. Trauma Divsn. to Tech. Reinvestment Project, 1993—. Contbr. to profl. jours. Fellow Coll. Chest Physicians, Coll. Critical Care Medicine (task force on tech. assessment 1993—); mem. Am. Trauma Soc., Pan Am. Trauma Soc., Soc. for Computer Clin. Data Mgmt. Sys. Office: LAC & USC Med Ctr Dept Surgery 1200 N State St Rm 9900 Los Angeles CA 90033-4525

BENACH, SHARON ANN, physician assistant; b. New Orleans, Aug. 28, 1944; d. Wilbur G. and Freda Helen (Klaas) Cherry; m. Richard Benach, Dec. 6, 1969 (div. Oct. 1976); children: Craig, Rachel. Degree, St. Louis U., 1978. Physician asst. VA Hosp., St. Louis, 1982-84, Maricopa County Health Svcs., Phoenix, 1984—. Served with USPHS, 1978-82. Recipient Outstanding Performance award HHS. Mem. Maricopa Faculty Assn. (div. internal medicine), Mensa. Jewish. Home: 5726 N 10th St No 5 Phoenix AZ 85014-2273

BEN-ASHER, M. DAVID, physician; b. Newark, June 18, 1931; s. Samuel Irving and Dora Ruth (Kagan)B.; m. Bryna S. Zeller, Nov. 22, 1956. BA, Syracuse U., 1952; MD, U. Buffalo Sch. Med., 1956. Intern E.J. Meyer Mem. Hosp., Buffalo, N.Y., 1956-57; resident Jersey City Med. Ctr., 1957-58; asst. chief med. service U.S. Army Hosp., Ft. McPherson, Ga., 1958-60; resident Madigan Gen. Hosp., Tacoma, Wash., 1960-62; chief gen. med. service Walson Army Hosp., Ft. Dix, N.Y., 1962-64; attending staff St. Mary's Hosp., Tucson, Ariz., 1964—; pvt. practice Tucson, 1964—; mem. Ariz. State Bd. Med. Examiners, 1978-88. Bd. dirs. Tucson Symphony, 1971-73; mem. Ariz. State Bd. Med. Examiners, 1978-88 (joint bd. for regulation of physicians' assts. 1990-97); bd. trustees United Synagogue Am., 1981-87, nat. adv. bd., 1987-91. Mem. Pima County Med. Soc. (bd. dirs. 1971-77, pres. 1976), Ariz. Med. Assn., AMA, ACP. Democrat. Home: 3401 N Tanuri Dr Tucson AZ 85715-6735 Office: So Ariz Med Specialists 4711 N 1st Ave Tucson AZ 85718-5610

BENAVIDES, MARY KATHLEEN, anesthesiologist, nutritional consultant; b. Alhambra, Calif., Sept. 10, 1958; d. Duane Joseph B. and Janet Leona Johnson; m. John Gerard Migliori, May 27, 1946. BS, U. Calif., 1980, MD, 1985. Diplomate Nat. Bd. Med. Examiners, Am. Bd. Anesthesiology. Intern Wadworths-VA Adminstrn. Hosp., Los Angeles, Calif., 1985-86; resident Loma Linda (Calif.) Med. Ctr., 1986-89; Attending physician L.A. Children's Hosp., 1989-90; anesthesiologist Inland Valley Regional Med. Ctr., Wildomar, Calif., 1990-91, Mission Bay Hosp., San Diego, 1991-96, Treasure Valley Hosp., Boise, 1996—; nutritional cons. BodyWise Internat., San Diego, 1989—, Boise, 1996—. Fellow Am. Bd. Anesthesiology; mem. Am. Soc. Anesthesiologists, Soc. Ambulatory Care Anesthesiology, Idaho State Soc. Anesthesiology. Home: PO Box 418 Boise ID 83701-0418

BENBOW, RICHARD ADDISON, psychological counselor; b. Las Vegas, Dec. 27, 1949; s. Jules Coleman and Bonnie Ray B. BBA, U. Nev. 1972, MS in Counseling, 1974; AAS in Bus. Mgmt. and Real Estate, Clark County Community Coll., 1980; PhD in Clin. Psychology, U. Humanistic Studies, 1986. Cert. tchr., Nev.; cert. clin. mental health counselor, secondary sch. counselor, Nev., substance abuse counselor, Nev., substance abuse program adminstr., Nev.; nat. cert. counselor. Jud. svcs. officer Mcpl. Ct. City of Las Vegas, 1983-88, pretrial program coord., 1988—; inmate classification technician Detention and Correctional Svcs., 1982-83; stress mgmt. cons. Mem. Biofeedback Soc. Am., Assn. Humanistic Psychology, Nat. Assn. Psychotherapists, Am. Counseling Assn., Am. Mental Health Counselors Assn., Am. Acad. Crisis Interveners, Jr. C. of C., U.S. Jaycees (presdl. award of honor 1978-79), Delta Sigma Phi. Democrat. Christian Scientist. Office: Mcpl Ct Intake Svcs City of Las Vegas 400 Stewart Ave Las Vegas NV 89101-2942

BENDEL, ADRIENNE ANTINK, association manager, writer; b. Santa Fe, Aug. 26, 1946; d. James and Josephine Cecilia (Granito) Antink; div.; 1 child, Joseph. BA, U. N.Mex., 1968; MBA, U. Wash., 1979. Substitute tchr. Ridgecrest (Calif.) Sch., 1970-71; shipping and receiving mgr. Montaldo's, Denver, 1980-84; dept. dir. Med. Group Mgmt. Assn., Denver, 1984—; chair Colo. Alliance of Bus. Task Force on Healthcare Professions, Denver, 1991-93. Contbr. articles to profl. jours. Precinct com. co-chair Rep. Party, Jefferson County, Colo., 1988, 92, 96; del. Jefferson County Rep. Party Conv., 1988, Rep. State Assembly, Colo., 1996; spl. exhibits vol. Nat. History Mus. 1st lt. U.S. Army, 1968-70. Mem. Colo. Soc. Assn. Execs. (membership svcs. com.), Nat. Book Critics Cir., Colo. Authors League, Phi Beta Kappa (Colo. Alpha Assn. newsletter editor 1993—, pres. 1994-96, del. to Triennial Conf. 1996). Lutheran. Home: 582 S Carr St Lakewood CO 80226 Office: Med Group Mgmt Assn 104 Inverness Ter E Englewood CO 80112-5313

BENDING, DAVID ALEXANDER GLEN, mining executive, geoscientist; b. Chicoutimi, Quebec, Can., Dec. 12, 1954; came to U.S., 1962; s. Glen Charles Bending and Beatress Elizabeth (Long) Wilkinson; m. Ginette Lilianne Bourdeau, May 10, 1986; children: Michael David, Katherine Marie. BSc in Geology, U. Oreg., 1976; MSc iin Geology, U. Toronto, Can., 1979. Mine and exploration geologist GRC Exploration Co., Metaline Falls, Wash., 1976-77; field party chief geologist Rio Tinto Can. Exploration, Vancouver, 1978-79; project geologist Tex. Gulf Exploration, Vancouver, 1979-82; rsch. assoc., cons. U. Toronto, 1982-84; exploration geologist, mgr. Homestake Mining Co., 1985-96; v.p. no. S.Am. Homestake Mining Co., Reno, 1993—; pres. D. Bending & Assoc., Ltd., Toronto, 1982-85; v.p. Homestake Venezuela, Puerto Ordaz, 1993—, Minera Rio Carichapo, Puerto Ordaz, 1993—, Minera Rio Marwani, Puerto Ordaz, 1993—. Fellow Soc. Econ. Geologists, Geol. Assn. Can.; mem. Can. Inst. Mining. Republican.

BEN-DOR, GISÈLE, conductor, musician; b. Montevideo, Uruguay; came to U.S., 1982; m. Eli Ben-Dor; children: Roy, Gabriel. Student, Acad. of Music, Tel Aviv; artist diploma, Rubin Acad. Music, Tel Aviv; M, Yale Sch. of Music, 1982. Music dir. Annapolis Symphony, Md., Pro Arte Chamber Orch. of Boston; condr. Norwalk (Conn.) Youth Symphony; conducting fellow L.A. Philharm. Inst., 1984, Tanglewood Music Ctr., 1985; resident condr. Houston Symphony, 1991; music dir. Santa Barbara Symphony, Calif., 1994—; resident condr. Houston Symphony; condr. variety conducting activities including prestigious summer festivals, competitions, 1983-87, Hungarian Nat. Symphony, Budapest Philharm., others; guest condr. orchs. in Uruguay, Ea. Europe, Israel and U.S. including Barvarian Radio Orch., Boston POPS, New World Symphony, Women's Philharm, San Francisco, Minn. Orch. in Summerfest Festival, 1986, N.Y. Philharm., 1993, 95, Orquestra del Teatro Nacional, Brazil, Ulster Orch., Israel Philharm., 1991, Carnegie Hall, 1991, others; past music dir. Houston Youth Symphony; past acting orch. dir. Shepherd Sch. Music Rice U.; music dir. Boston ProArte Chamber Orch., Annapolis Symphony. Condr. Israel Philharm. Orch. (play) The Rite of Spring; recs. with London Symphony, Israel Chamber Orch., (CD) London Symphony Orch., Sofia Soloists, Boston ProArte Chamber Orch.; numerous TV appearances. Am.-Israel Cultural Found scholar, Frances Wickes scholar; Leonard Bernstein fellow; recipient Bartók prize Hungarian TV Internat. Condrs. Competition, 1986. Office: Santa Barbara Symphony Orch Arlington Theatre 1900 State St Ste G Santa Barbara CA 93101-2429

BENES, ANDREW CHARLES, professional baseball player; b. Evansville, Ind., Aug. 20, 1967. Student, U. Evansville. With San Diego Padres, 1988-95, St. Louis Cardinals, 1995—; mem. U.S. Olympic Baseball Team, 1988, Nat. League All-Star Team, 1993. Named Sporting News Rookie Pitcher of Yr., 1989. *

BENEŠ, NORMAN STANLEY, meteorologist; b. Detroit, July 1, 1921; s. Stanley and Cecelia (Sereneck) B.; m. Elinor Simson, May 5, 1945 (div. Feb. 1972); children: Gregory, Heather, Michelle, Francine; m. Celia Sereneck, Mar. 3, 1972. BS, U. Wash., 1949; postgrad., U. Calif., Davis, 1963, U. Mich., 1966. Chief meteorologist Hawthorne Sch. of Aero., Moultrie, Ga., 1951-55; meteorologist U.S. Weather Bur., Phoenix, 1955-57, 59-60; meteorologist in charge NSF, Hallett, Antarctica, 1958; sta. sci. leader NSF, Byrd, Antarctica, 1960-61; meteorologist Nat. Weather Service, Sacramento, Calif., 1962-84; mem. Exec. Com. Range Benes Peak, Antarctica. Contbr. articles to profl. jours. Pres. local chpt. PTA, 1965. With USN, 1943-46, PTO. Mem. AAAS, Am. Meteorol. Soc., Am. Geophys. Union, Nat. Weather Assn., Masons. Home: 3311 Holiday Ln Placerville CA 95667-9076

BENET, CAROL ANN, journalist, career counselor, teacher; b. Albany, N.Y., Mar. 21, 1939; d. Morton Harold and Ethel Leona (Maitland) Levin; m. Leslie Z. Benet, Sept. 8, 1960; children: Reed Michael, Gillian Vivia. AB, U. Mich., 1961, MA, 1964; PhD, U. Calif., Berkeley, 1987. Journalist, arts critic Ark newspaper, Belvedere, Calif., 1975—; book seminar tchr. U. Calif. Extension, Berkeley, San Francisco, 1991-93; book group leader several different univs., Marin County, San Francisco, 1987—; PhD career advisor/counselor U. Calif., Berkeley, 1990—; journalist, arts critic Bay City News Svc., San Francisco, 1993—; adj. prof. Antioch Coll., Yellow Springs, Ohio, 1995-96, lectr. grad. humanities program, Dominican Coll, San Raphael, Calif., 1996—. Author: The German Reception of Sam Shephard, 1990. Docent Asian Art Mus., San Francisco, 1987, De Young Mus., San Francisco, 1984. Jewish. Home: 53 Beach Rd Belvedere CA 94920 Office: U Calif 2111 Bancroft Way Spc 4350 Berkeley CA 94720-4350

BENGELSDORF, IRVING SWEM, science writer, consultant; b. Chgo., Oct. 23, 1922; s. Jacob and Frieda (Wiener) B.; m. Beverly Devorah Knapp, June 12, 1949; children: Ruth, Lea, Judith. BS in Chemistry with highest honors, U. Ill., 1943; student, Cornell U.; MS, U. Chgo., 1948, PhD, 1951. Mem. chemistry faculty UCLA, 1952-54; rsch. chemist Gen. Electric Rsch. Lab., Schenectady, N.Y., 1954-59; rsch. group leader Texaco-U.S. Rubber Rsch. Ctr., Parsippany, N.J., 1959-60; sr. scientist U.S. Borax Rsch. Corp., Anaheim, Calif., 1960-63; sci. editor L.A. Times, 1963-70; dir. sci. communication Calif. Inst. Tech., Pasadena, 1971-80; contbg. sci. columnist L.A. Herald-Examiner, 1978-86; tech. writer, specialist Jet Propulsion Lab., Calif. Inst. Tech., Pasadena, 1980-88; contb. sci. columnist North County Times, Calif., 1992—; cons. Jet Propulsion Lab., 1988—; Disting. vis. prof. U. So. Calif., L.A., 1971-90; tchr. TV course in Russian lang. Gen. Electric Rsch. Lab., Schenectady, 1958; cons. NASA, 1979. Author: Spaceship Earth: People and Pollution, 1969; co-author: Biology: A Unique Science, 1978; contbr. chpts. to books, articles to profl. jours.; patentee in field. Participant 19th Pugwash Conf. on Sci. and World Affairs, Sochi, USSR, 1969; mem. cabinet U. Chgo. Alumni Cabinet, 1968-71; mem. U. Calif. Ctrs. for Water and Wildland Resources Adv. Coun., Davis, 1973—; mem. Mayor Bradley's Energy Policy Com., L.A., 1974; mem. Am. Fedn. TV and Radio Artists, 1971-73. With USN, 1944-46. Recipient Claude Bernard Sci. Journalism award Nat. Soc. for Med. Rsch., 1968, Bicentennial Humanitarian award City of L.A., 1981. Mem. AAAS (Westinghouse Writing award 1967, 69), Am. Chem. Soc. (James T. Grady award 1967), Nat. Assn. Sci. Writers, U. Chgo. Alumni Club L.A. (Disting. Alumnus award 1975), Soc. for Tech. Communication (hon.), Sigma Xi. Home and Office: 3778 Via Las Villas Oceanside CA 92056-7258

BENHAM, JAMES H., state official; b. Twin Falls, Idaho, July 14, 1944; s. James Henry and Matilda (Riggs) B.; m. Ann Elizabeth McIntosh, Mar. 28, 1965; 2 children. BA in Polit. Sci., Idaho State U., 1990, MPA, 1992. From police officer to chief of police Pocatello (Idaho) Police Dept., 1988-94; marshal dept. justice U.S. Dist. Idaho, Boise, 1994—. Contbr. articles to profl. jours. Bd. dirs. Nat. Criminal Justice Assn., 1992-93. Mem. Idaho Peace Officers Assn. (pres. 1986), Idaho Chief of Police Assn. (pres. 1990-91), Pocatello Police Relief Assn., Lions, Phi Kappa Phi. Methodist. Office: US Marshal for Dist Idaho Dept Justice Rm 777 550 W Fort St MSC 010 Boise ID 83724

BENI, GERARDO, electrical and computer engineering educator, robotics scientist; b. Florence, Italy, Feb. 21, 1946; came to U.S., 1970; s. Edoardo and Tina (Bazzanti) B.; m. Susan Hackwood, May 24, 1986; children: Catherine Elizabeth, Juliet Beatrice. Laurea in Physics, U. Firenze, Florence, Italy, 1970; PhD in Physics, UCLA, 1974. Research scientist AT&T Bell Labs., Murray Hill, N.J., 1974-77; research scientist AT&T Bell Labs., Holmdel, N.J., 1977-82, disting. mem. tech. staff, 1982-84; prof. elec. and computer engring. U. Calif., Santa Barbara, 1984-91, dir. Ctr. for Robotic Systems in Microelectronics, 1985-91; prof. elec. engring., dir. distbn. robotic system lab. U. Calif., Riverside, 1991—. Founder, editor: Jours. Robotic Systems, 1983 (Jour. of Yr. award 1984); editor: Recent Advances in Robotics, 1985, Vacuum Mechatronics, 1990; contbr. more than 130 articles to tech. jours.; 16 patents in field. Fellow Am. Physics Soc. Office: U Calif-Riverside Coll Engring Riverside CA 92521 *Produce in freedom; give in freedom; and in freedom enjoy.*

BENIRSCHKE, KURT, pathologist, educator; b. Glueckstadt, Germany, May 26, 1924; came to U.S., 1949, naturalized, 1955; s. Fritz Franz and Marie (Luebcke) B.; m. Marion Elizabeth Waldhausen, May 17, 1952; children: Stephen Kurt, Rolf Joachim, Ingrid Marie. Student, U. Hamburg, Germany, 1942, 45-48, U. Berlin, Germany, 1943, U. Wuerzburg, Germany, 1943-44; M.D., U. Hamburg, 1948. Resident Teaneck, N.J., 1950-51, Peter Bent Brigham Hosp., Boston, 1951-52, Boston Lying-in-Hosp., 1952-53, Free Hosp. for Women, Boston, 1953, Children's Hosp., Boston, 1953; pathologist Boston Lying-in-Hosp., 1955-60; teaching fellow, assoc. Med. Sch. Harvard, 1954-60; prof. pathology, chmn. dept. pathology Med. Sch. Dartmouth, Hanover, N.H., 1960-70; prof. reproductive medicine and pathology U. Calif. at San Diego, 1970-94; chmn. dept. pathology U. Calif. at San Diego (Sch. Med.), La Jolla, 1976-79; ret. U. Calif. at San Diego, 1994; dir. research San Diego Zoo, 1975-86, trustee, 1986—; cons. NIH, 1957-70. Served with German Army, 1942-45. Mem. Am. Soc. Pathology, Internat. Acad. Pathology, Am. Coll. Pathology, Am. Acad. Arts and Scis., Teratol. Soc., Am. Soc. Zool. Vets. Home: 8457 Prestwick Dr La Jolla CA 92037-2023 Office: Univ Calif San Diego Pathology Dept San Diego CA 92013-8321

BENJAMIN, KARL STANLEY, art educator; b. Chgo., Dec. 29, 1925; s. Eustace Lincoln and Marie (Klamsteiner) B.; m. Beverly Jean Paschke, Jan. 29, 1949; children: Beth Marie, Kris Ellen, Bruce Lincoln. Student, Northwestern U., 1943, 46; BA, U. Redlands, 1949; MA, Claremont Grad. Sch., 1960. With dept. arts Pomona Coll., Claremont, Calif., 1979-97, Loren Barton Babcock Miller prof., artist-in residence, 1978-94, prof. emeritus, 1997—; prof. art Claremont Grad. Sch. Traveling exhbns. include New Talent, Am. Fedn. Arts, 1959, 4 Abstract Classicists, Los Angeles and San Francisco museums, 1959-61, West Coast Hard Edge, Inst. Contemporary Arts, London, Eng., 1960, Purist Painting, Am. Fedn. Arts, 1960-61, Geometric Abstractions in Am, Whitney Mus., 1962, Paintings of the Pacific, U.S., Japan and Australia, 1961-63, Artists Environment, West Coast, Amon Carter Mus., Houston, 1962-63, Denver annual, 1965, Survey of Contemporary Art, Speed Mus., Louisville, 1965, The Colorists, San Francisco Mus., 1965, Art Across Am, Mead Corp., 1965-67, The Responsive Eye, Mus. Modern Art, 1965-66, 30th Biennial Exhbn. Am. Painting, Corcoran Gallery, 1967, 35th Biennial Exhbn. Am. Painting, 1977, Painting and Sculpture in California: The Modern Era, San Francisco Mus. Modern Art, 1976-77, Smithsonian Nat. Collection Fine Arts, Washington, 1976-77, Los Angeles Hard Edge: The Fifties and Seventies, Los Angeles County Mus. Art, 1977, Corcoran Gallery, Washington, Cheney Cowles Mus., Spokane, 1980, Calif. State U., Bakersfield, 1982, Henry Gallery, U. Wash., 1982, U. Calif., Santa Barbara, 1984, L.A. Mcpl. Art Galleries, Barnsdall Park, 1986, Turning the Tide: Early Los Angeles Modernists, Santa Barbara Mus. Art, Oakland Mus., others, 1989-91; rep. permanent collections, Whitney Mus., L.A. County Mus. Art, San Francisco Mus. Art, Santa Barbara (Calif.) Mus. Art, Pasadena (Calif.) Art Mus., Long Beach (Calif.) Mus. Art, La Jolla (Calif.) Mus. Art, Fine Arts Gallery San Diego, U. Redlands, Mus. Modern Art, Israel, Pomona Coll., Scripps Coll., Univ. Mus., Berkeley, Calif., Wadsworth Atheneum, Nat. Collection Fine Arts, Seattle Mus. Modern Art, Newport Harbor Mus., U. N.Mex. Mus. Art, Wash. State U., L.A. Mus. Contemporary Art; retrospective exhbn. covering yrs. 1955-87 Calif State U. at Northridge, 1989, retrospective exhbn. 1979-94, Pomona Coll., 1994. Served with USNR, 1943-46. Visual Arts grantee NEA, 1983, 89. Office: Pomona Coll Dept Arts 333 N College Way Claremont CA 91711-6182 also: Claremont Grad Sch Art Dept 251 E 10th St Claremont CA 91711

BENJAMIN, LORNA SMITH, psychologist; b. Rochester, N.Y., Jan. 7, 1934; d. Lloyd Albert and Esther (Tack) Smith; children: Laureen, Linda. AB, Oberlin Coll., 1955; PhD, U. Wis., 1960. NIMH fellow dept. psychiatry U. Wis., 1958-62, clin. psychology intern, 1960-64, asst. prof., 1966-71, assoc. prof., 1971-77, prof. psychiatry, 1977-88; prof. psychology U. Utah, 1988—; research asso. Wis. Psychol. Inst., Madison, 1962-66. Contbr. articles to profl. jours. Mem. Am. Psychol. Assn., Soc. Psychotherapy Research, Phi Beta Kappa. Office: U Utah Dept Psychology Salt Lake City UT 84112 *I attribute my success to a high energy level, and to some teachers and friends who supported me in times and places women were unwelcome.*

BENN, JULIE EVE AREND, writer, communications specialist; b. Highland Park, Ill., Mar. 11, 1971; d. Robert Lee Arend and Andrea Diann (Pries) Kuipers; m. John Tyler Benn, Oct. 21, 1995. Assoc. in Psychology, Mira Costa Coll., 1994; B Journalism, San Diego State U., 1996. Editl. intern San Diego Mag., 1993; reporter The Beach News, Encinitas, Calif., 1993-96; intern KGTV Channel 10, San Diego, 1994, KOCT Oceanside (Calif.) Cmty. TV, 1996; comms. specialist Try J Advt., Carlsbad, Calif., 1996—; newsrm. asst. Rep. Convention programming CBS News, San Diego, 1996; media advisor Married Students Club, San Diego State U., 1995-96. Commentator Morning Edition program Nat. Pub. Radio, 1996. Mem. Radio-TV News Dirs. Assn., Soc. Profl. Journalists.

BENNER, RICK, professional basketball team executive; m. Diann Benner. Grad. magna cum laude, U. Mo., Columbia, 1978. CPA. Acct.

Coopers and Lybrand, Kansas City, 1978-83; contr., pres. fin., exec. v.p. bus. ops. King ARCO Arena, Sacramento, 1983-89; pres. Capital Sports and Entertainment, Sacramento, 1989—. Mem. adv. bd. Salvation Army, People Reaching Out. Mem. Sacramento Metro C. of C. (mem. adv. bd.), Rotary Club. Office: Sacramento Kings One Sports Pkwy Sacramento CA 95834*

BENNETT, BARBARA ESTHER, accountant, tax professional; b. Norfolk, Nebr., Nov. 24, 1953. AA, Northeastern Nebr. Community Coll., Norfolk, Nebr., 1973; student, U. Nebr., 1980, U. Colo., Denver, 1985. Bookkeeper McIntosh, Inc., Norfolk, 1971-77; credit, office mgr. Goodyear Service Stores Inc., Norfolk, 1977-81; pvt. practice acct. Norfolk, 1971-81; base adminstr. Evergreen Helicopters Inc., Greeley, Colo., 1981-82; pvt. practice acctg. and tax service Denver, 1984—; acctg. supr, asst. controller Saltzgitter Machinery, Inc., Louviers, Colo., Saltzgitter, Fed. Republic Germany., 1982-85; corp. controller Satter, Inc., Denver, 1985-95; fin. mgr. LMS Group, Inc., Denver, 1996—. Past Sunday sch. tchr., past chmn. bd. fin. Redeemer Luth. Ch. Mem. Am. Soc. Women Accts., Am. Legion Aux., Phi Theta Kappa, Phi Beta Lambda. Republican. Home and Office: 963 S Patton Ct PO Box 19070 Denver CO 80219-0070

BENNETT, BRENDA G., secondary school counselor, mathematics educator; b. Portland, Oreg., July 17, 1940; d. Edwin E. and Mable Maru (Wilhelm) Osgood; m. Steven L. Bennett, June 18, 1961; children: Sheryl Born, Laura Navarro, Katherine. BA in Math., Portland State U., 1962, MS in Counseling, 1976. Registered counselor, Wash.; lic. counselor, Oreg.; cert. advanced math. tchg., Oreg. Lab. asst. U. Oreg. Med. Sch., Portland, 1961-64; math. and science tchr. Franklin H.S., Portland, 1973-74; math. tchr. Grant H.S., Portland, 1974-79, counselor, 1979—; counselor Counseling Ctr. Vancouver, Wash., 1984-93; math. instr. Portland C.C., 1987—.

BENNETT, CHARLES LEON, vocational and graphic arts educator; b. Salem, Oreg., Feb. 5, 1951; s. Theodore John and Cora Larena (Rowland) B.; m. Cynthia Alice Hostman, June 12, 1976 (div.); m. Lynn Marie Toland, Aug. 12, 1977 (div.); children: Mizzy Marie, Charles David; m. Christina M. Crawford, Dec. 19, 1987 (div.). AS in Vocat. Tchr. Edn., Clackamas C.C., 1977; AS in Gen. Studies, Linn Benton C.C., 1979; BS in Gen. Studies, Ea. Oreg. State Coll., 1994. Tchr. printing Tongue Point Job Corps, Astoria, Oreg., 1979-80; tchr., dept. chmn. Portland (Oreg.) pub. schs., 1980—; owner, mgr. printing and pub. co., Portland, 1981-87. With AUS, 1970-72. Mem. NRA, Oreg. Vocat. Trade-Tech. Assn. (dept. chmn., pres. graphic arts div., Indsl. Educator of Year 1981-82), Oreg. Vocat. Assn. (Vocat. Tchr. of Yr. 1982-83), Graphic Arts Tech. Found., In-Plant Printing Mgmt. Assn., Internat. Graphic Arts Edn. Assn. (v.p. N.W. region VI), Oreg. Assn. Manpower Spl. Needs Personnel, Oreg. Indsl. Arts Assn., Internat. Platform Assn. Nat. Assn. Quick Printers, Am. Vocat. Assn., Pacific Printing & Imaging Assn., Inplant Printing Mgmt. Assn., Portland Club Lithographers and Printing House Craftsmen. Republican. Home: 20295 S Unger Rd Beavercreek OR 97004-9758 Office: 546 NE 12th St Portland OR 97213

BENNETT, CHARLES TURNER, social welfare administrator; b. Egypt, Ark., June 17, 1932; s. Charley Clower and Lois LaJoy (Turner) B.; m. Ella Jane Fye, July 6, 1962; children: Rebeca Joy, Lisa Anne. Grad., Moody Bible Inst., Chgo., 1953; student, UCLA, 1970; MA, Fuller Theol. Seminary, Pasadena, Calif., 1972, Claremont (Calif.) Grad. Sch., 1983. Bush pilot Mission Aviation, Mexico, 1955-68; dir. research Mission Aviation Fellowship, Fullerton, Calif., 1968-72; pres., chief exec. officer Mission Aviation Fellowship, Redlands, Calif., 1973-85; exec. dir. Presby. Ctr. for Mission Studies, Fullerton, 1972-73; exec. v.p. Food for the Hungry Internat., Geneva, Switzerland, 1985-88, Scottsdale, Ariz., 1988-91; pres. Ptnrs. Internat., San Jose, Calif., 1992—; bd. dirs. Air Svc. Internat. Redlands, Evang. Fgn. Missions Assn., Washington, 1976-82; founder Redlands Aviation Corp., 1980. Author: Tinder in Tabasco, 1968, Pantano Ardiente, 1989, Heroes on the Frontlines, 1995, God in the Corners, 1997, (with others) From Nairobi to Berkeley, 1967, God, Man and Church Growth, 1973. Chmn. world service Redlands Rotary Club., 1982-85. Named Alumnus of Yr. Fuller Theol. Seminary, 1985; recipient Outstanding Sr. Achievement award, Claremont Grad. Sch., 1997. Democrat. Home: 2395 Delaware-Sp 161 Santa Cruz CA 95060-5726 Office: Ptnrs Internat 2302 Zanker Rd San Jose CA 95131

BENNETT, EUGENE PEART, artist; b. Central Point, Oreg., Dec. 20, 1921; s. Edward Carl and Mable Ann (Peart) B. Student, U. Oreg., 1940-43, Park Coll., 1943; student evening classes, DePaul U., 1949-50; BA in Art Edn., Art Inst. Chgo., 1951; student evening classes, U. Chgo., 1951-53; MA in Art Edn., Art Inst. Chgo., 1954; student, Florence, Italy, 1954-55. Tchr. Eugene Bennett Summer Art Classes, Medford, Oreg., 1948-53; tchr. jr. sch. Art Inst. Chgo., 1950-51; tchr. New Trier Twp. H. S., Winnetka, Ill, 1951-54, Abbott Labs., N. Chgo., 1951-53, Katharine Lord's Studio, Evanston, Ill., 1952-53; tchr. life drawing Art Inst. Chgo., 1953-54; tchr. 414 Art Workshop, Chgo., 1953-54, 1955-58; tchr. New Trier Twp. H. S., Winnetka, Ill., 1955-58; co-dir. 414 Art Workshop Gallery, Chgo., 1956-58; pvt. classes Medford and Jacksonville, Oreg., 1959-69; bd. dirs., founder Rogue Valley Art Assn., Medford, Oreg., 1959—, pres. 1959-60. One man shows include Portland (Oreg.) Art Mus., 1950, 60, Mus. of Art U. Oreg., Eugene, 1969, 82, So. Oreg. Hist. Soc., Jacksonville, 1983, Schneider Mus. Art So. Oreg. State Coll., Ashland, 1994; group shows include Mcpl. Art Gallery, Jackson, Miss., 1948, Portland Art Mus., 1950, Bklyn. Mus., 1951, Mus. Modern Art, N.Y.C., 1953, Art Inst. Chgo., 1954, 56, Madison Square Garden, 1958, San Francisco Mus. Art, 1961, Meml. Union Art Galleries Oreg. State U., Corvallis, 1963, Alba, Italy, 1963, State Capital Mus., Olympia, Wash., 1964, Oreg. Arts. Commn., 1986, Expo 86, Seattle, 1986, Galleria State Capitol, Salem, Oreg., 1991; represented in pub. collections Mus. Modern Art, Mus. Art. U. Oreg., Haseltine Collection of N.W. Art, Coos Art Mus., Schneider Mus. Art, Bundy Art Mus., Miss. Art Mus., Pacific Power; prin. work includes Oreg. Pavillion, Seattle Worlds Fair, 1962; executed two groups of wood sculpture U.S. Nat. Bank of Oreg., Eugene, 1961, bas relief, wood screens Salishan Lodge, Gleneden, Oreg. Bd. dirs. So. Oreg. Hist. Soc., Medford, 1969-73; chmn. Jacksonville (Oreg.) Historic Preservation Commn., 1968-70; mem. Jacksonville (Oreg.) Planning Commn., Oreg. Arts Commn. With USN, 1943-46. Recipient Pauline Palmer prize Art Inst. Chgo, 1956, Renaissance prize, 1957, award of merit Am. Assn. Mus., 1984; honrable mention Oreg. Centennial Exhibn., 1959. Mem. So. Oreg. Soc. of Artists (hon. life), Sch. of Art Inst. Chgo. (alumni), Oreg. Advs. for Arts, Schneider Mus. Art. Home: P O Box 328 355 S Oregon St Jacksonville OR 97530

BENNETT, FRED LAWRENCE, engineering educator; b. Troy, N.Y., Apr. 4, 1939; s. Fred A. and Dorothy (Lee) B.; m. Margaret Ann Musgrave, Aug. 25, 1962; children: Matthew Lawrence, Andrew Lee. BCE, Rensselaer Poly. Inst., 1961; MS, Cornell U., 1963, PhD, 1965. Registered profl. engr., Alaska, Pa., N.H. Planning and scheduling engr. United Engrs. & Cons. Inc., Phila., 1965-68; assoc. prof. engring. mgmt. U. Alaska, Fairbanks, 1968-74, prof. engring. mgmt., 1974—, asst. to chancellor, 1977-79, vice chancellor acad. affairs, 1979-82, acting v.p. for acad. affairs, 1982-83, head dept. engring. and sci. mgmt., 1969-80, 83—; owner F. Lawrence Bennett, P.E., Engring. and Mgmt. Cons., 1969—; vis. prof. engring. Luleå, Sweden, 1992. Author: Critical Path Precedence Networks, 1977, (with others) Construction in Cold Regions, 1991, The Management of Engineering, 1996; contbr. papers and articles on engring. mgmt. and cold regions constrn. to profl. publs. Mem. coun. exec. bd. Boy Scouts Am., Fairbanks, 1982-92. Fellow ASCE (Peyton Cold Regions Engring. award 1996); mem. NSPE, Am. Soc. Engring. Edn., Am. Soc. Engring. Mgmt., Project Mgmt. Inst., Soc. Logistics Engrs., Sigma Xi, Phi Kappa Phi, Tau Beta Pi, Chi Epsilon. Home: PO Box 83009 Fairbanks AK 99708-3009 Office: U Alaska PO Box 755900 Fairbanks AK 99775-5900

BENNETT, JAMES CHESTER, computer consultant, real estate developer; b. Chico, Calif., May 14, 1932; s. George Clerk and Georgia Mae (James) B.; m. Grace M. Schutrum, Feb. 14, 1955 (div. 1967); children: Ronald, Becky Ann, Todd Bryant. BA in Bus., Calif. State U., Long Beach, 1965. Sgt. USAF, 1947-62; customer engr. IBM, L.A., 1962-70; mgr. computer systems Continental Airlines, L.A., 1970-82; instr. ITT Tech. Inst., Buena Park, Calif., 1982-84; dir. Ramasat Comm., LTD, Bangkok, Thailand, 1984-89; instr. ITT Tech. Inst., San Diego, 1989-90; pres. The Systems Group, Inc., Ramona, Calif., 1990—. Home: PO Box 2032 209 Tenth St Ramona CA 92065-2032

BENNETT, JAMES P., construction executive; b. 1936. Pres. J.A. Jones Co. SA, Tenn., 1959-78, Rogers Cons., Nashville, 1978-87; with PCL Enterprises Inc., Denver, 1987—, now pres. Office: PCL Enterprises Inc 2000 S Colorado Blvd Ste 400 Denver CO 80222-7911*

BENNETT, KENNETH R., oil company executive, school board executive; b. Tucson, Aug. 1, 1959; s. Archie Roy and Donna Lucille (Bulechek) B.; m. Jeanne Tenney Bennett, Mar. 13, 1982; children: Ryan, Dana, Clifton. BS, Ariz. State U., 1984. Ceo Bennett's Oil Co., 1984—; mem. Ariz. State Bd. Edn., Phoenix, 1992—, pres., 1996-97; Ariz. State Bd. for Charter Schs., Phoenix, 1994—, Governor's Task Force Edn. Reform, Phoenix, 1991-92. Mayor Pro Tempore City of Prescott (Ariz.), 1988; councilman City of Prescott (Ariz.), 1985-89; scoutmaster Boy Scouts of Am., 1993—. Republican. LDS. Home: 1826 Oaklawn Prescott AZ 86301 Office: Bennett Oil Co 810 E Sheldon Prescott AZ 86301

BENNETT, NOËL, artist, author; b. San Jose, Dec. 23, 1939; d. Charles Faris and Merton (Meyer) Kirkish; m. John N. Bennett, II; children: John N. III, Brockington LeLeand; m. Jim Wakeman. BA cum laude with honors in humanities, Stanford U., 1961, MA in Edn. and Fine Art, 1962; postgrad., U. N.Mex., 1984-86. Art faculty Coll. Notre Dame, Belmont, Calif., 1963-67, U. N.Mex., Albuquerque, 1971-75; founder Navajo Weaving Restoration Ctr., 1978; faculty Internat. Coll., L.A., 1979-84; rschr. A Place in the Wild, N.Mex., 1984—; founder, dir. Shared Horizons, 1981—; condr. multimedia presentations, workshops on Navajo weaving and Native Am. concepts to numerous mus., univs. and guilds; coord. seminars on S.W. textiles, culture, fiber and dye identification, storage and conservation, 1980, 82. Author: Working With the Wool -- How to Weave a Navajo Rug (with Tiana Bighorse), 1971, Genuine Navajo Rug -- Are You Sure?, 1973, 2d edit. 1980, The Weaver's Pathway -- A Clarification of the "Spirit Trail" in Navajo Weaving, 1974, Designing with the Wool -- Advanced Navajo Weaving Techniques, 1979, Shared Horizons/Navajo Textiles (with Susan McGreevy and Mark Winters), 1981, Patterns of Power -- Art, Life, Self (cassette), 1982, Halo of the Sun -- Stories Told and Retold, 1987, Navajo Weaving Way -- The Path From Fleece to Rug (with Tiana Bighorse), 1997; editor: Bighorse The Warrior, 1990; contbr. articles to profl. jours.; exhbns. include Univ. Art Ctr., Stanford U., Coll. Notre Dame, Mus. No. Ariz., Flagstaff, Convergence, San Francisco, St. John's Episc. Cathedral, Albuquerque, Denver Mus. Natural History, U. N.Mex., Statements 86, Albuquerque, Ansel Adams Gallery, Yosemite, Calif., 1990, Art Ctr. Los Alamos, N.Mex., 1996, Woman Made Gallery, Chgo., 1996; works in permanent collections of Sheehan, Sheehan and Stelzner, P.A., Albuquerque, Corrales (N.Mex.) Pub. Libr., San Jose State Coll., Grant St. Apts., San Francisco, Viking Apts., Eugene, Oreg., Simmons Inst. Human rels., Redwood City, Calif., Padre House, Carmel, Calif. and numerous private collections. Recipient Comm. Arts award, 1982, Mortimer C. Levintritt award for most outstanding work in dept. of art and arch., Stanford U., 1961; grantee Weatherhead Found., 1975, Tenn. Humanities Found., 1982, L.J. and Mary C. Skaggs Found., 1986, 89, Richard C. and Susan B. Ernst Found., 1989, NEA, 1990. Home: 976 Vallecitos Rd Jemez Springs NM 87025-9380

BENNETT, PAUL ALAN, artist, educator; b. Bozeman, Mont., Dec. 4, 1949; s. Ben Theodore and Elizabeth Prudence (Johnston) B.; m. Carolyn Plat, Aug. 25, 1992; 1 child, Parker Daniel Alan. BFA, Md. Inst. Art, 1972; MA, U. LaVerne, Athens, Greece, 1982. Artist-in-edn. Regional Arts Coun., Portland, Oreg., 1983—; instr. art history Ctrl. Oreg. C.C., Bend, 1993-96; artist Artist-In-Edn. Com., Salem, Oreg., 1995—. One man exhibns. include The White Bird Gallery, Cannon Beach, Oreg., 1983, 84, The White Gallery Portland (Oreg.) State U., 1984, The Unitarian Ch., Portland, 1985, 93, The Gango Gallery, Portland, Oreg., 1988, 89, 90, Progress, Oreg., 1990, 91, 93, Oreg. Sch. Arts and Crafts, Portland, 1989, Artfolio Gallery, Portland, 1996; group exhibns. U. Oreg., Corvallis, 1992, Allied Arts Assn., Richland, Wash., 1992, Ea. Wash. Watercolor Soc., 1994, 95, N.W. Watercolor Soc., Wash., 1994, 97, Sunbird Gallery, Bend, Oreg., 1995, Columbia Gorge Art Gallery, Hood River, Oreg., 1996, Mirror Pond Gallery, Bend, 1996; illustrator (software CD) Greece, 1996, greeting cards, short stories, CD covers, poster for Sisters (Oreg.) Folk Festival, poster for Humane Soc., Bend; featured in Northwest Arts mag., Oreg. Focus Mag. Recipient 3rd Place Wallowa Arts Fesival, 1992, 5th Place Art in the Mountains Nat. Watercolor Shco, 1992, Battelle Purchase award Allied Arts Assn., 1992, Honorable Mention Ea. Washington Watercolor Soc. show, 1994, 95, Award of Excellence Ariz. Acqueous 95 Nat. Watercolor Show, 1995, 1st Pl. award Beaverton Showcase, 1991, 93, Award of Excellence, Ariz. Aqueous 95 Nat. Watermedia Show, 1995, People's Choice award Co-Arts, 1995. Home and Office: PO Box 1301 Sisters OR 97759

BENNETT, PAUL GROVER, agribusiness executive; b. Ancon, C.Z., Panama, Sept. 1, 1940; s. Arden Lamont and Mercedes (Reluz) B.; m. Diane Huarte, Dec. 17, 1967; children: Courtney, Kimberly, Christopher, Michael. BA, Northwestern U., 1962; MBA, Stanford U., 1968. Fin. analyst, research supt. Standard Fruit Co. (Dole Food Co.), Limon, Costa Rica, 1968-70, research dir., La Ceiba, Honduras, 1970-72, asst. gen. mgr., Guayaquil, Ecuador, 1972-73; v.p., regional controller Castle & Cooke Foods (Dole Food Co.), San Francisco, 1973-74, v.p., gen. mgr., Davao, Philippines, 1974-76, v.p., gen. mgr., Medellin, Colombia, 1977-78; v.p., gen. mgr. Mauna Loa Macadamia Nut Corp., Hilo, Hawaii, 1978-81, pres., 1981-83; group v.p. diversified services Internat. Air Service Co. Ltd., Foster City, Calif., 1983-86; pres. Hawaiian Holiday Macadamia Nut Co., Honolulu, 1986-89; sr. ptnr. Agricon Hawaii, Honolulu, 1989-91; pres., CEO Calif. Ammonia Co., Stockton, Calif., 1991-93, Nature Berry Growers, Watsonville, Calif., 1993-96; mng. ptnr. Agri-Food Internat., 1996—; dir. Agrl. Coun. of Calif.; alt. dir. Calif. Strawberry Commn.; mem. adv. bd. Agribus. Inst., St. Clara U. Served to lt. comdr. USN, 1962-66. Mem. Stanco, Stanford Alumni Assn., Phi Gamma Delta. Republican.

BENNETT, ROBERT F., senator; b. Salt Lake City, Utah, 1933; s. Wallace F. Bennett; m. Joyce McKay; 6 children. BS, U. of Utah, 1957. Various staff positions U.S Ho. of Reps., U.S. Senate, Washington; CEO Franklin Quest, Salt Lake City, 1984-90; U.S. senator from Utah, 1993—; chmn. legis. br. appropriations subcom. Senate GOP; chmn. fin. svcs. and tech. subcom.; mem. banking, housing, urban affairs ocm., appropriations com., joint economic com., small bus. com.; chmn. task force Senate reorganization; lobbyist various orgns., Washington; head Dept. Transp.'s Congl. Liaison. Author: Gaining Control. Chmn. Education Strategic Planning Commn. Utah State Bd. Edn. (mem. Edn. Strategic Planning Com.). Recipient Light of Learning award for Outstanding Contbns. to Utah edn., 1989; named Entrepreneur of Yr. for Rocky Mtn. region INC. magazine, 1989. Republican. Office: US Senate Office Of Senate Mems Washington DC 20510

BENNETT, RONALD THOMAS, photojournalist; b. Portland, Oreg., Nov. 6, 1944; s. E.E. Al and Donna Mae (Thomas) B.; children: R. Thomas, Gardinas. Student, Portland State U., 1964-67; student in photojournalism, U. Wash., 1965; student pre-law and bus. mgmt, Multnomah Coll., Portland, 1963-64. Lab. technician, photographer Sta. KATU-TV, Portland, 1963-65; staff photographer Oreg. Jour., Portland, 1965-68, UPI Newspictures, L.A., 1968-70; staff photojournalist UPI at White House, 1970-88; sr. photo editor The San Diego Union, 1988-89; owner, CEO Capital TV, La Jolla, Calif., 1989—; instr. photojournalism Portland State U., 1967; mem. standing com. U.S. Senate Press Photographers Gallery, 1980-89, sec.-treas.; CEO, Ronald T. Bennett Photography Frameable Original Photos & Note Cards, 1995—. Photographer: Assassination, 1968; one-man show Lake Oswego, Oreg., 1979; group exhbns. Libr. of Congress, 1971-89. Mem. coun. Town of La Jolla, Calif., active Associated Volume Buyers, chmn. Brown Goods. Recipient 1st prize World Press Photo Assn., 1969, Calif. Press Photographers, 1968, 69, Gold Seal competition, 1968, 69; nominated for Pulitzer prize, 1968, 76, 77, 78. Mem. White House News Photographers (bd. dirs. photo exhbn. com. 1974-78, 1st prize 1976, 77, 78, 80, 84, 86, 87), Nat. Headliner Club (1st prize 1969, 78), Nat. Press Photographers Assn. (1st prize 1972), Rotary (staff photographer La Jolla chpt., Achievement award Am. Project 1992, 93). Baptist. Home: 12907 La Tortola San Diego CA 92129-3057

BENNETT, SHOSHANA STEIN, post partum counselor, consultant, lecturer; b. N.Y.C., Sept. 5, 1954; . Herman David and Charmion Kerr (Goldfarb) S.; m. Henry Joseph Bennett, May 24, 1981; children: Elana Michelle, Aaron Daniel. BA, Grinnell Coll., 1975; MA, San Francisco State U., 1977; postgrad. Clin. Psychology, Calif. Coast U., Santa Ana, 1991—. Cert tchr. learning handicapped, multiple subjects, Calif.; cert. c.c. tchr., Calif.; cert. in clin. hypnotherapy. Founder, coord. Postpartum Assistance for Mothers, Castro Valley, Calif., 1987—; instr. in handling postpartum depression Hayward (Calif.) Adult Sch., 1988-90; group leader Acalanes Adult Sch., Walnut Creek, Calif., 1988-90; guest spkr., cons. Western Regional Postpartum Support Internat. Seminar, Oakland (Calif.) Children's Hosp., 1990, ASPO Lamaze Conf., Walnut Creek, Calif., 1990, Nat. Assn. Postpartum Care Svcs. Conf., Oakland, 1992, Ob.Gyn. Conf., Kaiser Oakland Med. Ctr., 1992, 95, Calif. Healthy Mothers, Healthy Babies Conf., Oakland, 1993, Calif. Diabetes and Pregnancy Program, Warrack Hosp., Santa Rosa, Calif., 1994, San Joaquin County Comprehensive Perinatal Svc. Program, Stockton, Calif., 1995, Family Practitioner Grand Rounds, San Joaquin Gen. Hosp., Stockton, 1995, Dept. Psychiatry Kaiser Permanente Med. Group, Redwood City, Calif., 1995, Kaiser Lactation Assocs. Conf., Hayward Med. Ctr., 1996. Speaker on People are Talking TV program, 1987, KLOK radio From Birth and Beyond, 1992; author hosp. manuals on postpartum depression. Mem. Sch. Site Coun., Castro Valley, Calif., 1995—. Mem. Am. Counseling Assn., Postpartum Health Alliance (v.p.), Postpartum Support Internat. (bd. dirs.), Depression After Delivery. Office: Postpartum Assistance for Mothers PO Box 20513 Castro Valley CA 94546

BENNETT, WILLIAM GORDON, casino executive; b. Glendale, Ariz., Nov. 16, 1924. Gen. mgr. Del Webb Corp., Las Vegas, 1965-70; with Western Equities Inc., Reno, Nev., 1971-78; chmn. Circus Circus Enterprises Inc., 1974—, dir.; pres. Circus Circus Enterprises, 1995—. Office: c/o Sierra Hotel Casino 2535 Las Vegas Blvd S Las Vegas NV 89109-1137

BENNETT, WILLIAM PERRY, lawyer; b. Inglewood, Calif., Aug. 28, 1938; s. George William and Lenora (Perry) B.; m. Linda L. Schneider, Aug. 19, 1961; children: Greg, Mark, Carin. BA, Calif. State U., Long Beach; MA in Specialized Ministry magna cum laude, Grace Theol. Sem.; JD, U. So. Calif.; DMin. magna cum laude, Reformed Theol. Sem. Lic. real estate broker; cert. real estate investment specialist, real estate mgmt. specialist, family law specialist; life time teaching credential specialized subject; bar: Calif. 1965, U.S. Ct. Appeals (9th cir.) 1965, U.S. Supreme Ct. 1993. Ptnr. Powars, Tretheway & Bennett Law Corp., 1965-78; sr. ptnr. William P. Bennett Law Corp., 1978-97; sr. real estate atty. Wise, Wiezorek, Timmons & Wise, 1991-94; owner, broker Century 21 Pacific Coast Realty, 1979-88, Pacific Coast Properties, Long Beach, 1988—; assoc. prof. bus. and real estate law Calif. State U., Long Beach, 1965-86; gen. counsel Campus Crusade for Christ, 1991-93; alumni pres., univ. adv. bd. Calif. State U., Long Beach; real estate arbitrator Am. Arbitration Assn. Panel, 1965—, L.A. County Superior Ct. Arbitrator/Pro Tem Judge, Christian Conciliation Svc., L.A. and Orange Counties; bus. adv. bd. Long Beach City Coll.; legal adv. Internat. Christian Leadership U.; spl. counsel numerous chs. and religious orgns. including Chs. Uniting in Global Mission, Crystal Cathedral Ministries, Calvary Chapel; adj. prof. of law Simon Greenleaf U. Bd. dirs., leagl advisor Long Beach Area March of Dimes, 1973-90; exec. dir. Legal Ministry Campus Crusade for Christ, dir. property mgmt. Campus Crusade, exec. mgmt. team Arrowhead Springs Conf Ctr., 1991-94. Mem. Long Beach Bar Assn. (bd. govs. 1970-76), Long Beach Area C. of C. (bd. dirs. 1985-86, Bus. Person of Yr. award 1987), Seal Beach C. of C. (pres. 1985-86, 89-90), Kiwanis Internat. (pres., lt. gov., Kiwanian of Yr.), Century 21 Orange County Brokers Coun. (pres. 1984), So. Calif. Investment Soc. (pres. 1988). Republican. Home: PO Box 2460 Seal Beach CA 90740-1460 Office: 333 City Blvd W Ste 1810 Orange CA 92868

BENNEY, GHISLAINE FRANÇOISE, religious organization executive; b. Montreal, Que., Can., Mar. 8, 1944; came to U.S., 1973; d. Henri Rosaire and Andréa Annonciade (Côté) Trudeau; m. John J. Spires, Aug. 28, 1966 (dec. Oct. 1969); m. Charles Henry Benney, May 24, 1975. Sales mgr. Ontario and Western Provinces Lancôme Can., Toronto, Ont., Can., 1970-72; tng. mgr. Estée Lauder Can., Toronto, 1972-73; dir. tng. and mgmt. devel. Estée Lauder Internat., N.Y.C., 1973-77; asst. v.p tng. and mgmt. devel. Citibank, N.Y.C., 1977-81, v.p. human resources, 1981-84, v.p. mktg., 1984; dir. support svcs. divsn. Ethiopia World Vision Internat., Arcadia, Calif., 1984-86; mission vol. Presbyn. Ch. U.S.A., N.Y.C., 1986-91; dir. comm. Mission Aviation Fellowship, Redlands, Calif., 1991—. Editor-in-chief LifeLink and LifeLink Digest, 1991—; editor, contbg. author: Giving Wings to the Gospel, 1995. Mem. Mayor Ed Koch's N.Y.C. Sr. Employment Adv. Coun., N.Y.C. Dept. Aging, 1981. Recipient Outstanding Use of Graphic Arts in Effective Comm. award Strathmore, 1992. Mem. ASTD (chmn. sales tng. divsn. 1979-81), Am. Mgmt. Assn., 1974-84. Baptist. Office: Mission Aviation Fellowship Box 3202 1849 Wabash Redlands CA 92373

BENNINGTON, LESLIE ORVILLE, JR., insurance agent; b. Sedalia, Mo., Dec. 29, 1946; s. Leslie Orville Sr. and Eunice May Marguerite (Cole) B.; m. Susan Frances Grotha, June 1, 1968; children: Leslie O. III, Jeremy Lawrence. BSME, U. Mo., Rolla, 1968; postgrad., U. Tenn. Space Inst., 1969; ChFC, Am. Coll., 1988. CLU; chartered fin. cons.; registered profl. engr., Wash., Wyo. Design engr. Arnold Research Orgn., Tullahoma, Tenn., 1968-70; engr. Pacific Power & Light, Glenrock, Wyo., 1973-75; agt., asst. gen. agt. Am. Nat. Ins. Co., Casper, Wyo., 1975-85; gen. agt. Ins. Sales, Glenrock, 1985—; pres. Cen.Wyo. Estate Planning Coun., Casper, 1985-86. Mem. Glenrock Vol. Fire Dept., 1973—, asst. chief, 1982, pres., 1993-97; pres., v.p. Converse County Recreation Bd., Douglas, Wyo., 1980-90; judge dist. h.s. speech contests, Glenrock; bd. dirs. Converse County Sch. Dist. 2, 1976; bd. dirs. Glenrock Cmty. Recreation Dist., 1990-97, pres., 1992-94; guide Helluva Hunt for physically disabled hunters, 1986—, bd. dirs., 1991—; bd. dirs. Nat. Bow Hunt, Glenrock, 1994—; baseball coach Little League and Babe Ruth, 1983-93. Mem. Nat. Assn. Life Underwriters (Nat. Quality award, Health Ins. Quality award, Nat. Sales Achievement award), Cen. Wyo. Life Underwriters (pres. 1978-80), Wyo. Life Underwriters Assn. (chmn. membership com. 1985-87, nat. com. 1982-87, v.p. 1986-87, bd. dirs. 1980-90, Ins. Agt. of Yr., 1980, pres. 1988-89), West Cen. Wyo. CLUs (pres. 1986-88), Million Dollar Round Table, Nat. Pony Express Assn. (pres. Ea. Wyo. div. 1985—, v.p. Wyo. div. 1989—), KC (grand knight, faithful navigator). Republican. Roman Catholic. Home: 6 Shannon Dr Glenrock WY 82637 Office: PO Box 2049 1260 Hwy 20-26-87 Glenrock WY 82637-9509

BENNION, JOHN STRADLING, engineering educator, consultant; b. Salt Lake City, Sept. 19, 1954; s. Mervyn S. Jr. and LaRee (Stradling) B. BS in Chemistry, U. Utah, 1987, BSChemE, 1987, MS in Nuclear Engring., 1990, PhD in Nuclear Engring., 1996. Lic. profl. engr., Utah, Idaho; registered radiation protection technologist Nat. Registry of Radiation Protection Technologists; lic. sr. reactor operator U.S. Nuclear Regulatory Commn. Carpenter various cos. Utah, 1974-86; sr. reactor engr. U. Utah Nuclear Engring. Lab., Salt Lake City, 1987-93; instr. mech. engring. dept. U. Utah, Salt Lake City, 1992—; asst. prof. Coll. Engring. Idaho State U., Pocatello, 1995—; reactor adminstr. Idaho State U. Coll. Engring., 1996—. Author tech. papers and reports. Mem. AAAS, ASME, NSPE, IEEE, Am. Chem. Soc., Am. Soc. Engring. Edn., Nuclear and Plasma Scis. Soc. of IEEE, Am. Nuclear Soc., Am. Soc. Quality Control, N.Y. Acad. Scis., Health Physics Soc., Internat. Soc. Radiation Physics, Utah Acad. Arts and Scis. (Order of the Engr. award), Phi Kappa Phi, Alpha Nu Sigma, Pi Tau Sigma, Tau Beta Pi, Sigma Xi. Republican. Mem. LDS Church. Office: Idaho State U Coll of Engring Campus Box 8060 Pocatello ID 83209

BENNION, JOHN WARREN, urban education educator; b. Salt Lake City, Nov. 25; s. M. Lynn and Katherine Bennion; m. Sylvia Lustig; children: Philip, Stanford, David, Bryan, Grant, Andrew. BS in Philosophy, English, U. Utah, 1961, MA in Edn. Adminstrn., 1962; PhD in Edn. Adminstrn., Ohio State U., 1966. Tchr. Granite High Sch., Salt Lake City, 1961-63; asst. instr. Ohio State U., Columbus, 1963-64, adminstrv. asst., 1965-66; adminstrv. intern Parma (Ohio) Sch. Dist., 1964-65; asst. supt. Elgin (Ill.) Pub. Schs., 1966-68; asst. prof. edn. adminstrn. Ind. U., Bloomington, 1968-69; supt. Brighton Cen. Schs., Rochester, N.Y., 1969-79, Bloomington (Minn.) Pub. Schs., 1979-80, Provo (Utah) Sch. Dist., 1980-85, Salt Lake City Schs., 1985-94; prof. urban edn., dir. Utah Edn. Consortium U. Utah, Salt Lake City, 1994—. Recipient Nat. Superintendent of the Yr. award, Utah, Am. Assn. of School Administrators, 1992. Mem. Assn. Supervision and Curriculum Devel., Assn. Early Childhood Edn., Am. Assn. Sch. Adminstrs., Phi Delta Kappa, Rotary. Home: 1837 Harvard Ave Salt

Lake City UT 84108-1804 Office: Univ Utah Grad Sch of Edn 225 Milton Bennion Hall Salt Lake City UT 84112-1169

BENNIS, WARREN GAMELIEL, business administration educator, author, consultant; b. N.Y.C., Mar. 8, 1925; s. Philip and Rachel (Landau) B.; m. Clurie Williams, Mar. 30, 1962 (div. 1983); children: Katharine, John Leslie, Will Martin; m. Mary Jane O'Donnell, Mar. 8, 1988 (div. 1991); m. Grace Gabe, Nov. 29, 1992. A.B., Antioch Coll., 1951; hon. cert. econs., London Sch. Econs., 1952; Ph.D., MIT, 1955; LL.D. (hon.), Xavier U., Cin., 1972, George Washington U., 1977; L.H.D. (hon.), Hebrew Union Coll., 1974, Kans. State U., 1979; D.Sc. (hon.), U. Louisville, 1977, Pacific Grad. Sch. Psychology, 1987, Gov.'s State U., 1991; LHD (hon.), Doan Coll., 1993. Diplomate Am. Bd. Profl. Psychology. Asst. prof. psychology MIT, Cambridge, 1953-56, prof., 1959-67; asst. prof. psychology and bus. Boston U., 1956-59; prof. Sloan Sch. Mgmt., 1959-67; provost SUNY-Buffalo, 1967-68, v.p. acad. devel., 1968-71; pres. U. Cin., 1971-77; U.S. prof. corps. and soc. Centre d'Etudes Industrielles, Geneva, Switzerland, 1978-79; exec.-in-residence Pepperdine U., 1978-79; George Miller Disting. prof.-in-residence U. Ill., Champaign-Urbana, 1978; Disting. prof. Bus. Adminstrn. Sch. Bus., U. So. Calif., L.A., 1980-88; univ. prof. U. So. Calif., L.A., 1988—; vis. lectr. Harvard U., 1958-59, Indian Mgmt. Inst., Calcutta; vis. prof. U. Lausanne (Switzerland), 1961-62, INSEAD, France, 1983; bd. dirs. The Foothill Group. Author: Planning of Change, 4th edit., 1985, Interpersonal Dynamics, 1963, 3d and 4th edits., 1975, Personal and Organizational Change, 1965, Changing Organizations, 1966, repub. in paperback as Beyond Bureaucracy, 1974, The Temporary Society, 1968, Organization Development, 1969, American Bureaucracy, 1970, Management of Change and Conflict, 1972, The Leaning Ivory Tower, 1973, The Unconscious Conspiracy: Why Leaders Can't Lead, 1976, Essays in Interpersonal Dynamics, 1979; (with B. Nanus): Leaders, 1985, On Becoming a Leader, 1989, (with I. Mitroff) The Unreality Industry, 1989, Why Leaders Can't Lead, 1989, Leaders on Leadership, 1992, An Invented Life: Reflections on Leadership and Change, 1993, Beyond Bureaucracy, 1993, (with J. Goldsmith) Learning to Lead, 1994, (with M. Mische) Reinventing the 21st Century, 1994, Beyond Leadership, 1994, Herding Cats: Bennis on Leadership, 1996, Organizing Genius, 1997; cons. editor Jour. Higher Edn., Calif. Mgmt. Rev., Mgmt. Series Jossey-Bass Pubs. Mem. Pres.' White House Task Force on Sci. Policy, 1960-70; mem. FAA study task force U.S. Dept. Transp., 1975; mem. adv. com. N.Y. State Joint Legis. Com. Higher Edn., 1970-71; mem. Ohio Gov.'s Bus. and Employment Coun., 1972-74; mem. panel on alt. approaches to grad. edn. Coun. Grad. Schs. and Grad. Record-Exam Bd., 1971-73; chmn. Nat. Adv. Commn. on Higher Edn. for Police Officers, 1976-78; adv. bd. NIH, 1978-84; trustee Colo. Rocky Mountains Sch., 1978-82; bd. dirs. Am. Leadership Forum, 1984-89; mem. vis. com. for Humanities MIT, 1975-81; trustee Antioch Coll., Salk Inst. Capt. AUS, World War II. Decorated Bronze Star, Purple Heart; recipient Dow Jones award, 1987, McKinsey Fedn. award, 1967, 68. Mem. Am. Acad. Arts and Scis. (co-chmn. policy coun. 1969-71), Am. Mgmt. Assn. (dir. 1974-77), U.S. C. of C. (adv. group scholars). Office: U So Calif Sch Bus University Park Los Angeles CA 90089-1421

BENREY, JEFF MICHAEL, marketing professional; b. Istanbul, Turkey, Sept. 8, 1962; came to the U.S., 1980; s. Michael and Denise Liliana B. BS in Engring. cum laude, Princeton U., 1984; MBA, UCLA, 1989. R&D engr. Imagen Corp., Santa Clara, Calif., 1984-87; project mgr. Sun Microsystems, Mountain View, Calif., summer 1988; product mktg. mgr. Apple Computer Inc., Cupertino, Calif., 1990-93; v.p. mktg. Ductus Inc., Mountain View, 1993-95; entertainment mktg. mgr. Silicon Graphics, Mountain View, 1995—. Mem. Tau Beta Pi, Beta Gamma Sigma. Office: Silicon Graphics 2011 N Shoreline Blvd Mountain View CA 94043

BENSCH, KLAUS GEORGE, pathology educator; b. Miedar, Germany, Sept. 1, 1928; (married); 3 children. M.D., U. Erlangen, Germany, 1953. Diplomate: Am. Bd. Pathology. Intern U. Hosps. of Erlangen, 1953-54; resident in anat. pathology U. Tex. and; M.D. Anderson Hosp., Houston, 1954-56, Yale, 1956-57; instr. pathology Yale Med. Sch., 1958-61, asst. prof., 1961-64, assoc. prof., 1964-68; prof. pathology Stanford Med. Sch., 1968—, acting chmn. dept. pathology, 1984-85, chmn. dept. pathology, 1985—. Office: Stanford U Med Sch Dept Pathology 300 Pasteur Dr Stanford CA 94305

BENSICK, CAROL MARIE, English literature educator. BA summa cum laude, Wellesley Coll., 1977; MA, Cornell U., 1980, PhD, 1982. Asst. prof. U. Denver, 1982-85; asst. prof. U. Ore., 1985-88, assoc. prof., 1988—; asst. prof. U. Calif., Riverside, 1988—; vis. asst. prof. UCLA, 1988, 89, 91, 92, Cornell U., 1983, 84, 86; planning com. Am. Lit. Pacific Northwest Renaissance Conf., 1988; asst. dir. grad. studies U. Denver, 1984-85; adj. faculty dept. religious studies U. Ore., post-tenure review com. dept. religious studies, cons. history dept. search in colonial Am. History, participating faculty honors coll., ctr. for humanities, dept. comparative lit., faculty mem. philosophy club, search coms. English Dept., 1985-86, 86-87, curriculum, qualifying exam., creative writing and computer coms., participant student advising, judge creative writing contests, 1987, 88; mem. com. on courses U. Calif., Riverside, faculty mem. honors program, adj. faculty mem. dept. religious studies, dept. women's studies, guest lectr., mem. undergrad. coun., chair search com. in Black Am. Lit., English Dept., interviewing mem. search com. Am. Lit. to 1900, mem. grad. com., panel on feminism and pedagogy, undergrad. com., com. nonsalaried appointments, chair grad. prize essay com., mem. writing courses com.; chair panel early Am. lit. Rocky Mount. Modern Lang. Assn., 1989-90; reader Vanderbilt U. Press, 1989, Northeastern U. Press, 1993, numerous profl. jours. Author: La Nouvelle Beatrice: Renaissance and Romance in "Rappaccini's Daughter," 1985; contbr. chpts. to books, articles and reviews to profl. jours., poems to Sparrowgrass Poetry Forum, Nat. Libr. Poetry. Contest/award winner Nat. Libr. of Poetry, 1997. Mem. MLA, AAUW, Am. Philosoph. Assn., Am. Lit. Assn., Nat. Women's Studies Assn., Nathaniel Hawthorne Soc., Soc. for Early Americanists, Soc. Women in Philosophy, Soc. for the Study of Women Philosophers, Soc. for Advancement of Am. Philosophy, Assn. for Advancement of Philosophy and Psychiatry, Nat. Coun. for Rsch. on Women, Internat. Soc. Poets (disting. mem.). Office: U Calif Dept English Riverside CA 92521

BENSON, ALLEN B., chemist, educator, consultant; b. Sioux Rapids, Iowa, Oct. 1, 1936; s. Bennett and Freda (Smith) B.; m. Marian Richter, Aug. 24, 1959; children: Bradley Gerard, Jill Germaine. BS in Secondary Edn. magna cum laude, Western Mont. U., 1960; postgrad., U. Mont., Missoula, 1960-61, Seattle U., 1962-63; M in Natural Sci., Highlands U., 1965; postgrad., Ill. Inst. Tech., 1969; PhD in Chemistry, U. Idaho, 1970. Chemistry instr. U. Wis., Whitewater, 1968-69, Spokane (Wash.) Falls Community Coll., 1969—; mem. steering com. Hanford Edn. Action League, Spokane, 1984-86; energy and nuclear cons., 1970—; mem. Hanford Health Effects Panel, Richland, Wash., 1986; numerous speeches, interviews and pub. articles on energy and nuclear issues, including speaker nat. conv. Physicians for Social Responsibility, Denver, 1990; lead sci. cons. Hanford Radiation Litigation Lawsuit for Hanford Downwinders against GE, Du-Pont and Rockwell, Wash., 1991, 93; sci. conf. leader UNLV on radiation and health effects, 1992; advisor internat. team of experts of contamination and health affects Simultec Ltd., Zurich, 1996—. Author: Hanford Radioactive Fallout: Are There Observable Health Effects?, 1989; co-author: Benson-Nguyen Proposal on Kazakhstan's Nuclear Test Site and the Human Health Effects, 1994, On Practical Application of the Yakima Holistic Concept to Environmental Restoration, 1995. Active Spokane County Dem. Platform Com., 1980, 84; prepared and gave testimony for Yakama Nation to U.S. Pres.'s Risk assessment Com., Seattle, 1995. With U.S. Army, 1955-57. Roman Catholic. Home: 4528 N Windsor Dr Spokane WA 99205-2052 Office: Spokane Falls Community Coll Spokane WA 99204

BENSON, ALVIN K., geophysicist, consultant, educator; b. Payson, Utah, Jan. 25, 1944; s. Carl William and Josephine Katherine (Wirthlin) B.; m. Connie Lynn Perry, June 17, 1966; children: Alauna Marie, Alisa Michelle, Alaura Dawn. BS, Brigham Young U., 1966, PhD in Physics, 1972. Cert. environmentalist. Nuclear group physicist Phillips Petroleum Co., Arco, Idaho, 1966; assoc. prof. physics Ind. U., New Albany, 1972-78, head physics dept., 1976-78; sr. rsch. geophysicist Conoco, Inc., Ponca City, Okla., 1978-81, supr. geophysical rsch., 1981-85; geophysics rsch. assoc. DuPont, Ponca City, 1985-86; prof. geophysics Brigham Young U., Provo, Utah, 1986—; tenured, 1991; cons. Dames and Moore Engring., Salt Lake City, 1987-88, DuPont, Ponca City, 1989-91, Kuwait U., 1991-92, Coleman Rsch., Laurel, Md., 1991, Centennial Mine, Boise, 1990-91, Certified Environ., Salt Lake City, 1991-92, EPA, Washington, 1992, Digital Exploration Ltd., East Grinstead, Eng., 1993-94, Paterson, Grant & Watson Ltd., Toronto, 1994, Ground Water Tech., Norwood, Mass., 1995; Inst. for Geology and Geotechnical Engring., Lyngby, Denmark, 1995-96; developer vis. geoscientist program Brigham Young U. Author: Seismic Migration, 1986, Theory and Practice of Seismic Imaging, 1988, The birth and Growth of Planet Earth, 1996; contbr. 160 articles to publs. including Geophysics, Jour. Computational Physics, Geophys. Prospecting, Jour. Applied Geophysics, Engring. Geology. Bishop LDS Ch., New Albany, 1976-78, Stake High Coun., Tulsa, 1979-81; active polit. adv. com. Rep. Party, Provo, 1990; polit. cons. Guatemala, 1991-92. Recipient Hon. Sci. award Bausch and Lomb, Rochester, N.Y., 1966, Disting. Leadership award Am. Biog. Inst., 1994, Citation of Meritorious Achievement in Geophysics, Soc. Exploration Geophysicists, 1994, Alcuin award Brigham Young Univ., 1994; named Geosci. Prof. of Yr. Brigham Young U., 1994-95; geophysics grantee Rotary, Provo, 1987, Am. Assn. Petroleum Geologists, Tulsa, 1988, Geol. Soc. Am., Boulder, Colo., 1988, Bur. of Reclamation, Washington, 1994, Nat. Pk. Svc., Washington, 1995. Mem. Am. Phys. Soc., Am. Geophys. Union, Soc. Exploration Geophysicists (referee 1980-96), Environ. and Engring. Geophys. Soc., Utah Geol. Assn. Home: 249 W 1100 S Orem UT 84058-6709 Office: Brigham Young U Dept Geophysics Provo UT 84602

BENSON, DEE VANCE, federal judge; b. Salt Lake City, Aug. 25, 1948; s. Gilbert and Beryl Butler (Despain) B.; m. Patricia Brown; children: Angela, Natalie, Lucas, Katherine. BA, Brigham Young U., 1973, JD, 1976. Bar: Utah 1976, U.S. Dist. Ct. Utah 1976, U.S. Ct. Appeals (10th cir.) 1976, U.S. Supreme Ct. 1984, U.S. Ct. Appeals (5th cir.) 1988. Ptnr. Snow, Christensen & Martineau, Salt Lake City, 1976-84; legal counsel Senate Judiciary Com., Washington, 1984-86; chief of staff Senator Orrin Hatch's Office, Washington, 1986-88; legal counsel U.S. Senate Select Com., Washington, 1987; assoc. dep. atty. gen. U.S. Dept. Justice, Washington, 1988; U.S. atty. dist. Utah U.S. Dept. Justice, Salt Lake City, 1989-91; judge U.S. Dist. Ct., Salt Lake, 1991—; legal counsel Iran-Contra Congl. Investigating Com., Washington, 1987. Contbg. author univ. law rev. Mem. ABA, Utah State Bar (com. on cts. and judges), Salt Lake County Bar Assn., Phi Alpha Delta. Mem. LDS Ch. Office: US Dist Ct 350 S Main St # 112 Salt Lake City UT 84101-2106*

BENSON, FRANCIS M., production engineer, radio producer; b. Bklyn., Oct. 7, 1958; s. Francis Gerald Benson and Grace Angela (Superty) Brothers; children: Megan Kristine, Lindsey Nicole. Student, Palmdale High Sch., Calif. Cert. Airframe & Powerplant Mechanic, Calif. Structure mechanic B Lockheed Aircraft Co., Palmdale, Calif., 1979-80, final assembly mechanic, 1980-83, structure mechanic B, 1985-86, mfg. supr., 1986-87; structure mechanic B Rockwell Internat., Palmdale, Calif., 1983-85, hydraulic checkout mechanic, 1985; structure mechanic A Northrop B-2 Division, Palmdale, Calif., 1987-88, mfg. supr., 1988, mfg. planner, 1988-89, mfg. engr., 1989-92; program coord., prodr. Disney/ABC, 1992-94, prodn. coord./prodr., 1994—; union steward Internat. Assn. Machinists & Aerospace, Palmdale Calif. Democrat. Roman Catholic. Home: 3520 Maricopa St Unit 19 Torrance CA 90503-4994 Office: 3321 S La Cienega Blvd Los Angeles CA 90016-3114

BENSON, JOAN, musician, music educator; b. St. Paul; d. John Raymond and Frances (Ostergren) B. MusM, U. Ill., 1952; performer's cert., Ind. U., 1953; pvt. studies with Edwin Fischer, Switzerland, 1953-57; pvt. studies with Fritz Neumeyer, Fed. Republic Germany, 1958-59; pvt. studies with Santiago Kastner, Portugal, 1960. Concert musician worldwide, 1962—; lectr. early keyboard Stanford Univ., Palo Alto, Calif., 1970-76; asst. prof. U. Oreg., Eugene, 1976-82; mem. artist faculty Aston Magna Acad., Mass., 1980, 82; adj. prof. U. Oreg., 1982—. Albums: Repertoire, 1962, Music of C. P. E. Bach for Piano and Clavichord, 1972, Pasquini and Haydn on Clavichords of the Boston Museum of Fine Arts, 1982, Kuhnau and C.P.E. Bach on Clavichord, 1988; contbr. music notes to Titanic and Focus record labels; contbr. articles to profl. jours. Recipient Kate Nell Kinley award. Mem. Am. Musicol. Soc. Home: 2795 Central Blvd Eugene OR 97403-2528

BENSON, JOHN ALEXANDER, JR., physician, educator; b. Manchester, Conn., July 23, 1921; s. John A. and Rachel (Patterson) B.; m. Irene Zucker, Sept. 29, 1947; children: Peter M., John Alexander III, Susan Leigh, Jeremy P. BA, Wesleyan U., 1943; MD, Harvard Med. Sch., 1946. Diplomate Am. Bd. Internal Medicine (mem. 1969-91, sec.-treas. 1972-75, pres. 1975-91, pres. emeritus 1991—), Subsplty. Bd. Gastroenterology (mem. 1961-66, chmn. 1965-66). Intern Univ. Hosps., Cleve., 1946-47; resident Peter Bent Brigham Hosp., Boston, 1949-51; fellow Mass. Gen. Hosp., Boston, 1951-53; rsch. asst. Mayo Clinic, Rochester, Minn., 1953-54; instr. medicine Harvard U., 1956-59; head divsn. gastroenterology U. Oreg. Med. Sch., Portland, 1959-75, prof. medicine, 1965-93; prof. emeritus Oreg. Health Sci. U., Portland, 1993—; interim dean Sch. Medicine Oreg. Health Sci. U., 1991-93, dean emeritus, 1993—; cons. VA Hosps., Madigan Gen. Army Hosp., John A. Hartford Found. Editorial bd.: Am. Jour. Digestive Diseases, 1966-73; Contbr. articles to profl. jours. Mem.Oreg. Med. Ednl. Found., 1967-73; dir. Oreg. Med. Ednl. Found., 1967-73, pres., 1969-72; bd. dirs. N.W. Ctr. for Physician-Patient Comm., 1994—, Am. Acad. on Physician and Patient, 1994—, Found. for Med. Excellence, 1996—. With USNR, 1947-49. Mem. AAS, AMA, ACP (master), Am. Gastroenterol. Assn. (sec. 1970-73, v.p. 1975-76, pres.-elect. 1976-77, pres. 1977-78), Am. Clin. and Climatol. Assn., Am. Soc. Internal Medicine, Western Assn. Physicians, North Pacific Soc. Internal Medicine, Am. Fedn. Clin. Rsch., Federated Coun. for Internal Medicine, Am. Assn. Study Liver Disease, Western Soc. Clin. Investigation, Soc. Health and Human Values, Assn. Health Svcs. Rsch., Inst. Medicine NAS (sr.), Phi Beta Kappa, Sigma Xi, Alpha Omega Alpha. Office: Oreg Health Scis U Sch Medicine L102 Portland OR 97201

BENSON, SHARON JOAN, mathematics educator; b. Glendale, Calif., Aug. 23, 1964; d. Paul John and Arleen Camille (Green) B. BS in Math., Calif. Poly. State U., 1987; MST in Math., U. N.H., 1992. Cert. single subject clear math., Calif. Tchr. math. Victor Valley Union High Sch. Dist., Victorville, Calif., 1988—; part-time instr. Victor Valley C.C., Victorville, 1993—. Mem. Nat. Coun. Tchrs. Math., Calif. Math. Coun., Oreg. Coun. Tchrs. of Math., Assn. Women in Math. Republican. Roman Catholic. Office: Victor Valley High Sch 16500 Mojave Dr Victorville CA 92392-3822

BENSON, STEPHEN R., editorial cartoonist. BA in Polit. Sci. cum laude, Brigham Young U., 1979. With Senate Rep. Policy Com., 1979-80; cartoonist The Ariz. Republic, Phoenix, 1980-90, 91—, The Morning-News Tribune, Tacoma, Wash., 1990-91. Author: Fencin' with Benson, 1984, Evanly Days, 1988, Back at the Barb-B-Cue, 1991, Where Do You Draw the Line?, 1992. Recipient Nat. Headliner award, 1984, 1st Place Best of the West, 1991, 92, 93, Pulitzer Prize finalist editorial cartooning, 1984, 89, 92, 94, Pulitzer Prize for editorial cartooning, 1993. Office: The Arizona Republic 200 E Van Buren St Phoenix AZ 85004-2226*

BENSON, STEVEN DONALD, shop owner, sheet metal mechanic, author; b. Longview, Wash., Oct. 11, 1953; s. Steven Hughes Benson and Donna Ruth (Johnson) McKinney; m. Patricia Joyce Krauss, Feb. 14, 1982; children: Steven William, Patricia Ann. A in Drafting, Salem (Oreg.)Indsl. Arts Coll., 1973. Precision sheet metal mechanic Ariz. Precision Sheet Metal, Phoenix, 1980-86, Neilson Mfg. Inc., Salem, Oreg., 1986—; owner, operator Time Honored Gifts, Salem, 1988—; instr. Oreg. Advanced Tech. Consortium, Wilsonville, Oreg., 1990—. Author: (textbooks) Introduction to Precision Press Brake, 1991, Intermediate Press Brake, 1992, Advanced Press Brake, 1994; (software) Advanced Sheet Metal Applications, 1994. Sec., treas. Bike PAC of Oreg., Salem, 1989—; minister Universal Life Ch., Modesto, Calif., 1990—. Home: 395 23rd St NE Salem OR 97301-4440 Office: Bike PAC of Oreg PO Box 5612 Salem OR 97304

BENTLEY, KENTON EARL, aerospace scientist, researcher; b. Detroit, June 1, 1927; s. Kenneth and Marion Isabel (Tillman) B.; m. Elizabeth Montrose, Apr. 18, 1953 (dec.). B.S. in Chemistry, U. Mich., 1950; Ph.D. in Analytical Chemistry, U. N.M., 1959. Research phys. chemist Consol. Electrodynamics Corp., Pasadena, Calif., 1956-57; research scientist Lockheed Calif. Co., Burbank, 1962-63; scientist, task leader Jet Propulsion Lab., Calif. Inst. Tech., Pasadena, 1963-65; head electrochemistry group Hughes Aircraft Co., Culver City, Calif., 1965-67; dir. sci. and applications br., dir. Iran earth resources programs Lockheed Electronics Co., Inc., Houston, 1967-88; mgr. life scis. flight payload integration program Lockheed Engring. & Scis. Co., Moffett Field, Calif., 1988-94; pres. Kiva Enterprises, Boulder City, Nev., 1994—; Vis. prof. chemistry Highlands (N.M.) U., 1959; asst. prof. chemistry Am. U. Beirut, Lebanon, 1959-61. Contbr. numerous articles to profl. jours. Served with USNR, 1945-46. Los Alamos research fellow, 1954-56. Mem. Am. Chem. Soc., AAAS (life), AAUP, Am. Astronautical Soc. (sr.; dir. 1969-73), Nat. Mgmt. Assn., Sigma Xi (life), Alpha Chi Sigma. Home: 325 N Gibson Rd # 815 Henderson NV 89014

BENTLEY, SARA, newspaper publishing executive. Pres. Gannett Northwest Newspaper Group, Salem, Oreg., 1988—. Office: Statesman-Journal Co Inc PO Box 13009 280 Church St NE Salem OR 97301*

BENTLY, DONALD EMERY, electrical engineer; b. Cleve., Oct. 18, 1924; s. Oliver E. Bently and Mary Evelyn (Conway) B.; m. Susan Lorraine Pumphrey, Sept. 1961 (div. Sept. 1982); 1 child, Christopher Paul. BSEE with distinction, U. Iowa, 1949, MSEE, 1950; DS (hon.), U. Nev., 1987. Registered profl. engr., Calif., Nev. Pres. Bently Nev. Corp., Minden, 1961-85, chief exec. officer, 1985—; chief exec. officer Bently Rotor Dynamics and Research Corp., Minden, 1985—; also chmn. bd. dirs. Bently Nev. Corp., Minden; chief exec. officer Gibson Tool Co., Carson City, Nev., 1978—; bd. dirs. Sierra Pacific Resources, 1982-83. Contbr. articles to profl. jours.; developer electronic instruments for the observation of rotating machinery, and the algorithm for rotor fluid-induced instability; inventor in field. Trustee Inst. World Politics. With USN, 1943-46, PTO. Named Inventor of Yr., State of Nev. Innovation and Tech. Coun., 1983; recipient first Decade award Vibration Inst., Myklestad award; inducted to Jr. Achievement of Northern Nev. Bus. Leaders' Hall of Fame. Mem. ASME (industry adv. bd.), Am. Petroleum Inst., St. Petersburg (Russian Fedn.) Acad. Engring., Sigma Xi, Eta Kappa Nu, Tau Beta Pi, Sigma Alpha Epsilon. Episcopalian. Office: Bently Nev Corp 1711 Orbit Way Minden NV 89423

BENTON, EUGENE ALFRED, school system administrator; b. Tucson, Apr. 16, 1942; s. Robert Lee Jr. and Amelia (Tellez) B.; m. Barbara Camacho, July 22, 1967 (div. Mar. 1987); children: Steven Eugene, Santiago Xavier, Damián Vicente. BA, U. Ariz., 1966, MA, 1968; postgrad., N.Mex. State U., Las Cruces, 1976-78. Cert. elem. edn., bilingual edn., ednl. adminstrn. Elem. sch. tchr. Tucson Unified Sch. Dist., 1966-74, resource tchr. K-12, 1974-75, elem. sch. tchr., 1975-76, asst. prin., 1978-79, elem. sch. prin., 1979-80, asst. supt., 1980—; mem. U. Ariz. Press Adv. Bd. Mem. Our Town Family Svcs., Tucson, 1988-96, chairperson bd., 1996-97; chairperson Lohse YMCA, Tucson, 1988-96, 96-97; mem. Hispanic Profl Action Com., Tucson, 1987-96. Mem. Ariz. Hispanic Sch. Adminstrs. Assn. (pres. 1994-95, Outstanding Educator 1995), U. Ariz. Hispanic Alumni Assn. Democrat. Roman Catholic. Home: PO Box 26070 Tucson AZ 85726 Office: Tucson Unified Sch Dist PO Box 40400 Tucson AZ 85717

BENTON, FLETCHER, sculptor; b. Jackson, Ohio, 1931. BFA, Miami U., Oxford, Ohio, 1956, DFA (hon.), 1993; DFA (hon.), Rio Grande U., 1994. Mem. faculty Calif. Coll. Arts and Crafts, 1959, San Francisco Art Inst., 1964-67; prof. art Calif. State U., San Jose, 1967-81; prof. Calif. State U., 1981-86. One-man shows include, San Francisco Mus. Modern Art, 1965, Albright-Knox Mus., Buffalo, 1970, Galeria Bonino, N.Y.C., 1969, Galerie Francoise Mayer, Brussels, San Francisco Mus. Modern Art, 1970, London Arts Gallery, Detroit, 1970, Galeria Bonino, Buenos Aires, Estudio Actual, Caracas, Venezuela, 1970, Landry-Bonino Gallery, N.Y.C., 1972, Phoenix Mus. Art, 1973, Galeria Bonino, Rio de Janiero, 1973, Calif. State U.-Berkeley, 1973, Neuberger Mus., N.Y., 1974, Hirshhorn Mus., 1974, Phila. Art Alliance, 1974, Elvehejem Mus. Art, Wis., 1976, San Francisco Modern Mus. Art, 1976, Huntsville Mus. Modern Art, Ala., 1977, Alrich Mus. Contemporary Art, Conn., John Berggruen Gallery, San Francisco, 1978, 84, 89, 96, Am. Acad. and Inst. Arts and Letters, N.Y.C., 1979, Chgo. Arts Club, 1979, Milw. Art Ctr., 1980, Suermondt-Ludwig Mus., Asschen, Fed. Republic Germany, Klingspor Mus., Offenbach, Fed. Republic Germany, 1981, 96, Kunsthandling Brigitte Haasner, Wiesbaden, Fed. Republic Germany, 1987, 92, 96, Sung Dem Fine Arts, Seoul, Korea, 1991, Dorothy Goldeen Gallery, Santa Monica, Calif., 1988, 93, Gallerie Simone Sterne, New Orleans, 1990, 93, Riva Yares Gallery, Scottsdale, 1991, Miami U., Oxford, 1993, Gallery Camino Real, Boca Raton, Fla.; group shows include San Francisco Art Inst., 1964, San Francisco Modern Mus. Art, 1964, Calif. Pal. of Legion of Honor, 1964, Whitney Mus. Am. Art, N.Y.C., 1966, 68, Los Angeles County Mus., 1967, Phila. Art Mus., 1967, Walker Art Ctr., Mpls., 1968, Art Inst. Chgo., 1968, Internat. Mus. Fine Arts, Osaka, Japan, 1970, Hayward Gallery, London, 1970, Stanford (Calif.) Mus., 1971, Am. Acad. and Inst. Arts and Letters, N.Y.C., 1981, Amerika Haus, Frankfurt, 1981, Whitney Mus. Am. Art, N.Y.C., 1981, Oakland Mus., 1982, John Berggruen Gallery, 1983, Olympic Arts Festival, Los Angeles, France, Fed. Republic Germany, Eng., Norway, 1984, John Berggruen Gallery, 1985, 89, 92, Chapman Coll. (Calif.), 1985, The Adrich Mus. Contemporary Art, Conn., 1985, Centro de Arte Moderna, Lisbon, Portugal, 1986, Kleinewefers, Krefeld, Fed. Repbulic Germany, 1987, Kundsthandlung Brigitte Haasner, Wiesbaden, Fed. Republic Germany, 1987, 88, Dorothy Goldeen Gallery, Santa Monica, Calif., 1988, Andre Emmerich Gallery, 1991, 92, Rio Grande (Ohio) U., 1994, Miami Art Mus., Oxford, Ohio, 1996, others; major collections Euroclear Hdqs. Brussels, Belgium, 1993, Modernesstadt Cologne, 1993, Gothaer, Cologne, Top Gallant, 1994, Pauling, N.Y., 1994; subject of book, Fletcher Benton by Paul Karlstrom and Edward Lucie-Smith, 1990. Served with USN, 1949-50. Recipient Disting. Svc. award to arts Am. Acad. and Inst. Arts and Letters, 1979, Career award Ohioana Libr. Assn., 1994; Pres.'s Scholar award San Jose State U., 1980.

BENTON, LEE F., lawyer; b. Springfield, Ohio, Feb. 18, 1944. AB, Oberlin Coll., 1966; JD, U. Chgo., 1969. Bar: Calif. 1970. Ptnr., chmn. bus. dept. Cooley, Godward, Castro, Huddleson & Tatum, Palo Alto, Calif.; teaching fellow Stanford Law Sch., 1969-70. Mem. Order Coif, Phi Beta Kappa. Office: Cooley Godward Castro Huddelson & Tatum 5 Palo Alto Sq 3000 El Camino Real Palo Alto CA 94306-2120

BENTY, CAMERON TODD, magazine editor; b. Highland Park, Mich., Dec. 4, 1956; s. John Louis and Florence May (Bailey) B.; m. Suzanne Margo Acosta, Apr. 11, 1987; children: Jenna Marie, Jordan Cameron. BA in Journalism, U. Pacific, 1978. Assoc. editor Hot Rod Mag., L.A., 1978-81; editor Argus Pub., L.A., 1981-87, Car Craft Mag., L.A., 1987-90; editor, dir. devel. Custom Pub., L.A., 1990-91; editor SPORT, L.A., 1991—, Petersen's Golfing, L.A., 1995—; mem. nominating com. ESPN Espy Awards, 1992—; mem. Victor Awards com., 1991—. Author 12 books of sports facts. Office: Petersen Publishing 6420 Wilshire Blvd Los Angeles CA 90048-5502

BENZING, DAVID WARREN, semiconductor equipment company executive; b. Perth Amboy, N.J., Feb. 11, 1953; s. Walter Charles and Ruth E. (McBride) B.; m. Pamela Jean Drummond, Dec. 28, 1972 (div. 1982); 1 child, Thor A.; m. Cathleen Lynn Hays, Sept. 12, 1985 (div. 1988); 1 child, Allison G. BSChemE, U. Calif., Berkeley, 1974; PhD in Chem. Engring., Princeton U., 1978. Sr. engr. Signetics Corp., Sunnyvale, Calif., 1978-81, Applied Materials, Inc., Santa Clara, Calif., 1981-82; dir. research and devel. Anelva Corp., San Jose, Calif., 1982-84; pres., founder Benzing Technologies, Inc., Santa Clara, 1984—; v.p., gen. mgr. Direction Inc., Sunnyvale, 1994-97, lectr. Sci. and Tech. Inst., Mountain View, Calif., 1981-83; cons. Ube Industries, Ltd., Tokyo, 1984-87, Plasma Sys. Corp., Tokyo, 1993—. Contbr. articles to profl. jours.; patentee in field. Mem. Electrochem. Soc., Thin Film Soc., Semiconductor Equipment and Materials Inst. Republican. Office: Benzing Techs Inc 1203 Foxworthy Ave San Jose CA 95118-1212

BENZLER, BRUCE C., healthcare executive; b. 1941. With Guide Dogs for the Blind, 1963—, exec. dir., 1988. Office: Guide Dogs for the Blind PO Box 151200 San Rafael CA 94915-1200*

BERANEK, DAVID JOHN, educational administrator, educator; b. Portland, Oreg., Oct. 17, 1960; s. Marvin Ray and Betty Rae (Larson) B.; m. Kim Marie Frosland, Dec. 20, 1985; children: Jonathan, Timothy, Samuel. Deuxième degré, U. Poitiers, France, 1980; student, U Guadalajara, Mexico, 1981; BA in French/Spanish, Edn., Oreg. Coll. Edn., Monmouth,

1983; MA in Romance Langs., U. Oreg., 1985; Attestazzione, U. Italiana per Stranieri, Perugia, Italy, 1985; MA in Curriculum & Instrn., U. Oreg., 1992, PhD in Curriculum & Instrn., 1993. Grad. tchg. fellow U. Oreg., Eugene, 1983-85; tutor in Romance langs., math., sci. Oreg. Coll. Edn., Monmouth, 1978-83; tchr. Spanish, French, Italian, ESL St. Mary's Sch., Medford, Oreg., 1985-90; romance lang. specialist Salem-Keizer Sch. Dist. #24J, Oreg., 1991-96, talented and gifted program asst., 1996—; adj. prof. Western Oreg. State Coll., Monmouth, 1996; cons. in gifted edn., 1985-96; rschr. in gifted edn. World Coun. on Gifted and Talented, 1993. Editor: Jackson County Historical Society History, 1990; editor TAG Parent Update, 1996; author: (poems) Le Coeur Solitaire, Northwest Passage, 1983, La naturaleza, El Gato Garaboto, 1980. Senator, chairperson Associated Students Oreg. Coll. of Edn., Associated Students Western Oreg. State Coll., Monmouth, 1978-83; exec. sec. Confedn. Oreg. Fgn. Lang. Tchrs., Salem, 1990-93; vol. YMCA, Salem, 1996; dir. children's Ch., Ch. of the Nazarene, Salem, 1995-96. Mem. Confedn. Oreg. Fgn. Lang. Tchrs. (exec. sec. 1990-93, editor), Am. Coun. Fgn. Lang. Tchg., World Coun. Gifted and Talented Children, Oreg. Assn. Tchrs. Spanish and Portuguese (bd. mem.), Oreg. Assn. Tchrs. French (bd. mem.), Oreg. Assn. Talented and Gifted (conf. presenter). Home: 842 Maine Ave NE Keizer OR 97303-4650 Office: Salem Keizer Sch Dist PO Box 12024 Salem OR 97309

BERDJIS, FAZLOLLAH, physicist; b. Soley, Kurdistan, Iraq, Feb. 4, 1943; came to U.S., 1982; s. Muzaffar and Monireh Berdjis; divorced; children: Vahid, Monireh. Vordiplom in Physics, Univ. Munich, 1967, diplom in Physics, 1972, D in Physics, 1978. Sci. co-worker Max-Planck Inst., Germany, 1978-82; asst. prof. physics U. Ill., Chgo., 1982-85; prof. physics and maths. Orange Coast Coll., Costa Mesa, Calif., 1990—; vis. physicist, UCLA, 1985-90; mem. faculty U. Phoenix, 1990—; conducted seminars U. Munich, 1979, 80; reviewer Math. Revs. Contbr. articles to profl. jours. Mem. Internat. Assn. Math. Physicists, Am. Math. Soc., Am. Phys. Soc., UN Assn., Assn. for Baha'i Studies. Office: Orange Coast Coll PO Box 5005 2701 Fairview Rd Costa Mesa CA 92628

BERENS, E. ANN, writer, mental health and youth advocate; b. Worthing, Eng., Sept. 28, 1930; came to U.S., 1962; d. Samuel Lister and Edith Emily (Harragin) James; m. Robin Hugh Berens, Sept. 22, 1956; children: Carolyn, Keith. Student, Bedford (Eng.) Tng. Coll., 1949-52. Tchr.'s cert. Nat. Froebel Found. Kindergarten and primary tchr. Copythorne Sch. and Ringwood Sch., Hampshire, Eng., 1952-55; childcare worker Protestant Children's Homes, Toronto, Ont., Can., 1956-59; v.p. Berens Assocs. Inc., Emeryville, Calif., 1966-92; presenter 5th World Congress Logotherapy, 1985, 8th,, 1991. Contbr. articles to profl. publs. Vol., chmn. mini course program Claremont Jr. H.S., Oakland, Calif., 1972; vol. for mentally ill Creative Living Ctr., Berkeley, Calif., 1975—, chmn. adv. bd., 1996—; group facilitator search for meaning Life Plan Ctr., San Francisco, 1996—; sec. bd. dirs. The Orgn. for Youth Svcs. Toys, Lafayette, Calif., 1994-97, editor newsletter, 1995-97. Mem. Inst. Logotherapy (bd. dirs. 1985-89). Mem. United Ch. of Christ. Home: 56 Camino del Diablo Orinda CA 94563

BERETTA, GIORDANO BRUNO, computer scientist, researcher; b. Brugg, Aargau, Switzerland, Apr. 14, 1951; came to U.S., 1984; PhD, ETH, Zurich, Switzerland, 1984. Mem. rsch. staff Xerox Palo Alto (Calif.) Rsch. Ctr., 1984-90; charter mem., sr. scientist Canon Info. Systems, Palo Alto, 1990-93; mem. tech. staff Hewlett-Packard Labs., 1994—; chmn. various confs. Contbr. articles to profl. jours.; patentee digital color reprodn. and colorimetry. Mem. The Internat. Soc. for Optical Engring., Inter-Soc. Color Coun., Soc. for Imaging Sci. and Tech., Swiss Math. Soc., Alumni Orgn. of Swiss Fed. Inst. of Tech. Zurich. Office: Hewlett-Packard Labs 1501 Page Mill Rd Palo Alto CA 94304-1126

BEREZNAY, FRANK M., information systems specialist; b. Inglewood, Calif., Mar. 22, 1948; s. Francis Regis and Dorothy Louise (Brown) B.; m. Shana Jean Sweeney, July 9, 1977; 1 child, Catherine Louise. BA in Bus. Adminstrn., Calif. State U., Fullerton, 1975, BA in Econs., 1975; postgrad., UCLA, 1975-77. Project mgr. Rand Info. Systems, San Francisco, 1977-80; systems programme, mgr. systems mgmt. Santa Fe Internat., Orange and Alhambra, Calif., 1980-86; mgr. tech. svcs. Bergen Brunswig, Orange, 1986; data ctr. mgr. Automobile Club of So. Calif., Costa Mesa, 1986—; presenter, speaker in field; developer tech. tng. programs. Mem. editorial rev. bd. Enterprise Systems Jour. With USN, 1967-71. Mem. Computer Measurement Group (mem. editorial bd. for procs. 1988-92, chmn. program com. nat. conf. 1994, program chmn. So. Calif. region 1988-91, pres. So. Calif. region 1991-94, nat. treas. 1994—, Legent Resource Mgr. of Yr. award 1993). Home: 528 S Cardiff St Anaheim CA 92806-4334 Office: Automobile Club of So Calif 3333 Fairview Rd Costa Mesa CA 92626-1610

BERG, DAVE, television producer, writer; b. Hollywood, Calif., June 1, 1948; s. David Bernard and Beverly May (Sparks) B.; m. Mary Khourie, Sept. 24, 1983; children: Melissa, David. BA in Polit. Sci., Northwestern U., 1970; MS in Journalism, Kans. State U., 1974. Writer, producer Sta. KCUR-FM, Kansas City, Mo., 1971-73; anchor, reporter Sta. WFRV-TV, Green Bay, Wis., 1974-76; assignment mgr., anchor Sta. KTIV-TV, Sioux City, Iowa, 1976-78; assignment mgr., reporter Sta. KETV-TV, Omaha, 1978-80; exec. producer Sta. KOVR-TV, Sacramento, 1980-82; writer, producer NBC News-Burbank, 1982-89; bur. chief L.A. CNBC (cable div. NBC), Ft. Lee, N.J., 1989-92; segment producer The Tonight Show With Jay Leno, Burbank, Calif., 1992—; instr. writing TV news Coll. of Canyons, Valencia, Calif., 1991-93. Songwriter: (country songs) Gonna Walk, 1990, Can't Make Up My Heart, 1990. Liturgist, adult Sunday sch. tchr. United Meth. Ch., Valencia. NIMH fellow, 1973-74. Republican. Office: The Tonight Show 3000 W Alameda Ave # 2190 Burbank CA 91523-0001

BERG, HANS FREDRIK, lawyer; b. St. Paul, Mar. 28, 1936; s. Ejner and Alphild (Hortelius) B.; m. Gail Andrews, Nov. 11, 1971; children: Heather, Sonja. BA, Fairleigh Dickinson U., 1961; LLB, Blackstone Sch. Law, Chgo., 1973. Bar: Calif. 1973, U.S. Dist. Ct. (cen. dist.) Calif. 1976, U.S. Supreme Ct. 1985. Sr. appraiser L.A. County Assessor, 1964-74; sr. dep. dist. atty. Los Angeles County, Calif., 1974-89; pvt. practice law, Lancaster, Calif., 1989—; mem. faculty Trade Tech. Coll., L.A., 1974-76. Chmn. Quartz Hill Sch. Site Coun., 1982-83, chmn. ad hoc com., 1983; v.p. AV Criminal Def. Bar Assn., 1993-94; pres. AV Dependency Bar Assn., 1994-95. Served with U.S. Army, 1954-56. Honored by resolution Calif. Assembly, 1980, Westside Union Sch. Bd. Quartz Hill, 1983, L.A. City Bd. Suprs., 1989. Mem. AV Bar Assn., Calif. Dist. Attys. Assn., Assn. Dep. Dist. Attys., Smithsonian Inst., Nat. Geog. Soc., Ocean Soc., Fairwind Yacht Club (L.A.). Office: 44421 10th St W Ste H Lancaster CA 93534-3335

BERG, KENNETH LLOYD, purchasing agent, writer, historian, educator; b. Vancouver, B.C., Can., Aug. 14, 1933; s. Lloyd Kenneth and Lauretta Margaret (Morgan) Bradley; m. Angela Joan Hughes, May 17, 1958; children: Steven Henry, Karen Louise, Christine Marie. Comml. diploma, U. Toronto, Ont., Can., 1960; Canadian Assn. of Purchasing Agent diploma, U. B.C., 1962; postgrad., U. Western Ont., 1979. Logger, cat skinner B.C., Can., 1951-55; buyer, expediter Heavy Constrn., B.C., Can., 1955-59; mgr. purchasing Prince George (B.C.) Pulp and Paper, 1959-70; dir. purchasing Kaiser Resources, Sparwood, B.C., 1970-84; purchasing mgr. Island Creek Coal, Lexington, Ky. and Ping Shuo, China, 1985-86; purchasing specialist Nystrom Lee and Kobayashi, Vancouver, Melbourne, Australia, 1988-90; writer, tchr. K&A Berg Assocs. Ltd., Vancouver and Mesa, Ariz., 1990—; cons. K&A Berg Assocs. Ltd., 1984—; capt. cruise boat European Canals and Waterways, Europe, France and Germany, 1986-87. Contbr. articles to profl. jours. Mem. libr. bds., Fernie, B.C., 1980s; mem. commemorative event U.S. 4th Armored Divsn., Bastogne, Belgium, 1995. Recipien Buyer of Yr. award Purchasing Mgmt. assn. of Canada Dofasco Steel, 1978, Civic medal Gov. Gen. Can., 1992, Civilian medal 4th Armored Divsn., Bastogne, 1995. Mem. Western Mining Purchasing Mgmt. Group (founder), Forest Industry Purchasing Mgmt. Group. Home: K&A Berg Assocs Ltd, 115 Hamptons Park NW, Calgary, AB Canada T3A 5A6

BERG, PAUL, biochemist, educator; b. N.Y.C., June 30, 1926; s. Harry and Sarah (Brodsky) B.; m. Mildred Levy, Sept. 13, 1947; 1 son, John. BS, Pa. State U., 1948; PhD (NIH fellow 1950-52), Western Res. U., 1952; DSc (hon.), U. Rochester, 1978, Yale U., 1978, Wash. U., St. Louis, 1986, Oreg. State U., 1989, Pa. State U., 1995. Postdoctoral fellow Copenhagen (Denmark) U., 1952-53; postdoctoral fellow sch. medicine Washington U., St. Louis, 1953-54; Am. Cancer Soc. scholar cancer research dept. microbiology sch. medicine Washington U., 1954-57, from asst. to assoc. prof. microbiology sch. medicine, 1955-59; prof. biochemistry sch. medicine Stanford U., 1959—, Sam, Lulu and Jack Willson prof. biochemistry sch. medicine, 1970-94; Robert W. Cahill prof. cancer rsch., 1994—; chmn. dept. sch. medicine Stanford U., 1969-74; dir. Stanford U. Beckman Ctr. for Molecular and Genetic Medicine, 1985—, Affymetrix, 1993—, Nat. Found. Biomed. Rsch., 1994—; non-resident fellow Salk Inst., 1973-83; adv. bd. NIH, NSF, MIT; vis. com. dept. biochemistry and molecular biology Harvard U.; bd. sci. advisors Jane Coffin Childs Found. Med. Rsch., 1970-80; chmn. sci. adv. com. Whitehead Inst., 1984-90; bd. sci. adv. DNAX Rsch. Inst., 1981—; internat. adv. bd. Basel Inst. Immunology; chmn. nat. adv. com. Human Genome Project, 1990-92. Contbr. profl. jours.; Editor: Biochem. and Biophys. Research Communications, 1959-68; editorial bd.: Molecular Biology, 1966-69. Trustee Rockefeller U., 1990-92. Served to lt. (j.g.) USNR, 1943-46. Recipient Eli Lilly prize biochemistry, 1959; V.D. Mattia award Roche Inst. Molecular Biology, 1972; Henry J. Kaiser award for excellence in teaching, 1969, 72; Disting. Alumnus award Pa. State U., 1972; Sarasota Med. awards for achievement and excellence, 1979; Gairdner Found. annual award, 1980; Lasker Found. award, 1980; Nobel award in chemistry, 1980; N.Y. Acad. Sci. award, 1980; Sci. Freedom and Responsibility award AAAS, 1982; Nat. Medal of Sci., 1983; named Calif. Scientist of Yr. Calif. Museum Sci. and Industry, 1963; numerous disting. lectureships including Harvey lectr., 1972, Lynen lectr., 1977, Priestly lectrs. Pa. State U., 1978, Dreyfus Disting. lectrs. Northwestern U., 1979, Lawrence Livermore Dir.'s Disting. lectr., 1983, Linus Pauling lectr., 1993. Fellow AAAS; mem. NAS, Inst. Medicine, Am. Acad. Arts and Scis., Am. Soc. Biol. Chemists (pres. 1974-75), Am. Soc. Cell Biology (chmn. pub. policy com. 1994—), Am. Soc. Microbiology, Am. Philos. Soc., Internat. Soc. Molecular Biology, Japan Biochem. Soc. (elected fgn. mem. 1978), French Acad. Sci. (elected fgn. mem. 1981), Royal Soc. (elected fgn. mem. 1992). Office: Stanford Sch Medicine Beckman Ctr B-062 Stanford CA 94305-5425*

BERG, ROBERT ALLEN, pediatrician, educator; b. Detroit, Dec. 12, 1949; s. Aaron and Mildred (Schuff) B.; m. Catherine Locke, May 8, 1982 (dec. Mar. 1994); children: David, Carolyn; m. Rochelle Bagatell, Jan. 5, 1997. BS, U. Mich., 1971; MD, U. Calif., San Francisco, 1975. Pediatric intern U. Calif., San Francisco, 1975-76, pediatric resident, 1976-77; chief resident dept. pediatrics Good Samaritan Hosp., Phoenix and San Francisco, 1977-78; dir. pediatric clinic and emergency rm. Maricopa Med. Ctr., Phoenix, 1978-84, dir. pediatric ICU, 1984-88; dir. pediatric ICU Tucson (Ariz.) Med. Ctr., 1989-91, U. Med. Ctr., Tucson, 1988—; asst. prof., clin. lectr. U. Ariz. Coll. Medicine, Tucson, 1983-88, clin. asst. prof., 1988-92, clin. assoc. prof., 1992-94, assoc. prof. with tenure, 1994—; chief med. staff Univ. Med. Ctr., Tucson, 1996; pres.-elect Phoenix Pediat. Soc., 1987-88; nat. faculty Pediat. Advanced Life Support, 1990-94, rsch. com., 1991-94, chmn. pediat. advance life support task force; mem. Am. Heart Assn.-Ariz. affiliate, 1990-94, rsch. com., 1991, chmn. pediat. advanced life support task force, 1989-91; vis. prof. U. Hawaii, Okinawa, Japan, 1991, Ohio State U., 1992, Kazakastan, 1994. Contbr. articles to profl. jours. Med. dir. Pilot Parents, Phoenix, 1979-88; chmn. Child Care Safety Seat Task Force, Ariz., 1983; bd. dirs. Congregation Chaverim, Tucson, 1993-96; med./exec. com. U. Med. Ctr., Tucson, 1994—. Rsch. grantee Ariz. Disease Control Rsch. Commn., 1994—, Ariz. affiliate Am. Heart Assn., 1996—. Fellow Am. Acad. Pediat., Am. Coll. Critical Care Medicine, Soc. Critical Care Medicine; mem. Am. Heart Assn. (pediat. subcom. and rsch. working group emergency cardiac care 1994—). Office: U Med Ctr Dept Pediatrics PO Box 245073 1501 N Campbell Ave Tucson AZ 85724-5073

BERGÉ, CAROL, author; b. N.Y.C., 1928; d. Albert and Molly Peppis; m. Jack Bergé, June 1955; 1 child, Peter. Asst. to pres. Pendray Public Relations, N.Y.C., 1955; disting. prof. lit. Thomas Jefferson Coll., Allendale, Mich., 1975-76; instr. adult degree program Goddard Coll. at Asilomar, 1976; tchr. fiction and poetry U. Calif. Extension Program, Berkeley, 1976-77; assoc. prof. U. So. Miss., Hattiesburg, 1977-78; vis. prof. Honors Ctr. and English dept. U. N.Mex., 1978-79, 87; vis. lectr. Wright State U., 1979, SUNY, Albany, 1980-81; tchr. Poets and Writers, Poets in the Schs. (N.Y. State Council on Arts), 1970-72, Poets in the Schs. (Conn. Commn. Arts); proprietor Blue Gate Gallery of Art and Antiques, 1988—. Author: (fiction) The Unfolding, 1969, A Couple Called Moebius, 1972, Acts of Love: An American Novel, 1973 (N.Y. State Coun. on Arts CAPS award 1974), Timepieces, 1977, The Doppler Effect, 1979, Fierce Metronome, 1981, Secrets, Gossip and Slander, 1984, Zebras, or, Contour Lines, 1991; (poetry) The Vulnerable Island, 1964, Lumina, 1965, Poems Made of Skin, 1968, The Chambers, 1969, Circles, as in the Eye, 1969, An American Romance, 1969, From a Soft Angle: Poems About Women, 1972, The Unexpected, 1976, Rituals and Gargoyles, 1976, A Song, A Chant, 1978, Alba Genesis, 1979, Alba Nemesis, 1979, (reportage) The Vancouver Report, 1965; editor Ctr. Mag., 1970-84, pub., 1991—; editor Miss. Rev., 1977-78, Subterraneans, 1975-76, Paper Branches, 1987, LIGHT YEARS: The N.Y.C. Coffeehouse Poets of the 1960's, 1997; contbg. editor Woodstock Rev., 1977-81, Shearsman mag., 1980-82, S.W. Profile, 1981; editor, pub. CENTER Press, 1991-93; pub.: Medicine Journeys (Carl Ginsburg), Coastal Lives (Miriam Sagan), 1991; co-pub.: Zebras (Carol Berge). Nat. Endowment Arts fellow, 1979-80. Mem. Authors' League, Poets and Writers, MacDowell Fellows Assn., Nat. Press Women. Home: 562 Onate Pl Santa Fe NM 87501-3674

BERGEL, PETER ROBIN, editor; b. Bishop, Calif., Apr. 27, 1944; s. Kurt and Alice Rose (Berger) B.; m. Parry Pierce; 1 child, Shanti Pierce. BA in Physics, Reed Coll., 1965. Mem. process devel. staff Precision Castparts, Portland, Oreg., 1965-66; rsch. apparatus operator Atomic Energy Commn., Berkeley, Calif., 1966-70; mem. staff Energy Conservation Orgn., Eugene, Oreg., 1975-76; legis. intern Oreg. Legislature, Salem, 1979, legis. asst., 1981; dir. Citizens Allied for Responsible Energy, Salem, 1979-81; co-dir. Citizen Action for Lasting Security, Salem, 1981-86; nat. staff person Am. Peace Test, Salem, Las Vegas, 1986-88; editor Oreg. PeaceWorker, Salem, 1988—; columnist Stateman Jour. Newspaper, 1994—; editor Civilian Based Defense, 1995—; trained cmty. mediator; founding bd. dirs. McKenzie River Gathering, Eugene, 1975-78; bd. dirs. polit. action com. Oreg. PeaceWorks; pres. bd. Ctr. for Energy Rsch.; bd. dirs. Shundahai Network. Founder, participant Dr. Atomic's Medicine Show, Salem, Eugene, 1974—; founder Ch. of Ithilien, Willamina, Oreg., 1969-72; co-founder Am. Peace Test, 1985, Peace Tng. Inst., Salem, 1993; co-chmn. COPRED Nat. Conf., 1995. Recipient Human Rights award City of Salem, 1985, Award of Distinction Oreg. Mag., 1985. Democrat. Taoist. Office: Ctr for Energy Rsch 333 State St Salem OR 97301-3533

BERGEN, CANDICE, actress, writer, photojournalist; b. Beverly Hills, Calif., May 9, 1946; d. Edgar and Frances (Westerman) B.; m. Louis Malle, Sept. 27, 1980 (dec. 1995); 1 dau., Chloe. Ed., U. Pa. Model during coll. Films include The Group, The Sand Pebbles, The Day the Fish Came Out, Live for Life, The Magus, Soldier Blue, Getting Straight, The Hunting Party, Carnal Knowledge, T.R. Baskin, The Adventurers, 11 Harrowhouse, Bite the Bullet, The Wind and the Lion, The Domino Principle, The End of the World in Our Usual Bed in a Night Full of Rain, Oliver's Story, Starting Over, Rich and Famous, Gandhi, 1982, Stick, 1985; TV series: Murphy Brown, 1988— (Emmy award, Leading Actress in a Comedy Series, 1988-89, 89-90, 91-92, 93-94, 94-95); TV films Arthur the King, 1985, Murder by Reason of Insanity, 1985, Mayflower Madam, 1987, Tim, 1996; TV miniseries Hollywood Wives, 1985, Trying Times, Moving Day; author Knockwood; photojournalist credits include articles for Life, Playboy; dramatist: (play) The Freezer (included in Best Short Plays of 1968). Recipient Emmy awards for lead actress in a comedy series, 1989, 90, 92, 94, 95.

BERGEN, CHRISTOPHER BROOKE, opera company administrator, translator, editor; b. L.A., Jan. 11, 1949; s. Edward Grinnell Bergen and Alvina Ellen (Temple) Stevens; m. Tessa Jennifer von Grunebaum, May 7, 1972. BA, UCLA, 1971; MA, Yale U., 1977. Conf. officer IAEA, Vienna, Austria, 1973-75, data analyst, 1979-81; import mgr. COBEC Trading Corp., N.Y.C., 1978-79; assoc. Geissler Engring. Co., Oakland, Calif., 1982-83; dir. Yale Cons. Assocs., San Francisco, 1983-84; editor INPUT, Mountain View, Calif., 1984; adminstr. surtitles San Francisco Opera, 1985—. Editor profl. jours.; translator operatic texts for projection during performances at San Francisco Opera, Met. Opera, Lyric Opera of Chgo., many other opera cos., symphonies and conservatories in U.S., abroad. Mem. Dolphin Swimming and Boating Club of San Francisco, Amnesty Internat., Sierra Club. Democrat. Home: 707 Stockton St # 506 San Francisco CA 94108-1466 Office: San Francisco Opera War Meml Opera House San Francisco CA 94102

BERGEN, POLLY, actress; b. Bluegrass, Tenn.; d. William and Lucy (Lawhorn) Burgin; m. Freddie Fields, Feb. 13, 1956 (div. 1976); children: Kathy, Pamela, Peter. pres. Polly Bergen Cosmetics, Polly Bergen Jewelry, Polly Bergen Shoes; exec. cons. Chantal Skin Care Corp., 1996. Author: Fashion and Charm, 1960, Polly's Principles, 1974, I'd Love To, But What'll I Wear, 1977; actor, producer for TV: Leave of Absence, 1994; Broadway plays include Champagne Complex, John Murray Andersons' Almanac, First Impression, Plaza Suite, Love Letters; films include Cape Fear, Move Over Darling, Kisses for My President, At War with the Army, The Stooge, That's My Boy, The Caretakers, A Guide for the Married Man, Making Mr. Right, Cry-Baby, 1990, Dr. Jekyll and Ms. Hyde, When We Were Colored, 1994; performed in one woman shows in Las Vegas, Nev., and Reno; albums: Bergen Sings Morgan, The Party's Over, All Alone By the Telephone, Polly and Her Pop, The Four Seasons of Love, Annie Get Your Gun and Do Re Mi, My Heart Sings, Act One Sing Too; numerous TV appearances including star of The Polly Bergen Show, NBC-TV; other TV appearances include The Helen Morgan Story, 1957 (Emmy award as best actress), To Tell the Truth, The Lightning Field, The Surrogate, For Hope; miniseries include The Winds of War (Emmy nomination), 79 Park Ave, War and Remembrance, 1988 (Emmy nomination); writer, prodr. NBC movie Leave of Absence, 1994. Bd. dirs. Martha Graham Dance Ctr., The Singer Co., Soc. Singers, Calif. Abortion and Reproductive Rights Action League, Show Coalition; hon. canister campaign chairperson Cancer Care, Inc., Nat. Cancer Found.; founder Nat. Bus. Coun. for ERA; mem. Planned Parenthood Fedn., Am. Bd. Advs.; mem. nat. adv. com. NARAL, Hollywood Women's Polit. Com. Recipient Fame award Top Ten in TV, 1957-58, Troupers award Sterling Publs., 1957, Editors and Critics award Radio and TV Daily, 1958, Outstanding Working Woman award Downtown St. Louis, Inc., Golden Plate award Am. Acad. Achievement, 1969, Outstanding Mother's award Nat. Mothers' Day Com., 1984, Best Achievement in New Jewelry Design award, 1986, Cancer Care award, 1989, Woman of Achievement award LWV, 1990, Extraordinary Achievement award Nat. Women's Law Ctr., 1991, Freedom of Choice award Calif. Abortion and Reproductive Rights Action League, 1992; Polly Bergen Cardio-Pulmonary Rsch. Lab., Children's Rsch. Inst. and Hosp., Denver dedicated, 1970. Mem. AFTRA, AGVA, SAG, Actors Equity. Office: c/o Jan McCormack 11342 Dona Lisa Dr Studio City CA 91604-4315

BERGER, ARTHUR ASA, broadcast communication educator; b. Boston, Jan. 3, 1933; s. Simon and Frances (Savel) B.; m. Phyllis Wolfson, June 25, 1961; children: Miriam Frances, Gabriel. BA, U. Mass., 1954; MA, U. Iowa, 1956; PhD, U. Minn., 1965. Prof. broadcast and electronic communication arts San Francisco State U., 1965—. Author: Television as an Instrument of Terror, 1978, Media Analysis Techniques, 1982, Signs in Contemporary Culture, 1984, Television in Society, 1986, Semiotics of Advertising, 1987, Media USA, 1988, Political Culture and Public Opinion, 1989, Agitpop: Political Culture and Communication Theory, 1990, Scripts: Writing for Radio and Television, 1990, Media Research Techniques, 1991, Reading Matter, 1992, Popular Culture Genres, 1992, An Anatomy of Humor, 1993, Improving Writing Skills, 1993, Blind Men & Elephants, 1995, Cultural Criticism, 1995, Essentials of Mass Communication Theory, 1995, Manufacturing Desire, 1996, Bloom's Morning, 1997, The Genius of the Jewish Joke, 1997, Narratives in Popular Culture, Media and Everyday Life, 1997, The Genius of the Jewish Joke, 1997, Bloom's Morning, 1997, The ARt of Comedy Writing, 1997; film and TV editor Society; editor Classics in Communication, Transaction Books; contbg. editor Jour. of Communication, 1974-94. With AUS, 1956-58. Fulbright scholar, 1963-64. Office: San Francisco State Univ 1600 Holloway Ave San Francisco CA 94132-1722

BERGER, BONNIE G., sport psychologist, educator; b. Champaign, Ill., May 20, 1941; d. Bernard G. and Mildred W. Berger; 1 son, Stephen Casher. BS, Wittenberg U., 1962; MA, Columbia U., 1965, EdD, 1972. Tchr., George Rogers Clark Jr. High Sch., Springfield, Ohio, 1962-64; supr. phys. edn. Agnes Russell Elem. Sch., N.Y.C., 1964-65; asst. prof. SUNY, Geneseo, 1965-66; asst. prof. Dalhousie U., Halifax, N.S., Can., 1969-71; asst. prof. Bklyn. Coll., 1971-77, assoc. prof., 1978-81, prof., 1982-93, dir. Sport Psychology Lab., master degree program in psychosocial aspects of physical activity; dep. chair dept. phys. edn. Bklyn. Coll., 1989-93; prof., assoc. dean coll. health scis., sch. physical and health edn. U. Wyo., Laramie, 1993-96, assoc. dean coll. health scis., 1996—; cons. sport psychology. Fellow Assn. for the Advancement of Applied Sport Psychology (exec. bd.), Am. Acad. Kinesiology and Phys. Edn.; mem. Am. Psychol. Assn., AAHPERD, Internat. Soc. Sports Psychology, N.Am. Soc. Psychology Sport and Phys. Activity. Author: Free Weights for Women, 1984; contbr. articles to profl. jours., chpts. to books. Home: 1673 Apache Dr Laramie WY 82070-6967 Office: U Wyo Coll Health Scis Quinson Bldg Laramie WY 82070

BERGER, DALE EDMUND, psychologist, educator; b. Perham, Minn., Feb. 21, 1943; s. Albert D. and Evelyn E. (Pausch) B.; m. Peggy Marie Seaver, Dec. 16, 1978; children: Laura, Eric. BS in Math., U. Minn., 1964; MA in Psychology, UCLA, 1966, PhD, 1970. Math. tchr. Torrance (Calif.) Unified Sch. Dist., 1964-65; asst. prof. Claremont (Calif.) Grad. Sch., 1970-77, assoc. prof., 1977-83, prof., 1983—, chair grad. faculty in psychology, 1989—, dir. Ctr. for Orgnl. and Behavioral Scis., 1993—. Author, editor: Applications of Cognitive Psychology, 1987; contbr. articles to profl. jours. Mem. Phi Beta Kappa. Office: Claremont Grad Sch 123 E 8th St Claremont CA 91711-3955

BERGER, JAY VARI, executive recruiter; b. San Francisco, Aug. 31, 1944; s. Jack Vari and Ruth (Wasserman) B.; m. Margareta Ahlberg, June 14, 1969; children: Karin Britta Margareta, John Vari Sten. BS, U. So. Calif., 1966, MS, 1967, PhD, 1971. Assoc. dean admissions U. So. Calif., L.A., 1969-76, dir. admissions, 1976-82, asst. v.p. devel., 1982-86; prin. ptnr. Morris & Berger, Pasadena, Calif., 1986—; chmn. bd. Berger & Berger Internat., Pasadena, 1976-96. Author: (juvenile) Willie the Worm, 1986; columnist Venture Connections, 1988. Chair bd. dirs. The Sycamores, Pasadena, 1985-94; bd. dirs. Foothill Friends of Music, 1989-92; bd. dirs. Covenant House Calif., pres., trustee Chandler Sch., Pasadena, 1987-89; trustee Flintridge Preparatory Sch., 1992—, chmn. bd. dirs. 1996—. Mem. Calif. Exec. Recruiters Assn., Calif. Assn. Ind. Schs. (bd. trustees 1988-91), Annandale Golf Club, Rotary (bd. dirs. Pasadena chpt. 1988-92). Home: 1550 Arroyo View Dr Pasadena CA 91103-1903 Office: Morris & Berger Cons Exec Search 201 S Lake Ave Ste 700 Pasadena CA 91101-3015

BERGER, JOHN MILTON, state agency administrator; b. Marysville, Ohio, June 24, 1943; s. John Howard and Betty Louise (Mossbarger) B. BSBA, Franklin U., 1971; postgrad., Ohio State U., 1972. Cert. hazard control mgr., assoc. Ins. Inst. Am. risk mgmt. designation. Claims adjuster State Compensation Ins. Fund, Denver, 1974-78, loss control cons., 1978-84; adminstrv. officer Indsl. Commn., Denver, 1984-86; self-ins. adminstrn. Colo. Div. Labor, Denver, 1986-91; ins. complaince mgr. divsn. workers' compensation Colo. Dept. Labor and Employment, Denver, 1991-97, mgr. employer svcs. divsn., 1997—; mem. legis. com. Colo. Div. Ins., Denver, 1989-91; mem. self-ins. subcom. of Internat. Assn. Indsl. Accident Bds. and Commns. Author: Workers' Compensation Loss Prevention and Loss Control Manual, 1990; contbr. article to profl. jour. With USN, 1961-64. Recognized for Outstanding Svc. to State Govt., 1986. Mem. Colo. Self-Insurers Assn. Republican. Home: 675 Dudley St Lakewood CO 80215-5406 Office: Colo Dept Labor & Employment Employer Svcs Divsn 1515 Arapahoe St Denver CO 80202-3150

BERGER, LELAND ROGER, lawyer; b. N.Y.C., Feb. 3, 1956; s. Albert and Audrey Sybil (Ellenbogen) B.; m. Lisa M. Burk, Feb. 15, 1987; 1 child, Robert Samson. Student, Am. U., 1977; BA, Dickinson Coll., 1978; JD, Lewis & Clark Coll., 1982. Bar: Oreg. 1983, U.S. Dist. Ct. Oreg. 1983, U.S. Ct. Appeals (9th cir.) 1990. Pvt. practice Portland, Oreg., 1983-84; assoc. Rieke, Geil & Savage, P.C., Portland, 1984-94; pvt. practice Portland, 1995—. Mem. Oreg. Bar Assn. (ad hoc com. to study multi-state bar exam. 1983-84, uniform criminal jury instrn. com. 1989-90, sec. 1990-91, criminal law sect., appellate law sect.), Multnomah County Bar Assn. (corrections com. 1987), Oreg. Young Attys. Assn. (bd. dirs. 1983-84), Nat. Lawyers Guild (co-chair criminal justice com. Portland chpt. 1983-84), Oreg. Criminal Def. Lawyers Assn., Nat. Criminal Def. Lawyers Assn. Democrat. Jewish.

Home: 2817 NE 12th Ave Portland OR 97212-3219 Office: 950 Lloyd Ctr Ste 3 Portland OR 97232-1262

BERGER, NEWELL JAMES, JR., security professional; b. Pitts., Oct. 26, 1926; s. Newell James and Marjorie Ikler (Herndon) B.; m. Darlene Ingram, Sept. 6, 1950 (dec. Nov. 1990). BS, Mich. State U., 1958; grad., U.S. Army Command and Gen. Staff Coll., 1963, U.S. Army War Coll., 1972; MA, Webster U., 1993. Enlisted man U.S. Army, 1944, advanced through grades to staff sgt., 1948, commd. 2d lt., 1948, advanced through grades to col., 1970; chief corrections hdqrs. U.S. Army, Washington, 1970-72, dir. security Office Surgeon Gen., 1972-73; dir. security Health Svcs. Command U.S. Army, Ft. Sam Houston, Tex., 1973-78; ret. U.S. Army, 1978; security cons. Phoenix and San Diego, 1979-84; chief plant security Teledyne Ryan Aero. Co., San Diego, 1985-86; dep. dir. security GDE Systems, Inc., San Diego, 1986—. Decorated Legion of Merit with two oak leaf clusters. Mem. (life) Internat. Assn. Chiefs Police, Am. Soc. for Indsl. Security (cert. protection profl.). Republican. Episcopalian. Home: 11872 Caminito Corriente San Diego CA 92128-4550 Office: GDE Systems Inc PO Box 1198 Poway CA 92074-1198

BERGER, PAUL ERIC, artist, photographer; b. The Dalles, Oreg., Jan. 20, 1948; s. Charles Glen and Virginia (Nunez) B. B.A., UCLA, 1970; M.F.A., SUNY-Buffalo, 1973. Vis. lectr. U. Ill., 1974-78; prof. art U. Wash.-Seattle, 1978—. Exhibited one-man shows, photographs, Art Inst. Chgo., 1975, Light Gallery, N.Y.C., 1977, Seattle Art Mus., 1980, Light Gallery, N.Y.C., 1982, Univ. Art Mus., Santa Barbara, Calif., 1984, Cliff Michel Gallery, 1989, Seattle Art Mus., 1990, Fuel Gallery, 1993, Galerie Lichtblick GFFK, Cologne, Germany, 1996. NEA Photographer's fellow, 1979, NEA Visual Artist's fellow, 1986; recipient Artist's Commn., Wash. State Arts Commn., 1990. Mem. Soc. Photographic Edn. Office: U Wash Sch Art Box 353440 Seattle WA 98195-3440

BERGER, RICHARD EUGENE, urologist, educator; b. Auburn, Nebr., Nov. 6, 1946; s. Arthur Albert and Nelda Jean (Shoemaker) B.; m. Deborah M. Erlick, Aug. 26, 1974; 1 child, Benjamin R. BA in Biology, U. Chgo., 1969, MD, 1973. Diplomate Am. Bd. Urology. Gen. surgery resident U. Colo. Affiliated Hosps., Denver, 1973-75; urology resident U. Wash. Affiliated Hosps., Seattle, 1975-76, 77-79, fellowship in infectious disease, 1976-77, instr. dept. urology, 1978-79, attending physician, 1979—, asst. prof. dept. urology, 1979-83, assoc. prof. dept. urology, 1983-92, prof. dept. urology, 1992—; affiliate, regional primate rsch. ctr. U. Wash., Seattle, 1980-85, dir. male fertility lab., 1981—; dir. Harborview Reproductive and Sexual Medical Clinic, Seattle, 1987-89, U. Wash. Reproductive and Sexual Medicine Clinic, Seattle, 1989—; chief urology svc. VA Med. Ctr., Seattle, 1981-84; chief dept. urology Harborview Med. Ctr., Seattle, 1984-89; cons. venereal disease control divsn. Ctr. for Disease Control, Atlanta, 1982; ad hoc reviewer Jour. Urology, 1984—, Urology, 1988—, Fertility Sterility, 1988—; mem. AUA ad hoc com. on sexually transmitted diseases, 1991—; assoc. editor Clin. Care of Prostatic Diseases, 1994—. Contbr. numerous papers to profl. jours. Named Best Drs. in Am., 1994. Mem. Am. Andrology Soc., Am. Fertility Soc., Am. Venereal Disease Assn., King County Med. Soc., Wash. State Med. Soc., Am. Urol. Assn., N.W. Urol. Soc., Am. Assn. Sex Educators, Counselors and Therapists, Soc. Study of Impotence, Soc. Study Male Reproduction. Office: U Wash PO Box 356150 Seattle WA 98195

BERGER, ROBERT SYDNEY, paper company executive; b. N.Y.C., Feb. 13, 1917; s. Matthew M. and Deborah Jeanette (Newblatt) B.; m. Nancy Mock, Sept. 23, 1952; children: Jill DeJong Gross, Kathy DeJong Albert. BA, U. Pa., 1936; MA, Columbia U., 1939; JD, Harvard U., 1939. Bar: N.Y. Assoc. office A.L. Pomerantz, N.Y.C., 1939-41; v.p. McKenna & Phelps Inc., N.Y.C., 1946-47; chmn. bd. Rittenhouse Paper Co., Chgo., Los Angeles, 1948—. Mem. bd. edn. Highland Park, Ill., 1960-66. Served to capt. USN, 1941-46, 51-53, USNR, 1954-77. Home: 10375 Wilshire Blvd Los Angeles CA 90024-4728 Office: Rittenhouse Paper Co 2440 E 38th St Los Angeles CA 90058-1708

BERGER, WOLFGANG H., oceanographer, marine geologist; b. Erlangen, Bavaria, Fed. Republic of Germany, Oct. 5, 1937; came to U.S., 1961; s. Helmut and Emilie Berger; m. Karen J. Thomas, June 9, 1966; children: Karl, Katrina. MS in Geology, U. Colo., 1963; PhD in Oceanography, U. Calif., San Diego, 1968. Wissensch. asst. Universität Kiel, Fed. Republic of Germany, 1969-71; rsch. asst. Scripps Inst. Oceanography U. Calif., La Jolla, 1963-68, asst. researcher, 1968-69, asst. prof., 1971-74, assoc. prof., 1974-80, prof. oceanography, 1980—; interim dir. Scripps Inst. Oceanography Scripps Inst. Oceanography U. Calif., 1996-97; vice-chancellor for marine scis. San Diego, 1996—; vis. prof. geology Universität Kiel, 1977, 80; guest researcher Universität Bremen, Fed. Republic of Germany, 1986—; interim dir. Scripps Inst. Oceanography, 1996-97. Editor: Abrupt Climatic Change, 1987, Ocean Productivity, 1989. Mem. geology adv. bd. U. Colo., Boulder, 1989-92. Recipient Bigelow medal Woods Hole (Mass.) Oceanographic Inst., 1979, Huntsman medal Bedford Oceanographic Inst., Can., 1984, Humboldt award German Sci. Found., Bonn, Fed. Republic of Germany, 1986, Albert I medal, Paris, 1991, Balzan prize, 1993. Fellow AAAS, Am. Geophysical Union (Ewing medal 1988), Geol. Soc. Am., European Geophysical Soc. Office: U Calif San Diego Scripps Inst Oceanography 510-UCSD-0215 La Jolla CA 92093

BERGERON, PAUL PHILLIP, internist; s. Roger Joseph and Jean Marie (Campiola) B.; m. Margaret Alice Pothier, June 4, 1994. BA, Coll. of the Holy Cross, 1987; MD, U. Vt., 1994. Cert. BLS, ACLS. Teenage counselor Worcester Youth Guidance Assn., 1985-86; developmentally-delayed children camp counselor Greater Lawrence Ednl. Collaborative, 1986; mental health technician Holy Family Hosp., 1985-87; pharm. co. rep. 3M Pharms./3M Health Care, 1988-90; resident in internal medicine Stanford (Calif.) Health Svcs., 1994—. Mem. ACP (assoc.), Psi Chi. Office: Stanford Health Svcs Dept of Medicine S102 325 Pasteur Stanford CA 94305

BERGH, DAVID MORGAN, entrepreneur; b. Boise, Idaho, Aug. 8, 1947; s. Rolfe Roald and Margaret Rose (Morgan) B.; m. Jan R. Seda, May 17, 1975; children: Hillary Lauren, Benjamin Morgan, Salle Alberta. BS in Mgmt., U. Idaho, 1972. Chpt. cons., then dir. expansion, asst. exec. dir. Kappa Sigma Internat. Fraternity, Charlottesville, Va., 1972-75; propr. Morgan's Exchange, Boise, 1975-79, Strato Lanes, Mountain Home, Idaho, 1979—; concessionaire various recreational concerns, Alaska and Idaho; supr. com. P.F. Credit Union. Chmn. Cen. Dist. Health, Idaho, 1983—; pres. Mountain Home Mil. Affairs Com., 1985—; sec., treas. Silver City Hist. Soc. Mem. Nat. Restaurant and Beverage Assn., Kappa Sigma (dist. prs. 1975—), Elks. Republican. Roman Catholic. Home and Office: PO Box 9 Mountain Home ID 83647-0009

BERGIN, ALLEN ERIC, clinical psychologist, educator; b. Spokane, Wash., Aug. 4, 1934; s. Bernard F. and Vivian Selma (Kullberg) B.; m. Marian Shafer, June 4, 1955; children: David, Sue, Cyndy, Kathy, Eric, Ben, Patrick, Daniel, Michael. BS, Brigham Young U., 1956, MS, 1957; PhD, Stanford U., 1960. Diplomate Am. Bd. Profl. Psychology. Postdoctoral fellow U. Wis., Madison, 1960-61; prof. psychology and edn. Tchrs. Coll., Columbia U., N.Y.C., 1961-72; prof. psychology Brigham Young U., Provo, Utah, 1972—, dir. Values Inst., 1976-78, dir. clin. psychology, 1989-93; sr. rsch. fellow Nat. Inst. Health Care Rsch., 1992—; assessment officer Peace Corps, Washington, 1961-66; cons. NIMH, Rockville, Md., 1969-75, 90. Co-author: Changing Frontiers in Psychotherapy, 1972; co-editor: Handbook of Psychotherapy, 1971, 4th edit., 1994 (citation classic 1979). Bishop LDS Ch., Emerson, N.J., 1970-72, Provo, 1981-84, stake pres., 1992-95; mem. steering com. Utah Gov.'s Conf. on Families, Salt Lake City, 1979-80. Recipient Biggs-Pine award AACD, 1986, Maeser rsch. award Brigham Young U. Alumni Assn., 1986, exemplary paper award Templeton Found., 1996. Fellow APA (Disting. Contbn. to Knowledge award 1989, William James award div. 36, 1990); mem. Soc. for Psychotherapy Integration (adv. bd.), Soc. for Sci. Study Religion, Soc. for Psychotherapy Rsch. (pres. 1974-75), Assn. Mormon Counselors (pres. 1979-80). Republican. Office: Brigham Young U 285 Tlrb Provo UT 84602-1052

BERGIN, COLLEEN JOAN, medical educator; b. Foxton, New Zealand, May 13, 1953; came to U.S., 1981; d. Joseph Bernard and Mary Catherine (Butel) B.; m. Niall C.T. Wilton, May 22, 1992; children: Tessa, Sophie. MBChB, Auckland Med. Sch., 1979. Resident U. B.C., Vancouver, Can., 1981-87; faculty Stanford (Calif.) U., 1989-92; assoc. prof. U. Calif., San Diego, 1992—. Contbr. articles to profl. jours. NIH Rsch. grantee, 1992—; Thoracic Radiology fellow Duke U., 1988. Mem. Am. Roentgen Ray Soc., Radiologic Soc. N.Am., Soc. Thoracic Radiology (stds. com. 1990-96), Soc. Magnetic Resonance. Democrat. Roman Catholic.

BERGMAN, DANIEL CHARLES, county official, lawyer, environmental manager; b. Corpus Christi, Tex., Aug. 18, 1943; s. Benjamin and Pearl H. B.; m. Susan Lee Axall, Aug. 15, 1965 (div. 1987); children: Erica Catherine, Kelli Lorraine. B.S. in Biology, San Diego State U., 1965, M.S., 1971; J.D., U. San Diego, 1975. Bar: Calif. 1976, U.S. Dist. Ct. (so. dist.) Calif. 1976, U.S. Ct. Appeals (9th cir.) 1977; registered environ. health specialist Calif., Ill.; cert. community coll. tchr., vector ecologist, 1971-72, supervising environ. health specialist Dept. Health Services, 1972-79, chief div. environ. health mgr., 1979-81; environ. health cons. Contra Costa (Calif.) Dept. Health Services, 1981, asst. health services dir. Div. Environ. Health, 1981-89; pres., CFO Pyrite Canyon Group, Inc., 1991—; sole practice law, San Diego and Danville, Calif., 1976—; lectr. in field. Recipient Am. Jurisprudence awards. Mem. Am. Pub. Health Assn., Nat. Environ. Health Assn. (Presdl. citation 1977), Calif. Environ. Health Assn. (Presdl. citation 1977, 78), ABA, Calif. State Bar Assn. Office: 3200C Pyrite St Riverside CA 92509

BERGMAN, ELLEN MARIE, state legislator; b. Lincoln, Nebr., Mar. 19, 1942; d. Ralph Celestine and Barbara Ellen (McGinley) Roach; m. Paul Albert Berman, Nov. 9, 1963; children: Barry, Patrick, Bradley, Christopher. Grad. parochial high sch., Beatrice, Nebr. Hairdresser various shops, Lincoln, 1961-65; checker Henry's Market, Scottsbluff, Nebr., 1974-76; sales clk. J.C. Penney Co., Miles City, Mont., 1977-81; prosthesis technician Home Health Spltys., Miles City, 1990—; mem. Mont. Ho. of Reps., Helena, 1992—. Reporter Family Issues Forum, Miles City, 1988—; vol. local nursing home and retirement home; vol. reach to recovery Am. Cancer Soc. Republican. Mem. Assembly of God. Home: 1019 S Strevell Ave Miles City MT 59301-4917*

BERGMAN, YAACOV, performing company executive; m. Joan Behrens. Degree in conducting and composition, Rubin Acad., Hebrew U., Jerusalem; studied with Richard Westenburg, Mannes Coll. Music; studied with Charles Bruck, Leonard Bernstein. Music dir. Colorado Springs (Colo.) Symphony; music dir. Walla Walla (Wash.) Symphony; founder, music dir., condr. Heritage Orch. N.Y.; condr. Osaka (Japan) Opera Co., 1996. Office: Colorado Springs Symphony PO Box 1692 Colorado Springs CO 80901

BERGMANN, FREDRICK LOUIS, English language educator, theater historian; b. Tecumseh, Kans., Sept. 27, 1916; s. Curt and Minna (Herrmann) B.; m. Jean Marshall, July 6, 1941; children: Juliann, John Fredrick. A.B., Washburn Coll., 1937; M.A., State Coll. Wash., 1939; postgrad., Columbia, 1941; Ph.D., George Washington U., 1953. Asst. Washburn Coll., 1939-40; instr. English DePauw U., 1940-43, asst. prof., 1943-46, assoc. prof., 1946-54, prof., 1954-82, prof. emeritus, 1982—, head dept. English, 1956-78, dir. Conf. Am. Studies, 1956-78, James Whitcomb Riley prof. English lit., 1969-83, also chmn. internat. edn. com. Author: (with R.W. Pence) Writing Craftsmanship, 1956, Paragraph Rhetoric, 1967, Sentence Rhetoric, 1969, Essays: Method, Content, Conscience, 1970, Essays 2, 1975, (with H.W. Pedicord) The Plays of David Garrick, 7 vols, 1979-82; contbr. articles to profl. jours. Founder Greencastle Summer Theater, 1962; pres. English dept. chmn. Gt. Lakes Colls. Assn., 1968-69. Fellow Folger Shakespeare Library, 1951; fellow grad. Council George Washington U. Mem. Ind. Coll. English Assn. (pres. 1956, 63), MLA, Am. Soc. 18th Century Studies, Societe francaise d'Etude du XVIIe Siecle, Johnson Soc. of Central Region, Am. English-Speaking Union, Sigma Delta Chi (Leather Medal award for greatest service to DePauw U. 1962), Delta Chi. Episcopalian. Home: 9823 W Taro Ln Peoria AZ 85382-2689

BERGMANN, MICHAEL DEAN, financial services company executive; b. St. Paul, Feb. 7, 1944; s. Edmund Karl and Karolyn Edna (Moyer) B.; m. Alma Jean Fleck, Sept. 9, 1967; children: Nathan, Kelley. BS magna cum laude, U. Minn., 1966; MS, Stanford U., 1969, PhD, 1970. Group mgr. Irwin Mgmt. Co., Columbus, Ind., 1970-72; cons. coord. Shearson, Hayden Stone, Beverly Hills, Calif., 1972-76; co-founder, sr. exec. v.p. Asset Mgmt. Group, Denver, 1976—. Author: Expectations, Inflation and the Term Structure of Interest Rates, 1970. McCarthy fellow Stanford U., 1967. Mem. Am. Econ. Assn., Am. Fin. Assn., Nat. Assn. Bus. Econs., Phi Beta Kappa. Home: 5200 Lakeshore Dr Bow Mar CO 80123-1540 Office: Asset Mgmt Group 6200 S Syracuse Way Ste 100 Englewood CO 80123-4738

BERGMANN, PETER JAY, television director and producer, educator; b. N.Y.C., Oct. 2, 1949; s. Otto Bergmann and Rose Marie Wasserman. AB, NYU, 1966, MFA, 1968, PhD, 1975; PhD, U. Pa., 1969. V.p. ABC Cir. Films, L.A., 1973-75; asst. pres. ABC Network, L.A., N.Y.C., 1975-78; assto to COB ABC Inc., L.A., N.Y.C., 1978-81; pres. Film Co., L.A., N.Y.C., 1981-86, Odyssey Filmakers, Hollywood, Calif., 1986-90, Bergmann Films, L.A., 1990—; prof. electronic filmmaking Fairleigh Dickinson U., Madison, N.J., 1994—; cons. CBS, L.A., N.Y.C., 1987. Prodr. (film) Boys in Band; (TV movie) Eleanor & Franklin, 1976, Victory at Entebbe, 1976; dir. The Great Stone Balloon, 1987. Bd. dirs. Make-A-Wish Found., L.A., 1990-94, Starlight, L.A., N.Y.C., 1993-95. Mem. Dirs. Guild Am., nat. Acad. TV Arts & Scis. Office: Film Co 520 Washington Blvd Marina Del Rey CA 90292-5442

BERGNER, LANNY MICHAEL, sculptor; b. Anacortes, Wash., Dec. 4, 1952; s. Paul Chris and Catherine Ann (Theisen) B.; m. Eve Deisher Loughran, May 22, 1994. BFA in Sculpture, U. Wash., 1981; MFA in Sculpture, Tyler Sch. Art, 1983. Sculpture asst. to Philip McCracken Guemes Island, Wash., 1976; sculpture fabricator Fabrication Specialties Inc., Seattle, 1978-81; exhbn. designer Nat. Mus. Am. Jewish History, Phila., 1983, Balch Inst. for Ethnic Studies, Phila., 1984-86; gallery coord. Fleisher Art Meml., Phila., 1986-94; instr. C.C. of Phila., 1993, 94; juror art competition Percent for Art, Phila., 1994; lectr. Md. Art Inst., Balt., 1991, Kutztown (Pa.) U., 1994, Skagit Valley Coll., Mt. Vernon, Wash., 1995. Prin. works include sculptures at Del. Art Mus., 1989, Phila. Internat. Airport, 1994, Seattle Water Dept., 1995, Seattle ARt Mus., 1996. Sgt. USAF, 1971-75. Visual arts fellow Pa. Coun. on Arts, 1987, 91; recipient scupture prize Contemporary Phila. Artists, 1990, Artist prize N.W. Internat. Art Competition, 1995, Betty Bowen Meml. award Seattle Art Mus., 1995. Mem. Artist Trust, Allied Arts of Whatcom County, Am. Craft Coun., Internat. Sculpture Ctr. Home and Studio: 498 Miller Rd Anacortes WA 98221

BERGQUIST, PETER (ED P. JR.), music educator emeritus; b. Sacramento, Aug. 5, 1930; s. Ed Peter and Margaret (Rogers) B.; m. Dorothy Catherine Clark, June 16, 1956; children: Carolyn, Emily (dec.). Student, Eastman Sch. Music, Rochester, N.Y., 1948-51; BS, Mannes Coll. Music, N.Y.C., 1958; MA, Columbia U., 1960, PhD, 1964. Asst. prof. Sch. Music, U. Oreg., Eugene, 1964-69, assoc. prof., 1969-73, prof., 1973-95, prof. emeritus, 1995—. Editor: Orlando di Lasso, The Complete Motets, 21 vols., 1995—, Orlando di Lasso, Samtliche Werke neue Reihe, vol. 22-25, 1992-93; contbr. articles to profl. jours. Sr. warden, jr. warden, vestryman St. Mary's Episcopal Ch., Eugene. With USAF, 1951-55. Recipient Ersted award for disting. teaching U. Oreg., 1973; Fulbright sr. rsch. awardee, 1985; Nat. Endowment for Humanities grantee, 1994-97; rsch. and travel awardee DAAD, ACLS. Mem. AAUP, Am. Musicol. Soc., Internat. Musicol. Soc., Soc. for Music Theory, Music Libr. Assn., Coll. Music Soc. Democrat. Home: 3195 Portland St Eugene OR 97405-5140 Office: Sch Music 1225 U Oreg Eugene OR 97403-1225

BERGREN, HELEN DUFFEY, retired nurse; b. Tacoma, Aug. 7, 1928; d. Joseph Clifford and Nancy Margaret (Johnson) Duffey; m. Bill G. Hollingsworth, Oct. 29, 1955 (dec. Sept. 1962), 1 child, Clint L.; m. Alfred C. Bergren, May 23, 1963. AA, Wenatchee (Wash.) Valley Coll., 1955. Supr. Ctrl. Wash. Deaconess Hosp., Wenatchee, 1955-56, Cascade Sanitarium, Leavenworth, Wash., 1957-60; 3-11 supr. Ctrl. Wash. Deconess Hosp., Wenatchee, 1961-66; pub. health nurse Chelan-Douglas Helath Dist., Wenatchee, 1966-75; staff nurse Cascade Gen. Hosp., Leavenworth, Wash., 1977-83, asst. dir. nursing, 1983-88, dir. nursing, 1988-90, ret., 1990; nurse Leavenworth Sch. Dist., 1966-72. Elizabeth Sterling Soule scholar, 1952; Pub. Health Dept. grantee, 1973-75. Mem. Ctrl. Wash. Deaconess Alumni Assn., Back Country Horsemen of Wash. and Am., Leavenworth Winter Sports Club, Phi Theta Kappa. Home: 7675 Icicle River Rd Leavenworth WA 98826

BERGRUN, NORMAN RILEY, aerospace executive; b. Green Camp, Ohio, Aug. 4, 1921; s. Theodore and Naomi Ruth (Stemm) B.; m. Claire Michaelson, May 23, 1943; children: Clark, Jay, Joan. BSME, Cornell U., 1943; LLB, LaSalle U. Ext., 1955; DSc, World U., 1983. Registered profl. mech. engr. Thermodynamicist Douglas Aircraft Co., El Segundo, Calif., 1943-44; rsch. scientist NACA Ames Rsch. Lab., Mt. View, Calif., 1944-56; mgr. analysis Lockheed Missile & Space Co., Sunnyvale, Calif., 1956-67, staff scientist, 1967-69; dir. mgmt. systems Nielsen Engring. and Rsch., Mt. View, 1969-71; CEO, scientist Bergrun Rsch. and Engring., Los Altos, Calif., 1971—; guest on radio and TV programs in the U.S., Can., Australia and Europe; spkr. L'Academie Europeene, 1987; Expo West lectr., 1996, CompuServe Conf. lectr. Author: Ringmakers of Saturn, 1986, Tomorrow's Technology Today, 1972, A Warming Trend for Icing Research, 1995; photographer including the Sir Francis Drake Collection, 1990; contbr. more than 80 articles and reports of profl. jours. Incorporator Aurora Singers Found., Palo Alto, Calif., 1989; co-founder NSPE Edn. Found., Sacramento, Calif., advisor to bd., 1985-92; mem. Steinman Coun., 1988—. Chief USN, 1944-46. Named Man of Yr., Am. Biog. Assn.; recipient Archimedes award, 1988, Cert. of Appreciation, Eglin AFB, 1961. Fellow AIAA (assoc., sr. judge 7th and 8th grade essay contest 1992, 93, 94, 95, 97, chair nat. pub.-policy comm. subcom. 1992—, regional dep. dir.-at-large 1995—, spl. svc. citation 1994, advisor Airline Safety Initiative 1997); mem. NSPE (life), Profl. Engrs. Soc. (Calif. pres. 1988-89, Integrity award 1989, Outstanding Exec. Performance award 1986, Disting. Contbns. award 1985-86, 86-87). Office: Bergrun Rsch and Engring 26865 Saint Francis Rd Los Altos CA 94022-1910

BERGSTEDT, ANDERS SPENCER, lawyer; b. Södertälje, Sweden, May 15, 1963; came to U.S., 1965; s. Jan-Eric Oskar and Vivianne (Sanfridsson) B. BA cum laude, U. Wash., 1985, JD, 1988. Bar: Wash. 1990, U.S. Dist. Ct. (we. dist.) Wash. 1990. Exec. dir. The Tenants Union, Seattle, 1988-90; mng. atty. Hyatt Legal Svcs., Seattle, 1990-92; pvt. practice Seattle, 1992—. Co-founder, treas. FTM Conf. and Edn. Project, Seattle, 1996—; mem. Vol. Attys. for People with AIDS, 1992—; bd. dirs. The Pride Found, 1993-95, Internat. Conf. Transgender Law & Employment Project, 1996—; co-chair Seattle Commn. Lesbians and Gays, 1989-91; mem. adv. bd. Office Crime Victim Advs., Olympia, Wash., 1989-92. Mem. Wash. State Bar Assn., Golden Key, Pi Sigma Alpha, Phi Beta Kappa. Office: 1211 Smith Tower 506 2nd Ave Seattle WA 98104

BERGSTROM, MARIANNE ELISABETH, program coordinator, special education educator; b. Sodertalje, Sweden, Aug. 18, 1941; came to U.S., 1967; d. Uno G. Bergstrom and Agnes (L.B.) Gustafsson. BA, Linkopings Tchrs. Coll., Sodertalje, 1964, Pacific Luth. U., 1973; MA, Pacific Luth. U., 1979; EdD, Seattle U., 1988; profl. mediation cert., U. Wash. Cert. tchr., prin., program adminstr., Wash.; cert. in profl. meditation skills tng. Tchr. spl. edn. Jarna and Botkyrka Sch. Dists., Sweden, 1964-67; tchr. spl. edn. Bellevue (Wash.) Sch. Dist., 1969-80, head tchr., 1980-91, program coord., 1991—; ednl. advisor Swedish Sch., Bellevue, 1991-92, pres. bd. dirs., 1993-94. Recipient Outstanding Guardian Ad Litem for abused and neglected children King County Superior Ct., Seattle, 1967-91, Outstanding Tchrs. in Exceptional Edn. award Acad. Therapy Publs., 1975. Mem. ASCD, Coun. for Exceptional Children. Lutheran. Office: Bellevue Sch Dist Bellevue WA 98009-9010

BERK, KAREN M., marketing and communications professional; b. Bklyn., Mar. 29, 1943; d. Harry and Minerva G. (Liptzin) Sternberg. BA, UCLA, 1964. Field office mgr. Employment Devel. Dept., Sacramento, 1970-73, asst. dep. dir., 1973-76, adminstr. evaluations div., 1976-84; v.p. Pvt. Industry Coun., L.A., 1984-88; dep. dir. mktg. svcs. Employment Devel. Dept., L.A., 1988-90; regional v.p. Jud. Arbitration & Mediation Svcs., Sacramento, 1990-91; exec. dir. March of Dimes, 1991-96; sr. v.p. Ruder-Finn, Inc., L.A., 1997—; ptnr. Ideas In Motion, Los Angeles, 1988-91; exec. dir. Mirch of Times of So. Calif., 1991-96; bd. dirs. Rykoff-Sexton Funding Inc., Evaluation and Tng. Contbr. to profl. publs. Mem. Orgn. Women Execs. (past pres.), Aerospace Human Resources Network. Home: 1842 Greenfield Ave Apt 302 Los Angeles CA 90025-4479

BERKE, IRVING, obstetrician-gynecologist, military officer; b. Bklyn., June 21, 1924; s. Abraham and Adela (Soffer) Berkowitz; m. Ruth E. Miller, Dec. 28, 1947 (dec. Feb. 1996); children: David, Laura, Nancy. Student, U. Wis., 1943; MD, Case Western Res. U., 1949. Cert. in obstetrics and gynecology; recert. Commd. 1st lt. U.S. Army, 1949, advanced through grades to col., 1972; ret., 1984; med. officer U.S. Army M.C., 1949-56; pvt. practice Youngstown, Ohio, 1956-63; med. officer USAR, Youngstown and L.A., 1956-84; pvt. practice Long Beach, Calif., 1963-83; physician Long Beach Dept. Health and Human Svcs., 1992—; med. advisor Calif. Blue Shield, L.A., 1967-73, Med. Bd. Calif., L.A., 1985-93; expert witness in ob-gyn., L.A., 1985—; asst. clin. prof. ob-gyn. Sch. Medicine, U. Calif., Irvine, 1977-83. Fellow ACOG, Internat. Coll. Surgeons; mem. Am. Acad. Anti Aging Medicine. Home and Office: 6430 Mantova St Long Beach CA 90815

BERKE, JUDIE, publisher, editor; b. Mpls., Apr. 15, 1938; d. Maurice M. and Sue (Supak) Kleyman; student U. Minn., 1956-60, Mpls. Sch. Art, 1945-59. Free lance illustrator and designer, 1959—; pres. Berke-Wood, Inc., N.Y.C., 1971-80, Manhattan Rainbow & Lollipop Co. subs. Berke-Wood, Inc., 1971-80; pres. Get Your Act Together, club act staging, N.Y.C., 1971-80; pres. Coordinator Pubs.,Inc., 1982-87; pres., chief exec. officer, Health Market Communications, 1987—; pres. Pub. and Media Services, Burbank, 1987—; pub., editor Continuing Care Coordinator, Health Watch mags.; pres. Continuing Care Coordinator Convs. and Seminars; pres. Rainbow and Lillipop Prodns., 1994—; cons. to film and ednl. cos.; guest lectr. various colls. and univs. in Calif. and N.Y., 1973—; cons., designer Healthy Lifestyles mag.; writer, illustrator, dir. numerous ednl. filmstrips, 1972—, latest being Focus on Professions, 1974, Focus on the Performing Arts, 1974, Focus on the Creative Arts, 1974, Workstyles, 1976, Wonderworm, 1976, Supernut, 1977; author, illustrator film Fat Black Mack (San Francisco Ednl. Film Festival award, part of permanent collection Mus. Modern Art, N.Y.C.), 1970; designer posters and brochures for various entertainment groups, 1963—; composer numerous songs, latest being Time is Relative, 1976, Love Will Live On in My Mind, 1976, My Blue Walk, 1976, You Make Me a Baby, 1982, Let's Go Around Once More, 1983, Anytime Anyplace Anywhere, 1987, Bittersweet, 1987, Sometimes It Pays, 1987, Gimme Back My Money Blues, Everybody Wants Me But the One I Love, Skin to Skin, It's Your Turn to Sing the Blues, Deny Till You Die, Men Just Call It Woman Talk, Poor Me, Women's Work is Never Done, 1993; composer/author off-Broadway musical Street Corner Time, 1978; producer: The Real Estate TV Shows 1988-89; contbr. children's short stories to various publs., also articles. Trustee The Happy Spot Sch., N.Y.C., 1972-75. Mem. Nat. Fedn. Bus. and Profl. Women, NAFE, Am. Acad. Polit. and Social Sci., Women in Animation.

BERKHOFER, ROBERT FREDERICK, JR., history educator; b. Teaneck, N.J., Nov. 20, 1931; s. Robert Frederick and Elsa Berkhofer; m. Genevieve Patricia Zito, June 9, 1962; 1 child, Robert Frederick III. BA, SUNY, Albany, 1953; MA, Cornell U., 1955, PhD, 1960. Instr. Ohio State U., Columbus, 1959-60; instr., asst. prof. U. Minn., Mpls., 1960-69; prof. U. Wis., Madison, 1969-73, U. Mich., Ann Arbor, 1973-91; grad. rsch. prof. U. Fla., Gainesville, 1984-85; prof. history U. Calif., Santa Cruz, 1991—. Author: Salvation and the Savage, 1965, A Behavioral Approach to Historical Analysis, 1969, The White Man's Indian, 1978, Beyond the Great Story, 1995. Recipient fellowships Social Sci. Rsch. Coun., 1957-59, Nat. Endowment for Humanities, 1973-74, John Simon Guggenheim Found., 1978-79, Stanford Humanities Ctr., 1987-88. Mem. Am. Studies Assn. (pres. 1980-82), Orgn. Am. Historians (exec. bd. 1981-84), Am. Hist. Assn. Office: U Calif Merrill Coll Santa Cruz CA 95064

BERKICH, JOHN, city manager; b. Johnstown, Pa., Jan. 21, 1948; s. Nicholas and Ann B.; m. Jamie Mae Jeffries, May 20, 1974 (div. Aug. 2, 1976); m. Angela Marie, June 11, 1978; children: Michael, Garret, Ryan. BA, Elmhurst Coll., 1971; MBA, Golden Gate U., 1986. Cert. mgmt.

acct. Cost acctg. supr. Western Elec. Co., Chgo., 1967-76; systems analyst supr. Wickes Corp., Wheeling, Ill., 1976-79; controller, data processing mgr. Frontier Enterprises, Carson City, Nev., 1979-83; audit divsn. mgr. Pub. Svc. Commn., Carson City, Nev., 1983-90; city mgr. City of Carson City, 1990—; cons. in field; coll. instr. Western Nev. C.C., Carson City, 1987-90. Recipient Disting. Svc. award No. Nev. Devel. Authority, 1992, Appreciation award U. Nev. Coop. Ext., 1993, Feed the Hungry award Friends in Svc. Helping, 1993. Mem. Internat. City Mgrs. Assn., Nat. Acctg. Assn., Am. Acctg. Assn., Inst. Mgmt. Accts., Rotary Club (Carson City). Republican. Methodist. Office: City of Carson City 2621 Northgate Ln Ste 2 Carson City NV 89706-1619

BERKLAND, JAMES OMER, geologist; b. Glendale, Calif., July 31, 1930; s. Joseph Omer and Gertrude Madelyn (Thompson) B. m. Janice Lark Keirstead, Dec. 19, 1966; children: Krista Lynn, Jay Olin. AA, Santa Rosa Jr. Coll., 1951; AB, U. Calif., Berkeley, 1958; MS, San Jose State U., 1964; postgrad., U. Calif., Davis, 1969-72. Registered geologist, Calif.; cert. engrng. geologist, Calif. With U.S. Geol. Survey, 1958-64; engrng. geologist U.S. Bur. Reclamation, 1964-69, cons. geologist, 1969-72; asst. prof. Appalachian State U., Boone, N.C., 1972-73; county geologist Santa Clara County, San Jose, Calif., 1973-94; ret., 1994; mem. geotech. adv. com. San Jose; adj. prof. San Jose State U., 1973-75, lectr. Gen. Edn. Conf., Sci. and Tech. Soc., 1985-89, coord. com. Calif. Conv., 1978; mem. evening faculty San Jose City Coll.; mem. West Valley Legis. Com., 1979-90; lectr. ann. deposit receipt seminar San Jose Real Estate Bd., 1980-85; discoverer in field; featured spkr. Keynote Speakers, Inc.; role model San Jose Sch. Dist., 1995-97. Contbr. numerous articles to profl. jours.; originator seismic window theory for earthquake prediction, 1974; numerous TV and radio appearances including PBA, Frontline, Evening Mag., People are Talking, 48 Hours, Sightings, You Bet Your Life, Science Faction, Science Fiction Cable, Two on the Town, CNN News, WGN, KIRO, KSL, KIEV, KGO, KCBS, KNYV, KOA, KOGO, KVEN, KSCO, Two at Noon, weekly interview show on Sta. KPFA-FM Radio, The Other Side, Northwest Afternoon, Art Bell's Coast to Coast, Town Meeting, Ron Owens Show, Laura Lee Show, Art Bell Show, Kathi Gori Show, Extra, Strange Universe; articles on work featured in OMNI, STERN, Wall St. Jour., Bergen's Tidende, San Francisco Examiner, San Francisco Chronicle, L.A. Times, Nat. Geog., Am. Health, The Astrology Ency., Old Farmers Almanac, 1991, Gilroy Dispatch, Bakersfield Californian, San Jose Mercury News, Sonoma Index Tribune, Intuition, Farmers Almanac, others; editor, pub. newsletter SYZYGY-An Earthquake Newsletter, 1990—; co-founder Quakeline. Treas. Creekside/Park Place Homeowners Group; v.p. West Coast Aquatics, Creekside/Park Place Swim Team; mem. various city and county adv. bds.; mem. Ctr. for Study Early Man, East Valley YMCA, legis. com. West Valley, 1980—, Route 85 Task Force, Earthquake Watch, 1979-82, New Weather Observer, Nat. Wildlife Fedn.; mem. Found. for the Study of Cycles, invited lectr. monthly and ann. meeting; active Statue of Liberty Found; mem. tech. and soc. San Jose Sch. Dist., 1980—, mem. role model program, 1996-97; mem. Sonoma Land Trust; active The Nature Conservancy, Nat. Wildlife Fed.; charter mem. The Dolphin Inst. Recipient Resolution of Commendation Santa Clara Bd. Suprs., 1994. Mem. Smithsonian Inst. (assoc.), Ret. Pub. Employee Assn. Calif., Alumni Assn. San Jose State U. Democrat. Home: 14927 E Hills Dr San Jose CA 95127-2536

BERKLEY, ROBERT JOHN, federal agency professional; b. Albion, Mich., Oct. 2, 1933; s. Paul Clifford and Ina Muriel (Burroughs) B.; m. Sharon Irene Haynes, Sept. 9, 1955 (div. 1965); children: Thomas Alan, Richard Jon, Luann Michele; m. Jacquelyn Jane (Lewis) Ballou, Jan. 14, 1966. AA, Jackson (Mich.) Jr. Coll., 1953; BS in Police Adminstrn., Calif. State U., L.A., 1962. Police officer City of Claremont, Calif., 1959-62, 63-66; investigator U.S. Civil Svc. Commn., Washington and L.A., 1962-63, 66-72; spl. agt. FAA, Seattle, 1972—, office mgr., 1973—. Local chmn. Selective Svc. Bd., Wash., 1981—. Sgt. USMC, 1953-56, Korea. Mem. SAR (chpt. pres. 1989-90, state sec. 1989-91, state pres. 1992, Patriots medal 1990, Law Enforcement medal 1991, 92), Am. Legion, Eastern Star (patron 1989-90), Masons (master 1984, life), Scottish Rite, Shriners. Home: 4403 192d Pl SE Issaquah WA 98027-9708 Office: FAA SEA-CASFO 1601 Lind Ave SW Rm 230 Renton WA 98055-4056

BERKLEY, STEPHEN MARK, computer peripherals manufacturing company executive; b. N.J., 1944; s. Irving S. and Goldie A. Berkley; student London Sch. Econs., 1964-65; BA in Econs., Colgate U., 1966; MBA, Harvard U., 1968; children: David, Michael.Mgmt. cons. Boston Cons. Group, 1968, 71-73; mgr. strategic planning Potlatch Corp., 1973-77; v.p. bus. devel. Qume Corp. subs. ITT, Hayward, Calif., 1977-80, v.p., gen. mgr. memory products div., 1980-81; v.p. mktg. Quantum Corp., Milpitas, Calif., 1981-83, chmn., CEO, 1987-92, chmn., 1992-93, 95—; chmn., CEO Coactive Computing Corp., 1993-94; pres. Plus Devel. Corp. (Quantum subs.), 1983-87, chmn., CEO, 1987-92; pres., The Rosewood Found.; bd. dirs. Quantum Corp., Edify Corp., Coactive Computing Corp.; instr. bus. and econs. E. Carolina U., 1969-71. Served to lt. USNR, 1968-71. Mem. Corp. Planners Assn. (dir.), Harvard Bus. Sch. Club No. Calif., Phi Beta Kappa. Office: Quantum Corp 500 Mccarthy Blvd Milpitas CA 95035-7908

BERKMAN, JAMES L., bicycle builder, publisher; b. Cleve., Jan. 12, 1952; m. Renee Eileen Lee, Oct. 15, 1994. BA in Philosophy, Youngstown State U., 1974; MA in Philosophy, Kent State U., 1975. Cert. bicycle mechanic, United Bicycle Inst. Instr. philosophy Lewis-Clark State Coll., Lewiston, Idaho, 1976-79; bicycle builder Ashland, Oreg., 1989—; owner Jim Berkman's Bikx, Ashland, 1989—; owner, pub. Runaway Publs., Ashland, 1977—. Author, editor poetry. Mem. Am. Philos. Assn., Christian Motorcyclists Assn. Republican. Office: Runaway Publs PO Box 1172 Ashland OR 97520

BERKUS, DAVID WILLIAM, venture capitalist; b. Los Angeles, Mar. 23, 1941; s. Harry Jay and Clara S. (Widess) B.; m. Kathleen McGuire, Aug. 6, 1966; children: Eric, Matthew, Amy. BA, Occidental Coll., 1962. Pres. Custom Fidelity Inc., Hollywood, Calif., 1958-74, Berkus Compusystems Inc., Los Angeles, 1974-81; pres., chief exec. officer Computerized Lodging Systems Inc. and subs., Los Angeles, 1981-93; pres. Berkus Tech. Ventures, venture capital, L.A., 1993—. Author: Better Than Money, 1994; author software Hotel Compusystem, 1979; creator 1st artificial intelligence-based yield mgmt. sys., 1987. Chmn. bd. Boy Scouts Am., San Gabriel Valley, 1986, v.p. area IV, 1993-94, pres. 1995—; trustee Occidental Coll., L.A. Lt. USNR, 1963-72. Recipient Dist. award of merit Boy Scouts Am., 1986, INC. mag. 500 award, 1986, Silver Beaver award Boy Scouts Am., 1988. Mem. Am. Hotel-Motel Assn., Audio Engring. Soc. (chmn. Los Angeles sect. 1973-74). Office: 1430 Glencoe Dr Arcadia CA 91006-1909

BERLAK, HAROLD, writer, educator, consultant; b. Cambridge, Mass., July 31, 1932; s. William and Dora Berlak; m. Ann Carol Abramson, Sept. 23, 1962; children: Mariam, Rachel, Lev. BA, Boston U., 1954; AMT, Harvard U., 1956, EdD, 1963. Cert. secondary tchr., Mass. Tchr. social studies Wenham (Mass.) Schs., 1957-59; tchr. social studies Concord (Mass.) Pub. Schs., 1959-63, supr., 1962-63; asst. prof. U. Calif., Santa Barbara, 1963-64; prof. Wash. U., St. Louis, Mo., 1964-92; freelance writer, consultant Oakland, Calif., 1992-94; co-dir. Wash. U. Social Studies project, St. Louis, 1965-74; dir. Met. St. Louis Social Studies Ctr., St. Louis, 1965-75. Author: People, Choices, Decisions, 1978, Dilemmas of Schooling, 1982; author, editor: Democracy, Pluralism, and Social Studies, 1968, Toward New Science of Educational Testing and Measurement, 1992; bd. editors Havard Edn. Rev., 1961-62. Organizer, sec. Dem. Schs. Network, 1982-86. With U.S. Army, 1954-56. Home and Office: 1127 Wellington St Oakland CA 94602-1342

BERMAN, DANIEL K(ATZEL), educational consultant, university official; b. Detroit, Nov. 17, 1954; s. Louis Arthur and Irene (Katzel) B. BS, Northwestern U., 1976, MS, 1977; AM, Harvard U., 1983; MA, U. Calif., Berkeley, 1984, PhD, 1991; cert. study, U. Paris, 1973, Peking (China) Normal U., 1981, Nat. Taiwan U., 1982. Subscription mgr. The N.Y. Times, 1983-84; editorial and rsch. asst. Inst. for Contemporary Studies, San Francisco, 1984-85; lang. cons. Berlitz Translation Svcs., San Francisco, 1986-89; v.p. Golden Gate Investment, San Francisco, 1985-87; lectr. St. Mary's Coll., Moraga, Calif., 1987; instr. U. Calif., Berkeley, 1984-90; chief exec. officer Pacific Fin. Svcs., San Francisco, 1987-92; editor Credit Report Newsletter for Consumer Edn., San Francisco, 1989-92; sales and mktg. cons. The Deerwood Corp./MRI, San Ramon, Calif., 1989-91; lectr. dept. mass comm. Calif. State U., Hayward, 1993—; founder/dir. Acad. Cons. Internat., San Francisco, 1993—; assoc. provost Summit U. La., New Orleans, 1995—. Author: The Hottest Summer in Peking, 1982, The Credit Power Handbook for American Consumers, 1988, 89, Words Like Colored Glass: The Role of the Press in Taiwan's Democratization Process, 1992; editor, translator: The Butterfly's Revenge and Other Chinese Mystery Stories. Edn. scholar Rep. of China Ministry of Edn., 1979-82; rsch. grantee Pacific Cultural Found., 1981; fgn. lang. and area studies fellow in Chinese U. Calif., 1983-84. Fellow John F. Kennedy Libr. Found.; mem. The Harvard Club of San Francisco, Soc. of Profl. Journalists, Acad. of Polit. Sci., Nat. Ctr. for Fin. Edn. (profl. sponsor), Kappa Tau Alpha (grantee). Jewish. Office: Acad Cons Internat PO Box 4489 Foster City CA 94404-0489

BERMAN, GEOFFREY LOUIS, credit manager; b. L.A., July 15, 1953; s. Geoffrey M. and Patricia A. (Meyer) B.; m. Autumn Joy Patton, Mar. 26, 1983; children: Arielle Louise, Michelle Elise. BA/BS in Bus. Adminstrn., U. of the Pacific, 1975; JD, Southwestern U., 1985. Loan officer Union Bank, L.A., 1975-80; adminstrv. asst. Credit Mgrs. Assn., L.A., 1980-82; loan officer Mitsui Mfrs. Bank, L.A., 1982-86; asst. sec., mgr. adjustment bur. Credit Mgrs. Assn., Burbank, Calif., 1986—; dir. Comml. Fin. Conf. Calif., L.A., 1978-80; co-chair insolvency laws com. Am. Bankruptcy Inst., Alexandria, Va., 1994—; mem. panel of mediators Ctrl. Dist. Bankruptcy Ct., L.A., 1996—. Co-author: (manual) ABI Creditor's Com. Manual, 1995; contbr. articles to profl. jours. Task force mem. City of Buena Park (Calif.) Investment Policy Rev. Com., 1995. Recipient Recognition award Fed. Bar Assn., L.A., 1986. Mem. L.A. Bankruptcy Forum, Bay Area Bankruptcy Forum, Orange County Bankruptcy Forum. Office: Credit Mgrs Assn Calif 40 E Verdugo Ave Burbank CA 91502

BERMAN, HOWARD LAWRENCE, congressman; b. L.A., Apr. 15, 1941; s. Joseph M. and Eleanor (Schapiro) B.; m. Janis Berman, 1979; children: Brinley Ann, Lindsey Rose. BA, UCLA, 1962, LLB, 1965. Bar: Calif. 1966. Vol. VISTA, Balt., San Francisco, 1966-67; assoc. Levy, Van Bourg & Hackler, L.A., 1967-72; mem. Calif. State Assembly from 43d dist., 1972-82 (majority leader); with 98th-104th Congresses from 26th Calif. dist.; freshman rep. steering and policy com., 1983, mem. jud. com., internat. law, immigration and refugees, intellectual property and jud. adminstrn., mem. internat. rels. com., ranking mem. Asia and Pacific, internat. ops., ranking mem. com. on stds. of ofcl. conduct. Pres. Calif. Fedn. Young Democrats, 1967-69 (budget com.); mem. adv. bd. Jewish Fund for Justice, Valley Internat. Trade Assn. Office: US Ho of Reps Rm 2330 Rayburn House Office Bldg Washington DC 20515

BERMAN, JEROME, museum director, curator. Dir., curator Calif. Mus. Ancient Art, Beverly Hills, 1983—. Office: Calif Mus Ancient Art PO Box 10515 Beverly Hills CA 90213

BERMAN, MORRIS, historian, author; b. Rochester, N.Y., Aug. 3, 1944; s. Harry and Libbie Berman. BA, Cornell U., 1966; PhD, Johns Hopkins U., 1971. Asst. prof. Rutgers U., New Brunswick, N.J., 1970-75, Concordia U., Montreal, Que., 1980-82; Lansdowne professorship U. Victoria, B.C., 1982-88; free-lance writer, 1988—; vis. prof. Seattle U., 1990, Evergreen State Coll., Olympia, Wash., 1991, U. Kassel, Germany, 1991-92; Amy Freeman Lee chair in humanities Incarnate Word Coll., San Antonio, 1993, Garrey Carruthers chair in honors U. N.Mex., 1994-95, Eccles chair in honors Weber State U., Ogden, Utah, 1997. Author: Social Change and Scientific Organization, 1978, The Reenchantment of the World, 1981, Coming to Our Senses, 1989. Recipient Gov.'s Writers award Wash. State, Olympia, 1990, Rolla May Ctr. grant Rollo May Ctr., San Francisco, 1992. Mem. Am. Hist. Assn. Democrat. Jewish. Home: 8015 Greenwood Ave N Apt 305 Seattle WA 98103-4241

BERMAN, MYLES LEE, lawyer; b. Chgo., July 11, 1954; s. Jordan and Eunice (Berg) B.; m. Mitra Moghimi, Dec. 19, 1981; children: Elizabeth, Calvin, Justin. BA, U. Ill., 1976; JD, Chgo.- Kent Coll. of Law, 1979. Bar: Ill. 1980, Calif. 1987, U.S. Dist. Ct. (no. dist.) Ill. 1980, U.S. Dist. Ct. (cen. dist.) Calif. 1988, U.S. Supreme Ct. 1992. Asst. state's atty. Cook County State's Atty.'s Office, Chgo., 1980-82; pvt. practice law offices of Myles L. Berman, Chgo., 1982-91, L.A., 1988—; traffic ct. judge pro tem Beverly Hills Mcpl. Ct., 1990—, Culver Mcpl. Ct., 1992—, traffic ct. judge pro tem adminstr., 1991—; probation monitor State Bar of Calif., 1992—. Editor: Century City Lawyer, 1992—. Mem. ABA, Santa Monica Bar Assn., Los Angeles County Bar Assn., Calif. Attys. for Criminal Justice, Nat. Assn. Criminal Def. Lawyers, Beverly Hills Bar Assn., Century City Bar Assn. (chmn. criminal law sect. 1989—, bd. govs. 1991—, Outstanding Svc. award 1990, 92, 93, 94, Spl. Recognition 1994, treas. 1994, sec. 1995, v.p. 1996, pres.-elect 1997), Criminal Cts. Bar Assn., Orange County Bar Assn., South Orange County Bar Assn., Cyberspace Bar Assn., Calif. Deuce Defenders. Office: 9255 Sunset Blvd Ste 720 Los Angeles CA 90069-3304 also: 4630 Campus Dr Ste 200 Newport Beach CA 92660-1805 also: 100 E Thousand Oaks Blvd Ste 259 Thousand Oaks CA 91360-5713

BERMAN, SANFORD SOLOMON, motion picture sound designer, composer, arranger, artist; b. Long Branch, N.J., Nov. 14, 1951; s. Jerome Sidney and Marion (Solomon) B. BFA, Phila. Coll. Art, 1974. Freelance sound designer, record prodr./arranger, musician/composer. Sound designer, supr. (features) The Flood, Kilronan, Multiplicity, Jade, Virtuosity, Wings of Courage, Bad Girls, Tombstone, Striking Distance Aladdin (Golden Reel winner, FX Editl., Oscar nomination), Love Field, Unlawful Entry, J.F.K. (FX Editl., Brit. Acad. award, Golden Reel nominee), Hot Shots!, Back to the Future (The Ride), Revenge (Golden Reel nominee), Immediate Family, Oliver & Company (Golden Reel winner), The Princess Bride (Golden Reel nominee), The Seventh Sign (Golden Reel nominee), da, Big Bad John, Going Under Cover, Mac & Me, Weeds, Jaws III, Cloak & Dagger, The Stone Boy, Wolfen, Strange Invaders, That Championship Season, The Sword & The Sorcerer, History of the World Part I, Miss Lonelyhearts, Ten to Midnight, The House on Sorority Row, Evilspeak, Q, Summerspell, Suburbia, Roar, Sweet Sixteen, The Fatal Game, Radioactive Dreams, The Glory of Khan, (short subjects) A Hard Rain, Ballet Robotique (Oscar nomination), The Wizard of Change, The Quest, A Trip to Tomorrow, Bird & The Robot, The Water Engine, Lean Machine, Wind Tunnel, Environmental Effects, New Magic, The Collector, Niagara, Lets Go!, Tour of the Universe, Runaway Train, Zargon, Deep Water Rescue, Rollercoaster, Monte Carlo Race, Alpine Highway, Toyota, Chevrolet, Jet Helicopter, Call from Space; keyboardist for James Brown "Static", 1996; creator comic effects Eat It (Grammy nomination), Like a Surgeon (Grammy nomination), New Duck (Grammy nomination); prodr., arranger, keyboardist Secret Smiles; composer (feature film scores) Screamers, Cataclysm, (commls.) Toyota, 1986, Celica, 1986; appeared with Bruce Springsteen, Steel, Hall & Oates, Chuck Berry, Dwayne Eddy, Jr. Walker & The All-Stars, James Brown, others. Mem. ACLU, So. Calif., 1985—, People for the Am. Way, So. Calif., 1985—, Am. Jewish Congress, 1982—. Recipient Brit. Acad. award Brit. Acad. of Film and TV Arts, Gt. Britain, 1992. Mem. Motion Picture Sound Editors (pres. 1992—, Golden Reel award 1988, 92), Acad. of Motion Picture Arts and Scis., Nat. Acad. Recording Arts and Scis., Am. Soc. Music Arrangers and Composers, Motion Picture Editors Guild. Democrat.

BERMAN, SAUL JAY, strategic consultant; b. Phila., Jan. 1, 1946; s. Sherwood and Leona (Habelson) B.; m. S. Jann Gillen, June 6, 1980; 1 child, Ashley Scott. BS in Econs., U. Pa., 1967; MBA, Columbia U., 1969, PhD, 1973. Asst. prof. U. So. Calif., L.A., 1972-77; divisional v.p. Broadway Dept. Stores, L.A., 1977-82; case leader Boston Consulting Group, L.A., 1982-86; mng. ptnr. Price Waterhouse Strategic Change Group, 1986—; active Internat. Planning Forum, 1986—. Bd. dirs. Love is Feeding Everyone, L.A., 1988-89; mem. L.A. County Beach Commn., 1978-80, Planning Forum, L.A., 1987—, Town Hall, L.A., 1987-94. Mem. U. Pa. Alumni Club (bd. dirs. 1986-88, So. Calif. assoc. alumni trustee 1990—), Columbia Bus. Sch. Club of So. Calif. (bd. dirs. 1992-95). Office: Price Waterhouse 1880 Century Park E Los Angeles CA 90067-1600

BERMINGHAM, PETER, museum director; b. Buffalo, Nov. ; s. Donald Michael and Margaret Anne (Murphy) B.; m. Eleanor Joan Sigborn, Sept. 5, 1964; children: Christopher, Jason, Alexander, Noelle, Nicholas. B.A., U. Md., 1964, M.A., 1968; Ph.D. (Smithsonian Instn. fellow 1971-72), U. Mich., 1972. Teaching asst. U Mich., 1968-71; vis. prof. art history U. Cin., 1972-73; curator edn. Nat. Collection Fine Arts, Smithsonian Instn., 1973-78; dir., chief curator U. Ariz. Mus. Art, Tucson, 1978—; mem. mus. policy panel Nat. Endowment Arts. Author exhbn. catalogues. Served with USAF, 1956-60. Mus. tng. fellow Nat. Endowment Humanities, 1967-68. Mem. Western Assn. Art Museums, Coll. Art Assn. Roman Catholic. Home: 3585 E Thimble Peak Pl Tucson AZ 85718-2230 Office: U Ariz Mus Art Park And Speedway Tucson AZ 85718

BERN, HOWARD ALAN, science educator, research biologist; b. Montreal, Que., Can., Jan. 30, 1920; m. Estelle Bruck, 1946; children: Alan, Lauren. BA, UCLA, 1941, MA, 1942, PhD in Zoology, 1948; D (hon.), U. Rouen, France, 1996; LLD (hon.), U. Hokkaido, Japan, 1996. Nat. Rsch. Coun. predoctoral fellow in biology UCLA, 1946-68; instr. in zoology U. Calif., Berkeley, 1948-50, asst. prof., 1950-56, assoc. prof., 1956-60, prof., 1960-89, prof. integrative biology, 1989-90, prof. emeritus, 1990—; rsch. endocrinologist Cancer Rsch. Lab., U. Calif., Berkeley, 1960—; chair group in endocrinology U. Calif., Berkeley, 1962-90, faculty rsch. lectr., 1988; rsch. prof. Miller Inst. for Basic Rsch. in Sci., 1961; vis. prof. pharmacology U. Bristol, 1965-66, U. Kerala, India, 1967, Ocean Rsch. Inst., U. Tokyo, 1971, 86, U. P.R., 1973, 74, U. Tel Aviv, 1975, Nat. Mus. Natural History, Paris, 1981, Toho U., Funabashi, Japan, 1982-84, 86-89, U. Hawaii, 1986, 91-93, Hokkaido U., 1992, 94, U. Fla., 1991, 92; James vis. prof. St. Francis Xavier U., Antigonish, N.S., 1986; Walker-Ames prof. U. Wash., 1977; disting. visitor U. Alta., Edmonton, Can., 1981; John W. Cowper Disting. vis. lectr. SUNY-Buffalo, 1984; Watkins vis. prof. Wichita (Kans.) State U., 1984; vis. scholar Meiji U., Tokyo, 1986; internat. guest prof. Yokohama City U., Japan, 1988, 95; lectr., spkr. in field; mem. adv. com. on instl. rsch. grants Am. Cancer Soc., 1967-70; mem. adv. com. Nat. Cancer Inst., 1975-79; mem. NIH adv. com. in Endocrinology and Metabolism, 1978-79; mem. GM Cancer Rsch. Found., Sloan Medal Selection Com., 1984-85, Japan Internat. Prize in Biology Selection Com., 1987, 92, 96. Mem. editl. bd. Endocrinology, 1962-74, Gen. and Comparative Endocrinology, Jour. Exptl. Zoology, 1965-69, 86-89, Internat. Rev. Cytology, Neuroendocrinology, 1974-80, Cancer Rsch., 1975-78, Jour. Comparative Physiology B, 1977-84, Am. Zoologist, 1978-83, Acta Zoologica, 1982-96, Zool. Sci., Tokyo, Animal Biol., Italy; contbr. articles to profl. publs. Assoc. Nat. Mus. Natural History, Paris, 1980; mem. adv. com. Contra Costa Cancer Rsch. Fund, 1984—, Stazione Zoologica Anton Dohrn de Napoli, 1987-92. Recipient Disting. Tchg. award U. Calif., Berkeley, 1979, The Berkeley Citation, 1990, Disting. Svc. award Soc. Adv. Chicanos and Native Americans in Sci., 1990; Guggenheim fellow, 1951-52, NSF fellow U. Hawaii, 1958-59, fellow Ctr. for Advanced Study in Behavioral Scis., Stanford U., 1960, NSF fellow Stazione Zoologica, Naples, 1965-66, Japan Soc. Promotion of Sci. Rsch. fellow U. Toyama, Japan, 1993. Fellow NAS, AAAS, Am. Acad. Arts and Scis., Indian Nat. Sci. Acad. (fgn.), Società Nazionale di Scienze Lettere e Arti Napoli (fgn.), Calif. Acad. Sci., Accademia Nazionale dei Lincei (fgn.); mem. Soc. Integrative Comparative Biology (hon., pres. 1967), Am. Assn. Cancer Rsch., Am. Physiol. Soc., Endocrine Soc., Internat. Soc. Neuroendocrinology (coun. 1977-80), Exptl. Biology and Medicine (coun. 1980-83), Am. Soc. Molec. Marine Biol. Biotech., Western Soc. Naturalists, Japan Soc. Zootech. Sci. (hon.), Japan Soc. Comparative Endocrinology (hon.), Cosmos Club. Home: 1010 Shattuck Ave Berkeley CA 94707-2626 Office: U Calif Dept Integrative Biology Berkeley CA 94720-3140

BERNABE, GRETTA MARIE DOMINGO, company officer; b. Manila, Oct. 23, 1965; came to U.S., 1991; d. Emmanuel Ilagan and Editha Domingo Bernabe. BS in Acctg., De La Salle U., Manila, 1987. Jr. acct. Far East Bank, Manila, 1988; staff auditor II Sycip, Gorres Velayo & Co., Makati, The Philippines, 1988-91; corp. sec./treas. Pleasant Care Corp., La Canada, Calif., 1991—. Mem. Philippine Inst. CPAs. Home: 751 Orchard Loop Azusa CA 91702 Office: Pleasant Care Corp 2258 Foothill Blvd La Canada CA 91011-1457

BERNARD, ALEXANDER, airport police official; b. L.A., Apr. 23, 1952; s. Louis and Hannah (Bergman) B.; m. Diana LoRee Winstead, Dec. 17, 1976; children: Michael Alexander, Andrew Alexander. AA magna cum laude, Los Angeles Valley Coll., 1976; BS summa cum laude, Calif. State U., L.A., 1989. Parking meter collector L.A. City Clk.'s Office, 1973-79; police officer L.A. Airport, 1979-95; sgt. Police Svcs. Divsn. L.A. Airport, Ontario, Calif., 1995—. Contbr. articles to profl. jours. Active Boy Scouts Am. Mem. NRA (life), Internat. Police Assn. (life), Indsl. Rels. Rsch. Assn., Calif. Peace Officers Assn., Peace Officers Rsch. Assn. Calif. (chpt. pres. 1982-84, 85-87, state bd. dirs. 1984-85, 88—, ethnic rels. com. 1993-94, exec. com. 1994—), L.A. Airport Peace Officers Assn. (pres. 1981-89, 94-95, bd. dirs. 1992-94), Airport Supervisory Police Officers' Assn. L.A. (bd. dirs. 1996, v.p. 1997—), Fraternal Order of Police, Calif. Rifle and Pistol Assn. (life), Golden Key (life), Phi Kappa Phi (life). Democrat. Mem. Assemblies of God Ch. Office: Ontario Internat Airport Police Svcs Divsn 1070 S Vineyard Ave Ontario CA 91761-8007

BERNARD, RICHARD MONTGOMERY, physician; b. Long Beach, Calif., Feb. 21, 1925; s. Francis M. and Irma V. (Phillips) B.; m. Virginia Marie Thompson, Sept. 19, 1946 (div. Mar. 1971); children: Richard Jr., David, Mary, Danielle; m. Nancy Johnston, Nov. 18, 1971; children: Vivienne Kouba, N. Catherine Thompson. BS in Chemistry, U. Calif. Berkeley, 1945; MD, U. Chgo., 1950. Charter Diplomate Am. Bd. Family Practice. Assoc. physician Dr. G. Alan Fisher, Gresham, Oreg., 1953-54; pvt. practice Westslope, Portland, Oreg., 1954-60, Beaverton, Oreg., 1960-86; assoc. with Dr. D. Graham R.M. Bernard, MD P.C., Beaverton, 1986-90; family practitioner St. Vincent Tanesbourne Med. Plz., Beaverton, 1990-91; locum tenens Oreg., 1991-92; family practitioner Providence Health Sys., Wilsonville, Oreg., 1992—; clin. prof. Med. Family Practioneror. dept., 1997—; clin. prof. medicine, family practice dept., Oreg. Health Sci. U., Portland, 1994—. Commr. Wilsonville Long Range Planning Commn. Capt. USNR, WWII, 1942-46, Korea, 1950-53, ret., 1985. Recipient Meritorious Achievement award Oreg. Health Science U., 1988. Mem. Wilsonville Rotary, Wilsonville C. of C. Republican. Home: 31530 SW Village Green Ct Wilsonville OR 97070-8426 Office: Providence Health Sys Ste E 29890 SW Town Center Loop W Wilsonville OR 97070-9494

BERNARD, THELMA RENE, property management professional; b. Phila.; d. Michael John and Louise Thelma (Hoffman) Campione; m. Gene Bernard (div.). Sec. Penn. Mut. Life Ins. Co., Phila., Suffolk Franklin Savs. Bank, Boston, Holmes and Narver, Inc., Las Vegas; constrn. site office mgr. Miles R. Nay, Inc., Las Vegas; adminstrv. asst to pres. N.W.S. Constrn. Corp., Inc., Las Vegas, 1982-86, corp. sec., 1982-86; gen. mgr., corp. sec. D.A.P., Inc. property mgmt. com, Las Vegas, pres., 1991—. Author: Blue Marsh, 1972, Winds of Wakefield, 1972, Moonshadow Mansion, 1973, 2d edit., 1976, Spanish transl., 1974, German transl., 1977; contbr. articles to Doll Reader, Internat. Doll World, other mags.; past editor Cactus Courier; editor, pub. The Hoyer Enthusiastic Ladies Mail Assn., 1980-90, 96—; Friendly Tymes, 1991—, Lady Charleen, 1995—; writer song lyrics. Mem. Nat. League Am. Pen Women (v.p. Red Rock Canyon br. 1986-88), Original Paper Doll Artists Guild, Heritage Rose Soc., Bookmark Collector Club, Seed Savers Exch. Office: PO Box 14002 Las Vegas NV 89114-4002

BERNASCONI, RICHARD, mayor; b. Modesto, Calif., Feb. 2, 1948; m. Joanne Bernasconi, 1973; children: Jennifer, Kevin. AABA, Modesto Jr. Coll., 1969; BS in Recreation, Calif. State U., 1973. Cert. tchr., Calif. Warehouse worker Tri Valley Cannery and Calpine Boxing Co., Modesto, 1966-67; from recreation leader to program supr. City of Modesto, 1966-73; recreation supr. recreation and parks dept. City of Merced, Calif., 1973-89; tchr. Merced Union H.S. Dist., 1990—; mayor City of Merced, 1993—; teen mentor advisor, student svc. advisor Merced Union H.S. Dist., 1995—. chmn. Castle Joint Powers Authority, 1996—, vice-chmn. 1995-96; active Merced City Coun., 1989-91; vol. Merced Girls Softball Assn., 1990-92, Octoberfest-Merced United Way, 1989-91, Merced Triathlon, 1989-91, Merced Youth Soccer Bd., 1988-90; commr. Jr. Baseball, Merced, 1973-80, Merced Youth Soccer Assn., 1974-76; coach Jr. Football, Merced, 1973-76, Little League, Modesto, 1968; purchasing agt. Little Guys Baseball, Merced, 1975. Mem. Amateur Softball Assn. (dep. commr.), Calif. Football Officials Assn. (bd. dirs.), Italo-Am. Lodge (pres. 1984, bd. dirs. 1986-91), Alpha Gamma Rho (intramural chmn.). Home: 2887 Santa Cruz Merced CA 95340 Office: City of Merced 678 W 18th St Merced CA 95340

BERNDT, NORBERT, biochemist; b. Dusseldorf, Germany, Dec. 22, 1953; came to U.S., 1989; s. Franz and Irma (Rockstroh) B.; m. Ingrid Bahner, Nov. 24, 1989. MS, Heinrich Heine U., Düsseldorf, 1982; PhD, Heinrich Heine U., Dusseldorf, 1986. Postdoctoral rsch. asst. U. Dundee, Scotland, 1986-89; asst. prof. U. So. Calif., L.A., 1990—; cons. Upstate Biotechnology, Inc., Lake Placid, N.Y., 1993—. Contbr. articles to profl. jours. Rsch. grantee Tobacco-Related Disease Rsch. Program, Berkeley, Calif., 1993, NIH, Bethesda, 1993. Mem. AAAS, Am. Soc. Cell Biology. Office: Childrens Hosp LA 4650 W Sunset Blvd Los Angeles CA 90027-6062

BERNE, STANLEY, author; b. Staten Island, N.Y., June 8, 1923; s. William and Irene (Daniels) B.; m. Arlene Zekowski, May 17, 1952. BS, Rutgers U., 1951; MA, N.Y.U., 1952; postgrad. fellow, La. State U., 1954-59. Cert. tchr. of mentally retarded, N.Y. Tchg. fellow La. State U., Baton Rouge, La., 1954-59; assoc. prof. English Ea. N. Mex. U., Portales, 1960-80, rsch. assoc. prof. in English, 1980—; chmn. of the bd. Am.-Canadian Publishers, Inc., Santa Fe, N. Mex., 1980-97; bd. dirs. New Arts Found., Inc., Santa Fe, N. Mex., 1990—; guest lectr. U. Ams., 1965, U. S.D., 1968, Styrian Hauptshulen Paedagogische Akademie, Graz, Austria, 1969. Author: A First Book of the Neo-Narrative, 1954, Cardinals and Saints, 1958, The Dialogues, 1962, The Multiple Modern Gods and Other Stories, 1964, The Unconscious Victorious and Other Stories, 1969, The New Rubaiyat of Stanley Berne, 1973, Future Language, 1976, The Great American Empire, 1981, Every Person's Little Book of Plutonium, 1992, To Hell with Optimism!!, 1996; (inclusion in anthologies) Trace, 1965, First Person Intense, 1978, Breakthrough Fictioneers, 1979, American Writing Today, 1992, Dictionary of the Avant-Gardes, 1993, New World Writing (11), 1957, The Living Underground, 1996; prodr. and co-host (with Arlene Zekowski) 9 Part TV Series for PBS, Future Writing Today. With USAF, 1942-46 PTO. Recipient Rsch. awards Ea. N. Mex. U., 4 awards. Mem. PEN, Com. of Small Mags., Editors, Poets, New Eng. Small Press Assn., Rio Grande Writers Assn., Santa Fe Writers Coop. Home: PO Box 4595 Santa Fe NM 87502-4595 Office: Rising Tide Press PO Box 6136 Santa Fe NM 87502

BERNER, JUDITH, mental health nurse; b. Tamaqua, Pa., June 19, 1938; d. Ralph Edgar and Ethel Mary (Williams) B. Diploma in nursing, Temple U. Hosp., 1959; AS, Coll. of Ganado, 1975, MS in Community Health, D of Med. Adminstrn. (hon.); BA, Stephens Coll., 1977; MEd, U. Ariz., 1980; LD (hon.), U. Iceland. RN, Ariz., N.Mex., Pa. Nursing adminstr. Project HOPE Internat. Office & Hosp. Ship, Washington, 1970-72; assoc. adminstr. Navajo Nation Health Found., Ganado, Ariz., 1972-79; clin. instr. psychiat. nursing Mo. So. State Coll., Joplin, 1986; nurse/therapist Presbyn. Kaseman Hosp., Albuquerque, 1986-93; emergency svcs. clinician for mental health svcs. Presbyn. Healthcare Systems, 1994-95, Hts. Psychiat. Hosp., 1994-95; charter Hts. Behavioral Health Sys., Albuquerque, 1995—; regional clin. coord. Mental Health Svcs., Inc., 1995—. Mem. ANA (cert. in psychiat. and mental health nursing), AACD, Internat. Acad. Behavioral Medicine, Counseling and Psychotherapy, Inc.

BERNHARD, PETER, publishing executive. Pres., publ. The Oakland (Calif.) Tribune. Office: The Oakland Tribune 66 Jack London Sq Oakland CA 94607

BERNHEIMER, MARTIN, music critic; b. Munich, Germany, Sept. 28, 1936; came to U.S., 1940, naturalized, 1946; s. Paul Ernst and Louise (Nassauer) B.; m. Lucinda Pearson, Sept. 30, 1961 (div. Feb. 1989); children: Mark Richard, Nora Nicoll, Marina and Erika (twins); m. Linda Winer, Sept. 27, 1992. MusB with honors, Brown U., 1958; student, Munich Conservatory, 1958-59; MA in Musicology, NYU, 1961. Free-lance music critic, 1958—; contbg. critic N.Y. Herald Tribune, 1959-62; mem. music faculty NYU, 1959-62; contbg. editor Mus. Courier, 1961-64; temporary music critic N.Y. Post, 1961-65; N.Y. corr. for Brit. Publ. Opera, 1962-65, L.A. corr., 1965—; corr. West Coast Brit. Opera Mag., 1965—; asst. to music editor Saturday Rev., 1962-65; mng. editor Philharmonic Hall Program, N.Y.C., 1962-65; music editor, chief critic L.A. Times, 1965-96; mem. faculty U. So. Calif., 1966-71, music faculty UCLA, 1969-75, Calif. Inst. Arts, 1975-82, Calif. State U., Northridge, 1978-81, Rockefeller Program for Tng. of Music Critics; mem. Pulitzer Prize Music Jury, 1984, 86, 90; L.A. corr. for Swiss publ. Opernwelt, 1984—. Contbg. author New Groves Dictionary; contbr. liner notes for recordings; appearances on radio and TV, Met. Opera Broadcasts; contbr. articles to Vanity Fair, Music Quar., The Critic, Opera News, Mus. Am., others. Recipient Deems Taylor award ASCAP, 1974, 78, Headliners award, 1979, Pulitzer Prize for disting. criticism, 1981, Lifetime Achievement award Svc. to Music, Calif. Assn. Profl. Music Tchrs., 1990. Mem. Nat. Opera Inst. (ind. selection com. 1980), Pi Kappa Lambda (hon.). Home: # 702-C 17350 Sunset Blvd #702-C Pacific Palisades CA 90272

BERNHOFT, FRANKLIN OTTO, psychotherapist, psychologist; b. Fargo, N.D., Aug. 12, 1944; s. Otto and Irene Bernhoft; m. Dorothy Ann Larsen, Aug. 11, 1973; children: Kimberley, Brady, Heather. BA in English, N.D. State U., 1966; MA in Counseling Psychology, U. N.D., 1970; MA in English, Calif. State U., 1978; PhD in Counseling Psychology, Brigham Young U., 1985. Cert. therapist, hypnotherapist, counselor, secondary tchr.; lic. marriage, family and child counselor, ednl. psychologist. Instr. Chapman Coll., Brigham Young U., U. N.D., U.S. I.U.; staff trainer Sacramento (Calif.) County Office Edn., 1977-82; therapist Lodi and Stockton, Calif., 1985—; therapist, family fitness trainer, master trainer systematic helping skills, devel. capable people trainer U. Pacific Behavioral Medicine Clinic; cofounder prevention/intervention project, Sacto County, 1977; presenter in field. Contbr. articles to profl. jours. Lt. U.S. Army, 1967-69. H.H. Kirk R. Askanase scholar; cert. achievement Ft. Carson; decorated Bronze star, combat med. badge Nat. Def. Svc. Vietnam. Mem. Am. Assn. Counseling and Devel., Children with Attention Deficit Disorders, Nat. Assn. Sch. Psychologists, Assn. Mormon Counselors and Psychotherapists, Calif. Assn. Marriage and Family Therapists,Sacramento Area Sch. Psychologists Assn., Calif. Continuation Edn. Assn. (past treas.), Calif. Assn. Lic. Edn. Psychologists, Mensa, Blue Key, Phi Eta Sigma. Office: Creative Therapy 310 W Lockeford St Lodi CA 95240-2033

BERNING, PAUL WILSON, lawyer; b. Marceline, Mo., Apr. 22, 1948; s. Harold John and Doris (Wilson) B. BJ, U. Mo., 1970; JD with honors, U. San Francisco, 1986. Bar: Calif. 1986, U.S. Dist. Ct. (no. dist., ea. dist., so. dist.) Calif. 1986, U. S. Dist. Ct. (cen. dist.) Calif. 1989, U.S. Ct. Appeals (9th cir.) 1986, U.S. Ct. Claims 1992, U.S. Supreme Ct. 1992. Copy editor Chgo. Sun-Times, 1970-74, nat., fgn. editor, 1974-78; asst. news editor San Francisco Examiner, 1978-83; law clerk San Francisco dist. atty. Consumer Fraud Divsn., 1984; extern Calif. Supreme Ct., San Francisco, 1985, San Francisco Superior Ct., 1986; assoc. Thelen, Marrin, Johnson & Bridges, San Francisco, 1986-94, ptnr., 1995—. Co-author: (book chpt.) Proving and Pricing Construction Claims, 1990; contbr. speeches and papers to profl. confs. Mem. ABA (forum on constrn. industry 1986—), State Bar Assn. Calif., Bar Assn. San Francisco (coord. legal assistance for mil. pers. 1991-92, assoc. liaison to San Francisco lawyers com. for urban affairs 1987-92), High Speed Ground Transp. Assn., Modern Transit Soc. Office: Thelen Marrin Johnson & Bridges 2 Embarcadero Ctr Ste 2100 San Francisco CA 94111-3823

BERNOCO, DOMENICO, immunogeneticist, educator; b. Cherasco, Cuneo, Italy, Apr. 6, 1935; s. Giuseppe and Lucia (Merlo) D.; m. Marietta Magdelene von Diepow, July 20, 1972. DVM, U. Torino, Italy, 1959; lic. vet. medicine, Rome, 1961; Libera Docenza, Ministry Pub. Instrn., Rome, 1971. Asst. prof. med. genetics U. Torino, 1961-70; mem. staff Basel (Switzerland) Inst. Immunology, 1970-76; assoc. rsch. immunologist dept. surgery UCLA, 1977-81; assoc. prof. vet. medicine reproduction U. Calif., Davis, 1981-94, prof. emeritus, 1994—. Contbr. 105 articles to profl. jours. Fellow Italian Nat. Coun. Rsch., 1962-63, Italian Ministry for Pub. Instrn., 1963-64, fellow for fgn. countries NATO, 1967-68. Mem. Am. Assn. Immunologists, Internat. Soc. Animal Genetics, Am. Soc. Histocompatibility and Immunogenetics. Home: 1002 Deodara Ct Davis CA 95616-5037 Office: U Calif Sch Vet Medicine Dept Population Health & Reproduction Davis CA 95616-8743

BERNSTEIN, ARTHUR HAROLD, venture capital executive; b. N.Y.C., June 8, 1925; s. Charles and Eva (Aronson) B.; m. Barbara R. Ettinger, June 24, 1951; children: Jeffrey R., Diane. B of Chem. Engring., Cornell U., 1947, JD, 1950. Bar: N.Y. 1950, Fla. 1956, U.S. Supreme Ct. 1962, Calif. 1972. Staff atty. N.Y. Cen. R.R. Co., N.Y.C., 1950-55; gen. counsel Ryder System, Inc., Miami, 1955-58, v.p., treas., 1958-65; sr. assoc. Lazard Freres & Co., N.Y.C., 1966-68; v.p. Norton Simon, Inc., Los Angeles, 1968-70; sr. v.p. Max Factor & Co., Los Angeles, 1970-77; mgr. gen. ptnr. Calif. Capital Investors, Ltd., L.A., 1980-93; pres. Bancorp Capital Group Inc., Bancorp Venture Capital Inc., L.A., 1988—, also bd. dirs.; bd. dirs. Ryder System, Inc., Miami, Sierra Trust Funds, Sierra Variable Annuity Trust Funds. Chmn., bd. dirs. Phillips Grad. Inst., Encino, Calif. With USN, 1943-46, PTO. Mem. ABA, Fla. Bar Assn., State Bar Calif. Jewish. Office: 11661 San Vicente Blvd Ste 405 Los Angeles CA 90049-5103

BERNSTEIN, GERALD WILLIAM, management consultant, researcher; b. Boston, Nov. 25, 1947; s. Alan Irwin and Anne (Fine) B.; m. Kathleen Ann Chaikin, Jan. 12, 1985. BS in Aero. Engring., Rensselaer Poly. Inst., 1969; MS in Engring., Stanford U., 1978. Transp. engr., dept. transp. State of N.Y., Albany, 1969-70; transp. planner Kennebec Regional Planning Com., Winslow, Me., 1974-77; dir. transp. dept. SRI Internat., Menlo Park, Calif., 1979-95; v.p. BACK Mgmt. Svcs., San Francisco, 1995—; session chmn. aviation workshop NSF, 1985, 91; profl. conf. chmn.; bd. dirs. Glob-Tran Corp., 1993—. Contbr. articles to profl. jours. Chmn. transp. com. Glenn Park Neighborhood Assn., San Francisco, 1982-85; dir. Balboa Terrace Neighborhood Assn., San Francisco, 1986-88; trustee Congregation Beth Israel-Judea, 1991-93. With U.S. Army, 1970-72. Recipient Cert. Appreciation City of Waterville, Maine, 1977. Mem. Am. Inst. Aeronautics and Astronautics (sr. mem.), Transp. Research Bd. of Nat. Research Council. Democrat. Jewish. Club: Toastmasters (Menlo Park, pres. 1986). Office: BACK Mgmt Svcs 236 W Portal Ave Ste 359 San Francisco CA 94127-1423

BERNSTEIN, GIORA, artistic director; b. Vienna, Austria. Studied with Igor Markevitch; doctorate, Boston U. Mem. Boston Symphony; founder, dir. Boston Chamber Orch., Claremont (Calif.) Music Festival; founding music dir., condr. Colo. Music Festival; guest condr. Liege Philharmonic, Stuttgart Philharmonic, Netherlands Chamber Orch., Tonkunstler Orch. Vienna, Berlin Symphony Orch., Basel Radio Orch., St. Gallen Symphony, San Remo Symphony, Haifa Symphony Orch., Seattle Symphony Orch., Colo. Symphony Orch. Recipient Westinghouse Debut Recital award, City of Claremont commendation, County of L.A. commendation, Calif. Fedn. of Music Club award, Nat. Fedn. of Music Club award, Coleman Chamber Music award, six ASCAP awards, Excellence in the Arts award Gov. of Colo.; Internat. Acad. at Mozarteum fellow, Salzburg, Austria; Juilliard Sch. of Music scholar, Brandeis U. scholar, Boston U. scholar. Office: Colo Music Festival Orch 1525 Spruce St Ste 101 Boulder CO 80302

BERNSTEIN, ROBERT DAVID, design engineer; b. Manchester, Conn., Nov. 25, 1958; s. Emil Oscar and Eleanor Rose (Mordell) B. Student, U. Calif., Berkeley, 1977-78; BS in Physics, MIT, 1980; MS in Sci. Instrumentation, U. Calif., Santa Barbara, 1984. Summer asst. Nat. Mus. Natural History, Washington, 1972-76; geodetic aide, programmer U.S. Geodetic Survey, Rockville, Md., 1976-77; rsch. asst. High Voltage Rsch. Lab., Cambridge, Mass., 1979; sr. technician CalDetect, Richmond, Calif., 1980-82; rsch. asst. U. Calif. Santa Barbara Instrumentation Lab., 1982-84; devel. engr. Nicomp Instruments, Goleta, Calif., 1984-86; sr. design engr. Digital Instruments, Santa Barbara, 1986—; bd. dirs. Amrita Corp., Menlo Park, Calif. Events coord. Ctrl. Am. Response Network, Goleta, 1984—; v.p. Santa Barbara Bicycle Coalition, 1992—; organizer Californians for Health Security, Santa Barbara, 1994. Mem. IEEE, ACLU, Sierra Club, Amnesty Internat., Am. Inst. Physics, MIT Alumni Assn. Democrat. Secular Humanist. Home: 448 Mills Way Apt B Goleta CA 93117-4047 Office: Digital Instruments 520 E Montecito St Santa Barbara CA 93103-3252

BERNSTEIN, SANDRA MARIE, county official; b. Brown City, Mich., Dec. 12, 1946; d. Raymond John and Margaret Helen (Hadrich) Tompsett; 1 child, Tammy Lynn; m. Charles Marc Bernstein, Dec. 30, 1988. AS, Ferris State U., 1983, BS, 1984; MBA, Calif. Coast U., 1992, PhD in Mgmt., 1995. Lic. registered social worker. Protective svcs. worker State of Mich., Stanton, 1984-88, facility mgr., 1987-88; North County coord. San Diego Svc. Ctr. for the Blind, 1988; protective svcs. worker County of San Diego, Calif., 1988-89; program specialist County of San Diego, 1989-90, contract analyst, 1990-91, budget, fiscal, procurement and chargeback mgr., 1991—; com. chair San Diego Commn. on Children and Youth, 1989-92. Exec. bd. County Employees Charitable Orgn., San Diego, 1993-94. Mem. San Diego Folk Heritage (bd. dirs. 1989-90). Office: County of San Diego 1600 Pacific Hwy San Diego CA 92101-2429

BERNSTEIN, SOL, cardiologist, educator; b. West New York, N.J., Feb. 3, 1927; s. Morris Irving and Rose (Leibowitz) B.; m. Suzi Maris Sommer, Sept. 15, 1963; 1 son, Paul. AB in Bacteriology, U. Southern Calif., 1952, MD, 1956. Diplomate Am. Bd. Internal Medicine. Intern Los Angeles County Hosp., 1956-57, resident, 1957-60; practice medicine specializing in cardiology L.A., 1960—; staff physician dept. medicine Los Angeles County Hosp. U. So. Calif. Med. Center, L.A., 1960—, chief cardiology clinics, 1964, asst. dir. dept. medicine, 1965-72; chief profl. services Gen. Hosp., 1972-74; med. dir. Los Angeles County-U So. Calif. Med. Center, L.A., 1974-94; med. dir. central region Los Angeles County, 1974-78; dir. Dept. Health Services, Los Angeles County, 1978; assoc. dean Sch. Medicine, U. So. Calif., L.A., 1986-94, assoc. prof., 1968—; med. dir. Health Rsch. Assn., L.A., 1995—; cons. Crippled Childrens Svc. Calif., 1965—. Contbr. articles on cardiac surgery, cardiology, diabetes and health care planning to med. jours. Served with AUS, 1946-47, 52-53. Fellow A.C.P., Am. Coll. Cardiology; mem. Am. Acad. Phys. Execs., Am. Fedn. Clin. Research, N.Y. Acad. Sci., Los Angeles, Am. heart assns., Los Angeles Soc. Internal Medicine, Los Angeles Acad. Medicine, Sigma Xi, Phi Beta Phi, Phi Eta Sigma, Alpha Omega Alpha. Home: 4966 Ambrose Ave Los Angeles CA 90027-1756 Office: 1640 Marengo St Los Angeles CA 90033-1015

BERRIAN, JAMES EDWIN, biology teacher; b. Pasadena, Calif., Jan. 4, 1951; s. James Henry and Bette Jo (Durant) B.; m. Robyn M. Garcia, Nov. 11, 1989; 1 child, Nathaniel James. AA in Zoology with honors, Southwestern Coll., 1976; BS in Zoology, San Diego State U., 1978, postgrad., 1979-83; cert. tchr., Nat. U., San Diego, 1984. Sr. vet. technician Chula Vista (Calif.) Vet. Clinic, 1978-79; agrl. technician aide San Diego County Dept. Agr., 1980-81; curatorial asst., rsch. asst., field assoc. in herpetology San Diego Natural History Mus., 1981-83, 93; sci. tchr. Emerald Jr. H.S., El Cajon, Calif., 1984, Montgomery Mid. Sch., El Cajon, 1984-85, Bonita Vista High Sch., Chula Vista, 1985-92; sci. tchr. El Cajon Valley H.S., 1993—, chair dept. sci.; presenter workshops, seminars in field. Contbr. articles to profl. publs. Initiator schoolwide/cmty. paper recycling and water conservation projects; guest speaker to various cmty. groups. With USN, 1970-74. Mem. Nat. Ctr. for Sci. Edn., Am. Arachnological Soc., Nature Conservancy, U.S. Naval Inst. Home: 4881 Hawley Blvd San Diego CA 92116

BERRY, DAWN BRADLEY, lawyer, writer; b. Peoria, Ill., Mar. 11, 1957; d. Raymond Coke and Clarette (Williams) Bradley; m. William Lars Berry, July 12, 1980. BS, Ill. State U., 1979, MS, 1982; JD, U. Ill., 1988. Bar: N.Mex. 1988, U.S. Dist. Ct. N.Mex. 1988, U.S. Ct. Appeals (10th cir.) 1993. Assoc. Modrall, Sperling, Roehl, Harris and Sisk, Albuquerque, 1988-90; pvt. practice Tijeras and Albuquerque, 1990—; assoc. Hinkle Law Offices, Albuquerque, 1995-96. Author: Equal Compensation for Women, 1994, The Domestic Violence Sourcebook, 1995, The Divorce Sourcebook, 1995, The Fifty Most Influential Women in American Law, 1996. Pres., bd. dirs. Talking Talons Youth Leadership, Inc., Tijeras, 1993—. Recipient Outstanding Young Alumni award Ill. State U., 1996; Rickert scholar for pub. svc. U. Ill., 1988. Mem. NAFE, N.Mex. Women's Bar Assn., S.W. Writer's Workshop, N.Am. Falconers Assn., Parrot Heads of N.Mex., Women's Wine Soc. N.Mex., F. Scott Fitzgerald Soc., Sisters in Crime. Home: 222 Raven Rd Tijeras NM 87059-8016 Office: 222 Raven Rd Tijeras NM 87059-8016

BERRY, GLENN, educator, artist; b. Glendale, Calif., Feb. 27, 1929; s. B. Franklin and Heloise (Sloan) B.; BA magna cum laude, Pomona Coll., 1951; BFA (Honnold fellow), MFA, Sch. Art Inst. Chgo., 1956. Faculty, Humboldt State U., Arcata, Calif., 1956-81, prof. art, 1969-81, emeritus, 1981—. Exhibited one-man shows Ingomar Gallery, Eureka, Calif., 1968, Ankrum Gallery, L.A., 1970, Esther Bear Gallery, Santa Barbara, Calif., 1971, Coll. Redwoods, Eureka, Calif., 1989; exhibited in group shows Palace of Legion of Honor, San Francisco, Pasadena (Calif.) Art Mus., Rockford (Ill.) Coll., Richmond (Calif.) Art Mus., Henry Gallery U. Wash., Seattle; represented in permanent collections at Storm King Art Center, Mountainville, N.Y., Kaiser Aluminum & Chem. Corp., Oakland, Calif., Palm Springs (Calif.) Desert Mus., Hirshhorn Mus., Washington, others; mural Griffith Hall, Humboldt State U., 1978. Mem. Phi Beta Kappa. Home: PO Box 2241 Mckinleyville CA 95519-2241

BERRY, JOHN CHARLES, clinical psychologist, educational administrator; b. Modesto, Calif., Nov. 29, 1938; s. John Wesley and Dorothy Evelyn (Harris) B.; A.B., Stanford, 1960; postgrad. Trinity Coll., Dublin, Ireland, 1960-61; Ph.D., Columbia, 1967; m. Arlene Ellen Sossin, Oct. 7, 1978; children—Elise, John Jordan, Kaitlyn. Research assoc. Judge Baker Guidance Center, Boston, 1965-66; psychology asso. Napa State Hosp., Imola, Calif., 1966-67, staff psychologist, 1967-75, program asst., 1975-76; program dir. Met. State Hosp., Norwalk, Calif., 1976-77; asst. supt. Empire Union Sch. Dist., Modesto, Calif., 1977-93, dep. supt., 1993—. Mem. Am. Psychol. Assn., Assn. Calif. Sch. Adminstrs., Sigma Xi. Contbg. author: Life History Research in Psychopathology, 1970. Home: 920 Eastridge Dr Modesto CA 95355-4672 Office: Empire Union Sch Dist 116 N Mcclure Rd Modesto CA 95357-1329

BERRY, KATHRYN ALLEN, editor in chief science publication; b. Binghamton, N.Y., July 9, 1958; d. William Earl Berry and Barbara (Ellis) Dickay; m. Mark Robert Bertram, Aug. 17, 1996. BA, Wittenberg U., 1980; M in Pub. Adminstrn., Ind. U., 1983. Assoc. instr. Ind. U., Bloomington, 1980-81; ranger, spokesperson U.S. Park Svc. Denali (Alaska) Nat. Park and Preserve, 1981-84 summers; sci. and investigative reporter Fairbanks (Alaska) Daily News Miner, 1984-88; publs. editor, br. mgr. Alaska Natural History Assn., Denlai Park, 1988-89; free lance writer and editor Alaska Bus. Monthly, Anchorage Daily News, Alask Geographic, Fairbanks, Alaska, 1989-91; sci. editor-in-chief Geophys. Inst. U. Alaska, Fairbanks, 1991—. Co-author, editor: (book) Black Tides: The Alaska Oil Spill, 1989; editor: (books) A Backcountry Companion, 1989, The Geology of Denali National Park, 1989; editor Geophys. Inst. Quarterly Newsletter, 1991— (1st pl. writing and editing Alaska Press Women, 1995, Nat. Press Women, 1995, Bronze award Coun. for Advancement and Support of Edn., 1994). Officer United Way, Fairbanks, Alaska, 1994—; bd. dirs. Presbn. Hospitality House, Fairbanks, 1995—. Recipient Alaska Legislature citation for publ. excellence, 1994, 95, 96, First Place Nat. award for editing and producing "Global Change and Polar Regions" Jour. of Govt. Info., 1995. Mem. Alaska Press Women, Nat. Press Women, Soc. Profl. Journalists. Democrat. Presbyterian. Office: Geophys Inst U Alaska 903 Koyukuk Dr Fairbanks AK 99775-7320

BERRY, KENNETH J., sociology educator. Prof. dept. sociology Colo. State U. Recipient Banner I. Miller award Am. Meteorol. Assn., 1994. Office: Colorado St Univ Dept Sociology Fort Collins CO 80523*

BERRY, KIM LAUREN, artist; b. Hollywood, Calif., June 5, 1962; d. Gary and Judith Debra (Epstein) B.; m. Stanley Mark Carroll, Dec. 2, 1990. Studied with Jon Serl, Lake Elsinore, Calif., 1983-90; cert. in biomed. art, Calif. State U., Long Beach, 1985, BFA in Illustration, 1985; MFA in Painting, Claremont (Calif.) Grad. Sch., 1990. Instr. visual art Bixby Sch., Long Beach, Calif., 1993-94; cons. visual art, artist Fullerton (Calif.) Sch. Dist., 1990-91. Art dir.: (film) The Secret of Easter Island, 1991 (Cine Golden Eagle award 1991); one-man show West Gallery, Claremont Grad. Sch., 1990; represented in group shows Double Rocking G Gallery, L.A., 1983, Coll. Bd., Princeton, N.J., 1984, Gallery C Calif. State U., Long Beach, 1985, DA Gallery, Pomona, Calif., 1988, West and East Galleries Claremont Grad., 1989, Helen Lindhurst Gallery, U. So. Calif., L.A., 1990, Am. Film Inst. Warner Theatre,L.A., 1991, Out of Darkness Gallery, Long Beach, 1991, 92, IPSO FACTO Gallery, Fullerton, Calif., 1992, Found. Art Resources, L.A., 1993, The Caged Chameleon Gallery, Santa Ana, Calif., 1993, A.R.C. Gallery William Rainey Harper Coll., Palatine, Ill., 1993, Nat. Congress Art Design, Salt Lake City, 1995, Aids Resource Ctr., Milwaukee, 1995, Fairfield (Calif.) Cultural Ctr., 1995, Huntington Beach (Calif.) Cultural Ctr., 1996, Orange County Ctr. Contemporary Art, Santa Ana, 1997, The Seaside Gallery, San Pedro Art Assn., 1997; contbr. to profl. jours. Active benefit exhibit Art for AIDS, AIDS Resource Ctr. of Wis., Milw., 1995, Animal Assistance League Benefit Exhibit, Ipso Facto Gallery, Fullerton, 1992, Homeless Benefit Exhibit, The Caged Chameleon Gallery, Santa Ana, Calif., 1993. Calif. State Grad. fellow in Humanities, 1990; Claremont Grad. Sch. Travel and Rsch. grantee, 1989. Home and Studio: 5891 Pinon Dr Huntington Beach CA 92649

BERRY, MARY DOUGLAS POINDEXTER, university official; b. Kanawha County, W.Va., July 21, 1943; d. Walter Douglas and Roberta (Backus) Poindexter; m. William J. Berry, Nov. 16, 1973. BA, Madison Coll., Harrisonburg, Va., 1965; MA, U. Ariz., 1972; PhD, N.Mex. State U., 1993. Cert. tchr., secondary sch. adminstr., N.Mex. Tchr. Fairfax County Pub. Schs., Fairfax, Va., 1965-80; dean edn. N.Mex. Adult Correctional System, Las Cruces, 1984-88; coord. secondary student teaching N.Mex. State U., Las Cruces, 1988-90, adminstrv. asst. to dean Coll. Edn., 1990-93, dir. pub. sch. adminstrn. internship program, 1994—, dir. vocat.-tech. insvc. Coll. Agr. and Home Econs., 1995-96; statis. analyst El Paso (Tex.) C C., 1993-95; instr. U.S.AID L.Am. Partnership Program, 1988-90; asst. to south ctrl. regional coord. Holmes Group ednl. Consortium, Las Cruces, 1991-93. Dep. voting registrar Dona Ana County, Las Cruces, 1984—. Named Corrections Edn. Tchr. of Yr., State of N.Mex., 1985. Mem. ASCD, AAUW (coord. teen esteem Las Cruces br. 1988-90, chmn. N.Mex. legal advocacy fund 1993-95, pres. N.Mex. 1995-97), N.Mex. ASCD (bd. dirs. 1990-93, sec. 1992-93, Excellence in Edn. award 1996), Nat. Coun. Rsch. on Women (affiliate), Assn. Women in Higher Edn., Phi Delta Kappa, Phi Mu.

BERRY, ROBERT WORTH, lawyer, educator, retired army officer; b. Ryderwood, Wash., Mar. 2, 1926; s. John Franklin and Anita Louise (Worth) B. B.A. in Polit. Sci., Wash. State U., 1950; J.D., Harvard U., 1955; M.A., John Jay Coll. Criminal Justice, 1981. Bar: D.C. 1956, U.S. Dist. Ct. (D.C.) 1956, U.S. Ct. of Appeals (D.C. cir.) 1957, U.S. Ct. Mil. Appeals 1957, Pa. 1961, U.S. Dist. Ct. (ea. dist.) Pa. 1961, U.S. Dist. Ct. (ctrl. dist.) Calif. 1967, U.S. Supreme Ct. 1961, Calif. 1967, U.S. Ct. Claims 1975. Research assoc. Harvard U., 1955-56; atty. Office Gen. Counsel U.S. Dept. Def., Washington, 1956-60; staff counsel Philco Ford Co., Phila., 1960-63; dir. Washington office Litton Industries, 1967-71; gen. counsel U.S. Dept. Army, Washington, 1971-74, civilian aide to sec. army, 1975-77; col. U.S. Army, 1978-87; prof., head dept. law U.S. Mil. Acad., West Point, N.Y., 1978-86; retired brigadier gen. U.S. Mil. Acad., 1987; mil. asst. to asst. sec. of army, Manpower and Res. Affairs Dept. of Army, 1986-87; asst. gen. counsel pub. affairs Litton Industries, Beverly Hills, Calif., 1963-67; chair Coun. of Def. Space Industries Assns., 1968; resident ptnr. Quarles and Brady, Washington, 1974-78; dir., corp. sec., treas., gen. counsel G.A. Wright, Inc., Denver, 1987-92, dir., 1987—; pvt. practice law Fort Bragg, Calif., 1993—; foreman Mendocino County Grand Jury, 1995-96; spl. counsel Messner Pavek & Reeves, LLC, Denver. Served with U.S. Army, 1944-46, 51-53, Korea. Decorated Bronze Star, Legion of Merit, Disting. Service Medal; recipient Disting. Civilian Service medal U.S. Dept. Army, 1973, 74, Outstanding Civilian Service medal, 1977. Mem. Fed. Bar Assn., Bar Assn. D.C., Calif. State Bar Assn., Pa. State Bar Assn., Army-Navy Club, Army-Navy Country Club, Phi Beta Kappa, Phi Kappa Phi, Sigma Delta Chi, Lambda Chi Alpha. Methodist.

BERRYHILL, GEORGIA GENE, graphic designer, educator; b. Wlliamsport, Ind., Aug. 27, 1947; d. Detro Horace and Bliss Bernice (Bilbrey) Sells; m. Robert Earl Berryhill, Aug. 10, 1966; children: Deven Earl, Joel Eugene. BA in Biomed. Illustration, Calif. State U., Long Beach, 1979; MA in Graphic Design, Calif. State U., L.A., 1986; PhD, Walden U., Mpls., 1993. Graphic designer, art dir. Illustrated Sci., Seal Beach, Calif., 1976-86; bio-med. illustrator UCLA Med. Ctr., Torrance, Calif., 1979-80; design instr., curriculum developer Glendale (Calif.) C.C., 1984-88; creative dir. Berryhill Prodns., Laguna Beach, Calif., 1986—; art/design instr. Biola U., La Mirada, Calif., 1987-89, Art Inst. of So. Calif., Laguna Beach, 1991-93; instr. computer graphics U. Calif., Irvine, 1992—; cons. Martin Luther King Hosp., L.A., 1980, U. So. Calif., L.A., 1980, UCLA Med. Ctr., 1980-86, Beckman Found., 1996; program adminstr. Beckman Found., 1997. Author: The Social Impact of Graphic Symbolism, 1993; contbr. articles to profl. jours.; spkr. in field. Mem. Am. Inst. of Graphic Arts, Soc. of Environ.

Graphic Design, Orange County Multimedia Users Group, Assn. for Advancement of Policy Rsch. Devel. in the 3d World, Kappa Pi Internat. Republican. Office: U Calif PO Box 6050 Irvine CA 92716

BERSIN, ALAN DOUGLAS, prosecutor, lawyer; b. Bklyn., Oct. 15, 1946; s. Arthur and Mildred (Laikin) B.; m. Elisabeth Van Aggelen, Aug. 17, 1975 (div. Dec. 1983); 1 child, Alissa Ida; m. Lisa Foster, July 20, 1991; children, Madeleine Foster, Amalia Rose. AB magna cum laude, Harvard U., 1968; student, Oxford U., 1968-71; JD, Yale U., 1974. Bar: Calif. 1975, U.S. Dist. Ct. (ctrl. dist.) Calif. 1975, U.S. Ct. Appeals (9th cir.) 1977, Alaska 1983, U.S. Dist. Ct. Alaska 1983, U.S. Dist. Ct. Hawaii 1992, U.S. Dist. Ct. (so. dist.) Calif. 1992, U.S. Supreme Ct., 1996. Exec. asst. Bd. Police Commrs., L.A., 1974-75; assoc. Munger, Tolles & Olson, L.A., 1975-77, ptnr., 1978—; spl. dep. dist. atty. Counties of Imperial and San Diego, Calif., 1993—; adj. prof. of law U. So. Calif. Law Ctr.; vis. prof. Sch. Law U. San Diego, 1992—; named spl. rep. for U.S. s.w. border by U.S. Atty. Gen., 1995—; mem. Atty Gen.'s adv. com. of U.S. Attys.,tech. adv. panel Nat. Inst. of Justice Law Enforcement, adv. com. FCC/NTIA Pub. Safety Wireless; founder U.S./Mex. Binat. Lab. Program; chmn. bd. dirs. U.S. Border Rsch. Tech. Ctr., S.W. Border Coun. Named Rhodes scholar 1968; recipient Resolution of Merit award Mayor and City Coun. L.A., 1991, Spl. Achievement award Hispanic Urban Ctr., 1992. Mem. Assn. Bus. Trial Lawyers (bd. govs. 1986-88), Inner City Law Ctr. (chmn. bd. dirs. 1987-90). Democrat. Jewish. Office: Office of US Atty 880 Front St Rm 6293 San Diego CA 92101-8893 also: U San Diego Sch Law 5998 Alcala Park San Diego CA 92110-2429

BERST, CHARLES ASHTON, English educator; b. Seattle, Sept. 30, 1932; s. Charles Ashton and Esther Anna (Weage) B.; m. Roelina Gerda den Ouden, June 8, 1962; children: Nelina, Caroline. BA, U. Wash., 1955, PhD, 1965. Asst. prof. U. Alta., Edmonton, Can., 1965-67; asst. prof. UCLA, 1967-73, assoc. prof., 1973-81, prof., 1981-94, prof. emeritus, 1994—; chair Coll. Letters & Sci. Faculty UCLA, 1977-81, vice chair and chair faculty senate, 1987-89. Author: Bernard Shaw and the Art of Drama, 1973, Pygmalion: Shaw's Spin on Myth and Cinderella, 1995; editor: Shaw and Religion, 1981. Office: UCLA Dept English PO Box 951530 Los Angeles CA 90095-1530

BERTAIN, G(EORGE) JOSEPH, JR., lawyer; b. Scotia, Humboldt County, Calif., Mar. 9, 1929; s. George Joseph and Ellen Veronica (Canty) B.; m. Bernardine Joy Galli, May 11, 1957; 1 child, Joseph F. AB, St. Mary's Coll. Calif., 1951; JD, Cath. U. Am., 1955. Bar: Calif. 1957. Assoc. Hon. Joseph L. Alioto, San Francisco, 1955-57, 59-65; asst. U.S. Atty. No. Dist. Calif., 1957-59; pvt. practice of law San Francisco, 1966—; panel mem. Theodore Granik's Am. Forum of The Air, Washington, 1955. Editor-in-Chief, Law Rev. Cath. U. Am. (vol. 5), 1954-55. Mem. bd. regents St. Mary's Coll. Calif., 1980—; chmn. San Francisco Lawyers Com. for Ronald Reagan, 1966-78, San Francisco lawyers com. for elections of Gov./U.S. Pres. Ronald Reagan, 1966, 70, 80, 84; spl. confidential advisor to Gov. Reagan on jud. selection, San Francisco, 1967-74; chmn. San Francisco Lawyers for Better Govt., 1978—; confidential advisor to Senator Hayakawa on judicial selection, 1981-82, to Gov. Deukmejian, 1983-90, to Gov. Wilson, 1991-92. Recipient De La Salle medal St. Mary's Coll. Calif., 1951, Signum Fidei award, 1976. Mem. ABA, Calif. Bar Assn., Fed. Bar Assn. (del. to 9th cir. jud. conf. 1967-76), St. Thomas More Soc. San Francisco, U.S. Supreme Ct. Hist. Soc., Assn. Former U.S. Attys and Asst. U.S. Attys. No. Calif. (past pres.), Commonwealth Club, Wester Assn., Knights of Malta, KC. Republican. Roman Catholic. Office: 22 Battery St Ste 1100 San Francisco CA 94111-5525

BERTAPELLE, ALLEN LOUIS, air force officer, flight test engineer; b. Greeley, Colo., Apr. 8, 1970; s. Anthony Louis and Connie Belle (Sayre) B.; m. Karen Louise Rogowski, May 29, 1993. BS in Elec. Engring., U. Colo., 1992. EIT, Colo. Commd. capt. USAF, 1992; flight test engr. 4950th Test Wing USAF, Wright-Patterson AFB, 1992-94; flight test project mgr. 418th Flight Test Squadron USAF, Edwards AFB, Calif., 1994—. Mem. Co. Grade Officers Coun., U. Colo. Alumni Assn. Home: 30 Glasgow Cir Edwards CA 93523-1714

BERTE, MARJORIE MARIE, state agency administrator; b. Oakland, Calif., Sept. 28, 1952; d. D. William and Betty A. Berte; m. Jerry O'Kane. BA in English, Stanford U., 1974. Exec. v.p. Profl. Ins. Agts. of Calif. and Nev., Van Nuys, Calif., 1978-88; dep. campaign dir. Citizens for No-Fault (Proposition 104) Campaign, San Francisco, 1988; media rels., strategic planning cons. San Francisco, 1989-91; dir. Calif. Office Ins. Advisor, Sacramento, 1991-95, Calif. Dept. Consumer Affairs, Sacramento, 1995—. Author: Hit Me - I Need the Money, 1991. Bd. dirs. Ins. Coun.-City of Hope Med. Rsch. Found.; counselor, arrangements chair Hugh O'Brien Youth Leadership Found.; founding dir., treas., sec. Jeffrey Nordhaus Meml. Scholarship Fund. Office: Calif Dept Consumer Affairs 400 R St Ste 3000 Sacramento CA 95814

BERTHELSDORF, SIEGFRIED, psychiatrist; b. Shannon County, Mo., June 16, 1911; s. Richard and Amalia (Morschenko) von Berthelsdorf; m. Mildred Friederich, May 13, 1945; children: Richard, Victor, Dianne. BA, U. Oreg., 1934, MA, MD, 1939. Lic. psychiatrist, psychoanalyst. Intern U.S. Marine Hosp., Staten Island, N.Y., 1939-40; psychiat. intern Bellevue Hosp., N.Y.C., 1940-41; psychiat. resident N.Y. State Psychiat. Hosp., N.Y.C., 1941-42; research assoc. Columbia U. Coll. Physicians and Surgeons, N.Y.C., 1942-43; asst. physician Presbyn. Hosp. and Vanderbilt Clinic, N.Y.C., 1942-51; supervising psychiatrist Manhattan (N.Y.) State Hosp., 1946-50; asst. adolescent psychiatrist Mt. Zion Hosp., N.Y.C., 1950-52; psychiat. cons. MacLaren Sch. for Boys, Woodburn, Oreg., 1952-84, Portland (Oreg.) Pub. Schs., 1952-67; clin. prof. U. Oreg. Health Scis. Ctr., 1956—; tng. and supervising analyst Seattle Psychoanalytic Inst., 1970—. Author: Treatment of Drug Addiction in Psychoanalytic Study of the Child, Vol. 31, 1976, Ambivalence Towards Women in Chinese Characters and Its Implication for Feminism, American Imago, 1988, (with others) Psychiatrists Look at Aging, 1992. Bd. dirs., v.p. Portland Opera Assn., 1960-64, Portland Musical Co., 1987-92; bd. dirs., pres. Portland Chamber Orch., 1964-70, 92-94, 96—. Maj. USAF, 1943-46. Recipient Henry Waldo Coe award U. Oreg. Med. Sch., Portland, 1939, citation Parry Ctr. for Children, Portland, 1970. Fellow Am. Psychiat. Assn. (life), Am. Geriatrics Soc. (founding fellow); mem. Am. Psychoanalytic Assn. (life), Portland Psychiatrists in Pvt. Practice (charter, pres. 1958), Mental Health Assn. (bd. dirs., chmn. med. adv. com. 1952-60), Multnomah County Med. Soc. (pres.'s citation 1979), Oreg. Psychoanalytic Found. (founding mem.), Am. Rhododendron Soc. (bd. dirs., v.p. Portland chpt. 1956-58, Bronze medal and citation 1974), Am. Rhododendron Species Found. (bd. dirs. 1960-75), Phi Beta Kappa, Sigma Xi, Phi Sigma. Home and Office: 1125 SW St Clair Ave Portland OR 97205-1127 *Life's challenge is to close the hiatus between what we are and what we aspire to: "Edel sei der Mensch, Hilfreich und gut!--".*

BERTHOLF, NEILSON ALLAN, JR., aviation executive; b. Morristown, N.J., Jan. 6, 1933; s. Neilson Allan Sr. and Marion Edna (Tiger) B.; m. Geraldine Henrietta Crabtree, Aug. 6, 1955; children: Mark Allan, Karen Jo. BS in Bus. Mgmt., Fairleigh Dickinson U., Rutherford, N.J., 1960, MBA, 1966. Flight dispatcher Lockheed Aircraft Svc., Inc., Atlantic City, N.J., 1958-59; chief airport ops. and safety Fed. Aviation Agy., Atlantic City, 1959-64; airport ops. mgr. City of Kansas City, Mo., 1965-67, asst. dir. aviation, 1967-79; airport dir. County of Milw., 1979-82; aviation dir. Sky Harbor Airport, Phoenix, 1982—. V.p. programs Boy Scouts Am., Phoenix, 1983—; com. mem. Fiesta Bowl Com., Phoenix, 1983—. With USN, 1951-55. Mem. Am. Assn. Airport Execs. (accredited; bd. dirs. S.W. chpt. 1988—), Airport Operators Coun. Internat. (official rep.; bd. dirs. 1981-84), Ariz. Airport Assn. (pres. 1983-84). Home: 3804 E Briarwood Ter Phoenix AZ 85044-7956 Office: Phoenix Aviation Dept 3400 E Sky Harbor Blvd Phoenix AZ 85034-4403*

BERTIGER, KAREN LEE, real estate broker, asset manager, consultant; b. Louisville, Aug. 25, 1954; d. Joseph Henry and Phyllis June (Hupp) Dickhaus; m. Paul Robert Kastensmith, June 3, 1978 (div. June 1980); children: Christine, Jennifer; m. Bary Robert Bertiger, Dec. 28, 1985; stepchildren: Karen, Jeff. Student, Miami U., 1972-73, U. Cin., 1973-75, Am. Open U., 1986-88. Pres. Seville Realty and Investment Co., Phoenix, 1983-84; realtor Realty Execs., Scottsdale, Ariz., 1984-89; CEO Landvest Securities, Ltd., Scottsdale, 1987—, Landvest, Ltd., 1989-92, Golden Desert Capital Corp., Scottsdale, 1992—; designated broker Landvest Ltd., Scottsdale, 1989-92, Golden Desert Capital Corp., Scottsdale, 1992—. Leader Ariz. Cactus-Pine Girl Scouts, Phoenix, 1985-86; co-founder The McDowell Sonoran Land Trust, 1991—, dir., treas., 1991-92. Mem. Nat. Assn. Realtors (grad. Realtor's Inst. 1986, cert. residential specialist 1989), Ariz. Assn. Realtors (registered lobbyist, chair fin., taxation subcom. 1995—, vice chair legis. com. 1996-97, chair 1997—), Urban Land Inst., World Future Soc., Scottsdale Assn. Realtors (grievance com. 1989-96, commun. rels. com. 1989-91, local city govt. com. 1988-89, govt. affairs com. 1989-90). Republican. Office: Golden Desert Capital Corp 8711 E Pinnacle Peak Rd # 247 Scottsdale AZ 85255-3555

BERTIN, JOHN JOSEPH, aeronautical engineer, educator, researcher; b. Milw., Oct. 13, 1938; s. Andrea and Yolanda G. (Pasquali) B.; m. Ruth Easterbrook; children: Thomas Alexander, Randolph Scott, Elizabeth Anne, Michael Robert. BA, Rice Inst., Houston, 1960; MS, Rice U., 1962, PhD, 1966. Aerospace technologist NASA Johnson Space Ctr., Houston, 1962-66; prof. U. Tex., Austin, 1966-89; program mgr. for space initiative MTS, Sandia Nat. Labs., Albuquerque, 1989-94; vis. prof. USAF Acad., Colorado Springs, Colo., 1988-89, prof. aero. engring., 1994—; cons. McGinnis, Lochridge & Kilgore, Austin, 1978-83, Sandia Nat. Labs., Albuquerque, 1980-89, BPD Difesa e Spazio, Rome, 1980-82, NASA, 1994-96, Sci. Applications Internat. Corp., 1996; detailed to Office of Space, U.S. Dept. Energy Hdqs., 1991-92; dir. Ctr. Excellence for Hypersonic Tng. and Rsch., 1985-89; mem. sci. adv. bd. USAF, 1989-93, mem. adv. group Flight Dynamics Labs., 1989-93. Author: Engineering Fluid Mechanics, 1987, Hypersonic Aerothermodynamics, 1994; co-author: Aerodynamics for Engineers, 1987; editor: Hypersonics, 1989, Advances in Hypersonics, 1992. Pres. Western Hills Little League, Austin, 1975; mem. arts subcom. NASA, 1987-91. Recipient Gen. Dynamics tchg. award U. Tex. Coll. Engring., 1978, Tex. Exec. tchg. award Ex-Students Assn. U. Tex., 1982, faculty award Tau Beta Pi, 1986, award for meritorious civilian svc. Dept. Air Force, 1993, Gen. Daley award USAFA, 1996, Exemplary Civilian Svc. Award medal, 1996. Fellow AIAA (dir. region IV 1983-86, Disting. Lectr., Thermophysics award 1997).

BERTMAN, ROGER BRUCE, management executive; b. Portland, Oreg., Apr. 29, 1944; s. Arwid W. and Edna L. (Jackson) B.; m. Julie Pershin, Aug. 29, 1965; children: Jason M., Justin R. BA in Math., Portland State U., 1966; MS in Math. and Computer Sci., Stevens Inst. Tech., 1969. Mem. tech. staff Bell Labs., Holmdel, N.J., 1966-75; staff engr. AT&T Long Lines, N.Y.C., 1975-78; software support mgr. AT&T Long Lines, San Francisco, 1978-81; nat. account mgr. AT&T Long Lines, Boise, Idaho, 1981-84; dir. mktg. Rolm Corp., Santa Clara, Calif., 1984-89; v.p. mktg. Ungermann-Bass, Santa Clara, 1989-92; v.p., gen. mgr. VeriFone, Inc., Redwood City, Calif., 1992—. Home: 1250 Estate Dr Los Altos CA 94024-6100 Office: VeriFone Inc 3 Lagoon Dr Redwood City CA 94065-1565

BERTOCH, RICHARD KEITH, electrical engineer, consultant; b. Salt Lake City, Mar. 4, 1924; s. Vivian Cutcliffe and Hazel (Hemenway) B.; m. Carol Venus Grondel, Aug. 20, 1949; children: Henry, Richard, Mary Kaye. BSEE, U. Utah, 1947. Registered profl. engr., Utah, Nev. Test engr. GE Co., Schenectady, N.Y., 1947-48; elec. engr. Graybar Electric, Salt Lake City, 1948-60, Wasatch Electric, Salt Lake City, 1960—; cons. in field; expert witness in field; bd. dirs. Micro Securities, Salt Lake City. Contbr. articles to profl. jours. Bd. dirs. Salt Lake City Hosp., 1964-84; chmn. Granger Hunter Civic Group, Salt Lake City, 1984-85; mem. Utah State Electric Bd., 1978-88; bishop LDS Ch., Salt Lake City, 1980-84. Named to West Valley City Hall of Fame, 1993, Cyprus H.S. Hall of Fame, 1985. Fellow Nat. Elec. Contrs. (com. chmn. 1980-85); mem. NSPE, IEEE (vice chmn. 1977-79). Republican. Home: 6089 W 3500 S West Valley City UT 84120

BERTOLDO, JOSEPH RAMON, lawyer; b. Safford, Ariz., Nov. 24, 1950; s. Joe M. Bertoldo and Virginia (Burrell) Simmons. BS, U. Ariz., 1973, JD, 1976. Bar: Ariz. 1977, U.S. Dist. Ct. Ariz. 1977, U.S. Ct. Appeals (9th cir.) 1980, U.S. Supreme Ct. 1980. Asst. city atty. City of Flagstaff (Ariz.), 1977-81, city atty., 1981-. Bd. dirs. IMPACT, victim-witness advocacy group, Flagstaff, 1986; active Flagstaff unit Am. Cancer Soc. Mem. Ariz. Bar Assn., Coconino County Bar Assn. (v.p. 1989, pres. 1990), Ariz. City Attys. Assn. (pres. 1995-96), Internat. Mcpl. Lawyers Assn. (Ariz. state chair 1991-94, regional v.p. 1994—), Phi Delta Phi. Democrat. Roman Catholic. Home: 1345 N Foxhill Rd Flagstaff AZ 86004-7881 Office: City of Flagstaff 211 W Aspen Ave Flagstaff AZ 86001-5359

BERTON, PETER ALEXANDER MENQUEZ, emeritus international relations educator, lecturer; b. Bialystok, Poland, June 11, 1922; came to U.S., 1949, naturalized, 1956; s. Claude Myron and Raissa (Menquez) B.; m. Michele Strick, Aug. 29, 1957 (dec. Dec. 1987); children: David Adrian Strick, Jonathan Claude Kurier. Diploma, YMCA Coll., Harbin, Manchuria, 1940, First Harbin Music Acad., 1941; grad., Waseda U., Tokyo, 1946; MA, Columbia U., 1951, PhD, 1956; Diploma, L.A. Psychoanalytic Inst., 1987. Dep. asst. censor Allied Hdqrs., Japan, 1945-47; instr. Japanese and Russian 8th Army Edn. Ctr., Yokohama, Japan, 1947-49; cons. Libr. of Congress, Washington, 1951; interpreter Asian leaders program Depts. State and Def., 1952; rsch. assoc., lectr. U. So. Calif., 1953-56, asst. prof., 1956-57, assoc. prof. internat. rels. and Asian studies, 1962-69, prof. internat. rels., 1969-91, coord. Asia/Pacific Regional Studies Program, 1961-91, prof. emeritus of internat. rels., lectr. Emeriti Coll., 1991—; rsch. cons. Columbia U., 1956-58; acting curator, asst. prof. Hoover Instn., Stanford, 1957-59, Ford Found., Stanford, 1960-61; vis. prof. polit. sci. UCLA, 1985; vis. prof. internat. rels., assoc. dean internat. divsn. Waseda U.; resident dir. Calif. Pvt. Univs. and Colls. Year-in-Japan Program, 1987-88; project assoc. John F. Kennedy Sch. Govt., Harvard U., 1992-93; vis. prof. Internat. Rsch. Ctr. for Japanese Studies, Kyoto, 1995; cons. Japanese Labor History Projects U Tokyo, 1957-60, Am. U., 1958-59. Author: Japanese-English Dictionary of Wartime Contributions to the Japanese Language, 1946, Manchuria: An Annotated Bibliography, 1951, The Secret Russo-Japanese Alliance of 1916, 1956, Soviet Works on China, 1959, The Chinese-Russian Dialogue, 2 vols., 1964, The Russo-Japanese Boundary, 1967, Japanese-Russian Territorial Dilemma: Historical Background, Disputes, Issues, Questions, Solution Scenarios, 1992; (with others) Japanese Training and Research in the Russian Field, 1956, Contemporary China: A Research Guide, 1967, Soviet Works on Southeast Asia, 1967, Symposium on the Comparative Study of Communist Foreign Policies, 1975, The Fateful Choice: Japan's Advance into Southeast Asia, 1939-1941, 1980, The Russian Impact on Japan: Literature and Social Thought, 1981; editor: The Japanese Penetration of Korea, 1894-1910, 1959, Far Eastern and Russian Rsch. Series, Internat. Subsys., 1969, Soviet Works on Korea, 1945-70, 1973; editor Studies in Comparative Communism, 1970-83, editor emeritus, 1983—; contbr. chpt. to Ency. Americana, more than 100 articles to profl. jours. Mem. AAUP, Assn. Asian Studies, Am. Assn. Advancement Slavic Studies, Internat. Studies Assn., Japan Soc. N.Y. Home: 320 S Rodeo Dr Beverly Hills CA 90212

BERTRAM, CHRISTOPHER D., artificial intelligence researcher; b. Colorado Springs, Colo., Nov. 17, 1963; s. David Frederick and Carmen B. AS in Math., Merritt Coll., 1990, AA in Social and Behavioral Sci., 1990; AS, Am. River Coll., 1994; AAS in Electronics Tech., Heald Inst. Tech., 1996, AAS in Network Tech., 1997. Numistic die finisher Treasury Dept., San Francisco, 1991-94; with TYN Rsch., Berkeley, Calif., 1994—; electronics engring. technician Applied Software Tech., Inc., San Carlos, Calif., 1996—. Editor/pub.: Bay Area Rock Mag., 1989-92; inventor passive prosthetic bionic light interpreter. With USN, 1985-90. Mem. IEEE, Assn. Computing Machinery. Office: TYN Rsch 48 Shattuck Sq # 163 Berkeley CA 94704

BERTRAM, JACK RENARD, information systems company executive; b. Lincoln, Nebr., Nov. 20, 1943; s. John Lewis and Emma Louise (Doerr) B.; m. Ingrid Frieda Reschke, Feb. 14, 1975; children: Deborah Geniene, Kenneth Brian. BS, Stanford U., 1966, MA, 1971; MS, Santa Clara U., 1988. Scientific programming specialist Lockheed Missles & Space Co., Sunnyvale, Calif., 1980-92; pres. Hansatech Internat., Redwood City, Calif., 1993—. Mem. AIAA, IEEE Computer Soc., Am. Assn. for Artificial Intelligence, Am. Astronautical Soc., Assn. for Computing Machinery, Computer Profls. for Social Responsibility, Inst. Cert. Profl. Mgrs. (cert. mgr.), Space Studies Inst. Democrat. Home: 1580 Alameda De Las Pulgas Redwood City CA 94061 Office: Hansatech Internat PO Box 554 Redwood City CA 94064-0554

BERTRAND, KEITH JAY, electrical engineer; b. Newton, Kans., Dec. 16, 1963; s. Helmut and Helen Alice Bertrand. BSEE, MIT, 1985. Hoser Sub Zero Systems Corp., Toronto, Ont., Can., 1985-86; engr. Delta Rsch. Group, Mountain View, Calif., 1986-87; staff engr. Ampex Corp., Redwood City, Calif., 1987—. Patentee in field. Mem. IEEE. Home: 214 Hamilton Ave Mountain View CA 94043-4207 Office: Ampex Corp 500 Broadway Redwood City CA 94063

BERTSCH, BRENDA R., flight nurse; b. Parkston, S.D., June 24, 1953; d. Ruben Henry and Frances Martha B.; m. Ken Safe, Mar. 12, 1977 (div. Oct. 1982); 1 child, John Safe; m. Brian Cratty, June 1987 (div. July 1993). BS, U. N.D., 1980; ADN, Casper Coll., 1983; BSN, U. Wyo., 1990. RN; cert. emergency med. tech., BLS, ACLS; CEN; cert. critical care RN, flight RN, neonatal resuscitation provider. State dir. Older Ams. Act Sr. Companion Program, Casper, Wyo., 1980-81; charge nurse emergency dept. Wyo. Med. Ctr., Casper, 1982-93; flight nurse AIREVAC, Phoenix, 1994—; emergency svcs. and ground ambulance nurse Wyo. Med. Ctr., 1985-93, nursing exec. com. 1991-92; flight nurse Wyo. LifeFlight, Casper, 1985-93; charge nurse ER St. Alphonsus Regional Med. Ctr., Boise, Idaho, 1993-94, emergency svcs. edn. coord., 1994. Mem. Nat. Flight Nurses Assn. (bd. dirs. Rocky Mtn. chpt. 1990-94, edn. com. chair), Emergency Nurses Assn., Ariz. Flight Nurses Assn., Phi Kappa Phi. Lutheran. Office: AIREVAC 2360 Sky Harbor Blvd Phoenix AZ 85034

BERWANGER, EUGENE HARLEY, history educator; b. Calumet City, Ill., June 8, 1929; s. Henry Nicholas and Cornelia (Benschop) B.; m. Elizabeth A. Kohl, June 12, 1967; children: Anne E., Thomas E. BA, Ill. State U., 1951, MA, 1952; PhD, U. Ill., 1964. Asst. prof. history Ill. Coll., Jacksonville, 1964-67; prof. history Colo. State U., Ft. Collins, 1967—. Bd. editors Pacific Hist. Rev., 1970-73; author: British Foreign Service and American Civil War, 1993, My Diary North and South, 1981, West and Reconstruction, 1980, Frontier Against Slavery, 1967. Cpl. U.S. Army, 1952-54. Office: Colorado State Univ Dept History Fort Collins CO 80523

BESHUR, JACQUELINE E., pet training consultant, writer; b. Portland, Oreg., May 8, 1948; d. Charles Daniel and Mildred (Domreis) Beshears. BA, UCLA, 1970; MBA, Claremont Grad. Sch., 1980; postgrad., City U., Seattle, 1989-90. Dir. and founder L.A. Ctr. for Photog. Studies, 1972-76; precious gem distbr. Douglas Group Holdings, Australia, 1976-78; small bus. owner BeSure Cleaning, 1981-90; animal trainer, exotic livestock farmer, 1990—. Author: Good Intentions Are Not Good Enough, 1992. Dir. County Citizens Against Incineration, 1987—, Ames Lake Protection Com., 1989—. Mem. Bridges for Peace, Nature Conservancy, Wash. Wilderness Coalition, Issaquah Alps Club, Inland Empire Pub. Lands Coun. Republican. Fundamentalist. Office: BeSure Tng PO Box 225 Carnation WA 98014-0225

BESSE, ROBERT GALE, food technologist; b. Calgary, Alta., Can., Feb. 11, 1923 (parents Am. citizens); s. Rene A. and Doria (Bray) B.; student N.Mex. State Tchrs. Coll., 1941-42; B.S., Oreg. State Coll., 1948; m. Mary A. McKay, Sept. 11, 1948; children—Rene A., Madeleine E., Leon J., Alan G., Michele M., Marc P., Angelique C. Supt., also in quality control Alderman Farms Frozen Foods, Dayton, Oreg., 1948-50, plant supt., 1950-54; chief food technologist Kuner Empson Co., Brighton, Colo., 1954-60; food technologist Northwest Packing Co., Portland, Oreg., 1960-62; food technologist research and devel. Nat. Can Corp., San Francisco, 1962-67, mgr. Pacific Area tech. research service, 1967-70; mgr. tech. services Western Can Co., 1970-86 ; customer tech. services Continental Can Co., 1986-88; cons. to food and can industries, RGB Cons., 1988—; dir. Material Metrics. Pres. St. Gregory's Theatre Guild; vol. hunting safety instr. Calif. Fish and Game Dept., 1972—. Served with Signal Corps, AUS, 1942-45. Mem. Soc. Plastic Engrs., Pacific Fish Tech. (pres.), Inst. Food Technologists (emeritus, sec.-treas. Rocky Mountain sect.; exec. com. Oreg. sect.), Confraternity of Christian Doctrine Cath. (pres.), N.W. Canners and Packers, Packaging Inst. (profl. mem.), Nat. Canners Assn. (mem. Western lab. adv. com.), No. Calif. Metal Decorating Assn. (pres.), Western Packaging Assn.; Soc. Mfg. Engrs. Club: Elks. Home and Office: 264 Portola Dr San Mateo CA 94403-2327

BEST, ANGELA KAYE, dietitian; b. Ogden, UT, Feb. 26, 1970; d. Richard Brown and Sharon Kaye (Harris) B. A in Home Econ., Ricks Coll., 1990; BS in Dietetics magna cum laude, Brigham Young U., 1993. Registered and cert. dietitian, Utah. Clin. and outpatient dietitian Ogden Regional Med. Ctr., Utah, 1993-97; chief clin. dietitian Columbia Lakeview Hosp., Bountiful, Utah, 1997—; cons. Pvt. Inds. Coun., Ogden, 1993—. Organist LDS ch., Weber State U., Ogden, 1993—. Mem. Am. Dietetic Assn. Mem. LDS ch. Home: 2182 E Eastwood Blvd Ogden UT 84403 Office: Ogden Regional Med Ctr 5475 S 500 E Ogden UT 84405

BEST, BARBARA, personal manager, publicist; b. San Diego, Dec. 2, 1921; d. Charles Lewis and Leila Harrison (Sanders) B. BA in Journalism, U. So. Calif., Los Angeles, 1943. Unit publicist 20th Century Fox Co., Los Angeles, 1943-50; reporter San Diego Jour., 1950; asst. to publicity dir. Stanley Kramer Co., Los Angeles, 1950-53; owner, mgr. Barbara Best & Assocs., Los Angeles, 1953-66; ptnr. Freeman and Best Pub. Rels., Los Angeles, 1967-75; owner, pres. Barbara Best, Inc., Pub. Relations, Los Angeles, 1975-87; personal mgr. Barbara Best Mgmt., Los Angeles, 1987—; exec. v.p. Maribar Prodns., Hollywood, Calif., 1986-. Co-founder, exec. dir. Vikki Carr Scholarship Found., Hollywood, 1971-82; pres. Publicists Fed. Credit Union, Hollywood, 1976-85. Mem. Hollywood Womens Press Club (past pres., bd. dirs.), Women in Film. Democrat. Episcopalian. Office: Barbara Best Mgmt 14159 Riverside Dr Sherman Oaks CA 91423-2362

BEST, DANA JO, primary school educator; b. Ajo, Ariz., Aug. 1, 1952; d. Leo Gibson and Evelyn Louise (Westerbrook) B. BA in Elem. Edn., No. Ariz. U., 1974, Reading Specialist Endorsement, 1989; MEd in Counseling, U. Ariz., 1983. Cert. elem. edn., Ariz. Elem. tchr. Picacho (Ariz.) Schs., 1974-75; bookkeeper Kelly-Springfield, Tucson, 1976-77; various sec. positions Ins. and Adv. Co., Tucson, 1977-78; libr. clk. II U. Ariz. Libr., Tucson, 1978-80, libr. clk., student asst., 1980-83; rehab. counselor Winslow, Ariz., 1983-84; primary sch. tchr. Chinle (Ariz.) Unified Sch. Dist., 1989—; mem. gifted edn. com. Chinle Unified Sch. Dist., 1992-93. Co-founder Project Pals, Chinle Unified Sch. Dist., 1991-92, founder sch. gardening project, 1991-92. Recipient award Chinle Future Famers Am., 1993. Mem. Chinle Edn. Assn. (negotiations team 1990-96, chmn. 1996), Lions. Methodist. Home: PO Box 1765 Chinle AZ 86503 Office: Chinle Unified Sch Dist PO Box 587 Chinle AZ 86503

BEST, GARY ALLEN, special education educator; b. Oceanside, Calif., July 27, 1939; s. Charles Richard and Vivian Elaine (Misner) B.; m. Shirley Joanne Seelhammer, Dec. 18, 1962; 1 child, Joanna Elaine Best Lefave. BA, Calif. State U., L.A., 1961, MA, 1965; PhD, U. Minn., 1968. Spl. edn. tchr. L.A. Unified Schs., 1961-65; instr. U. Minn., Mpls., 1966-68, Duluth, 1966-68; prof. Wis. State U., Eau Claire, 1966; asst. prof. Calif. State U., L.A., 1968—, chmn. div. spl. edn., 1986-91, acting dean, grad. studies, 1986-87, assoc. dean student svcs. Charter Sch. of edn., 1996—; vis. prof. U. Victoria, B.C., 1970, 74, Western Mich. U., Kalamazoo, 1973; bd. dirs. Calif. State U. Found., Crippled Children's Soc. So. Calif.; mem. spl. edn. adv. com. Calif. Commn. on Tchr. Credentialing. Author: Individuals With Physical Disabilities, 1978; contbr. articles and chpts. to profl. jours. and books on phys. disability and sex edn. for exceptional populations. Registered reader Huntington Rare Books/Manuscript Libr., San Marino, Calif., 1980-81. Recipient Outstanding Prof. award Calif. State U., L.A., 1983, named Disting. Alumnus, 1992; named Alumnus of Yr. Riverside C.C., 1994; Fulbright scholar Taipei, Taiwan, 1991. Mem. Coun. for Exceptional Children (parliamentarian 1991-94, pres. divsn. physically handicapped 1984-85). Office: California State Univ LA 5151 State University Dr Los Angeles CA 90032-4221

BEST, MARY LANI, university program coordinator; b. Hilo, Hawaii, June 3, 1944; d. Stanley Clark and Emma Holokahiki (Martinson) Brooks; m. Leningrad Elarionoff, Aug. 14, 1965 (div. 1981); children: Kimberly

Kehaunani, Grad. Ikaika; m. Gary Dean Best, Dec. 7, 1984 (div. 1996). BA, U. Hawaii, Hilo, 1988; MS, Creighton U., 1991. Substitute tchr. Hilo High Sch., 1990; counselor secondary alternative program Westside High Sch., Omaha, 1991; coord. Ctr. for Gifted & Talented Native Hawaiian Children U. Hawaii, Hilo, 1991—. Contbr.: (book) Sociology of Hawaii, 1992; co-editor: Glimpses of Hawaiian Daily Life and Culture, 1994. Active Hale O Na Alii, Hilo, 1988—. Mem. AACD. Republican. Home: 84 Pukihae St Apt 304 Hilo HI 96720-2402 Office: U Hawaii 200 W Kawili St Hilo HI 96720-4075

BEST, ROGER NORMAN, real estate investment manager; b. L.A., Apr. 16, 1949; s. Norman Frank and Muriel Noreen (Atkinson) B.; m. Sheri Lyn Kruyer, Oct. 16, 1982. BA, U. Wash., 1971. Lic. Real Estate Broker, Calif., 1985. Musician, entertainer, 1963-69; pres. Best Enterprises, L.A., 1969—; head electronic media svcs. Cedars-Sinai Med. Ctr., L.A., 1971-73; pres. Tazio Prodns., L.A., 1973-76; v.p. Video Disco & Assocs., L.A., 1975-76, DSL Constrn. Corp., L.A., 1977-85; v.p., chief operating officer Scott Properties, Inc., L.A., 1978-85; pres., chief exec. Tazio Properties, Inc., L.A., 1980—. Inventor correctable typewriter ribbon; creator original music videos concept with Visual Music, 1974; featured columnist Apt. Age Mag., L.A., 1989—. Mem. Van Nuys Airport Adv. Coun., 1987-94. Citation of Appreciation, City of L.A., 1988, 89, 94. Office: Tazio Properties Inc 3580 Wilshire Blvd Fl 17 Los Angeles CA 90010-2501

BEST, SUSAN KIMBERLY, gifted education educator; b. Tonasket, Wash., Dec. 17, 1954; d. Hubert Edwards and Bertha Alberta (Michel) Matt; m. Dennis Eugene Best, Nov. 23, 1979; children: Devin Gene, Danyal Denise. BE, Heritage Coll., 1987, MEd, 1994. Cert. tchr., Wash. Tchr. Paschal Sherman Indian Sch., Omak, Wash., 1987—, coord. gifted program, 1991—. Contbr. poetry to anthologies. Lifetime mem. Okanagan/Lakes Band Enrollment # 1721-C, Colville Confederated Tribes, Colville Indian Reservation. Mem. ASCD, Nat. Assn. for Gifted Children, Colville Tribal Artists. Home: PO Box 1149 181 Haley Creek Rd Omak WA 98841 Office: Paschal Sherman Indian Sch Soaring Eagles Gifted Program Omak Lake Rd Omak WA 98841

BEST-MARTINI, ELIZABETH M., recreation therapist; b. Long Beach, Calif., Sept. 10, 1948; d. Isaac Shelby Best and Margaret Mary (Hughes) Lockett; m. John Arturo Martini, June 16, 1990. BS, Sonoma State U., 1975; MS, San Francisco State U., 1979. Cert. recreation therapist. Intern in recreation therapy U. Calif., San Francisco, 1978; recreation therapist Bayside Convalescent Ctr., Greenbrae, Calif., 1978-82; tchr., instr. Coll. of Marin, Kentfield, Calif., 1983—; instr. Santa Rosa (Calif.) Jr. Coll., 1983—, San Francisco State U., 1996; owner, cons. Recreation Cons., San Rafael, Calif., 1983—. Mem. Nat. Lita Assn. (sec. 1990—), Lita Inc. of Marin (chmn. bd. dirs. 1982-86), Am. Therapeutic Recreation Assn., Nat. Therapeutic Recreation Assn., Calif. Parks and Recreation Soc., Am. Soc. on Aging, Nat. Assn. Activity Profls. Democrat. Office: Recreation Cons 714 C St Ste 207 San Rafael CA 94901

BESTWICK, WARREN WILLIAM, retired construction company executive; b. Missoula, Mont., June 27, 1922; s. William Andrew and Beatrice Anna (Eddy) B.; student Glendale Coll., 1941, U. Mont., 1942; BA, U. Wash., 1949, postgrad., 1950; m. Glenette Haas, Sept. 11, 1949; children: Sharon Kaye, Carol Eddy, Jan Marie. Sr. acct. Frederick & Nelson, Seattle, 1950; controller, bus. mgr. Virginia Mason Hosp., Seattle, 1958-64; contr. Bumstead Woolford Co., Seattle, 1964-68; contr., treas. Wash. Asphalt Co., Seattle, 1968-72; exec. v.p., sec. treas. Wilder Constrn. Co., Inc., Bellingham, Wash., 1972-77, pres., 1977-89, vice chmn., 1989-92, also bd. dirs., ret., 1992; past bd. dirs. Consumers Choice, Bellingham; bd. govs. Va. Mason Med. Ctr., Seattle; past chmn. Area IV advisory bd. Wash. Dept. Commerce and Econ. Devel.; past dir., vice chmn. Mt. Baker Bank, Bellingham. Past bd. dirs., adv. bd. Mt. Baker coun. Boy Scouts Am.; past pres., bd. dirs. Shuckson Found. Whatcom County. Served to col., pilot USMCR, 1942-74. Decorated DFC (3), Air medal (7). Mem. Assn. Wash. Bus. (past. dir.), Whatcom County Devel. Council (past dir. and pres.), Bellingham C. of C. (past dir.), Marine Res. Officers Assn. (past dir. Seattle), Res. Officers Assn., Marine Corps League, The Beavers Constrn. (hon.), United For Wash., U. Wash. Alumni Assn., Ret. Officers Assn., Marine Aviation Assn., World Affairs Coun., Wash. Athletic Club (Seattle), Bellingham Golf and Country Club, Bellingham Yacht Club, Rotary (past pres.). Home: 233 N State St Bellingham WA 98225-5323 also: PO Box 2032 Rancho Santa Fe CA 92067-2032

BETANCOURT, HECTOR MAINHARD, psychology scientist, educator; b. Chile, Sept. 1, 1949; came to U.S. 1979; s. Hector and Eleonora (Mainhard) B.; m. Bernardita Sahli; children: Paul, Daniel. BA, Cath. U., Santiago, Chile, 1976; MA, UCLA, 1981, PhD in Psychology, 1983. From asst. prof. to assoc. prof. psychology Cath. U., Santiago, Chile, 1977-79, 83-85; from assoc. prof. to prof. of psychology Loma Linda U., Riverside, Calif., 1985-93, chmn., 1990-93; chmn., prof. psychology Grad. Sch. Loma Linda (Calif.) U., 1993—. Editor Interam. Psychologist, 1982-86; mem. edit. bd. Jour. Cmty. Psychology, 1986-89, Spanish Jour. Social Psychology, 1986—, Conflict and Peace, 1993—, Jour. Personality and Social Psychology, 1997-98; contbr. articles to profl. jours. Recipient Rotary Found. award for Internat. Understanding, Rotary Internat., 1976-77; Fulbright fellow, UCLA, 1979-80. Mem. APA (exec. com. and chmn. task force on ethnicity, divsn. 48 peace psychology 1994-95, pres.-elect 1996-97), Internat. Soc. Polit. Psychology, Internat. Soc. Cross-Cultural Psychology (exec. com. 1984-86), Interam. Soc. Psychology (sec.-gen. 1983-87), Soc. for Psychol. Study Social Issues, Soc. Personality and Social Psychology. Office: Loma Linda U Dept Psychology Grad S Loma Linda CA 92350

BETANCOURT, NELLIE, physician; b. San Juan, May 13, 1951; d. Ricardo and Nellie (Jimenez) B.; m. Alejandro Salicrup, July 1971 (div. Sept. 1988); children: Alejandro Salicrup, Ricardo Salicrup, Jose Enrique Salicrup; m. Rene Torres, Aug. 16, 1990. BA in Art/English Lit. magna cum laude, U. P.R., 1972, BS in Chemistry magna cum laude, 1975, MD, 1985; postgrad., Med. Coll. Wis., 1993—. Diplomate Am. Bd. Internal Medicine; cert. physician, Calif., P.R., Ga., qualified med. examiner; cert. med. rev. officer; expert evaluator Med. Bd. Calif. Intern, resident in internal medicine VA Hosp., Rio Piedras, P.R., 1985-88; pvt. practice internal medicine Ashford Meml. Hosp., San Juan, 1988-90; staff physician occupational medicine Howell Indsl. Clinic, Atlanta, 1990-91; dir. Hanover Network Indsl. Clinic, City of Industry, Calif., 1992-93; assoc. dir. indsl. medicine Friendly Hills HealthCare Network, La Habra, Calif., 1993-95; med. dirs. BusinessHealth Network, 1995—; bd. dirs. EarthBond, Inc. Mem. Am. Coll. Occupl. and Environ. Medicine, OccMed, Inc. (pres. 1995—), Alpha Omega Alpha. Office: PO Box 2615 Bakersfield CA 93303-2615

BETLACH, MARY CAROLYN, biochemist, molecular biologist; b. Madison, Wis., June 12, 1945; d. William Thompson Stafford and Carolyn Jesse Gillette McCormick; m. Charles J. Betlach, Nov. 14, 1970 (div. 1978); children: John F., Melanie Carolyn. Student, U. Wis., 1963-68; PhD, U. Calif., San Francisco, 1992. Staff rsch. assoc. dept. pediatrics U. Calif., San Francisco, 1970-72, staff rsch. assoc. dept. microbiology/biochemistry, 1972-83, rsch. specialist dept. biochemistry, 1983-93; sr. scientist Parnassus Pharms., Alameda, Calif., 1993-94; dir. molecular biology Kosan Bioscis., Burlingame, Calif., 1995—; adj. asst. prof. dept. pharm. chemistry, U. Calif., San Francisco, 1993—; mem. various grant rev. panels. Contbr. chpts. to books, articles to Gene, Microbiology, Nucleic Acids Rsch., Biochemistry, Jour. Bacteriology, others. Mem. AAAS, Am. Soc. for Microbiology.

BETTIS, JOHN GREGORY, songwriter; b. Long Beach, Calif., Oct. 24, 1946; s. Wayne Douglas and Nellie Jane (House) B. Songwriter, music pub. Warner/Chappel Music, 1976-82; songwriter, pub. John Bettis Music, Santa Monica, Calif., 1982—. Lyricist: (songs) Yesterday Once More, 1973 (Gold Record), Top of the World, 1974 (Gold Record), Heartland, Can You Stop the Rain, 1991, (Grammy nominee 1991), Promise Me You'll Remember, 1990 (acad. awards nominee 1991), One Moment In Time, 1988 (Emmie 1989), Crazy for You, 1985 (Gold Record), Slow Hand, 1981 (Gold Record), Human Nature, 1983 (Grammy cert.-Album of Yr. 1984); lyricist songs for movies including Say Anything, Star Trek V, Cocktail, Nothing in Common, Godfather Part III; lyricist TV theme songs. Recipient Top TV Series award for Growing Pains, ASCAP, 1986, for Just the Ten of Us, ASCAP, 1987, for Empty Nest, ASCAP, 1990, 34 Gold Records, Rec. Industry Assn. Am., 1970-90, 7 Platinum Records, Rec. Industry Assn. Am., 1970-90, 32 Performance awards ASCAP, 1970-90. Mem. ASCAP (bd. rev. 1982-88, bd. dirs. 1995—), Nat. Acad. Songwriters (bd. dirs. 1980-94, chmn. bd. dirs. 1985-87). Office: John Bettis Music PO Box 668 Sunset Beach CA 90742-0668

BETTS, BARBARA LANG (MRS. BERT A. BETTS), lawyer, rancher, realtor; b. Anaheim, Calif., Apr. 28, 1926; d. W. Harold and Helen (Thompson) Lang. BA magna cum laude, Stanford U., 1948; LLB, Balboa U., 1951; m. Roby F. Hayes, July 22, 1948 (dec.); children: John Chauncey IV, Frederick Prescott, Roby Francis II; m. Bert A. Betts, July 11, 1962; 1 child, Bruce Harold; stepchildren: Bert Alan, Randy W., Sally Betts Joynt, Terry Betts Marsteller, Linda Betts Hansen, LeAnn Betts Wilson. Bar: Calif. 1952, U.S. Supreme Ct. 1978; pvt. practice law, Oceanside, Calif., 1952-68, San Diego, 1960—, Sacramento, 1962—; ptnr. Roby F. Hayes & Barbara Lang Hayes, 1952-60; city atty., Carlsbad, Calif., 1959-63; v.p. Isle & Oceans Marinas, Inc., 1970-80, W. H. Lang Corp., 1964-69; sec. Internat. Prodn. Assos., 1968—, Margaret M. McCabe, M.D., Inc., 1977-88 . Chmn. Traveler's Aid, 1952-53; pres. Oceanside-Carlsbad Jr. Chambrettes, 1955-56; vice chmn. Carlsbad Planning Commn., 1959; mem. San Diego Planning Congress, 1959; v.p. Oceanside Diamond Jubilee Com., 1958. Candidate Calif. State Legislature, 77th Dist., 1954; mem. Calif. Dem. State Central Com., 1958-66; co-chmn. 28th Congl. Dist., Dem. State Central Com., 1960-62; alt. del. Dem. Nat. Conv., 1960; co-sponsor All Am. B-24 Liberator Collings Found. Named to Fullerton Union High Sch. Wall of Fame, 1986; recipient Block S award Stanford U. Mem. Am. Judicature Soc., Nat. Inst. Mcpl. Officers, ABA, Calif. Bar Assn., San Diego County Bar Assn., Oceanside C. of C. (sec. 1957, v.p. 1958, dir. 1953-54, 57-59), AAUW (legis. com. 1958-59; local pres. 1959-60; asst. state legis. chmn. 1958-59), Heritage League (2d div. 8th Air Force), No. San Diego County Assn. Cs. of C. (sec.-treas.), Bus. and Profl. Women's Club (So. dist. legislation chmn. 1958-59), DAR (regent Oceanside chpt. 1960-61), San Diego C. of C., San Diego Hist. Soc., Fullerton Jr. Assistance League, Calif. Scholarship Fedn. (life), Loyola Guild of Jesuit High Sch., Phi Beta Kappa. Clubs: Soroptimist Internat. (pres. Oceanside-Carlsbad 1958-59, sec. pub. affairs San Diego, Imperial Counties 1954; pres. of pres.'s council San Diego and Imperial counties and Mexico 1958-59), Barristers, Stanford (Sacramento), Stanford Mothers, Heritage League (2nd air divsn. USAAF). Author: (with Bert A. Betts) A Citizen Answers. Home: 441 Sandburg Dr Sacramento CA 95819-2559 Office: Betts Ranch PO Box 306 Elverta CA 95626-0306 also: 1830 Avenida Del Mundo Apt 1608 Coronado CA 92118-3022

BETTS, BARBARA STOKE, artist, educator; b. Arlington, Mass., Apr. 19, 1924; d. Stuart and Barbara Lillian (Johnstone) Stoke; m. James William Betts, July 28, 1951; 1 child, Barbara Susan (dec.). BA, Mt. Holyoke Coll., 1946; MA, Columbia U., 1948. Cert. tchr., N.Y., Calif., Hawaii. Art tchr. Walton (N.Y.) Union Schs., 1947-48, Presidio Hill Sch., San Francisco, 1949-51; free-lance artist San Francisco, 1951; art tchr. Honolulu Acad. Arts, summer 1952, 59, 63, 85, spring 61, 64; libr. aide art rm. Libr. of Hawaii, Honolulu, 1959; art tchr. Hanahauoli Sch., Honolulu, 1961-62, Hawaii State Dept. Edn., Honolulu, 1958-59, 64-84; owner Ho'olaule'a Designs, Honolulu, 1973—. Illustrator: Cathedral Cooks, 1964, In Due Season, 1986; exhibited in Hawaii Pavilion Expo '90, Osaka, Japan, State Found. of Culture and Arts, group shows since 1964, one person shows 1991, 96; represented in Arts of Paradise Gallery, Waikiki, 1990—; traveling exhbns. include Pacific Prints, 1991, Printmaking East/West, 1993-95, Hawaii/Wis. Watercolor Show, 1993-94. Mem. Hawaii Watercolor Soc. (newsletter editor 1986-90), Nat. League Am. Pen Women (art chmn. 1990-92, sec. 1992-94, nat. miniature art shows 1991, 92, 93, 95), Honolulu Printmakers (dir. 1986, 87), Assn. Hawaii Artists. Republican. Episcopalian. Home: 1520 Ward Ave Apt 203 Honolulu HI 96822-3550

BETTS, JAMES WILLIAM, JR., financial analyst, consultant; b. Montclair, N.J., Oct. 11, 1923; s. James William and Cora Anna (Banta) B.; m. Barbara Stoke, July 28, 1951; 1 child, Barbara Susan (dec.). BA, Rutgers U., 1946; postgrad. New Sch. for Social Rsch., 1948-49; MA, U. Hawaii, 1957. With Dun & Bradstreet, Inc., 1946-86, svc. cons., 1963-64, reporting and svc. mgr., 1964-65, sr. fin. analyst, Honolulu, 1965-86; owner Portfolio Cons. of Hawaii, 1979—; cons. Saybrook Point Investments, Old Saybrook, Conn., 1979—; owner James W. Betts and Co., 1996—. Contbr. articles to mag. Served with AUS, 1943. Mem. Am. Econ. Assn., Nat. Assn. Bus. Economists, Western Econ. Assn., Atlantic Econ. Soc., Col. Henry Rutgers Soc. Republican. Episcopalian. Office: Portfolio Cons Hawaii 126 Queen St Ste 222 Honolulu HI 96813-4411

BETZ, RICHARD, agricultural products executive; b. 1943. Sec.- treas. Royal Pak Produce Inc., Hermiston, Oreg., 1968-74; with Bud-Rich Potato Inc., Hermiston, 1974—, now pres./treas. With U.S. Army, 1964-68. Office: Bud-Rich Potato Inc Butter Creek Hwy Hermiston OR 97838*

BETZ-ZALL, JONATHAN RICHARD, librarian; b. Boston, June 28, 1950; s. Paul M. and Elisabeth (Weisz) Zall; m. Rose E. Betz, Oct. 5, 1973; children: Marissa, David. BA, Swarthmore Coll., 1972; M of Librarianship, U. Wash., 1976. Head libr. Aircraft Tech. Pubs., San Francisco, 1976-77; libr. San Francisco Pub. Libr., 1977-78, Upper Merion Twp. Libr., King of Prussia, Pa., 1978-79, Free Libr. Phila., 1979-85, Sno-Isle Regional Libr. Sys., Marysville, Wash., 1985—. Contbr. book revs. and articles to libr. jours. Co-chmn. Greenwood Family Sing!, 1987—. Mem. Wash. Libr. Assn. (interest group rep. 1994-95, chmn. social responsibilites round table 1988-91, 93-94, chmn. intellectual freedom interest group 1996—), N.W. Internat. Cmtys. Assn. (bd. dirs., pres.). Office: Edmonds Libr 650 Main St Edmonds WA 98020-3056

BEVERETT, ANDREW JACKSON, marketing executive; b. Midland City, Ala., Feb. 21, 1917; s. Andrew J. and Ella Levonia (Adams) B.; m. Martha Sophia Landgrebe, May 26, 1951; children: Andrew Jackson III, James Edmund, Faye A. BS, Samford U., 1940; MBA, Harvard U., 1942. Various exec. positions in corporate planning and mgmt. United Air Lines, Chgo., 1946-66; dir. aviation econs., sr. mktg. and econ. cons. Mgmt. and Econs. Research, Inc., Palo Alto, Calif., 1966-71; sr. economist Stanford Research Inst., Menlo Park, 1971-72; pres. Edy's on the Peninsula stores, 1973-78; real estate broker, fin. and tax cons., Saratoga and San Jose, Calif., 1979—. Ensign to lt. USNR, 1942-46. Mem. Nat. Assn. Enrolled Agts., Nat. Assn. Realtors, Pi Gamma Mu, Phi Kappa Phi. Home: 6325 Whaley Dr San Jose CA 95135-1447

BEVERSDORF, ANNE ELIZABETH, author, astrologer, educator; b. Houston, Tex., Aug. 14, 1949; d. S. Thomas and Norma (Beeson) B. BA, U. Tex., 1972; MLS, Ind. U., 1974. Founding librarian Social Studies Devel. Ctr. Ind. U., Bloomington, 1975-79, info. specialist, 1980-82; co-founder Ind. Clearinghouse for Computer Edn., Indpls., 1983-86; Calif. mktg. rep. Minn. Ednl. Computing Corp., San Marcos, Calif., 1986-88; pres., chief exec. officer Beversdorf Assocs., Ltd., Vista, Calif., 1988-93; writer, lectr., astrologer Vista, Calif., 1993—; cons. Procter & Gamble Ednl. Services, Cin., 1981-85, Brazil Office of Tech. Edn., Rio de Janeiro, Porto Alegre, 1986; mem. faculty Ind. U., Indpls., 1986, San Diego State U., 1988-91. Contbr. over 30 articles to U.S. and internat. profl. jours. Mem. Am. Coun. Vedic Astrology, Am. Fedn. Astrologers, San Diego Astrol. Soc., So. Calif. Astrol. Network. Home and Office: 1119 Anza Ave Vista CA 92084-4517

BEYERL, PAUL VINCENT, priest, educator; b. Colby, Wis., Sept. 2, 1945; s. Jacob Beyerl and Rosemary Bitter. Attended, Wis. State U., Stevens Point, 1963-66, Minn. State U., Winona, 1970-71. Founder, pres. The Rowan Tree Ch., Mpls., 1976—, elder, 1993—; dir. The Hermit's Grove, Kirkland, Wash., 1993-96. Author: The Holy Books of Devas, 1980, rev. and expanded edit., 1993, The Master Book of Herbalism, 1984, A Wiccan Bardo: Initiation and Self-Transformation, 1996, Painless Astrology, 1993, A Compendium of Herbal Magick, 1996; editor The Unicorn, 1977—. Office: The Rowan Tree Ch 9724 B2 Ave NE Kirkland WA 98033

BEYERS, WILLIAM BJORN, geography educator; b. Seattle, Mar. 24, 1940; s. William Abraham and Esther Jakobia (Svendsen) B.; m. Margaret Lyn Rice, July 28, 1968. B.A., U. Wash., 1962, Ph.D., 1967. Asst. prof. geography U. Wash., Seattle, 1968-74, assoc. prof., 1974-82, prof., 1982—, chmn. dept. geography, 1991-95. Mem. Assn. Am. Geographers, Regional Sci. Assn., Am. Econs. Assn., Western Regional Sci. Assn. Home: 7159 Beach Dr SW Seattle WA 98136-2077 Office: U Wash Dept Geography Dept Geography DP 10 Box 353550 Seattle WA 98195-3550

BEYERSDORF, MARGUERITE MULLOY, educator; b. Terry, Mont., Apr. 20, 1922; d. John William and Laura Agnes (Mahar) Mulloy; m. Curtis Alexander Beyersdorf, 1946; 1 child, Mary Jo Wright. Kindergarten-Primary Cert., Coll. St. Catherine, St. Paul, 1942; PhB, Marquette U., 1945; postgrad., Gonzaga U., Spokane, Wash., 1957-62, Ea. Wash. State U., 1977-79. Tchr. grade 3 Sacred Heart Sch., Oelwein, Iowa, 1942-43; tchr. grades 1 and 2 Jr. Mil. Acad., Chgo., 1943-44; tchr. history, English Fairfield (Wash.) High Sch., 1945-46; substitute tchr. Riverside High Sch., 1957; tchr. Mead (Wash.) Sch. Dist., 1958-75; owner/mgr. First Ave. Parking Lot, Spokane, Wash., 1957—. Vol. Spokane N.W. Communities Found., 1982—; active United Way Spokane, 1950, ARC, Am. Cancer Soc., Multiple Sclerosis Soc., others; vol. coord. Dominican Outreach Found. to Domicile Single Parent Families; canteen vol. Spokane Blood Bank, 1981—; vol. Miryam's House of Transition, 1989—. Recipient Vol. of Yr. Golden Rule award J.C. Penney Co., 1993; grantee NSF, Whitworth Coll., 1967. Mem. NEA, APGA, AAUW (bd. dirs. Spokane br., chmn. scholarship com.), Wash. Edn. Assn.-Retired (del. rep. assembly, mem. comm. com 1993—, chmn. comm. commn. 1993—), Mead Edn. Assn. (sec., exec. bd., former bldg. rep., mem. curriculum com.).

BEYLKIN, GREGORY, mathematician; b. St. Petersburg, USSR, Mar. 16, 1953; came to U.S., 1980; naturalized citizen, 1985; s. Jacob and Raya (Pripshtein) B.; m. Helen Simontov, 1974; children: Michael, Daniel. Diploma in Math., U. St. Petersburg, Leningrad, 1975; PhD in Math., NYU, 1982. Assoc. rsch. sci. NYU, 1982-83; mem. profl. staff Schlumberger-Doll Research, Ridgefield, Conn., 1983-91; prof. dept. applied math. U. Colo., Boulder, 1991—. Contbr. articles to profl. jours. Mem. Am. Math. Soc., Soc. for Indsl. and Applied Math., Soc. Exptl. Geophysicists. Home: 3897 Promontory Ct Boulder CO 80304 Office: U Colo Dept Applied Math Boulder CO 80309

BEYMER, DALE ALLEN, manufacturing executive; b. Van Nuys, Calif., July 31, 1957; s. Lawerence Elmos and Patricia Anne (Bryce) B.; m. Anna Louise Beverage, June 3, 1984. Foreman Ronlo Engring. Ltd., Camarillo, Calif., 1975-79; gen. mgr. prodn. Alonian Enterprises Inc., Newbury Park, Calif., 1979-87; v.p. ops. J.M. Precision Inc., Chatsworth, Calif., 1987-88; mgr. machine shop Crane Co. Hydro-Aire Divsn., Burbank, Calif., 1988—; owner, pres. Dycal Systems, Newbury Park, 1982-92. Patentee torque limiting vise handle, 1985. Recipient Geometric Dimensioning and Tolerancing award Tech. Cons., Inc., 1993. Mem. Assn. for Integrated Mfg. Tech. Home: 11 E Avenida De Las Flores Thousand Oaks CA 91360-3104 Office: Crane Co Hydro-Aire Divsn PO Box 7722 Burbank CA 91510-7722

BEZEMER, CAL GENE, composer; b. Lynnville, Iowa, Dec. 9, 1936; s. Arie Edward Bezemer and Deana Berdena (Kuipers) Hanen; m. Penelope Kraner, Nov. 14, 1965 (div. June 1969); children: John, Mark, Kristy: 1 adopted child, Christopher. BA in Music Theory-Composition-Piano, Kansas City Conservatory, 1962; grad., Iowa State U., 1965; ThD, Internat. Theol. Sem., 1985. Pvt. practice, 1976—; music dir., pianist Yma Sumac and Herb Jeffries, 1988—; founder, dir. Wholy Cow, 1997—; v.p. Hollywood-Wilshire Symphony, 1978-92, So. Calif. Motion Picture Coun., 1978-92, Hollywood Opera Club, 1978-92. Ptnr. with Leo Savalas, 1997, Dorothy Donnegan, 1997; leader, sideman, Hollywood Bowl, Palladium, Coconut Grove, Music Center, Cinegrill, House of Blues; piano and sax aboard USS Pocono, Admiral's Flagship for Atlantic Fleet; with Al Jarreau, David Sanborn, Debbie Reynolds, Eddie Jefferson, "Scatman" Crothers, Ralph Marterie, Ray McKinley (Glen Miller Band), "Wolfman" Jack, Alan Jones, Four Lads, Art Lund, Gene Bell, Arthur Duncan; columnist Spotlite on Las Vegas (Angel City Jazz Beat). Exec. v.p. Music and Performing Arts Angels, 1978—; assoc. min., organist Internat. Evangelism Crusades, 1983—; v.p. Hollywood Bowl Easter Sunrise Svc. Guild, 1992-95. With USN, 1954-57. Recipient 1st Composers award Matinne Musical Club, 1978. Mem. Am. Soc. Music Arrangers and Composers, Musician's Union, Hollywood Men's Comedy Club, Troupers, Navy League, Am. Legion Film League, Dexter Grey Found. Film Adv. Bd. of Elaine Blythe. Republican. Mem. Christian Ch. Home: 222 S Mariposa Ave # 301 Los Angeles CA 90004-5415 Office: Music Angels Prodn 222 S Mariposa Ave # 301 Los Angeles CA 90004-5415

BHADURI, RAHUL SANKAR, metallurgical engineer; b. Calcutta, India, Aug. 23, 1956; came to U.S., 1981; s. Ajit and Sujita (Bhattacharjee) B.; m. Debjani Purkayastha, Jan. 4, 1985. BS in Metall. Engring., Jadavpur U., Calcutta, India, 1979; MS in Metall. Engring., U. Nev., 1987. Reg. profl. engr., Nev. Sales engr. Greaves-Foseco Ltd., Bombay, India, 1980; rsch., teaching asst. U. Nev., Reno, 1981-84; assayer, metallurgist Angst Inc., Gold Bar Mine, Beatty, Nev., 1987-88, metall. engr., 1988-89; metallurgist Atlas Gold-Gold Bar Mine, Eureka, Nev., 1990-92; metall. engr. Gold Fields Ops. Co.-Chimney Creek, Golconda, Nev., 1992-93; metall. engr. Santa Fe Pacific Gold-Twin Creeks Mine, Golconda, Nev., 1993-96, prof. cons. on arsenical water treatment, 1996—. Contbr. papers to profl. publs. Mem. Am. Inst. Mining, Metall. & Petroleum Engrs., Soc. Mineral Analysts, Toastmasters Internat. Office: Santa Fe Pacific Gold Twin Creeks Mine PO Box 492 Winnemucca NV 89446

BHAGWAN, SUDHIR, computer industry and research executive, consultant; b. Lahore, West Pakistan, Aug. 9, 1942; came to U.S., 1963; s. Vishan and Lakshmi Devi (Arora) B.; m. Sarita Bahl, Oct. 25, 1969; children: Sonia, Sunil. BSEE, Punjab Engring. Coll., Chandigarh, India, 1963; MSEE, Stanford U., 1964; MBA with honors, Golden Gate U., 1977. Engr. Gaylor Products, North Hollywood, Calif., 1964-68, Burroughs Corp., Pasadena, Calif., 1968-70; engring. mgr. Burroughs Corp., Santa Barbara, Calif., 1970-78; engring. mgr. Intel Corp., Hillsboro, Oreg., 1978-81, chmn. strategic planning, 1981-82, gen. mgr., 1983-88; pres., exec. dir., bd. dirs. Oreg. Advanced Computing Inst., Beaverton, 1988-90; strategic bus. mgr. INTEL Corp., Hillsboro, Oreg., 1990-92, gen. mgr. bus. multimedia products, 1992-93, bus. area mgr., 1993-94, dir. internat. mktg., 1995—; spkr. to high tech. industry, Oreg., 1988—; mem. organizing com. Distributed Memory Computing Conf., 1989-90, gen. chmn., 1990-91; chmn. computer tech. adv. bd. Oreg. Mus. Sci. and Industry, 1991-93; bd. dirs. II-Tracker Inc. Cons. Oreg. Econ. Devel. Dept., 1988-91; bd. dirs. St. Mary's Acad., Portland,, 1989-92. Mem. Am. Electronics Assn. (higher edn. com. Oreg. chpt. 1989-90, exec. com. 1990). Home: 13940 NW Harvest Ln Portland OR 97229-3653 Office: INTEL Corp 5200 NE Elam Young Pky Hillsboro OR 97124-6463

BHAT, BAL KRISHEN, geneticist, plant breeder; b. Srinagar, India, May 3, 1940; came to U.S. 1989; s. Justice Janki Nath and Dhanwati (Kaul) B.; m. Sarla Kaul, Sept. 23, 1966; children: Arun Bhat, Anupama Bhat. MSc, Indian Agrl. Rsch. Inst., New Delhi, 1963; PhD, I.A.R.I., New Delhi, 1967. Rsch. assoc. Rockefeller Found., New Delhi, 1967; plant breeder in charge of rsch. Birla Inst. of Sci. Rsch., Rupar, Punjab, India, 1967-68; scientist C Reg. Rsch. Lab. Coun. of Sci. and Indsl. Rsch., Srinagar, India, 1968-74, head, 1972-79, 87-89, scientist E I, 1974-79, scientist E II, 1981-85, deputy dir., 1985-89; v.p., dir. rsch. Bot. Resources, Inc., Independence, Oreg., 1989-95; cons., 1995—; rsch. fellow U. Tasmania, Hobart, Australia, 1979-81, sr. rsch. fellow, 1981-86; cons. in field. Contbr. over 100 articles to profl. jours. Named Scientist of the Yr., Reg. Rsch. Lab., Srinagar, 1976. Fellow Indian Soc. Genetics and Plant Breeding; mem. Am. Soc. Agronomy, Crop Sci. Soc. Am., Soc. for Advancement of Breeding Rsch. in Asia and Oceania, Coun. for Agrl. Sci. and Tech.

BHATIA, PETER K., editor, journalist; b. Pullman, Wash., May 22, 1953; s. Vishnu N. and Ursula Jean (Dawson) B.; m. Elizabeth M. Dahl, Sept. 27, 1981; children: Megan Jean, Jay Peter. BA, Stanford U., 1975. Polit. reporter, asst. news editor Spokesman Rev., Spokane, Wash., 1975-77; news editor Dallas Times Herald, 1980-81; asst. news editor San Francisco Examiner, 1977-80, news editor, 1981-85, dep. mng. editor/news, 1985-87; mng. editor Dallas Times Herald, 1987-88; editor York Dispatch, York, Pa., 1988-89; mng. editor The Sacramento Bee, 1989-93; exec. editor The Fresno Bee, 1993; mng. editor The Oregonian, Portland, 1993—; Pulitzer Prize juror, 1992-93. Mem. Stanford U. Alumni Assn., Am. Soc. Newspaper Editors (bd. dirs. 1997—), AP Mng. Editors (bd. dirs. 1991—), Asian Am. Journalists Assn., Nat. Assn. Minority Media Execs., Sigma Delta Chi, Theta Delta Chi. Office: The Oregonian 1320 SW Broadway Portland OR 97201-3411

BHAYANI, KIRAN LILACHAND, environmental engineer, programs manager; b. Bhavnagar, Gujarat, India, Dec. 2, 1944; came to U.S., 1968, naturalized; s. Lilachand Premchand and Rasila (Chhotalal Shah) B.; m. Chandra Vasantlal Gandhi, June 24, 1971; children: Nikhil K., Mihir K. BEng with honors, U. Bombay, India, 1965, MEng, 1968; MS, U. R.I., 1970. Diplomate Am. Acad. Environ. Engrs.; registered profl. engr., Va., Ga., Utah. San. engr. Greeley & Hansen, N.Y.C., 1971-72, Hayes, Seay, Mattern & Mattern, Roanoke, Va., 1972-77; environ. engr. Hussey, Gay & Bell, Inc., Savannah, Ga., 1977-80; engring. mgr., Utah Div. Water Quality, Dept. Environ. Quality, Salt Lake City, 1980—; tech. transfer and sludge mgmt. coord., 1982—; mem. fair employment com. Dept. Health, Salt Lake City, 1982-90, adv. 1991-93, chmn., 1988-89, cons., 1989-91; mem. Utah Engrs. Coun., 1989—, vice-chmn., 1992-93, chmn. 1993-94, awards chmn., 1994-95; chmn. Engr's. Week, 1992; v.p. Gujarati Samaj of Utah, 1992-93. Reviewer (practice manual) Financing Sewer Projects, 1984; reviewer for biennial conf. Internat. Assn. on Water Quality, 1995— and manuscripts for Water Rsch., 1994—; design of Municipal Wastewater Treatment Plants, 1990-91. Fellow ASCE (profl. coordination com. 1981-88, reviewer Jour. Environ. Engring. Div., Proceedings ASCE 1988—); mem. NSPE, Am. Acad. Environ. Engrs. (state chmn. 1988—), Am. Water Works Assn., Internat. Assn. Water Quality, Water and Environ. Fedn. (internat. com. 1984, mem. tech. rev. com. for manual of practice, 1990-95), MATHCOUNTS (chmn. 1985-88, bd. govs. 1988—, regional coord. 1988-95). Office: Utah Div Water Quality 288 N 1460 W Salt Lake City UT 84116-3100

BIALOSKY, MARSHALL HOWARD, composer; b. Oct. 30, 1923. Student, Converse Coll., 1942-43, 46, Colo. Coll., 1948; MusB cum laude, Syracuse U., 1949; MusM, Northwestern U., 1950. Asst. prof. music Milton (Wis.) Coll., 1950-54; asst. conductor Milton Coll. Band, 1954; asst. prof. humanities and music U. Chgo., 1956-61; assoc. prof. music and humanities, conductor chorale SUNY, Stony Brook, 1961-64; prof., chmn. dept. fine arts Calif. State U., Dominguez Hills, 1964-77, founding chmn. dept. music, 1977-78, prof. dept. music, 1978-86, prof. emeritus dept. music, 1986—; mem. Calif. State Coll. Employee Assn. Statewide Acad. Coun., 1968-71; mem. Calif. State Coll. Internat. Program Acad. Coun. and Exec. Com., 1967-73; bd. dirs. Monday Evening Concerts, L.A., 1966-77; dir. Saturday Conservatory Music, L.A. chpt., 1967-71; coord. humanities M.A. program Calif. State U., Dominguez Hills; composer-in-residence Chamber Music Conf. and Composer's Forum of the East, Bennington Coll., 1989. Performer various cities, radio stas. and schs. Composer piano music including An Album for the Young, Five Western Scenes, mixed chorus including American Names, A Sight in Camp in the Daybreak Gray and Dim, Women's Chorus including American Poets Suite, At Last, Vocal Music including Two Songs to Poems of Howard Nemerov, folk songs, spirituals, Christmas music, music for wind instruments, string instruments, brass instruments, guitar and percussion instruments. Contbr. articles to jours. Fulbright award, 1954-56; Wurlitzer Found. grantee, 1979, N.Y.C. Meet-the-Composer grantee, 1984, 86; recipient Career Achievement award Profl. Fraternity Assn. Am., 1980. Mem. ASCAP (creative grant award 1976—), Coll. Music Soc., Am. Soc. Univ. Composers (nat. chmn. 1974-77), Nat. Assn. Composers U.S.A. (pres. 1978—), Soc. Composers Inc., Am. Assn. Choral Conductor. Office: Nat Assoc Composer USA PO Box 49256 Los Angeles CA 90049-0652

BIAN, RANDY XINDI, research scientist; m. Shiyuan Zhong, July 1, 1985; 1 child, Jessica. BS, Nanjing (China) U., 1982, MS, 1985; MS, Iowa State U., 1993. Tchg. asst. Nanjing U., 1982-86; lectr. Nanjing Inst. Meteorology, 1987-88; rsch. asst. Iowa State U., Ames, 1989-92; scientist Pacific N.W. Nat. Lab., Richland, Wash., 1993—. Contbr. articles to profl. jours. Mem. AAAS, Am. Geophys. Union, Am. Meteorol. Soc. Office: Pacific NW Nat Lab PO Box 999 K9-30 Richland WA 99352

BIANCHI, RICHARD, food products executive; b. 1947. With Bianchi Land Co., Merced, Calif., 1968—, v.p., 1971—, now v.p., sec., CFO. Office: Bianchi Land Co 1975 W Olive Ave Merced CA 95348-1206*

BIANCO, JAMES A., research and development executive; b. 1956. BS cum laude with honors, NYU, 1979; MD, Mt. Sinai Sch. of Medicine, 1983. Intern, then resident Mt. Sinai Med. Ctr., N.Y.C., 1983-87; fellow in oncology U. Wash., Seattle, 1987-91, asst. prof. medicine 1991-92; dir. bone marrow transplant program VA Med. Ctr., Seattle, 1990-92; asst. mem. Fred Hutchinson Cancer Rsch. Ctr., Seattle, 1991-92; pres., CEO Cell Therapeutics, Inc., Seattle, 1992—. Mem. Alpha Omega Alpha. Office: Cell Therapeutics Inc 201 Elliott Ave W Ste 400 Seattle WA 98119-4230*

BIBEL, BARBARA MITA, librarian; b. N.Y.C., Oct. 30, 1945; d. Seeling Isaac and Lillian (Serebreny) Chaikin; m. David J. Bibel, 1970 (div. 1977); 1 child, Sara. BA summa cum laude in French, UCLA, 1967; MA in Romance Lang., Johns Hopkins U., 1970; MLS, U. Calif., Berkeley, 1971. Cert. tchr., Calif. Libr. Fitz Hugh Ludlow Meml. Libr., San Francisco, Calif., 1972-75; reference libr. Info. Unlimited, Berkeley, 1977-79; indsl. safety trainer Chevron U.S.A., Richmond, Calif., 1980-82; asst. unit head humanities grad. svc. Gen. Libr. U. Calif., Berkeley, 1983-87; reference libr. IIsci, bus., sociology dept. Oakland (Calif.) Pub. Libr., 1986—; book reviewer Booklist, Chgo., 1988—, Libr. Jour., N.Y.C., 1989—, Am. Ref. Books Ann., Englewood, Colo., 1993—, R.R. Bowker, 1994; translator Berkeley Sci. Translation, 1977-79; instr. health edn. Vista Coll., Berkeley, 1977-81; reference libr. Bay Area Libr. Info. System, 1984-91, Berkeley Pub. Libr., 1984—; libr. Congregation Beth El., Berkeley, 1985-86; instr. sch. libr. and info. studies U. Calif., Berkeley, 1984-87; contbr. Encyclopedias, Dictionaries, Atlases for the 1990's. Editor: Reference Sources for Small and Medium-Sized Libraries, 6th edit., 1995. asst. coord. safety svcs. ARC, Berkeley, 1977-79. John Hopkins U. fellow, 1967-70; Calif. State U. scholar, 1963-67, UCLA Alumni scholar, 1963-67. Mem. ALA (editorial bd. Reference Books Bulletin), ACLU, Calif. Libr. Assn., Nat. Assn. Emergency Med. Technicians, Phi Beta Kappa. Office: Oakland Pub Libr 125 14th St Oakland CA 94612-4310

BIBLE, FRANCES LILLIAN, mezzo-soprano, educator; b. Sackets Harbor, N.Y.; d. Arthur and Lillian (Cooke) B. Student, Juilliard Sch. Music, 1939-47. Artist-in-residence Shepherd Sch. of Music Rice U., Houston, 1975-91. Appeared throughout U.S., Australia, Europe including Vienna Staatsoper, Karlsruhe Staatsoper, Dublin Opera Co., N.Y.C. Opera, NBC-TV Opera, San Francisco Opera, Glyndebourne Opera, San Antonio Opera Festival, New Orleans Opera, Houston Grand Opera, Miami Opera, Dallas Opera; appeared in concer with major symphonies; world premiers (opera): The Ballad of Baby Doe, The Crucible, The Troubled Island, The Dybuk. Named Woman of the Yr. in Opera, Mademoiselle, 1949. Mem. Am. Guild Mus. Artists (past 3d v.p., bd. dirs. 1989-91), Sigma Alpha Iota (hon.), Beta Sigma Pi (hon.). Republican. Episcopalian. Home: 2377 Thata Way Hemet CA 92544-7009 *Always try to do your very best with the talent you were given but keep your sense of humor, and don't take yourself too seriously!.*

BICE, SCOTT HAAS, lawyer, educator; b. Los Angeles, Mar. 19, 1943; s. Fred Haas and Virginia M. (Scott) B.; m. Barbara Franks, Dec. 21, 1968. B.S., U. So. Calif., 1965, J.D., 1968. Bar: Calif. bar 1971. Law clk. to Chief Justice Earl Warren, 1968-69; successively asst. prof., assoc. prof., prof. law., Carl Mason Franklin prof. U. So. Calif., Los Angeles, 1969—; assoc. dean U. So. Calif., 1971-74, dean, 1980—; vis. prof. polit. sci. Calif. Inst. Tech., 1977; vis. prof. U. Va., 1978-79; bd.dirs. Western Mut. Ins. Co., Residence Mut. Ins. Co., Imagine Films Entertainment Co., Jenny Craig, Inc. Mem. editl. adv. bd. Calif. Lawyer, 1989-93; contbr. articles to law jours. Bd. dirs. L.A. Family Housing Corp., 1989-93, Stone Soup Child Care Programs, 1988—. Affiliated scholar Am. Bar Found., 1972-74. Fellow Am. Bar Found.; mem. Am. Law Inst., Calif. Bar, Los Angeles County Bar Assn., Am. Judicature Soc., Calif. Club, Chancery Club, Long Beach Yacht Club. Home: 787 S San Rafael Ave Pasadena CA 91105-2326 Office: U So Calif Sch of Law 699 Exposition Blvd Los Angeles CA 90089-0071*

BICK, ISRAEL, collectables and memorabilia company executive; b. Bronx, N.Y., Nov. 3, 1937; s. Benjamin and Sylvia (Berger) B.; m. Ida Hirsch, Feb. 8, 1970 (div. 1980); children: Benjamina, Mayer. BA, Yeshiva U., 1959. Founder, owner, CEO Bick Internat., Van Nuys, Calif., 1952—; cons. numerous charitable orgns.; appraiser for state, city, banks, and estates. Chmn. stamp and coin divsn. United Jewish Fund L.A. With U.S. Army, 1961-63. Named Soldier of Yr., U.S. Army, 1962; recipient plaque U.S. Postal Svc. Mem. Internat. Stamp Collectors Soc. (exec. dir.). Office: PO Box 854 Van Nuys CA 91408-0854

BICKEL, PETER JOHN, statistician, educator; b. Bucharest, Romania, Sept. 21, 1940; came to U.S., 1957, naturalized, 1964; s. Eliezer and P. Madeleine (Moscovici) B.; m. Nancy Kramer, Mar. 2, 1964; children: Amanda, Stephen. AB, U. Calif., Berkeley, 1960, MA, 1961, PhD, 1963; PhD (hon.), Hebrew U. Jerusalem, 1988. Asst. prof. stats. U. Calif., Berkeley, 1964-67, assoc. prof., 1967-70, prof., 1970—, chmn. dept. stats., 1976-79, dean phys. scis., 1980-86, chmn. dept. stats., 1993—; vis. lectr. math. Imperial Coll., London, 1965-66; fellow J.S. Guggenheim Meml. Found., 1970-71, J.D. and Catherine T. MacArthur Found., 1984-89; NATO sr. sci. fellow, 1974. Author: (with K. Doksum) Mathematical Statistics, 1976, (with C. Klaassen, Y. Ritov and J. Wellner) Efficient and Adaptive Estimation in Semiparametric Models, 1993; assoc. editor Annals of Math. Stats., 1968-76, 86-93; contbr. articles to profl. jours. Fellow J.D. and Catherine T. MacArthur Found., 1984-89. Fellow AAAS (chair sect. U 1996-97), Inst. Math. Stats. (pres. 1980), Am. Statis. Assn.; mem. NAS, Royal Statis. Soc., Internat. Statis. Inst., Am. Acad. Arts and Scis., Royal Netherlands Acad. Arts and Scis., Bernoulli Soc. (pres. 1990). Office: U Calif Dept Stats Evans Hall Berkeley CA 94720

BICKERSTAFF, BERNARD TYRONE, SR., professional basketball team coach; b. Benham, Ky., Nov. 2, 1943; m. Eugenia King; children: Tim, Robin, Cydni, Bernard, John. Grad., U. San Diego. Former head coach U. San Diego; then asst. coach Washington Bullets, Nat. Basketball Assn., Landover, Md.; head coach Seattle SuperSonics, 1985-90, v.p. ops., 1990; pres., gen. mgr., head coach Denver Nuggets Profl. Basketball Team, 1990-97; head coach Washington Bullets Profl. Basketball Team, 1997—. Office: Washington Bullets 1 Harry S Truman Dr Landover MD 20785 also: Washington Bullets 9 US Air Arena Landover MD 20785*

BICKMORE, EDWARD CLIFTON, JR., risk management consulting executive; b. Upland, Calif., Oct. 12, 1929; s. Edward Clifon and Vira Jean (Sechrist) B.; m. Kennieth Jean Nasalrond, Edward Charles, Denise Lee. BS in Acctg., Calif. State U., 1974. Contr. Kings View Corp., Reedley, Calif., 1974-77; gen. mgr. Orange Cove (Calif.) Irrigation Dist., 1977-81, Calif. Water Agy. Joint Powers, Sacramento, 1981-94; founder, pres. Bickmore & Assocs. Inc., Citrus Heights, Calif., 1984—. Lt. comdr. USN, 1947-70. Mem. Pub. Agy. Risk Mgrs. Assn., Calif. Assn. Joint Powers Authorization (bd. dirs. 1986-87), Phi Kappa Phi, Beta Sigma Sigma. Republican. Home: 6444 Pretty Girl Ct Citrus Heights CA 95621-4743 Office: Bickmore & Assocs Inc 6371 Auburn Blvd Citrus Heights CA 95621-5274

BIDDLE, DONALD RAY, aerospace company executive; b. Alton, Mo., June 30, 1936; s. Ernest Everet and Dortha Marie (McGuire) B.; m. Nancy Ann Dunham, Mar. 13, 1955; children: Jeanne Kay Biddle Bednash, Mitchell Lee, Charles Alan. Student El Dorado (Kans.) Jr. Coll., 1953-55, Pratt (Kans.) Jr. Coll., 1955-56; BSME, Washington U., St. Louis, 1961; postgrad. computer sci. Pa. State U. Extension, 1963; cert. bus. mgmt. Alexander Hamilton Inst., 1958. Design group engr. Emerson Elec. Mfg., St. Louis, 1957-61; design specialist Boeing Vertol, Springfield, Pa., 1962; cons. engr. Ewing Tech. Design, Phila., 1962-66; chief engr. rotary wing Gates Learjet, Wichita, Kans., 1967-70; dir. engring./R & D BP Chems., Inc. Advanced Materials Div., Stockton, Calif., 1971-93; prin. Biddle & Assocs., Consulting Engrs., Stockton, 1993—; pres., CEO Big Valley Aviation, Inc., Stockton, Calif., 1997—. Guest lectr. on manrated structures, devel. proprietary designs, small bus. devel. to various univs. and tech. socs. Cons. engr. Scoutmaster , counselor, instl. rep. Boy Scouts Am., St. Ann, Mo., 1958-61; mem. Springfield Sch. Bd., 1964. Mem. ASME, ASTM, AIAA, Am. Helicopter Soc. (sec.-treas. Wichita chpt. 1969), Am. Mgmt. Assn., Exptl. Pilots Assn., Soc. for Advancement of Metals and Process Engring. Republican. Methodist (trustee, chmn. 1974-76, 84-86, staff parish 1987-90, fin. 1991-96, video and interiors 1990—). Patentee landing gear designs, inflatable rescue system, glass retention systems, adjustable jack system, cold weather start fluorescent lamp, paper honeycomb core post-process systems. Home: 1140 Stanton Way Stockton CA 95207-2537 Office: Big Valley Aviation Inc ESOP/T 7535 S LIndbergh St Stockton CA 95206

BIDWILL, WILLIAM V., professional football executive; s. Charles W. and Violet Bidwill; m. Nancy Bidwill; children: William Jr., Michael, Patrick, Timothy, Nicole. Grad., Georgetown U. Co-owner St. Louis Cardinals Football Team (now known as Phoenix Cardinals), 1962-72, owner, 1972—, also chmn., 1972—; pres. St. Louis Cardinals Football Team (now known as Phoenix Cardinals), Phoenix, Ariz. Office: Ariz Cardinals P O Box 888 Phoenix AZ 85001-0888*

BIEDERMAN, DONALD ELLIS, lawyer; b. N.Y.C., Aug. 23, 1934; s. William and Sophye (Groll) B.; m. Marna M. Leerburger, Dec. 22, 1962; children: Charles Jefferson, Melissa Anne. AB, Cornell U., 1955; JD, Harvard U., 1958; LLM in Taxation, NYU, 1970. Bar: N.Y. 1959, U.S. Dist. Ct. (so. dist.) N.Y. 1967, Calif. 1977. Assoc. Hale, Russell & Stentzel, N.Y.C., 1962-66; asst. corp. counsel City of N.Y., 1966-68; assoc. Delson & Gordon, N.Y.C., 1968-69; ptnr. Roe, Carman, Clerke, Berkman & Berkman, Jamaica, N.Y., 1969-72; gen. atty. CBS Records, N.Y.C., 1972-76; sr. v.p. legal affairs and adminstrn. ABC Records, L.A., 1977-79; ptnr. Mitchell, Silberberg & Knupp, L.A., 1979-83; exec. v.p., gen. counsel bus. affairs Warner/Chappell Music Inc. (formerly Warner Bros. Music), L.A., 1983—; adj. prof. Sch. Law Southwestern U., L.A., 1982—, Pepperdine U., Malibu, Calif., 1985-87, Loyola Marymount U., L.A., 1992; lectr. Anderson Sch. Mgmt. UCLA, 1993, U. So. Calif. Law Ctr., 1995—. Editor: Legal and Business Problems of the Music Industry, 1980; co-author: Law and Business of the Entertainment Industries, 1987, 2d edit., 1991, 3d edit., 1995. Bd. dirs. Calif. Chamber Symphony Soc., L.A., 1981-92; dir. Entertainment Law Inst. U. So. Calif., 1993—. 1st lt. U.S. Army, 1959. Recipient Hon. Gold Record, Recording Industry Assn. Am., 1974, Trendsetter award Billboard mag., 1976. Mem. N.Y. Bar Assn., Calif. Bar Assn., Riviera Country Club, Cornell Club. Democrat. Jewish. Home: 2406 Pesquera Dr Los Angeles CA 90049-1225 Office: Warner/Chappell Music Inc 10585 Santa Monica Blvd Los Angeles CA 90025-4921

BIER, JESSE, literature educator; b. Hoboken, N.J., July 18, 1925; s. Benjamin Arthur and Lenore (Greenberg) B.; m. Laure Victoria Darsa, July 21, 1950; children: Ethan, Leslie, Lilian. BA, Bucknell U., 1949; MA, Princeton U., 1952, PhD, 1956. From instr. to prof. lit. U. Mont., Missoula, 1955-90; Fulbright prof. U. Lyon and Clermont-Ferrand, France, 1957-58; vis. lectr. Bucknell U., Lewisburg, Pa., 1965-66; vis. prof. San Diego State Coll., 1971; chair in Am. lit. Université de Lausanne, Switzerland, 1971-72; vis. lectr. Sorbonne, 1995; cons. editor Bucknell U. Press, 1975-77; cons. Swiss Univ. System, Switzerland, 1978, U. Ottowa, Can., 1983. Author: The Rise and Fall of American Humor: Criticism, History, 1968, 81, Resistant Essays, 1993, criticism; novels: Trial at Bannock: 1963-64, A Hole in the Lead Apron, 1964, Year of the Cougar, 1976. Cpl. U.S. Army, 1943-45, ETO. Decorated Purple Heart. Home: 5850 Wildcat Rd Missoula MT 59802

BIERBAUM, JANITH MARIE, artist; b. Evanston, Ill., Jan. 14, 1927; d. Gerald Percy and Lillian (Sullivan) Turnbull; m. J. Armin Bierbaum, Apr. 17, 1948; children: Steve, Todd, Chad, Peter, Mark. BA, Northwestern U., 1948; student, Mpls. Art Inst., 1964; postgrad., St. Paul Art Inst., 1969-70. Rsch. asst. AMA, Chgo., 1948-49; tchr. Chgo. high schs., 1949-51; freelance artist Larkspur, Colo., 1951—. Exhibited in group shows at Foot Hills Art Ctr., 1985, 86, 87, Palmer Lake (Colo.) Art Assn., 1986-87, 88-89, Gov.'s Mansion, Bismarck, N.D., 1960; oil painting appeared in 1989 Women in Art Nat. calendar pub. by AAUW. Recipient 1st Place Purchase award U. Minn., Mpls., 1966, Coors Classic award Coors Beer, Golden, Colo., 1987. Mem. Colo. Artist Assn. Republican. Home and Office: 7787 S Perry Park Blvd Larkspur CO 80118-9005

BIERMAN, HOWARD RICHARD, physician; b. Newark, Jan. 27, 1915; m. Doris Simmons, May 16, 1946; children: Barry, Tracey, Dana. BS in Medicine, Washington U. St. Louis, 1939, MD, 1939. House officer Barnes Hosp., 1938-39, resident and fellow in hematology, 1939-41; prin. clin. investigator Nat. Cancer Inst., NIH, Bethesda, Md., 1946-53; chief clin. sect. lab. experimental oncology & medicine U. Calif., San Francisco, 1947-53; dir. hosp. for tumors and allied diseases City of Hope Med. Hosp., Duarte, Calif., 1953-59; chmn. dept. medicine City of Hope Med. Hosp., Durate, Calif., 1954-59, med. and scientific dir., 1955-59; dir. Bierman Med. Group, Inc., 1959—; scientific dir. Inst. for Cancer and Blood Rsch., Beverly Hills, Calif., 1959—; sr. attending physician L.A. County Gen. Hosp., 1959-68, sr. attending physician emeritus, 1968—; attending physician Cedars of Lebanon Hosp. and Mt. Sinai Hosp., L.A., 1959-76, Cedars-Sinai Med. Ctr., L.A., 1967—; attending physician, cons. Century City Hosp., Midway Hosp., 1976—; cons. hematology-oncology White Meml. Hosp., 1959—; vis. prof. Bangkok Sanitarium and Hosp., 1960, 63. Editor: Leukopoiesis and Disease, 1964, Am. Lectrs. Series in Tumors, 1970-72; author of 5 books; contbr. over 250 articles to profl. jours.; patentee in field. Comdr. USN, 1941-47, USNR, 1947-65. Fellow AAAS, Am. Coll. Physicians, Am. Coll. Angiology; mem. AMA, Am. Soc. Internal Medicine, Am. Soc. Clin. Oncology, Am. Soc. Pharmacology and Experimental Therapeutics, Am. Assn. Cancer Rsch., Am. Soc. Hematology, Calif. Med. Assn., So. Calif. Acad. Clin. Oncology, Los Angeles County Med. Assn., Internat. Assn. Study Lung Cancer, Internat. Union Cancer, Internat. Soc. Preventive Oncology, Internat. Soc. Experimental Hematology, Cell Kinetics Soc., Alpha Omega Alpha (Mo. chpt.). Office: Bierman Med Group 150 N Robertson Blvd Beverly Hills CA 90211-2142

BIERMAN, JACK VICTOR, magazine editor, publisher; b. Bklyn., Oct. 15, 1942; s. Sam and Freda (Adler) B.; m. Susan Toshiko Owaki, Mar. 26, 1983; children: Lisa, Clare. BA, Calif. State U., 1979. Editor-in-chief Games Mag., L.A., 1980-83, Parenting Mag., Orange County, Calif., 1986—, San Diego Parent, 1988—; editor, publisher L.A. Parent Mag., 1980—; founder Nat. Parenting Publ. awards, L.A., 1990. Editor, publisher: The Guide for Families Directory, 1996; editor: (cookbook) I Want More, 1994. Founder Children's Playwright Festival, L.A., 1996; advisor Theatre Arts Festival, L.A., 1990-94, Ednl. TV Network, L.A., 1993—, Nursery Nature Walks, L.A., 1993—; mem. adv. bd. Monte Vista Sch., La Crescenta, Calif., 1994. Recipient Mayor's award City L.A., 1982. Mem. Parenting Publs. Am. (honoree 1995). Office: LA Parent Mag 443 Irving Dr Burbank CA 91504-2447

BIERMAN, SANDRA L., artist; b. Bklyn., N.Y., 1938; d. John Charles Riesberg and Martha Lee (Blair) Davies; m. William Raymond Bumgardner, Feb. 8, 1958 (div. Oct. 1969); children: Cheryl, Steven, James; m. Arthur Bierman, Oct. 1, 1983. Student, Md. Inst. Art, Balt., 1957-58, Art Students League, N.Y.C., 1981-83, Woodstock (N.Y.) Sch. Art, 1986-88. oil painter represented by Moondance Gallery, Santa Fe, N.Mex., 1992-94, David Haslam/Montgomery, Boulder, Colo., 1992-96, Galerie du Bois, Aspen, Colo., 1993—, Contemporary S.W. Gallery, Santa Fe, 1994—, Merrill Gallery, Denver, 1995—, Ruthl Linton-David Haslam, Boulder, 1996—, Gallery East, Loveland, Colo., 1996—; art workshop instr. West'n Acad. Women Artists, Boulder, 1996—, Suzanne Brown Gallery, Scottsdale, Ariz., 1997—, Jack Meier Gallery, Houston, Tex., 1997—; instr. workshop Nat. Acad. Women Artists, Wickenburg, Ariz., 1997. One-person shows include Nat. Ctr. for Atmospheric Rsch., Boulder, 1992, Columbine Gallery, Loveland, Colo., 1995, Montgomery House Gallery, 1994, 95, Contemporary S.W. Galleries, 1996; group shows include Biola U., 1994, Alwin House Found., Phoenix, 1992, Moondance Gallery, 1993, B & R Gallery, Canyon Country, Calif., 1995, La Galleria D'Arte, Newport Beach, Calif., 1995, Merrill Gallery, 1996, 97, O'Brian's Art Emporium, Scottsdale, 1996, Colo. History Mus., Denver, 1996, Queens Coll. Gallery, Cambridge, Eng., 1994, Nat. Arts Club, N.Y.C., 1995, Salmagundi Club, N.Y.C., 1995, Maison du Terroir, Genouilly, France, 1996, Loveland Mus., 1997, Clymer Mus., Ellensburg, Wash., 1997, Desert Caballeros Mus., Wickenburg, Ariz., 1997; works in permanent collections at City of Boulder, CSI Ltd., Cambridge, Eng., El Pomar Found., Colorado Springs, Colo., Gilford, Inc., N.Y.C., Herzog & Adams, N.Y.C., Harlow Club Hotel, Palm Springs, Calif., Telluride Gallery of Fine Art, Colo., Kaiser Permanente, Denver, Kohn Family Trust, Balt., Mfrs.-Hanover trust, N.Y.C., Mayo Women's Clinic, Scottsdale, NAMI, Washington, Penrose Conf. Ctr., Colorado Springs, Philip Chamberlan Inc., Madison, Conn., Sidney and Joanna Poitier, Beverly Hills, Calif., Walters Mus., Balt., Women of the W. Mus., Boulder; featured in Southwest Art Mag., N.Y. Graphics Soc., ArtBeats, Roman Art Creations, Ltd., Blue Sky Publ. Recipient Best of Show award Western Images, Boulder, 1993. Mem. West'n Acad. Women Artists (signature mem., nominating juror 1997—), Am. Artist s Profl. League (Medal of Honor 1995), Nat. Mus. of Women in the Arts, Katharine Lorillard Wolfe Art Club, Oil Painters of Am. Home: 542 Arapahoe Boulder CO 80302

BIERSTEDT, PETER RICHARD, lawyer, entertainment industry consultant; b. Rhinebeck, N.Y., Jan. 2, 1943; s. Robert Henry and Betty (MacIver) B.; m. Carol Lynn Akiyama, Aug. 23, 1980 (div. Oct. 1995). AB, Columbia U., 1965, JD cum laude, 1969; cert., U. Sorbonne, Paris, 1966. Bar: N.Y. 1969, U.S. Supreme Ct. 1973, Calif. 1977. Atty. with firms in N.Y.C., 1969-74; pvt. practice cons. legal and entertainment industry, 1971, 75-76, 88—; with Avco Embassy Pictures Corp., L.A., 1977-83; v.p., gen. counsel Avco Embassy Pictures Corp., 1978-80, sr. v.p., 1980-83, dir., 1981-83; gen. counsel New World Entertainment (formerly New World Pictures), L.A., 1984-87, exec. v.p., 1985-87, sr. exec. v.p. Office of Chmn., 1987-88, also bd. dirs.; pres. subs. New World Prodns. and New World Advt. New World Pictures, 1985-88; guest lectr. U. Calif., Riverside, 1976-77, U. So. Calif., 1986, 91, UCLA, 1987, 95, 96; bd. dirs. New World Pictures (Australia) Ltd., FilmDallas Pictures, Inc., Cinedco, Inc. Exec. prodr. (home video series) The Comic Book Greats. Mem. Motion Picture Assn. Am. (dir. 1980-83), Acad. Motion Picture Arts and Scis. (exec. br.), N.Y. State Bar Assn., L.A. County Bar Assn., ACLU. Democrat. Home and Office: 6201 Quebec Dr Los Angeles CA 90068-2219

BIES, ROGER DAVID, cardiologist; b. Athens, Ohio, May 28, 1956; s. Ronald Kenneth and Genivieve H. (Parlow) B.; m. Rhonda Jean Pope; children: Lucas, Tyler, Wade. BA, U. Colo., 1979, MD, 1986. Intern, resident U. Pitts., 1986-89; fellow in cardiology Baylor Coll. Medicine, Houston, 1987-92; asst. prof. medicine U. Colo. Health Scis. Ctr., Denver, 1993—; vis. asst. prof. Inst. Molecular Genetics, Houston, 1993; assoc. dir. cardiology U. Colo. Health Sci. Ctr., 1995—; dir. heart failure/transplant clinic VA Med. Ctr., Denver, 1993—, dir. pacemaker clinic, 1993—. Author: A Primer of Molecular Biology, 1992; contbr. articles to profl. jours., chpts. to books. Grantee: VA Rsch. , Am. Heart Assn. Fellow Am. Coll. Cardiology; mem. Am. Fedn. Clin. Rsch. (grantee), Am. Heart Assn, VA Rsch. Office: VA Med Ctr 1055 Clermont St Denver CO 80220-3808

BIGGERS, ROBERT DAVID, urologist, nutritionist; b. Hartford City, Ind., Dec. 18, 1947; s. Frederick Leigh and Betty Jo (Bennett) B.; m. Nancy Carol Henry, Jan. 23, 1971 (div. Dec. 1973); 1 child, Sarah; m. Maureen Ann Maloy, Jan. 19, 1974; children: Amy, Shannon, Jennifer. BA, U. So. Calif., 1968, MD, 1972. Intern U.S. Spl. Forces, Persidio San Francisco, 1973, Ft. Bragg, N.C., 1973-75; resident in urology U.S. Spl. Forces, Honolulu, 1975-79; chief of urology U.S. Army, Ft. Bragg, N.C., 1979-81; chief urology USAF Acad., Ft. Carson, Colo., 1981-93; ptnr. Pikes Peak Urology, Colorado Springs, Colo., 1993—; cons. USAF Surgeon Gen., 1982-85; codel. Am. Assn. Clin. Urologists, Balt., 1994-96; lectr. nutrition, 1984-96. Contbr. over 20 articles to profl. jours. Chmn. Victim's Compensation Bd., Colorado Springs, Colo., 1992-96; pres. St. Francis Men's Club, Colorado Springs, 1983, 86, 91. Named to Order Mil. Med. Merit, U.S. Army, 1991, Legion of Merit, 1993. Fellow ACS; mem. Soc. Govt. Svc. Urologists, Colo. Med. Soc., El Paso County Med. Soc., Rocky Mountain Urology Soc. Republican. Roman Catholic. Home: 1915 Oak Hills Dr Colorado Springs CO 80919 Office: Pikes Peak Urology PC 6208 Lehman Dr Colorado Springs CO 80918-8408

BIGGS, THOMAS WYLIE, chemical company executive; b. Seattle, Oct. 28, 1950; s. Ray Wylie and Mildred Virginia (Ramsey) B.; m. Marcia Jean Holts, Aug. 4, 1973; children: Jennifer Tamar, Jordan Wylie. BA, U. Wash., 1972. Chemisty tchr. Samammish High Sch, Bellevue, Wash., 1972-74; sales rep. Litton Industries, Seattle, 1974-75; sales rep. Van Waters & Rogers, Kent, Wash., 1975-80, area chem. mgr., 1988-90, br. mgr., 1990-94; nat. raw materials mgr. Van Waters & Rogers, Kirkland, 1995—; field sales mgr. Van Waters & Rogers, Kent, Wash., 1980-85; sales mgr. Van Waters &

Rogers, South Bend, Ind., 1985-86; mgr. chem. dept. Van Waters & Rogers, Indpls., 1986-88; dir. materials mgmt. URECO (subs. Univar), Indpls., 1996—. 1st lt. USAR, 1973-80. Mem. Chgo. Drug and Chem. Assn., N.W. Paint and Coating Assn., Nat. Petroleum Refiners Assn. Office: Van Waters and Rogers 6100 Carillon Pt Kirkland WA 98033-7357

BIGLIN, KAREN EILEEN, library director; b. Hastings, Nebr., Apr. 23, 1954; d. James Eugene and Mary Ann (Truhlar) B.; m. Richard Jeffrey, Turnier, Aug. 4, 1979. BA, U. Ariz., 1976, MLS, 1978. Reference libr. No. Ariz. U., Flagstaff, 1978-80, sr. reference libr., 1980-84; reference libr. Tempe (Ariz.) Pub. Libr., 1984; circulation libr. Phoenix Coll., 1984-85; tech. svcs. libr. Scottsdale (Ariz.) C.C., 1985-93, libr. dir., 1993—, pres. faculty senate, 1994-95. Alice B. Good scholar U. Ariz., 1977. Mem. ALA, Ariz. Libr. Assn., Ariz. Online Users Group (pres. 1984-86), Phi Beta Kappa, Phi Kappa Phi, Beta Phi Mu. Office: Scottsdale CC 9000 E Chaparral Rd Scottsdale AZ 85250

BIGONY, F. RANDALL, leasing company executive; b. Natick, Mass., Dec. 14, 1957; s. Frederick and Katherine (Meinig) B.; m. Cynthia Gaylin, Nov. 25, 1989; children: Kendell, Courtney. BBA, U. Mass., 1981; MBA in Fin., U. Calif., Berkeley, 1983. Mgr. Ernst & Whinney, San Francisco, 1983-87; pres. F. Randall Bigony & Co., San Francisco, 1987-92; dir. ops. Atel Fin. Corp., San Francisco, 1992-94; sr. v.p., CFO Atel Capital Group, San Francisco, 1994—. Dir., treas. I Have A Dream Found., 1987—, founding bd. dirs. Bay area chpt., San Francisco. Recipient Wall St. Jour. Student Achievement award, 1981. Mem. Phi Kappa Phi. Office: Atel Fin Corp 235 Pine St Fl 6 San Francisco CA 94104-2701

BIKLE, DANIEL DAVID, research physician; b. Harrisburg, Pa., Apr. 25, 1944; s. Charles Augustus and Sarah Elizabeth (Yaukey) B.; m. Mary Elizabeth Wanner, June 20, 1965; children: Christine, Hilary. BA, Harvard U., 1965; MD, U. Pa., 1969, PhD, 1974. Diplomate Am. Bd. Internal Medicine; cert. Nat. Bd. Med. Examiners. Research intern Letterman Army Inst. Research, San Francisco, 1974-79; asst. prof. medicine U. Calif., San Francisco, 1979-86, assoc. prof. medicine, 1986-91, prof. medicine, 1991—, prof. dermatology, 1993—; co-dir. spl. diagnostic treament unit VA Med. Ctr., San Francisco, 1979—. Editor: Assay of Calcium Regulating Hormones, 1982, Hormonal Regulation of Bone Mineral Homeostasis, 1995; contbr. articles to profl. jours., chpts. to books. Served to col. USAR, 1974—. Research grantee NIH, 1979—, NASA, 1979—, VA, 1979—. Fellow ACP; mem. Endocrine Soc. (mem. editl. bd. 1984—), Am. Soc. Clin. Investigation, Am. Soc. Clin. Nutrition, Am. Fedn. Clin. Rsch., Assn. Am. Physicians. Republican. Mem. Christian Ch. Clubs: Commonwealth of Calif., Harvard (San Francisco). Office: VA Med Ctr 4150 Clement St San Francisco CA 94121-1545

BILBRAY, BRIAN P., congressman; b. San Diego, Calif.; m. Karen; 5 children. Supr.ctrl. and so. coastal regions San Diego County, Calif.; mem. Congress from 49th Calif. dist., 1994—; mem. fin. & hazardous materials, health & environment, oversight & investigations coms. Mem. San Diego County Air Pollution Control Bd., State Air Resources Bd., San Diego County Internat. Trade Com., Calif. Coastal Com., San Diego Bay Water Quality Panel, San Diego Coun. Literacy. Office: US Ho of Reps 1530 Longworth HOB Washington DC 20515-0549

BILBRAY, JAMES HUBERT, former congressman, lawyer, consultant; b. Las Vegas, May 19, 1938; s. James A. and Ann E. (Miller) B.; m. Michaelene Mercer, Jan. 1960; children: Bridget, Kevin, Erin, Shannon. Student, Brigham Young U., 1957-58, U. Nev., Las Vegas, 1958-60; BA, Am. U., 1962; JD, Washington Coll. Law, 1964. Bar: Nev. 1965. Staff mem. Senator Howard Cannon U.S. Senate, 1960-64; dep. dist. atty. Clark County, Nev., 1965-68; mem. Lovell, Bilbray & Potter, Las Vegas, 1969-87; mem. Nev. Senate, 1980-86, chmn. taxation com., 1983-86, chmn. interim com. on pub. broadcasting, 1983; 100th-103d U.S. Congresses from 1st Nev. dist.; mem. 100th-103rd Congresses from 1st Nev. dist., 1987-95; mem. fgn. affairs com., 1987-88, mem. house armed svs. com., subcom. procurement, mil. contracts, sea power, mem. small bus. com., chmn. procurement, taxation and tourism subcom., 1989-95; ptnr. Alcalde & Fay, Arlington, Va., 1995—; mem. Spl. Panel on NATO and North Atlantic Alliance, fgn. affairs com., select com. on hunger, 1987-88, select com. on aging, 1988-93, subcoms. Africa, trade exports and tourism, select com. on intelligence, 1993-95; alt. mcpl. judge City of Las Vegas, 1987-89; del. North Atlantic Alliance, 1989-95; bd. visitors U.S. Mil. Acad., West Point, 1995—, vice chmn., 1996-97; mem. adv. bd. Ex-Import Bank of U.S., 1996—. Bd. regents U. Nev. Sys., 1968-72; mem. Nat. Coun. State Govts. Commn. on Arts and Historic Preservation; mem. bd. visitors USAF Acad., 1991-93; mem. Dem. Nat. Com., 1996-97. Named Outstanding Alumnus U. Nev., Las Vegas, 1979, Man of Yr. Am. Diabetes Assn., 1989, Man of Yr. Haddassah (Nev.), 1990. Mem. Nev. State Bar Assn., Clark county Bar Assn., U. Nev.-Las Vegas Alumni Assn. (pres. 1964-69, Humanitarian of Yr. 1984), Phi Alpha Delta, Sigma Chi, KC. Democrat. Roman Catholic. Lodges: Elks, Rotary.

BILBRUCK, DANIEL WAYNE, investment company executive; b. Portland, Sept. 22, 1946; s. William Wayne Bilbruck and JoAnn Irene (Black) Bellomy; m. Jodell Girrard, 1966 (div. 1968); children: Curtis, Scott. Pres., CEO Azaru Corp., Washougal, Wash., 1989-94, Global Tech. Group, Vancouver, Wash., 1993—; CEO Global Tech. Group, Plymouth, Eng., 1995—, Global Advanced Recycling, Plymouth, 1995—; pres., CEO Global Tech. Group, Port Moresby, New Guinea, 1993—; gen. mgr. Rootco, Inc., Kent, Wash., 1990-95. editor Foc'sle Hints by Captain Dan, 1976-78. Served with USN, 1965. Mem. Moose. Home and Office: 3702 NE 83rd Ave Vancouver WA 98662-7226

BILBY, RICHARD MANSFIELD, federal judge; b. Tucson, May 29, 1931; s. Ralph Willard and Marguerite (Mansfield) B.; m. children: Claire Louise, Ellen M. Moore; m. Elizabeth Alexander, May 25, 1996. BS, U. Ariz., 1955; JD, U. Mich., 1958. Bar: Ariz. 1959. Since practiced in Tucson; law clk. to Chief Judge Chambers, 9th Circuit Ct. Appeals, San Francisco, 1958-59; mem. firm Bilby, Thompson, Shoenhair & Warnock, 1959-79, partner, 1967-79; judge U.S. Dist. Ct., Dist. Ariz., Tucson, 1979-96; chief judge U.S. Dist. Ct., Dist. Ariz., 1984-90; sr. judge U.S. Dist. Ct., 1996—; conscientious objector hearing officer Dept. Justice, 1959-62; chmn. Pima County Med.-Legal panel, 1968-70; Mem. Tucson Charter Revision Com., 1965-70. Chmn. United Fund Profl. Div., 1968; chmn. Spl. Gift Div., 1970, St. Joseph Hosp. Devel. Fund Drive, 1970; Republican state chmn. Vols. for Eisenhower, 1956; Rep. county chmn., Pima County, Ariz., 1972-74; Past pres. Tucson Conquistadores; bd. dirs. St. Josephs Hosp., 1969-77, chmn., 1972-75. Served with AUS, 1952-54. Fellow Am. Coll. Trial Lawyers; mem. Ariz. Acad., Town Hall (dir. 1976-79). Office: US Dist Ct US Courthouse Rm 301 45 E Broadway Blvd Tucson AZ 85701-1711*

BILEZIKJIAN, EDWARD ANDREW, architect; b. Los Angeles, Mar. 29, 1950; s. Andrew and Alice (Dardarian) B. BSArch, U. So. Calif., 1973, MArch, 1977. Registered architect, Calif. Project mgr. RMA Archtl. Group, Inc., Costa Mesa, Calif., 1977-78; dir. architecture Donald De Mars Assocs., Inc., Van Nuys, Calif., 1978-85; prin. architect EAB Architects, Sepulveda, Calif., 1985-87, Laguna Hills, Calif., 1988—; architect, planner III Trammell Crow Co., Irvine, Calif., 1986-88; prin. architect Fluor Daniel, Inc., Irvine, Calif., 1989—. Chmn. parish coun. Armenian Apostolic Ch. Newport Beach, 1988-91, 94-95. Mem. AIA, Triple-X Fraternity of Calif. (corresponding sec. 1984-85), Nat. Coun. Archtl. Registration Bds. (cert.). Democrat. Mem. Armenian Apostolic Ch.

BILLIG, FRANKLIN ANTHONY, chemist; b. L.A., Feb. 11, 1923; s. Frank Henry and Hazel (Rockwell) B.; m. Tetsuko Morinaga, Apr. 23, 1957; 1 child, Patricia Ann Kikuko Billig-Harvey. BS, U. So. Calif., L.A., 1954. CPC, CSS. Sr. rsch. chemist Am. Potash & Chem. Corp., Whittier, Calif., 1954-64; rsch. chemist/lab. mgr./safety officer, Dept. Chemistry U. So. Calif., L.A., 1964—; cons. Flintridge Cons., Inc., Calif., 1980—, Hanson Lab. Furniture, Newberry Park, Calif., 1989; cons./staff assoc. Enterprise Environ. Svcs., L.A., 1981—. Author: Advances in Chemistry, 1959, 61, Organic Synthesis, 1959, Infra Red Spectra of Organic Sulfur Compounds, 1964, Infra Red Spectra of Sulfur Compounds, 1966; patentee in field. Master sgt. USAF, 1942-53, PTO, Korea. Fellow AAAS, L. Pasteur Inst. Advanced Med. Studies, Am. Inst. Chemists; mem. Sigma Xi. Republican. Roman Catholic. Home: 12722 Spindlewood Dr La Mirada CA 90638-2735 Office: U So Calif Dept Chemistry University Park Los Angeles CA 90089-1062

BILLIG, SHELLEY HIRSCHL, educational research and training consultant; b. Canton, Ohio, June 23, 1951; d. Alex T. and Flora H. Hirschl; m. Stephen M. Billig, Aug. 7, 1977; children: Lisa, Joshua. BA, Boston U., 1973; MA, Tufts U., 1975, PhD, 1978. Prof. U. R.I., Kingston, 1977-78, Northeastern Coll., Boston, 1978-80, Regis Coll., Weston, Mass., 1980-82, Merrimack Coll., N. Andover, Mass., 1982-86; rsch. assoc. N.W. Region Ednl. Lab., Denver, Colo., 1987-88; office dir. RMC Rsch. Corp., Denver, 1988—; mem. editl. bd. JESPAR, Johns Hopkins, Balt., 1995—, adv. bd. Colo. Parent Involvment Ctr., 1995—; prin. investigator Region VIII Comprehensive Ctr. and svc.-learning project. Contbg. author Parent Involvment in the Middle Grades; also articles. Office: RMC Rsch Corp 1512 Larimer St Ste 540 Denver CO 80202-1620

BILLING, RONALD JAMES, immunologist, researcher; b. U.K., July 23, 1943; came to U.S., 1970; s. James Jackson and Margaret Isobel (O'Connor) B.; m. Angela Mary Gillett, July 9, 1965; children: Peter, Michael, Janet. BS, U. Liverpool, 1965; PhD, U. Glasgow, 1969. Postdoctoral fellow Cal Inst. Tech., Pasadena, 1970-72; asst. prof., assoc. prof. UCLA, 1972-85; rsch. dir. C V Cancer Ctr., San Marcos, Calif., 1985—; rschr. in field. Patentee in field; contbr. numerous articles to profl. jours. Gosney fellow, 1970-72; grantee NIH, 1974-77, 77-88. Office: C V Cancer Ctr PO Box 456 San Marcos CA 92079

BILLINGS, JUDITH DIANE, elementary education educator; b. San Jose, Calif., Feb. 11, 1944; d. Milton Edward and Dorothy M. (Dunston) McConnell; m. Gary William Billings, July 11, 1965; children: Keri Kustin, Michael, Alyssa Duncan. BA in Edn., San Jose State U., 1965. Cert. K-8 elem. edn. Tchr. 2d and 3d grade Cupertino (Calif.) United Sch. Dist., 1965-67; tchr. pre-sch. Calif. Young World, Sunnyvale, 1969-70; tchr. extended learning Oak Grove Sch. Dist., San Jose, 1972-73; tchr. 2d and 3d grade San Lorenzo Valley Unified Sch. Dist., Ben Lomond, Calif., 1978-87; tchr. 6th grade San Lorenzo Valley Unified Sch. Dist., Boulder Creek, Calif., 1991—; supr. student tchrs. U. Calif., Santa Cruz, 1987-89; coord. Life Lab, Santa Cruz, 1990-91. Recipient award Schs. Plus, 1987, 90, Calif. Tchg. Innovations Program, State of Calif., 1984, Golden Apple, 1982. Mem. NEA, San Lorenzo Valley Tchrs. Assn. Home: 1747 Quail Hollow Rd Ben Lomond CA 95005-9581 Office: Redwood Elem Sch 16900 Highway 9 Boulder Creek CA 95006-9626

BILLINGS, RICHARD BRUCE, economics educator, consultant; b. Waukesha, Wis., Dec. 5, 1938; s. Floyd Henry and Edessa Mary (Burmeister) B.; m. Patricia Christy Barnum, Mar. 31, 1961; children: Stephen Michael, David Christopher. BA in Econs. and Math., U. Ariz., 1962, MA in Econs., 1963; PhD in Econs, Claremont (Calif.) Coll., 1969. Asst. prof. U. Ariz., Tucson, 1965-69; lectr. in econs. U. Ariz., 1970—; rsch. economist State of Ariz., Phoenix, 1969-70; cons. State of Hawaii, Honolulu, 1984, Bur. Reclamation, Boulder, Colo., 1986, Tucson Water, 1988-89, State of Ariz., Phoenix, 1989. Author: Forecasting Urban Water Demand, 1996; contbr. articles to profl. jours. Pres. Campus Christian Ctr., Tucson, 1971, 75; pres., bd. dirs. 1st United Meth. Ch., Tucson, 1992-94, chair fin. com., 1989-93, 95-96; scoutmaster Boy Scouts Am., Tucson, 1981-86. Mem. Soc. Govt. Economists, Nat. Tax Assn. Democrat. Home: 660 N Circle D Way Tucson AZ 85748 Office: U Ariz Dept Econs McClelland Hall 401 Tucson AZ 85721

BILLINGS, THOMAS NEAL, computer and publishing executive, management consultant; b. Milw., Mar. 2, 1931; s. Neal and Gladys Victoria (Lockard) B.; m. Barta Hope Chipman, June 12, 1954 (div. 1967); children: Bridget Ann, Bruce Neal; m. Marie Louise Farrell, Mar. 27, 1982. AB with honors, Harvard U., 1952, MBA, 1954. V.p. fin. and adminstrn. and technol. innovation Copley Newspapers Inc., La Jolla, Calif., 1957-70; group v.p., dir. tech. Harte-Hanks Comm. Inc., San Antonio, 1970-73; exec. v.p. United Media, Inc., Phoenix, 1973-75; asst. to pres., dir. corp. mgmt. systems Ramada Inns, Inc., Phoenix, 1975-76; exec. dir. NRA, Washington, 1976-77; pres. Ideation Inc., N.Y.C., 1977-81; chmn. Bergen-Billings Inc., N.Y.C., 1977-80; pres. The Assn. Svc. Corp., San Francisco, 1978-91; pres. Recorder Printing and Pub. Co. Inc., San Francisco, 1980-82; v.p. adminstrn. Victor Techs. Inc., Scotts Valley, Calif., 1982-84; mng. dir. Saga-Wilcox Computers Ltd., Wrexham, Wales, 1984-85; chmn. Thomas Billings & Assocs., Inc., Reno, 1978—, Intercontinental Travel Svc. Inc., Reno, 1983-88, Oberon Optical Character Recognition, Ltd., Hemel-Hemstead, Eng., 1985-86; bd. dirs. 5M Corp., San Francisco, Intercontinental Rsch. Coun., London, Corp. Comm. Coun., Alameda; dir., CEO Insignia Software Solutions group, High Wycombe, Eng., Cupertino, Calif., 1986-89; chmn. Intercontinental News Svc. Inc., London and Alameda, Calif., 1989—; v.p. Cromer Equipment Co., Oakland, Calif., 1991-94; chmn. Newton Group of Cos., Las Vegas, 1993—, Info. Integrity Internat., Inc., Las Vegas, London, 1994—, WordMaster Corp., Reno, 1995—; bd. dirs. Digital Broadcasting Corp., Mountain View, Calif., Lenny's Restaurants Inc., Wichita, Kans., Tymyndr Corp., Dover, Del., Zzyzzyx Corp., Reno, Harrod's Hotel & Casino Corp., Las Vegas, Pandemonium Pictures, Inc., San Mateo, Calif., Bonanza Enterprises, Inc., Virginia City, Nev., Quillmill Ltd., London, Better Betting Systems, Inc., Alameda, Calif., Video Stream, Inc., Cupertino, Calif., ResuMaster Corp., Walnut Creek, Calif., 1995—, ProcessMaster Corp., Pleasanton, Calif., Enterprise Ho., Alameda, People Finders, Inc., Walnut Creek, Calif., Chut! Cheri's Chic Chit Choppe, S.A., Laguna Beach, Calif., Waters Equiptment Co., Inc., San Francisco, 1996—, Goldstein Miller and Assocs. Inc., San Bruno, Calif., Silicon World Search Group, Inc., 1997—; speaker and seminar leader; co-inventor StrokSavr Software, 1994. Bd. dirs. Nat. Allergy Found., 1973—, The Wilderness Fund, 1978—, San Diego Civic Light Opera Assn., 1965-69; chief exec. San Diego 200th Anniversary Expn., 1969; founder, exec. dir. Am. Majority Party, 1993—. The Millenium Three Found., 1996—, The Rememberance Soc., 1996—, People Finders' Inc., 1996—, Corp. Comm. Counsel Inc., 1996—. Served with U.S. Army, 1955-57. Recipient Walter F. Carley Meml. award, 1966, 69. Fellow U.K. Inst. Dirs.; mem. Am. Newspaper Pubs. Assn., Inst. Execs. Inc. (dir.), Inst. Newspaper Fin. Officers, Sigma Delta Chi. Clubs: West Side Tennis, LaJolla Country; Washington Athletic; San Francisco Press; Harvard (N.Y.C.); Elks. Author: Creative Controllership, 1978, Our Credibility Crisis, 1983, Non-Euclidean Theology, 1987, Ruminations on Meta Mentality, 1990, Fixing our Broken System, 1992, (series) The Ethnic Epicure, 1995—; editor: The Vice Presidents' Letter, 1978-92; pub. The Microcomputer Letter, 1982-94, Synthetic Hardware Update, 1987-93, Windows on Tomorrow Magazine, 1994—; editor: Intercontinental News Svc., London and Alameda, Calif., 1985—. Office: PO Drawer I Alameda CA 94501-0262 also: 100 W Grove St Ste 360 Reno NV 89509

BILLINGSLEY, LARON KENT, financial planner; b. Lynnwood, Calif., Oct. 8, 1947; s. Aaron P. and Myrtle (Bates) B.; m. Shirley Julia Jacobson, June 19, 1971; children: Lisa Julia, Traci Jennifer, Michael Laron, Melanie Jenae, Matthew Kent, Bryce Jacob. BS in Edn., Brigham Young U., 1973; MS in Sch. Adminstrn., Calif. State U., Fullerton, 1978; MBA, U. Phoenix, Ogden, Utah, 1989. Cert. life and disability ins. and securities, Utah, Calif., Tex. Coach Santa Fe H.S., Santa Fe Springs, Calif., 1973-74; tchr., coach Mayfair H.S., Lakewood, Calif., 1974-79; program mgr. Thiokol Corp., Brigham City, Utah, 1979-95; sr. analyst Dynmeridian Corp., Alexandria, Va., 1995—; registered rep. WMA Securities, Inc., Logan, Utah, 1995—; facility prodn. cons. Strategic Arms Reduction Treaty Start, Brigham City, 1989-95. Republican. Mem. LDS Ch. Home: 634 N Highland Blvd Brigham City UT 84302

BILODEAU, GENE PAUL, student services administrator, counselor; b. Helena, Mont., June 10, 1955; s. Eugene Paul and Eva Lyda (Pearson) B.; m. Kim Ann Landers, July 16, 1960; children: Jacob Paul, Tucker Allen. BS in Sociology, U. Mont., 1979; MEd in Counseling, Mont. State U., 1984. Lic. profl. counselor, Wyo. Counselor Inter-Mountain Deaconess Home for Children, Helena, Mont., 1980-84; therapist Carbon County Counseling Ctr., Rawlins, Wyo., 1984-87, Casper (Wyo.) Psychol. Svcs., 1988-90; dir. counseling, student devel. Casper Coll., 1990-94; assoc. dean for student svcs. Colo. Northwestern C.C., Craig, 1994—; mem. adv. bd. Grand Futures, Craig, 1995—, Christian Counseling Ctr., Casper, 1993-94. Mem. ACA, Nat. Bd. Cert. Counselors (cert. counselor), Wyo. Counseling Assn. (pres. 1993-94, Outstanding Svc. award 1994). Roman Catholic. Home: 3436 Riford Ct Craig CO 81625 Office: Colo Northwestern CC 50 College Dr Craig CO 81625-3685

BIMBER, BRUCE ALLEN, political science educator; b. Warren, Pa., Oct. 26, 1961; s. Gail E. and Joyce Kathleen B.; m. Laura L. Mancuso. BSEE, Stanford U., 1983; PhD, MIT, 1992. Mktg. engr. Hewlett-Packard Co., Palo Alto, Calif., 1983-86; assoc. pol. scientist Critical Techs. Inst., RAND Corp., Washington, 1992-93; asst. prof. polit. sci. U. Calif., Santa Barbara, 1993—; cons. NAS, Washington, Nat. Rsch. Coun., Washington, Carnegie Corp., N.Y.C., Critical Techs. Inst., Washington, ISyS Forum, Palo Alto, Calif. Contbr. articles to profl. jours. Rsch. fellow Brookings Inst., 1990-91. Mem. Tau Beta Pi. Home: 946 W Campus Ln Goleta CA 93117-4345 Office: U Calif Dept Polit Sci Santa Barbara CA 93106

BINDER, BETTYE B., author, lecturer; b. New Rochelle, N.Y., Feb. 12, 1939; d. Alex and Leah (Binder) B.; div. BA, Barnard Coll., 1960; MA in Pub. Law and Govt., Columbia U., 1962. Free lance writer, lectr. Culver City, Calif., 1980—; speaker Whole Life Expo, 1985—; exec. producer Brain and Mind Symposium, L.A., 1992-94. Author: (books) Past Life Regression Guidebook, 1985, Past Lives Present Karma Workbook, 1985, Discovering Past Lives and Other Dimensions, 1994; publisher, author (mini mag.) Who Were You in Past Lives?, 1992. Coord. Students for Kennedy-Johnson, N.Y. State, 1960; rschr., writer, Dem. Nat. Com., Washington, 1963-65; assoc. dir. Fight Inflation Together, L.A., 1973-76. Mem. Assn. for Past Life Rsch. and Therapies (bd. dirs. 1991-97, pres. 1993-97), Assn. Past Life Rsch. and Therapies, New Age Pub. and Retailing Alliance, numerous environ. orgns. Democrat. Jewish. Office: PO Box 7781 Culver City CA 90233-7781

BINDER, GORDON M., health and medical products executive; b. St. Louis, 1935. Degree in elec. engring., Purdue U., 1957; MBA, Harvard U., 1962. Formerly with Litton Industries, 1962-64; various fin. mgmt. positions Ford Motor Co., 1964-69; CFO Sys. Devel. Corp., 1971-81; v.p., CFO Amgen, Thousand Oaks, Calif., 1982-88, CEO, 1988—, chmn. bd., 1990—. Baker scholar Harvard U. Office: Amgen 1840 De Havilland Dr Thousand Oaks CA 91320-1701*

BINDER, JAMES KAUFFMAN, computer consultant; b. Reading, Pa., Nov. 20, 1920; s. Paul Burdette and Edna (Kauffman) B.; B.A., Lehigh U., 1941; M.A., Johns Hopkins U., 1952; profl. cert. in systems mgmt. U. Calif.-San Diego, 1976; A.S. in Data Processing, San Diego Evening Coll., 1979, A.A. in Fgn. Lang., 1979; A.A. in Spanish, Mira Costa Coll., Oceanside, Calif., 1981. Instr. English, Notre Dame U., South Bend, Ind., 1948-49; prof. English, Athens (Greece) Coll., 1950-51; CARE rep., Greece, 1951-52; reporter, staff writer Athens News, 1952-53; dir. lang. tng. World Council Chs. Refugee Service, Athens, 1953-54; co-editor Am. Overseas Guide, N.Y., West Berlin, 1957-58; lectr. English, U. Md. Overseas Program, European and Far East divs., 1958-66; successively supr. Cen. Info. Ctr., supt. documents, sr. systems analyst GA Techs., Inc., La Jolla, Calif., 1968-85. Recipient Williams Prize, Lehigh U., 1939, 41; Johns Hopkins U. Grad. Sch. Pres. scholar, 1945-48. Roman Catholic. Clubs: Tudor and Stuart, Automobile of So. Calif. Author: The Correct Comedy, 1951; contbg. translator Modern Scandinavian Poetry, 1948; editor: (with Erwin H. Tiebe) American Overseas Guide, 1958.

BINDER, MARC DAVID, neuroscientist, educator; b. Brookline, Mass., June 8, 1949; m. Karin Kalff; 2 children. AB, Columbia U., 1971; MS, U. So. Calif., 1972, PhD, 1974. Rsch./teaching asst. biol. scis. and biomed. engring. U. So. Calif., 1972-74; rsch. cons. Ocean Sci. and Engring., Inc., Long Beach, Calif., 1972-73; rsch. assoc. Pacific Med. Ctr., San Francisco, 1974-75; instr. U. Calif. Extension, Davis, 1975; rsch. assoc. in physiology U. Ariz., Tucson, 1975-78; asst. prof. dept. physiology and biophysics U. Washington, Seattle, 1978-81, assoc. prof., 1981-86, prof., 1986—; vis. asst. prof. dept. physiology U. Ariz., 1978-81; vis. assoc. prof. dept. physiology and biophysics Harvard U., 1982-83; adj. prof. dept. oral biology U. Washington, 1990—. Editorial assoc.: Courts, Health Sci. and the Law, Brain and Behavioral Scis.; manuscript reviewer: Sci., Jour. Neurophysiology, Experimental Brain Rsch., Neurosci. Letters, Experimental Neurology, Jour. Neurosci., Muscle & Nerve, Jour. Applied Physiology, IEEE Transactions in Biomed. Engring.; contbr. articles to profl. jours. Recipient Tchr.-Investigator Devel. award Nat. Inst. Neurol. Diseases and Stroke, 1978-83, Neurosci. Teaching award U. Ariz., 1980, Jacob Javits Neurosci. Investigator award, 1992; fellow Arthur Vining Davis Found., 1972, Postdoctoral fellow Nat. Eye Inst., 1975, Muscular Dystrophy Assn., 1975, 76, Regents fellow U. Calif., 1975, Chancellor's fellow U. Calif., Davis, 1975; Biele grantee for grad. rsch., 1972, Internat. travel grantee Nat. Rsch. Coun., 1977. Mem. AAAS, Internat. Brain Rsch. Orgn., Internat. Soc. Myochemistry, Am. Physiol. Soc., Soc. Neurosci., Sigma Xi. Home: 15930 41st Ave NE Seattle WA 98155-6739 Office: U Wash Sch Medicine Dept Physiology & Biophys SJ-40 Seattle WA 98195

BINDSCHADLER, BRIAN CHARLES, gifted and talented education educator, writer; b. St. Louis, Apr. 21, 1964; s. Darryl Duane and Helga Harriet (Prostel) B.; m. Katherine Linn Wallace, Aug. 1, 1987; children: Caitlyn Ann, Carrie Nicole. BA in Elem. and Spl. Edn., U. Wyo., 1987; MA in Gifted Edn., U. Ariz., 1993. Cert. edn. and gifted endorsement, Ariz. Elem. tchr. Crane Sch. Dist., Yuma, Ariz., 1987-90; elem. tchr. Catalina Foothills Sch. Dist., Tucson, 1990—, coord. gifted edn., 1996—. Contbr. short stories and poetry to lit. publs. Winner essay contest VFW, 1989. Mem. Phi Beta Kappa. Democrat.

BINGAMAN, JEFF, senator; b. El Paso, Tex., Oct. 3, 1943; s. Jesse and Beth (Ball) B.; m. Anne Kovacovich, Sept. 13, 1968. BA in Govt., Harvard U., 1965; JD, Stanford U., 1968. Bar: N.Mex. 1968. Asst. atty. gen., 1969; atty. Stephenson, Campbell & Olmsted, 1971-72; ptnr. Campbell, Bingaman & Black, Santa Fe, 1972-78; former atty. gen. State of N.Mex.; now U.S. senator from N.Mex., mem. armed svcs. com., mem. joint econ. com., mem. Senate Dem. steering and coordination com., mem. Senate Den. tech. and comm. com., ranking minority mem., mem. energy and natural resources subcom. of energy prodn. and regulation. U.S. Army 1968-74. Democrat. Methodist. Home: PO Box 5775 Santa Fe NM 87502-5775 Office: US Senate 703 Hart Senate Bldg Washington DC 20510

BINGHAM, PARIS EDWARD, JR., electrical engineer, computer consultant; b. Aurora, Colo., Sept. 26, 1957; s. Paris Edward and Shirley Ann (Blehm) B.; m. Laurie Sue Piersol, May 9, 1981 (div. Sept. 1987); m. Helen Naef, Aug. 7, 1993. BS in Elec. Engring. and Computer Sci., U. Colo., 1979. Mem. tech. staff Western Electric Co., Aurora, 1979-81, system engr., 1981; mem. electronic tech. staff Hughes Aircraft Co., Aurora, 1981-83, staff engr., 1983-86, sr. staff engr., 1986-93, scientist, engr., 1993-94; area systems support engr. Sun Microsystems, Inc., Englewood, Colo., 1994—; cons. RJM Assocs., Huntington, N.Y., 1987-91; cons. Aurora, 1988—. Mem. IEEE, Assn. for Computing Machinery. Republican. Presbyterian. Office: Sun Microsystems Inc 5251 Dtc Pky Ste 500 Englewood CO 80111-2734

BINKIEWICZ, ANNA I.S., pediatrician; b. Lwów, Poland, Apr. 14, 1938; came to U.S., 1957; d. Carl W. and Anna W. (Wysocka) Zisch; m. Longin W. Binkiewicz, Aug. 17, 1964 (dec. Dec. 1992). BA, Clark U. Womens Coll., 1961; MD, Tufts U., 1965. Diplomate Am. Bd. Pediat., Am. Bd. Pediat. Endocrinology. Intern Boston Floating Hosp., 1965-66, resident in pediat., 1966-68, fellow in emotional and social aspects in pediat., 1968-69, fellow in pediat. endocrinology, 1969-71; asst. in endocrinology New Eng. Med. Ctr., Boston, 1971-77, from coord. student edn. in pediat. to staff pediatrician, 1978-86; from instr. to assoc. prof. pediat. Tufts U. Sch. Medicine, Boston, 1971-86, prof. clin. pediat., 1986—; chief sect. gen. pediat. U. Ariz. Health Scis. Ctr., Tucson, 1986—; ednl. com. dept. pediat. U. Ariz. Coll. Medicine, 1988—, co-founder, child advocate group dept. pediat., 1987—; asst. endocrinologist New Eng. Med. Ctr., Boston, 1977-86, chief div. gen. pediat., 1978-86; coord. student edn. in pediatrics Tufts U. Sch. Medicine, Boston, 1980-86; acting med. dir. U. Affiliated Programs, 1991—; lectr. in field. Contbr. articles to profl. jours. Active Govs. Task Force for Prevention Child Abuse in Ariz., 1989, Ariz. Coun. for Mothers and Children, 1989—. Recipient grants in field, 1994—, 1993—. Mem. Ambulatory Pediat. Assn., Am. Acad. Pediat., Am. Diabetes Assn., Pediat. Endocrine Soc., Nat. Com. for Prevention Child Abuse, Soc. for Prevention Child Abuse and Neglect, Am. Profl. Soc. on Abuse of Children, Ariz. Acad. Pediat. (steering com. mem. ann. conf. 1990—), Boston Floating Alumni

Assn. Office: Univ Ariz Health Sci Ctr 1501 N Campbell Ave Tucson AZ 85724-0001

BINKLEY, JOAN VIVIAN (JODY BINKLEY), artist, educator, gallery owner; b. Hanford, Calif., July 8, 1933; d. Albert Henry Lohse and Alice (Day) Romdall; m. Henry Alson Binkley, Sept. 20, 1958; children: Cameron, Brock, Clayton. Student, Colo. State U., 1951-53; studied with, Frederick Van Twente, Mary Ann Lohman, Larry Webster, Delbert Gish, Leslie B. Demille. Owner, instr. Studio West Galleries, Wheatridge, Colo., 1973-80; owner Studio West Galleries, Littleton, Colo., 1975-80; owner, instr. Country Lane Art Gallery, Lakewood, Colo., 1983-85, Lakewood Arts Studio Gallery, 1988—; workshop instr. Wheatridge Art Club, 1987, 89, 91. Exhbns. include Denver Cancer League Spring Benefit, 1989, 90, 91, 92, also Studio West Galleries, Wheatride and Littleton, Emily Ingram Galleries, Steamboat, Colo., 1984-92, Santa Fe Impressions, Littleton, 1987—, Gallery of Western Art, 1987—, Parade of Homes, 1988-89; pub. work in North Light Book Club's The Best of Flower Painting, 1997. Mem. Colo. Artist Assn., Lakewood Arts Coun., Foothills Art Ctr. Home: 12588 W 1st Pl Lakewood CO 80228-5004 Studio: Lakewood Arts Studio 85 S Union Blvd Lakewood CO 80228-2207

BINNIE, NANCY CATHERINE, retired nurse, educator; b. Sioux Falls, S.D., Jan. 28, 1937; d. Edward Grant and Jessie May (Martini) Larkin; m. Charles H. Binnie. Diploma, St. Joseph's Hosp. Sch. Nursing, Phoenix, 1965; BS in Nursing, Ariz. State U., 1970, MA, 1974. Intensive care charge nurse Scottsdale (Ariz.) Meml. Hosp., 1968-70, coordinator critical care, 1970-71; coordinator critical care John C. Lincoln Hosp., Phoenix, 1971-73; prof. nursing GateWay Community Coll., Phoenix, 1974-96; coord. part-time evening nursing programs Gateway Community Coll., 1984-97, interim dir. nursing, 1989, 91. Mem. Orgn. Advancement of Assoc. Degree Nursing, Practical and Assoc. Coun. Nursing Educators, Ariz. Coun. Nurse Educators. Office: Gateway C C 104 N 40th St Phoenix AZ 85034-1704

BIRBECK, STEPHEN ANTHONY, city official; b. Washington, Sept. 14, 1947; s. Richard Wellington and Louise (Keebler) B.; m. Sharon Langmaid, July 28, 1979; children: Stephen Anthony, Walter Alexander, Amanda Rose. BA, U. Calif., Riverside, 1974; MA, U. Redlands, 1987. Adminstrv. asst. Coachella Valley Assn. Govts., Palm Desert, Calif., 1974-78; asst. city mgr. City of Rancho Mirage, Calif., 1978-83, city mgr., 1984-85; exec. dir. Rancho Mirage Redevel. Agy., 1985-86; mng. dir. Riverside County Redevel. Agy., 1986-88; asst. city mgr. City if Rancho Mirage, 1988-95, mcpl. cons., 1995—. Mem. Eastside Adv. Coun., Riverside, 1973; bd. dirs. One-way Outreach Ctr., Coachella, 1979; mem. fin. com. Calvary Chapel, Cathedral City, Calif., 1987-92. Recipient Resolution of Appreciation Palm Desert City Coun., 1982, Rancho Mirage Parks Commn., 1985, Cove Communities Fire Commn., 1985, Rancho Mirage City Coun., 1995. Republican. Home and Office: 78430 Discovery Bay Indio CA 92201-1393

BIRCHER, ANDREA URSULA, psychiatric mental health nurse, educator, clinical nurse specialist; b. Bern, Switzerland, Mar. 6, 1928; came to U.S., 1947; d. Franklin E. Bircher and Hedy E. Bircher-Rey. Diploma, Knapp Coll. Nursing, Santa Barbara, Calif., 1957; BS, U. Calif., San Francisco, 1961, MS, 1962; PhD, U. Calif., Berkeley, 1966. RN, Calif., Ill. Staff nurse, head nurse Cottage Hosp., Santa Barbara, 1957-58; psychiatric nurse, jr., sr. Langley-Porter Neuropsychiatric Inst., San Francisco, 1958-66; asst. prof. U. Ill. Coll. Nursing, Chgo., 1966-72; prof. U. Okla. Coll. Nursing, Oklahoma City, 1972-93, prof. emeritus, 1993—. Contbr. articles and papers to profl. jours. Recipient award for Outstanding Contributions to Faculty Governance U. Okla. Faculty Senate 1985, 93, others. Mem. AAUP, ANA, AAUW, Soc. for Edn. and Rsch. in Psychiat. Nursing, Nat. League for Nursing, N.Am. Nursing Diagnosis Assn., Internat. Platform Assn., Ventura County Writers Club, Sigma Theta Tau, Phi Kappa Phi. Republican. Home: 1161 Cypress Point Ln Apt 201 Ventura CA 93003-6074

BIRDSALL, BRIAN, food products executive; b. 1956. Grad., Wash. State U., 1979. With Pannell Kerr Foster Acctg., Wenatchee, Wash., 1979-88; pres., treas. Chief Wenatchee, 1988—. Office: Chief Wenatchee 1705 N Miller St Wenatchee WA 98801-1585*

BIRENBAUM, MARC ALLEN, editor, writer; b. Balt., Jan. 26, 1959; s. David and Irene (Gerstl) B.; m. Barbara Sue Lemerman, July 28, 1991; 1 child, Rachel Sara. BA in Journalism and Polit. Sci., Washington and Lee U., 1980. Editor AQUA Mag., Santa Ana, Calif., 1989-91; assoc. editor Dental Equipment Rental Mag., Culver City, Calif., 1991-93, Dimensional Stone Mag., Woodland Hills, Calif., 1993-95; editor Tile and Decorative Surfaces, Woodland Hills, 1993-95; mng. editor Nat. Notary Assn., Canoga Park, Calif., 1995—. Democrat. Jewish. Home: 636 Bienveneda Ave Pacific Palisades CA 90272 Office: Nat Notary Assn 8236 Remmet Ave Canoga Park CA 91309

BIRKBY, WALTER HUDSON, forensic anthropologist, consultant; b. Gordon, Nebr., Feb. 28, 1931; s. Walter Levy and Margery Hazel (Moss) B.; m. Carmen Sue Gates, Aug. 18, 1955; children: Jeffrey Moss, Julianne. BA, U. Kans., 1961, MA, 1963; PhD, U. Ariz., 1973. Diplomate Am. Bd. Forensic Anthropology (pres. 1985-87, exec. com. 1980-87). Med. and X-ray technician Graham County (Kans.) Hosp., Hill City, 1955-58; phys. anthropologist Ariz. State Mus., Tucson, 1968-85; lectr. anthropology U. Ariz., Tucson, 1981-90, adj. rsch. prof. anthropology, 1990-96; curator phys. anthropology Ariz. State Mus., Tucson, 1985-96; forensic anthropologist Pima County Med. Examiner's Office, Tucson, 1981—, Recovery of Victims of Alfred G. Packer party (1874), Lake City, Colo., 1989; dental cons. USAF Hosp., Davis Monthan AFB, Tucson, 1984-96; human osteologist U. Ariz.-Republic of Cyprus Archaeol. Expdn., 1984-87, Lugnano in Teverina (Italy) Expdn., 1990-91; dir. dept. anthropology masters program in forensic anthropology, 1984-96; cons. to Chief Armed Svcs. Graves Registration Office U.S. Army, 1987-93; mem. disaster mortuary team Nat. Disaster Med. Sys., 1994—. Mem. editorial bd. (jour.) Cryptozoology, 1982—; bd. editors Am. Jour. Forensic Medicine and Pathology, 1992-97; co-author video tng. film Identification of Human Remains, 1980; contbr. articles to profl. jours. Served as sgt. USMCR, 1951-52, Korea. Recipient Achievement medal for meritiorious svc. Pima County Sheriff's Dept., 1992, Spl. Recognition award, 1995; NIH fellow U. Ariz., 1966-68. Fellow Am. Acad. Forensic Scis. (exec. com. 1978-81, T. Dale Stewart award in anthropology 1991); mem. Am. Assn. Phys. Anthropologists, Calif. Assn. Criminalists, Ariz. Identification Coun. of the Internat. Assn. for Identification, Ariz. Homicide Investigators Assn., Sigma Xi (pres. local chpt. 1984-85). Republican. Home: 7349 E 18th St Tucson AZ 85710-4904 Office: Forensic Sci Ctr 2825 E District Tucson AZ 85714

BIRKENBACH, ADAM STEPHEN, engineer; b. Grant Twp., Mich., Jan. 26, 1937; s. Adam Christopher and Mary (Askey) B.; m. Fern Ellen Fox, Dec. 14, 1956 (div. June 1974); children: Stephanie, Jennifer; m. Angela Rivera, July 22, 1982; children: Frank, Michael Salvador. AA in Engring., E. L.A. Coll., 1960; BSEE, Calif. State U., L.A., 1962; MPA, Calif. State U., Long Beach, 1987. Jr. engr. IMC Magnetics, Maywood, Calif., 1960-62; assoc. elec. engr. Dept. of Water and Power, L.A., 1962-68; chief elec. engr. Port of L.A., San Pedro, Calif., 1968-79, chief of design, 1979-85, asst. chief harbor engr., 1985-95; chief harbor engr. Port of L.A., 1995—; port facilities cons. Asia/Am., Monterey Park, Calif., 1992-94, elec. engring. cons., San Pedro, 1968—. Contbg. author: (books) American National Standard Practice for Industrial Lighting, 1967, rev. edit. 1994, IESNA Lighting Handbook, 1980, rev. edit. 1994. Res. commdr. L.A. Sheriff Dept., Los Angeles County, 1968-94; pres. Penninsula Pointe Homeowners Assn., Rancho Palos Verdes, Calif., 1992-94; mem. Empty Saddle Club, Palos Verdes Estates, Calif., 1983-94. With USN, 1954-58, Asia, Korea. Mem. Illuminating Engring. Soc. of N.Am. (chmn. various coms. 1965-94), Permanent Internat. Assn. of Navigation Congress, Am. Soc. Civil Engrs., Propeller Club of U.S. (com. chmn. 1980-94), Soc. Port Engrs., Elks. Republican. Home: PO Box 532 San Pedro CA 90733-0532 Office: Worldport LA PO Box 151 San Pedro CA 90733

BIRKHEAD, JOHN ANDREW, political science educator; b. Anchorage, Jan. 10, 1954; s. Herbert Cecil and Eugenia Clarke (McChesney) B.; children: Nathaniel Andrew, Colin Michael. BA, U. Colo., 1975; MA, U. Calif., Davis, 1984; PhD, Stanford U., 1994. Commd. 2d lt. USAF, 1975, advanced through grades to maj., 1987; navigator USAF, Little Rock, 1976-82; instr. polit. sci. USAF Acad., Colorado Springs, 1984-85; sr. navigator USAF, Okinawa, Japan, 1988-91; assoc. prof. USAF Acad., Colorado Springs, 1991-96; mem. polit. sci. faculty Pikes Peak C.C., 1994, U. So. Colo., 1994, Colo. Coll., 1996. Named Outstanding Young Men of Am., 1985. Mem. Pi Sigma Alpha. Democrat. Home: 3703 S Hudson St Denver CO 80237

BIRKINBINE, JOHN, II, philatelist; b. Chestnut Hill, Pa., Mar. 29, 1930; s. Olaf Weimer and Gertrude Marie (Tyson) B.; m. Ausencia Barrera Elen, Dec. 19, 1969; children: John III, Bayani Royd. Chmn., chief exec. officer Am. Philatelic Brokerages, Tucson, 1946—; chmn. bd. dirs. Ariz. Philatelic Rangers, Tucson, 1987—; bd. dirs. Confederate Stamp Alliance, 1987-88; bd. dirs. Postal History Found., 1991—. Chmn. bd. 1869 Pictorial Rsch. Assn., 1969, bd. dirs., 1970-76, chmn. Baha'i Faith Adminstrv. Body, Pima County, Ariz., 1977-81, 83-91; sheriff, chmn. Santa Catalina Corral of Westerners Internat., Tucson, 1986. Recipient Large Gold and Spl. award Spanish Soc. Internat., San Juan, P.R., 1982, New Zealand Soc. Internat., Auckland, 1990, Large Internat. Gold award Australian Soc. Internat., Melbourne, 1984, Swedish Soc. Internat., Stockholm, 1986, Singapore Soc. Internat., 1995, Internat. Gold award U.S. Soc. Internat., Chgo., 1986, Bulgarian Soc. Internat., Sofia, 1989. Mem. Am. Philatelic Soc. (U.S. Champion of Champions award 1985), U.S. Philatelic Classics Soc. (disting. philatelist award 1995), Am. Philatelic Congress (McCoy award 1969), Scandinavian Collectors Club, Collectors Club N.Y., Western Cover Soc. Office: Am Philatelic Brokerages PO Box 36657 Tucson AZ 85740-6657 Address: PO Box 36657 Tucson AZ 85740-6657 *To look for and appreciate the good qualities in each individual, to have sympathy and empathy for their problems, and to provide exceptional service in an attempt to satisfy their needs and desires.*

BIRNBAUM, STEVAN ALLEN, investment company executive; b. L.A., Apr. 21, 1943; s. Eugene David and Bessie (Holtzman) B.; m. Barbara Patricia Ostroff, June 29, 1971 (div. Aug. 1991); children: Marc, Jill. BS in Engring., UCLA, 1965; MBA, Harvard U., 1967. Dir. advanced programs Whittaker Corp., L.A., 1967-69; v.p. Hohenberg & Assocs., Beverly Hills, Calif., 1969-74; dir. adminstrv. mgmt. Dames & Moore, L.A., 1974-77; prin. Xerox Venture Capital, L.A., 1977-81; venture capitalist, L.A., 1981-83; ptnr. Oxford Ptnrs., Santa Monica, Calif., 1983-95; pres. Oxcal Venture Corp., Santa Monica, 1981—; founder, bd. dirs. Brentwood Savs. Bank, 1982; bd. dirs. Quintar Corp., Torrance, Calif. Republican. Jewish.

BIROC, SANDRA LYN, bilogical scientist; b. L.A., Dec. 14, 1947; d. Robert Biroc and Doris Lynell (Haven) Rast; m. Daniel Bernard Unger, Mar. 27, 1982; children: Elizabeth Kaye, Douglas Gustav. BA in Biology, Calif. State U., Northridge, 1970; PhD in Biology, Johns Hopkins U., 1975. Postdoctoral fellow U. Calif., Davis, 1975-78; instr. Calif. State U., Sacramento, 1978-80; lab. coord., asst. prof. biology U. Colo., Boulder, 1980-91; founding mem., staff scientist Khepri Pharms., South San Francisco, 1992-95; pharmacologist Arris Pharm., South San Francisco, 1995—. Author: Developmental Biology, 1986. Dem. del., Colo., 1988. Mem. AAAS, Boulder Internat. Folk Dancers (pres. 1985-90), Masons (state rep. 1965-66), Assn. Women in Sci. Office: Arris Pharmaceuticals Inc 180 Kimball Way South San Francisco CA 94080

BISHOP, BETTY JOSEPHINE, financial consultant, expert witness; b. Seattle, Wash., Feb. 27, 1947; d. Arthur Joseph and Julia Teresa (Azzolina) Lovett; children: Deborah, Scott. BS, Wash. State U., 1969; postgrad., Ohio State U., 1983; JD, Santa Barbara Coll. of Law, 1994. Cert. real estate appraiser. Tchr. Seattle Sch. Dist., 1973-75; appraiser Pacific First Fed., Tacoma, 1977-78, asst. v.p., mgr., secondary market ops., 1978-82; regional exec. United Guaranty, Westlake Village, Calif., 1982-83; sr. v.p. comml. secondary mktg. FCA Am. Mortgage Corp./ Am. Savs., Santa Monica, Calif., 1983-85; v.p., mgr. secondary market ops. County Savs. Bank, Santa Barbara, Calif., 1985-88; pres., fin. cons. SMC Fin. Svcs., Montecito, Calif., 1988—; mem. conf. subcom., sec. mktg. com. Calif. Savs. and Loan League, L.A., 1985-88; document subcom., sec. mktg. subcom. U.S. Savs. and Loan League, Chgo., 1987-88. Contbr. articles to profl. jours. Fund drive chmn. Easter Seal Soc., Olympia, 1972. Mem. Consumer Atty.'s Assn., Santa Barbara Assocs., Conejo Ski Club (past woman of yr.), Santa Barbara Ski Club (past pres., past L.A. coun. rep.). Republican. Roman Catholic.

BISHOP, C. DIANE, state agency administrator, educator; b. Elmhurst, Ill., Nov. 23, 1943; d. Louis William and Constance Oleta (Mears) B. BS in Maths., U. Ariz., 1965, MS in Maths., MEd in Secondary Edn., 1972. Lic. secondary educator. Tchr. math. Tucson Unified Sch. Dist., 1966-86, mem. curriculum council, 1985-86, mem. maths. curriculum task teams, 1983-86; state supt. of pub. instrn. State of Ariz., 1987-95, gov. policy advisor for edn., 1995—, dir. gov.'s office workforce devel. policy, 1996—; mem. assoc. faculty Pima C.C., Tucson, 1974-84; adj. lectr. U. Ariz., 1983, 85; mem. math. scis. edn. bd. NRC, 1987-90, mem. new standards project governing bd., 1991; dir. adv. bd. sci. and engring. ednl. panel, NSF; mem. adv. bd. for arts edn. Nat. Endowment for Arts. Active Ariz. State Bd. Edn., 1984-95, chmn. quality edn. commn., 1986-87, chmn. tchr. crt. subcom., 1984-95, mem. outcomes based edn. adv. com., 1986-87, liaison bd. dirs. essential skills subcom., 1985-87, gifted edn. com. liaison, 1985-87; mem. Ariz. State Bd. Regents, 1987-95, mem. com. on preparing for U. Ariz., 1983, mem. high sch. task force, 1984-85; mem. bd. Ariz. State Community Coll., 1987-95; mem. Ariz. Joint Legis. Com. on Revenues and Expenditures, 1989, Ariz. Joint Legis. Com. on Goals for Ednl. Excellence, 1987-89, Gov.'s Task Force on Ednl. Reform, 1991, Ariz. Bd. Regents Commn. on Higher Edn., 1992. Woodrow Wilson fellow Princeton U., summer 1984; recipient Presdl. Award for Excellence in Teaching of Maths., 1983, Ariz. Citation of Merit, 1984, Maths. Teaching award Nat. Sci. Research Soc., 1984, Distinction in Edn. award Flinn Found., 1986; named Maths. Tchr. of Yr. Ariz. Council of Engring. and Sci. Assns., 1984. Mem. AAUW, NEA, Nat. Coun. Tchrs. Math., Coun. Chief State Sch. Officers, Women Execs. in State Govt. (bd. dirs. 1993), Ariz. Assn. Tchrs. Math., Women Maths. Edn., Math. Assn. Am., Ednl. Commn. of the States (steering com.), Nat. Endowment Arts (adv. bd. for arts edn.), Nat. Forum Excellence Edn., Nat. Honors Workshop, Phi Delta Kappa. Republican. Episcopalian. Office: Ariz Gov's Office 1700 W Washington St Phoenix AZ 85007-2812

BISHOP, CAROL WARD, dean; b. Sewickley, Pa., July 10, 1936; d. Earl Dawson and Wilma Henrietta (Obenour) Ward; m. Jack Lynn Bishop, Mar. 29, 1958; children: Lori Diane Bishop Dagg, Jeffrey Lynn. BS in Home Econs. and Journalism, Kans. State U., 1958; MS in Nutrition, Va. Poly. Inst., 1961. Registered dietitian. Asst. editor Household Mag., Topeka, 1958-59; rsch. instr. Va. Poly. Inst., Blackburg, 1964-67; instr. nutrition Modesto (Calif.) Jr. Coll., 1967-70; instr. nutrition Solano Coll., Suisun City, Calif., 1970-78, divsn. chair fine arts, 1978-90, dean fine and applied arts, 1990—; grant writer Tech-Prep State Presch., Fed. Block Grant, Child Devel. Consortium, Fed. Food Program, Foster Parent, Ind. Living, Nutrition Edn. Tng., Child Devel. Renovation and Repair; chair Tech. Prep. Adv. Com. Mem. Am. Dietetic Assn., Calif. Dietetic Assn., Diablo Valley Dietetic Assn., Danas Women's Club (bridge chmn.), Phi Kappa Phi, Delta Sigma Gamma. Home: PO Box 267 Bethel Island CA 94511-0267 Office: Solano Coll 4000 Suisun Valley Rd Suisun City CA 94585-4017

BISHOP, JOHN MICHAEL, biomedical research scientist, educator; b. York, Pa., Feb. 22, 1936; married 1959; 2 children. AB, Gettysburg Coll., 1957; MD, Harvard U., 1962; DSc (hon.), Gettysburg Coll., 1983. Intern in internal medicine Mass. Gen. Hosp., Boston, 1962-63, resident, 1963-64; rsch. assoc. virology NIH, Washington, 1964-66, sr. investigator, 1966-68; from asst. prof. to assoc. prof. U. Calif. Med. Ctr., San Francisco, 1968-72, prof. microbiology and immunology, 1972—, prof. biochemistry and biophysics, 1982—; prof., dir. G.W. Hooper Rsch. Found. G.W. Hooper Rsch. Found., 1981—; Univ. prof. U. Calif. Med. Ctr., San Francisco, 1994—. Recipient Nobel prize in physiology or medicine, 1989, Biomed. Rsch. award Am. Assn. Med. Colls., 1981, Albert Lasker Basic Med. Rsch. award, 1981, Armand Hammer Cancer award, 1984, GM Found. Cancer Rsch. award, 1984, Gairdner Found. Internat. award, Can., 1984, Medal of Honor, Am. Cancer Soc., 1984; NIH grantee, 1968—. Fellow Salk Inst. (trustee 1991—); mem. NAS, Inst. Medicine. Office: U Calif Medical Ctr Dept Microbiology Box 0552 San Francisco CA 94143-0552*

BISHOP, ROBERT CHARLES, architect, metals and minerals company executive; b. Butte, Mont., June 6, 1929; s. Lester Farragut and Helen Katherine (Bauman) B.; m. B. Jean Rausch, June 29, 1957; children: Desta Fawn Bishop O'Connor, Valerie Dawn. BS in Gen. Engring., Mont. State U., 1958, BArch., 1960. Assoc. architect various firms, Mont., 1960-64; owner, architect R.C. Bishop & Assocs., Butte, Great Falls and Missoula, Mont., 1965-69; owner, chief exec. officer Val-Desta 4M, Butte, 1980—, Val-Desta Mines and Minerals, Louisville, Ky., 1985—; prin. Archtl. Assocs., 1969—; chief exec. officer, pres. Cove-Lock Log Home Mfrs., Inc., Butte, 1986-72, Busy Beaver Enterprises, Great Falls, 1968-72, New Horizon Homes, Missoula, 1968-72; asst. contracts adminstr. Davy-McKee Constrn. Engrs., Butte, 1982-83. Developer 9 major and 2 minor algorithms for mineral prospecting, valid for over 100 areas in Mont. and Idaho; discoverer 100 to 300 million tons of high grade bull quarts and rock crystal, copper and molybdenum, potential world class deposits; discoverer naturally occurring minerals that when infused in a water medium are capable with electrolysis to produce 3.5 times the hydrogen as available from the electrolysis of sea water; co-patentee in field. Advisor, Kiwanis, Jaycees, Nat. Res., 1960-72, Am. Legion, 1976. With U.S. Army, 1953-55. Named One of 2, 000 Men of Achievement Melrose Press, 1970, 73. Mem. Internat. Platform Assn., Nat. Hist. Soc. (founding assoc. 1971), Elk Bow Hunting Club (bugle tchr. 1970-84), Butte Mulitlist Club (real estate tchr. 1978-84), Nat. Coun. Archtl. Registeration Bds. (registered architect seismic design 1965—). Presbyterian. Home and Office: 1008 W Galena St Butte MT 59701-1420

BISHOP, TILMAN MALCOLM, state senator, retired college administrator; b. Colorado Springs, Jan. 1, 1933; B.A., M.A., U. No. Colo.; m. Pat Bishop, 1951; 1 son, Barry Alan. Retired adminstr., dir. student services Mesa State Coll., Grand Junction, Colo.; mem., pres. pro tem Colo. Senate. World series com. Nat. Jr. Coll. Baseball. Served with U.S. Army. Mem. Am. Sch. Counselors Assn., Nat. Assn. for Counseling and Devel., Colo. Assn. for Counseling and Devel. Republican. Methodist. Lodges: Elks, Lions. Avocations: fishing, small game hunting. Office: State Capitol Bldg Denver CO 80203 Home: 2697 G Rd Grand Junction CO 81506-8367

BISHOP, VIRGINIA WAKEMAN, retired librarian and humanities educator; b. Portland, Oreg., Dec. 28, 1927; d. Andrew Virgil and Letha Evangeline (Ward) Wakeman; m. Clarence Edmund Bishop, Aug. 23, 1953; children: Jean Marie Bishop Johnson, Marilyn Joyce. BA, Bapt. Missionary Tng. Sch., Chgo., 1949, Linfield Coll., McMinnville, Oreg., 1952; MEd, Linfield Coll., McMinnville, Oreg., 1953; MA in Librarianship, U. Wash., 1968. Ch. worker Univ. Bapt. Ch., Seattle, 1954-56, 59-61, pre-sch. tchr. parent coop presch., 1965-66; libr. N.W. Coll., Kirkland, Wash., 1968-69; undergrad. libr. U. Wash., Seattle, 1970; libr., instr. Seattle Cen. Community Coll., 1970-91. Leader Totem coun. Girl Scouts U.S., 1962-65; pres. Wedgwood Sch. PTA, Seattle, 1964-65; chair 46th Dist. Dem. Orgn., Seattle, 1972-73; precinct com. officer Dem. Party, 1996—; candidate Wash. State Legislature, Seattle, 1974, 80; bd. dirs. Univ. Bapt. Children's Ctr., 1989-95, chair, 1990-95; vol. Ptnrs. in Pub. Edn., 1992-96. Recipient Golden Acorn award Wedgwood Elem. Sch., 1966. Mem. LWV of Seattle (2d v.p. 1994-96), U. Wash. Grad. Sch. Libr. and Info. Sci. Alumni Assn. (1st v.p. 1986-87, pres. 1987-88). Baptist. Home: 3032 NE 87th St Seattle WA 98115-3529

BISHOP-GRAHAM, BARBARA, secondary school educator, journalist; b. Angwin, Calif., Apr. 22, 1941; d. Will Francis and Esther Clara (Blisserd) Bishop; children: Gregory Mark, Steven Bishop. *Father, Will Francis Bishop, was the leading custom home builder in world-renowned wine country, Napa Valley, from the 1930's to 1972. He built his business and also constructed custom homes and apartment buildings in the North San Francisco Bay area, as well as suburban areas of Walnut Creek and Lafayette. He was noted for his well-built homes and the then-unique talent for designing and drawing his own plans, in which the influence of Frank Lloyd Wright could be seen. The majority of these homes are standing today. An original second floor feature was his own "airplane" beadroom suite, a light, airy finishing touch.* BA in Journalism, BA in English, BA in Art Hist., U. Hawaii, 1975, BFA in Painting and Drawing, 1975; nat. cert. in journalism, Kans. State U., 1994. Cert. tchr., Hawaii. Photography instr., art tchr. Hawaii Sch. for Girls, Honolulu, 1974-76; substitute tchr. English State Dept. Edn., Oahu, 1977-78; English and grammar instr. Hawaii Sch. for Bus., Honolulu, 1979-80; media dir., exec. asst., historian Oriental Treasures and Points West, Honolulu, 1981-82; legal asst. Goodsill, Anderson, Quinn, Honolulu, 1983-84; lang. arts and photography tchr. Lodi (Calif.) H.S., 1984-88, writing and lang. arts tchr., 1988-93, journalism adviser, lang. arts tchr., 1993—, Brit. lit. tchr., 1996—; mem. curriculum coun. Lodi Unified Sch. Dist., 1989-92; liaison to PTSA Lodi H.S., 1991-92, mentor tchr., 1991-94; student literary mag. advisor Lodi H.S., 1989—. Sportswriter Oakland Tribune, 1957-60; contbr. articles to profl. publs. Fundraiser chmn. Big Bros. of Am., San Francisco, 1967; media dir. Clements (Calif.) Cmty. Cares, 1985-89. Recipient Edn. Contbn. award Masonsm 1988-92; grantee Nat. Endowment of Arts, 1989; social rschr. grantee Brazil, U. So. Calif., 1992, grantee, 1992. Mem. NEA, Calif. Tchrs. Assn. (mem. state coun. rep. 1996—), Lodi Edn. Assn. (conf. fund chair 1989—). Republican. Seventh-Day Adventist. Office: Lodi HS 3 S Pacific Ave Lodi CA 95242-3020

BISSELL, CYNTHIA L., artist; b. N.Y.C., Mar. 31, 1924; d. Leonard Bissell and Mary G. Hubbell. Student, Colo. Coll. Salesperson Macy's, San Francisco and N.Y.C.; with record dept. Grabe Electric Sales, Tucson; med.-allergy Kaiser Hosp., San Francisco; salesperson Dohrmanns, San Francisco. Exhibited in group shows Lebant Gallery, San Francisco, Navajo Gallery, Taos, N.Mex., Artist's Loop, Santa Fe, U. N.Mex., Las Cruces. Home: # 11-E 2720 N Swan Tucson AZ 85712

BISSONETTE, JOHN ALFRED, research scientist; b. Colchester, Vt., July 9, 1941; s. Kenneth Joseph and Diane Marie (Gamache) B.; m. Mary Elizabeth Poe, Oct. 1, 1966; children: Nicole Elizabeth, Gabriel Jared. BA, U. Vt., 1964; MFS, Yale U., 1970; PhD, U. Mich., 1976. Vertebrate zoologist Ariz. State U., Tempe, 1975-77; asst. unit leader Okla. State U., Stillwater, 1977-81; asst. unit leader, act. leader U. Maine, Orono, 1981-85; leader Utah coop. fish & wildlife res. unit Utah State U., Logan, 1985—; mem., chmn. bd. govs. SNR-U. Mich., Ann Arbor, 1985-91; mem., bd. dirs. Natural Res. Coun. Maine, Augusta; bd. scientists Chihuahuan Desert Res. Inst., Alpine, Tex., 1987—; bd. dirs. N.Am. Loon Fund, N.H.; mem. Utah Nat. Resources Coordinating Coun., 1995—. Home: 1960 N 1380 E Logan UT 84541 Office: Utah State U US Geol Survey Divsn Biol Resources Coll Natural Resources Logan UT 84522-5290

BISTLINE, STEPHEN, retired state supreme court justice; b. Pocatello, Idaho, Mar. 12, 1921; s. Ray D. and Martha (Faber) B.; m. Sharon Mooney; children: Patrick, Claire, Susan, Shelley, Diana, Paul, Leslie, Arthur. LL.B., U. Idaho, 1949. Bar: Idaho 1949. Pvt. practice law Sandpoint, Idaho, 1950-76; justice Idaho Supreme Ct., Boise, 1976-94. Served with USN, 1941-45. •

BITTENBENDER, BRAD JAMES, environmental safety and health administrator; b. Kalamazoo, Dec. 4, 1948; s. Don J. and Thelma Lu (Bacon) B.; m. Patricia Stahl Hubbell, June, 1992. BS, Western Mich. U., 1972; Cert. Hazardous Material Mgmt., U. Calif., Irvine, 1987; Cert. Environ. Auditing, Calif. State U., Long Beach, 1992. Cert. safety profl. of the Ams.; cert. hazardous materials mgr. Supr. mfg. Am. Cyanamid, Kalamazoo, 1973-77; supr. mfg. Productol Chem. div. Ferro Corp., Santa Fe Springs, Calif., 1977-79, environ. adminstr., 1979-80; sr. environ. engr. Ferro Corp., Los Angeles, 1980-87; mgr. environ. safety and indsl. hygiene dept. Composites divsn. Ferro Corp., Los Angeles, 1988-91, Structural Polymer Systems, Inc., Montedison, Calif., 1991-95; dir. environ. safety and health dept. Culver City (Calif.) Composites Corp., 1996—; bd. dirs., mem. adv. bd. safety and health extension program U. Calif. Irvine, 1985—. Bd. dirs. adv. com. hazardous materials Community Right to Know, Culver City, Calif., 1987—; mem. Calif. Mus. Found., L.A., 1985—, Mus. Contemporary Art, L.A., 1985—; founding sponsor Challenger Ctr. Mem. Am. Inst. Chem. Engrs., Nat. Assn. Environ. Mgmt., Acad. Cert. Hazardous Materials Mgrs., Suppliers of Advanced Composites Materials Assn. (mem. environ. health and safety com. 1989-92), Am. Indsl. Hygiene Assn., Am. Soc. Safety Engrs., Nat. Fire Protection Assn., Beta Beta Beta. Republican. Presbyterian. Office: Culver City Composites Corp 5915 Rodeo Rd Los Angeles CA 90016-4312

BITTERMAN, MELVIN LEE, real estate developer; b. Yankton, S.D., Dec. 9, 1938; s. Edward Phillip and Amanda Bertha (Moke) B.; m. Constance Winfried Mann, Nov. 7, 1970; 1 child, Janet Amanda. BA, N. Tex.

State U., 1967. Librarian City of Glendale, Calif., 1967-71; sales rep. Allstate Ins. Co., Glendale, 1971-86; property mgr./developer Glendale, 1986—. With U.S. Army, 1961-64. Mem. Rotary (sec. 1985), Alpha Beta Alpha. Republican. Roman Catholic. Address: 1400 Beaudry Blvd Glendale CA 91208-1708

BITTERMAN, MORTON EDWARD, psychologist, educator; b. N.Y.C., Jan. 19, 1921; s. Harry Michael and Stella (Weiss) B.; m. Mary Gayle Foley, June 26, 1967; children—Sarah Fleming, Joan, Ann. B.A., NYU, 1941; M.A., Columbia U., 1942; Ph.D., Cornell U., 1945. Asst. prof. Cornell U., Ithaca, N.Y., 1945-50; assoc. prof. U. Tex., Austin, 1950-55; mem. Inst. for Advanced Study, Princeton, N.J., 1955-57; prof. Bryn Mawr Coll., Pa., 1957-70, U. Hawaii, Honolulu, 1970—; dir. Békésy Lab. Neurobiology, Honolulu, 1991—. Author: (with others) Animal Learning, 1979; editor: Evolution of Brain and Behavior in Vertebrates, 1976; co-editor: Am. Jour. Psychology, 1955-73; cons. editor Jour. Animal Learning and Behavior, 1973-76, 85-88, Jour. Comparative Psychology, 1988-92. Recipient Humboldt prize Alexander von Humboldt Found., Bonn, W.Ger., 1981; Fulbright grantee; grantee NSF, Office Naval Research, NIMH, Air Force Office Sci. Research, Deutsche Forschungsgemeinschaft. Fellow Soc. Exptl. Psychologists, Am. Psychol. Assn., AAAS; mem. Psychonomic Soc. Home: 229 Kaalawai Pl Honolulu HI 96816-4435 Office: Univ Hawaii Bekesy Lab of Neurobiology 1993 E West Rd Honolulu HI 96822-2321

BITTERS, CONRAD LEE, biological sciences educator; b. Waco, Tex., Jan. 2, 1946; s. E. Conrad and Margaret Lee (Miles) B.; m. Karen Kay, May 1, 1970; children: Rebecca, Brian. BA, Calif. State U., Fresno, 1969. Life Credential, Biol./Phys. Sciences, Calif. Biology/zoology tchr. Clovis (Calif.) High Sch., 1970—, science dept. chmn., 1973-80, biology coordinator, 1980—; founder, sponsor Clovis (Calif.) High Ecology club, 1970—, Clovis High Fgn. Studies Club, 1978-87, 92-97; jr. div. judge Cen. Valley Sci. Fair, Fresno, Calif., 1975—; coach-sr. div. Cen. Valley Sci. Fair, Fresno, 1972—; dist. rep. Jr. Sci. and Humanities Symposium, Berkeley, Calif., 1974—; Calif. Ednl. Initiatives Fund Grant Dir., 1986. Recipient Faculty award Eastman Kodak Co., 1980, Nat. Jr. Sci. and Humanities Symposium, 1985, 93, 94, Merit award Rotary Club Fresno, 1985, 88, 93-94, Faculty Commendation Lawrence Hall of Sci., 1985, 87, 94, John D. Isaacs Scholarship Com., 1985, Outstanding Sci. Tchrs. Fresno County, Dow Chem. Co., 1986, Presdl. award in sci. tchg. Calif. State Dept. Edn., 1986, Faculty Commendation award Calif. Sci. Fair, 1988, 94, commendation Internat. Sci. Engring. Fair, 1982, 93-94, Commendation for Dept. Energy award, 1993. Mem. Nat. Sci. Teachers' Assn. Republican. Mem. LDS Ch. Home: 2695 Armstrong Ave Clovis CA 93611-4167 Office: Clovis High Sch 1055 Fowler Ave Clovis CA 93611-2062

BITTLINGMAYER, GEORGE, educator; b. Heidelberg, Germany, May 29, 1951; came to U.S., 1957; s. Jakob and Theresia (Bieber) B.; m. Elizabeth Ann Nunn, Aug. 22, 1981; children: Adam, Stefan, Eric. BA, Lehigh U., 1975; AM, U. Chgo., 1977, PhD, 1981. Asst. prof. U. Mich., Ann Arbor, 1980-85; vis. economist Fed. Trade Commission, Washington, 1983-84; vis. assoc. prof. Washington U., St. Louis, Mo., 1984-85; rsch. fellow Sci. Cen. Berlin, 1986-88; prof. U. Calif., Davis, 1988—; vis. prof. John M. Olin Found. U. Chgo., 1993. Assoc. editor Econ. Inquiry, Jour. Corporate Fin.; contbr. articles to profl. jours. Mem. Am. Econ. Assn., Am. Fin. Assn., Western Econ. Assn. (nominating com. 1993). Office: U Calif Grad Sch Mgmt Davis CA 95616

BITTNER, EGON, sociology educator; b. Skrecon, Czechoslovakia, Apr. 16, 1921; came to U.S., 1949, naturalized, 1955; s. Zygmunt and Hermine (Lewkowicz) B.; m. Jean G. Kline, Dec. 24, 1951; children—Thomas J., Debora H. B.A., Los Angeles State Coll., 1955, M.A., 1958; Ph.D., U. Calif. at Los Angeles, 1961. Instr., then asst. prof. sociology U. Calif., Riverside, 1960-63; asst. prof., then asso. prof. U. Calif. Med. Sch., San Francisco, 1963-68; prof. sociology Brandeis U., Waltham, Mass., 1968—; prof. emeritus, 1991—. Author: The Functions of the Police in Modern Society, 1970, Aspects of Police Work, 1990. Mem. Am. Sociol. Assn., Soc. Study Social Problems, Law and Soc. Assn., AAUP. Jewish. Home: 411 Saddlebrook Ln Pleasant Hill CA 94523 Office: Brandeis U Waltham MA 02154

BJELETICH, JOHN GEORGE, metallurgical engineer; b. Butte, Mont., Mar. 19, 1933; s. George Perov and Andja (Lalic) B.; m. Nancy Jean Hall, June 19, 1965; children: Peter, Marko. BSMetE, Mont. Sch. Mines, 1960, MSMetE, 1962. Cert. metall. engr., Calif. Assoc. engr. Theratest Labs., Inc., Sunnyvale, Calif., 1962, engring. supr., 1962-64; scientist Lockheed Missiles & Space Co., Inc., Palo Alto, Calif., 1964-66, sr. scientist, 1966-68, rsch. scientist, 1968-77, staff scientist, 1977-84, sr. staff scientist, 1984-96, materials engr. cons., 1996—; instr. Deanza C.C., Cupertino, Calif., 1971—. Inventor: Automated Crack Follower, NDE Device for Solid Rocket Motor. Treas. Sant Sava Serbian Orthodox Ch., 1984-86, pres. 1986-88. With U.S. Army, 1953-55. Mem. VFW (q.m. 1959, vice comdr. 1960). Office: Lockheed Martin Missile and Space Co Inc 3251 Hanover St Bldg 204 Palo Alto CA 94304

BJORHOVDE, PATRICIA ORDONEZ, university development director; b. Summit, N.J., May 20, 1944; d. Carlos Midence and Beatrice Ellery (Graves) Ordonez; m. Reidar Bjorhovde, Oct. 30, 1972; children: Ian Douglas, Heather Leah Bebee. MusB, Bucknell U., 1966; postgrad., U. Alberta, Edmonton, Can., 1978-80; diploma in arts mgmt., Banff Ctr. Sch. Mgmt., Banff, Alberta, Can., 1981. Cert. fund raising exec. Mid. sch. music tchr. Mt. Laurel (N.J.) Bd. Edn., 1966-67; elem. tchr. Somerville (N.J.) Bd. Edn., 1967-72; ednl. evaluator Saal Lesser Assocs., Mt. Vernon, N.Y., 1974-76; music officer Alberta Culture, Edmonton, Can., 1979-81; gen. mgr. Ariz. Touring Orch., Tucson, 1982; dir. devel. Tucson Symphony Orch., 1982-87; mng. dir. Dance Alloy, Pitts., 1987-91; dir. ann. support Pitts. Symphony Soc., 1991-92; dir. devel., fine arts U. Ariz., Tucson, 1992—; cons. various arts orgn., Ariz., Pa., 1981—; adj. asst. prof. Carnegie Mellon U., Pitts., 1992; art grant panelist Ariz. Commn. on the Arts, Phoenix, 1986, 87, 93, 95, Tucson Pima Arts Coun., 1993—; co-chair mgrs. coun. Dance USA, Washington, 1990-91. Bd. dirs. Cultural Alliance of Tucson, 1981-85, Catalina Foothills Sch. Found., Tucson, 1983-85, Cultural Alliance of Pa., Harrisburg, 1988-92, Friends of Carnegie Music Libr., Pitts., 1990-91, Ariz. Friends of Chamber Music, Tucson, 1994—, Ariz. Town Hall, Phoenix, 1995—; mem. Tucson Symphony Soc., 1996—. Mem. Nat. Soc. Fund Raising Execs. (So. Ariz. chpt. bd. dirs., co-chair state conf. 1984, v.p. 1986, pres. 1987, treas. 1994, pres. 1995, 96, Western Pa. chpt. bd. dirs., asst. treas. 1990, 91, 92, nat. del. assembly 1994-96). Democrat. Office: Univ Ariz Fine Arts Adminstrn Music Bldg Rm 111 Tucson AZ 85721

BJORK, ROBERT ERIC, language professional educator; b. Virginia, Minn., Feb. 19, 1949; s. George Emanual and Alice Celinda (Sandberg) B. BA, Pomona Coll., 1971; MA, UCLA, 1974, PhD, 1979. Adj. lectr. Writing Programs and Medicine UCLA, 1979-83; asst. prof., assoc. prof. English Ariz. State U., Tempe, 1983-89, prof., 1989—; vis. scholar St. Catharine's Coll. Cambridge U., 1997. Author: Old English Saints' Lives, 1985; transl. Holme Trilogy, 1989-90, Only a Mother, 1991; co-editor Studies in Scandinavian Lit. and Culture, 1992—; gen. editor Modern Scandinavian Lit. in Translation, 1984-94. Recipient Tchg. award Burlington No. Found., 1988. Mem. Medieval Acad. Am. (dir. data project), Renaissance Soc. Am. (coun.). Office: Ariz State Univ Ctr Medieval Renaissance Tempe AZ 85287

BJORKLUND, JANET VINSEN, speech pathologist; b. Seattle, July 31, 1947; d. Vernon Edward and Virginia Lea (Rogers) B.; m. Dan Robert Young, Dec. 04, 1971; children: Emery Allen, Alanna Vinsen, Marisa Rogers. Student, U. Vienna, Austria, 1966-67; BA, Pacific U., 1969; student, U. Wash., 1970-71; MA, San Francisco State U., 1977. Cert. clin. speech pathologist, audiologist. Speech pathologist, audiological cons. USN Hosp., Rota, Spain, 1972-75; traineeship in audiology VA Hosp., San Francisco, 1976; speech pathologist San Lorenzo (Calif.) Unified Schs., 1975-77, 78-81; dir. speech pathology St. Lukes Speech and Hearing Clinic, San Francisco, 1977-78; audiologist X.O. Barrios, M.D., San Francisco, 1977-81; cons. Visually Impaired Infant Program, Seattle, 1981-82; speech pathologist Everett (Wash.) Schs., 1982-94; speech-lang. pathologist, supr. Sultan (Wash.) Schs., 1995—; supr. pediat. programs speech pathology Group Health Coop. Puget Sound, Seattle, 1994; cons. Providence Hosp. Childrens Ctr., Everett, 1985-93, Pacific Hearing and Speech, 1988-93; rep. audiology adv. com. Ednl. Staff Assocs. Speech-Lang. Pathology, Wash., 1995—. Author: (with others) Screening for Bilingual Preschoolers, 1977, (TV script), Clinical Services in San Francisco, 1978, Developing Better Communication Skills, 1982. Chair Washington Mid. Sch. Site Coun., 1995—. Mem. Am. Speech-Lang. and Hearing Assn., Wash. Speech and Hearing Assn. (regional rep. 1985-86, chair licensure task force 1986-88, rep. Birth to Six Project 1988-91, pres. 1993), Pub. Edn. Adv. Com. (rep. 1995—), Phi Lambda Omicron (pres. Pacific U. chpt. 1968). Congregationalist.

BJURING, GÖRAN LENNART, engineering executive; b. Linköping, Sweden, Mar. 6, 1937; came to U.S., 1987; s. Gerhard and Ester Amalia (Karlsson) B.; m. Birgitta Krän, June 7, 1960 (div. Feb. 1975). MBA, Gothenburg (Sweden) U., 1963; postgrad. exec. program, Stanford U., 1984. V.p. fin. Nynäs Petroleum, Sweden, 1970-85; CEO Axel Johnson Engring., San Francisco, 1985-86; v.p. fin. Johnson Constrn. Co., Sweden, 1986-87; pres. Santa Fe Engring. Inc., Lancaster, Calif., 1987—. Sgt. Swedish Army, 1956-57. Home: 39812 Golfers Dr Palmdale CA 93551-2948 Office: Santa Fe Engring Inc 44733 Date Ave Lancaster CA 93534-3101

BLACHER, JOAN HELEN, psychotherapist, educator; b. L.A., Aug. 10, 1928; d. Albert Scribner and Isabel (Marriott) Oakholt; m. Norman Blacher, July 27, 1973; stepchildren: Eric, Steven, Mark. BA, U. Calif., Berkeley, 1950; MEd, U. So. Calif., 1971, PhD, 1981. Lic. ednl. psychologist, Calif.; lic. marriage, family and child counselor, Calif. Elem. tchr. L.A. Unified Sch. Dist., 1962-71, sch. psychologist, 1971-72, 73-74; sch. psychologist Pasadena (Calif.) Unified Sch. Dist., 1972-73; sch. psychologist Ventura (Calif.) County Supt. Schs., 1974-79, prin., 1979-86; assoc. prof. sch. edn., dir. counseling and guidance program Calif. Luth. U., Thousand Oaks, 1987—; pvt. practice, Ventura, 1984—. Bd. dirs. Coalition Against Household Violence, Ventura, 1984-85, Camarillo Hosp., 1994—. Mem. APA, Am. Counselors Assn., Am. Ednl. Rsch. Assn., Calif. Assn. Counselors, Educators, Suprs. (past pres.), Calif. Assn. Marriage and Family Therapists, Calif. Assn. Counseling Devel., Phi Delta Kappa. Republican.

BLACK, ALAN, author; b. Chgo., Nov. 16, 1970. Author: (novels) Mosquito, 1994, Astoria 1881, Spiritus Mundi (novella), 1995; author screenplay: Blade Runner Two, 1995. Home: 1000 S Coast Dr Unit H-201 Costa Mesa CA 92626

BLACK, ANDERSON DUANE, writer, business consultant; b. Jackson, Mich., May 15, 1928; s. Walter Ward and Mary Christmas (Anderson) B.; m. Sheila Eiko Ueda, Dec. 26, 1962. BS, Northwestern U., 1954; MA, U. Hawaii, 1959, MBA, 1979. Instr. U. Hawaii, Honolulu, 1959-62; mgr. Castle & Cooke, Inc., Honolulu, 1963-84; pres. A.D. Black Assocs., Lanai City, Hawaii, 1984—; adminstr. Lanai Cmty. Hosp., Lanai City, Hawaii, 1989-92. Author: (play) Tsunami!, 1960, (play) Year of the Great Poy Shortage, 1961, Golden Children of Hawaii, 1987. Bd. dirs. State Comprehensive Health Planning Coun., Honolulu, 1969-75; pres., bd. dirs. Pacific and Asian Affairs Coun., Honolulu, 1964-70. Recipient Pacific House award Pacific and Asian Affairs Coun., 1969. Mem. Lanai City Lions Club (pres. 1963—), Lions Internat. (state sec. dist. 50 1983-84). Home: 1634 Makiki St #102 Honolulu HI 96822-4437 Office: AD Black Assocs PO Box 765 Lanai City HI 96763-0765

BLACK, CAROLYN BICKNELL, science and education educator. MS, Emory U., 1970; PhD, U. Tex., 1990. Cert. secondary edn. and biology tchr., Tex. Teaching asst. Emory U., Atlanta, 1968-70; tchr. secondary sci. Overseas Dependent Schs., Ankara, Turkey, 1966-67; tchr. sci. Fairfax County Schs., Fairfax, Va., 1972-75; ednl. specialist U. Tex., San Antonio, 1980-84; supr. tchrs. 2d level U. Tex., Austin, 1989—; instr. sci. U. of the Incarnate Word, San Antonio, 1992-94; lectr. undergrad. sci. U. Incarnate Word, San Antonio, 1993-94; instr. Ft. Lewis Coll., Durango, Colo., 1995—. Mem. AAAS, ASCD, Nat. Sci. Tchrs. Assn., Sigma Xi (chmn. publicity com. Alamo chpt. 1985-90), Phi Beta Kappa, Kappa Delta Pi.

BLACK, DAVID R., superintendent; b. Albuquerque, Apr. 19, 1950; s. Robert E. and Ethyl M. (Nutt) B.; m. Trudy Rae Letts, June 12, 1971; children: Kasey Ellin, Joanna Kate. BS in Edn., No. Ariz. U., 1972, MA in Edn., 1975; EdD, Nova Southeastern U., 1994. Tchr./coach Ajo (Ariz.) Schs., 1972-75; coach/tchr./counselor Show Low (Ariz.) Schs., 1976-82; prin. Blue Ridge Schs., Pinetop, Ariz., 1983-85; vice-prin. Show Low Schs., 1985-88, prin., 1988-93; supt. schs. Winslow (Ariz.) Unified Sch. Dist. # 1, 1993-96, supt. schs., 1997—; mem. state curriculum task force Ariz. Dept. Edn., Phoenix, 1991-92; chmn. Winslow Personnel Bd. Mem. Gov.'s Alliance Against Drugs, Phoenix, 1988-92, Gov.'s Alliance Against Gangs, Phoenix, 1992—; chmn. Parks/Recreation Commn., Show Low, 1982-92, Winslow Parks/recreation chmn., 1995; mem. Ch. Fin. Planning, Roman Cath. Ch., Show Low, 1987; bd. dirs. Am. Heart Assn., 1992; mem. Native Am. adv. com. Johnson OMalley; active La Posada Gardening Angel, 1993-94, La Posada Found., 1995. Named Ariz. Regional Coach of the Yr. Ariz. Interscholastic Assn., 1980, Ariz. Coach-All Stars Ariz. Coaches Assn., 1980. Mem. Ariz. Sch. Adminstrs., Boy Scouts of Am. Eagle Scout Assn., Kiwanis, Phi Delta Kappa. Republican.

BLACK, EILEEN MARY, elementary school educator; b. Bklyn., Sept. 20, 1944; d. Marvin Mize and Anne Joan (Salvia) B. Student, Grossmont Coll., El Cajon, Calif., 1964; BA, San Diego State U., 1967; postgrad., U. Calif., San Diego, Syracuse U. Cert. tchr., Calif. Tchr. La Mesa (Calif.)-Spring Valley Sch. Dist., 1967—. NDEA grantee Syracuse U., 1968; recipient 30 Yrs. Svc. award La Mesa-Spring Valley Sch. Dist., 1997. Mem. Calif. Tchrs. Assn., Greenpeace, San Diego Zoological Soc., Wilderness Soc. Roman Catholic. Home: 9320 Earl St Apt 15 La Mesa CA 91942-3846 Office: Northmont Elem Sch 9405 Gregory St La Mesa CA 91942-3811

BLACK, KAREN L., not-for-profit administrator, social worker, advocate; b. Moscow, Idaho, June 5, 1950. BA in Social Work, Ea. Wash. U., 1990, MA in Social Work, 1992, MA in Pub. Adminstrn., 1993. Cert. in chem. dependency counseling. Community organizer N.Y. Tenant Assn., N.Y.C., 1972-80; word processing supr. KTI Miller, Irvine, Calif., 1980-85, Assn. Retarded Citizens, Spokane, Wash., 1986-87; cons., founder Cheney Coop. Gardens, Cheney, Wash., 1990-96; cons., adminstr. Cheney Outreach, Cheney, Wash., 1991-92; social work case mgr., counselor, educator Salvation Army CD Outpatient Svcs., Spokane, Wash., 1997—. Recipient Community Svc. award Seattle Jaycees, 1992. Mem. Nat. Assn. Social Workers, Am. Soc. Pub. Adminstrs., Assn. Community Organizers and Social Adminstrs.

BLACK, KAY CHERENE, clinical nurse specialist; b. Blackwell, Okla., May 25, 1954; d. Joseph Douglas Boyer and Velva Dean (Foetisch) Oathout; divorced; 1 child, Jesse Lane Black. AD, No. Okla. Coll., Tonkawa, 1979; BS, N.W. Okla. State U., Alva, 1990; MSN, U. Okla., 1993. Cert. psychiat. and mental health nurse. Staff nurse St. Mary's Hosp., Enid, Okla., 1979-86; unit mgr. Meadowlake Hosp., Enid, 1986-90; head nurse St. Anthony Hosp., Oklahoma City, 1990-91; dir. nursing Okla. Youth Ctr., Norman, 1991-93; clin. nurse specialist, owner, dir. Counseling and Emotional Wellness Svcs., Chama, N.Mex., 1993—; speaker Meadowlake Hosp., Enid, 1986-90; trainer CONTACT, Enid, 1980-83. Named to Outstanding Young Women of Am., 1986; Parry Merit scholar U. Okla., 1991-92. Mem. C. of C. (sec., bd. dirs.), Rio Arriba Family Care Network (bd. dirs.), Crisis Intervention Task Force. Home: PO Box 799 Chama NM 87520-0799 Office: TLC Enterprises Inc PO Box 790 Chama NM 87520

BLACK, KRISTINE MARY, physicist; b. St. Paul, July 11, 1953; d. Jaurd Oliver and Dorothy Helen (Amos) B. B in Physics, U. Minn., 1975, MS in Cell Biology, 1978, MS in Metallurgy and Materials Sci., 1981. Analytical physicist Cardiac Pacemakers, St. Paul, 1978, qualifications engr., 1978-81; biomaterials engr. St. Jude Med., Inc., St. Paul, 1981-83; mgr. quality assurance Unisys Semicondr. Ops., St. Paul, 1983-88; sys. assurance sect. mgr. Unisys, 1988-90, quality assurance mgr. SMPO divsn., San Diego, 1990-91; mgr. reliability and quality assurance Carborundum Co., Phoenix, 1991-93; supplier quality assoc. Hamilton Std. Comml. Aircraft Products, Mesa, Ariz., 1993-94; mgr. materials QA Micro-Rel. divsn. Medtronics, 1994—. Contbr. articles to profl. jours. Mem. Am. Soc. for Quality Control, Am. Soc. Metals, U. Minn. Inst. Tech. Alumni Soc. (dir. 1980-87, v.p. 1986-87, pres. 1987-88). Office: Medtronic-Micro-Rel 2343 W 10th Pl Tempe AZ 85281

BLACK, LAVONNE PATRICIA, special education educator; b. West Palm Beach, Fla., Sept. 28, 1924; d. Harvey Francis Paul and Elsie Marguerite (Theegarten) B. Diploma, Palm Beach Jr. Coll., 1945; BA in Edn., Fla. State Coll. for Women, 1947; MA in Edn., George Peabody Coll. Tchrs., 1964. Cert. tchr. elem. edn. reading, hearing disabilities, motor disabilities, Fla.; cert. tchr. social studies, elem. edn., Kans.; cert. elem. edn. spl. hard of hearing-orthopedic, Ky. Tchr. physically handicapped Bd. Pub. Instr., West Palm Beach, 1947-58; tchr. deaf and hard of hearing Royal Palm Sch., West Palm Beach, 1952-58; tchr. physically handicapped/learning disorders Bd. Pub. Instrn. Exceptional Child Ctr., Ft. Lauderdale, Fla., 1958-69; dir., tchr. Scenicland Sch., Chattanooga, 1969-70; occupational edn. tchr. John Currie Jr. High Sch., Jacksonville, Fla., 1970-71; substitute tchr. Iliff Pre-Sch., Denver, 1972, University Park Coop., Denver, 1973, Austin Presch., 1973; house mother Sigma Alpha Epsilon Fraternity, U. Denver, 1971—; organizer, mgr. Sigma Alpha Epsilon Summer Rental Program, 1976—. Inventor portable sound chart for Lang., reading, speech, 1964. Active Jr. Welfare League, Inc., Palm Beach and Ft. Lauderdale.; secret spl. messenger Morrison Field, West Palm Beach, World War II, summer 1942. Recipient Thomas G. Goodale award for disting. svc. U. Denver, 1991. Mem. Coun. Exceptional Children, PEO, Palm Beach Jr. Coll. Alumni Assn., Kappa Alpha Theta. Democrat. Methodist. Home and Office: Sigma Alpha Epsilon 2050 S Gaylord St Denver CO 80210-4306

BLACK, NOEL ANTHONY, television and film director; b. Chgo., June 30, 1937; s. Samuel Abraham and Susan (Quan) B.; m. Catherine Elizabeth Cownie, June 1, 1988; children: Marco Eugene, Nicole Alexandra, Carmen Elizabeth, Catherine Ellen. BA, UCLA, 1959, MA, 1964. Ind. fil, TV dir., 1966—; asst. prof. grad. program Inst. Film and TV, Tisch Sch. of Arts, NYU, 1992-93. Dir. (TV films) Trilogy: The American Boy, 1967 (Outstanding Young Dir. award Monte Carlo Internat. Festival of TV, Silver Dove award Internat. Cath. Soc. for Radio and TV), I'm a Fool, 1977, Mulligan'e Stew, 1977, The Golden Honeymoon, 1979, The Electric Grandmother, 1981 (George Foster Peabody award 1982), The Other Victim, 1981, prime Suspect, 1981, Happy Endings, 1982, Quarterback Princess, 1983, Deadly Intentions, 1985, Promises to Keep, 1985, A Time to Triumph, 1985, My Two Loves, 1986, Conspiracy of Love, 1987, The Town Bully, 1988, Hollow Boy, 1991, (short films) Skaterdater, 1966 (Grand Prix award Cannes XX Film Festival, Grand Prix Tech. Cannes XX Internat. Film Festival, awards Cork Film Festival, Silver medal Moscow Internat. Film Festival, others), Riverboy, 1967 (Lion of St. Mark awrad Venice Internat. Film Festival, 1st prize Vancouver Internat. Film Festival), (feature films) Pretty Poison, 1968, Mirrors, 1974, A Man, A Woman and A Bank, 1978; screenwriter, exec. prodr. Mischief, 1984. Mem. Writers Guild Am., Dirs. Guild Am., Acad. Motion Picture Arts and Scis., Acad. TV Arts and Scis. Office: Starfish Prodns 126 Wadsworth Ave Santa Monica CA 90405-3510

BLACK, PETE, state legislator, educator; b. Ansbach, Germany, Sept. 16, 1946; came to U.S., 1948; s. Howard and Kadi (Fietz) B.; m. Ronda Williams, July 12, 1970; 1 child, Darin. BS, Idaho State U., 1975; postgrad., 1991—. Cert. elem. tchr. Tchr. Pocatello (Idaho) Sch. Dist., 1975—; mem. Idaho Ho. Reps., Boise, 1983—, asst. minority leader, 1987—; mem. edn. tech. coun.; mem. adv. coun. chpt. II ESEA. Bd. dirs. Arts for Idaho. With USNR, 1964. Mem. NEA, Idaho Edn. Assn., Idaho Libr. Assn. Democrat. Home: 2249 Cassia St Pocatello ID 83201-2059 Office: Idaho Ho Reps Statehouse Mail Boise ID 83720

BLACK, RICHARD, government adminstrator; b. L.A., 1944. BS in Human Rels. and Orgnl. Behavior, U. San Francisco, 1983. Exec. officer Ct. Reporters Bd. Calif., Sacramento. Decorated Bronze star. Mem. KC, Rotary (Natomas club svc. dir. 1995-96). Office: Ct Reporters Bd Calif 2535 Capitol Oaks Dr Ste 230 Sacramento CA 95833-2919

BLACK, RICHARD BRUCE, business executive, consultant; b. Dallas, July 25, 1933; s. James Ernest and Minerva Iantha (Braden) B.; children: Kathryn Braden, Paula Anne (dec.), Erica Lynn. BS in Engring., Tex. A&M U., 1954; MBA, Harvard U., 1958; postgrad., Northwestern U., 1960-62. With Vulcan Materials Co., Birmingham, Ala., 1958-62; v.p. fin. Warner Electric Brake & Clutch Co., Beloit, Wis., 1962-67, dir., 1973-85; pres. automotive group, exec. v.p. corp. Maremont Corp., Chgo., 1967-72, pres. corp., COO, 1972-76, pres., chmn., CEO, 1976-79; pres., CEO, dir. Alusuisse of Am., Inc., N.Y.C., 1979-81; chmn., CEO, dir. AM Internat., Inc., Chgo., 1981-82; owner R. Black & Assocs., 1983—; chmn. ECRM, Boston, 1983—; ptnr. King Black Assocs., Jackson, Wyo., 1987—, KBA Ptnrs. L.P., Jackson, Wyo., 1987—; bd. dirs. Gabelli Group Inc., Oak Tech. Inc., Gen. Scanning Corp., Morgan Group Inc., Benedetto Gartland & Greene; lectr. econs. Beloit (Wis.) Coll., 1964-67. Author: (with Jack Pierson) Linear Polyethylene-Propylene: Problems and Opportunities, 1958. Trustee Beloit Coll., Am. Indian Coll. Fund., N.Y.C., Bard Ctr. for Curatorial Studies, Inst. for Advanced Study, Princeton, N.J., Snake River Conservancy Found. 1st lt. USAF, 1954-56. Mem. Am. Alpine Club, Harvard Club (N.Y.C.).

BLACK, ROBERT CLIFFORD, III, history educator; b. N.Y.C., Feb. 11, 1914; s. Robert Clifford and Beatrice (Cluett) B.; B.A., Williams Coll., 1937; M.A., U. Denver, 1947; Ph.D., Columbia U., 1951; m. Regina Ann Maleham, Sept. 5, 1939; children: Maleham C., R. Clifford, Beatrice (Mrs. Rolland W. Hoverstock), John N., Peter N., James A. Instr. history Rensselaer Poly. Inst., Troy, N.Y., 1945-48; instr. history Trinity Coll., Hartford, Conn., 1950-52, assoc. prof., 1952-66; prof. history Colo. Women's Coll., Denver, 1965-79, emeritus, 1979—; lectr. in field. Dist. committeeman West Hartford Republican Com., 1954-66; bd. dirs. Hist. Denver Inc., 1974-76. Served to capt. AUS, 1942-45. Recipient Merit award Am. Assn. State and Local History, 1970. Mem. Am., Can., Conn., Colo. hist. assns., Assn. Am. Historians, Colo. Hist. Soc. (dir. 1969-88), Friends of Denver Pub. Library, Alpha Delta Phi., Pi Gamma Mu. Episcopalian. Clubs: Denver Country, Denver, Williams. Author: The Railroads of The Confederacy, 1952, The Younger John Winthrop, 1966, Island in the Rockies, 1969, Railroad Pathfinder, 1988. Home: 1510 E 10th Ave Apt 8E Denver CO 80218-3105

BLACK, TRUDY RAE LETTS, education educator; b. Winslow, Ariz., Jan. 29, 1950; d. O. Wade Letts and Helen (Mooney) Letts Copsey; m. David Roderick Black, June 12, 1971; children: Kasey Ellin, Joanna Kate. BS in Edn., No. Ariz. U., 1972, MA in Edn., 1976. Tchr. Ajo (Ariz.) Sch. Dist., 1972-75; educator Show Low (Ariz.) Sch. Dist., 1975-93, Winslow (Ariz.) Sch Dist., 1993—. Active Girl Scouts U.S., 1994, Winslow PTA, 1994, Ariz. Leadership Acad., 1994-95, La Posada Gardening Angels, 1993-94, La Posada Found., 1995. Mem. NEA, P.E.O. (rec. sec.), Ariz. Edn. Assn., Winslow Edn. Assn., Phi Delta Kappa, Delta Kappa Gamma. Republican. Roman Catholic. Home: 137 Papago Blvd Winslow AZ 86047-2021

BLACK, WILLIAM REA, lawyer; b. N.Y.C., Nov. 4, 1952; s. Thomas Howard and Dorothy Chambers (Dailey) B.; m. Kathleen Jane Owen, June 24, 1978; children: William Ryan, Jonathan Wesley. BSBA, U. Denver, 1978, MBA, 1981; JD, Western State U., Fullerton, Calif., 1987. Bar: Calif., U.S. Ct. Appeals (fed. cir.), U.S. Dist. Ct.; lic. real estate broker. Bus. mgr. Deere & Co., Moline, Ill., 1979-85; dir. Mgmt. Resource Svcs. Co., Chgo., 1985-86; sr. v.p. Geneva Corp., Irvine, Calif., 1986-91; pvt. practice Newport Beach, Calif., 1991—; gen. counsel Sunclipse, Inc., 1992—; spl. counsel Amcor, Ltd., 1992—; dir. gen. Amcor de Mex., S.A. de C.V., 1993—; secretario KHL de Mex. S.A. de C.V., 1995—; dir. gen. counsel, LL Knickerbocker Co., Inc., Anle Paper Co., Mann-Craft, Inc., Pyraponic Industries; sec. Pure Energy Corp., Krasner Group, Raymark Container, Inc., Georgetown Collection, Inc. Mng. editor Western State U. Law Rev., Fullerton, 1984-87. Instr. U.S. Judo Assn., Denver, 1975-80. Recipient Am. Jurisprudence award Bancroft-Whitney Co., 1984, 85, 86; Pres.'s scholar full acad. merit scholarship, 1983. Mem. ABA, Am. Soc. Appraisers, Inst. Bus. Appraisers, Assn. Productivity Specialists, Am. Employment Law Coun., Profls. in Human Resources Assn., Am. Mgmt. Assn., Orange County Bar Assn., L.A. County Bar Assn., Mu Kappa Tau. Office: Sunclipse Inc 30055 Comercio Rancho Santa Margarita CA 92688

BLACKBURN, ALEXANDER LAMBERT, author, English literature educator; b. Durham, N.C., Sept. 6, 1929; s. William Maxwell and Elizabeth Cheney (Bayne) B.; m. Jane Allison, 1957 (div. 1974); children: David Alexander, Philip William Rhodes; m. Inés Dölz, Oct. 14, 1975. BA, Yale U., 1951; MA, U. N.C., 1956; PhD, Cambridge (Eng.) U., 1963. Instr. Hampden-Sydney (Va.) Coll., 1960-61, U. Pa., Phila., 1963-65; lectr. U. Md., RAF, Upper Heyford, England, 1967-73; prof. English U. Colo., Colorado Springs, 1973-95; prof. emeritus, 1996—. Author: The Cold War of Kitty Pentecost, 1979, The Myth of the Picaro, 1979, A Sunrise Brighter Still: The Visionary Novels of Frank Waters, 1991, Suddenly a Mortal Splendor, 1995; editor: The Interior Country: Stories of the Modern West, 1987, Higher Elevations: Stories from the West, A Writers' Forum Anthology, 1993; editor-in-chief Writers' Forum, vols. 1-21, 1974-95; author essays, revs. and articles. 1st lt. U.S. Army, 1951-53. Recipient Chancellor's award U. Colo., 1994, Faculty Book award, 1993, Am. Acad. Poets award, 1959. Mem. Authors Guild, Colo. Authors League, Western Lit. Assn., Rocky Mountain MLA, Frank Waters Soc., Coun. Lit. Mags. and Presses. Home: 6030 Twin Rock Ct Colorado Springs CO 80918

BLACKBURN, CHARLES EDWARD, manufacturing executive; b. Detroit, June 19, 1939; s. Wallace Manders and Elva Jean (Beetham) B.; m. Judith Ann Brady, June 30, 1979. BS, Baldwin-Wallace Coll., 1961; MBA, Pepperdine U., 1990. Assoc. rsch. chemist Parke-Davis and Co., Ann Arbor, Mich., 1963-71; mgr. Mallinckrodt Chem. Works, St. Louis, 1971-74; sr. product mgr. Packard Instrument Co., Downers Grove, Ill., 1974-77; product mktg. mgr. Beckman Instruments, Fullerton, Calif., 1977-80; gen. sales mgr. Wahl Instruments, Culver City, Calif., 1980-84; v.p. Signet Sci. Co., El Monte, Calif., 1984-91; chmn., CEO "C" Enterprises, San Marcos, Calif., 1991—. Contbr. articles to profl. jours. Mem. Rotary Internat. (sec. 1983, pres. 1984). Office: "C" Enterprises 540 S Pacific St San Marcos CA 92069-4056

BLACKBURN, JOHN LEWIS, consulting engineer; b. Kansas City, Mo., Oct. 2, 1913; s. John Ealy and Lela (Garnett) B.; m. Margaret Bailey, Sept. 12, 1943; children: Susan T., Joan Blackburn Krist, Margot A. Blackburn Jahns. BSEE with high honors, U. Ill., 1935. With Westinghouse Electric Corp., Newark, 1936-78, cons. engr., 1969-78; pvt. practice cons., Bothell, Wash., 1979-97; adj. prof. Poly. Inst. N.Y., 1949-65, Poly. Inst. N.J., Newark, 1958-71; spl. lectr. IEEE Ednl. Activities, 1952-80; affiliate prof. U. Wash., 1988; instr. North Seattle Community Coll., 1988-93. Author, editor: Applied Protective Relaying, 1978; author: Protective Relaying Principles and Application, 1987, Symmetrical Components for Power Systems Engineering, 1993. Trustee, treas. Millington Bapt. Ch., N.J., 1952-69. Recipient Order of Merit award Westinghouse Electric Corp., 1971, Attwood Assocs. award U.S. Nat. Com. Internat. Conf. for Large High Voltage Electric Systems, 1986. Fellow IEEE (life, chmn. publ. dept. Power Engring. Soc. 1972-76, sec., 1977-79, chmn. power system relaying com. 1969-70, Disting. Service award 1978, Outstanding Service award IEEE ednl. bd. 1979, Centennial medal 1984); mem. China Stamp Soc. Inc. (Meritorious Svc. award, treas. 1961-82, dir. 1968-77, pres. 1980-97), Am. Soc. Polar Philatelists (bd. dirs., treas. 1967—), Sigma Xi, Tau Beta Pi, Eta Kappa Nu, Phi Kappa Phi. Died Feb. 23, 1997. Home: 21816 8th Pl W Bothell WA 98021-8153

BLACKETER, JAMES RICHARD, artist; b. Laguna Beach, Calif., Sept. 24, 1931; s. Cleo Toby and Ida Hattie (Renter) B.; m. Gloria Jean Blacketer, June 20, 1971 (div. Aug. 1975); children: Susan Elizabeth Glover, Mary Jane Kelsey. Owner Blacketer Sign Co., Laguna Beach, 1950-53; designer/art dir. Fed. Sign and Signal Corp., Santa Ana, Calif., 1953-73; owner The Studio Antiques, Laguna Beach, 1973-95. Exhibited in group shows at Showcase 21, L.A., 1959, The Studio Gallery, Laguna Beach, Ferguson Gallery, La Jolla, Long Beach Art Mus., Porth Gallery, Laguna Beach, Pasadena Art Mus., Los Angeles County Fair, Laguna Beach Art Festival, Fresno Art Mus., Ebell Club, L.A., Wells Gallery, Laguna Beach, others; represented in permanent collections at Norton Simon Art Mus., Laguna Beach Art Assn., South Coast Med. Ctr. Bd. dirs. festival of Arts, Laguna Beach, 1965-66. Recipient Nat. Award for Outdoor Advertising, Nat. Elec. Sign Assn., 1970, 71, 72, Nat. Award for Design, Nat. Interscholastic Art Assn., Pitts., 1950, Calif. Award for poster design Am. Legion, State of Calif., 1946; winner various painting awards, 1950—. Mem. Laguna Beach Art Assn. (art dir. 1968-69, bd. dirs. 1969-70). Home: 266 Canyon Acres Dr Laguna Beach CA 92651-1106

BLACKFIELD, CECILIA MALIK, civic volunteer, educator; b. Oakland, Calif., Jan. 18, 1915; d. Benjamin Malik and Mollie Saak; m. William Blackfield, Dec. 25, 1941; children: Leland Gregory, Pamela Esther, Karen Ann. BA, U. Calif., Berkeley, 1936; MEdn., San Francisco State Tchrs. Coll., 1937. cert. elem. tchr. Calif. (lifetime). Tchr. Albany (Calif.) Sch. Dist., 1938-43; rep. NEA, Alameda County, Calif., 1938-43. Pres. Calif. Tchrs. Assn., Alameda County, Calif., 1939; mem. (charter) Territorial Hosp. Aux., Kauikeolani Children's Hosp. (bd. dirs.); bd. dirs. Hastings Law Sch. Found., San Francisco, Calif., McCoy Pavilion Park, Honolulu, Hi., Daughters of the Nile, Honolulu, Temple Emmanuel; mem. Mayor's Citizen Advisory Com. for Diamond Head, Wakiki, Honolulu, Mayor's Adv. Com. for Community & Urban Renewal, Beautification Com., League of Women Voters; chmn. Hawaii Cancer Fund Crusade and many more; mem. master planning com. Vision for Waikiki 2020; mem. Preservation Rev. Com. Hist. Hawaii. Named Woman of the Year for Nat. Brotherhood Week, Honolulu, 1972. Mem. Nat. Assn. Home Builders (pres. Hawaii chpt. women's aux.), Outdoor Circle (pres.), Friends of Foster Gardens, Washington Palace State Capitol, Hadassah (past pres. Oakland chpt.), Women's Com. Brandeis U. (life mem.). Home: 901 Kealaolu Ave Honolulu HI 96816-5416

BLACKHAM, LEONARD MOYLE, state senator; b. Mt. Pleasant, Utah, Aug. 26, 1949; m. Laura Bagley, Feb. 20, 1970; 6 children. AS, Snow Coll., 1969; BS, Utah State U., 1971. Turkey prodr. agrl. co-op bus.; mem. Utah Ho. of Reps., 1992-94; mem. Utah State Senate, 1994—, majority whip, 1995-96; chmn. bd. dirs. Moroni Feed Co.; bd. dirs. Norbest; mem. various coms. including energy, natural resources, agrl. standing. Past county commr. Republican. Office: PO Box 337 Moroni UT 84646

BLACKSTOCK, JOSEPH ROBINSON, newspaper editor; b. L.A., Dec. 8, 1947; s. Joseph Richard McCall and Doris Louise (Robinson) B.; m. Nancy Ruth Frederiksen, Feb. 9, 1974; children: Miriam, Susan, Cynthia, Catherine. BA, Calif. State U., L.A., 1970, MA, 1977. Sports writer Monterey Park Californian, 1967-72; sports and news writer, mng. editor San Gabriel Valley Tribune, West Covina, Calif., 1972-89; exec. editor Pasadena (Calif.) Star-News, 1989-93; layout editor Riverside (Calif.) Press-Enterprise, 1993—. With USAR, 1970-78.

BLACKWELL, CHARLES CURTIS, writer, visual artist; b. San Francisco, Aug. 11, 1950; s. Curtis H. and Gertrude Lizzie (Tinsley) B.; divorced. Student, Sacramento City Coll., 1968-70, American River Coll., Sacramento, 1972-74; BA in Sociology, Calif. State U., Chico, 1975; postgrad., Calif. State Sacramento U., 1975-76. Artist County of Sacramento and Calif. State U., Sacramento, 1977-78; tchr./counselor, art instr. Washington Therapeutic Arts for Handicapped, 1984; organizer in arts, performer Employment Support Ctr., Washington, 1987-90; art isntr./counselor D.C. Child Family Svcs., Washington, 1989; resident playwright Calif. Original Theatre, Sacramento, 1993—; writer instr. workshop William James Assn. Arts in Prison, Santa Cruz, Calif., 1992-94; organizer cultural arts The Cane Leaves Sway, Sacramento, 1994, The Bulu Project, Washington, 1987-88. Author: (plays) I's the Color of Mississippi Mud, 1985, I'm a Boxer, 1989, also poems. Mem. Nat. Conf. Artists, Z.I.C.A. Home: PO Box 417730 Sacramento CA 95841-7730

BLACKWELL, GARLAND WAYNE, retired military officer; b. Roxboro, N.C., July 8, 1956; s. Garland and Mattie (Wright) B.; m. Juanita M. Downell, Dec. 6, 1996. BSBA, U. N.C., 1978; MBA, N.Mex. Highlands U., 1982; postgrad., Willamette U., 1995. CPA, cert. internal auditor. Commd. 2d lt. USAF, 1979, advanced through grades to major, 1990; dep. acctg. and fin. officer 1606 Air Base Wing USAF, Kirtland AFB, N.Mex., 1979-82; staff auditor Air Force Audit Agy., Vandenberg AFB, Calif., 1982-83, Torrejon AB, Spain, 1983-85; audit office chief Air Force Audit Agy., Castle AFB, Calif., 1985-89; audit mgr. Air Force Audit Agy., Norton AFB, Calif., 1989-92; comptroller 432 Fighter Wing USAF, Misawa AB, Japan, 1992-94. Active Caring By Sharing Maranatha Community Ch., L.A., 1989-92; bd. dirs. project alpha March of Dimes, San Bernadino, Calif., 1990-91; bd. dirs. Portland Habilitation Ctr., 1996—. Decorated Commendation medal (3), Meritorious Svc. medal (2), Nat. Defense medal; named one of Outstanding Young Men Am., 1984, 86, 89, Most Eligible Bachelor Ebony Mag., 1989. Mem. Nat. Soc. Tax Profls., Inst. Internal Auditors, Am. Soc. Mil. Comptrollers (chpt. v.p. 1986-88), Nat. Black Masters in Bus. Adminstrn. Assn. (life), Air Force Assn., Tuskegee Airmen, Inc., Alpha Phi Alpha (life, chpt. v.p. 1981-82). Home: 2526 SW Abigail Ct Portland OR 97219

BLAINE, DOROTHEA CONSTANCE RAGETTÉ, lawyer; b. N.Y.C., Sept. 23, 1930; d. Robert Raymond and Dorothea Ottilie Ragetté; BA, Barnard Coll., 1952; MA, Calif. State U., 1968; EdD, UCLA, 1978; JD, Western State U., 1981; postgrad. in taxation Golden Gate U. Bar: Calif. 1982, U.S. Dist. Ct. (ea., so. and cen. dists.) Calif., 1982. Mem. tech. staff Planning Rsch. Corp., L.A., 1964-67; assoc. scientist Holy Cross Hosp., Mission Hills, Calif., 1967-70; career devel. officer and affirmative action officer County of Orange, Santa Ana, Calif., 1970-74, sr. adminstrv. analyst, budget and program coord., 1974-78; spl. projects asst. CAO/Spl. Programs Office, 1978-80, sr. adminstrv. analyst, 1980-83; pvt. practice, 1982—; instr. Am. Coll. Law, Brea, Calif., 1987; judge pro tem Orange County Mcpl. Ct., 1988—. Bd. dirs. Deerfield Community Assn., 1975-78, Orange YMCA, 1975-77. Mem. ABA, ACLU, Trial Lawyers Am., Calif. Trial Lawyers Assn., Orange County Trial Lawyers Assn., Calif. Women Lawyers, Nat. Women's Polit. Caucus, Calif. Bar Assn., Orange County Bar Assn. (Orange County del. to Calif. State Bar Conv. 1985-96, bd. dirs. Orange County lawyers referral svc. 1988-92, mandatory fee arbitration com. 1996), Delta Theta Phi, Phi Delta Kappa. Office: 3 Imperial Promenade Fl 4 Santa Ana CA 92707-5908

BLAIR, FREDERICK DAVID, interior designer; b. Denver, June 15, 1946; s. Frederick Edward and Margaret (Whitely) B. BA, U. Colo., 1969; postgrad. in French, U. Denver, 1981-82. Interior designer The Denver, 1969-76, store mgr., 1976-80; v.p. Hartley House Interiors, Ltd., Denver, 1980-83; pvt. practice interior design Denver, 1983—; com. mem. Ice House Design Ctr., Denver, 1985-86, Design Directory Western Region, Denver, 1986; edn. com. for ASID Nat. Conf., Denver, 1991. Designs shown in various mags. Mem. Rep. Nat. Com.; bd. dirs. One Day, orgn. for children with AIDS, Very Spl. Arts, 1993; bd. dirs. Supporters of Children, 1996—, mem. steering com., 1994, pres.-elect, 1996-97. Mem. Am. Soc. Interior Designers (co-chmn. com. profl. registration 1986, edn. com. nat. conf. 1991, bd. dirs. Colo. chpt. 1990—), Denver Art Mus., Nat. Trust Historic Preservation, Historic Denver, Inc. Christian Scientist.

BLAIR, MARY B., education educator; b. L.A., Aug. 28, 1956. MEd, Univ. San Diego, 1980. Behavior cons. Jay Nolan Cmty. Svc., L.A., 1982—; cons. L.A. Unified Schs., 1985—, mentor, tchr., 1985-89, program specialist, 1994—; part time prof. Calif. State Univ., Northridge, 1993—. Author, editor: Crisis Intervention, 1989, Behavior Intervention for Students with Serious Behavior Problems, 1986, Case Manager Notebook, 1994. Chairperson fundraising St. Euphrasia ch., Granada Hills, Calif., 1996; mem. com. spl. edn. consent decree L.A. Unified Sch. Dist., 1996. Mem. Autism Soc. L.A., Coun. Exceptional Children, Coun. Children Behavior Disorders. Office: LA Unified Schs Spl Edn Svc Unit EV 15530 Hesby St Encino CA 91436-1519

BLAIR, SANDY JEAN, author, publisher; b. Denver, Apr. 14, 1938; d. Harold Eugene Blair and Elizabeth Mae (Alexander) Blair Dodd. Student, Phoenix Coll., 1969. Tchr. Arthur Murray Studio, Denver, 1956-57; supr. Dalcs Dance studio, Denver, 1958-60; with New Eng. Advt. Dow, Denver, 1960-65; owner, mgr. Copper Penny Bar, Phoenix, 1965-71; tchr., salesperson Bobby Ball Agy., Phoenix, 1976-78; salesperson KMOG Radio, Payson, Ariz., 1982-84; owner Inspired Pub. Co., Payson, 1994—. Author/editor: It Is Time to Try Paradise, 1995. Mem. Payson Lightworker Assn., Payson Area Writers Soc. (sec.-treas. 1993-96), Ariz. Psychic Alliance, Payson Love Corp., Payson Tennis Club (pres. 1984-92).

BLAIR, STEVEN DOUGLAS, development director; b. San Diego, Apr. 24, 1960; s. James Franklin and Nita (Thurman) B.; m. Shelly Blair; 1 child, Travis Jordan. AA, Glendale (Calif.) Community Coll., 1984; BA, Calif. Polytech., 1988. Tour guide Universal Studios Tour, Universal City, Calif., 1979-87; cons. Lambda Chi Alpha Fraternity, Indpls., 1988-89, assoc. dir. of chapter svc., 1989. Spl. events coord. March Dimes, 1990-92; dir. devel. Am. Heart Assn., 1992-96, U. Calif. Cardiovascular Ctr., San Diego, 1996—. Mem. Order of Omega (pres. 1987-88). Republican. Mem. Christian Ch. Home: 14847 Fox Hunt Ln San Diego CA 92128-3731

BLAIR, VIRGINIA FREY, public health service officer; b. Platte, S.D., Aug. 17, 1941; d. Immanuel Gustave and Dorothea Edith (Schlegel) Frey; m. Douglas Daykin Blair, May 27, 1965; children: Marjorie, Mark, Alexandra. Diploma in nursing, Good Samaritan Hosp. Sch. Nursing, Phoenix, 1962; BS, St. Francis Coll., Joliet, Ill., 1990. RN, Ariz. From staff nurse to asst. head nurse Good Samaritan Hosp., Phoenix, 1962-65; pediat. nurse Phoenix, 1965-68; staff nurse Maryvale Samaritan Hosp., Phoenix, 1983-88; health facilities inspection specialist Ariz. Dept. Health Svcs., Phoenix, 1988-90, health facilities inspection team leader, 1990-91, health program mgr., 1991-93, office chief, 1993, asst. dir., 1994-95, health program mgr., 1995-96, bur. chief, 1996—. Recipient Genie Eide award Ariz. Assn. for Homecare, 1993, Gov.'s award for excellence, State of Ariz., 1995. Republican. Lutheran. Office: Ariz Dept Health Svcs 1647 E Morten Ste 220 Phoenix AZ 85020

BLAIRE, STEPHEN E., bishop; b. L.A., Dec. 22, 1941. Grad., St. John's Sem., Camarillo, Calif. Ordained priest Roman Cath. Ch., 1967, titular bishop of Lamzella. Aux. bishop L.A., 1990—. Office: Our Lady of Angels Pastoral Ctr 2636 S Mansfield Ave Los Angeles CA 90016-3512

BLAIS, ROBERT HOWARD, lawyer; b. Muskegon, Mich., May 14, 1955. BA with high honors, Mich. State U., 1977; JD cum laude, U. Notre Dame, 1980. Ptnr. Bogle & Gates, Seattle, 1988-93; shareholder Gores & Blais, Seattle, 1993—; adj. prof. estate and tax planning Seattle U., 1982-83; chairperson Wash. State U. Planned Giving Adv. Bd., 1989-96. Mem. ABA, Wash. State Bar Assn. (real property, probate and trust coun. 1987-88), , Seattle-King County Bar Assn., Estate Planning Coun. Seattle (pres. 1996-97), Am. Coll. Trust and Estate Counsel. Office: Gores & Blais 1420 5th Ave Ste 2600 Seattle WA 98101-2333

BLAKE, BAMBI REVA, international fine artist; b. Douglaston, N.Y., Sept. 26, 1955; d. Martin and Eva Mae Blake; 1 child, Star Ray. BFA, Sch. Visual Arts, 1977. Founder Star Light Studios, Internat., N.Y., S.C., 1985-89; art dir. Bernstein Film Prodn., Hollywood, Calif., 1990-92; founder Spirit Dancer Fine Art, N.Mex., 1990-94; founder Spirit Dancer Fine Art, Boulder, Colo., 1993-97, internat. fine artist, 1970—. Author: Prince Star Ray Flys to Earth on his Magic Carpet of Birds, 1984, (screenplay) The Forbidden Galaxy, 1984; producer, dir. (movie) A Touch of Class, 1989, (video) Bambi Blake in Action, 1989; prin. works included in numerous collections including The Rhodes Collection Met. Mus. Art, N.Y.C., (TV) Art Auction, 1997. Active Childrite Art Auction, Taos, N.Mex., 1991, 92, 94, Santa Fe Opera Art Auction, 1992, Taos Valley Sch. Art Auction, 1994. Recipient Phillip Frankel Meml. award Art Chmns. Assn., 1973, Art award Master Eagle Family, 1973, Achievement award Colo. Divsn. Wildlife, 1994; scholar Sch. Art League, 1973. Mem. Mem. Santa Fe Art Alliance, Santa Fe Coun. for Arts, Longmont Artist Guild (1st place blue ribbon for sculpture 1994), Catron County Fair, Catron County Art Guild, Delaware Valley Arts & Alliance. Office: Spirit Dancer Fine Art PO Box 20036 Boulder CO 80308-3036

BLAKE, D. STEVEN, lawyer; b. Saginaw, Mich., June 2, 1940. BA, Mich. State U., 1963; JD, U. Calif., Davis, 1971. Bar: Calif. 1972. With Downey, Brand, Seymour & Rohwer, Sacramento; adj. prof. law U. Pacific, 1983. Co-author: California Real Estate Finance and Construction Law, 1995. Mem. ABA (bus. law sect.), Am. Arbitration Assn. (arbitrator), State Bar Calif. (fin. instns. com., bus. law sect., panelist, presenter numerous seminars Calif. State Bar Continuing Edn. Bar 1981-91, co-chair corps. com. bus. law sect. 1997), Yolo County Bar Assn. Office: Downey Brand Seymour & Rohwer 555 Capitol Mall Ste 1050 Sacramento CA 95814-4601

BLAKELEY, JAMES EDWARD, III, interior designer; b. L.A., June 15, 1945; s. James Edward and Mary Ann (Carlise) B. BS, Woodbury U., 1964. Prin. Blakeley Bazeley Ltd., Beverly Hills, Calif., 1982—. Contbr. chpts. to books, articles to profl. jours. and mags. Adv. bd. Venice (Calif.) Family Clinic, Valley Coll., Van Nuys, Calif. Dorothy Peterson Edn. grantee, 1994. Mem. Am. Soc. Interior Designers (L.A. chpt. pres. 1993-94, nat. bd. dirs. 1995—), Designers Lighting Forum (bd. dirs. 1990-92). Office: Blakeley Bazeley Ltd PO Box 5173 Beverly Hills CA 90209-5173

BLAKELY, DAVID ALBERT, county supervisor; b. Cali, Colombia, Oct. 8, 1950; s. Everett E. Blakely and Margaret Ann Spence; m. Naomi Gross, Mar. 29, 1980; children: Daniel Ryan, Colin Palmer. BS in Social Scis., Calif. Poly. Inst., 1973, secondary teaching credential, 1974. Tchr. Atascadero (Calif.) Unified Schs., 1975-89; county supr. County of San Luis Obispo, Calif., 1989—; adj. prof. Calif. Poly. Inst., San Luis Obispo, 1978-86. Area coord. Spl. Olympics, San Luis Obispo, 1980-81; chmn. Santa Margarita (Calif.) Adv. Coun., 1975-89, Friday Night Live, San Luis Obispo, 1990—; dir. Econ. Opportunity Commn., San Luis Obispo, 1989-94, San Luis Obispo Coun. Govts., 1989—. Mem. Calif. State Assn. Counties, Local Govt. Commn., Santa Margarita Moose. Home: PO Box 909 Santa Margarita CA 93453-0909 Office: San Luis Obispo Bd Suprs Rm 370 Government Center San Luis Obispo CA 93453

BLAKELY, EDWARD JAMES, economics educator; b. San Bernardino, Calif., Apr. 21, 1938; s. Edward Blakely and Josephine Elizabeth (Carter) Proctor; m. Maaike C. Vander Sleesen, July 1, 1971; children: Pieta C., Brette D. BA, U. Calif., Riverside, 1960; MA, U. Calif., Berkeley, 1964; MBA, Pasadena Nazerene Coll., 1967; EdD in Edn. and Mgmt., UCLA, 1971. Mgr. Pacific Telephone Co., Pasadena, Calif., 1960-65; exec. dir. Western Community Action Tng., Los Angeles, 1965-69; spl. asst. U.S. Dept. State, Washington, 1969-71; asst. chancellor, assoc. prof. U. Pitts., 1971-74; assoc. dean and prof. applied econs. and behavioral scis. U. Calif., Davis, 1974-77; asst. v.p. U. Calif., Berkeley, 1977-85, prof., chmn. dept. city and regional planning, 1985—; expert advisor Orgn. Econ. Cooperation and Devel., asst. to Mayor Elihu Harris, City of Oakland. Author: Rural Communities in Advanced Industrial Society, Community Development Research, Taking Local Development Initiative, Planning Local Economic Development SAGE, 1988, Separate Societies: Poverty and Inequality in U.S. Cities (Paul Davidoff award 1993), 1992. Chmn. fin. com. Pvt. Industry Council of Oakland (Calif.), 1978-85; vice chmn. Ecole Bilingue Sch., Berkeley, 1982-85, chmn., 1988—; chmn. bd. Royce Sch., Oakland, Calif., 1988—; sec., treas. Econ. Devel. Corp., Oakland, 1983; expert advisor Orgn. Econ. Corp. and Devel., Paris, 1986. Served to 1st lt. USAF, 1961-63. Recipient San Francisco Found. award, 1991, Paul Davidoff award, 1993; Guggenheim fellow, 1995-96, fellow Urban Studies Australian Inst. Urban St., 1985, German Acad. Exch., 1984; Fulbright St. scholar Internat. Exch. of Scholars, 1986, John Simon Guggenheim fellow, 1995-96; named to Athlete Hall of Fame, U. Calif. Riverside Alumni Press, 1992, 125th Anniversay Prof. U. Calif. at Riverside Berkeley Campus, 1992; apptd. by Pres. Bill Clinton to the Pres. Trust. Mem. Cmty. Devel. Soc. (bd. dirs. 1980-84, svc. award 1983, disting. svc. award 1990), Calif. Local Econ. Devel. (standing com. 1980-81), Am. Planning Assn. (accreditation com.), Am. Assn. Collegiate Schs. of Planning, Nat. Assn. State and Land Grant Colls. (exec. com. 1987), Phi Delta Kappa, Lambda Alpha. Club: Rueful Order. Home: 855 Old Mill Rd San Marino CA 91108-1741 Office: Univ So Calif Sch Urban Reg Planning & Devel Los Angeles CA 90089-0042

BLAKEMORE, PAUL HENRY, JR., retired publishing executive; b. Des Moines, Mar. 7, 1925; s. Paul Henry and Mabel (Evstace) B.; m. Barbara Jane Spargur, Oct. 24, 1952; children: Paul H. III, John E. BSBA, Northwestern U., 1950. Regional dir. First Fin. Group, Brookline, Mass., 1955-62; sr. v.p. TV/Radio Age, N.Y.C., 1963-87, cons., 1987—. Capt. USMC, 1943-47. Mem. Lions. Republican. Home: PO Box 4024 Malibu CA 90264-4024

BLAKENEY, ALLAN EMRYS, Canadian government official, lawyer; b. Bridgewater, N.S., Can., Sept. 7, 1925; s. John Cline and Bertha (Davies) B.; m. Mary Elizabeth Schwartz, 1950 (dec. 1957); m. Anne Louise Gorham, May 1959; children: Barbara, Hugh, David, Margaret. BA, Dalhousie U., 1945, LLB, 1947, LLD (hon.); BA (Rhodes scholar), Oxford U., 1949, MA, 1955; DCL (hon.), Mount Allison U.; LLD (hon.), York U., Toronto, U. Western Ont., London, 1991, U. Regina, 1993, U. Sask., 1995. Bar: N.S. 1950, Sask. 1951. Queen's counsel, 1961; sec. to govt. fin. office Govt. Sask., 1950-55; chmn. Sask. Securities Commn., 1955-58; ptnr. Davidson, Davidson & Blakeney, Regina, Sask., 1958-60, Griffin, Blakeney, Beke, Koskie & Lueck, Regina, 1964-70; premier of Sask., 1971-82; Mem. Sask. Legislature, 1960-88; Officer of the Order of Can., 1992; leader of the opposition Sask. Legislature, 1970-71, 82-87; prof. Osgoode Hall Law Sch., York U., 1988-90, U. Sask., 1990—; minister of edn., Sask., 1960-61, provincial treas., 1961-62, minister pub. health, 1962-64; mem. Royal Commn. on Aborginal Peoples, 1991-93. Home: 1752 Prince of Wales Ave, Saskatoon, SK Canada S7K 3E5 Office: U Saskatchewan Coll Law, 15 Campus Dr, Saskatoon, SK Canada S7N 5A6

BLAKEY, SCOTT CHALONER, journalist, writer; b. Nashua, N.H., Nov. 19, 1936; s. Elmer F. and Mildred Livingstone (Chaloner) B.; m. Lone Erting, July 18, 1970 (div.); 1 child, Nicholas Scott; m. Caroline M. Scarborough, June 28, 1985 (div.); children: Alexandra Scarborough, Susannah Chaloner. BA, U. N.H., 1960. Reporter, photographer Nashua (N.H.) Telegraph, 1960-62, polit. reporter, 1963-64; legis. asst. Congressman James C. Cleveland, Washington, 1963; mng. editor Concord (N.H.) Monitor, 1964-68; urban affairs corr. San Francisco Chronicle, 1968-70, reporter, asst. city editor, 1979-84, TV corr., 1985-87; corr., asst. news dir. KQED-TV, San Francisco, 1970-74; free-lance writer San Francisco, 1974-79; news editor KRON-TV (NBC), San Francisco, 1987-89; nationally syndicated columnist KidVid L.A. Times Syndicate, 1990—; sr. news rep. div. corp. communications Pacific Gas & Electric Co., San Francisco, 1991—. Writer, field producer TV documentary 2251 Days, 1973 (2 Emmy awards 1974); author (books) San Francisco, 1976, Prisoner at War, 1978, Kid Vid, 1995; contbr. articles to profl. jours. Recipient Best Polit. Writing award New Eng. AP News Editors Assn., 1965, Dupont Columbia award, 1974. Mem. Authors Guild, Am. Air Mail Soc., Audubon Soc. Democrat. Home: 1801 Turk St Apt 17 San Francisco CA 94115-4429 Office: Pacific Gas & Electric 77 Beale St Ste 2935A San Francisco CA 94105-1829

BLALOCK, ANN BONAR, policy analyst, evaluation researcher; b. Parkersburg, W.Va., Apr. 16, 1928; d. Harry and Fay (Conley) Bonar; m. Hubert Blalock, Jr., 1951; children: Susan Blalock Lyon, Kathleen Blalock McCarrell, James W.; m. Gerhard E. Lenski, 1996. AB, Oberlin Coll., 1950; MA, U. N.C., 1954; MSW, U. Wash., 1978. Pvt. cons. Admiralty Inlet Consulting, Hansville, Wash. Sr. author: Introduction to Social Research, 2d edit., 1970; co-editor: Methodology in Social Research, 1968; editor Evaluation Forum, 1986-97, Evaluating Social Programs, 1990. Recipient research award Partnership for Employment and Tng. Careers. Mem. NASW (past pres. Wash. State chpt.), Am. Eval. Assn. (past com. chair), Assn. Pub. Policy Analysis and Mgmt. Home: PO Box 409 Hansville WA 98340-0409

BLANCHARD, WILLIAM HENRY, psychologist; b. St. Paul, Mar. 25, 1922; s. Charles Edgar and Ethel Rachael (Gurney) B.; m. Martha Ida Lang, Aug. 11, 1947; children: Gregory Marcus, Mary Lisa. Diploma in Sci. Mason City Jr. Coll., 1942; BS in Chemistry, Iowa State U., 1944; PhD in Psychology, U. So. Calif., 1954. Lic. clin. psychologist, Calif. Shift chemist B.F. Goodrich Chem. Co., Port Neches, Tex., 1946-47; court psychologist L.A. County Gen. Hosp., 1954-55; psychologist, dir. rsch. So. Reception Ctr. and Clinic, Calif. Youth Authority, Norwalk, 1955-58; social scientist Rand Corp., 1958-60, System Devel. Corp., 1960-70; mem. faculty Calif. State U.-Northridge, L.A., 1970; assoc. prof. UCLA, 1971; faculty group leader urban semester U. So. Calif., L.A., 1971-75; sr. rsch. assoc. Office of Chancellor, Calif. State U., L.A., 1975-76; sr. fellow Planning Analysis and Rsch. Inst., Santa Monica, Calif., 1976-96; pvt. practice psychologist, Calif., 1976-96; clin. assoc. dept. psychology U. So. Calif., 1956-58. Author: Rousseau and the Spirit of Revolt, 1967; Aggression American Style, 1978; Revolutionary Morality, 1984; Neocolonialism American Style, 1996; contbr. articles to profl. jours. Mem. com. on mental health West Area Welfare Planning Council, L.A., 1960-61; bd. dirs. L.A. County Psychol. Assn., 1969; commr.

Bd. Med. Examiners, Psychology Exam. Com., State of Calif., 1969; v.p. Parents and Friends of Mentally Ill Children, 1968-69, pres., 1966-68, trustee, 1968-69. Mem. APA, AAAS, Internat. Soc. Polit. Psychology. Home: 4307 Rosario Rd Woodland Hills CA 91364-5546

BLANCHE, JOE ADVINCULA, aerospace engineer, consultant, educator; b. Rizal, Santa, Ilocos Sur, Philippines, Sept. 11, 1954; came to U.S. 1976; s. Emilio Peralta and Concepcion (Advincula) B.; m. Albine Selerio Lansangan, Oct. 9, 1982; children: Emmanuel Joseph, Earl Jordan. Cert. in mil. sci., U. Philippines, 1973; BS in Math., Adamson U., Manila, 1976; postgrad., Calif. State U., Long Beach, 1982-85; AAS in Avionics Systems Tech., Community Coll. Air Force, Maxwell AFB, Ala., 1990; cert. in mgmt., Cen. Tex. Coll., 1990; PhD in Mgmt., Pacific Western U., 1993; MA in Orgnl. Mgmt., U. Phoenix, 1995. Lic. real estate broker, Calif.; registered tax preparer, Calif.; notary pub., Calif. Assoc. engr./scientist McDonnell Douglas Corp., Long Beach, Calif., 1981-84; engr./scientist McDonnell Douglas Corp., 1984-86, engr./scientist specialist, 1987-88, sr. engr./scientist, 1988-94; lead aerospace engr. Sikorsky Aircraft-UTC, Stratford, Conn., 1986-87; founder, pres. J. & A. Blanche Ventures', Inc., Corona Hills, Calif., 1990-96; cons. aerospace engring. McDonnell Douglas/Shin Maywa, 1996—; avionics maint. inspector USAFR, 1983-86, 87-97, ret., 1997. Eucharistic min. St. Edward's Ch., Corona. With USAF, 1976-80. Bur. Forestry grantee and scholar U. Philippines, 1971-73, USVA scholar Calif. State U., 1982-85. Mem. AIAA (sr.), Nat. Notary Assn., NRA, So. Calif. Profl. Engrs. Assn., Corona-Norco Bd. Realtors, Internat. Soc. Allied Weight Engrs. (sr.), Adamson U. Alumni Assn. So. Calif. (v.p., chmn. bd. 1997-98), Santanians USA Inc. (bd. dirs. 1984-87, pres. 1994-96, pres., chmn. bd. 1997-98), Marinduque Assn. So. Calif., Fil-Am. Assn. Corona (auditor 1993-94, bd. dirs. 1995-96, parliamentarian 1997-98). Republican. Office: J & A Blanche Ventures Inc 420 N Mckinley St Ste 111-333 Corona CA 91719-6504

BLAND, DOROTHY ANN, construction executive, real estate agent; b. Black Township, Pa., Jan. 12, 1945; d. Homer Charles and Edith Birdie Colflesh; m. Jonathan Lee Sharp, Sept. 28, 1963 (dec. Dec. 31, 1979); children: Deborah, Todd, Wade; m. Brian C. Bland, Nov. 2, 1985; stepchildren: Paulette, Kelli. Lic. Real Estate Agent, Utah. Beauty coll. recruiter, sec. Continental Coll. of Beauty, Salt Lake City, 1968-72; exec. sec. Vaughn Hansen Assoc., Salt Lake City, 1973-82; v.p., co-owner Bland Bros., Inc., West Jordan, Utah, 1985—; co-owner Blands Sand & Gravel, Utah, 1990—; real estate agent Preferred Properties, Salt Lake City, 1982-90, Mansell, Salt Lake City, 1990—. Office: Bland Brothers Inc 8630 Redwood Rd West Jordan UT 84088-9226

BLAND, JANEESE MYRA, editor; b. Evanston, Ill., Feb. 20, 1960; d. James Milton and Jeanette Malisa (Bryant) B. BA, U. Ark., 1980. Cert. tchr., Ark., Ill. Tutor counselor U. Ark., Pine Bluff, 1979; tchr. Pine Bluff High Sch., 1980, Chgo. Bd. Edn., 1981-84; editor, author, columnist, creator Beautiful Images Hollywood (Calif.) Gazette Newspaper, 1985—; VIP organizer People's Choice Awards, Beverly Hills, 1984—; exec. prodr. stas. Chgo. Access Corp., Century Cable Comms., L.A., BH-TV, Beverly Hills; hostess The Janeese Bland Show. Proof editor: Nursing Rsch. Jour., 1989. Polit. vol. Rep. Party, Santa Monica, 1988—; vol. organizer Windfeather, Inc., Beverly Hills, 1983—, United Negro Coll. Fund, L.A., 1984—, Sickle Cell Disease Rsch. Found., L.A., 1985—; pres., founder June Maria Bland Scholarship Found. Recipient Image award Fred Hampton Scholarship Found., 1983, Wiley W. Manuel award State Bar Calif., Cert. Merit, Bet Tzedek Legal Svcs. Mem. SBA (pres.). Republican. Baptist. Office: Sta Century Cable TV JMB Show PO Box 1387 Beverly Hills CA 90213

BLANEY, LOREN FRANCIS, JR., software engineer; b. Los Alamos, N.Mex., Oct. 22, 1948; s. Loren Francis and Elizabeth Caldwell (Jones) B.; m. Monique Gene Didero, Nov. 12, 1988. BS in Physics, So. Colo. State Coll., 1970; BS in Elec. Engring., Colo. State. U., 1973. Registered profl. engr., Colo. Assoc engr. Viking mission to Mars Martin Marietta, Denver, 1974-75, engr., 1976-78; software engr. jet propulsion lab. Viking lander simulation team NASA, Pasadena, Calif., 1975-76; software cons. Nederland, Colo., 1979—. Software developer and creator. Mem. Assn. Computing Machinery. Home and Office: Magnolia Star Rt Nederland CO 80466

BLANEY, SUZANNE AVERY, artist; b. Washington, Nov. 12, 1931; d. Edward Frederick Avery and Marba Jean (Woolhiser) Randlemon; m. William Deshields Winder, June 12, 1950 (div. Feb. 1966); 1 child, Dale Beverly; m. Floyd Earl Blaney, June 1966. Student, U. Miami, 1949-50, Fredden Goldberg Art Acad., San Francisco, 1970-73, Calif. Sch. Arts and Crafts, 1981-82. Exec. sec. Bechtel Corp., San Francisco, 1953-58, J.C. Penney Regional Office, San Francisco, 1960-64, Parsons-Brinckerhoff-Tudor-Bechtel, San Francisco, 1964-66; realtor Coldwell Banker, Walnut Creek, Calif., 1980-81; profl. artist, 1981—; lectr. on pastels, 1991—. Solo shows include Artist Alley, San Francisco, 1971, San Francisco Coop. Gallery, 1973, New Masters Gallery, Walnut Creek, Calif., 1974, Beecher Room Gallery, Calif., 1991, 94, Tuttle Masion Gallery, Alburn, Calif., 1991, Old Ch. Gallery, Meadow Vista, Calif., 1991, Graphic Designs Gallery, Old Town Auburn, Calif., 1993, Placer County Civic Arts League, Auburn, 1994, Chapa De Indian Facility, Auburn, 1995, Gregory's Historic Bistro, Auburn, 1996, Lou LaBonte's, Auburn, 1996; group shows include Las Juntas Artists, Pleasant Hill, Calif., 1987 (1st place award), 1988 (2d place award), 88 (hon. mention), 1991 (1st place award), Scaramento Fine Arts Ctr., 1989, 90, 91 (merit award), 92, 93, 94, 95, League of Carmichael Artists Exhb., 1993, 96, AAUW Ann. Exhbn., 1993, 95, 96 (1st place), Pastel Soc. of the West Coast Exhibition, 1988, 89, 90, 91 (merit award), 92, 93, 94, 96 (1st place), Placer Arts League Exhibition, 1991 (hon. mention), 93 (1st place), 94 (1st place), 1995 (hon. mention); represented in permanent collections throughout U.S. and Europe. Recipient awards for oil and pastel paintings. Fellow Royal Soc. Arts (London); mem. Pastel Soc. West Coast (signature mem., pres. 1989-91, bd. dirs. 1988—, mem. adv. bd. 1991—, editor quar. newsletter 1991—), Nat. Mus. Women in Arts, Placer Arts League, Placer County Arts Coun., ArtCetera. Home and Studio: 1250 Grizzly Flat Ct Auburn CA 95603-5835

BLANK, CARLA MARIA, performance director, author; b. Pitts., Aug. 14, 1941; d. Marcus Blank and Ethel (Snider) Strasser; m. Ishmael Reed, June 6, 1970; 1 child, Tennessee Maria. Student, Carnegie-Mellon U., 1959-61; BA, Sarah Lawrence Coll., 1963; MA, Mills Coll., 1972. cert. instr., Calif. Tchr. dance and drama Convent of the Sacred Heart, San Francisco, 1974-76; co-dir. Roberts & Blank Dance Theater, Inc., Berkeley, 1977-92; tchr. dance and drama Arrowsmith Acad., 1990—; artist in residence Home for Jewish Parents Calif. Arts Coun., Oakland, 1979-80; guest lectr., workshop leader various colls. and arts coun., 1981—; artist in residence Calif. Arts Council and East Bay Schs., Oakland and Berkeley, 1984-91; co-dir. Roberts & Blank Dance Theater, Inc., Berkeley, 1981—; vis. prof. Dartmouth Coll., Hanover, N.H., 1981, U. Wash., Seattle, 1989; adj. prof. U. Calif., Berkeley, 1994, 97. Choreographer: Kore at Eleusis, 1979-81, Kitchen Cabinet, 1980-83, Skydiving, 1985, East Bay Dance Series, Manifest Destiny, Oakland, 1986, Bay Area Dance Series, 1990-91, Songs from texts by Ishmael Reed, 1985-90, St. Mark's Danspace Project, 1989; author: (with Jody Roberts) Live On Stage!, 1997. Founding mem. Bay Area Youth Theater Consortium, San Francisco, 1984; mem. Dance Bay Area. Recipient Performance award Exptl. Intermedia Found., N.Y.C., 1981, Sakai Kinu award, 1993, Children's Troupe award Zellerbach Family Fund, San Francisco, 1985-92; grantee Foremost McKesson Found., 1982-83, Wells Fargo Bank, 1984, Fleishhaker Found., 1990-91, San Francisco Found., 1991, 92, Morris Stulshaft Found., 1986. Office: 870 53rd St Oakland CA 94608-3257

BLANKENBURG, HEINZ HORST, vocalist, director; b. N.Y.C., Jan. 15, 1931; 3 children from a previous marriage; m. Gayle Cameron-McComb, Dec. 14, 1986. D in Performing Arts (hon.), Calif. State U., 1977, U. Calif., 1986. Operatic debut San Francisco Opera, 1955, leading baritone, 1955-66; leading baritone Glyndenbourne Festival Opera, 1957-70, as Papageno and Figaro, Rimbaud, Arlecchino, Hamburg (Germany) State Opera, 1959-79, as Beckmesser, Schaunard, Fra Melitone in La Forza del Destino, Paolo in Simon Boccanegra; sang in Brit. premiere Die Frau ohne Schatten, Hamburg State Opera, 1966; guest baritone opera cos. in Munich, Berlin, Vienna, Paris, Frankfurt, Met., Amsterdam, Rome, Brussels, Lausanne, Basle, Strasbourg, Naples, N.Z., St. Louis, Portland, numerous others; recordings include CD's, TV, radio for BBC, RAI, ZDF. Recipient Kammersänger Hamburg State Opera, 1966, Maori Welcome, N.Z., 1971. Office: Calif State U Opera Theatre 5151 State U Dr Los Angeles CA 90032

BLANKENSHIP, JULIE RENEE, artist, educator; b. La Jolla, Calif., Dec. 2, 1957; d. Upton Duane and Janice (Palmer) B. BFA, San Francisco Art Inst., 1985, MFA, 1987; Cert., Arts Leadership Iniative, San Francisco, 1995. vis. artist San Francisco Art Inst., 1994-96; vis. lectr. San Francisco State U.-Inter-Arts Ctr., 1995-97; lectr. in field. Artist outdoor installation: The Tower, Secession Gallery, 1992; photographs at San Francisco Camerawork Gallery, 1995, San Francisco Art Inst., 1996. Bd. trustees San Francisco Art Inst., 1986-87, chmn. artists com. 1993—; bd. trustees, exec. com. Secession Gallery, San Francisco, 1992-94.

BLANKFORT, LOWELL ARNOLD, newspaper publisher; b. N.Y.C., Apr. 29, 1926; s. Herbert and Gertrude (Butler) B.; m. April Pemberton; 1 child, Jonathan. BA in History and Polit. Sci., Rutgers U., 1946. Reporter, copy editor L.I. (N.Y.) Star-Jour., 1947-49; columnist London Daily Mail, Paris, 1949-50; copy editor The Stars & Stripes, Darmstadt, Germany, 1950-51, Wall St. Jour., N.Y.C., 1951; bus., labor editor Cowles Mags., N.Y.C., 1951-53; pub. Pacifica (Calif.) Tribune, 1954-59; free-lance writer, Europe, Asia, 1959-61; co-pub., editor Chula Vista (Calif.) Star-News, 1961-78; co-owner Paradise (Calif.) Post, 1977—, Monte Vista (Colo.) Jour., Ctr. (Colo.) Post-Dispatch, Del Norte (Colo.) Prospector, 1978-93, Plainview (Minn.) News, St. Charles (Minn.) Press, Lewiston (Minn.) Jour., 1980—, Summit (Colo.) Sentinel, New Richmond (Wis.) News, 1981-87, Yuba City Valley Herald, Calif., 1982-85, TV Views, Monterey, Calif., 1982-87, Summit County Jour., Colo., 1982-87, Alpine (Calif.) Sun, 1987-93. Columnist, contbr. articles on fgn. affairs to newspapers. Mem. Calif. Dem. Cen. Com., 1963. Named Outstanding Layman of Yr. Sweetwater Edn. Assn., 1966, Citizen of Yr. City of Chula Vista, 1976, Headliner of Yr. San Diego Press Club, 1980. Mem. ACLU (pres. San Diego chpt. 1970-71), Calif. Newspaper Pubs. Assn., World Affairs Council San Diego (pres. 1996—), Ctr. Internat. Policy (bd. dirs. 1991—), Internat. Ctr. Devel. Policy (nat. bd. 1985-90), UN Assn. (pres. San Diego chpt. 1991-93, nat. coun. 1992—), World Federalist Assn. (nat. bd., pres. San Diego chpt. 1984-86), Soc. Profl. Journalists, East Meets West Found. (nat. v.p. 1992—), Inst. of the Ams. (assoc. 1989—, mem. internat. coun. 1994—). Home: Old Orchard Ln Bonita CA 91902 Office: 315 4th Ave Ste S Chula Vista CA 91910-3816

BLANNING, WILLIAM ANDREW, media specialist. BA in Am. History, Yale U., 1976. Asst. editor Bedford (Mass.) Minuteman, 1979-80; reporter Beverly (Mass.) Times, 1980-83; freelance reporter, writer, 1983-84; reporter St. Petersburg (Fla.) Times, 1984-87, United Press Internat., L.A., 1987-89; bur. mgr. PR Newswire/L.A. Bur., 1989-92; mgr. media rels. Rockwell Internat. Corp., 1992-95; dir. media rels. Rockwell Internat. Corp., Seal Beach, Calif., 1995—. Home: 9782 Hampton Ct Fountain Valley CA 92708-5862 Office: PO Box 4250 2201 Seal Beach Blvd Seal Beach CA 90740-8250

BLANTON, JOHN ARTHUR, architect; b. Houston, Jan. 1, 1928; s. Arthur Alva and Caroline (Jeter) B.; m. Marietta Louise Newton, Apr. 10, 1954 (dec. 1976); children: Jill Blanton Milne, Lynette Blanton Rowe, Elena Diane. BA, Rice U., 1948, BS in Architecture, 1949. With Richard J. Neutra, L.A., 1950-64; pvt. practice architecture, Manhattan Beach, Calif., 1964—; lectr. UCLA Extension, 1967-76, 85, Harbor Coll., Los Angeles, 1970-72. Archtl. columnist Easy Reader newspaper, 1994-96. Mem. Capital Improvements Com., Manhattan Beach, 1966, city commr. Bd. Bldg. Code Appeals; chmn. Zoning Adjustment Bd., 1990; active Planning Commn., 1993, chmn., 1996. Served with Signal Corps, U.S. Army, 1951-53. Recipient Best House of Year award C. of C., 1969, 70, 71, 83, Preservation of Natural Site award, 1974, design award, 1975, 84. Mem. AIA (contbr. book revs. to jour. 1972-76, recipient Red Cedar Shingle/AIA nat. merit award 1979). Designed nine bldgs. included in L.A.: An Architectural Guide; works featured in L'architettura mag., 1988; design philosophy included in American Architects (Les Krantz), 1989. Office: John Blanton AIA Architect 1456 12th St # 4 Manhattan Beach CA 90266-6113

BLASE, NANCY GROSS, librarian; b. New Rochelle, N.Y.; d. Albert Philip and Elsie Wise (May) Gross; m. Barrie Wayne Blase, June 19, 1966 (div.); 1 child, Eric Wayne. BA in Biology, Marietta (Ohio) Coll., 1964; MLS, U. Ill., 1965. Info. scientist brain info. svc. Biomed. Libr., UCLA, 1965-66; libr. Health Sci. Libr., U. Wash., Seattle, 1966-68, Medlars search analyst, 1970-72, coord. Medline, 1972-79, head Natural Scis. Libr., 1979—; mem. libr. adv. com. Elizabeth C. Miller Libr., Ctr. for Urban Horticulture, Seattle, 1986-90. Contbr. articles to profl. jours. NSF fellow interdept. tng. program for sci. info. specialists U. Ill., 1964-65. Mem. Am. Soc. for Info. Sci. (pres. personal computer spl. interest group 1993-94, chair constn. and bylaws com. 1994-97, rsch. grantee Pacific N.W. chpt. 1984-85), Geosci. Info. Soc., Internat. Tng. in Comm. (pres. Pacific N.W. region 1994-95), Phi Beta Kappa pres. chpt. 1993-96). Home: 10751 Durland Ave NE Seattle WA 98125-6945 Office: U Wash Natural Scis Libr Box 352900 Seattle WA 98195-2900

BLASOR-BERNHARDT, DONNA JO, screenwriter, poet, author, photographer; b. Pittsburg, Kans., May 8, 1944; d. Donald Archie and Bessie Beryl (Tatham) Blasor; m. Richard Wayne Bernhardt, Oct. 29, 1964 (dec. Feb. 1987); children: Erik Wayne, Katherine Elizabeth. Student, U. Alaska, Anchorage, 1963-64. Reporter, poet Mukluk News Paper, Tok, Alaska, 1977—; interior, coord., technical advisor Alaska Nitty Gritty Dirty Band Alcan Caravan, 1992—; interior coord. Up With People Internat. Show, 1992, 94, 96; interior Alaska coord. and tech. advisor Nitty Gritty Dirt Band Alcan Caravan TV spl., 1992, regional rep. Internat. Women's Writing Guild, 1996, 97; field editor Birds & Blooms Mag., 1996, 97. Author: (books) A Tent in Tok, 1980, More...A Tent in Tok, 1982, Friends of the Tent in Tok, 1987, (short story) K'hann De G'hann, 1989 (1st pl. adult writing 1989), (book) Beyond the Tent in Tok, 1990, The Tent, 1991, Before the Tent in Tok, 1992, Love and the Tent in Tok, 1994, Tok-The Real Story, 1996, Going to the End of the World, 1992, (audio tape mus. drama) Gettysburg, Fields of Love and Honor, 1993, (radio show play) The River, 1997; writer featured story (TV) Paul Harvey's News and Commentary, 1978; featured writer Alaska's S.W. Regional Newsletter, Juneau, 1985, Sta. WAMU Pub. Radio, 1990; featured profile writer Fairbanks (Alaska) Northland News, 1985; featured guest Senator Frank Murkowski's Show, 1988, CBS TV Night Watch, 1989, Tok River Fire Exhibit Dedication, 1992, Channel 11-TV News, Anchorage, 1992, KTVA-TV Norma Goodman Show, Anchorage, 1992, 10th Ann. show Highway Daze, 1992; featured profiles in various publs.; contbr. articles, short stories and poetry pub. in Anchorage Times, Anchorage News, Haiku Highlights, Copper River Jour., Delta News, Mukluk News, Fairbanks Northland News, State of Alaska Newsletter, Divsn. of Forestry, Country mag., Fireweed Jour., Bell's Alaska/Yukon Travel Guide, Alaska Mag., The S.C. Observer, Seattle Times, Santa Monica Daily Breeze, Ark. Dem. Gazette, Chgo. Daily News, Angoon Yearbook, Gettysburg Times, RV Today, Fairbanks Heartland Newspaper. Named winner of Alaska State Diving Championship, 1958-62, Poet Laureate, 1990, Internat. Woman of Yr., Internat. Biol. Ctr., 1991-92, Poet Laureate of the Alaska Hwy., 1994; recipient 1st pl. Tok River Fire Writing Competition, 1990, 1st pl. Tok River Wildfire Photo Competition, 1990. Named Poet Laureate of the Alaska Highway, 1990, 1994, 96; winners of Alaska State Diving Championship, 1958-62, Internat. Biological Ctr. Internat. Woman of Yr., 1991-92; recipient 1st pl. Tok River Fire Writing Competition, 1990, 1st pl. Tok River Wildfire Photo Competition, 1990. Office: A Tent in Tok Winter Cabin Prodns PO Box 110 Tok AK 99780-0110

BLATNER, KEITH ALLAN, forest economics educator, consultant; b. Gowanda, N.Y., Feb. 9, 1952; s. William Francis and Marian Johanna (Smith) B.; m. Betty Joyce Cross, May 14, 1977; children: Justin Heath, Sean Brandon. BS in Natural Resources, Ohio State U., 1975; MS in Forestry, Miss. State U., 1977; PhD in Forestry, Va. Poly. Inst. and State U., 1983. Forestry trainee Container Corp. Am., Circleville, Ohio, 1974; forestry intern U.S. Forest Svc., Washington, 1975; forestry inst. Northwest Ala. State Jr. Coll., Phil Campbell, 1977-78; rsch. specialist, forester U. Ark., Monticello, 1978-80; asst. prof. Wash. State U., Pullman, 1983-89, assoc. prof., 1989-96; prof. Wash. State U., 1996—; sec./treas. Northwest Wood Products Clinic, Spokane, Wash., 1994—. Author: (book chapter) Socioeconomic Issues Pertaining to Forest Health, 1966, Forest Health Management Case Study in Southwestern Idaho, 1994; contbr. articles to profl. jours.; assoc. editor Canadian Jour. of Forest Rsch., 1991-94, Western Jour. of Applied Forestry, 1993—. Mem. Soc. Am. Foresters, Forest Products Soc. (sec. Inland Empire sect. 1985-87, vice chair 1987-90, chair 1990-91), Western Forest Economists (v.p. 1989-90, pres. 1990-91). Republican. Episcopalian. Home: 259 NW Sunrise Dr Pullman WA 99163 Office: U Wash Dept Natural Resource Scis Svcs PO Box 646410 Pullman WA 99164-6410

BLATT, MORTON BERNARD, medical illustrator; b. Chgo., Jan. 9, 1923; s. Arthur E. and Hazel B. Student Central YMCA Coll., 1940-42, U. Ill., 1943-46. Tchr., Ray-Vogue Art Schs., Chgo., 1946-51; med. illustrator VA Center, Wood, Wis., 1951-57, Swedish Covenant Hosp., Chgo., 1957-76; med. illustrator Laidlaw Bros., River Forest, Ill., 1956-59; cons., allied health textbooks, 1956-59; illustrator Standard Edn. Soc., Chgo., 1960; art editor Covenant Home Altar, 1972-83, Covenant Companion, 1958-82. Served with USAAF, 1943-44. Mem. Art Inst. Chgo. Club: Chgo. Press. Illustrator: Atlas and Demonstration Technique of the Central Nervous System, also numerous med. jours.; illustrator, designer Covenant Hymnal, books, record jackets. Address: 373 Eliseo Dr Greenbrae CA 94904-1326

BLATTNER, MEERA MCCUAIG, computer science educator; b. Chgo., Aug. 14, 1930; d. William D. McCuaig and Nina (Spertus) Klevs; m. Minao Kamegai, June 22 1985; children: Douglas, Robert, William. BA, U. Chgo., 1952; MS, U. So. Calif., 1966; PhD, UCLA, 1973 . Rsch. fellow in computer sci. Harvard U., 1973-74; asst. prof. Rice U., 1974-80; assoc. prof. applied sci. U. Calif. at Davis, Livermore, 1980-91, prof. applied sci., 1991—; adj. prof. U. Tex., Houston, 1977—; vis. prof. U. Paris, 1980; program dir. theoretical computer sci. NSF, Washington, 1979-80. Co-editor: (with R. Dannenberg) Multimedia Interface Design, 1992. NSF grantee, 1977-81, 93—. Mem. Soc. Women Engrs., Assn. Computing Machinery, IEEE Computer Soc. Contbr. articles to profl. jours. Office: U Calif Davis/Livermore Dept Applied Sci Livermore CA 94550

BLAWIE, JAMES LOUIS, law educator; b. Newark, Mar. 26, 1928; s. Louis Paul and Cecelia Ruth (Grish) B.; m. Marilyn June Beyerle, May 30, 1952; children: Elias J., Cecelia R., Christiana L. BA, U. Conn., 1950; AM, Boston U., 1951, PhD, 1959; JD, U. Chgo., 1955. Bar: Conn. 1956, Calif. 1965, U.S. Dist. Ct. (no. dist.) Calif. 1965, U.S. Ct. Appeals (9th cir.) 1967, U.S. Supreme Ct. 1968. Instr. polit. sci. Mich. State U., East Lansing, 1955; assoc. prof. U. Akron, Ohio, 1956-57, Kent State U., 1956-57; asst. prof. bus. law U. Calif., Berkeley, 1958-60; assoc. prof. law Santa Clara U., Calif., 1960-63, prof. law, 1963—; vis. prof. polit. sci. Calif. State U., Hayward, 1966-67; adminstrv. law judge U.S. Equal Employment Opportunity Commn., Washington, 1982-85; complaints examiner U.S. Equal Employment Opportunity Agy., Office Equal Employment Opportunity; cons. in field. Author: (handbook) The Michigan Township Board, 1957; contbr. articles to profl. jours. Mem. Citizen's Adv. Com. on Capital Improvements, 1962-65; bd. dirs. Washington Hosp., 1964-68. Maj. U.S. Army, 1963-74. Boston U. Faculty fellow, 1951-53; U. Chgo. Law Sch. scholar, 1953-55; grantee Mich. State U. grantee, 1955-56, Helsinki Govt. Ministry Edn. grantee, 1980-81. Mem. ABA, Fairfield County Bar Assn., Mensa. Republican. Home: 41752 Marigold Dr Fremont CA 94539-4779 also: PO Box 1102 Fremont CA 94538-0110 Office: Santa Clara U Sch Law Santa Clara CA 95053

BLAZEY, MICHAEL ALAN, educator; b. Rochester, N.Y., Jan. 5, 1952; s. Charles Henry and Kathryn Blazey; m. Jennifer Anne Nestegard, July 6, 1991; 1 child, Amanda Rose. BA, U. Oreg., 1974; MS, S.D. State U., 1977; PhD, Pa. State U., 1984. Recreation supt. Brookings (S.D.) Parks and Recreation, 1974-77; instr. Kans. State U., Manhattan, 1977-79; recreation dir. Ketchikan (Alaska) Parks and Recreation, 1979-80; grad. asst. Pa. State U., University Park, 1980-83; instr. Western Carolina U., Cullowhee, 1983-84; assoc. prof. Wash. State U., Pullman, 1984-90, Calif. State U., Long Beach, 1990—; cons. Queen Mary, Long Beach, 1989-92; rsch. proposal cons. Am. Assn. Ret. Persons Andrus Found., Washington, 1993—; cons. Calif. Parks and Recreation, Sacramento, 1993, Wash. Tourism Devel., Olympia, 1985-90. Contbr. articles to profl. jours. Mem. Housing and Cmty. Devel. Citizen Participation Commn., La Habra, Calif., 1995—; bd. dirs. United Meth. Ch. Campus Ministry, Long Beach, 1991—. Named Glenn E. Robinson lectr. S.D. State U., 1991; recipient Rsch. award Am. Assn. Ret. Persons/Andrus, 1988. Mem. Nat. Recreation and Parks Assn., Calif. Parks and Recreation Soc., World Leisure and Recreation Assn., Soc. Park and Recreation Educators (comm. chmn. 1995-96), Am. Assn. Higher Edn. Office: Calif State U 1250 Bellflower Blvd Long Beach CA 90840-4903

BLECHMAN, ELAINE ANN, psychology educator; b. Orange, Calif., Sept. 15, 1943; 1 child, Reva Blechman Sing. BA in Psychology with honors, UCLA, 1966, MA in Devel. Psychology, 1968, PhD in Clin. and Social Psychology, 1971. Diplomate Am. Bd. Behavioral Psychology; lic. psychologist, Conn., N.Y., Colo. Asst. prof. psychology U. Md., 1971-73; asst. prof. psychiatry Yale U., New Haven, 1973-77; rsch. assoc. prof. Wesleyan U., Conn., 1977-83, rsch. prof., 1983-84; prof. psychiatry Albert Einstein Coll. Medicine, 1984-89; sr. rsch. scientist N.Y.C. Dept. Health, 1990; prof. psychiatry SUNY Health Scis. Ctr., Bklyn., 1990; prof. psychology U. Colo., Boulder, 1990—; cons. in field. Contbr. articles to profl. jours.; ad hoc reviewer. Grantee Sigma Xi, 1973, NIMH, 1977-80, 82-84, 85-90, 90-93, NIH, U. Colo., others. Fellow APA (award for rsch. on women 1986), Assn. for Clin. Psychosocial Rsch.; mem. Am. Psychol. Soc., Assn. for Advancement of Behavior Therapy, Nat. Register Health Svc. Providers, Soc. for Behavioral Medicine, Soc. for Clin. and Preventive Psychology (founding), Soc. for Psychotherapy Rsch., Soc. for Rsch. on Adolescence, Soc. for Rsch. on Child and Adolescent Psychopathology, Soc. for Rsch. on Psychopathology, Sigma Xi. Home: 220 Green Rock Dr Boulder CO 80302 Office: U Colo Muenzinger Psychology Bldg Campus Box 345 Boulder CO 80309-2967

BLEIBERG, LEON WILLIAM, surgical podiatrist; b. Bklyn., June 9, 1932; s. Paul Pincus and Helen (Epstein) B.; m. Beth Daigle, June 7, 1970; children: Kristina Noel, Kelley Lynn, Kimberly Ann, Paul Joseph. Student, L.A. City Coll., 1950-51, U. So. Calif., 1951, Case Western Res. U., 1951-53; DSc with honors, Temple U., 1955; PhD, U. Beverly Hills, 1970. Served rotating internship various hosps., Phila., 1954-55; resident various hosps., Montebello, L.A., 1956-58; surg. podiatrist So. Calif. Podiatry Group, Westchester (Calif.), L.A., 1956-75; health care economist, researcher Drs. Home Health Care Svcs., 1976—; chmn. bd. Unltd. Healthcare, Metro Manila, Philippines; podiatric cons. U. So. Calif. Athletic Dept., Morningside and Inglewood (Calif.) High Schs., Internet Corp., Royal Navy Assn., Long Beach, Calif. Naval Sta.; exec. cons. Thomas Med. Group, Pomona, Calif., 1995, Cardiotel, Van Nuys, Calif., 1995; lectr. in field; healthcare affiliate Internat. divsn. CARE/ASIA, 1987; pres. Medica, Totalcare, Cine-Medics Corp., World-Wide Health Care Svcs.; exec. dir. Internat. Health Trust, developer Health Banking Program; adminstr. Orthotic Concepts, 1993; prof. health care econs. and med. rehab. Global U., Ontario, Calif., chmn. dept. health care econs., chmn. dept. biomechanics and phys. rehab. Producer (films) The Gun Hawk, 1963, Terrified, Day of the Nightmare; contbr. articles to profl. jours. Hon. Sheriff Westchester 1962-64; commd. mem. Rep. Senatorial Inner Circle, 1984-86; co-chmn. health reform com. United We Stand Am., Thousand Oaks, Calif.; mem. exec. coun. State of Calif., United We Stand Am.; active 1st Security and Safety, Westlake Village, Calif., 1993—; lt. comdr. med. svcs. corps Brit.-Am. Sea Cadet Corps, 1984—; track coach Westlake High Sch., Westlake Village. With USN, 1955-56. Recipient Medal of Merit, U.S. Presdl. Task Force. Mem. Philippine Hosp. Assn. (Cert. of Appreciation 1964, trophy for Outstanding Svc. 1979), Calif. Podiatry Assn. (hon.), Am. Podiatric Med. Assn. (hon.), Acad. TV Arts and Scis., Royal Soc. Health (Eng.), Western Foot Surgery Assn., Am. Coll. Foot Surgeons, Am. Coll. Podiatric Sports Medicine, Internat. Coll. Preventive Medicine, Hollywood Comedy Club, Sts. and Sinners Club, Westchester C. of C., Hals Und Beinbruch Ski Club, Beach Cities Ski Club, Orange County Stamp Club, Las Virgenes Track Club, Masons, Shriners. Home: 30856 Agoura Rd # J-16 Agoura Hills CA 91301

BLESSING-MOORE, JOANN CATHERINE, physician; b. Tacoma, Wash., Sept. 21, 1946; d. Harold R. and Mildred (Benson) Blessing; m. Robert Chester Moore; 1 child, Ahna. BA in Chemistry, Syracuse U., 1968; MD, SUNY, Syracuse, 1972. Diplomate Am. Bd. Pediatrics, Am. Bd. Allergy Immunology, Am. Bd. Pediatric Pulmonology. Pediatric intern, then resident Stanford U. Sch. Medicine, Palo Alto, Calif., 1972-75, allergy pulmonology fellow, 1975-77; co-dir. pediatric allergy pulmonology dept.

Stanford U. Children's Hosp., Palo Alto, Calif., 1977-84; clin. asst. prof. dept. pediatrics Stanford U. Sch. Medicine, Palo Alto, Calif., 1977-84, co-dir. pediatric pulmonology lab., 1977-84; clin. asst. prof. dept. immunology Stanford U. Hosp., 1984—; allergist Palo Alto Med. Clinic, 1984-90; pvt. practice allergy immunology-pediatric-pulmonary Palo Alto, Calif., 1990—; dir. ednl. program for children with asthma Camp Wheeze, Palo Alto, 1975—; cons. FDA, 1992—; cons. in field. Author handbooks, camp program manuals; co-editor jour. supplements; mem. edit. bd. Allergy jours.; contbr. articles to sci. publs. Fellow Am. Acad. Allery, Asthma, Immunology (various offices 1980—, task force parameters of care asthma and allergy 1989—), Am. Coll. Chest Physicians (com. mem. 1980—), Am. Coll. of Asthma, Allergy and Immunology (regent 1995-98); mem. Am. Thoracic Soc., Am. Lung Assn., No. Calif. Allergy Found. (bd. dirs., pres.), Peninsula Women's Assn., Santa Clara and San Mateo County Med. Soc., Chi Omega. Republican. Presbyterian. Office: 770 Welch Rd Ste 301 Palo Alto CA 94304-1513 also: 100 S Ellsworth Ave Ste 309 San Mateo CA 94401-3931 also: Stanford Univ Hosp Dept Immunology Palo Alto CA 94304

BLETHEN, FRANK A., newspaper publisher; b. Seattle, Apr. 20, 1945. B.S. in Bus., Ariz. State U.; P.M.D., Harvard U. Pub. Walla Walla Union-Bulletin, Wash., 1975-79; circulation mgr. Seattle Times, 1979-81, v.p. sales and mktg., 1982-85, pub., chief exec. officer, 1985—; chmn. Walla Walla Union-Bull., Yakima (Wash.) Herald Republic. Mem. adv. bd. Wash. State U. Mem. Am. Newspaper Pubs. Assn. (bd. dirs., chmn. telecomm. com.), Bellevue Athletic Club, Sigma Delta Chi. Office: Seattle Times Fairview Ave N & John St PO Box 70 Seattle WA 98111-0070

BLEVINS, WILLARD AHART, electrical engineer; b. Jonben, W.Va., Nov. 20, 1949; s. Oakley Cameron and Peggy Jane (Agee) B.; m. Nancy Phyllis Bailey, June 26, 1971; children: Maria Dawn, Teresa Lynn. AA in Elec. Tech. with honors, N.D. State Sch. Sci., 1974; BSEE with honors, Ariz. State U., 1988. Technician Sperry Flight Systems, Phoenix, 1974-88; engr. Sperry/Honeywell, Phoenix, 1988—. Patentee out of lock detector. With USAF, 1968-72. Recipient Honeywell Tech. Achievement award, 1995; named Parent of Yr., Phoenix Children's Chorus, 1985. Home: 15810 N 47th Ln Glendale AZ 85306-2602 Office: Honeywell PO Box 21111-w33C Phoenix AZ 85036

BLEWETT, STEPHEN DOUGLAS, journalism educator, public relations consultant; b. Bremerton, Wash., Feb. 21, 1942; s. Wesley Edgar and Christina (Ball) B.; m. Judith Marie Mohr, June 17, 1967; children: Mark Joseph, Christina Marie, Susan Renee. BA in Journalism, Ea. Wash. U., 1969, MA in English, 1981. Newspaper reporter/editor The Spokesman-Rev., Spokane, Wash., 1970-73; pub. rels. coord. Wash. Water Power Co., Spokane, 1973-88; prof./program dir. Ea. Wash. U., Spokane, 1988—; prin. Comm. Concepts, Spokane, 1989—; mem. cmty. adv. bd., mktg. com. Jr. League Spokane, 1996—. Author: A History of The Washington Water Power Company: 1889-1989, 1989, (with Jeffrey L. Stafford) Hitting the Bricks: A College Student's Practical Guide to Finding Work as a Communication Professional, 1995, (one act play) Pancakes to Go, 1985; cons. editor Inland, 1993-96; contbr. articles to profl. jours. Active Spokane Pub. Rels. Coun., 1995—, mktg. com. Cath. Diocese Found., 1996—. With USAF, 1961-65. Recipient Max award of merit Spokane Advt. Fedn., 1982, 83 85, cert. excellence for spl. events United Way of Am., 1983. Mem. Internat. Assn. Bus. Communicators (accredited, bd. dirs., past pres. Metro Spokane chpt. 1982-95, ethics com. 1992-95, award of merit 1985, Gold Quill award of merit 1986), Pacific Northwest Assn. Journalism Educators (past pres.), Immaculate Heart Retreat Ctr. Dirs. Club. Democrat. Roman Catholic. Office: Ea Wash U 705 W 1st Ave Spokane WA 99204

BLEY, JOHN L., state agency administrator. Dir. fin. instns. State of Wash., Olympia. Office: State of Wash Rm 300 210 11th Ave SW 3rd Fl Olympia WA 98504

BLIESNER, JAMES DOUGLAS, municipal/county official, consultant; b. Milw., Mar. 19, 1945; s. Milton Carl and Dorothy (St. George) B.; m. Phyllis Jean Byrd, June 15, 1966 (div. 1985); children: Tris, Cara. BA in Philosophy, Ea. Nazarene Coll., 1968; MA in Social Ethics, Andover, Newton Theol. Sch., 1973; postgrad., Boston U., 1969-70; student, N.Y. Studio Sch./Delordoua, Mus. Sch., Milw. Tech. Art Sch. Exec. dir. San Diego Youth and Community Svcs., 1974-78; cons., analyst San Diego Housing Commn., 1979-84; dir. San Diego City-County Reinvestment Task Force, 1984—; bd. dirs. Calif. Cmty. Reinvestment Corp.; vice chmn. Calif. Reinvestment Com., 1989—; founder, chmn. City Heights Cmty. Devel. Corp., San Diego, 1980-89; fin. com. chairperson Mid-City Revitalization Com., San Diego, 1988; instr. San Diego State U. Author monographs, 1979; visual arts exhbns. include San Diego Arts Inst., Soc. Western Artists, Santa Barbara Contemporary Arts Forum, Calif. Coun. for Humanities; films exhibited in Centro Cultural, Tijuana, Mexico, Venice, Paris, Jerusalem, Mexico, Eng., China exhbns. Coun. appointee City of San Diego Com. on Reapportionment, 1990, Com. on Growth and Devel., San Diego, 1989; gov. appointee Gov.'s Office of Neighborhoods, Calif., 1987; mem. City Heights Redevel. Project Com., San Diego, 1992; pres. San Diego Housing Consortium. Recipient Award of Honor, Am. Planning Assn., 1987, Spl. Project award, 1987, Merit award, 1989, Lifetime Achievement award Non-Profit Fedn. San Diego; named Citizen of Yr. Mid-City C. of C., 1986, award Calif. Coun. Humanities. Mem. Urban Land Inst. Methodist. Home: 4106 Manzanita Dr San Diego CA 92105-4508 Office: City County Reinvestment Task Force 1600 Pacific Hwy # A6 San Diego CA 92101-2429

BLINDER, JANET, art dealer; b. L.A., Sept. 21, 1953; d. Joseph and Margaret (Nadel) Weiss; m. Martin S. Blinder, Dec. 10, 1983. Founder Nationwide Baby Shops, Santa Monica, Calif., 1976-82; adminstr. Martin Lawrence Ltd. Editions, Van Nuys, Calif., 1982-90; art dealer L.A., 1990—. Mem. benefit com. AIDS Project L.A., 1988, prin. sponsor ann. fundraiser, 1990; mem. benefit com. Art Against AIDS, L.A., 1989; patron, sponsor Maryvale Orphanage, Rosemead, Calif., 1984—; patron Scottsdale Ctr. for the Arts. Recipient Commendation for Philanthropic Efforts City of L.A. Mayor Tom Bradley, 1988. Mem. Mus. Modern Art, Whitney Mus. Am. Art, Guggenheim Mus., Palm Springs (Calif.) Mus. Art, Mus. of Contemporary Art, Scottsdale (Ariz.) Ctr. for the Arts.

BLINDER, MARTIN S., business consultant, art dealer; b. Bklyn., Nov. 18, 1946; s. Meyer and Lillian (Stein) B.; m. Janet Weiss, Dec. 10, 1983. BBA, Adelphi U., 1968. Account exec. Bruns, Nordeman & Co., N.Y.C., 1968-69; v.p. Blinder, Robinson & Co., Westbury, N.Y., 1969-73; treas. BHB Prodns., L.A., 1973-76; pres. Martin Lawrence Ltd. Edits., Van Nuys, Calif., 1976-94, chmn., 1986-94, bd. dirs., 1994—; pres., dir. Corp. Art Inc., Visual Artists Mgmt. Corp., Art Consultants Inc.; lectr. bus. symposia. Contbr. articles to mags. and newspapers; appeared on TV and radio. Mem. Dem. Nat. Com.; mem. benefit com. AIDS project, L.A., 1988; bd. dirs. Very Spl. Arts, 1989—, chmn. visual arts Internat. Very Spl. Arts Festival, 1989; patron Guggenheim Mus., N.Y.C., Mus. Modern Art, N.Y.C., L.A. County Mus. Art, L.A. Mus. Contemporary Art (hon. founder), Whitney Mus. Am. Art, Palm Springs Mus. Art, Hirschhorn Mus., Washington, Skirball Mus., L.A., Diabetes Found. of City of Hope, B'nai B'rith Anti-Defamation League, Very Spl. Arts, Scottsdale Ctr. for the Arts; mem. Citizens for Common Sense; bd. dirs., pres. Rsch. Found. for Crohns Disease; mem. benefit com. Art Against AIDS, 1989; co-chair artists com. for Don't Bungle the Jungle Companions of Arts and Nature, 1989; prin. sponsor, ann. fundraiser AIDS Project, L.A., 1990. Read into Congl. Record, 1981, 83, 86, 88, 91; recipient resolution of commendation L.A. City Coun., 1983, State of Calif. resolution for contbn. to arts in Calif., 1983, Merit award Republic Haiti for contbn. to arts, 1985, U.S. Senate commendation, 1983, County of L.A. Bd. Suprs. resolution for Contbn. to arts in So. Calif., 1983, Gov. of R.I. resolution for contbns. to arts, 1985, commendation County of Los Angeles-Supr. Ed Edelman, 1991, commendation for contbns. to the arts and the healing arts City of L.A., 1991, commendation for contbns. to arts and philanthropy Mayor David Dinkins, N.Y.C., 1992; Nov. 18, 1985 declared Martin S. Blinder Day in L.A. in his honor by Mayor Tom Bradley; recipient spl. award San Diego Youth and Cmty. Svcs. Mem. Fine Art Pub.'s Assn. (bd. dirs. 1990-94), Med. Art Assn. at UCLA. Office: MSB Fine Art 7000 E Shea Blvd Ste 1390 Scottsdale AZ 85254-5229

BLISH, EUGENE SYLVESTER, trade association administrator; b. Denver, Oct. 9, 1912; s. George Joseph and Lillian Lenox (O'Neill) B.; m. Susan M. Monti, Feb. 21, 1950; children: Eugene A., Mary, Susan Blish Clarke, Julia Blish Gordon. BSC, U. Notre Dame, 1934. Advt. dir. Colo. Milling and Elevator Co., Denver, 1934-45; advt. and mktg. cons., Denver, 1945-57; asst. exec. dir. Am. Sheep Producers Council, Denver, 1957-74; merchandising rep. Nat. Potato Bd., Denver, 1974-87. Mem. alumni bd. dirs. U. Notre Dame, 1947-49. Mem. Soc. Mayflower Desc., Barnstable Hist. Soc. (Mass.). Clubs: Denver Athletic, Mt. Vernon Country, Denver Notre Dame. Home and Office: 1370 Madison St Denver CO 80206-2613

BLISS, LEE, English language educator; b. Buffalo, Aug. 9, 1943; d. Charles Perry and Louise (Ramseyer) B. PhD, U. Calif., Berkeley. Asst. prof. U. Calif., Santa Barbara, 1977-82, prof., 1988—; vis. asst. prof. Scrips Coll., Pomona, Calif., 1972-73; part time lectr. UCLA, 1973-75; vis. assoc. prof. Claremont Grad. Sch., Pomona, 1980. Author: The World's Perspective, 1983, Francis Beaumont, 1987. Summer fellow NEH, 1974, Folger fellow, 1992-93. Mem. MLA, Renaissance Soc. Am., Shakespeare Assn. Am., Malone Soc. Office: U Calif Dept English Santa Barbara CA 93106

BLISSITT, PATRICIA ANN, nurse; b. Knoxville, Tenn., Sept. 23, 1953; d. Dewitt Talmadge and Imogene (Bailey) B. BSN with high honors, U. Tenn., 1976, MSN, 1985; postgrad., U. Wash., 1996—. RN; cert. in case mgmt.; cert. trauma nurse core course, ACLS, pediat. advanced life support. Staff nurse neurosci. unit City of Memphis Hosp., 1976-78, head nurse neurosci. unit, 1978-79; physician's asst. Dr. John D. Wilson, Columbus, Miss., 1979-81; staff nurse med.-surg.-trauma ICU U. Tenn. Meml. Hosp., Knoxville, 1982-83; staff nurse neurosci. ICU Bapt. Meml. Hosp., Memphis, 1985-86, clin. nurse specialist neurosci., 1986-94, trauma coord., 1991-93, neuro case mgr., 1993-94; staff nurse neurosurg. ICU Harborview Med. Ctr., Seattle, 1994—; nurse cons. neurosci. VA Hosp., Memphis, 1986; mem. adv. com. Tenn. Bd. Nursing Practice. Author: (with others) Critical Care Nursing in Clinics of North America, 1990, Jour. Neurosci. Nursing, 1986, 92, 96, Guidelines for Critical Care Nursing; abstractor: Nursing SCAN in Critical Care, 1995—; contbr. articles to sci. jour., chpt. to book; mem. editl. cons. bd. Focus on Critical Care, 1990-92. Mem. ANA (mem. coun. med.-surg. nurses, mem. coun. clin. nurse specialists), Am. Assn. Neurosci. Nurses (cert. neurosci. nurse, pres. local chpt. 1989-90, treas. local chpt. 1987-89, mem. neurosci. nursing test devel. com. Am. Bd. Neurosci. Nursing 1996—, nat. lectr., mem. and chair resource devel. com., mem. continuing edn./ann. sci. program com., program/seminar chairperson local chpt. 1990-93, mem. nurse practice com., chairperson patient edn. project 1991-92, mem. program/seminar com., program/seminar chairperson mid-South chpt. 1990-93, chairperson nat. resource devel. com. 1992-94, pres. local chpt. 1995—), AACN (life, cert. critical care nurse, lectr., mem. CCRN corp. exam. devel. com. 1989-92, NTI spkr. 1992, editl. cons. bd. 1990-92, pres.-elect Greater Memphis area chpt. 1989-90, pres. 1990-91, immediate past pres., chairperson nat. critical care awareness week 1990-93, chpt. cons. Region II 1991-93, chpt of yr. com. chairperson 1992-94, chairperson-elect Puget Sound chpt. program 1995-96, chairperson program com. 1996-97, editor elect newsletter Puget Sound chpt. 1997—, mem. program com. 1997—), Am. Assn. Spinal Cord Injury Nurses, Wash. Nurses Assn., Tenn. Nurses Assn. (mem. com. on practice 1992-93), Tenn. Nursing Congress (pres. 1990-94), Am. Assn. Neurol. Surgeons (assoc.), Western Inst. Nursing, Sigma Theta Tau. Methodist. Avocation: music. Home: 1105 Spring St Apt 405 Seattle WA 98104-3513

BLITZ, IRA ALLEN, obstetrician-gynecologist; b. Bklyn., July 4, 1944; s. Julius and Sylvia (Weprinsky) B.; m. Virginia Louise Johnson, June 9, 1974; children: Matthew, Daniel. BA, UCLA, 1966, MD, 1970. Intern UCLA Affiliated Hosps., 1970-71; resident Cedars-Sinai Med. Ctr., L.A., 1974-77; staff gynecologist Kaiser-Permanente, L.A., 1978-86, San Gabriel Valley, Calif., 1986—. Exec. v.p. Temple Shaarei Tikvah, Arcadia, Calif., 1987-91; ritual chmn. Congregation Shaarei Torah, Arcadia, 1994-95. Fellow ACOG; mem. Am. Soc. Reproductive Medicine, L.A. Ob.-Gyn. Soc. Office: Kaiser-Permanente 1011 Baldwin Park Blvd Baldwin Park CA 91706-5806

BLITZ-WEISZ, SALLY, speech pathologist; b. Buffalo, Nov. 9, 1954; d. Isaac and Paula (Goldstein) Blitz; m. Andrew Weisz, Dec. 16, 1984; 1 child, Naomi Ariel Weisz. BA in Speech Pathology, Audiology, SUNY, Buffalo, 1976, MA in Speech Pathology, 1978; MS Sch Counseling, pupil pers credential, U. LaVerne, 1991. Lic. speech/lang. pathologist, Calif. Speech, lang. pathologist Lang. Devel. Program, Tonawanda, N.Y., 1978-82, Bailey and Drown Assocs., La Habra, Calif., 1982-83; speech, lang. specialist, cons. Pasadena (Calif.) Unified Schs., 1983-94, L.A. Unified Schs., 1996—. Active Anti-Defamation League, San Fernando Valley, 1985-86; mem. 2d Generation Holocaust Survivors, Los Angeles, 1986—. Recipient Excellence in Studies award Temple Shaarey Zedek, Buffalo, 1968. Mem. Am. Speech-Lang.-Hearing Assn. Democrat. Club: Jewish Young Adults. Lodge: B'nai Brith. Home: 11671 Amigo Ave Northridge CA 91326-1849 Office: L A Unified Sch Dist Mid City-SESU Los Angeles CA 91101-3507

BLIZINSKY, MARLIN JOEL, lawyer; b. St. Paul, Dec. 16, 1947; s. Irwin M. and Jeannie (Weisberg) B.; m. Ellen E. Bert, Sept. 24, 1979; 1 child, Katherine D. BA, U. Minn., 1969; AM, U. Chgo., 1974; JD, U. Puget Sound Sch. Law, 1985. Bar: Wash. 1985. With King County Real Property Div., Seattle, 1986-90; mgr. King County Office Cable Comm., Seattle, 1990—; adj. prof. law Albers Sch. Bus., 1993—.

BLOCH, ERNEST, II, foundation administrator; b. Portland, Oreg., Nov. 15, 1938; s. Ivan and Mariana (Trotel) B.; m. Laurie M. Munro, Mar. 5, 1993; children by previous marriage: Peter Ernest, Suzanne M. Bloch-St. Clair. BS, Portland State U., 1961. Pricing mgr. Western Airlines, L.A., 1961-74; dir. pricing Tex. Internat., Houston, 1974-76; pres. Bus. Exch., Houston, 1976-79; v.p. Air Oreg., Portland, 1979-80; dir. corp. comms. NERCO, Portland, 1981-91; exec. dir. Pacific Corp. Found., Portland, 1991—. Pres. Chamber Music N.W. Portland, 1996; advisor Portland Art Mus, 1995; mem. bus. mktg. com. Oreg. Symphony; bd. dirs. 1998 World Masters Games, World Affairs Coun.; mem. United Way Cabinet; spl. projects advisor Oreg. Mus. Sci. and Industry. Mem. Grant Makers of Oreg. and S.W. Wash. (pres. 1993-94), Pacific N.W. Grant Makers Forum. Democrat. Jewish. Office: Pacific Corp Found 700 NE Multnomah 1600 Portland OR 97232

BLOCK, ALVIN GILBERT, journal editor; b. Moline, Ill., Sept. 15, 1946; s. Sylvan Emory Block and Pauline (Kutten) Salzman; m. Sarah Cannon Michael, June 17, 1977 (div. 1984); m. Ellen Marie Chapman, Jan. 19, 1992; children: Will Chapman, Thomas Chapman. BA, Bradley U., 1968. Editl. asst. Playboy mag., Chgo., 1970; exec. Salzman & Co., Davenport, Iowa, 1971-74; editor Ketchum (Idaho) Tomorrow, 1975-77; reporter Idaho Statesman, Ketchum, 1978-80; freelance writer, Sacramento, 1980-82; mng. editor Calif. Jour., Sacramento, 1983-94, editor, columnist, 1995—; commentator Sta. KXPR-FM, Sacramento, 1985-88. Councilman City of Ketchum, 1979. With U.S. Army, 1969-74. Recipient award for column Soc. Profl. Journalists, 1995. Home: 1133 Marian Way Sacramento CA 95818 Office: Calif Jour 2101 K St Sacramento CA 95816

BLOCK, M. JULIANN MCCARTHY, school psychologist; b. Lewistown, Mont., Jan. 5, 1957; d. John Joseph and Helen Patricia (Ryan) McCarthy; m. David William Block, Jan. 8, 1993; step-children: Will Jacob, Bret Roman. BA, Carroll Coll., 1979; MA, U. Mont., 1983, 84. Cert. tchr., sch. psychologist, Ariz.; nat. cert. sch. psychologist. English tchr. Garfield County H.S., Jordan, Mont., 1979-81; sch. psychologist Cassia County Joint Sch. Dist., Burley, Idaho, 1984-85, Ednl. Svc. Dist. #112, Vancouver, Wash., 1985-92, Chandler (Ariz.) Unified Sch. Dist., 1992-94, Fountain Hills (Ariz.) Unified Sch. Dist., 1994—. Del. Wash, Dem. Party Clark County, Olympia, 1992. Mem. ASCD, Nat. Assn. Sch. Psychologists. Roman Catholic. Home: 1026 N Portland Ave Gilbert AZ 85234 Office: McDowell Mountain Elem Sch 14825 N Fayette Fountain Hills AZ 85268

BLOCK, MICHAEL KENT, economics and law educator, public policy association executive, former government official, consultant; b. N.Y.C., Apr. 2, 1942; s. Philip and Roslyn (Klein) B.; m. Carole Arline Polansky, Aug. 30, 1964 (div.); children: Robert Justin, Tamara Nicole; m. Olga Vyborna, Dec. 1, 1996. A.B., Stanford U., 1964, A.M., 1969, Ph.D., 1972. Research analyst Bank of Am., San Francisco, 1965-66; research assoc. Planning Assocs., San Francisco, 1966-67; asst. prof. econs. U. Santa Clara, 1969-72; asst. prof. econs. dept. ops. research and adminstrv. sci. Naval Postgrad. Sch., Monterey, Calif., 1972-74, assoc. prof., 1974-76; research fellow Hoover Instn., Stanford U., 1975-76, sr. research fellow, 1976-87; dir. Center for Econometric Studies of Justice System, 1977-81; ptnr. Block & Nold, Cons., Palo Alto, Calif., 1980-81; assoc. prof. mgmt., econs. and law U. Ariz., Tucson, 1982-85, prof. econs. and law, 1989—; mem. U.S. Sentencing Commn., Washington, 1985-89; exec. v.p. Cybernomics, Tucson, 1991—; pres. Goldwater Inst. for Pub. Policy, Phoenix, Ariz., 1992—; sr. policy adviser State of Ariz. Gov. Symington, 1996-97; mem. Ariz. Residential Utility Consumer Bd., 1995-96, chmn. Ariz. Constl. Def. Coun., 1994—; seminar dir. Econ. Devel. Inst./World Bank, 1992-95; cons. in field. Author: (with H.G. Demmert) Workbook and Programmed Guide to Economics, 1974, 77, 80, (with James M. Clabault) A Legal and Economic Analysis of Criminal Antitrust Indictments:, 1955-80; contbr. articles to profl. publs. Fellow NSF, 1965, Stanford U., sr. fellow Progress and Freedom Found., Washington, 1995—. Mem. Am. Econ. Assn., Phi Beta Kappa. Office: U Ariz Dept Econs Tucson AZ 85721

BLODGETT, ELSIE GRACE, association executive; b. Eldorado Springs, Mo., Aug. 2, 1921; d. Charles Ishmal and Naoma Florence (Worthington) Robison; m. Charles Davis Blodgett, Nov. 8, 1940; children: Carolyn Doyel, Charleen Bier, Lyndon Blodgett, Daryl (dec.). Student Warrensburg (Mo.) State Tchrs. Coll., 1939-40; BA, Fresno (Calif.) State Coll., 1953. Tchr. schs. in Mo. and Calif., 1940-42, 47-72; owner, mgr. rental units, 1965—; exec. dir. San Joaquin County (Calif.) Rental Property Assn., Stockton, 1970-81; prin. Delta Rental Property Owners and Assocs., 1981-82; propr. Crystal Springs Health World, Inc., Stockton, 1980-86; bd. dirs. Stockton Better Bus. Bur. Active local PTA, Girl Scouts U.S., Boy Scouts Am.; bd. dirs. Stockton Goodwill Industries; active Vols. in Police Svc., 1993; capt. Delaware Alpine Neighborhood Watch, 1994—. Named (with husband) Mr. and Mrs. Apt. Owner of San Joaquin County, 1977. Mem. Nat. Apt. Assn. (state treas. women's div. 1977-79), Calif. Ret. Tchrs. Assn. Republican. Methodist. Lodge: Stockton Zonta. Home and Office: 2285 W Mendocino Ave Stockton CA 95204-4005

BLODGETT, FORREST CLINTON, economics educator; b. Oregon City, Oreg., Oct. 6, 1927; s. Clinton Alexander and Mabel (Wells) B.; m. Beverley Janice Buchholz, Dec. 21, 1946; children: Cherine (Mrs. Jon R. Klein), Candis Melis, Clinton George. BS, U. Omaha, 1961; MA, U. Mo., 1969; PhD, Portland State U., 1979. Joined C.E. U.S. Army, 1946, commd. 2d lt., 1946, advanced through grades to lt. col., 1965, ret., 1968; engrng. assignments U.S. Army, Japan, 1947-49, U.K., 1950-53, Korea, 1955-56, Alaska, 1958-60, Vietnam, 1963; staff engr. 2d Army Air Def. Region U.S. Army, Richards-Gebaur AFB, Mo., 1964-66; base engr. Def. Atomic Support Agy., Sandia Base, N.Mex., 1966-68; bus. mgr., trustee, asst. prof. econs. Linfield Coll., McMinnville, Oreg., 1968-73, assoc. prof., 1973-83, prof., 1983-90, emeritus prof. econs., 1990—; pres. Blodgett Enterprises, Inc., 1983-85; founder, dir. Valley Community Bank, 1980-86, vice chmn. bd. dirs., 1985-86. Commr., Housing Authority of Yamhill County (Oreg.), chmn., 1980-83; mem. Yamhill County Econ. Devel. Com., 1978-83; bd. dirs. Yamhill County Found., 1983-91, Oreg. Internat. Coun., 1995—. Decorated Army Commendation medal with oak leaf cluster; recipient Joint Service Commendation medal Dept. of Def. Mem. Soc. Am. Mil. Engrs. (pres. Albuquerque post 1968), Am. Econ. Assn., Western Econ. Assn. Internat., Nat. Ret. Officers Assn., Res. Officers Assn. (pres. Marion chpt. 1976), SAR (pres. Oreg. soc. 1985-86, v.p. gen. Nat. Soc. 1991-93), Urban Affairs Assn., Soc. for The History of Tech., Pi Sigma Epsilon, Pi Gamma Mu, Omicron Delta Epsilon (Pacific NW regional dir. 1978-88), Rotary (pres. McMinnville club 1983-84, dir. Gregor Internat. Coun. 1995—). Republican. Episcopalian. Office: Linfield Coll Mcminnville OR 97128

BLOEDE, VICTOR CARL, lawyer, academic executive; b. Woodwardville, Md., July 17, 1917; s. Carl Schon and Eleanor (Eck) B.; m. Ellen Louise Miller, May 9, 1947; children—Karl Abbott, Pamela Elena. A.B., Dartmouth Coll., 1940; J.D. cum laude, U. Balt., 1950; LL.M. in Pub. Law, Georgetown U., 1967. Bar: Md. 1950, Fed. Hawaii 1958, U.S. Supreme Ct. 1971. Pvt. practice Balt., 1950-64; mem. Goldman & Bloede, Balt., 1959-64; counsel Seven-Up Bottling Co., Balt., 1958-64; dep. atty. gen. Pacific Trust Ter., Honolulu, 1952-53; asst. solicitor for ters. Office of Solicitor, U.S. Dept. Interior, Washington, 1953-54; atty. U.S. Justice, Honolulu, 1955-58; assoc. gen. counsel Dept. Navy, Washington, 1960-61, 63-64; spl. legal cons. Md. Legislature, Legis. Council, 1963-64, 66-67; assoc. prof. U. Hawaii, 1961-63, dir. property mgmt., 1964-67; house counsel, dir. contracts and grants U. Hawaii System, 1967-82; house counsel U. Hawaii Research Corp., 1970-82; legal counsel Law of Sea Inst., 1978-82; legal cons. Rsch. Corp. and grad. rsch. divsn. U. Hawaii, 1982-92; spl. counsel to Holifield Congl. Commn. on Govt. Procurement, 1970-73. Author: Hawaii Legislative Manual, 1962, Maori Affairs, New Zealand, 1964, Oceanographic Research Vessel Operations, and Liabilities, 1972, Hawaiian Archipelago, Legal Effects of a 200 Mile Territorial Sea, 1973, Copyright-Guidelines to the 1976 Act, 1977, Forms Manual, Inventions: Policy, Law and Procedure, 1982; writer, contbr. Coll. Law Digest and other publs. on legislation and pub. law. Mem. Gov.'s Task Force Hawaii and The Sea, 1969, Citizens Housing Com. Balt., 1952-64; bd. govs. Balt. Cmty. YMCA, 1954-64; bd. dirs. U. Hawaii Press, 1964-66, Coll. Housing Found., 1968-80; appointed to internat. rev. commn. Canada-France Hawaii Telescope Corp., 1973-82, chmn., 1973, 82; cofounder, incorporator First Unitarian Ch. Honolulu. Served to lt. comdr. USNR, 1942-45, PTO. Grantee ocean law studies NSF and NOAA, 1970-80. Mem. ABA, Balt. Bar Assn., Fed. Bar Assn., Am. Soc. Internat. Law, Nat. Assn. Univ. Attys. (founder & 1st chmn. patents & copyrights sect. 1974-76). Home: 635 Onaha St Honolulu HI 96816-4918

BLOEMKER, E. FREDRICK, physician, ophthalmologist; b. Indpls., Feb. 26, 1939; s. Albert W. and Kathleen (Cain) B.; m. Frances Ellen Hume, June 23, 1962; children: Anne, Kathleen, Jane. BS, St. Louis U., 1961; MD, Ind. U., 1965. Intern Meth. Hosp., Indpls., 1965-66; resident in ophthalmology Ind. U., Indpls., 1969-71; ophthalmologist Affiliated Eye Surgeons, Phoenix, 1971—; chmn. dept. ophthalmology St. Joseph's Hosp., Phoenix, 1975-85. Capt. USAF, 1966-68. Fellow ACS, Am. Acad. Ophthalmology. Republican. Home: 3500 E Lincoln Dr Phoenix AZ 85013 Office: Affiliated Eye Surgeons 222 W Thomas Rd Phoenix AZ 85013-4419

BLOM, JEFFREY LEWIS, publishing executive; b. Phila., Oct. 24, 1946; s. Charles Nils and Alice Honey (Bartok) B.; m. Valerie Wasson, Aug. 1969 (div. July 1975). BA in Math., U. Washington, Seattle, 1974. Owner Blue Dove Press, San Diego, Calif., 1993—. With U.S. Army, 1966-68. Office: Blue Dove Press 10141 Maya Linda Rd #105 San Diego CA 92126

BLOMQUIST, CARL ARTHUR, medical and trust company executive, insurance executive; b. L.A., Feb. 2, 1947; s. Carl Arthur and Delphine Marie (Forcier) B.; m. Diane Leslie Nunez, May 5, 1973 (div. Dec. 1979); 1 child, Kristin; m. Patricia Marie Johnson, Feb. 3, 1984 (div. Dec. 1988), m. Sharon Elaine Fromwiller, Oct. 14, 1995. BS, U. San Diego, 1969; MPH, UCLA, 1973. Auditor Naval Area Audit Svc., San Diego, 1969-71; trainee USPHS, Washington, 1971; asst. adminstr. Northridge (Calif.) Hosp., 1973-76; asst. adminstr. fin. and facilities St. Vincent Med. Ctr., L.A., 1976-77; asst. v.p. 1st Interstate Mortgage, Pasadena, Calif., 1977-79; chief exec. officer Coop. Am. Physicians/Mut. Protection Trust, L.A., 1979-94; spl. dep. Calif. ins. commr. Exec. Life Ins. Co., L.A., 1991-94, acting CEO, 1991-92; prin. Carl A. Blomquist Cons., Playa Del Rey, Calif., 1994-95; mgr., CEO Head Injury Rehab. Svcs., LLC, 1995—; mem. instl. review bd. Motion Picture Hosp. Woodland Hills, Calif., 1993—; bd. dirs. Risk Mgmt. Assurance Corp., Dallas, 1996—; profl. adv. com. L.A. Posada Home Health, Pasadena, 1996—. Mem. Calif. Health Facilities Financing Authority, Sacramento, 1981—; co-chmn. Adv. Commn. on Malpractice Ins., Calif. Senate, Sacramento, 1984-92, mem. Commn. on Cost Containment in State Govt., 1984—; bd. dirs. Chaminade Coll. Prep. Sch., West Hills, Calif., 1988. Journalism grantee Helms Found., 1965. Mem. Am. Coll. Healthcare Execs., Am. Hosp. Assn., President's Assn. of Am. Mgmt. Assn., Health Care Execs. So. Calif., Hosp. Coun. So. Calif., UCLA Health Care Mgmt. Alumni Assn. (bd. dirs. 1987-94), Case Mgmt. Soc. Am., Am. Congress of Rehab. Med., Big Brothers Am. Republican. Roman Catholic. Office: Carl A Blomquist Cons 6641 Vista Del Mar Playa Del Rey CA 90293-7545

BLOMSTROM, BRUCE A., healthcare executive; b. Salem, Mass., July 4, 1937; m. Anne Blomstrom; children: Jeffrey, Kristin. BS, MIT, 1959, MS in Indsl. Mgmt., 1962. Asst. sec. Ministry of Commerce and Industry, Govt. of

Uganda, Kampala, 1962-64; regional dir., Far East dir., internat. product mgmt., Libby McNeil & Libby, Chgo., 1965-73; dir. corp. planning, exec. mng. dir. Nippon Abbott; gen. mgr. South Africa Abbott Labs., North Chicago, Ill., 1973-82; v.p. Alpha Therapeutic, L.A., 1982-84; v.p.corp. devel. Whittaker Corp., L.A., 1984-85; pres., CEO Guardian Products divsn. Sunrise Med., Arleta, Calif., 1985-90, Clinishare, Inc. divsn. Unihealth, Chatsworth, Calif., 1991—; pres., dir. Unihealth Investment, Burbank, Calif., 1995—; bd. dirs. Cedaron, Davis, Calif. Contbr. articles to profl. jours. Mem. alumni fund bd. MIT, 1996—; bd. dirs., v.p. Pasadena (Calif.) Symphony Assn., 1985—; mem. Pacific Coun. on Internat. Policy, L.A., 1996—. 1st lt. USAR, 1959-67. Mem. Calif. Assn. for Health Svcs. at Home (legis. com. 1992—), Adaptive Bus. Leaders, 1992—, San Marino (Calif.) City Club (bd. dirs. 1994-96), Japan Am. Soc., 1983—, Delta Tau Delta. Home: 1440 Kensington Rd San Marino CA 91108-1922 Office: Clinishare 20600 Nordhoff St Chatsworth CA 91311-6114

BLONSHINE, SHEENA KAY, medical, surgical nurse; b. Traverse City, Mich., Oct. 15, 1945; d. LeRoy H. and Arta M. (Terry) Blonshine. Diploma, Orange Meml. Sch. Nursing, 1966; BSN cum laude, Boise State U., 1994. RN, Idaho, Fla. Staff nurse Tampa (Fla.) Gen. Hosp., 1966-72; pvt. scrub nurse Blank, Pupello, Bessone, M.D., Tampa, 1972-82; staff nurse St. Luke's Regional Med. Ctr., Boise, 1982-84, asst. head nurse, 1984-86, dir. cardiovasc. surgery, 1986—; Bd. dirs. Heart Inst. St. Luke's Regional Med. Ctr. Nagel scholar Boise State U. Mem. NAFE, Assn. Nurses Execs., Assn. Oper. Rm. Nurses (CNOR nat. cert. bd., ednl. lectr. nat. meeting 1988, bd. dirs. Treasure Valley chpt. 1990, 94,), Sigma Theta Tau (Mu Gamma chpt.). Home: 12184 W Hickory Dr Boise ID 83713-2465 Office: Saint Luke's Regional Med Ctr 190 E Bannock St Boise ID 83712-6241

BLOOD, PEGGY A., college administrator; b. Pine Bluff, Ark., Feb. 8, 1947; d. Roscoe C. and Zelphia (Mayo) B.; m. Lawrence A. Davis, May 31, 1975; children: Lauren A., Pawnee A., Zelana P. BS, U. Ark., Pine Bluff, 1969; MFA, U. Ark., 1971; PhD, Union Inst., Cin., 1986; MA, Holy Names Coll., 1987. Art dir. Office Econ. Opportunity, Altheimer, Ark., 1969; acting. dept. chair, asst. prof. art Univ. Ark., Pine Bluff, 1971-74; activity coord. Good Samaritan Home, Oakland, Calif., 1978-80; art instr. Chabot Community Coll., Hayward, Calif., 1980-81, Solano Community Coll., Suisun, Calif., 1980-90; prin. Palma Ceia Christian Elem. Sch., Hayward, Calif., 1983-84; curriculum chmn., instr. Calif. IMPACT, Oakland, 1985-87; ctr. dir. Chapman U., Fairfield, Calif., 1988—; art cons. Sch. bd. trustee Benicia (Calif.) Unified Sch. Dist., 1989-93; bd. mem. Nat. Inst. Art & Disabilities, Richmond, Calif., 1988-90, Girl Scouts Am., Solano County, Calif., 1995-96. Recipient Ledalle Morehead scholarship, U. Ark., Pine Bluff, 1968; named first Afro-Am. grad. MFA in Art, U. Ark., Fayetteville, 1971, Outstanding Bay Area Artist, Oakland (Calif.) Arts, 1985. Mem. AAUW, Nat. Art Edn. Assn., Coll. Art Assn., Calif. Sch. Bd. Assn., C. of C., LWV (bd. mem. 1980-82), Rotary, Alpha Kappa Alpha (first prize art award 1982-83). Roman Catholic. Office: Chapman U 230 Link Rd Suisun City CA 94585-1672

BLOOM, JOHN W., counselor, educator; b. Cleve., Mar. 15, 1945; s. William Warren and Audrey (Rebscher) B.; m. Susan Beth Staley, Apr. 6, 1968; children: Kristi Ann, Lori Beth. BA, Miami U. Ohio, 1967, MEd, 1967; PhD, Purdue U., 1973. Cert. profl. counselor, Ariz. English tchr. Mad River Jr. H.S., Dayton, Ohio, 1967-69; counselor Spinning Hills Jr. H.S., Dayton, Ohio, 1969-70, Stebbins H.S., Dayton, Ohio, 1970-71; counselor Placement Ctr. Purdue U., West Lafayette, Ind., 1972-73; counselor Hershey Elem. Sch., Lafayette, Ind., 1972-73, Lindbergh H.S., St. Louis, 1973-76; counselor educator Ctrl. Mich. U., Mt. Pleasant, 1976, Iowa State U., Ames, 1976-77, No. Ariz. U., Flagstaff, 1977-96, Butler U., Indpls., 1996—; chair, bd. dirs. Nat. Bd. for Cert. Counselors, Greensboro, N.C., 1995-96; 1st chair counseling Ariz. Bd. Behavioral Health Examiners, Phoenix, 1989. Editor Ariz. Counseling Jou., 1988-89, 91-92. Recipient Outstanding Rsch. award Am. Assn. State Counseling Bds., 1991-92, Profl. Svc. award Ariz. Counselors Assn., 1991. Mem. Am. Counseling Assn., Assn. for Counselor Edn. and Supervision, Am. Sch. Counselors Assn. (bd. dirs. 1989-91), Kiwanis (disting. pres. 1992-93). Methodist.

BLOOM, JULIAN, artist, editor; b. Cleve., May 6, 1933; s. John Bernard and Lillian Judith (Finkel) B.; m. Shirley Ann Harper, Nov. 29, 1954; children: Sandra Layne Walker, Andrea Sue Wells. AA, Cypress Coll., 1972; student, U. LaVerne (Calif.), 1983-86. Lab tech. Harvey Aluminum, Torrance, Calif., 1956-64, foreman, 1964-66; draftsman Northrop Corp., Anaheim, Calif., 1966-67; designer Northrop Aircraft, Anaheim, Calif., 1967-69, facilities engr., 1969-81, design to corp. cost designer, 1982-84; mfg. engring. mgr. Northrop Aircraft, Anaheim, 1984-85, mfg. mgr., 1985-92; artist, owner Realistic Watercolors, Cypress, 1992—. Featured in The Best of Watercolor, 1995. Co-chmn. Cypress (Calif.) Cultural Arts Planning Com., 1993-95; pres. Cypress Art Art League, 1993-96. Served with U.S. Army, 1954-56. Fellow Am. Artists Profl. League (Signature award 1993); mem. Nat. Watercolor Soc. (assoc., editor newsletter 1994-97). Republican. Jewish. Home and Office: 4522 Cathy Ave Cypress CA 90630-4212

BLOOM, MICHAEL EUGENE, consulting executive; b. Pittsburg, Calif., Jan. 16, 1947; s. Benjamin Bernard and Mildred (Haims) B.; m. Deborah Ann Bresler, Aug. 6, 1977; children: Benjamin Solomon Bresler, Miriam Hannah Bresler. BA in Sociology, U. Calif.-Santa Barbara, 1969, postgrad. elec. engring., 1969-71; MBA, Stanford U., 1979. Broadcaster, Sta. KCSB-FM, Santa Barbara, 1964-68, gen. mgr., 1968-69; broadcaster KKIS-AM, Pittsburg, Calif., 1965, KMUZ-FM, Santa Barbara, 1965-67, KTMS-AM-FM, Santa Barbara, 1967-69; mem. tech. staff Gen. Rsch. Corp., Santa Barbara, 1970-72; mgmt. scientist, cons. Sci. Applications, Inc., LaJolla, Calif., 1973-74, Planning and Mgmt. Cons. Corp., Cleve., 1974, Bloom Enterprises, Santa Monica, Calif., 1975-77; project team leader, sr. programmer Bendix Field Engring. Corp., Sunnyvale, Calif., 1977; retail product planner Crocker Nat. Bank, San Francisco, 1978; dir. corp. devel. Am. TV & Communications Corp., Englewood, Colo., 1979-82, dir. new bus. devel., 1983-84, dir. bus. and tech. devel., 1984-85; dir. video svcs. devel. Pacific Bell, San Francisco, 1985-86, dir. product strategy and devel., San Ramon, Calif., 1986-87, dir. market strategy group, 1986-88, dir. customer premises Broadband Mktg. div., 1988-90, dir. customer premises Broadband Applications div., 1990-92, Japan task force, 1988-92; dir. business devel. Kaleida Labs, Inc., 1992-94, co-founder, v.p., gen. mgr. Power TV Inc., 1994-95, founder, pres. Comm. Ventures, 1995—; chmn. comm., bd. U. Calif.-Santa Barbara; v.p., bd. dir. Intercollegiate Broadcasting System, Inc., 1967-70; founder, dir. U. Calif. Radio Network, 1967-69; chmn. systems standards task force on teletext Nat. Cable TV Assn., 1980-81. Adv. coun. Coll. Info. Studies, U. Denver, 1982-85; treas. Camp Arazim, Inc. 1993—; mem. tech. com. The Coll. Prepatory Sch., 1993—. Recipient Pres.'s Merit award U. Calif., 1965. Mem. IEEE, Am. Mktg. Assn. (exec.), Soc. Cable TV Engrs., Nat. Cable TV Assn., U. Calif.-Santa Barbara Alumni Assn. (life), Stanford U. Bus. Sch. Alumni Assn. (program chmn. Rocky Mountain chpt. 1982-85), Stanford U. Alumni Assn. (life)., San Francisco Multi Media Devel. Group, Interactive Svs., Assn., Author: (with L.A. Sibley) Carrier Current System Design, 1967.

BLOOM, ROBERT, language professional educator; b. N.Y.C., May 28, 1930; s. Michael and Fannie (Hecker) B.; m. Gloria Loebenson, Aug. 19, 1953; children: Claudia, Madeline, Jonathan. BA, NYU, 1951; MA, Columbia U., 1952; PhD, U. Mich., 1960. Asst. prof., assoc. prof. English U. Calif. Berkeley, 1960-72, prof. English, 1972—. Author: The Indeterminate World: A Study of the Novels of Joyce Cary, 1962, Anatomies of Egotism: A Reading of the Last Novels of H.G. Wells, 1977; contbr. articles to profl. jours. Lt. j.g. U.S. Coast Guard, 1952-54. Bruern fellow in Am. Civilization U. Leeds, 1963. Mem. Modern Lang. Assn., Phi Beta Kappa. Office: Univ Calif Dept English Berkeley CA 94720

BLOOM, ROSE ELLEN GIEHL, engineer; b. Des Moines, Mar. 20, 1951; d. Francis Richard and Geraldine Eunice (Dietrich) Giehl; m. James William Bloom, May 18, 1974; children: Brian (dec.), Emily, Catherine. BS, Iowa State U., 1972; MS, U. Mich., 1976. Lic. NRC sr. reactor operator. Rsch. technician GM Rsch. Labs, Warren, Mich., 1973-74; reactor operator Ford Nuclear Reactor, Ann Arbor, Mich., 1974-76; assoc. engr. Westinghouse, Pitts., 1976-77; tng. engr. Commonwealth Edison, Chgo., 1980-81; assoc. scientist Stone & Webster Engring., Boston, 1981-82; computer specialist Kankakee (Ill.) C.C., 1983-84; cons. El Sobrante, Calif., 1985—. Bd. dirs. Birthright, El Sobrante, Calif., 1987-94. Mem. St. Anne's #78 Young Ladies Inst., Soc. Physics Students (pres. Ames, Iowa chpt. 1969, v.p. 1970). Republican. Roman Catholic. Home: 3663 May Rd El Sobrante CA 94803-2019

BLOOM, STEPHEN MICHAEL, lawyer, judge; b. San Francisco, June 10, 1948; s. Alan I. and Wilma (Morgan) B.; m. Rebecca J. Nelson, June 19, 1976; children: Benjamin Jacob, Molly Marie, John Robert. Student, Dartmouth Coll., 1966-68; BA in English, Stanford U., 1970; student, Calif. State U., Sacramento, 1973-74; JD, Willamette Coll. Law, 1977. Bar: Oreg. 1977, U.S. Dist. Ct. Oreg. 1979. Adminstrv. asst. Calif. Dept. Edn., Sacramento, 1973-74; atty. Joyce & Harding, Corvallis, Oreg., 1977-78; dep. dist. atty. Umatilla County, Pendleton, Oreg., 1978-79; atty. Morrison & Reynolds, Hermiston, Oreg., 1979-81, Kottkamp & O'Rourke, Pendleton, 1981—; appointed U.S. magistrate, 1988. Bd. dirs. Edn. Svc. Dist., Pendleton, 1982-89. Lt. (j.g.) USN, 1970-72. Mem. ABA, Oreg. Bar Assn., Rotary (pres. 1990-91, bd. dirs. 1991). Office: US Dist Ct PO Box 490 Pendleton OR 97801-0490 also: Kottkamp & O'Rourke 331 SE 2nd St Pendleton OR 97801-2224

BLOOMFIELD, ARTHUR JOHN, music critic, food writer; b. San Francisco, Jan. 3, 1931; s. Arthur L. and Julia (Mayer) B.; m. Anne Buenger, July 14, 1956; children: John, Cecily, Alison. AB, Stanford U., 1951. Music and art critic San Francisco Call-Bull., 1958-59, San Francisco News Call-Bull., 1962-65; co-music and art critic San Francisco Examiner, 1965-79; corr. Mus. Am. mag., 1958-61, 63-64, Opera mag., 1964-91; restaurant critic Focus mag., San Francisco, 1979-83; program note writer Mus. and Arts Records, 1996. Author: The San Francisco Opera, 1923-61, 61, Fifty Years of the San Francisco Opera, 1972, Guide to San Francisco Restaurants, 1975, The San Francisco Opera 1922-78, 1978, Arthur Bloomfield's Restaurant Book, 1987. With AUS, 1953-55. Home: 2229 Webster St San Francisco CA 94115-1820

BLOOMFIELD, MASSE, publishing executive, writer; b. Franklin, N.H., Aug. 20, 1923; s. Harry and Ida Minnie (Steinberg) B.; m. Fay Koenigsberg, Feb. 21, 1954; children: Beth A., Ellen J., Dina A. BS, U. N.H., 1948; MLS, Carnerie Inst. of Tech., Pitts., 1951. Libr. USDA libr., Washington, 1951-53, U.S. Naval Ordnance Test Sta., China Lake, Calif., 1953-56, Atomics Internat., Canoga Park, Calif., 1956-62; head tech. libr. Hughes Aircraft Co., El Segundo, Calif., 1962-85; pres. Masefield Books, Canoga Park, Calif., 1991—. Author: How to Use a Library, 1991, Mankind in Transition, 1993, The Automated Society, 1995, How to Publish Your Own Book for Less Than $575, 1996; contbr. over 100 book revs. to profl. jours., over 30 articles to profl. jours. Lt. Col. USAF, 1943-45, ETO. Recipient Disting. Flying Cross, Air medal with 4 clusters USAF, 1945. Mem. World Future Soc., Nat. Space Soc., The Planetary Soc. Office: Masefield Books 7210 Jordan Ave Ste B-54 Canoga Park CA 91303-1223

BLOOMFIELD, SUZANNE, artist; b. Cleve., June 23, 1934. BSED, Ohio U., 1955; MEd, U. Ariz, 1975. Exhibited in group shows at Cleve. Mus. Art, 1950, U. Ariz., 1968, 72, No. Ariz. U., 1968, Walker Art Inst., N.Y.C., 1976, Ford Found., 1976, Fordham U., 1976, New Sch. Social Rsch., 1976, Ariz. Invitational, Flagstaff, 1980, Ohio U., 1981, U. S.D., 1981, U. Innsbruck, Austria, 1982, Iowa State U., 1983, Idaho State U., 1984, Grove Gallery U. Calif. San Diego, 1985, SUNY, Alfred, 1986, UN World Conf. on Women, Nairobi, Kenya, 1987, Pa. State U., 1987, U. Portland, 1987, Nat. Assn. Women Artists, N.Y.C., 1988, San Francisco Women Artists Gallery, 1990, Nat. Mus. Women in the Arts, Washington, 1990, City of Tucson, 1992-94, Ariz. State Capitol, 1994, Jain Marunouchi Gallery, N.Y.C., 1995; executed mural U. Ariz. Dept. Counseling & Guidance, 1975. Mailing Address: 1830 E Broadway Blvd Tucson AZ 85719

BLOOMQUIST, RODNEY GORDON, geologist; b. Aberdeen, Wash., Feb. 3, 1943; s. Verner A. and Margaret E. (Olson) B.; m. Linda L. Lee, Dec. 19, 1964 (div. July 1968); m. Bente Brisson Jørgensen, Aug. 4, 1977; 1 child, Kira Brisson. BS in Geology, Portland State U., 1966; MS in Geology, U. Stockholm, 1970, PhD in Geochemistry, 1977. Rschr. U. Stockholm, 1974-77; asst. prof. Oreg. Inst. Tech., Klamath Falls, 1978-80; geologist Wash. State Energy Office, Olympia, 1980-96, sr. scientist, 1995; sr. scientist Wash. State U., Olympia, 1996—; vis. prof. Internat. Sch. Geothermics, Pisa, Italy, 1990—; adj. prof. Evergreen State Coll., Olympia, 1996—; cons. U.S. Dept. Energy, Washignton, 1990, Govt. of Can., 1984, Aesa-Stal Geoenergy, Lund, Sweden, 1985-86, City and County of San Francisco, 1988-89, Lake County, Calif., 1992, San Francisco State U., 1993, Internat. Geoenergy Consortium, Springfield, Mo., 1996—. Author: Regulatory Guide to Geothermics, 1991; mem. editl. bd. Geothermics, 1985-88; also numerous books and articles. Smitts fellow, Sweden, 1974, Royal Rsch. fellow, Sweden, 1975-77; rsch. grantee U. Stockholm, 1975-77. Mem. Geothermal Resources Coun. (bd. dirs. 1985-92, pres. 1989, pres. Pacific N.W. sect. 1982-85), Internat. Dist. Energy Assn. (western sect. bd. dirs. 1990—, bd. dirs. 1994—), Internat. Geothermal Assn. (bd. dirs. 1988-92, 95—), N.Am. Dist. Heating and Cooling Inst. (bd. dirs. 1986-88), Am. Blade Smith Soc. (bd. dirs. 1989—). Democrat. Lutheran. Office: Wash State Energy Office 925 Plum St SE Olympia WA 98501-1529

BLOUIN, SCOTT E., engineering company executive; b. 1943. BS, MS, MIT, 1966. Rsch. engr. USA CRREL, Hanover, N.H., 1971-79; with CSI Inc., South Royalton, Vt., 1979-80; v.p. Applied Rsch. Assoc. Inc., Albuquerque, 1980—. With USAF, 1967-71. Office: Applied Rsch Assoc Inc 4300 San Mateo Blvd NE Albuquerque NM 87110-1229*

BLOUKE, MILTON BAKER, lawyer; b. Chgo., Jan. 18, 1946; s. Pierre and Jessie (Scott) B.; m. Christine Hunt, Nov. 25, 1971; children: Scott M., Katie M. BS, U. Wash., 1970; JD, Lewis and Clark Law Sch., 1974; LLM in Taxation, Boston U., 1978. Bar: Oreg. 1974, U.S. Tax Ct. Atty. Dist. Counsel IRS, Boston, 1974-78, San Francisco, 1978-82; staff atty. Regional Counsel IRS, San Francisco, 1982-84; atty. Dist. Counsel IRS, San Jose, Calif., 1984-86; asst. dist. counsel Dist. Counsel IRS, San Jose, 1986-88, Seattle, 1988-91; atty. Dist. Counsel IRS, Las Vegas, Nev., 1991—. 1st lt. U.S. Army, 1966-69. Mem. ABA, Oreg. Bar Assn. Home: 2026 Grafton Ave Henderson NV 89014-0625 Office: Dist Counsel IRS 4750 W Oakey Blvd Las Vegas NV 89102-1500

BLOUNT, KERRY ANDREW, defense analyst; b. Lubbock, Tex., Sept. 1, 1949; s. Andrew William Blount and Evelyn Ruth (Caldwell) Anderson; m. Barbara Jean Massey, May 21, 1971; children: Tanis Andra, Zeitel Elizabeth. BA in Internat. Studies, West Tex. State U., 1971; MA in Russian Area Studies, Georgetown U., 1973; grad. in Soviet studies, U.S. Army Russian Inst., Garmisch, Germany, 1984. Commd. 2d lt. U.S. Army, 1971, advanced through grades to maj., 1982; comdr. Counterintelligence Spl. Ops., Frankfurt, Germany, 1975-77; intelligence analyst Intelligence Ctr. Pacific, Honolulu, 1978-81; diplomatic courier U.S. Dept. State, Helsinki, Finland, 1983; intelligence instr. Brit. Intelligence Ctr., Ashford, Eng., 1984-86; sr. intelligence analyst Army Intelligence and Threat Analysis Ctr., Washington, 1986-89; resigned U.S. Army, 1989; sr. def. analyst Sci. Applications Internat. Corp., Denver, 1989-94, mgr. C2 warfare program, 1994-97. Contbr. articles to profl. jours. Mem. bd. elders S.E. Ch. of Christ, Aurora, Colo., 1995-97. Mem. Armed Forces Comm. and Electronics Assn., Assn. of U.S. Army.

BLOW, JOHN NEEDHAM, social services educator; b. Whitby, Ont., Can., Nov. 30, 1905; came to U.S., 1952; s. Ezekiel Richard and Edith May (Correll) B.; m. Emma Jane White, June 6, 1942; children: Carol Anne, Brenda Jane, Mary Roberta, Elizabeth Diane. BA, McMaster U., 1939; MSW, U. Toronto, Ont., 1948. Cert. elem. tchr., Toronto, community colls. instr., Calif. Exec. sec. Community Welfare Planning Council Ont., Toronto, 1948-52; exec. v.p. Motel Corp., Las Vegas, Nev., 1952-54; exec. dir. Nev. div. Am. Cancer Soc., 1954-56, assoc. exec. dir. Los Angeles County br., 1956-70; program assoc. Am. Heart Assn., Los Angeles, 1970-74; project dir., coordinator sr. community service employment program Orange County, Calif., 1974-75; instr. community service programs for adults North Orange County Community Coll. Dist. and Coastline Coll., 1976-79, Mira Costa and Palomar Community Colls., 1979-85. Author: (poems) New Frontiers, 1984. Vol. Arthritis Found.; asst. commr. tng. Boy Scouts Can., Ottawa, 1934-41; Chaplain Tri-City Coun. Navy League. Wing comdr. RCAF, 1941-46. Recipient Commendation for Outstanding Svc. to Srs., Orange County Sr. Citizens Coun., 1977, Gold award Orange County United Way, 1977, Golden Poet award, 1991, World of Poetry, 1989, 90. Mem. Nat. Assn. Social Workers, Acad. Cert. Social Workers, San Luis Rey Officers Club, Valley Sr. Ctr., North County Concert Assn., So. Calif. McMaster U. Alumni Assn. (past pres., inducted Alumni Gallery 1986), Can. Soc. Los Angeles (charter, past pres.), U. Toronto Alumni Assn. (exec. com., past pres. So. Calif. br.). Presbyterian. Lodge: Elks. Home: 3725 Sesame Way Oceanside CA 92057-8328

BLOWER, JOHN GREGORY, special education educator; b. Orange, Calif., Mar. 18, 1952; s. James Girard and Juanita Mae (Pierce) B.; 1 child, Becky Renee. BS in Psychology, Pacific Christian, 1975; MEd in Spl. Edn., Idaho State U., 1982. Assoc. minister edn. 1st Christian Ch., Santa Ana, Calif., 1972-75; spl. edn. tchr. Fremont County Schs., St. Anthony, Idaho, 1977—; vice chmn., con. People for Spl. People, St. Anthony, 1986—. Program coord. Idaho Spl. Olympics, St. Anthony, 1978—, bd. dirs., Boise, 1982-88, chmn. bd. dirs., Boise, 1987-88. Mem. Coun. for Exceptional Children, Nat. Edn. Assn. Office: South Fremont High Sch 550 N 1st W Saint Anthony ID 83445-1151

BLOYD, STEPHEN ROY, environmental manager, educator, consultant; b. Alameda, Calif., Aug. 17, 1953; s. William Allen and Alice Louella (Scott) B. Grad. high sch., Reedley, Calif., 1971. Cert. environ. mgr., Nev.; registered hazardous substances specialist. Reagent tech. Tenneco Corp., Gold Hill, Nev., 1982; environ. tech. Pierson Environ. Drilling, Modesto, Calif., 1982-84; pres. Bloyd and Assocs., Dayton, Nev., 1986—. Author: Hazardous Waste Site Operations for General Site Workers, 1992; editor: (newsletter) Pumper, 1991. Firefighter Dayton Vol. Fire Dept., 1975, capt., 1976-78, chief, 1978-83, tng. officer, 1984-96; mem. Silver City (Nev.) Fire Dept., 1996—; asst. prof. Dodd/Beals Fire Protection Tng. Acad. U. Nev., Reno, 1990-96; instr. chemistry hazardous materials Nat. Fire Acad., Emmitsburg, Md., 1989—, instr. hazardous materials incident mgmt., 1996—; mem. bylaw com. Dayton Regional Adv. Coun., 1989. Named Firefighter of Yr., City of Dayton, 1992. Mem. NRA, Nat. Environ. Tng. Assn., Nat. Environ. Health Assn., Nev. State Firemen's Assn. (1st v.p. 1992-93, 2d v.p. 1991-92, pres. 1993-94, chmn. hazardous materials com. 1987-93, legis. com. 1991, bylaws com. 1986), Nev. Fire Chief's Assn., Internat. Platform Assn., Soc. Nat. Fire Acad. Instrs. Libertarian. Office: PO Box 113 Silver City NV 89428-0113

BLUE, JAMES GUTHRIE, veterinarian; b. Flora, Ind., Oct. 22, 1920; s. Van C. and Florence A. (Guthrie) B. AB, Wabash Coll., 1943; postgrad., Northwestern U., 1943; DVM, Ohio State U., 1950; AA in Labor Negotiation/Rels., L.A. Trade Tech. Coll., 1989. Pvt. practice cons., 1950-80; field vet. City of L.A., 1980—, acting chief vets., 1992, chief vets., 1992-95; rsch. project cons. Calif. State U. Northridge, 1980-87; pro med. svcs. sec.-negtiator AFSCME, L.A., 1983—; sec. Ariz. Bd. Vet. Med. Examiners, 1973-79. Mem. wellness com. Drug Free Work Place, 1989-97. Lt. comdr. USN, 1943-46. Mem. AMVA, N.Y. Acad. Scis., Am. Soc. Lib. Animal Practitioners, L.A. World Affairs Coun., San Diego Vet. Med. Assn., So. Ariz. Vet. Med. Assn., Calif. Vet. Med. Assn. (environ. and pub. health ecology com. 1986-97, state ethics com. 1986—, wellness com. 1990—), So. Calif. Vet. Med. Assn. (coun. mem., polit. action com., continuing edn. com. 1980—), Am. Legion, Navy League, Shriners, Mil. Order World War, U.S. Naval Rsch. Assn., Navy League Coun. Tucson. Democrat. Episcopalian. Home: 2121 E 2nd St Tucson AZ 85719-4928

BLUESTONE, STUART MICHAEL, lawyer; b. Pitts., Oct. 17, 1946; s. Max L. and Charlotte G. (Goldfarb) B.; m. Judith E. Naumburg, May 24, 1987; children: Tahlia Jane, Darren Michael. BA, Trinity Coll., 1968; MPA, Harvard U., 1988; JD, Georgetown U., 1972. Bar: D.C. 1973, Pa. 1975, U.S. Supreme Ct. 1978, N.Mex. 1984. Assoc. Berlin, Roisman & Kessler, Washington, 1972-74; advisor, litigator Fed. Energy Adminstrn., Washington, 1974-76; assoc. Miller & Chevalier, Washington, 1978-83, asst. mng. ptnr., 1983-84; dir. consumer protection and econ. crimes divsn. N.Mex. Atty. Gen.'s Office, Santa Fe, 1984-87; chief counsel judiciary com. N.Mex. Ho. of Reps., Santa Fe, 1987; dep. dir. N.Mex. Legis. Coun. Svc., Santa Fe, 1988—. Bd. dirs. No. N.Mex. Legal Svcs., 1995—; mem. code of profl. conduct com. N.Mex. Supreme Ct., 1996—, v.p., 1996—. With USCGR, 1968-74. Mem. N.Mex. Bar Assn. (chmn. bd. pub. law sect. 1992-93, Outstanding Contbn. award 1992)), Pi Gamma Mu, Phi Psi. Jewish. Office: Legis Coun Svc 311 State Capitol Santa Fe NM 87503

BLUM, ARTHUR MARVIN, academic administrator; b. Bklyn., Aug. 29, 1934; s. Albert R. and Lucy Blum; m. Joanne L. Finkelor, June 14, 1959; children: Sherry R., Laurie J., Katie J. BA in Psychology, U. Pa., 1956; MS in Speech Pathology, U. Pitts., 1958. Lic. speech pathologist, Calif. Grad. asst. dept. speech and theatre arts U. Pitts., 1956-58, clin. supr., instr. dept. speech and theatre arts, 1958-59; assoc. prof. psychology Point Park Coll., 1960-73; sec. of coll., dir. admissions Point Park Coll., Pitts., 1960-65, exec. v.p., sec. of coll., 1965-67, pres., 1967-73; gen. mgr., CEO San Francisco Ballet Assn., 1973-74; cons. Development, 1975-77; pres. San Francisco Sch. of Arts, San Anselmo, Calif., 1976-78; pres., bd. dirs. Marin Civic Ballet Assn., San Rafael, Calif., 1976-77; pres. New England Summer Programs in Arts, Pittsfield, Mass., 1978-83; speech pathologist, pvt. cons. San Anselmo, Calif., 1983-84; v.p. Columbia Pacific U., San Rafael, Calif., 1984—; lectr. Berkshire C.C., Pittsfield, 1979-80, San Francisco State U., 1983-84; cons. Bur. Measurement and Guidance, Carnegie Mellon U., 1959; assoc. dir. Camp Cascade, Eagle Bay, N.Y., 1956-59; pres. New Eng. Summer Programs in the Arts; chmn. bd. dirs., CEO Pitts. Playhouse; cons. on ednl. facility and theatre design Gismondi and Arnold, Architects, White Plains, N.Y.; cons., mem. evalaution teams Mid. State Assn. Colls. and Univs.; author/participant assembly on univ. goals and governance AAAS. V.p. Am. Wind Symphony Orch., 1968-73; past mem. sponsoring com. Allegheny Conf. on Cmty. Devel.; past bd. dirs. Waterways Wind Orch. of N.Y., C. of C. of Greater Pitts., Mt. Lebanon Civic League, Pa. Jr. Acad. Sci., Pitts. Chamber Music Soc., Pitts. Coun. on Higher Edn., Pitts. Symphony Soc.; incorporator, pres. bd. trustees San Francisco Sch. of Arts; active Marin Civic Ballet Assn. Mem. NEA, Am. Cleft Palate Assn., Am. Speech and Hearing Assn., Am. Acad. Polit. and Social Scis., Calif. Speech and Hearing Assn., Pa. Acad. Sci., Pa. Speech and Hearing Assn., Speech Assn. Am., Urban League Pitts., World Affairs Coun. Pitts., Young Pres.'s Orgn., Pa. Sports Hall of Fame, Scottish Rite. Home: 1090 Butterfield Rd San Anselmo CA 94960-1148 Office: Columbia Pacific U 1415 3rd St San Rafael CA 94901-2860

BLUM, DEBORAH, reporter. Sr. writer The Sacramento (Calif.) Bee; sci. writer in residence U. Wis., Madison, 1993. Author: The Monkey Wars, 1994. Recipient Pulitzer Prize for beat reporting, 1992. Mem. Nat. Assn. Sci. Writers (bd. dirs.), Sigma Xi. Office: Sacramento Bee 2100 Q St Sacramento CA 95816-0779

BLUM, JOAN KURLEY, fundraising executive; b. Palm Beach, Fla., July 27, 1926; d. Nenad Daniel and Eva (Milos) Kurley; m. Robert C. Blum, Apr. 15, 1967; children: Christopher Alexander, Martha Jane, Louisa Joan, Paul Helmuth, Sherifa. BA, U. Wash., 1948. Cert. fund raising exec. U.S. dir. Inst. Mediterranean Studies, Berkeley, Calif., 1962-65; devel. officer U. Calif. at Berkeley, 1965-67; pres. Blum Assocs., Fund-Raising Cons., San Anselmo, Calif., 1967-92, The Blums of San Francisco, 1992—; mem. faculty U. Calif. Extension, Inst. Fund Raising, SW Inst. Fund-Raising U. Tex., U. San Francisco, U.K. Vol. Movement Group, London, Australasian Inst. Fund Raising. Contbr. numerous articles to profl. jours. Recipient Golden Addy award Am. Advt. Fedn.; Silver Mailbox award Direct Mail Mktg. Assn., Best Ann. Giving Time-Life award, others; decorated commdr. Sovereign Order St. Stanislas. Mem. Nat. Soc. Fund-Raising Execs. (dir.), Nat. Assn. of Hosp. Devel., Women Emerging., Rotary (San Francisco), Fund Raising Inst. (Australia), Tahoe Yacht Club. Office: 202 Evergreen Dr Kentfield CA 94904-2708 also: 73 Albert Ave Ste 8, Chatswood Sydney NSW 2067, Australia

BLUM, JOANNE LEE, development executive, educator; b. Pitts., Aug. 30, 1932; d. L. Herbert and Dorothy Ruth (Cimberg) Finkelhor; m. Arthur Marvin Blum, June 14, 1959; children—Sherry Ruth Blum-Becker, Laurie Jill Blum Glodowski, Katie Jo Blum Berryhill. Student U. Chgo., 1947-49, Chatham Coll., Pitts., 1949-51; B.A., Brandeis U., 1953; M.Ed., Harvard U., 1954; postgrad. U. Pitts., 1963-65. Cert. fundraising exec. Tchr., Mt. Diablo

Unifed Sch. Dist., Walnut Creek, Calif., 1954-55; asst. dir. Fgn. Policy Assn. Pitts. (now World Affairs Council Pitts.), 1955-57, assoc. dir., 1957-61, assoc. producer Focus on World Affairs, 1959-61; pres. Pitts. Internat. Travel, 1961-62; founder, chmn. dept. edn. Point Park Coll., Pitts., 1962-69, dir. preschool Lab. Program, 1964-69, dir. intermediate level Lab. Sch., 1972-73; co-founder, dean San Francisco Sch. Arts, San Anselmo, Calif., 1976-78; co-owner, dir. Camps Wahconah and Potomac and New Eng. Summer Programs in the Arts, Pittsfield, Mass., 1978-82; devel. and membership coordinator World Affairs Council of No. Calif., San Francisco, 1983-85; pvt. practice devel. cons., Calif., 1986-89; dir. devel. Project SEED, Berkeley, Calif., 1989—; cons. The Lighthouse for the Blind and Visually Impaired, San Francisco, Goodwill Industries Devel. Office, Internat. Visitors Ctr., 1985, Devel. Médecins du Monde, Paris; co-founder Pitts. Area Preschool Assn., 1965; lectr. Headstart program Carnegie-Mellon U., Pitts., 1965. Founding dir. Pitts. Ballet Theatre, 1965; cons. arts program for handicapped children Renaissance Ctr. for Arts, Mt. Lebanon, Pa., 1967. Mem. Am. Edn. Rsch. Assn., Edn. Excellence Network, Nat. Soc. Fund Raising Execs. (sec. 1987), Devel. Execs. Roundtable (v.p. 1988, pres. 1989), Rotary. Jewish.

BLUMBERG, NATHAN(IEL) BERNARD, journalist, educator, writer and publisher; b. Denver, Apr. 8, 1922; s. Abraham Moses and Jeannette Blumberg; m. Lynne Stout, June 1946 (div. Feb. 1970); children: Janet Leslie, Jenifer Lyn, Josephine Laura; m. Barbara Farquhar, July 1973. B.A., U. Colo., 1947, M.A., 1948; D.Phil. (Rhodes scholar), Oxford (Eng.) U., 1950. Reporter Denver Post, 1947-48; assoc. editor Lincoln (Nebr.) Star, 1950-53; asst. to editor Ashland (Nebr.) Gazette, 1954-55; asst. city editor Washington Post and Times Herald, 1956; from asst. prof. to assoc. prof. journalism U. Nebr., 1950-55; asso. prof. journalism Mich. State U., 1955-56; dean, prof. Sch. Journalism, U. Mont., 1956-68, prof. journalism, 1968-78, prof. emeritus, 1978—; pub. Wood FIRE Ashes Press, 1981—; vis. prof. Pa. State U., 1964, Northwestern U., 1966-67, U. Calif., Berkeley, 1970; Dept. State specialist in Thailand, 1961, in Trinidad, Guyana, Surinam and Jamaica, 1964. Author: One-Party Press?, 1954; The Afternoon of March 30: A Contemporary Historical Novel, 1984, also articles in mags. and jours.; co-editor: A Century of Montana Journalism, 1971; editor: The Mansfield Lectures in International Relations, Vols. I and II, 1979; founder: Mont. Journalism Rev, 1958—; editor, pub. Treasure State Rev., 1991—. Served with arty. U.S. Army, 1943-46. Bronze Star medal. Mem. Assn. Am. Rhodes Scholars, Brasenose Soc., Kappa Tau Alpha (nat. pres. 1969-70). Home: PO Box 99 Bigfork MT 59911-0099

BLUMBERG, ROBERT LEE, manufacturing executive; b. Bklyn., Apr. 1, 1942; s. William T. and Hazel Blumberg; m. Joyce T. Yavner, Mar. 29, 1969; children: Matthew Y., Michael L. BS, MIT, 1964, MS, 1965; MBA, Harvard U., 1967. Assoc. J.H. Whitney & Co., N.Y.C., 1970-72; ptnr. Idanta Ptnrs., N.Y.C. and San Diego, 1972-80; pres., chief exec. Spectragraphics Corp., San Diego, 1981—; mem. vis. com. MIT Mech. Engring. Dept., Cambridge, 1986-92; mem. corp. devel. com. MIT, 1993—; regional chmn. MIT Ednl. Coun., San Diego, 1978-88; chmn. MIT Enterprise Forum San Diego, 1989-92, 94—, bd. dirs. 1990—; trustee Francis W. Parker Sch., 1984-89; bd. dirs. Pacific Comm. Sci., Inc., San Diego, 1987-93; bd. dirs. Cong. Beth Israel, 1987-96. Served to lt. U.S. Army, 1967-69. Republican. Jewish. Office: Spectragraphics Corp 9877 Waples St San Diego CA 92121-2954

BLUME, JAMES BERYL, financial advisor; b. N.Y.C., Apr. 9, 1941; s. Philip Franklin Blume and Mary Kirschman Asch; m. Kathryn Weil Frank, Jan. 20, 1984; 1 child, Zachary Thomas Philip. BA, Williams Coll., Williamstown, Mass., 1963; MBA, Harvard U., Boston, 1966; M. Psychology, The Wright Inst., Berkeley, Calif., 1983, PhD in Psychology, 1986. Security analyst Faulkner, Dawkins & Sullivan, N.Y.C., 1966-68; sr. v.p. Faulkner, Dawkins & Sullivan Securities, Inc., N.Y.C., 1968-73; ptnr. Omega Properties, N.Y.C., 1973-74; exec.v.p. Arthur M. Fischer, Inc., N.Y.C., 1974-77; psychotherapist in pvt. practice Berkeley, 1985-91, fin. cons., 1987—; pres. James B. Blume, Inc., fin. counsel and mgmt., Berkeley, 1993-94; bd. dirs. RHL/Golden State Pub. San Francisco, 1991-92. Bd. dirs. ACLU No. Calif., San Francisco, 1988-94, treas., 1993-94; bd. dirs. East Bay Clinic for Psychotherapy, Oakland, Calif., 1981-85, Marin Psychotherapy Inst., Mill Valley, Calif., 1986-87; trustee The Wright Inst., 1981-85. Mem. Berkeley Tennis Club, Williams Club (bd. govs. 1968-72). Democrat. Jewish. Office: 1708 Shattuck Ave Berkeley CA 94709-1700

BLUMENAUER, EARL, congressman; b. Portland, Oreg., Aug. 16, 1949. BA, Lewis and Clark Coll., 1970, JD, 1976. Asst. to pres. Portland State U., 1971-73; mem. Oreg. Ho. of Reps., 1973-79; county commr. Multnomah County, Portland, 1979-87; mem. Portland City Coun., 1987-96; U.S. senator from Oreg., 1996—; U.S. congressman and mem. transp. com. Oreg., 1991—; mem. early childhood and oversight subcoms. Econ. and Ednl. Opportunities Com. Office: 516 SE Morrison Ste 250 Portland OR 97214

BLUMENKRANZ, MARK SCOTT, surgeon, researcher, educator; b. N.Y.C., Oct. 23, 1950; s. Edward and Helene (Cymberg) B.; m. Recia Kott, June 10, 1975. AB, Brown U., 1972, MD, 1975, MMS, 1976; postgrad., Stanford U., 1975-79, U. Miami, 1979-80. Intern, resident Stanford (Calif.) U. Med. Ctr., 1975-79; fellow Bascom Palmer Eye Inst. U. Miami, Fla., 1979-80; asst. prof. Bascom Palmer Eye Inst., Miami, 1980-85; assoc. prof. Wayne State U., Detroit, 1985-92; clin. prof. Stanford U., 1992—, dir. of retina, 1992—, dir. clin. programs, chief ophthalmology Stanford Health Svcs.; chmn. sci. adv. bd. Escalon Ophthalmics, 1990—; assoc. examiner Am. Bd. Ophthalmology; bd. dirs. OIS, Midlabs. Mem. editl. bd. Ophthalmology, Retina, Vitreoretinal Tech., Graefes Archives; contbr. chpts. to books and articles to profl. jours.; inventor ophthalmic devices. Mem. bd. overseers Brown U. Sch. Medicine. Recipient Visual Scis. medal in Visual Scis. Rosenthal Found., 1990, Heed award Heed Found., 1988, Manpower award Rsch. to Prevent Blindness. Mem. Am. Acad. Ophthalmology (mem. preferred practice com., others), Macula Soc. (chmn. rsch. com. 1986-90), Assn. Rsch. in Vision and Ophthalmology (chmn. retina sect. 1987-90), Retina Soc. (mem. membership com.), Maimonodes Soc. (mem. exec. com.). Office: Stanford Univ Dept Ophthalmology Boswell A-157 Stanford CA 94305 Also: 1225 Crane St Menlo Park CA 94025-4253

BLUMENTHAL, RICHARD CARY, construction executive, consultant; b. Bklyn., Dec. 18, 1951; s. Mervin Harold and Barbara June (Engelson) B.; m. Ginnilyn Hawkins; children: Aaron Joseph, Meredith Taylor. BS, U. N.H., 1974. Planner RECON Assocs., Hamilton, Mont., 1976-77; project mgr. Grizzly Mfg., Hamilton, 1977-78; profl. carpenter Ed Brown Constrn., Bainbridge Island, Wash., 1978-79; pres. Richard Blumenthal Constrn., Inc., Bainbridge Island, 1979—; instr. Bainbridge Island Community Sch., 1993—. Mem. pk. bd. coun. City of Winslow, 1989-90; bd. dirs. Bainbridge Island Pub. Libr., 1992—; mem. Land Use Profls. Forum, 1992—; mem. advisory com. Bainbridge Band Park & Rec. Gymnastics Com., 1993—. Mem. Ind. Bus. Assn., C. of C. Home: 330 Nicholson Pl NW Bainbridge Island WA 98110-1702 Office: 10140 NE High School Rd Bainbridge Island WA 98110-1913

BLUMER, HARRY MAYNARD, architect; b. Stillwater, Okla., Aug. 27, 1930; s. Harry H. and Nona A. (Ftizpatrick) B.; m. C. Sue Linebaugh, Sept. 2, 1952; children: Eric W., Laura B., Martha L. BArch, Okla. State U., 1953; BS in Bus., Ariz. State U., 1976. Designer, draftsman Norman Byrd Architect, Oklahoma City, Okla., 1952, Overend & Boucher Architects, Wichita, Kans., 1953-54; archtl. designer, draftsman Louis G. Hesselden Architect, Albuquerque, 1956; project designer, planner, constrn. & contract adminstr. Flatow, Moore, Bryan & Fairburn Architects, Albuquerque, 1956-61; regional architect U.S. Forest Svc., Albuquerque, 1961-62; v.p. prodn. Guirey, Srnka, Arnold & Sprinkle, Phoenix, 1962-82, Guirey, Srnka, Arnold & Sprinkle Architects, Phoenix, 1962-82; cons., architect pvt. practice, Paradise Valley, Ariz., 1982—; lectr. architecture Ariz. State U., Tempe, 1968-69; speaker in field. Contbr. articles to profl. publs. Bd. dirs., camping com., camp master plan design Maricopa County Coun. Campfire Girls, 1962-69; pres. N.Mex. Cactus and Succulent Soc., 1959-60; sec. Advancement Mgmt., Phoenix, 1972-73, dir., 1971-72; bd. govs. Amateur Athletic Union U.S., 1972-75, chmn. nat. conv. registration com., 1975; v.p. Ariz. Assn. Bd. MGrs., 1972-73, pres., 1973; treas. Pop Warner Football Assn., 1975; pres. parents club Scottsdale YMCA Judo Club, 1970-80. 1st lt. U.S. Army, 1954-56. Recipient Edn. Commendation award Constrn. Specifications Inst., 1980. Fellow AIA, Constrn. Specification Inst.; mem. ASTM. Office: 8517 N 49th St Paradise Valley AZ 85253-2002*

BLUMHARDT, JON HOWARD, college official; b. Ft. Benning, Ga., Oct. 3, 1951; s. Howard Jerome and Joan (Tisdal) B.; m. Lisette Susan Vinet, Jan. 26, 1973; children: Matthew, Malia, Mark. BA in History, U. Hawaii, 1973, MA in Sociology, 1978, MEd, 1979, postgrad.; EdS, U Va., 1984. Media specialist U.S. Army JAG Sch., Charlottesville, Va., 1980-85; adminstr. officer OPM Fed. Exec. Inst., Charlottesville, 1985-86; chief resources mgmt. IRS Honolulu Dist., 1986-87; dir. ednl. media svcs. Honolulu C.C., 1987—. Advisor, Explorer Post 311, Aloha coun. Boy Scouts Am., 1996. Named one of Outstanding Young Men in Am., 1989, Eagle Scout, 1965; recipient Mahalo award Mayor of Honolulu, 1978, Cert. of Merit Aloha Coun. Boy Scouts Am., 1978, Scoutmaster award of Merit Nat. Eagle Scout Assn., 1990. Mem. DAV (life), German Benevolent Soc. (Honolulu), 4th degree KC Coun. 6307, Am. Legion, U. Va. Alumni Assn. (life), Pan Pacific Distance Learning Assn. (pres. 1996), Am. Legion (post 0009). Republican. Roman Catholic. Home: 1140 Lauloa St Kailua HI 96734-4065 Office: Honolulu Community Coll 874 Dillingham Blvd Honolulu HI 96817-4505

BLUMMER, KATHLEEN ANN, counselor; b. Iowa Falls, Iowa, Apr. 17, 1945; d. Arthur G. and Julia C. (Ericson) Thorsbakken; m. Terry L. Blummer, Feb. 13, 1971 (dec. 1980); 1 child, Emily Erica. AA, Ellsworth Coll., Iowa Falls, 1965; BA, U. Iowa, 1967; postgrad., Northeastern Ill. U., 1969-70, U. N.Mex., 1980—; MA, Western N.Mex. U., 1973. Asst. buyer Marshall Field & Co., Chgo., 1967-68; social worker Cook County Dept. Pub. Aid, Chgo., 1968-69; tchr. Chgo. Pub. Schs., 1968-69; student fin. aid counselor Western N.Mex. U., Silver City, 1971-72; family social worker, counselor Southwestern N.Mex. Svcs. to Handicapped Children and Adults, Silver City, 1972-74; career edn. program specialist Galluo McKinley County (N.Mex.) Schs., 1974-76; dir. summer sch. Loving (N.Mex.) Mcpl. Schs., 1977; counselor, dept. chmn. Carlsbad (N.Mex.) Pub. Schs., 1977-82; counselor Albuquerque Pub. Schs., 1982—. Mem. AAUW (topic chmn. Carlsbad chpt., v.p. Albuquerque chpt.), N.Mex. Personnel and Guidance Assn., Theos Club, Highpoint Swim and Racquet Club (Albuquerque), Elks. Democrat. Lutheran.

BLUS, LAWRENCE JOHN, biologist; b. Tilden, Ill., Dec. 23, 1933; s. Frank and Anna (Lentkis) B.; m. Donna Darlene Weil, Apr. 25, 1964; children: Denise, Emily, Daniel. BS, So. Ill. U., 1959, MA, 1963. Rsch. biologist Nebr. Game Commn., Thedford, 1961-66; biologist wildlife rsch. U.S. Fish and Wildlife Svc., Laurel, Md., 1966-77, Corvallis, Oreg., 1977-93; biologist wildlife rsch. Nat. Biol. Svc., Corvallis, 1993—. Contbr. chpts. in books and articles to profl. jours. Pres. Aid Assn. for Luths., Corvallis, 1988—. With U.S. Army, 1953-55. Mem. Am. Ornithologists Union, Soc. Environ. Toxicology and Chemistry, Wildlife Soc. (bd. dirs. ctrl. sect. 1963-64), Toastmasters Beltsville Md. (v.p. 1975-77, Disting. Svc. award 1977), Sigma Xi. Democrat. Home: 1845 NW Division Pl Corvallis OR 97330-2108 Office: Nat Biological Svc 3080 SE Clearwater Dr Corvallis OR 97333-2100

BLUTH, JOHN FREDERICK, archivist, oral historian; b. Ogden, Utah, Mar. 18, 1944; s. Weyman John and Thelma Lavon Bluth; m. Patricia Harmer, June 1, 1971; 1 child, Sarah. BS, Weber State Coll., Ogden, 1966; MA, Brigham Young U., 1968, PhD, 1978. Cert. archivist. Oral historian Charles Redd Ctr., Provo, Utah, 1973-78; manuscript curator Brigham Young U., Provo, 1979-86; dir. Dalton (Pa.) Libr., 1988-91; archivist Jet Propulsion Lab., Pasadena, Calif., 1991—; cons. Bur. Land Mgmt., Salt Lake City, 1975-81, Pa. Hist. Commn., Harrisburg, 1986-91; oral historian Kaiser-Permanente, Pasadena, 1994—. Pres. Project: Art, Scranton, Pa., 1990-91. A.W. Mellon fellow Bentley Libr. U. Mich., 1984, NDEA Title IV fellow, 1968-72. Mem. S.W. Oral History Assn. Mem. LDS Ch. Home: 1367 Brookhaven Ave Camarillo CA 93010 Office: Jet Propulsion Lab MS512-110 4800 Oak Grove Dr Pasadena CA 91109-8099

BOADO, RUBEN JOSE, biochemist; b. Buenos Aires, Argentina, Feb. 8, 1955; came to U.S., 1985; s. Osvaldo Ruben and Lucia B.; m. Adriana Graciela Swiecicki, Jan. 11, 1980; children: Augusto Ruben, Lucrecia Adriana. MS, U. Buenos Aires, 1979, Diploma in Biochemistry, 1980, PhD, 1982. Rsch. fellow endocrinology Nat. Coun. Scientific Rsch., Buenos Aires, 1979-81, postdoctoral rsch. fellow in endocrinology, 1981-83, established investigator, 1983-89; internat. fellow UCLA Sch. Medicine, 1985-88, asst. rsch. endocrinologist, 1988-91, asst. prof. medicine, 1991-97, assoc. prof. medicine, 1997—. Author numerous scientific publs. Recipient Best Scientific Paper award Internat. Assn. Radiopharmacology, Chgo., 1981, Cross-Town Endocrine Soc., L.A., 1988. Mem. AAAS, European Neurosci. Assn., Argentine Soc. Clin. Rsch., Am. Thyroid Assn. (travel award 1987), Endocrine Soc. (travel award 1984), Brain Rsch. Inst., Soc. Neurosci. Office: UCLA Dept Medicine/Endocrin Rsch Labs C-Lot Rm 104 Los Angeles CA 90024-1682

BOARDMAN, DAVID, newspaper editor; m. Barbara Winslow; children: Emily, Madeline. BS in Journalism, Northwestern U., 1979; M in Comm., U. Wash., 1983. Copy editor Football Weekly, Chgo., 1977-79; reporter Anacortes (Wash.) American, 1979-80, Skagit Valley Herald, Mt. Vernon, Wash., 1980-81; reporter, copy editor The News Tribune, Tacoma, 1981-83; copy editor The Seattle Times, 1983, editor, reporter, 1984, nat. editor, 1984-86, local news editor, 1986-87, asst. city editor, 1987-90, regional editor, 1990-96, metro. editor, 1997—; vis. faculty Poynter Inst. Media Studies, St. Petersburg, Fla. Recipient Goldsmith Prize in Investigative Reporting JFK Sch. Govt. Harvard U., 1993, Worth Bingham prize, 1993, Investigative Reporters and Editors award, 1993, AP Mng. Editors Pub. Svc. award, 1992, 1st place nat. reporting Pulitzer Prize, 1990, lead editor Pulitzer Prize in investigative reporting, 1997; named finalist Pulitzer Prize for Pub. Svc., 1993; fellow Japan-IBCC fellowship Ctr. Fgn. Journalists, 1995. Office: The Seattle Times PO Box 70 1120 John St Seattle WA 98111

BOAS, FRANK, lawyer; b. Amsterdam, North Holland, The Netherlands, July 22, 1930; came to U.S., 1940; s. Maurits Coenraad and Sophie (Brandel) B.; m. Edith Louise Bruce, June 30, 1981 (dec. July 1992); m. Jean Scripps, Aug. 6, 1993. AB cum laude, Harvard U., 1951, JD, 1954. Bar: U.S. Dist. Ct. D.C. 1955, U.S. Ct. Appeals (D.C. cir.) 1955; U.S. Supreme Ct. 1958. Atty. Office of the Legal Adviser U.S. State Dept., Washington, 1957-59; pvt. practice, Brussels and London, 1959-79; of counsel Patton, Boggs & Blow, Washington, 1975-80; pres. Frank Boas Found., Inc., Cambridge, Mass., 1980—. Mem. U.S. delegation to UN confs. on law of sea, Geneva, 1958, 60; vice chmn. Commn. for Ednl. Exch., Brussels, 1980-87; mem. vis. com. Harvard Law Sch., 1987-91, Ctr. for Internat. Affairs, 1988—; dir. Found. European Orgn. for Research and Treatment of Cancer, Brussels, 1978-87, Paul-Henri Spaak Found., Brussels, 1981—, East-West Ctr. Found., Honolulu, 1990-96, Law of the Sea Inst., Honolulu, 1992-97, Pacific Forum CSIS, Honolulu, 1996—, Honolulu Acad. Arts, 1997—; hon. sec. Am. C. of C. in Belgium, 1966-78. With U.S. Army, 1955-57. Decorated Officer of the Order of Leopold II, comdr. Order of the Crown (Belgium), comdr. Order of Merit (Luxembourg); recipient Tribute of Appreciation award U.S. State Dept., 1981, Harvard Alumni Assn. award, 1996. Mem. ABA, Fed. Bar Assn., Pacific and Asian Affairs Coun. (v.p.), Honolulu Com. Fgn. Relations, Pacific, Outrigger Canoe (Honolulu), Travelers (London), Am. and Common Market (Brussels pres. 1981-85), Honolulu Social Sci. Assn. Home: 4463 Aukai Ave Honolulu HI 96816-4858

BOAT, RONALD ALLEN, business executive; b. Dayton, Ohio, Nov. 16, 1947; s. Robert Mallory and Elvetta June (Smith) B. Student, Naval Acad./Army Sch. Music, Norfolk, Va., 1968-69, Ariz. State U., 1966-68. Pres. Prodn. Svcs., Phoenix, 1968—, Greek Specialties Corp., Phoenix, 1980-94; v.p. Am. Baby Boomers, San Diego, 1984-93; co-founder, v.p. Internat. Food Network, San Diego, 1985-90; founder, pres. AMC Food Svcs. Corp., 1991-94; pres. The Natural Light Co., 1994-96; ind. prodr. Intel, Honeywell, Best Western, Sperry, Phoenix, 1985—; mem. Lund Team Real Estate Adv. Bd., 1991-95; bd. dirs. Lund Real Estate Corp., 1990-95. Founder, pres. Group AMC, Inc., 1995—. With U.S. Army, 1968-71. Named Outstanding sales rep. Club Am., Dallas, 1972-73, Top Distbr. Club Am., Dallas, 1973; recipient Top Restaurant award Am. Heart Assn., Phoenix, 1988, Best of Phoenix restaurant award, 1991. Mem. Am. Radio Relay League, Internat. Platform Assn., Phi Mu Alpha Sinfonia. Republican. Office: P S A 14628 N 48th Way Scottsdale AZ 85254-2203

BOATNER, JAMES WILLIAM, trial court administrator; b. Randolph County, Ark., Nov. 4, 1936; s. John H. and Birdie L. (Brooks) B.; m. Phyllis K. Scott, Dec. 30, 1955; children: Debra K., James R., John Scott. BSBA, Ark. State U., 1967; MPA, City U., Bellevue, Wash., 1990, MBA, 1991. Data processing technician IBM/Univac, 1959-65; programmer mgr. Neiman Marcus, Dallas, 1967-69; data processing mgr. Crown Zellerbach Corp., Portland, Oreg., 1969-75; profl. photographer Boatner's Portrait Studio, McMinnville, Oreg., 1975-78; real estate salesman Shasta Real Estate, Klamath Falls, Oreg., 1978-80; systems coord. Oreg. Jud. Dept., Portland, 1980-84; info. analyst Oreg. Jud. Dept., Salem, 1984-89; dir. exec. svcs. Oreg. Jud. Dept., Portland, 1989-91; trial ct. adminstr. Oreg. Jud. Dept., Albany/Corvallis, 1991—; mem. Juvenile Svcs. Commn., Linn County, Albany, 1993—, Linn/Benton (Oreg.) Mediation Commn., 1991—, Linn County Criminal Justice Coun., 1993—, Willamette Criminal Justice Coun., Corvallis, Oreg., 1993—. Mem. Young Reps., Jonesboro, Ark., 1966-67, Kiwanis, McMinville, 1975-78, C. of C., McMinnville, 1975-78. Served with USAF, 1955-59. Mem. Oreg. Assn. Ct. Adminstrs. Mem. Ch. of Christ. Office: Oreg Jud Dept PO Box 1749 Albany OR 97321-0491

BOBB, RICHARD ALLEN, non-profit executive; b. Gahanna, Ohio, Oct. 27, 1937; s. Everett Leo and Mary Ennetta (Dunlap) B.; m. Betty Lee Knechtly, Oct. 21, 1960; 1 son, Michael Allen. B.Sc. in Bus, Ohio State U., 1959. With Pure Oil Co., 1963-65, Gen. Electric Co., 1965-79; exec. v.p., dir. ops. ITT Comml. Fin. Corp., St. Paul, 1979-86, Ford Motor/USL Capital, San Francisco, 1986-92, Guide Dogs for the Blind, 1995—. Served with USNR, 1960-63. Republican. Presbyterian. Office: Guide Dogs for the Blind 350 Los Ranchitos Rd San Rafael CA 94915

BOBOIA, HORIA, artist, educator; b. Bucharest, Romania, Mar. 31, 1955; came to U.S., 1977; s. Simion and Maria (Manescu) B.; m. Irena Karin Boboia, Dec. 28, 1982; children: Maya Bianca, Anna Carmem. BFA, Calif. Inst. Arts, Valencia, 1983, MFA, 1985. Asst. prof. Hochschule der Kunst, Berlin, 1984-85; illustrator Xianu Design, L.A., 1987-90; master printer Har-El Printers and Pubs., Jaffa, Israel, 1992-96; artist Portland, 1995—. DAAD travel grantee, Berlin, 1984-85.

BOBRICK, STEVEN AARON, property manager; b. Denver, Apr. 11, 1950; s. Samual Michael and Selma Gertrude (Birnbaum) B.; m. Maria Diane Boltz, Oct. 5, 1980. Attended, U. Colo., 1968-72. Registered apt. mgr. Owner Bobrick Constrn., Denver, 1969-72; with Bell Mtn. Sports, Aspen, Colo., 1972-75; mgr. Compass Imports, Denver, 1975-80, Aurora (Colo.) Bullion Exch., 1980-81; contr. Bobrick Constrn., Aurora, 1981-85; appraiser Aurora, 1985-89; property mgr. Aurora (Colo) Cmty. Mental Health, 1989—, active real estate and constrn., facilities mgr., 1989—. Co-author: Are You Paying Too Much in Property Taxes, 1990. Coun. mem. City of Aurora, 1981-89; chmn. Explore Commercial Opportunities, Aurora, 1986-89, bd. dirs.; bd. dirs. Adam County Econ. Devel. Commn., Northglenn, Colo., 1985-89; vice chair Aurora Urban Renewal Authority, 1982-89; chmn. Aurora Enterprise Zone Found., 1991—; bd. dirs. Aurora Community Med. Clinic, 1987-88. Office: Aurora Cmty Mental Health 1290 Chambers Aurora CO 80011

BOBROW, SUSAN LUKIN, lawyer; b. Cleve., Jan. 18, 1941; d. Adolph and Yetta (Babkow) Lukin; m. Martin J. Bolhower, Nov. 28, 1986 (div. Dec. 1988); children from previous marriage: Elizabeth Bobrow Pressler, Erica, David. Student, Antioch Coll., Yellow Springs, Ohio, 1958-61; BA, Antioch Coll., L.A., 1975; JD, Southwestern U., L.A., 1979. Bar: Calif., 1980. Owner, ptnr. Mediation Assocs., Beverly Hills, Calif., 1982; atty. Law Offices of Susan Bobrow, Beverly Hills, Calif., 1983-88; assoc. Schulman & Miller, Beverly Hills, 1988-89; staff counsel Fair Polit. Practices Commn., Sacramento, Calif., 1990-96; sr. counsel Calif. State Lottery, 1996—; mem. panel for paternity defense L.A. Superior Ct., 1984. Exhibited paintings at Death and Trasnfiguration Show, Phantom Galleries, Sacramento, 1994. Bd. dirs. San Fernando Valley Friends of Homeless Women and Children, North Hollywood, Calif., 1985-88, Jewish Family Svcs., 1997; mem. adv. bd. Project Home, Sacramento Interfaith Svc. Coun., 1990-91; v.p. cmty. affairs B'nai Israel Sisterhood, Sacramento, 1991-93. Recipient commendation Bd. Govs. State Bar of Calif., 1984. Mem. Inst. Noetic Scis., Sacramento Inst. Noetic Scis. (steering coun. 1994), Los Angeles County Bar Assn. (Barristers com. on adminstrn. of justice 1985), Sacramento County Bar Assn. (com. on profl. responsibility 1993-94, alt. del. to state bar conv. 1991). Democrat. Office: Calif State Lottery Commn 600 N 10th St Sacramento CA 95814-0393

BOCHIN, HAL WILLIAM, speech communication educator; b. Cleve., Feb. 23, 1942; s. Harold Washington and Miriam Rita (Sherer) B.; m. Janet Suzanne Schindler, June 7, 1975; 1 child, Christopher. BA, John Carroll U., 1964; MA, U. Wis., 1967; PhD, Ind. U., 1970. Asst. prof. Calif. State U., Fresno, 1969-74, assoc. prof., 1974-78, prof., 1978—. Author: Richard Nixon: Rhetorical Strategist, 1990; co-author: Hiram Johnson: Political Revivalist, 1995, Hiram Johnson: A Bio-Bibliography, 1988, (with others) The Inaugural Addresses of 20th Century American Presidents, 1993, U.S. Presidents as Orators, 1995, African-American Orators, 1996. Mem. Speech Communication Assn. Roman Catholic. Home: 2776 W San Ramon Ave Fresno CA 93711-2752 Office: Calif State U Dept Speech Communication Fresno CA 93740

BOCK, RUSSELL SAMUEL, author; b. Spokane, Wash., Nov. 24, 1905; s. Alva and Elizabeth (Mellinger) B.; m. Suzanne Ray, Feb. 26, 1970; children: Beverly A. Bock Wunderlich, James Russell. B.B.A., U. Wash., 1929. Part-time instr. U. So. Calif., UCLA, 1942-50; with Ernst & Ernst, CPAs, Los Angeles, 1938, ptnr., 1951-69; cons. Ernst & Young, 1969—. Author: Guidebook to California Taxes, annually, 1950—, Taxes of Hawaii, annually, 1964—; also numerous articles. Dir., treas. Cmty. TV So. Calif., 1964-74; dir., v.p. treas., So. Calif. Symphony-Hollywood Bowl Assn., 1964-70; bd. dirs. Cmty. Arts Music Assn., 1974-76, 78-84, Santa Barbara Symphony Assn., 1976-78, Santa Barbara Boys and Girls Club, 1980-93, UCSB Affiliates, 1983-85, Santa Barbara Civic Light Opera, 1995—. Mem. Am. Inst. C.P.A.s (council 1953-57, trial bd. 1955-58, v.p. 1959-60), Calif. Soc. C.P.A.s (past pres.), Los Angeles C. of C. (dir. 1957-65, v.p. 1963), Sigma Phi Epsilon, Beta Alpha Psi, Beta Gamma Sigma. Clubs: Birnam Wood Golf, Santa Barbara Yacht. Office: 300 Hot Springs Rd Apt 190 Santa Barbara CA 93108-2069

BOCK, S. ALLAN, physician, educator; b. Balt., Apr. 28, 1946; s. Sam and Charlotte Bock; m. Judith Lloyd, Oct. 19, 1985; children: Sam, Lea. AB, Washington U., 1968; MD, U. Md., 1972. Diplomate Am. Bd. Pediatrics, Am. Bd. Allergy and Immunology; lic. physician, Colo. Intern U. Md. Hosp., Balt., 1972-73; resident in pediatrics U. Colo. Med. Ctr., Denver, 1973-74, asst. prof. pediatrics; fellow in pediatric allergy and immunology Nat. Jewish Hosp. and Rsch. Ctr., Denver, 1974-76; assoc. clin. prof. pediatrics U. Colo. Health Scis. Ctr., Boulder, 1982-90, clin. prof. pediatrics, 1990—; sr. staff physician Nat. Jewish Ctr. Immunology and Respiratory Medicine, 1976—; pediatric allergist Dept. Health and Hosps., 1976-84. Contbr. numerous articles to profl. jours. Recipient Jacob E. Finesinger prize for excellence in psychiatry, 1972. Fellow Am. Acad. Allergy and Immunology, Am. Acad. Pediatrics; mem. Alpha Omega Alpha. Office: Boulder Valley Asthma Allergy Clinic 3950 Broadway St Boulder CO 80304-1104

BOCKUS, HERMAN WILLIAM, JR., artist, educator, writer; b. Frazee, Minn., Feb. 21, 1915; s. Herman William and Emma (Kimmerle) B.; m. Janet Davidson Fisher, Jan. 15, 1944; children: Genevieve, Kim, William, Heidi, Jill. BBA, U. Minn., 1937, BS, 1948, MEd, 1949. Salesman Food Warehouse, New Ulm, Minn., 1937-39; interpreter U.S. Govt., Colon, Canal Zone, 1939-42; art tchr. Highlands U., Las Vegas, N.Mex., 1948; art prof. Pasadena City Coll., 1950-75, head dept. art, 1965-66; tech. writer Calif. Inst. Tech., Pasadena, 1960-64. author: Advertising Graphics, 1969, 4th edit. 1986, Checklist for Better Tennis, 1973, Designers Notebook, 1977, Life Science Careers, 1991, Boys, 1995.. Capt. USMC, 1942-45. Recipient Cert. of Merit, L.A. Art Dirs. Show, 1965. Home: 1943 N Coolidge Ave Altadena CA 91001

BOCZKAJ, BOLESLAW FRANCISZEK, electrical engineer, consultant; b. Zabrze, Poland, May 16, 1957; came to U.S., 1973, naturalizaed, 1979; s. Bohdan Karol and Teresa Marcela (Bieniosek) B. BSEE, U. Rochester,

1979; MS, Ga. Inst. Tech., 1988. Registered profl. engr., Pa. Mgmt. assoc. U.S. Steel Corp., Rankin and Duquesne, Pa., 1979-83; elec. engr. Internat. Paper Co., Lewisburg, Pa., 1984; elec. and instrumentation engr. Belcan Corp., Bridgeville, Pa., 1984-86; elect. design engr. Centerline Engring. Corp., Wexford, Pa., 1988-89; elec. engr. Voest-Alpine Industries, Pitts., 1989-91; PLC programmer AEG Automation Systems Corp., Oakdale, Pa., 1991-92; elec. engr. John Carollo Engrs., Santa Ana, Calif., 1992; software engr. Varco Drilling Systems, Orange, Calif., 1993-96. Co-author: Obrona Polski Dzis i Jutro, 1993, Wizja Polski, Pierwsze Przyblizenie, 1995; contbr. articles to profl. jours. and conf. publs. Mem. IEEE, Instrument Soc. Am. (stds. com. 1994—), SME. Home: 21 Greco Aisle Irvine CA 92614 Office: PO Box 17027 Irvine CA 92623-7027

BODDIE, LEWIS FRANKLIN, obstetrics and gynecology educator; b. Forsyth, Ga., Apr. 4, 1913; s. William F. and Luetta T. (Sams) B.; m. Marian Bernice Claytor, Dec. 27, 1941; children: Roberta Boddie Miles, Lewis Jr., Bernice B. Jackson, Pamela, Kenneth, Fredda, Margaret. BA, Morehouse Coll., 1933; MD, Meharry Med. Sch., 1938. Diplomate Am. Bd. Ob-Gyn (proctor parti exam Los Angeles area 1955-63). Intern Homer-Phillips Hosp., St. Louis, 1938-39, resident in ob-gyn, 1939-42; mem. attending staff Grace Hosp., Detroit, 1944-48, Parkside Hosp., Detroit, 1944-48, Los Angeles County Gen. Hosp., 1952-79; sr. mem. attending staff Queen of Angels Hosp., Los Angeles, 1964-91, chmn. dept. ob-gyn, 1968-70; asst. clin. prof. U. So. Calif. Sch. Medicine, L.A., 1953-79, prof. emeritus, 1979—; assoc. clin. prof. U. Calif., Irvine, 1956-81; sec. Verndro Med. Corp., 1952-90. vice chmn. bd. mgrs. 28th St. YMCA, Los Angeles 1960-75; steward African Meth. Episc. Ch., Los Angeles, 1949—. Fellow ACS (life), Am. Coll. Ob-Gyn (life), Los Angeles Ob-Gyn Soc. (life): mem. Los Angeles United Way (priorities and allocations coms., 1985-95, standards com. 1987-95, new admission com. 1988-95), Children's Home Soc. (bd. dirs. 1952-89, trustee 1989—, v.p. 1963-68, pres. 1968-70), Child Welfare League Am. (bd. d irs. 1969-76). Republican.

BODENSIECK, ERNEST JUSTUS, mechanical engineer; b. Dubuque, Iowa, June 1, 1923; s. Julius Henry and Elma (Sommer) B.; BSME, Iowa State U., 1943; m. Margery Elenore Sande, Sept. 9, 1943; children: Elizabeth Bodensieck Eley, Stephen. Project engr. TRW Inc., Cleve., 1943-57; supr. rocket turbomachinery Rocketdyne div. Rockwell Internat., Canoga Park, Calif., 1957-60, supr. nuclear turbomachinery Rocketdyne div., 1964-70; advance gear engr. Gen. Electric Co., Lynn, 1960-64; asst. mgr. engine components Aerojet Nuclear Systems Co., Sacramento, 1970-71; gear and bearing cons. AiResearch div. Garrett Corp., Phoenix, 1971-81; transmission cons. Bodensieck Engring. Co., Scottsdale, Ariz., 1981—. Registered profl. engr., Ariz. Mem. ASME, AIAA, Soc. Automotive Engrs. (various coms.), Aircraft Industries Assn. (various coms.), Am. Gear Mfrs. Assn. (mem. aerospace, gear rating and enclosed epicyclic coms.), Nat. Soc. Profl. Engrs., Pi Tau Sigma. Lutheran. Patentee in field. Home: 7133 N Via De Alegria Scottsdale AZ 85258-3812

BODEY, BELA, immunomorphologist; b. Sofia, Bulgaria, Jan. 18, 1949; came to U.S., 1985, naturalized, 1994; s. Joseph and Rossitza (Derebeeva) B.; m. Victoria Psenko, Aug. 29, 1979; children; Bela Jr., Vivian. MD, Med. Acad., Sofia, 1973; PhD in Immuno-Biology, Inst. Morphology, Bulgarian Acad. Sci., Sofia, 1977. Lic. physician, exptl. pathologist, embryologist, immuno-morphologist, thymologist, exptl. oncologist. Asst. prof. Semmelweis Med. U., Budapest, 1977-80; prof. Inst. Hematology, Budapest, 1980-83; rsch. assoc. Tufts U., Boston, 1985; rsch. fellow immuno-pathology Mass. Gen. Hosp./Harvard U., Boston, 1986; rsch. fellow Childrens Hosp. L.A., 1987-90, rsch. scientist, 1991-92; asst. prof. rsch. pathology, Sch. of Medicine Univ. Southern Calif., 1992—; vis. prof. Alexander von Humboldt Found., Ulm, Fed. Republic Germany, 1984. Mem. Am. Assn. Cancer Rsch., Am. and Can. Acad. Pathology, French Soc. Cell Biology, French Soc. Electronmicroscopy, Internat. Soc. Exptl. Hematology, Internat. Soc. Comparative Oncology, N.Y. Acad. Scis., Free Masons. Roman Catholic. Home: 15745 Saticoy St Van Nuys CA 91406-3155 Office: U So Calif Sch Medicine 2011 Zonal Ave Los Angeles CA 90033-1034

BODI, F. LORRAINE, lawyer; b. Newport, R.I., Nov. 5, 1951. BA, U. Pa., 1972, MS, 1972; JD, George Washington U., 1976. Atty. U.S. EPA, Washington, 1976-78, U.S. NOAA, Seattle, 1978-91; dir. N.W. office Am. Rivers, Seattle, 1992; pres., bd. mem. Save Our World Salmon Coalition, Seattle, 1992—; adv. bd. mem. NAFTA Environ. Adv. Coun., Washington, 1994-95; bd. mem. Sustainable Fisheries Found., Seattle, 1995—, N.W. Renewable Resources Ctr., Seattle, 1996—. Co-author: Our Common Lands, 1988, Salmon Documentary History, 1996, Ecology Management of Streams and Rivers of the Pacific Eco Region, 1997; contbr. articles to profl. jours. Mem. State of Washington Citzen's Adv. Com. on Trust Water Rights, 1993-94. Mem. Phi Beta Kappa. Office: Am Rivers 400 E Pine # 225 Seattle WA 98122

BODIN, ARTHUR M., clinical psychologist; b. N.Y.C., July 11, 1932; s. Harry S. and Rose B.; m. Miriam Irene, June 25, 1961; children: Douglas Adam, Laura June. BA in Zoology, Swarthmore Coll., 1954; MA in Edn., NYU, 1957; PhD in Psychology, SUNY, Buffalo, 1966. Lic. psychologist, Calif.; lic. marriage, family & child counselor, Calif.; diplomate in clin. psychology Am. Bd. Profl. Psychology; diplomate in forensic psychology Am. Bd. Profl. Psychology. Sr. rsch. fellow Mental Rsch. Inst., Palo Alto, Calif., 1965—; ind. practice clin. psychology Palo Alto, 1967—; bd. dirs. Silicon Valley Ind. Practice Assn., Santa Clara County, Calif., Mental Rsch. Inst., Palo Alto. Editor: (newsletter) Calif. State Psychologist, 1973-74, (bulletins) Bull. Am. Acad. Forensic Psychologists, 1980-83, State Psychol. Assoc. Affairs, 1990-91; contbr. numerous chpts. to books, articles to profl. jours. Mem. early childhood edn. com. Palo Alto Unified Sch. Dist., Palo Alto, 1970. Elected Disting. Practitioner in Psychology, Nat. Acads. of Practice, 1993; recipient Disting. Achievement in New Directions in Family Therapy award Am. Family Therapy Acad., 1981. Fellow APA (coun. of reps. 1979-81, 83-85, 91, 93, 96—, Karl F. Heiser Presdl. award 1993, pres. divsn. family psychology 1988, pres. divsn. of state psychol. assn. affairs 1993, Family Psychologist of Yr. award 1990, pub. rels. and communications bd., chair comm. on human resources, 1996), Acad. Clin. Psychology, Profl. Acad. Custody Evaluators, Am. Orthopsychiat. Assn.; mem. Calif. Psychol. Assn. (pres. 1976, Disting. Svc. award 1978, Silver Psi award). Office: 555 Middlefield Rd Palo Alto CA 94301-2124

BODINSON, HOLT, conservationist; b. East Orange, N.J., Nov. 14, 1941; s. Earl Herdien and Hermoine (Holt) B. BA, Harvard, 1963; m. Ilse Marie Maier, Feb. 29, 1970. Sr. asso. Am. Conservation Assn., Inc., N.Y.C., 1966-70; dir. Office of Policy Analysis, N.Y. State Dept. Environ. Conservation, Albany, 1970-71, dir. div. ednl. services, 1971-77; dir. Ariz.-Sonora Desert Mus., 1977-78; exec. dir. Safari Club Internat./Safari Club Internat. Conservation Fund, Tucson, 1980-89; conservation dir. Safari Club Internat., Tucson, 1991-94, dir. wildlife and govtl. affairs, 1994-96; committeeman, Montgomery Twp. Conservation Commn., 1967-70; sec. N.Am. del. Conseil Internat. de la Chasse et de la Conservation du Gibier, 1988—; gen. sec. World Hunting and Conservation Congress, 1988; dir. Internat. Wildlife Mus., 1991-96; nat. sec. United Conservation Alliance, 1994-96. Served with arty. AUS, 1964-66. Mem. Stony Brook-Millstone Watershed Assn. (dir.), Safari Club Internat. (dir. Ariz. chpt.), N.Y. Outdoor Edn. Assn. (dir.), Outdoor Writers Assn. of Am., N.Y. State Rifle and Pistol Assn. (dir.). Episcopalian. Club: Harvard of So. Ariz. (pres.). Author: (with Clepper and others) Leaders in American Conservation, 1971. Contbg. editor Jour. Environmental Edn., 1968-94; dir. Conservationist mag. 1971-77, N.Y. State Environment newspaper, 1971-74. Home: 4525 N Hacienda Del Sol Tucson AZ 85718-6619 Office: 5605 E River Rd Ste 219 Tucson AZ 85750

BODNAR, JACKIE SUE, molecular biologist, geneticist; b. Provo, Utah, Oct. 11, 1972; d. Jack Earl and Suzanna (Steele) Perry; m. James D. Bodnar, Aug. 27, 1994. Student, U. Utah, 1988; BS, Brigham Young U., 1993; postgrad., UCLA. Lab. technician Brigham Young U., Provo, 1990-1993; computer scientist, programmer Lawrence Livermore (Calif.) Nat. Labs., 1992, molecular biology rsch. scientist, 1993; rsch. scientist new tech. and automation Incyte Pharm., Inc., Palo Alto, Calif., 1994—. Mem. Mapleton (Utah) Youth City Coun., 1989. Mem. AAAS, Assn. Women in Sci., Am. Soc. Biochemistry and Molecular Biology, Fedn. Am. Socs. Exptl. Biology (contbr. articles to jour.). Office: Incyte Pharm Inc 3330 Hillview Ave Palo Alto CA 94304

BOEHM, PAUL EUGENE, health medical products executive, pharmacist; b. Bismarck, N.D., Sept. 4, 1937; m. Judith Ann Boehm; children: Noelle, Scott, Kevin. BS, N.D. State U., 1959, MS, 1972. Commd. 2d lt. USAF, 1959, advanced through grades to capt., 1964; maj. USAFR, 1974-90, ret., 1990; asst. chief pharmacy svc. Bismarck Med. Ctr., 1959-60; asst. chief pharmacy sci. USAF Med. Ctr., Lackland AFB/San Antonio, Tex., 1960-63; chief pharmacy svc. USAF Med. Ctr., Wiesbaden, Germany, 1963-66, Wright Patterson/Dayton, Ohio, 1966-68; asst. chief pharmacy svc. VA Med. Ctr., Fargo, N.D., 1968-70, chief pharmacy svc., 1968-70; asst. chief pharmacy svc. VA Med. Ctr., Palo Alto, Calif., 1974-77, chief pharmacy svc., 1977-96; dir. Sunburst Unltd., 1996—; pharmacy cons. to USAF Surgeon Gen., Wiesbaden, 1963-66; mem. USAF Inspector Gen. Team, Dayton, 1966-68. Coach children's soccer team Am. Soccer Assn., Cupertino, Calif., 1983-89, children's basketball team, YMCA, Cupertino, 1983-89, children's baseball team, Cupertino, 1987-89. Capt. USAF, 1960-68, Europe. Mem. N.D. Hosp. Pharmacists Assn. (v.p. 1969-70), N.D. Pharm. Assn., Am. Soc. Hosp. Pharmacists, Am. Pharm. Assn., Calif. Soc. Hosp. Pharmacists, Calif. Pharm. Assn., Quatra County Hosp. Pharmacists Assn.

BOEKHOUDT-CANNON, GLORIA LYDIA, business education educator; b. Portsmouth, Va., Jan. 18, 1939; d. William and Clara (Virgil) Boekhoudt; m. George Edward Cannon, Dec. 27, 1959. AB in Sociology/Psychology, Calif. State U., San Diego, 1977; MA in Spl. Edn./Learning Disabilities, Calif. State U., Sacramento, 1981; EdD in Orgn. and Leadership of Higher Edn. and Curriculum and Instrn., U. San Francisco, 1989. Instr. bus. edn. Midway Adult Sch. extension San Diego City Coll., San Diego, 1974-78, San Diego City Coll., 1974-78, Sacramento City Coll., 1979—. Author: Fundamentals of Business English, 1986. Mem. Women in Community Colls., Phi Delta Kappa. Democrat. Jewish. Office: Sacramento City Coll Dept Bus 3835 Freeport Blvd Sacramento CA 95822-1318

BOERSMA, LAWRENCE ALLAN, animal welfare administrator; b. London, Ontario, Can., Apr. 24, 1932; s. Harry Albert and Valerie Kathryn (DeCordova) B.; m. Nancy Noble Jones, Aug. 16, 1952 (div. 1962) children: Juliana Jaye, Dirk John; m. June Elaine Schiefer McKim, Nov. 22, 1962; children: Kenneth Thomas McKim, Mark Rennie McKim. *Wife June writes non-fiction under the pen name Jalma Barrett. She's written for Ladies' Home Journal, Dog Fancy, Cat Fancy, Dog World, Horse Illustrated, Popular Photography, MotoFocus, Petersen's Photographic, Studio Photography, and others. She is co-owner, photographer of Allan/The Animal Photographers, San Diego, 1980—; and served as VP/Board Member of The Photographic Institute International, 1982-86. She has addressed the national convention of the Professional Photographers of America, Western States Professional Photographers Association, and the Professional Photographers of Nevada and New Mexico .* BA, U. Nebr., Omaha, 1953, MS, 1955; PhD, Sussex U., 1972; postgrad., U. Oxford, Eng., 1996. Journalism tchr. Tech. High Sch., Omaha, Nebr., 1953-55; dir. pub. rels., chair journalism dept. Adams State Coll., Alamosa, Colo., 1955-59; advt. sales analyst, advt. salesman Better Homes and Gardens, Des Moines, N.Y.C., 1959-63; advt. account exec. This Week Mag., N.Y.C., 1963-66; eastern sales dir., mktg. dir. Ladies' Home Jour., N.Y.C., 1966-75; v.p. assoc. pub., v.p. pub. Saturday Evening Post and The Country Gentleman, N.Y.C., 1975; v.p., dir. mktg. and advt. sales Photo World Mag., N.Y.C., 1975-77; advt. mgr. LaJolla (Calif.) Light, 1977-80; owner, photographer Allan/The Animal Photographers, San Diego, 1980—; pres., CEO The Photographic Inst. Internat., 1982-86; dir. comty. rels. San Diego Humane Soc./Soc. for Prevention Cruelty to Animals, 1985-94; assoc. exec. dir. The Ctr. for Humane Edn. for So. Calif., 1994—; adj. asst. prof. Grad. Sch. Bus., Pace U., N.Y.C., 1964-65; adj. instr. N.Y. Inst. of Advt., 1974-77, others; adj. prof. Sch. Bus. Mesa Coll., San Diego, 1981-84, City Coll., San Diego, 1982-86; adj. prof. Coll. Bus. Adminstrn. U. LaVerne, San Diego, 1985; pres., CEO United Animal Welfare Found., San Diego, 1992-94; bd. dirs. Escondido Humane Soc. Found., 1994—; chmn., CEO Internat. Dolphin Project, 1995. Author: Strange Events at the House on Park Avenue: A Jack and Jimmy Mystery, 1996; contbr. and photographer articles to mags. Spokesperson Coalition for Pet Population Control, San Diego, 1990, 93, Com. Against Proposition C-Pound Animals for Med. Rsch., San Diego, 1990; spokesperson Spay-Neuter Action Project, 1991, mem. steering com., 1991, bd. dirs., 1992-93; mem. evaluation subcom. County of San Diego Dept. Animal Control Adv. Com.; founder, chair Feral Cat Coalition of San Diego County, 1992-93; vol. in pub. info. San Diego/Imperial Counties chpt. ARC, 1993—, mem. chpt. centennial com., 1996-97; mem. pub. info. officers San Diego County Emergency Svcs. Orgn., 1993-95. Fellow Royal Photographic Soc. of Gt. Britain, Profl. Photographers Am. (Master of Photography award 1985, Photographic Craftsman award 1986), Profl. Photographers of Calif.; mem. PRSA (chmn. So. Tier N.Y. chpt. 1972), Soc. Animal Welfare Adminstrs., Nat. Soc. Fund Raising Execs. (cert., bd. dirs. 1988-89, treas. San Diego chpt. 1990-91, mem. nat. faculty 1992-93), Shriners (pres. Al Bahr chpt., Businessmen's Club), Masons. Republican. Presbyterian. Home: 3503 Argonne St San Diego CA 92117-1009

BOERSMA, P. DEE, zoology educator; d. Henry W. and Vivian (Anspach) B. BS, Ctrl. Mich. U., 1969; PhD, Ohio State U., 1974. Asst. prof. Inst. Environ. Studies, U. Wash., Seattle, 1974-80, assoc. prof., 1980-88, prof. environ. studies, 1988-93, prof. zoology, 1988—, adj. prof. women's studies, 1993—, assoc. dir., 1987-93, acting dir., 1990-91; mem. sci. adv. com. for outer continental shelf Environ. Studies Program, Dept. Interior, 1980-83; prin. investigator Magellanic Penguin Project, N.Y. Zool. Soc., 1982-; Evans vis. fellow U. Otago, New Zealand, 1995. Contbr. articles to profl. jours. Mem. adv. U.S. del. to UN Status Women Commn., N.Y.C., 1973, UN World Population Conf., Romania, 1974; mem. Gov. Lowry's Task Force on Wildlife, 1993; sci. adv. EcoBios, 1985-95; bd. dirs. Zero Population Growth, 1975-82, Washington Conservancy, 1995—; mem. scholar diplomatic program Dept. of State, 1977. Recipient Outstanding Alumni award Cen. Mich. U., 1978, Matrix award Women in Comm., 1983; named to Kellogg Nat. Leadership Program, 1982-85; recipient Top 10 Outsiders of Yr. award Outside Mag., 1987, Outstanding Centennial Alumni award Ctrl. Mich. U., 1993. Fellow Am. Ornithol. Union (regional rep. Pacific seabird group 1981-85); mem. AAAS, Ecol. Soc. Am., Wilson Ornithol. Soc., Cooper Ornithol. Soc., Soc. Am. Naturalists, Soc. for Conservation Biology (bd. govs. 1991-94, pres. elect 1995—). Club: Gopher Brokers (Seattle pres. 1982-83). Office: U Wash Dept Zoology Box 351800 Seattle WA 98195-1800

BOESPFLUG, JOHN F., JR., lawyer; b. 1944. AB, Whitman Coll.; JD, U. Wash. Bar: 1969. Mem. Bogle & Gates, Bellevue, Wash., 1994—. Mem. ABA. Office: Bogle & Gates 10500 NE 8th St Ste 1500 Bellevue WA 98004-4398

BOGART, FRANK JEFFREY, system and product planning engineer; b. Johnson City, Tenn., May 17, 1942; s. Frank Lavon and Mary Stein (Hattan) B.; m. JoAnne Ruth Hodgson, Aug. 1, 1964; children: Christopher Alan, Timothy Andrew. BS, U. R.I., 1963; MS, Rutgers U., 1965; postgrad., U. Colo., 1970-74. Disting. mem. tech. staff Lucent Techs. Bell Labs., Holmdel, N.J., 1963-65, 68-69; mem. tech. staff Lucent Techs. Bell Labs., Denver, 1969—; participant Career Awareness Program, AT&T, Denver, 1985—. Patentee in field. Various positions Boy Scouts Am., 1951—; treas. 1st Congl. Ch., United Ch. of Christ, 1994-96; moderator 1st Congrl. Ch., UCC, 1997-99. Served to capt. U.S. Army, 1965-67, Vietnam. Decorated Bronze Star; recipient God and Svc. award United Ch. of Christ, 1990, Silver Beaver award Boy Scouts Am., 1976, Disting. Commr. award Boy Scouts Am., 1991. Mem. Telephone Pioneers Am. Home: 4796 Devonshire St Boulder CO 80301-4137 Office: Lucent Technologies Bell Labs 11900 Pecos St Denver CO 80234-2703

BOGART, LOUISE BERRY, education educator; b. N.Y.C., July 15, 1942; d. Herbert George and Flora Louise (Porcelli) Berry; m. Burton Stanley Bogart, Aug. 29, 1965; children: Samuel Isaac, Jonathan Douglas. BA, Kans. State U., 1964; MEd, Coll. Notre Dame, Belmont, Calif., 1973; postgrad., U. Hawaii-Manoa, 1991—. Cert. Montessori tchr.; cert. pvt. tchr., Hawaii; cert. tchr., prin., Ohio; cert. neurolinguistic profl., neurolinguistic master. Field advisor, sr. program dir., day camp dir. Kaw Valley Girl Scout Coun., Topeka, 1964-65; field advisor Seal of Ohio Girl Scout Coun., Columbus, 1966-67; elem. tchr. St. Joseph Mntessori Sch., Columbus, 1970-78; pre-kindergarten tchr. Maryknoll Grade Sch., Honolulu, 1978-80; head tchr. elem. classes Montessori Cmty. Sch., Honolulu, 1980-82; asst. prof. edn. Chaminade U. of Honolulu, 1982-92, assoc. prof. edn., 1993—, acting chair dept. edn., 1988-90, Montessori Program dir., 1986-92. Active Girl Scouts U.S., Honolulu, 1978—. Eisenhower grantee U.S. Dept. Edn., 1989-90, 90-91, 91-92, 95-96, others. Mem. ASCD, Am. Montessori Soc. (vice chair 1987-91), Montessori Assn. Hawaii (v.p. 1980-81), Nat. Assn. Edn. of Young children, Hawaii Assn. Edn. of Young Children, Hawaii Coun. Tchrs. Math., Internat. Inst. Peace Educators, World Coun. for Curriculum and Instrn. Home: 1131 Kaumoku St Honolulu HI 96825-1303 Office: Chaminade U Honolulu 3140 Waialae Ave Honolulu HI 96816-1510

BOGART, REBECCA A., musician, educator; b. Palo Alto, Calif., Sept. 6, 1960. BS in Bus. Adminstrn. summa cum laude, Univ. Calif., Berkeley, 1981; MusM in Piano Performance, San Francisco Conservatory, 1985. Tchr., owner Rebecca Bogart Piano Studio, various, 1977—; rsch. analyst First Deposit Corp., San Francisco, 1982-87; concert pianist, 1983—; group mgr. Preeman Music, Arcadia, Costa Mesa, Mission Viego, San Diego, 1993. Recipient prize Carmel Music Soc. Competition, 1986, Pacific Internat. Piano Competition, 1987, 2 prizes San Francisco Bay Area Keyboard Arts Competition, 1996; Alfred Hertz fellow U. Calif., Berkeley, 1986, Montalvo fellow Villa Montalvo Ctr. Arts, Saratoga, Calif., 1989. Mem. Chamber Music Am., Music Tchrs. Nat. Assn. (cert.), Music Tchrs. Assn. Calif. (v.p. Alameda County br. 1996—), Phi Beta Kappa.

BOGATAY, TODD CUNNINGHAM, architect; b. Columbus, Ohio, Mar. 1, 1937; s. Paul Josef and Henrietta Beecher (Cunningham) B. AB cum laude, Harvard U., 1959, MArch, 1962. Lic. architectural, Ariz., Mass. Designer, draftsman William Lescaze FAIA, N.Y.C., 1962-63, 65-66, Antonin Raymond FAIA, Tokyo, 1963-65; designer, planner San Juan, 1966; designer I.M. Pei and Ptnrs., N.Y.C., 1967, Richard Meier, FAIA, N.Y.C., 1967-69; prin. Bogatay, Architect, N.Y.C., 1970-71, Boston, 1972-80, Bisbee, Ariz., 1981—; instr. Pratt Inst., Bklyn., 1969-70, Boston Archtl. Ctr., 1973-76. Designer Residence for Chief of State of Cambodia, 1962; arch. American Plywood Assn., 1970 (Design award). Recipient Heritage Fund Grant Ariz. State Parks, Bisbee, 1993. Mem. Nat. Coun. of Archtl. Registration Bds. Office: Bogatay Archs PO Box Z 1011 West Blvd Bisbee AZ 85603-0209

BOGDAN, JAMES THOMAS, secondary education educator, electronics researcher and developer; b. Kingston, Pa., Aug. 14, 1938; s. Fabian and Edna A. (Spray) B.; m. Carolyn Louetta Carpenter, May 5, 1961; 1 child, Thomas James. BS in Edn., Wilkes U., Wilkes-Barre, Pa., 1960. Cert. chemistry and physics tchr., Calif. Tchr. Forty Fort (Pa.) Sch. Dist., 1960-63; tchr., chmn. sci. dept. L.A. Unified Sch. Dist., 1963-96; owner, mgr. Bogdan Electronic Rsch. & Devel., Lakewood, Calif., 1978—; cons. Lunar Electronics, San Diego, 1978-83, T.E. Systems, L.A., 1988-89. Author, pub. The VHF Reporter newsletter, 1967-76. Tng. officer Los Angeles County Disaster Comm., 1968-91, UHF and microwave sys. staff officer, 1991-94, dep. chief comm. officer, 1994—; pin chmn. Tournament of Roses Comm. Group, Pasadena, Calif., 1985—. Republican. Office: PO Box 62 Lakewood CA 90714-0062

BOGENSBERGER, JOAN HELEN HESS, school administrator, consultant; b. Ft. Collins, Colo., Aug. 18, 1939; d. Eugene Vernon and Margaret Rose (Mantey) Hess; m. Robert R. Bogensberger, Aug. 20, 1960; children: John Andrew, Margaret Rose, Helen Marie. BA, Colo. State Coll., Greeley, 1961; MA, Western Wash. U., 1976; postgrad. U. Wash., 1964. Cert. tchr., Wash. Tchr., elem. schs. South Cen. Sch. Dist., Seattle, Wash., 1960-68; vol. music tchr. Immaculate Comception Sch., Mt. Vernon, 1968-71; libr. Mt. Vernon Christian Sch., 1971-76; founder, tchr., prin. Floyd Paxton Sch., Mt. Vernon, 1977—; chair program state edn. conv. Wash. Fedn. Ind. Schs., 1989-90; cons. in field; developer art curriculum; pres. Skagit Community Band Bd. Wash. State Homeschs. Mem. Skagit Performing Arts Coun., IDEAS, Spokane, 1997. Mem. ASCD, Internat. Reading Assn., Nat. Coun. Tchrs., Assn. Childhood Edn., Tau Beta Sigma, Delta Omicron. Roman Catholic. Office: Floyd Paxton Elem Sch 1340 Avon Allen Rd Mount Vernon WA 98273-8204

BOGER, DAN CALVIN, economics educator, statistical and economic consultant; b. Salisbury, N.C., July 9, 1946; s. Brady Cashwell and Gertrude Virginia (Hamilton) B.; m. Gail Lorraine Zivna, June 23, 1973; children: Gretchen Zivna, Gregory Zivna. BS in Mgmt. Sci., U. Rochester, 1968; MS in Mgmt. Sci., Naval Postgrad. Sch., Monterey, Calif., 1969; M.A. in Stats., U. Calif., Berkeley, 1977, Ph.D. in Econs., 1979. Cert. cost analyst, profl. estimator. Research asst. U. Calif., Berkeley, 1975-79; asst. prof. econs. Naval Postgrad. Sch., Monterey, Calif., 1979-85, assoc. prof., 1985-92, prof., 1992—, chair dept. command, control and comm., 1995—; bd. dirs. Evan-Moor Corp., 1992—; cons. econs. and statis. legal matters CSX Corp, others, 1977—. Assoc. editor The Logistics and Transportation Rev., 1981-85, Jour. of Cost Analysis, 1989-92; mem. editorial rev. bd. Jour. Transp. Research Forum, 1987-91; contbr. articles to profl. jours. Served to lt. USN, 1968-75. Flood fellow Dept. Econs., U. Calif.-Berkeley, 1975-76; dissertation research grantee A.P. Sloan Found., 1978-79. Mem. Am. Econ. Assn., Am. Statis. Assn., Econometric Soc., Math. Assn. Am., Inst. Mgmt. Sci., Ops. Research Soc. Am. (sec., treas. mil. applications sect. 1987-91), Sigma Xi. Home: 27 Cramden Dr Monterey CA 93940-4145 Office: Naval Postgrad Sch Code SM/Bo Monterey CA 93943

BOGGS, STEPHEN TAYLOR, cultural anthropologist, researcher, consultant; b. Chgo., July 13, 1924; s. Judge and Jeannette Francina (Neligh) B.; m. Joan Whitehorn, Feb. 15, 1929; children: Christofer H., Ellen E., Andrew K. AB summa cum laude, Harvard Coll., 1947; PhD, Washington U., St. Louis, 1954. Acting asst. prof. sociology Stanford (Calif.) U., 1953-56; social anthropologist NIMH, Bethesda, Md., 1957-60; exec. sec. Am. Anthrop. Assn., Washington, 1961-66; prof. anthropology U. Hawaii, Honolulu, 1966-83; emeritus U. Hawaii, Manoa, 1984—; expert witness on Hawaiian culture; rschr., cons. KEEP, Kamahameha Schs., Honolulu, 1971-73, Bishop Mus. Nanakuli Community Study, Hawaii, 1966-68, various native Hawaii groups. Author: Speaking, Relating, and Learning: A Study of Hawaiian Children at Home and at School, 1985; contbr. articles to profl. jours. Mem. Low Income Housing Coalition, Honolulu, 1989-94; vol. Amnesty Internat. Nederland, Colo., 1990—. With U.S. Army, 1943-46. Recipient Shaw fellowship Harvard Coll., 1947-48, Social Sci. Rsch. Coun. fellow, 1951-52. Fellow Am. Anthrop. Assn. Roman Catholic. Home: # 1922 46 033 Aliianela Pl Kaneohe HI 96744-3707

BOGGS, STEVEN EUGENE, lawyer; b. Santa Monica, Calif., Apr. 28, 1947; s. Eugene W. and Annie (Happe) B. BA in Econ., U. Calif., Santa Barbara, 1969; D of Chiropractic summa cum laude, Cleveland Chiropractic, L.A., 1974; PhD in Fin. Planning, Columbia Pacific U., 1986; JD in Law, U. So. Calif., 1990. Bar: Calif. 1990, U.S. Dist. Ct. (cen. dist.) Calif. 1990, Hawaii 1991, U.S. Ct. Appeals (9th cir.); CFP; lic. chiropractor Hawaii, Calif.; lic. radiography X-ray supr. and operator. Faculty mem. Cleveland Chiropractic Coll., 1972-74; pres. clinic dir. Hawaii Chiropratic Clinic, Inc., Aiea, 1974-87; pvt. practice Honolulu, 1991—; cons. in field; seminar presenter 1990—. Contbr. articles to profl. jours. Recipient Cert. Appreciation State of Hawaii, 1981-84. Fellow Internat. Coll. of Chiropractic; mem. ABA, Am. Trial Lawyers Assn., Am. Trial Lawyers Assn. of Hawaii, Am. Chriopractic Assn., Hawaii State Chiropractic Assn. (pres. 1978, 85, 86, v.p. 1977, sec. 1979-84, treas. 1976, other coms., Valuable Svc. award 1984, Cert. Appreciation 1986, Cert. Achievement 1986, Chiropractor of Yr. 1986, Outstanding Achievement award 1991), Consumer Lawyers of Hawaii (bd. dirs.). Democrat. Office: 804 Fort Street Mall Honolulu HI 96813-4318

BOGGS, WILLIAM S., lawyer; b. Toledo, Ohio, May 17, 1946. AB summa cum laude, Wittenberg U., 1968; JD cum laude, Harvard U., 1972. Bar: Calif. Ptnr. Gray, Cary, Ware & Freidenrich, San Diego. Mem. ABA, San Diego County Bar Assn., Internat. Assn. Defense Counsel, Assn. So. Calif. Defense Counsel, San Diego Defense Lawyers, Lincoln's Inn. Office: Gray Cary Ware & Freidenrich 401 B St Ste 1700 San Diego CA 92101-4240

BOHANNON, LINDA SUE, special education educator; b. L.A., July 19, 1954; d. Hearold Eugene and Ruth Ella (Sanders) Paisley; divorced; children: David Eugene, Jamie Lyn. AS, Mt. San Antonio C.C., Walnut, Calif., 1974; AA, Antelope Valley C.C., Lancaster, Calif., 1990; BA, Calif. State U., Northridge, 1992; MA, Chapman U., Orange, Calif., 1994. Cert. tchr. Calif.; learning handicapped tchr., Calif. Paraeducator L.A. County Office of Edn., Downey, Calif., 1987-93; tchr. Westside Sch. Dist., Lancaster, Calif., 1993-

96, Lancaster Sch. Dist., Lancaster, 1996—; dir. Awana Girls Club, Leona Valley, Calif., 1993-95; advisor Calif. Jr. Scholarship Fedn., Lancaster, 1994-96. Mem. Cristian Educators Assn., Calif. Educators Assn. Republican. Office: Sierra Elem Sch 747 W Ave J-12 Lancaster CA 93534

BOHMAN, HAROLD RAY, surgeon; b. Galesburg, Ill., Oct. 26, 1949; s. Raymond Harold and Eileen Angela (Calmer) B.; m. Cathleen Lynn Carlson, May 22, 1976; children: Eisha Lynn, Erik Raymond. BA magna cum laude, Bethany Coll., 1971; MD, U. Okla., 1975; cert. gen. surgery, Naval Med. Ctr., Oakland, Calif., 1980; cert. colon and rectal surgery, U. Medicine & Dentistry N.J., 1985. Diplomate Am. Bd. Surgery, Am. Bd. Colon and Rectal Surgery. Staff surgeon U.S. Naval Hosp., Guam, 1980-82, Nat. Naval Med. Ctr., Bethesda, Md., 1983-85; pvt. practice Sacramento, Calif., 1985-88; staff surgeon Naval Med. Ctr., Oakland, Calif., 1988-92; capt., chief profl. svcs. 1st Med. Bn. USN 1st Force Svc. Support Group, Camp Pendleton, Calif., 1992—; staff surgeon Naval Hosp., Camp Pendleton, 1992—; specialty advisor Bur. Medicine and Surgery USN, Washington, 1995—. Contbr. articles to profl. jours. Fellow ACS, Am. Soc. Colon and Rectal Surgeons; mem. Soc. Am. Gastrointestinal Endoscopic Surgeons. Lutheran. Office: Naval Hosp Dept Surgery Box 555191 Camp Pendleton CA 92055-5191

BOHN, DENNIS ALLEN, electrical engineer, executive; b. San Fernando, Calif., Oct. 5, 1942; s. Raymond Virgil and Iris Elouise (Johnson) B.; 1 child, Kira Michelle; m. Patricia Tolle, Aug. 12, 1986. BSEE with honors, U. Calif., Berkeley, 1972, MSEE with honors, 1974. Engring. technician GE Co., San Leandro, Calif., 1964-72; research and devel. engr. Hewlett-Packard Co., Santa Clara, Calif., 1973; application engr. Nat. Semicondr. Corp., Santa Clara, 1974-76; engring. mgr. Phase Linear Corp., Lynnwood, Wash., 1976-82; v.p. rsch. and devel., ptnr. Rane Corp., Mukilteo, Wash., 1982—; founder Toleco Systems, Kingston, Wash., 1980. Suicide and crisis ctr. vol., Berkeley, 1972-74, Santa Clara, 1974-76. Served with USAF, 1960-64. Recipient Am. Spirit Honor medal USAF, 1961; Math. Achievement award Chem. Rubber Co., 1962-63. Editor: We Are Not Just Daffodils, 1975; contbr. poetry to Reason mag.; tech. editor Audio Handbook, 1976; contbr. articles to tech. jours.; columnist Polyphony mag., 1981-83; 2 patents in field. Fellow Audio Engring. Soc.; mem. IEEE, Tau Beta Pi. Office: Rane Corp 10802 47th Ave W Mukilteo WA 98275-5000

BOHN, PAUL BRADLEY, psychiatrist, psychoanalyst; b. Santa Monica, Calif., Apr. 11, 1957; m. Pamela Summit, Nov. 17, 1990. BA in Pharmacology, U. Calif., Santa Barbara, 1980; MD, U. Calif., Irvine, 1984; postgrad. in Psychoanalysis, L.A. Psychoanalytic Inst., 1988-93; PsyD, Grad. Inst. Contemporary Psychoanalysis, 1995. Diplomate Am. Bd. Psychiatry and Neurology. Psychiat. resident UCLA, 1984-88, assoc. dir. anxiety disorders clinic, 1989-95, dir. social anxiety clinic, 1993-95; fellow U. So. Calif., L.A., 1988-89; v.p. Pacific Psychopharmacology Rsch. Inst., Santa Monica, 1990—; pvt. practice psychiatry Santa Monica, 1988—; expert reviewer, Med. Bd. Calif. Grantee Ciba-Geigy, Santa Monica, 1992. Mem. Am. Psychiat. Assn., So. Calif. Psychiat. Assn., Anxiety Disorders Assn. of Am., Obsessive Compulsive Found.. Office: 2730 Wilshire Blvd Ste 325 Santa Monica CA 90403-4747

BOHRER, RICHARD WILLIAM, religious writer, editor, educator; b. N.Y.C., June 17, 1926; s. Jacob William and Elsie Marie (Wahlstad) B.; m. Elizabeth Anne Spencer, July 8, 1955; children: Joel Stephen, Janice Joy Bohrer Pruitt. BA, Westmont Coll., 1947; MSc, U. So. Calif., L.A., 1956; MA, Calif. State U., Long Beach, 1962. Tchr. grades 3, 4, 5 Haile Selassie I Elem. Sch., Gondar, Ethiopia, 1947-50; tchr. grades 9, 10, 11 Alhambra (Calif.) High Sch., 1954-55; tchr. grade 6 Maple Ave. Sch., Fullerton, Calif., 1955-56; tchr. grades 9, 10, 11 Orange (Calif.) High Sch., 1956-63; news editor Anaheim (Calif.) Gazette, 1961-62; prof., dir. journalism Multnomah Sch. of the Bible, Portland, Oreg., 1963-79; broker Dick Bohrer Realty Inc., Portland, 1968-81; sr. editor, mng. editor Moody Monthly mag., Chgo., 1979-83; pub. Glory Press, 1981—; prof. Liberty U., Lynchburg, Va., 1983-89, 91-94; asst. prof., head mag. sequence Ball State U., Muncie, Ind., 1989-90; dir. Maranatha Writers Conf., Muskegon, Mich., 1980-89; prof. Inst. Bibl. Studies, Lake Grove, Oreg., 1996-97. Author: Easy English, 1977, Edit, Yourself and Sell, 1980, They Called Him Shifta, 1981, 21 Ways to Write Stories for Christian Kids, 1980, 3d edit., 1997, John Newton, 1983, Bill Borden, 1984, How to Write What You Think, 1985, How to Write Features Like a Pro, 1986, Be an Editor Yourself, 1987, J. Edgar Beanpole: Football Detective, 1991, J. Edgar Beanpole: Volleyball Spy, 1991, J. Edgar Beanpole: Soccer Sleuth, 1991, J. Edgar Beanpole: Night Watcher, 1991, No Frills Editing Skills, 1993, John G. Mitchell: Lion of God, 1994, J. Edgar Beanpole: Stage Snoop, 1997, J. Edgar Beanpole: Basketball Hawk, 1997; editor: The Battle for Your Faith (Willard M. Aldrich), The Schemer and the Dreamer (Luis Palau), Down to Earth (John Lawrence), Parables by the Sea (Pamela Reeve), An Everlasting Love (John G. Mitchell), Plague in Our Midst (Gregg Albers, MD), Right With God (John G. Mitchell), What Do You Say When.... (Nellie Pickard), Counseling the Terminally Ill (Gregg Albers, MD), The Self-Study of Liberty University, Maranatha, Our Lord, Come! (Renald Showers), Let's Revel in John's Gospel (John G. Mitchell), Let's Revel in Romans (John G. Mitchell), Priceless Pearls (John and Esther Nader Smit); acting editor Moral Majority Report, 1983-85, copy editor, 1985-88. Recipient Pres.'s Svc. award Liberty U., 1985, Tchr. of Yr. award, 1987, 89. Mem. Northwest Assn. of Book Publ. Republican. Mem. Plymouth Brethren Ch. Home: PO Box 624 West Linn OR 97068

BOLAÑOS, MARY CATHERINE, infection control coordinator; b. Berkeley, Calif., Dec. 25, 1954; d. Robert L. and Carolyn M. (Hicks) Luis; m. José R. Bolaños, June 24, 1978; children: Maria C.O., José R.M. AS, L.A. City Coll., 1976; B of Health Sci., Chapman Coll., 1983; MPH, U. Wash., 1994. RN, Calif., Wash. Staff nurse Hollywood Presbyn. Hosp., L.A., 1976-77; charge nurse Good Samaritan Hosp., L.A., 1977-78, Glendale (Calif.) Adventist Med. Ctr., 1978-80; infection control coord. Great West Hosps., Inc., L.A., 1980-85, VA Med. Ctr., Tacoma, 1985-87; nurse cons. State of Wash. Dept. Health, Olympia, 1987-89; DON Reach Nursing, Seattle, 1989-90; infection control coord. Highline Comty. Hosp., Seattle, 1990-94; coord. infection control, nurse cons. advisor Wash. Dept. Social and Health Svcs., Olympia, 1994—; cons. in field, L.A., 1984-85, Seattle, 1985—. Named Outstanding Career Woman, City of Pomona, 1982. Mem. Assn. for Practitioners of Infection Control (pres. 1986-87, bd. dirs. 1987-88, nominating com. 1993-94), State Expert Panel on Infection Control (panel mem. 1992—). Democrat. Roman Catholic. Home: 31526 45th Ct SW Federal Way WA 98023-2189

BOLDON, ALLIFEE, aerospace company executive; b. Streetman, Tex., July 27, 1941; s. James Paul and Izora (English) B.; children: Latrina, Dwyane, Keith. BA, Dominguez Hills U., 1969; JD, Loyola U., 1975. Mgr. McDonnell Douglas, Santa Monica, Calif., 1962-69, Edison, Rosemead, Calif., 1969-75, Hughes Aircraft, El Segundo, Calif., 1975-79; dir. TRW, Redondo Beach, Calif., 1979—. Bd. dirs. GLAAACC, L.A., 1997, Compton (Calif.) Coll. Exec. Bd., 1997, BBA, L.A., 1997. Mem. Nat. Soc. Am. Indians (dir., Cert. 1997), Nat. Tech. Assn. (dir., Cert. 1996), NASA Prime Contractor Round Table (dir. 1993-97, Cert. 1997). Democrat. Methodist.

BOLDREY, EDWIN EASTLAND, retinal surgeon, educator; b. San Francisco, Dec. 8, 1941; s. Edwin Barkley and Helen Burns (Eastland) B.; m. Catherine Rose Oliphant, Oct. 20, 1973; children: Jennifer Elizabeth, Melissa Jeanne. BA with honors, De Pauw U., 1963; MD, Northwestern U., Chgo., 1967. Diplomate Am. Bd. Ophthalmology. Rotating intern U. Wash., Seattle, 1967-68; resident in gen. surgery U. Minn., Mpls., 1968-69; resident in ophthalmology U. Calif., San Francisco, 1971-74; Heed Found. fellow in retinal and vitreous surgery Washington U., St. Louis, 1974-75; mem. staff dept. ophthalmology Palo Alto (Calif.) Med. Clinic, 1975-91; dept. chmn., 1989-91; pvt. practice, San Jose, Mountain View, Calif., 1991—; clin. instr. Stanford (Calif.) U. Med. Sch., 1975-79, asst. clin. prof., 1979-87, assoc. clin. prof., 1987—; cons. VA Hosp., Palo Alto, Calif., 1976—; vice chmn. dept. ophthalmology Good Samaritan Hosp., San Jose, 1993-95, chmn., 1995-97. Contbr. articles to med. jours., chpt. to book. Lt. comdr. M.C., USNR, 1969-71. Recipient Asbury award dept. ophthalmology U. Calif., San Francisco, 1973. Fellow ACS, Am. Acad. Ophthalmology (honor award 1989); mem. AMA, Retina Soc., Vitreous Soc. (charter), Peninsula Eye Soc. (pres. 1987-88), Western Retina Study Club (charter, exec. sec.-treas. 1983-95), Cordes Eye Soc. (pres. 1995-96), also others. Office: Retina Vitreous Assocs Inc 2512 Samaritan Ct Ste A San Jose CA 95124-4002

BOLEN, MICHAEL D., construction executive; b. 1949. BS in Gen. Engring., USAF Acad., 1970; MA, U. No. Colo. Supt. Kitchell Contractors, Inc., Phoenix, 1973-81; pres. Newport Beach (Calif.) divsn. McCarthy Brothers, Inc. Office: Mc Carthy Brothers Inc Newport Beach Divsn 100 Bayview Cir Newport Beach CA 92663*

BOLES, THOMAS LEE, medical technician; b. Chgo., Sept. 6, 1946; s. Millard Martin and Gayle Alberta (Salley) B. BS, N.M. State U., 1971; MA, Calif. State U., Long Beach, 1989. Mech. engr. U.S. Army Engr. Dist., Ft. Worth, 1972-74; aerospace engr. Naval Air Rework Facility North Island, San Diego, 1974-80; mech engr. 11th Coast Guard Dist., Long Beach, 1980-83; EEG/magnetoencephalography technician VA Med. Ctr., Albuquerque, 1990-91; EEG technician Gerald Champion Hosp., Alamogordo, N.M., 1992—; cons. HydroNuc. Corp., Albuquerque, 1971. Vol. docent, exhibitor Toy Train Depot, Alamogordo, 1993—; active Sierra Club, N.M., Tex., Calif., 1967-96. Mem. APA (assoc.), Am. Soc. Electroneurodiagnostic Technicians. Democrat. Methodist.

BOLEY, DENNIS LYNN, construction company executive; b. Lima, Ohio, Aug. 27, 1951; s. James Cloyral and Joan Marie (Bevington) B.; m. Marjorie Ann Ribic, Dec. 13, 1975; children: Lisa Marie, Amanda Michelle. BSCE, Tri State Coll., 1974; MSCE, Ga. Inst. Tech., 1977. Registered profl. engr., Pa., Ohio; registered profl. land surveyor, Pa. Staff engr. D'Appolonia Cons. Engrs., Inc., Pitts., 1974-77, asst. project engr., 1977-78, project engr., 1978-82, mgr. civil group, 1982-83; dir. engring. research and devel. Nicholson Constrn. Co., Pitts., 1983-87, v.p., 1987-89; pres. Nicholson Constrn. Inc., Atlanta, 1989-92; mgr. Bauer-Nicholson Joint Venture, Atlanta, 1992-96; pres., gen. mgr. Denver Grouting Svcs., Inc., 1996—. Contbr. more than 25 articles to profl. jours. Lay speaker, councilman Alpha Luth. Ch., Turtle Creek, Pa., 1986-87; coun. pres. St. Thomas Luth. Ch., Roswell, Ga., 1991-93. Mem. ASCE (sec. Pitts. sect. 1980-83, bd. dirs. 1984-85, v.p. 1985-86, pres. 1986-87, past pres. 1987—, Outstanding Young Civil Engr. of Yr. 1987), Engrs. Soc. West Pa. Republican. Home: 1800 Belshire Ct Roswell GA 30075-5252

BOLIN, RICHARD LUDDINGTON, industrial development consultant; b. Burlington, Vt., May 13, 1923; s. Axel Birger and Eva Madora (Luddington) B.; m. Jeanne Marie Brown, Dec. 18, 1948; children: Richard Luddington, Jr., Douglas, Judith, Barbara, Elizabeth. BSChemE, Tex. A&M U., 1947; MSChemE, MIT, 1950; postgrad. advanced mgmt. program Harvard Bus. Sch., 1969. Jr. rsch. engr. Humble Oil & Refining Co., Baytown, Tex., 1947-49; staff mem. Arthur D. Little, Inc., Cambridge, Mass., 1950-56, Caribbean office mgr. San Juan, 1957-61, gen. mgr., Mex., 1961-72; pres. Internat. Parks, Inc., Flagstaff, Ariz., 1973-94, chmn., 1995—; bd. dirs. Parque Indsl. de Nogales, Nogales, Sonora, Mex.; dir. The Flagstaff Inst., 1976—, Secretariat World Export Processing Zones Assn., 1985—; mem. adv. bd. Lowell Obs., Flagstaff, 1993-94. With U.S. Army, 1942-46. Mem. Univ. Club of Mex. Office: PO Box 986 Flagstaff AZ 86002

BOLIN, VERNON SPENCER, microbiologist, consultant; b. Parma, Idaho, July 9, 1913; s. Thadeus Howard Bolin and Jennie Bell Harm; m. Helen Epling, Jan. 5, 1948 (div. 1964); children: Rex, Janet, Mark; m. Barbara Sue Chase, Aug. 1965; children: Vladimir, Erik. BS, U. Wash., 1942; MS, U. Minn. 1949. Teaching asst. U. Minn.-Mpls., 1943-45; rsch. assoc. U. Utah, Salt Lake City, 1945-50, fellow in surgery, 1950-52; rsch. virologist Jensen-Salsbery Labs., Inc., Kansas City, Mo., 1952-57; rsch. assoc. Wistar Inst. U. Pa., 1957-58; rsch. virologist USPHS, 1958-61; founder Bolin Labs., Phoenix, 1959—, also bd. dirs. Contbr. articles to profl. jours. Served with U.S. Army, 1931-33. Mem. N.Y. Acad. Scis., Phi Mu Chi. Home: 36629 N 19th Ave Phoenix AZ 85027

BOLIN, VLADIMIR DUSTIN, chemist; b. Inglewood, Calif., Feb. 25, 1965; s. Vernon Spencer and Barbara Sue (Chase) B.; m. Elizabeth Lynne Boswood, May 18, 1985; children: Ragnar Spencer, Roark Morgan. BS, U. Ariz., 1987. Chemist, microbiologist Bolin Labs., Inc., Phoenix, 1987-93; bd. dirs., pres. Aerotech Labs., Inc., Phoenix, 1993—, pres., 1993—; pres. Kalmar Labs., Inc., Pheonix, 1993—, also bd. dirs.; v.p. lab ops. Aqualab Inc.; bd. dirs., pres. Kalmar Labs., Inc., Phoenix; bd. dirs. Aqualab Inc., v.p., 1996—; bd. dirs. Ariz. Indoor Quality Coun., v.p. 1995—. Mem. ASTM, AAAS, Am. Water Works Assn. (pres.), Assn. Official Analytical Chemists, Am. Soc. Microbiolgoy, Am. Chem. Soc., N.Y. Acad. Scis. Home: 2020 W Lone Cactus Dr Phoenix AZ 85027-3537 Office: Aerotech/Kalmar Labs Inc 2020 W Lone Cactus Dr Phoenix AZ 85027-2624

BOLING, JUDY ATWOOD, civic worker; b. Madras, India, June 19, 1921 (parents Am. citizens); d. Carroll Eugene and Marion Frances (Ayrer) Atwood; m. Jack Leroy Boling, Apr. 8, 1941 (dec. July 1988); children: Joseph Edward, Jean Ann, James Michael, John Charles. AA, San Antonio Jr. Coll., 1940; student Rogue Community Coll., Grants Pass, Oreg., 1978-79, So. Oreg. State Coll., Ashland, 1982—. Contbr. articles to profl. jours. First aid instr. ARC, various locations, 1940-65, chmn. vols., Calif., 1961-62, Eng., 1964-65; den mother cub scouts Boy Scouts Am., Monterey, Calif., 1951-52; active Girl Scouts U.S., 1953—, coun. pres., Winema (Oreg.) Coun., 1971-73, 79-82, historian, 1990—, del. to nat. coun., 1966, 72, 81, cons. for nat. pubs., 1971, 79; Sunday sch. tchr. Base Chapel, Pyote, Tex., 1949-51, choir dir., 1951; Sunday sch. adminstr. Base Chapel, Morocco, 1954-55; Sunday sch. tchr. Hermon Free Meth. Ch., L.A., 1956-57; active United Way campaign, 1967-84, Childrens Festival, 1974-88; former liaison with local people in Japanese-Am., Franco-Am., Anglo-Am. orgns.; mem., patron Rogue Craftsmen Bd., Grants Pass, 1972-85, sec., 1972-78, v.p., 1978-85; bd. dirs. Rogue Valley Opera Assn., 1978-85, sponsor/mem., 1978—; bd. dirs. Community Concert, 1979-88, 92—, mem. Grants Pass Friends of the Symphony, 1989— (bd. dirs. 1992—); vol. RSVP, 1982—; historian Josephine County Rep. Women, 1982-86, treas., 1986-94, sec., 1994-96; elected Rep. precinct committeeperson, 1991—; sustaining mem. Sta. KSYS pub. TV; mem. Sta. KSOR pub. radio; frequent pub. speaker. Recipient Thanks badge Girl Scouts U.S., 1957, 60, 73, Girl Scouts Japan, 1959, U.K. Girl Guides, 1982; others; cert. of appreciation USAF, 1959, City of Hagi, City of Fukuoka (Japan), Gov. of Fukuoka Prefecture; 2 citations Internat. Book Project; Oreg. Vol. award Sen. Packwood, 1983; Community Woman of Year award Bus. and Profl. Women, 1984, Nat. award Juliette Gordon Low World Friendship medal Girl Scouts Am., 1995. Mem. Josephine County Hist. Soc. (bd. dirs. 1991—), So. Oreg. Resources Alliance, Am. Host Found., Friends of Libr., Grants Pass Art Mus., Knife and Fork Club (bd. dirs. 1994—), Phi Theta Kappa. Address: 3016 Jumpoff Joe Creek Rd Grants Pass OR 97526-8778

BOLITHO, LOUISE GREER, educational administrator, consultant; b. Wenatchee, Wash., Aug. 13, 1927; d. Lon Glenn and Edna Gertrude (Dunlap) Greer; m. Douglas Stuart, June 17, 1950 (div. Dec. 1975); children: Rebecca Louise, Brian Douglas. BA, Wash. State U., 1949. With Stanford (Calif.) U., 1967-91, adminstrv. asst. physics labs., 1974-77, mgr. ctr. for research in internat. studies, 1977-84, law sch. fin. and adminstrv. services dir., 1984-86; computer cons., Palo Alto, Calif., 1984—; acting mgr. Inst. for Internat. Studies, 1987-88, fin. analyst, 1988-91. Mem. Peninsula vols., Menlo Park, Calif., 1986-94; budget com. chmn., bd. dirs. Mid-Peninsula Support Network, Mountain View, Calif., 1984-86; chairperson active older adults com. YMCA; pres. 410 Sheridan Ave. Homeowners Assn., 1989-93, treas., 1993—. Mem. AAUW (bd. dirs. 1987-88). Home and Office: 410 Sheridan Ave Condo 445 Palo Alto CA 94306-2020

BOLLES, CHARLES AVERY, librarian; b. Pine Island, Minn., Aug. 10, 1940; s. Arthur Marston and Clarice Ione (Figy) B.; B.A., U. Minn., 1962, M.A. in Library Sci., 1963, M.A. in Am. Studies, 1969, Ph.D. in Library Sci., 1975; m. Marjorie Elaine Hancock, May 17, 1964; children: Jason Brice, Justin Brian. Catalog and serials librarian U. Iowa, Iowa City, 1964-67; asst. prof. Emporia (Kans.) State U., 1970-76; dir. library devel. div. Kans. State Library, 1976-78; dir. Sch. Library Sci., Emporia State U., 1978-80; state librarian State of Idaho, Boise, 1980—. Mem. ALA, Chief Officers State Library Agys., Western Council State Libraries (chmn. 1985-86), Pacific N.W. Library Assn. (pres. 1990-91), Idaho Library Assn. Office: Idaho State Libr 325 W State St Boise ID 83702-6055

BOLOCOFSKY, DAVID N., lawyer, psychology educator; b. Hartford, Conn., Sept. 29, 1947; s. Samuel and Olga Bolocofsky. BA, Clark U., 1969; MS, Nova U., 1974, PhD, 1975; JD, U. Denver, 1988. Bar: Colo. 1988; cert. sch. psychologist, Colo., Fla., cert. counselor, Fla. Tchr. high sch. Univ. Sch., Ft. Lauderdale, Fla., 1972-73; ednl. coord. Living and Learning Ctr., Ft. Lauderdale, 1972-75; asst. prof. U. No. Colo., Greeley, 1975-79, assoc. prof., 1979-90, dir. sch. psychology program, 1979-82; assoc. Robert T. Hinds Jr. & Assocs., Littleton, Colo., 1988-93; hearing officer State of Colo., 1991—; pres. David N. Bolocofsky, P.C., Denver, 1993—; psychol. cons. Clin. Assocs., Englewood, Colo., 1978—. Author: Enhancing Personal Adjustment, 1986, (chpts. in books) Children and Obesity, 1987, Obtaining and Utilizing a Custody Evaluation, 1989; contbr. numerous articles to profl. jours. Mem. Douglas-Elbert Bar Assn., Arapahoe Bar Assn., Nat. Assn. Sch. Psychologists (ethics com. 1988-91), Colo. Soc. Sch. Psychologists (bd. dirs. 1978-96, treas. 1993-96), Interdisciplinary Commn. on Child Custody (pro bono com. 1988—), Colo. Bar Assn. (family law sect., sec. juvenile law sect. 1990-92), Colo. Soc. Behavioral Analysis Therapy (treas. 1990-96), Arapmhc (bd. mem. 1993—, bd. pres.1995—). Home: 9848 E Maplewood Cir Englewood CO 80111-5401 Office: 5353 W Dartmouth Ave Ste 500 Denver CO 80227-5517

BOLTON, BRADFORD L., court clerk; b. Greenfield, Mass.; s. Norman Irwin and Jean Francis (Sibley) B.; 2 children. BA in Polit. Sci., Calif. State U., L.A., 1974; MPA Judicial Adminstrn., U. So. Calif., 1976. Security adminstr. Dept. Def., 1972-74; dir. adminstrv. svcs. U.S. Dist. Ct., L.A., 1974-79; clk. U.S. Bankruptcy Ct. Colo., Denver, 1979—. Mem. Evergreen Chorale, Colo. Symphony Orch. With USAF, 1969, Calif. Air Nat. Guard until 1975. Mem. Nat. Conf. Bankruptcy Clks., Rotary Internat. Methodist. Office: US Custom House 721 19th St Denver CO 80202-2508

BOLTON, LEON LESLIE, plastic surgeon; b. Memphis, Sept. 4, 1954. BA summa cum laude, U. Tenn., 1976; MD, U. Tenn., Memphis, 1980. Diplomate Am. Bd. Surgery, Am. Bd. Plastic Surgery. Resident in gen. surgery Emory U. Hosps., Atlanta, 1980-83, U. Ky. Hosps., Lexington, 1983-85; resident in plastic and reconstructive surgery U. So. Calif., L.A., 1985-87; pvt. practice Aesthetic Surgery Ctr., Long Beach, Calif., 1987—; clin. instr. surgery U. So. Calif., L.A., 1987—; spkr. in field. Contbr. articles to profl. jours. Fellow ACS; mem. AMA, Am. Assn. for Accreditation of Ambulatory Surgery Facilities (chair oper. com. 1995—), Am. Soc. Plastic and Reconstructive Surgeons, Am. Soc. Aesthetic Plastic Surgery, Calif. Soc. Plastic Surgeons, Lipoplasty Soc. N.Am., Los Angeles County Med. Assn., Calif. Med. Assn., Phi Beta Kappa, Phi Kappa Phi, Alpha Omega Alpha. Office: Aesthetic Surgery Ctr 4300 N Long Beach Blvd Ste 150 Long Beach CA 90807-2011*

BOLTON, MARTHA O., writer; b. Searcy, Ark., Sept. 1, 1951; d. Lonnie Leon and Eunice Dolores Ferren; m. Russell Norman Bolton, Apr. 17, 1970; children: Russell Norman II, Matthew David, Anthony Shane. Grad. high sch., Reseda, Calif. Freelance writer for various comedians, 1975-86; newspaper columnist Simi Valley Enterprise, Simi, Calif., 1979-87; staff writer Bob Hope, 1986—, The Mark and Kathy Show, 1995-96. Author: A Funny Thing Happened to Me on My Way Through the Bible, 1985, A View from the Pew, 1986, What's Growing Under Your Bed?, 1986, Tangled in the Tinsel, 1987, So. How'd I Get To Be in Charge of the Program?, 1988, Humorous Monologues, 1989, Let My People Laugh, 1989, If Mr. Clean Calls Tell Him I'm Not In, 1989, Journey to the Center of the Stage, 1990, If You Can't Stand the Smoke, Get Out of My Kitchen, 1990, Home, Home on the Stage, 1991, TV Jokes and Riddles, 1991, These Truths Were Made for Walking, 1991, When the Meatloaf Explodes It's Done, 1993, Childhood Is a Stage, 1993, Honey, It's Time To Weed the Carpets Again, 1994, Walk A Mile in His Truths, 1994, The Cafeteria Lady on the Loose, 1994, On the Loose, 1994, If the Pasta Wiggles, Don't Eat It, 1995, Bethlehem's Big Night, 1995, Club Family, 1995, When the Going Gets Tough, The Tough Start Laughing, 1995, Who Put The Pizza in the VCR?, 1996, And Now a World from Our Maker, 1997, (lyrics) Mouth in Motion. Pres. Vista Elem. Sch. PTA, Simi, 1980-81. Recipient Emmy nomination for outstanding achievement in music and lyrics, 1988, Internat. Angel award, 1991, Amb. award Media Fellowship Internat., 1995. Mem. ASCAP, NATAS, Nat. League Am. Pen Women (pres. Simi Valley br. 1984-86, 96—, Woman of Achievement award 1984, Pen Woman of Yr. award 1995), Writers Guild Am. West, Soc. Children's Book Writers. Office: PO Box 1212 Simi Valley CA 93062-1212

BOLTON, ROBERT FLOYD, construction executive; b. Dunlap, Iowa, Oct. 18, 1942; s. Russel J. And Mary Jane (Lacey) B.; m. Mary Louise Hartman, May 15, 1988. Lic. residential/comml. gen. bldg. contractor. Sole practice farming Dunlap, Iowa, 1967-72; supr. Phillips Constrn. Co., Cottonwood, Ariz., 1972-84; contractor Bolton Bldg. and Devel. Co., Sedona, Ariz., 1984—; cons. in field. With U.S. Army, 1964-66. Mem. Nat. Assn. Home Builders, Am. Soc. Home Inspectors, C. of C., VFW, Meth. Mens Fellowship Club. Republican. Methodist. Home & Office: 90 Evening Glow Pl Sedona AZ 86351-7912

BONA, MARY JO, English educator; b. Chgo., July 5, 1959; d. Vincent J. and Florence L. (Orlando) B. BA, Loyola U., Chgo., 1981, MA, 1983; PhD, U. Wis., 1989. Tchg. asst. LoyolaU., 1981-83; adj. faculty U. Wis., Madison, 1983-88; mem. faculty Edgewood Coll., Madison, 1988-89, Lakeland Coll., Madison, 1989; prof. English, Gonzaga U., Spokane, Wash., 1989—, mem. rsch. coun., 1991. Editor: The Voice We Carry: Recent Italian/American Women's Fiction, 1994 (Guernica Edits. Bestseller award 1995), (with Anthony Tamburri) Through the Looking Glass: Italian and Italian/American Images in the Media, 1996; contbr. articles to profl. jours. Vol., reader, monitor, capt. The NAMES Quilt Project Found., Spokane, 1993, 96. Wash. Ctr. grantee Evergreen State Coll., 1993. Mem. MLA, Am. Italian Hist. Assn. Office: Gonzaga U E 502 Boone Spokane WA 99258-0001

BONAFEDE, R. PETER, rheumatologist; b. Cape Town, South Africa, Aug. 12, 1950; came to U.S., 1986; m. Janet Jones, Deb. 15, 1981; children: Sebastian, Caroline. MB, Ch. B, U. Cape Town, S. Africa, 1974; MD, U. Cape Town, 1979; MBA, U. Oreg., 1996. Diplomate Am. Bd. Internal Medicine, Am. Bd. Rheumatology; lic. Brit. Med. Coun., S. Africa Med. Coun., Wash., Oreg. Intern ob/gyn. and surgery Groote Schuur Hosp., Captetown, South Africa, 1975-76; resident internal medicine Groote Schuur Hosp., Captetown, 1982-86; fellow in rheumatology Oreg. Health Scis. U., Portland, 1986-89; dir. Arthritis Ctr. Providence Hosp. and Med. Ctr., Portland, 1989-92; med. dir. Arthritis Ctr. Providence Hosp. & Med. Ctr., Portland, 1992—; clin. asst. prof. medicine divsn. arthritis, rheumatic diseases Oreg. Health Scis. U., Portland, 1989—; med. officer S. Africa nat. svc., 1976-77, internal medicine Addington Hosp., Durban, S. Africa, 1978; rsch. fellow human genetics U. Cape Town, 1976-78; emergency physician Groote Schuur Hosp., Capetown, 1979; tutor in internal medicine, U. Cape Town, 1983-86; attending physician Somerset Hosp., Cape Town, 1986; mem. planninc com. of ctrs. for bone and joint care, Providence Hosp. Ctr., 1989—; chmn. edn. com. Providence Ctrs. for Bone and Joint Care, 1993—. Contbr. articles and abstracts to profl. jours. Bd. dirs. Oreg. chpt. Arthritis Found., 1990—, med. and sci. com., 1990—, chmn. 1992-94. Recipient Univ. scholarship S. African Coll., 1969; named hon. pres. S. African Univs. Judo Assn., 1975, 76. Fellow ACP, Am.Coll. Rheumatology; mem. AMA, Multnomah County Med. Soc., S. African Arthritis and Rheumatism Assn. Home: 10560 SW 161st Ct Beaverton OR 97007-8171 Office: Providence Arthritis Ctr 5050 NE Hoyt St Ste 155 Portland OR 97213-2956

BOND, WARD CHARLES, mathematics and computer educator; b. Sidney, Nebr., June 3, 1961; s. Eugene R. and Clara Kay (Meyer) B.; m. Anna M. Angaiak, July 1993; 1 child, Baxter Wayne. BS, U. Wyo., 1985, student, 1994—. Cert. tchr., Wyo., Kans., Nebr., Alaska. Math. tchr. Laramie (Wyo.) High Sch., Decatur Commuity High Sch., Oberlin, Kans.; math. and computer tchr., coach Carbon County Sch. Dist. 2, Hanna, Wyo.; high sch. math. and sci. tchr. Lower Kuskokwim Sch. Dist., Tununak, Alaska, 1989-94, 94—, mentor tchr. coach phys. edn., art, geography, econs. Mem. ASCD, NEA, Nat. Platform Assn., Alaska Coun. Tchrs. Math., Alaska Edn. Assn., Lower Kuskokwim Edn. Assn., Sigma Nu (Epsilon Delta chpt. Outstanding Sr. Man). Home: PO Box 7 Tununak AK 99681-0007

BOND, WENDELL ANSON, petroleum geologist, oil company executive; b. Columbus, Ohio, Mar. 13, 1947; s. Ralph Hurd and Virginia (Barker) B.;

m. Laurel J. Etkin, Apr. 25, 1987; children: Ryan, Erin, Sydney. BS in Geology, Capital U., 1969; MS in Geology, U. Colo., 1973. Registered profl. geologist, Wyo. Project geologist Intrasearch, Inc., Denver, 1973-74; corp. geologist Bond Exploration Co., Denver, 1974-76; project geologist Webb Resources, Inc., Denver, 1976-80; dist. geologist Sohio Petroleum Co., Denver, 1980-81; chief geologist Bird Oil Corp., Denver, 1981-82; pvt. practice cons. petroleum geologist Denver, 1982-84; chief geologist Samuel Gary Jr. and Assocs., Denver, 1984-88; pres. Bond Petroleum Corp., Boulder, 1988—, Wendell A. Bond, Inc., Boulder, 1989—; bd. mem. Denver (Colo.) Earth Resources Libr. Mem. Am. Assn. Petroleum Geologists, Denver Internat. Petroleum Soc., Rocky Mountain Assn. Geologists. Home and Office: Bond Petroleum Corp 1137 Barberry Ct Boulder CO 80303

BONDAR, RICHARD JAY LAURENT, biochemist; b. N.Y.C., Sept. 4, 1940; s. Kelliher H. and Helen (Halper) B.; m. Enid Sue Teicher, Dec. 21, 1961; children: Randal, Karen. BS, McGill U., Montreal, Que., Can., 1962; MS, Calif. Inst. Tech., 1965; PhD, U. Calif., Riverside, 1969. Tech. dir. Worthington Biochem. =Corp., Freehold, N.J.; prin. devel. chemist Beckman, Brea, Calif.; mgr. Abbott Labs, South Pasadena, Calif.; v.p. Internat. Medication Systems, South El Monte, Calif.; mgr. pharm. devel. Banner Pharmacaps, Chatsworth, Calif.; mgr. quality control lab. 3M Pharmaceuticals, Northridge, Calif. Contbr. over 30 refereed articles to profl. jours. Fellow Am. Inst. chemists; mem. Am. Chem. Soc., Am. Assn. Pharm. Scientists, Sigma Xi. Office: 3M Pharmaceuticals 19901 Nordhoff Northridge CA 91328

BONDI, BERT ROGER, accountant, financial planner; b. Portland, Oreg., Oct. 2, 1945; s. Gene L. and Elizabeth (Poynter) B.; m. Kimberley Kay Higgins, June 18, 1988; children: Nicholas Stone, Christopher Poynter. BBA, U. Notre Dame, 1967. CPA, Colo., Calif., Wyo. Sr. tax acct. Price Waterhouse, Los Angeles, 1970-73; ptnr. Valentine Adducci & Bondi, Denver, 1973-76; sr. ptnr. Bondi & Co., Englewood, Colo., 1977—; dir. Citizens Bank. Bd. govs. Met. State Coll. Found.; bd. dirs. Am. Cancer Soc. Denver; mem. adv. bd. Jr. League of Denver. Served with U.S. Army, 1968-70. Mem. C. of C., Community Assns. Inst., Govt. Fin. Officers Assn., Colo. Soc. Assn. Execs. (edn. com.), Home Builders Assn., Am. Inst. CPAs, Colo. Soc. CPAs, Wyo. Soc. CPAs., Rotary (Denver), Notre Dame Club, Metropolitan Club (Denver), Castle Pines Country Club. Roman Catholic. Home: 49 Glenalla Pl Castle Rock CO 80104-9026 Office: Bondi & Co 44 Inverness Dr E Englewood CO 80112-5410

BONDI, HARRY GENE, lawyer; b. Sheridan, Wyo., Apr. 3, 1948; s. Gene and Elizabeth (Poynter) B; divorced; 1 child, Bert Gene. BS in sci., fin., Fairfield U., 1970; JD, U. Wyo., 1974; postgrad., Georgetown U. Law Ctr., 1977. Bar: Wyo. 1974, U.S. Dist. Ct. D.C. 1976, U.S. Tax Ct. 1976, U.S. Ct. Claims 1975, U.S. Supreme Ct. 1980, D.C. 1975, Colo. 1988, U.S. Dist. Ct. Wyo. 1977, U.S. Ct. Appeals (10th cir.) 1980. Trial atty. U.S. Renegotiation Bd., Washington, D.C., 1974-77; pub. defender Wyo. State Pub. Defender Office, Casper, 1978-79; pvt. practice Harry G. Bondi, P.C., Casper, 1977—. Author: Wyoming Labor and Employment Law, 1992, Workers Compensation in Wyoming, 1993, Wrongful Discharge Claims Under Wyoming Law, 1994, 95. Chmn. City of Casper Housing and Cmty. Devel. Commn., 1977-81; past pres. Natrona County Meals of Wheels, Inc., 1988-90, Meals on Wheels Found., 1991-94; bd. dirs. Casper Jr. Baseball League, 1994—. Mem. Wyo. Bar Assn., Natrona County Bar Assn., Am. Trial Lawyers Assn., Wyo. Trial Lawyers Assn., Wyo. Criminal Defense Lawyers Assn., Colo. Bar Assn., D.C. Bar Assn., Federal Bar Assn., Criminal Justice Adminstrn. Panel Dist. Wyo.

BONDS, BARRY LAMAR, professional baseball player; b. Riverside, Calif., July 24, 1964; s. Bobby B. Student, Ariz. State U. With Pitts. Pirates, 1985-92, San Francisco Giants, 1992—. Named MVP Baseball Writers' Assn. Am., 1990, 1992, 1993, Maj. League Player Yr. Sporting News, 1990, Nat. League Player Yr. Sporting News, 1990, 91, mem. Sporting News Coll. All-Am. team, 1985, mem. All-Star team, 1990, 1992-95; recipient Gold Glove award, 1990-94, Silver Slugger award, 1990-94. Office: San Francisco Giants Candlestick Park San Francisco CA 94124*

BONFIELD, ANDREW JOSEPH, tax practitioner; b. London, Jan. 26, 1924; s. George William and Elizabeth Agnes B.; came to U.S., 1946, naturalized, 1954; m. Eleanor Ackerman, Oct. 16, 1955; children: Bruce Ian, Sandra Karen. Gen. mgr. Am. Cushion Co., Los Angeles, 1948-50, Monson Calif. Co., Redwood City, 1951-58; mfrs. mktg. rep., San Francisco, 1958-62; tax practitioner, bus. cons., Redwood City, San Jose, Los Gatos, Calif., 1963—. Past treas., dir. Northwood Park Improvement Assn.; mem. exec. bd. Santa Clara County council Boy Scouts Am., 1971—, past council pres., mem. Nat. council; mem. Santa Clara County Parks and Recreation Commn., 1975-81, 82-86; mem. County Assessment Appeals Bd., 1978-86; mem. Hawaii Bd. Taxation Review, 1992—. Served with Brit. Royal Navy, 1940-46. Decorated King George VI Silver Badge; recipient Silver Beaver award, Vigil honor award Boy Scouts Am.; enrolled to practice before IRS. Mem. Nat. Soc. Public Accts., Nat. Assn. Enrolled Agts., Calif. Soc. Enrolled Agts., Hawaii Assn. Pub. Accts., Hawaii Soc. Enrolled Agrs., Royal Can. Legion (past state parliamentarian, past state 1st vice comdr.). Club: Rotary (pres. San Jose E. 1977-78, pres. Kihei-Wailea 1993-94). Home: 760 S Kihei Rd Apt 215 Kihei HI 96753-7517

BONHAM, CHARLIE LEONARD, college official; b. Richmond, Calif., Sept. 26, 1939; s. Leonard Shelby and Lavern Luella (McKay) B.; m. Pamela Ann Prahl, Feb. 23, 1963; children: Stephen Shelby, Karen Elizebeth, Tracy Michelle. BS in Marine Engring., Calif. Maritime Acad., 1960; BA in Internat. Rels., Navy Postgrad. Sch., Monterey, Calif., 1970. Lic. engr. U.S. Mcht. Marine. 3d asst. engr. Mil. Sea Transport Svc., San Francisco, 1960; commd. ensign USN, 1961, advanced through grades to capt., 1982, comdr. 4 USN ships; ret., 1989; v.p. adminstrn. and student svcs. Calif. Maritime Acad., Vallejo, 1989—, pres. Calmaritime Acad. Found., 1990-97. Mem. Propeller Club U.S. (pres. San Francisco 1989-91). Republican. Office: Calif Maritime Acad 200 Maritime Academy Dr Vallejo CA 94590-8181

BONNELL, VICTORIA EILEEN, sociologist; b. N.Y.C., June 15, 1942; d. Samuel S. and Frances (Nassau) B.; m. Gregory Freidin, May 4, 1971. B.A. Brandeis U., 1964; M.A., Harvard U., 1966, Ph.D., 1975. Lectr. politics U. Calif.-Santa Cruz, 1972-73, 74-76; asst. prof. sociology U. Calif.-Berkeley, 1976-82, assoc. prof., 1982-91, prof., 1991—; chair Berkeley Ctr. for Slavic and East European Studies, U. Calif.-Berkeley, 1994—. Recipient Heldt prize in Slavic women's studies, 1991, editor Identities in Transition: Eastern Europe and Russia after the Collapse of Communism, 1996; AAUW fellow, 1979; Regents faculty fellow, 1978; Fulbright Hays faculty fellow, 1977; Internat. Research and Exchanges Bd. fellow, 1977, 88; Stanford U. Hoover Instn. nat. fellow, 1973-74; Guggenheim fellow, 1985; fellow Ctr. for Advanced Study in Behavioral Scis., 1986-87; Pres.' Rsch. fellow in humanities, 1991-92; grantee Am. Philos. Soc., 1979, Am. Council Learned Socs., 1976, 90-91. Mem. Am. Sociol. Assn., Am. Assn. Advancement Slavic Studies. Am. Hist. Assn. Author: Roots of Rebellion: Workers' Politics and Organizations in St. Petersburg and Moscow, 1900-1914, 1983; editor: The Russian Worker: Life and Labor under the Tsarist Regime, 1983, (with Ann Cooper and Gregory Freidin) Russia at the Barricades: Eyewitness Accounts of the August 1991 Coup, 1994; contbr. articles to profl. jours.

BONNELL, WILLIAM CHARLES, secondary education educator; b. L.A., Aug. 28, 1959. BA in English and History, San Francisco State U., 1983, MA in Classics, 1986; Diploma in Theology, Oxford (Eng.) U., 1992. Cert. English, history, Latin tchr. Tchr. English and Latin San Mateo (Calif.) Union Dist. High Sch., 1986—. Contbr. articles to profl. jours. Scholar Rotary Internat., 1991-92. Mem. Am. Classical League, Calif. Classical Assn. (sec. 1996—), Classical Assn. of Mid. West & South, Dickens Fellowship. Anglican. Office: San Mateo High Sch 506 N Delaware San Mateo CA 94401

BONNER, ROBERT CLEVE, lawyer; b. Wichita, Kans., Jan. 29, 1942; s. Benjamin Joseph and Caroline (Kirkwood) B.; m. Kimiko Tanaka, Oct. 11, 1969; 1 child, Justine M. B.A., Md. U., 1963; J.D., Georgetown U., 1966. Bar: D.C. 1966, Calif. 1967, U.S. Ct. Appeals (no. so., ctrl. dists.) Calif., U.S. Ct. Appeals (4th, 5th, 9th, 10th cirs.), U.S. Supreme Ct. Law clk. to judge U.S. Dist. Ct., L.A., 1966-67; asst. U.S. atty. U.S. Atty's Office (cen. dist.) Calif., L.A., 1971-75, U.S. atty., 1984-89; judge U.S. Dist. Ct. (cen. dist.) Calif., L.A., 1989-90; ptnr. Kadison, Pfaelzer, et al, Los Angeles, 1975-84; dir. Drug Enforcement Adminstrn., Washington, 1990-93; ptnr. Gibson, Dunn & Crutcher, L.A., 1993—. Served to lt. comdr. USN, 1967-70. Fellow Am. Coll. Trial Lawyers, Fed. Bar Assn. (pres. Los Angeles chpt. 1982-83). Republican. Roman Catholic. Office: Gibson Dunn & Crutcher 333 S Grand Ave Los Angeles CA 90071-1504

BONNEY, JOHN DENNIS, retired oil company executive; b. Blackpool, Eng., Dec. 22, 1930; s. John P. and Isabel (Evans) B.; four children from previous marriage; m. Elizabeth Shore-Wilson, Aug. 1986; two children. B.A., Hertford Coll., Oxford U., Eng., 1954, M.A., 1959; LL.M., U. Calif., Berkeley, 1956. Oil adviser Middle East, 1959-60; fgn. ops. adviser, asst. mgr., then mgr. Chevron Corp. (formerly Standard Oil Co. of Calif.), San Francisco, 1960-72, v.p., from 1972, vice chmn., dir., 1987-95. Clubs: Commonwealth; World Trade (San Francisco); Oxford and Cambridge (London). Office: care Chevron Corp 555 Market St San Francisco CA 94105-2870

BONO, SONNY SALVATORE, congressman, singer, composer, former mayor; b. Detroit, Feb. 16, 1935; m. Donna Rankin; 1 child, Christy; m. Cher LaPiere, Oct. 27, 1964 (div.); 1 child, Chastity; m. Susie Coehlo (div.); m. Mary Whitaker, Mar. 1986; children: Chesare Elan, Chianna Maria. Congressman, Calif. 44th Dist. U.S. Ho. of Reps., Washington, 1995—, mem. Nat. Security and Judiciary coms. Songwriter, later artist and repertoire man for Speciality Records; singer with Cher as team Sonny and Cher, 1964-74, co-star The Sonny and Cher Show, 1971-74; now solo night club act; numerous recs., TV, concert and benefit appearances; has appeared on numerous TV series; composer, lyricist, appearance in Good Times, 1966; films include: Escape to Athena, 1979, Airplane II-The Sequel, 1982, Hairspray, 1988; producer film: Chastity, 1969; composer: A Cowboy's Work is Never Done, The Beat Goes On, I Got You, Babe, Needles & Pins, others; TV video Nitty Gritty Hour with Cher, 1992; autobiography: And The Beat Goes On, 1991. Restaurateur; mayor Palm Springs, Calif., 1988-92; ran, defeated U.S. Senate, 1992.

BONOWITZ, ABRAHAM JACOB, human rights activist; b. Columbus, OH, Dec. 29, 1966; s. Marvin Hersh and Anne B. AS in Photgraphic Tech., Ohio Inst. Photography, Dayton, 1986. Owner, operator Abe Bonowitz, Photographer, Columbus, 1986-94; spl. asst. Ohio Pub Defender Commn., Columbus, 1993; dep. exec. dir. Cesar E. Chavez Found., Keene, Calif., 1994-96; acting exec. dir. Cesar E. Chavez Found., L.A., 1996-97; co-founder, co-dir. Citizens United for Alternatives to Death Penalty, 1997—. Actor: extra (movie) Teachers, 1994, Dead Man Walking 1996. Bd. dirs. U.S. sect. Amnesty Internat., 1994-96; organizer/convenor Abolitionist Action Com., also other death penalty abolitionist orgns. Jewish. Home: PO Box 65675 Los Angeles CA 90065-0675

BONSELL, THOMAS ALLEN, journalist, publisher; b. Lusk, Wyo., Mar. 17, 1935; s. Dee V. and Neoma Vada (Bevens) B. BBA, Woodbury U., 1963; postgrad., Georgetown U., 1964-65. Journalist, reporter The Portland (Oreg.) Reporter, 1963-64; intelligence analyst Nat. Security Agy., Ft. Meade, Md., 1964-65; journalist, editor The Utica (N.Y.) Daily Press, 1965-67, The Denver Post, 1967-80; journalist, writer Port Orchard, Wash., 1980—; founder, editor Country Cottage Pub., Port Orchard, 1995—. Author: The Un-Americans, 1995. With USAF, 1956-60. Mem. Phi Gamma Kappa. Home and Office: Country Cottage Pub 285 SE Rim Rd Port Orchard WA 98367

BONSER, QUENTIN, surgeon; b. Sedro Wooley, Wash., Nov. 1, 1920; s. George Wayne and Kathleen Imogene (Lynch) B.; BA in Zoology, UCLA, 1943; MD, U. Calif., San Francisco, 1947; m. Loellen Rocca, Oct. 20, 1945; children: Wayne, Gordon, Carol, Patricia (Mrs. Martin Sanford). Intern U. Calif. Hosp., San Francisco, 1947-49, resident gen. surgery, 1949-56; practice gen. surgery, Placerville, Calif., 1956—; ret.; surgeon King Faisal Splty. Hosp., Saudi Arabia, Sept.-Oct., 1984; vis. prof. surgery U. Calif., San Francisco, 1968. Capt. M.C., USAF, 1950-51. Vol. physician, tchr. surgery Vietnam, 1971, 72, 73. Diplomate Am. Bd. Surgery. Fellow A.C.S.; mem. H.C. Naffziger Surg. Soc. (pres. 1974-75). Home: 2590 Northridge Dr Placerville CA 95667-3416

BOOCHEVER, ROBERT, federal judge; b. N.Y.C., Oct. 2, 1917; s. Louis C. and Miriam (Cohen) B.; m. Lois Colleen Maddox, Apr. 22, 1943; children: Barbara K., Linda Lou, Ann Paula, Miriam Deon. AB, Cornell U., 1939, LLD, 1941; HD (hon.), U. Alaska, 1981. Bar: N.Y. 1944, Alaska 1947. Law clk. Nordlinger, Riegel & Cooper, 1941; asst. U.S. atty. Juneau, 1946-47; partner firm Faulkner, Banfield, Boochever & Doogan, Juneau, 1947-72; asso. justice Alaska Supreme Ct., 1972-75, 78-80, chief justice, 1975-78; chief justice U.S. Ct. Appeals (9th cir.), Pasadena, Calif., 1980-86; sr. judge U.S. Ct. Appeals, Pasadena, Calif., 1986—; mem. 9th cir. rules com. U.S. Ct. Appeals, 1983-85, chmn. 9th cir. libr. com., 1995—; chmn. Ala. Jud. Coun., 1975-78; mem. appellate judges seminar NYU Sch. Law, 1975; mem. Conf. Chief Justices, 1975-79, vice chmn., 1978-79; mem. adv. bd. Nat. Bank of Ala., 1968-72; guest spkr. Southwestern Law Sch. Disting. Lecture Series, 1992. Chmn. Juneau chpt. ARC, 1949-51, Juneau Planning Commn., 1956-61; mem. Alaska Devel. Bd., 1949-52, Alaska Jud. Qualification Commn., 1972-75; mem. adv. bd. Juneau-Douglas Community Coll. Served to Capt. U.S. Army, 1941-45. Named Juneau Man of Year, Rotary, 1974; recipient Disting. Alumnus award Cornell U., 1989. Fellow Am. Coll. Trial Attys.; mem. ABA, Alaska Bar Assn. (pres. 1961-62), Juneau Bar Assn. (pres. 1971-72), Am. Judicature Soc. (dir. 1970-74), Am. Law Inst., Juneau C. of C. (pres. 1952, 55), Alaskans United (chmn. 1972). Clubs: Marine Meml., Cornell Club of L.A., Altadena Town and Country. Office: US Ct Appeals PO Box 91510 125 S Grand Ave Pasadena CA 91105-1652

BOOKER, JAMES AVERY, JR., surgeon; b. Richmond, Va., May 26, 1936; s. James Avery and Thelma Martha (Morton) B.; m. Rita M. Booker, Nov. 24, 1984; children: James A. III, Karla L., Michael J., Ja Rita B. BS, Hampton (Va.) U., 1957; DDS, Med. Coll. Va., 1961; MD, Howard U., Washington, 1968. Diplomate Am. Bd. Surgery, Am. Bd. Quality Assurance and UR Physicians (mem. fin. com. 1989-91). Pvt. practice gen. surgery Oakland, Calif., 1976-90; v.p., med. dir. Family Health Found., Alviso, Calif., 1989-90; pvt. practice gen. surgery Torrance, Calif., 1991—. USAF, 1962-66, col. ret. Decorated Air Force Commendation medal, 1988. Fellow ACS, Am. Coll. Med. Quality (membership and credentials com. 1990-91), Internat. Coll. Surgeons (exec. com. So. Calif. chpt. 1991—), Southwestern Surg. Congress; mem. Am. Coll. Physician Execs. Office: 3655 Lomita Blvd Ste 115 Torrance CA 90505-3932

BOOKIN, DANIEL HENRY, lawyer; b. Ottumwa, Iowa, Oct. 16, 1951. BA, U. Iowa, 1973; JD, Yale U., 1976. Bar: Calif. 1978. Law clk. U.S. Dist. Ct. (no. dist.) Calif., 1976-77; asst. U.S. atty. U.S. Dist. Ct. (so. dist.) N.Y., 1978-82; ptnr. O'Melveny & Myers, San Francisco, 1982—. Mem. bd. editors Yale Law Jour., 1975-76. Fellow Am. Coll. Trial Lawyers, Phi Beta Kappa. Office: O'Melveny & Myers Embarcadero Ctr W Tower 275 Battery St San Francisco CA 94111-3305

BOOKKEY, GERALD C., agricultural products executive; b. 1925. With C.A. Swanson & Sons, Seattle, 1952-56; prin. Jumbo Corp., Seattle, 1952-78, 1956—; CEO Nat. Food Corp. Office: Nat Food Corp 16740 Aurora Ave N Seattle WA 98133-5311*

BOOKMAN, MARK ANDREW, business educator, consultant; b. June 12, 1948; s. Milford Norman and Barbara Doris (Goffman) B.; m. Dena Sara Goldberg Bookman; children: Aron, Noah. BA in History, UCLA, 1970; JD, 1973. Pres. Srpoul Hall Residents Assn., U. Calif., L.A., 1968-69; adminstrv. v.p. Undergrad. Student Assn. U. Calif., L.A., 1969-70; asst. to dean Campus Programs and Activities U. Calif., L.A., 1970-71, pres. Grad. Student Assn., 1971-72, rsch. asst., 1972-73; dir. U. Calif., San Diego, 1973-76; gen. mgr. Calif. State U., 1976-84; asst. v.p. Student Affairs U. Houston, 1984-88; cons., author, pres. Edn. and Non-Profit Consulting, Inc., 1986—; vis. scholar Inst. for Higher Edn. Law and Governance U. Houston, 1989-90; prof. bus. U. Judaism, 1990—, v.p. adminstrn., 1997—; Bar: Calif., 1973. Contbr. numerous articles to profl. jours. Pres., pres. Congregation Beth Israel, 1978, 1983-84; moderator Chico Unified Sch. Dist., 1982-84; trustee Chico Women's Crisis Fund, 1983-84; youth soccer coach. Recipient Outstanding Svc. to UCLA cert., Chancellor Young, 1973; named Honor Sr., 1970. Mem. Citizens Adv. Com. North Shore Adult Sch., Calif. Bar Assn., UCLA Alumni Assn.. Home: 5438 Micaela Dr Agoura Hills CA 91301-4060 Office: University of Judaism 15600 Mulholland Dr Los Angeles CA 90077-1519

BOOMER, DEBORAH LYNN, counselor, educator; b. Yakima, Wash., Sept. 30, 1952; d. William Henry and Jean Eleanore (McHugh) B.; 1 child, Annalee Boomer Millar. BA in Sociology, U. Wash., 1985; MA in Psychology, Antioch U., 1992. Tech. support U.S. West Comms., Seattle, 1970-91; mktg. support Arthur Anderson, N.Y.C., 1986; pvt. practice counselor Seattle, 1993—; Title I tutor Seattle Pub. Schs., 1996. Mem. ACA, Wash. Assn. for Masters in Psychology (pres. 1995-96, v.p., legis. coord. 1996-97). Office: 180 Nickerson St Ste 303 Seattle WA 98109-1631

BOONE, BIRTHE SCHNOHR, nurse practitioner; b. Denmark, Jan. 7, 1945; came to U.S., 1980; d. Otto Johannes and Inger Sofie (Schnohr) Kristensen; m. Erik Højstrup Christensen, June 24, 1963 (div. 1968); 1 child, Peter Højstrup; m. Earle Marion Boone, Oct. 16, 1979. BSN, Calif. State U., L.A., 1986; MSN, Calif. State U., Long Beach, 1989. RN, Calif.; cert. adult nurse practitioner, gerontological nurse practitioner. Supr. Danish Nat. Svc. for Mentally Retarded, Copenhagen, 1968-77; dir. Mental Health Soc. for Developmentally Disabled Children, Amman, Jordan, 1977-79; staff nurse neurology Los Angeles County-U. So. Calif. Med. Ctr., 1984-85; staff nurse Torrance (Calif.) Meml. Hosp. Med. Ctr., 1985-87; clin. educator Kaiser Permanente Med. Ctr., L.A., 1987-88; nurse practitioner VA Med. Ctr., Long Beach, 1988-91, Phoenix, 1991—; adj. prof. Calif. State U., Long Beach, 1990-91; clin. preceptor U. Ariz., Tucson, 1993-94. Mem. Ariz. Geriatrics Soc., Sigma Theta Tau. Office: VA Med Ctr 650 E Indian School Rd Phoenix AZ 85012-1839

BOONE, EARLE MARION, business executive; b. Panama City, Fla., Apr. 25, 1934; s. Earle Alpha and Lucy Marian (Jerkins) B.; m. Birthe Schnohr Kristensen Boone, Oct. 16, 1979; children: Tina Boone Broderick, Darlene Boone Moseley, Earle Marion Jr. BS in Aviation Mgmt., So. Ill. U., 1977; MS in Pub. Adminstrn., Calif. State U., 1983. Lic. airline transport pilot. USAF pilot, 1954-75; corp. pilot pvt. practice, 1975-78, aviation mgmt. cons., 1978-80; mktg. dir. Northrop Corp., Hawthorne, Calif., 1980-92; v.p. mktg. Cognitive Neurometrics, Scottsdale, Ariz., 1992-95; pres., CEO Cognitive Neurometrics Inc., Scottsdale, Ariz., 1995—; SR-71 pilot 9th Strat Recon Wing, Beale AFB, Calif., 1966-68; F4-E combat fighter pilot 388 Tactical Fighter Wing, Thailand, 1970-71; mktg. dir. Northrop Corp., Hawthorne, 1980-92. lt. col. USAF, 1954-75, Vietnam. Recipient The Disting. Flying Cross, The Air medal, Bronze Star medal, Meritorious Svc. medal, Sec. Air Force, Vietnam, 1970-71,. Mem. Ret. Officers Assn., Order of Daedalians, Sierra Club, Phi Alpha Alpha. Republican. Home: 8607 E Lariat Ln Scottsdale AZ 85255-1456 Office: Cognitive Neurometrics Inc Scottsdale AZ 85255

BOONE, KAREN, nutritionist, oriental medicine physician; b. L.A., Apr. 27, 1949; d. Elton Daniel Jr. and Barbara (Lombard) Boone; m. Paul Lester Doupe, Dec. 25, 1970 (div. Nov. 1989); children: Priscilla, Tyler. Student, Scripps Coll., Claremont, Calif., 1967-69; BA in Sociology, Willamette U., Salem, Oreg., 1971; OMD in Acupuncture, Herbs, Calif. Acupuncture Coll., L.A., 1986; PhD in Nutrition, Internat. U., Los Altos, Calif., 1990. Diplomate in acupuncture; lic. acupuncturist, Calif.; cert. hypnotherapist, nutritional cons., iridologist, Acu-Quit therapist for smoking termination, wellness counselor; qualified med. examiner State of Calif., 1990. Pvt. practice oriental medicine and nutrition Bonsall, Calif., 1986—; v.p., adv. bd. Reverse Speech Enterprises, Inc., Bonsall, 1996—; prof. Irvine U., Westminster, Calif., 1996—. Author: Taoist Book of Days, A Treatment Formulary, 1986, The Sacred Path of Pregnancy, 1993; contbr. articles to profl. jours. Mem. Am. Assn. Acupuncture and Oriental Medicine, Nat. Health Fedn., Calif. Assn. Acupuncture and Oriental Medicine, Leeds Club (dir. 1995-96).

BOOTH, FORREST, lawyer; b. Evanston, Ill., Oct. 31, 1946; s. Robert and Florence C. (Forrest) B.; m. Louise A. Hayes, June 14, 1980; 1 child, Kristin A. BA, Amherst Coll., 1968; JD, Harvard U., 1975. Bar: D.C. 1976, U.S. Ct. Appeals (D.C. cir.) 1976, Calif. 1977, U.S. Dist. Ct. (no. dist.) Calif. 1977, U.S. Ct. Appeals (9th cir.) 1977, U.S. Supreme Ct. 1979. Assoc. Graham & James, Washington, 1975-76, Mccutchen, Doyle, Brown & Emersen, San Francisco, 1976-78; ptnr. Hancock, Rothert & Bunshoft, San Francisco, 1978-89, Rice, Fowler, Booth & Banning, San Francisco, 1990—; faculty mem. S.E. Admiralty Law Inst., Savannah, Ga., 1990; chmn. Pacific Admiralty Seminar, San Francisco, 1983-97; advisor U. San Francisco Maritime Law Jour., 1992—. Contbr. articles to profl. jours. Lt. USN, 1968-72, Vietnam. Mem. Maritime Law Assn. U.S. (proctor), World Trade Club of San Francisco, Marine Club London, Assn. Average Adjusters U.K., St. Francis Yacht Club. Office: Rice Fowler Booth & Banning 275 Battery St Fl 27 San Francisco CA 94111-3305

BOOTH, JOHN LOUIS, service executive; b. Danville, Va., May 15, 1933; s. William Irvine and Melba (Harvey) B.; m. Ann Fennell, May 23, 1959; children: Mark, Robin. BA, U. Richmond, 1958; ThM, Dallas Theol. Sem., 1962, ThD, 1965, PhD, 1993; postgrad., Ariz. State U., 1972, 79. Pastor Skyway Bible Ch., Seattle, 1964-66, Mount Prospect (Ill.) Bible Ch., 1966-71, Camelback Bible Ch., Paradise Valley, Ariz., 1971-78; counselor Camelback Counseling Ctr., Phoenix, 1978-79; dir. Paradise Valley Counseling, Inc., Phoenix, 1980—; chmn. bd. Paradise Valley Counseling, Inc., 1980—; chmn. bd. Paradise Valley Counseling Found., Inc., Phoenix, 1982—; adj. prof. Grand Canyon U., 1981-96, Southwestern Coll., Phoenix, 1979-97, Talbott Theol. Sem. Phoenix Ext., 1983-85; seminar speaker frequent engagements, 1965—. Author: Understanding Today's Problems, 1980, Marriage by the Master Plan, 1980, Equipping for Effective Marriage, 1983, 95, (tape series) Starting Over, 1982, Enjoying All God Intended, 1988, 95, 96. Precinct committeeman Rep. Party, Phoenix, 1983-84, 87-88, 90-91; chaplain Ariz. State Senate, Phoenix, 1973. Mem. Am. Psychol. Soc., Christian Assn. for Psychol. Studies, Am. Assn. Christian Counselors. Baptist. Office: Paradise Valley Counseling Inc 10210 N 32nd St Ste 211 Phoenix AZ 85028-3848

BOOTH, MARK WARREN, university dean; b. Mt. Vernon, Wash., Mar. 17, 1943; s. Norman Given and Blanche Edith (Pearce) B.; m. Cleta Kay Smith, Aug. 27, 1965; children: Robert Craig, Michael Raymond. BA, Rice U., Houston, 1965; MA, Harvard U., 1966, PhD, 1971. Asst. prof. Lehman Coll., Bronx, 1971-76; from asst. to assoc. prof. Va. Commonwealth U., Richmond, 1976-87; prof., chmn. dept. English U. Wyo., Laramie, 1987-93, assoc. dean, 1993—; assoc. Nat. Network for Ednl. Renewal, Seattle, 1995-96. Author: Experience of Songs, 1981, American Popular Music, 1983. Woodrow Wilson fellow, 1965-66, Danforth Found. fellow, 1965-71. Mem. Phi Beta Kappa. Home: 2359 Ames Ct Laramie WY 82070 Office: Univ of wyoming Dept English Laramie WY 82071

BOOTH, STEPHEN WALTER, English language educator; b. N.Y.C., Apr. 20, 1933; s. Frank and Ruth Joan (Friedman) B.; m. Susan Patek, June 20, 1959; children: Jason Michael, Mary. AB, Harvard U., 1955, PhD, 1964; BA, Cambridge (Eng.) U., 1957; LHD, Georgetown U., 1991. Asst. prof. U. Calif., Berkeley, 1962-69, assoc. prof., 1969-74, prof., 1974—. Author: An Essay on Shakespeare's Sonnets, 1969, paperback, 1972, The Book Called Holinshed's Chronicles, 1969, Shakespeare's Sonnets, Edited with Analytic Commentary, 1977, rev. edit., 1978, paperback, 1979, King Lear, Macbeth, Indefinition and Tragedy, 1983, (pamphlet) Liking Julius Caesar, 1991; mem. editorial bd. S.E.L., 1978—, Assays, 1979—, Mississippi Studies in English, 1979—, Shakespeare Quar., 1981—. Decorated Order Brit. Empire; recipient Marshall scholarship British govt., Cambridge, 1955-57; Guggenheim fellow, 1970-71. Mem. MLA (James Russell Lowell prize 1978). Democrat. Episcopalian. Home: 98 The Uplands Berkeley CA 94705-2815 Office: Univ of Calif Dept English 322 Wheeler Hall Berkeley CA 94720-1030

BOOZE, THOMAS FRANKLIN, toxicologist; b. Denver, Mar. 4, 1955; s. Ralph Walker and Ann (McNatt) B.; children: Heather N., Ian T. BS, U. Calif., Davis, 1978; MS, Kans. State U., 1981, PhD, 1985. Registered environ assessor, Calif. Asst. instr. Kans. State U., Manhattan, 1979-85; consulting toxicologist Chevron Corp., Sacramento, 1985-92; sr. toxicologist Radian Corp., Sacramento, 1992—; cons. in field, Manhattan, Kans., 1981-83. contbr. articles to profl. jours. Vol. Amigos de las Americas, Marin

County, Calif., 1973, Hospice Care, Manhattan, 1985. Mem. N.Y. Acad. Sci., Soc. Toxicology, Soc. for Risk Analysis, Sigma Xi. Home: 8338 Titian Ridge Ct Antelope CA 95843-5627 Office: Radian Corp 10389 Old Placerville Rd Sacramento CA 95827-2506

BOPP, THOMAS THEODORE, university administrator, chemistry educator; b. Glendale, Calif., Nov. 29, 1941; s. Clarence Hardecke and Mildred Lorine (Eggers) B.; m. Judith May Creamer, June 9, 1962 (div. 1972); children: William Richard, Christopher Paul; m. Georgia Ann Kinney, Apr. 22, 1973; children: Patricia Jayne, Jon Scott. BS, Calif. Inst. Tech., 1963; PhD, Harvard U., 1968. Asst. prof. chemistry U. Hawaii, Manoa, Honolulu, 1967-72, assoc. prof. chemistry, 1972-85, prof. chemistry, 1985—, asst. v.p., 1995—; chair chemistry dept., U. Hawaii, Manoa, 1992-95, chair faculty senate, 1991-92. Mem. Oahu Choral Soc. Office: Univ Hawaii OSVP/EVC 2444 Dole St Bachman 105 Honolulu HI 96844-2302

BORCHARDT, MARILYN, development administrator; b. Clintonville, Wis., Aug. 13, 1944; d. Millard E. and Rena (Schneiderwent) Gerbig; m. Glenn Borchardt, June 12, 1965; children: Nina, Natalie. BS, U. Wis., 1966; MS, Oreg. State U., 1969. Exec. dir. JACKIE, San Francisco, 1974-84; devel. dir. Lighthouse for the Blind, San Francisco, 1985-86; dep. dir. Inst. for Food and Devel. Policy, Oakland, Calif., 1986—; bd. dirs. Alameda County Community Food Bank, Oakland; founding dir. San Francisco Environ. Film Festival, 1993—. Mem. Devel. Execs. Roundtable. Office: Inst for Food & Devel Policy 398 60th St Oakland CA 94618-1212

BORCHERDING, THOMAS EARL, economist; b. Cin., Feb. 18, 1939; s. Earl Schaff and Vivian Joan (Miller) B.; m. Rhoda Jean Larson, Nov. 23, 1968; children: Matthew James, Benjamin Adam. BA, U. Cin., 1961; PhD, Duke U., 1966. Asst. prof. U. Wash., Seattle, 1966-71; assoc. prof. Va. polytech Inst., Blacksboro, 1971-73; prof. econs. Simon Fraser U., Burnaby, B.C., Can., 1973-83; prof. law and econs. U. Toronto (Ont., Can.), 1978-79; prof. econs. Claremont (Calif.) Grad. Sch., 1983—; editl. bd. CATO Jour., Washington; bd. of advisors Ind. Inst., Oakland, Calif., 1990—. Author: The Egg Board: The Social Cast of Monopoly, 1981; contbr. articles to profl. jours. NDEA fellow Duke U., 1961-64, postdoctoral fellow U. Va., 1965-66, Hoover Instn., Stanford U., 1974-75, Avery fellow Claremont U. Ctr., 1988—. Mem. Am. Econ. Assn., Western Econ. Assn. (editor 1980-96), Pub. Choice Soc., Mont Pelern Soc., Phi Beta Kappa, Omicron Delta Epsilon, Phi Delta Theta. Republican. Home: 1374 Tulane Rd Claremont CA 91711-3420 Office: Claremont Grad Sch Ctr for Politics & Econs Claremont CA 91711

BORCHERS, MARY AMELIA, middle school educator; b. Miles City, Mont., July 6, 1935; d. Earl Gordon and Lulu Irene (Ankerman) Forgaard; m. Justus Charles Borchers, Nov. 25, 1960; 1 child, James Gordon. AA, Lassen Jr. Coll., 1955; BA, Chico State Coll., 1960. Cert. tchr., Calif. Tchr. Loyalton (Calif.) High Sch., 1957-60, Point Arena (Calif.) High Sch., 1960-64, Nelson Ave Sch., Oroville, Calif., 1965-81; math. tchr. Weaver Elem. Sch., Merced, Calif., 1986—; mem. math. educators del. People to People, Russia and Estonia; AIMS trainer Fresno (Calif.) Pacific Coll., 1988-90. Mem. Calif. Tchrs.' Assn., Weaver Tchrs.' Assn., Phi Delta Kappa.

BORCHERT, WARREN FRANK, elementary education educator; b. Faribault, Minn., Mar. 5, 1948; s. Harold C. and Beata J. (Hoffmann) B.; m. Mari L. Runquist, Aug. 7, 1971 (div. Oct. 1985); children: Nicholas, Kyle, Megan. BA, Gustavus Adolphus Coll., 1971; postgrad., Boise State U., 1975—, U. Idaho, 1979—; MEd, Coll. Idaho, 1983; cert. instr. leader level, Nat. Fedn. Interscholastic Coaches Edn. Program-Am. Coaching Effectiveness Program, 1991. Cert. advanced elem. and phys. edn. tchr. Phys. edn. tchr. Hopkins (Minn.) Sch. Dist., 1972-73; elem. tchr., phys. edn. tchr. Mountain Home (Idaho) Sch. Dist. 193, 1974-84, phys. edn. tchr., 1984—; coach boys basketball Mountain Home Jr. High Sch., 1986—; coach girls softball Mountain Home High Sch., 1993—; instr. Intermountain Environ. Edn. Tng. Team, Salt Lake City, 1979—. Instr., mgr. ARC-pool, Mountain Home, 1975-83; pres. Men's Slo Pitch Softball Assn., Mountain Home, 1975-79; bd. dirs., coach Elmore County Youth Baseball Assn., Mountain Home, 1989-92; treas., bd. dirs. Grace Luth. Ch., Mountain Home, 1991-95. Mem. AAHPERD, Idaho Assn. Health, Phys. Edn, Recreation and Dance, Idaho ASCD, Idaho Soc. for Energy and Environ. Edn. (treas. 1985-87). Democrat. Office: Base Primary Sch 100 Gunfighter Ave Mountain Home AFB ID 83648-1022

BORDA, RICHARD JOSEPH, management consultant; b. San Francisco, Aug. 16, 1931; s. Joseph Clement and Ethel Cathleen (Donovan) B.; m. Judith Maxwell, Aug. 30, 1953; children: Michelle, Stephen Joseph. AB, Stanford U., 1953, MBA, 1957. With Wells Fargo Bank, San Francisco, 1957-70; mgr. Wells Fargo Bank, 1963-66, asst. v.p., 1966-67, v.p., 1967-70; exec. v.p. adminstrn. Wells Fargo Bank, San Francisco, 1973-85; asst. sec. Air Force Manpower Res. Affairs, Washington, 1970-73; vice chmn., chief fin. officer Nat. Life Ins. Co., Montpelier, Vt., 1985-90, also bd. dirs.; chmn., chief exec. officer Sentinal Group Funds, Inc., 1985-90, also bd. dirs.; mgmt. cons., 1990—. Former pres. Air Force Aid Soc., Washington; trustee Monterey Inst. Internat. Studies; govs. coun. Boys and Girls Club of Monterey Peninsula. Recipient Exceptional Civilian Svc. award, 1973, 95. Mem. USMC Res. Officers Assn., Air Force Assn., Bohemian Club, Monterey Peninsula Country Club (bd. dirs., pres.), Old Capital Club, Air Force Aid Soc. (disting. counselor), Phi Gamma Delta. Republican. Episcopalian.

BORDELON, SCOTT LEE, computer systems engineer; b. Fullerton, Calif., May 23, 1967; s. Sidney Augusten and Carolyn Ann (Dobsky) B. BSEE, U. Calif., 1989, MS in Computer Engring., 1990. Registered profl. engr., Calif. Designer analog circuits Western Instrument Corp., Ventura, Calif., 1988; software engr. Rockwell Internat., Irvine, Calif., 1989; computer architecture rschr. UCSB Computer Architecture Lab., Goleta, Calif., 1988-90; systems design engr. Amdahl Corp., Sunnyvale, Calif., 1990-93; mgr. applications engring. Duet Techs., Inc., San Jose, Calif., 1993-97, VLSI Librs., Inc., 1997—; networks cons. U. Calif., Santa Barbara, 1990-91; expert in field integrated circuit test methodologies. Inventor in field. Vol. homeless shelter Cmty. Found. Santa Clara, Calif., 1991-92; vol. Second Harvest Food Bank, 1993-94. Mem. IEEE, Assn. Computing Machinery, Eta Kappa Nu. Unitarian. Office: Duet Techs Inc 2833 Junction Ave Ste 100 San Jose CA 95134-1920

BORDERS, KAREN LYNN, police officer; b. Glendale, Calif., Mar. 10, 1960; d. Denison Lee and Diane Arlyce (Shapiro) Baldwin; m. Steven Henry Holtz, June 1, 1985 (div. Dec. 1992); m. Donald Eugene Borders, Apr. 29, 1995; children: Ashley, Stacey. AS, Coll. of the Desert, 1985; BS, U. Redlands, 1992. Police officer Palm Springs (Calif.) Police Dept., 1982—, explorer advisor, 1985-89, detective, 1989-94, field tng. officer, 1994-96, domestic violence detective, 1996—. Recipient Medal of Valor, Am. Legion, 1989. Republican. Roman Catholic. Office: Palm Springs Police Dept 200 S Civic Dr Palm Springs CA 92262-7201

BORDNER, GREGORY WILSON, chemical engineer; b. Buffalo, Aug. 16, 1959; s. Raymond Gordon and Nancy Lee (Immegart) B.; m. Margaret Patricia Toon, June 14, 1981; children: Eric Lawrence, Heather Rae. BSChemE, Calif. State Poly. U., 1982; MS in Sys. Mgmt., U. So. Calif., 1987. Registered profl. engr., Calif. Commd. 2nd lt. USAF, 1983, advanced through grades to capt., 1987; engr., mgr. various air launched missile, antisatellite and strategic def. initiative projects Air Force Rocket Propulsion Lab., Edwards AFB, Calif., 1983-86; asst. mgr. space transp. Air Force Astronautics Lab., Edwards AFB, 1986-87; chief small intercontinental ballistic missiles ordnance firing system br. Hdqrs. Ballistic Missile Orgn., San Bernardino, Calif., 1987-90; sr. plant environ. engr. Filtrol Corp./Akzo Chems. Inc., L.A., 1991-92; water/soils project engr. TABC, Inc., Long Beach, Calif., 1992—. Author: (manual) Pyrotechnic Transfer Line Evaluation, 1984, (with others) Rocket Motor Heat Transfer, 1984. Mem. AIChE, Am. Water Works Assn. Home: 10841 Ring Ave Alta Loma CA 91737-4429

BORDY, MICHAEL JEFFREY, lawyer; b. Kansas City, Mo., July 24, 1952; s. Marvin Dean and Alice Mae (Rostov) B.; m. Marjorie Enid Kanof, Dec. 27, 1973 (div. Dec. 1983); m. Melissa Anne Held, May 24, 1987; children: Shayna Robyn, Jenna Alexis. Bar: Calif., 1986, U.S. Dist. Ct. (cen. dist.) Calif., 1986, (so. dist.) Calif., 1987, U.S. Ct. Appeals (9th cir.), 1986. Tchg. asst. biology U. Kans., Lawrence, 1975-76, rsch. asst. biology, 1976-80; post-doctoral fellow Johns Hopkins U., Balt., 1980-83; tchg. asst. U. So. Calif., L.A., 1984-86; assoc. Thelen, Marrin, Johnson & Bridges, L.A., 1986-87, Wood, Lucksinger & Epstein, L.A., 1987-89, Cooper, Epstein & Hurewitz, Beverly Hills, Calif., 1989-93; ptnr. Jacobson, Runes & Bordy, Beverly Hills, 1994-96, Jacobson, Sanders & Bordy, LLP, Beverly Hills, 1996—. Bd. govs. Beverly Hills (Calif.) Bar Barristers, 1988-90, Cedars-Sinai Med. Ctr., L.A., 1994—; cabinet United Jewish Fund/Real Estate, L.A., 1995—; mem. planning com. Am. Cancer Soc.; mem. Guardians of the Jewish Home for the Aging, 1995—; active Lawyers Against Hunger, 1995—. Pre-Doctoral fellow NIH, Lawrence, 1977-80; post-doctoral fellow Mellon Found., Balt., 1980-83. Mem. ABA, State Bar Calif., L.A. County Bar Assn., Beverly Hills Bar Assn. (gov., barrister 1988—), Profl. Network Group. Democrat. Jewish. Office: Jacobson Sanders & Bordy LLP 9777 Wilshire Blvd Beverly Hills CA 90212

BOREL, JAMES DAVID, anesthesiologist; b. Chgo., Nov. 15, 1951; s. James Albert and Nancy Ann (Sieverson) B. BS, U. Wis., 1973; MD, Med. Coll. of Wis., 1977. Diplomate Am. Bd. Anesthesiology, Nat. Bd. Med. Examiners, Am. Coll. Anesthesiologists. Research asst. McArdle Lab. for Cancer Research, Madison, Wis., 1972-73, Stanford U. and VA Hosp., Palo Alto, 1976-77; intern. The Cambridge (Mass.) Hosp., 1977-78; clin. fellow in medicine Harvard Med. Sch., Boston, 1977-78, clin. fellow in anesthesia, 1978-80, clin. instr. in anaesthesia, 1980; resident in anesthesiology Peter Bent Brigham Hosp., Boston, 1978-80; anesthesiologistt Mt. Auburn Hosp., Cambridge, 1980; fellow in anesthesiology Ariz. Health Scis. Ctr., Tucson, 1980-81; research assoc. U. Ariz. Coll. Medicine, Tucson, 1980-81, assoc. in anesthesiology, 1981—; active staff Mesa (Ariz.) Luth. Hosp., 1981—; courtesy staff Scottsdale (Ariz.) Meml. Hosp., 1982—; vis. anaesthetist St. Joseph's Hosp., Kingston, Jamaica, 1980. Contbr. numerous articles to profl. jours. Mem. AMA, AAAS, Ariz. Anesthesia Alumni Assn., Ariz. Soc. Anesthesiologists, Am. Soc. Regional Anesthesia, Can. Anesthestists' Soc., Internat. Anesthesia Rsch. Soc., Am. Soc. Anesthesiologists. Office: Valley Anesthesia Cons 2950 N 7th St Phoenix AZ 85014-5404

BOREN, KENNETH RAY, endocrinologist; b. Evansville, Ind., Dec. 31, 1945; s. Doyle Clifford and Jeannette (Koerner) B.; m. Rebecca Lane Wallace, Aug. 25, 1967; children: Jennifer, James, Michael, Peter, Nicklas, Benjamin. BS, Ariz. State U., 1967; MD, Ind. U., Indpls., 1972; MA, Ind. U., Bloomington, 1974. Diplomate Am. Bd. Endocrinology, Am. Bd. Nephrology, Am. Bd. Internal Medicine. Intern in pathology Ind. U. Sch. Medicine, Indpls., 1972; intern in medicine Ind. U. Sch. Medicine, 1972-73, resident in medicine, 1975-77, fellow in endocrinology, 1977-79, fellow nephrology, 1979-80, instr., 1980; physician East Valley Nephrology, Mesa, Ariz., 1980—; chief medicine Mesa Luth Hosp., 1987-89, chief staff, 1990-91. Bd. dirs. Ariz. Kidney Found., Phoenix, 1984—, pres. 1993-94. Lt. USN, 1973-75. Fellow ACP, Am. Coll. of Clin. Endocrinology; mem. AMA, Maricopa County Med. Assn., Ariz. Med. Assn., Am. Soc. Nephrology, Internat. Soc. Nephrology, Am. Diabetes Assn. Republican. Latter Day Saints. Home: 4222 E Mclellan Rd Ste 10 Mesa AZ 85205-3119 Office: East Valley Nephrology 560 W Brown Rd Ste 3006 Mesa AZ 85201-3225

BORENSTEIN, DANIEL ASA, newspaper political editor; b. Berkeley, Calif., Sept. 23, 1955; s. Martin and Betty (Aron) B.; m. Susan Watkins, Jan. 3, 1982 (div. June 1996); 1 child, Crystal Fawn Knight. BA in Journalism, U. Calif., Berkeley, 1978, BA in Polit. Sci., 1978, Master of Journalism, 1985, Master of Pub. Policy, 1985. Reporter Antioch (Calif.) Daily Ledger, 1980-83; reporter, asst. city editor Valley Times, Pleasanton, Calif., 1983-85; reporter, asst. city editor Contra Costa Times, Walnut Creek, Calif., 1986-90, polit. editor, 1990—; free-lance commentator Sta. KRON-TV, San Francisco, 1995—, Sta. KQED-TV, San Francisco, 1994—; free-lance writer Calif. Jour., Sacramento, 1986, 91. Mem. Better Govt. task force Contra Costa County, 1995-96. Recipient Pub. Svc. award Calif. Newspaper Pubs. Assn., 1993, Investigative Reporting award, 1994, Third place pub. svc. award Nat. Headliner Club, 1994, Golden Medallion award for legal reporting State Bar of Calif., 1985, 93, Third place investigative reporting award Nat. Newspaper Assn., 1987, numerous others. Mem. Soc. of Profl. Journalists (co-chair Freedom of Info. com. No. Calif. Chpt., 1996—, invesigative reporting award 1992-93, James Madison Freedom of Info. award 1994). Office: Contra Costa Times 2640 Shadelands Dr Walnut Creek CA 94598-2513

BORESI, ARTHUR PETER, author, educator; b. Toluca, Ill.; s. John Peter and Eva (Grotti) B.; m. Clara Jean Gordon, Dec. 28, 1946; children: Jennifer Ann Boresi Hill, Annette Boresi Pueschel, Nancy Jean Boresi Broderick. Student, Kenyon Coll., 1943-44; BSEE, U. Ill., 1948, MS in Mechanics, 1949, PhD in Mechanics, 1953. Research engr. N. Am. Aviation, 1950; materials engr. Nat. Bur. Standards, 1951; mem. faculty U. Ill., Urbana, 1953—, prof. theoretical and applied mechanics and nuclear engring., 1959-79; prof. emeritus U. Ill. at Urbana, Urbana, 1979; Disting. vis. prof. Clarkson Coll. Tech., Potsdam, N.Y., 1968-69; NAVSEA research prof. Naval Postgrad. Sch., Monterey, Calif., 1978-79; prof. civil engring. U. Wyo., Laramie, 1979-95, head, 1980-94, prof. emeritus, 1995—; vis. prof. Naval Postgrad. Sch., Monterey, Calif., 1986-87.; cons. in field. Author: Engineering Mechanics, 1959, Elasticity in Engineering Mechanics, 3d edit., 1987, Advanced Mechanics of Materials, 5th edit., 1993, Approximate Solution Methods in Engineering Mechanics, 1991; also articles. Served with USAAF, 1943-44; Served with AUS, 1944-46. Fellow ASME, ASCE, Am. Acad. Mechanics (founding, treas.); mem. Am. Soc. Engring. Edn. (Archie Higdon Disting. Educator award 1993), Soc. Exptl. Mechanics, Sigma Xi. Office: U Wyo Box 3295 Univ Station Laramie WY 82071

BORGES, STEPHANY PATRICIA, English language educator; b. Oakland, Calif., June 12, 1948; d. Harold Borges and Elsie (Hansen) Marron; children: Sofia Borges Waitzkin, Daren Borges. MA, Sonoma State U., 1980; MFA in Fiction, U. Calif., Irvine, 1985, PhD, 1990. Tchg. assoc. U. Calif., Irvine, 1983-90; vis. asst. prof. Harvey Mudd Coll., Claremont, Calif., 1990-91; tchg. assoc. Irvine (Calif.) Valley Coll., 1991-94; English tchr. Cornelia Connelly Sch., Anaheim, Calif., 1994—; pvt. practice writer and tchr., Santa Ana, Calif., 1993—. Author: Rebels and Old Maids, 1990; author short stories. Recipient Best Essay awards Friends of the Libr., Corona del Mar, Calif., 1983, 85. Fellow MLA, Coll. English Assn., D.H. Lawrence Soc. Home: 2108 Greenleaf St Santa Ana CA 92706-2534 Office: Cornelia Connelly Sch 2323 W Broadway Anaheim CA 92804-2306

BORGES, WILLIAM, III, environmental scientist; b. Long Beach, Calif., Nov. 21, 1948; s. William Borges Jr. and Dorothy Mae (Raymond) Morris; m. Rosalind Denise Marye, Nov. 23, 1968; children: William IV, Blake Austin. BA in Geography, Calif. State U., Sonoma, 1973. Environ. planner Mendocino County Planning Dept., Ukiah, Calif., 1976; project mgr. Engring. Sci., Inc., Berkeley, Calif., 1976-79, Santa Clara County Planning Dept., San Jose, Calif., 1979-81, Internat. Tech. Corp., San Jose, 1985-88; mgr. sales ops. Adac Labs., Milpitas, Calif., 1983-85; prin. WT Environ. Cons., Phoenix, 1988-91; project mgr. Dynamac Corp., Newport Beach, Calif., 1991-93; prin. environ. scientist Midwest Rsch. Inst., Scottsdale, Ariz., 1993-96. Contbr. photographs to various mags. Coord. pub. rels. Stellar Acad. for Dyslexics, Fremont, Calif., 1988. With M.I., U.S. Army, 1967-70. Mem. Am. Mensa.

BORGESON, BET, artist; b. Mpls., Feb. 12, 1940; d. Claire Vernon and Adelaide Pauline (Zwiefel) Chamberland; m. Edwin George Borgeson, Jan. 21, 1920; children; Richard Raphael Sands, Scott Eric Sands. BS, Portland State U., 1978. One-woman shows include Maveety Gallery, Salishan, Oreg., 1989, 91, Lawrence Gallery, Portland, Oreg., 1983, 84; author: The Colored Pencil, 1983, 93, Color Drawing Workshops, 1984, Colored Pencil Fast Techniques, 1988, Basic Colored Pencil Techniques, 1997. Home: 3977 SW Condor Ave Portland OR 97201-4103

BORIK, ANNE, osteopath; b. Pitts., Jan. 5, 1964; d. Nicolaus Charles and Norma (Budway) B. Student, Duquesne U., 1983-84; BS in Exercise Physiology, Temple U., 1987; DO, Phila. Coll. Osteo. Medicine, 1991. Rotating intern Grandview Hosp. and Med. Ctr., Dayton, Ohio, 1991-92; resident in internal medicine Allegheny Gen. Hosp., Pitts., 1992-95; internal medicine physician Casa Blanca Clinic, Apache Junction, Ariz., 1995—; emergency room physician Shadyside Hosp., Pitts., 1993, Urgicare of Pitts., 1993—, Mercy Providence Hosp., Pitts., 1993—; tchr. karate and self-defense Shitoryo Dotokushin Assn., Phila. Coll. Osteo. Medicine. Founder, tchr. Pitts. Blind Karate Club. Mem. AMA, ACP, Pa. Med. Assn., Allegheny County Med. Assn. Office: Casa Blanca Clinic 2050 W Southern Ave Apache Junction AZ 85220-7305

BORIN, BORIS MICHAYLOVITCH, writer, publisher; b. Kamenets-Dodolsky, Ukraine, June 25, 1935; came to U.S., 1980; s. Meshilim Shlemovitch and Maria Shoel (Keiser) Oykhman; m. Galina Israilovna Goykhenberg, Sept. 19, 1946; children: Marat, Felix (twins). Diploma in mech. engring., Tech. Coll., Tchernovits, Ukraine, 1952-57; diploma in history, St. Petersburg U., St. Petersburg, Leningrad, 1962-67. Tchr., instr. Indsl. coll., Semiluki, Russia, 1968-71; tchr. high sch. Surgut, Russia, 1971-80, Kurganinsk, Russia, 1981-86; tchr., instr. Russian lang. Def. Lang., San Antonio, Tex., 1986—; writer L.A., 1995—; publisher Borin B.M. Publs., L.A., 1995—. Author: Volens and Nolens, 1993, Aesop, 1995; inventor exercise and portable grill. Home: 7545 Hampton Ave # 314 Los Angeles CA 90046

BORN, ROBERT HEYWOOD, consulting civil engineer; b. L.A., Nov. 7, 1925; s. Robert Bogle and Mignon Mary (Heywood) B.; m. Marilyn Alice Simpson, Aug. 15, 1947; 1 child, Stefanie Born. Student, Stanford U., 1943; BE, U. So. Calif., 1949, MSCE, 1956. Registered civil engineer Calif., Ariz., Nev., Utah, Tenn., Guam; registered agriculture engr. Calif. Assoc. hydraulic engr. Calif. Dept. of Water Resources, L.A., 1949-58; chief engr., county hydraulic engr. County Flood Control/Water Conservation Dist., San Luis Obispo, Calif., 1958-70; dir., exec. v.p., regional mgr. Camp, Dresser & McKee, Inc., Pasadena, Calif., 1970-78; v.p., regional mgr. Born, Barrett & Assoc./Barrett Cons. Group, Newport Beach, Calif., 1978-86, Memphis, 1978-86; prin. Robert H. Born Cons. Engrs., Memphis, 1986—, Irvine, Laguna Niguel, Calif., 1986—. Chmn. World Affairs Coun., San Luis Obispo, 1965. 1st lt. U.S. Army, 1943-47. Decorated Bronze star medal, 1944. Fellow ASCE (life, Engr. of Merit 1994); mem. Am. Water Works Assn. (com. chmn.), U.S. Com. on Large Dams, Am. Pub. Works Assn. (cert. outstanding pub. works achievement 1969, Floodplain Mgmt. Assn. Calif. Democrat. Presbyterian. Home: 15 Anacapri Laguna Niguel CA 92677-8630 Office: Robert H Born Cons Engrs 15 Anacapri Laguna Niguel CA 92677-8630

BORNELL, CECIL JEAN, computer graphics designer, small business owner; b. Alliance, Ohio, Oct. 31, 1929; d. William Cecil and Ethel Elizabeth (Borton) Headrick; m. Donald Gustave Bornell; 1 child, Gaynet Lee. BS, Ill. State U., 1951; postgrad., Tchrs. Coll., Columbia U., 1952, U. Ill., 1955-56; MA, UCLA, 1967. Art supv. Bement (Ill.) Union Sch. Dist., 1951-53; art tchr. North Hollywood H.S., L.A., 1955-56, Sequoia Jr. H.S., L.A., 1957-62, Hale Jr. H.S., L.A., 1963-65, Samoana H.S., Am. Samoa, 1971-72, Westmont Coll., Montecito, Calif., 1974-75; art instr. L.A. Pierce Coll., 1965-69; environ. designer Montecito, Calif., 1975-80, Santa Ynez, Calif., 1980-84; graphics designer MII, Santa Ynez, 1985—; feature artist Channel 7 TV, L.A., 1963; mem. art jury Litton Sys., L.A., 1969. Author: Sense Perception, Basis for Education, 1967; co-author: Body Friendly, 1989, Tap Dancing-The Body's Beat, 1990; editor, designer: What is Man?, 1969. Rsch. asst. Earthwatch, 1982—; mem. com. Friends of Ethnic Arts, 1983—. Mem. Am. Craft Coun., Ctr. Sci. in Public Interest. Home: 3901 Long Valley Rd Santa Ynez CA 93460-9588 Office: MII Internat 3901 Long Valley Rd Santa Ynez CA 93460-9588

BORNEMAN, JOHN PAUL, pharmaceutical executive; b. Darby, Pa., Oct. 18, 1958; s. John A. III and Ann (Conway) B.; m. Anne Marie Albert, July 18, 1980; 1 child, Elizabeth Anne. BS in Chemistry, St. Joseph's U., Phila., 1980, MS in Chemistry, 1983, MBA in Fin., 1986. V.p. Boiron-Borneman Inc., Norwood, Pa., 1980-86; dir. mktg. Standard Homeopathic Co., L.A., 1986-89, v.p., 1989-96, exec. v.p., 1996—; pres. P&S Labs., L.A., 1996—; chmn. FDA liaison com. Am. Homeopathic Pharm. Assn., 1986—. Editor Homeopathic Pharmacopoeia U.S., 1983—; columnist Resonance mag., 1986-95; contbr. articles to homeopathic jours. Bd. dirs. Internat. Found. for Homeopathy, 1986-92, Nat. Ctr. for Homeopathy, 1987—. Mem. Am. Chem. Soc., Am. Pharm. Assn., Nat. Nutritional Foods Assn. (mem. legis. affairs com. 1996—), Sigma Xi. Office: Standard Homeopathic Co Box 61067 210 W 131st St Los Angeles CA 90061

BORNSTEIN, ELI, artist, sculptor; b. Milw., Dec. 28, 1922; dual citizen, U.S. and Can.; m. Christina Bornstein; children: Sarah, Thea. BS, U. Wis., 1945, MS, 1954; student, Art Inst. Chgo., U. Chgo., 1943, Academie Montmartre of Fernand Leger, Paris, 1951, Academie Julian, 1952; DLitt, U. Sask., Can., 1990. Tchr. drawing, painting and sculpture Milw. Art Inst., 1943-47; tchr. design U. Wis., 1949; tchr. drawing, painting, sculpture, design and graphics U. Sask., Can., 1950-90; prof. U. Sask., 1963-90, prof. emeritus, 1990—, head art dept., 1963-71. Painted in France, 1951-52, Italy, 1957, Holland, 1958; exhibited widely, 1943—; retrospective exhbn. (works 1943-64), Mendel Art Gallery, Saskatoon, 1965, one man shows, Kazimir Gallery, Chgo., 1965, 67, Saskatoon Pub. Library, 1975, Can. Cultural Center, Paris, 1976, Glenbow-Alta. Inst. Art, Calgary, 1976, Mendel Art Gallery, Saskatoon, 1982, York U. Gallery, Toronto, 1983, Confedn. Ctr. Art Gallery, Charlottetown, P.E.I., 1983, Owens Art Gallery, Mt. Allison U., Sackville, N.B., 1984, Fine Arts Gallery, U. Wis.-Milw., 1984, Mendel Art Gallery, Saskatoon, 1996; represented in numerous pvt. collections; executed marble sculpture now in permanent collection, Walker Art Center, Mpls., 1947, aluminum constrn. for Sask. Tchrs. Fedn. Bldg., 1956, structurist relief in painted wood and aluminum for, Arts and Scis. Bldg., U. Sask., 1958, structurist relief in enamelled steel for, Internat. Air Terminal, Winnipeg, Man., Can., 1962, four-part constructed relief for, Wascana Pl., Wascana Ctr. Authority, Regina, Sask., 1983; also structurist reliefs exhibited, Mus. Contemporary Art, Chgo., Herron Mus. Art, Indpls., Cranbrook Acad. Art Galleries, Mich., High Mus., Atlanta, Can. House, Cultural Centre Gallery, London, 1983, Can. Cultural Ctr., Paris, 1983, Brussels, 1983, Milw. Art Mus., 1984, Bonn, 1985; model of aluminium construction, 1956 and model version of structurist relief in 5 parts, 1962, now in collection, Nat. Gallery, Ottawa, Ont., others in numerous collections.; Co-editor: periodical Structure, 1958; founder, editor: ann. publ. The Structurist, 1960—; Contbr. biennial articles, principally on Structurist art to various publs. Recipient Allied Arts medal Royal Archtl. Inst. Can., 1968; honorable mention for 3 structurist reliefs 2d Biennial Internat. Art Exhbn., Colombia, S.Am., 1970. Address: 3625 Saskatchewan Cres S, Corman Park, SK Canada S7T 1B7 Office: U Sask, Box 378 RPO U, Saskatoon, SK Canada S7N 4JB

BOROVANSKY, VLADIMIR THEODORE, librarian; b. Prague, Czechoslovakia, May 25, 1931; came to U.S., 1968; s. Ladislav and Karla (Uttlova) B.; m. Dagmar Korbelova, July 12, 1961; children: Dominika, Herbert. Cert., Czechoslavic Acad., Prague, 1946-49, 56-57; Grad. Libr., Charles U., Prague, 1965, PhD, 1990. Lab. mgr. Rsch. Inst. Ferrous Metal, Prague, 1955-65, asst. dir. info. ctr., 1965-67; sci. reference head Ariz. State U., Tempe, 1968-78; reference dept. head U. Petroleum and Minerals, Dhahran, Saudi Arabia, 1978-79; reference dept. head Ariz. State U., Tempe, 1979-82, Noble sci. libr. head, 1982-94; sci. bibliographer, 1994—; vis. prof. Charles U., spring and fall, 1991; Fulbright lectr. to Czechoslovakia, 1991. Contbr. articles to profl. jours.; editor Meteoritics, 1971-87. Academic Specialist grantee Charles U., 1993, IREX Travel grantee, 1994. Mem. Am. Soc. Eng. Edn. (Engring Library divsn.), Am. Soc. for Metals, Czechoslovak Soc. Arts and Sci., Internat. Assn. of Tech. U. Libraries. Republican. Roman Catholic. Home: 7026 N 14th St Phoenix AZ 85020-5409 Office: Ariz State U Hayden Libr Tempe AZ 85287-1006

BORSCH, FREDERICK HOUK, bishop; b. Chgo., Sept. 13, 1935; s. Reuben A. and Pearl Irene (Houk) B.; m. Barbara Edgeley Sampson, June 25, 1960; children: Benjamin, Matthew, Stuart. AB, Princeton U., 1957; MA, Oxford U., 1959; STB, Gen. Theol. Sem., 1960; PhD, U. Birmingham, 1966; DD (hon.), Seabury Western Theol. Sem., 1978, Gen. Theol. Sem., 1988; STD (hon.), Ch. Div. Sch. of Pacific, 1981, Berk Div. Sch. Yale U., 1983. Ordained priest Episcopal Ch., 1960; curate Grace Episcopal Ch., Oak Park, Ill., 1960-63; tutor Queen's Coll., Birmingham, Eng., 1963-66; asst. prof. N.T. Seabury Western Theol. Sem., Evanston, Ill., 1966-69, assoc. prof. N.T., 1969-71; prof. N.T. Gen. Theol. Sem., N.Y.C., 1971-72; pres., dean Berk Div. Sch. Yale U., Berkeley, Calif., 1972-81; dean of chapel, prof. religion Princeton U., 1981-88; bishop Episc. Diocese, L.A., 1988—; rep.

Faith and Order Commn., Nat. Coun. Chs., 1975-81; mem. exec. coun. Episc. Ch., 1981-88, Anglican Cons. Coun., 1984-88; chair bd. of govs. Trinity Press Internat., 1989—. Author: The Son of May in Myth and History, 1967, The Christian and Gnostic Son of Man, 1970, God's Parable, 1976, Introducing the Lessons of the Church Year, 1978, Coming Together in the Spirit, 1980, Power in Weakness, 1983, Jesus: The Human Life of God, 1987, Many Things in Parables, 1988, Christian Discipleship and Sexuality, 1993, Outrage and Hope, 1996; editor: Anglicanism and the Bible, 1984, The Bible's Authority in Today's Church, 1993. Keasbey scholar, 1957-59. Fellow Soc. Arts, Religion and Contemporary Culture; mem. Am. Acad. Religion, Soc. Bibl. Lit., Studiorum Novi Testamenti Societas, Phi Beta Kappa. Home: 2930 Corda Ln Los Angeles CA 90049-1105 Office: Episcopal Diocese of LA PO Box 2164 Los Angeles CA 90051-0164

BORSON, DANIEL BENJAMIN, physiology educator, inventor, researcher, lawyer; b. Berkeley, Calif., Mar. 24, 1946; s. Harry J. and Josephine F. (Esterly) B.; m. Margaret Ann Rheinschmidt, May 22, 1974; children: Alexander Nathan, Galen Michael. BA, San Francisco State Coll., 1969; MA, U. Calif., Riverside, 1973; PhD, U. Calif., San Francisco, 1982; JD, U. San Francisco, 1995. Lic. comml. pilot, flight instr. FAA; lic. atty., Calif. Musician Composer's Forum, Berkeley, San Francisco, 1961-70; flight instr. Buchanan Flying Club, Concord, Oakland, Calif., 1973-77, pres., 1975-77; physiology U. Calif., San Francisco, 1984-92, asst. rsch. physiologist Cardiovascular Rsch. Inst., 1988-92; vis. scientist Genentech Inc., South San Francisco, Calif., 1990-92. Contbr. articles, rev. chpts. and abstracts to profl. jours., legal periodicals and law rev. Fellow NIH, 1976-84, grantee, 1988-93; fellow Cystic Fibrosis Found., 1985, grantee, 1989-91; fellow Parker B. Francis Found., 1985-87; grantee Am. Lung Assn., 1985-87. Mem. ABA, Am. Physiol. Soc. (editl. bd. Am. Jour. Physiology 1990-92), Am. Soc. Cell Biology, Am. Chem. Soc., Am. Intellectual Property Law Assn., San Francisco Intellectual Property Law Assn., Bay Flute Club (pres. 1978). Home: 146 San Aleso Ave San Francisco CA 94127-2531

BORTELL, LINDA LEE, clinical psychologist; b. Harrisburg, Pa., Jan. 25, 1963; d. Joseph Thomas and Ruth Janet (Mengel) B. BA, Ind. U. Pa., 1985; MA, Fairleigh Dickinson U., Morristown, N.J., 1987; PsyD in Psychology, Calif. Sch. Profl. Psychology, 1993. Charge person, psychiat. emergency team Kimball Med. Ctr., Lakewood, N.J., 1988-89; counselor Chabad Rehab., Culver City, Calif., 1989-92; hotline counselor Open Quest Inst., Pasadena, Calif., 1990-91; intern The Switzer Ctr., Torrance, Calif., 1991-92; program coord., instr. Santa Anita Family Svc., Monrovia, Calif., 1991—; intern The Wright Inst., L.A., 1992-93; hotline counselor Child Help USA, Hollywood, Calif., 1991-96; postdoctoral assoc. The Wright Inst., L.A., 1993-94; psychologist Santa Anita Family Svc., Monrovia, Calif., 1993—; pvt. practice, 1994—; assoc. prof. Calif. State U., 1996—; mem. adj. faculty Calif. Sch. Profl. Psychology, Alhambra, 1994—; cons. "The Leeza Show", 1996, Children's Inst. Internat., 1995—; bd. dirs. Wright Inst. Author: What About Me, 1993. Mem. mental health team. ARC, 1996—. Recipient Psychology scholarship, Lucille Walker scholarship, Outstanding Doctoral Project Calif. Sch. Profl. Psychology, Alhambra, Calif., 1992, 93. Mem. APA, Calif. State Psychol. Assn., Pasadena Area Psychol. Assn., Div. 39 Psychoanalysis. Office: 1961 W Huntington Dr Ste 202 Alhambra CA 91801-1222

BORTON, GEORGE ROBERT, airline captain; b. Wichita Falls, Tex., Mar. 22, 1922; s. George Neat and Travis Lee (Jones) B.; m. Anne Louise Bowling, Feb. 5, 1944 (dec.); children: Trudie T., Robert B., Bruce M. AA, Hardin Coll., Wichita Falls, 1940. Cert. airline transport pilot, FAA flight examiner. Flight sch. operator Vallejo (Calif.) Sky Harbor, 1947-48; capt. S.W. Airways, San Francisco, 1948-55; check capt. Pacific Airlines, San Francisco, 1955-68, Hughes Air West, San Francisco, 1968-71; capt. N.W. Airlines, Mpls., 1971-82, ret., 1982. Col. USAF, 1943-73, ret. Decorated Air medal. Mem. Airline Pilots Assn., Res. Officers Assn., Air Force Assn., Horseless Carriage Club, Model T of Am. Club (San Jose, Calif.). Republican. Home: 325 Denio Ave Gilroy CA 95020-9203

BORUCHOWITZ, STEPHEN ALAN, health policy analyst; b. Plainfield, N.J., Sept. 24, 1952; s. Robert and Earla Louise (Sloat) B.; m. Linda Susan Grant, Sept. 16, 1989; 1 child, Grant Stephen. BA in Internat. Affairs, George Washington U., Washington, 1974; MA in Sci., Tech. and Pub. Policy, George Washington U., 1981. Food prog. specialist U.S. Food & Nutrition Svc., Washington, 1978-81; internat. affairs specialist Office Internat. Cooperation & Devel., Washington, 1981-87; legis. analyst Wash. State Senate, Olympia, 1986-89; project dir. Wash. 2000 Project, Olympia, 1989-92; sr. health policy analyst Wash. Dept. Health, Olympia, 1992—; mem. Pew Commn. task force on regulation of health professions, 1994-95. Editor newsletter: Project Update, 1990-92. Study team mem. Gov.'s Efficiency Commn., 1990-91; com. mem. Coun. of State Govts. Strategic Planning Subcom., Lexington, Ky., 1990-92; chmn. Montclair Divsn. IV Neighborhood Assn., 1989-92, Shadywood Homeowner's Assn., 1992-94; bd. dirs. Classical Music Supporters, Seattle, 1987-89. Recipient Superior Performance award, U.S. Dept. Agr., 1986. Mem. World Future Soc., Internat. Health Futures Network. Office: Wash Dept Health PO Box 47851 Olympia WA 98504-7851

BOS, JOHN ARTHUR, aircraft manufacturing executive; b. Holland, Mich., Nov. 6, 1933; s. John Arthur and Annabelle (Castelli) B.; m. Eileen Tempest, Feb. 15, 1974; children: John, James, William, Tiffany. BS in Acctg., Calif. State Coll., Long Beach, 1971. Officer 1st Nat. Bank, Holland, Mich., 1954-61; dir. bus. mgmt. McDonnell Douglas, Long Beach, 1962—. Mem. Inst. Mgmt. Accts. (cert. mgmt. acct. 1979), Nat. Assn. Accts. Office: McDonnell Douglas Aircraft Co 3855 N Lakewood Blvd Long Beach CA 90846-0003

BOSKIN, MICHAEL JAY, economist, government official, university educator, consultant; b. N.Y.C., Sept. 23, 1945; s. Irving and Jean B.; m. Chris Dornin, Oct. 20, 1981. AB with highest honors, U. Calif., Berkeley, 1967, MA in Econs., 1968, PhD in Econs., 1971. Asst. prof. Stanford (Calif.) U., 1970-75, assoc. prof., 1976-78, prof., 1978—, dir. Ctr. for Econ. Policy Rsch., 1986-89, Wohlford prof. econs., 1987-89; chmn. Pres.'s Coun. Econ. Advisors, The White House, Washington, 1989-93; Friedman Prof. Econs. Stanford (Calif.) U., 1993—; pres. Boskin & Co., Menlo Park, Calif., 1993—; vis. prof. Harvard U., Cambridge, Mass., 1977-78; disting. faculty fellow Yale U., 1993, scholar Am. Enterprise Inst., 1993—; rsch. assoc. Nat. Bur. Econ. Rsch., 1976—; bd. dirs. Oracle Corp., Exxon Corp., Healthcare Compare Corp., Airtouch Comm., Inc.; chmn. Congl. Adv. Commn. on the Consumer Price Index; advisor, cons. numerous govt. agencies, pvt. businesses. Author: Too Many Promises: The Uncertain Future of Social Security, 1986, Reagan and the Economy: Successes, Failures Unfinished Agenda, 1987, Frontiers of Tax Reform, 1996; contbr. articles to profl. jours., popular media. Mem. several philanthropic bds. dirs. Faculty Rsch. fellow Mellon Found., 1973; recipient Outstanding Rsch. award Nat. Assn. Bus. Economists, 1987. Fellow Nat. Assn. Bus. Econs. (Presdl. medal Italian Republic). Office: Stanford U 213 HHMB Stanford CA 94305-6010

BOSKOVICH, GEORGE, JR., food products executive; b. 1946. Chmn. Boskovich Farms. Office: Boskovich Farms Inc 711 Diaz Ave Oxnard CA 93030-7247

BOSSERT, PHILIP JOSEPH, information systems executive; b. Indpls., Feb. 23, 1944; s. Alfred Joseph and Phyllis Jean (Cashen) B.; m. Jane Elizabeth Shade, June 29, 1968 (div. Dec. 1990); m. ChaoYing Deng, May 22, 1992; 1 child, Lian Brittni. BA in Econs., Rockhurst Coll., 1968; cert. in Philosophy, U. Freiburg, Fed. Republic Ger., 1970; MA in Philosophy, Washington U., St. Louis, 1972, PhD in Philosophy, 1973. Asst. prof. philosophy Hawaii Loa Coll., Honolulu, 1973-76, pres., 1978-86; dir. Hawaii com. for the humanities Nat. Endowment for the Humanities, Honolulu, 1976-77; dir. long range planning Chaminade U., Honolulu, 1977-78; pres. Strategic Info. Solutions, Honolulu, 1986—; mgr. strategic info. systems GTE Hawaiian Telephone, Honolulu, 1987-91; asst. supt. info. & telecom. svcs. Hawaii State Dept. Edn., 1991-94; project dir. Hawaii Edn. and Rsch. Network, 1994-97; chmn. bd. dirs., dir. Media Design & Devel., Inc., 1996—; chmn. bd. dirs., CEO Baden Wines Internat., Ltd., 1997—; cons. Ssangyong Bus. Group, Seoul, Korea, 1987-90, Nat. Assn. Colls. Univs. and Bus. Officers, Washington, 1980-90. Author: Strategic Planning and Budgeting, 1989; author, editor numerous books on philosophy; contbr. articles to profl. jours. V.p. bd. dirs. Hawaii Childrens Mus.; pres. bd. dirs. Friends of the East West Ctr.; treas. bd. dirs. Hawaii Alliance for the Arts. Fulbright-Hays fellow, 1968-70, Woodrow Wilson fellow, 1972-73, Nat. Endowment for Humanities fellow, 1976. Mem. Data Processing Mgmt. Assn., Pacific Telecom. Coun. (bd. dirs.), Honolulu Com. on Fgn. Relations, Honolulu Rotary Club. Office: Strategic Info Solutions Inc 239 Merchant St Honolulu HI 96813

BOSTWICK, TODD WILLIAM, city archaeologist; b. Seattle, Dec. 18, 1952; s. Michael and Roxie Marilynn (Byers) B.; m. Heidi Bostwick. BA, U. Nev., Reno, 1979; MA, Ariz. State U., 1985. Rsch. asst. Nev. Archaeol. Survey, Reno, 1977; archaeol. technician U.S. Forest Svc., Plumas Nat. Forest, Calif., 1978; asst. crew chief Black Mesa project So. Ill. U., Carbondale, 1980-81; project dir. Northland Rsch., Inc., Flagstaff, Ariz., 1981-85; staff archaeologist, dept. anthropology Ariz. State U., Tempe, 1985-87; asst. city archaeologist City of Phoenix, 1987-90; city archaeologist City of Phoenix, Pueblo Grande Mus., 1990—; mem. adv. com. Deer Valley Rock Art Ctr., Phoenix, 1994—; mem. exec. com. Ariz. Archaeol. Coun., Phoenix, 1994—. Co-author: First Street and Madison: Historical Archaeology of the Second and Phoenix Chinatown, 1992; co-editor, co-author 2 books; author articles. Bd. dirs. Ariz. Preservation Found., Phoenix, 1991-96, Pioneer Cemetery Assn., Phoenix, 1993—. With USAF, 1972-74. Recipient Gov.'s awards in hist. preservation State of Ariz., 1995, Spl. Recognition award State of Ariz., 1995, City Mgr.'s Excellence award City of Phoenix, 1996, others. Mem. Soc. for Am. Archaeology, Ariz. Archaeol. Soc., Ariz. Archaeol. and Hist. Soc., Sigma Xi. Democrat. Office: Pueblo Grande Mus 4619 E Washington St Phoenix AZ 85034

BOSWELL, DAN ALAN, health maintenance organization executive, health care consultant; b. Upland, Calif., July 25, 1947; s. Paul Leslie and Jana Delores (Thompson) B.; m. Lona Kathalene Bentley, Dec. 26, 1969; children: Bethanie Laurel, Daniel Alan II. Grad. in Mktg. and Sales Mgmt., UCLA. Mktg. dir. Maxicare Co., L.A., 1974-78; v.p. Gen. Med, Santa Ana, Calif., 1978-81; exec. v.p. IMC Health Maintenance Orgn., Miami, Fla., 1981-83, Protective Health Providers, San Diego, 1981-83; CEO U.S. Health Plan, San Diego, 1982-84; pres., CEO Serra Health Plan, Sun Valley, Calif., 1984-85, Amerimed (formerly Serra Health Plan), Burbank, Calif., 1985; pres. The Wellstarr Group, Inc., Upland, Calif., 1986-89, pres., CEO, 1990-93; pres., CEO Humantics Managed Care Corp., 1989-92; pres. The Garvey Group, Calif., Upland, 1993—, Managed Care Specialists, Upland, 1993-97; nat. dir. corp. devel. Axiom Inc., Chatsworth, Calif., 1997—; faculty fellow Nat. HMO George Washington U., 1982-83; teaching asst. expert market devel., fed. reviewer health maintenance qualification HHS, Rockville, Md., 1982-84. Mem. governing body Healthsys. Agy., San Diego and Imperial Counties, Calif., 1981-85, pres. trauma task force, San Diego, 1984; mem. adv. bd. Calif. Med. Asst. Commn., San Fernando Valley, 1986; dist. dir. Pony Baseball, Inc.; mgr. Upland Black Am. Legion Baseball, 1992-94. Mem. Am. Mgmt. Assn., Am. Mktg. Assn., Group Health Assn. Am., Marine Corps Assn. Am., El Prado Men's Club (Chino, Calif., bd. dirs. 1985-86), Sierra Laverne Country Club, Towns Club (Pomona, Calif.). Republican. Home: 851 Emerson St Upland CA 91784-1227 Office: Axiom Inc 21601 Devonshire Ste 219 Chatsworth CA 91311

BOSWELL, SUSAN G., lawyer; b. El Paso, Tex., June 26, 1945. BA, U. Ariz., 1972, JD, 1976. Bar: Ariz. 1977, Nev. 1992. Mem. Streich & Lang P.C., Phoenix; instr., faculty mem. Nat. Inst. Trail Advocacy, 1991; bd. vis. U. Ariz. Coll. of Law. Fellow Am. Coll. Bankruptcy; mem. State Bar of Ariz. (peer review com., assistance com.), Ariz. Women Lawyers Assn, Phi Kappa Phi. Office: Streich Lang PC 1 S Church Ave Ste 1700 Tucson AZ 85701-1621

BOSWORTH, BRUCE LEIGHTON, school administrator, educator, consultant; b. Buffalo, Mar. 22, 1942; s. John Wayman and Alice Elizabeth Rodgers; children: David, Timothy, Paul. BA, U. Denver, 1964; MA, U. No. Colo., 1970; EdD, Walden U., 1984. Elem. tchr. Littleton (Colo.) Pub. Schs., 1964-67, 70-81; bldg. prin. East Smoky Sch. Div. 54, Valleyview, Alta., Can., 1967-70; pres., tchr. Chatfield Sch., Littleton, 1981—; adoption cons. hard-to-place children; ednl. cons. spl. needs children. St. Andrew Presbyn. Ch. (USA). Mem. ASCD, Council Exceptional Children, Masons, Shriners, York Rite. Home and Office: 3500 S Lowell Blvd # 316 Sheridan CO 80236

BOTELHO, BRUCE MANUEL, state official, mayor; b. Juneau, Alaska, Oct. 6, 1948; s. Emmett Manuel and Harriet Iowa (Tieszen) B.; m. Guadalupe Alvarez Breton, Sept. 23, 1988; children: Alejandro Manuel, Adriana Regina. Student, U. Heidelberg, Federal Republic of Germany, 1970; BA, Willamette U., 1971, JD, 1976. Bar: Alaska 1976, U.S. Ct. Appeals (9th cir.), U.S. Supreme Ct. Asst. atty. gen. State of Alaska, Juneau, 1976-83, 87-90, dep. commr., acting commr. Dept. of Revenue, 1983-86; mayor City, Borough of Juneau, 1988-91, dep. atty. gen., 1991-94, atty. gen., 1994; atty. gen. State of AK, 1994—. Editor: Willamette Law Jour., 1975-76; contbr. articles profl. jours. Assembly mem. City, Borough of Juneau, 1983-86; pres. Juneau Human Rights Commn., 1978-80, Alaska Coun. Am. Youth Hostels, 1979-81, Juneau Arts and Humanities Coun., 1981-83, SE Alaska Area Coun. Boy Scouts Am., 1991-93; bd. dirs. Found. for Social Innovations, Alaska, 1990-93, Alaska Econ. Devel. Coun., 1985-87, Alaska Indsl. Devel. Corp., 1984-86, Juneau World Affairs Coun.; chair adminstrv. law sect. Alaska Bar Assn., 1981-82; chair Alaska Resources Corp., 1984-86, Gov.'s Conf. on Youth and Justice, 1995-96; trustee Alaska Children's Trust, 1996—. Democrat. Methodist. Home: 401 F St Douglas AK 99824-5353 Office: State Alaska Dept Law PO Box 110300 Juneau AK 99811-0300

BOTELLO, TROY JAMES, arts administrator, counselor; b. Long Beach, Calif., Sept. 2, 1953; s. Arthur P. and Jayme Alta (McBride) B. AA in Spl. Edn., Cerritos Coll., 1979; BA in Music Therapy, Calif. State U., Long Beach, 1984; cert. in arts adminstrn., U. So. Calif., Orange County, 1988; MA in Adminstrn., Calif. Polytech. Inst., Pomona, 1992. Cert. tchr., Calif. Asst. music dir. St. John Bosco High Sch., Bellflower, Calif., 1969-72; music dir. Bellflower Unified Schs., 1971-74; tchr. severely handicapped L.A. County Office of Edn., 1974-88; vocat. rehab. counselor Tesseler Counseling Group, Anaheim, Calif., 1988-91; dir. edn. Orange County Performing Arts Ctr., Costa Mesa, Calif., 1991—; exec. dir., co-founder Project: Arts in Motion, Bellflower, 1983-92; ednl. cons. Edn. Div. Music Ctr., L.A., 1986—; vice chmn. La Mirada (Calif.) Community Concerts, 1976-79; v.p. grants Master Symphony Orch., Norwalk, Calif. Chairperson La Mirada Hist. Com., 1977-78; rep. Edn. Adv. Com., L.A., 1981; exec. prod., bd. dirs. Imagination Celebration of Orange County, 1991—; pres. Anaheim Cultural Arts Found., 1993-95; state pres., bd. dirs Very Special Arts Calif., 1992—. Mem. Assn. for Music Therapy Profls., So. Calif. Band and Field Judges, Profl. Arts Mgmt. Inst., Calif. Assn. Rehab. Profls., Am. Assn. Orff Schwelrk, Young Composers of Am., Alumni of Drum Corps Internat. Home: 14216 Neargrove Rd La Mirada CA 90638-3854 Office: Orange County Performing Arts Ctr 600 Town Center Dr Costa Mesa CA 92626-1916

BOTIMER, ALLEN RAY, retired surgeon, retirement center owner; b. Columbus, Miss., Jan. 30, 1930; s. Clare E. and Christel J. (Kalar) B.; m. Dorris LaJean, Aug. 17, 1950; children: Larry Alan, Gary David. BS, Walla Walla Coll., 1951; MD, Loma Linda U., 1955. Diplomate Am. Bd. Surgery. Intern U.S. Naval Hosp., San Diego, 1955-56, surg. resident, 1955-60; asst. chief surgery U.S. Naval Hosp., Guam, 1960-62, Bremerton, Wash., 1962-64; chief surgery Ballard Community Hosp., Seattle, 1970, chief of staff, 1972, chief surgery, 1986-87; pvt. practice Seattle, 1964-87; ret., 1987; ptnr. Heritage Retirement Ctr., Nampa, Idaho, 1972-82, owner, 1982—. Lt. comdr. USN, 1955-64. Fellow ACS, Seattle Surg. Soc.; mem. Wash. State Med. Soc., King County Med. Soc. Home and Office: 1319 Torrey Ln Nampa ID 83686

BOTKIN, DANIEL BENJAMIN, biologist, environmental scientist; b. Oklahoma City, Aug. 19, 1937; s. Benjamin Albert and Gertrude (Fritz) B.; m. Ellen Chase, Dec. 22, 1962 (div. 1976); children: Nancy, Jonathan; m. Erene Victoria Youngberg, Apr. 7, 1978 (dec. Mar. 1994). BA, U. Rochester, 1959; MA, U. Wis., 1962; PhD, Rutgers U., 1968. From asst. to assoc. prof. Yale U., New Haven, 1968-76; assoc. scientist Marine Biol. Lab., Woods Hole, Mass., 1976-78; prof. biology U. Calif., Santa Barbara, 1978-92, chmn. environ. studies program, 1978-85; dir. program on global change biology dept. George Mason U., Fairfax, Va., 1993—; pres. The Ctr. for the Study of the Environment, 1992—. Author: Discordant Harmonies: A New Ecology for the 21st Century, 1990, Forest Dynamics: An Ecological Model, 1993, Environmental Science: Earth As A Living Planet, 1995, Our Natural History: The Lessons of Lewis and Clark, 1995; (software) JABOWA, 1970, Timber: model of forest growth, 1983, 87, JABOWA-II, 1992; co-author: Forest Succession, 1981, Environmental Studies, 1982, 87, Changing the Global Environment, 1989; contbr. articles to profl. jours. Trustee Santa Barbara Bot. Garden, 1987-93. Recipient Fernow prize for Internat. Forestry, 1995, First Prize, Mitchell Internat. Prize for Sustainable Devel., 1991; named to Environ. Hall of Fame, Calif. Polytechnic U., 1995; fellow Rockefeller Bellagio (Italy) Inst., 1985, East-West Ctr., Honolulu, 1985-87, Woodrow Wilson Internat. Ctr. for Scholars, Washington, 1977-78; grantee EPA, NSF, NASA, NOAA, Mellon Found., Pew Charitable Trusts, W. Alton Jones Found., World Wildlife Fund, SOHIO Alaska Corp. Fellow AAAS; mem. Am. Soc. Naturalists, Brit. Ecol. Soc., Sigma Xi (lectr. 1981-83). Office: Ctr in Study of Environment PO Box 93160 Santa Barbara CA 93160

BOTKIN, MONTY LANE, computer company executive; b. Lubbock, Tex., Mar. 26, 1951; s. Louis A. and Geneva O. (Marlin) B.; 1 child, Nicholas L.; m. Ayami Honda, Oct. 26, 1996. BA, Tex. Tech U., 1975. Supr. Tex. Instruments, Inc., Lubbock, 1976-77, Abilene, Tex., 1977-78; electronic ctr. mgr. Tex. Instruments Supply Co., Palo Alto, Calif., 1978-81; mfg. mgr. home computers Tex. Instruments, Inc., Lubbock, 1981-83, mfg. mgr. calculator, 1983-87, mfg. mgr. ednl. products, 1987-90; Semi-Conductor Grp. photolithography ops. mgr. Tex. Instruments, Inc., 1990-91, total quality control mgr. Lubbock Mos Memory, 1991-93; dir. mfg. Brother Industries U.S.A., Bartlett, Tenn., 1993-96, also bd. dirs.; dir. ops. Taiwan Semiconductor Mfg. Co., San Jose, Calif., 1996—. Mem. Inst. Indsl. Engrs. (sr.), Am. Soc. for Quality Control (chmn. West Tex. sect.), Am. Prodn. and Inventory Control Soc. Home: 1735 Colony Way Gilroy CA 95020 Office: Taiwan Semiconductor Mfg Co 1740 Technology Dr Ste 660 San Jose CA 95110

BOTSAI, ELMER EUGENE, architect, educator, former university dean; b. St. Louis, Feb. 1, 1928; s. Paul and Ita May (Cole) B.; m. Patricia L. Keegan, Aug. 28, 1955; children: Donald Rolf, Kurt Gregory.; m. Sharon K. Kaiser, Dec. 5, 1981; 1 dau., Kiana Michelle. AA, Sacramento Jr. Coll., 1950; A.B., U. Calif.-Berkeley, 1954. Registered architect, Hawaii, Calif. Draftsman, then asst. to architect So. Pacific Co., San Francisco, 1953-57; designer J.H. Ferguson Co., San Francisco, 1955; project architect Anshen & Allen Architects, San Francisco, 1957-63; prin. Botsai, Overstreet & Rosenberg, Architects and Planners, San Francisco, 1963-79, Elmer E. Botsai FAIA, Honolulu, 1979—; chmn. dept. architecture U. Hawaii, Manoa, 1976-80, dean Sch. Architecture, 1980-90, prof., 1990—; lectr. U. Calif., Berkeley, 1976, dir. Nat. Archtl. Accrediting Bd., 1972-73, 79; adminstrv. and tech. cons. Wood Bldg. Rsch. Ctr., U. Calif., 1985-90, mem. profl. preparation project com. at U. Mich., Ann Arbor, 1986-87; co-author water infiltration seminar series for Bldg. Owners and Mgrs. Rsch. Ctr., 1986-87; chief investigator effects of Guatemalan earthquake for NSF and AIA, Washington, 1976; steering com. on structural failures Nat. Bur. Standards, 1982-84; chmn., dir. gen. svcs. Adv. Com. State of Calif. Co-author: Architects and Earthquake, Research Needs, 1976, ATC Seismic Standards for National Bur. of Standards, 1976, Architects and Earthquakes: A Primer, 1977, Seismic Design, 1978, Wood-Detailing for Performance, 1990, Wood as a Building Material, 2d edit., 1991; contbr. articles and reports to profl. jours.; prin. works include expansion of Nuclear Weapons Tng. Facility at Lemoore Naval Air Sta., Calif., LASH Terminal Port Facility Archtl. Phase, San Francisco, Incline Village (Nev.) Country Club, 1365 Columbus Ave. Bldg., San Francisco, modernization Stanford Ct. Hotel, San Francisco; monument area constrn. several Calif. ceneteries. With U.S. Army, 1946-48. Recipient Cert. Honor Fedn. Archtl. Colls. Mex. Republic, 1984; NSF grantee for investigative workshop project, San Diego, 1974-80. Fellow AIA (bd. dirs., 1966-71, treas. No. Calif. chpt. 1968-69, pres. 1971, nat. v.p., 1975-76, nat. pres. 1978, pres. Hawaii 1985); hon. fellow Royal Can. Inst. Architects, N.Z. Inst. Architects, Royal Australian Inst. Architects, La Societed de Arquitectos Mexicano; mem. Archtl. Secs. Assn. (hon.), Soc. Wood Sci. and Tech., Internat. Conf. Bldg. Ofcls. Home: 321 Wailupe Cir Honolulu HI 96821-1524 Office: 2560 Campus Rd # 2B Honolulu HI 96822-2217

BOTTEL, HELEN ALFEA, columnist, writer; b. Beaumont, Calif.; d. Alpheus Russell and Mary Ellen (Alexander) Brigden; m. Robert E. Bottel; children: Robert Dennis, Rodger M., R. Kathryn Bottel Bernhardt, Suzanne V. Bottel Peppers. AA, Riverside Coll. Calif.; student, Oreg. State U., 1958-59, So. Oreg. Coll., 1959. Writer, editor Illinois Valley News, Cave Junction, Oreg., 1950-56; writer Grants Pass (Oreg.) Courier, Portland Oregonian, Medford (Oreg.) Mail Tribune, 1952-58; daily columnist Helen Help Us and Generation Rap King Features Syndicate, N.Y.C., 1958-83, columnist (with Sue Bottel), 1969-83; adv. bd. Internat. Affairs Inst., N.Y.C., Tokyo, 1986—; freelance mag. writer, author, lectr., 1956—. Author: To Teens with Love, 1969, Helen Help Us, 1970, Parents Survival Kit, 1979; contbg. editor, columnist Real World mag., 1978-84; weekly columnist Yomiuri Shimbun, Tokyo, 1982-90; thrice weekly columnist Sacramento Union, 1986-88; newspaper and mag. columnist Look Who's Aging (with dau. Kathy Bernhardt), 1992-96; contbr. nonfiction to books and nat. mags. Staff mem. ACT Handicapped Children Games, Sacramento, 1986—; bd. dirs. Ill. Valley Med. Ctr., 1958-62, Childrens Ctr., Sacramento, 1969, Family Support Programs, Sacramento, 1991-95; active Grants Pass Br. Oreg. Juvenile Adv. Com., 1960-62, Nat. Spina Bifida Assn.; charter patron Cosumnes River Coll., Sacramento, 1972—; nat. adv. bd. Nat. Anorexic Aid Soc., 1977-83; scholarship com. judge Exec. Women Internat., 1985. Recipient Women's Svc. Cup Riverside Coll., citation for aid to U.s. servicemen in Vietnam Gov. Ga., 1967, Disting. Merit citation NCCJ, 1970, 1st place award for books Calif. Press Women, 1970, Sacramento Regional Arts Coun. Lit. Achievement award, 1974, Alumna of Yr. award Riverside Coll., 1987, Gold and Silver medals Calif. Sr. Games (tennis), 1990-91. Mem. Am. Soc. Journalists and Authors, Internat. Affairs Inst. Presbyterian. Clubs: Calif. Writers, Southgate Tennis. Home: 2060 56th Ave Sacramento CA 95822-4112 *"Leap before you look." That's for me. My best moments and finest achievements have resulted from spur-of-the-moment impulses on which I've acted before second thoughts or considered judgment could persuade me they were impossible.*

BOTTI, RICHARD CHARLES, association executive; b. Brockton, Mass., May 1, 1939; s. Alfred Benecchi and Elizabeth Savini; stepson Ernest Botti; student Pierce Jr. Coll., 1959, Orange Coast Coll., 1964; m. Gwen Botti; children—Randolph K., Douglas S., Richard II. Pres., Legis. Info. Services Hawaii, Inc., Honolulu, 1971—; exec. dir., profl. lobbyist Hawaii Food Industry Assn., Honolulu, Hawaii Automotive & Retail Gasoline Dealers Assn., Inc., Honolulu, Hawaii Bus. League, Retail Liquor Dealers Assn. Hawaii, Liquor Dispensers of Hawaii, Hawaii Pubs. Assn., Automotive Body and Painting Assn.; gen. mgr. Hawaii Fashion Industry Assn. Mem. Food Industry Assn. Execs., Am. Soc. Assn. Execs., Aloha Soc. Assn. Execs. (dir. Hawaii Foodbank). Address: Legis Info Services 677 Ala Moana Blvd Ste 815 Honolulu HI 96813-5416

BOTTOMS, DAVID TIMOTHY, editor, journalist; b. Athens, Ala., Aug. 9, 1970; s. Robert Garvin and Gwendolyn J. (Vickers) B. BA, Denison U., 1992. Bus. mgr., mktg. mgr. Electronics mag. Penton Pub., Cleveland, 1992-94; bus. mgr., mktg. mgr. Computer-Aided Engineering mag., 1992-94, asst. editor Industry Week mag., 1994-95; assoc. editor Industry Week mag. West Coast bur. San Francisco, 1995-96; pub. rels. specialist Netscape Comm. Corp., Mountain View, Calif., 1996—. Contr. articles to profl. jours. (nominee: Nat. Bus. Press award, 1996). Mem. Press Club of San Francisco. Republican. Episcopalian. Office: Netscape Communications Industry Week 501 E Middlefield Rd Mountain Fiew CA 94043

BOTWINICK, MICHAEL, museum director; b. N.Y.C., Nov. 14, 1943; s. Joseph and Helen (Shlisky) B.; m. Harriet Maltzer, Aug. 14, 1965; children: Jonathan Seth, Daniel Judah. B.A., Rutgers Coll., 1964; M.A., Columbia U., 1967. Instr. Columbia U., N.Y.C., 1968-69, CCNY, CUNY, 1969; asst. curator medieval art Cloisters Met. Mus. Art, N.Y.C., 1969; asso. curator medieval art Cloisters Met. Mus. Art, 1970, asst. curator-in-chief, 1971—;

asst. dir. art Phila. Mus. Art, 1971-74; dir. Bklyn. Mus., 1974-83, Corcoran Gallery Art, 1983-87; sr. v.p. Knoedler-Modarco, S.A., N.Y.C., 1987-88; pres. Fine Arts Group, Chgo., 1989-91; dir. Newport Harbor Art Mus., Newport Beach, Calif., 1991—; dir. Ctr. Orange County Regional Studies U. Calif., Irvine, 1997—; pres. Cultural Instns. Group, 1975-76; mem. N.Y.C. Adv. Commn. Cultural Affairs, 1975-76, N.Y.C. Urban Design Coun., 1975; mem. adv. bd. WNET, N.Y.C., 1979-83; mem. Nat. Conservation Adv. Coun., 1979-80, exec. com. U.S. Com.-Internat. Coun. Mus., 1982-87, Yale U. Coun. Com. on the Art Gallery, 1983-88, Internat. Rsch. and Exch. Bd., fine arts com. German Dem. Republic, 1984-87, fine arts com. U.S. State Dept. Arts in Embassies Program, 1986-88; arts adminstrn. adv. com. U. Calif.-Irvine, 1993—. Mem. Assn. Art Mus. Dirs., Am. Assn. Museums, Coll. Art Assn., Steppenwolf Theater Co., Chgo. (bd. dirs. 1990-91). Office: U Calif PO Box 6050 Irvine CA 92616*

BOTZLER, RICHARD GEORGE, wildlife educator; b. Detroit, Jan. 27, 1942; s. Otto and Elfriede (Nolte) B.; m. Sally Jo Nelson, Oct. 5, 1942; children: Emilisa, Tin, Dorothy, Sarah, Thomas. BS, Wayne State U., 1963; M of Wildlife Mgmt., U. Mich., 1967, PhD, 1970. Asst. prof. wildlife Humboldt State U., Arcata, Calif., 1970-74, assoc. prof., 1974-79, prof., 1979—; chair wildlife dept. Humboldt State U., 1977-80, 96—. Editor: Environmental Ethics: Divergence and Convergence, 1993; contbr. articles to profl. jours. Co-founder Humboldt County Coun. on Adoptable Children, 1971—. Recipient Outstanding Prof. for Calif. State U. System, 1992. Mem. Wildlife Disease Assn. (coun. mem. 1991-96, asst. editor jour. of wildlife disease 1990-91, editor 1991-96, mem. editl. bd. 1991—), Fulbright Assn. (life, fellow 1981-82), The Wildlife Soc., Soc. Conservation Biology, Soc. Vector Ecology, Sigma Xi. Office: Humboldt State U Dept Wildlife Arcata CA 95521

BOUCHARD, PAUL EUGENE, artist; b. Providence, Sept. 26, 1946; s. Marcel Paul and Anna Theresa (Dullea) B., m. Ann Marie, Nov. 18, 1972 (div. 1977); 1 child Michael Paul; m. R. Jane Bouchard, Apr. 11, 1997. BFA, Calif. State U., Long Beach, 1978. bd. dir, Angeles Gate Cultural Ctr., San Pedro, Calif., 1983-85. One-man show at Rogue Coll., Grants Pass, Oreg., 1996, El Camino Coll., 1997; exhibited in group shows at Rental Gallery, Oakland Mus., 1984, Rental Gallery, L.A. County Mus. of Art, 1985, Sixth St. Gallery, San Pedro, Calif., Aquarius Gallery, Cambria, Calif., 1986, St. Andrew's Priory, Valyermo, Calif., Riverside (Calif.) Art Mus., Rental Gallery, 1987, Vietnam Vet.'s Art Exhibit, 1988, Coos Art Mus., Coos Bay, Oreg., 1989, Grants Pass Mus. of Art, 1991, Eastern Wash. U., 1992, Dept. Vets. Affairs Hdqrs., Sydney, Australia, 1992-93, Australian Nat. Gallery, Brisbane County Hall Gallery, Nat. Vietnam Vets. Art Mus., Chgo., others. Recipient Contribution to the Arts, City of Torrance, Calif., 1985; grantee Franklin Furnace, N.Y.C., 1989-90, Artist Space, N.Y.C., 1989-90. Home and Studio: 30268 Mersey Ct Temecula CA 92591

BOUGHTON, IRENE, elementary education educator; b. Kincaid, Kans., Mar. 14, 1901; d. William Gauf and Alice Mae (Trout) Frazer; m. Reuben Byron Boughton, June 15, 1924; children: Alice, Nova Jean, Keith, Lynn. BA, U. No. Colo., 1953. Cert. lifetime tchg., Colo. Reading lab. tchr. Ft. Mesa Pub. Schs., Fruita, Colo., 1965-66; reading technician Pub. Sch. Dist., Mt. Shasta, Weed, Calif., 1966-68. Author: (short stories) Growing Up On the Homestead, 1994, (poems) People Pomes, 1988. Deaconess Grace Cmty. Ch., 1983-91. Mem. IEA, Silver Rebekah Lodge. Republican. Home: 245 Encanto Ct Fruita CO 81521

BOUGHTON, LESLEY D., library director; b. New Haven, Conn., Jan. 21, 1945; d. Robert and Marjorie (Anderson) D.; m. Charles E. Boughton, Sept. 5, 1964 (dec. 1991); children: Michael, James, Gregg. AB, Conn. Coll., 1971; MLS, So. Conn. State U., 1978. Dir. Platte County Library, Wheatland, Wyo., 1980-88, Carbon County Library, Rawlins, Wyo., 1988-93, Natrona County Pub. Library, Casper, Wyo., 1993—; mem. Gov's. Telecommunications Coun., Wyo., 1994—. Mem. ALA (chpt. councilor 1988, 91), Wyo. Library Assn. (pres. 1985, Disting. Svc. award 1991). Office: Natrona County Pub Libr 307 E 2nd St Casper WY 82601-2505*

BOUKIDIS, CONSTANTINE MICHAEL, lawyer; b. Burbank, Calif., Nov. 16, 1959; s. Michael A. and Frances (Mavros) B.; m. Eugenia Demetra Rodinos, May 17, 1987; children: Michael Constantine, Frances Anastasia, Katherine Elizabeth, Evan Constantine. BA in Econs., Northwestern U., 1981; JD, Loyola Law Sch., L.A., 1984. Bar: Calif. 1985, U.S. Dist. Ct. (cen. dist.) Calif. 1985, U.S. Ct. Appeals (9th cir.), 1985. Investigator Harney & Moore, L.A., 1980-82; assoc. Law Offices of David M. Harney, L.A., 1985-92; pvt. practice, 1992—. Treas., chmn. cathedral planning com. St. Sophia Greek Orthodoc Cathedral Cmty., L.A., 1989, pres. cmty., 1994-96; apptd. St. Sophia Cathedral Found., asst. sec., 1997—; bd. dirs. Glendale (Calif.) YMCA, 1997—, Glendale Bar Assn. Lawyer Referral Svc., 1995—. Mem. ABA, Glendale Bar Assn., Phi Kappa Sigma (treas. 1980-81). Democrat. Home: 1641 Country Club Dr Glendale CA 91208-2038 Office: 144 N Glendale Ave Ste 101 Glendale CA 91206-4903

BOULDEN, JUDITH ANN, federal judge; b. Salt Lake City, Dec. 28, 1948; d. Douglas Lester and Emma Ruth (Robertson) Boulden; m. Alan Walter Barnes, Nov. 7, 1982; 1 child, Dorian Lisa. BA, U. Utah, 1971, JD, 1974. Bar: Utah 1974, U.S. Dist. Ct. Utah 1974. Law clk. to A. Sherman Christianson U.S. Cts., Salt Lake City, 1974; assoc. Roe & Fowler, Salt Lake City, 1975-81, McKay Burton Thurman & Condie, Salt Lake City, 1982-83; trustee Chpt. 7, Salt Lake City, 1976-82, Standing Chpt. 12, Salt Lake City, 1987-88, Standing Chpt. 13, Salt Lake City, 1979-88; sr. ptnr. Boulden & Gillman, Salt Lake City, 1983-88; U.S. Bankruptcy judge U.S. Cts., Salt Lake City, 1988—. Mem. Utah Bar Assn. *

BOULEY, JOSEPH RICHARD, pilot; b. Fukuoka, Japan, Jan. 7, 1955; came to U.S., 1955; s. Wilfrid Arthur and Minori Cecelia (Naraki) B.; m. Mi Sun Chang, Dec. 19, 1980 (div. June 1990); children: Denise Marie, Janice Elizabeth; m. Sara Elizabeth Caldwell, July 6, 1991. BA in English, U. Nebr., 1977; MAS, Embry Riddle Aeronautical U., 1988. Commd. 2d lt. USAF, 1977; advanced through grades to lt. col. USAFR, 1996; F-117A Stealth Fighter pilot USAF, Persian Gulf, 1991; pilot United Airlines, 1992—. Ct. apptd. spl. advocate Office of Guardian Ad Litem, Salt Lake City, 1996. Decorated Disting. Flying Cross, 4 Air medals, 3 Meritorious Svc. medals, 2 Aerial Achievement medals, 3 Air Force Commendation medals, Air Force Achievement medal. Mem. VFW, Am. Legion, Disting. Flying Cross Soc., Airline Pilots Assn., Red River Valley Fighter Pilots Assn., Aircraft Owners & Pilots Assn. Republican. Roman Catholic. Home: 1544 E Emerson Ave Salt Lake City UT 84105

BOULWARE, RICHARD STARK, airport administrator; b. Chgo., Aug. 28, 1935; s. John Stark and Ellen Bradley (Bowlin) B.; m. Sylvia Grace Panaro, Sept. 17, 1960 (div. Jan. 1980); children: Susan Bradley, Robert Stark; M. Janice Gilliland Wells, Oct. 1, 1992. BFA, Art Ctr. Coll., 1967. Photographer Hughes Aircraft, Los Angeles, 1960-61; chief photographer U. Iowa, Iowa City, 1962-67; dir. audio/visual media TransWorld Airlines, N.Y.C., 1968-70; owner, mgr. RBA Prodns., Denver, 1970-80; dir. photography Colo. Inst. Art, Denver, 1980-84; dep. dir. aviation Stapleton Internat. Airport and Denver Internat. Airport, Denver, 1984—, Denver Internat. Airport, 1984—. Served with USN, 1954-58. Recipient Golden Eagle award CINE, 1976, award Bus. and Profl. Advt. Assn., Alfie award Denver Advt. Fedn., Christensen Meml. award Iowa Press Photographers Assn., award Art Dirs. Club Denver; named Nat. Photographer of Yr. U. Profl. Photographers Assn. Am., 1967. Mem. Pub. Relations Soc. Am. (award Colo. chpt.), Colo. Broadcasters Assn. Colo. Press Assn., Am. Assn. Airport Execs., Art Dirs. Club Denver (v.p.). Home: 9112E E Amherst Dr Denver CO 80231-4006 Office: Denver Internat Airport Airport Office Bldg 8500 Pena Blvd Denver CO 80249-6205

BOUNDS, M. BETSY, educational administrator, consultant; b. Phila., Oct. 4, 1944; d. Richard V. and Marion (Anderson) Bond; m. James Monty Bounds, Dec. 18, 1965 (div. July 1987); children: Brian, Lisa. BA, U. Ariz., 1967, MEd, 1969, EdS, 1975, PhD, 1988. Cert. in elem. edn., spl. edn., counseling and guidance adminstrn., Ariz. Tchr. Cartwright Sch. Dist., Phoenix, 1967-69; resource tchr. Tucson Unified Sch. Dist., 1975-76, supportive tchr., 1976-82, clin. coord., 1982-84, asst. dir., 1984-88, exec. dir., 1988—; adj. prof. U. Ariz., Tucson, 1992-94, No. Ariz. U., 1997—. Mem. joint legis. com. on extended sch. yr. Ariz. Legislature, Phoenix, 1988-89; mem. mayor's sch. dist. action force City of Tucson, 1994—. Recipient award of excellence Spl. Needs Pers. Assn. Ariz. Mem. Ariz. Coun. Adminstrs. in Spl. Edn. (pres. 1994-96), Tucson Residence Found. (pres. 1996—), Ariz. Coun. for Exceptional Children (pres.-elect 1997—), Am. Assn. Sch. Adminstrs. (cons., workshop presenter). Office: Tucson Unified Sch Dist 1010 E 10th St Tucson AZ 85719-5813

BOURKE, LYLE JAMES, electronics company executive, small business owner; b. San Diego, May 28, 1963; s. Robert Victor and Virginia (Blackburn) B. Cert. in electronics, Southwestern Coll., San Diego, 1984; cert. in microelectronics, Burr Brown, Miramar, Calif., 1985; student, NACS, Scranton, Pa., 1988; AA in Econs., Cuyamaca Coll., 1991, postgrad., 1991-92; student, Wendelstedt Umpire Sch., 1992-93. Counselor Dept. Parks and Recreation City of Imperial Beach, Calif., 1979-80; warehouse worker Seafood Cannery, Cordova, Alaska, 1981, Nat. Beef Packing, Liberal, Kans., 1983; night mgr. Southland Corp., San Diego, 1983-85; tech. developer Unisys Corp., San Diego, 1985-92; process technician Ben & Jerry's Homemade, Inc., Springfield, Vt., 1994-95; technician Laser Power Corp, San Diego, Calif., 1996-97; founder Sparrells Ltd., 1992; instr. Harmonium Enrichment Program, 1993. Editor (handbook) College Policies, 1991; contbr. Cleanrooms mag., 1992; inventor Jacuzzi pillow, no-sit snowboard bindings. Vol. United Way, San Diego, 1987—; donor Imperial Beach Boys and Girls Club, 1988-93, Cal Farley's Boys Ranch, 1985-93, Assn. Handicapped Artists, 1988—, San Diego Jr. Theatre, 1992, Cabrillo Elem. Sch. Found., 1992. Chulsa Vista Lit. Team, 1996-97. Named Most Valuable Player Mex. Amateur Baseball League, San Diego-Tijuana, 1990. Mem. Am. Assn. Ret. Persons, Am. Mgmt. Assn. (charter), Prognosticators Club. Democrat. Office: Unisys 8011 Fairview Ave La Mesa CA 91941-6416

BOURQUE, LINDA ANNE BROOKOVER, public health educator; b. Indpls., Aug. 25, 1941; d. Wilbur Bone and Edna Mae (Eberhart) Brookover; m. Don Philippe Bourque, June 3, 1966 (div. Nov. 1974). BA, Ind. U., 1963; MA, Duke U., 1964, PhD, 1968. Postdoctoral researcher Duke U., Durham, N.C., 1968-69; asst. prof. sociology Calif. State U., Los Angeles, 1969-72; asst. prof. to assoc. prof. pub. health UCLA, 1972-86, prof. pub. health, 1986—, acting assoc. dir. Inst. for Social Sci. Research, 1981-82, vice chair dept. community health scis., 1991-94. Author: Defining Rape, 1989, (with Virginia Clark) Processing Data: The Survey Example, 1992, (with Eve Fielder) How to Conduct Self-Administered and Mail Surveys, 1995; contbr. articles to profl. jours. Violoncellist with Santa Monica (Calif.) Symphony Orch., 1978—, Los Angeles Doctors' Symphony, 1981—. Mem. AAAS, Am. Sociol. Assn. (mem. med. sociology sect. council 1975-78, co-chmn. com. freedom research and teaching, 1975-78, cert. recognition 1980), Pacific Sociol. Assn. (co-chmn. program com. 1982, v.p. 1983), Am. Pub. Health Assn. (mem. standing com. on status of women 1974-76), Sociologists for Women in Society, Am. Assn. Pub. Opinion Rsch., Assn. Rsch. in Vision and Ophthalmology, Delta Omega, Phi Alpha Theta. Office: UCLA Sch Pub Health Box 957220 Los Angeles CA 90095-1772

BOURRIE, SALLY RUTH, writer; b. Denver, Nov. 5, 1958; d. Lawrence John and Helen Leone (Atkins) B. AB, Vassar Coll., 1980; MA, U. So. Calif., 1983. Freelance writer Chgo. and Denver, 1987—. Author: (catalog) Art of Paul Landacre, 1983. V.p. Vassar Coll. Class of 1980, 1995—. Recipient 1st pl. award for individual writing Chgo. Women in Publishing, 1993, Hon. Mention award Writer's Digest, 1991. Mem. Colo. Vassar Club (v.p. 1995—), Haviland Collectors Club Internat.

BOUTELL MOONIER, SYLVIA, artist; b. Phila., Dec. 13, 1921; d. Harry Littman and Rose Myers; 2 children. BA, Okla. U. Tchr. Garden Grove H.S., Calif., 1975; owner art restoration co. Moonier Galleria, Newport Beach, Calif., 1977. Group shows include Garden Grove Whitehouse Mus., 1980; represented in the permanent collections of John Wayne, Joan Irvine Smith, Olive Nohel, Lindsey Crosby, Price Waterhouse, among others. Recipient trophies (2) L.A. Radio Broadcasting, 1985. Home: 101 Havenview Ln Oceanside CA 92056-4829

BOUTILIER, NANCY W., writer, secondary English educator; b. Worcester, Mass., Feb. 6, 1961; d. Richard James and Janet (Kallgren) B. AB, Harvard/Radcliffe, 1984; MA, Bread Loaf Sch. of English, 1990. Tchr. Phillips Acad., Andover, Mass., 1984-90, San Francisco U. High Sch., 1991—; columnist Bay Area Reporter, 1991—. Author: According to Her Contours, 1992; contbr. articles to profl. jours. Co-founder Phillips Acad. Gay/Straight Alliance, 1988, Bay Area Ind. Sch. Gay and Lesbian Caucus, 1992. Recipient Outstanding Columnist Cable Car award, 1992, 94. Home: 151 Bonview St San Francisco CA 94110-5146 Office: San Francisco U HS 3065 Jackson St San Francisco CA 94115-1022

BOUTONNET, EDWARD, food products executive; b. 1938. V.p. Boutonnet Farms, Inc., Castroville, Calif.; sec. Kleen Globe,Inc., Castroville, Calif., 1972—; pres. Calif. Artichoke, Castroville, Calif., 1982—. Office: Ocean Mist Farms 11500 Del Monte Ave Castroville CA 95012-3155*

BOUVIER, MARSHALL ANDRE, lawyer; b. Jacksonville, Fla., Sept. 30, 1923; s. Marshall and Helen Marion B.; m. Zepha Windle, July 11, 1938; children: Michael A., Debra Bouvier Williams, Mark A., Marshall André III, Suzanne, John A. (dec.), Wendy Bouvier Clark, Jennifer Lynn. AB, Emory U., LLB, 1949. Bar: Ga. 1948, Nev. 1960. Commd. USN, 1949; naval aviator, judge advocate; ret., 1959; atty. State of Nevada, 1959-60; pvt. practice, Reno, 1960-82, 88—; dist. atty. County of Storey, Nev., 1982-88, spl. cons. to Nev.Dist. Atty., 1991—, Storey County Dist. Atty., 1991—; cons. on corp. securites problems. Mem. Judge Advocates Assn., Am. Bd. Hypnotherapy, Ancient and Honorable Order Quiet Birdmen, Rotary, E Clampus Vitus, Phi Delta Phi, Sigma Chi.

BOVEN, DOUGLAS GEORGE, lawyer; b. Holland, Mich., Aug. 11, 1943. BSE, U. Mich., 1966, JD, 1969. Bar: Calif. 1970. With Crosby, Heafy, Roach & May PC, San Francisco; arbitrator Fed. and Superior Ct. Panel of Arbitrators, 1980—; panelist Superior Ct. Early Settlement Program, 1987. Mem. ABA (mem. bus. bankruptcy, Chpt. 11 and secured creditors coms.), Am. Bankruptcy Inst., Comml. Law League Am., State Bar Calif. (insolvency law and real estate sects.), Alameda County Bar Assn., Sonoma County Bar Assn., Bay Area Bankruptcy Forum, Bar Assn. San Francisco (comml. law and bankruptcy sect., mem. arbitrator fee disputes com. 1973—), Tau Beta Pi. Office: Crosby Heafey Roach & May PC One Market Plz Spear Tower # 1800 Spear St San Francisco CA 94105-1000

BOVEY, TERRY ROBINSON, insurance executive; b. Oregon, Ill., May 13, 1948; s. John Franklin and Frances (Robinson) B.; m. Diana Carmen Rodriguez, Aug. 29, 1970 (div. 1980); 1 child, Joshua; m. Kathy Jo Johnston, Sept. 14, 1985; children: Courtney, Taylor. Student, Ariz. Western Coll., 1966-68, Grand Canyon Coll., 1968-69; BBA, U. Ariz., 1972. Salesman All-Am. Dist. Co., Yuma, Ariz., 1972-76; dist. asst. mgr. Equitable Life Ins., Yuma, 1976-81; gen. sales mgr. Ins. Counselors, Yuma, 1981-83; mng. gen. agt. First Capital Life Ins. Co., Ariz., Calif., Nev., N.C., 1983-90; master gen. agt. Comml. Union Life Ins. Co., Tucson, 1990—; regional commr. Ariz. Interscholastic Assn., Yuma, 1972-88; umpire Nat. League, Major League Baseball, 1979, 95, crew chief, 95, Nat. League playoffs, 1984, baseball supr. Ariz. C.C. Athletic Conf., 1992—. mem. Century Club, Boy's Club of Yuma. Mem. Million Dollar Round Table, Nat. Assn. Life Underwriters (numerous sales achievement awards, Nat. Quality awards), Life Underwriters Polit. Action Com., Tucson City Assn. Republican. Presbyterian.

BOWDEN, GEORGE NEWTON, lawyer; b. East Orange, N.J., Nov. 21, 1946; s. W. Paul and Catherine A. (Porter) B. BA, Bowdoin Coll., 1971; JD, U. Maine, 1974. Bar: Wash. 1974, Maine 1975, U.S. Dist. Ct. (we. dist.) Wash. 1978, U.S. Ct. Appeals (9th cir.) 1980, U.S. Supreme Ct. 1982. Asst. county atty. Lincoln County, Wiscasset, Maine, 1974; dep. pros. atty. Grays Harbor County, Montesano, Wash., 1974-76, King County, Seattle, 1976, Snohomish County, Everett, Wash., 1976-79; ptnr. Senter & Bowden, Everett, Wash., 1979—; judge pro tempore Snohomish County Superior and Dist. Cts.; arbitrator, mediator Settlement Now. Bd. dirs. Everett Symphony Orch. 1993—, pres. 1996—; v.p. Driftwood Players, Edmonds, Wash., 1978. Sgt. USMC, 1966-68. Mem. ATLA, Nat. Assn. Criminal Def. Attys., Wash. State Bar Assn. (CLE com., fee arbitration bd.), Wash. Assn. Criminal Def. Lawyers (bd. govs., sec. 1993), Wash. State Trial Lawyers Assn., Snohomish County Bar Assn. (pres. 1995). Office: Senter and Bowden 2817 Wetmore Ave Everett WA 98201-3517

BOWDEN, RANDALL GLEN, academic adminstrator; b. Council, Idaho, Sept. 26, 1959; s. Rocky Smith and Barbara (Chilcott) Loftis; m. Donna Michelle Kniss, July 1, 1978; children: Nikki, Sarah. BA, Colo. Christian Univ., 1987; MA, Univ. Colo., 1990; student, Univ. Denver, 1993—. Glazier All Glass Svc., Lakewood, Colo., 1983-87; sales rep. Kwik Temp Glass, Aurora, Colo., 1988-89; gen. mgr. United Glass Co., Aurora, 1989-90; acad. advisor Colo. Christian Univ., Colorado Springs, 1990-91, acad. coord., 1991-92, dir., 1992-96; exec. dir. Colo. Christian Univ., Lakewood, 1996-97; dean Colo. Christian U., 1997—; pres. Vintage Quest, Colorado Springs, 1995—. Contbr. articles to profl. publs. Campaign media rels. rep. Mary Ellen Epps for State Rep., Colorado Springs, 1996. Mem. C. of C. Office: Colo Christian Univ 685 Citadel Dr E Ste 225 Colorado Springs CO 80909-5315

BOWE, ROGER LEE, small business owner; b. Pueblo, Colo., Aug. 30, 1954; s. William Roy and Ruth Ann (Penn) B.; 1 child, Patrick William; m. Wendy C. Kempf, June 5, 1981. Grad. high sch., Denver. Mechanic Crest Motors, Denver, 1970-74; svc. mgr. Grand Prix Imports, Denver, 1974-76; line tech. Kerlin & Son, Denver, 1976-80; owner, operator Wheels of Fortune, Inc., Littleton, Colo., 1981—. Past mem. Vat. Fedn. Ind. Bus., 1988. Mem. Z Car Club Colo. (tech. advisor), Better Bus. Bur. Office: Wheels of Fortune Inc 2659 1/2 W Main St Littleton CO 80120-1914

BOWEN, BYRON ROLLAND, writer, educator; b. Seattle, Feb. 24, 1937; s. Victor Roland Bappy and Lela Ila (Edwards) Bappy-Bowen; m. Shirley Ann Zuppe-Bowen, June 18, 1961; children: Debra Lynn, David Byron, Tram Christopher. MA in English Edn., Ctrl. Wash. U., 1975. Lifetime cert. tchr. Subs. tchr. Tacoma (Wash.) Pub. Schs., 1964-66, Ellensburg (Wash.) Pub. Sch. Dist., 1977-85; with cost & estimating Boeing Co. MM, Seattle, 1967-68; owner Cattle/Hay Ranch, Ellensburg, 1968-73, Safeway Cement Fin. Co., Ellensburg, 1970-85; fin. rep. Boeing Fin., Seattle, 1986-92; writer, inventor Ellensburg, 1992—; tchr. Longview (Wash.) Pub. Schs., 1961-62. Author: A Philosophy of Unified Field Theory of Life, Mass, Matter & Energy, 1993, The People of Forrs, 1994, The Holy Bible (A Social Literary Criticism), 1994, The City of Shaern, 1994, Elmira, 1994, Vergrailan, 1996, Project-H, 1996; inventor hygenic pad for optical use, 1995. Pvt. U.S. Army, 1955-57. Home and Office: 312 W 11th Ave Ellensburg WA 98926-2410

BOWEN, CLOTILDE DENT, retired army officer, psychiatrist; b. Chgo., Mar. 20, 1923; d. William Marion Dent and Clotilde (Tynes) D.; m. William N. Bowen, Dec. 29, 1945 (dec.). BA, Ohio State U., 1943, MD, 1947. Intern, Harlem Hosp., N.Y.C., 1947-48; resident and fellow in pulmonary diseases, Triboro Hosp., Jamaica, L.I., N.Y., 1948-50; resident in psychiatry VA Hosp., Albany, N.Y., 1959-62; pvt. practice, N.Y.C. 1950-55; chief pulmonary disease clinic, N.Y.C. 1950-55; asst. chief pulmonary disease svc., Valley Forge Army Hosp., Pa., 1956-59; chief psychiatry VA Hosp., Roseburg, Oreg., 1962-66, acting chief of staff, 1964-66; asst. chief neurology and psychiatry Tripler Gen. Hosp., Hawaii, 1966-68; psychiat. cons. and dir. Rev. Br., Office Civil Health and Med. Program, Uniform Svcs., 1968-70; commd. capt. U.S. Army, 1955, advanced through ranks to col., 1968; neuropsychiat. cons. U.S. Army Vietnam, 1970-71; chief dept. psychiatry Fitzsimons Army Med. Ctr., 1971-74; chief dept. psychiatry. Tripler Army Med. Ctr., 1974-75; comdr. Hawley Army Clinic, Ft. Benjamin, Harrison, Ind., 1977-78, chief dept. primary care and cmty. medicine, 1978-83, chief psychiat. consultation svc., Fitzsimons Army Med. Ctr., 1983-85; chief psychiatry svc. med./regional office ctr. VA, Cheyenne, Wyo., 1987-90; staff psychiatrist Denver VA Satellite Clinic, Colorado Springs, Colo., 1990-96, ret., 1996; vol. staff physician, 1996—; Locum Tenums practice psychiatry, 1996—; surveyor, Joint Commn. on Accreditation Healthcare Orgns., 1985-92; assoc. prof. psychiatry U. Colo. Med. Ctr., Denver, 1970-83. Decorated Legion of Merit, several other medals; recipient Colo. Disabled Am. Vets. award, 1994-95. Fellow Am. Psychiat. Assn. (life), Acad. Psychosomatic Medicine; mem. AMA, Nat. Med. Assn., Menninger Found. (charter). Home: 1020 Tari Dr Colorado Springs CO 80921-2257 *To be successful one must always aspire to a goal just beyond his or her immediate reach.*

BOWEN, MARIA ANTONIA, artist; b. San Francisco, Dec. 17, 1963; d. Patrick Gordon Bowen and Maria Dolores Morales; m. Pavl Mica, Sept. 8, 1990. BFA, U. San Francisco, 1988. Artist, card designer Hallmark, Kansas City, Mo., 1988-89; mural artist Envirographics, San Francisco, 1990-93; computer artist Mondo Media, San Francisco, 1994, Lucas Arts, San Rafael, Calif., 1995—. Recipient award N.Y. Soc. Illustrators, 1988. Mem. Greenpeace, Sierra Club.

BOWEN, PETER GEOFFREY, investment advisor, writer, business management lecturer; b. Iowa City, Iowa, July 10, 1939; s. Howard Rothmann and Lois Berntine (Schilling) B.; m. Shirley Johns Carlson, Sept. 14, 1968; children: Douglas Howard, Leslie Johns. BA in Govt. and Econs., Lawrence Coll., 1960; postgrad. U. Wis., 1960-61, U. Denver. cert. expert real estate witness, Denver Dist. Ct., 1987. Dir. devel. Mobile Home Communities, Denver, 1969-71; v.p. Perry & Butler, Denver, 1972-73; exec. v.p., dir. Little & Co., Denver, 1973; pres. Builders Agy. Ltd., Denver, 1974-75; pres. The Investment Mgmt. Group Ltd., Denver, 1975-87; independent investor, writer, Vail, Colo., 1987—; gen. ptnr. 8 real estate ltd. ptnrships.; bus. faculty mem. Colo. Mt. Coll.; lectr. on real estate syndications and entrepreneurships. Contbr. articles to profl. pubs. Mem. Colo. Coun. Econ. Devel., 1964-68; vice-chmn. Greenwood Village (Colo.) Planning and Zoning Commn., 1983-85; mem. Vail Planning and Environ. Commn., 1992-93; dir. Vail Alliance for Environ. Edn. 1993—; elected mem. City Council Greenwood Village, 1985-86, also mayor pro tem, 1985-86; trustee Vail Mountain Sch. Found., 1987-88; bd. dirs. Colo. Plan for Apportionment, 1966; speaker Forward Metro Denver, 1966-67. Mem. Rotary Club (bd. dirs. Vail chpt., named Rotarian of Yr. 1991-92), Lawrence U. Alumni Assn. (bd. dirs. 1966-72, 82-86). Home: 4950 S Beeler St Greenwood Village CO 80111

BOWEN, RICHARD LEE, academic administrator, political science educator; b. Avoca, Iowa, Aug. 31, 1933; s. Howard L. and Donna (Milburn) B.; m. Connie Smith Bowen, 1976; children: James, Robert, Elizabeth, Christopher; children by previous marriage—Catherine, David, Thomas. B.A., Augustana Coll., 1957; M.A., Harvard, 1959, Ph.D., 1967. Fgn. service officer State Dept., 1959-60; research asst. to U.S. Senator Francis Case, 1960-62; legis. asst. to U.S. Senator Karl Mundt, 1962-65; minority cons. sub-com. exec. reorgn. U.S. Senate, 1966-67; asst. to pres., assoc. prof. polit. sci. U. S.D., Vermillion, 1967-69, pres., 1969-76; pres. Dakota State Coll., Madison, 1973-76; commr. higher edn. Bd. Regents State S.D., Pierre, 1976-80; Disting prof. polit. sci. U. S.D., 1980-85; pres. Idaho State U., Pocatello, 1985—. Served with USN, 1951-54. Recipient Outstanding Alumnus award Augustana Coll., 1970; Woodrow Wilson fellow, 1957, Congl. Staff fellow, 1965; Fulbright scholar, 1957. Office: Idaho State U Office of Pres Campus Box 8310 Pocatello ID 83209-0009

BOWEN-FORBES, JORGE COURTNEY, artist, author, poet; b. Queenstown, Guyana, May 16, 1937; came to U.S., 1966; s. Walter and Margarita V. (Forbes) Bowen. BA, Queens Coll., Eve Leary, Guyana, 1969; MFA, Chelsea (Eng.) Sch. Design, 1972. Comml. artist Guyana Litographic, Georgetown; art dir. Corbin Advt. Agy., Bridgetown, Barbados; tech. advisor Ministry of Info. and Culture, Georgetown; nat. juror Nat. Arts Club, N.Y.C., 1985, Nat. Soc. Painters in Casein and Acrylic. Major exhbns. include Expo 67, Can., Nat. Acad. Design, N.Y., Frye Mus., El Paso (Tex.) Mus., Wichita (Kans.) Centennial, Caribbean Festival of the Arts, Newark Mus.; 10-one-man exhbns. worldwide; works in collections including Nat. and Colgrain Collections, Guyana, El Paso Mus. Art, Kindercare Internat., Leon Loards Gallery, The McCreery Cummings Fine Art Collection, Bomani Gallery, San Francisco; poetry and articles pub. various jours.; author: Best Watercolors, 1996, Creative Watercolor, 1996; published in Best in Watercolor, Best in Oil Painting, Best in Acrylic Painting, Creative Watercolor, Splash 11, Best Contemporary Watercolors, American Poetry Annual. Recipient Silver medal of honor Allied Artists of N.Y., 1978, Gold medal of honor, 1975. Mem. Nat. Watercolor Soc. (signature mem.), Nat. Soc. Painters in Casein and Acrylics, Audubon Artists, Knickerbocker Artists (Gold Medal of Honor 1977, 79), Am. Watercolor Soc. (signature mem.,

High Winds medal 1984). Studio: 10410 Foothill Blvd Apt 18 Oakland CA 94605-5150

BOWER, DEBBY RAE, nursing administrator; b. Denver, Dec. 31, 1950; d. Lee Norwood and Wanda Jean (Winkelman) B. BSN, Augustana Coll., Sioux Falls, S.D., 1973. RN, Calif. Nurse paraplegic, urology unit Vets. Hosp., Long Beach, Calif., 1978-80; charge nurse, relief nurse supr. Midwood Cmty. Hosp., Anaheim, Calif., 1980-82; head nurse med., surg. unit, alcohol and drug rehab unit Costa Mesa (Calif.) Med. Ctr., 1982-85; asst. head nurse security unit Riverside (Calif.) Gen., 1985—. Active Special Olympics, Riverside, 1987-91; care provider for handicapped, Riverside, 1987—; mem. adult advisory Ability Counts Sheltered Workshop, Riverside, 1990—. Lt. USN Nurse Corps., 1972-78.

BOWER, DONALD EDWARD, author; b. Lockport, N.Y., July 19, 1920. BA, U. Nebr., 1942. D.E. Bower & Co., Inc., Denver, 1945-60; editor, pub. Arapahoe Tribune, 1960-62; editor Adams County Almanac, Adams County Dispatch, Jefferson County Herald, 1962-65; freelance staff Writer Fawcett Publs., 1962-64, lit. cons., 1962-67; editor, pub. Buyer's Showcase mag. and FURN Club News 1965-66; exec. editor Colo. mag., 1966-69; editor-in-chief, v.p., dir. Am. West Pub. Co., editor Am. West mag., 1970-74; pres. Colo. Authors League, 1975-76; dir. Nat. Writers Club, Denver, 1974-86; dir. Assoc. Bus. Writers Am., 1978-86, also pres. Assn. Hdqrs., 1978-86; editorial dir. Nat. Writers Press, 1982-86; lit. agent Don Bower Lit. Agy., 1991—. Author: Roaming the American West, 1970; Ghost Towns and Back Roads, 1972; intro. to The Magnificent Rockies, 1972; Fred Rosenstock: A Legend in Books and Art, 1976; The Professional Writers' Guide, 1984, rev. edition, 1990;Ten Keys to Writing Success, 1987, Sex and Espionage, 1990; also 4 paperback detective novels, 1960-64; editor: Living Water, Living Earth, 1971; Anasazi: Ancient People of the Rock, 1973; The Great Southwest, 1972; Edge of a Continent, 1970; The Mighty Sierra, 1972; The Magnificent Rockies, 1972; The Great Northwest, 1973; Gold and Silver in the West, 1973; Steinbeck Country, 1973; contbr. Western Writers Handbook, 1988, articles to mags. Mem. Authors Guild Am., Western Writers Assn. Am., Friends of Denver Pub. Libr., Sigma Delta Chi. Office: 3082 S Wheeling Way Apt 209 Aurora CO 80014-5611

BOWERS, BONNIE JEAN, writer; b. Conneaut, Ohio, June 8, 1955; d. Richard Eugene and Alvina Ruth (Simmons) Van Tassell; m. David Eugene Bowers; children: Jason Patrick, Justin Timothy. Dipl., N.Am. Sch. Animal Scis., 1981. Sales rep. Vancouver, Wash., 1991-96; demonstrator House of Lloyd, Victorville, Calif., 1996—. Participant Am. Poetry Ann. 1994, Remembrances, 1994, Literary Excellence award, 1994, Best New Poems, 1994, And Time Stood Still, 1994, Musing, 1995, Hon. Mention, 1995, Voices, 1995, Literary award, 1995. Mem. Internat. Soc. Poets (Poet of Yr. 1996), Nat. Poetry Assn. (Editor's Choice award 1994), Nat. Authors Registry (Pres.'s award 1995, 96), Poets Soc. (Artistic Merit award 1994), Amherst Soc. (Poetic Achievement award 1994), Pacific Northwest Writers Assn. Home: 15251 Village Dr Sp #4 Victorville CA 92394

BOWERS, ZELLA ZANE, real estate broker; b. Liberal, Kans., May 24, 1929; d. Rex and Esther (Neff) Powelson; m. James Clarence Bowers, Aug. 12, 1949; (div. 1977); 1 child: Dara Zane. BA, Colo. Coll., 1951. Cert. real estate brokerage mgr. Sec. Bowers Ins. Agy., Colorado Springs, Colo., 1955-59, Cen. Colo. Claims Svc., Colorado Springs, 1959-63; pres. Premium Budgeting Co., Colorado Springs, 1962-67; pres., owner Monument Valley Realty, Inc., Colorado Springs, 1981-89; mng. broker The Buick Co. Buyer's Market; broker assoc. Haley Realty, Inc., Colorado Springs, 1990—; pres. Realtor Svcs. Corp., 1989. Hon. trustee The Palmer Found., Colorado Springs, 1980—, pres., 1983-84; trustee Pikes Peak United Way, 1988-91; pres. Vis. Nurse Assn., Colorado Springs, 1966-67, 74; dir. Colo. League Nurses, Denver, 1968; steering com. The Kennedy Ctr. Imagination Celebration, Colorado Springs, 1989-93, chmn., 1990-92; sec. Care & Share, Colorado Springs, 1984; chmn. McAllister House Mus., Colorado Springs, 1973-74; docent chmn. Colorado Springs Fine Arts Ctr., 1969-70; mem. historic preservation bd. City of Colorado Springs, 1989-94, chmn. 1989-92, mem. Comprehensive Plan Task Force City of Colorado Springs, 1990-91; charter rev. commn. City of Colorado Springs, 1991-92; commr. Colo. Springs City Planning, 1995—; pres. Friends of the Libr., 1971-72; pres. Woman's Ednl. Soc. Colo. Coll., 1974-77; civil adminstrv. staff asst. Air Def. Filter Ctr., 1956-57, ground observer, 1956, others. Recipient Women's Trade Fair Recognition award, 1987. Mem. Nat. Assn. Realtors, Colo. Assn. Realtors (dir. 1987-91, 96—, v.p. S.E. dist. 1992, trustee edn. found. 1988-92, dir. housing opportunity found. 1991-93, Disting. Svc. award 1991, Polit. Svc. award 1992), Colorado Springs Bd. Realtors (pres. 1987-88, named Realtor of Yr. 1989), Pikes Peak Assn. Realtors, Children of the Am. Revolution (pres. 1956-57), Gamma Phi Beta. Avocations: genealogy, travel. Home: 128 W Rockrimmon Blvd # 104 Colorado Springs CO 80919-1876 Office: Haley Realty Inc 109 E Fontanero St Colorado Springs CO 80907-7452

BOWES, FLORENCE (MRS. WILLIAM DAVID BOWES), writer; b. Salt Lake City, Nov. 19, 1925; d. John Albreckt Elias and Alma Wilhelmina (Jonasson) Norborg; student U. Utah, 1941-42, Columbia, 1945-46, N.Y. U., 1954-55; grad. N.Y. TV Workshop, 1950; m. Samuel Ellis Levine, July 15, 1944 (dec. July 1953); m. William David Bowes, Mar. 15, 1958 (dec. 1976); 1 son, Alan Richard. Actress, writer Hearst Radio Network, WINS, N.Y.C., 1944-45; personnel and adminstrv. exec. Mut. Broadcasting System, N.Y.C., 1946-49, free-lance editor, writer, 1948-49; freelance writer NBC and ABC, 1949-53; script editor, writer Robert A. Monroe Prodns., N.Y.C., Hollywood, Calif., 1953-56; script and comml. dir. KUTV-TV, Salt Lake City, 1956-58; spl. editor, writer pub. relations dept. U. Utah, Salt Lake City, 1966-68, editor, writer U. Utah Rev., 1968-75; author: Web of Solitude, 1979; The MacOrvan Curse, 1980; Interlude in Venice, 1981; Beauchamp, 1983. Mem. Beta Sigma Phi. Home: 338 K St Salt Lake City UT 84103-3562

BOWIE, HERBERT HUGHES, JR., magazine editor, publisher, writer; b. Washington, May 5, 1951; s. Herbert Hughes, Doris Elnora (Brown) B.; m. Pauline Marie Hendrickson, Sept. 13, 1980; 1 child, Stephen Lee. BA in English, U. Mich., 1973. Editor People Forever, Scottsdale, Ariz., 1989-96; owner PowerSurge Pub., Scottsdale, 1996—. Editor: Together Forever: An Invitation to Physical Immortality, 1990, (mag.) Forever Alive, 1989-96; author, pub.: Why Die?-A Beginner's Guide to Living Forever, 1997. Office: PowerSurge Pub PO Box 14707 Scottsdale AZ 85267-4707

BOWLEN, PATRICK DENNIS, holding company executive, lawyer, professional sports team executive; b. Prairie du Chien, Wis., Feb. 18, 1944; s. Paul Dennis and Arvella (Woods) B. B.B.A., U. Okla., 1966, J.D., 1968. Bar: Alta. 1969. Read law Saucier, Jones, Calgary, Alta., Can., assoc., 1969-70; asst. to pres. Regent Drilling Ltd., 1970-71; pres. Batoni-Bowlen Enterprises Ltd., 1971-79, Bowlen Holdings Ltd., Edmonton, Alta., Can., 1979—; pres., chief exec. officer, owner Denver Broncos, 1984—. Mem. Law Soc. Alta., Can. Bar Assn., Young Presidents Orgn. Roman Catholic. Clubs: Mayfair Golf and Country; Edmonton Petroleum; Outrigger Canoe (Honolulu). Office: Denver Broncos 13655 Broncos Pky Englewood CO 80112-4004*

BOWLER, LEWIS J., communications executive; b. St. George, Utah, Sept. 8, 1930; s. Charles E. and Mary (Riding) B.; m. Dorcus Nower, Sept. 23, 1955; children: LuAnn, Mary Alice, Nancy, Scott L. Student, So. Utah State Coll., 1975, Dixie Coll., St. George, 1992. Lineman Mountain Bell Tel. Co., Salt Lake City, 1949-53, constrn. foreman, 1954-58; PBX and key technician Mountain Bell Tel. Co., St. George, 1958-60, ctrl. office technician, 1960-64, network mgr., 1964-79; owner Bowler's C Com, St. George, 1980—. Chmn. bd. dirs. Vocat. Adv. Bd., St. George, 1976-78; bd. dirs. So. Utah Alcohol Recovery, Cedar City, 1961-80; leader Boy Scouts Am., St. George, 1956—; mem. adv. bd. Washington County Sch. Dist., St. George, 1976-78; homeless adv. So. Utah Social Svc., St. George, 1981-85. With Signal Corps, U.S. Army, 1951-55. Recipient Svc. award Boy Scouts Am., 1988. Mem. Lions Internat. (club pres. 1991-92, lt. gov. 1992-93, zone chmn. 1992-93, dist. gov. 1994-95, past dist. gov. 1995—, 100% Pres. award 1992, Lion of Yr. 1993, 96, Gov. award 1993, Excel award 1995). Office: Bowlers C Com 289 N Bluff St Saint George UT 84770

BOWLIN, GREGORY LEE, marketing professional; b. Denver, June 1, 1955; s. Robert Lee and Beryl Audrey (Carter) B.; m. Rebecca Ann Richardson, July 29, 1978; children: Paul Matthew, John Michael. AA, Columbia Coll., 1983; BS in Tech. Mgmt. magna cum laude, Regis Coll., 1987; postgrad., Stanford U., 1994. Pvt. pilot's lic., FAA. Flight info. drafter Jeppesen Sanderson, Inc., Englewood, Colo., 1973-77; flight info. compiler Jeppesen Sanderson, Inc., Englewood, 1977-80, airline tech. acct. exec., 1980-83, mgr. air carrier mktg./sales/svc., 1983-88, dir. ops. info. svcs., 1988-90, dir. chart svcs. mktg., 1990-91, dir. airline svcs., 1991-94, dir. mktg., sales and svc., 1995-, v.p. flight info. svcs. mktg., 1990-96; pres., treas. Highpoint Neighborhood Partnership, Aurora, Colo., 1988—. Mem. Am. Mktg. Assn. (exec. mem.), Aircraft Owners and Pilots Assn. Republican. Baptist. Office: Jeppesen Sanderson Inc 55 Inverness Dr E Englewood CO 80112-5412

BOWLIN, MICHAEL RAY, oil company executive; b. Amarillo, Tex., Feb. 20, 1943; m. Martha Ann Rowland; 1 child, John Charles. BBA, North Tex. State U., 1965, MBA, 1967. Scheduler prodn. and transp. A. Brant Co., Ft. Worth, 1965-66; mktg. rep. R.J. Reynolds Tobacco Bo., 1967-68; personnel generalist Atlantic Richfield Co., Dallas, 1969-71; coll. relations rep. Atlantic Richfield Co., Los Angeles, 1971-72, mgr. internal profl. placement, 1973, mgr. corp. recruiting and placement, 1973-75, mgr. behavioral sci. services, 1975, sr. v.p. ARCO resources adminstrn., 1985, sr. v.p. ARCO internat. oil and gas acquisitions, 1987, sr. v.p., 1987—; employee relations mgr. Atlantic Richfield Co., Alaska, 1975-77; v.p. employee relations Anaconda Copper Co. (div. Atlantic Richfield Co.), Denver, 1977-81; v.p. employee relations ARCO Oil & Gas (div. Atlantic Richfield Co.), Dallas, 1981-82, v.p. fin. planning and control, 1982-84; sr. v.p. Atlantic Richfield Co., 1985-92; pres. ARCO Coal Co., 1985-87, ARCO Internat. Oil & Gas Co., 1987-92; CEO Atlantic Richfield Co., 1994—; pres., COO ARCO Internat. Oil & Gas Co., 1993, 1993, pres., CEO, 1994-95, chmn., CEO, 1995—. Office: Atlantic Richfield Co 515 S Flower St Los Angeles CA 90071-2201*

BOWMAN, ALISON FRANCES, writer; b. Pasadena, Calif., Feb. 15, 1968; d. Allen Paul and Frances Ann Bowman. BA in Politics, U. Calif., Santa Cruz, 1991; MA in Radio and TV, San Francisco State U., 1995. Radio news journalist KZSC-FM, Santa Cruz, 1986-87; radio news dir. KXSC-FM, Santa Cruz, 1987-88; print journalist City on a Hill Press, Santa Cruz, 1988-89; city editor Cityona Hill Press, Santa Cruz, 1989-90; editor-in-chief Primer Mag., Santa Cruz, 1990; market rschr. Larry Wisch Assocs., San Francisco, 1992-96. Prodr. documentary film Green Dreams, 1994; contbr. articles to Santa Cruz Mag., Urban Tempo, Might mag. Mem. Soc. Profl. Journalists, Media Alliance. Home: 624 Brooklyn Ave # 204 Oakland CA 94606 Office: 390 Townsend St # 252 San Francisco CA 94107

BOWMAN, BRUCE, art educator, writer, artist; b. Dayton, Ohio, Nov. 23, 1938; s. Murray Edgar Bowman and Mildred May (Moler) Elleman; m. Julie Ann Gosselin, 1970 (div. 1980); 1 child, Carrie Lynn. AA, San Diego City Coll., 1962; BA, Calif. State U.-Los Angeles, 1964, MA, 1968. Tchr. art North Hollywood Adult Sch., Calif., 1966-68; instr. art Cypress Coll., Calif., 1976-78, West Los Angeles Coll., 1969—; tchr. art Los Angeles City Schs., 1966—; seminar leader So. Calif., 1986—. Author: Shaped Canvas, 1976; Toothpick Sculpture and Ice Cream Stick Art, 1976; Ideas: How to Get Them, 1985, (cassette tape) Develop Winning Willpower, 1986, Waikiki, 1988. Contbr. articles to profl. jours. One-man shows include Calif. State U.-Los Angeles, 1968, Pepperdine U., Malibu, Calif., 1978; exhibited in group shows McKenzie Gallery, Los Angeles, 1968, Trebor Gallery, Los Angeles, 1970, Cypress Coll., Calif., 1977, Design Recycled Gallery, Fullerton, Calif., 1977, Pierce Coll., Woodland Hills, Calif., 1978, Leopold/Gold Gallery, Santa Monica, Calif., 1980. Served with USN, 1957-61. Avocation: karate (black belt Tang Soo Do). Home: 28322 Rey De Copas Ln Malibu CA 90265-4463

BOWMAN, DAVID WINSLOW, mechanical engineer; b. McRae, Ga., Nov. 25, 1964; s. David W. and Jewll M. (Geiger) B. BS in Agrl. Engring., U. Ga., 1988; MME, Tex. A&M, 1991. Mem. tech. staff Los Alamos (Calif.) Nat. Lab., 1991—.

BOWMAN, GARY MARTIN, social worker; b. Chatham, Ont., Can., July 13, 1943; came to U.S., 1960; s. John Martin and Hilda Ruth (Shaw) B.; m. Gwendolyn Yit-Wah Lee, July 3, 1970 (div. Dec. 1982); m. Jacqueline Custis Miller Lien, Mar. 17, 1984; 1 child, Alexander Stewart Bauman-Bowman. BA, Graceland Coll., 1965; MSW, U. Hawaii, 1972. Pub. social service worker Linn County Dept. Social Svcs., Cedar Rapids, Iowa, 1965-67; dir. Joint Services Recreation Assn. for Handicapped, Honolulu, 1967-69, 71-72; social group worker Adolescent Unit Hawaii State Hosp., Kaneohe, 1970-73, 81-83; coordinator adolescent mental health svcs. St. Joseph's Hosp. Health Ctr., Syracuse, N.Y., 1973-74; community services coordinator Elmcrest Children's Svcs., Syracuse, 1974-75; psychiat. social worker Santa Rosa County Mental Health ctr., Milton, Fla., 1975-80, St. Francis Hosp. Health Care, Honolulu, 1980-81, Los Angeles County Coastal Community Mental Health Ctr., Carson, Calif., 1984-86, West-Cen. Family Mental Health Svcs., Los Angeles, 1986-90; pvt. practice cons., therapy and tng. Burbank, 1986-90, L.A., 1990—; clin. coord. Inglewood, Lawndale, Hollywood and Santa Clarita Med. Ctrs., 1995—, Med. Men Health Palmdale-Lancaster, Venice, Calif., 1995—; adj. faculty mem. U. Syracuse, Western Fla. U. at Pensacola, U. Hawaii, 1974-83; trainer crisis mgmt. Syracuse Police Dept., 1974; presentor Hawaii-Pacific Gerontology Conf., 1981, Happy Valley Singles Camp, Santa Cruz, Calif., 1984, Stas. KRLA-AM, KBZT-FM Separation/Divorce Trauma, Pasadena, Calif., 1986, Parenting By Men Cable TV, 1988, Buckhorn Women's Camp on Grief and Reconnection, Idlewild, Calif., 1988, Erie Beach Camp Families, Ont., Can., 1989, 96, Nurturing Adolescent Nonconformists to Help Group, Van Nuys, Calif., 1989, Parents Without Ptnrs., Glendale, Calif., 1991, St. Luke's Hosp., Pasadena, 1991; examiner Consumer Svcs. for Licensing Social Workers, State of Calif., 1995-96. Author: Joys, Fears, Tears, 1968; editor (newsletter) The Javelin, 1967-69; co-producer, dir. an interfaith gospel, country, western and contemporary music concert Spring Info Action - Reach Out for Excellence, Burbank, Calif., 1991, The Hope of a New Tomorrow-Home & Family Reunion Improvement, 1996; spkr. in field; contbr. articles and poems to mags. Bd. dirs., program chmn. Summer Action Vol. Youth Program, Honolulu, 1972-73, 80-83; pres. Friends of Libr. Santa Rosa County, Milton, 1979-80; founder singles separated divorced support group Reorganized Ch. Jesus Latter-day Saints, Burbank, Calif., 1985-92, founder, dir. Solid Rock Cafe and Coffee House, Burbank, 1995—; founder Camp In Search Of, 1978—; coord. Concert for Dr. Sharma-Candidate for Inglewood City Coun., 1993—. Named Citizen for Day Sta. KGU, Honolulu, 1972; recipient Unheralded Humanitarianism, Dist. 1 Mental Health Bd., 1980. Mem. NASW (diplomate clin. social work, cert., steering con. region H&I Calif. 1983—, alt. dir. region H Calif. 1984-85, chmn. licensing com. 1979-80, mem. program and continuing edn. coms. 1980-83, Loyal and Dedicated Leadership award 1980), Kiwanis (co-dir. Surrender Outreach Sports program 1991 Burbank club), Optimist (youth ctr. dir. Hiawatha, Iowa club 1966-67). Home: 4433 Sinova St Los Angeles CA 90032-1452

BOWMAN, JEAN LOUISE, lawyer, civic worker; b. Albuquerque, Apr. 3, 1938; d. David Livingstone and Charlotte Louise (Smith) McArthur; student U. N.Mex., 1956-57, U. Pa., 1957-58, Rocky Mountain Coll., 1972-74; B.A. in Polit. Sci. with high honors, U. Mont., 1982, J.D., 1985; children—Carolyn Louise, Joan Emily, Amy Elizabeth, Eric Daniel. Dir. Christian edn. St. Luke's Episcopal Ch., 1979-80; law clk. to assoc. justice Mont. Supreme Ct., 1985-87; exec. v.p. St. Peter's Community Hospital Found., 1987-91; exec. dir. Harrison Hosp. Found., Bremerton, Wash., 1991-93, St. Patrick Hosp. and Health Found., 1993—, Missoula Symphony Bd., 1993—; pres. Missoula Symphony Assn., 1996—; dir. 1st Bank West. Bd. trustees Rocky Mountain Coll., 1972-80; bd. dirs. Billings (Mont.) Area C. of C., 1977-80; mem. Internat. Women's Forum, 1996—, City-County Air Pollution Control Bd., 1969-74, chmn., 1970-71; del. Mont. State Constnl. Conv., 1971-72, sec. conv., 1971-72; chmn. County Local Govt. Study Commn., 1973-76; mem. Billings Sch. Dist. Long Range Planning Com., 1978-79; former pres. Billings LWV, dir., 1987-91, pres. Helena LWV, 2d v.p. Mont. LWV; former pres. Silver Run Ski Club. Named one of Billings' most influential citizens, Billings Gazette, 1977; Bertha Morton Scholar, 1982. Rotary (pres. 1997-98). Republican. Home: 1911 E Broadway St Missoula MT 59802-4901

BOWMAN, JEFFREY R., protective services official; b. Akron, Ohio, Apr. 24, 1952; s. Roger Heath and Ruth Ann (Corrigan) B.; divorced; children: Katie, Andrew, Brian. BS in Orgnl. Behavior, U. San Francisco, 1986. Firefighter Anaheim (Calif.) Fire Dept., 1973-75, paramedic, 1975-79, capt., 1979-83, battalion chief, 1983-85, div. chief, 1985-86, fire chief, 1986—. Pres. bd. dirs. Anaheim Boys and Girls Club, 1988—; chmn. fundraising Boy Scouts Am., Anaheim, 1988. Mem. Internat. Assn. Fire Chiefs, Calif. Fire Chiefs Assn. Office: Anaheim Fire Dept 201 S Anaheim Blvd Ste 301 Anaheim CA 92805-4099*

BOWMAN, JON ROBERT, editor, film critic; b. Spokane, Wash., Nov. 9, 1954; s. Donald Ken and Carolyn Joyce (Crutchfield) B.; m. Geraldine Maria Jaramillo, Jan. 27, 1979 (div. Dec. 1985); m. Amy Farida Siswayanti, May 23, 1992 (div. Jan. 1994). BA, U. N.Mex., 1976. Reporter, arts editor, news editor N.Mex. Daily Lobo, Albuquerque, 1972-76; film critic Albuquerque Jour., 1974-76; reporter Alamogordo (N.Mex.) Daily News, 1976; sci. writer, editor Los Alamos (N.Mex.) Monitor, 1976-81; reporter, arts editor New Mexican, Santa Fe, 1981-86, film critic, 1987—; editor New Mexico Mag., Santa Fe, 1986—; guest lectr. U. N.Mex., Coll. Santa Fe, 1976—. Author: (with others) Explore New Mexico, 1988, A New Mexico Scrapbook, 1990, Day Trip Discoveries: Selected New Mexico Excursions, 1993, The Allure of Turquoise, 1995; contbr. articles to mags. and newspapers; author salutes for Greer Garson, James Coburn, Ben Johnson, and John Huston for festivals honoring them. Vol. tchr. Albuquerque pub. schs., 1972-76; organizer film festivals Albuquerque and Santa Fe. 1972-91, benefits including Ctr. for Contemporary Arts, Santa Fe; program cons. Taos Talking Picture Festival, 1995—. Recipient Sci. Writing award AP, 1978, citation AP, 1979, others. Home: 602 Aqua Fria St Santa Fe NM 87501 Office: NMex Mag Lew Wallace Bldg 495 Old Santa Fe Trl Santa Fe NM 87503

BOWMAN, MICHAEL O., interior designer; b. Bluffton, Ind., Mar. 24, 1946; s. Daniel B. and Hilda M. (Steffen) B.; m. Rachel Valencia Bowman, Mar. 20, 1971; children: Catharine M. Bowman-French, Rachel Anne. Student, Parson's, Paris, 1979. Designer/mgr. Saxton's Inc., Tacoma, Wash., 1968-81, owner, 1981-91; owner Michael Bowman Interiors, Seattle, 1989-91; designer/mgr. Greenbaum's Home Furnishing, Bellevue, Wash., 1992-93, Westbay Interiors, Gig Harbor, Wash., 1994-95; freelance designer Tacoma, 1995—. With U.S. Army, 1965-68. Recipient Design for Better Living award Am. Wood Coun., 1990. Mem. Am. Soc. Interior Designers (cert., bd. dirs. 1994-96, pres.-elect 1996—), Rotary, Elks, Tacoma C. of C. (mem. Pres.'s Club 1989-90). Roman Catholic. Home and Office: 4420 Elwood Dr W Tacoma WA 98466-7536

BOWMAN, NAOMA SUSANN, elementary school educator; b. Dublan, Mex., Feb. 17, 1951; d. Samuel Keith and Mary Naoma (Haynie) B. BS in Elem. Edn., Brigham Young U., 1984. Cert. tchr., Utah. Tchr. Escuela Manuel Dublan, 1972-81; tchr. Spanish adult edn. program Mission Tng. Ctr., Provo, Utah, 1981-84, teacher trainer, 1984-85; tchr. Spanish immersion Meadow Elem. Sch., Lehi, Utah, 1985-89, Northridge Elem. Sch., Orem, Utah, 1989—; asst. dir. Spanish immersion curriculum com. Alpine Sch. Dist., American Fork, Utah, 1986-89, new-tchr. orienter, 1987-92, chair Spanish Immersion Conf., 1989-91, dir. Spanish immersion summer camp, 1991—, rep. Orem Cluster, 1991—, peer evaluator, 1991—, mem. prin. screening com., 1989-90; tchr. summer migrant program, Nebo Sch. Dist., 1992, 93. Grantee Utah Humanities Coun., 1992, City of Orem, 1992. Fellow NEA, ASCD, Alpine Edn. Assn., Utah Edn. Assn., Utah Educators of Tchrs. Assn., Utah Fgn. Lang. Assn. (sec. 1988-90), Utah Fgn. Lang. in Elem. Assn. (pres. 1987-88, Tchr. of Yr. 1989), Phi Delta Kappa. Republican. Mormon. Office: Cherry Hill Elem Sch 250 W 1650 S Orem UT 84058

BOWNE, MARTHA HOKE, publishing consultant; b. Greeley, Colo., June 9, 1931; d. George Edwin and Krin (English) Hoke; children: Gretchen, William, Kay, Judith. BA, U. Mich., 1952; postgrad., Syracuse U., 1965. Tchr. Wayne (Mich.) Pub. Schs., 1953-54, East Syracuse and Minoa Cen. Schs., Minoa, N.Y., 1965-68; store mgr. Fabric Barn, Fayetteville, N.Y., 1969-77; store owner Fabric Fair, Oneida, N.Y., 1978-80; producer, owner Quilting by the Sound, Port Townsend, Wash., 1987—, Quilting by the Lake, Cazenovia, N.Y., 1981—; organizer symposium Am. Quilters Soc.; founder, pres. Quilter's Quest Video Prodns., 1994; workshop prodn. organizer. Contbr. articles to profl. jours. Mem., pres. Minoa Library, 1960-75; mem. Onondaga County Library, Syracuse, 1968-71. Mem. Nat. Quilting Assn., Am. Quilters Soc. (editor Am. Quilter mag. 1985-95), new Eng. Quilt Mus. Home: 4445 Oden Bay Dr Sandpoint ID 83864

BOWSER, M. GAYL, special education coordinator; b. St. Louis, Dec. 20, 1948; d. George Winston and Mary Hulda (Bagale) Cloyd; 1 child, Nathan Christopher. BA, U. Mo., 1966-71; MA, U. Iowa, 1971-72. Cert. spl. edn. tchr., Oreg. Spl. edn. tchr. Camp Lab. Sch., Cullowhee, N.C., 1971-73; spl. edn. tchr. West High Sch., Iowa City, 1974-79, Fir Grove Sch., Roseburg, Oreg., 1979-81, Community Exptl. Edn. Ctr., Iowa City, 1976-79; mainstream specialist Douglas Edn. Svc. Dist., Roseburg, 1981-88; project coord. Oreg. Tech. Access Project, Roseburg, 1988-90; coord. Oreg. tech. access program Oreg. Dept. Edn., Roseburg, 1990—; assistive tech. cons., 1986—; mem. transition task force Oreg. Dept. Edn., 1986-88. Author: Computers in Early Intervention, 1988, Computers in Special Education Curriculum, 1989, Computers in Mainstream, 1990, Famous People Stories, 1980. Bd. dirs. Umpqua Homes for Handicapped, Coalition for Assistive Tech. in Oreg. Recipient Oreg. Disting. Educator award Milken Nat. Educator Awards, 1993, Disting. Svc. award Coalition in Oreg. for Parent Edn., 1997; named Tchr. of Yr., Oreg. Fedn. Coun. for Exceptional Children, 1992; Transition grantee Oreg. Dept. Edn., 1987-88, project Tech Trans grantee, 1996—, Coop. and Innovative Models grantee, 1988-90. Mem. Internat. Soc. for Tech. in Edn., Assn. for Severely Handicapped Coun. for Exceptional Children (nat. fedn. tech. and media divsn. 1993, Svc. award Nat. fedn. 1993, Tech. and Media Divsn. Svc. award 1992). Home: 203 W Bowden St Roseburg OR 97470-5311 Office: Oreg Tech Access Program 1871 NE Stephens St Roseburg OR 97470-1433

BOWYER, JANE BAKER, science educator; b. Dayton, Ohio, Mar. 16, 1934; d. Homer Kenneth and Helen Elizabeth (Brown) Baker; m. Charles Stuart Bowyer, Feb. 27, 1957; children: William Stuart, Robert Baker, Elizabeth Ann. BA, Miami U., Oxford, Ohio, 1956; MA, U. Calif., Berkeley, 1972, PhD, 1974. Abbie Valley prof. Mills Coll., Oakland, Calif., 1974—, head dept. edn., 1985—; cons. Lawrence Hall Sci., U. Calif., Berkeley, 1975—, Nat. Assn. Ednl. Progress, 1975-78, Utah State Bd. Edn., 1985-86; mem. Calif. Round Table's Math/Sci. Task Force, 1983-85; dir. ednl. research Industry Initiatives in Sci. and Math Edn., 1985-86, bd. dirs., 1985—; dir. Mills Coll./Oakland Unified Sch. Dist. Partnership, 1985—; dir. midcareer math. and sci. tchr. R&D, NSF, 1987—, prin. investigator and dir. systemic reform program, 1994—, Leadership Inst. Teaching Elem. Sci., Mills and Oakland, Calif., 1994—. Author: Science and Society, 1984, Science and Society Activity Book, 1984; contbr. articles to profl. jours. Bd. dirs. Oakland Sci. and Art Sch., 1979-82, Eric Erickson Sch., San Francisco, 1983-85; prin. investigator Projects in Sci. Edn.; cons. UNESCO, Paris Div. Sci. Edn., 1989-90, 93. Fulbright Research fellow, Germany, 1982-83. Mem. AAAS, Nat. Assn. Research in Sci. Teaching (mem. editorial bd. 1980-82, bd. dirs. 1985-88, Outstanding Paper award, 1979, 81), Am. Ednl. Research Orgn., Mortar Bd. Home: 34 Seascape Dr Muir Beach CA 94965-9765

BOX, JAMES M., newspaper editor. Exec. editor Daily Breeze, Torrance, Calif. Office: Daily Breeze 5215 Torrance Blvd Torrance CA 90503

BOXER, ALAN LEE, accountant; b. Denver, Sept. 9, 1935; s. Ben B. and Minnette (Goldman) B.; m. Gayle, Dec. 21, 1958; children: Michael E., Jodi S., Richard S. BSBA in Acctg., U. Denver, 1956. CPA, Colo. Audit mgr. Touche, Ross & Co. CPAs, Denver, 1956-60, Ballin, Milstein & Feinstein CPAs, Denver, 1960-61; prin. Alan L. Boxer, CPA, Denver, 1961-69; v.p and treas. Pawley Co., Denver, 1969-78; pres. Sci-Pro Inc., Denver, 1978-82; regional mgr. A.T.V. Systems, Inc., Denver, 1982-83; prin. The Enterprise Group, Denver, 1983-86; shareholder, pres. Allerdice, Baroch, Boxer & Co., CPAs, Denver, 1986-87; prin. Alan L. Boxer, CPA, Denver, 1987—. Bd. dirs. Anti-Defamation League, Denver, 1986-90, BMH Congregation, Denver, 1986—, treas. 1990-93, v.p. 1993—. Mem. Am. Inst. CPAs, Colo. Soc. CPAs, Bnai Brith #171 (pres. 1982, trustee 1983-89). Democrat. Jewish.

BOXER, BARBARA, senator; b. Bklyn., Nov. 11, 1940; d. Ira and Sophie (Silvershein) Levy; m. Stewart Boxer, 1962; children: Doug, Nicole. BA in Econ., Bklyn. Coll., 1962. Stockbroker, econ. rschr. N.Y. Securities Firm, N.Y.C., 1962-65; journalist, assoc. editor Pacific Sun, 1972-74; congl. aide to rep. 5th Congl. Dist. San Francisco, 1974-76; mem. Marin County Bd. Suprs., San Rafael, Calif., 1976-82; mem. 98th-102d Congresses from 6th Calif. dist., mem. armed services com., select com. children, youth and families; majority whip at large, co-chair Mil. Reform Caucus, chair subcom. on govt. activities and transp. of house govt. ops. com., 1990-93, U.S. senator from Calif., 1993—, mem. banking, housing and urban affairs com., mem. budget com., mem. environ. and pub. works com. Pres. Marin County Bd. Suprs., 1980-81; mem. Bay Area Air Quality Mgmt. Bd., San Francisco, 1977-82, pres., 1979-81; bd. dirs. Golden Gate Bridge Hwy. and Transport Dist., San Francisco, 1978-82; founding mem. Marin Nat. Women's Polit. Caucus; pres. Dem. New Mems. Caucus, 1983. Recipient Open Govt. award Common Cause, 1980, Rep. of Yr. award Nat. Multiple Sclerosis Soc., 1990, Margaret Sanger award Planned Parenthood, 1990, Women of Achievement award Anti-defamation League, 1990. Jewish. Office: US Senate 112 Hart Senate Office Bldg Washington DC 20510-0505*

BOXER, JEROME HARVEY, computer and management consultant, vintner; b. Chgo., Nov. 27, 1930; s. Ben Avrum and Edith (Lyman) B.; AA magna cum laude, East L.A. Coll., 1952; m. Sandra Schaffner, June 17, 1980; children by previous marriage: Michael, Jodi. AB with honors, Calif. State U., L.A., 1954. CPA, Calif; cert. computing profl. Lab. instr. Calif. State U., L.A., 1953-54; staff acct. Dolman, Freeman & Buchalter, L.A., 1955-57; sr. acct. Neiman, Sanger, Miller & Beress, L.A., 1957-63; ptnr. firm Glynn and Boxer, CPAs, L.A., 1964-68; v.p., sec. Glynn, Boxer & Phillips Inc., CPA's, L.A.and Glendale, 1968-90, pvt. practice cons., 1990—; owner Oak Valley Vineyard; pres. Echo Data Svcs., Inc., 1978-90; instr. data processing L.A. City Adult Schs.; tchr. lectr., cons. wines and wine-tasting; instr. photography. Mem. ops. bd. Everywoman's Village; bd. dirs., v.p. So. Calif. Jewish Hist. Soc., v.p. Jewish Hist. Soc. of the Ctrl. Coast; co-founder Open Space Theatre; former officer Ethel Josephine Scantland Found.; past post adviser Explorer Scouts, Boy Scouts Am., also Eagle Scout. Recipient Youth Svc. award Mid-Valley YMCA, 1972-73; Mem. Am. Inst. CPAs, Calif. Soc. CPAs, Assn. for Systems Mgmt., Data Processing Mgmt. Assn., Am. Fedn. Musicians, Am. Jewish Hist. Soc., Friends of Photography, L.A. Photog. Ctr., Acad. Model Aeros., Nat. Model Railroad Assn., Maltese Falcons Home Brewing Soc., San Fernando Valley Silent Flyers, San Fernando Valley Radio Control Flyers, Associated Students Calif. State U., Los Angeles (hon. life), Acad. Magical Arts, Internal Brotherhood of Magicians, Soc. Preservation of Variety Arts, Am. Wine Soc., Knights of the Vine, Soc. Wine Educators, Napa Valley Wine Libr. Alumni Assn., L.A.-Bordeaux Sister City Affiliation, Soc. Bacchus Am., Paso Robles Dem. Club (pres. 1993), Ctrl. Coast Winegrowers Assn., Wines and Steins, Cellarmasters, Paso Robles Vintners and Growers Assn., German Shepherd Dog Club Am., German Shepherd Dog Club Los Angeles County, Blue Key, Alpha Phi Omega. Clubs: Verdugo, Exchange, Kiwanis (pres. Sunset-Echo Park 1968), Braemar Country, Pacific Mariners Yacht, S.Coast Corinthian Yacht (former dir., officer), B'nai B'rith. Cons., contbr. Wine World Mag., 1974-82. Home and Office: 1660 Circle B Rd Paso Robles CA 93446-9595

BOXER, LESTER, lawyer; b. N.Y.C., Oct. 19, 1935; s. Samuel and Anna Lena (Samovar) B.; m. Frances Barenfeld, Sept. 17, 1961; children: Kimberly Brett, Allison Joy. AA, UCLA, 1955, BS, 1957; JD, U. So. Calif., 1961. Bar: Calif. 1962; U.S. Dist. Ct. (cen. dist.) Calif. 1962. Assoc. Bautzer & Grant, Beverly Hills, Calif., 1961-63; pvt. practice Beverly Hills, 1963-65, 69—; ptnr. Boxer & Stoll, Beverly Hills, 1965-69. Mem. Calif. Bar Assn., L.A. County Bar Assn., Beverly Hills Bar Assn. Office: 1875 Century Park E Ste 2000 Los Angeles CA 90067-2521

BOXLEITNER, WARREN JAMES, electrical engineer, researcher; b. Lewiston, Idaho, Jan. 8, 1948; s. Paul Henry and Lois Genelle (Samsel) B.; m. Linda Jane Schraufnagel, Aug. 23, 1969; 1 child, Kirk Lee. BSEE, U. Idaho, 1971. Design engr. Keytronic Corp., Spokane, Wash., 1975-79, project engr., 1981-83, sr. engr., 1983-86, tech. svcs. mgr., 1986-87; internat. sales mgr. Eurokey, Ravensberg, Fed. Republic Germany, 1979-81; dir. engring. Keytek Instrument Corp., Wilmington, Mass., 1987-89, v.p. engring., 1989-92, v.p. tech. and ventures, 1992-94; pres. The Boxleitner Group, Kirkland, Wash., 1994—; U.S. del. to IEC Working Group for EMC Immunity; participant symposia in field. Author: ESD and Electronic Equipment, 1989; also articles. 1st lt. USAF, 1971-75. Mem. IEEE (sr., chmn. working group 1989). Office: The Boxleitner Group 218 Main St Unit 428 Kirkland WA 98033-6199

BOYAJIAN, TIMOTHY EDWARD, public health officer, educator, consultant; b. Fresno, Calif., Feb. 22, 1949; s. Ernest Adam and Marge (Medzian) B.; m. Tassanee Bootdeesri, Apr. 23, 1987. BS in Biology, U. Calif., Irvine, 1975; M of Pub. Health, UCLA, 1978. Registered environ. health specialist, Calif. Rsch. asst. UCLA, 1978-81; lectr. Chapman U., 29 Palms, Calif., 1982-84, 88-89; refugee relief vol. Cath. Relief Svcs., Surin, Thailand, 1985-86; lectr. Nat. Univ., L.A., 1989-91; environ. health specialist Riverside County Health Svcs. Agy., Palm Springs, Calif., 1991-96; cons. parasitologist S. Pacific Commn., L.A., 1979; pub. health cons. several vets. groups, L.A., 1981-84, 97—, Assn. S.E. Asian Nations, Bangkok, Thailand, 1988. Veterans rights activist, Vietnam Vet. Groups, L.A., 1981-84. With USMC, Vietnam, 1969-71. Recipient U.S. Pub. Health Traineeship, U.S. Govt., L.A., 1977-81. Mem. So. Calif. Pub. Health Assn.,. Home: PO Box 740 Palm Springs CA 92263-0740

BOYARSKI, ADAM MICHAEL, physicist; b. North Bank, Alberta, Can., Apr. 14, 1935; came to U.S., 1963; s. Albert and Mary (Roskiewich) B.; m. Lorretta Sramek, June 1, 1968; children: Lisa A., Mike A. BA in Sci., U. Toronto, 1958; PhD, M.I.T., 1962. Rsch. assoc. M.I.T., Cambridge, 1962-63; staff physicist Stanford (Calif.) Linear Accelerator Ctr., 1963—; cons. in field; mem. team discovering psi family of elem. particles. Author: (software) HANDYPAK, A Histogram and Display Package, 1980; contbr. articles to scientific jours. Mem. Am. Phys. Soc. Office: SLAC 2575 Sand Hill Rd Menlo Park CA 94025-7015

BOYCE, JAMES DANIEL, ophthalmologist; b. Rutland, Vt., Sept. 1, 1947; s. George Potter and Mary Emma (Bree) B.; m. Janet Muff, July 26, 1975. BA, Columbia Coll., 1969; MD, Columbia U., 1973. Diplomate Am. Bd. Ophthalmology. Intern medicine U. So. Calif., L.A., 1974-77; resident ophthalmology Columbia U., N.Y.C., 1977; pvt. practice L.A., 1977-78; ophthalmologist Orange County Ophthalmology Group, Garden Grove, Calif., 1978-79; pvt. practice Garden Grove, 1979-95; ptnr. Orange County Ophthalmology Group, Garden Grove, 1995—; instr. U. So. Calif. Doheny Eye Inst., L.A., 1983—; team ophthalmologist L.A. Rams Football Team, L.A., 1983-95. Pres. Rotary, Garden Grove, 1992-93. Recipient Cmty. Svc. award Sister City Assn., Garden Grove, 1993. Mem. L.A. Soc. Ophthalmology (program chair 1994-95, treas. 1995-96), Orange County Soc. Ophthalmology (program chair 1993-95). Republican. Office: Orange County Ophthalmology 12665 Garden Grove Blvd Garden Grove CA 92843-1901

BOYCE, KER, electrophysiologist, cardiologist; b. Augusta, Ga., Mar. 30, 1961; s. Andrew Summers and Monique Dechezelle (Davis) B. BS with high honors, Ga. Inst. Tech., 1979; MD, Emory U., 1983. Internship Emory U., Atlanta, 1983-84, resident in internal medicine, 1983-86; commd. ens. USN, 1979, advanced through grades to comdr., 1994; force med. officer U.S. Naval Support Force Antarctica, 1987-89; cardiology fellow Naval Hosp., San Diego, 1989-92; staff cardiology Naval Med. Ctr., San Diego, 1992-93, cardiology divsn. head, 1993—; electropsychology fellow U. Calif. San Diego Med. Ctr., 1991-92. Contbr. articles to profl. jours. Fellow ACP, Am. Coll. Cardiology; mem. Undersea and Hyperbasic Med. Soc., Aerospace Medicine Assn., Am. Heart Assn., Am. Soc. Circumpolar Health. Republican. Episcopalian. Office: Naval Med Ctr Cardiology Divsn San Diego CA 92134

BOYD, DAWN ANDREA WILLIAMS, airline official, artist; b. Neptune, N.J., Mar. 9, 1952; d. John Arthur Williams and Narvie Denise (Hill) Puls; m. Joseph L. Boyd II, July 19, 1980 (separated); children: Dziko Ain Williams, Iyabo Kijakazi. BFA, Stephens Coll., 1974. Saleswoman Neusteters, Denver, 1976-77; instr. Opportunities Industrialization Ctr., Denver, 1977-78; reservations and sales agt. United Airlines, Inc., Denver, 1978—. Pres. ULOZI, African-Am. artists collective, Denver, 1995-97. Recipient cmty. art award Colo. Black Women for Polit. Action, 1995, award of merit Colo. '96 Art Exhibit, 1996. Mem. Rocky Mountain Women's Inst. (assoc.), ULOZI Art Ctr. Office: ULOZI Art Ctr 2818 Welton St Denver CO 80205

BOYD, EDWARD HASCAL, retired military officer; b. Kevil, Ky., Sept. 4, 1934; s. Lloyd E. and D. Irene (Steinbeck) B.; m. D. Ann Creecy, Jan. 13, 1956 (dec. Mar. 1970); children: Lawrence H., Debra A.; m. Margaret Lorene Hogan, Nov. 7, 1970; 1 child, Laura Irene. AA, Phoenix Coll., 1954; BS, Ariz. State U., 1956, MBA, 1972. Cert. secondary tchr., Ariz. Commd. 2d lt. USMC, 1956, advanced through ranks to col., 1980, exec. officer Marine Detachment USS Helena, 1959-60; assigned Marine Corps Recruit Depot, San Diego, 1961-63; instr. ops. and intelligence Landing Force Tng. Command USMC, 1963-65, mem. 1st Bn. 4th Marines, 1966-67, instr. Amphibious Warfare Sch., 1967-70, Hdqrs. USMC, 1973-76; assigned to Devel. Ctr. Marine Corps Devel. and Edn. Command, 1977-80; comdr. Hdqrs. Bn., Camp Pendleton, Calif., 1981-84; ret. USMC, 1984; substitute tchr. Mesa (Ariz.) Unified Sch. Dist., 1984-86. Mem. Marine Corps Assn., Ret. Officers Assn., SAR, Magna Charta Barons, Alta Mesa Country Club, Alpha Tau Omega. Home: 5851 E Elmwood St Mesa AZ 85205-5833

BOYD, HARRY DALTON, lawyer, former insurance company executive; b. Huntington Park, Calif., June 13, 1923; s. Randall and Thelma L. (Lewis) B.; m. Margaret Jeanine Gamewell, June 13, 1948; children—Leslie Boyd Cotton, Wayne, Lynn Boyd Denby, Evan, Lance. LL.B., U. So. Calif., 1949, LL.M., 1960; Asso. in Mgmt., Ins. Inst. Am., 1972. Bar: Calif. bar 1950. Pvt. practice Los Angeles; assoc. Harvey & Viereck, Los Angeles, 1952-55; assoc. gen. counsel, corp. sec. Farmers Ins. Group, Los Angeles, 1955-77; group v.p., gen. counsel Swett & Crawford Group, Los Angeles, 1977-83; gen. counsel, dir. Harbor Ins. Co., 1983-89; Calif. counsel Continental Ins. Co., 1987-89; of counsel Fidler & Bell, Burbank, Calif., 1990-93, Richard E. Garcia, Atty. at Law, L.A., 1994-96; bd. dirs. FIG Fed. Credit Union, 1958-61, pres., 1960-61; mem. Sherman Oaks Property Owners Assn., 1967—, pres., 1969, 72; mem. Western Ins. Info. Svc., Spkrs. Bur., 1971-77; bd. dirs. Buffalo Reins. Co., 1983-87; expert witness in ins. litigation, 1990—; arbitrator reins., 1990—. Mem. adv. council Chandler Elementary Sch., 1970-73; mem. adv. council Milliken Jr. High Sch., 1973-74. Served with USAAF, 1943-46. Mem. Calif. Ins. Guarantee Assn. (bd. govs. 1972-77), Los Angeles County Bar Assn. (chmn. exec. com. corp. law depts. sect. 1971-72), Reins. Assn. Am. (legal com. 1979-81), Nat. Assn. Ind. Insurers (chmn. surplus lines com. 1980-82), Calif. Assn. Ins. Cos. (exec. com. 1979-83), Wilshire C. of C. (bd. dirs. 1971-79, pres. 1975), Nat. Assn. Ins. Commrs. (industry adv. com. on reins. regulation 1983-90), Am. Arbitration Assn. (arbitrator). Republican. Lutheran (pres. council 1964-65). Home: 13711 Weddington St Van Nuys CA 91401-5825

BOYD, J. MICHAEL, dentist; b. Charlotte, N.C., Oct. 13, 1943; s. James Marion and Alice Purcell Boyd; m. Sharyl McCoy, Dec. 29, 1967; children: Michael Brent, Erin Elizabeth. BS in Dentistry, Ind. U., 1965; DDS, Ind. U., Indpls., 1968. Lic. dentist, Ind., Calif. Dentist Manteca (Calif.) Dental Group, 1970-71; pvt. practice Modesto, Calif., 1971—; regional cons. Delta Dental, San Francisco, 1990—, Stanislaus Dental Found., Modesto, 1990—, v.p., 1988—, bd. dirs., 1985—, continuing edn. chmn. 1985-88; hosp. staff Meml. Hosp. Med. Ctr., 1975-85, Drs. Med. Courtesy, 1975-85, Stanislaus Med. Ctr., 1993-95. Bd. dirs. Am. Cancer Soc., Modesto, 1973-75, chmn. oral cancer screening, 1977; asst. dir. commr. Boy Scouts Am., Modesto, 1974-75; bishop's warden St. Dinstan's Episc. ch., 1972-73, 87-90, bishop's com., 1987-90, 94-96, stewardship chmn., 1995-97; diocesan coun. Diocese of San Joaquin, 1980-85. Capt. USAF, 1968-70. Pierre Fauchard Acad. fellow, 1995. Fellow Internat. Coll. Dentists, Am. Coll. Dentists; mem. ADA (alt. del. 1984, del. 1995-97), Acad. Gen. Dentistry, Calif. Dental Assn. (trustee 1990-96, del. 1983-84, screening com. 1992-95, chmn. 1994-95), Midvalley Dental Health Found. (bd. dirs. 1979-87), Stanislaus Dental Soc. (pres. 1984, v.p. 1983, sec. 1982, treas. 1981, bd. dirs. 1981-85, 90-96, adv. com. 1989-93, peer rev. chmn. 1979, ethics com. 1988-89, dental liaison chmn. 1974), Ind. U. Alumni Assn., Input Dental Study Club, North Modesto Kiwanis (sec. 1989, Disting. Sec. award 1990, chmn. Pre Concours Party 1980-90), Delta Sigma Delta, Omicron Kappa Upsilon, Delta Upsilon. Republican. Episcopalian. Home: 3712 Almond Blossom Ct Modesto CA 95356-1805 Office: 2813 Coffee Rd Ste B2 Modesto CA 95355-1755

BOYD, JOHN FRANKLIN, orthopaedic surgeon; b. Jamestown, N.D., Sept. 7, 1920; s. Ward Franklin and Ellen Gittings (Pugh) B.; m. Jane Cotton, July 24, 1944 (dec. Apr. 1991); children: Jay F., Jeffrey C., James Curtis; m. Edna Wells, Sept. 9, 1995. BA, Coll. of Wooster, Ohio, 1942; MD, U. Mich., 1945. Diplomate Am. Bd. Orthopedic Surgery. Intern Grace Hosp., Detroit, 1945-46; resident in orthopaedic surgery Cleve. Clinic, 1948-52; pvt. practice Albuquerque Orthopaedics Assocs., P.A., 1953-92; clin. assoc. prof. orthopaedic dept. U. N.Mex. Previously bd. dirs., elder First Presbyn. Ch.; bd. dirs. All Faith Receiving Home; trustee Coll. of Wooster. Served to capt. M.C., AUS, 1946-48. Recipient awards C. of C., 1992, Albuquerque Sports Hall of Fame, 1992, others. Fellow ACS; mem. AMA, Am. Acad. Orthopaedic Surgeons, Western Orthopaedic Assn., Clin. Orthopaedic Soc., Southwestern Surg. Soc., Southwestern Med. Soc., Pan Pacific Surg. Assn., Am. Orthopaedic Soc. for Sports Medicine. Republican. Presbyterian. Home: 1514 Plaza Encantada NW Albuquerque NM 87107

BOYD, LEONA POTTER, retired social worker; b. Creekside, Pa., Aug. 31, 1907; d. Joseph M. and Belle (McHenry) Johnston. Grad. Ind. (Pa.) State Normal Sch., 1927, student Las Vegas Normal U., N.Mex., 1933, Carnegie Inst. Tech. Sch. Social Work, 1945, U. Pitts. Sch. Social Work, 1956-57; m. Edgar D. Potter, July 16, 1932 (div.); m. Harold Lee Boyd, Oct. 1972. Tchr. Creekside (Pa.) Pub. Schs., 1927-30, Papago Indian Reservation, Sells, Ariz., 1931-33; caseworker, supr. Indiana County (Pa.) Bd. Assistance, 1934-54, exec. dir., 1954-68, ret. Bd. dirs. Indiana County Tourist Promotion, hon. life mem.; former bd. dirs. Indiana County United Fund, Salvation Army, Indiana County Guidance Ctr., Armstrong-Indiana Mental Health Bd.; cons. assoc. Community Rsch. Assocs., Inc.; mem. Counseling Ctr. Aux., Lake Havasu City, Ariz., 1978-80; former mem. Western Welcome Club, Lake Havasu City, Sierra Vista Hosp. Aux., Truth or Consequences, N.Mex. Recipient Jr. C. of C. Disting. Svc. award, Indiana, Pa., 1966, Bus. and Profl. Women's Club award, Indiana, 1965. Mem. Am. Assn. Ret. Persons, Daus. Am. Colonists. Lutheran. Home: 444 S Higley Rd Apt 219 Mesa AZ 85206-2186

BOYD, MALCOLM, minister, religious author; b. Buffalo, June 8, 1923; s. Melville and Beatrice (Lowrie) B. B.A., U. Ariz., 1944; B.D., Ch. Div. Sch. Pacific, 1954; postgrad., Oxford (Eng.) U., 1955; S.T.M., Union Theol. Sem., N.Y.C., 1956; DD (hon.), Ch. Div. Sch. of Pacific, 1995. Ordained to ministry Episcopal Ch., 1955. V.p., gen. mgr. Pickford, Rogers & Boyd, 1949-51; rector in Indpls., 1957-59; chaplain Colo. State U., 1959-61, Wayne State U., 1961-65; nat. field rep. Episcopal Soc. Cultural and Racial Unity, 1965-68; resident fellow Calhoun Coll., Yale U., 1968-71, assoc. fellow, 1971—; writer-priest in residence St. Augustine-by-the Sea Episcopal Ch., 1982-95; chaplain to commn. on AIDS Ministries of Episcopal Diocese of L.A., 1993—; lectr. World Council Chs., Switzerland, 1955, 64; columnist Pitts. Courier, 1962-65; resident guest Mishkenot Sha'ananim, Jerusalem, 1974; chaplain AIDS Commn. Episcopal Diocese L.A., 1989—; poet-in-residence Cathedral Ctr. of St. Paul, L.A., 1996—. Host: TV spl. Sex in the Seventies, CBS-TV, Los Angeles, 1975; author: Crisis in Communication, 1957, Are You Running with Me, Jesus?, 1965, rev. 25th anniversary edit., 1990, Free to Live, Free to Die, 1967, Book of Days, 1968, As I Live and Breathe: Stages of an Autobiography, 1969, Human Like Me, Jesus, 1971, The Lover, 1972, When in the Course of Human Events, 1973, The Runner, 1974, The Alleluia Affair, 1975, Christian, 1975, Am I Running with You, God?, 1977, Take Off the Masks, 1978, rev. edit. 1993, Look Back in Joy, 1981, rev. edit., 1990, Half Laughing, Half Crying, 1986, Gay Priest: An Inner Journey, 1986, Edges, Boundaries and Connections, 1992, Rich with Years, 1993; plays Boy, 1961, Study in Color, 1962, The Community, 1964, others; editor: On the Battle Lines, 1964, The Underground Church, 1968, Amazing Grace: Stories of Gay and Lesbian Faith, 1991; book reviewer: Los Angeles Times.; contbr. articles to numerous mags. including Newsday, Parade, Modern Maturity, also newspapers. Active voter registration, Miss., Ala., 1963, 64; mem. Los Angeles City/County AIDS Task Force. Malcolm Boyd Collection and Archives established Boston U., 1973; Recipient Integrity Internat. award, 1978; Union Am. Hebrew Congregations award, 1980. Mem. Nat. Council Chs. (film awards com. 1965), P.E.N. (pres. Los Angeles chpt. 1984-87), Am. Center, Authors Guild, Integrity, Nat. Gay Task Force, Clergy and Laity Concerned (nat. bd.), NAACP, Amnesty Internat., Episc. Peace Fellowship, Fellowship of Reconciliation (nat. com.). Office: PO Box 2164 Los Angeles CA 90051-2145 *The years have taught me the cost of getting involved in life. It is all a risk. One is on stage in an ever-new set without a script. The floor may give way without warning, the walls abruptly cave in. One may die at the hand of an assassin acting on blind impulse. Security, for which men sell their souls, is one of the few real jests in life. Yet the cost of not getting involved in life is higher; one has merely died prematurely. When one has stripped power of its mystique, its robes and artifices, it becomes vulnerable. When you stand up to power, you stand up to one or more individuals. Look an individual, then, in the eye, laugh, if you feel like it. This may be rightly received as a much-needed expression of human solidarity.*

BOYD, WILLIAM HARLAND, historian; b. Boise, Idaho, Jan. 7, 1912; s. Harland D. and Cordelia (Crumley) B.; AB, U. Calif.-Berkeley, 1935, MA, 1936, PhD, 1942; m. Mary Kathryn Drake, June 25, 1939; children: Barbara A. Boyd Voltmer, William Harland, Kathryn L. Boyd Nemeyer. Tchr. Fall River High Sch., McArthur, Calif., 1937-38, Watsonville (Calif.) High Sch., 1941-42, San Mateo (Calif.) High Sch., 1942-44; prof. history Bakersfield Coll., 1946-73, chmn. social sci. dept., 1967-73. Pres., Kern County Hist. Soc., 1950-52; adv. com. Kern County Mus., 1955-60; chmn. Fort Tejon Restoration Com. Bakersfield, 1952-55, sec., 1955-60; mem. Kern County Hist. Records Commn., 1977—, Bakersfield Hist. Preservation Commn., 1984-87. Recipient Merit award Kern County Bd. Trade, 1960, Doctor Waddingham award Conf. Calif. Hist. Socs., 1996; commendation Kern County Bd. Suprs., 1952, 76, 78. Mem. Calif. Tchrs. Assn., Am. Hist. Assn., Phi Alpha Theta. Republican. Baptist. Author: Land of Havilah, 1952, (with G.J. Rogers) San Joaquin Vignettes, 1955, (with others) Spanish Trailblazers in the South San Joaquin, 1957, A Centennial Bibliography on the History Kern County, California, 1966, A California Middle Border, 1972, A Climb Through History, 1973, Bakersfield's First Bapt. Church, 1975, Kern Country Wayfarers, 1977, Kern County Tall Tales, 1980, The Shasta Route, 1981, Stagecoach Heyday in the San Joaquin Valley, 1983, Bakersfield's First Baptist Church A Centennial History, 1989, Lower Kern River Country, 1997. Contbr. to Ency. Brit. Home: 1301 New Stine Rd Apt 216 Bakersfield CA 93309-3501

BOYDSTON, JAMES CHRISTOPHER, composer; b. Denver, July 21, 1947; s. James Virgal and Mary June (Wiseman) B.; m. Ann Louise Bryant, Aug. 20, 1975. BA in Philosophy, U. Tex., 1971. Lutenist and guitarist Collegium Musicum, U. Tex., Austin, 1968-70; tchr. classical guitar Extension div. The New Eng. Conservatory of Music, Boston, 1972-73. Arranger music: S. Joplins, "The Entertainer," 1976; arranger/composer/performer cassette recording: Wedding Music for Classical Guitar, 1988; inventor classical guitar bridge-saddle, 1990; author original poetry included in: The World of Poetry Anthology, 1991. Home: 4433 Driftwood Pl Boulder CO 80301-3104

BOYD-VERQUER, ROBYN GAYLE, medical technologist, executive; b. Pueblo, Colo., Jan. 24, 1962; d. Robert Henry Boyd and Betty Ernestine Martin; m. Robert Joseph Verquer, Mar. 27, 1993. BS in Biology, U. So. Colo., 1989. Cert. med. technologist, clin. lab. scientist. Med. technologist Advantage Lab, Golden, Colo., 1991-92; dir. MLT program Pima Med. Inst., Denver, 1992; owner Precision Concepts, Arvada, Colo., 1992—; clin. lab. scientist Met West Lab, Denver, 1993-94; med. technologist Boulder (Colo.) Med. Ctr., 1994-95, Vencor Hosp., Denver, 1995; tech. cons. lab. Compliance Cons. N.C., 1995—, Quality Am., Va., 1995—, Aurora (Colo.) Eye Physicians, 1996—. Author: CLIA 88 Manual, 1995; contbr. articles to profl. jours. Mem. Am. Soc. for Clin. Pathologists, Nat. Cert. Agy. Office: Precision Concepts 1667 Cole Blvd Ste 400 Golden CO 80401-3313

BOYER, CARL, III, mayor, city official, secondary education educator; b. Phila., Pa., Sept. 22, 1937; s. Carl Boyer Jr. and Elizabeth Campbell Timm; m. Ada Christine Kruse, July 28, 1962. Student, U. Edinburgh, Scotland, 1956-57; BA, Trinity U., 1959; MEd in Secondary Edn., U. Cin., 1959; postgrad., Calif. State U., Northridge, 1964-72. Tchr. Edgewood High Sch., San Antonio, Tex., 1959-60; libr. U. Cin., Cincinnati, Ohio, 1960-61; tchr. Eighth Avenue Elem. Sch., Dayton, Ky., 1961-62, Amelia High Sch., Amelia, Ohio, 1962-63; instr. Kennedy San Fernando Comm. Adult Sch., San Fernando, Calif., 1964-74, Mission Coll., San Fernando, 1971; tchr. San Fernando High Sch., San Fernando, Calif., 1963—; faculty chmn. San Fernando High Sch., dept. chmn.; cons. Sofia (Bulgaria) City Coun., 1991. Author, compiler 14 books on genealogy and family history; contbr. articles to profl. jours. Councilman City of Santa Clarita, Calif., 1987—, mayor pro tem, 1989-90, 94-95, mayor, 1990-91, 95-96; mem. Nat. League Cities Internat. Mcpl. Consortium, 1992—; mem. revenue and taxation com. League Calif. Cities, 1992-95; sec. Calif. Contract Cities Assn., 1992-93; trustee Santa Clarita C.C. Dist., 1973-81, pres., 1979-81; bd. dirs. Castaic Lake Water Agy., 1982-84, pres. Newhall-Saugus-Valencia Fedn. Homeowners Assn., 1969-70, 71-72; pres. Del Prado Condo. Assn., Inc., Newhall, Calif.; exec. v.p. Canyon County Formation Com.; chmn. Santa Clarita City Formation Com., 1987; pres. Santa Clarita Valley Internat. Program, 1991-97; treas. Healing the Children Calif., 1994-96, pres., 1996—. Mem. United Tchrs. L.A., New Eng. Hist. Geneal. Soc. Republican. Methodist. Home: PO Box 220333 Santa Clarita CA 91322-0333 Office: Santa Clarita City Hall 23920 Valencia Blvd Ste 300 Santa Clarita CA 91355-2175

BOYER, FORD SYLVESTER, relationship consultant; b. Cadet, Mo., Jan. 12, 1934; s. Wilford Robert and Mary Elizabeth (DeClue) B.; m. Juelle-Ann Rupkalvis, May 2, 1970. BA in Psychology, USAF Inst., 1957; DD, Am. Bible Inst., Kansas City, Mo., 1977; MA, John F. Kennedy U., 1994. Cert. alcohol specialist. Adminstr. Getz Bros., San Francisco, 1969-73; supr. word processing U.S. Leasing Corp., San Francisco, 1977-82, dir. tng. and applications-word processing, 1982-84; computer cons Petaluma, Calif., 1984-87; massage therapist Petaluma, 1985-87; pvt. practice hypnotherapy Alameda, Calif., 1987—; cons. for chem. dependency Alameda, 1987—. Contbr. articles to profl. publs.; writer, pub.: (newsletter) Starfire, 1988—. With USAF, 1953-57, Korea. Mem. Am Coun. Hypnotist Examiners, Nat. Assn. Alcohol and Drug Abuse Counselors, Calif. Assn. Alcohol and Drug Abuse Counselors, Calif. Assn. Alcohol Recovery Homes. Home and Office: Spiritual Comm Sys 3327 Cook Ln Alameda CA 94502-6939

BOYER, NANCY GAIL, language educator; b. Martinez, Calif., July 15, 1950; d. John Marcus and Esther (Mabey) B. BA in Spanish, Oreg. State U., 1972; MA in Tchr. ESL, Brigham Young U., 1976. ESL instr. Briam Inst./Am. Cultural Ctr., Madrid, 1972-73, Ch. Coll. of Western Samoa, Pesega, 1977-78; ESL instr. Brigham Young U., Laie, Hawaii, 1979-80, Provo, Utah, 1980-83; ESL instr. Ark. State U., Jonesboro, 1983-84, Kuwait U., 1984-90, Pasadena (Calif.) City Coll., 1990-91, Golden West Coll., Huntington Beach, Calif., 1991—. Mem. TESOL, Calif. TESOL. Republican. Mem. LDS Ch. Office: Golden West Coll 15744 Golden West St Huntington Beach CA 92647

BOYETT, JOAN REYNOLDS, arts administrator; b. L.A., May 2, 1936; d. Clifton Faris Reynolds and Jean Margaret (Howard) Hauck; m. Harry William Boyett, Oct. 5, 1956; children: Keven William, Suzanne Marie Boyett Liebherr. Student, Occidental Coll., 1954-55, Pasadena Playhouse, 1955-57. Mgr. youth activities L.A. Philharm. Orch., 1970-79; dir., founder edn. divsn. Music Ctr. Los Angeles County, 1979—, v.p. edn., 1988—; mem. supt.'s task force on arts edn., 1997; cons. NEA, Washington; chmn. arts edn. task force Calif. Arts Coun., Sacramento, 1993-95; arts edn. mem. Nat. Working Group, Washington, 1992-95. Active various coms. and task forces, L.A., Sacramento. Named Woman of Yr. L.A. Times, 1976; recipient Labor's award of honor County Fedn. Labor, L.A., 1984, Susan B. Anthony award Bus. and Profl. Women, 1986, Gov.'s award Calif. Arts Coun. and Gov., 1989. Mem. Calif. Art Edn. Assn. (Behind the Scenes award 1985), Calif. Dance Educators Assn. (Svc. award 1985), Calif. Ednl. Theatre Assn. (Outstanding Contbn. award 1990). Republican. Presbyterian. Home: PO Box 1805 Studio City CA 91614-0805 Office: The Music Ctr 717 W Temple St Ste 400 Los Angeles CA 90012-2615

BOYKIN, WILLIAM EDWARD, principal; b. Clarendon, Tex., June 27, 1932; s. Garland Lester and Lucy Edna (Matthews) B.; m. Bobby Jo Irving,

July 26, 1958 (dec. Apr. 1992); children: Martha Anne, Douglas Irving, Kenneth Garland; m. Jane Ellen Larson, Mar. 1, 1996; stepchildren: Mike, Todd, Phillip Woods. BA in Journalism, N.Mex. State U., 1954, MA in English, 1964, ednl. adminstr., 1976. Tchr., coach, adminstr. Las Cruces (N.Mex.) H.S., 1958-70; asst. football coach N.Mex. State U., Las Cruces, 1970-73; agt., state dir. Fidelity Union Life Ins. Co., Albuquerque, 1973-76; vice-prin., prin. Farmington (N.Mex.) H.S., 1976-86; adminstr. Mesilla Valley Christian Sch., Las Cruces, 1996—. Contbr. articles to profl. jours. Mem. Fields of Dreams Com., Las Cruces, 1994—. Capt. USAF, 1954-58. Recipient Secondary Adminstr. of Yr. N.Mex. Adminstrs. Assn., 1986, Leadership award, 1986. Mem. Am. Legion. Republican. Methodist. Home: 3035 Hillrise Dr Las Cruces NM 88011 Office: Mesilla Valley Christian Sch 3850 Stern Dr Las Cruces NM 88001

BOYLAN, MICHELLE MARIE OBIE, medical surgical nurse; b. St. Louis, Jan. 22, 1962; d. James Martin and Yvonne Marie (DeLoof) Obie; m. Steven Arthur Boylan, June 5, 1962; children: Paige Brittany, Courtney Marie, Brandon James. BSN, Marquette U., 1984; MA, Webster U., 1996. RN. Commd. 2d lt. U.S. Army, 1984, advanced through grades to maj., 1994; pediatrics charge nurse William Beaumont Army Med. Ctr., El Paso, 1984-86, neonatal ICU charge nurse, 1986-87; asst. head nurse pediatrics 98th Gen. Hosp., Neurenberg, Germany, 1987-88; head nurse 98th Gen.Hosp., Neurenberg, Germany, 1987-90, U.S. Army Ft. Huachuca, Sierra Vista, Ariz., 1990-92; head nurse Winn Army Cmty. Hosp., Ft. Stewart, Ga., 1992—, infection control/quality improvement nurse, 1994—, chief patient support divsn., chief quality mgmt. divsn., 1996—; lectr. in field. Decorated Army Commendation medal with 4 oak leaf clusters, Meritorious Svc. medal with 2 oak leaf clusters. Mem. Am. Profls. in Infection Control. Roman Catholic. Home: 870 Piros Dr Colorado Springs CO 80922 Office: Evans Army Cmty Hosp Fort Carson CO 80913

BOYLAN, RICHARD JOHN, psycologist hypnotherapist, researcher, behavioral scientist; b. Hollywood, Calif., Oct. 15, 1939; s. John Alfred and Rowena Margaret (Devine) B.; m. Charnette Marie Blackburn, Oct. 26, 1968 (div. June 1984); children: Christopher J., Jennifer April, Stephanie August; m. Judith Lee Keast, Nov. 21, 1987; stepchildren: Darren Andrew, Matthew Grant. BA, St. John's Coll., 1961; MEd, Fordham U., 1966; MSW, U. Calif., Berkeley, 1971; PhD in Psychology, U. Calif., Davis, 1984. Lic. psychologist, Calif.; lic. clin. social worker, Calif.; lic. marriage, family and child counselor, Calif.; cert. clin. hypnotherapist. Assoc. pastor Cath. Diocese of Fresno, 1965-68; asst. dir. Berkeley (Calif.) Free Ch., 1970-71; psychiat. social worker Marin Mental Health Dept., San Rafael, Calif., 1971-77; dir. Calaveras Mental Health Dept., San Andreas, Calif., 1977-85; prof., coord. Nat. U., Sacramento, 1985-86; instr. Calif. State U., Sacramento, 1985-90, U. Calif., Davis, 1984-88; assoc. prof. Chapman Univ., Sacramento, 1997—; dir. U.S. Behavioral Health, Sacramento, 1988-89; pvt. practice psychotherapy, Sacramento, 1974-95, assoc. prof. Chapman U., 1997—; hypnotherapy practice, Sacramento, 1996—. Author: Extraterrestrial Contact and Human Responses, 1992, Close Extraterrestrial Encounters, 1994, Labored Journey to the Stars, 1996, Project Epiphany, 1997. Bd. dirs. Marin Mcpl. Water Dist., 1975-77; cons. Calif. State Legis., Sacramento, 1979-80; chmn. Calaveras County Bd. Edn., Angels Camp, Calif., 1981-84. Recipient Geriatric Medicine Acad. award NIH, 1984, Experiment Station grant USDA, Calif., 1983. Mem. APA, ACA, Am. Assn. for Humanistic Edn. and Devel., Nat. Bd. Hypnotherapy and Med. Anaesthesiology, Calif. Psychol. Assn., Sacramento Valley Psychol. Assn. (past pres.), Sacramento Soc. Profl. Psychologists (past pres.), Nat. Resources Def. Coun., Acad. Clin. Close-Encounter Therapists (founder, sec., treas.). Democrat. Office: 2826 O St Ste 2 Sacramento CA 95816-6400

BOYLAN, STEVEN ARTHUR, career officer; b. N.Y.C., June 5, 1962; s. Louis Kruegar and Barbara Elaine (Stein) B.; m. Michelle Marie Obie, July 23, 1992; children: Courtney, Brandon, Paige. BA in Comm., Mercer U., 1984; MA in Mgmt., Webster U., 1997. Commd. 2d lt. U.S. Army, 1984, advanced through grades to maj., 1995; spkr. in field. Media, disting. visitor rep. Pueblo (Colo.) Medal Honor Soc., 1995-96. Decorated Meritorious Svc. medal, Army Commendation medal with 2 oak leaf clusters, Army Achievement medal with 2 oak leaf clusters, Multinational Forces and Observer medal with number 2; recipient Bronze medal Excellence in Competition, 1994. Mem. NRA (life), Assn. U.S. Army. Home: 870 Piros Dr Colorado Springs CO 80922 Office: NORAD Dir Pub Affairs 250 S Peterson Blvd Ste 116 Peterson AFB CO 80914

BOYLE, CAROLYN MOORE, public relations executive, marketing communications manager; b. Los Angeles, Jan. 29, 1937; d. Cory Orlando Moore and Violet (Brennan) Baldock; m. Robert J. Ruppelt, Oct. 8, 1954 (div. Aug. 1964); children: Cory Robert, Traci Lynn; m. Jerry Ray Boyle, June 1, 1970 (div. 1975). AA, Orange Coast Coll., 1966; BA, Calif. State U., Fullerton, 1970; student, U. Calif., Irvine, 1970-71. Program coord. Newport Beach (Calif.) Cablevision, 1968-70; dir. pub. rels. Fish Communications Co., Newport Beach, 1970-74; mktg. rep. Dow Pharm. div. Dow Chem. Co., Orange County, Calif., 1974-77, Las Vegas, Nev., 1980-81; mgr. product publicity Dow Agrl. Products div. Dow Chem. Co., Midland, Mich., 1977-80; mgr. mktg. communications Dowell Fluid Services Region div. Dow Chem. Co. Houston, 1981-84; adminstr. mktg. communications Swedlow, Inc., Garden Grove, Calif., 1984-85; cons. mktg. communications, 1985-86; mgr. mktg. communications Am. Convertors div. Am. Hosp. Supply, 1986-87; mgr. sales support Surgidev Corp., Santa Barbara, Calif., 1987-88; owner Barrel House, Victorville, Calif., 1988-91, Saratoga Fences, Las Vegas, 1991; pub. info. officer nuc. waste divsn. Clark County Comprehensive Planning, Las Vegas, 1992-96; pub. info. officer Clark County, Las Vegas, 1996—; guest lectr. Calif. State U., Long Beach, 1970; seminar coordinator U. Calif., Irvine, 1972; mem. Western White House Press Corps, 1972; pub. relations cons. BASF Wyandotte, Phila., 1981-82. Author: Agricultural Public Relations/Publicity, 1981; editor Big Mean AG Machine (internal mag.), 1977; contbr. numerous articles to trade publs.; contbg. editor Dowell Mktg. Newsletter, 1983; creator, designer Novahistine DMX Trial Size nat. mktg. program, 1977. Com. mem. Dow Employees for Polit. Action, Midland, 1978-80; bd. dirs. Dowell Employees for Polit. Action Com., Houston, 1983-84. World Campus Afloat scholar, U. Seven Seas, 1966-67; recipient PROTOS award, 1985. Mem. Pub. Relations Soc. Am. (cert.), Soc. Petroleum Engrs., Internat. Assn. Bus. Communicators. Episcopalian. Recipient first rights to televise President Nixon in Western White House. Office: 6340 Lanning Ln Las Vegas NV 89108-2605

BOYLE, (CHARLES) KEITH, artist, educator; b. Defiance, Ohio., Feb. 15, 1930. Student, Ringling Sch. Art; B.F.A., U. Iowa. Prof. painting and drawing Stanford U., Calif., 1962-88. Group shows include Stanford U. Mus., 1964, San Francisco Mus. Art, 1965, Ann Arbor, Mich., 1965, Joslyn Art Mus., Omaha, 1970, San Jose Mus. Art, Calif., 1978; represented in permanent collections: San Francisco Mus. Art, Stanford U. Mus., Mead paper Corp., Atlanta, Nat. Fine Arts Collection, Washington, Oakland Mus., Continental Bank, Chgo., Seton Med. Ctr., Daily City, Calif., Schneider Mus., Ashland, Oreg. Grantee NEA, 1981-82, Pew Meml. Trust, 1986-87. Address: 6285 Thompson Creek Rd Applegate OR 97530-9639

BOYLE, LARRY MONROE, federal judge; b. Seattle, June 23, 1943; s. Thomas L. and Winona (Green) B.; m. Beverly Rigby, Jan 31, 1969; children: Brian, Jeffery, Bradley, David, Melissa, Layne. BSc, Brigham Young U., 1968; JD, U. Idaho, 1972. Bar: Idaho 1973, U.S. Dist. Ct. Idaho 1973. Atty. Hansen, Boyle, Beard & Martin, P.A., Idaho Falls, Idaho, 1973-86; dist. judge 7th Jud. Dist., Idaho Falls, 1986-89; judge U.S. Supreme Ct. Idaho, Boise, 1989-92; magistrate judge U.S. Dist. Ct. Idaho, Boise, 1992—. Office: US Courthouse 550 W Fort St Rm 518 Boise ID 83724-0101*

BOYLE, STEVEN LEONARD, secondary school educator; b. Yakima, Wash., Dec. 6, 1954; s. Leonard Lavern and Lillith Ernestine (Lueck) B.; m. Tracy Lynn Achziger, June 15, 1991. BA in Music Edn., Ctrl. Wash. U., 1979, MA in Adminstrv. Edn., 1992. Cert. K-12 music tchr., Wash. Music tchr. Housel Mid. Sch., Prosser, Wash., 1979-89; 6th-12th grade band tchr. Housel and Prosser H.S., 1989—. Leader Boy Scouts Am., Prosser, 1980—. Mem. NEA, Music Educators Assn., Wash. Music Educators Assn., Prosser Edn. Assn. (pres. 1989-90), Wash. Edn. Assn. (Hon. Mention Tchr. of Yr. 1982). Home: 1116 Budd Ave Prosser WA 99350-1306 Office: Housel Mid Sch 2001 Highland Dr Prosser WA 99350-1522

BOYNTON, DONALD ARTHUR, retired title insurance company executive; b. Culver City, Calif., Sept. 6, 1940; s. A.A. and Margaret Lena (Slocum) B.; m. Jean Carolyn Ferrulli, Nov. 10, 1962; children: Donna Jean, Michael Arthur; m. Sharon C. Burns, Nov. 18, 1984; children: Cynthia, David, Sharie. Student, El Camino Jr. Coll., 1960-62, Antelope Valley Jr. Coll., 1963-64, Orange Coast Coll., 1969-72; BA, Bradford U., 1977. With Title Ins. & Trust Co., 1958-63; sales mgr. Title Ins. & Trust Co., Santa Ana, Calif., 1980-81; dep. sheriff County of Los Angeles, 1963-65; with Transamerica Title Ins. Co., L.A., 1965-69, state coord., 1981-82; sr. title officer Calif. Land Title Co., L.A., 1969-72; asst. sec., systems analyst Lawyers Title Ins. Corp., 39 states, 1972-77; county mgr. Am. Title Co., Santa Ana, Calif., 1977-79; v.p., mgr. Orange County ops. Chgo. Title Ins. Co., Tustin, Calif., 1979-80; pres. Stewart Title Co. of Fresno, 1985-86; supr. builder svcs. Orange Coast Title Co., Santa Ana, 1986-89; sr. title officer TSG dept. Orange Coast/Record Title, Whittier, Calif., 1990-94; sr. title officer, ednl. coord. State of Calif. for Orange Coast Title, 1993; sr. nat. coord. Chgo. Title and Ins., Irvine, Calif., 1993-96; title officer, claims officer N.Am. Title Ins., Orange, Calif., 1996. Mem. Calif. Trustees Assn., Orange County Escrow Assn., Optimists (sec.-treas.), Elks (life, chaplain), Rotary. Home: 9061 Bermuda Dr Huntington Beach CA 92646-7812 Office: 701 S Parker # 100 Orange CA 92868

BOYNTON, ROBERT GRANVILLE, computer systems analyst; b. North Bend, Oreg., Aug. 11, 1951; s. Granville Clarence Jr. and Leatrice Anne (Yoder) B.; m. Sandra Lynn Harrold, Aug. 17, 1991. Student, Central Oreg. Community Coll., 1969-70. cert. career data processing Heald Coll. Bus., 1972. Computer operator Coca-Cola Bottling Co. Calif., San Francisco, 1973-76, data processing mgr., 1977-78; computer operator Warn Industries, Milwaukie, Oreg., 1979-81, computer programmer, 1981-85, analyst, 1983-85, computer systems analyst, 1985-90, info. systems team leader, 1990—, sr. bus. analyst, 1993—. Vol. Oreg. Spl. Olympics, 1985-86. Democrat. Home: 5712 SE 130th Pl Portland OR 97236-4175 Office: Warn Industries 13270 SE Pheasant Ct Portland OR 97222-1277

BOYNTON, WILLIAM LEWIS, electronic manufacturing company official; b. Kalamazoo, May 31, 1928; s. James Woodbury and Cyretta (Gunther) B.; ed. pub. schs.; m. Kei Ouchi, Oct. 8, 1953. Asst. mgr. Speigel J & R, Kalamazoo, 1947-48; with U.S. Army, 1948-74, ret., 1974; with Rockwell/Collins div., Newport Beach, Calif., 1974-78, supr. material, 1978-81, coord., 1981-88; supr. coord. Rockwell/CDC, Santa Ana, Calif., 1981—, coord. investment recovery, 1982-86, shipping and material coord., 1987-88, material coord., 1988, environ. coord. Rockwell/DCD, Newport Beach, 1988-89, ret.; mem. faculty Western Mich. U., 1955-58. Trustee Orange County Vector Control Dist., 1980—, bd. sec. 1991, bd. v.p. 1992—; pres., 1993; v.p. Calif. Mosquito and Vector Control Assn. Trustee Corp. Bd., 1993, pres., 1993-94, mem. exec. bd. dirs., 1994, mem. bd.; mem. adv. panel for bus./econ. devel. Calif. State Legislature, 1979-86. Decorated Bronze Star. Mem. Assn. U.S. Army, Assn. U.S. Army, Non-Commd. Officers Assn., Nat. Geog. Soc. Republican. Roman Catholic. Home and Office: 5314 W Lucky Way Santa Ana CA 92704-1048

BOYUM, KEITH OREL, political scientist, consultant; b. Lakota, N.D., Aug. 20, 1945; s. Orel A. and Doris Marie (Craig) B.; m. Renae Ruth Pieri, June 19, 1971; children: Nicole, Andrew. BA, U. N.D., 1967; MA, U. Minn., 1971, PhD, 1974. Asst. prof. Calif. State U., Fullerton, 1972-76, assoc. prof., 1976-80, prof. polti. sci., 1980—, acting assoc. v.p., 1983-84, chair acad. senate, 1984-85, 95-96, chair divsn. polit. sci. and criminal justice, 1996—; study dir. Nat. Rsch. Coun./NAS, Washington, 1977-79; coord. edn. policy fellowship program Inst. for Ednl. Leadership, Washington, 1985-95; cons., evaluator Jud. Coun Calif., San Francisco, 1991-95; lectr. Young Pres.'s Orgn., Dallas, 1992, 96; mem. statewide adv. bd. Ctr. for Calif. Studies, Sacramento, 1992—. Editor-in-chief Justice Sys. Jour., 1989-94; co-editor: Empirical theories about Courts, 1983, California Government in National Perspective, 1989, Forecasting the Impact of Legislation on Courts, 1980. Pres. Good Shepherd Luth. Ch., Irvine, Calif., 1984; mem. policy bd. Luth. Office Pub. Policy, Sacramento, 1995—; mem., chair govt. affairs Acad. Senate of Calif. State U., Long Beach, 1986-96; faculty, 1st nat. conf. on eliminating bias in the cts. Nat. Ctr. for State Cts., Williamsburg, Va., 1995. Recipient Warren E. Burger award for achievement in ct. adminstrn. Nat. Ctr. for the Cts., 1994. Mem. Am. Polit. Sci. Assn., Law and Soc. Assn., Western Polit. Sci. Assn., Phi Beta Kappa. Democrat. Office: Calif State U Divsn Polit Sci/Crim Just PO Box 34080 Fullerton CA 92834-6848

BOZARTH, GEORGE S., historian, musicologist, pianist; b. Trenton, N.J., Feb. 28, 1947. MFA, Princeton U., 1973; PhD, Princeton U., 1978. Assoc. prof. music U. Wash.; dir. Brahms Archive, Seattle, Internat. Brahms Conf., Washington, 1983; co-artistic dir. Gallery Concerts, Seattle. Editor: Johannes Brahms, Orgelwerke, The Organ Works, Munich, G Henle, 1988, J.S. Bach Cantata, Ach Gott vom Himmel sieh darein, BWV2, Neue Bach Augabe, 1/16, 1981, 84, The Correspondence of Johannes Brahms and Robert Keller, 1996, facsimile editions Brahms' Lieder and Duets, the genesis and chronology of Brahms's works, Brahms' piano sonatas and First Piano Concerto, editl. problems, questions of authenticity, Brahms's pianos and piano music. Fullbright-Hayes scholar to Austria, 1975-77; fellow ACLS, 1982; NEH Rsch. Conf. grantee, 1983. Mem. Am. Brahms Soc. (exec. dir.), Am. Musicol. Soc., Early Music Am., Classical Consort. Office: Sch Music U Wash Box 353450 Seattle WA 98195-3450

BRAASCH, BARBARA LYNN, banker; b. Santa Monica, Calif., Apr. 14, 1958; d. C. Duane and René Barbara (Siegel) B. Student, Golden Gate U., 1989-91. Opers. mgr. Bank of Am., Fresno, Calif., 1976-87; v.p., mgr. Bank of Am., San Francisco, 1996—; ops. officer Bank of Am., Fresno, Calif., 1976-87; v.p., mgr. Wells Fargo Bank, San Francisco, 1994-96, v.p. mgr., 1994-96; v.p., mgr. Bank of Am., San Fransisco, 1996—; mentor Jr. Achievement, L.A., 1980-83. 1st class scout Girl Scouts Am., 1976, leader, asst. leader, 1976-79, 84-87; vol. Open Hand, San Francisco, 1991-92, San Francisco AIDS Found., various women's groups, 1989—. Mem. Am. Compensation Assn. Democrat. Jewish. Office: Bank of Am 185 Berry St 3rd Fl San Francisco CA 94107

BRACEY, EARNEST NORTON, political science educator; b. Jackson, Miss., June 8, 1953; s. Willard and Odessa Manola (Ford) B.; m. Atsuko Konuma, Apr. 2, 1995; children: Dominique, Princess, Omar. MPA, Golden Gate U., 1979; MA, Cath. U., Washington, 1983; D of Pub. Adminstrn., George Mason U., 1993. Commd. 2d lt. U.S. Army, 1975, advanced through grades to lt. col., 1992; ret., 1995; instr. polit. sci. C.C. of So. Nev., Las Vegas, 1996—; adj. prof. Ctrl. Tex. Coll., Camp Zama, Japan, 1993-95; mem. Nev. faculty alliance C.C. of So. Nev., Las Vegas, 1996—. Author: Choson, 1994. Mem. NAACP, Am. Soc. of Mil. Comptrs., Assn. of the U.S. Army, Retired Officer Assn.

BRACHER, GEORGE, radiologist; b. Portland, Oreg., Mar. 20, 1909; s. George Michael and Anna (Ris) B.; m. Helen Arndt, Oct. 6, 1936; children: Randall W., Ann Louise. BS, U. Oreg., 1932, MD, 1934. Diplomate Am. Bd. Radiology. Intern St. Vincent's Hosp., Portland, 1935; resident fellow U. Chgo., 1936-38; asst. prof. radiology U. Oreg. Med. Sch., Portland, 1938-39; radiologist King County Hosp. System, Seattle, 1939-41, Hilo (Hawaii) Hosp., 1960-85, Lucy Henriques Med. Ctr., Kamuela, Hawaii, 1985—; pvt. practice Seattle and Spokane (Wash.), 1941-60; cons. radiologist Honokaa (Hawaii) Hosp., 1960—, Kohala (Hawaii) Hosp., 1960—, Kau Hosp., Pahala, Hawaii, 1960—; attending physician U. Hawaii Peace Corps Project, 1962-70. Pres. Hawaii County unit Am. Cancer Soc., Hilo, 1970, Hawaii Pacific div. Honolulu, 1972, chmn. Pacific and related islands com., 1975; founder Hawaii County Med. Soc. Scholarship Fund, Cancer Care Trust, Hilo. Mem. AMA, Hawaii Med. Assn., Hawaii County Med. Soc. (pres. 1969), Am. Coll. Radiology, Hawaii Radiologic Soc., Wash. Athletic Club, Hilo Yacht Club. Home: 134 Puako Beach Dr Kamuela HI 96743-9709

BRACKNER, JAMES WALTER, accounting educator, consultant; b. Selma, Ala., Aug. 6, 1934; s. James Oscar and Ruby Belle (Langston) B.; m. Gayle Linton, Sept. 11, 1959; children: James L., Betsy, Joseph L., David L., Susan, Daniel L., Nancy. BS in Acctg., Brigham Young U., 1961, MS in Acctg., 1962; PhD in Accountancy, U. Ala., 1985. CPA, Cert. Mgmt. Acct. Staff acct. Arthur Andersen, L.A., 1962-65; controller, asst. sec. Teledyne-WIW, L.A., 1965-68; CFO Phaostron Electronics, South Pasadena, Calif., 1968-69; instr., asst. prof. Brigham Young U., Provo, Utah, 1969-78; CFO Deseret Mgmt. Corp.-Farms Divsn., Salt Lake City, 1978-81; from asst. prof. to assoc. prof. Utah State U., Logan, 1981-93, prof., 1993—; cons., expert witness Richards Brandt Miller Nelson, Salt Lake City, 1988-91. Author: Management Accounting/Manufacturing Excellence, 1996; contbr. articles to profl. jours., chpt. to book. Scout leader, merit badge counselor Boy Scouts Am., Logan, 1982—. With U.S. Army 1954-56. Mem. AICPA, Inst. Mgmt. Accts. (nat. v.p. 1996-97, bd. regents 1995-96, edn. com. 1994-95, ethics com. 1991-94), Am. Acctg. Assn., Utah Assn. CPAs (chpt. pres. 1995-96). Republican. Mormon. Home: 760 Stewart Hill Dr Logan UT 84321 Office: Utah State Univ Sch Accountancy Logan UT 84322-3540

BRADAC, THOMAS FRANK, theater educator; b. South Gate, Calif., July 30, 1947; s. Thomas Frank Sr. and Pearl Evelyn (Bloodgood) B.; m. Anne Sara Barolet, Apr. 25, 1987; children: Alyssa Dianne, Caitlin Jean. BA, Calif. State U., Long Beach, 1969, MA, 1971. Cultural arts coord. City of Garden Grove (Calif.), 1979-80; founder, artistic dir. Grove Shakespeare Fest, Garden Grove, 1980-81, Shakespeare Orange County, Orange, Calif., 1992—; theater prof. Chapman U., Orange, 1990—; bd. dirs. So. Calif. Ednl. Theatre Assn., 1996—. Commr. Art in Public Places, City of Garden Grove, 1987; bd. dirs. Shakespeare Theatre Assn. Am., 1990-93. Recipient Pub.'s award for Exceptional Achievement in Theatre Hollywood Drama-Logue mag., 1991. Democrat. Roman Catholic. Office: Chapman U 333 N Glassell Orange CA 92866

BRADBURY, STEPHEN DOUGLAS, judge, rancher; b. Long Beach, Calif., Jan. 25, 1950; m. Karen Lee Taylor, Aug. 14, 1971; children: William, Michael, Amedee. BA with honors, San Diego State U., 1973; JD, U. Calif., San Francisco, 1976. Bar: Calif. 1976, U.S. Dist. Ct. (ea. dist.) Calif. 1977, U.S. Supreme Ct. 1982. Ptnr. Harvey & Bradbury, Susanville, Calif., 1977-79, Bradbury, Kellison and Cady, PC, Susanville, 1979-84; v.p., gen. counsel Five Dot Land & Cattle Co., Inc., Susanville, 1984-86; judge Lassen Consolidated Jud. Dist., Lassen County, Calif., 1986-96; judge Superior Ct. State of Calif., Lassen County, 1996—; presiding judge, 1997—; mem. jud. faculty Calif. Jud. Coll., U. Calif., Berkeley (mcpl. ct. seminar leader 1992, rural cts. course 1993, 94-96), Calif. Rural Cts. Conf. (ethics session 1992, 93, mem. planning com. 1992, 93, 94-95), Mcpl. and Justice Cts. Inst., San Diego (contempt and sanctions 1993, jud. chairperson 1993, mem. planning com. 1992); apptd. by chief justice to standing com. jud. performance Jud. Coun. Calif., 1994-95. Trustee Lassen C.C. Dist., 1978-86, Shaffer Union Sch. Dist., 1980-86; bd. chairperson City of Susanville Mcpl. Energy Corp., 1981-82; capt. Lassen County Sheriff's Posse, 1984; bd. dirs. Nev. area coun. Boy Scouts Am., 1992—, chair rural scouting com., 1997; bd. dirs. Sierra, Nev. coun. Girl Scouts Am., 1997—. With USAF, 1968-70. Recipient Dist. award of Merit, Boy Scouts Am., 1993. Mem. Calif. Judges Assn. (justice cts. mgmt. com. 1987-93, jud. chairperson rural mcpl. and justice cts. forum 1993-94, ethics com. 1995—), Lassen County Cattlemens Assn., Lassen County Farm Bur., Rotary Club (bd. dirs. Susanville chpt. 1990-94, pres. 1994-95), Pi Sigma Alpha, Phi Delta Phi. Office: Courthouse 200 S Lassen St Susanville CA 96130-4350

BRADEN, GEORGE WALTER, II (LORD OF CARRIGALINE), company executive; b. L.A., Sept. 1, 1936; s. Paul Sumner and Evelyn Widney (Traver) B.; m. Trina Rose Thomas, July 3, 1964; children: Barbara Diane, Beverly Eileen Braden Christensen. BS, Calif. State U., 1963; grad. cert., U. So. Calif., 1990, Harvard U., 1991; postgrad., UCLA, 1990—; MBA, Chadwick U.; JA, Blackstone Law Sch. Mgr. western region vet. div. Bristol-Myers, Syracuse, N.Y., 1970-79; pres. Braden Sales Assocs. Internat., Apple Valley, Calif., 1980—. Mem. Friends of Hoover Inst., Stanford, Calif.; charter mem. Rep. Presdl. Task Force, Washington, 1989—; commr. Rep. Presdl. Adv. Com., Washington, 1991—; active Nat. Rep. Senatorial Com. Capt. USMB, 1985-93, maj., 1993—. Recipient Presdl. order of Merit, Heritage Found., Rep. Presdl. award, 1994; numerous awards Boy Scouts of Am.; named Lord of North Bovey, Lord of Newton Bushel. Mem. Am. Mktg. Assn., Tex. A&M U. Internat. Assn. of Agri-Bus., Curia Baronis Build for Barons, Lords of Manor, Pres.'s Club. Mem. LDS Ch.

BRADFORD, CRAIG SNOW, corporate executive; b. San Francisco, Feb. 10, 1944; s. Lowell W. and Mauvia S. (Tracy) B.; m. Sharon A. Cokely, July 27, 1973; children: Matthew, Daniel, Anna-Marie. BS in Biology, U. Utah, 1968; MA in Internat. Law, U. So. Calif., Cambridge, Eng., 1980. Commd. 2d lt. USAF, 1968, advanced through grades to col., 1987; U.S. diplomat, Chief Aviation, Office Mil. Cooperation USAF, Cairo, 1988-90; chief staff 57th Fighter Weapons Wing, dep. inspector gen. USAF, Nellis AFB, Nev., 1990-91, dir. quality improvement Fighter Weapons Ctr., 1991-93; pres. Bradford & Assocs Internat., Las Vegas, Nev., 1993—; dir. project adminstrn. City of North Las Vegas, Nev., 1992-93, dep. city mgr., 1994-95; bd. dirs. Quality and Productivity Inst., Nev., 1991-96; mem. Gov.'s Task Force for Reinventing Govt., Nev., 1993-94; chmn. bd., CEO Ensotech, Inc. Author, producer video Rebirth of a City: A Total Quality Challenge, 1994. Mem. election bd. Clark County, Nev., 1993; Eagle Scout advisor, mem. com. Boy Scouts Am., 1993-94. Decorated Legion of Merit, DFC (7), Bronze Star with "V", Purple Heart, Air medals (16), Vietnamese Cross of Gallantry with bronze star, Vietnamese Cross of Gallantry with Gold Palm. Mem. Indsl. Rels. Rsch. Assn. Republican. Mem. LDS Ch. Home: 323 Oliveiro Ct Henderson NV 89014-5100

BRADFORD, DAVID PAUL, judicial assistant; b. Lynwood, Calif., Mar. 23, 1955; s. William H. and Barbara E. (O'Leary) Johnson. AA, Citrus Coll., Azusa, Calif., 1975; BA in Polit. Sci., UCLA, 1978; postgrad., Calif. State U., L.A., 1984-85, U. West L.A., 1990-91. Prin. clerk UCLA Brain Rsch. Inst., 1977-81; adminstrv. asst., supr. UCLA Hosp. and Clinics, 1977-81; dep. to atty. in residence matters office of registrar UCLA, 1981-85; office of clerk L.A. County Bd. Suprs., L.A., 1987-88; judicial asst., ct. clerk L.A. Superior Ct., L.A., 1988—; founder Bradford & Assocs., L.A., 1987—; rsch. dir. citizens Protection Alliance, Santa Monica, 1992—. Active L.A. County Domestic Violence Coun. Recipient Cert. of Appreciation, Domestic Violence Coun., 1990, commendation Los Angeles County Bd. Suprs., 1993, L.A. Police Dept. and Assn. Threat Assessment Profls. award, 1994. Mem. N.Y. Acad. Scis., Los Angeles County Superior Ct. Clks. Assn. (local 575 AFSCME pres. 1993, 94), N.Y. Acad. Polit. Scis., Calif. Profl. Ct. Clks. Assn. (exec. dir.). Office: Bradford & Assocs 3921 Wilshire Blvd Ste 303V Los Angeles CA 90010-3317

BRADFORD, G. ERIC, animal science educator emeritus; b. Kingsey, Que., Can., Nov. 2, 1929; came to U.S., 1957, naturalized, 1989; m. Elizabeth Ann Engelke, June 19, 1954; children: Anne, Kenneth, Margaret, Ellen. BSc in Agr., McGill U., Montreal, 1951; MS, U. Wis., 1952, PhD, 1956. Asst. prof. McGill U., 1955-57; asst. prof. U. Calif. Davis, 1957-64, assoc. prof., 1964-69, prof. animal sci., 1969-93, chair dept. animal sci., 1973-78, 90-93, prof. emeritus, 1993—, dir. Animal Agr. Rsch. Ctr., 1993-95; vis. asst. prof. Cornell U., Ithaca, N.Y., 1963; vis. scientist Am. Breeding Rsch. Orgn., Edinburgh, 1970-71, Winrock Internat., Morrilton, Ark., 1978-79. Author some 135 articles on animal sci. and animal genetics. Bd. dirs. Internat. House, Davis, 1993—. Recipient Svc. awrd Calif. Wool Growers Assn., 1990. Fellow AAAS; mem. Am. Soc. Animal Sci. (Rockefeller-Prentice award 1984), Brit. Soc. Animal Sci., Coun. Agrl. Sci. and Tech. Presbyterian. Office: U Calif Dept Animal Sci Davis CA 95616

BRADIC, ZDRAVKO, chemist; b. Ugarci, Croatia, Sept. 3, 1947; came to U.S., 1981; naturalized; s. Dusan and Marija Bradic; m. Connie Lynn Zothman; children: Daniela L., Ryan J. BS in Pharmacy, Zagreb U., Croatia, 1970, MS in Instrumental Methods, 1972, PhD in Chemistry, 1974. Rsch./teaching asst., assoc. Zagreb U., 1970-81; postdoctoral fellow N.Mex. State U., Las Cruces, 1976-77, 82-84, asst. prof. chemistry, 1984-85; postdoctoral fellow U. Minn., Mpls., 1977-78; rsch. scientist Hyland div. Baxter, L.A., 1985-88; sr. scientist Chiron Diagnostics, Irvine, Calif., 1988—. Contbr. over 20 articles to profl. jours. Fellow Am. Inst. Chemists; mem. AAAS, Am. Chem. Soc., Am. Assn. Clin. Chemists. Office: Chiron Diagnostics Corp 17392 Daimler St Irvine CA 92614

BRADLEY, CHARLES WILLIAM, podiatrist, educator; b. Fife, Tex., July 23, 1923; s. Tom and Mary Ada (Cheatham) B.; m. Marilyn A. Brown, Apr. 3, 1948 (dec. Mar. 1973); children: Steven, Gregory, Jeffrey, Elizabeth, Gerald. Student, Tex. Tech., 1940-42; D. Podiatric Medicine, Calif. Coll. Podiatric Medicine U. San Francisco, 1949, MPA, 1987, D.Sc. (hon.). Pvt.

practice podiatry Beaumont, Tex., 1950-51, Brownwood, Tex., 1951-52, San Francisco, San Bruno, Calif., 1952—; assoc. clin. prof. Calif. Coll. Podiatric Medicine, 1992—; chief of staff Calif. Podiatry Hosp., San Francisco; mem. surg. staff Sequoia Hosp., Redwood City, Calif.; mem. med. staff Peninsula Hosp., Burlingame, Calif.; chief podiatry staff St. Luke's Hosp., San Francisco; chmn. bd. Podiatry Ins. Co. Am.; cons. VA; assoc. prof. podiatric medicine Calif. Coll. Podiatric Medicine. Mem. San Francisco Symphony Found.; mem. adv. com. Health Policy Agenda for the Am. People, AMA; chmn. trustees Calif. Coll. Podiatric Medicine, Calif. Podiatry Coll., Calif. Podiatry Hosp.; mem. San Mateo Grand Jury, 1989. Served with USNR, 1942-45. Mem. Am. Podiatric Med. Assn. (trustee, pres. 1983-84), Calif. Podiatry Assn. (pres. No. div. 1964-66, state bd. dirs., pres. 1975-76, Podiatrist of Yr. award 1983), Nat. Coun. Edn. (vice-chmn.), Nat. Acads. Practice (chmn. podiatric med. sect. 1991-96, sec. 1992, 96), Am. Legion, San Bruno C. of C. (bd. dirs. 1978-91, v.p. 1992, bd. dir. grand jury assoc. 1990), Olympic Club, Commonwealth Club Calif., Elks, Lions. Home: 2965 Trousdale Dr Burlingame CA 94010-5708 Office: 560 Jenevein Ave San Bruno CA 94066-4408

BRADLEY, JEAN ELEANOR, newspaper executive, public relations consultant; b. North York, Ontario, Can., Apr. 14, 1928; d. Archer and Eleanor (Aitkin) Wardle; m. Kenneth Gordon Bradley, Nov. 26, 1949; children: Jill (dec. 1964), Anne Marjorie Bradley Jaeger. Grad., Earl Haig Coll., North York, Ont., Can., 1945; student bus. mgmt., Portland (Oreg.) C.C., 1981-85; student computer sci., U. Oregon, Rock Creek, 1987-88. Underwriter, office mgr. A.B. Ferguson, Ins., Toronto, Ont., Can., 1946-55; asst. editor, co-owner Estevan (Sask., Can.) Mercury, 1964-66; pub. rels. mgr. Kaiser Permanente N.W. region, Portland, Oreg., 1968-88; v.p., co-owner Daily Shipping News, Portland, 1985-95; pres. Braeward Pub., Portland, 1996—; exec. com. Kaiser Permanente Retirees, Portland, 1989—. Contbg. author: Oregon Writers Colony Anthology, 1993; author: A Home Across the Water, 1996; contbr. articles to various newspapers and mags. Bd. Dirs. Vol. Ctr., Portland, 1989-95. Recipient writing awards Nat. Fedn. Press Women, Oreg. Press Women, 1994; named Outstanding Profl. of Yr., Women in Comms., Portland, 1986. Mem. Pub. Rels. Soc. Am. (accredited, chpt. pres. 1980, dist. chmn. 1985, president's citation 1985, William Marsh lifetime achievement award Columbia River chpt. 1988), Oreg. Press Women (various coms.), Oreg. Writers Colony (bd. dirs. 1994), Daus. Brit. Empire (v.p. state bd. dirs. 1989-93).

BRADLEY, MARK CHARLES, defender; b. Detroit, Dec. 28, 1965; s. Roger Wilson and Phyllis Marian (Readhead) B. BA, Hope Coll., 1988; JD, Northwestern U. Sch. of Law, 1993. Bar: Wash. Info. systems cons. Andersen Consulting, Detroit, 1988-90; community organizer North River Commn., Chgo., 1990; asst. pub. defender The Defender Assn., Seattle, 1993—. Mem. ACLU, Nat. Lawyers Guild. Home: 80 S Jackson St # 201 Seattle WA 98104-2855 Office: The Defender Assn 810 3rd Ave Fl 8 Seattle WA 98104-1614

BRADLEY, OMAR, mayor. Mayor City of Compton, Calif. Office: 205 S Willowbrook Compton CA 90220

BRADLEY, WADE HARLOW, acquisitions specialist; b. Mpls.; s. Robert Douglas and Florence (Wells) B.; m. Alessandra Maria Benitez, June 30, 1984; children: Isabella Andrea, Francesca Alessandra. BS, U. Minn., 1983; postgrad., LaJolla Acad. Advt., 1984. Bus. cons. A.B.A. Investment Corp., La Jolla, Calif., 1987-88; pres. The Harlow Co., San Diego, 1987—; acquisitions specialist Pacific Capital Ptnrs., San Diego, 1989-90; sr. v.p. corp. devel. Sundance Resources Inc., San Diego, 1990-95, sr. v.p., 1995—; sr. analyst La Jolla Securities Corp, 1995—. Republican. Roman Catholic. Office: La Jolla Securities Corp 1020 Prospect St # 200 La Jolla CA 92037

BRADLEY, WALTER D., lieutenant governor, real estate broker; b. Clovis, N.M., Oct. 30, 1946; s. Ralph W. and M. Jo (Black) B.; m. Debbie Shelly, Sept. 17, 1977; children: Tige, Lance, Nicole, Kristin. Student Eastern N.M. U., 1964-1967. Supr. Tex. Instruments, Dallas, Tex. 1967-73; mgr., salesman Nat. Chemsearch, Irving, Tex., 1973-76; real estate broker Colonial Real Estate, Clovis, 1976; real estate broker Realtors Assn. N.Mex., Clovis, N.Mex., 1976—; state senator Curry County, State of N.Mex., 1989-93; Lt. Governor State of N.Mex., Santa Fe, N. Mex., 1995—. mem. N.Mex. Senate, 1989-92; lieutenant governor State N.Mex., 1995—. V.p., bd. dirs. Clovis Indsl. Commn., 1983-86, pres. econ. devel., 1987; bd. dirs. United Way, Clovis, 1984-86, Curry County Blood Adv. Bd., Clovis, 1980-85; chmn. Curry County Reps., Clovis, 1984-88; Cosmos Soccer, Clovis, 1984. Mem. Realtors Assn. N.Mex. (v.p., bd. dirs. 1982-85, v.p. 1987-88), Clovis Bd. Realtors (pres. 1982, 93), Clovis C. of C., Curry County Jaycees, N.M. Jaycees. Baptist. Lodge: Lions. Office: Office Lt Governor PO Box 2106 Santa Fe NM 87503

BRADSHAW, RALPH ALDEN, biochemistry educator; b. Boston, Feb. 14, 1941; s. Donald Bertram and Eleanor (Dodd) B.; m. Roberta Perry Wheeler, Dec. 29, 1961; children: Christopher Evan, Amy Dodd. BA in Chemistry, Colby Coll., 1962; PhD, Duke U., 1966. Asst. prof. Washington U., St. Louis, 1969-72, assoc. prof., 1972-74, prof., 1974-82; prof., chair dept. U. Calif., Irvine, 1982-93, prof., 1993—; study sect. chmn. NIH, 1979, mem., 1975-79, 80-85; mem. sci. adv. bd. Hereditary Disease Found., 1983-87, ICN Nucleic Acids Rsch. Inst., 1986-87; rsch. study com. physiol. chem. Am. Heart Assn., 1984-86, mem. Coun. on Thrombosis, 1976-90; fellowship screening com. Am. Cancer Soc. Calif., 1984-87; chmn. adv. com. Western Winter Workshops, 1984-88; dir., chmn., mem. organizing com. numerous symposia, confs. in field including Proteins in Biology and Medicine, Shanghai, Peoples Republic of China, 1981, Symposium Am. Protein Chemists, San Diego, 1985, chmn. exec. com. Keystone Symp. Mol. Cell. Biol., 1991-94, Keystone Ctr. bd. trustees, 1991—; mem. exec. com. Internat. Union Biochem. Mol. Biol., 1991-97, U.S. Nat. Commn. Biochem., 1987-96, chmn., 1992-96; bd. dirs. Fed. Am. Soc. Exptl. Biology, 1992-96, v.p., 1994-95, pres., 1995-96. Mem. editorial bd. Archives Biochemistry and Biophysics, 1972-88, Jour. Biological Chemistry, 1973-77, 78-79, 81-86, assoc. editor, 1989—, Jour. Supramolecular Structure/Cellular Biochemistry, 1980-91, Bioscience Reports, 1980-87, Peptide and Protein Reviews, 1980-86, Jour. Protein Chemistry, 1980-90, IN VITRO Rapid Communication in Cell Biology, 1984—; editor Trends in Biochemical Sciences, 1975-91, editor-in-chief, 1986-91, J. Neurochem, 1986-90, Proteins: Structure, Functions & Genetics, 1988-92, Growth Factors, 1989—; assoc. editor: Protein Science, 1990-92, mem. editl. bd., 1992—; contbr. numerous articles to scientific jours. Recipient Young Scientist award Passano Found., 1976. Fellow AAAS; mem. Am. Chem. Soc. (Sect. award 1979), Am. Soc. Biochem. Molecular Biologists (coun. 1987-90, treas. 1991-97), Am. Peptide Soc., N.Y. Acad. Scis., Protein Soc. (acting pres. 1986-87), Am. Soc. for Cell Biology, Soc. for Neuroscience, The Endocrine Soc., Am. Soc. Bone Mineral Rsch., Sigma Xi. Home: 25135 Rivendell Dr Lake Forest CA 92630-4134 Office: U Calif Irvine Dept Biol Chemistry CCM D240 Irvine CA 92697

BRADY, JOHN PATRICK, JR., electronics educator, consultant; b. Newark, Mar. 20, 1929; s. John Patrick and Madeleine Mary (Atno) B.; m. Mary Coop, May 1, 1954; children: Peter, John P., Madeleine, Dennis, Mary G. BSEE, MIT, 1952, MSEE, 1953. Registered profl. engr., Mass. Sect. mgr. Hewlett-Packard Co., Waltham, Mass., 1956-67; v.p. engring. John Fluke Mfg. Co., Inc., Mountlake Terrace, Wash., 1967-73; v.p. engring. Dana Labs., Irvine, Calif., 1973-77; engring. mgr., tech. advisor to gen. mgr. Metron Corp., Upland, Calif., 1977-78; ptnr. Resource Assocs., Newport Beach, Calif., 1978-86; prof. electronics Orange Coast Coll., Costa Mesa, Calif., 1977—, faculty fellow, dean technology, 1983-84, chmn. electronics tech. dept., 1994-96; instr. computers and electric engring. Calif. State U., Long Beach, 1982-84. Mem. evaluation team Accrediting Commn. for Community and Jr. Colls., 1982-92; mem. blue ribbon adv. com. on oversees technology transfer U.S. Dept. of Commerce, 1974-76. With USN, 1946-48. Mem. Measurement Sci. Conf. (dir. 1982-83), MIT (L.A.). Contbr. articles in field to profl. jours.; mem. Eta Kappa Nu, Tau Beta Pi, Sigma Xi. Office: Orange Coast Coll Costa Mesa CA 92626

BRADY, RODNEY HOWARD, broadcast company executive, holding company executive, former college president, former government official; b. Sandy, Utah, Jan. 31, 1933; s. Kenneth A. and Jessie (Madsen) B.; m. Carolyn Ann Hansen, Oct. 25, 1960; children: Howard Riley, Bruce Ryan, Brooks Alan. BS in Acctg. with high honors, U. Utah, MBA with high honors, 1957; DBA, Harvard U., 1966; postgrad., UCLA, 1969-70; PhD (hon.), Weber State Coll., 1986, Snow Coll., 1991. Missionary Ch. Jesus Christ of Latter-day Saints, Great Britain, 1953-55; teaching assoc. Harvard U. Bus. Sch., Cambridge, Mass., 1957-59; v.p. Mgmt. Systems Corp., Cambridge, 1962-65, Center Exec. Devel., Cambridge, 1963-64; v.p., dir. Center Exec. Devel., Boston, 1964-65; v.p. Tamerand Reef Corp., Christiansted, St. Croix, V.I., 1963-65; v.p., dir. Am. Inst. Execs., N.Y.C., 1963-65; v.p., mem. exec. com. aircraft div. Hughes Tool Co., Culver City, Calif., 1966-70; asst. sec. adminstrn. and mgmt. Dept. HEW, Washington, 1970-72; chmn. subcabinet exec. officers group of exec. br., 1971-72; exec. v.p., chmn. exec. com., dir. Bergen Brunswig Corp., Los Angeles, 1972-78; chmn. bd. Unimgrs. Internat., Los Angeles, 1974-78; pres. Weber State Coll., Ogden, Utah, 1978-85; pres., CEO Bonneville Internat. Corp., Salt Lake City, 1985-96, also dir.; pres., CEO Deseret Mgmt. Corp., Salt Lake City, 1996—; bd. dirs. Bergen Brunswig Corp., 1st Security Bank Corp., Mgmt. and Tng. Corp., Deseret Mut. Benefit Assn., chmn.; bd. dirs. Maximum Svc. Television, Inc., Intermountain Health Care Found., Nat. Assn. Broadcasters TV Bd., Utah Opera Co.; bd. advisors Mountain Bell Telephone, 1983-87; chmn. Nat. Adv. Com. on Accreditation and Instl. Eligibility, 1984-86, mem., 1983-87; chmn. Utah Gov.'s Blue Ribbon Com. on Tax Recodification, 1984-90; cons. Dept. Def., Dept. State, Dept. Commerce, HEW, NASA, Govt. of Can., Govt. of India (and indsl. firms), 1962—. Author: An Approach to Equipment Replacement Analysis, 1957, Survey of Management Planning and Control Systems, 1962, The Impact of Computers on Top Management Decision Making in the Aerospace and Defense Industry, 1966, (with others) How To Structure Incentive Contracts—A Programmed Text, 1965, My Missionary Years in Great Britain, 1976, An Exciting Start Along an Upward Path, 1978; contbr. articles to profl. jours. Mem. exec. com. nat. exec. bd. Boy Scouts Am., 1977—; chmn. nat. Cub Scout commn., 1977-81, pres. Western region, 1981-83, chmn. nat. ct. of honor, 1984-88; mem. adv. com. program for health sys. mgmt. Harvard U., 1973-78, mem. nat. adv. coun. U. Utah, 1971—, chairperson, 1974-76, nat. adv. bd. Coll. Bus., 1985—, chmn., 1989-93, mem. adv. com. Brigham Young U. Bus. Sch., 1972—; mem. dean's round table UCLA Grad. Sch. Mgmt., 1973-78; trustee Ettie Lee Homes for Boys, 1973-79; mem. gov. bd. McKay Dee Hosp., Ogden, Utah, 1979-87; bd. dirs. Utah Endowment for Humanities, 1978-80, Nat. Legal Ctr. for the Pub. Interest, 1991—, vice chmn., 1994-95, chmn., 1995—, Utah Shakespeare Festival, 1992—, Ogden C. of C., 1978-83; bd. dirs. Utah Opera Co., 1997—. 1st lt. USAF, 1959-62. Recipient Silver Antelope award Boy Scouts Am., 1976; recipient Silver Beaver award Boy Scouts Am., 1979, Silver Buffalo award Boy Scouts Am., 1982, Disting. Alumni award U. Utah, 1990. Mem. Nat. Assn. TV Broadcasters (bd. dirs.), Am. Mgmt. Assn. (award 1969), L.A. C. of C. (tax structure com. 1969-70), Salt Lake Area C. of C. (bd. dirs. 1985-88), SAR (pres. Utah chpt. 1986-87), Sons of Utah Pioneers, Freedoms Found. at Valley Forge (nat. bd. dirs. 1986—), L.A. Country Club, Ft. Douglas County Club, Alta Club, Rotary, Phi Kappa Phi, Tau Kappa Alpha, Beta Gamma Sigma. Mem. LDS Ch. (past pres. L.A. stake). Office: Deseret Mgmt Corp Eagle Gate Twr 60 E South Temple Ste 575 Salt Lake City UT 84111

BRADY, STEPHEN R.P.K., physician; b. New London, Conn., Oct. 13, 1955; s. Richard Harris and Jeanne Margaret (Halpin) B.; m. Marsha Anne Erickson, June 18, 1978 (div. Jan. 1993); 1 child, Ericka Anuhea; m. Elizabeth Ada Rewick, Dec. 27, 1994. AB cum laude, Harvard U., 1977; MPH, U. Hawaii, 1978, postgrad., 1979; MD, U. Pa., 1982. Intern U. Hawaii, 1982-83, resident, 1983-85; physician Kaiser Clinics, Honolulu, 1985-86; physician, med. dir. Kokua Kalihi Valley, Honolulu, 1986-89; clin. instr. Sch. Medicine U. Hawaii, Honolulu, 1986—, chair dept. continuing med. edn. Sch. Medicine, 1993—; physician Waianae (Hawaii) Coast Health Svc., 1989-94; asst. med. dir., physician Am. Hawaii Cruises, Honolulu, 1989—; physician Straub Clinic & Hosp., Honolulu, 1984—; founding chair Hawaii Consortium for Continuing Med. Edn. U. Hawaii Sch. of Medicine, 1993—. Host weekly Ask the Dr. program KHON-Fox 2 News, Hawaii, 1996—. Cubmaster Boy Scouts Am., Kailua, Hawaii, 1995—. Comdr. U.S. Merchant Marine, 1989—. Rsch. grantee Kuakini Med. Rsch. Inst., Honolulu, 1971, Pacific Health Rsch. Inst., Honolulu, 1972-78, Children's Hosp., Phila., 1979; Paul Harris fellow, 1995. Mem. AMA, Am. Coll. Physicians, Am. Soc. Internal Medicine, Am. Pub. Health Assn, Am. Statistical Assn., Hawaii Soc. Internal Medicine, Hawaii Med. Assn. (chair continuing med. edn. com. 1987—), Soc. Epidemiologic Rsch., Rotary, Soroptimiss (v.p. 1993—), Aumoana Cmty. Assn., (v.p. 1996—); Kaneohe Yacht Club, Plaza Club. Congregationalist. Home: Ste A #731 2357 S Beretania St Honolulu HI 96826-1413 Office: Straub Clinic & Hosp 888 S King St Honolulu HI 96813-3009

BRAGDON, LYNN LYON, library administrator; b. Kansas City, Mo., Dec. 22, 1944; d. Chester Willard and Frances Helen (Bechtold) Lyon; m. James Albert Bragdon, Jr., June 16, 1969. BS in Edn., Central Mo. State U., 1967; cert., U. Paris at Sorbonne, 1966; MLS, U. Okla., 1968. Rsch. libr. E.I. DuPont de Nemours, Wilmington, Del., 1968-72; asst. libr. North Cobb H.S., Marietta, Ga., 1972-74; head cataloging U. Miss. Med. Ctr., Jackson, 1975-76, assoc. dir. libr. ops., 1976-77; mgr. reference svcs. Miss. R & D Ctr., Jackson, 1977-79; chief libr. svc. VA Med. Ctr., Grand Junction, Colo., 1980-96, mgr. libr. sect., 1996—; mem. governing bd. Pathfinders Regional Libr. System, 1985—; mem. regional adv. com. Midcontinental Regional Med. Libr. Program, Omaha, 1988-92; mentor new chiefs libr. svc. Dept. Vets. Affairs, Washington, 1992—. Mem. Jr. Svc. League, Grand Junction,, 1984—, bd. dirs., 1986-94, sec., 1988-90, coord. park, 1991-94; active Western Colo. Mus., 1984—; asst. lay leader Meth. Ch., 1996—. Mem. Acad. Health Info. Profls. (sr.), Med. Libr. Assn., Colo. Coun. Med. Librs., Colo. Nat. Monument Assn. (v.p., bd. dirs. 1986-87, mem. bd. dirs. 1986-92), Grand Junction Gem and Mineral Soc. (libr. 1983), Western Colo. Botanic Soc. Methodist. Avocations: travelling, wildflower photography, cross-country skiing, music. Home: 610 Broken Spoke Rd Grand Junction CO 81504-5270 Office: Library 142D VA Med Ctr 2121 North Ave Grand Junction CO 81501-6428

BRAGG, ALBERT FORSEY, retired airline captain; b. Providence, Oct. 25, 1932; s. Horatio Frederick Roy and Olive Lavinia (Bardsley) B.; m. Anne Dana Bernard, Mar. 22, 1955 (div. 1977); children: Steven Keith, Gail Marie; m. Anita Bürki, Aug. 6, 1983. Student, Duke U., 1950-53. Lic. air transport pilot, flight engr., FAA, numerous ratings. First officer-capt. N.Y. Airways, Inc., N.Y.C., 1959-64; flight ops. instr. United Air Lines, Denver, 1964-65; flight engr. United Air Lines, Chgo., 1965-66; co-pilot United Air Lines, N.Y.C., Denver, 1967-83; capt. United Air Lines, 1983-92; check airman United Air Lines, Denver, 1984-85, 86-89, flight check mgr., 1985-86; internat. capt. United Air Lines, N.Y.C., 1991-92; aerospace edn. officer Civil Air Patrol, Boonton, N.J., 1972-74, Denver, 1974-79. Designer, builder dome for astronomic obs., Sheep Hill Obs., Boonton, N.J., 1973. Mem. sch. bd. Town of Boonton, 1972-75; active Colo. Motor Sports Coun. Comdr. USN, 1954-59. Recipient life saving award Civil Air Patrol, Denver, 1977, first place short take off contest Nat. Stearman Fly-In, Galesburg, Ill., 1992, 93, 94, 96. Mem. Exptl. Aircraft Assn. (safety lectr., tech. counselor Rocky Mountain Builder Forum, instr. Young Eagles program; v.p. chpt. 301 1995-97), Tail Hook Assn., Am. Navion Soc., Antique Aircraft Assn., Stearman Restorers Assn., Mercedes Benz Club (bd. dirs. 1989—, treas. 1992-94, pres. 1994—, Mem. of Yr. 1991, Otto Saborsky award 1994, Officer of Yr. 1996), Ret. United Pilots Assn. Republican. Home: 10695 W Rowland Ave Littleton CO 80127-2941

BRAGG, DARRELL BRENT, nutritionist, consultant; b. Sutton, W.Va., May 24, 1933; s. William H. and Gertrude (Perrine) B.; m. Elizabeth Hosse, Dec. 28, 1957; children: Roger, Larry, Teresa. BSc, W.Va. U., 1959, MSc, 1960; PhD, U. Ark., 1966. Instr. dept. animal sci. U. Ark., Fayetteville, 1965-67; asst. prof. U. Man., Winnipeg, Can., 1967-68, assoc. prof., 1968-70; assoc. prof. dept. poultry sci. U. B.C., Vancouver, Can., 1970-74, prof., head dept., 1975-86; industry cons., Vancouver, 1986-89; nutritionist, dir. quality assurance Rangen Aquaculture Feeds, Buhl, Idaho, 1990-92; sr. rsch. scientist Rangen Aquaculture Rsch. Ctr., Hagerman, Idaho, 1991-92; indsl. biochem. cons. Deutrel Labs. Inc., Palmdale, Calif., 1991—. Contbr. numerous articles to sci. jours. With U.S. Army, 1954-56. Recipient numerous rsch. grants from industry, univs. and govts. Mem. Poultry Sci. Assn. (nat. bd. dirs., v.p., pres. 1978-84), World Poultry Sci. Assn. (bd. dirs., v.p. 1975-86), Sigma Xi, numerous others. Home: PO Box 38 Payette ID 83661-0038

BRAIG, BETTY, artist, educator; b. Naylor, Mo., Apr. 21, 1932; d. Earnest R. and Polly A. (Tyson) Rideout; m. Russell C. Braig, July 27, 1951; 1 child, Rebecca L. AA, Phoenix Coll., 1964; BA, Ariz. State U., 1970, MA, 1973. Cert. elem. and secondary tchr., Ariz. Tchr. art, dir. gallery Phoenix Union High Sch. Dist., 1970—; mem. State Adv. Com. on Visual Arts, 1976; dir. gallery South Mountain Ctr. for the Arts, Phoenix, 1988—. One-woman shows in various galleries; exhibiting artist Levy Gallery, Scottsdale, Ariz., 1975—, Magadini Gallery, Scottsdale, 1980; May Gallery, Scottsdale, 1990, Carlson Gallery, 1992. Active Citizens Amb. Program, People to People, Internat., Russia, Czechslovakia, 1992. Recipient Asilomar Faculty award Watercolor West, David Gail award Western Fedn. Watercolor. Mem. Soc. Exptl. Art, Assn. Am. Watercolor Soc., Ariz. Artist Guild (officer 1978—, Grumbacher award), Ariz. Watercolor Assn. (officer 1975—, Travel Exhbn. award 1978, 80, 83), 22-30 Watercolor Ariz., Classroom Tchrs. Assn. Lutheran. Home and Studio: 5271 S Desert Willow Dr Gold Canyon AZ 85219

BRAITHWAITE, WALT WALDIMAN, aircraft manufacturing company executive; b. Kingston, Jamaica, Jan. 19, 1945; s. Ivanhoe Alexander and Ivy Mary (Green) B.; m. Edwina Gerell Patrick, Apr. 7, 1967 (div. March 1976); 1 child, Charlene Maria; m. Rita Cecelia Wood, May 4, 1974; children: Catherine Cecelia, Rachel Christine. BS in Electromech. Engring., Am. Inst. Engring. & Tech., Chgo., 1965; MS in Computer Sci., U. Wash., Seattle, 1975; SM in Mgmt., MIT, Cambridge, 1981. Cert. computer tech. Systems engr. engring. div. The Boeing Co., Renton, Wash., 1979-80; Sloan fellow MIT The Boeing Co., 1980-81; program mgr. bus. planning and commitments 7/7/7 div. The Boeing Co., Renton, Wash., 1981-82, mgr. CAD/CAM integration engring. div., 1982-83; dir. program tech. mgmt. Nat. Airspace Systems Co. div. Boeing/Lockheed, Kent, Wash., 1983-84; chief engr. CAD/CAM integration engring. div. The Boeing Co., Renton, Wash., 1984; chief engr. engring. ops. 747/767 div. The Boeing Co., Everett, Wash., 1984-85, dir. computing systems 747/767 div., 1985-86; dir. program mgmt. 707/737/757 div. The Boeing Co., Renton, 1986-91, v.p. info. systems Boeing Comml. Airplane Group, 1991—, v.p. info., support svcs., 1996—, v.p. co. offices adminstrn., 1997—; initial graphics exchange specification Nat. Bur. Standards, Calif., 1980. Author: Design and Implementation of Interpreters, 1978. Bd. dirs. City Art Works, Seattle, 1981-85. Recipient Joseph Marie Jacquare Meml. award Am. Inst. Mfg. Tech., Mass., 1987, leadership award Computer and Automated Systems Assn., Seattle, 1987, Black Achievers award YMCA, Seattle, 1990. Mem. Soc. Mfg. Engrs., Greater Renton C. of C. (pres. 1990-91), Boeing Mgmt. Assn. (pres. 1994, Black Engr. of Yr. 1995). Episcopalian. Office: The Boeing Co PO Box 3707 Seattle WA 98124-2207

BRAKHAGE, JAMES STANLEY, filmmaker, educator; b. Kansas City, Mo., Jan. 14, 1933; s. Ludwig and Clara (Dubberstein) B.; m. Mary Jane Collom, Dec. 28, 1957 (div. 1987); children: Myrrena, Crystal, Neowyn, Bearthm, Rarc; m. Marilyn Jull, Mar. 30, 1989; children: Anton, Vaughn. Ph.D., San Francisco Art Inst., 1981; Doctorate (hon.), Calif. Arts, 1994. Lectr. Sch. Art Inst. Chgo., 1969-81; prof. U. Colo., Boulder, 1981; mem. Filmmakers Coop., N.Y.C., Canyon Cinema Coop., San Francisco, London Filmmakers Coop., Can. Filmmakers' Distbn. Ctr., Toronto, Lightcome, Paris, France; Faculty lectr. U. Colo., 1990-91. Films include Interim, 1952, Anticipation of the Night, 1958, The Dead, 1960, Blue Moses, 1962, Dog Star Man, 1964, Songs in 8mm, 1964-69, Scenes from Under Childhood, 1967-70, The Weir Falcon Saga, 1970, The Act of Seeing with One's Own Eyes, 1971, The Riddle of Lumen, 1972, Sincerity and Duplicity, 1973-80, The Text of Light, 1974, Desert, 1976, The Governor, 1977, Burial Path, 1978, Nightmare Series, 1978, Creation, 1979, Made Manifest, 1980, Salome, 1980, Murder Psalm, 1980, Roman Numeral Series, 1979-81, the Arabic series, 1980-82, Unconscious London Strata, 1982, Tortured Dust, 1984, The Egyptian Series, 1984, The Loom, 1986, Nightmusic, 1986, The Dante Quartet, 1987, Faust, parts I-IV, 1987-89, Marilyn's Window, 1988, Visions in Meditation, 1989-90, City Streaming, 1990, Glaze of Cathexis, 1990, Babylonian Series, 1989-90, Passage Through: A Ritual, 1990, A Child's Garden and the Serious Sea, 1991, Delicacies of Molten Horror Synapse, 1991, Christ Mass Sex Dance, 1991, Crack Glass Eulogy, 1992, Boulder Blues and Pearls and For Marilyn, Interpolations 1-5, 1992, Blossom Gift Favor, The Harrowing, Tryst Haunt, Study in Color and Black and White, Stellar, Atumnal, 1993, Three Homerics, 1993, Naghts, Chartres Series, Ephemeral Solidity, Elementary Phrases, Black Ice, First Hymn to the Night—Novalis, 1994, In Consideration of Pompeii, 1994, The Mammals of Victoria, 1994, Paranoia Corridor, 1994, Can Not Exist, 1994, Can Not Not Exist, 1994, I Take These Truths, 1994, We Hold These, 1994, I..., 1995, Earthen Aerie, 1995, Spring Cycle, 1995, The Lost Films, 1995, The B Series, 1995, Preludes 1-6, 1995, The Fur of Home, 1996, Preludes 7-12, 1996, Preludes 13-18, 1996, Preludes, 19-24, 1996, Beautiful Funerals, 1996, Yggdrasill Whose Roots Are Stars in the Human Mind, 1997; author: Metaphors on Vision, 1963, A Moving Picture Giving and Taking Book, 1971, The Brakhage Lectures, 1972, Seen, 1975, Film Biographies, 1977, Brakhage Scrapbook, 1982, Film at Wits End, 1989, I...Sleeping, 1989. Recipient Brussels Worlds Fair Protest award, 1958, Brandeis citation, 1973, Colo. Gov.'s award for arts and humanities, 1974, Jimmy Ryan Morris Meml. Found. award, 1979, Telluride Film Festival medallion, 1981, Maya Deren award Am. Film Inst., 1986, medal U. Colo., 1988, Outstanding Achievement award Denver Internat. Film Festival, 1988, MacDowell medal, 1989, Libr. Congress Nat. Film Registry, 1992, Anthology Film Archives honor, 1993, The Colo. 100 Cert. of Recognition, 1993, Disting. Prof. award U. Colo., 1994; retrospective Mus. Modern Art, 1995; grantee Avon Found., 1965-69, NEA, 1974-75, 77, 80, 83, 88, U. Colo. Coun. Rsch. and Creative Work, 1983, Rocky Mountain Film Ctr., 1985; Rockefeller fellow, 1967-69, Guggenheim fellow, 1978. Democrat. Home: 2142 Canyon Blvd Apt 203 Boulder CO 80302-4517 Office: U Colo Film Studies Hunter 102 Campus Box 316 Boulder CO 80309

BRALEY, JEAN (J. MCNEIL SARGENT), artist, educator; b. North Wilkesboro, N.C., 1925; d. Sargent Duffield and Agnes A. Student, Sch. Profl. Art, N.Y.C., 1942-45, Art Students League, 1957, La Reparata Graphic Ctr., Florence, Italy, 1975, Pratt Graphic Ctr., N.Y.C., 1976. Dir. Atelier for Calif. Printmakers; instr. art C.C. San Diego, Mira Costa Coll., Oceanside, Calif., Corcoran Mus., Washington; cons. Calif. Art Commn.; founder, 1st pres. Artists Equity Assn. San Francisco; comml. illustrator, N.Y.C. and Washngton. Exhibited in one-person shows at Yogesh Gallery, Bombay, Spectrum Gallery, San Diego, Prestige Gallery, Boston, Riverside (Calif.) Mus., The Gallery, Washington, others; mus. shows include Long Beach (Calif.) Mus., Palm Springs Desert Mus., San Diego Mus., Palace of Fine Arts, Mexico City, Smithsonian Inst., Washington, De Young Mus., San Francisco; group exhbns. include Art Nold, Nice, France, Galerie Cezanne, Laguna Beach, Calif., Plaza Gallery, N.Y.C., Agra Gallery, Washington;. Recipient awards San Diego Art Inst., S.W. Annual Art Festival, Washington, Fairfax (Va.) Art Ann., Ajax Nat. Art Exhibit, numerous others. Mem. Nat. Assn. Women Artists. Address: 12245 Carmel Vista Rd Apt 193 San Diego CA 92130-2532

BRAMAN, DONALD WILLIAM, public relations consultant; b. Mpls., June 19, 1917; s. Maurice I. and Ida (Garber) B.; m. Sally Davidson, June 16, 1946; children: Stuart, Sandra, Richard. BA cum laude, U. Minn., 1937. With Mpls. Star, 1937-41; dir. public relations Manson-Gold Advt. Agy., Mpls., 1946-47; public relations staff, publs. editor Toni Co., St. Paul, 1947-49; assoc. dir. public relations Olmsted & Foley, Mpls., 1950-58; co-founder, pres. Don Braman & Assos., Inc., Mpls., 1958-77; v.p. Doremus & Co., N.Y.C. 1977-82; pub. relations cons., 1982—; cons. Internat. Exec. Service Corps., Service Corps Retired Execs.; teaching asst., lectr. Sch. Journalism U. Minn.; dir. Minn. Advt. Fedn. Chmn. Mayor's Com. for Employment of Handicapped, 1950's; chmn. Mpls. Symphony Orchestra Guaranty Fund Campaign, 1960's; fin. com. Mpls. LWV, 1970's; dir. Am.-Israel Chamber of Commerce & Industry of Minn., 1980's; bd. dirs. Keep Sedona Beautiful. Served with USMC, 1941-45. Mem. Public Relations Soc. Am. (dir., pres. Minn. chpt., mem. exec. com. counselors acad., Disting. Service award 1973, accredited fellow), Nat. Investor Rels. Inst. (dir., pres. Minn. chpt.), Mpls. Area C. of C. (chmn. coms. various dates), Marine Corps Combat Correspondents Assn., Nat. Audubon Soc., Ariz. Archeol. Soc., Masons, Scottish Rite, Shrine, Zeta Beta Tau. Contbr. articles in field to profl. publs., travel articles to popular publs. Home and Office: 1865 Gun Fury Rd Sedona AZ 86336-3948

BRAME, MARILLYN A., hypnotherapist; b. Indpls., Sept. 17, 1928; d. David Schwalb and Hilda (Riley) Curtin; 1 child, Gary Mansour. Student, Meinzinger Art Sch., Detroit, 1946-47, U. N.Mex., 1963, Orlando (Fla.) Jr. Coll., 1964-65, El Camino Coll., Torrance, Calif., 1974-75; PhD in Hypnotherapy, Am. Inst. Hypnotherapy, 1989. Cert. and registered hypnotherapist. Color cons. Pitts. Plate Glass Co., Albuquerque, 1951-52; owner Signs by Marillyn, Albuquerque, 1952-53; design draftsman Sandia Corp., Albuquerque, 1953-56; designer The Martin Co., Orlando, 1957-65; pres. The Arts, Winter Park, Fla., 1964-66; supr. tech. publs. Gen. Instrument Corp., Hawthorne, Calif., 1967-76; pres. Camart Design, Westminster, Calif., 1977-86, Visual Arts, El Toro, Calif., 1978—; mgr. tech. publs. Archive Corp., Costa Mesa, Calif., 1986-90; adj. instr. Orange Coast Coll., Costa Mesa, 1985-90; hypnotherapist, Lake Forest, 1986—; bd. dirs. Orange County chpt. Am. Bd. Hypnotherapy. Author: Lemon and Lime Scented Herbs, 1994, (textbook) Folkdancing is for Everybody, 1974, Innovative Imagery, 1996, Changing Your Mood, 1997; inventor, designer dance notation sys. MS Method. Mem. bd. govs. Lake Forest II Showboaters Theater Group, 1985-88, 90-95; mem. cultural arts com. City of Mission Viejo, 1995—. Mem. Soc. Tech. Communication (v.p. programs, 1987, newsletter editor 1986-87, newsletter prodn. editor 1985-86).

BRANCH, ANNE HEATHER, fund raiser; b. Fresno, Calif., Feb. 7, 1960; d. John Donald and Laurie Anne McFeeters; m. Kelly Christopher Branch, Dec. 23, 1987; children: Patrick Simpson, Spenser Morse. BA, U. So. Calif., L.A., 1982, cert. in bus. planning, 1989; M in Internat. Bus. Adminstrn., Monterey Inst. Internat. Study, 1984. Sales mgr. Hyatt Hotels, Inc., Washington, 1985-87; assoc. dir. devel. U. So. Calif., L.A., 1987-91; dir. devel. The Heart Inst., L.A., 1991-93, Northridge Hosp. Found., L.A., 1993-94; asst. dir. devel. Braille Inst. Am., Inc., L.A., 1995-96; Hathaway Children Family Svc., 1996—; pro-bono cons. Jonathan Art Found., L.A., Cmty. Counseling Svc., L.A., World Children's Transplant Fund, L.A. Recipient scholarship to attend nat. conf. Assn. Hosp. Devel., 1993, commendation U. So. Calif. Annenberg Sch. Comm., L.A., 1995. Mem. Nat. Soc. Fund Raising Execs., Nat. Com. on Planned Giving, Planned Giving Roundtable So. Calif. (scholarship to nat. conf. 1985). Office: 8955 Gold Creek Rd Sylmar CA 91342

BRANCH, MICHAEL PAUL, humanities educator; b. Wyandotte, Mich., Dec. 6, 1963; s. Stuart Elton and Sharon Eileen (Shuck) B. BA in English, Coll. William and Mary, 1985; MA in English, U. Va., 1987, PhD of English, 1993. Tchr. U. Va., Charlottesville, 1986-93; asst. prof. English Fla. Internat. U., Miami, 1993-95; asst. prof. lit. and environment U. Nev., Reno, 1995-96, assoc. prof. lit. and environment, 1997—; pres. Assn. for Study of Lit. and Environment, 1995-96. Book rev. editor Interdisciplinary Studies in Lit. and Environment, 1996-98; assoc. editor Am. Nature Writing Newsletter, 1993-95; contbr. articles to profl. jours. Fellow State Coun. Higher Edn., 1988, 90; grantee Knapp Found., 1994. Mem. Modern Lang. Assn., Am. Lit. Assn., Am. Soc. Environ. History, Soc. Early Americanists, We. Lit. Assn., Sierra Club, Wilderness Soc., Wild Earth, Orion Soc., Phi Beta Kappa. Office: Univ Nevada Dept English 098 Reno NV 89557

BRANCH, TAYLOR, writer; b. Atlanta, Jan. 14, 1947; s. Franklin T. and Jane (Worthington) B.; m. Christina Macy; 2 children. AB, U. N.C., 1968; postgrad., Princeton U., 1968-70. Staff member Washington Monthly mag., Washington, D.C., 1970-73, Harper's mag., N.Y.C., 1973-75, Esquire mag., N.Y.C., 1975-76. Author: (with Bill Russell) Second Wind: The Memoirs of an Opinionated Man, 1979, The Empire Blues, 1981, (with Eugene M. Propper) Labyrinth, 1982, Parting the Waters: America in the King Years, 1954-63, 1988 (Pulitzer Prize for history 1989, Nat. Book Critics Circle award for non-fiction 1988, Christopher award 1988, Nat. Book award nomination 1989); editor, contbr.: (with Charles Peters) Blowing the Whistle: Dissent in the Public Interest, 1972. Office: Diskant & Assocs 116 E De La Guerra St # 7 Santa Barbara CA 93101-2205*

BRAND, GERHARD, retired English educator; b. Vienna, Austria, Aug. 18, 1927; came to U.S., 1939; s. Leo and Gertrude (Scharf) B.; m. Alice Mary Godfrey, Aug. 25, 1962 (div. May 1973); children: Madeleine, Rachel; m. Ann Kempe Lodwig, Nov. 26, 1983. BA, Trinity Coll., Hartford, Conn., 1949; MA, UCLA, 1953, PhD, 1969. Instr. Cornell U., Ithaca, N.Y., 1957-60; prof. Calif. State U., L.A., 1960-92. Contbr. articles to profl. jours. With U.S. Army, 1953-54. Democrat. Home: 2589 Magnolia Blvd W Seattle WA 98199

BRAND, LARRY MILTON, biochemist; b. Mpls., Sept. 18, 1949; s. Arthur Leonard and Raleigh (Murphy) B.; m. Regina Fenster, Jan. 27, 1974; children: Ilana Michele, Sarah Eve, Alicia Leah. BS magna cum laude, U. Minn., 1971; PhD, U. Wis., 1975. NIH rsch. fellow Brandeis U., Waltham, Mass., 1975-77; rsch. biochemist Procter and Gamble Co., Cin., 1977-81, head sect. toxicology, 1981-83, head sect. inflammation, 1983-85, assoc. dir. R&D, 1985-90, assoc. dir. licensing and acquisitions, 1990-95; sr. licensing mgr. U. Calif., San Diego, 1995—. Contbr. articles to Biochemistry, Agents and Actions, other jours. Babcock fellow U. Wis., 1972; recipient Nat. Rsch. Svc. award NIH, 1976. Mem. Am. Coll. Toxicology, Assn. Chemoreception Scis., Inflammation Rsch. Assn., Licensing Execs. Soc., Am. Assn. Pharm. Scientists (charter), Phi Lambda Upsilon. Jewish. Home: 3598 Wellesly Ave San Diego CA 92122-2341 Office: U Calif 9500 Gilman La Jolla CA 92093-0910

BRANDENBURG, CARLOS HENRY, clinical psychologist; b. Crisobal Colon, Panama, May 17, 1948; s. James Gilbert and Aura Raquel (Mayorga) B.; 1 child, Frank. BA, U. Nev., Las Vegas, 1969, MA, 1971; PhD, U. Nev., Reno, 1975. Psychologist Lakes Crossing Ctr., Sparks, Nev., 1975-78; dir. Forensic Svcs., Sparks, 1978-95; adminstr. Divsn. Mental Hygiene and Mental Retardation, Carson City, Nev., 1995—; mental health cons. Sierra Nevada Corp., 1978-84. Bd. dirs. Juvenile Justice Com., Reno, 1991—; mem. Criminal Justice Com., Reno, 1992—; mem. United Way, Reno, 1991—. Recipient Leadership award NAMI, 1996, Am. Bd. Mental Health, 1996. Mem. APA, Internat. Coun. Psychologists, Am. Soc. Clin. Psychologists. Democrat. Roman Catholic. Home: 7390 Pinehurst Reno NV 89502 Office: Divsn MH/MR 505 E King St Carson City NV 89710

BRANDES, STANLEY HOWARD, anthropology educator, writer; b. N.Y.C., Dec. 26, 1942; s. Emanuel Robert and Annette (Zalisch) B.; divorced; children: Nina Rachel, Naomi Carla. BA, U. Chgo., 1964; MA, U. Calif., Berkeley, 1969, PhD, 1971. Asst. prof. anthropology Mich. State U., East Lansing, 1971-75; asst. prof. anthropology U. Calif., Berkeley, 1975-78, assoc. prof., 1978-82, prof. anthropology, 1982—, chmn. dept., 1990-93; dir. Barcelona Study Ctr., U. Calif. and Ill., Spain, 1981-82, Mexico City Study Ctr., 1995—, U. Calif. Author: Migration, Kinship and Community, 1975, Metaphors of Masculinity, 1980, Forty: The Age and the Symbol, 1985, Power and Persuasion, 1988; co-editor: Symbol as Sense, 1980. NIH fellow, 1967-71; NICHD Rsch. fellow, 1975-77; fellow John Carter Brown Libr., 1994; Am. Council Learned Socs. grantee, 1977. Fellow Am. Anthrop. Assn.; mem. Am. Ethnological Soc., Soc. for Psychol. Anthropology. Office: U Calif Dept Anthropology Berkeley CA 94720

BRANDMEIR, CHRISTOPHER LEE, hospitality and food service consultant; b. Seattle, Mar. 6, 1950; s. Jack W. and Betty G. (Lyman) B. BA, U. San Francisco, 1972. Dir. coll. rels. Cogswell Coll., San Francisco, 1983-86; exec. dir. San Lorenzo (Calif.) Village, 1986-88; owner Inn Sight, Seattle, 1996—; pres., co-owner HBH Mgmt., Lopez Island, Wash., 1993-96, Inn at Swifts Bay, Lopez Island, Wash., 1988-96. Chair San Juan Islands Tourism Resource Coun.; bd. dirs., past chair San Juan Islands Visitor Info. Svc.; bd. dirs., fundraiser Lopez Island Cmty. Ctr.; pres. Lopez Island Chamber. Recipient Lyons Club Svc. award. Mem. Internat. Assn. Culinary Profls. Republican. Roman Catholic. Home and Office: 2415 2nd Ave #737 Seattle WA 98121

BRANDON, GARY KENT, physician, health facility administrator; b. Pueblo, Colo.; s. Vernon Charles and Eva M. (Hachey) B.; m. D.J. Harris, May 21, 1976; children: Terry, Belinda, John, Tracye, Sherry, Kimberly. BA, U. So. Colo., 1968; MS, N.Mex. Highlands U., 1969; DO, U. Health Scis., 1973; MPH, Johns Hopkins U., 1979; postgrad., Nat. War Coll., 1989-90. Diplomate Am. Bd. Preventive Medicine, Am. Bd. Med. Mgmt. Intern Lake Side Hosp., Kansas City, Mo., 1973-74; resident Johns Hopkins, 1978-79, USAF Sch. Aerospace Medicine, 1979-80; commd. capt. USAF, 1976, advanced through grades to col., 1986; hosp. comdr. Barksdale AFB, Shreveport, La., 1987-89, MacDill AFB, Tampa, Fla., 1990-93; dir. med. inspection USAF, Albuquerque, 1993-95; ret. USAF, 1995; med. dir. Valley Wide Health Svc., Alamosa, Colo., 1995—; sr. examiner Malcolm Baldridge Nat. Quality Award, Washington, 1993-96. Author: Aviation, Space and Environmental Medicine, 1980, co-author 2d edit., 1983. V.p. Rocky Mountain HMO, Grand Junction, Colo., 1975, Western Colo. Physicians, Inc., Grand Junction, 1975; pres. Mesa County Osteo. Assn., Grand Junction, 1976. Recipient Med. Leadership award Strategic Air Command USAF, Aboline, Tex., 1986, USAF award for profl. excellence, Washington, 1994. Fellow Am. Coll. Preventive Medicine; mem. APHA, Am. Coll. Occupl. and Environ. Medicine, Am. Soc. Quality Control, Nat. Assn. Managed Care Physicians. Home: 778 23rd Rd Grand Junction CO 81505

BRANDON, KATHRYN ELIZABETH BECK, pediatrician; b. Salt Lake City, Sept. 10, 1916; d. Clarence M. and Hazel A. (Cutler) Beck; MD, U. Chgo., 1941; BA, U. Utah, 1937; MPH, U. Calif., Berkeley, 1957; children: John William, Kathleen Brandon McEnulty, Karen (dec.). Intern, Grace Hosp., Detroit, 1941-42; resident Children's Hosp. Med. Center No. Calif., Oakland, 1953-55, Children's Hosp., L.A., 1951-53; pvt. practice, La Crescentia, Calif., 1946-51, Salt Lake City, 1960-65, 86—; med. dir. Salt Lake City public schs., 1957-60; dir. Ogden City-Weber County (Utah) Health Dept., 1965-67; pediatrician Fitzsimmons Army Hosp., 1967-68; coll. health physician U. Colo., Boulder, 1968-71; student health physician U. Utah, Salt Lake City, 1971-81; occupational health physician Hill AFB, Utah, 1981-85; child health physician Salt Lake City-County Health Dept., 1971-82; cons. in field; clin. asst. U. Utah Coll. Medicine, Salt Lake City, 1958-64; clin. asst. pediatrics U. Colo. Coll. Medicine, Denver, 1958-72; active staff emeritus Primary Children's Hosp., LDS Hosp., and Cottonwood Hosp., 1960-67. Diplomate Am. Bd. Pediatrics. Fellow Am. Pediatric Acad., Am. Pub. Health Assn., Am. Sch. Health Assn.; mem. Utah Coll. Health Assn. (pres. 1978-80), Pacific Coast Coll. Health Assn., AMA, Utah Med. Assn., Salt Lake County Med. Soc., Utah Public Health Assn. (sec.-treas. 1960-66), Intermountain Pediatric Soc. Home and Office: PO Box 58482 Salt Lake City UT 84158-0482

BRANDON, MICHAEL JAMES, legislative aide; b. King City, Calif., July 13, 1968; s. James Ross and Judith Ann (Jeffrey) B. BA in Philosophy, Calif. State U., Fresno, 1991, MA in Internat. Rels., 1994. Advisor internat. rels. Sho Ei Kan, Nagoya, Japan, 1991-92; rsch. assoc. U.S. Senator Dianne Feinstein, San Francisco, 1994—. Mem. adv. bd. Pacifica Radio KPFA, Berkeley, Calif., 1996—. Mem. Am. Polit. Sci. Assn., Am. Philos. Assn., Assn. Asian Studies, Internat. Studies Assn. Home: 10096 N Fowler Ave Clovis CA 93611 Office: US Senator Dianne Feinstein 525 Market St Ste 3670 San Francisco CA 94105

BRANDT, ALAN ERWIN, insect biotechnology company executive, consultant; b. Norfolk, Va., Jan. 13, 1944; s. Erwin L. and Ruth I. (Prescott) B.; m. Susan J. Rapport, June 10, 1983; 1 child, Aaron E. BS in Chemistry, U. Mich., 1966, PhD in Biochemistry, 1971. Postdoctoral fellow U. Calif., Davis, 1972-73; sr. biochemist SRI Internat., Menlo Park, Calif., 1973-86; pres., CEO, Growth Source, Woodside, Calif., 1985—; chmn., CEO, Insect Biotech., Redwood City, Calif., 1992—. Contbr. articles to sci. jours.; patentee in field. Mem. Nat. Ski Patrol, San Francisco Peninsula, 1981—, patrol dir., 1988-90, sect. chief Bay Area region, 1992-94. Grantee NIH, 1981. Mem. Am. Chem. Soc.

BRANDT, BEVERLY KAY, design educator; b. Evanston, Ill., Aug. 26, 1951; d. Richard Charles Brandt and Edith Elaine (Uhrenholdt) Littler. BFA, U. Mich., 1973; MA, Mich. State U., 1977; PhD, Boston U., 1985. Cert. designer Nat. Coun. Interior Design Qualification. Asst. prof. Iowa State U., Ames, 1984-87; asst. prof. Ariz. State U., Tempe, 1987-92, assoc. prof., 1992—, dir., 1992-95; cons. Phoenix Art Mus., 1993; dir.-at-large Ariz. Design Inst., Tempe, 1992-93. Book reviewer; author (chpts.) Encyclopedia of Arts and Crafts, 1989, The Ideal Home, 1993, Innovation and Derivation, 1995, The Substance of Style, 1996, Inspiring Reform, 1997; contbr. articles to profl. jours. Wakonse fellow, 1992—, Lincoln Ctr. fellow, 1996—; recipient Faculty Achievement award Burlington Resources Found., 1991, Rsch. citation Progressive Architecture, 1995; Travel-to-Collections grantee NEH, 1985-86, Attingham grantee-in-aid Am. Soc. Interior Designers, 1987. Mem. AAUW, Decorative Arts Soc., Furniture History Soc., Nat. Trust for Hist. Preservation, Soc. Archtl. Historians, Internat. Interior Design Assn., William Morris Soc., Victorian Soc. Am., Kappa Omicron Nu. Office: Arizona State U Sch of Design PO Box 872105 Tempe AZ 85287-2105

BRANDT, IRA KIVE, pediatrician, medical geneticist; b. N.Y.C., Nov. 9, 1923; s. Charles Zachary and Hilda Eleanor (Moss) B.; m. Dorothy Godfrey, Nov. 26, 1947; children—Elizabeth, Laura, William, Rena. A.B., NYU, 1942; M.D., Columbia U., 1945. Diplomate Am. Bd. Pediatrics, Am. Bd. Med. Genetics. Intern Morrisania City Hosp., N.Y.C., 1945-46; resident Lincoln Hosp., N.Y.C., 1948-50; fellow pediatrics Yale U., New Haven, 1955-57, asst. prof., 1957-61, assoc. prof., 1961-68; chmn. dept. pediatrics Children's Hosp., San Francisco, 1968-70; clin. prof. pediatrics U. Calif., San Francisco, 1970; prof. pediatrics and med. genetics Ind. U. Sch. Medicine, Indpls., 1970-89, prof. emeritus, 1989—. Served to capt. U.S. Army, 1946-47, 52. Mem. Am. Pediatric Soc., Am. Acad. Pediatrics, Soc. Pediatric Rsch., Soc. Inherited Metabolic Disorders, Am. Soc. Human Genetics, Am. Coll. Med. Genetics. Office: Ind U Sch Medicine Dept Pediatrics 702 Barnhill Dr # 0907 Indianapolis IN 46202-5128

BRANDT, MARYCLARE, interior designer, educator; b. Winona, Minn., Aug. 30, 1950; 1 child, Laran Clare. Student, Academie DePort Royal, Paris, France, 1970-71; BA in Art, Coll. St. Teresa, Winona, 1972; MA in Interior Design, Kans. State U., 1976. Cert. interior designer, Calif. V.p., designer Environ. Concepts, San Marcos, Tex., 1980-86; owner, designer M.C. Brandt, La Jolla, Calif., 1986—; instr. S.W. Tex. State U., San Marcos, 1985-86, U. Calif., San Diego, 1990-93. Works have appeared in numerous mags. including Austin Homes and Gardens, Designer Mag., Better Homes and Gardens. Mem. Am. Soc. Interior Designers (bd. dirs. 1988-90, 94—, Outstanding Design award 1990, 1st place award 1990, 3rd place award 1994). Office: MC Brandt Interior Design PO Box 8276 La Jolla CA 92038-8276

BRANDWAJN, ALEXANDRE, software company executive; b. Hohne, Fed. Republic of Germany, Apr. 13, 1948; came to U.S., 1978; s. Rachmiel and Liba (Goldziuk) B.; m. Marlene Francette Chabbat, May 22, 1974; children: Elise Sophie, Xavier Marc. Telecommunications Engring. Diploma, ENST, Paris, 1971; D of Engring., U. Paris, 1972, BA in Lit., 1973, Docteur d'Etat, 1975. Researcher Inst. Rsch. Automatique and Informatique, Rocquencourt, France, 1971-75; prof. computer sci. Ecole Nat. Superieure des Telecommunications, Paris, 1975-79; sr. computer architect Amdahl Corp., Sunnyvale, Calif., 1979-82, mgr. performance analysis, 1982-85; pres. Pallas Internat. Corp., San Jose, Calif., 1983—; prof. computer engring. U. Calif., Santa Cruz, 1985—; cons. UCCEL Corp., Dallas, 1986-87, MCC, Austin, Tex., 1986-87, Amdahl Corp., Sunnyvale, 1985—. Contbr. articles to profl. jours. Mem. Assn. for Computing Machinery, Computer Measurement Group. Office: Pallas Internat Corp 1744 Maysong Ct San Jose CA 95131

BRANKOVICH, MARK J., restaurateur; b. Rijeka, Yugoslavia, Mar. 4, 1922; came to U.S., 1951; s. Joseph M. and Rose (Haydin) B.; m. Marilyn J. Severin, Jan. 4, 1957; children: Mark, Laura. BA in Philosophy, U. Zurich, 1944; student, U. Geneva, 1945, U. Padua, Italy, 1947. Owner The Golden Deer, Chgo., 1953-55; mgr. Gaslight Club, N.Y.C., 1955-57; gen. mgr., exec. v.p., dir. Gaslight Club, Chgo., 1959-63; owner, mgr. Franchise Gaslight Club, L.A., 1963-66; owner Monte Carlo Italian Deli, Burbank, Calif., 1969—, Pinocchio Restaurant, Burbank, 1970—, Pinocchio West, Santa Monica, 1972—, Pinocchio Westwood (Calif.), 1978, Italia Foods Wholesale, Burbank, 1972. Mem. Presdl. Task Force, Washington, 1980—, Rep. Senatorial Inner Circle, 1986. Mem. Internat. Platform Assn. Serbian Orthodox. Home: 1250 Hilldale Ave West Hollywood CA 90069-1826 Office: Monte Carlo Italia Foods Inc 3103 W Magnolia Blvd Burbank CA 91505-3046

BRANN, ALTON JOSEPH, oil field services executive; b. Portland, Maine, Dec. 23, 1941; s. Donald Edward and Marjorie Margaret (Curran) B. B.A., U. Mass., 1969. Mgr. advanced programs Dynamics Research Corp., Wilmington, Mass., 1969-73; dir. engring. Litton Guidance & Control Systems, L.A., 1973-79, dir. program mgmt., 1979-81, v.p. engring., 1981-83, pres., 1983-86; group exec. Navigation Guidance and Control Systems Group, Beverly Hills, Calif., 1986-88; sr. v.p. Components and Indsl. Products Group Litton Industries, Beverly Hills, 1988-90, pres., COO, 1990-92, CEO, 1992-94, chmn., 1994-96; chmn., CEO Western Atlas Inc., Beverly Hills, 1994—; trustee Mfrs. Alliance Productivity and Innovation, coun. fgn. diplomacy, U.S.-Russia bus. coun. Mem. IEEE (sr. mem.), Soc. Petroleum Engrs., Optical Soc. Am., L.A. World Affairs Coun., Town Hall of L.A. Office: Western Atlas Inc 360 N Crescent Dr Beverly Hills CA 90210-4802*

BRANNEN, JEFFREY RICHARD, lawyer; b. Tampa, Fla., Aug. 27, 1945; s. Jackson Edward and Tobiah M. (Lovitz) B.; m. Mary Elizabeth Strand, Nov. 24, 1972; 1 child, Samuel Jackson. BA in English, U. N.Mex., 1967, JD, 1970. Bar: N.Mex. 1970, U.S. Dist. Ct. N.Mex. 1970, U.S. Ct. Appeals (10th cir.) 1976, U.S. Supreme Ct. 1978. Law clk. N.Mex. State Supreme Ct., Santa Fe, 1970-71; from assoc. to pres., shareholder Montgomery & Andrews, pa, Santa Fe, 1972-93; pres. Jeffrey R. Brannen, P.A., Santa Fe, 1993—; with Carpenter, Comeau, Maldegan, Nixon & Templeman, Santa Fe; faculty Nat. Inst. Trial Advocacy, Hastings Ctr. for Trial & Appellate Advocacy, 1980-93; co-chmn. Pers. Injury Inst., Hastings, 1992. Mem. ABA, Am. Bd. Trial Advocates, Assn. Def. Trial Attys. (state chmn. 1992—), Def. Rsch. Inst. (Exceptional Performance Citation 1989), N.Mex. Def. Lawyers Assn. (pres. 1989). Democrat. Office: Carpenter Comeau et al 141 E Palace Ave Santa Fe NM 87501-2041

BRANSBY, ERIC JAMES, muralist, educator; b. Auburn, N.Y., Oct. 25, 1916; s. Charles Carson and Lillian Holland (Dowsett) B.; m. Mary Antoinette Hemmie, Nov. 23, 1941; 1 dau., Fredericka Jo. Profl. cert., Kansas City Art Inst., 1938-42; BA, Colo. Coll., 1947, MA, 1949; MFA, Yale U., 1952; DFA (hon.), Park Coll., 1995; DHL (hon.), U. Colo., 1997. Instr. U. Ill., Urbana, 1950-52; asst. prof. art Western Ill. U., Macomb, 1963-65; assoc. prof. art U. Mo., Kansas City, 1965-70; prof. U. Mo., 1970—; authority on history and theory of mural painting. One-man shows include, Okla. Art Center, Oklahoma City, 1973, U. Mo., Kansas City, 1971, 77, Denver U., 1966, Brigham Young U., 1966, Colorado Springs (Colo.) Fine Arts Center, 1968, U. Mo., Columbia, 1979, Loveland Musuem, Loveland, Co, 1989; Pikes Peak Ctr., Colorado Springs, 1995, 50 yrs. retrospective (incl. spouse). nat. and internat. group shows, murals include, U.S. Command and Gen. Staff Sch., 1945, Mech. Engring. Bldg., U. Ill., 1953, NORAD Hdqrs., Colorado Springs, 1956, Brigham Young U., 1958, Mcpl. Bldg., Liberty, Mo., 1982 (Nat. Mural Competition award), Luth. Ch., Mo. Synod, Internat. Ctr., St. Louis, 1983 (Nat. Mural Competition award), planetarium, USAF Acad., Colorado Springs, 1961-70, Western Ill. U., Macomb, 1965, Rockhurst Coll., Kansas City, 1968, F.D. Roosevelt Meml. Competition, 1961, HUD Nat. Community Art Competition, 1974, U. Mo., Kansas City, 1973-75, Mcpl. Bldg., Sedalia, Mo., 1977, Kans. State Capitol Nat. Mural Competition, 1978, St. Paul Sch., Chgo., 1985, Colo. Springs Fine Arts Ctr., 1986, Kans. State U., 1986, Loveland (Colo.) Mus., 1988, Park Coll., Kansas City, 1991, City of Colorado Springs (Colo.) Mus., 1994, Colo. Springs Mcpl. Airport, 1996; contbr. chpt. to book; producer of video tapes in field; represented in permanent collections; pub. Art Do-It. Served with inf. AUS, 1942-45. Edwin Austin Abbey Found. mural painting fellow, 1952; grantee applied and theoretical studies in mural painting field U.S., Turkey, Mex., Italy; recipient Veatch award U. Mo., 1977. Mem. Nat. Soc. Mural Painters, Phi Kappa Phi. Home: 9080 S State Highway 115 Colorado Springs CO 80926-9716 Office: Univ Mo Dept Art Kansas City MO 64110
At the center of my personal direction in art is the belief that it belongs in the public environment, performing a socio-cultural function. Corollary to this is the belief that a great number of the highest achievements in art are represented by those works attaining a complex but successful synthesis with architecture.

BRANSCOMB HARMON, HAZEL MARIE, training specialist, consultant; b. Chgo., Mar. 5, 1942; d. John Henry Branscomb and Marion (Yeager) Webb; children: Kenneth Ivan, William Cornell, David Lamarr Harmon. BS, U. Calif., Davis, 1984. Cert. grantmanship and proposal writing. Project coord. Dept. Food/Agr., Sacramento, 1983-85; tchr. exptl. coll. U. Calif., Davis, 1990-92; exec. cons. S.E.M. Cons., Beaverton, Oreg.; tng. cons. north campus Portland (Oreg.) C.C., 1992—. Author: (instrnl. books) Proposal Writing Work Book, 1995, Communication Skills/Techniques, 1995. Mem. AAUW, Am. Assn. Women in C.C., U. Calif.-Davis Aggie Alumni Assn. Office: S E M Cons 14720 SW Grayling Ln Beaverton OR 97007-3673

BRANSON, ALBERT HAROLD (HARRY BRANSON), magistrate judge, educator; b. Chgo., May 20, 1935; s. Fred Brooks and Marie (Vowell) B.; m. Siri-Anne Gudrun Lindberg, Nov. 2, 1963; children: Gunnar John, Gulliver Dean, Hanna Marie, Siri Elizabeth. BA, Northwestern U., 1957; JD, U. Chgo., 1963. Bar: Pa. 1965, Alaska 1972. Atty. Richard McVeigh law offices, Anchorage, 1972-73; ptnr. Jacobs, Branson & Guetschow, Anchorage, 1973-76, Branson & Guetschow, Anchorage, 1976-82; pvt. practice Law Offices of Harry Branson, Anchorage, 1982-84, 85-89; atty. Branson, Bazeley & Chisolm, Anchorage, 1984-85; U.S. magistrate judge U.S. Dist. Ct., Anchorage, 1989—; instr., adj. prof. U. Alaska Justice Ctr., 1980-93; U.S. magistrate, Anchorage, 1975-76. With U.S. Army, 1957-59. Mem. Alaska Bar Assn. (bd. dirs., v.p. bd. govs. 1977-80, 83-86, pres. bd. govs. 1986, Disting. Svc. award 1992, Spl. Svc. award 1988, editor-in-chief Alaska Bar Rag 1978-86), Anchorage Bar Assn. (bd. dirs., bd. govs. 1982-86), Anchorage Inn of Ct. (pres. 1995). Democrat. Office: US Dist Ct 222 W 7th Ave Unit 33 Anchorage AK 99513-7504

BRANSON, HARLEY KENNETH, finance executive, motion picture producer; b. Ukiah, Calif., June 10, 1942; s. Harley Edward and Clara Lucile B.; 1 child, Erik Jordan. BS in Acctg. and Fin., San Jose State U., 1965; JD, Santa Clara U., 1968. Bar: Calif. 1969. Law clk. to judge U.S. Ct. Appeals (9th cir.), San Diego, 1968-69; pvt. practice San Diego, 1969-78; div. counsel Ralston Purina Co., San Diego, 1978-83; group gen. counsel Castle & Cooke, Inc., San Diego, 1983-85; exec. v.p., gen. counsel, corp. sec., bd. dirs. Bumble Bee Seafoods, Inc., San Diego, 1985-89; pres., CEO Flying Palms LLC, San Diego, 1995—; bd. dirs., asst. corp. sec. Network Resource Corp., San Jose, Calif., 1990-95; bd. dirs. Wind & Weather, Inc. Exec. prodr. (feature motion picture) Love Always, 1997. Bd. dirs. U. C. Univ. Art Gallery, 1995—.

BRANTHAVER, JAN FRANKLIN, research chemist; b. Davenport, Iowa, Mar. 12, 1936; s. Franklin Inglis and Ruth Matilda (Doering) B. BA, Millikin U., 1958; PhD, N.D. State U., 1976. Rsch. aide N.D. State U., Fargo, 1964-76; rsch. chemist Laramie (Wyo.) Energy Tech. Ctr., 1976-83; program mgr. Western Rsch. Inst., Laramie, 1983—. Editor Metal Complexes in Fossil Fuels, 1987; contbr. numerous articles to profl. publs. With U.S. Army, 1959. Mem. Am. Chem. Soc. (sec. Wyo. sect. 1986-87, treas. 1990-97), Sigma Xi. Lutheran. Home: 1000 E Garfield St Apt 17 Laramie WY 82070-4065 Office: Western Rsch Inst 365 N 9th St Laramie WY 82070-3380

BRANZEI-VELASQUEZ, SYLVIA CAROL, secondary education educator; b. Royal Oak, Mich., Aug. 20, 1958; d. Alexander and Sylvia Jean (Anderson) Branzei; m. Brian Pascal Dunstan, Sept. 18, 1982 (div. Mar. 1989); m. Byron William Velasquez, July 14, 1990; stepchildren: Ian Mantha, Alison Mantha, Aaron Montgomery, Jon Robin Montgomery. BS, U. Mich., 1980, tchg. cert., 1982; MEd, Calif. State Poly., 1986. Cert. tchr., Calif. Sci. tchr. The Buckley Sch., Sherman Oaks, Calif., 1983-85, Marin Acad., San Rafael, Calif., 1986-87; sci. tchr. and coord. Corden Redwood Sch., Alameda, Calif., 1987-88; chemistry outreach coord. Lawrence Hall of Sci., Berkeley, Calif., 1988-91; editor, writer Addison-Wesley, Menlo Park, Calif., 1992-94; project co-mgr. Project CREATE, Oakland, Calif., 1993-95; sci. tchr. Whale Gulch Sch., Whitethorn, Calif., 1995-97; ednl. cons. Hughes Galaxy Classroom, L.A., 1990; curriculum cons. NASA-SETI, Mountain View, Calif., 1991-92, Alameda County Office Edn., Hayward, 1995; mus. cons. Davis St. Transfer Sta., San Leandro, Calif., 1995. Author: Environmental Science, 1995, Grossology, 1995 (Pub. Weekly Best Seller 1996), Animal Grossology, 1996 (Pub. Weekly Best Seller 1997); editor: Science Insights—Exploring Earth and Space, 1994, Science Insights—Exploring Matter and Energy, 1994; co-author (play) A Soap Opera, 1991; contbr.

articles to profl. jours. Active Green Party, Oakland, 1989—; sec. Clover Gardens Neighborhood Assn., Oakland, 1993-95. Norse Civic Assn. scholar, Detroit, 1976, Minority Edn. scholar Calif. State Poly., Pomona, 1985. Mem. Nat. Sci. Tchrs. Assn. Home: PO Box 216 Redway CA 95560-0216

BRASSELL, ROSELYN STRAUSS, lawyer; b. Shreveport, La., Feb. 19, 1930; d. Herman Carl and Etelka (McMullan) Strauss. BA, La. State U., 1949; JD, UCLA, 1962. Bar: Calif. 1963. Atty. CBS, Los Angeles, 1962-68, sr. atty., 1968-76, asst. gen. atty., 1976-83, broadcast counsel, 1983-91; pvt. practice law L.A., 1991—; instr. TV Prodn. Bus. and Legal Aspects, UCLA Extension, 1992. Co-writer: Life After Death for the California Celebrity, 1985; bd. editors U. Calif. Law Rev., 1960-62. Named Angel of Distinction Los Angeles Cen. City Assn., 1975. Mem. Calif. Bar Assn., L.A. County Bar Assn. (exec. com. 1970—, sect. chmn. 1980-81), Inst. Corp. Counsel (adv. bd. 1980—), L.A. Copyright Soc. (treas. 1977-78, sec. 1978-79, pres. 1981-82), Am. Women in Radio and TV (nat. dir.-at-large 1971-73, nat. pub. affairs chmn. 1977-78, Merit award So. Calif. chpt. 1989), NATAS, Women in Film, Orange County World Affairs Coun. (trustee 1995—), U. Calif. Law Alumni Assn. (dir. 1971-74), Order of Coif, Alpha Xi Delta, Phi Alpha Delta. Republican. Home: 33331 Cockleshell Dr Monarch Beach CA 92629-4451 Office: 645 Wilcox Ave Ste 1-D Los Angeles CA 90004-1131

BRATMAN, DAVID STEPHEN, librarian; b. Chgo., Mar. 31, 1957; s. Robert Louis and Nancy Ellin (Bylan) B.; m. Bernadette Cecile Phillips, June 12, 1994. BA, U. Calif. Berkeley, 1979; MLS, U. Wash., 1983. Cataloger Stanford (Calif.) U., 1983-89, 96—, Santa Clara (Calif.) U., 1989-91, Coll. of Notre Dame, Belmont, Calif., 1992-93; libr. cons. Hillel Found., Stanford, Calif., 1991—. Editor: (periodical) Mythprint, 1980-95; contbr. articles to profl. jours. Mem. The Mythopoeic Soc. (bd. dirs. 1980—, chmn. 1986-87, 93, 97, conf. chair 1988, awards adminstr. 1992—), The World Sci. Fiction Soc. (awards adminstr. 1993-94, 96), The Tolkien Soc., Friends of the English Regency, No. Calif. Tech. Processing Group. Home: 1161 Huntingdon Dr San Jose CA 95129-3124

BRATSPIS, NED DAVID, marriage and family therapist; b. Phila., Dec. 28, 1951; s. Gerald and Edith (Neff) B.; m. Leslie Jane Shulman, June 5, 1983; 1 child, Gail Eddy. BA in Philosophy, Pa. State U., 1973; MA in Ednl. Psychology and Counseling, Calif. State U., Northridge, 1989. Cert. in clin. hypnosis; lic. marriage and family therapist, Calif. Marriage and family therapist intern Forte Found., Van Nuys, Calif., 1986-89; children's social worker L.A. County Dept. Children and Family Svcs., Sherman Oaks, Calif., 1989-95; marriage and family therapist West Valley Psychology Clinic, Encino, Calif., 1989—; geriatric counselor Beverly Manor, Canoga Park, Calif., 1995-96; individual couple, child, and family therapist Newhall, Calif., 1995—. Recipient Belle Dubnoff Lecture award Calif. State U. Northridge, 1987. Mem. ACA, Employee Assistance Profl. Assn., Calif. Assn. Marriage and Family Therapists (clin.). Office: 23030 Lyons Ave Ste 205 Newhall CA 91321

BRATTON, HOWARD CALVIN, federal judge; b. Clovis, N.Mex., Feb. 4, 1922; s. Sam Gilbert and Vivian (Rogers) B. B.A., U. N.Mex., 1941, LL.D., 1971; LL.B., Yale U., 1947. Bar: N.Mex. 1948. Law clk. U.S. Cir. Ct. Appeals, 1948; ptnr. Grantham & Bratton, Albuquerque, 1949-52; spl. asst. U.S. atty. charge litigation OPS, 1951-52; assoc., then ptnr. Hervy, Dow & Hinkle, Roswell, N.Mex., 1952-64; judge U.S. Dist. Ct. N.Mex., Las Cruces, 1964—, chief judge, 1978-87, sr. judge, 1987—; chmn. N.Mex. Jr. Bar Assn., 1952; pres. Chaves County (N.Mex.) Bar Assn., 1962; chmn. pub. lands com. N.Mex. Oil and Gas Assn., 1961-64, Interstate Oil Compact Commn., 1963-64; mem. N.Mex. Commn. Higher Edn., 1962-64, Jud. Conf. of U.S. Com. on Operation of Jury Sys., 1966-72, 79—, Jud. Conf. U.S. Com. on Ethics, 1987-92; mem. Ad Hoc Com. on Internat. Jud. Rels., 1992-94. Bd. regents U. N.Mex., 1958-68, pres., 1963-64; bd. dirs. Fed. Jud. Ctr., 1983-87. Served to capt. AUS, 1942-45. Mem. Trial Judges Assn. 10th Circuit (pres. 1976-78), Nat. Conf. Fed. Trial Judges (exec. com. 1977-79), Sigma Chi. Home: 6760 Via Emma Dr Las Cruces NM 88005-4977 Office: US Dist Ct 200 E Griggs Ave Las Cruces NM 88001-3523

BRAULT, G(AYLE) LORAIN, healthcare executive; b. Chgo., Jan. 3, 1944; d. Theodore Frank and Victoria Jean (Pribyl) Hahn; m. Donald R. Brault, Apr. 29, 1971; 1 child, Kevin David. AA, Long Beach City Coll., 1963; BS, Calif. State U.-Long Beach, 1973, MS, 1977. RN, Calif; cert. nurse practitioner. Dir. nursing Canyon Gen. Hosp., Anaheim, Calif., 1973-76; dir. faculty critical care masters degree program Calif. State U., Long Beach, 1976-79; regional dir. nursing and support svcs. Western region Am. Med. Internat., Anaheim, Calif., 1979-83; v.p. Hosp. Home Care Corp. Am., Santa Ana, Calif., 1983-85; pres. Healthcare Assn. So. Calif., Torrance, 1986-92; v.p. Hosp. Coun. So. Calif., L.A., 1993—; invited lectr. China Nurses Assn., 1983; cons. AMI, Inc., Saudi Arabia, 1983; advisor dept. grad. nursing Calif. State U., L.A., 1988, advisor Nursing Inst., 1990-91; guest lectr. dept. pub. health UCLA, 1986-87; assoc. clin. prof. U. So. Calif., 1988—; lectr. Calif. State U., L.A., 1996-97; editl. advisor RN Times, Nurseweek, 1988—, chmn. editl. adv. bd. Contbr. articles to profl. jours., chpts. to books. Commr. HHS, Washington, 1988. HEW advanced nurse tng. grantee, 1978. Mem. Women in Health Adminstrn. (sec. 1989, v.p. 1990), Nat. Assn. Home Care, Am. Orgn. Nursing Execs., Calif. Assn. Health Svcs. at Home (task force chmn. 1988, bd. dirs. 1988-93, chmn. bd. dirs. 1990-93), Calif. League Nursing (bd. sec. 1983, program chmn. 1981-82), Am. Coll. Health Care Execs., ASAE, AONE, Phi Kappa Phi, Sigma Theta Tau. Republican. Methodist. Home: 1032 E Andrews Dr Long Beach CA 90807-2406

BRAULT, MARGUERITTE BRYAN, theatre organization administrator; b. Hutchinson, Kans., Sept. 18, 1930; d. George Wilson and Maude Alice (Vancil) Bryan; m. James William Brault, June 27, 1952 (div. May 1986); children: Stephen Michael, Lisa Lynn, Jennifer Elaine. BS with high honors, U. Wis., 1952; BA with highest distinction, U. Ariz., 1975, MA, 1979. Adminstrv./rsch. asst. Ednl. Testing Svc., Princeton, N.J., 1959-64; cons., scorer trainer Ednl. Testing Svc., Tucson, 1964-65; psychometrician Sunnyside Sch. Dist., Tucson, 1965-66; psychometrician U. Ariz., Tucson, 1966, rsch. asst., 1984-86; prodr., writer Sci-Expo, Tucson, 1985; program dir., writer Sci. Alive!/Discovery Alive, Inc., Tucson, 1986—; actor, 1988—; mem. Arts Edn. Working Group, Tucson, 1992. Writer video: An Apple Did Not Fall on My Head, 1985; co-author drama/musical prodn. The Fate of the Earth, 1982; writer, dir. plays: How Do We Discover?, the Fascinating World of Electricity, Secrets of the Heart, What is the World Made Of?; contbr. poetry to profl. publs. Bd. dirs. LifeQuest Interfaith Cmty., Tucson, 1990—; toy project dir. Am. Friends Svc. Com., Tucson, 1983-90. Semifinalist in Nat. Libr. of Poetry contest, 1995. Mem. Ariz. Reading Assn., Tucson Area Reading Coun., Inst. Noetic Scis., Phi Beta Kappa. Office: Sci Alive Discovery Alive 3331 N Wilson Ave Tucson AZ 85719-2452

BRAUN, STEPHEN BAKER, academic administrator; b. Cleve., Nov. 3, 1942; s. William B. and Louise M. (Baker) B.; m. Retta F. Kriefall, June 16, 1974; children: Elizabeth Rachel, Christopher Baker. BS, Xavier U., 1964; MBA, Fairleigh Dickinson U., 1976; postgrad., Imperial Coll., U London, 1996—. Regional mgr. Northwest Airlines, Inc., St. Paul, Minn., 1967-72; v.p. Inflight Motion Pictures, Inc., N.Y.C., 1972-78; v.p., gen. mgr. Columbia Pipe & Supply, Inc., Portland, Oreg., 1978-79; exec. v.p. Golby Mfg. Co., Portland, 1979-80; v.p. fin. Timberline Software, Inc., Portland, 1980-82; pres., founder Computer Systems Supplyware, Inc., Portland, 1982-87; dean Coll. Bus. Concordia U., Portland, 1987-92, exec. v.p., 1993—; CEO Concordia U. Found., Portland, 1993—, vice chmn., dir., 1985—; mem. bd. regents Concordia U., 1986-87, 92—; bd. dirs. Alameda Resources Co., Tigard, Oreg. Com. chmn. United Way, Boston, 1966; bd. dirs. German Am. Found., 1990—. With USN, 1964-67. Mem. Oreg. Ctr. for Entrepreneurship (pres., founder, 1986), Am. Mktg. Assn. (panelist 1985-88), Assn. Data Processing Systems Orgn., Rotary (long-range planning com. 1985—). Lutheran. Office: Concordia U 2811 NE Holman St Portland OR 97211-6067 also: Imperial Coll/Mgmt Sch, 53 Princes Gate Exhibition Rd, London SW7 2PG, England

BRAUN, STEPHEN HUGHES, psychologist; b. St. Louis, Nov. 20, 1942; s. William Lafon and Jane Louise B.; BA, Washington U., St. Louis, 1964, MA, 1965; PhD (USPHS fellow in Clin. Psychology), U. Mo., Columbia, 1970; 1 son, Damian Hughes. Asst. prof. psychology Calif. State U., Chico, 1970-71; dir. social learning div. Ariz. State Hosp., Phoenix, 1971-74; chief bur. planning and evaluation Ariz. Dept. Health Svcs., Phoenix, 1974-79; pres. Braun and Assocs., human svc. program cons.'s, Scottsdale, Ariz., 1979—; v.p. Ariz. Healthcare, 1991-95; dir. clin. svcs. Cmty. Partnership So. Ariz., 1995-97; asst. prof. psychology Ariz. State U., 1971-79, vis. asst. prof. Ctr. of Criminal Justice, 1974-79, Ctr. for Pub. Affairs, 1979-81; v.p. Value Behavioral Health, Falls Church, Va., 1997—; cons. Law Enforcement Assistance Adminstrn., NIMH, Alcohol, Drug Abuse, and Mental Health Adminstrn., Ariz. Dept. Health Svcs., Ariz. Dept. Corrections, Ariz. Dept. Econ. Security, local and regional human svc. agys. NIMH rsch. grantee, 1971-74; State of Calif. rsch. grantee, 1971; lic. clin. psychologist, Ariz. Mem. Am. Psychol. Assn., Sigma Xi. Editorial cons.; contbr. articles to profl. publs. Office: 3110 Fairview Park Dr Falls Church VA 22042-0988

BRAUNSTEIN, GLENN DAVID, physician, educator; b. Greenville, Tex., Feb. 29, 1944; s. Mervin and Helen (Friedman) B.; m. Jacquelyn D. Moose, July 5, 1965; children: Scott M. Braunstein, Jeffrey T. Braunstein. BS summa cum laude, U. Calif. San Francisco, 1965, MD, 1968. Diplomate Am. Bd. Internal Medicine, subspecialty endocrinology, diabetes, metabolism. Intern, resident Peter Bent Brigham Hosp., Boston, 1968-70; clin. fellow in medicine Harvard U. Med. Sch., Boston, 1969-70; clin. assoc., reproduction rsch. br. NIH, Bethesda, Md., 1970-72; chief resident in endocrinology Harbor Gen. Hosp. UCLA, 1972-73; dir. endocrinology Cedars-Sinai Med. Ctr., L.A., 1973-86, chmn., dept. medicine, 1986—; asst. prof. medicine UCLA Sch. Medicine, 1973-77, assoc. prof., 1977-81, prof., 1981—, vice chair dept. medicine, 1986—; cons. for AMA drug evaluations, 1990—; mem. internat. adv. com. Second World Conf. on Implantation and Early Pregnancy in Human, 1994; mem. endocrinologic and metabolic drugs adv. com. FDA, 1991-95, chmn., 1994-95, spl. advisor, 1995—; bd. mem. Am. Bd. Internal Medicine Endocrinology, Diabetes, Metabolism Subspecialty, 1991—, chmn., 1995—, bd. dirs., 1995—. Editl. bd. Jour. Clin. Endocrinology & Metabolism, 1978-80, editor, 1980-83; editl. bd. Mt. Sinai Jour. Medicine, 1984-88, Early Pregnancy: Biology and Medicine, 1994—, Am. Family Physician, 1995—. Bd. dirs. Israel Cancer Rsch. Fund, 1991-94; mem. Jonsson Comprehensive Cancer Ctr., 1991—. Recipient Gold Headed Cane Soc. award U. Calif. San Francisco Med. Ctr., 1968, Merck scholarship, 1968, Mosby scholarship, 1968, Soc. of Hacham award Cedars-Sinai Med. Ctr., 1976, Morris Press Humanism award Cedars-Sinai Med. Ctr., 1984. Fellow ACP (mem. adv. com. to gov., So. Calif. region 1989—, credentials com. So. Calif. region 1993); mem. AAAS, Am. Diabetes Assn., Cross Town Endocrine Club (chmn. 1982-83), Endocrine Soc. (publs. com. 1983-89, long range planning com. 1986-87, recent progress hormone rsch. com. 1993—, ann. meeting steering com. 1993—), Pacific Coast Fertility Soc. (pres. 1988), Western Soc. for Clin. Rsch., Am. Fedn. for Clin. Rsch., Am. Fertility Soc., Western Assn. Physicians, Assn. Am. Physicians, Am. Soc. Clin. Investigations (mem. nominating com. 1989), USCF Sch. Medicine Alumni Faculty Assn. (regional v.p. so. Calif., mem. bd. dirs. Israel Cancer Rsch. Fund 1991-94, mem. Jonsson Comprehensive Cancer Ctr. 1991—), Phi Delta Epsilon, Alpha Omega Alpha. Office: Cedars Sinai Med Ctr Dept Med Pla Level B118 8700 Beverly Blvd Los Angeles CA 90048-1804

BRAUNSTEIN, TERRY MALIKIN, artist; b. Washington, Sept. 18, 1942; d. Hiram and Dorothy (Malakoff) Malikin; m. David R. Braunstein, Jan. 17, 1965; children: Samantha, Matthew. BFA, U. Mich., 1964; MFA, Md. Inst. Art, 1968. vis. prof. Calif. State U., Long Beach, 1989; asst. prof. Corcoran Sch. Art, 1978-86; lectr. in field. One-woman shows include Franklin Furnace, N.Y.C., 1977-79, Fendrick Gallery, Washington, 1980, Washington Project for Arts, 1976-82, Marcuse Pfeifer, N.Y.C., 1987, Tartt Gallery, Washington, 1986, 88, U. Mich., Ann Arbor, 1990, Hampshire Coll., Amherst, Mass., 1990, Hampshire Coll., Amherst, Mass., 1990, Almediterranea '92, Almeria, Spain, 1990, Long Beach (Calif.) Mus. of Art, 1991, Turner/Krull Gallery, L.A., 1992, Troyer, Craig Krull Gallery, L.A., 1994, Fiktzpatrick, Lassman Gallery, Washington, 1995, U. Salamanca (Spain), 1996; exhibited in group shows at Bronx Mus., 1976, Corcoran Gallery of Art, 1973, 85, Gallery Miyazaki, Osaka, Japan, 1983, Bertha Udang Gallery, N.Y.C., 1985, Calif. State U., Long Beach, Calif., 1987, Ctr. Georges Pompidou, Paris, 1985, Calif. Mus. Photography, Riverside, 1990, Long Beach Mus. Art., 1992, Sala Arcs Gallery, Barcelona, Spain, 1990, Salas de Arenal and traveling exhibition, Seville, Madrid, Spain and Marseille, France, 1992—, Centro Esposito della Rocca Paotina, Italy, 1994, L.A. County Mus. Art, 1995, Dirty Windows, Berlin, Germany, 1996; commd. works include L.A. County Met. Transp. Authority MetroRail, 1992; represented in permanent collections at Mus. Modern Art, N.Y.C., Corcoran Gallery of Art, Washington, Long Beach Mus. Art, Mus. Contemporary Art, Chgo., Bibliotheque Nationale, Paris, Libr. of Congress, Washington, Bruce Peel Spl. Collections Libr., U. Alberta, Can., Nat. Mus. Am. Art, Washington, Mills Coll. Spl. Collections Libr., Oakland, Calif., U. Art Mus., Calif. State U., Long Beach, Getty Ctr. for Arts & Humanities, Victoria and Albert Mus., others. Recipient Visual Artists fellowship Nat. Endowment for Arts, 1985, Disting. Artist award City of Long Beach, 1992, video grant Long Beach Mus. Art, 1992, Nat. Artist's Book award Nat. Mus. Women in Arts, 1994; named disting. Vis. Prof., Calif. State U., 1989. Home: 262 Belmont Ave Long Beach CA 90803-1522

BRAWLEY, EDWARD ALLAN, academic administrator; b. Edinburgh, Scotland, Nov. 20, 1935; came to U.S., 1964; s. Edward and Elizabeth Swan Berwick (Allan) B.; m. Emilia Esther Martinez, Nov. 9, 1963; children: Stephen, Ewan. Cert., Heriot-Watt U., Edinburgh, 1958, Langside Coll., Glasgow, Scotland, 1960, Strathclyde U., Glasgow, Scotland, 1963; DSW, U. Pa., 1973. Cert. social worker. Social worker Larchgrove House, Glasgow, 1960-61, Dr. Guthrie's Boys Sch., Edinburgh, 1963-64; dir. residential life The Glen Mills (Pa.) Schs., 1965-68; div. dir. social scis. Community Coll. Phila., 1968-78; prof. social work Pa. State U., University Park, 1978-92; prof. social work Ariz. State U. W, Phoenix, 1992—, vice provost for acad. affairs, 1996—; cons. Bur. Labor Stats., Washington, 1986-88, Nat. Inst. Alcohol Abuse and Alcoholism, Rockville, Md., 1978-81; vis. prof. U. Regina (Can.) Faculty Social Work, 1983; vis. rsch. fellow U. East Anglia Sch. Econ. and Social Studies, Norwich, Eng., 1985; scholar-in-residence Bar-Ilan U., Ramat-Gan, Israel, 1987. Co-author: Community and Social Service Education in the Community College, 1972, Social Care at the Front Line, 1987; author: The New Human Service Worker, 1975, Mass Media and Human Services, 1983, Human Services and the Media, 1995. Mem. Pa. Transp. Adv. Com., Harrisburg, 1986-92; mem. Gov. of Pa. Task Force on Human Svcs., Harrisburg, 1970-71; mem. Pa. Legis. Audit Adv. Commn., Harrisburg, 1978. Mem. Nat. Assn. Social Workers, Coun. Social Work Edn., Internat. Coun. Social Welfare, Internat. Assn. Schs. Social Work. Home: 4523 E La Mirada Way Phoenix AZ 85044-7510 Office: Ariz State U 4701 E Thunderbird Rd Phoenix AZ 85069-7100

BRAWNER, SHARON LEE, bilingual education educator, researcher; b. Marietta, Ga., Jan. 26, 1951; d. Robert Felton and Ruby Lee (Burks) B.; div.; 1 child, Marion Eugene Sealy III. BA, Clemson U., 1975; MEd, U. S.C., 1987; EdD, U. Ga., 1994. ESL cert., gifted and talented tchg. cert. English tchr. grades 7-12 Columbia, S.C., 1981-88; English instr. U. Ga., Athens, 1990, grad. asst., 1990-94; asst. prof. No. Ariz. U., Yuma, 1994-96; adj. sr. faculty English U. Ariz., 1997—; presenter Ga. Children's Lit. Conf., Athens, 1991, Ga. Coun. Tchrs. English Conf., 1991, TESOL Nat. Conf., Balt., 1994. Author: New Ways in Teaching Listening, 1995. Pres., governing bd. Yuma County Juvenile Ct. Sys. Charter Sch., 1995-96; mem. San Luis, Ariz./San Luis, Sonora, Mex. Edn. Commn., 1994-96; essay judge Ga. Acad. Decathlon, Athens, 1991; vol. tutor Athens Regional Libr., 1993-94. Mem. Internat. Reading Assn. (rsch. com. No. Ariz. U. 1994-96), Nat. Council for Tchrs. of English, mem., Tchrs. of English to Speakers of other Languages.

BRAY, R(OBERT) BRUCE, music educator; b. La Grande, Oreg., July 24, 1924; s. Ernest C. and Leta M. (Haight) B.; m. Donna Marie Siegman, July 2, 1949 (div. 1980); children: Stephen Louis, Ruth Elizabeth, Katherine Ernestine, Anne-Marie. BA, U. Oreg., 1949, MMus, 1955; postgrad., U. Strasbourg, France, 1949-50, U. Wash., 1960-61. Music tchr. Helen McCune Jr. High Sch., Pendleton, Oreg., 1951-54; dir. choral music Albany (Oreg.) Union High Sch., 1954-56; elem. music supr. Ashland (Oreg.) Public Schs., 1956-57; asst. prof. music Cen. Wash. U., Ellensburg, 1957-60; from asst. to prof. U. Idaho, Moscow, 1961-89, prof. emeritus, 1989—; sec. faculty U. Idaho, Moscow, 1968-88, sec. emeritus, 1988—. Editor: Oreg. Music Educator, 1954-57, Wash. Music Educator, 1957-60, U. Idaho Music, 1961-68, Idaho Music Notes, 1963-68, U. Idaho Register, 1974-88 ; editorial bd. Music Educators Jour., 1964-68. With USNR, 1942-46. Mem. Music Educators Nat. Conf. (bd. dirs., pres. N.W. divsn. 1963-65, nat. exec. com. 1964-66), Phi Mu Alpha Sinfonia. Democrat. Episcopalian. Home and Office: 2614 E Everett Ave Spokane WA 99207-6210

BRAZIER, ROBERT G., transportation executive. Student, Stanford U. With Airbone Aircraft Service Inc., 1953-63; v.p. ops. Pacific Air Freight Inc., 1963-68; sr. v.p. ops. Airborne Freight Corp., Seattle, 1968-73, exec. v.p., 1973-78, COO, 1973—, pres., dir, COO, 1978—. Office: Airborne Freight Corp PO Box 662 Seattle WA 98111-0662*

BRECHBILL, SUSAN REYNOLDS, lawyer, educator; b. Washington, Aug. 22, 1943; d. Irving and Isabell Doyle (Reynolds) Levine; B.A., Coll. William and Mary, 1965; J.D., Marshall-Wythe Sch. Law, 1968; children—Jennifer Rae, Heather Lea. Admitted to Va. bar, 1969, Fed. bar, 1970; atty. AEC, Berkeley, Calif., 1968-73, indsl. relations specialist AEC, Las Vegas, 1974-75; atty. ERDA, Oakland, Calif., 1976-77; atty. Dept. Energy, Oakland, 1977-78, dir. procurement div. San Francisco Ops. Office, 1978-85, asst. chief counsel for gen. law, 1985-93, acting asst. mgr. environ. mgmt. and support, 1992, acting asst. mgr. def. programs, 1993; chief counsel Dept. Energy Richland Ops. Office, 1994—; mem. faculty U. Calif. Extension; speaker Nat. Contract Mgmt. Assn. Ann. Symposiums, 1980, 81, 83, 84, 88; speaker on doing bus. with govt. Leader Girl Scouts U.S.A., San Francisco area. Named Outstanding Young Woman Nev., 1974; recipient Meritorious Svc. award Dept. Energy, 1992. Mem. NAFE, Va. State Bar Assn., Fed. Bar Assn., Nat. Contract Mgmt. Assn. (pres. Golden Gate chpt. 1983-84, N.W. regional v.p. 1984-86). Republican. Contbr. articles to profl. jours.

BREDA, MICHAEL ALEXANDER, surgeon; b. Vienna, Austria, Dec. 18, 1959; came to the U.S., 1963; m. Susan A. Huang; 1 child, Sonja Breda. BS in Chemistry magna cum laude, U. Wash., 1981; MD, Johns Hopkins U., 1985; postgrad., UCLA, 1992. Diplomate Am. Bd. Surgery, Am. Bd. Surgery Critical Care; lic. physician, Calif, Oreg.; cert. ACLS. From jr. to chief resident in surgery U. Calif., L.A., 1985-92; fellowship liver transplantation and hepatobiliary surgery Cedars-Sinai Med. Ctr., L.A., 1992-94; staff surgeon Health First, Portland; clin. faculty Oreg. Health Scis. U.; researcher Fred Hutchinson Cancer Rsch. Ctr. Dept. Tumor Virology, Seattle, 1979-80, U. Wash. Dept. Biochemistry, Seattle, 1981, Johns Hopkins U. Div. Cardiothoracic Surgery, Balt., 1984-85, UCLA div. cardiothoracic surgery, 1987-89; instr. UCLA Program Endovascular Surgery, 1989; presenter in field. Co-author: (with H. Lakes) Thoracic and Cardiovascular Surgery, 1991; contbr. articles to profl. jours. Biomed. Rsch. Support grantee; Nat. Rsch. Svcs. scholar; recipient Philip K. Caves award Internat. Soc. for Heart Transplantation, 1985, Paul C. Samson prize Western Thoracic Surg. Assn., 1989. Mem. ACS, Phi Beta Kappa, Alpha Omega Alpha. Office: Health First 1130 NW 22nd Ave Ste 220 Portland OR 97210-2976

BREDDAN, JOE, systems engineering consultant; b. N.Y.C., Sept. 18, 1950; s. Hyman and Sylvia (Hauser) B. BA in Math. and Psychology, SUNY, Binghamton, 1972; MS in Ops. Research, U. Calif., Berkeley, 1975; PhD in Systems Engring., U. Ariz., 1978. Teaching and research assoc. Dept. Systems and Indsl. Engring. U. Ariz., Tucson, 1975-79; project engr. B.D.M. Services Co., Tucson, 1979-80; mem. tech. staff Bell Labs., Am. Bell, AT&T Info. Systems, Denver, 1980-86; staff mgr. AT&T, Denver, 1986-91; pvt. practice cons. Boulder, Colo., 1991—. Patentee in field. Home and Office: 2120 Goddard Pl Boulder CO 80303-5616

BREDE, ANDREW DOUGLAS, research director, plant breeder; b. Pitts., Feb. 4, 1953; s. James Faris and Adele Katherine (Konefal) B.; m. Linda Davis Rudd, Jan. 11, 1992; children from previous marriage: Loralee Elizabeth, Michael Douglas. BS, Pa. State U., 1975, MS, 1978, PhD, 1982. Asst. golf course supt. Valley Brook Country Club, McMurray, Pa., 1975-76; grad. rsch. asst. Pa. State U., University Park, 1976-82; assoc. prof. Okla. State U., Stillwater, 1982-86; dir. rsch. Jacklin Seed Co., Post Falls, Idaho, 1986—; v.p. Turfgrass Breeders Assn., Tangent, Oreg., 1989-91; chmn. variety rev. Lawn Inst., Marietta, Ga., 1990—; bd. dirs. Nat. Turfgrass Evaluation Program; golf course supr. Assn. Am. Rsch. Com., 1996—. Assoc. editor Agronomy Jour., 1993—; contbr. articles to Agronomy Jour., 150 articles to mags.; prodr. 15 ednl. videos. Rsch. grantee, 1983-86. Mem. Am. Soc. Agronomy. Republican. Office: Jacklin Seed Co 5300 W Riverbend Rd Post Falls ID 83854-9499

BREDFELDT, JAMES EDWARD, gastroenterologist; b. Spearville, Kans., Feb. 17, 1948; s. Everett I. and Evelyn Mary (Stehwien) B.; m. Elaine Marie Riley, Aug. 28, 1982. B.A., U. Kans.-Lawrence, 1970; M.D., U. Kans.-Kansas City, 1974. Diplomate Am. Bd. Internal Medicine and Gastroenterology. Intern U. Kans.-Kansas City, 1974-75, resident in internal medicine, 1975-77; fellow in gastroenterology U. Mo., Columbia, 1977-79; fellow in hepatology Yale U., New Haven, 1979-81, instr. in medicine, 1981-83; gastroenterologist, hepatologist Lovelace Med. Ctr., Albuquerque, 1983-88, Va. Mason Med. Ctr., Seattle, 1988—; research assoc. VA, Med. Ctr., West Haven, Conn., 1981-83; clin. asst. prof. medicine U. N.Mex., Albuquerque, 1983-88. Contbr. articles, abstracts to profl. publs. Fellow ACP, Am. Coll. Gastroenterology; mem. Am. Gastroenterol. Assn., Am. Assn. for Study Liver Diseases, Am. Soc. Gastrointestinal Endoscopy, Alpha Omega Alpha. Office: Virginia Mason Med Ctr 1100 9th Ave Seattle WA 98101-2756

BREDLOW, THOMAS GAYLE, metals designer, craftsman; b. Pontiac, Mich., Oct. 18, 1938; s. Warren Kenneth and Elizabeth (La Ponsa) B. BA in Math., Tex. A&M U., 1960; postgrad., U. Ariz., 1960-61. Machinist, designer physics dept. Tex. A&M U., 1958-60, U. Ariz., Tucson, 1960-61, 64; owner, sole craftsman Tom Bredlow's Blacksmith Shop, Tucson, 1964-86; designer, craftsman, preservationist Tucson, 1986—; guest speaker Sch. Arch., U. Ariz., Tucson, 1964-86, Sch. Anthropology, 1964-86. Prin. woirks include Washington Cathedral, Mt. St. Albans, Washington, 1968, Barrio to Historico, Tucson, 1970, Pima County Parks and Recreation, Tucson, 1981, Fred Harvey Bldgs., Grand Canyon, Ariz., 1983-91, McCormick residence entry, Houston, 1978, Santa Fe, 1993, Antique Indian Jewelry Restoration, Pauline Bircher Collection, Tucson, 1993—, Architectural Ironwork, Tornabene Residence, Tucson, 1997, Porch and Garden Screens, Stephens Residence, Tucson, 1997. Mem. Mountain Oyster Club (hon. artist life mem.). Home: 3524 N Olive Rd Tucson AZ 85719-1830

BREECHER-BREEN, SHEILA RAE, lawyer; b. Nephi, Utah, Aug. 14, 1953; d. Leo Neil and Jeannine (Cole) Van Ausdal; m. Jerome P. Breen, Aug. 11, 1995; children: Michael Erin, Anthony Edward, Kelsey Nichole. BS, Utah State U., 1974, MS, 1974; JD, Brigham Young U., 1984. Bar: Ariz. 1985, U.S. Dist. Ct. Ariz. 1985, U.S. Ct. Appeals (9th cir.) 1985. Speech pathologist Maricopa Spl. Svcs. Consortium, Buckeye, Ariz., 1974-75; speech pathologist Phoenix Union High Sch. Dist. (Ariz.), 1975-81; assoc. Charles, Smith & Bellah, Glendale, Ariz., 1986; speech pathologist Phoenix Union High Sch. Dist., 1986-88; judge pro tem City of Peoria (Ariz.) Mcpl. Ct., 1987—; of counsel Smith & Breecher, Scottsdale, Ariz., 1987—; tchr. Legal Magnet High Sch. Program Phoenix Union High Sch. Dist., 1988-89; coord. policy and legal assistance, spl. edn. sect. Ariz. Dept. Edn., Phoenix, 1989-94, dir. adult edn., 1995-96; CEO SolED, PLLC, Phoenix, 1996—; cons. Ednl. Mgmt. Group, Scottsdale, 1997—; legal cons. Flagstaff (Ariz.) Pub. Schs., 1987-89, Phoenix Union High Sch. Dist., 1986-89; mem. legis. team Ariz. Dept. Edn., Phoenix, 1991-95. Editor: Criminal Procedure, 1983. Precinct committeeperson Dem. Party, Glendale, Ariz., 1979-81; adv. Ariz. Dept. Edn., Phoenix, 1988-90; dep. registrar Maricopa County Elections Dept., Phoenix, 1987-92; authorized pub. lobbyist, 1989-95; mem. Edn. Policy Fellowship Program, 1991-92; bd. dirs. Phoenix Day, 1992-96; bd. dirs. Cmty. Info. and Referral, 1992-96; mem. hon. bd. Tempe Ctr. Habilitation, 1994—; mem. adv. bd. Inst. Cultural Affairs, 1995—. Mem. Ariz. Bar Assn., Valley Leadership Class XII (Phoenix), Soroptimist Internat. Home: 4512 E Thistle Landing Phoenix AZ 85044 Office: SolEd 4512 E Thistle Landing Dr Phoenix AZ 85044-6847

BREEDEN, TOWNSEND DEAN, electronics company executive, consultant; b. Washington, Aug. 27, 1932; s. Harry Clinton and Ethel (Townsend) Breeden; m. Wanda Louise Riddle, June 25, 1960; children: Townsend Paul, Edward Dean. BSEE, U. Md., College Park, 1960; MSEE, Drexel U., 1965. Engr. Radio Corp. of Am., Hightstown, N.J., 1960-65; dir. Fairchild Industries, Germantown, Md., 1965-77; v.p. Am. Satellite Co., Rockville, Md., 1977-82, Hekimian Labs., Gaithersburg, Md., 1982-88; cons. Townsend

Group, 1988-89; gen. mgr. Keltec Fla., Inc., Ft. Walton Beach, 1989-92; pres., gen. mgr. Fairchild Data Corp., 1992—. Served with USN, 1952-56. Recipient Ranger Program Citation, NASA, 1964. Fellow AIAA (assoc., chmn. com. 1977-78), IEEE, Armed Forces Comms. and Electronics Assn., Izaak Walton League of Am. (nat. dir. 1984-85, pres. Rockville chpt. 1982-84), NRA (life mem.). Republican. Episcopalian. Home: PO Box 7 Boyds MD 20841-0007 Office: Fairchild Data Corp 350 N Hayden Rd Scottsdale AZ 85257-4601

BREEN, ROY EUGENE, physician; b. Bethesda, Md., Mar. 18, 1952; s. Roy Eugene and Winifred (Legg) B.; m. Nancy Ann Nicklas, Jan. 8, 1956. BS, U. Calif., Davis, 1974; MD, U. Calif., Irvine, 1978. Diplomate Am. Bd. Colon and Rectal Surgery, Am. Bd. Surgery. Intern Good Samaritan Hosp., Portland, Oreg., 1978-79; resident in gen. surgery Oreg. Health Scis. U., Portland, 1979-84; fellow in colon and rectal surgery Sansum Med. Clinic, Inc., Santa Barbara, Calif., 1984-85; active staff Providence Med. Ctr.; courtesy staff Good Samaritan Hosp., St. Vincent Hosp. Coach baseball, basketball, soccer West Linn, Oreg. Fellow ACS, Am. Soc. Colon and Rectal Surgeons; mem. AMA, Portland Surg. Soc., N.W. Soc. Colon and Rectal Surgeons, Oreg. Med. Assn., Multnomah County Med. Soc. Episcopalian. Office: 511 SW 10th Ave Ste 714 Portland OR 97205-2708

BREESKIN, MICHAEL WAYNE, lawyer; b. Washington, Dec. 25, 1947; s. Nathan and Sylvia (Raine) B.; m. Frances Cox Lively, May 29, 1982; children: Molly Louise, Laura Rose. BA cum laude, U. Pitts., 1969; JD, Georgetown U. Law Ctr., 1975. Bar: D.C. 1975, Colo. 1983, U.S. Dist. Ct. D.C. 1977, U.S. Dist. Ct. Colo. 1983, U.S. Ct. Appeals (D.C. cir.) 1978, U.S. Ct. Appeals (10th cir.) 1984, U.S. Supreme Ct. 1995. With The Legal Ctr. for People with Disabilities and Older People; mng. atty. Tobin & Covey, Washington, 1977-79; assoc. Donald M. Murtha & Assocs., Washington, 1979-80; counsel NLRB Office Rep. Appeals, Washington, 1980-83; trial atty. NLRB Denver Regional Office, 1983-88; assoc. Wherry & Wherry, Denver, 1989-91; sr. atty. The Legal Ctr. for People with Disabilities and Older People (formerly The Legal Ctr. Serving Persons with Disabilities), Denver, 1991—; presenter, lectr. Denver, 1991—. Recipient Outstanding Work for People with Disabilities acknowledgement Very Spl. Arts Colo., 1996; named Advocate of Yr. Assn. for Cmty. Living in Boulder County, Inc. (formerly, Assn. for Retarded Citizens in Boulder County, Inc.), 1996. Mem. ABA (litigation sect.). Office: Legal Ctr for People with Disabilities-Older People 455 Sherman St Ste 130 Denver CO 80203-4403

BREHOVE, THERESA M., physician; b. Burbank, Calif., Oct. 3, 1959; d. Stephen and Joan (Froelich) McDonough; m. Richard S. Brehove, July 9, 1983; children: Matthew Steven, Christina Marie, Lisa Ann. BS in Biology, Loyola Marymount U., 1980; MD, St. Louis U., 1984. Diplomate Am. Bd. Family Practice. Resident in family medicine Glendale (Calif.) Adventist Hosp., 1984-87; family physician Bay Shores Med. Group, San Pedro, Calif., 1987-96, Venice (Calif.) Family Clinic, 1996—. Mem. Am. Acad. Family Physicians. Roman Catholic.

BREITELS, BARBARA RENEE, engineer; b. San Jose, Calif., Dec. 9, 1970; d. Diana C. Burns; m. David Morgan Breitels, Aug. 3, 1991. BS in aerospace engring., San Jose State U., 1994. Sales supr. Emporium, Santa Clara, Calif., 1988-94; database adminstr. Desktop Strategies, Los Altos, Calif., 1994; product engr. Caere Corp., Los Gatos, Calif., 1994—. Mem. Soc. Women Engrs. Office: Caere Corp 100 Cooper Ct Los Gatos CA 95030

BREITENBACH, MARY LOUISE MCGRAW, psychologist, chemical dependency counselor; b. Pitts., Sept. 26, 1936; d. David Evans McGraw and Louise (Schoch) Neel; m. John Edgar Breitenbach, Apr. 15, 1960 (dec. 1963); m. Joseph George Piccoli III, Aug. 15, 1987; 1 dau. Kirstin Amethyst. Postgrad., Oreg. State Coll., 1960-61; BA, Russell Sage Coll., Troy, N.Y., 1958; MEd, Harvard U., 1983. Lic. profl. counselor, Wyo.; lic. chem. dependency specialist, Wyo.; cert. addiction specialist, level III; nat. cert. addiction counselor II, master addiction counselor, 1995. Paraprofessional psychologist St. John's Episc. Ch., Jackson, Wyo., 1963-94; pvt. practice Wilson, Wyo., 1983—; counselor Curran/Seeley Found. Addiction Svcs., Jackson, 1989-91, Van Vleck House/Tri-County Group Home, Jackson, 1986-89, others; provider multiple employee assistance programs local and nat. cos.; mem. adv. com. The Learning Ctr., 1997—. Trustee Teton Sci. Sch., Kelly, Wyo, 1960-76; pres. bd. govs. Teton County Mus., 1989-91, Jackson; vestry mem. St. John's Ch., Jackson. Mem. APA, LWV, Wyo. Psychol. Assn., Wyo. Assn. Counseling and Devel., Wyo. Assn. Addiction Specialists, Nat. Assn. Alcohol and Drug Addiction Counselors. Democrat. Episcopalian. Home and Office: Star Rte Wilson WY 83014

BREMS, JOHN JOSEPH, surgeon; b. Cedar Rapids, Iowa, Sept. 21, 1954; s. George Frederick and Anne Delores (Kennedy) B.; m. Catherine Suzanne Edwards, June 27, 1980; children: Daniel Edward, Julie Anne, Mark Joseph. BS in Chemistry, Rockhurst Coll., 1979; MD, St. Louis U., 1981. Gen. surgery resident Sch. Medicine St. Louis U., 1981-86, dir. liver transplantation dept. surgery, 1988-90; transplant fellow UCLA, 1986-87, asst. prof. surgery, asst. dir. liver transplantation, 1987-88; dir. multi-organ transplantation program Scripps Clinic, La Jolla, Calif., 1990—, mem. network devel. adv. bd. Green Cancer Ctr.; chmn. scientific bd. Exten Corp., San Diego; med. dir. Organ and Tissue Ctr. of So. Calif., San Diego, 1992-94. Co-developer artificial liver; contbr. chpts. to books. Bd. dirs. Am. Liver Found., San Diego, 1990-94; mem. adv. panel on transplantation Calif. Med. Assn., Sacramento, 1992; mem. nat. edn. com. United Network Organ Sharing, Richmond, Va., 1992-93; active environ. and social issues San Diego County Med. Soc., 1992-94. Fellow ACS, Southwestern Surg. Congress (program 1992-94), Pacific Coast Surg. Soc.; mem. San Diego Surg. Soc. (v.p. 1993-94, pres. 1995-96), San Diego Surg. Soc., Am. Soc. Transplant Surgeons (chmn. bylaws com. 1993-94), Am. Assn. for Study of Liver Diseases. Roman Catholic. Home: 3719 Newcrest Pt San Diego CA 92130-2033 Office: Scripps Clinic & Rsch Found 10666 N Torrey Pines Rd La Jolla CA 92037-1027

BREMSER, GEORGE, JR., electronics company executive; b. Newark, May 26, 1928; s. George and Virginia (Christian) B.; m. Marie Sundman, June 21, 1952 (div. July 1979); children: Christian Fredrick II, Priscilla Suzanne, Martha Anne, Sarah Elizabeth; m. Nancy Kay Woods, Oct. 27, 1983 (div. Feb. 1989). BA, Yale U., 1949; postgrad., U. Miami, 1959; MBA, NYU, 1962. With McCann-Erickson Inc., N.Y.C., 1952-61; asst. gen. mgr. McCann-Erickson Inc., Bogota, Columbia, 1955, gen. mgr., 1955-57; account supr. McCann-Erickson Inc., N.Y.C., 1958; v.p., mgr. McCann-Erickson Inc., Miami, Fla., 1959-61; with Gen. Foods Corp., White Plains, N.Y., 1961-71; v.p., gen. mgr. internat. div. Gen. Foods Europe, White Plains, N.Y., 1967; pres. Gen. Foods Internat., White Plains, 1967-71; group v.p. Gen. Foods Corp., White Plains, 1970-71; chmn., pres., chief exec. officer Texstar Corp., Grand Prairie, Tex., 1971-81; exec. v.p. Shaklee Corp., San Francisco, 1981-82; chmn., pres., chief exec. officer Etak Inc., Menlo Park, Calif., 1983-88, 96, chmn., 1989-96, 97—; chmn., pres., CEO Etak, Inc., Menlo Park, Calif., 1996—, chmn., 1997—; bd. dirs. PBI Industries Inc. Trustee Union Ch., Bogota, 1956-57; Dem. county committeeman, Ridgewood, N.J., 1962-63; mem. New Canaan (Conn.) Town Council, 1969-73; founder, past pres. Citizens Com. for Conservation, New Canaan; mem. coun. Save the Redwoods League, 1987—. Served to 2d lt. USMC 1950-52, capt. Res. Mem. New Canaan Country Club, Brook Club, Yale Club (N.Y.C.), Block Island Club, Casino Club (Nantucket, Mass.), Explorers Club, Phi Beta Kappa, Beta Gamma Sigma, Beta Theta Pi. Home: 535 Everett Ave Palo Alto CA 94301-1547 also: Mansion Beach Rd Block Island RI 02807 Office: care Etak Inc 1430 Obrien Dr Menlo Park CA 94025-1432

BRENNAN, CIARAN BRENDAN, accountant, independent oil producer, real estate developer; b. Dublin, Ireland, Jan. 28, 1944; s. Sean and Mary (Stone) B. BA with honors, Univ. Coll., Dublin, 1966; MBA, Harvard U., 1973; MS in Acctg., U. Houston, 1976. Lic. real estate broker, Calif.; CPA, Tex. Auditor Coopers & Lybrand, London, 1967-70; sr. auditor Price Waterhouse & Co., Toronto, Ont., Can., 1970-71; project acctg. specialist Kerr-McGee Corp., Oklahoma City, 1976-80; contr. Cummings Oil Co., Oklahoma City, 1980-82; CFO Red Stone Energies, Ltd., 1982, Leonoco, Inc., 1982-87; treas., chief fin. officer JKJ Supply Co., 1983-87, Saturn Investments Inc., 1983-87, JFL Co., 1984-87, Little Chief Drilling & Energy Inc., 1984-85; pres. Ciaran Brennan Corp., 1990, Rathgar Securities, Inc., 1989-90; CFO Nationwide Industries, 1991-93, Cinema Internat. Inc., 1993—; bd. dirs., cons. small oil cos.; adj. faculty Oklahoma City U., 1977-86; vis. faculty Ctrl. State U., 1977-86. Contbr. articles to profl. jours. Mem. AICPA, Inst. Chartered Accts. Eng. and Wales, Inst. Chartered Accts. Can., Inst. Chartered Accts. Ireland, Tex. Soc. CPAs, Clf. Soc. CPAs. Democrat. Roman Catholic.

BRENNAN, JERRY MICHAEL, economics educator, statistician, reseacher, clinical psychologist; b. Grosse Pointe, Mich., July 17, 1944; s. Walter X. and Aretta May (Gempler) B. Student Kalamazoo (Mich.) Coll., 1962-64, Pasadena (Calif.) City Coll., 1966-67; B.A., UCLA, 1969; M.A., U. Hawaii, 1973, Ph.D., 1978. Researcher, UCLA, 1968-69; researcher U. Hawaii, 1972, 74-78, cons., 1975, 77, 78, data analyst and statis. cons., 1979-80, lectr., 1976-80, asst. prof. econs., 1980—; pres. Sugar Mill Software, 1986—; cons. WHO; v.p. Forest Inst. Profl. Psychology. Light scholar, 1964-66. Mem. Am. Psychol. Assn., Soc. Multivariate Exptl. Psychology, Psychometric Soc., Western Psychol. Assn., AAUP, Hawaii Ednl. Research Assn. Contbr. psychol. articles to profl. jours. Address: 651 Kaumakani St Honolulu HI 96825-1827

BRENNAN, JOAN STEVENSON, federal judge; b. Detroit, Feb. 21, 1933; d. James and Betty (Holland) Stevenson; m. Lane P. Brennan, June 26, 1954 (div. 1970); children: Suzanne, Steven, Clayton, Elizabeth, Catherine. BA, Skidmore Coll., 1954; JD, Santa Clara U., 1973. Bar: Calif. Dep. dist. atty. Dist. Attys. Office, Santa Clara, Calif., 1974-78; legal counsel U.S. Leasing Internat., San Francisco, 1978-79; asst. U.S. atty. U.S. Dist. Ct. (no. dist.) Calif., San Francisco, 1980-82, U.S. Magistrate judge, 1982—. Mem. Nat. Assn. Women Judges, Nat. Assn. Magistrate Judges. Democrat. Office: US Dist Ct PO Box 36054 450 Golden Gate Ave San Francisco CA 94102*

BRENNAN, JUDITH, mayor. Mayor City of Norwalk, Calif. Office: 12700 Norwalk Blvd Norwalk CA 90651-1030

BRENNEN, STEPHEN ALFRED, international business consultant; b. N.Y.C., July 7; s. Theodore and Margaret (Pembroke) B.; m. Yolanda Alicia Romero, Sept. 28, 1957; children: Stephen Robert, Richard Patrick. AB cum laude, U. Americas, Mexico City, 1956; MBA, U. Chgo., 1959. Supr. Montgomery Ward, Chgo., 1956; credit mgr. Aldens, Chgo., 1956-59; gen. mgr. Purina de Guatemala, 1964-66; pres. Purina Colombiana, Bogotá, 1967-69; founding pres. Living Marine Resources, Inc., San Diego, 1969-70; mng. dir. Central and S. Am. Ralston Purina, Caracas, Venezuela, Coral Gabels, Fla., 1970-74; pres. Van Camp Seafood Co., San Diego, 1974-79; chmn. P.S.C. Corp., Buena Park, Calif., 1979-81; pres. Inter-Am. Cons. Group, San Diego, 1981-85; chmn. Beta Enterprises Inc., 1986-91; advisor Nat. Productivity Exch.; spl. asst. C.A.O., County of San Diego, Calif., 1987-95; mng. ptnr. Interam. Cons. Group, 1983-95; ptnr. Acad. Interpreting & Translations, Internat., 1995; assoc., owner the Montgomery Group, Inc., La Jolla. Author: Successfully Yours. Past mem. adv. bd. Mexican-Am. Found. Served with USAF. Mem. Am. Soc. Profl. Cons. Roman Catholic. Club: U. Chgo. in San Diego (past pres.).

BRENNER, ESTHER LERNER, fundraiser; b. Washington, July 27, 1931; d. Mayer and Ethel Sarah (Kawarsky) Lerner; children: Mayer Alan, Saul Daniel, Matthew Hy. BA with distinction, George Washington U., 1953; MBA, U. Judaism, L.A., 1987. Speech therapist Alexandria area schs. for handicapped, Va., 1952-54; speech therapist, pvt. practice L.A., 1954-62; tchr. L.A. area pvt. schs., 1962-72; exec. dir., lobbyist Mfrs. Assn., L.A., 1980-82; exec. dir. Citizens for Constl. Rights, Beverly Hills, Calif., 1982-86; regional coord. U.S. Holocaust Meml. Council, Washington, 1986-89; pres. L.A. Hebrew High Sch., 1987-89; dir. devel. Aviva Ctr., L.A., 1992—; bd. dirs. Bur. Jewish Edn., L.A. Pres. Beverly-Angeles Homeowners Assn., 1978-87, bd. chair, 1992-97; sec., bd. dirs. Westside Civic Fedn., L.A., 1978-89; bd. dirs. Meals on Wheels, Beverly Hills, Friends of Beverly Hills Pub. Libr.; bd. dirs., v.p. 1939 Club. Mem. Nat. Soc. Fund Raising Execs., Jewish Communal Profls. of So. Calif., Phi Beta Kappa. Home: 1264 Beverly Green Dr Beverly Hills CA 90212-4106

BRENNER, GERRY, English educator; b. Seattle, Oct. 7, 1937; s. Eugene Nansen and Gladys Marie (Western) Brenner; m. Teresa Joan Mays, June 11, 1960; children: Patrick Mays, Kyle Frederick, John Keegan. BA, U. Wash., 1961, MA, 1962, PhD, 1965. Asst. prof. U. Idaho, Moscow, 1965-67; assoc. prof. Boise (Idaho) State U., 1967-68; asst. prof. U. Mont., Missoula, 1968-71, assoc. prof., 1971-78, prof. English, 1978—; Fulbright sr. lectr. U. Cyril & Methodius, Skopje, Macedonia, 1980-81; exch. prof. lit. LaTrobe U., Bendigo, Vic., Australia, 1994-95. Author: Concealments in Hemingway's Works, 1983, The Old Man and the Sea: Story of a Common Man, 1991; co-author: Ernest Hemingway, 1986; contbr. articles to profl. jours. Mem. adv. bd. Inst. Medicine and Humanities, Missoula, Mont., 1989-93, exec. bd., 1995—; trustee Hemingway Found./Soc., 1996—; exec. com. U.S. Healthcare-Reform Symposium, Missoula, 1990-91; mem. air-pollution adv coun. Missoula City-County Health Dept., 1988-92. With U.S. Army, 1955-57. Mem. MLA, The Hemingway Soc., Rocky Mountain MLA, Soc. for Study of Narrative Lit., Phi Kappa Phi (treas. 1997—). Democrat. Home: 670 E North Ave Missoula MT 59801 Office: Univ of Montana Dept of English Missoula MT 59812

BRENT, PAUL LESLIE, mechanical engineering educator; b. Douglass, Okla., July 3, 1916; s. Paul Leslie and Ruth (McKee) B.; m. Aledo Render, May 29, 1938; children: Carolyn J., Paul Richard; m. E. Ferne McCoy, Nov. 19, 1984. BS, Central State U., 1938; MEd, U. Okla., 1949, EdD, 1959. Tchr. math. and sci. public schs. Adair, Okla., 1938-40; prin. Alden Public Schs., Carnegie, Okla., 1940-43; supt. Alden Public Schs., 1950-58; tchr. public schs. Cooperton, Okla., 1946-47; prin. high sch., public schs. Washita, Okla., 1947-48; supt., 1948-50; asst. prof. Calif. State U., Long Beach, 1959-63, assoc. prof. edn., 1963-72, asst. to chmn. div. edn., 1961-67, prof. instructional media, 1972-86, coordinator graphics support sect. dept. mech. engring., 1981-86, prof. emeritus, 1986—; mem. Baptist Edn. Study Task, 1966-67; trustee Calif. Bapt. Coll., 1969-74. Co-Author: Point, Line, Plane and Solid, 1984. Served with USNR, 1943-46. Mem. NEA, Am. Assn. Sch. Adminstrs., Congress of Faculty Assns., Calif. Faculty Assn. (pres. elect), Calif. Media and Libr. Educators, Calif. State U. Emerigus and Ret. Faculty Assn. (pres. Long Beach chpg. 1993-96), Phi Delta Kappa, Kappa Delta Pi, Phi Kappa Phi, Phi Beta Delta. Republican. Baptist. Home: 11112 Bos Pl Cerritos CA 90703-6426 Office: Calif State U 1250 N Bellflower Blvd Long Beach CA 90840-0006

BRERETON, ALYN ROBERT, behavioral primatologist, researcher; b. Turlock, Calif., June 29, 1948; s. Robert Young and Gladine Harriet (Unger) B. BA, Stanislaus State Coll., Turlock, 1971; MA, Calif. State U., Sacramento, 1976; PhD, U. Stirling, Scotland, 1989. Rschr. Cayo Santiago, P.R., 1977; observer Gilgil, Kenya, 1982; rschr. Tanaxpillo, Catemaco, Mex., 1983-84; observer Arashiyama West, Dilley, Tex., 1989-90, Cayo Santiago, P.R., 1991-92; ind. scholar Modesto, Calif., 1992-94; adj. asst. prof. anthropology Calif. State U., Stanislaus, Turlock, 1994—. Author articles on primates. Sigma Xi grantee, 1981; L.S.B. Leakey Found. grantee, 1982. Mem. Am. Anthrop. Assn., Internat. Primatological Soc., Am. Soc. Primatologists, Animal Behavior Soc. Democrat. Home: 913 Carrigan Ave Modesto CA 95350-3608

BRES, PHILIP WAYNE, automotive executive; b. Beaumont, Tex., Mar. 6, 1950; s. Roland Defrance Bres and Edna Gene (Griffith) Seale; m. Janet Vivian Meyer, May 16, 1987; children: Rachel Elizabeth, Rebecca Claire. BA, Lamar U., Beaumont, Tex., 1972; MBA, Stephen F. Austin State U., 1973. Distbn. mgr., bus. mgmt. mgr. Mazda Motors of Am., Houston, 1973-75; analyst, cons. C.H. McCormack and Assocs., Houston, 1975-76; assoc. Frank Gillman Pontiac/GMC/Honda, Houston, 1976-79, David Taylor Cadillac Co., Houston, 1979-80; pres. Braintrust Inc., Houston, 1980-83; sales mgr. Mossy Oldsmobile, Inc., Houston, 1983-84; gen. mgr. Mossy Nissan/Ford, Bellevue, Wash., 1984-86; dir. ops. Mossy Co., Encinitas, Calif., 1986-91; gen. mgr. Performance Nissan, Duarte, Calif., 1991—; seminar lectr. Rice U., Houston, 1980-83. Author: The Entrepreneurs Guide for Starting a Successful Business., 1982; contbr. (book) Business Planning for the Entrepreneur, 1983. Mem. Houston C. of C. (small bus. coun.), Opt Astron. Soc., Univ. Club, Phi Eta Sigma, Phi Kappa Phi. Office: Performance Nissan PO Box 1500 Duarte CA 91009-4500

BRESHEARS, GUY RUBEN, social studies educator, researcher; b. Spokane, June 15, 1962; s. Howard Patrick and B. Jane (Seeley) B. AA, Spokane Falls C.C., 1990; BA in Edn., Ea. Wash. U., 1993, postgrad., 1995-96. Cert. tchr., Wash. Maintenance supr. McDonald's Corp., Spokane, 1981-94; tchr. social studies Mt. St. Michael's, Spokane, 1994-95. Co-author: Voices From the Darkness, 1991, Treu Bis In Den Tod: A History of the 13th New York Independent Light Artillery Battery, 1992; rsch. asst. book: American Realities, 1993; contbr. to profl. publs. Mem. U.S. Naval Inst., Air Force Assn., Kennesaw Mountain Hist. Assn. Republican. Home: 6706 N Washington St Spokane WA 99208-4027

BRESLAUER, GEORGE WILLIAM, political science educator; b. N.Y.C., Mar. 4, 1946; s. Henry Edward and Marianne (Schaeffer) B.; m. Yvette Assia, June 5, 1976; children: Michelle, David. BA, U. Mich., 1966, MA, 1968, PhD, 1973. Asst. prof. polit. sci. U. Calif., Berkeley, 1971-79, assoc. prof., 1979-90, prof., 1990—, chmn. dept., 1993-96, chmn. Ctr. for Slavic and East European Studies, 1982-94; vice chmn. bd. trustees Nat. Coun. for Soviet and East European Rsch., Washington, 1988-91. Author: Khrushchev and Brezhnev as Leaders, 1982, Soviet Strategy in the Middle East, 1989; editor: Can Gorbachev's Reforms Succeed?, 1990, Learning in U.S. and Soviet Foreign Policy, 1991. Grantee Ford Found., 1982-84, Carnegie Corp., 1985-94. Mem. Am. Assn. for Advancement Slavic Studies (bd. dirs., exec. com. 1990-93). Office: U Calif Dept Polit Sci 210 Barrows Hall Berkeley CA 94720-1950

BRESLAW, CATHY LEE, artist, graphic designer, educator; b. Coral Gables, Fla.; d. William Howard and Miriam Roberts (Lasker) B.; m. Paul K. Cohen, Nov. 24, 1986; children: Adam, Micah. BA, George Washington U., 1973; MSW, Howard U., 1978. Graphic designer, artist Lee Press, Encinitas, Calif., 1992—; instr. fine art Jewish Cmty. Ctr., Encinitas, North County Quail Gardens, Encinitas; represented by La Jolla (Calif.) Gallery and Cafe, Wagner Fine Art, Del Mar, Calif. Exhibited in group shows San Diego Watercolor Soc., 1996, Nat. Watercolor Ann. Exhbn. and Travel Show, 1996-97, Gallery Contemporary Art U. Colo., 1997, Tubac Ctr. Arts, 1997, Downey (Calif.) Mus. Art, 1997, Calif. Watercolor Assn., San Francisco, 1997; one-woman shows include Curbside Cafe, Vista, Calif., 1996, Emerald Plaza, San Diego, 1996, Off Track Gallery, 1997. Bd. dirs., sec. United Cerebral Palsy Bay Area, San Francisco, 1978-82. Mem. Nat. Watercolor Soc. (signature mem.), San Diego Watercolor Soc. Office: PO Box 231122 Encinitas CA 92023

BRESLOW, BRUCE, mayor; b. Boston, 1956; 1 child, Matt. BJ, U. Mo., 1977. Mayor City of Sparks, Nev., 1991—; acct. exec. Minor Advt.; chmn. bd. Reno-Sparks Convention and Vis. Authority, 1995. Active MDA, Easter Seals, Heart Assn., Make-a-Wish; bd. dirs. Truckee Meadows Boys and Girls Club. Named Nev. Sportscaster of Yr., 1986-87, 89-90; recipient Peabody award, Emmy award. Office: 431 Prater Way Sparks NV 89431

BRESSAN, ROBERT R., accountant; b. Yonkers, N.Y., Feb. 8, 1945; s. Alfred D. and Antionette (Desivo) B.; m. Florence L. Vigna, June 9, 1968 (dec.); children: Anne Marie, Robert A., Tiffany L. BBA in Acctg., Iona Coll., 1967. CPA; cert. tax profl. Am. Inst. Tax Studies. Staff to sr. Coopers & Lybrand, N.Y.C., 1967-70; sr. to audit mgr. Fox & Co., Colorado Springs, 1970-80; ptnr., owner Robert R. Bressan, Colorado Springs, 1980—; mem. exec. com. GAO Intergovtl. Audit Forum. Mem. charity rev. com. BBB. Mem. Sertoma, AICPA, Inst. Mgmt. Accts., Govtl. Fin. Officers Assn., Colo. Govtl. Fin. Officers, Nat. Assn. Counties. Office: 829 N Circle Dr Ste 214 Colorado Springs CO 80909-5008

BREST, PAUL A., law educator; b. Jacksonville, Fla., Aug. 9, 1940; s. Alexander and Mia (Deutsch) B.; m. Iris Lang, June 17, 1962; children: Hilary, Jeremy. AB, Swarthmore Coll., 1962; JD, Harvard U., 1965; LLD (hon.), Northeastern U., 1980, Swarthmore Coll., 1991. Bar: N.Y. 1966. Law clk. to Hon. Bailey Aldrich U.S. Ct. Appeals (1st cir.), Boston, 1965-66; atty. NAACP Legal Def. Fund, Jackson, Miss., 1966-68; law clk. Justice John Harlan, U.S. Supreme Ct., 1968-69; prof. law Stanford U., 1969—, Kenneth and Harle Montgomery Prof. pub. interest law, Richard E. Lang prof. and dean, 1987—. Author: Processes of Constitutional Decisionmaking, 1992. Mem. Am. Acad. Arts and Scis. Home: 814 Tolman Dr Palo Alto CA 94305-1026 Office: Stanford U Sch Law Nathan Abbott Way at Alvarado Row Stanford CA 94305

BRETERNITZ, CORY DALE, archaeological company executive, consultant; b. Tucson, Apr. 9, 1955; s. David Alan and Barbara Blair (Myers) B.; m. Adrian Sue White, May 21, 1981; children: Jessie Lynn, Dylan Blair. BA, U. Ariz., 1978; MA, Wash. State U., 1982. Archaeologist Mus. No. Ariz., Flagstaff, 1973; lab. technician Lab. of Tree-Ring Rsch., Tucson, 1973-78; archaeologist Ariz. State Mus., Tucson, 1978, Nat. Pk. Svc., Albuquerque, 1976-79, Dolores (Colo.) Archaeol. Program, 1980-81; project dir. Navajo Nation Archaeology Program, Window Rock, Ariz., 1981-82, Profl. Svc. Industries, Inc., Phoenix, 1982-84; pres. Ctr. for Indigenous Studies in Ams., Phoenix, 1991—; pres., owner Soil Systems, Inc., Phoenix, 1984—. Mem. Ariz. Archaeol. Coun. (exec. com. 1976, editor 1989-94), N.Mex. Archaeol. Coun., Am. Cultural Resources Assn. (bd. dirs. 1995—), Colo. Coun. Profl. Archaeologists, Utah Profl. Archaeol. Coun., Am. Quaternary Assn., Soc. for Am. Archaeology (chmn. 1996—), Am. Anthrop. Assn. Office: Soil Systems Inc 1121 N 2nd St Phoenix AZ 85004-1807

BRETH, CHARLES ANDREW, artist; b. N.Y.C., Feb. 28, 1946; s. Fred Ernest and Adele (Lang) B. BA, U. Calif., Berkeley, 1969, MA in Sculpture, 1971; MFA in Ceramics, Ohio State U., 1993. Photography instr. U. Calif., Berkeley, 1967-71, ceramics instr., 1969-71; photographer Mendocino (Calif.) Art Ctr., 1970; head ceramics and sculpture Malispana U. Coll., Nanaimo, B.C., Can., 1987-88; drawing instr. Ohio State U., Columbus, 1991-93; head ceramics dept. U. Cin., 1993-94; lectr. U. Alta. Extension, Edmonton, Can., 1985-87; lectr. Alta. Culture, Edmonton, 1986, mem. jury, 1987; Roswell (N.Mex.) Artist in Residence, 1995-96; resident Archit Bray Found., Helena, 1994-95, Banff (Alta.) Ctr., 1990. One man shows include Courthouse Gallery, Red Deer, Alta., 1990, The Works, Edmonton, 1990, U. Mont., Missoula, 1995, U. Tex., El Paso, 1995, Paris Gibson Sq. Art Gallery, Great Falls, Mont., 1995, in situ Gallery, Cin., 1995, Bray Found., Helena, Mont., 1995; exhibited in group shows at Alta. Culture, 1990, Medicine Hat (Alta.) Mus., 1990, Muttart Gallery, Calgary, Alta., 1990, Ohio U., 1991, Big Ten Conf., Chgo., 1993, Columbus (Ohio) Art League, 1993, Archie Bray Found., Mont., 1994, 95, Ctrl. Mich. U., Mt. Pleasant, 1994, Holter Mus. Art, Helena, 1995, 96, San Angelo (Tex.) Nat. Ceramic Competition, 1996 (merit award); represented in permanent collections at Mus. Modern Art, N.Y.C., U. Calif., Berkeley, Fed Deer Coll., Anderson Mus. Contemporary Art, also pvt. collections. Grantee Alta. Culture, 1983, 86, Can. Coun., 1994, ; recipient Jury award Alta. Potters Assn., 1990, Edith Fergus Gilmore Materials award Ohioo State U., 1993. Home: 221 Harbourside Pl, Salt Spring Island, BC Canada Office: 30 S Harrison Ave Helena MT 59601

BRETT-ELSPAS, JANIS ELLEN, fashion designer, public relations executive; b. Hackensack, N.J., Sept. 6, 1956; d. Charles and Jean Estelle (Hawrey) Brett; m. Shlomo Elspas, Sept. 14, 1986; 1 child, Raphael Isaac Elspas. BA in Polit. Sci., U. Ariz., 1978; postgrad., UCLA, 1983. Asst. dir. pub. rels. SSC&B Advt., L.A., 1978-81; sr. pub. rels. specialist Informatics Gen. Corp., Woodland Hills, Calif., 1981-83; sr. account exec. Hill & Knowlton, San Jose, Calif., 1983-84; corp. account exec. Rogers & Cowan, L.A., 1984-86; artist, fashion designer self-employed, Lomita, Calif., 1990—; pres., founder Rachel PR Svcs., Redondo Beach, Calif., 1984—. Author feature articles for PR Jour., Profl. Communicator, Communication World; writer syndicated column Copley News Svc., 1986-87. Mem. Pub. Rels. Soc. Am., Internat. Assn. Bus. Communicators (Feature Writing award 1991), Publicity Club L.A., Ind. Writers So. Calif., Delta Zeta. Office: Rachel PR Svcs # 200C 1650 S Pacific Coast Hwy Redondo Beach CA 90277

BREUER, STEPHEN ERNEST, temple executive; b. Vienna, Austria, July 14, 1936; s. John Hans Howard and Olga Marion (Haar) B.; came to U.S., 1938, naturalized, 1945; BA cum laude, UCLA, 1959, gen. secondary credential, 1960; m. Gail Fern Breitbart, Sept. 4, 1960 (div. 1986); children: Jared Noah, Rachel Elise; m. Nadine Bendit, Sept. 25, 1988. Tchr. L.A. City Schs., 1960-62; dir. Wilshire Blvd. Temple Camps, L.A., 1962-86; exec. dir. Wilshire Blvd. Temple, 1980—; dir. Edgar F. Magnin Religious Sch., Los Angeles, 1970-80. Instr. Hebrew Union Coll., Los Angeles, 1965-76, 92—,

U. Judaism, 1991; field instr. San Francisco State U., 1970-80, Calif. State U., San Diego, Hebrew Union Coll., 1977-81, U. of Judaism UCLA extension. Vice pres. L.A. Youth Programs Inc., 1967-77; youth adviser L.A. County Commn. Human Rels., 1969-72. Bd. dirs. Cmty. Rels. Conf. So. Calif., 1965-85; bd. dirs. Alzheimer's Disease and Related Disorders Assn., 1984-95, v.p. L.A. County chpt., 1984-86, pres., 1986-88, nat. exec. com., 1987-95, nat. devel. chair, 1992-95, Calif. state coun. pres. 1987-92, chmn. of Calif. gov.'s adv. com. on Alzheimer's disease, 1988—; mem. goals program City of Beverly Hills, Calif., 1985-91; bd. dirs. Pacific SW regional Union Am. Hebrew Congregations, 1985-88, mem. nat. bd. , exec. com., 1993—; bd. dirs. Echo Found., 1986-88, Mazon-Jewish Response to Hunger, 1993—, Wilshire Stakeholders, exec. com., 1987-94; treas. Wilshire Community Prayer Alliance, 1986-88; active United Way. Recipient Service awards Los Angeles YWCA, 1974, Los Angeles County Bd. Suprs., 1982, 87, Ventura County Bd. Suprs., 1982, 87, Weinberg Chai Lifetime Achievement award Jewish Fed. Council Los Angeles, 1986, Nat. Philanthropy Day L.A. Medallion, 1993, L.A. County Redevel. Agy. recognition, 1994; Steve Breuer Conference Ctr. in Malibu named in his honor Wilshire Blvd. Temple Camps, 1990. Mem. So. Calif. Camping Assn. (dir. 1964-82), Nat. Assn. Temple Adminstrs. (nat. bd. dirs. 1987—, v.p. 1991-93, pres. 1993—, Svc. to Judaism award 1989, Svc. to the Community award 1990), Nat. Assn. Temple Educators, Los Angeles Assn. Jewish Edn. (dir.), Profl. Assn. Temple Adminstrs. (pres. 1985-88), Jewish Communal Profls. So. Calif., Assn. Supervision and Curriculum Devel., Am. Mgmt. Assn., So. Calif. Conf. Jewish Communal Workers, Jewish Profl. Network, Amnesty Internat., Jewish Resident Camping Assn. (pres. 1976-82), World Union for Progressive Judaism, UCLA Alumni Assn., Wilderness Soc., Center for Environ. Edn., Wildlife Fedn., Living Desert, Maple Mental Health Ctr. of Beverly Hills, Los Angeles County Mus. Contemporary Art, People for the Am. Way, Assn Reform Zionists Am. (bd. dirs. 1993—). Office: Wilshire Blvd Temple 3663 Wilshire Blvd Los Angeles CA 90010-2703 *You do not know at what moment you may touch the life of a child. It is rarely at the moment of plan or choice.*

BREUER, WERNER ALFRED, retired plastics company executive; b. Sinn, Hessia, Germany, Jan. 30, 1930; came to U.S., 1959; s. Christian and Hedwig (Cunz) B.; m. Gertrud Ackermann, June 21, 1950; children: Patricia, Julia, Eva-Maria. BS in Human Rels. and Orgnl. Behavior, U. San Francisco, 1983; MS in Bus. Mgmt., U. La Verne, 1985, DPA, 1988. Musician, bandleader BBT Dance Orch., various cities, Germany, 1950-54; lab. technician Firma E. Leitz GMBH, Wetzlar, Germany, 1954-59; lab. supr. Dayco Corp. (Am. latex divsn.), Hawthorne, Calif., 1959-65; tech. ops. mgr. Olin Corp., Stamford and New Haven, Conn., 1965-69; gen. mgr., exec. v.p. Expanded Rubber and Plastics Corp., Gardena, Calif., 1969-96; ret., 1996; gen. mgr. Schlobohm Co. Inc., Dominguez Hills, Calif., 1989-96; ret.; cons. human resources Stabond Corp., Gardena, 1988-95. Author/composer various popular and sacred recordings, 1970s; contbr. articles to jours. Active Town Hall of Calif., L.A., 1972—, World Affairs Coun., L.A., 1975—. Recipient William of Orange Gymnasium scholarship, Dillenburg, Germany, 1940, Portfolio award U. San Francisco, 1983-84. Mem. ASTM, ASCAP, Am. Soc. for Metals, Soc. for Plastics Engrs., N.Y. Acad. Scis., U. La Verne Alumni Assn. Republican. Home: 564 E Sage Circle Highlands Ranch CO 80126

BREWER, DAVID L., sociologist; b. Tucson, Mar. 11, 1933; s. Leslie O. and Nina (Brinkerhoff) B.; m. Sue Mansfield; children: Phillip, Brent, Robin. BS, Brigham Young U., 1957; MS, Purdue U., 1959; PhD in Sociology, U. Utah, 1966. Various teaching and rsch. positions including Fresno (Calif.) State U., Calif. State U./Hayward, Newark State Coll, others, 1964-71; rsch. analyst Calif. Dept. Corrections, Chino, 1972-82; various to assoc. govtl. program analyst Calif. Dept. Corrections, Sacramento, 1982-88, correctional counselor, 1988-89; correctional counselor Calif. Dept. Corrections, Chino, 1989-90, clin. sociologist, 1990-92, correctional counselor, 1992-94; rsch. assoc. Dem. Processes Ctr., Tucson, 1995—. Contbr. articles to profl. jours., publs. Mem. Am. Sociol. Assn., Assn. Criminal Justice Rsch., Soc. for Study of Symbolic Interaction, Calif. Sociol. Assn., Sociol. Practice Assn. Office: Dem Processes Ctr 4349 N Linda Lee Dr Tucson AZ 85705-2399

BREWER, JANICE KAY, state legislator, property and investment firm executive; b. Hollywood, Calif., Sept. 26, 1944; d. Perry Wilford and Edna Clarice (Bakken) Drinkwine; m. John Leon Brewer, Jan. 1, 1963; children: Ronald Richard, John Samuel, Michael Wilford. Med. asst. cert. Valley Coll., Burbank, Calif., 1963, practical radiol. technician cert., 1963; D in Humanities (hon.) L.A. Chiropractic Coll., 1970. Pres., Brewer Property & Investments, Glendale, Ariz., 1970—; mem. Ariz. Ho. of Reps., Phoenix, 1983-86, Ariz. Senate, 1987-96, majority whip, 1993-96; mem. Maricopa County Bd. Suprs., 1997—. State committeeman, Rep. Party, Phoenix, 1970, 1983; legis. liaison Ponderosa Rep. Women, Phoenix, 1980; bd. dirs. Motion Picture & TV Commn. Active NOW. Recipient Freedom award Vets. of Ariz., 1994; named Woman of Yr., Chiropractic Assn. Ariz., 1983, Legislator of Yr., Behaviour Health Assn. Ariz., 1991, NRA, 1992. Mem. Nat. Fedn. Rep. Women, Am. Legis. Exch. Coun. Lutheran. Home: 6835 W Union Hills Dr Glendale AZ 85308-8058*

BREWER, LIA HARPER, marriage and family therapist; b. San Luis Obispo, Calif., June 4, 1962; d. Jeremy More and Althea (Harper); m. David Wayne Brewer, Oct. 15, 1988; 1 child, Alyssa Michelle; stepchildren: Anthony, Rebecca. Student, Lewis and Clark Coll., 1980-82; BA in Devel. Psychology, U. Calif., Santa Barbara, 1984; MA in Counseling, Calif. Family Study Ctr., Burbank, 1986. Lic. marriage, family, and child counselor. Play therapy intern Internat. Inst. for Transpersonal Studies, Ojai, Calif., 1986-87; marriage, family, and child counseling intern Interface Family Svcs., Ventura, Calif., 1986-87; intern, assoc. play therapist Ventura Family Ctr., 1986-93; pvt. practice Ventura, Ojai, 1993-94; pvt. practice, sch. cons. Taft, Calif., 1994—. Author: Digger Gets Help - A Story About Sexual Abuse for Children, 1996, Digger's Secret Fear - A Story About Divorce for Children, 1993. Mem. Am. Assn. Marriage, Family Therapists, Am. Psychotherapy Assn., Step-Family Assn., Calif. Assn. Marriage, Family Therapists. Republican. Mem. Christian Ch. Office: 503 6th St Taft CA 93268-2704

BREWER, RONALD RAY, religious organization administrator; b. Bethany, Okla., May 9, 1951; s. Walter Ray and Bertha Lou (Stepp) B.; m. Nancey Anne Boyd, Aug. 22, 1972; children: Phillip Wayne, Allison Marie. AA, Southwestern Coll., 1972; BA, So. Nazarene U., 1974; MA, Southwestern Sem., Ft. Worth, 1978. Cert. ch. bus. adminstr. Min. youth, music Cherokee Hills Bapt. Ch., Oklahoma City, 1972-74; min. youth, family Pleasantview Bapt. Ch., Crowley, Tex., 1974-79; min. adminstrn. Trinity Bapt. Ch., Oklahoma City, 1979-85, First Bapt. Ch., Lawton, Okla., 1985-90, Wieuca Rd. Bapt. Ch, Atlanta, 1990-93, First Bapt. Ch., Amarillo, Tex., 1993-95, Village Christian Schs., Sun Valley, Calif., 1995—; mem. christian ethics com. Comanche-Cotton Bapt. Assn., Lawton, 1986, pers. com., 1987-88, chmn. bylaws revision com., 1989. Pres. Christian Family Counseling Ctr. Bd., Lawton, 1987-88, treas., 1988-89, chmn. fin. com., 1988-90; v.p. Bapt. edn., Music Assn. Okla., 1984-85. Named one of Outstanding Young Men Am., OYMA/Jaycees, 1981. Fellow Nat. Assn. Ch. Bus. Adminstrs. (cert.); mem. So. Bapt. Assn. for Ch. Bus. Adminstrn. (cert.), Christian Ministries Mgmt. Assn., Atlanta Bapt. Assn. (bd. dirs. 1990). Democrat. Home: 30654 Yosemite Dr Castaic CA 91384-3738 Office: Village Christian Schs 8930 Village Ave Sun Valley CA 91352-2129

BREWER, THOMAS BOWMAN, retired university president; b. Fort Worth, July 22, 1932; s. Earl Johnson and Maurine (Bowman) B.; m. Betty Jean Walling, Aug. 4, 1951; children: Diane, Thomas Bowman Jr. B.A., U. Tex., 1954, M.A., 1957; Ph.D., U. Pa., 1962. Instr. St. Stephens Episcopal Sch., Austin, Tex., 1955-56, S.W. Tex. State Coll., San Marcos, 1956-57; from instr. to asso. prof. N. Tex. State U., Denton, 1959-66; asst. prof. U. Ky., 1966-67; asso. prof. Iowa State U., 1967-68; prof. history, chmn. dept. U. Toledo, 1968-71; dean Tex. Christian U., Fort Worth, 1971-72, vice chancellor, dean univ., 1972-78; chancellor E. Carolina U., Greenville, N.C., 1978-82; v.p. acad. affairs Ga. State U., Atlanta, 1982-88; pres. Met. State Coll. of Denver, 1988-93. Editor: Views of American Economic Growth, 2 vols, 1966, The Robber Barons, 1969; gen. editor: Railroads of America Series. Home: 104 Javelin Dr Austin TX 78734-5016

BREWER, TIMOTHY FRANCIS, III, retired cardiologist; b. Hartford, Conn., Oct. 30, 1931; s. Timothy F. Jr. and Catherine Marie (Sullivan) B.; m. Norma Rae Flicker, June 14, 1954 (div. 1980); children: Raymond, Donna, Timothy, Kevin, William; m. Barbara Grace Bagdasarian, May 28, 1983. BA, Yale Coll., 1953; MD, N.Y. Med. Coll., 1957. Diplomate Am. Bd. Internal Medicine Cardiovascular Diseases. Intern St. Francis Hosp., Hartford, 1957-58; resident in internal medicine VA Ctr., L.A., 1958-60; spl. fellow in cardiovascular diseases Cleve. (Ohio) Clinic, 1960-62; pvt. practice St. Francis Hosp., Hartford, 1962-64; assoc. dir. clin. rsch. Pfizer Inc., Groton, Conn., 1964-71; dir. Clin. Pharmacology Miles Lab., West Haven, Conn., 1971-74; pvt. practice Middlesex Hosp., Middletown, Conn., 1974-96, ret., 1996; pres. med. staff Middlesex (Conn.) Hosp., 1981-83, chief sect. cardiology, 1988-95. Fellow ACP, Am. Coll. Cardiology (emeritus), Am. Coll. Chest Physicians, Coun. on Clin. Cardiology; mem. AMA (pres. South Ctrl. Conn. chpt. 1982, bd. dirs. 1980), Am. Heart Assn. (Conn. affiliate).

BREWINGTON, ARTHUR WILLIAM, retired English language educator; b. Bklyn., Nov. 10, 1906; s. Oscar and Julia (Wenisch) B.; m. Thelma Sherman, Aug. 18, 1955. AB, Asbury Coll., 1928; MA, Cornell U., 1931; PhD, Vanderbilt U., 1941. Head English dept. Tenn. Wesleyan Coll., Athens, 1929-31; instr. English Pa. State U., State College, 1932-33; prof. English and speech Memphis State U., 1940-43; inspector quality control Glenn Martin Co., Balt., 1943-45; head English and speech dept. Towson State U., Balt., 1945-71; dir. drama and theater Towson State U., 1946-69. Contbr. rsch. to profl. publs. Fund-raiser, bd. dirs. Am. Heart Assn., Green Valley, 1995-96. Fulbright grantee U.S. State Dept., 1955-56, Danforth grantee, 1963. Mem. Kiwanis (com. chmn. 1971-95), Masons (chaplain lodge 171 1972-75), Cornell Club., Green Valley Shrine Club (pres. 1974). Democrat. Episcopalian. Home: 69 W Cedro Dr Green Valley AZ 85614

BREWSTER, RUDI MILTON, federal judge; b. Sioux Falls, S.D., May 18, 1932; s. Charles Edwin and Wilhemina Therese (Rud) B.; m. Gloria Jane Nanson, June 27, 1954; children: Scot Alan, Lauri Diane (Alan Lee), Julie Lynn Yahnke. AB in Pub. Affairs, Princeton U., 1954; JD, Stanford U., 1960. Bar: Calif. 1960. From assoc. to ptnr. Gray, Cary, Ames & Frye, San Diego, 1960-84; judge U.S. Dist. Ct. (so. dist.) Calif., San Diego, 1984—. Served to capt. USNR, 1954-82 Ret. Fellow Am. Coll. Trial Lawyers; mem. Am. Bd. Trial Advs., Internat. Assn. Ins. Counsel, Am. Inns of Ct. Republican. Lutheran. Office: US Dist Ct 940 Front St San Diego CA 92101-8994

BREYTSPRAAK, JOHN, JR., management consultant; b. Chgo., May 24, 1929; s. John and Grace Willets (Merrick) B.; m. Charlotte Helfand, Dec. 27, 1958. BA in Econs., Lake Forest (Ill.) Coll., 1950. Mgr. mktg. communications fibers div. Am. Cyanamid, N.Y.C., 1964-67; merchandising mgr. Vectra Fiber, Standard Oil Co. N.J., N.Y.C., 1967-69; account supr. Doyle Dane Bernbach, N.Y.C., 1969-73; mgr. mktg. svcs. Formica Corp., Am. Cyanamid, Cin., 1973-76; pres. Sanitas Wallcoverings, Am. Cyanamid, Wayne, N.J., 1976-80; gen. mgr. Chem. Light, Am. Cyanamid, Wayne, 1980-81; pres. Simmons Wallcoverings, Gulf & Western, N.Y.C., 1981-84; cons. New Bern, N.C., 1984—; pres. Composers Music Co., New Bern, 1987—. Composer 12 musical works, 1985-89; contbr. hist. articles to Jour. of New Bern Hist. Soc., 1988-89. Pres., Craven Concerts Inc., Craven County, N.C., 1987-89; instr. U.S. Power Squadron, Craven County, 1985-87; mem. New Bern Hist. Soc., 1986-89. Home and Office: 1414 Sleater Kinney Rd SE Lacey WA 98503-2537

BREZZO, STEVEN LOUIS, museum director; b. Woodbury, N.J., June 18, 1949; s. Louis and Ella Marie (Savage) B.; m. Dagmar Grimm, Aug. 10, 1975. B.A., Clarion State Coll., 1969; M.F.A., U. Conn., 1973. Chief curator La Jolla Mus. Contemporary Art, Calif., 1974-76; asst. dir. San Diego Mus. Art, 1976-78, dir., 1978—. Mem. Am. Assn. Mus. (del. to China 1981, to Italian mus. study trip 1982), Calif. Assn. Mus. (pres. 1992—), La Jolla Library Assn. (pres. 1980). Club: University (San Diego). Lodge: Rotary. Office: San Diego Museum of Art PO Box 2107 San Diego CA 92112-2107*

BRIAN, BRAD D., lawyer; b. Merced, Calif., Apr. 19, 1952. BA, U. Calif., Berkeley, 1974; JD magna cum laude, Harvard U., 1977. Bar: Calif. 1977, U.S. Ct. Appeals (3d cir.) 1978, U.S. Dist. Ct. (ctrl. dist.) Calif. 1978, U.S. Ct. Appeals (9th cir.) 1980. Law clk. to Hon. John J. Gibbons U.S. Ct. Appeals (3d cir.), 1977-78; asst. U.S. atty. Office U.S. Atty. (ctrl. dist.) Calif., 1978-81; hearing examiner L.A. City Police Commn., 1982; atty. Munger, Tolles & Olson, L.A.; lectr. in law U. So. Calif. Law Ctr., 1983; instr. Nat. Inst. Trial Advocacy, 1986; guest instr. Harvard Law Sch. Trial Advocacy Program, 1983. Bd. editors Harvard Law Rev., 1975-77, mng. editor and treas., 1976-77. Mem. ABA (chmn. pre-trial practice and discovery, litigation sect. 1987-89, liaison with fed. jud. confs. 1989-91, chair task force on civil justice reform act of 1990), State Bar Calif., L.A. County Bar Assn. (mem. fed. practice standards com. 1980-82). Office: Munger Tolles & Olson 355 S Grand Ave Fl 35 Los Angeles CA 90071-1560

BRICKER, LAUREN WEISS, historian; b. Bethesda, Md., Aug. 6, 1954; d. Arnold and Elaine (Aldino) Weiss; m. David Bricker, Apr. 26, 1981; 1 child, Thalia Rae. BA, Swathmore Coll., 1977; MA, U. Calif., Santa Barbara, 1983; PhD, U. Calif., Santa Barabara, 1992. Archtl. historian Found. San Francisco's Archtl. Heritage, 1989-91; archtl. historian, cons. various cities, So. Calif., 1993—; adj. faculty Riverside (Calif.) C.C., 1995—, Calif. State Poly. U., Pomona, 1996—, U. Redlands (Calif.), 1996—; guest curator Palm Springs (Calif.) Desert Mus., 1996-97. Author: (with others) Architectural Historian in America, 1990. Mem. Calif. Preservation Found., 1989— (Design award 1994, 95); trustee Redlands (Calif.) Conservancy, 1994—; hist. advisor La Quinta (Calif.) Hist. Preservation Commn., 1995—; trustee Kimberly-Shirk Assn., Redlands, 1996—. Samuel H. Kress Found. fellow art history dept., U. Calif., Santa Barbara, 1981, 83, 85, 86; Andrew Mellon Found. fellow Huntington Libr., 1994-95. Mem. Soc. Archtl. Historians (mem. presentation com. 1990—). Home and Office: 1405 Garden St Redlands CA 92373

BRICKMAN, HARRY RUSSELL, psychiatrist, psychoanalytic institute dean; b. N.Y.C., Feb. 16, 1924; s. Lewis and Rose (Oxman) B.; m. Beatrice Helen Krane, May 29, 1948; children: Mark, Marianne. BS, NYU, 1944, MD, 1947; PhD, So. Calif. Psychoanalytic Inst., 1972. Intern Fresno (Calif.) County Hosp., 1947-48; resident in psychiatry Menninger Found., Topeka, 1948-50, Palo Alto (Calif.) Hosp., 1950-51, Langley Porter Clinic, San Francisco, 1950-51; dir. Riverside (Calif.) State Mental Hygiene Clinic, 1951-52; pvt. practice L.A., 1951—; dir. So. Calif. Reception Ctr., Calif. Youth Authority, Norwalk, 1954-56; dir. outpatient svcs. dept. psychiatry UCLA Sch. Medicine, 1956-60; founding dir. Los Angeles County Mental Health Dept., L.A., 1960-76; dean So. Calif. Psychoanalytic Inst., L.A., 1991-96. Contbr. articles to profl. jours. Lt. USNR, 1950-52. Fellow Am. Psychiat. Assn. (life); mem. Am. Psychoanalytic Assn. (life), Internat. Psychoanalytic Assn. (life). Office: 1100 Glendon Ave Ste 1210 Los Angeles CA 90024-3516

BRIDE, ROBERT FAIRBANKS, lawyer; b. Washington, July 18, 1953; s. Noel Crawford and Jeanne Marie (Rafferty) B.; m. Tracy Viles Johnson, 1992. BA, Northwestern U., 1974; JD, U. Mich., 1978. Bar: Calif. Assoc. Sullivan, Jones and Archer, San Diego, 1978-80, Kosmo, Cho and Brown, Ventura, Calif., 1980-85; assoc. McGahan and Engle, Ventura, 1985-87, ptnr., 1987-88; founding ptnr. Engle and Bride, Ventura, 1988—; judge pro tempore Ventura County Superior Ct. and Mcpl. Ct., 1989—; arbitrator Ventura County Superior Ct., 1983—; prof. Pacific Legal Arts Coll., Camarillo, Calif., 1981-84; lectr. Assn. of So. Calif. Def. Counsel, 1992—. Sponsor Save the Children, 1988—, Santa Barbara Civic Light Opera, 1988—, Cato Inst., 1991—. Mem. ABA, Assn. Soc. Calif. Def. Counsel, Am. Bd. Trial Advocates, Am. Soc. Law, Medicine and Ethics, Ventura County Bar Assn., Bar Assn. U.S. Supreme Ct., Mensa, Phi Beta Kappa, Pierpont Racquet Club. Republican. Roman Catholic. Home: 508 W Eucalyptus St Ojai CA 93023 Office: Engle and Bride 353 San Jon Rd Ventura CA 93001-3250

BRIDGE, SHERRY, clinical dietitian; b. Magrath, Alta., Can., Apr. 4, 1952; came to U.S., 1954; d. Malcolm Ririe and Elizabeth (McBride) B. BS, Utah State U., 1974. Registered dietitian, Utah. Dietitian/supr. Lakeview Hosp., Bountiful, Utah, 1975-76; dietitian/food svc. dir. Brigham City (Utah) Cmty. Hosp., 1977-79; adminstrv. dietitian Lakeview Hosp., an affiliate of Columbia/HCA, Bountiful, 1978-93; clin. dietitian Lakeview Hosp., an affiliate of HealthTrust, Inc., Bountiful, 1993—; cons. dietitian Davis County Coun. on Aging, Farmington, Utah, 1979-81; adj. prof. Brigham Young U., Provo, Utah, 1992—. Organist LDS Ch., Bountiful, 1974-95, mem. presidency of local women's soc. orgn.; data entry operator LDS Geneol. Soc., Salt Lake City, 1990-93. Mem. Utah Dietetic Assn. (coun. on practice 1981-89, sec. 1989-91, 92, pres. 1994-95, reimbursement issues com. 1995—), Am. Heart Assn. (Davis County affiliate).

BRIDGES, DOUGLAS M., musician, small business owner; b. Belleville, Ill., Jan. 22, 1958; s. Donald Miles and Geneva (Verduce) B.; m. Laura L. Missey, Oct. 21, 1978. Ordained to ministry Universal Life Ch., 1993. Musician Easy St., Belleville, 1981, Cimmaron, Las Vegas, Nev., 1981-85; co-owner Cimarron Music Works, Estes Park, Colo., 1990-94; composer, music adv. Horizon Video Prodn., Denver, 1995—. Author: Banjo Owners Notebook, 1989; composer; patentee in field. Park watcher nat. Parks Conservation Assn., 1994—. Office: DM Bridges PO Box 2186 Estes Park CO 80517

BRIDGES, EDWIN MAXWELL, education educator; b. Hannibal, Mo., Jan. 1, 1934; s. Edwin Otto and Radha (Maxwell) B.; m. Marjorie Anne Pollock, July 31, 1954; children: Richard, Rebecca, Brian, Bruce. BS, U. Mo., 1954; MA, U. Chgo., 1956, PhD, 1964. English tchr. Bremen Community High Sch., Midlothian, Ill., 1954-56; asst. prin. Griffith (Ind.) High Sch., 1956-60, prin., 1960-62; staff assoc. U. Chgo., 1962-64, assoc. prof., 1967-72; assoc. dir. Univ. Coun. for Edn. Adminstrn., Columbus, Ohio, 1964-65; asst. prof. Washington U., St. Louis, 1965-67; assoc. prof. U. Chgo., 1967-72; prof. U. Calif., Santa Barbara, 1972-74; prof. edn. Stanford (Calif.) U., 1974—; mem. nat. adv. panel Ctr. for Rsch. on Ednl. Accountability and Tchr. Evaluation, 1990-95; external examiner U. Hong Kong, 1990-92; vis. prof. Chinese U., Hong Kong, 1976, 96; cons. World Bank, China, 1986, 89; dir. Midwest Adminstrn. Ctr., Chgo., 1967-72. Author: Managing the Incompetent Teacher, 1984, 2d edit., 1990, The Incompetent Teacher, 1986, 2d edit., 1991, Problem Based Learning for Administrators, 1992; co-author: Introduction to Educational Adminstration, 1977, Implementing Problem-based Leadership Development, 1995; contbr. articles to profl. jours. Recipient of the R.F. Campbell Lifetime Achievement award, 1996; named Outstanding Young Man of Ind., C. of C., 1960; named hon. prof. and cert. of honor So. China Normal U., 1989. Mem. Am. Ednl. Rsch. Assn. (v.p. 1974-75). Office: Stanford U Sch Edn Stanford CA 94305

BRIDGES, KATHLEEN ERICKSON, communication disorders specialist; b. Mojave, Calif., June 3, 1944; d. John Stahlberg and Evelyn Lyle (Shriver) Erickson. BA cum laude, U. Utah, 1968, MA, 1969. Lic. speech pathologist, Utah, Calif. Resource tchr. Salt Lake City Schs., 1971-76, communication disorders specialist, 1969-70, 76-89; communication disorders specialist Orange (Calif.) Unified Schs., 1970-71, 89-91, Tustin Unified Schs., 1991-92; spl. day class tchr. Capistrano Unified Sch. Dist., 1992-95, comm. disorders specialist, 1995—; clin. instr. U. Utah Dept. Communication Disorders, Salt Lake City, 1976-89, mem. adv. bd.; chmn. com. for practical examination speech pathology licensure Utah Dept. Bus. Regulations, Salt Lake City, 1984, 86. Mem. Salt Lake Jr. League, 1973-85, rec. sec., 1980-81, project chmn., 1976-77; chmn. Youth Svcs. Adv. Bd., 1976-78; treas., trustee Parent Support, Inc., 1976-89; bd. dirs., coms. chmn. Salt Lake Jr. Achievement, 1974-78; tchr. leader Salt Lake Dist. Career Ladder, 1985-87, tchr. specialist, 1987-88; mem. adv. bd. Pi Beta Phi, U. Calif., Irvine, 1993-95. Named Vital Vol., Salt Lake County Commn., 1986. Mem. NEA, Calif. Tchrs. Assn., Am. Speech Lang. Hearing Assn. (cert.), Calif. Speech Lang. Hearing Assn., Capistrano Unified Tchrs. Assn., Pi Beta Phi Alumnae Club (sec. 1971-72, chmn. 1982-83, philanthropy chmn. 1973-75, pledges advisor 1978-80, house advisor 1985-86, adv. com. chmn. 1986-88, PSI province coord. 1988-89), Cen. Orange County Alumnae Club (v.p. membership 1995-97, pres. 1996—), Golden Key, Phi Kappa Phi. Democrat. Mem. Christian Scientist Ch. Home: 15 Telura Rancho Santa Margarita CA 92688-3024 Office: Wood Canyon Elementary 23431 Knowland Aliso Viejo CA 92656

BRIDGES, ROBERT MCSTEEN, mechanical engineer; b. Oakland, Calif., Apr. 17, 1914; s. Robert and Josephine (Hite) B.; BS cum laude in Mech. Engring., U. So. Calif., 1940; postgrad. UCLA; m. Edith Brownwood, Oct. 26, 1945; children: Ann, Lawrence, Robert. Registered profl. engr., Calif. Engr. Nat. Supply Co., Torrance, Calif., 1940-41; design engr. landing gear and hydraulics Lockheed Aircraft Corp., Burbank, Calif., 1941-46; missile hydraulic controls design engr. Convair, San Diego, 1946-48; sr. staff engr. oceanic systems mech. design Bendix Corp., Sylmar, Calif., 1948—; adv. ocean engring. U.S. Congress. Com. chmn. Boy Scouts Am., 1961. Recipient award of Service Am. Inst. Aero. Engrs., 1965. Mem. Marine Tech. Soc. (charter; com. cables, connectors 1969), Tau Beta Pi. Republican. Patentee in field of undersea devices (54 internat., 14 U.S.), including deep ocean rubber band moor; inventor U.S. Navy sonobuoy rotochute; contbr. articles to profl. jours. and confs. Home: 10314 Vanalden Ave Northridge CA 91326-3326 Office: Allied Signal Ocean Systems Corp Bendix Sylmar Divsn 15825 Roxford St San Fernando CA 91342-3537

BRIDGES, ROY DUBARD, JR., career officer; b. Atlanta, July 19, 1943; s. Roy D. and Elizabeth A. (Roberson) B.; m. Benita L. Allbaugh, Mar. 26, 1967; children: Tanya M., Brian N. BS in Engring. Sci., USAF Acad., 1965; MS in Astronautical Engring., Purdue U., 1966. Commd. 2d lt. USAF, 1965, advanced through grades to maj. gen., 1992; test pilot Air Force Flight Test Ctr., Edwards AFB, Calif., 1970-75; student Air Command and Staff Coll., Maxwell AFB, Ala., 1975-76; staff officer Hdqrs. USAF, Pentagon, Washington, 1976-79; dep. dir. plans Detachment 3, Air Force Flight Test Ctr., Henderson, Nev., 1979-80; astronaut (pilot) Johnson Space Ctr., NASA, Houston, 1980-86; comdr. 6510th Test Wing, Edwards AFB, Calif., 1986-89; comdr., Ea. Space and Missile Ctr., Patrick AFB, Fla., 1989-90; dep. chief of staff for test and resources Air Force Systems Command, Andrews AFB, Md., 1990-91; comdr. Air Force Flight Test Ctr. Edwards AFB, Edwards AFB, Calif., 1991-93; dir. requirements Air Force Materiel Command, Wright Patterson AFB, Ohio, 1993-96; ret. USAF, 1996; dir. NASA-Kennedy Space Ctr., Fla., 1997—; pilot space shuttle Challenger, NASA,1985. Named to Ga. Aviation Hall of Fame, 1995; recipient Space Flight award Am. Astronautical Soc., 1986, Astronaut Engring. Alumnus award Purdue U., 1990. Fellow Soc. Exptl. Test Pilots (assoc.); mem. Air Force Assn., Assn. of Space Explorers. Methodist.

BRIDGFORTH, ROBERT MOORE, JR., aerospace engineer; b. Lexington, Miss., Oct. 21, 1918; s. Robert Moore and Theresa (Holder) B.; student Miss. State Coll., 1935-37; BS, Iowa State Coll., 1940; MS, MIT, 1948; postgrad. Harvard U., 1949; m. Florence Jarnberg, November 7, 1943; children: Robert Moore, Alice Theresa. Asst. engr. Standard Oil Co., of Ohio, 1940; teaching fellow M.I.T., 1940-41, instr. chemistry, 1941-43, research asst., 1943-44, mem. staff div. indsl. cooperation, 1944-47; asso. prof. physics and chemistry Emory and Henry Coll., 1949-51; rsch. engr. Boeing Airplane Co., Seattle, 1951-54, rsch. specialist 1954-55, sr. group engr., 1955-58, chief propulsion systems sect. Systems Mgmt. Office, 1958-59, chief propulsion rsch. unit, 1959-60; founder, chmn. bd. Rocket Rsch. Corp., 1960-69, Explosives Corp. Am., 1966-69. Fellow AIAA (assoc.), Brit. Interplanetary Soc., Am. Inst. Chemists; mem. AAAS, Am. Astronautical Soc. (dir.), Am. Chem. Soc., Am. Rocket Soc. (pres. Pacific NW 1955), Am. Ordnance Assn., Am. Inst. Physics, Am. Assn. Physics Tchrs., Tissue Culture Assn., Soc. for Leukocyte Biology, N.Y. Acad. Scis., Combustion Inst., Sigma Xi. Achievements include U.S. patents for rocket tri-propellants and explosives. Home: 4325 87th Ave SE Mercer Island WA 98040-4127

BRIDGMAN, RICHARD DARRELL, lawyer; b. Madison, S.D., Mar. 1, 1929; s. Lloyd Alton and Fay Catherine (Turner) B.; m. Marilyn Elizabeth Smith, May 25, 1952 (div. June 1987); 1 child: Richard Darrell. AB, U. Calif., 1951; JD, Golden Gate U., 1958. Bar: Calif. 1958, U.S. Dist Ct. (no. dist.) Calif. 1958, U.S. Dist. Ct. (ea. dist.) Calif. 1982, U.S. Dist Ct. (cen. dist.) Calif. 1985, U.S. Ct. Appeals (9th cir.) 1958. Ptnr. Ericksen, Ericksen, Kincaid & Bridgman, Oakland, Calif., 1959-69; ptnr. O'Neill & Bridgman, Oakland, Calif., 1969-86, San Francisco, 1986-88; pvt. practice Richard D. Bridgman, San Francisco, 1988-92; ptnr. Bridgman & Bridgman, San Francisco, 1992—; mem., bd. dirs. Lawyer's Mutual Ins. Co., Burbank, Calif., 1978-88; faculty Golden Gate U., San Francisco, 1963-69, Hastings Coll. Trial & Appellate Advocacy, San Francisco, 1978-91. Co-author: Legal Malpractice-Suing & Defending Lawyers, 1984; contbr. articles to profl. jours. Lt. U.S. Navy, 1951-54, Korea. Named Lawyer of Yr. Lawyers Club of Alameda Co., 1980. Mem. Inner Cir. Advocates, Am. Bd Trial Advocates, Am. Bd. Profl. Liability Attys. (diplomate), Calif. Trial Lawyers Assn.

(bd. govs. 1976-83, sec. 1978-81), Alameda Conta Costa Trial Lawyers Assn. (pres. 1982). Office: Bridgman & Bridgman 5 Marietta Dr San Francisco CA 94127-1839

BRIDWELL, C. JOSEPH, computer systems analyst; b. Greenville, S.C., Feb. 4, 1955; s. Gordon William and Vera Mae (Whisenant) B.; m. Clemeth Ray Saylor, May 2, 1987 (dec. July 1994). BS, Furman U., 1977; MA, Ga. State U., 1983; client server cert., Bellevue C.C., 1997. Programmer, analyst Daniel Internat., Greenville, S.C., 1977-80, C&S Nat. Bank, Atlanta, 1980-83; DBA So. Motor Carriers, Atlanta, 1983-87; analyst, cons. Options Clearing Corp., Chgo., 1987-88, Seafirst Nat. Bank, Seattle, 1988-91, Ernst, Seattle, 1991-96; bd. dirs. Urdd Arleisiau'r Ddraig, Seattle, 1993-97. Contbr. articles to mags. Mem. Hands Off Washington, Seattle, 1994-97, Human Rights campaign, Washington, 1994-97. Fellow TRUST; mem. Ariz. Gay Rodeo Assn., Nat. Leather Assn. Home: 2501 E Madison St # 302 Seattle WA 98112-4754

BRIER, JAMES ROY, airplane manufacturing company official; b. Scranton, Pa., Aug. 27, 1931; s. William and Lillian May (Mundy) B.; m. Natalie Mary Pantle, Aug. 8, 1953; 1 child, Susan Paige Brier Chang. BS in Econs., U. Richmond, 1954; MBA in Prodn. Mgmt., Mich. State U., 1965. Helicopter pilot U.S. Army, 1956-86; program mgr. McDonnell Douglas, Mesa, Ariz., 1986—, program mgmt. adminstr., 1989-90. Contbr. articles to profl. jours. Col. U.S. Army, 1957-86. Decorated Bronze Star with two oak leaf clusters, Legion of Merit. Republican. Presbyterian. Home: 2622 E Fountain St Mesa AZ 85213

BRIER, PETER A., English literature educator; b. Vienna, Austria, Mar. 5, 1935; came to U.S., 1940; s. Francis Simon and Stella Rose Brier; m. Nurith Goldschmidt, May 29, 1975; children: Jonathan, Moriah. BA, Yale U., 1956; MA, Harvard U., 1958; PhD, Intercoll. Program Grad. Stds., 1971. Instr. Occidental Coll., L.A., 1966-70; from instr. to assoc. prof. English lit. Calif. State U., L.A., 1968-81, prof., 1981—; Author: (biography) Howard Mumford Jones and the Dynamics of Liberal Humanism, 1994; co-author: (bibliography) American Prose and Criticism 1990-1950, 1981. Mem. Phi Kappa Phi. Democrat. Jewish. Home: 1847 Craig Ave Altadena CA 91001-3429 Office: Calif State U Calif State U Los Angeles CA 90032

BRIERLEY, JAMES ALAN, research administrator; b. Denver, Dec. 22, 1938; s. Everette and Carrie (Berg) B.; m. Corale Louise Beer, Dec. 21, 1965. BS in Bacteriology, Colo. State U., 1961; MS in Microbiology, Mont. State U., 1963, PhD, 1966. Research scientist Martin Marietta Corp., Denver, 1968-69; asst. prof. biology N.Mex. Inst. Mining and Tech., Socorro, 1966-68, from asst. prof. to prof. biology, chmn. dept. biology, 1969-83; research dir. Advanced Mineral Techs., Golden, Colo., 1983-88; chief biologist Newmont Metall. Svcs., Englewood, Colo., 1988—; vis. fellow U. Warwick, Coventry, Eng., 1976, vis. prof. Catholic U., Santiago, Chile, 1983; adj. prof. dept. metallurgy U. Utah, 1994-96; cons. Mountain State Mineral Enterprises, Tucson, 1980, Sandia Nat. Lab., Albuquerque, 1976, Bechtel Civil and Minerals, Scottsdale, Ariz., 1984. Contbr. numerous articles to profl. jours.; patentee in field. Served to staff sgt. Air N.G., 1956-61. Recipient 32 research grants. Fellow AAAS; mem. Am. Soc. Microbiology, Soc. Gen. Microbiology, Sigma Xi. Home: 2074 East Terrace Dr Highlands Ranch CO 80126-2692 Office: Newmont Tech Facility 10101 East Dry Creek Rd Englewood CO 80112

BRIGGS, DINUS MARSHALL, agriculturist; b. Stillwater, Okla., Mar. 5, 1940; s. Hilton Marshall and Lillian (Dinusson) B.; m. June Elaine Wolf, Sept. 2, 1962; children: Denise, Deborah. BS, S.D. State U., 1962; MS, Iowa State U., 1969, PhD, 1971. Asst. pastor Stroudsburg (Pa.) Meth. Ch., 1962-64; grad. asst. Iowa State U., Ames, 1964-66, research assoc., 1966-70; asst. prof. N.C. State U., Raleigh, 1970-75; asst. dir. Ark. Agrl. Expt. Sta., Fayetteville, 1976-82; assoc. dir. N.Mex. Agrl. Expt. Sta., Las Cruces, 1982—. Co-author: Modern Breeds of Livestock, 1980. Mem. Poultry Sci. Assn. (resolutions com. 1972-73), Am. Assn. Animal Sci., World's Poultry Sci., Sigma Xi. Lodge: Rotary. Home: 1927 Francine Ct Las Cruces NM 88005-5509 Office: NMex Agrl Experiment Sta PO Box 30003 # 3bf Las Cruces NM 88003-8003

BRIGHAM, GERALD ALLEN, research physicist, consultant; b. Burlington, Vt., June 9, 1928; s. Francis Wilbur and Thelma Mary (Peria) B.; m. Sondra Claire Kay Brigham, Dec. 21, 1960; children: Stacia, Thaisa (Mrs. Jeffrey Kendall), David Allen. BS in Applied Math, U. R.I., 1954; MS in Physics, 1957; postgrad., U. Conn., 1958-62. Mathematician Aberdeen (Md.) Proving Grounds, 1954-55; student instr. U. R.I., Kingston, 1955-57; rsch. physicist Electric Boat Divsn., Groton, Conn., 1957-60; cons. in acoustics Wakefield Rsch. Assn., New London, Conn., 1960-62; rsch. physicist Naval (Underwater) Ordinance Station, Newport, R.I., 1962-66; staff scientist Autonetics Divsn./Rockwell, Anaheim, Calif., 1966-71; rsch. physicist Naval Underseas Sys. Ctr., New London, 1971-73; cons., CEO, Gerald A. Brigham & Assocs. Inc., Anaheim, Calif., 1973-79; rsch. physicist Sanders Assocs., Nashua, N.H., 1979-80; cons., CEO Aquasonics, Inc., Anaheim, Calif., 1980-88; prin. engr. SubSig Divsn./Raytheon, Portsmouth, R.I., 1988-94; instr. elec. engring. Calif. State U., Long Beach, 1968-71; cons. in applied scis., noise control acoustics, sonar, and marine engring., 1960-62, 69-71, 73-79, 80-88. Contbr. articles to profl. jours. Sgt. USAF, 1946-49. Recipient outstanding achievement award Naval Underseas Sys. Ctr., 1973, Sanders Assn., 1981, author's award Raytheon, 1992, 93. Mem. Acoustical Soc. Am., Sigma Pi Sigma. Home and Office: 2543 E Ames Ave Anaheim CA 92806-4702

BRIGHAM, SAMUEL TOWNSEND JACK, III, lawyer; b. Honolulu, Oct. 8, 1939; s. Samuel Townsend Jack, Jr. and Betty Elizabeth (McNeil) B.; m. Judith Catherine Johnson, Sept. 3, 1960; children: Robert Jack, Bradley Lund, Lori Ann, Lisa Katherine. B.S. in Bus. magna cum laude, Menlo Coll., 1963; J.D., U. Utah, 1966. Bar: Calif. 1967. Asso. firm Petty, Andrews, Olsen & Tufts, San Francisco, 1966-67; accounting mgr. Western sales region Hewlett-Packard Co., North Hollywood, Calif., 1967-68; atty. Hewlett-Packard Co., Palo Alto, Calif., 1968-70; asst. gen. counsel Hewlett-Packard Co., 1971-73, gen. atty., asst. sec., 1974-75, sec., gen. counsel, 1975-82, v.p., gen. counsel, 1982-85, v.p. corp. affairs, gen. counsel, mgr./dir. law dept., 1985—; lectr. law Menlo Coll.; speaker profl. assn. seminars. Bd. dirs. Palo Alto Area YMCA, 1974-81, pres., 1978; bd. govs. Santa Clara County region NCCJ; trustee Menlo Sch. and Coll.; bd. dirs. Just Say No. Served with USMC, 1957-59. Mem. ABA, Calif. Bar Assn., Peninsula Assn. Gen. Counsel, MAPI Law Council, Am. Corp. Counsel Assn. (chmn. 1985, bd. dirs. 1983—), Am. Soc. Corp. Secs. (pres. No. Calif. Chpt. 1983—), Assn. Gen. Counsel (sec.-treas. 1991—). Home: 920 Oxford Dr Los Altos CA 94024-7032 Office: Hewlett-Packard Co 3000 Hanover St Palo Alto CA 94304-1112*

BRIGHTON, JOAN KATHLEEN, psychologist; b. Urbana, Ill., July 10, 1954; d. Gerald David and Lois (Robbins) B. BA in Sociology, So. Ill. U., 1974; MA in Psychology, U. Nev., 1982. VISTA vol. Oper. Life, Las Vegas, 1974-75; grad. asst. U. NEv., Las Vegas, 1978-80; psychologist So. Nev. Adult Mental Health Svcs., Las Vegas, 1984-92; vocational rehab. counselor State Indsl. Ins. System, Las Vegas, 1992—. Treas. Spiritual Assembly of Baha'is, North Las Vegas, 1977-92; vice chmn. Baha'is, Sunrise Manor, 1993—. Pres. scholar So. Ill. U., 1971-74. Mem. Nat. Alliance for Mentally Ill, Nat. Wildlife Fedn., World Wlidlife Fund, Nev. Alliance for Mentally Ill (liaison 1986-89), AAUW, Amnesty Internat., Sierra Club (Toiyabe chpt.), Habitat for Humanity, Phi Kappa Phi, Psi Chi. Home: 3648 Rochester Ave Las Vegas NV 89115-0229 Office: State Indsl Ins System 1700 W Charleston Blvd Las Vegas NV 89102-2335

BRILL, YVONNE THERESA, marketing research company executive, consultant; b. Redwood City, Calif., Oct. 13, 1960; d. Fred and Hedy (Buhler) Schneider; m. Michael Clark Brill, May 1, 1982; children: Laura, Katherine, Jeff. BS in Biol. Scis., U. Calif., Davis, 1982; MBA, Santa Clara U., 1987. Biologist I Syntex, Palo Alto, Calif., 1982-84, biologist II, 1984-85, regulatory affairs assoc., 1985-87, regulatory affairs project adminstr., 1987-89, regulatory affairs group mgr., 1989-90, product devel. mgr., 1990-91; mgr. strategic devel. Nycomed Salutar, Sunnyvale, Calif., 1991-92, dir. mktg., 1992-93; dir. ops. MedSearch, Los Altos, Calif., 1993-94, v.p., 1994—. Sunday sch. tchr. Queen of Apostles Ch., San Jose, Calif., 1990-95. Office: 10075 Pasadena Ave Cupertino CA 94015

BRIMMER, CLARENCE ADDISON, federal judge; b. Rawlins, Wyo., July 11, 1922; s. Clarence Addison and Geraldine (Zingsheim) B.; m. Emily O. Docken, Aug. 2, 1953; children: Geraldine Ann, Philip Andrew, Andrew Howard, Elizabeth Ann. BA, U. Mich., 1944, JD, 1947. Bar: Wyo. 1948. Pvt. practice law Rawlins, 1948-71, mcpl. judge, 1948-54; U.S. commr., magistrate, 1963-71; atty. gen. Wyo. Cheyenne, 1971-74; U.S. atty., 1975; chief judge U.S. Dist. Ct. Wyo., Cheyenne, 1975-92, dist. judge, 1975—; mem. panel multi-dist. litigation, 1992—; mem. Jud. Conf. U.S., 1994—, exec., 1995—. Sec. Rawlins Bd. Pub. Utilities, 1954-66; Rep. gubernatorial candidate, 1974; trustee Rocky Mountain Mineral Law Found., 1963-75. With USAAF, 1945-46. Mem. ABA, Wyo. Bar Assn., Laramie County Bar Assn., Carbon County Bar Assn., Am. Judicature Soc., Masons, Shriners, Rotary. Episcopalian. Office: US Dist Ct PO Box 985 Cheyenne WY 82003-0985

BRINGMAN, JOSEPH EDWARD, lawyer; b. Elmhurst, N.Y., Jan. 31, 1958; s. Joseph Herman and Eileen Marie (Sheehy) B.; m. Laurie Lynn Cunningham, July 11, 1992; 1 child, Joseph Edward Bringman Jr. BA, Yale U., 1980; JD, Stanford U., 1983. Bar: N.Y. 1984, Wash. 1985, U.S. Dist. Ct. (we. dist.) Wash. 1986, U.S. Ct. Appeals (9th cir.) 1986, U.S. Ct. Appeals (fed. cir.) 1988. Acting asst. prof. U. Wash. Law Sch., Seattle, 1983-85; assoc. Perkins Coie, Seattle, 1985-91, of counsel, 1992—; dir. Perkins Cole Cmty. Fellowship, Seattle, 1990-96. Editor: Stanford Jour. Internat. Law, 1980-83. Mem. Yale Alumni Schs. Com., Seattle, 1983—, Palo Alto, Calif., 1980-83. Nat. Merit scholar, 1976; recipient Pro Bono Publico award Trumbull Coll. (Yale U.), 1980. Mem. ABA, Wash. State Bar Assn., King County Bar Assn. (mem. judicial screening com., fair campaign practices com.). Democrat. Roman Catholic. Office: Perkins Coie 1201 3rd Ave Fl 40 Seattle WA 98101-3099

BRINK, GLEN ARTHUR, publisher, wholesaler; b. Boulder, Colo., Mar. 26, 1944; m. Gloria Jean Savage, 1979 (div. 1983); 1 child, Holly Francesca; m. Alice Lorraine O'Dell. BS in Applied Math., U. Colo., 1967, MS in Computer Sci., 1977. Statistician U. Colo. Med. Ctr., Denver, 1967-69; computer cons. CIBAR, Colorado Springs, 1977-83; wholesaler The Radiant Expression, Colorado Springs, 1981—; pub. The Fly Fishing Catalog, Boulder, 1991—. Author: (booklets) The Bidding Apercu', 1977, Mail Order Multilevel Marketing, 1992, How to Get Anything You Want, 1993. With U.S. Army, Vietnam, 1969-70. Recipient Tipton scholarship U. Colo., 1962. Mem. Stars Edge Rsch., Wisdom Soc., Four Sigma, Sigma Tau. Office: The Fly Fishing Catalog PO Box 6101 Boulder CO 80306-6101

BRINKERHOFF, LORIN C., nuclear engineer, management and safety consultant; b. St. Anthony, Idaho, June 4, 1929; s. James Byron and Bessie Hazel (Miller) B.; m. Donna Lee Lords, Nov. 27, 1951; children: Kathleen Rae, Diane Lee, Sandra Lynne, Bonnie Jo, Dirk Lorin, Michael Lorin. B-SChemE, U. Utah, 1955; postgrad. MIT, 1970, Safety and Reliability Directorate (Eng.), 1974, Nuclear Power Devel. Establishment (Scotland), 1981. Rsch. specialist GE, Hanford, Wash., 1952-53; reactor ops. foreman Phillips Petroleum Co., Idaho Falls, Idaho, 1955-58; critical facility mgr. Lawrence Radiation Lab., Nevada Test Site, 1958-62; sr. nuclear engr. Aerojet Gen. Corp., Nevada Test Site, 1962-69; sr. reactor safety specialist AEC, Germantown, Md., 1969-81; chief reactor safety br. U.S. Dept. Energy, Germantown, 1981-86; mgr. tech. safety appraisal team, 1986-89; ind. nuclear safety cons., 1989—. With U.S. Army, 1950-51. Mem. Am. Nuclear Soc. (standards com. 1980-89), Am. Nat. Standards Inst. (standards com. 1978-85). Republican. Mem. Ch. of Jesus Christ of Latter-day Saints (bishop). Home and Office: 9671 Countess Way South Jordan UT 84095-3465

BRINNER, WILLIAM MICHAEL, Near Eastern studies educator; b. Alameda, Calif., Oct. 6, 1924; s. Fred Kohn and Sadie (Weiser) B.; m. Lisa Johanna Kraus Brinner, Sept. 23, 1951; children: Benjamin E., Leyla A., Rafael J. BA, U. Calif., Berkeley, 1948, MA, 1950, PhD, 1956; DHL (hon.), Hebrew Union Coll., 1992. Asst. prof. U. Calif., Berkeley, 1957-61, assoc. prof., 1961-64, prof., 1964-91, prof. emeritus, 1991; vis. prof. U. San Francisco, 1985, U. Wash., 1991; lectr. Harvard U., 1960-61; dir. Ctr. for Arabic Study Abroad, Cairo, Egypt, 1967-70, Study Ctr. U. Calif., Jerusalem, Israel, 1973-75; acting dir. Annenberg Rsch. Inst., Phila., 1992-93. Editor, translator: A Chronicle of Damascus, 2 vols., 1963; translator: An Elegant Composition Concerning Relief After Adversity, 1978 (Jewish Book Coun. award 1979), History of Al-Tabari vols. 2 and 3, 1987, 91; editor, contbr.: Studies in Islamic & Judaic Traditions 2 vols., 1986, 89. Commentator World Press, Pub. Broadcasting, 1967-77; mem. Steering Com. World Affairs Coun., Oakland, Calif., 1979-82, Bd. Trustees Judah Magnes Mus., Berkeley, Calif., 1981-95; chmn. Steering Com. Bay Area Academic Consortium, San Francisco, 1989—. Guggenheim Fellowship Guggenheim Fdn., 1965-66. Mem. Am. Oriental Soc. (pres. 1976), Am. Acad. for Jewish Rsch. (exec. com. 1992—), Am. Hist. Assn., Middle East Studies Assn. (pres. 1970), Assn. for Jewish Studies (bd. dirs. 1986-92), Soc. for Judeo-Arabic Studies (bd. dirs. 1984—). Home: 753 Santa Barbara Rd Berkeley CA 94707-2045

BRINTON, BYRON CHARLES, publishing executive, editor; b. Fessenden, N.D., Jan. 28, 1912; s. Charles Mackay and Elizabeth Rose (Mueller) B.; m. Roberta Lee Wright, Sept. 14, 1935 (dec. Jan. 1993); children: Lynn Ann, Ross Burr, Byron Dorsy, Alice Kathleen, Greg Charles. Jr. cert. with honors, U. Oreg., 1933. Co-owner, co-editor Weekly North Powder News and Haines Record, Haines, Oreg., 1928-34; co-owner, co-editor Record-Courier, Baker City, Oreg., 1934-57, owner, 1957—, editor, 1934—; bd. dirs. Oreg. Geographic Names, Oreg. Trail Regional Mus.; pres., organizing exec. Anthony Lakes Ski Area Corp., 1961-64. Active Bonneville Adv. Bd., 1940—, Oreg. State Water Bd., 1958-59; com. sec. City of Baker Mgr. Charter Form Govt., 1950-57; co-founder, dir. Sumpter Valley R.R. Restoration, Baker City, 1980; sec. Hells Canyon Devel. Assn., Baker City, 1944—; mem. devel. com. Oreg. Trail Regional Mus.; mem. Baker County Mus. Commn. With USN, 1944-46. Recipient Baker County Cattlemens Assn. Svc. plaque, 1993, Outstanding Svc. plaque Baker County Fair, 1993, Oreg. State Coll. Diamond Agr. Achievement Registry award, 1993; named Baker County Man of Yr., 1995. Mem. Oreg. Cattlemens Assn., Baker County Livestock Assn. (Outstanding Svc. plaque), Future Farmers Am. (hon.), Kiwanis (life), Powder River Sportsmens Club (life). Democrat. Baptist. Home: PO Box 70 2517 Valley Ave Baker City OR 97814 Office: The Record Courier 1718 Main St Box 70 Baker City OR 97814

BRINTON, GREGORY S., ophthalmologist, educator; b. Salt Lake City, Aug. 2, 1950; s. Sherman S. and Susan Bonna (Ashby) B.; m. Sally Jean Peterson, Apr. 7, 1976; children: Jonathan, Jason, Eric, Jessica, Stephanie, Lindsey, Samuel. Student, Stanford U., 1968-69; BA, U. Utah, 1973, MD, 1976, MBA, 1995. Diplomate Am. Bd. Ophthalmology; lic. Fla., Wis., Utah. Intern Beth Israel Hosp., Boston, 1976-77; resident Bascom Palmer Eye Inst., Miami, Fla., 1977-80; fellow Med. Coll. Wis., Milw., 1980-81, asst. prof., 1981-84; clin. assoc. prof. U. Utah, Salt Lake City, 1984-94, clin. prof., 1994—; staff physician Cottonwood Med. Ctr., LDS Hosp., Salt Lake Regional Hosp., U. Utah Med. Ctr., Primary Children's Med. Ctr., Utah Valley Regional Med. Ctr., Ogden Regional Hosp., Logan Regional Med. Ctr. Contbr. articles to profl. jours. Fellow Am. Acad. Ophthalmology; mem. Retina Soc., Vitreous Soc., Utah State Med. Assn., Utah Ophthalmol. Soc., Bascom Palmer Alumni Assn., Alpha Omega Alpha. Office: 5810 S 300 E Ste 210 Salt Lake City UT 84107-6178 Also: 359 8th Ave Ste 210 Salt Lake City UT 84103

BRINTON, RICHARD KIRK, marketing executive; b. Hanover, Pa., Apr. 21, 1946; s. James Henry and Mabel (Adelung) B.; m. Joan Marita Ayo, Mar. 21, 1970; children: Katherine, Mark, Michael. BA in Liberal Arts, BS in Indsl. Engring., Pa. State U., 1968. Registered profl. engr., Ohio. From systems engr. to dir. mktg. AccuRay/ABB, Columbus, Ohio, 1968-82; group mktg. dir. AccuRay/ABB, London, 1982-84; internat. sales mgr. Flow Systems, Seattle, 1984, v.p. sales and mktg., 1985-87; dir. mktg. and bus. devel. UTILX Corp., Seattle, 1987-90, v.p. mktg. and bus. devel., 1990-93, v.p. internat. ops., 1993-96; chmn. Nippon FlowMole, Tokyo, 1991-93; dir. mktg. and sales Lamb-Grays Harbor, Hoquiam, Wash., 1996—. Mem. World Trade Club Seattle (bd. dirs. 1993-95). Home: 18137 149th Ave SE Renton WA 98058-9654 Office: Lamb-Grays Harbor Co Box 359 Blaine & Firman Sts Hoquiam WA 98550-0359

BRISBIN, ROBERT EDWARD, insurance agency executive; b. Bklyn., Feb. 13, 1946; m. Sally Ann Tobler-Norton. BSBA, San Francisco State U., 1968. Cert. safety exec. Field rep. Index Research, San Mateo, Calif., 1969-82; mgr. loss control Homeland Ins. Co., San Jose, Calif., 1982-87; ins. exec. Morris and Dee Ins. Agy., San Luis Obispo, Calif., 1987—; prin., cons. Robert E. Brisbin & Assocs., Pismo Beach, Calif., 1972—; mgt. cons.; pres. Profl. Formulas Amino Acid Food Supplements, 1987-90. Author: Amino Acids, Vitamins and Fitness, 1986, Loss Control for the Small- to Medium-Sized Business, 1989, (with Carol Bayly Grant) Workplace Wellness, 1992; composer: Country Songs and Broken Dreams, 1978, America the Land of Liberty, 1980. Mem. Am. Soc. Safety Engrs., World Safety Orgn. (cert. safety exec.), UN Roster Safety Cons. Republican. Office: PO Box 341 Pismo Beach CA 93448-0341

BRISCOE, AGATHA DONATTO, data processing executive, instructor; b. Liberty, Tex., Feb. 21, 1947; d. Alton Peter and Audrey Mary (Broussard) Donatto; m. Edward Gans Briscoe, Jan. 23, 1976; 1 child, Allison Marie. BS in Math. summa cum laude, Tex. So. U., 1969; student, UCLA, 1967-68, 69-70. Cert. secondary tchr., Tex. Scientific programmer The Aerospace Corp., El Segundo, Calif., 1971-73; tech. staff TRW Def. and Space Systems Group, El Segundo, 1973-76; instr. data processing Hawaii C.C., Hilo, 1979-86; analyst, programmer Cayman Islands Govt., Grand Cayman, 1986-87; dir. mgmt. info. svcs. V.I. Dept. Health, St. Thomas, 1987-89; systems analyst V.I. Telephone Co., St. Thomas, 1989-90; sr. applications specialist InfoTech (Kapioloni Health Care Systems), Honolulu, 1990-93, new projects coord., 1993-95; sr. programmer/analyst Sutter Health, Sacramento, 1995-96; advanced programmer-analyst Shared Med. Systems, Sacramento, 1996—; pres. Hawaii Vocat. Assn., Hilo, 1983-85; coord. data processing program Hawaii C.C., Hilo, 1979-86. Supr. com. mem. Big Island Ednl. Fedn. Credit Union, Hilo, 1979-86; troop leader Girl Scouts Am., Hilo, 1984-85; cmty. rep. African-Am. adv. com. U. Hawaii, Manoa, 1994; vol. tutor, Honolulu, 1991-94. Equipment grantee U. Hawaii Pres.'s Fund, Honolulu, 1985. Home: 2964 Bridlewood Dr Cameron Park CA 95682-4232 Office: Sutter Health 2901 L St Sacramento CA 96816

BRISCOE, JOHN, lawyer; b. Stockton, Calif., July 1, 1948; s. John Lloyd and Doris (Olsen) B.; divorced; children: John Paul, Katherine. JD, U. San Francisco, 1972. Bar: Calif. 1972, U.S. Dist. Ct. (no., ea. and ctrl. dists.) Calif. 1972, U.S. Supreme Ct. 1978. Dep. atty. gen. State of Calif., San Francisco, 1972-80; ptnr. Washburn and Kemp, San Francisco, 1980-88, Washburn, Briscoe and McCarthy, San Francisco, 1988—; bd. dirs. San Francisco Bay Planning coalition, chmn., 1990-93; vis. scholar U. Calif., Berkeley, 1990—. Author: Surveying the Courtroom, 1984; editor: Reports of Special Masters, 1991; contbr. articles to profl. and lit. jours. Mem. ABA, San Francisco Bar Assn., Law of the Sea Inst. Roman Catholic. Office: Washburn Briscoe & McCarthy 55 Francisco St San Francisco CA 94133-2122

BRISLAIN, JUDY ANN, psychologist; b. Hawthorne, Nev., Apr. 24, 1947; d. Margaret Johnson; m. Gregory Brislain, July 4, 1976. BA in English Edn., U. Nev., 1969; MA in Spl. Edn., Calif. State U., 1972; EdD in Ednl. and Counseling Psychology, U. Pacific, 1984. Lic. ednl. psychologist, marriage, family child therapist; lic. secondary tchr., Calif., learning handicapped tchg. specialist, Calif., pupil pers. svcs., Calif., C.C. instr., Calif. Tchr. English, forensic coach Placer Joint Union High Sch. Dist., Auburn, Calif., 1969-70; disgnostic clinician Melvin-Smith Sch., Sacramento, Calif., 1970-71, tchr., 1971-74, resource specialist, program coord., 1974-75, program and behavior guidance coord., 1975-77; clin. edn. dir. Brislain Learning Ctr., 1977—; pvt. practice, 1980—; cons. Dept. Grants and Rsch. Devel. Calif. State U., Chico, others. Author: Diagnosis in the Classroom: Program for Success, 1973, Ready, Set Go: A Language Program, 1974. Bd. dirs. Campfire, Inc., 1984, Chico Mus. Found.; co-chair Chico Tomorrow, 1986; mem. steering com. Sch. Bond Election, 1988, Butte County Literacy Coun., 1990; bd. dirs. Chico Community Found., Project Child; mem. steering com. Chico Unified Sch. Dist. Hall of Fame; apptd. by Gov. Pete Wilson to Calif. State Bd. Behavioral Sci. Examiners, 1992, chair, 1994-96. Mem. Am. Psychol. Assn., Am. Assn. Marriage & Family therapy, Calif. Assn. Marriage, Family and Child Counselors, Calif. State Psychol. Assn., P.G. & E. Caribou Group for Women Leaders, Rotary Internat. (bd. dirs. Chico chpt.), Greater Chico C. of C. (chair edn. com. 1987, bd. dirs., chair bus.-sch. partnership subcom., Athena award 1991). Office: Brislain Learning Ctr 1550 Humboldt Rd Ste 3 Chico CA 95928-9115

BRISTOL, STANLEY DAVID, mathematics educator; b. Mankato, Minn., Dec. 30, 1948; s. Robert Frederick Bristol and Ruth Charlotte (Buckeye) Bristol Bond; m. Elaine Metzer, Jan. 30, 1970; children: Thomas Alan, Jennifer Elise. BS, Ariz. State U., 1969, MA, 1970. Cert. secondary tchr. with gifted endorsement. Math. tchr. Saguaro H.S., Scottsdale, Ariz., 1973-74, Poston Jr. H.S., Mesa, Ariz., 1974-77, Corona del Sol H.S., Tempe, Ariz., 1977—, Ariz. State U., Tempe, 1989—. Sunday sch. tchr. 1st United Meth. Ch., Tempe, 1983-93. With U.S. Army, 1970-73. Named Tchr. of Yr., Tempe Diablos (C. of C.), 1987, Tribune Educator of Yr., 1995; recipient Presdl. award for Excellence in Math. Teaching, 1990. Mem. Nat. Coun. Tchrs. Math., Ariz. Assn. Tchrs. Math., Nat. Edn. Assn., Ind. Order of Foresters, Math. Assn. Am. Office: Corona del Sol High Sch 1001 E Knox Rd Tempe AZ 85284-3204

BRITTI, JULIE MCGREGOR, communications director; b. Grants Pass, Oreg., Jan. 13, 1962; d. Bruce and Ruth McGregor; m. Michael A. Britti, Dec. 6, 1996. BA, George Washington U., 1990. Legis. aide U.S. Senator Mark O. Hatfield, Washington, 1984-90; dir. internat. policy U.S. Senator Mark O. Hatfield, 1990-94, comm. dir., 1994-95; comm. dir. N.Mex. Human Svcs. Dept., Santa Fe, 1996—. Pres. Oreg. State Soc. of D.C., Washington, 1989. Recipient Leadership award Oreg. Mental Health Divsn., 1988, Svc. award U.S. Senate, 1995.

BRITTON, THOMAS WARREN, JR., management consultant; b. Pawhuska, Okla., June 16, 1944; s. Thomas Warren and Helen Viola (Haynes) B.; BS in Mech. Engring., Okla. State U., 1966, MS in Indsl. Engring. and Mgmt., 1968; m. Jerlyn Kay Davis, 1964 (div. 1970); 1 child, Natalie Dawn; m. Deborah Ann Mansour, Oct. 20, 1973; 1 child, Kimberly Ann. Cons., Arthur Young & Co., Los Angeles, 1968-72, mgr., 1972-76, prin., 1976-79, ptnr., 1979-88, office dir. mgmt. svcs. dept., Orange County, Calif., 1980-87; ptnr. West Region Mfg., 1987-88, Price Waterhouse; ptnr.-in-charge west coast mfg. cons. practice, Nat. Aerospace and Def. Industry, 1988-95; part-in-charge west coast products and logistics practice, 1995—; lectr. in field. Mem. City of San Dimas Creative Growth Bd., 1976-77, chmn. planning commn., 1977-83; trustee World Affairs Council of Orange County, 1980; benefactor, founders com., v.p. ann. fund, pres., chair long range planning, trustee South Coast Repertory Theater, 1982-92; trustee Providence Speech and Hearing Ctr., 1985-90, Spl. Olympics of So. Calif., 1995—; mem. devel. com. U. Calif.-Irvine Med. Sch.; chmn. Costa Mesa Arts Council. Served to capt. USAR, 1971-86. Cert. mgmt. cons. Mem. Los Angeles Inst. CPAs, Mgmt. Adv. Svcs. Com., Am. Prodn. and Inventory Control Soc., Am. Inst. Indsl. Engrs., Greater Irvine Indsl. League, Okla. State Alumni Assn., Kappa Sigma Alumni Assn. Clubs: Jonathan, Ridgeline Country, Santa Ana Country. Home: 18982 Wildwood Cir Villa Park CA 92861-3137

BROAD, ELI, financial services executive; b. N.Y.C., June 6, 1933; s. Leon and Rebecca (Jacobson) B.; m. Edythe Lois Lawson, Dec. 19, 1954; children: Jeffrey Alan, Gary Stephen. BA in Acctg. cum laude, Mich. State U., 1954. CPA, Mich. 1956. Co-founder, chmn., pres., CEO SunAmerica Inc. (formerly Kaufman & Broad, Inc.), L.A., 1957; chmn. Sun Life Co. Am., Anchor Nat. Life Ins. Co., First SunAmerica Life Ins. Co.; chmn. Kaufman and Broad Home Corp., L.A., 1986-93, chmn. exec. com., 1993-95, founder, chmn., 1993—; chmn. Stanford Ranch Co.; mem. exec. com. adv. bd. Fed. Nat. Mortgage Assn., 1972-73; active Calif. Bus. Roundtable, 1986—; co-owner Sacramento Kings and Arco Arena, 1992—; trustee Com. for Econ. Devel., 1993-95; mem. real estate adv. bd. Citibank, N.Y.C. Mem. bd. dirs. L.A. World Affairs Coun., 1988—, chmn., 1994—, DARE Am., 1989-95, hon. mem. bd. dirs. 1995—; founding trustee Windward Sch., Santa Monica, Calif., 1972-77; bd. trustees Pitzer Coll., Claremont, Calif., 1970-82, chmn. bd. trustees, 1973-79, life trustee, 1982—, Haifa U., Israel, 1972-80, Calif. State U., 1978-82, vice chmn. bd. trustees, 1979-80, trustee emeritus, 1982—, Mus. Contemporary Art, L.A., 1980-93, founding chmn., 1980, Archives

Am. Art, Smithsonian Instn., Washington, 1985—, Am. Fedn. Arts, 1988-91, Leland Stanford Mansion Found., 1992—, Calif. Inst. Tech., 1993—, Armand Hammer Mus. Art and Cultural Ctr. UCLA, 1994—; pres. Calif. Non-Partisan Vote Registration Found., 1971-72; chancellor's assoc. UCLA, 1971—, mem. vis. com. Grad. Sch. Mgmt., 1972-90, trustee UCLA Found., 1986—, co-chair bd. visitors Sch. of the Arts & Architecture, 1995—; assoc. chmn. United Crusade, L.A., 1973-76; chmn. Mayor's Housing Policy Com., L.A., 1974-75; del., spkr. Fed. Econ. Summit Conf., 1974, State Econ. Summit Conf., 1974; mem. contemporary coun. L.A. County Mus. Art, 1973-79, bd. trustees acquisitions com., 1978-81, trustee, 1995—; bd. fellows, mem. exec. com. The Claremont (Calif.) Colls., 1974-79; nat. trustee Balt. Mus. Art, 1985-91; mem. adv. bd. Boy Scouts Am., 1982-85, L.A. Bus. Jour., 1986-88; mem. adv. coun. Town Hall of Calif., 1985-87; trustee Dem. Nat. Com. Victory Fund, 1988, 92, 96; mem. painting and sculpture com. Whitney Mus., N.Y.C., 1987-89; chmn. adv. bd. ART/LA, 1989; bd. overseers The Music Ctr. of L.A. County, 1991-92, mem. bd. govs., 1996—; mem. contemporary art com. Harvard U. Art Mus., Cambridge, Mass., 1992—; mem. internat. dirs. coun. Guggenheim Mus., N.Y.C., 1993—; active Nat. Indsl. Pollution Control Coun., 1970-73, Maeght Found., St. Paul de Vence, France, 1975-80, Mayor's Spl. Adv. Com. on Fiscal Adminstrn., L.A., 1993-94. Recipient Man of Yr. award City of Hope, 1965, Golden Plate award Am. Acad. Achievement, 1971, Housing Man of Yr. award Nat. Housing Coun., 1979, Humanitarian award NCCJ, 1977, Am. Heritage award Anti Defamation League, 1984, Pub. Affairs award Coro Found., 1987, Honors award visual arts L.A. Arts Coun., 1989; Eli Broad Coll. Bus. and Eli Broad Grad. Sch. Bus. named in his honor Mich. State U., 1991; knighted Chevalier in Nat. Order Legion of Honor, France, 1994. Mem. Beta Alpha Psi, Regency Club and Hillcrest Country Club (L.A.). Home: 75 Oakmont St Los Angeles CA 90049-1901 Office: SunAmerica Inc 1 Sun America Ctr Los Angeles CA 90067-6022*

BROADBENT, BERNE STEVEN, lawyer; b. Macon, Ga., Feb. 15, 1955; s. Berne D. and Miriam Sarah (Fullmer) B.; m. Suzanne Claybrook, Oct. 27, 1978; children: David, John, Heidi, Rebecca. BS in Physics cum laude, Brigham Young U., 1979, JD cum laude, 1982. Bar: Utah 1982, U.S. Dist. Ct. Utah 1982, U.S. Patent and Trademark Office 1982. Assoc. Fox, Edwards & Gardiner, Salt Lake City, 1982-84; assoc. Workman, Nydegger & Jensen, Salt Lake City, 1984-87, ptnr., 1987-89; pres., founder, pvt. practice Salt Lake City, 1989—. Bd. mem. Magna Mosquito Abatement Dist., Salt Lake County, Utah, 1987-88; dist. varsity scout chair Boy Scouts Am. Great Salt Lake Coun., Salt Lake City, 1988-89. Mem. ABA, Utah State Bar Assn., Am. Intellectual Property Assn., Copyright Soc. of the U.S.A. (editl. bd. 1986-89). Office: 1045 Key Bank Tower 50 S Main St Salt Lake City UT 84144-0103

BROADHEAD, RONALD FRIGON, petroleum geologist, geology educator; b. Racine, Wis., July 22, 1955; s. Ronald Leslie and Thereise (Frigon) B. BS, N.Mex. Tech. U., 1977; MS, U. Cin., 1979. Geologist, Cities Svc. Oil Co., Oklahoma City and Tulsa, 1979-81; sr. petroleum geologist, asst. dir. N.Mex. Bur. Mines, Socorro, 1981—, asst. dir., 1994—; mem. adj. faculty N.Mex. Tech. Coll., 1983—; mem. potential gas com. Potential Gas Agy. Union Oil Co. summer fellow Duke U. Marine Lab., 1977. Mem. Am. Assn. Petroleum Geologists (Ho. of Dels.), Soc. Econ. Paleontologists and Mineralogists, N.Mex. Geol. Soc. (past pres.) , Roswell Geol. Soc., Four Corners Geol. Soc., West Tex. Geol. Soc., Sigma Xi. Office: NMex Bur Mines Campus Sta Socorro NM 87801

BROADHURST, NORMAN NEIL, foods company executive; b. Chico, Calif., Dec. 17, 1946; s. Frank Spencer and Dorothy Mae (Conrad) B.; BS, Calif. State U., 1969; MBA, Golden Gate U., 1975; m. Victoria Rose Thomson, Aug. 7, 1976; 1 child, Scott Andrew. With Del Monte Corp., San Francisco, 1969-76, product mgr., 1973-76; product mgr. Riviana Foods, Inc., div. Colgate Palmolive, Houston, 1976-78; new products brand devel. mgr. foods div. Coca Cola Co., Houston, 1978-79, brand mgr., 1979-82, mktg. dir., 1982-89, v.p. mktg. Beatrice Foods Co., Chgo., 1983-86; pres., COO Famous Amos Chocolate Chip Cookie Co., Torrance, Calif., 1986-88; corp. sr. v.p., gen. mgr. Kerr Group Inc., L.A., 1988-92, corp. sr. v.p., pres. Kerr Group Consumer Products, 1992-95; chmn. dir. Double Eagle Holdings, Inc., 1995—; chmn., pres. and CEO Trusted Brands, Inc., 1995—. Home: 5009 Queen Victoria Rd Woodland Hills CA 91364-4757 Office: Double Eagle Holdings Inc 19528 Ventura Blvd # 420 Tarzana CA 91356-2917

BROADLEY, HUGH T., art history educator; b. Sacramento, Calif., June 5, 1922; s. Harold S. and Isabella J. (Taylor) B.; m. Jean V. Brown, May 31, 1946; children: Hugh T., Jr., Mark A. AB, Park Coll., 1947; MA, Yale U., 1949; PhD, NYU, 1961. Mus. curator and lectr. Nat. Gallery of Art, Washington, 1954-61; asst. prof. art Bowling Green (Ohio) State U., 1961-65; curator Univ. Art Collections/assoc. prof. art Ariz. State U., Tempe, 1965-67, prof. art, 1969-88, prof. art emeritus, 1988, faculty assoc., 1992; dir. Phoenix Art Mus., 1967-69; mem. numerous acad. coms., including Fulbright-Hays screenin com., 1974-81, faculty senate, others. Contbr. articles to profl. jours. Vis. com. mem. Am. Assn. Mus., 1970-90, sr. examiner, 1980-90; adv. bd. Alliance of Ariz. Opera Guilds, 1968-78; mem. commn. Ariz. Gov.'s Ariz.-Mexico Commn., 1972-75; past treas. Ariz. Humanities Coun., 1973-79; numerous others. With U.S. Army, 1942-46. Mem. Am. Assn. Mus., Coll. Art Assn. Am., Internat. Coun. Mus., Phi Kappa Phi.

BROADWATER, BRUCE A., mayor; b. Columbus, Ohio, Sept. 1, 1938; m. Peggy Broadwater; children: Josh, Jeremy. AA, East L.A. Coll.; BA in Human Rels., U. San Francisco. Owner ins. agy., Garden Grove, Calif.; consumer complaint analyst Calif. Dept. Ins.; elected Garden Grove City Coun., 1992-94; elected mayor City of Garden Grove, 1994—. Bd. dirs. Am. Host Found.; active scouting programs, Boy Scouts Am. With U.S. Army, 1957-59, Germany. Mem. Garden Grove C. of C. Office: Office of Mayor PO Box 3070 Garden Grove CA 92842

BROCA, LAURENT ANTOINE, aerospace scientist; b. Arthez-de-Bearn, France, Nov. 30, 1928; came to U.S., 1957, naturalized, 1963; s. Paul L. and Paule Jeanne (Ferrand) B.; B.S. in Math., U. Bordeaux, France, 1949; Lic. es Scis. in Math. and Physics, U. Toulouse (France), 1957; grad. Inst. Technique Professionnel, France, 1960; Ph.D. in Elec. Engring., Calif. Western U., 1979; postgrad. Boston U., 1958, MIT, 1961, Harvard U., 1961; m. Leticia Garcia Guerra, Dec. 18, 1962; 1 dau., Marie-There Yvonne. Teaching fellow physics dept. Boston U., 1957-58; spl. instr. dept. physics N.J. Inst. Tech., Newark, 1959-60; sr. staff engr. advanced research group ITT, Nutley, N.J., 1959-60; examiner math. and phys. scis. univs. Paris (France) and Caen, Exam. Center, N.Y.C., 1959-69; sr. engr. surface radar div. Raytheon Co., Waltham, Mass., 1960-62, Hughes Aircraft Co., Culver City, Calif., 1962-64; asst. prof. math. Calif. State U., Northridge, 1963-64; prin. engr. astrionics lab. NASA, Huntsville, Ala., 1964-65; fellow engr. Def. and Space Center, Westinghouse Electric Corp., Balt., 1965-69; cons. and sci. adv. electronics, phys. scis. and math. to indsl. firms and broadcasting stations, 1969-80; head engring. dept. Videocraft Mfg. Co., Laredo, Tex., 1974-75; asst. prof. math. Laredo State U., summer, 1975; engring. specialist dept. systems performance analysis ITT Fed. Electric Corp., Vandenberg AFB, Calif., 1980-82; engring. mgr. Ford Aerospace and Communications Corp., Nellis AFB, Nev., 1982-84; engring. mgr. Arcata Assocs., Inc., North Las Vegas, Nev., 1984-85; sr. scientific specialist engring. and devel. EG&G Spl. Projects, Inc., Las Vegas, 1985—. Served with French Army, 1951-52. Recipient Published Paper award Hughes Aircraft Co., 1966; Fulbright scholar, 1957. Mem. IEEE, Am. Nuclear Soc. (vice chmn. Nev. sect. 1982-83, chmn. 1983-84), Am. Def. Preparedness Assn., Armed Forces Communications and Electronics Assn., Air Force Assn. Home: 5040 Lancaster Dr Las Vegas NV 89120-1445 Office: EG&G Spl Projects Inc PO Box 93747 Las Vegas NV 89193-3747

BROCCHINI, RONALD GENE, architect; b. Oakland, Calif., Nov. 6, 1929; s. Gino Mario and Yoli Louise (Lucchesi) B.; m. Myra Mossman, Feb. 3, 1957; 1 child, Christopher Ronald. B.A. in Architecture with honors, U. Calif., Berkeley, 1953, M.A. in Architecture with honors, 1957. Registered architect, Calif., Nev. Architect, designer SMP, Inc., San Francisco, 1948-53, designer, assoc., 1956-60; assoc. architect Campbell & Wong, San Francisco, 1961-63; prin. architect Ronald G. Brocchini, Berkeley, Calif., 1964-67, Worley K Wong & Ronald G Brocchini Assocs., San Francisco, 1968-87, Brocchini Architects, Berkeley, 1987—; lectr. Calif. Coll. Arts and Crafts, Oakland, 1981-83; commr. Calif. Bd. Archtl. Examiners, 1961-89; mem. exam. com. Nat. Coun. Archtl. Registration Bds., 1983-85. Author: Long Range Master Plan for Bodega Marine Biology, U. Calif., 1982; prin. works include San Simeon Visitor Ctr., Hearst Castle, Calif., Mare Island Med.-Dental Facillity, IBM Ednl. and Data Processing Hdqrs., San Jose, Calif., Simpson Fine Arts Gallery, Calif. Coll. Arts, Ceramics and Metal Crafts, Emery Bay Pub. Market Complex, Analytical Measurement Facility, U. Calif., Berkeley, Bodega Marine Biology Campus, U. Calif., Berkeley, Fromm & Sichell (Christian Bros.) Hdqrs., The Nature Co., Corp. Offices, Berkeley, Merrill Coll., Athletic Facilities, U. Calif., Santa Cruz, Coll. III Housing, U. Calif., San Diego, Ctr. Pacific Rim Studies, U. San Francisco, married student housing Escondido II, III, IV, Stanford (Calif.) U. With U.S. Army, 1953-55. Recipient Bear of Yr. award U. Calif., Berkeley, 1987, Alumni Citation, 1988; recipient 18 Design Honor awards for architecture, Design award State of Calif. Dept. Rehab., 1995. Fellow AIA (bd. dirs. Calif. coun., pres. San Francisco chpt. 1982); mem. Bear Backers Club (bd. dirs. U. Calif.-Berkeley athletic coun.), Berkeley Breakfast Club (bd. govs.), Order of the Golden Bear, Chi Alpha Kappa. Republican. Roman Catholic. Office: Brocchini Architects Inc 2748 Adeline St Berkeley CA 94703

BROCK, JAMES MELMUTH, engineer, futurist; b. Brockton, Mass., Jan. 12, 1944; s. James Melmuth and Ruth Eleanor (Copeland) B.; student U. Hawaii, 1964-65, 1982, Taiwan Normal U., 1969; m. Mary Soong, June 24, 1964; 1 dau., Cynthia. Survey apprentice Malcolm Shaw, Hanson, Mass., 1959-62; with Peace Corps, N. Borneo, 1962-64; engr. Austin, Smith & Assocs., Honolulu, 1964-65, Trans-Asia Engrs., Vietnam, 1965-67; ops. mgr. Teledyne, Bangkok, Thailand, 1967-69; chief surveys Norman Saito Engrs. Hawaii, 1970-73; sr. prin. Brock and Assocs., Maui, Hawaii, 1973-82; pres. Honolulu Cons. Group, Honolulu, 1982-88; dir. Koolau Brewery, Inc., 1985-88; pres., dir. First Pacific Capital, Inc., 1984-88; v.p., dir., ceo, Seaculture Inc., 1988-90; prin. ECM, Inc., 1989-92; v.p., dir., and ceo, USA-China Tech. Corp., 1992-95; ind. cons., 1996—; Del. White House Conf. Small Bus., 1980, 86. Registered land surveyor, Hawaii, registered profl. engr.; mem. NSPE, ASCE, World Futures Studies Fedn. Address: PO Box 4586 Honolulu HI 96812-4586

BROCK, JAMES WILSON, drama educator, playwright, researcher; b. Greensfork, Ind., May 23, 1919; s. Virgil Prentiss and Blanche (Kerr) B.; m. Martha Faught, June 1942 (div. Mar. 1956); m. Patricia Anne Clemons, Mar. 1956 (div. Nov. 1966); children: Lisa Anne, Tamsen Lee, Julie Michele; m. Marjorie Mellor, Feb. 1, 1969 (dec. Jan. 1995); m. Esther Arzoo, Dec. 18, 1996. AB, Manchester Coll., 1941; MA, Northwestern U., 1942, PhD, 1950. Assoc. prof. Albion (Mich.) Coll., 1946-56; asst. prof. Mich. State U., East Lansing, 1956-57, U. Mich., Ann Arbor, 1957-58; assoc. prof. Fla. State U., Tallahassee, 1958-59; prof. Calif. State U., Northridge, 1959-89; mng. dir. Plymouth (Mass.) Drama Festival, 1956-58. Author: (plays) Modern Chancel Dramas, 1964, (musical dance drama) The Summons, 1964; contbr. articles to profl. jours. Sgt. USAAF, 1942-45, Middle East, ETO. Decorated Bronze Star; fellow Ch. Soc. for Coll. Work, Eng., 1964; rsch. grantee Calif. State U. Found., 1964, 66, 67. Mem. Am. Soc. Theatre Rsch., Nat. Theatre Conf., Nat. Trust for Historic Preservation, Internat. Found. Theatre Rsch., Theta Alpha Phi (sec.-treas. 1952-57), Delta Sigma Rho. Democrat. Episcopalian. Home: 2716 Beaver Ave Simi Valley CA 93065

BROCKERT, JOHN EARL, state official; b. Madison, Wis., Feb. 11, 1934; s. Claude O. and Geneva C. (Smith) B.; m. Mary O'Connor, May 19, 1962; children: Mary C., Chris S. BS, Ariz. State U., 1956; MS, U. Idaho, 1958; MPH, U. Calif., 1965. Clk. unemployment ins. claims Ariz. Dept. Employment Security, Casa Grande, 1958-59; survey field mgr. Ariz. Dept. Employment Security, Phoenix, 1959; statistican vital records Ariz. Dept. Pub. Health, Phoenix, 1960; statistician health statistics Alaska Dept. Health & Welfare, Juneau, 1960-64; statistician vital records Calif. Dept. Pub. Health, Sacramento, 1965-66, statistician, cons., 1966-67, asst. dir. vital records, 1968-69; dir. vital records and health statistics Utah Dept. of Health, Salt Lake City, 1969-96; cons. Vital Records, 1996—. Commr. Not-Too Serious Softball League, Salt Lake City, 1972-92; mgr. beverage booths Carmelite Fair, Salt Lake City, 1974—; mem. Nat. Com. for Vital Records and Health Statistics, Washington, 1979-82; chair birth cert. sub-com. Panel to Revise U.S. Standard Ctrs., Washington, 1983-86. Fellow Am. Pub. Health Assn. (sect. rep. 1965—, Disting. Svc. award 1985); mem. Utah Pub. Health Assn. (pres. 1972-74, Betty award 1987), Utah Child Abuse and Neglect Coun. (chair, trust com. 1986—, Recognition Cert. 1989), Assn. Vital Records and Health Stattistics (pres. 1978-80, Halbert Dunn award 1988), Hibernian Soc. (founding mem., trustee, pres. 1982-83, chair 1st st. Patrick's day parade 1979, Grand marshall parade 1985, Hibernian of Yr. award 1984), Friends of St. Joseph's Villa (chair 1990—). Home: 2183 Evergreen Ave Salt Lake City UT 84109-2940 Office: Utah Dept Health Bur Vital Records PO Box 16700 Salt Lake City UT 84116

BROCKMAN, KEVIN MICHAEL, broadcast network executive; b. Cin., Aug. 1, 1965; s. Allen Joseph and Mary Ann (Volle) B.; m. Daniel James Berendsen, Sept. 16, 1995. BS, U. Fla., 1987. Mgr. theatricals Cromarty & Co., N.Y.C., 1987-90; mgr. pub. rels. and promotion Radio City Music Hall, N.Y.C., 1990-93; dir. pub. rels. and promotion Fox TV, L.A., 1993-94; v.p. publicity and talent United Paramount Network, L.A., 1994-97; v.p. media and talent rels. ABC, L.A., 1997—. Mem. NATAS, Assn. of Theatrical Press Agts. and Mgrs. (TV publicity execs. com.). Democrat. Episcopalian. Office: United Paramount Network 11800 Wilshire Blvd Los Angeles CA 90025

BRODERICK, DONALD LELAND, electronics engineer; b. Chico, Calif., Jan. 5, 1928; s. Leland Louis and Vera Marguerite (Carey) B.; m. Constance Margaret Lattin, Sept. 29, 1957; children: Craig, Eileen, Lynn. BSEE, U. Calif., Berkeley, 1950; postgrad., Stanford U., 1953-54. Jr. engr. Boeing Co., Seattle, 1950-52; design engr. Hewlett-Packard Co., Palo Alto, Calif., 1952-59; sr. staff engr. Ampex Computer Products, Culver City, Calif., 1959-60; dir. engring. Kauke & Co., Santa Monica, Calif., 1960-61; program mgr. Space Gen. Corp., El Monte, Calif., 1961-68, Aerojet Electronics Div., Azusa, Calif., 1968-89; prin. D.L. Broderick, Arcadia, Calif., 1989—. Contbr. articles to profl. jours. Mem. Jr. C. of C., Woodland Hills, Calif., 1963-64. With USN, 1945-46. Fellow Inst. for Advancement of Engring.; mem IEEE (chmn. profl. group on audio 1955-59, mem. exec. com. San Francisco sect. 1957-59, chmn. San Gabriel Valley sect. 1964-71, chmn. sects. com. L.A. coun. 1971-72, chmn. L.A. coun. 1972-76, chmn. bd. WESCON conv. 1976-80, bd. dirs. IEEE Electronics Conv. Inc. 1981-84, 1995—, Centennial medal 1984), AIAA (sec. L.A. sect. 1986-88, sec. nat. tech. com. on command control comm. and intelligence, Washington, 1985-89, chmn. devel. com. L.A. coun. 1986-94). Home: 519 E La Sierra Dr Arcadia CA 91006-4321

BRODERICK, HAROLD CHRISTIAN, interior designer; b. Oakland, Calif., Apr. 8, 1925; s. Harold Christian and Laura Jane (Lloyd) B. BA, U. Tex., 1947. A founder Arthur Elrod Assos., Inc., Palm Springs, Calif., 1954, now pres.; bd. dirs. The Living Desert. Mem. Planning Commn., City of Palm Springs, 1972-74; trust Palm Springs Desert Mus.; mem. devel. com. Barbara Sinatra Children's Ctr. Mem. Am. Soc. Interior Designers. Republican. Office: Arthur Elrod Assocs Inc PO Box 2890 Palm Springs CA 92263-2890

BRODERICK, JON PALMER, geologist, mining company executive; b. Sheboygan, Wis., Dec. 23, 1941; s. John James Broderick and Viola Madelaine (Maigret) Walsh; m. Margaret Carol Bobo, June 7, 1969 (div. Mar. 15, 1995); children: Amy Erin, Cristopher Kelly, Jeffry Palmer. BSc, Union Coll., Schenectady, N.Y., 1964; MSc, U. Ariz., 1967. Cert. profl. geologist. Exploration geologist The Hanna Mining Co., various locations, 1966-69; sr. geologist NL Industries, Inc., various locations, 1969-78, Labrador Mining & Exploration, various locations, 1978-85; cons. geologist Reno, Nev., 1985-92; pres. Silver Eagle Resources Ltd., Reno, 1992—; dir. Silver Eagle Resources Ltd., Vancouver, B.C., Reno, Reese River Resources, Inc., Battle Mountain, Nev.; dir., pres. Exploration Mgmt. Svcs., Inc., Reno, 1990—. Fellow Soc. Econ. Geologists; mem. Am. Assn. Petroleum Geologists, Am. Inst. Profl. Geologists, Geol. Soc. Nev. (membership chair 1984-85, v.p. 1985, pres. 1985-86), Assn. Exploration Geochemists (organizing com. and treas. Reno Symposium 1983-85), Reno C. of C. Office: Silver Eagle Resources Ltd 2420 N Huachuca Dr Tucson AZ 85745-1202

BRODERICK, MICHAEL JOSEPH, radio news director; b. Chgo., July 30, 1949; s. William Anthony and Frances Ruth (McKevitt) B.; m. Donna Simmons, May 19, 1979 (div. Feb. 1981). BA in Speech with deptl. distinction, U. Ill., 1976. Color analyzer Newell Photo, L.A., 1981-92; reporter Burns (Oreg.) Times Herald, 1992-94; news dir. Sta. KBOO, Portland, Oreg., 1994—; instr. vol. work Sta. KBOO, 1991—. Author audio prodn. manual, 1996. Barnhard & Acad. scholar U. Ill., 1976. Office: KBOO Radio 20 SE 8th Ave Portland OR 97214

BRODIE, HOWARD, artist; b. Oakland, Calif., Nov. 28, 1915; s. Edward and Anna (Zeller) B. Student, Art Inst. San Francisco, Art Student's League, N.Y.C., U. Ghana, Accra; LHD (hon.), Acad. Art Coll., San Francisco, 1984. Mem. staff Life mag., Yank: the Army Weekly, Collier's, AP, CBS News, 1969-89; freelance artist, journalist, 1990—. Author: (book) Howard Brodie War Drawings, 1963, Drawing Fire, A Combat Artist At War, 1996; art journalist: (major wars) World War II, Korea, French Indo-China, Vietnam, (trials) Jack Ruby, Ray, Sirhan, My Lai, Charles Manson, Chicago Seven, Watergate, John Hinckley, Klaus Barbie in France, (famous people) John Wayne, Pres. Kennedy, James Jones; art at White House, 1946, 48; work represented in permanent collections Calif. Palace of the Legion Hon., San Francisco, Soc. Illustrators, N.Y., Libr. Congress, Washington, Air Force Acad., Colo.; prints, books: U.S. Army Infantry Mus., Ft. Benning, Ga., U.S. Army Mus., Presidio, Monterery, Oreg. Nat. Mil. Mus., The Hoover Instn. on War, Revolution and Peace, Anne S.K. Brown Mil. Collection Brown U. Libr., The Mus. of Books, Lenin Libr., Moscow, Gorky Sci. Libr., Moscow ., Admiral Nimitz State Hist. Pk., Tex., Henry E. Huntington Libr. (award), San Marina, New Britain Mus. Am. Art, Conn., West Point Libr., N.Y., Brown U. Libr., R.I.; guest on Merv Griffin Show, Charles Kuralt Sunday Morning program, Ted Koppel program, Night Line; featured Andy Rooney CBS Sunday Morning program, Nostagia Network, Dennis Wholey Am. Program. Sgt., U.S. Army. Decorated Bronze Star; recipient honor medals Freedom Found., 1957, 58, 60, 61.

BRODSKY, BART LOU, publisher; b. Toledo, Ohio, Nov. 3, 1949; s. Robert L. and Anne M. (Shoched) B.; m. Janet E. Geis, Feb. 14, 1985; 1 child, Audrey Lane Geis. BA, U. Calif., Berkeley, 1974. Exec. dir. Community Resource Inst., Berkeley, 1973—; founder, pub. Open Exch. Mag., Berkeley, 1974—. Author: The Teaching Marketplace, 1991, Finding Your Niche...Marketing Your Professional Service, 1992. Office: Open Exch Mag 1442A Walnut St # 51 Berkeley CA 94709-1496

BRODSKY, E. JASON, audio engineer; b. L.A., Feb. 15, 1970; s. Harvey and Harriet (Plotnick) B. A of Audio Arts, Inst. Audio Rsch., N.Y.C., 1991. Audio engr. Knitting Factory, N.Y.C., 1991-92; audio engr., prodn. mgr. Slims, San Francisco, 1992—; prodn. mgr. Box Set, 1993—. Contbr. essays and articles to mags. Children's edn. activist St. John's Ednl. Presch. Ctr., San Francisco, 1992—. Mem. Audio Engring. Soc. Home and Office: 861 40th Ave San Francisco CA 94121

BRODSKY, JAY BARRY, medical educator; b. N.Y.C., Nov. 11, 1946; s. Irving and Ann (Sapir) B.; m. Solveg Jensen, Aug. 12, 1973; children: Sonja Brodsky, Noah Brodsky. BS, CCNY, 1967; MD, Upstate Med. Ctr., Syracuse, N.Y., 1971. Diplomate Am. Bd. Anesthesiology. Asst. prof. Stanford U. Sch. Medicine, Stanford, Calif., 1977-82; assoc. prof. Stanford U. Sch. Medicine, Stanford, 1982-88, prof., 1988—; bd. dirs. Interplast, Inc., Palo Alto, 1984-86. Editor: (books) Oxygen--a Drug, The Pregnant Surgical Patient, Thoracic Anesthesia; contbr. 80 articles to profl. jours.; author 20 book chpts. Maj. U.S. Army, 1975-77. Mem. Am. Soc. Anesthesiologists, Calif. Soc. Anesthesiologists, Internat. Anesthesia Rsch. Soc., Assn. Univ. Anesthesiologists. Jewish. Home: 852 Pine Hill Rd Stanford CA 94305-1018 Office: Dept Anesthesia Stanford U Med Ctr Stanford CA 94305

BRODY, BONNIE, clinical social worker; b. N.Y.C., Dec. 1, 1947; d. Richard and Edith (Tranes) Mechlowe; m. A. William Brody, June 22, 1969; children: Laura, Davya, Sol. BA, Ripon (Wis.) Coll., 1973; MEd, U. Alaska, 1983; MSW, Washington U., St. Louis, 1992. Lic. clin. social worker; lic. marriage and family therapist. Dir. Alaska Tchr. Placement, Fairbanks, 1987-90; sr. clinician Human Affairs Alaska, Fairbanks, 1992-95; pvt. practice Fairbanks, 1992—; mem. adj. faculty U. Alaska, Fairbanks, 1996. Mem. Alaska Mental Health Bd., 1996—; mem. sch. bd. Fairbanks North Star Borough Sch. Dist., 1984-90. Mem. NASW (state Com. On Gay and Lesbian Issues com. 1995—). Home and Office: PO Box 82533 Fairbanks AK 99708

BRODY, JACOB JEROME, art history educator; b. Bklyn., Apr. 24, 1929; s. Aladar and Esther (Kraiman) B.; m. Jean Lindsey, Feb. 13, 1956; children: Jefferson, Jonathan, Allison. Cert. fine arts, Cooper Union, 1950; B.A., U. N.Mex., 1956, M.A., 1964, Ph.D., 1970. Curator of art Everhart Mus., Scranton, Pa., 1957-58; curator collections Isaac Delgado Mus. Art, New Orleans, 1958-60; Mus. Internat. Folk Art, Santa Fe, 1960-61; prof. anthropology U. N.Mex., 1965-85, prof. art history, 1972-89; prof. emeritus, 1989—; curator Maxwell Mus., U. N.Mex., Albuquerque, 1962-72; dir. Maxwell Mus., U. N.Mex., 1972-85; mem. adv. bd. Ghost Ranch Mus., N.Mex. Mus. Natural History, 1981-84, Wheelwright Mus. of the Am. Indian, 1989-92, Zuni Pueblo Mus., 1992—; rsch. curator Maxwell Mus., Sch. of Am. Rsch., Lab. of Anthropology; mem. fine arts bd. City of Albuquerque, vice chmn., 1970-74; mem. Gov. N.Mex. Task Force Paleontol. Resources, 1978-79. Author: Indian Painters and White Patrons, 1971, Mimbres Painted Pottery, 1977, Between Traditions, 1977, Yazz: Navajo Painter, 1982, The Chaco Phenomenon, 1983, The Anasazi, 1990, Beauty From the Earth, 1990, Anasazi and Pueblo Painting, 1991, Pueblo Indian Painting: Tradition and Modernism in New Mexico 1990-1930, 1997; co-author: Mimbres Pottery: Ancient Art of the American Southwest, 1983, To Touch the Past: The Painted Pottery of the Mimbres People, 1996. Recipient Tom L. Popejoy Dissertation award U. N.Mex., 1970, Gov.'s award of honor N.Mex. Hist. Com., 1978; Non-Fiction award Border-Regional Library Assn., 1972; Art Book award, 1979; resident scholar Sch. Am. Research, 1980-81; honoree Archeol. Soc. N.Mex., 1990. Mem. Am. Assn. Museums, Soc. Am. Archaeology, Council Mus. Anthropology, N.Mex. Mus. Assn.

BROENING, ELISE HEDWIG, writer; b. Bronx, N.Y., Feb. 10, 1941; d. Herman Berhardt and Lillian Marie (Kraft) B. BS in English, NYU, 1962, MA in Ednl. Psychology, 1969; postgrad., NYU Reading Inst., 1968-69, SUNY, Binghamton, 1986-87, Cornell U., Ithaca Coll., P.R., Cin. U. Tchr. English Jr. High Sch. # 104, N.Y.C., 1961-62, Union Endicott (N.Y.) Cen., 1962-63; tchr. English and Reading Johnson City (N.Y.) Schs., 1963-87; freelance writer San Diego, 1987—. Contbr. articles to profl. jours. Mem. Met. Opera Guild, San Diego Opera Guild, Tri-Cities Opera Guild, NYU Alumni Assn., Kappa Delta Pi. Home and Office: 606 3rd Ave Apt 201 San Diego CA 92101-6838

BROESAMLE, JOHN JOSEPH, history educator; b. Long Beach, Calif., Feb. 10, 1941; s. Otto Albert and Josephine (Young) B.; m. Katharine Sue Warne, June 12, 1963; children: Carolyn Jo, Robert Alan. BA, U. of the Pacific, Stockton, Calif., 1964; MA, Columbia U., 1965, PhD, 1970. Prof. history Calif. State U., Northridge, 1968—. Author: William Gibbs McAdoo 1863-1917, 1973, Reform and Reaction in 20th Century American Politics, 1990, Suddenly a Giant, 1993. Coord. Growth Control Initiative, Thousand Oaks, Calif., 1979-80; vol. reading tutor Ojai (Calif.) Unified Sch. Dist., 1993—; v.p. Ojai Valley Land Conservancy, 1995—; active Dem., 1968—. Woodrow Wilson fellow, 1964-65, Woodrow Wilson Dissertation fellow, 1966-67; Columbia U. fellow, 1965-67. Mem. AAUP, Am. Hist. Assn., Orgn. Am. Historians, Acad. Polit. Sci., Nat. Parks and Conservation Assn., Danforth Found. Assoc. Program, Phi Kappa Phi. Home: 3945 Thacher Rd Ojai CA 93023-9368 Office: Calif State U Northridge Dept History 18111 Nordhoff St Northridge CA 91330-8250

BROGDEN, STEPHEN RICHARD, library administrator; b. Des Moines, Sept. 26, 1948; s. Paul M. and Marjorie (Kueck) B.; m. Melinda L. Raine, Jan. 1, 1983; 1 child, Nathan. BA, U. Iowa, 1970, MA, 1972. Caretaker Eya Fechin Branham Ranch, Taos, N.Mex., 1970-72; dir. Harwood Found. U. N.Mex., Taos, 1972-75; vis. lectr. U. Ariz., Tucson, 1975-76; rd. mgr. Bill and Bonnie Hearne, Austin, Tex., 1976-79; head fine arts Pub. Libr. Des Moines, 1980-90; dep. dir. Thousand Oaks (Calif.) Libr., 1990—. Author book revs., Annals of Iowa, 1980; columnist Taos News, 1973. Mem. Am.

Libr. Assn., Calif. Libr. Assn., Films for Iowa Librs. (pres. 1983-86), Metro Des Moines Libr. Assn. (pres. 1980). Office: Thousand Oaks Libr 1401 E Janss Rd Thousand Oaks CA 91362-2134

BROGLIATTI, BARBARA SPENCER, television and motion picture executive; b. L.A., Jan. 8, 1946; d. Robert and Lottie Spencer; m. Raymond Haley Brogliatti, Sept. 19, 1970. BA in Social Scis. and English, UCLA, 1968. Asst. press. info. dept. CBS TV, L.A., 1968-69, sr. publicist, 1969-74; dir. publicity Tandem Prodns. and T.A.T. Comm. (Embassy Comm.), L.A., 1974-77, corp. v.p., 1977-82, sr. v.p. worldwide publicity, promotion and advt. Embassy Comm., L.A., 1982-85; sr. v.p. worldwide corp. comm. Lorimar Telepictures Corp., Culver City, Calif., 1985-89; pres., chmn. Brogliatti Co., Burbank, Calif., 1989-90; sr. v.p. worldwide TV publicity, promotion and advt. Lorimar TV, 1991-92; sr. v.p. worldwide TV publicity, promotion and pub. rels. Warner Bros. Inc., Burbank, 1992—. Mem. bd. govs. TV Acad., L.A., 1984-86; bd. dirs. KIDSNET, Washington, 1987—, Nat. Acad. Cable Programming, 1992-94; mem. Hollywood Women's Polit. Com., 1992-93; mem. steering com. L.A. Free Clinic, 1997—. Recipient Gold medallion Broadcast Promotion and Mktg. Execs., 1984. Mem. Am. Diabetes Assn. (bd. dirs. L.A. chpt. 1992-93), Am. Cinema Found. (mem. bd. dirs. 1994—), Dirs. Guild Am., Publicists Guild, Acad. TV Arts and Scis. (vice chmn. awards com.). Office: Warner Bros Studios 4000 Warner Blvd Burbank CA 91522

BROKAW, NORMAN ROBERT, talent agency executive; b. N.Y.C., Apr. 21, 1927; s. Isadore David and Marie (Hyde) B.; children—David M., Sanford Jay, Joel S., Barbara M., Wendy E., Lauren Quincy. Student pvt. schs., Los Angeles. With William Morris Agy., Inc., Beverly Hills, Calif., 1943—, sr. agt. and co. exec., 1951-74, v.p. world-wide ops., 1974-80, exec. v.p., dir., 1980—, co-chmn. bd., 1986-91, pres., CEO, 1989-91, chmn. bd., CEO, 1991—. Pres. Betty Ford Cancer Center, Cedars-Sinai Med. Center, Los Angeles, 1978—; bd. dirs. Cedars-Sinai Med. Center; industry chmn. United Jewish Welfare Fund, 1975. With U.S. Army, World War II. Mem. Acad. Motion Picture Arts and Scis. Clubs: Hillcrest Country (Los Angeles). Office: William Morris Agy 151 El Camino Dr Beverly Hills CA 90212-2704 also: William Morris Agy Inc 1325 Avenue Of The Americas New York NY 10019-6026

BROM, ROBERT H., bishop; b. Arcadia, Wis., Sept. 18, 1938. Ed., St. Mary's Coll., Winona, Minn., Gregorian U., Rome. Ordained priest Roman Catholic Ch., 1963, consecrated bishop, 1983. Bishop of Duluth Minn., 1983-89; coadjutor bishop Diocese of San Diego, 1989-90, bishop, 1990—. Office: Diocese of San Diego Pastoral Ctr PO Box 85728 San Diego CA 92186-5728*

BROMMER, GERALD FREDERICK, artist, writer; b. Berkeley, Calif., Jan. 8, 1927; s. Edgar C. and Helen (Wall) B.; m. Georgia Elizabeth Pratt, Dec. 19, 1948. BS in Edn., Concordia Coll., Nebr., 1948; MA, U. Nebr., 1955; postgrad., UCLA, U. So. Calif., Otis Art Inst., Chouinard Art Inst.; D.Litt., Concordia U., 1985. Instr., St. Paul's Sch., North Hollywood, Calif., 1948-55, Lutheran High Sch., Los Angeles, 1955-76; one-person shows throughout country; exhibited in numerous group shows including Am. Watercolor Soc., NAD, Royal Watercolor Soc., London; represented in permanent collections Claremont Colls. (Calif.), Pacific Telesis, Epcot Ctr., Orlando, Hilton Hotels, Inc., Reno, Anaheim, Las Vegas, San Francisco, Intercontinental Hotel, L.A., Harvey Mudd Coll., Claremont, Calif., Laguna Beach Mus. Art, TRW, Cola Cola Co., Ky., Concordia Coll., Nebr., Ill., Mo., Utah State U., Provo; books include: College Techniques, 1994, Discovering Art History, 1981, 3rd edit., 1995, The Art of Collage, 1978, Drawing, 1978, Understanding Transparent Watercolor, 1993, Landscapes, 1977, Art in your World, 1977, Watercolor and Collage Workshop, 1986, Exploring Painting, 1989, Exploring Drawing, 1990, Art: Your Visual Environment, 1977, Movement and Rhythm, 1975, Space, 1974, Transparent Watercolor, 1973, Relief Printmaking, 1970, Wire Sculpture, 1968, Careers in Art, 1984, and others; editor: The Design Concept Series, 10 vols., 1974-75, Insights to Art series, 1977—; various texts; 8 video art presentations for Crystal Prodns., Inc.; set of 14 design posters for schs. for Crystal Prodns., Inc.; assoc. Hewitt Painting Workshops, Artist Workshop Tour Agy. Grand Strand Watercolor workshops, Jade Fun Watercolor Workshops, Hudson Valley Art Workshops. Recipient prizes Am. Watercolor Soc., 1965, 68, 71, Watercolor U.S.A., 1970, 73, Los Angeles City Art Festival, 1970, 75, Calif. State Fair, 1975. Mem. Nat. Watercolor Soc. (treas., v.p., pres., awards 1972, 74, 78, 80), West Coast Watercolor Soc., Nat. Arts Club, Rocky Mountain Nat. Watermedia Soc., Watercolor USA Honor Soc., Nat. Art Edn. Assn., Nat. Arts (N.Y.C.), Phila. Water Color Club, La. Watercolor Soc. Republican. Lutheran. Address: 11252 Valley Spring Ln North Hollywood CA 91602-2611

BRONESKY, JOSEPH J., lawyer; b. Milw., Aug. 6, 1947; s. Joseph Francis and Rita Cornelia B.; m. Jacquelin A. Medina, Mar. 15, 1985; children: Jessica, Amanda, Antoinette. BA, Marquette U., 1969; JD, U. Chicago, 1972. Bar: Wis. 1972, U.S. Ct. Mil. Appeals 1974, U.S. Supreme Ct. 1975, Colo. 1977, U.S. Dist. Ct. Colo. 1977. Law clk. to judge Latham Castle U.S. Ct. Appeals 7th cir., Chgo., 1972-73; assoc. Sherman & Howard, Denver, 1976-80, ptnr., 1980—. Asst. editor U. Chgo. Law Review, 1971-72. Bd. dirs. Camp Fire Denver area coun. 1983-86, Montessori Sch. Denver, 1992-94, Mile Hi coun. Girl Scouts U.S., Denver, 1992—, fin. com. 1989—. Lt. JAGC USN, 1973-76. Mem. ABA, Colo. Bar Assn., Colo. Trial Lawyers Assn. Democrat. Roman Catholic. Office: Sherman & Howard 633 17th St Ste 3000 Denver CO 80202-3660

BRONSTER, MARGERY S, attorney general; b. N.Y., Dec. 12, 1957; married; 1 child. BA in Chinese Lang., Lit. and History, Brown U., 1979; JD, Columbia U., 1982. Assoc. Sherman & Sterling, N.Y., 1982-87; ptnr. Carlsmith, Ball, Wichman, Murray, Case & Ichiki, Honolulu, 1988-94; atty. gen. State of Hawaii, 1994—; bd. dirs. Hawaii Lawyers Care, past pres., 1992; co-chair planning com. Citizens Conf. Judicial Selection, 1993. Bd. dirs. Ballet Hawaii. Office: Office Attorney General 425 Queen St Honolulu HI 96813-2903*

BROOK, WINSTON ROLLINS, retired audio-video design consultant; b. Cameron, Tex., Aug. 20, 1931; s. Winston Marshall and Maude Katherine (Woody) B. BA, U. Denver, 1955. Lic. radiotelephone operator, FCC. Engr. Sta. WKNO-TV, Memphis, 1965-67; instr. Memphis State U., 1967-69; audio-visual dir. So. Coll. Optometry, Memphis, 1968-73; sr. cons. Bolt Beranek and Newman, Chgo. and L.A., 1973-87; prin. RB Sys., L.A., 1987-97; ret., 1997; instr. various seminars and workshops; assoc. editor Theater Design & Tech. mag., N.Y.C., 1981-87; tech. cons. Sound & Video Contractor mag., Overland, Kans., 1987—. Co-author: Handbook for Sound Engineers, 1987; contbr. articles to profl. jours., 1978—. Mem. Audio Engrng. Soc., Acoustical Soc. Am., U.S. Inst. for Theatre Tech. Democrat. Mormon. Home: 5715 Calvin Ave Tarzana CA 91356-1108

BROOKBANK, JOHN W(ARREN), retired microbiology educator; b. Seattle, Apr. 3, 1927; s. Earl Bruce and Louise Sophia (Stoecker) B.; m. Marcia Ireland, Sept. 16, 1950 (div. 1978); children: Ursula Ireland, John W. Jr., Phoebe Bruce; m. Sally Satterberg Cahill, Aug. 6, 1983. BA, U. Wash., 1950, MS, 1953; PhD, Calif. Inst. Tech., 1955. Asst. prof. biology U. Fla., Gainesville, 1955-58, assoc. prof., 1958-68, prof. microbiology and cell sci., 1968-85, prof. emeritus, 1985—; vis. assoc. prof. U. Fla. Coll. Medicine, Gainesville, 1961-63, U. Wash., Seattle, 1965; cons. in field, Friday Harbor, Wash. 1986—. Author: Developmental Biology, 1978, (with W. Cunningham) Gerontology, 1988; editor: Improving Quality of Health Care of the Elderly, 1977, Biology of Aging, 1990; contbr. articles to profl. jours. Pres. Griffin Bay Preservation Com., Friday Harbor, 1985—, Bridge Council on Narcotics Addiction, Gainesville, 1974, Marine Environ. Consortium, 1986-89; founding pres. Gainesville Regional Council on Alcoholism, 1976; mem devel. adv. bd. U. Wash. Friday Harbor Lab., 1995—. Research grantee NIH, 1957-80, NSF, 1972-73. Mem. Gerontol. Soc. Am., Seattle Tennis Club. Republican. Episcopalian. Home: PO Box 2688 Friday Harbor WA 98250-2688

BROOKE, EDNA MAE, retired business educator; b. Las Vegas, Nev., Feb. 10, 1923; d. Alma Lyman and Leah Mae (Ketcham) Shurtliff; m. Bill T. Brooke, Dec. 22, 1949; 1 child, John C. BS in Acctg., Ariz. State U., 1965, MA in Edn., 1967, EdD, 1975. Grad. teaching asst. Ariz. State U., Tempe, 1968-69; prof. bus. Maricopa Tech. Coll., Phoenix, 1967-72, assoc. dean instl. services, 1972-74; prof. bus. and acctg. Scottsdale (Ariz.) Community Coll., 1974-93; ret., 1993; cons. in field. Author: The Effectiveness of Three Techniques Used in Teaching First Semester Accounting Principles to Tech. Jr. College Students, 1974. Home: 1330 E Calle De Caballos Tempe AZ 85284-2404

BROOKE, PEGAN STRUTHERS, artist, art educator; b. Santa Ana, Calif., July 19, 1950; d. Lee Edwin and Maxine (Jones) Struthers; children: Marshall Payne, Clara Payne. BA in Lit., U. Calif., San Diego, 1972; BFA in Painting, Drake U., 1976; MA in Painting, U. Iowa, 1977; MFA in Painting, Stanford U., 1980. Instr. Sonoma (Calif.) State U., 1983; vis. artist U. Calif., Berkeley, 1982, Davis, 1984; prof. art, grad. dir. San Francisco Art Inst., 1985—; guest artist Calif. Coll. Arts and Crafts, Oakland, 1983. One-woman shows include Hansen Fuller Gallery, San Francisco, 1981, 83, Fuller Goldeen Gallery, San Francisco, 1985, 87, Parnas Gallery, Santa Monica, Calif., 1994, Terrain Gallery, San Franciso, 1995, Joan Roebuck Gallery, Lafayette, Calif., 1996, R.B. Stevenson Gallery, La Jolla, Calif., 1996; exhibited in group shows Guggenheim Mus., N.Y.C., 1987, Documenta, Sao Paulo, Brazil, 1994, Washburn Gallery, N.Y.C., 1995, R.B. Stevenson Gallery, 1996. Grantee Tiffany Found., 1983-84, Marin Arts Coun., 1992, U.S. Govt., 1995—. Home: PO Box 857 Bolinas CA 94924-0857 Office: San Francisco Art Inst 800 Chestnut St San Francisco CA 94133-2206

BROOKE, TAL (ROBERT TALIAFERRO), company executive, author; b. Washington, Jan. 21, 1945; s. Edgar Duffield and Frances (Lea) B. BA, U. Va., 1969; M in Theology/Philosophy, Princeton (N.J.) U., 1986. V.p. pub. rels. nat. office Telecom Inc., 1982-83; pres., chmn. Spiritual Counterfeits Project, Inc., Berkeley, 1989—; guest lectr. Cambridge U., Eng., 1977, 86, Oxford and Cambridge U., 1979, 84. Author: Lord of the Air, 1990, When the World Will Be As One, 1989 (bestseller 1989-90), Riders of the Cosmic Circuit, 1986, Avatar of Night, 1987 (bestseller in India 1981-84), The Other Side of Death, Lord of the Air: The International Edition, 1976, America's Warning Light, 1994, Virtual Gods, 1997. Mem. Internat. Platform Assn., Soc. of The Cincinnati. Office: SCP Inc PO Box 4308 Berkeley CA 94704-0308

BROOKES, VALENTINE, retired lawyer; b. Red Bluff, Calif., May 30, 1913; s. Langley and Ethel (Valentine) B.; m. Virginia Stovall Cunningham, Feb. 11, 1939; children: Langley Brookes Brandt, Lawrence Valentine, Alan Cunningham. A.B., U. Calif., Berkeley, 1934, J.D., 1937. Bar: Calif. 1937, U.S. Supreme Ct. 1942. Asst. franchise tax counsel State of Calif., 1937-40; dep. atty. gen. Calif., 1940-42; spl. asst. to U.S. atty. gen., asst. to solicitor gen. U.S., 1942-44; partner firm Kent & Brookes, San Francisco, 1944-70, Alvord & Alvord, Washington, 1944-50, Lee, Toomey & Kent, Washington, 1950-79; partner firm Brookes and Brookes, San Francisco, 1971-88, of counsel, 1988-90; legal cons. Orinda, Calif., 1990—; lectr. Hastings Coll. Law, U. Calif., 1941-48, U. Calif. Law Sch., Berkeley, 1948-70; cons. fed. taxation. Author: The Continuity of Interest Test in Reorganizations, 1946, The Partnership Under the Income Tax Laws, 1949, The Tax Consequences of Widows Elections in Community Property States, 1951, Corporate Trasactions Involving Its Own Stock, 1954, Litigation Expenses and the Income Tax, 1957. Bd. dirs. Children's Hosp. Med. Center of N. Calif., 1963-74, v.p., 1968-70; trustee Oakes Found., 1957-70; regent St. Mary's Coll., Calif., 1968-88, pres bd., 1970-72, emeritus mem., 1988—. Fellow Am. Bar Found. (life); mem. Am. Law Inst. (life), ABA (chmn. com. on statute of limitations 1954-57, mem. coun., tax sect. 1960-63), Calif. Bar Assn. (chmn. com. on taxation 1950-52, 60-61), Soc. Calif. Pioneers (v.p. 1964, 75-86), Phi Kappa Sigma, Phi Delta Phi. Republican. Clubs: Pacific Union, Orinda Country, World Trade. Home and Office: 7 Sycamore Rd Orinda CA 94563-1418

BROOKLER, HARRY AARON, retired physician; b. Winnipeg, Man., Can., Jan. 16, 1915; came to U.S., 1954; s. Samuel David and Rachel (Farbstein) B.; m. Gertrude Mandel, Jan. 1, 1941; children: Jerome, Rickey, Jackie, Resa, Maxwell. MD, Man. U., 1938. Diplomate Am. Bd. Anesthesiology. Resident in surgery Winnipeg Gen. Hosp., 1937-39; pvt. practice Lemberg, Sask., 1940-41, Weyburn, Sask., 1941-54, San Diego, 1954-59, 61-85; resident in anesthesia Harbor Gen. Hosp.-UCLA, Torrance, 1959-61; med. dir. skilled nursing facilities Casa Blanca Corp., San Diego, 1976—; surg. cons. Weyburn Mental Hosp., Sask., 1942-54; chief of staff Weyburn Gen. Hosp., Sask., 1945-50, Doctors (Sharp Cabrillo) Hosp., San Diego, 1964-66; coroner Sask. Govt., 1944-54; cons. Can. Pacific Railway, Weyburn, 1941-54. Bd. dirs. Beth Jacob Congregation, San Diego, 1958-60, Jewish Family Svc., San Diego, 1960-62; workshipful master Masons, Weyburn, 1952; chmn. bd. dirs. Jewish Family Svc., San Diego, 1961. Recipient Isbister scholarships Man. Govt., 1931, 32, 33. Fellow Am. Geriatrics Soc., Am. Coll. Anesthesia; mem. AMA, Calif. Med. Assn., San Diego County Med. Assn. (chmn. skilled nursing com. 1961-66, staff survey com. 1967—), Calif. Assn. Med. Dirs. (bd. dirs., founder 1980—, treas. 1980-85). Home and Office: 5310 Prosperity Ln San Diego CA 92115-2145

BROOKMAN, ANTHONY RAYMOND, lawyer; b. Chgo., Mar. 23, 1922; s. Raymond Charles and Marie Clara (Alberg) B.; m. Marilyn Joyce Brookman, June 5, 1982; children: Meribeth Brookman Farmer, Anthony Raymond, Lindsay Logan Christensen. Student, Ripon Coll., 1940-41; BS, Northwestern U., 1947; JD, U. Calif., San Francisco, 1953. Bar: Calif. 1954. Law clk. to presiding justice Calif. Supreme Ct., 1953-54; ptnr. Nichols, Williams, Morgan, Digardi & Brookman, 1954-68; sr. ptnr. Brookman & Talbot, Inc. (formerly Brookman & Hoffman, Inc.), Walnut Creek, Calif., 1969-92, Brookman & Talbot Inc., Sacramento, 1992—. Pres. Young Reps. Calif., San Mateo County, 1953-54. 1st lt. USAF. Mem. ABA, Alameda County Bar Assn., State Bar Calif., Lawyers Club Alameda County, Alameda-Contra Costa County Trial Lawyers Assn., Assn. Trial Lawyers Am., Calif. Trial Lawyers Assn., Athenian Nile Club, Masons, Shriners. Republican. Office: 901 H St Ste 200 Sacramento CA 95814-1808 also: 1990 N California Blvd Walnut Creek CA 94596-3742 also: 1746 Grand Canal Blvd Ste 11 Stockton CA 95207-8111

BROOKS, DENNIS EUGENE, electrician; b. Wheatridge, Colo., Dec. 22, 1963; s. Jerome Rodney and Marilyn Althea (Egelhoff) B. Grad., Adult H.S., Wheatridge, 1982. 2d yr. apprentice Gould & Preisner Electric, Denver, 1984-86; svc. driver Crist Truck Tire Svc., Fontana, Calif., 1986-91; salesman, warehouse mgr. The Carpet Barn, Denver, 1991-95; 3d yr. apprentice Duro Electric, Englewood, Colo., 1994-95; 4th yr. apprentice Kenny Electric Svc., Englewood, Colo., 1995—. Author poetry. Home: 6237 Fenton St Arvada CO 80003

BROOKS, DONALD LEE, civil engineering and scientific consulting firm executive; b. Boston, 1956; s. Douglas Lee and Elizabeth Brooks; m. Terry O'Sullivan, 1987 (div. 1989); m. Jill Blondin, 1991; children: Nathan Donald, Kylie Elizabeth. BA in Biology, Earlham Coll., Richmond, Ind., 1979; postgrad., U.Ariz., 1984. Registered profl. engr., Ariz.; profl. hydrologist. Field biologist/vegetation mgr. Colo. River Projects Ariz. State U. Ctr., 1980-81; resch. asst. U. Ariz., Tucson, 1982-84; subdivsn. engr., devel. divsn. mgr. Pima County Dept. Transp., Tucson, 1984-89; mgr. water resources Anderson-Passarelli, Tucson, 1989; v.p. URBAN Engrng., Tucson, 1989-92; project mgr. Johnson-Brittain Assocs., Tucson, 1992; client mgr. David Evans & Assocs., Tucson, 1992-93; pres., prin. engr. ICON Cons. USA, Inc., Tucson, 1993—. Contbr. articles to profl. jours. Mem. ASCE, Am. Inst. Hydrology, Ariz. Floodplain Mgmt. Assn. (Outstanding Svc. award 1990-91), Assn. State Flood Plains Mgrs., Am. Water Resources Assn., So. Ariz. Home Builders Assn. Quaker. Home: 1514 N Plaza de Lirios Tucson AZ 85745 Office: ICON Cons USA Inc 1870 W Prince Rd # 11 Tucson AZ 85705

BROOKS, EDWARD HOWARD, college administrator; b. Salt Lake City, Mar. 2, 1921; s. Charles Campbell and Margery (Howard) B.; m. Courtaney June Perren, May 18, 1946; children: Merrillee Brooks Runyan, Robin Anne (Mrs. R. Bruce Pollock). B.A., Stanford U., 1942, M.A., 1947, Ph.D., 1950. Mem. faculty, adminstrn. Stanford U., 1949-71; provost Claremont (Calif.) Colls., 1971-81; v.p. Claremont U. Center, 1979-81; sr. v.p. Claremont McKenna Coll., 1981-84; provost Scripps Coll., 1987-89, pres., 1989-90; ret., 1990. Trustee EDUCOM, 1978-80, Webb Sch. of Calif., 1979-90, Menlo Sch. and Coll., 1985-88; bd. overseers Hoover Instn., 1972-78; bd. dirs. Student Loan Mktg. Assn., 1973-77; mem. Calif. Student Aid Commn., 1984-88, chmn., 1986-88. Served with AUS, 1942-45. Clubs: Manhattan Country. Home: 337 8th St Manhattan Beach CA 90266-5629 *Looking back since retirement, I have concluded that the most useful and, perhaps, enduring contribution an institutional leader can make is clearly committed efforts to make the institution better and the individuals within it better; holding everyone to even higher standards.*

BROOKS, JAMES SPRAGUE, retired national guard officer; b. Los Angeles, Feb. 16, 1925; s. Julian Chesney and Louise Heegaard (Sprague) B.; m. Loa Mae Woolf, June 17, 1947; children—Georgia Lee (stepdau.), Kerri Louise (dec.), James Patrick. B.C.E., Oreg. State Coll., 1951. Commd. lt. Idaho N.G., 1947, advanced through grades to maj. gen., 1975; engrng. staff officer Idaho Mil. Dept. Idaho N.G., Boise, 1951-64, engr. Budget and Property Office, 1953-64, chief staff, 1965-74, adj. gen., chief Bur. Disaster Svcs., state dir. Selective Svc., 1975-85; chmn. army res. forces policy com. Dept. Army, 1979. Contbr. articles to Aviation Digest. Nat. Guard Mag. Mem. Boise Mcpl. Airport Commn., 1963-90, Idaho Law Enforcement Planning Commn., 1975, Boise Met. Plan Steering Com., 1976, Boise County Comprehensive Planning Task Force, 1989—, Idaho Pub. Transp. Adv. Coun., 1994—; chmn. Boise Mayor's Transit Adv. Com., 1991-94. With USAAF, 1943-46. Decorated Legion of Merit, D.S.M.; recipient Idaho Safe Pilot award, 1974; named Disting. Citizen, Idaho Statesman, 1977. Mem. N.G. Assn., U.S. Army, AF Assn., Retired Officers Assn., Tau Beta Pi, Sigma Tau.

BROOKS, JOHN SCOTT, county official; b. Ventura, Calif., June 9, 1964; s. John Wilburn and Carolyn Ruth (Hartley) B.; m. Maria Acela Nunez, May 8, 1990; children: Sierra Lynn, Shasta Lee. AA, Ventura (Calif.) C.C., 1987; BS in Environ. Planning and Comms., Humboldt State U., Arcata, Calif., 1990. Econ. devel. fin. profl. Waste mgmt. specialist Calif. Integrated Waste Mgmt. Bd., Sacramento, 1990-93, assoc. waste mgmt. specialist, 1993-96; program dir. Regional Coun. Rural Counties, Environ. Svcs. Joint Powers Authority, Sacramento, 1996—; pres., founder Ventura Coll. Biol. Assn., 1986. Co-author, editor: The Rural Cookbook-Recipes for Successful Waste Prevention, 1994. V.p., co-founder Ventura Indian Student Assn., 1985. Recipient Customer Svc. award Calif. EPA, Sacramento, 1995, Outstanding Achievement award Calif. Integrated Waste Mgmt. Bd., Sacramento, 1994, Rural County Assistance award Regional Coun. of Rural Counties, Sacramento, 1994. Mem. Solid Waste Assn. N.Am., Toastmasters (sgt. at arms 1994, edn. v.p. 1995, Toastmasters on TV 1995). Republican. Office: Regional Coun Rural Counties Environ Svcs Joint Powers 1020 12th St Ste 400 Sacramento CA 95814-3917

BROOKS, MARIAN, retired comptroller and credit manager; b. Baker, Oreg., Nov. 23, 1930; d. Paul and Florence (Cornman) Seiffert; m. Gregg Brooks, Oct. 29, 1955; 1 child, Wayne. Office mgr. Redmond (Oreg.) Motor Co., 1952-53, Morris-Nelson Pontiac, Redmond, 1953-54; comptr., credit mag. McCaulou's Inc., Madras, Oreg., 1955-1994; ret., 1994—; past pres. bd. dirs. Consumer Credit Counseling Svc. Oreg., Bend. Bd. dirs. United Way Jefferson County, Madras, 1985-96. Mem. Internat. Credit Assn. Ctrl. Orgn. (pres.), Credit Assn. Oreg. (hon. life, past pres. bd. dirs.), Soc. Cert. Credit Execs. Home: 743 SE Hull St Madras OR 97741

BROOKS, SAMUEL EVERETT, purchasing agent; b. Connellsville, Pa., Jan. 19, 1946; s. J. Melvin and Ruth Pearl (Firestone) B.; m. Martha Jane Peters, May 28, 1966; children: Kristine, Kimberly, Kerrie, Jason. Student, W.Va. U., 1963-64, Ann Arundel C.C., 1964-66. Data compiler Westinghouse, Balt., 1965-70; buyer, dept. head Leggetts, Waynesboro, Va., 1970-74; asst. mgr. Cranes Men's Shop, Connellsville, 1974-77; buyer Volkswagen of Am., New Stanton, Pa., 1977-88; mgr. indirect purchasing New United Motors Mfg. Inc., Fremont, Calif., 1988—; bd. dirs. No. Calif. Purchasing Coun.; MRO purchasing spkr. Youth worker local ch., Balt., 1965-70, Waynesboro, 1971-74. Republican. Home: 4844 Sterling Hill Dr Antioch CA 94509-7667 Office: New United Motors Mfg Inc 45500 Fremont Blvd Fremont CA 94538-6326

BROOKS, SCOTT DAVID, health facility administrator; b. Burbank, Calif., Aug. 22, 1962. BA, UCLA, 1985; MA, Calif. Grad. Inst., 1990. From rsch. asst. to dir. HIV Intervention Project Edelman Health Ctr., L.A., 1988-92; program asst. Children's Hosp. L.A., 1993-94; adminstrv. analyst clin. rsch. unit UCLA, 1994-96; with dept. clin. rsch. Kraus Med. Ptnrs., L.A., 1996—; dir. cmty. adv. bd. Edelman Health Ctr., 1990-92. Mem. Am. Psychol. Assn., Am. Counseling Assn., Calif. Psychol. Assn., L.A. Gay Psychotherapists Assn. Home: PO Box 461586 Los Angeles CA 90046

BROOKS, SHELLEY, middle school educator; b. Boston, Aug. 20, 1955; d. Bernard and Carol Florence (Klass) B. BEd, U. Miami, Coral Gables, Fla., 1977; cert. in reading, U. Fla., Gainesville, 1978; postgrad., U. Tex., Dallas, 1990, U. Nev., Las Vegas, 1993. Cert. early childhood edn., elem., K-12 reading tchr., Nev. Elem. curriculum libr. U. Miami, 1977-78; classroom tchr. Citrus County Sch. Dist., Homosassa, Fla., 1978-80; reading tchr. Dallas Ind. Sch. Dist., 1982-90, Clark County Sch. Dist., Las Vegas, 1990—. Tchr. rep. Clark County Sch. Dist., 1991-93, Dallas Ind. Sch. Dist., 1982-90. Mem. Internat. Reading Assn. Jewish. Office: James Cashman Mid Sch 4622 W Desert Inn Rd Las Vegas NV 89102-7115

BROOKS, SIDNEY B., judge; married; 2 children. BA in Polit. Sci., U. Colo.; JD, U. Denver Coll. Law. Assoc. atty. Nelson and Haridng, Denver, 1971-73; asst. atty. gen. Office of Atty. Gen., Denver, 1973-75; ptnr. Nelson & Harding, Denver, 1975-80, Smart DeFurio Brooks Eklund and McClure, Denver, 1980-84; pres. Brooks and Krieger P.C., 1984-87; judge U.S. Bankruptcy Ct. Colo., 1988—; guest spkr. Russian Law Conf., Russian Rsch. Ctr., Harvard U. Law Sch., 1994, Russian Bankruptcy Conf., Moscow, 1994; participant Conf. on Chinese Bankruptcy Law REform, Internat. Rep. Inst., Beijing, 1995. Contbr. over 50 articles to profl. jours. in The Colorado Lawyer, The Denver Post, The Rocky Mountain News, and others. Office: US Bankruptcy Ct Colo 721 19th St Rm 560 Denver CO 80202-4045

BROOKS, STUART DALE, building consultant; b. Honolulu, July 5, 1952; s. Clarence Mathew and Beatrice Miyoko (Okamoto) B.; m. Charlene Naomi Juarez, Aug. 25, 1973; children: Kaleinani S., Stuart K. AS in Drafting Tech., U. Hawaii, 1973; BS in Bus. and Constrn., U. Oreg., 1980. Cert. bldg. inspector. Archtl. draftsman Honolulu, 1972-75; archtl. designer Brooks & Assoc., Eugene, Oreg., 1980-82; sr. cost estimator Hanscomb Assoc., Inc., Anchorage, Alaska, 1983-84; energy programs mgr. State of Alaska, Anchorage, 1984-92; pres., CEO Energy Design Assocs., Inc., Eagle River, Alaska, 1992—; tech. advisor Energy Rated Homes of Alaska, Anchorage, 1985-90; tech. energy advisor Alaska Housing Fin. Corp., Anchorage, 1995-96. Author: State of Alaska Building Energy Efficiency Standard, 1992; tech. advisor, editor: State of Alaska Energy Conservation Work Book, 1988. Founder, bd. dirs. Alaska Craftsman Home Program, 1986-87. Mem. Internat. Conf. Bldg. Ofcls., Matsu Homebuilders Assn., Alaska Ctr. for Appropriate Tech. Office: Energy Design Assocs Inc 17526 Rachel Cir Eagle River AK 99577

BROOKS, TIMOTHY JOE, career military officer; b. Marietta, Ohio, Mar. 17, 1954; s. Joseph Canada and Katherine (Harris) B.; m. Suzanne Rene Craig, Aug. 15, 1982; children: Thomas Joe, Patrick Craig. BS in Recreation, Ind. State U., 1976; AS in Aviation Tech., Thomas A. Edison State U., 1994. Cert. Comml. helicopter pilot FAA. Commd. 2d lt. U.S. Army, 1976, advanced through grades to lt. col., 1995. Vol. Boy Scouts Am.; scoutmaster Troop 181 Security, Colo. 1997—. Mem. Army Aviation Assn. Am. (v.p. programs Calif. chpt., treas. Pike's Peak chpt. Colo., life mem.), Res. Officers Assn. (v.p. Conn. chpt. 1991-92, life), Masons, Scottish Rite, Eastern Star, Phi Delta Theta. Baptist. Home: 5560 Pickering Ct Colorado Springs CO 80911

BROOKS-KORN, LYNNE VIVIAN, artist; b. Detroit, July 6, 1951; d. Loren Edward and Edith Zona (Gaub) Brooks; m. Howard Allen Korn, Apr. 17, 1977. BFA magna cum laude, U. Mich., 1973, MFA, 1976. Teaching fellow U. Mich. Sch. Art, Ann Arbor, 1976; vis. lectr. various history of art depts.; over 150 solo and group shows since 1992. Numerous one-woman shows, including Grants Pass (Oreg.) Mus. Art, 1993, Red River Valley Mus., Vernon, Tex., 1993, Red River Valley Mus., Vernon, Tex., 1993, Coll. Ea. Utah, 1994, Aberdeen (Scotland) Arts Ctr., 1995, Napa

County Librs., 1996, MacLaurin Art Gallery, Ayr, Great Britain, 1996, Carlsbad (N.Mex.) Mus., 1994; group shows include Foster City (Calif.) Mus. Gallery, 1993, San Bernardino County Mus., Redlands, Calif., 1993, Ohio State U., 1994, Bryn Mawr (Pa.) Coll., 1995, Haggin Mus., Stockton, Calif., 1996; represented in permanent collections San Bernardino County Mus., Longwell Mus., Downey Mus. Art, Red River Valley Mus., Yosemite Mus., Brit. Mus., Bryn Mawr Coll., others; work reviewed in numerous publs.; various commns. Recipient numerous awards for art, including Internat. Art Competition, 1987, 88, 89, Nepenthe Munki Soc., Wichita, Kans., 1989, Haggin Mus., Stockton, Calif., 1990, Menlo Park Civic Ctr., 1991, San Bernardino County Mus., 1992, Sweetwater County Art Guild, 1993, East Tex. State U., 1993, Breckenridge Fine Arts Ctr., 1993, Lake Worth Art League, Inc., 1993, 94, Amador County Arts Coun., 1993, Coastal Ctr. for Arts, St. Simons Island, Ga., 1993, Soc. We. Artists Signature Mem., 1994, Ea. Washington WC Soc., 1994, San Jacinto Coll., Pasadena, Tex., 1995, Peninsula Art Assn., Burlingame, Calif., 1996; Rackham grantee U. Mich., 1975. Mem. Coll. Art Assn. Democrat. Studio: 700 Loma Vista Ter Pacifica CA 94044-2425

BROPHY, DENNIS RICHARD, psychology and philosophy educator, administrator, clergyman; b. Milw., Aug. 6, 1945; s. Floyd Herbert and Phyllis Marie (Ingram) B.; BA, Washington U., St. Louis, 1967, MA, 1968; M.Div., Pacific Sch. Religion, 1971; PhD in Indstrl. and Orgnl. Psychology, Texas A & M U., 1995. Cert. coll. tchr., Calif. Edn. rschr. IBM Corp., White Plains, N.Y., 1968-71; edn. minister Cmty. Congl. Ch., Port Huron, Mich., 1971-72, Bethlehem United Ch. of Christ, Ann Arbor, Mich., 1972-73, Cmty. Congl. Ch., Chula Vista, Calif., 1974; philosophy instr. Southwestern Coll., Chula Vista, 1975; assoc. prof. psychology and philosophy Northwest Coll., Powell, Wyo., 1975-96, prof., 1996—, chmn. social sci. divsn., 1992-95; religious edn. cons. Mont.-No. Wyo. Conf. United Ch. of Christ. Mem. APA (Daniel Berlyne award 1996), Wyo. Coun. for Humanities, Soc. Indsl. Orgnl. Psychology, Yellowstone Assn. of United Ch. of Christ, Phi Kappa Phi, Phi Beta Kappa, Sigma Xi, Omicron Delta Kappa, Theta Xi, Golden Key Nat. Honor Soc. Home: 533 Avenue C Powell WY 82435-2401 Office: Northwest Coll 231 W 6th St Powell WY 82435-1898

BRORBY, WADE, federal judge; b. 1934. BS, U. Wyo., 1956, JD with honor, 1958. Bar: Wyo. County and prosecuting atty. Campbell County, Wyo., 1963-70; ptnr. Morgan Brorby Price and Arp, Gillette, Wyo., 1961-88; judge U.S. Ct. Appeals (10th cir.), Cheyenne, Wyo., 1988—. With USAF, 1958-61. Mem. ABA, Campbell County Bar Assn., Am. Judicature Soc., Def. Lawyers Wyo., Wyo Bar Assn. (commr. 1968-70). Office: US Ct Appeals 10th Cir O'Mahoney Fed Bldg Rm 2016 PO Box 1028 Cheyenne WY 82003*

BROSNAN, PETER LAWRENCE, documentary filmmaker; b. Bklyn., July 6, 1952; s. John Joseph and Audrey Barbara (Holran) B. BFA, NYU, N.Y.C., 1974; MA, U. So. Calif., 1979, Pepperdine U., 1995. Documentary filmmaker, writer L.A., 1980—; dir. DeMille Project, Hollywood Heritage, L.A., 1988—. Author: (screenplays) Heart of Darkness, 1992, The Ark, 1994, Perfect Target, 1996; co-author: (book) PML Report, 1989; writer: (documentary film) Ghosts of Cape Horn, 1980 (World Ship Trust award); prodr., dir.: (TV documentary) The Lost City, 1992; writer, segment prodr.: (PBS series) Faces of Culture, 1983-84 (Emmy award 1984), Writer Marketing, 1984 (Emmy award 1985); dir.: (documentary) Sand Castles, 1995. Democrat. Home: 1709 N Fuller Ave Apt 25 Los Angeles CA 90046-3012

BROTMAN, CAROL EILEEN, adult education educator, advocate; b. L.A., Feb. 17, 1955; d. Hyman and Beverly Joanne (Krause) B. AA, L.A. Pierce Coll., 1977; BA, U. So. Calif., L.A., 1984; postgrad., UCLA, 1990, cert. legal asst., 1991. Cert. adult edn. tchr., Calif. Tchr. divsn. adult and career edn. L.A. Unified Sch. Dist., 1986—; tchr. adult edn. and ESL North Hollywood (Calif.) Adult Sch., 1987-94, dept. chair, 1990-91; pre-employment trainer Refugee Employment Tng. Project, 1995—; tchr. ESL Met. Skills Ctr., L.A. Founder Families for Quality Care, San Fernando Valley, Calif., 1983-86; mem. com. L.A. Pub. Libr. Ctrl. Libr., internat. langs. dept. Langs. Expertese and Resources Network, 1991; vol. paralegal Harriet Buhai Ctr. for Family Law, 1992-94; organizer adult-student cmty. group Thanksgiving dinner for new immigrants St. Patrick's Ch., North Hollywood, 1987-90. Recipient Mayor's Commendation, 1984, Older Women's League, 1985, Cert. of Tribute, Harriet Buhai Ctr. for Family Law, 1992, 93, Cert. of Appreciation for Outstanding Vol. Work, Family Law Sect., L.A. County Bar Assn. and Superior Ct. of L.A., 1993. Mem. AAUW, NAFE, United Tchrs. of L.A., Rare Fruit Gardenrs Assn. Home: 10921 Reseda Blvd Northridge CA 91326-2803

BROTMAN, JEFFREY H., variety stores executive; b. 1942. JD, U. Wash., 1967. Ptnr. Lasher-Brotman & Sweet, 1967-74; with ENI Exploration Co., 1975-83; co-founder Costco Wholesale Corp., 1983, chmn. bd., chief exec. officer, 1983-88; chmn. bd. Price/Costco, 1988—. Office: Price/Costco 999 Lake Dr Issaquah WA 98027-5367*

BROTMAN, RICHARD DENNIS, counselor; b. Detroit, Nov. 2, 1952; s. Alfred David and Dorothy G. (Mansfield) B.; m. Debra Louise Hobold, Sept. 9, 1979. AA, E. L.A. Jr. Coll., 1972; AB, U. So. Calif., 1974, MS, 1976. Instructional media coord. Audio-Visual Div., Pub. Library, City of Alhambra, Calif., 1971-78; clin. supr. Hollywood-Sunset Community Clinic, L.A., 1976—; client program coord. N. L.A. County Regional Ctr. for Developmentally Disabled, 1978-81; sr. counselor Eastern L.A. Regional Ctr. for Developmentally Disabled, 1981-85; dir. community svcs. Almansor Edn. Ctr., 1985-87; tng. and resource devel. Children's Home Soc. Calif., 1987-90; program supr. Pacific Clinics-East, 1990-94; dir. clin. svcs. Alma Family Svcs., 1994—; probable cause hearing officer Orange County (Calif.) Healthcare Agy., 1986—; intern student affairs div., U. So. Calif., 1976. Corp. dir. San Gabriel Mission Players, 1973-75. Lic. marriage, family and child counselor, Calif.; cert. counselor Calif. Community Coll. Bd. Mem. Am. Assn. For Marriage and Family Therapy (approved supr.), Calif. Personnel and Guidance Assn. (conv. participant, 1976, 77, 79), Calif. Rehab. Counselors Assn. (officer), San Fernando Valley Consortium of Agys. Serving Developmentally Disabled Citizens (chmn. recreation subcom.), L.A. Aquarium Soc. Democrat. Home: 3515 Brandon St Pasadena CA 91107-4542 Office: Alma Family Svcs 6505 Rosemead Blvd Ste 300 Pico Rivera CA 90660-3544

BROTT, BORIS, orchestra conductor; b. Montreal, Que., Can., Mar. 14, 1944; m. Ardyth Webster; children: Alexandra, David, Benjamin. Student Conservatoire de Musique, Montreal, McGill U., Montreal; studies with Pierre Monteux, Igor Markevitch, Leonard Bernstein, Alexander Brott; LLD (hon.) McMaster U., 1990. Debut as violinist Montreal Symphony, 1949; debut as condr. Nat. Symphony Orch., Mex., 1958; founder, condr. Philharm. Youth Orch. Montreal, 1959-61; asst. condr. Toronto (Ont., Can.) Symphony, 1963-65, N.Y. Philharm., 1968-69; music dir. No. Sinfonia Orch., Eng., 1964-69, Lakehead Univ., Thunder Bay, Ont., 1967-72; interim music dir. Kitchener (Ont.) Waterloo Symphony, 1970-71; music dir. Regina (Sask., Can.) Symphony, 1970-73; music dir., condr. Hamilton (Ont.) Philharm., 1969-90, Ont. Place Pops Orch., Toronto, 1987—, Ventura (Calif.) County Symphony Orch., 1992-95, Boris Brott Summer Music Festival, 1988—, New West Symphony, Ventura; co-conductor, McGill Chamber Orch., Montreal, 1989—; pres. Great Music Can., 1977—; chief condr. BBC Welsh Symphony Orch., Cardiff, Wales, 1972-77, CBC Winnipeg Orch., 1976-83; prin. guest condr., music advisor Symphony N.S., Halifax, Can., 1981-87; co-condr. McGill Chamber Orch., 1989—; guest condr. major orchs. in Can., U.K., U.S.A., Italy, Germany, and Israel; numerous guest appearances on TV; numerous recs. for various cos.; artistic dir. Stratford (Ont.) Summer Music Festival, 1983—, Boris Brott Summer Music Festival, 1988—. Recipient Pan Am. Condr.'s prize, Mexico City, 1958, Gold medal for 1st prize Dimitri Mitropoulos Internat. Competition N.Y.C., 1968, Award for Innovative Programming PRO CAL, 1983, 85, Am. Music award, 1986, Officer of Order of Can. award, 1987; named One of Outstanding Young Men in Can., Jaycees, 1969, 73. Mem. Jeunesses Musicales (nat. pres. 1987), Knight of Malta. Home: 301 Bay St S, Hamilton, ON Canada L8P 3J7

BROUDY, VIRGINIA CONSTANCE, hematologist, educator; b. Stockholm, Sweden, Nov. 7, 1954; came to U.S., 1955; d. Lloyd Hollingsworth and Margaret Constance (Avery) Smith; m. David Robert Broudy, June 19, 1983; children: Sarah, Laura, Daniel. BA in Biochemistry cum laude, Harvard U., 1976; MD, U. Calif., San Francisco, 1980. Diplomate in internal medicine, hematology and oncology Am. Bd. Internal Medicine. Med. intern Oreg. Health Scis. U., Portland, 1980-81, resident in medicine, 1981-83, fellow in oncology, 1983-85; fellow in hematology U. Wash., Seattle, 1985-87, asst. prof. medicine, 1987-92, assoc. prof. medicine, 1992—; mem. biol. response modifiers adv. com. FDA, Bethesda, Md., 1994—; mem. pers. for rsch. sci. adv. com. Am. Cancer Soc., Atlanta, 1994-96, chair leukemia and blood cell devel. com., 1997—. Contbr. more than 50 articles to profl. jours. Mem. U.S. Nat. Championship Team, U.S. Rowing Assn., 1973; Am. Cancer Soc. grantee, 1991, NIH grantee, 1992. Mem. Am. Soc. Hematology (chair membership com. 1994), Am. Soc. Clin. Oncology, Western Soc. for Clin. Investigation, Am. Soc. Clin. Investigation. Office: U Wash Divsn Hematology/Dept Med Box 357710 Seattle WA 98195

BROUGH, BRUCE ALVIN, public relations and communications executive; b. Wayland, N.Y., Nov. 22, 1937; s. Alvin Elroy and Marjorie Huberta (McDowell) B.; m. Jane Virginia Koethen, Aug. 9, 1958; children: John David, Pamela Marjorie, Robert Bruce. BS in Pub. Rels., U. Md., 1960; MS in Mass Communications, Am. U., Washington, 1967. Comm. mgr. IBM Corp., various locations, 1965-74; owner, pres. Bruce Brough Assocs., Inc., Boca Raton, Fla., 1974-75; worldwide press rels. rep. Tex. Instruments Inc., 1975-76; v.p. pub. rels. Regis McKenna Inc., 1976-77; pres., prin. Pease/Brough Assocs., Inc., Palo Alto, Calif., 1978-80, Franson/Brough Assocs., Inc., San Jose, Calif., 1980-81; sr. v.p., dir. Advanced Tech. Network Hill and Knowlton, Inc., San Jose, 1981-86; sr. v.p., gen. mgr. Hill and Knowlton, Inc., Santa Clara, Calif., 1989; mgr. corp. pub. rels. Signetics Corp., 1986-87; mktg. comm. mgr. Corp. Ctr. Philips Components divsn. Philips Internat., B.V., Eindhoven, The Netherlands, 1987-89; dir. corp. comm. Centigram Comm. Corp., San Jose, Calif., 1989-90; prin. Brough Comm., Santa Cruz, Calif., 1994—; lectr. San Jose State U., 1977-83, 91—; cons. comm. and pub. rels., 1986—. Author: Publicity and Public Relations Guide for Business, 1984, revised edit., 1986, The Same Yesterday, Today and Forever, 1986; contbg. editor Family Bible Ency., 1973. Recipient Sustained Superior Performance award NASA, 1964, award Freedom's Found., 1963. Mem. Pub. Rels. Soc. Am. (accredited), Soc. Tech. Comm., Nat. Press Club, Sigma Delta Chi. Republican. Roman Catholic. Home: 155 Rabbits Run Rd Santa Cruz CA 95060-1526 Office: Brough Comms 4113 Scotts Valley Dr Ste 200 Scotts Valley CA 95066

BROUGHTON, RAY MONROE, economic consultant; b. Seattle, Mar. 2, 1922; s. Arthur Charles and Elizabeth C. (Young) B.; BA, U. Wash., 1947, MBA, 1960; m. Margret Ellen Ryno, July 10, 1944 (dec.); children: Linda Rae Broughton Silk, Mary Catherine Broughton Boutin; m. Carole Jean Packer, 1980. Mgr. communications and managerial devel. Gen. Electric Co., Hanford Atomic Products Ops., Richland, Wash., 1948-59; mktg. mgr., asst. to pres. Smyth Enterprises, Seattle, 1960-62; dir. rsch. Seattle Area Indsl. Council, 1962-65; v.p., economist (mgr. econ. rsch. dept.) First Interstate Bank of Oreg., N.A., Portland, 1965-87; ind. economic cons., 1987—; mem. econ. adv. com. to Am. Bankers Assn., 1980-83; mem. Gov.'s Econ. Adv. Council, 1981-88; dir. Oregonians for Cost Effective Govt., 1989-90; instr. bus. communications U. Wash., Richland, 1956-57. Treas., dir. Oreg. affiliate Am. Heart Assn., 1972-78, chmn., 1980-81, dir., 1980-84. Served to 1st lt. U.S. Army, 1943-46; ETO. Mem. Western Econ. Assn., Pacific N.W. Regional Econ. Conf. (dir. 1967-94), Nat. Assn. Bus. Economists (co-founder chpt. 1971), Am. Mktg. Assn. (pres. chpt. 1971-72), Alpha Delta Sigma. Author: Trends and Forces of Change in the Payments System and the Impact on Commercial Banking, 1972; contbg. editor Pacific Banker and Bus. mag., 1974-80. Home and Office: 10127 SW Lancaster Rd Portland OR 97219-6302

BROWER, DAVID ROSS, conservationist; b. Berkeley, Calif., July 1, 1912; s. Ross J. and Mary Grace (Barlow) B.; m. Anne Hus, May 1, 1943; children: Kenneth David, Robert Irish, Barbara Anne, John Stewart. Student, U. Calif., 1929-31; DSc (hon.), Hobart and William Smith Colls., 1967; DHL (hon.), Claremont Colls. Grad. Sch., 1971, Starr King Sch. for Ministry, 1971, U. Md., 1973; PhD in Ecology (hon.), U. San Francisco, 1973, Colo. Coll., 1977; other hon. degrees, New Sch. for Social Rsch., 1984, Sierra Nev. Coll., 1985, Unity Coll., Maine, 1989. Editor U. Calif. Press, 1941-52; exec. dir. Sierra Club, 1952-69, bd. dirs., 1941-43, 46-53, 83-88, mem. editorial bd., 1935-69, hon. v.p., 1972—; dir. John Muir Inst. Environ. Studies, 1969-71, v.p., 1968-72; pres. Friends of the Earth, 1969-79; founder, chmn. Friends of the Earth Found., 1972-84, bd. dirs.; founder Environ. Liaison Ctr., Nairobi, 1974; founder, chmn. Earth Island Inst., San Francisco, 1982—; founder, pres. Earth Island Action Group, 1989; founder biennial Fate and Hope of the Earth Confs., N.Y.C., 1982, Washington, 1984, Ottawa, 1986, Managua, 1989; activist in conservation campaigns, Kings Canyon Nat. Pk., 1938-40, Dinosaur Nat. Monument, 1952-56, Alaska parks and forests, 1954—, North Cascades Nat. Pk., 1955-94, Cape Cod, Fire Island, Point Reyes nat. seashores, 1960-68, Redwood Nat. Pk., 1963-68, Great Basin Nat. Park, 1965, Galapagos Islands World Heritage, 1965-68, Grand Canyon 1952-68, Snowdonia Nat. Park, 1970, 71, population and growth control and nuclear proliferation issues, Nat. Wilderness Preservation System, 1951-64, James Bay defense, 1991-94, conservation lectr., U.S., 1939—, Finland, 1971, Sweden, 1972, Kenya, 1972, 74, Italy, 1972, 74, 79, 82, 91, 94, Australia and N.Z., 1974, Japan, 1976, 78, 90, 92, U.K., 1968, 70, 93, USSR, 1985, 88, 90, 91, 92, France, 1970, 90-91, Fed. Republic Germany, 1989, Berlin, 1990, Nicaragua, 1988, 89, Brazil, 1992, The Netherlands, 1993-94; founder Trustees for Conservation, 1954, sec., 1960-61, 64-65; founder Sierra Club Found., 1960; bd. dirs. Citizens Com. Natural Resources, 1955-78; chmn. Natural Resources Coun. Am., 1955-57; bd. dirs. North Cascades Conservation Coun., from 1957, Rachel Carson Trust for Living Environment, 1966-72, cons. expert, from 1973; founder, steering com. League Conservation Voters, 1969-80; founder Les Amis de la Terre, Paris, 1970; founder, guarantor Friends of the Earth U.K., 1970-88; chmn. Earth Island Ltd., London, 1971-74; active Restoring-the-Earth movement, from 1986, founder Global CPR Svc., 1990, leader del. to Lake Baikal, Siberia, 1988, 90, 91, 92, mem. various adv. bds. including Found. on Econ. Trends, Nat. Strategy, Coun. Econ. Priorities, Zero Population Growth, Yosemite Concessions Svc., Earth Day 1990, 94; mem. Com. on Nat. Security. Initiator, designer, gen. editor: Sierra Club Exhibit Format Series, 20 vols., 1960-68, Friends of the Earth series The Earth's Wild Places, 10 vols., 1970-77, Celebrating the Earth series, 3 vols., 1972-73; numerous other films and books, biographee in Encounters with the Archdruid (John McPhee), 1970; (autobiography) Vol. 1, For Earth's Sake: The Life and Times of DAvid Brower, 1990, Vol. 2, Work in Progress, 1991; co-author: (Steve Chapple) Let the Mountains Talk, Let the Rivers Run, 1995; contbr. articles to nat. mags., profl. publs., others; subject video documentary produced for Sta. KCTS, Seattle, shown nationally on PBS; contbr. to U.S. Army mountain manuals, instruction, 1943-45. Participant in planning for 1992 UN Conf. on Environment, Rio de Janiero, 1987-92. Served as 1st lt. with 10th Mountain div. Inf. AUS, 1943-45; maj. Inf.-Res. ret. Decorated Bronze Star; recipient awards Calif. Conservation Coun., 1953, Nat. Parks Assn., 1956, Bklyn. Coll. Libr. Assn., 1970, also Carey-Thomas award, 1964, Paul Bartsch award Audubon Naturalist Soc. of Cen. Atlantic States, 1967, Golden Ark award the Prince of The Netherlands, 1979, Golden Gadfly award Media Alliance, San Francisco, 1984, Rose award World Environment Festival, Ottawa, Can., 1986, Strong Oak award New Renaissance Ctr., 1987, Lewis Mumford award Architects Designers Planners for Social Responsibility, 1991, Robert Marshall award, 1994; hon. fellow John Muir Coll., U. Calif., San Diego, 1986. Nominated Nobel Peace Prize, 1978, 79. Mem. Nat. Parks and Conservation Assn. (hon.), The Mountaineers (hon.), Appalachian Mountain Club (hon.), Sierra Club (1933—, John Muir award 1977), Am. Alpine Club (hon.). Office: Earth Island 300 Broadway St San Francisco CA 94133-4545 *It is true that some major resources of wildlife and wilderness, and all they mean to people, are still intact thanks to conservation battles I have shared. For this I can only be grateful—for the help, and the hope that future battles for these irreplaceable things will be as successful as well as the global efforts to restore what we can. They will succeed if enough people realize that this generation is not required to race through all the resources it can find, if humanity comprehends that this is the only earth, and there is no spare.*

BROWN, ALAN JOHNSON, chemicals executive; b. Alnwick, Eng., June 18, 1951; came to U.S., 1987; s. George and Margaret Mary (Johnson) B.; m. Cathy Sturlis, May 14, 1988 (div. Feb. 1993); m. Nueva G. Buck, Oct. 18, 1996. BS in Chemistry, U. East Anglia, Eng., 1974; MS in Enzymology, U. Warwick, Eng., 1975, PhD in Molecular Sci., 1977. Chartered chemist. Group leader ICI Corp. Rsch., Runcorn, Eng., 1977-81; group leader ECC Internat. Cen. Rsch., St. Austell, Eng., 1981-87; rsch. mgr. ECC Internat. Tech. Ctr., Sandersville, Ga., 1987-92; tech. dir. Columbia River Carbonates, Woodland, Wash., 1993—. Patentee in field. Mem. Royal Soc. Chemistry (S.W. Region com. 1986-87), Am. Chem. Soc., Clay Minerals Soc., Tech. Assoc. Pulp and Paper Inst., Chem. Mfrs. Assn. (chmn. analytical methods group 1991, 92), Soc. Mining Engrs. Office: Columbia River Carbonates PO Box D Woodland WA 98674-1103

BROWN, ALAN WHITTAKER, accountant; b. Pullman, Wash., Mar. 21, 1950; s. Richard Maurice and Kathryn (Doane) B.; adopted s. Waynona (Newcom) B; m. Carmen Lee Morales, Oct. 13, 1990. BS, U. Ill., 1987. CPA, Calif. Sr. staff acct. Brookside Hosp., San Pablo, Calif., 1987-90; acct. S.J. Gallina & Co., Walnut Creek, Calif., 1990-94; fin. analyst Kaiser Permanente, Oakland, Calif., 1994—. Mem. AICPA, Balloon Fedn. Am. Office: Permanente Med Group 901 Nevin Ave Richmond CA 94801-3143

BROWN, ALISON K., aeronautics company executive; b. Edinburgh, Scotland, Jan. 14, 1957; came to the U.S., 1980; d. Kenneth Robson and Margery (Kay) B.; m. Bruce Graham Johnson, June 26, 1993. BA, MA in Engring., Cambridge U., 1979; MS in Aero. Engring., MIT, 1981; PhD in Mechanics and Aerospace, UCLA, 1985. Draper fellow Draper Lab., Cambridge, Mass., 1980-81; mem. tech. staff Litton Industries, Woodland Hills, Calif., 1981-86; pres. NAVSYS Corp., Monument, Colo., 1986—. Patentee in field; contbr. articles to profl. jours. Mem. com. USAF Scientific Adv. Bd., Washington, 1994—. Scholar Sidney Sussex Coll., 1979, DuPont scholar, 1980; recipient Sir George Nelson prize Cambridge U., 1979, Cert. of Appreciation Radio Tech. Com. for Aviation. Mem. Inst. Navigation (coun. mem., conf. chair), IEEE, AIAA. Office: NAVSYS 14960 Woodcarver Rd Colorado Springs CO 80921-2370

BROWN, ANTHONY B., finance executive; b. Mpls., Apr. 5, 1922; s. Wayland Hoyt and Adele (Birdsall) B.; m. Mary Alice Ann Anderson, July 28, 1956. BS, Rutgers U., 1949; postgrad. U. So. Calif., 1968-69; PhD, U. Beverly Hills, 1986. Cert. data processing systems profl. Sr. system analyst Thrifty Corp., L.A., 1957-69; system engr. Informatics Gen., Inc., L.A., 1969-73; contract instr. computer software York U., 1970, McGill U., U. Victoria, 1971, USMC, Boston U., W.Va. U., U. Guelph, 1972; sr. system engr. Jet Propulsion Lab., La Canada, Calif., 1974-76; sr. system engr. Informatics Gen., Inc., Anchorage, L.A., Washington, 1976-78; supr. project control Hughes Aircraft Co., L.A., 1978-81; contr. western ops. Contel Corp., Redondo Beach, Calif., 1981-88. Author: A Century of Blunders--America's China Policy 1844-1949. Rep. precinct capt., presdl. election, 1964; vol. Reason Found.; chmn. bd. govs. La Brea Vista Townhouses, 1967-68; active numerous animal welfare orgns. Served with Finance Corps, U.S. Army, 1951-57. Decorated Bronze Star. Fellow Brit. Interplanetary Soc.; mem. AAAS, The Planetary Soc., Nature Conservancy, Town Hall of Calif., Assn. Computer Machinery (chpt. sec. 1973-74), Assn. Systems Mgmt., Mensa, Intertel, Armed Forces Communications and Electronics Assn., Assn. Inst. Cert. Computer Profls., Am. Assn. Fin. Profls., Am. Def. Preparedness Assn., Washington Legal Found., Am. Security Council (mem. nat. adv. bd.), Calif. Soc. SAR, Mil. Order World Wars, Aircraft Owners and Pilots Assn., Internat. Platform Assn., Theodore Roosevelt Assn., Res. Officers Assn., Delta Phi Epsilon. Republican. Club: Los Angeles Athletic. Lodges: Masons, Shriners, Nat. Sojourners. Home: 4333 Redwood Ave Marina Del Rey CA 90292-6424

BROWN, ARTHUR CARL, JR., retired minister; b. Stockton, Calif., Dec. 16, 1915; s. Arthur Carl and Maud (Twitchings) B.; m. Inez Lundquist, May 10, 1940 (dec. Aug. 1982); 1 child, Arthur Carl III. BA, Coll. of the Pacific, 1937; MA, San Francisco Theol. Sem., 1939, BD with honors, 1940; postgrad., Stanford U., 1949-50. Ordained to ministry Presbyn. Ch., 1940. Pastor Presbyn. Ch., Sedro Woolley, Wash., 1940-44, Community Ch., Santa Clara, Calif., 1944-46; assoc. pastor First Presbyn. Ch., San Jose, Calif., 1946-49; minister edn. First Presbyn. Ch., Palo Alto, Calif., 1949-51; organizing pastor Covenant Presbyn. Ch., Palo Alto, 1951-74; pastor Trinity Presbyn. Ch., Santa Cruz, Calif., 1974-78; outreach assoc. Los Gatos (Calif.) Presbyn. Ch., 1978-81; commr. to gen. assembly United Presbyn. Ch., 1947, 52, 59; moderator San Jose Presbytery, 1950, chmn. various coms., 1950-78; mem. Synod Golden Gate and Synod of Pacific coms. Synod of Calif., 1947-82; pastor emeritus Covenant Presbyn. Ch.; moderator Bellingham Prebytery-Synod of Wash., 1943. Treas., chmn. fin. com., bd. dirs. Internat. House, Davis, Calif., 1984-90, chmn. nominating com., 1990-96, mem. devel. com., 1991—. Home: 4414 San Ramon Dr Davis CA 95616-5018

BROWN, BARBARA BLACK, publishing company executive; b. Eureka, Calif., Dec. 11, 1928; d. William Marion and Letitia (Brunia) Black; m. Vinson Brown, June 18, 1950; children—Tamara Pinn, Roxana Hodges, Keven. B.A., Western State Coll., Gunnison, Colo. Owner, mgr. Naturegraph Pubs., Inc., Los Altos, Calif., 1950-53, San Martin, Calif., 1953-60, Healdsburg, Calif., 1960-76, Happy Camp, Calif., 1976—. Author: Barns of Yesteryear; co-author: Sierra Nevadan Wildlife Region. Mem. Baha'i World Faith. Office: Naturegraph Pubs Inc 3543 Indian Creek Rd Happy Camp CA 96039-9706

BROWN, BART A., JR., consumer products company executive; b. Louisville, 1933. LLB, U. Louisville, 1955; LLM, Georgetown U., 1957, JD. With Irs, 1970-76, with Keating, Muething, Klekamp, Brown & Gardner, 1976-90; past CEO Circle K Corp., Phoenix, 1971—, chmn., also bd. dirs. Office: Circle K Corp Box 52084 1601 N 7th St Phoenix AZ 85072-2084*

BROWN, CAROLYN SMITH, communications educator, consultant; b. Salt Lake City, Aug. 12, 1946; d. Andrew Delbert and Olive (Crane) Smith; m. David Scott Brown, Sept. 10, 1982. BA magna cum laude, U. Utah, 1968, MA, 1972, PhD, 1974. Instr. Salt Lake Ctr., Brigham Young U., Salt Lake City, 1976-78; vis. asst. prof. Brigham Young U., Provo, 1978; asst. prof. Am. Inst. Banking, Salt Lake City, 1977—; prof., chmn. English, communication and gen. edn. depts. Latter Day Saints Bus. Coll., Salt Lake City, 1973—, dean acad. affairs, 1986-96, v.p. for acad. affairs, 1996—; founder, pres. Career Devel. Tng., Salt Lake City, 1979—; cons. in-house seminars 1st Security Realty Svcs., USDA Natural Resource Conservation Svc., Utah Power & Light, Utah Soc. Svcs., Adminstrv. Office of Cts., HUD, Intermountain Health Care, Fidelity Investments, Am. Inst. Banking; mem. NW Assn. Schs. & Colls. Liaison, 1980—, Utah Bus. Coll. Dean's com., 1990—. Author: Writing Letters & Reports That Communicate, 8th edit., 1994; contbr. articles to profl. jours. Demi-soloist Utah Civic Ballet (now Ballet West), Salt Lake City, 1964-68; active Mormon Ch.; C. of C. Bus. Edn. com., 1991-92. Named Tchr. of Month, Salt Lake City Kiwanis, 1981; NDEA fellow, U. Utah, 1972. Mem. Am. Bus. Communications Assn. (lectr. West/N.W. regional chpt. 1987), Delta Kappa Gamma (2d v.p. 1977-79), Lambda Delta Sigma (Outstanding Woman of Yr. 1983), Kappa Kappa Gamma (Outstanding Alumnus in Lit. 1974). Republican. Clubs: Alice Louise Reynolds Literary (Salt Lake City) (v.p. 1978-79, sec. 1985-86). Office: LDS Bus Coll 411 E South Temple Salt Lake City UT 84111-1302

BROWN, CATHIE, city official; b. Seattle, Mar. 23, 1944; d. G. Warren and Dorothy (Patterson) Cryer; m. Tom Brown, July 1, 1967; children: Amy, James W. BA in Criminology, U. Calif., Berkeley, 1966; MPA, Calif. State U., Hayward, 1985. Juvenile probation officer Santa Clara (Calif.) County, 1967-72; founder, dir. Tri-Valley Haven for Women, Livermore, Calif., 1976-79; planning commr. City of Livermore, 1980-82, city coun. mem., 1982-89; exec. dir. Alameda County Project Intercept, Hayward, 1986—; dir. Svcs. for Families of Inmates, Pleasanton, Calif., 1981-82; mayor City of Livermore, 1989—; active County Justice System Adv. Group, Oakland, Calif., 1990—; co-founder Tri-Valley Community Fund, Pleasanton. Active Alameda County Mayors' Conf., 1989—; del. Assn. Bay Area Govts., 1982-89; founder Youth For Action, Livermore, 1984-86, Youth Task Force, Livermore, 1989-90. Named Woman of Yr. Calif. State Legislature, 1990. Mem. League Calif. Cities (pres. East Bay div. 1982-89), MPA Alumni Assn. (pres. Calif. State U. chpt. 1989—). Democrat. Home: 1098 Angelica Way Livermore CA 94550-5701*

BROWN, CHRISTOPHER, artist; b. Camp Lejeune, N.C., 1951. BA, U. Ill., 1972; MFA, U. Calif., Davis, 1976. Prof. art U. Calif., Berkeley, 1981-92. One-person shows include Madison (Wis.) Art Ctr., 1985-86, Matrix

Gallery, U. Art Mus., Berkeley, Calif., Des Moines Art Ctr., 1985-86, U. Tex., Arlington, 1988, Ctr. Res. Contemporary Art, 1988, Gallery Paule Anglim, San Francisco, 1990, Edward Thorp Gallery, N.Y., 1992, 95, Modern Art Mus. Ft. Worth, 1995, Inst. Arts and Letters, N.Y., 1988, Blum Helman, L.A., 1989, others; represented in permanent collections San Francisco Mus. Modern Art, U. Art Mus., Calif., Fine Arts Mus. San Francisco, Security Pacific Nat. Bank, Calif., Chase Manhattan Bank, N.Y., Met. Mus., N.Y., N.Y. Pub. Libr., Grey Art Gallery, N.Y., NYU, Gen. Mills, Mpls., Walker Art Ctr., Mpls., Sheldon Meml. Art Gallery, Lincoln, Nebr., Coca-Cola Corp., Atlanta, Kemper Mus., Kansas City. Fellow Nat. Endowment Arts, 1987; recipient award Am. Acad. and Inst. Art and Letters, 1988. Address: 770 Camelia St Berkeley CA 94710 Office: 214 E 12th St Apt 2 New York NY 10003-9100*

BROWN, CHRISTOPHER PATRICK, health care administrator, educator; b. Phoenix, June 7, 1951; s. Charles Francis and R. Patricia (Quinn) B.; m. Tracey Ann Wallenberg, May 23, 1987; 1 child, Ryan Matthew. AA in Biol. Scis., Shasta Coll., Redding, Calif., 1976; AS in Liberal Arts, SUNY, Albany, 1977; grad. Primary Care Assoc. Program, Stanford U., 1978; BA in Community Svcs. Adminstrn., Calif. State U., Chico, 1982; M. in Health Svcs., U. Calif., Davis, 1984. Gen. mgr. Pacific Ambulance Svc., El Cajon, Calif., 1974; primary care assoc. Family Practice, Oregon-Calif., 1978-82; cons. Calif. Health Profls., Chico, 1982-84; bus. ops. mgr. Nature's Arts, Inc., Seattle, 1985-86; instr. North Seattle C.C., 1984-89, program dir., 1986-89; asst. dir. Pacific Med. Clinic North, Seattle, 1990-92; dir. Pacific Med. Clinic Renton (Wash.), Pacific Med. Ctr., 1992-95; dir. ops./physician svcs. St. Luke's Regional Med. Ctr., Boise, Idaho, 1995—; accreditation syrveyor Accreditation Ass. Ambulatory Health Care, 1996—. Mem. Butte County Adult Day Care Health Coun., Chico, 1982-84; bd. dirs., pres. Innovative Health Care Svcs., Chico, 1982-84; bd. dirs. Highline W. Seattle Mental Health Ctr., 1985-90, v.p. 1988-90; tech. adv. com. North Seattle C.C., 1992-93. With U.S. Navy, 1970-74. Mem. Internat. Platform Assn., Soc. Ambulatory Care Profls., Med. Group Mgmt. Assn., Multispecialty Group Exec. Soc., Accreditation Assn. for Ambulatory Health Care (accreditation surveyor 1996—). Home: 1480 W Pintail Dr Meridian ID 83642 Office: St Lukes Regional Med Ctr 190 E Bannock St Boise ID 83712-6241

BROWN, CRAIG WILLIAM, physical chemist; b. Denver, Aug. 3, 1953; s. Clarence William and Gail Margaret (Farthing) B.; 1 child, Russell Corey. BS in Chemistry, Colo. State U., 1975; MS, Fla. State U., 1977, PhD, 1980. Dep. dir. picosecond and quantum radiation lab. Tex. Tech. U., Lubbock, 1980-83; systems engr. Internat. Marine Systems, Inc., Seattle, 1983-87; freelance cons., 1987-88; staff scientist Heart Interface Corp., Kent, Wash., 1988-91, sr. project engr., 1991-93; cons. scientist Brooks Rand Ltd., Seattle, 1992-93, sr. scientist, 1993—; cons. Environ. Protection Agy., Dept. Energy, 1995—; mem. battery charger/inverter project tech. com. Am. Boat and Yacht Coun., Edgewater, Md., 1989-92; cons. on mercury speciation Environ. Protection and Dept. Energy, 1995—; mgr. of inert anode aluminum prodn. rsch. project, 1996—. Contbr. articles to Phys. Rev. Letters and Jour. Chem. Physics; contbr. book revs. to Photochemistry and Photobiology; contbr. to conf. proceedings. Whiteford scholar Colo. State U., 1974-75, Honors scholar U. Denver, 1971-72, Gustavson fellow Colo. State U., 1974-75, Welch postdoctoral fellow Tex. Tech U., 1980-83; Dept. Energy rsch. grantee, 1994-96. Mem. AAAS, Am. Chem. Soc., N.Y. Acad. Scis., Internat. Platform Assn. Office: Brooks Rand Ltd 3950 6th Ave NW Seattle WA 98107-5056

BROWN, DAVID GERARD, author, actor, air trafic controller; b. Lubbock, Tex., Aug. 18, 1957; s. Thomas Duane and Shirley Ann (Prokop) B.; m. Deborah Ann Thompson, June 25, 1976; children Danielle Jené, Lindsy Nichele. enroute radar air traffic control specialist, FAA. Author: Gold Buckle Dreams - The Rodeo Life of Chris LeDoux (Pulitzer nomination 1987), 1987, paperback edit., 1989. Mem. Author's Guild, Profl. Rodeo Cowboy's Assn., Screen Actor's Guild, Nat. Air Traffic Controller's Assn. Home: P.O. Box 91772 Henderson NV 89009

BROWN, DAVID R., academic administrator. Pres., dir. Art Ctr. Coll. Design, Pasadena, Calif. Office: Art Ctr Coll of Design Office of Pres 1700 Lida St Pasadena CA 91103-1924

BROWN, DAVID W., lawyer; b. Seattle, Jan. 29, 1955. Student, Albion Coll.; BS, U. Oreg., 1977, JD, 1980. Bar: Oreg. 1980. Ptnr. Miller, Nash, Wiener, Hager & Carlsen, Portland, Oreg. Mem. Oreg. State Bar. Office: Miller Nash Wiener Hager & Carlsen 111 SW 5th Ave Portland OR 97204-3604

BROWN, DON, museum director. Dir. Internat. Wildlife Mus., Tucson, Ariz. Office: Internat Wildlife Mus 4800 W Gates Pass Rd Tucson AZ 85745

BROWN, DONALD MALCOLM, plastic surgeon; b. Nelson, N.Z., May 28, 1945; came to U.S., 1947; s. Donald Roland and Edna M. (McPherson) B.; m. Susan E. Boeing, Sept. 3, 1989. MD, U. B.C., 1970. Diplomate Am. Bd. Otolaryngology and Plastic Surgery. Resident in otolarngology Manhattan Eye and Ear Hosp., N.Y.C., 1976; resident in plastic surgery Columbia U., N.Y.C., 1980; pvt. practice San Francisco, 1981—; vis. prof. plastic surgery U. Liberia, Africa, 1980-81. Mem. AMA, Calif. Med. Assn., San Francisco Med. Assn., Am. Soc. Plastic and Reconstructive Surgery, Am. Soc. Aesthetic Surgery, Pacific Union Club, St. Francis Yacht Club. Office: 2100 Webster St Ste 429 San Francisco CA 94115-2380

BROWN, DONALD RAY, school system administrator; b. Culver City, Calif., Oct. 15, 1946; s. Clarence Otis and Velma Lucile (Osborn) B.; m. Carol Jane Maple; children: David, Christopher, Michael. BA in Psychology, Calif. State U., 1969, MS in Sch. Adminstrn., 1976; PhD in Edn., U. Calif., Santa Barbara, 1993. Cert. elem. tchr., Calif. Tchr. La Habra (Calif.) City Sch. Dist., 1969-76; prin. Oakley (Calif.) Union Sch. Dist., 1976-79; prin., pers. asst. Orcutt (Calif.) Union Sch. Dist., 1979-90; asst. supt. Lompoc (Calif.) Unified Sch. Dist., 1990—. Treas. Assn. Sch. Adminstrs., Santa Maria, 1985-87. Mem. ASCD, Assn. Calif. Sch. Adminstrs. (Adminstr. of Yr. award 1988). Democrat. Methodist. Home: 432 Garnet Way Santa Maria CA 93454-3244 Office: Lompoc Unified Sch Dist 1301 N A St Lompoc CA 93438

BROWN, GARY HUGH, artist, art educator; b. Evansville, Ind., Dec. 19, 1941. BA, DePauw U., 1963; MFA, U. Wis., 1966. Prof. art U. Calif., Santa Barbara, 1966—; mem. faculty Coll. Creative Studies, 1984-85, Courtyard of Hope and Fountain of Tears Aids Home, 1994, Venice Biennale: Art Against AIDS, 1993; judge 9th ann. competition Bristol-Myers Squibb Co., 1991. One-man shows include Comsky, Beverley Hills, 1974, United Arts Club, Dublin, Ireland, 1975, Source, San Francisco, 1976, New Harmony Gallery of Contemporary Art, 1977, Santa Barbara City Coll. Art Gallery, 1979, Atelierhaus, Worpswede, Germany, George Eastman House, Cooper-Hewitt Mus., N.Y.C., 1980, Life Gallery Santa Barbara, 1982, The Frameworks and De La Guerra Gallery, Santa Barbara, 1984, Art Space, Nishunomiya, Japan, 1980, Allan Hancock Coll. Art Gallery, Santa Maria, Calif., 1991, Gallery 2, Ventura Coll., Calif., 1992; Evansville Mus. Arts & Scis., 1988, De La Guerra Gallery, 1989,. Bd. dirs. Santa Barbara Contemporary Arts Forum, 1988; statewide liaison com. Creative Arts, 1971-73. Recipient purchase prize Nat. Endowment for Arts, 1971; fellow U. Calif. Inst. Creative Art, 1977-78; grantee E.T. Greenshields Found., 1963-64. Home: 8 W Mountain Dr Santa Barbara CA 93103-1624 Office: U Calif Art Studio Dept Santa Barbara CA 93106-7120

BROWN, GAY WEST, school psychologist; b. L.A., Nov. 20, 1953; d. James Dale and Ola Maye (Daniels) West; m. Lorenzo Hubbard, Nov. 26, 1977 (dec. Feb. 1990); 1 child, Loren Rochelle; m. Fred Lyndle Brown, Jr., Dec. 28, 1992. BA, Calif. State U., Dominguez Hills, 1975; MS, U. So. Calif., 1976; PhD, UCLA, 1991. Lic. ednl. psychologist; cert. sch. psychologist. Student counselor Dignity Ctr. for Drug Abuse, L.A., 1974-76; community health worker Am. Indian Free Clinic, Compton, Calif., 1974-76; student psychologist Martin Luther King Hosp., L.A., 1976-77; counselor aide Washington High Sch., L.A., 1974-77; vocat. counselor Skill Ctr., L.A., 1977-78; sch. psychologist L.A. Unified Sch. Dist., 1978—, tchr., advisor, 1988-90; psychol. asst. Verdugo Hills (Calif.) Mental Health, 1984-85; counselor, coord. Crenshaw High Sch., L.A., 1985-87; part-time instr. Calif. State U., Dominguez Hills, 1996—; asst. behavior sci. cons. Coalition Mental Profls., L.A., 1992-93; psychol. asst. Martin Luther King Hosp., L.A., 1992-93; part-time prof. Calif. State U., L.A., 1994-95. Mem. APA, Nat. Assn. Sch. Psychologists, Calif. Assn. Sch. Psychologists, L.A. Assn. Sch. Psychologists, Assn. Black Psychologists (sec. 1992-93, historian 1995-96), Pan African Scholars Assn., United Tchrs. L.A., Delta Sigma Theta (chair teen lift com. 1994—). Democrat. United Methodist. Office: Sch Mental Health Clinic 439 W 97th St Los Angeles CA 90003-3968

BROWN, GEORGE EDWARD, JR., congressman; b. Holtville, Calif., Mar. 6, 1920; s. George Edward and Bird Alma (Kilgore) B.; m. Marta Macias. B.A., UCLA, 1946; grad. fellow, Fund Adult Edn., 1954. Mgmt. cons. Calif., 1957-61; v.p. Monarch Savs. & Loan Assn., Los Angeles, 1960-68; mem. Calif. Assembly from 45th Dist., 1959-62; former mem. 88th-91st congresses from 29th Dist. Calif., 93d Congress from 38th Dist. Calif.; mem. 94th-105th Congresses from 36th (now 42nd) Dist. Calif.; mem. standing com. on agr., chmn. sci. space and tech. com. 94th-101st Congresses from 36th Dist. Calif., 1987; mem. agriculture com., ranking dem. mem. sci. com.; chmn. Office of Tech. Assessment; coll. lectr., radio commentator, 1971. Mem. Calif. Gov.'s Adv. Com. on Housing Problems, 1961-62; mem. Mayor Los Angeles Labor-Mgmt. Com., 1961-62, Councilman, Monterey Park, Calif., 1954-58, mayor, 1955-56; candidate for U.S. Senate, 1970. Served to 2d lt., inf. AUS, World War II. Recipient Chairman's award Am. Assn. Engring. Socs., 1993. Mem. Am. Legion, Colton C. of C., Urban League, Internat. Brotherhood Elec. Workers, AFL-CIO, Friends Com. Legislation, Ams. for Dem. Action. Democrat. Methodist. Lodge: Kiwanis. Office: US Ho of Reps 2300 Rayburn HOB Washington DC 20515-0542

BROWN, GEORGE STEPHEN, physics educator; b. Santa Monica, Calif., June 28, 1945; s. Paul Gordon and Frances Ruth (Moore) B.; m. Nohema Fernandez, Aug. 8, 1981 (div. 1992); 1 child, Sonya; m. Julie Claire Dryden, Mar. 22, 1997. BS, Calif. Inst. Tech., 1967; MS, Cornell U., 1968, PhD, 1973. Mem. tech. staff Bell Labs., Murray Hill, N.J., 1973-77; sr. research assoc. Stanford (Calif.) U., 1977-82, rsch. prof. applied physics, 1982-91; prof. physics U. Calif., Santa Cruz, 1991—; assoc. dir. Stanford Synchrotron Radiation Lab., Stanford, 1980-91. Mem. editorial bd. Rev. Sci. Instruments, 1983-86; contbr. articles to profl. jours. Fellow Am. Phys. Soc. Home: 404 Village Cir Santa Cruz CA 95060-2461 Office: U Calif Dept Physics Santa Cruz CA 95064

BROWN, H. WILLIAM, urban economist, private banker; b. L.A., Sept. 6, 1933; s. Homer William Brown and Carol Lee (Thompson) Weaver; m. Verlee Nelson, Aug. 1953 (div. 1955); 1 child, Shirlee Dawn; m. Shirley Rom, Jan. 18, 1955 (div. 1962). BA in Pub. Adminstrn., Calif. State U., 1956; MA in Bus. Adminstrn., Western States U., 1983, Phd in Urban Econs., 1984. Pres. Real Estate Econs., Sacramento, 1956-60; dir. spl. projects Resource Agy. Calif., Sacramento, 1960-65; program planning officer U.S. Dept. Housing and Urban Devel., Washington, 1965-66; asst. dir. regional planning U.S. Dept. Commerce, Washington, 1967-69; dir. internat. office Marshall and Stevens, Inc., L.A., 1970-72; vice chmn., CEO Investment Property Econ. Cons., 1972—; chmn., CEO The Northpoint Investment Group, San Francisco, 1986—; chmn. Trade and Devel. Ctr. For UN, N.Y. 1983-88, pres. Ctr. for Habitat and Human Settlements, Washington 1977-90. Author: The Changing World of the Real Estate Market Analyst-Appraiser, 1988. Mem. Appraisal Inst., Le Groupe (charge d'affaires, pvt. bankers assn.). Office: Northpoint Investment Group 350 Bay St Ste 100-111 San Francisco CA 94133-1902

BROWN, HANK, former senator; b. Denver, Feb. 12, 1940; s. Harry W. and Anna M. (Hanks) B.; m. Nana Morrison, Aug. 27, 1967; children: Harry, Christy, Lori. BS, U. Colo., 1961, JD, 1969; LLM, George Washington U., 1986, M in Tax Law, 1986. Bar: Colo. 1969; CPA, 1988. Tax acct. Arthur Andersen, 1967-68; asst. pres. Monfort of Colo., Inc., Greeley, 1969-70; corp. counsel Monfort of Colo., Inc., 1970-71; v.p. Monfort Food Distbg., 1971-72, v.p. corp. devel., 1973-75, v.p. internat. ops., 1975-78, v.p. lamb div., 1978-80; mem. 97th-101st Congresses from Colo. 4th dist., 1981-90; mem. Colo. State Senate, 1972-76, asst. majority leader, 1974-76; U.S senator from Colo. Washington, 1991-96; chmn. Fgn. Rel. subcom. Near Ea. and South Asian affairs, Judicorp subcom. on constl. law. With USN, 1962-66. Decorated Air medal, Vietnam Svc. medal, Nat. Defense medal, Naval Unit citation. Republican. Congregationalist. address: 1322 43d Ave Greeley CO 80634*

BROWN, HARRY PARKER, JR. (BUTCH BROWN), program manager; b. Providence, Oct. 22, 1943; s. Harry Parker and Helen Elizabeth (Cates) B.; m. Jennifer Lee Bubul, Dec. 10, 1970 (div. June 1990); 1 child, David Parker. BS, U. Colo., 1971; MA, U.S. Naval War Coll., 1986. Lic. comml. pilot FAA. Commd. officer USN, 1970, advanced through grades to comdr.; pers. officer Tactical Electronic Warfare Squadron 136, Oak Harbor, Wash., 1972-76; tng. dept. head Tactical Electronic Warfare Squadron 129, Oak Harbor, 1976-80; adminstrv. dept. head Tactical Electronic Warfare Squadron 130, Oak Harbor, 1980-83; officer-in-charge fleet aviation specialized ops. detachment Naval Air Sta. Whidbet Island, Oak Harbor, 1983-86; ops. officer Tactical Electronic Warfare Squadron 138, Oak Harbor, 1986-88; comdg. officer Tactical Electronic Warfare Squadron 134, Oak Harbor, 1988-90; ret., 1990; strike warfare program mgr. U.S. Naval Strike and Air Warfare Ctr., Fallon, Nev., 1990—. Author, editor: EA-6B Naval Aviation Training and Operating Procedures, 1978. Mem. Old Crows.

BROWN, JACK EDWARD, lawyer; b. Omaha, Mar. 15, 1927; B.S. with distinction, Northwestern U., 1949; LL.B., Harvard U., 1952. Bar: N.Y. 1954, Ariz. 1959. Law clk. to presiding justice Ariz. Supreme Ct., 1959, U.S. Dist. Ct., Mass., 1952-53; assoc. Cravath, Swaine & Moore, N.Y.C., 1953-59, Evans, Kitchel & Jenckes, Phoenix, 1959-60; sr. ptnr. Brown & Bain, P.A., Phoenix, 1960—; lectr. in field. Pres. Phoenix Jewish Community Ctr., 1963-64; Ariz. region NCCJ, 1969—, nat. del., 1971, vice chmn., 1976-82, chmn., 1983-84; adv. mem. Navajo Tribal Fair Commn., 1971; bd. dirs. Ariz. Acad., 1975—, Friends of KAET-TV, 1975—, Reading is Fundamental, 1976—; trustee Lawyers Com. Civil Rights Under Law, 1976—, Law and Tech. Inst., 1982—. Recipient Disting. Service award Ariz. State U. Sch. Law, 1983. Mem. ABA, Ariz. Bar Assn., Maricopa County Bar Assn., Am. Arbitration Assn. Contbr. articles on law to profl. jours. Office: Brown & Bain PO Box 400 Phoenix AZ 85001-0400

BROWN, JAMES CARRINGTON, III (BING BROWN), public relations and communications executive; b. Wilmington, Del., May 17, 1939; s. James Carrington Jr. and Virginia Helen (Miller); m. Carol Osman, Nov. 3, 1961. Grad. security mgmt. group, Indsl. Coll. of the Armed Forces; BBA, Ariz. State U., 1984. Accredited, Pub. Rels. Soc. Am., 1988. Newsman, disc jockey, program dir. various radio stas., Ariz., 1955-60; morning news editor Sta. KOY, Phoenix, 1960-61; staff writer, photographer Prescott (Ariz.) Evening Courier, 1961; bus. editor, staff writer, photographer Phoenix Gazette, 1961-65; various communications positions Salt River Project, Phoenix, 1965-89; pres. Carrington Communications, Phoenix, 1989—; cons. comm., freelance writing, photography The Browns, Phoenix, 1965—; pub. info. officer Water Svcs. Dept., City of Phoenix, 1991—; instr. Rio Salado C.C., Phoenix, 1989—; guest lectr. various colls. and univs., 1975—; prof. Walter Cronkite Sch. Journalism and Telecomm., Ariz. State U., 1990—. Bd. dirs. Grand Canyon coun. Boy Scouts Am., 1985-89, mem. adv. coun., 1990—; mem. exec. com. Cmty. Svc. Fund Drive, 1992—; mem. environment com. Phoenix Futures Forum, 1991-93; mem. project adv. com. for Am. Waterworks Assn. Rsch. Found. study of Pub. Involvement Strategies, 1994-95; deacon Meml. Presbyn. Ch., 1980-82, elder, 1985-87; mem. spl. gifts com. United Way, Phoenix, 1986-89. Recipient Golden Eagle award Boy Scouts Am., 1992. Mem. Western Systems Coordinating Coun. (chmn. pub. info. com. 1969-89), Ariz. Newspapers Assn. (Billy Goat award, Allied Mem. of Yr. 1985), Ariz. Broadcasters Assn., Western Coalition Arid States (chmn. comm. subcom. 1991-93, chmn. com. and mem. com. 1993—, editor WESTCAS News 1991—, Disting. Performance award 1996), Western Energy Supply and Transmission Assocs. (mem. pub. info. com. 1967-89), Phoenix Press Club (pres. 1982-83), PRSA, Nat. Acad. TV Arts/Scis., Ariz. Zool. Soc., Heard Mus. Anthropology And Primitive Art. Republican. Home and Office: Carrington Comm 3734 E Campbell Ave Phoenix AZ 85018-3507 also: Phoenix Water Svcs Dept 200 W Washington St Phoenix AZ 85003-1611

BROWN, JAMES CHANDLER, college administrator; b. Garden City, N.Y., Aug. 5, 1947; s. Harry Chandler and Lillian Marie (Cutter) B. BA, Susquehanna U., Selinsgrove, Pa., 1970; License es Lettres, Geneva U., 1978; postgrad., Stanford U., 1984. Rsch. asst. Geneva (Switzerland) U., 1972-79; asst. Galerie Jan Krugier, Geneva, 1978-81; coord. pubs. So. Oreg. State Coll., Ashland, 1982-84; dir. pubs. So. Oreg. State Coll., 1984—; cons. in field. Author: How to Sharpen Your Publications (brochure, Case award) 1985, College Viewbook (booklet), 1985. Sec. bd. dirs. Schneider Mus. Art, Ashland, 1985-94. Canton of Geneva grantee, 1974-79; awardee, Coun. for Advancement and Support of Edn., 1987-88, 95. Mem. Coun. for Advancement and Support of Edn., Omicron Delta Kappa Leadership Soc. Methodist. Home: 385 Guthrie St Ashland OR 97520-3023 Office: So Oreg State Coll 1250 Siskiyou Blvd Ashland OR 97520-5001

BROWN, JAMES COOKE, nonprofit organization administrator, game and language inventor, educational administrator, writer; b. Tagilarin, Bohol, The Philippines, July 21, 1921; came to U.S., 1929; s. Bryan Burtis and Violet Mary (Cooke) B.; m. Evelyn Ruth Hamburger, July 21, 1985; children: Jefferson O'Reilly, Jill O'Reilly, Jennifer Fuller. BA in Philosophy and Math., U. Minn., 1946, PhD in Sociology, Philosophy and Math. Stats., 1952. Instr. sociology Wayne State U., Detroit, 1949-50; asst. prof. Ind. U., Bloomington, 1950-52; dir. statis. controls Inst. for Motivation Rsch., Croton-on-Husdon, N.Y., 1954-55; asst. prof. sociology and humanities, assoc. prof. sociology, philosophy U. Fla., Gainesville, 1955-63, 70; dir., then chmn. Loglan Inst., Inc., Gainesville and San Diego, 1964—. Author: Loglan 1: A Logical Language, 1966, 4th edit., 1989; (novel) The Troika Incident, 1970; inventor game Careers, 1956, Loglan lang., 1960. Home and Office: 3009 Peters Way San Diego CA 92117-4313

BROWN, JAMES MICHAEL, writer, educator; b. San Jose, Calif., Nov. 14, 1957; s. Donald Bernand and Vivien (Agrillo) B.; m. Heidi Ann Whited, June 19, 1982; children: Andrew James, Logan Michael, Nathaniel Henry. BA, San Francisco State U., 1980; MFA, U. Calif., Irvine, 1985. Prof. English Calif. State U., San Bernardino. Author: Hot Wire, 1985, Final Performance, 1988, Lucky Town, 1994, (story collection) Second Story and Two Encores, 1994. NEA grantee, 1995; recipient Nelson Algren award in short fiction Chicago Tribune, 1992. Office: Calif State U Dept English 5500 University Pkwy San Bernardino CA 92407-2318

BROWN, JAMES RANDALL, mechanical engineer; b. Aug. 12, 1958; m. Reina Brown; children: Jacqueline, Sonya, Danielle. BS in mech. engring., Rensselaer Poly. Inst., 1983; BS in computer sci., U. N.C., 1986. Engr. Stone & Webster Engring. Corp., Boston, 1981-83; mfg. engr. Digital Equipment Corp., Maynard, Mass., 1988-94; engr. PRI Automation, Inc., Billerica, Mass., 1994—. Mem. ASME, ACM, IEEE, SME. Home: 6401 Prairie Sage Dr NW Albuquerque NM 87120 Office: PRI Automation Inc 1380 Rio Rancho Dr SE Albuquerque NM 87124-1006

BROWN, J'AMY MARONEY, journalist, media relations consultant; b. L.A., Oct. 30, 1945; d. Roland Francis and Jeanne (Wilbur) Maroney; m. James Raphael Brown, Jr., Nov. 5, 1967 (dec. July 1982); children: James Roland Francis, Jeanne Raphael. Attended U. So. Calif., 1963-67. Reporter L.A. Herald Examiner, 1966-67, Lewisville Leader, Dallas, 1980-81; editor First Person Mag., Dallas, 1981-82; journalism dir. Pacific Palisades Sch., L.A., 1983-84; free-lance writer, media cons., 1984-88; press liaison U.S. papal visit, L.A., 1987; media dir., chief media strategist Tellem Inc., 1990-92, communication cons., issues mgr. 1992—; pres., CEO and owner PRformance Grp. Communications, 1995—; pres. PRformance Group. Auction chmn. Assn. Pub. Broadcasting, Houston, 1974, 75; vice chmn. Dallas Arts Council, 1976-80; vice chmn. Met. March of Dimes, Dallas, 1980-82; del. Dallas Council PTAs, 1976-80; coord. specialist World Cup Soccer Organizing Com. Recipient UPI Editors award for investigative reporting, 1981. Mem. NAFE, Pub. Rels. Soc. Am. (accredited), Women Meeting Women, Women in Comm., Am. Bus. Women's Assn. Republican. Roman Catholic. Home: 1143 High Rd Santa Barbara CA 93108-2430

BROWN, JANICE ROGERS, state judge. Assoc. justice Calif. Supreme Ct., San Francisco. Office: Calif Supreme Ct 303 2nd St 8th Fl South Tower San Francisco CA 94107*

BROWN, JEFFREY CHARLES, rental company executive; b. Alma, Mich., May 23, 1965; s. Jerry and Emma Jane (McBride) B. BBA, Univ. Mich., 1987; MBA, Pepperdine Univ., 1993. Sr. acct. mgr. NCR Corp., Irvine, Calif., 1987-92; owner, CEO Eagle Rider Motorcycle Rental, Torrance, Calif., 1992—. Home: 616 Esplanade # 304 Redondo Beach CA 90277 Office: Eagle Rider Mortorcycle Rental 20917 Western Ave Torrance CA 90501

BROWN, JODY TOUCHTON, arts and sciences organization administrator; b. Sept. 18, 1971; d. John Michael and Clree Leona (Robinson) Touchton; m. Dudley Wooten Brown, III, Dec. 29, 1995. BA in Journalism cum laude, U. No. Colo., 1994. Tutor, rsch. asst. Disabled Student Svcs. U. No. Colo., Greeley, 1992-94, acad. adv. journalism dept., 1993-94; exec. dir. heartland regional Nat. Acad. TV Arts and Scis., Denver, 1996—; press sec. Congressman Bob Schaffer, 1996. Broadcast TV scholar Colo. Press Women, 1993-94. Mem. Nat. Fedn. Press Women (scholar 1993), Soc. Profl. Journalists (bd. local awards chair, nat. convention com. Colo. profl. chpt., sec., chair ethics U. No. Colo. student chpt., journalism scholarship 1993). Republican. Home: 15478 E Oberlin Pl Aurora CO 80013 Office: Nat Acad TV Arts & Scis Colo/Heartland Chpt 1550 Park Ave #103 Denver CO 80218

BROWN, JOHN VINCENT, gynecologic oncologist; b. Kansas City, Mo., Feb. 11, 1958; s. John Vincent and Celia Ann (Kilgore) B.; m. Katharine Fry, May 19, 1984; children: Michael Overton, Katharine Kilgore, Anne McCune. BS, U. Kans., 1980, MD, 1980-84. Diplomate Am. Bd. Ob-Gyn.; cert. spl. qualification gynecol. oncology. Intern/resident U. Wash., Seattle, 1984-88; fellow Divsn. of Gynecology/Oncology, UCLA, 1988-90; ptnr. Gyn Oncology Assocs., Newport Beach, Calif., 1990—; asst. clin. prof. UCLA Harbor Sch. Medicine, Torrance, 1990—. Contbr. articles to profl. jours. Recipient J. George Moore award Western Assn. Gynecologic Oncologists, 1990; U. Kans. Summerfield scholar, 1977; Bristol Myers Pharm. Co. grantee, 1994. Fellow ACOG, ACS; mem. AMA, Soc. Gynecologic Oncologists, Am. Soc. Clin. Oncologists, Western Assn. Gynecologic Oncologists, Internat. Soc. Gynecologic Cancer, Soc. Surg. Oncologists, Phi Kappa Phi. Office: Gynecologic Oncology Assocs 351 Hospital Rd Newport Beach CA 92663-3509

BROWN, JOSEPH E., landscape architecture executive; b. 1947. BA, Cath. U., 1970; M in Landscape Architecture and Urban Design, Harvard U., 1972. With Edaw, Inc., San Francisco, 1973—, now pres. Office: Edaw Inc 753 Davis St San Francisco CA 94111-1405*

BROWN, KATE, state legislator; b. Torrejon de Ardoth, Spain, 1960. BA, U. Colo.; JD, Lewis and Clark Northwestern. Mem. Oreg. Ho. of Reps., 1991-96, Oreg. Senate, 1996—; atty. Democrat. Address: PO Box 82699 Portland OR 97282-0699 Office: Oreg State Senate State Capitol Senate 310 Salem OR 97301

BROWN, KEITH LAPHAM, retired ambassador; b. Sterling, Ill., June 18, 1925; s. Lloyd Heman and Marguerite (Briggs) B.; m. Carol Louise Liebmann, Oct. 1, 1949; children: Susan, Briggs (dec.), Linda, Benjamin. Student, U. Ill., 1943-44, Northwestern U., 1946-47; LLB, U. Tex., 1949. Bar: Tex., Okla., Colo. Assoc. Lang, Byrd, Cross & Ladon, San Antonio, 1949-55; v.p., gen. counsel Caulkins Oil Co., Oklahoma City, 1955-70, Denver, 1955-70; founder, developer Vail Assocs., Colo., 1962; pres. Brown Investment Corp., Denver, 1970-87; developer Colo. State Bank Bldg., Denver, 1971; amb. to Lesotho Dept. State, 1982-84; amb. to Denmark Dept. State, Copenhagen, 1988-92; ret., 1992; chmn. Brown Investment Corp., Denver, 1993—. Chmn. Rep. Nat. Fin. Com., 1985-88; hon. trustee, past pres. bd. Colo. Acad. Served with USN, 1943-46. Mem. Denver Country Club, San Antonio Country Club, Univ. Club, Bohemian Club. Presbyterian. Address: PO Box 1172 Edwards CO 81632 Office: 1490 Colo State Bank Bldg 1600 Broadway Denver CO 80202-4927

BROWN, LAWRENCE LEONARD, III, city official; b. Boston, June 23, 1957; s. Lawrence Leonard Jr. and Jean Ann (Lee) Brown; m. Celeste Lynn Mizerock, Feb. 18, 1984; children: Lawrence L. IV, Johnna, Shannon. B Govt., Harvard U., 1979. Profl. baseball player San Diego Padres, Inc., Las Vegas, Nev., 1979-85; chief, supr. City of Las Vegas, 1985-87; mgr. Nev. Beverage Co., Las Vegas, 1987-90; dir. Las Vegas Valley Water Dist., 1990—. Vice chmn. Planning Commn., Las Vegas, 1993—; bd. mem. Opportunity Village, Las Vegas, 1986—; com. chair Bus. Edn. Collaborative, Las Vegas, 1994—. Mem. Am. Water Works Assn., Am. Soc. Pub. Adminstrs., Las Vegas C. of C. (bd./com. mem. 1988—), Harvard Varsity Club, KC, Elks, Eagles. Democrat. Roman Catholic. Office: Las Vegas Valley Water Dist 1001 S Valley View Blvd Las Vegas NV 89107-4447

BROWN, LEONID S., biophysicist researcher; b. Moscow, Jan. 9, 1966; came to U.S., 1992; s. Sergey I and Nina I (Slutskaya) B.; m. Mariya N Kozhevnikova, Jun. 9, 1990. MS in Biology, Moscow State U., Russia, 1988, PhD in Biophysics, 1991. Rschr. Moscow State U., Russia, 1991-92, U. Calif., Irvine, 1992—. Contbr. articles to profl. jours. Mem. Am. Biophysical Soc. Office: U Calif Coll Medicine Dept Physiology and Biophysics Irvine CA 92697

BROWN, LESTER B., social work educator; b. Whitmire, S.C., Jan. 11, 1943; s. William Barney and Minnie Eugenia (Vaughn) B. AB in Psychology, U. Chgo., 1969, AM, 1971, PhD, 1980. Sr. child care counselor, therapist Nicholas J. Pritzker Ctr. and Hosp., Chgo., 1964-68, 69; social worker I, Ill. Dept. Children and Family Services, Chgo., 1967-70, social worker II, 1971; group homes social worker Jewish Children's Bur., Chgo., 1971-73; social worker, field instr. Jackson Park Hosp., Chgo., 1973, clin. dir., 1973-74, cons., 1975-77; cons. SUNY-Albany, 1981, asst. prof. social work, chmn. under-grad. social welfare program, 1981-86; assoc. prof. social work Wayne State U., 1986-89; assoc. prof. social work Calif. State U., Long Beach, 1989-95, assoc. prof. social work and Am. Indian studies, dir. Am. Indian studies, 1995—; lectr. U. Wis.-Milw., 1977-78, instr., 1978-70; lectr. U. Chgo., 1977-78; guest lectr. Boston Coll., 1981; cons., presenter in field. Author: Two Spirit People: American Indian Lesbian Women and Gay Men, 1997, Aging Gay Men, 1997; contbr. articles to profl. jours., chpts. to books; mem. editl. bd. Health Care Mgmt. Rev., 1981-84. Condr. workshops on ethnic sensitive work Pittsfield Sch. Dist., Mass., 1984; participant workshops on mental health and child welfare; bd. dirs. Capital Dist. Travelers Aid Soc., 1983-86; mem. com. Urban League. Grantee Sch. Social Welfare, 1982, SUNY, 1981, U.S. Dept. HHS, 1981. Mem. NASW, Acad. Cert. Social Workers, Coun. Social Work Edn. Democrat. Avocation: baking/cooking. Office: Calif State Univ Long Beach Am Indian Studies and Social Work 1250 Bellflower Blvd Long Beach CA 90840-0902

BROWN, LILLIAN ERIKSEN, retired nursing administrator, consultant; b. Seattle, Feb. 7, 1921; d. Peter Louis and Lena (Lien) Eriksen; m. Jan. 21, 1942 (div. Nov. 1963); children: Patricia Lee, Michael Gregory, Kevin William. Student, U. Calif., Berkeley, 1939-40; diploma, St. Luke's Hosp. Sch. Nursing, San Francisco, 1943; AB, Calif. State U., San Francisco, 1952; MPA, U. So. Calif., 1975. RN, Calif. Pub. health nurse San Francisco Dept. Health, 1946-50; asst. dir. nursing San Francisco Gen. Hosp., 1950-56; dir. nursing Weimar (Calif.) Med. Ctr., 1956-62, Orange County Med. Ctr., Orange, Calif., 1962-76; assoc. dir. hosp. and clins., dir. nursing, lectr. U. Calif. Med. Ctr., Irvine, 1976-82; assoc. hosp. adminstr. King Khalid Eye Specialist Hosp., Riyadh, Saudi Arabia, 1982-86; cons. AMI-Saudi Arabia Ltd., Jeddah, 1986-90; chmn. Western Teaching Hosp. Coun. Dirs. Nursing, 1972-75, 80-81; mem. planning project com. Calif. Dept. Rehab., 1967-69, mem. adv. com., 1970-73; mem. ad hoc president's com. on hosp. governance U. Calif., 1981-82; pres. dirs. nursing coun. Hosp. Coun. So. Calif., 1972-74, mem. pers. practices com., 1976-78, 80-83, area rep., 1975-82; mem. dept. nursing adv. com. to establish baccalaureate program U. So. Calif., 1980-82; mem. adv. bd. various coll. nursing programs. Contbr. articles to profl. jours. Sec. Olive (Calif.) Little League, 1967-72; mem. com. on emergency med. svcs. Orange County Health Planning Coun., 1977-78, mem. health promotion task force, 1978-79. 2d lt. Nurse Corps, U.S. Army, 1944-45. Recipient Lauds and Laurels award U. Calif., Irvine, 1981. Fellow Am. Acad. Nurses; mem. ANA (cert. nurse adminstr. advanced), Nat. League for Nursing, APHA, Am. Orgn. Nurse Execs., Nat. Critical Care Inst. Edn., Calif. Nurses Assn. (Lillian E. Brown award named in her honor 1989), Calif. Orgn. for Nurse Execs. (hon.), Calif. Soc. for Nursing Svc. Adminstr., NOW. Republican. Home: 1806 N Nordic Pl Orange CA 92865-4637

BROWN, LINDA LOUISE, trade association executive, communication consultant; b. Trenton, Mo., Oct. 7, 1946; d. Herbert Shanklin and Dorothy Mae (French) B.; m. Raymon Dan Prewitt, Aug. 1990; 1 child, Russell Prewitt. BA, Tex. Christian U., 1968; MBA, U. Tex., 1975. Coord. legis. and regulations Chevron U.S.A., San Francisco, 1975-94; prin. Haz Masters, Oakland, Calif., 1994—; regional mgr. Assn. Gen. Contractors of Calif., Inc., Concord, 1995—; cons. Nat. Edn. Internat., Cairo and other cities in Egypt, 1994. Prodr. variolus videos and multi media programs; contbr. articles to profl. jours. Active Big Bros./Big Sisters, San Francisco, 1983-90; organizer Himalyan Fair, Berkeley, Calif., 1996; participant Skyline Parents Tchrs. Students Assn., Oakland, 1996—. Mem. AAUW, Bay Area Tex. Execs. Assn. (pres. 1978—), Ex-Student Assn. Democrat. Home: 2609 Chelsea Dr Oakland CA 94611 Office: Assn Gen Contractors Calif Inc Ste 1030 1390 Willow Pass Rd Concord CA 94520

BROWN, MARC M., civil engineer; b. Elko, Nev., Apr. 13, 1953; s. Marshall M. and Jean Brown; m. Karen J. Brown, Nov. 17, 1975; children: Douglas, David, Monica. Diploma in civil and environ. engring., Utah State U., 1975. Registered profl. engr., Nev., Utah. Bridge design engr. Wyo. Hwy. Dept., Cheyenne, 1975-77; design engr. Montgomery Watson, Salt Lake City, 1977-80; mgr. civil dept. Montgomery Watson, 1980-84, mcpl. mgr., 1984-88, mgr. Las Vegas office, 1988-94; Desert S.W. regional mgr. Montgomery Watson, Las Vegas, 1994—; bd. dirs. Agnavision, Las Vegas. Scoutmaster Boy Scouts Am., Las Vegas, 1988-96, unit commr., 1996. Mem. Am. Consulting Engr. Coun. (bd. dirs. 1980—), Am. Pub. Works Assn. (various coms. 1980-94), Am. Water Works Assn. (various coms. 1984—), Colorado River WAter User Assn., Nev. Water Resource Assn. (pres. bd. dirs. 1994-95), Las Vegas C. of C., Henderson C. of C. (com. 1988—). Republican. Mem. LDS Ch. Office: Montgomery Watson 3014 W Charleston Las Vegas NV 89102

BROWN, MARIAN VAN DE WATER, utilities executive; b. Oakland, Calif., June 28, 1946; d. Gilbert Raymond and Florence (Culbertson) Van de Water; m. Kenneth Spiers Brown, June 16, 1968; children: Monica Suzanne, Patricia Hawley. BA in Econs. cum laude, Pomona Coll., 1968; PhD in Econs., Stanford U., 1979. Vol. Peace Corps, Ghana, 1968-70; sr. rsch. analyst Nat. Bur. Econ. Rsch.-West, Stanford, Calif., 1975-77; asst. prof. econs. Pomona Coll., Claremont, Calif., 1977-86; sr. analyst market rsch. and program evaluation So. Calif. Edison, San Dimas, 1986-89, mgr. measurement and evaluation Energy Efficiency Divsn., 1989—; vis. scholar Divsn. Econ. Rsch., Social Security Adminstrn., Washington, 1984-85; chair Calif. Demand-Side Mgmt. Measurement Adv. Com., 1993, 97, Edison rep., 1994—; bd. dirs., treas. Assn. Energy Svcs. Profls., 1994—; bd. dirs. Clinebell Inst. Vol., bd. dirs. United Campus Christian Movement, Stanford U., 1970-73; Lay leader Claremont United Meth. Ch., 1991—, chair adminstrv. bd., 1986-88, 94—, chair various coms., 1981-91; bd. dirs., alumni coun. Pomoma Coll., 1989-90; sec.-treas. involvement corps Palo Alto (Calif.) 1st United Meth., 1975-77, youth leader, 1971-73. NSF fellow, 1970-73. Mem. Am. Econ. Assn., Assn. Energy Svc. Profls., Nat. Coun. Returned Peace Corps Vols., Stanford Profl. Women L.A. Democrat. Methodist. Home: 434 W 12th St Claremont CA 91711-3835 Office: So Calif Edison 300 N Lone Hill Ave San Dimas CA 91773-1741

BROWN, MARILYNNE JOYCE, emergency nurse; b. Algona, Iowa, Sept. 26, 1932; d. Michael Henry and Enid Hazel (Bonnette) Miller; m. Vaughn Hardgrove Brown; children: Jeffery Von, Steven Michael, Sindy Lynne, Timothy Ralph. Diploma in Nursing, St. Mary's Sch. Nursing, Rochester, Minn., 1953; AA, Grossmont C.C., El Cajon, Calif., 1981; BS in Health Sci. Edn., San Diego State U., 1983. Cert. emergency nurse. Dir. Algona Osteo. Clinic, 1953-55; staff nurse St. Ann's Hosp., Algona, 1955-60; emergency/relief charge nurse El Cajon Valley Hosp., 1960-65; emergency nurse MICN Grossmont Hosp., La Mesa, Calif., 1965-90; ret.; coord. EMT program Grossmont C.C., El Cajon, 1970-83; cons. and lectr. in field. Mem. Emergency Nurses Assn. (life, past sec., v.p., pres.), Beta Sigma Phi. Home: 596 Dichter St El Cajon CA 92019-2572

BROWN, MARK STEVEN, medical physicist; b. Denver, July 12, 1955; s. Clarence William and Gail Margaret (Farthing) B.; m. Mary Linda Avery, Oct. 9, 1988 (div. July 1995). Student, Northwestern U., 1973-74; BS, Colo. State U., 1977; PhD in Phys. Chemistry, U. Utah, 1984. GE postdoctoral fellow Yale U. Sch. Medicine, New Haven, 1984-86, assoc. rsch. scientist, 1986-87; rsch. asst. prof. U. N.Mex. Sch. Medicine, Albuquerque, 1987-89; med. physicist Swedish Med. Ctr. Porter Meml. Hosp., Englewood, Colo., 1989-92; instr. C.C. Denver, Denver, 1990, 91; asst. clin. prof. radiology U. Colo. Sch. Medicine, Denver, 1991-92, asst. prof. radiology, 1992—. Author: (with others) NMR Relaxation in Tissues, 1986; contbr. articles to profl. jours. Mem. Am. Chem. Soc., Soc. Magnetic Resonance. Home: PO Box 61344 Denver CO 80206 Office: Univ Colo Health Scis Ctr Dept Radiology Box A034 4200 E 9th Ave Denver CO 80220-3706

BROWN, MARTA MACÍAS, legislative staff member, executive assistant; b. San Bernardino, Calif., Nov. 29, 1944; m. George E. Brown Jr., Mar. 27, 1989. BA, Calif. State U., San Bernardino, 1970; postgrad., U. Calif., Riverside, 1971. Publ., editor El Chicano Cmty. Newspaper, San Bernardino, 1968-75; cmty. edn. specialist human resources agy. County of San Bernardino, 1972-73, dir. of info. and referral svcs., 1973-75; student affirmative action officer U. Calif., Riverside, 1975-80; exec. asst., dist. press sec. to Congressman George Brown, Calif., 1980—; bd. dirs. Casa Ramona Inc., San Bernardino, Ramona Sr. Complex, San Bernardino. Mem. Senator Barbara Boxer's judicial appts. com., 1992—; adv. bd., sponsor, Peacebuilders, 1994—; mem. Calif. Dem. Party Ctrl. Com., 1994—, family preservation planning com. County of San Bernardino, 1995—. U. Calif. grad. fellow, 1970. Mem. LWV, Democratic Spouses, Kiwanis (bd. dirs. greater San Bernardino chpt. 1990—). Roman Catholic. Home: 873 Bernard Way San Bernardino CA 92404-2413 Office: Congressman George E Brown Jr 2300 Rayburn HOB Washington DC 20515

BROWN, MELVIN R., state legislator. Spkr. Utah Ho. of Reps., Midvale. Office: 165 E 7430 S Midvale UT 84047

BROWN, PAUL FREMONT, aerospace engineer, educator; b. Osage, Iowa, Mar. 10, 1921; s. Charles Fremont and Florence Alma (Olson) B.; m. Alice Marie Culver, Dec. 5, 1943; children—Diane, Darrell, Judith, Jana. BA in Edn. and Natural Sci., Dickinson State Coll., 1942; BS in Mech. Engring., U. Wash., 1948; MS in Cybernetic Systems, San Jose State U., 1971. Profl. quality engr., Calif., 1978; cert. reliability engr., Am. Soc. Quality Control, 1976. Test engr., supr. Boeing Aircraft Corp., Seattle, 1948-56; design specialist, propulsion systems, Lockheed Missiles and Space Co., Sunnyvale, Calif., 1956-59; supr. system effectiveness, 1959-66, staff engr., 1966-76, mgr. product assurance Hubble Space Telescope Program, 1976-83; v.p. research, devel. Gen. Agriponics Inc. of Hawaii, 1971-76; owner Diversatek Engring. and Product Assurance Conss., 1983—; coll. instr., lectr., San Jose State U. Active in United Presbyn. Ch., 1965—; scoutmaster, Boy Scouts Am., 1963-65. Served to 1st lt., USAF, 1943-46. Recipient awards for tech. papers, Lockheed Missiles and Space Co., 1973-75. Mem. Am. Soc. Quality Control, AIAA. Clubs: Toastmasters (Sunnyvale, Calif.), Calif. Writers' (pres. South Bay br. 1993-94). Author: From Here to Retirement, 1988; contbr. articles to profl. jours. Home and Office: 19608 Braemar Dr Saratoga CA 95070-5046

BROWN, RANDY LEE, systems engineer; b. Yakima, Wash., Oct. 9, 1963; s. Jack Leroy Brown and Carol Ann (Litchtenburg) Myers. Student, Yakima Valley Vocat. Skills Ctr., 1980-82, Phoenix Inst. Tech., 1982-83. Cert. electronic technician Easy Enterprises Amusements, Yakima, 1983-84; svc. mgr. Cliff Miller's Computers Inc., Yakima, 1984—. Named State Champion radio TV repair Vocat. Industries Clubs Am., 1982. Home: 608 S Yakima Ave Wapato WA 98951-1261 Office: Cliff Millers Computers Inc 22 N 2nd St Yakima WA 98901-2612

BROWN, RICHARD ELWOOD, educator; b. Kansas City, Mo., Feb. 11, 1946; s. Lester J. and Frances M. (Brizendine) B. AB, Stanford U., 1968; PhD, Cornell U., 1972. Asst. to assoc. to prof. U. Nev., Reno, 1972—. Author: Chester's Last Stand, 1988, (short story collection) Fishing for Ghosts, 1994. Office: U Nev Reno English Dept 098 Reno NV 89557

BROWN, ROBERT MUNRO, museum director; b. Riverside, N.J., Mar. 4, 1952; s. James Wendell and Janet Elizabeth (Munro) B.; m. Mary Ann Noel, June, 1973 (div. 1977); m. Claudia Leslie Haskell, Jan. 14, 1978. BA in Polit. Sci. cum laude, Ursinus Coll., 1973; MA in Social Scis., Rivier Coll., 1978; PhD in Early Am. History, U. N.H., 1983. Grad. asst. dept. history U. N.H., Durham, 1979-83, instr., 1983-84; site curator T.C. Steele State Hist. Site Ind. State Mus. System, Nashville, Ind., 1984-91; dir. Hist. Mus. at Ft. Missoula, Mont., 1991—; hist. interpreter Strawberry Banke, Portsmouth, N.H., 1980-83; instr. Rivier Coll., Nashua, N.H., 1986-91, N.H. Coll., Nashua and Salem, 1986-91; supr. pub. programs Mus. Am. Textile History, North Andover, Mass., 1985-91; sec.-treas. Western Mont. Heritage Ctr./No. Rockies Heritage Ctr., 1992-93; mem. grad. com. U. Mont., 1993; mem. steering com. Ft. Missoula, 1993; reviewer Inst. Mus. Svcs., 1993, 94, 95; lectr., presenter, chair panels in field. Contbr. articles to profl. jours. Trustee Historic Harrisville, N.H., 1989-91; bd. dirs. United Peoples Found., 1991-93, v.p., 1993; mem. planning com. Western Mont. Heritage Ctr., 1991, U. Mont. Centennial Celebration, 1992, Leadership Missoula, 1992; active open space, parks and resource planning and mgmt. project team City of Missoula, 1993; mem. blue ribbon task force Five Valleys Luth. Retirement Community Planning Com., 1994. Scholar U. N.H., 1979-83, rsch. grantee, 1982; grantee Mass. Coun. on Arts and Humanities, 1986, 87, 88, Int. Mus. Svcs., 1988, 89, 90, 91, AT&T, 1988, Am. Wool Coun., 1988, BayBank, 1989, Am. Yarn Assn., 1989, North Andover Arts Lottery Coun., 1989, 90, Mass. Cultural Coun., 1990, Greater Lawrence Cmty. Found., 1991, Mass. Arts Lottery Coun., 1991, Gallery Assn. for Greater Art, 1991, 92, 94, 95, 96, Mont. Com. for Humanities, 1991, 92, 93, 94, 95, 96, Sinclair Oil Co., 1991, Mont. Rail Link, 1992, U. Mont. Found., 1992, Pepsi-Cola Co., 1992, 93, 94, 95, 96, U.S. WEST Found., 1992, 95, The Missoulan, 1992, 95, Champion Internat., 1992, Mont. Cultural Trust, 1993, 95, Missoula Rotary, 1993, Tex. Mus. Assn., 1993, Inst. Mus. Svcs., 1993, 95, Zip Beverage Co., 1994, Bitterroot Motors, 1994, 95, 96, Grizzly Hackle, 1994, University Motors, 1995, 96, Earl's Distributing, 1996; Kellogg Found. fellow, 1987. Mem. Am. Assn. Mus., Am. Assn. State and Local History (state membership rep. 1996—), Am. Hist. Assn., Assn. Records Mgrs. and Adminstrs. (charter Big Sky chpt. 1992-94), Mont. Hist. Soc., Mus. Assn. Mont. (panelist 1994), Western Mont. Fundraisers Assn. (charter 1991, v.p. 1993-95, pres. 1995—), Mtn. Plains Mus. Assn. (Mont. state rep. 1995—), Greater Boston Mus. Educator's Roundtable (steering com. 1988-90), Masons (Missoula chpt.), Kiwanis (Sentinel chpt.), Phi Alpha Theta (Psi Pi chpt.). Democrat. Home: 216 Woodworth Ave Missoula MT 59801-6052 Office: Hist Mus at Ft Missoula Ft Missoula Bldg 322 Missoula MT 59801

BROWN, RONALD MALCOLM, engineering corporation executive; b. Hot Springs, S.D., Feb. 21, 1938; s. George Malcolm and Cleo Lavonne (Plumb) B.; m. Sharon Ida Brown, Nov. 14, 1964 (div. Apr. 1974); children: Michael, Troy, George, Curtis, Lisa, Brittney. AA, Southwestern Coll., 1970; BA, Chapman Coll., 1978. Commd. USN, 1956, advanced through grades to master chief, 1973, ret., 1978; engring. mgr. Beckman Inst., Fullerton, Calif., 1978-82; mech. engring. br. mgr. Northrop Corp., Hawthorne, Calif., 1982-83; dir. of ops. Transco, Marina Del Rey, Calif., 1983-85; v.p. ops. Decor Concepts, Arcadia, Calif., 1985—; design dir. Lockheed Aircraft Corp., Ontario, Calif. Mem. Soc. Mfg. Engrs., Inst. Indsl. Engrs., Nat. Trust for Hist. Preservation, Fleet Res. Assn., Am. Film Inst., Nat. Mgmt. Assn.

BROWN, SHIRLEY KERN (PEGGY BROWN), interior designer; b. Ellensburg, Wash., Mar. 30, 1948; d. Philip Brooke and Shirley (Dickson) Kern; m. Ellery Kliess Brown, Jr., Aug. 7, 1970; children: Heather Nicole Coco, Rebecca Cherise, Andrea Shirley Serene, Ellery Philip. B.A. in Interior Design, Wash. State U., 1973. Apprentice, then interior designer L.S. Higgins & Assocs., Bellevue, Wash., 1969-72; interior designer ColorsPlus Interiors, Inc., Bellevue, 1972, Strawns Office Furniture & Interiors, Inc., Boise, Idaho, 1973-75, Empire Furniture Inc., Tulsa; owner Inside-Out Design Co. Ltd., Boise, 1973-82; interior designer Architekton, Inc., Tulsa, 1984-86; Johnson Brand Design Group, Inc., 1986-87; Ellery Brown & Assoc. Arch. AIA, 1987—; Seattle Design Ctr.-Visions & Studio Programs, 1994—; lectr. schs., Meridian, Idaho, 1976, 78, Boise, 1980-81, Oral Roberts U., Tulsa. Contbr. articles to profl. jours. Pres. PTA, co-chair capital bond prin. selection com., enrollment rev. com., 1989-95. Mem. Am. Soc. Interior Designers (presdl. citation Oreg. chpt. 1977, 95, 96, dir. chpt. 1976-77, chmn. Boise subchpt. 1977-79, sec. 1980-81, Wash. chpt. workshop chmn., NCIDQ chmn. 1993—), Nat. Soc. Interior Designers, Idaho Hist. Co., AAUW, Wash. State U. Alumni Assn., Jr. League, Alpha Gamma Delta. Republican. Presbyterian. Club: Zonta. Office: 506 S 17th St Renton WA 98055-4264

BROWN, STEPHANIE CECILE, librarian, writer; b. Pasadena, Calif., Mar. 23, 1961; d. Harry Francis and Anne Catherine (Murray) B.; m. Derek Lawrence Christiansen, Dec. 1, 1991; children: Nathaniel, Thomas. BA, Boston U., 1984; MFA, U. Iowa, 1986; MLS, U. Calif., Berkeley, 1987. Libr. specialist Orange County Pub. Libr., San Juan Capistrano, Calif., 1989-97, sr. libr. specialist collection devel., 1997—. Contbr. poetry to profl. publs. Recipient Jessica Maxwell Meml. Poetry prize Am. Poetry Rev., 1994. Roman Catholic. Home: 2818 Via Blanco San Clemente CA 92673 Office: Orange County Pub Libr Adminstrn 1501 Saint Andrew Pl Santa Ana CA 92707

BROWN, STEVEN BRIEN, radiologist; b. Ft. Collins, Colo., Jan. 18, 1952; s. Allen Jenkins and Shirley Irene (O'Brien) B.; m. Susan Jane DiTomaso, Sept. 10, 1983; children: Allison Grace, Laura Anne. BS, Colo. State U., 1974; MD, U. Calif., San Diego, 1978. Diplomate Am. Bd. Radiology. Intern U. Wash., Seattle, 1978-79; resident in radiology Stanford (Calif.) U., 1979-82; fellow in interventional and neuro-radiology Wilford Hall, USAF Med Ctr., San Antonio, 1982-83; staff radiologist Wilford Hall, USAF Med Ctr., 1983-86, Luth. Med. Ctr., Wheat Ridge, Colo., 1986—; chief angiography and interventional radiology Luth. Med. Ctr., 1987-94; chief dept. med. imaging Luth. Med. Ctr. Joint Venture, 1994-96; pres. Luth. Med. Ctr. Joint Venture, 1992-95; mem. bd. mgrs. Primera HealthCare LLC, 1995—; pres. HealthCare Select Inc., 1995-97. Contbr. articles to profl. jours. Mem. Rep. Nat. Com., Washington, 1984—, Nat. Rep. Senatorial Com., 1985—, Rep. Presdl. Task Force, 1986—; bd. dirs. The Health Care Initiative. Maj. USAF, 1982-86. Fellow Radiol. Soc. N.Am.; mem. Colo. Radiol. Soc. (pres. 1995-96), Rocky Mt. Radiol. Soc. (pres. 1994-95), Am. Coll. Radiology, Soc. Cardiovasc. and Interventional Radiology, Western Neuroradiol. Soc., Am. Soc. Neuroradiology, Colo. Preferred Physicians Orgn. (bd. dirs. 1987-89), World Wildlife Orgn., Colo. Angio Club. Republican. Presbyterian. Office: Luth Med Center 8300 W 38th Ave Wheat Ridge CO 80033-6005

BROWN, THEOPHILUS, artist; b. Moline, Ill., 1919. BA, Yale U., 1941; MA, U. Calif., Berkeley, 1952; studied with Ozenfant, New York, 1948; studied with Leger, Paris, 1949. Instr. U. Calif., Berkeley, 1954-56, San Francisco Art Inst., 1955-57, U. Calif., Davis, 1956-60, 75-76, U. Kans., Lawrence, 1967, Stanford U., 1967. One man shows include San Francisco Mus. Modern Art, 1957, Felix Landau Gallery, L.A., 1958, 60, 63, 65, 67, Kornblee Gallery, N.Y.C., 1961, Barone Gallery, N.Y.C., 1961, Crocker Art Gallery, Sacramento, 1965, Hollis Gallery, San Francisco, 1965, Ester Bear Gallery, Santa Barbara, Calif., 1965, U. Kans. Art Mus., 1967, Landau Alan Gallery, N.Y.C., 1968, Charles Campbell Gallery, San Francisco, 1972, 75, 78, Smith Gallery U. Calif., Santa Cruz, 1982, John Berggruen Gallery, San Francisco, 1983, 87, Maxwell Davidson Gallery, N.Y., 1989, Koplin Gallery, L.A., 1989, 91, 94, Tatistcheff & Co., Inc., N.Y., 1990, 92, Natsoulas Gallery, Davis, Calif., 1991, Harcourts Gallery, San Francisco, 1993; included in public collections at Metropolitan Mus. Art, Joseph H. Hirshhorn Mus., U. Kansas, Oakland Art Mus., San Francisco Mus. Modern Art, Sheldon Mus. U. Nebr., Capitol Records Inc., Commerce Trust Co., Davenport Mcpl. Art Gallery, Readers Digest Assn., Koplin Gallery, L.A.

BROWN, THOMAS ADAMS, aviation executive; b. Phoenix, May 3, 1948; s. James Granville and Billie Kathryn (Adams) B.; m. Christine Ann Hajjar; children: Mark, Adam, Matthew. Student in aero. engring., U. Colo., 1966-69; BS in Bus., U. Tex., 1970. Regional dir. sales and svcs. Tex. Internat. Airlines, Houston, 1968-79; dir. material sys. and controls Tiger Internat., Burbank, Calif., 1979-81; exec. v.p. Aerotron AirPower, Inc., Long Beach, Calif., 1981—, LaGrange, Ga.; pres. Long Beach Airport Assn. Mem. Nat. Aviation Assn., Aero Club of So. Calif., Nat. Bus. Aircraft Assn., Aero. Repair Sta. Assn. (bd. dirs.), Long Beach Area C. of C. (bd. dirs.). Home: 880 Whitebook Dr La Habra CA 90631-6410 Office: Aerotron AirPower 456 Aerotron Pkwy LaGrange GA 30240

BROWN, THOMAS JOSEPH, immunologist; b. Washington, Iowa, Feb. 6, 1947; s. William Wright and Marjorie Lois (Walker) B. BS, Iowa State U., 1971. Registered microbiologist. Rsch. assoc. U. Iowa Hosp. and Clinic, Iowa City, 1972-85; rsch. scientist Bristol-Myers Squibb Pharm. Rsch. Inst., Seattle, 1985—. Author: book chpt., 1990; contbr. articles to profl. jours. Patentee in field. Mem. Am. Soc. Microbiology, Inflammation Rsch. Assn. Office: Bristol-Myers Squibb Co 3005 1st Ave Seattle WA 98121-1010

BROWN, TIMOTHY CHARLES, social science professional; b. June 9, 1938; s. Gilbert Edgar Brown and Frances G. (Shaw) Milum; m. Leda Moraima Zuniga Fernandez, Sept. 11, 1958; children: Barbara, Rebecca, Tamara, Timothy Patrick. BA in Internat. Rels., U. Nev., 1965; MA in Internat. Trade and Econs., Fgn. Svc. Inst. Dept. State, 1974; PhD, N.Mex. State U., 1997. Staff State Dept., 1965-92; Orgn. Econ. Coop. desk Orgn. Economic Coop. & Devel., 1980-81; dep. coord. for Cuban affairs Dept. State, Coord. Cuban Embargo and Radio Marti, Washington, 1981-83; U.S. consul gen. French Caribbean Depts., Martinique, 1983-87; sr. liaison in C.Am. Nicaraguan Dem. Resistance, Tegucigalpa, Honduras, 1987-90, UN Observer Force in C.Am. and OAS Internat. Commn. Cease-Fire Verification and Assistance, 1989-90; sr. fellow Border Rsch. Inst. N.Mex. State U., Las Cruces, 1990-92; ind. scholar, trade cons., internat. and nat. lectr., 1992-97; rsch. fellow Hoover Instn. on War, Revolution and Peace, Stanford U., 1994; presenter in field. Contbr. articles to profl. jours. and major press, Wall St. Jour. Sgt. USMC, 1954-64. Recipient Marine Corps. Commendations, Nicaragua, 1959, Thailand, 1963, State Dept. Commendations, Disting. Svc. award, Vietnam, 1967, Meritorious Honor awards, 1978, 82, Commendation Dir. Gen.s' Reporting awards, 1985, 89, Superiour Honor medal, 1990. Mem. Rotary Club, Marine Corps Assn. Home: 1025 Marilissa Ln Las Cruces NM 88005-3816 Office: Ctrl Am Found PO Box 1266 Mesilla NM 88046-1266

BROWN, TIMOTHY DONELL, professional football player; b. Dallas, July 22, 1966. BA, U. Notre Dame, 1988. Wide receiver L.A. Raiders, 1988—. Recipient Heisman trophy, 1987; named Wide Reciever on The Sporting News Coll. All-Am. team, 1986, 87; Coll. Football Player of the Yr. The Sporting News, 1987, Kick Returner The Sporting News NFL All-Pro Team, 1988. Office: LA Raiders 332 Center St El Segundo CA 90245-4047

BROWN, TOD DAVID, bishop; b. San Francisco, Nov. 15, 1936; s. George Wilson and Edna Anne (Dunn) B. BA, St. John's Coll., 1958; STB, Gregorian U., Rome, 1960; MA in Theology, U. San Francisco, 1970, MAT in Edn., 1976. Dir. edn. Diocese of Monterey, Calif., 1970-80, vicar gen., clergy, 1980-82, chancellor, 1982-89, vicar gen., chancellor, 1983-89; pastor St. Francis Xavier, Seaside, Calif., 1977-82; bishop Roman Catholic Diocese of Boise, Idaho, 1989—. Named Papal Chaplain Pope Paul VI, 1975. Mem. Cath. Theol. Soc. Am., Cath. Biblical Assn., Canon Law Soc. Am., Equestrian Order of the Holy Sepulchre in Jerusalem. Office: Diocese of Boise 303 Federal Way Boise ID 83705-5925

BROWN, VALERIE, state legislator; b. Kansas City, Mo., Oct. 30, 1945; divorced; 1 child, Lisa Davis. BS, U. Mo., 1972, MA, 1978. Former mayor City of Sonoma; mem. Calif. State Assembly, 1993—; marriage, family and child counselor. Mem. Sonoma Valley C. of C. (v.p.). Democrat. Presbyterian. Home: 299 1st St West Sonoma CA 95476 Office: State Capitol Rm 2130 Sacramento CA 95814-4906*

BROWN, WALTER CREIGHTON, biologist; b. Butte, Mont., Aug. 18, 1913; s. D. Frank and Isabella (Creighton) B.; m. Jeanette Snyder, Aug. 20, 1950; children: Pamela Hawley, James Creighton, Julia Elizabeth. AB, Coll. Puget Sound, 1935, MA, 1938; PhD, Stanford U., 1950. Chmn. dept. Clover Park High Sch., Tacoma, Wash., 1938-42; acting instr. Stanford U., Calif.,

1949-50; instr. Northwestern U., Evanston, Ill., 1950-53; dean sci. Menlo Coll., Menlo Park, Calif., 1955-66, dean instrn., 1966-75; rsch. assoc., fellow Calif. Acad. Sci., San Francisco, 1978—; lectr. Sillman U., Philippines, 1954-55, dir. rsch. Program on Ecology and Systematics of Philippine Amphibians and Reptiles, 1958-74; rschr. rels. of amphibian faunas of Philippines & Indo-Australian Archipelago; vis. prof. biology Stanford U., 1962, 64, 66, 68, Harvard U., Cambridge, Mass., 1969, 72. Author: Philippine Lizards of the Family Gekkonidae, 1978, Philippine Lizards of the Family Scincidae, 1980, Lizards of the Genus Emoia (Scincidae) with Observations of Their Evolution and Biogeography, 1991; contbr. over 80 articles to profl. jours. Served with U.S. Army, 1942-46. Fellow AAAS; mem. Am. Soc. Ichthyologists and Herpetologists, Am. Inst. Biol. Scis., Sigma Xi. Office: Calif Acad Scis Dept Herpetology Golden Gate Park San Francisco CA 94118

BROWN, WAYNE J., mayor; b. 1936. BS, Ariz. State U. Staff acct. Arthur Andersen & Co. CPA's, 1960-63; mng. ptnr. Wayne Brown & Co. CPA's, 1964-79; dir. acctg. Ariz. State Dept. Adminstrn., 1979-80; chmn. Brown Evans Distbg. Co., Mesa, Ariz., 1980—; mayor City of Mesa, 1996—. Office: Office of the Mayor 20 E Main St Ste 750 Mesa AZ 85201

BROWN, WILLIAM CARROLL, plastic surgeon, microsurgeon; b. St. Paul, Mar. 16, 1954; s. Jerry W. and M. Suzanne (Stussi) B.; m. Sandra J. Hansen Brown, Nov. 12, 1977; children: Amanda B., Ryan W. BS and BA in biochemical genetics and physiological psychology magna cum laude, U. Minn., 1976, student, 1978, postgrad., 1978-79; MD CM, McGill U. Faculty of Medicine, Montreal, Que., Can., 1983. Diplomate Am. Bd. Plastic Surgery in Surgery of the Hand, Am. Bd. Plastic Surgery, Am. Bd. Surgery, Nat. Bd. of Med. Examiners. Resident, gen. surgery Boston's Beth Israel Hosp. Dept. of Surgery, 1983-88; postdoctoral tng. Boston Mass Dept. of Surgery, 1984-86, Royal Cornwall Hosp., Truro, Cornwall, England, 1986-88; resident, fellow Duke U. Med. Ctr. Dept of Plastic Surgery, Durham, N.C., 1988-91; resident, hand and microsurgery fellow Christine M. Kleinert Inst. for Hand and Microsurgery, Louisville, 1989; rsch. Plastic and Reconstructive Surgery Duke U. Med. Ctr., Physiological Psychology U. Minn., 1973-76, Biochemical Genetics U. Minn., 1974-76, Gastrointestinal Physiology U. Minn., 1977-78, Microciculatory Physiology U. Minn., 1978-82. Contbr. articles to profl. jours. Capt. M.C., U.S. Army, 1990—. Mem. AMA, ACS, Am. Soc. of Plastic and Reconstructive Surgeons, Am. Soc. for Surgery of the Hand, Am. Cleft Palate-Craniofacial Assn., Colo. State Soc. Plastic and Reconstructive Surgeons, Colo. Cleft Palate Assn., Denver Med. Assn., Rose Cleft Palate Assn. Office: Plas Surg Clinic 1578 Humboldt St Denver CO 80218-1638*

BROWN, WILLIE LEWIS, JR., mayor, former state legislator, lawyer; b. Mineola, Tex., Mar. 20, 1934; s. Willie Lewis and Minnie (Boyd) B.; children: Susan, Robin, Michael. B.A., San Francisco State Coll., 1955; LL.D., Hastings Coll. Law, 1958; postgrad. fellow, Crown Coll., 1970, U. Calif.-Santa Cruz, 1970. Bar: Calif. 1959. Mem. Calif. State Assembly, Sacramento, 1964-95; speaker Calif. State Assembly, 1980-95, chmn. Ways and Means Com., 1971-74; chmn. revenue and taxation com., 1976-79; Democratic Whip Calif. State Assembly, 1969-70, majority floor leader, 1979-80, chmn. legis. black caucus, 1980, chmn. govtl. efficiency and economy com., 1968-84; mayor San Francisco, 1995—. Mem. U. Calif. bd. regents, 1972, Dem. Nat. Com., 1989-90; co-chmn. Calif. del. to Nat. Black Polit. Conv., 1972, Calif. del. to Nat. Dem. Conv., 1980; nat. campaign chmn. Jesse Jackson for Pres., 1988. Mem. State Legis. Leaders Found. (dir.), Nat. Conf. State Legislatures, NAACP, Black Am. Polit. Assn. Calif. (co-founder, past chmn.), Calif. Bar Assn., Alpha Phi Alpha, Phi Alpha Delta. Democrat. Methodist. Office: Office of the Mayor 401 Van Ness Ave Ste 336 San Francisco CA 94102-4527 also: 1388 Sutter St Ste 820 San Francisco CA 94109-5453

BROWNE, GRETCHEN LYNN, interior designer; b. Seattle, Dec. 6, 1969; d. Ivan Len and Judy Lynn (Gott) A. BA, We. Wash. U., 1992. Interior designer Village Interiors, Inc., Issaquah, Wash., 1992-96, pvt. practice, Bothell, Wash., 1996—, Design Fit, Edmonds, Wash., 1997—. Mem. Associated Soc. Interior Designers. Home and Office: 10005 NE 201st St Bothell WA 98011-2437

BROWNE, JOSEPH PETER, retired librarian; b. Detroit, June 12, 1929; s. George and Mary Bridget (Fahy) B.; A.B., U. Notre Dame, 1951; S.T.L., Pontificium Athenaeum Angelicum, Rome, 1957, S.T.D., 1960; MS in L.S., Cath. U. Am., 1965. Joined Congregation of Holy Cross, Roman Cath. Ch., 1947, ordained priest, 1955; asst. pastor Holy Cross Ch., South Bend, Ind., 1955-56; libr., prof. moral theology Holy Cross Coll., Washington, 1959-64; mem. faculty U. Portland (Oreg.), 1964-73, 75—, dir. libr., 1966-70, 76-94, dean Coll. Arts and Scis., 1970-73, assoc. prof. libr. sci. 1967-95, prof. emeritus, 1995—, regent, 1969-70, 77-81, chmn. acad. senate, 1968-70, 1987-88; prof., head dept. libr. sci. Our Lady of Lake Coll., San Antonio, 1973-75; chmn. Interstate Libr. Planning Coun., 1977-79. Mem. Columbia River chpt. Huntington's Disease Soc. Am., 1975-90, pres., 1979-82; pastor St. Birgitta Ch., Portland, 1993—; chmn. Archdiocesan Presbyteral Coun., 1994—; mem. coll. of cons. Archdiocese of Portland, 1995—. Recipient Culligan award U. Portland, 1979. Mem. Cath. Libr. Assn. (life, pres. 1971-73), ALA, Cath. Theol. Soc. Am., Pacific N.W. Libr. Assn. (pres. 1985-86), Oreg. Libr. Assn. (life, pres. 1967-68), Nat. Assn. Parliamentarians, Oreg. Assn. Parliamentarians (pres. 1985-87), Mensa Internat., All-Ireland Cultural Soc. Oreg. (pres. 1984-85). Democrat. Club: KC. Home: 11820 NW Saint Helens Rd Portland OR 97231-2319

BROWNE, VEE F., writer; b. Ganado, Ariz., Sept. 4, 1956; d. William T. Sr. and Sarah F. (Tsosie) Brown Gorman; m. (div. 1983); children: Tye O'Harris Brown, Delilah Violet Brown. BS, No. Ariz. U., 1985; MA (hon.) in counseling, Western N.M. U., 1990. Writer U. Ariz., Tucson, 1987—; drama coach Cottonwood Jr. High, Chinle, Ariz., 1985-90. Author children's book Monster Slayer, 1988. Counselor Northland Crisis Nursery-Abused Children, Flagstaff, Ariz., 1979. Mem. Ariz. Tchrs. Assn., Delta Epsilon, Beta Phi Gamma. Home: PO Box 1085 Chinle AZ 86503-1085

BROWNFIELD, SHELBY HAROLD, soil scientist; b. Ava, Ill., June 12, 1931; s. William Edward and Mabel (Ditzler) B.; m. Lois Marie Landreth, Apr. 27, 1952 (dec. 1991); children: Susan, Nancy, David, Judy, Lori; m. Joyce Marilyn Bland-Gasperson, Dec. 11, 1993. BS in Agriculture, U. Ill., 1954; postgrad., Iowa State U., 1968. Lab. tech. USDA, Urbana, Ill., 1952-54; soil conservation tech. USDA, Joliet, Ill., 1954; soil scientist soil conservation svc. USDA, Greencastle, Ind., 1954-56, Spencer, Ind., 1957-60; soil survey party leader USDA, Franklin, Ind., 1960-65, Shelbyville, Ind., 1965-67, North Vernon, Ind., 1967-72; area soil scientist and party leader USDA, Kendallville, Ind., 1972; soil correlator USDA, Bozeman, Mont., 1972-77; state soil scientist USDA, Boise, 1977-86; cons. soil scientist Idaho Divsn. Environ. Quality, Boise, 1986-88, Associated Earth Scis., Boise, 1988—; Author: Soil Survey of Shelby County, Indiana, 1968, Soil Survey of Bartholomew County, Indiana, 1972; co-author: Soil Survey of Owen County, Indiana, 1960; contbr. articles to profl. jours. Mem. Am. Soc. Agronomy, Idaho Soil Scientist Assn. (pres. 1993), Masons, Elks. Baptist. Home and Office: 7689 Stirrup Boise ID 83709 also: PO Box 418 Bunker Hill IL 62014-0418

BROWNING, JAMES ROBERT, federal judge; b. Great Falls, Mont., Oct. 1, 1918; s. Nicholas Henry and Minnie Sally (Foley) B.; m. Marie Rose Chapell. BA, Mont. State U., Missoula, 1938; LLB with honors, U. Mont., 1941, LLD (hon.), 1961; LLD (hon.), Santa Clara U., 1989. Bar: Mont. 1941, D.C. 1950, U.S. Supreme Ct. 1952. Spl. atty. antitrust div. Dept. Justice, 1941-43, spl. atty. gen. litigation sect. antitrust div., 1946-48, chief antitrust dept. N.W. regional office, 1948-49; asst. chief gen. litigation sect. antitrust div. Dept. Justice (N.W. regional office), 1949-51, 1st asst. civil div., 1951-52; exec. asst. to atty. gen. U.S., 1952-53; chief U.S. (Exec. Office for U.S. Attys.), 1953; pvt. practice Washington, 1953-58; lectr. N.Y.U. Sch. Law, 1953, Georgetown U. Law Center, 1957-58; clk. Supreme Ct. U.S., 1958-61; judge U.S. Ct. Appeals 9th Circuit, 1961-76, chief judge, 1976-88, judge, 1988—; mem. Jud. Conf. of U.S., 1976-88, exec. com. of conf., 1978-87, com. on internat. conf. of appellate judges, 1987-90, com. on ct. adminstrn., 1969-71, chmn. subcom. on jud. stats., 1969-71, com. on the budget, 1971-77, adminstrn. office, subom. on budget, 1974-76, com. to study U.S. jud. conf., 1986-88, com. to study the illustrative rules of jud. misconduct, 1985-87, com. on formulation of standard of conduct of fed. judges, 1969, Reed justice com. on cont. edn., tng. and adminstrn., 1967-68; David T. Lewis Disting. Judge-in-residence, U. Utah, 1987; Blankenbaker lectr. U. Mont., 1987, Sibley lectr. U. Ga., 1987, lectr. Human Rights Inst. Santa Clara U. Sch. Law, Strasbourg. Editor-in-chief, Mont. Law Rev. Dir. Western Justice Found.; chmn. 9th Cir. Hist. Soc. 1st lt. U.S. Army, 1943-46. Decorated Bronze Star; named to Order of the Grizzly, U. Mont., 1973; scholar in residence Santa Clara U., 1989, U. Mont., 1991; recipient Devitt Disting. Svc. to Justice award, 1990. Fellow ABA (judge adv. com. to standing com. on Ethics and Profl. Responsibility 1973-75); mem. D.C. Bar Assn., Mont. Bar Assn., Am. Law Inst., Fed. Bar Assn. (bd. dirs 1945-61, Nat. council 1958-62), Inst. Jud. Adminstrn., Am. Judicature Soc. (chmn. com. on fed. judiciary 1973-74, bd. dirs. 1972-75), Herbert Harley award 1984), Am. Soc. Legal History (adv. bd. jour.), Nat Lawyers Club (bd. govs. 1959-63). Office: US Ct Appeals 9th Cir 121 Spear St San Francisco CA 94119-3939 *Notable cases include: pro bono case Bell vs. U.S., 349 U.S. 81, 1955.**

BROWNING, JESSE HARRISON, entrepreneur; b. Kingsville, Mo., July 27, 1935; s. Jesse Harrison and Anna Love (Swank) B.; m. Vicki Carol Thompson, Dec. 21, 1957; children: Caroline Kaye, Marcia Lynn, Nanci Ann, Susan Louise. MPA, U. So. Calif., 1988; PhD, U. Wash., 1995. Cert. mfg. engr. Field engr. The Boeing Co., Los Angeles, 1961-64; gen. mgr. SPI, Los Angeles, 1964-70; chmn. Browning Inc., Los Angeles, 1970-95; dir. global trade, transp. and logistic studies U. Wash., Seattle, 1995—; chmn. Vapor Engring., Los Angeles, 1979-87. Patentee in field. Mem. ASPA, World Coun. on Internat. Trade, World Affairs Coun., Am. Helicopter Soc., Am. Assn. Geographers, Soc. Mgr. Engrs., Propellor Club. Lutheran.

BROWNING, NORMA LEE (MRS. RUSSELL JOYNER OGG), journalist; b. Spickard, Mo., Nov. 24, 1914; d. Howard R. and Grace (Kennedy) B.; m. Russell Joyner Ogg, June 12, 1938. A.B., B.J., U. Mo., 1937; M.A. in English, Radcliffe Coll., 1938. Reporter Los Angeles Herald-Express, 1942-43; with Chgo. Tribune, from 1944, Hollywood columnist, 1966-75; Vis. lectr. creative writing, editorial cons., mem. nat. adv. bd. Interlochen Arts Acad., Northwood Inst. Author: City Girl in the Country, 1955, Joe Maddy of Interlochen, 1963, (with W. Clement Stone) The Other Side of the Mind, 1965, The Psychic World of Peter Hurkos, 1970, (with Louella Dirksen) The Honorable Mr. Marigold, 1972, (with Ann Miller) Miller's High Life, 1972, Peter Hurkos: I Have Many Lives, 1976, Omarr: Astrology and the Man, 1977, (with George Masters) The Masters Way to Beauty, 1977, (with Russell Ogg) He Saw A Hummingbird, 1978, (with Florence Lowell) Be A Guest At Your Own Party, 1980, Face-Lifts: Everything You Always Wanted to Know, 1981, Joe Maddy Of Interlochen: Portrait of A Legend, 1991; Contbr. articles to nat. mags. Recipient E.S. Beck award Chgo Tribune. Mem. Theta Sigma Phi, Kappa Tau Alpha. Address: 226 E Morongo Rd Palm Springs CA 92264-8402

BROWNING, WILLIAM DOCKER, federal judge; b. Tucson, May 19, 1931; s. Horace Benjamin and Mary Louise (Docker) B.; m. Courteny Browning (div.); children: Christopher, Logan, Courtenay; m. Zerilda Sinclair, Dec. 17, 1974; 1 child, Benjamin. BBA, U. Ariz., 1954, LLB, 1960. Bar: Ariz. 1960, U.S. Dist. Ct. Ariz. 1960, U.S. Ct. Appeals (9th cir.) 1965, U.S. Supreme Ct. 1967. Pvt. practice Tucson, 1960-84; judge U.S. Dist. Ct., Tucson, 1984—; mem. jud. nominating com. appellate ct. appointments, 1975-79. Del. 9th Cir. Jud. Conf., 1968-77, 79-82; trustee Inst. for Ct. Mgmt., 1978-84; mem. Ctr. for Pub. Resources Legal Program. 1st lt. USAF, 1954-57, capt. USNG, 1958-61. Recipient Disting. Citizen award U. Ariz., 1995. Fellow Am. Coll. Trial Lawyers, Am. Bar Found.; mem. ABA (spl. com. housing and urban devel. law 1973-76, com. urban problems and human affairs 1978-80), Ariz. Bar Assn. (chmn. merit selection of judges com. 1973-76, bd. gove. 1968-74, pres. 1972-73, Outstanding Mem. 1980), Pima County Bar Assn. (exec. com. 1964-68, med. legal screening panel 1965-75, pres. 1967-68), Am. Bd. Trial Advocates, Am. Judicature Soc. (bd. dirs. 1975-77), Fed. Judges Assn. (bd. dirs.). Office: US Dist Ct US Courthouse Rm 301 55 E Broadway Blvd Tucson AZ 85701-1719

BROWNLEE, WILSON ELLIOT, JR., history educator; b. Lacrosse, Wis., May 10, 1941; s. Wilson Elliot Sr. and Pearl (Woodings) B.; m. Mary Margaret Cochran, June 25, 1966; children: Charlotte Louise, Martin Elliot. BA, Harvard U., 1963; MA, U. Wis., 1965, PhD, 1969. Asst. prof. U. Calif., Santa Barbara, 1967-74, assoc. prof., 1974-80, prof. history, 1980—, spl. advisor to systemwide provost, 1995, assoc. systemwide provost, 1996; vis. prof. Princeton (N.J.) U., 1980-81; chmn. dept. history U. Calif., Santa Barbara, 1984-87, acad. senate, 1983-84, 88-90, systemwide acad. senate, 1992-93; dir. U. Calif.-Santa Barbara Ctr., Washington, 1990-91; chmn. exec. com. dels. Am. Coun. Learned Socs., N.Y.C., 1988-90, bd. dirs.; bd. dirs. Nat. Coun. on Pub. History, Boston; bicentennial lectr. U.S. Dept. Treasury, 1989; faculty rep. U. Calif. Bd. Regents, 1991-93. Author: Dynamics of Ascent, 1974, 2nd edit., 1979, Progressivism and Economic Growth, 1974, Federal Taxation in America: A Short History, 1996; co-author: Essentials of American History, 1976, 4th edit., 1986, America's History, 1987, 3rd edit., 1997; editor: Women in the American Economy 1976, Funding the American State, 1996; contbr. numerous articles to profl. jours., chpts. to books. Chmn. schs. com. Harvard Club, Santa Barbara, 1971-80, 85, 86; pres. Assn. for Retarded Citizens, Santa Barbara, 1982-84; 1st v.p. Assn. for Retarded Citizens Calif., Sacramento, 1983-84; pres. Santa Barbara Trust for Hist. Preservation, 1986-87, 95—; trustee Las Trampas Inc., 1994—. Charles Warren fellow Harvard U., 1978-79, fellow Woodrow Wilson Ctr., Washington, 1987-88; recipient Spl. Commendation, Calif. Dept. Pks. and Recreation, 1988. Mem. Am. Hist. Assn., Orgn. Am. Historians, Econ. History Assn., Am. Tax Policy Inst. Office: U Calif Dept History Santa Barbara CA 93106

BROWNSON, JACQUES CALMON, architect; b. Aurora, Ill., Aug. 3, 1923; s. Clyde Arthur and Iva Kline (Felter) B.; m. Doris L. Curry, 1946; children—Joel C., Lorre J., Daniel J. BS in Architecture, Ill. Inst. Tech., 1948, MS, 1954. Instr., asst. prof. architecture Ill. Inst. Tech., 1949-59; prof. architecture, chmn. dept. U. Mich., 1966-68; chief design C.F. Murphy Assocs., Chgo., 1959-61; project architect, chief designer Chgo. Civic Ctr. Architects, 1961-68; dir. state bldg. div. State of Colo., Denver, 1986-88; pvt. practice Denver, 1988—; former mng. architect Chgo. Pub. Bldg. Commn.; past dir. planning and devel. Auraria Ctr. for Higher Edn., Denver; bd. dirs. Capital Constrn., Denver; guest lectr. architecture in U.S. and Europe. Prin. works include Chgo. Civic Ctr., Lake Denver, Colo., 1985, Chgo. Tribune/Cabrini Green Housing, 1993; author: History of Chicago Architects, 1996, Oral History of Jacuqes Calmon Brownson, 1996. Recipient award for Geneva House Archtl. Record mag., 1956; Design award for steel framed factory Progressive Architecture mag., 1957. Home and Office: 659 Josephine St Denver CO 80206-3722

BROWN-STIGGER, ALBERTA MAE, nurse; b. Columbus, Ohio, Nov. 11, 1932; d. Sylvester Clarence and Malinda (Mason) Angel; grad. Antelope Valley Coll., 1961; AA, L.A. Valley Coll., 1975; BS, Calif. State U., Dominguez Hills, 1981; m. Norman Brown, Dec. 29, 1967 (dec. Jan. 1989); children: Charon, Charles, Stevan, Carole; m. A.C. Stigger, June 14, 1992. RN, Calif.; lic. vocat. nurse. Nurses aid, vocat. nurse, respiratory therapist St. Bernardines Hosp., 1965-69, Good Samaritan Hosp., L.A., 1969-70, Midway Hosp., L.A., 1973-81; allergy nurse, instr. respiratory therapy VA Hosp., L.A., 1970-93, also acting dept. head; nurse, respiratory splty. unit Jerry L. Pettis Meml. Hosp., Loma Linda, Calif., 1984-93; with Wadley Regional Med. Ctr., Texarkana, Tex., 1993-94; rehab. nurse Robert H. Ballard Rehab. Hosp., San Bernardino, Calif., 1994—; instr. L.A. Valley Med. Technoogists Sch., Compton Coll. seminar instr., 1979. Active Arrowhead Allied Arts Coun. of San Bernardino; CPR instr. Am. Heart Assn. Mem. Am. Assn. Respiratory Therapy, Nat. Honor Soc., Eta Phi Beta. Democrat. Baptist. Clubs: Social-Lites, Inc. of San Bernardino, Order Ea. Star. Patentee disposable/replaceable tubing for stethoscope. Home: Orangewood Estates 1545 Hancock St San Bernardino CA 92411-1667

BROZOWSKI, LAURA ADRIENNE, mechanical engineer; b. Yokohama, Japan, May 12, 1960; came to U.S., 1961; d. John and Muriel Sydney (Jackson) B. BSME, U. Calif., 1982; MSME, Calif. State U., 1987; MBA, Pepperdine U., 1988. Registered profl. engr.; cert. profl. mgr. Mem. tech. staff Rocketdyne divsn. Boeing N.Am., Inc., Canoga Park, Calif., 1982—. Author in field. Fellow Inst. Advancement Engring.; mem. ASME, NSPE, Nat. Mgmt. Assn. Home: 22036 Collins St # 230-n Woodland Hills CA 91367-4713

BRUBAKER, WILLIAM ROGERS, sociology educator; b. Evanston, Ill., June 8, 1956; s. Charles William and Elizabeth (Rogers) B. BA summa cum laude, Harvard U., 1979; MA, Sussex U., Eng., 1980; PhD, Columbia U., 1990. Prof. UCLA, 1994—, assoc. prof. sociology, 1991-94. Author: The Limits of Rationality, 1984, Citizenship and Nationhood in France and Germany, 1992, Nationalism Reframed, 1996; editor: Immigration and Politics of Citizenship in Europe and North America, 1989. Jr. fellow Soc. Fellows Harvard U., 1988-91; MacArthur fellow, 1994—; NSF Young Investigator awardee. Office: U Calif Dept Sociology 264 Haines Hall 405 Hilgard Ave Los Angeles CA 90095-1301*

BRUCE, DOUGLAS E., real estate investor; b. L.A., Aug. 26, 1949; s. Carl Edward and Marjorie Louise (Atkinson) B. BA, Pomona Coll., 1970; JD, U. So. Calif., 1973. Bar: Calif. State Bar 1973. Dep. dist. atty. L.A. county, 1973-79; pvt. practice real estate investor, 1975—. Author Colo. state constl. amendment limiting state and local govt. taxes, revenue and debt, 1992, Colorado Springs tax cuts, 1991, capital improvements petition, 1997; co-author Colo. state constnl. term limits amendments, 1990, 96. Named Coloradoan of the Yr. Rocky Moutain News, 1992, Friend of Liberty Colo. Libertarian Party, 1993, 95. Republican. Office: PO Box 26018 Colorado Springs CO 80936

BRUCE, JOHN ALLEN, foundation executive, educator; b. Kansas City, Mo., Sept. 17, 1934; BA, Wesleyan U., Middletown, Conn., 1956; MDiv, Gen. Theol. Sem., N.Y.C., 1959; PhD, U. Minn., 1972. Ordained to ministry Episcopal Ch., 1959. Clergyman, 1959-68; prof. U. Ala., Tuscaloosa, 1972-74; exec. dir. E.C. Brown Found., Portland, Oreg., 1974—; cons. to philanthropies and corp. programs; clin. prof. community medicine Sch. Medicine, Oreg. Health Scis. U., Portland, 1976—. Author, editor various scholarly publs. Exec. producer various ednl. films on family life, health and values. Bd. dirs. various community orgns. Served to lt. USN, 1964-67. Recipient various awards and grants from med. orgns. and related groups. Mem. Nat. Coun. on Family Rels. (Disting. Service to Families award 1979), Oreg. Coun. on Family Rels. (pres. 1981), Cosmos Club. Republican. Office: EC Brown Found 101 SW Main St Ste 500 Portland OR 97204-3213

BRUCE, NORMAN RICHARD, manufacturing executive; b. Rockford, Ill., May 30, 1924; s. John Alonzo and Grace Elizabeth (Gilmore) B.; m. Bettie Jane McCormick, July 28, 1950; children: Paul Richard, John Edward. Student, L.A. Valley Coll., 1956-58. Technician and buyer Shasta Trailer Co., L.A., 1946-52; customer engr. IBM, L.A., 1952; mech. lab. technician AMF, L.A., 1952-54, RCA, Vandenburg AFB, Calif., 1954, Collins Radio, Burbank, Costa Mesa, Calif., 1954-63; owner Bruce Constrn., Central Point, Oreg., 1963-66; pres. Granada Pitching Machines, Inc., Central Point, 1966—. Patents include 2 Wheel Pitching Machine and Polyball Use, Self-Orienting Pitching Machine; patent pending for 3-Wheel Programmable Pitching Machine; co-inventer Urethane Baseball-P.M. Use. V.p. Central Point C. of C., 1975-78; mem. sch. bd. Grace Christian Sch., Medford, Oreg., 1985-94; committeeman Reps., Medford, 1997—. Mem. Am. Baseball Coaches Assn., Am. Legion (comdr. post 129 1984—).

BRUCE, ROBERT KIRK, college administrator; b. Evanston, Ill., Nov. 7, 1942; s. Robert Kirk and Irma Bertha (Roese) B.; m. Judith Lee Chlopecki, July 13, 1968; children: Michael, James, Suzanne, Gary, Meredith. BS in Edn., No. Ill. U., DeKalb, 1967; MA, Ctrl. Mich. U., Mt. Pleasant, 1972, EdS, 1974. Edn. writer Rockford (Ill.) Morning Star, 1969-70; coord. News Bur. Ctrl. Mich. U., Mt. Pleasant, 1970-75; dir. News Bur. U. Oreg., Eugene, 1975-78; dir. univ. rels. Kans. State U., Manhattan, 1978-82; dir. univ. info. U. Nebr., Lincoln, 1982-89; asst. v.p. Oreg. State U., Corvallis, 1989-94, interim chief instl. advancement officer, 1994-96, exec. dir. comms. and mktg., 1996—; cons. U. Ariz., Tucson, 1984, Barton County C.C., Great Bend, Kans., 1984, Glassboro (N.J.) State Coll., 1988. Mem. Mayor's Task Force on Pub. Artwork, Manhattan, Kans., 1981; bd. dirs. Lincolnfest Celebration, Lincoln, Nebr., 1983-87, Oreg. Spl. Olympics, 1976-78. With USNR, 1965-73. Recipient Pub. Rels. awards ACPRA, AAC, Washington, 1971-74. Mem. Coun. for Advancement and Support of Edn. (medal awards 1980—), Am. Legion, Lincoln C. of C. (chmn. com. 1983-89), Century Club (bd. dirs. 1990—). Democrat. Roman Catholic. Home: 1075 NW Charlemagne Pl Corvallis OR 97330-3643 Office: Oreg State U Ads # 634 Corvallis OR 97331

BRUCE, THOMAS EDWARD, psychology educator, thanatologist; b. Vinton, Iowa, Dec. 3, 1937; s. George Robert and Lucille Etta (Aurner) B.; children: Scott Thomas and Suzanne Laura. BA, U. No. Iowa, 1961, MA, 1964; postgrad., U. Colo., 1968-71; MA, U. San Francisco, 1985. Lic. psychology educator, counselor, Calif. Tchr. various Iowa high schs., 1961-65; sociologist, counselor Office Econ. Opportunity, Denver, 1965-66; social sci. educator Arapahoe Coll., Littleton, Colo., 1966-69; lectr. U. Colo., Boulder, 1968-71; psychology educator Sacramento City Coll., Calif., 1972—; thanatology cons. for hospices, survivor support groups, No. Calif., 1984—. Author: Grief Management: The Pain and the Promise, 1986, Thanatology: Through the Veil, 1992; contbr. articles to profl. publs. Co-founder, bd. dirs. Bereavement Resources Network, Sacramento, 1983-87; profl. dir. Children's Respite Ctr., Sacramento, 1985-88; pres.-elect., bd. dirs. Hospice Care of Sacramento, 1979-85. With U.S. Army, 1955-58. Recipient Pres.'s award Nat. Hospice Orgn., 1985. Mem. Sacramento Mental Health Assn. (Vol. Svc. award 1985, 87), Assn. for Death Edn. and Counseling, Thanatology Found., Am. Fedn. Tchrs., Faculty Assn. Calif. C.C.'s, Pi Gamma Mu, Phi Delta Kappa. Presbyterian. Office: Sacramento City Coll 3835 Freeport Blvd Sacramento CA 95822-1318

BRUCH, BARBARA RAE, artist, educator; b. Seattle, Apr. 15, 1940; d. Willard Ray and Zephyr Eloise (Tull) B. BA, U. Wash., 1962, MFA, 1964. Children's art instr. Cornish Coll. Art, Seattle, 1965-67; artist-in-residence City of Seattle, 1967-78; lectr. art Seattle Pacific U., 1974-78; gallery dir. Husted Gallery, Seattle, 1978-94; art instr. Sev-Shoon Art Ctr., Seattle, 1994—; recording agt. Kappeler Inst., Seattle, 1995—; art restorer Husted Gallery/Studio Tara, 1978—; gallery coord. A New Space Gallery, Seattle, 1986-88; condr. art workshops. Illustrator: Stocks and Commodities mag., 1994—; one woman exhbns. include Seattle Pacific U., 1993, New Space Gallery, 1986, Husted Gallery, 1983, 85. Illustrator/mem. Friends of the Earth, Seattle, 1972-76, Wash. Wildlife Study Coun., Seattle, 1974-76. Recipient Editor's Choice award Nat. Libr. Poetry, 1995; Bank of Am. scholar, 1958. Mem. Seattle Women's Caucus for Art (pres. 1991-94, Kathe Kollwitz award 1996), No Limits for Women Artists. Office: Kappeler Inst PO Box 9229 Seattle WA 98109

BRUCKER, CONNIE, police officer, consultant; b. Detroit, June 29, 1946; d. Joseph Schwenk and Errawanna Coates; 1 child, Debra June Huegel. Student San Jose State Coll., 1980, East Los Angeles Coll., 1978. Legal sec. Lapin & Chester, West Los Angeles, Calif., 1972-75; police officer Santa Monica Police Dept., Calif., 1977—, mem. "K9 bite" rev. bd., mem. various award coms.; instr. Santa Monica Jr. Coll.; speaker, lectr. Lady Beware Programs, Los Angeles Area; cons. Safety Products, Calgary, Can., Calif. Council Hosps., Los Angeles, TV movies and spls. and interviews, Los Angeles. Author writings in field. Bd. dirs. ARC, Santa Monica, 1984—. Recipient Medal of Courage, City of Santa Monica, 1979, Mayor's Commendation, 1982, medals of Merit, Santa Monica Police Dept./City of Santa Monica, 1994, 96. Mem. Internat. Police Assn., Women Peace Officers Assn., Los Angeles Peace Officers Assn., Santa Monica Police Officers Assn., Sexual Assault Investigators Assn., Calif. Sexual Assault Investigators Assn. (pres. 1987). Office: Santa Monica Police Dept 1685 Main St Santa Monica CA 90401-3248

BRUECHERT, BEVERLY ANN, sales executive, recording artist, pianist; b. Oregon City, Oreg., May 3, 1960; d. Robert Wayne and Bonnie Helen (Troutner) B. BS in Applied Design with honors, Portland State U., 1986. Sales exec. iin interior furnishing MW End Store, Portland, Oreg.; fabric designer Daisy Kingdom, Portland; sales exec. in design firm Chase Internat., Portland; music dir. Waverly United Ch. of Christ, Portland; asst. music dir. Sunset Presbyn. Ch., Portland. Recorded album/CD, Twilight, a solo piano experience, 1994; vocal and piano compositions. Mem. Fashion

Group Internat. Republican. Christian. Home: 6605 W Burnside 144 Portland OR 97210

BRUESKE, CHARLOTTE, poet, composer; b. Plainview Township, Minn., Jan. 1, 1934; d. Layton Floyd and Berneta Dallas (Thompson) B. AA, Pasadena City Coll., 1976; BA, Calif. State U., Fullerton, 1984; postgrad., Fuller Theol. Sem. Author: Once in a Coon's Age, 1989, The Ancestors of Gottlob August Bruss and Bertha Pauline Goede, 1989, A Search for the Records of the Orphans of Dannan, 1990; composer, lyricist numerous works, including Evergreen, 1990, Every New Day, 1991, Lift Up One Another, 1991, Where the Red Ferns Abound, 1995. Recipient Cert. of Merit Virginia Baldwin/Talent Assocs., 1977. Democrat. Presbyterian. Home: 260 Streamwood Irvine CA 92620

BRUGGEMAN, LEWIS LEROY, radiologist; b. N.Y.C., Sept. 9, 1941; s. Louis LeRoy and Edwina Jane (Mickel) B.; m. Ann Margaret Kayajan, May 28, 1966; children: Gretchen Ann, Kurt LeRoy. AB, Dartmouth Coll., 1963, B in Med. Sci., 1965; MD, Harvard U., 1968. Intern Los Angeles County Harbor Gen. Hosp., Torrence, Calif., 1968-69; resident in diagnostic radiology Columbia Presbyn. Med. Ctr., N.Y.C., 1969-72; chief dept. radiology Bremerton (Wash.) Naval Regional Med. Ctr., 1972-74; pvt. practice diagnostic radiology South Coast Med. Ctr., South Laguna, Calif., 1974-96, dir. dept. radiology, 1983-95, hosp. bd. trustees, 1985-87; pvt. practice diagnostic radiology Saddleback Community Hosp., Laguna Hills, Calif., 1974-95; pres., chmn. bd. dirs. South Coast Med. Group Inc., South Laguna, Calif., 1983-95; ret., 1996; pres. So. Coast Radiol. Med. Group Inc., South Laguna, 1986-95; vice-chmn. and bd. trustees South Coast Med. Ctr. Found., 1993—. Lt. comdr. Med. Corps USN, 1972-74. Mem. Am. Coll. Radiology, Dartmouth Club Orange County. *Happiness emanates from a good job, well done. Focus on your goals, enjoy your work, and your rewards will not be far behind.*

BRUGGEMEYER, MARK EDWARD, career officer; b. Fla., Mar. 18, 1956; s. Roger Allen and Elizabeth Ann (Templeton) B.; m. Marilyn Jean McRae, June 30, 1984; children: Daniel Mark, Diane Marilyn. BS, USAF Acad., Colorado Springs, Colo., 1978; MA, Calif. State U., San Bernardino, 1987, Johns Hopkins U., Washington, 1994. Grad. USAF Fighter Weapons Sch. Commd. 2d lt. USAF, 1978, advanced through grades to lt. col.; flight comdr. 3d Fight Squadron, Clark AFB, The Philippines, 1987-88; chief squadron weapons and tactics 3d Fight Squadron, The Philippines, 1988-89, 562d Fighter Squadron, Victorville, Calif., 1989-90; asst. chief wing weapons and tactics 35th Fighter Wing, Victorville, Calif., 1990-92; base closure program mgr. The Pentagon, Washington, 1992-95; ops. officer 561st Fighter Squadron, Las Vegas, 1995—. Decorated Air medal, Meritorious Svc. medal, Aerial Achievement medal, Air Force Commendation medal. Mem. Soc. Wild Weasels.

BRUGGERE, THOMAS H., computer science company executive; b. Berkeley, Calif., 1946; m. Kelley Bruggere; 2 children. BA in Math., U. Calif., Santa Barbara; MS in Computer Sci., U. Wis.; MBA, Pepperdine U. Founder Mentor Graphics Corp.; computer tech. exec. Tektronix, Wilsonville, Oreg., 1977—; mem. Oreg. State Bd. Higher Edn.; bd. dirs. Will Vinton Studios, Reed Coll. Bd. dirs. Oreg. Symphony. Mem. Am. Electronics Assn. (bd. dirs.), Portland C. of C. (bd. dirs.). Office: 30000 SW 35th Dr Wilsonville OR 97070

BRULOTTE, BENNETT, agricultural products executive; b. 1944. With A/B Hop Farms, Inc., Prosser, Wash., 1968—, now sec. With U.S. armed forces, 1965-68. Office: A/B Hop Farms Inc 4456 Evans Rd Prosser WA 99350*

BRUMBAUGH, KEVIN JAMES, electronics executive; b. Pitts., July 21, 1955; s. James B. and Marjorie K. (Kuhn) B.; m. Candace A. Barr, May 21, 1977; 1 child, Andrew K. BSME, W.Va. U., 1977. Various mgmt. positions GE, 1977-87; ops. mgr., plant mgr. Westinghouse Electric, 1987-92; v.p., gen. mgr. Nelco Tech., Tempe, Ariz., 1992—. Mem. Sports Club Car of Am. (Ariz. region exec. 1995—, chief driving instr. 1994—). Republican. Roman Catholic. Home: 3915 East Mountain Vista Dr Phoenix AZ 85044 Office: Nelco Tech 1104 W Geneva Dr Tempe AZ 85282-3431

BRUMBAUGH, ROLAND JOHN, bankruptcy judge; b. Pueblo, Colo., Jan. 21, 1940; s. Leo Allen and Ethel Marie (Brummett) B.; m. Pamela Marie Hultman, Sept. 8, 1967; children—Kenneth Allen, Kimberly Marie. B.S. in Bus. with honors, U. Colo., 1968, J.D., 1971. Bar: Colo. 1971, U.S. Dist. Ct. Colo. 1972, U.S. Ct. Appeals (10th cir.) 1973, U.S. Supreme Ct. 1980. Legal intern HUD, Denver, 1971-72; sole practice, Denver, 1972-75; chief dep. city atty. City of Lakewood, Colo., 1975; dep. dir. Colo. Dept. of Revenue, Denver, 1975-78; asst. U.S. atty. Dist. of Colo., Denver, 1978-82; judge U.S. Bankruptcy Ct. Dist. of Colo., Denver, 1982—; lectr. in field. Author: Colorado Liquor and Beer Licensing-Law and Practice, 1970; Handbook for Municipal Clerks, 1972. Contbr. articles to profl. jours. Served with USAF, 1962-65. Recipient numerous awards for excellence in law. Mem. Colo. Bar Assn., Alpha Kappa Psi, Beta Gamma Sigma, Rho Epsilon, Sigma Iota. Home: 1845 Sherman St Ste 400 Denver CO 80203-1167 Office: US Dist Ct 721 19th St Denver CO 80202*

BRUMMER, STEVEN E., police chief. Chief of police Bakersfield, Calif. Office: PO Box 59 1601 Truxtun Ave Bakersfield CA 93302

BRUMMETT, ROBERT EDDIE, pharmacology educator; b. Concordia, Kans., Feb. 11, 1934; s. Gordon Legonia and Gladys Leona (Anderson) B.; m. Naomi Deen Weaver, Dec. 19, 1955; children: Randall, Wendy, Robin, Philip. BS, Oreg. State U., 1959, MS, 1960; PhD, U. Oreg., 1964. Registered pharmacist, Oreg. Asst. prof. pharmacology Oreg. State U., Corvallis, 1961-62; asst. prof. otolaryngology Oreg. Health Scis. U., Portland, 1964-70, assoc. prof. otolaryngology and pharmacology, 1970-80, prof. otolaryngology and Pharmacology, 1981-97, prof. emeritus, 1997—; mem. Oreg. Coun. on Alcohol and Drug Problems, Salem, 1979-85; instr. Am. Acad. Otolaryngology, Washington, 1964—; mem. adv. panel otorhinolaryngology U.S. Pharmacopeia, 1985—, mem. drug info. adv. panel, 1988—, mem. coun. on naturopathic physicians formulary, 1990—. Contbr. more than 100 articles to profl. jours.; patentee in field. Comdr. U.S. Power Squadron, Portland, 1988-89, adminstrv. officer, 1987, dist. ednl. officer, 1991-94, dist. adminstrv. officer, 1994-95, dist. exec. officer, 1995-96, dist. comdr. 1996-97, nat. comdr., 1997—. Grantee NIH, 1969—, Deafness Research Found., 1970, Med. Research Found., 1979, 83. Mem. AAAS, Am. Acad. Otolaryngology (instr. 1964—), Head and Neck Surgery, Associated Rschrs. in Otolaryngology, Hayden Island Yacht Club, Elks, Sigma Xi. Republican. Home: 2366 N Menzies Ct Portland OR 97217-8219 Office: Oreg Health Scis U 3181 SW Sam Jackson Park Rd Portland OR 97201-3011

BRUN, MARGARET ANN CHARLENE, semiconductor industry buyer, planner; b. Toledo, Ohio, June 19, 1945; d. John Joseph and Maude Elizabeth (Harrell) Bartos; m. Paul Joseph Brun, June 17, 1967. Student, Phoenix Coll., 1964-67, Glendale C.C., 1991-93; Assocs., Mesa C.C., 1996. Cert. purchasing mgr. Contr. material inventory Digital Equipment Corp., Phoenix, 1975-76, contr. prodn. inventory, 1976-77, prodn. control planner, 1977-79, inventory control planner, 1979, buyer, 1979-91; buyer, planner ASM Am., Inc., 1991-95, sr. buyer, 1996—. Named Buyer of Yr., Purchasing World mag., 1987. Mem. Purchasing Mgmt. Assn. Ariz. affiliate of Nat. Assn. Purchasing Mgmt. Democrat. Methodist.

BRUNACINI, ALAN VINCENT, fire chief; b. Jamestown, N.Y., Apr. 18, 1937; s. John N. and Mary T. Brunacini; B.S., Ariz. State U., 1970, M.P.A., 1975; m. Rita McDaugh, Feb. 14, 1959; children—Robert Nicholas, John Nicholas, Mary Candice. Mem. Phoenix Fire Dept., 1959—, bn. chief, then asst. fire chief, 1971-78, fire chief, 1978—; condr. nat. seminar on fire dept. mgmt., 1970—. Redford scholar, 1968. Mem. Am. Soc. Public Adminstrn. (Superior Service award 1980), Nat. Fire Protection Assn. (chmn. fire service sect. 1974-78, dir. 1978), Internat. Assn. Fire Chiefs, Soc. Fire Service Instrs. Author: Fireground Command; also articles in field. Office: Office of Fire Chief 150 S 12th St Phoenix AZ 85034-2110*

BRUNDIN, BRIAN JON, lawyer; b. St. Paul, Oct. 11, 1939; s. Milton E. Brundin and LuVerne (Johnson) Roddan; m. Carolyn Bagley, June 30, 1961; children: Iana L. Sayer, Ian S., Dane E. BBA in Acctg. cum laude, U. Alaska, 1961; JD, Harvard U., 1964. Bar: Alaska 1966, U.S. Ct. Appeals (9th cir.) 1966, U.S. Supreme Ct. 1986; CPA, Alaska. Assoc. Hughes, Thorsness, Gantz, Powell & Brundin, Anchorage, 1966-70, ptnr., 1970-96, prin. ptnr., 1975-96, chair comml. div. and corp. sect., 1970-96, from vice-chmn. to chmn., 1972-82, mgmt. group, 1994-96; vis. asst. prof. acctg. Sch. Bus. and Pub. Policy, U. Alaska, Anchorage, 1996—; instr. acctg. and law U. Alaska, 1965-69; bd. dirs., pres. Brundin, Inc., 1979—, Kyak Oil, Inc., 1985-90; bd. dirs., sec. Far North Fishermen, Inc., 1981-85; trustee Humana Hosp. Alaska, 1982-83; adv. bd. World Trade Ctr. Alaska, 1992—. Chmn. subcom. on sales taxes Operation Breakthrough, Anchorage, 1968; mem. U. Alaska Bd. Regents, 1969-77, chmn. fin. com., 1970-75, v.p. 1973-75, pres., 1975-77; mem. Alaska Postsecondary Commn., 1973-75; founder, trustee U. Alaska Found., 1974-95, trustee emeritus, 1995—, pres., 1974-77, mem. exec. com., 1987—, chmn. Bullock prize for execellence com., 1989—; Alaska chmn. Harvard U. Law Sch. Fund, 1975-78; mem. adv. bd. alaska Ctr. for Internat. Bus., 1986-88; trustee AnchorAGE Sr. Ctr., Inc. Endowment Fund, 1996—. Capt. U.S. Army, 1964-66. Mem. ABA, AICPA, Anchorage Bar Assn. (legis com.), Alaska Bar Assn. (ethics and client security, corp. banking, bus. law and taxation WICHE, higher edn.), Am. Acad. Hosp. Attys., Am. Soc. Atty./CPAs, Alaska Soc. CPAs, U. Alaska Alumni Assn. (pres. Anchorage chpt. 1968-69), Sons of Norway, Pioneers of Alaska Igloo 15, Am. Legion, Amvets, Lions, Rotary, Ancient Teachings of Masters (bd. dirs., treas.).

BRUNELL, DAVID H., information systems manager; b. 1946. BA in History, U. N.Mex., 1970, MA in European History, 1974; MLS, U. Mich., 1976. Rsch. asst. U. Mich., Ann Arbor, 1974-76; sys. specialist U. N.Mex., Albuquerque, 1976-79; network libr. Libr. Congress, Washington, 1979-83; exec. dir., sec., treas. Bibliog. Ctr., Aurora, Colo., 1983—. Office: Bibliog Ctr 14394 E Evans Ave Aurora CO 80014-1408

BRUNELLO-MCCAY, ROSANNE, sales executive; b. Cleve., Aug. 26, 1960; d. Carl Carmello and Vivan Lucille (Caranna) B.; divorced, 1991; m. Walter B. McCay, Feb. 26, 1994; 1 child, Angela Breanna. Student, U. Cin., 1978-81, Cleve. State U., 1981-82. Indsl. sales engr. Alta Machine Tool, Denver, 1982; mem. sales./purchases Ford Tool & Machine, Denver, 1982-84; sales/ptnr. Mountain Rep. Enterprises, Denver, 1984-86; pres., owner Mountain Rep. Ariz., Phoenix, 1986—; pres. Mountain Rep. Oreg., Portland, 1990—, Mountain Rep. Wash., 1991—; sec. Computer & Automated Systems Assoc., 1987, vice chmn., 1988, chmn., 1989. Active mem. Rep. Party, 1985—; mem. Phoenix Art Mus., Grand Canyon Minority Coun., 1994; vol. Make-A-Wish Found., 1995-96. Named Mrs. Chandler Internat. by Mrs. Ariz. Internat. orgn., 1996, Mrs. East Valley U.S., 1997; finalist Mrs. Ariz. Internat., 1996. Mem. NAFE, Soc. Mfg. Engrs. (pres. award 1988), Computer Automated Assn. (sec. 1987, vice chmn. 1988 chmn. 1989), Nat. Hist. Soc., Italian Cultural Soc., Tempe C. of C., Vocat. Ednl. Club Am. (mem. exec. bd., pres. 1987—). Roman Catholic. Office: Mountain Rep Ariz 410 S Jay St Chandler AZ 85224-7668

BRUNER, CINDY HULL, judge; b. Waterbury, Conn., Apr. 26, 1949; d. Harry Garfield Jr. and Ella Betsey (Houghton) Hull (dec.); m. Jack Dennis Bruner, Sept. 24, 1988; children. BS, U. Vt., 1979; JD, U. Colo., 1984. Bar: Colo. 1984, U.S. Dist. Ct. Colo., 1985. Law clk. U.S. Dist. Ct., Denver, 1984-85; dep. dist. atty. Adams County, Brighton, Colo., 1985-91; count. ct. judge 17th Jud. Dist., Brighton, 1991—; mem. Colo. Supreme Ct. Criminal Rules Com., 1995—. coach h.s. mock trial competition, 1986-88, judge, 1990-97, judge nat. semi-finals and finals, 1994; mem. Vol. Probation Bd., 1995—; mem. adv. com. Almost Home, 1995—; vol. scripter Pub. TV Art Auction, 1992—; vol. host. refugee families Ecumenical Refugee Svcs., 1996—. Mem. Colo. Bar Assn. (criminal law sect. exec. coun. 1993—), Adams County Bar Assn. Office: Hall of Justice 17th Jud Dist 1931 E Bridge St Brighton CO 80601-1937

BRUNETT, ALEXANDER J., bishop; b. Detroit, MI, Jan. 13, 1958. ordained priest July 13, 1958. Ordained bishop Diocese of Helena, 1994. Office: Chancery Diocesan Pastoral Office 515 North Ewing PO Box 1729 Helena MT 59624*

BRUNETTI, MELVIN T., federal judge; b. 1933; m. Gail Dian Buchanan; children: Nancy, Bradley, Melvin Jr. Student, U. Nev.; JD, U. Calif., San Francisco, 1964. Mem. firm Vargas, Bartlett & Dixon, 1964-69, Laxalt, Bell, Allison & Lebaron, 1970-78, Allison, Brunetti, MacKenzie, Hartman, Soumbeniotis & Russell, 1978-85; judge U.S. Ct. Appeals (9th cir.), Reno, 1985—. Mem. Council of Legal Advisors, Rep. Nat. Com., 1982-85. Served with U.S. Army N.G., 1954-56. Mem. ABA, State Bar of Nev. (pres. 1984-85, bd. govs. 1975-84). Office: US Ct Appeals US Courthouse 400 S Virginia St # 506 Reno NV 89501-1948

BRUNK, PATRICK CHARLES ROY, mental health professional, counselor; b. Tonasket, Wash., June 5, 1959; s. Charles H. and Margie J. (Stockham) B. BS in Psychology, Warner Pacific Coll., 1983; MEd, Heritage Coll., 1991. Cert. counselor, child and adolescent treatment specialist, Wash. Social worker, mental health counselor II Carondelet Psychiat. Care Ctr., Richland, Wash., 1985-88; county designated mental health profl. Carondelet Psychiat. Care Ctr., Richland, Wash., 1988-91; co-therapist Inner Directions Counselling, Kennewick, Wash., 1990-94; county designated mental health profl. Benton County, Kennewick, Wash., 1992—; employee assistance counselor Personal Counselling Svc., Hermiston, Oreg., 1994—; pvt. practitioner Umatilla County Anger Mgmt. Program, Hermiston, Oreg., 1994—; co-instr. psychology Yakima Valley C.C., Grandview, Wash., 1990-91, Columbia Basin Coll., Pasco, Wash., 1990-93. Office: Personal Counselling Svc 955 W Orchard Ave Hermiston OR 97838-1536

BRUNNER, HOWARD WILLIAM, professional land surveyor; b. Mobile, Ala., July 24, 1946; s. Joseph Edward and Beaulah (Howard) B.; m. Linda Marie Parker, Dec. 20, 1963 (div. June 1978); children: Leah Marie, Anne Marie; m. Catherine Cecilia Byrnes, June 27, 1981; 1 child, Jordan Thomas Howard. Grad. high sch., Santa Rosa, Calif. Lic. profl. land surveyor, Calif., Wash., Nev. Survey technician Roemer & Estes, Mill Valley, Calif., 1964-65, Ken Frost & Assocs., Mill Valley, 1965-66; engring. aide County of Marin, San Rafael, Calif., 1966-75; pres. Engring. Field Svcs., San Rafael, 1975-77, Brunner, Phelps & Assocs., Inc., Cotati, Calif., 1977-80; v.p. Ray Carlson & Assocs., Inc., Santa Rosa, Calif., 1980-92; ptnr. Bedford Brunner, Santa Rosa, 1993-96; prin. Howard W. Brunner, Profl. Land Surveyor, Santa Rosa, 1996—; expert examiner, profl. land surveyor, cons., registrar, tech. adv. com. mem., expert witness, chmn. item writing com. Bd. Registration for Profl. Engrs. and Land Surveyors, Sacramento, 1985-96. Mem. Geysers Geothermal Assn. (bd. dirs. 1985-92), Calif. Land Surveyors Assn. (treas. 1987-88, sec. 1988-89, pres. 1990), Am. Consulting Engrs. Coun. (chmn. coun. profl. land surveyors 1995-96). Roman Catholic. Home: 1161 Valley View Dr Healdsburg CA 95448-4540 Office: 320 College Ave Ste 220 Santa Rosa CA 95401

BRUNO, HAROLD ROBINSON, III, lawyer; b. Chgo., Oct. 7, 1960; s. Harold Robinson Jr. and Margaret (Christian) B.; m. Brenda Joy Johnson, Dec. 30, 1982; children: Claire, Madeline. BS in Fin. with honors, U. Ill., 1982; JD, U. Colo., 1985. Bar: Colo. 1985, D.C. 1988, Va. 1991, U.S. Dist. Ct. Colo. 1985, U.S. Dist. Ct. D.C. 1989, U.S. Ct. Appeals (4th, 10th, and fed. cirs.) 1989. Assoc. Koronsky, Friedman & Cohen, P.C., Denver, 1985-88, Hopper, Kanouff et al, Denver, 1988-89, Ward, Lazarus & Grow, Washington, 1989-92, Hopper & Kanouff, P.C., Denver, 1992-96; dir. Smith, McCullough and Ferguson P.C., Denver, 1996—. Atty. U. Colo. Legal Aid, Boulder, 1984-85. Mem. ABA, Colo. Bar Assn., Denver Bar Assn., D.C. Bar Assn., Fairfax Bar Assn., Forum on Franchising. Home: 2309 Birch St Denver CO 80207-3130 Office: Smith McCullough & Ferguson 1610 Wynkoop St Ste 300 Denver CO 80202-1135

BRUNO, JUDYTH ANN, chiropractor; b. Eureka, Calif., Feb. 16, 1944; d. Harold Oscar and Shirley Alma (Farnsworth) Nelson; m. Thomas Glenn Bruno, June 1, 1968; 1 child, Christina Elizabeth. AS, Sierra Coll., 1982; D of Chiropractic, Palmer Coll. of Chiropractic West, Sunnyvale, Calif., 1986. Diplomate Nat. Bd. Chiropractic Examiners. Sec. Bank Am., San Jose, Calif., 1965-67; marketer Memorex, Santa Clara, Calif., 1967-74; order entry clk. John Deere, Milan, Ill., 1977; system analyst Four Phase, Cupertino, Calif., 1977-78; chiropractic asst. Dr. Thomas Bruno, Nevada City, Calif., 1978-81; chiropractor Chiropractic Health Care Ctr., Nevada City, 1987—; pvt. practice Cedar Ridge, Calif., 1991—. Area dir. Cultural Awareness Coun., Grass Valley, Calif., 1977—; vol. Nevada County Libr., Nevada City, 1987-88, Decide Team III, Nevada County, 1987-92, Active Parenting of Teen Facilitator Nev. Union H.S., 1989-93, judge sr. projects, 1992—; noetic scis. mem. women's forum, 1995—. Mem. Am. Chiropractic Assn., Women Health Practitioners of Nevada County (founder 1993—), Nevada County C. of C. (vol. task force health care 1993), Toastmasters (sec. 1988, pres. 1989, edn. v.p. 1990), Women's Forum, Noetic Scis. Republican. Office: Chiropractor Health Care PO Box 1718 Cedar Ridge CA 95924-1718

BRUNO, PETER JACKSON, counselor, consultant, pastor; b. White Plains, N.Y., Dec. 27, 1945; s. Charles Fredrick and Barbara (Jackson) B.; m. Barbara Suesens; 1 child, Linda; 2d m. Corky Jean Brown, July 3, 1976; children: Benjamin, Elizabeth. BA in Psychology, Brown U., 1968; MEd in Counseling, Mont. State U., 1978. Lic. min. Evangelical Ch.; lic. profl. counselor, Mont.; nat. cert. counselor. Addictive disease counselor Mont. State Hosp., Galen, 1973-76; tchg. asst. Mont. State U., Bozeman, 1977-78; psychologist V Ea. Mont. Mental Health, Miles City, 1979-92; pvt. practice counselor Glendive, Mont., 1992—; clin. cons. Dept. Damily Svcs., Miles City, Home on the Range, Sentinel Butte, N.D., Pine Hills Sch., Miles City, all 1992-94; lead clin. staff Big Sky Ranch, Glendive, 1992—. Author: New Ways Workbook, 1992. Pres. Montanans for Children, Youth and Families, Inc.; leader, pastor, tchr. Evangelical Ch. Named Mont.'s Outstanding Direct Svc. Provider, Mental Health Assn. Mont., 1982. Mem. Am. Profl. Soc. on the Abuse of Children, Great Plains Counseling Assocs. (dir.), Toastmasters Internat. (Disting. Leadership award 1995), Nat. Spkrs. Assn., Internat. Platform Assn. Office: Great Plains Christian Counseling PO Box 684 513 N Merrill Ave Glendive MT 59330

BRUNS, JUDSON LEROY, III, diplomat; b. Hollywood, Calif., Apr. 27, 1954; s. Judson Leroy Jr. and Virginia Lee (Edwards) B.; m. Katherine Tully Breer, July 15, 1989; children: Timothy, Lucas, Virginia. BA, Colo. Coll., 1976; postgrad., U. Copenhagen, 1974-75; MA, George Washington U., 1979. Vice consul U.S. Embassy, Oslo, 1979-81; 2d sec. U.S. Embassy, Bonn, Germany, 1981-83; spl. asst. to dep. sec. U.S. State Dept., Washington, 1986-87; dir. for investment U.S. Trade Reps. Office, Washington, 1987-88; 1st sec., charge d'affaires U.S. Embassy, Port-of-Spain, Trinidad and Tobago, 1988-91; 1st sec. U.S. Embassy, Tokyo, 1992-96; U.S. consul gen. U.S. Consulate Gen., Vancouver, B.C., Can., 1996—; mem. adv. bd. coun. for N.Am. bus. studies Simon Fraser U., Vancouver, 1996—. Mem. Pacific Corridor Enterprise Coun. (hon.), Vancouver Lawn Tennis and Badminton Club, Pallisades Tennis and Swim Club.

BRUNSON, MABEL (DIPPER), researcher; b. Oshoto, Wyo., Mar. 24, 1934; d. Robert Emmet and Gennevieve Mae (Irwin) Brislawn; m. Donald George Brunson, Jan. 1, 1959; children: Daniel F., David G. Student, Nieman's Bus. Coll., 1956. Rschr., sec. Bob Brislawn, Spanish Mustang Registry Inc., Oshoto, 1943-79; legal sec. Scotty Gladstone/Richard Macy law offices, Sundance, Wyo., 1957-58; cons. Bob Brislawn, Spanish Mustang Registry Inc., 1957—; sec., clk. Farmers Home Adminstrn., Sundance, 1958-59, Soil Conservation Svc., Sundance, 1975-82. Co-author: Spanish Mustang Registry, Inc., 1996; author: Mr. Mustang, Life of Bob Brislawn, 1997, also brochures in field. Sec., treas. Homemaker's Clubs, Wyo., 1959-76; religious tchr. Cath. Chs., Upton and Sundance, Wyo., 1965-80, eucharistic min., Sundance, 1984-97; cub scout leader Boy Scouts Am., Sundance, 1972-79. Recipient Svc. award Boy Scouts Am., 1979; named Centennial Woman of Yr. St. Paul's Cath. Ch., 1990. Avocations: history, genealogy, western art, writing. Office: Brunson Enterprises 1310 Oak Creek Rd Aladdin WY 82710

BRUNSTAD, MICHAEL LEWIS, elementary education educator; b. Aberdeen, Wash., Nov. 17, 1956; s. William Ray and Diane (Mason) B.; m. Kathleen Rochelle Close, Apr. 8, 1989; children: Roger Russell Tryon, Mason Ray. Student, Grays Harbor Coll., 1975-77; BA in Edn., Western Wash. U., 1981; postgrad., Ctrl. Wash. U., 1984-86, U. Alaska, 1992—. Cert. tchr. Alaska, Wash. Subs. tchr. Renton (Wash.), Kent (Wash.) and Auburn (Wash). Sch. Dists., 1981-84; tchr. jr.-sr. high sch. Wishram (Wash.) Sch. Dist., 1984-86; tchr. phys. edn. K-12 Quinault Lake Sch. Dist., Amanda Park, Wash., 1986-87; mgr. Nautilus Fitness Ctr., Aberdeen, 1987-88; recreation supr. Clallam Bay (Wash.) Correction Ctr. for Men, 1988-90; tchr. elem. edn. Cape Flattery Sch. Dist., Sekiu, Wash., 1990-91, Anchorage (Alaska) Sch. Dist., 1991—; head coach girl's basketball team Wishram High Sch., 1984-85, head coach volleyball team, 1984, 85; head coach football team Lake Quinault High Sch., Amanda Park, 1986; asst. coach wrestling Clark Jr. High Sch., Anchorage, 1992; summer Day camp dir. Anchorage Parks and Recreation, Municipality of Anchorage, 1993; asst. football coach Nea Bay (Wash.) H.S., 1990. Contbr. articles to profl. jours. Soccer and football coach Boys & Girls Club, 1993—. Named Eagle Scout Boy Scouts Am., 1973. Mem. Elks (dir. hoop shoot lodge # 1351 1995—). Home: 3812 Deborah Ln Anchorage AK 99504 Office: Anchorage Sch Dist 4600 Debarr Rd Anchorage AK 99508-3126

BRUST, DAVID, physicist; b. Chgo., Aug. 24, 1935; s. Clifford and Ruth (Klapman) B.; BS, Calif. Inst. Tech., 1957; MS, U. Chgo., 1958, PhD, 1964. Rsch. assoc. Purdue U., Lafayette, Ind., 1963-64; rsch. assoc. Northwestern U., Evanston, Ill., 1964-65, asst. prof. physics, 1965-68; theoretical rsch. physicist U. Calif., Lawrence Radiation Lab., Livermore, Calif., 1968-73; cons. Bell Telephone Lab., Murray Hill, N.J., 1966. Campaign co-ordinator No. Calif. Scientists and Engrs. for McGovern, 1972. NSF travel grantee, 1964; NSF rsch. grantee, 1966-68. Mem. Am. Phys. Soc., Am. Assn. Coll. Profs., Internat. Solar Energy Soc., Astron. Soc. of Pacific, Nature Conservancy, Calif. Acad. Sci., Commonwealth Club of Calif., World Affairs Coun. No. Calif. Commonwealth Club Anza Borrego Desert, Natural History Assn., Planetary Soc., Sierra Club, Sigma Xi. Office: PO Box 13130 Oakland CA 94661-0130

BRYA, WILLIAM JOHN, anesthesiologist; b. Chgo., Mar. 30, 1938; s. William George and Julie Anne (Mikalansky) B.; m. Catherine Anne Froehlich, June 26, 1965; children: Jacqueline Anne, Lara Michele, Jennifer Rene, Kristen Elisabeth. B of Engring. Sci., Johns Hopkins U., 1960, PhD, 1966; MD, U. Miami, 1975. Diplomate Am. Bd. Anesthesiology. Postdoctoral fellow Bell Tel. Labs., Murray Hill, N.J., 1966-69; staff scientist Sandia Labs., Albuquerque, 1969-73; intern U. Calif., San Diego, 1975-76, resident in anesthesiology, 1976-78; pvt. practice, Albuquerque, 1978—. Mem. AMA, Tau Beta Pi, Eta Kappa Nu, Omicron Delta Kappa. Republican. Roman Catholic. Office: Surgery Ctr Albuquerque 1720 Wyoming Blvd NE Albuquerque NM 87112-3855

BRYAN, A(LONZO) J(AY), service club official; b. Washington, N.J., Sept. 17, 1917; s. Alonzo J. and Anna Belle (Babcock) B.; student pub. schs.; m. Elizabeth Elfreida Koehler, June 25, 1941 (div. 1961); children: Donna Elizabeth, Alonzo Jay, Nadine; m. Janet Dorothy Onstad, Mar. 15, 1962 (div. 1977); children: Brenda Joyce, Marlowe Francis, Marilyn Janet. Engaged as retail florist, Washington, N.J., 1941-64. Fund drive chmn. ARC, 1952; bd. dirs. Washington YMCA, 1945-55, N.J. Taxpayers Assn., 1947-52; mem. Washington Bd. Edn., 1948-55. Mem. Washington Grange, Sons and Daus. of Liberty, Soc. Am. Florists, Nat. Fedn. Ind. Businessmen, Florists Telegraph Delivery Assn., C. of C. Methodist. Clubs: Masons, Tall Cedars of Lebanon, Jr. Order United Am. Mechanics, Kiwanis (pres. Washington (N.J.) 1952, lt. gov. internat. 1953-54, gov. N.J. dist. 1955, sec. N.J. dist. 1957-64, sec. S.E. area Chgo. 1965-74; editor The Jersey Kiwanian 1958-64, internat. staff 1964-85); Breakfast (pres. 1981-82) (Chgo.); sec., treas. Rocky Mtn. Kiwanis Dist., 1989; pres. South Denver, 1990-91; editor Rocky Mountain Kiwanian, 1990-96. Home: 8115 S Poplar Way Englewood CO 80112-3174 Office: 8859 Fox Dr # 100 Denver CO 80221

BRYAN, GORDON REDMAN, JR., nuclear power engineering consultant; b. Cleve., Dec. 1, 1928; s. Gordon Redman and Iola (Schecter) B.; m. Janet Louise McIntyre, Aug. 1, 1951 (div. Oct. 1985); children: Gordon L., Steven G.; m. Judith Hager, July 5, 1987. BA, Brown U., 1951; MS, George Washington U., 1970. Commd. ensign USN, 1951, advanced through grades to capt., 1971; comdg. officer 4 navy ships and 5 shore commands, 1965-78, submarine squadron, 1972-74; ret., 1978; marine design cons. various aerospace and engring. cos., Seattle, 1979-81; engring. cons. U.S. Nuc. Regulatory Commn. and U.S. Dept. Energy, Seattle, 1982-95. Decorated Legion of Merit. Mem. Am. Nuclear Soc., Am. Radio Relay League, N.Y. Acad. Scis.,

Rotary. Republican. Home and Office: Saddle Brook Country Club 37810 S Rolling Hills Dr Tucson AZ 85739 also: PO Box 1285 Bay View MI 49770-1285

BRYAN, JOHN RODNEY, management consultant; b. Berkeley, Calif., Dec. 29, 1953; s. Robert Richard and Eloise (Anderson) Putz; m. Karen Nelson, Jan. 20, 1990. BA in Chemistry, U. Calif., San Diego, 1975; MBA, Rutgers U., 1985. Agt. Prudential, San Diego, 1975-79; sales mgr. Herman Schlorman Showrooms, L.A., 1980-83; pvt. practice mgmt. cons. Basking Ridge, N.J., 1983-85; mgmt. cons. The Brooks Group, Hollywood, Fla., 1985—; pvt. practice San Diego, 1988—; with Western Productivity Group, 1990-95. Elder La Jolla Presbyn. Ch., 1991—. Mem. ASPA, Inst. Indsl. Engring., Rutgers Club So. Calif., Beta Gamma Sigma. Office: Applied Control Mgmt Effectiveness Sys 6265 Hurd Ct San Diego CA 92122

BRYAN, RICHARD H., senator; b. Washington, July 16, 1937; married; 3 children. B.A., U. Nev., 1959; LL.B., U. Calif.-San Francisco, 1963. Bar: Nev. 1963. Dep. dist. atty. Clark County, Nev., 1964-66; public defender Clark County, 1966-68; counsel Clark County Juvenile Ct., 1968-69; mem. Nev. Assembly, 1969-73, Nev. Senate, 1973-79; atty. gen. State Nev., 1979-83, gov., 1983-89; senator from Nevada U.S. Senate, 1989—; mem. U.S. Senate coms. on commerce, sci. and transp.; mem. Dem. Policy Com.; mem. Fin. Com.; mem. Banking, Housing and Urban Affairs Com.; mem. Sen. Nom. Steering and Coor. Com.; mem. select. Com. on Intelligence. Bd. dirs. March of Dimes; former v.p. Nev. Easter Seal Soc.; former pres. Clark County Legal Aid Soc. Served with U.S. Army, 1959-60. Recipient Disting. Svc. award Vegas Valley Jaycees. Mem. ABA, Clark County Bar Assn., Am. Judicature Soc., Council of State Govts. (past pres.), Phi Alpha Delta, Phi Alpha Theta. Democrat. Clubs: Masons, Lions, Elks. Office: US Senate 364 Russell Senate Bldg Washington DC 20510

BRYAN, ROBERT J., federal judge; b. Bremerton, Wash., Oct. 29, 1934; s. James W. and Vena Gladys (Jensen) B.; m. Cathy Ann Welander, June 14, 1958; children: Robert James, Ted Lorin, Ronald Terence. BA, U. Wash., 1956, JD, 1958. Bar: Wash. 1959, U.S. Dist. Ct. (we. dist.) Wash. 1959, U.S. Tax Ct. 1965, U.S. Ct. Appeals (9th cir.) 1985. Assoc., then ptnr. Bryan & Bryan, Bremerton, 1959-67; judge Superior Ct., Port Orchard, Wash., 1967-84; ptnr. Riddell, Williams, Bullitt & Walkinshaw, Seattle, 1984-86; judge U.S. Dist. Ct. (we. dist.) Wash., Tacoma, 1986—; mem. State Jail Comm., Olympia, Wash., 1974-76, Criminal Justice Tng. Com., Olympia, 1978-81, State Bd. on Continuing Legal Edn., Seattle, 1984-86; mem., sec. Jud. Qualifications Commn., Olympia, 1982-83. Author: (with others) Washington Pattern Jury Instructions (civil and criminal vols. and supplements), 1970-85, Manual of Model Criminal Jury Instructions for the Ninth Circuit, 1992, Manual of Model Civil Jury Instruction for the Ninth Circuit, 1993. Chmn. 9th Ct. Jury Com., 1991-92. Served to maj. USAR. Office: US Dist Ct 1717 Pacific Ave Rm 4427 Tacoma WA 98402-3234

BRYANT, ARTHUR STEVEN, public relations executive; b. Warner Robins, Ga., June 8, 1956; s. Arthur Bowman Bryant and Betty Sue (Doke) Golden; m. Demian, Sept. 1, 1981. BS in Music, Psychology and Sociology, U. State N.Y., Albany, 1987. Accredited bus. communicator. Profl. singer classical music San Francisco, 1980-85; co-dir. Ptnrs. Task Force for Gay and Lesbian Couples, Seattle, 1986—; sr. v.p. gen. mgr., health mktg. Evans Group, Seattle, 1986—. Bd. mem. Seafair, Seattle, 1995-96. Recipient award of merit Soc. Tech. Comm. 1988, award of merit for videotape L.A. Bus./Profl. Advt. Assn., 1988, 2nd pl. for non-for-profit comm. rels. Wash. Press Assn., 1988, 3rd pl. for media kits Wash. Press Assn., 1989, 2nd pl. for one-to-three color bus. newsletters Wash. Press Assn., 1989, 1st pl. for one-to-three color bus. newsletters Wash. Press Assn., 1989, Totem award Pub. Rels. Soc. Am., 1989, award for achievement in poster design Soc. Tech. Comm. 1991-92, 3rd pl. for news releases Wash. Press Assn., 1990, 2nd pl. for advt. BioMed. Mktg. Assn., 1991, award of merit for outside newsletters Soc. Tech. Comm., 1992, Best of Show and Disting. award for newsletters Soc. Tech. Comm., 1993, 1st pl. Totem award Pub. Rels. Soc. Am., 1993, 1st pl. for original film or video Wash. Press Assn., 1993, 2nd pl. for original film or video Wash. Press Assn., 1993, 2nd pl. Totem award Pub. Rels. Soc. Am., 1993, 2nd pl. for four-color brochures Wash. Press Assn., 1993, 1st pl. for video Nat. Fedn. Press Women 1994, 1st pl. for pub. svc. Wash. Press Assn., 1994, 2nd pl for comm. rels. Wash. Press Assn., 1994, 2nd pl. for mktg. campaign for new product Wash. Press Assn., 1994, award of merit for publs. Soc. Tech. Comm., 1994-95, 1st pl. for video Pub. Rels. Soc. Am., 1995, 1st pl. for spl. print comm. Pub. Rels. Soc. Am., 1995. Mem. Med. Mktg. Assn., Internat. Assn. Bus. Communicators (award of excellence for sales promotion brochures 1989, award of merit for tech. writing 1992, award of excellence for sales/mktg. videos 1994, award of merit 1994, award of merit for sales/mktg. videos 1994, award of merit for multimedia 1995, award of merit 1995, awards for excellence and merit for print comm. 1995, award of merit for brochure design 1995, award of merit for brochure writing 1995, awards of excellence for corp. image video, brochures and materials for spl. events and external comm. programs, awards of merit for pub. svc. announcements, sales video and pro bono video 1996). Democrat. Office: Evans Group 190 Queen Anne Ave N Seattle WA 98109-4926

BRYANT, CAROL LEE, public health educator, psychotherapist, consultant; b. L.A., Aug. 17, 1946; d. John Thomas and Janice Hathaway (Haislip) B.; m. Norman Alexander, June 4, 1966 (div. 1975); children: Ian Alexander, Colin Alexander; m. Reinhard Alexander Fritsch, June 14, 1983; 1 child, Briana Noelle Fritsch-Bryant. AA, Diablo Valley Jr. Coll., Pleasant Hill, Calif., 1975; BA, San Francisco State U., 1978; MA in Transpersonal Counseling, John F. Kennedy U., Orinda, Calif., 1982, MA in Clin. Psychology, 1982; PhD in Clin. Psychology, Sierra U., 1986. Lic. marriage, family, and child counselor, Calif. Instr., tchr. Community Recreation YWCA, Walnut Creek, Calif., 1970-80, John F. Kennedy U., Orinda, Calif., 1980-81; adminstrv. dir. Touchstone Counseling Svc., Walnut Creek, 1981-83; tchr. Diablo Valley Jr. Coll., 1984; exec. dir. Battered Women's Alternatives, Concord, Calif., 1984-85, Child Abuse Prevention Coun., Walnut Creek, 1985-90; psychotherapist InVision Assocs., Lafayette, Calif., 1984-94; pub. health educator Mariposa (Calif.) Health Dept., 1990—; cons. Computer Using Educators, Menlo Park, Calif., 1988-90; lectr. in field; mem., chairperson Mariposa Mental Health Adv. Bd.; vice chairperson Mariposa Drug and Alcohol Adv. Bd., maternal child health adv. bd., mem. John C. Fremont Hosp. Found. Contbr. articles to profl. jours. and books. Chmn. No. Calif. Legis. Children and Family Coalition, Berkeley, 1987-90; adv. bd., chmn. Women's Recovery Ctr., Bass Lake, Calif., 1990-92; coord./mem. No. Calif. Child Death Review Coalition, San Francisco, 1988-90, Children and Family Trust Fund Com., Concord, 1989-90. Mem. Assn. Marriage Family Therapists. Home: 4821 Crystal Aire Dr Mariposa CA 95338-9039 Office: Mariposa Pub Health Dept PO Box 5 Mariposa CA 95338-0005

BRYANT, DON ESTES, economist, scientist; b. Truman, Ark., May 18, 1917; s. James Monroe and Olivia (Mayfield) B.; m. Jess Ann Chailer, Jan. 27, 1956; children: Stephen Williamson (dec.), Patrice Ann. Student, Cass Tech. Trade Coll., 1938-41. Pres., founder Consol. Aircraft Products, El Segundo, Calif., 1949-57, Trilan Corp., El Segundo, 1957-62, The Am. Inventor, Palos Verdes Estates, Calif., 1962-68; chmn., founder Message Control Crop., Palos Verdes Estates, 1968-70; scientist Econ. Rsch., Palos Verdes Estates and Lake Arrowhead, Calif., 1970—; cons. Svc. Corps. Ret. Execs. Assn.-SBA, L.A., 1965-67; founder Bryant Inst. and Club U.S.A. (United to Save Am.), 1991, J. Ayn Bryant and Assocs., 1991. Inventor missle and satellite count-down systems for USAF, 1958; formulator sci. of human econs.; host TV talk show World Peace Through Free Enterprise, 1985; author: 10-book children's series The 1, 2, 3's of Freedom and Economics, 1988. Served with USN, 1935-37. Republican. Roman Catholic. Home: 329 Greenview Ln Fallbrook CA 92028

BRYANT, THOMAS LEE, magazine editor; b. Daytona Beach, Fla., June 15, 1943; s. Stanley Elson and G. Bernice (Burgess) B.; m. Patricia Jean Bryant, June 30, 1979. BA in Polit. Sci., U. Calif., Santa Barbara, 1965, MA in Polit. Sci., 1966. Fgn. svc. officer U.S. Dept. State, Washington, Buenos Aires, 1967-69; radio broadcaster KDB Sta., Santa Barbara, Calif., 1969-72; magazine editor, now editor-in-chief Road & Track, Newport Beach, Calif., 1972—. Mem. Internat. Motor Press Assn., Motor Press Guild, Sports Car Club of Am. Office: Road & Track 1499 Monrovia Ave Newport Beach CA 92663-2752*

BRYANT, WOODROW WESLEY, architect; b. San Jose, Calif., June 5, 1949; s. Foy Eldean and Loraine (McKee) B.; m. Becky Ann Hoffmaster, June 27, 1981; 1 stepson: Jeremy Saul Martin. Student, Am. River Coll., Sacramento, Calif., 1968; BArch, Calif. State Polytechnic U., 1973. Registered architect, Calif., Nev., Utah, Idaho, Ariz. Designer, project mgr. Angello & Vitiello Assoc., Sacramento, 1971-75; draftsman Caywood, Nopp & Ward, Sacramento, 1975; architect W. Bryant Enterprises, Sacramento, 1975-76, Wright, Bryant & Johnson, Ketchum, Idaho, 1976—; bd. dirs. Elkhorn Archtl. Design Commn., Uniform Bldg. Code Bd. Appeals, Ketchum, Uniform Fire Code Bd. Appeals, Ketchum, Blaine County, Idaho. Recipient Best Archtl. Interior Detailing award, Custom Builder mag., 1993. Mem. AIA. Office: Wright Bryant & Johnson PO Box 21 Sun Valley ID 83353-0021*

BRYCE, MARK ADAMS, artist, painter; b. San Francisco, July 4, 1953; s. James Mayo and Corinne (Howe) B.; m. Shirley Lynn Grant, 1972 (div. 1985). Cert., Pa. Acad. of Fine Art, 1975. Tchr. Pa. Acad. of Art, Phila., 1978-82. Solo painting exhbns. include Butler Inst. Am. Art, 1982, Del. Art Mus., Wilmington, 1983, Marian Locks Gallery, 1988, James Corcoran Gallery, Santa Monica, Calif., 1992, Brian Gross Fine Arts, San Francisco, 1995; group show include Phila. Mus. Art, 1990, Contemporary Landscapes Larry Evans Gallery, San Francisco, 1994, Palm Springs Mus., 1995; permanent collection De Young Mus. Recipient Outstanding Landscape award Calif. State Fair, Outstanding Painting award Phila. Civic Ctr. Mus., 1994, Best of Show N.J. State Mus. Home and Office: 1625 Balboa St San Francisco CA 94121-3114

BRYCHEL, RUDOLPH MYRON, engineer, consultant; b. Milw., Dec. 4, 1934; s. Stanley Charles and Jean Ann (Weiland) B.; m. Rose Mary Simmons, Sept. 3, 1955; children: Denise, Rita, Rudolph Myron Jr., Patrick, Bradford, Matthew. Student, U. Wis., Stevens Point, 1953, U.S. Naval Acad., 1954-55, U. Del., 1957, Colo. State U., 1969, North Park Coll., Chgo., 1973, Regis U., Denver, 1990-91. Lab. and quality tech. Thiokol Chem. Co., Elkton, Md., 1956; final test insp. Martin Aircraft Co., Middle River, Md., 1956-57; system final insp. Delco Electronics Co., Oak Creek, Wis., 1957-58; test equipment design engr. Martin Marietta Co., Littleton, Colo., 1958-64; prodn. supr. Gates Rubber Co., Denver, Colo., 1964-65; freelance mfr., quality and project engr. Denver and Boulder, Colo., Raton, N.Mex., 1965-67; quality engr. IBM, Gaithersburg (Md.), Boulder (Colo.), 1967-73; sr. quality engr. Abbott Labs., North Chicago, Ill., 1973-74; instrumentation and control engr. Stearns Roger Co., Glendale, Colo., 1974-81; staff quality engr. Storage Tech., Louisville, Colo., 1981-83; sr. quality engr. Johnson & Johnson Co., Englewood, Colo., 1983-84; quality engr., cons. Staodynamics Co., Longmont, Colo., 1984-85; sr. engr. for configuration and data mgmt. Martin Marietta Astronautics Group, Denver, 1985-91; freelance cons. Littleton, Colo., 1991—. With USN, 1953-56. Mem. Am. Soc. Quality Control (cert. quality engr.), Regulatory Affairs Profl. Soc., Soc. for Tech. Communications (regional chpt. chmn. 1970), KC. Democrat. Roman Catholic. Home and Office: 203 W Rafferty Gardens Ave Littleton CO 80120-1710

BRYDON, HAROLD WESLEY, entomologist, writer; b. Hayward, Calif., Dec. 6, 1923; s. Thomas Wesley and Hermione (McHenry) B.; m. Ruth Bacon Vickery, Mar. 28, 1951 (div.); children: Carol Ruth, Marilyn Jeanette, Kenneth Wesley. AB, San Jose State Coll., 1948; MA, Stanford U., 1950. Insecticide sales Calif. Spray Chem. Corp., San Jose, 1951-52; entomologist, fieldman, buyer Beech-Nut Packing Co., 1952-53; mgr., entomologist Lake County Mosquito Abatement Dist., Lakeport, Calif., 1954-58; entomologist, adviser Malaria Eradication Programs AID, Kathmandu, Nepal, 1958-61, Washington, 1961-62, Port-au-Prince, Haiti, 1962-63; dir. fly control research Orange County Health Dept. Santa Ana, Calif., 1963-66; free-lance writer in field, 1966—; research entomologist U. N.D. Sch. Medicine, 1968; developer, owner Casierra Resort, Lake Almanor, Calif., 1975-79; owner Westwood (Calif.) Sport Shop, 1979-84; instr. Lassen Community Coll., Susanville, Calif., 1975—; bio control cons., 1980—. Mem. entomology and plant pathology del. People to People Citizen Ambassador Program, China, 1986; citizen ambassador 30th Anniversary Caravan to Soviet Union, 1991, Vietnam Initiative Del., 1992, Initiative for Edn., Sci. and Tech. to The Republic of South Africa, 1995; mem. Bus. Intelligence Bd., 1995. Contbr. profl. jours. and conducted research in field. Served with USNR, 1943-46. Recipient (with others) Samuel Crumbine award to Orange County Health Dept., Calif., 1964, Meritorious Honor award for work in Nepal, AID, U.S. Dept. State, 1972. Mem. Entomol. Soc. Am., Am. Mosquito Control Assn., Pacific Coast Entomol. Soc., Am. Legion. Republican. Methodist. Club: Commonwealth of California. Lodges: Masons, Rotary. Home: PO Box 312 Westwood CA 96137-0312

BRYDON, RUTH VICKERY, history educator; b. San Jose, Calif., June 2, 1930; d. Robert Kingston and Ruth (Bacon) Vickery; m. Harold Wesley Brydon, Mar. 28, 1951 (div.); children: Carol Ruth Brydon Koford, Marilyn Jeanette, Kenneth Wesley. BA, Stanford U., 1952; student San Jose State Coll., 1964-65, MA, Calif. State Coll., Chico, 1987. Cert. tchr., Calif., cert. sch. adminstr. Tchr., Lincoln Sch., Kathmandu, Nepal, 1959-60; tchr. Am. Sch., Port-au-Prince, Haiti, 1962-63; tchr. social studies Norte Vista High Sch., Riverside, Calif., 1965-67, chmn. social studies dept., 1966-67; tchr. home econs., social studies Westwood (Calif.) H.S., 1967-90, mentor tchr., 1984-85; media specialist Lake Havasu H.S., 1990-91; history instr. Mohave C.C., Lake Havasu Campus, 1990—; instr. Elderhostel, 1992—; coord. extended day classes Lassen Coll., 1977-84. Author: Westwood, California: A Company Town in Comparative Perspective, 1900-1930, 1995. Co-chairperson Almanor Art Show, 1980-84. NDEA grantee, 1967. Mem. Archeol. Soc. Ariz. and Lake Havasu, Lake Havasu City Hist. Soc. (bd. dirs.). Episcopalian. Home: 2681 N Cisco Dr Lake Havasu City AZ 86403-5020

BRYNGELSON, JIM, educational administrator; b. Billings, Mont., Mar. 8, 1941; s. Ivan Carl and Clarie (Ellingwood) B.; m. Judy Bryngelson, June 29, 1969; children: Joy, Nick. Home: 1144 Henry Rd Billings MT 59102-0811 Office: Youth Dynamics 2601 Uir Ln Billings MT 59102

BRYSON, DOROTHY PRINTUP, retired educator; b. Britton, S.D., Dec. 2, 1894; d. David Lawrence and Marion Harland (Gamsby) Printup; m. Archer Butler Hulbert, June 16, 1923 (dec. Dec. 1933); children: Joanne Woodward, Nancy Printup; m. Franklin Fearing Wing, Oct. 15, 1938 (dec. Mar. 1942); m. Arthur Earl Bryson, Feb. 15, 1964 (dec. Apr. 1979). AB, Oberlin Coll., 1915; AM, Radcliffe Coll., 1916; LHD (hon.), Colo. Coll., 1989. Instr. Latin, Tenn. Coll., Murfreesboro, 1916-18; tchr. Latin, prin. high sch., Britton, 1918-20; instr. classics Colo. Coll., Colorado Springs, 1921-22, 23-25, sec., instr., head resident, 1951-60; tchr. latin San Luis Prep. Sch., Colorado Springs, 1934-36, 41-42, Sandia Sch., Albuquerque, 1937-39, Westlake Sch., L.A., 1946-49; exec. dir. YWCA, Colorado Springs, 1942-46, 49-51; editor western history Stewart Commn., Colorado Springs, 1934-41; ret., 1960. Editor: Overland to the Pacific, 5 vols., 1934-41. Bd. dirs. Day Nursery, Colorado Springs 1933-37. Fellow Aelioian Lit. Soc., 1920-21; scholar U. Chgo., 1920-21. Mem. LWV (v.p., bd. dirs. Colorado Springs 1943-45), Women's Edn. Soc. Colo. Coll. (pres., bd. dirs. 1955—), Reviewers Club, Tuesday Discussion Club, Pikes Peak Posse Westerners, Women's Literary Club, Phi Beta Kappa, Gamma Phi Beta. Republican. Episcopalian. Home: 107 W Cheyenne Rd Apt 610 Colorado Springs CO 80906-2509

BRYSON, GARY SPATH, cable television and telephone company executive; b. Longview, Wash., Nov. 8, 1943; s. Roy Griffin and Marguerite Elizabeth (Spath) B.; m. Bobbi Bryson; children: Kelly Suzanne, Lisa Christine. AB, Dartmouth Coll., 1966; MBA, Tuck Sch., 1967. With Bell & Howell Co., Chgo., 1967-79; pres. consumer and audio-visual group Bell & Howell Co., 1977-79; chmn. bd., CEO Bell & Howell Mamiya Co., Chgo., 1979-81; exec. v.p. Am. TV & Communications Corp., subs. Time, Inc., Englewood, Colo., 1981-88; v.p. diversified group US West, Englewood, 1988-89, pres. cable communications div., 1989-92; pres., CEO TeleWest Internat., 1992-93; pres. SkyConnect, Boulder, 1994-96; comm. cons., 1996—. Mem. Phi Beta Kappa, Sigma Alpha Epsilon. Republican. Lutheran. Home: 2221 Carriage Hills Dr Boulder CO 80302-9476

BRYSON, JOHN E., utilities company executive; b. N.Y.C., July 24, 1943; m. Louise Henry. B.A. with great distinction, Stanford U., 1965; student, Freie U. Berlin, Federal Republic Germany, 1965-66; J.D., Yale U., 1969. Bar: Calif., Oreg., D.C. Asst. in instrn. Law Sch., Yale U., New Haven, Conn., 1968-69; law clk. U.S. Dist. Ct., San Francisco, 1969-70; co-founder, atty. Natural Resources Def. Council, 1970-74; vice chmn. Oreg. Energy Facility Siting Council, 1975-76; assoc. Davies, Biggs, Strayer, Stoel & Boley, Portland, Oreg., 1975-76; chmn. Calif. State Water Resources Control Bd., 1976-79; vis. faculty Stanford U. Law Sch., Calif., 1977-79; pres. Calif. Pub. Utilities Commn., 1979-82; ptnr. Morrison & Foerster, San Francisco, 1983-84; sr. v.p. law and fin. So. Calif. Edison Co., Rosemead, 1984; exec. v.p., chief fin. officer Edison Internat. and So. Calif. Edison Co., 1985-90; chmn. of bd., CEO Edison Internat. and So. Calif. Edison Co., Rosemead, 1990—; lectr. on pub. utility, energy, communications law.; former mem. exec. com. Nat. Assn. Regulatory Utility Commrs., Calif. Water Rights Law Rev. Commn., Calif. Pollution Control Financing Authority; former mem. adv. bd. Solar Energy Research Inst., Electric Power Research Inst., Stanford Law Sch.; bd. dirs. Pacific Am. Income Shares Inc. Mem. bd. editors, assoc. editor: Yale U. Law Jour. Bd. dirs. World Resources Inst., Washington, Calif. Environ. Trust, Claremont U. Ctr., Grad. Sch., Stanford U. Alumni Assn.; trustee Stanford U., 1991. Woodrow Wilson fellow. Mem. Calif. Bar Assn., Oreg. Bar Assn., D.C. Bar Assn., Nat. Assn. Regulatory Utility Commrs. (exec. com. 1980-82), Stanford U. Alumni Assn. (bd. dirs. 1983-86), Phi Beta Kappa. Office: Edison Internat 2244 Walnut Grove Ave Rosemead CA 91770-3714

BUCCOLA, VICTOR ALLAN, physical education educator, sports association executive; b. L.A., June 20, 1933; s. Carl and Josephine (Canzoneri) B.; m. Sally Louise Ward, Jan. 17, 1959; children: David, Anna, Victoria. BS in Phys. Edn., Calif. Polytechnic State U., 1956, MS in Edn., Phys. Edn., 1957; EdD, Ariz. State U., 1972. Phys. edn. instr., football, boxing and track coach Coll. Idaho, Caldwell, 1958-61; health and sci. instr., asst. football and track coach Mark Keppel High Sch., Alhambra, Calif., 1961-62; phys. edn. instr., asst. football coach Calif. Polytechnic State U., San Luis Obispo, 1962-73, prof. phys. edn., 1981-86, athletics dir., 1973-81; commr. Western Football Conf., San Luis Obispo, 1982-93, Am. W. Conf., 1993-96; chair divsn. II Football Com. NCAA, 1980-83, mem. championship com. divsn. II, 1986-92. Contbr. articles to jours. in field. Mem. bd. dirs. SESLOC Fed. Credit Union, San Luis Obispo, 1980-90, v.p. 1984-90; mem. Youth Football Bd., San Luis Obispo, 1972; asst. coach Little League Baseball Team, San Luis Obispo, 1971-73. Capt. Artillary, 1957. Mem. AAHPERD, Calif. Assn. Health, Phys. Edn., Recreation and Dance. Office: Cal Poly San Luis Obispo CA 93407

BUCHANAN, JAMES DOUGLAS, lawyer; b. Modesto, Calif., Aug. 7, 1941; s. James Monroe and Gladys Marian (Crowell) b.; m. Claudia Anne Dukes, May 26, 1963; children: Sarah, Jennifer, Amy, Andrew. BA in Journalism, U. Nev., 1963; JD, U. of Pacific, Sacramento, 1975. Bar: Calif. 1975, U.S. Dist. Ct. (ea. dist.) Calif. 1976. Dep. dist. atty. Inyo County, Independence, Calif., 1976-77, pub. defender, 1977-78; ptnr. Smith & Buchanan, Bishop, Calif., 1978-86; legal counsel No. Inyo Hosp. Dist., Bishop, 1980—; ptnr. Berger, Buchanan and Berger, 1989-91. Pipe major Loch Ness Scots Pipe Band, Bishop, 1982-97; chmn. Selective Svc. Bd. 87, Bishop, 1983-97; deacon Episc. Ch., 1995. Served to 1st lt. USAR, 1963-65. Mem. Inyo-Mono Bar Assn. (pres. 1980). Office: 459 W Line St Bishop CA 93514-3333

BUCHANAN, LEE ANN, public relations executive; b. Albuquerque, July 6, 1955; d. William Henry Buchanan and Juanita Irene (Pilgrim) Wood; m. Charles Stanton Wood, Jan. 17, 1987. BA, U. Calif., Irvine, 1977. Exec. asst. to Congressman William Thomas, U.S. Ho. of Reps., Washington, 1979-83; dep. chief staff Gov. George Deukmejian, Sacramento, 1983-84; sr. v.p., ptnr. Nelson Comm., Costa Mesa, Calif., 1985-95. Bd. govs. Rep. Assocs. of Orange County, 1985—; founding sec. Orange County Young Reps., 1985. Mem. Internat. Assn. Bus. Communicators, Am. Assn. Polit. Cons., Pub. Relations Soc. Am., U. Calif.-Irvine Alumni Assn. Address: PO Box 1741 Mammoth Lakes CA 93546-1741

BUCHANAN, PAUL WILLIAM, English language educator; b. Belfast, Ireland, Oct. 4, 1959; s. William and Ruth (Lowry) B.; m. Revelation Versoza, Aug. 15, 1981; children: Ryan, Heather, Dylan. BA, Biola U., 1981; MA, U. Calif., Riverside, 1985; MPW, U. So. Calif., 1997. Lectr. in English Biola U., La Mirada, Calif., 1989—; chief editor Biola U., 1991—; prin. Petersen & Buchanan Graphic Design, Whittier, Calif., 1993—. Author: Return of the Eagle, 1992; fiction and poetry editor Ratio: Essays in Christian Thought, Fullerton, 1994—. Dir. campus chpt. Habitat for Humanity, Whittier, 1993—. Recipient awards for distinction and excellence Coun. for Advancement and Support of Edn., 1993. Mem. PEN. Democrat. Office: Biola U 13800 Biola Ave La Mirada CA 90639-0002

BUCHANAN, TERI BAILEY, communications executive; b. Long Beach, Calif., Feb. 24, 1946; d. Alton Hervey and Ruth Estelle (Thompson) Bailey; m. Robert Wayne Buchanan, Aug. 14, 1964 (div. May 1979). BA in English with highest honors, Ark. Poly. Coll., 1968. With employee communications AT&T, Kansas City, Mo., 1968-71; freelance writer Ottawa, Kans., 1971-73; publs. dir. Ottawa U., 1973-74; regional info. officer U.S. Dept. Labor, Kansas City, 1974; owner, operator PBT Communications, Kansas City, 1975-79; sr. pub. affairs rep., sr. editor, exhibit supr., communications specialist Standard Oil/Chevron, San Francisco, 1979-84; owner The Resource Group/Comms., Napa, Calif., 1984—; mem. faculty pub. rels. master's program Golden Gate U., San Francisco, 1987. Pub. rels. trainer Bus. Vols. for Arts, San Francisco, 1985-93; mem. Nat. trust for Hist. Preservation, Napa County Landmarks. Recipient Internat. Assn. Bus. Communicators Bay Area Gold and Silver awards, 1984. Mem. Yountville C. of C., North Bay Assn. Realtors. Democrat. Episcopalian. Office: The Resource Group 134 Golden Gate Cir Napa CA 94558

BUCHANAN, WALTER WOOLWINE, electrical engineer, educator and administrator; b. Lebanon, Ind., Oct. 6, 1941; s. Eugene Neptune and Amy Malvina (Woolwine) B.; m. Carol Ann Saunders, Dec. 28, 1968 (div. 1978); children: William Saunders, John Douglas; m. Charlotte Jane Drake, 1985. BA, Ind. U., 1963, JD, 1973, PhD, 1993; BS in Engring., Purdue U., 1982, MS in Elec. Engring., 1984. Bar: Ind.; registered profl. engr., Ind., Fla., Oreg. Aerospace engr. Martin Co., Denver, 1963-64, Boeing Co., New Orleans, 1964-65; audit coord. Ind. Tax Bd., Indpls., 1970-73; atty. VA, Indpls., 1973-79; electronics engr. Naval Avionics, Indpls., 1979-86; asst. prof. Ind. U.-Purdue U., Indpls., 1986-93, U. Ctrl. Fla., Orlando, 1993-95; assoc. prof., chair Mid. Tenn. State U., Murfreesboro, 1995-96; prof., dean Oreg. Inst. Tech., Klamath Falls, 1996—; cons. Benjamin/Cummings Pubs., Menlo Park, Calif., Holt, Rinehart & Winston, N.Y.C., Houghton Mifflin Co., Boston, MacMillan Pub. Co., Columbus, Delmar Pub. Co., Albany, Prentice Hall, Simon & Schuster, Columbus, Oxford U. Press, N.Y.C.; evaluator Accreditation Bd. for Engring. and Tech., Balt.; alt. mem. Tech. Accreditation Commn.; grants reviewer NSF, Washington. Contbr. articles to profl. jours., numerous papers in field. Com. chair theater adv. bd. Ind. U.-Purdue U., Indpls., 1985-91, mem. faculty coun., 1989-92, mem. exec. com., 1991-92; fundraiser Ind. U. Found., Indpls.; mem. tech. com. Ind. Bus. Modernization Corp., Indpls., 1990-93. Lt. comdr. USN, 1965-69, Vietnam. Recipient Glenn W. Irwin award, Peter Marbaugh award Ind. U.-Purdue U. Indpls., 1988; Wright scholar Ind. U., 1961; rsch. grantee Ctr. on Philanthropy, 1992, Fla. Engring. and Indsl. Experimentation Sta., 1993. Mem. NSPE (educator, exec. bd. 1991-92, 95—, Profl. Engr. in Edn. award 1993), IEEE (sr., com. tech. accreditation activities, press electronics tech. editl. bd.), Soc. Mfg. Engrs. (sr.), Am. Soc. for Engring. Edn. (exec. bd. ednl. rsch. and methods divsn. 1986-92, exec. com. engring. tech. divsn. 1994—, rsch. grantee, Centennial award 1993), Engring. Tech. Leadership Inst. (exec. coun. 1995—), Ind. Soc. Profl. Engrs. (chair engring. edn. 1988-92), Fla. Engring. Soc. (chair engring. edn. 1993-95), Tenn. Soc. Profl. Engrs. (chair engring. edn. 1996), Indpls. Sci. and Engring. Found. (bd. dir. 1988-92), Scientech Club (bd. dirs. 1990-92), Univ. Faculty Club (bd. dirs. 1988-93), Engring. and Sci. Hall of Fame, Order of Engr., Tau Alpha Pi. Republican. Episcopalian. Office: Oreg Inst Tech Sch Engring and Indsl Tech 3201 Campus Dr Klamath Falls OR 97601-8801

BUCHBINDER, MAURICE, cardiologist; b. June 23, 1953; came to U.S., 1979; s. Jacob and Henriette (Jejati) B.; m. Lani Susan, May 5, 1956; children: Jaimie Lauren, Natalie Cara. BS, McGill U., 1974, MD, 1978. Cert. specialist in cardiovascular disease. Intern in internal medicine Montreal, 1980; resident in cardiology Stanford, Calif., 1981-83; asst. prof. of medicine/cardiology Stanford U., 1985-95; dir. interventional cardiology U. Calif., San Diego, Calif., 1995—, Sharp Healthcare, San Diego, 1995—; founder Versaflex, Inc., San Diego, 1983-88; cons., chief of cardiology Scripps Hosp., San Diego, 1995-97. Fellow Am. Coll. Cardiology. Office: Found Cardiovascular Medicine 7901 Frost St San Diego CA 92123

BUCHSER, JOHN ROBERT, computer scientist; b. Fairbanks, Alaska, Feb. 25, 1954; s. Robert D. Buchser and Alberta (Rumpp) Allesandro; m. Linda W. Dutcher, July 4, 1985. BS in Basic Scis., N.Mex. Inst. Mining and Tech., 1982. Software engr. Los Alamos (N.Mex.) Nat. Lab., 1977-87, Sandia Nat. Lab., Albuquerque, 1988-92; systems analyst Lincoln Lab. MIT, Socorro, N.Mex., 1993-94; mgmt. analyst State of N.Mex. Dept. of Health, Santa Fe, 1994—; v.p. engring. Mentron, Santa Fe, 1992—; mem. summer sci. tng. program Fla. State U., Tallahassee, 1971. Mem. IEEE, AAAS, Assn. for Computing Machinery (v.p. 1985-87, 93, pres. 1990-91), Sierra Club. Home: 606 Alto St Santa Fe NM 87501 Office: Pub Health Office 605 Letrado St Santa Fe NM 87505-4162

BUCHTA, EDMUND, engineering executive; b. Wostitz, Nikolsburg, Czechoslovakia, May 11, 1928; came to U.S., 1979; Kaufmann, Deutsche Wirtschaftoberschule, Bruenn, Czechoslovakia, 1942-45. Shop foreman Messerklinger, Ernsting, Austria, 1949-51; constrn. foreman Hinteregger, U.S. Mil. Project, Salzburg, Siezenheim, Austria, 1951-52, Auserehl Constrn. Corp., N.Y.C., 1963; pres. Grout Concrete Constrn. Ltd., Edmonton, Alta., Can., 1966-73; pioneer & explorer Canol Project Parcel B and Land Ownership N.W. Can., 1968—; pres. Barbarosa Enterprises Ltd., Yellowknife, Can., 1971—; owner (with Barbarosa Enterprises Ltd.) Canol Project Parcel B, 1968—. Mem. Dem. Senatorial Campaign Com. With German Mil., 1943-45. Named Emperor of the North, McLean Mag., Can., 1976. Mem. Internat. Platform Assn., Dem. Senatorial Campaign Com. Home: PO Box 7000-713 Redondo Beach CA 90277

BUCHTEL, MICHAEL EUGENE, optical mechanical engineer; b. Denver, Jan. 29, 1939; s. William Paxton and Lorraine Edith (Hammond) B.; m. Gloria Jean Guerrero, Sept. 29, 1967. BS, West Coast U., Compton, Calif., 1972. Sr. engr. Ford Aerospace Corp., Newport Beach, Calif., 1972-92; pres. The Techtel Co., Costa Mesa, Calif., 1992—; cons. Internat. Orgn. for Standards, Pforzheim, Switzerland, 1993—. Patentee for optical scanner in U.S. and Japan. With U.S. Army, 1962-64. Mem. Internat. Soc. for Optical Engrs., Am. Soc. Design Engrs. Republican. Roman Catholic. Office: The Techtel Co 1666 Newport Blvd Costa Mesa CA 92627-3717

BUCK, ANNE MARIE, library director, consultant; b. Birmingham, Ala., Apr. 12, 1939; d. Blaine Alexander and Marie Reynolds (McGeorge) Davis; m. Evan Buck, June 17, 1961 (div. Apr. 1977); children: Susan Elizabeth Buck Rentko, Stephen Edward. BA, Wellesley (Mass.) Coll., 1961; MLS, U. Ky., 1977. Bus. mgr. Charleston (W.Va.) Chamber Music Soc., 1972-74; dir. Dunbar (W.Va.) Pub. Libr., 1974-76; tech. reference libr. AT&T Bell Labs., Naperville, Ill., 1977-79; group supr. libr. AT&T Bell Labs., Reading, Pa., 1979-83; group supr. support svcs. AT&T Bell Labs., North Andover, Mass., 1983; dir. libr. network Bell Communications Rsch. (Bellcore), Morristown, N.J., 1983-89; dir. human resources planning Bell Communications Rsch. (Bellcore), Livingston, N.J., 1989-91; univ. libr. N.J. Inst. Tech., Newark, 1991-95, Calif. Inst. of Tech., Pasadena, 1995—; adj. prof. Rutgers U., New Brunswick, N.J., 1989-90; instr. U. Wis., Madison, 1988-90; v.p. Engring. Info. Found., N.Y.C., 1994—; mem. Engring. Info. Inc (bd. dirs.), Castle-Point-on-the-Hudson, Hoboken, N.J., 1988—; spkr. profl. assn. confs., 1982—; libr. cons. North Port (Fla.) Area Libr., 1990-91. Mem. editorial adv. bd. Highsmith Press, 1991—; contbr. articles to profl. jours. Sect. mgr. United Way of Morris County, Cedar Knolls, N.J., 1984-85; advisor Family Svc. Transitions Coun., Morristown, 1987-90; libr. trustee Lisle (Ill.) Pub. Libr. Dist., 1978-80; bd. dirs. Kanawha County Bicentennial Commn., Charleston, W.Va., 1974-76; personnel com., denominational affairs com., Neighborhood Ch., Pasadena, Calif., 1996—. Recipient Vol.'s Gold award United Way, 1991, Disting. Alumna award U. Ky. Sch. Libr. and Info. Sci., 1996. Mem. ALA (Grolier Nat. Libr. Week grantee 1975), Am. Soc. Info. Sci. (chpt. chmn. 1987-89, Chpt. of Yr. award 1988, treas. 1992-95), Conf. Bd. Inc. (chmn. info. svcs. adv. coun. 1987-89), Spl. Libr. Assn., Am. Soc. Engring. Edn., Archons of Colophon, Indsl. Tech. Info. Mgrs. Group, Wellesley Coll. Alumni Assn. (class rep. 1986-91), N.J. Wellesley Club (regional chmn. 1986-89, corr. sec. 1994-95), Beta Phi Mu. Unitarian. Home: 2254 Loma Vista St Pasadena CA 91104-4906 Office: Calif Inst Tech Mail Stop 1-32 Pasadena CA 91125 *Perhaps the greatest skill one can develop is the ability to identify genuine opportunities and the willingness to incur risk in pursuing them.*

BUCK, FRANCIS SCOTT, pathologist, educator; b. Eskridge, Kans., Oct. 6, 1921; s. Robert Willard Buck and Helen Miriam Dill; m. Dorothy Irene Hollenbeck, Sept. 10, 1948; children: Ronald Scott, Richard Allen, Robert Grant, Dottiann Irene Pino Buck. Student, Fresno State Coll., 1939-43, 45-47; DO, Coll. Osteo. Physicans/Surgeon, L.A., 1951; MD, Calif. Coll. Medicine, 1962. Cert. anatomic and clin. pathology Am. Bd. Pathology. Dir. pathology L.A. County Hosp., 1955-68; chief physician, pathologist L.A. County/U. So. Calif. Med. Ctr., L.A., 1968-85, attending physician, 1985—; mem. profl. staff assn. L.A. County/U. So. Calif. Med. Ctr., L.A., 1968-85; v.p., bd. govs. Am. Osteopathic Coll. Pathology, 1961-62. Contbr. articles to med. jours. Mem. donor recruitment com. L.A./Orange County ARC Blood Bank, 1980-81; bd. trustees Reformed Presbyn. Ch. N.Am., 1972-79; elder Reformed Presbyn. Ch. L.A., 1971—. Capt. U.S. Army Air Force, 1942-45. Mem. AMA, Calif. Med. Assn., Calif. Soc. Pathologists, L.A. Soc. Pathologists, Grad. Soc. Pathologists, L.A. County/U. So. Calif. Med. Ctr. (sec., pres. 1979-85). Republican. Home: 240 Cherry Dr Pasadena CA 91105 Office: LA County/U So Calif Med Ctr Box 55 1200 N State St Los Angeles CA 90033

BUCK, G. WENDELL, library director; b. Medford, Oreg., Jan. 7, 1950; s. Gilbert Wallace and Mildred Fern (Miracle) B.; m. Judy Ann Syphers, Aug. 17, 1975 (div. 1995); children: Emily Rose, Geoffrey Wycliffe. BA, Walla Walla Coll., 1973; M Libr. Info. Scis., U. Alt., Edmonton, Can., 1991. Tchr., libr. Columbia Acad., Battleground, Wash., 1975-78, Broadview Acad., La Fox, Ill., 1978-80; asst. libr. Can. Union Coll., College Heights, Alta., 1980-88; libr. technician Lacombe (Alta.) Composite H.S., 1989-91; tech. svcs. libr. Wapiti Regional Libr., Prince Albert, Sask., 1992; libr. dir. Oreg. Trail Libr. Dist., Boardman, 1993-96, Fern Ridge Libr. Dist., Veneta, Oreg., 1996—. V.p. Ctrl. Alta. AIDS Network, Red Deer, 1990. Mem. ALA, Oreg. Libr. Assn. Democrat. Home: 1480 W 12th # 15 # D2 Eugene OR 97402 Office: Fern Ridge Libr Dist PO Box 397 Veneta OR 97487

BUCK, GENE, graphics company executive, satirist, historian; b. Seattle, July 4, 1946; s. Gene Cecil and Theodosia Ann (Burr) B. Student, U. Hawaii, 1975-76, U. Wash., 1976-79, Kingswork Inst., Honolulu, 1979-80. Owner Buck & Assocs. Advt. Agy., Monterey, Calif., 1980-85, Cypress Fine Arts, Monterey, 1981-87, Gene Buck, Publicist, Monterey, 1983-87; dir. Aaron Burr Accord, Seattle, 1987—; chmn. Aaron Burr Commemorative Stamp Com., Seattle, 1981—; owner Storyville Graphics, Seattle, 1990—; cons. Spencer Prodns., Inc., N.Y.C., 1975—, Bing Crosby Hist. Soc., Tacoma, 1975-94; dir. Brotherhood for Respect, Elevation, and Advancement of Dishwaters, Monterey, 1983-85. Author: (children's book) On the Sidewalks of New York, 1995, ABC Color and Learn Book, 1997, (satire/cartoon book) The Penguin Papers, 1993, (with Gerald E. Mowery) Who's Who in the Slow-Lane, 1997, (hist. sci. fiction) The First ET—Aaron Burr, 1996. Chmn. Rose St. Commons, Seattle, 1992-96, Stop the Train!, Seattle, 1993-96; dir. Soc. of Disenfranchised, Seattle, 1987-96, dir., 1980-87. With USNR, 1974-78. Office: Storyville Graphics PO Box 4644 Seattle WA 98104-0644

BUCK, LINDA DEE, recruiting company executive; b. San Francisco, Nov. 8, 1946; d. Sol and Shirley D. (Setterberg) Press; student Coll. San Mateo (Calif.), 1969-70; divorced. Head hearing and appeals br. Dept. Navy Employee Rels. Svc., Philippines, 1974-75; dir. human resources Homestead Savs. & Loan Assn., Burlingame, Calif., 1976-77; mgr. VIP Agy., Inc., Palo Alto, Calif., 1977-78; exec. v.p., dir. Sequent Personnel Svcs., Inc., Mountain View, Calif., 1978-83; founder, pres. Buck & Co., San Mateo, 1983-91. Publicity mgr. for No. Calif., Osteogenesis Imperfecta Found. Inc., 1970-72; cons. Am. Brittle Bone Soc., 1979-88; active Florence (Oreg.) Area Humane Soc., 1994—, Friends of Libr., Florence, 1994—; bd. dirs. Florence Festival Arts, 1995; mem. Florence Area C. of C.; bd. dir., dir. women Rhododendron Scholarship Program, Florence, Oreg., 1995. Jewish.

BUCK, LOUISE BRYDEN, psychiatrist; b. St. Louis, Mo., Apr. 26, 1943; d. Robert Ervin and Jane Bookings (Bryden) Buck; m. Adolph Pfefferbaum, June 11, 1967 (div. Feb. 1973); m. Randolph Seville Charlton, Feb. 14, 1975; children: Genevieve Lynn, Blake Randolph. BS, U. Calif., San Francisco, 1965, MD, 1968. Diplomate Am. Psychoanalytic Assn. Internal medicine intern Barnes Hosp.-Washington U., St. Louis, 1968-69; gen. practice Olney, Md., 1969-70; resident in psychiatry U. Md., Balt., 1970-72, Stanford U., Palo Alto, Calif., 1971-73; pvt. practice specializing in psychiatry Palo Alto, 1974—; mem. clin. fculty Stanford U., 1973—. Mem. Am. Psychoanalytic Assn., Peninsula Psychoanalytic Group (chmn.), San Francisco Psychoanalytic Inst. Office: 690 Waverley St Palo Alto CA 94301-2549

BUCKINGHAM, MICHAEL JOHN, oceanography educator; b. Oxford, Eng., Oct. 9, 1943; s. Sidney George and Mary Agnes (Walsh) B.; m. Margaret Penelope Rose Barrowcliff, July 15, 1967. BSc with hons., U. Reading (Eng.), 1967, PhD, 1971. Postdoctoral rsch. fellow U. Reading, 1971-74; sr. sci. officer Royal Aircraft Establishment, Farnborough, Eng., 1974-76; prin. sci. officer Royal Aircraft Establishment, 1976-82; exchange scientist Naval Rsch. Lab., Washington, 1982-84; vis. prof. MIT, Cambridge, 1986-87; sr. prin. sci. officer Royal Aircraft Establishment, 1983-86, 1987-90; prof. oceanography Scripps Instn. of Oceanography, La Jolla, Calif., 1990—; vis. prof. Inst. Sound and Vibration rsch., Southampton, Eng., 1990—; cons. Commn. of European Communities, Brussels, Belgium, 1989—; dir. Arctic rsch. Royal Aerospace Establishment, Farnborough, 1990—. Author: Noise in Electronic Devices and Systems, 1983; editor: Sea Surface Sound '94, Proceedings of the III Internat. Mtg. on Natural Phys. Processes Related to Sea Surface Sound; sr. editor Jour. Computational Acoustics; editor Phys. Acoustics; contbr. articles to profl. jours.; patentee in field. Recipient Clerk Maxwell Premium, Inst. Electronic and Radio Engrs. London, 1972, A.B. Wood Medal, Inst. Acoustics, Bath, Eng., 1982, Alan Burman Pub. award, Naval Rsch. Lab., 1988, Commendation for Disting. Contbns. to ocean acoustics Naval Rsch. Lab., 1986. Fellow Inst. Acoustics (U.K.), Inst. Elec. Engrs. (U.K.), Acoustical Soc. Am. (chmn. acoustical oceanography tech. com. 1991—); mem. Am. Geophys. Union, Sigma Xi. Home: 7921 Caminito Del Cid La Jolla CA 92037-3404 Office: Scripps Inst Oceanography Marine Phys Lab La Jolla CA 92093-0213

BUCKLEY, VIKKI, state official. Sec. of state State of Colo., 1995—. Office: Office of the Sec of State 1560 Broadway Ste 200 Denver CO 80202-6000*

BUCKLIN, LOUIS PIERRE, business educator, consultant; b. N.Y.C., Sept. 20, 1928; s. Louis Lapham and Elja (Barricklow) B.; m. Weylene Edwards, June 11, 1956; children: Randolph E., Rhonda W. Student, Dartmouth Coll., 1950; MBA, Harvard U., 1954; PhD, Northwestern U., 1960. Asst. prof. bus. U. Colo., Boulder, 1954-56; instr. in bus. Northwestern U., Evanston, 1958-59, assoc. dean Grad. Sch. Bus. Adminstrn., 1981-83; prof. bus. adminstrn. U. Calif., Berkeley, 1960-93, prof. emeritus, 1993—; vis. prof. Stockholm Sch. Econs., 1983, INSEAD, Fontainebleau, France, 1984, Erasmus U., Rotterdam, Netherlands, 1993-94, Cath. U. Leuven, Belgium, 1994; prin. Bucklin Assocs., Lafayette, Calif., 1975—;mem. adv. bd. Gemini Cons., San Francisco, 1987-94. Author: A Theory of Distribution Channel Structure, 1966, Competition Evolution in The Distributive Trades, 1972, Productivity in Marketing, 1979; editor: Vertical Marketing Systems, 1971, Channels and Channel Institutions, 1986, Jour. of Retailing, 1996—. Mem. City of Lafayette Planning Commn., 1990-93. Capt. USMC, 1951-53, Korea. Recipient Alpha Kappa Psi Found. award for best paper in Jour. Mktg., 1993. Mem. Am. Mktg. Assn. (Paul D. Converse award 1986), Inst. for Ops. Rsch. and Mgmt. Scis., European Acad. Mktg., Lafayette-Langeac Soc. (bd. dirs. 1988-92). Democrat. Office: U Calif Haas Sch Bus Berkeley CA 94720-1900

BUCKMAN, FREDERICK W., gas utility executive. Pres., COO Consumers Power Co., Jackson, Mich., 1988—. Recipient George Westinghouse Gold medal, ASME, 1993. Office: Consumers Power Co 212 W Michigan Ave Jackson MI 49201-2236

BUCKNER, KAY LAMOREUX, artist; b. Seattle, Dec. 26, 1935; d. H.D.W. and Eunice (Coble) Lamoreux; m. Paul Buckner, Aug. 15, 1959; children: Matthew, Nathan. BA, U. Wash., 1958; MFA, Claremont Grad. Sch., 1961. One-woman shows include Frye Art Mus., Seattle, 1979, Oreg. Mus. Art, Eugene, 1981, Jadite Galleries, N.Y.C., 1988, Spokane Arts commn., 1996, Chase Gallery, Spokane, 1996; exhibited in group shows at Marietta (Ohio) Coll., 1974, 76, Ea. N.Mex. U., Portales, 1981 (1st prize), U. Wash., Seattle, 1984, Austen Peay U., Clarksville, Tenn., 1989, Md. Fedn. Art, Annapolis, 1991, U. Md., Balt., 1994; rep. in permanent collections Olympic Coll., Bremerton, Wash., Georgia-Pacific Co., Portland, Oreg., Wash. State Dept. Corrections, Emanuel Hosp., Portland.

BUCKNER, MATTHEW ERIC, sculptor; b. Pomona, Calif., Jan. 15, 1961; s. Paul Eugene and Kay Shirley (Lamoreux) B. BA, CUNY, N.Y.C., 1984; MFA, Boston U., 1988. Apprentice carver Intagliatori Bertolozzi, Florence, Italy, 1980-81; carving restorer Regency Restorations, Ltd., N.Y.C., 1983-86; supervisor gilding, painting Fine Art Decorating Co., N.Y.C., 1986; sculpture finisher Tallix Sculptuer Foundry, N.Y.C., 1988-91; art instr. U. Oreg., Eugene, 1991—; gallery dir. Howland Art Ctr., Beacon, N.Y., 1990. Collections include Mugar Meml. Libr., Boston, 1988, Lawrence Hall, U. Oreg., 1991, Thunderbird Sch., Phoenix, 1994. Mem. Nat. Sculpture Soc. (Louis Bennett prize 1989, Gloria medal 1988). Home and Studio: 2332 Rockwood St Eugene OR 97405-1413

BUCKNER, PHILIP FRANKLIN, newspaper publisher; b. Worcester, Mass., Aug. 25, 1930; s. Orello Simmons and Emily Virginia (Siler) B.; m. Ann Haswell Smith, Dec. 21, 1956 (div. Nov. 1993); children: John C., Frederick S., Catherine A.; m. Mary Emily Aird, Dec. 15, 1995. AB, Harvard U., 1952; MA, Columbia U., 1954. With Bay State Abrasive Products Co., 1954-59; Reporter Lowell (Mass.) Sun, 1959-60; pub. East Providence (R.I.) Post, 1960-62; asst. to treas. Scripps League Newspapers, Seattle, 1964-66, divsn. mgr., 1966-71; pres. Buckner News Alliance, Seattle, 1971—; pub. daily newspaper group including Carlsbad (N.Mex.) Current-Argus, 1971-90, Pecos (Tex.) Enterprise, 1971—, Fontana (Calif.) Herald-News, 1971-89, Banning and Beaumont (Calif.) Gazette, 1971-74, Lewistown (Pa.) Sentinel, 1971-93, Tiffin (Ohio) Advertiser-Tribune, 1973-93, York (Pa.) Daily Record, 1978—, Winsted (Conn.) Citizen, 1978, Excelsior Springs (Mo.) Standard, 1978, Oroville (Calif.) Mercury-Register, 1983-89, Corona (Calif.) Independent, 1984-89, Minot (N.D.) News, 1989-93. Office: Buckner News Alliance 2101 4th Ave Ste 2300 Seattle WA 98121-2317

BUCKSTEIN, CARYL SUE, writer; b. Denver, Aug. 10, 1954; d. Henry Martin and Hedvig (Neulander) B. BS in Journalism, U. Colo., 1976. Editor Rifle (Colo.) Telegram, 1976; corr. So. Colo. Pueblo (Colo.) Star-Jour. and Chieftain, 1977-84; corr. The Denver Post, 1985; staff editor Nat. Over-the-Counter Stock Jour., Denver, 1985-89; writer Rocky Mountain News, Denver, 1990-92; editor Urban Spectrum, Denver, 1993; contbg. writer Boulder (Colo.) County Bus. Report, 1992—. Bd. mem. Holiday Project, Denver, 1996. Recipient 1st Place Gen. Assignment Bus. Articles, Colo. Press Women, Denver, 1985, 90, 91. Mem. Colo. Soc. Profl. Journalists (sec.-treas. 1988).

BUDD, BARBARA TEWS, sculptor; b. Milw., Jan. 4, 1935; d. Herbert Albert and Helen Estelle (Dieman) Tews; m. John Marshall Budd Jr., June 29, 1957; children: Elizabeth, John Marshall III, Peter, Benjamin. BA, Smith Coll., 1957; student of art, Yale U., 1958-59, Mpls. Inst. Art, 1960-73, Mpls. Sch. of Art, 1960-73, U. Minn., 1960-73. Co-author, illustrator: The Uncommon Guide to Twin Cities, 1970, The Uncommon Guide to Dining in the Twin Cities, 1970, The Uncommon Guide to Minnesota, 1971, co-author: Colorado Springs Today, 1982, 2d edit., 1985; sculpture exhibits include The Tactile Gallery, Colo. Springs, Colo., 1990, Loveland Invitational Sculpture Show, Loveland, Colo., 1992-96, Pioneer Mus., Colo. Springs, Colo., 1993, New England Fine Arts Inst., Boston, 1993, Cottonwood Festival Sculpture Internat. Show, Hastings, Nebr., 1994, USAF Permanent Profs. Mus., 1995, Collector's Choice Show, Colorado Springs Fine Arts Ctr., 1997; participated in numerous other group shows; represented in various permanent collections. Co-founder Minn. Children's Mus., 1971; bd. dirs. Colo. Springs Goals, 1975-84, Colo. Springs Sch., 1974-80, Cheyenne Village, Manitou Springs, Colo., 1974-80, Colo. chpt. Nat. Mus. Women in Art, Washington, D.C., 1988-96, Pikes Peak Art Council, 1991-96, St. Paul Arts and Sci. Coun., 1972, 1984-87, Penrose Hosp. Aux., 1984-87; mem. Pikes Peak Arts Commn., 1993-95. Mem. Internat. Sculpture Ctr. (Washington), Colo. Artists Registry, Nat. Sculpture Soc. Republican. Episcopalian. Home: 10 Thayer Rd Colorado Springs CO 80906-4221

BUDDRESS, LOREN A.N., state agency administrator; b. Seattle, July 7, 1945; s. E.N. and Miriam Louise B.; m. Patricia Ann Wenner, June 2, 1976; 1 child. AA, Coll. San Mateo, 1966; BA with honors, San Jose State U., 1969, MA with honors, 1970. Eligibility worker San Mateo County Welfare Dept., 1971-74; adult probation officer III San Mateo County Probation Dept., 1974-80; from probation officer to supr. probation officer U.S. Probation Office No. Dist. Calif., San Francisco, 1980-89, chief, 1989—. With USCG, 1968-69, with res., 1969-74. Recipient Pub. Svc. award Calif. State Congress Parents, Tchrs. and Students, 1988. Mem. Fed. Probation and Pretrial Svcs. Officer Assn., Fed. Probation and Pretrial Clks. Coun., Am. Correctional Assn., U.S. Probation and Pretrial Svcs. Officers Chiefs Adv. Coun., Nat. Sociology and Psychology Honor Soc. Office: US Probation Office No Calif Ste 17-6884 450 Golden Gate Ave San Francisco CA 94102

BUDEK, ALLIN ALLA, artist; b. Kiev, Ukraine, June 19, 1923; came to U.S., 1948; d. Igor W. and Olga G. (Intelman) Domansky; m. Herbert E. Budek, June 1, 1946; 2 children. BA in Creative Studies, U. Calif., Santa Barbara, 1981. Exhibited in group shows at COAL Art Gallery, Carlsbad, Calif., 1995-96, San Dieguito Art Guild, Leucadia, Calif., 1993-95 (1st pl. award 1993, 94, 95), La Jolla (Calif.) Art Assn. Gallery, 1995-96, Hellenic Arts Inst., N.Y.C., 1995-96, Musee D'Art Moderne de la Commanderie, Unets, France, 1994, Oceanside Art Mus., Calif., 1996, Art Prospects, La Jolla, Calif., 1995. Recipient 1st Pl. awards Art Vision, 1993, 94, COAL Spring Show, 1993, 95, San Dieguito Art Guild, 1993, 94, 95, 96. Home: 133 Smart Ct Encinitas CA 92024-2934

BUDINGTON, WILLIAM STONE, retired librarian; b. Oberlin, Ohio, July 3, 1919; s. Robert Allyn and Mabel (Stone) B.; m. Irma Johnson. B.A., Williams Coll., 1940, L.H.D., 1975; B.S. in L.S, Columbia U., 1941, M.S., 1951; B.S. in Elec. Engring, Va. Poly. Inst., 1946. Reference librarian Norwich U., 1941-42; librarian, engring. and phys. scis. Columbia, 1947-52; asso. librarian John Crerar Library, Chgo., 1952-65; librarian John Crerar Library, 1965-69, exec. dir., librarian, 1969-84; Mem. U.S.-USSR Spl. Libraries Exchange, 1966; bd, dirs. Center for Research Libraries, 1970-72, chmn., 1972; mem. vis. com. on libraries Mass. Inst. Tech., 1972-77. Served with AUS, 1942-46. Fellow AAAS, Med Library Assn.; mem. ALA, Am. Soc. Info. Sci., Spl. Libraries Assn. (pres. 1964-65, Hall of Fame 1984), Am. Soc. Engring. Edn., Assn. Research Libraries (dir. 1970-74, pres. 1973), Assn. Coll. and Research Libraries (Acad. Research Librarian of Year 1982), Phi Beta Kappa, Tau Beta Pi, Eta Kappa Nu. Clubs: Caxton, Arts. Home: 211 Wood Terrace Dr Colorado Springs CO 80903-2337

BUDZINSKI, JAMES EDWARD, interior designer; b. Gary, Ind., Jan. 4, 1953; s. Edward Michael and Virginia (Caliman) B. Student U. Cin., 1971-76. Mem. design staff Perkins & Wills Architects, Inc., Chgo., 1973-75, Med. Architectonics, Inc., Chgo., 1975-76; v.p. interior design Interior Environs., Inc., Chgo., 1976-78; pres. Jim Budzinski Design, Inc., Chgo., 1978-80; dir. interior design Robinson, Mills & Williams, San Francisco, 1980-87, dir. design, interior architecture Whisler Patri, San Francisco, 1987-90; v.p. design sales and mktg. Deepa Textiles, 1990—; instr. design Harrington Inst. Design, Chgo.; cons. Chgo. Art Inst., Storwal Internat., Inc.; speaker at profl. confs. Designs include 1st Chgo. Corp. Pvt. Banking Ctr., 1st Nat. Bank Chgo. Monroe and Wabash Banking Ctr., 1978, IBM Corp., San Jose, Deutsch Bank, Frankfort, Crowley Maritime Corp., San Francisco, offices for Brobeck, Phleger and Harrison, offices for chmn. bd. Fireman's Fund Ins. Cos., Nob Hill Club, Fairmont Hotel, San Francisco, offices for Cooley, Godword, Castro, Huddleson, and Tatum, Palo Alto, Calif, offices for Pacific Bell Acctg. div., San Francisco, showroom for Knoll Internat., San Francisco, lobby, lounge TransAm. Corp. Hdqrts, San Fransisco, offices for EDAW, San Francisco, showroom for Steelcase Inc., Bally of Switzerland, N.Am. Flagship store, San Francisco; corp. Hqrs. Next Inc., Redwood City, Calif., Schafer Furniture Design, Lobby Renovation 601 California, San Francisco, Bennedetti Furniture Inc. Furniture Design. Pres. No. Calif. chpt. Design Industries Found. for AIDS. Office: Deepa Textiles 333 Bryant St San Francisco CA 94107-1421

BUECHLER, RALPH WOLFGANG, German language and literature educator; b. Winsen, Germany, July 21, 1948, came to U.S., 1958; s. William Emil and Hilde (Blümchen) B. BA in German, Washington U., St. Louis, 1971; MA in German, U. Ill., 1973, MAS in Acctg., 1976; PhD in German, U. Wis., 1988. Tchg. asst. U. Ill., Urbana, 1971-76; auditor Price Waterhouse & Co., St. Louis, 1977-79; tchg. asst. U. Wis., Madison, 1979-83, instr., 1983-88, lectr., 1988-89; assoc. prof. German lang. and lit. U. Nev., Las Vegas, 1989—, chair dept. fgn. langs., 1995—; libr. Goethe Haus Pub. Libr., Milw., summer 1981; bibliographer U. Wis., 1981-82, adminstrv. asst., 1983-85, vis. asst. prof., 1990, 92. Author: The Essays of Lichtenberg, 1990; contbr. articles to profl. publs. Mem. MLA, Soc. for Eighteenth-Century Studies, Soc. for Lit. and Sci. Democrat. Office: U Nev Dept Fgn Langs 4505 Maryland Pkwy Las Vegas NV 89154

BUECHNER, JOHN C., academic administrator. Dir. govtl. rels., then dir. pub. affairs U. Colo. System Office, Denver, until 1989; chancellor U. Colo., Denver, 1988-96, pres., 1996—. Office: U Colo-Denver PO Box 35 1200 Larimer St Boulder CO 80309*

BUEHLER, MARILYN KAY HASZ, secondary education educator; b. Garden City, Kans., July 19, 1946; d. Benjamin Bethel and Della Marie (Appel) Hasz; m. Brice Edward Buehler, July 23, 1966. BA in English, Washburn U., 1970; MA in Reading Edn., Ariz. State U., 1976; DHL (hon.), No. Ariz. U., 1989. Cert. tchr. English and secondary edn. Vol. probation officer, co-facilitator Maricopa County Probation Office, Phoenix, 1972; adult edn. tchr. Phoenix Union High Sch., 1972-73; tchr. English Trevor G. Browne High Sch., Phoenix, 1973; tchr. Title I Carl Hayden High Sch., Phoenix, 1974; tchr. English Camelback High Sch., Phoenix, 1975, Central High Sch., Phoenix, 1976-85, North High Sch., Phoenix, 1985—; internat. baccalaurate English instr., 1986—; chmn. awareness facilitator Phoenix Union High Sch. System, 1986-95; speaker Partnrships in Edn., Phoenix, 1991—, adv. bd. Phoenix Coll. Creative Writing, 1995-96. Bd. dirs. Ariz. Edn. Found., Phoenix, 1990-95, North High-Ariz. Pub. Svc. Partnership Com., 1991-95. Named Ariz. State Tchr. of Yr., State of Ariz./AEF, 1989; recipient award of honor for outstanding contbns. to edn. Nat. Sch. Pub. Rels. Assn., 1989, others. Mem. NEA, Nat. Coun. Tchrs. English, Classroom Tchrs. Assn., Nat. Writers Club, Nat. State Tchrs. of Yr., Ariz. State Tchrs. of Yr. (pres. 1993-95), Phoenix Zoo Bd. (edn. com, 1995-96). Democrat. Office: North High Sch 1101 E Thomas Rd Phoenix AZ 85014-5447

BUEL, BOBBIE JO, editor. Mng. editor Tucson. Office: 4850 S Park Ave Tucson AZ 85726-6807

BUELL, JAMES RICHARD, JR., investment management company executive; b. Flint, Mich., Feb. 4, 1947; s. James Richard and Frances Luella (Budd) B.; m. Barbara Jean Van Fleet, July 19, 1969; children: Melanie Lyn, Kristin Elizabeth; m. Laura Marguarite Bestor, Aug. 4, 1990; children: Brenda Joanne, Karina Hinton. BA in Comm., U. Mich., 1969; MA in Comm., Bowling Green State U., 1970; MBA, Mich. State U., 1975. CFP. Dir. info. svc. William C. Brown Co., Dubuque, Iowa, 1975-77; group product mgr. new products Stroh Brewery Co., Detroit, 1977-82; dir. new product devel. Anheuser-Busch, Inc., St. Louis, 1982-87; sr. v.p. mktg. Southtrust (Bank) Corp., Birmingham, Ala., 1987-89, Fla. Nat. (Bank) Corp., Jacksonville, 1989-90; pres. Greenfield Cons. Group, St. Louis, 1990-92; v.p. sales and mktg. Agribank, FCB, St. Paul, 1992-94; gen. securities prin. Planners Fin. Svcs., Mpls., 1994—; registered investment adviser Montgomery Investment Mgmt., Mpls., 1994-95; pres., CEO Greenfield Fin.

Svcs., St. George, Utah, 1995—; adj. faculty fin. svcs. mktg. U. St. Thomas, Mpls., 1993—; adj. faculty mem. consumer behavior Maryville U., St. Louis, 1990-92; adj. faculty mktg. Wayne State U., Detroit, 1978-80. Author articles, monograph in field. Loaned corp. exec. United Way, St. Joseph, Mich., 1974. Maj. USAR, 1969-90. Mem. Inst. CFPs, Internat. Assn. Fin. Planning, Bank Mktg. Assn., Am. Mktg. Assn. (chpt. pres. 1981), Sales and Mktg. Execs., Res. Officers Assn., Masons, Shriners, Town and Country Club.

BUELL, THOMAS ALLAN, retired lumber company executive; b. Toronto, Ont., Can., Nov. 14, 1931; s. Allan Foster and Jessie L. (Stayner) B.; m. Phyllis Ann Lee, Aug. 27, 1955; children: Elizabeth, Christopher, Michael, Robert. BSCF in Forestry, U. Toronto, 1956. Forester Kimberly Clark of Can., 1956-61; mgr. No. Plywoods Co., 1961-64; with Weldwood of Can. Ltd., Vancouver, B.C., 1964—; v.p. mfg. Weldwood of Can. Ltd., 1970-75, pres., chief exec. officer, 1975-79, chmn., pres., CEO, 1979-92, chmn., 1992-96, CEO, 1992-93, ret. CEO, 1993; co-chmn. Canfor-Weldwood Distbn. Ltd.; bd. dirs. B.C. Gas Inc., Placer Dome Inc., Swiss Bank Corp. (Can.), Mayne Nickless Can. Inc., Lafarge Corp. Chmn. dean's adv. coun. faculty of forestry U. B.C., mem. adv. coun. faculty of commerce and bus. adminstrn.; mem. citizens bd. Forest Alliance B.C.; mem. forestry sector adv. coun.; bd. dirs. Vancouver Found., Trans Mountain Pipeline Ltd., Can. Liquid Air. Mem. Royal Vancouver Yacht Club, Vancouver Club.

BUESCHER, BERNARD, air transportation executive; b. 1949. Attended, U. Colo., 1970-73. With Williams, Turner & Holmes P.C., Grand Junction, Colo., 1973-87; ptnr. Buescher Family Ltd. Partnership, Grand Junction, 1982—; officer West Star Engine Corp., Grand Junction, 1987-92; pres. West Star Aviation, Grand Junction, 1987—. Office: West Star Aviation Inc 768 Heritage Way Grand Junction CO 81506-8643*

BUESCHER, LOUIS, airport service executive. With Mesa Beverage Co., Grand Junction, Colo., 1971-82; gen. ptnr. Buescher Family L.P., Grand Junction, Colo., 1982—; with Pipeline Service, Inc., Grand Junction, Colo., 1983-87; officer West Star Engine Corp., Grand Junction, Colo., 1987-92; with West Star Aviation, Inc., Grand Junction, Colo., 1987—. Office: West Star Aviation Inc 796 Heritage Way Grand Junction CO 81506-8643*

BUFFA, PETER, mayor. Mayor Costa Mesa, Calif. Address: 77 Fair Dr Costa Mesa CA 92626

BUFFINGTON, GARY LEE ROY, safety standards engineer, construction executive; b. Custer, S.D., Dec. 6, 1946; s. Donald L. B. and Madge Irene (Selby) Lampert; m. Kathleen R. Treloar, Aug. 3, 1965; children: Katherine, Lowell, Gary Jr. BS in Bus. Edn., Black Hill State Coll., 1971; AA in Criminal Justice, U. S.D., 1972, MS, 1974. Cert. safety profl., EMT, law enforcement officer, mine safety and health adminstrn. instr., OSHA instr.; Canadian registered safety profl.; lic. pvt. investigator. Contract miner Homestake Mining Co., Lead, S.D., 1966-72; dep. sheriff, criminal investigator Pennington County Sheriff's Dept., Rapid City, S.D., 1972-77; fed. mine inspector U.S. Dept. of Labor, Mine Safety and Health Adminstrn., Birmingham, Ala., 1977-79; supr., spl. investigator U.S. Dept. of Labor, Mine Safety and Health Adminstrn., Birmingham, 1979-81; supr., mine inspector U.S. Dept. of Labor, Mine Safety and Health Adminstrn., Grand Junction, Colo., 1981-83; safety and security mgr. Black & Veatch Engrs. Stanton Energy Ctr., Orlando, Fla., 1983-87; loss control mgr. Black & Veatch Engrs. AES Thames Cogeneration Plant, Uncasville, Conn., 1987-90; loss control mgr. Trans-Mo. River Tunnel project Black & Veatch, Engrs.-Architects, Kansas City, Mo., 1990-92; mgr. safety and security. metro rail constrn. mgr. Parsons-Dillingham, L.A., 1992-95; asst. dir. constrn. safety L.A. Metro Rail Project Met. Transp. Authority, 1995—; owner Safety Expert Witness Am. Safety Cons., L.A., 1991—; mem. ANSI A-10 Accredited Standards Com., Washington, 1984—, Mine Safety and Health Adminstrn. Standards Com., Arlington, Va., 1981-83. Named Police Officer of the Year, Sundown Optimist Club, Rapid City, 1975; recipient Meritorious Achievement award, U.S. Dept. of Labor, Arlington, 1979, Monetary Spl. Achievement award, U.S. Dept. Labor, Arlington, 1980. Mem. Am. Soc. Safety Engrs., World Safety Orgn., Am. Indsl. Hygiene Assn., Am. Soc. for Indsl. Security, Nat. Safety Council, Moose Lodge. Republican. Lutheran. Home: 20025 W Jacana Ct Santa Clarita CA 91351-5562 Office: LA County Met Transp Auth 1 Gateway Plz Fl 17 Los Angeles CA 90012-2932

BUFFINGTON, LINDA BRICE, interior designer; b. Long Beach, Calif., June 21, 1936; d. Harry Bryce and Marguerite Leonora (Tucciarone) Van Bellehem; student El Camino Jr. Coll., 1955-58, U. Calif., Irvine, 1973-75; children: Lisa Ann, Phillip Lynn. Cert. interior designer and gen. contractor, Calif.; lic. gen. contractor, Calif. With Pub. Fin., Torrance, Calif., 1954-55, Beneficial Fin., Torrance and Hollywood, Calif., 1955-61; interior designer Vee Nisley Interiors, Newport Beach, Calif., 1964-65, Leon's Interiors, Newport Beach, 1965-69; ptnr. Marlind Interiors, Tustin, Calif., 1969-70; owner, designer Linda Buffington Interiors, Villa Park, Calif., 1970—, LBI, Contractors, 1993—; cons. builders, housing developments. Mem. Bldg. Industry Assn. (past pres. Orange County chpt. 1989, 90), Internat. Soc. Interior Designers, Nat. Assn. Home Builders. Republican. Office: 17853 Santiago Blvd Ste 107 Villa Park CA 92861-4113

BUFFORD, SAMUEL LAWRENCE, federal judge; b. Phoenix, Ariz., Nov. 19, 1943; s. John Samuel and Evelyn Amelia (Rude) B.; m. Julia Marie Metzger, May 13, 1978. BA in Philosophy, Wheaton Coll., 1964; PhD, U. Tex., 1969; JD magna cum laude, U. Mich., 1973. Bar: Calif., N.Y., Ohio. Instr. philosophy La. State U., Baton Rouge, 1967-68; asst. prof. Ea. Mich. U., Ypsilanti, 1968-74; asst. prof. law Ohio State U., Columbus, 1975-77; assoc. Gendel, Raskoff, Shapiro & Quittner, L.A., 1982-85; atty. Paul, Weiss, Rifkind, Wharton & Garrison, N.Y.C., 1974-75, Sullivan Jones & Archer, San Francisco, 1977-79, Musick, Peeler & Garrett, L.A., 1979-81, Rifkind & Sterling, Beverly Hills, Calif., 1981-82, Gendel, Raskoff, Shapiro & Quittner, L.A., 1982-85; U.S. bankruptcy judge Ctrl. Dist. Calif., 1985—; bd. dirs. Fin. Lawyers Conf., L.A., 1987-90, Bankruptcy Forum, L.A., 1986-88; lectr. U.S.-Romanian Jud. Delegation, 1991, Internat. Tng. Ctr. for Bankers, Budapest, 1993, Bankruptcy Technical Legal Assistance Workshop, Romania, 1994, Comml. Law Project for Ukraine, 1995-96, Ea. Europe Enterprise Restructuring and Privitization Project, U.S. AID, 1995-96; cons. Calif. State Bar Bd. Examiners, 1989-90. Editor-in-chief Am. Bankruptcy Law Jour., 1990-94; contbr. articles to profl. jours.; columnist Norton Bankruptcy Advisor, 1988—. Younger Humanist fellowship NEH. Mem. ABA, L.A. County Bar Assn. (past chmn. ethics com.), Order of Coif. Office: US Bankruptcy Ct 255 E Temple St Ste 1582 Los Angeles CA 90012-3334

BUGBEE-JACKSON, JOAN, sculptor; b. Oakland, Calif., Dec. 17, 1941; d. Henry Greenwood and Jeanie Lawler (Abbot) B.; m. John Michael Jackson, June 21, 1973; 1 child, Brook Bond. BA in Art, U. Calif., San Jose, 1964, MA in Art/Ceramics, 1966; student Nat. Acad. Sch. Fine Arts, N.Y.C., 1968-72, Art Students League, N.Y.C., 1968-70. Apprentice to Joseph Kiselewski, 1970-72; instr. art Foothill (Calif.) Jr. Coll., 1966-67; instr. design De Anza Jr. Coll., Cupertino, Calif., 1967-68; instr. pottery Greenwich House Pottery, N.Y.C., 1969-71, Craft Inst. Am., N.Y.C., 1970-72, Cordova (Alaska) Extension Center, U. Alaska, 1972-79, Prince William Sound Community Coll., 1979—; one-woman exhbns. in Maine, N.Y.C., Alaska and Calif.; group exhbns. include Allied Artists Am., 1970-72, Nat. Acad. Design, 1971, 74, Nat. Sculpture Soc. Ann., 1971, 72, 73, Alaska Woman Art Show, 1987, 88, Cordova Visual Artists, 1991-96, Alaska Artists Guild Show, 1994, Am. Medallic Sculpture Nat. Travelling Exhbn., 1994-95; pres. Cordova Arts and Pageants Ltd., 1975-76; commns. include Merle K. Smith Commemorative plaque, 1973, Eyak Native Monument, 1978, Anchorage Pioneer's Home Ceramic Mural, 1979, Alaska Wildlife Series Bronze Medal, 1980, sculpture murals and portraits Alaska State Capitol, 1981, Pierre De Ville Portrait commn., 1983, Robert B. & Evangeline Atwood, 1985, Armin F. Koernig Hatchery Plaque, 1985, Cordova Fishermen's Meml. Sculpture, 1985, Alaska's Five Govs., bronze relief, Anchorage, 1986, Reluctant Fisherman's Mermaid, bronze, 1987, Charles E. Bunnell, bronze portrait statue, Fairbanks, 1988, Alexander Baranof Monument, Sitka, Alaska, 1989, Wally Noerenberg Hatchery Plaque, Prince William Sound, Alaska, 1989, Russian-Alaskan Friendship Plaque (edit. of 4), Kayak Island, Cordova, Alaska and Vladivostok & Petropavlovsk-Kamchatskiy, Russia, 1991, Sophie-Last Among Eyak Native People, 1992, Alaska Airlines Medal Commn. 1993, Hosp. Aux. plaque, 1995; also other portraits. Bd. dirs. Alaska State Coun. on the Arts, 1991-95. Scholarship student Nat. Acad. Sch. Fine Arts, 1969-72; recipient J.A. Suydam Bronze medal, 1969; Dr. Ralph Weiler prize, 1971; Helen Foster Barnet award, 1971; Daniel Chester French award, 1972; Frishmuth award, 1971; Allied Artists Am. award, 1972; C. Percival Dietsch prize, 1973; citation Alaska Legislature, 1981, 82, Alaskan Artist of the Yr., 1991. Fellow Nat. Sculpture Soc. Address: PO Box 374 Cordova AK 99574-0374

BUGLI, DAVID, conductor. Conductor Carson City Chamber Orch., Nev. Office: Carson City Chamber Orchestra PO Box 2001 Carson City NV 89702-2001*

BUHLER, DAVID L., senator, institute director; b. Salt Lake City, July 13, 1957; s. Robert E. and Phyllis (Liddle) B.; m. Lori Goaslind, July 7, 1982; children: Jennifer, Matthew, Spencer, Emily. BS in History, BS in Polit. Sci., U. Utah, 1983; MPA, Brigham Young U., 1985. Staff asst. Office of U.S. Senator Orrin Hatch, Salt Lake City, 1979-83, dir. constituent svcs., 1983-85; adminstrv. asst. State of Utah Gov.'s Office, Salt Lake City, 1985-88; exec. dir. Utah Dept. Commerce, Salt Lake City, 1989-92; v.p. Nat. Assessment Inst., Salt Lake City, 1992—; instr. polit. sci. U. Utah, 1990—. Del. Rep. Nat. Conv., Houston, 1992, San Diego, 1996; presdl. elector Utah Electoral Coll., 1992; mem. Utah State Senate, Dist. 7, Salt Lake City, 1994—. Mem. LDS. Home: 1436 S Yuma St Salt Lake City UT 84108 Office: National Assessment Inst 560 E 200 S #300 Salt Lake City UT 84102

BUHLER, JILL LORIE, editor, writer; b. Seattle, Dec. 7, 1945; d. Oscar John and Marcella Jane (Hearing) Younce; 1 child, Lori Jill Kelly; m. John Buhler, 1990; stepchildren: Christie, Cathie Vsetecka, Mike. AA in Gen. Edn., Am. River Coll., 1969; BA in Journalism with honors, Sacramento State U., 1973. Reporter Carmichael (Calif.) Courier, 1968-70; mng. editor Quarter Horse of the Pacific Coast, Sacramento, 1970-75, editor, 1975-84; editor Golden State Program Jour., 1978, Nat. Reined Cow Horse Assn. News, Sacramento, 1983-88, Pacific Coast Jour., Sacramento, 1984-88, Nat. Snaffle Bit Assn. News, Sacramento, 1988; pres., chief exec. officer Communications Plus, Port Townsend, Wash., 1988—; mag. cons., 1975—. Interviewer Pres. Ronald Regan, Washington, 1983; mng. editor Wash. Thoroughbred, 1989-90. Mem. 1st profl. communicators mission to USSR, 1988; bd. dirs. Carmichael Winding Way, Pasadena Homeowners Assn., 1985-87; mem. scholarship com. Thoroughbred Horse Racing's United Scholarship Trust; hosp. commr. Jefferson Gen. Hosp., 1995—, chair bd. dirs. 1997—. Recipient 1st pl. feature award, 1970, 1st pl. editorial award Jour. Assn. Jr. Colls., 1971, 1st pl. design award WCHB Yuba-Sutter Counties, Marysville, Calif., 1985, Photography awards, 1994, 95, 96. Mem. Am. River Jaycees (Speaking award 1982), Am. Horse Publs. (1st Pl. Editl. award 1983, 86), Port Townsend C. of C. (trustee, v.p. 1993, pres. 1994, officer 1996, 97, 98), Mensa (bd. dirs., asst. local sec., activities dir. 1987-88, membership chair 1988-90), Kiwanis Internat. (chair MEP com., treas. 1992—), 5th Wheel Touring Soc. (v.p. 1970). Republican. Roman Catholic. Home: 440 Adelma Beach Rd Port Townsend WA 98368-9605

BUI, TUAN SY, biomedical company executive, researcher; b. Thanh Hoa, Vietnam, Oct. 16, 1950; came to U.S., 1991; s. Thi Sy and Kim Yen (Tran) B.; m. Chau Bich Phan, Nov. 6, 1973; 1 child, Tuan Huy. BE, Canterbury U., Christchurch, New Zealand, 1972, PhD in Electronics, 1979; MBA, MacQuarie U., Sydney, Australia, 1984. Group leader Ausonics, Sydney, 1980-83, prodn. mgr., 1983-84, chief rsch. engr., 1984-87, mktg. exec., 1987-89; group product mgr. Telectronics, Sydney, 1989-91; internat. product mgt. Telectronics Pacing Systems, Denver, 1991-92, project mgr., 1992-93, dir. ops., 1993—. Patentee in field. Colombo scholar New Zealand Govt., 1968-78. Mem. IEEE (sr.). Office: Telectronics Pacing Systems 7400 S Tucson Way Englewood CO 80112-3938

BUIDANG, GEORGE (HADA BUIDANG), educator, administrator, consultant, writer; b. Danang, Vietnam, Dec. 30, 1924; came to U.S., 1981; s. Bui Dang Do and Ha Thi Yen; m. Pham Thi Hong, Feb. 25, 1951; children: Bui Tu Long, Bui Nguyen Khanh, Bui Minh Hoang, Bui Thi Tuong Vi. G-rad., Providence Inst., Vietnam, 1944. Head translator USMC, 1956-61; dep. employment officer Hdqrs. Support Activity Saigon USN, 1962-65; asst. dir. Ctrl. Tng. Inst. U.S. Army, Vietnam, 1966; pers. dir. Foremost Dairies Vietnam of Foremost-McKesson Internat., 1966-75; instr. of French Un Bateau Pour L'Asie Du Sud-Est, Brussels, Belgium, 1980; asst. dir. edn. Career Resources Devel. Ctr., Inc., San Francisco, 1981-93; ind. cons. San Francisco, 1993—. Author: Using WordPerfect 5.0, 1989, Using Lotus 1-2-3 Release 2.2., 1991, Using WordPerfect 5.1, 1991, Using Microsoft Windows 3.1, 1993, Using WordPerfect 6.0 for DOS, 1994, Using Lotus 1-2-3 for Windows, 1995, Using WordPerfect for Windows, 1996, Using Microsoft Word 97 for Windows 95, 1997. Nominated Internat. Man of Yr. for 1992/1993 Internat. Biog. Ctr. of Cambridge, Eng., Man of Yr. Am. Biog. Inst. Internat. Bd. Rsch., 1996. Republican. Roman Catholic. Home: 565 Geary St Apt 411 San Francisco CA 94102-1660 Office: 655 Geary St San Francisco CA 94102-1646

BUIST, NEIL ROBERTSON MACKENZIE, medical educator, medical administrator; b. Karachi, India, July 11, 1932; m. Sonia Chapman; children: Catriona, Alison, Diana. Degree with commendation, U. St. Andrews, Scotland, MB, ChB, 1956; Diploma of Child Health, London U., England, 1960. Diplomate Am. Bd. Med. Genetics, Am. Bd. Clinical Genetics. House physician internal medicine Arbroath Infirmary, 1956-57; house physician externe cardiopulmonary dept. Hosp. Marie Lannelongue, Paris, 1957; house surgeon Royal Hosp. Sick Children, Edinburgh, Scotland, 1957; commd. far east med. officer Regimental Military Svc., 1957-60; house physician Royal Infirmary, Dundee, Scotland, 1960; registrar internal medicine Maryfield Hosp., Dundee, Scotland, 1960-62; lectr. child health U. St. Andrews, Dundee, Scotland, 1962-64; rsch. fellow pediatric microchemistry, Sch. Health Sci. U. Colo., Denver, 1964-66; asst. prof. pediatrics, Sch. Medicine U. Oreg., Portland, 1966-70; dir. Pediatrics Metabolic Lab, Oreg. Health Sci. U., Portland, 1966-93, Metabolic Birth Defects Ctr., Oreg. Health Sci. U., Portland, 1966—; assoc. prof. pediatrics and med. genetics Health Sci Ctr., U. Oreg., Portland, 1970-76; prof. pediatrics and med. genetics Oreg. Health Scis. U., 1976—; med. cons. Northwest Regional Newborn Screening Program, Portland, 1970—; vis. prof. WHO, China, 1988, U. Colo., 1990, Wesley Med. Ctr., Kans., 1991, Phoenix Children's Hosp., Ariz., 1991, Tucson Med. Ctr., Ariz., 1991, U. Ill., Chgo., 1991, Kapoiolani Med. Ctr., Hawaii, 1992, Shriners Hosp. for Crippled Children., Hawaii, 1992, Ark. Children's Hosp., 1993, Australasian Soc. for Human Genetics, New Zealand, 1994, LBJ Med. Ctr., Americas Samoa, 1994, Mahidol U., Bangkok, 1996, U. P.R., 1996, U. Auckland (New Zealand), 1997. Author: (with others) Textbook of Pediatrics, 1973, Inherited Disorders of Amino Acid Metabolism, 1974, 1985, Clinics in Endocrinolog and Metabolism: Aspects of Neonatal Metabolism, 1976, Textbook of Pediatrics, 1978, Practice of Pediatrics, 1980, Management of High-Risk Pregnancy, 1980, Current Occular Therapy, 1980, Practice of Pediatrics, 1981, Clinics in Endocrinology and Metabolism: Aspects of Neonatal Metabolism, 1981, Textbook of Pediatrics, 1984, Disorders of Fatty Acid Metabolism in the Pediatric Practice, 1990, Birth Defects Encyclopedia, 1990, 1991, Treatment of Genetic Disease, 1991, Pediatric Clinics of North Americs Medical Genetics II, 1992, Forfar & Arneil's Textbook of Paediatrics, 1992, 97, Galactosemia New Frontiers in Research, 1993, New Horizons in Neonatal Screening, 1994, New Trends in Neonatal Screening, 1994, Alpha-1-Antitrypsin Deficiency, 1994, Diseases of the Fetus and Newborn, 1995, Inborn Metabolic Diseases: Diagnosis and Treatment, 1995; cons. editor: Inborn Metabolic Disease Text, 1995; editorial bd. mem.: Jour. of Inherited Metabolic Diseases, 1977—, Kelley Practice of Pediatrics, 1980-87, Screening, 1991-96; jour. reviewer: Am. Jour. of Human Genetics, Jour. of Pediatrics, Pediatric Rsch., Screening. Adv. com. Tri County March of Dimes, Portland, 1977—; physician Diabetic Children's Camp, 1967—, Muscle Biopsy Clinic Shriners Hosp., 1989—; bd. dirs. Mize Info. Enterprises, Dallas, 1987—. Fellow Royal Coll. Physicians Edinburgh, Fogarty Internat. Vis. Scientist, Royal Coll. Physicians Edinburgh; mem. Brit. Med. Assn., Western Soc. Pediatric Rsch. (coun. mem. 1966—), Pacific North West Pediatric Soc., Am. Pediatric Soc., Soc. for the Study of Inborn Errors of Metabolism, Soc. for Inherited Metabolic Disorders (treas. 1977—), Oreg. Pediatric Soc., Oreg. Diabetes Assn., Portland Acad. Pediatrics, Internat. Newborn Screening Soc. Coun. (founding mem. 1988—). Office: Oreg Health Sci U Ste 303 3181 SW Sam Jackson Park Rd # L473 Portland OR 97201-3011

BULKLEY, ROBERT DE GROFF, JR., lawyer; b. Toledo, Ohio, June 19, 1943; s. Robert De Groff and Loretta (Coburn) B.; m. Linda Gail Throp, June 20, 1964 (div. May 1982); children: Joanna Eleanor, Katrina Elisabeth; m. Joyce Lorraine MacWilliamson, Feb. 10, 1985. BA, Lewis & Clark Coll., 1964; MA, Princeton U., 1966, PhD, 1971; JD, U. Oreg., 1977. Bar: Oreg. 1977, U.S. Dist. Ct. Oreg. 1978, U.S. Ct. Appeals (9th cir.) 1978, U.S. Supreme Ct. 1990. Instr. history Benedict Coll., Columbia, S.C., 1966-67; asst. prof. history Rocky Mountain Coll., Billings, Mont., 1968-74; law clk. U.S. Ct. Appeals, 9th Cir., Portland, Oreg., 1977-78; asst. atty. gen. Oreg. Dept. Justice, Portland, 1978-83; staff atty. Oreg. Ct. Appeals, Salem, 1983-90, 95—; assoc. Markowitz, Herbold et al, Portland, 1990-92, of counsel, 1992-95. Clk. of session First Presbyn. Ch., Portland, 1986-89, mem. various coms., 1980—; mem. peace and justice com. Presbytery of the Cascades, Portland, 1989-95; mem. cmty. ministries com. Ecumenical Ministries of Oreg., Portland, 1995—. Woodrow Wilson fellow, 1964. Mem. Oreg. State Bar. Democrat. Home: 11585 SW Denfield Beaverton OR 97005 Office: Oregon Court of Appeals 300 Justice Bldg Salem OR 97310

BULL, BRIAN STANLEY, pathology educator, medical consultant, business executive; b. Watford, Hertfordshire, Eng., Sept. 14, 1937; came to U.S., 1954, naturalized, 1960; s. Stanley and Agnes Mary (Murdoch) B.; m. Maureen Hannah Huse, June 3, 1963; children: Beverly Velda, Beryl Heather. B.S. in Zoology, Walla Walla Coll., 1957; M.D., Loma Linda (Calif.) U., 1961. Diplomate: Am. Bd. Pathology. Intern Yale U., 1961-62, resident in anat. pathology, 1962-63; resident in clin. pathology NIH, Bethesda, Md., 1963-65; fellow in hematology and electron microscopy NIH, 1965-66, staff hematologist, 1966-67; research asst. dept. anatomy Loma Linda U., 1958, dept. microbiology, 1959, asst. prof. pathology, 1968-71, assoc. prof., 1971-73, prof., 1973—, chmn. dept. pathology, 1973—, assoc. dean for acad. affairs sch. medicine, 1993-94, dean sch. medicine, 1994—; cons. to mfrs. of med. testing devices; mem. panel on hematology FDA; mem. Nat. Com. on Clin. Lab. Standards; mem. Internat. Commn. for Standardization in Hematology, pres., 1996-97. Mem. bd. editors Blood Cells, Molecules and Diseases, 1995—; contbr. chpts. to books, articles to med. jours.; patentee in field; editor-in-chief Blood Cells N.Y. Heidelberg, 1985-94. Served with USPHS, 1963-67. Nat. Inst. Arthritis and Metabolic Diseases fellow, 1967-68; recipient Daniel D. Comstock Meml. award Loma Linda U., 1961, Merck Manual award, 1961, Mosby Scholarship Book award, 1961; Ernest B. Cotlove Meml. lectr. Acad. Clin. Lab. Physicians and Scientists, 1972; named Alumnus of Yr., Walla Walla Coll., 1984, Honored Alumnus, Loma Linda U. Sch. Medicine, 1987, Humanitarian award, 1991, Citizen of Yr., C. of C. of Loma Linda. Fellow Am. Soc. Clin. Pathologists, Am. Soc. Hematology, Coll. Am. Pathologists, FDA Panel on Hematology, Nat. Com. on Clin. Lab. Standards, Internat. Commn. for Standards in Hematology, N.Y. Acad. Scis.; mem. AMA, Calif. Soc. Pathologists, San Bernadino County Med. Soc. (William C. Cover Outstanding Contbn. to Medicine award 1994), Acad. Clin. Lab. Physicians and Scientists, Am. Assn. Pathologists, Sigma Xi, Alpha Omega Alpha. Seventh-day Adventist. Office: Loma Linda U Sch Medicine 11234 Anderson St Loma Linda CA 92354-2804

BULL, HENRIK HELKAND, architect; b. N.Y.C., July 13, 1929; s. Johan and Sonja (Geelmuyden) B.; m. Barbara Alpaugh, June 9, 1956; children: Peter, Nina. B.Arch., Mass. Inst. Tech., 1952. With Mario Corbett, San Francisco, 1954-55; pvt. practice, 1956-68; ptnr. Bull, Field, Volkmann, Stockwell, Calif., 1968-82, Bull, Volkmann, Stockwell, Calif., 1982-90, Bull Stockwell and Allen, Calif., 1990-93, Bull, Stockwell, Allen & Ripley, San Francisco, 1993—; Vis. lectr. Syracuse U., 1963; Mem. adv. com. San Francisco Urban Design Study, 1970-71. Works include Sunset mag. Discovery House, Tahoe Tavern Condominiums, Lake Tahoe, Calif., Snowmass Villas Condominiums, Aspen, Colo., Northstar Master Plan Village and Condominiums, Moraga Valley Presbyn. Ch., Calif., Spruce Saddle Restaurant and Poste-Montane Hotel, Beaver Creek, Colo., Bear Valley visitor ctr., Point Reyes, Calif., The Inn at Spanish Bay, Pebble Beach, Calif., Taluswood Cmty., Whistler, B.C. Served as 1st lt. USAF, 1952-54. Winner competition for master plan new Alaska capital city, Willow, 1978. Fellow AIA (pres. N. Calif. chpt. 1968, Firm award Calif. chpt. 1989). Democrat. Office: Bull Stockwell Allen Ripley 350 Pacific Ave San Francisco CA 94111-1708*

BULL, JOHN CARRAWAY, JR., plastic surgeon; b. Raleigh, Sept. 21, 1934; s. John Carraway and Coralee Bull; m. Ann Bull, June 28, 1958; children: Virginia S., Kristin L., Natalie E., John C. III. MD, Harvard U., 1960. Diplomate Am. Bd. Surgery, Am. Bd. Plastic Surgery. Intern med. sch. hosp. U. Oreg.; resident in gen. surgery U. Calif., San Francisco; resident in plastic surgery Johns Hopkins; pvt. practice specializing in plastic surgery Phoenix, 1970-86; v.p. med. affairs St. Joseph Hosp. & Med. Ctr., Phoenix, 1986—. Bd. dirs. U. Ariz. Health Sci. Ctr. Lt. USN, 1961-64. NIH awardee, 1970. Fellow ACS; mem. Am. Coll. Physician Execs., Am. Coll. Health Care Execs., Ariz. Med. Assn. (Disting. Svc. award 1986), Maricopa County Med. Soc. (Disting. Svc. award 1981), Harvard Club. Office: Saint Joseph Hosp & Med Ctr 350 W Thomas Rd Phoenix AZ 85013-4409

BULLARD, SHARON WELCH, librarian; b. San Diego, Nov. 4, 1943; d. Dale L. and Myrtle (Sampson) Welch; m. Donald H. Bullard, Aug. 1, 1969. B.S.Ed., U. Central Ark., 1965; M.A., U. Denver, 1967. Media specialist Adams County Sch. Dist. 12, Denver, 1967-69; tchr., libr. Humphrey pub. schs., Ark., 1965-66, libr., 1969-70; catalog libr. Ark. State U., Jonesboro, 1970-75; head documents cataloging Wash. State U., Pullman, 1979-83; head serials cataloging U. Calif.-Santa Barbara Davidson Libr., 1984-88, head circulation svcs., 1988—; cons. Ctr. for Robotic Systems Microelectronics Rsch. Libr., Santa Barbara, 1986, Calif. State Libr. retrospective conversion project, 1987, Ombudsman's Office U. Calif., Santa Barbara, 1988; distributor Amway, 1985-91. Canvasser, Citizens for Goleta Valley, 1985-86; adv. bd. Total Interlibr. Exch., 1994-96. Mem. ALA, Calif. Libr. Assn. (tech. svcs. chpt. southern Calif. sect.), Libr. Assn. U. Calif.-Santa Barabara (mem. subcom. on advancement and promotion 1987-91, 1995-96, chmn. subcom. advancement and promotion 1996—), NAFE, So. Calif. Tech. Processes Group (membership com. 1987), Assn. Coll. and Rsch. Librs. (intern membership com. 1993-94, extended campus libr. sect. guidelines com. 1995-96), Libr. Adminstrn. and Mgmt. Assn. (mem. circulation/access svcs. systems and svcs. sect. 1993—, mem. equipment com. bldg. and equipment sect. 1993—), Notis Users Circulation Interest Group (presenter meeting 1992, mem. CIRC SIG steering com. 1993-97, moderator meeting 1993-95, chair elect 1994-95, chair 1995-96, program com. 1996-97), Pi Lambda Theta (exec. bd., sec. Santa Barbara chpt. 1990-91, hospitality com. 1991-92). Avocations: walking, camping, boogey boarding, swimming.

BULLICK, KAREN FAYE, dietitian; b. L.A., Aug. 11, 1964; d. Ralph and Pearl Ellen (Harris) B. BS in Psychology, Brigham Young U., 1987; BS in Nutrition summa cum laude, Calif. State U., Long Beach, 1990; MS in Nutrition, U. Wash., 1993. Registered dietitian. Nutrition specialist Evans-Kraft Advt. and Pub. Rels. Agy., Seattle, 1991-92; cons. dietitian in pvt. practice Huntington Beach, Calif., 1992—; cons. dietitian for long-term health care facilities Huntington Beach, 1992—; speaker in field. Brigham Young U. scholar, 1983-87, U. Wash. scholar, 1993. Mem. Am. Dietetic Assn. (legis. network 1992-93), Am. Soc. Parenteral and Enteral Nutrition, Sierra Club, Toastmasters Internat., Phi Kappa Phi. Mormon. Home: 34026 Selva Rd Unit 66 Dana Point CA 92629-3762

BULLIS, MICHAEL A., hotel executive; b. Pensacola, Fla., Aug. 24, 1947; s. Jerell W. Sr. and W. Joyce (Watson) B.; children: Shannon Renee Bullis Ray, Katrina Celeste. BBA, Sam Houston State U., 1969. Gen. mgr. Nat. Hotel Co., Galveston, Tex., 1969-74, Hospitality Mgmt. Corp., Dallas, 1974-78; mng. dir. Claremont Resort Hotel & Tennis Club, Oakland, Calif., 1978-82; pres. Wrather Hotels & Wrather Mgmt. Co., Anaheim, Calif., 1982-89, Destination Properties, Inc., Newport Beach, Calif., 1989-94; v.p. Hanjin Internat., gen. mgr. Omni L.A. Hotel & Ctr., 1995—. Dir. Gov.'s Coun. on Tourism, Calif.; mem. Calif. Tourism Bd.; dir. Disney Pigskin Classic and Freedom Bowl. 1st lt. U.S. Army Nat. Guard. Mem. Calif. Hotel & Motel Assn. (pres., chmn., co-chmn. polit. action com., mem. strategic planning com., mem. ednl. inst. audit com., chmn. mktg. task force and membership com.), Orange County Sports Assn., Anaheim Visitor & Convention Bur. (chmn.), Huntington Beach Conf. & Visitors Bur. (dir.), Huntington Beach

C. of C. Republican. Home and Office: 2133 Miramar Dr Newport Beach CA 92661-1518

BULLOCK, DONALD WAYNE, elementary education educator, educational computing consultant; b. Tacoma Park, Md., Mar. 24, 1947; s. B.W. and Margaret (Harris) B.; m. Pamela Louise Hatch, Aug. 7, 1971. AA in Music, L.A. Pierce Coll., Woodland Hills, Calif., 1969; BA in Geography, San Fernando Valley State Coll., 1971; Cert. Computer Edn., Calif. Luth. U., 1985, MA in Curriculum-Instrn., 1987. Tchr. music Calvary Luth. Sch., Pacoima, Calif., 1970-71; elem. tchr. 1st Luth. Sch., Northridge, Calif., 1971-73; elem. tchr. Simi Valley (Calif.) Unified Sch. Dist., 1973—, computer insvc. instr., 1982-85, computer mentor tchr., 1985-87, mentor tchr. ednl. tech., 1992-95; lectr. Calif. Luth. U., Thousand Oaks, 1985-92; ednl. computer cons. DISC Ednl. Svcs., Simi Valley, 1985—; speaker profl. confs. Contbr. articles to profl. publs. Pres. Amen Choir, Van Nuys, Calif., 1981-83. Recipient Computer Learning Month grand prize Tom Snyder Prodns., 1988, Computer Learning Found., 1990, Spl. Commendation of Achievement, Learning mag. profl. best tchr. excellence awards, 1990, Impact II Disseminator award Ventura County Supt. of Schs. and Ventura County Econ. Devel. Assn., 1995; grantee Tandy-Radio Shack, Inc., 1985, Calif. Dep. Edn., 1985. Mem. NEA, ASCD, Internat. Soc. Tech. in Edn., Computer Using Educators Calif., Gold Coast Computer Using Educators (bd. dirs. 1988-89, 95-96), Basset Hound Club am., Basset Hound Club So. Calif. (bd. dirs. 1994-95, pres. 1995—). Home: 2805 Wanda Ave Simi Valley CA 93065-1528 Office: Garden Grove Elem Sch 2250 Tracy Ave Simi Valley CA 93063-2753

BULLOCK, JAMES BENBOW, sculptor; b. St. Louis, Feb. 6, 1929; s. James Absalom and Rosalind Julia (Hausberger) B.; m. Jean Audrey Fegeans, May 31, 1952; children: Richard Benbow, Sarah Jean, Carol Ann. BA, Wesleyan U. Prin. works exhibited in numerous one-man and group shows including Gensler & Assocs., 1993, Marathon Plaza, San Francisco, 1993, Art Concepts Gallery and Contra Costa Coun., Walnut Creek, Calif., 1992, Pacific Design Ctr., L.A., 1992, Contract Design Ctr., San Francisco, 1991, Palm Springs Desert Mus., 1994, SOMAR Gallery, San Francisco, 1993, Dominical Coll., San Rafael, Calif., 1997, James A. Michener Mus. Sculpture Park, Doylestown, Pa., 1996-97, others; works represented in numerous collections including AT&T, San Francisco, Gov.'s Mansion, Santa Fe, N.Mex., Bramalea Pacific Corp., Oakland, Calif., Tower-Perrins Corp., N.Y.C. With USCG, 1951. Recipient Royal Mus. award Hakone Open Air Mus., 1989, 2d prize Festival des Arts, France, 1994. Home: 12 Sandy Beach Rd Vallejo CA 94590-8122

BULLOCK, MOLLY, retired elementary education educator; d. Wiley and Annie M. Jordan; m. George Bullock; children: Myra A. Bauman, Dawn M. BS in Edn., No. Ariz. U., 1955, postgrad., 1958; postgrad., LaVerne U., 1962, Claremont Grad. Sch., 1963, Calif. State U. L.A., 1966. Tchr. Bur. Indian Affairs, Kaibeto, Ariz., 1955-56, Crystal, N.Mex., 1956-59; tchr. Covina (Calif.) Valley Unified Sch. Dist., 1961-95, supervising master tchr. for trainees of LaVerne U. and Calif. State U. - L.A., 1961-71, mem. curriculum devel. adv. bd., 1977-79; ret., 1995; mem. voting com. Excellence in Edn. awards Lawry's Foods. Poet: A Tree (Golden Poet 1991), What is Love (Golden medal of honor). Vol., visitor area convalescent hosps. Mini grantee Hughes/Rotary Club/Foothill Ind. Bank, Covina, 1986-90. Mem. ASCD, NEA, NAFE, AAUW (treas. 1972), Internat. Platform Assn., Internat. Soc. Poets (hon. charter), Calif. Tchrs. Assn. Home: 2175 Victoria Way Pomona CA 91767-2371

BULLOCK, WELDON KIMBALL, health facility administrator, pathologist, pathology educator; b. Vernal, Utah, Jan. 6, 1908; s. John Kimball and Adelaide (Arnold) B.; m. Dosia Opal Newton, Dec. 26, 1931; children: John, Jim. BA, U. Utah, 1930; MD, Northwestern U., 1934, MSc in Pathology, 1942. Diplomate Am. Bd. Pathology; lic. MD, Calif., Idaho, Utah. Intern Alameda County Hosp., 1933-34; resident in medicine Cook County Hosp., 1940-41; resident in surgery L.A. County-U. So. Calif. Med. Ctr., 1946-47; head surg. pathology LAC-U. So. Calif. Med. Ctr., 1949-69; instr. pathology Sch. Medicine U. So. Calif., 1947-48, asst. prof., 1955-62, clin. prof., 1963-74, clin. prof. emeritus, 1974—; exec. dir. Calif. Tumor Tissue Registry, various locations, 1955-95; dir. emeritus Calif. Tumor Tissue Registry, 1995—; chief pathology svc. Orthop. Hosp., 1956-63; assoc. pathologist St. Luke Hosp., 1963-70, chief pathologist, 1970-77, assoc. pathologist, 1977-81; clin. prof. pathology Sch. Medicine Loma Linda U., 1992—; James Ewing fellow in pathology Meml. Hosp. for Cancer and Allied Disease, 1948-49; cons. Calif. Assn. Cytotechnologists, 1962—, So. Calif. Acad. Oral Pathology, 1963—, Orthop. Hosp., 1963—; mem. Am. Joint Com. Cancer Staging and End Result Reporting, 1963-69, chmn. audio-visual task force, 1966-69, mem. exec. com., 1969; mem. rev. com. clin. cancer tng. grants Nat. Cancer Inst., 1965-68; mem. cancer planning com. Calif. Regional Med. Program, Area V, U. So. Calif., 1967-69; mem. pub. health svc. spl. project rev. com. HEW, State of Calif., 1967-69; meml. lectr. Arthur Purdy Stout Soc. Surg. Pathologists, 1979. Author: Oral Cancer & Tumors of the Jaws, 1956; contbr. articles to profl. jours. Lt. Col. U.S. Army Res., 1941-45, PTO. Decorated Bronze Star. Mem. AMA, Coll. Am. Pathologists (mem. com. cancer 1965-70), Am. Soc. Clin. Pathologists, Soc. Surg. Oncology, Calif. Med. Assn., Calif. Soc. Pathologists (mem. exec. com. 1960-62, sec.-treas. 1962-65, pres.-elect 1965-66, pres. 1966-67), L.A. County Med. Assn. (chmn. com. med. examiner 1968-72), L.A. Soc. Pathologists (past pres. exec. com. 1961-62), Soc. Grad. Pathologists-L.A. County-U. So. Calif. Med. Ctr., Soc. Grad. Surgeons-L.A. County-U. So. Calif. Med. Ctr. Home: 1460 Van Dyke Rd San Marino CA 91108 Office: Calif Tumor Tissue Registry 11021 Campus Ave AH 335 Loma Linda CA 92350

BULTMANN, WILLIAM ARNOLD, historian; b. Monrovia, Calif., Apr. 10, 1922; s. Paul Gerhardt and Elsa (Johnson) B.; AB, UCLA, 1943, PhD, 1950; m. Phyllis Jane Wetherell, Dec. 28, 1949; 1 child, Janice Jane. Assoc. prof. history Central Ark. U., Conway, 1949-52, prof., 1954-57; assoc. prof. Ohio Wesleyan U., Delaware, 1957-61, prof., 1961-65; prof. Western Wash. U., Bellingham, 1965-87, chmn. dept., 1968-70, dean arts and scis., 1970-72, provost, 1971-73; vis. assoc. prof. U. Tex., Austin, 1952-53; vis. prof. U. N.H., summers 1965, 66; acad. cons. Wash. Commn. for Humanities, 1973-87, Nat. Endowment for Humanities, 1976-87; reader Ednl. Testing Service Princeton, 1973-85. Bd. dirs. Bellingham Maritime Heritage Found., 1980-85; mem. The Nature Conservancy, 1992—, Washington Arboretum Found., 1992—; adminstrv. officer Bellingham Power Squadron, 1981-82, comdr., 1982-84. Fulbight sr. lectr. Dacca (Bangladesh) U., 1960-61; Ohio Wesleyan U. rsch. fellow, 1964; Fund for Advancement Edn. fellow for fgn. study, 1953-54; recipient rsch. award Social Sci. Rsch. Coun., 1957. Mem. AAUP. Am. Hist. Assn., Nat. Tropical Botanical Garden Soc., Nat. Boating Fedn., Ch. Hist. Soc., Conf. Brit. Studies, Pacific, Pacific N.W. confs. Brit. studies, Mystery Writers of Am., Interclub Boating Assn. Washington, Seattle Power Squadron, Phi Beta Kappa, Phi Delta Kappa, Pi Gamma Mu. Episcopalian. Clubs: Park Athletic Recreation, Bellingham Yacht (chmn. pub. rels. com. 1981-86), Squalicum Yacht (trustee 1979-82), Birch Bay Yacht; Wash. Athletic. Co-author: Border Boating, 1978; co-founder, mem. editorial bd. Albion, 1968-84; mng. editor Brit. Studies Intelligencer, 1973-80; co-editor Current Research in British Studies, 1975; editor Jib Sheet, 1981-86; feature writer, columnist Sea mag., 1974-93; feature writer Venture mag., 1981-85, Poole Publs., 1988-92. Home: 1600 43rd Ave E Apt 101 Seattle WA 98112-3245

BUMBAUGH, ROBERT WARREN, SR., oil industry executive; b. L.A., Sept. 8, 1937; s. Warren Herbert and Nina May (Browning) B.; m. Betty Jean Harkless, Apr. 14, 1956; children: Robert Warren Jr., Scott Arthur, Cheryllyn Jean. Student, Santa Ana (Calif.) Jr. Coll., 1960-62, Orange Coast Coll., 1965-66, Kenai Peninsula Coll., 1989-92. Cert. journeyman painter, CPR, internat. coating inspector. Painter Garden Grove (Calif.) Unified Sch. Dist., 1964-67, Kent (Ohio) U., 1968-69, Nicholas and Nicholas Painting, Orange, Calif., 1969-70, Stockwell Painting Contractors, 1970-71; owner, operator Bumbaugh's Painting, 1971-79; painter Sledge & Son Painting, 1979-81; painter, foreman Roger's Alaskan Painting, 1981-83; owner, operator Bumbaugh's Alaskan Enterprises, 1983-86; foreman Wade Oilfield Svc. Co., Inc., 1986-89; supr. Alaska Petroleum Contractors, Nikiski, 1989—. Bd. dirs. Ch. of Nazarene, Coeur d' Alene, Idaho, 1947-94. Home: PO Box 3727 Soldotna AK 99669-3727 Office: Alaska Petroleum Contractor PO Box 8113 Nikiski AK 99635-8113

BUMGARDNER, LARRY G., foundation administrator, law and political science educator; b. Chattanooga, June 10, 1957; s. Walter G. and Kathryn (Hamrick) B. BA, David Lipscomb Coll., 1977; JD, Vanderbilt U., 1981. Bar: Tenn. 1981, U.S. Dist. Ct. (cen. dist.) Tenn. 1982, Calif. 1984, U.S. Dist. Ct. (cen. dist.) Calif. 1985. From reporter to copy editor Nashville (Tenn.) Banner, 1975-79; editor Tenn. Attorneys Memo, Tenn. Jour., Nashville, 1979-83; dir. founds. Pepperdine U., Malibu, Calif., 1983-85, asst. v.p. comm. and grants, 1985-92, assoc. vice chancellor for founds. and rsch., asst. prof. comms., 1992-94, adj. prof. law and polit. sci., 1994—; dep. dir. Ronald Reagan Presdl. Found., Simi Valley, Calif., 1994-95; exec. dir. Ronald Reagan Presdl. Found. and Reagan Ctr. Pub. Affairs, 1995—. Contbr. numerous articles to various publs. Mem. ABA, Calif. Bar Assn. Home: 2700 Westham Cir Thousand Oaks CA 91362-5379 Office: 40 Presidential Dr Simi Valley CA 93065-0600

BUNCHMAN, HERBERT HARRY, II, plastic surgeon; b. Washington, Feb. 23, 1942; s. Herbert H. and Mary (Halleran) B.; m. Marguerite Fransioli, Mar. 21, 1963 (div. Jan. 1987); children: Herbert H. III., Angela K., Christopher. BA, Vanderbilt U., 1964; MD, U. Tenn., 1967. Diplomate Am. Bd. Surgery, Am. bd. Plastic Surgery. Resident in surgery U. Tex., Galveston, 1967-72, resident in plastic surgery, 1972-75; practice medicine specializing in plastic surgery Mesa, Ariz., 1975—; chief surgery Desert Samaritan Hosp., 1978-80. Contbr. articles to profl. jours. Eaton Clin. fellow, 1975. Mem. AMA, Am. Soc. Plastic and Reconstructive Surgery, Am. Soc. Aesthetic Plastic Surgery, Singleton Surgical Soc., Tex. Med. Assn., So. Med. Assn. (grantee 1974), Ariz. Med. Assn. Office: Plastic Surgery Cons PC 1520 S Dobson Rd Ste 314 Mesa AZ 85202-4727

BUNDE, CON, communication educator, state legislator; b. Mankato, Minn., Aug. 4, 1938; s. Ralph Louis and Leona Dorothy (Lehman) B.; m. Angelene Hammer, Aug. 22, 1964; children: Joy, Kurt. BA, Ctrl. Wash. U., 1966, MS, 1970; AA, Anchorage C.C., 1970. Cert. speech pathologist. Speech therapist Gig Harbor (Wash.) Schs., 1967-68, Anchorage Sch. Dist., 1968-70; asst. prof. speech comm. Anchorage C.C., 1970-88; prof. U. Alaska, Anchorage, 1988-93; mem. Alaska Ho. of Reps., Juneau, Anchorage, 1993—; pilot Ketchum Air Svc., Anchorage, 1975—; seminar leader in field. Mem. citizens adv. coun. Dept. Fish and Game, Anchorage, 1991-92, instr. bowhunter edn. program; active Anchorage Community Theater; mem. citizen's adv. bd. U. Alaska Anchorage Aviation Airframe and Power Plant degree program. With U.S. Army, 1956-59. Mem. Alaska Sled Dog Racing Assn. (pres. 1970-78), Alaska Airmen's Assn., Alaska Bowhunter Assn. (bd. dirs. 1991-92), Alaska Sportfishing Assn., Alaska Outdoor Coun. Republican. Office: Alaska State Legislature Ho of Reps 716 W 4th Ave Ste 200 Anchorage AK 99501-2107*

BUNDESEN, FAYE STIMERS, investment and management company owner, educator; b. Cedarville, Calif., Sept. 16, 1932; d. Floyd Walker and Ermina Elizabeth (Roberts) Stimers; m. Allen Eugene Bundesen, Dec. 27, 1972 (dec. 1991); children: William, David, Edward Silvius; Ted, Eric Bundesen. BA, Calif. State U.-Sacramento, 1955; MA, Calif. State U.-San Jose, 1972. Licensed real estate broker, Calif. Elem. sch. tchr. San Francisco Pub. Schs., 1955-60; elem. and jr. h.s. tchr., lang. arts specialist Sunnyvale (Calif.) Schs., 1978-83; cons. Santa Clara County Office of Edn. and Sunnyvale Sch. Dist., 1983-86; v.p. Bundesen Enterprises, Elk Grove, Calif., 1975-81, pres., 1981—. Bd. dirs. Sunnyvale Sch. Employees' Credit Union, 1983-86, v.p., 1984-86; co-chmn. Elk Grove Taxpayers Assn. for Incorporation, 1994; pres. Elk Grove/Laguna Civic League, 1994—; pers. chmn. Bethany Presbyn. Ch., 1992-95; mem. City of San Jose Tenant/Landlord Hearing Com., 1983-86, v.p., 1984-85. Mem. Assn. Supervision and Curriculum Devel., Calif. Scholarship Fedn. (life), AAUW, Calif. Apartment Assn., Nat. Apartment Assn., Calif. Assn. Realtors, Nat. Assn. Realtors, Sacramento Assn. Realtors, Sacramento Valley Apt. Assn., Soroptimist Internat. Rio Cosumnes, Elk Grove C. of C. Presbyterian. Office: PO Box 2006 Elk Grove CA 95759-2006

BUNDY, ROBERT C., prosecutor; b. Long Beach, Calif., June 26, 1946; s. James Kenneth and Kathleen Ilene (Klosterman) B.; m. Virginia Bonnie Lembo, Feb. 3, 1974; 2 children. BA cum laude, U. So. Calif., L.A., 1968; JD, U. Calif., Berkeley, 1971. Bar: Alaska 1972, Calif. 1972. Supervising atty. Alaska Legal Svcs. Corp., Nome, Alaska; dist. atty. Second Jud. Dist., Nome; asst. dist. atty. Alaska Dept. Law, asst. atty. gen. antitrust sect.; ptnr. Bogle & Gates, Anchorage, Alaska; now U.S. atty. for Alaska U.S. Dept. Justice, Anchorage. Mem. Trout Unlimited, Alaska Flyfishers. Office: Office US Atty for Alaska Rm C-253 222 W 7th Ave Unit 9 Anchorage AK 99513-7504*

BUNGE, ROBERT ALEXANDER, JR., educational administrator; b. Tacoma, Wash., Nov. 15, 1956; s. Robert Alexander and Margie Ann (Berry) B.; m. Patrice Melinda Gibble, Aug. 23, 1980; children: Katarina, Matthew. BA in History magna cum laude, U. Wash., 1979; AM in History, Stanford U., 1982, AM in Edn., 1984. Lic. prin., tchr., Wash. Tchr. Castilleja Sch., Palo Alto, Calif., 1983-84, Upward Bound, San Jose (Calif.) State U., 1984, Los Gatos (Calif.) H.S., 1984-85, Ferndale (Wash.) H.S., 1985-92; asst. prin. Mt. Vernon (Wash.) H.S., 1992-95, coord. extended learning, 1995-96, dir. opportunities program, 1996—; cons., trainer Corp. Edse Computer Learning Ctr., Bellingham, Wash., 1995—. Author: Exploring Solutions to World Problems, 1991. Vol. Star Task Force, Bellingham, 1987-89. Mem. ASCD, Phi Beta Kappa. Home: 2811 Ontario St Bellingham WA 98226-6111 Office: Mt Vernon HS 314 N 9th St Mount Vernon WA 98273

BUNGE, RUSSELL KENNETH, writer, poet, editor; b. Long Beach, Calif., Apr. 28, 1947; s. Kenneth Duncan Bunge and Mona Irene (Deleree) Coker; ptnr. Mr. Kelly A. Quiros. BA in Creative Writing, Calif. State U., Long Beach, 1972; MA in Humanities, Calif. State U., Dominguez Hills, 1985. Cert. C.C. tchr., Calif. Spl. svcs. cons. AT&T Comms., San Luis Obispo, Calif., 1973-90; info. cons. Obispo Info. Group, San Luis Obispo, 1990-95; pub., exec. editor Deleree & Co., San Luis Obispo, Calif., 1996—; mem. adv. bd. Calif. Online Resources for Edn., Long Beach, 1993-94; edn. coord. SLONET Info. Network, 1993-95, dir., 1997—. Author: Double Lives: Poems 1984-85, 1985; editor: Obispo Web Digest: on the World Wide Web; contbr. poems to profl. publs. Founding mem. AIDS Support Network, San Luis Obispo, 1984. Mem. MLA, Assn. for Computers and Humanities. Office: Delerre & Co Box 771 Mission Station San Luis Obispo CA 93406-0771

BUNKER, JOHN BIRKBECK, cattle rancher, retired sugar company executive; b. Yonkers, N.Y., Mar. 28, 1926; s. Ellsworth and Harriet (Butler) B.; m. Emma Cadwalader, Feb. 27, 1954; children: Emma, Jeanie, Harriet, John C., Lambert C. BA, Yale U., 1950. With Nat. Sugar Refining Co., 1953-62; pres. Gt. Western Sugar Co., Denver, 1966; pres., CEO Holly Sugar Co., Colorado Springs, Colo., 1967-81, chmn., CEO, 1971-81; pres., CEO Calif. and Hawaiian Sugar Co., San Francisco, 1981-88, vice chmn., 1988-89, ret., 1989; gen. ptnr. Bunker Ranch Co., 1989—; chmn. Wheatland Bankshares and First State Bank of Wheatland, 1992—. Trustee Colo. Coll., 1973-94, Asia Found., 1985-94. Mem. Wyo. Nature Conservancy, Wyo. Stockgrowers Assn., Wyo. Heritage Found., Wyo. Farm Bur., Colo.-Wyo. Nat. Farmers Union. Home: 1451 Cottonwood Ave Wheatland WY 82201-3412*

BUNKIS, JURIS, plastic surgeon; b. Lubeck, Germany, Aug. 27, 1949; came to the U.S., 1974; s. Janis and Jadviga (Buzinskis) B.; m. Ruta Sternbergs, Oct. 12, 1974; children: Justin S., Jessica S. Degree, U. Toronto, 1970, MD, 1974. Intern gen. surgery Mary Imogene Bassett Hosp., Columbia U., Cooperstown, N.Y., 1974-75, jr. resident gen. surgery, 1975-76; jr. resident gen. surgery Beth Israel Hosp., Mass. Gen. Hosp. & Shriner's Burn Inst., Harvard U., Boston, 1976-77; sr. resident gen. surgery Mary Imogene Bassett Hosp., Columbia U., Cooperstown, 1977-78, chief resident gen. surgery, 1978-79; sr. resident, chief resident plastic surgery Peter Bent Brigham & Children's Hosps., Harvard U., Boston, 1979-81; clin. instr. in surgery Harvard U., 1979-81; asst. prof. surgery divsn. plastic surgery U. Calif., San Francisco, 1981-83, asst. clin. prof. surgery, 1983-85; asst. chief plastic surgery San Francisco Gen. Hosp. U. Calif., 1981-82, chief plastic surgery, 1983; chmn. bd. dirs., pres. Juris Bunkis M.D., Inc., Danville, Calif., 1983—; chmn. bd. dirs., pres., med. dirs. Blackhawk Surgery Ctr., Inc., Danville, 1989—; chmn. bd. dirs., pres., sec. United Bridges, Inc., 1994—; invited lectr. numerous confs. Contbr. chpts. to books and articles to med. jours. Knight, Cavalieri di San Marco (Knights of San Marco), venice, 1995. Mem. Am. Assn. Hand Surgery (mem. program com. 1983-84, socioecons. com. 84-85), Am. Soc. Plastic and Reconstructive Surgery (mem. Tel Med subcom. 1986-87), Am. Soc. Aesthetic Surgery, Calif. Med. Soc., Calif. Soc. Plastic Surgeons (mem. program com. 1984-85, mem. ethics com. 86-87, mem. newsletter com. 87-89, mem. B.M.Q.A. liaison com. 87-89), Alameda-Contra Costa Med. Assn., Lipoplasty Soc. N.Am., Internat. Soc. Aesthetic Plastic Surgery, Pan Pacific Surg. Assn., Latvian Med. and Dental Assn., Plastic Surgery Rsch. Coun., Assn. Medicorum Bohemoslovacorum J.E. Purkyne (hon.), Soc. Bohemoslovaca Chirurgiae Plasticae (hon., Prague). Office: United Bridges Inc 4165 Blackhawk Plaza Cir Danville CA 94506-4691

BUNN, CHARLES NIXON, strategic business planning consultant; b. Springfield, Ill., Feb. 8, 1926; s. Joseph Forman and Helen Anna Frieda (Link) B.; student U. Ill., 1943-44; BS in Engring., U.S. Mil. Acad., 1949; MBA, Xavier U., Cin., 1958; m. Cecine Cole, Dec. 26, 1951 (div. 1987); children: Sisene, Charles; m. Marjorie Fitzmaurice, Apr. 5, 1988. Flight test engr. Gen. Electric Co., Cin., also Edwards AFB, Calif., 1953-59; sr. missile test engr., space systems div. Lockheed Aircraft Corp., USAF Satellite Test Center, Sunnyvale, Calif., 1959-60, 63-70, economist, advanced planning dept., 1961-63; economic and long-range planning cons., Los Altos, Calif., 1970-73; head systems planning, economist, strategic bus. planning, Western Regional hdqrs. U.S. Postal Service, San Bruno, Calif., 1973-78; strategic bus. planning cons., investment analysis cons., 1978-79; strategic bus. planning Advanced Reactor Systems dept. Gen. Electric Co., Sunnyvale, Calif., 1979-84; strategic planning cons., 1984—. Served with inf. paratroops U.S. Army, 1944-45, with inf. and rangers, 1949-53, Korea. Decorated Battle Star (5). Mem. Nat. Assn. Bus. Economists, World Future Soc., Sigma Nu. Episcopalian. Home and Office: 222 Incline Way San Jose CA 95139-1525

BUNN, DOROTHY IRONS, court reporter; b. Trinidad, Colo., Apr. 30, 1948; d. Russell and Pauline Anna (Langowski) Irons; m. Peter Lynn Bunn; children: Kristy Lynn, Wade Allen, Russell Ahearn. Student No. Va. Community Coll., 1970-71, U. Va., Fairfax, 1971-72. Registered profl. reporter; cert. shorthand reporter. Pres., chief exec. officer Ahearn Ltd., Springfield, Va., 1970-81, Bunn & Assocs., Glenrock, Wyo., 1981—; cons. Bixby Hereford Co., Glenrock, 1981-89, co-mgr., 1989—. Del., White House Conf. on Small Bus., Washington, 1986, 95, state chair, 1995; mem. Wyo. adv. coun. Small Bus. Adminstrn., 1994-96. Mem. NAFE, Am. Indian Soc., Nat. Ct. Reporters Assn., Nat. Fedn. Ind. Bus., Xcel Internat. (1st v.p., 1994-95, dir. 1995-96), Wyo. Shorthand Reporters Assn. (chmn. com. 1984-85), Nat. Cattlewomen, Wyo. Cattlewomen (Converse County), Nat. Fedn. Ind. Businesses (guardian 1991-96), Nat. Fedn. Bus. and Profl. Women (1st v.p. Casper 1994-95, pres. 1995-96, pub. rels. chair, Choices chair), Xscribe Users Assn. Avocation: photography. Office: Bixby Hereford Co PO Box 1618 Glenrock WY 82637 also: Bunn & Assocs 81 Bixby Rd Glenrock WY 82637

BUNN, JAMES LEE, congressman; b. Gleneden Beach/Depoe Bay, Oreg., Dec. 12, 1956; s. Benjamin Adam and Viola Mae (Fulgham) B.; children: James Jr., Matthew, Phillip, Malachi, Caleb. AA, Chemeketa Community Coll., Salem, Oreg., 1977; BA in Biology, N.W. Nazarene Coll., Nampa, Idaho, 1979. Farmer Oreg.; senator from dist. 15 Oreg. State Senate, 1987-95, Rep. whip, 1990-95; mem. 104th Congress from 5th Oreg. dist., 1995-96; lobbyist Message Ctr Lobbyist, Newberg, 1997—; exec. dir. Oreg. Rep. Party.; mem. appropriations com., interior, water and energy, fgn. ops. subcom. U.S. Congress. With Oreg. Criminal Justice Coun., Commn. Hispanic Affairs, Oreg. Hunger Task Force, Yamhill Cmty. Action Program Bd. Dirs., Oreg. N.G. Res. Recipient Minuteman citation Non-Commd. Officers Assn. U.S.A., 1989, cert. of appreciation Cmty. Action Agy. Yamhill County, 1990, Nat. Sr. Citizen Hall of Fame award, 1992, cert. of appreciation County Planning Dirs. Assn. Oreg., 1993. Mem. Nazarene Ch. Office: 738 Hawthorne Ave NE Salem OR 97301-4674 also: 408 E 1st Newberg OR 97132*

BUNN, PAUL A., JR., oncologist, educator; b. N.Y.C., Mar. 16, 1945; s. Paul A. Bunn; m. Camille Ruoff, Aug. 17, 1968; children: Rebecca, Kristen, Paul H. BA cum laude, Amherst Coll., 1967; MD, Cornell U., 1971. Diplomate Nat. Bd. Med. Examiners, Am. Bd. Internal Medicine, Am. Bd. Med. Oncology. Intern U. Calif., H.C. Moffitt Hosp., San Francisco, 1971-72, resident, 1972-73; clin. assoc. medicine br. Nat. Cancer Inst., NIH, Bethesda, Md., 1973-76; sr. investigator med. oncology br. Nat. Cancer Inst., Washington VA Hosp., 1976-81; asst. prof. medicine med. sch. Georgetown U., 1978-81; head cell kinetic sect., Navy med. oncology br. Nat. Cancer Inst., Bethesda, 1981-84; assoc. prof. medicine uniformed svcs. Univ. Health Scis., Bethesda, 1981-84; prof. medicine health scis. ctr. U. Colo., Denver, 1984—, head divsn. med. oncology, 1984-94, dir. cancer ctr., 1987—; mem. instl. rev. bd. NIH, Nat. Cancer Inst., 1982-84; mem. intramural support contract rev. com. Nat. Cancer Inst., 1982-84; cons. Coulter Immunology, 1984-89, Abbott Labs., 1992-94, Seragen, 1993—, others; mem. cancer com. U. Colo., 1984—, mem. faculty senate health scis. ctr., 1985-94, mem. exec. com. sch. medicine, 1987—; mem. fin. com. Univ. Physicians, Inc., 1986-91; mem. med. bd. Univ. Hosp., 1987—; external sci. advisor cancer ctr. U. Miami, 1988-92, U. Ark., 1989-94, U. Va., 1991-94, others; mem. oncology drug adv. com. FDA, 1992—; mem. sci. secretariat 7th World Conf. Lung Cancer, 1994; bd. dirs. Univ. Hosp. Resource Coun.; mem. oncology drug adv. com. FDA, 1993—. Author: Carboplatin (JM-8) Current Perspectives and Future Directions, 1990, Clinical Experiences With Platinum and Etoposide Therapy in Lung Cancer, 1992, (with M.E. Wood) Hematology/Oncology Secrets, 1994; assoc. editor Med. and Pediatric Oncology, 1984—, Jour. Clin. Oncology, 1991—, Cancer Rsch., 1992—, others; contbr. chpts. to books and articles to profl. jours. Bd. dirs. Colo. divsn. Am. Cancer Soc., 1989—, Leukemia Soc. Am., 1991—; bd. dirs. The Cancer Venture, 1993-94, Fair Share Colo., 1993-94; chmn. Solid Tumor Oncology Edn. Found., 1996—. With USPHS, 1973-84. Decorated Medal of Commendation; recipient Sci. of Yr. award Denver chpt. ARCS, 1992; named one of 400 Best Drs. in Am., Good Housekeeping Mag., 1991, 92; grantee Schering Plough, 1988-89, Burroughs Wellcome, 1991—, Bristol-Myers Squibb, 1993—, others. Fellow ACP; mem. AAAS, Am. Soc. Hematology (mem. sci. subcom. neoplasia 1989-92), Am. Assn. Cancer Rsch., Am. Soc. Clin. Oncology (chair program subcom. 1985-86, 90), Am. Fedn. Clin. Rsch., Am. Assn. Cancer Insts. (bd. dirs. 1992—), Internat. Assn. Study Lung Cancer (bd. dirs. 1988—, pres. 1994—), Wesstern Assn. Physicians, S.W. Oncology Group (mem. lung and leukemia com. 1986—, mem. biologic response modifier com. 1987—), Lung Cancer Study Group, Alpha Omega Alpha. Office: U Colo Cancer Ctr Box B188 4200 E 9th Ave Denver CO 80220-3706

BUNTAIN, JEANNINE, agricultural products executive; b. 1939. Various positions Inland Fruit & Produce Co., Wapato, Wash., 1968-92, pres., 1992—. Office: Inland Fruit & Produce Co Frontage Rd Wapato WA 98951*

BUNTING, KENNETH FREEMAN, newspaper editor; b. Houston, Dec. 9, 1948; s. Willie Freeman and Sarah Lee (Peterson) B.; m. Juliana Amy Jafvert, July 13, 1989; 1 child, Maxwell Freeman. Student, U. Mo., 1966-67; AA in Journalism, Lee Coll., 1968; BA in Journalism and History, Tex. Christian U., 1970; advanced exec. program, Northwestern U., 1996. Mgmt. trainee, reporter Harte-Hanks Newspapers Inc., Corpus Christi, Tex., 1970-71; reporter, then copy editor San Antonio Express-News, 1971-73; exec. asst. to Hon. G.J. Sutton Tex. Ho. of Reps., San Antonio, 1973-74; reporter Cin. Post, 1974-78, Sacramento Bee, 1978; reporter, asst. city editor, state capitol corr. L.A. Times, 1978-87; capitol bur. chief, city editor, dep. mng. editor, sr. editor Ft. Worth Star-Telegram, 1987-93; mng. editor Seattle Post-Intelligencer, 1993—; journalism instr. Orange Coast Coll., Costa Mesa, Calif., 1981-82; mem. adv. bd. Maynard Inst., Oakland, Calif., 1994—. Bd. dirs. Seattle Symphony, 1995—; mem. commn. Woodland Park Zoo, Seattle, 1995-96; mem. Leadership Ft. Worth; mem. journalism adv. bd. Tex. Christian U.; former mem. minorities task force Assn. for Edn. in Journalism and Mass Comms.; past pres. Press Club, Orange County, Calif.; past bd. dirs. Covington (Ky.) Cmty. Ctr.; past 1st v.p. Young Dems. of Tex.; past treas., mem. exec. bd. Freedom of Inro. Found. of Tex. Mem. Nat. Assn. Black Journalists, AP Mng. Editors Assn. (mem. ethics com. 1995-96), Am. Soc. Newspaper Editors (mem. minorities com.), APME (bd. dirs. 1996—), Soc. Profl. Journalists (bd. dirs. western Wash. chpt. 1995-96), Seattle C. of C.

(mem. cmty. devel. roundtable 1994—), Tex. Christian U. Alumni Assn. (bd. dirs.), Freedom of Info. Found. Tex., Rainier Club, Washington Athletic Club. Unitarian. Office: Seattle-Post Intelligencer 101 Elliott Ave W Seattle WA 98119-4220

BUNTON, CLIFFORD ALLEN, chemist, educator; b. Chesterfield, Eng., Jan. 4, 1920; came to U.S., 1963, naturalized, 1978; s. Arthur and Edith (Kirk) B.; m. Ethel Clayton, July 28, 1945; children—Julia Margaret, Claire Jennifer. B.Sc., Univ. Coll., London, 1941, Ph.D., 1945; hon. degree, U. Perugia, Italy, 1986. Successively asst. lectr., lectr., reader Univ. Coll., 1944-63; prof. chemistry U. Calif., Santa Barbara, 1963-90, prof. emeritus, 1990—, chmn. dept., 1967-72; Commonwealth Fund fellow U. Columbia, 1948-49; Brit. Coun. vis. lectr., Chile and Argentina, 1960; vis. prof. UCLA, 1961, U. Toronto, 1962, U. Sao Paolo, Brazil, 1973, U. Lausanne, Switzerland, 1976, 79; adj. prof. U. Chile, Santiago, 1990—; mem. policy com. U. Chile-U. Calif. Coop. Program, chmn. sci. and engring. sub-com., 1969—; mem. sci. com., U.S.-Mexico Found. for Sci., 1993—. Contbr. articles to profl. jours. Recipient Tolman medal, So. Calif. sect. Am. Chem. Soc., 1987. Fellow AAAS; mem. N.Y. Acad. Sci., Am. Chem. Soc. (Calif. sect.), Chem. Soc. (London); corr. mem. Chilean Acad. Scis. (1974). Home: 935 Cocopah Dr Santa Barbara CA 93110-1204 Office: U Calif Dept Chemistry Santa Barbara CA 93106

BURAS, NATHAN, hydrology and water resources educator; b. Barlad, Romania, Aug. 23, 1921; came to U.S., 1947; s. Boris and Ethel (Weiser) B.; m. Netty Stivel, Apr. 13, 1951; 1 child, Nir H. BS with highest honors, U. Calif., Berkeley, 1949; MS, Technion, Haifa, Israel, 1957; PhD, UCLA, 1962. Registered profl. engr., Israel. Prof. hydrology and water resources Technion, 1962-80, dean, 1966-68; vis. prof. Stanford (Calif.) U., 1976-81; prof., head of dept. hydrology and water resources U. Ariz., Tucson, 1981-89, prof. hydrology and water resources, 1989—; cons. Tahal, Ltd., Tel Aviv, 1963-73, World Bank, Washington, 1972-76, 79-81, Regional Municipality of Waterloo, Ont., Can., 1991-93, U.S. AID, Washington, 1992-93, Great No. Paper Co., 1992—; apptd. mem. standing com. on terminology Internat. Glossary of Hydrology UNESCO, 1996. Author: Scientific Allocation of Water Resources, 1972; editor: Control of Water Resources Systems, 1976, Management of Water Resources in North America, 1995. Mem. Israel-Mex. Mixed Commn. on Sci. Cooperation, 1976, So. Ariz. Water Resource Assn., 1982—; active Pugwash Workshops, 1991, 92, 93. Named Laureat du Congres, Internat. Assn. Agrl. Engring., 1964; recipient Cert. of Appreciation, USDA., 1970. Fellow ASCE (life), Ariz.-Nev. Acad. Sci., Internat. Water Resources Assn.; mem. Am. Geophys. Union, Am. Water Resources Assn. (charter). Jewish. Home: 5541 E Circulo Terra Tucson AZ 85750-1003 Office: U Ariz Dept Hydrology and Water Resources Tucson AZ 85721

BURBACK, RONALD LEROI, computer scientist; b. Brush, Colo., Feb. 1, 1952; s. William and Pauline (Cook) B.; m. Sandra Ann Rockwell, Aug. 14, 1971; children: Jennifer, Christy, Katy. BA, U. Colo., 1974; MS in Engring., Stanford U., 1982, postgrad., 1993. Physicist Los Alamos (N.Mex.) Labs., 1974-78, Stanford Rsch. Inst., Menlo Park, Calif., 1978-82; prin. engr. Digital, Colorado Springs, Colo., 1982-86; artificial intelligence rschr. Lawrence Livermore (Calif.) Labs., 1987; sr. corp. cons. TDS Healthcare, San Jose, Calif., 1988-90; researcher Stanford (Calif.) U., 1991, tchr., 1993—; CEO Tableau Software, Stanford, 1988-92; dir. engring. Oceania Healthcare, Palo Alto, Calif., 1992-93; pres. Object Plus Software, Pleasanton, Calif., 1993—. Author: Using the Tableau System, 1991; patentee in field. Bloodorn Found. scholar, 1970, Phi Beta Kappa scholar, 1974; recipient Outstanding Artificial Intelligence Rschr. award U.S. Pentagon, 1988. Mem. AAAI, IEEE. Home: 1944 Paseo Del Cajon Pleasanton CA 94566-5913 Office: Stanford U Computer Sci Dept Stanford CA 94305-3068

BURBICK, JOAN, English educator; b. Chgo., June 20, 1946; d. Michael and Eileen Burbick; 1 child, Claire Burbick Huntsberry. BA, Boston Coll., 1968; MA, Brandeis U., 1969, PhD, 1974; MA, Wesleyan U., Middleton, Conn., 1976. Asst. prof. Wash. State U., Pullman, 1978-83, assoc. prof., 1983-88, prof. English, 1988—, Edward R. Meyer prof., 1996—; vis. prof. U. Colo., Boulder, 1988-89. Author: Thoreau's Alternative History, 1987, Healing the Republic, 1994; mem. adv. bd. Legacy jour., 1985—; mem. editl. bd. ESQ jour., 1978—; contbr. articles, essays, revs. to profl. jours. (Foerster award Am. Lit. 1986). Andrew Mellon fellow Ctr. for Humanities, Wesleyan U., 1976-77, Martha Sutton Weeks fellow Stanford U. Humanities Ctr., 1987-88; recipient Norman Foerster award MLA/Am. Lit. assn., 1986. Mem. Pacific N.W. Am. Studies Assn. (v.p., pres. 1980's). Office: Wash State U English Dept Pullman WA 99164-5000

BURBIDGE, E. MARGARET, astronomer, educator; b. Davenport, Eng.; d. Stanley John and Marjorie (Stott) Peachey; m. Geoffrey Burbidge, Apr. 2, 1948; 1 child, Sarah. B.S., Ph.D., U. London; Sc.D. hon., Smith Coll., 1963, U. Sussex, 1970, U. Bristol, 1972, U. Leicester, 1972, City U., 1973, U. Mich., 1978, U. Mass., 1978, Williams Coll., 1979, SUNY, Stony Brook, 1985, Rensselaer Poly. Inst., 1986, U. Notre Dame, 1986, U. Chgo., 1991. Mem. staff U. London Obs., 1948-51; rsch. fellow Yerkes Obs. U. Chgo., 1951-53, Shirley Farr fellow Yerkes obs., 1957-59, assoc. prof. Yerkes Obs., 1959-62; rsch. fellow Calif. Inst. Tech., Pasadena, 1955-57; mem. Enrico Fermi Inst. for Nuclear Studies, 1957-62; prof. astronomy dept. physics U. Calif. San Diego, 1964—, univ. prof., 1984—; dir. Royal Greenwich Obs. (Herstmonceux Castle), Hailsham, Sussex, Eng., 1984-90; rsch. prof. dept. physics U. Calif., San Diego, 1990—; Lindsay Meml. lectr. Goddard Space Flight Ctr., NASA, 1985; Abby Rockefeller Mauze prof. MIT, 1968; David Elder lectr. U. Strathclyde, 1972; V. Gildersleeve lectr. Barnard Coll., 1974; Jansky lectr. Nat. Radio Astronomy Observatory, 1977; Brode lectr. Whitman Coll., 1986. Author: (with G. Burbidge) Quasi-Stellar Objects, 1967; editor: Observatory mag., 1948-51; mem. editorial bd.: Astronomy and Astrophysics, 1969—. Recipient (with husband) Warner prize in Astronomy, 1959, Bruce Gold medal Astronomy Soc. Pacific, 1982; hon. fellow Univ. Coll., London, Girton Coll., Lucy Cavendish Coll., Cambridge; U.S. Nat. medal of sci., 1984; Sesquicentennial medal Mt. Holyoke Coll., 1987, Einstein medal World Cultural Coun., 1988. Fellow Royal Soc., Nat. Acad. Scis. (chmn. sect. 12 astronomy 1986), Am. Acad. Arts and Scis., Royal Astron. Soc.; mem. Am. Astron. Soc. (v.p. 1972-74, pres. 1976-78; Henry Norris Russell lectr. 1984), Internat. Astron. Union (pres. commn. 28 1970-73), Grad. Women Sci. (nat. hon. mem.). Office: U Calif-San Diego Ctr Astrophysics Space Scis Mail Code # 0111 La Jolla CA 92093

BURCH, BARBARA JEAN, special education educator; b. Seattle, Dec. 16, 1948; d. Robert and Jean Frances (Richards) Griesbach; m. John Mitchell Burch, Aug. 2, 1975; children: Adam John, Joshua Robert. BA, U. Wash., 1973, MEd, Idaho State U., 1978. Cert. tchr., Alaska. Substitute educator Seattle Sch. Dist. 1, 1972-73; edn. educator Butte County Sch. Dist. 111, Arco, Idaho, 1973-76, Pocatello (Idaho) Sch. Dist. 1, 1977-86; educator Fairbanks (Alaska) Northstar Borough Schs., 1986—, dir. spl. edn., 1995—; instr. in continuing edn. U. Alaska, Fairbanks, 1986-87. Mem. ASCD, Coun. for Exceptional Children (pres. 1987-88, 90-91), Internat. Reading Assn., S.E. Idaho Coun. (treas. 1985-86), Golden Heart Reading Coun. (treas. 1987-91), NEA, Am. Fedn. Tchrs. (pres. Pocatello chpt. 1984-86), Phi Delta Kappa. Home: 891 Gold Mine Trl Fairbanks AK 99712-2070 Office: Fairbanks Northstar Borough 520 5th Ave Fairbanks AK 99701

BURCH, MARY LOU, organization consultant, housing advocate; b. Billings, Mont., Apr. 4, 1930; d. Forrest Scott Sr. and Mary Edna (Hinshaw) Chilcott; m. J. Sheldon Robinson, June 18, 1949 (div. 1956); m. G. Howard Burch, Nov. 27, 1957 (div. 1984); children: Julie Lynne Scully, Donna Eileen, Carol Marie Kimball, Alan Robert, Christine Philips Spruill Enomoto. AA, Grant Tech. Coll., Sacramento, 1949; AB, Sacramento State Coll., 1955; student, U. Alaska, 1976-78, Santa Rosa (Calif.) Jr. Coll., 1987. Diagnostic tchr. Calif. Youth Authority, Perkins, 1955-57; com. chmn. on pub. info. Sequoia Union High Sch. Dist., So. San Mateo County, Calif., 1970-72; exec. dir. Presbyn. Hospitality House, Fairbanks, Alaska, 1979-80; realtor Century 21 Smith/Ring, Renton, Wash., 1980-81; cons. Fairbanks, Alaska, 1981-84; exec. dir. Habitat for Humanity of Sonoma County, Santa Rosa, Calif., 1986-89, Affordable Housing Assoc., Santa Rosa, Calif., 1989-90; pvt. cons. in housing and orgn. Scottsdale, Ariz., 1991-92, Prescott and Dewey, Ariz., 1992—; bd. dirs. Hosp. Chaplaincy Svcs, Santa Rosa, Villa Los Alamos Homeowners Assn.; cons. Access Alaska, Anchorage, 1983; contractor Alaka Siding, Fairbanks, 1982-83; founder Let's Get Organized!. Local coord. fgn. exch. student program Acad. Yr. in Am., 1993-94; acad. coord. fgn. exch. student program Cultural Homestay Internat., 1994—; vol. Habitat for Humanity coms. Named vol. of the year, Hosp. Chaplaincy Svcs., 1987. Democrat. United Ch. of Christ. Home and Office: 1288 Tapadero Dr #D-PCC Dewey AZ 86327-5823

BURCHFIELD, DON R., counselor, youth services administrator; b. Yuba City, Calif., May 24, 1952; s. Ray and Myrtle (Whitecotton) B.; m. Connie L. Hendrix, July 18, 1975; children: Christina, Kailee. BA in Edn., N.N.C., 1975; MA in Counseling, Liberty U., 1996. Youth counselor Peoples Ch., Phoenix, 1976-78, Valley Cathedral, Phoenix, 1978-82; counselor Terros, Phoenix, 1987-92; grad. counselor Grand Canyon, Phoenix, 1992-93; life counselor Life Counseling, Phoenix, 1993-94; counselor Tri City Counseling, Phoenix, 1994—; mem. steering com. Ariz. Adolescent Coalition, Phoenix, 1994-96; charter mem. Ariz. Gun Safety Com., Phoenix, 1994-96; presenter Mothers for Healthy Babies, 1995; chairperson Conf. on Self-Esteem, 1993, 94, 95, 96. Author: Surviving Adolescent City of Phoenix, 1994-95, (prevention program) Give It a Day, 1994-95, (bill) Gun Safety Bill for Safety, 1991, 92, 93, 94, 95. Charter pres. Offering Parents Info. on Needless Suicide; homeless/runaway youth assessor, Phoenix; chairperson Red Ribbon Youth Rally, Phoenix; charter mem. Gov.'s Office Youth Suicide Task Force, 1994-95; mem., chairperson, contact person Hope Coalition, Advocates Against Adolescent Suicide, pres., 1993—; mem. Ch. Alive, pres., 1980—; mem. Ariz. Adolescent Health Coalition, steering com., 1993—. Recipient Gov.'s Office for Children award, Gov. of Ariz., 1993, Cert. Appreciation, Nat. Orgn. Adolescent Pregnancy, 1995, Cert. Appreciation, Dept. Health Svcs., 1996; named Vol. of Yr., Terros Health Ctr., 1987. Democrat. Home and Office: 4547 N 17th Ave Phoenix AZ 85015

BURD, STEVE, food service executive; b. 1949. BS, Carroll Coll., 1971; MA in Econs., U. Wis., 1973. With fin. and mktg. So. Pacific Transp. Co., San Francisco; with Arthur D. Little, N.Y.C., 1982-87; mgmt. cons., 1986-91; cons. Stop & Shop Cos., Boston, 1988-89, Fred Meyer Inc., Portland, Oreg., 1989-90, Safeway Inc., Oakland, Calif., 1986-87, 91—; pres., CEO Safeway Inc., 1992—. Office: Safeway Inc 5918 Stoneridge Mall Rd Pleasanton CA 94588-3229*

BURDEN, JAMES EWERS, lawyer; b. Sacramento, Oct. 24, 1939; s. Herbert Spencer and Ida Elizabeth (Brosemer) B.; m. Kathryn Lee Gardner, Aug. 21, 1965; children: Kara Elizabeth, Justin Gardner. BS, U. Calif., Berkeley, 1961; JD, U. Calif., Hastings, 1964; postgrad., U. So. Calif., 1964-65. Bar: Calif. 1965, Tax Ct. U.S. 1969, U.S. Supreme Ct. 1970. Assoc. Elliott and Aune, Santa Ana, Calif., 1965, White, Harbor, Fort & Schei, Sacramento, 1965-67; assoc. Miller, Starr & Regalia, Oakland, Calif., 1967-69, ptnr., 1969-73; ptnr. Burden, Aiken, Mansuy & Stein, San Francisco, 1973-82, James E. Burden, Inc., San Francisco, 1982—; of counsel, Aiken, Kramer & Cummings, Oakland and San Francisco; bd. dirs. Roofing Equipment, Inc., Indsl. Products, San Leandro, Calif.; pres. Austex, Oil and Gas Co., Inc., Luling, Tex.; underwriting mem. Lloyds of London, 1986-93; instr. U. Calif., Berkeley, 1968-74, Merritt Coll. Contbr. articles to profl. jours. Mem. ABA, Inst. Dirs. (London), Lutine Golf Soc. (London), Claremont Country Club, San Francisco Grid Club, Commonwealth of Calif., The Naval Club (London), Inst. Dirs. (London). Office: Ste 3005 50 California St San Francisco CA 94111-4344

BURDGE, RICHARD JAMES, JR., lawyer; b. Long Beach, Calif., Dec. 4, 1949; s. R. James and Jean Margaret (Steele) B.; children: Kristin Alexis, Lindsay Michelle, Margaret Lynn, Kelly Anne. BS, Yale U., 1972; JD, UCLA, 1979. Bar: Calif. 1979, U.S. Dist. Ct. (cen. dist.) Calif. 1979, U.S. Ct. Appeals (9th cir.) 1980, U.S. Dist. Ct. (no. dist.) Calif. 1984, U.S. Supreme Ct. 1984, U.S. Dist. Ct. (ea. dist.) Calif. 1987, U.S. Dist. Ct. (so. dist.) Calif. 1990. Assoc., then ptnr. Lillick, McHose & Charles, L.A., 1979-86; ptnr. Dewey Ballantine and predecessor firms, L.A., 1986—; del. L.A. County Bar Del. to Calif. State Bar Conf. of Dels., 1988—. Mng. editor UCLA Law Rev., 1978-79, mem. editl. staff, 1977-78. Chmn. UCLA Law Ann. Fund, 1989-91; co-chair UCLA Law Libr. Alumni Campaign, 1994—. Lt. USN, 1972-76. Mem. Assn. Bus. Trial Lawyers (gov. 1989-91, 93-95, ann. seminar chair 1992, jud. coll. chair 1995, treas. 1995-96, sec. 1996-97), Chancery Club. Office: Dewey Ballantine 333 S Hope St Ste 3000 Los Angeles CA 90071-3039

BURDICK, ROBERT W., newspaper editor; b. Feb. 11, 1948; m. Patty Burnett; 1 child, David. B in Polit. Sci., Fla. Atl. U., 1969. Reporter Miami Herald, Fla. Today; night city editor Palm Beach (Fla.) Post; mng. editor Palm Beach Daily News; asst. mng. editor Wichita (Kans.) Eagle; city editor/metro editor/asst. to exec. editor San Jose (Calif.) Mercury News, 1978-82; asst. mng. editor Denver Post, 1982-84; asst. mng. editor/mng. editor/editor L.A. Daily News, 1984-94; mng. editor, editor Rocky Mountain News, Denver, 1994—. Mem. Am. Soc. Newspaper Editors, Soc. Profl. Journalists, AP News Execs. Coun. (past bd. mem., past pres. Calif., Nev. chpt., past editor AP Mng. Editors News). Office: Rocky Mountain News 400 W Colfax Denver CO 80204

BURE, PAVEL, professional hockey player; b. Moscow, Mar. 31, 1971. Wing Vancouver (Can.) Canucks. Recipient Calder Meml. trophy, 1991-92; NHL regular season and playoff Top Goal Scorer, 1993-94. Office: Vancouver Canucks, 800 Griffiths Way, Vancouver, BC Canada V6B 6G1

BURFORD, RICHARD S., agricultural products executive; b. 1931. Graduate, U. Tenn., 1953. Pvt. practice Fresno, Calif., 1957-79; with Richard S. Burford, Inc., Fresno, Calif., 1967—. With U.S. Army, 1953-57. Office: 1443 W Sample Ave Fresno CA 93711-1948

BURG, JEROME STUART, financial planning consultant; b. N.Y.C., Aug. 2, 1935; s. Norman and Ruth (Schkurman) B.; m. Janis Elaine Lyon, May 26, 1974; children: Jeffrey Howard, David Matthew, Audree, Harriet, Robert, Stephanie. Student, Temple U., 1953-56; CLU, Am. Coll., 1973, chartered fin. cons., 1984; cert. fin. planner, Coll. Fin. Planning, 1983. Pres., CEO Jerome Burg Assoc., Inc., Cherry Hill, N.J., 1963-79, Contemporary Fin. Planning, Scottsdale, Ariz., 1979-89; sr. acct. mgr. Acacia Group, Phoenix, 1989—; instr. Glendale and Scottdale C.C., 1983—, Nat. Inst. Fin., N.J., 1984-90. Host (radio program) Money Talks Sta. KFNN, Phoenix, 1993—. Pres. N.J. Assn. Life Underwriters, Trenton, 1963-65; instr. Jr. Achievement, Scottsdale, 1985-89; 1st v.p. Pres. Cabinet-Acacia Group, Washington, 1991, 93, co-pres., 1992. With U.S. Army, 1956-58. Mem. Internat. Assn. Fin. Planning (bd. dirs. Greater Phoenix chpt. 1982—), Inst. Cert. Fin. Planners. Office: Acacia Group 3200 E Camelback Rd Ste 245 Phoenix AZ 85018-2320

BURG, WALTER A., airport terminal executive. Gen. manager, ceo Tucson Airport Authority, Ariz., 1966—. Office: Tucson Internat Airport 7005 S Plumer Ave Tucson AZ 85706-6926*

BURGARINO, ANTHONY EMANUEL, environmental engineer, consultant; b. Milw., July 20, 1948; s. Joseph Francis Burgarino and Mardelle (Hoeffler) T.; m. Gail Fay DiMatteo, Mar. 13, 1982; children: Paul Anthony, Joanna Lynn. BS, U. Wis., 1970; MS, Ill. Inst. Tech., 1974, PhD, 1980. Registered profl. engr., Ariz. Sales engr. Leeds & Northrup, Phila., 1970-72; rsch. asst. Ill. Inst. Tech., Chgo., 1972-75; chemist City of Chgo., 1975-79; instr. Joliet (Ill.) Jr. Coll., 1978-79; sr. project engr. Carollo Engrs., Walnut Creek, Calif., 1980—; cons. City of Clovis, Calif., 1981-83, City of Fresno, Calif., 1983-96, City of Phoenix, 1981-90, City of Yuma, Ariz., 1989—, City of Santa Maria, Calif., 1991-95, City of Vallejo, Calif., 1992—, City of Peoria, Ariz., 1996—. Contbr. articles to profl. jours. EPA grantee, 1970-72; NSF fellow, 1973, Ill. Inst. Tech. Rsch. Found. fellow, 1974. Mem. Am. Water Works Assn. Roman Catholic. Home: 2321 Lafayette Dr Antioch CA 94509-5871 Office: Carollo Engrs 2700 Ygnacio Valley Rd Ste 300 Walnut Creek CA 94598-3464

BURGE, WILLARD, JR., software company executive; b. Johnson City, N.Y., Oct. 2, 1938; s. Willard Sr. and Catherine Bernice (Matthews) B.; m. Carol Crockenberg, June 16, 1961; children: Willard III, Pennie Lynn. Registered profl. engr., Ohio. Indsl. engr. Harnischfeger Corp., Escanaba, Mich., 1966-67; sr. indsl. engr. Gen. Electric, Ladson, S.C., 1968-74; advanced mfg. engr. Gen. Electric, Mentor, Ohio, 1971-74; corp. staff engr. Eaton Corp., Willoughby Hills, Ohio, 1974-79, supr. N/C programming, 1979-80, supr. mfg. engring., 1980-82, mgr. mfg. systems engring., 1982-87; bus. unit mgr. MSC Products, Eaton Corp., Costa Mesa, Calif., 1987-91; pres., CEO CAM Software, Inc., Provo, Utah, 1991-93; chief exec. officer Key Svcs., Cypress, Calif., 1993—; bd. dirs. CAM Software, Inc.; presenter in field. With U.S. Army, 1957. Mem. Soc. Mfg. Engrs. Republican. Home and Office: Key Svcs 13280 Saint Andrews Dr Seal Beach CA 90740-3796

BURGER, EDMUND GANES, architect; b. Yerington, Nev., Mar. 28, 1930; s. Edmund Ganes and Rose Catherine (Kobe) B.; m. Shirley May Pratini, Jan. 21, 1968; 1 dau., Jane Lee. B.M.E., U. Santa Clara, 1951; B.Arch., U. Pa., 1959. Engr. Gen. Electric Co., 1951-52; design engr. U. Calif. Radiation Lab., 1952-57; John Stewardson fellow in architecture, 1959; architect Wurster, Bernardi & Emmons, San Francisco, 1960-63; founder Burger & Coplans, Inc. (Architects), San Francisco, 1964; pres. Burger & Coplans, Inc. (Architects), 1964-79; owner Edmund Burger (Architect), 1979—; guest lectr. U. Calif., Berkeley. important works include Acorn Housing Project, Oakland, Calif., Crescent Village Housing Project, Suisun City, Calif., Coplans residence, San Francisco, Betel Housing Project, San Francisco, Grand View Housing Project, San Francisco, Albany (Calif.) Oaks Housing, Grow Homes, San Pablo, Calif., Mariposa Housing, Dunleavy Plaza Housing, Potrero Ct. Housing, San Francisco, Lee residence, Kentfield, Calif., Burger residences, Lafayette, Calif., Oceanside, Oreg., and El Cerrito, Calif., Yamhill Valley Vineyards Winery, McMinneville, Oreg., Portico De Mar, shop and restaurant complex, Barcelona, Spain, Hendrickson residence, Newport Beach, Calif., Hamilton residence, Winters, Calif., Sanders residence, Yuba City, Calif.; author: Geomorphic Architecture, 1986. Recipient citation for excellence in community architecture AIA, 1969, award of merit AIA, award of merit Homes for Better Living, 1970, 79, 1st Honor award, 1973, 81, Holiday award for a beautiful Am., 1970, Honor award 4th Biennial HUD awards for design excellence, 1970, Bay Area awards for design excellence, 1969, 74, 78, Apts. of Year award Archtl. Record, 1972, Houses of Year award, 1973, Calif. Affordable Housing Competition award, 1981, HUD Building Value into Housing award, 1981, Community Design award Calif. Council AIA, 1986; design grant Nat. Endowment for Arts, 1980, HUD, 1980; constrn. grant HUD, 1981. Office: PO Box 10193 Berkeley CA 94709-5193

BURGER, EMIL FERDINAND, allergist, medical group executive; b. Dallas, June 7, 1934; s. Emil Ferdinand and Florance Helen (Hays) B. BA, Rice U., 1955; MD, U. Tex., 1961. Diplomate Am. Bd. Allergy and Immunology. Pediatrician Kaiser Permanente Med. Group, L.A., 1964-66, 68-70; pvt. practice allergy, Downey, Calif., 1970—; med. dir. Am. Techs., Paramount, Calif., 1993—; guest prof. Chulalongkorn U. Sch. Dentistry, Bangkok, 1992. Capt. U.S. Army, 1966-68. Fellow Am. Acad. Allergy, Am. Coll. Allergy. Office: 8301 Florence Ave Ste 104 Downey CA 90240-3946

BURGESS, CURT, psychologist, computer scientist, educator; b. Phila., June 19, 1953; s. Clarke Jacob and Barbara B.; m. Catherine Helen Decker, May 25, 1991. BGS, Univ. Nebr., 1982, MA, 1985; MA, Univ. Rochester, 1989, PhD, 1991. Asst. prof. psychology Syracuse (N.Y.) Univ., 1989-92; asst. prof. psychology Univ. Calif., Riverside, 1992-97, assoc. prof. psychology, 1997—; faculty computational neurosc. program Syracuse Univ., 1991-92, affiliate prof. dept. computer sci., 1990-92; chair admissions Univ. Calif., Riverside, 1994—, coop. faculty dept. computer sci., 1996—. Contbr. over 30 chpts. to books, articles to jours. Presdl. Faculty fellow U.S. Pres./NSF, 1994. Mem. APA, Cognitive Sci. Soc., Psychonomic Soc., Assn. Computational Linguistics, Western Psychol. Assn., Sigma Xi (v.p. 1996—). Office: U Calif Dept Psychology 1419 LIfe Sci Bldg Riverside CA 92521

BURGESS, DAVID BRUCE, pediatrician; b. Waukegan, Ill., Apr. 15, 1947; s. Samuel George and Jane Catherine (Menzel) B.; 1 child, Sarah Elizabeth. BS, U. Ill., 1969; MD, U. Wis., 1973. Resident Tulane U., New Orleans, 1973-77, asst. prof., 1977-78, 1980-85; fellow in child development U. Colo., Denver, 1978-80; med. dir. Exceptional Family Member Program Fitzsimons Army Med. Ctr., Aurora, Colo., 1985—. Mem. Soc. for Devel. Pediatrics, Soc. for Behavioral Pediatrics, Soc. for Pediatric Rsch., Am. Acad. for Cerebral Palsy and Devel. Medicine. Office: Fitzsimons Army Med Ctr Bldg 506 Aurora CO 80045-5501

BURGESS, LARRY LEE, aerospace executive; b. Phoenix, May 13, 1942; s. Byron Howard and Betty Eileen (Schook) B.; m. Sylvia Wynnell, Sept. 30, 1964 (div. Dec. 1984); children: Byron, Damian; m. Mary Jane Ruble, Mar. 9, 1985; children: Christopher, Patrick. BSEE, MSEE, Naval Postgrad. Sch. Officer USN, Washington, 1964-85; corp. exec. Lockheed-Martin, Denver, 1985—; pres. L & M Capital Investments, Denver, 1987—; CEO L&M Property Mgmt. Co.; pub. 2 papers 4th Internat. Conf. on Tethers, 1995. V.p. Denargo Market Neighborhood Assn.; co-pres. Upper Larimer Neighborhood Assn.; coach Youth Activities, Corpus Christi, 1976-78; coach youth basketball Littleton (Colo.) YMCA, 1994, 95, 96-97, Columbine Basketball, 1996; speaker in local schs., Littleton, 1987-90. Inducted into the Kans. Basketball Hall of Fame, 1993. Mem. AIAA (dir.), SASA, Armed Forces Comm. and Electronic Agy. Republican. Home: 3 Red Fox Ln Littleton CO 80127-5710 Office: Martin Marietta PO Box 179 # 4001 Denver CO 80201-0179

BURGESS, MARY ALICE (MARY ALICE WICKIZER), publisher; b. San Bernardino, Calif., June 21, 1938; d. Russell Alger and Wilma Evelyn (Swisher) Wickizer; m. Michael Roy Burgess, Oct. 15, 1976; children from previous marriage: Richard Albert Rogers, Mary Louise Rogers Reynnells. AA, Valley Coll., San Bernardino, 1967; BA, Calif. State U., San Bernardino, 1975, postgrad., 1976-79; postgrad., U. Calif., Riverside, 1976-79. Lic. real estate salesman, Calif.; real estate broker, Calif. Sec.-treas. Lynwyck Realty & Investment, San Bernardino, 1963-75; libr. asst. Calif. State U., San Bernardino, 1974-76, purchasing agt., 1976-81; co-pub. The Borgo Press, San Bernardino, 1975—. Co-pub: (with Robert Reginald) Science Fiction and Fantasy Book Review, 1979-80; co-author (with M.R. Burgess) The Wickizer Annals: The Descendents of Conrad Wickizer of Luzerne County, Pennsylvania, 1983, (with Douglas Menville and Robert Reginald) Futurevisions: The New Golden Age of the Science Fiction Film, 1985, (with Jeffrey M. Elliot and Robert Reginald) The Arms Control, Disarmament and Military Science Dictionary, 1989, (with Michael Burgess) The House of the Burgesses, 2d edit., 1994; author: The Campbell Chronicles: A Genealogical History of the Descendants of Samuel Campbell of Chester County, Pennsylvania, 1989, (with Boden Clarke) The Work of Katherine Kurtz, 1992-93, (with Michael Burgess and Daryl F. Mallett) State and Province Vital Records Guide; editor: Cranberry Tea Room Cookbook, Still The Frame Holds, Defying the Holocaust, Risen from the Ashes: A Story of the Jewish Displaced Persons in the Aftermath of World War II, Being a Sequel to Survivors (Jacob Biber), 1989, Ray Bradbury: Dramatist (Ben P. Indick), 1989, Across the Wide Missouri: The Diary of a Journey from Virginia to Missouri in 1819 and Back Again in 1821, with a Description of the City of Cincinnati, (James Brown Campbell), Italian Theatre in San Francisco, Into the Flames: The Life Story of a Righteous Gentile, Jerzy Kosinski: The Literature of Violation, The Little Kitchen Cookbook, Victorian Criticism of American Writers, 1990, The Magic That Works: John W. Campbell and The American Response to Technology, 1993, Libido into Literature: The "Primèra Época" of Benito Pérez Galdós, 1993, A Triumph of the Spirit: Stories of Holocaust Survivors, 1994, A Way Farer in a World in Upheaval, 1993, William Eastlake: High Desert Interlocutor, 1993, The Price of Paradise: The Magazine Career of F. Scott Fitgerald, 1993, The Little Kitchen Cookbook, rev. edit., 1994, An Irony of Fate: William March, 1994, Hard-Boiled Heretic: Ross Macdonald, 1994, We The People!, 1994, The Chinese Economy, 1995, Voices of the River Plate, 1995, Chaos Burning on My Brow, 1995; co-editor and pub. (with Robert Reginald) of all Borgo Press publs.; also reviewer, indexer, researcher and editor of scholarly manuscripts. Chmn. new citizens Rep. Women, San Bernardino, 1967; libr. San Bernardino Geneal. Soc., 1965-67; vol. Boy Scout Am., Girl Scouts U.S., Camp Fire Girls, 1960s. Recipient Real Estate Proficiency award Calif. Dept. Real Estate, San Bernardino, 1966. Mem. City of San Bernardino Hist. and Pioneer Soc., Calif. State U. Alumni Assn., Cecil County (Md.) Hist. Soc., Gallia County (Ohio) Hist. and Geneal. Soc., DAR (membership and geneal. records chmn. 1964-66, registrar and vice regent San Bernardino chpt. 1965-67). Office: The Borgo Press PO Box 2845 6980 Perris Hill Rd San Bernardino CA 92404-2845*

BURGESS, STEPHEN ANDREW, company executive; b. San Francisco, May 6, 1951; s. Roy Walter and Betty Jane (Kapel) B.; m. Gina Rae Mann, Mar. 16, 1974; children: Allison Renae, Andrew Ryan. BS in Biology, So. Oreg. State U., 1975. Br. mgr. Transamerica, Beaverton, Oreg., 1976-77; field mgr. Southland Corp., Portland, Oreg., 1977-79; bus. mgr. Clark Bros. Equipment Co., Portland, 1979-83; franchising/bus. cons. B & B Enterprises, San Diego, 1983-84; br. mgr. Businessland Inc., San Diego, 1984; corp. tng. mgr. Businessland Inc., San Jose, Calif., 1985-86; dir. bus. ops. Businessland Inc., San Jose, 1987-89; v.p. ops. Krause's Sofa Factory, Fountain Valley, Calif., 1989-91; sr. v.p. sales and ops. Krause's Sofa Factory/Castro Convertibles, Brea, Calif., 1991—; sr. v.p. franchise ops. Krause's Furniture Inc., Brea, 1994—. Contbr. articles to profl. jours. Contbr., vol. Olive Crest Homes for Children, Newport Beach, 1989—, City of Hope, L.A., 1990—. Mem. Canyon Crest Country Club, Gonzaga Preparatory Alumni Club. Home: 5360 Via Zopapo Yorba Linda CA 92887-3130 Office: Krauses Sofa Factory Castro Convertibles 200 N Berry St Brea CA 92821-3903

BURGESS, WES, neuropsychiatrist, psychopharmacologist; b. Dumas, Tex., Mar. 5, 1952; s. Wes and Dorothea Inez Burgess. BS, Purdue U., 1974; PhD, N.C. State U., 1979; MD, U. Miami, Fla., 1987. Lic. physician, Calif. Mem. faculty dept. psychology U. Calif., Davis, 1979-81; fellow, rsch. faculty dept. psychiatry UCLA, 1981-83; fellow, instr. Stanford (Calif.) U. Med. Sch., 1990, chief resident, 1990; dir. adolescent divsn. Mood Disorders Ctr., L.A., 1991-93; pvt. practice, cons. L.A. and Brentwood, Calif., 1994—; with faculty Pacific Grad. Sch., Calif. Profl. Sch., Western Sch. Psychology; cons. L.A. County Law Assn., 1991—; mem. expert witness bd. Superior Mcpl. and Juvenile Cts., L.A., 1991-96; dir. NIMH clin. rsch. on depression. Contbr. articles to profl. jours. Mem. State Bd. Rehab. and Disability, Sacramento, 1989—. Recipient Rsch. award No. Calif. Psychiat. Soc., 1990. Mem. AMA, Am. Psychiat. Assn., Am. Anxiety Assn., Nat. Assn. Depression and Manic Depression, Soc. Clin. Psychopharmacology, OCD Soc., Calif. Med. Assn., Calif. Psychiat. Assn., So. Calif. Psychiat. Assn., L.A. County Med. Assn., U. Miami Alumni Bd., Soc. Magical Arts and Scis. Office: 11980 San Vincente Ste 620 Los Angeles CA 90049

BURGOIN, CATHERINE ANN, management, personnel consultant; b. Council Bluffs, Iowa, May 27, 1949; d. Clarence Ward and Nellie Charlotte (Godfrey) B.; m. Russell Wayne Dealy, May 21, 1983 (div. May 1994). BA, Kansas City (Mo.) Art Inst., 1970. Info. specialist, editor U. Mo., Kansas City, 1970-72, asst. dir. pub. rels., 1972-73; dir. mktg. and communications Kansas City Art Inst., 1973-78; pvt. practice cons. Kansas City, 1978-79; sales svc. rep. Lowell Press, Kansas City, 1979-81, prodn. mgr., 1981-85, v.p. mfg., 1985-86; v.p. mfg. Lieb Graphics Corp., Kansas City, Kans., 1987-90; gen. mgr. X-Press div. Spangler Inc., Kansas City, Kans., 1990-92; pres. Essential Solutions, Merriam, Kans., 1993-96, Blaine, Wash., 1996—; presenter workshops in field. Author, editor, mgr. Marketing Publications and Film, 1974-76 (Excellence award). Kansas City Regional Coun. for Higher Edn. grantee, 1976. Mem. Coun. for Advt. and Support Edn. (chmn. com. 1977).

BURISCH, DANNY B. CATSELAS, microbiologist; b. Lynwood, Calif., Feb. 2, 1964; s. John Dennis and Doreen Aglaie (LaPierre) C.; m. Deborah Kay Burisch, July 17, 1990; children: Tiffany Nicole Burisch, Victoria Nicole Burisch. BA, U. Nev., Las Vegas, 1986; PhD, NYU, 1989. Lab. asst. Bunyan Rsch., Inc., Dover, Eng., 1980-81, U. Nev., Las Vegas, 1982-85; owner, biologist Burisch Rsch., Las Vegas, 1987—; adj. cons. Space Biospheres, Tucson, 1989—; coord. Planetary Soc., Las Vegas, 1989-90; speaker Young Astronauts Nev., Las Vegas, 1990—, del. NASA Space Sta. Freedom Utilization Conf., 1993. Tchr. Jr. Girl Scouts Las Vegas, 1988-89; tchr. environ. sci. Las Vegas Boys and Girls Club, 1993—. Recipient Hon. Young Astronaut award, cert. appreciation Young Astronauts Nev., Las Vegas, 1990; fellow Huntingdon (Eng.) Rsch. Inst., 1980; scholar Harry S Truman Scholar Found., Las Vegas, 1984. Mem. AAAS, Aris. Acad. Sci., Am. Inst. Biol. Scis., Nev. Acad. Sci., Am. Soc. Naturalists, N.Y. Acad. Scis.

BURK, GARY MAURICE, health care facility planner; b. Dallas, Nov. 8, 1943; s. Houston Maurice and Evelyn (Howell) B. BArch, Tex. Tech U., 1968; MArch, U. Ill., 1970. Registered architect; NCARB cert. Asst. prof. Tex. Tech U., Lubbock, 1970-79; project designer Hellmuth, Obata & Kassabaum, Dallas, 1979-80; assoc. Richard Ferrara, Architect, Dallas, 1980-83; cons. designer Myrick, Newman, Dahlberg, Dallas, 1982-83; assoc. prof. Calif. State U., Pomona, Calif., 1983-85; sr. facility planner Am. Med. Internat., L.A., 1985-86; dir. facilities planning URS Cons., Cleve., 1986-88, URS Consultants, N.Y. and N.J., 1988-91; sr. med. planner Ellerbe Becket, Inc., L.A., 1991-95; v.p. Ellerbe Becket, Inc., San Francisco, 1995-96; prin. Ratcliff Architects, Berkeley, Calif., 1996—; owner Strategic & Facility Planning for Healthcare, San Francisco, 1996—; cons. City Hosp./St. Thomas Med. Ctr., Merger Task Force, Akron, 1988-89, L.A. County Pub. Health Programs and Svcs., 1992-94, Palo Alto (Calif.) Med. Found., 1992-96, U. Tex. med. br., Galveston, 1994-96; dir. Hosp. of the Future research studio, 1985. Mem. Dallas Civic Chorus, 1980-83, St. Alban's Parish Choir, Cleveland Heights, Ohio, 1987-88, All Saints Parish Choir, Hoboken, N.J., 1988-90, Cleve. Opera Assocs., 1987-88; mem. steering com. Judith Resnik Women's Health Ctr., Summa Health System, Akron, 1989-91, Friends of N.Y. Philharm, 1990-91. Research grantee Tex. Tech U., 1976. Mem. AIA (ednl. fellow 1968, Calif. coun.), AIA Acad. on Architecture for Health (steering com.), San Francisco AIA (health facilities, program com.), Health-Care Strategies and Perspectives. Democrat. Episcopalian. Home: 155 Jackson St Apt 2204 San Francisco CA 94111-1940 Office: Ratcliff Architects Box 1022 Berkeley CA 94701

BURKE, ARTHUR THOMAS, engineering consultant; b. Pueblo, Colo., Nov. 26, 1919; s. Daniel Michael and Naomi Edith (Brashear) B.; BS, U.S. Naval Acad., 1941; postgrad. UCLA; m. Regina Ahlgren Malone, June 15, 1972 (dec. July 1996); children: Arthur Thomas, Craig Timothy, Laura Ahlgren, Scott Ahlgren. With USN Electronics Lab. Center, San Diego, 1947-72, sr. satellite communications cons., 1964-72, satellite communications engring. cons., 1974—. Sweepstakes judge, San Diego Sci. Fair, 1960—. With USN, 1938-46; comdr. Res., ret. Recipient Presdl. Unit citation, 1942, Superior Performance award USN Electronics Lab. Center, 1967. Mem. IEEE (mem. San Diego membership com. 1958-68), AAAS, San Diego Astronomy Assn., San Diego Computer Assn., Am. Radio Relay League. Patentee electronic bathythermograph. Home and Office: 4011 College Ave San Diego CA 92115-6704

BURKE, DONALD WARREN, anesthesiologist; b. Ridgecrest, CA, Aug. 1, 1960; s. Kenneth Wayne and Elsie Juanita (Pannell) B. BS in Biochemistry cum laude, U. Calif., Davis, 1981; MD, Baylor U., 1986. Diplomate Am. Bd. Anesthesiology. Resident in anesthesiology Cornell Med. Ctr., N.Y.C., 1986-90; staff anesthesiologist Long Beach (Calif.) Comty. Med. Ctr., 1991—; provider BLS, ACLS, and PALS, Am. Heart Assn., Long Beach, Calif., 1987—, instr. Pediatric Advanced Life Support, Am. Heart Assn., Long Beach, Calif., 1995—. Med. vol. Mission to Ensenada, Mex., 1000 Smiles Found., Carlsbad, Calif., 1995; sponsor Charity Golf Found., Comty Hosp. Found., Long Beach, Calif., 1996. Mem. AMA, Am. Soc. Anesthesiologists, Long Beach Surgical Soc., U. Calif. Davis Alumni Assn. (life), Sierra Club (life), MENSA (life), Sigma Xi (Rsch. award 1976). Republican. Home and Office: 5318 E 2nd St Apt 504 Long Beach CA 90803-5354

BURKE, DOUG, author, inventor; b. July 25, 1963; s. Robert Louis and Joan Mary (Rowbotham) B. BS, U. Calif., Irvine, 1986, MS, 1987, PhD in Physics, 1990; D of Sci. of Drama (hon.), Case Western Res. U., 1991. Co-author: (novel) The Dark Prophet, 1995; author: (textbook) Psychophysics and Drama, 1991, (play) Rebel King, 1995, (screenplay) Gull, 1995; patentee in the field of three-dimensional image creation and display systems. Office: PO Box 4254 Newport Beach CA 92661-4254

BURKE, EDMOND WAYNE, retired judge; b. Ukiah, Calif., Sept. 7, 1935; s. Wayne P. and Opal K. B.; children from previous marriage: Kathleen R., Jennifer E.; m. Anna M. Hubbard, Dec. 29, 1990. A.B., Humboldt State Coll., 1957, M.A., 1958; J.D., U. Calif., 1964. Bar: Calif., Alaska, Mont. Individual practice law Calif. and Alaska, 1965-67; asst. atty. gen. State of Alaska, 1967; asst. dist. atty. Anchorage, Alaska, 1968-69; judge Superior Ct., Alaska, 1970-75; justice Supreme Ct. State of Alaska, Anchorage, 1975-93, chief justice, 1981-84; of coun. Bogle & Gates, 1994-95; mem. Burke, Bauermeister & Brelsford, Anchorage, 1996—. Republican. Presbyterian.

BURKE, KRISTIN MARIE, costume designer; b. Orange, Calif., Mar. 20, 1970; d. Bruce Lennont and Patricia Ann (Mullin) B. Grad., Northwestern U., 1991. Owner, designer KB Creates Fashion Design, Chico, Calif., 1982—; wardrobe runner Tri-Star Hudson Hawk, L.A., 1990—, asst. prodn. coord., 1990—; prodn. designer Niteskool, Northwestern U., 1987, 88, 89, 90, exec. producer, 1989—. Dir. La Madeleine, 1990 (Judge's Pick Seattle Video Shorts); costume designer: Varsity Cafe, 1989; (feature films) The Skate Board Kid, 1992, Street Wise, 1992, Carnosaur, 1992, Human Target, 1993, The Unborn II, 1993, Furious Angel, 1993, Revenge of the Red Baron, 1993, Criminal Passion, 1993, Ground Zero, 1993, Munchie Strikes Back, 1993, Sweet Dreams, 1994, Force on Force, 1994, Red Ribbon Blues, 1995, Within the Rock, 1995, The Corporate Ladder, 1996, Ravager, 1996, Casper II: Ghost Central Station, 1997; (short films) Lucky Peach, 1992, Showdown on Rio Road, 1992, Judgement, 1994; also music videos; wardrobe asst. Dracula, 1991; writer screenplay Mes Jours San Popcorn, 1990; writer, dir. Ascent, 1990, To Whom It May Concern, 1990, I Am A Red Cat Flipping, 1990. Calif. State art scholar, 1987; finalist USA-Dallas Filmfest, 1991. Mem. Costume Designers Guild (local IATSE 892 designer category). Office: PO Box 492553 Los Angeles CA 90049-8553

BURKE, LARRY DRYDEN, public relations administrator; b. Ritzville, Wash., Dec. 10, 1946; s. Berwyn Frank and Dorothy Edith (Dryden) B. BA, U. Idaho, 1970. Corp. clk. Office of Sec. of State, Boise, Idaho, 1973-74; info. specialist Boise State U., 1974-81, dir. univ. rels., 1981—; mem. case regional bd. Coun. Advancement and Support of Edn., Washington, 1984-85. Editor: Idaho Entrepreneurs, 1992, Snake, 1994 (Idaho Book award 1995), Broncos, 1994; editor (mag.) Focus, 1978— (numerous state, regional and nat. awards). Dir. pub. rels. Jackson for Gov., Boise, 1978; pub. rels. specialist Fundsy, Boise, 1983; bd. dirs. City Arts Commn., Boise, 1985-86. Mem. City Club, Idaho Press Club, Capital City Communicators, Am. Polit. Items Collectors. Home: 3008 Leadville Boise ID 83706 Office: Boise State Univ 1910 University Dr Boise ID 83725-0001

BURKE, MARIANNE KING, state agency administrator, financial executive; b. Douglasville, Ga., May 30, 1938; d. William Horace and Evora (Morris) King; divorced; 1 child, Kelly Page. Student, Ga. Inst. Tech., 1956-59, Anchorage C.C., 1964-66, Portland State U., 1968-69; BBA, U. Alaska, 1976. CPA, Alaska. Sr. audit mgr. Price Waterhouse, 1982-90; v.p. fin., asst. sec. NANA Regional Corp., Inc., Anchorage, 1990-95; v.p. fin. NANA Devel. Corp., Inc., Anchorage, 1990-95; sec.-treas. Vanguard Industries, J.V., Anchorage, 1990-95, Alaska United Drilling, Inc., Anchorage, 1990-95; treas. NANA/Marriott Joint Venture, Anchorage, 1990-95; v.p. fin. Arctic Utilities, Inc., Anchorage, 1990-95, Tour Arctic, Inc., Anchorage, 1990-95, Purcell Svcs., Ltd., Anchorage, 1990-95, Arctic Caribou Inn, Anchorage, 1990-95, NANA Oilfield Svcs., Inc., Anchorage, 1990-95, NANA Corp. Svcs., Inc., Anchorage, 1992-95; dir. divsn. ins. State of Alaska, 1995—; mem. State of Alaska Medicaid Rate Commn., 1985-88, State of Alaska Bd. Accountancy, 1984-87; bd. dirs. Nat. Assn. Ins. Commrs. Edn. and Rsch. Found. Bd. dirs. Alaska Treatment Ctr., Anchorage, 1978, Alaska Hwy. Cruises; treas. Alaska Feminist Credit Union, Anchorage, 1979-80; mem. fund raising com. Anchorage Symphony, 1981. Mem. AICPA, Alaska Soc. CPAs, Govtl. Fin. Officers U.S. and Can., Fin. Execs. Inst. (bd. dirs.), Nat. Assn. of Ins. Commrs. Home: 7241 Foxridge Cir Anchorage AK 99518-2702 Office: State Office Bldg PO Box 110805 333 Willoughby Ave Juneau AK 99811-0805 also: 3601 C St Ste 1324 Anchorage AK 99503-5948

BURKE, MICHAEL JOHN, dean, academic programs director; b. Chgo., July 7, 1942; s. John J. and Rejean P. (Ough) B.; m. Mary Ellen Mueller, Aug. 4, 1964; children: Mara Jean, John Edmund. BA, Blackburn Coll., 1964; PhD, Iowa State U., 1969. Asst. prof. U. Minn., St. Paul, 1972-76; assoc. prof. Colo. State U., Ft. Collins, 1976-79; prof., chairperson U. Fla., Gainesville, 1979-84; assoc. dean Oreg. State U., Corvallis, 1984—; bd. dirs. E.R. Jackman Found., Agrl. Research Found. Recipient Hon. State Farmer degree Oreg. Future Farmers of Am., Salem, 1986. Mem. Am. Chem. Soc., Am. Soc. Hort. Sci. (Darrow award 1979), Am. Soc. Plant Physiologists, AAAS, Cryobiology Soc. Home: 3510 NW Dimple Hill Rd Corvallis OR 97330-3295 Office: Oreg State Univ Straud 137 Corvallis OR 97331

BURKE, PATRICK GEORGE, financial executive; b. Lansing, Mich., May 8, 1946; s. Edward L. and B. Marian (Hull) B.; m. Valerie J. Zuber, Sept. 10, 1967 (div. June 1982); m. Johnnie Ruth Whitten, Apr. 8, 1984; children: Rita V., Regina D., Daniel P. Assoc. degree, Lansing C.C., 1968; BA, Mich. State U., 1972. Lic. broker, Ariz. Nat. wholesale mgr. Firestone Car Care, San Francisco, 1989-92; loan officer, dir. ops. Javazon Fin. Svcs., Tucson, 1993-96; pres., broker Sabino Fin. Group, Tucson, 1996—. Mem. So. Ariz. Home Builders Assn. With USMC, 1964-65. Mem. Nat. Employee Svc. Recreation Assn., Ariz. Assn. Mortgage Brokers. Republican. Office: Sabino Fin Group 7278 N Oracle Rd Tucson AZ 85704

BURKE, RICHARD JAMES, optical physicist, consultant; b. Barberton, Ohio, Apr. 19, 1917; s. Edward Richard Joseph and Mary Margaret (Hildum) B.; m. Louise Morgan, Nov. 9, 1940 (div. 1961); children: Richard Lewis, Pamela Jean Zwehl-Burke; m. Polly Pring Deveau, Dec. 21, 1985. BS in Engring. Physics, U. Ill., 1940; MS in Solid State Physics, U. Md., 1950, PhD in Optical Physics, 1954. Devel. engr. Eastman Kodak Co., Rochester, N.Y., 1937-40; devel. physicist Naval Ordnance Lab., Silver Spring, Md., 1940-56; dept. mgr. Lockheed Missiles and Space Co., Palo Alto, Calif., 1956-60; pres., founder Applied Systems Corp., Palo Alto, 1960-64, h nu Systems, Inc., Menlo Park, Calif., 1964-68; dept. mgr. Coherent Inc., Palo Alto, 1972-80; pres., founder Burke Concepts Unltd., San Mateo, Calif., 1980—. Author: Alternatives to Economic Disaster, 1972, Song of Angels, 1984, The Fifth Force, 1988, Boundaries of Knowledge, 1991, No Shadow of Doubt, 1994, Order of the Universe, 1995. Mem. Tau Beta Pi, Phi Kappa Phi, Sigma Xi, Phi Eta Sigma, Phi Lambda Upsilon. Home and Office: 741 Cuesta Ave San Mateo CA 94403-1203

BURKE, RUTH, writer; b. L.A., Jan. 16, 1933; d. Thomas Arthur and Bertha Morgan King; children: D. Julian Montelbano, Alan D., Carol Burke Ward, Michael L., Laurel, Abram D. AA, East L.A. Coll., 1957; AB, San Diego State U., 1967; postgrad., Western N.Mex. U., 1996—. Cert. tchr., Ariz. English instr. Reed Christian Coll., Compton, Calif., 1985; writing instr. Cochise Coll., Benson, Ariz., 1996; book reviewer Interrace Mag., Atlanta, 1993, Lambda Book Report, Washington, 1996—. Mem. editl. staff True Romance, True Experience; columnist Ariz. Range News, Willcox, 1995-96; contbr. numerous works to profl. publs. Mem. sch. coun. Bowie (Ariz.) Schs., 1996. Libertarian. Roman Catholic. Home: PO Box 247 Bowie AZ 85605

BURKEE, IRVIN, artist; b. Kenosha, Wis., Feb. 6, 1918; s. Omar Lars and Emily (Quardokas) B.; diploma Sch. of Art Inst. Chgo., 1945; m. Bonnie May Ness, Apr. 12, 1945; children: Brynn, Jill, Peter (dec.), Ian (dec.). Owner, silversmith, goldsmith Burkee Jewelry, Blackhawk, Colo., 1950-57; painter, sculptor, Aspen, Colo., 1957-78, Cottonwood, Ariz., Pietrasanta, Italy, 1978—; instr. art U. Colo., 1946, 50-53, Stephens Coll., Columbia, Mo., 1947-49. John Quincy Adams travel fellow, Mex., 1945. Executed copper mural of human history of Colo. for First Nat. Bank, Englewood, Colo., 1970, copper mural of wild birds of Kans. for Ranchmart State Bank, Overland Park, Kans., 1974; exhibited Art Inst. Chgo., Smithsonian Instn. (award 1957), Milw. Art Inst., Krannert Mus., William Rockhill Nelson Gallery, St. Louis Art Mus., Denver Art Mus.; represented in southwestern galleries, also pvt. collections throughout U.S.; work illustrated in books Design and Creation of Jewelry, Design through Discovery, Walls. Mem. Nat. Sculpture Soc., Sedona Chamber Music Soc. Address: PO Box 5361 Lake Montezuma AZ 86342-5361

BURKETT, JOHN DAVID, professional baseball player; b. New Brighton, Mass., Nov. 28, 1964. With San Francisco Giants, 1983-94, Tex. Rangers, 1994—. *

BURKETT, WILLIAM ANDREW, banker; b. nr. Herman, Nebr., July 1, 1913; s. William H. and Mary (Dill) B.; m. Juliet Ruth Johnson, Oct. 5, 1940 (dec. Mar. 1976); children: Juliet Ann Burkett Hooker, Katherine C. Burkett Congdon, William Cleveland; m. Nancy Schallert Morrow, June 20, 1992. Student, U. Nebr., 1931-32, Creighton U. Law Sch., 1932-33; LL.B., U. Omaha, 1936. Exec. trainee Bank Am., 1937-38; Sr. spl. agt., intelligence unit Treasury Dept., 1945-50; exec. v.p. Calif. Employers Assn. Group, Sacramento, 1950-53; dir. Calif. Dept. Employment, 1953-55; chmn. Calif. Employment Stabilization Commn., 1953-55; supt. banks, chmn. Dept. Investments Calif., 1955-59; dir. Liquidation Yokohama Specie Bank; also Sumitomo Bank, San Francisco, 1955-59; cons. Western Bancorp, San Francisco, 1959-61; chmn. bd., pres. Security Nat. Bank Monterey County, Monterey-Carmel, Calif., 1961-66, Burkett Land Co., Monterey, 1966—; chmn. bd. Securities Properties Corp., Monterey; witness Calif. Crime Com., U.S. Senate Kefauver Crime Com., 1950-52, U.S. Congress Banking Com., 1991; nat. chmn., founder Bank Savs. & Loan Depositor's League, 1991. Author: Mount Rushmore National Memorial's History of America, 1776-1904, 1971. Elected nominee Nebr. Sec. State, 1936; witness Calif. Crime Commn. and U.S. Senate Kefauver Crime Commn., 1950-52, U.S. Congress Banking Com., 1991; dir. banking and investments, cabinet gov., Calif., 1953-59; dir. Calif. Emergency Manpower Commn., 1953-55; chmn. Gov. Calif. Com. Refugee Relief, 1953-55; mem. Calif. Securities Commn., 1955-59; mem. financial bd. Pine Manor Jr. Coll., Chestnut Hill, Mass., 1967—; mem. Monterey County Hist. Commn., Nat. Trust Found., Royal Oak Found.; bd. dirs. Monterey Symphony Assn.; chmn. bd. trustees Nat. Hist. Found.; trustee Monterey Mus. Art, Bishop Kip Sch., Carmel Valley, Calif.; co-chmn., trustee Mt. Rushmore Hall of Records Commn., 1987; mem. adv. bd. Robert Louis Stevenson Sch., Pebble Beach, Calif., 1971-74, candidate for gov. Calif., 1978 . Served as officer USCGR, 1943-45. Mem. Am., Calif., Ind. bankers assns., Nat. Assn. Supts. State Banks (pres. 1958-59), Monterey History and Art Assn., Mt. Rushmore Nat. Meml. Soc. (life mem., trustee), Amvets (dept. comdr. Calif. 1947, nat. vice comdr. 1948), Soc. Calif. Pioneers, Bank and Savs. and Loan Depositor's League (nat. chmn. 1991—), Monterey Peninsula Mus. Art, Mt. Rushmore Hall of Records Commn. Inc. (nat. co-chmn.1990—). Episcopalian. Clubs: Monterey Peninsula Golf and Country (Pebble Beach), Beach and Tennis (Pebble Beach), Stillwater Yacht (Pebble Beach); Carmel Valley Golf and Tennis; Commonwealth (San Francisco), Rotary (San Francisco); Sutter Lawn (Sacramento). Home: PO Box 726 Pebble Beach CA 93953-0726 Office: Viscaino Rd Pebble Beach CA 93953

BURKHART, BRAD JOHN, horticulturist, landscape architect; b. Ann Arbor, Mich., Jan. 24, 1949. BA in Fine Art, Kalamazoo Coll., 1971; student, Washington U., St. Louis, 1972-74; cert. completition horticulture, City Coll. San Francisco, 1979; M Landscape Architecture, U. Mich., 1982. Mgr. Weber Native Plant Nursery, San Diego County, 1983-86, Habitat Restoration and Mgmt. Group, San Diego, 1987-96; tchr. native plant lendscaping 3 colls., San Diego County, 1984-94; lectr. on habitat restoration and native plant landscaping; presenter Soc. Ecol. Restoration confs., 1989—. Prin. works include 1st San Diego River Improvement Project Horticultural Supervision and Monitoring, La Paloma Brodiaea Filifolia Mitigation Program - Baldwin Co., Twin Oaks Valley Ranch Riparian Mitigation Plans - Brock Devel., North Mission Valley Interceptor Sewer Riparian Mitigation Plans - City of San Diego Water Utilities Dept., Black Mountain Rd. San Diego Thornmint Mitigation - Pardee Devel., Sabre Springs Disturbed Hillside Chaparral Revegetation Program - Pardee Constrn.; contbr. articles to profl. jours. Recipient San Diego Xeriscape award, 1990. Mem. Soc. Ecol. Restoration, Assn. Wetland Mgrs., Internat. Erosion Control Assn., Calif. Native Plant Soc., Native Grassland Assn. Calif. Home: 9836 Rimpark Way San Diego CA 92124-1627 Office: Ogden Environ & Energy Svcs 5510 Morehouse Dr San Diego CA 92121-3720

BURKHART, RICHARD HENRY, mathematician; b. Tacoma, Wash., Dec. 17, 1946; s. Perry Needham and Dorothy Alice (Shoff) B.; m. Saowalak Sutharalais, Aug. 3, 1971 (div. Oct. 1987); children: Sanyaalak D., Sandra S., Diana P.; m. Mona Lee Southerland, June 11, 1988. BA, Reed College, 1969; AM, Dartmouth Coll., 1974, PhD, 1976. Asst. prof. U. N.C., Wilmington, 1976-80; mathematician Boeing Co., Seattle, 1981—. Dir. Auburn (Wash.) Sch. Bd., 1993—; editor 31st Dist. Democrats Newsletter, Auburn, 1992—; mem. govtl. affairs com. Cascade Bicycle Club, Seattle, 1993—. Mem. Am. Math. Soc., Soc. for Indsl. and Applied Math. Democrat. Unitarian - Universalist. Home: 4802 S Othello St Seattle WA 98118-3851 Office: Boeing Info & Support Systems PO Box 3707 MS 7L-21 Seattle WA 98124

BURKHART, SANDRA MARIE, art gallery director; b. Cleve., Dec. 29, 1942; d. John Joseph Norris and Audrey Eleanor Kegg McGuire Marshall; m. Thomas Henry Burkhart, Oct. 29, 1960 (div. Sept. 26, 1979); children: Bryan, Brad, Lisa, Michelle. Student, Evergreen Valley Coll., San Jose, 1978-80, San Jose City Coll., 1978-80, West Valley Coll., Saratoga, Calif., 1978-79. Med. technician Eye Med. Clinic, San Jose, 1980-83; ind. corp. art salesperson San Jose, 1983-92; corp. sales dir. Phoenix Gallery, San Jose, 1986-88; v.p. mktg. Whittlers Mother, San Francisco, 1989-90; dir. Martin Lawrence Galleries, Santa Clara, Calif., 1990—. Home: 1353 Greenwich Ct San Jose CA 95125-5964

BURKLE, RONALD, consumer products company executive. CEO Smith's Food & Drug Ctr., Salt Lake City. Office: 1550 S Redwood Rd Salt Lake City UT 84104*

BURKS, JACK SHELDON, neurologist; b. Charleston, W.Va., Nov. 28, 1943; s. Jack Sheldon Burks and Monica Louise (Long) Ghent; m. Susan Dawn Ayarbe, Aug. 19, 1989; children: Jonathan, Ryan, Jacqueline. BA, W.Va. U., 1965, MD with honors, 1969. Lic. physician, Colo. Intern U. Cin., 1969-70; resident in neurology U. Colo., Boulder, 1970-73; postdoctoral fellow in virology/immunology Johns Hopkins U., Balt., 1973-75, instr. neurology, 1974-75; asst. prof. neurology/microbiology/immunology U. Colo., Boulder, 1975-81, assoc. prof., 1981-88; pres. Rocky Mountain Multiple Sclerosis Ctr., Englewood, Colo., 1978—; lectr. in field; vis. prof. numerous med. schs., hosps., med. socs.; chief neurology Swedish Med. Ctr., 1993—. Contbr. numerous articles and abstracts to profl. jours.; editl. bd. Rehab Mgmt., 1994, Jour. Neurologic Rehab., 1986—; ad hoc reviewer various jours.; co-editor: Interdisciplinary Rehabilitation of Multiple Sclerosis and Neuromuscular Disorders, 1985. Bd. trustees Nat. Easter Seal Rsch. Found., 1990-91, mem. rsch. com., 1992—. Recipient Speedy award Paralyzed Vets. of Am., 1988; fellow Am. Cancer Soc., 1965, Nat. Multiple Sclerosis Soc., 1973. Fellow Am. Acad. Neurology (sec.-treas. sect. neurologic rehab. 1985-87, chmn./co-chmbn. various sci. sessions on neurologic rehab., vice chmn. sect. neurologic rehab. 1987-89, chmn. 1990-92, rep. to Am. Acad. Phys. Medicine and Rehab. 1993—, exec. com. 1985-94); mem. Am. Acad. Med. Dirs., Am. Congress Rehab. Medicine, Am. Neurol. Assn., Am. Soc. Neurorehab. (pres.-elect 1990-93, pres. 1994-96, bd. dirs. 1990—), Colo. Soc. Clin. Neurologists, Consortium of Multiple Sclerosis Ctrs. (co-chmn. com. on patient care 1986-92, exec. com. 1985-92, fin. com. 1987-91, membership rev. com. 1987-91, treas.), Multiple Sclerosis Soc. Colo. (med. dir. 1975-84, med. advisor 1988-91), Clin. Neurosci. Soc. (pres. 1979-80), Natl. Multiple Sclerosis Soc. (bd. dirs. Ctrl. Colo. chpt. 1976-78, med. adv. bd. 1985-89, com. on unitorm data base for multiple sclerosis 1986-89, clinic com., profl. adv. com. 1991-93, edn. com. 1991-94, med. adv. bd. 1991—), Colo. Neurol. Inst. (rsch. com. 1988—, edn. com. 1988—, sec. bd. dirs. 1990-94, chmn. clin. programs and outreach com. 1988-92), Arapahoe Med. Soc. (coun. mem.), Colo. Med. Soc. (ho. of dels. 1990—), Rotary, Alpha Omega Alpha. Office: Rocky Mountain MS Ctr 701 E Hampden Ave Ste 420 Englewood CO 80110-2760

BURKS, ROCKY ALAN, social services executive, consultant; b. San Bernardino, Calif., June 12, 1952; s. Lloyd Jackson and Vivian Elnora B.; m. Nikki Ann Stone (div. 1974); 1 child, Gannon LeRoy; m. Lydia Ann Deatherage, Aug. 20, 1983. BA in Social Welfare, Calif. State U., Chico, 1979, BA in Sociology, 1979. Instrument flight instr. USAF, Del Rio, Tex., 1971-75; dir. outreach and recruitment, Office of Vets. Affairs Calif. State U., Chico, 1976-81; exec. dir. Easter Seal Soc. of Butte County, Chico, 1981-82, No. Calif. Ind. Living Program, Chico, 1982-85, Ind. Living Svcs. of N. Calif., Inc., Chico, 1988—; social worker, Adult Protective Svcs. Butte County Welfare Dept., Oroville, Calif., 1985-87; bd. dirs. Calif. Coalition of Ind. Living Ctrs., Sacramento, Calif., pres., 1991-94; bd. dirs. Pub. Interest

Ctr. on Long-term Care, Sacramento, treas., 1994—; mem. disability access adv. bd. Divsn. of the State Arch., Sacramento, 1995—, Disabled Access Bd. of Appeals, Butte County Building Divsn., Oroville, 1994—. Editor: (newsletter) Independent Life, 1988—, Voice, 1976-81. Mem. Transp. Adv. Comm., Butte County Assn. of Govts., Oroville, 1992—; disability adv. Calif. Assn. of Persons with Handicaps, Sacramento, 1994. With USAF, 1971-75. Recipient cert. of Congl. recognition, Congressman Wally Herger, Chico, 1993, 96, Master Instr. award Calif. Assn. Persons with Handicaps. Mem. Chico Breakfast Lions (pres. 1991-92, Lion of the Year 1990), Lions Eye Found. of Calif. Nev., Freemasons, Scottish Rite, Ben Ali Shrine, Melvin Jones Fellow, Lions Internat., Chickasaw Indian Nation. (citizen), Am. Leg. Vietnam Vets. Am. Home: 4135 Keefer Rd Chico CA 95973-8956 Office: Ind Living Svcs No Calif 555 Rio Lindo Ave Ste B Chico CA 95926

BURLAND, BRIAN BERKELEY, novelist, poet, painter, scenarist; b. Paget, Bermuda, Apr. 23, 1931; s. Gordon Hamilton and Honor Alice Croydon (Gosling) B.; m. Charlotte Ann Taylor, 1952 (div. 1957); children: Susan, Anne, William; m. Edwina Ann Trentham, 1962 (div. 1979); 1 child, Benjamin; m. Isabella Petrie, 1990. Grad., Aldenham Sch., Elstree, Eng., 1948; student, U. Western Ont., Can., 1948-51. Mng. dir. Burland Estates, Ltd., Gosling Estates, Ltd.; 1st v.p. G.H. Burland & Co., Ltd., 1951-56; assoc. editor Bermudian Mag., 1957; lectr. Am. Sch., London, 1974, Washington and Lee U., Va., 1973; writer in residence So. Sem., Va., 1973, Bermuda Writers Conf., 1978, U. Hartford, Conn., 1981-82; guest fellow Yale U., 1982-83; vis. prof. Conn. Coll., 1986-87; judge P.E.N. Syndicated Fiction Project, 1985; narrator stories and poems BBC, 1968—; condr. poetry and fiction readings Yale U., Washington and Lee U., U. Hartford, U. Mass., Amherst, Arts Coun. Princeton, 1990-93; writer, painter-in-residence Melville Coll., 1992, Shotts (Scotland) Prison; lectr. Bermuda Coll., 1995-96. Author: A Fall from Aloft, 1968, A Few Flowers for St. George, 1969, Undertow, 1970, The Sailor and the Fox, 1973, Surprise, 1975, Stephan Decatur, 1976, The Flight of the Cavalier, 1980, Love is a Durable Fire, 1985 (children's book), St. Nicholas the Tub, 1964; (poetry) To Celebrate a Happiness That is America, 1971; represented in various pvt. collections worldwide. Mem. Princeton Arts coun. Served with Brit. Mcht. Svc., 1944. Recipient Lifetime Achievement award Bermuda Arts Coun., 1993. Fellow Royal Soc. Lit., Acad. Am. Poets; mem. PEN, Poetry Soc. Am., Authors Guild, Am. Ctr. Soc., Princeton Writers Group (founder), Royal Bermuda Yacht Club, Chelsea Arts Club (London). Mem. Bah'ai World Faith. Office: care Mary Cunnane W W Norton & Co 550 Fifth Ave New York NY 10036-5001

BURLESKI, JOSEPH ANTHONY, JR., information services professional; b. Poughkeepsie, N.Y., June 30, 1960; s. Joseph Anthony Burleski Sr. and Fredeline Cyr; m. Judith Ann Lezon, June 10, 1989; children: Joseph Anthony III, Jessica Ann. BSBA, Marist Coll., 1982; MBA Mktg., U. Phoenix, 1992; grad. in human rels. and effective speaking, Dale Carnegie, 1990. Cert. project mgmt. profl. Project Mgmt. Inst. Computer operator IBM Corp., Poughkeepsie, 1982-83, lead/sr. computer operator, 1983-84, systems programmer, 1984-85, assoc. systems programmer, 1985-86, mgr. offshift computer ops., 1986-87; mgr. info. processing IBM Corp., Boulder, Colo., 1987-88, mgr. MVS systems programming, 1988-91; mgr. location and field svcs. devel. Integrated Systems Solutions Corp. (subs. IBM), Boulder, 1991-93, mgr. location and field svc. devel. ind. test, 1992-93; mgr. VM/VSE svcs. Integrated Sys. Solutions Corp. subs. IBM Corp., Boulder, 1993-94; account mgr. Integrated Sys. Solutions Corp., Boulder, 1994-96; delivery project exec. IBM, Boulder, 1997—; mem. IBM Data Processing Ops. Coun., Poughkeepsie, 1983-92, Project Mgmt. Inst., 1995—, Am. Mgmt. Assn., 1991—; grad. asst. Dale Carnegie Inst., Boulder, 1990—; mem. Help Desk Inst., 1996—. Coach Spl. Olympics, 1987—; mem. Order of the Arrow Hon. Soc., sec., editor, 1976-77, pres. 1977-78, treas. 1980-81; patrol leader, store dir., asst. camp dir. Boy Scouts Am., Cub Scouts Summer Camp, 1985-87. Mem. Marist Coll. Alumni Assn. (contbr.), Vigil Nat. Honor Soc., IBM Runners' Club. Roman Catholic. Home: 1826 Lashley St Longmont CO 80501-2061 Office: 5600 N 63d St Boulder CO 80301-9269

BURLINGAME, ALMA LYMAN, chemist, educator; b. Cranston, R.I., Apr. 29, 1937; s. Herman Follett Jr. and Rose Irene (Kohler) B.; children: Mark, Walter; m. Marilyn F. Schwartz, Feb. 14, 1993; 1 stepchild, Corey Schwartz. BS, U. R.I., 1959; PhD, MIT, 1962. Asst. prof. U. Calif., Berkeley, 1963-68, assoc. chemist, 1968-72, rsch. chemist, 1972-78; prof. U. Calif., San Francisco, 1978—, Univ. Coll., London, 1996—; vis. prof. Ludwig Inst. for Cancer Rsch., London, 1993-94. Editor: Topics in Organic Mass Spectrometry, 1970, Mass Spectrometry in Health and Life Science, 1985, Biological Mass Spectrometry, 1990, Mass Spectrometry in the Biological Sciences, 1995; contbr. articles to profl. jours. With USAR, 1954-62. Guggenheim Found. fellow, 1970. Fellow AAAS. Office: U Calif Dept Pharms and Chemistry San Francisco CA 94143-0446

BURLINGHAM, ARAGON, aerospace engineer; b. Ipswich, Eng., Feb. 25, 1968; came to U.S., 1986; s. Richard and Haleh (Mojibi) B. BS in Aeronautics/Astronautics, U. So. Calif., L.A., 1990; MS in Aerospace Engring., Stanford U., 1992. Rsch. technologist GEC-Alsthom, Whetstone, Eng., 1990-91; customer support engr. RASNA Corp., San Jose, Calif., 1992-93; cons. engr. Food & Machinery Corp., San Jose, 1993; engr. Modeling & Computing Svcs., Boulder, Colo., 1993—. Contbr. papers to tech. publs. Mem. AIAA (events coord. U. So. Calif. chpt. 1989), ASME (assoc.), Bakersfield Coll. Engrs. Club (v.p. 1987-88), Tau Beta Pi.

BURMAN, SHEILA FLEXER ZOLA, special education educator; b. N.Y.C., May 1, 1935; d. Jack and Edna (Eagle) Flexer; m. Eugene Lee Zola, July 7, 1957 (div. Aug. 1973); children: Leslie Sheldon, Sharon Joanne; m. Milton Burman, Mar. 19, 1978. Student, Hunter Coll., 1952-55; BA in Edn., BS, UCLA, 1957, 85, spl. edn. cert. for Learning Handicapped, 1985; and Severely Handicapped; MS in Counseling, U. LaVerne, 1983; resource specialist cert., Calif. Luth. U., 1988. Tchr. L.A. Unified Sch. Dist., 1957-81, spl. edn. tchr., 1981-88, resource specialist jr. high sch., 1988-89, resource specialist elem. sch., 1989-96, commr. spl. edn. commn.; Cert. tchr., spl. edn. tchr., resource specialist, pupil pers. credential. Grantee CTIP 1988, Computer 1989. Mem. Coun. for Exceptional Children, Assn. Ednl. Therapists, United Tchrs. L.A., Calif. Tchrs. Assn., UCLA Alumni Assn., UCLA Grad. Sch. Edn. Alumni Assn., Hunter Coll. Alumni Assn., Pi Lambda Theta. Home: 15455 Hamner Dr Los Angeles CA 90077-1802

BURNETT, ELIZABETH (BETSY BURNETT), counselor; b. Columbus, Ohio, July 17, 1953; m. Gilbert C. Burnett, Jan. 2, 1973; children: Jeffrey, Stephanie. BS in Med. Tech. with honors, Rutgers U., 1976; MA in Counseling with honors, Denver Sem., 1992. Med. technologist various hosps., Denver and Plainfield, N.J., 1976-92; missions dir. Bear Creek Ch. and Family of Faith Ch., Denver, 1985-89; counseling dir. Providence Homes, Denver, 1989—; dir. Providence Counseling Ministry, Denver, 1993—; program cons. various urban counseling svcs. and rehabs., Denver, Colorado Springs, Mich., Calif., Australia, 1992—; urban ministry cons. Denver Sem., 1991-95; contract counselor So. Gables Ch., Littleton, Colo., 1992-96, presenter divorce recovery workshops, 1992-96; spkr. in field. Author: Handbook of Urban Christian Counseling, 1992. Children's dir. mothers of preschoolers, vacation Bible sch., and missions edn. program Bear Creek Ch., Denver, 1982-85; deaconess, lay leader So. Gables Ch., Littleton, 1992-96. Recipient med. tech. award Muhlenberg Hosp., 1976. Mem. ACA, Am. Assn. Christian Counselors, Internat. Assn. Addictions & Offender Counselors, Assn. Multicultural Counseling and Devel., Christians for Bibl. Equality, Am. Soc. Clin. Pathologists. Office: Providence Homes 801 Logan St Denver CO 80203-3114

BURNETT, ERIC STEPHEN, environmental consultant; b. Manchester, Eng., Apr. 5, 1924; s. William Louis and Edith Winifred (Gates) B.; came to U.S., 1963; naturalized, 1974; BSc in Physics (with honors), London U., 1954; MS in Environ. Studies, Calif. State, Dominguez Hills, 1976; PhD in Environ. Engring., Calif. Coast U., 1982. children: Diana, Ian, Brenda, Keith. Program mgr. Brit. Aircraft Corp., Stevenage, Eng., 1953-63; sr. systems engr. RCA, Princeton, N.J., 1963-66; project mgr. Gen. Electric Co., Valley Forge, Pa., 1966-67; dept. head TRW systems Group, Redondo Beach, Calif., 1967-72; dir. energy and pollution control ARATEX Svcs., Inc., Calif., 1974-81, dir. tech. devel., 1981-83, staff cons., 1983-91; cons., lectr. in spacecraft sensor tech., energy conservation, environ. and contamination controls. With Royal Air Force, 1942-47. Assoc. fellow AIAA; mem. Inst. Environ. Scis. (sr.). Contbr. articles in field to profl. jours. Home and Office: 3423 Excalibar Rd Placerville CA 95667-5418

BURNETT, JOHN LAURENCE, geologist; b. Wichita, Kans., Aug. 28, 1932; s. Virgil Milton and Bertha Maurine (Van Order) L.; m. Annetta J. Saywell, July, 2, 1954 (div. 1975); children: John Forrester, Laurence Gregory. AB in Geology, U. Calif., Berkeley, 1957, MS in Mining, 1960. Cert. engring. geologist; registered geologist. Geologist Calif. Div. Mines and Geology, Sacramento, Calif., 1958-95; cons. geologist, 1996—; courts expert superior ct. of L.A., 1967-71; instr. geology U. Calif. Extension, Berkeley, 1967-75, Cosumnes River Coll., 1981-88, 96. Pvt. U.S. Army, 1955. Fellow Geol. Soc. of Am. Unitarian. Office: Calif Div Mines and Geology 801 St Ms 12 # 31 Sacramento CA 95814

BURNEY, VICTORIA KALGAARD, business consultant, civic worker; b. Los Angeles, Apr. 12, 1943; d. Oscar Albert and Dorothy Elizabeth (Peterson) Kalgaard; children: Kim Elizabeth, J. Hewett. BA with honors, U. Mont., 1965; MA, U. No. Colo., 1980; postgrad. Webster U., St. Louis, 1983-84. Exec. dir. Hill County Community Action, Havre, Mont., 1966-67; community orgn. specialist ACCESS, Escondido, Calif., 1967-68; program devel. and community orgn. specialist Community Action Programs, Inc., Pensacola, Fla., 1968-69; cons. Escambia County Sch. Bd., Fla., 1969-71; pres. Kal Kreations, Kailua, Hawaii, 1974-77; instr., dir. office human resources devel. Palomar Coll., San Marcos, Calif., 1978-81; chief exec. officer IDET Corp., San Marcos, 1981-87; cons. County of Riverside, Calif., 1983. Mem. San Diego County Com. on Handicapped, San Diego, 1979; cons. tribal resource devel., Escondido, Calif., 1979; mem. exec. com. Social Services Coordinating Council, San Diego, 1982-83; mem. pvt. sector com. and planning and rev. com. Calif. Employment and Tng. Adv. Council, Sacramento, 1982-83; bd. mgrs. Santa Margarita Family YMCA, Vista, Calif., 1984-86; bd. dirs. North County Community Action Program, Escondido, 1978, Casa de Amparo, San Luis Rey, Calif., 1980-83; mem. San Diego County Pub. Welfare Adv. Bd., 1979-83, chairperson, 1981; mem. Calif. Rep. Cen. Com., Sacramento, 1989—; ofcl. San Diego County Rep. Cen. Com., 1985-93, exec. com., 1987-92, 2nd vice-chmn. 1991-92; chmn. 74th Assembly Dist. Rep. Caucus, 1989-90; chmn. Working Ptnrs., 1987-90; trustee Rancho Santa Fe Community Ctr., 1991-92; active Nat. Assistance League, 1993—; bd. dirs. Assistance League North Coast, 1994—, mem. 1993—. Mem. Nat. Assn. County Employment and Tng. Adminstrs. (chairperson econ. resources com. 1982-85), Calif. Assn. Local Econ. Devel., San Diego Econ. Devel. Corp., Oceanside Econ. devel. Council (bd. dirs. 1983-87), Oceanside C. of C., San Marcos C. of C. (bd. dirs. 1982-85), Carlsbad C. of C. (indsl. council 1982-85), Escondido C. of C. (comml. and indsl. devel. council 1982-87), Vista C. of C. (vice chairperson econ. devel. com. 1982-83), Vista Econ. Devel. Assn., Nat. Job Tng. Partnership, San Diego County Golden Eagle Club.

BURNINGHAM, KIM RICHARD, former state legislator; b. Salt Lake City, Sept. 14, 1936; s. Rulon and Margie (Stringham) Burningham; m. Susan Ball Clarke, Dec. 19, 1968; children: Christian, Tyler David. BS, U. Utah, 1960; MA, U. Ariz., 1967; MFA, U. So. Calif., 1977. Cert. secondary tchr., Utah. Tchr. Bountiful (Utah) High Sch., 1960-88; mem. Utah Ho. of Reps., Salt Lake City, 1979-94; cons. Shipley Assocs., Bountiful, 1989-94, Franklin Quest Cons. Group, 1994—; gubernatorial appointee as exec. dir. Utah Statehood Centennial Commn., 1994-96. Author dramas for stage and film, also articles. Mem. state strategic planning com. Utah Tomorrow, 1989—; mem. exec. bd. Utah Heritage Found. Mem. NEA, PTA (life), Utah Edn. Assn., Davis Edn. Assn., Nat. Forensic League. Republican. Mem. LDS Ch. Home: 932 Canyon Crest Dr Bountiful UT 84010-2002

BURNISON, BOYD EDWARD, lawyer; b. Arnolds Park, Iowa, Dec. 12, 1934; s. Boyd William and Lucile (Harnden) B.; m. Mari Amaral; children: Erica Lafore, Alison Katherine. BS, Iowa State U., 1957; JD, U. Calif., Berkeley, 1961. Bar: Calif. 1962, U.S. Supreme Ct. 1971, U.S. Dist. Ct. (no. dist.) Calif. 1962, U.S. Ct. Appeals (9th cir.) 1962, U.S. Dist. Ct. (ea. dist.) Calif. 1970, U.S. Dist. Ct. (ctrl. dist.) Calif., 1992. Dep. counsel Yolo County, Calif., 1962-65; of counsel Davis and Woodland (Calif.) Unified Sch. Dists., 1962-65; assoc. Steel & Arostegui, Marysville, Calif., 1965-66, St. Sure, Moore & Hoyt, Oakland, 1966-70; ptnr. St. Sure, Moore, Hoyt & Sizoo, Oakland and San Francisco, 1970-75; v.p. Crosby, Heafey, Roach & May, P.C., Oakland, 1975—, also bd. dirs. Adviser Berkeley YMCA, 1971—; adviser Yolo County YMCA, 1962-65, bd. dirs. 1965; bd. dirs. Easter Seal Soc. Crippled Children and Adults of Alameda County, Calif., 1972-75, Moot Ct. Bd., U. Calif., 1960-61; trustee, sec., legal counsel Easter Seal Found., Alameda County, 1974-79, hon. trustee, 1979—. Fellow ABA Found. (life); mem. ABA (labor rels. and employment law sect., equal employment law com. 1972—), Nat. Conf. Bar Pres.'s, State Bar Calif. (spl. labor counsel 1981-84, labor and employment law sect. 1982—), Alameda County Bar Assn. (chmn. memberships and directory com. 1973-74, 80, chmn. law office econs. com. 1975-77, assn. dir. 1981-85, pres., 1984, vice chmn. bench bar liaison com. 1983, chmn. 1984, Disting. Svc. award 1987), Alameda County Bar Found. (bd. dirs. 1993-95), Yolo County Bar Assn. (sec. 1965), Yuba Sutter Bar Assn., Bar Assn. San Francisco (labor law sect.), Indsl. Rels. Rsch. Assn., Sproul Assoc. Boalt Hall Law Sch. U. Calif. Berkeley, Iowa State Alumni Assn., Order Knoll, Round Hill Country Club, Rotary (Paul Harris fellow), Pi Kappa Alpha, Phi Delta Phi. Democrat. Home: PO Box 743 2500 Caballo Ranchero Dr Diablo CA 94528 Office: Crosby Heafey Roach & May 1999 Harrison St Oakland CA 94612-3517

BURNS, CONRAD RAY, senator; b. Gallatin, Mo., Jan. 25, 1935; s. Russell and Mary Frances (Knight) B.; m. Phyllis Jean Kuhlmann; children: Keely Lynn, Garrett Russell. Student, U. Mo., 1952-54. Field rep. Polled Hereford World Mag., Kansas City, Mo., 1963-69; pub. rels. Billings (Mont.) Livestock Com., 1969-73; farm dir. KULR TV, Billings, 1974; pres., founder No. Ag-Network, Billings, 1975-86; commissioner Yellowstone County, Billings, 1987-89; U.S. Senator from Montana, 1989—; Mem. Aging Com., Small Bus. Com., Nat. Rep. Senatorial Com., chmn. Appropriations Subcom. of Military Constrn., Chmn. Com. Sci. and Transp. Subcom. of Sci. Tech. and Space, chmn. Energy and Nat. Rescs. Subcom. of Energy Rsch & Devel. With USMC, 1955-57. Mem. Nat. Assn. Farm Broadcasters, Am. Legion, Rotary, Masons, Shriners. Republican. Lutheran. Office: US Senate 183 Dirksen Bldg Washington DC 20510

BURNS, DAN W., manufacturing company executive; b. Auburn, Calif., Sept. 10, 1925; s. William and Edith Lynn (Johnston) B.; 1 child, Dan Jr. Dir. materials Menasco Mfg. Co., 1951-56; v.p., gen. mgr. Hufford Corp., 1956-58; pres. Hufford div. Siegler Corp., 1958-61; v.p. Siegler Corp., 1961-62, Lear Siegler, Inc., 1962-64; pres., dir. Electrada Corp., Culver City, Calif., 1964, pres., chief exec. officer Sargent Industries, Inc., L.A., 1964-85, chmn. bd. dirs., 1985-88; now chmn. bd. dirs., CEO Arlington Industries, Inc.; bd. dirs. Gen. Automotive Corp., Dover Tech. Internat., Inc., Kistler Aerospace Corp. Bd. dirs. San Diego Aerospace Mus., Smithsonian Inst., The Pres.'s Cir., Nat. Acad. Scis., Atlantic Coun. of U.S., George C. Marshall Found. Capt. U.S. Army, 1941-47; prisoner of war Japan; asst. mil. attache 1946, China; adc to Gen. George C. Marshall 1946-47. Mem. OAS Sports Com. (dir.), L.A. Country Club, St. Francis Yacht Club, Calif. Club, Conquistador del Cielo, Cosmos Club Washington. Home: 7400 Bryan Canyon Rd Carson City NV 89704

BURNS, DENISE RUTH, artist; b. Bellville, N.J., Oct. 17, 1943; d. A. Richard and Ruth Jean (Landers) Culkin; m. Robert P. Burns Jr., Apr. 8, 1960; children: Michael R, David R. Studied, Sergei Bongart Sch. Art, 1971-73; studied with Dan McCaw, Scottsdale Sch. Art, 1980, 89, studied with, 1988; studied with, Harley Brown, 1994, Michael Lynch and, Ovanes Berberian, 1995. One-woman shows include Off White Gallery, 1984, 85, 86, 93; two-woman show May Gallery, Scottsdale, Ariz., 1993; group shows include May Gallery, 1987-92, 94-95, Roy Miles Gallery, London, 1993, Art du Monde, Japan, 1993, N.C. Mus. History, 1995, N.C. Mus. Hist. Spring Show, 1995, Oil Tips, London-Quarto Pub., 1995, How To Put Movement in Your Paintings, 1996, Plein Air Painters Show Oakland Mus. 1996, How to Put Movement in Your Paintings, 1996; featured in Swart Mag., 1992. Instr. Chambersburg (Pa.) Art Alliance, 1985-86, 87-89, Omaha Artist Group, 1988, Pocono Pines (Pa.), 1994, Catalina Art Assn., Avalon, Calif., 1990-91; dir. Plein Air Painters Show, Catalina Island, 1986-97; judge Big Bear Art Festival, 1986, Children's Show, L.A. County Libr., Avalon, 1990. Recipient 2nd Pl. award Scottsdale Art Sch., 1991; named Emerging Artist by Am. Artist Mag., 1984, Best of Show by Catalina Art Festival, 1984, 86, 87, 89-91, Oil Painters of Am. Regional Best of Show, 1994; Gold medal artist award May Galleries, 1994. Mem. Plein Air Painters Am. (dir., founder), Catalina Art Assn. (pres. 1985-86), Oil Painters of Am., Calif. Art Club, Western Acad. Women Artists, Palos Verde Art Ctr. Home: PO Box 611 Avalon CA 90704-0611

BURNS, DENVER P., forestry research administrator; b. Bryan, Ohio, Oct. 27, 1940; married; 1 child. BS, Ohio State U., 1962, MS, 1964, PhD in Entomology, 1967; MPA, Harvard U., 1981. Asst. entomologist So. Forest Experiment Sta., 1962-68, rsch. entomologist, 1968-72, asst. dir., 1972-74; staff asst. to dep. chief for rsch. U.S. Forest Svc., 1974-76; dep. dir. North Ctrl. Experiment Sta., 1976-81; dir. Northeastern Forest Experiment Sta., Radnor, Pa., 1981-92, Rocky Mountain Sta., 1992—. Mem. AAAS. Office: US Forest Service 240 W Prospect Rd Fort Collins CO 80526-2002

BURNS, DONALD SNOW, registered investment advisor, financial and business consultant; b. Cambridge, Mass., July 31, 1925; s. Jules Ian and Ruth (Snow) B.; m. Lucy Lee Keating, July 15, 1947 (div.); childen: Julie Ann Wrigley, Patti B. Boyd, Laurie Bidegain, Wendi Collins, Loni Monahan, Robin Alden. Student, Williams Coll., 1943-44; M in Baking, Am. Inst. of Baking, 1947. Baker O'Rourke Baking Co., Buffalo, 1946-49; gen. mgr. Glaco Co. of So. Calif., L.A., 1949-51; regional mgr. Glaco Div. of Ekco Prodn. Co., Chgo., 1951-53, gen. mgr., 1953-56; pres. McClintock Mfg. Div. Ekco Prodn. Co., Chgo., 1956-61; v.p. Ekco Products Co., Chgo., 1961-67; pres., chmn. Prestige Automotive Group, Garden Grove, Calif., 1967-78; chmn. Prestige Holdings Ltd., Newport Beach, Calif., 1978—; chmn. bd. Newport Nat. Bank, Newport Beach, 1961-67; bd. dir. Securitas Trust, Monte Carlo, Monaco, Am. Safety Equipment Co., Glendale, Calif., Internat. Tech. Corp., Torrance, Calif., Escorp, San Luis Obispo, Calif.; dir. Internat. Rectifier, El Segundo. Author: (short story) The Goose that Neighed, 1967, (books) Two and a Half Nickels, 1970, Light My Fire, 1979. Mem. Calif. State U. Adv. Bd., Fullerton, 1973-76; bd. dirs. Santiago Coll. Found., Santa Ana, Calif., 1989-90, Orange County Sheriff's Adv. Coun., Calif., 1978—, pres., 1987-88; chmn. bd. trustees Orme Sch. Mayer Ariz., 1976-78. With USNR, 1943-46. Mem. Jonathan Club. Office: Prestige Holdings Ltd 16 Tech Way Ste 114 Irvine CA 92718

BURNS, LOUIS FRANCIS, retired history educator; b. Elgin, Kans., Jan. 2, 1920; s. Lee Robert and Bessie Pearl (Tinker) B.; m. Ruth Blake, Apr. 24, 1945; chldren: Alice Bettie Burns Thomas, Keith Lee. BS in Edn., Kans. State U., 1949, MS, 1950. Cert. secondary educator, jr. coll. educator, Kans., Mo., Calif. Teaching fellowship Kans. State U., Emporia, 1950; instr. geography, U.S. history Shawnee-Mission (Kans.) Sr. High Sch., 1950-60; instr. U.S. history Santa Ana (Calif.) Coll., 1965-76; author, speaker self-employed Fallbrook, Calif., 1977-94; ret., 1994; presenter and speaker in field; advisor Osage Tribal Mus., Pawhuska, Okla., 1990-94. Author: (book) Osage Indian Customs & Myths, 1984, A History of the Osage People, 1989, Symbolic & Decorative Art of the Osage People, 1994 and related books; editor Osage News, 1982-84, Osage Hist. Feature Writer; contbr. related articles to profl. jours. Rep. Osage Indian Nation, Montauban, France, 1990, 92. Staff sgt. USMC, 1942-45. Recipient Chevalier de L'Hypocras du Foix, Companions of L'Hypocras, 1992; named in Mottled Eagle Clan, Osage Indian Tribe, 1988; admitted to I'n Lon Schka, Pawhuska Camp, Osage Tribe, 1988. Mem. NEA, Okla. Hist. Soc., Kans. State Hist. Soc., Western History Assn. Democrat. Roman Catholic. Home: 654 Golden Rd Fallbrook CA 92028-3452

BURNS, MARY FERRIS, finance executive; b. Corpus Christi, Tex., Aug. 24, 1952; d. Wilbur Glenn and Lena (Faught) Ferris; m. Douglas Keith Burns, Dec. 26, 1975. BA, Baylor U., 1974; MLS, U. Tex., Austin, 1975; BS, U. Tex., Dallas, 1982; MA, U. Fla., 1978. CPA, Tex., Wash.; human resources profl. Reference libr., Latin Am. collection U. Fla., Gainesville, 1975-78; reference libr., Fondren Libr. So. Meth. U., Dallas, 1978-79; libr. Tex. A&M U., College Station, 1979-81; auditor, provider reimbursement divsn. Blue Cross & Blue Shield Tex., Dallas, 1983-84; internal auditor U. Tex. Health Sci. Ctr. at Dallas, 1984-85, adminstrv. svcs. officer Biomed. Comm. Resource Ctr., 1985-87; adminstrv. svcs. mgr. Div. of Lab. Animal Medicine Stanford U., 1988-89, adminstrv. svcs. mgr. Dept. of Microbiology and Immunology, 1989; dir. fin. and adminstrn. RIDES for Bay Area Commuters, Inc., San Francisco, 1989-93, Children's Home Soc. Wash., Seattle, 1993—; cons. Centro Intenacional de Desarrollo Humano en America Latina, Cuernavaca, Mex., 1975. Contbg. editor: Hispanic American Periodicals Index, 1975, 76. Trustee, treas. Cmty. Svcs. for Blind, King County Libr. Sys. Found. Mem. AICPA, Wash. Soc. of CPA's., Soc. for Human Resource Mgmt.

BURNS, MICHAEL EDWARD, technology company executive; b. Long Beach, Calif., July 11, 1943; s. Troy A. Burns and Vivian F. (Clay) Clifton; m. Jane K. Slothower, Apr. 18, 1965; 1 child, Heather Anne. BA, Western State Coll., 1966; exec. cert., U. Va., 1976. Dir. pro ski patrol Crested Butte (Colo.) Ski Area, 1966-70; sales rep. The North Face, Berkeley, Calif., 1970-85; cons. Learning Internat., Washington, 1985-90; N.Am. sales mgr. Patagonia, Ventura, Calif., 1990-92; dir. sales and mktg. The North Face, Berkeley, 1992-93; v.p. sales Sweetwater, Inc., Boulder, Colo., 1993—. Contbr. articles to profl. mags. Republican. Office: Sweetwater Inc 2505 Trade Center Ave Longmont CO 80503-7664

BURNS, RICHARD GORDON, retired lawyer, writer, consultant; b. Stockton, Calif., May 15, 1925; s. Earl Gordon and Alberta Viola (Whale) B.; m. Eloise Estelle Beil, June 23, 1951 (div. May 25, 1985); children: Kenneth Charles, Donald Gordon. AA, U. Calif., Berkeley, 1948; AB, Stanford U., 1949, JD, 1951. Atty. Clausen & Burns, San Francisco, 1951-61; pvt. practice Corte Madera, Calif., 1961-86; cons. Wyo. Pacific Oil Co., L.A., 1986—; pub. Good Book Pub., Kihei, Hawaii, 1991—. Author: New Light on Alcoholism: The A.A. Legacy from Sam Shoemaker, 1994, The Akron Genesis of Alcoholics Anonymous, 1994, (with Bill Pittman) Courage To Change, 1994, Anne Smith's Journal, 1995, Dr. Bob's Library, 1995, The Good Book and The Big Book: AA's Roots in the Bible, 1995, Design for Living: The Oxford Group's Contribution to Early A.A., 1995, That Amazing Grace, 1996, The Books Early AAs Read for Spiritual Growth, 1996, Good Morning! Quiet Time, Morning Watch, Meditation, and Early A.A., 1996; Turning Point: A History of Early A.A.'s Spiritual Roots and Successes, 1997; case editor Stanford Law Rev., 1950. Dir. Almonte Sanitary Bd., Marin County, Calif., 1962-64; v.p./sec. Lions Club, Corte Madera, 1961-86; pres. Almonte Improvement Club, Mill Valley, Calif., 1960, Cmty. Ch., Mill Valley, 1971, C. of C., Corte Madera, 1972, Corte Madera Ctr. Merchant Co., 1975, Redwoods Retirement Ctr., Mill Valley, 1980. Sgt. U.S. Army, 1943-46. Mem. Am. Hist. Assn., Author's Guild, Maui Writers Guild, Phi Beta Kappa. Office: Box 959 Kihei HI 96753-0959

BURNS, ROBERT IGNATIUS, historian, educator, clergyman; b. San Francisco, Aug. 16, 1921; s. Harry and Viola Marie (Whearty) B. B.A., Gonzaga U., 1945, M.A., 1947; M.A., Fordham U., 1949; Phil.B., Jesuit Pontifical Faculty, Spokane, Wash., 1946, Phil.Lic., 1947; S.Th.B., Jesuit Pontifical Faculty, Alma, Calif., 1951, S.Th.Lic., 1953; postgrad., Columbia U., 1949, Oxford (Eng.) U., 1956-57; Ph.D. summa cum laude, Johns Hopkins U., 1958; Doc.ès Sc.Hist., Fribourg (Switzerland) U. (double summa cum laude), 1961; hon. doctorates, Gonzaga U., 1968, Marquette U., 1977, Loyola U., Chgo., 1978, Boston Coll., 1982, Georgetown U., 1982, U. San Francisco, 1983, Fordham U., 1984, U. Valencia, 1985. Mem. Jesuit order; ordained priest Roman Catholic Ch., 1952. Asst. archivist Jesuit and Indian Archives Pacific N.W., Province, Spokane, 1945-47; instr. history dept. U. San Francisco, 1947-48, asst. prof., 1958-62, assoc. prof., 1963-66, prof., 1967-76; sr. prof. dept. history UCLA, 1976—, named overscale (chair), 1987—; dir. Inst. Medieval Mediterranean Spain, 1976—; prof. methodology, faculty history Gregorian U., Rome, 1955-56; guest lectr. humanities honors program Stanford U., 1960; vis. prof. Coll. of Notre Dame, Belmont, Calif., 1963; James chair Brown U., Providence, 1970; faculty mem. Inst. Advanced Study, Princeton, N.J., 1972; Levi della Vida lectr. UCLA, 1973; vis. prof., Hispanic lectr. U. Calif. at Santa Barbara, 1976; staff UCLA Near Eastern Center, 1979—, UCLA Center Medieval-Renaissance Studies, 1977—; Humanities Coun. lectr. NYU, 1992; Columbus Quincentennial Commn. of Calif. State Legislature, 1992. Author: The Jesuits and the Indian Wars of the Northwest, 1966, reprinted 1985, The

Crusader Kingdom of Valencia: Reconstruction on a Thirteenth-Century Frontier, 1967, Islam Under the Crusaders: Colonial Survival in the Thirteenth-Century Kingdom of Valencia, 1973, Medieval Colonialism: Post-Crusade Exploitation of Islamic Valencia, 1975, Moors and Crusaders in Mediterranean Spain, 1978, Jaume I i els Valencians del segle XIII, 1981, Muslims, Christians and Jews in the Crusader Kingdom of Valencia, 1983, El reino de Valencia en el siglo XIII, 1983, Society and Documentation in Crusader Valencia, 1985, The Worlds of Alfonso the Learned and James the Conqueror, 1985, Emperor of Culture: Alfonso X, 1990, Foundations of Crusader Valencia, 1991, rev. transl. Els fonaments del regne croat de València, 1995, El Regne Croat de Valencia, 1994, Jews in the Notarial Culture, 1996; bd. editors: Trends in History, 1979—, Anuario de Estudios Medievales (Spain), 1985—, Bull. of the Cantigueiros, 1986—, Catalan Rev., 1986—; co-editor: Viator, 1980-93; assoc. editor Ency. of Medieval Iberia; mem. editl. bd. U. Calif. Press, 1985-88, chair, 1987-88, mem. bd. of control, 1987-88; contbr. articles to profl. jours. Trustee Hill Monastic Manuscript Library, 1977-81; mem. adv. bd. Am. Bibliog. Center, 1982—. Recipient Book award Am. Hist. Assn. Pacific Coast Br., 1968, Am. Assn. State Local History, 1967, Am. Cath. Hist. Assn., 1967, 68, Book award Inst. Mission Studies, 1966, Am. Cath. Press Assn., 1975, Phi Alpha Theta, 1976; Haskins medal Medieval Acad. Am., 1976; Premi de la Critica, 1982; Premi Catalonia, 1982, Premi Internacional Llull, 1988; Cross of St. George Catalan Govt., 1989; Guggenheim fellow, 1963-64; Ford Found. and Guggenheim grantee, 1980; NEH fellow, 1971, 73, 75-83, 88, Am. Coun. Learned Socs. fellow, 1972; travel grantee, 1975; Robb Publ. Grantee, 1974; Darrow Publ. grantee, 1975; Consejo Superior de Investigaciones Cientificas (Spain) travel grantee, 1975, 82; Valencia province and Catalan region publ. grantee, 1981; Del Amo Grantee, 1983; U.S.-Spain treaty grantee, 1983-85; grantee Consejo Superior de Investigaciones Cientificas (Spain), 1985; Mellon Publ. grantee, 1985. Fellow Medieval Acad. Am. (trustee 1975-77, prize com. 1980, scribe 1987—), Accio Cultural del Pais Valencia; mem. Hispanic Soc. Am. (hon.), Am. Cath. Hist. Assn. (pres. 1975, coun. 1976—), Soc. Spanish Portuguese Hist. Studies (exec. coun. 1974-77), Am. Hist. Assn. (del. Internat. Congress Hist. Scis. 1975, 80, pres. Pacific Coast br. 1979-80, exec. coun. 1981-83), Medieval Assn. Pacific (exec. coun. 1975-77), Acad. Rsch. Historians Medieval Spain (pres. 1976), N.Am. Catalan Soc., Tex. Medieval. Office: UCLA History Dept Los Angeles CA 90095

BURNSIDE, MARY BETH, biology educator, researcher; b. San Antonio, Apr. 23, 1943; d. Neil Delmont and Luella Nixon (Kenley) B. BA, U. Tex., 1965, MA, 1967, PhD in Zoology, 1968. Instr. med. sch. Harvard U., Boston, 1970-73; asst. prof. U. Pa., Phila., 1973-76; asst. prof. U. Calif., Berkeley, 1976-77, assoc. prof., 1977-82, prof., 1982—, dean biol. scis., 1984-90, chancellor prof., 1996—; mem. nat. adv. eye coun. NIH, 1990-94; mem. sci. adv. bd. Lawrence Hall of Sci., Berkeley, 1983—, Whitney Labs., St. Augustine, Fla., 1993—; mem. bd. sci. councillors Nat. Eye Inst., 1994—. Mem. editl. bd. Invest. Ophthalmol. Vis. Sci., 1992-94; contbr. numerous articles to profl. jours. Mem. sci. adv. bd. Mills Coll., Oakland, Calif., 1986-90; trustee Bermuda Biol. Sta., St. George's, 1978-83; dir. Miller Inst., Berkeley, Calif., 1995—. Recipient Merit award NIH, 1989—, rsch. grantee, 1972—; rsch. grantee NSF. Fellow AAAS; mem. Am. Soc. Cell Biology (coun. 1980-84). Office: U Calif Dept Molecular & Cell Biology 335 Life Scis Addn Berkeley CA 94720-3200

BURR, JOHN CHARLES, software engineer; b. Ft. Huachuca, Ariz., May 16, 1934; s. John Charles and Willa Victoria (Walker) B.; m. Caroline Janet O'Shaughnessy, Aug. 26, 1961; children: Elizabeth, Michael. BS, Colo. State U., 1957; PhD, U. Minn., 1969. R&D coord. Redstone arsenal U.S. Army, Huntsville, Ala., 1964-66; chemist B.F. Goodrich Rsch. Ctr., Brecksville, Ohio, 1966-69; air quality mgr. Ohio EPA, Columbus, 1969-76; sr. environ. scientist Dames & Moore, North Ridge, Ill., 1976-82; postdoctoral fellow Colo. State U., Ft. Collins, 1982-84; software test & quality assurance mgr. ITT FSI, Colorado Springs, 1984-87; sr. software engr. Sci. Applications Internat. Corp., Boulder, Colo., 1987-92; prin. Sagatech, Boulder, 1992-94; software engr. Inst. Tel. Sci., Boulder, 1994—. Capt. U.S. Army, 1963-65. GE fellow, 1960. Mem. IEEE, Kappa Mu Epsilon, Phi Kappa Phi. Democrat. Episcopalian. Home: 8343 Westfork Rd Boulder CO 80302 Office: ITS/DOC 325 S Broadway St Boulder CO 80303-3464

BURR, ROBERT LYNDON, information services specialist; b. Boonville, N.Y., May 9, 1944; s. James Isaac and Virginia Ellen (Davidson) B.; m. Angela Delores Tucci, June 26, 1965; 1 son, Robert Anthony. Student, U. Rochester, 1962-65; A.B., Canisius Coll., 1972; M.S. in L.S, Case-Western Res. U., 1973; Ed.D., Gonzaga U., 1981. Asst. prodn. mgr., purchasing mgr. Carleton Controls Corp., Buffalo, 1966-71; asst. to pres. Audn Corp., Buffalo, 1971-72; circulation services librarian Coll. William and Mary, Williamsburg, Va., 1973-77; dean libr. svcs. Gonzaga U., Spokane, 1977—, adj. asso. prof. edn., 1979—, assoc. acad. v.p., 1996—; library cons. Contbr. articles to profl. jours. Trustee Mus. Native Am. Cultures, 1979—. Served with AUS, 1967-69. Mem. ALA (nat. research award 1974), Nat. Libraries Assn., Wash. Library Assn., Pacific N.W. Library Assn., AAUP, Mensa, Moses Lake Golf and Country Club. Office: Gonzaga U Foley Ctr 502 E Boone Ave Spokane WA 99258-1774

BURRELL, CALVIN ARCHIE, minister; b. Fairview, Okla., June 22, 1943; s. Lawrence Lester and Lottie Edna (Davison) B.; m. Barbara Ann Mann, May 29, 1966; children: Debra, Darla, Donna. BS, Northwestern State U., 1965; MA, So. Nazarene U., Bethany, Okla., 1978. Ordained to ministry Ch. of God. tchr., prin., dean of boys, Spring Vale Acad., Owosso, Mich., 1964-76; Pastor Ch. of God (Seventh Day), Ft. Smith, Ark., 1970-73, Shawnee, Okla., 1976-78, Denver, 1978-88; pastor Ch. of God, Galena Park, Tex., 1996—; pres. gen. conf. Ch. of God, Denver, 1987—; instr. Summit Sch. Theology, Denver, 1978-95; officer Bible Sabath Assn., 1983-96. Office: Ch of God 330 W 152nd Ave PO Box 33677 Denver CO 80233-0677

BURRELL, GARLAND E., JR., federal judge; b. L.A., July 4, 1947. BA in Sociology, Calif. State U., 1972; MSW, Washington U., Mo., 1976; JD, Calif. Wes. Sch. Law, 1976. Bar: Calif. 1976, U.S. Dist. Ct. (ea. dist.) Calif. 1976, U.S. Ct. Appeals (9th cir.) 1981. Dep. dist. atty. Sacramento County, Calif., 1976-78; dep city atty. Sacramento, 1978-79; asst. U.S. atty., dep. chief civil divsn. Office of U.S. Atty. for Ea. Dist. Calif., 1979-85, asst. U.S. atty., chief civil divsn., 1990-92; litigation atty. Stockman Law Corp., Sacramento, Calif., 1985-86; sr. dep. city atty. Office of City Atty., Sacramento, 1986-90; judge U.S. Dist. Ct. (ea. dist.) Calif., Sacramento, 1992—. With USMC, 1966-68. Office: Dist Ct 650 Capitol Mall Sacramento CA 95814-4708*

BURRI, BETTY JANE, research chemist; b. San Francisco, Jan. 23, 1955; d. Paul Gene and Carleen Georgette (Meyers) B.; m. Kurt Randall Annweiler, Dec. 1, 1984. BA, San Francisco State U., 1976; MS, Calif. State U., Long Beach, 1978; PhD, U. Calif. San Diego, La Jolla, 1982. Research asst. Scripps Clinic, La Jolla, 1982-83, research assoc., 1983-85; research chemist Western Human Nutrition Rsch. Ctr., USDA, San Francisco, 1985—; adj. prof. nutrition dept. U. Nev., 1993—; mem. steering com. Carotenoid Rsch. Interaction Group, 1994—. Co-editor Carotenoid News; contbr. articles to profl. jours. Grantee NIH, 1982, 85, USDA, 1986-97; affiliate fellow Am. Heart Assn., 1983, 84. Mem. Assn. Women in Sci. (founding dir. San Diego chpt.), N.Y. Acad. Sci., Carotenoid Rsch. Interaction Group, Am. Soc. Nutrition Sci. Office: Western Human Nutrition Rsch Ctr PO Box 29997 San Francisco CA 94129-0997

BURRIS, VALLON LEON, JR., sociologist, educator; b. Beeville, Tex., May 8, 1947; s. Vallon Leon, Sr. and Phyllis Bertha (Tatro) B.; m. Beverly Lynn Hudeck, Mar. 8, 1969 (div. 1978).; BA, Rice Univ., 1969; MA, Princeton Univ., 1972, PhD, 1976. Asst. prof. CUNY, N.Y.C., 1976-77; from asst. prof. to prof. Univ. Oreg., Eugene, 1977-92, prof., 1992—. Editor Critical Sociology, 1991—; assoc. editor Social Sci. Quar., 1983-93, Am. Sociol. Rev. 1992-95; contbr. over 30 articles to profl. jours. Mem. Am. Sociol. Assn., Phi Beta Kappa. Office: U Oreg Dept Sociology Eugene OR 97403

BURROUGHS, JAMES TRAVIS, state agency administrator; b. Seattle, Dec. 31, 1955; s. Robert Walter and Mary Elizabeth (Gowan) B.; m. Carrie Lowe, June 24, 1995. BA, Whitman Coll., 1978; MA, U. Wis., 1981; JD, Georgetown U., 1990. Bar: Calif. 1990, U.S. Dist. Ct. (no. dist.) Calif. 1990, U.S. Dist. Ct. (ea. dist.) 1992, D.C. 1992. Legis. asst. U.S. Congressman Norm Shumway, Washington, 1981-83, Senator Pete Wilson, Washington, 1983-89; assoc. Beveridge & Diamond, Washington and San Francisco, 1989-94; dep. sec., gen. counsel State of Calif. Resources Agy., Sacramento, 1994-96; chief dep. dir. Calif. Dept. Forestry and Fire Protection, Sacramento, 1996—. Commr. San Francisco Bay Conservation and Devel. Commn., 1994-96, Calif. Coastal Conservancy, San Francisco, 1994-96. Mem. Calif. State Bar (environ. law sect.), Order of Coif. Republican. Office: Calif Dept Forestry/Fire Protection 1416 9th St Sacramento CA 95814

BURROWS, E. MICHAEL, art educator, artist; b. Denver, Oct. 18, 1952; s. Edwin Harry and Beverly Mae (Hopley) B.; m. Leilani Haubner, Nov. 1977 (div. Mar. 1983); children: Ian, Leila; m. Jann Bell Simpson, Oct. 15, 1983; children: Kristan, Erika. BFA, U. Colo., Denver, 1974, postgrad., 1985-86; MFA, U. Colo., Boulder, 1977. Tchr. U. Colo., Boulder, 1976-77; artist Boulder Art Assn., 1978-79; picture framer Montgomery House, Boulder, 1979-81; tchr. Kent Denver Sch., Englewood, Colo., 1981—; substitute tchr. U. Colo., Denver, 1981—; sec. Media Svcs. Inc., Denver, 1989—. Exhibited in shows at Greenwood Village, 1988-91, Arvada Ctr., Aspen Mus., 1989, Lake Oswego Festival of Arts, 1994, Stable Gallery, Taos, N.Mex., 1996. Recipient 2d prize Boulder Art Assn., 1975, 1st pl., Jurors Choice award Colo. Inst. Art, 1989, Merit award Northwestern Colo. Art Mus., 1995, 2d prize, 1996. Mem. Assn. Colo. Ind. Schs., Am. Numis. Assn., Colored Pencil Soc., Spark Gallery (assoc.; historian). Home: 6464 Montview Blvd Denver CO 80207 Office: Kent Denver Sch 4000 E Quincy Englewood CO 80110

BURROWS, JAMES, television and motion picture director, producer; b. L.A., Dec. 30, 1940; s. Abe Burrows. BA, Oberlin Coll.; MFA, Yale U. Off-Broadway prodns.: dir. (motion picture) Partners, 1982, (TV film) More Than Friends, 1978, (TV series episodes) Mary Tyler Moore Show, Bob Newhart, Taxi, Lou Grant, Dear John, Night Court (pilot), Wings (pilot), Roc (pilot), Frasier (pilot), Friends (pilot), Newsradio (pilot), Third Rock from the Sun (pilot), Caroline in the City (pilot); co-creator, co-exec. producer, dir. (TV series) Cheers. Recipient Dirs. Guild Am. award for comedy direction, 1984, 91, 94, Emmy awards NATAS for dir. in comedy series Taxi, 1979-80, 81-82 seasons, Cheers, 1982-83, 90-91 seasons; Emmy award as co-producer Cheers, 1982-83, 83-84, 89-90, 90-91 seasons; Emmy award as director of a Comedy Series for Fraiser, 1994. Office: care Paramount TV Prodns 5555 Melrose Ave Los Angeles CA 90038-3112

BURROWS, ROBERT PAUL, optometrist; b. Chehalis, Wash.; s. Fremont O. and Pauline A. (Kostick) B.; m. Marilyn Burrows. BS in Visual Sci., Pacific U., 1979, OD, 1981. Assoc. optometric physician L.E. Hedgen, O.D. & Assocs., Chehalis, 1981-86; ptnr. L.E. Hedgen, R.P. Burrows, O.D. & Assocs., Chehalis, 1986—. Mem. United Way, 1981—. PTU Rsch. grantee, 1980. Mem. Am. Optometric Assn. (charter contact lens sect., recognition award 1984-97), Wash. Assn. Optometric Physicians, Kiwanis (dir. 1984-85, 89-90), Twin City C. of C., Omega Epsilon Phi. Methodist. Office: 1179 S Market Rd Chehalis WA 98532

BURSTEIN, ALVIN C., physician; b. Bronx, N.Y., Sept. 14, 1950; s. Samuel and Rima (Sacks) B.; m. Lisa Fran Berger, July 14, 1974; children: Zachary, Adam. BS, Johns Hopkins U., 1972; MD, Wayne State U., 1976. Diplomate Am. Bd. Psychiatry and Neurology. Clin. instr. Harvard Med. Sch., Boston, 1980-85; asst. prof. psychiatry Tufts Med. Sch., Boston, 1980-84; attending psychiatrist Hampstead, N.H., 1985-91; med. dir. St. Luke's Behavioral Health, Phoenix, 1992-96, chief of staff, 1992—; med. dir. Ariz. Biodyne, Phoenix, 1994-96; psychiatrist Phoenix, 1992—. Mem. Am. Psychiat. Assn., Am. Coll. Physicians Execs. Office: Well Being Systems 2701 E Camelback Rd Ste 391 Phoenix AZ 85016-4307

BURSTEN, STUART LOWELL, physician, biochemist; b. L.A., Jan. 19, 1953; s. Leo and Goldie (Zeff) B.; m. Colleen Sue Thompson, May 4, 1980; children: Elisa Michelle, Shawna Mariel, Tiana Marie. BS in Biology, Stanford U., 1975, AB Psychology, 1975; MD, Yale U., 1980. Diplomate Am. Bd. Internal Medicine, Am. Bd. Nephrology. Intern Boston City Hosp., 1980-81; resident internal medicine U. Wash., Seattle, 1981-83, fellow nephrology, 1983-85, postdoctoral rsch. fellow, nephrology, 1985-86; acting instr. U. Wash. Sch. Medicine, 1986-88, asst. prof. medicine, 1988-92, clin. asst. prof. medicine, 1992-94, clin. assoc. prof. medicine, 1994—. Contbr. articles to profl. jours.; patentee. Rsch. dir. Friends of Snoqualmie Valley, Wash., 1986-89. Nat. Merit Found. scholar 1971, Nat. Grocers Assn. scholar, 1971, S&H Green Stamps Assn. scholar 1971; grantee NIH, 1975-78; recipient Northwest Kidney Found. Rsch. award, 1988-89, Nat. Inst. Arthritis, Diabetes, Digestive, and Kidney Diseases fellowship, 1985-86, others. Mem. Am. Heart assn., Am. Fedn. Med. Rsch., N.Y. Acad. Scis., AAAS, Am. Soc. Nephrology. Home: 36116 SE 89th Pl Snoqualmie WA 98065 Office: Cell Therapeutics Inc 201 Elliott Ave W Seattle WA 98119-4230

BURT, EUGENE CLINTON, art historian, library director; b. Phila., July 31, 1948; s. William John and Jean (Kirschmann) B.; m. Darlene Marilyn Schmidt, May 24, 1974; 1 child, Malaika Camille. BA, Temple U., 1970; MA, U. Wash., 1973, PhD, 1980, MLS, 1984. Faculty Kenyatta U., Nairobi, Kenya, 1975-77, Tufts U., Sommerville, Mass., 1980-82, Cornish Coll. of the Arts, Seattle, 1984-87, Evergreen State Coll., Olympia, Wash., 1991-92; libr. dir. Art Inst. Seattle, 1994—. Editor: Ethno Arts Index Cumulative Bibliographies Africa, Oceania, Native American, Latin America, 1990, Preliminary Study of the Arts of East Africa, 1992; compiler: Bibliography of the Visual Art of East Africa, 1982, Erotic Art Bibliography, 1989; editor Data Arts, Seattle, 1983—; contbr. articles to profl. jours. Home: PO Box 30789 Seattle WA 98103

BURT, THOMAS WILLIAM, lawyer; b. Spokane, Wash., Jan. 24, 1955; s. Jack Wallace and Peggy (Windes) B.; m. Ann Darling, Apr. 2, 1989; children; Trevor D. Welling, Griffin D., Caroline D. AB in Human Biology, Stanford U., 1976; JD, U. Wash., 1979. Bar: Wash. 1979, U.S. Ct. Appeals (9th cir.) 1979, U.S. Dist. Ct. (we. dist.) Wash. 1980. Law clk. to judge Ozell Trask U.S. Ct. Appeals (9th cir.), Phoenix, 1979-80; ptnr., atty. Riddell, Williams, Bullitt & Walkinshaw, Seattle, 1980-95; sr. corp. atty. litigation Microsoft Corp., Redmond, Wash., 1995—. Bd. dirs. Bainbridge Island (Wash.) Land Trust, 1990-91. Mem. ABA, Wash. Bar Assn., Seattle-King County Bar. Office: Microsoft Corp One Microsoft Way Redmond WA 98052

BURTNER, ROGER LEE, research geologist; b. Hershey, Pa., Mar. 31, 1936; s. Bruce Lemmuel and Bernetta Viola (Quigle) B.; m. Carol Ann Spitzer, Aug. 1, 1965; 1 child, Pamela Sue. BS cum laude, Franklin and Marshall Coll., 1958; MS, Stanford U., 1959; PhD, Harvard U., 1965. Assoc. research geologist Calif. Research Corp. div. Standard Oil Co. of Calif., La Habra, 1963-64, research geologist, 1964-68; exploration geologist Tex. div. Standard Oil Co. of Calif., Corpus Christi and Houston, 1968-69; research geologist Chevron Oil Field Research Co. div. Chevron Corp., La Habra, 1969-74, sr. research geologist, 1974-77, sr. research assoc., 1977-92, petrology group project leader, 1975-80, supr. electron microscopy lab., 1977-82; sr. assoc. TerraSpec Assocs., La Habra, 1992-95; dir., v.p. Remote Sensing Exploration, Ltd., Denver, 1996—; mem. Pres. west coast regional adv. coun. Franklin & Marshall Coll., 1992—; adj. prof. Case Western Reserve U., Cleveland, 1992—. Contbr. articles to sci. jours. Founder Concordia U., Irvine, 1976, Orange County Performing Arts Ctr., Costa Mesa, Calif., 1979; trustee Concordia U. Found., 1989—, found. sec., 1990, v.p., 1991—, chmn. found., 1992-95; mem. Friends of Concordia U., Cmty. Chorale, 1983—; mem. Fullerton Arboretum, 1983—, Orange County Master Chorale, 1978-81; bd. dirs. Luth. H.S. Assn., Orange County, Calif., 1975-81, 88-94, pres., 1977-79, v.p., 1979-81, 92-94; v.p. Prince of Peace Luth. Ch., Anaheim, Calif., 1980-86, 89-91, 93-95, pres., 1972-74, 86-89, 95-96, v.p., 1996—; mem. energy and resource mgmt. com. City of Fullerton, 1995—; bd. dirs. Good Shepherd Luth. Home of the West, 1996—; mem. North County Leadership Inst., 1996; dir. Job Devel. Coun., North Orange County, 1996—. NSF fellow, 1958-60. Fellow Geol. Soc. Am.; mem. Am. Assn. Petroleum Geologists, Soc. Sedimentary Geology, Clay Minerals Soc. (councilor 1981-84), Geochem. Soc., Los Angeles Basin Geol. Soc., Audubon Soc., Rocky Mountain Assn. Geologists, South Coast Geological Soc., Sierra Club, Internat. Assn. Geochemistry and Cosmochemistry, Sigma Xi, Phi Beta Kappa. Republican. Home: 721 Harmony Ln Fullerton CA 92831-1865

BURTON, EDWARD LEWIS, industrial procedures and training consultant, educator; b. Colfax, Iowa, Dec. 8, 1935; s. Lewis Harrison and Mary Burton; m. Janet Jean Allan, July 29, 1956; children: Mary, Cynthia, Katherine, Daniel. BA in Indsl. Edn., U. No. Iowa, 1958; MS in Indsl. Edn., U. Wis.-Stout, 1969; postgrad., Ariz. State U., 1971-76. Tchr. apprentice program S.E. Iowa Community Coll., Burlington, 1965-68; tchr. indsl. edn. Keokuk (Iowa) Sr. H.S., 1965-68, Oak Park (Ill.)-River Forest High Sch., 1968-70; tchr. Rio Salado Community Coll., Phoenix, 1972-82; tchr. indsl. edn. Buckeye (Ariz.) Union High Sch., 1970-72; cons. curriculum Westside Area Career Opportunities Program - Ariz. Dept. Edn.; instr. vocat. automotive Dysart High Sch., Peoria, Ariz., 1979-81; tng. adminstr. Ariz. Pub. Service Co., Phoenix, 1981-90; tng. devel. cons. NUS Corp., 1991-95; vocat. auto instr. Holbrook (Ariz.) H.S., 1995-96, Gila Bend (Ariz.) H.S., 1996—; mem. dispatcher tng. com. Western Systems Coord. Coun., Salt Lake City, 1986-90; owner Aptitude Analysis Co., 1987—; mem. IEEE Dispatcher Tng. Work Group, 1988-91. Editor: Bright Ideas for Career Education, 1974, More Bright Ideas for Career Education, 1975. Mem. Citizens Planning Com., Buckeye, 1987-90, Town Governing Coun., Buckeye, 1990-91. NDEA grantee, 1967. Mem. NEA (life), NRA (life, endowment), Ariz. Rifle and Pistol Assn., Ariz. Indsl. Edn. Assn. (life), Mensa (test proctor 1987—), Masons. Republican. Methodist. Home: 19845 W Van Buren St Buckeye AZ 85326-5601

BURTON, FREDERICK GLENN, laboratory director; b. Greensburg, Pa., Nov. 30, 1939; s. Frederick Glenn and Vivian Baird (Chambers) B.; m. Jeanne Marie Nesper, May 29, 1968. BA, Coll. Wooster, 1962; MA, Wesleyan U., 1966; PhD, U. Rochester, 1971. Instr. Ohio Agrl. Experiment Sta., Wooster, 1962-64; postdoctoral fellow Salk Inst., San Diego, 1971-73; from rsch. scientist to sr. rsch. scientist Battelle N.W., Richland, Wash., 1974-85; project mgr. Battelle Meml. Inst., Columbus, Ohio, 1985-89; lab dir. Battelle Tooele (Utah) Ops., 1990—; project mgr., 1994—; cons. Immunodiagnostics Inc., Oceanside, Calif., 1973-74. Mayor City of West Richland, 1976-81. With USAR, 1964-70. Recipient honor Fed. Lab. Consortium, 1986. Mem. Am. Chem. Soc., Controlled Release Soc. Home: 90 Lakeview Tooele UT 84074-9668 Office: Battelle Tooele Ops 11650 Stark Rd Tooele UT 84074-9712

BURTON, JOHN PAUL (JACK BURTON), lawyer; b. New Orleans, Feb. 26, 1943; s. John Paul and Nancy (Key) B.; m. Anne Ward; children: Jennifer, Susanna, Derek, Catherine. BBA magna cum laude, La. Tech. U., 1965; LLB, Harvard U., 1968. Bar: N.Mex. 1968, U.S. Dist. Ct. N.Mex. 1968, U.S. Ct. Appeals (10th cir.) 1973, U.S. Supreme Ct. 1979. Assoc., Rodey, Dickason, Sloan, Akin & Robb, Albuquerque, 1968-74, dir., 1974—, chmn. comml. dept., 1980-81, mng. dir. Santa Fe, N.Mex., 1986-90. Co-author: (book) Boundary Disputes in New Mexico, 1992, Unofficial Update on the Uniform Ltd. Liab. Co. Act., 1994. Mem. Nat. Coun. Commrs. on Uniform State Laws, 1989—, drafting com. UCC Article 5, 1990-95, UCC Article 9, 1993-95, Uniform Ltd. Liability Co. Act, 1993-95, legis. coun., 1991—, divsn. chair, 1993-95, chair legis. com., 1995—, exec. com., 1995—; liaison for exec. com. to joint editorial bd. Unincorporated Bus. Orgns., 1994-95; pres. Brunn Sch., 1987-89. Fellow Am. Coll. Real Estate Lawyers, Lex Mundi Coll. of Mediators, State Bar Found.; mem. ABA, N.Mex. State Bar Assn. (chmn. comml. litigation and antitrust sect. 1985-86), Am. Law Inst. (rep. to UCC Article 5 drafting com. 1992-95), Am. Coll. Mortgage Attys., Am. Arbitration Assn. (panel arbitrators). Office: Rodey Dickason Sloan Akin & Robb PA PO Box 1357 Santa Fe NM 87504-1357

BURTON, KATHLEEN T., mental health professional; b. Lynn, Mass., Jan. 29, 1962; d. Charles W. and Mary L. (Mayer) B. BA in Psychology/Comms., Notre Dame Coll., South Euclid, Ohio, 1985; MEd in Counseling, Cleve. State U., 1990, EdS in Counseling Psychology, 1991; postgrad., Saybrook Inst., San Francisco, 1992—. Cert. cognitive-behavioral therapist. Human rels. & devel. coord. Kaiser Permanente, Cleveland Heights, Ohio, 1984-87; counselor Cleve. Treatment Ctr., 1989-90; tchg. asst., counselor intern Cleve. State U., 1989-91; community trainer Woodland (Calif.) Community Options, 1991-95; mental health profl., psychologist intern Davis, Calif., 1992-95; psychologist pvt. practice, 1995—; group facilitator for human sexuality course dept. psychiatry Davis Med. Sch., 1994—; group leader, facilitator anxiety, phobias and panic Woodland Sr. Ctr., 1993—; mental health cons., creator "Mental Health Matters" Pub. TV, 1995; founder Sr./Youth Fair, Woodland, 1995; mental health writer Davis Enterprise; lectr. anxiety, phobias, panic, drug addictions, Moscow, Kiev, 1994. Author (poem) Hold on Tight; contbr. article to medical jour. 1st place winner Nat. Future Design competition, Washington, 1984. Mem. ACA, Internat. Assn. for Addictions & Offender Counselors, Ohi Counseling Assn. (past rep.), Am. Family Assn. Roman Catholic.

BURTON, LAWRENCE DEVERE, agriculturist, educator; b. Afton, Wyo., May 27, 1943; s. Lawrence VanOrden and Maybell (Hoopes) B.; m. Arva Merrill, Nov. 20, 1967; children: LauraLee, Paul, Shawn, Renee, Kaylyn, Kelly, Brett. BS, Utah State U., 1968; MS, Brigham Young U., 1972; PhD, Iowa State U., 1987. Agr. tchr. Box Elder County Sch. Dist., Brigham City, Utah, 1967-68, Morgan County Sch. Dist., Morgan, Utah, 1968-70, Minidoka County Sch. Dist., Rupert, Idaho, 1972-79, Cassia County Sch. Dist., Declo, Idaho, 1979-84; instr. Iowa State U., Ames, 1984-87; area vocat. edn. coord. Idaho State Div. Vocat. Edn., Pocatello, 1987-88; state supr. agrl. sci. and tech. Idaho State Div. Vocat. Edn., Boise, 1988—; biochem. cons. rep. Ctr. for Occupational Rsch. and Devel., Waco, Tex., 1989-94; chmn. Nat. Task Force, Agrl. Edn. Ind. Study Honors program, 1993. Author: Agriscience and Techology, 1991, 97, Ecology of Fish and Wildlife, 1995, Forestry Science, 1997; contbr. articles to profl. jours. Vice chmn. Minidoka County Fair Bd., Rupert, Idaho, 1977-80. Mem. Am. Vocat. Assn., Nat.Vocat. Agrl. Tchrs. Assn., Idaho Vocat. Agrl. Tchrs. Assn. (pres. 1981-82, Adminstr. of Yr. 1989), Nat. Assn. Suprs. Agrl. Edn. (western v.p. 1990-91, nat. pres. 1993-94), Gamma Sigma Delta, Alpha Zeta. Mem. Ch. of Jesus Christ of Latter Day Saints. Home: 10966 Highlander Rd Boise ID 83709-5243 Office: State Div Vocat Edn PO Box 83720 Boise ID 83720-0095

BURTON, MARIE DINIE, principal; b. Escondito, Calif., June 8, 1952; d. William J. and Sylvia D. (Powell) Mattenklodt; m. Larry A. Burton, Sept. 9, 1972; 1 child, Lindsey M. BA in Art Edn., Univ. No. Colo., 1974, MA in Elem. Edn., Spl. Edn., 1980. Cert. elem. tchr., spl. edn. tchr., art edn. tchr., school adminstr. Spl. edn. tchr. Lower Yukon Sch. Dist., Hooper Bay, Alaska, 1977-80, Anchorage Sch. Dist., 1981-83, Mutunusku Sustina Sch. Dist., Palmer, Alaska, 1984—. mem. Mutunausku Sustina Prin. Assn. Office: Cottonwood Creek Elem Sch 800 N Seward Meridian Rd Wasilla AK 99654-7267

BURTON, PAUL FLOYD, social worker; b. Seattle, May 24, 1939; s. Floyd James and Mary Teresa (Chovanak) B.; BA, U. Wash., 1961, MSW, 1967; m. Roxanne Maude Johnson, July 21, 1961; children: Russell Floyd, Joan Teresa. Juvenile parole counselor Div. Juvenile Rehab. State of Wash., 1961-66; social worker VA, Seattle, 1967-72, social worker, cons. Work Release program King County, Wash., 1967-72; supr., chief psychiatry sect. Social Work Svc. VA, Topeka, Kans., 1972-73; pvt. practice, Topeka and L.A., 1972—; chief social work svc. VA, Sepulveda, Calif., 1974—, EEO coord. Med. ctr., 1974-77. Mem. APHA, NASW (newsletter editor Puget Sound chpt. 1970-71), Acad. Cert. Social Workers, Ctr. for Studies in Social Functioning, Am. Sociol. Assn., Am. Hosp. Assn., Soc. Social Work Adminstrs. in Health Care, Assn. VA Social Work Chiefs (founder 1979, charter mem. and pres. 1980-81, newsletter editor 1982-83, 89-91, pres. elect 1993-95, pres. 1995—). Home: 14063 Remington St Arleta CA 91331 Office: 16111 Plummer St Sepulveda CA 91343-2036

BURTON, RANDALL JAMES, lawyer; b. Sacramento, Feb. 4, 1950; s. Edward Jay and Bernice Mae (Overton) B.; children: Kelly Jacquelyn, Andrew Jameson; m. Kimberly D. Rogers, Apr. 29, 1989. BA, Rutgers U., 1972; JD, Southwestern U., 1975. Bar: Calif. 1976, U.S. Dist. Ct. (ea. dist.) Calif. 1976, U.S. Dist. Ct. (no. dist.) Calif., 1990, U.S. Supreme Ct, 1991. Assoc. Brekke & Mathews, Citrus Heights, Calif., 1976; pvt. practice, Sacramento, 1976-93; ptnr. Finch, Burton & White, Sacramento, 1993—; judge pro tem Sacramento Small Claims Ct., 1982—. Bd. dirs. North Highlands Recreation and Park Dist., 1978-86, Family Svc. Agy. of Sacramento, 1991-96; active Local Bd. 22, Selective Svc., 1982—, Active 20-30 Club of Sacramento, 1979-90, pres., 1987. Recipient Disting. Citizen award, Golden Empire Council, Boy Scouts Am. Mem. Sacramento Bar Assn., Sacramento

Young Lawyers Assn. Presbyterian. Lodge: Rotary (pres. Foothill-Highlands club 1980-81). Office: 1540 River Park Dr Ste 224 Sacramento CA 95815-4609

BURTON, ROBERT LYLE, accounting firm executive; m. Lee Sanders; 2 children. Diploma, Kinman Bus. U. CPA. With LeMaster & Daniels, Spokane, Wash., 1963-86; mng. ptnr. LeMaster & Daniels, 1986—; mem. adv. bd. acctg. dept. U. Wash.; chmn. The Am. Group of CPA Firms. Trustee Econ. Devel. Coun.; past chmn. Samaritan Hosp. Found., Moses Lake, Wash. Mem. AICPA (agri-bus. com., adv. group B), Washington Soc. CPAs (former dir., v.p., com. chmn., legis. com.), Spokane Club, Inland Empire Fly Fishermen, Moses Lake Golf and Country Club, Rotary. Office: LeMaster & Daniels 601 W Riverside Ave Ste 700 Spokane WA 99201-0611

BURTON, THOMAS ROGHAAR, English language educator; b. Ogden, Utah, Oct. 7, 1933; s. Laurence S. and Marguerite E. (Roghaar) B.; m. Sharon Slater, June 11, 1959; children: Thomas, Julie, Matthew, James. AS, Weber Coll., 1953; BS, Brigham Young U., 1959, MA, 1960; PhD, U. Wash., 1967. Chair English dept. Weber State U., Ogden, 1972-74, assoc. v.p. for acad. affairs, 1974-80, prof. English dept., 1963—, chair faculty senate, 1989-95; treas., bd. dirs. Weber State Credit Union; chair, bd. dirs. Utah State Divsn. of Youth Correction, Salt Lake City; active numerous coms. including salary com., strategic planning task force and steering com., deans coun., search com. for pres., Weber State U., chair gen. edn. com., curriculum com., admissions, stds. and student affairs com. Contbr. articles to profl. jours. With USN, 1953-55. Mem. AAUP (pres. Utah conf.), Assn. for Mormon Letters (exec. bd.), Phi Kappa Phi. Republican. Mem. Ch. LDS. Home: 839 Vista Dr Ogden UT 84403-3038 Office: Weber State U 3800 Harrison Blvd Ogden UT 84403-2027

BUSCH, ANITA M., journalist; b. Granite City, Ill., May 31, 1961; d. J. Patrick and Catherine Busch. BA in Comms., Ea. Ill. U., 1983. Typewetter, keyliner Crain Comms., Chgo., 1984-85; assoc. editor Crain News Svc./AP, Chgo., 1985-86; prodn. editor Advt. Age, Chgo., 1986-87, assoc. editor, 1987-90; midwest editor Backstage/Shoot, Chgo., 1990; film and mktg. reporter The Hollywood Reporter, L.A., 1990-94; film editor, sr. film reporter Variety/Daily Variety, L.A., 1994—. Recipient William H. Donaldson Editl. Achievement award BPI Comms., N.Y.C., 1990. Office: Variety Inc 839 S Sycamore Ave Los Angeles CA 90036

BUSCH, ANN MARIE HERBAGE, medical/surgical clinical nurse specialist; b. Roseburg, Oreg., Jan. 24, 1958; d. Robert Canfield and Magdaline Mary (Tuchscherer) Herbage; m. John Patrick Busch, June 27, 1981; children: Rebecca Ann, Michael Robert. BSN summa cum laude, U. Portland, 1980; MSN, U. Calif., San Francisco, 1985. RN, Oreg., Calif.; cert. clin. specialist in med.-surg. nursing; cert. enterostomal therapy nurse; cert. CPR instr. Staff nurse IV Stanford (Calif.) U. Hosp., 1981-88, acting nursing ednl. coord., 1986-87; coord./educator RN refresher program DeAnza Coll., Cupertino, Calif., 1986-88; med-surg. clin. nurse specialist Cmty. Hosp. Los Gatos (Calif.), 1988-92; surg. clin. nurse specialist Palo Alto VA Med. Ctr., 1992-95; liver transplant clin. nurse specialist Vet. Affairs Med. Ctr., Portland, Oreg., 1995—; cons. for patient pathways U. So. Calif. Hosp., 1990-91; asst. clin. prof. dept. physiol. nursing U. Calif., San Francisco, 1993—; primary faculty Oreg. Health Scis. U. Sch. Nursing, 1995—; spkr. in field. Contbr. articles to profl. jours. Recipient dist. nursing rsch. utilization award VA, 1993. Mem. ANA (coun. nurses advanced practice), Wound, Ostomy and Continence Nurses Soc., Am. Soc. Parenteral and Enteral Nutrition, Internat. Transplant Nurses Assn., Nat. League for Nursing, Oreg. Nurses Assn., Oreg. Coun. Clin. Nurse Specialists Group, Blue Key, U. Portland Nursing Honor Soc., Sigma Theta Tau, Delta Epsilon Sigma. Home: 1310 Stonehaven Dr West Linn OR 97068-1867 Office: Portland Vet Affs Med CtrLiver Transplant (112L) PO Box 1034 3710 SW US Veterans Hosp Rd Portland OR 97207

BUSCH, JOYCE IDA, small business owner; b. Madera, Calif., Jan. 24, 1934; d. Bruno Harry and Ella Fae (Absher) Toschi; m. Fred O. Busch, Dec. 14, 1956; children: Karen, Kathryn, Kurt. BA in Indsl. Arts & Interior Design, Calif. State U., Fresno, 1991. Cert. interior designer Calif. Stewardess United Air Lines, San Francisco, 1955-57; prin. Art Coordinates, Fresno, 1982—, Busch Interior Design, Fresno, 1982—; art cons. Fresno Community Hosp., 1981-83; docent Fresno Met. Mus., 1981-84. Treas. Valley Children's Hosp. Guidance Clinic, 1975-79, Lone Star PTA, 1965-84,; mem. Mothers Guild Jan Joaquin Mem. Hosp., 1984-88. Mem. Am. Soc. Interior Designers, Illuminating Engring. Soc. N.Am. Republican. Roman Catholic. Club: Sunnyside Garden (pres. 1987-88).

BUSCHA, RALPH VICTOR, security firm executive; b. Houston. AA, Phoenix Coll., 1973. Undercover investigator, 1968-70, gen. investigator, 1970-75, from br. mgr. to dist. mgr., 1978—; v.p. ESS Inc., Phoenix; investigator Pinkerton's Inc. With USAF, 1964-68. Mem. Am. Soc. Indsl. Security. Republican. Lutheran. Home: 4825-2 E Euclid Ave Phoenix AZ 85044 Office: ESS Inc PO Box 51507 Phoenix AZ 85076

BUSH, JUNE LEE, real estate executive; b. Philippi, W.Va., Sept. 20, 1942; d. Leland C. and Dolly Mary (Costello) Robinson; m. Jerry Lee Coffman, June 15, 1963 (div. 1970); 1 child, Jason Lance; m. Richard Alfred Bush, May 20, 1972. Grad., Fairmont State Coll., 1962, Dale Carnegie, Anaheim, Calif., 1988. Exec. sec. McDonnell Douglas, Huntington Beach, Calif., 1965-72; adminstrv. asst. Mgmt. Resources, Inc., Fullerton, Calif., 1978-80; bldg. mgr. Alfred Gobar Assocs., Brea, Calif., 1980-95; treas. Craig Park East, Fullerton, 1982, bd. dirs., 1982-84. Author instrn. manual Quality Assurance Secretarial Manual, 1971. Sec. PTA, La Palma, 1974. Mem. Gamma Chi Chi. Home: 563 Highland Ave Half Moon Bay CA 94019-1703

BUSH, MARIA WESTY, artist, educator; b. Schenectady, N.Y., Feb. 15, 1934; d. Willem F. and Mary (Andrews) Westendorp; 2 children. BFA, U. Colo., 1956; MFA, U. Wash., 1958. Cert. tchr., Colo. Elem. multicultural bilingual art specialist Colorado Springs (Colo.) Sch. Dist. #11, 1977-81, jr. h.s. art tchr., 1982-87; acad. art tchr. Dept. of Corrections, Cañon City, Colo., 1987-90; prof. art Regis U., Denver, Cañon City, 1990-94; art tchr. Sange de Cristo Arts & Conf. Ctr., Pueblo, Colo., 1995-96, Teen Devel. Awareness Program, Colorado Springs, Colo., 1995-96. Author, illustrator 4 books of drawings & poems; contbr.: Ethnic Autonomy, 1978; exhbns. include Colo. State Fair, Colorado Springs Fine Arts Ctr., Pueblo Art Guild Gallery, Staircase 22, Pueblo, Sharon's Gallery, Colorado Springs, Bus. Art Ctr., Manitou Springs; illustrator 7 children's books; artist info. displays USDA Forest Svc., Pueblo, 1994-95. Artist, voter registrar King's Movement Equality Now, Nacogdoches, Tex., 1968-71. Recipient Purchase award Utah State Inst. Art, 1964, Outstanding Young Woman U.S. award, 1969, Best of Show award Colorado Springs Art Guild, 1994, 12 art ribbons. Mem. Friends El Pueblo Mus., Bus. Art Ctr., Native Am. Women's Assn., Pueblo Arts Coun., Pueblo Art Guild, Pueblo African Am. Concerns Orgn., Phi Beta Kappa. Unitarian.

BUSH, MARY ELIZABETH, mechanical engineer; b. Gary, Ind., June 11, 1963; m. William H. Bush, Aug. 10, 1984. BS in Mech. Engring., Purdue U., 1984, MS in Biology, 1986. Registered profl. engr., Calif. Registered patent agt., U.S. Patent Office. Anatomy and physiology tchg. asst. Purdue U., West Lafayette, Ind., 1984-85; neurobiology tchg. asst. Purdue U., West Lafayette, 1986; rsch. asst. Purdue U. Biomed. Engring. Ctr., West Lafayette, 1985-86; mech. engr. Pacesetter Systems, Inc., Sylmar, Calif., 1986-89; mech. devel. engr. Siemens-Pacesetter, Inc., Sylmar, 1989; leads engr. Ventritex, Inc., Sunnyvale, Calif., 1989-91; sr. mech. engr. Ventritex, Inc., Sunnyvale, 1991—. Patents include implantation of leads, apparatus for attaching implanted materials to body tissue, multiple electrode deployable lead, double jaw apparatus for attaching implanted material to body tissue, electrical connection for medical electrical stimulation electrode, defibrillation lead with improved mechanical and electrical characteristics, lead adapter, flexible defibrillation electrode of improved construction, cardiac lead having defibrillation and atrial sensing electrodes, osmotic control of drug elution, nonshunting endocardial defibrillation lead, method of making a flexible defibrillation electrode. Recipient Pres.'s Honor award Purdue U., 1981. Mem. Assn. for the Advancement of Med. Instrumentation. Home: 2068 Mento Dr Fremont CA 94539-4625

BUSH, REX CURTIS, lawyer; b. Longview, Wash., Oct. 21, 1953; s. Rex Cole Bush and Arline (Quanstrom) Fitzgerald; m. Joy Ann Pallas, July 22, 1977 (div.); children: Alicia, Angela, Carrie; m. Janet Rae Hicks July 2, 1988; children: Jeni, Mykal. BA cum laude, Brigham Young U., 1980; JD, U. Utah, 1983. Bar: Utah 1983, U.S. Dist. Ct. (no. dist.) Utah 1983, U.S. Tax Ct. 1985. Tax atty. Arthur Andersen & Co., Houston, 1983-84; assoc. Mortensen & Neider, Midvale, Utah, 1984-85; in-house counsel Fin. Futures, Salt Lake City, 1985-87; registrar Hollander Cons., Portland, Oreg., 1987-88; in-house counsel Bennett Leasing, Salt Lake City, 1987-88; pres. Bush Law Firm, Sandy, Utah, 1988—; judge pro tempore 3d Cir. Ct., Salt Lake City, 1985-87. Author: (booklet) What To Do in Case of an Automobile Accident, 1994. Mayor University Village, U. Utah, 1981-82; Rep. candidate Utah state senate, 1992; Rep. voting dist. sec., treas., 1992. Recipient Meritorious Leadership award, Nat. Com. for Employer Support of Guard and Reserve, 1990. Mem. ATLA, Utah Trial Lawyers Assn., Utah State Bar (chmn. small firm and solo practitioners com. 1994-96, honored for outstanding svc. to legal profession 1996). Office: Bush Law Firm 9615 S 700 E Sandy UT 84070-3557

BUSH, SARAH LILLIAN, historian; b. Kansas City, Mo., Sept. 17, 1920; d. William Adam and Lettie Evelyn (Burrill) Lewis; m. Walter Nelson Bush, June 7, 1946 (dec.); children: William Read, Robert Nelson. AB, U. Kans., 1941; BS, U. Ill., 1943. Clk. circulation dept. Kansas City Pub. Library, 1941-42, asst. librarian Paseo br., 1943-44; librarian Kansas City Jr. Coll., 1944-46; substitute librarian San Mateo County Library, Woodside and Portola Valley, Calif., 1975-77; various temporary positions, 1979-87; owner Metriguide, Palo Alto, Calif., 1975-78. Author: Atherton Lands, 1979, rev. edition 1987. Editor: Atherton Recollections, 1973. Pres., v.p. Jr. Librarians, Kansas City, 1944-46; courtesy, yearbook & historian AAUW, Menlo-Atherton branch (Calif.) Br.; asst. Sunday sch. tchr., vol. Holy Trinity Ch., Menlo Park, 1955-78; v.p., membership com., libr. chairperson, English reading program, parent edn. chairperson Menlo Atherton High Sch. PTA, 1964-73; founder, bd. dirs. Friends of Atherton Community Library, 1967—, oral historian, 1968—, chair Bicentennial event, 1976; bd. dirs. Menlo Park Hist. Assn., 1979-82, oral historian, 1973—; bd. dirs. Civic Interest League, Atherton, 1978-81; mem. hist. county commn. Town of Atherton, 1980-87; vol. Allied Arts Palo Alto Aux. to Children's Hosp. at Stanford, 1967—, oral historian, 1978—, historian, 1980—; vol. United Crusade, Garfield Sch., Redwood City, 1957-61, 74-88, Encinal Sch., 1961-73, program dir., chmn. summer recreation, historian, sec.; vol. Stanford Mothers Club, 1977-81, others; historian, awards chairperson Cub Scouts Boy Scouts Am.; founder Atherton Heritage Assn. 1989, bd. dirs., 1989—; mem. Guild Gourmet, 1971—. Recipient Good Neighbor award Civic Interest League, 1992. Mem. PTA (life). Episcopalian.

BUSH, STANLEY GILTNER, secondary school educator; b. Kansas City, Mo., Nov. 4, 1928; s. Dean Thomas and Sallie Giltner (Hoagland) B.; m. Barbara Snow Adams, May 23, 1975 (dec. Mar. 1994); stepchildren: Deborah Gayle Duclon, Douglas Bruce Adams. BA, U. Colo., 1949, MA, 1959, postgrad., 1971; postgrad., U. Denver, 1980, 85, 90. Tchr. Gering (Nebr.) Pub. Schs., 1949-51, 54-57, Littleton (Colo.) Pub. Schs., 1957-91; emergency plan dir. City of Littleton, 1961—; safety officer Littleton Pub. Schs., 1968—; founder, chief Arapahoe Rescue Patrol, Inc., Littleton, 1957-92, search mission coord., 1975—; pres. Arapahoe Rescue Patrol, Inc., 1957—, Expedition, Inc., Littleton, 1973—; owner Emergency Rsch. Cons., 1990—. Contbr. chpts. to Boy Scout Field Book, 1984; co-author: Managing Search Function, 1987; contbr. articles to profl. jours. Safety advisor South Suburban Parks Dist., Littleton, 1985-96; advisor ARC, Littleton, 1987—, Emergency Planning Com., Arapahoe County, Colo., 1987—; coord. search and rescue Office of Gov., Colo., 1978-82; state judge Odyssey of the Mind, 1996-97. Sgt. U.S. Army, 1951-54. Shell Oil Co. fellow, 1964; recipient Silver Beaver award Boy Scouts Am., 1966, Vigil-Order of Arrow, 1966, Award of Excellence Masons, 1990. Mem. Nat. Assn. for Search and Rescue (life, Hall Foss award 1978), Colo. Search and Rescue Bd., NEA (life). Methodist. Home: 2415 E Maplewood Ave Littleton CO 80121-2817 Office: Littleton Ctr 2255 W Berry Ave Littleton CO 80120-1151

BUSHEE, WARD, newspaper editor; b. Redding, Calif., 1949; m. Claudia Bushee; children: Ward Gardiner, Mary Standish. BS in History, San Diego State U., 1971. Sports editor Gilroy (Calif.) Dispatch, 1972-75; asst. city editor/sports editor/reporter/copy editor Salinas (Calif.) Californian, 1975-80; sports editor Marin County (Calif.) Ind. Jour., 1980-82; startup staff, including asst. sports editor profl. sports USA Today, Arlington, Va., 1982-85; asst. mng. editor Westchester (N.Y.) Suburban Newspapers, 1985-86; exec. editor Sioux Falls (S.D.) Argus Leader, 1986-90; editor Reno (Nev.) Gazette-Jour., 1990—. Named Editor of Yr., 1992, Gannett Co., Inc., finalist 1991, 95, Pres.'s Ring winner 1992, 93, 94, 95. Mem. Nev. Press Assn. (pres. 1993, 94, API discussion leader 1996). Office: Reno Gazette-Journal PO Box 22000 Reno NV 89520

BUSHMAN, EDWIN FRANCIS ARTHUR, engineer, plastics consultant, rancher; b. Aurora, Ill., Mar. 16, 1919; s. George J. and Emma (Gengler) B.; B.S., U. Ill., 1941, postgrad., 1941-42, Calif. Inst. Tech., 1941; m. Louise Kathryn Peterson, Jan. 3, 1946; children: Bruce Edwin, Gary Robert, Joan Louise, Karen Rose, Mary Elisabeth, Paul George. Jr. engr, Gulf Refining Co. Gulf Oil Corp., Mattoon, Ill., 1940-41; engr. radio and sound lab. war rsch. div. U. Calif. at Navy Electronics Lab., Pt. Loma, San Diego, 1942-45; project engr. Bell and Howell Co., Lincolnwood, Ill., 1945-46; research cons., Scholl Mfg. Co., Inc., Chgo., 1946-48; project engr. deepfreeze div. Motor Products Corp., North Chicago, Ill., 1948-50; research and product design engr. Bushman Co., Aurora, Ill. also Mundelein, Ill., 1946-55; with Plastics div. Gen. Am. Transp. Corp., Chgo., 1950-68, tech. dir., 1950-55, mgr. sales and sales engring. Western states, Compton, Calif., 1955-68, sales and sales engring. research and devel. div., 1962-64; with USS Chems., 1968-70; plastics cons. E.F. Bushman Co., 1970—, Tech. Conf. Assocs., 1974-80. Program mgr. Agriplastics Symposium Nat. Agrl. Plastics Conf., 1966; program mgr. Plastics in Hydrospace, 1967; originator Huisman Plastics awards, 1970, Un-Carbon Polymer prize and Polymer Pool Preserve Plan, 1975, Polymer Independence award, 1977, 78. Bd. dirs. Coastal Area Protective League, 1958-66, Lagunita Community Assn., 1959-66 (pres. 1964-65), Calif. Marine Parks and Harbors Assn., 1959-69. Sr. editor Plastic Trends mag., 1985-90. Recipient Western Plastics Man of Yr. award, 1972. Mem. Soc. Plastics Industry Inc. (chpt. pres. 1971-72), Soc. Plastic Engrs. (Lundberg award 1981), Western Plastics Pioneers, Western Plastics Mus. and Pioneers, Plastics Pioneers Assn., Sunkist Growers, Cal. Citrus Nurserymen's Soc., Calif. Farm Bur. Fedn. U. Ill. Alumni Assn., Soc. for Advancement Materials and Process Engring., Geopolymers Inst. Roman Catholic. Author various profl. and strategic resource papers. Patentee in field of plastics, carbon and colored glass fibers, process, and applications. Home: 19 Lagunita Ln Laguna Beach CA 92651-4237 Office: PO Box 581 Laguna Beach CA 92652-0581

BUSHNELL, KENNETH WAYNE, artist, educator; b. L.A., Oct. 16, 1933; s. George Lilburn and Luella Mae (Bivens) B.; m. Reneé Hazel Laufer, Mar. 15, 1956 (div. 1973); children: Blake, Dale; m. Helen O. Gilbert, Apr. 5, 1977. BA, UCLA, 1956; MFA, U. Hawaii, 1961. Prof. art U. Hawaii at Manoa, Honolulu, 1961—; exch. prof. in painting L.I. U., C.W. Post Ctr., 1979-80, 83; chmn. dept. art U. Hawaii, Manoa, 1990-92. Shows include Mus. Modern Art, N.Y., 1962, Balt. Mus. Art, 1962, Gima's Gallery, Honolulu, 1963, 66, 69, 72, 75, Pa. Acad. Fine Arts, 1963, United Fedn. Graphic Arts, Phila., 1964, Contemporary Arts Ctr, Honolulu, 1965, 77, 86, Honolulu Acad. Arts Mus., 1968, 73, Ariel Gallery, Milan, 1976, N.Y. Horticultural Soc. Gallery, N.Y.C., 1980, Wallnut Gallery, Phila., 1980, 81, Galerie Meissner Editions, Hamburg, West Germany, 1984, Taller Fort Gallery, Cadaques, Spain, 1984, 90, 91, Sande Webster Gallery, Phila., 1985, 88, Maronier Gallery, Kyoto, Japan, 1986, Wacoal Ginza Gallery, Tokyo, 1986, Richards Gallery, Boston, 1986, The Contemporary Mus., Honolulu, 1992, others; exhibited in group shows at Contemporary Arts Ctr., 1977, 78, Honolulu Internat. Ctr., Honolulu Acad. Arts, 1963-75, 78, 79, 82, 84, 86, 89, 91, 93, 95, 96, Honolulu Hale, 1979, Contemporary Museum, Honolulu, 1990, Queen Emma Gallery, Honolulu, 1990, Galerie Karin Fesel, Dusseldorf, West Germany, 1990, Sande Webster Gallery, 1992, Galerie Carlos Lozano, Cadaques, Spain, 1995, 97, others; represented in permanent collections Portland Museum, Contemporary Art Ctr., The Honolulu Acad. Arts Museum, Bibliotheque Nationale, Corcoran Museum, Library of Congress, numerous others. Chmn. dept. pers. com. U. Hawaii, 1986, dept. curriculum com., 1987; mem. Manoa Writing Bd.; juror in field. Lt. USNR, 1956-60. Recipient Honolulu Acad. of Arts Purchase award, 1973, Melusine award for painting, 1996, Hawaii State Found. on Culture and Arts puchase award, 1973, 75, 79, 81, Bibliotheque Nationale purchase award, 1976; paintings commissioned by Harmonie Club of N.Y., 1980, Mr. and Mrs. Alan Hunt of Honolulu, 1983; print commissioned by Hawaiian Diptych for Waiohai Gallery; site specific relief painting commissioned by Sande Webster Gallery, 1986 and others. Mem. AAUP, Coll. Art Assn., Honolulu Printmakers Assn. (pres. of the bd. 1961), Am. Abstract Artists. Democrat. Home: 2081 Keeaumoku Pl Honolulu HI 96822-2553 Office: U Hawaii at Manoa 2535 The Mall Honolulu HI 96822-2233

BUSHNELL, RODERICK PAUL, lawyer; b. Buffalo, Mar. 6, 1944; s. Paul Hazen and Martha Atlee B.; m. Suzann Yvonne Kaiser, Aug. 27, 1966; 1 child, Arlo Phillip. BA, Rutgers U., 1966; JD, Georgetown U., 1969. Bar: Calif. 1970, U.S. Supreme Ct. 1980. Atty. dept. water resources Sacramento, 1969-71; ptnr. Bushnell, Caplan & Fielding, San Francisco, 1971—; adv. bd. dirs. Bread & Roses, Inc., Mill Valley, Calif. Bd. dirs. Calif. Lawyers for the Arts, Ft. Mason, San Francisco, 1985—. Mem. ATLA, San Francisco Bar Assn. (arbitrator), San Francisco Superior Ct. (arbitrator), Calif. Bar Assn., Lawyers Club of San Francisco, Calif. Trial Lawyers Assn., San Francisco Trial Lawyers Assn., No. Calif. Criminal Trial Lawyers Assn., San Francisco Bay Club, Commonwealth Club. Democrat. Office: Bushnell Caplan & Fielding 221 Pine St Ste 600 San Francisco CA 94104

BUSIG, RICK HAROLD, mining executive; b. Vancouver, Wash., June 21, 1952; s. Harold Wayne and Ramona (Riley) B. AA, Clark Coll., Vancouver, 1972; BA in Econs., U. Wash., 1974. CPA, Wash. Acct., Universal Svcs., Seattle, 1975-78; acct., acctg. mgr., controller Landura Corp., Woodburn, Oreg., 1978-80; asst. controller Pulte Home Corp., Laramie, Wyo., 1980-81; treas., controller Orcal Cable, Inc., Sparks, Nev., 1981-82; controller Saga Exploration Co., Reno, Nev., 1982—; acct. Sterling Mine Joint Venture, Beatty, Nev., 1982-95. Del. Nev. State Dem. Conv., Reno, 1984, 94, Las Vegas, 1988. Recipient Spaatz award CAP. Mem. AICPA, Wash. Soc. CPA's, Oreg. Soc. CPA's. Home: 2735 Lakeside Dr # A Reno NV 89509-4203 Office: Saga Exploration Co 2660 Tyner Way Reno NV 89503-4926

BUSS, JERRY HATTEN, real estate executive, sports team owner; Children: John, Jim, Jeanie, Jane. BS in Chemistry, U. Wyo.; MS, PhD in Chemistry, U. So. Calif., 1957. Chemist Bur. Mines; past mem. faculty dept. chemistry U. So. Calif.; mem. missile div. McDonnell Douglas, Los Angeles; partner Mariani-Buss Assos.; former owner Los Angeles Strings; chmn. bd., owner Los Angeles Lakers (Nat. Basketball Assn.), 1979—; until 1988 owner Los Angeles Kings (Nat. Hockey League), 1979—. Office: care LA Lakers PO Box 10 3900 W Manchester Blvd Inglewood CA 90306-0010*

BUSSELEN, STEVEN CARROLL, journalist, editor; b. Midland, Mich., Aug. 14, 1971; s. Harry Julius Jr. and Carroll (Kincaid) B. BA in English, Santa Clara U., 1993. Reporter, photographer The Daily Press, Paso Robles, Calif., 1993-94; reporter The Bus. Jour., Fresno, Calif., 1994, copy editor, 1994-96, asst. editor, 1996-97; spl. projects editor The Bus. Jour., Fresno, 1997—. Mem. Soc. Am. Bus. Editors and Writers. Office: The Business Jour 807 Skyline Dr San Luis Obispo CA 93405-1053

BUSSEY, GEORGE DAVIS, psychiatrist; b. Salta, Argentina, Apr. 14, 1949; s. William Harold and Helen (Wygant) B.; m. Moira Savage, July 26, 1975; children: Andrew Davis, Megan Elizabeth. BS, U. Denver, 1969; MD, Ea. Va. Med. Sch., 1977; JD, U. Hawaii, 1993. Intern Eastern Va. Grad. Sch. Medicine, 1977-78; resident Ea. Va. Grad. Sch. Medicine, 1978-79, Vanderbilt U. Hosp., Nashville, 1979-81; staff psychiatrist Hawaii State Hosp., Kaneohe, 1981-82; asst. prof. dept. psychiatry U. Hawaii, Honolulu, 1982-84; dir. adult svcs. Kahi Mohala Hosp., Ewa Beach, Hawaii, 1983-89; assoc. med. dir. Queens Healthcare Plan, Honolulu, 1988-94; med. dir. Managed Care Mgmt., Inc., 1994—; clin. assoc. prof. Dept. Psychiatry U. Hawaii, Honolulu, 1990—. Mem. U. Hawaii Law Rev., 1991-93; contbr. articles to profl. jours. Fellow Am. Psychiat. Assn., Hawaii Psychiat. Soc. (treas. 1982-83, pres. 1985-87).

BUSSIERE, JEANINE LOUISE, toxicologist; b. Winona, Minn., May 29, 1962; d. Eugene Albert and Ruth Margaret (Utecht) B. BS, U. Idaho, 1984; MS, Western Wash. U., 1986; PhD, Wash. State U., 1989. Diplomate Am. Bd. Toxicology. Rsch. asst. U. Idaho, Moscow, 1982-84, Western Wash. U., Bellingham, 1985-86; rsch. aide U. Idaho, Moscow, 1986-89; postdoctoral fellow Temple U., Phila., 1990-92; toxicologist Genentech, Inc., San Francisco, 1992—; tng. program lectr. SmithKline Beecham, Phila., 1991; peer rev. on Boron Neutron Capture Therapy, Dept. Energy, Chgo., 1992; in vitro toxicology task force Pharm. Mfrs. Assn., Bethesda, Md., 1993-94. Contbr. chpt. to book and articles to profl. jours. Recipient Travel awards Nat. Inst. Drug Abuse, 1991, Comm. Problems of Drug Dependence, 1992; postdoctoral fellow Nat. Inst. Drug Abuse, Temple U., 1990-92. Mem. Am. Soc. for Pharmacology and Exptl. Therapeutics, Soc. for Neurosci., Soc. Environ. Toxicology and Chemistry, Soc. Toxicology (Travel award 1988). Office: Genentech Inc Dept Toxicology 460 Point San Bruno Blvd South San Francisco CA 94080-4918

BUTCHER, JACK ROBERT (JACK RISIN), manufacturing executive; b. Akron, Ohio, Dec. 10, 1941; s. William Hobart and Marguerite Bell (Dalton) B.; m. Gloria Jean Hartman, June 1, 1963; children: Jack R. II, Charlotte Jean. BA in Math., Jacksonville U., 1964; cert. mgmt. consulting, Akron U., 1979; cert. paralegal, CCT Inst., 1990; cert. radio broadcasting, Chaffey Coll., 1994. Pres. Portableacher Corp., Hesperia, Calif., 1977—; v.p. Nice Day Products, Hesperia, 1980-85; pres. The Mark of Profl. Mgmt. and Design Co., Hesperia, 1983—, Nice Day Products, Hesperia, 1985—; bd. govs. Internat. Platform Assn., 1996—; co-owner JB Scale Co., Hesperia, Calif., 1991—; acting, voice-overs and commls. Film Industry Workshop Sch. of Acting, 1995—. Author: (poems) Something Good, 1978, Forever My Valentine, 1996; patentee in field. Mem. Internat. Platform Assn. (bd. govs. 1996—, Silver Bowl award 1995), Screen Actors Guild, Masons, Shriners, Royal Order of Jesters. Office: PO Box 402540 Hesperia CA 92340-2540

BUTENHOFF, SUSAN, public relations executive; b. N.Y.C., Jan. 13, 1960. BA with honors in Internat. Rels., Sussex U., Eng.; MPhil, Wolfson Coll., Cambridge U., Eng. Account exec. Ellen Farmer Prodns., 1984-85; account exec. Ketchum Pub. Rels., N.Y.C., 1988-90, v.p., account supr., 1990-91; prin., CEO Access Pub. Rels., San Francisco, 1991—. Mem. Pub. Rels. Soc. Am. Office: Access Pub Rels 101 Howard St San Francisco CA 94105-1629*

BUTH, DONALD GEORGE, biology educator; b. Chgo., Feb. 23, 1949; s. Werner George and Arlene Dolores (Kreier) B. BS in Zoology, U. Ill., 1971, AB in Anthropology, 1972, MS in Zoology, 1974, PhD in Ecology, Ethol. and Evolution, 1978. Research, teaching asst. U. Ill., Urbana, 1971-78; postdoctoral researcher UCLA, 1978-79, instr. biology, 1980, asst. prof., 1980-86, assoc. prof., 1986-92, prof., 1992—; coord. bd. U. Calif. Water Resources, 1990-97. Contbr. articles to profl. jours. Fellow AAAS, Willi Hennig Soc. (councilor 1981-82); mem. Am. Soc. Ichthyologists and Herpetologists (bd. govs. 1984—, exec. com. 1983-86, assoc. editor COPEIA, 1985-93, editl. bd. 1993-96, System Biol., 1994-95, editor Isozyme Bull. 1991-93), So. Calif. Acad. Sci. (bd. dirs. 1992-96, editl. bd. bull. 1995-96). Office: UCLA Dept Biology Los Angeles CA 90095-1606

BUTLER, ANNE M., history educator; b. Somerville, Mass., Dec. 4, 1938; d. Thomas Francis Maroney and Katherine Jean (Atkins) Posey; children: Daniel Ryan Porterfield, Katherine Anne Porterfield. BS, Towson State U., 1973; MA, U. Md., 1975, PhD, 1979. Assoc. editor/historian U.S. Capitol Hist. Soc., Washington, 1980-81; assoc. prof. history Gallaudet U., Washington, 1981-88; assoc. prof., then prof. Utah State U., Logan, 1989—; co-editor Western Hist. Quar., Logan, 1989—. Author: Gendered Justice in the American West: Women Prisoners in Male Penitentiaries, 1997; Daughters of Joy, Sisters of Misery: Prostitutes in the American West, 1985; co-author: Uncommon Common Women: Ordinary Lives in the West, 1996; co-editor: Major Problems in the American West, 1996; contbr. chpt. to: Oxford History of the American West, 1994; contbr. articles to hist. publs.; mem. editorial bd. Western Hist. Quar., 1987-89. Mem. Western History Assn.,

Phi Kappa Phi. Office: Western Hist Quar Utah State Univ Logan UT 84322

BUTLER, ARTHUR MAURICE, university administrator; b. Osaka, Japan, Mar. 18, 1947; came to U.S. 1949; s. John Elzie Jr. and Connie Mae (Hartzel) B.; m. Celine Marie Bell, Sept. 19, 1970. BA in Polit. Sci., Calif. State Coll., San Bernadino, 1977. Asst. dir. pub. safety Calif. State Coll., 1975-81, dir. pub. safety, 1981-87, dir. adminstrv. svcs., 1987—; exec. dir. Found. for Calif. State U., San Bernardino, 1987—; bd. dirs. Western Assn. Coll. Aux. Svcs., Calif., Inland Bus. Coun. on Emergency Preparedness, San Bernadino. Vice chair City Personnel Bd., Riverside, Calif., 1981-88; chair Selective Svc. Bd., Riverside, 1980—; active Calif. Rep. Cen. Com. Sacramento, 1982-84; bd. dirs. CSU Risk Mgmt. Authority, 1996—. mem. Nat. Assn. Coll. Aux. Svcs. (dir. region 1 1988-89), Newcomen Soc., Serra Club (trustee, sec. Riverside chpt. 1985-90), Victoria Club, Pi Sigma Alpha. Roman Catholic. Office: Calif State U San Bernardino 5500 University Pky San Bernardino CA 92407-2318

BUTLER, BYRON CLINTON, obstetrician, gynecologist; b. Carroll, Iowa, Aug. 10, 1918; s. Clinton John and Blance (Prall) B.; m. Jo Ann Nicolls; children: Marilyn, John Byron, Barbara, Denise; 1 stepdau., Marriane. MD, Columbia Coll. Physicians and Surgeons, 1943; ScD, Columbia U., 1952; G.G. grad. gemologist, Gemol. Inst. Am., 1986. Diplomate Am. Bd. Ob/Gyn. Intern Columbia Presbyn. Med. Ctr.; resident Sloane Hosp. for Women; instr. Columbia Coll. Physicians and Surgeons, 1950-53; dir. Butler Rsch. Found., Phoenix, 1953-86, pres., 1970—; ret. as gyn. surgeon, 1989; pres. World Gems/G.S.G., Scottsdale, Ariz., 1979—, World Gems Software, 1988, World Gems Jewelry, 1990—; cosmologist, jewelry designer Extra-Terrestrial-Alien Jewelry & Powerful Personal Talismans, 1992—, 3rd Mellineum Line of Tektite Jewelry, 1994—. Patentee in field. Bd. dirs. Heard Mus., Phoenix, 1965-74; founder Dr. Byron C. Butler, G.G., Fund for Inclusion Research, Gemol. Inst. Am., Santa Monica, Calif., 1987. Served to capt. M.C. AUS, 1944-46. Grantee Am. Cancer Soc., 1946-50, NIH, 1946-50, 50-53. Fellow AAAS; mem. Am. Gemstones Trade Assn., Ariz. Jewelers Assn., Mufon, Mutual UFO Networks. Home: 77 E Missouri Ave Unit #20 Phoenix AZ 85012

BUTLER, DASCHEL E., protective services official. Chief of police Berkeley, Calif. Office: 2171 McKinley Ave Berkeley CA 94703

BUTLER, EDWARD EUGENE, plant pathology educator; b. Wilmington, Del., Dec. 8, 1919; s. Edward Harry and Julia (Ennis) B.; m. Mildred Norene Godden, Dec. 20, 1947; children: David, Stephen, Susan, Thomas, James. BS, U. Del., Newark, 1943; MS, Mich. State U., 1948; PhD, U. Minn., 1954. Instr. plant pathology U. Minn., St. Paul, 1951-54; jr. plant pathologist U. Calif., Davis, 1955-56; asst. plant pathologist U. Calif., 1957-61, assoc. prof. plant pathology, 1961-68, prof. plant pathology, 1968-90, prof. emeritus, 1990—; vis. prof. U. P.R., 1966-67; vis. scientist Rancho Santa Ana Bot. Garden, Claremont, Calif., 1983-84. Assoc. editor Phytopathology, 1973-76; editorial bd. Mycologia, 1978-88, Mycopathologia, 1992—; contbr. to profl. jours. Capt. U.S. Army, 1943-46, PTO. Named to U. Del. Wall of Fame, 1996. Fellow AAAS; mem. Mycol. Soc. Am. (W.H. Weston award 1981), Am. Phytopathol. Soc. (Lifetime Achievement award Pacific divsn. 1996), Brit. Mycol. Soc. Democrat. Home: 402 12th St Davis CA 95616-2023 Office: U Calif Dept Plant Pathology Davis CA 95616

BUTLER, GERALD JOSEPH, English and comparative literature educator; b. San Francisco, Feb. 24, 1942; s. Dale and Marian Elizabeth (Watchler) B.; m. Evelyn Anne Kelly, Feb. 3, 1964; children: James Dale, Marian Margaret, Wayne Anthony. AA, San Francisco City Coll., 1961; AB with honors, U. Calif., Berkeley, 1963; PhD, U. Wash., 1969. Prof. English & comparative lit. San Diego State U., 1968—; maitre de conf. U. Nice, France, 1987-88; prof. U. Orleans, France, 1990-91, U. Rennes, France, 1996; mem. exec. com. Inst. for History of Mentalities, Hamilton, New Zealand, 1992—. Author: Love and Reading, 1989, Henry Fielding and Lawrence's Old Adam, 1991, Fielding's Unruly Novels, 1996; editor: Recovering Literature, 1972—; contbr. articles to profl. jours. Mem. Phi Beta Kappa. Home: PO Box 805 Alpine CA 91903-0805 Office: San Diego State U Dept English and Comparative Lit San Diego CA 92182

BUTLER, KATY (KATHERINE ANNE BUTLER), editor, freelance writer; b. Grahamstown, South Africa, Jan. 21, 1949; d. Jeffrey Ernest and Valerie Joy (de la Harpe) B.; m. Robert Steenrod Britton, Oct. 17, 1984 (div. Nov. 1995). Student, Sarah Lawrence Coll., Bronxville, N.Y., 1967-69; BA, Wesleyan U., Middletown, Conn., 1971, MA (hon.), 1981. Freelance corr. Washington Post, 1974-75; reporter San Francisco Bay Guardian, 1973-77, San Francisco Chronicle, 1977-95; writer, editor Family Therapy Networker, Washington, 1989—; resident Blue Mountain (N.Y.) Ctr., 1989, 92; spkr. Investigative Reporters and Editors, (I.R.E.) Providence, 1996. Contbr. articles and revs to nat. mags. and newspapers, including New Yorker, L.A. Times, N.Y. Times, Vogue. Mem. awards com. Media Alliance, San Francisco, 1992, 93, 94. Recipient feature writing and investigative reporting awards and hon. mentions San Francisco Press Club, 1973, 75, 86; fellow Wesleyan Writers Conf., Middletown, Conn., 1992, Bay Area Writers Workshop, Mills Coll., 1992. Mem. Authors Guild, Soc. Profl. Journalists. Buddhist. Office: PO Box 832 Mill Valley CA 94942

BUTLER, LESLIE ANN, advertising agency owner, artist, writer; b. Salem, Oreg., Nov. 19, 1945; d. Marlow Dole and Lala Ann (Erlandson) Butler. Student Lewis and Clark Coll., 1963-64; BS, U. Oreg, 1969; post-grad. Portland State U. 1972-73, Lewis & Clark Coll., 1991. Creative trainee Ketchum Advt., San Francisco, 1970-71; asst. advt. dir. Mktg. Systems, Inc., Portland, Oreg., 1971-74; prodn. mgr., art dir., copywriter Finzer-Smith, Portland, 1974-76; copywriter Gerber Advt., Portland, 1976-78; freelance copywriter, Portland, 1983-84, 83-85; copywriter McCann-Erickson, Portland, 1980-81; copy chief Brookstone Co., Peterborough, N.H., 1981-83; creative dir. Whitman Advt., Portland, 1984-87; prin. L.A. Advt., 1987—. Co-founder, v.p., newsletter editor Animal Rescue and Care Fund, 1972-81; Bd. dir. Big Brothers Big Sisters of Am.; active mem. Oregon Ballet Theatre, Portland Art Mus., Oreg. Humane Soc. Recipient Internat. Film and TV Festival N.Y. Finalist award, 1985, 86, 87, 88, Internat. Radio Festival of N.Y. award, 1984, 85, 88, Hollywood Radio and TV Soc. Internat. Broadcasting award, 1981, TV Comml. Festival Silver Telly award, 1985, TV Comml. Festival Bronze Telly, 1986, AVC Silver Cindy, 1986, Los Angeles Advt. Women LULU, 1986, 87, 88, 89 Ad Week What's New Portfolio, 1986, N.W. Addy award Seattle Advt. Fedn., 1984, Best of N.W. award, 1985, Nat. winner Silver Microphone award, 1987, 88, 89. Mem. ASPCA, Portland Advt. Fedn. (Rosey Finalist award 1986), , People for Ethical Treatment of Animals. Home and Office: 7556 SE 29th Ave Portland OR 97202-8827

BUTLER, PATRICIA LACKY, mental health nurse, educator, consultant; b. Galesburg, Ill., Aug. 31, 1943; d. Allen Dale and Mary Lacky; m. Glen William Butler, Mar. 14, 1964 (div. Apr. 1974); children: Scott Lewis, Andrew William, Suzanne Elizabeth; m. Keith Warren Turner, Oct. 13, 1992. AA in Nursing/Journalism, Sacramento City Coll., 1965; BS in Sociology/Psychology, SUNY, Albany, 1992. Clin. nurse Mercy Gen. Hosp., Sacramento, Sacramento Med. Ctr.; Davis (Calif.) Cmty. Hosp.; clin. nurse Woodland (Calif.) Meml. Hosp., 1965-74; dir. nurses Woodland Skilled Nursing, 1978-79; head nurse/psychiatry St. Croix Mental Health, Christiansted, U.S. V.I., 1974-79; clin. program coord. Yolo County Mental Health, Woodland, 1980—; instr. Yuba C.C., Marysville, Calif., 1988—. Author curriculum; mem. editl. adv. bd. Daily Democrat. Bd. dirs. Concilio of Yolo County, Woodland, 1984-87; mem. Red Cross Nat. Disaster Mental Health, 1996—. Recipient Bell award Mental Health Assn. Yolo County, 1993; NIMH grantee, 1989-90. Mem. Forensic Mental Health Assn. Calif. (sec. 1991-93, conf. planning 1990-91, dir. edn. and tng. 1996—). Democrat. Roman Catholic. Home: McKinney-Rasicon Rd Homewood CA 96141 Office: Yolo County Mental Health 213 W Beamer St Woodland CA 95695-2510

BUTLER, PETER, JR., retired educator; b. New Orleans, Dec. 28, 1929; s. Peter and Ada (Smith) B.; m. Annie Mae Darrington, Dec. 24, 1956; children: Simone Walton, Daryl R., Phyllis E. Young, Deidre M. Hudson, Myra A. Cuff. BA, So. U., Baton Rouge, 1954; MEd, La. State U., 1959; EdD, U. So. Calif., 1976. Cert. elem. tchr., secondary sch. tchr., gen. adminstrv. svcs., Calif. Tchr. English, New Orleans Pub. Schs., 1954-56, 59-63; tchr. English Archdiocese Schs., New Orleans, 1956-59; tech. writer The Boeing Co., New Orleans, 1963-64; tchr. English, Inglewood (Calif.) Unified Sch. Dist., 1964-67, asst. prin., 1967-69, prin., dir. secondary edn., asst. supt. pers. svcs., 1969-89; adj. prof. Chapman U., Orange, Calif., 1994—. Contbr. articles to profl. jours. With U.S. Army, 1947-50. Mem. ASCD, Kappa Alpha Psi. Methodist. Home: 19202 Hillford Ave Carson CA 90746-2656

BUTLER, VIGGO M., airport terminal executive; b. 1942. BBD, Calif. State Poly U., 1964; MBA, Pepperdine U., 1980. Ops. mgr. Kansas City (Mo.) Internat. Airport, 1969-73; various positions to pres. Lockheed Air Terminal Inc., Burbank, Calif., 1973-95; corp. v.p. Lockheed Corp., 1973-95; now chmn. United Airports Ltd., Chatsworth, Calif. With USAF, 1964-69. Office: United Airports Ltd 10801 Winnetka Ave Chatsworth CA 91311

BUTLER-THOMAS, JANNETTE SUE, human resources professional; b. Eugene, Oreg., Mar. 15, 1960; d. Robert Eugene and Dorothy Marilyn (Irvin) Butler; m. Robert Alan Thomas, Oct. 3, 1992. BS in Hotel Adminstrn., U. Nev., Las Vegas, 1982. Cert. health promotion dir., sr. profl. in human resources. Pers. mgmt. trainee The Sheraton Corp., San Diego, 1982-83; dir. pers. The Sheraton Corp., Palm Coast, Fla., 1983-85; dir. human resources The Sheraton Corp., Dallas, 1985-89; corp. dir. human resources Hilton Reservations Worldwide, Carrollton, Tex., 1989-95; human resource cons. Symantec Corp., Eugene, Oreg., 1995-97; mgr. human resource Microsoft Corp., Redmond, Wash., 1997—. Mem., vol. Nat. Multiple Sclerosis Soc., Dallas, 1991—; mem. steering com. Lane County Career Ctrs. Recipient Volunteerism award Lodging Industry Tng. Ctr., 1988. Mem. Soc. for Human Resource Mgmt., Northwest Human Resource Mgmt. Assn. (pres. elect 1997), Inst. for Internat. Human Resource Mgmt., Eugene C. of C. (edn. com.). Episcopalian. Office: Microsoft One Microsoft Way Redmond WA 98052

BUTTERWORTH, ROBERT ROMAN, psychologist, researcher, media therapist; b. Pittsfield, Mass., June 24, 1946; s. John Leon and Martha Helen (Roman) B. BA, SUNY, 1972; MA, Marist Coll., 1975; PhD in Clin. Psychology, Calif. Grad. Inst., 1983. Asst. clin. psychologist N.Y. State Dept. Mental Hygiene, Wassaic, 1972-75; pres. Contemporary Psychology Assocs., Inc., L.A. and Downey, Calif., 1976—; cons. L.a. County Dept. Health Svc.; staff clinician San Bernardino County Dept. Mental Health, 1983-85; staff psychologist State of Calif. Dept. Mental Health, 1985—; media interviews include PA, L.A. Times, N.Y. Times, USA Today, Wall St Jour., Washington Post, Redbook mag., London Daily Mail and many others; TV and radio interviews include Larry King Live, CBA, NBA and ABC networks, Oprah Winfrey Show, CNN Newsnight, Can. Radio Network, Mut. Radio Network and many others. Served with USAF, 1965-69. Mem. Am. Psychol. Assn. for Media Psychology, Calif. Psychol. Assn., Nat. Accreditation Assn. Psychoanalysis. Office: Contemporary Psychology Assocs Inc PO Box 76477 Los Angeles CA 90076-0477

BUTTS, EDWARD PERRY, civil engineer, environmental consultant; b. Ukiah, Calif., July 29, 1958; s. Edward Oren Butts and Orvilla June (Daily) Hutcheson; m. JoAnne Catherine Zellner, Aug. 14, 1978; children: Brooke C., Adam E. Cert. continuing studies in Irrigation Theory and Practices, U. Nebr., 1980. Registered profl. engr., Oreg., Wash.; cert. water rights examiner, Oreg.; registered control sys. engr., Oreg. Technician Ace Pump Sales, Salem, Oreg., 1976; technician Stettler Supply Co., Salem, 1976-78, assoc. engr., 1978-86, chief engr., 1986-90, v.p. engring., 1990-97, pres., 1997—; profl. engr. exam. question reviewer Nat. Coun. Engring. Examiners, Clemson, S.C., 1989—; profl. engr. exam. supr. Oreg. State Bd. Engring. Examiners, Salem, 1986—; lectr. various water works profl. groups; mem. Marion County Water Mgmt. Coun., 1993—. Contbr. articles to Jour. Pub. Works Mag., AWWA Opflow, Water Well Jour. Coach Little League Cascade Basketball Leage, Turner, Oreg., 1990—. Recipient Merit award Am. City and County Mag., 1990, Cmty. Vol. citation City of Keizer, Oreg., 1993, Cert. of appreciation Oreg. State Bd. Engring. Examiners, 1996, Letter of Commendation for flood assistance City of Salem, 1996, Appreciation Design award Spraying Systems Co., 1996. Mem. ASCE, NSPE, Am. Pub. Works Assn., Assn. Groundwater Scientists and Engrs., Profl. Engrs. Oreg. (mid-Willamette chpt. v.p. 1990-91, pres. 1992-93, state v.p. 1993-95, state pres.-elect 1995-96, state pres. 1996-97, Young Engr. of Yr. award 1993-94), Am. Water Works Assn. Republican. Office: 1810 Lana Ave NE Salem OR 97303-3116

BUURSMA, WILLIAM F., architect. BArch, U. Mich., 1964; MArch, U. Pa., 1965. Lic. arch. With various archtl. design firms; joined John Graham Assocs/DLR Group, Seattle, 1976—, prin.; tchg. fellow U. Tenn., also assoc. prof. France program. Prin. works include Madigan Army Med. Ctr., Ft. Lewis, Wash., Clackamas Town Ctr., Portland, Oreg., Kauai Hilton Resort and Condominium Complex, Hawaii, high-rise office bldgs., retail shopping malls, and numerous other complexes. Mem. AIA. Office: John Graham Assoc 900 4th Ave Ste 700 Seattle WA 98164-1001*

BUXBAUM, RICHARD M., law educator, lawyer; b. 1930. A.B., Cornell U., 1950, LL.B., 1952; LL.M., U. Calif.-Berkeley, 1953; Dr. (hon.) U. Osnabrück, 1992, Eötvös Lorand U., Budapest, 1993. Bar: Calif. 1953, N.Y. 1953. Practice law, pvt. firm, Rochester, N.Y., 1957-61; prof. U. Calif.-Berkeley, 1961—, dean internat. and area studies. Editor-in-chief Am. Jour. Comparative Law. Recipient Humboldt prize, 1991, German Order of Merit, 1992. Mem. German Soc. Comparative Law (corr.), Coun. on Fgn. Rels. Office: U Calif Internat & Area Studies 260 Stephens Hall Berkeley CA 94720-2301

BUXTON, MARION WEST, middle school education educator; b. Amory, Miss., Aug. 17, 1949; d. O.M. and Corinne (Todd) West; m. George Glenton Buxton, Sept. 6, 1969; children: William Glenton, Jonathan West. BS, Miss. State U., 1970. Cert. tchr., La., Miss., Calif. Elem. tchr. St. Tammany Schs., Slidell, La., 1984-88; tchr. honors lang. arts Moorpark (Calif.) Unified Schs., 1989—; state mentor for gifted edn. State of Calif., Sacramento, 1995—. Author: Simply Successful, 1993. V.p. United Meth. Women, Slidell, 1987; deacon, mem. worship com., mem. fellowship com. Presbyn. Ch., Moorpark, 1995, small group chair, 1996. Impact II grantee Ventura (Calif.) County Dept. Edn., 1994, Tri-County Gifted Edn. grantee; recipient Tchg. award WHO, 1997, Pres.'s award Edn., 1997; nominee AMGEN Tchr. Yr. award. 1997. Mem. Delta Kappa Gamma. Republican. Home: 4093 Little Hollow Pl Moorpark CA 93021 Office: Moorpark Unified Schs 280 Poindexter Ave Moorpark CA 93021-1833

BUYERS, JOHN WILLIAM AMERMAN, agribusiness and specialty foods company executive; b. Coatesville, Pa., July 17, 1928; s. William Buchanan and Rebecca (Watson) B.; m. Elsie Palmer Parkhurst, Apr. 11, 1953; children: Elsie Buyers Viehman, Rebecca Watson Buyers-Basso, Jane Palmer Buyers-Russo. B.A. cum laude in History, Princeton U., 1952; M.S. in Indsl. Mgmt., MIT, 1963. Div. ops. mgr. Bell Telephone Co. Pa., 1964-66; dir. ops. and personnel Gen. Waterworks Corp., Phila., 1966-68; pres., chief exec. officer Gen. Waterworks Corp., Phila, 1971-75; v.p. adminstrn. Internat. Utilities Corp., Phila., 1968-71; pres., chief exec. officer, dir. C. Brewer and Co., Ltd., Honolulu, 1975—, chmn. bd., 1982—; chmn. Calif. and Hawaiian Sugar Co., 1982-84, 86-90; pres. Buyco, Inc., 1986—; mem. Hawaii Joint Coun. Econ. Edn., Japan-Hawaii Econ. Coun.; bd. dirs. 1st Hawaiian Inc., John B. Sanfilippo & Sons, Inc., Outrigger Hotels and Restors; chmn. bd. C. Brewer Homes, Inc.; vice chmn. Pacific Internat. Ctr. for High Tech. Rsch., 1976—. Trustee U. Hawaii Found., Hawaii Prep. Acad., 1986—; chmn. bd. dirs. Hawaii Visitors Bur., 1990-91; mem. Gov.'s Blue Ribbon Panel on the Future of Healthcare in Hawaii; bd. dirs. Hawaii Sports Found., 1990—; mem. adv. group to U.S. Dist. Ctr. With USMC, 1946-48. Sloan fellow, 1963. Mem. Hawaiian Sugar Planters Assn. (chmn. bd. dirs. 1980-82, dir.), c. of C. Hawaii (chmn. bd. dirs. 1981-82), Nat. Alliance Bus. (chmn. Hawaii Pacific Metro chpt. 1978), Cap and Gown Club (Princeton), Hilo Yacht Club, Oahu Country Club, Pacific Club, Waialae county Club, Prouts Neck (Maine) County Club, U.S. C. of C. (mem. food and gr. com. 1991—), Beretania Tennis Club. Presbyterian. Clubs: Cap and Gown (Princeton); Hilo Yacht, Oahu Country, Pacific, Waialae Country; Prouts Neck (Maine) Country. Home: Grand Penthouse West 1080 S Beretania St Honolulu HI 96814-1400 Office: C Brewer & Co Ltd PO Box 1826 Honolulu HI 96805-1826 also: Buyco Inc 827 Fort Street Mall Honolulu HI 96813-4317*

BUZBEE, JOHN D., JR., sales executive; b. Jonesboro, Ark., Dec. 19, 1958; s. John D. and Louise (Tice) B.; m. Jana Denise Brown, Jan. 26, 1991; children: Jillian, Caitlin. BS, BA in Mgmt. and Gen. Bus., U. Ark., 1981. Acct. mgr. Consolidated Holding Co., Tulsa, Okla., 1981-83; sls. rep. Davis and Geck, Tulsa, Okla., 1983-86, Jobst Inst., Inc., Tulsa, Okla., 1986-88; dist. sls. mgr. Jobst Inst., Inc., L.A., 1989-90, regional sls. mgr., 1990-93, regional bus. mgr., 1994-95; nat. acct. mgr. Beiersdorf-Jobst, Inc., L.A., 1996—. Republican. Home: 32315 Via Cordoba Temecula CA 92592 Office: Beiersdorf-Jobst Inc 32315 Via Cordoba Temecula CA 92592

BUZUNIS, CONSTANTINE DINO, lawyer; b. Winnipeg, Man., Can., Feb. 3, 1958; came to U.S., 1982; s. Peter and Anastasia (Ginakes) B. BA, U. Man., 1980; JD, Thomas M. Cooley Law Sch., 1985. Bar: Mich. 1986, U.S. Dist. Ct. (ea. and we. dists.) Mich. 1986, Calif. 1986, U.S. Dist. Ct. (so. dist.) Calif. 1987, U.S. Supreme Ct. 1993. Assoc. Church, Kritselis, Wyble & Robinson, Lansing, Mich., 1986; assoc. Neil, Dymott, Perkins, Brown & Frank, San Diego, 1987-94, ptnr., 1994—. Sec., treas. Sixty Plus Law Ctr., Lansing, 1985; active Vols. in Parole, San Diego, 1988—; bd. dirs. Hellenic Cultural Soc., 1993—. Mem. ABA, FBA, ATLA, Mich. Bar Assn., Calif. Bar Assn., San Diego County Bar Assn., San Diego Trial Lawyers Assn., So. Calif. Def. Coun., State Bar Calif. (gov. 9th dist. young lawyers divsn. 1991-94, 1st v.p. 1993-94, pres. 1994-95, bd. govs. 1995-96) San Diego Barristers Soc. (bd. dirs. 1991-92), Pan Arcadian Fedn., Order of Ahepa (chpt. bd. dirs., v.p. 1995—), Phi Alpha Delta. Home: 3419 Overpark Rd San Diego CA 92130-1865 Office: Neil Dymott Perkins Brown & Frank 1010 2nd Ave Ste 2500 San Diego CA 92101-4913

BYBEE, JOAN LEA, linguistics educator; b. New Orleans, Feb. 11, 1945; d. Robert William and Elizabeth Mai (Rachal) B.; 1 child, Brody. BA in Spanish and English, U. Tex., 1966; MA in Linguistics, San Diego State U., 1970; PhD in Linguistics, UCLA, 1973. Prof. linguistics SUNY, Buffalo, 1973-89; Regents' prof. linguistics U. N.Mex., Albuquerque, 1989—, assoc. dean Coll. Arts and Scis., 1992-93; dir. 1995 Linguistic Inst., U. N.Mex., 1995. Author: Introduction to Natural Generative Phonology, 1976, Morphology, 1985, The Evolution of Grammar, 1994, Modality in Grammar and Discourse, 1995. Fellowship Guggenheim Meml. Found., 1987-88, Netherlands Inst. of Advanced Study, 1983-84; recipient Disting Alumni award San Diego State U., 1976. Mem. Linguistic Soc. of Am. (chair program com. 1982-83, exec. com. 1988-91). Office: Univ New Mexico Dept Linguistics Humanities 526 Albuquerque NM 87131

BYBEE, PAUL RALPH, psychiatrist; b. Cin., Sept. 5, 1931; s. Earl Lee and Sara Frances (Hays) B.; m. Margaret Pauline Knepper, Aug. 13, 1955 (div. Mar. 1972); children: Paul Daniel, Victoria Lynn, Tammy Lou, Guy Adam; m. Matilda Gaio, June 15, 1985. BS, E. Ky. U., 1954; MD, Ohio State U., 1958. Diplomate Am. Bd. Psychiatry and Neurology. Intern St. Joseph's Hosp., Phoenix, 1958-59; psychiat. resident Walter Reed Army Hosp., Washington, 1959-62; chief of psychiatry Ft. Campbell Army Hosp., Ky., 1962-66; pvt. practice Phoenix, 1966-85; chief psychiat. svcs. VA Hosp., Cheyenne, Wyo., 1985-86, Prescott, Ariz., 1986-87, Temple, Tex., 1987-91; locum tenens assignments, 1991—. Author: What's Psychotherapy?, 1977. Maj. U.S. Army, 1957-66. Mem. APA (life). Home: 8101 N 12th Pl Phoenix AZ 85020-3867

BYDALEK, DAVID ALLEN, educator; b. Kankakee, Ill., June 14, 1943; s. Paul Daniel and Earleen Doris (Shrontz) B.; m. Karen Mildred Gebauer, Jan. 24, 1968; children: Karin, Peggy, Gabriel. BS in Edn., Ea. Ill. U., 1965; MS in Edn., No. Ill. U., 1967; EdD, Ariz. State U., Tempe, 1979. Instr. Ind. U., Ft. Wayne, 1967-69; instr., dept. chair Gateway C.C., Phoenix, 1969-90; instr. Mesa (Ariz.) C.C., 1990—, chair dept., 1992—. Author: A Means for Individualized Progression in Bookkeeping, 1972, A Supplement to Teach Accounting Principles, 1977. Mem. Maricopa County Colls. Faculty Assn. (pres. 1979), Delta Pi Epsilon (pres. 1978). Office: Mesa CC 1833 W Southern Ave Mesa AZ 85202-4822

BYERS, BRECK EDWARD, geneticist, educator; b. St. Louis, July 4, 1939; s. F. Donald and Melba Constance (Boothman) B.; m. Margaret Tyler Read, Nov. 26, 1964; children: Mark Andrew, Carl Bradford. BS, U. Colo., 1961; MS, Harvard U., 1963, PhD, 1967. Researcher Univ. of Geneva, Geneva, Switzerland, 1968-70; asst. prof. dept. genetics U. Washington, Seattle, 1970—, chair., prof. dept. genetics, 1990—. Contbr. articles to profl. jours. Recipient Merit award Nat. Inst. Health, 1993. Democrat. Office: U Wash Dept Genetics Box 357360 Seattle WA 98195-7360

BYERS, CHARLES FREDERICK, public relations executive, marketing executive; b. Johnstown, Pa., Jan. 30, 1946; s. Walter Hayden and Mary Ann Elizabeth (Succop) B.; m. Vicki Louise Beard, June 3, 1967 (div. Apr. 1992); children: Natalie L., Tamara N., Valerie A.; m. Janette Lanora Buck, Apr. 23, 1993. BS in Journalism, Ohio U., 1968; MA in Mass Comms., U. Tex., 1969. Accredited pub. rels. practitioner. Gen. reporter Springfield (Ohio) Daily News, 1967-68; promotion specialist Gen. Electric Co., Chgo., 1969-71; account supr. Burson-Marsteller, Chgo., 1971-78; group v.p. Carl Byoir & Assocs., Chgo., 1978-82; gen. mgr. Carl Byoir & Assocs., Atlanta, 1982-85; pres. Camp-Byers Pub. Rels., Atlanta, 1985-91; client svc. dir. Kalman Comm., L.A., 1991-92; v.p., COO Hayes Pub. Rels., San Jose, Calif., 1992-95; mktg. comms. mgr. Actel Corp., San Jose, Calif. Pres. Hoffman Estates (Ill.) Jaycees, 1976; dir., treas. Brookcliffe Home Owners Assn., 1988-89; comm. chair Ga. Heart Assn., Atlanta, 1990. Recipient Golden Trumpet, Chgo. Publicity Club, 1980. Mem. Pub. Rels. Soc. Am. (dir. Silison Valley chpt. 1993, v.p. Silicon Valley chpt. 1994, pres.-elect 1995, pres. 1996, del. nat. assembly 1997, dir. L.A. chpt. 1992, Silver Anvil 1978). Office: Actel Corp 955 E Arques Ave Sunnyvale CA 94086

BYLECKIE, SCOTT ANDREW, SR., health facility coordinator; b. Plainfield, N.J., June 20, 1962; s. George Christopher and Barbara Ann B.; m. Pamela Gasperini, Apr. 25, 1992; 1 child, Scott Andrew Jr.; 1 stepchild, Justin Michael Gasperini. BS in Health Edn., Ohio U., 1984; MS in Phys. Edn., West Chester U., 1987. Student trainer Ohio U., Athens, 1980-84; grad. asst. athletic trainer West Chester (Pa.) U., 1984-85, grad. asst. human performance rsch. lab., 1985-86; asst. athletic trainer Lafayette Coll., Easton, Pa., 1986, U. Nev., Las Vegas, 1986-90; coord. sports medicine svcs. St. Rose Dominican Hosp., Henderson, Nev., 1991—; co-clin. coord. Weigand Cardiac Rehab. Program St. Rose Dominican Hosp., Henderson, 1995-96. Mem. Nat. Athletic Trainers Assn. (cert., Nev. rep. secondary sch. athletic trainers com. Far West Athletic Trainers Assn. Dist. 8 1994—), Nev. Athletic Trainers Assn. (licensure com. 1992—, treas. 1996—, conv. com. 1996). Republican. Roman Catholic. Home: 810 Chimney Rock Dr Henderson NV 89015 office: St Rose Dominican Hosp 102 E Lake Mead Dr Henderson NV 89015-5575

BYMEL, SUZAN YVETTE, talent manager, film producer; b. Chgo.; d. Howard Behr and Jacqueline Shirley (Richards) B. Student, U. Ill., Chgo. Exec. asst. Kenny Rogers Prodns., 1981; prodn. exec. Pinehurst Prodns., 1982; music mgmt. assoc. Frontline Mgmt., 1983; pres. Suzan Bymel & Assocs., 1985-94; oper. ptnr. Bymel/O'Neill Mgmt., 1995—, Meg Ryan Prodns. (a.k.a. Fandango Films), 1988-93, Bymel/O'Neill Mgmt., 1995—; freelance screenwriter, actress. Mem. Hollywood Woman's Polit. Com., L.A. Office: 1724 N Vista St Los Angeles CA 90046-2235

BYRD, MARC ROBERT, florist; b. Flint, Mich., May 14, 1954; s. Robert Lee and Cynthia Ann (Poland) B.; m. Bonnie Jill Berlin, Nov. 25, 1975 (div. June 1977). Student, Ea. Mich. U., 1972-75; grad., Am. Floral Sch., Chgo., 1978. Gen. mgr., dir. flowers shop; designer Olive Tree Florist, Palm Desert, Calif., 1978-79, Kayo's Flower Fashions, Palm Springs, 1979-80; owner, designer Village Florist, Inc., Palm Springs, 1980-85; pres. Mon Ami Florist, Inc., Beverly Hills, 1986-87; gen. mgr. Silverio's, Santa Monica, 1987; gen. mgr., hotel florist, creative dir. Four Seasons Hotel, Beverly Hills, 1988-90; pres. Marc Fredericks, Inc., Beverly Hills, 1990—. Author: Celebrity Flowers, 1989. Del., Dem. County Conv., 1972, Dem. County Conv., 1972, Dem. State Conv., 1972, Dem. Nat. Conv., 1972. Mem. Soc. Am. Florists, So. Calif. Floral Assn., Desert Mus., Robinson's Gardens. Republican. Mem. Dutch Reformed Ch. Home: 2350 N Vermont Ave Los Angeles CA 90027-1239 Office: Marc Fredericks Inc 8445 Warner Dr Culver City CA 90232-2428

BYRD, RONALD DALLAS, civil engineer; b. Reno, Nov. 30, 1934; s. Eugene Richard and Helen Madelyn (Hursh) B.; m. Irene Josephine Phenix, Sept. 19, 1953; children: Kevin Gregory, Helen Christine, Stephanie Irene. BSCE, U. Nev., 1960. Registered profl. engr., Nev., Calif., Oreg., Wash., Idaho., Wyo. Staff engr. Sprout Engrs., Sparks, Nev., 1960-64, design engr., 1964-67; office mgr. Sprout Engrs., Seattle, 1967-70; exec. v.p. Sea, Inc., Seattle, 1970-72, Sparks, 1972—; also bd. dirs. SE&A Engrs.; bd. dirs. ABS Land Co.; bd. dirs. Am. Cons. Engrs. Coun. Nev., 1987-95, pres., 1993-94, nat. dir. 1994-95. Fellow ASCE (sec. 1966-67); mem. NSPE (bd. dirs. 1983-86), Am. Pub. Works Assn., U. Nev. Reno Engring. Alumni Assn. (sec. 1985-86), U. Nev. Reno Alumni Assn. (pres. 1989-90), Kiwanis (pres. Sparks club 1971-72), Rotary (pres. Federal Way, Wash. club 1971-72, bd. dirs. Reno Sunrise 1992—, pres. 1996-97), Elks, Masons. Republican. Methodist. Home: 30 Ocelet Way Reno NV 89511 Office: SEA Inc 950 Industrial Way Sparks NV 89431-6092

BYRNE, GEORGE MELVIN, physician; b. San Francisco, Aug. 1, 1933; s. Carlton and Esther (Smith) B.; BA, Occidental Coll., 1958; MD, U. So. Calif., 1962; m. Joan Stecher, July 14, 1956; children: Kathryne, Michael, David; m. Margaret C. Smith, Dec. 18, 1982. Diplomate Am. Bd. Family Practice, 1971-84. Intern, Huntington Meml. Hosp., Pasadena, Calif., 1962-63, resident, 1963-64; family practice So. Calif. Permanente Med. Group, 1964-81, physician-in-charge Pasadena med. office, 1966-81; asst. dir. Family Practice residency Kaiser Found. Hosp., L.A., 1971-73; clin. instr. emergency medicine Sch. Medicine, U. So. Calif., 1973-80; v.p. East Ridge Co., 1983-84, sec., 1984; dir. Alan Johnson Porsche Audi, Inc., 1974-82, sec., 1974-77, v.p., 1978-82. Bd. dirs. Kaiser-Permante Mgmt. Assn., 1976-77; mem. regional mgmt. com. So. Calif. Lung Assn., 1976-77; mem. pres.'s circle Occidental Coll., L.A. Drs. Symphony Orch, 1975-80; mem. profl. sect. Am. Diabetes Assn. Fellow Am. Acad. Family Physicians (charter); mem. Am., Calif., L.A. County Med. Assns., Calif. Acad. Family Physicians, Internat. Horn Soc., Quarter Century Wireless Assn., Am. Radio Relay League (Pub. Service award), Sierra (life), So. Calif. Dx Club. Home: 528 Meadowview Dr La Canada Flintridge CA 91011

BYRNE, JOHN VINCENT, higher education consultant; b. Hempstead, N.Y., May 9, 1928; s. Frank E. and Kathleen (Barry) B.; m. Shirley O'Connor, Nov. 26, 1954; children: Donna, Lisa, Karen, Steven. AB, Hamilton Coll., 1951, LLD (hon.), 1994; MA, Columbia U., 1953; PhD, U. So. Calif., 1957; JD (hon.), Hamilton Coll., 1994. Research geologist Humble Oil & Refinery Co., Houston, 1957-60; assoc. prof. Oreg. State U., Corvallis, 1960-66, prof. oceanography, 1966—, chmn. dept., 1968-72, dean Sch. Oceanography, 1972-76, acting dean research, 1976-77, dean research, 1977-80, v.p. for research and grad. studies, 1980-81, pres., 1984-95; pres., 1984-95; adminstr. NOAA, Washington, 1981-84; pres. Oreg. State U., 1984-95; higher edn. cons. Corvallis, 1996—; Program dir. oceanography NSF, 1966—; exec. dir. Kellogg Commn. on Future of State and Land Grant Univs.; dir. Oreg. Coast Aquarium, Harbor Br. Ocean Inst. Recipient Carter teaching award Oreg. State U., 1964. Fellow AAAS, Geol. Soc. Am., Am. Meteorol. Soc.; mem. Am. Assn. Petroleum Geologists, Am. Geophys. Union, Sigma Xi, Chi Psi. Home: 3190 NW Deer Run Corvallis OR 97330-1746 Office: Autzen House 811 SW Jefferson Corvallis OR 97333

BYRNE, NOEL THOMAS, sociologist, educator; b. San Francisco, May 11, 1943; s. Joseph Joshua and Naomi Pearl (Denison) B.; m. Dale W. Elrod, Aug. 6, 1989. BA in Sociology, Sonoma State Coll., 1971; MA in Sociology, Rutgers U., 1975, PhD in Sociology, 1987. Instr. sociology Douglass Coll., Rutgers U., New Brunswick, N.J., 1974-76, Hartnell Coll., Salinas, Calif., 1977-78; from lectr. to assoc. prof. dept. mgmt. Sonoma State U., Rohnert Park, Calif., 1978-94, chmn. dept. of mgmt., 1990-91, from. assoc. prof. to prof. sociology dept., 1994—, chmn. dept. sociology, 1997—; cons. prof. Emile Durkheim Inst. for Advanced Study, Grand Cayman, B.W.I., 1990-93. Contbr. articles and revs. to profl. lit. Recipient Dell Pub. award Rutgers U. Grad. Sociology Program, 1976, Louis Bevier fellow, 1977-78. Mem. AAAS, Am. Sociol. Assn., Pacific Sociol. Assn., N.Y. Acad. Sci., Soc. for Study Symbolic Interaction (rev. editor Jour. 1980-83), Soc. for Study Social Problems, Commonwealth Club. Democrat. Home: 4773 Ross Rd Sebastopol CA 95472-2114 Office: Sonoma State U Dept Sociology Rohnert Park CA 94928

BYRNE, RAYMOND HARRY, electrical engineer, educator; b. Baton Rouge, Dec. 12, 1965; s. Harry C. and Judita K. (Kamarauskas) B. BSEE, U. Va., 1987; MSEE, U. Colo., 1989; PhDEE, U. N.Mex., 1995. Engr.-in-tng., N.Mex. Sr. mem. tech. staff Sandia Nat. Labs., Albuquerque, 1989—; adj. prof. elec. engring. U. N.Mex., Albuquerque, 1996—. Bd. dirs. North Eubank Ski Club, Albuquerque, 1989—. Mem. IEEE (bd. dirs. Albuquerque sect. 1992—), Sigma Xi, Tau Beta Pi, Eta Kappa Nu. Office: Sandia Nat Labs 1515 Eubank SE Albuquerque NM 87185

BYRNE, WILLIAM MATTHEW, JR., federal judge; b. L.A., Sept. 3, 1930; s. William Matthew Sr. and Julia Ann (Lamb) B. BS, U. So. Calif., 1953, LLB, 1956; LLD, Loyola U., 1971. Bar: Calif. 1956. Ptnr. Dryden, Harrington & Schwartz, 1960-67; asst. atty U.S. Dist. Ct. (so. dist.) Calif., 1958-60; atty. U.S. Dist. Ct. (cen. dist.) Calif., Los Angeles, 1967-70, judge, 1971—; now chief judge U.S. Dist. Ct. (cen. dist.) Calif.; exec. dir. Pres. Nixon's Commn. Campus Unrest, 1970; instr. Loyola Law Sch., Harvard U., Whittier Coll. Served with USAF, 1956-58. Mem. ABA, Fed. Bar Assn., Calif. Bar Assn., Los Angeles County Bar Assn (vice chmn. human rights sect.), Am. Judicature Soc. Office: US Dist Ct RM 110 312 N Spring St Los Angeles CA 90012-4701*

BYRNE-DEMPSEY, CECELIA, journalist; b. L.A., Aug. 7, 1925; d. John Joseph and Margaret Agnes (Frakell) B.; m. John Dempsey, Mar. 25, 1951 (dec. June 1981); children: Margaret, Elizabeth, John, Cecelia, Cathrine, Patricia, Bridget, Charles, Mary Teresa. Student, Immaculate Heart Coll., 1944; BA in Psychology, Calif. State U., Northridge, 1975, BA in Journalism, 1978, MA in Mass Communication, 1992. Staff Lockheed Aircraft Corp., Burbank, Calif., 1943—, Office Naval Rsch., San Francisco, 1947—; with Sisters of Mercy, Burlingame, Calif., 1945—, Sisters of Presentation, San Francisco, 1949—; mem. staff Calif. State U., Calif., 1976—. Mentor 4-H Club; past mem. Urban Corp., L.A. Mem. Mensa, Kappa Gamma Delta. Republican. Jewish.

CABOT, HUGH, III, painter, sculptor; b. Boston, Mar. 22, 1930; s. Hugh and Louise (Melanson) C.; m. Olivia P. Taylor, Sept. 8, 1967; student Boston Museum, 1948, Ashmolean Mus., Oxford, Eng., 1960, Coll. Ams., Mexico City, 1956, San Carlos Acad., Mexico City. Portrait, landscape painter; sculptor in bronze; one-man shows: U.S. Navy Hist. and Recreation Dept., U.S. Navy Art Gallery, The Pentagon, Nat. War Mus., Washington, La Muse de la Marine, Paris; group shows include: Tex. Tri-state, 1969 (1st, 2d, 3d prizes), Starmont Vail Med. Ctr. Topeka, Kans., Tucson Med. Ctr. Ariz., Harwood Found. Taos, N.Mex., Washburn U. Topeka, Kans., U. Ariz. Tucson, Ariz. Served as ofcl. artist USN, Korean War. Named Artist of Yr., Scottsdale, Ariz., 1978, 30th ann. Clubs: Salmagundi (N.Y.C.). Author, illustrator: Korea I (Globe).

CADA, RONALD LEE, laboratory administrator, consultant; b. Clarkson, Nebr., June 10, 1944; s. Jerome John and Blanche Ann (Polodna) C.; m. Bernice Ann Studnicka, Aug. 4, 1966; children: Debra Ann Cada King, Craig Jerome. BS, Colo. State U., 1966, MS, 1968; PhD, U. Tex., Houston, 1974. Microbiologist Colo. Dept. Pub. Health, Denver, 1968-72; asst. prof. Sch. Pub. Health U. Tex., Houston, 1974-79; asst. dir. Univ. Hygienic Lab., Iowa City, Iowa, 1979-85; dir. labs. Colo. Dept. Pub. Health and Environment, Denver, 1985—; cons. Tng., Consultation Mgmt. Resources, Inc., Dover, Del., 1995—; workgroup chair EPA, Washington, 1993-95; mem. clin. lab. improvement adv. com. Ctrs. for Disease Control, Atlanta, 1995—. Co-author: (book chpt.) Introduction to Public Health Administration, 1977; contbr. articles to profl. jours. Mem. Assn. State of Territorial Pub. Health Lab. Dir. (sec./treas. 1991-94). Roman Catholic. Office: 8100 Lowry Blvd Denver CO 80220

CADDY, EDMUND H.H., JR., architect; b. N.Y.C., Apr. 17, 1928; s. Edmund Harrington Homer and Glenna Corinne (Garratt) C.; m. Mary Audrey Ortiz, Dec. 22, 1951; children—Edmund Harrington Homer III, Mary Elizabeth. B.A., Princeton, 1952, M.F.A. (grad. sch. fellow), 1955. With Louis E. Jallade, N.Y.C., 1949-53, Eggers & Higgins, N.Y.C., 1953-55; dir. design Dalton-Dalton Assocs., Cleve., 1955-60; assoc. Raymond & Rado, N.Y.C., 1960-68; gen. ptnr. Raymond & Rado and Ptnrs., N.Y.C., 1968-72, Raymond, Rado, Caddy & Bonington, P.C., N.Y.C., 1972-80; pres. Raymond, Rado, Caddy & Bonington, P.C., 1980-83; project mgr. Robinson, Mills & Williams, San Francisco, 1983-87, McCue, Boone, Tomsick, San Francisco, 1987-88, O'Brien-Kreitzberg, San Francisco, 1988-90; Sverdrup Corp., 1990-94; archtl. design cons., 1994—; apptd. by Pres. John F. Kennedy to adv. com. arts John F. Kennedy Ctr. Performing Arts, 1963-70; mem. archtl. adv. commn. N.Y.C. C.C., CUNY, 1979-83. Works include Suburban Hosp. Cleve., 1957, J.M. Smucker Co, Salinas, Cal., 1957, Brookpark (Ohio) City Hall, 1959; Cleve. Transit System addition, 1959, adminstrn. bldg., Met. Water Treatment System, Saigon, 1960, Franklin D. Roosevelt High Sch, N.Y.C., 1963, Crown Heights Intermediate Sch, N.Y.C., 1966, engring. complex, Stony Brook Campus, State U. N.Y., 1970, Sibley's dept. stores, Syracuse, N.Y., 1973, Rochester Downtown Devel. Study, 1975, R.H. Macy & Co. dept. store, Stamford, Conn., 1979; project mgr. Main Postal Facility, San Francisco, 1985, Univ. Ctr., U. Calif., Irvine, 1987, Santa Clara (Calif.) County CourtHouse, Ft. Mojave Resort Devel., 1991-94. Pres. bd. trustees Montclair (N.J.) Cmty. Hosp., 1973-80. Served with USMC, 1946-48, USMCR, 1948-53. Mem. AIA, NCARB, Calif., N.J., Ohio, N.Y. State architects Assns., Tower Club (Princeton), Racquet and Tennis Club (N.Y.C.). Home: PO Box 22 Dillon Beach CA 94929-0022

CADELLO, JAMES PETER, philosopher, educator; b. Westfield, Mass., June 29, 1958; s. Peter Michael and Madelyn (Jeglewicz) C. BA, Westfield State Coll., 1982; MA, Purdue U., 1984, PhD, 1990. Vis. prof. Purdue U.-Calumet, Hammond, Ind., 1988-89; asst. prof. Regis U., Denver, 1989-95; assoc. prof. philosophy Ctrl. Wash. U., Ellensburg, 1995—; mem. summer seminar for coll. tchrs. NEH, 1991; sec. Philosophy in Context, 1994—, Social Philosophy Rsch. Inst., 1987—. Mng. editor Social Philosophy Rsch. Inst. book series, 1990—; contbr. articles to profl. publs. Grantee Ctrl. Wash. U., 1996. Mem. Am. Philos. Assn., N.Am. Soc. Social Philosophy, N.Am. Nietzsche Soc., Am. Assn. Philosophy Tchrs. (program chair 1994-96). Home: 1005 D St Ellensburg WA 98926 Office: Ctrl Wash U Dept Philosophy Ellensburg WA 98926-7555

CADY, JOSEPH HOWARD, management consultant; b. Dallas, Feb. 2, 1959. BSBA, San Diego State U., 1981, MBA, 1988. Cert. profl. cons. to mgmt. Project coord. Mitsubishi Bank of Calif., Escondido and L.A., 1979-82; ind. mgmt. cons. San Diego, 1985-87; sr. cons. Deloitte & Touche, San Diego, 1989-90; mng. ptnr. CS Cons. Group, San Diego, 1990—; guest lectr. U. San Diego, 1987-97, Southwestern Coll., Chula Vista, Calif., 1990; instr. San Diego State U., 1996—; spkr. in field. Contbr. articles to profl. jours. Mem. Cons. Roundtable of San Diego. Office: CS Cons Group 3150 Sandrock Rd San Diego CA 92123-3064

CAETANO, RAUL, psychiatrist, educator; b. São Paulo, Brazil, May 5, 1945; came to U.S., 1978; s. Silvestre Vieira and Vera Vieira (Barbosa) C.; m. Patrice Vaeth, Sept. 30, 1995; children: Izabel, Lauren. MD, U. Rio de Janeiro, 1969, diploma in psychiatry, 1971; MPH, U. Calif., Berkeley, 1979, PhD, 1983. Psychiatrist Pine Hosp., Rio de Janeiro, 1969-73; asst. prof. State U., Rio de Janeiro, 1969-73; rsch. psychiatrist Inst. Psychiatry U. London, 1973-76; asst. prof. Inst. Psychiatry, Rio de Janeiro, 1976-78; vis. scholar Alchohol Rsch. Group, Berkeley, 1978-83, assoc. scientist to sr. scientist, 1983-94, dir., 1992—; assoc. adj. prof. Sch. Pub. Health, U. Calif., Berkeley, 1991—; assoc. dir. Calif. Pacific Med. Ctr. Rsch. Inst., San Francisco, 1992-93. Contbr. numerous sci. papers to profl. jours. WHO fellow, 1973-76; rsch. grantee Nat. Inst. Alcohol Abuse and Alcoholism, 1985—. Mem. APHA, Am. Coll. Epidemiology, Rsch. Soc. Alcoholism. Roman Catholic. Office: Alcohol Rsch Group 2000 Hearst Ave Berkeley CA 94709-2130

CAFFEY, H. DAVID, music educator; b. Austin, Tex., June 2, 1950; s. Howard Lee and Dorthy May (Mangum) C.; m. Linda Kay Larson, June 13, 1970; children: Heather Leigh, Sean Efraim. BMus, U. Tex., 1972, MMus, 1974; postgrad., Calif. State U., Northridge, 1973. Asst. prof. music So. Oreg. State Coll., Ashland, 1974-76; dir. jazz studies, instr. Sam Houston State U., Huntsville, Tex., 1976-79; asst. prof. music U. Denver, 1979-83, assoc. prof., 1983-84; asst. prof. music Calif. State U., L.A., 1984-86, assoc. prof., 1986-91, prof., 1991—, chmn. dept., 1993—; mem. adv. bd. Luckman Fine Arts Ctr., L.A., 1993-96; bd. dirs. Friends of Music, Calif. State U., L.A., 1993—; mem. adv. bd. L.A. County H.S. of Arts, 1993—; mem. bd. advisors Calif. Inst. for Preservation Jazz, Calif. State U., Long Beach, 1996—; mem. adv. bd. cultural arts coun. Mt. San Antonio Coll., 1996—. Composer over 40 compositions, 1975—; prodr. 9 record albums, 1979-90; contbr. articles to profl. jours. Com. chair Troop 448 Boy Scouts Am., Covina, Calif., 1991-92. Mem. ASCAP (award for composition 1981-85), Internat. Assn. Jazz Educators (Calif. state pres. 1991-96, winner composition contest 1978), Comml. Music Educators (nat. bd. 1992—), Music Educators Nat. Conf., Am. Fedn. Musicians, Nat. Assn. Schs. Music (region vice chair, instn. rep. 1995-97). Office: Calif State U Music Dept 5151 State University Dr Los Angeles CA 90032

CAGIN, TAHIR, physicist; b. Izmir, Turkey, Nov. 27, 1956; came to U.S. 1984; s. Mehmet and Bahriye (Teksoz) C.; m. Gul Yenici, Sept. 18, 1980; children: Elif, Kerem. BS, Middle East Tech. U., Ankara, Turkey, 1981, MSc in Physics, 1983; PhD in Physics, Clemson (S.C.) U., 1988. Rsch. assoc. chemistry U. Houston, 1988-89; rsch. scientist Systran Corp., Dayton, Ohio, 1989-90; sr. scientist, project mgr. Molecular Simulations, Inc., Pasadena, 1990-95; dir. high performance simulationTech., Materials, and Process Simulation Ctr. Calif. Inst. Tech., Pasadena, 1995—; vis. scientist Matls. Lab., Wright Paterson AFB, Dayton, 1989-90; vis. assoc. chemistry Calif. Tech., 1991—. Contbr. articles to profl. jours. Mem. AAAS, Am. Phys. Soc., Am. Chem. Soc., Matls. Rsch. Soc. Office: Calif Inst Tech Material Simulation Ctr 139-74 Pasadena CA 91125

CAHAN, ROBERT BARMACH, psychiatrist, educator; s. Jacob Morris and Hilda G. (Barmach) C.; m. Bernice Alpert, Mar. 20, 1955; 1 child, James Samuel. AB, Syracuse U., 1949, MA, JD, 1950, JD; MD, Jefferson Med. Coll., 1954. Diplomate Am. Bd. Psychiatry and Neurology, Am. Bd. Forensic Psychiatry. Intern Nazareth (Pa.) Hosp., 1954-55; resident in psychiatry Norristown (Pa.) State Hosp., 1955-60; pvt. practice San Francisco, 1960—; sr. psychiatrist, cons. geriatrics rsch. project, U. Calif., San Francisco, 1960-65; dir. Immediate Psychiat. Aid and Referral Ctr., 1961-67; mem. clin. faculty, assoc. clin. prof. U. Calif., San Francisco, 1961—; clin. assoc. San Francisco Psychoanalytic Inst., 1962-74; psychiat. cons. Jail Med. Svc., San Francisco, 1974-76; med. dir. Consulting Med. Specialists, San Francisco, 1987—; adj. prof. U. Calif. San Francisco Mt. Zion Med. Ctr., 1964—; dir. Worker's Compensation Psychiat. Evaluation Program, 1983; faculty expert Hastings Coll. Advocacy, 1984—; mem. forensic panel U.S. Dist. Ct., U.S. Atty., Fed. Pub. Defender, U.S. Dept. Labor, U.S. Dept. Commerce, U.S. Dept. Interior, FAA, Calif. Med Bd., Nev. Med. Bd., Retirement System City and County San Francisco. Mem. AMA, San Francisco Ind. Practice Assn. (bd. dirs., ins. mediation com.), San Francisco Med. Soc., Calif. Med. Assn., Calif. Psychiat. Assn., No. Calif. Psychiat. Soc., Am. Acad. Psychiatry and Law (pres. No. Calif. chpt. 1984-90, dir. psychiat. cross-examination video workshop 1988, 90, 91), Calif. Soc. Indsl. Medicine and Surgery (exec. bd. dirs. 1982-88). Office: 825 Van Ness Ave # 401 San Francisco CA 94109-7837

CAHILL, EILEEN MARY, secondary education educator; b. Norwich, N.Y., Nov. 3, 1950; d. Kevin Tracey and Martha Sue (Eckard) C. BA, D'Youville Coll., Buffalo, 1972; MA, U. Toronto, 1974; PhD, SUNY, Buffalo, 1987. Cert. tchr., N.Y. English tchr. North Collins (N.Y.) Ctrl. Sch., 1972-85; curator of lit. Rosenbach Mus. and Libr., Phila., 1988-89; instr. English Temple U., Phila., 1987-88, Bryn Mawr (Pa.) Coll., 1987-88; English tchr. Marlborough Sch., L.A., 1989-96; mem. Stanford (Calif.) Ctr. for Rsch. on Women, 1990-94. Author articles. Coun. for Basic Edn. Nat. fellow for ind. study in humanities, 1993. Mem. MLA, Am. Conf. for Irish Studies, Irish Am. Cultural Inst. Democrat. Home: 7825 Fair Oaks Dr Clemmons NC 27012

CAHILL, LAWRENCE GLENN, JR., investigation firm owner; b. Modesto, Calif., Aug. 13, 1934; s. Lawrence Glenn and Marjorie Ellen (Malone) C.; m. Vera Louise Bettes, Apr. 11, 1955; children: Edwin James, Larry Allan, Joseph Lloyd, John Michael. AS, Modesto Jr. Coll.; BS, Stanislaus State U., Turlock, Calif., 1977; postgrad., FBI Acad./U. Va., 1978. Lic. pvt. investigator, Calif. Enlisted USAF, 1953, rose through ranks to master sgt., intelligence analyst, 1953-73, retired, 1973; sr. criminal investigator Dist. Atty.'s Office, Modesto, 1973-89; ret.; owner, investigator, cons. Larry Cahill & Assocs., Modesto, 1989—. Fellow Internat. Coll. Pvt. Police Practitioners, FBI Acad. Grads. Assn., Calif. Assn. Lic. Investigators, Calif. Pub. Defenders Assn., Nat. Assn. Investigative Specialists, Calif. Inst. Profl. Investigators, K.C. Office: Larry Cahill & Assocs PO Box 3150 Modesto CA 95353-3150

CAHILL, RICHARD FREDERICK, lawyer; b. Columbus, Nebr., June 18, 1953; s. Donald Francis and Hazel Fredeline (Garbers) C.; m. Helen Marie Girard, Dec. 4, 1982; children: Jacqueline Michelle, Catherine Elizabeth, Marc Alexander. Student, Worcester Coll., Oxford, 1973; BA with highest honors, UCLA, 1975; JD, U. Notre Dame, 1978. Bar: Calif. 1978, U.S. Dist. Ct. (ea. dist.) Calif. 1978, U.S. Dist. Ct. (cen. dist.) Calif. 1983, U.S. Dist. Ct. (so. dist.) Calif. 1992, U.S. Ct. Appeals (9th cir.) 1992. Dep. dist. atty. Tulare County Dist. Atty., Visalia, Calif., 1978-81; staff atty. Supreme Ct. of Nev., Carson City, 1981-83; assoc. Acret & Perochet, Brentwood, Calif., 1983-84, Thelen, Marrin, Johnson & Bridges, L.A., 1984-89; ptnr. Hammond Zuetel & Cahill, Pasadena, Calif., 1989—. Mem. Pasadena Bar Assn., Los Angeles County Bar Assn., Assn. So. Calif. Defense Counsel, Notre Dame Legal Aid and Defender Assn. (assoc. dir.), Phi Beta Kappa, Phi Alpha Delta (charter, v.p. 1977-78), Pi Gamma Mu, Phi Alpha Theta (charter pres. 1973-74), Phi Eta Sigma, Sigma Chi. Republican. Roman Catholic. Home: 201 Windwood Ln Sierra Madre CA 91024-2677 Office: Hammond Zuetel & Cahill 180 S Lake Ave Ste 540 Pasadena CA 91101-2619

CAHN, ROBERT NATHAN, physicist; b. N.Y.C., Dec. 20, 1944; s. Alan L. and Beatrice (Geballe) C.; m. Frances C. Miller, Aug. 22, 1965; children: Deborah, Sarah. BA, Harvard U., 1966; PhD, U. Calif., Berkeley, 1972. Rsch. assoc. Stanford (Calif.) Linear Accelerator Ctr., 1972-73; rsch. asst. prof. U. Wash., Seattle, 1973-76; asst. prof. U. Mich., Ann Arbor, 1976-78; assoc. rsch. prof. U. Calif., Davis, 1978-79; sr. staff physicist Lawrence Berkeley Nat. Lab, 1979-91; div. dir. Lawrence Berkeley Lab., 1991-96. Author: Semi Simple Lie Algebras and Their Representations, 1984; co-author: Experimental Foundations of Particle Physics, 1989. Fellow Am. Phys. Soc. (sec.-treas. divsn. particles and fields 1992-94).

CAI, XING YI, art historian, educator; b. Macao, China, July 16, 1939; came to U.S., 1988; s. Jun Guang and Ling Fang (Huang) C.; m. Kock Wah Lum, Oct. 1, 1970; children: Franklin Cai, Lance Cai. BA, Tchr's. U. of South China, 1963; MA, The Art Acad. of China, 1981. Vice chief editor History and Theory of the Fine Arts, Beijing, 1981-83; dir. ancient art divsn. The Art Acad. of China, Beijing, 1983-85; dean dept. of art history grad. sch. The Art Acad. of China, Beijing, 1985-87; vis. scholar, prof. U. Belgium, 1987-88, U. Kans., 1988-89, Stanford U., 1989-90, U. Calif. Berkeley, 1989-90; honor rsch. fellow Fine Arts Inst., Art Acad. of China, Beijing, 1990—; art cons., Oakland, San Francisco, 1993—. Author, editor: Dictionary of Connoisseur of Caligraphy and Painting, 1988; contbr. to Great Ency. of China, 1986-90; contbr. articles to profl. jours. Mem. Artists Assn. of China. Office: Pacific Renaissance Plz 388 9th St Ste 216 Oakland CA 94607

CAIN, PATRICIA JEAN, accountant; b. Decatur, Ill., Sept. 28, 1931; d. Paul George and Jean Margaret (Horne) Jacka; m. Dan Louis Cain, July 12, 1952; children: Mary Ann, Timothy George, Paul Louis. Student, U. Mich., 1949-52, Pasadena (Calif.) City Coll., 1975-76; BS in Acctg., Calif. State U., L.A., 1977, MBA, 1978; M in Taxation, Golden Gate U., Los Angeles, 1988; Diploma in Pastry, Hotel Ritz, France, 1991. CPA, Calif.; cert. personal fin. planner; cert. advanced fin. planner. Tax supr. Stonefield & Josephson, L.A., 1979-87; CFO Loubella Extendables, Inc., L.A., 1987-96; pvt. practice Pasadena, Calif., 1996—; participant program in bus. ethics U. So. Calif., L.A., 1986; trainer for A-Plus in house tax Arthur Andersen & Co., 1989-90; instr. Becker CPA Rev. Course, 1989-93. Bd. dirs. Sierra Madre coun. Girl Scouts U.S.A., 1968-73, treas., 1973-75, nat. del., 1975; mem. Town Hall, L.A., 1987—, L.A. Bus. Forum, 1991—. Listed as one of top six tax experts in L.A. by Money mag., 1987. Mem. AICPA (chair nat. tax teleconf. 1988, taxation com./forms subcom. 1994—), Am. Women's Soc. CPAs (bd. dirs. 1986-87, v.p. 1987-90), Calif. Soc. CPAs (chair free tax assistance program 1983-85, high road com. 1985-86, chair pub. rels. com. 1985-89, microcomputer users discussion group taxation com., fin. com./speaker computer show and conf. 1987-93, planning com. and speaker San Francisco Tax and Microcomputer show 1988, state com. on taxation 1991—, speaker Tax Update 1992, dir. L.A. chpt. 1993-95, v.p. 1995-96), Internat. Arabian Horse Assn., Wrightwood Country Club, Beta Alpha Psi. Democrat. Episcopalian.

CAIN, ROBERT JOSEPH, elementary school educator; b. Floral Park, N.Y., June 18, 1947; s. Edwin Thomas and Cecilia Marie (Dunn) C. BA in English, Hofstra U., 1972; BA in Edn., Ariz. State U., 1978, MEd, 1988. Cert. elem. tchr. Auditor Williamsburgh Savs. Bank, Bklyn., 1973-74; skip tracer, adjuster Ariz. Bank, Phoenix, 1974-75; 1st grade tchr. Paradise Valley Unified Sch. Dist. #69, Phoenix, 1979—. Actor City of Phoenix Shakespeare, 1978, Janus Theatre, Phoenix, 1980-81; actor, dir. Glendale Little Theatre, 1974-80; cantor St. Joseph's Ch., 1974—; benefactor Ariz. Opera, 1989—; supporter Met. Opera, 1980—; mem. Titanic Hist. Soc., 1980—. With U.S. Army, 1968-69. Republican. Roman Catholic. Home: 11012 N 45th St Phoenix AZ 85028-3013 Office: Quail Run Elem Sch 3303 E Utopia Rd Phoenix AZ 85024-3900

CAIN, SEYMOUR, historian, philosopher and writer; b. Chgo., May 1, 1914; s. Michael Max and Sarah Annabelle (Rabinowitz) Caann; m. Betty Jean Binder, Oct. 27, 1951; children: Henry George Binder, Robert Victor Binder, Michael Soren. PhD, U. Chgo., 1956. Mem., editor Inst. for Philos. Rsch., San Francisco, 1958-63; cons. to pres. Ctr. for Study of Dem. Instns., Santa Barbara, Calif., 1963-65; contbg. editor Annals of Am., Chgo., 1965-67; sr. editor Ency. Britannica, Chgo., 1967-73; humanist emeritus Tri-Coll. Univ., Moorhead, Minn., 1974-75; asst. prof. Indiana U. of Pa., 1977-78; ind. scholar and writer, San Diego, 1978—; vis. scholar U. Calif.-San Diego, La Jolla, 1990—; vis. prof. Western Mich. U., Kalamazoo, 1975-76, Kalamazoo Coll., 1975-76; organizer, participant Internat. Interdisciplinary Conf. on Martin Buber's Impact on Human Scis., San Diego State U., 1991; columnist Light Newspapers, San Diego, 1983-85. Author: Gabriel Marcel, 1963, 79, Gabriel Marcel's Theory of Religious Experience, 1995; assoc. editor, contbr. Martin Buber and the Human Sciences, 1996; contbg. author: The Persistence of Religions: Essays in honor of Kees W. Bolle, 1996; author guides to classic texts in theology, philosophy, lit., ethics, 1961-63; poetry pub. in Midstream, Christian Century, others; short stories pub. in Cosmopolitan, San Diego Writers monthly, others. Organizer, active various civil rights groups, Pacifica, Calif.; organizer, publicist University City Residents for Equity, San Diego. With Signal Corps, USAAF, 1941-45. U. Chgo. fellow, 1954-55, NEH fellow, 1978-79, 94. Mem. Am. Acad. Religion, Am. Soc. for Study of Religion, Soc. for Sci. Study of Religion, Mormon History Assn., San Diego Ind. Scholars, Nat. Writers Union. Democrat. Jewish. Home and Office: 2845 Arnoldson Ave San Diego CA 92122-2132

CAIN, SHANNON MARGARET, fundraising executive; b. Denver, June 3, 1964; d. Kathleen Margaret (Day) Day-Cain; 1 child, Brennan Margaret Cain-Nuccio. BA, U. Ariz., 1988. Mgr. special projects Fgn. Policy Assn., N.Y.C., 1989-91; fundraising assoc. Shakin, Lichty & Boreyko, N.Y.C., 1991-92; exec. dir. Women's Health Edn. Project, N.Y.C., 1992-94; pres. Cain & Co. Fundraising, Tucson, 1994—. Bd. dirs. Primavera Found., Tucson, 1995-97, Rose F. Kennedy Family Ctr., New York, 1993-95; active WHAM! Women's Health Action and Mobilization, New York, 1991-94. Mem bd. dirs., Southern Ariz. Women's Fund, 1997—.

CAIN, WILLIAM STANLEY, psychologist, educator; b. N.Y.C., Sept. 7, 1941; s. William Henry and June Rose (Stanley) C.; m. Claire Murphy, Oct. 30, 1993; children: Justin, Alison, Michael, Jennifer, Courtney. BS, Fordham U., 1963; MSc, Brown U., 1966, PhD, 1968. From asst. fellow to fellow John B. Pierce Lab., New Haven, 1967-94; from instr. to assoc. prof. depts. Epidemiology, Pub. Health, and Psychology Yale U., New Haven, 1967-84, prof. dept. epidemiology, pub. health, psychology, 1984-94; prof. surgery (otolaryngology) U. Calif., San Diego, 1994—; mem. sensory disorders study sect. NIH, Bethesda, Md., 1991-95; mem. sci. adv. bd. Ctr. Indoor Air Rsch., Linthicum, Md., 1991—. Mem. editl. bd. Chem. Senses,

1985-94; editl. adv. bd. Indoor Air, 1990—, Physiology and Behavior, 1995-96; editor 5 books, 1971—; contbr. numerous articles to profl. jours. Recipient Crosby Field award ASHRAE, 1984, Jacob Javits/Claude Pepper award NIH, 1984, Sense of Smell award, Fragrance Rsch. Fund, 1986. Fellow APA, ASHRAE, Am. Psychol. Soc., Acad. Indoor Air Rsch.; mem. Assn. Chemoreception Scis. (exec. chmn. 1983-84), N.Y. Acad. Scis. (pres. 1986). Home: 4459 Nabal Dr La Mesa CA 91941-7168 Office: U Calif Dept Surgery 9500 Gilman Dr # Mc0957 La Jolla CA 92093-5003

CAINE, CAROLYN MOORE, activist, publishing executive, author, consultant; b. Oakland, Calif., June 10, 1922; d. Rollin Bascom and Mildred (Knox) M.; m. George Eccles Caine, Jan. 24, 1946 (dvi. July 1, 1972); children: Lynda, George Jr., Lisa. Student, Berkeley (Calif.) H.S., 1940. Asst. to dir. ARC, Oakland, Calif., 1943-44; social worker Children's Hosp., Oakland, Calif., 1944-45; asst. to treas. Markle Found., N.Y.C., 1947-49; rsch. dir. Data Rsch. Inst., Salt Lake City, 1970-71; cons., mem. panel NEA, Washington, 1974-78; bd. dirs., pres. Utah Environ. Ctr., Salt Lake City, 1973-79. Author: On Your Own in San Francisco, 1988, rev. edit., 1996. State chair ARTRAIN, Salt Lake City, 1972-73, Utah's Festival of Arts for Young, Salt Lake City, 1972-78; bd. dirs., chair Women's Coun. U. Utah, Salt Lake City, 1972-77; adv. Congressman Lloyd, Salt Lake City, 1975-77; mem., officer Sister City Com., Salt Lake City, 1974-79; cons. Sustainable San Francisco, 1995-96. Recipient Civic Beautification award Salt Lake City, 1971, award of Merit Met. Transp. Commn., San Francisco, 1996; named Most Admired Woman Phi Mu Sorority, 1977. Mem. Internat. Diplomacy Coun., Sr. Action Network, Jr. League, San Francisco Planning and Urban Rsch. Assn. Office: Blue Pearl Press PO Box 460548 San Francisco CA 94146

CAINE, STEPHEN HOWARD, data processing executive; b. Washington, Feb. 11, 1941; s. Walter E. and Jeanette (Wenborne) C. Student Calif. Inst. Tech., 1958-62. Sr. programmer Calif. Inst. Tech., Pasadena, 1962-65, mgr. sys. programming, 1965-69, mgr. programming, 1969-70; pres. Caine, Farber & Gordon, Inc., Pasadena, 1970—; lectr. applied sci. Calif. Inst. Tech., Pasadena, 1965-71, vis. assoc. elec. engring., 1976, vis. assoc. computer sci., 1976-84. Dir. San Gabriel Valley Learning Ctrs., 1992-95. Mem. Pasadena Tournament of Roses Assn., 1976—. Mem. AAAS, Nat. Assn. Corrosion Engrs., Am. Ordnance Assn., Assn. Computing Machinery, Athanaeum Club (Pasadena), Houston Club. Home: 77 Patrician Way Pasadena CA 91105-1039

CAIRNS, DIANE PATRICIA, motion picture executive; b. Fairbanks, Alaska, Mar. 2, 1957; d. Dion Melvin and Marsha Lala (Andrews) C. BBA, U. So. Calif., 1980. Literary agt. Sy Fischer Agy., L.A., 1980-85; sr. v.p. Internat. Creative Mgmt., L.A., 1985-96; sr. v.p. prodn. Universal Pictures, L.A., 1996—. Mem. NOW, Acad. Motion Picture Arts and Scis., Women in Film, Amnesty Internat., L.A. County Mus. of Art, Mus. of Contemporary Art (L.A.).

CAIRNS, ELTON JAMES, chemical engineering educator; b. Chgo., Nov. 7, 1932; s. James Edward and Claire Angele (Larzelere) C.; m. Miriam Esther Citron, Dec. 26, 1974; 1 dau., Valerie Helen; stepchildren: Benjamin David, Joshua Aaron. B.S. in Chemistry, Mich. Tech. U., Houghton, 1955; B.S. in Chem. Engring, 1955; Ph.D. in Chem. Engring. (Dow Chem. Co. fellow, univ. fellow, Standard Oil Co. Calif. grantee, NSF fellow), U. Calif., Berkeley, 1959. Phys. chemist GE Rsch. Lab., Schenectady, 1959-66; group leader, then sect. head chem. engring. div. Argonne (Ill.) Nat. Lab., 1966-73; asst. head electrochemistry dept. GM Rsch. Labs., 1973-78; assoc. lab. dir., dir. energy and environment divsn. Lawrence Berkeley Nat. (Calif.) Lab., 1978-96, head, Energy Conversion and Storage Program, 1982—; prof. chem. engring. U. Calif., Berkeley, 1978—; cons. in field; mem. numerous govt. panels; Croft lectr. U. Mo., 1979. Author: (with H.A. Liebhafsky) Fuel Cells and Fuel Batteries, 1968; mem. editor bd. Advances in Electrochemistry and Electrochm. Engring., 1974—; div. editor Jour. Electrochem. Soc., 1968-91; regional editor Electrochimica Acta, 1984—; contbr. articles to profl. jours. Recipient IR-100 award, 1968, Centennial medal Case Western Res. U., 1980, R&D 100 award, 1992; named McCabe lectr. U. N.C., 1993; grantee DuPont Co., 1956. Fellow Am. Insts. Chemists, Electrochem. Soc. (chmn. phys. electrochem. divsn. 1981-84, v.p. 1986-89, pres. 1989-90, Francis Mills Turner award 1963); mem. AIChE (chmn. energy conversion com. 1970-94), AAAS, Am. Chem. Soc., Internat. Soc. Electrochemistry (chmn. electrochem. energy conversion divsn. 1977-85, U.S. nat. sec. 1983-89, v.p. 1984-88, pres.-elect 1997-98), Intersoc. Energy Conversion Engring. Conf. (steering com. 1970—, gen. chmn. 1976, 90, 97, program chmn. 1983). Home: 239 Langlie Ct Walnut Creek CA 94598-3615 Office: Lawrence Berkeley Lab 1 Cyclotron Rd Berkeley CA 94720

CALAS, NAPOLEON EVANS, medical laboratory administrator; b. Pontiac, Mich., June 12, 1951; s. Angelo and Anna Louise (O'Brien) C.; m. Carolyn Ann Cooper, Sept. 24, 1977 (div. 1992); children: Megan Ann, Christopher Evans; m. Lonna Rae Bernhard, Aug. 7, 1992; 1 child, Hannah Beth. BS in Zoology, Mich. State U., 1973, BS in Med. Tech., 1974; MBA, U. Mich., 1979. Fin. analyst Hospital Affiliates, Nashville, 1979-80; administr. Rogers City (Mich.) Hosp., 1980-84; divsn. pres. Internat. Clin. Labs., Seattle, 1984-88; divsn. mgr. Nat. Health Labs., Kent, Wash., 1989-94; v.p., owner Sterilchek Laboratories, 1995—; v.p. corp. devel. Dynacare Labs., 1996—. Home: 20314 42nd Ave NE Lake Forest Park WA 98155-1616

CALDER, ROBERT MAC, aerospace engineer; b. Vernal, Utah, Oct. 16, 1932; s. Edwin Harold and Sydney (Goodrich) C.; m. Yoshiko Iemura, Feb. 14, 1959; children: Suzanne, Alexis, Irene, John. BSChemE, U. Utah, 1956, M.S. in Math. and Geology (NSF grantee), 1967; postgrad., U. Wash., 1964, Utah State U., 1965, U. Iowa, 1966. Cert. secondary tchr., Utah. Tchr. Utah Pub. Schs., 1958-79. V.p. Sydney Corp., Bountiful, Utah, 1958-82; sr. engr. aero. div. Hercules Inc., Magna, Utah, 1979—; owner RMC Enterprises, Nations Imports; cons. in field, 1960—; cultural exchange participant to Israel, Egypt, 1983, 87. Active Boy Scouts Am., 1945-75, instr., Philmont Scout Ranch, 1972, asst. scoutmaster Nat. Jamboree Troop, 1973; instr. hunter safety and survival, Utah Dept. Fish and Game, 1964-74; state advisor U.S. Congl. Adv. Bd., 1982—; mem. Rep. Nat. Com. Capt. USAF, 1956-70. Mem. AIAA, NRA (life), Am. Quarter Horse Assn., Internat. Platform Assn., Oratorio Soc. Utah, The Planetary Soc., Hercules Toastmasters Club (treas. 1980, v.p. edn. 1981, pres. 1982), N.Am. Fishing Club (life). Mormon. Home: PO Box 268 Bountiful UT 84011-0268 Office: PO Box 194 Kaysville UT 84037-0194

CALDERWOOD, NEIL MOODY, retired telephone traffic engineer, consultant; b. Vinalhaven, Maine, June 19, 1910; s. Austin Shirley and Eliza Louise (Carver) C.; m. Katherine Foster Mariani, Oct. 13, 1940; children: John Carver, James Foster, Bruce Glidden. BSCE, U. Maine, Orono, 1932, MS in Math., 1935. Sr. engr. Resettlement Adminstrn., Camden, Maine, 1935-37; sr. engr. Pacific Telephone, San Francisco, 1937-42, staff engr., dist. traffic engr., gen. traffic engr., staff dir. network ops., 1946-75; telecom. expert Internat. Telecom. Union, UN, Geneva, 1975-76; cons. telephone numbering plans Libyan Govt., Benghazi, Tripoli, 1976; traffic engring. cons. Las Vegas Telephone Co., 1952, Hawaiian Telephone Co., 1963; expert witness Public Utilities Commn. of Calif. hearings on all number calling cases, San Francisco and L.A., 1962-64. Lt. comdr. USNR, 1942-46. Mem. Am. Rose Soc., Pierce-Arrow Soc., Telephone Pioneers, Phi Gamma Delta. Republican. Home: 49 Dolores Way Orinda CA 94563-4154

CALDERWOOD, WILLIAM ARTHUR, physician; b. Wichita, Kans., Feb. 3, 1941; s. Ralph Bailey and Janet Denise (Christ) C.; m. Nancy Jo Crawford, Mar. 31, 1979; children: Lisa Beth, William Arthur II. MD, U. Kans., 1968. Diplomate Am. Bd. Family Practice. Intern Wesley Med. Ctr., Wichita, 1968-69; gen. practice family medicine Salina, Kans., 1972-80, Peoria, Ariz., 1980—; med. dir. First Am. Home Care, 1994—, First Am. Homecare, 1995—; pres. staff St. John's Hosp., Salina, 1976; 28th jud. dist. coroner State of Kans., Wichita, 1978-80; cons. in addiction medicine VA Hosp., 1989-94; bd. dirs. Pelms House. Inventor, patentee lighter-than-air-furniture. Bd. dirs. Pelms House (For Chem. Dependence), 1995—, Gen. Health Medcare, 1995—. Fellow Am. Acad. Family Physicians; mem. AMA, Ariz. Med. Soc. (physicians med. health com., exec. com. 1988-92), Maricopa County Med. Soc., Ariz. Acad. Family Practice (med. dir. N.W. Orgn. Vol. alternatives 1988-91), Am. Med. Soc. on Alcoholism and Other Drug Dependencies (cert.), Shriners. Home: 7015 W Calavar Rd Peoria AZ 85381-4706 Office: 14300 W Granite Valley Dr Sun City West AZ 85375-5783

CALDWELL, CAREY TERESA, museum curator; b. McMinnville, Tenn., July 24, 1954; d. Harold Glenn Caldwell and Nancy Perkins (Bragg) Caldwell-Tedesco. BA in History, Queens Coll., Charlotte, N.C., 1974; postgrad., U. S.C., 1974-75, U. N.C., 1976; MA in Anthropology/Museology, U. Wash., 1987. Archaeology, field, lab. and rsch. asst. Ninety Six (S.C.) Hist. Site, 1974-75; tribal curator Suquamish (Wash.) Indian Tribe, 1977-78, dir. Suquamish Tribal Cultural Ctr. and Mus., 1979-85; cons. Bainbridge Island (Wash.) Japanese-Am. Heritage Project, 1986-87; cons. Fed. Cylinder Project Am. Folklife Ctr., Libr. of Congress, Washington, 1986-87; sr. curator history Oakland Mus. of Calif., 1987-96, chief curator history, 1996—; cons., strategic planner, advisor to numerous mus., orgns., Indian tribes and cmty. groups including Nat. Mus. of Am. Indian, Smithsonian Instn., NEH, Wash. State Heritage Coun., 1978-85; panelist, reviewer NEH, 1986—; grants reviewer Inst. Mus. Svcs., 1986; cons. United Indians of All Tribes Found., Seattle, 1992-96; evaluator, cons. Osage Tribal Mus., 1993; cons. Native Am. Archives Project, 1981-82; cons. Minn. Hist. Soc., 1984-85, 94-95, Western Alliance of Art Adminstrs., 1993-95. Fellow Am. Anthropol. Assn.; mem. Am. Assn. Mus., Western Mus. Assn. (v.p. 1990-92), Coun. for Mus. Anthropology (bd. dirs. 1988-89), Internat. Coun. Mus., Am. Assn. for State and Local History (edn. com. 1981-82, publs. com. 1987-92, program com. 1989, ann. mtg., common agenda adv. bd. 1990-92, award of merit 1993), Wash. Mus. Assn. Democrat. Office: Oakland Mus Calif 1000 Oak St Oakland CA 94607-4820

CALDWELL, COURTNEY LYNN, lawyer, real estate consultant; b. Washington, Mar. 5, 1948; d. Joseph Morton and Moselle (Smith) C. Student, Duke U., 1966-68, U. Calif., Berkeley, 1967, 1968-69; BA, U. Calif., Santa Barbara, 1970, MA, 1975; JD with highest honors, George Washington U., 1982. Bar: D.C. 1984, Wash. 1986, Calif. 1989. Jud. clk. U.S. Ct. Appeals for 9th Cir., Seattle, 1982-83; assoc. Arnold & Porter, Washington, 1983-85, Perkins Coie, Seattle, 1985-88; dir. western ops. MPC Assocs., Inc., Irvine, Calif., 1988-91, sr. v.p., 1991—. Bd. dirs. Univ. Town Ctr. Assn., 1994; bd. dirs. Habitat for Humanity, Orange County, 1993-94, chair legal com., 1994. Named Nat. Law Ctr. Law Rev. Scholar, 1981-82. Mem. Calif. Bar Assn., Wash. State Bar Assn., D.C. Bar Assn., Urban Land Inst. Office: MPC Assocs Inc 1451 Quail St Ste 102 Newport Beach CA 92660-2747

CALDWELL, DAN EDWARD, political science educator; b. Oklahoma City, May 12, 1948; s. John Edward and Hester Evelyn (Kiehn) C.; m. Lora Jean Ferguson, Mar. 21, 1970; children: Beth Christine, Ellen Claire, John Ferguson. BA in History, Stanford U., 1970, MA in Polit. Sci., PhD in Polit. Sci., 1978; MA in Internat. Rels., Tufts U., 1971. Staff mem. Office Emergency Preparedness, Exec. Office of Pres., Washington, 1972; rsch. and teaching fellow Stanford (Calif.) U., 1975-78; assoc. dir. Ctr. for Fgn. Policy Devel., Brown U., Providence, 1982-84; prof. polit. sci. Pepperdine U., Malibu, Calif., 1978-82, 84—, pres. faculty orgn., 1980-81, 89-90; dir. Forum for U.S.-Soviet Dialogue, Washington, 1984—, pres., 1989-91. Author: American-Soviet Relations, 1981, The Dynamics of Domestic Politics and Arms Control, 1991; editor: Henry Kissinger, 1985. Elder Pacific Palisades (Calif.) Presbyn. Ch. With USN, 1971-74. Named Prof. of Yr., Pepperdine U. Student Alumni Assn., 1992.; rsch. fellow U.S. Inst. Peace, 1987, Pew faculty fellow Harvard U. Kennedy Sch. Govt., 1990. Mem. Internat. Inst. Strategic Studies (London), Am. Polit. Sci. Assn., Internat. Studies Assn. (sect. exec. com. 1982-87, dir. sect. on Am.-Soviet rels. 1984-86, fellow 1977), Coun. on Fgn. Rels. Home: 654 Radcliffe Ave Pacific Palisades CA 90272-4331 Office: Pepperdine U Social Sci Divsn 24255 Pacific Coast Hwy Malibu CA 90263-0001

CALDWELL, HOWARD BRYANT, English language educator; b. London, Ky., Jan. 28, 1944; s. Stratton and Linda Emily (Bryant) C. BA, Berea (Ky.) Coll., 1966; MA, U. Calif., Berkeley, 1977. Cert. adult edn. tchr. Tchr. L.A. Unified Sch. Dist., 1977—. Mem. L.A. County Mus. Art, N.Y. Met. Mus. Art, L.A. World Affairs Coun. With USAF, 1966-70, The Philippines. Mem. United Tchrs. L.A., London Victory Club. Republican. Baptist.

CALDWELL, JOHN WINSTON, III, petroleum engineer; b. Gainesville, Fla., Nov. 21, 1955; s. John Winston Jr. and Barbara T. (Thostenson) C.; m. Melissa Ann Myers, June 26, 1981; children: Graham Colin, Alexandra Alyssa, Evan Benjamin. BSCE, U. Idaho, 1977. Registered profl. engr., Okla. Prodn. engr. Texaco, Inc., Hobbs, N.Mex., 1978-80; drilling/prodn. engr. Southland Royalty Co., Farmington, N.Mex., 1980-82; reservoir engr. Southland Royalty Co., Oklahoma City, Okla., 1982-84, Houston, Tex., 1985; sr. reservoir engr. Meridian Oil Inc., Billings, Mont., 1986, regional joint interest engr., 1987; regional reservoir engr. Meridian Oil Inc., Farmington, N.Mex., 1988-89, regional drilling engr., 1990-95, regional planning engr., 1996—; expert witness on reservoir issues in Okla., Tex., Colo., N.D., Mont., N.Mex., Ark. State Oil Commns. Mem. Soc. of Petroleum Engrs. Home: 4109 St Michaels Dr Farmington NM 87401 Office: Meridian Oil Inc 3535 E 30th St Farmington NM 87402-8801

CALDWELL, JONI, psychology educator, small business owner; b. Chgo., Aug. 8, 1948; d. Bruce Wilber and Eloise Ethel (Ijams) C. BS in Home Econs. Edn., Mich. State U., 1970; MA in Psychology, U. San Francisco, 1978. Cret. high sch. and coll. tchr., Mich. Instr. Northwestern Mich. Coll., Traverse City, 1972-78, Mott Community Coll., Flint, Mich., 1974-78; tchr. Grand Blanc (Mich.) High Sch., 1970-73, Clio (Mich.) High Sch., 1974-78; parent educator, vol. coord. Family Resource Ctr., Monterey, Calif., 1981-82; owner, gen. mgr. Futons & Such, Monterey, 1982—; instr. psychology Hartnell Coll., Salinas, Calif., 1993-96; spl. project dir. YWCA, 1996-97; instr. women's studies Monterey Peninsula Coll., 1997. Bd. dirs., v.p., pres. Ch. Religious Sci., Monterey, 1984-87; mem. bd. stewards Pacific Coast Ch., Monterey, 1988-92, v.p.; bd. dirs. YWCA, Monterey, 1986-88, mem. nominating com., 1995—; vol., fund raiser Buddy Program, 1992—; membership com. Profl. Womens Network, 1989—. Mem. New Monterey Bus. Assn. (past pres., bd. dirs. 1984-95, v.p. 1993—), Monterey C. of C. (cons. workshop com. 1985-87, Small Bus. Excellence award 1990). Home: 29 Portola Ave Monterey CA 93940-3731 Office: Futons & Such 475 Alvarado St Monterey CA 93940-1457

CALDWELL, MARCIA DIANE, nurse; b. Turlock, Calif., June 12, 1947; d. Stanley Ellsworth Oie and Lydia Cornelia (Coey) Hammer; m. Gary Allen Caldwell, Dec. 21, 1968; children: David Alan, Michael Benjamin. BS in Bus., Fresno State U., 1969; AS in Nursing, Coll. Sequoias, 1985; cert. lactation educator, UCLA, 1994. Cert. inpatient obstetric nurse. CNA-OB Visalia (Calif.) Cmty. Hosp., 1977-85, RN II family birthing, 1987-95; RN med./surg. Kaweah Delta Hosp., Visalia, Calif., 1985-87, RN II Family Birthing Ctr., 1994—; breastfeeding instr., prenatal classes Sierra Med. Group, 1979-85; lectr. La Leche League, Calif., 1995. Mem. Assn. Women's Health, Obstetric and Neonatal Nurses, Internat. Lactation Cons. Assn. Home: 11971 Avenue 274 Visalia CA 93277-9301 Office: Kaweah Delta Hosp Family Birthing Ctr 400 W Mineral King Ave Visalia CA 93291-6237

CALDWELL, STRATTON FRANKLIN, kinesiologist; b. Mpls., Aug. 25, 1926; s. Kenneth Simms and Margaret Mathilda (Peterson) C.; m. Mary Lynn Shaffer, Aug. 28, 1955 (div. May 1977); children: Scott Raymond, Karole Elizabeth; m. Sharee' Deanna Ockerman, Aug. 6, 1981; 1 stepchild, Shannon Sharee' Calder. Student, San Diego State Coll., 1946-48; BS in Edn. cum laude, U. So. Calif., 1951, PhD in Phys. Edn., 1966; MS in Phys. Edn., U. Oreg., 1953. Teaching asst. dept. phys. edn. UCLA, 1953-54, assoc. in phys. edn., 1957-65, vis. asst. prof. phys. edn., 1967; dir. phys. edn. Regina (Sask., Can.) Young Men's Christian Assn., 1954-56; tchr. sec. grades, dir. athletic Queen Elizabeth Jr.-Sr. High Sch., Calgary, Alta., Can., 1956-57; asst. prof. phys. edn. San Fernando Valley State Coll., Northridge, Calif., 1965-68, assoc. prof., 1968-71; prof. phys. edn. dept. kinesiology Calif. State U., Northridge, 1971-90, prof. kinesiology, 1990-92, prof. kinesiology emeritus, 1992; vis. asst. prof. phys. edn. UCLA, 1967; vis. assoc. prof. phys. edn. U. Wash., Seattle, 1968, U. Calif., Santa Barbara, 1969. Author (with Cecil and Joan Martin Hollingsworth) Golf, 1959, (with Rosalind Cassidy) Humanizing Physical Education: Methods for the Secondary School Movement Program, 5th edit., 1975; also poetry, book chpts., articles in profl. jours., book revs. With USN, 1944-46. Recipient Meritorious Performance and Profl. Promise award Calif. state U., 1986, 87, 89, Disting. Teaching award, 1992; AAPHERD fellow, 1962, Am. Coll. Sports Medicine fellow, 1965, Can. Assn. for Health, Phys. Edn., and Recreation fellow, 1971. Fellow Am. Alliance for Health, Phys. Edn., Recreation and Dance (Centennial Commn. 1978-85, cert. appreciation 1985), Am. Coll. Sports Medicine; mem. Calif. Assn. for Health, Phys. Edn., Recreation and Dance (pres. L.A. coll. and univ. unit 1969-70, v.p. phys. edn. com. 1970-71, mem. editorial bd. CAHPER Jour. 1970-71, mem. forum 1970-71, Disting. Svc. award 1974, Honor award 1988, Verne Landreth award 1992), Nat. Assn. for Phys. Edn. in Higher Edn. (charter), Sport Art Acad., Nat. Assn. for Sport and Phys. Edn., N.Y. Acad. Scis., N.Am. Soc. for Sports History, Sport Lit. Assn., Acad. Am. Poets, Phi Epsilon Kappa (Svc. award 1980), Alpha Tau Omega (charter,Silver Circle award 1976), Phi Delta Kappa, Phi Kappa Phi, others. Republican. Mem. Christian Ch. Home: 80 N Kanan Rd Oak Park CA 91301-1105 *The consumate teacher is the artist who consistently attempts to deepen and enrich human experience, to weave the fabric of feeling, mood, attitude and idea into a tailor-made garment of personal meaning.*

CALDWELL, THOMAS MICHAEL, facilities director; b. Beardstown, Ill., June 29, 1946; s. Carl and E. Lou (Bullard) C.; children: Tamera Lynn, Thomas Adam, Elizabeth R., Benjamin T. BS, U. N.Mex., 1975. Ptnr. Solar Retrofit Inc., Albuquerque, N.Mex., 1978-81; maint. data collections W.B.C. Consultants, Tucson, 1981-82; facilities dir. EG&G, Albuquerque, 1983-90; owner T's Weldry, Los Lunas, N.Mex., 1988--; ptnr. D&T Solar Lazers, Albuquerque, 1983; exec. v.p. Solar Detox. Corp., Albuquerque, 1990—. Co-designer human powered vehicle, Boing 888. With USN, 1965-69. Mem. Rio Grande Human Powered Vehicle Assn. (pres.). Democrat. Roman Catholic. Home and Office: 2291 Hwy 304 # 4 Belen NM 87002

CALDWELL, WALTER EDWARD, editor, small business owner; b. L.A., Dec. 29, 1941; s. Harold Elmer and Esther Ann (Fuller) C.; m. Donna Edith Davis, June 27, 1964; 1 child, Arnie-Jo. AA, Riverside City Coll., 1968. Sales and stock professional Sears Roebuck & Co., Riverside, Calif., 1963-65; dispatcher Rohr Corp., Riverside, Calif., 1965-67; trainee Aetna Fin., Riverside, 1967-68; mgr. Aetna Fin., San Bruno, Cal., 1968-70, Amfac Thrift & Loan, Oakland, Calif., 1970-74; free lance writer San Jose, Calif., 1974-76; news dir. Sta. KAVA Radio, Burney, Cal., 1977-79; editor-pub. Mountain Echo, Fall River Mills, Calif., 1979—. Contbg. author Yearbook of Modern Poetry, 1976. Del. Farmers and Ranchers Congress, St. Louis, 1985; participant Am. Leadership Conf., San Diego, 1989; pres. United Way, Burney, 1979, co-chmn., 1977, chmn., 1979; disaster relief worker ARC, Redding, Calif., 1988-91, disaster action team leader, 1991-95; bd. dirs. Shasta County Women's Refuge, Redding, 1988-91, Shasta County Econ. Devel. Corp., 1986-90, Crossroads, 1985; bd. dirs. Shasta County Econ. Devel. Task Force, 1985-86, exec. bd. dirs., 1988; pres. Intermountain Devel. Corp., 1989; leader Girl Scouts U.S.A., San Jose, 1973-76; announcer various local parades; trustee Mosquito Abatement Dist., Burney, 1978-87, 89—, chmn., 1990—; commr. Burney Fire Protection Dist., 1987-91, v.p., 1990, pres., 1991; chmn. Burney Basin Days Com., 1984-95, Hay Days Com., 1995-96; candidate for Shasta County Bd. Suprs., 1992; alt. commr. Local Agy. Formation Commn. Shasta County, 1995—. With USMC, 1959-63. Mem. Burney Basin C. of C. (advt. chmn. 1982, Cmty. Action award 1990, 93), Fall River Valley C. of C. (bd. dirs. 1991, pres. 1995), Internat. Platform Assn., Am. Legion (citation of recognition 1987, Cmty. Action award 1989, 93), Calif. Newspaper Pubs. Assn., Profl. Journalism Assn., Rotary (pres. 1977-78, chmn. bike race 1981-85), Lions (student spkr. chmn. Fall River 1983—, 1st v.p. 1991, pres. 1992, co-chmn. disaster com., newsletter chmn. dist. 4-C1 1989-91), Moose, Masons (master 1995), Shriners (sec.-treas. 1992-94), Nat. Press Club, Calif. Press Assn. Republican. Office: Mountain Echo Main St Fall River Mills CA 96028 also: PO Box 224 Fall River Mills CA 96028-0224

CALDWELL, WILLIAM MACKAY, III, business executive; b. Los Angeles, Apr. 6, 1922; s. William Mackay II and Edith Ann (Richards) C.; BS, U. So. Calif., 1943; MBA, Harvard U., 1948; m. Mary Louise Edwards, Jan. 16, 1946 (dec. 1980); children: William Mackay IV, Craig Edwards, Candace Louise; m. Jean Bledsoe, Apr. 27, 1985. Sec.-treas., dir. Drewry Photocolor Corp., 1957-60, Adcolor Photo Corp., 1957-60; treas., dir. Drewry Bennetts Corp., 1959-60; sr. v.p., chief fin. officer Am. Cement Corp., 1960-67; sr. v.p. corp., 1966-70, pres. cement and concrete group, 1967-70; pres., chmn. bd., chief exec. officer Van Vorst Industries, 1969; pres. Van Vorst Corp., Washington, 1969-77; chmn. bd., pres. So. Cross Industries, U.S. Bedding Co., 1979-84, St. Croix Mfg. Co., 1979-81, Hawaiian Cement Corp.; pres. Englander Co., 1979-84; v.p., dir. Am. Cement Internat. Corp., Am. Cement Properties; chmn. Kyco Industries Inc., 1982—; pres. BHI Inc., 1984—; cons. prof. U. So. Calif. Mem. men's com. Los Angeles Med. Center; bd. dirs. Commerce Assocs., Calif. Mus. Sci. and Industry, U. So. Calif. Assocs., bd. dirs. Pres.'s Circle; bd. dirs. Am. Cement Found. Served to lt. USNR, 1943-46. Mem. Newcomen Soc., Friends Huntington Library, L.A. Country Club, Town Hall Club, Calif. Club (L.A.), Trojan Club, Annandale Golf Club, Eldorado Country Club, Chaparral Golf Club, Harvard Bus. Sch. of So. Calif. (dir. 1960-63), Kappa Alpha, Alpha Delta Sigma, Alpha Pi Omega. Presbyterian. Office: PO Box 1151 Pasadena CA 91102-1151

CALDWELL-PORTENIER, PATTY JEAN GROSSKOPF, advocate, educator; b. Davenport, Iowa, Sept. 28, 1937; d. Bernhard August and Leontine Virginia (Carver) Grosskopf; m. Donald Eugene Caldwell Mar. 29, 1956 (dec. Feb. 1985); children: John Alan, Jennifer Lynn Caldwell Lear; m. Walter J. Portenier, Oct. 3, 1992. BA, State U. Iowa, 1959. Hearing officer Ill. State Bd. Edn., Springfield, 1979-91, Appellate Court, 1986-91; pres., bd. dirs. Tri-County Assn. for Children With Learning Disabilities, Moline, Ill., 1972-79; adv. vol., Iowa and Ill., 1979-91; mem. adv. coun. Prairie State Legal Svcs., Inc., Rock Island, Ill., 1984-91; mem. profl. svcs. com. United Cerebral Palsy N.W. Ill., Rock Island, 1986-88; arbitrator Am. Arbitration Assn., Chgo., 1986-91, Better Bus. Bur., Davenport, 1986-91. Founder, pres. Quad Cities Diabetes Assn., Moline, 1969-72, bd. dirs., 1973—; mem. com. Moline Internat. Yr. Disabled, 1981; mem. Assn. for Retarded Citizens, Rock Island, 1987; mem. vol. Coun. on Children at Risk, Moline, 1988-91; reader for the blind Sta. WVIK, Rock Island, 1989-91. Mem. Ill. Assn. for Children with Learning Disabilities (bd. dirs., adv. 1980-83). Methodist. Home and Office: 2443 La Condessa Dr Los Angeles CA 90049-1221

CALECA, JOHN EDWARD, secondary education educator; b. Salinas, Calif., Feb. 18, 1947; s. Vito Peter and Irene Ellen (Mandarini) C.; children: Justen Edward Thomas, Brendan Peter. BA, Calif. State U., San Jose, 1969, MA, 1973; MA, U. Santa Clara, 1975, postgrad., 1977. Lic. fin. real estate and fin. guide coun. Budget asst. Santa Clara County Office of Edn., 1976; v.p. adminstrv. svcs. King City Joint Union H.S. Dist., 1978-79; cons., instr. Los Gatos (Calif.) Joint Union H.S. Dist., 1978-79; pers. asst., prin., counselor Fremont Union H.S. Dist., Sunnyvale, Calif., 1974-77, govt. projects adminstr., 1977-78, tchr., 1971-84, 86—. Mem. Calif. Tchrs. Assn. Home: 16110 Matilija Dr Los Gatos CA 95030-3083 Office: Fremont Union H S Dist PO Box F Sunnyvale CA

CALHOUN, JOHN JOSEPH, advertising executive; b. Lafayette, Ind., May 27, 1964; s. Robert James and Elizabeth (Callaghan) C. BS, Purdue U., 1987; MBA, Harvard, 1992. Asst. brand mgr. Procter & Gamble, Cin., 1987-90; cons. Corp. Decision, Boston, 1991; asst. brand mgr. Procter & Gamble, Hunt Valley, Md., 1992-93; mktg. mgr. Levi Strauss & Co., San Francisco, 1993-94; acct. supr. Foote, Conc & Belding, San Francisco, 1994-95; v.p., mgmt. supr. Citron Haligman Bedecarre, San Francisco, 1995-96, v.p., acct. dir./dir. acct. mgmt., 1997—.

CALIENDO, THEODORE JOSEPH, pediatrician, neonatalogist; b. Bklyn., Nov. 9, 1941; s. Leo J. and Anna C.; m. Arlene Mann, Jan. 7, 1970 (div. Aug. 1984); children: Michael, Robert, Barbra, David. BS, St. John's U., Bklyn., 1962; MD, N.Y. Med. Coll., 1966. Intern, resident Cedars Sinai Med. Ctr., L.A., 1966-69; pediatrician, neonatalogist Kaiser-Permanente, Mission Viejo, Calif., 1973—; attending physician Cedars Sinai Med. Ctr., L.A., 1971-81, Kaiser Hosp., Anaheim, Calif., 1979—; asst. prof. pediatrics UCLA Med. Sch., 1971-82. Lt. comdr. USN, 1969-71. Fellow Am. Acad. Pediatrics; mem. L.A. Pediatric Soc., Ritz Bros., Monarch Bay Club, Rancho Niquel Club, Ferarri Club Am. Office: Kaiser Permanente 23781 Maquina Mission Viejo CA 92691-2716

CALKINS, BRUCE EDGAR, computer company executive; b. Sacramento, Mar. 9, 1952; s. Dixon H. and Kathryn L. Calkins; m. Nancy Greig, Jan. 11, 1976; 1 child, Matthew Ryan. AA in Drafting Tech., Am. River Coll., Sacramento, 1978; BS, U. San Francisco, 1983. Drafter, CAD operator Lawrence Livermore (Calif.) Nat. Lab., 1978-81; CAD designer Bechtel Petroleum, San Francisco, 1981-84; CAD support mgr. USN, Mare Island, Calif., 1984-93; sr. mgr., fed. SIG chmn. Intergraph Corp., Bellevue, Wash., 1993-95; exec. mgr. vehicle design dept. Intergraph Corp., Huntsville, Ala., 1995—; chmn. architecture, engring. and constrn. group Comutervision U.G., Mare Island, 1985-87; mem. initial graphics exch. std. Navy Industry Digital Data Exch. Stds. Com., Mare Island, 1987-90. With U.S. Army, 1972-75. Home: 5013 Laura St SE Olympia WA 98501

CALLAGHAN, JOHN W., state agency administrator; b. Sept. 18, 1951; m.; 2 children. AB cum laude, Harvard U., 1973; MA, U. Chgo., 1978, PhD, 1981. Dir. program svcs. Hopi Ctr. for Human Svcs., Second Mesa, Ariz., 1977-79; spl. projects officer Cerritos Coll., Norwalk, Calif., 1979-81; supr., planner planning and policy devel. sect. N.Mex. Health and Environment Dept., 1981-84; chief dirs. office planning social svcs. divsn. N.Mex. Human Svcs. Dept., Santa Fe, 1984-85, from dep. dir. to dir. social svcs. divsn., 1986-89, dir. divsn. mental health, 1989—; presenter in field. Home: 117 Mateo Cir Santa Fe NM 87505 Office: Divsn Mental Health PO Box 26110 1190 St Francis Dr Santa Fe NM 87502-6110

CALLAGHAN, MARY ANNE, secondary school educator; b. Seattle, Mar. 14, 1947; d. John Joseph and Catherine Clara (Emard) C.; m. David Michael Buerge, Mar. 8, 1975; children: David John, Catherine Emily. BA in English Lit., U. Wash., 1970, Teaching Cert., 1973. Standard Wash. state teaching certification. Tchr. tng. intern Hazen H.S., Renton, Wash., 1968-70, tchr. English, 1970-71; tchr. English, theology Forest Ridge Sch. of the Sacred Heart, Bellevue, Wash., 1971-93, dean of students, 1988-92; tchr. English, theology Holy Cross H.S., Everett, Wash., 1993—; student life v.p., 1995—; chair English dept. Forest Rdige H.S. and Holy Cross H.S., 1980—; mem. accreditation team Holy Name Acad., Seattle, 1991, O'Dea H.S., Seattle, 1995; insvc. presenter for Archdiocese of Seattle, 1992, 93. Vol. Christian Movement for Peace, Montreal, Quebec, 1972; sch. bd. mem. St. Catherine Parish, Seattle, 1984-90. Recipient grants to initiate ethnic awareness programs Religious of the Sacred Heart, 1982, grant to study Asian lit. NEH, 1988. Mem. Nat. Cath. Edn. Assn., Nat. Coun. Tchrs. English. Roman Catholic. Office: Holy Cross Sch 2617 Cedar St Everett WA 98201-3137

CALLAHAN, GARY BRENT, lawyer; b. Ashland, Oreg., Apr. 24, 1942; s. Donald Burr and Joyce Valeri (Powers) C.; m. Nancy Kay King, Feb. 1967 (div. 1978); children: Shawn, Christopher; m. Sally Kornblight, Jan. 18, 1983; 1 child, Zachary. Student, Sacramento State U.; JD, U. of Pacific, 1970. Bar: Calif. 1971, U.S. Dist. Ct. (ea. dist.) Calif. 1971. Assoc. Rust & Mills, Sacramento, Calif., 1971-73, Barrett, Matheny & Newlon, Sacramento, 1973-77; ptnr. Westley & Callahan, Sacramento, 1977-80, Wilcoxen, Callahan, Montgomery & Harbison, Sacramento, 1980-94, Callahan & Deacon, Sacramento, 1994—; instr., lectr. Continuing Edn. Bar, Berkeley, Calif., 1978—; faculty mem. advocacy skills workshop Sch. Law Stanford U., 1994—, Sch. Law U. San Francisco, 1994—. Served with USN, 1960-63. Mem. Calif. Bar Assn., Assn. Trial Lawyers Am. (sustaining), Consumer Attys. Calif., Capitol City Consumer Attys. (pres. 1984-85), Am. Bd. Profl. Liability Attys., Am. Bd. Trial Advs., Nat. Bd. Trial Advs. Democrat. Office: Callahan & Deacon 77 Cadillac Dr # 240 Sacramento CA 95825

CALLAHAN, LEEANN LUCILLE, psychologist; b. San Diego, Calif., Dec. 7, 1950; d. Charlie A. Olsen and Delores A. (Libke) Turner; m. Chuck Callahan, Oct. 31, 1970; children: Clint, Devin, Chet. BS/MS in Psychology, San Diego State U., 1983; PhD in Psychology, USIU, San Diego, 1990. Lic. clin. psychologist. Clin. dir. Sharp Cabrillo Hosp., San Diego, 1989-91, Charter Hosp., San Diego, 1991-93; psychologist San Diego, 1989—; preferred provider Charter Hosp., San Diego, 1990—, speakers bur., 1990—; staff psychologist Sharp Cabrillo Hosp., San Diego, 1989-92. Editor Parentteen Mag.; contbr. articles to profl. jours. Pres. PTA, San Diego, 1985; citizen adv./city coun. City of San Diego, 1987; vol. Poway Unified Sch. Dist., San Diego, 1975—; speaker Rotary, San Diego, 1994. Recipient Citizen of Yr. award, Sigma Chi, 1997. Mem. APA, Calif. State Psychol. Assn. Office: 9320 Carmel Mountain Rd Ste D San Diego CA 92129-2159

CALLAHAN, MARILYN JOY, social worker; b. Portland, Oreg., Oct. 11, 1934; d. Douglas Q. and Anona Helen Maynard; m. Lynn J. Callahan, Feb. 27, 1960 (dec.); children: Barbara Callahan Baer, Susan Callahan Sewell, Jeffrey Lynn. BA, Mills Coll., 1955; MSW, Portland State U., 1971, secondary teaching cert., 1963. Bd. cert. diplomate in clin. social work. Developer, adminstr. ednl. program Oreg. Women's Correctional Ctr., Oreg. State Prison, Salem, 1966-67; mental health counselor Benton County Mental Health, Corvallis, Oreg., 1970-71; inst. tchr. Hillcrest Sch., Salem, Oreg., 1975-81; social worker protective svcs. Mid Willamette Valley Sr. Svcs. Agy., Salem, 1981-88; psychiat. social worker dept. forensics Oreg. State Hosp., 1988-93; pvt. practice treatment of adult male and female sexual offenders Salem, 1993—; pvt. practice in care/mgmt. of elderly, 1993—; panel mem. Surgeon Gen.'s N.W. Regional Conf. on Interpersonal Violence, 1987; speaker in field; planner, organizer Seminar on Age Discrimination, 1985. Mem. NASW (bd. dirs. Oreg. chpt.), Nat. Org. Forensic Social Work, Am. Acad. Forensic Scis., Acad. Cert. Social Workers (lic. clin. social worker), Oreg. Gerontol. Assn., Catalina 27 Nat. Sailing Assn. Office: Ste 304 780 Commercial St SE Salem OR 97301-3455

CALLAHAN, RONALD, federal investigator, historian; b. San Francisco, Jan. 8, 1947; s. Raymond Edward and Camille (Masucci) C.; m. Delores Leona Cody Callahan, Nov. 15, 1986; children: Randell James Stowe, Miranda Dawn Stowe, Christopher Ronald Callahan, Kimberly Ann Callahan. BS, Calif. State U., 1973, student, 1987-91. Cert. spl. agt. Air traffic controller USAF, Davis-Monthan AFB, Ariz., 1967-68; air trafic controller USAF, Kadena AB, Japan, 1968-70; clk. Franchise Tax Bd., Sacramento, 1973; acct. clk. Employment Devel. Dept., Sacramento, 1973-74; air cargo specialist 82nd Aerial Port Squadron, Travis AFB, Calif., 1978-80; adjudicator VA, San Francisco, 1974-82; historian 349th Mil. Airlift Wing, Travis AFB, Calif., 1980-82, Fourth Air Force, McClellan AFB, Calif., 1986-90; investigator Def. Investigative Svc., Sacramento, 1982—. Author: Annual Histories of McClellan and Travis Air Bases, 1980-82, 86-90, Airpower Journal, 1991-93. Vol. El Dorado County Juvenile Svc. Coun., Placerville, Calif., 1992, Calvary Refuge, Sacramento, Marysville, Calif., 1992—; mem. Grace Cmty. Ch., Pleasant Valley, Calif., 1993—; adult literacy tutor El Dorado County Literacy Action Coun., Placerville, 1994—; mem. bd. elders Calvary Refuge, 1996—. Sgt. USAF, 1966-70. Named Dean's Honors list Calif. State U., Sacramento, 1971, 72; recipient Spl. Act award Def. Investigative Svc., Sacramento, 1983, Air Force Commendation medal USAF, McClellan AFB, Calif., 1989. Mem. Air Force Assn., Orgn. Am. Historians, Am. Christian History Inst., Friends of Libr., Grace Cmty. Ch., Calvary Refuge, Phi Alpha Theta. Republican. Home: 1640 Glen Dr Placerville CA 95667-9302 Office: Defense Investigative Svc 1860 Howe Ave Ste 330 Sacramento CA 95825-1073

CALLAN, JOSI IRENE, museum director; b. Yorkshire, Eng., Jan. 30, 1946; came to U.S., 1953; d. Roger Bradshaw and Irene (Newbury) Winstanley; children: James, Heather, Brett Jack; m. Patrick Marc Callan, June 26, 1984. BA in Art History summa cum laude, Calif. State U., Domingues Hills, 1978, MA in Behavioral Scis., 1981. Dir. community rels./alumni affairs Calif. State U., Dominguez Hills; adminstrv. fellow office chancellor Calif. State U., Long Beach, assoc. dir. univ. svcs. office chancellor, 1979-85; dir. capital campaign, assoc. dir. devel. Sta. KVIE-TV, Sacramento, 1985-86; dir. project devel. Pacific Mountain Network, Denver, 1986-87; dir. mktg. and devel. Denver Symphony Orch., 1988-89; assoc. dir. San Jose (Calif.) Mus. Art, 1989-91, dir., 1991—; asst. prof. sch. social and behavioral scis. Calif. State U., Dominguez Hills, 1981—; mem. adv. com. Issues Facing Mus. in 1990s JKF U., 1990-91. Mem. com. arts policy Santa Clara Arts Coun., 1990-92; chair San Jose Arts Roundtable, 1992-93; active ArtTable, 1992—, Community Leadership San Jose, 1992-93, Am. Leadership Forum, 1994; mem. adv. bd. Bay Area Rsch. Project, 1992—; mem. Calif. Arts Coun., Visual Arts Panel, 1993-95, Santa Clara Arts Coun. Visual Arts Panel, 1993; bd. dirs. YWCA, 1993—. Recipient Leadership award Knight Found., 1995; fellow Calif. State U., 1982-83. Mem. AAUW, Am. Assn. Mus., Nat. Soc. Fund Raising Execs. (bd. dirs. 1991), Colo. Assn. Fund Raisers, Art Mus. Devel. Assn., Assn. Art Mus. Dirs., We. Mus. Assn., Calif. State U. Alumni Coun. (pres. 1981-83), Rotary Internat., Knight Found. (leadership award, 1995). Office: San Jose Mus Art 110 S Market St San Jose CA 95113-2307

CALLAWAY, JOHN CHARLES, wetland ecologist; b. Santa Monica, Calif., Sept. 16, 1962; s. Daniel Blayne and Carol Joy (Champion) C.; m. Patricia Ann Cruse, Dec. 31, 1991. BA, U. Calif., Berkeley, 1985; MA, San Francisco State U., 1990; PhD, La. State U., 1994. Rsch. asst. Romberg Tiburon Ctr. San Francisco State U., 1987-90; rsch. asst. prof. dept. biology San Diego State U., 1994—; postdoctoral fellow Pacific Estuarine Rsch. Lab., San Diego, 1994-96; asst. dir. Pacific Estuarine Rsch. Lab., 1996—. Contbr. articles to profl. jours. Mem. Estuarine Rsch. Fedn., Calif. Bot. Soc. (bd. editors Madroño jour. 1996—), Soc. Wetland Scientists, Ecol. Soc. Am., Am. Geophys. Union, Soc. Ecol. Restoration. Office: San Diego State U Pacific Estuarine Rsch Lab San Diego CA 92182

CALLAWAY, LINDA MARIE, special education educator; b. Upland, Calif., June 21, 1940; d. Elwyn T. and Fladger Idell (Flake) Bice; m. David Barry Callaway, May, 1957 (div. sept. 1962); children: Tess Callaway Tyler, Darren Francis. B in English, Calif. State U., Fullerton, 1975; MEd Adminstrn., Calif. State U., L.A., 1991. Cert. tchr., Calif. Tchr. multiply-handicapped children L.A. County Office Edn., Downey, 1984-88; tchr. spl. day class Pomona (Calif.) Unified Sch. Dist., 1988-90, resource specialist spl. edn., 1990—; mem. subcom. Master Plan, Claremont, Calif., 1994. Writer, editor Tempo Jour. Inland Valley, 1993, 94. Calif. State U. monetary grantee, 1990-91. Mem. Am. Inst. Wine and Food (assoc.). Republican. Soc. of Friends. Home: 1071 E Alvarado Ave Pomona CA 91767-5137 Office: Pomona HS Pomona Unified Sch Dist 475 Bangor Pomona CA 91767

CALLEN, LON EDWARD, county official; b. Kingman, Kans., Mar. 31, 1929; s. Cleo Paul and Josephine Nell (Mease) C.; BA in Math. and Physics, U. Wichita (Kans.), 1951; m. Barbara Jean Sallee, Oct. 12, 1954; children: Lon Edward, Lynnette J. Commd. 2d lt. USAF, 1951, advanced through grades to lt. col., 1968; comdr. Tuslog Detachment 93, Erhac, Turkey, 1966-67; sr. scientist Def. Atomic Support Agy., Washington, 1967-71; ret., 1971; dir. emergency preparedness City-County of Boulder, Colo., 1976—; bd. dirs. Boulder County Emergency Med. Svcs. Coun., 1977, Boulder County Amateur Radio Emergency Svcs., 1978—. Mem. hon. awards com. Nat. Capital Area council Boy Scouts Am., 1971; chmn. Boulder County United Fund, 1976-82; mem. asst. staff Indian Princesses and Trailblazer programs Boulder YMCA, 1974-78. Decorated Joint Svc. Commendation medal; recipient cert. achievement Def. Atomic Support Agy., 1970. Mem. AAAS, Am. Ordnance Soc., Am. Soc. Cybernetics, Planetary Soc., Math. Assn. Am., N.Y. Acad. Scis., Fedn. Am. Scientists, Nat. Assn. Atomic Vets., Union Concerned Scientists, Boulder County Fire Fighters Assn., Colo. Emergency Mgmt. Assn., Ret. Officers Assn., Colo. Front Range Protective Assn., Mensa, Sigma Xi, Pi Alpha Pi. Clubs: Boulder Knife and Fork, Boulder Gunbarrel Optimists, Denver Matrix, U. Colo. Ski, U. Wichita. Author articles in field. Home: 4739 Berkshire Ct Boulder CO 80301-4055 Office: County Courthouse Box 471 Boulder CO 80306

CALLENDER, JONATHAN FERRIS, environmental engineer, consultant; b. L.A., Nov. 7, 1944; s. Robert Ford and Ruth Merigold (Ferris) C.; m. Cynthia E. Bennett, Aug. 16, 1967 (div. Apr. 1982); children: Katherine, Elizabeth, Jennifer, Sarah. BS, Calif. Inst. Tech., 1966; AM, Harvard U., 1968, PhD in Geology, 1975. Asst. prof. U. N.Mex., Albuquerque, 1972-77, assoc. prof., 1977-84, asst. chmn. geology dept., 1979-81, adj. prof. geology, 1985-90; chief sci. programs N.Mex. Mus. Natural History, Albuquerque, 1983-84, dir., 1984-90, also bd. dirs.; v.p., prin. Adrian Brown Cons., Denver, 1990-96; sr. project engr. Kennecott Utah Copper Corp., Magna, 1996—; adj. prof. geology N.Mex. Inst. Mining and Tech., Socorro, 1985-90. Editor numerous books on N.Mex. geology; author numerous tech. papers in field. Active N.Mex. First, 1986-90, Hispanic Cultural Found., Albuquerque, 1986-90; bd. dirs. N.Mex. Mus. Found., 1984-90. Nat. Sci. Found. fellow, 1971-72; recipient Presdl. Recognition award U. N.Mex., 1982. Fellow Geol. Soc. Am.; mem. Am. Assn. Petroleum Geologists, Am. Geophys. Union (chmn. transl. bd. 1985-96), N.Mex. Geol. Soc. (hon., pres. 1977). Home: 9300 S Redwood Rd Apt 5-09 West Jordan UT 84088 Office: Kennecott Utah Copper Corp PO Box 112 Bingham Canyon UT 84006-0112

CALLIER, CECILE, writer, actress. BA in English Edn., U. No. Colo., 1979. Cert. secondary tchr. English. Broadcast journalist and prodr. various TV and pub. radio stas., Colo., 1983—; freelance writer Colo., 1993—; pub. rels. dir. and grantwriter Grand River Hosp. Dist., Rifle, Colo., 1997—; tchr. various schs. in Denver area and Roaring Fork Valley, 1979-96; sales and mktg. rep. various cos., Colo., 1986—; local coord. and cmty. counselor, Acad. Yr. Am., 1991—, Am. Inst. Foreign Study, 1991—, Au Pair in Am., 1992—. Appeared in (films) Christmas Vacation '95, Murder in High Places, He's Still There, Endangered Species; (TV shows) Unsolved Mysteries, Sky Merchant Home Shopping Program; provides voiceover and narration for various TV and radio commls. Mem. SAG, NAFE, Nat. Writer's Union. Home and Office: 1609 Cooper Ave # 2 Glenwood Springs CO 81601

CALLIES, QUINTON CARL, allergist; b. Lomira, Wis., Sept. 16, 1930. MD, U. Wis. Intern Metro Gen. Hosp., Cleve., 1960-61; immunologist U. Mich. Hosp., Ann Arbor, 1961-64, fellow in allergy medicine, 1964-66; now allergist Scottsdale (Ariz.) Meml. Hosps.; asst. prof. medicine Mayo Med. Sch. Office: Scottsdale Memorial Hospital 9003 E Shea Blvd Scottsdale AZ 85260-5404*

CALLISON, JAMES R., plastic surgeon; b. Columbia, Ky., 1933. MD, Vanderbilt U., 1958. Intern Vanderbilt Hosp., Nashville, 1958-59; surgeon Mass. Gen. Hosp., Boston, 1959-60, 62-65; plastic surgeon Pitts. Med. Ctr., 1965-67; now plastic surgeon St. Joseph's Hosp., Phoenix. Fellow ACS. Office: 2218 N 3rd St Phoenix AZ 85004-1401

CALLISON, NANCY FOWLER, nurse administrator; b. Milw., July 16, 1931; d. George Fenwick and Irma Esther (Wenzel) Fowler; m. B.G. Callison, Sept. 25, 1954 (dec. Feb. 1964); children: Robert, Leslie, Linda. Diploma, Evanston Hosp. Sch. Nursing, 1952; BS, Northwestern U., 1954. RN, Calif.; cert. case mgr. Staff nurse, psychiat. dept. Downey VA Hosp., 1954-55; staff nurse Camp Lejeune Naval Hosp., 1955, 59-61; obstet. supr. Tri-City Hosp., Oceanside, Calif., 1961-62; pub. health nurse San Diego County, 1962-66; sch. nurse Rich-Mar Union Sch. Dist., San Marcos, Calif., 1966-68; head nurse San Diego County Community Mental Health, 1968-73; dir. patient care services Southwood Mental Health Ctr., Chula Vista, Calif., 1973-75; program cons. Comprehensive Care Corp., Newport Beach, Calif., 1975-79; dir. Manpower Health Care, Culver City, Calif., 1979-80; dir. nursing services Peninsula Rehab. Ctr., Lomita, Calif., 1980-81; clinic supr., coordinator utilization and authorizations, acting dir. provider relations Hawthorne (Calif.) Community Med. Group, 1981-86; mgr. Health Care Delivery Physicians of Greater Long Beach, Calif., 1986-87; cons. Quality Rev. Assocs., West L.A., 1988-93; case mgr. Mercy Physicians Med. Group, 1992-93; rehab. nurse coord. network The Zenith Ins., 1993—; clin. coord., translator Flying Samaritans, 1965—, mem. internat. bd. dirs., 1975-77, 79-86, 89—, dir. San Quentin project, 1991-93, dir. univ. program, 1996—, pres. South Bay chpt., 1975-81, v.p., 1982-85, bd. dirs. San Diego chpt., 1987-90, pres. San Diego chpt. 1991-92, adminstr. Clinica Esperanza de Infantil Rosarito Beach 1990-93. Mem. Rehab. Nurse Coord. Network, U.S.-Mex. Border Health Assn., Cruz Roja Mexicana (Delegacion Rosarito 1986-92).

CALLISON, RUSSELL JAMES, lawyer; b. Redding, Calif., Sept. 4, 1954; s. Walter M. and Norma A. (Bruce) C. BA in Polit. Sci., U. of Pacific, 1977, JD cum laude, 1980. Bar: Calif. 1980, U.S. Dist. Ct. (ea. dist.) Calif. 1981, U.S. Dist. Ct. (no. dist.) Calif. 1986, U.S. Ct. Appeals (9th cir.) 1989. Assoc. Memering & DeMers, Sacramento, Calif., 1980-85; pres. DeMers, Callison & Donovan, P.C., Sacramento, 1985-95; ptnr. Lewis, D'Amato, Brisbois & Bisgaard, 1995—; spl. master Calif. State Bar, 1991—; arbitrator, judge pro tem Sacramento County Superior Ct., 1986—. Co-author: Premises Liability in California, 1996. Mem. ABA (litigation sect.), SAR (chpt. pres. 1992-93), Am. Arbitration Assn. (panel of arbitrators), Sacramento County Bar Assn., Assn. Def. Counsel No. Calif., Commonwealth Club, Natomas Racquet Club, Order ofCoif, Phi Alpha Delta. Republican. Episcopalian. Home: 1891 11th Ave Sacramento CA 95818-4142 Office: Lewis D'Amato Brisbois & Bisgaard 2500 Venture Oaks Way Ste 200 Sacramento CA 95833-3501

CALLISTER, LOUIS HENRY, JR., lawyer; b. Salt Lake City, Aug. 11, 1935; s. Louis Henry and Isabel (Barton) C.; m. Ellen Gunnell, Nov. 27, 1957; children: Mark, Isabel, Jane, Edward, David, John Andrew, Ann. BS, U. Utah, 1958, JD, 1961. Bar: Utah 1961. Asst. atty. gen. Utah, 1961; sr. ptnr. Callister Nebeker & McCullough (formerly Callister, Duncan & Nebeker), Salt Lake City, 1961—; bd. dirs. Am. Stores Co., Quailbluff Devel. Co. Vice-chmn. Salt Lake City Zoning Bd. Adjustment, 1979-84; bd. govs. Salt Lake Valley Hosps., 1983-91; treas. exec. com. Utah Rep. Com., 1965-69; chmn. Utah chpt. Rockefeller for Pres. Com., 1964-68; sec., trustee Salt Lake Police/Sheriff Hon. Cols., 1982—; trustee, mem. exec. com. Utah Econ. Devel. Corp., 1992—; trustee U. Utah, 1987—, vice-chmn., 1989—, bd. dirs. U. Utah Hosp., 1993—. Mormon. Home: 22 S Ironwood Dr North Salt Lake UT 84054 Office: Callister Nebeker & McCullough Gateway Tower E Ste 900 Salt Lake City UT 84133-1102

CALLISTER, MARION JONES, federal judge; b. Moreland, Idaho, June 6, 1921; m. Nina Lynn Hayes, June 7, 1946; children—Nona Lynn Callister Haddock, Lana Sue Callister Meredith, Jenny Ann Callister Thomas, Tamara Callister Banks, Idonna Ruth Callister Andersen, Betty Patricia Callister Carr, Deborah Jean Hansen, Mary Clarice Fowler, David Marion, Nancy Irene Callister Garvin, Michelle Burk, Kimberly Jane Simmons. Student, Utah State U., 1940-41; B.S.L., U. Utah, 1950, J.D., 1951. Bar: Idaho 1951. Dep. pros. atty. Bingham County, Idaho, 1951-52; asst. U.S. atty. Dist. of Idaho, 1953-57, U.S. atty., 1975-76; pvt. practice, 1958-69; judge Idaho Dist. Ct. 4th Jud. Dist., 1970-75; judge U.S. Dist. Ct. Idaho, Boise, 1976—, chief judge, 1981-88, sr. judge, 1989—. Served with U.S. Army, 1944-46. Decorated Purple Heart. Republican. Mormon. Office: US Dist Ct MSC 040 550 W Fort St Boise ID 83724-0101

CALMAN, CRAIG DAVID, writer, actor, director; b. Riverside, Calif., June 11, 1953. Student, Pacific U., Forest Grove, Oreg., 1971-72, U. de Querétaro, Mex., 1972-73; BA in Motion Picture/TV, UCLA, 1975. Sr. admitting worker UCLA Med. Ctr., 1974-76; actor/playwright Old Globe Theatre, San Diego, 1977-78, Off Broadway and regional, N.Y.C. and East Coast, 1979-86; exec. asst. various film/TV studios and law firms, L.A., 1986-89, Orion Pictures Corp., L.A., 1989-90; dir. staged readings L.A., 1991—; Actor with starring roles (TV and film) ADP Industrial, Teamwork, Macbeth, Flesteron in Amazonia, co-starring roles in Commercial Break, Sullivan's Travels; actor with co-starring/lead roles (theatre) in Book of the Dead, Dark Lady of the Sonnets, Hamlet, Rosencrantz and Guildenstern are Dead, Much Ado About Nothing, Too True to be Good, Henry V, The Counterfeit Rose, Richard III, The Rivals, Merchant of Venice, A Day for Surprises, The Tavern, Madame De..., and others; columnist World Wide Web mag. Filmzone, 1995—. Author play/screenplays: The Turn of the Century, 1982/89, Strangled Nocturne, 1977/91, Skidoo Ruins, 1987/92; author novel: The Turn of the Century, 1994; author one-act plays, screenplays, full-length plays, poetry; writer asst. Hal Roach, Bel Air, Calif., 1987-88. Vol. book reader Recording for the Blind, L.A., 1991—. Recipient Old Globe Theatre Atlas award for best actor in a comedy role for Too True to be Good, 1977-78; Helene Wurlitzer Found. of N.Mex. Writers Residency grantee, 1988; finalist Walt Disney fellowship program, 1992, Chesterfield Film Co. Writers Project, 1997. Mem. Screen Actors Guild, Actors Equity Assn. Office: 6632 Lexington Ave Ste 77 Los Angeles CA 90038-1306

CALVANO-SMITH, RITA, journalist, small business owner; b. Pasadena, Calif., Jan. 11, 1948; d. Alfred Augustus and Rose Lucille (DeFazio) Calvano; m. Clifford R. Smith, Nov. 6, 1992. BA in Journalism, San Diego State U., 1972, MA in Am. Studies, 1976. Reporter The Daily Californian, El Cajon, Calif., 1972-76, San Diego Tribune, 1977-92; instr. Fashion Careers of Calif., San Diego, 1993-95, Fashion Inst. Design & Merchandising, San Diego, 1993, Mira Costa C.C., Oceanside, Calif., 1992-93; pres., owner Make Mine Petite, San Diego, 1992—; vol. instr. San Diego Journalism Project, 1996; mem. fashion prodn. com. Crawford H.S., 1994—. Editor/writer PS Features, San Diego, 1996—. Recipient Cmty. Svc. award AAUW, LaMesa, Calif., 1970's, Feature Writing award AP, 1970's, Ring of Truth award Copley Press, 1980's. Democrat.

CALVERT, KEN, congressman; b. Corona, Calif., June 8, 1953. AA, Chaffey Coll., 1973; BA Econs., San Diego State U., 1975. Corona/ Norco youth chmn. for Nixon, 1968, 82; county youth chmn. rep. Vesey's Dist., 1970, 43d dist., 1972; congl. aide to rep. Vesey, Calif., 1975-79; gen. mgr. Jolly Fox Restaurant, Corona, Calif., 1975-79, Marcus W. Meairs Co., Corona, Calif., 1979-81; pres., gen. mgr. Ken Calvert Real Properties, Corona, Calif., 1981—; Reagan-Bush campaign worker, 1980; co chmn. Wilson for Senate Campaign, 1982, George Deukmejian election, 1978, 82, 86, George Bush election, 1988, Pete Wilson senate elections, 1982, 88, Pete Wilson for Gov. election, 1990; mem. 104th Congress from 43rd Calif. dist., 1993—; mem. natural resources com., sci., space and tech. com., 1993—, also mem. ag. com.; former v.p. Corona/ Norco Rep. Assembly; chmn. Riverside Rep. Party, 1984-88, County Riverside Asset Leasing; bd. realtors Corona/ Norco. Exec. bd. Corona Community Hosp. Corp. 200 Club; mem. Corona Airport adv. commn.; adv. com. Temescal/ El Cerrito Community Plan. Mem. Riverside County Rep. Winners Circle (charter), Lincoln Club (co-chmn., charter, 1986-90), Corona Rotary Club (pres. 1991), Elks, Navy League Corona Norco, Corona C. of C. (pres. 1990), Noroco C. of C., Monday Morning Group, Corona Group (past chmn.), Econ. Devel. Ptnrship., Silver Eagles (March AFB support group, charter). Office: US Ho of Reps 1034 Longworth HOB Washington DC 20515*

CALVERT, LEONARD JAMES, editor, writer; b. Eugene, Oreg., Aug. 14, 1933; s. Ross Mark Calvert and Florence A. (Brooks) Ball; m. Janet K. Lohrenz, Nov. 19, 1960; children: Timothy Leonard, Douglas Jacob. BA, U. Oreg., 1955, MA, 1976. News editor Valley Sentinel, Coquille, Oreg., 1955-58; editor Argur-Observer, Ontario, Oreg., 1958-60, Headlight-Herald, Tillamook, Oreg., 1960-61; comm. specialist ext. svc. Oreg. State U., Corvallis, 1961-65, 69-95; pub. affairs officer U. Oreg., Eugene, 1967-69; editor Jour. of Ext., Eugene, 1996—. Recipient Writing Award of Excellence, Agrl. Communicators in Edn., 1995. Mem. Soc. Profl. Journalists, Lions, Epsilon Sigma Phi (chpt. pres. 1997, Regional Disting. Svc. award 1995). Episcopalian. Home and Office: 1062 Woodside Dr Eugene OR 97401

CALVERT, PATRICIA VIOLA, dietitian; b. Richmond, Oreg., Apr. 28, 1940; d. Oliver Raymond Trent and Clara Hester (Brooks) Reynolds; m. Lyle Lavern Calvert, Sept. 9, 1962; children: Lyla Dalene Calvert Keithley. BS, Walla Walla Coll., 1961. Registered dietitian, Oreg. Intern Loma Linda U., 1962; clin. dietitian, chief Good Samaritan Hosp., Portland, Oreg., 1963-68; food and nutrition supr., clin. rsch. dietitian, chief St. Charles Med. Ctr., Bend, Oreg., 1971-95; with Pioneer Meml. Hosp., 1996—; nutrition cons., 1996—; food and nutrition cons. Pioneer Meml. Hosp., Prineville, Oreg., 1968-74, 87-92, Cen. Oreg. Dist. Hosp., Redmond, 1974-75, Batchelor Butte Nursing Home, Bend, 1968-70, Harney Dist. Hosp., Burns, Oreg., 1987-92; menu cons. Soroptimist Sr. Mealsite, Prineville, Oreg., 1992—. City budget com. Redmond City Coun., 1970, 71; deaconess Powell Butte Christian Ch., 1994-95. Mem. Am. Dietetic Assn., Oreg. Dietetic Assn. (treas., pres.-elect, pres., nominating chair 1963—).

CALVIN, ALLEN DAVID, psychologist, educator; b. St. Paul, Feb. 17, 1928; s. Carl and Zelda (Engelson) C.; m. Dorothy VerStrate, Oct. 5, 1953; children—Jamie, Kris, David, Scott. B.A. in Psychology cum laude, U. Minn., 1950; M.A. in Psychology, U. Tex., 1951, Ph.D. in Exptl. Psychology, 1953. Instr. Mich. State U., East Lansing, 1953-55; asst. prof. Hollins Coll., 1955-59, assoc. prof., 1959-61; dir. Britannica Center for Studies in Learning and Motivation, Menlo Park, Calif., 1961; prin. investigator grant for automated teaching fgn. langs. Carnegie Found., 1960; USPHS grantee, 1960; pres. Behavioral Research Labs., 1962-74; prof., dean Sch. Edn., U. San Francisco, 1974-78; Henry Clay Hall prof. Orgn. and leadership, 1978—; pres. Pacific Grad. Sch. Psychology, 1984—. Author textbooks. Served with USNR, 1946-47. Mem. Am. Psychol. Assn., AAAS, Sigma Xi, Psi Chi. Home: 1645 15th Ave San Francisco CA 94122-3523 Office: U San Francisco Psychology Dept San Francisco CA 94117

CALVIN, MELVIN, chemist, educator; b. St. Paul, Minn., Apr. 8, 1911; s. Elias and Rose I. (Hervitz) C.; m. Genevieve Jemtegaard, 1942; children: Elin, Karole, Noel. BS, Mich. Coll. Mining and Tech., 1931, DSc, 1955; PhD, U. Minn., 1935, DSc, 1969; hon. rsch. fellow, U. Manchester, Eng., 1935-37; Guggenheim fellow, 1967; DSc, Nottingham U., 1958, Oxford (Eng.) U., 1959, Northwestern U., 1961, Wayne State U., 1962, Gustavus Adolphus Coll., 1963, Poly. Inst. Bklyn., 1962, U. Notre Dame, 1965, U. Gent, Belgium, 1970, Whittier Coll., 1971, Clarkson Coll., 1976, U. Paris Val-de-Marne, 1977, Columbia U., 1979, Grand Valley U., 1986. With U. Calif., Berkeley, 1937—; successively instr. chemistry, asst. prof., prof., Univ. prof., dir. Lab. Chem. Biodynamics U. Calif., 1963-80, assoc. dir. Lawrence Berkeley Lab., 1967-80; Peter Reilly lectr. U. Notre Dame, 1949; Harvey lectr. N.Y. Acad. Medicine, 1951; Harrison Howe lectr. Rochester sect. Am. Chem. Soc., 1954; Falk-Plaut lectr. Columbia U., 1954; Edgar Fahs Smith Meml. lectr. U. Pa. and Phila. sect. Am. Chem. Soc., 1955; Donegani Found. lectr. Italian Nat. Acad. Sci., 1955; Max Tishler lectr. Harvard U., 1956; Karl Folkers lectr. U. Wis., 1956; Baker lectr. Cornell U., 1958; London lectr., 1961, Willard lectr., 1982; Vanuxem lectr. Princeton U., 1969; Disting. lectr. Mich. State U., 1977; Prather lectr. Harvard U., 1980; Dreyfus lectr. Grinnell Coll., 1981, Berea Coll., 1982; Barnes lectr. Colo. Coll., 1982; Nobel lectr. U. Md., 1982; Abbott lectr. U. N.D., 1983; Gunning lectr. U. Alta., 1983; O'Leary disting. lectr. Gonzaga U., 1984; Danforth lectr. Dartmouth Coll., 1984, Grinnell Coll., 1984; R.P. Scherer lectr. U. S. Fla., 1984; Imperial Oil lectr. U. Western Ont., Can., 1985; disting. lectr. dept. chemistry U. Calgary, Can., 1986; Melvin Calvin lectr. Mich. Tech. U., 1986; Eastman prof. Oxford (Eng.) U., 1967-68. Author: (with G.E.K. Branch) The Theory of Organic Chemistry, 1940, (with others) Isotopic Carbon, 1949, (with Martell) Chemistry of Metal Chelate Compounds, 1952, (with Bassham) Path of Carbon in Photosynthesis, 1957, (with Bassham) Photosynthesis of Carbon Compounds, 1962, Chemical Evolution, 1969, Following the Trail of Light: A Scientific Odyssey, 1992; contbr. articles to chem. and sci. jours. Recipient prize Sugar Research Found., 1950, Flintoff medal prize Brit. Chem. Soc., 1953, Stephen Hales award Am. Soc. Plant Physiologists, 1956, Nobel prize in chemistry, 1961, Davy medal Royal Soc., 1964; Virtanen medal, 1975, Priestley medal, 1978, Am. Inst. Chemists medal, 1979, Feodor Lynen medal, 1983, Sterling B. Hendricks medal, 1983, Melvin Calvin Medal of Distinction Mich. Tech. U., 1985, Nat. Medal of Sci., 1989, John Ericsson Renewable Energy award U.S. Dept. Energy, 1991. Mem. Britain's Royal Soc. London (fgn. mem.), Am. Chem. Soc. (Richards medal N.E. chpt. 1956, Nichols medal N.Y. chpt. 1958, award for nuclear applications in chemistry, pres. 1971, Gibbs medal Chgo. chpt. 1977, Priestley medal 1978, Desper award Cin. chpt. 1981), Am. Acad. Arts and Scis., Nat. Acad. Scis., Royal Dutch Acad. Scis., Japan Acad., Am. Philos. Soc., Sigma Xi, Tau Beta Pi, Phi Lambda Upsilon. Office: U Calif Dept Chemistry Berkeley CA 94720

CALVO, DEBRA LEE GOFF, public relations executive; b. Inglewood, Calif., May 21, 1957; d. Francis Lee and Grace Mae (Finfrock) Goff; m. Angel Luis Calvo, Sept. 15, 1990. BA, UCLA, 1981. V.p. The Dolphin Group, L.A., 1981-87, 88—; asst. mgr. govt. rels. First Interstate Bank, L.A., 1987-88. Coord.: (resource notebook) Medfly Task Force Resource Book, 1990, Disaster in The Wings: Medfly Threat, 1994; contbg. writer World Cup Curriculum, 1994; editor Issues in Food Safety, 1990—. Administrv. asst. to campaign mgr. Deukmejian for Gov., L.A., 1981-82; mem. steering com. govt. rels. UCLA, 1981—, bd. dirs. UCLA Prytanean, 1987—; mem./sponsor Results, 1982-88; mgr. Crime Victims for Ct. Reform, L.A., 1983-86; campaign mgr. No On K Campaign, Newport Beach, Calif., 1988; exec. dir. Alliance for Food & Fiber, L.A., 1989—; mem. Gov. Wilson's Women's Adv. Com., Calif., 1990—; mem. Jr. League of L.A., 1991—; mem. internat. adv. coun. World Food Day, 1992—; bd. dirs. Friends of Coro Found., L.A., 1993—. Recipient Prism award Pub. Rels. Soc. L.A., 1992, 95; named one of Outstanding Young Women of Am. Republican. Presbyterian. Office: The Dolphin Group 10866 Wilshire Blvd Ste 550 Los Angeles CA 90024-4313

CALZA, ROGER ERNEST, animal science genetics and cell biology educator; b. Meriden, Conn., July 10, 1951; m. Stella Margaret Caesar; children: Gina Marguerite, Laura Elizabeth, Paula Therese, Olivia Mary. BS, U. N.H., 1974; PhD, Wash. State U., 1981. Teaching asst. Wash. State U., Pullman, 1976-81; grad. rsch. asst. Yale U., 1977, 80; postdoctoral rsch. fellow Albert Einstein Sch. Medicine, N.Y.C., 1982-83; rsch. asst. Cornell U., 1983-85, French Nat. Rsch. Inst., 1985-86; grad. faculty Wash. State U., 1990, asst. prof., 1986-92, assoc. prof., 1992—. Contbr. some 35 articles to profl. jours. Coach Greater Ithaca Activity Ctr. Boxing Program, 1983-84; bd. dirs., mem. steering com. St. Mary's Cath. Sch., 1989-92, mem. parish coun., 1994—. Mem. Am. Soc. Animal Sci., KC (4th degree), Phi Sigma, Alpha Zeta. Office: Wash State U Dept Animal Sci Genetics & Cell Biol Pullman WA 99164-6320

CALZOLARI, ELAINE, sculptor; b. Albertson, N.Y., Dec. 30, 1950; d. Oswald Henry and Edith (Jackson) C.; m. Robert A. Paley, May 2, 1986; 1 child, Miranda. Student, Sarah Lawrence Coll., Lacoste, France, 1972; BA magna cum laude, Hofstra U., 1973. artist design team New Denver Airport, 1990, artful cities panelist pub. art symposium Urban Design Forum, Denver, 1990; rules and regulations com. art in pub. places program Colo. Coun. on Arts, Denver, 1991-92; cons. CityTime, 1992—; guest critic pub. art course Colo. Coll., Colorado Springs, 1993. Exhbited in two-person shows and group shows at Denver Art Mus., 1980, 82, Sante Fe Festival of Arts, 1983, Mus. of N.Mex., Santa Fe, 1985, Robinschon Gallery, Denver, 1986, The New Gallery, Houston, 1986, The Aspen (Colo.) Inst., 1986, Gerald Peters Gallery, Dallas, 1986, Internat. Symposium on Electronic Art, Mpls., 1993, etc.; represented in permanent collections including Colo. State U., Ft. Collins, Bosher Assocs., Palm Springs, Calif., Mesa Coll., Grand Junction, Colo., Denver Art Mus., Auraria Higher Edn. Complex, Denver, Piper Jaffary, Mpls., City and County of Denver, etc. Vol. Community Caring Project, Denver, 1991—. Fellow Eagle Valley Arts Coun., 1974, Colo. Coun. on Arts and Humanities, 1984. Mem. Internat. Sculpture Ctr., Urban Design Forum.

CAMACHO, DIANNE LYNNE, mathematics educator, administrator; b. Dundas, Ontario, Can., Mar. 21, 1948; d. Leslie Benjamin and Helen Isobel (Don) DeMille; m. Tate Stanley Casey, June 16, 1971 (div. June, 1975); 1 child, Marie Anne; m. Thomas John Camacho, Aug. 30, 1980; children: Patricia Suzanne, Tara Lynne. BA in Math., Whittier Coll., 1970, secondary tchg. cert., 1972; postgrad., Walden U. Math. tchr. Mater Dei H.S., Santa Ana, Calif., 1972-79, Santa Ana (Calif.) H.S., 1979; instr. math. Coast C.C., Costa Mesa, Calif., 1979-81; math. tchr. East Middle Sch., Downey, Calif., 1979-81, South Middle Sch., Downey, 1981-82, Warren H.S., Downey, 1982-93; specialist So. Calif. Regional Algebra Project Orange County Dept. Edn., Costa Mesa, 1993—; mem. math. adv bd. Downey Unified Sch. Dist., 1983—; cons., presenter confs., Orange County Dept. Edn., Costa Mesa, 1986—, Calif. State Dept. of Edn., Sacramento, 1989—; chief math devel. team Calif. Learning Assessment Sys.; chief reader, table leader Stds. Adv. Golden State Math. Exam.; mem. devel. team, chief reader Calif. State Regional Lead Assessment; reviewer Am. Coll. Testing. Author: (book) Batch Basic, 1973; author and project specialist (series of books and workbooks) So. Calif. Regional Algebra Project Focus on Algebra, Focus on Geometry, 1989—, (units in book) Math A, Investigating Mathematics, 1989. Recipient Wright Bros. Innovative Tchrs. award, Rockwell Co., L.A., 1991; grantee Rockwell Co., 1992. Mem. ASCD, Nat. Coun. Tchrs. of Math., Calif. Math. Coun. (Nominee Presidential award 1986). Home: 5243 Hersholt Ave Lakewood CA 90712-2732 Office: Orange County Dept Edn 200 Kalmus Dr Costa Mesa CA 92626-5922

CAMARA, JORGE DE GUZMAN, ophthalmologist, educator; b. Ann Arbor, Mich., May 21, 1950; s. Augusto A. and Feliciana (de Guzman) C.; m. Virginia Valdes, June 23, 1977; 1 child, Augusto Carlos. BS in Pre-Medicine, U. Philippines, 1972, MD cum laude, 1976. Diplomate Am. Bd. Ophthalmology. Surg. intern U. Tex, Houston, 1977-78; resident in ophthalmology Baylor Coll. Medicine, Houston, 1978-81, fell in ophthalmic plastic and reconstructive surgery, 1981-82; ophthalmologist Straub Clinic and Hosp., Honolulu, 1982-88; pvt. practice Honolulu, 1988—; asst. prof. U. Hawaii Sch. Medicine, Honolulu, 1982—; cons. Tripler Army Hosp., Honolulu, 1982—; chmn. dept. ophthalmology and otorhinolaryngology, bd. dirs. St. Francis Med. Ctr.; bd. dirs. Am. Savs. Bank, Hawaiian Electric Industries. Bd. dirs. Aloha Med. Mission, Honolulu, 1988—. Fellow Am. Acad. Ophthalmology; mem. AMA, Hawaii Ophthal. Soc. (pub. rels. officer 1984-85, pres. 1992, chmn. com. for indigent svcs. 1994—), Philippine Med. Assn. Hawaii (pres. 1988—). Roman Catholic. Office: 2228 Liliha St Ste 106 Honolulu HI 96817

CAMBIO, IRMA DARLENE, nursing consultant; b. Belleville, Kans., July 23, 1936; d. James and Agnes Marie (Morehead) Dooley; m. Anderson Cambio (div.); children: Jim, Connie Rae. AA, East L.A. Coll., 1960; student continuing ednl. courses, UCLA, 1966-69; student Coll. Nursing, U. Md., 1985. RN, Calif., Colo., Washington, N.Mex., Wyo. Nurse oper. rm. Beverly Cmty. Hosp., Montebello, Calif., 1960-63; DON Pico Rivera (Calif.) Cmty. Hosp., 1963-64, Burbank (Calif.) Convalescent Hosp., 1964-66; staff nurse oper. rm., then head nurse, insvc. instr. Huntington Meml. Hosp., Pasadena, Calif., 1966-68; staff nurse oper. rm. Sunrise Hosp., Las Vegas, Nev., 1969-71; supr. oper. rm. Valley Hosp., Las Vegas, 1971-72; head nurse med./surg. fl. Chino (Calif.) Gen. Hosp., 1972-73; staff nurse emergency rm. Dr.'s Hosp. Montclair, Calif., 1972-73; head nurse med. fl. Boulder (Nev.) Cmty. Hosp., 1973; staff nurse recovery rm. Holy Cross Hosp., Ft. Lauderdale, Fla., 1973; float nurse, then house shift supr. Imperial Point Hosp., Ft. Lauderdale, 1973-74; staff nurse oper. rm. Lauderdale Lakes (Fla.) Hosp., 1973-74; patient care coord. oper. rm., recovery rm. Imperial Point Hosp., Ft. Lauderdale, 1974-78; asst. head nurse level IV open heart surgery/transplant surgery dept. and transplant divsn. St. Anthony's Hosp., Denver, 1978-80; oper. rm. cons., equipment planner internat. divsn. Nat. Med. Enterprises, 1980-85; mem. oper. rm. staff, float nurse Rocky Mountain Hosp., Denver, 1985; mem. oper. rm. staff St. Joseph Hosp., Denver, 1985-86; head nurse level IV oper. rm. King Faisal Splty. Hosp., Riyadh, Saudi Arabia, 1986-93; cons. oper. rm., recovery rm. and ctrl. sterile supply mgmt. Denver, 1993—; cons. Gortex Graft Co., 1978-80; on-call staff nurse Nursefinders Nurses' Registry, L.A., 1984-85, Olsten Nurses' Registry, Denver, 1985—; travel nurse oper. rm. Georgetown U. Hosp., Washington, 1994, Penrose/St. Francis Hosp., Colorado Springs, Colo., 1994-95; past mem. commissioning team for start-up ops. of 5 new acute care hosps. Taif, Dhahran and Riyadh, Saudi Arabia, 1 acute care hosp. Kuala Lumpur, Malaysia; compiler book for new hosps. detailing equipment, instrumentation and supplies necessary for oper. suite and recovery rm., 1982; rschr./developer policy and procedure manuals for nursing svcs. several hosps., Saudi Arabia, 1983; cons. commd. hosps. and Royal Family Pvt. Med. Clinics, Saudi Arabia, 1986-87; cons. equipment purchase for expansion, cons. materials flow and mgmt. svs. various hosps., Saudi Arabia, 1986-91, NME New Hosp., Malaysia, 1991—, mem. commn. team. Contbr. articles to profl. publs. Participant Health Vols. Overseas, Washington. Mem. Assn. Oper. Rm. Nurses (pres. Las Vegas chpt. 1978-79, mem. mgmt. splty. assembly/divsn. 1994—, rschr. new products, developer plan for presentation and integration to hosps.). Republican. Methodist. Home and Office: 439 Wright St Apt 26 Lakewood CO 80228-1152

CAMBRE, ATHLEO LOUIS, JR., plastic surgeon; b. L.A., Feb. 21, 1954. MD, Case Western Res. U., 1981. Intern U. Colo. Sch. Medicine, Denver, 1981-82, gen. surgeon, 1982-86; burn surgery fellow Cornell-N.Y. Hosp., N.Y.C., 1986-87; plastic surgeon UCLA, 1987-89, Cedars-Sinai Med. Ctr., L.A., 1989—; asst. clin. prof. plastic surgery UCLA. Office: Plastic and Recostruction Surgery 436 N Roxbury Dr Ste 207 Beverly Hills CA 90210-5017*

CAMENZIND, MARK J., research chemist; b. Palo Alto, Calif., Nov. 17, 1956; s. Paul V. and Mildred Martha Camenzind; m. Dorothy L. Hassler. SB in Chemistry, MIT, 1978; PhD in Inorganic Chemistry, U. Calif., Berkeley, 1983. Postdoctoral fellow U. B.C., Vancouver, 1983-86; rsch. chemist Salutar, Inc., Sunnyvale, Calif., 1987, Balazs Analytical Lab., Sunnyvale, 1987—. Contbr. rsch. papers to profl. jours. Mem. ASTM, Semicondr. Equipment and Materials Internat., Am. Chem. Soc., Am. Vacuum Soc., Inst. Environ. Scis., Internat. Disk Drive Equipment and Materials Assn. Office: Balazs Analytical Lab 252 Humboldt Ct Sunnyvale CA 94089-1315

CAMERON, CHARLES HENRY, petroleum engineer; b. Greeley, Colo., Oct. 21, 1947; s. Leo Leslie and Naomi Tryphena (Phillips) C.; m. Cheryl Christine Debelock, Aug. 30, 1969; 1 child, Ericka Dawn. AS, Mesa State Coll., 1968; BS in Geology, Mesa Coll., 1978; AS in Hazardous Materials Tech., Front Range C.C., Wesminister, Colo., 1990. Retardation technician Colo. State Home and Tng. Sch., Grand Junction, 1967-69; journeyman carpenter Brotherhood of Carpenters and Joiners, Grand Junction, 1969-76; hydrocompaction mgr. Colo. Dept. Hwys., Grand Junction, 1975-77; rsch. geologist Occidental Oil Shale, Inc., Grand Junction, 1977-78; geol. engr. Cleveland Cliffs Iron Co., Morgantown, W.Va., 1978-81; tech. advisor Ute Indian Tribe, Ft. Duchesne, Utah, 1981-86; ops. mgr. Charging Ute Corp., Golden, Colo., 1986-87; cons. Golden, 1987-90; petroleum engr. U.S. Dept. Interior/Bur. of Indian Affairs, Ft. Duchesne, 1990—, hazardous material mgr., freedom of info./privacy act coord., 1990—, natural resources officer, 1996—, ADP com. chmn. LAN adminstr., PL 93-638 com. chmn. grants/loan mgr., 1990—, LAN adminstr., 1996—. Contbr. articles to profl. jours. Mem. Colo. Oil Field Investigators Assn., Vernal (Utah) C. of C., Internat. Platform Assn. Home: 255 E 200 N Vernal UT 84078-1713 Office: BIA Uintah Ouray Agy Fort Duchesne UT 84026

CAMERON, GARY MICHAEL, real estate construction and development executive; b. San Mateo, Calif., Dec. 10, 1961; s. Robert Clyde and Shirley Irene (Bayer) C.; m. Melinda Cathrine Mason, June 3, 1988; children: Hunter Michael, Kyler John. BS in Engring., U. Nev., 1990. Pres. Bonanza Co., Reno, 1992—. Mem. Nat. Assn. Home Builders, Builders Assn. Western Nev. (bd. dirs. 1995—). Republican. Roman Catholic. Office: Bonanza Co PO Box 18600 Reno NV 89511

CAMERON, JANICE CAROL, legal regulatory administrator; b. Pitcairn, N.Y., Feb. 16, 1940; d. Lawrence Baird and Alice Irene (Manchester) Morgan; m. Albert A. Cameron, III, June 11, 1960 (div. Oct. 26, 1967); children: Albert A. IV, Richard D. AA, Jefferson C.C., Watertown, 1978; BA in Mgmt., St. Mary's Coll., Moraga, Calif., 1984. Nat. dir. Howard Ruff Cmty Forums Target, Inc., 1982-86; sr. mktg. adminstr. IPF divsn. The Pacific Bank N.A./Providian Bancorp, San Francisco, 1989-96; with legal dept. Nat. IPF, Mesa, Ariz., 1996—; notary public. Contbr. articles to profl. jours. Founder, chair First Support Group for Parents of Gay Mormons LDS, Social Svcs. Divsn., Fremont, Calif., 1986-94, Utah Gen. Authorities for Soc. Svcs. Program; 1st chpt. dir. Parents, Families and Friends of Lesbians and Gays, Danville-San Ramon chpt., Calif., 1993-94. Mem. Dobson Bay Club. Democrat. Home: 1331 W Baseline Rd #357 Mesa AZ 85202 Office: National IPF 1750 S Mesa Dr Mesa AZ 85210

CAMERON, JUDITH LYNNE, secondary education educator, hypnotherapist; b. Oakland, Calif., Apr. 29, 1945; d. Alfred Joseph and June Estelle (Faul) Moe; m. Richard Irwin Cameron, Dec. 17, 1967; 1 child, Kevin Dale. AA in Psychol., Sacramento City Coll., 1965; BA in Psychol., German, Calif. State U., 1967; MA in Reading Specialization, San Francisco State U., 1972; postgrad., Chapman Coll.; PhD, Am. Inst. Hypnotherapy, 1987. Cert. tchr., Calif. Tchr. St. Vincent's Catholic Sch., San Jose, Calif., 1969-70, Fremont (Calif.) Elem. Sch., 1970-72, LeRoy Boys Home, LaVerne, Calif., 1972-73; tchr. Grace Miller Elem. Sch., LaVerne, Calif., 1973-80, resource specialist, 1980-84; owner, mgr. Pioneer Take-out Franchises, Alhambra and San Gabriel, Calif., 1979-85; resource specialist, dept. chmn. Bonita High Sch., LaVerne, Calif., 1984—; mentor tchr. in space sci. Bonita Unified Sch. Dist., 1988—, rep. LVTV; owner, therapist So. Calif. Clinic Hypnotherapy, Claremont, Calif., 1988—; bd. dirs., recommending tchr., asst. dir. Project Turnabout, Claremont, Calif.; Teacher-in-Space cons. Bonita Unified Sch. Dist., LaVerne, 1987—; advisor Peer Counseling Program, Bonita High Sch., 1987—; advisor Air Explorers/Edwards Test Pilot Sch., LaVerne, 1987—; mem. Civil Air Patrol, Squadron 68, Aerospace Office, 1988—; selected amb. U.S. Space Acad.-U.S. Space Camp Acad., Huntsville, Ala., 1990; named to national (now internat.) teaching faculty challenger Ctr. for Space Edn., Alexandria, Va., 1990; regional coord. East San Gabiel Valley Future Scientists and Engrs. of Am.; amb. to U.S. Space Camp, 1990; mem. adj. faculty challenger learning ctr. Calif. State U., Dominguez Hills, 1994; rep. ceremony to honor astronauts Apollo 11, White House, 1994. Vol. advisor Children's Home Soc., Santa Ana, 1980-81; dist. rep. LVTV Channel 29, 1991; regional coord. East San Gabriel Valley chpt. Future Scientists and Engrs. of Am., 1992; mem. internat. invesigation Commn. UFOs, 1991. Recipient Tchr. of Yr., Bonita H.S., 1989, continuing svc. award, 1992; named Toyolaa Tchr. of Yr., 1994. Mem. NEA, AAUW, Internat. Investigations Com. on UFOs, Coun. Exceptional Children, Calif. Assn. Resource Specialists, Calif. Elem. Edn. Assn., Calif. Tchrs. Assn., Calif. Assn. Marriage and Family Therapists, Planetary Soc., Mutual UFO Network, Com. Sci. Investigation L5 Soc., Challenger Ctr. Space Edn., Calif. Challenger Ctr. Crew for Space Edn., Orange County Astronomers, Chinese Shar-Pei Am., Concord Club, Rare Breed Dog Club (L.A.). Republican. Home: 3257 La Travesia Dr Fullerton CA 92835-1455 Office: Bonita High Sch 115 W Allen Ave San Dimas CA 91773-1437

CAMERON, PAUL DRUMMOND, research facility administrator; b. Pitts., Nov. 9, 1939; s. Nelson Drummond and Veronica (Witco) C.; m. Virginia May Rusthoi. BA, L.A. Pacific Coll., 1961; MA, Calif. State U., L.A., 1962; PhD, U. Colo., 1966. Asst. prof. psychology Stout State U., Menomonie, Wis., 1966-67, Wayne State U., Detroit, 1967-69; assoc. prof. psychology U. Louisville, 1970-73, Fuller Grad. Sch. Psychology, Pasadena, Calif., 1976-79; assoc. prof. marriage and family therapy U. Nebr., Lincoln, 1979-80; pvt. practice psychologist Lincoln, 1980-83; chmn. Family Rsch. Inst., Washington, 1982-95, Colo. Springs, 1995—; reviewer Am. Psychologist, Jour. Gerontology, Psychol. Reports; presenter, witness, cons. in field. Author: Exposing the AIDS Scandal, 1988, The Gay 90's, 1993; contbr. articles to profl. jours. Mem. Ea. Psychol. Assn., Nat. Assn. for Rsch. and Treatment of Homosexuality. Republican. Lutheran. Office: Family Rsch Inst PO Box 62640 Colorado Springs CO 80962-2640

CAMERON, RICHARD IRWIN, property manager; b. Twin Falls, Idaho, Feb. 12, 1941; s. Wilbur Richard and Rose (Steinberg) C.; m. Judith Lynne Moe, Dec. 17, 1967; 1 child, Kevin Dale. Student, U. Idaho; BA, Idaho State U., 1963. Lic. real estate broker. Owner, mgr. Four C Ranches, Twin Falls, 1962-65, Cameron's Marina and Garage, Twin Falls, 1965-67; mgr. Doggie Diner Restaurants, Oakland, Calif., 1967-68; mgr. Bartels & Blaine A&W Restaurant, San Mateo, Calif., 1968-70, supr., gen. mgr., 1970-73; area supr. McDonalds Corp., L.A., 1973-78; pres. CamWal Enterprises, Inc., Alhambra, Calif., 1978-84, Four C Svcs., Inc., San Gabriel, Calif., 1979-85, Four C Properties, Fullerton, Calif., 1979—; cons. Enterprise Pub. Co., La Mirada, Calif., 1989—; v.p. pub. rels. Infinity Hyponosis Group, Orange County Calif., 1992—, So. Calif. Hypnotherapy, L.A. County, Orange County, 1993-95, pub. rels. officer Earth Angel Enterprises. Vol. counselor Children's Home Soc., Santa Ana, Calif., 1980-84; mem. Friends of the Observatory, Air/Space Mus., San Diego, Calif. With U.S. Air Guards, 1963-64. Recipient Nat. Franchisee of Yr. award Pioneer Take-Out Corp., L.A., 1984. Mem. Nat. Franchisees Assn. (bd. dirs. 1980-85), Nat. Restaurant Assn., Rotary, Elks. Republican. Home and Office: Four C Properties 3257 La Travesia Dr Fullerton CA 92835-1455

CAMMALLERI, JOSEPH ANTHONY, financial planner, retired air force officer; b. Bronx, N.Y., Feb. 2, 1935; s. Leo Anthony and Angela Marie (Mirandi) C.; BS, Manhattan Coll., 1956; M.S., Okla. State U., 1966; post-grad. Golden Gate U., 1974; children: Anthony R., Aaron L., Thomas K., Jeffrey A. Cert. life ins. instr., Calif. Commd. 2d lt. USAF, 1956, advanced through grades to lt. col., 1973; trainee flight crew, 1956-58; crew mem. B-52, 1958-64; behavioral scientist Aerospace Med. Rsch. Labs., Wright-Patterson AFB, Ohio, 1966-68; EB-66 crew mem. Tahkli AFB, Thailand, 1968-69; faculty mem. dept. life and behavioral scis. USAF Acad. (Colo.), 1969-74, assoc. prof., dir. operational psychology div., 1972-74, B-1 human factors engring. mgr. Air Force Flight Test Center, Edwards AFB, Calif., 1974-76, chief handbook devel., 1976-77; ret., 1977; account exec. Merrill Lynch, Pierce, Fenner & Smith, Sherman Oaks, Calif., 1977-80; acad. program rep. U. Redlands (Calif.), 1980-84, regional dir. admissions, 1984-86, mem. faculty Whitehead Coll., 1979—, assoc. dean admissions, 1986-89; faculty Golden Gate U., 1975-80; account exec. Humanomics Ins., 1989-90; corp. dir. tng. and edn. Fin. West Group, 1990-92, prin. CEO Spectrum Securities, Inc., Westlake Village, Calif., 1992-95; assoc. dean admission Alfred North Whitehead Coll. U. of Redlands, 1996—; registered gen. securities prin. Thomas F. White & Co., Inc., 1996—; CFO, registered prin. PLC Securities Corp., Ventura, Calif., 1996—; adj. faculty Calif. Luth. U., 1990—, Antioch U., 1992—; sec., 7th Ann. Narrow Gauge Conv. Com., Pasadena, Calif., 1986. Contbr. articles to profl. jours. Sec. com. centennial celebration Rio Grande So. Ry., Dolores, Colo., 1991; USAF Acad. Liason Officer, North Los Angeles County, 1992—. Decorated D.F.C., Air medal (5), Meritorious Service medal. Mem. Nat. Ry. Hist. Soc., Ry. and Locomotive Hist. Soc., Rocky Mountain R.R. Club, L.A. Live Steamers, Nat. Model R.R. Assn., Colo. R.R. Hist. Found. (life), Santa Fe Ry. Hist. Soc., USAF Acad. Athletic Assn. (life), DAV, Psi Chi. Home: 601 Hampshire Rd Apt 550 Westlake Village CA 91361-2303 Office: PLC Securities Corp 1727 Mesa Verde Ave Ste 203 Ventura CA 93003 also: Thomas F White & Co Inc 1727 Mesa Verde Ave Ste 203 Ventura CA 93003

CAMOUS, LOUISE MICHELLE, secondary education educator, sister; b. San Francisco, Oct. 21, 1954; d. Eugene Paul and Anna Elizabeth (Shay) C. BA, San Francisco State Univ., 1975. Cert. tchr., Calif. Tchr. Santa Barbara Sch., Dededo, Guam, 1975-76, Our Lady Mt. Carmel Sch., Agat, Guam, 1976-77, Our Lady of Visitacion, San Francisco, 1977-80, St. Vincent de Paul Sch., Phoenix, 1982-85, Marian Sch., Montebello, Calif., 1985-87, Notre Dame Regional Sch., Price, Utah, 1987-96. Founding bd. dirs. Habitat for Humanity of Castle Country, Price, 1989-92. Recipient Dedication to Youth Carbon County award Nat. Honor Soc. Carbon H.S. Chpt., Price, 1994, Notre Damean award from Notre Dame Regional Sch., 1995. Mem. Nat. Cath. Edn. Assn., Nat. Coun. Tchrs. Math. Democrat. Home: 26000 Altamont Rd Los Altos CA 94022-4317

CAMP, DELPHA JEANNE, counselor; b. Yakima, Wash., Apr. 20, 1937; d. George Emerson and Emilie Loraine (Rivard) Stevens; m. George Ernest Mills, Aug. 13, 1960 (dec. 1975); children: Adriene Phillips, Stacey Harcus, Ryan, Tiffany; m. James Clell Camp, June 24, 1978; children: Catherine Thompson (dec.), Wayne (dec.), Darla Coolman, John, Janna Barnes. BEd, Gonzaga Univ., 1959; MS, Univ. Oreg., 1977. Lic. profl. counselor; cert. grief counselor and death educator. Tchr. Riverside Sch. Dist., Milan, Wash., 1959-61, Cheney (Wash.) Sch. Dist., 1968-70; asst. prof. Univ. Oreg., Eugene, 1979-92; pvt. practice Eugene, 1992—; adj. faculty Marylhurst (Oreg.) Coll., 1992—. Mem. ACA, Assn. for Death Edn. and Counseling (bd. dirs. 1990-93, co-chair conf. 1994, Svc. award 1990), Am. Mental Health Counselors Assn., Oreg. Counseling Assn., Oreg. Mental Health Counselors Assn. Home: 440 E 39th Ave Eugene OR 97405-4722 Office: 317 W Broadway Ste 217 Eugene OR 97401-2890

CAMPANA, SAM KATHRYN, mayor. Exec. dir. Arizonans for Cultural Devel., Scottsdale, 1983—; mem. Scottsdale City Coun., 1986-94; mayor City of Scottsdale, 1996—. Office: Office of Mayor 3939 Civic Center Blvd Scottsdale AZ 85251

CAMPBELL, ADDISON JAMES, JR., writer; b. Dilliner, Pa., Dec. 16, 1933; s. Addison James Campbell and Nora Lee (Marshall) Reynolds; m. Fumie Murashige, Oct. 13, 1962; 1 child, Gary Clark Campbell. Pres. Action Bolt Corp., Houston, 1965-72. Author: Nanci's World, Ukelele Lil of Lihue, The Object; co-author: Fumie Murashige Campbell, 1994; contbr. numerous articles and research papers to profl. jours. Sgt. USMC, 1952-55. Recipient recognition award for Adult Correction Officer for Island of Kauai, State of Hawaii, 1987, 88.

CAMPBELL, ARTHUR WALDRON, lawyer, educator; b. Bklyn., Mar. 29, 1944; s. Wilburn Camrock and Janet Louise (Jobson) C.; m. Drusilla Newlon Green, June 7, 1969; children: Wilburn Camrock, Matthew Patrick. BA, Harvard U., 1966; JD, W.Va. U., 1971; M in Criminal Justice, Georgetown U., 1975. Bar: W.Va. 1971, D.C. 1971, Calif. 1974. Asst. U.S. atty. U.S. Justice Dept., Washington, 1971-73; clin. instr. D.C. Consortium Univs., 1973-76; law prof. Calif. Western Sch. Law, San Diego, 1976—; cons. W.Va. State Legis. Com. to Rewrite Criminal Code, 1972-73; chmn. Va. sect. Nat. Assn. Criminal Def. Lawyers Strike Force on Grand Jury Abuse, 1975-76; mem. ABA Com. on Privacy, Washington, 1974, D.C. Bar Landlord and Tenant Com., 1975, Neighborhood Legal Svcs., San Diego, 1982; pvt. prac. 1976—; chief exec. officer Trudar Prodns. Inc., San Diego, 1981—. Author: (legal treatise) Law of Sentencing, 1978, 2d edit., 1991, (coursebook) Entertainment Law, 1993, 4th edit., 1997, (books) Discoveries of a Workaholic, 1988, Meditations for Recovering Workaholics, 1990. Pres. Peace Store, San Diego, 1986. Recipient Harvard Nat. scholarship, 1962-63, Am. Jurisprudence awrd Lawyers Coop. Pub. Co., 1970-71, Prettyman Fellowship,

Georgetown U., 1971-73; middle weight boxing champion Harvard U., 1964-65. Mem. Fed. Defenders, Appellate Defenders, Peace Through Law Inst. Home: 4891 Sparks Ave San Diego CA 92110-1358 Office: Calif Western Sch Law 225 Cedar St San Diego CA 92101-3046

CAMPBELL, BARBARA ANN, podiatrist; b. Seattle, July 31, 1959; d. Mahlon Erb and Barbara Lee (Welch) C.; m. Allan Gray Dyer, Apr. 23, 1988. BS in Pre-medicine, Kans. State U., 1981; D of Podiatric Medicine, Calif. Coll. Podiatric Medicine, 1986. Diplomate Am. Bd. Podiatric Orthopedics and Primary Podiatric Medicine. Resident in podiatric surgery Cmty. Hosp. Med. Ctr., Phoenix, 1986-87; assoc. podiatrist Quinlan Foot and Ankle Ctr., Scottsdale, Ariz., 1987-95; pvt. practice podiatrist Barbar A. Campbell, DPM, Paradise Valley, Ariz., 1995—. Mem., vol. Internat. Soc. for Protection of Wild Mustangs and Burros-Bur. Land Mgmt., Scottsdale, 1991. Fellow Am. Coll. Foot and Ankle Orthopedics and Medicine; mem. Am. Coll. Foot and Ankle Surgeons (assoc.); mem. Am. Podiatric Med. Assn., Ariz. Podiatric Med. Assn. (sec. 1994-95, v.p. 1995-96), Am. Assn. for Women Podiatrists (regiona XIV rep. 1991-94, membership chair 1994-96). Lutheran. Office: Barbara A Campbell DPM 10575 N Tatum Blvd Ste C-123 Paradise Valley AZ 85253-1027

CAMPBELL, BEN NIGHTHORSE, senator; b. Auburn, Calif., Apr. 13, 1933; m. Linda Price; children: Colin, Shanan. BA, Calif. U., San Jose, 1957. Educator Sacramento Law Enforcement Agy.; mem. Colo. Gen. Assembly, 1983-86, U.S. Ho. Reps., 1987-93; U. S. Senator from Colorado, 1993—; rancher, jewelry designer, Ignacio, Colo. Chief No. Cheyenne Tribe. Named Outstanding Legislator Colo. Bankers Assn., 1984, Man of Yr. LaPlata Farm Bur., Durango, Colo., 1984; named one of Ten Best Legislators Denver Post/Channel 4, 1986. Mem. Am. Quarter Horse Assn., Am. Brangus Assn., Am. Indian Edn. Assn. Republican. Office: US Senate Senate Bldg 380 Russell Washington DC 20510

CAMPBELL, BRAD LEE, financial executive; b. Emmett, Idaho, Aug. 4, 1960; s. Worth and Carol (Smith) C.; m. Margaret R. Nelson, July 26, 1991. BBA in Acctg., Boise State U., 1982. Sr. auditor Ernst & Whinney, Anchorage, 1983-87; asst. contr. Alaska Housing Fin. Corp., Anchorage, 1987-94; contr. Key Bank of Alaska, Anchorage, 1994-95, Goldbelt, Inc., Juneau, Alaska, 1995—. Contbr. poetry to Am. Poetry Anthology, 1987/88. Bd. dirs., treas. Standing Together Against Rape, Anchorage, 1992-95. Republican. Office: Goldbelt Inc 9087 Glacier Hwy Ste 200 Juneau AK 99801

CAMPBELL, CAROLE ANN, sociology educator; b. Gallup, N.Mex., July 6, 1949; d. Albert James and Dorothy Elaine (Kauzlarich) Baumgardner; m. John H. Campbell (div.); 1 child, Jameel. BA summa cum laude, U. Albuquerque, 1978; MA, U. Colo., Denver, 1979; PhD, U. Colo., Boulder, 1984. Teaching and rsch. asst. U. Albuquerque, 1976-78; teaching and rsch. asst. U. Colo., Denver, 1978-79, Boulder, 1980-84; instr. sociology U. Nev., Las Vegas, 1985-86; assoc. prof. sociology Calif. State U., Long Beach, 1986—. Contbr. articles to profl. jours. AIDS educator, field placement coord. Calif. State U., Long Beach, 1986—. Mem. Am. Med. Writers Assn. Democrat. Office: Calif State U Dept Sociology 1250 N Bellflower Blvd Long Beach CA 90840-0006

CAMPBELL, CAROLYN MARGRET, communications consultant; b. Washington, Sept. 11, 1949; d. Donald Herman and Josephine Anne (Conrad) C. BA in Interior Design summa cum laude, Md. Inst. Coll. Art, 1971. Dir. spl. events Corcoran Gallery Art, Washington, 1977-79, dir. pub. rels., 1977-83; pub. rels. cons. Washington, 1983-85; dir. pub. info. Am. Film Inst., L.A., 1985; v.p. Josh Baran & Assocs., Venice, Calif., 1986-88; pres. Campbell Comms., L.A., 1988-94; dir. comms. Sch. of Arts and Arch. UCLA, 1995—. Named one of Outstanding Young Women Am., 1982, 83. Mem. Pub. Rels. Soc. Am. (Thoth Cert. Excellence 1979), ArtTable (membership and program coms.), Calif. & West Coast New Art Assn. (founder 1985, bd. dirs. 1985-90). Home and Office: 8530 Holloway Dr Apt 226 Los Angeles CA 90069-2477

CAMPBELL, CHARLES CURTIS, healthcare consultant; b. Orange, Calif., Dec. 16, 1944; s. J.M. Bill Campbell and Elizabeth M. (Burnham) Davis; m. Grace Lyn Buttermore, Nov. 7, 1965 (div. 1969); m. Sara Moores, Mar. 2, 1970; children: Brett James, Thomas Edward. BA, U. N.C., Asheville, 1974; postgrad., Harvard U., 1975-80. Dir. admissions Warren Wilson Coll., Asheville, N.C., 1974-79; dir. admissions Sch. Pub. Health Harvard U., Boston, 1979-82; ptnr. Burnham-Campbell, Greenport, N.Y., 1982-86; dir. MidAtlantic Med. Svcs., Inc.-Healthcare, Rockville, Md., 1986-89, Am. Psychmgmt., Arlington, Va., 1989-91; ptnr. Campbell & Assocs., Santa Barbara, Calif., 1991—; cons. numerous hosps., Md., Va., 1986-91. Trustee L.I. Hosp., Greenport, 1982-86; mem. exec. com. Santa Barbara Hospice, 1992—. Mem. Univ. Club (Santa Barbara). Unitarian-Universalist. Office: Campbell & Assocs 2330 Skyline Way Santa Barbara CA 93109-1245

CAMPBELL, C(HARLES) ROBERT, architect. BS in Archtl. Engrng., U. N.Mex., 1958. Registered architect, N.Mex., Tex., Ariz., Colo., Okla. With SMPC Architects, Albuquerque, 1955—, prin., 1969—, pres., CEO, 1991—; mem. State Bd. Examiners Architects, 1992-93, vice chmn., 1994, chmn., 1995-96; mem. adv. com. sch. architecture U. N.Mex.; vis. critic U. N.Mex. Profl. mem. Bernalillo County Bd. Appeals; bd. dirs. Presbyn. Healthcare Found. Mem. AIA (corp., pres., v.p., sec. Albuquerque chpt., mem. joint practice com. 1989—), Am. Arbitration Assn., Nat. Coun. Archtl. Registration Bd. (cert., juror/grader architecture registration exam, mem. architecture registration exam com. 1993-94, 94-95, 95-96), N.Mex. Soc. Architects (sec. 1974, pres. 1975-76). Office: 115 Amherst Dr SE Albuquerque NM 87106-1425*

CAMPBELL, CINDY IRENE, social service administrator; b. Alameda, Calif., Jan. 27, 1955; d. Reginald Marvin Corum and LeOsa Riley; m. David James Campbell, June 12, 1977. BS in Psychology and Social Work, Gallaudet U., Washington, 1977; MS in Rehab. Counseling, U. Md., 1992. Vocat. evaluation supr. Ctrs. for the Handicapped, Silver Spring, Md., 1978-81; outreach specialist Ardmore Industries, Hyattsville, Md., 1981-82; vocat. evaluator Nat. Assn. of the Deaf, Silver Spring, 1982-85; vocat. rehab. specialist Md. State Divsn. of Vocat. Rehab., Landover, Md., 1985-90; asst. dir. Inst. on Deaf-Blindness, Hyattsville, 1990-91; placement specialist Electronics Industries Found., Washington, 1991-92; exec. dir. S.W. Wash. Ctr. of the Deaf and Hard of Hearing, Vancouver, Wash., 1992—; dir. social svcs. North Lincon Hosp., 1996—; Wash. state rep. for ADA rev. and renewal, 1995. Cons. to Am. Deafness Assn. gov.'s coms. on ADA compliance, Olympia, Wash., 1992—, com. on employment, 1992; cons. Clark County Steering Com. on Social Health Svcs., Vancouver, 1992—, Columbia River Mental Health Svcs., Vancouver, 1993—. Named Counselor of the Yr., Md. Divsn. of Vocat. Rehab., 1987; mem. Nat. Disting. Svc. Registry, Libr. of Congress, 1987, 89. Mem. Nat. Assn. Rehab., Wash. Assn. Rehab., Am. Deafness and Rehab. Assn., Order Ea. Star. Office: North Lincoln Hosp Social Svcs 3043 NE 28th St Lincoln City OR 97367

CAMPBELL, COLIN HERALD, former mayor; b. Winnipeg, Man., Can., Jan. 18, 1911; s. Colin Charles and Aimee Florence (Herald) C.; m. Virginia Paris, July 20, 1935; children: Susanna Herald, Corinna Buford, Virginia Wallace. BA, Reed Coll., 1933. Exec. sec. City Club of Portland, 1934-39; alumni sec., dir. endowment adminstrn. Reed Coll., 1939-42, exec. sec. N.W. Inst. Internat. Rels. 1940-42, instr. photography, 1941-42; contract supr. engr. Kaiser Co., Inc., 1942-45; asst. pers. dir. Portland Gas & Coke Co., 1945-48; dir. indsl. rels. Pacific Power & Light Co., Portland, 1948-76. Mem. Oreg. Adv. Com. on Fair Employment Practices Act, 1949-55; trustee, chmn., pres. Portland Symphonic Choir, 1950-54; trustee Portland Civic Theater, 1951-54; bd. dirs. Portland Symphony Soc., 1957-60, Community Child Guidance Clinic, 1966-68; active United Way, 1945-75; bd. dirs. Contemporary Crafts Assn., 1972-76, treas., 1975-76; bd. dirs. Lake Oswego Corp., 1961-65, 71-73, 74-76, corp. sec., 1964, pres., 1973-74, treas., 1975-76; mem. com. on Citizen Involvement, City of Lake Oswego, 1975-77; chmn. Bicentennial Com., Lake Oswego; sec.-treas. Met. Area Communications Commn., 1980-85; treas. Clackamas County Community Action Agy., 1980-82, chmn., 1982-85; mem. fin. adv. com. W. Clackamas County LWV, 1974-76, 78-80; councilman City of Lake Oswego, 1977-78, mayor, 1979-85, chmn. libr. growth task force, 1987-89, chmn. hist. rev. bd., 1990-92; chmn. energy adv. com. League Oreg. Cities, 1982-84; mem. adv. bd., chmn. fin. com. Lake Oswego Adult Community Ctr. 1985-88; pres. Oswego Heritage Coun., 1992-95, sec., 1995-96, treas., 1997—; mem. County Blue Ribbon Com. on Law Enforcement, 1987-89; mem. fee arbitration panel Oreg. State Bar Assn., 1995—. Mem. Edison Electric Inst. (exec. com.), N.W. Electric Light and Power Assn., Lake Oswego C. of C. (v.p. 1986-87, chmn. Land Use com. 1990-91), Nat. Trust for Hist. Preservation, Hist. Preservation League Oreg., Portland Art Mus., Pacific N.W. Pers. Mgmt. Assn. (past regional v.p.), St. Andrews Soc., Oreg. Hist. Soc., Rotary (treas. Lake Oswego chpt. 1990-93). Republican. Presbyterian. Home: 398 Furnace St Lake Oswego OR 97034-3917

CAMPBELL, DAVID CHARLES, economist; b. Edmonton, Alberta, Can.; s. Gordon Alexander Campbell and Margaret Rosemary (Lacroix) Forbes; m. Joyce Claire Berney, June 13, 1964; children: Allan Douglas, Michael-Ramsey. B Commerce, U. B.C., Vancouver, Can., 1965; MA, San Francisco State U., 1967; MS, U. Calif., Berkeley, 1969, PhD, 1972. Acct. Sagadahoc Oil & Gas Corp., San Francisco, 1959-71; assoc. prof. econs. U. Idaho, Moscow, 1972-80; econ. advisor OAS, Port of Spain, Trinidad, 1973-74; vis. assoc. prof. govt. and pub. adminstrn. The Am. U., Washington, 1978-79; sr. economist U.S. Water Resources Coun., Washington, 1979-82; staff economist Nat. Wildlife Fedn., Washington, 1982-93; cons. economist, 1993—; vis. assoc. prof. govt. and pub. adminstrn. U. Md., 1993. Mem. Am. Water Resource Assn. (nat. capital sec., pres. 1988-89). Office: 2126 Mayview Dr Los Angeles CA 90027-4636

CAMPBELL, DEMAREST LINDSAY, artist, designer, writer; b. N.Y.C.; d. Peter Stephen III and Mary Elizabeth (Edwards) C.; m. Dale Gordon Haugo, 1978. BFA in Art History, MFA in S.E. Asian Art History, MFA in Theatre Design. Art dir., designer murals and residential interiors Campbell and Haugo Design Consultants, 1975—; chargeman scenic artist Am. Conservatory Theatre, 1976—. Designed, painted and sculpted over 200 prodns. for Broadway, internat. opera, motion pictures. Mem. NOW, Asian Art Mus. Soc., San Francisco. Mem. United Scenic Artists, Scenic & Title Artists and Theatrical Stage Designers., Sherlock Holmes Soc. London, Amnesty Internat., Nat. Trust for Hist. Preservation (Gt. Brit. and U.S.A. chpt.), Shavian Malthus Soc. (charter Gt. Brit. chpt.).

CAMPBELL, DIANE RITA, biologist, educator; b. Washington, Jan. 25, 1956; m. Theodore Mark Porter, Aug. 19, 1979; 1 child, David Campbell Porter. BS in Biology, Stanford U., 1977; PhD in Zoology, Duke U., 1983. Postdoctoral fellow U. Calif., Riverside, 1983-84; asst. prof. U. Va., Charlottesville, Va., 1984-89; asst. prof. U. Calif., Irvine, 1989-93, assoc. prof., 1993—. Contbr. articles to profl. jours. Mem. Am. Soc. Naturalists, Bot. Soc. Am., Ecol. Soc. Am., Soc. Study Evolution (assoc. editor 1992-94), Rocky Mountain Biol. Lab. Office: U Calif Dept Ecology & Evolutionary Biology Irvine CA 92717

CAMPBELL, DOUGLAS L., communications company executive, consultant; b. Pasadena, Calif., Jan. 29, 1954; s. Cecil Lewis and Georgia Mae (Frick) C.; m. Karen Elaine Palin, June 30, 1979; children: Kacie, Caleb. BA, Calif. State U., L.A., 1980. V.p. ops. Knight Enterprises, Burbank, Calif., 1975-81; field dir. Far East Broadcasting Co., Inc., Saipan, Marianas Islands, 1981-93; v.p. internat. adminstrn. Far East Broadcasting Co., Inc., La Mirada, Calif., 1993—. Mem. Soc. Profl. Journalists, Am. Mgmt. Assn. Republican. Office: Far East Broadcasting Co Inc 15700 E Imperial Hwy La Mirada CA 90638

CAMPBELL, FREDERICK HOLLISTER, lawyer, historian; b. Somerville, Mass., June 14, 1923; s. George Murray and Irene Ivers (Smith) C.; A.B., Dartmouth, 1944; J.D., Northwestern U., 1949; postgrad. Indsl. Coll. Armed Forces, 1961-62; M.A. in History, U. Colo., 1984, PhD in History, 1993; m. Amy Holding Strohm, Apr. 14, 1951; 1 dau., Susan Hollister. Served with USMCR, 1944-46; joined USMC, 1950, advanced through grades to lt. col., 1962; admitted to Ill. bar, 1950, U.S. Supreme Ct. bar, 1967, Colo. bar, 1968; judge adv. USMC, Camp Lejeune, N.C., Korea, Parris Island, S.C., El Toro, Calif., Vietnam, Washington, 1950-67; asso. editor Callaghan and Co., Chgo., 1949-50; practiced law, Colorado Springs, Colo., 1968-88; ptnr. firm Gibson, Gerdes and Campbell, 1969-79; pvt. practice law, 1980-88; gen. counsel 1st Fin. Mortgage Corp., 1988-96, vice chmn., corp. sec., 1993-96; hon. instr. history U. Colo., Colorado Springs, 1986—; vis. instr., Colo. Coll., 1993-95, asst. prof., 1996—. Mem. Estate Planning Coun., Colorado Springs, 1971-81, v.p., 1977-78. Rep. precinct committeeman, 1971-86; del. Colo. Rep. State Conv., 1972, 74, 76, 80, alt., 1978; trustee Frontier Village Found., 1971-77; bd. dirs. Rocky Mountain Nature Assn., 1975—, pres., 1979-92; dir. Rocky Mountain Nat. Park Assocs. 1986—, v.p. 1986-92, sec. 1992-95. Mem. Colo. Bar Assn., El Paso County Bar Assn., Am. Arbitration Assn., Marines Meml. Club, Phi Alpha Theta. Congregationalist. Author: John's American Notary and Commissioner of Deeds Manual, 1950. Contbr. articles to profl. jours. Home and Office: 2707 Holiday Ln Colorado Springs CO 80909-1217

CAMPBELL, GEOFFREY HAYS, materials scientist; b. Berkeley, Calif., Aug. 16, 1962; s. Graham Hays and Patricia Helen C.; m. Andrea Regina Berger, Aug. 20, 1992. BS, MIT, 1984; MS, U. Calif., Berkeley, 1986; PhD, U. Calif., Santa Barbara, 1990. Postdoctoral fellow Max Planck Inst. fur Metallforschung, Stuttgart, Germany, 1990-91; postdoctoral assoc. Lawrence Livermore (Calif.) Nat. Lab., 1991-93, metallurgist, 1993—. Mem. Am. Ceramic Soc., Materials Rsch. Soc., Microscopy Soc. Am., Inst. Mechanics and Materials (Young Investigator adv. com. 1993—). Democrat. Office: Lawrence Livermore Nat Lab L-356 Livermore CA 94551

CAMPBELL, GORDON MUIR, mayor; b. Vancouver, B.C., Can., Jan. 12, 1948, s. Charles Gordon and Margaret Janet (Muir) C.; m. Nancy J. Chipperfield, July 4, 1970; children: Geoffrey Gordon, Nicholas James. AB, Dartmouth Coll., 1970; MBA, Simon Fraser U., 1978. Tchr. Can. Univ. Service Overseas, Yola, Nigeria, 1970-72; exec. asst. to mayor City of Vancouver, 1972-76, alderman, 1984-86, mayor, 1986-94; project mgr. Marathon Realty Devel. Co., Vancouver, 1976-81; pres. Citycore Devel. Corp., Vancouver, 1981-86; leader Ofcl. Oppostion Liberal Caucus, B.C. Recipient Outstanding Alumni award Simon Fraser U., 1987. Office: 865 Hornby St Ste 907, Vancouver, BC Canada V6Z 2G3

CAMPBELL, HARRY WOODSON, geologist, mining engineer; b. Carthage, Mo., Jan. 14, 1946; s. William Hampton and Elizabeth Verle (LeGrand) C. BSEE, Kans. State U., 1969; MBA, U. Oreg., 1973, BS in Geology, 1975; MS in Geology, Brown U., 1978. Registered profl. engr., Wash.; cert. profl. geologist, Va. Geologist, mining engr. and phys. scientist U.S. Bur. Mines, Spokane, 1980-96; geologist U.S. Geol. Survey, Spokane, 1996—. Served with U.S. Army, 1969-71. Recipient Spl. Achievement award U.S. Bur. Mines, 1983, 86, 88. Mem. Geol. Soc. Am., Soc. Mining Engrs. Office: US Bur Mines 4257 E 26th Ave Spokane WA 99223-5623

CAMPBELL, JAMES, VII, patent lawyer; b. St. Louis, Oct. 12, 1934; s. James VI and Dorothy Lila (Brown) C.; m. Anne Elizabeth Jaudon, July 19, 1957; children: Elizabeth, Douglas, Kevin, Carolyn. BSEE, U. Colo., 1956; LLB, George Washington U., 1960. Bar: Oreg. 1961, U.S. Dist. Ct. Oreg. 1961, U.S. Ct. Appeals (fed. cir.) 1982, U.S. Ct. Appeals (9th cir.) 1968, U.S. Supreme Ct. 1989. Patent examiner U.S. Patent Office, Washington, 1956-60; patent atty. Klarquist, Sparkman, Campbell, Leigh & Whinston (and predecessor firms), Portland, Oreg., 1960—. Contbr. chpt. to Patent Law Essentials. Mem. ABA, IEEE, Oreg. Bar Assn. (contbr. chpt. to book), Am. Intellectual Property Law Assn., Oreg. Patent Assn. (pres.), Licensing Execs. Soc., Kiwanis. Republican. Baptist. Home: 18460 Ray Ridge Dr Lake Oswego OR 97034-7527 Office: Klarquist Sparkman Campbell Leigh & Whinston 1600 One World Trade Bldg 121 SW Salmon St Portland OR 97204-2901

CAMPBELL, JOHN ARTHUR, geology educator, researcher; b. Muskogee, Okla., Nov. 2, 1930; s. John Cope and Leda (Diffendaffer) C.; m. Patricia B. Bartlett, May 26, 1953; children: Keith, Allyn, Karyn. B of Geology, U. Tulsa, 1955; MS, U. Colo., 1957, PhD, 1966. Instr. geology Colo. State U., Ft. Collins, 1957-60, asst. prof., 1960-66, assoc. prof., 1966-74; rsch. geologist U.S. Geol. Survey, Denver, 1974-81; prof. geology Ft. Lewis Coll., Durango, Colo., 1981—, dept. chair, 1986-89; rsch. geologist U.S. Geol. Survey, Durango, Colo., 1981-85, 91-94; hon. prof. U. Colo., Denver, 1978-80; appointed by Gov. of Colo. to Minerals, Energy, Geology Adv. Bd., State of Colo., 1992-94, Oil and Conservation Com., 1990-94. Contbr. over 85 articles to profl. jours. Commr. Oil and Gas Conservation Commn., 1990-94. Served with USN, 1952-56. Recipient NSF Faculty fellowship, 1962-63, fellowship U. Colo., 1963. Fellow Geol. Soc. Am.; mem. Am. Assn. Petroleum Geologists, Soc. Econ. Paleontologists and Mineralogists, Four Corners Geol. Soc., Sigma Xi. Home: 195 Aspen Ln Durango CO 81301-8594 Office: Ft Lewis Coll Dept Geology Durango CO 81301

CAMPBELL, JOHN D., religious organization administrator. Media contact, coord. ch. svc. mission Ch. God. Office: Ch God We Can Assembly, 4717 56th St, Camrose, AB Canada T4V 2C4

CAMPBELL, JOHN HYDE, laser materials researcher, consultant; b. Ithaca, N.Y., Dec. 2, 1947. BS in Chemistry, Rochester Inst. of Tech., 1970; PhD in Phys. Chemistry, U. Ill., 1975. Rsch. chemist Lawrence Livermore (Calif.) Lab., 1975-77, nuclear waste project leader, 1977-80, laser material rsch. leader, 1980-88, BEAMLET project leader, 1989-94, laser glass project leader, 1994—. Patentee in field; contbr. over 35 articles to profl. jours. Recipient R&D-100 award R&D Mag., 1987, 88. Home: 2136 Westbrook Ln Livermore CA 94550 Office: Lawrence Livermore Nat Lab PO Box 808 Livermore CA 94550

CAMPBELL, KRISTINE KOETTING, pediatric nurse, administrator; b. Arcadia, Wis., Feb. 22, 1952; d. John Joseph and Dorothy Ann (Vogel) Koetting; m. Douglas William Campbell, Feb. 1, 1980; children: Colin William, Ryan Joseph. BSN, Viterbo Coll., La Crosse, Wis., 1974; MS in Nursing, Ohio State U., 1983; postgrad. studies in nursing, Oregon Health Scis. U., Portland, 1988—. RN Oreg., Wash.; TNCC (Emergency Nurses Assn.). Staff nurse Natal ICU Madigan Army Med. Ctr., Tacoma, Wash., 1974-76; head nurse nursery US Army Hosp., Augsburg, Germany, 1976-79; head nurse pediatrics US Army Hosp., Ft. Campbell, Ky., 1979-81; instr. pediatric and nursey nurses Columbus (Ohio) Tech. Inst., 1983-84; instr. pediatric nursing Ohio State U., Columbus, 1984-87; grad. rsch. asst. Oreg. Health Scis. Univ., Portland, 1988—; nursing supr. Landstuhl (Germany) Army Med. Ctr., 1990-91; chief nurse 396th Combat Support Hosp., Vancouver, Wash., 1995—; child educator tng. adults in positive parenting, Longview, Wash., 1992—. Co-author: (computer simulation) Lucy Web a four year old with Down's Syndrome undergoing a tonsillectomy. Mem. PTO, Longview, Wash., 1988—. Capt. U.S. Army, 1974-81; col. USAR. Recipient Instnl. Nat. Rsch. Svc. award, Oreg. Health Scis. U., 1990. Mem. ANa, Nat. Coun. on Family Rels., Res. Officers Assn., Assn. Mil. Surgeons U.S., Sigma Theta Tau. Democrat. Home: 3 Country Club Dr Longview WA 98632-5424 Office: Oreg Health Scis U Sch Nursing 3181 SW Sam Jackson Park Rd Portland OR 97201-3011

CAMPBELL, LEE ANN, microbiology educator; b. Altoona, Pa., Sept. 12, 1955; d. Ronald Charles Crain and Ruth Ann Hooper Crain Saleme. BS in Microbiology, Pa. State U., 1977, MS in Microbiology, 1979, PhD in Microbiology, 1982. Grad. teaching asst. dept. microbiology Pa. State U., 1977-82; postdoctoral fellow U. Rochester, N.Y., 1982-83; scientist dept. microbiology U. Rochester, 1984-85; asst. prof. dept. pathobiology U. Wash., Seattle, 1985-91, mem. grad. sch. faculty, 1985—, faculty mem. interdisciplinary molecular/cell biology prog., 1990—, assoc. prof. dept. pathobiology, 1991-96, prof. pathobiology, 1996—; ad hoc grant reviewer The Wellcome Trust, London, 1992, The Israel Sci. Found., 1993; ad hoc grant reviewer Dept. Vets. Affairs, 1994; ad hoc mem. site visit com. BM-1 Study Sect., NAIAD/NIH, 1992, ad hoc mem. BM-1 Study Sect., 1995, mem. BM-1 Study Sect. 1996—; cons. Microprobe, Bothel, Wash., 1989-90; lectr. in field. Contbr. numerous articles to profl. jours.; patentee in field; reviewer Jour. Clin. Microbiology, Gene, Am. Jour. Vet. Medicine, Jour. Immunology, Jour. Infectious Disease, Clin. Infectious Disease, European Jour. Epidemiology, European Jour. Clin. Microbiology and Infectious Diseases; mem. Wash. Pub. Health Editl. Bd., 1987—. Pa. State U. Alumnae Award scholar, 1975; grantee N.Y. State Health Rsch. Coun., 1982-83, Edna McConnell Clark Found., 1985-87, 88, 89-90, NIH, 1986-91, 88-93, 90-91, 91—, 92—, 93—, USDA, 1992-96, Pfizer Labs., 1991-94. Mem. Am. Soc. Microbiology, Sigma Xi, Phi Kappa Phi. Home: 17515 8th Ave NE Seattle WA 98155-3603 Office: Univ of Wash Dept Pathobiology Box 357238 Seattle WA 98195

CAMPBELL, MARILYN B., judge; b. Wendell, Idaho, Dec. 11, 1944. BA, U. Idaho, 1967; MA in French Lit. with honors, Ariz. State U., 1970, JD, 1977. Bar: Utah 1977, U.S. Dist. Ct. Utah 1977, U.S. Ct. Appeals (10th cir.) 1982. Tchr. French Twin Falls (Idaho) Sch. Dist., 1967-69, Tempe (Ariz.) H.S., Phoenix Jr. Coll., 1972-73; assoc. atty. Johnson Durham and Moxley, Salt Lake City, 1977-79, Fabian and Clendenin, Salt Lake City, 1979-81; dep. county atty. Salt Lake County, Salt Lake City, 1981; asst. U.S. atty. criminal divsn. Office of U.S. Atty. Dist. Utah, 1981-95; judge U.S. Dist. Ct. Utah, 1995—. Mem. Utah Bar Assn., Ft. Douglas HIdden Valley Country Club. Office: US Dist Ct Utah Rm 110 US Ct House 350 S Main St Salt Lake City UT 84101

CAMPBELL, PATRICK MILTON, internist, educator; b. Vancouver, Wash., Mar. 17, 1955; s. Robert Owen Campbell and Phyllis June (Mattison) Lindsley; m. Carolyn Ann Lintner, May 23, 1989; children: Thomas S., Jessica M. Student, Lewis and Clark Coll., 1973-75; BA in Chemistry and Biology, U. Calif., Santa Cruz, 1981; MD, U. Calif., Irvine, 1988. Diplomate Am. Bd. Internal Medicine. Resident primary care internal medicine program U. Calif., Davis, 1988-91; assoc. med. dir. MED Ctr., Sacramento, 1991-92; pvt practice in internal medicine Redding, Calif., 1993—; staff dept. Medicine Redding Med. Ctr., Redding Splty. Hosp., Redding, 1993—; staff Mercy Med. Ctr., Redding, Calif., 1993—; med. dir. Mercy Preventive Cardiology and Diabetes Ctr., 1995—; clin. instr. U. Calif. Davis, Sacramento, 1991-92; staff dept. Medicine Sutter Cmty. Hosps., Sacramento, 1992—. Contbr. articles to profl. jours. U. Calif. MacKenzie scholar, 1986-88, Fight for Sight Inc. fellow, summer 1982, 83. Mem. ACP, ADA, Am. Heart Assn. Home: 8250 Muscat Ct Redding CA 96001-9575 Office: 1555 East St Ste 300 Redding CA 96001-1153

CAMPBELL, RICHARD ALDEN, electronics company executive; b. Bend, Oreg., July 31, 1926; s. Corlis Eugene and Lydia Amney (Peck) C.; m. Edna Mary Seaman, June 12, 1948; children: Stephen Alden, Douglas Niall (dec.), Carolyn Joyce. B.S. in Elec. Engring., U. Ill., 1949, M.S. in Elec. Engring., 1950. With TRW Inc., Redondo Beach, Calif., 1954-87, exec. v.p., 1979-87; bus. cons., profl. co. dir. Rolling Hills Estates, Calif., 1987—; bd. dirs. Novadyne Computer Systems, Inc. Patentee in radio communications. Bd. dirs. U. Ill. Found., Hugh O'Brian Youth Found. With USN, 1944-46. Recipient Alumni Honor award U. Ill. Coll. Engring. Mem. IEEE (life), Am. Electronics Assn. (pres. 1969, dir. 1970), Phi Kappa Phi, Tau Beta Pi, Eta Kappa Nu, Sigma Tau, Pi Mu Epsilon, Phi Eta Sigma, Rolling Hills Country Club, Rancheros Visitadores Club, Los Caballeros Club. Republican.

CAMPBELL, ROBERT ALLEN, pediatrician; b. Toledo, Dec. 21, 1924; s. Glenn Harold and Harriet Mae (Kintzley) C.; m. Mary Christine Muchka, Sept. 21, 1949; children: Robert Perry, Mary Ellen, Catherine Anne. BA, U. Calif., Berkeley, 1954; MD, U. Calif., San Francisco, 1958. Rsch. asst. dept. zoology U. Calif., Berkeley, 1950-54; intern. resident U. Calif., San Francisco, 1954-58; instr. pediatrics U. Oreg. Med. Sch., Portland, 1961-63, asst. prof., 1963-67, assoc. prof., 1967-72, prof., 1972-91, prof. emeritus, 1991—; dir. pediat. renal-metabolic rsch. lab. OHSU, Portland, 1963—. Editor: Advances in Polyamine Research, 1978; contbr. articles to profl. jours., chpts. to books. Mem. World Coun., Portland, 1988—, Am. Chinese Orgn., Portland, 1988—; trustee, dir. Cystic Fibrosis Soc. Oreg., Kidney Assn. Oreg., Kerr Ctr. for Children, Portland. USPHS fellow U. Oreg. Med. Sch., 1961-63, Am. Pediat. Soc., Wyeth fellow, 1960-61. Fellow Am. Acad. Pediatrics, Am. Pediatric Soc., Am. Soc. Nephrology, Am. Soc. Pediat. Nephrology, Internat. Soc. Nephrology, Internat. Pediat. Nephrology Assn. Office: Oreg Health Sci U 3181 SW Sam Jackson Park Rd Portland OR 97201-3011

CAMPBELL, ROBERT CHARLES, clergyman, religious organization administrator; b. Chandler, Ariz., Mar. 9, 1924; s. Alexander Joshua and Florence (Betzner) C.; m. Lotus Idamae Graham, July 12, 1945; children:

Robin Carl, Cherry Colleen. AB, Westmont Coll., 1944; BD, Eastern Bapt. Theol. Sem., 1947, ThM, 1949, ThD, 1951, DD (hon.), 1974; MA, U. So. Calif., 1959; postgrad., Dropsie U., 1949-51, U. Pa., 1951-52, NYU, 1960-62, U. Cambridge, Eng., 1969; DLitt (hon.), Am. Bapt. Sem. of West, 1972; HHD (hon.), Alderson-Broaddus Coll., 1979; LHD (hon.), Linfield Coll., 1982; LLD (hon.), Franklin Coll., 1986. Ordained to ministry Am. Bapt. Ch., 1947; pastor 34th St. Bapt. Ch., Phila., 1945-49; instr. Eastern Bapt. Theol. Sem., Phila., 1949-51; asst. prof. Eastern Coll., St. Davids, Pa., 1951-53; assoc. prof. N.T. Am. Bapt. Sem. of West, Covina, Cal., 1953-54, dean, prof., 1954-72; gen. sec. Am. Bapt. Chs. in U.S.A., Valley Forge, Pa., 1972-87; pres. Eastern Bapt. Theol. Sem., Phila., 1987-89, ret.; Vis. lectr. Sch. Theology at Claremont, Calif., 1961-63, U. Redlands, Calif., 1959-60, 66-67, Fuller Theology Seminary, Calif., 1992—; Bd. mgrs. Am. Bapt. Bd. of Edn. and Publ., 1956-59, 65-69; v.p. So. Calif. Bapt. Conv., 1967-68; pres. Am. Bapt. Chs. of Pacific S.W., 1970-71; Pres. N.Am. Bapt. Fellowship, 1974-76; mem. exec. com. Bapt. World Alliance, 1972-90, v.p., 1975-80; mem. exec. com., gov. bd. Nat. Council Chs. of Christ in U.S.A., 1972-87; del. to World Council of Chs., 1975, 83, mem. central com., 1975-90. Author: Great Words of the Faith, 1965, The Gospel of Paul, 1973, Evangelistic Emphases in Ephesians, Jesus Still Has Something To Say, 1987. Home: 125 Via Alicia Santa Barbara CA 93108-1769

CAMPBELL, ROBERT HEDGCOCK, investment banker; b. Ann Arbor, Mich., Jan. 16, 1948; s. Robert Miller and Ruth Adele (Hedgcock) C.; m. Katherine Kettering, June 17, 1972; children: Mollie DuPlan, Katherine Elizabeth, Anne Kettering. BA, U. Wash., 1970, JD, 1973. Bar: Wash. 1973, Wash. State Supreme Ct. 1973, Fed. 1973, U.S. Dist. Ct. (we. dist.) Wash. 1973, U.S. Ct. Appeals (9th cir.) 1981. Assoc. Roberts & Shefelman, Seattle, 1973-78, ptnr., 1978-85; sr. v.p. Lehman Bros., Inc., Seattle, 1985-87, mng. dir., 1987—; dir., treas. Nat. Assn. Bd. Lawyers, Hinsdale, Ill., 1982-85; pres., trustee Wash. State Soc. Hosp. Attys., Seattle, 1982-85; mem. econs. dept. vis. com. U. Wash., 1995—. Contbr. articles to profl. jours. Trustee Bellevue (Wash.) Schs. Found., 1988-91, pres., 1989-90; nation chief Bellevue Eastside YMCA Indian Princess Program, 1983-88; trustee Wash. Phikeia Found., 1983-91, Sandy Hook Yacht Club Estates, Inc., 1993—; mem. Wash. Gov.'s Food Processing Coun., 1990-91. Republican. Home: 8604 NE 10th St Medina WA 98039-3915 Office: Lehman Bros Columbia Seafirst Ctr 701 5th Ave Ste 7101 Seattle WA 98104-7016

CAMPBELL, SCOTT, newspaper publishing company executive; b. May 25, 1956. BS, U. Oreg., 1979. Pub. The Columbian, Vancouver, Wash., 1980-86, pres., COO, 1986-88, pub., 1988—. Chair adv. coun. Wash. State U.; chair S.W. Wash. Higher Edn. Consortium; mem. exec. bd. Columbia River Econ. Devel. Coun. Mem. Newspaper Assn. Am. (mem. bus. devel. com.), Pacific N.W. Newspaper Assn. (pres.), Allied Daily Newspapers Wash. Office: Columbian Pub Co PO Box 180 701 W 8th St Vancouver WA 98660-3008

CAMPBELL, STEWART CLAWSON, retired sales executive, artist; b. Salt Lake City, Aug. 18, 1903; s. Alexander Stewart and Alice Young (Clawson) C.; m. Mary M. McIntyre, June 27, 1942 (dec. July 1983); children: Stewart, Jeffrey, David (dec.), James, Scott, Judith. Student, U. Utah, 1928-31. Pres. Mormon Mission Conf., Dresden, Germany, 1924-28; surveyor Wasatch Gas Co., Salt Lake City, 1928-31, United Gas Sys., Houston, 1931-32; warehouse supr. Maceys Dept. Store, N.Y.C., 1932-35; overseer Alaska Rural Rehab. Corp., Palmer, 1935-39; regional adminstr. Nat. Youth Adminstrn., Cleve., 1939-41; spl. asst. Fed. Civil Def. Emergency Adminstrn., Washington, 1941-42; pres. Utah Wonderland Stages, Salt Lake City, 1946-51; regional adminstr. Fed. Civil Def. Adminstrn., 1952-56; gen. sales mgr. O.C. Tanner Co., Salt Lake City, 1956-75; ret., 1975. One-man shows include Wilma Wayne Gallery, London; maker Petrohlyphs replicas (ancient Indian images in stone); concieved combinationmosaic (new art form) for Human Rights Space Movement and Tower. Lt. col. USAF, 1942-46. Named to Hon. Order of Ky. Colonels, 1953. Mem. LDS Ch. Home: 777 E So Temple 10A Salt Lake City UT 84102

CAMPBELL, THOMAS J., congressman, law educator; b. 1952. BA, U. Chgo., 1973, MA, 1973, PhD, 1980; JD, Harvard U., 1976. Bar: Ill. 1976, D.C. 1977. Law clk. to Hon. George E. MacKinnon U.S. Ct. Appeals (D.C. cir.), 1976-77; law clk. U.S. Supreme Ct., Washington, 1977-78; atty. Winston & Strawn, Chgo., 1978-80; White House fellow Office Chief of Staff, Washington, 1980-81; exec. asst. to the Dep. Atty. Gen. U.S. Dept. of Justice, Washington, 1981; dir. Bur. of Competition FTC, D.C., 1981-83; assoc. prof. Stanford (Calif.) U., 1983-87, prof. law, 1987—. Editor Harvard Law Rev. Mem. U.S. Congress, 1989-93, 95—; Calif. state senator, 1993-95. Mem. ABA (antitrust sect., program chmn. 1984); Phi Beta Kappa. Office: care Joel Starr Congress Rayburn House Rm 2442 Washington DC 20515 also: Stanford Law Sch Nathan Abbott Way Stanford CA 94305

CAMPBELL, WILLIAM JOSEPH, academic director; b. Bklyn., N.Y., Nov. 26, 1944; s. William Joseph and Loretta Jane (Graessle) C. BA in Philosophy, U. Dayton, 1966; MS in Edn., Fordham U., 1972; MA in Theology, St. John's U., 1977; MA in Pvt. Sch. Adminstrn., U. San Francisco, 1986; EdD in Ednl. Mgmt., U. LaVerne, 1990. Cert. sch. adminstr., Calif.; cert. guidance counselor, N.Y. Tchr., dean students Most Holy Trinity H.S., Bklyn., 1966-68; tchr., coach Charlotte (N.C.) Cath. H.S., 1968-69; tchr., dir. freshman guidance Chaminade H.S., Mineola, N.Y., 1969-82; tchr., counselor Junipero Serra H.S., Gardena, Calif., 1982-84; academic asst. prin. Archbishop Riordan H.S., San Francisco, 1984-87; prin. Chaminade Coll. Prep., West Hills, Calif., 1987-90; dir. edn. Marianists, Cupertino, Calif., 1990-95; asst. supt. Archdiocese of Portland, Oreg., 1996—. Bd. dirs. Regis H.S., Staton, Oreg. Mem. ASCD, Nat. Assn. Secondary Sch. Prins., Nat. Cath. Edn. Assn., World Future Soc., Assn. for Religious and Values Issues in Counseling, Phi Delta Kappa. Office: Archdiocese of Portland 2838 E Burnside St Portland OR 97214

CAMPER, JOHN SAXTON, public relations and marketing executive; b. Trenton, N.J., Apr. 24, 1929; s. Thomas Emory and Mildred Ruth (Burke) C.; m. Ferne Arlene Clanton; children: Susan Jennifer, John Saxton III. BS in History and Econs., U. Nebr., 1968. Enlisted U.S. Army, 1948, commd. to 1st lt., advanced through ranks to maj., 1972, ret., 1972; regional mktg. officer First Bank System, Mont., 1978-83; lectr., instr. mktg. and advt. pub. rels.; pres. Camper Comm., Helena, 1983—; dir. Profl. Devel. Ctr., Mont., 1984-91. Decorated Legion of Merit. Mem. Helena Advt. Fedn. (1st pres., founder), Rotary Internat. Republican. Methodist.

CAMPESE, VITO MICHELE, nephrologist; b. May 23, 1942; m. Stefania; 1 child, Paola. MD, U. Bari, Italy, 1966. Diplomate Am. Bd. Nephrology, Am. Bd. Internal Medicine; cert. in nephrology, Italy. Internship, residency Policlinico, Bari, Italy, 1966-67, 67-69; fellowship in nephrology U. Bari, Italy, 1971-73, asst. prof. Inst. of Nephrology, 1973-74; fellowship hypertension svc. U. So. Calif., 1974-75; asst. prof. hypertension svc. L.A. County-U. So. Calif. Med. Ctr., L.A., 1975-77, asst. prof. divsn. nephrology, 1977-80, assoc. prof. divsn. nephrology, 1980-85, prof. medicine divsn. nephrology, 1985—, assoc. chief divsn. nephrology, 1987—; physician specialist L.A. County-U. So. Calif., L.A.; reviewer for various journs. in field; invited speaker in field. Mem. editorial bd. Hypertension, Jour. of the Am. Soc. of Nephrology, Clin. and Exptl. Pharmacology and Physiology, Jour. of Nephrology, Jour. of Human Hypertension, Clin. Advances in the Treatment of Hypertension; asst. editor Am. Jour. of Nephrology; contbr. numerous articles to profl. jours. Mem. adv. coun. Kidney Found. So. Calif., 1977—; mem. promotion com. dept. medicine U. So. Calif., 1989—, mem. med. student rsch. com., 1990—; mem. Nat. High Blood Pressure Edn. Program, 1991—. Recipient The Domenico Cotungo medal and award in Nephrology, 1988, The Regione Puglia Targa D'oro award for contbn. to Sci., 1991; grantee NIH, 1988-92, 92-95, 91-95, Baxter, 1994-97, Pfizer Lab, 1991-93. Mem. Internat. Soc. Nephrology, Internat. Soc. Hypertension, Coun. for High Blood Pressure Rsch., Am. Soc. Nephrology, Am. Soc. Renal Biochemistry and Metabolism, The Endocrine Soc., Western Soc. Clin. investigation, Italian-Am. Soc. Nephrologists, Am. Soc. Hypertension. Office: U So California Dept Nephrology 2025 Zonal Ave # 4250 Los Angeles CA 90033-4526

CAMPIONE, MARY ELLEN, software engineer, consultant, writer; b. Salinas, Calif., Aug. 30, 1963; d. David Arthur Sr. and Ellen Loraine (Loughran) McNabb; m. Richard James Campione, Oct. 2, 1993; 1 child, Sophia Ann. BS in Computer Sci., Calif. Poly., 1985. Programmer Ford Aerospace, Palo Alto, Calif., 1985-88; software engr. Sun Microsystems, Mountain View, Calif., 1988-89; developer support engr. Next Computer Inc., Redwood City, Calif., 1990-91; ind. software cons., writer San Francisco, 1991-96; tech. writer Sun Microsystems, Mountain View, Calif., 1996—. Author: Typesetting Tables on The Unix System, 1990, Postscript By Example, 1992, The Java Tutorial, 1996.

CAMPISI, DOMINIC JOHN, lawyer; b. San Jose, Calif., Apr. 30, 1944; s. Dominic Albert and Mary Elizabeth (Lukes) C.; m. Mary Beth Gillick, Jan. 5, 1969; children: Anne Elizabeth, Megan Moran, Catherine Marie. BA, U. Santa Clara, Calif., 1966; M in Pub. Affairs, Princeton U., 1968; JD, Yale U., 1974. Nat. field rep. Cmty. Rels. Svc., Washington, 1968, 71; clk. U.S. Ct. Appeals, Seattle, 1974-75; assoc. Morrison & Foerster, San Francisco, 1975-80; ptnr. Evans Latham Harris & Campisi, San Francisco, 1980—; dir. Cuvaison Winery, Calistoga, Calif., 1989—; chmn., vice chmn. trust and estate litigation com. sect. Real Property Probate and Trust, Chgo., 1984—. Author: Estate & Trust Litigation, 1981-96; contbr. chpt. to book, articles to Jour. Real Property Probate and Trust. With U.S. Army, 1969-71. Fellow Am. Coll. Trust & Estate Counsel; mem. Nat. Coll. Probate Judges. Office: Evans Latham Harris & Campisi 1 Post St Ste 600 San Francisco CA 94104-5210

CAMPO, CATHERINE (SAUTER), computer programmer; b. Balt., Oct. 16, 1969; d. Donald and Anna (Pillar) S. BA in Physics, U. Md., Balt., 1991. Rsch. analyst Areté Assocs., Sherman Oaks, Calif., 1991-93; test engr. Centronic, Inc., Newbury Park, Calif., 1993-94; computer scientist Trandes Corp., San Diego, 1995-96; programmer Orincon Corp., San Diego, 1996, Gen. Atomics, San Diego, 1996—. Mem. Am. Phys. Soc., Sigma Pi Sigma, Pi Mu Epsilon. Democrat. Roman Catholic. Home: 10545 Sea Mist Way San Diego CA 92121 Office: Gen Atomics 3550 General Atomics Ct San Diego CA 92121

CAMPOBASSO, CRAIG, casting director; b. Sun Valley, Calif., Oct. 5, 1959; s. Fred Vierow and Marie Donna King Campobasso; stepson of Louis V. Campobasso. Acting coach L.A., 1987—; casting dir. for motion pictures: Dickwad--A Comedy, 1993, The Silence of the Hams, 1993, Innocent Adultery, 1993, Prancer, 1994, Red Palms, 1995, Stigmata. 44, 1994, Stick Fighter, 1994, L.A.'s Finest--To Protect and Serve, 1994, McNelly's Rangers, 1994, Timebomb, Endless Descent, 1994, Watch the Skies, 1995, Joe's Wedding, 1996, Original Gangsters, 1996, Critical Move, 1996, The Good Bad Guy, 1996, May Day!, 1997, Clear Target, 1997, Boy Meets Girl, 1997, Shattered Illusion, 1997; TV credits include Cinemax's Payback, 1994, Picket Fences, 1995-96 (nominated for Emmy for outstanding achievement in casting for a TV series); assoc. casting dir. for TV, Steven Spielberg's Amazing Stories. Author: Autobiography of an Extraterrestrial: The Star-Seed Journals, 1995—.(Films) Mayday, 1997, Clear Target, 1997, Boys Meet Girls, 1997, ShatteredIllusion, 1997. Vol. Babies with AIDS, L.A., 1992.

CAMPOS, JOAQUIN PAUL, III, chemical physicist, regulatory affairs analyst; b. L.A., Feb. 16, 1962; s. Joaquin Reyna and Maria Luz (Chavez) C.; m. Barbara Ann Esquivel, Oct. 31, 1987; children: Courtney Luz, Nathaniel Alexander. Student, U. Calif., Santa Cruz, 1980-85, UCLA, 1985-86. Tutor U. Calif., Santa Cruz, 1980-82, admissions liaison, 1982-84; chem. teaching assoc. L.A. Unified Sch. Dist., 1985-87; pvt. tutor Santa Clara, L.A., 1987-89; tech. specialist Alpha Therapeutics Corp., L.A., 1989-95; regulatory affairs specialist III Gensia Labs., Ltd., Irvine, Calif., 1995-96; sr. assoc. Genentech, Inc., South San Francisco, 1996—; cons. L.A. Unified Sch. Dist., 1985-87. Docent in tng. L.A. Mus. of Sci. and Industry, 1989. Scholar, grantee So. Calif. Gas Co., L.A., 1980-84, Sloan Rsch. fellow, 1981-82. Mem. Am. Chem. Soc., N.Y. Acad. Sci., Am. Inst. Chemists, Am. Assn. Physics Tchrs., AAAS, Fed. Am. Scientists, Pharm. Rsch. Mfrs. Am., Internat. Union of Pure and Applied Chemistry, Drug Info. Assn., Math. Assn. Am., Soc. Hispanic Profl. Engrs., IEEE. Office: Genentech Inc 460 Pt San Bruno Blvd South San Francisco CA 94080-4990

CAMPOS, SANTIAGO E., federal judge; b. Santa Rosa, N.Mex., Dec. 25, 1926; s. Ramon and Miquela Campos; m. Patsy Campos, Jan. 27, 1947; children: Theresa, Rebecca, Christina, Miquela Feliz. J.D., U. N.Mex., 1953. Bar: N.Mex. 1953. Asst., 1st asst. atty gen. State of N.Mex., 1955-57; judge 1st Jud. Dist. N.Mex., 1971-78; judge U.S. Dist. Ct. N.Mex., Santa Fe, 1978—, sr. judge, 1992—. Served as seaman USN, 1944-46. Mem. State Bar of N.Mex., First Jud. Dist. Bar Assn. (hon.), Hon. Order of Coif. Office: US Dist Ct PO Box 2244 Santa Fe NM 87504-2244*

CANADA, STEPHEN ANDREW, writer; b. Portland, Maine, Apr. 20, 1941; s. Andrew Jackson and Hazel Maude (Archibald) C.; divorced. Student, Upsala (Sweden) U., 1964-65, Alliance Francaise, Paris, 1967; BA, Calif. State Coll., 1969; MA, Calif. State U., L.A., 1977. lcetr. in field. Author: Crop Circle Language 10 vols., 1990-91, UFOs' Origin Identified, 1993, The Mars Structures--Who Made Them?, 1993, UFOs Crop Circles and Mars Structures--Their Common Origin, 1993, Crop Circles Series, Communication, 4 vols., 1993, Crop Cirles: The End of Time, 1996, Crop Circles: A Convergence of Narrative, 1996; and 31 other books; also poetry; paintings exhibited at various group shows, 1969-86. Home: 111 W Romie Ln #8 Salinas CA 93901

CANADA, WILLIAM H., plastic surgeon; b. Huntington, W.Va., Sept. 5, 1930. MD, W.Va. U., 1956. Intern Meml. Hosp., Charleston, W.Va., 1956-57, gen. surgeon, 1957-59; plastic surgeon Baylor U. Med. Ctr., Houston, 1959-61; chief plastic surgeon Las Vegas Surgery Ctr., 1987—; attending surgeon Univ. Med. Ctr., Las Vegas; clin. instr. plastic surgery Baylor U., Houston. Fellow ACS. Office: 8068 W Sahara Ave Ste G Las Vegas NV 89117-1973

CANADAY, NICHOLAS, retired English educator; b. N.Y.C., Dec. 22, 1928; s. Nicholas and Nadine (Mueller) C.; m. Amelia Crossland, Mar. 1, 1952; children: Ellen, Nicholas III, Thomas. BA, Princeton U., 1950; MA, U. Fla., 1955, PhD, 1957. Instr. English, asst. prin. The Bolles Sch., Jacksonville, Fla., 1952-54; grad. tchg. asst. U. Fla., Gainesville, 1954-57; instr. English La. State U., Baton Rouge, 1957-59, asst. prof. English, 1959-65, assoc. prof. English, 1965-73, prof. English, 1973-86, prof. emeritus English, 1986—; Fulbright Lectr. in Am. lit. Kanazawa (Japan) U., 1963-64, Trondheim (Norway) U., 1977-78, Shandong U., Jinan, China, 1986-87; Danforth Black Studies fellow Yale U., New Haven, 1970-71. Author: Melville and Authority, 1968; contbr. articles to profl. jours. Vol. Downtown Emergency Svc. Ctr., Seattle, 1987-93; precinct com. officer Dem. Party, Seattle, 1988—; vestry mem. St. Mark's Cathedral, Seattle, 1993-96. Cpl. U.S. Infantry, 1950-52. Episcopalian. Home: 228 11th Ave E Apt 301 Seattle WA 98102-5784

CANADAY, RICHARD A., lawyer; b. Alton, Ill., Aug. 26, 1947. AB, Stanford U., 1969; JD, U. Calif., 1973. Bar: Oreg. 1973, Wash. 1987. Ptnr. Miller, Nash, Wiener, Hager & Carlsen, Portland, Oreg. Mem. ABA, Oreg. State Bar, Wash. State Bar Assn. Office: Miller Nash Wiener Hager & Carlsen 111 SW 5th Ave Portland OR 97204-3604

CANALES, FRANCISCO LUIS, hand surgeon; b. Mexico City, July 20, 1957. MD, Stanford U., 1982. Intern Stanford (Calif.) U. Hosp., 1982-83, surgeon, 1983-87, plastic surgeon, 1987-90; microsurgery fellow Davies Med. Ctr., San Francisco, 1989; hand surgery fellow San Francisco Hand Fellowship, 1988; now hand surgeon Santa Rosa (Calif.) Meml. Hosp. Office: Plastic Surgery Assoc 2465 Summer Field Santa Rosa CA 95405-4816*

CANALES, JAMES EARL, JR., foundation administrator; b. San Francisco, Nov. 6, 1966; s. James Earl Canales Sr. and Maritsa M. (Solorzano) Espinoza. BA, Stanford U., 1988, MA, 1989. English tchr., class dean San Francisco Univ. H.S., 1989-91, dir. admissions, 1991-93; program assoc. The James Irvine Found., San Francisco, 1993-95, program officer, spl. asst. to pres., 1995—; mem. Calif. adv. com. Aspen Inst. Nonprofit Sector Rsch. Fund, Washington, 1995—; bd. dirs. Nat. Ctr. for Nonprofit Bds., Washington. Vice chair, bd. dirs. Larkin St. Youth Ctr., San Francisco, 1992—; bd. dirs., Nat. Assn. for Cmty. Leadership, Indpls., 1994—; trustee San Francisco Day Sch., 1996—. Andrew W. Mellon Edn. Found. fellow, 1988-89. Democrat. Roman Catholic. Home: 5 Buena Vista Ter Apt B San Francisco CA 94117-4110 Office: The James Irvine Found Spear 1715 One Market San Francisco CA 94105

CANALIS, RINALDO FERNANDO, surgeon, educator, researcher; b. Peru, Sept. 15, 1938; came to U.S., 1965; s. Fernando and Andreina (Oneto) C.; m. Sandra Ciotola, Apr. 5, 1970; children: John, Elizabeth. BS, U. Nacional Mayor San Marcos, Lima, Peru, 1959, MD, 1965. Asst. chief otolaryn. Harbor-UCLA Med. Ctr., Torrance, Calif., 1973-78, assoc. chief otolaryn., 1979, chief otolaryn., 1979—; vice chief head and neck surgery UCLA Sch. Medicine, 1979—; acting chair surgery, Harbor-UCLA Med. Ctr., Torrance, 1992-93; acting vice chair surgery UCLA Sch. Medicine, 1992-93, prof. surgery, 1981—; cons. phys. anthropology lab. San Diego Mus. of Man, 1980—. Contbr. chpt. to book, numerous sci. papers to profl. jours. Prin. advisor Meniere's Patients Support Group, West L.A., 1985—. Mem. ACS, Am. Acad. Otolaryn./Head and Neck Surgery (Honor award 1983, cert. of appreciation 1979, 82), Am. Laryngological, Rhinological and Otological Soc., Am. Laryngological Assn., Am. Otological Soc., N.Am. Base of the Skull Soc. (funding mem.). Democrat. Roman Catholic. Home: 457 15th St Santa Monica CA 90402-2231 Office: Harbor-UCLA Med Ctr PO Box 2910 Torrance CA 90509-2910

CANBY, WILLIAM CAMERON, JR., federal judge; b. St. Paul, May 22, 1931; s. William Cameron and Margaret Leah (Lewis) C.; m. Jane Adams, June 18, 1954; children—William Nathan, John Adams, Margaret Lewis. A.B., Yale U., 1953; LL.B., U. Minn., 1956. Bar: Minn. 1956, Ariz. 1972. Law clk. U.S. Supreme Ct. Justice Charles E. Whittaker, 1958-59; asso. firm Oppenheimer, Hodgson, Brown, Baer & Wolff, St. Paul, 1959-62; asso., then dep. dir. Peace Corps, Ethiopia, 1962-64; dir. Peace Corps, Uganda, 1964-66; asst. to U.S. Senator Walter Mondale, 1966; asst. to pres. SUNY, 1967; prof. law Ariz. State U., 1967-80; judge U.S. Ct. Appeals (9th cir.), Phoenix, 1980-96, sr. judge, 1996—; chief justice High Ct. of the Trust Ter. of the Pacific Islands, 1993-94; bd. dirs. Ariz. Center Law in Public Interest, 1974-80, Maricopa County Legal Aid Soc., 1972-78, D.N.A.-People's Legal Services, 1978-80; Fulbright prof. Makerere U. Faculty Law, Kampala, Uganda, 1970-71. Author: American Indian Law, 1988; also articles; note editor: Minn. Law Rev, 1955-56. Precinct and state committeeman Democratic Party Ariz., 1972-80; bd. dirs. Central Ariz. Coalition for Right to Choose, 1976-80. Served with USAF, 1956-58. Mem. State Bar Ariz., Minn. Bar Assn., Maricopa County Bar Assn., Phi Beta Kappa, Order of Coif. Office: US Ct Appeals 9th Cir US Courthouse Rm 6445 230 N 1st Ave Phoenix AZ 85025-0230

CANDELARIA, ANGIE MARY, special education educator; b. Durango, Colo., July 13, 1939; d. Angelo and Lucia (Mattevi) Dallabetta; m. David Candelaria, Sept 24, 1958 (div. Mar. 1964); children: David D., Craig D.; m. Richard James McMullen, July 3, 1982. BA, Ft. Lewis Coll., Durango, 1965. Cert. tchr. spl. edn., Colo. Tchr. Sch. Dist. R25, Loveland, Colo., 1967-68; tchr. spl. edn. Sch. Dist. 9R, Durango, 1968—, mem. profl. devel. com., 1990-94; ind. rschr. Josten Integrated Computer Edn. Co. Colo. Dept. Edn. spl. edn. grantee, 1966, cross-cultural inst. grantee, 1972-74, Sch. Dist. 9R grantee, 1992. Mem. ASCD, NEA, Colo. Edn. Assn., Durango Edn. Assn., Internat. Reading Assn., VFW Aux. (life), Am. Legion Aux., Elks, Colombo Lodge. Republican. Roman Catholic. Home: PO Box 1897 485 Florida Rd D-13 Durango CO 81302

CANE, WILLIAM EARL, nonprofit organization executive; b. San Francisco, Aug. 15, 1935; s. Joseph Earl and Mae M. (McDermott) C.; m. Patricia Ann Mathes. MDiv, St. Patrick's Sem., 1973; ThD, San Francisco Theol., 1976. Assoc. pastor St. Joseph Ch., Cupertino, Calif., 1960-65; dir. St. Benedict Ctr., San Francisco, 1966-72; prof. Grad. Theol., Berkeley, Calif., 1973-79; dir. IF, Santa Cruz, Calif., 1975—; editor Integrities, Santa Cruz, 1985—; pres. Assn. Priests Union, San Francisco, 1970-72; bd. dirs. Gaia Ctr., Santa Cruz, Friends of Cantera, Santa Cruz; lectr. in field. Author: Thru Crisis to Freedom, 1980, Circles of Hope, 1992; contbr. articles to profl. jours. Founder Friends of the Deaf, San Francisco, 1970; cofounder Santa Cruz (Calif.) Sanctuary, 1987. Grantee Rascob Found., San Francisco, 1970, Santa Cruz (Calif.) Cmty. Found., 1988, Mervyn's Found., 1988, Eschaton Found., Santa Cruz, 1994. Home and Office: 3015 Freedom Blvd Watsonville CA 95076-0436

CANFIELD, GRANT WELLINGTON, JR., management consultant; b. L.A., Nov. 28, 1923; s. Grant Wellington and Phyllis Marie (Westland) C.; m. Virginia Louise Bellinger, June 17, 1945; 1 child, Julie Marie. BS, U. So. Calif., 1949, MBA, 1958. Personnel and indsl. relations exec., L.A., 1949-55; employee relations cons., regional mgr. Mchts. and Mfrs. Assn. L.A., 1955-60; v.p., orgnl. devel. cons. Hawaii Employers Council, Honolulu, 1960-75; pres., dir. Hawaiian Ednl. Council, 1969-92, chmn., CEO, 1989-92, chmn. emeritus, 1992; prin. cons. Grant W. Canfield CMC, 1993—; faculty assignments Calif. State U., L.A., 1957-59, U. So. Calif., 1958-59, U. Hawaii, 1963-72; exec. v.p. Hawaii Garment Mfrs. Assn., 1965-75, Assn. Hawaii Restaurant Employers, 1966-75; exec. dir. Hawaii League Savs. Assns., 1971-78; exec. dir. Pan-Pacific Surg. Assn., 1980-81, exec. v.p., 1982-83; exec. dir. Hawaii Bus. Roundtable, 1983-89; sec., treas. Econ. Devel. Corp. Honolulu, 1984-85; sec., treas. Hawaii Conv. Park Council, Inc., 1984-86, hon. dir., 1986-88. Co-author: Resource Manual for Public Collective Bargaining, 1973. Bd. dirs. Hawaii Restaurant Assn., 1974-76, bd. dirs. Hawaii chpt. Nat. Assn. Accts., 1963-67, nat. dir., 1965-66; bd. dirs. Vol. Service Bur. Honolulu, 1965-66, pres., 1966-68; bd. dirs. Vol. Info. and Referral Service Honolulu, 1972-75, Goodwill Vocat. Tng. Ctrs. of Hawaii, 1973-81, Girl Scout council Pacific, 1961-65, 71-72; bd. dirs. Hawaii Com. Alcoholism, 1962-71, co-chmn., 1964-68; pres., dir. Friends of Punahou Sch., 1972-75; mem. community adv. bd. Jr. League Honolulu, 1968-70; exec. bd. Aloha council Boys Scouts Am., 1962-65; bd. regents Chaminade U., 1983-85. Served to 1st lt. inf. AUS, 1943-46. Decorated Bronze Star, Purple Heart, Combat Inf. badge. Mem. ASTD, Am. Soc. Assn. Execs. (cert. assn. exec.), Inst. Mgmt. Cons. (cert.), Soc. for Human Resource Mgmt., Pacific Club, Healdsburg Mus. and Hist. Soc. (chmn. exec. com. 1993-95, dir. 1994—, pres. 1995—), Santa Rosa Symphony Assn. (bd. dirs. 1993—, mem. exec. com. 1995—), Rotary, Masons. Home: 1950 W Dry Creek Rd Healdsburg CA 95448-9747

CANFIELD, JAMES, art director. Art dir. Oreg. Ballet, Portland. Office: Oregon Ballet 1120 SW 10th St Portland OR 97205*

CANFIELD, J(OHN) DOUGLAS, English language educator; b. Washington, Feb. 4, 1941; s. Austin Francis and Gertrude (MacBride) C.; m. Pamela Eden Crotty, Sept. 7, 1963; children: Robert Alan, Bret Douglas, Colin Geoffrey. BA, U. Notre Dame, 1963; MA in Tchg., Yale U., 1964; MA, Johns Hopkins U., 1966; PhD, U. Fla., 1969. Tchr. Radnor (Pa.) Sr. H.S., 1964-65; grad. asst. tchg. Johns Hopkins U., Balt., 1965-66; asst. prof. U. Calif., L.A., 1969-74; assoc. prof. U. Ariz., Tucson, 1974-79, prof., 1979-94, Regents' prof., 1994—. Author: Nicholas Rowe and Christian Tragedy, 1977, Word as Bond in English Literature from the Middle Ages to the Restoration, 1989, Tricksters and Estates: On the Ideology of Restoration Comedy, 1997; editor: Twentieth-Century Interpretations of Sanctuary, 1982; co-editor: Rhetorics of Order/Ordering Rhetorics, 1989, Cultural Readings of Restoration and Eighteenth-Century-English Theater, 1995; contbr. articles to profl. jours. Coach, referee Am. Youth Soccer Orgn., Tucson, 1984—. Recipient Excellence in Tchg., Burlington Resources Found., 1991; named Ariz. Prof. of the Yr., Coun. for the Advancement and Support of Edn., Washington, 1993. Mem. MLA (chair divsn. restoration and early eighteenth century English lit. 1994), Am. Soc. for Eighteenth Century Studies (chair 1990-91, Clifford prize com.). Office: Univ Ariz Dept English Tucson AZ 85721

CANIN, STUART VICTOR, violinist; b. N.Y.C., Apr. 5, 1926; s. Monroe H. and Mary (Becker) C.; m. Virginia Yarkin, June 8, 1952; children: Aram Roy, Ethan Andrew. Student, Juilliard Sch. Music, 1946-49. Asst. prof. violin State U. Iowa, Iowa City, 1953-57; assoc. prof. State U. Iowa, 1957-61; prof. Oberlin Conservatory, 1961-66; concertmaster Chamber Symphony of Phila., 1966-68, San Francisco Symphony Orch., 1970-80, various Hollywood (Calif.) film and TV studio Orchs., 1980—; Fulbright prof. Staatliche Musikhochschule, Freiburg, Germany, 1956-57; sr. lectr. U. Calif., Santa Barbara, 1983-92. Chamber music artist Aspen (Colo.) Summer Music Festival, 1962, 63, 64, Santa Fe Chamber Music Festival, 1975, Spoleto Festival Two Worlds, Charleston, S.C., and Spoleto Italy, 1980, Music Acad.

of West, Summer Music Festival, Santa Barbara, 1983-91, Waterloo Festival and Sch. Music, Waterloo Village, N.J., 1987, 88; concert master Casals Festival Orch., San Juan, P.R., 1977, 78, Mostly Mozart Summer Festival, Lincoln Ctr., 1980; condr. master classes Shanghai (China) Conservatory Music, 1989. Served with U.S. Army, 1944-46. Recipient 1st prize Paganini Internat. Violin Competition, Genoa, Italy, 1959; Handel medal N.Y.C., 1960.

CANNON, CHRISTOPHER B., congressman; b. Salt Lake City, Oct. 20, 1950; m. Claudia Fox, 1978; 7 children. BA, Brigham Young U., JD. Atty., 1979-83; dep. assoc. solicitor U.S. Dept. Interior, 1983, assoc. solicitor, 1984-86; owner Cannon Industries, 1987—; mem. 105th Congress from 3d Utah dist., 1996—; mem. Resources, Judiciary, and Sci. coms. Republican. Office: 440 Cannon Washington DC 20515-4403

CANNON, CHRISTOPHER JOHN, lawyer; b. Milw., Feb. 12, 1954; s. John and Delphine (Bruckwick) C.; m. Anne E. Libbin, July 20, 1985; children: Abigail, Rebecca. Student, U. Sophia, Tokyo; BA, U. Notre Dame; JD, Southwestern U., 1979. Bar: Calif. 1979, U.S. Dist. Ct. (so. and no. dists.) Calif. 1979, U.S. Ct. Appeals (9th cir.) 1979, U.S. Dist. Ct. (cen. and ea. dists.) Calif. 1990, U.S. Supreme Ct. 1992. Law clk. to Hon. William J. Swiegart U.S. Dist. Ct., San Francisco, 1979-81; asst. pub. defender Santa Clara (Calif.) Cts., 1981-82; asst. fed. pub. defender San Francisco Cts., 1982-89; ptnr. Sugarman & Cannon, San Francisco, 1989—. Contbr. articles to profl. jours. Recipient Cert. of Appreciation Fed. Practice Program, San Francisco, 1989. Mem. Fed. Bar Assn., Nat. Assn. Criminal Def. Lawyers, ACLU, Calif. Attys. Criminal Justice Assn., San Francisco Bar Assn. Democrat. Home: 18 Mateo Dr Belvedere Tiburon CA 94920-1046 Office: Sugarman & Cannon 600 Harrison St Ste 535 San Francisco CA 94107-1370

CANNON, GARY CURTIS, lawyer, publishing executive; b. Ft. Worth, May 28, 1951; s. Curtis Warfield and Lucile (Curran) C. BA, U.S. Internat. U., 1974; MBA, Nat. U., 1984, JD, 1987. Bar: Calif. 1987, U.S. Dist. Ct. (so. dist.) Calif. 1987, U.S. Dist. Ct. (ctrl. dist.) Calif. 1993, U.S. Ct. Appeals (9th cir.) 1993, U.S. Ct. Internat. Trade 1993, U.S. Supreme Ct. 1993. Pvt. practice, San Diego, 1987-89; v.p. Am. Pub., San Diego, 1988-89; pres. Emerald Bay Pub. Inc., San Diego, 1989—; sr. ptnr. Cannon, Potter & Scott, 1989-93, Cannon, Potter & Day, 1993-94; pvt. practice, 1994-95; gen. and corp. counsel Builders Staff Corp., 1995—, F.Y. Partnership Inc., MUG Corp., Lexo Ins. Brokers Inc., 1995—; chmn. bd. Fin. Svcs. and Investments Corp., 1994-96; adj. prof. bus. law Nat. Univ., 1990—. Mem. ABA, Calif. Bar Assn., San Diego County Bar Assn., San Diego Trial Lawyers Assn. Republican. Presbyterian. Office: 9868 Erma Rd # 17 San Diego CA 92131

CANNON, LOUIS SIMEON, journalist, author; b. N.Y.C., June 3, 1933; s. Jack and Irene (Kohn) C.; m. Virginia Oprian, Feb. 2, 1953 (div. 1983); children: Carl, David, Judy, Jack; m. Mary L. Shinkwin, Sept. 7, 1985. Student, U. Nev., 1950-51, San Francisco State U., 1951-52. Reporter Lafayette Sun, Calif., 1957; editor Newark (Calif.) Sun, 1957-58, Merced Sun Star, Calif., 1958-60, Contra Costa Times, Calif., 1960-61, San Jose (Calif.) Mercury News, Calif., 1961-69; Sacramento corr. San Jose Mercury News, Calif., 1965-69; Washington corr. Ridder Pubs., Washington, 1969-72; reporter The Washington Post, Washington, 1972-96; spl. corr. The Washington Post, L.A., 1997—. Author: President Reagan: the Role of a Lifetime, 1991, Reagan, 1982, Ronnie and Jesse, 1969, Reporting: An Inside View, 1977, The McCloskey Challenge, 1972. Recipient Gerald R. Ford prize Gerald Ford Libr., 1988, Merriman Smith award White House Corrs. Assn., 1986, Aldo Beckman award, 1984, Washington Journalism Rev. award, 1985, Disting. Reporting of Pub. Affairs award Am. Polit. Sci. Assn., 1968. Mem. Soc. of Profl. Journalists, Authors Guild. Home: PO Box 436 Summerland CA 93067-0436

CANNON-WILSON, MARGARET ELIZABETH, art educator, artist; b. Marquette, Mich., May 26, 1923; d. Carl Arthur and Elizabeth Justina (Jacobson) Erickson; m. John Pershing Cannon, Sept. 4, 1947 (dec. Aug. 1983); children: Miguel, Colleen Nicholson, Ericka Kramer; m. Robert Carlton Wilson, Aug. 16, 1992. BA in Art Edn., U. Ams., Mexico City, 1953, postgrad., 1954; MFA in Drawing and Painting, Calif. State U., Fullerton, 1967; studies with Aniela Jaffe, C.J. Jung Inst., Zürich, Switzerland; studied with Diego Rivera, studied with Jose Guitierrez. Lecturer U. of the Americas, Mexico City, 1954; art lecturer Adult School, Fullerton, Calif., Cerritos, Cypress and Fullerton Jr. Colls., Calif. (Fullerton) State U., 1967, Chapman U., San Diego, Calif., 1982-92. Author: Patriots-Female Version, 1961, The Great Painting Escape, 1996; one-woman shows include Paideia Gallery, La Cienega, L.A. and others; exhibited in group shows at Laguna Museum of Art, Cerritos Coll. Gallery, Calif. U. at Fullerton, U. Americas, Mexico, La Mirada Festival of Arts, Orange County Art Assn., L.A. Art Assn., Fine Arts Assn. Invitational, Warsaw, Poland, U. Calif., Irvine, San Diego Art Inst., 1996 others. With USNR, 1944-52. Mem. U.S. Former Mems. of Congress Wives, Aerospace Mus., San Diego Mus. of Art, San Diego Art Inst., San Diego Watercolor Soc. Home: 1640-65 Maple Dr Chula Vista CA 91911

CANO, LARRY RAYMOND, film maker; b. Chgo., July 25, 1949; s. Ramon L. and Lorraine B. (Habes) C.; m. Lee C. Healy, June 21, 1991; 1 child, Corey. BA, Calif. State U., Fullerton, 1972; MFA, UCLA, 1983. Film maker Larry R. Cano, Inc., Newport Beach, Calif., 1982—; film instr. Pasadena (Calif.) City Coll., 1986, 87. Exec. prodr. (motion picture) Silkwood, 1983 (5 Acad. award nominations 1983); prodr., dir. (video documentary) Trouble in Paradise, 1996; co-author: Stretch and Strenghten Your Way to Great Golf, 1996. Address: Box 10095 Newport Beach CA 92658

CANOFF, KAREN HUSTON, lawyer; b. Medford, Oreg., May 15, 1954; d. Loyd Stanley and Donna Lou (Wall) Huston; m. Lawrence Scott Canoff, May 30, 1981; children: Vincent Jared, Alyssa Rae. BS, U. Oreg., 1977; JD cum laude, Lewis & Clark Coll., 1981. Bar: Oreg. 1981, U.S. Dist. Ct. Oreg. 1982, U.S. Ct. Appeals (9th cir.) 1985, Calif. 1985, U.S. Dist. Ct. (so. dist.) Calif. 1985, U.S. Dist. Ct. (cen. dist.) Calif. 1986, U.S. Ct. Appeals (fed. cir.) 1991. Fin. cons. Stretch & Sew, Inc., Eugene, Oreg., 1975-78; assoc. Margaretta Eakin P.C., Portland, Oreg., 1981-82, 83, Gary M. Bullock, Portland, 1982-83, Markowitz & Herbold, Portland, 1983-86; ptnr. Dorazio, Barnhorst & Bonar, San Diego, 1986-89, shareholder, 1989; ptnr. Hyde & Canoff, San Diego, 1990-96; divsn. counsel Nielsen Dillingham Builders, Inc., San Diego, 1996—; instr. People's Law Sch., Eugene, Oreg., 1978. Author: (with others) Legal Resource Guide, 1983; contbr. articles to profl. jours. Mem. Multnomah County Vol. Lawyers, Portland, Oreg., 1982-83, San Diego Vol. Lawyers Program, 1985-96, Vols. in Parole, San Diego, 1986-87, Charlotte Baker Soc., 1992-93; judge pro tem San Diego County mcpl. Ct., 1988—, San Diego Superior Ct, 1991—, 4th Dist. Ct. Appeals, 1995—; mem. nat. panel comml. arbitrators Am. Arbitration Assn., 1991-96. Finalist San Diego Women Who Mean Bus. awards, 1995, 96; recipient Am. Jurisprudence award, 1979. Mem. Calif. State Bar Assn. (bus. law, labor and employment, pub. law and real property sects.), San Diego County Bar Assn. (appellate ct. com. 1987—, editor It's the Law 1987, alternative dispute resolution sec. 1990-95, arbitration com. 1990-96, client rels. com. 1990-96, bus. law, comml. law, constrn. law, corp. counsel and labor and employment law sects., editor Bar Briefs 1992, mem. ethics com. 1996—), Lawyers Club San Diego (bd. dirs. 1988-91, editor Lawyers Club News 1986-88), Assn. Bus. Trial Lawyers, Am. Corp. Counsel Assn., Associated Gen. Contractors (legal issues com., constrn. defect def. action coalition), Nat. Assn. Women Bus. Owners (bd. dirs. 1993-96, sec. 1993-94, chair govt. affairs 1995-96), Mortgage Bankers Assn. Am. (legal issues com. 1987-89), Phi Beta Kappa.

CANOVA-DAVIS, ELEANOR, biochemist, researcher; b. San Francisco, Jan. 18, 1938; d. Gaudenzio Enzio and Catherine (Bordisso) Canova; m. Kenneth Roy Davis, Feb. 10, 1957; children: Kenneth Roy Jr., Jeffrey Stephen. BA, San Francisco State U., 1968, MS, 1971; PhD, U. Calif., San Francisco, 1977. Lab. asst. Frederick Burk Found. for Edn., San Francisco, 1969-71; rsch., tchg. asst. U. Calif., San Francisco, 1972-77, asst. rsch. biochemist, 1980-84; NIH postdoctoral fellow U. Calif., Berkeley, 1977-80; sr. scientist Liposome Tech., Menlo Park, Calif., 1984-85, Genentech, Inc., South San Francisco, 1985—. Contbr. articles to profl. jours. Recipient Nat. Rsch. Svc. award NIH, 1977-80, Honors Convocation award San Francisco State U., 1966; grantee Chancellor's Patent Fund, U. Calif., San Francisco, 1976, Earl C. Anthony Trust; grad. div. fellow U. Calif., San Francisco, 1972-73. Mem. Am. Chem. Soc., Calif. Scholarship Fedn., Sequoia Woods Country Club, Protein Soc., Am. Peptide Soc., Am. Soc. Mass Spectrometry. Roman Catholic. Home: 1203 Edgewood Rd Redwood City CA 94062 Office: Genentech Inc 460 Point San Bruno Blvd South San Francisco CA 94080-4918

CANTER, BARRY MITCHELL, electronics specialist, musician; b. Mineola, N.Y., Feb. 24, 1950; s. Robert Ackley and Lillian Georgette (Cook) C.; m. Janice Marie Cantone, Aug. 25, 1974; children: Eric Vincent, Laura Marie. Student, Nassau C.C., 1968-70, Clark County C.C., 1980-82, Nat. U., 1987, Mesa Coll., 1991-92; BS in Electronics Tech., U. of Berkley, 1995; M in Comm. Tech., Nat. Radio Examiners, 1995. Lic. FCC Gen. Radio Telephone Operator, 1994, FCC amateur tech., 1994, FCC radar endorsement, 1995, gen. radio telephone operators lic. FCC. Rec. producer, engr., musician Accutrack Rec. Studios, Garden City, N.Y., 1971-73; musical dir., performer Assoc. Booking Corp., N.Y.C., 1973-75; entertainer, performer various major hotels, San Diego and Las Vegas, Nev., 1975—; electronics repair technician Wilson Electronics, Inc., Las Vegas, 1980-83, Motorola Comms., Inc., Las Vegas, 1986-87; nat. tech. svc. advisor Regency Landmobile, Inc., Las Vegas, 1983-86; nat. customer svc. mgr. Celltronics-Neutec-Trilectric, San Diego, 1987-89, asst. nat. sales mgr., 1989-90; nat. customer svc. mgr. Hitec RCD Inc., Santee, Calif., 1991-96; support engr. Qualcomm Inc., San Diego, 1996—; music tchr., San Diego, 1990—; band leader Third Degree, San Diego, 1991—, Material Witness, San Diego, 1995—. Composer various songs; contbr. articles to profl. publs. Vol. Sundance Elem. Sch., 1989-90, Deer Canyon Elem. Sch., 1990-91, disabled children's basketball and baseball league, San Diego, 1991—. Mem. Musicians Union of Las Vegas. Office: Qualcomm Inc 6455 Lusk Blvd San Diego CA 92121-2779

CANTERBURY, LESLIE JOHN, librarian; b. Hancock, Mich., June 9, 1958; s. Leslie Blaine and Ellen Ann (Järvenpää) C.; m. Alisa Marie Slaughter, July 20, 1991. BA, U. Ariz., 1986, MLS, 1988. Librarian U. Ariz. Main Libr., Tucson, 1989-90, U. Redlands (Calif.) Armacost Libr., 1990—. Mem. ALA (various coms.), Calif. Libr. Assn. (various coms.), Ariz. State Libr. Assn. (various coms.). Democrat. Office: Univ Redlands Armacost Libr 1200 E Colton Ave Redlands CA 92374-3755

CANTOR, JAMES ELLIOT, lawyer; b. Detroit, Mar. 14, 1958; s. Bernard J. and Judith (Levin) C.; m. Susan Elaine Finger, Dec. 26, 1983; 1 child, Tilly Samantha. BS in Natural Resources, U. Mich., 1980; JD, Cornell U., 1986. Bar: Alaska 1986. Assoc. Perkins Coie, Anchorage, 1986-91; asst. atty. gen. environ. sect. State of Alaska, Atty. Gen.'s Office, Anchorage, 1991—. Mem. Eagle River (Alaska) Pk. and Recreation Bd. of Suprs., 1989-95, chmn., 1991-92; dir. Anchorage (Alaska) Trails and Greenways Coalition, 1994—. Mem. Anchorage Inn of Ct. Office: Atty Gen Office 1031 W 4th Ave Ste 200 Anchorage AK 99501-5903

CANTOR, RUSTY SUMNER, artist; b. N.Y.C., Aug. 6, 1927; s. Charles and Mollie (Kaufman) Sumner; m. Paul Arthur Cantor, Aug. 30, 1953 (dec. Sept. 1980); children: Lesley Cantor-Fallihee, Matt Geoffrey. presenter in field. Solo exhibits include Inst. of Am. Indian Art Mus., Santa Fe, 1984, Christenson-Heller-Lowe, Berkeley, 1990, Mill Valley (Calif.) City Hall, 1991, AIA, Oakland, Calif., 1994, Bade Mus., Berkeley, Calif., 1996, SoMar, San Francisco, 1997, others; two-person show Gallery on the Rim, San Francisco, 1995; group exhibits include Lynnhouse Gallery, East Bay Bronze, Antioch, Calif., 1995, Fourth World Congress on Women, Beijing, 1995, Berkeley (Calif.) Art Ctr., 1995, Ritz Carlton Sculpture Gallery, San Francisco, 1995, NAWA Lever House, N.Y.C., 1995, ACCI Gallery, Berkeley, 1996, ISE Art Found., N.Y.C., 1996, Bechtel Gallery Stanford U., 1996, NAWA Traveling exhibit, 1996—; Prieto Gallery, Mills Coll., Oakland, 1996, Design Ctr., San Francisco, 1996, Ctr. for the Visual Arts, Oakland, 1996, NAWA, N.y.C., 1996, NAWA Traveling Exhbn., 1996—, numerous others; represented in collections Nat. Mus. Women in the Arts, Washington, Inst. Am. Indian Art Mus., Santa Fe, Am. Embassy, New Delhi, Art in Embassies Program, Washington, Many Horses Gallery, L.A., numerous pvt. collections. Group leader Noetic Soc.; advisor, past pres. N.C. Womens Caucus for the Arts. Mem. Nat. Assn. Women Artists, Alliance Women Artists, Women's Caucus for Art, Pacific Rim Sculptor Group, Union des Femmes Peintres et Sculpteurs. Home and Studio: 2512 Ninth St #14 Berkeley CA 93710

CANTWELL, CHRISTOPHER WILLIAM, artist; b. Atwater, Calif., Dec. 24, 1960; s. Donald Byron and Ann Louise Cantwell; m. Susan Rebecca Moore, Sept. 19, 1982; children: Claire Elyse Moore, Katie Lynn Moore. Owner, artist Christopher W. Cantwell Woodworks, Modesto, Calif., 1979-82, Oakhurst, Calif., 1982—; cons. Internat. Union for conservation of Natural Resources, Cambridge, Eng., 1991—. Contbr. art book Jewelry Boxes, 1996; exhibited at Del Mano Gallery, 1990; represented in permanent collections Irving Lipton Collection, White House Ornament Collection. Youth advisor Oakhurst Luth. Ch., 1992—. Mem. Am. Craft Coun., World Wildlife Fund, Program for Belize, Good Wood Alliance (CITES Liaison 1994—). Democrat. Home and Office: PO Box 1736 Oakhurst CA 93644

CANTWELL, MARIA E., congresswoman. Grad., Miami U. Former rep. Dist. 44 State of Wash.; mem. 103rd Congress from 1st Wash. dist., Washington, D.C., 1993—; owner pub. rels. firm. *

CAO, THAI-HAI, industrial engineer; b. Saigon, Republic of Vietnam, July 8, 1954; came to U.S., 1975; s. Pho Thai and Anh Ngoc (Nguyen) C.; m. Hue Thi Tran, June 29, 1979; children: Quoc-Viet Thai, Quoc-Nam Thai, Huyen-Tran Thai, Uyen-Phuong Thai. BS in Indsl. Engring., U. Wash., 1980; grad., Gen. Electric Mfg. Mgmt. Prgm., 1982. Mfg. engr. GE, San Jose, Calif., 1980-82; mgr. mfg. engring. and quality assurance Broadcast Microwave div. Harris Corp., Mountain View, Calif., 1982-85; mgr. mfg. engring. John Fluke Mfg. Co., Everett, Wash., 1986-90; mgr. quality engring. Advanced Tech. Labs., Bothell, Wash., 1990—; prin. electronic process engr. Primex Aerospace Co.; cons. total quality mgmt. Vinatek. Mem. Am. Soc. Quality Control (chmn. membership com. 1987-88), Soc. Vietnamese Profls. (pres. 1988), Soc. Mfg. Engrs., Inst. Indsl. Engrs., Am. Prodn. and Inventory Control. Home: 23502 22nd Ave SE Bothell WA 98021-9553

CAPANNA, ALBERT HOWARD, neurosurgeon, neuroscientist; b. Utica, N.Y., May 12, 1947; m. Dawn McLouth; children: Christine, Alicia, Albert II, Danielle, Gabriella, Guy, Brianna, Gianna. BA, U. Tex., 1970; MD, Wayne State U., 1974. Med. intern St. John Hosp., Detroit, 1974, resident in gen. surgery, 1974-75; resident in neurosurgery Wayne State U., Detroit, 1975-79; fellow in microneurosurgery U. Zurich, 1979; stereotactic fellow U. Paris, 1980; fellow in pediatric neurosurgery Hosp. for Sick Children, Toronto, 1980; pvt. practice Internat. Neurosci. Cons., Las Vegas, 1983—; chief staff Sunrise Hosp., Las Vegas, 1993-94; chief neurosurgery Univ. Med. Ctr., Las Vegas; clin. prof. U. Nev. Sch. Medicine, 1991—. Office: 1111 Shadow Ln Las Vegas NV 89102-2314

CAPELL, CYDNEY LYNN, editor; b. Jacksonville, Fla., Dec. 20, 1956; d. Ernest Clary and Alice Rae (McGinnis) Capell; m. Garrick Philip Martin, July 16, 1983 (div. Jan. 1988). BA, Furman U., 1977. Mktg. rep. E.C. Capell & Assocs., Greenville, S.C., 1977-80; sales rep. Prentice-Hall Publs., Cin., 1980-81; sales, mktg. rep. Benjamin/Cummings, Houston, 1981-83; sales rep. McGraw-Hill Book Co., Houston, 1983-85, engring. editor, N.Y.C., 1985-87; acctg. and infosystems editor Bus. Pubs., Inc., Plano, Tex., 1988-89; sr. editor Gorsuch Scarisbrick Pubs., Scottsdale, Ariz., 1989-90; editor-in-chief rsch. dept. Rauscher, Pierce, Refsnes Stock Brokers, 1990-94; editor-in-chief, dir. mktg. Marshall & Swift, L.A., 1994—; editor lit. mag. Talon, 1972; news editor Paladin newspaper, 1977. Named Rookie of Yr., McGraw-Hill Book Co., 1985. Mem. NOW, NAFE, Women in Pub., Women in Communications, Mensa. Republican. Avocations: tennis, ballet.

CAPELLE, MADELENE CAROLE, opera singer, educator, music therapist; b. Las Vegas, Nev., July 29, 1950; d. Curtis and Madelene Glenna (Healy) C. BA, Mills Coll., 1971; MusM, U. Tex., 1976; postgrad., Ind. U., 1976-77; diploma cert., U. Vienna, Austria, 1978; postgrad. in creative arts, Union Coll. Cert. K-12 music specialist, Nev. Prof. voice U. Nev., C.C. So. Nev., Nev. Sch. for the Arts, Las Vegas, 1986—; music therapist Charter Hosp., Las Vegas, 1987—; pvt. practice music therapy, Las Vegas, 1989—; music specialist Clark County Sch. Dist., Las Vegas, 1989—; contract music therapist Nev. Assn. for Handicapped, Las Vegas, 1990; guest voice coach U. Basel, Switzerland, 1992; presenter concerts in Kenya, self-esteem workshops for children and adult women; artist-in-residence, Nev., Wyo., S.D., Oreg., Idaho, N.D., Utah, 1988—; mem. cons. roster Wyo. Arts Cou., 1988—; cons. U.S. rep. Princess Margaret of Romania Found.; workshops in music therapy and humor therapy Germany, Austria, Switzerland; workshop day treatment program dir. Harmony Health Care; judge Leontyne Price Nat. Voice Competition; creative arts cons. Utah Festival Opera; artistic cons. Utah Fest Opera. Opera singer, Europe, Asia, S.Am., U.S., Can., Australia, 1978—; roles include Cio Cio San in Madama Butterly, Tosca, Turandot and Fidelio, Salome Electra; community concerts artist; featured PBS artist Guess Who's Playing the Classics; featured guest All Things Considered PBS radio, 1985; co-writer (one-woman show) The Fat Lady Sings, 1991 (Women's Awareness award), The Undone Divas: Hysterical/Historical Perspective (Nev. Humanities grant) ; concerts Africa, Kenya, Somalia; concerts for Jugaslavian Relief throughout Europe; guest soloist national anthem San Francisco 49ers. Pres., founder, cons. Children's Opera Outreach, Las Vegas, 1985—; artist Musicians Emergency Found., N.Y.C., 1978-82; vol. Zoo Assn., Allied Arts, Ziegfeld Club (first Junior Ziegfeld Young Woman of Yr.), Las Vegas, 1979—; clown Very Spl. Arts, Nev., Oreg., S.D., 1989-90; goodwill and cultural amb. City of Las Vegas, 1983; panelist Kennedy Ctr., Washington, 1982; artist Benefit Concerts for Children with AIDS; mem. Nev. Arts Alliance, Make a Wish Found., Lyric Opera of Las Vegas; CEO Outreach for Creative Arts, DBA Opera Piccolo. Named Musician of Yr. Swiss Music Alliance, 1993; recipient Congl. Cert. of Merit for work in the arts, 1993, 96. Mem. Internat. Platform Assn., Nat. Assn. Tchrs. Singing (featured guest spkr.), Performing Arts Soc. Nev., Cultural Arts Soc. (co-founder 1995), Brown Bag Concert Assn. (bd. dirs.), Make a Wish Found., Las Vegas Lyric Opera (bd. dirs.). Democrat. Home: 3266 Brentwood St Las Vegas NV 89121-3316

CAPENER, REGNER ALVIN, minister, electronics engineer, author, inventor; b. Astoria, Oreg., Apr. 18, 1942; s. Alvin Earnest and Lillian Lorraine (Lehtosaari) C.; divorced; children: Deborah, Christian, Melodie, Ariella; m. Della Denise Melson, May 17, 1983; children: Shelley, Danielle, Rebekah, Joshua. Student, U. Nebr., 1957-58, 59-60, Southwestern Coll., Waxahachie, Tex., 1958-59, Bethany Bible Coll., 1963-64. Ordained minister Full Gospel Assembly Ch., 1971. Rsch. engr. Lockheed Missiles & Space Corp., Palo Alto, Calif., 1962-64; engr., talk show host Sta. KHOF-FM, Glendale, Calif., 1966-67; youth min. Bethel Union Ch., Duarte, Calif., 1966-67; pres. Intermountain Electronics, Salt Lake City, 1967-72; assoc. pastor Full Gospel Assembly, Salt Lake City, 1968-72, Long Beach (Calif.) Christian Ctr., 1972-76; v.p. Refuge Ministries, Inc., Long Beach, 1972-76; pres. Christian Broadcasting Network-Alaska, Inc., Fairbanks, 1977-83; gen. mgr. Action Sch. of Broadcasting, Anchorage, 1983-85; pres., pastor House of Praise, Anchorage, 1984-93; chief engr. KTBY-TV, Inc., Anchorage, 1988-93; pres. R & DC Engring., Anchorage, 1993—; area dir. Christian Broadcasting Network, Virginia Beach, 1977-83; cons., dir. Union Bond and Trust Co., Anchorage, 1985-86; author, editor univ. courses, 1984-85; dep. gov. Am. Biog. Inst. Rsch. Assn., 1990—. Author: Spiritual Maturity, 1975, Spiritual Warfare, 1976, The Doctrine of Submission, 1988, A Vision for Praise, 1988, Ekklesia, 1993, For the Marriage of the Lamb Has Come, 1996, Open Letters to the Ekklesia, 1997; author, composer numerous gospel songs; creator numerous broadcasting and electronic instrument inventions. Sec., Christian Businessmen's Com., Salt Lake City, 1968-72; area advisor Women's Aglow Internat., Fairbanks, 1981-83; local co-chmn. campaign Boucher for Gov. Com., Fairbanks, 1982; campaigner for Boucher, Anchorage, 1984, Clark Gruening for Senate Com., Barrow, Alaska, 1980; TV producer Stevens for U.S. Senate, Barrow, 1978; fundraiser City of Refuge, Mex., 1973-75; statewide rep. Sudden Infant Death Syndrome, Barrow, 1978-82; founder Operation Blessing/Alaska, 1981; mem. resch. bd. advisors Am. Biog. Inst., 1990—; advisor Anchorage chpt. Women's Aglow Internat., 1990-91. Mem. Soc. Broadcast Engrs., Internat. Soc. Classical Guitarists (sec. 1967-69), Alaska Broadcaster's Assn., Nat. Assn. Broadcasters, Anchorage C. of C. Republican. Office: R & DC Engring 709 S 7th St Sunnyside WA 98944-2218 *The word "impossible" need never be a part of the vocabulary of one whose life is intertwined with the Lord Jesus Christ. I have learned that there are no problems in life which do not have clear and definitive solutions when approached from the standpoint of a personal relationship with Jesus Christ.*

CAPILLUPO, JEAN NADY, public school administrator, educator; b. Des Moines, Aug. 17, 1943; d. Xavier Wray and Wanda Pauline (Hendrickson) Nady; m. Vincent Paul Capillupo, June 20, 1964. BA, U. No. Colo., Greeley, 1965, MA, 1971; EdD, U. Denver, 1980. Cert. supt. and elem. sch. prin., Colo. Tchr. and/or acting prin. Colo. and Nebr., 1965-81; prin. Homestead Elem. Sch., Cherry Creek Schs., Englewood, Colo., 1981-84; exec. adminstrv. asst. Cherry Creek Schs., Englewood, 1984-86; prin. Ponderosa Elem. Sch., Cherry Creek Schs., Englewood, 1986-90; north area exec. dir. Cherry Creek Schs., Englewood, 1990-91; area supt. Jefferson County Schs., Golden, Colo., 1991-94; supt. Brighton (Colo.) Sch. Dist., 1994—; prof. Weekend Sch. Exec. program U. Denver, 1994—. Participant Leadership Denver, 1988; bd. dirs. Colo. I Have a Dream Found., Denver, 1988—. Named Alumnus of Yr., St. Mary's Acad., Englewood, 1996; IDEA fellow Kettering Found., 1986, 88, 90, 92; Fulbright-Hays Group Projects Abroad grantee, 1985. Mem. ASCD, Am. Assn. Sch. Adminstrs., Phi Delta Kappa. Democrat. Office: Brighton Sch Dist 630 S 8th Ave Brighton CO 80601-3257

CAPLAN, DAVID LEON, brokerage house executive; b. Pitts., Jan. 21, 1946; s. Norman and Esther (Samuels) C.; m. Linda Bowman, Jan. 27, 1973; children: Carole, Daniel. BA, Pa. State U., 1967; JD, Am. U., 1970. Bar: Calif. Pvt. practice law Malibu, Calif., 1972-75; pvt. practice real estate syndication broker Malibu, 1975-76; dir. futures/options dept. Bateman & Elchler, L.A., 1976-78; futures/options dept. head Jessup & LaMont, L.A., 1978-82; pres., founder Opportunities in Options, Oxnard, Calif., 1982—; lectr. in field. Contbr. articles to profl. jours. Office: Opportunities in Options 300 E Esplanade Dr Ste 200 Oxnard CA 93030-1261

CAPLAN, EDWIN HARVEY, university dean, accounting educator; b. Boston, Aug. 24, 1926; s. Henry and Dorothy (Nathanson) C.; m. Ramona Hootner, June 20, 1948; children—Gary, Dennis, Jeffrey, Nancy. B.B.A., U. Mich., 1950, M.B.A., 1952; Ph.D., U. Calif., 1965. C.P.A., Calif., Mich. Ptnr. J.J. Gotlieb & Co., C.P.A.s, Detroit, 1953-56; prof. acctg. Humboldt State U., 1956-61; prof. acctg., emeritus U. Oreg., 1964-67; prof. U. N.Mex., Albuquerque, 1967-91, assoc. dean Sch. Mgmt., 1982-83, dean Sch. Mgmt., 1989-90, prof. emeritus, 1991—; cons. in field. Contbr. articles to profl. jours. Served to 1st lt. U.S. Army, 1944-46. Mem. AICPA, Am. Acctg. Assn., Inst. Mgmt. Accts. Home: 8201 Harwood Ave NE Albuquerque NM 87110-1517 Office: Univ N Mex Anderson Sch Mgmt Albuquerque NM 87131

CAPORASO, KAREN DENISE, financial planner; b. Alhambra, Calif., May 23, 1953; d. Robert S. and Vivian J. (Scharff) Kuhle; m. Fredric Caporaso, Dec. 5, 1981; children: Allison Marie, Eric Duncan. BS in Fin., Chapman U., 1988, BS in Bus. Econs., 1988. CFP. Supr. payroll and acctg. Am. Med. Optics, Irvine, Calif., 1983-85; acct. Liberty Capital Markets, Newport Beach, Calif., 1985-89; stock broker Baraban Securities, Inc., Anaheim, Calif., 1990-92; registered rep. First Fin. Planners/FFP Securities, Tustin, Calif., 1992-95; with Orange Capital Mgmt., Orange, Calif., 1995—; registered rep. FFP Adv. Svcs., Inc.; cons. Fed. Employees Benefit Group, 1996—. Mem. Internat. Assn. Fin. Planners, Orange County Soc. of Inst. CFPs, So. Calif. Profl. Women in Bus. Office: Orange Capital Mgmt 333 S Anita Dr # 625 Orange CA 92868

CAPOZZI, ANGELO, surgeon; b. Solvay, N.Y., Apr. 20, 1933; s. Angelo and Daminana (Pirro) C.; m. Louise Armanetti, June 18, 1960; children: Angelo III, Leonard, Jeanne. BS, U. Notre Dame, 1956; MD, Loyola U., Chgo., 1960. Diplomate Am. Bd. Plastic Surgery. Intern St. Francis Hosp., Evanston, Ill., 1960-61, resident in gen. surgery, 1962-64; resident in plastic surgery U. Wis., Madison, 1964-66; chief plastic surgery USAF, Travis AFB, Calif., 1966; chief dept. plastic surgery St. Marys Hosp., San Francisco, 1974-77; assoc. clin. prof. dept. surgery U. Calif., San Francisco; chmn. dept.

plastic and reconstructive surgery St. Francis Meml. Hosp., San Francisco, 1987—, dir. plastic surgery residency program, 1987—; mem. tchg. staff St. Francis Meml. Hosp., Bothin Burn Ctr., San Francisco, 1968—; cons. Shriners Hosp., San Francisco. Author: Change of Face, 1984; contbr. articles to profl. jours. Mem. parks and recreation com. City of Tiburon, Calif., 1973. Capt. USAF, 1966-68. Recipient Alumni citation Loyola U., 1983, Bru Brunnier fellow award San Francisco Rotary Found., 1996; named Man of Yr., U. Notre Dame Alumni, 1983. Mem. San Francisco Olympic Club, San Francisco Rotary (Outstanding Svc. award 1993, Svc. Above Self award 1995), Rotoplast, Inc. (founding mem.). Office: 1199 Bush St Ste 640 San Francisco CA 94109-5999

CAPPELLO, A. BARRY, lawyer; b. Bklyn., Feb. 21, 1942; s. Gus and Ann (Klukoff) C.; children: Eric Rheinschild, Blythe, Brent. AB, UCLA, 1962, JD, 1965. Bar: Calif. 1966, U.S. Dist. Ct. (cen. dist.) Calif. 1966, U.S. Ct. Appeals (9th cir.) 1974, U.S. Dist. Ct. (no. dist.) Calif. 1981, U.S. Ct. Appeals (7th cir.) 1985, U.S. Supreme Ct. 1985, U.S. Dist. Ct. (ea. dist.) Calif. 1986, U.S. Ct. Appeals (10th cir.) 1986. Dep. atty. gen. State of Calif., L.A., 1965-68; chief trial dep. Santa Barbara County, 1968-70, asst. dist. atty., 1970-71; city atty. Santa Barbara, 1971-77; pvt. practice, mng. ptnr., 1977-85; with Cappello & McCann, Santa Barbara, 1977—; lectr. complex bus. litigation, lender liability, adv. trial techniques. Author: Lender Liability, 2d edit., 1994, Lender Liability: A Practical Guide, 1987, AmJur Model Trials and Proofs of Facts; contbr. more than 100 articles to profl. legal and bus. jours. Mem. ABA, ATLA, Consumer Attys. of Calif., Santa Barbara Inns of Ct. (master). Office: Cappello & McCann 831 State St Santa Barbara CA 93101-3227

CAPPELLO, EVE, international business consultant; b. Sydney, Australia; d. Nem and Ethel Shapira; children: Frances Soskins, Alan Kazdin. BA, Calif. State U.-Dominguez Hills, 1974; MA, Pacific Western U., 1977, PhD, 1978. Singer, pianist, L.A., 1956-76; profl. devel., mgmt./staff tng., 1976—; instr. Calif. State U., Dominguez Hills, 1977-95; counselor Associated Tech. Coll., L.A. instr. Mt. St. Mary's Coll., U. of Judaism, U. So. Calif., Loyola Marymount U.; founder, pres. A-C-T Internat.; invited speaker World Congress Behavior Therapy, Israel, Melbourne U., Australia. Mem. Internat. Platform Assn., Book Publicists So. Calif., Pasadena C. of C., Alpha Gamma. Author: Let's Get Growing, 1979, The New Professional Touch, 1988, 2d edit., Dr. Eve's Garden, 1984, Act, Don't React, 3d edit., 1988, The Game of the Name, 1985, The Perfectionist Syndrome, 1990, Why Aren't More Women Running The Show?, 1994; newspaper columnist, 1976-79; contbr. articles to profl. jours. Home: 518 S El Molino Ave # 303 Pasadena CA 91101

CAPPS, WALTER HOLDEN, religion educator; b. Omaha, May 5, 1934; s. Holden Frances and Mildred Linnea (Bildt) C.; m. Lois Ragnhild Grimsrud, Aug. 21, 1960; children: Lisa Margarit, Todd Holden, Laura Karolina. BS, Portland (Oreg.) State U., 1957; BD, Augustana Theol. Sem., Rock Island, Ill., 1960; STM, Yale U., 1961, MA, 1963, PhD, 1965. Prof. religious studies U. Calif., Santa Barbara, 1964—. Author: The Unfinished War, 1982, The Monastic Impulse, 1983, New Religious Right, 1990, Thomas Merton, 1990. Bd. dirs. Pacific Luth. Sem., Berkeley, Calif., 1965-73, La Casa de Maria Retreat Ctr., Santa Barbara, 1966-84; chair Calif. Coun. for Humanities, San Francisco, 1984-87; pres. Fedn. State Humanities Couns., Washington, 1985-87. Lutheran. Home: 1724 Santa Barbara St Santa Barbara CA 93101-1025 Office: U Calif Santa Barbara Dept Religious Studies Santa Barbara CA 93106

CAPURRO, FRANK L., food products executive; b. 1945. Ptnr. Watsonville (Calif.) Produce, 1974—; treas. Ocean Organic Produce, Inc., Castroville, Calif., 1988—, now ptnr. Office: 2250 Salinas Rd Watsonville CA 95076-9232*

CAPUTO, GARY RICHARD, radiology educator; b. Newark, Nov. 26, 1951. AB in Chemistry, Coll. of the Holy Cross, 1973; MD, Mt. Sinai Sch. Medicine, 1977. Diplomate Am. Bd. Internal Medicine, Am. Bd. Nuclear Medicine. Intern in internal medicine Mt. Sinai Hosp., 1977-78, resident in internal medicine, 1978-79; fellow in cardiology U. Wash., Seattle, 1979-81, 82-83; resident in internal medicine St. Vincent's Hosp. & Med. Ctr., Portland, Ore., 1981-82; resident in nuclear medicine U. Wash., 1983-85; fellow in cardiovascular imaging U. Calif., San Francisco, 1985-86; asst. prof. internal medicine, adj. prof. med. informatics U. Utah Sch. Medicine, Salt Lake City, 1986-89; asst. prof. U. Calif., San Francisco, 1989-92; assoc. prof. U. Calif., 1992—; clin. instr. U. Wash., 1982-83; dir. advanced cardiac imaging svc. LDS Hosp., Salt Lake City, 1986-89; supr. clin. cardiovascular magnetic resonance rsch. program and vis. fgn. scholars, 1989—; adminstr. NIH tng. grant, 1989-92; coord. in-svc. tng. program, 1990-91; mem. com. on human rsch., 1991-93; lectr. Fla. Radiol. Soc., 1988—; cons. GE Med. Sys., Milw., 1991—; dir. nuclear cardiology fellowship tng. program U. Utah Sch. of Medicine, 1987-89, mem. PhD candidate com. dept. med. informatics, 1987-91; apptd. bioengring. grad. group U. Calif., Berkeley, San Francisco, 1992—, staff scientist Lawrence Berkeley Nat. Lab., 1992—, U. Calif. San Francisco Lab. for Radiolog. Informatics, 1993—, U. Calif. San Francisco Magnetic Resonance Sci. Ctr., 1993-95, assoc. dir., staff scientist, 1993-95, U. Calif. San Francisco Position Emission Tomography Ctr., 1993—, assoc. dir., staff scientist 1993—. Grantee Deseret Found., 1987, Am. Heart Assn., 1988, Richards Meml. Med. Found., 1988, Merritt-Peralta Rsch. Found., 1990, NIH, 1986—, numerous others. Fellow Am. Heart Assn. Coun. Cardiovascular Radiology; mem. Radiol. Soc. N.Am., N.Am. Soc. Cardiac Imaging, Soc. Nuclear Medicine, San Francisco Radiol. Soc. Office: U Calif Dept Radiology Box 0628 San Francisco CA 94143-0628

CARATAN, ANTON G., food products executive; b. 1955. With Anton Caratan & Son, Delano, Calif., 1976—, ptnr., 1984—. Office: Anton Caratan & Son 1625 Road 160 Delano CA 93215*

CARATAN, GEORGE, food products executive; b. 1929. With Anton Caratan & Son, Delano, Calif., 1952—. Office: Anton Caratan & Son 1625 Road 160 Delano CA 93215*

CARDEN, THOM(AS) RAY, psychologist; b. Indpls.; s. Howard Ray Carden and Mary Ola Eacret; m. Shirley A. Towles, 1953 (div. 1968); m. Anita Van Natter, May 26, 1973; children: Thom H., Kevin L., Shawn D., Dennis P., Suzanne M., Marlene, Cindy, Lorrie, Linda, Alayne. AA in Psychology, Cerritos Coll., 1973; BA in Psychology, Calif. State U., Northridge, 1975; MS in Psychology, U. So. Calif., 1976; PhD in Psychology, Walden U., 1980. Tchr. spl. edn. L.A. Unified Schs., 1976-81; spl. cons. Torrance (Calif.) Unified Sch. Dist., 1977-78; pvt. practice Northridge, Calif., 1977—, Durango, Colo. Author: Birth Control for Disabled, 1977, V.D. is Very Dangerous, 1977, Sexuality Tutoring for Developmentally Disabled Persons, 1976, (computer program) Personality Index Spectral Analysis, 1987; contbr. articles to profl. jours. With USN, 1950-51. Republican. Mormon.

CÁRDENAS, ANTONIO CONTRERAS, foreign language educator; b. Gómez Fariaz Jalisco, Mex., Feb. 4, 1954; came to U.S., 1974; s. Manuel and Teresa (Contreras) C.; m. Luz María Figueroa, Aug. 14, 1992; 1 child, Laura Janet. AA, Laney Coll., Oakland, Calif., 1983; BA, San Francisco State U., 1985, MA, 1990. Cert. tchr. Spanish, Calif., Spanish and anthropology, Ariz. Instr. Spanish San Francisco State U., 1988-90, Ariz. State U., Tempe, 1992-94, Mesa (Ariz.) C.C., 1993—; Spanish tutor, dir. Univ. Tutorial Ctr., San Francisco State U., 1987-90; rschr. sociocultural anthropology Jungle of Chiapas, Mex., 1988; rschr. Spanish lit. Nat. Philippino Libr., Manila, 1989. Contbr. articles to profl. jours. Vol. Spanish instr. H.S. for Adult Hispanics, Oakland, 1980-81. Recipient Cert. of Recognition and Appreciation, San Francisco State U., 1989-90, grad. fellow, 1988. Mem. Ariz. Assn. Chicanos for Higher Edn. (treas. 1985—, Outstanding Leadership award 1996), Hispanic Journalism Sch. (Outstanding Leadership award 1996). Office: Mesa Community College 1833 W Southern Ave Mesa AZ 85202-4822

CARDINALLI, MARC PATRICK, lawyer; b. Ft. Lewis, Wash., Nov. 19, 1954; s. Guy Fredrick and Patricia Marie (DeWalt) C.; m. Deane Peacock, May 10, 1992. BA in Journalism, U. Nev., 1979; JD, U. of the Pacific, Sacramento, 1986. Bar: Nev. 1986, Calif. 1987. Student atty. Sacramento County Pub. Defender's Office, 1983-86; assoc. David Allen & Assocs., Sacramento and Reno, 1980-88; pvt. practice Reno, 1988; dep. atty. gen. State of Nev., Carson City, 1989-94; asst. gen. counsel U. and C.C. Sys. of Nev., Las Vegas, 1994-96; sr. asst. gen. counsel U. and C.C. Sys. of Nev., 1996—; mem. Nev. Atty. Gen.'s Com on Alt. Dispute Resolution, Com. on Continuing Legal Edn., 1990-94; instr. Nev. Atty. Gen.'s office continuing legal edn., 1994. Contbg. editor: Nevada Evidence Bench Book, 1985; contbg. author: So You Want to Go to Law School, 1989. Mem. Carson City Gang Task Force, 1989-91; mem., atty. gen.'s rep. Nev. Fed./State Jud. Com., 1990-94; rep. U.S. Justice Dept. Summit on Corrections, 1992; chair edn. com. Temple Emanuel, Reno, 1993-94; co-chair Nat. RFRA Lobbying Com., Carson City, 1993; pres. 5th Ave. Townhouse Owners Assn., Carson City, 1993-94; bd. dirs. Carson City United Way, 1993-94; instr. Congregation Ner Tamid post b'nai mitzvah class, Las Vegas, 1996—. Scholar Ahamson Found., Sacramento, 1985, Sacramento Bee, 1985. Mem. Nat. Assn. Coll. and University Attys. (com. on info. svcs. 1994—, reporter com. on litig. and alt. dispute resolution 1995—). Democrat. Jewish. Office: UCCSN 5550 W Flamingo Rd Ste C1 Las Vegas NV 89103

CARDINE, GODFREY JOSEPH, state supreme court justice; b. Prairie Du Chien, Wis., July 6, 1924; s. Joseph Frederick and Mary (Kasparek) C.; m. Janice Irene Brown, Sept. 14, 1946; children: Susan, John, Lisa. BS in Engring., U. Ill., 1948; JD with honors, U. Wyo., 1954. Bar: Wyo. 1954, U.S. Dist. Ct. Wyo. 1954, U.S. Ct. Appeals (10th cir.) 1954. Assoc. Schwartz, Bon & McCrary, Casper, Wyo., 1954-66; dist. atty. Natrona County, Wyo., 1966-70; ptnr. Cardine, Vlastos & Reeves, Casper, 1966-77; prof. law U. Wyo., Laramie, 1977-83; justice Wyo. Supreme Ct., Cheyenne, 1983-88, 90-94, chief justice, 1988-90; mem. Wyo. State Bd. Law Examiners, 1973-77; faculty dir. Western Trial Advocacy Inst., Laramie, 1981—; bd. advisors Land and Water Law Rev., 1985-90; mem. ad hoc com. to rev. bar assn. rules and by-laws, 1987-88; jud. assoc. editor Georgetown U. Cts., Health Sci. and the Law, 1989-91; adj. prof. trial advocacy Harvard U. Law Sch., 1991;. Contbr. articles to profl. jours. Active Little League Baseball, Casper, 1960-62; mem. Gov.'s Com. on Dangerous Drugs, 1968-71; initiator Alternative Dispute Resolution Program State of Wyo., 1989, chmn., 1990—. Fellow Internat. Soc. Barristers; mem. ABA (jud. adminstrn. divsn.), Assn. Trial Lawyers Am., Wyo. State Bar (pres. 1977-78), Phi Alpha Delta, Potter Law Club (pres. 1953-54), Rotary. Home: 2040 Rustic Dr Casper WY 82609-3405 Office: Wyo Supreme Ct Supreme Ct Bldg Cheyenne WY 82002

CARDONA-LOYA, OCTAVIO, plastic surgeon; b. San Diego, Nov. 28, 1946. MD, Med. U. of Guadalajara, Mex., 1972. Intern Regina Grey Nuns Hosp., 1972-73; plastic surgeon Tulane U., New Orleans, 1979-81; now plastic surgeon Sharp, Chula Vista, Calif.; clin. asst. prof. U. Calif., San Diego. Surgeon USPHS, 1975-79. Fellow ACS. Office: 750 Med Ctr Ct # 4 Chula Vista CA 91911-6634*

CARDWELL, MICHAEL RICHARD, land use planner; b. Tacoma, Wash., Aug. 27, 1954; s. Mary Bumgardner. BA in Govt., Eastern Wash. U., Cheney and Spokane, 1987, MPA, 1990, M of Urban and Regional Planning, 1990. Cert. planner. Program mgmt. intern Am. Indian Cmty. Ctr., Spokane, 1988; office asst. Spokane County DCD, Spokane, 1988-89; tribal planner Coeur d'Alene, Idaho, 1989-90; rschr. Dept. Energy, Richland, Wash., 1990; cmty. planner Muckleshoot Indian Tribe, Auburn, Wash., 1990-91; cons. Port of Seattle, 1991-92; land use planner Quinault Indian Nation, Taholah, Wash., 1993—; founder The Native Project, Spokane, 1988, 7 Feathers Art Coop., Taholah, 1993—, Kla Wow Ya, Taholah, 1994—, SNQHEP, Taholah, 1992—. Artist, photographer. Del. to county conv. Republican Party, Spokane County, Wash., 1988, King County, Wash., 1992. Am. Planning Assn. fellow, 1988-89, Am. Inst. Cert. Planners scholar, 1993, Presbyn. Ch. scholar, 1983-85. Mem. Am. Planning Assn., Am. Inst. Cert. Planners, N.W. Tribal Planners Forum, Ind. Order Foresters, Grays Harbor Regional Planning Commn. (bd. dirs., exec. sec.). Home: 1304 Chai-Chu PO Box 40 Taholah WA 98587-0040 Office: Quinault Indian Nation 1214 Aalis PO Box 189 Taholah WA 98587

CAREN, ROBERT POSTON, aerospace company executive; b. Columbus, Ohio, Dec. 25, 1932; s. Robert James and Charlene (Poston) C.; m. Linda Ann Davis, Mar. 27, 1963; children: Christopher Davis, Michael Poston. B.S., Ohio State U., 1953, M.S., 1954, Ph.D., 1961. Sr. physicist N.Am. Aviation, Columbus, 1959-60; assoc. research scientist research and devel. div. Lockheed Missiles and Space Co., Inc., Palo Alto, Calif., 1962-63, research scientist, 1963-66, sr. mem. research lab., 1966-69, mgr. def. systems space systems div., 1969-70, mgr. infared tech. R & D div., 1970-71, research dir., 1972-76, chief engr., 1976-86, v.p. gen. mgr. R & D div., 1986—, corp. v.p. sci. and engring., 1987—; bd. dirs. LITEX Corp., Superconducting Tech. Inc. Contbr. articles to profl. jours. Mem. dean's adv. coun. Ohio State U., Calif. Poly. State U.-St. Louis Obispo, U. So. Calif., U. Calif., L.A., U. Calif., Davis. Fellow AIAA, AAAS, AAS; mem. NAE, IEEE (sr.), Am. Astron. Soc., Am. Def. Preparedness Assn. (past chmn. rsch. divsn.), Am. Phys. Soc., Aerospace Industries Assn. (past chmn. tech. and ops. coun.), Calif. Coun. on Sci. and Tech., Sigma Pi Sigma, Pi Mu Epsilon. Home: 5616 Blackbird Ave Thousand Oaks CA 91362-5019 Office: 4500 Park Granada Calabasas CA 91399-0001

CARET, ROBERT LAURENT, university president; b. Biddeford, Maine, Oct. 7, 1947; s. Laurent J. and Anne (Santorsola) C.; m. Elizabeth Zoltan; children: Colin Ready, Katherine Ready, Katalyn Ford, Kellen Ford. BA, Suffolk U., 1969; PhD, U. N.H., 1974; DSc (hon.), Suffolk U., 1996. Dean Coll. Natural and Math. Scis. Towson (Md.) State U., 1981-87, prof. chemistry, 1994—, assoc. v.p., 1985-86, exec. asst. to pres., 1986-87, provost, exec. v.p., 1987-95; pres. San Jose (Calif.) State U., 1995—. Author: (with A.S. Wingrove) Quimca Organica, 1984, Study Guide and Answer Book to Organic Chemistry, 1981, Organic Chemistry, 1981, (with P. Plante) Myths and Realities in Higher Education Administration, 1990, (with K. Denniston and J.J. Topping) Principles and Applications of Organic and Biological Chemistry, 1995, 2d edit., 1997, Principles and Applications of Inorganic, Organic and Biological Chemistry, 1992, 2d edit., 1997, Foundations of Inorganic, Organic and Biological Chemistry, 1995; contbr. articles to profl. jours. Chmn. Baltimore County Higher Edn. Adv. Bd., Towson, 1989—; co-chmn. Balt. Sci. Fair/Kiwanis, Towson, 1983-88; bd. dirs. San Jose Repertory Theater, San Jose Opera, Calif. State U. Inst., Mesa. Recipient Employee Incentive award State of Md., 1987, Outstanding Chemistry Tchr. award Md. Inst. Chemists, 1971, Award for Excellence Suffolk U. Gen. Alumni Assn., 1986; Lester A. Pratt fellow U. N.H., 1972, Albert W. Diniak fellow, U. N.H., 1972. Mem. AAUP (Towson State U. chpt., mem. exec. com. 1978-81, v.p. 1975-80, divsn. and dept. rep. 1975-80), Am. Assn. Higher Edn., Am. Assn. Univ. Adminstrs. (Md. membership rep. 1986—), Am. Coun. on Edn., Am. Assn. Coll. Deans, Coun. Colls. of Arts and Scis., EDUCOM (instl. rep. 1986-87), Am. Chem. Soc. (Chesapeake sect. alt. counselor 1979-87, mem. exec. com. 1978-87, mem.-at-large 1978-79, various coms. 1978-87), Am. Assn. State Colls. and Univs. (adv. bd. 1986—, Kellogg Leadership bd. 1989—, state rep. 1989—, joint venture Silicon Valley bd. dirs. 1997, co-chair econ. devel. team 1996—), Md. C. of C., Balt. County C. of C., San Jose C. of C. (bd. dirs.), Sigma Xi (Towson State U. chpt. pres. 1975-76), Sigma Zeta, Phi Beta Chi, Omicron Delta Kappa. Office: San Jose State U One Washington Sq San Jose CA 95192-0002

CAREY, AUDREY LANE, interior designer, motivational speaker, educator; b. Spokane, Wash., Sept. 26, 1936; d. Glen Howard and Beatrice M. (Olsen) L.; m. Willard Keith Carey, July 4, 1959; children—Natalie Kay, Robert Lane, Willard Arthur. B.S. with honors in Home Econs., Wash. State U., 1958; postgrad. U. Wash., 1958, Eastern Oreg. State Coll., 1960—. High sch. home econs. tchr. Coulee City, Wash., 1958, Reardan, Wash., 1958-59; substitute tchr. LaGrande pub. schs. (Oreg.), 1960-65; nutrition instr. Eastern Oreg. State Coll., 1968-71; owner, mgr. Audrey Lane Carey Studio of Interior Design, LaGrande, 1973-85; vol. mgmt. tng. U. Colo., 1988, Nat. Vol. Conf., 1987, 88; family task force rep. 13 western states and Guam N.G. Assn. U.S., 1986-89; speaker in field. Active local Episcopal Ch., 1960—; youth activities dir. City of LaGrande, 1959-60; v.p., bd. dirs. Grande Ronde Symphony, 1960-64; den mother Blue Mountain council Boy Scouts Am., 1970; leader 4-H Clubs, 1971-73; pres. DeMolay Mothers Club, 1983; advisor EOSC Canterbury Club, 1961-65; campaign chmn. Union County, Sec. State, 1976, 80; pres. Union County Rep. Women, 1968; advisor Rainbow Girls, 1974-78; sponsor S.E. Asian Family, 1980-84; mem. Gov.'s Higher Edn. Mission, 1985; Eastern Oreg. chmn. Employer Support of Guard and Res. Family Readiness Program, 1985; mem. bd. trustees Oreg. State Library, 1986-94, chair, 1993-94. Viola Coulter scholar, 1957; recipient Patrick Henry citation Nat. Guard Assn. U.S., 1994. Mem. Am. Soc. Interior Designers, Kappa Alpha Theta (rush bd. chmn. 1960-84), Phi Kappa Phi, Pi Lambda Theta, Omicron Nu. Republican. Episcopalian. Club: PEO (past pres., charter mem. 1962—) (La Grande).

CAREY, JAMES C., JR., plastic surgeon; b. Chgo., 1932. MD, Northwestern U., 1957. Intern Cook County Hosp., Chgo., 1957-58, resident in gen. surgery, 1958-63; plastic surgeon U. Mo., Kansas City, 1980-82; now plastic surgeon Twin Cities Cmty. Hosp., Templeton, Calif. Office: 959 Las Tablas Rd Ste B3 Templeton CA 93465-9703

CAREY, KATHRYN ANN, advertising and public relations executive, editor, consultant; b. Los Angeles, Oct. 18, 1949; d. Frank Randall and Evelyn Mae (Walmsley) C.; m. Richard Kenneth Sundt, Dec. 28, 1980. BA in Am. Studies with honors, Calif. State U., L.A., 1971; postgrad. Georgetown U., Boston Coll. Cert. commercial pilot instrument rated. Tutor Calif. Dept. Vocat. Rehab., L.A., 1970; teaching asst. U. So. Calif., 1974-75, UCLA, 1974-75; claims adjuster Auto Club So. Calif., San Gabriel, 1971-73; corp. pub. rels. cons. Carnation Co., L.A., 1973-78; cons., adminstr. Carnation Community Svc. Award Program, 1973-78; pub. rels. cons. Vivitar Corp., 1978; sr. advt. asst. Am. Honda Motor Co., Torrance, Calif., 1978-84; exec. dir. Am. Honda Found., 1984—, Honda Philanthropy, Office of the Ams., 1996—; adminstr. Honda Matching Gift and Vol. Program, Honda Involvement Program; mgr. Honda Dealer Advt. Assns., 1978-84, Honda Philanthropy Office of the Americas, 1996—; cons. advt., pub. rels., promotions. Editor: Vivitar Voice, Santa Monica, Calif., 1978, Rod Machado's Instrument Pilots' Survival Manual, c. 1991; editor Honda Views, 1978-84, Found. Focus, 1984—; asst. editor Friskies Research Digest, 1973-78; contbg. editor Newsbriefs and Momentum, 1978—, Am. Honda Motor Co., Inc. employees publs. Calif. Life Scholarship Found. scholar, 1967; recipient Silver award, Wilmer Shields Rich award Coun. Founds. Excellence in Comm., 1995, award of Excellence, Soc. Tech. Comm., 1995, Merit award, 1996. Mem. Advt. Club L.A., Pub. Rels. Soc. Am., So. Calif. Assn. Philanthropy, Coun. on Founds., Affinity Group on Japanese Philanthropy (pres.), Ninety-Nines, Am. Quarter Horse Assn., Aircraft Owners and Pilots Assn., Los Angeles Soc. for Prevention Cruelty to Animals, Greenpeace, Ocicats Internat., Am. Humane Assn., Humane Soc. U.S., Elsa Wild Animal Appeal. Office: Am Honda Found 1919 Torrance Blvd Torrance CA 90501-2722

CAREY, KEITH GRANT, editor, publishing executive; b. Oakland, Calif., Jan. 13, 1958; s. Richard William and Juanita May (Yost) C.; m. Lois Lynn Schuricht, Oct. 15, 1994. BA in History with honors, San Jose State U., 1980. Tchr. Chaparral H.S., Las Vegas, 1981-82; pers. mgr. Grecian Health Spa, Palo Alto, Calif., 1982-83, Palos Verdes Health Spa, San Pedro, Calif., 1983-86; prodn. mgr., mng. editor U.S. Ctr. World Mission, Pasadena, Calif., 1986—. Mng. editor Global Prayer Digest, 1992—. Office: USCWM Global Prayer Digest 1605 E Elizabeth St Pasadena CA 91104-2721

CAREY, MARGARET THERESA LOGAN, newspaper education consultant; b. Phila., May 8, 1931; d. Michael Francis and Margaret Mary (Meehan) Logan; m. William Emmett Carey, June 21, 1952; children: William Edward, Michael Patrick, Peggy Ann. AA, Bucks County Community Coll., 1968; student, Temple U., 1968-69; BS, U. Bridgeport, 1971; MEd in Reading, U. N.C., 1973. Reading resource tchr. Wake County Sch. Dist., Raleigh, N.C., 1971-76; newspaper in edn. cons. The News & Observer, Raleigh, 1976-77; ednl. cons. U.S. News and World Report, Washington, 1977-78; newspaper in edn. cons. N.Y. Times, N.Y.C., 1978, Times Newspaper, Trenton-Princeton, N.J., 1979-91, Mitchellville, Md., 1991-93; cons. N.J. Dept. Edn., Trenton, 1978-79, Newspaper Assn. Am., 1992-93, Washington Post, 1992-93. Author: The Aft Summer Learning Calendar, 1992, 93, Getting Ready to Read with the New York Times, 1978; editor, founder (children's page) Funtimes, 1981-88, (supplement) Create-An-Ad, 1984-88. Newspaper in Edn. State rep. for N.J. Am. Newspaper Pubs. Assn. Found., Reston, Va., 1983-91; active Reading is Fundamental, Mercer County, N.J., 1984-91. Mem. Internat. Reading Assn. (literacy 1986), N.J. Reading Assn. (award 1986), Tri-County Reading Assn. (award 1986), N.J. Press Assn. (chmn. newspaper in edn. com. 1983-91), Assistance League of Denver, Denver Botanic Gardens, U.S. Golf Assn., Nat. Trust for Historic Preservation, Am. Hort. Soc., Country Club Castle Pines, Colo. Hist. Soc., Denver Art Mus., The Nature Conservancy. Roman Catholic.

CAREY, PETER KEVIN, reporter; b. San Francisco, Apr. 2, 1940; s. Paul Twohig and Stanleigh M. (White) C.; m. Joanne Dayl Barker, Jan. 7, 1978; children: Brendan Patrick, Nadia Marguerite. BS in Econs., U. Calif., Berkeley, 1964. Reporter San Francisco Examiner, 1964; reporter Livermore (Calif.) Ind., 1965-67, editor, 1967; aerospace writer, spl. projects and investigative reporter San Jose (Calif.) Mercury, 1967—. Recipient Pulitzer prize for internat. reporting Columbia U., 1986, George Polk award L.I. U., 1986, Investigative Reporters and Editors award, 1986, Jessie Meriton White Svc. award Friends World Coll., 1986, Mark Twain award Calif.-Nev. AP, 1983, staff team Pulitzer prize for gen. reporting, Columbia U., 1990, Thomas L. Stokes award Washington Journalism Ctr., 1991, Malcolm Forbes award Overseas Press Club of Am., 1993, Gerald Loeb award UCLA Grad. Sch. Mgmt., 1993, Best of the West, First Amendment Funding Inc., 1993, 95, Pub. Svc. award Calif. Newspapers Pub. Assn., 1996, Fairbanks award for pub. svc. AP, 1996; profl. journalism fellow NEH, 1983-84. Mem. Soc. Profl. Journalists, Investigative Reporters and Editors. Office: San Jose Mercury-News 750 Ridder Park Dr San Jose CA 95131-2432

CAREY, SHIRLEY ANNE, nursing consultant; b. Syracuse, N.Y., Sept. 27, 1939; d. John Crotty and Eva Mae (Pratt) Walsh; m. John Paul Carey, July 23, 1966; children: Jason Leo, Jonathan Paul, Jennifer Anne. BSN, Nazareth Coll., 1961. RN, Calif. Charge nurse surg. svcs. L.A. County Hosp., 1962-64; instr. nursing L.A. County-U. So. Calif. Med. Ctr. Sch. Nursing, 1964-70; rschr./developer nursing edn. films Concept Media, Irvine, Calif., 1971-78; cmty. health educator Huntington Beach (Calif.) Hosp. and Med. Ctr., 1983—; nursing cons., health educator, writer Huntington Beach, 1988—; dir. staff devel. Columbia Huntington Beach, 1995—, Columbia San Clemente Hosp. and Med. Ctr., San Clemente, Calif., 1995—; instr. basics of babysitting Huntington Beach Hosp. and Med. Ctr., 1986Y; instr. basic life support Am. Heart Assn., Huntington Beach, 1986—; HIV/AIDS educator ARC, Tustin, Calif., 1991—; bd. dirs. W. Orange County Consortium Spl. Edn., Huntington Beach, 1991-92, clk., 1992, 97, alt., 1993; bd. trustees Huntington Beach City Sch. Dist., 1990-94, 94—, clk., 1992, 97, pres., 1993. Author, rschr.: (film series) Impaired Mobility, 1993, Basic Patient Care, 1994, Infection Control, 1995; film coord.: (film series) Human Development: Conception to Neonate, 1992, Human Development: First 2 1/2 Years, 1992, Human Development 2 1/2 to 6 Years, 1993. Pres., bd. dirs. Harry W. Montague Basketball Meml. Scholarship Com., Huntington Beach, 1989—, sec., bd. dirs. Huntington Beach Sister City Assn., 1993-95; mem., past officer Orange County (Calif.) Adoptive Parents, 1975-96; active Girl Scouts Am., Costa Mesa, Calif., 1984-96, PTA, Huntington Beach, 1976—; commr. Huntington Beach Cmty. Svcs. Commn., 1994—; mem. Huntington Beach Children's Needs Task Force, 1995—, com. Orange County Sch. Orgn., 1994—, v.p., 1997; exec. bd. dirs. Huntington Beach PRIDE/DARE Found., 1995—. Recipient Hon. Svc. award PTA, 1989, 2d Pl. award Am. Jour. Nursing Film Festival, 1994, 96, Finalist AMA Internat. Film Festival, 1994, 96. Mem. AAUW (exec. bd. dirs. 1996-97, co-pres. 1997—), AHA (bd. dirs. Huntington Valley divsn. 1996—), Nat. Sch. Bd. Assn. (mem. fed. rels. network 1993-97), Calif. Sch. Bd. Assn. (mem. legis. network 1990—, del. assembly 1993—). Home and Office: 21142 Brookhurst St Huntington Beach CA 92646-7407

CARINO, LINDA SUSAN, business consultant; b. San Diego, Nov. 4, 1954; d. DeVona (Clarke) Dungan. Student, San Diego Mesa Coll., 1972-74, 89-90. Various positions Calif. Can. Bank, San Diego, 1974-77, ops. supr., 1977-80, ops. mgr., 1980-82; asst. v.p. ops. mgr. First Comml. Bank (formerly Calif. Can. Bank), San Diego, 1982-84; v.p. data processing mgr. First Nat. Bank, San Diego, 1984-91; v.p. conversion adminstr. Item Processing Ctr. Svc. Corp., Denver, 1991-92; mgr. computer ops. FIserv, Inc., Van Nuys, Calif., 1992-93; v.p., data processing mgr. So. Calif. Bank, La Mirada, Calif., 1993-94, v.p. tech. support mgr., 1994-96; ind. cons. First Nat. Bank of Ctrl. Calif., Salinas, Calif., 1996—; project mgr. EDS Corp., Burbank, Calif., 1996—. Democrat. Home and Office: 8400 Edinger Ave # X104

Huntington Beach CA 92647 Office: EDS Corp 8400 Edinger Ave #X104 Huntington Beach CA 92647

CARL, JOAN STRAUSS, sculptor, painter; b. Cleve., Mar. 20, 1926. Student, Cleve. Sch. Art, Chgo. Art Inst., New Sch. Art, L.A. Lectr. Fed. Visual Arts Program, Title Three, 1961-64; faculty Valley Ctr. of the Arts, 1960-64; tchr. Univ. of Judaism. One-woman shows inlcude Paideia Gallery, L.A., Bel Air Ext. Gallery, Beverly Hills, Calif., Laguna Beach (Calif.) Art Mus., Courtney Collins Gallery, Raleigh, N.C., Linden-Kicklighter Gallery, Cleve., Muskegon (Mich.) C.C., Bakersfield (Calif.) Coll., Fresno (Calif.) Art Ctr. Mus., Brand Libr. Gallery, Glendale, Calif., Thinking Eye, L.A., Courtright Gallery, L.A.; group shows include Cerritos (Calif.) Coll., L.A. Art Assn., So. Calif. Exposition, San Diego, Santa Cruz (Calif.) Art Show, West End Gallery, N.Y.C., Stuart Kingston Galleries, Naples, Fla., Laguna Beach Art Mus., Mint Mus., Charlotte, N.C., Paideia Gallery, Oborn Gallery, Kansas City Kans., Gallery Judaica, L.A., Feldheim Libr. Gallery, San Bernardino, Calif., Feingood Gallery, Milkin Ctr., Northridge, Calif., Judson Gallery, L.A., Laukershimz Gallery, North Hollywood, Calif.; comms. and collections include Zinkal Ltd., Tel Aviv, Raleigh (N.C.) Mus., No. Ohio Mus., Cleve., Sinai Meml. Pk., L.A., Govt. of Japan, Internat. Cultural Ctr. Youth, Jerusalem, others. Recipient Design award Ceramic Tile Inst. Mem. Calif. Confedn. of Arts (founding mem.), Artists Equity Assn. (past pres. L.A. chpt.), L.A. Art Assn. (past pres.). Home and Office: 4808 Mary Ellen Ave Sherman Oaks CA 91423-2120

CARLE, HARRY LLOYD, social worker, career development specialist; b. Chgo., Oct. 26, 1927; s. Lloyd Benjamin and Clara Bell (Lee) C.; BSS, Seattle U., 1952; MSW, U. Wash., 1966; m. Elva Diana Ulrich, Dec. 29, 1951 (div. 1966); adopted children: Joseph Francis, Catherine Marie; m. Karlen Elizabeth Howe, Oct. 14, 1967 (dec. Feb. 1991); children: Kristen Elizabeth and Sylvia Ann (twins), Eric Lloyd; m. Diane Wyland Gambs, May 23, 1993. Indsl. placement and employer rels. rep. State of Wash., Seattle, 1955-57, parole and probation officer, Seattle and Tacoma, 1957-61, parole employment specialist, 1961-63, vocat. rehab. officer, 1963-64; clin. social worker Western State Hosp., Ft. Steilacoom, Washington and U.S. Penitentiary, McNeil Island, Wash., 1964-66; exec. dir. Shohomish County Community Action Council/Social Planning Council, Everett, Wash., 1966-77; employment and edn. counselor Pierce County Jail Social Services, Tacoma, 1979-81; dir. employment devel. clinic, coord. vocat. program North Rehab. Facility, King County Div. Alcoholism & Substance Abuse, Seattle, 1981-90; counselor Northgate Outpatient Ctr. Lakeside Recovery , Inc., Seattle, 1991; staff devel. cons. Counseling for Ind. Living, Newport, R.I., 1992; community orgn./agy. problems mgmt. cons., 1968—; mem. social service project staff Pacific Luth. U., Tacoma, 1979-81. Cons. to pres. Geneal. Inst., Salt Lake City, 1974-78. Served with USN, 1944-46. U.S. Office Vocat. Rehab. scholar, 1965-66, named First Honoree Hall of Success Iowa Tng. Sch. for Boys, 1969. Mem. NASW, Seattle Geneal. Soc. (pres. 1974-76), Soc. Advancement Mgmt. (chpt. exec. v.p. 1970-71), Acad. Cert. Social Workers, Pa. German Soc., Henckel Family Nat. Assn., various hist. and geneal. socs. in Cumberland, Perry and Lancaster counties, Pa., Peoria and Fulton Counties, Ill., Seattle Japanese Garden Soc. (v.p. 1993-96), Hakone Found. (Saratoga, Calif.), Olympia-Yashiro Sister City Assn., Puget Sound Koi Soc., Dr. Sun Yat-sen Garden Soc. Vancouver (B.C., Can.), Kubota Garden Found. (Seattle), Bloedel Reserve (Banbridge Island, Wash.). Roman Catholic. Home: Karlensgarten Retreat 1425 10th Pl N Edmonds WA 98020-2629

CARLEONE, JOSEPH, aerospace executive; b. Phila., Jan. 30, 1946; s. Frank Anthony and Amelia (Ciaccia) C.; m. Shirley Elizabeth Atwell, June 29, 1968; children: Gia Maria, Joan Marie. BS, Drexel U., 1968, MS, 1970, PhD, 1972. Civilian engring. trainee, mech. engr. Phila. Naval Shipyard, 1963-68; grad. asst. in applied mechanics Drexel U., Phila., 1968-72, postdoctoral rsch. assoc., 1972-73, NDEA fellow, 1968-71, adj. prof. mechanics, 1974-75, 77-82; chief rsch. engr. Dyna East Corp., Phila., 1973-82; chief scientist warhead tech. Aerojet Ordnance Co., Tustin, Calif., 1982-88. v.p., gen. mgr. warhead systems div. GenCorp. Aerojet Precision Weapons, Tustin, 1988-89; v.p., dir. armament systems, Aerojet Electronics Systems Divsn., Azusa, Calif., 1989-94, v.p. tactial def. and armament products., Aerojet, Calif. 1994—. Editor: Tactical Missile Warheads, 1993. Mem. ASME, Sigma Xi, Tau Beta Pi, Pi Tau Sigma, Phi Kappa Phi. Contbr. articles to profl. jours.; rschr. explosive and metal interaction, ballistics, projectile penetration, impact of plates. Home: 2112 Campton Cir Gold River CA 95670-8302 Office: Aerojet PO Box 13222 Sacramento CA 95813-6000

CARLESIMO, P. J. (PETER J. CARLESIMO), former college basketball coach, professional basketball coach; b. Scranton, Pa.. Grad., Fordham U., 1971. Asst. basketball coach Fordham U., Bronx, N.Y., N.H. Coll., Manchester; mem. staff Wagner Coll., Staten Island, N.Y.; head coach Seton Hall U., South Orange, N.J., 1982-94, Portland Trailblazers, 1994—. Office: Portland Trailblazers 1 N Center Court St Ste 200 Portland OR 97227-2103*

CARLESON, ROBERT BAZIL, public policy consultant, corporation executive; b. Long Beach, Calif., Feb. 21, 1931; s. Bazil Upton and Grace Reynolds (Wilhite) C.; m. Betty Jane Nichols, Jan. 31, 1954 (div.); children: Eric Robert, Mark Andrew, Susan Lynn; m. Susan A. Dower, Feb. 11, 1984. Student, U. Utah, 1949-51; B.S., U. So. Calif., 1953, postgrad., 1956-58. Adminstrv. asst. City of Beverly Hills, Calif., 1956-57; asst. to city mgr. City of Claremont, Calif., 1957-58; sr. adminstrv. asst. to city mgr. City of Torrance, Calif., 1958-60; city mgr. City of San Dimas, Calif., 1960-64, Pico Rivera, Calif., 1964-68; chief dep. dir. Calif. Dept. Public Works, 1968-71; dir. Calif. Dept. Social Welfare, 1971-73; U.S. commr. welfare Washington, 1973-75; pres. Robert B. Carleson & Assocs., Sacramento, Calif. and Washington, 1975-81; chmn. Robert B. Carleson & Assocs., Washington, 1987-93, San Diego, 1993—; pres. Innovative Environ. Svcs. Ltd., Vancouver, B.C., Can., 1992; spl. asst. to U.S. pres. for policy devel. Washington, 1981-84; prin., dir. govt. rels. Main Hurdman KMG, Washington, 1984-87; dir. transition team Dept. Health & Human Services, Office of Pres.-Elect, 1980-81; spl. adviser Office of Policy Coordination; sr. policy advisor, chmn. welfare task force Reagan Campaign, 1980; bd. dirs. Fed. Home Loan Bank of Atlanta, 1987-90, I.E.S., Ltd., Can., Transenviro Co., USA, Churchill Co., USA; adv. com. Fed. Home Loan Mortgage Corp., 1985-87; pres. Nat. Tax Limitation Found., Washington, 1991—; mem. strengthening family policy coun. Nat. Policy Forum, Washington, 1994—. Adv. coun. gen. govt. Rep. Nat. Com., Washington, 1980-81; sr. fellow Free Congress Found., 1994—. Officer USN, 1953-56. Clubs: Masons, Rotary (pres. 1964), Army & Navy (Washington), Capitol Hill, Fairfax Hunt. Home and Office: 1911 Willow St San Diego CA 92106-1823

CARLETON, MARY RUTH, dean, consultant; b. Sacramento, Feb. 2, 1948; d. Warren Alfred and Mary Gertrude (Clark) Case; m. Bruce A. Hunt, Jan. 21, 1989. BA in Polit. Sci., U. Calif.-Berkeley, 1970, MJ, 1974; postgrad., San Diego State U. TV news anchorwoman, reporter Sta. KXAS-TV, Ft. Worth, 1974-78, Sta. KING-TV, Seattle, 1978-80, Sta. KOCO-TV, Oklahoma City, 1980-84; news anchor, reporter Sta. KTTV-TV, L.A., 1984-87; news anchor Sta. KLAS-TV, Las Vegas, Nev., 1987-91, KTNV-TV, 1991-93, Sta. UNLV-TV, 1993-94; broadcast instr. Okla. Christian Coll., 1981-84, UCLA, 1985-87, U. Nev.-Las Vegas, 1991-94; pub. speaking cons.; dir. UNLV Women's Ctr., 1991-94; news dir. univ. news Sta. UNLV-TV, 1992-94; asst. dean devel. San Diego State U., 1994—. Bd. dirs. World Neighbors, Oklahoma City, 1984-89, Allied Arts Coun. So. Nev.-Las Vegas, 1988-94, Nev. Inst. for Contemporary Art, 1988-94; bd. dirs. United Way, Las Vegas, 1991-94, secret witness bd., 1991-94, Las Vegas Women's Coun., 1993-94, Friends of Channel 10, 1991-94. Named Best Environ. Reporter, Okla. Wildlife Fedn., 1983, Disting. Woman of So. Nev., Woman of Achievement Las Vegas Women's Coun., 1990; recipient Broadcasting award UPI, 1981, Nat. award for best documentary, 1990, Tri-State award for best newscast, 1990, Emmy award, L.A., 1986, L.A. Press Club award 1986, 90, Nat. award for documentaries UPI, 1990, Woman of Achievement Media award Las Vegas C. of C., 1990. Mem. AARP (mem. nat. econ. issues team 1992-94, state legis. com.)Women in Comm. (Clarion award 1981, Best Newscaster 1990), Soc. Prol. Journalists, Press Women, Investigative Reporters, Sigma Delta Chi. Democrat. Roman Catholic. Avocations: tennis, gourmet cooking. Office: San Diego State U Coll Health & Human Svcs 5500 Canpanile San Diego CA 92182-4124

CARLIN, JEAN EFFAL, physician, psychiatrist, psychologist; b. Hibbing, Minn., July 24; d. Earl William and Effal Octavia (Anderson) C. BA, U. Minn., 1950, BS, 1952, MA, 1953, MD, 1954; PhD, 1959. Faculty North Park Coll., Chgo., 1956-58, Long Beach (Calif.) U., 1958-61; physician pvt. practice, 1961-67; staff mem. Orange County Hosp., 1969-80; faculty U. Calif., Irvine, 1969-80, assoc. dean med. sch., 1974-78; mem. faculty and staff Fairview Hosp. for Devel. Disabled, Costa Mesa, Calif., 1969-75, 78-80; dir. psychiatry resident edn. Martin Luther King Med. Sch., L.A., 1980-82; dir. resident edn. U. Okla., Oklahoma City, 1982-86; fellowship in forensic psychiatry U. So. Calif., L.A., 1986-87; psychiatrist So. regional office Conditional Release Program State of Calif., L.A., 1987-88; cons. L.A. County Mental Health Dept., 1979-80. Contbr. chpts. to books and articles to profl. jours. Col. U.S. Army Nat. Guard, Okla., 1982-86, Calif., 1981-82, 86-95. Recipient Am. Bus. Women's Assn. award, Cambodian Assn. Am. awards, 1976-78, Viet Nam Govt. awards, 1969, 72. Mem. Covenant Ch. Office: 500 Pacific Coast Hwy Ste 208 Seal Beach CA 90740-6601

CARLIP, HILLARY, author, screenwriter; b. L.A., Oct. 20, 1956; d. Allen Robert and Miriam Rhea (Lieverman) C. Student, U. Calif., Santa Cruz, 1975-76. Various positions as actress, juggler, fire-eater, comedienne, sketch writer, TV writer, screenwriter, artist; chair fundraising and publicity Aviva Ctr.-Sterlings, L.A., 1991—. Author: Girl Power, 1995, Zine Scene, 1998. Mem. SAG, AFTRA, Writers Guild Am., Actors Equity, Am. Soc. Composers and Pubs., BMI. Office: PO Box 2635 Los Angeles CA 90078

CARLISLE, DANIEL JAMES, announcer; b. Garden City, N.Y., Sept. 9, 1943. Announcer Radio Sta. WRIF-FM, Detroit, Radio Sta. WABX-FM, Detroit, Radio Sta. KSAN-FM, San Francisco, Radio Sta. WMMR-FM, Phila., Radio Sta. KROQ-FM, L.A., Radio Sta. KLOS-FM, L.A., Radio Sta. WNEW-FM, N.Y.C., Radio Sta. KKCY-FM, San Francisco, Radio Sta. KOFY-FM, San Francisco, Radio Sta. KFOG, San Francisco; Unistar Corp., L.A.; writer, asst. to sr. prodr. NBC TV, L.A.; news reporter KICU-TV, San Jose, Calif., ABC World News Tonight, N.Y.C.; dir. Grande Ballroom, Detroit, 1971-72; TV anchor Electric City, San Francisco, 1986-90. Author: (poetry) Greenwood Review, 1982, Religion Weaves A Dress, 1983. Home: 4020 19th St # 4 San Francisco CA 94114-2524

CARLQUIST, JOHN FREDERICK, microbiologist, immunologist; b. Salt Lake City, May 25, 1948; s. John Howard and Beatrice (Degenkolbe) C.; m. Pamela Woodbury, Aug. 22, 1975; children: John David, William Christopher. BS, U. Utah, 1971, PhD, 1977. Rsch. asst. dept. microbiology U. Utah Coll. of Medicine, Salt Lake City, 1967-69; microbiologist Utah State Dept. Health, Salt Lake City, 1970-71; microbiologist, curator Pure Culture Lab. U. Utah Coll. of Medicine, Salt Lake City, 1972-73, teaching asst. Dept. Microbiology, 1973-75, teaching fellow Dept. Microbiology, 1976-77; postdoctoral fellow Dept. Bioengring. U. Utah, Salt Lake City, 1977-78; rsch. asst. Dept. Pathology LDS Hosp., Salt Lake City, 1979-82, rsch. assoc. Dept. Medicine Divsn. Cardiology, 1982-86; rsch. scientist head cardiology rsch. lab., sci. dir. molecular pathology LDS Hosp., Salt Lake City, 1986—, 92—; rsch. instr., rsch. assoc. prof. Dept. Internal Medicine U. Utah Sch. of Medicine, Salt Lake City, 1988-91, 91—. Contbr. numerous articles to profl. jours. English instr. Guadalupe Cultural Ctr., Salt Lake City, 1971; youth councilor, chaperone St. Mary's Cath. Ch., Park City, Utah, 1979; dist. rep. Park City Cmty. Citizens Coun., 1980. Recipient Am. Soc. for Microbiology Student Rsch. award, 1976, 77, Frat. Order of Eagles award for Cardiovascular Rsch., 1990, Grad. fellowship U. Utah, 1973; grantee Deseret Found. Rsch., 1980, 85, 88, Am. Heart Assn., 1984, 87, 90, NIH, 1989, 90. Mem. AAAS, Am. Soc. for Microbiology, Transplantation Soc., Park City Ski Patrol (avalanche advisor 1990—, Outstanding Patroller award 1990, 91), Nat. Ski Patrol, Am. Assn. Immunologists, Fedn. of Am. Socs. for Exptl. Biology, Kappa Sigma. Office: LDS Hosp Divsn Cardiology 8th Ave C St Salt Lake City UT 84132

CARLS, JUDITH MARIE, physical education educator, golf coach; b. Moline, Ill., Aug. 16, 1940; d. Orville Allen and Eleanor Lou (Shollenberger) Meyers; m. Larry Michael, Dec. 21, 1966 (div. June 1971). BA in Phys. Edn., U. No. Iowa, 1962; MA, Western Ill. U., 1982. Cert. educator/adminstr. K-14, Ill. Phys. edn. instr. John Deere Jr. H.S., Moline; dep. chmn. phys. edn. Moline H.S., 1965-93; dir. golf schs. Recreation Pk. Golf Course, Long Beach, Calif., 1993—; part-time instr., student tchr. supr. Calif. State U., Fullerton, 1994—; dir. jr. golf City of Long Beach, Calif., 1996—; cons. LPGA Jr. Golf Program, L.A., 1993-94; dir. Jr. Golf. in the City of Long Beach, 1997—. Campaign, fundraiser Tim Bell State Rep., Moline, 1980-84. Named to Ill. Coaches Hall of Fame, 1993. Mem. NEA, Ladies Profl. Golf Assn. (mid-west sect. 1982—), Ill. Phys. Edn. Assn. (govt. affairs office 1989-93), Phi Kappa Phi. Republican. Lutheran. Home: 2814 32nd Avenue Dr Moline IL 61265-6956

CARLSEN, JANET HAWS, insurance company owner, mayor; b. Bellingham, Wash., June 16, 1927; d. Lyle F. and Mary Elizabeth (Preble) Haws; m. Kenneth M. Carlsen, July 26, 1952; children: Stephanie L. Chambers, Scott Lyle, Sean Preble, Stacy K., Spencer J. Cert., Armstrong Bus. Sch., 1945; student, Golden Gate Coll., 1945-46. Office mgr. Cornwall Warehouse Co., Salt Lake City, 1950-55, Hansen's Ins., Newman, Calif., 1969-77; owner Carlsen Ins., Gustine, Calif., 1978-97. Mem. city coun. City of Newman, 1980-82, mayor, 1982-94; bd. dirs. ARC, Stanislaus, Calif., 1982-83, Tosca, 1993—; bd. dirs. Stanislaus County Area Agy. on Aging, 1995—, chairperson, 1996-97; bd. dirs. Calif. state com. TACC Commn. on Aging, 1996—; grand marshal Newman Fall Festival, 1989; v.p. ctrl. divsn. League of Calif. Cities, 1989-90, pres. 1990, 91; bd. dirs. Sr. Opportunity Svc. Ctr., 1993-96, 97—, Sr. Opportunity Svc. Program of Stanislaus County, 1995-96; chairperson Ctrl. Valley Opportunity Ctr., 1996—. Named Soroptimist Woman of Achievement, 1987, Soroptimist Woman of Distinction, 1988, Outstanding Woman, Stanislaus County Commn. for Women, 1989, Newman Rotary Club Citizen of Yr., 1993-94, Woman of Yr. Calif. State Assembly Dist. 26, 1994, Ambassador, City of Newman, 1997—. Morman. Club: Booster (Newman). Lodge: Soroptimist. Home: 1215 Amy Dr Newman CA 95360-1003 Office: 377 5th St Gustine CA 95322-1126

CARLSEN, MARY BAIRD, clinical psychologist; b. Salt Lake City, Utah, Aug. 31, 1928; d. Jesse Hays and Susannah Amanda (Bragstad) Baird; m. James C. Carlsen, May 1, 1949; children: Philip, Douglas, Susan, Kristine. Student, St. Olaf Coll., 1946-47; BA, Whitworth Coll., 1950; MA, U. Conn., 1967; PhD, U. Wash., 1973. Profl. organist, piano tchr. Wash., Oreg., Ill., Conn., 1949-68; staff counselor Presbyn. Counseling Svc., Seattle, 1976-79; pvt. practice clin. psychologist, marriage therapist, cognitive, devel. psychology, career devel. Seattle, 1978-95; cons. creative aging Walla Walla, 1996—; chmn. sr. adult adv. coun. Seattle Parks Dept., 1975-76; adv. bd. Northwest Ctr. for Creative Aging, 1995—. Author: Meaning-Making: Therapeutic Processes in Adult Development, 1988, Creative Aging: A Meaning-Making Perspective, 1991, 2d edit., 1996, Transformational Meaning-Making and the Practices of Career Counseling, 1991; editl. bd. Jour. Constructivist Psychology, 1994—; contbr. chpt. to book. Grantee PEO Rsch., 1972, U. Wash. Women's Guidance Ctr., 1972. Mem. APA, Am. Soc. Aging, Assn. Humanistic Psychology, N.Am. Personal Construct Network.

CARLSON, CURTIS EUGENE, orthodontist, periodontist; b. Mar. 30, 1942; m. Dona M. Seely; children: Jennifer Ann, Gina Christine, Erik Alan. BA in Divisional Scis., Augustana Coll., 1965; BDS, DDS, U. Ill., 1969; cert. in periodontics, U. Wash., 1974, cert. in orthodontists, 1976. Dental intern Oak Knoll Navy Hosp., Oakland, Calif., 1969-70; dental officer USN, 1970-72; part-time dentist VA Hosp., Seattle, 1972-73; part-time periodontist Group Health Dental Coop., Seattle, 1973-76, part-time orthodontist, 1976-78; clin. instr. U. Wash., 1976; prin. Bellevue (Wash.) Orthodontic and Periodontic Clinic, 1976—; clin. instr., trainer Luxar Laser Corp., Bothell, Wash., 1992—; presenter in field. Master of ceremonies Auctioneer Friendship Fair, Augustana Coll., 1965, orientation group leader, 1965, mem. field svcs. com. for high sch. recruitment, 1965. Fellow Am. Coll. Dentists; mem. ADA, Am. Acad. Periodontology, Am. Assn. Orthodontics, Western Soc. Periodontology (bd. dirs. 1984-85, 86, program chmn. 1986, v.p. 1988, pres. elect 1989, pres. 1990), Seattle King County Dental Soc. (grievance, ethics and pub. info. coms.), Wash. State Dental Assn., Wash. State Soc. Periodontists (program chmn., pres. elect 1987, pres. 1988, 89), Wash. Assn. Dental Specialists (com. rep. 1987, 88, 89), Omicron Kappa Upsilon (dental hon. fraternity), Pi Upsilon Gamma (social chmn. 1964, pres. 1965). Home: 16730 Shore Dr NW Seattle WA 98155-5634 Office: Bellevue Orthodontic Periodontic Clinic 1248 112th Ave NE Bellevue WA 98004-3712

CARLSON, FREDERICK PAUL, electronics executive; b. Aberdeen, Wash., May 26, 1938; s. Edwin Gustaf and Anna Amelia (Anderson) C.; m. Alice A. Mercer, July 22, 1960 (div. Dec. 1969); 1 child, David Michael; m. Judith Kathryn Maxner, Dec. 12, 1970; children: Paul John, Britt Anna, Corrie Kathryn. Cert. advanced nuclear engring., Bettis Reactor Engring. Sch., 1962; BSEE, U. Wash., 1960, PhD, 1967; MS, U. Md., 1964; cert. exec. program, Stanford U., 1987, Aspen Inst., 1990, MIT, 1991. Registered profl. engr., Oreg., Wash. Rsch. engr. Boeing Aerospace Co., Seattle, 1965-66; prof. elec. engring. U. Wash., Seattle, 1967-77; pres., chief exec. officer Oreg. Grad. Ctr. Corp., Beaverton, 1977-88; v.p. strategy and bus. devel. Honeywell, Inc., Mpls., 1988-91; pres., chief exec. officer Carlson Cons., Inc., Tacoma, 1991—, pres., 1991—; bd. dirs. Synektron, Inc., Portland, Oreg., Tektronix, Inc., Beaverton, Logic Automation, Inc., Portland, Frank Russell Trust Co., Tacoma, Wash., PacifiCorp, Portland; vis. prof. elec. engring. Stanford (Calif.) U., 1975-76; mem. Commn. for Internat. Union Radio Sch., NRC. Author: Introduction to Applied Optics for Engineers, 1977; editor: Man, His Capabilities and Limitations in Systems, 1968; patentee low-frequency detection system, 1978, blood cell analyzer, 1979. Mem. Gov.'s Task Force on Econ. Recovery, Portland, 1982, Bus. Task Force on Trasnp. Systems, Portland, 1988. Officer electronics command USN, 1960-64; capt. USNR, 1964-83. Recipient High Tech. Industry's Good Scout award, Boy Scouts Am., Portland, 1986. Mem. IEEE, Optical Soc. Am. (chpt. pres. 1976), Arlington Club, Waverly Club, Tacoma Club. Office: 1201 Pacific Ave Ste 1702 Tacoma WA 98402-4301

CARLSON, GARY LEE, public relations executive, director, producer; b. Yakima, Wash., Oct. 15, 1954; s. Glenn Elmer and Helen Mary (McLean) Carlson. AA, Yakima Community Coll., 1975; BA in Communications, U. Wash., 1977. Dir. pub. affairs Sta. KCMU, Seattle, 1976-77; dir. programming and promotions Sta. KAPP-TV, Yakima, 1978-80; dir. promotions Sta. WBZ-TV, Boston, 1980-84; producer Sta. KCBS-TV, Los Angeles, 1985; dir. creative services Metromedia Producers, Los Angeles, 1985-86; dir. promotion publicity 20th Century Fox, Los Angeles, 1986—. Writer: (TV animation program) Bruno, the Kid, 1996; writer, co-prodr. (TV movie) Coaching a Murder, 1994; prodr., dir. M*A*S*H* 15th Ann. Campaign, 1987 (Internat. Film and TV Festival N.Y. award), The Fox Tradition, 1988 (Internat. Film and TV Festival N.Y. award, Clio finalist award 1988, Telly award 1988, B.P.M.E. award 1988); prodr., writer, dir. Consumer Reports, 1983 (Internat. Film and TV Festival N.Y. award, Houston Internat. Film and TV award). Mem. Broadcast Promotion and Mktg. Execs., Nat. Assn. TV Program Execs., Beta Theta Pi. Home: 1510 Rock Glen Ave Glendale CA 91205-2063 Office: 20th Century Fox Film Corp PO Box 900 Beverly Hills CA 90213-0900

CARLSON, KAY MARIE, artist, educator; b. Marshfield, Wis., Aug. 29, 1948; d. Delmer Roland and Florence (Biechler) C.; m. Robert Vigil, Jan. 1, 1982 (div. Aug. 1987). BA in English Lit., U. Wis., 1970; postgrad., San Francisco Art Inst., 1971-74. English tchr. Antioch West Coll., San Francisco, 1973; gallery asst. Source Gallery, San Francisco, 1978-79; art dir., sales mgr. Vorpal Gallery, San Francisco, 1979-81; artist in residece Tomales (Calif.) Bay Schs., 1986; art tchr. Talampais Cmty. Edn., Mill Valley, Calif., 1992—; cons. to artists Amsterdam Art Sight and Insight Ctr., Marin County, Calif., 1985—, bd. dirs., 1997; founder, project dir. Marin Open Studios, Sausalito, Calif., 1993-96; art curator Concordia Argonaut Club, San Francisco, 1988—; artist trip leader Wilderness Tours, Bolinas, Calif., 1987-88; sec., mem. com. Indsl. Ctr. Bldg., Sausalito, Calif., 1994-97; represented by Mus. Modern Art Gallery, San Francisco, Interart Gallery, Walnut Creek, Calif., The Art Club, Oakland, Calif. One woman shows include BankAm World Hdqrs., San Francisco, 1979, Henry Gifford Hardy Gallery, San Francisco, 1987, Mill Valley Libr. Gallery, 1990, Jessup OrangeWorks Gallery, San Anselmo, Calif, 1991, U. Wis. Marshfield Wood County Ctr., 1991, Ames Corp., San Rafael, 1992, Pt. Reyes Seashore Lodge, Olema, Calif., 1992, CCC Gallery, Tiburon, 1993, Bank of Marin, 1994, U. San Francisco, 1994; exhibited in group shows at Escalle Winery, Bank of Marin, Coll. of Marin, 1991, Bolinas (Calif.) Mus., 1991, Artisans Gallery, Mill Valley, 1991, Marin County Fair, San Rafael, 1991, 93 (1st Pl.), San Francisco Artists Guild, 1991, Grants Pass (Oreg.) Mus. Art, 1991, 92, Indsl. Ctr. Bldg., 1992, Marin Agrl. Land Trust, Ross, Calif., 1992, Marin Open Studios, Sausalito, 1993, Mill Valley City Hall, 1993, Shorebirds Gallery, Tiburon, 1994, Artisans Gallery, 1995, numerous others; executed mural St. Francis Hosp.; represented in permanent collections at BankAm., Itel Corp., Boston, U.S. Dept. Labor, EPA, San Francisco, Fireman's Fund Ins. Co., Seattle, numerous others. Sec. bd. dirs. Marin Art Coun., San Rafael, Calif., 1991-96. Home: 15 Linda Vista Tiburon CA 94920 Studio: # 33 Indsl Ctr Bldg 480 Gate 5 Rd Sausalito CA 94965

CARLSON, MARGARET EILEEN (PEGGY CARLSON), counselor, hypnotherapist; b. Seattle, July 20, 1946; d. Patrick William and Dorothy Christina (DeMello) Hurley; m. Jerome Cathey, Sept. 6, 1968 (div. Feb. 1994); 1 child, Michael Patrick; m. Eric VictorCarlson, Jan. 20, 1996; children: Grace, Nick. BS, Bastyr U., 1995. Retail store owner Seattle, 1973-94; counselor, hypnotherapist pvt. practice, Seattle, 1995—. Named for Outstanding Cmty. Svc. U. C. of C., Seattle, 1992. Home: 4808 NE 41st St Seattle WA 98105-5112 Office: 2800 E Madison St Seattle WA 98112-4859

CARLSON, NANCY LEE, English language educator; b. Spokane, Wash., June 1, 1950; d. Catherine Esther Paight. BS, Wash. State U., 1973; MEd, curriculum specialist, Ea. Wash. U., 1987. Tchr. Stevenson-Carson Sch. Dist., Wash., 1973-74, Spokane Sch. Dist., 1974—; vis. faculty Ea. Wash. U., 1989-91, 93—; active steering com. Spokane County Children's Alliance, 1992—. Spokane County co-chmn. Sen. Slade Gorton campaign, 1988, mem. adv. bd., 1989—; Rep. precinct committeeperson, 1988-90, 92-94; bd. dirs. West Ctrl. Cmty. Ctr., Spokane Civic Theater, sec., 1992-94; mem. affordable housing com. Spokane County, 1990-91; treas. Inland Empire for Africa, Spokane, 1985-86; vice chmn. Ea. Wash. phone bank for Sen. Dan Evans, Spokane, 1984; mem. Mayor's Task Force on the Homeless, 1987-88; mem. Spokane County adv. bd. City of Spokane Cmty. Ctr., 1990-92; lay min. First Presbyn. Ch., deacon, 1994—, sec. bd. deacons, 1994-96, vice moderator bd. deacons, 1996—. Mem. NEA, ASCD, Nat. Coun. Tchrs. English, Wash. Coun. Tchrs. English, Wash. Edn. Assn., Spokane Edn. Assn., Wash. State U. Alumni Assn. (area rep. 1987-90). Republican. Presbyterian. Office: Rogers High Sch Sch Dist # 81 1622 E Wellesley Ave Spokane WA 99207-4261

CARLSON, ROBERT ERNEST, freelance writer, architect, lecturer; b. Denver, Dec. 6, 1924; s. Milton and Augustine Barbara (Walter) C.; m. Jane Frances Waters, June 14, 1952 (div. June 1971); children: Cristina, Bob, Douglas, Glenn, James. BS in Archtl. Engring., U. Colo., 1951. Registered architect, Colo. Architect H.D. Wagener & Assocs., Boulder, Colo., 1953-75; pvt. practice architect Denver, 1975-82; health and promotion cons. Alive & Well Cons., Denver, 1982-85; freelance writer Denver, 1985—; mem. Colo. Gov.'s Coun. for Fitness, Denver, 1975—; state race walking chmn. U.S. Track & Field, Denver, 1983—; bd. dirs. Colo. Found. for Phys. Fitness, Denver, 1987—; lectr. in field. Author: Health Walk, 1988, Walking for Health, Fitness and Sport, 1996. Vol. Colo. Heart Assn., 1985—, Better Air Campaign, 1986-87, Cystic Fibrosis, 1989-91, Multiple Sclerosis Soc., 1988-91, Qualife, 1989—, March of Dimes, 1989, United Negro Coll. Fund, 1989, bd. trustees, 1990. With U.S. Army, 1943-46, ETO. Decorated Bronze Star; named One of Ten Most Prominent Walking Leaders in U.S.A., Rockport Walking Inst., 1989. Mem. Colo. Author's League, Phidippides Track Club (walking chmn. 1981-85), Rocky Mountain Rd. Runners (v.p. 1983-84), Front Range Walkers Club (founder, pres. Denver chpt. 1985—), Lions (bd. dirs. 1965-72). Episcopalian. Home and Office: 2261 Glencoe St Denver CO 80207-3834

CARLSON, ROBERT MICHAEL, artist; b. Bklyn., Nov. 19, 1952; s. Sidney Carlson and Vickey (Mihaloff) Woodward; m. Linda Schneider; m. Mary Elizabeth Fontaine, Feb. 24, 1984; 1 child, Nora. Student, CCNY, 1970-73; studied with Flora Mace and Joey Kirkpatrick, Pilchuck Glass Sch., 1981, studied with Dan Dailey, 1982. Teaching asst. Pilchuck Sch., Stanwood, Wash., 1986, 88, mem. faculty, 1989-90, 92, 95; mem. faculty Pratt Fine Arts Ctr., Seattle, 1988-90, Penland (N.C.) Sch. Crafts, 1994,

Bild-Werk Sch., Germany, 1996; mem. artists adv. com. Pilchuck Sch., 1989, 90; vis. artist Calif. Coll. Arts and Crafts, Oakland, 1989, Calif. State U., Fullerton, 1991, blossom summer program Kent State U., Ohio, 1991, U. Ill., Urbana-Champaign, 1993, Toledo Mus. of Art Sch., 1994; visual-artist-in-residence Centrum Found., Port Townsend, Wash., 1992. One-man shows include Foster White Gallery, Seattle, 1987, 90, 92, The Glass Gallery, Bethesda, Md., 1988, Heller Gallery, N.Y.C., 1989, 95, Betsy Rosenfield Gallery, Chgo., 1991, 92, MIA Gallery, Seattle, 1994, others; exhibited in group shows at Traver Gallery, Seattle, 1984, 89, Mindscape Gallery, Evanston, Ill., 1984, 86, Tucson Mus. Art., 1984 (Purchase award), 86 (Award of Merit), Hand and Spirit Gallery, Scottsdale, Ariz., 1985, 86, Craftsman Gallery, Scarsdale, N.Y., 1985, Robert Kidd Gallery, Birmingham, Mich., 1985, 88, Gazebo Gallery, Gatlinburg, Tenn., 1985, The Glass Gallery, Bethesda, Md., 1986 (Jurors award), 91, 92, 94, Artists Soc. Internat., San Francisco, 1987 (Critics Choice award), William Traver Gallery, Seattle, 1987, 90, 91, 92, Japan Glass Artcrafts Assn., Tokyo, 1987, Heller Gallery, 1988, 89, 90, 91, 93, 94, 95, 96, 97, Washington Sq. Ptnrs., 1988, Foster White Gallery, 1988, 90, Bellvue Art Mus., Wash., 1988, 91, 94, Am. Arts and Crafts Inc., San Francisco, 1989, Mus. Craft and Folk Art, San Francisco, 1989, Great Am. Gallery, Atlanta, 1989, Dorothy Weiss Gallery, San Francisco, 1989, Habitat Gallery, Farmington Hills, Mich., 1990, 93, Philabaum Gallery, Tucson, 1990, Greg Kucera Gallery, Seattle, 1990, Connell Gallery, Atlanta, 1990, Net Contents Gallery, Bainbridge Island, Wash., 1991, Seattle Tacoma Internat. Airport Installation, 1991, 95, Pratt Fine Arts Ctr., Seattle, 1991, Crystalex, Novy Bor, Czechoslovakia, 1991, Whatcom County Mus., Bellingham, Wash., 1992, Art Gallery West Australia, 1992, 1004 Gallery, Port Townsend, 1992, Bainbridge Island Arts Coun., 1992, MIA Gallery, 1993, Betsy Rosenfield Gallery, Chgo., 1993, Blue Spiral Gallery, Asheville, N.C., 1995, Huntington Mus., 1996, Salem Art Assn., 1996, Judy Yovens Gallery, Houston, 1997, Internat. Glass Art Exchange, Tucson, 1997; represented in permanent collections Corning (N.Y.) Mus. Glass, Tucson Mus. Art, Toledo Mus. Art, Glasmuseum Frauenau, Germany, Glasmuseum Ebeltoft, Denmark, Valley Nat. Bank, Phoenix, Fountain Assocs., Portland, Oreg., Iceland Air Co., Reykjavik, Iceland, Crocker Banks, L.A., Davis Wright Tremain, Seattle, Meiwa Trading Co., Tokyo, Safeco Ins. Corp., Seattle, Crystalex Corp., L.A. County Mus. Art. Fellow Tucson Pima Arts Coun., 1987, NEA, 1990. Mem. Glass Art Soc. (conf. lectr. 1991, bd. dirs. 1992-94, v.p. 1993-94, pres. 1995). Office: PO Box 11590 Bainbridge Island WA 98110-5590

CARLSON, RONALD FRANK, educator, fiction writer; b. Logan, Utah, Sept. 15, 1947; s. Ed and Verna (Mertz) C.; m. Georgia Elaine Craig, June 14, 1969; children: Nicholas George Carlson, Colin Edwin. BA, U. Utah, 1970, MA, 1972. English tchr. Hotchkiss Sch., Lakeville, Conn., 1971-81; artist in edn. Utah Arts Coun., Salt Lake City, 1982-87, Idaho Arts Com., Boise, 1983-89, Alaska Arts Com., Anchorage, 1984-87; instr. continuing edn. U. Utah, Salt Lake City, 1982-86; writer-in residence Ariz. State U., Tempe, 1986-87, asst. prof. English, 1987-88, assoc. prof. English, 1988-94, prof. English, 1994—, dir. creative writing, 1989-96, prof. English, 1994—. Author: (novels) Betrayed by F. Scott Fitzgerald, 1977, Truants, 1981, (collection of stories) The News of the World, 1987, Plan B for the Middle Class, 1992, The Hotel Eden, 1997, (story) Milk (Best Am. Stories 1987), Blazo Norton Anthology, 1997. Bd. dirs., founder Class of '65 West High Schlarship Fund, Salt Lake City, 1985—. Mem. Writers Guild of Am. West. Office: Ariz State Univ Dept English Tempe AZ 85287

CARLSON, THOMAS E., judge; m. Cynthia Hustad. BA, Beloit Coll., 1969; JD, Harvard U., 1975; LLM, NYU, 1985. Bar: Calif. 1976; U.S. Dist. Ct. (no. dist.) Calif. 1977, U.S. Dist. Ct. (cen. dist.) Calif. 1984, U.S. Ct. Appeals (9th cir.) 1978. Law clk. to Hon. Thomas Roberts U.S. Supreme Ct., R.I., 1976-77; law clk. to Hon. Donald Wright Supreme Ct. Calif., 1977-78; assoc. atty. Cooper, White & Cooper, San Francisco, 1978-84; dep. staff dir. Ninth Cir. Ct. Appeals, San Francisco, 1984; judge U.S. Bankruptcy Ct. No. Dist. Calif., San Francisco, 1997—. Mem. Nat. Conf. Bankruptcy Judges. Office: US Bankruptcy Ct Calif PO Box 7341 235 Pine St San Francisco CA 94120-7341

CARLSTROM, R. WILLIAM, retired special education educator; b. Seattle, Oct. 22, 1944; s. Roy Albert Carlstrom and Dorothy (Anderson) Hart; m. Ann Scheffer, July 29, 1967; children: Trina Anderson Carlstrom, Paul Scheffer. BA, Lewis & Clark Coll., 1967; MA, U. Wash., 1970. Tchr. Shoreline Pub. Schs., Seattle, 1968-71; program coordinator fo adult handicapped City of Seattle, 1971-72; spl. edn. tchr. South Shore Middle Sch., Seattle, 1972-75, Sharples Jr. High, Seattle, 1975-78, Ryther Child Ctr., Seattle, 1978-89; edn. specialist Therapy Clinic of Whidbey Island, Oak Harbor, Wash., 1995—; sec., treas., bd. dirs. Glaser Found., Inc., Edmonds, Wash., 1974-86, exec. dir., 1983-91, trustee, 1983—; dir. adminstrn. First Place Sch. for Homeless Children, 1994-95; adv. com. mem. U. Wash. Dentistry for Handicapped, Seattle, 1979-94, pres., cons. Funding Resources Group, Inc., Edmonds, 1984-94; co-founder, trustee Snohomish County Youth Cmty. Found., 1992-93; pres. Current Health Techniques, Inc., 1992-93, N.P. Mktg.; trustee St. Regis Clinics, 1992-93; French tchr. Edmonds Cybersch., 1996—; pres., bd. dirs. Whidbey Clinic Inc., 1995—. Coun. mem. U. Wash. Grad. Sch. for Dentistry, 1979-94; trustee Edmonds Unitarian Ch., 1980-81, Pub. Edn. Fund, Dist. 15, Edmonds, 1986-88, Home Care Wash.; pres. Madrona Mid. Sch. PTA, Edmonds, 1983-84; v.p., bd. dirs. South Whidbey Schs. Found., 1995—. Grantee Seattle Masonic Temple, 1974-75, Fed. Govt., 1970-71. Mem. Pacific N.W. Grantmakers Forum. Democrat. Office: Therapy Clinic of Whidbey Island 520 E Whidbey Ave # 206 Oak Harbor WA 98277

CARLTON, THOMAS GRANT, psychiatrist; b. San Diego, Nov. 9, 1943; s. Edwin Thomas and Theda Miriam (Waddell) C. BA, San Jose State U., 1966; MD, U. Wis., 1970. Commd. ensign USN, 1969, advanced through grades to capt., 1985, ret., 1993; pvt. practice psychiatry Moses Lake, Wash., 1993-95; med. dir. Ctr. for Emotional Trauma Recovery, Lake Chelan Cmty. Hosp., 1995—; asst. prof. Eastern VA Med. Sch., Norfolk, Va., 1979-83, George Washington U., Washington, 1979-83, Chgo. Med. Sch., 1988-90. Mem. AMA, Am. Psychiatric Assn., Internat. Soc. for Traumatic Stress Studies, Internat. Soc. for Study of Dissociation, Am. Soc. Clin. Hypnosis, Rotary. Office: Ctr for Emotional Trauma Recovery Lake Chelan Cmty Hosp PO Box 908 Chelan WA 98816

CARLTON-ADAMS, DANA GEORGIA MARIE ANNE, psychotherapist; b. Kansas City, Mo.; d. George Randolph Carlton and Harriett Marie (Smith) Carlton-Witt; m. John Adams; 1 child, J.J. II. Student, Kansas City (Mo.) Jr. Coll., Rockhill Coll., Trinity Coll., Dublin, Ireland, 1973, City U. of London (Eng.), 1978. Owner Pure White Electric Light and Magic, Lakewood, Calif., 1985—; dir., owner Trauma Buddy's, Lakewood, 1988—; clin. hypotherapist Inner Group Mgmt., Cerritos, Calif., 1989—; cons. Rockwell, McDonnell Douglas, Long Beach, Calif., 1987-90; assoc. staff, instr. Talbert Med. Group; owner In Print mag., 1990—; staff counselor FHP. Author: Who Calls on Pandora, 1969, Jupiter in Scorpio, 1974, Burma Route, 1989, Counterstrike: Dimitri Manulski, 1990, Kitty-Morphis, 1982, Mouse Tails, 1991, Bookish Miss Emma, 1993, A Little Trip Through the Universe, 1993, Handbook for the Living, 1990. Adv. Greater Attention Victims Violent Crimes; active Animal Rights Pet Protection Soc., Calif. Preventive Child Abuse Orgn., Sierra Club, Women's Abuse Shelters. Mem. Calif. Astronomy Assn., Acoustic Brain Rsch., Inner Group Mgmt., NLP Integration Soc. (pres. 1988-89), British Psychol. Assn., C. of C., Willmore Heritage Ctr. for Neighborhood Downtown Preservation. Home and Office: 243 W 8th St Long Beach CA 90813-4157

CARMACK, MILDRED JEAN, retired lawyer; b. Folsom, Calif., Sept. 3, 1938; d. Kermit Leroy Brown and Elsie Imogene (Johnston) Walker; m. Allan W. Carmack, 1957 (div. 1979); 1 child, Kerry Jean Carmack Garrett. Student, Linfield Coll., 1955-58; BA, U. Oreg., 1967, JD, 1969. Bar: Oreg. 1969, U.S. Dist. Ct. Oreg. 1980, U.S. Ct. Appeals (9th and fed. cirs.) 1980, U. S. Claims Ct. 1987. Law clk. to Hon. William McAllister Oreg. Supreme Ct., Salem, 1969-73, asst. to ct., 1976-80; asst. prof. U. Oreg. Law Sch., Eugene, 1973-76; assoc. Schwabe, Williamson & Wyatt, Portland, Oreg., 1980-83, ptnr., 1984-96, ret., 1996; writer, lectr., legal educator, Oreg., 1969—; mem. exec. bd. Appellate sect. Oreg. State Bar, 1993-95. Contbr. articles to Oreg. Law Rev., 1967-70. Mem. citizen adv. com. State Coastal Planning Commn., Oreg., 1974-76, State Senate Judiciary Com., Oreg., 1984; mem. bd. visitors Law Sch. U. Oreg., 1992-95. Mem. Oreg. State Bar Assn., Multnomah County Bar Assn., Order of Coif.

CARNEY, RICHARD EDGAR, foundation executive; b. Marshall, Tex., Dec. 11, 1923; s. Edgar Lester and Lillian (Sansom) C.; m. Adrienne McAndrews, 1973 (div. 1981). Student, Culver-Stockton Coll., 1942, 46, Washington U., St. Louis, 1946-48; Taliesin fellow, Spring Green, Wis. and Scottsdale, Ariz., 1948-55. Aide to Frank Lloyd Wright, 1952-59; asst. to sec.-treas. Frank Lloyd Wright Found., Scottsdale, 1959-62, exec. asst. to pres., 1962-85, treas., 1962-95, mng. trustee, ceo, 1985-96; chmn. Frank Lloyd Wright Found., Scottsdale, Ariz., 1996—; dir. admissions, student advisor Frank Lloyd Wright Sch. Architecture, Scottsdale, 1962—, bd. dirs. Taliesin Architects, Scottsdale, 1962—, treas. 1962—; exhbn. com. Scottsdale Ctr. for Arts, 1985-91; mem. Gov.'s Commn. on Taliesin, State of Wis., 1988-89; organizer, bd. dirs. Taliesin Preservation Commn., Spring Green, 1990—; pres., 1991—. Set designer, performer theatrical prodns., Taliesin West, Scottsdale, 1960—. Trustee Unity Chapel, Inc., Spring Green, 1980—; mem. Task Force on Higher Edn., Scottsdale, 1991-92; trustee Ariz. Vision Weavers, Phoenix, 1994—. Sgt. U.S. Army, 1942-46, ETO. Recipient Alumni of Yr. award Culver-Stockton Coll., 1963. Home and Office: Frank Lloyd Wright Found Taliesin W Scottsdale AZ 85261

CARNICKE, SHARON MARIE, drama educator, theatre specialist and director; b. Bridgeport, Conn., July 28, 1949; d. Stephen J. and Evelyn (Furjesz) C. Cert. Russian Lang., Moscow U., USSR, 1970; AB, Barnard Coll., 1971; MA, NYU, 1973; PhD, Columbia U., 1979. Asst. prof. Sch. Visual Arts, N.Y.C., 1980-83; coord. core curriculum Columbia U., N.Y.C., 1978-83; asst. dean curriculum NYU, 1983-86, asst. prof. English, 1984-87; assoc. prof. theatre U. So. Calif., L.A., 1987—; Russian evaluator, NEA, Washington, 1984-87; cons. core curriculum Sch. Visual Arts, N.Y.C., 1980-83; interpretor Soviet Dirs. at Actors Studio, N.Y.C., 1978. Contbr. articles to profl. jours.; author: The Theatrical Instinct, 1989; translator plays from Russian, Chekhov and New Soviet, 1970—; adaptor, trans. plays: The Storm, Blackforest, 1978, 89; head editor project to publish English translation of Collected Works of Stanislavsky. Interpretor Am. Soviet Youth Forum, USA, USSR, 1973-74. Fellowship Am. Coun. Learned Socs., 1988-89, Rockefeller Found., U. Wis., Madison, 1988, Mogilat-Mihaly fellowship, USSR, 1978; grantee Institut d'etudes slaves, La Sorbonne, France, 1979. Mem. MLA, Am. Lit. Translators Assn., Dramatists Guild. Office: U So Calif MC0791 Sch Theatre Los Angeles CA 90089

CARNINE, DOUGLAS WAYNE, education educator, author; b. Sullivan, Ill., Oct. 7, 1947; s. Wayne J. and Olive F. (Emel) C.; m. Linda M. McRoberts, June 10, 1970; children: Berkley, Leah. BS, U. Ill., 1969; MS, U. Oreg., 1970; PhD, U. Utah, 1974. Asst. prof. U. Oreg., Eugene, 1975-81, assoc. prof., 1981-87, prof., 1987—. Author: Theory of Instruction, 1982, Learning Pascal, 1989. Office: U Oreg 805 Lincoln St Eugene OR 97401-2810

CARO, EVELYN INGA ROUSE, writer; b. Monterey Park, Calif., June 2, 1956; d. Coburn Whitehead and Marcelaine (Ulvick) Rouse; m. Johnny Caro, Dec. 19, 1982; children: Jessica Lynn, Juan Abram, Matthew Jason, Ruben Emmanuel. Author: A Prelude to Summer, 1990, (novel) The Trial of Adam Smith, 1995 (play); contbr. poetry to various publs. Elder 7th-day Adventist Ch., 1995—. Home: 9266 Valley View Ave Whittier CA 90603

CARO, MIKE, writer, editor, publisher; b. Joplin, Mo., May 16, 1944; s. Peter Klaus and Marguerite (Zuercher) C.; m. Bonita Marie Polniak, June 6, 1965 (div. June 1972); m. Phyllis Marsha Goldberg. Gen. mgr. Huntington Park (Calif.) Casino, 1985; chief strategist Bicycle Club, Bell Gardens, Calif., 1984-85; editor, pub. Mike Caro's Pro Poker monthly, 1993; gaming author, cons., 1993—; founder Mad Genius Brain Trust; actor, instr. video tape Play to Win Poker, 1988. Author: Caro on Gambling, 1984, Mike Caro's Book of Tells-The Body Language of Poker, 1985, Poker for Women-A Course in Destroying Male Opponents at Poker and Beyond, 1985, New Poker Games, Gambling Times Quiz Book, Bobby Baldwin's Winning Poker Secrets, Caro's Fundamental Secrets of Poker, 1991; editor-in-chief Poker Player; poker editor Gambling Times; mng. editor B&G Pub.; contbr. articles to gambling mags.; programmer ORAC: Artificially Intelligent Poker Player, 1983; developer programming tools Mike Caro's Poker Engine, audio tapes Real Life Strategy, Positive Poker, Pro Poker Secrets, Pro Hold 'em Secrets, 1992, four-color deck, 1992; video Caro's Power Poker Seminar, 1995, Caro's Pro Poker Tells, 1995, Caro's Pro Poker Tells, 1995. Address: 4535 W Sahara Ave Ste 105 Las Vegas NV 89102-3733

CARPARELLI, PETER LOUIS, education educator; b. Passaic, N.J., Sept. 7, 1943; s. Peter N. and Frances Anne (Scarfo) C.; m. Mary Louise DuPont, June 18, 1966; children: Keith Allen Carparelli, Lisa Maria Carparelli Schuma. BA, Montclair State U., 1966; MS, Mich. State U., 1971; EdD, U. Mont., 1979. Cert. sci. tchr., N.J., N.D., sch. adminstr., Mont. Sci. tchr., coach Red Cloud Indian Sch., Pine Ridge, S.D., 1964-65, West Morris Regional H.S., Chester, N.J., 1966-69; sci. tchr., sci. dept. chmn. U.S. Bur. Indian Affairs, Belcourt, N.D., 1970-72; tchr. supr. U.S. Bur. Indian Affairs, Belcourt, 1972-75; sci. methods instr. U. Mont., Missoula, 1975-76; vice prin. Helena (Mont.) H.S., 1976-79, prin., 1979-84; prin. Helena Mid. Sch., 1984-87; supt. Butte (Mont.) Pub. Schs., 1987-90, Billings (Mont.) Pub. Schs., 1990-95; prin. ptnr. Synergetics Consulting Svcs., Bozeman, 1992—; bd. dirs. N.W. Regional Edn. Lab., Portland, Oreg., 1992-95; mem. Gov.'s Edn. Adv. Com., Helena, 1989-91. Editor: (jour.) Big Sky Administrator, 1985; contbr. articles to profl. jours. Bd. dirs. Billings Family YMCA, 1993-95, Job Svc. Employers Com., Billings, 1990-94, Jobs for Mont.'s Grads., Helena, 1989-93, Yellowstone United Way, Billings, 1990-93. Recipient G.V. Erickson award Sch. Adminstrs. Mont., 1994, Excellence award Mont. State U.-Billings, 1993, Golden Apple award Butte Area C. of C., 1990; named Outstanding Adminstr. Yr. Billings Edn. Assn., 1994. Mem. Mont. Assn. Sch. Supts. (membership com. 1987—), Am. Assn. Sch. Adminstrs. (com. on state nat. rels. 1994—), Elks. Roman Catholic. Home: 2200 W Dickerson # 82 Bozeman MT 59718 Office: Mont State Univ Dept Edn 116 Reid Hall Bozeman MT 59717

CARPENTER, ARTHUR ESPENET, furniture designer; b. N.Y.C., Jan. 20, 1920; s. Flora Dunn (Welch) C.; children: Victoria, Arthur III. BA, Dartmouth Coll., 1942. Furniture craftsman, 1948—; tchr. San Francisco State U., 1975-79, Anderson Ranch, Snowmass, Colo., 1976-88; workshop tchr. in field. Pres. Sch. Bd., Bolinas, 1960-63. Lt. USNR, 1942-45. NEA fellow, 1976; Fulbright lectr. tour, 1985; recipient Calif. Living Treasure award, 1985. Fellow Am. Craft Coun.; mem. Calif. Craft Assn. (hon.). Home: 1100 Olema Bolinas Rd Bolinas CA 94924-9615

CARPENTER, DONALD BLODGETT, real estate appraiser; b. New Haven, Aug. 20, 1916; s. Fred Donald and Gwendolen (Blodgett) C.; m. Barbara Marvin Adams, June 28, 1941 (dec. Aug. 1978); m. 2d, Lee Burker McGough, Dec. 28, 1980 (div. Apr. 1987); children—Edward G., John D., William V., Andrew J., Dorothy J. and James J. McGough. PhB, U. Vt., 1938; postgrad., Sonoma State U., 1968-69, Mendocino C. Coll., 1977, Coll. of Redwoods, 1984-85. Reporter Burlington (Vt.) Daily News, 1938-39; guide chair operator Am. Express Co., N.Y. World's Fair, 1939; underwriter G.E.I. Corp., Newark, 1939-40; sales corr. J. Dixon Crucible Co., Jersey City, 1940-41, asst. office mgr., priorities specialist, 1941-42; sales rep. J. Dixon Crucible Co., San Francisco, 1946-52; field supr. Travelers Ins. Co., San Francisco, 1952-58; gen. agt. Gen. Am. Life Ins. Co., San Francisco, 1958-59; western supr. Provident Life & Accident Ins. Co., San Francisco, 1959-60; brokerage supr. Aetna Life Ins. Co., San Francisco, 1960-61; maintenance cons. J.I. Holcomb Mfg. Co., Mill Valley, Calif., 1961-68; ednl. svc. rep. Marquis Who's Who, Inc., 1963-68; sales rep. Onox, Inc., Mendocino, Calif., 1965-68; tchr., coach Mendocino Jr.-Sr. High Sch., 1968; real property appraiser Mendocino County, 1968-81; instr. Coll. of Redwoods, 1985-87; real estate appraiser Carpenter Appraisal Svcs., 1982-88, ret. Active numerous civic orgns.; co-chmn. Citizens for Sewers, 1971-72; mem. Mendocino County Safety Coun., 1981; sponsor mem. Mendocino Art Ctr., 1965-96. With USNR, 1942-46; lt. comdr., comdg. officer res. unit, 1967-68, ret., 1968. Sec. of Navy Commendation with ribbon, 1946, other awards, certificates; companion Mil. Order World Wars (life); named Cmty. Sportsman of Yr., 1971. Mem. Res. Officers Assn. U.S. (life, chpt. pres. 1954-56, state v.p. 1958-61), Ret. Officers Assn. (life, chpt. survivors assistance area counselor 1979-97, chpt. scholarship com. 1986-91), Save-the-Redwoods League, Marines Meml. Assn., Mendocino County Employees Assn. (dir. 1981), Mendocino County Hist. Soc., Mendocino Hist. Rsch. Inc. (docent 1982-88), Nat. Assn. Uniformed Svcs. (life), Mendocino Coast Geneal. Soc. (pres. 1991-93), Nat. Ret. Tchrs. Assn., Calif. Ret. Tchrs. Assn., Naval Order U.S. (life), Naval Res. Assn. (life), Navy League U.S. (life), U.S. Naval Inst. (life), Am. Diabetes Assn., Alumni Assn. U. Vt. (founding pres. San Francisco Alumni Club 1964), Mendocino Coast Stamp Club (charter, dir. 1983-96, pres. 1994, v.p. 1995), Rotary Internat. (club pres. 1975-76, dist. gov. area rep. 1977-78, dist. ambassadorial scholarship com. 1978-81, 89-90, dist. group study exchange com. 1981-88, 90-93, club historian 1989—, dist. foun. alumni com. 1991-92, Paul Harris fellow 1979—, Rotarian of Yrs. 1969-88, Dist. Gov. award 1974, 76, 96, Cert. Achievement for outstanding svc. 1993-94), Am. Legion (post comdr. 1972-73, State Citation for outstanding cmty. svc. 1972, past comdrs. Calif., life), Mendocino Coast Land Devel. Corp. (dir. 1991-97, exec. v.p. 1995-97), Mendocino Cardinal Booster Club (charter, life, pres. 1971), U. Vt. Catamount Club (charter), Old Mill Club, Kappa Sigma (Scholarship-Leadership award 1937-38). Republican. Congregationalist. Home: PO Box 87 10801 Gurley Ln Mendocino CA 95460-0087

CARPENTER, FRANK CHARLES, JR., retired electronics engineer; b. L.A., June 1, 1917; s. Frank Charles and Isobel (Crump) C.; A.A., Pasadena City Coll., 1961; B.S. in Elec. Engring. cum laude, Calif. State U.-Long Beach, 1975, M.S. in Elec. Engring., 1981; m. Beatrice Josephine Jolly, Nov. 3, 1951; children—Robert Douglas, Gail Susan, Carol Ann. Self-employed design and mfgr. aircraft test equipment, Los Angeles, 1946-51; engr. Hoffman Electronics Corp., Los Angeles, 1951-56, sr. engr., 1956-59, project mgr., 1959-63; engr.-scientist McDonnell-Douglas Astronautics Corp., Huntington Beach, Calif., 1963-69, spacecraft telemetry, 1963-67, biomed. electronics, 1967-69, flight test instrumentation, 1969-76; lab. test engr. Northrop Corp., Hawthorne, Calif., 1976-82, spl. engr., 1982-83; mgr. transducer calibration lab. Northrop Corp., Pico-Rivera, Calif., 1983-86. Served with USNR, 1941-47. Mem. IEEE (life), Amateur Radio Relay League. Contbr. articles to profl. jours. Patentee transistor squelch circuit; helicaland whip antenna. Home: 2037 Balearic Dr Costa Mesa CA 92626-3514

CARPENTER, JAMES FARLIN, press secretary; b. Denver, Apr. 1, 1960; s. Charles H. and Lillian R. (Griffith) C.; m. Nancy Rhyme, Aug. 15, 1987; children: Emma, Nicholas. BA in Polit. Sci., U. Colo., 1985. Staff asst. U.S. Rep. Timothy E. Wirth, Washington, 1980-84; ops. dir. Wirth for U.S. Senate, Denver, 1985-86; assoc., cons. Nat. Strategies, Washington, 1987-88; dep. state dir. U.S. Senator Timothy Wirth, Denver, 1988-93; cons. Pub. Decisions, Denver, 1993-94; press sec. Gov. Roy Romer, Denver, 1995—. Active Dem. Party, Denver, 1978—. Mem. Denver Athletic Club.

CARPENTER, JEANNINE NUTTALL, nurse; b. Safford, Ariz., Feb. 10, 1934; d. Joseph Heber and Alma (Woolsey) Nuttall; m. Jerry K. Carpenter, Apr. 1, 1953; children: Jeffrey, Joe, Jan, Jason, Julie. ADN, Mesa Community Coll., 1973; BSN, U. Phoenix, Tucson, Ariz., 1990. Cert. profl. health care quality, Ariz. Dental asst. Safford, Ariz., 1952-69; staff nurse Maricpa Med. Ctr., Phoenix, 1973, Mt. Graham Community Hosp., Safford, 1973-75; dance instr. Ea. Ariz. Coll., Thatcher, 1978-91, instr. cert. nursing asst., 1984-90; nurse supr. Mt. View Nursing Ctr., Safford, 1975-77; RN/EMT Caldwell's Ambulance, Safford, 1974-86; nurse supr. No. Cochise Hosp., Willcox, Ariz., 1977-79; dir. nurses Safford Care Ctr., 1986-87; swing bed coord. Mt. Graham County Hosp., Safford, 1987—; quality coord. nursing Mt. Graham Hosp., Safford, 1989—, interim dir. nursing, 1994, quality resources dept. dir., 1993—; v.p. Ariz. Bd. Adminstrs., Phoenix, 1987-90; clin. preceptor U. Phoenix, Tucson, 1990—; publ. bd. Ariz. Assn. Healthcare Quality, Tucson, 1990-93; coord. Joint Commn. Accreditation and State Dept. of Health Svcs. Licensure, 1991—. Actress mus. theater, 1974. Sec. Am. Heart Assn., Safford. Republican. Mormon. Office: Mt Graham Community Hosp 1600 S 20th Ave Safford AZ 85546-4011

CARPENTER, JOHN EVERETT, retired principal, educational consultant; b. Tarrytown, N.Y., Nov. 27, 1923; s. Everett Birch and Mary (Avery) C.; student Union Coll., 1943; B.A., Iona Coll., 1946; M.A., Columbia, 1949, profl. diploma, 1961; m. Marie F. McCarthy, Nov. 14, 1944; 1 son, Dennis Everett. Tchr., Blessed Sacrament High Sch., New Rochelle, N.Y., 1946-50; tchr., adminstr. Armonk (N.Y.) pub. schs., 1950-62; dir. guidance Ridge Street Sch., Port Chester, N.Y., 1962-64; counselor Rye (N.Y.) High Sch., 1964-66, prin., 1966-78, ret.; guest lectr. Served to lt. USNR; now lt. comdr. ret. Res. Decorated Bronze Star medal. Mem. Middle States Assn. Colls. and Schs. (commn. on secondary schs.), Am. (life), Westchester-Putnam-Rockland (past pres.) personnel and guidance assns., NEA, Am. Legion (past comdr.), Phi Delta Kappa, Kappa Delta Pi. Rotarian (past pres., Paul Harris fellow). Clubs: Tarrytown Boat (past commodore). Home: 321 N Paseo De Los Conquistadores Green Valley AZ 85614-3140

CARPENTER, MARGARET WILSON, mayor; b. Danielson, Conn., Nov. 24, 1930; married 1951 (div.). BA, Ottawa (Kans.) U., Ont., Can., 1952; MA, Colo. State Coll., 1962; EdD, U. No. Colo., 1971. Tchr. Mapleton (Colo.) Pub. Schs., 1957-70, reading and lang. arts coord., 1970-72, exec. dir. instrn., 1972-84, asst. supt. planning and devel., 1984-87; apptd./elected/re-elected Thornton (Colo.) City Coun., 1973-79; elected mayor City of Thornton, 1979-83, re-elected, 1987, 91, 95; mem. Colo. Mcpl. League policy com., 1974-81, chmn., 1977-78, mem. police and fire pension com., 1976-79, chmn., 1979, vice chmn. mayors and councilmen's sect., 1977-79, chmn., 1979-81, exec. bd., 1981-83, 84-85, 87-91, sec., 1982, 88, v.p., 1989, pres., 1990; mem. Colo. Water Roundtable, 1981, Transp. Roundtable, 1986, Growth Summit, 1995, Supreme Ct./Ct. Appeals Nom. com., 1995; exec. bd. Denver Regional Coun. Govts., 1992—, chmn., 1995, legis. com., 1992—; mem. E-470 Highway Authority, 1992—, chmn., 1994-95. Bd. dirs. Nat. League of Cities, 1988-90, chair initial conf. planning com., 1995, mem. fin., adminstrn., intergovtl. rels. steering coms., 1980-87, vice chair, 1986-87, mem. leadership tng. coun., 1992—, strategic planning task force, 1988-89, Women in Mcpl. Govt., 1988—, adv. coun., 1991—, vice chair, 1993, chair, 1994. Recipient Denver Water Dept. Great Gildersleeve award, 1983, North Suburban Bus. and Profl. Women Woman of Yr. award, 1986, Fed. Exec. Bd. Disting. Denver Metro Svc. award, 1983, North Suburban Bd. Realtors Citizen of Yr. award, 1986-87, Front Range Toastmaster Communication Achievement award. Mem. Colo. Assn. Sch. Execs., Phi Delta Kappa (Leadership award 1983), Delta Kappa Gamma. Office: Office of Mayor 9500 Civic Ctr Dr Thornton CO 80229

CARPENTER, PETER ROCKEFELLER, bank executive; b. Sunbury, Pa., Apr. 18, 1939; s. Alvin Witmer and Katharine (Rockefeller) C.; m. Janet Ross Buck, Aug. 24, 1963; children: Karen Louise Althaus, Jean Ellen Chronis, Peter Alvin. BA, Pa. State U., 1962. Mgr. dept. J.C. Penney Co., Menlo Park, N.J., 1964-67; ops. mgr. Allstate Ins. Co., Summit, N.J., 1967-73; adminstrv. mgr. Prudential Property & Casualty, Scottsdale, Ariz., 1973-75; v.p. Fortune Properties, Scottsdale, 1975-76; life underwriter Conn. Mutual Life, Phoenix, 1976-81; v.p. and dir. sales and mktg. No. Trust Bank, Phoenix, 1981-89; v.p. M&I Marshall & Ilsley Trust Co., 1989-94; dir. planned giving Luth. Social Svcs. of the S.W., 1994-95; v.p. trust dept. Founders Bank of Ariz., Scottsdale, 1995-96; v.p. dir sales & mktg. Southwest Region Wells Fargo, 1996—. Sec. exec. bd. Samuel Gompers Rehab. Ctr., 1981-84, chmn. bd., 1984-91; div. chmn. Phoenix United Way, 1981, 82, 86, 90; Rep. committeeman, Phoenix, 1978-86; bd. dirs. Scottsdale Boys and Girls Club, bd. govs., 1997—; bd. dirs. Scottsdale Cultural Coun. Adv., Herberger Theatre Ctr. With USN, 1962-64. Mem. Nat. Assn. Planned Giving Roundtable, Pa. State U. Alumni Assn. (dir. 1979-86), Son of Am. Revolution, Ariz. Club (bd. dirs.), U.S. Navy League, Kiwanis (Disting. lt. gov.), Sigma Alpha Epsilon. Lutheran. Home: 13076 N 101st St Scottsdale AZ 85260 Office: Wells Fargo PCS 7501 E McCormick Pky Scottsdale AZ 85258

CARPENTER, RICHARD NORRIS, lawyer; b. Cortland, N.Y., Feb. 14, 1937; s. Robert P. and Sylvia (Norris) C.; m. Elizabeth Bigbee, Aug. 1961 (div. June 1975); 1 child, Andrew Norris; m. Leslie Nordby, July, 1992. BA magna cum laude, Syracuse U., 1958; LLB, Yale U., 1962. Bar: N.Y. 1962, N.Mex. 1963, U.S. Dist. Ct. (no. dist.) N.Y., U.S. Dist. Ct. N.Mex., U.S. Ct. Appeals (D.C. and 10th cirs.), U.S. Supreme Ct. Assoc. Breed, Abbott & Morgan, N.Y.C., 1962-63, Bigbee & Byrd, Santa Fe, 1963-67; ptnr. Carpenter, Comeau, Maldegan, Nixon & Templeman, Santa Fe, 1967—; spl. asst. atty. gen., State of N.Mex., 1963-74, 90—; sec. Bokum Corp., Miami,

Fla., 1969-70. Mem. adv. bd. Interstate Mining Compact, N.Mex., 1981-88; elder 1st Presbyn. Ch., Santa Fe, 1978-80, 86-89, trustee, 1975-77, pres., 1977; bd. dirs. Santa Fe Community Coun., 1965-67, St. Vincent Hosp. Found., Santa Fe, 1980-84; trustee Santa Fe Prep. Sch., 1981-84, pres., 1982-84; trustee St. Vincent Hosp., 1980-86, 87—, chmn. 1985-86, 90-93; bd. dirs. Santa Fe YMCA, 1964-69, pres., 1969; trustee Santa Fe Prep. Permanent Endowment Fund., 1987-90. Rotary Found. fellow, Panjab U., Pakistan, 1959-60. Mem. ABA, N.Mex. Bar Assn., 1st Jud. Bar Assn., N.Y. State Bar Assn., Phi Beta Kappa, Pi Sigma Alpha, Phi Beta Phi. Home: 1048 Bishops Lodge Rd Santa Fe NM 87501-1009

CARR, ADRIAN WALTER, film director, editor; b. Melbourne, Australia, Oct. 2, 1952; s. Walter Hugo and Marie (McCarthy) C.; m. Joyce Singh, 1975 (div. 1976); m. Ann Lyons, 1976; 1 child, Anthony James Lyons; m. Rosemary Marks. Student, Royal Melbourne Inst. Tech., 1970-71. Asst. film editor Australian Broadcasting Commn., Melbourne, 1970-73; editor Crawford Film Prodns., Melbourne, 1973-77, Film House P/L, Melbourne, 1977-82; free-lance editor, director, 1982—. Dir. (feature films) The Sword of Bushido, 1989, Now and Forever, (Interactive CD Rom) The Pandora Directive, 1995, The Poisoned Pawn, 1997, (short film) Spiders, Permanent Stays, 1990 (ACS Gold award); editor (films) Dark Age, Prisoners, The Lighthorsemen, D.A.R.Y.L., The Aviator, The Man for Snowy River 1, Harlequin, (TV movies) Mr. B Says No, Stopover, (mini-series) The Far Country; automatic dialogue replacement editor: Crocodile Dundee, Sky Pirates; effects editor: Anzacs; dir. additional scenes (feature) 13th Floor, 1987; sup. film editor: Quigley Down Under, 1989. Roman Catholic. Home and Office: 1047 S Orange Grove Ave #1 Los Angeles CA 90019

CARR, GERALD FRANCIS, German educator; b. Pitts., Dec. 29, 1930; s. James Patrick and Hannah (Sweeney) C.; m. Irmengard Rauch, June 12, 1965; children: Christopher, Gregory. BEd, Duquesne U., 1958; MA, U. Wis., 1960, PhD, 1968. Instr. in German Duquesne U., Pitts., 1960-62, asst. prof. German, 1964-68; tchg. asst. U. Wis., Madison, 1962-64; asst. prof. German Ea. Ill. U., Charleston, 1968-70, assoc. prof. German, 1970-75, prof. German, 1975-87; prof. German Calif. State U., Sacramento, 1987—. Co-editor: The Semiotic Bridge, 1989, Insights in Germanic Linguistics I, 1995, II, 1996, Semiotics Around the World, 1996. Cpl. USMC, 1951-54. Mem. MLA, Semiotic Soc. Am., Am. Assn. Tchrs. of German. Office: Calif State U 6000 J St Sacramento CA 95819

CARR, NOEL, food products executive; b. 1943. BS in Farm Mgmt., Calif. State Poly U., 1967. Mgr. Spreckels Sugar, Salinas, Calif., 1967-71; sales mgr. Bruce Church, Inc., Salinas, 1971-75, harvest mgr., 1975-81; v.p. Fresh Western Marketing, Salinas, 1981—; pres. Harvest Tek Inc., Salinas, 1981—; v.p. Pacific Freezers, Salinas, 1989-94. Office: Harvest Tek Inc 1156 Abbott St Salinas CA 93901-4503*

CARR, PAUL WALLACE, actor; b. New Orleans, Jan. 31, 1934; s. Edward Sidney and Elaine Grace Carr; children: Alexandra, Christina, Michael. Grad., Am. Theatre Wing, 1953. Actor, dir. L.A. Repertory Co., 1990—. Actor over 50 feature films, over 300 guest starring TV roles, over 100 stage prodns. Broadway, off-Broadway, L.A. and regional theatres. Recipient awards L.A. Weekly Newspaper, 1987, Dramalogue Mag., L.A., 1994. Democrat.

CARR, PETER EMILE, publisher; b. La Habana, Cuba, Oct. 16, 1950; came to U.S., 1962; s. Pedro Emilio Carr and Carmen Emelina Luaces; m. Sheryl A. Strayer, Nov. 18, 1995. BA in Anthropology, Calif. State U., Long Beach, 1986. Asst. mgr. Hides & Skins Unltd., L.A., 1976-85; archaeol. cons. Archaeol. Enterprises, L.A., 1985-91; pres. The Cuban Index, San Luis Obispo, Calif., 1991—; cons. Soc. for Hispanic Hist. and Ancestral Rsch., Westminster, Calif., 1992—, Calif. Geneal. Alliance, San Francisco, 1992—. Author: Guide to Cuban Genealogical Research, 1991 (reference book series) San Francisco Passenger Departure Lists, Vols. I-V, 1992, 93, 94, Censos, Padrones y Matriculas de la Poblacion de Cuba, 1993, Genealogical Resources of Hispanic Central and South America, 1996; author, editor jours. Caribbean Hist. and Geneal. Jour., 1993-94. Recipient Spl. Honor award Anthropology Students Assn., 1985, Gold Poet award Internat. Poetry, 1988. Mem. Nat. Geneal. Soc., Coun. for Genealogy Columnists, Inc. (co-editor newsletter 1992-95), Manchester and Lancashire Family History Soc., Cercle Genealoguique de la Brie, Mortar Bd. Honor Soc. Mem. Humanist Party. Roman Catholic. Office: TCI Genealogical Resources PO Box 15839 San Luis Obispo CA 93406-5839

CARR, ROXANNE MARIE, mortgage company executive; b. Mpls., Jan. 26, 1940; d. John A. and Lyla Jeannette (Coombs) Johnson; m. Rodney R. Levin, Sept. 7, 1993; children: Kurt Allen Carr, Karen Lee Carr Davis. BA, Calif. State U., Long Beach, 1968. Lic. real estate broker; cert. Dept. Real Estate approved instr. West coast regional v.p. ARCS Mortgage, Inc., San Luis Obispo, Calif., 1973-94; divsn. pres. and corp. sr. v.p. The Mortgage House, Inc., San Luis Obispo, 1995—; instr. real estate fin. Cuesta Coll.; bd. dirs. Cuesta Title Guaranty Co., San Luis Obispo, 1995—, Building Industry Assn., San Luis Obispo, 1996—, Econ. Forecast Project, U. Calif., Santa Barbara, 1996—. Author: Financing Workbook for Real Estate Professionals, 1972, rev., 1994. Active various cmty. orgns.; bd. dirs. United Way of San Luis Obispo, 1994—, chairperson The Giving Tree Alliance; vol. 1995 Kiss the Pig Fund Raiser; chair bus. support campaign Cuesta, San Luis Obispo, 1996-97; bd. dirs. Cure 2000. Named Bus. Woman Yr. Telegram-Tribune, 1994. Mem. Rotary (various). Lutheran. Office: The Mortgage House Inc 742 B Marsh St San Luis Obispo CA 93401

CARR, RUTH MARGARET, plastic surgeon; b. Waco, Tex., July 2, 1951. MD, U. Okla., 1977. Intern U. Okla. Med. Sch., Oklahoma City, 1977-78; resident U. Okla. Health Sci. Ctr., Oklahoma City, 1978-81, UCLA, 1981-83; plastic surgeon St. John's Hosp., 1989—, Santa Monica (Calif.) Hosp., 1989—; clin. asst. prof. UCLA, 1983—. Office: 1301 20th St Ste 470 Santa Monica CA 90404-2054

CARRARA, PAUL EDWARD, geologist, researcher; b. San Francisco, Sept. 16, 1947. BA in Geology, San Francisco State Coll., 1969; MSc in Quaternary Geology, U. Colo., 1972. Snow avalanche cons. Inst. Arctic and Alpine Rsch., U. Colo., Boulder, 1972-74; geologist U.S. Geol. Survey, Denver, 1974—. Contbr. articles to profl. jours. Recipient Antarctic Svc. medal NSF, 1980. Fellow Geol. Soc. Am.; mem. Am. Quaternary Assn., Colo. Sci. Soc., N.W. Sci. Assn. Office: US Geol Survey Denver Fed Ctr Mail Stop 913 Denver CO 80225

CARREL, ANNETTE FELDER, writer; b. San Francisco, Dec. 11, 1929; m. Robert E. Carrel (dec. 1989); 3 children. AA, Notre Dame Coll.; BA, Lone Mountain Coll.; MA in Spl. Edn., U. Calif., San Francisco. Home: 210 Garden St Santa Barbara CA 93105-3615

CARREL, MARC LOVIS, lawyer, legislative policy consultant; b. Buffalo, Aug. 31, 1967; s. Jerome D. and Judith E. (Fish) C. BA with distinction, U. Mich., 1988; JD, U. Pa., 1993. Bar: Calif., 1993, D.C., 1995. Staff asst. U.S. Senate Com. Agriculture, Nutrition, and Forestry, Washington, 1989, calender clk., 1989-90; assoc. cons. Office of Calif. State Assemblyman Richard Polanco, Sacramento, 1994; legis. cons. Office of Calif. State Senator Richard Polanco, Sacramento, 1994-96; counsel Calif. State Senate Dem. Caucus, Sacramento, 1995-96; legis. policy cons. to Cruz Bustamante Office of Calif. Assembly, Sacramento, 1997—; mem. Legis. Task Force Land Use, Sacramento, 1995, L.A. Fiscal Crisis Working Group, Sacramento, 1995, Calif. Organized Investment Network Econ. Devel. Com., 1996; co-chair Ins. Reinvestment Task Force, Sacramento, 1995; mem. rural devel. strategic plan steering com. USDA. Sec. Pa. Law Equal Justice Found., Phila., 1990-92; comm. dir. Arlo Smith for Atty. Gen. '94, San Francisco, 1993; co-chair Young Leadership Divsn., Sacramento, 1996-97; trustee Jewish Fedn. Sacramento Region, 1996-97; bd. dirs. Jewish Cmty. Rels. Coun., Sacramento, 1997—. Recipient U.S. Atty.'s Office Spl. Achievement award, Buffalo, 1991; William J. Branstrom Freshman prize, 1986. Mem. Am. Polit. Items Collectors, State Bar Calif., D.C. Bar, Sacramento Bar Assn., U. Mich. Alumni Assn. Office: Office of Spkr State Capitol Rm 219 Sacramento CA 95814

CARRELL, HEATHER DEMARIS, foundation executive; b. Bryn Mawr, Pa., Jan. 4, 1951; d. Jeptha J. and J. Demaris (Affleck) C.; m. Peter F. Brazitis, June 27, 1981; children, Evan, Victoria. BA, Oberlin Coll., 1973; MEd, U. Wash., 1976, PhD, 1982. Cert. tchr., Wash. Head tchr., trainer Exptl. Edn. Unit U. Wash., Seattle, 1976-80, tchr. trainer, 1976-80, supr. early childhood and spl. edn. tchrs. in tng., 1980, coord. classrooms behavior disorders, 1980-81, coord. interdisciplinary tng., 1979-82, asst. prin., 1981-82, cons. Transition Rsch. Problems Handicapped Youth, 1986-88; self-employed cons., 1983-96; cons. North Kitsap Sch. Dist., Poulsbo, Wash., 1984; presenter edn. and spl. edn. various groups from U.S., Can., Australia, 1977-82; pres., co-founder Hansville (Wash.) Coop. Presch., 1982, 84-89; mem. diversity and multicultural advocacy team Wash. State Sch. Dirs. Assn.; rep. to U. Wash. Tchr. Profl. Edn. Adv. Bd., 1992-95; mem. WSSDA Fin. Task Force, 1994; mem. Intertribal Coun. Com. on Racism, North Kitsap, Wash., 1993-94. Author: (with others) The Experimental Education Training Program, 1977; contbr. articles to profl. publs. Commr. North Kitsap Dept. Parks and Recreation, 1983-84; dir. North Kitsap Sch. Bd., 1990-95, v.p., 1992-93, pres., 1993-95; trustee North Kitsap Tchr. of Yr. Found., 1989-90; bd. dirs. North Kitsap Juvenile Diversion Bd., 1987-91; co-founder, v.p. bd. dirs. Kitsap Cmty. Found., 1993-96. Bur. Edn. Handicapped fellow, 1974-75, 77-78.

CARREY, NEIL, lawyer, educator; b. Bronx, N.Y., Nov. 19, 1942; s. David L. and Betty (Kurtzburg) C.; m. Karen Krysher, Apr. 9, 1980; children: Jana, Christopher; children by previous marriage: Scott, Douglas, Dana. BS in Econs., U. Pa., 1964; JD, Stanford U., 1967. Bar: Calif. 1968. Mem. firm, v.p. corp. DeCastro, West, Chodorow & Burns, Inc., L.A., 1967—; instr. program for legal paraprofls. U. So. Calif., 1977-89; lectr. U. So. Calif. Dental Sch., 1987—, Employee Benefits Inst., Kansas City, Mo., 1996. Author: Nonqualified Deffered Compensation Plans-The Wave of the Future, 1985. Officer, Vista Del Mar Child Care Center, L.A., 1968-84; treas. Nat. Little League of Santa Monica, 1984-85, pres., 1985-86, coach, 1990-95, coach Bobby Sox Team, Santa Monica, 1986-88, bd. dirs. 1988, umpire in chief, 1988; referee, coach Am. Soccer Youth Orgn., 1989-95; curriculum com. Santa Monica-Malibu Sch. Dist., 1983-84, comm. health adv. com., 1988-95, chmn., 1989-95, athletic adv. com., chmn., 1993—, dist. com. for sch. based health ctr., 1991-94, gender equity com., chmn., 1992—, athletic study com., chmn., 1989-91, fin. adv. com., 1994; dir. The Santa Monica Youth Athletic Found., 1995—; dir. The Small Bus. Coun. of Am., 1995—, Santa Monica Police Activities League, 1995—, Santa Monica H.S. Booster Club, 1995—, Santa Monica Bay Rep. Club, 1995-96, Santa Monica PAL; pres. Gail Dorin Music Found., 1994—; v.p. Sneaker Sisters, 1996—; pres. Santa Monica Bay Jr. Rowing. Mem. U. Pa. Alumni Soc., So. Calif. (pres. 1971-79, dir. 1979-87), Alpha Kappa Psi (life), Mountaingate Tennis Club. Republican. Jewish. Home: 616 23rd St Santa Monica CA 90402-3130 Office: 10960 Wilshire Blvd Fl 18 Los Angeles CA 90024-3702

CARRICO, DONALD JEFFERSON, public transit system manager; b. Dallas, June 15, 1944; s. Ivan and Helen Mae (Jefferson) C.; m. Prudence Louise Cornish, Aug. 17, 1968; children: Bryan Jefferson, Alan Jefferson. BSBA, Ohio State U., 1967; MA in Bus. Mgmt., Cen. Mich. U., 1977. Commd. 2d lt. USAF, 1967, advanced through grades to maj., 1979; various supervisory positions USAF Air Freight Terminals, 1967-72; mgr. passenger travel and cargo br. USAF Transp. Div., Rickenbacker AFB, Ohio, 1972-74; transp. and air terminal insp. USAF Insp. Gen. Team, Hawaii, 1974-76; liaison officer US Naval Supply Ctr., Pearl Harbor, Hawaii, 1976-78; transp. staff officer USAF Hdqrs. Tactical Air Command, Langley AFB, Va., 1978-83; chief transp. USAF Transp. Div., Incirlik AB, Turkey, 1983-85, Williams AFB, Ariz., 1986-88; vehicle fleet mgr. V&B Svcs., Phoenix, 1989-91; asst. mgr. dispatch svcs. Phoenix Transit System, 1991-92, ops. mgr., 1993-95, logistics mgr., 1996—. Logistics chief Gilbert Food Bank Cmty. Food Dr., Gilbert, Ariz., 1987, chmn., 1988; asst. cubmaster Pack 282 Boy Scouts Am., Gilbert, 1987; mem. Town of Gilbert Gen. Plan Rev. Task Force, 1992-93, total quality mgmt. rsch. panel Transp. Rsch. Bd., Washington, 1992-95; transp. coord. Super Bowl XXX, Tempe, 1995-96. Decorated Bronze Star. Home: 683 E Washington Ave Gilbert AZ 85234-6401

CARRICO, STEPHEN J., construction company executive; b. 1954. Grad., Ctrl. Mich. U., 1977. CPA. With Straka, Jarackas & Co., Detroit, 1977-84; various positions Hensel Phels Constrn. Co., Greeley, Colo., 1984—, now v.p. fin. Office: Hensel Phelps Construction Co 420 6th Ave Greeley CO 80631-2332*

CARRIGAN, CHARLES ROGER, geophysicist; b. Altadena, Calif., Sept. 7, 1949; s. Charles Francis and Alyce (Krosley) C.; m. Suzanne Lundin, Feb. 21, 1976; children: Alisa Lynn, Charles Jonathan. BA in Astronomy and Physics, UCLA, 1971, MS in Geophysics, 1973, PhD in Geophysics, 1977. Rsch. assoc. UCLA, 1979-80; tech. staff mem. Sandia Nat. Labs., Albuquerque, 1980-89; physicist Lawrence Livermore Nat. Lab., Livermore, Calif., 1989—. Patentee in field; contbr. articles to profl. jours. Deacon Grace Bapt. Ch., Tracy, Calif., 1993-94, chmn. bd. 1994-95, 97—. Fellow Cambridge (Eng.) U., 1977-79, NATO, 1977. Mem. Am. Geophys. Union, Sigma Xi, Sigma Pi Sigma. Office: Lawrence Livermore Nat Lab PO Box 808 Livermore CA 94551-0808

CARRIGAN, JIM R., arbitrator, mediator, retired federal judge; b. Mobridge, S.D., Aug. 24, 1929; s. Leo Michael and Mildred Ione (Jaycox) C.; m. Beverly Jean Halpin, June 2, 1956. Ph.B., J.D., U. N.D., 1953; LL.M. in Taxation, NYU, 1956; LLD (hon.), U. Colo., 1989, Suffolk U., 1991. Bar: N.D. 1953, Colo. 1956. Asst. prof. law U. Denver, 1956-59; vis. assoc. prof. NYU Law Sch., 1958, U. Wash. Law Sch., 1959-60; jud. administr. State of Colo., 1960-61; prof. law U. Colo., 1961-67; partner firm Carrigan & Bragg (and predecessors), 1967-76; justice Colo. Supreme Ct., 1976-79; judge U.S. Dist. Ct. Colo., 1979-95; mem. Colo. Bd. Bar Examiners, 1969-71; lectr. Nat. Coll. State Judiciary, 1964-77, 95; bd. dirs. Nat. Inst. Trial Advocacy, 1978—, Environ. Law Inst., chmn. bd. 1986-88, also mem. faculty, 1972—; adj. prof. law U. Colo, 1984, 1991—; commr. Denver Broncos Stadium Dist., 1996—. Editor-in-chief: N.D. Law Rev., 1952-53, Internat. Soc. Barristers Quar., 1972-79; editor: DICTA, 1957-59; contbr. articles to profl. jours. Bd. regents U. Colo., 1975-76; bd. visitors U. N.D. Coll. Law, 1983-85. Recipient Disting. Svc. award Nat. Coll. State Judiciary, 1969, Outstanding Alumnus award U. N.D., 1973, Regent Emeritus award U. Colo., 1977, B'nai Brith Civil Rights award, 1986, Thomas More Outstanding Lawyer award Cath. Lawyers Guild, 1988, Oliphant Disting. Svc. award Nat. Inst. Trial Advocacy, 1993, Constl. Rights award Nat. Assn. Blacks in Criminal Justice (Colo. chpt.), 1992, Disting. Svc. award Colo. Bar Assn., 1994, Amicus Curiae award ATLA, 1994. Fellow Colo. Bar Found., Boulder County Bar Found.; mem. ABA (action com. on tort system improvement 1985-87, TIPS sect. long range planning com., 1986—; coun. 1987-91, task force on initiatives and referenda 1990-92, size of civil juries task force 1988-90, class actions task force 1995—), Am. Law Inst., Colo. Bar Assn., Boulder County Bar Assn., Denver Bar Assn., Cath. Lawyers Guild, Inns. of Ct., Internat. Soc. Barristers, Internat. Acad. Trial Lawyers (bd. dirs. 1995—), Fed. Judges Assn. (bd. dirs. 1985-89), Am. Judicature Soc. (bd. dirs. 1985-89), Tenth Circuit Dist. Judges Assn. (sec. 1991-92, v.p. 1992-95, pres. 1994-95), Order of Coif, Phi Beta Kappa. Roman Catholic. Office: Judicial Arbiter Group 1601 Blake St Ste 400 Denver CO 80202-1328

CARRIKER, ROBERT CHARLES, history educator; b. St. Louis, Aug. 18, 1940; s. Thomas B. and Vivian Ida (Spaunhorst) C.; m. Eleanor R. Gualdoni, Aug. 24, 1963; children: Thomas A., Robert M., Andrew J. BS, St. Louis U., 1962, AM, 1963; PhD, U. Okla., 1967. Asst. prof. Gonzaga U., Spokane, Wash., 1967-71, assoc. prof., 1972-76, prof. history, 1976—. Author: Fort Supply, Indian Territory, 1970, 90, The Kalispel People, 1973, Father Peter De Smet, 1995; editor: (with Eleanor R. Carriker) Army Wife on the Frontier, 1975; book rev. editor Columbia mag., 1987—. Mem. Wash. Lewis and Clark Trail Com., 1978—; commr. Wash. Maritime Bicentennial, Olympia, 1989-92; bd. dirs. Wash. Commn. for Humanities, Seattle, 1988-94. Burlington No. Found. scholar, 1985, 96; recipient Disting. Svc. award Lewis and Clark Trail Heritage Found., 1989. Mem. Wash. State Hist. Soc. (trustee 1981-90, v.p. 1993—), Western Hist. Assn., Phi Alpha Theta (councilor 1985-87). Roman Catholic. Office: Gonzaga U 502 E Boone Ave Spokane WA 99258-1774

CARROLL, DAVID TODD, computer engineer; b. West Palm Beach, Fla., Apr. 8, 1959; s. David Irwin and Lois Ellen (Spriggs) C. Student, U. Houston, 1978-81. Lab. technician Inst. for Lipid Rsch., Baylor Coll. Medicine, Houston, 1978-81; software specialist Digital Equipment Corp., Colorado Springs, Colo., 1982-86, systems engr., 1986-91, systems support cons., 1991-94; systems cons. Mentec, Inc., Colorado Springs, 1994—. Mem. AAAS, Digital Equipment Corp. Users Soc. Home: 7332 Aspen Glen Ln Colorado Springs CO 80919-3024 Office: Mentec Inc 305 S Rockrimmon Blvd Colorado Springs CO 80919-2303

CARROLL, EARL HAMBLIN, federal judge; b. Tucson, Mar. 26, 1925; s. John Vernon and Ruby (Wood) C.; m. Louise Rowlands, Nov. 1, 1952; children—Katherine Carroll Pearson, Margaret Anne. BSBA, U. Ariz., 1948, LLB, 1951. Bar: Ariz., U.S. Ct. Appeals (9th and 10th cirs.), U.S. Ct. of Claims, U.S. Supreme Ct. Law clk. Ariz. Supreme Ct., Phoenix, 1951-52; assoc. Evans, Kitchel & Jenckes, Phoenix, 1952-56, ptnr., 1956-80; judge U.S. Dist. Ct. Ariz., Phoenix, 1980—; spl. counsel City of Tombstone, Ariz., 1962-65, Maricopa County, Phoenix, 1968-75, City of Tucson, 1974, City of Phoenix, 1979; designated mem. U.S. Fgn. Intelligence Surveillance Court by Chief Justice U.S. Supreme Ct., 1993—; chief judge Alien Terrorist Removal Ct., 1996—. Mem. City of Phoenix Bd. of Adjustment, 1955-58; trustee Phoenix Elem. Sch. Bd., 1961-72; mem. Gov.'s Council on Intergovtl. Relations, Phoenix, 1970-73; mem. Ariz. Bd. Regents, 1978-80. Served with USNR, 1943-46; PTO. Recipient Nat. Service awards Campfire, 1973, 75, Alumni Service award U. Ariz., 1980, Disting. Citizen award No. Ariz. U., Flagstaff, 1983, Bicentenial award Georgetown U., 1988, Disting. Citizen award U. Ariz., 1990. Fellow Am. Coll. Trial Lawyers, Am. Bar Found.; mem. ABA, Ariz. Bar Assn., U. Ariz. Law Coll. Assn. (pres. 1975), Phoenix Country Club, Sigma Chi (Significant Sig award 1991), Phi Delta Phi. Democrat. Office: US Dist Ct US Courthouse & Fed Bldg 230 N 1st Ave Ste 6000 Phoenix AZ 85025-0005

CARROLL, JEREMIAH PATRICK, II, auditor; b. Akron, Ohio, Feb. 9, 1955; s. Jeremiah Patrick and Kathleen Mary (Kilroy) C.; m. Anne Marie Mollica; children: Dawn Renee, Patricia Eileen, Bridget Kathleen, Jeremiah Joseph. BS in Acctg., U. Akron, 1979. CPA, Nev., Mont. Benefits supr. Roadway Express, Akron, Ohio, 1976-80; auditor Clark County Nev., Las Vegas, 1980-86, dir. internal audit, 1986—. Contbr. articles to profl. jours. Mem. Am. Soc. Pub. Adminstrs., Nat. Assn. Local Govt. Auditors, Nev. State Bd. Accountancy (pres., past sec.-treas.), Nev. Soc. CPAs, Nat. Assn. Local Govt. Auditors, Western Intergovtl. Audit Forum, Sons of Erin (pres. 1984-86). Republican. Roman Catholic. Home: 7185 Del Rey Ave Las Vegas NV 89117-1526 Office: Clark County Nev Internal Audit 301 Clark Ave Ste 265 Las Vegas NV 89101-6533 also: PO Box 551120 Las Vegas NV 89155-1120 also: 500 S Grand Central Pkwy Las Vegas NV 89106

CARROLL, JON, newspaper columnist. Columnist San Francisco Chronicle. Office: Chronicle Pub Co 901 Mission St San Francisco CA 94103-2988*

CARROLL, KIM MARIE, nurse; b. Ottawa, Ill., Feb. 13, 1958; d. John J. and Charin E. (Reilley) Marmion; m. Thomas Christopher Carroll, Aug. 25, 1979; children: Christopher John, Meaghan Elizabeth. BSN, U. Denver, 1983; diploma Copley Meml. Hosp. Sch. Nursing, Aurora, Ill., 1979. RN, Ill., Ind., Colo.; critical care practitioner. Staff nurse Penrose Hosp., Colorado Springs, Colo., 1979-83, asst. head nurse cardiac floor, 1983-84; asst. dir. nurses Big Meadows Nursing Home, Savanna, Ill., 1985-86, dir. nurses, 1986-88; clin. dir. Ind. Heart Physicians, Inc., Beech Grove, Ind., 1989-95; ambulatory care adminstr. The Gates Clinic, Denver, 1995—. Mem. Soc. Ambulatory Care Profls., Profls. In Workers' Compensation, Beta Sigma Phi (chpt. pres. 1988-89, rec. sec. 1991-92, treas. 1996—), Sigma Theta Tau. Roman Catholic. Avocation: skiing. Home: 5293 S Cathay Way Aurora CO 80015-4859 Office: The Gates Clinic 1000 S Broadway Denver CO 80209-4012

CARROLL, PAT, actress; b. Shreveport, La., May 5, 1927; d. Maurice Clifton and Kathryn Angela (Meagher) C.; children: Sean, Kerry, Tara. Student, Immaculate Heart Coll., 1944-47, Catholic U., 1950; Litt.D. (hon.), Barry Coll., Miami, Fla., 1969. pres. Sea-Ker, Inc., Beverly Hills, Calif., 1979—; pres. CARPA Prodns., Inc., N.Y.C. Profl. debut in stock prodn. A Goose for the Gander, 1947; supper club debut at Le Ruban Bleu, N.Y.C., 1950; appeared on numerous television shows, 1950—, including: Red Buttons Show, 1951, Caesar's Hour, 1956-57 (Emmy award), Danny Thomas Show, 1961-63, Getting Together, 1971-72, Busting Loose, 1977, The Ted Knight Show, 1985, She's the Sheriff, 1987-1988; (TV movie) Second Change, 1972; Broadway debut in Catch a Star, 1955 (Tony nomination); appeared in motion picture With Six You Get Eggroll, 1968, The Brothers O'Toole, 1973; producer, actress: Gertrude Stein Gertrude Stein Gertrude Stein for colls. and univs. (Grammy award 1980, Drama Desk award, Outer Critics Circle award); Shakespeare debut as nurse in Romeo and Juliet and Falstaff in The Merry Wives of Windsor (Helen Hayes award, 1990), Shakespeare Theater at the Folger, 1986 (Helen Hayes award 1987); voice of Ursula, the Wicked Squidwitch, in The Little Mermaid, 1989; appeared in The Show-Off, 1992, Roundabout Theater Company. Pres. Center of Films for Children, 1971-73; bd. regents Immaculate Heart Coll., Hollywood, Calif., 1970. Mem. AFTRA, SAG, Actors Studio, Actors Fund (life), Actors Equity Assn., Acad. TV Arts and Scis. (trustee 1958-59), Am. Youth Hostel (life), Del. and Hudson Canal Hist. Soc., The Players, George Heller Meml. Fund.

CARROLL, ROBERT LLOYD, orthopaedic surgeon; b. L.A., Sept. 2, 1931; s. Robert Lide and Jean Livingston (Wilson) C.; m. Sally Britton Richardson, Aug. 28, 1954; children: John Fielding, Lynne Wilson Carroll Taylor. BS, UCLA, 1954; MD, U. So. Calif., 1958. Diplomate Am. Bd. Orthopaedic Surgery. Intern L.A. County Gen. Hosp., 1958-59; resident Orthop. Hosp., L.A., 1961-65; pvt. practice Orthop. Med. Group Pasadena (Calif.) Inc., 1965—. Capt. U.S. Army, 1959-61. Fellow Am. Orthop. Surgeons, Western Orthop. Surgeons Assn.; mem. AMA, Calif. Med. Assn., L.A. County Med. Assn. Republican. Episcopalian. Home: 1490 Charlton Rd San Marino CA 91108-1908 Office: Orthop Med Grou Pasadena 50 Bellefontaine St Ste 101 Pasadena CA 91105-3132

CARROLL, ROSSYE O'NEAL, college administrator; b. Corsicana, Tex., Sept. 27, 1929; s. Thearon Andrew and Elnora (Cook) C.; m. Neverro Jean Randle, June 6, 1958 (div. June 1982); children: Arnett, Brenda, Marvin, Stephen, Rossye Jr., Sheila, Vicky, Karen, Edwin; m. Bertha Lee Johnson, Aug. 23, 1982. BA, U. Nev., Las Vegas, 1982; AAS, C.C. of So. Nev., North Las Vegas, 1989. Cert. secondary edn. tchr., Nev. Instr. 523 Field Tng. Squadron USAF, Las Vegas, 1969-75, propulsion supt. 247th Field Maintenance, 1975-76; propulsion supt. 2d Field Maintenance USAF, Shreveport, La., 1976-78; supr. maintenance Meadows Mall, Las Vegas, 1978-79; substitute tchr. Clark County Sch. Dist., Las Vegas, 1979-84; asst. to dean for Nellis Zone continuing edn. C.C. of So. Nev., North Las Vegas, 1984—. Mem. choir 2d Bapt. Ch., Las Vegas, 1990—. Sr. master sgt. USAF, 1950-78. Recipient Air Force Commendation medal, 1975, Meritorious Svc. medal, 1978. Mem. AAUP, NEA, Nat. Coun. Instructional Adminstrs., Nev. Faculty Alliance. Democrat. Baptist. Home: 1305 Jackson St Las Vegas NV 89106 Office: C C So Nev 4475 England Ave Ste 217 Las Vegas NV 89191

CARROLL, STEPHEN GRAHAM, university communications administrator, writer; b. St. Joseph, Mo., July 18, 1942; s. Lecil R. and Lelah M. (Ketchum) C.; m. Sharon Ann Kelly, Sept. 9, 1962; children: Stephen G., Kathryn; m. Louise Ann Purrett, Feb. 18, 1978. BJ, U. Mo., 1964; MA, Drake U., 1968; PhD, U. Colo., 1970. Asst. prof. Mo. Western State Coll., St. Joseph, 1970-74; sr. ptnr. R&D Cons., Boulder, Colo., 1974-77; corp. editor Storage Tech. Corp., Louisville, Colo., 1977-79; comms. project leader Solar Energy Rsch. Inst., Golden, Colo., 1979-81; exec. mgr. Market Media Svcs., Inc., Boulder, 1981-87; dir. engring. publs. Coll. Engring. and Applied Sci. U. Colo., Boulder, 1987-94, dir. engring. comm. Coll. Engring. and Applied Sci., 1995—; cons. CU Comms. Roundtable, Boulder, 1993—; co-instr. Sch. Journalism and Mass Comms., Boulder, 1994-95, mem. chancellor's pubs. commn., 1995. Co-author: The Rushing Tide, 1983; reviewer IEEE Transactions on Tech. Comms., 1990—; newsletter editor Boys' Club of Boulder, 1974-79. Cons. Meals on Wheels of Boulder, 1992—; bd. dirs., sec. Boulder Press Club, 1988-89. Recipient APEX Nat. awards of excellence Comms. Concepts, Inc., 1991, 92, 93, 94, 95, 96. Mem. Soc. for Tech. Comm. (sr. mem., Disting., Excellence and Merit awards, Internat. award of distinction 1996), Am. Soc. for Engring. Edn., Coun. for Advancement and Support of Edn. (Nat. Bronze medal awards 1990, 93, Exceptional Achievement award 1992, award for Excellence 1994), IEEE Profl. Comm. Soc. Home: 3331 Sentinel Dr Boulder CO 80301-5474 Office: U Colo Coll Engring & Applied Sci Campus Box 422 Regents Dr and Colorado Ave Boulder CO 80309-0422

CARROLL, WALLACE B., allergist, immunologist; b. Oakland, Calif., 1946. MD, U. Autonoma de Guadalajara, Mex., 1975. Intern Valley Med. Ctr., Fresno, Calif., 1976-77, resident pediatrician, 1977-79; resident in allergy and immunology Children's Hosp., Stanford, Calif., 1979-81; now allergist and immunologist Meml. Hosp., Modesto, Calif. Office: Gould Med Group 600 Coffee Rd Modesto CA 95355-4201

CARR-RUFFINO, NORMA, management educator; b. Ft. Worth, Dec. 15, 1932; d. Robert L. and Lorene D. (Dickeson) Carr; m. Randell H. Smith, July 20, 1951 (div. Jan. 1973); children: Randell H. II, Brian F., Carrie F.; m. Alfredo Ruffino, Jan. 6, 1979. BBA, Tex. Wesleyan U., 1968; M Bus. Edn., U. North Tex., 1969, PhD, 1973. V.p. Randy's, Inc., Ft. Worth, 1965-69; vocat. office edn. coord. Ft. Worth Pub. Schs., 1969-72; prof. mgmt. San Francisco State U., 1973—. Author: Writing Short Business Reports, 1980, Promotable Woman, 1982, rev. edit., 1985, 3rd edit., 1997, Business Student Guide, 1987, 2d edit., 1991, Managing Diversity, 1996, Managing Diversity Skill Builder, 1996. Referee Calif. State Bar Ct., 1985—. Named Alumna of Yr. Tex. Wesleyan U., 1988, one of Top 100 Women Alumna (100th anniversary), 1991. Mem. Acad. of Mgmt., Women's Leadership Forum of Dem. Party, World Future Soc., Internat. Assn. of Bus. and Soc., 21st Century World. Home: 1414 Alameda San Mateo CA 94402 Office: San Francisco State U Coll of Bus 1600 Holloway Ave San Francisco CA 94132-1722

CARSON, CLAYBORNE, history educator; b. Buffalo, June 15, 1944; s. Clayborne Sr. and Louise (Lee) C.; m. Susan Ann Beyer, Aug. 29, 1967; children: David Malcolm, Temera Lea. BA, UCLA, 1967, MA, 1971, PhD, 1975. Acting asst. prof. history UCLA, 1971-74; asst. prof. history Stanford (Calif) U., 1974-81, assoc. prof., 1981-90, prof., 1990—; vis. assoc. prof. Dept. Afro-Am. Studies U. Calif., Berkeley, 1982-83; Landmarks Scholar in History, Am. U., Washington, 1990; fellow Ctr. Advanced Study in Behavioral Scis., Stanford, 1993-94; advisor Chicano! TV documentary, 1994—, Freedom on My Mind documentary, 1990-94; vis. scholars program Woodwrow Wilson Nat. Fellowship Found, 1988-90, series advisor Eyes on the Prize documentary, 1985-89; chair Am. History and Social Studies Test Devel. Com. Coll. Bd., 1979-83. Author: In Struggle: SNCC and the Black Awakening of the 1960s, 1981, 2d edit., 1995 (Frederick Jackson Turner award Orgn. Am. Historians 1981), (with Carol Be rkin, et al) American Voices: A History of the United States, 1992; editor. Andrew Mellon fellow 1977, Ctr. Advanced Study Behavioral Scis., 1993-94; Ctr. Study Civil Rights and Race Rels. Duke U., Durham, N.C. vis. fellow, 1978. Mem. Am. Hist. Assn. (mem. program com. 1988-89, Pacific Coast Br. program com. 1980-81), Am. Studies Assn., Assn. Documentary Editing, Assn. Study Afro-Am. Life and History, Nat. Coun. Black Studies, Orgn. Am. Historians (lectr. Lectureship Program, 1988—, elected mem. nominating bd. 1986-87, mem. program com. 1981-82), Soc. Am. Historians, So. Hist. Assn. Office: King Papers Project Cypress Hall D Stanford CA 94305-4146

CARSON, ELIZABETH LORRAINE NEAL, small business owner, civilian military employee; b. Glendale, Calif., Oct. 2, 1958; d. Harold Dean and Viola Gertrude (Neal) Donaldson; m. Robert Lawrence Chally, Aug. 7, 1981 (div. Sept. 1985); m. Richard Wayne Carson, Oct. 5, 1992. BS, Spring Arbor Coll., 1979; MS, Air Force Inst. Tech., 1988. Loan sec. Sacramento (Calif.) Savs. and Loan, 1979, acctg. clk., 1979-81; equipment specialist trainee Civil Svc. USAF, McClellan AFB, 1981-84, equipment specialist, 1984-86; logistics specialist Civil Svc. USAF, L.A. AFB, 1986-88; dep. systems program mgr. Civil Svc. USAF, Sacramento, 1988-89, chief, resource and plans, 1989-90, program mgr., 1990-93, integrated weapon system mgr., program mgmt. process action team rep., 1991-92; adj. prof. Colo. Tech. Coll., Colorado Springs, 1989-91; advisor Logistics Adv. Bd., Colorado Springs, 1988-92; integrated weapon sys. mgmt. program mgr., process action team mem. Air Force Material Command, 1991-93; co-owner Colors of Nature Gallery, In Home. Organist/pianist Orangevale Free Meth. Ch., 1971-76, fin. com. 1981-82, music com., 1971-76, 80-85, chmn. music com., 1984. Mem. Soc. Reliability Engrs., Soc. Logistics Engrs., Sigma Iota Epsilon. Republican. Office: Colors of Nature Gallery 3865 Soft Breeze Way Colorado Springs CO 80918-4814

CARSON, HARRY GLENN, II, writer, editor, retired educator; b. Mooreland, Okla., June 2, 1930; s. Harry Glenn Sr. and Mary Capitola (Hoover) C.; m. Mary Carolyn Lee, June 9, 1950; children: Leanne Marie Boyd, Carol Lynnette Rivera, Harry Glenn III, Kenneth Wayne, Patricia Louise Shaheen. BA, U. Colo., 1963, MA, 1965. Tchr. elem. pub. schs. Emblem, Wyo., 1950-51, Ft. Sumner, N.Mex., 1953-60, Boulder, Colo., 1960-81. Author, pub.: Coinshooting How and Where, 1971, Coinshooting II, 1982, Coinshooting III, 1994, Cache Hunting, 1984, Cache Hunting II, 1987, Backroads to Adventure, 1986, Treasure Hunting, Modern Search for Adventure, 1973, Hunting the Ghost Town, 1971, New Guide to Treasure Hunting, 1992, Malpais Gold, 1978, Pilar La Dura, 1993, Some Paths to Sudden Wealth, 1992, Southwest New Mexico Ghost Towns, 1991, Lost Ledges of the West, 1991, Hedge Yourself Against Disaster, 1973, Guide to Treasure in Colorado, 1995, Guide to Treasure in Idaho, 1996; contbg. editor: Eastern and Western Treasure Mag., 1971—. Home and Office: PO Box 71 Deming NM 88030

CARSON, STANLEY DAVID, cardiothoracic surgeon; b. Blackwell, Okla., June 6, 1946; s. David and Belva Irene (Scott) C.; m. Bonita Ann Synar, June 15, 1968; 1 child, Bryan David. BS in Chemistry with honors, Tulane U., 1968, MD with honors, 1972. Diplomate Am. Bd. of Surgery, Am. Bd. of Thoracic Surgery. Asst. prof. of Surgery, Health Sci's. Ctr. Univ. Colo., Denver, 1978-82; asst. clin. prof. surgery U. Colo. Health Scis. Ctr., Denver, 1982—; attending surgeon St. Joseph's Hosp., Denver, 1982—, Presbyn.-St. Luke's Med. Ctr., Denver, 1982-92. Contbr. articles to med. jours. Mem. Gov's. Task Force on Med. Malpractice, 1987. Fellow Am. Coll. of Chest Physicians, Am. Coll. of Surgeons, Am. Coll. of Cardiology; mem. Denver Acad. of Surgery, Rocky Mountain Cardiac Surgical Soc. (pres. 1988-89), Western Thoracic Surg. Assn., Soc. of Thoracic Surgeons, Alpha Omega Alpha. Office: Denver Cardiac Surgery PC 2005 Franklin St Ste 700 Denver CO 80205-5401

CARSON, WALLACE PRESTON, JR., state supreme court chief justice; b. Salem, Oreg., June 10, 1934; s. Wallace Preston and Edith (Bragg) C.; m. Gloria Stolk, June 24, 1956; children: Scott, Carol, Steven (dec. 1981). BA in Politics, Stanford U., 1956; JD, Willamette U., 1962. Bar: Oreg. 1962, U.S. Dist. Ct. Oreg. 1963, U.S. Ct. Appeals (9th cir.) 1968, U.S. Supreme Ct. 1971, U.S. Ct. Mil. Appeals 1977; lic. comml. pilot FAA. Pvt. practice law Salem, Oreg., 1962-77; judge Marion County Cir. Ct., Salem, 1977-82; assoc. justice Oreg. Supreme Ct., Salem, 1982-92, state chief justice, 1992—. Mem. Oreg. Ho. of Reps., 1967-71, maj. leader, 1969-71; mem. Oreg. State Senate, 1971-77, minority floor leader, 1971-77; dir. Salem Area Community Council, 1967-70, pres., 1969-70; mem. Salem Planning Commn., 1966-72, pres., 1970-71; co-chmn. Marion County Mental Health Planning Com., 1965-69; mem. Salem Community Goals Com., 1965; Republican precinct commiteeman, 1963-66; mem. Marion County Rep. Central Exec. Com., 1963-66; com. predinct edn. Oreg. Rep. Central Com., 1965; vestryman, acolyte, Sunday Sch. tchr., youth coach St. Paul's Episcopal Ch., 1935—; task force on cts. Oreg. Council Crime and Delinquency, 1968-69; trustee Willamette U., 1970—; adv. bd. Cath. Ctr. Community Services, 1976-77; mem. comporehensive planning com. Mid-Willamette Valley Council of Govts., 1970-71; adv. com. Oreg. Coll. Edn. Tchr. Edn., 1971-75; pres. Willamette regional Oreg. Lung Assn., 1974-75, state dir., exec. com., 1975-77; pub. relations com. Williamette council Campfire Girls, 1976-77; criminal justice adv. bd. Chemeketa Community Coll., 1977-79; mem. Oreg. Mental Health Com., 1979-80; mem. subcom. Gov's Task Force Mental Health, 1980; you and govt. adv. com. Oreg. YMCA, 1981—. Served to col. USAFR, 1956-59. Recipient Salem Disting. Svc. award, 1968; recipient Good Fellow award Marion County Fire Svc., 1974, Minuteman award Oreg. N.G. Assn., 1980; fellow Eagleton Inst. Politics, Rutgers U., 1971. Mem. Marion County Bar Assn. (sec.-treas. 1965-67, dir. 1968-70), Oreg. Bar Assn., ABA, Willamette U. Coll. Law Alumni Assn. (v.p. 1968-70), Salem Art Assn., Oreg. Hist. Soc., Marion County Hist. Soc., Stanford U. Club (pres. Salem chpt. 1963-64), Delta Theta Phi. Home: 1309 Hillendale Dr SE Salem OR 97302-3347 Office: Oreg Supreme Ct Supreme Ct Bldg 1163 State St Salem OR 97310-1331

CARSTEN, ARLENE DESMET, financial executive; b. Paterson, N.J., Dec. 5, 1937; d. Albert F. and Ann (Greutert) Desmet; m. Alfred John Carsten, Feb. 11, 1956; children: Christopher Dale, Jonathan Glenn. Student Alfred U., 1955-56; Exec. dir. Inst. for Burn Medicine, San Diego, 1972-81, adv. bd. mem., 1981-92; founding trustee, bd. dirs. Nat. Burn Fedn., 1975-83; chief fin. officer A.J. Carsten Co. Inc., San Diego, 1981-91; CFO A.J. Carsten Co., Ltd., Powell River, B.C., Can., 1992-97, cons., 1997—. Contbr. articles to profl. jours. Organizer, mem. numerous cmty. groups; chmn. San Diego County Mental Health Adv. Bd., 1972-74, mem., 1971-75; chmn. cmty. rels. subcom., mem. exec. com. Emergency Med. Care Com., San Diego, Riverside and Imperial Counties, 1973-75; pub. mem. psychology exam. com. Calif. State Bd. Med. Quality Assurance, 1976-80, chmn., 1977; mem. rep. to Health Svcs. Agy. San Diego County Govt., 1980; mem. Calif. Dem. Cen. Com., 1968-74, exec. com., 1971-72, 73-74; treas. San Diego Dem. County Cen. Com., 1972-74; chmn. edn. for legislation com. women's div. So. Calif. Dem. Com., 1972; dir. Muskie for Pres. Campaign, San Diego, 1972; organizer, dir. numerous local campaigns; councilwoman City of Del Mar, Calif., 1982-86, mayor, 1985-86; bd. dirs. Gentry-Watts Planned Indsl. Devel. Assn., 1986-90, pres., 1987-90; v.p. Okeover Rate Payers Assn., 1996-97, pres., 1997—; commencement speaker Alfred U., 1984. Recipient Key Woman award Dem. Party, 1968, 72, 1st Ann. Community award Belles for Mental Health, Mental Health Assn. San Diego, 1974, citation Alfred U. Alumni Assn., 1979. Home: RR# 2 Malaspina Rd C-68, Powell River, BC Canada V8A 4Z3

CARSTENS, DIANE YVONNE, retirement housing consultant; b. Vancouver, B.C., Can., Apr. 9, 1955; d. Hans Wilfred Otto Carstens and Louise Marie (Kennedy) Voloshin; m. Edward Christie Lubieniecki, Mar. 24, 1983. Student, Stanford U., 1976; BA, Mills Coll., 1979; M in Landscape Architecture, U. Ill., 1982. Researcher U. Ill. Housing Research Program, Champaign, 1981-83; project mgr. Project for Pub. Spaces, N.Y.C., 1983-85; dir. planning and research Leisure Tech. and Care Inc., Lakewood, N.J., 1985-86; v.p. planning and design Gerontol. Services, Inc., Santa Monica, Calif., 1986—; cons., manuscript reviewer Van Nostrand Reinhold, N.Y.C.; lectr., speaker at various univs.; conductor seminars in field. Author: Site Planning and Design for the Elderly, 1985, (with others) Housing the Elderly: A Review of Selected References, (contbg.) Retirement Housing in Australia, 1986. Mem. ad hoc com. Dept. of Health, Bur. Licensure and Certification- State of Ala., 1986. Recipient Honor award Am. Soc. Landscape Architects, Ill., 1981. Mem. Am. Assn. Homes for Aging, Am. Soc. Aging, Environ. Design Research Assn. (Honor award 1986), Am. Assn. Homes and Svcs. for Aging. Home: 1407 Jonesboro Dr Los Angeles CA 90049-3626 Office: Gerontol Svcs Inc 320 Wilshire Blvd Ste 100 Santa Monica CA 90401

CARTÉ, GEORGE WAYNE, geophysicist, mayor; b. Buhl, Idaho, Sept. 8, 1940; s. Harold D. Carte and Reba E. (Lammert) Magoon; m. Katherine I. Williams, Sept. 8, 1962; children: Charles M., Theresa L., Jeannette M., Suzanne E. AAS, Columbia Basin Coll., Wash., 1962; BS in Geol. Engring., U. Idaho, 1964; postgrad. U. Hawaii, 1978-79. Hydraulic engr. U.S. Geol. Survey, Anchorage, 1964-66; seismologist AK Tsunami Warning Ctr., Palmer, Alaska, 1966-97; instr. Mat-Su Community Coll., Palmer, 1971-72, 81; instr. English Saroma Kyoikuiiukai, Japan, 1997—; instr. elem. Japanese lang. and culture. Mayor City of Palmer, 1981-95, councilman, 1980-81, 95-96; chmn. Palmer Planning and Zoning Commn., 1968-78; mem. Mat-Su Borough Planning Commn., 1975-78. Mem. Alaska Conf. of Mayors, 1982-95, Mat-Su Borough Econ. Devel. Commn., 1989-95; chmn. Palmer-Saroma Japan Sister City; trustee Joint Ins. Assn., 1989-96, chmn., 1994-96. Recipient cert. of achievement Anchorage Fed. Exec. Assocs., 1981, 87. Mem. Alaska Mcpl. League (bd. dirs. 1983-96, pres. 1986-87, trustee joint ins. arrangement 1989-96, chmn. 1992-96), Earthquake Engring. Rsch. Inst., Am. Geophys. Union, Tsunami Soc., Alaska Geol. Soc. Mem. Pentecostal Ch. Home: 367 N Valley Way Palmer AK 99645-6137 Office: Eidai-cho, Saroma-cho Tokoro-gun, Hokkaido 093-05, Japan

CARTER, C. CRAIG, sales consultant; b. Warwick, N.Y., Oct. 3, 1959; s. Charles R. and Michelle B. (Cohen) C.; m. Kelley R. Ward, June 25, 1983; children: C. Cameron, Colin M. Student, USCG Acad., 1977-79; BBA in Mktg. Comms., U. Puget Sound, 1984. Restaurant mgr. Pioneer, Warwick, N.Y., 1980; store mgr. Farrell's, Tacoma, Wash., 1982-83; retail sales rep. Ted Brown Music, Tacoma, 1983-84; sales rep. Print Northwest, Tacoma, 1984-90; sales mgr. Mercury Press, Tacoma, 1990-91; sales rep., sales mgr. Johnson-Cox, Tacoma, 1991-95; sales rep. Printing Control, Seattle, 1995—. Spkr. Visitor and Convention Bur., Tacoma, 1988-90; bd. dirs. Tacoma Young Life, 1994-95, Broadway Ctr. for Performing Arts, Tacoma, 1987-90; mem. sch. centered decision making com. Sherman Elem. Sch., Tacoma, 1995—; mem. design com. Tacoma Sch. Dist., 1996—. Scholar Up With People, 1981, U. Puget Sound, 1983, 84. Mem. Adv. Prodn. Assn. (program com. 1989-91), Tacoma Ad Fedn. (pres. 1989, treas. 1990-91). Presbyterian. Home: 3620 N Stevens Tacoma WA 98407 Office: Printing Control 1011 Andover Park East Seattle WA 98188-7615

CARTER, DAVID MACCORMICK, marketing professional; b. Oakland, Calif., Nov. 22, 1964; s. Robert Melvin and Marjorie Claire (Lee) C.; m. Vickie Williams, Feb. 9, 1991. BS in BA, U. So. Calif., 1986, MBA in Fin., 1991. Mktg. rep. L.A. Athletic Club, 1987-88, L.A. Clippers, 1988-89; sports mgmt. cons. Redondo Beach, Calif., 1989-96; licenser Walt Disney Co., 1996—; faculty mem. U. So. Calif. Grad. Sch. Bus., 1994—. Author: You Can't Play the Game if You Don't Know the Rules, 1994, Keeping Score, 1996. Bd. dirs. Help the Homless Help Themselves, Palos Verdes, Calif., 1992-93. Republican. Roman Catholic.

CARTER, DENNIS LEE, marketing professional; b. Louisville, Oct. 23, 1951; s. Bernard Lee and Opal Delores (Jaggers) C.; m. Janice Lea Herbert, Dec. 31, 1976; children: Serra Kimberly, Scott Winston. BSEE, BS in Physics, Rose Hulman Inst., Terre Haute, Ind., 1973; MSEE, Purdue U., 1974, DSc (hon.), 1996; MBA, Harvard U., 1981. Instr. elec. engring. tech. Purdue U., West Lafayette, Ind., 1975; collateral engr. Rockwell-Collins, Cedar Rapids, Iowa, 1975-76, design engr., 1976-79; product mktg. engr. Intel Corp., Santa Clara, Calif., 1981-83, software products mktg. mgr., 1983-85, tech. asst. to pres., 1985-89, end-user mktg. mgr., 1989-90, gen. mgr. end-user components divsn., 1990-91, dir. corp. mktg., 1991-92, v.p., dir. corp. mktg., 1992—. Inventor radio reception path monitor for a diversity sys., 1985. Episcopalian. Office: Intel Corp RN5-20 2200 Mission College Blvd Santa Clara CA 95054-1537

CARTER, GEORGE KENT, oil company executive; b. Toledo, Ohio, Nov. 5, 1935; s. Fred S. and Charlotte J. (Horen) C.; children from previous marriage: Caitlin, Seth; m. Kathleen Anne McKenna, July 22, 1990. AB, Stanford U., 1957, MBA, 1961. Various fin. positions Standard Oil of Calif., San Francisco, 1962-74, asst. treas., 1974, asst. comptroller, 1974-81; comptroller Chevron U.S.A., Inc., San Francisco, 1981-83, v.p. fin., 1986-89; comptroller Chevron Corp. (formerly Standard Oil of Calif.), San Francisco, 1983-86, v.p. and treas., 1989—. Mem. Stanford Bus. Sch. Assn., Stanford U. Alumni Assn., Bankers Club. Office: Chevron Corp 575 Market St San Francisco CA 94105-2856 also: Chevron Corp PO Box 7643 San Francisco CA 94120-7643

CARTER, JANICE JOENE, telecommunications executive; b. Portland, Oreg., Apr. 17, 1948; d. William George and Charline Betty (Gilbert) P.; m. Ronald Thomas Carter, June 13, 1968; children: Christopher Scott, Jill Suzanne. Student, U. Calif., Berkeley, 1964, U. Portland, 1966-67, U. Colo., Boulder, 1967-68; BA in Math, U. Guam, 1970; postgrad., Golden Gate U., 1996—. Computer programmer Ga.-Pacific Co., Portland, 1972-74; systems analyst ProData, Seattle, 1974-79; systems analyst, mgr. Pacific Northwest Bell, Seattle, 1979-80; data ctr. mgr. Austin Co., Renton, Wash., 1980-83; developer shared tenent svcs. Wright-Runstad, Seattle, 1983-84; system adminstr. Hewlett-Packard, Bellevue, Wash., 1984; telecom. dir. Nordstrom, Inc., Seattle, 1984-96; telecom. engring. mgr. Hewlett-Packard Co., Palo Alto, Calif., 1996—; mem. large customer panel AT&T, Seattle, 1987—. Ski instr. Alpental, Snoqualmie Pass, Wash., 1984-87; bd. dirs. Educationally Gifted Children, Mercer Island, Wash., 1978-80; mem. curriculum com. Mercer Island Sch. Bd., 1992-95; mem. Sweet Adelines. Mem. Telecom. Assn., Internat. Comm. Assn., System 85/ETN User Group. Office: Hewlett-Packard 3000 Hanover MS 20CX Palo Alto CA 94304

CARTER, JOY EATON, electrical engineer, consultant; b. Comanche, Tex., Feb. 8, 1923; d. Robert Lee and Carrie (Knudson) Eaton; m. Clarence J. Carter, Aug. 22, 1959; 1 child, Kathy Jean. Student, John Tarleton Agrl. Coll., 1939-40; B Music cum laude, N. Tex. State Tchrs. Coll., 1943, postgrad., 1944-45; postgrad., U. Tex., 1945; MSEE, Ohio State U., 1949, PhDEE and Radio Astronomy, 1957. Engr. aide Civil Service Wright Field, Dayton, Ohio, 1945-46; instr. math. Ohio State U., Columbus, 1946-48, asst., then assoc. Rsch. Found., 1947-49, from instr. to asst. prof. elec. engring., 1949-58; rsch. engr. N.Am. Aviation, Columbus, 1955-56; mem. tech. staff Space Tech. Labs. (later TRW Inc.), Redondo Beach, Calif., 1958-68; sect. head, staff engr. electronics rsch. labs. The Aerospace Corp., El Segundo, 1968-72, staff engr. and mgr. system and terminals, USAF Satellite Communications System Program Office, 1972-77, mgr. communications subsystem Def. Satellite Communications System III Program Office, 1978-79; cons. Mayhill, N.Mex., 1979—. Active Mayhill Vol. Fire Dept., 1986—; bd. dirs. Mayhill Cmty. Assn., 1988—, sec. bd. dirs., 1988—; co-chair music com. Mayhill Bapt. Ch., 1988—, trustee, 1989-92, 94-97; bd. dirs. Otero County Farm Bur., 1987—. Named Cow Belle of Yr., Otero CowBelles, 1988. Mem. IEEE (sr., life), Am. Astron. Soc., Am. Nat. Cattlewomen (sec. Otero CowBelles chpt. 1986-87, 1st v.p. 1988, historian 1989), Calif. Rare Fruit Growers, Native Plant Soc. N.Mex., Sacramento Mountains Hist. Soc. (bd. dirs. 1986—, treas. 1997—), High Country Horseman's Assn., Sigma Xi (life), Eta Kappa Nu (life), Sigma Alpha Iota (life), Alpha Chi, Kappa Delta Pi, Pi Mu Epsilon, Sigma Delta Epsilon. Home and Office: PO Box 23 Mayhill NM 88339-0023

CARTER, LARRY ALEXANDER, brokerage firm executive; b. Joplin, Mo., Nov. 9, 1940; s. Samuel E. and Laura L. (House) C.; m. Jan. 24, 1962 (div.); children: Larry Vince, Donna Diane, Mitchell Alexander. Student, Cerritos Coll., Long Beach State Coll., UCLA, Calif. Orange Coast Coll. Police officer South Gate (Calif.) Police Dept., 1963-65; narcotics expert Long Beach (Calif.) Police Dept., 1965-75; pvt. practice constrn., 1975-76; v.p., office mgr. Diversified Securities, Inc., El Toro, Calif., 1976-89; v.p. Diversified Securities, Inc., Crestline, 1989—; speaker in field. Recipient Calif. Commn. on Police Officer Standards and Tng. Advanced cert., 1974; named DSI Top Ten Mem., 1977—. Mem. NRA, Calif. Rifle & Pistol Assn., Calif. State Sheriffs Assn., Lake Arrowhead C. of C., Crestline C. of C., Narcotics Officers Assn., Crest Forest Cmty. Assn. (bd. dirs.). Republican. Baptist. Address: PO Box 3271 Crestline CA 92325-3271 Office: 396 Hartman Cir # A Cedarpines Park CA 92322

CARTER, LARRY VINCE, financial planner; b. Long Beach, Calif., July 5, 1962; s. Larry Alexander and Patricia Ruth (Gabriel) C. Grad. high sch., El Toro, Calif. Lead technician Mini Lab Maintenance, Inc., Laguna Hills, Calif., 1983-85, Taylor Photo/Technician Support, Cypress, Calif., 1985-87; mgr., registered prin., fin. planner Diversified Securities Inc., Crestline, Calif., 1987—. Republican. Home: 392 Hartman Circle Cedarpines Park CA 92322 Office: Diversified Securities Inc PO Box 3271 Crestline CA 92325-3271

CARTER, MELVIN WHITSETT (MEL CARTER), artist, educator; b. Ill., Nov. 19, 1941; s. Mallory and Claudia (Whitsett) C. BFA, U. Ill., 1963; MFA, U. Gunajuato, Mex., 1968. Tchr. art Denver Pub. Schs., 1963-68; instr. Fine Arts Community Coll., Denver, 1968-71; coord. Fine Arts Community Auraria, Denver, 1971-89; artist, instr. Art Students League Denver, 1987—; guest prof. art Western N.Mex. U., summer 1994; artist cons., bd. dirs. Cherry Creek Arts Festival, Denver, 1991-92. Numerous one-man shows and group exhbns., 1964-96, including residence U.S. amb. to Austria, Vienna; illustrator: Occupational Communications, 1969; artist (withothers) Figure Drawing Workshop, 1985; featured artist New Choices mag., 1995, How to Sell Your Art (Carole Katchen), 1996; solo exhibn. (AIDS rsch. benefit) Celebration of Life, Denver, 1996. Commr. art Mayors Commr. Art, Culture, Film, 1992; artist advisor, bd. dirs. Cherry Creek Arts Festival, Denver, 1991. Sgt. USAF, 1959-61. Named Prof. Art, Colo. Community Colls. Abroad, Rome, Paris, London, 1970, Outstanding Educator Am., Bd. Dirs., Washington, 1974, State of Colo., 1987; recipient medal Excellence in Higher Edn., U. Tex., Austin, 1989; Fulbright scholar USIA, Netherland Am. Agy., 1987. Home: 1330 Gilpin St Denver CO 80218-2511 Office: Art Students League Denver 200 Grant St Denver CO 80203-4020

CARTER, NANCY CAROL, legal educator, law librarian; b. Tacoma, Wash., Nov. 12, 1942; d. Walter Martin and Lois (Wilson) Schwebel. BS, Tex. A&I, 1963, MS, 1967; MLS, U. Okla., 1965, JD, 1975. Asst. acquisitions libr. U. Okla., Norman, 1967-71; law libr. dir., prof. law Golden Gate U., San Francisco, 1975-86; legal rsch. ctr. dir., prof. law U. San Diego, 1987—. Mem. Am. Assn. Law Librs., Okla. State Bar Assn. Office: U San Diego Legal Rsch Ctr 5998 Alcala Park San Diego CA 92110-2429

CARTER, PAUL EDWARD, publishing company executive; b. Spokane, Wash., July 7, 1925; s. Richard Bert and Lula Selena (Jones) C.; m. Helen Barbara crosby, Nov. 2, 1950; children: Nancy, Thomas, Richard, Robert. BA in English and Journalism, Wash. State U., 1949. Advt. mgr. The Spokesman-Rev. and Spokane Daily Chronicle, 1949-87; advt. dir. Hobbs (N.Mex.) Daily News-Sun, 1987-91; western sales mgr. Slike Pub. Co., Harrisburg, Pa., 1983—; cons. various daily newspapers. Editor numerous ch., coll., club pubs., 1948—. Pres. Inland Empire coun. Boy Scouts Am., Spokane, 1971-73; divsn. chmn. United Way of Spokane County, 1955-68; pres. adv. bd. Spokane City U., 1943-46; bishopric LDS Ch., mem. high coun., young men's program leader, Sunday sch. supt., Elders Quorum pres., High Priest quorum leader, scoutmaster, explorer scout adviser. 1st lt. USAF, 1950-52, Korea, USAAF, WWII. Recipient Ramsey Oppenheim award Advt. Assn. of the West, 1962, Silver Beaver award Boy Scouts Am., 1973, Demolay Legion of Honor, 1955, Don Dirstine award Spokane Jr. C. of C., 1950, Disting. Svc. award Spokane Ctrl. Lions Club, 1958, 60 Yrs. Svc. Recognition award, 1997. Mem. Internat. Newspaper Advt. Execs. (dist. dir. 1989-92), Pacific N.W. Newspaper Advt. Execs. (pres. 1973-74), Soc. Profl. Journalists (pres. Coll. chpt.), Am. Press Inst. (del. 1958), SAR (pres. Salt Lake City chpt. 1997—), Spokane Advt. Club (pres. 1961-62, Advt. Man of the Yr. 1962, hon. life), Hobbs Rotary (pres. 1991-92, Rotarian of the Yr. 1989-90). Republican. LDS. Home: 6280 S Castleford Dr West Jordan UT 84084

CARTER, PAUL EDWARD, contractor, construction company executive; b. Lakeview, Oreg., Mar. 9, 1952; s. John Clifford and Theresa (McAllister) C.; m. Laura Marie Brewen, May 17, 1986; 2 children: Heather, Sharresa. Student, Cuesta Coll., 1976-77. Buckaroo cowboy Monroe Ranch, Likely, Calif., 1971-72; meat cutter Safeway, Klamath Falls, Oreg., 1974-76; rodeo cowboy Profl. Cowboy Assn., San Luis Obispo, Calif., 1976-80; carpenter Bordonaro Constrn., Paso Robles, Calif., 1981-87; owner, contractor Cont. State Lic. Bd., Paso Robles, 1988—; gen. contractor Paul Carter Constrn., Paso Robles, 1988—. With U.S. Army, 1972-74. Home and Office: 235 Via Ramona Paso Robles CA 93446

CARTER, PAUL RICHARD, physician; b. St. Louis, Apr. 14, 1922; s. Paul William and Lily Edith (Kreutzer) C.; m. Lenora Martha Parker, Dec. 24, 1944; children: Richard Brian, Janet Carol Becker. BA in English and History, Union Coll., 1944; MD, Loma Linda U., 1947. Diplomate Am. Bd. Gen. Surgery & Thoracic Surgery. Intern L.A. County Gen. Hosp., 1947-49, surg. resident, 1949-52, 54-56, head physician surgery, 1957-67; resident in chest surgery Olive View Sanitarium, 1956-57; chief of surgery Rancho Los Amigo Hosp., Downey, Calif., 1967-69; prof. of surgery Loma Linda (Calif.) U., 1960—; clin. prof. of surgery U. Calif., Irvine, 1960—; pvt. practice surgery Covina, Calif., 1960—; chief thoracic surgery Pettis VA Hosp., Loma Linda, 1978-94. Author about 90 articles and book chpts. in field; co-author: (2 vol.) History of the Pacific Coast Surgical Association, 1982, 88. Capt. USAMC, 1952-54, Korea. Recipient Fulbright scholarship, Oxford, 1959; named to editorial bd., Annals of Thoracic Surgery for 11 yrs. Fellow. ACS (recorder, sec., treas., pres. So. Calif. chpt. 1989, gov. 1991); mem.

Pacific Coast Surgical Assn. (v.p. 1987—, historian), Am. Assn. Thoracic Surgery, Soc. Thoracic Surgeons, Western Surgical Assn., Societe Internat. Chirurgie, Coll. Chest Physicians, Gen. Thoracic Surgical Club, Internat. Soc. Diseases of the Esophagus. Republican. Home: 75-310 14th Green Dr Indian Wells CA 92210-7421

CARTER, PETER LENN, electrical engineer; b. Albany, Calif., Sept. 28, 1938; s. Lennard James and Emogene (West) C.; m. Barbara Randolph, Apr. 1959 (div. June 1969); children: Kimberly, Kiersten, Katherine, James. AA, Contra Costa (Calif.) Coll., 1961; BS, U. Calif., Berkeley, 1963. Registered profl. engr., Calif. Engrng. positions Bechtel Corp., San Francisco, 1966-73; project engr. Bechtel Corp., Beruit, Lebanon, 1973-75; chief engr. Bechtel Corp., San Francisco, 1975-79; owner Pacific Bldg., Oakland, Calif., 1979—; real estate developer and investor, Calif., 1979—. Lt., Alameda County (Calif.) Underwater Rescue Unit, 1963-70. Mem. IEEE, NSPE, Calif. Soc. Profl. Engrs., Augustan Soc. (bd. dirs.), Def. Orientation Conf. Assn., Soc. Mayflower Decendants, Pilgrim Soc., Order of Wash., Shriners, Magna Charta Barons (Somerset chpt.), Soc. Descs. of Knights of Garter, Colonial Soc. Ams. of Royal Descent, Commonwealth Club.

CARTER, RAYMOND (BEAU), healthcare association executive; b. Montclair, N.J., Nov. 28, 1943; s. Raymond Hitchings and Katharine (Gribbel) C.; children: John Hitchings, Matthew Gribbel. BA, Princeton U., 1965; postgrad., Am. U., 1965-66. Program analyst U.S. Dept. HEW, Washington, 1970-72; Calif. liaison officer U.S. Dept. HEW, San Francisco, 1972-74, 76-86; exec. dir. Fed. Regional Coun., San Francisco, 1974-76; v.p. govt. affairs Hosp. Coun., San Mateo, Calif., 1987-94; sr. v.p. pub. policy Hosp. Coun., Pleasanton, Calif., 1994-95; exec. dir. Integrated Healthcare Assn., Pleasanton, 1995—. Bd. chair Cen. Br. YMCA, San Francisco, 1985-87; chair inter-br. coun. Met. YMCA, San Francisco, 1986-87; cub master Cub Scout Pack 351, San Francisco, 1987-89; ch. pres. West Portal Luth. Ch., San Francisco, 1992-94. 1st lt. U.S. Army, 1967-69. Recipient Unsung Hero award San Francisco Vol. Ctr., 1983; named Vol. of Yr., Cen. Br. YMCA, 1985. Mem. Am. Soc. Pub. Adminstrn. (chpt. pres. 1983-84, Chpt. Contbr. award 1981, 85). Episcopalian. Home: 1435 41st Ave San Francisco CA 94122-3033 Office: Integrated Healthcare Assn 7901 Stoneridge Dr Pleasanton CA 94588-3600

CARTER, RICHARD BERT, retired church official, retired government official; b. Spokane, Wash., Dec. 2, 1916; s. Richard B. and Lula Selena (Jones) C.; BA in Polit. Sci., Wash. State U., 1939; postgrad. Georgetown U. Law Sch., 1941, Brown U., 1944, Brigham Young U. Extension, 1975-76; m. Mildred Brown, Sept. 6, 1952; children: Paul, Mark, Janis, David. Advt. credit mgr. Elec. Products Consol., Omaha, 1939-40; pub. affairs ofcl., investigator FBI, Washington, 1940-41, Huntington, W.Va., 1941, Houston, 1942, Boston, 1943, S. Am., 1943, Providence, 1944-45, N.Y.C., 1945, Salt Lake City, 1945, P.R., 1946-48, Phoenix, 1948-50, Washington, 1950-51, Cleve., 1952-55, Seattle, 1955-75, ret., 1975; assoc. dir. stake and mission pub. affairs dept. Ch. Hdqrs., Ch. of Jesus Christ of Latter-day Saints, Salt Lake City, 1975-77. Dist. chmn. Chief Seattle coun. Boy Scouts Am., 1967-68, coun. v.p., 1971-72, coun. commr., 1973-74, nat. coun. rep., 1962-64, 72-74, area II, Eagle Scout Assn., 1984—. Mem. Freedoms Found. Valley Forge, Utah chpt., 1988—; bd. dirs. Salvation Army, 1963, United Way, 1962-63, mem. allocations com., 1962, 1987-88, JayCees, Omaha, Neb., 1939-40; organizer First Family History Lib., Seattle, 1971. Served to lst lt., Intelligence Corps, U.S. Army, 1954. Recipient Silver Beaver award Boy Scouts Am., 1964, Vigil Honor, 1971, Alumni Achievement award for Disting. Svc. Wash. State U., 1997; named Nat. Media Man-of-Month Morality in Media, Inc., N.Y.C., 1976. Mem. Profl. Photographers Am., Internat. Assn. Bus. Communicators, Am. Security Council (nat. adv. bd.), Internat. Platform Assn., Sons Utah Pioneers (pres. 1982, Disting. Svc. award 1985), SAR (pres. Salt Lake City chpt. 1987-88, Law Enforcement Commendation medal 1987, Meritorious Svc. medal 1989, Pres.-Gen.'s Program Excellence award, Oliver R. Smith medal 1990, Grahame T. Smallwood award 1990, Liberty medal 1991, Patriot medal 1992), Utah State Soc. (pres. 1989-90), Amicus Club of Deseret Found., chmn. membership com. 1988—, Gold Caduceus award, 1993), World Sr. Games (adv. com, 1987—), William Carter Family Orgn. (nat. pres.), Nat. Assn. Chiefs of Police (Am. Police Hall of Fame, John Edgar Hoover Distin. Pub. Svc. medal 1991, Nat. Patriotism medal 1993), Scabbard and Blade, Crimson Circle, Am. Media Network (nat. adv. bd.), Assn. Former Intelligence Officers, Soc. Profl. Journalists, Alpha Phi Omega, Pi Sigma Alpha, Phi Delta Theta. Mem. LDS Ch. (coord. pub. affars council Seattle area 1973-75, br. pres. 1944-45, seventies quorum pres. 1952, dist. pres. 1954-55, high priest 1958—, stake pres. counselor 1959-64, stake Sunday Sch. pres. 1980-81, temple staff 1987—). Clubs: Bonneville Knife and Fork (bd. dirs. 1982-85), Rotary (dir., editor The Rotary Bee, 1982-83, Paul Harris fellow 1982, Richard L. Evans fellow 1987, Best Club History in Utah award 1988, Best Dist. Newsletter award 1983, Rotarian of Month 1988, membership com. 1995—, club 24 found. bd. 1995—). Author: The Sunbeam Years-An Autobiography, 1986; assoc. editor FBI Investigator, 1965-75; contbg. author, editor: Biographies of Sons of Utah Pioneers, 1982; contbr. articles to mags. Home: 2180 Elaine Dr Bountiful UT 84010-3120 *Receiving good gifts brings happiness. Giving your time to serve others bring true joy.*

CARTER, ROBERT SPENCER, private investor; b. Oakmont, Pa., Aug. 18, 1915; s. Robert Spencer and Adele Rebecca (Crowell) C.; m. Cynthia Root, Dec. 31, 1937; children—Lief Hastings, Delight Carter Willing. B.A., Harvard U., 1937. Underwriter, Atlantic Mutual Ins. Co., N.Y.C., 1939-51; marine mgr. Gen. Ins. Co. of Am., Seattle, 1951-59; pvt. investor, Medina, Wash., 1959—. Author: Sail Far Away, 1978. Contbr. articles to profl. jours. Trustee, Archaeol. Inst. Am. Boston, 1980-87. Clubs: Cruising of Am., Seattle Yacht, Corinthian, Explorers. Achievements include accredited discoverer submerged seaport of Aperlae, Turkey.

CARTER, ROBERTA ECCLESTON, therapist, counselor; b. Pitts.; d. Robert E. and Emily B. (Bucar) Carter; divorced; children: David Michael Kiewlich, Daniel Michael Kiewlich. Student Edinboro State U., 1962-63; BS, California State U. of Pa., 1966; MEd, U. Pitts., 1969; MA, Rosebridge Grad. Sch., Walnut Creek, Calif., 1987. Tchr., Bethel Park Sch. Dist., Pa., 1966-69; writer, media asst. Field Ednl. Pub., San Francisco, 1969-70; educator, counselor, specialist Alameda Unified Sch. Dist., Calif., 1970—; master trainer Calif. State Dept. Edn., Sacramento, 1984—; personal growth cons., Alameda, 1983—. Author: People, Places and Products, 1970, Teaching/Learning Units, 1969; co-author: Teacher's Manual Let's Read, 1968. Mem. AAUW, NEA, Calif. Fedn. Bus. and Profl. Women (legis. chair Alameda br. 1984-85, membership chair 1985), Calif. Edn. Assn., Alameda Edn. Assn., Charter Planetary Soc., Oakland Mus., Exploratorium, Big Bros. of East Bay, Alameda C. of C. (svc. award 1985). Avocations: acrobics, gardening, travel. Home: 1516 Eastshore Dr Alameda CA 94501-3118

CARTER, SHIRLEY RAEDELLE, retired elementary school educator; b. Pueblo, Colo., Oct. 28, 1937; d. John Clay and Velda Edythe (Bussard) Apple; m. Carrol Joseph Carter, Apr. 26, 1958; children: Margaret Carol, Norma Katherine, Michael Clay. AA in Edn., Pueblo Jr. Coll., 1957; BA in Elem. Edn., Adams State Coll., 1960, MA in Elem. Edn., 1971. Cert. tchr., Colo. 2d and 3d grade tchr. Beulah (Colo.) Elem. Sch., 1957-58; 3d grade tchr. Westcliffe (Colo.) Elem. Sch., 1961-62; substitute tchr. Dist. RE 11J, Alamosa, Colo., 1974-77; 6th grade English tchr. Evans Intermediate Sch., Alamosa, 1977-78, 5th grade English tchr., 1978-80; 5th grade tchr. Evans Elem. Sch., Alamosa, 1980-90, 4th grade tchr., 1990-95; ret., 1995; owner Shirley's Selectables Joe's Junk, Creede, Colo., 1993—.k. Editor, pub. newspaper Evans Eagle, 1984, newspaper anns. Tasanti, 1957, El Conquestor, 1959. Leader San Luis Valley Girl Scout Columbine Coun., 1972-77, adult trainer, 1974-87; dir. San Luis Valley Girl Scout Camp, 1974-75, program dir., 1976-87; parish Coun. Sacred Heart Ch., Alamosa, Colo., 1982-84. Mem. Creede C. of C. (bd. dirs. 1994-96), Internat. Reading Assn. (bd. dirs. San Luis Valley chpt. 1980-90, pres., 1983-84, presenter Colo. Coun. 1982-88, Sweetheart 1985-86, 90-91). Democrat. Roman Catholic. Home: P O Box 53 Creede CO 81130

CARTER, SUSIE GLORIA, publisher, editor, television and radio personality; b. Indpls., Dec. 5, 1942; d. Frederick Milton Rash and Dorothy Josephine (Fox) DeLellis; m. Warren Muench, Mar. 30, 1965 (div. May 1972); children: Cheryl Anne, Ephraim Adam, Robin Ruth, Shirlee Dawn; m. Davis Rush Carter, Sept. 7, 1972 (div. May 1995); children: Aaron Wayne, Amber Noelle, Bruce Allen, Rich Ben. Day care/foster parent, 1965-87; pub., editor Alaskamen Mag., Anchorage, 1987—; mem. adv. bd. Citizens of the Future, L.A. Chmn. Safe Haven Non-Profit Orgn. Home and Office: Alaskamen 205 E Dimond Blvd # 522 Anchorage AK 99515

CARTER, WILLIAM GEORGE, III, army officer; b. Buffalo, June 18, 1944; s. William George Jr. and Elaine Ruth (Weber) C.; m. Linda Fay Yener, Oct. 2, 1965; children: Kris Ann, William George. BS, U. Tampa, 1972; MA, U. Shippensberg, 1982; MPE, U. Pitts., 1984. Commd. 2d. lt. U.S. Army, 1965, advanced through grades to lt. gen., 1995; various command and staff positions, 1964-77; exec. officer 3d Brigade, 1st Armored Div., Bamberg, Fed. Republic Germany, 1977-79; comdr. 1st Bn., 52d Inf., Bamberg, 1979-81, G3 1st Armored Div., VII U.S. Corps, Ansbach, Fed. Republic Germany, 1981-83; chief Plans and Integration Office, Hdqrs. U.S. Army, Washington, 1983-86; comdr. 1st Brigade, 4th Inf. Div., Ft. Carson, Colo., 1986-88; exec. asst. Office Chief of Staff Army, Washington, 1988-89; asst. div. comdr. 1st Inf. Div., Ft. Riley, Kans., 1989-91; comdr. Nat. Tng. Ctr., Ft. Irwin, Calif., 1991-93, 1st Armored Divsn., 1993-95; chief of staff Allied Forces So. Europe, 1995—. Decorated DDSM, DSM, Legion of Merit with six oak leaf clusters, Bronze Star with V device and two oak leaf clusters, Purple Heart with oak leaf cluster. Mem. Soc. of the Big Red One, Alpha Chi.

CARTER, WILLIAM GERALD, non-profit corporation executive; b. Bethany, Mo., Jan. 12, 1929; s. William Young and Leah Genevieve (Cover) C.; m. Geralyn Gail Finlay, July 22, 1951; children: Kathryn Carter Gee, Karen Carter Winn, William Ralph. BSc, U. Mo., 1950. Assoc. editor Nat. Livestock Prodr., Chgo., 1950-51; comm. specialist Farmland Industries, Kansas City, Mo., 1953-54; advt. dir. MFA Oil Co., Columbia, Mo., 1954-58; ptnr. Neds & Wardlow Advt. Agy., Springfield, Mo., 1958-68; chmn., pres. Tri-State Pharm Co., Oklahoma City, 1968-81; real estate broker W.G. Carter Real Estate, Oklahoma City & Foster City, Calif., 1981-96; founder, chmn. Am. Acad. Vols. in Edn., Foster City, Calif., 1994-97. Spl. agent intelligence U.S. Army, 1951-53. Named Young Man of Yr., C. of C., Springfield, 1964. Mem. Optimist Internat. (mem. various coms. 1981-89, v.p., bd. dirs. 1984, chair numerous coms. 1985-87, v.p. Optimist Vols. for Youth, Inc. 1992-97). Republican. Methodist. Home and Office: 247 Boothbay Ave Foster City CA 94404

CARVALHO, WAYNE G., protective services official. Chief of police Hilo, Hawaii. Office: City of Hilo Police Dept 349 Kapiolani St Hilo HI 96720

CARVER, JOHN GUILL, physicist; b. Mt. Juliet, Tenn., Feb. 10, 1924; s. Henry Gilliam and Inez (Cook) C.; m. Elva Emily Kattelman, Apr. 21, 1956; children: John Jr., Linda Lee Samaripa, Karen Emily Cushing, Susan Aline. BS in Physics, Ga. Inst. Tech., 1950; MS, Yale U., 1951, PhD, 1955. Registered profl. elec. engr., Ohio, registered profl. nuclear engr., Calif. Field svc. engr. Philco Corp., Phila., 1946-48; nuclear engr. dept. atomic power equipment Gen. Electric, Cin., 1955-60; nuclear engr., mgr. irradiations physics Gen. Electric, San Jose, Calif., 1960-67; mgr. advanced rsch. Rockwell Internat., Downey, Calif., 1967-72; supr. electro-optics Rockwell Internat., Seal Beach, Calif., 1972-78; prin. engr. Rockwell Internat., Downey, 1978-84; prin. cons. Rockwell Internat., Seal Beach, 1984-89; cons. in electro-optical physics Karsulin Enterprises, Orange, Calif., 1989—. Contbr. articles to profl. jours. Elder Forest Dale Ch. of Christ, Cin., 1957-60, Valley Ch. of Christ, Livermore, Calif., 1964-67, East Anaheim (Calif.) Christian Ch., 1969—. 1st lt. USAAF, 1943-46, maj. USAFR. Rockefeller Found. fellow, 1955-56. Fellow AAAS, AIAA (assoc.); mem. Am. Phys. Soc., Soc. Photo-Optical Instrumentation Engrs., N.Y. Acad. Scis., Am. Nuclear Soc. Office: Karsulin Enterprises PO Box 3774 Orange CA 92865-0774

CARVER, JUANITA ASH, plastic company executive; b. Indpls., Apr. 8, 1929; d. Willard H. and Golda M. Ashe; children: Daniel Charles, Robin Lewis, Scott Alan. Student Ariz. State U., 1948, 72, Mira Mar Coll., 1994. Cons. MOBIUS, 1983—; pres. Carver Corp., Phoenix, 1977—. Bd. dirs. Scottsdale Meml. Hosp. Aux., 1964-65, now assoc. Republican. Methodist. Patentee latch hook rug Yarner, Pressure Lift. Home: 9866 Reagan Rd Apt 126 San Diego CA 92126-3143

CARVER, LOYCE CLEO, clergyman; b. Decaturville, Tenn., Dec. 13, 1918; s. Oscar Price and Mae Joanne (Chumney) C.; m. Mary Rebecca Frymire, Dec. 14, 1940; children—Judith Ann Carver Tyson, Linda Carver Sheals, Rebecca Carver Bishop. Ordained to ministry Apostolic Faith, 1947; real estate appraiser, dep. county tax assessor Klamath County, Oreg., 1943-44; bookkeeper Pacific Fruit Co., Los Angeles, Klamath Falls, Oreg., 1945-47; pastor Apostolic Faith Ch., Dallas, Oreg., 1948-49, San Francisco, 1949-52, Los Angeles, 1952-56, Medford, Oreg., 1956-65; chmn. bd. dirs. Apostolic Faith, Portland, Oreg., 1965-93; chmn. bd. dirs. World-Wide Movement, 1965-93, trustee, 1959—, pres., 1993. Served with USNR, 1944. Home: 5411 SE Duke St Portland OR 97206-6841 Office: 6615 SE 52nd Ave Portland OR 97206-7660*

CASABURI, RICHARD, respiratory and critical care physician; b. Queens, N.Y., Apr. 28, 1947; m. Mary Jane Molitor, July 3, 1976; children: James, Anne. BSEE, Rensselaer Poly. Inst., 1968, M of Engring. in Biomed. Engring., 1969, PhD in Biomed. Engring., 1971; MD, U. Miami, 1980. Bd. cert. in internal medicine and pulmonary medicine. Rsch. asst. dept. surgery Albany (N.Y.) Med. Coll., 1968-69, rsch. asst. dept. physiology, 1969-71; rsch. assoc. dept. biomed. engring. U. So. Calif., L.A., 1971-73, postdoctoral fellow in biomed. engring., 1971-73; rsch. assoc. divsn. respiratory physiology and medicine Harbor-UCLA Med. Ctr., Torrance, Calif., 1973-74, asst. prof. medicine divsn. respiratory physiology and medicine, 1974-78, 84-88, intern, 1980-81, resident in internal medicine, 1981-83, pulmonary fellow divsn. respiratory and critical care physiology and medicine, 1983-84, dir. clin. respiratory physiology lab., 1986—, assoc. prof. medicine divsn. of respiratory and critical care physiology and medicine, 1988-94, prof. medicine, 1994—, assoc. chief divsn. of respiratory and critical care physiology and medicine, 1989—; lectr. in field. Mem. editl. rev. bd. Jour. Cardiopulmonary Rehab., 1992—; mem. editl. bd. Jour. Applied Physiology, 1993-96, Am. Jour. Respiratory Critical Care Medicine, 1996—; contbr. articles to profl. jours. Pres. Pulmonary Edn. and Rsch. Found., 1993—; mem. cardiopulmonary coun. Am. Heart Assn. Tng. fellow Am. Lung Assn., 1983-85, Trudeau scholar, 1985-88; established investigator Am. Lung Assn. Calif., 1991-93. Fellow Am. Coll. Chest Physicians; mem. Am. Physiol. Soc., Am. Thoracic Soc. (respiratory and structure function assembly program com., chmn. long-range planning com. and nominating com. 1992—, co-chmn. combined Am. Thoracic Soc./Calif. Thoracic Soc. blood gas proficiency testing program 1989-94, mem. com. on proficiency stds. for clin. pulmonary function labs.), Calif. Thoracic Soc. (blood gas proficiency testing program 1987—, treas. 1994-95, sec. 1995-96, pres. elect 1996—), Sigma Xi, Tau Beta Pi, Eta Kappa Nu. Office: Harbor-UCLA Med Ctr Divsn Resp & Crit Care Mail Box 24 Torrance CA 90509-2910

CASALS, ROSEMARY, professional tennis player; b. San Francisco, Sept. 16, 1948. Profl. tennis player, 1968—; nat. championships and major tournaments include U.S. Open singles (finalist), 1970, 71, U.S. Open doubles, 1967, 71, 74, 82, U.S. Open mixed doubles, 1975, Wimbledon doubles, 1967, 68, 70, 71, 73; nat. championships and major tournaments include Wimbledon mixed doubles, 1971, 73, finalist with Dick Stockton, 1976; finalist with Dick Stockton Italian doubles, 1967, 70; finalist with Dick Stockton Family Circle Cup (winner), 1973, Wightman Cup, 1967, 76-81; Wightman Cup Bridgeston doubles championships (finalist), 1975, Spalding mixed doubles, 1976, 77, U.S. Tennis Assn. Atlanta doubles, 1976, Fedn. Cup, 1967, 76-81; winner 1st Virginia Slims tournament, 1970; 3d place Virginia Slims Championships, 1976, 4th place, 1977, 78; winner Murjani-WTA championship, 1980; Fla. Fed. Open doubles, 1980; pres. sports promotion co. Sportswoman, Inc., Sausalito, Calif., 1981—; Virginia Slims Legends Tour, 1995—. Mem. Los Angeles Strings team, World Team Tennis, 1975-77. Virginia Slims Event tennis winner, 1986, doubles winner (with Martina Navratilova), 1988, 89; inducted in to Internat. Tennis Hall of Fame, Newport, R.I., 1996. Mem. Women's Internat. Tennis Assn. (bd. dirs.). Office: Sportswoman Inc PO Box 537 Sausalito CA 94966-0537

CASANO, SALVATORE FRANK, physician; b. Chgo., Aug. 16, 1948; s. Salvatore and Rose Mary Casano; m. Freda Lois, Aug. 19, 1978; children: Ashley Rae, Sebastian Ross. BS in Biology, John Carroll U.; MD, Automous U., Guadalajara, Mex., 1975. Diplomate in gen. surgery and surg. critical care Am. Bd. Surgery. Intern Maricopa County Med. Ctr., Phoenix, 1977, resident in gen. surgery, 1978-82; pvt. practice in gen. surgery Phoenix, 1982—; trauma surgeon St. Joseph's Hosp., Phoenix, 1985—, Good Samaritan Hosp., Phoenix, 1989—. Fellow ACS, Southwestern Surg. Congress; mem. Phoenix Surg. Soc. (pres. 1993-94), Maricopa County Med. Soc., Ariz. Med. Assn. Democrat. Roman Catholic. Home: 600 W Berridge Ln Phoenix AZ 85013 Office: 333 E Virginia Ave Ste 201 Phoenix AZ 85004-1210

CÁSAREZ-LEVISON, ROSA, psychologist; b. L.A., Jan. 30, 1951; d. Juan Garcia and Felicitas (Najera) Cásarez; m. Philip M. Levison, Nov. 6, 1983 (div. Dec. 1990). BA, Pitzer Coll., 1973; MA, Claremont Grad. Sch., 1977; PhD, Stanford U., 1991. Tchr. Compton (Calif.) Unifed Sch. Dist., 1973-75; instr. San Jose (Calif.) State U., 1976-80, 82-83; rsch. asst. Stanford (Calif.) U., 1982-83; asst. prof. San Jose State U., 1991-92, Santa Clara U., 1992—; dir. student life U. Calif., Santa Cruz, 1992-93; asst. prof. San Francisco State U., 1993—; pres., founder Casarez & Assocs., Palo Alto, Calif., 1985—; expert psychologist media/TV; presenter, cons. in field; adv. mem. L.A. Piensalo Drug Prevention Campaign, 1990-91. Contbr. articles, short stories, poems to profl. publs., chpt. to book. Mem. exec. bd. San Francisco Sch. Vols., 1990-93; vol. ARC; bd. dirs. YWCA, Palo Alto, 1987-88. Digital Power grantee, 1984, Pitzer Coll. grantee, 1971-73; fellow Ford Found., 1979-81, Irvine Found., 1989. Mem. APA, Am. Coll. Forensic Examiners, Am. Ednl. Assn., Nat. Assn. Victim Assistance, Nat. Soc. Study of Edn., Nat. Assn. Gifted Children, Internat. Soc. Arts and Tech. (exec. bd. dirs. 1987—). Democrat. Roman Catholic. Office: Casarez & Assocs 360 College Ave # 1 Palo Alto CA 94306-4444 also: Casarez & Assocs PO Box 5490 Palo Alto CA 94309-5490

CASE, CHARLES CALVIN, anthropology educator; b. Tulare, Calif., Oct. 20, 1922; s. Charles Calvin and Evelyn K. (Sells) C.; m. Ramona Davis (div. 1972); children: Lisa, Cosette. BA, UCLA, 1947; MA, U. So. Calif., 1961; PhD, U. Oreg., 1968. Prof. anthropology No. Ariz. U., 1963—, U.S. Internat., Calif., 1970—. Author: Culture: The Human Plan, 1977, The Yankee Generations, 1982. With USAF, 1942-43. Fellow Am. Anthropol. Assn., Current Anthropology; mem. Am. Inst. Archeology, Etruscan Soc. Home: D-10 7858 Cowles Mountain Ct San Diego CA 92119-2543

CASE, CHARLES G., II, federal bankruptcy judge; b. Phoenix, Ariz., Jan. 17, 1948. BA cum laude, Harvard U., 1969; JD magna cum laude, Ariz. State U., 1975. Bar: Ariz. 1975. With Lewis and Roca, Phoenix, 1975-88, Meyer, Hendricks, Victor, Osborn & Maledon P.C., Phoenix, 1988-93; judge U.S. Bankruptcy Ct., Phoenix, 1994—; judge pro tempore Ariz. Ct. Appeals; adj. prof. law Ariz. State U., 1988-91, 97—. Contbg. author Comml. Law and Practice Guides, 1991. Mem. ABA.

CASE, LEE OWEN, JR., retired academic administrator; b. Ann Arbor, Mich., Nov. 5, 1925; s. Lee Owen and Ava (Comin) C.; m. Dolores Anne DeLoof, July 1950 (div. Feb. 1958); children: Lee Douglas, John Bradford; m. Maria Theresia Breninger, Feb. 27, 1960; 1 adopted dau., Ingrid Case Dunlap. AB, U. Mich., 1949. Editor Washtenaw Post-Trib, Ann Arbor, 1949; dir. pub. rels. Edison Inst., Dearborn, Mich., 1951-54; field rep. Kersting, Brown, N.Y.C., 1954-58; campaign dir. Cumerford Corp., Kansas City, Mo., 1958-59; v.p. devel., pub. rels. U. Santa Clara, 1959-69; v.p. planning, devel., Occidental Coll., L.A., 1969-90, ret., 1990; interim v.p. Inst. Advance Calif. State U., L.A., 1994.Mem. Sr. Cons. Network. Chmn. Santa Clara City Proposition A, 1966; mem. Santa Clara County Planning Com. on Taxation and Legis., Santa Clara, 1968. Served to 1st lt. USAAF, 1943-46. Mem. Am. Coll. Pub. Relations Assn. (bd. dirs. 1968-74), Council for Advancement and Support Edn. (founding bd. dirs. 1974-75), 1st Tribute for Distinction in Advancement, Dist. VII, 1985), Santa Clara C. of C. (pres. 1967), Santa Clara County C. of C. (founding bd. dirs. 1968), Aviation Pioneers Assn. Republican. Lodge: Rotary. Home and Office: 2633 Risa Dr Glendale CA 91208-2355

CASE, PATRICIA SULLIVAN, mental health counselor, educator; b. Ft. Worth, Aug. 1, 1946; d. Elmer Dudley Sullivan and Minnie Jo Crittenden Bennett; m. John Philip Case, July 5, 1985. AA, Scottsdale (Ariz.) C.C., 1978; BS, Ariz. State U., 1980, M of Counseling, 1984; PhD, Walden U., Mpls., 1993. Diplomate Nat. Bd. Cert. Counselors; cert. counselor, Ariz.; cert. cmty. coll. counselor. Counselor in pvt. practice Scottsdale, 1984-88; adj. faculty Maricopa C.C.s, Phoenix, 1984-90; area ctrl. cons. Rio Salado C.C., Phoenix, 1987-89, adminstr. asst., 1989-90, faculty, counselor, dept. chair., 1990—; treas. Ariz. Behavioral Health Credentialing Task Force, 1987-89, chair, 1989-91. Mem. ACA, Ariz. Counselors (pres. Ctrl. chpt. 1986-87, govt. liaison 1987-88, pres.-elect 1989), Outstanding Contbn. to Counseling Profession award 1987), Ariz. Mental Health Counselors Assn. (treas. 1985-86), Rio Salado C.C. Faculty Assn. (pres. 1994-96). Office: Rio Salado Coll 2323 W 14th St Tempe AZ 85281

CASE, ROCKY CECIEL, finance company executive; b. Worland, Wyo., Aug. 12, 1949; s. Leslie Charles and Helen Jewel (Williams) C.; m. Judy Ann Agee, Aug. 25, 1971; children: Tiffany Jo Mossey, Eric William, Rocky Shane. AA, Laramie County C.C., Cheyenne, Wyo., 1986. CFP, Wyo. Plant mgr. Cheyenne Cable TV, 1969-84; v.p. Wyo. Deferred Compensation, Inc., Cheyenne, 1985—; chmn. publicity com. U.S.S. Cheyenne. Author numerous poems and short stories. Dir. Boys & Girls Club Cheyenne, 1997—. Mem. Nat. Assn. Life Underwriters, Cheyenne C. of C. (vice chmn. USS Cheyenne com. 1997, mil. affairs com.), Rotary (chmn. youth exch. 1992-95, bd. dirs. 1995—), Nat. Assn. Govt. Deferred Compensation Adminstrs. (audit and fin. com.). Home: 1201 W 8th Ave Cheyenne WY 82001

CASERIO, MARJORIE CONSTANCE, academic administrator; b. London, Feb. 26, 1929; came to U.S., 1953; d. Herbert C. and Doris May (House) Beckett; m. Frederick F. Jr. Caserio, Mar. 9, 1957; children: Brian, Alan. BSc in Chemistry, U. London, 1950; MA in Organic Chemistry, Bryn Mawr Coll., 1951, PhD in Organic Chemistry, 1956. Rsch. chemist Fulmer Rsch. Inst., Buckinghamsnire, Eng., 1952-53; post-doctoral fellow Calif. Inst. Tech., Pasadena, 1956-59, sr. rsch. fellow, 1959-65; from. asst. prof. to prof. chemistry U. Calif., Irvine, 1965-90, chair dept. chemistry, 1987-90; vice-chancellor academic affairs U. Calif., San Diego, 1990-95, interim chancellor, 1995-96, prof. emeritus, 1990—. Contbr. articles to profl. jours. Recipient Cert. of Achievement, Leadership of Women Orange County, 1983; Sir John Dill scholar, 1950; Fulbright travel award, 1950; Guggenheim fellow, 1975-76. Fellow AAAS; mem. Am. Chem. Soc. (Garvan medal 1975) Grad. Women in Sci. (hon.), Sigma Xi. Office: U Calif San Diego Dept Chemistry/Biochemistry La Jolla CA 92093

CASEY, DANIEL E., psychiatrist, educator; b. West Springfield, Mass., Jan. 24, 1947; s. Arthur and Gloria Casey; m. Lenka Casey. BA in Psychology, U. Va., 1969, MD, 1972. Resident in psychiatry U. Oreg., Portland, 1973-74, Brown U., Providence, 1974-76; affiliate sci. Oreg. Regional Primate Rsch. Ctr., Portland, 1980—; staff psychiatrist VA. Med. Ctr., Portland, 1976—, chief psychiatry rsch., psychopharmacology, 1980—; prof. psychiatry Oreg. Health Scis. U., Portland, 1985—, prof. neurology, 1992—; pres., bd. dirs. Danicas Found., Portland. Author books; Contbr. over 165 articles to profl. jours. Office: VA Med Ctr Psychiatry Svc 3710 SW Us Veterans Hospital Rd Portland OR 97201-2964

CASEY, JAMES LEROY, curriculum director; b. Bigham, Ill., July 6, 1942; s. Truman Alva and Juanita Clara (Boaz) C.; m. Kazuko Casey, Dec. 26, 1963. BA, Sophia U., Tokyo, 1974; MS in Edn., U. Soc. Calif., 1976, EdD, 1992. Enlisted USAF, 1959, rose through ranks to Master Sgt., retired, 1983; tchr. English as a fgn. lang. Wakanai H.S., Japan, 1964, Chitose (Japan) Am. Lang. Inst., 1970-72, Tomakami (Japan) Jr. Coll., 1972, Sophia U., Tokyo, 1973-75; pers. mgr. and tchr. English as fgn. lang. Berkeley House Lang., Tokyo, 1982-88; curriculum dir. Mid Pacific Coll., Honolulu, Hawaii, 1992—. Mem. VFW, Tokyo, (cmmdr. post 9450 Tokyo 1984-85, cmmdr. Japan dist. 1985-86, chaplin dept. Pacific area 1987-88), Elks (scholarship chmn. 1995—, dist. scholarship chmn. 1996—). Lutheran. Home: 94 619 Palai St Waipahu HI 96797

CASEY, JOSEPH T., corporate executive; b. 1931; married. B.S., Fordham U. With Arrow Surgical Supply Co., 1947-51, Am. Lumberman's Mutual Casualty Co. of Ill., 1951-52, Thoroughbred Racing Protective Bur. Inc., 1952-55; mgr. audits Touche, Ross, Bailey & Smart, 1955-63; controller Litton Industries Inc., Beverly Hills, Calif., 1963-67, v.p. fin., 1967-69, sr. v.p. fin., 1969-76, exec. v.p. fin., 1976-91, CFO, 1991-94, chmn. exec. com., 1994-96, also bd. dirs.; vice chmn. and CFO Western Atlas, Inc., Beverly Hills, Calif., 1994-96; bd. dirs. Litton Industries, Inc., Western Atlas Inc. Bd. trustees Don Bosco Tech. Inst., 1971—, Claremont McKenna Coll., 1989—. Office: Western Atlas Inc 360 N Crescent Dr Beverly Hills CA 90210-4802

CASEY, PAUL ARNOLD, writer, composer, photographer; b. Inglewood, Calif., Dec. 10, 1934; s. Paul Franklyn and Orilee Corinne (Gray) C. AA, UCLA, BA. Pres., genetics cons. CSCA Internat., Sun Valley, Calif.; pres., tech. advisor Solenz Corp., Wilmington, Del.; dramaturg L.A. Playwrights Group, 1996. Author poetry: Songs of Youth, 1951; photographer wildlife: Girl Scouts Calendar, 1995; developer breed of cat: Calif. Spangled, 1971-86; inventor power lens, 1967. With USN, 1953-54. Recipient Nat. Humane Soc. award, 1965; U.S. Govt. scholar, 1954. Mem. L.A. Playwrights Group (gen. sec. 1995-96). Office: CSCA International PO Box 368 Sun Valley CA 91352

CASH, R. D., natural gas and oil executive; b. Shamrock, Tex., 1942. BSIE, Tex. Tech U., 1966. With Amoco Prodn. Co., 1966-76; v.p. Mountain Fuel Supply Co. subs. Questar Corp., 1976-79, pres., CEO, 1980-84, now also chmn. bd.; pres. Wexpro Co., 1979-80; pres., CEO Questar Corp., 1984—, also chmn. bd., 1985—. Office: Questar Pipeline Co 79 S State St Salt Lake City UT 84111-1517*

CASHATT, CHARLES ALVIN, retired hydro-electric power generation company executive; b. Jamestown, N.C., Nov. 14, 1929; s. Charles Austin and Ethel Buren (Brady) C.; m. Wilma Jean O'Hagan, July 10, 1954; children: Jerry Dale, Nancy Jean. Grad. high sch., Jamestown. Bldg. contractor, Jamestown, 1949-50; 1954-58; powerhouse foreman Tri-Dam Project, Strawberry, Calif., 1958-66; power project mgr. Merced Irrigation Dist., Calif., 1966-92; ret. 1992; mem. U.S. com. large dams, 1988-92. Contbr. articles to ASCE pub. and books. Pres. Merced County Credit Union, 1981-82. Served with USAF, 1950-54. Mem. Am. Legion. Republican. Lodge: Elks, Odd Fellows.

CASHMAN, MICHAEL RICHARD, small business owner; b. Owatonna, Minn., Sept. 26, 1926; s. Michael Richard and Mary (Quinn) C.; m. Antje Katrin Paulus, Jan. 22, 1972 (div. 1983); children: Janice Katrin, Joshua Paulus, Nina Carolin. BS, U.S. Mcht. Marine Acad., 1947; BA, U. Minn., 1951; MBA, Harvard U., 1953. Regional mgr. Air Products & Chems., Inc., Allentown, Pa., 1959-64; then pres. so. div. Air Products & Chems., Inc., Washington, 1964-68; mng. dir. Air Products & Chems., Inc. Europe, Brussels, 1968-72; internat. v.p. Airco Indsl. Gasses, Brussels, 1972-79; pres. Continental Elevator Co., Denver, 1979-81; assoc. Moore & Co., Denver, 1981-84; prin. Cashman & Co., Denver, 1984—. Committeeman Denver Rep. Com., 1986—, congl. candidate, 1988; chmn. "Two Forks or Dust" Ad Hoc Citizens Com.. Lt. (j.g.) USN, 1953-55. Mem. Bldg. Owners and Mgrs. Assn., Colo. Harvard Bus. Sch. Club, Am. Rights Union, Royal Golf de Belgique, Belgian Shooting Club, Rotary, Soc. St. George, Phi Beta Kappa. Home: 2512 S University Blvd Apt 802 Denver CO 80210-6152

CASPER, GERHARD, academic administrator, law educator; b. Hamburg, Germany, Dec. 25, 1937; s. Heinrich and Hertha C.; m. Regina Koschel, Dec. 26, 1964; 1 child, Hanna. Legal state exam., U. Freiburg, U. Hamburg, 1961; LL.M., Yale U., 1962; Dr.iur., U. Freiburg, Germany, 1964. Asst. prof. polit. sci. U. Calif., Berkeley, 1964-66; assoc. prof. law and polit. sci. U. Chgo., 1966-69, prof., 1969-76, Max Pam prof. law, 1976-80, William B. Graham prof. law, 1980-87, William B. Graham Disting. Svc. prof. law, 1987-92, dean law sch., 1979-87, provost, 1989-92; prof. law Stanford (Calif.) U., 1992—, pres., 1992—; vis. prof. law Cath. U., Louvain, Belgium, 1970, U. Munich, 1988, 91; bd. dirs. Ency. Britannica. Author: Realism and Political Theory in American Legal Thought, 1967, (with Richard A. Posner) The Workload of the Supreme Court, 1976; co-editor: The Supreme Ct. Rev., 1977-91. Fellow Am. Acad. Arts and Scis.; mem. Internat. Acad. Comparative Law, Am. Bar Found. (bd. dirs. 1979-87), Coun. Fgn. Rels., Am. Law Inst. (coun. 1980—), Oliver Wendell Holmes Devise (permanent com. 1985—). *

CASPERS, CORLYN MARIE, adult nurse practitioner; b. Breckenridge, Minn., Aug. 24, 1964; d. Wilbur Richard Caspers and Coralee Meredith (Warner) Fries; m. Rodney Ralph Kolkow, May 1, 1993; children: Megan, Laura. BSN, Oreg. Inst. Tech., 1986; MS, U. Portland (Oreg.), 1994. RN, registered adult nurse practitioner. Hospice primary care nurse Klamath (Oreg.) Hospice, 1985-93; clin. mgr. Merle West Med. Ctr., Klamath Falls, 1989, primary care nurse, 1986-94; home health nurse Merle West Med. Ctr., 1988-94; nurse practitioner, clinician coll. health svcs. Oreg. Inst. Tech., Klamath Falls, 1994—; sub-chmn. quality assurance and standards com., 1989, nursing edn. coun., preceptor Merle West Med. Ctr., 1988-94; interim nursing instr. Oreg. Health Scis. U. Sch. Nursing, Oreg. Inst. Tech., 1996.

CASSEL, SUSIE LAN, literature educator; b. Monrovia, Liberia, Sept. 30, 1966; d. Russell Napoleon and Lan Mieu (Dam) C. BA, U. So. Calif., 1986, U. So. Calif., 1987; MA in English, Harvard U., 1988; PhD in English Lit., U. Calif., Riverside, 1996. Prof. English Calif. State U., San Marcos, 1996—. Capt. USAF, 1988-91, res. Mem. Mod. Lang. Assn., Asian Am. Studies Assn., Chinese Hist. Soc. Am., Multi-ethnic Lit. of U.S. Assn.

CASSELL, BEVERLY ANNE, artist, art association executive; b. Montgomery, Ala., Jan. 20, 1936; d. William Duhenfort and Mildred Lucile (Taylor) Bach; m. Dennis Don Cassell, May 17, 1968 (div. Mar. 1972); m. Jesiah C. Venger, Aug. 30, 1989; stepchildren: Jamie Lewis, Tad, Ty Venger. BA, Birmingham So. Coll., 1958; MFA, U. Ga., 1960; postgrad., NYU, 1963. Tchr. drawing and painting U. Colo., Denver, 1967-69, Temple-Buell Coll., Denver, 1968-71; tchr. drawing and painting U. Calif., Santa Cruz, 1972-81, L.A., 1986-89; founder, dir. Artist Conf. Network, 1983—; lectr. art Getty Mus. Edn. Series, L.A., 1992. Works have appeared in shows including Art Mus. of Santa Cruz, Calif., 1984, 85, Taiwan Mus. Art, Taichung, 1989, Nagasaki (Japan) Mus. Art, 1992, 93, 94, 95, 96, L.A. (Calif.) County Mus. Art, 1992, Hanlim Gallery, Tae Jeon, Korea, 1994; spl. guest: (tv show) Women in Contemporary Art, L.A., 1988; set design: Disney Studios, 1990. Bd. dirs. Judson Arts Coun., N.Y.C., 1961-64, L.A. Artcore, 1990-92; mem. L.A. (Calif.) Arts Coun., 1986-89; youth enrollment team Youth at Risk, L.A., 1987-89; dir. L.A. (Calif.) Inner-City Youth Water Sculpture Project, 1990-92. Mem. Mortar Bd. Home and Office: Artist Conf Network 2202 W 20th St Los Angeles CA 90018-1408

CASSENS, NICHOLAS, JR., ceramics engineer; b. Sigourney, Iowa, Sept. 8, 1948; s. Nicholas and Wanda Fern (Lancaster) C.; B.S. in Ceramic Engring., Iowa State U., 1971, B.S. in Chem. Engring., 1971; M.S. in Material Sci. and Engring., U. Calif., Berkeley, 1979; m. Linda Joyce Morrow, Aug. 30, 1969; 1 son, Randall Scott, Jr. research engr. Nat. Refractories and Minerals Corp., Livermore, Calif., 1971-72, research engr., 1972-74, sr. research engr., 1974-77, staff research engr., 1977-84, sr. staff research engr., 1984—. Mem. Am. Ceramic Soc. Democrat. Patentee in field, U.S., Australia, S.Am., Japan, Europe. Home: 4082 Suffolk Way Pleasanton CA 94588-4117 Office: 1852 Rutan Dr Livermore CA 94550-7635

CASSIDY, BARRY ALLEN, physician assistant, clinical medical ethicist; b. Chgo., Aug. 28, 1947; s. Frank Thomas and Ann Marie (Panek) C.; m. JoAnn DeRue (div.); m. Robin G. Lacher (div.); children: Colleen Osmond, Jason Lacher, Nathaniel Austin; m. Barbie A. Cassidy. Cert. physician assoc., Duke U., 1971; BS, Univ. State N.Y., Albany, 1992; PhD, Union Inst., 1995. Cert. physician asst. Physician assoc. Med. Offices of T.C. Rozema, MD, Waukegan, Ill., 1971-73; instr. in healthcare sci. Sch. Medicine George Washington U., Washington, 1973-75; med. cons. Medicolegal Rsch., Washington, 1975-79; CEO, dir. health svcs. Occucare, Inc., Research Triangle Park, N.C., 1979-81; v.p. Coastal Group, Inc., Durham, N.C., 1981-82; exec. v.p. So. Emergency Med. Assocs., Research Triangle Park, 1982-83; physician asst. Ariz. Heart Inst., Phoenix, 1983-86; pres. West Health Corp., Phoenix, 1986-87; thoracic and cardiovascular surgery asst. Mayo Clinic, Scottsdale, Ariz., 1987-96; assoc. prof., assoc. dir. physician asst. program Coll. Allied Health Scis. Midwestern U., Glendale, Ariz., 1996—; adj. faculty S.W. Ctr. for Osteo. Med. Edn. and Health Scis., 1995-96. Mem. editl. bd. Physician Assts. in Primary Care, 1985-88; inventor break-away catheter sys. Advisor on allied health Ill. Med. Soc., Chgo., 1972; advisor Gov.'s Health Licensure Commn., State of Ill., Chgo., 1972. Sgt. USAF, 1965-69. Mem. Ariz. Med. Assn., Ariz. Acad. Physician Assts., Hastings Ctr. for Med. Ethics (assoc.), Am. Soc. Law, Medicine and Ethics, Am. Acad. Physician Assts. (chmn. jud. affairs com., v.p. 1974). Jewish. Home: 6630 E Lafayette Scottsdale AZ 85251 Office: Midwestern U Coll Allied Health Scis 19555 N 59th Ave Glendale AZ 85308

CASSIDY, DONALD LAWRENCE, former aerospace company executive; b. Stamford, Conn., May 26, 1933; s. John Dingee and Ursula Agnes (Lynch) C. BS, MIT, 1954; grad. mgmt. policy inst., U. Southern Calif., L.A., 1973. Jr. exec. Johns-Manville Corp., N.Y.C., 1954-55; contracting officer U.S. Army Signal Corps Electric Lab., Ft. Monmouth, N.J., 1955-57; with contract dept. field svc. and support div. Hughes Aircraft Co., L.A., 1957-69, mgr. contracts support systems, 1969-78; dir. contracts Hughes Aircraft Co., Long Beach, Calif., 1978-87, group v.p. bus. ops., 1987, v.p., chief contracts officer, 1987-92. 1st lt. U.S. Army, 1955-57. Mem. Am. Def. Preparedness Assn. (L.A. chpt. bd. dirs.), Nat. Contract Mgmt. Assn., Nat. Security Indsl. Assn., Aerospace Industries Assn. (procurement finance coun. exec. group). Republican.

CASSIDY, RICHARD ARTHUR, environmental engineer, governmental water resources specialist; b. Manchester, N.H., Nov. 15, 1944; s. Arthur Joseph and Alice Ethuliette (Gregoire) C.; m. Judith Diane Maine, Aug. 14, 1971; children: Matthew, Amanda, Michael. BA, St. Anselm Coll., 1966; MS, U. N.H., 1969, Tufts U., 1972. Field biologist Pub. Service Co. of N.H., Manchester, 1968; jr. san. engr. Mass. Div. Water Pollution Control, Boston, 1968-69; aquatic biologist Normandeau Assocs., Bedford, N.H., 1969-70; hydraulic engr. New Eng. div. U.S. Army C.E., Waltham, Mass., 1972-77, environ. engr., Portland Dist., Oreg., 1977-81, supr., environ. engr., 1981—. Contbr. articles to books and profl. jours. Den leader Pack 164 and 598 Columbia Pacific council Cub Scouts Am., Beaverton, Oreg., 1982-83, Webelos leader, 1984-85, 90-91, troop 764 committeeman, 1985-87, asst. scoutmaster, 1992, scoutmaster, 1993-94 troup 598 scoutmaster, 1995—, Columbia Pacific council Boy Scouts Am., 1985-87; mem. Planning Commn. Hudson, N.H., 1976-77. Recipient commendation for exemplary performance Mo.-Miss. flood, 1973, commendation for litigation defense, 1986, commendation for mgmt. activities, 1987, 91. Mem. Am. Inst. Hydrology (cert., profl. ethics com. 1986, v.p. Oreg. sect. 1987-89, pres. Oreg. sect. 1990-92, nat. treas. 1995—), Internat. Tng in Communication (pres. West Way Club 1989-90), N.Am. Lake Mgmt. Soc. Democrat. Roman Catholic. Home: 7655 SW Belmont Dr Beaverton OR 97008-6335 Office: Portland Dist CE Chief Reservoir Reg & Water Quality PO Box 2946 Portland OR 97208

CASSIDY, SAMUEL H., lawyer, lieutenant governor, state legislator; m. Jillian Jacobellis; children: Rachael Kathryn, Sarah Woyneve, Alexandra, Samuel H. IV. BA, U. Okla., 1972; JD, U. Tulsa, 1975; postgrad., Harvard U., 1991. Bar: Okla., 1975, U.S. Supreme Ct. 1977, U.S. Ct. Appeals (10th cir.), 1977, Colo. 1982. Ptnr. Cassidy, Corely & Ganem, Tulsa, 1975-77, Seigel, Cassidy & Oakley, Tulsa, 1977-79, Beustring, Cassidy, Faulkner & Assocs., Tulsa, 1979-82; pvt. practice Pagosa Springs, Colo., 1982-94; mem. Colo. State Senate, 1991-94; lt. gov. State of Colo., 1994-95; pres. Jefferson Econ. Coun., 1995—; bd. dirs. Capital Reporter; instr. U. Tulsa, 1978-81, Tulsa Jr. Coll., 1979; owner High Country Title Co.; developer Townhome Property, Mountain Vista; ptnr. Hondo's Inc.; pres. Sam Cassidy, Inc., mem. agriculture and natural resources com. 1991-92, state, mil. and vet. affairs com., 1991-92, local govt. com. 1991, legal svcs. com. 1991-92, hwy. legis. review com. 1991-93, nat. hazards mitigation coun., 1992-93, appropriations com., 1993, judiciary com., 1993; v.p. Econ. Devel. Coun. of Colo., 1993—;exec. com. legis. coun., 1993-94, senate svcs. com. 1993; elected Senate Minority Leader, 1993-94, exec. com. Colo. Gen. Assembly. Mem. State Dem. Ctr. Com., 1987-95; bd. dirs. Colo. DLC, 1993-95, Leadership Jefferson County, Rocky Flats Local Impacts Initiative, dir.; chmn. bd. Arts Comm., Inc.; v.p. Econ. Devel. Coun. Colo. Named Outstanding Legislator for 1991 Colo. Bankers Assn., ACLU Outstanding Legis. 1994; recipient Outsatnding Legis. Efforts award Colo. Counties, Guardian of Small Bus. award, NFIB, 1992, 94; fellow Gates Found., 1991, U. Denver sr. fellow. Mem. Colo. Bar Assn. (bd. gov. 1993-94), S.W. Colo. Bar Assn., Nat. Conf. State Legis. (Colo. rep., task force on state-tribe rels.), Rotary (hon. mem., sustaining Paul Harris fellow), Club 20 (bd. dirs.), San Juan Forum (chmn., bd. dirs.). Home: 1390 Ash St Denver CO 80220-2409 Office: 1536 Cole Blvd Ste 100 Golden CO 80401-3413 *Leaders must nurture the positive in people's characters, their concern for the whole community, not just their personal welfare; the future of their grandchildren, not their own tomorrow. This is a vision which is hard to sell next November but which clearly distinguishes leaders from politicians.*

CAST, PATRICIA WYNNE, writer, former nun, executive secretary; b. London, July 2, 1931; came to U.S., 1952; d. Albert James and Norah (Wynne) C. BA in Modern Lang. with honors, Birmingham U., 1952. Sec. Exec. Office of Sec. Gen., UN, N.Y.C., 1953-57; novice mistress Carmelite Monastery, N.Y.C., 1957-70; personnel dir. Knutsen Cos., Inc., Mpls., 1973-74; mgr. Working Horse Trust, Sussex, Eng., 1988-91; ret., 1993. Author: Trees for the Forest, 1978, Diptych, 1993, Writings of the Sun, 1994, Arts of Decay, 1995, Shadows of the Moon, 1996; translator: Life of Céline Martin, 1962; contbr. articles to mags. Organizer UNICEF, Robertsbridge, Sussex, 1987. Mem. Assn. Contemplative Sisters (founder). Roman Catholic. Home: 120 B Fiesta St Santa Fe NM 87501

CASTALDI, GWEN, journalist; b. Cleve., Mar. 15, 1952; d. John Wilson and Anna Marie (Dawley) Rupert; m. Ralph Anthony Toddre, May 9, 1981 (div. 1988). Student, Cleve. State U., 1970-71. Reporter, photographer Euclid (Ohio) News Jour., 1971; musician, pianist, singer, 1971-74; reporter, copy editor Sta. KBMI All News Radio, Las Vegas, 1975-76, reporter, assignment editor, 1976; reporter, news anchor Sta. KSHO TV, Las Vegas, 1976; promotion asst. Las Vegas Rev.-Jour., 1977; news dir. Sta. KNUUS All News Radio, Las Vegas, 1977; news reporter, pub. affairs show host Sta. KLAS TV, Las Vegas, 1977-80; news reporter Sta. WBBM-TV, Chgo., 1980; news reporter, anchor Sta. KVBC-TV, Las Vegas, 1981—. Contbr. articles to newspapers and mags. Judge Bicentennial Com., Las Vegas, 1987—; bd. dirs. Arthritis Found., Las Vegas, 1986-87; mem. historic preservation com. City of Las Vegas, 1993-95; mem. mus. and history bd. State of Nev., 1992-93; panel moderator Gov.'s Conf. on Victim's Rights, 1986; panelist numerous orgns.; speaker, host for numerous community groups including United Blood Svcs., Am. Cancer Soc., Am. Heart Assn., C. of C., Children's Miracle Network Telethons, United Way, others. Recipient numerous awards for journalism So. Nev. Journalism awards, UPI, AP, Emmy, 1995, NATAS (San Diego chpt.). Mem. NATAS (San Diego chpt.), Women in Comm., Profl. Soc. Journalists, Sigma Delta Chi (past pres., v.p.). Office: Sta KVBC TV 3 1500 Foremaster Ln Las Vegas NV 89101-1103

CASTANEDA, CARLOS, anthropologist, author; b. Sao Paulo, Brazil, Dec. 25, 1931; s. C.N. and Susana (Aranha) C. BA, UCLA, Los Angeles, 1962; MA, UCLA, 1964, PhD, 1970. Apprentice to Yaqui Indian sorcerer, five years; now anthropologist. Author: The Teachings of Don Juan: A Yaqui Way of Knowledge, 1968, A Separate Reality: The Phenomenology of Special Consensus, 1971, Journey to Ixtlan, 1974, Tales of Power, 1975, The Second Ring of Power, 1977, The Eagle's Gift, 1982, The Fire from Within, 1984, The Power of Silence: Further Lessons of Don Juan, 1987, The Art of Dreaming, 1993. Office: TOHCC Artists 813 N Martel Ave Los Angeles CA 90046-7508

CASTBERG, ANTHONY DIDRICK, political science educator, researcher; b. San Francisco, Apr. 1, 1941; s. Robert Stabell and Juliet Louise (Evans) C.; m. Harolyn Dang, Dec. 22, 1963 (div. Feb. 1977); 1 child, Beth Kehaulani Mei-Lin; m. Juan Kazu Eguchi, Dec. 30, 1977. BA, U. Hawaii, 1963, MA, 1966; PhD, Northwestern U., 1968. Asst. prof. polit. sci. Calif. State U., L.A., 1968-72, assoc. prof. polit. sci., 1972-76; prof. polit. sci. U. Hawaii, Hilo, 1974—. Author: Cases on Constitutional Law, 1973, Japanese Criminal Justice, 1990; contbr. articles to profl. jours. Russell Sage Found. fellow Northwestrn U., 1966-68, Fulbright Found. fellow, 1987-88. Mem. Law and Soc. Assn., Res. Officers Assn., U.S. Naval Inst. Office: U Hawaii at Hilo 200 W Kawili St Hilo HI 96720-4075

CASTBERG, EILEEN SUE, construction company owner; b. Santa Monica, Calif., Mar. 12, 1946; d. George Leonard and Irma (Loretta) Conroy; m. David Christopher Castberg, Oct. 27, 1967; children: Eric, Christopher. Grad. high sch., U. High Sch., L.A., 1964; certificate, Anthony Schs., 1990. Lic. real estate agt., Calif. Exec., co-founder Advanced Connector Telesis, Inc., Santa Ana, Calif., 1986-87; exec. Western Energy Engrs., Inc., Costa Mesa, Calif., 1987-89; owner Dave Castberg and Assoc., Inc., Ramona, Calif., 1989 --; cons. Watt Asset Mgmt., Santa Monica, 1990-91. Mem. choir Ramona Luth. Ch.; 3d v.p. Holy Cross Luth. Ch. Women's League, Cypress, Calif., 1983; adv. dir. San Diego Country Estates Timeshare. Mem. San Diego Bd. Realtors, Ramona Real Estate Assn. (bd. dirs.), Intermountain Rep. Women's Fedn. (pres.), Ramona Christian Women's Club, San Vicente Valley Club (corr. sec.). Republican.

CASTELLANO, JOSEPH ANTHONY, chemist, management consulting firm executive; b. N.Y.C., Oct. 28, 1937; s. Joseph John and Marie Antoinette (Gallo) C.; m. Rosalie Ann Fantaci, Aug. 28, 1960; children: Joseph, Thomas, Laura. BS in Chemistry, CCNY, 1959; MS in Chemistry, Poly. Inst. N.Y., 1964, PhD in Chemistry, 1969. Cert. profl. chemist; cert. community coll. instr. Research chemist Witco Chem. Co., Paterson, N.J., 1959-62; sr. research chemist Thiokol Chem. Corp., Denville, N.J., 1962-65; mem. tech. staff, project mgr. RCA Labs., Princeton, N.J., 1965-73; chmn., CEO Princeton Materials Sci., 1973-75; ops. mgr. Fairchild Camera and Inst. Corp., Palo Alto, Calif., 1975-77; mgr. ops. Kylex, Mt. View, Calif., 1977-78; pres. Stanford Resources, San Jose, Calif., 1978—; cons. scientist Princeton U., 1970-72; lectr. Rutgers U., Kent State U., SUNY-Binghamton, NASA Research Ctr., USAF Materials Lab., Office Naval Research, IBM Research Ctrs., RCA Labs., Motorola and various profl. and trade assns. Author: Handbook of Display Technology, 1992; publisher: Electronic Display World, The Electronic Display Industry Svc.; contbr. articles to profl. jours.; patents in field. Recipient RCA Doctoral Study award, RCA Labs. Outstanding Achievement award Indsl. Rsch. mag.'s IR-100 award, David Sarnoff Team award in Sci. Fellow Am. Inst. Chemists; mem. AAAS, Am. Chem. Soc., Am. Assn. Advancement Sci., N.Y. Acad. Sci., Royal Chem. Soc., Soc. Info. Display, Profl. and Tech. Cons. Assn., Soc. Tech. Comm., N.Y. Acad. Sci., Sigma Xi. Roman Catholic. Home: 7017 Elmsdale Dr San Jose CA 95120-3225 Office: Stanford Resources Inc PO Box 20324 San Jose CA 95160-0324

CASTELLANO, MICHAEL ANGELO, research forester; b. Bklyn., June 26, 1956; s. Biagio and Mildred Anne (Cucco) C.; m. Elizabeth Marie Phillips, July 14, 1979; children: Nicholas Aaron, Daniel Robert Feller, Kelly Marie, Katlyn Morgan. AAS, Paul Smiths Coll., 1978; BS, Oreg. State U., 1982, MS, 1984, PhD, 1988. Forest technician Weyerhauser Co., Columbus, Miss., 1979; forester trainee USDA Forest Svc., Pacific N.W., Corvallis, Oreg., 1980-84, forester, 1984-87, rsch. forester, 1987—; cons. CSIRO, Div. of Forestry, Australia, 1988-95, Spanish-Am. Binational Prog., Barcelona, 1987, 91. Author: Key to Hypogeous Fungi, 1989, (agr. handbook) Mycorrhizae, 1989; contbr. articles to profl. jours. Bishop LSD Ch. Named one of Outstanding Young Men, Am. JayCees, 1984. Mem. Soc. Am. Foresters, N.Am. Truffling Soc. (advisor), Soil Ecology Soc., Mycol. Soc. of Am. (nomenclature 1986), Sigma Xi. Home: 1835 NW Garfield Ave Corvallis OR 97330-2535 Office: USDA Forest Svc 3200 SW Jefferson Way Corvallis OR 97331-8550

CASTELLANO, VALEN EDWARD, biologist; b. Seattle, July 4, 1954; s. Edward Joseph and Florence Marie(Beaudette) C.; m. Mary Joan Coakley, Mar. 5, 1989. BS, Humboldt State U., 1980; MPA, Calif. State U., Turlock, 1995. Fisheries Aide Calif. Dept. Fish & Game, Eureka, 1980-81; rsch. asst. Oreg. Coop. Wildlife Rsch. Unit, Corvallis, 1981-84; fisheries tech. Coastal Fisheries Divsn. Tex. Parks & Wildlife Dept., Seabrook, 1984-86; fgn. fisheries observer Oreg. State U. Nat. Marine Fisheries Svc., Seattle, 1986-87; wildlife control agt. Wash. Dept. Wildlife, Olympia, 1988-89; agrl. biologist Merced Co. Dept. Agrl., Los Banos, Calif., 1989—. Mem. Am. Soc. Pub. Adminstrn., The Wildlife Soc. Office: Merced County Dept Agrl 342 D St Los Banos CA 93635-5402

CASTELLINI, PATRICIA BENNETT, business management educator; b. Park River, N.D., Mar. 25, 1935; d. Benjamin Beekman Bennett and Alice Catherine (Peerboom) Bennett Breckinridge; m. William McGregor Castellini; children: Bruce Bennett Subhani, Barbara Lea Ragland. AA, Allan Hancok Coll., Santa Maria, Calif., 1964; BS magna cum laude, Coll. Great Falls, 1966; MS, U N D., 1967, PhD, 1971. Fiscal acct. USIA, Washington, 1954-56; pub. acct., Bremerton, Wash., 1956; statistician USN, Bremerton, 1957-59; med. svcs. accounts officer U.S. Air Force, Vandenberg AFB, Calif., 1962-64; instr. bus. adminstrn. Western New Eng. Coll., 1967-69; vis. prof. econs. Chapman Coll., 1970; vis. prof. U. So. Calif. systems Griffith AFB, N.Y., 1971-72; assoc. prof., dir. adminstrv. mgmt. program Va. State U., 1973-74; assoc. prof. bus. adminstrn. Oreg. State U., Corvallis, 1974-81, prof. mgmt., 1982-90, emeritus prof. mgmt., 1990—, univ. curriculum coord., 1984-86, dir. adminstrv. mgmt. program, 1974-81, pres. Faculty Senate, 1981, Interinstl. Faculty Senate, 1986-90, pres., 1989-90; exec. dir. Bus. Enterprise Ctr., 1990-92, Enterprise Ctr. L.A., Inc., 1992-95, Castellini Co., 1995—; commr. Lafayette Econ. Devel. Authority, 1994—, treas., 1995-96, vice chm. 1996-97; cons. process tech. devel. Digital Equipment Corp., 1982. Pres., chmn. bd. dirs. Adminstrv. Orgnl. Svcs., Inc., Corvallis, 1976-83, Dynamic Achievement, Inc., 1983-92; bd. dirs. Oreg. State U. Bookstores, Inc., 1987-90, Internat. Trade Devel. Group, 1992-97, BBB of Acadiana, 1994—, sec., 1995, vice chmn. 1996, chmn. 1997; cons. Oregonians in Action, 1990-91. Cert. adminstrv. mgr. Pres. TYEE Mobil Home Park, Inc., 1987-92. Fellow Assn. Bus. Communication (mem. internat. bd. 1980-83, v.p. Northwest 1981, 2d v.p. 1982-83, 1st v.p. 1983-84, pres. 1984-85); mem. Am. Bus. Women's Assn. (chpt. v.p. 1979, pres. 1980, named Top Businesswoman in Nation 1980, Bus. Assoc. Yr. 1986), Assn. Info. Systems Profls., Adminstrv. Mgmt. Soc., AAUP (chpt. sec. 1973, chpt. bd. dirs. 1982, 84-89, pres. Oreg. conf. 1983-85, profls. chpt. 1985-86, administrv.), Am. Vocat. Assn. (nominating com. 1976), Associated Oreg. Faculties, Nat. Bus. Edn. Assn., Nat. Assn. Tchr. Edn. for Bus. Office Edn. (pres. 1976-77, chmn. public relations com. 1978-81), La. Bus. Incubation Assn. (sec.-treas. 1993-95), Corvallis Area C. of C. (v.p. chamber devel. 1987-88, pres. 1988-89, chmn. bd. 1989-90, Pres.' award 1986), Boys and Girls Club of Corvallis (pres. 1991-92), Sigma Kappa, Rotary Corvallis (bd. dirs. 1990-92, dir. voc. svcs. 1991-92, pres.-elect 1992), Rotary Lafayette (bd. dirs. 1993—, cmty. svc. dir. 1993-94, treas. 1995-96, sec. 1996-97, v.p. 1997—), Lafayette Rep. Women's Club (first v.p. 1997, gen. chmn. La. Fedn. Rep. Women's Clubs State Conv. 1997). Roman Catholic. Contbr. numerous articles to profl. jours. Office: Castellini Co 1007 W St Mary Blvd Lafayette LA 70506-3427

CASTER, RONALD LYNN, fire chief; b. Medford, Oreg., May 16, 1954; s. Otto R. and Patricia A. (Hopkins) C.; m. Rosanne D. Green, Nov. 15, 1975 (div. 1991); children: Amanda M., Anna L. AA in fire sci., Rogue Cmty. Coll., Grants Pass, Oreg., 1990. Firefighter U.S. Air Force, Mountain Home AFB, Idaho, 1975-79; fire dept. crew chief U.S. Air Force, RAF Fairford, Eng., 1979-81; fire chief U.S. Air Force, Calumet AFS, Mich., 1981-84; firefighter U.S. Army, Hermiston,' Oreg., 1984-85; fire chief Medford/ Jackson County Airport, Medford, Oreg., 1985-90; trainer Oreg. State Fire Marshal's Office, Medford, Oreg., 1990-91; fire chief Grays Harbor Fire Dist. 2, Aberdeen, Wash., 1991—; adv. fire sci. South Puget Sound Cmty. Coll., Olympia, Wash., 1992—. Mem. Nat. Fire Protection Assn., Internat. Assn. Fire Chiefs, Washington State Fire Chiefs Assn., Twin Harbor Chiefs Assn. (v.p. 1991-94, pres. 1995-97). Democrat. Office: Grays Harbor Fire Dist #2 6317 Olympic Hwy Aberdeen WA 98520-5723

CASTILLO, RICHARD JOSEPH, psychiatric anthropologist, educator; b. Long Beach, Calif., Aug. 17, 1951; s. Celestino Ledesma and Elvira Alarcon (Gloria) C. BA in Philosophy magna cum laude, U. Hawaii, 1983, MA in Asian Religions, 1985; MA in Psychiat. Anthropology, Harvard U., 1989, PhD in Psychiat. Anthropology, 1991. Tchg. fellow Harvard U., Cambridge, Mass., 1986-88, resident tutor, 1987-89; vis. colleague U. Hawaii Manoa, Honolulu, 1989-90; lectr. psychiat. anthropology U. Hawaii West Oahu, Pearl City, 1990-93, asst. prof., 1993-95, assoc. prof., 1995—; clin. assoc. prof. psychiatry U. Hawaii Sch. Medicine, Pearl City, 1996—; advisor Diagnostic & Statis. Manual Mental Disorders, 4th edit. task force Am.

Psychiat. Assn., Washington, 1992-94; mem. cultural study group, dept. of psychiatry U. Hawaii Sch. of Medicine; rsch. anthropologist WHO Psychiat. Rsch. Ctr., U. Hawaii, Manoa. Author: Culture and Mental: A Client-Centered Approach, 1996. Ford Found. dissertation fellow, 1989-90; grad. fellow NSF, 1986-89, Harvard U., 1985-91. Fellow Am. Anthrop. Assn.; mem. NIMH (mem. group on culture and diagnosis 1992—), Am. Ethnol. Soc., Internat. Soc. for Study of Dissociation, Soc. for Anthropology of Consciousness (Volney Stefflre award 1993), Soc. Med. Anthropology, Phi Beta Kappa. Office: Univ Hawaii West Oahu 96-043 Ala Ike St Pearl City HI 96782-3366

CASTLE, ALFRED, administrator; b. Washington, Dec. 22, 1948; m. Mary Ann Slagle (div. 1979); m. Lilia Kruglova, 1992. BA, Colo. State U., 1971, MA, 1972; postgrad., U. N.Mex., Columbia U., 1980, U. N.Mex. Chmn., div. humanities Sunset Hill Sch., Kansas City, 1973-75; teaching asst. U. N.Mex., Alburquerque, 1975; prof., history N.Mex. Mil. Inst., Roswell, 1976-83; exec. dir. NMMI Fedn. N.Mex. Mil. Inst., 1983-87; v.p. devel. Hawaii Pacific U., Honolulu, 1987-95; v.p. U. advancement Calif. State U., San Marcos, 1995—; trustee Samuel N. and Mary Castle Found., Honolulu, 1987—, pres.-elect, 1992—; trustee Acad. Pacific, Honolulu, 1987—, Hawaiian Hist. Soc., Honolulu, 1988—. Author: Century of Philanthropy, 1992; contbr. articles to profl. jours., chpts. to books. Trustee Hawaii Food Bank, Honolulu, 1987—, Hawaii Sch. Girls, Honolulu, 1987—, Henry Dorothy Castle Fund, Robert Black Meml. Trust, Trimble Charitable Trust; trustee, pres. Samuel N. and Mary Castle Found. NEH fellow, 1978, 79-80, 81, 86, 91, Hoover fellow, 1983, 86, 90, 93, 96, Coolidge fellow, 1988. Mem. Assn. Grantmakers Hawaii, Govrs. Coun. Children Youth, Coun. Founds., San Diego Coun. Grantmakers. Episcopalian. Home: 206 Alta Mesa Dr Vista CA 92084

CASTLE, EMERY NEAL, agricultural and resource economist, educator; b. Eureka, Kans., Apr. 13, 1923; s. Sidney James and Josie May (Tucker) C.; m. Merab Eunice Weber, Jan. 20, 1946; 1 dau., Cheryl Diana Delozier. B.S., Kans. State U., 1948, M.S., 1950; Ph.D., Iowa State U., 1952. Agrl. economist Fed. Res. Bank of Kansas City, 1952-54; from asst. prof. to prof. dept. agrl. econs. Oreg. State U., Corvallis, 1954-65; dean faculty Oreg. State U., 1965-66, prof., head dept. agrl. econs., 1966-72, dean Grad. Sch., 1972-76, Alumni disting. prof., 1970, prof. univ. grad. faculty econs., 1986—; v.p., sr. fellow Resources for the Future, Washington, 1976-79; pres. Resources for the Future, 1979-86; vice-chmn. Environ. Quality Commn. Oreg., 1988-95. Editor: The Changing American Countryside: Rural People and Places, 1995; mem. editl. bd. Land Econs., 1969—. Recipient Alumni Disting. Service award Kans. State U., 1976; Disting. Service award Oreg. State U., 1984. Fellow AAAS, Am. Assn. Agrl. Economists (pres. 1972-73), Am. Acad. Arts and Scis. Home: 1112 NW Solar Pl Corvallis OR 97330-3640 Office: Oreg State U 307 Ballard Extension Hall Corvallis OR 97331-8538

CASTLE, TERRY JACQUELINE, English language educator; b. San Diego, Oct. 18, 1953; d. Richard P. Castle and Mavis K. (Goodhead) Parker. BA in English, U. Puget Sound, 1975; MA in English, U. Minn., 1978, PhD in English, 1980. Jr. fellow Soc. Fellows, Harvard U., Cambridge, Mass., 1980-83; asst. prof. English Stanford (Calif) U., 1983-85, assoc. prof. English, 1985-88, prof. English, 1988—. Author: Clarissa's Ciphers: Meaning and Disruption in Richardson's "Clarissa", 1982, Masquerade and Civilization: The Carnivalesque in 18th-Century English Culture and Fiction, 1986, The Apparitional Lesbian: Female Homosexuality and Modern Culture, 1993, The Female Thermometer: Eighteenth-Century Culture and the Invention of the Uncanny, 1995, Noel Coward and Radclyffe Hall: Kindred Spirits, 1996. Fellow Stanford U., 1987-88, Guggenheim Found., 1989-90. Mem. MLA (William Riley Parker prize 1985), Am. Soc. 18th Century Studies (James Clifford prize 1988). Office: Stanford Univ Dept English Stanford CA 94305-2087

CASTLEBERRY, ARLINE ALRICK, architect; b. Mpls., Sept. 19, 1919; d. Bannona Gerhardt and Meta Emily (Veit) Alrick; m. Donald Montgomery Castleberry, Dec. 25, 1941; children: Karen, Marvin. B in Interior Architecture, U. Minn., 1941; postgrad., U. Tex., 1947-48. Designer, draftsman Elizabeth & Winston Close, Architects, Mpls., 1940-41, Northwest Airlines, Mpls., 1942-43, Cerny & Assocs., Mpls., 1944-46; archtl. draftsman Dominick and Van Benscotten, Washington, 1946-47; ptnr. Castleberry & Davis Bldg. Designers, Burlingame, Calif., 1960-65; prin. Burlingame, 1965-90. Recipient Smith Coll. scholarship. Mem. AIA, Am. Inst. Bldg. Designers (chpt. pres. 1971-72), Commaisini, Alpha Alpha Gamma, Chi Omega. Democrat. Lutheran. Home and Office: 1311 Parrott Dr San Mateo CA 94402-3630

CASTLEMAN, BREAUX BALLARD, health management company executive; b. Louisville, Aug. 19, 1940; s. John Pryor and Mary Jane (Ballard) C.; m. Sue Ann Foreman (div. 1995); children: Matthew B., Shea B. BA in Econs., Yale U., 1962; postgrad., NYU, 1963. Mgmt. trainee Bankers Trust Co., N.Y.C., 1963-65; mng. dir. Castleman and Co., Houston, 1965-71; dir. program planning, econ. U.S. Dept. HUD, Ft. Worth, Dallas, 1971-73; v.p., office mgr. Booz Allen and Hamilton, Dallas, Houston, 1973-85; mng. dir. Castleman Group, Houston, 1985-87; mng. dir., chief exec. officer Kelsey-Seybold Clinic, P.A., Houston, 1987-95; pres. physician resources divsn. Caremark Internat., Inc., 1994-96; pres. Scripps Clinic, La Jolla, Calif., 1996—. Contbr. articles to profl. jours. Candidate state legislature, Houston, 1968. Mem. Planning Forum (chmn. 1985-86), Inst. for Mgmt. Cons., Coronado Club, Yale Club of NYC. Office: Scripps Clinic 10666 N Torrey Pines Rd La Jolla CA 92037

CASTON, JONATHON CRAIG, talk radio producer, engineer; b. McCloud, Calif., Dec. 13, 1948; s. John Harding and Joanne Louise (Maddock) C.; m. Lucy V. Palkina, July 12, 1991; (div.); 1 child, Irina G. BA in Polit. Sci., Calif. State U., Northridge, 1972, BA in Journalism, 1977. Cert. broadcast engr. AM and FM. Staff mem. Sta. KEDC-FM Pub. Radio Broadcasting, Northridge, 1969-72; intern pub. affairs dept. Sta. KCET-TV Pub. TV, L.A., 1971-72; early morning anchor, reporter Sta. KORK-TV, Las Vegas, 1976; talk radio producer, engr. KIEV Radio, Glendale, L.A., Calif., 1984—; cons. Caston Internat., Littlerock, Calif., 1992—; owner, co-founder Orion Bus. Internat., Canoga Park, Calif., 1985-90. Active Littlerock Town Coun., 1992-93. Mem. Am. Radio Relay League (life), Amateur Radio Satellite Orgn. (life). Democrat. Office: Caston Internat PO Box 74 Littlerock CA 93543-0074

CASTOR, JON STUART, management consultant; b. Lynchburg, Va., Dec. 15, 1951; s. William Stuart and Marilyn (Hughes) C.; m. Stephanie Lum, Jan. 7, 1989; 1 child, David Jon. BA, Northwestern U., 1973; MBA, Stanford U., 1975. Mgmt. cons. Menlo Park, Calif., 1981-96, pres. Tera Logic Inc., 1996—. Dir. Midwest Consumer Adv. Bd. to FTC, 1971-73; v.p., bd. dirs. San Mateo coun. Boy Scouts Am., 1991-93; bd. dirs. Pacific Skyline Coun. Boy Scouts Am., 1994—; trustee Coyote Point Mus. Environ. Edn., San Mateo, 1992-95. Office: TeraLogic Inc 707 California St Mountain View CA 94041

CASTOR, WILBUR WRIGHT, futurist, author, consultant; b. Harrison Twp., Pa., Feb. 3, 1932; s. Wilbur Wright and Margaret (Grubbs) C.; m. Donna Ruth Schwartz, Feb. 9, 1963; children: Amy, Julia, Marnie. BA, St. Vincent Studies, 1959; PhD, Calif. U. Advanced Studies, 1990. Sales rep. IBM, Pitts. and Cleve., 1959-62; v.p. data processing ops. Honeywell, Waltham, Mass., 1962-80; pres., chief exec. officer Aviation Simulation Tech., Lexington, Mass., 1980-82; sr. v.p. Xerox Corp., El Segundo, Calif., 1982-89; freelance cons., 1989—. Author: (play) Un Certaine Soirire, 1958, (mus. comedy) Breaking Up, 1960, (book) The Information Age and the New Productivity, 1990; contbr. articles to profl. jours. Mem. Presdl. Rep. Task Force; pres., bd. dirs. Internat. Acad., Santa Barbara; active Town Hall Calif. Served to capt. USN, 1953-58, with USAFR, 1958-76. Recipient Disting. Alumnus of Yr. award St. Vincent Coll., 1990. Mem. World Bus. Acad., The Strategy Bd., U. Denver "Netthink", World Future Soc., Aircraft Owners and Pilots Assn., Caballeros Country Club, Rolling Hills (Calif.) Club, Tennis Club, U.S. Senator's Club. Home: 19 Georgeff Rd Rolling Hills Estates CA 90274-5274

CASTRO, DAVID ALEXANDER, construction executive; b. L.A., Dec. 30, 1950; s. Victor A. and Guadalupe (Valadez) C.; m. Katherine Winfield Taylor, Sept. 30, 1990; children: Sarah Taylor, Kyle Christian, Andrew Joseph. A Liberal Arts, U. Md., 1976, BS in Bus. and Mgmt., 1978; A Engring. Asst., C.C. USAF, 1986; MS in Systems Mgmt., Golden Gate U., 1991. Enlisted USAF, 1970, advanced through grades to Chief Master Sgt., 1989; quality control mgr. 6950 security wing USAF, Royal AFB Chicksands, U.K., 1976-79; supr. engring. support 2851 civil engring. squadron USAF, McClellan AFB, Calif., 1979-82, inspector major projects 2851 civil engring. squadron, 1982-85, supt. engring. svcs. 2851 civil engring. squadron, 1985-87; dep. dir. pub. works tech. assistance team USAF, Beni Seuf, Egypt, 1987-88; contract mgr., then program mgr. 60 civil engring squadron USAF, Travis AFB, Calif., 1988-91; ret. USAF, 1991; acct. rep. Met. Life Ins. Co., Fairfield, Calif., 1991-92; construction mgr. Pacifica Svcs. Inc., Travis AFB, Calif., 1992-96; constrn. program mgr. CAL Inc., Vacaville, Calif., 1996-97, chief construction divsn., 1997—; mem. USAF Enlisted Coun., Washington, 1984-86. Group leader Neighborhood Watch, North Highlands, Calif., 1983-86; vol. Loaves and Fishes, Sacramento, 1984-86, Christman Promise, Sacramento, 1983-85; coach Little League Baseball, U.K. and Sacramento, 1976-81. Mem. Air Force Assn. (named Outstanding Airman 1985), Air Force Sgts. Assn., Travis Chiefs Group (treas. 1990-92), Am. Legion. Republican. Roman Catholic. Home: 1143 Araquipa Ct Vacaville CA 95687

CASTRO, DIANA MARIA, writer; b. Horta, Fayal, Portugal, Mar. 22, 1958; came to U.S., 1960; d. Raymond do Conte Castro and Alvarina (Soares de Melo) Castro. Diploma, B.M.C. H.S., Fall River, Mass., 1976; student, L.A. City Coll., 1980-82, Sonoma State U., 1990-94. tchr. writing workshops The Sitting Room: A Common Women's Libr., 1991-94, leader pro-women's writing support group, 1991-94, beginning women's writing, 1993. Contbr. short stories, essays, poems, book revs. to The Sun: A Magazine of Ideas, The Healing Woman, The Abiko Lit. Quarterly. Susan C. Petrey scholar Oreg. Sci. Fiction Soc., 1989. Democrat. Buddhist. Home: 4310 SE 52nd St Portland OR 97206

CASTRO, JOSEPH ARMAND, music director, pianist, composer, orchestrator; b. Miami, Ariz., Aug. 15, 1927; s. John Loya and Lucy (Sanchez) C.; m. Loretta Faith Haddad, Oct. 21, 1966; children: John Joseph, James Ernest. Student, San Jose State Coll., 1944-47. Mus. dir. Herb Jeffries, Hollywood, Calif., 1952, June Christy, Hollywood, 1959-63, Anita O'Day, Hollywood, 1963-65, Tony Martin, Hollywood, 1962-64, Tropicana Hotel, Las Vegas, Nev., 1980—, Desert Inn, Las Vegas, 1992-93; orch. leader Mocambo Night Club, Hollywood, 1952-54; soloist Joe Castro Trio, L.A., N.Y.C., Honolulu, 1952-65, Sands Hotel, Desert Inn, Las Vegas, 1975-80; mus. dir. Folies Bergere, 1980-89. Recs. include Cool School with June Christy, 1960, Anita O'Day Sings Rodgers and Hart, 1961, Lush Life, 1966, Groove-Funk-Soul, Mood Jazz, Atlantic Records, also albums with Teddy Edwards, Stan Kenton, Jimmy Borges with Joe Castro Trio, 1990, Loretta Castro with Joe Castro Trio, 1990, Honolulu Symphony concerts; command performance, Queen Elizabeth II, London Palladium, 1989, Concerts with Jimmy Borges and Honolulu Symphony Pops Concerts, 1991; jazz concert (with Nigel Kennedy) Honolulu Symphony, 1990; jazz-fest, Kailua-Kona, Hawaii, 1990; leader orch. Tropicana Hotel, 1989-94. With U.S. Army, 1946-47. Roman Catholic. Home: 2812 Colanthe Ave Las Vegas NV 89102-2026 Office: Tropicana Hotel 3801 Las Vegas Blvd S Las Vegas NV 89109-4325

CASTRO, LEONARD EDWARD, lawyer; b. L.A., Mar. 18, 1934; s. Emil Galvez and Lily (Meyers) C.; 1 son, Stephen Paul. A.B., UCLA, 1959, J.D., 1962. Bar: Calif. 1963, U.S. Supreme Ct. 1970. Assoc. Musick, Peeler & Garrett, Los Angeles, 1962-68, ptnr., 1968—. Mem. ABA, Internat. Bar Assn., Los Angeles County Bar Assn. Office: Musick Peeler & Garrett 1 Wilshire Blvd Ste 2000 Los Angeles CA 90017-3806

CASTRUITA, RUDY, school system administrator. BA in Social Sci., Utah State U., 1966, MS in Sch. Adminstrn., 1967; EdD, U. So. Calif., 1983. Cert. adminstrv. svcs., std. secondary, pupil svcs. Dir. econ. opportunity program City of El Monte, Calif., 1966-67; secondary tchr., counselor, program coord. El Monte Union High Sch. Dist., 1967-75, asst. prin. Mountain View High Sch., 1975-80; prin. Los Alamitos (Calif.) High Sch. Los Alamitos Unified Sch. Dist., 1980-85; asst. supt. secondary divsn. Santa Ana (Calif.) Unified Sch. Dist., 1985-87, assoc. supt. secondary divsn., 1987-88, supt., 1988-94; supt. schs. San Diego County, 1994—; adj. prof. Calif. State U., Long Beach, 1981-88, mem. adv. com. dept. ednl. adminstrn., 1983-86; adj. prof. U. San Francisco, 1984-88; mem. State Tchr. of Yr. Selection Com., 1988, Student Tchr. Edn. Project Coun., SB 620 Healthy Start Com., SB 1274 Restructuring Com., Joint Task Force Articulation, State High Sch. Task Force; mem. Latino eligibility study U. Calif., mem. ednl. leadership inst.; mem. state adv. coun. Supt. Pub. Instrn.; Delta Epsilon lectr. U. So. Calif.; rep. Edn. Summit; mem. selection com. Calif. Ednl. Initiatives Fund; co-chair subcom. at risk youth Calif. Edn. Com., 1989; mentor supt. Harvard Urban Supt.'s Program, 1993—. Chair Orange County Hist. Adv. Coun., South El Monte Coordinating Coun.; mem. exec. coun. Santa Ana 2000; mem. articulation coun. Rancho Santiago C.C. Dist.; active Hacienda Heights Recreation and Pks. Commn., Santa Ana City Coun. Stadium Blue Ribbon Com.; exec. dir. Orange County coun. Boy Scouts Am.; mem. adv. com. Bowers Mus.; mem. exec. bd. El Monte Boys Club; hon. lifetime mem. Calif. PTA; bd. dirs. Santa Ana Boys and Girls Club, Orange County Philharm. Soc., Santa Ana Pvt. Industry Coun., El Monte-South El Monte Consortium, Drug Use is Life Abuse, EDUCARE sch. edn. U. So. Calif. Named Supt. of Yr. League United Latin Am. Citizens, 1989; state finalist Nat. Supt. Yr. award, 1992. Mem. ASCD, Assn. Calif. Sch. Adminstrs. (rep. region XVII secondary prins. com. 1981-85, presenter region XVII 1984, Calif. Supt. of Year award 1991, Marcus Foster award 1991), Calif. Sch. Bds. Assn. (mem. policy and analysis com.), Assn. Calif. Urban Sch. Dists. (pres. 1992—), Orange County Supts. (pres.), Santa Ana C. of C. (bd. dirs.), Delta Epsilon (pres. 1990-91), Phi Delta Kappa. *

CASTY, ALAN HOWARD, author, retired humanities educator; b. Chgo., Apr. 6, 1929; s. Louis and Gertrude (Chaden) C.; m. Marilyn McPheeters, Aug. 10, 1956 (div. Dec. 1970); children: Lisa, David, Erica; m. Jill Herman, Jan. 7, 1971. BA, U. Calif., Berkeley, 1950; MA, U. Calif., L.A., 1956, PhD, 1973. Sports reporter The Richmond (Calif.) Ind., 1950-51; publicist Natural Vision Film Corp., Hollywood, Calif., 1953-54; prof. English and cinema Santa Monica (Calif.) Coll., 1956-92, prof. emeritus, 1992—. Author: Robert Rossen, 1967, The Shape of Fiction, 1967, 2d edit., 1973, Mass Media and Mass Man, 1968, 2d edit., 1973, 3d edit., 1975, The Films of Robert Rossen, 1969, A Mixed Bag, 1970, 2d edit., 1975, Building Writing Skills, 1971, The Dramatic Art of the Film, 1971, Development of the Film: An Interpretive History, 1973, Let's Make It Clear, 1977, Improving Writing, 1981, The Writing Project, 1983, others; contbr. articles to profl. jours. Sgt. U.S. Army, 1951-53. Jewish. Home: 225 17 Mile Dr Pacific Grove CA 93950-2442 Office: Santa Monica Coll 1900 Pico Blvd Santa Monica CA 90405-1628

CATCHPOLE, JUDY, state agency administrator; m. Glenn Catchpole; children: Glenda, Fred, Katie. BA in Edn., U. Wyo. CEO, state supt. public schs. State Dept. Edn., Cheyenne. Exec. dir. Wyoming Rep. Party. Mem. Wyo. Sch. Bds. Assn. (vice chmn.), Wyo. Early Childhood Assn. (pres.), Natrona County Bd. Trustees (chmn., treas.), Bd. Coop. Edn. Svcs. (treas.), Natrona County C. of C. Office: Wyo Dept Edn Hathaway Bldg 2nd Fl 2300 Capitol Ave Cheyenne WY 82002-0050

CATE, BENJAMIN WILSON UPTON, journalist; b. Paris, France, Sept. 28, 1931; s. Karl Springer and Josephine (Wilson) C.; children: Christopher, Stephanie. B.A., Yale U., 1955. Reporter St. Petersburg (Fla.) Times, 1955-60; corr. Time mag., Los Angeles, 1960-61, Detroit, 1961-65; chief Houston bur. Time mag., 1965-68; corr. Time mag., Paris, 1968-69; chief Bonn. (Fed. Republic of Germany) bur. Time mag., 1969-72; dep. chief of corrs. Time mag., N.Y.C., 1972-75; chief Midwest bur. Time mag., Chgo., 1975-81; chief West Coast bur. Time mag., Beverly Hills, Calif., 1981-85; spl. asst. to pub. Time mag., Los Angeles, 1985-86, sr. corr., 1987; polit. editor Sta. KCRW-FM, Santa Monica, Calif., 1987-88; freelance writer, editorial cons., 1989—. Served with U.S. Army, 1955-57. Home: 10583 Dunleer Dr Los Angeles CA 90064-4317

CATE, FLOYD MILLS, electronic components executive; b. Norfolk, Va., Aug. 2, 1917; s. Floyd Mills and Ellen (Lewis) C.; m. Ann Willis, Jan. 31, 1943; 1 child Carol Cate Webster. B.A. U. Tenn., 1940; student exec. program UCLA, 1958; B.A. (hon.) Calif. Inst. Tech., 1947. With special sales dept. Cannon Electric Co., Los Angeles, 1940-46, western sales mgr., 1946-50, with internat. sales dept., 1950-57, v.p. sales, mktg., 1957-62, pres. internat. sales, 1958-62, v.p. sales and mktg. electronics, 1962-69; v.p. sales, mktg. divsn. Japan Aviation Electronics Zemco, Irvine, Calif., 1977-80, cons., 1977-80; pres., owner F.E.S. Cons., San Clemente, Calif., 1968-94; 2R engring. cons. dir., San Marcos, Calif., 1987-94; consulting agent LHC Shorecliff Golf Club; U.S.A. agent Ocean Resources Engr. Co-chmn. Ron Packard for Congress, San Clemente, 1984; chmn. ad hoc com. Sea Sade Village, 1986-94; pres. Assn. Shorecliffs Residence, San Clemente, 1986-94; dir. La Christianitos pageants Samaritan Hosp. Guild. Mem. IEEE, Internat. Electric Electronic Engrs., San Clemente C. of C., San Clemente Hist. Soc. Democrat. Roman Catholic. Club: Shorecliff Golf (bd. dirs. San Clemente). Office: 205 Via Montego San Clemente CA 92672-3625

CATO, ROBERT GEORGE, financial company manager; b. Portland, Oreg., Mar. 30, 1933; s. Archie Barnes and Etta Marie (Yager) C.; BA, U. Portland, 1954; postgrad. Portland State Coll., 1959-60, U. Portland, 1959-60, Johns Hopkins U., 1983; m. Nancy Louise Foord, Sept. 18, 1954; children: Cheryl, Sandra, Sharon. With Eastman Kodak Co., Portland, 1950-55; field rep. Gen. Motors Acceptance Corp., Portland, 1957-62, credit rep., Boise, Idaho, 1962-65, dist. rep., The Dalles, Oreg., 1965-66, credit supr., Seattle, 1966-69, credit mgr., 1969-72, sales mgr., 1972-74, staff asst., N.Y.C., 1974-77, asst. br. mgr., Norfolk, Va., 1977-79, Balt., 1979-85, control br. manager, Buffalo, 1985-86, Pitts., 1986-89, Mpls., 1989-92, ret., 1992. Served with U.S. Army, 1955-57. Mem. Elks, Masons, Shriners. Republican. Home: 15915 NW Tullamorrie Way Portland OR 97229-7853

CATRAMBONE, EUGENE DOMINIC, public relations consultant; b. Chgo., June 5, 1926; s. Nicola and Maria Theresa (Catrambone) C.; m. Mary Gloria Gaimari, Mar. 26, 1951; children: Mary, Eugene Jr., Jane, David, Jill. BA, St. Benedict Coll., 1950; postgrad., Kans. State U., 1952-54; MA, DePaul U., 1960; postgrad., UCLA, 1962-63. Cert. secondary tchr., coll. instr., Calif. Tchr. high schs. Chgo., 1950-62, L.A., 1963-88; cons. pub. rels. Westlake Village, Calif., 1986—; tech. writer U. Chgo., 1956-59, Douglas Missile div. USN, L.A. and Ventura, Calif., 1962-75; reporter, editor Las Virgenes Enterprise, Calabasas, Calif., 1968-75; evening instr. L.A. City Coll., 1965-68. Author: Requiem for a Nobody, 1993, The Golden Touch: Frankie Carle, 1981; poems "Exit dust", 1982, "Tender Moments", 1996; contbr. articles on edn. to profl. publs., 1959-60, feature stories to local newspapers, 1968-75. Sgt. U.S. Army, 1944-46. Recipient Fostering Excellence award L.A. Unified Sch. Dist., 1986-87, nominee Apple award, 1986. Mem. NEA (life), Calif. Tchrs. Assn., Book Publicists So. Calif., United Tchrs. L.A., Am. Legion, Westlake Village Men's Golf Club (pub. rels. editor 1986—, bd. dirs., pres. 1989—). Democrat. Roman Catholic. Home: 31802 Tynebourne Ct Westlake Village CA 91361-4132 Office: Golden Touch Assocs 31802 Tynebourne Ct Westlake Village CA 91361-4132

CATTANDO-HELD, DONNA, school director; b. Chicago Heights, Ill., June 13, 1949; d. Frank and Betty Cattando; m. Edward A. Held, May 10, 1979; 1 child, Julia Held. BA cum laude, San Francisco State U., 1985. Tchr. Discovery Ctr., San Francisco, 1975-77; dir. Newbridge Elem. Sch., L.A., 1977-90, The Country Sch., North Hollywood, Calif., 1990-92; adminstr. Children Now, L.A., 1992; founder, head sch. Tarzana Hills Elem. Sch., Tarzana, Calif., 1992—, tech. and sci. specialist, 1993—. Vol. George Moscone senate and mayorial campaigns, San Francisco, 1971-76. Office: Tarzana Hills Elem Sch 5562 Reseda Blvd Tarzana CA 91356-2608

CATTANEO, JACQUELYN ANNETTE KAMMERER, artist, educator; b. Gallup, N.Mex., June 1, 1944; d. Ralph John and Gladys Agnes (O'Sullivan) Kammer; m. John Leo Cattaneo, Apr. 25, 1964; children: John Auro, Paul Anthony. Student Tex. Woman's U., 1962-64. Portrait artist, tchr. Gallup, N. Mex., 1972; coord. Works Progress Adminstrn. art project renovation McKinley County, Gallup, Octavia Fellin Performing Arts wing dedication, Gallup Pub. Library; formation com. mem. Multi-modal/Multi-Cultural Ctr. for Gallup, N.Mex.; exch. with Soviet Women's Com., USSR Women Artists del., Moscow, Kiev, Leningrad, 1990; Women Artists del. and exch. Jerusalem, Tel Aviv, Cairo, Israel; mem. Artists Del. to Prague, Vienna and Budapest.; mem. Women Artists Del. to Egypt, Israel and Italy, 1992, Artist Del. Brazil, 1994, Greece, Crete and Turkey, 1996, Spain, 1996. One-woman shows include Gallup Pub. Libr., 1963, 66, 77, 78, 81, 87, Gallup Lovelace Med. Clinic, Santa Fe Station Open House, 1981, Gallery 20, Farmington, N.Mex., 1985—, Red Mesa Art Gallery, 1989, Soviet Restrospect Carol's Art & Antiques Gallery, Liverpool, N.Y., 1992, N.Mex. State Capitol Bldg., Santa Fe, 1992, Lt. Govt. Casey Luna-Office Complex, Women Artists N.Mex. Mus. Fine Arts, Carlsbad, 1992, Rio Rancho Country Club, N.Mex., 1995; group shows include: Navajo Nation Library Invitational, 1978, Santa Fe Festival of the Arts Invitational, 1979, N.Mex. State Fair, 1978, 79, 80, Catharine Lorillard Wolfe, N.Y.C., 1980, 81, 84, 85, 86, 87, 88, 89, 91, 92, 4th ann. exhbn. Salmagundi Club, 1984, 90, 3d ann. Palm Beach Internat., New Orleans, 1984, Fine Arts Ctr. Taos, 1984, The Best and the Brightest O'Brien's Art Emporium, Scottsdale, Ariz., 1986, Gov.'s Gallery, 1989, N.Mex. State Capitol, Santa Fe, 1987, Pastel Soc. West Coast Ann. Exhbn. Sacramento Ctr. for Arts, Calif., 1986-90, gov.'s invitational Magnifico Fest. of the Arts, Albuquerque, 1991, Assn. Pour La Promotion Du Patrimone Artistique Français, Paris, Nat. Mus. of the Arts for Women, Washington, 1991, Artists of N.Mex., Internat. Nexus '92 Fine Art Exhbn., Trammell Corw Pavilion, Dallas, Carlsbad (N.Mex.) Mus. Fine Art; represented in permanent collections: Zuni Arts and Crafts Ednl. Bldg., U. N.Mex., C.J. Wiemar Collection, McKinley Manor, Gov.'s Office, State Capitol Bldg., Santa Fe, Historic El Rancho Hotel, Gallup, N.Mex., Sunwest Bank. Fine Arts Ctr., En Taos, N.Mex., Armand Hammer Pvt. Collection, Wilcox Canyon Collections, Sadona, Ariz., Galaria Impi, Netherlands, Woods Art and Antiques, Liverpool, N.Y., Stewarts Fine Art, Taos, N.Mex. Mem. Dora Cox del. to Soviet Union-U.S. Exchange, 1990. Recipient Cert. of Recognition for Contbn. and Participation Assn. Pour La Patrinome Du Artistique Français, 1991, N.Mex. State Senate 14th Legislature Session Meml. # 101 for Artistic Achievements award, 1992, Award of Merit, Pastel Soc. West Coast Ann. Membership Exhbn., 1993. Mem. Internat. Fine Arts Guild, Am. Portrait Soc. (cert.), Oil Painters of Am., Pastel Soc. of W. Coast (cert.), Mus. N.Mex. Found., N.Mex. Archtl. Found., Mus. Women in the Arts, Fechin Inst., Artists' Co-op. (co-chair), Gallup C. of C., Gallup Area Arts and Crafts Council, Am. Portrait Soc. Am., Pastel Soc. N.Mex., Catharine Lorillard Wolfe Art Club of N.Y.C. (oil and pastel juried membership), Chautaugua Art Club, Knickerbocker Artists and Oil Painters of Am., Soroptimists (Internat. Woman of Distinction 1990). Address: 210 E Green St Gallup NM 87301-6130

CATTERTON, MARIANNE ROSE, occupational therapist; b. St. Paul, Feb. 3, 1922; d. Melvin Joseph and Katherine Marion (Bole) Maas; m. Elmer John Wood, Jan. 16, 1943 (dec.); m. Robert Lee Catterton, Nov. 20, 1951 (div. 1981); children: Jenifer Ann Dawson, Cynthia Lea Uthus. Student, Carleton Coll., 1939-41, U. Md., 1941-42; BA in English, U. Wis., 1944; MA in Counseling Psychology, Bowie State Coll., 1980; postgrad., No. Ariz. U., 1987-91. Registered occupational therapist, Occupational Therapy Cert. Bd. Occupational therapist VA, N.Y.C., 1946-50; cons. occupational therapist Fondo del Seguro del Estado, Puerto Rico, 1950-51; dir. rehab. therapies Spring Grove State Hosp., Catonsville, Md., 1953-56; occupational therapist Anne Arundel County Health Dept., Annapolis, Md., 1967-78; dir. occupational therapy Eastern Shore Hosp. Ctr., Cambridge, Md., 1979-85; cons. occupational therapist Kachina Point Health Ctr., Sedona, Ariz., 1986; regional chmn. Conf. on revising Psychiat. Occupational Therapy Edn., 1958-59; instr. report writing Anne Arundel Community Coll., Annapolis, 1974-78. Editor Am. Jour. Occupational Therapy, 1962-67. Active Md. Heart Assn., 1959-60; mem. task force on occupational therapy Md. Dept. of Health, 1971-72; chmn. Anne Arundel Gov. Com. on Employment of Handicapped, 1959-63; mem. gov.'s com. to study vocat. rehab., Md., 1960; com. mem. Annapolis Youth Ctr., 1976-78; mem. ministerial search com. Unitarian Ch. Anne Arundel County, 1962; curator Dorchester County Heritage Mus., Cambridge, 1982-83; v.p., officer Unitarian-Universalist Fellowship Flagstaff, 1988-93, v.p., 1993-97; co-moderator, founder Unitarian-Universalist Fellowship of Sedona, 1994—, respite care vol., 1994—; citizen interviewer Sedona Acad. Forum, 1993, 94; vol. Care Givers, 1996—. Mem. P.R. Occupl. Therapy Assn. (co-founder 1950), Am. Occupl. Therapy Assn. (chmn. history com. 1958-61), Md. Occupl. Therapy Assn. (del. 1953-59), Ariz. Occupl. Therapy Assn., Pathfinder Internat., Dorchester County Mental Health Assn. (pres. 1981-84), Internat. Platform Assn., Ret. Officers

Assn., Air Force Assn. (Barry Goldwater chpt., sec. 1991-92, 94-97), Severn Town Club (treas. 1965, sec. 1971-72, 94-95), Internat. Club (Annapolis, publicity chmn. 1966), Toastmasters, Newcomers (Sedona, pres. 1986), Pathfinder, Zero Population Growth, Delta Delta Delta. Republican. Home: 415 Windsong Dr Sedona AZ 86336-3745

CATTS, LOIS MAY, critical care nurse specialist; b. Portland, Oreg., May 3, 1952. BSN, Seattle Pacific U., 1974; MSN, U. Calif., 1989. CCRN. Staff nurse, charge nurse Good Samaritan, Portland, 1974-87; staff nurse U. Calif., San Francisco, 1987-90; critical care educator Sequoia Hosp., Redwood City, Calif., 1990; critical care CNS Providence Yakima (Wash.) Med. Ctr., 1990-96; dir. Providence Regional Heart Care Ctr., Yakima, 1997—. Mem. AACN, Am. Heart Assn. (chmn. ACLS task force 1992—). Office: Providence Yakima Med Ctr 110 S 9th Ave Yakima WA 98902-3315

CATZ, BORIS, endocrinologist, educator; b. Troyanov, Russia, Feb. 15, 1923; s. Jacobo and Esther (Galbmilion) C.; came to U.S., 1950, naturalized, 1955; m. Rebecca Schechter; children: Judith, Dinah, Sarah Lea, Robert. BS, Nat. U. Mexico, 1941, MD, 1947; MS in Medicine, U. So. Calif., 1951. Intern, Gen. Hosp., Mexico City, 1945-46; prof. adj., sch. medicine U. Mexico, 1947-48; research fellow medicine U. So. Calif., 1949-51, instr. medicine, 1952-54, asst. clin. prof., 1954-59, assoc. clin. prof., 1959-83, clin. prof., 1983—; pvt. practice, Los Angeles, 1951-55, Beverly Hills, Calif., 1957—; chief Thyroid Clinic Los Angeles County Gen. Hosp., 1955-70; sr. cons. thyroid clin. U. So. Calif.-Los Angeles Med. Center, 1970—; clin. chief endocrinology Cedars-Sinai Med. Ctr., 1983-87. Served to capt. U.S. Army, 1955-57. Boris Catz lectureship named in his honor Thyroid Research Endowment Fund, Cedars Sinai Med. Ctr., 1985. Fellow ACP, Am. Coll. Nuclear Medicine (pres. elect 1982), Royal Soc. Medicine; mem. AMA, AAAS, Cedars Sinai Med. Ctr. Soc. for History of Medicine (chmn.), L.A. County Med. Assn., Calif. Med. Assn., Endocrine Soc., Am. Thyroid Assn., Soc. Exptl. Biology and Medicine, Western Soc. Clin. Research, Am. Fedn. Clin. Research, Soc. Nuclear Medicine, So. Calif. Soc. Nuclear Medicine, N.Y. Acad. Scis., L.A. Soc. Internal Medicine, Collegium Salerni, Cedar Sinai Soc. of History of Medicine, Beverly Hills C. of C., Phi Lambda Kappa. Jewish. Mem. B'nai B'rith. Club: The Profl. Man's (past pres.). Author: Thyroid Case Studies, 1975, 2d edit., 1981. Contbr. numerous articles on thyroidology to med. jours. Home: 300 S El Camino Dr Beverly Hills CA 90212-4212 Office: 435 N Roxbury Dr Beverly Hills CA 90210

CAUDRON, JOHN ARMAND, accident reconstructionist, technical forensic investigator; b. Compton, Calif., Sept. 26, 1944; s. Armand Robert and Evelyn Emma (Hoyt) C.; m. Marilynn Edith Fairfield, Mar. 16, 1968; children: Melita, Rochelle. AA, Ventura Coll., 1965; BA, Calif. State U., Fullerton, 1967; postgrad., U. Nev., 1975-78; MS, U. So. Calif., 1980. Dist. rep. GM, Reno, 1969-75; mgr. Snyder Rsch. Lab., Reno, 1976-78, v.p., El Monte, Calif., 1978-82, pres., 1982-85; prin. Fire and Accident Reconstruction, Rowland Heights, Calif., 1985—. Pub. accident reconstrn. newsletter. With U.S. Army, 1967-69. Mem. ASCE, Am. Bd. Forensic Examiners (bd. cert.), Inst. Forensic Examiners, Am. Soc. Safety Engrs., Nat. Fire Protection Assn., Geol. Soc. Am., Firearms Rsch. and Identification Assn. (pres. 1978—), Am. Soc. Metals, Nat. Safety Coun., Nat. Soc. Profl. Engrs., Nat. Assn. Profl. Accident Redonstruction Specialists, Ft. Tejon Hist. Assn. (info. adviser 1983—). Republican. Baptist. Avocations: hiking, traveling, photography. Office: Fire & Accident Reconstruction 21465 E Fort Bowie Dr Walnut CA 91789-5106

CAUFIELD, MARIE CELINE, religious organization administrator; b. Chgo., Aug. 11, 1929; d. John Patrick and Anna Marie (Clear) C. MA in Religious Edn., Fordham U., 1975; DMin in Creative Ministry, Grad. Theol. Found., Bristol, Ind., 1989. Elem. prin. St. Martin's Sch., Kankakee, Ill., 1952-64; missionary Congregation de Notre Dame, Guatemala, Ctrl. Am., 1964-71; dir. religious edn. St. Colomba, N.Y.C., 1971-75, St. Bernard, Pirtleville, Ariz., 1975-76; dir. Hispanic ministry Diocese of Providence (R.I.), Central Falls, 1976-81; dir. of the Office of Hispanic ministry Roman Cath. Diocese of Boise, 1981-96; nat. exec. dir. The Cath. Migrant Farmworker Network, 1996—. Author numerous poems; contbr. articles to profl. jours. Bd. dirs. Cath. Migrant Farmworkers' Network, Toledo, 1992—; founder Idaho's Cath. Golden Age Chpt., Boise, 1983-87. Grantee Am. Bd. Cath. Missions, 1991. Mem. Nat. Writers Assn., Fedn. of Returned Overseas Missioners (N.W. contact person 1990-94). Roman Catholic. Home: 1111 N 17th St Boise ID 83702-3306 Office: Catholic Migrant Farmworker Network 1915 University Dr Boise ID 83706

CAUGHLIN, STEPHENIE JANE, organic farmer; b. McAllen, Tex., July 23, 1948; d. James Daniel and Betty Jane (Warnock) C. BA in Family Econs., San Diego State U., 1972, MEd, 1973; M. in Psychology, U.S. Internat. U., San Diego, 1979. Cert. secondary life tchr., Calif. Owner, mgr. Minute Maid Svc., San Diego, 1970-75; prin. Rainbow Fin. Svcs., San Diego, 1975-78; tchr. San Diego Unified Sch. Dist., 1973-80; mortgage broker Santa Fe Mortgage Co., San Diego, 1980-81; commodity broker Premex Commodities, San Diego, 1981-84; pres., owner Nationwide Futures Corp., San Diego, 1984-88; owner, sec. Nationwide Metals Corp.; owner, gen. mgr. Seabreeze Organic Farm, 1984—. Sec. Arroyo Sorrento Assn., Del Mar, Calif., 1978—. Mem. Greenpeace Nature Conservancy, DAR, Sierra Club, Jobs Daus. Republican. Avocations: horseback riding, swimming, skiing, gardening. Home and Office: 3909 Arroyo Sorrento Rd San Diego CA 92130-2610

CAULEY, LINDA MARILYN, high school counselor; b. Farmington, Iowa, Nov. 14, 1942; d. Raymond R. and Alice M. (Jones) Harnagel; m. Paul K. CAuley, Nov. 27, 1965; children: Kevin, Brian. BA, Parsons Coll., Fairfield, Iowa, 1964; MS, Mt. St. Mary's Coll., L.A., 1991. Calif. life tchg. credential, puplil pers. cert. Tchr. Walter Reed Jr. H.S., North Hollywood, Calif., 1964-66, 68-71, Queens Lake Sch., Williamsburg, Va., 1967-68; dir. counseling Notre Dame H.S., Sherman Oaks, Calif., 1984—. Mem. ACA. Office: Notre Dame HS 13645 Riverside Dr Sherman Oaks CA 91423-2407

CAULFIELD, CARLOTA, education educator; b. Havana, Cuba, Jan. 16, 1953; came to U.S., 1981; d. Francis and Ada (Robaina) C.; m. Servando Gonzalez, May 1973; 1 child, Franco Caulfield Gonzalez. BA, U. Havana, 1979; MA, San Francisco State U., 1986; PhD, Tulane U., 1992. Lectr. San Francisco State U., 1985-86; publ., editor Literary Gazette/El Gato Tuerto, San Francisco, 1984-88; from teaching asst. to rsch. asst. Tulane U., New Orleans, 1988-92; asst. prof. Hispanic studies Mills Coll., Oakland, Calif., 1992—; free-lance acquisitions editor Mercury House, San Francisco, 1988-90; free-lance copy editor John Wiley & Sons, Inc., N.Y.C., 1988. Author: Visual Games for Words and Sounds, 1993, (poems) Angel Dust, 1990, Oscurita Divina, 1990, 34th Street, 1987, A las Puertas del Papel Con Amoroso Fuego, 1996. Recipient Internat. Poetry prize Ultimo Novecento, 1988, hon. mention Premio Plural, Mex., 1993, hon. mention poetry prize Federico Garcia Lorca, 1994, Italy poetry prize Riccardo Machi-Torre di Calafuria, 1995; Cintas fellow, 1988, 96, Quigley fellow Mills Coll., 1994; Nat. Hispanic scholar, 1991; Mellon Summer Rsch. grantee Tulane U., 1990. Mem. MLA, Latin Am. Jewish Studies Assn., Philol. Assn. the Pacific Coast, PEN Internat., Gruppo Internat. Lettura (hon., pres. U.S. chpt. 1988—), Libera Acad. Galileo Galilei (hon.). Office: Mills Coll 5000 Macarthur Blvd Oakland CA 94613-1301

CAULFIELD, W. HARRY, health care industry executive, physician; b. Waverly, N.Y., Aug. 22, 1936; m. Mary Sisk; children: Mary, Harry, James, Michael. AB, Harvard U., 1957, postgrad., 1976; MD, U. Pa., 1961. Diplomate Am. Bd. Internal. Medicine, Am. Bd. Cardiology. Rotating intern Hosp. U. Pa., 1961-62; resident Pa. Hosp., 1962-64; fellow in cardiology Georgetown U. Hosp., 1964-66; dir. ICU Kaiser Found. Hosp., San Francisco, 1969-75, asst. chief of staff, 1971-75, chief of staff, 1975-80; physician-in-chief, mem. exec. com. Permanente Med. Group, San Francisco, 1975-80, mem. internal medicine staff cardiology, 1968—, from exec. dir.-elect to exec. dir., 1990—; assoc. clin. prof. medicine U. Calif., San Francisco, 1971-96. Capt. U.S. Army Med. Corps, 1966-68. Fellow Am. Coll. Cardiology, Am. Heart Assn.; mem. AMA (adv. com. on group practice physicians 1994—, fedn. study consortium 1994—), San Francisco Med. Soc. (alt. del. to Calif. Med. Assn. 1992, del. 1993-94, managed care task force, leadership devel. com.), Calif. Med. Assn., Calif. Hosp. Assn. (membership com. 1987), Am. Hosp. Assn., Calif. Acad. Medicine, Am. Med. Group Assn. (trustee 1994—, vice chmn. bylaws com. 994, fin. com. 1996—), Soc. Med. Adminstrs., Am. Assn. Health Plans (bd. dirs. 1994—). Office: Permanente Med Group Inc 1950 Franklin St Oakland CA 94612-5103

CAUSEY, GILL TERRY, recreation company executive; b. L.A., May 22, 1950; s. Gill B. and June Celeste (Hillman) C. BA, Whittier Coll., 1972. With Causey & Rhodes Devel. Co., Newport Beach, Calif., 1972-75, Causey Investment Co., Laguna Beach, Calif., 1973-80, B&C Wines Importers, Kamuela, Hawaii, 1980-86; pres. Charter Locker, Inc., Kailua-Kona, Hawaii, 1986—, Big Island Yacht Sales, Inc., Kailua-Kona, Hawaii, 1986-93, Paradise Rafting Adventures, Inc., Agana, Guam, 1991—; v.p. Atoll Express, Inc., Kailua-Kona, 1988—; dir. Pelorus Maritime Ltd., Rarotonga, Cook Islands, Causey Trust Investments, newport Beach. Vice pres. Nancy Griffith, Inc., Kailua-Kona, 1987—. Mem. Pacific Ocean Rsch. Found., nat. Assn. Charterboat Operators, Kona Sailing Club, Hawaii Yacht Club. Presbyterian. Office: Charter Locker Inc 74-425 Kealakehe Pky Kailua Kona HI 96740-2708

CAVANAGH, JOHN CHARLES, advertising agency executive; b. San Francisco, Dec. 19, 1932; s. John Timothy and Alicia Louise (McDowell) C.; m. Mary Ann Anding, Apr. 10, 1959; children: Karen, Brad. Student, U. Hawaii, 1950; BS, U. San Francisco, 1954. Pub. rels. rep. Kaiser Industries Corp., Oakland, Calif., 1956-58; pub. rels. mgr. Kaiser Cement & Gypsum Corp., Oakland, 1958-63; pub. relations dir. Fawcett-McDermott Assos. Inc., Honolulu, Hawaii, 1964-66; ops. v.p. Fawcett-McDermott Assos. Inc., 1966-69, exec. v.p., 1969-73, pres., dir., 1973-75; pres., dir. Fawcett McDermott Cavanagh Inc., Honolulu, 1975-87, Fawcett McDermott Cavanagh Calif., Inc., San Francisco, 1975-87; pres. The Cavanagh Group/Advt. Inc., San Francisco, Calif., 1987—. Served to 1st. lt. 740th Guided Missile Bn. AUS, 1954-56. Named Advt. Man of Yr. Honolulu Advt. Fedn., 1985. Mem. Pub. Rels. Soc. Am. (accredited, v.p. 1970, pres. Hawaii chpt. 1971), Advt. Agy. Assn. Hawaii (pres. 1973), Am. Assn. Advt. Agys. (chmn. Hawaii coun. 1980-81), Affiliated Advt. Agys. Internat. (chmn. 1984-85), Sonoma County Ad Club, Fountaingrove Country Club, Outrigger Canoe Club, Commonwealth Club of Calif. Home: 3750 St Andrews Dr Santa Rosa CA 95403-0945 Office: The Cavanagh Group 505 Sansome St 10th Fl San Francisco CA 94111

CAVANAUGH, MICHAEL ARTHUR, education administrator, retired sociologist; b. Tacoma, Feb. 16, 1953; s. Robert Paul and Lorraine Florence Bertha (Teske) C. AA, Fla. Keys C.C., Key West, 1973; BA in Religion, Fla. State U., 1975, MA in Religion, 1977; PhD in Sociology, U. Pitts., 1983. Instr. Temple U., Phila., 1983-85; co-adjutant prof. Rutgers U., Camden, N.J., 1983-85; sr. wine cons. Emissary/Aura Ltd., Orange, Calif., 1986; instr. L.A. (Calif.) Cmty. Coll. Dist., 1986—, Calif. State U., Northridge, 1988-90; certificated employee L.A. (Calif.) Unified Sch. Dist., 1989—. Contbr. articles to profl. jours. Charles E. Merrill fellow Fla. State U., 1975-76, Andrew W. Mellon fellow U. Pitts., Pa., 1981-83, Vis. fellow UCLA, L.A., 1985-86. Mem. Assn. for Sociology Religion. Home: 1851 W 11th Pl Los Angeles CA 90006-4101

CAVIGLI, HENRY JAMES, petroleum engineer; b. Colfax, Calif., Mar. 14, 1914; s. Giovanni and Angelina (Giachi) C.; m. Ruth Loree Denton, June 11, 1942; children: Henry James Jr., Robert D., Paul R., Loree Ann McIntire. BS in Petroleum Engring., U. Calif., Berkeley, 1937, MS in Mech. Engring., 1947. Sr. engr. Chevron Corp., Rio Vista, Calif., 1954-57, supt. No. Calif., 1958-69; mgr. non operated joint ventures Chevron Corp., LaHabra, Calif., 1970-76; cons. Cavigli & Mee, petroleum cons., Sacramento, Calif., 1976—. Author: Escapades in the Blue, 1996. Mem. sch. bd. Rio Vista High Sch., 1962-67. Maj. USAF, 1942-47. Decorated Bronze Star with 4 oak leaf clusters. Mem. Soc. Petroleum Engrs., Petroleum Prodn. Pioneers, Calif. Conservation Commn. Oil Producers (chmn. 1971-72), Sutter Club, C. of C., Lion, Sigma Xi, Theta Tau Epsilon. Republican. Roman Catholic. Home: 6271 Eichler St Sacramento CA 95831-1864 Office: Cavigli & Mee PO Box 22815 Sacramento CA 95822-0815

CAVNAR, MARGARET MARY (PEGGY CAVNAR), business executive, former state legislator, nurse, consultant; b. Buffalo, July 29, 1945; d. James John and Margaret Mary Murtha Nightengale; BS in Nursing, D'Youville Coll., 1967; MBA, Nat. U., 1989; m. Samuel M. Cavnar, 1977; children: Heather Anne Hicks, Heide Lynn Gibson, Dona Cavnar Hambly, Judy Cavnar Bentrim. Utilization rev. coord. South Nev. Meml. Hosp., Las Vegas, 1975-77; v.p. Ranvac Publs., Las Vegas, 1976—; ptnr. Cavnar & Assocs., Reseda, Calif., 1976—, C & A Mgmt., Las Vegas, 1977—; pres. PS Computer Svc., Las Vegas, 1978-86; bd. mem. Nev. Eye Bank, 1987-89, exec. dir., 1990-91; dir. of health fairs Centel & CH13TV, 1991-94; bd. dirs. Bridge Counseling Assocs., 1992—, pres., 1994-95. Mem. Clark County Republican Cen. Com., 1977-87, Nev. Rep. Cen. Com., 1978-80; mem. Nev. Assembly, 1979-81; Rep. nominee for Nev. Senate, 1980; Rep. nominee for Congress from Nev. 1st dist., 1982, 84; bd. dirs., treas. Nev. Med. Fed. Credit Union; v.p. Cmty. Youth Activities Found., Inc., Civic Assn. Am.; mem. utilization rev. bd. Easter Seals; trustee Nev. Sch. Arts, 1980-87; nat. adviser Project Prayer, 1978—; co-chmn. P.R.I.D.E. Com., 1983—; co-chmn. Tax Limitation Com., 1983, Personal Property Tax Elimination Com., 1979-82, Self-Help Against Food Tax Elimination Denial Com., 1980; mem. nat. bd. dirs., co-chmn. Nev. Pres. Reagan's Citizens for Tax Reform Com., 1985-88; mem. Nev. Profl. Stds. Rev. Orgn., 1984; co-chmn. People Against Tax Hikes, 1983-84; bd. dirs. Nev. Eye Bank, 1988-90. Mem. Nev. Order Women Legislators (charter, parliamentarian 1980—), Cosmopolitanly Hers Info. (pres.), Sigma Theta Tau.

CAVNAR, SAMUEL MELMON, author, publisher, activist; b. Denver, Nov. 10, 1925; s. Samuel Edward and Helen Anita (Johnston) C.; m. Peggy Nightengale, Aug. 14, 1977; children by previous marriage: Dona Cavnar Hambly, Judy Cavnar Bentrim; children: Heather Anne Hicks, Heide Lynn MacLeod. Student pub. schs., Denver. Dist. mgr. U.S. C. of C., various locations, 1953-58; owner Cavnar & Assocs., mgmt. cons., Washington, Las Vegas, Nev., Denver and Reseda, Calif., 1958—; v.p. Lenz Assoc. Advt., Inc., Van Nuys, Calif., 1960—; dist. mgr. Western States Nu-Orm Plans, Inc., Los Angeles, 1947-52; cons. to architect and contractor 1st U.S. Missile Site, Wyo., 1957-58; prin. organizer Westway Corp. and subsidiaries, So. Calif. Devel. Co., 1958—; chmn. bd. Boy Sponsors, Inc., Denver, 1957-59; pres. Continental Am. Video Network Assn. Registry, Inc., Hollywood, Calif., 1967—; pres. United Sales Am., Las Vegas and Denver, 1969—; sr. mgmt. cons. Broadcast Mgmt. Cons. Service, Hollywood, Las Vegas, Denver, Washington, 1970—; pres., dir., exec. com. Am. Ctr. for Edn., 1968—; pub. Nat. Ind., Washington, 1970—, Nat. Rep. Statesman, Washington, 1969—, Nat. Labor Reform Leader, 1970—, Nat. Conservative Statesman, 1975—; owner Ran Vac Pub., Las Vegas and Los Angeles, 1976—; ptnr. P.S. Computer Services, Las Vegas, 1978—, C & A Mgmt., Las Vegas, 1978—, Westway Internat., 1983—; lectr. in field; spl. cons. various U.S. senators, congressmen, 1952—. Author: Run, Big Sam, Run, 1976, The Girls on Top, 1978, Big Brother Bureaucracy, The Cause and Cure, 1977, Kiddieland West, 1980, Games Politicians Play: How to Clean Up Their Act, 1981, A Very C.H.I.C. President, 1981, How to Clean Up Our Act, 1982, Assassination By Suicide, 1984, How to Get Limited Government, Limited Taxes, 1985, Tax Reform or Bust, 1985, At Last: Real Tax Reform, 1986, On the Road to a Real Balanced Budget, 1989, It's Time for Term Limitation, 1990, Clinton's "Investments": Just More Taxes, 1993, Hillary-Billary's New Road to Socialism, 1993, The Cause and the New Cure, 1995, Messin' With My Mind and Body, 1995, Reaction to Messin With My Mind, 1996. Nat. gen. chmn. Operation Houseclean, 1966-81; nat. candidate chmn. Citizens Com. To Elect Rep. Legislators, 1966, 68, 70, 72-74, 85—; mem. Calif. and Los Angeles County Rep. Cen. Coms., 1964-70; nat. gen. chmn. Project Prayer, 1962—; exec. dir. Project Alert, 1961—; nat. chmn. Nat. Labor Reform Com., 1969—; sustaining mem. Rep. Nat. Com., 1964—; Western states chmn. and nat. co-chmn. Am. Taxpayers Army, 1959—; area II chmn. Calif. Gov.'s Welfare Reform Com., 1970; chmn. Com. Law and Order in Am., 1975; mem. Nev. State Rep. Com., 1972—; mem. Clark County Rep. Com., 1972—; bd. dirs. Conservative Caucus, Las Vegas, 1974, 76, 82, 92; Rep. candidat for U.S. Senate from Nev., 1976, 82, 92; Rep. nominee for U.S. Congress from 30th dist. Calif., 1968, 70; nat. chmn. Return Pueblo Crew, 1968, Citizens League for Labor Reform, 1984—; nat. co-chmn. U.S. Taxpayers Forces, 1985—; pres., trustee Community Youth Activities Found., 1977—; nat. chmn. Operation Bus Stop, 1970—, P.R.I.D.E. Com., 1981—, Positivics Program, 1982—; co-chmn. Question 8 Com., 1980-82, S.H.A.F.T.E.D. Tax Repeal Com., 1982 C.H.I.C. Polit. Edn. Com., 1977—, People Against Tax Hikes Com., 1983—; bd. dirs., Nev. co-chmn. Pres. Reagan's Citizen's Com. for Tax Reform, 1985-86; nat. chmn. Term Limitation Com., 1988—; nat. chmn. Combined Coms. for Republican's Contract With Am., 1994—; chmn. Citizen's To Return Barloon and Daliberti, 1995—. Served with USN, 1942-45, USAF, 1950-53, Korea; comdr. USCG Aux., 1959-60. Recipient Silver medal SAR. Mem. Am. Legion (comdr. 1947-48, mem. nat. conv. disting. guest com. 1947-52), DAV, VFW, Am. Security Council (nat. adviser 1966—), U.S. C. of C. (sr. mem. rep. 1986—). Home: 301A Misty Isle Ln Las Vegas NV 89107-1117 Office: 1615 H St NW Washington DC 20062-0001

CAWLEY, LEO PATRICK, pathologist, immunologist; b. Oklahoma City, Aug. 11, 1922; s. Pat Bernard and Mary Elizabeth (Forbes) C.; m. Joan Mae Wood, May 20, 1948; children: Kevin Patrick, Karin Patricia, Kary Forbes. BS in Chemistry, Okla. State U., 1948; MD, Okla. Sch. Medicine, 1952. Diplomate Am. Bd. Pathology, Am. Bd. Nuclear Medicine, Am. Bd. Allergy and Immunology, Am. Bd. Med. Lab. Immunology, Am. Bd. Pathology in immunopathology. Intern Wesley Med. Ctr., Wichita, 1952-53, resident in pathology, 1953-54; resident in pathology Wayne County Gen. Hosp., Eloise, Mich., 1954-56, chief resident in pathology, 1956-57; clin. pathologist, asst. dir. lab. Wesley Med. Ctr., Wichita, Kans., 1957-69, dir. sci., 1965-86, dir. labs., 1969-77, dir. clin. immunology, 1979-86; med. dir. Roche Biomed. Lab., Wichita, Kans., 1979-86; dir. clin. labs. Iatric Corp., Tempe, Ariz., 1988—; pres. Kilcawley Enterprises, 1986—. Author: Electrophoresis/Immunoelectric Phoresis, 1969; editor series Lab Med Little Brown, 1965-81; contbr. 210 articles to profl. jours. Pfc. USM, 1942-45. Fellow Am. Soc. Clin. pathologist (bd. dirs. 1968, Disting. Svc. award 1980), Coll. Am. Pathologist; mem. AAAS, ACS, Am. Assn. Clin. Chemists, Alpha Pi Mu, Phi Lambda Upsilon, Alpha Omega Alpha. Office: KilCawley Enterprises 7135 E Main St Scottsdale AZ 85251

CAYETANO, BENJAMIN JEROME, governor, former state senator and representative; b. Honolulu, Nov. 14, 1939; s. Bonifacio Marcos and Eleanor (Infante) C.; children: Brandon, Janeen, Samantha. B.A., UCLA, 1968; J.D., Loyola U., 1971. Bar: Hawaii 1971. Practiced in Honolulu, 1971-86; mem. Hawaii Ho. of Reps., 1975-78, Hawaii Senate, 1979-86; lt. gov. State of Hawaii, 1986-95, gov., 1994—; bar examiner Hawaii Supreme Ct., 1976-78, disciplinary bd., 1982-86; arbitration panel 1st Cir. Ct. State of Hawaii, 1986; adv. U. Hawaii Law Rev., 1982-84. Mem. bd. regents Chaminade U., 1980-83; mem. adv. council U. Hawaii Coll. Bus. Adminstrn., 1982-83. Recipient Excellence in Leadership Medallion Asia-Pacific Acad. Consortium for Pub. Health, 1991, UCLA Alumni award for excellence in pub. svc., 1993. Democrat. Office: Office of Gov State Capitol 415 S Ave Beretenia 5th Flr Honolulu HI 96813*

CAYNE, DOUGLAS ANDREW, computer company executive; b. Cambridge, Mass., Mar. 8, 1958; s. Bernard Stanley and Helen Marie (Burgard) C.; m. Madoka Etoh, Aug. 20, 1977 (div. 1981). BA, Stanford U., 1980. Analyst Hudson Inst., Croton-on-Hudson, N.Y., 1978-80; rsch. analyst McKinsey & Co., L.A., 1980-81; v.p. Gartner Group, Inc., Stamford, Conn., 1981-91; group v.p., gen. mgr. Gartner Group, Inc., San Jose, Calif., 1992—. Office: Gartner Group Inc 251 River Oaks Pkwy San Jose CA 95134-1913

CAYSE, PHYLLIS, federal mediator; b. Newark, N.J., Oct. 7, 1930; d. Isadore Helen (Blackman) Smith; m. Aaron H. Schectman, Dec. 24, 1950 (div. Apr. 1973); children: David, Hal; m. Raymond T. Cayse, July 25, 1976. BA, Douglass Coll., 1952. Cert. tchr., N.J.; commd. Fed. Mediation and Conciliation. Libr. asst. Newark Pub. Libr., 1952-54; tchr. Metuchen (N.J.) Pub. Schs., 1954-56, Woodbridge Pub. Schs., Colonia, N.J., 1964-67, Ocean Twp. Pub. Schs., Ocean Twp., N.J., 1967-68; hearing officer N.J. Pub. Employee Rels., Trenton, 1968-72; field agt. Nat. Labor Rels. Bd., Newark, 1973-74; commr. Fed. Mediation and Conciliation Svc., St. Louis and L.A., 1974—; nominating com. mem. Soc. for Profls. in Dis. Res., St. Louis, L.A., 1974-80. Mem. Indsl. Rels. Rsch. Assn. (exec. bd. mem., sec.-treas. L.A. 1990-93), Nat. Trust for Historic Preservation, Smithsonian, Holocaust Mus. Office: Fed Mediation/Conciliation Svc 225 W Broadway Glendale CA 91204-1331

CAZIER, BARRY JAMES, electrical engineer, software developer; b. Phoenix, May 10, 1943; s. James Henry and Dorothy Marie (Lynton) C.; m. Susan Arline Shewey, June 13, 1964 (dec. July 1979); children: Suzanne, Bryan; m. Illene D. Miller, Dec. 19, 1994. Student, Colo. Sch. Mines, 1961-62; BSEE, U. Colo., 1965; student advanced bus. adminstrn., Ariz. State U., 1974-77. Mfg. mgmt. Gen. Electric, Richland, Wash., 1965-66, Warren, Ohio, 1966-67; system engr. Gen. Electric, Schenectady, N.Y., 1967-69; project mgr. Honeywell, Phoenix, 1970-80, dir. field ops., 1980-85, program mgr., 1985—; prin. Cazier Software Designs, Scottsdale, Ariz., 1985—. adv. Jr. Achievement, Phoenix, 1972. Club: IBM PC Users (Phoenix). Home: 8508 E Via Montoya Scottsdale AZ 85255-4936 Office: Honeywell 16404 N Black Canyon Hwy Phoenix AZ 85023-3033

CECH, THOMAS ROBERT, chemistry and biochemistry educator; b. Chgo., Dec. 8, 1947; m. Carol Lynn Martinson; children: Allison E., Jennifer N. BA in Chemistry, Grinnell Coll., 1970, DSc (hon.), 1987; PhD in Chem., U. Calif., Berkeley, 1975; DSc (hon.), U. Chgo., 1991; Drury Coll., 1994. Postdoctoral fellow dept. biology MIT, Cambridge, Mass., 1975-77; from asst. prof. to assoc. prof. chemistry U. Colo., Boulder, 1978-83, prof. chemistry and biochemistry also molecular cellular and devel. biology, 1983—, disting. prof., 1990—; rsch. prof. Am. Cancer Soc., 1987—; investigator Howard Hughes Med. Inst., 1988—; co-chmn. Nucleic Acids Gordon Conf., 1984; Phillips disting. visitor Haverford Coll., 1984; Vivian Ernst meml. lectr. Brandeis U., 1984, Cynthia Chan meml. lectr. U. Calif., Berkeley; mem. Welch Found. Symposium, 1985; Danforth lectr. Grinnell Coll. 1986; Pfizer lectr. Harvard U., 1986, Hastings lectr., 1992; Verna and Marrs McLean lectr. Baylor Coll. Medicine, 1987; Harvey lectr., 1987; Mayer lectr. MIT, 1987, HHMI lectr., 1989, T.Y. Shen lectr., 1994; Martin D. Kamen disting. lectureship, U. Calif., San Diego, 1988; Alfred Burger lectr. U. Va., 1988; Berzelius lectr. Karolinska Inst., 1988; Osamu Hayaishi lectr. Internat. Union Biochemistry, Prague, 1988; Beckman lectr. U. Utah, 1989; Max Tishler lectr. Merck, 1989; Abbott vis. scholar U. Chgo., 1989; Herriott lectr. Johns Hopkins U., 1990; J.T. Baker lectr., 1990; G.N. Lewis lectr. U. Calif., Berkeley, 1990; Sonneborn lectr. Ind. U., 1991; Sternbach lectr. Yale U., 1991; W. Pauli lectr., Zürich, 1992; Carter-Wallace lectr. Princeton U., 1992; Stetten lectr. NIH, 1992; Dauben lectr. U. Wash., 1992; Marker lectr. U. Md., 1993; Hirschmann lectr. Oberlin Coll., 1993; Beach lectr. Purdue U., 1993; Abe White lectr. Syntex, 1993; Robbins lectr. Pomona Coll., 1994; Bren lectr. U. Calif., Irvine, 1994; Wawzonek lectr. U. Iowa, 1994; Sumner lectr. Cornell U., 1994; Steenbock lectr. U. Wis., 1995; Murachi lectr. FAOB Congress, Sydney, 1995; Streck award lectr. U. Nebr., 1996; Gardner-Davern lectr. U. Utah, 1996, Priestley lectr. Pa. State U., 1996; Beckman lectr. Calif. Inst. Tech., 1996, Lemieux lectr. U. Alta., Can., 1997, Hogg Award lectr. MD Anderson Cancer Ctr., 1997. Assoc. editor Cell, 1986-87, RNA Jour.; mem. editl. bd. Genes and Development; dep. editor Sci. mag. NSF fellow, 1970-75, Pub. Health Svc. rsch. fellow Nat. Cancer Inst. 1975-77, Guggenheim fellow, 1985-86; recipient medal Am. Inst. Chemists, 1970, Rsch. Career Devel. award Nat. Cancer Inst., 1980-85, Young Sci. award Passano Found., 1984, Harrison Howe award, 1984, Pfizer award, 1985, U.S. Steel award, 1987, V.D. Mattia award, 1987, Louisa Gross Horowitz prize, 1988, Newcombe-Cleveland award AAAS, 1988, Heineken prize Royal Netherlands Acad. Arts and Scis., 1988, Gairdner Found. Internat. award, 1988, Lasker Basic Med. Rsch. award, 1988, Rosenstiel award, 1989, Warren Triennial prize, 1989, Nobel prize in Chemistry, 1989, Hopkins medal Brit. Biochem. Soc., 1992, Feodor Lynen medal, 1995, Nat. Sci. medal, 1995; named to Esquire Mag. Register, 1985, Westerner of Yr. Denver Post, 1986. Mem. AAAS, Am. Soc. Biochem. Molecular Biology, NAS, Am. Acad. Arts and Scis., European Molecular Biology Orgn., RNA Soc. (v.p. 1993-96). Office: U Colo Dept Chemistry & Biochemistry Boulder CO 80309

CECI, JESSE ARTHUR, violinist; b. Phila., Feb. 2, 1924; s. Luigi Concezio and Catherine Marie (Marotta) C.; m. Catherine Annette Stevens, Aug. 5, 1979. BS, Juilliard Sch. Music, 1951; license de concert, L'Ecole Normale de Musique, Paris, 1954; MusM, Manhattan Sch. Music, 1971. Assoc. concertmaster New Orleans Philharm. Orch., 1953-54; violinist Boston Symphony Orch., 1954-59, N.Y. Philharm. Orch., N.Y., 1959-62, Esterhazy

Orch., N.Y.C., 1962-68; concertmaster Denver Symphony Orch., 1974-89, Colo. Symphony Orch., 1989-95; over 50 performances of 22 major works; mem. Zimbler Sinfonietta, Boston, 1957-59; participant Marlboro Festival Chamber Orch. Vt., summmers 1960-62, 65, Marlboro Festival Chamber Orch. European-Israeli tour, 1965, Grand Teton Festival, Wyo., 1972, N.Mex. Festival, Taos, 1980, Carmel (Calif.) Bach Festival, 1987—, Whistler (B.C., Can.) Mozart Festival, 1989-90, Bear Valley (Calif.) Festival, 1995—, Mendocino (Calif.) Festival, 1996—; mem. faculty Congress of Strings, Dallas, 1985, N.Y. Coll. Music, 1961-71, NYU, 1971-74, U. Colo., 1975-79; guest mem. faculty Univ. Denver, 1986; mem., assoc. concertmaster Casals Festival Orch., San Juan, P.R., 1963-77; violinist Cleve. Orch. fgn. tours, 1967, 73, 78, Cin. Symphony Orch. world tour, 1966; 1st violinist N.Y. String Quartet in-residence at U. Maine, Orono, summer 1969; guest violinist Fla. West Coast Symphony, Sarasota, 1993—; concertmaster Minn. Orch., summers 1970-71, Denver Chamber Orch., 1985-90; guest concertmaster Pitts. Symphony Orch., Pitts., L.A., 1988, mem. N.Y. Philharmonia Chamber Ensemble in-residence at Hopkins Ctr., Dartmouth U., summer 1973; recitalist, Paris, 1963, Amsterdam, 1963, recitalist Carnegie Recital Hall, N.Y.C., 1963, Town Hall, N.Y.C., 1968, 70, Alice Tully Hall, N.Y.C., 1972; fgn. tour Pitts. Symphony Orch., 1989. Cpl. U.S. Army, 1943-46, PTO. Fulbright fellow Paris, 1951-52. Democrat. Roman Catholic. Office: Colo Symphony Orch 1031 13th St Denver CO 80204-2156

CEDOLINE, ANTHONY JOHN, psychologist; b. Rochester, N.Y., Sept. 19, 1942; s. Peter Ross and Mary J. (Anthony) C.; m. Clare Marie De Rose, Aug. 16, 1964; children: Maria A., Antonia C., Peter E. Student, U. San Francisco, 1960-62; BA, San Jose State U., 1965, MS, 1968; PhD in Ednl. Pscyhology, Columbia Pacific U., 1983. Lic. ednl. psychologist, sch. adminstr., marriage, family, child counselor, sch psychologist, sch. counselor, social worker, Calif.; Lic. real estate broker, Calif. Mng. ptnr. Cienega Valley Vineyards and Winery (formerly Almaden Vineyards) and Comml. Shopping Ctrs., 1968—; coord. psychol. svcs. Oak Grove Sch. Dist., San Jose, Calif., 1968-81, asst. dir. pupil svcs., 1977-81; dir. pupil svcs. Oak Grove Sch. Dist., San Jose, 1981-83; pvt. practice, ednl. psychologist Ednl. Assocs., San Jose, 1983—; co-dir. Biofeedback Inst. of Santa Clara County, San Jose, 1976-83; ptnr. in Cypress Ctr.-Ednl. Psychologists and Consultancy, 1978—; cons., program auditor for Calif. State Dept. Edn.; instr. U. Calif., Santa Cruz and LaVerne Coll. Ext. courses; guest spkr. San Jose State U.; lectr., workshop presenter in field. Author: Occupational Stress and Job Burnout, 1982, A Parents Guide to School Readiness, 1971, The Effect of Affect, 1975; contbr. articles to profl. jours. and newspapers. Founder, bd. dirs. Lyceum of Santa Clara County, 1971—. Mem. NEA, Calif. Tchrs. Assn., Calif. Assn. Sch. Psychologists, Nat. Assn. Sch. Psychologists, Coun. for Exceptional Children, Calif. Assn. for Gifted, Assn. Calif. Sch. Adminstrs., Calif. Personnel & Guidance Assn., Biofeedback Soc. Am., Nat. Assn., Tau Delta Phi. Home and Office: 1183 Nikulina Ct San Jose CA 95120-5441

CELLA, JOHN J., freight company executive; b. 1940; married. BBA, Temple U., 1965. Regional mgr. Japan ops. Airborne Freight Corp., Seattle, 1965-71, v.p. Far Ea. ops., 1971-72, sr. v.p. internat. div., from 1982, now exec. v.p. internat. div. Office: Airborne Freight Corp 3101 Western Ave Seattle WA 98121-1024*

CENARRUSA, PETE T., secretary of state; b. Carey, Idaho, Dec. 16, 1917; s. Joseph and Ramona (Gardoqui) C.; m. Freda B. Coates, Oct. 25, 1947; 1 son, Joe Earl. B.S. in Agr., U. Idaho, 1940. Tchr. high sch. Cambridge, Idaho, 1940-41, Carey and Glenns Ferry, Idaho, 1946; tchr. vocat. agr. VA, Blaine County, Idaho, 1946-51; farmer, woolgrower, nr. Carey, 1946-95; mem. Idaho Ho. of Reps., 1951-67, speaker, 1963-67; sec. state Idaho, 1967-90, 91—; mem. Idaho Bd. Land Commrs., Idaho Bd. Examiners; pres. Idaho Flying Legislators, 1953-63; chmn. Idaho Legis. Council, 1964—, Idaho Govt. Reorgn. Com.; Idaho del. Council State Govts., 1963—. Elected ofcl., mem. BLM Adv. Coun., Boise Dist.; Rep. adminstr. Hall of Fame, 1978; sr. mem. State Bd. Land Commrs., 1967-96. Maj. USMCR, 1942-46, 52-58. Named Hon. Farmer Future Farmers Am., 1955; named to Agrl. Hall of Fame, 1973; Idaho Athletic Hall of Fame, 1976, Basque Hall of Fame, 1983. Mem. Blaine County Livestock Mktg. Assn., Idaho Wool Growers Assn. (chmn. 1954), Carey C. of C. (pres. 1952), U. Idaho Alumni Assn., Gamma Sigma Delta, Tau Kappa Epsilon. Republican. Office: Office of Sec State PO Box 83720 Boise ID 83720-0080*

CENTERWALL, WILLARD RAYMOND, physician; b. Missoula, Mont., Jan. 16, 1924; s. Willard Raymond Centerwall, Sr. and Charlotte Amanda (Brandon) Wood; m. Siegried Louise Achorn Centerwall, Sept. 2 , 1949 (dec. July 1992); children: Theodore, Brandon, Krista, Alison, Jennifer, Rebecca; m. Arlene Rudd Centerwall, Aug. 27, 1994. BS in Zoology, Yale U., 1949, MD, 1952; MPH in Maternal & Child Health, U. Mich., 1967, MS in Human Genetics, 1968; D in Cultural Anthropology (hon.), World U., 1983. Diplomate Am. Bd. Pediatrics, Am. Bd. Preventive Medicine, Am. Bd. Med. Genetics. Rotating internship White Meml. Hosp., L.A., 1952-53; first yr. pediatric residency White Meml. Hosp., L.A. County Gen. Hosp., 1953-54; sr. yr. pediatric residency L.A. Children's Hosp., 1954-55; instr., asst. clin. prof., asst. prof. pediatrics Coll. Med. Evangelists Sch. of Medicine, L.A., 1955-61; lectr., reader, assoc. prof. pediatrics Christian Med. Coll., Vellore, South India, 1961-66; organizer, first head of dept. pediatrics Miraj Med. Sch., Maharashtra State, India, 1965; assoc. prof. pediatrics Loma Linda U. Sch. Medicine, 1968, prof. pediatrics, 1970-78; assoc. prof. pub. health Loma Linda U. Sch. Health, Calif., 1968, prof. maternal & child health, 1970-78, gen. cons., 1982—; prof. anthropology Loma Linda U. Grad. Sch., Calif., 1976-78; prof. emeritus of pediatrics and genetics Loma Linda U. Sch. Medicine, 1986; prof. pediatrics and genetics U. Calif. Sch. Medicine, Davis, 1978-85; prof. in residence dept. reproduction U. Calif. Sch. Veterinary Medicine, Davis, 1981-85; prof. emeritus of pediatrics and genetics U. Calif., Davis, 1986; clin. prof. depts. med. genetics & pediatrics Oreg. Health Scis. U. & Sch. Medicine, Portland, 1986—; ret.; dir. Satellite Genetic Diagnostic and Counseling Clinic, Reno, 1983-85, State Newborn Metabolic Screening Program at U. Calif., Davis, 1980-85, Chico-Oroville (Calif.) Satellite Genetic Diagnostic and Counseling Clinic, 1980-85, Satellite Genetic Diagnostic & Counseling Clinic, Redding, Calif., 1980-83, Genetic Disorders and Birth Defects Clinic Alta Regional Ctr., Sacramento, Calif., 1978-83; civilian med. specialist cons. in pediatrics David Grant USAF Med. Ctr., Travis AFB, 1982-85; organizer, 1st med. dir. Birth Defects and Genetics Clinic, Lakeport, Calif., 1978-84, Birth Defects and Genetics Diagnostic and Counseling Svc. Riverside County Health Dept., Calif., 1978, Birth Defects and Genetics Diagnostic and Counseling Svc. Loma Linda U. Med. Ctr., Calif., 1969-78, Birth Defects and Genetics Svc. Clarke County Dept. Pub. Health, Las Vegas, 1972, Birth Defects and Chromosome Lab. Svcs. Loma Linda U. Med. Ctr., Calif., 1969-78; organizer, 1st dir. Birth Defects and Genetics Clinic at Regional Ctr. for Devel. Disabilities, San Bernardino, Calif., 1976-78; spl. cons. to genetic disease section maternal & child health branch State Calif. Dept. Health, 1977-85, mem. adv. com. on inherited disorders, 1976; med. dir. Orthopedically Handicapped Clinic, Redlands, Calif., 1971-78; med. cons. Calif. Sch. for the Deaf, Riverside, Calif., 1969-78; pediatric cons. Pacific State Hosp. for Mentally Retarded, Pomona, Calif., 1955-60, 69-78, Sch. for Cerebral Palsied Children of Southern Calif., Altadena, 1956-60, and numerous others; vol. clin./acad. positions in Oreg., 1985—. Med. editor: Introduction series of booklets, 1958—; speaker in field. 1st lt. U.S. Army Corps of Engrs., 1943-47. Recipient of rsch. grants NIH, U.S. Pub. Health Svc., Meda Johnson & Co., Alumni Assn. of the Coll. of Med. Evangelists, Nat. Assn. for Retarded Children, Walter E. MacPherson Soc., The Nat. Found. March of Dimes, The Nat. Cancer Inst. and HEM Rsch., Inc., Calif. State Dept. Health; recipient Outstanding Svc. award for Excellence in the Provision of Med. Svcs. to Mentally Retarded Sacramento Assn. for the Retarded, Inc., 1982, 1st J.B.S. Haldane Oration medal Soc. Bionaturalists, 1985, Children's Bur. fellowship in Pub. Health and Human Genetics U. Mich., Ann Arbor, 1966-68. Home: 101 Silverwood Ln Silverton OR 97381-9739

CENTORINO, JAMES ROCCO, science educator; b. Salem, Mass., Aug. 16, 1949; s. James Joseph and Nicoletta Nancy (DiFine); m. Susan Virginia Hasson, Aug. 26, 1989. BS, Boston Coll., 1971, MS, 1975; MusB, Boston Conservatory Music, 1981, MusM, 1994. Calif. state tchg. credential, secondary sch. phys. sci. Asst. mgr., clk. Danvers (Mass.) News Agy., 1963-75; music arranger, instr. mus. marching groups, Northeastern U.S.A., 1964-84; tchg. fellow Boston Coll., 1972-74; substitute sci. and music tchr. Boston area schs., 1974-80; sci. tchr. Winchester (Mass.) Pub. Schs., 1980-81, Needham (Mass.) Pub. Schs., 1982; physics and music tchr. Weston (Mass.) Pub. Schs., 1982-84; physics tchr. Natick (Mass.) H.S., 1984-85, El Camino Real H.S., Woodland Hills, Calif., 1985—; music and sci. coach Acad. Decathlon Team, Woodland Hills, 1991—; music composing cons. bands, drum and bugle corps, mus. groups, 1965—. Composer: Notes on a Triangle, 1983 (ASCAP award 1993), Christmas Love, 1984 (ASCAP award 1985), others, 1975—; composer, performer, prodr.: (mus. album) Footsteps in the Sand, 1991 (Album of Yr. 1991), Ivory, 1993 (Genesis award recognition 1994), It's Christmas Everywhere, 1997, Three Dreams For Solo Cello and Piano. Mem. ASCAP, Nat. Assn. Rec. Arts and Scis., Nat. Sci. Tchrs. Assn., Calif. Tchrs. Assn., United Tchrs. L.A., Sigma Xi, Pi Kappa Lambda, Phi Mu Alpha Sinfonia. Roman Catholic. Home: 23278 Aetna St Woodland Hills CA 91367-3101 Office: Centorino Prodns PO Box 4478 West Hills CA 91308

CEREZO, ABRAHAM JOHNSON, marriage and family counselor; b. San Francisco, Dec. 1, 1966; s. Abelardo Sumijit and Mapuana Jane (Kanoho) C.; m. Carrie Ann Warner; children: Brandon Keli'i, Cameron Kekoa. BA in Psychology, Sacramento State U., 1992, MS in Counseling, 1995. Youth care worker St. Patrick's Home for Children, Sacramento, 1990-92; field rsch. worker Inst. for Social Rsch., Sacramento, 1991-92; anger mgmt. spkr. South Sacramento Counseling Ctr., 1995—, intern in marriage, family and child counseling, 1995—; owner Cerezo's Martial Arts, Sacramento, 1995—; sch. age coord., trainer and curriculum specialist McClelland AFB, Calif., 1996—; conflict mgmt. coord., spkr. Mark Hopkins Elem. Sch., Sacramento, 1994-95, conflict mgmt. coord., 1994-95; cmty. liaison South Sacramento Counseling Ctr., 1995—. Bd. dirs. South Sacramento Interfaith Partnership, 1995-96; mem. strategic planning com. Childrens Health, Sacramento, 1995—. Mem. ACA, Assn. for Multicultural Counseling and Devel., Calif. Assn. Marriage and Family Therapists. Office: Cerezos Martial Arts 7213B Florin Mall Dr Sacramento CA 95823

CERNAK, KEITH PATRICK, health care and financial consultant; b. Northampton, Mass., Mar. 17, 1954; s. Samuel and Geraldine (Dykstra) C.; m. Kristin Freedman, Sept. 10, 1983; children: Emily Samantha, Melanie Kristin. BA magna cum laude, U. Mass., 1976; MPH, U. Hawaii, 1980; MBA, UCLA, 1984. Healthcare researcher U. Hawaii, Honolulu, 1978; health planning cons. Guam Health Planning Agy., Agana, 1979; rsch. dir. Hawaii Dept. Health, Honolulu, 1980-81; grad. instr. UCLA Sch. Pub. Health, 1981; mgmt. cons. Am. Med. Internat., Beverly Hills, Calif., 1982; v.p. Crocker Bank, L.A., 1984-86; v.p. fin. Weyerhaeuser, San Francisco, 1986-91; dir. cmty. partnership, outcome mgmt. and health care provider consortium Evergreen Med. Ctr., Seattle, 1992—; health care cons.; nat. presenter in field. Author papers in field. Health Svc. scholar U. Hawaii, 1978. Mem. UCLA Sch. Mgmt., Beta Gamma Sigma. Home: 24503 SE 43rd Pl Issaquah WA 98029-7542

CERNY, CHARLENE ANN, museum director; b. Jamaica, N.Y., Jan. 12, 1947; d. Albert Joseph and Charlotte Ann (Novy) Cerny; children: Elizabeth Brett Cerny-Chipman, Kathryn Rose Cerny-Chipman. BA, SUNY, Binghamton, 1969. Curator Latin-Am. folk art Mus. Internat. Folk Art, Santa Fe, 1972-84, mus. dir., 1984—; adv. bd. C.G. Jung Inst., Santa Fe, 1990—. Mem. Mayor's Commn. on Children and Youth, Santa Fe, 1990-93, adv. bd. Recipient Exemplary Performance award State of N.Mex., 1982, Internat. Ptnr. Among Mus. award; Smithsonian Instn. travel grantee, 1976; Florence Dibell Bartlett Meml. scholar, 1979, 91; Kellogg fellow, 1983. Mem. Am. Assn. Mus. Internat. Coun. Mus. (bd. dirs. 1991—, exec. bd. 1991-95), Am. Folklore Soc., Mountain-Plains Mus. Assn., N.Mex. Assn. Mus. (chair membership com. 1975-77). Office: Mus Internat Folk Art PO Box 2087 Santa Fe NM 87504-2087

CERULLO, RUDY MICHAEL, II, psychology, theology educator, minister; b. Phila., Feb. 25, 1952; s. Rudy and Edith Elizabeth (Cullen) C.; m. Kathleen Marie Evans, June 10, 1993. BA, Oral Roberts U., Tulsa, 1973; MDiv, Fuller Theol. Sem., Pasadena, Calif., 1976, ThM, 1984; DMin, ThD, So. Calif. Theol. Sem., 1990; PhD, Vision Internat. U., Ramona, Calif., 1996; DDiv, Kingsway Theol. Sem., Des Moines, 1989. Ordained to ministry Assemblies of God, 1977; cert. pastoral counselor. Assoc. pastor Orange (Calif.) Covenant Ch., First Presbyn. Ch., Alhambra, Calif., Tri-City Assembly Ch., Covina, Calif., Woodland Hills (Calif.) Neighborhood Ch., Palm View Assembly of God Ch., Whittier, Calif., En Agape Christian Fellowship Ch., Alta Loma, Calif.; psychiat. hosp. program dir., clinician in pvt. practice Brea (Calif.) Hosp. Neuropsychiat. Ctr., Terrace Plaza Med. Ctr., Baldwin Park, Calif., Manor West Hosp., L.A., Buena Park (Calif.) Med. Ctr., Agape Counseling and Therapy Svcs., Anaheim; prof. theology So. Calif. Coll., Costa Mesa, Calif., 1979-83; prof. psychology/theology, acad. dean So. Calif. Theol. Sem., Stanton, 1989-92, Trinity Coll. of Grad. Studies, Orange, 1989-92; assoc. pastor Harmony Christian Fellowship Ch., Anza, Calif., 1994-96; pastor Discipleship Regency Christian Ctr., Downey, Calif., 1996—; prof. psychology/theology, psychology dept. dir. Vision Internat. U., Pomona, 1991—, Calif. Union U., Fullerton, 1991—, Calif. Grad. Sch. Theology, Rosemead, 1991—, New Hope U., Stanton, 1991—, Ctrl. U., Palos Verdes, Calif., 1991—. Named Disting. counselor in field of Psychiat. Hosp. Devel., U.S. Pubs., Inc., 1990. Fellow ACA (student cert. sponsor 1988—). Republican. Home and Office: 3218 S Linda Way Santa Ana CA 92704-6140

CERVANTES, JAMES VALENTINE, English language educator; m. Leilani Wright, Mar. 31, 1995. BA, U. Wash., 1972; MFA, U. Iowa, 1974. Tchng. asst. U. Iowa, 1972-74; tchr. humanities dept. C.C. of Vt., Brattleboro, 1974-76; lectr., English dept. Ariz. State U., 1978-81; instr. English dept. Yavapai C.C., 1987-88, No. Ariz. U., 1985-88; asst. prof. Learning Skills Ctr., English dept. Calif. State U., Sacramento, 1988-92; prof. English dept. Mesa C.C., 1992—; poet-in-residence Ariz. Commn. on the Arts, 1994-95; presenter confs. in field; presenter poetry readings; cellist, Air Force Orchestra, 1963-67; psychiat. aide at pvt. mental hosp., 1974-75. Author: The Headlong Future, 1990, The Year is Approaching Snow, 1981, The Firesin Oil Drums, 1980; editor: (with Leilani Wright) Fever Dreams: Contemporary Arizona Poets, 1997; editor Porch Mag., 1977-81; contbr. poetry to anthologies; contbr. articles to profl. jours. Faculty profl. devel. minigrantee, Calif. State U., Sacramento, 1990-91; recipient The Capricorn award The Writer's Voice and the West Side Y Writer's Ctr., N.Y.C., 1987. Office: Mesa CC 1833 W Southern Ave Mesa AZ 85202-4866

CERVANTEZ, GIL LAWRENCE, venture capital company executive; b. Concord, Calif., July 14, 1944; s. Val J. and Laura E. (Verdugua) C.; m. Pamela A. Richmond, Feb. 14, 1965; children: Jeffrey, Thomas. BS, U. Oreg., 1965; MBA, U. Calif., Berkeley, 1972. V.p. Gt. Western Nat. Bank, Portland, Oreg., 1971-74, Heller Internat., San Francisco, 1975-76; dir. Control Data, San Francisco, 1976-79; sr. v.p. Century Bank, San Francisco, 1979-85; dir. syndications Pacificorp Ventures, Portland, 1988-90; pres. Latipac Fin., San Francisco, 1985-90; pres. A G & T Investments, Inc., Walnut Creek, Calif., 1990—, also bd. dirs.; exec. v.p. Terameth Industries, Inc., Walnut Creek, 1990—, also bd. dirs. Lt. comdr. USN, 1965-71, Vietnam. Mem. Robert G. Sproul Assocs., U. Calif. Alumni Assn., Libr. Assocs., Smithsonian Assocs., Bear Backers, Commonwealth Club Calif. Republican. Roman Catholic. Home: 177 Ardith Ct Orinda CA 94563-4344 Office: A G & T Investments Inc 1331 N California Blvd Ste 730 Walnut Creek CA 94596-4536

CESARO, WAYNE ROBERT, maritime technology educator; b. Newark, Apr. 28, 1952; s. Robert Julian Cesaro and Threasa Elizabeth (Rizzo) Racioppi; m. Catherine Elizabeth Gough, Jan. 4, 1990. Lead instr., skipper Seattle O.I.C., 1980-82; deck officer Port of Seattle, 1982-83; mil. command Able Seaman, Oakland, Calif., 1983-86; deck officer Western Geo Phys., Houston, 1986-87; vessel capt. Argosey, Seattle, 1987-91; instr. Seattle Pub. Schs., 1991—; chmn. VHF Survey Com., Seattle, 1987-89, Seaward Bound Adv. Bd., Seattle, 1991—. With USN, 1975-81. Mem. Propeller Club Port Seattle. Democrat. Roman Catholic. Office: Work Tng Program 13720 Roosevelt Way N Seattle WA 98133-7233

CEVENINI, ROBERTO MAURO, gas and oil industry executive, educator, author, athlete, inventor, consultant, speaker; b. Bologna, Emilia, Italy, Oct. 28, 1957; came to U.S., 1985; s. Romano and Camilla Cevenini; m. Carol Jean Porter, Aug. 9, 1985; children: Dino, Marco, Franco. BSME, Cath. U., Venezuela, 1979; BS in Indsl. Engring. cum laude, U. Miami, Fla., 1983, MS in Indsl. Engring., 1985, MBA, 1986, MS in Mgmt. Sci., 1992. Registered profl. engr., Fla.; cert. project mgr.; cert. cost/scheduling engr.; cert. reliability engr.; cert. quality engr.; cert. prodn. and inventory control engr.; cert. power plant control ctr. operator. Prodn. engr. GM Metalmaster-Prodenca, Valencia & La Victoria, Venezuela, 1978; quality control and design engr. Metalmaster-Prodenca, Sao Paulo, Rio de Janeiro, Brazil, 1979; mfg. and mktg. engr. Metal Master Prodenca, Buenos Aires, Mendoza, Argentina, 1980-83; quality control and mfg. engr. Rolls-Royce Aerospace Mfg., Inc., Derby, Eng., 1983-85, Miami, Fla., 1983-85; corp. mgmt. cons. Fla. Power & Light Co., Miami, 1986, nuclear plant ops. coord., 1987, prin. plant engr., 1988-89, power plant supt., 1989-90; project mgr. and internat. cons. Qualtec Quality Svcs., West Palm Beach, 1991; pres. Dynatek, 1991—; exploration/prodn. dir. total quality mgmt. sys./engring. Texaco, Inc., Denver, 1992—; dir. business alliances, joint ventures and acquisitions, Texaco, Denver, 1994—; cons. Goodwill Industries, Miami, 1983; cons. 43 major multinat. corps. in 14 countries, 1980—; adj. faculty Broward C.C., Miami, 1987, Fla. Internat. U., Miami, 1987-92, U. Miami, 1990-92, Denver U., 1993—, Phoenix U., 1995—; examiner Malcolm Baldridge Nat. Quality Award (ISO 9000 auditor), Deming Overseas Quality Medal Award. Author 18 tech. manuals translated into five langs. on integration of engring. reliability and indsl. statis. applications that include: Statistical Team Leader Training, Statistical Team Member Training, Reliability Engineering, 1 & 2, Statistical Process Control, 1 & 2 Process Management, Team Facilitator, Applications Expert Engineering, Benchmarking in the Technical and Business Fields, Policy Management Systems, Managing Process Improvement Teams, Concurrent Engineering, Valve Added Analysis, Business Alliances and International Joint Ventures, Business Acquisitions, Business Development; author 38 tech. papers; inventor rectangular fan; expert witness 3 cases. Mem. Fla. Power and Light Track Team, Miami, 1986, Golf League, 1986; head coach Denver Little League Soccer, 1993—; mem. North Miami Beach City Coun., 1987-89; corp. team leader Multiple Sclerosis Soc. Am., March of Dimes, United Way, Global Relief. Recipient Gold medal Swimming Fedn., 1971, 41 profl. awards for outstanding contbns. to 9 fields and industries. Mem. ASME, IEEE, NSPE, Soc. Petroleum Engrs., Am. Inst. Indsl. Engrs., Am. Nuclear Soc., Inst. Mgmt. Sci., Am. Soc. for Quality Control, Soc. of Profl. Engrs., Internat. Platform Assn., Texaco Athletic Corp. Team, Golden Key, Phi Kappa Phi, Tau beta Pi, Alpha Pi Mu. Roman Catholic. Office: Texaco Inc 4601 Dtc Blvd Denver CO 80237-2549

CHABOT, AURORE, art educator, artist; b. Nashua, N.H., July 30, 1949; d. Paul Emile and Simone Bernadette (Miville) C. B.F.A., Pratt Inst., 1971; M.f.A., U. Colo., 1981. Coordinator ceramics program Women's Interart Ctr., N.Y.C., 1978-79; teaching asst. U. Colo., Boulder, 1980; vis. head ceramics U. Minn.-Duluth, 1981-82; asst. prof. art U. Vt., Burlington, 1982-88; asst. prof. U. Ariz., Tucson, 1988-91, assoc. prof., 1991—; exhbn. juror Helen Day Art Ctr., Stowe, Vt., 1984; accreditation evaluator Commn. on Instns. Higher Edn., New Eng. Assn. Schs. and Colls., Inc., 1985, 87; artist-in-residence Artpark, Lewiston, N.Y., 1984, Sun Valley Ctr. Arts and Humanities, Idaho, 1985, J.M. Kohler Arts Ctr., Sheboygan, Wis., 1985, Banff Ctr. Sch. Fine Arts, Can., 1987, Watershed Ctr, Ceramic Arts, North Edgecomb, Maine, 1987, MacDowell Artists Colony, Peterboro, N.H., 1991, Ceramic Symposium, Dzinteri, Latvia, 1991, Archie Bray Found., Helena, Mont., 1993, 95, Va. Ctr. Creative Arts, Sweet Briar, 1994. One-woman shows WARM Gallery, Mpls., 1982, Jane Hartsook Gllery of Greenwich House Pottery, N.Y.C., 1983, John Michael Kohler Art Ctr., Sheboygan, 1984, The Gallery at the Living and Learning Ctr., U. Vt., Burlington, 1986; group shows include Bennington Coll., 1983, Brattleboro Mus., 1984, Skidmore Coll., 1984, Taipei Fine Arts Mus., Taiwan, 1985, U. Mass., 1985, Jane Corkin Gallery, Toronto, 1985, Chgo. Library Cultural Ctr., 1986, AIR Gallery, N.Y.C., 1986, Monmouth Mus., Lincroft, N.J., 1986, Scripps Coll., Claremont, Calif., 1986, Wellesley Coll. Mus., Mass., 1986, T.W. Wood Art Gallery, Montpelier, Vt., 1986, Maudslay State Park outdoor sculpture installation, Newburyport, Mass., 1986, Fashion Inst. Tech. Artisan Space Gallery, N.Y.C., 1987, U. N.Mex., Las Cruces, 1987, others. Vt. Council on Arts grantee, 1983-84, 86; Nat. Endowment for Arts grantee, 1983. Mem. Coll. Art Assn., Nat. Council on Edn. for Ceramic Arts, Am. Crafts Council, Women's Caucus for Art. Democrat.

CHACON, MICHAEL ERNEST, computer networking specialist; b. L.A., Feb. 14, 1954; s. Ernest Richard and Teresa Marie (Venegas) C.; m. Virginia Marie; children: Mylan Graham, Aubrie Sarah, Christina Nabseth, Caitlyn Nabseth, Julia Anna. Student, Pierce Coll., 1972-74, Boise State U., 1980-82; BSBA, U. Phoenix, 1997. Systems cons. MEC & Assocs., Riverside, Calif., 1986-91; regional mgr. Inacom Corp., Garden Grove, Calif., 1991—; chief tech. officer Ascolta Tng. Co., Irvine, Calif.; cons. in field; lectr. Microsoft Corp., Bellvue, Wash., 1990-92; chief tng. officer Ascolta Tng. Co., Irvine, Calif. Author: Understanding Networks, 1991; contbr. articles to profl. jours. Named to Dean's List, Pierce Coll., 1973, 74. Mem. Lake Elsinore Sportsman Assn., L.A. World Affairs Coun., 3Com Adv. Coun. (pres. tech. adv. bd. 1986-92). Office: Inacom Corp 11842 Monarch St Garden Grove CA 92841-2113

CHADEY, HENRY F., museum director; b. Superior, Wyo., Feb. 20, 1924; s. Frank and Anna (Glogovsek) C.; m. Helen Putz, Aug. 3, 1957; children: Michael, Katherine, Mary Jo, Jeanne. BA, U. Wyo., 1949, MA, 1955. Tchr. Dist. No. 7, Reliance, Wyo., 1956; sch. supt. Dist. No. 7, Reliance, 1956-59; asst. supt. Wyo. State Dept. Edn., Cheyenne, Wyo., 1959-61; high sch. prin. Dist. No. 8, Glenrock, Wyo., 1961-62, Dist. No. 4, Rock Springs, Wyo., 1962-67; mus. dir. Sweetwater City Mus., Green River, Wyo., 1967-90; ret., 1990; instr. in field. Author: Rock Springs Chinese, 1985; author jour. Wyoming Geological Assistant Guidebook, 1973, Annals of Wyoming, 1978. Clk. Sch. Dist. No. 1, Sweetwater County, 1967—; pres. Wyo. State Hist. Soc., 1972-73; chmn. Wyo. Sch. Bd. Assn., 1977-78; mem. Wyo. State Sch. Bd., 1977-78. Mem. Am. Assn. Mus., Am. Assn. for State and Local History, Mt. Plains Mus. Assn., Colo.-Wyo. Mus. Assn. (dir. 1986-88), Lions (pres. 1976-77, clk. 1980-86), Wyo. Ret. Tchrs. (v.p.). Democrat. Roman Catholic. Home: 413 Fremont St Rock Springs WY 82901-6627

CHADWICK, CYDNEY MARIE, writer, art projects executive; b. Oakland, Calif.. MA, Kootenay Sch. of Writing, Vancouver, B.C., Can., 1996. Exec. dir. Syntax Projects for Arts, Penngrove, Calif., 1990—; writer Penngrove, Calif., 1993—. Author: Enemy Clothing, 1993 The Gift Horse's Mouth, 1994, Oeuvres, 1995, Persistent Disturbances, 1995, Interims, 1997. Office: AVEC Box 1059 Penngrove CA 94951

CHADWICK, WHITNEY, writer, art historian, educator; b. Niagara Falls, N.Y., July 28, 1943; d. Cecil George and Helen Louise (Reichert) C.; m. Robert Alan Bechtle, Nov. 5, 1983. BA, Middlebury Coll., 1965; MA, Pa. State U., 1968, PhD, 1975. From asst to assoc. prof. MIT, Cambridge, Mass., 1972-78; prof. of art San Francisco State U., 1978—; vis. asst. prof. U. Calif., Berkeley, 1977; vis prof. Stanford (Calif.) U., 1990. Author: Myth in Surrealist Painting, 1980, Women Artists and the Surrealist Movement, 1985, Women, Art and Society, 1990; co-editor: Significant Others, 1995; (monograph) Leonora Carrington, 1995. Named NEH fellow, 1981, ACLS fellow, 1987, Mary Ingraham Bunting Inst. fellow, Cambridge, Mass., 1992-93. Mem. Coll. Art Assn. (bd. dirs. 1987-93). Office: San Francisco State U 1600 Hollaway Ave San Francisco CA 94132

CHAFFEE, JAMES ALBERT, protective services official; b. Balt., Aug. 14, 1952; s. John Dempster and Elizabeth May (Holden) C.; m. Virginia Rose Braun, Oct. 4, 1980; children: Andrew James, Thomas John, Elizabeth Mary. AA, Alan Hancock Coll., 1973; BA, Chapman Coll., 1980; MBA, St. Thomas Coll., 1986. Lic. EMT, L.A. County; lic. police officer, Minn. Police officer Minnetonka (Minn.) Police Dept., 1976-87, police supr., 1982-87; pub. safety dir. City of Chanhassen, Minn., 1987-90; dir. security Walt Disney Co., Burbank, Calif., 1990—; dir. S.W. Metro Drug Task Force, Chanhassen, 1988-90; adv. com. 1991 U.S. Open, Chaska, Minn., 1989-90. Founding mem. Chanhassen Rotary Club, 1987, v.p., 1990; pres. Emblem Sch. Site Coun., Saugus, Calif., 1992. With USAF, 1972-76. Mem. Chief Spl. Agts. Assn. (dir. 1991—), Am. Soc. for Indsl. Security, Community Police and Security Team. Republican. Roman Catholic. Office: Walt Disney Co 500 S Buena Vista St Burbank CA 91521-0001

CHAFFEE, STEVEN HENRY, communication educator; b. South Gate, Calif., Aug. 21, 1935; s. Edwin Wilbur and Nancy Marion (Kinghorn) C.; m. Sheila M. McGoldrick, Sept. 20, 1958 (div. Apr. 1987); children: Laura,

Adam, Amy; m. Debra Lieberman, Mar. 25, 1989; 1 child, Eliot. BA, U. Redlands, 1957; MS, U. Calif., 1962; PhD, Stanford U., 1965. News editor Angeles Mesa News Advertiser, L.A., 1957; reporter Santa Monica (Calif.) Evening Outlook, 1962; rsch. assoc. Stanford (Calif) U., 1963-65, prof. communication, 1981—, Janet M. Peck prof., 1986—; asst. prof. to assoc. prof. U. Wisconsin, Madison, 1965-72, prof., 1972-82, 85-86, Vilas rsch. prof., 1974-81; mem. com. on mass communication and polit. behavior Soc. Sci. Rsch. Coun., N.Y.C., 1973-77; sci. adv. com. on TV and behavior NIMH, Washington, 1979-82. Author: Communication Concepts I: Explication, 1991; co-author: Television and Human Behavior, 1978, To See Ourselves, 1994; author, editor: Political Communication, 1972; co-author, co-editor: Handbook of Communication Science, 1986; co-editor: The Beginnings of Communication Study in the United States, 1996; contbr. numerous articles to profl. jours. Campaign pollster Dem. Party, Dane Co., Wis., 1966-84. Lt (j.g.) USNR, 1958-61. Fellow Internat. Comm. Assn. (pres. 1982-83); mem. Am. Polit. Sci. Assn., Assn. for Edn. in Journalism and Mass Comm. (mem. exec. com. 1971-72, 86-87), Am. Assn. Pub. Opinion Rsch. Democrat. Office: Stanford U Dept Communication Bldg 120 Stanford CA 94305-2050

CHAFFEE, WILBER ALBERT, political science educator; b. L.A., Oct. 17, 1930; s. Wilber Albert Chaffee and Elene (Graham) Chaffee-Loebbecke; m. Alice Blake (div.); children: Graham Stewartson, Lyman Blake; m. Edivanir Fontanelli. BA, Occidental Coll., L.A., 1952; MA, U. Tex., 1970, PhD, 1975. Asst. prof. U. Tex., Austin, 1975-77; asst. prof. St. Mary's Coll., Moraga, Calif., 1978-82, assoc. prof., 1982-88, prof., 1988—; chair dept. govt. St. Mary's Coll., Moraga, 1991—, dir. internat. studies, 1992—. Author, editor: Cuba: a Different America, 1989; author: Economic of Violence, 1992, Desenvolvimento: Politics and Economics in Brazil, 1997. Sgt. U.S. Army, 1953-55, Korea. Fulbright grantee, Latin Am., 1985. Mem. Am. Polit. Sci. Assn., Latin Am. Studies Assn., Pan Am. Soc. Calif. (chair acad. adv. com. 1991-95). Presbyterian. Office: St Mary's Coll Calif PO Box 3356 SMC Moraga CA 94575

CHAGALL, DAVID, journalist, author; b. Phila., Nov. 22, 1930; s. Harry and Ida (Coopersmith) C.; m. Juneau Joan Alsin, Nov. 15, 1957. Student, Swarthmore Center Coll., 1948-49; B.A., Pa. State U., 1952; postgrad., Sorbonne, U. Paris, 1953-54. Social caseworker State of Pa., Phila., 1955-57; sci. editor Jour. I.E.E., 1959-61; pub. relations staff A.E.I.-Hotpoint Ltd., London, 1961-62; mktg. research assoc. Chilton Co., Phila., 1962-63; mktg. research project dir. Haug Assos., Inc. (Roper Orgn.), Los Angeles, 1964-74; research cons. Haug Assos., 1976-79; investigative reporter for nat. mags., 1975—; host TV series The Last Hour, 1994—. Author: Diary of a Deaf Mute, 1960, The Century God Slept, 1963, The Spieler for the Holy Spirit, 1972, The New Kingmakers, 1981, The Sunshine Road, 1988, Surviving the Media Jungle, 1996; pub.: Inside Campaigning, 1983; contbr. syndicated column, articles, revs., stories and poetry to mags., jours., newspapers; contbg. editor: TV Guide, L.A. Mag. Apptd. to Selective Svc. Bd., 1991; bd. dirs. Chosen Prophetic Ministries, 1991. Recipient U. Wis. Poetry prize, 1971; nominee Nat. Book award in fiction, 1972, Pulitzer prize in letters, 1973, Disting. Health Journalism award, 1978; Presdl. Achievement award, 1982; Carnegie Trust grantee, 1964. Home: PO Box 85 Agoura Hills CA 91376-0085

CHAI, WINBERG, political science educator, foundation chair; b. Shanghai, China, Oct. 16, 1932; came to U.S., 1951, naturalized, 1973; s. Ch'u and Mei-en (Tsao) C.; m. Carolyn Everett, Mar. 17, 1966 (dec. 1996); children: Maria May-lee, Jeffrey Tien-yu. Student, Hartwick Coll., 1951-53; BA, Wittenberg U., 1955, DHL, 1997; MA, New Sch. Social Rsch., 1958; PhD, NYU, 1968. Lectr. New Sch. Social Rsch., 1957-61; vis. asst. prof. Drew U., 1961-62; asst. prof. Fairleigh Dickinson U., 1962-65; asst. prof. U. Redlands, 1965-68, assoc. prof., 1969-73, chmn. dept., 1970-73; prof., chmn. Asian studies CCNY, 1973-79; disting. prof. polit. sci., v.p. acad. affairs, spl. asst. to pres. U. S.D., Vermillion, 1979-82; prof. polit. sci., dir. internat. programs U. Wyo., Laramie, 1988—; chmn. Third World Conf. Found., Inc., Chgo., 1982—; pres. Wang Yu-fa Found., Taiwan, 1989—. Author: (with Ch'u Chai) The Story of Chinese Philosophy, 1961, The Changing Society of China, 1962, rev. edit., 1969, The New Politics of Communist China, 1972, The Search for a New China, 1975; editor: Essential Works of Chinese Communism, 1969, (with James C. Hsiung) Asia in the U.S. Foreign Policy, 1981, (with James C. Hsiung) U.S. Asian Relations: The National Security Paradox, 1983, (with Carolyn Chai) Beyond China's Crisis, 1989, In Search of Peace in the Middle East, 1991, (with Cal Clark) Political Stability and Economic Growth, 1994, China Mainland and Taiwan, 1994; co-translator: (with Ch'u Chai) A Treasury of Chinese Literature, 1965. Haynes Found. fellow, 1967, 68; Ford Found. humanities grantee, 1968, 69, Pacific Cultural Found. grantee, 1978, 86, NSF grantee, 1970, Hubert Eaton Meml. Fund grantee, 1972-73, Field Found. grantee, 1973, 75, Henry Luce Found. grantee, 1978, 80, S.D. Humanities Com. grantee, 1980, Pacific Culture Fund grantee, 1987, 90-91. Mem. Am. Assn. Chinese Studies (pres. 1978-80), AAAS, AAUP, Am. Polit. Sci. Assn., N.Y. Acad. Scis., Internat. Studies Assn., NAACP. Democrat. Home: 1071 Granito Dr Laramie WY 82070-5045 Office: PO Box 4098 Laramie WY 82071-4098 *Born in China and educated in the United States, I feel privileged to have experienced two rich cultures. My goals include promoting better understanding of all cultures and peoples.*

CHAKRABARTI, AJOY CHUNI, biochemist, educator; b. Baton Rouge, La., Apr. 28, 1964; came to U.S., 1993; s. Chuni Lal and Vimal C. BSc in Biochemistry with honors, Carleton U., Ottawa, Ontario, Can., 1986, MSc, 1988; PhD in Biochemistry, U. British Columbia, Can., 1992. NASA Planetary Biology Intern U. Calif., Davis, 1991, fellow, 1993-94; fellow Scripps Rsch. Inst., La Jolla, Calif., 1993-95, U. Santa Cruz, Calif., 1994-95, NeXstar Pharms. Inc., San Dimas, Calif., 1995—. Contbr. articles to profl. jours.; patentee; lipid encapsulation of enzymes; accumulation of peptides into liposomes; metal ion accumulation in liposomes. Recipient summer rsch. award Nat. Sci. & Engring. Rsch. Coun., Can., 1984, grad. fellowship U. B.C., Can., 1989-91, grad. award Sci. Coun. B.C., 1990-91, NASA internship U. Calif. Davis, 1991, postdoctoral fellowship NASA exobiology, 1993-95, MRC of Can., 1993-95; fellow Human Frontiers of Sci. Rsch. Program, 1995. Mem. AAAS. Office: NeXstar Inc Chem Devel/Formation 650 Cliffside Dr San Dimas CA 91773

CHALK, EARL MILTON, retired art director; b. Deerlodge, Mont., Sept. 14, 1927; s. Forrest A. and Jeanette Curtis (Robinson) C.; m. Carole Estelle, Feb. 9, 1963 (div. 1974); children: Teri, Kevin, Quinn. BFA, U. Wash., 1953. Artist Facilities Boeing, Seattle, 1954-57; writer, artist Facilities Boeing, Renton, Wash., 1957-60; supr. mfg. Facilities Boeing, Seattle, 1960-65; sr. supr. planning Facilities Boeing, Auburn, Wash., 1965-71, art dir. mfg. engring., 1971-87; painter in oils, 1987—; co-mgr., owner Art Galary, 1967-74. Artist Puget Sound Group of North West Painters, Seattle, 1968-78, artist Puyallup, Wash., 1987—. 1st class petty officer USN, 1945-49. Recipient Rotary scholarship U. Wash., 1953. Mem. Grapha Techna. Home and Office: 1803 7th Ave SE Puyallup WA 98372-4010

CHALLEM, JACK JOSEPH, health, advertising/public relations writer; b. Montreal, Quebec, Can., May 29, 1950; came to U.S., 1954; s. Alex and Sara Bella (Novak) C.; m. Renate Lewin, Sept. 30, 1977; 1 child, Evan G. BA, Northeastern Ill. U., 1972. Advt. mgr. J.R. Carlson Labs., Arlington Heights, Ill., 1973-78; editor-in-chief Physician's Life Mag., Evanston, Ill., 1978; contbg. editor Health Quarterly, New Canaan, Conn., 1979-83, Your Good Health Rev., New Canaan, 1979-83; graphics mgr. Eberline Instrument Corp., Santa Fe, 1979-81; sci. writer, media rels. specialist Los Alamos (N.Mex.) Nat. Lab., 1981-88; contbg. editor Let's Live Mag., L.A., 1978—; writer KVO Advt. & Pub. Rels., Portland, Oreg., 1988-94; pres. The Virtual Writer. Author: What Herbs Are All About, 1979, Vitamin C Updated, 1983, Getting the Most out of Your Vitamins and Minerals, 1993, Homocysteine: The "New" Cholestorol, 1996, The Health Benefits of Soy, 1996, The Natural Health Guide to Beating the Supergerms, 1997; contbr. Natural Health Mag., 1992—; editor, pub.: The Nutrition Reporter Newsletter, 1992—; contbr. articles to profl. jours. Home: 6782 SW 167th Pl Beaverton OR 97007-6310

CHAMBERLAIN, OWEN, nuclear physicist; b. San Francisco, July 10, 1920; divorced 1978; 4 children; m. June Steingart, 1980 (dec.). AB (Cramer fellow), Dartmouth Coll., 1941; PhD, U. Chgo., 1949. Instr. physics U. Calif., Berkeley, 1948-50, asst. prof., 1950-54, assoc. prof., 1954-58, prof., 1958-89, prof. emeritus, 1989—; civilian physicist Manhattan Dist., Berkeley, Los Alamos, 1942-46. Recipient Nobel prize (with Emilio Segrè) for physics, for discovery anti-proton, 1959, The Berkeley citation U. Calif., 1989; Guggenheim fellow, 1957-58; Loeb lectr. at Harvard U., 1959. Fellow Am. Phys. Soc., Am. Acad. Arts and Scis.; mem. Nat. Acad. Scis., Berkeley Fellows. Office: U Calif Physics Dept Berkeley CA 94720*

CHAMBERLAIN, WILLIAM EDWIN, JR., management consultant; b. St. Louis, June 8, 1951; s. William Edwin Sr. and Grace (Salisbury) C. AA in Bus. Mgmt., Mesa (Ariz.) Community Coll., 1983; BBA, U. Phoenix, 1988. Tng. and human resources devel. specialist Motorola, Inc., Phoenix, 1979-87; pres., seminar speaker Chamberlain Cons. Svcs., Chino Valley, Ariz., 1987—. Curator, dir. ops. U.S. Wolf Refuge and Adoption Ctr. Mem. ASTD, Network for Profl. Devel. *Personal philosophy: Better people make better workers and better workers make better people. A company's workforce is often its biggest investment, therefore efforts to develop its workers will often bring the biggest returns.*

CHAMBERLAIN, WILTON NORMAN, retired professional basketball player; b. Phila., Aug. 21, 1936. Student, U. Kans., 1954-58. Player Harlem Globetrotters, 1958-59, Phila. (later San Francisco) Warriors, 1959-65, Phila. 76ers, 1965-68, Los Angeles Lakers, 1968-73; coach San Diego Conquistadors, Am. Basketball Assn., 1973-74. Actor, Conan The Destroyer, 1982; author: A View from Above, 1991. Player, Nat. Basketball Assn. All-Star Game, 1960-69, 71-73; rookie of yr. Nat. Basketball Assn., 1960; Most Valuable Player, Nat. Basketball Assn., 1960, 66-68, Nat. Basketball Assn. Playoffs, 1972; inducted Naismith Meml. Basketball Hall of Fame, 1978; named to Nat. Basketball Assn. 35th Anniversary All-Time Team, 1980; mem. Nat. Basketball Assn. Championship Team, 1967, 72; holder Nat. Basketball Assn. record for most points scored in one game with 100. Office: care Seymour Goldberg 11111 Santa Monica Blvd Los Angeles CA 90025-3333*

CHAMBERLIN, EUGENE KEITH, historian, educator; b. Gustine, Calif., Feb. 15, 1916; s. Charles Eugene and Anina Marguerite (Williams) C.; B.A. in History, U. Calif. at Berkeley, 1939, M.A., 1940, Ph.D., 1949; m. Margaret Rae Jackson, Sept. 1, 1940; children—Linda, Thomas, Rebecca, Adrienne (dec.), Eric. Tchr. Spanish, Latin, Lassen Union High Sch. and Jr. Coll., Susanville, Calif., 1941-43; tchr. history Elk Grove (Calif.) Joint Union High Sch., 1943-45; teaching asst. history U. Calif., Berkeley, 1946-48; instr. history Mont. State U., Missoula, 1948-51, asst. prof., 1951-54; asst. prof. to prof. San Diego City Coll., 1954-78; part time cab driver San Diego Yellow Cab Co., 1955-74, 79, 86; vis. prof. history Mont. State Coll., Bozeman, summer 1953, U. Calif. Extension, 1964-68, San Diego State Coll., 1965-68, others; instr., coordinator history lectures San Diego Community Colls.-TV, 1969-77; prof. San Diego Miramar Coll., 1978-83; prof. history San Diego Mesa Coll., 1983-86; mem. adv. com. Quechan Crossing Master Plan Project, 1989-90; historian San Diego First Ch. Of The Brethren, 1954—. Huntington Library-Rockefeller Found. grantee, 1952; Fulbright-Hays grantee, Peru, 1982; recipient merit award Congress of History San Diego County, 1978; Outstanding Educator award, San Diego City Coll., 1970; recipient award for dedicated svc. to local history San Diego Hist. Soc., 1991; Ben Dixon award Congress, 1997. Mem. AAUP (various coms., nat. council 1967-70, pres. Calif. conf. 1968-70, acting exec. sec. 1970-72), San Diego County Congress of History (pres. 1976-77, newsletter editor 1977-78), Am. Hist. Assn. (life, Beveridge-Dunning com. 1982-84, chmn. 1984), Pacific Coast Council on Latin-Am. Studies, Cultural Assn. of the Californias, The Westerners (Calif., S.D. chpts.), E Clampus Vitus Squibab Chpt. (historian 1970-96, emeritus historian and archivist 1996—, chpt. pres. 1972-73, ECV dir. proctor 1983-89, grand council mem. 1972-93, dir. T.R.A.S.H 1979-93, pres. 1983-84), Phi Alpha Theta (sec. U. Calif. Berkeley chpt. 1947-48, organizer and faculty adv., Mont. State U. chpt. 1948-54). Democrat. Mem. Ch. of the Brethren (del. 200th Annual Conf. 1986). Author numerous booklets on SW Am. history and numerous articles on Mexican NW to profl. jours. Home: 3033 Dale St San Diego CA 92104-4929

CHAMBERLIN, GORDON ROBERT, secondary education educator; b. Clark AFB, Philippines, Mar. 23, 1970; s. Robert Allyn and Marie Theresa (Kirsch) C.; m. Margaret Jeanette Thome, June 18, 1993. AA, Pima C.C., Tucson, 1992; BA in Edn., U. Ariz., Tucson, 1995. Cert. thcr. history and biology, Ariz., Alaska. Biology tchr. asst. Pima C.C., 1992-94, acad. advisor, 1994-95; tchr. Marana Pub. Schs., Tucson, 1996; tchr. history and sci. S.W. Region Sch. Dist., Dillinaham, Alaska, 1996—. Musician, singer on album Lost In Paradise, 1993; author, editor producer video documentary Modern Day Issues in Edn., 1994. Mem. ASCD, NEA, Nat. Coun. on Social Studies. Home: PO Box 89881 Tucson AZ 85752

CHAMBERS, CAROLYN SILVA, communications company executive; b. Portland, Oreg., Sept. 15, 1931; d. Julio and Elizabeth (McDonnell) Silva; widowed; children: William, Scott, Elizabeth, Silva, Clark. BBA, U. Oreg. V.p., treas. Liberty Comm., Inc., Eugene, Oreg., 1960-83; pres. Chambers Comm. Corp., Eugene, 1983-95, chmn., 1996—; chmn., bd. dirs. Chambers Constrn. Co., 1986—; bd. dirs., dep. chair bd. Fed. Res. Bank, San Francisco, 1982-92; bd. dirs. Portland Gen. Corp.; bd. dirs. U.S. Bancorp. Mem. Sacred Heart Med. Found., 1980—, Sacred Heart Gov. Bd., 1987-92, Sacred Heart Health Svcs. Bd., 1993-95, PeaceHealth Bd., 1995—; mem. U. Oreg. Found., 1980—, pres., 1992-93; chair U. Oreg. Found., The Campaign for Oreg., 1988-89; pres., bd. dirs. Eugene Arts Found.; bd. dirs., treas., dir. search com. Eugene Symphony; mem. adv. bd. Eugene Hearing and Speech Ctr., Alton Baker Park Commn., Pleasant Hill Sch. Bd.; chmn., pres., treas. Civic Theatre, Very Little Theatre; negotiator, treas., bd. dirs., mem. thrift shop Jr. League of Oreg. Recipient Webfoot award U. Oreg., 1986, U. Oreg. Pres.'s medal, 1991, Disting. Svc. award, 1992, Pioneer award, 1983, Woman Who Made a Difference award Internat. Women's Forum, 1989, U. Oreg. Found. Disting. Alumni award, 1995, Tom McCall awrd Oreg. Assn. Broadcasters, 1995, Disting. Alumni award U. Oreg., 1995, Outstanding Philanthropist award Oreg. chpt. Nat. Soc. Fund Raising Execs., 1994. Mem. Nat. Cable TV Assn. (mem. fin. com., chmn. election and by-laws com., chmn. awards com., bd. dirs. 1987-89, Vanguard award for Leadership 1982), Pacific Northwest Cable Comm. Assn. (conv. chmn., pres.), Oreg. Cable TV Assn. (v.p., pres., chmn. edn. com., conv. chmn., Pres.'s award 1986), Calif. Cable TV Assn. (bd. dirs., conv. chmn., conv. panelist), Women in Cable (charter mem., treas., v.p., pres., recipient star of cable recognition), Wash. State Cable Comm. Assn., Idaho Cable TV Assn., Community Antenna TV Assn., Cable TV Pioneers, Eugene C. of C. (first citizen award, 1985). Home: PO Box 640 Pleasant Hill OR 97455-0640 Office: Chambers Comm Corp PO Box 7009 Eugene OR 97401-0009

CHAMBERS, CLYTIA MONTLLOR, public relations consultant; b. Rochester, N.Y., Oct. 23, 1922; d. Anthony and Marie (Bambace) Capraro; m. Joseph John Montllor, July 2, 1941 (div. 1958); children: Michele, Thomas, Clytia; m. Robert Chambers, May 28, 1965. BA, Barnard Coll., N.Y.C., 1942; Licence en droit, Faculte de Droit, U. Lyon, France, 1948; MA, Howard U., Washington, 1958. Assoc. dir. dept. rsch. Coun. for Fin. Aid to Edn., N.Y.C., 1958-60; asst. to v.p. indsl. rels. Sinclair Oil Corp., N.Y.C., 1961-65; writer pub. rels. dept. Am. Oil Co., Chgo., 1965-67; dir. editorial svcs., v.p. Hill & Knowlton Inc., N.Y.C., 1967-77; sr. v.p., dir. spl. svcs. Hill & Knowlton Inc., L.A., 1977-90; sr. cons. Hill & Knowlton Inc., 1990—; cons. and trustee Childen's Inst. Internat., L.A., 1988-93. Co-author: The News Twisters, 1971; editor: Critical Issues in Public Relations, 1975. Mem. Calif. Rare Fruit Growers (editor Fruit Gardener 1979—). Home: 11439 Laurelcrest Dr Studio City CA 91604-3872

CHAMBERS, GARY LEE, lawyer; b. Inglewood, Calif., June 6, 1953; s. George Edmund and Beverly Jean (Shuler) C.; m. Dalyn Valerie Myhra, Dec. 7, 1985; children: Garrett Ryan, Brendan Kyle, Danielle Christine, Shalyn Nicole. BA, U. Redlands (Calif.), 1975; JD, Western State U., Fullerton, Calif., 1978. Bar: Calif. 1979, U.S. Dist. Ct. (cen. dist.) Calif. 1979, U.S. Supreme Ct. 1982. Assoc. Law Offices of Murray Palitz, Westminster, Calif., 1979; pvt. practice law Orange, Calif., 1979-80; assoc. Law Offices Giles, Callahan et al, Tustin, Calif., 1980-81, Law Offices of Mark E. Edwards, Tustin, 1981-82; ptnr. Edwards, Chambers & Hoffman, Tustin, 1983-88, Chambers, Hoffman & Noronha, Santa Ana, Calif., 1989-92, Chambers, Noronha & Lowry, Santa Ana, Calif., 1992—; mem. tech. adv. staff Impact Gen., 1990—. Editorial adv. bd. James Pub. Co., 1988—. Named to Hall of Fame, Western State U., 1994. Mem. Am. Bd. Trial Adv., Am. Trial Lawyers Assn., Orange County Trial Lawyers Assn. (bd. govs. 1984-92, pres. 1990), Consumer Attys. Calif. (bd. govs. 1986-93, sec. 1991-93, v.p. 1994-95, Chpt. Pres. of Yr. 1990, Presdl. award of merit 1987, 92, 93), Trial Lawyers Pub. Justice. Democrat. Christian Ch. Office: Chambers Noronha & Lowry 2070 N Tustin Ave Santa Ana CA 92705-7827

CHAMBERS, KENNETH CARTER, astronomer; b. Los Alamos, N.Mex., Sept. 27, 1956; s. William Hyland and Marjorie (Bell) C.; m. Jeanne Marie Hamilton, June 28, 1986; children: Signe Hamilton, William Hamilton. BA in Physics, U. Colo., 1979, MS in Physics, 1982; MA in Physics and Astronomy, Johns Hopkins U., 1985, PhD in Physics and Astronomy, 1990. Rsch. asst. dept. physics U. Colo., Boulder, 1982-83; rsch. asst. dept. physics and astronomy Johns Hopkins U., Balt., 1983-86; mem. instrument team Hopkins Ultraviolet Telescope, Balt., 1983-86; rsch. asst. Space Telescope Sci. Inst., Balt., 1986-90; postdoctoral fellow Leiden (The Netherlands) Obs. Leiden U., 1990-91; asst. prof. Inst. Astronomy U. Hawaii, Honolulu, 1991—; Contbr. articles to Astrophys. Jour., Nature mag., Phys. Rev.; contbr. conf. procs. in field. Mem. Am. Astron. Soc. (Chretein award 1989), Am. Phys. Soc. Office: U Hawaii Inst Astronomy 2680 Woodlawn Dr Honolulu HI 96822-1839

CHAMBERS, LOIS IRENE, insurance automation consultant; b. Omaha, Nov. 24, 1935; d. Edward J. and Evelyn B. (Davidson) Morrison; m. Peter A. Mscichowski, Aug. 16, 1952 (div. 1980); 1 child, Peter Edward; m. Frederick G. Chambers, Apr. 17, 1981. Clk. Gross-Wilson Ins. Agy., Portland, Oreg., 1955-57; sec., bookkeeper Reed-Paulsen Ins. Agy., Portland, 1957-58; office mgr., asst. sec., agt. Don Biggs & Assocs., Vancouver, Wash., 1958-88, v.p. ops., 1988-89, automation mgr., 1989-91, mktg. mgr., 1991-94; automation cons. Chambers & Assocs., Tualatin, Oreg., 1985—; chmn. adv. com. Clark Community Coll., Vancouver, 1985-93, adv. com., 1993-94. Mem. citizens com. task force City of Vancouver, 1976-78, mem. Block Grant rev. task force, 1978—. Mem. Ins. Women of S.W. Wash. (pres. 1978, Ins. Woman of Yr. 1979), Nat. Assn. Ins. Women, Nat. Users Agena Systems (charter; pres. 1987-89), Soroptimist Internat. (Vancouver)(pres. 1978-79, Soroptimist of the Year 1979-80). Democrat. Roman Catholic. Office: Chambers & Assocs 8770 SW Umatilla St Tualatin OR 97062-9338

CHAMBERS, MILTON WARREN, architect; b. L.A., Aug. 5, 1928; s. Joe S. and Barbara N. (Harris) C.; m. Elizabeth M. Smith, Nov. 27, 1949; children: Mark, Michael, Daniel, Matthew. Student, Coll. of Sequoias, 1948-49, Harvard U., 1990. Lic. architect, Calif., Nev., Colo., Hawaii, Mont.; cert. Nat. Coun. Archtl. Registration Bds. Apprentice architect Kastner & Kastner Architects, Visalia, Calif., 1950-57; project architect Wurster, Bernardi & Emmons, Architects, San Francisco, 1958-63, Claude Oakland, Architect, San Francisco, 1964-65; chief architect Bank of Am., San Francisco, 1965-68; pres., owner Milton W. Chambers, Architect, San Rafael, Calif., 1969-82, The Chambers Group, Architects, Rancho Mirage, Calif., 1983—. Architect, designer St. Margaret's Episcopal Church, 1988. Foreman Marin County Grand Jury, San Rafael, 1976; mem. Archtl. Design Rev. Bd., Rancho Mirage, 1986—; trustee Marywood Sch., Rancho Mirage, 1990—. Cpl. U.S. Army, 1946-48, PTO, 50-51. Mem. AIA (pres. Calif. Desert chpt. 1986-87, 96&, dir. Calif. coun. 1989-90, 96—), Rotary Internat., Terra Linda Rotary Club (pres. 1975-76, dist. gov. 1993-94), Rancho Mirage Rotary Club (pres. 1986-87). Republican. Episcopalian. Office: The Chambers Group 44267 Monterey Ave Ste B Palm Desert CA 92260-2710

CHAMP, STANLEY GORDON, scientific company executive; b. Hoquiam, Wash., Feb. 15, 1919; s. Clifford Harvey and Edna Winnifred (Johnson) C.; m. Anita Knapp Wegener, Sept. 6, 1941; children: Suzanne Winnifred Whalen, Colleen Louise Szurszewski. BS, U. Puget Sound, 1941; MS, U. Wash., 1950; postgrad., MIT, 1955, 57, UCLA, 1959. Cert. tchr., adminstr., Wash. Tchr. Lake Washington Sch. Dist., Kirkland, Wash., 1942-48; prof. math. U. Puget Sound, Tacoma, 1948-51; supr. mathematician Puget Sound Naval Shipyard, Bremerton, Wash., 1951-55; rsch. specialist Boeing Co., Seattle, 1955-68; v.p. R.M. Towne & Assocs., Seattle, 1968-75; founder, pres. Dynac Scis., Tacoma, 1975—; cons. R.M. Towne Assocs., Seattle, Yantis Assocs., Bellevue, Wash. Contbr. articles to profl. jours.; patent method and apparatus determination soil dynamics insitu. Mem. N.Y. Acad. Sci., Phi Delta Kappa. Presbyterian. Home: 2709-84th Ave Ct W #12 Tacoma WA 98466

CHAMPAGNE, DUANE WILLARD, sociology educator; b. Belcourt, N.D., May 18, 1951; m. Liana Marie Bruce, Aug. 16, 1973; children: Talya, Gabe, Demelza. BA in Math., N.D. State U., 1973, MA in Sociology, 1975; PhD in Sociology, Harvard U., 1982. Teaching fellow Harvard U., Cambridge, Mass., 1981-82, rsch. fellow, 1982-83; asst. prof. U. Wis., Milw., 1983-84; asst. prof. UCLA, 1984-91, assoc. prof., 1991—; publs. dir. Am. Indian Studies Ctr., UCLA, 1986-87, assoc. dir., 1990, acting dir., 1991, dir., 1991—; adminstrv. co-head interdepartmental program for Am. Indian studies UCLA, 1992-93; mem. grad. rsch. fellowship panel NSF, 1990-92, minority fellowship com. ASA; cons. Energy Resources Co., 1982, No. Cheyenne Tribe, 1983, Realis Pictures, Inc., 1989-90, Sta. KCET-TV, L.A., 1990, 92, Salem Press, 1992, Book Prodns. Systems, 1993, Readers Digest, 1993, Rattlesnake Prodns., 1993. Author: American Indian Societies, 1989, Social Order and Political Change, 1992; editor: Native North American Almanac, 1994, Chronology of Native North American, 1994, Native American of the peoples Portrait, 1994; co-author: A Second Century of Dishonor: Federal Inequities and California Tribes, 1996, Service Delivery for Native American Children in Los Angeles County, 1996; editor: Native Am. Studies Assn. Newsletter, 1991-92; co-editor: Native American Activism: Alcatraz to the Longest Walk, 1997; book rev. editor Am. Indian Culture and Rsch. Jour., 1984-86, editor, 1986—; book reviewer Contemporary Sociology, Am. Indian Quarterly, Cultural Survival Quarterly, Am. Ethnologist, Ethnohistory; reviewer Am. Sociol. Rev., Am. Indian Culture and Rsch. Jour., Social Sci. Quarterly, Social Problems, Am. Ethnologist, Families in Society, Am. Indian Quarterly, Demography, Ethnohistory, NSF, U. Calif. PRess, Oxford U. Press; contbr. over 20 articles to profl. jours. Mem. city of L.A. Cmty. Action Bd., 1993, L.A. County/City Am. Indian Commn., 1992—, chair, 1993, 95-97; mem. subcom. for cultural and econ. devel. L.A. City/County Native Am. Commn., 1992-93; bd. dirs. Ctr. for Improvement of Child Caring, 1993—, Greater L.A. Am. Indian Culture Ctr., Inc., 1993, Incorporator, 1993; bd. trustees Southwest Mus., 1994—; Master of Coll. of Humanities and Social Sci., N.D. State U., 1996. Recipient L.A. Sr. Health Peer Counseling Cmty. Vol. Cert. of Recognition, 1996; grantee Rockefeller Found., 1982-83, U. Wis. Grad Sch. Rsch. Com., 1984-85, Wis. Dept. Edn., 1984-85, 87-88, 88-89, NSF, 1985-88, 88-89), Nat. Endowment for Arts, 1987-88, 91-92, NRC, 1988-89, Nat. Sci. Coun., 1989-90, John D. and Catherine T. MacArthur Found., 1990-91, Hayes Found., 1990-91, 92-93, Calif. Coun. for Humanities, 1991-92, Ford Found., 1990-92, Gale Rsch. Inc., 1991-93, 93-95, Rockwell Corp., 1991-93, GTE, 1992-93; Am. Indian scholar, 1973-75, 80-82, Minority fellow Am. Sociol. Assn., 1975-78, RIAS Seminar fellow, 1976-77; Rockefeller Postdoctoral fellow, 1982-83, NSF fellow, 1985-88, Postdoctoral fellow Ford Found., 1988-89. Home: 28012 Ridgecove Ct N Rancho Palos CA 90275-3377 Office: UCLA Am Indian Studies Ctr 3220 Campbell Hall PO Box 951548 Los Angeles CA 90095-1548

CHAMPNEY, LINDA LUCAS, reading educator; b. El Paso, Tex., Dec. 18, 1946; d. William Franklin and Caroline (Clements) Lucas; m. Rod Wayne Champney, Aug. 4, 1967; children: Kimberley Anne, Krisa Marie, Kari Lyn. BA, U. Tex., 1968; MEd, U. Colo., 1989. Cert. lang. arts and elem. edn. educator; nat. bd. cert. tchr. early adolescent lang. Tchr. MacArthur Jr. H.S., El Paso, 1968-69, 78-79; dir., tchr. St. Paul's United Meth. Ch., El Paso, 1976-78; subs. tchr. Irvine (Calif.) Unified Sch. Dist., 1981; reading tutor Mark Twain Elem. Sch., Littleton, Colo., 1982-83; lang. arts, reading tchr. Powell Mid. Sch., Littleton, 1983-93; reading specialist, cons. EdSource, Inc., Littleton, 1996—; instr. C.C. Aurora, Colo., 1990-91, C.C. Denver, Colo., 1995—. Mem. ASCD, Internat. Reading Assn. (study & rsch. com., program com.), Littleton Edn. Assn. (faculty rep.). Home and Office: 1657 W Canal Ct Littleton CO 80120

CHAMPOUX, JAMES JOSEPH, biochemist, educator; b. Seattle, Nov. 6, 1942; s. Louis and Alice Louise (Stafford) C.; m. Esther Arceo, Aug. 30, 1968 (div. Sept. 1992); children: Angie Farmer, Erik; m. Sharon Schultz, June 25, 1994. BS in Chemistry, U. Wash., 1965; PhD in Biochemistry,

Stanford U., 1970. Postdoctoral fellow The Salk Inst., La Jolla, Calif., 1970-72; asst. prof. U. Wash., Seattle, 1972-78, assoc. prof., 1978-82, prof., 1982—; vis. scientist MIT, Cambridge, Mass., 1980-81; mem. study sect. Am. Cancer Soc., N.Y.C., 1979-84; sabbatical leace ISREC, Lausanne, Switzerland, 1992-93. Co-author: (book) Medical Microbiology-An Introduction to Infectious Diseases, 2d edit., 1990, 3rd edit., 1994; contbr. articles to profl. jours. Recipient Guggenheim fellowship Guggenheim Found., 1980-81, Disting. Teaching award U. Wash., 1985. Home: 4101 NE 186th St Seattle WA 98155-2851 Office: U Wash Dept Microbiology Seattle WA 98195

CHAN, ANTHONY BERNARD, university administrator, educator, filmmaker; b. Victoria, B.C., Can.. MA in Oriental Studies, U. Ariz., Tucson, 1973; diploma in Chinese, Beijing (China) Lang. Inst., 1975; PhD in History, York U., Toronto, 1980. Instr. Ferris State Coll., Big Rapids, Mich., 1969-70; asst. prof. St. Mary's U., Halifax, N.S., Can., 1979-80, U. Alta., Edmonton, 1980-81; lectr. U. Victoria, U. Sask., Saskatoon, 1982; asst. coord. China Project Office St. Mary's U., Halifax, 1982-83; TV reporter Can. Broadcasting Corp., Edmonton, Saskatoon, and Calgary, 1983-85; sr. prodr., TV journalist, anchor English divsn. TV Broadcasts Ltd., Hong Kong, 1985-87; assoc. prof. mass comm. Calif. State U., Hayward, 1987-90; assoc. prof. internat. studies U. Wash., Seattle, 1990—, dir. Can. Studies Ctr., 1995—, editor New Scholars-New Visions in Can. Studies, 1986—, mem. film/video program ext. divsn., 1990—; ind. prodr. Lindca Enterprises, Seattle, 1990—; lectr. U. Ariz., Tucson, 1972, York U., 1973-75, U. Sask., Saskatoon, Can., 1981. Author: Arming the Chinese, 1982, Gold Mountain, 1983, Li Ka-Shing: Hong Kong's Elusive Billionaire, 1996; (documentary film) American Nurse, 1992. Postdoctoral fellow Inst. Am. Culture, UCLA, 1983; recipient Best News Analysis award N.Y. Internat. Film/Video Festival, N.Y.C., 1987, Hon. Mention awward Am. Nurse, Hiroshima (Japan) Film Festival, 1993. Mem. Alliance Can. Cinema TV and Radio Artists. Home and Office: U Wash Can Studies Centre Box 353650 Seattle WA 98195

CHAN, DANIEL SIU-KWONG, psychologist; b. Swatow, China, June 6, 1952; came to U.S., 1973; s. Hon-Kwong and Suet-Hing (Wong) C.; m. Rosario Arroyo, Dec. 14, 1985; children: Nathaniel Arroyo, Jennifer Arroyo. BA, Buena Vista Coll., 1977; MS, U. La Verne, 1980; PhD, U.S. Internat. U., 1984. Lic. psychologist Calif. Dir. outreach program Chinese Cmty. Ch., San Diego, 1980-81; exec. dir. Chinese Social Svc. Ctr., San Diego, 1981-82; rehab. counselor Asian Rehab. Svcs., Inc., L.A., 1982-84; program dir. Hawthorne (Calif.) Cmty. Group Home, 1984-86; psychologist Pacific Clinics, Pasadena, Calif., 1986-89, Fairview Devel. Ctr., Costa Mesa, Calif., 1989—; pvt. practice, Monterey Park, Calif., 1989—; cons. psychologist Ingleside Hosp., Rosemead, Calif., 1991—, Garfield Med. Ctr., Monterey Park, 1993—, Asian Youth Ctr., Rosemead, 1993—, Allied Physicians of Calif., San Gabriel, 1993—, Project SHINE, Inc., Downey, Calif., 1982-88. Mem. APA, Am. Soc. Clin. Hypnosis, Calif. Psychol. Assn., Fairview Psychol. Assn. Republican. Presbyn. Home: 11107 Mcvine Ave Sunland CA 91040-2121 Office: ACRO Cons 943 S Atlantic Blvd Ste 221 Monterey Park CA 91754-1066

CHAN, DAVID RONALD, tax specialist; b. L.A., Aug. 3, 1948; s. David Yew and Anna May (Wong) C.; m. Mary Anne Chan, July 21, 1980; children: Eric, Christina. AB in Econs., UCLA, 1969, MS in Bus. Adminstrn., 1970, JD, 1973. Bar: Calif. 1973, U.S. Tax Ct. 1974, U.S. Ct. Appeals (9th cir.) 1974, U.S. Dist. Ct. (ctrl. dist.) Calif. 1980. Acct. Oxnard Celery Distbrs., L.A., 1968-73, Touche Ross & Co., L.A., 1970; tax prin. Kenneth Leventhal & Co. (name now E&Y Kenneth Leventhal Real Estate Group), L.A., 1973—. Contbr. chpts. to books and articles to profl. jours. Founder, dir. Chinese Hist. Soc. So. Calif., L.A., 1975—; mem. spkrs. bur. L.A. 200 Bicentennial, L.A., 1981; spkr. Project Follow Through, L.A., 1981. Recipient Forbes Gold medal Calif. Soc. CPAs, L.A., 1970, Elijah Watt Sells cert. AICPA, L.A., 1970, cert. recognition Chinese Hist. Soc. So. Calif., L.A., 1985. Mem. So. Calif. Chinese Lawyers Assn., L.A. County Bar Assn., Chinese Am. CPAs So. Calif., Asian Bus. League, Chinese For Affirmative Action. Republican. Office: E&Y Kenneth Leventhal Real Estate Group 2049 Century Park E Ste 1700 Los Angeles CA 90067-3119

CHAN, MICHAEL CHIU-HON, chiropractor; b. Hong Kong, Aug. 31, 1961; came to U.S., 1979; s. Fuk Yum and Chun Wai (Ma) C. D of Chiropractic, Western States Chiropractic Coll., 1985; fellow, Internat. Acad. Clin. Acupuncture, 1986. Assoc. doctor Widoff Chiropractic Clinic, Phoenix, 1986, Horizon Chiropractic Clinic, Glendale, Ariz., 1986-88; dir. North Ranch Chiropractic Assoc., Scottsdale, Ariz., 1988-91; pvt. practice Phoenix, 1991—; dir. Neighborhood Chiropractic, Phoenix, 1988-89. Contbr. articles to profl. jours. Mem. Am. Chiropractic Assoc., Internat. Platform Assn., Coun. on Diagnostic Imaging, Paradise Valley Toastmaster Club. Office: 3911 W McDowell Rd # 1 Phoenix AZ 85009 also: 3109 E Cactus Rd Phoenix AZ 85030

CHAN, PETER WING KWONG, pharmacist; b. L.A., Feb. 3, 1949; s. Sherwin T.S. and Shirley W. (Lee) C.; m. Patricia Jean Uyeno, June 8, 1974; children: Kristina Dionne, Kelly Alison, David Shoichi. BS, U. So. Calif., 1970, D in Pharmacy, 1974. Lic. pharmacist, Calif. Clin. instr. U. So. Calif., 1974-76; staff clin. pharmacist Cedars-Sinai Med. Ctr., L.A., 1974-76; 1st clin. pharmacist in ophthalmology Alcon Labs., Inc., Ft. Worth, 1977—, formerly in Phila. monitoring patient drug therapy, teaching residents, nurses, pharmacy students, then assigned to Tumu Tumu Hosp., Karatina, Kenya, also lectr. clin. ocular pharmacology tng. course, Nairobi, Cairo, Athens, formerly dist. sales mgr. Alcon/BP, ophthal. products div. Alcon Labs., Inc., Denver; v.p., gen. mgr. Optikem Internat., Sereine Products Div., Optacryl, Inc., Denver, 1980-91; product mgr. hosp. pharmacy products Am. McGaw div. Am. Hosp. Supply Corp., 1981-83; internat. market mgr. IOLAB subs. Johnson & Johnson, 1983-86, dir. new bus. devel. Iolab Pharms., 1986-87, dir. Internat. Mktg., 1987-89, dir. new products mktg., 1989; bus. and mktg. strategies cons. to pharm. and med. device cos. Chan & Assocs., Northridge, Calif., 1989—; ptnr., chmn., CEO PreFree Techs., Inc., 1992-96; med. dir., Clin Profl. Affairs, Nexstar Pharms., Inc., Boulder, 1996—; ptnr. Vitamin Specialties Corp., 1993-95, JSP Ptnrs., Ltd., 1992—; med. dir., clin. and profl. affairs, Nexstar Pharm. Inc., Boulder, Colo., bd, dirs. SUDCO Internat., L.A. Del. Am. Pharm. Assn. House of Dels., 1976-78, Calif. Youth Theatre at Paramount Studios, Hollywood 1986-87, 91-96; bd. councillors U. So. Calif. Sch. Pharmacy, 1995—. Recipient Hollywood-Wilshire Pharm. Assn. spl. award for outstanding svc., 1974. Mem. Chinese Am. Pharm. Assn., Am. Pharm. Assn., Calif. Pharm. Assn., Hollywood-Wilshire Pharm. Assn. (bd. dirs. 1972-76), Am. Soc. Hosp. Pharmacists, Am. Pharm. Assn. Acad. of Pharmacy Practice, U. So. Calif. Assocs. (life), U. So. Calif. Gen. Alumni Assn., U. So. Calif. (steering com. lifescis. info. networking coun.), Granada Hills H.S. Highlanders Booster Club (bd. dirs. 1991, 92, 93, chmn.-Project 2000), QSAD Centurions, U. So. Calif. Lifetime Assocs., Gamma Epsilon Omega Alumni Assn. (bd. dirs.), Phi Delta Chi, NRA (life), Golden Eagle, Calif. Rifle and Pistol Assn. (life mem.). Republican. Home: 10251 Vanalden Ave Northridge CA 91324-1240 Office: Nexstar Pharms Inc 2826 Wilderness Pl Boulder CO 80301

CHANCE, EDWARD WAYNE, administration and leadership studies educator; b. Richmond, Calif., Oct. 30, 1946; s. Wayne and Juanita (Bales) C.; m. Patti Lynn Bruza, Mar. 20, 1976. BA in History, U. Okla., 1969, MSS in Social Scis., 1976, MEd in Counseling, 1980, PhD in Adminstrn., 1985. Spl. instr. Univ. Lab. Sch., U. Okla., Norman, 1970-73; tchr. Lindsay (Okla.) Pub. Schs., 1974-81; asst. prin. Shawnee (Okla.) Schs., 1981-84; prin. Henryetta (Okla.) Schs., 1984-85; asst. prof. S.D. State U., Brookings, 1986-88; instr. Coll. Edn. U. Okla., Norman, 1985-86, assoc. prof. adminstrv. theory and leadership, 1988-95; prof. leadership and orgnl. theory U. Nev., Las Vegas, 1995—; dir. Ctr. for Study Small and Rural Schs., Norman, 1990-95; mem. exec. com. Okla. Commn. Ednl. Leadership, 1988-92; cons. Orgn. Rural Okla. Schs., Oklahoma City, 1988-95. Mem. editorial bd. Rural Educator, Nat. Forum Ednl. Adminstrn. and Supervision Jour., Jour. Sch. Leadership; contbr. articles to profl. jours.; author tng. program. Recipient Outstanding Svc. award Women and Minorities in Adminstrn., 1989, Coop. Coun. Sch. Adminstrs., 1991-95. Mem. Am. Assn. Sch. Adminstrs., Nat. Rural Edn. Assn. (rsch. ctr. dir. 1990, exec. bd., chair rsch. forum, chair rsch. com. 1994—), Am. Ednl. Rsch. Assn., Univ. Coun. Ednl. Adminstrn. (plenary rep. 1989-93), Phi Delta Kappa.

CHANCE, KENNETH DONALD, engineer; b. Denver, July 27, 1948; s. John Jefferson and Evelyn Pauline (Jacobs) C. AA, Red Rocks Coll., Golden, Colo., 1982. Stationery operating engr. EG&G Rocky Flats, Golden, 1980—.

CHANDLER, AL BART, state agency administrator; b. Spokane, July 28, 1942; s. Atlee Basil and Azalea Chandler-Schmer; m. Toni Lynn, Aug. 2, 1975; children: Chris, Amy. BA in Sociology, Linfield Coll., 1964; MS in Edn., Western Oreg. Coll., 1970, MS in Corrections Adminstrn., 1976. Counselor Oreg. Dept. Corrections, Salem, 1964-67, mgr. correctional programs, 1967-80; parole/probation supr. Oreg. Dept. Corrections, Portland, 1980-85; exec. asst. Oreg. Dept. Corrections, Salem, 1985-87, dir. classification, 1987-93, dep. asst. dir., 1993-94, asst. dir., 1994—; exec. sec. T.L. Chandler & Assocs., Salem, 1991—. Mem. Am. Corrections Assn., Oreg. Corrections Assn. Republican. Baptist. Office: Oreg Dept Corrections 2575 Center St NE Salem OR 97310

CHANDLER, ALLEN, food products executive; b. 1942. With Northwest Wholesale, Wenatchee, Wash., 1964-68; with No. Fruit Co., Wenatchee, Wash., 1968—, now v.p. Office: Northern Fruit Co 220 3rd St NE Wenatchee WA 98802-4856*

CHANDLER, BRIDGETT ANN, municipal government policy advisor; b. Spokane, Wash., Sept. 18, 1961; d. Leo Michael and Patricia Mae (Sterling) C.; m. Bear Silverstein, Aug. 13, 1993. BA in Comparative Lit. summa cum laude, Seattle U., 1983, BA in Fgn. Lang. summa cum laude, 1983; license sciences economiques, Université Paul Valéry, Montpellier, France, 1985; M in Internat. Studies, Claremont U., 1987; postgrad., Harvard U., 1996. Rsch. asst. Seattle City Light, 1982-83; paralegal King County Prosecuting Atty., Seattle, 1979-82, Wash. Atty. Gen., Seattle, 1984; statistics teaching asst. Claremont Grad. Sch., 1986-87; rsch. asst. U.S. EPA, Washington, 1984; planning and devel. specialist City of Seattle, Washington, 1987-91, sr. planner human svcs., 1992, sr. planner rapid transit, 1993, Sand Point base closure mgr. exec. office intergovtl. rels., 1993-96; chair-steering com. Student Conservation Assn., Seattle, 1993—, Earthwork. Contbg. author: Framework Policies, 1991; editor: Fragments, 1983; radio talk show host: Talking Book and Braille Libr., Seattle, 1990—. Pres. Seattle Women in Gov., 1989-90, program chair, 1988-89; panel discussion facilitator Seattle Women's Commn., 1992-93; grad. Leadership Tomorrow, Seattle, 1990-91; judicial candidate review Mcpl. League, Seattle, 1992; City of Seattle AIDS Walk Coord. NW Aids Found., Seattle, 1992—; bd. dirs. West Seattle Helpline, Friends of Cedar River; table capt. YWCA, 1991—. Named Outstanding Grad., Coll. Arts and Scis. Seattle U., 1983; Claremont Grad. Sch. fellow, 1985-87, Internat. scholar Rotary Internat., 1984-85. Mem. Am. Planning Assn., Seattle Women in Govt., Seattle Mgmt. Assn. Democrat. Home: 5436 48th Ave SW Seattle WA 98136-1009 Office: City of Seattle Mayor's Office Intergovtl Rels 600 4th Ave Ste 200 Seattle WA 98104-1826

CHANDLER, BRUCE FREDERICK, internist; b. Bohemia, Pa., Mar. 26, 1926; s. Frederick Arthur and Minnie Flora (Burkhardt) C.; m. Janice Evelyn Piper, Aug. 14, 1954; children: Barbara, Betty, Karen, Paul, June. Student, Pa. State U., 1942-44; MD, Temple U., 1948. Diplomate Am. Bd. Internal Medicine. Commd. med. officer U.S. Army, 1948, advanced through grades to col., 1967; intern Temple U. Hosp., Phila., 1948-49; chief psychiatry 7th Field Hosp., Trieste, Italy, 1950; resident Walter Reed Gen. Hosp., Washington, 1949-53; battalion surgeon 2d Div. Artillery, Korea, 1953-54; chief renal dialysis unit 45th Evacuation Hosp. and Tokyo Army Hosp., Korea, Japan, 1954-55; various assignments Walter Reed Gen. Hosp., Fitzsimons Gen. Hosp., Letterman Gen. Hosp., 1955-70; comdg. officer 45th Field Hosp., Vicenza, Italy, 1958-62; pvt. practice internist Ridgecrest (Calif.) Med. Clinic, 1970-76; chief med. svc. and out-patients VA Hosps., Walla Walla, Spokane, Wash., 1976-82; med. cons. Social Security Adminstrn., Spokane, Wash., 1983-87; ret. Panel mem. TV shows, 1964-70; lectr.; contbr. numerous articles to med. profl. jours. Decorated Legion of Merit. Fellow ACP, Am. Coll. Chest Physicians; mem. AMA, Am. Thoracic Soc., N.Y. Acad. Scis., So. European Task Force U.S. Army Med. Dental Soc. (pres., founder 1958-62). Republican. Methodist. Home: 6496 N Callisch Ave Fresno CA 93710-3902

CHANDLER, KRIS, computer consultant, educator; b. Cleveland Heights, Ohio, June 26, 1948; d. Gerhard A. and Hanna R. (Rittmeyer) Hoffmann; children: Karen, Heidi. BSBA with honors and spl. distinction U. So. Colo., 1984, postgrad., 1984-85; MBA, U. Ark., 1987; PhD in C.C. Adminstrn. Colo. State U, 1993. Owner, mgr. V&W Fgn. Car Svc., Canon City, Colo., 1970-80; prin. The Chandlers, Computer Cons., Pueblo, Colo., 1982-88; ptnr. Jak Rabbit Software, 1989—; faculty Pikes Peak Community Coll., chair computer info. systems dept., U. So. Colo., also mgr. Sch. Bus. microcomputer lab. Bd. dirs. Canon City Community Svc. Ctr., 1978-80, Canon City chpt. ARC, 1978-81. Mem. Assn. for Computing Machinery, Data Processing Mgmt. Assn. (advisor student chpt. Pikes Peak Community Coll. 1989—), U. So. Colo. Honors Soc. (pres.), U. So. Colo. Grad. Assn. (founder), Alpha Chi, Sigma Iota Epsilon. Home and Office: 401 S Neilson Ave Pueblo CO 81001-4238

CHANDLER, PAUL MICHAEL, Spanish and Portuguese educator, homeless advocate; b. Flora, Ill., Nov. 15, 1954; s. John Paul and Doris (O'Dell) C. BA, Ind.-Purdue U., Ft. Wayne, 1983; MA in Tchg., Ind. U., Bloomington, 1985, PhD, 1992. Instr. Spanish, Ind. U., 1983-89, coord. Spanish, 1989-90; asst. prof. San Jose (Calif.) State U., 1990-92; instr. Portuguese, Mission Coll., Santa Clara, Calif., 1992; asst. prof. and coord. Spanish, U. Hawaii, Honolulu, 1992—; vis. lectr. U. Seville, Spain, 1985-86; Portuguese translator Gen. Telephone, Honolulu, 1993. Editor, author: HALT Selected Papers and Language Teaching Ideas from Paradise, 1994; co-author: (Spanish textbook) Que te parece?, 1996; contbr. articles to profl. pubs. Travel grantee Ind. U., 1989-90, San Jose State U., 1990-92, U. Hawaii, 1992. Mem. MLA, Nat. Reading Conf., Am. Coun. on Tchg. Fgn. Langs. (nat. award com. for outstanding tchr. of culture 1993), Am. Assn. Tchrs. of Spanish and Portuguese, Calif. Lang. Tchrs. Assn., Hawaii Assn. Lang. Tchrs., Acad. Alliance (treas. 1992-95). Office: U Hawaii Moore Hall 483 1890 East-West Rd Honolulu HI 96822-2318

CHANDOR, STEBBINS BRYANT, pathologist; b. Boston, Dec. 18, 1933; s. Kendall Stebbins Bryant and Dorothy (Burrage) C.; m. Mary Carolyn White, May 30, 1959; children: Stebbins Bryant Jr., Charlotte White. B.A., Princeton U., 1955; M.D., Cornell U., 1960. Diplomate Am. Bd. Pathology. Intern Bellevue Hosp., N.Y.C., 1960-61, resident, 1965-66; resident Stanford U. Med. Ctr., Palo Alto, Calif., 1962-65; instr. Cornell U., Ithaca, N.Y., 1966; asst. prof. U. So. Calif. Med. Ctr., Los Angeles, 1969-73, assoc. prof., 1974-76; assoc. prof. SUNY, Stony Brook, 1976-80; prof., chmn. dept. pathology Marshall U. Sch. Medicine, Huntington, W.Va., 1981-91; assoc. dean for clin. affairs Marshall U. Sch. Medicine, 1990-91; prof., vice chmn. Sch. Medicine U. So. Calif., L.A., 1991—; pathologist Tripler Army Med Ctr, Honolulu, 1966-69; dir. immunopathology U. So. Calif., Los Angeles County Med. Ctr., 1969-76; dir. clin. lab. Univ. Hosp., Stony Brook, N.Y., 1978-80; dir. JMMS Labs., Huntington, W.Va., 1981-91; dir.labs. U. So. Calif. U. Hosp., L.A., 1991—. Contbr. articles to profl. jours. Pres. San Marino Tennis Found., 1975. Served to maj. USAR, 1966-69. Decorated Army Commendation medal; recipient Physicians Recognition award AMA, 1983, 86, 89, 93. Fellow Am. Soc. Clin. Pathologists (deputy commn, 1993— continuing edn., bd. dirs. 1990-96, chair by-law com., 1993-96, chmn. pathology group, 1993—), Coll. Am. Pathologists (state commr. I&A program 1987-91, dist. commr. 1991—); mem. Calif. Soc. Pathologists (sec.-treas. 1974-75, pres. elect. 1975-76), Assn. Am. Pathologists, W.Va. Assn. Pathologists (pres. 1985-86), Assoc. Pathol. Chmn. Acad. Clin. Lab. Physicians and Scientists (rep. CAS 1991—), L.A. Acad. Medicine, Princeton Club, Valley Club (v.p. 1975, bd. dirs. 1993), City Club (v.p. 1988-89, pres. 1989-90), San Gabriel Country Club, Valley Hunt Club. Republican. Episcopalian. Home: 855 S Oak Knoll Ave Pasadena CA 91106-4419 Office: U So Calif Sch Medicine 2011 Zonal Ave Los Angeles CA 90033-1034 *Have fun and make life enjoyable for those around you.*

CHANDRAMOULI, RAMAMURTI, electrical engineer; b. Sholinghur, Madras, India, Oct. 2, 1947; s. Ramamurti and Rajalakshmi (Ramamurti) Krishnamurti; m. Ranjani, Dec. 4, 1980; children: Suhasini, Akila. BSc, Mysore U., 1965, BE, 1970, MEE, Pratt Inst., 1972; PhD, Oreg. State U., 1978. Instr., Oreg. State U., Corvallis, 1978; sr. engr. R & D group, mem. tech. staff spacecraft datasystems sect. Jet Propulsion Lab., Pasadena, Calif., 1978-81; staff engr., design automation group Am. Microsystems Inc., Santa Clara, Calif., 1982-83; staff software engr. corp. computer-aided design Intel, Santa Clara, 1983-86; project leader computer-aided design Sun Microsystems, Mountain View, Calif., 1986-93; tech. mktg. engr. Mentor Graphics, San Jose, Calif., 1993-95; dir. Bist Products Logicvision, San Jose, 1995—; adj. lectr. Calif. State U.-Fullerton, 1987—. Sec., South India Cultural Assn., L.A., 1980-81; bd. dirs. Am. Assn. East Indians. Mem. IEEE, IEEE Computer Soc., Sigma Xi, Eta Kappa Nu. Home: 678 Tiffany Ct Sunnyvale CA 94087-2439 Office: LV Software Inc 1735 N 1st St San Jose CA 95112-4511

CHANDRAMOULI, SRINIVASAN (CHANDRA CHANDRAMOULI), management and systems consultant; b. Kumbakonam, Tamil Nadu, India, Nov. 14, 1952; came to U.S., 1978; s. Veda and Padmavathi Srinivasan; m. Janaki Chandramouli. BS in Math. and Physics, Ferguson Coll., Pune, India, 1973; postgrad., Indian Inst. Tech., New Delhi, 1973-74; MBA in Mktg. and Gen. Mgmt., Indian Inst. Tech., Ahmedabad, 1976; MBA in Fin. and Acctg., U. Chgo., 1980. CPA, Ill. Cons. Hindustan Petroleum Corp. Ltd., Bombay, India, 1975; fin. mgr. prodn. Associated Cement Cos., Bombay, 1976-77; cons., researcher The World Bank, Washington, 1979-80; v.p. Am. Mgmt. Systems Inc., Chgo., 1980—; vis. faculty mem. K.C. Coll. Mgmt. U. Bombay, 1976-77. Editor newsletter India Assn. Pitts., 1977-78. Gen. sec. Jawahar Mitra Mandal, Pune, 1970-74. Fellow Inst. Profl. Acctg. U. Chgo., 1979-80; Open Merit and Nat. Merit scholar Govt. of India U. Poona, 1969-73. Mem. Am. Inst. CPA's, Ill. CPA Soc., Beta Gamma Sigma. Republican. Hindu. Home: 16118 E Prentice Pl Aurora CO 80015-4172 Office: Am Mgmt Systems Inc 14033 Denver West Pkwy Golden CO 80401

CHANDRARATNA, PREMINDRA ANTHONY N., physician; b. Ceylon, July 27, 1941; came to U.S., 1971; m. Frances Roanne; children: Nirmal, Previn. MD, U. Ceylon, 1964. Diplomate Am. Bd. Internal Medicine, Am. Bd. Cardiovascular Disease. Rsch. fellow in cardiology U. Rochester Sch. Medicine; staff cardiologist Mt. Sinai Med. Ctr., Miami Beach, Fla., 1973-75; assoc. prof. medicine U. Okla. Health Scis. Ctr., 1975-77, U. Calif., Irvine, 1977-80; chief echocardiography lab., divsn. cardiology Los Angeles County/ U.So. Calif. Med. Ctr., 1990—; Bauer and Bauer Rawlins prof. cardiology, prof. medicine U. So. Calif. Sch. Medicine. Mem. editl. bd. Am. Jour. Non-Invasive Cardiology and Echocardiography; contbr. more than 180 articles to profl. jours.; patent for ultrasound microscope for imaging living tissues. Fellow ACP, Am. Coll. Cardiology, Am. Heart Assn. (coun. clin. cardiology), Royal Coll. Physicians; mem. Western Soc. for Clin. Investigation. Home: 30932 Marne Dr Palos Verdes Peninsula CA 90275-5612

CHANEN, STEVEN ROBERT, lawyer; b. Phoenix, May 15, 1953; s. Herman and Lois Marion (Boshes) C. Student, UCLA, 1971-73; BS in Mass Communications, Ariz. State U., 1975, JD, 1979. Bar: Ariz. 1980, U.S. Dist. Ct. Ariz. 1980, U.S. Ct. Appeals (9th cir.) 1980, Calif. 1981, U.S. Dist. Ct. (no. dist.) Calif. 1982. Ptnr. Wentworth & Lundin, Phoenix, 1980-86, of counsel, 1986-87; appointed bd. dirs. Ariz. Gov.'s Commn. on Motion Pictures and TV, 1986, chmn., 1990; appointed bd. dirs., exec. v.p. Chanen Corp.; fin. intermediary, chmn. bd. dirs. S.R. Chanen and Co, Inc.; pres. Chanen Constrn. Co., Inc. Bd. dirs. Anytown, Am., Phoenix, 1986—, COMPAS, Inc., Phoenix, 1986—, Ariz. Mus. Sci. and Tech., Phoenix, 1987—, Mus. Theater Ariz., Phoenix, 1988-89, Temple Beth Isreal, Ariz. Politically Interested Citizens, Jewish Fedn.; v.p. bd. dirs. Community Forum, Phoenix, Phoenix Children's Hosp., Maricopa County C.C. Dist. Found. Mem. ABA (forum com. entertainment and sports industries 1981—), Ariz. Bar Assn., Calif. Bar Assn., Maricopa County Bar Assn., Assn. Trial Lawyers Am. Republican. Jewish. Office: 3300 N 3rd Ave Phoenix AZ 85013-4304

CHANEY, G. P. RUSS, trade association administrator; m. Jutta Suzanne Kobia, Dec. 9, 1995. AA in Acctg., Brookdale Coll., Lincroft, N.J., 1981; BS in Pers. Mgmt., Glassborough (N.J.) State U., 1979. Master plumber, N.J., Tex.; plumbing inspector, N.J. Master plumber Garnet Plumbing, Jackson, N.J., 1981-91; dir. tech. svcs. Nat. Assn. Plumbing, Heating & Cooling Contractors, Falls Church, Va., 1991-95; exec. dir. Internat. Assn. Plumbing & Mech. Ofcls., Walnut, Calif., 1995—; cons. plumbing industry; developer plumbing and mech. codes. Mem. Am. Soc. San. Engrs. Roman Catholic. Office: Internat Assn Plumbing & Mech Ofcls 20001 E Walnut Dr S Walnut CA 91789-2825

CHANEY, JAMES ALAN, construction company executive; b. Portland, Oreg., Oct. 10, 1951; s. Frank Edmund and Marjorie Elizabeth (Holtham) C.; m. Elizabeth Coates, Feb. 19, 1971 (div. Oct. 1991); children: Raleigh, Richard, Curtis, Charles; m. Linda Marie Bowman, Dec. 11, 1993. Student, U. Oreg., 1969-70, 89-91. Carpenter, Eugene, Oreg., 1971-78; supt. Morris Kielty Contractor, Eugene, 1978-81; estimator, mgr. Hyland Bros. Constrn., Springfield, Oreg., 1981-83; pres., gen. mgr. McKenzie Comml. Gen. Contractors, Eugene, 1983—; constrn. cons., Eugene, 1984—; constrn. arbitrator, Eugene, 1987—; mem. Oreg. Constrn. Contractors Bd., Salem, 1994—. Mem. Eugene Constrn. Code Bd. Appeals, 1985-87, Lane County Constrn. Appeals and Adv. Bd., Eugene, 1987-90, Eugene Hist. Rev. Bd., 1990-92. Named Employer of Yr. Eugene chpt. Nat. Assn. Women in Constrn., 1987; recipient recognition award Lane County, 1989, continuing excellence award S.W. Oreg. chpt. AIA, 1993. Fellow Constrn. Specifications Inst. (chpt. pres. 1991, nat. bd. dirs. 1992-95, nat. treas. 1996—, chpt., regional and nat. awards 1986-93), Am. Arbitration Assn. (panel arbitrators 1986—), Am. Concrete Inst. Democrat. Office: McKenzie Comml Gen Contractors 865 W 2nd Ave Eugene OR 97402-4967

CHANEY, RONALD CLAIRE, environmental engineering educator, consultant; b. Tulsa, Okla., Mar. 26, 1944; s. Clarence Emerson and Virginia Margaret (Klinger) C.; m. Patricia Jane Robinson, Aug. 11, 1984. BS, Calif. State U., Long Beach, 1969; MS, Calif. State U., 1970; PhD, UCLA, 1978. Prof. engr., Calif.; geotech. engr., Calif. Structural engr. Fluor Corp. Ltd., L.A., 1968-70; rsch. engr. UCLA, 1972-74; lab. mgr. Fugro Inc., Long Beach, 1974-79; assoc. prof. Lehigh U., Bethlehem, Pa., 1979-81; dir. Telonicher Marine Lab. Humboldt State U., Trinidad, Calif., 1984-90, 96—; prof. Humboldt State U., Arcata, Calif., 1981—; geotech. engr. LACO Assocs., Eureka, Calif., 1988, 96; panel mem. Humboldt County Solid Waste Appeals, Eureka, 1992-96; mem. shipboard measurement panel Joint Oceanog. Instn., Washington, 1991-96. Co-editor Symposium on Marine Geotechnology and Nearshore/Offshore Structures, 1986, Symposium on Geotechnical Aspects of Waste Disposal in the Marine Environment, 1990, Symposium on Dredging, Remediation and Containment of Contaminated Sediments, 1995; editor Marine Geotech. Jour., 1981-92; co-editor Marine Georesources and Geotech. jour., 1992—, ASTM Geotech. Testing Jour., 1996—. Fellow ASTM (Hogentogler award 1988, Std. Devel. award 1991, Outstanding Achievement award 1992, Dudley medal 1994, Award of Merit 1995, vice chmn. D18), Seismological Soc. Am., Earthquake Engring. Rsch. Inst., Sigma Xi, Phi Kappa Phi. Office: Humboldt State U Dept Environ Engring Arcata CA 95521

CHANEY, VICTOR HARVEY, secondary education educator, historical dramatist; b. Chgo., Nov. 11, 1940; s. Charles and Libby (Siegel) C.; m. Meta Bowman, July 14, 1973; 1 child, Dana; stepchildren: Gary, Rick, Randy. BA in Polit. Sci., UCLA, 1963; MEd, Calif. State U., Northridge, 1973. Tchr. Simi Valley (Calif.) Unified Sch. Dist., 1972-89, Beaverton (Oreg.) Sch., 1989—. Author: (poetry volume) Passing Through, 1984; (novel) The Bernstein Projections, 1991; creator and actor of one man plays and guest speaker presentations. Mem. Oreg. Tchrs. Assn., Nat. Audubon Soc., Nature Conservancy. Home: 6940 SW 160th Ave Beaverton OR 97007-4883

CHANG, CINDY, writer; b. Taipei, Taiwan, Apr. 21, 1968; d. Edward Chang and Irene Kao. Author, reteller, editor Random House, Inc., N.Y.C., 1990; editor Price, Stern, Sloan, Inc., L.A., 1990-94, Intervisual Books, Santa Monica, Calif., 1994-96; dir. MCA Pub. Rights, Universal City, Calif., 1996—. Author: Good Night, Kitty!, 1994, Good Morning, Puppy!, 1994, What's for Lunch?, 1996, Where's the Mouse?, 1996, Jump! Jump! All the Games, Rhymes and Helpful Hints You'll Ever Need to Know about Jumping Rope!, 1996, Trucks All Around, 1996; reteller: The Seventh Sister: A Chinese Legend, 1994; adaptor: Balto: The Junior Novelization, 1995; compiler: (quote books) Food, 1995, Gardens, 1995, Golf, 1995, Reading, 1996, Nature, 1996, Thank You, 1996, Family, 1996; co-editor: (newsletter)

Kitetales. Mem. PEN USA West (editl. bd.), Soc. Children's Book Writers and Illustrators. Office: care MCA Pub Rights 100 Universal City Plz Universal City CA 91608

CHANG, HSU HSIN (SIDNEY H. CHANG), history educator; b. Wuchang, China, Jan. 1, 1934; came to U.S., 1957; s. Chung-ning C.; m. Elaine Pardue; children: Chi-chung, Chi-tung. BA, Nat. Taiwan U., 1956; MA, U. Mo., 1959; MS, Fla. State U., 1961; PhD, U. Wis., 1967. Asst. prof. history Calif. State U., Fresno, 1966-69, assoc. prof. history, 1969-74, prof. history, 1974—; post-doctoral fellow Harvard U., Cambridge, Mass., 1969-70. Co-author: Sun Yat-sen and His Revolutionary Thought, 1991; co-editor: Bibliography of Sun Yat-sen in China's Republican Revolution, 1885-1925, 1990, 2d edit., 1997, The Storm Clouds Clear over China: Memoir of Ch en Li-fu, 1900-93, 1994. Mem. Rep. Presdl. Task Force, 1984—. Mem. Am. Hist. Assn., Assn. for Asian Studies. Office: Calif State U Dept History Cedar and Shaw Fresno CA 93726

CHANG, I-SHIH, aerospace engineer; b. Taipei, Taiwan, Dec. 2, 1945; came to U.S., 1968; s. I.H. and T.C. Chang; m. O.J. Chang, May 25, 1974; children: Anna, Brandon. Degree in mech. engring., Taipei Inst. of Tech., 1965; MS, U. Kans., 1969; PhD, U. Ill., 1973. Scientist assoc.-rsch. Lockheed Missiles & Space, Huntsville, Ala., 1973-76; mem. tech. staff Rockwell Internat., Anaheim, Calif., 1976-77; mem. tech. staff The Aerospace Corp., El Segundo, Calif., 1977-80, engring. specialist, 1980-90, sr. engring. specialist, 1990-91, disting. engr., 1991—. Contbr. articles to profl. jours. Fellow AIAA (assoc.); mem. Phi Kappa phi. Democrat. Home: 890 S Calle Venado Anaheim CA 92807-5004 Office: The Aerospace Corp M4/967 2350 E El Segundo Blvd El Segundo CA 90245

CHANG, JANICE MAY, lawyer, law educator, naturopath, psychologist; b. Loma Linda, Calif., May 24, 1970; d. Belden Shiu-Wah and Sylvia (Tan) C. BA, Calif. State U, San Bernardino, 1990, cert. paralegal studies, 1990, cert. creative writing, 1991; JD, LaSalle U., 1993; D in Naturopathy, D in Herbal Medicine, Clayton Sch. Natural Healing, 1993; Dr. Psychology, Internat. U., 1993; DO, Anglo-Am. Inst. Drugless Ther., 1994, Anglo-Am. Inst. Drugless Ther., 1994; M of Herbology, Emerson Coll. Herbology, 1996; MS in Clin. Psychology, Calif. Coast U., 1997, postgrad., 1997—. Victim/witness contact clk.-paralegal Dist. Atty.'s Office Victim/Witness Assistance Program, San Bernardino, Calif., 1990; gen. counsel JMC Enterprises, Inc., 1993—; law prof. LaSalle U., 1994—. Contbr. poetry to anthologies, including Am. Poetry Anthology, 1987-90, The Pacific Rev., 1991, The Piquant, 1991, River of Dreams, 1994, Reflections of Light, 1994, Musings, 1994 (Honorable Mention award 1994), Best Poems of 1995 (Celebrating Excellence award 1995, Inspirations award 1995), Am. Poetry Annual, 1996, Best New Poems of 1996, Interludes, 1996, Meditations, 1996, Perspectives, 1996 (Honorable Mention award 1996), Keepsakes, 1997 (Honorable Mention award 1997), Best Poems of 1997, Poetic Voices of America, 1997, The Isle of View, 1997. Recipient Poet of Merit award Am. Poetry Assn., San Francisco, 1989, Golden Poet award World of Poetry, Washington, 1989, Publisher's Choice award Watermark Press, 1990, Editor's Choice award The Nat. Libr. of Poetry, 1990-96, Pres.'s award for lit. excellence Iliad Press, 1995, 96; fellow Emerson Coll. Rsch. Coun. on Bot. Medicine. Mem. APA, ATLA, Am. Psychology-Law Soc., Am. Coll. Legal Medicine, Am. Naturopathic Med. Assn., Am. Soc. Law, Medicine and Ethics, Brit. Guild of Drugless Practitioners (diplomate), Calif. Trial Lawyers Assn. (med. law sect.), Nat. Assn. for Poetry Therapy, Delta Theta Phi. Republican. Seventh-Day Adventist. Home: 11466 Richmont Rd Loma Linda CA 92354-3523

CHANG, JONATHAN LEE, orthopedist; b. Lebanon, Pa., Feb. 22, 1959; s. Timothy Scott and Annabelle (Yee) C. Ed., U. Mich., 1980; MD, Duke U., 1984. Intern in surgery U. Va., Charlottesville, 1984-85, resident in surgery, 1985-86, resident in orthopedics, 1986-90; fellow in sports medicine Ky. Sports Medicine, Lexington, 1991; pvt. practice Orthop. Surgery and Sports Med. Group, Monterey Park, Calif., 1991—; clin. instr. U. So. Calif., L.A., 1992—; bd. dirs. Anderson Unicom Group, Inc., Pasadena, 1996—; team physician El Monte (Calif.) H.S., 1991—. Editl. bd. Jour. Musculoskeletal Medicine, 1993—; contbr. articles to profl. jours. Mem. AMA, Calif. Med. Assn., Am. Acad. Orthop. Surgeons, Am. Coll. Sports Medicine, L.A. County Med.. Assn., Nat. Athletic Trainers Assn., The McCue Soc. Office: Orthopedic Surgery and Sports Medical Group 500 N Garfield Ave Ste 204 Monterey Park CA 91754-1242

CHANG, KUANG-YEH, microelectronics technologist; b. Nanjing, China, Sept. 1, 1948; came to U.S., 1971; s. Yi and Wen-Teh (Tang) C.; m. Huey-Lian Ding, June 30, 1975; children: Fen, Wendy, Sherry, Sean. BSEE, Nat. Taiwan U., 1970; MSEE, U. Tenn., 1973; PhD, U. Pitts., 1978. Mem. tech. staff Hughes Aircraft Co., Newport Beach, Calif., 1978-83; mem. tech. staff Advanced Micro Devices, Sunnyvale, Calif., 1983-85, tech. integration mgr., 1994-96; device mgr. Motorola, Austin, Tex., 1985-89; engring. mgr. VLSI Tech., San Jose, Calif., 1989-91; fellow Compass Design Automation, San Jose, 1991-94; dir. ops. United Microelectronics Corp. Science Park, Hsinchu, Taiwan, 1996—; com. mem. ASIC Conf., Rochester, 1993-94. Patentee in field. 2d lt. Chinese Army, 1970-71. Mem. IEEE, Phi Kappa Phi. Home: 125 Forest Hill Dr Los Gatos CA 95032-4023 Office: UMC Science Park, 10 Innovation Rd 1, Hsinchu Taiwan

CHANG, RODNEY EIU JOON, artist, dentist; b. Honolulu, Nov. 26, 1945; s. Alfred Koon Bo and Mary Yet Moi (Char) C.; m. Erlinda C. Feliciano, Dec. 4, 1987; children: Bronson York, Houston Travis, Rochelle Jessica. BA in Zoology, U. Hawaii, 1968; AA in Art, Triton Coll., 1972; DDS, Loyola U., 1972; MS in Edn., U. So. Calif., 1974; MA in Painting and Drawing, U. No. Ill., 1975; MA in Community Leadership, Cen. Mich. U., 1976; BA in Psychology, Hawaii Pacific U., 1977; MA in Psychology of Counseling, U. No. Colo., 1980; PhD in Art Psychology, The Union Inst., 1980; MA in Computer Art, Columbia Pacific U., 1989. Pvt. practice dentist Honolulu, 1975—; dir. SOHO too Gallery and Loft, Honolulu, 1985-89; freelance artist Honolulu, 1982—; curator Webfelt Mus. of Early Cyberart, Honolulu, 1996—; founder Pygoya Internat. Art Group, 1990—; founder Art Cap Group, Slap Caps Co., Honolulu, 1993; columnist Milk Cap News; dir. ann. Honolulu City Hall Hawaiian Computer Art Exhbn., 1990-92; speaker on art psychology and computer art, also numerous TV and radio interviews. Author: Mental Evolution and Art, 1980, Rodney Chang: Computer Artist, 1988, Commentaries on the Psychology of Art, 1980; host (radio show) Disco Doc Hour, Sta. KISA; one-man shows include Honolulu Acad. Arts, 1986, Shanghai State Art Mus., People's Republic of China, 1988, Retrospective Exhbn. 1967-87, Ramsay Gallery, Honolulu, 1987, Visual Encounters Gallery, Denver, 1987, The Bronx Mus. of the Arts, N.Y.C., 1987, Nishi Noho Gallery, N.Y.C., 1987, Eastern Wash. U. Gallery of Art, 1988, Salon de la Jeune Peinture, Paris, 1989, Holter Art Mus., Mont., 1989, Las Vegas Art Mus., 1990, Forum Art Sch. Gütershoh, Fed. Republic of Germany, 1990, Siggraph-Dallas, 1990, Tartu State Art Mus., Estonia/USSR, 1990, U. Oregon Continuation Ctr., Portland, 1991—, Kauai Art Mus., Hawaii, 1993, RC Gallery of Computer Art, Honolulu, 1994, Archtl. Design of the Pygoya Home Mus., 1994; conceived, produced 1st milk cap art exhbn., Arts of Paradise Gallery, Waikiki Beach, 1993. Judge Jr. Miss Contest, Honolulu, 1981. Served to capt., U.S. Army, 1973-74. Mem. ADA, Hawaii Dental Assn., Assn. of Honolulu Artists (pres. 1989), Nat. Computer Graphics, Acad. Gen. Dentistry, Hawaii Space Soc., Bernice Bishop Mus. Honolulu. Roman Catholic. Office: 2119 N King St Ste 206 Honolulu HI 96819-4550

CHANG, SHENG-TAI, English language educator; b. Shanghai, Dec. 12, 1951; came to the U.S., 1986; s. Shucheng and Miaoxin (Xu) C. BA in English, East China Normal U., 1982; MA, U. Calgary, 1986; PhD in Comparative Lit., U. So. Calif., 1993, MA in East Asian Langs. and Cultures, 1994. English tchr. East China Normal U., Shanghai, 1982-84; instr. Chinese L.A. Trade-Tech. Coll., 1991; asst. lectr. in Chinese U. So. Calif., L.A., 1991; adj. asst. prof. Occidental Coll., L.A., 1993; lectr. U. So. Calif., L.A., 1994; instr., prof. South Puget Sound C.C., Olympia, Wash., 1994—. Editor, translator: The Tears of Chinese Immigrants, 1990; contbr. articles to profl. jours. Grantee Can. Ministry Multiculturalism, 1986. Mem. MLA, Philological Assn. Pacific Coast, Am. Assn. for Asian Studies, Am. Comparative Lit. Assn., Internat. Soc. for Comparative Study Civilizations, Phi Kappa Phi. Office: South Puget Sound CC 2011 Mottman Rd SW Olympia WA 98512-6218

CHANG, SYLVIA TAN, health facility administrator, educator; b. Bandung, Indonesia, Dec. 18, 1940; came to U.S., 1963; d. Philip Harry and Lydia Shui-Yu (Ou) Tan; m. Belden Shiu-Wah Chang, Aug. 30, 1964; children: Donald Steven, Janice May. Diploma in nursing, Rumah Sakit Advent, Indonesia, 1960; BS, Philippine Union Coll., 1962; MS, Loma Linda (Calif.) U., 1967; PhD, Columbia Pacific U., 1987. Cert. RN, PHN, ACLS, BLS instr., cmty. first aid instr., IV, TPN, blood withdrawal/. Head nurse Rumah Sakit Advent, Bandung, Indonesia, 1960-61; critical care, spl. duty and medicine nurse, team leader White Meml. Med. Ctr., L.A., 1963-64; nursing coord. Loma Linda U. Med. Ctr., 1964-66; team leader, critical care nurse, relief head nurse Pomona (Calif.) Valley Hosp. Med. Ctr., 1966-67; evening supr. Loma Linda U. Med. Ctr., 1967-69, night supr., 1969-79, adminstrv. supr., 1979-94; sr. faculty Columbia Pacific U., San Rafael, Calif., 1986-94; dir. health svc. La Sierra U., Riverside, Calif., 1988—; site coord. Health Fair Expo La Sierra U., 1988-89; adv. coun. Family Planning Clinic, Riverside, 1988-94; blood drive coord. La Sierra U., 1988—. Counselor Pathfinder Club Campus Hill Ch., Loma Linda, 1979-85, crafts instr., 1979-85, music dir., 1979-85; asst. organist U. Ch., 1982-88. Named one of Women of Achievement YWCA, Greater Riverside C. of C., The Press Enterprise, 1991, Safety Coord. of Yr. La Sierra U., 1995. Mem. Am. Coll. Health Assn., Assn. Seventh-day Adventist Nurses, Pacific Coast Coll. Health Assn., Adventist Student Pers. Assn., Loma Linda U. Sch. Nursing Alumni Assn. (bd. dirs.), Sigma Theta Tau. Republican. Seventh-day Adventist. Home: 11466 Richmont Rd Loma Linda CA 92354-3523 Office: La Sierra U Health Svc 4700 Pierce St Riverside CA 92505-3331

CHANG, TAIPING, marketing executive, magazine publisher; b. Tainan, Taiwan, Apr. 20, 1949; came to U.S., 1975; d. Lanfeng Chang and Shuchun Liu; m. David R. Knechtges, June 7, 1976; 1 child, Jeanne Y. BA, Tunghai U., 1971, MA, 1974; PhD, U. Wash., 1981. Lectr. Tunghai U., Taichung, Taiwan, 1974-75; asst. prof. Pacific Luth. U., Tacoma, 1986-88; pub. Asia Pacific Bus. Jour., Seattle, 1988-94; pres. Asia Media Group, Inc., Seattle, 1989-94; asst. prof. Asian studies program U. Puget Sound, Tacoma, Wash., 1994-95; asst. prof. Asian langs. and lit. dept. U. Wash., Seattle, 1996—; bd. dirs. Chong-Wa Benevolent Assn., Seattle, No. Seattle (Wash.) C.C.; chmn. World Trade Club-Taiwan Forum, Seattle, 1991—. Editor: Editor-in-Chief, 1988. Named Woman of Yr., Asia Am. Soc., Seattle, 1990. Mem. Rotary Club. Office: Univ Wash Asian Lang Lit Dept Seattle WA 98195

CHANG, WUNG, researcher, lecturer, business advisor; b. Republic of Korea, Apr. 24, 1942; came to U.S., 1973; s. Jae Sun and Key Bok (Yoo) C.; m. Han Jin Yang, Nov. 14, 1970; children: Min, Won. MPA, Yon-Sei U., 1971; PhD in Bus. Mgmt., Union U., 1983. Editor-in-chief Korea Photo Times, Seoul, 1970-73; sec.-gen. Wum Found., L.A., 1986-87; sr. analyst Pacific Rsch. Inst., L.A., 1988-92; advisor Korea Travel News, Seoul, 1988-93; controller U.S. Top Capital Corp., L.A., 1991—; vice chmn. Mid-Wilshire Vocat. Tng. Ctr. divsn. Adult and Career Edn., L.A. Unified Sch. Dist. Adv. Coun., 1994-96; vol. lectr. The Korean Sr. Citizens Assn. of San Fernando Valley Coll, 1995-96; co-chmn. Internat. Rsch. Inst. Govt. and Pub. Adminstrn., L.A., 1995—. Mem. Rep. Presdl. Adv. Commn., Washington, 1991; active Rep. Senatorial Com., Washington, 1991; nat. campaign advisor Rep. Senatorial Inner Circle, Washington, 1995—. Capt. Korean Army, 1966-70. Recipient Presdl. Order of Merit, 1991, Rep. Presdl. Task Force Wall of Honor, 1992. Home: 7625 Radford Ave North Hollywood CA 91605-2858

CHAO, JAMES MIN-TZU, architect; b. Dairen, China, Feb. 27, 1940; s. T. C. and Lin Fan (Wong) C.; came to U.S., 1949, naturalized, 1962; m. Kirsti Helena Lehtonen, May 15, 1968. BArch, U. Calif., Berkeley, 1965. Registered architect, Calif., Ariz.; cert. instr. real estate, Calif. Intermediate draftsman Spencer, Lee & Busse, Architects, San Francisco, 1966-67; asst. to pres. Import Plus Inc., Santa Clara, Calif., 1967-69; job capt. Hammaberg and Herman, Architects, Oakland, Calif., 1969-71; project mgr. B A Premises Corp., San Francisco, 1971-79; constrn. mgr. The Straw Hat Restaurant Corp., 1979-81, mem. sr. mgmt., dir. real estate and constrn., 1981-87; mem. mktg. com. Straw Hat Coop. Corp., 1988-91; pvt. practice architect, Berkeley, Calif., 1987—; pres. Food Svc. Cons. Inc., 1987-89; pres., CEO Stratsac, Inc., 1987-92; prin. architect Alpha Cons. Group Inc., 1991—; v.p. Intersyn Industries Calif., 1993—; nat. tng. dir. Excel Telecommunications, Inc., 1995—; CEO Nuts and Bolts Books, 1997—; lectr. comml. real estate site analysis and selection for profl. real estate seminars; coord. minority vending program, solar application program Bank of Am.; guest faculty mem. N.W. Ctr. for Profl. Edn.; bd. dirs Ambrosia Best Corp., 1992—. Author: The Street-Smart Restaurant Development Handbook, 1996; patentee tidal electric generating system; author first comprehensive consumer orientated performance specification for remote banking transaction. Recipient honorable mention Future Scientists Am., 1955. Mem. AIA, Encinal Yacht Club (bd. dir. 1977-78). Republican.

CHAPELLE, GREGORY PHILIPPE, electronics engineer, researcher; b. Vitoria, Spain, July 28, 1961; came to U.S., 1963; s. Rene Adrien and Glenda Mae (Padgett) C.; m. Sonja Wischow, Aug. 8, 1986. BSEE, U. Calif. San Diego, 1985; MSEE, Purdue U., 1986; CPhil, U. Calif., San Diego, 1994. Lic. amateur radio operator, FCC. Teaching asst. U. Calif. San Diego, 1984-85; assoc. engr. La Jolla Scis., Solana Beach, Calif., 1984-85; mem. tech. staff avionics systems divsn. TRW, San Diego, 1987-95, digital design engr. avionics systems divsn., 1996—. Author: The Birdcage Review, 1985; author, editor: (newspaper) Hiatus, 1985. Radio merit badge counselor Boy Scouts Am., San Diego, 1993—; chmn. Friends of Canyon Country, San Diego, 1993—. Recipient TRW Doctorate fellowship, 1989. Mem. IEEE, IEEE Comm. Soc. (vice chmn. San Diego sect. 1988-90), Eta Kappa Nu, Tau Beta Pi. Presbyterian. Home: 10984 Canyon Hill Ln San Diego CA 92126-2056 Office: TRW Avionics Systems Divsn One Rancho Carmel San Diego CA 92126

CHAPLIN, GEORGE, newspaper editor; b. Columbia, S.C., Apr. 28, 1914; s. Morris and Netty (Brown) C.; m. Esta Lillian Solomon, Jan. 26, 1937; children: Stephen Michael, Jerry Gay. BS, Clemson Coll., 1935; Nieman fellow, Harvard U., 1940-41; HHD (hon.), Clemson U., 1989; LHD (hon.), Hawaii Loa Coll., 1990. Reporter, later city editor Greenville (S.C.) Piedmont, 1935-42; mng. editor Camden (N.J.) Courier-Post, 1946-47, San Diego Jour., 1948-49; mng. editor, then editor New Orleans Item, 1949-58; asso. editor Honolulu Advertiser, 1958-59, editor in chief, 1959-86, editor at large, 1986—; mem. selection com. Jefferson fellowships East-West Ctr.; chmn. Gov.'s Conf. on Year 2000, 1970; chmn. Hawaii Commn. on Year 2000, 1971-74; co-chmn. Conf. on Alt. Econ. Futures for Hawaii, 1973-75; charter mem. Goals for Hawaii, 1979-81; alt. U.S. rep. South Pacific Commn., 1978-81; chmn. search com. for pres. U. Hawaii, 1983; chmn. Hawaii Gov.'s Adv. Coun. on Fgn. Lang. and Internat. Studies, 1983-94; rep. of World Press Freedom Com. on missions to Sri Lanka, Hong Kong, Singapore, 1987. Editor, officer-in-charge: Mid-Pacific edit. Stars and Stripes World War II; Editor: (with Glenn Paige) Hawaii 2000, 1973. Bd. dirs. U. Hawaii Rsch. Corp., 1970-72, Inst. for Religion and Social Change, Hawaii Jewish Welfare Fund; mem. bd. govs. East-West Ctr., Honolulu, 1980-89, chmn., 1983-89; mem. bd. govs. Pacific Health Rsch. Inst., 1984-90, 93-97, pres., 1995-96; bd. govs. Straub Med. Found., 1989—, Hawaii Pub. Schs. Found., 1986-87; trustee Clarence T. C. Ching Found., 1986-95; Am. media chmn. U.S.-Japan Conf. on Cultural and Ednl. Interchange, 1978-86; co-founder, v.p. Coalition for Drug-Free Hawaii, 1987-90; panelist ABA Conf., 1989; mem. Civilian Adv. Group, U.S. Army, Hawaii, 1985-95; co-chair Hawaii State Commn. on Judicial Salaries, 1995—. Capt. AUS, 1942-46. Decorated Star Solidarity (Italy), Order Rising Sun (Japan), Prime Minister's medal (Israel). Recipient citations Overseas Press Club, 1961, 72, Headliners award, 1962, John Hancock award, 1972, 74, Distinguished Alumni award Clemson U., 1974, E.W. Scripps award Scripps-Howard Found., 1976, Champion Media award for Econ. Understanding, 1981, Judah Magnes Gold medal Hebrew U. Jerusalem, 1987, Herbert Harley award Am. Judicature Soc., 1991; inductee Honolulu Press Club Hall of Fame, 1987. Mem. Soc. Nieman Fellows, Honolulu Symphony Soc., Pacific and Asian Affairs Council (dir.), Internat. Press Inst., Am. Soc. Newspaper Editors (dir., treas. 1973, sec. 1974, v.p. 1975, pres. 1976), Friends of East-West Ctr. Clubs: Pacific, Waialae Country. Home: 4437 Kolohala St Honolulu HI 96816-4938 Office: care Honolulu Advertiser PO Box 3110 Honolulu HI 96802-3110

CHAPLINE, CLAUDIA BEECHUM, artist, art dealer; b. Oak Park, Ill., May 23, 1930; d. Jacob Burwell and Lillian Estella (Schell) C.; m. James Nicol Hood, Dec. 1955 (div. 1979); children: Craig Chapline Hood, Randall Jameson Hood; m. Harold Chambers Schwarm, Feb. 14, 1989. BA in Drawing and Painting cum laude with spl. honors, George Washington U., 1953; postgrad., Corcoran Sch. Art, 1948-53; MA in Dance Therapy, Washington U., St. Louis, 1956. Instr. dance Washington U., St. Louis, 1953-56, U. Mo., Columbia, 1956-57, Alhambra (Calif.) High Sch., 1959-60, El Camino Coll., L.A., 1960-61; dir. Shatto Drama Ctr., L.A., 1958-59; asst. prof. dance UCLA, 1960-61, Calif. State U., Northridge, 1961-64; founder, dir. Inst. for Design/Dance and Exptl. Art, Santa Monica/Sacramento, 1974-88; lectr. dance U. Calif. ext., L.A., 1981-82; owner Claudia Chapline Gallery & Sculpture Garden, Stinson Beach, Calif., 1987—; coord. Artists in Social Instns., Calif. Arts Coun., 1982-84, program mgr. Art in Pub. Bldgs., 1984-90; dir. Bolinas (Calif.) Mus. Devel., 1989. One-woman shows include Humanist Ctr., St. Louis, 1956, Hobart Gallery, 1966, 67, E.B. Crocker Art Gallery, Sacramento, 1967, Humboldt Galleries, San Francisco, 1969, Jacqueline Anhalt Gallery, L.A., 1973, Palos Verdes Mus. Art, 1975, Inst. for Dance and Experimental Art, Santa Monica, Calif., 1976, 78, 79, Shackelford and Sears Gallery, Davis, Calif., 1986, IDEA, Sacramento, 1990, Wilder Gallery, Los Gatos, Calif., 1992, Claudia Chapline Gallery, Stinson Beach, Calif., 1994, 96, JFK U., Orinda, Calif., 1994, Galerie Im Gassla, Erlangen, Germany, 1995, Anagma Arte Contemporaneo, Valencia, Spain, 1995, Bolinas Mus. (Calif.) Mus., 1996; exhibited in group shows at Corcoran Gallery of Art, Washington, 1952, Hobart Gallery, 1965, Ryder Gallery, L.A., 1967, Zachary Waller Gallery, L.A., 1970, Long Beach Mus. Art, 1971, L.A. County Mus. Art, 1973, L.A. Inst. Contemporary Art, 1975, Pasadena Artists Concern, 1976, Gray Whale, Sacramento, 1985, Bolinas (Calif.) Mus., 1990, 92, 93, 94, 95, 96, Marin Arts Coun., 1993, 94, 95, 96, Artisan's Gallery, Mill Valley, Calif., 1994, Somar Gallery, San Francisco, 1994, Falkirk Cultural Ctr., San Rafael, Calif., 1994, 95, Marin Civic Ctr., 1995, 96, Internat. Art Fair, Mexico City, 1995, Pub. Art Works (bd. dirs. 1995—); represented in numerous pub. and pvt. collections. Mem. San Francisco Art Dealers Assn., ArtTable (bd. dirs. 1993-95), Alliance Women Artists. Office: Claudia Chapline Gallery & Sculpture Garden PO Box 946 3445 Shoreline Stinson Beach CA 94970

CHAPMAN, ALGER BALDWIN, III, pediatrician, researcher; b. N.Y.C., June 13, 1957; s. Alger B. Chapman Jr. and Pauline Badham Pinto; m. Trina McKean, Sept. 25, 1988; children: Ryan, Samantha. BS cum laude, Yale U., 1979; PhD, Stanford U., 1986, MD, 1987. Diplomate Am. Bd. Pediatrics and Pediatric Infectious Disease. Pediatric intern U. Calif., San Francisco, 1987-88, resident in pediatrics, 1988-89, fellow in pediatric infectious disease, 1989-92, adj. asst. prof. pediatrics, 1992-95, asst. clin. prof., 1995-96; ptnr. ABC Pediat., San Mateo, Calif., 1995—. Contbr. articles to profl. jours. NIH fellow, 1979-88, 90-95. Fellow Am. Acad. Pediatrics; mem. Infectious Disease Soc. Am., Pediatric Infectious Disease Soc., Am. Soc. Tropical Medicine and Hygiene. Democrat. Office: ABC Pediatrics 50 S San Mateo Dr Ste 260 San Mateo CA 94401-3859

CHAPMAN, DONALD BRENT, computer network security consultant; b. Prescott, Ariz., July 23, 1968; s. Timothy James and Diana Patricia (Beasley) C. BS, U. Calif., Berkeley, 1989. Computer ops. mgr. Capital Market Tech., Berkeley, 1985-89; UNIX ops. mgr. Xerox Palo Alto (Calif.) Rsch. Ctr., 1989-90; computer ops. mgr. Ascent Logic Corp., San Jose, Calif., 1990-91; cons., owner Great Circle Assocs., Mountain View, Calif., 1988—. Mission coord., search & rescue pilot Civil Air Patrol, Palo Alto, 1991—. Mem. IEEE, Sys. Adminstrs. Guild (charter), Bay Area Large Installation Sys. Adminstrs., Assn. for Computing Machinery. Office: Great Circle Assocs 1057 W Dana St Mountain View CA 94041-1222

CHAPMAN, GEORGE J., agricultural products executive; b. 1936. With Magi Inc., Brewster, Wash., 1966—, now pres. Office: Magi Inc 26049 State Hwy 97 Brewster WA 98812*

CHAPMAN, GERALD WESTER, educator; b. Rusk, Tex., July 20, 1927; s. Gerald Benson and Eunice (Wester) C.; m. Ruth Rimmer, Dec. 31, 1950 (div. 1967); children: Robin Chapman Stacey, Gerald Wester Jr.; m. Karen Carbone, Dec., 1968 (div. 1972). BA, So. Meth. U., Dallas, 1949, MA, 1951; PhD, Harvard U., 1957. Instr. Northwestern U., Evanston, Ill., 1954-57; instr. Harvard U., Cambridge, Mass., 1957-60, lectr., 1960-61, vis. prof., summer 1968, 70; asst. prof. U. Tex., Austin, 1961-62; assoc. prof. English, U. Denver, 1962-65, prof., 1965—, Phipps prof., 1967-76; mem. vis. com. dept. English, Harvard Bd. Overseers, Cambridge, 1967-73. Author: Edmund Burke: The Practical Imagination, 1967, Literary Critic in England 1660-1800, 1966; editor: Essays on Shakespeare, 1965; co-founder, assoc. editor Denver Quar., 1966-76. John Simon Guggenheim fellow, 1977-78. Home: 2512 S University Blvd Denver CO 80210 Office: U Denver Denver CO 80208

CHAPMAN, JOYCE EILEEN, law educator, administrator; b. Red Bluff, Calif., June 11, 1940; d. Joseph L. and Elaine C. (Potter) Cole; m. William H. Chapman, July 15, 1961; 1 child, Gregory W. AA in Bus. Edn., Shasta Coll., Redding, Calif., 1960; BA in Bus. Edn., Chico (Calif.) State Coll., 1962; MA in Edn. with distinction, Calif. State U., Chico, 1991. Cert. C.C. instr., office svcs. and related techs., banking, fin., ct. reporting, office adminstr. Calif. Tchr. bus. edn. Red Bluff (Calif.) Union H.S., 1962-63; traffic mgr. WOHP Radio, Bellefontaine, Ohio, 1963; tchr. bus. edn. Indian Lake H.S., Lewistown, Ohio, 1963-64; adminstrv. and transp. supr. Tumpane Co., Inc., Adana, Turkey, 1964-66; telephone claims rep. Allstate Ins. Co., San Antonio, Tex., 1966-70; tchr. vocat. office edn. Somerset (Tex.) H.S., 1975-80; instr. bus. edn. Shasta Coll., Redding, Calif., 1980-94; instr. office info. systems Butte Coll., Oroville, Calif., 1987-90; instr. ct. reporting Butte Coll., Oroville, 1990—; mem. Butte Coll. Curriculum Com. Oroville, 1990-91; facilitator ct. reporting Adv. Com., Oroville, 1990—, Butte Coll. Ct. Reporting, Oroville, 1990—; mem. Butte FLEX Com. (staff devel.), Oroville, 1993-96. Author: (book) Introduction to Computer-Aided Transcription, 1991; (degree program) Court Reporting: A Macro Curriculum for Butte C.C. Dist., 1990. Mem. ASCD, NEA, Nat. Ct. Reporters Assn., Calif. Ct. Reporters Assn., Calif. Tchrs. Assn., North State Ct. Reporters Assn., Reporting Assn. Pub. Schs. Calif. (sec.-treas.). Republican. Office: Butte Coll 3536 Butte Campus Dr Oroville CA 95965-8303

CHAPMAN, LORING, psychology educator, neuroscientist; b. L.A., Oct. 4, 1929; s. Lee E. and Elinore E. (Gundry) Scott; children: Robert, Antony, Pandora (dec.). BS, U. Nev., 1950; PhD, U. Chgo., 1955. Lic. psychologist, Oreg., N.Y., Calif. Rsch. fellow U. Chgo., 1952-54; rsch. assoc., asst. prof. Cornell U. Med. Coll., N.Y.C., 1957-61; rsch. dir. Music Rsch. Found., N.Y.C., 1958-61; assoc. prof. in residence Neuropsychiat. Inst., UCLA, 1961-65; rsch. prof. U. Oreg., Portland, 1965; br. chief NIH, Bethesda, Md., 1966-67; prof., chmn. dept. behavioral biology, joint prof. human physiology Sch. Medicine U. Calif., Davis, 1967-81, prof. psychiatry and head Divsn. of Clin. Psychology, 1977-91; prof. emeritus Sch. Medicine U. Calif., 1991—, prof. neurology, 1977-81, prof. human physiology, 1977-81; asst. dean, rsch. affairs Sch. Medicine U. Calif., Davis, 1972-74; vice chmn. div. of sci. basic to medicine, 1976-79; Lic. psychologist, Calif. Author: Pain and Suffering, 3 vols, 1967, Head and Brain 3 vols, 1971, (with E.A. Dunlap) The Eye, 1981; assoc. editor courtroom medicine series updates, 1965—; contbr. sci. articles to publs. Fogarty Sr. Internat. fellow, 1980; grantee NASA, 1969-80; grantee NIH, 1956-91; grantee Nat. Inst. Drug Abuse, 1971-80; recipient Thornton Wilson prize, 1958, Career award USPHS, 1964, Commonwealth Fund award, 1970. Mem. Am. Acad. Neurology, Am. Physiol. Soc., Am. Psychol. Assn., Royal Soc. Medicine (London)., Am. Neurol. Assn., Am. Assn. Mental Deficiency, Aerospace Med. Assn., Soc. for Neurosci. Home: 7610 Rush River Dr Apt 121 Sacramento CA 95831-5517 Office: U Calif Med Ctr Dept Psychiatry 2315 Stockton Blvd Sacramento CA 95817-2201 *The first taste of the forbidden fruit in the distant gardens of genesis evoked a most deeply human question, beautifully phrased in antiquity, "And we, who are we, anyway?" I have been privileged to spend my working life sharing in the search for this understanding. The pace of progress has seemed rapid, but evil has come along with good, and now the terrible fragility of ourselves and our planet lies bare before us. We feel the need for immediate, practical, and wise answers ever more urgently, for our utmost yearning is to see the full flowering of who we, we human beings, are and can become.*

CHAPMAN, RICHARD LEROY, public policy researcher; b. Yankton, S.D., Feb. 4, 1932; s. Raymond Young and Vera Everette (Trimble) C.; m. Marilyn Jean Nicholson, Aug. 14, 1955; children: Catherine Ruth, Robert Matthew, Michael David, Stephen Raymond, Amy Jean. BS, S.D. State U., 1954; postgrad., Cambridge (Eng.) U., 1954-55; MPA, Syracuse U., 1958, PhD, 1967. With Office of Sec. of Def., 1958-59, 61-63; dep. dir. rsch. S.D. Legis. Rsch. Coun., 1959-60; mem. staff Bur. of the Budget, Exec. Office of Pres., Washington, 1960-61; profl. staff mem. com. govt. ops. U.S. Ho. of Reps., Washington, 1966; program dir. NIH, Bethesda, Md., 1967-68; sr. rsch. assoc. Nat. Acad. Pub. Adminstrn., Washington, 1968-72, dep. exec. dir., 1973-76, v.p., dir. rsch., 1976-82; sr. rsch. scientist Denver Rsch. Inst., 1982-86; mem. adv. com. Denver Rsch. Inst. U. Denver, 1984-86; ptnr. Milliken Chapman Rsch. Group Inc., Denver, 1986-88; v.p. Chapman Rsch. Group, Inc., Littleton, 1988—; cons. U.S. Office Pers. Mgmt., Washington, 1977-81, Denver, 1986—; cons. CIA, Washington, 1979, 80, 81, Arthur S. Fleming Awards, Washington, 1977-81; exec. staff dir., cons. U.S. Congressman Frank Denholm; lectr. on sci., tech., govt. and pub. mgmt. Author: (with Fred Grissom) Mining the Nation's Braintrust, 1992; contbr. over 60 articles and revs. to profl. jours. and congl. staff reports. Mem. aerospace com. Colo. Commn. Higher Edn., Denver, 1982-83; chmn. rules com. U. Denver Senate, 1984-85; bd. dirs. S.E. Englewood Water Dist., Littleton, 1984-88, pres. 1986-88; mem. strategic planning com. Mission Hills Bapt. Ch., 1986; bd. dirs. Lay Action Ministry Program, 1988-96, chmn. 1992-96; established Vera and Raymond Chapman Scholarship Fund, S.D. State U.; mem. Fairfax County Rep. Ctrl. Com., Va., 1969-71, Fairfax County Com. of 100, 1979-82. With U.S. Army, 1955-57, Korea, capt. Res. Syracuse U. Maxwell Sch. fellow, 1957-58, 63-64, Brookings Inst. fellow, 1964-65. Mem. AAAS, Tech. Transfer Soc. (bd. dirs. 1987-95, Pres.'s award 1991, founder Colo. chpt., Thomas Jefferson award 1996), Fed. Lab. Consortium (nat. adv. com. 1989—), S.D. State U. Found. (bd. dirs. 1992—, vice chmn. 1994-96, chmn. bd. 1996—), Masons, Knights Templar, Order of DeMolay (Cross of Honor 1982), Rotary (fellow Internat. Found. 1954-55, Paul Harris fellow 1989), Southglen Country Club. Republican. Office: Chapman Rsch Group 6129 S Elizabeth Way Littleton CO 80121-2647 *Treat all of life as an opportunity to learn and to contribute. As one enriches the lives of others, you receive great satisfaction and returns that cannot be imagined.*

CHAPMAN, ROBERT DALE, research chemist; b. Glendale, Calif., June 4, 1955; s. Forrest Dale and Berta (Jäger) C.; m. Debra Jay Cullen, Dec. 5, 1981. BA in Chemistry, U. Calif., Irvine, 1977, PhD, 1980. Research assoc. U. Colo., Boulder, 1981; research chemist Naval Weapons Ctr., China Lake, Calif., 1981-82; rsch. chemist Astronautics Lab., Edwards AFB, Calif., 1982-89; sr. rsch. chemist Fluorochem Inc., Azusa, Calif., 1989-91; staff scientist Unidynamics, Phoenix, 1991-92; sr. scientist TPL Inc., Albuquerque, 1992-95; rsch. chemist Naval Air Warfare Ctr., China Lake, Calif., 1995—. NRC fellow, 1981. Mem. Am. Chem. Soc., Internat. Pyrotechnics Soc., Sigma Xi. Methodist. Office: NAWC Code 4B2200D China Lake CA 93555

CHAPMAN, ROBERT GALBRAITH, retired hematologist, administrator; b. Colorado Springs, Colo., Sept. 29, 1926; s. Edward Northrop and Janet Galbraith (Johnson) c.; m. Virginia Irene Potts, July 6, 1956; childen: Lucia Tully Chapman Chatzky, Sarah Northrop Chapman Bohrer, Robert Bostwick. Student, Westminster Coll., 1944-45; BA, Yale U., 1947; MD, Harvard U., 1951; MS, U. Colo., 1958. Diplomate Am. Bd. Internal Medicine and Pathology; lic. physician, Colo., Calif. Intern Hartford (Conn.) Hosp., 1951-52; resident in medicine U. Colo. Med. Ctr., Denver, 1955-58; fellow in hematology U. Wash., Seattle, 1958-60; chief resident in medicine U. Colo., Denver, 1957-58, instr. medicine, 1960-62, asst. prof. medicine, 1962-68, assoc. prof., 1968-91; chief staff VA Hosp., Denver, 1968-70; dir. Belle Bonfils Meml. Blood Ctr., Denver, 1977-91; mem. regionalization com. Am. Blood Commn., Washington, 1985-87, Colo.sickle cell com., Denver, 1978-91, gov.'s AIDS Coun., 1987-88; trustee Coun. Community Blood Ctrs., v.p., 1979-81, pres., 1989-91, mem. rsch. inst. bd. Palo Alto Med. Found., 1991—. Contbr. articles to profl. jours. Served as capt. USAF, 1953-55. USPHS fellow, 1958-60. Fellow ACP; mem. Am. Assn. Blood Banks, Mayflower Soc., Denver Med. Soc., Colo. Med. Soc., Western Soc. Clin. Rsch., Am. Radio Relay League. Mem. United Ch. Christ. Home: 47 La Rancheria Carmel Valley CA 93924-9424

CHAPMAN, WILLIAM RYAN, history educator; b. Springfield, Vt., July 1, 1949; s. Howard Goodell and Mary Jane (Ryan) C.; m. Linda Louise Callahan, May 19, 1979 (div. 1981); m. Maria Elizabeth Ausherman, June 23, 1984; children: Chloe Amelia,Lydia Marie. BA in Anthropology, U. Va., 1971; MSt in Anthropology, U. Oxford, 1974; MS in Historic Preservation, Columbia U., 1978; DPhil, Oxford U., 1982. Archtl. historian Govt. of V.I., Charlotte, 1979-83; historian Nat. Park Svc., Phila., 1983-85; asst. prof. U. Ga., Athens, 1986-91, assoc. prof., 1991-93; assoc. prof., dir. historic preservation program U. Hawaii, Honolulu, 1993—; bd. trustees US/ICOMOS, Washington, 1989-95; bd. advisors Ga. Trust Historic Preservation, Atlanta, 1987-93. Author: Madison Historic Preservation Manual, 1991. Bd. dirs. Kaimuki Main St., Inc., Honolulu, 1996—; chmn. Hist.Assn. Commn. Athens-Clarke County, Ga., 1987-90. Rsch. grantee Graham Found., Chgo., 1994-95; Rsch. fellow Fulbright Found., Washington, 1985. Mem. Hawaiian Hist. Soc., Historic Hawaii Found., Victorian Soc. Am., William Morris Soc. Home: 1995 Wilhelmina Rise Honolulu HI 96816 Office: U Hawaii Dept Am Studies Moore 334 Honolulu HI 96822

CHAPNICK, ROBERT IAN, physician; b. N.Y.C., Oct. 23, 1951; s. Seymour and Laura Helene (Wilk) C.; m. Henny Gurewich, Dec. 8, 1979; 1 child, Daniel. BA, CUNY, 1972; MD, SUNY, Bklyn., 1976. Diplomate Am. Bd. Internal Medicine. Internal medicine intern Brookdale Med. Ctr., Bklyn., 1976-77, internal medicine resident, 1977-79; pvt. practice San Leandro, Calif., 1979-88; med. dir. City/County San Francisco Homeless Programs, 1988-95, Cmty. Med. Ctrs. Inc., Stockton, Calif., 1995—; asst. clin. prof. U. Calif., San Francisco, 1990—; co-chair San Francisco Dept. Pub. Health Joint Pharmacy & Therapeutics Com., 1994-95; mem. San Francisco Gen. Hosp. Pharmacy & Therapeutics Com., 1992-95; mem. San Francisco Dept. Pub. Health AIDS Com., 1990-95; med. expert, cons. State of Calif., Sacramento, 1995—; coord., bd. dirs. Su Salud Health Edn. Found. Mem. AMA, San Joaquin Med. Soc., Calif. Med. Assn. Home: 26551 Durham Way Hayward CA 94542-1740 Office: Cmty Med Ctrs Inc 701 E Channel St Stockton CA 95202-2628

CHAPPELL, DAVID WELLINGTON, religion educator; b. St. John, N.B., Can., Feb. 3, 1940; came to U.S., 1966; s. Hayward Lynsin and Mary Elvira (Mosher) C.; m. Bertha Vera Bidulock, Aug. 23, 1960 (div. Jan. 1976); children: Cynthia Joan, Mark Lynsin David; m. Stella Quemada, July 11, 1981. BA, Mt. Allison U., Sackville, N.B., 1961; BD, McGill U., Montreal, Que., Can., 1965; PhD, Yale U., 1976. Min. United Ch. Can., Elma, Ont., Can., 1964-66; prof. U. Hawaii, Honolulu, 1971—; asst. prof. U. Toronto, Toronto, Ont., 1977-78; vis. prof. U. Pitts., 1982; vis. lectr. Taisho U., Tokyo, 1986-88; dir. East West Religions Project, Honolulu, 1980—, Buddhist Studies Program, U. Hawaii, 1987-92. Editor: T'ien-t'ai Buddhism, 1983, Buddhist and Taoist Practice, 1987; editor Buddhist-Christian Studies jour., 1980-95. Mem. Am. Acad. Religion, Assn. Asian Studies, Internat. Assn. Buddhist Studies, Soc. Buddhist-Christian Studies (past pres.). Democrat. Home: 47-696 Hui Kelu St Apt 1 Kaneohe HI 96744-4636

CHAR, CARLENE, writer, publisher, editor; b. Honolulu, Oct. 21, 1954; d. Richard Y. and Betty S.M. Char. BA in Econs., U. Hawaii, 1977; MA in Bus. Adminstrn., Columbia Pacific U., 1984, PhD in Journalism, 1985, B in Gen. Studies in Computer Sci., Roosevelt U., 1986. Freelance writer, Honolulu, 1982—; editor Computer Book Rev., Honolulu, 1983—; instr. Chaminade U., Honolulu, 1996—.

CHARBONNEAU, JOANNE ADRIENNE, literature and humanities educator; b. Worcester, Mass., Sept. 9, 1950; d. Philip Paul and Stasia Marie (Poltorak) C.; m. Richard Eugene Rice, June 9, 1972. Student, St. John's Coll., Annapolis, Md., 1968-70; BA, U. Mass., 1972; MA, U. Mont., 1974; PhD, Mich. State U., 1981. Instr., writing specialist Mich. State U., East Lansing, 1978-79, asst. prof., English, 1981-82; mem. faculty, English dept. Md. Inst. Coll. of Arts, Balt., 1983-84; asst. prof. English Butler U., Indpls., 1984-88, dir. freshman English, 1986-89, assoc. prof. English, 1988-90; chmn. English dept. Fayetteville (N.C.) State U., 1990-91; vis. assoc. prof. U. Mont., Missoula, 1991—. Freelance editor; contbg. author: (book) Riverside Chaucer; author: (book) ME Romance: Annotated Bibliography, 1987; contbr. ency. entries, articles to profl. jours. Mem. Medieval Acad. of Am., MLA, Rocky Mountain Medieval and Renaissance Assn. Office: U Mont Liberal Studies Dept Missoula MT 59812

CHARD, CAROLYN DOBBS, physical therapist; b. New Haven, Conn., Mar. 28, 1939; d. William Gibson Hazard and Elizabeth Emily (Booth) Dobbs; m. Howard LeRoy Chard, Oct. 10, 1964 (div. Oct. 1975); 1 child, Sherrilee. BA, U. Rochester, 1961; MA in Phys. Therapy, Baylor U., 1962; MA in Edn., Ariz. State U., 1985. Registered phys. therapist, Ariz. Phys. therapist Mary Free Bed Hosp., Grand Rapids, Mich., 1963-65; head phys. therapy dept. Mesa (Ariz.) Luth. Hosp., 1968-70; phys. therapist Scottsdale (Ariz.) Meml. Hosp., 1970-74; pvt. practice Phoenix, 1975-86; vol. Peace Corps, Sierra Leone, West Africa, 1986-87; phys. therapist pvt. practice Phoenix, 1990—. Mem. Am. Phys. Therapy Assn. Home and Office: 1130 W Portland St Phoenix AZ 85007-2129

CHARLES, BLANCHE, retired elementary education educator; b. Spartanburg, S.C., Aug. 7, 1912; d. Franklin Grady and Alice Florida (Hatchette) C. BA, Humboldt State U., 1934; adminstrv. cert., U. So. Calif., 1940. Tchr. Jefferson Elem. Sch., Calexico (Calif) Unified Sch. Dist., 1958-94; libr. Calexico Pub. Libr., El Centro Pub. Libr. Elem. sch. named in her honor, 1987. Mem. NEA, ACT, Calif. Tchrs. Assn., Nat. Soc. DAR, Nat. Soc. Daus. of Confederacy, Delta Kappa Gamma. Home: 37133 Highway 94 Campo CA 91906-2809

CHARLES, CHERYL, non-profit executive, business owner; b. Seattle, Nov. 4, 1947; d. Tom E. Charles and Irene D. (Brown) Shelver; m. Robert E. Samples, Sept. 15, 1973; 1 child, Stician M. BA, U. Ariz., 1969; MA, Ariz. State U., 1971; PhD, U. Wash., 1982. Lic. secondary edn. Tchr. Phoenix Union H.S., 1969-71; staff assoc. Social Sci. Edn. Consortium, Boulder, Colo., 1971-72; social studies dept. chmn. Trevor Browne H.S., Phoenix, 1972-73; asst. dir. Essentia: Environ. Studies for Urban Youth, Olympia, Wash., 1973-75; nat. dir. Project Learning Tree, Tiburon, Calif. & Boulder, Colo., 1976-84; exec. dir. Project Wild, Boulder, 1981-93; pres. Sol y Sombra Found., Santa Fe, N.Mex., 1991—; exec. dir. Ctr. for Study of Cmty., Santa Fe, 1993—; prin. investigator MacArthur Found., Chgo., 1993-94, Bradley Found., Milw., 1995—, Ednl. Found. Am., Westport, Conn., 1995—; project dir. McCune Found., Santa Fe, N.Mex., 1995—. Co-author: The Whole School Book, 1977; editor: Project Wild Elementary and Secondary Guide, 1983-92, Project Wild Aquatic Guide, 1987-92; co-editor, designer Windstar Jour., 1987-90. Mem. nat. adv. com. U. Mich. Coll. Engring., East Lansing, Mich., 1990-93; nat. judge Seiko Youth Challenge, 1994; bd. advisors Aspen (Colo.) Global Change Inst., 1990—; bd. trustees Hispanic Culture Found., Albuquerque, 1995—; pres. bd. trustees Windstar Land Conservancy, 1996—; chair bd. trustees Windstar Found., 1995—. Recipient Leadership award U.S. Forest Svc., internat. region, 1985, L.B. Sharp award excellence in outdoor/environ. edn., 1993, Gold medal Pres. Environ. and Conservation Challenge award, Washington, 1991; named Profl. of Yr. Western Assn. Fish/Wildlife Agys., 1991. Mem. N.Am. Assn. Environ. Edn., Nat. Coun. Social Studies, N.Mex. First Town Hall, No. N.Mex. Grant Makers. Office: Ctr for Study of Cmty 4018 Old Santa Fe Trl Santa Fe NM 87505-4500

CHARLES, MARY LOUISE, newspaper columnist, photographer, editor; b. L.A., Jan. 24, 1922; d. Louis Edward and Mabel Inez (Lyon) Kusel; m. Henry Loewy Charles, June 19, 1946; children: Susan, Henry, Robert, Carol. AA, L.A. City Coll., 1941; BA, San Jose (Calif.) State U., 1964. Salesperson Bullock's, L.A., 1940-42, Roos Bros., Berkeley, Calif., 1945-46; ptnr. Charles-Martin Motors, Marysville, Calif., 1950-54; farm editor Indep. Herald, Yuba City, Calif., 1954-55; social worker Sutter County, Yuba City, 1955-57; social worker Santa Clara County, San Jose, 1957-61, manual coordinator, 1961-73, community planning specialist, 1973-81; columnist Sr. Grapevine various weekly newspapers, Santa Clara County, 1981-86; editor Bay area Sr. Spectrum Newspapers, Santa Clara, 1986-90; columnist, 1990-94; columnist Santa Clara Valley edit. Senior Mag., 1994-95; columnist San Jose Mercury News, 1994—, Prime Times Monthly Mag. (now Prime Monthly), 1994—; founder, pres. Triple-A Coun. Calif., 1978-80. Vice chmn. Santa Clara County Sr. Care Commn., 1987-89, chmn., 1989-91, mem. social svcs. com., 1993—; mem. adv. coun. Coun. on Aging of Santa Clara County, 1995—; mem. aging and disabled adv. com. Met. Transp. Commn., 1995—. With WAVES, USNR, 1942-45. Recipient Social Welfare award Daniel E. Koshland Found., 1973, Friends of Santa Clara County Human Rels. Commn. award, 1992, first ann. Angelina Aguilar Yates Humanitarian award, 1995; named 24th State Assembly Dist. Woman of Yr., 1990. Mem. NASW, APHA (Gerontol. sect.), LWV (San Jose/Santa Clara Bd. 1993-96, Bay Area bd. transp. chmn. 1996), Nat. Coun. Sr. Citizens (bd. dirs. 1988—), Svc. Employees Internat. Union (mem. local 535, state exec. bd. dirs. 1973—, pres. sr. mems. and retiree chpt. 1982—), Congress of Calif. Srs. (bd. dirs. 1987—, region IV pres. 1992—, trustee 1993-97, no. v.p. 1997—), Older Women's League (bd. dirs. 1980-84), Older Women's League of Calif. (edn./resource coord. 1987-89, pres. 1990-91, Golden Owl award 1995), Am. Soc. on Aging (co-chair women's concerns com. 1985-86, awards com. 1990-93), Nat. Coun. on the Aging, Calif. Specialists on Aging (treas. 1985-93), Calif. Srs. Coalition (chmn. 1986, treas. 1993—), Calif. Writers Club (cen. bd. dels. 1995—). Home and Office: 2527 Forbes Ave Santa Clara CA 95050-5547

CHARLESTON, STEVE, bishop. Bishop Diocese of Alaska, Fairbanks, 1991—.

CHARLTON, JOHN KIPP, pediatrician; b. Omaha, Jan. 26, 1937; s. George Paul and Mildred (Kipp) C. A.B., Amherst Coll., 1958; M.D., Cornell U., 1962; m. Susan S. Young, Aug. 15, 1959; children: Paul, Cynthia, Daphne, Gregory. Intern, Ohio State U. Hosp., Columbus, 1962-63; resident in pediatrics Children's Hosp., Dallas, 1966-68, chief pediatric resident, 1968-69; nephrology fellow U. Tex. Southwestern Med. Sch., Dallas, 1969-70; pvt. practice medicine specializing in pediatrics, Phoenix, 1970; chmn. dept. pediatrics Maricopa Med. Ctr., Phoenix, 1971-78, 84-93, assoc. chmn. dept. pediatrics, 1979-84, med. staff pres., 1991; med. dir., bd. dirs. Crisis Nursery, Inc., 1977—; dir. Phoenix Pediatric Residency, 1983-85, Phoenix Hosps. affiliated pediatric program, 1985-88; clin. assoc. prof. pediatrics U. Ariz. Coll Medicine. Pres. Maricopa County Child Abuse Coun., 1977-81; bd. dirs. Florence Critenton Svcs., 1980-83, Ariz. Children's Found, 1987-91; mem. Gov.'s Coun. on Children, Youth and Families, 1984-86. Officer M.C., USAF, 1963-65. Recipient Hon Kachina award for volunteerism, 1980, Jefferson award for volunteerism, 1980, Horace Steel Child Advocacy award, 1993; named Clin. Sci. Educator of Yr. U. Ariz., 1997. Mem. Am. Acad. Pediatrics, Ariz. Pediatric Soc., Maricopa County Pediatric Soc. (past pres.). Author articles, book rev. in field. Home: 6230 E Exeter Blvd Scottsdale AZ 85251-3060 Office: Maricopa Med Ctr 2601 E Roosevelt St Phoenix AZ 85008-4973

CHARLTON, (JAMES) PAUL(ETT JR.), information systems architect; b. Charlottesville, Va., Oct. 3, 1966; s. James P. and Jeannette Charlton; m. Consuelo Kaiser, May 29, 1993. BS in Computer and Systems Engring., Rensselaer Poly. Inst., 1988. Systems devel. mgr. MYARC Inc., Basking Ridge, N.J., 1986-88; devel. engr. Hewlett Packard, Greeley, Colo., 1988-90; dir. MCB advanced tech. lab. Chase Manhattan Bank, Garden City, N.Y., 1990-92; tech. contbr. D.E. Shaw & Co., N.Y.C., 1992-94; computer multimedia devel. Apple Computer, Cupertino, Calif., 1994-96; co-founder, v.p. tech. BeyondNews, Inc., Alamo, Calif., 1996—; pres. Orange Moon Prodns., Inc., 1995—, Charlton Innovations, Inc., 1996—. Author software: Fast Term, 1984, MYARC Disk Operating System, 1987, Quicktime for Windows, 1994. Mem. IEEE, Assn. Computing Machinery, World Affairs Coun., U.S. Chess Fedn. Home: 696 Windsor Ter Sunnyvale CA 94087-2328

CHARLTON, RANDOLPH SEVILLE, psychiatrist, educator; b. Salt Lake City, Nov. 16, 1944; s. Randolph Seville and Patricia Joy (Jensen) C.; m. Louise Bryden Buck, Feb. 14, 1975; children: Genevieve, Blake. BA, Wesleyan U., 1966; MD, Cornell U., 1970. Diplomate Am. Acad. Psychoanalysis. Intern U. Calif., San Francisco, 1970-71; resident psychiatry Stanford U., 1971-74; clin. faculty Standford Med. Sch., Palo Alto, Calif., 1974—; prof. clin. psychiatry Stanford (Calif.) U. Med. Ctr., 1990—; pvt. practice psychiatrist Palo Alto, 1974—. Editor: Treating Sexual Disorders, 1996; contbr. chpt. to book, articles to profl. jours. Bd. trustees Castilleja Sch., Palo Alto, 1992-96; bioethics com. Recovery Inn, Menlo Park, Calif., 1994—. Fellow Am. Acad. Psychoanalysis; mem. C.G. Jung Inst. (tng. analyst 1978—). Democrat. Office: 690 Waverley St Palo Alto CA 94301-2549

CHARNEY, PHILIP, dermatologist; b. N.Y.C., Dec. 15, 1939; s. Louis and Rose (Shay) C. BA cum laude, CUNY, Bklyn., 1960; MD, SUNY, Bklyn., 1964. Diplomate Am. Bd. Dermatology; lic. physician, N.Y., D.C., N.J., Calif., Nev., Ariz. Intern Interfaith Med. Ctr., Bklyn., 1964-65; resident dermatology USPHS Hosp., S.I., N.Y., 1965-67; vis. fellow dermatology Columbia-Presbyn. Med. Ctr., N.Y.C., 1967-68; asst. chief medicine dermatology outpatient clinic USPHS, Washington, 1968-70; asst. dir. clin. rsch. Schering Corp., Bloomfield, N.J., 1970-73, assoc. dir. clin. rsch., 1973; pvt. practice dermatology South Lake Tahoe, Calif., 1973-76, Lake Tahoe, Carson City, Nev., 1976-84, Phoenix, 1984-87, Castro Valley, Calif., 1987-94; career physician The Permanente Med. Group, Vallejo, Calif., 1994—; attending staff dept. dermatology Howard U. Washington, 1968-70; clinic asst. St. Luke's Hosp. Ctr., N.Y.C., 1971-73; attending staff Barton Meml. Hosp., South Lake Tahoe, 1973-84; courtesy staff Carson Tahoe Hosp., Carson City, 1978-84; active staff Chandler (Ari.) Regional Hosp., 1985-87, Eden Hosp. Ctr., Castro Valley, Calif., 1987-94, Kaiser Hosp., Vallejo, 1994—. Contbr. articles to profl. jours. Mem. AMA, Am. Acad. Dermatology, Am. Soc. Dermatologic Surgery, Internat. Soc. Dermatology, Pacific Dermatological Assn., San Francisco Dermatological Soc., Sacramento Valley Dermatological Soc., Alameda/Contra Costa County Med. Assn., Calif. Med. Assn., N.Y. Acad. Sci., ACLU, Sierra Club. Democrat. Jewish. Office: 975 Sereno Dr Vallejo CA 94589-2441

CHARTIER, VERNON LEE, electrical engineer; b. Ft. Morgan, Colo., Feb. 14, 1939; s. Raymond Earl and Margaret Clara (Winegar) C.; m. Lois Marie Schwartz, May 20, 1967; 1 child, Neal Raymond. BSEE, BS in Bus., U. Colo., 1963. Registered profl. engr., Pa.; cert. electromagnetic compatibility engr. Rsch. engr., cons. Westinghouse Electric Co., East Pittsburgh, Pa., 1963-75; principal engr. high voltage phenomena Bonneville Power Adminstrn., Vancouver, Wash., 1975-95; power sys. EMC cons., Portland, 1995—. Contbr. articles to profl. jours. Fellow IEEE (past mem. fellow com. 1993-96, Herman Halperin Transmission and Distribution award 1995); mem. IEEE Power Engring. Soc. (chmn. transmission and distribution com. 1987-88, chmn. fellows com. 1990-92), Internat. Conf. Large High Voltage Electric Systems (U.S. rep. to study com. 36 on power system electromagnetic compatibility), Bioelectromagnetics Soc., Internat. Electrotech. Commn. (U.S. rep. to subcom. on High Voltage Lines & Traction Systems), Chartier Family Assn. Baptist. Home and Office: 13095 SW Glenn Ct Beaverton OR 97008-5664

CHASE, KRISTINE LOUISE, economics educator, academic administrator; b. Oakland, CA, Jan. 16, 1949; d. Keith E. and Dorothea L. (Lodi) Terrill; m. Daniel P. Chase, June 9, 1973; children: Karen L., Michael S. BA in Econs., U. Calif., Davis, 1970, MA in Econs., 1972; PhD in Econs., U. Md., 1981. Instr. and asst. chair econs. dept. U. Md., College Park, 1973-79; vis. asst. prof. U.S. Naval Acad., Annapolis, Md., 1979-81; asst. prof. U. Md., Balt., 1981-82; assoc. prof. St. Mary's Coll., Moraga, Calif., 1985-93; prof., acting dean sch. econs. and bus. St. Mary's Coll., Moraga, 1993-94, prof., 1994—; cons. Irwin, Inc. Publishers, Homewood, Ill., 1988—. Contbr. articles to profl. jours., chpts. to books. Mem. planning commn. City of Larkspur, Calif., 1983-84; pres. Orinda (Calif.) Assn.; trustee Contra Costa C.C. Dist. Bd., 1996—. Mem. Am. Econs. Assn., Western Econs. Assn., Contra Costa Coun., Omicron Delta Epsilon (v.p. 1995—). Home: 37 Van Ripper Ln Orinda CA 94563-1117 Office: Saint Mary's Coll Econs Dept Moraga CA 94575

CHASE, RANDAL STUART, communication educator, consultant; b. Payson, Utah, Aug. 3, 1949; s. Irel Lynn and Louise (Barton); m. Deborah Johnsen, Feb. 1, 1971; children: Michelle, Randal Field, April, William Irel, Michael Darwin, Adam Paul. BS in Mass Comm. magna cum laude, U. Utah, 1987, MS in Comm., 1991, PhD in Comm., 1997. Program dir. Sta. KSL-FM, Salt Lake City, 1972-73; pres., CEO, Chase Media, Inc., Salt Lake City, 1973-83, Chase Cons. Inc., Salt Lake City, 1986—; instr. Sandy (Utah) Inst. LDS Ch. Ednl. System, 1994—; adj. prof. Westminster Coll., Salt Lake City, 1994—; assoc. prof. Salt Lake C.C., Salt Lake City, 1993—, comm. dept. head, 1996—; cons. media, bus. comm. and tech. to 30 firms, Salt Lake City, 1984—. Creator Internet Interactive Labs. on TV ratings, Telecomm., 1993; producer radio talk show KCPX Youth Talk, 1986-87. Bishop LDS Ch., Sandy, Utah, 1977-83, mem. high coun. LDS Granite Stake, 1994—. Recipient Farr scholarship U. Utah, Salt Lake City, 1988-89. Mem. Internat. Comm. Assn., Speech Comm. Assn., Assn. Educators in Journalism and Mass Comm., Western Speech Comm. Assn., Media History Soc., Utah Info. Tech. Assn., Kappa Tau Alpha, Phi Kappa Phi. Home: 9231 Solena Way Sandy UT 84093 Office: Salt Lake CC 4600 S Redwood Rd Salt Lake City UT 84130

CHASE, RICHARD BARTH, operations management educator; b. L.A., May 4, 1939; s. Louis R. and Sally (Barth) C.; m. Harriet Levine, Jan. 27, 1962; children: Laurie, Andrew, Glenn. BS, UCLA, 1962, MBA, 1963, PhD, 1966. Asst. prof. UCLA, 1966-68; assoc. prof. Pa. State U., University Park, 1968-69; assoc. prof. U. Ariz., Tucson, 1970-75, prof., 1975-85; prof. ops. mgmt. U. So. Calif. Sch. Bus., L.A., 1985—; vis. prof. Inst. for Mgmt. Devel., Lausanne, Switzerland, 1976-77, Harvard U., Boston, 1988-89; dir. Ctr. for Svc. Excellence, L.A., 1985—; examiner Malcolmb Baldridge Nat. Quality Award, 1989; bd. govs. Acad. Mgmt., 1985-87. Co-author: Management: A Life Cycle Approach, 1981, Production and Operations Management, 1989, Service Management Effect, 1990. Fellow Decision Scis. Inst., Acad. Mgmt.; mem. Ops. Mgmt. Assn. (bd. dirs. 1985-87), Beta Gamma Sigma, Omega Rho. Office: U So Calif Sch Bus Ctr Ops Mgmt Los Angeles CA 90089-1421

CHASON, LLOYD RALPH, corporate educator; b. Rocky Mount, N.C., Oct. 14, 1934; s. Charles Franklin and Katie Vera (Rich) C.; m. Joan Carolyn McKenzie, June 16, 1957; children: Allison Lynn, Michael Ralph. BS, East Carolina U., 1957; MA, Baylor U., 1962, PhD, 1968. Commd. 2d lt. USAF, 1957, advanced through grades to col., 1976, ret., 1982; mgr. tech. edn. and tng. Northrop Aircraft Svcs. Div., Hawthorne, Calif., 1982-85; dir. corp. edn. and tng. Northrop Corp., L.A., 1985-89; v.p., mgr. career devel. and tng. Bechtel Corp., San Francisco, 1989-95; v.p. worldwide exec. and employee devel. Sybase Corp., Emeryville, Calif., 1995—. Contbr. articles to profl. jours. Mem. exec. edn. adv. bd. U. Calif., Berkeley, also mem. univ. ext. bd. Mem. APA, ASTD, Am. Mgmt. Assn., The Conf. Bd., Inter-U. Seminar on Armed Forces, Sigma Xi, Alpha Chi, Phi Mu Alpha. Republican. Methodist. Home: 81 Amanda Ct Danville CA 94526-1262 Office: Sybase Corp 6425 Christie Ave Emeryville CA 94608-1010

CHATARD, PETER RALPH NOEL JR., aesthetic plastic surgeon; b. New Orleans, June 25, 1936; s. Peter Ralph Sr. and Alberta Chatard; m. Patricia Myrl White, Jan. 31, 1963; children: Andrea Michelle, Faedra Noelle, Tahra Deonne. BS in Biology, Morehouse Coll., 1956; MD, U. Rochester, 1960. Diplomate Am. Bd. Plastic Surgery, Am. Bd. Otolaryngology. Intern Colo. Gen. Hosp., 1960-61; asst. resident in gen. surgery Highland Gen. Hosp., Rochester, N.Y., 1963-64; resident in otolaryngology Strong Meml. Hosp., Rochester, 1964-67; resident in plastic and reconstructive surgery U. Fla., 1980-82; staff otolaryngologist Group Health Coop. of Puget Sound, Seattle, 1967-68; practice medicine specializing in otolaryngology Seattle, 1968-80, practice medicine specializing in plastic surgery, 1982—; clin. asst. prof. otolaryngology, head and neck surgery U. Wash., Seattle, 1975—; plastic surgery cons. western sec. Maxillofacial Rev. Bd. State of Wash., 1982-90, cons. Conservation of Hearing Program, 1968-80; trustee Physicians and Dentist Credit Bur., 1974-80, 84-87, pres. 1976-77, 84-85; active staff mem. Northwest Hosp., Seattle; courtesy staff Swedish Hosp., Children's Hosp. Med. Ctr., Seattle, Providence Hosp., Seattle, Stevens Meml. Hosp., Edmond, Wash., Seattle, Fifth Ave. Med. Ctr., Seattle, and others. Capt. USAF, 1961-63. Fellow ACS, Am. Rhinologic Soc., Seattle Surg. Soc., Am. Acad. Facial Plastic and Reconstructive Surgery, Am. Acad. Otolaryngology-Head and Neck Surgery, Northwest Acad. Otolaryngology and Head and Neck Surgery, Soc. for Ear, Nose and Throat Advances in Children, Pacific Oto-Ophthalmological Soc.; mem. Am. Soc. Plastic and Reconstructive Surgeons, Am. Soc. for Aesthetic Plastic Surgery, Inc., Lipoplasty

Soc. N. Am., Wash. Soc. Plastic Surgeons, Nat. Med. Assn., King County Med. Soc., Wash. Med. Assn., N.W. Soc. of Plastic Surgeons. Home: 20914 39th Ave SE Bothell WA 98021-7904 Office: Chatard Plas Surg Ctr 1200 N Northgate Way Seattle WA 98133-8916

CHATFIELD, MICHAEL, accounting educator; b. Seattle, June 13, 1934; s. Chester and Thelma (McCormick) C. BA in Bus. Adminstrn., U. Wash., 1957, MBA, 1962; D in Bus. Adminstrn., U. Oreg., 1966. CPA, Wash. Jr. acct. Yergen and Meyer CPAs, Astoria, Oreg., 1957-58; acct. Mill Factors Corp., N.Y.C., 1959; staff acct. R.C. Mounsey and Co. CPAs, Seattle, 1959-61; tchg. asst. acctg. U. Oreg., Eugene, 1962-63; instr. acctg. U. Oreg., 1963-65; asst. prof. acctg. UCLA, 1965-72; sr. lectr. acctg. U. Canterbury, New Zealand, 1972-73; prof. acctg. Calif. State U., Hayward, 1973-82, 84-90, Fresno, 1982-84; prof. acctg. So. Oreg. State Coll., Ashland, 1990—; mem. numerous coms. So. Oreg. State U., 1991-96; presenter confs. in field. Author: A History of Accounting Thought, 1974 (rev. edit. 1978, Japanese edit. 1979, Korean edit. 1985, Chinese edit. 1989); co-author: (with Denis Neilson) Cost Accounting, 1983, (with Richard Vangermeersch) The History of Accounting: An International Encyclopedia, 1996; editor: Contemporary Studies in the Evolution of Accounting Thought, 1968 (Spanish edit., 1970, 79), The English View of Accountants' Duties and Responsibilities, 1881-1902, 1978; mem. editl. bd. The Acctg. Rev., 1970-72, 74-75, The Accounting Historians Jour., 1976-95; contbr. articles to profl. jours. Mem. Am. Acctg. Assn., Acad. Acctg. Historians (Hourglass award 1974, 96), Beta Alpha Psi. Office: So Oreg State Coll Bus Sch Ashland OR 97520

CHATHAM, RUSSELL, landscape artist; b. San Francisco, Oct. 27, 1939; m. Mary Fanning (div.); m. Doris Meyer (div.); m. Suzanne Porter; children: Georgina, Lea, Rebecca, Paul. Ed., San Francisco. Painter, writer, Calif.; landscape artist, lithographer, Mont., 1972—. Address: PO Box 659 Livingston MT 59047-0659

CHATROO, ARTHUR JAY, lawyer; b. N.Y.C., July 1, 1946; s. George and Lillian (Leibowitz) C.; m. Christina Daly, Aug. 6, 1994. BChemE, CCNY, 1968; JD cum laude, New York Law Sch., 1979; MBA with distinction, NYU, 1982. Bar: N.Y. 1980, Ohio 1992, Calif. 1993. Process engr. Std. Oil Co. of Ohio, various locations, 1968-73; process specialist BP Oil, Inc., Marcus Hook, Pa., 1974-75; sr. process engr. Sci. Design Co., Inc., N.Y.C., 1975-78; mgr. spl. projects The Halcon SD Group, N.Y.C., 1978-82; corp. counsel, tax and fin. The Lubrizol Corp., Wickliffe, Ohio, 1982-85; sr. counsel spl. investment projects The Lubrizol Corp., Wickliffe, 1989-90; gen. counsel Lubrizol Enterprises, Inc., Wickliffe, 1985-89; chmn. Correlation Genetics Corp., San Jose, Calif., 1990-91; gen. counsel Agrigenetics Co., Eastlake, Ohio, 1990-92; gen. counsel, dir. comml. contracting Agrigenetics, L.P., San Diego, 1992-93; counsel Agrigenetics, Inc. dba Mycogen Seeds, San Diego, 1994—. Mem. Met. Parks Adv. com., Allen County, Ohio, 1973. Mem. ABA, Am. Inst. Chem. Engrs., N.Y. State Bar Assn., San Deigo County Bar Assn., Am. Corp. Counsel Assn., Jaycees (personnel dir. Lima, Ohio chpt. 1972-73), Toastmasters, Omega Chi Epsilon, Beta Gamma Sigma. Club: Toastmasters. Home: 3525 Del Mar Hts Rd # 285 San Diego CA 92130-2122 Office: Mycogen 5501 Oberlin Dr San Diego CA 92121-1718

CHAUVIN, YVES, cognitive scientist; b. Cholet, France, Dec. 20, 1956; came to U.S., 1982; s. Rene and Marie-Therese (Provost) C. BS in Engring., INPG, 1980; BA in Psychology, U. Calif., San Diego, 1983, PhD in Cognitive Sci., 1988. Rsch. scientist Thomson-CSF, Palo Alto, Calif., 1986-90, Stanford U., Palo Alto, Calif., 1986-90, Net-ID, Inc., San Francisco, 1991—; founder, pres. NEt-ID, Inc., 1991—. Author/editor: Back-Propagation: Theory, Architecture and Applications, 1995.

CHAVEZ, ALBERT BLAS, financial executive; b. L.A., Jan. 1, 1952; s. Albert Blas and Yolanda (Garcia) C.; m. Irma Laura Cavazos, Dec. 21, 1996. BA, U. Tex., El Paso, 1979; MBA, Stanford U., 1985. CPA, Calif. Mem. profl. staff Deloitte Haskins and Sells, L.A., 1980-83; planning analyst corp. fin. planning Boise (Idaho) Cascade Co., 1984; treasury analyst corp. treasury RCA Corp., N.Y.C., 1985; asst. contr. RCA/Ariola Records, Mexico City, 1986; fin. analyst corp. exec. office GE Co., Fairfield, Conn., 1987-90; fin. cons. Entertainment Industry and Litigation Support Svcs., L.A., 1990-91; co-founder, sr. v.p., CFO El Dorado Comm., Inc., L.A., 1991—, also bd. dirs. Bd. dirs., treas. L.A. Conservation Corps, 1990—. Mem. AICPA, Calif. Soc. CPAs. Democrat. Home: 18744 Strathern St Reseda CA 91335 Office: El Dorado Comm Inc 2130 Sawtelle Blvd Ste 307 Los Angeles CA 90025-6250

CHAVEZ, EDWARD, police chief; b. Stockton, Calif., Mar. 22, 1943; m. Nancy Ruhr; children: Eric, Jill. AA, San Joaquin Delta Coll., 1971; BA, Calif. State U., 1972; MS, Calif. Polytechnic Pomona, 1990; grad., POST Command Coll., Delinquency Control Inst., Leadership Stockton Program, FBI Nat. Acad. With USAF, 1962-70; officer Stockton Police Dept., 1973, sgt., 1980, lt., 1986, capt., 1990, dep. chief of police, 1990, acting chief of police, 1993, chief of police, 1993—. Bd. dirs. St. Joseph's Med. Ctr., San Joaquin United Way, Lilliput Childrens Svcs., Greater Stockton C. of C.; active Hispanics for Polit. Action; adv. com. Leadership, Stockton. With USAF, 1962-70. Mem. Calif. Peace Officers Assn., Hispanic Am. Police Command Officer's Assn., Mexican Am. C. of C., Stockton E. Rotary, Coun. for Spanish Speaking (past bd. dirs.), Leadership Stockton Alumni Assn. Office: Stockton Police Dept 22 E Market St Stockton CA 95202-2802

CHAVEZ, GILBERT ESPINOZA, bishop; b. Ontario, Calif., Mar. 19, 1932; ed. St. Francis Sem., El Cajon, Calif., Immaculate Heart Sem., San Diego, U. Calif., San Diego. Ordained priest Roman Cath. Ch., 1960; titular bishop of Magarmel and aux. bishop Diocese of San Diego, 1974—. Office: St Joseph Cathedral 1535 3rd Ave San Diego CA 92101-3192*

CHAVEZ, JOHN, mayor. Mayor City of Pico Rivera, Calif., 1996—. Office: 6615 S Passons Blvd Pico Rivera CA 90660

CHAVEZ, RONALD JOSEPH, business educator, chamber of commerce executive; b. Denver, Jan. 13, 1947; s. Eloy and Andrea Lillian (Gutierrez) C.; m. Sandra Ann DeLisle, Apr. 11, 1970; children: Dawn Elizabeth, Thomas Joseph. BA in Sociology, Regis U., Denver, 1975; MBA, Regis U., 1994; postgrad. in internat. bus., Southwest U., 1995. Vocat. and rehab. counselor Colo. State Dept. Social Svcs., Denver, 1976-86; pres., owner Consolidated Mgmt. and Acctg. Resources, Inc., Denver, 1986-94; prof. bus. C.C. Aurora, Colo., 1994-96; pres., CEO Albuquerque Hispano C. of C., 1996—; adv. bd. U. No. Colo., Greeley. Author: Strategic Analysis International Business, 1995. Mem. N.Mex. Gov.'s Task Force Internat. Bus., 1996. With USAF, 1967-71. Mem. Nat. Hispano C. of C., Petroleum Club. Roman Catholic. Home: Ste 1001 6303 Indian School Rd Albuquerque NM 87110 Office: Hispano Chamber of Commerce 202 Central Ave SE Ste 300 Albuquerque NM 87102-3459

CHÁVEZ, THOMAS ESTEBAN, curator; b. Las Vegas, Jan. 19, 1948. AA, Pasadena (Calif.) City Coll., 1968; BA, Calif. State Coll., 1970, U. N.Mex., 1974; MA, U. N.Mex., 1976, PhD, 1980. Instr. Coll. Santa Fe, 1979-82; from mus. coord. edn. bur. to dir. Palace of the Govs. Mus. of N.Mex., Santa Fe, 1978—; instr. U. N.Mex. No. Consortium, 1978. Author: Manuel Alvarez, 1974-1856: A Southwestern Biography, 1990, Illustrated History of New Mexico, 1992, In Quest for Quivera: Spanish Exploration on the Plains from 1540 to 1821, 1992; editor: Conflict and Acculturation: Manuel Alvarez' 1942 Memorial, 1989; contbr. articles to profl. jours. Served in U.S. Army, 1970-72. Mem. Hist. Soc. N.Mex. (bd. dirs., past chmn. membership com., past chmn. conf. com.), N.Mex. Assn. Mus. (pres. 1979-81), Western History Assn., Am. Assn. State and Local History, Conf. for Latin Am. History, The Old Santa Fe Assn. (bd. dirs. 1979-81, pres. 1981-84), The Westerners, N.Mex. Endowment for the Humanities (vice chmn. bd. dirs. 1990-91, chmn. 1991—), Hispanic Culture Found. (bd. dirs. 1989—). Office: Palace Govs PO Box 2087 Santa Fe NM 87504-2087

CHAYKIN, ROBERT LEROY, manufacturing and marketing executive; b. Miami, Fla., May 2, 1944; s. Allan Leroy and Ruth (Levine) C.; m. Patty Jean Patton, Feb. 1971 (div. May 1975); m. Evalyn Marcy Slodzina, Sept. 3, 1989; children: Stephanie Lee, Michelle Alee, Catrina Celia, Ally Sue, Stephanie Lee. BA in Polit. Sci., U. Miami, Fla., 1965, LLB, 1969. Owner, operator Serrating Svcs. Miami, 1969-71, Serrating Svcs. Las Vegas, Nev., 1971-84; pres. Ser-Sharp Mfg., Inc., Las Vegas, 1984—; nat. mktg. dir. Coserco Corp., Las Vegas, 1987—. Patentee in mfg. field. With U.S. Army, 1962. Recipient 2d degree black belt Tae Kwon Do, Profl. Karate Assn., 1954-61.

CHAZEN, MELVIN LEONARD, chemical engineer; b. St. Louis, Sept. 26, 1933; s. Saul and Tillie (Kramer) C.; m. Dorothea Glazer, June 29, 1958; children: Jamie Lynn, Avery Glazer. BS in Chem. Engring., Washington U., St. Louis, 1955. Registered profl. engr., Mo. Thermodynamics engr. Bell Aerospace Textron, Buffalo, 1958-59; devel. engr. Bell Aerospace Textron, 1959-62, project engr., 1962-65, chief sec. rocket engines, 1965-72, prog. mgr., tech. dir., 1972-74, project engr., 1974-84, chief engr. rocket devel., 1984-87; sr. staff engr. Space and Tech. div. TRW, Redondo Beach, Calif., 1987—; bd. dirs. Unimed Corp., Rochester. Contbr. articles to profl. jours. Recipient Innovation award Enterprise Devel. Inc., 1994, Recognition Cert. NASA, 1994, TRW Chmn.'s award, 1995. Mem. Alpha Chi Sigma. Home: 12522 Inglenook Ln Cerritos CA 90703-7837 Office: TRW Space and Tech Divsn One Space Park Redondo Beach CA 90278

CHAZEN, STEPHEN I., oil company executive; b. Buffalo, N.Y., Aug. 26, 1946; s. Michael M. and Marcia Chazen; m. Patricia L. Orr, Nov. 20, 1971. AB, Rutgers Coll., 1968; PhD, Mich. State U., 1973; MS, U. Houston, 1977. Lab. mgr. Northrop Svcs., Inc., Houston, 1973-77; dir. project evaluation Columbia Gas Devel. Corp., Houston, 1977-81; v.p. Merrill Lynch, Houston, 1982-86; mng. dir. Merrill Lynch, N.Y.C., 1987-93; exec. v.p. Occidental Petroleum Corp., L.A., 1994—; dir. Clark Oil Co., St. Louis, 1996—. Mem. L.A. C. of C. (dir. 1996—). Home: PO Box 427 Pacific Palisades CA 90272 Office: Occidental Petroleum Group 10889 Wilshire Blvd Los Angeles CA 90024

CHEAH, KEONG-CHYE, psychiatrist; b. Georgetown, Penang, West Malaysia, Mar. 15, 1939; came to U.S., 1959; s. Thean Hoe and Hun Kin (Keong) C.; m. Sandra Massey, June 10, 1968; children: Chylynn, Maylynn. BA in Psychology, U. Ark., 1962; MD, U. Ark., Little Rock, 1967, MS in Microbiology, 1968. Diplomate Am. Bd. Psychiatry and Neurology (examiner 1982, 85); cert. Ark. State Sci. Bd., Ark. State Med. Bd. Intern U. Ark. Med. Ctr., 1967-68; resident VA Med. Ctr. and U. Ark. Med. Ctr., Little Rock, 1968-72; chief addiction sect. Little Rock (Ark.) VA Med. Ctr., 1972-73, staff psychiatrist, 1975-80; chief psychiatry Am. Lake VA Med. Ctr., Tacoma, Wash., 1981-86; chief consultation, liason Am. Lake VA Med. Ctr., Tacoma, 1986-94; asst. prof. medicine, psychiatry U. Ark., Little Rock, 1975-81; asst. prof. psychiatry and behavioral scis. U. Wash., Seattle, 1981-86, clin. assoc. prof., 1987—; mem. dist. br. com. The CHAMPUS, 1977-91; site visitor AMA Continuing Med. Edn., 1979-83; book reviewer Jour. Am. Geriatrics Soc., 1984-85; mem. task force alcohol abuse VA Med. Dist. 27, 1984, survey mem. Sytematic External Rev. Process, 1985; mem. mental health plan adv. com. State of Ark., 1976-81, chmn. 1979-81, chmn. steering com., 1979; mem. Vietnamese Resettlement Program, 1979; many coms. Am. Lake VA Med. Ctr. including chmn. mental health coun. 1981-84, utilization rev. com., 1981-86. Contbr. articles and abstracts to profl. jours.; presenter to confs. and meetings of profl. socs. Mem. Parents Adv. Com., Lakes H.S., Wash., 1987-91; mem. Mayor's Budget and Fin. Foresight Com., 1992—, chmn. 1990-92; sch. cons. Child Study Ctr. U. Ark., 1972-74; bd. dirs. Crisis Ctr. Ark., 1974-79, chmn. pub. rels. com., 1975-79, mem. pers. com. 1974, vice chmn. bd. 1977; pres. Chinese Assn. Ctrl. Ark., 1977; mem. gifted edn. adv. coun. Clover Park Sch. Dist. 400, Wash., 1983-85, Parent Tchr. Student Orgn. Recipient U.S. Govt. scholarship 1959, cert. merit State of Ark., 1973, Leadership award, Mental Health Svcs. Divsn., State of Ark., 1980. Fellow Am. Psychiat. Assn. (sec. treas. Asian Am. caucus 1985-87, pres. 1987-94); mem. Assn. Mil. Surgeons U.S., Wash. State Psychiat. Assn. (mem. peer rev. com. 1982-92, chmn. pub. psychiatry com. 1985-93, exec. coun. 1985-93), N. Pacific Soc. Neurology and Psychiatry Assn. (sec.-treas. 1986—, pres. 1993), S. Puget Sound Psychiat. Assn., Assn. Chinese-Am. Psychiatrists, Ark. Caduceus Club, Alpha Epsilon Delta, Psi Chi, Phi Beta Kappa. Office: VA Med Ctr Am Lake Tacoma WA 98493

CHEAVENS, THOMAS HENRY, chemistry educator; b. Dallas, May 19, 1930; s. Tom H. and Sarah (Newsom) C.; m. Eleanor Louise Seemar, Dec. 30, 1955; children: Suzanne Cheavens Wontrobski, Tom Jr., Jeff W. BS in Chemistry, U. Tex., 1950, PhD in Chemistry, 1955. Rsch. chemist Am. Cyanamid Co., Bound Brook, N.J., 1955-57; group leader Am. Cyanamid Co., Stamford, Conn., 1957-67; rsch. supr. W.R. Grace & Co., Clarksville, Md., 1967-72; rsch. dir. W.R. Grace & Co., Clarksville, 1972-75; contract officer Energy R & D Adminstrn., Washington, 1976-78; rsch. dir. Quest Rsch. and Engring., Tyler, Tex., 1978-82; pres. Quest Rsch. and Engring., Tyler, 1982-86; rsch. assoc. chemistry U. Tex., Austin, 1986-89; assoc. prof. chemistry N.Mex. Highland U., Las Vegas, 1989—; v.p. Improtec, Inc., Tyler, 1981-86. Inventor in field. Rsch. grantee NSF, 1991, NIH, 1992—. Fellow AAAS, Am. Inst. Chemists; mem. Am. Chem. Soc., Sigma Xi, Phi Kappa Phi. Office: N Mex Highlands Univ National Ave Las Vegas NM 87701

CHEDID, JOHN G., bishop; b. Eddid, Lebanon, July 4, 1923. Educated, Sems. in Lebanon and Pontifical Urban Coll., Rome. Ordained priest Roman Cath. Ch., 1951. Titular bishop of Callinico and aux bishop St. Maron of Bklyn., 1981. Office: 333 S San Vicente Blvd Los Angeles CA 90048-3313*

CHEE, PERCIVAL HON YIN, ophthalmologist; b. Honolulu, Aug. 29, 1936; s. Young Sing and Den Kyau (Ching) C.; m. Carolyn Tong, Jan. 27, 1966; children: Lara Wai Lung, Shera Wai Sum. BA, U. Hawaii, 1958; MD, U. Rochester, 1962. Intern Travis AFB Hosp., Fairfield, Calif., 1962-63; resident Bascom Palmer Eye Inst., Miami, Fla., 1965-68, Jackson Meml. Hosp., Miami, 1965-68; partner Straub Clinic, Inc., Honolulu, 1968-71; practice medicine specializing in ophthalmology, Honolulu, 1972—; mem. staffs Queen's Med. Center, St. Francis Hosp., Kapiolani Children's Med. Center, Honolulu; clin. assoc. prof. surgery U. Hawaii Sch. Medicine, 1971—; cons. Tripler Army Med. Center. Mem. adv. bd. Services to Blind; bd. dirs. Lions Eye Bank and Makana Found. (organ bank), Multiple Sclerosis Soc. Served to capt. USAF, 1962-65. Fellow Am. Acad. Ophthalmology, ACS; mem. AMA, Pan Am. Med. Assn., Pan Pacific Surg. Assn., Am. Assn. Ophthalmology, Soc. Eye Surgeons, Hawaii Ophthal. Soc. Pacific Coast Ophthal. Soc., Am. Assn. for Study Headache, Pan Am. Ophthal. Found. Contbr. articles to profl. pubs. Home: 3755 Poka Pl Honolulu HI 96816-4409 Office: Kukui Pla 50 S Beretania St Ste C116 Honolulu HI 96813-2222

CHEESEMAN, DOUGLAS TAYLOR, JR., wildlife tour executive, photographer, educator; b. Honolulu, July 16, 1937; s. Douglas Taylor Cheeseman and Myra Bettencourt; m. Gail Macomber, Apr. 7, 1963; children: Rosie M., Ted F. BA, San Jose (Calif.) State U., 1959, MA, 1964. Cert. secondary tchr., Calif. Naturalist Crater Lake (Oreg.) Nat. Park, summers 1959-60; tchr. biology Woodside High Sch., Redwood City, Calif., 1961-65; teaching asst. U. Colo., Boulder, 1966-67; prof. biology De Anza Coll., Cupertino, Calif., 1967—, dir. environ. study area, 1970—, dir. Student Ecology Rsch. Lab., 1990—; pres. Cheeseman's Ecology Safaris, Saratoga, Calif., 1981—; instr. wildlife and natural history photography, Saratoga, 1984—; rsch. cooperator Fish and Wildlife Svc., 1972—, guest lectr. numerous conservation groups, No. Calif., 1978—; spkr. on rainforest destruction, zone depletion, global warming; participant, spkr. to save planet; spkr. Calif. Acad. Antarctic Ecology, Am. Acad. African Birds, 1996; expdn. leader Sengey Vavilov, Antarctic, 1994; active in saving flora and fauna in third workd; exptn. leader, Antarctica, 1996, ship Alla Tarasova, 1996, 98. Photographs represented in books and on calendars. Recipient Outstanding Svc. and Tchr. award, Pres.'s award De Anza Coll., 1988, Nat. Leadership award U. Tex., Austin, 1989; NSF fellow, 1969, 71; NEDA Title III grantee, 1970. Mem. Ecol. Soc. Am., Am. Ornithologists Union, Am. Soc. Mammalogists, Brit. Trust Ornitology, Brit. Ornithologists Union, AfricanWildlife Soc., Marine Mammal Soc. (founding), Calif. Native Plants Soc., Bay Area Bird Photographers (co-founder), Santa Clara Valley Audubon Soc. (bd. dirs., v.p., program chmn. 1983—), Cooper Soc. Home: 20800 Kittridge Rd Saratoga CA 95070-6322 Office: De Anza Coll Dept Biology Cupertino CA 95014

CHEIFETZ, LORNA GALE, psychologist; b. Phoenix, Mar. 22, 1953; d. Walter and Ruth Cheifetz. BS, Chapman Coll., Orange, Calif., 1975; D of Psychology, Ill. Sch. Profl. Psychology, 1981. Psychology intern Cook County Hosp., Chgo., 1979-80; clin. psychologist City of Chgo., 1980-84, Phoenix Inst. for Psychotherapy, 1984-87; pvt. practice Phoenix, 1987—; cons. to judges, attys., cts., 1984—; adj. faculty Met. U., Phoenix, 1984-88, Ill. Sch. Profl. Psychology, 1982-86. Contbr. chpt. to book Listening and Interpreting, 1984; contbg. editor Internat. Jour. Communicative Psychoanalysis and Psychotherapy, 1991-93. Cons., vol. Ariz. Bar Assn. Vol. Lawyer Program, 1985—; co-coord. Psychology Info. Referral Svc., Maricopa County, Ariz., 1984-96. Named Psychologist of Yr. Ariz. Bar Assn., 1987, 95. Mem. APA (activist 1989—), Nat. Register Health Svc. Providers in Psychology, Internat. Soc. for the Study of Dissociative Disorders. Office: 2211 E Highland Ave Ste 135 Phoenix AZ 85016-4833

CHEITLIN, MELVIN DONALD, physician, educator; b. Wilmington, Del., Mar. 25, 1929; s. James Cheitlin and Mollie Budman; m. Hella Hochschild, Aug. 4, 1952; children: Roger, Kenneth, Julie. AB, Temple U., 1950, MD, 1954. Intern, resident internal medicine Walter Reed Army Med. Ctr., Washington, 1954-59, cardiology fellow, 1959-60, chief cardiology, 1971-74; chief cardiology Madigan Army Med. Ctr., Tacoma, Wash., 1960-64, Tripler Army Med. Ctr., Honolulu, 1964-68, Letterman Army Med. Ctr., San Francisco, 1968-71; assoc. chief cardiology San Francisco Gen. Hosp., 1974-91, chief cardiology, 1991—; prof. medicine U. Calif., San Francisco, 1974—. Author: Clinical Cardiology, 1994; assoc. editor: Cardiology, 1988, rev. edit., 1993. Mem. ACP, Am. Coll. Cardiology. Democrat. Jewish. Home: 224 Castenada Ave San Francisco CA 94116-1445 Office: San Francisco Gen Hosp 1001 Potrero Avee San Francisco CA 94110

CHEN, BARBARA MARIE, anesthesiologist; b. Youngstown, Ohio, May 17, 1960; d. Ching Chi and Kim Lian Chen. BS summa cum laude, Youngstown State U., 1981; MD, St. Louis U., 1985. Diplomate Am. Soc. Anesthesiologists. Resident in surgery Bklyn.-Caledonian Hosp., Bklyn., 1985-88; resident in anesthesia Georgetown U. Hosp., Washington, 1989-92; staff anesthesiologist NIH, Bethesda, Md., 1992-93; staff anesthesiologist, researcher Georgetown U. Hosp., Washington, 1992-95; staff anesthesiologist Providence Hosp., Anchorage, Alaska, 1996—. Vol. Spl. Olympics, Arlington, Va., 1992, Cmty. for a Creative Nonviolence, Washington, 1989-95, Holiday Project, 1989-95, Martha's Table, 1994-95. Recipient Robert Dripps Meml. award Janssen Pharm., 1991. Mem. AMA, Am. Soc. Anesthesiologists, Am. Regional Soc. Anesthesiologists, Am. Heart Assn., Am. Med. Women's Assn., Soc. Cardiovascular Anesthesiologists. Office: Providence Hosp 3300 Providence Dr Ste 107 Anchorage AK 99508-4619

CHEN, CHING-HONG, medical biochemist, biotechnology company executive; b. Pingtung, Taiwan, July 15, 1935; came to U.S., 1963; s. Ching-Da and Jen-Mei (Yang) C.; m. Su-Wan Yang, Aug. 29, 1964; 1 child, Sung-Wei. BS in Biology, Taiwan Normal U., Taipei, 1959; MS in Biology, U. Wash., 1966, MS in Chemistry, 1972; PhD in Biochemistry, U. N.D., 1978. Instr. Taiwan Chung-Hsing U., Taichung, 1959-62; biologist U. Wash., Seattle, 1966-72, rsch. scientist dept. biology, 1972-75, rsch. assoc. dept. medicine, 1978-80, mem. rsch. faculty dept. medicine, 1980-88; pres., CEO Alpha Biomed. Labs., Bellevue, Wash., 1988—; vis. scientist Biophys. Inst. Boston U., 1982; cons. Bainbridge Lab., Bainbridge Island, Wash., 1984-87, Solomon Pk. Rsch. Inst., Kirkland, Wash., 1985-88, Medix Biotech., Inc., Foster City, Calif., 1988—. Contbr. articles to profl. jours. Recipient NSF award (Taiwan), 1957; NIH fellow, 1975-78. Fellow Am. Heart Assn. (sci. coun.); mem. AAAS, Am. Assn. for Clin. Chemistry, Wash. State Biotech. and Biomed. Assn. Home: 7248 29th Ave NE Seattle WA 98115-5852 Office: Alpha Biomed Labs 920 180th Ave NE # 1 Bellevue WA 98004

CHEN, EVE YING VONG, city official; b. Hong Kong, Oct. 7, 1958; came to U.S., 1975; d. George W.Y. and Ven-Yah E. (Szw) Chow; m. Yaw-Hwang Henry Chen, June 17, 1982; children: Ryan, Alan. BS in Bus. Adminstrn., Colo. State U., Ft. Collins, 1991. Budget technician Intel Corp., Santa Clara, Calif., 1983-84; budget analyst City of Loveland, Colo., 1985-93, budget officer, 1994—. Mem. Govt. Fin. Officers Assn. (budget reviewer 1990-95), Colo. Mcpl. League. Christian. Office: City of Loveland 500 E 3rd St Loveland CO 80537-5773

CHEN, JIAN HUA, medical physicist; b. Nan Jing, Jiang Su, China, June 3, 1948; came to U.S., 1985; s. Hei Yu Yuan and Ping Yan Cha; m. Yuan Fang Shen, Jan. 1978; 1 child, Serra. BS in Applied Physics, Beijing Poly. U., 1982; MS in Superconductivity, Bowling Green (Ohio) State U., 1989; PhD in Med. Physics, Med. Coll. Ohio, Toledo, 1993. Math. and physics tchr. Beijing 182nd H.S., 1972-78; physics and calculus tchr. Qing Hua U. Br. Coll., Beijing, 1982-85; teaching asst. U. Toledo, 1985-87, Bowling Green State U., 1987-89; rsch. asst. Med. Coll. Ohio, Toledo, 1989-92; med. physicist Med. Coll. Hosp. Ohio, Toledo, 1992-93, Cancer Ctr. No. Ariz., Flagstaff, 1993—. Co-author: Report to Cray Research Company #933724, 1991. Mem. Am. Asns. Med. Physicists. Home: 1460 E Everest Dr Flagstaff AZ 86004-1726 Office: 1329 N Beaver St Flagstaff AZ 86001-3121

CHEN, JOHN CALVIN, child and adolescent psychiatrist; b. Augusta, Ga., Apr. 30, 1949; s. Calvin Henry Chen and Lora (Lee) Liu. BA, Pacific Union Coll., 1971; MD, Loma Linda U., 1974; PhD in Philosophy, Claremont Grad. Sch., 1984; JD, UCLA, 1987. Bar: Calif. 1987, U.S. Dist. Ct. (ctrl. dist.) Calif. 1988; diplomate Am. Bd. Psychiatry and Neurology, Child and Adolescent Psychiatry. Resident in psychiatry Loma Linda U. Med. Ctr., 1975-77; fellow in child and family psychiatry Cedars-Sinai Med. Ctr., L.A., 1977-78; psychiat. cons. San Bernardino (Calif.) County Mental Health Dept., 1979-83; pvt. practice Claremont, Calif., 1980-84; fellow in child and adolescent psychiatry U. So. Calif., L.A., 1983-84; law clk. to Hon. William P. Gray U.S. Dist. Ct., L.A., 1987-88; mental health psychiatrist L.A. County Mental Health Dept., L.A., 1988-94, Alameda County Health Care Svcs. Agy., Fremont, Calif., 1994-97; psychiat. cons. Edgewood Children's Ctr., San Francisco, 1996-97; physician specialist L.A. County Health Care Svcs. Agy., L.A., 1997—; staff child psychiatrist Martin Luther King Hosp., L.A., 1997—; adj. instr. philosophy Fullerton (Calif.) Coll., 1989-90. Recipient Cert. Recognition Pub. Svc. L.A. County Mental Health Dept., 1993; univ. fellow Claremont Grad. Sch., 1980-81. Mem. ABA, Am. Philos. Assn., Chinese for Affirmative Action, Soc. for Exploration of Psychotherapy Integration, Chinese Hist. Soc. Am., Calif. Hist. Soc., Chinese Hist. Soc. So. Calif. Office: 745 E Valley Blvd #120 San Gabriel CA 91776-3549

CHEN, LEWAY, cardiologist; b. Kao-Hsiung, Taiwan, Apr. 15, 1967. BA, MD, U. Mo., Kansas City, 1991. Intern in internal medicine Beth Israel Hosp., Boston, 1991-92, resident in internal medicine, 1992-94; rsch. fellow Framingham Heart Study, 1994-95, cardiology fellow, 1995-99. Mem. ACP, AMA, Mass. Med. Soc., Alpha Omega Alpha. Methodist. Home: 7428 Gatewood Rd SW Seattle WA 98136-2117 Office: U Washington Med Ctr Seattle WA 98119

CHEN, LYNN CHIA-LING, librarian; b. Peking, China, Dec. 3, 1932; came to U.S., 1955; d. Shu-Peng Wang; m. Di Chen, June 14, 1958; children: Andrew A., Daniel T. BA, Nat. Taiwan U., 1955; MLS, U. Minn., 1957. Cataloger Hennepin County Libr., Edina, Minn., 1972-80; libr./programmer Prorodeo Hall of Champions, Colorado Springs, Colo., 1981-83; ref. libr. Meml. Hosp., Colorado Springs, 1983-85; asst. libr. Am. Numismatic Assn., Colorado Springs, 1985-90, head libr., 1991—. Mem. Colo. Libr. Assn., Spl. Libr. Assn. Home: 302 Sunbird Cliffs Ln W Colorado Springs CO 80919-8017 Office: American Numismatic Assn 818 N Cascade Ave Colorado Springs CO 80903-3208

CHEN, MARY YUN-CHUN, research engineer; b. Shanghai, China, Sept. 4, 1949; came to U.S., 1981; d. Donald Zhi-Chu and Grace (Fang) Chen; m. Paul D. Elliott. AA, Shanghai Tchr.'s Coll., China, 1980; BA magna cum laude, Mount Holyoke Coll., 1983; PhD, Cornell U., 1988. Rsch. asst. Cornell U., Ithaca, NY, 1983-87; sr. rsch. engr. Rsch. Triangle Inst., Research Triangle Park, N.C., 1987-91; sr. mem. tech. staff Comsat Lab., Clarksburg, Md., 1991-93; rsch. staff Hughes Rsch. Labs., Malibu, Calif., 1993-97; sr. scientist Rockwell Sci. Ctr., Thousand Oak, Calif., 1997—. Contbr. articles to profl. jours. Co-recipient Mary Lyon award Alumnae Assn. Mt. Holyoke Coll., 1996. Mem. IEEE, Phi Beta Kappa. Office: Rockwell Sci Ctr 1049 Camino Dos Rios Thousand Oaks CA 91360

CHEN, NAI-FU, finance educator; b. Hong Kong, Nov. 24, 1950; came to U.S., 1968; s. Lee (Wong) Chen;m. Victoria Ma, Feb. 1, 1975; children: Nicole, Ellen. AB in Math., U. Calif., Berkeley, 1972, PhD in Math., 1975; PhD in Finance, UCLA, 1981. Asst. prof. math. U. So. Calif., L.A., 1976-78; asst. prof. econs. U. Calif., Santa Barbara, 1980-81; asst. prof. finance U. Chgo., 1981-85, assoc. prof. finance, 1985-89; prof. finance U. Calif., Irvine, 1989—; prof., head fin. Hong Kong U. Sci. and Tech., 1990—; docent fin. Swedish Sch. Econs. and Bus. Adminstrn., Helsinki, 1991—; exec. cons. Roll & Ross Asset Mgmt., Culver City, Calif., 1989—. Contbr. articles to profl. jours. Mem. Am. Finance Assn.

CHEN, PETER WEI-TEH, mental health services administrator; b. Fuchow, Fukien, Republic of China, July 20, 1942; came to U.S., 1966; s. Mao-Chuang and Sheu-Lin (Wang) C.; m. Lai-Wah Mui, Nov. 8, 1969; children: Ophelia Mei-Chuang, Audrey Mei-Hui. BA, Nat. Chung Hsing U., Taipei, Taiwan, Republic of China, 1964; MSW, Calif. State U., Fresno, 1968; D of Social Work, U. So. Calif., 1976. Case worker Cath. Welfare Bur., L.A., 1968-69; psychiat. social worker L.A. County Mental Health Svcs., 1969-78, mental health svcs. coordinator, 1978; sr. rsch. analyst Jud. and Legis. Bur. L.A. County Dept. Mental Health, 1978-79; Forensic In-Patient Program dir. L.A. County Dept. Mental Health, 1979-86, chief Jail Mental Health Svcs., 1986-89, asst. dep. dir. Adult Svc. Bur., 1989, dir. cmty. care programs, 1989—; pres. Orient Social and Health Soc., Los Angeles, 1973-75; bd. dirs. Am. Correctional Health Assn., 1986-87. Author: Chinese-Americans View Their Mental Health, 1976. Bd. dirs. San Marino (Calif.) Cmty. Chest, 1986-87; trustee San Marino Schs. Found., 1987-90; advisor San Marino United Way, 1989-92, AIDS Commn. L.A. County, 1993; bd. dirs. Chinese Am. Profl. Soc., 1984. 2d lt. Chinese Marine Corps, Taiwan, Republic of China, 1964-65. Recipient several cmty. svc. awards, 3 spl. awards Nat. Assn. County Orgn. Mem. Nat. Assn. Social Workers (bd. dirs. Calif. chpt. 1979-80), Nat. Correctional Health Assn., Forensic Mental Health Assn. Calif., L.A. World Affairs Coun. Clubs: Chinese of San Marino (pres. 1987-88), San Marino City. Home: 2161 E California Blvd San Marino CA 91108-1348 Office: LA County Dept Mental Health 155 N Occidental Blvd Los Angeles CA 90026

CHEN, STEPHEN SHAU-TSI, psychiatrist, physiologist; b. Tou-Nan, Yun-Lin, Taiwan, Aug. 18, 1934; s. R-Yue and Pi-Yu (Huang) C.; m. Clara Chin-Chin Liu, Sept. 7, 1936; children: David, Timothy, Hubert. MD, Nat. Taiwan U., Taipei, 1959; PhD, U. Wis., 1968. Diplomate Am. Bd. Psychiatry and Neurology, also sub. bd. Geriatric Psychiatry. Intern Nat. Taiwan U. Hosp., 1959; instr. dept. physiology U. Wis., Madison, 1968-71, asst. prof., 1971-75; resident in psychiatry SUNY, Stony Brook, 1975-78; asst. prof. psychiatry dept. psychiatry U. Pitts., 1978-80; asst. prof. psychiatry dept. psychiatry and behavioral sci. U. Wash., Seattle, 1981-86, clin. asst. prof. psychiatry, 1986—; chief mental health clinic VA Med. Ctr., Tacoma, 1981-85. Contbr. articles to Am. Jour. Physiol., Jour. Physiology, Can. Jour. Physiology and Pharmacology, Acta Physiol. Fellow Wis. Heart Assn., 1966-68. Mem. APA, North Pacific Soc. Neurology and Psychiatry. Presbyterian. Office: VA Med Ctr Psychiatry Svc Tacoma WA 98493

CHEN, SUSIE, nursing educator; b. Taiwan, Republic of China, Nov. 13, 1959. ADN, Nat. Taipei Coll. Nursing, 1981; BSN, Kaohsiung Med. Coll., Taiwan, 1983; MEd, Oklahoma City U., 1988; M in Nursing, UCLA, 1994. BLS instr.; cert. dir. coun. for pvt. postsecondary and vocat.-edn., Calif. Floating staff nurse Mackay Meml. Hosp., Taipei, 1979-81; instr. Mackay Sch. of Nursing, Taipei, 1983-85; staff nurse Bapt. Med. Ctr., Oklahoma City, 1989-90; charge nurse Western Med. Ctr., Anaheim, Calif., 1990-91; instr. Pacific Coast Coll., Encino, Calif., 1991-92; home health nurse CSM Home Health Svc., Inc., L.A., 1993; clin. instr. Cerritos C.C., Calif., 1992-94; dir. nursing Southcal Nursing Ednl. Inst., El Monte, Calif., 1990—; instr. Biola Univ., La Mirada, Calif., 94—; affiliated faculty Am. Heart Assn., 1994—. Author: IV Therapy: A Student Handbook, 1993, Content Review of Psychiatric Nursing, 1986; editor: Textbook of Nursing I: Fundamental, 1986. Pres./founder Chinese Nurses Assn. of So. Calif., L.A., 1993. Named Ambassador-at-large Oklahoma City, Mayor Andy Coats, 1986, Excellent Youth in Taiwan, Pres. Chiang of Rep. of China, Taipei, 1980. Mem. Coun. on Cardiovascular Nursing, AACN, Intravenous Nurses Soc. Office: Biola Univ Dept Baccalaureat Nursing 13800 Biola Ave La Mirada CA 90639-0002

CHENEY, ANNA MARIE, medical, surgical nurse; b. Wishek, N.D., Nov. 27, 1935; d. Jacob Jangula and Eva Wald; m. Edwin J. Cheney, Feb. 6, 1965; children: Alan, Deborah, Darrell. Diploma, Sisters of St. Joseph Sch. Nursing, Grand Forks, N.D., 1957; BSN, St. Louis U., 1960; MSN, UCLA, 1965. Oper. rm. instr. Sisters of St. Joseph, Grand Forks, 1957-58; staff nurse Cardinal Glennon Meml. Hosp., St. Louis, 1958-60, VA Med. Ctr., St. Louis and L.A., 1960-62; head nurse VA Med. Ctr., West L.A., 1963-64; staff nurse UCLA Med. Ctr., 1964-65; head nurse Meml. Hosp., Culver City and L.A., 1965-66; staff nurse West Pk. Hosp., Canoga Park, Calif., 1980-84; staff nurse VA Med. Ctr., Sepulveda, Calif., 1984-89, clin. nurse specialist med./surg., 1989—, clin. nurse specialist ambulatory care, 1994; instr. CPR Am. Heart Assn., L.A., 1991-94; facilitator stop smoking Am. Cancer Soc., L.A., 1991-94, instr. breast self exam, 1991-94. Contbr. articles to profl. jours. Named Outstanding Pub. Spkr., Am. Cancer Soc., 1993; grantee UCLA, 1963-64. Mem. Toastmaster Internat. (v.p. edn. 1991-92, pres. 1992-93, Cert. of Appreciation 1992, competent toastmaster, Toastmaster Leadership Excellence award 1995). Democrat. Roman Catholic. Home: 23741 Highlander Rd West Hills CA 91307-1825

CHENEY, GALEN WALCOTT, artist; b. Northridge, Calif., Oct. 31, 1962; d. Marvin and Rosina (Chapin) C. Student, U. Florence, 1982-83; BA cum laude, Mt. Holyoke Coll., 1984; MFA, Md. Inst. Coll. Art, 1990. Assoc. editor Harcourt Brace Jovanovich Pub., N.Y.C., 1984-87; graphic artist Carlie's, Florence, Italy, 1990-91; instr. learning disabilities Harwood Union H.S., Moretown, Vt., 1992-94; rsch. asst. State of Vt., Waterbury, 1994-95; sculptor Maiden Foundry, Sandy, Oreg., 1995—; dir. visual arts Fernwood Camp, Oxford, Maine, 1993; guest curator Kristal Gallery, Warren, Vt., 1994-95; dir. aftersch. arts program Waitsfield (Vt.) Elem. Sch., 1993. Gallery artist Omni Gallery; guest artist. S.C. Gifted and Talented Program, Walterboro, 1993; guest artist, lectr. Harwood Union H.S., Moretown, 1995; exhibited works at Coll. Santa Fe, Woman Made Gallery, Chgo., Gallery 84, N.Y.C.; contbr. articles to profl. jours.

CHENEY, STEPHEN ALLEN, career officer, foreign policy analyst; b. Wareham, Mass., Aug. 7, 1949; s. Leroy Allen C. BS in Marine Engring., U.S. Naval Acad., 1971; MS in Systems Mgmt., U. So. Calif., 1978; postgrad., Nat. War Coll., Washington, 1990, Coun. on Fgn. Rels., N.Y.C., 1994. Commd. 2d lt. USMC, 1971, advanced through grades to col.; artillery officer Camp Pendleton, Calif., 1972-74; aerial obs. Okinawa, Japan, 1974-75; company cmmdr. San Diego, Calif., 1975-78; assignment officer Hdqtrs Marine Corps, Washington, 1979-83; force artillery officer III Marine Expeditionary Force, Okinawa, Japan, 1984-85; artillery battalion exec. officer Camp Pendleton, Calif., 1985-87; battalion cmmdr. Marine Recruit Depot, San Diego, 1987-89; ground plans officer Drug Enforcement Office Sec. Defense, Washington, 1990; dep. exec. sec. to Sec. Defense, Washington, 1991-93; mil. fellow Coun. on Fgn. Rels., N.Y.C., 1993-94; mil. liason to congrl. commn. on roles and missions Headquarters USMC, Washington, 1994-95; regimental cmmdr. Recruit Tng. Regiment, San Diego, 1995—. Decorated Legion of Merit medal, Defense Superior Svc. medal. Mem. Coun. on Fgn. Rels., Pacific Coun. on Internat. Policy, U.S. Naval Inst. Episcopalian. Office: Recruit Tng Regiment 1500 Iwo Ave (MCRD) San Diego CA 92140

CHENG, CARL FU KANG, artist; b. San Francisco, Feb. 8, 1942; s. Theodore and Sung Yuan (Kwan) C. BA, UCLA, 1963; postgrad., Folkwang Sch. Art, Essen, Germany, 1964-65; MA, UCLA, 1967. instr. Otis Art Inst., L.A., 1977-80; vis. lectr. UCLA, 1980-84, Claremont (Calif.) Grad. Sch., 1984-85. Pub. art commns. for City of Santa Monica, Calif., San Francisco, Tempe, Ariz., MTA, L.A., Kaiser Permanente, L.A., 1997-98, N.Y.C. Getty Museum fellow, L.A., 1990; grantee L.A. Cultural Affairs, 1990, 96; recipient award NEA, 1986, 92. Mem. Internat. Sculpture Ctr., Mus. Contemporary Art. Studio: 1518 17th St Santa Monica CA 90404-3402

CHENG, HENG-DA, computer scientist; b. Shenyang, Liaoning, China, May 1, 1944; came to U.S., 1980; s. Ji Cheng and Yu-Zhi Pan; m. Xiaohong Hao (Haybina Hao); children: Yang-Yang, Yue-Yue, Lydia. BS, Harbin (China) Inst. Tech., 1967; MS, Wayne State U., 1981; PhD, Purdue U., 1985. Instr. Harbin Shipbuilding Inst., 1971-76; rschr., technician Harbin Railway Sci. and Tech. Rsch. Inst., Harbin, 1976-78, Computing Tech. Inst., 1978-80; vis. asst. prof. U. Calif., Davis, 1985-86; asst. prof. Concordia U., Montreal, Que., Can., 1987-88; assoc. prof. Tech. U. N.S., Halifax, Can., 1988-91; assoc. prof. Utah State U., Logan, 1991-93, adj. assoc. prof., 1993—; co-chmn. Vision Interface '90, 4th Can. Conf., Halifax, 1990; com. mem. Vision Interface '92, 1992, Vision Interface '96, 1996; panelist 2d Internat. Conf. Fuzzy Theory and Tech., 1993; mem. best paper award evaluation com., session chmn. Internat. Joint Conf. on Info. Scis., 1994, 95; com. mem. Internat. Conf. on Tools with Artificial Intelligence, 1995, 17th Internat. Conf. on Computer Processing of Oriental Langs., 1997; lectr. in field. Co-editor Pattern Recognition: Architectures Algorithms and Applications, 1991; assoc. editor: Pattern Recognition and Info. Scis.; contbr. articles to profl. jours. and confs.; reviewer sci. jours. and cons. Recipient grants Nat. Scis. and Engring. Rsch. Coun. Can., NSF, 1987—, NSERC, 1989-93, Utah State U., 1992-93, Utah Dept. Transp., 1996—, others. Mem. IEEE (sr.), Computer Soc. of IEEE, Cirs. and Sys. Soc. of IEEE, Geosci. and Remote Sensing Soc. of IEEE, Robotics and Automation Soc. of IEEE, Sys., Man and Cybernetics Soc. of IEEE, Signal Processing Soc. of IEEE, Engring. in Medicine and Biology Soc. of IEEE, Assn. for Computing Machinery. Office: Utah State Univ Dept Computer Sci Logan UT 84322-4205

CHENOWETH, HELEN, congresswoman; b. Topeka, Kans., Jan. 27, 1938; 2 children. Attended, Whitworth Coll., 1975-79; cert. in law office mgmt., U. Minn., 1974; student, Rep. Nat. Com. Mgmt. Coll., 1977. Bus. mgr. Northside Med. Ctr., 1964-75; state exec. dir. Idaho Rep. Party, 1975-77; chief of staff Congressman Steve Symms, 1977-78; campaign mgr. Symms for Congress Campaign, 1978, Leroy for Gov., 1985-86; v.p. Consulting Assocs., Inc., 1978—; mem. House of Reps., Washington; mem. agriculture, resources, vets. affairs coms.; bd. dirs. Ctr. Study of Market Alternatives. Deacon Capitol Christian Ctr., Boise. Office: US Ho of Reps 1727 Longworth Washington DC 20515*

CHENOWETH, WILLIAM LYMAN, consulting geologist; b. Wichita, Kans., Sept. 16, 1928; s. Bertrum and Bessie (Lyman) C.; m. Miriam Bernadine Pawlicki, Jan. 6, 1955; children: Mary, Martin, Peter, Paul. AB, Wichita State U., 1951; postgrad., N.Mex. Sch. of Mines, 1949; MS, U. N.Mex., 1951. Registered profl. geologist Wyo. Geologist AEC, Navajo Indian Reservation, Ariz., 1953-55, project geologist, 1955-57, area geologist, 1957-62; project geologist AEC, Grand Junction, Colo., 1962-74, staff geologist, 1975-77; staff geologist U.S. Dept. of Energy, Grand Junction, 1977-81, chief geologist, 1981-83; pvt. practice cons. geologist Grand Junction, 1984—; rsch. assoc. N.Mex. Bur. Mines, Socorro, 1984—. Editor: Colorado Uranium, 1981. Staff sgt. USNG, 1955-59. Recipient Living Resource award Mus. Western Colo., 1994. Fellow Geol. Soc. Am.; mem. Am. Assn. Petroleum Geologists (chmn. nuclear minerals com. 1982—), Rocky Mountain Assn. Geologists (Cert. of Recognition 1980), N.Mex. Geol. Soc. Democrat. Roman Catholic. Home: 707 Brassie Dr Grand Junction CO 81506-3911

CHERESKIN, VALERIE LEE, marketing professional; b. Chgo., Aug. 2, 1954; d. Samuel and Rosalie (Marks) C.; m. John William Hansen Jr., July 18, 1987. MusB, Eastern Ill. U., 1976; MBA with honors, San Diego State U., 1996. Sales rep. Wurlitzer Piano and Organ, Westchester, Ill., 1976-77; office mgr. Carl Fischer, Inc., Chgo., 1977-78; regional tng. mgr. Motorola, Inc., Schaumburg, Ill., 1979-81, account mgr., 1981-83; sales engr. Motorola-Codex, Schaumburg, Ill., 1983-84; account exec. Computer Intelligence, La Jolla, Calif., 1984-87; dir. mktg. Chereskin Designs, La Jolla, 1987-90; prin. and owner Valerie Chereskin Mktg. and Pub. Rels. Strategies, Carlsbad, Calif., 1990—. Mem. Pub. Rels. Soc. Am., Carlsbad C. of C., Am.-Russian Bus. Coun. of So. Calif. (bd. dirs.), San Diego Flute Guild, Computer and Electronics Mktg. Assn., Beta Gamma Sigma. Democrat. Home: 1364 Calle Christopher Encinitas CA 92024-5511 Office: Ste 2B 7750 El Camino Real Carlsbad CA 92009-8519

CHERINGTON, MICHAEL, neurologist, educator; b. Pitts., Nov. 24, 1934; s. Maurice and Sybil (Young) C.; children: Claire, David, Jennifer. BS in Chemistry summa cum laude, U. Pitts., 1956, MD, 1960. Diplomate Am. Bd. Neurology and Psychiatry, Am. Bd. Electrodiagnostic Medicine. Intern Montefiore Hosp., Pitts., 1961; resident in internal medicine U. Colo. Med. Ctr., 1961-62, resident in neurology, 1963-66; instr. neurology U. Colo. Med. Ctr., Denver, 1966-68, asst. clin. prof. neurology, 1968-76, assoc. clin. prof. neurology, 1976-88, clin. prof. neurology, 1988—; dir. med. edn. Mercy Hosp., Denver, 1968-71; pres. staff Spalding Rehab. Ctr., 1976-77; chmn., founder Lightning Data Ctr., St. Anthony Hosp., Denver, 1992—. Contbr. articles to profl. jours. With M.C., U.S. Army, 1962-63, hon. discharge. Fellow ACP, Am. Acad. Neurology, Am. Geriatric Soc., Am. Assn. Electromyography and Electrodiagnosis; mem. Am. Neurol. Assn., Phi Beta Kappa, Alpha Omega Alpha, Phi Eta Sigma. Office: St Anthony Hosp Lightning Data Ctr 4231 W 16th Ave Denver CO 80204-1335

CHERIS, ELAINE GAYLE INGRAM, business owner; b. Ashford, Ala., Jan. 8, 1946; m. Samuel David Cheris, June 8, 1980; 1 child, Zachariah Adam Abraham. BS, Troy State U., 1971. Aquatics dir. Yale U., New Haven, 1976-79; owner, mgr. Cheyenne Fencing Soc., Denver, 1980—; chmn. organizing com. World Fencing Championships, 1989, World Jr./Cadet Fencing Championships, 1993. Author: Handbook for Parents - Fencing, 1988, 2d edit., 1992; editor Yofen Mag., 1988-90, 1992—. Mem. Gov.'s Coun. on Sports and Fitness, Colo., 1990—; commr. Colo. State Games-Fencing, 1989—. Mem. U.S. Olympic Foil Team, 1980, 88 (6th place fencing), U.S. Olympic Epee Team, 96 (8th place), mem. U.S. Pan-Am. Games Team, 1987 (Gold medal women's foil team), 1991 (Gold medal women's epee team); named Sportswoman of Yr. Fencing, YWCA, 1980, 81, 82, to Sportswoman Hall of Fame, 1982; mem. U.S. World Championship Fencing Team, 1982, 85, 87, 90, 91, 92, 93, U.S. Maccabiah Fencing Team, 1981 (1 gold, 1 silver medal); recipient Gold Medal of Honor from Fedn. Internat. d'Escrime, 1993. Mem. AAPHERD, U.S. Fencing Assn. (youth chmn. 1988-90, editor Youth mag., 1988-90, 92—, chmn. Colo. divsn., 1992-94), Fedn. Internat. d'Escrime (chmn. Atlanta fencing project '96, chmn. World Fencing Day 1994). Jewish. Office: Cheyenne Fencing Soc 5818 E Colfax Ave Denver CO 80220-1507

CHERKAS, MARSHALL S., psychiatrist, psychoanalyst; b. Savannah, Calif., Jan. 5, 1929; s. Meyer L. and Fanye (Robinson) C.; m. Patricia Mae Clemens, Dec. 20, 1958; children: Karen, Brian, Jonathan. BA, U. Ill., 1948; MS in Hosp. Adminstrn., Northwestern U., 1952, MD, 1959; PhD, So. Calif. Psychoanalytic Inst. Diplomate Am. Bd. Psychiatry and Neurology. Intern Cedars of Lebanon Hosp., L.A., 1959-60; resident VA Ctr., Mt. Sinai Hosp., L.A., 1960-63; pres. Marshall S. Cherkas Med. Corp., L.A., 1963—; panel psychiatrist L.A. County Superior Ct., 1967—; cons. L.A. County Dept. Mental Health, 1965-73. Fellow APA (life), Am. Coll. Forensic Psychiatry (bd. dirs. 1980—); mem. AMA, Am. Soc. Adolescent Psychiatry (L.A. chpt. pres. 1966—). Office: Marshall S Cherkas Med Corp 12304 Santa Monica Blvd Los Angeles CA 90025-2551

CHERKIN, ADINA, interpreter, translator; b. Geneva, Nov. 22, 1921; came to U.S., 1940; d. Herz N. and Genia (Kodriansky) Mantchik; m. Arthur Cherkin, Mar. 14, 1943 (div. Sept. 1980); children: Della Peretti, Daniel Craig. BA, UCLA, 1942, MA in Russian Linguistics, 1977. Pvt. practice med. interpreter L.A., 1942-80; translator UCLA Med. Sch., 1970-79; pres. acad. forum Jewish studies Herz Mantchik Amity Cir., L.A., 1973-94. Author numerous poems. Active L.A. Internat. Vis. Coun., 1991—; pub. rels. Judge Stanley Mosk's Campaign, L.A., 1960; vol. Gov. Cranston's Campaign, 1960. Recipient Community Svc. award L.A. City Coun., 1992. Mem. Am. Soc. for Technion Israel Inst. Tech. (bd. regents). Home and Office: 2369 N Vermont Ave Los Angeles CA 90027-1253

CHERMAK, GAIL DONNA, audiologist, speech and hearing sciences educator; b. N.Y.C., Sept. 30, 1950; d. Martin I. Chermak and Zelda Lax; children: Isaac Martin, Alina Marta. BA in Communication Disorders, SUNY, Buffalo, 1972; MA in Speech and Hearing Sci., Ohio State U., 1973, PhD in Speech and Hearing Sci., 1975. Cert. clin. competency in audiology. Asst. prof. speech So. Ill. U., Edwardsville, 1975-77; assoc. prof. and dir., communication disorders program Wash. State U., Pullman, 1977-89, prof., chmn. dept. speech and hearing scis., 1990—, coord. grad. program dept. speech and hearing scis., 1983-89, prof., chmn. speech and hearing scis., 1990—; feature editor Am. Jour. Audiology, 1991-95; editl. cons. Ear and Hearing Jour., Cin., 1984, 88, 89, 90, 91, 92, 93, 94, Internat. Jour. Disability Devel. and Edn., 1991, Lang. Speech and Hearing Svcs. in Schs., 1993, 94, 95, 96, 97, Jour. of Communication Disorders, 1994, Am. Jour. Audiology, 1994, 95; profl. advisor Palowe chpt. Self-Help for Hard of Hearing, Moscow, Idaho, 1984-89. Author: Handbook of Audiological Rehabilitation, 1981, Central Auditing Processing Disorders: New Perspectives, 1997; contbr. articles to profl. jours. Kellogg nat. fellow, 1986-89; Fulbright scholar, 1989-90. Fellow Soc. Ear, Nose and Throat Advances in Children; mem. AAAS, AAUW, Am. Assn. for Higher Edn., Am. Speech, Lang. and Hearing Assn. (cert. clin. competence in audiology), Acoustical Soc. Am., Am. Acad. Audiology, Am. Auditory Soc., Internat. Soc. Audiology, NOW (v.p. Moscow chpt. 1985-86), ACLU (human rights com.), Phi Beta Kappa. Office: Wash State U Dept Speech and Hearing Scis 201 Daggy Hall Pullman WA 99164-2420

CHERNOF, BRUCE, internist, educator; s. David and Lorna Jean (Laff) C. BA in Biology cum laude, Harvard U., 1984; MD, UCLA, 1988. Diplomate Am. Bd. Internal Medicine, Nat. Bd. Med. Examiners. Intern, then resident in internal medicine UCLA/Sepulveda VA Med. Ctr., 1988-91, chief resident in internal medicine, 1991-92; fellow med. edn. Ctr. for Ednl. R&D UCLA Sch. Medicine, 1992-93, clin. instr., instr. fundamentals of clin. medicine, 1991-92, asst. prof. medicine, 1992—, mem. faculty divsn. gen. internal medicine, 1992—; mem. nat. faculty managing for change TQI Leadership Tng., Cleve. Regional Med. Edn. Ctr., 1994; founding mem. Healthy Beginnings project UCLA Med. Ctr. Found., 1992—; lectr. in field. Contbr. articles, monographs to profl. publs. Fellow ACP; mem. AMA, Sog. Gen. Internal Medicine, Calif. Med. Assn., Harvard Radcliffe Club of So. Calif. (interviewer, mem. undergrad. admissions com. 1980—). Democrat. Office: Olive View UCLA Med Ctr Med Adminstrn Ste 2C-138 14445 Olive View Dr Sylmar CA 91342

CHERRY, BRADY DEAN, municipal government official; b. Burbank, Calif., Aug. 5, 1955; s. Eugene Ashton and Barbara J. (Brown) C.; m. Cynthia Lynn Grigsby, Nov. 4, 1989; children: Natasha, Brenna, Bryce. AA, El Camino Coll., 1975; BA in Fine Arts, U. Calif., Irvine, 1977; MA in Psychology, Pepperdine U., 1992. Dir. comty. svcs. City of Lawndale, Calif., 1973-88, City of Pt. Hueneme, Calif., 1988-94, City of Atascadero, Calif., 1994—; pks. and harbor commr. County of Ventura, Calif., 1992-94. Bd. dirs. Pt. Hueneme Boys and Girls Club, 1988-94; mem. Atascadero Hist. Soc., 1995-96, Friends of the Libr., 1996. Named Citizen of Yr., Pt. Hueneme C. of C., 1993. Mem. Calif. Pks. and Recreation Soc., So. Calif. Mcpl. Athletic Fedn. (bd. dirs. 1980, 84, 88, Citation award 1987). Office: City of Atascadero 6500 Palma Ave Atascadero CA 93422-7225

CHERRY, JAMES DONALD, physician; b. Summit, N.J., June 10, 1930; s. Robert Newton and Beatrice (Wheeler) C.; m. Jeanne M. Fischer, June 19, 1954; children—James S., Jeffrey D., Susan J., Kenneth C. BS, Springfield (Mass.) Coll., 1953; MD, U. Vt., 1957; MSc in Epidemiology, London Sch. Hygiene and Tropical Medicine, 1983. Diplomate Am. Bd. Pediat., Am. Bd. Pediat. Infectious Diseases. Intern, then resident in pediat. Boston City Hosp., 1957-59; resident in pediat. Kings County Hosp., Bklyn., 1959-60; rsch. fellow in medicine Harvard U. Med. Sch.-Thorndike Meml. Lab., Boston City Hosp., 1961-62; instr. pediatrics U. Vt. Coll. Medicine, also asst. attending physician Mary Fletcher DeGoesbriand Meml. hosps., Burlington, Vt., 1960-61; asst. prof., then assoc. prof. pediat. U. Wis. Med. Sch., Madison, 1963-66; assoc. attending physician Madison Gen., U. Wis. hosps., 1963-66; dir. John A. Hartford Rsch. Lab., Madison Gen. Hosp., 1963-66; mem. faculty St. Louis U. Med. Sch., 1966-73, prof. pediatrics, 1969-73, vice chmn. dept., 1970-73; mem. staff Cardinal Glennon Meml. Hosp. Children, St. Louis U. Hosp., 1966-73; prof. pediatrics, chief divsn. infectious diseases UCLA Med. Ctr. UCLA Sch. Medicine, 1973—; acting chmn. dept. pediatrics UCLA Med. Ctr., 1977-79; attending physician, chmn. infection control com. UCLA Med. Ctr.; cons. Project Head Start; vis. worker dept. cmty. medicine Middlesex Hosp. and Med. Sch., London, 1982-83; vis. worker Common Cold Rsch. Unit, 1969-70; mem. immunization adv. com. Los Angeles County Dept. Health Svcs., 1978—. Co-editor Textbook of: Pediatric Infectious Diseases, 1981, 2nd edit., 1987, 3rd edit., 1992; assoc. editor: Clin. Infectious Diseases, 1990—; Am. regional editor: Vaccine, 1991—; author numerous papers in field; editl. reviewer profl. jours. Bd. govs. Alexander Graham Bell Internat. Parents Orgn., 1967-69. With USAR, 1958-64. John and Mary R. Markle scholar acad. medicine, 1964. Mem. AAAS, APHA, Am. Acad. Pediat. (mem. exec. com. Calif. chpt. 2 1975-77, mem. com. infectious diseases 1977-83, assoc. editor 19th Red Book 1982), Am. Soc. Microbiology, Am. Fedn. Clin. Rsch., Soc. Pediat. Rsch., Infectious Diseases Soc. Am., Am. Epidemiol. Soc., Am. Pediat. Soc., L.A. Pediat. Soc., Soc. Exptl. Biology and Medicine, Internat. Orgn. Mycoplasmologists, Am. Soc. Virology, Soc. Hosp. Epidemiologists Am., Pediat. Infectious Diseases Soc. (pres. 1989-91), Alpha Omega Alpha. Office: UCLA Sch Medicine Dept Pediatrics Rm 22-442 10833 Le Conte Ave Los Angeles CA 90095-1762

CHERRY, LEE OTIS, scientific institute director; b. Oakland, Calif., Nov. 20, 1944; s. Knorvel and Lucy (Grayson) C.; m. Lauren Michelle Waters, Aug. 30, 1980; children: Aminah L., Jamilah L. AA, Merritt Community Coll., Oakland, Calif., 1965; BSEE, San Jose State U., 1968; cert. Hazardous Material Mgmt., U. Calif., Berkeley, 1995, cert. Site Assessment and Remediation, 1997. Registered Environ. Assessor, Calif. Systems analyst IBM, San Francisco, 1968-69; elec. engr. Pacific Gas & Elec., Oakland, Calif., 1969-79; project mgr. Navy Facility, Dept. Def., Washington, 1979-84; project mgr., environ. engr. NAVFACENGCOM and REA Navy Facility, Dept. Def., San Bruno, Calif., 1984—; co-founder, exec. dir. African Sci. Inst., Oakland, 1967—; sr. cons. Devel. Cons. & Assocs., Oakland, 1972—; proprietor L & L & Assocs., Oakland, 1980—. Pubr. mo. mag. "Technology Transfer", 1979-83, quar. newspaper "SciTech", 1988—; developer calendar: Blacks in Science, 1986—. Mem. AAAS, Ghanaian-Am. C. of C. (co-founder, bd. dirs. 1990—). Office: African Scientific Inst PO Box 12161 Oakland CA 94604-2161

CHESHIRE, WILLIAM POLK, retired newspaper columnist; b. Durham, N.C., Feb. 2, 1931; s. James Webb and Anne Ludlow (McGehee) C.; m. Lucile Geoghegan, Aug. 1, 1959; children—William Polk, Helen Wood Cheshire Elder, James Webb. A.B., U. N.C., Chapel Hill, 1958. Reporter Richmond News Leader, Va., 1958-61; assoc. editor Canton (N.C.) Enterprise, 1961-62, Charleston Evening Post, S.C., 1963-68, The State, Columbia, S.C., 1968-72; editorial dir. Capital Broadcasting Co., Raleigh, N.C., 1972-75; editorial page editor Greensboro Record, N.C., 1975-78; editor-in-chief Charleston Daily Mail, W.Va., 1978-84; editor, editorial pages Washington Times, 1984-87; editor, editorial pages The Ariz. Republic, Phoenix, 1987-93, sr. editorial columnist, 1993-96, ret., 1996; prof. journalism U. Charleston, 1979-83; commentator Voice of Am., 1986-87. Dir. comm. N.C. Senate Campaign, 1972; bd. dirs. Sunrise Mus., Charleston United Way, 1978-84. With USCG, 1952-56. Recipient Council for the Def. of Freedom award, 1980, George Washington Honor medal Freedoms Found., 1975; named Disting. Fellow in Journalism, Heritage Found., 1987; Media fellow Hoover Instn., 1991. Mem. N.C. Soc. Cin. (pres. 1988-91), Phila. Soc., Nat. Press Club, Phoenix Country Club, Ariz. Club, Sigma Delta Chi (pres. Piedmont chpt. 1978). Anglican. *

CHESNEY, MAXINE M., judge; b. 1942. BA, U. Calif., Berkeley, 1964, JD, 1967. Trial atty. Office Dist. Atty., San Francisco, 1968-69, sr. trial atty., 1969-71, prin. trial atty., 1971-76, head atty., 1976, asst. chief dep., 1976-79; judge San Francisco Mcpl. Ct., 1979-83, San Francisco Superior Ct., 1983-95, U.S. Dist. Ct. (no. dist.) Calif., San Francisco, 1995—. Bd. dirs. San Francisco Child Abuse Coun., 1976-79, Hosp. Audiences, 1978-81. Mem. Fed. Judges Assn., Nat. Assn. Women Judges, Calif. Women Lawyers, Edward J. McFetridge Am. Inn of Ct., U.S. Assn. Constl. Law, Queen's Bench. Office: US Dist Ct No Dist Calif PO Box 3606 450 Golden Gate Ave San Francisco CA 94102

CHESNEY, SUSAN TALMADGE, human resources specialist, technical writer; b. N.Y.C., Aug. 12, 1943; d. Morton and Tillie (Talmadge) Chesney; m. Donald Lewis Freitas, Sept. 17, 1967 (div. May 1976); m. Robert Martin Rosenblatt, Apr. 9, 1980. AB, U. Calif., Berkeley, 1967. Placement interviewer U. Calif., Berkeley, 1972-74, program coord., 1974-79; pers. adminstr. Hewlett-Packard Co., Santa Rosa, Calif., 1982-84; pres. Mgmt. Resources, Santa Rosa, 1984—; human resources mgr. BioBottoms Inc., Petaluna, Calif., 1990-91; human resources adminstr. Parker Compumotor, Rohnert Park, Calif., 1991-93; cons. Kensington Electronics Group, Healdsburg, Calif., 1984-85, Behavioral Medicine Assocs., Santa Rosa, 1985-86, M.C.A.I., Santa Rosa, 1986-87, Bowdon Designs, Santa Rosa, 1987-88, Bass & Ingram, Santa Rosa, 1988—, Eason Tech., Inc., Healdsburg, 1995—, Interim Svcs., Inc., Santa Rosa, 1995—, Flex Products, Inc., Santa Rosa, 1996—. Mem. Nat. Soc. Performance Instrn., No. Calif. Human Resources Coun., Pers. Assn. Sonoma County. Avocations: cooking, gardening, music.

CHESNUT, CAROL FITTING, lawyer; b. Pecos, Tex., June 17, 1937; d. Ralph Ulf and Carol (Lowe) Fitting; m Dwayne A. Chesnut, Dec. 27, 1955; children: Carol Marie, Stephanie Michelle, Mark Steven. BA magna cum laude, U. Colo., 1971; JD, U. Calif., San Francisco, 1994. Rsch. asst. U. Colo., 1972; head quality controller Mathematica, Inc., Denver, 1973-74; cons. Mincome Man., Winnipeg, Can., 1974; cons. economist Energy Cons. Assocs. Inc., Denver, 1974-79; exec. v.p. tng. ECA Intercomp, 1980-81; gen. ptnr. Chestnut Consortium, S.F., 1981—; sec., bd. dirs. Critical Resources, Inc., 1981-83. Rep. Lakehurst Civic Assn., 1968; staff aide Senator Gary Hart, 1978; Dem. precinct capt., 1982-88. Mem. ABA, ACLU, AAUW (1st v.p. 1989-90), Am. Mgmt. Assn., Soc. Petroleum Engrs., Am. Nuclear Soc. (chmn. conv. space activities for 1989, chair of spouse activities 1989), Am. Geophys. Union, Assn. Women Geoscientists (treas. Denver 1983-85), Associated Students of Hastings (rep. 1994), Calif. State Bar, Nev. State Bar, Canyon Ranch Homeowners Assn. (sec. bd. dirs. 1994—), Phi Beta Kappa, Phi Chi Theta, Phi Delta Phi. Unitarian. Office: 7537 Dry Pines Cir Las Vegas NV 89129-5932

CHESSER, STEVEN BRUCE, public relations executive; b. Lakeland, Fla., Sept. 28, 1951; s. Gordon Stuart and Shirley (Hoff) C.; m. Mary Sennholtz, 1972 (div. 1989); children: Bethany, Michelle; m. Karole Gwen Sense, Feb. 28, 1993; 1 child, Stephen Bryce. BA, U. S.C., 1973; MA, U. Okla., 1985. Commd. ensign USN, 1973, advanced through grades to lt. comdr., served on U.S.S. N.J., 1986-88, served with Naval Surface Group at Long Beach, Calif., 1988-93, ret., 1993; media rels. specialist Met. Transp. Authority, L.A., 1993-97; cmty. rels. sr. mgr. McDonnell Douglas Corp., Long Beach, 1997—; coord. publicity 1st battleship battlegroup deployment, 1986; condr. 23 press events Operation Desert Shield/Desert Storm, 1990-91; coord. MTA response to "60 Minutes" inquiry, 1995. Event chmn. Am. Cancer Soc., Long Beach, Calif., 1992-93; publicity dir. The Crossing Homeless Shelter, San Pedro, Calif., 1992-93; pres. Drug Abuse Resistance Edn., Long Beach, 1993-94. Recipient Key to the City, City of Long Beach, 1993. Office: McDonnell Douglas 3855 Lakewood Blvd Long Beach CA 90846

CHESSICK, CHERYL ANN, psychiatrist; b. Ft. Collins, Colo., July 30, 1960. BA, Colo. Coll., 1982; MD, U. Colo., 1986. Med. technologist, rsch. asst. Children's Hosp., Denver, 1983; intern U. Colo., Denver, 1986-87, resident in psychiatry, 1987-90; on-call physician Ft. Logan State Hosp., Denver, 1988-89; on-call psychiatrist Denver Gen. Hosp., 1989—; staff psychiatrist Colo. State Hosp., Pueblo, 1990-91, med. dir. psychiat. emergency rm., 1991-92; psychiatrist in pvt. practice Denver, 1992—; assoc. med. dir. Pro Behavioral Health, 1986—; expert witness Denver Civil Ct., Pueblo Civil Ct., Logan County Criminal Ct., El Paso Civil Ct., Adams County Criminal Ct., 1987—; presenter at profl. confs. co-coord. seminar on battered women U. Colo. Health Sci. Ctr., Denver, 1986; guest lectr. Boulder Community Hosp., 1989, Hosp. & Community Psychiat. Ctr., 1990; curriculum cons. Colo. AIDS Edn. and Tng. Ctr., Denver, 1989—. Mem. Am. Psychiat. Soc., Colo. Psychiat. Soc., Phi Gamma Mu. Office: 950 S Cherry St # 200 Denver CO 80222-2699

CHESTER, ELFI, artist; b. Cologne, Rheinland/Westfalen, Germany, Aug. 7, 1952; came to the U.S., 1977; d. Adolf and Elsbeth Bollert; m. Marvin Chester, July 30, 1977; children: Chaim Peter, Sadye Vera. Degree in Art Edn., Pädagogische Hochschule Berlin, 1976. Founder "Odd Thursday" group of figurative artists in Venice, Calif., 1990; co-founder COOP Fine Art Gallery, Occidental, Calif., 1993. Exhibits include: Collector's Choice, Laguna Beach, Calif., 1982, The House, Santa Monica, Calif., 1982, Arts in Motion, Laguna Beach Arts Commn. Alliance, Calif., 1982, Sculpture in the Park '83, '84, Peter Strauss Ranch, Agoura, Calif., Pierce Coll., Mainstage Theatre, Woodland Hills, Calif., 1983, Designs in Motion, San Francisco, 1983, Don Conrad Mobiles, Ghiradelli Square, 1983, Meditate Centrum DE KOSMOS, Amsterdam, 1983, Agoura Hills City Gallery, 1984, Exploratorium, San Francisco, Deplana Einrichtungshaus, Berlin, 1984, Star Magic, N.Y. and San Francisco, 1984, Gallo, Rome, 1986, Tropical Palm Gallery, Maui, 1988, Talpa Trangle Gallery, Taos, New Mexico, 1988, Santa Monica Main Library, 1990, Claudia Chapline Gallery, Stinson Beach, Calif., 1991, Sebastopol Ctr. for the Arts, 1992, Coop. FINE ART, Occidental, 1993; juried shows and awards: Small Works, Calif. Mus. of Art, 1993, Sonoma County Office of Edn., curated by CACSC, 1995, A Little Heat, Juror: Jack Stuppin Coop, 1996, Towards Abstraction, Juror: Michael Hayden, sculptor Coop, 1996, World Wide Web on-line exhibit, 1996; numerous pvt. collections; prodr. art performance Laguna Beach Arts Commn. Alliance and L.A. Choreographers and Dancers, 1982. Recipient Agoura Hills Art Contbn. award City of Agoura Hills, 1983. Mem. Sebastopol Ctr. for the Arts, Cultural Arts Coun. of Sonoma County, Donkey Barn Artists. Home: PO Box 324 Occidental CA 95465-0324

CHESTER, LYNNE, foundation executive, artist; b. Fargo, N.D., May 29, 1942; d. Harry Batten and Margaret Emily (White) Welliver; m. R. Craig Chester, Feb. 25, 1984; 1 child, Benjamin. BA in Music, Hillsdale Coll., 1964; MA in Guidance Counseling, Mich. State U., 1965; PhD in Psychology, U. Mich., 1971. Tchr. Warren (Mich.) Consol. Schs., 1965-70; curriculum advisor Royal Oak (Mich.) Pub. Schs., 1974-75; co-founder, exec. dir. Peace Rsch. Found., Carmel, Calif., 1993—; assoc. Hillsdale Coll., 1989—; guest lectr. ceramics James Milliken U., Decatur, Ill., 1991; guest lectr. creative covergence Carl Cherry Ctr. for Art, Carmel, 1991, Compton lectr., Monterey, Calif., 1996—, juror h.s. poetry contest Monterey County, 1997; co-founder, bd. mem. Monterey Peninsula Coll. Art Gallery, 1991—; fundraiser Monterey Peninsula Coll. Student Art Gallery, 1992-94; guest juror Monterey County Essay Contest, 1997. Artist of multiple commd. sculptures for pvt. collections; also ceramics, sculpture and photographs in pvt. and corp. collections; represented in permanent collection at Krammert Art Mus., Champaign, Ill., Fresno (Calif.) Mus. Art; juried show Ctr. for Photographic Art, Carmel, Calif., 1996; art represented at Who's Who in Art, Monterey, 1989—, Christmas Miniatures/Invitational Ctr. for Photographic Art, Carmel, 1996, Holiday Print Show Ctr. for Photographic Art, Carmel, 1996 (Dir.'s Choice 1996); author of poetry; juror essay contest Personal Heroes Monterey County K-12, 1997; juror poetry contest Monterey County 9-12 grades, Carl Cherry Ctr. for the Arts, 1993—. Co-founder Southfield (Mich.) Symphony, 1972, World Rhythms Festival, Carmel, 1996—; co-founder, bd. dirs. Monterey Bay Artists Day, KAZU-FM Radio Sta., 1987-89; pres., bd. dirs. Carl Cherry Ctr. for Arts, Carmel, 1988-94, 95—; bd. dirs. Monterey Peninsula Mus. Art, 1991-93, Carmel Pub. Libr. Found., 1992-93, Monterey Inst. for Rsch. in Astronomy, 1985-95, Monterey County Cultural Commn., 1994—. Recipient Citizens Adv. Coun. award City of Royal Oak, 1978-83, Best of Show award for monoprint Monterey Peninsula Coll., 1990, Poetry prizes Carl Cherry Ctr. for Arts, 1990-94, Benefactor of Arts award Monterey County Cultural Coun., 1992, 93, 94, Soccer Mgr./Coach of Yr. 1976-81; others. Mem. AAUW, Internat. Platform Assn., Internat. Sculpture Ctr., Nat. Soc. Fund Raising Execs., Nat. Mus. Women in Art (charter mem.), Am. Crafts Coun., Sigma Alpha Iota (Ruby Sword of Honor 1968). Home: 9645 Sandbur Pl Salinas CA 93907 Office: Peace Rsch Found 225 The Crossroads # 145 Carmel CA 93923-8649

CHESTER, MARVIN, physics educator; b. N.Y.C., Dec. 29, 1930; s. Herman and Sadye C.; m. Ruth Chester (div. 1960); 1 child, Karen; m. Sandra Chester (div. 1963); 1 child, Lisa; m. Elfi Bollert, July 30, 1977; children: Chaim Peter, Sadye Vera. BS, CCNY, 1952; PhD, Calif. Inst. Tech., 1961. Prof. physics U. Calif., L.A., 1961-92, prof. emeritus, 1992—; sr. rsch. fellow U. Sussex, Eng., 1973. Author: Primer of Quantum Mechanics, 1987; contbr. articles to profl. jours. Recipient Alexander von Humboldt award, Von Humboldt Stifftung, 1974-75. Mem. Am. Phys. Soc., N.Y. Acad. Sci. Office: UCLA Dept Physics Los Angeles CA 90024

CHESTER, SHARON ROSE, photographer, natural history educator; b. Chgo., July 12, 1942; d. Joseph Thomas and Lucia Barbara (Urban) C. BA, U. Wis., 1964; grad., Coll. San Mateo, 1972-74; postgrad., U. Calif., Berkeley, 1977; grad., San Francisco State U., 1989. Flight attendant Pan Am. World Airways Inc., San Francisco, 1965; free lance photographer San Mateo, Calif., 1983—; stock photographer Comstock, N.Y.C., 1987—; lectr. Soc. Expdns., Seattle, 1985-91, Abercrombie & Kent, Chgo., 1992-94, Seven Seas Cruise Line, San Francisco, 1994-95; owner Wandering Albatross, 1993. Author (checklist) Birds of the Antarctic and Sub-Antarctic, 1986, revised, 1994, Antarctic birds and Seals: A Pocket Guide, 1993, South to Antarctica, 1994, The Northwest Passage, 1994; author and illustrator, Birds of Chile, Aves de Chile, 1995; co-author: The Birds of Chile: A Field Guide, 1993, The Arctic Guide, 1996, The Marquesas Islands: Mave Mai, 1997; photos featured in Sierra club Book: Mother Earth Through the Eyes of Women Photographers and Writers, 1992; photographer mag. cover King Penguin and Chick for Internat. Wildlife Mag., 1985, Sierra Club Calendar, 1986; exhibited photos at Royal Geographic Soc. London. Mem. Calif. Acad. Sci. Home: 724 Laurel Ave Apt 211 San Mateo CA 94401-4131

CHESTON, MICHAEL GALLOWAY, airport executive; m. Laurie; children: Kenny, Geoffrey. AA in Gen. Edn., Catonsville (Md.) C.C., 1975; BA in English, St. Mary's Coll. of Md., 1977; MBA in Real Estate Devel., George Washington U., 1994. Cert. air traffic control specialist. Corporate recruiting supr., computer resource acquisition specialist Electronic Data Sys., Inc., Bethesda, Md., 1984-86; dir. European ops. Corporate Devel. Sys., Inc., Wellesley, Mass., 1986-87; acting mgr., ops. officer, bus. analyst Met. Washington Airports Authority, Alexandria, Va., 1987-93; airport mgr. Portland (Oreg.) Internat. Airport, 1993—, gen. mgr. ops., maintenance and aviation. Comdr. USMC, 1977-84; maj., USMCR. Mem. Am. Assn. Airports Execs., Airports Coun. Internat., Portland Highland Games Assn. (pub. safety mgr.), Marine Corps Assn., Marine Corps Res. Officers Assn. (chpt. pres.). Office: Portland Internat Airport PO Box 3529 Portland OR 97208-3529*

CHETTLE, A(LVIN) B(ASIL), JR., judge, lawyer, educator; b. Hollywood, Calif., Apr. 13, 1937; s. Alvin Basil Sr. and Evelyn Teresa (Olsen) C. BS, Georgetown U., 1959, JD, 1962, LLM, 1964. Bar: Va. 1962, D.C. 1962, U.S. Ct. Mil. Appeals 1962, U.S. Ct. Appeals (D.C. cir.) 1962, U.S. Ct. Claims 1963, U.S. Tax Ct. 1963, U.S. Ct. Appeals (9th cir.) 1964, Calif. 1965, U.S. Dist. Ct. (cen. dist.) Calif. 1965, U.S. Supreme Ct. 1975, U.S. Dist. Ct. (so. dist.) Calif. 1977. Adminstrv. asst. to dir. claims div. Nat. Canners Assn. (now Nat. Food Processors Assn.), Washington, 1962-64; assoc. Keel & Pressman, Hawthorne, Calif., 1964; ptnr. Keel & Chettle, Hawthorne, Calif., 1965, Keel, Chettle & Valentine, Hawthorne, Calif., 1966-71; city prosecutor City of Hawthorne, 1965-69; sr. ptnr. Chettle & Valentine, Manhattan Beach, Calif., 1971-92; lectr. Food Processors Inst., Washington, Massey U., New Zealand, 1983; spl. counsel City of Inglewood, Calif., 1971, City of Hawthorne, Calif., 1977-84, City of Torrance, Calif., 1979—; arbitrator South Bay Mcpl. Ct., Torrance; judge pro tem L.A. Jud. Dist., 1982—, South Bay Jud. Dist., Torrance, 1985—, L.A. County Superior Ct., 1990—; hearing officer City of Garden Grove, 1989-92, City of Hawthorne, 1992—. Active L.A. chpt. ARC, 1966-96, ARC Blood and Tissue Svcs., 1966-96; 1st chair emeritus bd. dirs. ARC Blood Svcs.-So. Calif. Region, 1997—; bd. dirs. Coalition of Food Industry Counsel. Recipient Life Time Achievements award Nat. Food Processors Assn. Mem. Am. Judicature Soc., D.C. Bar Assn., Calif. Bar Assn. (del. conf. of dels. 1969), Va. Bar Assn., Assn. So. Calif. Def. Counsel, Def. Rsch. Isnt., Ingelwood Dist. Bar Assn. (trustee 1967, 70, treas. 1967, nominating com. 1966, 75, 76, 77, v.p. 1968, pres. 1969), L.A. County Bar Assn. (conf. affiliated bar pres. 1969, parking lot com. 1969, 70). Office: PO Box 7 Manhattan Beach CA 90267

CHETWYND, LIONEL, screenwriter, producer, director; b. London, Jan. 29; s. Peter and Betty (Dion) C.; m. Gloria Carlin, June 2; children: Michael Anthony, Joshua Stephen. BA with honors, Sir George Williams U., Montreal, Que., 1963; B in Civil Law, McGill U., Montreal, Que., 1967; postgrad., Trinity Coll. of Oxford (Eng.) U., 1968. Bar: PQ 1967. With acquisition/distbn. dept. Columbia Pictures, London, 1968-72; screenwriter, 1971—; mem. faculty Grad. Film Sch., NYU; lectr. screenwriting Frederick Douglass Ctr., Harlem; appointed pres.. Am. Cinema Found. Writer: (stage prodns.) Maybe That's Your Problem, 1971, Bleeding Great Orchids, 1971, (feature films) The Apprenticeship of Duddy Kravatz, 1974 (also adaptor, Acad. award nomination 1974), Morning Comes, 1975 (also dir.), Two Solitudes, 1978 (also prodr., dir., Grand award Salonika 1979), Quintet, 1978, Hot Touch, 1981 (Genie nomination), The Hanoi Hilton, 1987 (also dir.), (TV films) Johnny, We Hardly Knew Ye, 1976 (also prodr., George Washington Honor medal Freedom Found. 1976), It Happened One Christmas, 1977 (citation Am. Women in Film and TV 1979), Goldenrod, 1977 (also prodr.), A Whale for the Killing, 1980, Miracle on Ice, 1981 (Christopher award 1981), Escape From Iran: The Canadian Caper, 1981, Sadat, 1983 (NAAPC Image award 1983), Children in the Crossfire, 1984 (Prix D'Association Mondiale des Amis de L'Enfants 1985, award Monte Carlo Internat. TV Festival 1985), To Heal a Nation, 1988 (also prodr., Vietnam Vets. Meml. Fund Patriots award, George Washington Honor medal Freedom Found. 1989), The American 1776 (ofcl. U.S. bicentennial film), The Man Who Captured Eichmann, 1996; co-writer, co-prodr. (stage prodn.) We The People...200, 1987; exec. prodr. Evil in Clear River, 1988 (Spl. award Am. Jewish Com., Christopher award); writer, dir., exec. prodr. So Proudly We Hail (Bnai Zion Creative Achievement award 1990), Heroes of the Desert Storm, 1991; exec. prodr., writer, creator (PBS documentary series) Reverse Angle, 1993, The Bible-Jacob, The Bible-Joseph (Emmy award), The Bible-Moses, (cable films) The Doom's Day Gun, Kissinger and Nixon, 1996. Cochair Arts and Entertainment Commn. for Reagan/Bush, L.A., 1978-80; exec. bd. dirs. Can. Ctr. for Advanced Cinema Studies, Toronto, 1986—; mem. exec. bd. L.A. chpt. Am. Jew Com.; named to panel on sexuality and social policy Am. Enterprise Inst.; bd. dirs. Profl. Friends of Dept. Film and Theatre UCLA; mem. nat. com. Vietnam Vets. Meml. Fund. Mem. Acad. Motion Picture Arts and Scis., Acad. TV Arts and Scis., Am. Cinema Found. (pres.), Writers Guild Am. (exec. bd. 1972-76, nat. exec. 1975, Writers Guild award 1974), Writers Guild Britain, Can. Bar Assn., Dirs. Guild Am., Broadcast Music, Inc., Assn. Can. TV and Radio Artists, UCLA Film TV and Edn. Assn. (bd. dirs.), Am. Cinema Found. (pres. 1996-97), Caucus of Writers, Prodrs. and Dirs. (steering com.). Jewish. Office: care Gang Tyre Raymer & Brown 6400 W Sunset Blvd Los Angeles CA 90028-7307

CHEUNG, JOHN B., research and development executive; b. 1943. COO Quest Integrated, Inc., Kent, Wash.; pres. Flow Dril Corp., Kent. Office: Flow Dril Corp 21414 68th Ave S Kent WA 98032-2416*

CHEUNG, KING-KOK, English language educator; b. Hong Kong, Jan. 11, 1954; came to U.S., 1973; m. Gerard M. Maré, Feb. 17, 1984. BA, Pepperdine U., 1975, MA, 1976; PhD, U. Calif., Berkeley, 1984. Asst. prof. English dept. UCLA, 1984-91, assoc. prof., 1991—. Author: Articulate Silences, 1993; editor: Asian American Literature: An Annotated Bibliography, 1988, Seventeen Syllables, 1993, An Interethnic Companion to Asian American Literature, 1996; mem. editl. bd. Asian America, Santa Barbara, Calif., 1991—. Recipient Rsch. fellowship Am. Coun. Learned Socs., 1987-88, Ctr. for Advanced Study in Behavioral Scis., Stanford U., 1995-96. Mem. MLA (chair publs. com. 1992-93, exec. com. divsn. of ethnic studies 1991-93, com. on the lit. and lang. of Am., 1995—), Soc. for the Study of Multi-Ethnic Lits. of the U.S. Office: UCLA Dept English Los Angeles CA 90024-1530

CHEVERS, WILDA ANITA YARDE, probation officer; b. N.Y.C.,; d. Wilsey Ivan and HerbertLee (Perry) Yarde; m. Kenneth Chevers, May 14, 1950; 1 child, Pamela Anita. BA, CUNY, 1947; MSW, Columbia, 1959; PhD, NYU, 1981. Probation officer, 1947-55; supr. probation officer, 1955-65; br. chief Office Probation for Cts. N.Y.C., 1965-72, asst. dir. probation, 1972-77, dep. commr. dept. probation, 1978-86; prof. pub. adminstrn. John Jay Coll. Criminal Justice CUNY, 1986-91; conf. faculty mem. Nat. Council Juvenile and Family Ct. Judges; mem. faculty N.Y.C. Tech. Coll., Nat. Coll. Juvenile Justice; mem. adv. com. Family Ct., First Dept. Sec. Susan E. Wagner Adv. Bd., 1966-70. Sec., bd. dirs. Allen Community Day Care Ctr., 1971-75; bd. dirs. Allen Sr. Citizens Housing, Queensboro Soc. for Prevention Cruelty to Children; chairperson, bd. dir. Allen Christian Sch., 1987-91. Named to Hunter Coll. Hall of Fame, 1983. Mem. ABA (assoc.), N.Y. Acad. Pub. Edn., Nat. Council on Crime and Delinquency, Nat. Assn. Social Workers, Acad. Cert. Social Workers. Middle Atlantic States Conf. Correction, Alumni Assn. Columbia Sch. Social Work, N.Y.U. Alumni Assn., NAACP, Am. Soc. Pub. Adminstrn. (mem. council), Counseliers, Hansel and Gretel Club (pres. 1967-69, Queens, N.Y.). Delta Sigma Theta. Home: 9012 Covered Wagon Ave Las Vegas NV 89117-7010

CHEVERTON, RICHARD E., newspaper editor. BSJ, Northwestern U., 1964, MSJ, 1965. Reporter Chgo. Today, 1970; editor Sunday Mag. Detroit Free Press, 1970-71; asst. editor Sunday Mag., editor review & opinion sect. Phila. Inquirer, 1972-75; mng. editor The New Paper, Phila., 1975; freelance Phila., 1975-76; features editor Phila. Daily News, 1976-79; newsfeatures editor Seattle Times, 1979-81; asst. mng. editor, features Orange County Reporter, Santa Ana, Calif., 1982-90, asst. mng. editor strategy and adminstrn., 1990-91, dep. editor strategy and adminstrn., 1991—; guest lectr. Poynter Inst., Am. Press Inst. Media mgr. Gray for Cong. campaign; speechwriter Friedman for Mayor campaign, Chgo., 1970. With US Army, 1967-69, Vietnam. Decorated Bronze Star; edited series that won Pulitzer Prize for Spl. Local Reporting, 1982. Mem. Am. Assn. Sunday and Feature Editors. Home: 7211 Monterey Ln La Palma CA 90623-1143 Office: The Orange County Register 625 N Grand Ave Santa Ana CA 92701-4347*

CHEW, LINDA LEE, fundraising management executive; b. Riverside, Calif., Mar. 3, 1941; d. LeRoy S. and Grace (Ham) Olson; m. Dennis W. Chew, July 23, 1965; children—Stephanie, Erica. B.Mus., U. Redlands, 1962. Cert. fund raising exec. Dir. pub. events U. Redlands (Calif.), 1962-69; dir. fin. and communications San Gorgonio council Girl Scouts U.S.A., Colton, Calif., 1969-71; exec. dir. United Cerebral Palsy Assn. Sacramento-Yolo Counties, 1972-73; fin. devel. dir. San Francisco Bay coun. Girl Scouts U.S.A., 1973-76; chief devel. and pub. info. East Bay Regional Park Dist., Oakland, Calif., 1976-86; cons. Chew & Assocs., Alamo, Calif., 1986-96; pres. Providence Hosp. Found., Oakland, 1991-92; dir. major gifts Alta Bates Found., Berkeley, Calif., 1996—. Bd. dirs. San Ramon Valley Edn. Found., 1984-88; Calif. Conservation Corps Bay Area Ctr. Adv. Bd., 1988-89; Mem. AAUW (pres. Redlands br. 1968-69), Nat. Soc. Fund Raising Execs. (nat. bd. dirs. 1981-90, nat. vice chmn. 1982-84, pres. Golden Gate chpt. 1979-80, bd. dirs. 1987-90, Abel Hanson Meml. award 1977, Outstanding Fund Raising Exec. 1988), Assn. Healthcare Philanthropy (Region 11 cabinet mem. 1991-94), Am. Guild Organists (dean Riverside-San Bernardino chpt. 1969-71), Pub. Rels. Soc. Am., Alamo Rotary, Oakland Rotary, Lamorinda Volleyball Club (pres. 1994-95). Office: 2450 Ashby Ave Berkeley CA 94705-2067

CHI, BERNADETTE SUN, educational administrator; b. San Francisco, Apr. 1, 1969; d. Yoon Sun and Kee Jae (Lee) C. Student, Yonsei U., Seoul, Korea, 1988; BA in Pub. Policy, Stanford U., 1991; postgrad., U. Calif., Berkeley. Rsch. asst. Integrated Family Svcs. Project, Sacramento, 1990; Stanford student coord. Youth Cmty. Svc., Jane Lathrop Stanford Mid. Sch., Palo Alto, Calif., 1990-91; Youth Engaged in Svc. amb. Points of Light Found., Washington, 1991-92; CalServe asst. coord. Calif. Dept. Edn., L.A. and Sacramento, 1992—; Summer of Svc. program mgr. East Bay Conservation Corps, Oakland, Calif., 1993; co-dir., counselor Camp K.I.T.E. (Korean Identity and Tradition Edn.), San Francisco, 1985-89; Stanford in Washington intern White House Office Nat. Svc., Washington, 1989; Sacramento summer fellows coord. Stanford in Govt., 1990. Contbr. articles to profl. publs. Bd. dirs. Points of Light Found., Washington, 1993—, Pub. Allies, Washington, 1993—; vol. various civic activities; grad. New Generation Tng. Program; mem. steering com. Youth Svc. Calif., 1990-93. George C. Hagen summer lab. fellow U. Calif., Berkeley, 1987, J.E. Wallace Sterling summer fellow, 1989. Mem. AAUW, Asian Ams./Pacific Islanders in Philanthropy, Comm. Network, Calif. Commonwealth Club. Democrat. Roman Catholic.

CHIANG, ALBERT CHIN-LIANG, electrical engineer; b. Putai, Taiwan, Jan. 25, 1937; s. San Chi and Chiu (Hsu) C.; BS in Elec. Engring., Nat. Taiwan U., 1959; MS in Elec. Engring., Chiaotung U., Taiwan, 1963; PhD, U. So. Calif., 1968; m. Steffie F.L. Huang, Dec. 24, 1966; children: Margaret, Stacy, Kathy, George. Came to U.S., 1963, naturalized, 1973. Research asst. U. So. Calif., Los Angeles, 1963-68; engr. specialist Litton Industries, Woodland Hills, Calif., 1968-70; dir. internat. sales Macrodata Co., Woodland Hills, Calif., 1970-77; pres. Tritek Internat. Co., Woodland Hills, Calif., 1977—. Mem. IEEE, Sigma Xi, Eta Kappa Nu. Home: 24132 Lupin Hill Rd Hidden Hills CA 91302-2430 Office: Tritek Internat Co 5000 N Parkway Calabasas Calabasas CA 91302

CHIANG, SAMUEL EDWARD, theological educator, humanities educator; b. Taipei, Taiwan, Republic of China, Oct. 20, 1959; s. William L. and Gladys (Chao) C.; m. Roberta Jean Bush, Dec. 31, 1987; children: Zachariah Asa, Micah Kaleem, Joni Abigail. B. Commerce, U. Toronto (Can.), 1982; MA in Bibl. Studies, Dallas Theol. Sem., 1989. Ordained minister Peoples' Ch., 1990. Writer, researcher Can. Broadcasting Co., Toronto, Ont., Can., 1980-81; audit automation coord. Can. nat. office Ernst & Young, Toronto, 1982-86; asst. to the pres. Dallas Sem. Found., 1988-91; East Asia regional dir. Ptnrs. Internat., San Jose, Calif., 1991—; tchr. Applied Principle of Learning-Walk Thru the Bible, 1990—; bd. dirs. Sharp Master Internat. Ltd. Contbr. articles to profl. jours.; editor, contbr. World Christian Perspective, 1988-91. Youth dir. jr. high The Peoples' Ch., Toronto, 1980-82; youth pastor Korean Philadelphia Presbyn. Ch., Toronto, 1983-85; youth dir. Dallas Chinese Fellowship Ch., 1987-90; bd. dirs. Dallas Chinese Ch. Youth Camps, 1987-91; adv. bd. dirs. I Too Have A Dream, Harare, Zimbabwe, 1989—, Foyer Fraternal, Ndjamena, Chad, 1990—, Student Christian Outreach for China, U.S., 1991; bd. dirs. Asian Impact Ministries, 1992-95, SALT, 1996—, Kingdom Trust, 1992—, BEE, Inc., 1995—; advisor The Tear Found., U.K., 1994—; dir. Sharpmaster Internat., 1996—; chmn. Pu Yang Heng Yuan Agritech Devel. Co. Ltd., 1997—. Mem. Evang. Missiological Soc. Office: PO Box 98583, TST Kowloon Hong Kong Hong Kong *Matters in this world are seldom urgent, except that which lasts for eternity—the souls of individuals.*

CHIAPPINELLI, ERIC ANDREW, law educator; b. Santa Monica, Calif., Mar. 22, 1953; s. Bruno Andrea and Evelyn Audrey (Oliver) C.; m. Gail Lorraine Miller, Apr. 18, 1985 (div. Oct. 1992); 1 child, Peter Miller. BA, Claremont (Calif.) Men's Coll., 1975; JD, Columbia U., 1978. Bar: Calif. Law clk. U.S. Dist. Ct., L.A., 1978-80; assoc. Munger, Tolles & Rickershauser, L.A., 1980-83, Jones, Day, Reavis & Pogue, L.A., 1983-84; law clk. Supreme Ct. of Calif., San Francisco, 1984-85; asst. prof. law U. Puget Sound, Tacoma, 1985-88; assoc. prof. law U. Puget Sound, 1988-94; prof. law Seattle U., Tacoma, 1994—. Republican. Episcopalian. Office: Seattle U Sch Law 950 Broadway Plz Tacoma WA 98402

CHIAPPONE, ROBERT CARL, orthodontist; b. Fresno, Calif., May 4, 1938; s. Carlo Paul and Clotilda Elena (Gaiato) C.; children: Tracy, Christopher, Cary, Craig. BA, U. Calif., Berkeley, 1960; DDS, U. Calif., San Francisco, 1966. Pvt. practice Concord, Calif., 1966—. Contbr. articles to profl. jours. Republican. Home: 1266 Panorama Dr Lafayette CA 94549-2413 Office: 1003 Willow Pass Rd Ste 201 Concord CA 94520-5817

CHIAT, JAY, advertising agency executive; b. N.Y.C., Oct. 26, 1931; s. Sam and Min (Kretchmer) C.; children: Debra, Marc, Elyse. BS, Rutgers U. Prodn. asst. NBC, New York, 1953-54; mgr. of recruit advertising Aero-Jet General Corp., Sacramento & Azusa, CA, 1956-57; v.p. & dir. Leland Oliver Co., Santa Ana, CA, 1957-62; founder, pres. Chiat & Associates, Inc., 1963-68; Chm. Bd., CEO Chiat Day Inc. Advertising, Venice, CA, 1968—. Served with USAF, 1956-57. Office: Chiat/Day Inc Advt 340 Main St Venice CA 90291-2524 Office: Chiat/Day/Mojo Advt 340 Main St Venice CA 90291-2524*

CHIATE, KENNETH REED, lawyer; b. Phoenix, June 24, 1941; s. Mac Arthur and Lillian (Lavin) C.; m. Jeannette Jensen, Aug. 21, 1965; children: Gregory Jensen, Carley McKay. B.A. with honors, Claremont Men's Coll., 1963; J.D., Columbia U., 1966; postgrad. U. So. Calif. Law Sch., 1967. Bar: Calif. 1967, U.S. Dist. Ct. (cen. dist.) Calif. 1967, Ariz. 1971, U.S. Dist. Ct. Ariz. 1971, U.S. dist. (no. dist.) Calif. 1982. Law clk. presiding justice U.S. Dist. Ariz., 1971; ptnr. Lillick McHose & Charles, L.A., 1966-91, Pillsbury Madison & Sutro, L.A., 1991—; arbitrator Los Angeles Superior Ct. Arbitration Panel, 1979-82; mcpl. ct. judge protem Los Angeles, 1979-81; mem.

Jury Instrn. Com. Los Angeles County, 1991—. Vice chmn. Los Angeles Open Com., 1969-71. Mem. ABA, Los Angeles County Bar Assn., Calif. State Bar Assn., Ariz. State Bar Assn., Maricopa County Bar Assn., So. Calif. Def. Assn., Am. Trial Lawyers Assn., Maritime Law Assn. of U.S.A., Los Angeles Port Propeller Club, mem. L.A. B.A.J.I. com., 1993-95. Office: Pillsbury Madison 725 S Figueroa St Ste 1200 Los Angeles CA 90017-5443

CHICOREL, MARIETTA EVA, publisher; b. Vienna, Austria; came to U.S., 1939, naturalized, 1945; d. Paul and Margaret (Gross) Selby. AB, Wayne State U., 1951; MALS, U. Mich., 1961. Asst. chief library acquisitions div. U. Wash., Seattle, 1962-66; project dir. Macmillan Info. Scis., Inc., N.Y.C., 1968-69; pres. Chicorel Library Pub. Corp., N.Y.C., 1969-79, Am. Library Pub. Co., Inc., 1979—; pub. cons. Creative Solutions Co., 1986—; asst. prof. dept. libr. sci. CUNY (Queens Coll.), 1986—; mem. edn. com. Gov.'s Commn. on Status of Women, Wash., 1963-65; instr. libr. scis. No. Ariz. U., Flagstaff, 1990; bd. dirs. Skills Devel. Tng. counseling; pub. cons. creative solutios. Chief editor: Ulrich's International Periodicals Directory, 1966-68; editor, pub.: Chicorel Indexes, 1969—; founding editor: Jour. Reading, Writing and Learning Disabilities International, 1985-90; contbr. chpt. on univs. to Library Statistics: A Handbook of Concepts, Definitions and Terminology, 1966. Mem. ALA (exec. bd. tech. svcs. divsn. 1965-68, chmn. libr. materials price index com. 1968-69, councillor 1969-73), Am. Assn. Profl. Cons., Am. Book Prodrs. Assn., Book League N.Y. (bd. govs. 1975-79), Am. Soc. for Info. Sci., Can. Libr. Assn., Pacific N.W. Libr. Assn., N.Y. Libr. Club, N.Y. Tech. Svcs. Librarians. Home and Office: PO Box 4272 Sedona AZ 86340-4272

CHIHOREK, JOHN PAUL, electronics company executive; b. Wilkes-Barre, Pa., June 22, 1943; s. Stanley Joseph and Caroline Mary C.; m. Cristina Maria Marroquin, Dec. 28, 1968; children: Jonathan, David, Crista, Daniel. BSEE, Pa. State U., 1965; postgrad., Calif. State U., San Diego, 1970-71; MBA, Calif. State U., Sacramento, 1972. Program officer Hdqrs. Air Force Logistic Command, Dayton, Ohio, 1972-75; sr. engr. Hdqrs. Air Force Space Div., L.A., 1975-78; mgr. software systems dept. Logicon Inc., San Pedro, Calif., 1978; mgr. software product assurance dept. Loral Aeronutronics, Rancho Santa Margarita, Calif., 1978-85, mgr. software engring., 1985—; pres. CMC Sys. Inc. Mem. Congl. Adv. Bd., 1980; active PTA, mem. Republican Nat. com. Served with USN, 1965-70, Vietnam. Decorated Bronze Star. Mem. IEEE (mgmt. bd. Computer Soc., exec. com. on standard), AAAS, Engring. Mgmt. Soc. (sec. bd. govs.), Air Force Assn., Internat. Platform Assn. Roman Catholic. Clubs: Lions, Odd Fellows. Office: Loral Aeronutronics Ford Rd Newport Beach CA 92633

CHIKALLA, THOMAS DAVID, retired science facility administrator; b. Milw., Sept. 9, 1935; s. Paul Joseph and Margaret Ann (Dittrich) C.; m. Ruth Janet Laun, June 20, 1960; children: Paul, Mark, Karyn. BS in Metallurgy, U. Wis., 1957, PhD in Metallurgy, 1966; MS in Metallurgy, U. Idaho, 1960. Research scientist Gen. Electric Co., Richland, Wash., 1957-62; sr. research scientist Battelle Pacific N.W. Labs., Richland, 1964-72, sect. mgr., 1972-80, programs mgr., 1980-83, dept. mgr., 1983-86, assoc. dir., 1986-95; ret., 1995; tchr. U. Wis., Madison, 1962-64. Contbr. articles to profl. jours. Fellow AEC. Fellow Am. Ceramic Soc. (counselor 1974-80); mem. AAAS, Am. Nuclear Soc., Sigma Xi. Republican. Roman Catholic. Clubs: Desert Ski (pres. 1958-59), Alpine. Home: 2108 Harris Ave Richland WA 99352-2021

CHILDRESS, DORI ELIZABETH, nursing consultant; b. Chgo., Jan. 25, 1945; d. John Fredrick and Doris Eleanor (Clark) Klafin; m. Larry Dunn, May 3, 1969 (div. Aug. 21, 1975); m. Terry Childress, May 17, 1986. BSN, Calif. State U., Chico, 1976; MSN, Calif. State U., Chica, 1983. Cert. prof. in healthcare quality; RN, Calif. Critical care nurse Kaiser Permanente, Sacramento, 1977-82; dir. nursing edn. Rancho Arroyo Vocat. Tech., Sacramento, 1979-86; nurse cons. State of Calif. Dept. Health, Sacramento, 1986—. With U.S. Army N.G., 1980-84, flight nurse USAFR, 1984-88, 94. Recipient State Pub. Health award Dept. Health Svcs., State of Calif., Sacramento, 1994, Superior Sustained award for outstanding performance, 1997. Mem. ANA (nat. com. curriculum devel. managed care program 1994), Nat. Assn. Healthcare Quality Profls., Calif. Assn. Healthcare Quality Profls., Toastmasters Internat. (area gov. 1992-93, dist. sgt.-at-arms 1989-90, Outstanding Area Gov. award 1993), Sigma Theta Tau. Home: 2510 Auburn Rd Lincoln CA 95648-9451 Office: State of Calif Dept Health Medi-Cal Managed Care Divsn 714 P St Rm 692 Sacramento CA 95814-6414

CHILDS, JOHN DAVID, computer hardware and services company executive; b. Washington, Apr. 26, 1939; s. Edwin Carlton and Catherine Dorothea (Angerman) C.; m. Margaret Rae Olsen, Mar. 4, 1966 (div.); 1 child, John-David. Student Principia Coll., 1957-58, 59-60; BA, Am. U., 1963. Jr. adminstr. Page Communications, Washington, 1962-65; account rep. Friden Inc., Washington, 1965-67; Western sales dir. Data Inc., Arlington, Va., 1967-70; v.p. mktg. Rayda, Inc., Los Angeles, 1970-73, pres., 1973-76, chmn. bd., 1976-84; v.p. sales Exec. Bus. Systems, Encino, Calif., 1981-87, sr. v.p. sales and mktg., 1987—; sr. assoc. World Trade Assocs., Inc., 1976—. Pres. Coll. Youth for Nixon-Lodge, 1959-60, dir. state fedn.; mem. OHSHA policy formulation com. Dept. Labor, 1967. Served with USAFR, 1960-66. Mem. Assn. Data Ctr. Owners and Mgrs. (chmn. privacy com. 1975, sec. 1972-74, v.p. 1974). Democrat. Christian Scientist. Office: 3089 Clairemont Dr # 213 San Diego CA 92117-6802

CHILES, WILTON RICHARDSON, electrical engineer; b. Greenville, S.C., Aug. 15, 1936; s. Wilton Richardson and Margaret Elizabeth (Skinner) C.; m. Dorothy Mae Stoky, Mar. 29, 1958; children: Derek Wilton, Devin Richardson. B in Elec. Engring. magna cum laude, U. Fla., 1960; MS in Elec. Engring., U. Pa., 1966. Design engr. RCA, Camden, N.J., 1960-66; sr. design engr. Gen. Elec., Phoenix, 1966-70; design engring. exec. Honeywell, Phoenix, 1970-88; sr. cons. engr. NCR, San Diego, 1988—; referee, session chair Internat. Test Conf., Washington, 1992—. Holder patent in field. Mem. IEEE (tech. working group 1991—). Republican. Home: 12658 Hickory Ct Poway CA 92064-3239 Office: NCR 17095 Via Del Campo San Diego CA 92127-1711

CHIMSKY, MARK EVAN, editorial executive; b. Cin., Jan. 24, 1955; s. Matthew and Jean (Berger) C.; life ptnr. Robert Ira Lustig. BA, Carnegie-Mellon U., 1976. Editor Anderson Pub. Co., Cin., 1977-79; copy editor Book-of-the-Month Club, Quality Paperback Book Club, N.Y.C., 1979-85; mng. editor Quality Paperback Book Club, N.Y.C., 1985-89, exec. editor, 1989-91; editor in chief Collier Books, Macmillan Co., N.Y.C., 1991-94; dir. trade paperbacks Little, Brown and Co., N.Y.C., 1994-96; exec. editor Harper, San Francisco, 1996, editl. dir., 1996—. Contbr. essays and poetry to lit. jours. Office: Harper San Francisco 353 Sacramento St Ste 500 San Francisco CA 94111-3653

CHIN, JANET SAU-YING, data processing executive, consultant; b. Hong Kong, July 27, 1949; came to U.S., 1959; d. Arthur Quock-Ming and Jenny (Loo) C. BS in Math, U. Ill., Chgo., 1970; MS in Computer Sci., U. Ill., Urbana, 1973. System programmer Lawrence Livermore (Calif.) Lab., 1972-79; sect. mgr. Tymshare Inc., Cupertino, Calif., 1979-83, Fortune Systems, Redwood City, Calif., 1983-85; div. mgr. Impell Corp, Berkeley, Calif., 1985; pres. Chin Assocs., Oakland, Calif., 1985-88; bus. devel. mgr. Sun Microsystems, Mountain View, Calif., 1988-92; engring. dir. Cadence Design Systems, San Jose, Calif., 1992-94, quality dir., 1994-95; asst. to CEO Avant! Corp., Sunnyvale, Calif., 1995—; provost World Inst. of Tech., Sunnyvale, 1996—; Vice-chmn. Am. Nat. Standards Inst. X3H3, N.Y.C., 1979-82, internat. rep. X3H3, 1982-88. Co-author: The Computer Graphics Interface, 1991; contbr. tech. papers to profl. publs. Mem. Assn. Computing Machinery, Sigma Xi.

CHIN, JENNIFER YOUNG, public health educator; b. Honolulu, June 22, 1946; d. Michael W.T. and Sylvia (Ching) Young; BA, San Francisco State Coll., 1969; M.P.H., U. Calif., Berkeley, 1971; m. Benny Chin, Nov. 16, 1975; children: Kenneth Michael, Lauren Marie, Catherine Rose. Edn. asst. Am. Cancer Soc., San Francisco, 1969-70; intern Lutheran Med. Ctr., Bklyn., 1971; community health educator Md. Dept. Health and Mental Hygiene, Balt., 1971-74; community health educator Northeast Med. Svcs., San Francisco, 1975; pub. health educator Child Health and Disability Prevention, San Francisco Public Health Dept., 1975-83; health educator maternal and child health, 1991-95, Breast and Cervical Cancer Control Program, 1995—. USPHS grantee, 1970-71. Mem. Soc. No. Calif. Pub. Health Edn. (treas. 1976, 77), Am. Public Health Assn. Office: 101 Grove St Rm 321 San Francisco CA 94102

CHIN, KELVIN HENRY, legal association executive, mediator, consultant; b. Boston, Jan. 7, 1951; s. Henry W.F. and King (Lee) C.; m. Peggy Abbott, July 26, 1987; children: Jesse, Samantha. Student, U. Strasbourg, France, 1971; AB cum laude, high distinction in French, Dartmouth Coll., 1973; MA, Yale U., 1974; JD, Boston Coll., 1983. Dir. in East Asia Found. for Creative Intelligence, Seelisberg, Switzerland, 1974-78; founding dir., corp. sec. Microtex Corp., Cambridge, Mass., 1978-83; life ins. agent Sun Life of Canada, Wellesley, Mass., 1979-81; law clerk Bingham, Dana & Gould, Boston, 1980-83; summer assoc. to assoc. Choate, Hall & Stewart, Boston, 1982-84; employee benefits cons. Hicks Pension Svcs., Lexington, Mass., 1984-86; founder The Mediation Office of Kelvin Chin, Boston, San Diego, 1986-92; mediation coord. AAA Ctr. for Mediation, Am. Arbitration Assn., San Diego, 1992-93; regional v.p. Am. Arbitration Assn., Las Vegas, Nev., 1993-96, L.A., 1996—; assoc. dir. Ctr. for Med. Ethics and Mediation, San Diego, 1992—; cons. Area Agy. on Aging, San Diego, 1991-93, San Diego Mediation Ctr., 1990-93, Continuing Edn. of the Bar, Calif. 1992—, Mediation Action Guide, 1993—, Bus. Practice Group, 1993—, Litigation Group, 1993—. Editor: International Law Dictionary, 1983. Ombudsman Calif. Dept. on Aging, San Diego, 1991-93; com. mem. Waldorf Sch. of San Diego PTA, 1992-93; vol. mediator Ctr. for Mcpl. Dispute Resolution City Atty.'s Office, San Diego, 1990-93. Rufus Choate scholar Dartmouth Coll., 1971-73; Nat. Def. Fgn. Language fellow U.S. Dept. Edn., 1973-74. Mem. ABA (dispute resolution sect.), Am. Arbitration Assn. (blue ribbon mediator panel 1992—), San Diego County Bar Assn. (treas. alternative dispute resolution sect. 1991-93), Soc. Profls. in Dispute Resolution, Dispute Resolution Forum, So. Calif. Mediation Assn., The Ombudsman Assn., Nat. Panel of Mediators, Nat. Assn. Securities Dealers. Office: Am Arbitration Assn 3055 Wilshire Blvd Los Angeles CA 90010-1108

CHIN, MING, judge; b. Klamath Falls, Oreg., Aug. 31, 1942; m. Carol Lyn Joe, Dec. 19, 1971; children: Jennifer, Jason. BA in Polit. Sci., U. San Francisco, 1964, JD, 1967. Bar: Calif., 1970, U.S. Fed. Ct., U.S. Tax Ct. Assoc., head trial dept. Aiken, Kramer & Cummings, Oakland, Calif., 1973-76, prin., 1976-88; dep. dist. atty. Alameda County, Calif., 1970-72; judge Alameda County Superior Ct., 1988-90; assoc. justice divsn. 3 Ct. Appeal 1st Dist., 1990-94; presiding justice 1st Dist. Ct. Appeal Divsn. 3, San Francisco, 1994-96; assoc. justice Calif. Supreme Ct., San Francisco, 1996—. Capt. U.S. Army, 1967-69, Vietnam, USAR, 1969-71. Mem. ABA, Calif. Judges Assn., State Bar Calif., Alameda County Bar Assn., San Francisco Dist. Atty.'s Commn. Hate Crimes, Asian Am. Bar Assn., Alpha Sigma Nu. Office: Supreme Ct Rm 8023 South Tower 8th Fl 303 Second St San Francisco CA 94107

CHIN, SUE SOONE MARIAN (SUCHIN CHIN), conceptual artist, portraitist, photographer, community affairs activist; b. San Francisco; d. William W. and Soo-Up (Swebe) C. Grad. Calif. Coll. Art, Mpls. Art Inst., (scholar) Schaeffer Design Ctr.; student, Yasuo Kuniyoshi, Louis Hamon, Rico LeBrun. Photojournalist, All Together Now show, 1973, East-West News, Third World Newscasting, 1975-78, Sta. KNBC Sunday Show, L.A., 1975, 76, Live on 4, 1981, Bay Area Scene, 1981; graphics printer, exhbns. include Kaiser Ctr., Zellerbach Pla., Chinese Culture Ctr. Galleries, Capricorn Asunder Art Commn. Gallery (all San Francisco), Newspace Galleries, New Coll. of Calif., L.A. County Mus. Art, Peace Pla. Japan Ctr., Congress Arts Communication, Washington, 1989; SFWA Galleries, Inner Focus Show, 1989—, Calif. Mus. Sci. and Industry, Lucien Labaudt Gallery, Salon de Medici, Madrid, Salon Renacimento, Madrid, 1995, Life Is a Circus, SFWA Gallery, 1991, 94, UN/50 Exhibit, Bayfront Galleries, 1995, Somar Galleries, 1997, Sacramento State Fair, AFL-CIO Labor Studies Ctr., Washington, Asian Women Artists (1st prize for conceptual painting, 1st prize photography), 1978, Yerba Buena Arts Ctr. for the Arts Festival, 1994; represented in permanent collections L.A. County Fedn. Labor, Calif. Mus. Sci. and Industry, AFL-CIO Labor Studies Ctr., Australian Trades Coun., Hazeland and Co., also pvt. collections; author (poetry) Yuri and Malcolm, The Desert Sun. 1994 (Editors Choice award 1993-94). Del. nat., state convs. Nat. Women's Polit. Caucus, 1977-83, San Francisco chpt. affirmative action chairperson, 1978-82, nat. conv. del., 1978-81, Calif. del., 1976-81. Recipient Honorarium AFL-CIO Labor Studies Ctr., Washington, 1975-76; award Centro Studi Ricerche delle Nazioni, Italy, 1985; bd. advisors Psycho Neurology Found. Bicentennial award L.A. County Mus. Art, 1976, 77, 78. Mem. Asian Women Artists (founding v.p., award 1978-79, 1st award in photography of Orient 1978-79), Calif. Chinese Artists (sec.-treas. 1978-81), Japanese Am. Art Coun. (chairperson 1978-84, dir.), San Francisco Women Artists, San Francisco Graphics Guild, Pacific/Asian Women Coalition Bay Area, Chinatown Coun. Performing and Visual Arts. Chmn., Full Moon Products; pres., bd. dir. Aumni Oracle Inc. Address: PO Box 421415 San Francisco CA 94142-1415

CHIN, WANDA WON, graphics designer; b. L.A., July 10, 1952; d. John Ah and Lui Shui (Leung) Chin; m. Terry Paul Dickey, Feb. 3, 1982; children: Emile, Pierre. BA, UCLA, 1974. Graphic designer KCOP-13 TV, L.A., 1977-78, KTTV-11 TV, L.A., 1978; exhibits designer U. Alaska Mus., Fairbanks, 1979-84, coord. exhibits, 1984—; U.S. judge World Ice Sculpture Competition, 1996. Artist fiber sculptures: Trading Ways, 1983, Magnetic Forces, 1985, Vuelo, 1986, Thrust Away, 1990; artist metal sculpture: Transformations, 1991. Panelist Dept. Natural Resources, Art in Pub. Places, Fairbanks, 1988-89; mem. State of Alaska Coun. on Arts, 1991-96; bd. dirs. Dance Omnium, 1982; mem. gov.'s tourism coord. com. State of Alaska, 1992; organizer, designer Arctic Winter Games, 1986. Fellow Kellogg Found., 1982, 87, NEA/Rockefeller Found., 1976. Mem. Nat. Assn. Mus. Exhibitors, Fairbanks Arts Assn., Am. Assn. of Mus., Mus. Alaska, Western Museums Assn. (bd. dirs. 1996—), Western States Arts Fedn. (trustee 1994-96), Inst. Alaska Native Arts, North Star Borough Chinese Assn., Asian Am. Women in Am. Office: Univ of Alaska Mus 907 Yukon Dr Fairbanks AK 99775

CHIÑAS, BEVERLY NEWBOLD, anthropologist, retired educator; b. Minden, Nebr., Sept. 1, 1924; d. Lewis Francis and Glennie Athel (Shoemaker) Newbold; m. Carlos Chiñas, Aug. 27, 1969. BA in Anthropology/Sociology, Fresno State Coll., 1963; MA in Anthropology, UCLA, 1965, PhD in Anthropology, 1968. Faculty dept. anthropology Calif. State U., Chico, 1968-94, prof. emerita, 1994—; vis. prof. dept. anthropology UCLA, 1981; vis prof. Oberlin (Ohio) Coll., 1981; organizer, chair various symposia. Author: Las Mujeres de San Juan: Los Papeles Economicos de Las Mujeres Zapotecas del Istmo de Tehuantepec, Mexico, 1975, The Isthmus Zapotecs, revised edit., 1992, La Zandunga: Of Fieldwork and Friendship in Southern Mexico, 1993; contbr. articles to profl. jours. John and Dora Haynes grad. fellow UCLA, 1963, NSF grad. fellow, 1966; NSF doctoral dissertation rsch. grantee, 1966, travel grantee Am. Coun. Learned Socs., Lima, Peru, 1970, Wenner-Gren Found. field rsch. grantee, 1982, NEH grantee, 1982. Mem. Southwestern Anthropol. Assn. (pres. 1984-85), Sigma Xi (chpt. pres. 1984-85). Office: Calif State U Dept Anthropology Chico CA 95929

CHINCHINIAN, HARRY, pathologist, educator; b. Troy, N.Y., Mar. 7, 1926; s. Ohaness and Armen (Der Arakelian) C.; m. Mary Corcoran, Aug. 22, 1952; children: Armen, Marjorie, Matthew. BA, U. Colo., 1952; MS, Marquette U., 1956, MD, 1959. Cert. anatomic and clin. pathologist. Co-dir. Pathologists Regional Labs., Lewiston, Idaho, 1964-96; chief of staff Tri-State Hosp., Clarkston, Wash., 1967, St. Joseph's Hosp., Lewiston, 1971; assoc. prof. pathology Wash. State U., Pullman, 1972-97. Author: Antigens to Melanoma, 1957, Parasitism and Natural Resistance, 1958, Pathologist in Peril, 1996, Immigrant Son, 1996, Murder in the Mountains, 1997; co-author: Malakoplakia, 1957, Pneumocystis, 1965. Pres. Am. Cancer Soc., Asotin County, Wash., 1968, Lewiston Roundup, 1972-73, N.W. Soc. Blood Banks, 1973-74. Sgt. U.S. Army, 1944-46. Fellow Am. Coll. Pathologists (cert., lab. inspector 1970—), Am. Soc. Clin. Pathologists; mem. Idaho Soc. Pathologists (pres. 1970). Home: 531 Silcott Rd Clarkston WA 99403-9784

CHINERY, JAMES PATRICK, marketing professional; b. Glendale, Calif., July 1, 1959; s. Donald William and Cateline Joan (Mishler) C.; m. Heather Marion Vincent, Nov. 16, 1996. BA, UCLA, 1982. Prodn. mgr. Banyan Design, Broomfield, Colo., 1985-88; cons. The Shibui Co., Denver, 1989; mktg. dir. Dieterich & Ball, Prescott, Ariz., 1990—; cons. Citizens for Health, Newport Beach, Calif., 1992-94. Contbr. articles to profl. jours. Office: Dieterich & Ball 624 Calero Ave San Jose CA 95123

CHING, ERIC SAN HING, health care and insurance administrator; b. Honolulu, Aug. 13, 1951; s. Anthony D.K. and Amy K.C. (Chong) C. BS, Stanford U., 1973, MS, MBA, 1977. Fin. analyst Mid Peninsula Health Service, Palo Alto, Calif., 1977; acting dep. exec. dir. Santa Clara County Health Systems Agy., San Jose, Calif., 1977-78; program officer Henry J. Kaiser Family Found., Menlo Park, Calif., 1978-84; dir. strategic planning Lifeguard Health Maintenance Orgn., Milpitas, Calif., 1984-90; v.p. strategic planning and dir. ops. Found. Life Ins. Co., Milpitas, 1986-90; sr. planning analyst Kaiser Found. Health Plan, Oakland, Calif., 1990-94, coord. product and competition analysis, 1994-95, mgr. ins. ops. and competitive intelligence cons., 1995—; adj. faculty Am. Pistol Inst., 1991-94. Mem. vol. staff Los Angeles Olympic Organizing Com., 1984; mem. panel United Way of Santa Clara County, 1985, panel chmn., 1986-87, mem. com. priorities and community problem solving, 1987-90, Project Blueprint, 1988-90. Mem. NRA, ACLU, Am. Soc. Law Enforcement Trainers, Internat. Assn. Law Enforcement Firearms Instrs., Internat. Wound Ballistics Assn., Soc. Competitive Intelligence Profls., Stanford Alumni Assn., Stanford Bus. Sch. Alumni Assn., Stanford Swordmasters (pres. 1980-89). Office: Kaiser Found Health Plan Inc One Kaiser Pla 25th Fl Oakland CA 94612

CHINN-HECHTER, MAMIE MAY, nonprofit organization executive; b. Oakland, Calif., Aug. 20, 1951; d. Bing T. and Georgia S. (Ong) C.; m. Marc S. Hechter. BS in Bus., U. Nev., 1974. Loan processor First Fed. Savs. and Loan, Reno, 1974-75, loan processor supr., 1975-76, sr. loan counselor, affirmative action officer, 1977-78; jr. loan officer First Fed. Savs. and Loan, Carson City, Nev., 1976-77; loan officer State of Nev. Housing Divsn., Carson City, 1978-79, loan adminstr., 1979-83, dep. adminstr., 1983-93; pres., CEO Nev. Comty. Reinvestment Corp., Las Vegas, 1993—; mem. exec. com. Housing and Devel. Fin., Ethics Com., Media and Comms. Com., Carson City, 1987-93. Bd. mem. Nev. Cmty. Reinvestment Corp., 1991—; bd. com. Nev. Housing and Neighborhood Devel., Inc., 1994—, state low income housing trust fund, 1994—; mem. United Way Planning Coun., 1995—; mem. cmty. adv. bd. Nev. State Bank; participant C. of C. Leadership Las Vegas, 1996. Mem. Capitol City (Carson City sec. 1984-88), Women's Bowling Assn. (bd. dirs. 1983-84), Nat. 600, Asian C. of C. Office: Nev Comty Reinvestment Corp 5920 W Flamingo Rd Ste 8 Las Vegas NV 89103-0109

CHIOLIS, MARK JOSEPH, television executive; b. Walnut Creek, Calif., Dec. 29, 1959; s. Richard Spiro and Muriel Marie (Kottinger) C. Student aeronautics, Sacramento Community Coll., 1980-82; student, American River Coll., 1982. With on-air ops. Sta. KRBK-TV, Sacramento, 1979-81; on-air ops. trainer, crew chief Sta. KVIE-TV, Sacramento, 1981-85; trainer on air ops., ops. crew chief Sta. KRBK-TV, Sacramento, 1981-84; producer, dir., ops. crew chief Sta. KVIE-TV, Sacramento, 1985-87, Sta. KRBK-TV, Sacramento, 1984-87; prodn. mgr., producer, dir. Sta. KVIE-TV, Sacramento, 1987—; production mgr., producer, dir. spl. programs, comml. productions Sta. KRBK-TV, Sacramento, 1987—; with on-air ops. Sta. KVIE-TV, Sacramento, 1980-82; regional sales mgr. BTS-Broadcast T.V. Systems, Inc., 1992—; promotion chmn. Capital Concour d'Elegance, Sacramento, 1984—, gen. chmn., 1987-89. Producer (music videos) Running Wild, Running Fee, 1984, Rocket Hot-/The Image, 1984 (Joey award 1985); producer, dir. (music video) Haunting Melodies, 1991; dir. (documentary) Behind Closed Doors, 1984; producer, dir. FLIGHTLOG, The Jerry Reynolds Show, CountryMile country music show, 1991; dir. (video camera) Reno Nat. Championship Air Races, 1992, 93, 94, 95, 96, Money Insights, 1993; tech. video dir. for state franchise bd. Tax Talk, 1992, 93, 94, 96, Teleconf. uplinks. Video producer Calif. N.G., 1980-82; video trainer Am. Cancer Soc., Sacramento, 1983-85; cons. Sacramento Sheriff's Dept., Sacramento, 1984—, United Way-WEAVE, Sacramento, 1984-85; bd. dirs. Woodside Homeowners Assn., 1989—. Recipient Gold Addy award, 1986, 87, Addy award, 1989. Mem. Calif. Broadcasters Assn. (bd. dirs. 1996—), Am. Advt. Fedn., Sacramento Advt. Club (awards video producer 1984—, chmn. judging 1988-89, bd. dirs. 1989—, co-chair awards banquet 1989-90), Aircraft Owners and Pilots Assn., Computer Users Group. Republican. Office: Philips Broadcast TV Sys 111 N 1st St Ste 100 Burbank CA 91502-1851

CHIPMAN, JACK, artist; b. L.A., Oct. 31, 1943; s. George Geotz and June Naomi (Hanson) C. BFA, Calif. Inst. Arts, 1966. Dealer Calif. pottery Calif. Spectrum, Redondo Beach, 1980-90; cons. Schroeder Pub., Paducah, Ky., 1982—. Author: Complete Collectors Guide Bauer Pottery, 1982, Collectors Encyclopedia California Pottery, 1992, Collector's Guide to Bauer Pottery, 1997, (periodicals) Antique Trader Weekly, 1981-83, Am. Clay Exch., 1982-88; one-person shows include Oakland Mus. Calif., Long Beach Mus. Art, U. Santa Clara Art Mus.; represented in permanent collections at Oakland (Calif.) Art Mus., Long Beach (Calif.) Mus. Art, U. Santa Clara (Calif.) Art Mus. Bd. dirs. Angels Gate Cultural Ctr., San Pedro, Calif., jour. editor, 1990-93. Office: PO Box 1079 Venice CA 90294-1079

CHIROT, DANIEL, sociology and international studies educator; b. Bélâbre, Indre, France, Nov. 27, 1942; came to U.S., 1949; s. Michel and Hélène C.; m. Cynthia Kenyon, July 19, 1974; children: Claire, Laura. BA in Social Studies, Harvard U., 1964; PhD in Sociology, Columbia U., 1973. Asst. prof. sociology U. N.C. Chapel Hill, 1971-74; asst. prof. to prof. internat. studies and sociology Henry M. Jackson sch. U. Wash., 1975—; mem. joint com. Ea. Europe of Am. Coun. Learned Socs. and Social Sci. Rsch. Coun., 1976-77, 82-88; acad. adv. bd. East European program Woodrow Wilson Ctr., 1990-95; chair Russian and East European studies program U. Wash., 1988-91; vis. prof. sociology Nat. Taiwan U., 1989; vis. prof. polit. sci. Northwestern U., Evanston, Ill., 1993, U. Calif., San Diego, 1996. Author: Social Change in a Peripheral Society, 1976, Social Change in the Twentieth Century, 1977, translations: Korean, 1984, Italian, 1985, Social Change inthe Modern Era, 1986, translations: Korean, 1984, Chinese, 1991, Modern Tyrants: The Power and Prevalence of Evil in Our Age, 1994, rev. edit., 1996, How Societies Change, 1994; translator: (with Holley Coulter Chirot) Traditional Romanian Villages (Henri H. Stahl), 1980; editor: The Origins of Backwardness in Eastern Europe, 1989, The Crisis of Leninism and the Decline of the Left, 1991; consulting editor Am. Jour. Sociology, 1986-88; founder and editor Ea. European Politics and Socs., 1986-89. Cons. for Radio Free Europe, 1985. John Simon Guggenheim fellow 1991-92; guest scholar Rockefeller Found. Study Ctr., Bellagio, Italy, 1992; vis. fellow Institut für die Wissenschaften vom Menschen, Vienna, 1992. Office: U Washington Jackson Sch Intl Studies 503 Thompson Hall Seattle WA 98195

CHISHOLM, DAVID HOLLISTER, German studies educator; b. New Rochelle, N.Y., Aug. 30, 1940; s. Robert Kerr and Margaret Sale (Covey) C.; m. Ana Carmen Valdés-Estay, May 9, 1971; children: Claudia Carmen, Andrew David. BA, Oberlin Coll., 1962; postgrad., U. Erlangen, Germany, 1962-63; MA, U. Chgo., 1965; PhD, Ind. U., 1971. Postdoctoral fellow U. Cin., 1971-72; vis. asst. prof. U. Ill., Urbana, 1972-73; asst. prof. German studies U. Ariz., Tucson, 1973-77, assoc. prof., 1977-83, prof., 1983—; vis. prof. German Summer Sch. of N.Mex., Taos, 1985, 86, 90, 93; lectr. U. Hamburg, Germany, 1967-68. Author: Goethe's Knittelvers, 1975; co-editor/compiler: Verse Concordance: C.F. Meyer, 1982, Concordance to Goethe's Faust, 1986; mem. editorial bd. Lit. and Linguistic Computing, 1986—. Alexander von Humboldt rsch. grantee, 1979-80, 81-82; Fulbright grantee, 1977, 82; Ctr. for Interdisciplinary Studies grantee, Bielefeld, Germany, 1983; ACLS grantee, 1973-74, 83. Mem. MLA, Am. Assn. Tchrs. German (tech. com. 1993—), Assn. for Computers and the Humanities, Assn. for Lit. and Linguistic Computing, Text-Encoding Initiative, Fulbright Alumni Assn. Office: U Ariz Dept German Studies Tucson AZ 85721

CHISHOLM, TOM SHEPHERD, environmental engineer; b. Morristown, N.J., Nov. 28, 1941; s. Charles Fillmore and Eileen Mary (Fenderson) C.; m. Mary Virginia Carrillo, Nov. 7, 1964; children: Mark Fillmore, Elaine Chisholm. Student, Northeastern U., Boston, 1959-61; BS in Agrl. Engring., N.Mex. State U., 1964; MS in Agrl. Engring., S.D. State U., 1967; PhD in Agrl. Engring., Okla. State U., 1970. Registered profl. engr., Ariz., La.; cert. Class A indsl. wastewater operator. Agrl. engr. U.S. Bur. Land Mgmt., St. George, Utah, 1964-65; asst. prof. U. P.R., Mayaguez, 1970-74, La. State U., 1974-77; assoc. prof. S.D. State U., 1977-81; environ. engr. Atlantic Richfield Subsidiary, Sahuarita, Ariz., 1981-86, Ariz. Dept. Environ. Quality, Phoenix,

1986-88; environ. mgr. Galactic Resources, Del Norte, Colo., 1988-91; v.p. M&E Cons., Inc., Phoenix, 1991-94; pres. Chisholm & Assocs., Phoenix, 1991—; v.p. 3R Resources, Tucson, 1994—; cons. various mfrs., Calif., Tex., Ill., Mex., 1980-91. Contbr. articles to profl. jours. NSF fellow, 1965-66, 68-69. Mem. Am. Soc. Agrl. Engrs. (faculty advisor student chpt. 1978-79), Phi Kappa Phi, Sigma Xi, Alpha Epsilon, Beta Gamma Epsilon. Office: Chisholm & Assocs PO Box 47554 Phoenix AZ 85068-7554

CHISHTI, NADEEM AHMAD, physician; b. Faisalabad, Pakistan, Aug. 15, 1961; came to U.S., 1988; s. Mumtaz A. and Zubeda B. (Begum) C.; m. Fazi Tubusam, Jan. 20, 1988 (div. Nov. 1993); m. Adeela Tufail, Dec. 31, 1995. Student, Govt. Coll., Pakistan, 1976-78; MD, Punjab Med. Sch., Pakistan, 1985. Rsch. asst. U. Calif. Davis Med. Ctr., Sacramento, 1989-90; intern U. So. Calif. Med. Ctr., L.A., 1990-91, resident, 1991-93, chief resident, 1993-94; fellow U. Calif. Irvine Med. Ctr., Orange, 1994—. Mem. AMA, ACP, Am. Coll. Chest Physicians. Home: 8623 E Canyon Vista Dr Anaheim CA 92808-1621 Office: 101 The City Dr S Orange CA 92868-3201

CHITTICK, ARDEN BOONE, steamship agency executive; b. Sunnyside, Wash., Aug. 5, 1936; s. Herbert Boone and Maude Ellen (George) C.; m. Nina Sorensen, Apr. 16, 1960; children: Kyle, Kirsten. BS, Wash. State U., 1964. Ops. mgr. Kerr Steamship Co. Inc., Seattle, 1979-81, marine mgr. PNW, 1981-84; dist. ops. mgr. Merit Steamship Agy. Inc., Seattle, 1984-86, Pacific N.W. ops. mgr., 1986-87; ops. mgr. Internat. Shipping Co. Inc., Seattle, 1987-89, v.p. ops., 1989-91, regional v.p. ops., 1991-96; v.p. Internat. Shipping Co. Inc., Portland, Oreg., 1991-96, bd. dirs., dir., 1996—; v.p. Marine Exch. of Puget Sound, Seattle, 1982-88; pres. Puget Sound Steamship Operators Assn., Seattle, 1987, v.p., 1983, 86, 95. Troop com. mem. Boy Scouts Am., Bainbridge Island, Wash., 1984. Capt. USMCR, 1957-64; comdr. USCG, 1964-79. Mem. Puget Sound Coast Guard Officers Assn. (pres. 1978), Propeller Club of U.S. (gov. Seattle chpt. 1984-87, 89-94). Republican. Methodist. Home: 8380 NE Blakely Heights Dr Bainbridge Is WA 98110-3200 Office: Internat Shipping Co Inc 1111 3rd Ave Ste 1825 Seattle WA 98101-3207

CHIU, JOHN TANG, physician; b. Macao, Jan. 8, 1938; s. Lan Cheong and Yau Hoon C.; m. Bonnie Doolan, Aug. 28, 1965 (div. Apr. 1986); children: Lisa, Mark, Heather. Student, Harvard U., 1959; BA, U. Vermont, 1960, MD, 1964. Diplomate Am. Bd. Allergy & Immunology. Pres. Allergy Med. Group, Inc., Newport Beach, Calif., 1969-72, 1972—; assoc. clin. prof. medicine U. Calif., Irvine, 1975—. Contbr. articles to profl. jours. Active Santa Ana Heights Adv. Commn., 1982-83; life mem. Orange County Sheriff's Adv. council, 1987—. Recipient Freshman Chem. Achievement award, Am. Chem. Soc., 1958. Fellow Am. Acad. Allergy and Immunology, Am. Coll. Allergy and Immunology, Am. Coll. Chest Physicians (sec. steering com. allergy 1977-81), Orange County Med. Assn. (chmn. communications com. 1985-88, communications com.). Office: Allergy Med Group Inc 400 Newport Center Dr Newport Beach CA 92660-7601

CHIU, PETER YEE-CHEW, physician; b. China, May 12, 1948; came to U.S., 1965; naturalized, 1973; s. Man Chee and Yiu Ying (Cheng) C. BS, U. Calif., Berkeley, 1969, MPH, 1970, DrPH, 1975; MD, Stanford U., 1983. Diplomate Am. Bd. Family Practice; registered profl. engr., Calif.; registered environ. health specialist, Calif. Asst. civil engr. City of Oakland, Calif., 1970-72; assoc. water quality engr. Bay Area Sewage Services Agy., Berkeley, 1974-76; prin. environ. engr. Assn. Bay Area Govts., Berkeley, 1976-79; intern San Jose (Calif.) Hosp., 1983-84, resident physician, 1984-86; ptnr. Chiu and Crawford, San Jose, 1986-89, Good Samaritan Med. Group, San Jose, 1989-90, The Permanente Med. Group, 1991—; adj. prof. U. San Francisco, 1979-83; clin. asst. prof. Stanford U. Med. Sch., 1987—. Contbr. articles to profl. publs.; co-authored one of the first comprehensive regional environ. mgmt. plans in U.S.; composer, pub. various popular songs Southeast Asia, U.S. mem. Chinese for Affirmative Action, San Francisco, 1975—; bd. dirs. Calif. Regional Water Quality Control Bd.,Oakland, 1979-84, Bay Area Comprehensive Health Planning Coun., San Francisco, 1972-76; mem. Santa Clara County Ctrl. Dem. Com., 1987—; mem. exec. bd. Calif. State Dem. Ctrl. Com.; commr. U.S. Presdl. Commn. on Risk Assessment and Risk Mgmt., Washington, 1993-97. Recipient Resident Tchr. award Soc. Tchrs. Family Medicine, 1986, Resolution of Appreciation award Calif. Regional Water Quality Control Bd., 1985. Fellow Am. Acad. Family Physicians; mem. Am. Pub. Health Assn., Chi Epsilon, Tau Beta Pi. Democrat. Office: The Permanente Med Group 770 E Calaveras Blvd Milpitas CA 95035-5491

CHIU, REBECCA OI-MUI, elementary education educator; b. Kowloon, Hong Kong, Oct. 16, 1953; came to U.S., 1971; d. David Chi-Kwong and Betty Wai-Lan (Kwok) Chan; m. Morson Mao-Sung Chiu, June 14, 1980; 1 child, Christian Enoch. BA in Music Edn., Azusa Pacific U., 1976, MA in Edn., 1977, cert. in teaching, 1989. Cert. adult edn. tchr., bi-lingual competency, Calif. Instr. Presbyn. Bible Coll., Hsinchu, Taiwan, 1978-80, Luth. Sem., Hsinchu, 1979-80, Christian Coll., Taipei, Taiwan, 1979-80; supr. INFO LIne, El Monte, Calif., 1980—; mentor/tchr. Emerson Sch./Garvey Sch. Dist., Rosemead, Calif., 1985—; lectr. Azusa Pacific U., 1987-88; mem. adv. bd. edn. dept. Azusa Pacific U., 1988—, instr. theol. sem., Chinese for Christ; founder Innovative Tchg. Inst., Rosemead, 1995—. Mem. Chinese Grace Ch., Duarte, Calif.; mem. Asian task force San Gabriel Valley, L.A.; mem. ethnic minority task force County of L.A. Mem. Nat. Tchrs. Assn., Calif. Tchrs. Assn., Calif. Music Tchrs. Assn., Suzuki Assn. Americas, Lions. Home: 132 Avila Way Claremont CA 91711-1823

CHIVERTON, LORRAINE MORGAN, developmental specialist; b. Vancouver, B.C., Can., Aug. 26, 1956; came to U.S., 1959; d. William Everard and Patricia Edith (Charlesworth) Turner; m. David Robert Beck (div. 1982). AA, Cabrillo Coll., 1977; AAS, Pima Coll., 1996. Presch. co-tchr. Desert Oasis, Tucson, 1989-91; counter person Bentleys, Tucson, 1991-93; constrn. worker William North Constrn., Tucson, 1992-94; sales counselor Bob's, Tucson, 1993-95; counselor TCWC, Tucson, 1994-96; developmental specialist NDRI, Tucson, 1997—. Vol. Pre-Trial Svcs., Tucson, 1988, Reid Park Zoo, Tucson, 1986. Recipient trophy Freedom Run-TJC, 1992, Tucson Roadrunners, 1994. Mem. Audubon Soc. (award 1997), Bodhistativa Inst., 5th St. Fitness.

CHO, DEAN DEUK, computer company executive; b. Teajon, South Korea, Oct. 27, 1963; came to the U.S., 1972; s. Seog Whan and Sahng Chun (Lee) C. BS, U. Calif., Riverside, 1986. Cert. Novell network adminstrn., Calif. Network sys. mgr. Managed Health Network, L.A., 1988-89; programmer analyst Blue Cross, Woodland Hills, Calif., 1989-91; dir. computing and info. sys. Internat. Studies and Overseas Programs UCLA, 1991—; pres., owner Beyond Techs., Torrance, Calif., 1988—. Pres., founder Korean Student Assn., U. Calif., Riverside, 1985-86. Recipient Outstanding Alumnus award U. Calif., Riverside, 1992, Svc. award U. Calif., Riverside, 1992. Mem. Asian Pacific Alumni Assn. (pres., founder U. Calif. Riverside 1991—, Svc. award 1992), UCLA Adminstrs. and Suprs. Assn., South Bay Network. Home: 4323 Artesia Blvd Torrance CA 90504-3107 Office: Univ Calif LA 11252 Bunche Hall Los Angeles CA 90024

CHO, LEE-JAY, social scientist, demographer; b. Kyoto, Japan, July 5, 1936; came to U.S., 1959; s. Sam-Soo and Kyung-Doo (Park) C.; m. Eun-Ja Chun, May 20, 1973; children: Yun-Kyong Nuy, Sang-Mun Ray, Han-Jae Jeremy. BA, Kookmin Coll., Seoul, Korea, 1959; MA in Govt., George Washington U., 1962; MA in Sociology (Population Council fellow), U. Chgo., 1964, PhD in Sociology, 1965; D in Econs. (hon.), Dong-A U., 1982; DSc in Demography, Tokyo U., 1983; D in Econs., Keio U., Tokyo, 1989. Statistician Korean Census Council, 1958-61; research assoc., asst. prof. sociology Population Research and Tng. Center, U. Chgo., 1965-66; asso. dir. Community and Family Study Center, 1969-70; sr. demographic adv. to Malaysian Govt., 1967-69; assoc. prof. U. Hawaii, 1969-73, prof., 1973-78; asst. dir. East-West Population Inst., East-West Center, Honolulu, 1971-74; dir. East-West Population Inst., East-West Center, 1974-92; pres. pro tem East-West Center, 1980-81, v.p., 1987—; cons. in field; mem. Nat. Acad. Scis. Com. on Population and Demography; mem. U.S. 1980 Census Adv. Com., Dept. Commerce. Author: (with others) Differential Current Fertility in the United States, 1970; editor: (with others) Introduction to Censuses of Asia and the Pacific: 1970-74, 1976, (with Kazumasa Kobayashi) Fertility Transition in East Asian Populations, 1979, (with Suharto, McNicoll and Mamas) Population Growth of Indonesia, 1980, The OWN Children of Fertility Estimation, 1986, (with Y.H. Kim) Economic Development of Republic of Korea: A Policy Perspective, 1989, (with Kim) Korea's Political Economy: An Institutional Perspective, 1994, (with Yada) Tradition and Change in the Asian Family, 1994; contbr. numerous articles on population and econ. devel. to profl. jours. Bd. dirs. Planned Parenthood Assn., Hawaii, 1976-77. Ford Found. grantee, 1977-79; Population Council grantee, 1973-75; Dept. Commerce grantee, 1974-78; recipient Award of Mugunghwa-Jang, govt. Republic of Korea, 1992. Mem. Internat. Statis. Inst. (tech. adv. com. World Fertility Survey), Internat. Union Sci. Study Population, Population Assn. Am., Am. Statis. Assn., Am. Sociol. Assn., N.E. Asia Econ. Forum (founding chmn.). Home: 1718 Halekoa Dr Honolulu HI 96821-1027 Office: 1777 E West Rd Honolulu HI 96822-2323 *The survival and welfare of the future generations will depend largely upon what we do today to plan and manage human population growth and sustainable development.*

CHO, SUNG-NEI CHARLES, physician; b. Kaesong, Korea, Nov. 10, 1934; came to U.S., 1954; naturalized, 1967; s. In-Jei and Kum-Sun (Kim) C.; m. Kyung-Jai Lee, Apr. 16, 1959; children: Irene, Wesley. BS magna cum laude, Piedmont Coll., 1957, D of Humanities, 1982; MD, U. Kans., 1962. Diplomate Am. Bd. Family Practice. Intern St. Joseph Hosp., Wichita, Kans., 1962-63, resident in pathology, 1963-64; resident in gen. practice Ventura (Calif.) County Med. Ctr., 1964-66; pvt. practice in family medicine, 1969—; attending and teaching staff family practice residency program Ventura County Med. Ctr., 1966-86, also courtesy staff mem., chmn. dept. family practice, 1976-77; mem. active staff St. John's Regional Med. Ctr., Oxnard, Calif., chmn. dept. ob-gyn., 1975-76, chmn. dept. family practice, 1980-81; pres., CEO Ventura County Ind. Physicians-IPA subs., 1981-93, med. cons. Found. Health, 1993—; founder, CEO Ventura County HMO, 1979-90, also bd. dirs. Bd. trustees Piedmont Coll., Demorest, Ga., 1984—. Lt. comdr. USN, 1967-69. Mem. AMA, Am. Acad. Family Physicians, Am. Acad. Physician Execs., Am. Coll. Occupational and Environ. Medicine, Calif. Med. Assn., Ventura County Med. Soc. (bd. govs. 1973-75, 81-83, treas. 1981-83), Kiwanis (pres. 1989-90). Home: 4372 Clubhouse Dr Somis CA 93066-9708

CHOCK, CLIFFORD YET-CHONG, family practice physician; b. Chgo., Oct. 15, 1951; s. Wah Tim and Leatrice (Wong) C. BS in Biology, Purdue U., 1973; MD, U. Hawaii, 1978. Intern in internal medicine Loma Linda (Calif.) Med. Ctr., 1978-79, resident in internal medicine, 1979; resident in internal medicine U. So. Calif.-L.A. County Med. Ctr., L.A., 1980; physician Pettis VA Clinic, Loma Linda, Calif., 1980; pvt. practice Honolulu, 1981—; physician reviewer St. Francis Med. Ctr., Liliha, Hawaii,, 1985—, chmn. Quality Care for Family Practice, 1990-93, 95; chmn. credentials Family Practice, 1990-93, 95-96, acting chmn. credentials com.; physician reviewer Peer Rev. Orgn. Hawaii, Honolulu, 1987-93; chmn. dept. family practice St. Francis Med. Ctr., Liliha, 1994—. Fellow Am. Acad. Family Physicians, Internat. Platform Assn. Office: 321 N Kuakini St Ste 513 Honolulu HI 96817-2361

CHODOROW, NANCY JULIA, sociology educator; b. N.Y.C., Jan. 20, 1944; d. Marvin and Leah (Turitz) C.; children: Rachel Esther Chodorow-Reich, Gabriel Issac Chodorow-Reich. BA, Radcliffe Coll., 1966; PhD, Brandeis U., 1975; grad., San Francisco Psychoanalytic, 1993. From lectr. to assoc. prof. U. Calif., Santa Cruz, 1974-86; from asst prof. sociology to prof. U. Calif., Berkeley, 1986—; faculty San Francisco Psychoanalytic Inst., 1994—. Author: The Reproduction of Mothering, 1978 (Jessie Bernard award 1979), Feminism and Psychoanalytic Theory, 1989, Femininities, Masculinities, Sexualities, 1994; contbr. articles to profl. jours. Fellow Russell Sage Found., NEH, Ctr. Advanced Study Behavioral Scis., ACLS, Guggenheim fellow. Mem. Am. Psychoanalytic Assn., San Francisco Psychoanalytic Soc. Office: U Calif Dept Sociology Barrows Hall Berkeley CA 94720

CHOI, JAI JOON, scientist, researcher, educator; b. Kyung-Joo, South Korea, Mar. 2, 1958; came to U.S., 1985; s. Byung-Ha and Kun-Sook (Lee) C.; m. Janice Chinki Min, June 23, 1985; children: Laura, Kathryn. BSE, Inha U., Inchon, Korea, 1979, MSE, 1981; MSEE, U. Wash., 1987, PhD in Elec. Engring., 1990. Mem. faculty Korean Air Force Acad., Seoul, 1981-85; sr. prin. scientist Boeing Info. and Support Svcs., Seattle, 1990—; affiliate asst. prof. and grad. faculty U. Wash., Seattle, 1992—; adj. faculty Henry Cogswell Coll., Everett, Wash., 1991—; cons. Flaw Industry, Kent, Wash., 1988; session chair World Congress on Computational Intelligence, Orlando, Fla., 1994, Internat. Symposium on Circuits and Sys., Seattle, 1995, Northcon Conf., Seattle, 1992, Internat. Conf. on Neural Networks, Washington, 1996. Assoc. editor: Fuzzy Logic Technology and Applications, 1994; contbr. articles to profl. jours.; 3 invention disclosures. Capt. Korean Air Force, 1981-85. Mem. IEEE (mem. tech. program com. Internat. Symposium on Circuits and Systems 1995, assoc. editor Trasn. on Neural Networks 1994), Eta Kappa Nu. Home: 24623 SE 37th St Issaquah WA 98029-6558 Office: Boeing Info & Support Svcs PO Box 24346 7L-44 Seattle WA 98124

CHOMKO, STEPHEN ALEXANDER, archaeologist; b. Bklyn., Nov. 18, 1948; s. Paul and Lucy Isabella (Bisaccio) C.; m. Leslie M. Howard, Aug. 1972 (div. 1980). BA in Anthropology cum laude, Beloit Coll., 1970; MA in Anthropology, U. Mo., 1976. Mem. rsch. staff Nassau County Mus. Natural History, Glen Cove, N.Y., 1969-71; grad. rsch. asst. U. Mo., Columbia, 1972-74, 75-78; rsch. asst. Ill. State Mus., Springfield, 1974-75; dist. archaeologist Bur. Land Mgmt., Rawlins, Wyo., 1978-80; archaeologist Office of Fed. Inspector, Denver, 1980-82; dir. Paleo Environ. Cons., Wheat Ridge, Colo., 1980-86; archaeologist Interagy. Archaeol. Svcs., Denver, 1982-92; chief rsch. and resource mgmt. Mesa Verde (Colo.) Nat. Park, 1992; chief tng. mgmt. Fort Carson, 1994—. Writer, dir. (video program) Our Past Our Future, 1992; contbr. articles to profl. jours. Grantee Cave Rsch. Found., Yellow Springs, Ohio, 1976; Anthropology scholar U. Mo., Columbia, 1978; recipient Quality Performance award Nat. Park Svc., Denver, 1992, 93, Environ. Quality award Dept. of Army, 1996, Environ. Stewardship award Dept. of Def., 1997. Mem. Soc. Am. Archaeology, Am. Anthropol. Assn., Am. Quaternary Assn., Wyo. Assn. Profl. Archaeologists (exec. com. 1979-82), Mont. Archaeol. Soc., Plains Anthropol. Soc. (v.p. 1988-89, bd. dirs. 1986-89). Home: 1144 Rock Creek Canyon Rd Colorado Springs CO 80926-9772 Office: Decam Attn AFZC-ECM Bldg 302 Fort Carson CO 80917

CHOMSKY, MARVIN J., director; b. N.Y.C., May 23, 1929. B.S., Syracuse U.; M.A., Stanford U. Dir. films including Evel Knievel, 1971, Murph the Surf, 1974, MacKintosh and T.J., 1975, Good Luck, Miss Wycoff, 1979, Tank, 1983; dir. TV movies Assault on the Wayne, 1971, Mongo's Back in Town, 1971, Family Flight, 1972, Fireball Forward, 1972, Female Artillery, 1973, The Magician, 1973, The FBI Story--Alvin Karpis, 1974, Mrs. Sundance, 1974, Kate McShane, 1975, Victory at Entebbe, 1976, Brink's: The Great Robbery, 1976, Law and Order, 1976, A Matter of Wife...and Death, 1976, Danger in Paradise, 1977, Little Ladies of the Night, 1977, Hollow Image, 1979, Inside Attica, 1980 (Emmy award), King Crab, 1980, I Was a Mail Order Bride, 1982, My Body, My Child, 1982, Nairobi Affair, 1984, Anastasia, 1986, Billionaire Boys Club, 1987, Angel Green, 1987, Telling Secrets, 1992, Hurricane Andrew, 1993; dir. TV mini-series including Attack on Terror, 1975, Roots, 1977, Holocaust, 1978 (Emmy award), Evita Peron, 1981, Inside the Third Reich, 1982 (Emmy award), RFK and His Times, 1985, The Deliberate Stranger, 1986, Peter the Great, 1986 (Emmy award), Brotherhood of the Rose, 1988, Strauss Dynasty, 1990, Catherine the Great, 1994. Office: care David B Cohen 131 Spinnaker Mall Marina Del Rey CA 90292-7263

CHOOK, EDWARD KONGYEN, university official, disaster medicine educator; b. Shanghai, Apr. 15, 1937; s. Shiu-heng and Shuiking (Shek) C.; m. Ping Ping Chew, Oct. 30, 1973; children by previous marriage: Miranda, Bradman. MD, Nat. Def. Med. Ctr., Taiwan, 1959; MPH, U. Calif., Berkeley, 1964, PhD, 1969; ScD, Phila. Coll. Pharmacy & Sci., 1971; JD, La Salle U., 1994. Assoc. prof. U. Calif., Berkeley, 1966-68; dir. higher edn. Bay Area Bilingual Edn. League, Berkeley, 1970-75; prof., chancellor United U. Am., Oakland and Berkeley, Calif., 1975-84; regional adminstr. U. So. Calif., L.A., 1984-90; provost Armstrong U., Berkeley, 1994—; pres. Shanghai Internat. Coll., 1997—; vis. prof. Nat. Def. Med. Ctr., Taiwan Armed Forces U., 1982—, Tongji U., Shanghai, 1992, Foshan U., China, 1992—; cons. specialist Beijing Hosp., 1988—; founder, pres. United Svc. Coun., Inc., 1971—; pres. Pan Internat. Acad., Changchun, China and San Francisco, 1979—, China Gen. Devel. Corp., U.S., 1992—; pub. Power News, San Francisco, 1979—; mem. NAS-NRC, Washington, 1968-71; spl. cons. cultural sensitivity seminars; spl. lectr. KPMG/Peat Warwick Accts., 1996. Assoc. editor U.S.-Chinese Times, 1996—; pub. US-China Times, 1996—; contbr. articles to profl. jours. Trustee Rep. Presdl. Task Force, Washington, 1978—; advisor on mainland China affairs Ctrl. Com. Chinese Nationalist party, Taiwan, 1994—; deacon Am. Bapt. Ch.; sr. advisor U.S. Congl. Adv. Bd.; mem. Presdl. Adv. Commn., 1991—; hon. dep. sec. of state State of Calif., 1990-93; spl. advisor to sec. of state, 1991—; pres. Yuen Kong Found. for Internat. Understanding, 1994-96, 96—; mem. Nat. Heart Coun., 1994—; senatorial commn. Rep. Senatorial Inner Cir., 1996. Mem. World Affairs Coun. San Francisco, Rotary (com. chmn. 1971—). Office: Adminstrn Office 555 Pierce St # B-2 Albany CA 94706-1044

CHOOLJIAN, LEO, food products executive; b. 1911. Now pres. Chooljian Bros. Packing Co., Inc., Sanger, Calif., 1949—. Office: 3192 S Indianola Ave Sanger CA 93657-9716*

CHOOLJIAN, MEHRAN, food products executive; b. 1918. Now v.p., sec. Chooljian Bros. Packing Co., Inc., Sanger, Calif., 1949—. Office: 3192 S Indianola Ave Sanger CA 93657-9716*

CHOPRA, INDER JIT, physician, endocrinologist; b. Gujranwala, India, Dec. 15, 1939; came to U.S., 1967; s. Kundan Lal and Labhwati (Bagga) C.; m. Usha Prakash, Oct. 16, 1966; children: Sangeeta, Rajesh, Madhu. B of Medicine and BS, All India Inst. Med. Scis., New Delhi, India, 1961, MD, 1965. Intern All India Inst. Med. Scis., New Delhi, 1961-62, clin. resident, 1962-65, registrar in medicine, 1966-67; resident Queens Med. Ctr., Honolulu, 1967-68; fellow in endocrinology Harbor Gen. Campus UCLA Sch. Medicine, 1968-71; asst. prof. of medicine UCLA, 1971-74, assoc. prof., 1974-78, prof., 1978—; mem. VA Merit Review Bd in Endocrinology, 1988-91. Contbr. more than 250 rsch. articles, revs. and book chpts. to profl. lit. Recipient Rsch. Career Devel. award, NIH, 1972. Fellow Am. Coll. Physicians; mem. Endocrine Soc. (Ernst Oppenheimer award 1980), Am. Thyroid Assn. (Van Meter-Armour award 1977, Parke-Davis award 1988), Am. Soc. Clin. Investigation, Assn. of Am. Physicians, Western Assn. Physicians, Am. Fed. for Clin. Rsch. Office: UCLA Sch Medicine Ctr for Health Scis 10833 Le Conte Ave Los Angeles CA 90024-1602

CHOPYAK-MINOR, CHRISTINE MARIE, school administrator, educator; b. Denver, Sept. 28, 1963; d. Joseph Leo and Angela Veronica (Augustine) Chopyak; m. Craig Baxter Minor, Jan. 20, 1991. BA in English, Lewis and Clark Coll., 1985. Mktg./pub. rels. specialist City Spirit Café, Denver; environ. edn. cons. Frederick County Parks and Recreation, Winchester, Va., 1988-90; adminstrv. coord. Forum Medicum, Inc., Berryville, Va., 1988-90; pastry chef Gaspard's Restaurant, Winchester, Va., 1989-90; environ. edn. cons. Va. State Arboretum, Blandy, Va.; adminstrv. coord. Forum Medicum, Inc., Berryville, Va.; field instr., asst. dir., dir. mktg. Keystone (Color.) Sci. Sch., 1990—; mem. edn. adv. bd. recruiting Colo. Bird Observatory, Brighton; prin. investigator NSF Young Scholar's Program, Keystone; active N.Am. Curriculum Survey-Nat. Fish and Wildlife Found. Ornithol. Curriculum Survey, Vt.; mem. com. on sci. edn. K-12 NRC-NAS, Washington, 1996; mem. edn. expo Environ. Edn. Pavillion, 1993-94. Author, editor: Jour. Nat. Sci. Edn. Standards-Informal Sci. Edn., 1996; author, creator: Environ. Awareness Programs Electronic Network for Tchrs., 1989-91. Recipient Va. State-Keeping Am. Beautiful award State of Va., 1990. Mem. NSTA, Colo. Alliance Environ. Edn. (bd. dirs.), Nat. Assn. Biology Tchrs., N.Am. Alliance Environ. Edn., Assn. Experiential Edn., 10th Mountain Hut Assn., Breckenridge Optimists. Office: Keystone Sci Sch PO Box 8606 1053 Soda Ridge Rd Keystone CO 80435

CHORLTON, DAVID, writer; b. Spittal-An-Der-Drau, Carinthia, Austria, Feb. 15, 1948; came to U.S., 1978; s. Frederick and Ernestine (Eder) C.; m. Roberta, June 21, 1976. Student, Stockport Sch. of Art, 1966-69. Graphic designer Pifco Co. Ltd., Manchester, Eng., 1969-71, Steinbock & Co., Vienna, Austria, 1971-72, Persil Ges-MBH, Vienna, 1972-75; editor The Current, Phoenix, 1991-93. Author: (poetry books) Outposts, 1994, Forget the Country You Came From, 1992; co-editor: (mag.) The Signal, 1986-92; dir. Alwun House Poetry Series, Phoenix, 1979-83. Bd. dirs. Ariz. Ctr. to Reverse the Arms Race, Phoenix, 1990-92, Ariz. Composers Forum, Phoenix, 1987-89; pres. Phoenix Early Music Soc., 1987-88. Home: 118 W Palm Ln Phoenix AZ 85003-1176

CHOU, TAI-YU, electrical engineer; b. Heng-Chun, Taiwan, China, Apr. 27, 1959; came to U.S., 1987; s. I-Kuan and Kue-Mei Chou; m. Chi-Ho Wang, July 26, 1986; 1 child, Robin Meng-Zoo. BSEE, Nat. Cheng-Kung U., Tainan, Taiwan, 1982; MSEE, Nat. Tsing-Hua U., Hsinchu, Taiwan, 1984; PhD, Carnegie Mellon U., 1991. Product and test engr. MOS Electronic Corp., Hsinchu, 1986-87; devel. engr. Ansoft Corp., Pitts., 1991-93; sr. staff engr. LSI Logic Corp., Fremont, Calif., 1993-96; dir. Express Packaging Systems, Inc., Palo Alto, Calif., 1996; staff engr. Sun Microsystems, Inc., Menlo Park, Calif., 1997—; conf. session chmn. 1st Internat. Symposium on Microelectronic Package and PCB Tech.; mem. com. Electronic Component and Tech. Conf.; chmn. Surface Mount Internat.; reviewer 1995 IEEE/ACM Design Automation Conf.; spkr. in field. Contbr. articles to profl. jours. Lt. Chinese Navy, 1982-84. Mem. IEEE, Internat. Electronic Packaging Soc., Chinese Inst. Engrs. (electronic packaging and mfg. com. mem. Bay Area chpt. 1993—), Circuit and System Soc., Microwave Technique and Tech. Soc. Home: 2371 Meadowlark Dr Pleasanton CA 94566-3116

CHOW, CHUEN-YEN, engineering educator; b. Nanchang, Jiangsi, China, Dec. 5, 1932; came to U.S., 1956; s. Pan-Tao and Huei-Ching (Yang) C.; m. Julianna H.S. Chen, June 26, 1960; children: Chi Hui, Chi Tu, Chi An. BSME, Nat. Taiwan U., 1954; MS in Aero. Engring., Purdue U., 1958; SM in Aeronautics and Astronautics, MIT, 1961; PhD in Aero. and Astro. Engring., U. Mich., 1964. Asst. prof. U. Notre Dame, Ind., 1965-67, assoc. prof., 1967-68; assoc. prof. U. Colo., Boulder, 1968-76, prof. engring., 1976—; aeronautics curriculum adv. com. USAF Acad., Colorado Springs, Colo., 1980—, disting. vis. prof., 1979-80. Author: An Introduction to Computational Fluid Mechanics, 1979; co-author: Foundations of Aerodynamics, 1986. Fellow AIAA (assoc.); mem. Sigma Xi. Office: Univ of Colorado Dept Aerospace Enging Sci Boulder CO 80309-0429

CHOW, FRANKLIN SZU-CHIEN, obstetrician, gynecologist; b. Hong Kong, Apr. 15, 1956; came to U.S., 1967; s. Walter Wen-Tsao and Jane Ju-Hsien (Tang) C. BS, CCNY, 1977; MD, U. Rochester, 1979. Diplomate Am. Bd. Ob-Gyn. Intern Wilmington (Del.) Med. Ctr., 1979-80, resident in ob-gyn, 1980-83; practice medicine specializing in ob-gyn Vail (Colo.) Valley Med. Ctr., 1983—, chmn. obstetrics com., 1984-85, 86-87, chmn. surg. com., 1987-88, vice chief of staff, 1989-91, chief of staff, 1991-92. Named to Athletic Hall of Fame, CCNY, 1983. Fellow Am. Coll. Ob-Gyn's; mem. AMA, Colo. Med. Soc., Intermountain Med. Soc. (pres. 1985-86), Internat. Fedn. Gynecol. Endoscopists, Am. Assn. Gynecol. Laparoscopists, Gynecologic Laser Soc., Am. Soc. Colposcopy and Cervical Pathology. Home: Box 5657 401 Winslow Rd Vail CO 81688-5657 Office: Vail Valley Med Ctr 181 W Meadow Dr Ste 600 Vail CO 81657-5058

CHOW, JUDY, library science and information sciences educator; b. Taipei, Taiwan, Feb. 13, 1954; came to U.S., 1964; d. Charles and Lucy (Chu) C.; m. Steve Lee, July 3, 1982; children: Andrew Chow Lee, Mike Chow Lee. BA, UCLA, 1975, MLS, 1977. Libr. L.A. County Pub. Libr., 1979-84, L.A. Pub. Libr., 1984-90; faculty mem. L.A. C.C., 1990—. Mem. Calif. Libr. Assn., Faculty Assn. of Calif. C.Cs. Buddhist. Office: LA CC 4800 Freshman Dr Culver City CA 90230-3519

CHOW, WINSTON, engineering research executive; b. San Francisco, Dec. 21, 1946; s. Raymond and Pearl C.; m. Lilly Fah, Aug. 15, 1971; children: Stephen, Kathryn. BSChemE, U. Calif. Berkeley, 1968; MSChemE, Calif. State U., San Jose, 1972; MBA cum laude, Calif. State U., San Francisco, 1985. Registered profl. chem. and mech. engr.; instr.'s credential Calif. Community Coll. Chem. engr. Sondell Sci. Instruments, Inc., Mountain View, Calif., 1971; mem. R & D staff Raychem Corp., Menlo Park, Calif., 1971-72; supervising engr. Bechtel Power Corp., San Francisco, 1972-79; sr. project mgr. water quality and toxic substances control program Electric

Power Rsch. Inst., Palo Alto, Calif., 1979-89, program mgr., 1990—. Editor: Hazardous Air Pollutants: State-of-the-Art, 1993; co-editor: Clean Water: Factors that Influence Its Availability, Quality and Its Use, 1996; co-author: Water Chlorination, vols. 4, 6; contbr. articles to profl. jours. Pres., CEO Directions, Inc., San Francisco, 1985-86, bd. dirs., 1984-87, chmn. strategic planning com., 1984-85; industry com. Am. Power Conf., 1988—; chmn. Dist. Cen. Com., 1992-94; strategic long-range planning and restructuring com. Sequoia Union H.S. Dist., 1990-93. Recipient Grad. Disting. Achievement award, 1985; Calif. Gov.'s Exec. fellow, 1982-83. Mem. ASME, AIChE (profl. devel. recognition award), NSPE, Calif. Soc. Profl. Engrs. (pres. Golden Gate chpt. 1983-84, v.p. 1982-83, state dir.), Water Environ. Fedn., Air and Waste Mgmt. Assn. (mem. electric utility com. 1990—), Calif. State U. Alumni Assn. (bd. dirs., treas. 1989-91), U. Calif. Alumni Assn., Beta Gamma Sigma. Democrat. Presbyterian. Office: Electric Power Rsch Inst 3412 Hillview Ave Palo Alto CA 94304-1395

CHOWNING, ORR-LYDA BROWN, dietitian; b. Cottage Grove, Oreg., Nov. 30, 1920; d. Fred Harrison and Mary Ann (Bartels) Brown; m. Kenneth Bassett Williams, Oct. 23, 1944 (dec. Mar. 1945); m. Eldon Wayne Chowning, Dec. 31, 1959. BS, Oreg. State Coll., 1943; MA, Columbia U., 1950. Dietetic intern Scripps Metabolic Clinic, LaJolla, Calif., 1944; sr. asst. dietitian Providence Hosp., Portland, Oreg., 1945-49; contact dietitian St. Lukes Hosp., N.Y.C., summer 1949; cafeteria food svc. supr. Met. Life Ins. Co., N.Y.C., 1950-52; set up food svc. and head dietitian McKenzie-Willamette Meml. Hosp., Springfield, Oreg., 1955-59; foods dir. Erb Meml. Student Union, Eugene, Oreg., 1960-63; set up food svc. and head dietitian Cascade Manor Retirement Home, Eugene, 1967-68; owner, operator Veranda Kafe, Inc., Albany, Oreg., 1971-80; owner, operator, sec.-treas. Chownings Adult Foster Home, Albany, 1984—. Contbr. articles to profl. jours. Lin County Women's chmn. Hatfield for Senator Spaghetti Rally, Albany H.S., 1966; food preparation chmn. Yi for You, Mae Yih for State Senate, Albany Lebanon, Sweet Home, 1982; Silver Clover Club sponsor Oreg. 4-H Found., Oreg. State U., Corvallis, 1994, 95, 96. Recipient coll. scholarship Nat. 4-H Food Preparation Contest, Chgo., 1939. Mem. Am. Dietetic Assn. (registered dietitian, gerontol. nutritionist dietetic practice group 1988—), Oreg. Dietetic Assn. (diet therapy chairperson, newsletter editor 1963-64), Willamette Dietetic Assn., Kappa Delta Pi (Kappa chpt.), Mu Beta Beta. Republican. Mem. Disciples of Christ. Home and Office: Chownings Adult Foster Home 4440 Woods Rd NE Albany OR 97321-7353

CHOY, HERBERT YOUNG CHO, judge; b. Makaweli, Hawaii, Jan. 6, 1916; s. Doo Wook and Helen (Nahm) C.; m. Dorothy Helen Shular, June 16, 1945. BA, U. Hawaii, 1938; JD, Harvard U., 1941. Bar: Hawaii 1941. Law clk. City and County of Honolulu, 1941; assoc. Fong & Miho, 1947-57; ptnr. Fong, Miho and Choy, 1957-58; atty. gen. Territory of Hawaii, 1958-71; ptnr. Fong, Miho, Choy & Robinson, Honolulu, 1958-71; sr. judge U.S. Ct. Appeals, Honolulu, 1971—; adv. com. on constrn. judiciary bldgs. Chief Justice Hawaii, 1970-71; compilation commn. to compile Revised Laws of Hawaii, 1955, 1953-57; com. to draft Hawaii rules of criminal procedure Supreme Ct., 1958-59; com. on pacific ocean territories Jud. Conf. the U.S., 1976-79. Dir. Legal Aid Soc. Hawaii, 1959-61; trustee Hawaii Loa Coll., 1963-79. Capt. U.S. Army, 1941-46, lt. col. Res. Recipient Order of Civil Merit award Republic of Korea, 1973. Fellow Am. Bar Found.; mem. ABA, Hawaii Bar Assn. (exec. com. 1953, 57, 61, legal ethics and unauthorized practices com. 1953, com. on legis. 1959). Office: US Ct Appeals PO Box 50127 Honolulu HI 96850

CHOYKE, GEORGE RAYMOND, safety educator, consultant; b. Ferndale, Mich., July 2, 1929; s. George Francis Choyke and Blanche Marie (Archambeau) Gordon; m. Ruth Marion Whaley, Jan. 8, 1982; children: Kip Noble Hayes, Falene Darby. Student, U. Mich., 1951-54, San Diego State U., 1967-70, U. Calif., La Jolla, 1961-63, 64-65; BS in Liberal Arts, Regents Coll., U. State N.Y., 1994. Spanish interpreter County of San Diego, 1959-67; bus. mgr. Gemstar Co., LaJolla, Calif., 1967-76, bus. owner, 1976-86; educator Nat. Safety Coun., San Diego, 1986-92, Robinsons May Sch., San Diego, 1986—; cons. Automobile Assn. of So. Calif., 1990-94; acad. advisor La Salle U.; instr. Coll. Extended Studies, San Diego State U. Contbr. articles to profl. jours. Mem. Rep. Ctrl. Com., San Diego, 1964. With U.S. Army, 1951-54. Bus. scholarship AIESEC, 1968; grantee U. Mich., 1953; recipient Achievement award Nat. Safety Coun., San Diego, 1988. Mem. Am. Numismatic Assn., Regents Coll.Alumni Assn., Heartland Numismatic Assn., Spinal Cord Soc. (asst. dir. regional 1988—), Mt. Helix Improvement Assn., Numismatic Soc. Mex., S.D. Numismatic Soc.; fellow Clements Libr. of Am. History, U. Mich. Republican. Roman Catholic. Home: 4410 Shade Rd La Mesa CA 91941-6953 Office: Robinson's May Sch 111 W Pomona Blvd Monterey Park CA 91754-7208

CHRISTENSEN, BRADFORD WILLIAM, state official; b. Green Bay, Wis., Feb. 6, 1951; s. William Gordon and Willow Margaret (Humphrey) C.; m. Roxann Mae VanParys, Aug. 4, 1979; children: Matthew, Melanie, Kimberly. BS in Geography, Ariz. State U., 1975, BS in Journalism, 1978. Reporter Ariz. Captol Times, Phoenix, 1978-83, legis. editor, 1983-88, mng. editor, 1988-93; comm. dir. Ariz. Dept. Health Svcs., Phoenix, 1993—; mem. Coalition Against Domestic Violence, Phoenix, 1994—; chmn. Ariz. Pub. Health Week Steering Com., Phoenix, 1994—; mem. ASTHO Drug Resistant Bacteria Com., Austin, Tex., 1996—, Youth Tobacco Prevention Media Com., Phoenix, 1996—. Editor Healthlink, 1993—, Pub. Health Week, 1995—; contbg. author Am. Jour. Health Comm., 1995—. Recipient Gov.'s award for excellence Ariz. Gov.'s Office, Phoenix, 1994, Gov.'s recognition award, 1995. Mem. Nat. Pub. Health Info. Coalition (v.p. 1996—, 4 awards for excellence in health comm.). Home: 6814 W Sunnyside Dr Peoria AZ 85345 Office: Ariz Dept Health Svcs 1740 W Adams St Rm 407 Phoenix AZ 85007-2602

CHRISTENSEN, BRENT J., surgeon; b. Salt Lake City, Apr. 21, 1954; s. James D. and Betty M. (Schoenfeld) C.; m. Sharon K. Lewis, June 29, 1979; children: Kelci, Jamie, Jordan, Chase, Dayne. BS, U. Utah, 1978, MD, 1984. Diplomate Am. Bd. Surgery. Intern St. Joseph Hosp., Denver, 1984-85, surg. resident, 1984-89; gen. surgeon Bryner Clinic, Salt Lake City, 1989—; dir. intermountain endosurg. inst. DS Hosp., Salt Lake City, 1991—, chair divsn. gen. surgery, 1994—, vice chair dept. surgery, 1994—; asst. clin. prof. U. Utah, Salt Lake City, 1994—; pres.-elect med. staff LDS Hosp., 1997, pres. 1998—; med. dir. LDS Hosp. Endocscopy Lab., 1996—. Fellow ACS; mem. AMA, Utah Med. Assn., Salt Lake County Med. Soc., Southwestern Surg. Congress, Soc. Am. Gastrointestinal Endoscopic Surgery, Soc. of Lapasoendoscopic Surgeons. Mormon. Office: Bryner Clinic 745 E 300 S Salt Lake City UT 84102-2256

CHRISTENSEN, CAROLINE, vocational educator; b. Lehi, Utah, Oct. 5, 1936; d. Byam Heber and Ruth (Gardner) Curtis; m. Marvin Christensen, June 16, 1961; children: Ronald, Roger, Robert, Corlyn, Richard, Chad. BS, Brigham Young U., 1958, MS, 1964. Sec. Brigham Young U., Provo, Utah, 1954-58; instr. bus. Richfield (Utah) H.S., 1958-61, Sevier Valley Applied Tech. Ctr., Richfield, 1970-92, dept. chairperson, 1988-92. Historian, Sevier Sch. Dist. PTA, 1968, 69; chmn. Heart Fund Dist., 1983, Voting Dist., 1988-90; dist. chmn. Am. Cancer Drive, 1994-95; guide Hist. Cove Fort, Utah, 1996—. Mem. Utah Edn. Assn., Am. Vocat. Assn., Utah Vocat. Assn., Nat. Bus. Edn. Utah Bus. Edn. Assn. (sec. 1986-87), NEA, Western Bus. Edn. Assn., Sevier Valley Tech. Tchrs. Assn. (sec. 1971-92, pres. 1986-87), Delta Pi Epsilon (historian), Delta Kappa Gamma (treas. 1975-90, pres. 1990-92, state nominating com. 1993-97, chmn. 95-97, state treas. 1993-95), Phi Beta Lambda (advisor 1988-92).

CHRISTENSEN, C(HARLES) LEWIS, real estate developer; b. Laramie, Wyo., June 3, 1936; s. Raymond H. and Elizabeth C. (Cady) C.; m. Sandra Stadheim, June 11, 1960; children: Kim, Brett. BS in Indsl. Engring., U. Wyo., 1959. Mgmt. trainee Gen. Mills, Chgo., 1959, Mountain Bell, Helena, Mont., 1962-63; data communications mgr. Mountain Bell, Phoenix, 1964-66, dist. mktg. mgr., So. Colo., 1970-73; seminar leader AT&T Co., Chgo., 1966-68, mktg. supr., N.Y.C., 1968-70; land planner and developer Village Assocs., Colorado Springs, Colo., 1973, exec. v.p., 1975-77; v.p. Cimarron Corp., Colorado Springs, 1974-75; pres. Lew Christensen & Assocs., Inc.; ptnr., gen. mgr. Briargate Joint Venture, 1977-90; pres. Vintage Communities, Inc. 1982-95. Bd. dirs. Pikes Peak council Boy Scouts Am., Citizens Goals, Colo. Council on Econ. Edn., Cheyenne Mountain Zoo, 1987-92, Penrose/St. Francis Hosp.; chmn. Colorado Springs Econ. Devel. Coun., 1977, 89 (named Colo. Springs Bus. Citizen of the Yr. 1993); bd. dirs. Penrose St. Francis Hosp., 1996—. Served with USAF, 1959-62. Mem. Colorado Springs Home Builders Assn. (bd. dirs.), Urban Land Inst., Colorado Springs C. of C. (bd. dirs. chmn. bd.). Republican. Presbyterian. Colorado Springs Country Club (bd. dirs.). Developer 1,000-acre Peregrine planned cmty., south of USAF Acad. Office: Lew Christensen & Assocs Inc 2948 Country Club Dr Colorado Springs CO 80909

CHRISTENSEN, DAVID EARL, architect; b. Seattle, Sept. 9, 1953; s. Poul and Jette Malka C.; m. Jean Renae Christensen; 1 child, Hannah. Student, Washington State U., 1971-72, Huxley Coll., 1973; BS in Indsl. Design, Western Wash. U., 1975; postgrad., U. Hawaii, 1978, Harvard U., 1985, 95, Urban Land Inst., 1987, 92. Registered architect, Wash. Civil engring. documentation Island County Engrs., 1969-71; constn. documents G.A. Davison Design, Mt. Vernon, Wash., 1971-72; project mgr., designer Stradling & Stewart Architects, 1972-77; project architect Wimberly, Allison, Tong & Goo, 1977-78; ptnr. in charge design Zervas Group Architects, 1978-87; project designer, marketer The Callison Partnership, 1985-87; owner Christensen Design Mgmt., Bellingham, Wash., 1988—; v.p. devel. Trillium Corp., 1990-91; mem. adv. com. Bellingham Internat. Airport; guest lectr. Western Washington U. Chmn. land use com. Port of Bellingham. Recipient Commendation award Bellingham Arts Commn., 1985, Excellence award Nat. Assn. Housing & Redevel. Officials, 1986, Nat. Judges Choice award Wolverine Technologies & Architecture Mag., 1992, Retail Store of Yr. award Chainstore Age Exec., 1992-93, Hotel of Yr. award Holiday Inn Worldwide, 1994, Nat. Grand award Best in Am. Remodeling Awards/Adaptive Reuse, 1994. Mem. N.W. AIA (bd. dirs., Merit award 1993, 95, 96, Citation award 1992-93, 94, 95, 96, Honor award 1980, 93), Urban Land Inst., Nat. Assn. Indsl. & Office Parks. Office: Christensen Design Mgmt 1151 Old Marine Dr Bellingham WA 98225-8447

CHRISTENSEN, DONN WAYNE, insurance executive; b. Atlantic City, Apr. 9, 1941; s. Donald Frazier and Dorothy (Ewing) C.; BS, U. Santa Clara, 1964; m. Marshella Abraham, Jan. 26, 1963 (div.); children: Donn Wayne, Lisa Shawn; m. Mei Ling Fill, June 18, 1976 (div.); m. Susan Kim, Feb. 14, 1987; stepchildren: Don Kim, Stella Kim. West Coast div. mgr. Ford Motor Co., 1964-65; agt. Conn. Mut. Life Ins. Co., 1965-68; pres. Christensen & Jones, Inc., L.A., 1968—; v.p. Rsch. Devel. Systems Inc.; investment advisor SEC, 1985—. Pres. Duarte Community Drug Abuse Coun., 1972-75; pres. Woodlyn Property Owners Assn., 1972-73; mem. L'Ermitage Found., 1985-90, Instl. Rev. Bd. White Meml. Hosp., L.A., 1975—, Friend's Med. Rsch., 1992—. Recipient Man of Yr. award L.A. Gen. Agts. and Mgrs. Assn., numerous. Mem. Nat. Life Underwriters Assn., Calif. State Life Underwriters Assn., Investment Co. Inst. (assoc.), Soc. Pension Actuaries, Foothill Community Concert Assn. (pres. 1970-73). Registered investment advisor, SEC, 1984. Office: 77 N Oak Knoll Ave Ste 101 Pasadena CA 91101-1812

CHRISTENSEN, DORIS ANN, antique dealer, researcher, writer; b. Safford, Ariz., Dec. 31, 1938; d. Joseph Solomon Welson and Bernice Beatrice (Blasius) Van Order; m. Donald Edward Christensen, April 22, 1967. Student, Ea. Ariz. Coll., 1961-66. Sec. to dean of admissions Ea. Ariz. Coll., Thatcher, 1963-67; sec. to pres. United Homes Corp., Fed. Way, Wash., 1969-89; office mgr. Heller Co. Realtors, Fed. Way, Wash., 1990-94; antique dealer All That & Everything, Buckley, Wash., 1995—; editor newsletter of Violin Bottle Collectors Assn., U.S. and Canada, 1995—. Author: Violin Bottles, Banjos, Guitars and Other Novelty Glass, 1995. Recipient: DAR Good Citizen's cert., 1957; Outstanding Citizenship award, Am. Legion, Safford, Ariz., 1957; Homemaker award, Betty Crocker, Mpls., 1957; attendee: Ariz. Girls' State, Tucson, 1956. Mem. Violin Bottle Collectors Assn. (editor newsletter U.S. and Can., 1995—). Office: All That & Everything 21815 106th St E Buckley WA 98321-9277

CHRISTENSEN, JAMES ARTHUR, middle school educator; b. Santa Monica, Calif., Mar. 31, 1945; s. Arthur Chris and Laura Louise (Wilken) C.; m. Linda J. Carlson, Dec. 19, 1967 (div. Feb. 1986); children: Darcie L., Gretta L., Corry J.; m. Virginia A. Woodruff, June 21, 1986. Student, Oreg. State U., 1963-64; BS in Edn., So. Oreg. State Coll., 1967, postgrad., 1980-82; postgrad., Coll. of Notre Dame, 1968-69. Cert. elem. tchr., Oreg. 6th grade tchr. Redwood City (Calif.) Sch. Dist., 1967-71; 5th-6th grade tchr. Manzanita Elem. Sch., Grants Pass, Oreg., 1971-75; 9th-10th grade English and reading tchr. Ill. Valley H.S., Cave Junction, Oreg., 1975-76; 8th grade math. and sci. tchr. Laurna Byrne Mid. Sch., Cave Junction, 1976-77; 7th-8th grade math. and sci. tchr. Fleming Mid. Sch., Grants Pass, 1977—; mem. tech. adv. bd. 3 Rivers Sch. Dist., Murphy, Oreg., 1994-95, mem. staff insvc. adv. bd., 1994-95. Vol. Visitors' Ctr., Grants Pass C. of C., 1993; mem. parish/staff rels. com. United Meth. Ch., Grants Pass, 1994-95. Recipient 3 Rivers Sch. Dist. Tchr. of the Year, 1995, Tech. Learning Challenge grant Through The Earth and Sea Investigators program, 1995—. Mem. ASCD, NEA, Rogue YAcht Club (trustee 1992-96). Democrat. Home: 2109 Shelly Cir Grants Pass OR 97526-3387 Office: Fleming Mid Sch 6001 Monument Dr Grants Pass OR 97526-8575

CHRISTENSEN, JON ALLAN, journalist; b. Northfield, Minn., May 17, 1960; s. Lauritz Christian and Barbara (Sheldon) C.; m. Carson Ann Miller, May 23, 1987; children: Annika Wesley, Lucia Rachel. Student, Stanford U., 1977-81; BA, San Francisco State U., 1985. Pub. affairs co-dir. KZSU-FM, Stanford, Calif., 1981-82; news and features producer KPFA-FM, Berkeley, Calif., 1983-85; news and info. asst. San Francisco State U., 1983-85; news and info. dir. Inst. for Food & Devel. Policy, San Francisco, 1985-87; assoc. editor Pacific News Svc., San Francisco, 1988—; Brazil corr. Pacific News Svc., Rio de Janeiro, 1989; corr. High Country News, Carson City, Nev., 1990—, regional editor, 1993-95; editor Great Basin News Svc., Carson City, Nev., 1996—; stringer The N.Y. Times, 1996—. Contbr. articles to profl. jours. Mem. Soc. Environ. Journalists. Home: 6185 Franktown Rd Carson City NV 89704-8529 Office: Great Basin News Svc 6205 Franktown Rd Carson City NV 89702-8529

CHRISTENSEN, MICHAEL E., foundation administrator; b. Logan, Utah, Feb. 26, 1947; s. J. Wesley and Beth Josephine (Tupl) C.; m. Denise Barrus, Mar. 12, 1969; children: Jennifer, Chad, John, Brandon. BS, Utah State U., 1971, MS, 1972; PhD, U. Utah, 1978. Assoc. instr. U. Utah, Salt Lake City, 1982—; rsch. analyst Utah State Legislature, Salt Lake City, 1983-85; state planning coord. State of Utah Office of Planning and Budget, Salt Lake City, 1985-91; exec. dir. Utah Found., Salt Lake City, 1991—; prof. U. Phoenix, Salt Lake City, 1993-94. Mem. adv. coun. This Is The Place State Park, Salt Lake City, 1985-94; chmn., mem. Utah Gov.'s Econ. Coordinating Com., 1987—; mem., pres. Wasatch Front Econ. Forum, 1993-94. Recipient Spl. Achievement award Govt. Rsch. Assn., 1993; named Outstanding Young Men in Am., U.S. Jr. C. of C., 1981. Mem. Rotary Club. Mem. LDS Ch. Home: 9445 Dunbar Cove South Jordan UT 84095 Office: Utah Found 10 W 100 S Salt Lake City UT 84101-1505

CHRISTENSEN, ROBERT WAYNE, oral maxillofacial surgeon, minister; b. N.Y.C., Apr. 6, 1925; s. Charles Joseph Brophy and Eva Sutherland (Hart) Christensen; m. Ann Forsyth (div.); children: Robert, Joan, Elizabeth, Peter, Mary, Colleen, Patricia, Michelle; m. Lynne Blindbury; children: Andrew, Matthew. DDS, NYU, 1948. Oral surgery tng. L.A. County Gen. Hosp., 1950; oral maxillofacial surgeon, 1950-88; pres. TMJ Implants, Inc., Golden, Colo., 1988—; minister, founder Covenant Marriages Ministry, Golden, 1988—; pres. Design Dynamics Internat., Golden, 1994—; R&D med. adv. bd. mem. Sch. Medicine LLU, Loma Linda, Calif.; pres.'s cabinet mem. Jerry Savelle Ministry, Ft. Worth, 1994—; adj. prof. bioengring. Sch. Engring., Clemson U. Inventor of 5 U.S. patents. Lt. USNR. Republican. Office: TMJ Implants Inc 17301 W Colfax Ave Ste 135 Golden CO 80401-4800

CHRISTENSEN, ROBERT WAYNE, JR., financial and leasing company executive; b. Chester, Calif., Nov. 11, 1948; s. Robert Wayne and Ann (Forsyth) C.; m. Debra Schumann, Dec. 6, 1988; 1 child, Heather. BA with honors, Coll. Gt. Falls, 1976; MBA, U. Puget Sound, 1978. Cert. flight instr. Corp. pilot Buttrey Food Stores, Gt. Falls, Mont., 1972-74; asst. to pres. Pacific Hide & Fur, Gt. Falls, 1974-76; fin. analyst Olympia Brewing Co., Olympia, Wash., 1977; chmn., CEO Westar Fin. Svcs. Inc., Olympia, 1978—; pres. PacWest Fin. Corp., Olympia, 1984—; bd. dirs. Westar Fin. Svcs., Inc., Olympia, Wash. Independent Bancshares, Olympia, 1982—, PacWest Fin. Corp., Olympia. Trustee CASR Trust, 1993—. Served to sgt. USAF, 1969-72. Mem. Nat. Vehicle Leasing Assn. (bd. dirs. 1978-88, 2d. v.p. 1984, pres. 1986), Western Assn. Equipment Lessors, Western Leasing Conf., Mensa, Rotary (bd. dirs. 1982-89, v.p. 1986-88, pres. 1988-89). Office: Westar Fin Svcs Inc The Republic Bldg PO Box 919 Olympia WA 98507-0919

CHRISTENSEN, STEVEN J., foreign language educator; b. L.A., June 12, 1945; s. Donald Roy and Jocile (Uresenbach) C.; m. Mary Bernice Anderson, Aug. 25, 1967; children: Jennifer, Matthew Alan, Mark Steven. BA, Brigham Young U., Provo, Utah, 1969; MEd, U. Nev., Las Vegas, 1977. Cert. tchr., adminstr., Utah. Camp dir. U.S. Youth Conservation Corps, Las Vegas, Nev., summers 1971-84; tchr. Nebo Sch. Dist., Spanish Fork, Utah, 1969-70; tchr., coach Clark County Sch. Dist., Las Vegas, 1970-78; tchr., coach adminstr. Washington County Sch. Dist., St. George, Utah, 1978—; Comm. specialist Nat. Coun. Tchrs. English, Las Vegas, 1977-78. Author: Population Resources Study Guide, 1975. Mem. S.W. Coun. Fgn. Lang. Tchrs., Utah Fgn. Lang. Assn. Democrat. Mem. Latter-Day Saints Ch. Home: 236 S 370 W Hurricane UT 84737 Office: Hurricane HS 345 W 100 S Hurricane UT 84737-1927

CHRISTENSEN, THOMAS CRAIG, engineering executive; b. Visalia, Calif., Feb. 22, 1953; s. Marvin Charlton and Charlotte Marie (Humbarger) C.; m. Elizabeth Monica Macias; children: Tristan James, Trevor John. AA in Auto Tech., Coll. of Sequoias, Visalia, 1977; BS in Mech. Engring., Calif. State Poly. Coll., 1978; MS in Mech. Engring., Stanford U., 1990. Registered mech. engr., safety engr., Calif. Staff engr. Chevron USA, Bakersfield/Concord, Calif., 1978-81; weapons engr. Lawrence Livermore Nat. Lab., Livermore, Calif., 1981-88; devel. engr. Hewlett-Packard, Palo Alto, Calif., 1988-91; owner, prin. San Ramon, Calif., 1990—; cons. accident reconstrn. and safety analysis. Mem. ASME, Am. Soc. Safety Engrs., Society Automotive Engrs., Soc. Forensic Engrs. and Scientists. Republican. Home and Office: Thomas C Christensen PE 601 Royal Coach Ct San Ramon CA 94583-5644

CHRISTENSON, ANDREW LEWIS, archaeologist; b. Seattle, Feb. 15, 1950; s. Carl James and Geraldine (Beleu) C. BA in Anthropology, UCLA, 1973, MA in Anthropology, 1976, PhD in Anthropology, 1981. Curator, archaeology Mus. of Cultural History, UCLA, L.A., 1980-83; assoc. scientist So. Ill. Univ., Carbondale, Ill., 1983-87; adj. faculty Prescott (Ariz.) Coll., 1988—; archaeologist CSWTA, Inc., Tuba City, Ariz., 1990-93; adj. faculty Yavapai Coll., 1995—; archaeology cons. U.S. Army, Washington, 1980, Zuni (N.Mex.) Archaeology Program, 1989-90, Nat. Park Svcs., 1990-93; assoc. editor Western U.S., Bull. of History of Archaeology, 1990—. Co-editor: (book) Modeling Change in Prehistoric Subsistence Economies, 1980; Co-author: (book) Prehistoric Stone Technology on Northern Black Mesa Arizona, 1987; editor: (book) Tracing Archaeology's Past, 1989. Bd. dirs. Smoki Mus., 1996—. Grantee Am. Philosophical Soc., 1985, NEH, 1985, S.W. Pks. and Monuments Assn., 1987. Mem. Soc. for Am. Archaeology (com. on the history of archaeology). Home and Office: 746 Redondo Rd Prescott AZ 86303-3724

CHRISTENSON, DANIEL PAUL, biologist, conservationist, educator; b. Montrose, Calif., Apr. 30, 1933; s. Clarence and Cecil Edna (Wells) C.; m. Maxine LaVon Parrish, Feb. 1, 1954 (div. Aug. 1980); children: Paul Daniel, Kenneth James, Glen Roger, Carl Edward, Julie Ann; m. Jennifer Lee Babcock, Jan. 10, 1981. AA, Glendale Coll., 1953; BS, Humboldt State Coll., 1956. Fish hatchery asst. Calif. Dept. Fish and Game, Bishop, 1956-57; from fisheries biologist to assoc. fisheries biologist Calif. Dept. Fish and Game, Fresno, 1957-84; biologist Calif. Dept. Fish and Game, Kernville, 1984-96; endangered species coord. Region 4 Calif. Dept. Fish and Game, Fresno, 1978-81; charter mem. Threatened Salmonids Com., Sacramento, 1972-96; mgr. Allen South Fork Preserve, Onyx, Calif., 1993—; prin. mgr. Little Kern Golden Trout Recovery Program, 1965-96; sub. tchr. sci. and math. Kean H.S. Dist., 1997—. Author: A Fisheries Management Plan for the Little Kern Golden Trout, 1978, rev., 1984; co-author: Blunt-nosed Leopard Lizard Recovery Plan, 1980, Upper Kern Basin Fisheries Management Plan, 1995. Founder Golden Valley Ecolog. Soc., Fresno, 1978-82; cmty. theater dir., pres. Kern Valley Players, Kernville, 1988—; conservation advisor Forest Alliance, Kernville, 1986—; dir. music Kernville United Meth. Ch., 1997—. Mem. Kern Valley Wildlife Assn. (conservation advisor 1983—), Sequoia Orgn. Llama Owners (founder, bd. dirs. 1988—).

CHRISTIAENS, CHRIS (BERNARD FRANCIS CHRISTIAENS), financial analyst, state senator; b. Conrad, Mont., Mar. 7, 1940; s. Marcel Jules and Virgie Jeanette (Van Spyk) C. BA in Chemistry, Coll. Gt. Falls, 1962, M in human svcs., 1994. Fin. and ins. mgr. Rice Motors, Gt. Falls, Mont., 1978-84; senator State of Mont., 1983-87, 1991—, majority whip 49th legis., 1985-86; fin. planner Jack Stevens CPA, Gt. Falls, 1984-85; adminstr., fin. analyst Gt. Falls Pre-Release, 1986-92; owner Oak Inn-Bed and Breakfast, 1989-95; mem. faculty U. Gt. Falls, part-time 1995—; bd. dirs. World Wide Press Inc., svc. rep., 1994—. Chmn. Balance of State Pvt. Industry Coun., Mont., 1984—; mem. Mont. Human Rights Commn., 1981-84; bd. dirs. St. Thomas Child and Family Ctr., Gt. Falls, 1983—, Coll. of Gt. Falls, 1984—, Cascade County Mental Health Assn., 1986—, Salvation Army, Habitat for Humanity, 1992-95; mem. adv. bd. State Drug and Alcohol Coun., State Mental Health Coun.; bd. dirs. treas. Gt. Falls Cmty. Food Bank, 1984-86; Dem. committeeman Cascade County, 1976-82; Mont. del. to Nat. Rules Conv., 1980; pub. chmn. Cascade County chpt. ARC, 1986; mem. adv. bd. Cambridge Court Sr. Citizen Apt. Complex, 1986; treas. Cascade County Mental Health Ctr.; vice chmn. Gov.'s Task Force on Prison Overcrowding, mem. regional jail com.; mem. Re-Leaf Gt. Falls Com., 1989—, mem. steering com.; mem. Gt. Falls and Cascade County Housing Task Force, 1995—. Recipient Outstanding Young Alumni award Coll. of Gt. Falls, 1979, Hon. Alumni Achievement award, 1994; Disting. Svc. award Rocky Mountain Coun. Mental Health Ctrs., 1995. Roman Catholic. Clubs: Gt. Falls Ski, Toastmasters. Lodge: Optimists. Address: 600 36th St S Great Falls MT 59405

CHRISTIAN, ANN SEGER, lawyer; b. Waterloo, Iowa, Oct. 11, 1954; d. David Edmund and Dorothy Ann (Reinhart) Seger; m. Thomas Embree Christian, July 21, 1978. BA in Social Work, U. Iowa, 1976, JD magna cum laude, 1980. Bar: Oreg. 1981. Worker income maintenance Iowa Dept. of Welfare, Cedar Rapids, 1976-77; assoc. Multnomah Defenders, Inc., Portland, Oreg., 1982-86, asst. dir., 1986-88; dir. Indigent Def. Svcs. divsn. Office of State Ct. Adminstrn., Salem, Oreg., 1988—. Bd. dirs. Vancouver (Wash.) Humane Soc., 1988-89. Mem. Oreg. Bar Assn., Phi Beta Kappa.

CHRISTIAN, ROLAND CARL (BUD CHRISTIAN), retired English and speech communications educator; b. LaSalle, Colo., June 7, 1938; s. Roland Clyde and Ethel Mae (Lattimer) C.; m. Joyce Ann Kincel, Feb. 15, 1959; children: Kathleen Marie Christian Dunham, Kristine May Christian Sweet. BA in English and Speech, U. No. Colo., 1962, MA, 1966. Cert. tchr., N.Y., Colo. Tchr. Southside Jr. High Sch., Rockeville Ctr., N.Y., 1962-63, Plateau Valley High Sch., Collbran, Colo., 1963-67; prof. English Northeastern Jr. Coll., Sterling, Colo., 1967-93, prof. emeritus, 1993—; presenter seminars, workshops, Sterling, 1967—; emcee/host Town Meeting of Am., Sterling, 1976. Author: Be Bright! Be Brief! Be Gone! A Speaker's Guide, 1983, Potpourrivia, A Digest of Curious Words, Phrases and Trivial Information, 1986, Nicknames in Sports: A Quiz book, 1986; lit. adv. New Voices mag., 1983—; contbr. Ways We Write, 1964, The Family Treasury of Great Poems, 1982, Our Twentieth Century's Greatest Poems, 1982, Anti-War Poems; vol. II, 1985, Impressions, 1986, World Poetry Anthology, 1986, American Poetry Anthology, 1986, Chasing Rainbows, 1988, The Poetry of Life, 1988, Hearts on Fire, 1988, Wide Open Magazine, 1986, 87, 88; columnist South Platte Sentinel, 1988—. Served with U.S. Army, 1956-59. Recipient Colo. Recognition of Merit scholarship, 1956, Merit cert. Poets Anonymous, 1983, Award of Merit (9), 1985, 86, Golden Poet of Yr. award World of Poetry Press, 1985, 86, 87, 88, Joel Mack Tchr. of Yr. award Northeastern Jr. Coll., 1986; Jr. Coll. Found. grantee, 1986, 87. Mem. NEA, AAUP, Jr. Coll. Faculty Assn. (sec./treas. 1970-72), Colo. Edn. Assn., Nat. Council Tchrs. of English, Poets of Foothills. Roman Catholic. Home: 603 Park St #105 Sterling CO 80751-3753

CHRISTIAN, SUZANNE HALL, financial planner; b. Hollywood, Calif., Apr. 28, 1935; d. Peirson M. and Gertrude (Engel) Hall; children: Colleen,

Carolyn, Claudia, Cynthia. BA, UCLA, 1956; MA, Redlands U., 1979; cert. in fin. planning, U. So. Calif., 1986. CFP. Instr. L.A. City Schs., 1958-59; instr. Claremont (Calif.) Unified Schs., 1972-84, dept. chair, 1981-84; fin. planner Waddell & Reed, Upland, Calif., 1982-96, sr. account exec., 1986; br. mgr. Hornor, Townsend & Kent, Claremont, 1996—; corp. mem. Pilgrim Place Found., Claremont; lectr. on fin., estate and tax planning for civic and profl. groups. Author: Strands in Composition, 1979; host Money Talks with Suzanne Christian on local TV cable, 1993—. Mem. legal and estate planning com. Am. Cancer Soc., 1988—; profl. adv. com. YWCA-Inland Empire, 1987; treas. Fine Arts Scripps Coll., 1993-94. mem. Inst. CFP's, Internat. Assn. Fin. Planners, Planned Giving Roundtable, Estate Planning Coun. Pomona Valley, Claremont C. of C. (pres., bd. dirs. 1994-95), Curtain Raisers Club Garrison (pres. 1972-75), Circle of Champions (pres.'s coun. 1994-95, Silver Crest award 1985-87, 94, 95), Rotary, Galileo Soc. Harvey Mudd Coll., Kappa Kappa Gamma (pres. 1970-74). Home: PO Box 1237 Claremont CA 91711-1237 Office: Hornor Townsend & Kent 419 Yale Ave Claremont CA 91711-4340

CHRISTIANSEN, ERIC ALAN, software development executive; b. Salt Lake City, May 14, 1958; s. Don Parley and Lilian Patricia (Clegg) C.; m. April Gay Willes, Jan. 9, 1988; children: Amber, Carly. BS in Computer Sci., West Coast U., L.A., 1981. Software engr. Lear Siegler Astronics, Santa Monica, Calif., 1980-82; sr. software specialist Digital Equipment Corp., Culver City, Calif., 1982-83; software cons. L.A., 1983-84; v.p. Mindcode Devel. Corp., Salt Lake City, 1984-85; software cons. Van Nuys, Calif., 1985-89; sr. software engr. ITT Gilfillan, Van Nuys, 1989-90; prin. Wells Fargo Nikko Investment Advisors, San Francisco, 1990—, Barclays Global Investors, San Francisco, 1996—; strategic advisor Tri-Pacific Cons. Corp., Alameda, Calif., 1991-93; guest lectr. George Mason U. and Joint Tactical Command, Control, and Comm. Agy., 1991; mem. rsch. team devel. quantitive stock market investment model. Developer (comml. software program) Structurer preprocessor enhancing command interface and language for VAX/VMS, 1989; contbr. articles to profl. jours. Mem. IEEE, Assn. for Computing Machinery, Digital Equipment Computer Users Soc. (local user group bd. 1988-90). Republican. Office: BZW Barclays Global Investors 45 Fremont St San Francisco CA 94105

CHRISTIANSON, ROGER GORDON, biology educator; b. Santa Monica, Calif., Oct. 31, 1947; s. Kyle C. and Ruby (Parker) C.; m. Angela Diane Rey, Mar. 3, 1967; children: Lisa Marie, David Scott, Stephen Peter. BA in Cell and Organismal Biology, U. Calif., Santa Barbara, 1969, MA in Biology, 1971, PhD in Biology, 1976. Faculty assoc. U. Calif., Santa Barbara, 1973-79, staff rsch. assoc., 1979-80; asst. prof. So. Oreg. U., Ashland, 1980-85, assoc. prof., 1985-93, prof., 1993—, coord. gen. biology program, 1980—, chmn. biology dept., 1996, 97—; instr. U. Calif., Santa Barbara, summers 1976, 78, 80. Contbr. articles to profl. jours. Active Oreg. Shakespeare Festival Assn., Ashland, 1983-87; mem. bikeway com. Ashland City Coun., 1986-88; coord. youth program 1st Bapt. Ch., Ashland, 1981-85, mem. ch. life commn., 1982-88, bd. deacons, 1993-95, mem. outreach com., 1994, 95; organizer Bike Oreg., 1982-92, Frontline staff, 1985—, Mex. Orphanage short-term mission work, 1986—; ofcl. photographer Ashland H.S. Booster Club, 1987-92; youth leader jr. and sr. H.S. students Grace Ch., Santa Barbara, Calif., 1973-80. Mem. AAAS (chair Pacific divsn. edn. sect. 1985—, coun. mem. Pacific divsn. 1985—), Am. Mus. Natural History, Oreg. Sci. Tchrs. Assn., Assn. for Biology Lab. Edn., Sigma Xi, Beta Beta Beta. Republican. Home: 430 Reiten Dr Ashland OR 97520-9724 Office: Southern Oregon U Dept Biology 1250 Siskiyou Blvd Ashland OR 97520-5010

CHRISTIE, HANS FREDERICK, retired utility company subsidiaries executive, consultant; b. Alhambra, Calif., July 10, 1933; s. Andreas B. and Sigrid (Falk-Jorgensen) C.; m. Susan Earley, June 14, 1957; children: Brenda Lynn, Laura Jean. BS in Fin., U. So. Calif., 1957, MBA, 1964. Treas. So. Calif. Edison Co., Rosemead, 1970-75, v.p., 1975-76, sr. v.p., 1976-80, exec. v.p., 1980-84, pres., dir., 1984-87; pres., chief exec. officer The Mission Group (non-utility subs. SCE Corp.), Seal Beach, Calif., 1987-89, ret., 1989, cons., 1989—; bd. dirs. Gt. Western Fin. Corp., L.A. Ducommun Inc., L.A., UntramarDiamond Shamrock Corp., C.T., Am. Mut. Fund, Inc., Am. Variable Ins., I.H.O.P. Corp., AECom Tech., L.A., Internat. House of Pancakes, Inc., Southwest Water Co., L.A., Smallcap World Fund, L.A., Bond Fund Am., Inc., L.A., Tax-Exempt Bond Fund Am., L.A., Ltd. Term Tax-Exempt Bond Fund Am., Am. High Income Mcpl. Bond Fund, Capital Income Builder, L.A., Capital World Bond Fund, L.A., Capital World Growth Fund, Capital World Growth and Income Fund, Intermediate Bond Fund Am., L.A., Intermediate Tax-Exempt Bond Fund Am., Capital World Growth 2d Income Fund, L.A.; trustee Cash Mgmt. Trust Am., New Economy Fund, L.A., Am. Funds Income Series, L.A., The Am. Funds Tax-Exempt Series II, Am. High Income Trust, L.A., Am. High-Inc Mun. Board Fund, Am. Variable Ins. Trust, U.S. Treasury Fund Am., L.A. Chmn. Nat. History Mus. L.A. County; bd. councillor sch. pub. adminstrn. U. So. Calif.; trustee Occidental Coll., 1984-96. With U.S. Army, 1953-55. Named Outstanding mem. Arthritis Found., L.A., 1975, Outstanding Trustee, Multiple Sclerosis Soc. So. Calif., 1979. Mem. Pacific Coast Elec. Assn. (bd. dirs. 1981-87, treas. 1975-87), L.A. C. of C. (bd. dirs. 1983-87), Calif. Club. Republican. Home: 548 Paseo Del Mar Palos Verdes Estates CA 90274-1260 Office: PO Box 144 Palos Verdes Estates CA 90274-0144

CHRISTINA, GRETA, book and film critic, writer, editor; b. Chgo., Dec. 31, 1961; d. Richard Hermann and Gretchen Lauranne (Wiant) M.; m. Richard Daniels, Mr. 16, 1985 (div. June 1986). BA, Reed Coll., 1983. News columnist On Our Backs, San Francisco, 1989-91; film critic San Francisco Bay Times, 1993-95, Bay Area Reporter, San Francisco, 1995, Spectator, Berkeley, 1995-96; book critic San Francisco Frontiers, 1996; mng. editor Fishnet (World Wide Web online mag.), 1996. Contbr. articles to newspapers, mags., jours. and anthologies.

CHRISTMAN, ALBERT BERNARD, historian; b. Colorado Springs, Colo., May 18, 1923; s. James S. and Olga Emelia (Nelson) C.; m. Kate Gresham, July 1945 (div. July 1952); 1 child, Lloyd James; m. Jean Stewart, Apr. 4, 1954 (dec. Sept. 1984); children: Neil Stewart, Laura Elizabeth. BA, U. Mo., 1949, BJ, 1950; MA, Calif. State U., Dominguez Hills, 1982. Reporter Comml. Leader, North Little Rock, 1950-51; tech. editor, writer Naval Ordnance Test Sta., China Lake, Calif., 1951-55, head presentation divsn., 1956-63; historian, info. specialist Naval Weapons Ctr., China Lake, Calif., 1963-72, head pubs., 1973-79; historian Navy Labs., San Diego, 1979-82; freelance historian, writer San Marcos, Calif., 1982—. Author: Sailors, Scientists and Rockets, 1971, Naval Innovators, 1776-1900, 1989; co-author: Grand Experiment at Inyokern, 1979; contbr. articles to profl. jours. Founding mem. Red Rock Canyon State Park Adv. Com., Tehachapi, Calif., 1969-74. Pvt. U.S. Army, 1942-45; maj. USAFR, ret. Recipient Robert H. Goddard Meml. award nat. Space, 1972, Superior Civilian Svc. award Dept. of The Navy, 1982, Helen Hawkins Meml. Rsch. grant, 1994. Mem. Maturango Mus. (trustee-sec. 1973-76), Naval Hist. Found., USN Inst., OX-5 Aviation Pioneers, Smithsonian Inst. (assoc.), Libr. of Congress Assn. (founding mem.). Democrat. Unitarian. Home and Office: 1711 Birchwood Dr San Marcos CA 92069-9609

CHRISTMAN, HELEN DOROTHY NELSON, resort executive; b. Denver, Nov. 25, 1922; d. Hector C. and Dorothy C. (Hansen) Russell; m. James Ray Christman, Aug. 7, 1942 (dec. June 1986); children: J. Randol, Linda Rae. Student, Colo. U., 1940-42. Producer Sta. KRMA-TV, Denver, 1960-62; resident mgr. Mana Kai Maui, Maui, Hawaii, 1974-76, exec. coord., 1976-78; pres. Resort Apts., Inc., 1986—; bd. dirs. Kihei Cmty. Assn. Pres. Stephen Knight PTA, Denver, 1957; radio and TV chmn. Colo. PTA, 1958-59; producer ednl. TV programs for PTA, Denver County, 1960-61; bd. dirs. Maui United Way, 1983—, Am. Lung Assn., chmn. Maui sect., 1995—, Hawaii State bd., 1995—; precinct pres. Maui Reps.; chmn. Maui County Rep. Com., 1989-91; mem. adv. bd. State of Hawaii Reapportionment Com., Maui, 1991—; bd. dirs. Hale Makua Found., 1994—, Hui No Eau, 1996—. Mem. Delta Delta Delta, Women's Golf Club (chmn. Silverswood chpt.), Maui Country Club (chmn. women's golf assn. 1987), Waiehu Women's Golf Assn. (pres. 1992-93), Maui Liquor Commn. Address: 3448 Hookipa Pl Kihei HI 96753-9216

CHRISTOPHER, JOHN CHAMBERS, counseling psychology educator; b. Balt., Mar. 29, 1962; s. John Francis and Anne Elizabeth (Chambers) C. AB, U. Mich., 1984; MEd, Harvard U., 1987; PhD, U. Tex., 1992. Intern U. Mo. Counseling Ctr., Columbia, 1991-92; asst. prof. U. Guam, Mangilao, 1992-95; asst. prof., mental health counseling program leader Mont. State U., 1995—. Contbr. chpts. to books and articles to profl. jours. Office: Montana State U Dept Health and Human Devel Herrich Hall Bozeman MT 59717

CHRISTOPHER, L. CAROL, communication researcher, freelance writer; b. Dallas, Dec. 11, 1953; d. Joe R. and S. Lanell Christopher. BA magna cum laude, U. Calif., San Diego, 1991, MA, 1993, Candidate of Philosophy, 1995. Systems editor The Dallas Morning News, 1978-84; systems editor, asst. to editor The Denver Post, 1984-86; tng. and comm. mgr. Newspaper Systems Support and Engring., San Diego, 1986-88; cons. Christopher Comm., Oakland, 1988—; tchg./rsch. asst. U. Calif., San Diego, 1991—; corr. The Cole Papers, San Francisco, 1991—; labor organizer Assn. Grad. Student Employees/UAW, Berkeley, 1995. Contbr. articles to profl. jours. Mem. exec. bd. Assn. Grad. Student Employees/UAW, Assn. Student Employees/UAW, Berkeley and San Diego, 1991—; precinct capt. Dukakis campaign, Dem. Nat. Party, San Diego, 1988. Mem. Internat. Comm. Ass., Speech Comm. Assn., Assn. of Educators in Journalism and Mass Comm. Office: U Calif Dept Communication 0503 9500 Gilman Dr La Jolla CA 92093

CHRISTOPHER, LINDA ELLEN, consultant, association executive; b. Flint, Mich., Aug. 26, 1949; d. Junion Homer Christopher and Mildred Ester Dare (Oldham) Burak; mem. Herald René Baxter, Dec. 21, 1994. BA, U. Mich., 1976; MPA, Sonoma State U., Rohnert Park, Calif., 1996. Cert. assn. exec. Med. transcriptionist Delta (Colo.) County Meml. Hosp., 1976-78; vocat. rehab. instr. Svc. Ctr. for Visually Impaired, Flint, Mich., 1978-81; med. record dept. supr. St. Joseph's Hosp., Flint, 1981-85; dir. edn. Am. Assn. Med. Transcription, Modesto, Calif., 1985-90; assoc. exec. dir. Sonoma County Med. Assn., Santa Rosa, Calif., 1990-94; cons. The Christopher Group, Santa Rosa, 1994—; CEO The Christopher Group, San Francisco, 1996—; exec. dir. Hand Therapy Cert. Commn., San Francisco, 1995-96; bd. dirs. Beginning Experience Inc., Flint, 1982-84; key contact Calif. Med. Assn., San Francisco, 1990-94, Am. Heart Assn., Calif., 1994—; exec. dir. Profl. and Personal Coaches Assn., San Francisco, 1996—. Calif. Coaliton of Nurse Practitioners, Sacramento, 1996—; speaker in field. Editor Jour. Sonoma County Med. Assn., 1990-94 (numerous awards); contbr. articles to profl. jours. Pres. Greater Santa Rosa divsn. Am. Heart Assn., 1996-97. Mem. Am. Heart Assn. (pres. elect 1995-96, pres. 1996—), Am. Soc. Assn. Execs. (mem. edn. coun. 1988-91, several awards), No. Calif. Soc. Assn. Execs. (bd. mem. 1993—, profl. recognition scholarships 1984, 89). Office: The Christopher Group 1275 4th St Ste 145 Santa Rosa CA 95404-4049

CHRISTOPHER, PERRY LEE, laboratory technician; b. Clinton, Mo., June 25, 1965; s. Leroy Alfred and Peggy Louretta (Houk) C. BS in Chemistry, Met. State Coll., Denver, 1991. Chem. lab. technician II Hauser Chem. Rsch., Boulder, 1992—. Author, editor, artist (book of poetry) Dreams and Realities a Collection of Poems, 1996. Home: 1406 Ashcroft Dr Longmont CO 80501

CHRISTY, THOMAS PATRICK, human resources executive, educator; b. Urbana, Ill., May 18, 1943; s. Edward Michael and Iona Theresa (Rogers) C.; m. Marjorie Anne McIntyre, June 1966 (div. May 1973); children: Thomas Patrick Jr., Derek Edward; m. Sandra Allen Stern, May 19, 1984 (div. Aug. 1996); children: Patrick Edward, Margaret Allen. BA in Psychology, Adams State Coll., 1965; MBA, Chapman U., 1997. Tchr. Colorado Springs Pub. Sch., 1965-69; regional personnel dir. Forest Service USDA, Washington, 1969-81; sr. account exec. Mgmt. Recruiters Inc., Costa Mesa, Calif., 1981-84; v.p. Coleman & Assoc. Inc., Santa Monica, Calif., 1984; asst. v.p. Union Bank, Los Angeles, 1984-88; v.p., human resources dir. TOPA Savs. Bank, Los Angeles, 1988-89, Cenfed Bank, Pasadena, Calif., 1989-91; v.p., regional human resources mgr., nat. dir. tng. Tokio Marine Mgmt., Inc., Pasadena, 1991-94; adj. prof. Coll. Bus. Mgmt., Northrop U., L.A., 1985-91, Coll. Bus. Mgmt., UCLA, 1991—; bd. dirs. Human Resources Mgmt. Inst., L.A., pres., 1993—; bd. dirs. The Employers Group; mem. editorial rev. bd. Calif. Labor Letter, L.A. Arbitrator Bus. and Consumer Arbitrator program Better Bus. Bur., Los Angeles and Orange County; mem. vestry St. Edmund's Episc. Ch., San Marino, Calif., 1995-96; mem. Calif. Lincoln Clubs. Mem. AAUP, Pers. and Indsl. Rels. Assn. (pres. 1993), Soc. Human Resources Mgmt. (Calif. state legis. affairs dir.), Employment Mgmt. Assn., Soc. Profls. in Dispute Resolution, Am. Compensation Assn., Japanese Am. Soc. So. Calif., Adams State Coll. Alumni Assn. (Calif. state pres.), Town Hall Calif., Valley Hunt Club, L.A. Athletic Club, Beach Club, Sigma Pi Alumni Assn. Episcopalian.

CHRITTON, GEORGE A., film producer; b. Chgo., Feb. 25, 1933; s. George A. and Dorothea (Goergens) C.; m. Martha Gilman, Aug. 26, 1956 (div. May 26, 1978); children: Stewart, Andrew, Douglas, Laura, Neil, Lyle. BA, Occidental Coll., 1955; postgrad., Princeton U., 1955-57. With CIA & various U.S. govt. agys., 1960-89; gen. ptnr. Margeo Investment Co., L.A., 1963-76; pres. Wildacre Prodns., Inc., L.A., 1990—; pres., CEO Fin. Svcs. Bancorp, Reno, 1990—; pres. Sycamore Prodns. Ltd., Nev. and Calif., 1994—. Mem. Am. Fgn. Svc. Assn., Washington, 1960—; chmn. bd. Neighborhood Learning Ctr., Capitol Hill, Washington, 1985-87; vol. Options House, Hollywood, Calif.; vol. coord. Rebuild L.A. Maj. USAF, 1957-60. Named Princeton Nat. Fellow, 1955-56, Vis. Fellow & Lectr. U. Calif., 1987-88. Mem. AFTRA, Am. Film Inst., Nat. Assn. Ind. Film & T.V. Prodrs., Phi Beta Kappa, Phi Gamma Delta, Alpha Mu Gamma, Alpha Phi Gamma, Princeton Club (So. Calif.). Office: Wildacre Prodns Inc PO Box 719 Beverly Hills CA 90213-0719

CHRONISTER, RICHARD DAVIS, physicist; b. Birmingham, Ala., Aug. 17, 1943; s. Richard D. and Mary Anne (Bealmear) C.; m. Vickie A. Bacon, Apr. 10, 1965; children: Susan K., Karen J. BS in Physics, U. Okla., 1965; MS in Nuclear Engring., Ohio State U., 1968. Cert. electromagnetic compatibility engr.; cert. environ. compliance mgr.; registered environ. profl. Commd. 2d lt. USAF, 1965; advanced through grades to maj., 1977; Project mgr. USAF Aeropropulsion Lab., Dayton, Ohio, 1965-69; electronics survivability officer Field Command Def. Nuclear Agy., Livermore, Calif., 1969-72; grad. student U. Okla., Norman, 1972-75; mgr., transient radiation effects on electronics USAF Weapons Lab., Albuquerque, 1975-78; chief, radiation analysis lab. USAF Tech. Applications Ctr., Sacramento, Calif., 1979-83; chief aircraft and space sys. USAF Nuclear Criteria Group Secretariat, Albuquerque, 1983-86; prin. engr./physicist BDM Internat., Albuquerque, 1986—. Author, co-author tech. reports. Sr. mem. Am. Inst. Aeronautics and Astronautics; mem. AAAS, Am. Phys. Soc., Nat. Assn. Radio and Telecommunications Engrs. Methodist. Home: 13005 Rebonito Rd NE Albuquerque NM 87112-4819 Office: BDM Internat 1801 Randolph Rd SE Albuquerque NM 87106-4230

CHRYSTAL, WILLIAM GEORGE, minister; b. Seattle, May 22, 1947; s. Frances Homer and Marjorie Isabell (Daubert) C.; m. Mary Francis King, Aug. 24, 1970; children: Shelley, Sarah, John, Philip. BA, U. Wash., 1969, MEd, 1970; MDiv, Eden Theol. Sem., 1978; MA, Johns Hopkins U., 1984. Ordained to ministry, United Ch. of Christ, 1977. Learning resources specialist Seattle C.C. Dist., 1970-71; dir. learning resources ctr. Whatcom C.C., Ferndale, Wash., 1971-73; minister St. Peter's United Ch. of Christ, Granite City, Ill., 1978-79; sr. minister 1st Congl. Ch., Stockton, Calif., 1979-83; minister Trinity United Ch. of Christ, Adamstown, Md., 1983-85; sr. minister Edwards Congl. Ch., Northampton, Mass., 1985-86, 1st Congl. Ch., Reno, Nev., 1991—; hosp. chaplain Washoe Med. Ctr., Reno, 1993—; host Thomas Jefferson Hour, on nat. pub. radio stas. Author: Young Reinhold Niebuhr: His Early Writings, 1911-1931, 1977, 2d edit., 1982, A Father's Mantle: The Legacy of Gustav Niebuhr, 1982, The Fellowship of Prayer, 1987, Goodby Forever: The First World War Diary of Orville A. "Tubby" Ralston, 1997; author monographs; contbr. articles to profl. jours. V.p. Reno-Sparks Met. Ministry, Reno, 1994—; Chautauqua scholar Great Basin Chautauqua, Reno, 1993, 94. Lt. comdr. USN, 1986-91, maj. Nev. Army N.G., 1992-96. Decorated (2) Meritorious Svc. medal. Mem. Am. Soc. Ch. History, Nev. Soc. Mayflower Descs. (gov.), Am. Legion, Disabled Vets. (life), VFW (life), Rotary Club (Paul Harris fellow 1997). Home: 3820 Bluebird Cir Reno NV 89509-5601 Office: 1st Congl Ch 627 Sunnyside Dr Reno NV 89503-3515

CHRYSTIE, THOMAS LUDLOW, investor; b. N.Y.C., May 24, 1933; s. Thomas Witter and Helen (Duell) C.; m. Eliza S. Balis, June 9, 1955; children: Alice B., Helen S., Adden B., James MacD. BA, Columbia U., 1955; MBA, NYU, 1960. With Merrill Lynch, Pierce, Fenner & Smith, Inc., N.Y.C., 1955-75, dir. investment banking divsn., 1970-75; sr. v.p. Merrill Lynch & Co., 1975-78, CFO, 1976-78; chmn. Merrill Lynch White Weld Capital Markets Group, 1978-81, Merrill Lynch Capital Resources, 1981-83; adv. on strategy Merrill Lynch & Co. Inc., 1983-88; pvt. investor Jackson, Wyo., 1988—; bd. dirs. Consumer Portfolio Svcs., Inc., Titanium Industries, Oreg. Metall. Corp. Trustee emeritus Columbia U.; trustee Nat. Mus. Wildlife Art, Middleton Place Found. Capt. USAF, 1955-58. Mem. N.Y. Athletic Club, Teton Pines Tennis Club. Home and Office: PO Box 640 Wilson WY 83014 *Whatever you are involved in, see it as part of a larger picture.*

CHRZANOWSKA-JESKE, MALGORZATA EWA, electrical engineering educator, consultant; b. Warsaw, Poland, Nov. 26, 1948; came to U.S., 1985; d. Waclaw and Halina (Siedlanowska) Chrzanowska; m. Witold Norbert Jeske, July 21, 1978; children: Marcin, Olaf. MS in Electronics, Warsaw Tech. U., 1972; MS in Elec. Engring., Tuskegee (Ala.) Inst., 1976; PhD in Elec. Engring., Auburn (Ala.) U., 1988. Rsch. and tchg. instr. Warsaw Tech. U., 1972-75; rsch. and tchg. asst. Tuskegee Inst., 1975-76; rsch. and tchg. asst. Auburn U., 1976-77, rsch. asst., postdoctoral fellow, 1985-89; sr. rschr. Inst. Electron Tech., Warsaw, 1977-82, CAD project leader, 1983-85; asst. prof. Portland (Oreg.) State U., 1989-95, assoc. prof. elec. engring., 1995—; cons. Inst. Electron Tech., Warsaw, 1985—; lectr. Tuskegee Inst., 1977; profl/lectr. Oreg. Ctr. for Advance tech., Beaverton, 1991-94. Contbr. articles to profl. jours. Troop leader Polish Scout Assn., Warsaw, 1958-66; sci. and activity com. chmn. Polish Student Assn., Warsaw, 1966-75; mem. Solidarity, Poland, 1980-85. Recipient First Level award Polish Dept. Sci., Higher Edn. and Tech., 1983; named to Women of Distinction in Engring. Columbia coun. Girl Scouts U.S., 1993. Mem. ACM, IEEE (Oreg. sect. exec. com. 1994—), IEEE Electron Device Soc. (chair edn. com. Oreg. sect. 1989—), IEEE Circuits and Sys. Soc., Eta Kappa Nu. Office: Portland State Univ Dept Elec Engring 1800 SW 6th Ave Portland OR 97201-5204

CHU, ALLEN YUM-CHING, automation company executive, systems consultant; b. Hong Kong, June 19, 1951; arrived in Can., 1972; s. Luke King-Sang and Kim Kam (Lee) C.; m. Janny Chu-Jen Tu, Feb. 27, 1993. BSc in Computer Sci., U. B.C., Vancouver, Can., 1977; BA in Econs., U. Alta., Edmonton, Can., 1986. Rsch. asst. dept. neuropsychology and rsch. Alta. Hosp., Edmonton, 1977-78; systems analyst dept. agr. Govt. of Alta., Edmonton, 1978-81; systems analyst for computing resources City of Edmonton, 1981-86; pres. ANO Automation Inc., Vancouver, 1986-92; v.p., bd. dirs. ANNOVA Bus. Group, Inc., Can., 1993—; mem. Vancouver Bd. Trade. Mem. IEEE Computer Soc., N.Y. Acad. Sci. Office: ANO Automation Inc, 380 W 2d Ave 2d Flr, Vancouver, BC Canada V5Y 1C8

CHU, CHRISTOPHER KAR FAI, graphic designer; b. Hong Kong, July 20, 1955; came to U.S., 1957; s. Joseph K. Woo and Marion Sui Sin Pau; m. Faye Allison Mark, July 30, 1988; children: Bethany Joy, Hannah Lynne, Sarah Michelle. AA, City Coll. San Francisco, 1981; BS, San Jose State U., 1984. Journeyman clk. Safeway Stores, Inc., San Francisco, 1974-85; creative dir. Neumeier Design Team, Palo Alto, Calif., 1985—. Recipient Silver award, Murphy awards, 1987, certificate of Distinction, N.Y. Creativity Show, 1988, 89, 90, 91, 92, 93, 94, 95, award of Excellence, Print Regional Design Ann., 1988, 91, 92, 93, Print Computer Art & Design Ann., 1991, 92, 93, Distinctive Merit award, N.Y. Art Dirs. Club, cert. of Design Excellence, Print Mag., award of Merit Brit. Designers & Art Dirs., and others. Home: 868 Boardwalk Pl Redwood City CA 94065-1809 Office: Neumeier Design Team 120 Hawthorne Ave Ste 102 Palo Alto CA 94301-1035

CHU, JULIA NEE, artist; b. Shanghai, China, Dec. 10, 1943; came to U.S., 1960; d. James and Chu-Non (Yang) Nee; m. Wesley W.C. Chu, 1961; children: Milton W., Christin M. BA, UCLA, 1978, MFA, 1981. curator Artistas Chineses da Calif., Leal Senado de Macau, Galeria de Exposicoe s Temporarias, Macau, 1992; grad. teaching fellow UCLA, 1980-81; lectr. UCLA Ext., Brandeis U. Women's Com., Orange Coast Coll., Westside Arts Ctr., L.A. County Mus. Art, Far Eastern Arts Coun.; panelist L.A. Dept. Cultural Affairs Grants. One-woman shows include Richard Green Gallery, Santa Monica, Calif., 1992, Galley Q, Tokyo, 1992, Memory Gallery, Nagoya, Japan, 1992, Richard Green Gallery, Santa Monica, Calif., 1992, 93, Andres Shire Gallery, L.A., 1992, Gallery Q, Tokyo, 1992, Occidental Coll., Glendale, Calif., 1993, Pierce Coll. Art Gallery, Woodland Hills, Calif., 1993, Tsubaki Gallery, Tokyo, 1994, Mandarin Oriental Fine Arts, Hong Kong, 1994, Bunkamura Gallery, Tokyo, 1995, Cmty. Focus Gallery, Santa Monica, 1995, Taipei Art Gallery, N.Y.C., 1996; represented in permanent collections at Hong Kong Mus., Macau Mus., MCA Music & Broadcast Co., Steve Chase Collecton Health Net; also pub. and pvt. collections. Ford Found. travel grantee, 1980; recipient award GTE, 1975. Home and Studio: 1520 17th St Santa Monica CA 90404-3402

CHU, SHIH-FAN (GEORGE CHU), economics educator; b. Hubei, China, Dec. 6, 1933; came to U.S., 1959; s. Teh-Chuan and Kuang-Hsin (Chou) C.; m. Li-Ming Kuo, Aug. 18, 1963; children: David Soo-lin, Diana Soo-Yin. BA, Nat. Taiwan U., 1955; MS, U. Ill., 1965, PhD, 1968. Asst. prof. econs. U. Nev., Reno, 1967-70, assoc. prof., 1970-77, prof., 1977—, chmn. dept. econs., 1992—; vis. prof. econs. Huazhong U. Sci. and Tech., Wuhan, China, 1981, Wuhan U., 1984, Nat. Taiwan U., Taipei, 1989. Contbr. numerous articles to econs. jours. Fulbright Travel grantee; Ford Found. Dissertation fellow; Inst. Internat. Edn. grad. scholar. Mem. numerous profl. orgns. in econs. Home: 4490 Gibraltar Dr Reno NV 89509 Office: U Nev Dept Econs Reno NV 89557

CHU, VALENTIN YUAN-LING, author; b. Shanghai, Republic of China, Feb. 14, 1919; came to U.S., 1956, naturalized, 1961; s. Thomas V.D. and Rowena S.N. (Zee) Tsu; m. Victoria Chao-yu Tsao, Sept. 25, 1954; 1 child, Douglas Chi-hua. BA, St. John's U, Shanghai, 1940. Asst. Shanghai Mcpl. Coun., 1940-42; asst. mgr., pub., printer Thomas Chu & Sons, Shanghai, 1943-45; chief reporter China Press, Shanghai, 1945-49; pub. rels. officer Cen. Air Transport Corp., Hong Kong, 1949; Hong Kong corr. Time & Life mags., Hong Kong, 1949-56; with Time, Inc., N.Y.C., 1956-76; writer, asst. editor Time-Life Books, N.Y.C., 1968-76; assoc. editor Reader's Digest Gen. Books, N.Y.C., 1978-83; lectr. on China. Author: Ta Ta, Tan Tan---Fight Fight, Talk Talk, 1963, Thailand Today, 1968, (with others) U.S.A., A Visitor's Handbook, 1969, The Yin-Yang Butterfly---Ancient Chinese Sexual Secrets for Western Lovers, 1993; contbr. articles to popular mags. Recipient spl. award UN Internat. Essay Contest, 1948. Mem. Authors League Am., Authors Guild, China Inst. in Am., Inst. Noetic Scis. Presbyterian. Home: 4520 Wildcat Cir Antioch CA 94509-7149

CHUA, CONSTANTINO PINA, electrical and instrument engineer, consultant; b. Cebu, The Philippines, Mar. 11, 1937; came to U.S., 1961; s. Francisco and Rosalia (Sy) C.; m. Monina M. Sanchez, Jan. 23, 1965; children: Margaret, Marie. BSEE, Cebu Inst. Tech., 1960, Heald's Coll., 1962. Elec. engr. Spreckels Sugar Co., Pleasanton, Calif., 1963-91; engring. cons. Pacific Gas Transmission, San Francisco, 1992-95, Bayer Corp., Berkeley, Calif., 1995—. Author: Beet Sugar Technology, 1982. Republican. Roman Catholic. Office: CPC Engring 1817 School St Moraga CA 94556

CHUA, KOON MENG, civil engineering educator; b. Singapore, Apr. 23, 1955; came to the U.S., 1982; s. Kim Yeow and Poh Choo Chua. BCE, U. Singapore, 1980; MS, Tex. A&M U., 1983, PhD, 1986. Registered profl. engr., Tex. Civil and structural engr. marine divsn. Brown & Root, Singapore, 1980-82; rsch. engr. Tex. Transp. Inst., College Station, 1986-88; prof. U. N.Mex., Albuquerque, 1988—; cons. Westinghouse Electric Corp., 1991—, N.Mex. State Hwy. and Transp. Dept., 1988—, NASA, 1990—. Contbr. articles to profl. jours. Mem. ASCE (chair subcom., mem. com. 19876), Transp. Rsch. Bd. (com. mem. 1988—), ASTM (com. mem. 1988—), SPIE (hon.). Methodist. Office: U NMex Dept Civil Engring Albuquerque NM 87131

CHUAN, RAYMOND LU-PO, scientific researcher, consultant; b. Shanghai, China, Mar. 4, 1924; came to U.S., 1941; s. Peter Shao-Wu and Katherine (Tao) C.; m. Norma Nicoloff, Dec. 21, 1951 (dec. 1973); m. Eugenia Nishimine Sevilla, Apr. 23, 1982; children: Jason, Alexander. BA,

Pomona Coll., 1944; MS, Calif. Inst. Tech., 1945, PhD, 1953. Rsch. assoc., then dir. Engring. Ctr. U. So. Calif., L.A., 1953-63, adj. prof. Sch. Engring., 1957-63; pres. Celestial Rsch. Corp., South Pasadena, Calif., 1963-68; staff scientist Atlantic Rsch., Costa Mesa, Calif., 1968-72, Celesco, Costa Mesa, 1972-76, Brunswick Corp., Costa Mesa, 1976-88; v.p. Femtometrics, Costa Mesa, 1985-93; ret., 1993; cons. NASA, Hampton, Va., 1972-82. Patentee in field; contbr. papers to sci. jours. Co-founder, chmn. bd. dirs. Sequoyah Sch., Pasadena, Calif., 1958-72. Mem. AAAS, Am. Geophys. Union. Home: PO Box 1183 Hanalei HI 96714-1183

CHUCK, WALTER G(OONSUN), lawyer; b. Wailuku, Maui, Hawaii, Sept. 10, 1920; s. Hong Yee and Aoe (Ting) C.; m. Marian Chun, Sept. 11, 1943; children: Jamie Allison, Walter Gregory, Meredith Jayne. Ed.B., U. Hawaii, 1941; J.D., Harvard U., 1948. Bar: Hawaii 1948. Navy auditor Pearl Harbor, 1941; field agt. Social Security Bd., 1942; labor law insp. Terr. Dept. Labor, 1943; law clk. firm Ropes, Gray, Best, Coolidge & Rugg, 1948; asst. pub. prosecutor City and County of Honolulu, 1949; with Fong, Miho & Choy, 1950-53; ptnr. Fong, Miho, Choy & Chuck, 1953-58; pvt. practice law Honolulu, 1958-65, 78-80; ptnr. Chuck & Fujiyama, Honolulu, 1965-74; ptnr. firm Chuck, Wong & Tonaki, Honolulu, 1974-76, Chuck & Pai, Honolulu, 1976-78; pres. Walter G. Chuck Law Corp., Honolulu, 1980-94; pvt. practice Honolulu, 1994—; dist. magistrate Dist. Ct. Honolulu, 1956-63; gen. ptnr. M & W Assocs., Kapalama Investment Co.; bd. dirs. Aloha Airlines, Inc., Honolulu Painting Co., Ltd. Chmn. Hawaii Employment Rels. Bd., 1955-59; bd. dirs. Nat. Assn. State Labor Rels. Bds., 1957-58, Honolulu Theatre for Youth, 1977-80; chief clk. Hawaii Ho. of Reps., 1951, 53, Hawaii Senate, 1959-61; govt. appeal agt. SSS, 1953-72; former mem. jud. coun. State of Hawaii; mem. exec. com. Hawaiian Open; former dir. Friends of Judiciary History Ctr. Inc., 1983-94; former mem. bd. dirs. YMCA. Capt. inf. Hawaii Terr. Guard. Recipient Ha'Aheo award for cmty. svc. Hawaii chpt. Am. Bd. Trial Advocates, 1995. Fellow Internat. Acad. Trial Lawyers (founder, dean, bd. dirs., state rep.), Am. Coll. Trial Lawyers; mem. ABA (former chmn. Hawaii sr. lawyers divsn., former mem. ho. of dels.), Hawaii Bar Assn. (pres. 1963), ATLA (former editor), U. Hawaii Alumni Assn. (Disting. Svc. award 1967, former dir., bd. govs.), Law Sci. Inst., Assoc. Students U. Hawaii (pres.), Am. Judicature Soc., Internat. Soc. Barristers, Am. Inst. Banking, Chinese C. of C., U. Hawaii Founders Alumni Assn. (v.p., bd. dirs., Lifetime Achievement award 1994), Harvard Club of Hawaii, Waialae Country Club (pres. 1975), Pacific Club, Oahu Country Club. Republican. Home: 2691 Aaliamanu Pl Honolulu HI 96813-1216 Office: Pacific Tower 1001 Bishop St Ste 2750 Honolulu HI 96813-3429

CHUNG, CHIN SIK, genetic epidemiologist; b. Taejon, Choongnam, Korea, May 6, 1924; came to U.S., 1949; s. Kyung Mo and Songja (Woo) C.; m. Hyun Sook, Aug. 31, 1957; children: Raymond T., Daniel C., Joyce A. BS, Oreg. State U., 1951; PhD, U. Wis., 1957. Rsch. asst. dept. genetics U. Wis., Madison, 1952-57, rsch. assoc. dept. med. genetics, 1957-61; vis. scientist NIH, Bethesda, 1961-64, rsch. biologist, 1964-65; prof. pub. health U. Hawaii, Honolulu, 1965-95, prof. genetics, 1969-95, chmn. pub. health scis., 1981-85, 90-91, 1990-92, assoc. dean Sch. Pub. Health, 1984-88; mem. EDC study sect. NIH, Bethesda, 1982-86. Assoc. editor: Am. Jour. of Human Genetics, Chgo., 1964-67; contbr. chpts. to mongraphs and over 80 articles to profl. jours. Recipient Rsch. grants NIH, NSF, Ctr. for Disease Control. Mem. APHA, AAAS, Am. Soc. Human Genetics, Am. Stats. Assn. Office: U Hawaii Sch Pub Health 1960 E West Rd Honolulu HI 96822-2319

CHUNG, HEON HWA, research and development executive; b. 1948. BEE, Younsai U.; M in Computer Sci., Mich. U., 1982. Engr. Signitic Korea, Seoul, Korea, 1973-77; mgr. PABC design Samsung GTE, Seoul, 1977-81; engr. hardware design Mohawk Data, 1983-84, ITT, 1984-87; with Samsung Info. Sys. Am., San Jose, Calif., 1990—, pres., 1994—. Office: Samsung Info Systems of Am 99 W Tasman Dr San Jose CA 95134-1707*

CHURCH, LORENE KEMMERER, retired government official; b. Jordan, Mont., Oct. 18, 1929; d. Harry F. and Laura (Stoller) Kemmerer; m. Scott Johnston, Sept. 8, 1948 (div. 1953); children: Linda M., Theodore O.; m. Fred C. Church, May 9, 1956 (dec. 1967); children: Ned B., Nia J.; m. Charles F. Gaultier, Oct. 1996. Student, Portland Community Coll., 1973-76, Portland State U., 1978-79. Sec. intelligence div. IRS, Portland, Oreg., 1973-75; trade asst. Internat. Trade Adminstrn., U.S. Dept. Commerce, Portland, 1975-84, internat. trade specialist, 1984-94; ret., 1995. Mem. NAFE, World Affairs Coun., N.W. China Coun., Portland C. of C. (Europe 1992 com. 1988-89, internat. trade adv. bd. 1988-89, treas. dist. export coun. 1996—), Western Internat. Trade Coun. Democrat. Roman Catholic. Home: 19725 SW Pike St Beaverton OR 97007-1446 Office: US Dept Commerce US&FCS 121 SW Salmon St Portland OR 97204-2901

CHURCHILL, DAVID BRIAN, claims services executive, lawyer; b. Montebello, Calif., Sept. 1, 1954; s. Wesley Byron and JoAnn (Hyland) C.; m. Laurie Lee Lathrop, Apr. 21, 1979; children: Brian Jeffrey, Paul David, Carly Denise. BS in Biology/Chemistry, No. Ariz. U., 1976, BS in Edn., 1977; JD, Western State U., 1979. Bar: Calif., U.S. Dist. Ct. (so. dist.) Calif.; tchg. credential, Calif., Ariz.; ins. lic., Calif. Tchr. biology, chemistry, physics Casa Grande (Ariz.) H.S., 1977; liability/malpractice adjuster Farmers Ins. Group, Las Vegas, Nev., 1980-81; claims mgr. Progressive Ins., Las Vegas, 1981-84; regional claims mgr. Progressive Ins., San Diego, 1984-90; CEO, gen. legal counsel, chmn. of bd. Profl. Claims Svcs., Inc., Poway, Calif., 1991—; bd. dirs. Reliant Gen. Ins., San Diego; mem. adv. bd. Vivid Net Comm., Inc., Nev., 1995—. Author: Casualty and Bodily Injury Claims, 1995. Mem. housing and devel. adv. bd. City Poway, 1991—. Recipient Hon. Svc. award PTA, 1992. Mem. ABA, State Bar Calif. Office: Profl Claims Svcs Inc 12759 Poway Rd # 201 Poway CA 92064-4446

CHURCHILL, WILLIAM DELEE, retired education educator, psychologist; b. Buffalo, Nov. 4, 1919; s. Glenn Luman and Ethel (Smith) C.; AB, Colgate U., 1941; MEd, Alfred U., 1951; EdD, U. Rochester, 1969; m. Beulah Coleman, Apr. 5, 1943; children: Cherylee, Christie. Tchr. secondary sci., Canaseraga, N.Y., 1947-56; dir. guidance Alfred-Almond Sch., Almond, N.Y., 1956-63; grad. asst. U. Rochester, 1963-65; asst. prof. psychology Alfred (N.Y.) U., 1965-66; assoc. prof. edn. Ariz. State U., Tempe, 1966-86. Lt. col. USAAF, 1942-79, PTO. Mem. Ariz. Psychol. Assn. Author: Career Survey of Graduates, 1973. Home: 11454 N 85th St Scottsdale AZ 85260-5727

CIA, MANUEL LOPEZ, artist; b. Las Cruces, N.Mex., Jan. 4, 1937; s. Anastacio Cea Lopez and Mercedes Rivera. Student, Am. Acad. Art, Chgo., 1958-61, Art Inst. San Francisco, 1962, L.A. Trade Tech., 1963-64, U. N.Mex., 1990. Author: Color Quest, 1991, Theory of Sophisticism, 1993; Exhibited in group shows at The Fundacion Teleton de Honduras, Teguicigalpa, 1989, France-USA, Paris, 1991, Arts and the Quincentennial, Albuquerque, 1992, U.S. Artists, Phila., 1993, State of the Art, Boston, 1993, Miniatures 1993, Albuquerque, 1993, Montserrat Gallery, N.Y.C., 1995; one man shows include El Prado Galleries, Sedonia, Ariz. and Santa Fe, N.Mex., 1989, 90, 95. With USAF, 1954-57. Recipient Outstanding Individual award Youth Devel., Albuquerque, 1991. Mem. Internat. Assn. Contemporary Art, Soc. Am. Impressionists. Home: PO Box 7332 Albuquerque NM 87194-7332

CIANFARANO, SAM ANTHONY, JR., principal, educator; b. Oswego, N.Y., Mar. 31, 1947; s. Samuel Anthony Sr. and Shirley Arlene (Chillson) C.; m. Lori Ann Nave, June 1981 (div. 1983); m. Linda Ann Easton, Dec. 21, 1985; children: Scott Andrew, Steven Michael. BS in Edn., SUNY, Geneseo, 1969; MEd in Adminstrn., U. Rochester, 1976; EdD in Adminstrn., No. Ariz. U., 1990. Cert. edn. adminstrn. Tchr. Rochester (N.Y.) City Sch. Dist., 1970-75, supervising tchr., sch.-cmty. rels. specialist, counselor, 1975-80; counselor, asst. prin. Murphy Elem. Sch. Dist., Phoenix, 1980-83; middle sch. prin. Osborn Sch. Dist., Phoenix, 1983-84; elem. prin. Deer Valley Unified Sch. Dist., Phoenix, 1984-92, Paradise Valley Unified Sch. Dist., Phoenix, 1992—; tchr. adminstrn. preperation, tchr. preparation courses U. Phoenix, Ariz., 1989—. Recipient celebrate literacy award Phoenix West Reading Coun., 1995, award for promoting literacy Ariz. State Reading Coun., 1995; named disting. prin. of yr. 1995 State of Ariz. Mem. ASCD, Nat. Assn. Elem. Sch. Prins., Internat. Reading Assn., Phi Delta Kappa. Lutheran. Home: 6102 E Blanche Dr Scottsdale AZ 85254-2535 Office: Paradise Valley USD #69 Liberty Elem Sch 5020 E Acoma Scottsdale AZ 85254

CICCIARELLI, JAMES CARL, immunology educator; b. Toluca, Ill., May 26, 1947; s. Maurice Cicciarelli and Helen Ippolito. BS, Tulane U., 1969; PhD, So. Ill. U., 1977. Lic. clin. lab. dir., Calif. Postdoctoral fellow dept. surgery UCLA, 1977-79, asst. prof. immunology, 1980-87, assoc. prof., 1987-91; prof. urology and microbiology U. So. Calif., L.A., 1992—; lab. dir. Metic Transplant Lab., Inc., L.A., 1984—; bd. dirs.. So. Calif. Organ Procurement Agy., 1987—; clin. lab. dir. Am. Bd. Bioanalysis, 1991—; mem. histocompatibility com. United Network Organ Sharing, 1991-94. Contbr. articles to sci. jours., chpts. to books. NIH rsch. grantee, 1985-88. Mem. Am. SOc. Histocompatibility and Immunogenetics, Internat. Transplant Soc., Am. Soc. Transplant Physicians, Internat. Soc. Heart Lung Transplantation. Libertarian. Roman Catholic. Home: 2524 Manhattan Ave Hermosa Beach CA 90254-2543 Office: USC Dept Urology Metic Transplant Lab 2100 W 3rd St Ste 280 Los Angeles CA 90057-1922

CICHANSKI, GERALD, golf course architect. B in Architecture and Engring., Ohio State U.; M in Architecture and Urban Planning, U. Wash. Registered arch., Wash. Prin. Mithun Ptnrs., Seattle; spkr., panelist Nat. Club Mgrs. Conv. Prin. works include Point Roberts (Wash.) Marina and Clubhouse, The Summit Athletic Club, Bellevue, Wash., Everett (Wash.) Gold & Country Club, Sunset Club, Seattle, Carnation (Wash.) Club, Snoqualmie (Wash.) Ridge Golf Club, Allen Island Resort & Clubhouse, San Juan Islands, Wash., Broadmoor Golf Club, Seattle, Newcastle Golf Club, Bellevue, Indian Summer Golf Club, Olympia, Wash., Meriwood at Hawks Prairie Golf Club, Olympia, Summer Golf & Country Club, Lacey, Wash., others. Mem. AIA, Nat. Golf. Found., Club Mgrs. Assn. Office: Mithun Partners Inc 414 Olive Way Ste 500 Seattle WA 98101-1132*

CICIONI, WALTER WILLIAM, traffic engineer; b. Shenandoah, Pa., Apr. 2, 1947; s. Giacamo Jack and Ann (Zemansky) C.; m. Ellen Marie Heaton, Jan. 31, 1970; children: Jennifer, Debora, Matthew. BS in Civil Engring., Pa. State U., 1969, MS in Traffic Engring., 1972. Registered profl. engr., Ariz. Traffic engring. asst. City of L.A., 1969-71; city traffic engr. City of Virginia Beach, Va., 1972-75; traffic engring. supr. City of Phoenix, 1975—. Mem. Inst. Transp. Engrs. Republican. Office: City of Phoenix 200 W Washington St Phoenix AZ 85003-1611

CICORA, MARY ANGELA, researcher, author; b. Ridgewood, N.J., Sept. 21, 1957; d. Samuel M. and Cecelia Cicora. BA, Yale U., 1979; MA, Cornell U., 1982, PhD, 1985. Vis. scholar Stanford (Calif.) U., 1986—. Author: Parsifal Reception, 1987, From History to Myth, 1992; contbr. articles to profl. jours. Mem. Phi Beta Kappa. Home: 707 Continental Cir Apt 1333 Mountain View CA 94040-3313

CILEK, JEFFREY ROBERT, nonprofit executive; b. Iowa City, June 5, 1958; s. Joseph Francis Cilek and Jean (Wilson) Adler; m. Katherine Ann Peck, Nov. 24, 1994; 1 child, Joseph Francis. BBA, U. Iowa, 1980. Legis. dir. U.S. Senator James A. McClure, Washington, 1982-84; staff dir. interior subcom. U.S. Senate, Washington, 1984-90; v.p. The Peregrine Fund, Boise, Idaho, 1992—; mem. adv. com. Nat. Fish and Wildlife Found., Washington, 1990-92. Editor: Congressional Candidates Briefing Book, 1984, Almanac of the Unelected, 1989-90. Del. Bush for Pres., Iowa City, 1980. Mem. Boise C. of C. (chmn. state affairs and natural resources). Roman Catholic.

CIMIKOWSKI, ROBERT JOHN, computer scientist; b. Norwich, Conn., Apr. 23, 1949; s. Stephen and Sophie (Sudik) C.; m. Linda E. Sankoski, Feb. 11, 1983. BA in Math., Fordham U., 1972; MS in Computer Sci., Worcester Poly., 1974; PhD in Computer Sci., N.Mex. State U., 1990. Systems analyst Burroughs Corp., East Hartford, Conn., 1974-77, Martin-Marietta Data Systems, Denver, 1978-81, AT&T Info. Systems, Denver, 1981-83; assoc. prof. Mont. State U., Bozeman, 1990—. Contbr. articles to Computers & Math. with Applications, Info. Processing Letter, Jour. Combinatorial Math. & Computing, Discrete Applied Math., Pattern Recognition Letters, Discrete Maths., others. Recipient Engring. Experiment Sta., Mont. State U., 1990, 91. Mem. Assn. for Computing Machinery, Spl. Interest Group on Automata Theory, European Assn. for Theoretical Computer Sci., Golden Key Honor Soc. Office: Montana State U Computer Sci Dept Bozeman MT 59717

CINNAMON, WILLIAM, III, elementary and special education educator; b. Kansas City, Mo., Aug. 19, 1953; s. William and Joan C. (Davidson) C. BA in Education, U. N.Mex., 1975; MA in Spl. Edn., Loyola Marymount U., 1990. Cert. Adult Multiple Subject, Calif., Single Subject, N.Mex. History, English tchr. Order of Friars Minor St. Elizabeth's High Sch., Oakland, Calif., 1975-83; elem. tchr. Archdiocese of L.A. Christ the King Sch., Hollywood, Calif., 1983-89, L.A. Unified Sch. Dist. Fernangeles Art St., Sun Valley, Calif., 1989-94; tchr. Richard E. Byrd Mid. Sch., 1994—, mentor tchr., 1992-95, dept. chairperson, 1994—; mem. Sch. Decision-Making Coun., Sun Valley, Calif., 1991—; cons. Spl. Edn. in Cath. Schs., L.A., 1985-89; participant, math. edn. leader FATHOM: Spl. Math. Edn. Leadership Tng., 1993-96. Contbr. articles to profl. jours. Mem. Christopher St. West, West Holywood, Calif., 1990, Mcpl. Elections Com., L.A.; vol. L.A. Olympic Orgn. Com., L.A., 1984, Stonewall Club. Recipient personal invitation to meet Pope John Paul II, Archdiocese of L.A., St. Vibiana's Cathedral. 1988. Mem. Gay and Lesbian Educators, L.A. City Math. Tchrs., United Tchrs. L.A., English Coun. L.A., Disneyland Alumni Club, Phi Delta Kappa. Roman Catholic. Home: 11601 Burbank Blvd # 3 North Hollywood CA 91601 Office: Byrd Mid Sch 9171 Telfair Ave Sun Valley CA 91352

CIOC, CHARLES GREGORY, information systems executive; b. Scottsbluff, Nebr., Apr. 16, 1951; s. Charles John and Beatrice Devona C.; children: Christopher, Connor. AA in Bus. Adminstrn., Casper (Wyo.) Coll., 1971; BA in Bus. Adminstrn., Wash. State U., 1973; M in Urban Planning, U. Wash., 1990. Indsl. engr. Boeing, Seattle, 1974-77, database adminstr., 1980-81; database analyst Transp. Sys. Ctr., Cambridge, Mass., 1978-80; systems officer Seafirst Bank, Seattle, 1981-83; airport planner TRA-Arch Engr., Seattle, 1986-90; sr. transp. planner King County Dept. Transp., Seattle, 1990-96, data devel. mgr. Puget Sound Regional Coun., 1997—. Home: 7534 NE Emerald Bainbridge Island WA 98110

CIOC, MARK, history educator; b. Havre, Mont., May 3, 1952; s. Charles John and Beatrice Devona (Watson) C. BA in History, U. Wyo., 1974, MA in History, 1978; PhD in History, U. Calif., Berkeley, 1986. Asst. prof. history U. Mass., Amherst, 1987-89; assoc. prof. history U. Calif., Santa Cruz, 1989—; provost Stevenson Coll., U. Calif., Santa Cruz, 1994—. Author: Pax Atomica, 1988. Grantee Fulbright Commn., 1978-79, 1993-94; peace fellow Hoover Inst., 1990-91. Home: Stevenson Provost House 101 McLaughlin Dr Santa Cruz CA 95064-1013 Office: U Calif 101 Mclaughlin Dr Santa Cruz CA 95064-1080

CIPRIANO, PATRICIA ANN, secondary education educator, consultant; b. San Francisco, Apr. 24, 1946; d. Ernest Peter and Claire Patricia (Croak) C. BA in English, Holy Names Coll., Oakland, Calif., 1967; MA in Edn. of Gifted, Calif. State U.-L.A., 1980. Cert. tchr., tchr. gifted, adminstrv. svc., lang. devel. specialist, Calif. Tchr. English, math. Bancroft Jr. High Sch., San Leandro, Calif., 1968-79, 83-85, coord. gifted edn., 1971-79; tchr. English, math., computers San Leandro High Sch., 1979-83, 85-96, mentor tchr., 1991-94, chmn. English dept., 1992-96, coord. gifted and talented edn., 1981-83; tchr. English, math. Los Cerritos Mid. Sch., Thousand Oaks, Calif., 1996—, chmn. English dept., 1996—; cons. Calif. State Dept. Edn., various Calif. sch. dists.; dir. Calif. Lit. Project Policy Bd. Recipient Hon. Svc. award Tchr. of Yr., Bancroft Jr. High Sch. PTA, 1973; bd. dirs. Calif. Curriculum Correlating Coun. Mem. NEA, Calif. Assn. for Gifted, World Coun. Gifted and Talented, Cen. Calif. Coun. Tchrs. English (past pres.), Calif. Assn. Tchrs. English (bd. dirs., past pres., disting. svc. award 1996), Nat. Coun. Tchr. English (bd. dirs.), San Leandro Tchrs. Assn., Calif. Tchrs. Assn., Computer Using Educators, Assn. for Supervision and Curriculum Devel., Calif. Math. Coun., Nat. Coun. Tchrs. Math., Curriculum Study Commn., Delta Kappa Gamma (past pres.). Roman Catholic. Avocations: reading, piano, calligraphy, tennis, photography. Contbr. articles to profl. jours. Office: Los Cerritos Mid Sch 2100 Avenida de Los Flores Thousand Oaks CA 91362

CIRIGLIANO, JOHN J(OSEPH), investment company executive; b. N.Y.C., Sept. 22, 1942; s. Michael and Ann T. (Lufrano) C.; m. Nancy B. Hughes, July 29, 1996. AB, Columbia U., 1964; JD, N.Y. Law Sch., 1968. Assoc. Longstreet Corp./Lazard Freres & Co., N.Y.C., 1968-72; v.p. Oppenheimer & Co., N.Y.C., 1972-73; pres. Copaquen Assocs., Inc., N.Y.C., 1973-75; v.p. Merrill Lynch, N.Y.C., 1976-81, mng. dir., 1981-86; pres. Clearbrook & Co. Ltd., Palo Alto, Calif., 1986—. Adv. bd. Outward Bound, Inc., Bedford, N.Y., 1986—, Columbia U., N.Y.C., 1990-93. Mem. Univ. Club, Sands Point Golf Club. Roman Catholic. Office: Clearbrook Cos 260 Sheridan Ave Ste 416 Palo Alto CA 94306-2011

CIRONE, WILLIAM JOSEPH, educational administrator; b. Bklyn., Dec. 27, 1937; s. Joseph Nicholas and Marie Ann (Basile) C.; m. Barbara Jane Skirkie, Dec. 22, 1962; 1 son, Peter Craig. BA, Providence Coll., 1959; MA, NYU, 1960; adminstrv. cert. U. Calif.-Santa Barbara, 1977. Tchr., N.Y.C. Pub. Schs., 1960-68; dir. product devel. ednl. div. Mead Corp., Atlanta, 1968-70, dir. mktg., 1970-73; founder/dir. Ctr. Community Edn. and Citizen Participation, Santa Barbara, Calif., 1973-82; supt. schs. Santa Barbara County, 1983—; vis. fellow Chisholm Inst. Technology, Melbourne, Australia, 1986; vis. scholar Ctr. for Excellence Tenn. State U., 1986. Contbg. editor New Designs for Youth Development, 1984—. Bd. dirs. Community Action Commn., 1973-81, Community Resource Info Service, 1978-82, Community Housing Corp., 1980-82; bd. dirs., sec. Pvt. Industry Council, Santa Barbara, 1983-89; bd. dirs. Industry Edn. Council, Santa Barbara, 1983—, pres., 1990—; bd. dirs. Santa Barbara Lung Assn., 1983-87, Philip Francis Siff Ednl. Found., 1986—; Community Devel. Assistance Corp., 1980—, Impact II, 1989—, pres., 1993; bd. dirs. Nat. Comm. Edn. Assn., 1989-92, pres., 1990; regional chair Calif. County Supt. Assn., 1990—, bd. dirs. media and values, 1989-92; hon. bd. dirs. So. Coast Spl. Olympics; mem. Gov.'s Commn. on Earthquake Hazards, 1981; mem. state bd. Common Cause, 1974-77, organizer and 1st state chmn., Ga., 1970-73; mem. voter accessibility adv. bd. Santa Barbara County, 1986—; mem. adv. bd. CALM, Peace Resource Ctr., Marymount Sch., Women's Community Bldg., Jodi House, commdrs. community liasion com. Vandenburg AFB; Access Theatre; Hon. Comm. for Goleta Valley Hosp.; mem. campaign cabinet Santa Barbara United Way, 1992—. Recipient Smallheiser award United Fedn. Tchrs., 1968, Hon. Svc. award 15th Dist. PTA, 1979, 81, Intercongregation Org. Project Action award, 1995, Anti-Defamation League, South Santa Barbara Disting. Svc. award, 1996. Meritorious Service award Community Action Com., Santa Barbara, 1981, Ind. Living Resource Ctr., 1985, Hon. Svc. award Calif. State PTA, 1995; named Calif. Community Educator Yr., Calif. Community Edn. Assn., 1984, Pub. Servant of Yr., Santa Barbara County, 1987. Mem. World Future Soc. (life), Am. Assn. Sch. Adminstrs., Assn. Calif. Sch. Adminstrs., So. Coast Coordinating Council (past chmn., past exec. com.), Nat. Soc. Fundraising Execs., Automobile Assn. Am. (So. Calif. adv. bd.), Phi Delta Kappa. Democrat. Unitarian. Home: 953 Elk Grove Ln Solvang CA 93463-9608 Office: PO Box 6307 Santa Barbara CA 93160-6307

CISMARU, PAT KLEIN, municipal official; b. N.Y.C., Sept. 27, 1933; children: Jay, David. BBA, CCNY, 1958; MEd, CUNY, 1960; MS, Tex. Tech U., 1985, PhD, 1991. Lic. social worker, Tex.; OAMT mgmt. cert.; notary public, Tex. Owner Masonry Constrn. Co., Lubbock, Tex., 1980—; dir. respite unit LRMHMR Ctr., Lubbock, 1980-89; acad. dir. Park Coll., Lubbock, 1985-90; programs adminstr. RRIP Lubbock Housing Authority, 1989-93; owner rental property, N.J., Vt., Tex., Colo., 1972—; owner residential and comml. laundromats, Colo., 1991; convenience store, Colo., 1993—; tanning salons, Tex., 1993—; galaxy grocer. Mem. NAFE, AARP, LWV, NASW, Goodwill Industries. Home and Office: PO Box 620693 Littleton CO 80162

CIVILIKAS, ROBERT GEORGE, naval officer; b. Needham, Mass., Dec. 30, 1959; s. Frank J. and Alice M. (Hampshire) C. BS in Aerospace Engring., U.S. Naval Acad., 1982; grad., Naval Fighter Weapons Sch., 1986, USAF Test Pilot Sch., 1988; MS in Sys. Mgmt., U. So. Calif., 1991. Ensign USN, 1982—, advanced through grades to lt. comdr., 1991. Mem. Sigma Xi. Home and Office: Strike Force S PSC 813 Box 172 Naples Italy FPO AE 09620-0172

CIVITELLO-JOY, LINDA JOAN, association executive; b. Sacramento, Jan. 21, 1951; d. Theodore Edward and Dorothy Mae (McCarnes) Civitello; m. David Franklin Joy, Nov. 14, 1981; children: Aileen F. Joy, Nicholas E. Joy. BA, Antioch West U., 1976; MA in Polit. Sci., San Francisco State U., 1985. Exec. dir. Tri-Cities Child Devel., Fremont, Calif., 1974-76; cmty. svcs. liaison U. Calif., San Francisco, 1976-91; sr. v.p. McClaughlin Young, San Francisco, 1991-93; exec. dir. Am. Lung Assn. San Francisco and San Mateo, Daly City, Calif., 1993—; bd. dirs. Am. Lung Assn. Contbr. articles to profl. jours. Mem. Am. Soc. Assn. Execs. Roman Catholic. Home: 3455 Sacramento St San Francisco CA 94118 Office: Am Lung Assn 2171 Junipero Serra Blvd Daly City CA 94014-1980

CLABAUGH, ELMER EUGENE, JR., lawyer; b. Anaheim, Calif., Sept. 18, 1927; s. Elmer Eugene and Eleanor Margaret (Heitshusen) C.; m. Donna Marie Organ, Dec. 19, 1960 (div.); children: Christopher C., Matthew M. BBA cum laude, Woodbury U.; BA summa cum laude, Claremont McKenna Coll., 1958; JD, Stanford U., 1961. Bar: Calif. 1961, U.S. Dist. Ct. (cen. dist.) Calif., U.S. Ct. Appeals (9th cir.) 1961, U.S. Supreme Ct. 1971. With fgn. svc. U.S. Dept. State, Jerusalem and Tel Aviv, 1951-53, Pub. Adminstrn. Svc., El Salvador, Ethiopia, U.S., 1953-57; dep. dist. atty. Ventura County, Calif., 1961-62; pvt. practice, Ventura, Calif., 1962-97; mem. Hathaway, Clabaugh, Perrett and Webster and predecessors, 1962-79, Clabaugh & Perloff, Ventura, 1979-97; state inheritance tax referee, 1968-78. Bd. dirs. San Antonio Water Conservation Dist., Ventura Community Meml. Hosp., 1964-80; trustee Ojai Unified Sch. Dist., 1974-79; bd. dirs. Ventura County Found. for Parks and Harbors, 1982-96, Ventura County Maritime Mus., 1982-94. With USCGR, 1944-46, USMCR, 1946-48. Mem. NRA, Calif. Bar Assn., Am. Arbitration Assn., Safari Club Internat., Mason, Shriners, Phi Alpha Delta. Republican. Home: 241 Highland Dr Oxnard CA 93035-4412 Office: 1190 S Victoria Ave Ventura CA 93003-6507

CLAES, DANIEL JOHN, physician; b. Glendale, Calif., Dec. 3, 1931; s. John Vernon and Claribel (Fleming) C.; AB magna cum laude, Harvard U., 1953, MD cum laude, 1957; m. Gayla Christine Blasdel, Jan. 19, 1974. Intern, UCLA, 1957-58; Bowyer Found. fellow for rsch. in medicine, L.A., 1958-61; pvt. practice specializing in diabetes, L.A., 1962—; med. cons. SIRA Techs., 1995—; v.p. Am. Eye Bank Found., 1978-83, pres., 1983—, dir. rsch., 1980—, chmn., CEO 1995—; pres. Heuristic Corp., 1981—. Mem. L.A. Mus. Art, 1960—. Mem. AMA, AAAS, Calif. Med. Assn., L.A. County Med. Assn., Am. Diabetes Assn. (profl. coun. on immunology, immunogenetics and transplantation), Internat. Diabetes Fedn., Internat. Pancreas & Islet Transplant Assn. Clubs: Harvard and Harvard Med. Sch. of So. Calif.; Royal Commonwealth (London). Contbr. papers on diabetes mellitus, computers in medicine to profl. lit. Office: Am Eyebank Found 15327 W Sunset Blvd Ste 236 Pacific Palisades CA 90272-3674

CLAES, GAYLA CHRISTINE, writer, editorial consultant; b. L.A., Oct. 17, 1946; d. Henry George and Glorya Desiree (Curran) Blasdel; m. Daniel John Claes, Jan. 19, 1974. AB magna cum laude, Harvard U., 1968; postgrad., Oxford (Eng.) U., 1971; MA, McGill U., Montreal, 1975. Administr. asst. U. So. Calif., L.A., 1968-70; teaching asst. English lit. McGill U., Montreal, 1970-71; editorial dir. Internat. Cons. Group, L.A., 1972-78; v.p. Gaylee Corp., L.A., 1978-81, CEO, 1981-88; writer, cons. L.A. and Paris, 1988—; dir. pub. rels. Centre Internat. for the Performing Arts, Paris and L.A., 1991—. Author: (play) Berta of Hungary, 1972, (novel) Christopher Derring, 1990; contbr. articles to lit. and sci. jours. Mem. Harvard-Radcliffe Club of So. Calif., Royal Commonwealth Soc. (London).

CLAIR, THEODORE NAT, educational psychologist; b. Stockton, Calif., Apr. 19, 1929; s. Peter David and Sara Renee (Silverman) C.; A.A., U. Calif. at Berkeley, 1949, A.B., 1950; M.S., U. So. Calif., 1953, M.Ed., 1963, Ed.D., 1969; m. Laura Gold, June 19, 1961; children: Shari, Judith. Tchr., counselor Los Angeles City Schs., 1957-63; psychologist Alamitos Sch. Dist., Garden Grove, Calif., 1963-64, Arcadia (Calif.) Unified Sch. Dist., 1964-65; head psychologist Wiseburn Sch. Dist., Hawthorne, Calif., 1966-69; asst. prof. spl. edn., coordinator sch. psychology program U. Iowa, Iowa City, 1969-72; dir. pupil personnel services Orcutt (Calif.) Union Sch. Dist., 1972-73; adminstr. Mt. Diablo Unified Sch. Dist., 1973-77; program dir., psychologist San Mateo County Office of Edn., Redwood City, 1977-91; assoc. prof. John F. Kennedy U. Sch. Mgmt., 1975-77; pvt. practice as ednl. psychologist and marriage and family counselor, Menlo Park, Calif., 1978—, Menlo Park, Calif., 1977-93, dir. Peninsula Vocat. Rehab. Inst., 1978—; psychologist Coll. Counseling Svc., Menlo Pk., 1992—, Calif. Pacific Hosp., San Francisco, 1993—. Served with USNR, 1952-54. Mem. APA, Nat. Assn. Sch. Psychologists, Calif. Assn. Marriage and Family Counselors, Nat. Rehab. Assn, Palo Alto B'nai B'rith Club (pres.). Author: Phenylketonuria and Some Other Inborn Errors of Amino Acid Metabolism, 1971; editor Jour. Calif. Ednl. Psychologists, 1992-94; contbr. articles to profl. jours. Home and Office: 56 Willow Rd Menlo Park CA 94025-3654

CLAIRE, FRED, professional baseball team executive. A.A., Mt. San Antonio Coll.; B.A. in Journalism, San Jose State Coll., 1957. Formerly sports writer and columnist Long Beach Ind. Press Telegram and Whittier News; sports editor Pomo Progress-Bull, Calif., until 1969; dir. publicity Los Angeles Dodgers, Nat. League, 1969-75, v.p. pub. relations and promotions, 1975-82, exec. v.p., from 1982, now exec. v.p. player personnel, 1987—; bd. dirs. Major League Baseball Promotion Corp. Bd. dirs. Greater Los Angeles Vistors and Conv. Bur. Named The Sporting News Major League Exec. of Yr., 1988. Mem. Echo Park C. of C. Lodge: Los Angeles Rotary. Office: LA Dodgers 1000 Elysian Park Ave Los Angeles CA 90012-1112*

CLANTON, PAUL DAVID, JR., management information systems director; b. Potsdam, N.Y., May 29, 1958; s. Paul David and JoAnne Carol (DeWitt) C.; m. Kimberly Jean Thuon, June 11, 1983; children: Ian, Adria. BA in Psychology, SUNY, Albany, 1980; AAS in Computer Sci., Parks Jr. Coll., 1986. Product integration mgr. Coral Group, Denver, 1986-92; sr. cons. Berger & Co., Denver, 1992-94; MIS dir. City of Thornton, Colo., 1994—. Mem. Data Processing Mgmt. Assn., Assn. Computer Machinery. Office: City of Thornton 9500 Civic Center Dr Thornton CO 80229-4326

CLARK, AARON LEE, environmental consulting executive; b. Fondulac, Wis., Sept. 24, 1955; s. Darrel R. and Geraldine M. (Vander Galien) C.; m. Gretchen L. Harrison, May 7, 1982. BA, Ind. U., 1977; MS, U. Louisville, 1979. Sr. scientist Woodward-Clyde Consultants, San Diego, 1979-81; coord. regulatory affairs Amoco Prodn. Co., Denver, 1981-87; pres. PIC Techs., Inc., Denver, 1987—. Trustee Black-Footed Ferret Recovery Found., Denver, 1996—. Office: PIC Techs Inc 1133 Pennsylvania St Denver CO 80203

CLARK, ARTHUR BRYAN, engineer; b. St. Paul, Aug. 26, 1964; s. Arthur Bryan and Frankie Lucy (Cartier) C.; m. Candace Lee Stutsman, Oct. 19, 1984; 1 child, Courtney Marie. Sr. engr. Eldyne, Inc., San Diego, 1987—. With USN, 1981—. Mem.Navy League (bd. dirs. 1995—), Naval Inst., Loyal Order Moose. Home: 603 Elaine Ave Oceanside CA 92057-3538

CLARK, ARTHUR JOSEPH, JR., mechanical and electrical engineer; b. West Orange, N.J., June 10, 1921; s. Arthur Joseph and Marjorie May (Courter) C.; BS in Mech. Engring., Cornell U., 1943; MS, Poly. Inst. Bklyn., 1948; MS in Elec. Engring., U. N.Mex., 1955; m. Caroline Katherine Badgley, June 12, 1943; children: Arthur Joseph, III, Durward S., David P. Design engr. Ranger Aircraft Engines Co., Farmingdale, N.Y., 1943-46; sr. structures engr. propeller div. Curtis Wright Co., Caldwell, N.J., 1946-51; mgr. space isotope power dept., also aerospace nuclear safety dept. Sandia Labs., Albuquerque, 1951-71, mgr. environ. systems test lab., 1971-79, mgr. mil. liaison dept., 1979-86; pres. Engring. Svcs. Cons. Firm, 1987; mem. faculty U. N.Mex., 1971-75; invited lectr. Am. Mgmt. Assn. Pres. Sandia Base Sch. PTA, 1960-61; chmn. finance com. Albuquerque chpt. Am. Field Svc., 1964-66; chmn. Sandia Labs. div. U.S. Savs. Bond drive, 1972-74, chmn. employee contbn. drive, 1973-75; active local Boy Scouts Am., 1958-66. Recipient Order Arrow, Boy Scouts Am., 1961, Order St. Andrew, 1962, Scouters Key award, 1964; cert. outstanding service Sandia Base, 1964. Fellow ASME (nat. v.p. 1975-79, past chmn. N.Mex. sect.); mem. IEEE (sr.), Cornell Engring. Soc., Theta Xi. Clubs: Kirtland Officers, Four Hills Country. Home: 905 Warm Sands Trail Albuquerque NM 87123-4332

CLARK, BEVERLY WYONE, nutritionist; b. Seattle, Sept. 10, 1948; d. Dean Voris and Gail Wyone (Whittaker) Babst; m. Roberto Medina Bernardo, Dec. 18, 1970 (div. June 1977); 1 child, Dolores; m. Barry Allan Clark, Dec. 30, 1978; children: Marcelina, Kevin. BS in foods & nutrition, Stout State U., 1970; MPH in nutrition, U. Calif., 1972; student, Merrill Palmer Inst., Mich., 1969. Registered dietitian. Dietary cons. various convalescent hosps., Bay Area, Calif., 1972-73; nutrition cons. Solano County Head Start, Fairfield, Calif., 1973-75; instr. home econs. San Jose (Calif.) City Coll., 1973; nutritionist Contra Costa County, Martinez, Calif., 1974-75, CARE, Manila, Philippines, 1975-76; dir., nutritionist Alameda County, Oakland, Calif., 1976-94, Contra Costa County, Concord, Calif., 1994—; rep. Task Force State WIC, Sacramento, 1986-88, 90-92; bd. rep. Calif. WIC Assn., 1992—; apptd. to adv. bd. Cambodian New Generation, Oakland, 1983-94. Vol. Lamorinda Dem. Club, Orinda, Calif., 1990—; apptd. adv. bd. Head Start, Contra Costa County. Mem. Calif. Dietetic Assn., Am. Dietetic Assn., Diablo Valley Dietetic Assn. Home: 400 Read Dr Lafayette CA 94549-5617 Office: Contra Costa County Health Svcs Dept 2355 Stanwell Cir Concord CA 94520-4806

CLARK, BRIAN THOMAS, mathematical statistician, operations research analyst; b. Rockford, Ill., Apr. 7, 1951; s. Paul Herbert and Martha Lou (Schlensker) C.; m. Suzanne Drake, Nov. 21, 1992. B.S. cum laude, No. Ariz. U., 1973; postgrad. Ariz. State U., 1980-82. Math. aide Center for Disease Control, Phoenix, 1973-74, math. statistician, 1979-83; math. Statistician Ctrs. for Disease Control, Atlanta, 1983-84 ops. research analyst U.S. Army Info. Systems Command, Ft. Huachuca, Ariz., 1984—; math. statistician U.S. Navy Metrology Engring. Center, Pomona, Calif., 1974-79. Republican. Mormon. Office: US Army Signal Command Dep Chief Staff Resource Mgmt G8 Managerial Acctg Pricing Fort Huachuca AZ 85613

CLARK, BURTON ROBERT, sociologist, educator; b. Pleasantville, N.J., Sept. 6, 1921; s. Burton H. and Cornelia (Amole) C.; m. Adele Halitsky, Aug. 31, 1949; children: Philip Neil (dec.), Adrienne. B.A., UCLA, 1949, Ph.D., 1954. Asst. prof. sociology Stanford U., 1953-56; research asso., asst. prof. edn. Harvard U., 1956-58; asso. prof., then prof. edn. and asso. research sociologist, then research sociologist U. Calif. at Berkeley, 1958-66; prof. sociology Yale U., 1966-80, chmn. dept., 1969-72; chmn. Higher Edn. Research Group, 1973-80, Comparative Higher Edn. Research Group, 1980-91; Allan M. Cartter prof. higher edn. UCLA, 1980-91, prof. emeritus, 1991—. Author: Adult Education in Transition, 1956, The Open Door College, 1960, Educating the Expert Society, 1962, The Distinctive College, 1970, The Problems of American Education, 1975, Academic Power in Italy, 1977, The Higher Education System, 1983, The Academic Life, 1987, Places of Inquiry, 1995; co-author: Students and Colleges, 1972, Youth: Transition to Adulthood, 1973, Academic Power in the United States, 1976, Academic Power: Patterns of Authority in Seven National Systems of Higher Education, 1978; editor: Perspectives on Higher Education, 1984, The School and The University, 1985, The Academic Profession, 1987, The Research Foundations of Graduate education, 1993; co-senior editor: Encyclopedia of Higher Education, 1992. Served with AUS, 1942-46. Mem. Internat. Sociol. Assn., Am. Sociol. Assn., Am. Ednl. Rsch. Assn. (Am. Coll. Testing award 1979, Divsn. J. Disting. Rsch. award 1988, Outstanding Book award 1989), Assn. Study Higher Edn. (pres. 1979-80, Rsch. Achievement award 1985), Am. Assn. Higher Edn., Nat. Acad. Edn. (v.p. 1989-93), Consortium Higher Edn. Rschrs., European Assn. for Instnl. Rsch., Brit. Soc. for Rsch. in Higher Edn. Home: 201 Ocean Ave Apt 1710B Santa Monica CA 90402-1476 Office: UCLA Dept Edn Los Angeles CA 90095

CLARK, CHARLES SUTTER, interior designer; b. Venice, Calif., Dec. 21, 1927; s. William Sutter and Lodema Ersell (Fleeman) C. Student Chouinard Art Inst., Los Angeles, 1950 51. Interior designer LM.H. Co., Gt. Falls, Mont., 1956-62, Andreason's Interiors, Oakland, Calif., 1962-66, Western Contact Furnishers Internat., Oakland, 1966-70, Design Five Assocs., Lafayette, Calif., 1972-73; owner, interior designer Charles Sutter Clark Interiors, Greenbrae, Calif., 1973-91, San Rafael, Calif., 1991—. Served with USAF, 1951-55. Recipient prizes Mont. State Fair, 1953-55. Mem. Am. Soc. Interior Designers. Home: 429 El Faisan Dr San Rafael CA 94903-4517

CLARK, EARL ERNEST, publisher; b. Corpus Christi, Tex., Nov. 1, 1958; s. Earl Rush and Erika Martha (Jacobs) C. BA, Oreg. State U., 1985. Pub. Horison Publs., Corvallis, Oreg., Avant-Garde Publs., Tigard, Oreg. Author: Magic of Credit Repair, 1994, (poetry) ...Bomb threat for general public, 1993 (award 1994). With USN, 1987-92. Mem. Masons. Home: 10000 SW Hall Blvd Apt 9 Tigard OR 97223-8847

CLARK, EARNEST HUBERT, JR., tool company executive; b. Birmingham, Ala., Sept. 8, 1926; s. Earnest Hubert and Grace May (Smith) C.; m. Patricia Margaret Hamilton, June 22, 1947; children: Stephen D., Kenneth A., Timothy R., Daniel S., Scott H., Rebecca G. BS in Mech. Engring, Calif. Inst. Tech., 1946, MS, 1947. Chmn., chief exec. officer Friendship Group, Baker Hughes, Inc. (formerly Baker Oil Tools, Inc.), L.A., 1947-89, v.p., asst. gen. mgr., 1958-62, pres., chief exec. officer, 1962-69, 75-79, chmn. bd., 1969-75, 79-87, 87-89, ret., 1989; ret. The Friendship Group, Newport Beach, Calif., 1989; bd. dirs. Honeywell, Inc., Kerr-McGee Corp., Beckman Instruments Inc., Regenesis Inc., Am. Mut. Fund. Past chmn., bd. dirs. YMCA of U.S.A.; past chmn. bd. YMCA for Met. L.A.; mem. nat. coun. YMCA; trustee Harvey Mudd Coll. With USNR, 1944-46, 51-52. Mem. AIME, Am. Petroleum Inst., Petroleum Equipment Suppliers Assn. (bd. dirs.), Tau Beta Pi. Office: Friendship Group 3822 Calle Ariana San Clemente CA 92672

CLARK, EDGAR SANDERFORD, insurance broker, consultant; b. N.Y.C., Nov. 17, 1933; s. Edgar Edmund, Jr., and Katharine Lee (Jarman) C.; student U. Pa., 1952-54; BS, Georgetown U., 1956, JD, 1958; postgrad. INSEAD, Fountainbleau, France, 1969, Golden Gate Coll., 1973, U. Calif., Berkeley, 1974; m. Nancy E. Hill, Sept. 13, 1975; 1 dau., Schuyler; children by previous marriages: Colin, Alexandra, Pamela. Staff asst. U.S. Senate select com. to investigate improper activities in labor and mgmt. field, Washington, 1958-59; underwriter Ocean Marine Dept., Fireman's Fund Ins. Co., San Francisco, 1959-62; mgr. Am. Fgn. Ins. Assn., San Francisco, 1962-66; with Marsh & McLennan, 1966-72, mgr. for Europe, resident dir. Brussels, Belgium, 1966-70, asst. v.p., mgr. captive and internat. div., San Francisco, 1970-72; v.p., dir. Risk Planning Group, Inc., San Francisco, 1972-75; v.p., dir. global constrn. group Alexander & Alexander Inc., San Francisco, 1975-94; exec. dir. The Surplus Line Assn. of Calif., 1995—; lectr. profl. orgns.; guest lectr. U. Calif., Berkeley, 1973, Am. Grad. Sch. Internat. Mgmt., 1981, 82, Golden Gate U., annually 1985-91. Served with USAF, 1956-58. Mem. Am. Mgmt. Assn., Am. Risk and Ins. Assn., Internat. Insurance Soc., Chartered Ins. Inst., Am. Soc. Internat. Law, Soc. Calif. Pioneers San Francisco, Meadow Club, Fairfax, Calif., World Trade San Francisco. Republican. Episcopalian. Mem. editorial adv. bd. Risk Mgmt. Reports, 1973-76. Home: 72 Millay Pl Mill Valley CA 94941-1501 Office: Surplus Line Assn of Calif 388 Market St Ste 1150 San Francisco CA 94111

CLARK, GLEN EDWARD, judge; b. Cedar Rapids, Iowa, Nov. 23, 1943; s. Robert M. and Georgia L. (Welch) C.; m. Deanna D. Thomas, July 16, 1966; children: Andrew Curtis, Carissa Jane. BA, U. Iowa, 1966; JD, U. Utah, 1971. Bar: Utah 1971, U.S. Dist. Ct. Utah 1971, U.S. Ct. Appeals (10th cir.) 1972. Assoc. Fabian & Clendenin, 1971-74, ptnr., 1975-81, dir., chmn. banking and comml. law sect., 1981-82; judge U.S. Bankruptcy Ct. Dist. Utah, Salt Lake City, 1982-86, chief judge, 1986—; bd. govs. nat. Conf. Bankruptcy Judges, 1988-94; mem. com. on bankruptcy edn. Fed. Jud. Ctr., 1989-92; vis. prof. U. Utah, Salt Lake City, 1977-79, 83; pres. Nat. Conf. Bankruptcy Judges, 1992-93; chair bd. trustees Nat. Conf. Bankruptcy Judges Endowment for Edn., 1990-92. vis. assoc. prof. law Univ. Utah; instr. adv. bus. law Univ. Utah. Articles editor: Utah Law Review. With U.S. Army, 1966-68. Finkbine fellow U. Iowa. Fellow Am. Coll. Bankruptcy (charter, mem. bd. regents 1995—); mem. Jud. Conf. U.S. (mem. com. jud. br. 1992—, 10th cir. bankruptcy appellate panel 1996—), Utah Bar Assn., Order of Coif. Presbyterian. Office: US Bankruptcy Ct US Courthouse Rm 361 350 S Main St Salt Lake City UT 84101-2106

CLARK, JAMES H., electronics executive; b. Ft. Worth, Tex., 1944. BS, U. New Orleans, 1971; MS, U. Utah, 1974, PhD. Founder, chmn. bd. Silicon Graphics, Inc., 1981—; bd. dirs. Paracomp. Home: 2040 Broadway St San Francisco CA 94115-1500

CLARK, JEFFREY RAPHIEL, research and development company executive; b. Provo, Utah, Sept. 29, 1953; s. Bruce Budge and Ouida (Raphiel) C.; m. Anne Margaret Eberhardt, Mar. 15, 1985; children: Jeffrey Raphiel, Mary Anne Elizabeth, Edward William Eberhardt. BS, Brigham Young U., 1977, MBA, 1979. CPA, Tex. Fin. analyst Exxon Coal USA, Inc., Houston, 1979-83; constrn. mgr. Gen. Homes, Inc., Houston, 1983-84; controller Liberty Data Products, Houston, 1984-86; v.p. Tech. Rsch. Assocs., Inc., Salt Lake City, 1987—; also dir. Tech. Rsch. Assocs., Inc. Scoutmaster Boy Scouts Am., Salt Lake City, 1989-91. Mem. AICPA, Utah Inst. CPAs, Salt Lake C. of C. (legis. action com.), Salt Lake Country Club. Republican. Mormon. Home: 1428 Michigan Ave Salt Lake City UT 84105-1609 Office: Technical Rsch Assocs 2257 S 1100 E Salt Lake City UT 84106-2320

CLARK, JOHN DEWITT, retired fine arts educator, sculptor; b. Kansas City, Mo., Mar. 11, 1925; s. Walter Perry and Anna Mae (Eubank) C. MA in Fine Art and Sculpture, San Diego State U., 1959. Prof. Southwestern Coll., 25 yrs. Exhibited works in numerous shows on West Coast, in N.Y. and Mex., others; represented in museums and pvt. collections throughout U.S. Served with U.S. Army, 1943-45, ETO. Decorated Silver Star. Democrat. Home: 10514 San Carlos Dr Spring Valley CA 91978-1037

CLARK, JOYCE LAVONNE, receptionist; b. Ashland, Oreg., Jan. 1, 1931; d. John Arthur and Minnie Lucille (Wisecarver) Freeman; m. Robert Glines (div. Aug. 1948); children: Judy Cabe, Jari Evelund, Cynthia Glines, Kevin Glines; m. L. A. Clark, June 1972 (div. 1983); children: Peter, John Freeman, Drew Freeman. BA in History, So. Oreg. State Coll., 1989, BA in Edn., 1989. Mgr. R/V trailer and laundromat, Soldotna, Alaska, 1981-84; substitute tchr. Kenai Peninsula Sch. Borough, Soldotna, 1989-91; receptionist Women in Crisis, Fairbanks, Alaska, 1991-95, Adult Learning Programs, Fairbanks, 1995—. Contbr. poem, articles to profl. publs. Sec. Lit. Arts Com., 1994-96. Democrat. Mem. Assembly of God.

CLARK, LLOYD, historian, educator; b. Belton, Tex., Aug. 4, 1923; s. Lloyd C. and Hattie May (Taylor) C.; m. Jean Reeves, June 17, 1950; children: Roger, Cynthia, Candyce. BSJ, So. Meth. U., 1948; B in Fgn. Trade, Am. Grad. Sch. Internat. Mgmt., 1949; MPA, Ariz. State U., 1972. String corr. A.P., Dallas, 1941-42; reporter Dallas Morning News, 1947; editor, pub. Ex-Press, Arlington, Tex., 1945-48; publicity mgr. Advt. Counselors Ariz., Phoenix, 1949; reporter Phoenix Gazette, 1949-65; asst. pub. Ariz. Weekly Gazette, 1965-66; founder Council on Abandoned Mil. Posts-U.S.A., 1966; project cons. City of Prescott, Ariz., 1971-72; dep. dir. adminstrv. svcs. No. Ariz. Coun. Govts., Flagstaff, 1972-73; regional adminstr. South Eastern Ariz. Govts. Orgn., Bisbee, 1973-75; local govt. assistance coordinator Ariz. Dept. Transp., Phoenix, 1975-80, program adminstr., 1980-83; history instr. Rio Salado Community Coll., Phoenix, 1983-89, Ariz. State U.-West, Sun City, 1995—; proprietor LC Enterprises, 1993—; editor and pub. Clark Biog. Reference, 1956-62. Bd. dirs. Friends of Channel 8, 1984-86; mem. transit planning com. Regional Pub. Transit Authority, 1988, Phoenix Citizen's Bond Com., 1987; bd. dirs. Friends of Ariz. Highways Mag., 1989-92; mem. Ariz. State Geographic and Historic Names Bd., 1994—. Served to lt. AUS, 1942-46; maj., 1966-70; col. Res. Recipient Ariz. Press Clubs exemplary gen. news coverage award, 1960, outstanding news reporting, 1961; Lloyd Clark Journalism scholarship named in honor U. Tex. at Arlington Alumni Assn., 1992. Mem. Am. Grad. Sch. Internat. Mgmt. Alumni Assn. (pres. Phoenix chpt. 1965), Ariz. Hist. Soc. (bd. dirs. cen. Ariz. chpt. 1992-93, state bd. dirs. 1993-95), Sharlot Hall Hist. Soc. (life), Res. Officers Assn. (life), Ex-Students Assn. No. Tex. Agrl. Coll. Arlington (pres. 1946-48), U. Tex. Arlington Alumni Assn. (life, bd. dir. 1994—), The Westerners (sheriff Phoenix Corral 1986-88), Sigma Delta Chi (pres. Valley of Sun chpt. 1964). Club: University (Phoenix). Author: Lloyd Clark's Scrapbook, Vol. 1, 1958, Vol. 2, 1960, Here's Looking at You, 1997. Address: PO Box 1537 Surprise AZ 85374-1489

CLARK, LOYAL FRANCES, public affairs specialist; b. Salt Lake City, July 16, 1958; d. Lloyd Grant and Zina (Okelberry) C. Student, Utah State U., 1976-78. Human resource coord. U.S. Forest Svc., Provo, Utah, 1984—, fire info. officer, 1987—, pub. affairs officer, interpretive svcs. coord., edn. coord., 1988—; mem. Take Pride in Utah Task Force, Salt Lake City, 1989—; chairperson Utah Wildlife Ethics Com., Provo, 1989—. Instr. Emergency Svcs., Orem, Utah, 1990—. Recipient Presdl. award for outstanding leadership in youth conservation programs Pres. Ronald Reagan, 1985, Superior Svc. award USDA, 1987, Exemplary Svc. award U.S. Forest Svc., 1992, Nat. Eyes on Wildlife Achievement award USDA Forest Svc., 1993. Mem. Nat. Wildlife Fedn., Nat. Assn. Interpretation, Utah Soc. Environ. Educators, Utah Wildlife Fedn. (bd. dirs. 1981-85, v.p. 1985-87, Achievement award 1983, 85, 87), Utah Wilderness Assn., Am. Forestry Assn., Nature Conservancy, Women in Mgmt. Coun. Office: Uinta Nat Forest 88 W 100 N Provo UT 84601-4452

CLARK, MARGARET, mayor. Mayor City of Rosemead, Calif. Office: City of Rosemead 8838 E Valley Blvd Rosemead CA 91770

CLARK, MICHAEL PHILLIP, English educator; b. Marlin, Tex., May 27, 1950; s. Burton Francis and Nelda (Blount) C.; m. Kathleen Mack, 1971 (div. 1973); m. Katherine Weber, May 26, 1977. BA magna cum laude, Rice U., 1972; MA, U. Calif., Irvine, 1973, PhD, 1977. Asst. prof. U. Mich., Ann Arbor, 1977-83; prof. in English and comparative lit. U. Calif., Irvine, 1983—. Author: Michael Foucault, 1983, Jacques Lacan, 1989; contbr. articles to profl. publs. Mem. MLA, Soc. Early Americanists. Office: U Calif Dept English & Comparative Lit Irvine CA 92697

CLARK, NANCI, elementary education educator; b. Reno, Apr. 11, 1957; d. Edwin Dail Baggett and Sharon Adair (Patterson) Marks; m. Rodney K. Clark, Oct. 25, 1986; children: Ashley Nichole, Sean Patrick. BS, Calif. State U., 1979, MS, 1983. Bilingual tchr. Moutain View Sch. Dist., 1979; resource specialist, bilingual tchr. Orange (Calif.) Unified Sch. Dist., 1980-88; resource specialist Alvord Unified Sch. Dist., Riverside, Calif., 1988-90, Rialto (Calif.) Unified Sch. Dist., 1990-93, Corona (Calif.)-Norco Unified Sch. Dist., 1993—. Mem. ASCD, Assn. Calif. Sch. Adminstrs. Office: Corona-Norco Unified Sch Dist 2350 Border Ave Corona CA 91720-5608

CLARK, R. BRADBURY, lawyer; b. Des Moines, May 11, 1924; s. Rufus Bradbury and Gertrude Martha (Burns) C.; m. Polly Ann King, Sept. 6, 1949; children: Cynthia Clark Maxwell, Rufus Bradbury, John Atherton. BA, Harvard U., 1948, JD, 1951; diploma in law, Oxford U., Eng., 1952; D.H.L., Ch. Div. Sch. Pacific, San Francisco, 1983. Bar: Calif. 1952. Assoc. O'Melveny & Myers, L.A., 1952-62, sr. ptnr., 1961-93; mem. mgmt. com., 1983-90; of counsel O'Melveny & Myers, L.A., 1993—; bd. dirs. So. Calif. Water Co., Econ. Resources Corp., Brown Internat. Corp., Automatic Machinery & Electronics Corp., John Tracy Clinic, also pres. 1982-88. Editor: California Corporation Laws, 6 vols, 1976—. Chancellor Prot. Episcopal Ch. in the Diocese of L.A., 1967—, hon. canon, 1983—. Capt. U.S. Army, 1943-46. Decorated Bronze Star with oak leaf cluster, Purple Heart with oak leaf cluster; Fulbright grantee, 1952. Mem. ABA (subcom. on audit letter responses, com. on law and acctg., task force on legal opinions), State Bar Calif. (chmn. drafting com. on gen. corp. law 1973-81, drafting com. on nonprofit corp. law 1980-84, mem. exec. com. bus. law sect. 1977-78, 84-87, sec. 1986-87, mem. com. nonprofit orgns. 1991—), L.A. County Bar Assn., Harvard Club, Chancery Club, Alamitos Bay Yacht Club (Long Beach, Calif.). Republican. Office: O'Melveny & Myers 400 S Hope St Los Angeles CA 90071-2801

CLARK, RAMONA RICHLI, radiologist; b. Camden, N.J., Jan. 24, 1940; m. Richard Norman Roger, June 24, 1961 (div. Sept. 1968); children: Gregory, Douglas, Nicholas; m. Guy Storman Clark, Sept. 24, 1972; children: Laura, Warren. Student, La Sierra U., 1957-59; MD, U. So. Calif., 1963. Diplomate Am. Bd. Pediatrics, Am. Bd. Radiology. Intern Glendale Adventist Med. Ctr., 1964-65; resident Children's Hosp. of L.A., 1964-65, L.A. County-U. So. Calif. Med. Ctr., 1968-69, Cedars-Sinai Med. Ctr., L.A., 1969-73; radiologist Alaska Native Svc. Hosp., Anchorage, 1973-74, Cmty. Meml. Hosp., Ventura, Calif., 1975-80; radiologist Pueblo Radiology Med. Group, Santa Barbara, Calif., 1980—, also bd. dirs.; dir. radiology svcs. Breast Care Ctr., Santa Barbara, Calif., 1995—; dir. med. staff edn. Cmty. Meml. Hosp., 1976-79; mem. quality care com. Goleta Valley Hosp., 1985—; chmn. Poeblo Radiology Pension Fund, 1987—; lectr. in field. Bd. dirs. Santa Barbara Chamber Orch., 1989-93, Monterey Bay Acad., 1992—; violinist with local cmty. groups; music dir. Seventh-Day Adventist Ch., 1988—. Mem. AMA, Calif. Med. Assn. (alt. del. 1992), Am. Coll. Radiology, Radiol. Soc. N.Am., Southcoast Radiol. Soc. (pres. 1988-89, sec.-treas. 1986-87), Santa Barbara County Med. Soc. (bd. dirs. 1990-95, treas. 1993, sec. 1994, pres.-elect 1995), Monterey Bay Acad. Alumni Assn. (bd. dirs. 1991-94, 1st fundraising chmn.). Office: Pueblo Radiology 2305 De La Vina St Santa Barbara CA 93105-3873

CLARK, RAYMOND OAKES, banker; b. Ft. Bragg, N.C., Nov. 9, 1944; s. Raymond Shelton and Nancy Lee (McCormick) C.; m. Patricia Taylor Slaughter; children: Matthew Patrick, Geoffry Charles. BBA, U. Ariz., 1966; postgrad., U. Wash., 1984-86. Mgmt. trainee First Interstate Bank, Phoenix, 1966, credit analyst, 1968-69, asst. br. mgr., Scottsdale, Ariz., 1969-72, asst. v.p., br. mgr., Tempe, Ariz., 1972-90, v.p. br. mgr. Scottsdale, 1990-92, v.p. mgr. main office Phoenix, 1992—. Pres., bd. dirs. Sun Devil Club, Tempe, 1975—; bd. dirs. Valley Big Brothers/Big Sisters, 1994—; pres. Tempe Diplomats, 1979-89; pres. Tempe Diablos, 1975—; major chmn. Fiesta Bowl, Tempe, 1975-79; bd. dirs. Maricopa County Bd. Mgrs., Phoenix, 1973, YMCA, Tempe, 1974, Tempe Design Rev. Bd., 1983-87. Named one of Outstanding Young Men of Am., 1978. Bd. dirs., treas. East Valley divsn. Am. Heart Assn., 1989-92. Served with U.S. Army, 1966-68. Mem. Tempe C. of C. (pres. 1979-80), Kiwanis (dist. lt. gov. 1972-87). Republican. Episcopalian.

CLARK, RICHARD WALTER, education consultant; b. Mt. Pleasant, Iowa, Apr. 14, 1936; s. Samuel Richard and Floreine Eunice (Walz) C.; m. Rosemary Helma Savage, June 10, 1958; children: Melissa O'Neal, Cameron Clark. BA, U. Wash., 1957, MA, 1963, PhD, 1970. Cert. tchr., prin., supt., Wash. Lectr., grad. asst. U. Wash., Seattle, 1960-61; tchr. Bellevue (Wash.) Pub. Schs., 1961-65, adminstr., 1965-91, dep. supt., to 1991; sr. assoc. Ctr. for Ednl. Renewal, U. Wash., Seattle, 1987—, Inst. for Ednl. Inquiry, Seattle, 1992—; cons. Pew Charitable Trusts, Phila., 1988—, MacArthur Found., Chgo., 1991-92, Coalition of Essential Schs., Brown U., Providence, 1990—, Ednl Commn. of the States, Denver, 1990-91, Calgary (Alta., Can.) Bd. Edn., 1990-91, others. Author: Effective Speech, 1982, 3d edit., 1994, (with others) Glencoe English 10, 11, 12, 1981, 2nd edit., 1985; contbbr. articles to profl. jours., chpts. to books. Pres. Youth Eastside Svcs., Bellevue, 1972. Capt. USMC, 1957-63. Recipient Outstanding Performance Pub. Svc. award Seattle King County Mcpl. League, 1987; named Educator of Yr., Lions Club, 1991. Mem. ASCD, Am. Edn. Rsch. Assn., Am. Assn. Sch. Adminstrs., Wash. Assn. Sch. Adminstrs., Speech Communication Assn., Nat. Soc. Study of Edn., Phi Delta Kappa. Methodist. Home and Office: 209 140th Ave Bellevue WA 98005

CLARK, RICHARD WARD, food industry executive, consultant; b. N.Y.C., Oct. 23, 1938; s. Richard Leal and Dorothy Jane (Whittaker) C. BA with honors, U. Rochester, N.Y., 1960; MBA in Fin., U. Pa., 1962. Corp. planning analyst Campbell Soup Co., Camden, N.J., 1965-67; asst. product mgr. Gen. Mills, Inc., Mpls., 1967-70; sr. fin. analyst McKesson Corp., San Francisco, 1970-71, asst. div. controller, 1971-72, div. controller, 1972-78, gen. mgr. grocery products devel., 1978-79; v.p., controller McKesson Foods Group/McKesson Corp., 1979-85, dir. strategic planning, 1985-87; v.p. fin., CFO, Provigo Corp. (Market Wholesale Grocery Co.), San Rafael, Calif., 1987-90; cons. on hotel devel., Napa Valley Assocs., S.A., San Francisco, 1990-92, health care cons., 1993-96; bd. dirs. Taylor Cuisine, Inc., San Francisco. Author: Some Factors Affecting Dividend Payout Ratios, 1962; musician (albums) Dick Clark at the Keyboard, I Love a Piano, 1990, I Play the Songs, 1993, On My Way to You, 1996. Adv. bd. Salvation Army, San Francisco, 1984—, chmn., 1993—; bd. dirs. Svcs. for Srs., San Francisco, 1990-93. Lt. (j.g.) USNR, 1962-64, PTO. Sherman fellow U. Rochester, 1960. Mem. Bohemian Club, Beta Gamma Sigma. Republican. Presbyterian. Home: 2201 Sacramento St Apt 401 San Francisco CA 94115-2314

CLARK, RUTH ANN, lay worker, educator; b. Columbus, Kans., July 18, 1935; d. Jacob Ellis Harold and Annie Lee Opal (Noel) Davidson; m. Ralph Francis Clark, July 10, 1965; children: Kristine Anna Jamison, Russell Kirk. BS, McPherson Coll., 1957; M in Religious Edn., Bethany Theol. Sem., Oak Brook, Ill., 1964. Commd. lay spkr. no. plains dist. Ch. of the Brethren. Vol. Brethren Vol. Svcs., Friedland, Kassel, Germany, 1957-60; youth fieldworker Cen. Region Youth Cabinet, North Manchester, Ind., 1960-62; dir. Christian edn. 1st Ch. of the Brethren, Roanoke, Va., 1964-65; substitute tchr. Froid/Medicine Lake (Mont.) Schs., 1984—. Sec., chair dist. bd. witness Ch. of Brethren, 1972-79, nat. standing com. 1978, 79, discipleship reconciliation, 1980-94, 96—, rep. to ch., local dist. for internat. heifer project, 1983—, Mon-Dak area com. chmn., 1979-89, mem. gen. bd., 1994—, no. plains dist. bd., 1994—, ex officio, 1994—, com. interch. rels. 1986-89; sec. PTO/PTA Medicine Lake, 1984; chairperson Music Mothers, Medicine Lake, 1983-85; judge county elections, Sheridan County, Mont., 1980-96. Recipient 15 Yrs. Leadership award 4-H, 1986, Class Agent of Yr. award McPherson Coll., 1987, Plaque of Appreciation from Com. on Interch. Rels., Ch. of Brethern, 1989. Mem. Inst. for Peace Studies (bd. dirs. 1990-96, vice chairperson 1990-96), Assn. Christian Educators (curriculum trainer 1994, curriculum cons. 1995). Home: HC 61 Box 36 Froid MT 59226-9601

CLARK, SCOTT H., lawyer; b. Logan, Utah, Jan. 7, 1946. BA with honors, U. Utah, 1970; JD, U. Chgo., 1973. Bar: Utah 1973. Ptnr. Ray, Quinney & Nebeker P.C., Salt Lake City. Mem. ABA, Utah State Bar, Salt Lake County Bar Assn., Phi Beta Kappa, Phi Kappa Phi, Pi Sigma Alpha. Office: Ray Quinney & Nebek PC Ste 400 Deseret Bldg 79 S Main St PO Box 45385 Salt Lake City UT 84145-0385

CLARK, SUSAN PATRICK, secondary English educator; b. L.A., Jan. 1, 1947; d. James Elliott Patrick and Rita Judy (Watkins) Garrett; m. David Graham Clark, July 19, 1969; children: Amy Michelle DuPuy, Aaron Stuart. BA in English with honors, Stanford U., 1968; MA in English, Columbia U., 1969. Cert. English tchr., N.Y., Oreg., Wash. English tchr. Brighton H.S., Rochester, N.Y., 1969-73; teller U.S. Bank, Portland, Oreg., 1973-75; English tchr. Meadow Park Middle Sch., Beaverton, Oreg., 1975; assessor, instr. Another Door to Learning, Tacoma, 1986-88; English tchr. Curtis Sr. H.S., University Place, Wash., 1990—; English dept. chair Curtis Sr. H.S., University Place, 1993-96, sch. improvement steering team, 1992-94, multi-cultural sub-com. chair, 1991-93; staff devel. com. University Place Sch. Dist., 1991-93; mem. Sch. Restructuring Com., 1997. Deacon University Place Presbyn. Ch., 1993-96, elder, 1986-89, deacon moderator, 1983-86; bd. dirs. Childrens Home Soc., Tacoma, 1987-90. Named Outstanding Influential Tchr., MIT, 1995, Recognition award Optimists Club, 1994. Mem. ASCD, NEA, Nat. Coun. Tchrs. English, Wash. Edn. Assn., Parent Tchr. Student Assn. (Outstanding Tchr. 1995). Democrat. Presbyterian. Office: Curtis Sr H S 8425 40th St W University Place WA 98466-2041

CLARK, SUZANNE, accountant; b. San Bernadino, Calif., Sept. 10, 1948; d. Richard Grant and Dorothy Jean (Gast) C.; children: Chelsea A. Clark-James, Graeme W. Clark-James. BS in Mktg. and Acctg., U. Colo., 1970, M in Urban Affairs, 1978. CPA/Personal Fin. Specialist, Colo., CFP, Colo. Dir. adminstrv. svcs. Suburban Cmty. Tng. & Svc. Ctr., Englewood, 1973-78; staff adminstr Solar Energy Rsch. Inst., Golden, Colo., 1979-80; rschr. Cmty. Coll. Denver, 1980-81; staff acct. R.E. Weise & Co., CPAs, Denver, 1982-83; owner Clark & Assoc., CPA, P.C., Denver, 1983—. Author: Providing Personal Financial Planning Services in Your CPA Practice, 1987, Providing Fiduciary Accounting and Tax Services, 1990, The Personal Financial Planning Process An Introduction, 1993, Personal Financial Planning in Crisis Situations, 1993, Estates and Trusts: A Guide to Fiduciary Advisors, 1996. Bd. dirs. Children's Ctr., Denver, 1982-84, Hospice of Peace, Denver, 1987-88. Mem. AICPA (personal fin. specialist edn. subcom. 1988-93), Colo. Soc. CPAs (specialization oversight bd. 1984-87, pres. fin. planning com. 1987-88, comms. com. 1994-97, bd. dirs. 1997—). Office: Clark & Assoc CPA PC 50 S Steele St Ste 430 Denver CO 80209-2808

CLARK, THOMAS P., JR., lawyer; b. N.Y.C., Sept. 16, 1943. AB, U. Notre Dame, 1965; JD, U. Mo., Kansas City, 1973. Bar: Calif. 1973. Ptnr. Stradling, Yocca, Carlson & Rauth P.C., Newport Beach, Calif. Editor-in-chief The Urban Lawyer, 1972-73; contbr. articles to profl. jours. Capt. USMC, 1966-70. Mem. State Bar Calif., Orange County Bar Assn., Phi Kappa Phi, Bench and Robe. Office: Stradling Yocca Carlson & Rauth PC 660 Newport Center Dr Newport Beach CA 92660-6401

CLARK, THOMAS RYAN, retired federal agency executive, business and technical consultant; b. Aberdeen, Wash., Sept. 16, 1925; s. George O. and Gladys (Ryan) C.; m. Barbara Ann Thiele, June 14, 1948; children: Thomas R. III, Kathleen Clark Sandberg, Christopher J.T. Student, U. Kans., 1943-44; BS, U.S. Mil. Acad., 1948; MSEE, Purdue U., 1955; cert., U.S. Army Command and Gen. Staff Coll., 1960, Harvard U., 1979. Commd. C.E., U.S. Army, 1948, advanced through grades to col., 1968; ret. U.S. Army, 1968; program mgr. U.S. AEC, Washington, 1968-75; dep. mgr. Dept. of Energy, Albuquerque, 1976-83; sr. exec. svc., 1977; mgr. Nev. ops. Dept. of Energy, Las Vegas, 1983-87, ret., 1987; cons. in field Las Vegas and Albuquerque, 1987—; mem. adv. bd. Dept. Chem. and Nuclear Engring., U. N.Mex., 1984—; mem. statewide adv. bd. Desert Research Inst., U. Nev., 1985-88. Editor, co-author: Nuclear Fuel Cycle, 1975. Trustee Nev. Devel. Authority, Las Vegas, 1984-88, Nat. Atomic Mus. Found., 1993—. Decorated Legion of Merit, Bronze Star; named Disting. Exec., Pres. of U.S., 1982. Mem. Las Vegas C. of C. (bd. dirs. 1983-87), Sigma Xi, Tau Beta Pi, Eta Kappa Nu, Rotary Club of Albuquerque (pres. 1993-94). Episcopalian. Lodge: Rotary.

CLARK, TIMOTHY JOHN, artist, educator; b. Santa Ana, Calif., June 30, 1951; s. Oliver Eugene and Bianca C.; m. Marriott Small, Aug. 18, 1991; children—Regina, Ginevra, Katherine. Student, Art Ctr. Coll., Pasadena, 1969-70, Otis Art Inst., 1974; B.F.A., Chounard Art Inst., 1972; B.F.A., Calif. Inst. Arts, 1975; M.A., Calif. State U., 1978. Artist, Disneyland, Anaheim, Calif., 1968-78; artist, Capistrano Beach, Calif., 1972—; prof. fine art Coastline C.C., Costa Mesa, Calif., 1974—; mem. faculty edn. program Worcester (Mass.) Art Mus., 1995—; lectr. Art Students League, N.Y.C., 1995; art instr. and lectr. T.J. Clark Painting Workshops, Hawaii and Europe, 1981—; guest lectr. U. of Hawaii, Hilo, 1982. Author: Learning from the Pros, 1984, Focus on Watercolor, 1987; artist/host PBS-TV series Focus on Watercolor, 1989 (Emmy nom.). Exhibited in one man shows at Eleventh Street Gallery, Santa Monica, Calif., 1991, Rosenfeld Gallery, Juarez, Mex., 1994, Fidelity Arts Gallery, Santa Monica, 1995, Missian San Juan Capistrano (Calif.) Mus., 1996, 97; group shows include: Am. Watercolor Soc., 1979, NAD, 1979, Butler Mus. Art, 1979-81, Challis Gallery, Esther Wells, 1979-84, Nat. Watercolor Soc., 1986, Art Expo, N.Y.C., L.A., 1990-92, Grand Ctrl. Art Galleries, N.Y.C., 1993, J. Todd Gallery, Wellesley, Mass., 1993-97. Pres. Acad. Senate, Coastline Coll., Fountain Valley, 1979-80; collections: El Paso Art Mus., San Juan Capistrano Mission Mus., Sherman Found. Recipient Spl. award, Traditional Artist Soc., 1976; Juror's award San Diego Watercolor Soc. Nat. Exhbn., 1979; Gallery award Rocky Mountain Watercolor Soc. nat. exhbn., 1981, Purchase award Nat. Original Print Exhbn., 1982, NISOD award 1997; named Tchr. of the Year Coastline Coll., 1997. Mem. Nat. Arts Club. Home: 27135 Paseo Pinzon Capistrano Beach CA 92624-1653 Office: Clark Studio PO Box 2728 Capistrano Beach CA 92624

CLARK, WALTER W., construction executive; b. 1947. With Arthur Young, Edmonton, Alta., Can., 1969-72, Levi-Strauss, Edmonton, Alta., Can., 1971-79, Westcan Group, Edmonton, Alta., Can., 1979-80, PCL Constrn. Group, Inc., Edmonton, Alta., Can., 1980-84; v.p. fin. administrn., sec., treas. PCL Enterprises, Inc., Denver, 1984—. Office: PCL Enterprises Inc 2000 S Colorado St Ste 400 Denver CO 80222*

CLARK, WOODROW WILSON, JR., strategic planner; b. Columbus, Ohio, July 13, 1945; s. Woodrow Wilson Sr. and Janet Jacobs (Berghiem) C.; m. Janis Lee Golden, Dec. 22, 1947; children: Woodrow Wilson III, Andrea Lee. BA, Wesleyan U., Delaware, Ohio, 1967; MA, Roosevelt U., 1970, Loyola U., Chgo., 1972, U. Ill., Urbana, 1974; PhD, U. Calif., Berkeley, 1977. Tchr. social studies Evanston (Ill.) Pub. Schs., 1967-70; head tchg. assoc. U. Ill., Urbana, 1970-72; rsch. assoc. U. Oreg., Eugene, 1972-75, Far West Edn. Lab., San Francisco, 1975-79; CEO, pres. Clark Comm. Inc., San Francisco, 1980-91; mgr. dir. ctr. for new ventures Calif. State U., Hayward, 1991-93; prof. Aalborg (Denmark) U., 1994; mgr. strategic planning Lawrence Livermore (Calif.) Nat. Lab., 1994—; lectr. U.S. State Dept., Europe, 1994; cons. Lockhead-Martin, Sunnyvale, Calif., 1994, Encyclopedia Brittanica, Chgo., 1994-95; mem. tech. adv. bd. Consortium Venture Capital, Palm Desert, Calif., 1995—. Producer various films and videos including The Workplace Hustle, Working Late, The Healing Force, English Language Series for NHK in Tokyo, 1980-91; contbr. numerous articles to profl. jours. Panelist Calif. Econ. Summit, 1993; mem. Calif. Def. Conversion Coun., Sacramento, 1993-96; econ. advisor Calif. Dem. Party, 1994-96. Fulbright fellow, 1994. Fellow Am. Anthrop. Assn. Home: PO Box 10407 Piedmont CA 94610-0407 Office: Lawrence Livermore Nat Lab 7000 East Ave # 2-644 Livermore CA 94550-9516

CLARKE, EVELYN WOODMAN, volunteer; b. National City, Calif., May 24, 1917; d. William Irving and Lena Edah (Crouse) Woodman; m. George Samuel Clarke, May 25, 1935 (dec. Nov. 1974); children: Peter Brian, August William, George Woodman. *A family member researched Durham town records and library research files, discovering that forebear Edward Woodman (born December, 1606) arrived June 3, 1635, and settled in Newbury, Massachusetts. He had sailed on the ship "James" on April 6 from his earlier life in Corsham, Wiltshire, England. His son, Captain John Woodman, born in 1630, built a garrisoned home on Stoney Brook near Oyster River. Each house was to be fortified for defense against raids. The unsuccessful Indian attack in 1694 was a sign of his foresight. His next door neighbor did not garrison. He and his family were massacred, along with 94 other victims, and 20 houses were burned.* Grad., Herbert Hoover H.S., San Diego, 1935; student, San Diego State Coll., 1935. Clk. U.S. Post Office, Grossmont, Calif., 1943-70. De. 49th Congl. Dist. White House Conf. on Aging, 1995-96; mem. San Diego County Dem. Ctrl. Com., 1978-83; chair 78th Assembly Dist. 1985-86; alt. del. Dem. Nat. Conv., N.Y., 1980; commr. San Diego City Pub. Utilities Adv. Commn., 1992—, San Diego County Commn. on Status of Women, 1980-83; mem. program/budget rev. panel United Way, 1980-83; observer U.S. Nat. Conf. for Women, Houston, 1977, UN Internat. Women's Yr. Tribunal, Mexico City, 1975; mem. U.S. Dem. Congl. Campaign Com., U.S. Dem. Senatorial Campaign Com., Clinton/Gore '96 Campaign. Recipient Vol.'s commendation United Way, San Diego, 1983, Susan B. Anthony cert. NOW, San Diego, 1982; named Hon. Life Mem. Calif. Congress Parents and Tchrs., 1948. Mem. YWCA, Uptown Dem. Club, Emily's List, Nat. Women's Polit. Caucus (Spl. Recognition award 1993, Alice Paul award 1985), Older Women's League (Wonderful Older Woman's award 1985), San Diego Hist. Soc., San Diego Opera, San Diego Zool. Soc., UN Assn. Home: 605 W Walnut Ave Apt A San Diego CA 92103-3987

CLARKE, MICHAEL WILLIAM, substance abuse professional, psychotherapist; b. Utica, N.Y., Dec. 4, 1955; s. William Jay and Marian (Wilcott) C.; m. Flowers; children: David M., Michael W. II. BA in Biopsychology, Calif. State U., Chico, 1979, MA in Counseling Psychology, 1983; PhD in Clin. Psychology, Calif. Grad. Sch. Psychology, 1994. Mental health asst., 1979, Ullerakers (Sweden) Mental Hosp., 1980; mental health counselor Santa Barbara County Mental Health, 1981-83; program dir. Cmty. Living Ctrs., Paradise, Calif., 1983-86; clin. supr. Butte County Mental Health, Chico, Calif., 1986-96; asst. dir. Butte County Alcohol Drug Mental Health, Chico, 1996—; pvt. practice A Step Forward, Chico. Office: 4 Williamsburg Ln # D Chico CA 95926-2225

CLARKE, RICHARD ALAN, electric and gas utility company executive, lawyer; b. San Francisco, May 18, 1930; s. Chauncey Frederick and Carolyn (Shannon) C.; m. Mary Dell Fisher, Feb. 5, 1955; children: Suzanne, Nancy C. Stephen, Douglas Alan. AB Polit. Sci. cum laude, U. Calif., Berkeley, 1952, JD, 1955. Bar: Calif. 1955. Atty. Pacific Gas and Electric Co., San Francisco, 1955-60;, 1970-74; asst. gen. counsel Pacific Gas and Electric Co., San Francisco, 1974-79, v.p., asst. to chmn., 1979-82, exec. v.p., gen. mgr. utility ops., 1982-85, pres., 1985-86, chmn. bd., CEO, 1986-94, chmn. bd., 1994-95; ptnr. Rockwell, Fulkerson and Clarke, San Rafael, Calif., 1960-69; bd. dirs. Pacific Gas & Electric Co., Potlach Corp., Bank Am. Corp., Consolidated Freightways; mem. Bus. Coun. Pres.' Coun. on Sustainable Devel. Bd. dirs., past chmn. Bay Area Coun.; trustee Boalt Hall Trust, Sch. Law U. Calif., Berkeley; mem. adv. bd. Walter A. Haas Sch. Bus., U. Calif., Berkeley; chmn. adv. bd. Ctr. for Orgnl. and Human Resource Effectiveness, U. Calif., Berkeley; bd. dirs. Nature Conservancy of Calif. Mem. Calif. C. of C. (past dir.), San Francisco C. of C. (past dir., v.p. econ. devel.), Edison Elect. Inst., Marin Tennis Club. Office: Pacific Gas & Electric Co 123 Mission St San Francisco CA 94105-1551

CLARKE, ROBERT F., utilities company executive; b. Oakland, Calif.. BA, U. Calif., Berkeley, 1965, MBA, 1966. Pres., CEO Hawaiian Electric, 1991—. Office: Hawaiian Electric Industries Inc 900 Richards St Honolulu HI 96813-2919*

CLARKE, URANA, writer, musician, educator; b. Wickliffe-on-the-Lake, Ohio, Sept. 8, 1902; d. Graham Warren and Grace Urana (Olsaver) C.; artists and tchrs. diploma Mannes Music Sch., N.Y.C., 1925; cert. Dalcroze Sch. Music, N.Y.C., 1950; student Pembroke Coll., Brown U.; BS, Mont. State U., 1967, M of Applied Sci., 1970. Mem. faculty Mannes Music Sch., 1922-49, Dalcroze Sch. Music, 1949-54; adv. editor in music The Book of Knowledge, 1949-65; v.p., dir. Saugatuck Circle Housing Devel.; guest lectr. Hayden Planetarium, 1945; guest lectr., bd. dirs. Roger Williams Park Planetarium, Providence; radio show New Eng. Skies, Providence, 1961-64, Skies Over the Big Sky Country, Livingston, Mont., 1964-79, Birds of the Big Sky Country, 1972-79, Great Music of Religion, 1974-79; mem. adv. com. Nat. Rivers and Harbors Congress, 1947-58; instr. continuing edn. Mont. State U. Chmn. Park County chpt. ARC, 1967-92, chmn. emeritus 1992—, co-chmn. county blood program, first aid instr. trainer, 1941-93; instr. ARC cardio-pulmonary resuscitation, 1976-84; mem. Mont. Commn. Nursing and Nursing Edn., 1974-76; mem. Park County Local Govt. Study Com., 1974-76, chmn., 1984-86, vice-chair, 94-96; chmn. Park County Red Cross, 1995—. Mem. Am. Acad. Polit. Sci., Am. Musicol. Soc., Royal Astron. Soc. Can., Inst. Nav., Maria Mitchell Soc. Nantucket, N.Am. Yacht Racing Union, AAAS, Meteoritical Soc., Internat. Soc. Mus. Research, Skyscrapers (sec.-treas. 1960-63), Am. Guild Organists, Park County Wilderness Assn. (treas.), Trout Unlimited, Nature Conservancy, Big Sky Astron. Soc. (dir. 1965—), Sierra Club. Lutheran. Club: Cedar Point Yacht. Author: The Heavens are Telling (astronomy), 1951; Skies Over the Big Sky Country, 1965; also astron. news-letter, View It Yourself, weekly column Big Skies, 1981—; contbr. to mags. on music, nav. and astronomy. Pub. Five Chorale Preludes for Organ, 1975; also elem. two-piano pieces. Inventor, builder of Clarke Adjustable Piano Stool. Address: Log-A-Rhythm 9th St Island Livingston MT 59047

CLARK-JACKSON, SUSAN, publishing executive. Pres., pub. Reno Gazette-Jour., 1985—; sr. group pres. Pacific Newspaper Group, Gannett; bd. dirs. Harrah's Entertainment, Inc.; bd. visitors John S. Knight Fellowships for Profl. Journalists, Stanford U. Office: Gannett Co Inc Box 22000 955 Kuenzli Reno NV 89520*

CLARK-LANGAGER, SARAH ANN, curator, director, university official; b. Lynchburg, Va., May 14, 1943; d. James Thomas and Mary Whitworth (Cooper) Clark; m. Craig T. Langager, 1979. BA in Art History, Randolph-Macon Woman's Coll., 1965; postgrad., U. Md., 1968; MA in Art History, U. Wash., 1970; PhD in Art History, CUNY, 1988. Assoc. edn. dept., lectr. Yale U. Art Gallery, New Haven, 1965-67, Albright-Knox Art Gallery, Buffalo, 1967-68; asst. to dir. Richard White Gallery, Seattle, 1969-70; curatorial asst. to curators painting and sculpture San Francisco Mus. Modern Art, 1970; assoc. edn. dept., lectr. Seattle Art Mus., 1971-73, 74-75; asst. curator, and then assoc. curator modern art, lectr. Seatle Art Mus., 1975-79; curator 20th century art, lectr. Munson-Williams-Proctor Inst., Utica, N.Y., 1981-86; asst. prof. art history, dir. Univ. Art Gallery, U. North Tex., Denton, 1986-88; dir. Western Gallery, curator outdoor sculpture collection Western Wash. U., Bellingham, 1988—, mem. adj. faculty, 1988—; lectr., cons. in edn. N.Y. Cultural Ctr., N.Y.C., 1973-74; editl. asst. October, MIT Press, N.Y.C., 1980; lectr. art history South Seattle C.C., 1975; lectr. 20th century art Cornish Inst. Fine Arts, Seattle, 1977-78; sole rep. for N.Y. State, Art Mus. Assn. Am., 1984-86; mem. Wash. Art Consortium, 1988—, v.p., 1989-90, pres., 1990-93, acting pres., 1996; mem. ad hoc del. concerning issues confronting Nat. Endowment for Arts, Bellingham, 1990; cons. State of Wash. SOS (Save Outdoor Sculpture), 1994—; also others. Contbr. articles to profl. jours.; curator exhbns., 1970—, including Rodney Ripps traveling exhbn., 1983, Sculpture Space: Recent Trends, 1984, Order and Enigma: American Art Between the Two Ward, 1984, Stars over Texas: Top of the Triangle, 1988, Master Works of American Art from the Munson-Williams-Proctor Institute, 1989, Public Art/Private Visions, 1989, Drawing Power, 1990, Audiophone Tour for Sculpture Collection-20 Interviews, 1991, Focus on Figure, 1992, Chairs: Embodied Objects, 1993, Northwest Native American and First Nations People's Art, 1993, New Acquisitions, 1995, Stars and Stripes: American Prints and Drawings, 1995, Photographs from America, 1996. Juror Arts in Pub. Places, Seattle Arts Commn., 1975, 78-79, Wash. State Arts Commn., 1976, 91, 92-93, King County Arts Commn., Seattle, 1979, Ctrl. N.Y. regional art exhbns., Syracuse, Utica, Rome, Potsdam, 1981-86, East Tex. State U., Commerce, 1987, Brookhaven C.C., Farmers Branch, Tex., 1988, Bellingham Mcpl. Arts Commn., 1989, 90; mem. adv. com. Steuben Park Fountain, Utica, 1985-86. Recipient Woman of Merit in Arts award Mohawk Valley C.C. and YWCA, Utica, 1985; Kress Found. fellow U. Wash., 1970; Helena Rubenstein Found. scholar CUNY Grad. Ctr., 1980. Office: Western Wash U Western Gallery Fine Arts Complex Bellingham WA 98225-9068

CLARKSON, LAWRENCE WILLIAM, airplane company executive; b. Grove City, Pa., Apr. 29, 1938; s. Harold William and Jean Henrietta (Jaxtheimer) C.; m. Barbara Louise Stevenson, Aug. 20, 1960; children: Michael, Elizabeth, Jennifer. BA, DePauw U., 1960; JD, U. Fla., 1962. Counsel Pratt & Whitney, West Palm Beach, Fla., 1967-72, program dep. dir., 1972-75, program mgr., 1974-75; v.p., mng. dir. Pratt & Whitney, Brussels, Belgium, 1975-78; v.p. mktg. Pratt & Whitney, West Palm Beach, 1978-80; v.p. contracts Pratt & Whitney, Hartford, Conn., 1980-82, pres. comml. products div., 1982-87; sr. v.p. Boeing Comml. Airplanes Group, Seattle, 1988-91; corp. v.p. planning and internat. devel. Boeing Co., Seattle, 1992-93, sr. v.p., 1994-97, pres., 1997—; dir. Partnership for Improved Air Travel, Washington, 1988-91. Trustee DePauw U., Greencastle, Ind., 1987—; overseer Tuck Sch. Dartmouth, Hanover, N.H., 1993—; corp. coun. Interlochen (Mich.) Ctr. for Arts, 1987, trustee, 1988—, chmn., 1996—; trustee Seattle Opera, 1990—, chmn., 1991—; pres. Japan-Am. Soc., Wash., 1993, pres. Wash. State China Rels. com., 1992-93; chmn. Nat. Bur. of Asia Rsch., Coun. Fgn. Rels.; vice chmn. U.S. Pacific Econ. Corp. Coun., 1993—. Capt. USAF, 1963-66. Mem. Nat. Assn. Mfrs. (bd. dirs.), N.Y. Yacht Club, Seattle Yacht Club, Met. Opera Club, Wings Club (bd. govs. 1987-91, Order of St. John (officer 1994—), Met. Club D.C. Episcopalian. Office: The Boeing Co MS 1F-26 PO Box 3707 Seattle WA 98124-2207

CLARREN, STERLING KEITH, pediatrician; b. Mpls., Mar. 12, 1947; s. David Bernard and Lila (Reifel) C.; m. Sandra Gayle Bernstein, June 8, 1970; children: Rebecca Pia, Jonathan Seth. BA, Yale U., 1969; MD, U. Minn., 1973. Pediatric intern U. Wash. Sch. Medicine, Seattle, 1973-74, resident in pediatrics, 1974-77, asst. prof. dept. pediatrics, 1979-83, assoc. prof., 1983-88, prof., 1988, Robert A. Aldrich chair in pediatrics, 1989—; head divsn. congenital defects U. Wash. Sch. Medicine, 1987-95; dir. dept. congenital defects Children's Hosp. and Med. Ctr., Seattle, 1987-96, dir. fetal alcohol syndrome clinic Child Devel. and Mental Retardation Ctr. U. Wash., 1992—, dir. Fetal Alcohol Syndrome Network, 1995—; dir. infant inpatient svcs. Children's Hosp. & Med. Ctr., Seattle, 1996—. Contbr. articles to profl. jours.; patentee for orthosis to alter cranial shape. Cons. pediatrician Maxillofacial Rev. Bd., State of Wash., Seattle, 1984—, chmn. Health-Birth Defects Adv. Com., Olympia, 1980—; mem. gov.'s task force on FAS State of Wash., 1994-95; mem. fetal alcohol adv. com. Children's Trust Found., Seattle, 1988—; mem. adv. bd. Nat. Orgn. on Fetal Alcohol Syndrome; mem. fetal alcohol com. Inst. Medicine, NAS, 1994-95. Rsch. grantee Nat. Inst. Alcohol Abuse & Alcoholism, 1982—, Ctrs. for Disease Control, 1992—. Fellow AAAS; mem. Am. Acad. Pediatrics, Soc. for Pediatric Rsch., Teratology Soc., Rsch. Soc. on Alcoholism (pres. fetal alcohol study group 1993), Am. Cleft Palate Assn., N.Y. Acad. Scis. Home: 8515 Paisley Dr NE Seattle WA 98115-3944 Office: Children's Hosp and Med Ctr Divsn Congenital Defects PO Box C-5371 Seattle WA 98105

CLASSEN, ALBRECHT, German language educator; b. Hesse, Germany, Apr. 23, 1956; s. Traugott Walter and Annemarie (Kraft) C.; m. Carolyn Aiko Sugiyama, June 16,1984; 1 child, Stephan. MA, U. Marburg, Germany, 1982; PhD, U. Va., 1986. Lectr. U. Va., Charlottesville, 1986-87; asst. prof. German U. Ariz., Tucson, 1987-92, assoc. prof., 1992-94, prof., 1994—. Author: Oswald von Wolkenstein, 1987, Utopie und Logos, 1990, Autobiographische Lyrik, 1991, The German Chapbook, 1995, Eroticism and Love in the Middle Ages, 1995; editor: Tristania vols. 13-17. Recipient El Paso Tchg. award El Paso Natural Gas, Tucson, 1995; rsch. grantee DAAD, 1996, U. ARiz., 1996. Mem. MLA, Am. Assn. Tchrs. German (chpt. pres. 1992-96, pres. Pres.' Assembly 1996—), German Studies Assn., South Eastern Medieval Assn. (exec. coun. 1993-96), Medieval Assn. of the Pacific. Democrat. Office: U Ariz Dept German Tucson AZ 85721

CLAUSEN, BRET MARK, industrial hygienist, safety professional; b. Hayward, Calif., Aug. 1, 1958; s. Norman E. and Barbara Ann (Wagner) C.; m. Cheryl Elaine Carlson, May 24, 1980; children: Kathrine, Eric, Emily. BS, Colo. State U., 1980, MS, 1983. Cert. indsl. hygienist, safety profl., hazard control mgr., hazardous materials mgr.; cert. in comprehensive practice Am. Bd. Inds. Hygiene; cert. in comprehensive practice and mgmt. aspects Bd. Cert. Safety Profls. Assoc. risk mgmt., indsl. hygienist, safety rep. Samsonite Corp., Denver, 1980-83, mgr. loss prevention, 1984-88; health, safety and environment rep. Storage Tech., Longmont, Colo., 1984; sr. project cons. Occusafe Inc., Denver, 1988; numerous indsl. hygiene and safety mgmt./tech. assignments Rocky Flats Environ. Tech. Site, Golden, Colo., 1988—; mem. radiol. assistance program team U.S. Dept. Energy, Region VI, 1994—. Local emergency planning com. Weld County, Colo., 1996—. Mem. Am. Indsl. Hygiene Assn. (pres. Rocky Mountain sect. 1988-89), Am. Soc. Safety Engrs. (prof.), Inst. Hazardous Materials Mgmt. (cert. sr. level), Ins. Inst. Am. (assoc. in risk mgmt.), Am. Nat. Stds. Inst. (com. on confined spaces 1993—), Am. Acad. Indsl. Hygiene (diplomate, acad. accreditation com. 1994—). Republican. Lutheran. Home: 16794 Weld County Rd # 44 La Salle CO 80645 Office: Safe Sites of Colo PO Box 464 Mail Stop T452A Golden CO 80402-0464

CLAUSON, GARY LEWIS, chemist; b. Peoria, Ill., Feb. 25, 1952; s. Cecil Lewis and Virgie Grace (Shryock) C. AAS, Ill. Cen. Coll., East Peoria, 1974; BA in Chemistry, U. Calif., San Diego, 1977; MS in Chem., Bradley U., Peoria, 1981; PhD in Organic Chemistry, U. Ill., 1987. Engring. technician U.S. Naval Sta., San Diego, 1974-75; lab. analyst Lehn & Fink Products Co., Lincoln, Ill., 1978-79; part-time faculty Bradley U., Peoria, 1980-81; sci. asst. Ill. State Geol. Survey, Urbana, 1986-87; sr. chemist Ciba-Geigy Corp., McIntosh, Ala., 1987-92; rsch. scientist Gensia, Inc., San Diego, 1992-95, cons., 1995-96; prin. scientist Alliance Pharm. Corp., San Diego, 1996—. Mem. Am. Chem. Soc. Home: 3277 Berger Ave Apt 20 San Diego CA 92123-1933

CLAUSS, JAMES JOSEPH, classics educator; b. Scranton, Pa., Sept. 1, 1953; s. James J. and Marion A. (Lynch) C.; m. Louise M. Betti, Aug. 12, 1978; children: Gerard, Michael, Elizabeth. BA, U. Scranton, 1974; MA, Fordham U., 1976; PhD, U. Calif., Berkeley, 1983; postgrad., Am. Sch. Classical Studies, Athens, 1982-83. Asst. prof. classics Creighton U., Omaha, 1983-84; asst. prof. classics U. Wash., Seattle, 1984-90, assoc. prof., 1990—. Author: The Best of the Argonauts, 1993; co-editor: Medea: Essays on Medea in Myth, Literature, Philosophy and Art, 1997; author numerous articles and revs. Mem. Seattle Perugia Sister City ASsn., 1991—. Thomas Day Seymour fellow Am. Sch. Classical Study, 1982-83. Mem. Am. Philol. Assn. (chmn. editorial bd. for textbooks, 1993-96), Classical Assn. Pacific N.W. (v.p. 1991-92, pres. 1992-93), Classical Assn. Middlewest and South, Am. Inst. Archaeology (v.p., pres. local chpt. 1990-92). Democrat. Roman Catholic. Office: U Wash Dept Classics Box 353110 Seattle WA 98195

CLAUSSEN, BONNIE ADDISON, II, aerospace company executive; b. Pueblo, Colo., Jan. 11, 1942; s. Bonnie A. I and Gertrude A. (Poe) C.; m. Charlotte J. Dipert, July 11, 1961; children: Christopher Addison, Raymond Dale. BS in Math., U. So. Colo., 1967; postgrad., Pa. State U., King of Prussia, 1968-69. Programmer Gen. Electric Corp., King of Prussia, 1967-69, sr. programmer, 1969-71; project mgr. Martin Marietta Aerospace Co., Denver, 1971-79; co-founder, exec. v.p. CTA, Inc., Englewood, Colo.,

1979—; co-founder, pres. CTA Simulation Systems, LLC, Greenwood Village, Colo., 1995—. Designer: (software) Real-Time Flight, 1967-78, Viking Mars Lander Flight, 1975; contbr: Real-Time Simulation Publs., 1975-78. Served with USAF, 1962-65. Recipient Pub. Service medal Nat. Aeronautics and Space Adminstrn., 1976. Republican. Office: CTA Simulation Systems LLC 7315 E Orchard Rd Cherry Hills Village CO 80111-2506

CLAY, SEAN COCHRANE, software development company executive; b. Oklahoma City, May 4, 1956; s. Robert Almonton and Maxine (Jackson) C.; m. Sharon Barlow, Jul. 14, 1984; children: Colby, Erin. AA, Saddleback C.C., 1977; student, Calif. State U., Fullerton, 1978, Riverside C.C., 1991. Programmer, software engr. Mai/Basic Four, Tustin, Calif., 1979-88; owner Clayco, Yucca Valley, Calif., 1988—; ptnr. Desert Gold, Yucca Valley, Calif.; cons. Priority Computer Sys., Irvine, Calif., 1988—, Venus Raches, Indio, Calif., 1991—. Author (software) Custom Password Utility, 1990, Bookstore Management Sys., 1994; inventor dynamic wheel balancer. Recipient Cert. of Appreciation Toastmasters Internat., 1983, Area Contest Highest Honors, 1982. Mem. Hi Desert Aero Barons, Yucca Mesa Improvement Assn., Channel Bandits, Yucca Mesa Adv. Coun., Masonic Lodge. Office: Clayco 2572 Yucca Mesa Rd Yucca Valley CA 92284-9272

CLAYTON, WAYNE CHARLES, protective services official, educator; b. Topeka, Kansas, Dec. 16, 1932; s. Alford Henry and Anna Ellen (Lynch) C.; m. Donna Marie Corrigan, March 3, 1962; Mark Wayne, Leslie Marie. AA in Liberal Arts, Mt. San Antonio Coll., 1959; BS, Calif. State U., L.A., 1968. cert. tchr., Calif. From reserve police officer to dep. chief El Monte Police Dept., 1957-1978, chief, 1978—; mem. session FBINA, 1980. With U.S. Navy, 1952-56. Recipient Golden Apple award West San Gabriel Valley Adminstrs. Assn., 1982, Spl. Medallion award Boys Club Am., 1982, Disting. Svc. award Dept. Youth Authority, 1983, Outstanding Svc. award C. of C., 1983, Spl. Appreciation award El Monte Police Officers Assn., 1985, Calif. Police Chief Officer of the Yr. award Internat. Union Police Assns. AFL-CIO, 1986, Exec. of Yr. award Exec. Mag., 1986, Dr. Byron E. Thompson Disting. Scouter award El Monte Explorer Post # 522, 1988, Appreciation award, 1992, Outstanding Svc. award Internat. Footprint Assn., 1991, award for continuing concern and dedication to the well being of Officers of El Monte Police Dept. Calif. Orgn. of Police and Sheriffs, 1991, Police Chief of the Yr. Perpetual award First Annual Shriners Club, 1994, C. of C. Citizen of Yr., 1994, Coord. Coun. Lifetime Achievement award, 1995. Mem. FBI Nat. Acad. Assocs., L.A. County Police Chiefs Assn., San Gabriel Valley Police Chiefs Assn., San Gabriel Valley Peace Officers Assn. (past pres.), Boys and Girls Club of San Gabriel Valley (v.p.), Civitan of El Monte (internat., charter pres. 1973). Democrat. Roman Catholic. Office: Police Dept Box 6008 11333 Valley Blvd El Monte CA 91731-3210

CLEARY, SEAN FULTON, radiation oncologist; b. Washington, Dec. 28, 1959; s. Thomas Fulton and Ruth Bernadette (Jarboe) C.; m. Anita Ruth Kirk, Sept. 3, 1988. BS, U. Notre Dame, 1982; MS in Pub. Health, U. N.C., 1983; PhD in Microbiology/Immunology, Med. Coll. of Va., 1986, MD, 1990. Diplomate Am. Bd. Radiology. Fellow Nat. Cancer Inst. Med. Coll. of Va., Richmond, 1985-86, intern in internal medicine, 1990-91; resident in radiation oncology Stanford (Calif.) U. Hosp., 1991-94, chief resident, 1993-94, Am. Cancer Soc. clin. oncology fellow, 1993-94; med. dir. radiation oncology Yakima (Wash.) Valley Meml. Hosp., 1995—; prin. investigator, nat. cancer clin. trials Radiation Therapy Oncology Group, NAt. Surg. Adjurant Breast Project, Southwestern Oncology Group; fellowship in high dose rate brachy therapy Calif. Endocurietherapy Ctr., Oakland, 1994. Contbr. articles to profl. jours. Mem. Nature Conservancy. Recipient Riffert award in Internal Medicine, Med. Coll. of Va. Hosp. and McGuire VA Hosp., 1991. Mem. Am. Coll. Radiology, Am. Soc. Therapeutic Radiology and Oncology, Am. Cancer Soc., Sigma Xi Rsch. soc. Office: Yakima Valley Meml Hosp Dept of Radiation Oncology 2811 Tieton Dr Yakima WA 98902-3761

CLEARY, SHIRLEY JEAN, artist, illustrator; b. St. Louis, Nov. 14, 1942; d. Frank and Crystal (Maret) C.; m. (Leo) Frank Cooper, June 18, 1982; stepchildren: Clay Cooper, Alicia Cooper, Curt Cooper. BFA, Wash. U., St. Louis, 1964; MFA, Tyler Sch. of Art of Temple U., Phila.. Rome, Italy, 1968; student, The Corcoran, Washington, 1967-71. mem. adv. coun. Mont. Trout Unlimited. Prin. works include illustrations in mags. Flyfishing Quar., Fly Fishers Mag., Flyfishing News, Mont. Outdoors, Flyfisherman, Flyfishing Heritage; contbr. articles to profl. jours.; exhibited in Am. in Paint and Bronze, Mo. Hist. Soc., St. Louis, 1987, Women in Wildlife, Wild Wings, Mpls., 1985-87, Am. Miniatures, Settlers West Galleries, Tucson, 1984, 96, Women Artists & The West, Tucson Mus. Art, 1995, 96; artist 1990 Oreg. Trout Stamp (Artist of Yr. award 1992, Assn. N.W. Steelheaders print winner 1992). Bd. mem. Mont. State Arts Coun., Mont., 1973-81, Helena Civic Ctr., Mont., 1983-89, mem. leadership Helena, 1985. Apprenticeship grantee Western Starts Art Found., Artist in Residence, River Meadow, Jackson, Wyo, 1989-94, Herning Hojskole, Herning, Denmark, 1981, Wyo. Artist in the Schools, Sheridan, Wyo., 1977; named Arts for Parks Top 100 ARtist, 1989, 94, Jackson One Fly Artist of Yr., 1990-92. Mem. Miniature Art Soc. of N.J., Mont. Assn. Female Execs., Pat Barnes Mo. River Chpt. of Trout Unlimited, Coll. Art Assn. Democrat. Home: 1804 Beltview Dr Helena MT 59601-5801

CLEARY, WILLIAM JOSEPH, JR., lawyer; b. Wilmington, N.C., Aug. 14, 1942; s. William Joseph and Eileen Ada (Gannon) C.; AB in History, St. Joseph's U., 1964; JD, Villanova U., 1967. Bar: N.J. 1967, U.S. Ct. Appeals (3d cir.) 1969, Calif. 1982, U.S. Ct. Appeals (9th cir.) 1983, U.S. Dist. Ct. (ctrl. dist.) Calif. 1983, U.S. Supreme Ct., 1992. Law sec. to judge N.J. Superior Ct. Jersey City, 1967-68; assoc. Lamb, Blake, H&D, Jersey City, 1968-72; dep. pub. defender State of N.J., Newark, 1972-73; 1st asst. city corp. counsel, Jersey City, 1973-76; assoc. Robert Wasserwald, Inc., Hollywood, Calif., 1984-86, 88-89, Gould & Burke, L.A., 1986-87; pvt. practice, 1989—. Mem. ABA, FBA, N.J. State Bar, Calif. Bar Assn., L.A. County Bar, Alpha Sigma Nu, Nat. Jesuit Honor Soc. Democrat. Roman Catholic. Office: 1853 1/2 Canyon Dr Los Angeles CA 90028-5607

CLECAK, DVERA VIVIAN BOZMAN, psychotherapist; b. Denver, Jan. 15, 1944; d. Joseph Shalom and Annette Rose (Dveirin) Bozman; m. Pete Emmett Clecak, Feb. 26, 1966 (div. 1993); children: Aimée, Lisa. BA, Stanford U., 1965; postgrad., U. Chgo., 1965; MSW, UCLA, 1969. Lic. clin. social worker, Calif.; lic. marriage, family and child counselor, Calif. Social work supr. Harbor City (Calif.) Parent Child Ctr., 1969-71; therapist Orange County Mental Health Dept., Laguna Beach, Calif., 1971-75, area coordinator, 1975-79; pvt. practice psychotherapy Mission Viejo, Calif., 1979—; founder, exec. dir. Human Options, Laguna Beach, 1981—; mem, co-chmn. domestic violence com. Orange County Commn. on Status of Women, 1979-81; mem. mental health adv. com. extension U. Calif., Irvine, 1983, counseling psychologist, 1980, lectr., 1984-85; lectr. Saddleback Community Coll., Mission Viejo, 1981-82, Chapman Coll., Orange, 1979; field instr. UCLA, 1970-71, 77-78. Co-chair Nat. Philanthropy Day, Orange County, 1996. Recipient Women Helping Women award Saddleback Community Coll., 1987, Cert. for child abuse prevention Commendation State of Calif. Dept. Social Svcs., 1988, Community Svc. award Irvine Valley Coll. Found., 1989, Disting. Svc. award in the field of domestic violence, Nicole Brown Simpson Found., 1996, Humanitarian of the Yr. award Alexis de Tocqueville Soc., United Way, 1997, Amelia Earhart award for disting. svc. to women Women's Opportunity Ctr./U. Calif.-Irvine, 1997; named Orange County Non-profit Exec. of Yr., 1994. Mem. NASW, Calif. Marriage Family and Child Counselors' Assn., Phi Beta Kappa.

CLEGHORN, JOHN H., protective services official. Chief police Corona (Calif.) Police Dept. Office: Corona Police Dept PO Box 940 Corona CA 91718

CLEMENS, CHARLES JOSEPH, insurance agent; b. Phila., Mar. 1, 1942; s. Charles Wesley and Jane Elizabeth (Nesselhauf) C.; m. Keiko Kobayashi, Aug. 12, 1965 (div. 1994); 1 child, Charles S. BA, Calif. State U., Fullerton, 1970; MBA, U. So. Calif., 1972. CLU. Asst. mgr. ins. N.Y. Life Ins. Co., Anaheim, Calif., 1971-74; ins. agt. Santa Ana, Calif., 1974-77; brokerage mgr. Alliance Ins. Co., Santa Ana, 1977-79; regional mgr. CIGNA, Orange, Calif., 1979-87; ins. agt. Garden Grove, Calif., 1987-93; ins. agt., broker Anaheim, 1993—. Major USAF-ANG, 1961—. Mem. NALU (pres. 1976, 80, Nat. Quality award). Republican.

CLEMENT, BETTY WAIDLICH, literacy educator, consultant; b. Honolulu, Aug. 1, 1937; d. William G. Waidlich and Audrey Antoinette (Roberson) Malone; m. Tom Morris, Jan. 16, 1982; 1 child, Karen A. Bratesani. BA in Elem. Edn., Sacramento State U., 1960; MA in Elem. Reading, U. No. Colo., 1973, MA in Adminstrn., EdD in Edn. & Reading, 1980. Elem. sch. tchr. pub schs., Colo., Calif., 1960-66; reading specialist, title I European area U.S. Dependent Schs., various locations, 1966-75; grad. practicum supr. U. No. Colo. Reading Clinic, Greeley, 1976-77; grant cons. Colo. Dept. Edn., Denver, 1978-81; adult edn. tutor, cons. various orgns., Boulder, Colo., 1983-87; student tchr. supr. U. San Diego, 1989-90; adult literacy trainer for vols. San Diego Coun. on Literacy, 1988—; adj. prof. U. Colo., Denver, 1981-82, U. San Diego, 1994—; adj. prof. comm. arts Southwestern Coll., Chula Vista, Calif., 1990—; presenter various confs. Co-author, editor: Adult Literacy Tutor Training Handbook, 1990. Grantee Fed. Right-to-Read Office Colo. Dept. Edn., 1979, curriculum writing Southwestern Coll., 1992. Fellow San Diego Coun. on Literacy (chair coop. tutor tng. com. 1991-93); mem. Whole Lang. Coun. San Diego, Calif. Reading Assn. Office: U San Diego Olin Hall Alcala Park San Diego CA 92110

CLEMENT, KATHERINE ROBINSON, social worker; b. Balt., Dec. 19, 1918; d. Alphonso Pitts and Sue Seymour (Ashby) Robinson; m. Harry George Clement, 1941 (dec. 1992). BA, Coll. of Wooster, Wooster, Ohio, 1940; MS in Social Work, Smith Coll., 1953; post grad., Washington Sch. of Psychiatry, 1951. Lic. clin. social worker, Calif. Social worker Family Svc., Cin., 1953-55, Hamilton, Ohio, 1955-57; social worker Orange County, Calif., 1957-60; counselor pvt. practice, Fullerton, Calif., 1959-63; social worker Family Svc., Long Beach, Calif., 1961-1963; child welfare worker San Mateo (Calif.) County Welfare Dept., 1963-1967; supr. child protection Yolo County Dept. Social Svcs., Woodland, Calif., 1967-79; pvt. practice Woodland, Calif., 1980—; cons. psychiatric social svc. State Dept. Social Svcs., Sacramento, 1984—. Active Yolo County Dem. Ctrl. Com.; treas. Feminist Legal Svcs.; founding bd. dirs. Yolo County Ct. Apptd. Spl. Advocates; bd. dirs. Yolo County ARC; mem. Yolo County Health Coun. Mem. NASW, NOW, LWV, Mensa, Toastmasters, Soroptimist Internat. Democrat. Unitarian. Home: 205 Modoc Pl Woodland CA 95695-6662

CLEMENT, SHIRLEY GEORGE, educational services executive; b. El Paso, Tex., Feb. 14, 1926; d. Claude Samuel and Elizabeth Estelle (Mattice) Gillett; m. Paul Vincent Clement, Mar. 23, 1946; children: Brian Frank, Robert Vincent, Carol Elizabeth, Rosemary Adele. BA in English, Tex. Western Coll., 1963; postgrad. U. Tex., El Paso, N.Mex. State U.; MEd in Reading, Sul Ross State U., 1987. Tchr. lang. arts Ysleta Ind. Schs., El Paso, 1960-62; tchr. adult edn., 1962-64, tchr. reading/lang. arts, 1964-77; owner, dir. Crestline Learning Systems, Inc., El Paso, 1980-90; dir. Crestline Internat. Schs. (formerly Crestline Learning Systems, Inc., now Internat. Acad. Tex. at El Paso), 1987-90; instr. Park Coll., Ft. Bliss, Tex., 1992—, U. Phoenix, 1995—; dir. tutorial for sports teams U. Tex., El Paso, 1984; bd. dirs. Southwest Inst., pres., 1993; dir. continuing edn. program El Paso Community Coll., 1985; mem. curriculum com. Ysleta Ind. Schs., El Paso, 1974; mem. Right to Read Task Force, 1975-77; mem. Bi-Centennial Steering Com., El Paso, 1975-76; presenter Poetry in the Arts, Austin, Tex., 1992, 97; judge student poetry contest, Austin, Tex., 1995; Poetry Soc. Tex. program presenter Mesilla Valley Writers, 1993-96, El Paso Writers, 1994-95, Poetry Soc. Tex., 1993; instr. writing Paris Am. Acad., summer 1994, 95; cons. Ysleta Schs. 1995; lectr. on reading in 4 states. Author: Beginning the Search, 1979, 2nd edit., 1997; contbr. articles to profl. jours.; contbr. poems to Behold Texas, 1983. Treas. El Paso Rep. Women, 1956; facilitator Goals for El Paso, 1975; mem. hospitality com. Sun Carnival, 1974, Cotton Festival, 1975. Mem. Internat. Reading Assn. (pres. El Paso County council 1973-74, presentor 1977-87), Assn. Children with Learning Disabilities (tchr. 1980), Poetry Soc. Tex. (Panhandle Penwomen's first place award 1981, David Atamian Meml. award 1991, judge, 1995), Nat. Fedn. State Poetry Soc. (1st place award ann. contest 1988, 1st prize El Paso Historical Essay contest 1991, 2nd prize 1995, honorable mention Writer's Digest Contest 1996, judge, 1997), Chi Omega Alumnae (pres. 1952-53). Home: PO Box 1645 114 Casas Bellas Ln Santa Teresa NM 88008-1645

CLEMENT, WALTER HOUGH, retired railroad executive; b. Council Bluffs, Iowa, Dec. 21, 1931; s. Daniel Shell and Helen Grace (Hough) C.; AA, San Jose (Calif.) City Coll., 1958; PhD, World U., 1983; m. Shirley Ann Brown, May 1, 1953; children: Steven, Robert, Richard. Designer, J.K. Konerle & Assocs., Salt Lake City, 1959-62; with U.P. R.R. Co., 1962—, class B draftsman, Salt Lake City, 1971-75, sr. right of way engr. real estate dept., 1975-80, asst. dist. real estate mgr., 1980-83, asst. engr. surveyor, 1983-87; owner, pres. Clement Sales and Svc. Co., Bountiful, Utah, 1987—. Mem. Republican Nat. Com., Rep. Congl. Com. With USN, 1950-54, Korea. Lic. realtor, Utah. Mem. Am. Ry. Engring. Assn., Execs. Info. Guild (assoc.), Bur. Bus. Practice. Methodist. Home: 290 W 1200 N Bountiful UT 84010-6826

CLEMENTS, GEORGE FRANCIS, mathematics educator; b. Colfax, Wash., Apr. 17, 1931; s. Harry Frank and Louise May (Schmidt) C.; m. Anna Bell, June 18, 1952; children: Ellen, Mark, Eric, Owen. BSME, U. Wis., 1953; MA, Syracuse U., 1957, PhD, 1962. Asst. prof. math. U. Colo., Boulder, 1962-68, assoc. prof. math., 1968-76, prof. math., 1976—. Contbr. articles to profl. jours. With U.S. Army, 1953-55. Mem. Am. Math. Soc. Unitarian. Home: 2954 3rd St Boulder CO 80304-3041 Office: U Colo Dept Math Box 395 Boulder CO 80309

CLEMENTS, JOHN ROBERT, real estate professional; b. Richmond, Ind., Nov. 2, 1950; s. George Howard and Mary Amanda (McKown) C. Grad. high sch., Phoenix. Sales assoc. Clements Realty, Inc., Phoenix, 1973-75; office mgr. Clements Realty, Inc., Mesa, Ariz., 1975-78; v.p., co-owner Clements Realty, Inc., Phoenix, 1978-80; broker, assoc. Ben Brooks & Assocs., Phoenix, 1980-88; pres. John R. Clements, P.C., 1984—; broker Keller Williams Realty, Phoenix and Mesa, Ariz., 1994-96; facilities dir. Outdoor Sys., Phoenix, 1996—. Real estate dir. Circle K Corp., Western Region, 1989-92; bd. dirs., v.p. Big Sisters Ariz., Phoenix, 1974-80; trustee Ariz. Realtors Polit. Action Com., 1975-85, Realtors Polit. Action Com., Ill., 1985-88; appointee Govtl. Mall Co., Ariz., 1986—, commr. chair, 1991-95. Mem. Ariz. Assn. Realtors (bd. dirs., pres. 1981), Mesa-Chandler-Tempe Bd. Realtors (past bd. dirs., pres., 1978), Nat. Assn. Realtors (past bd. dirs.), REsidential Sales Coun. Realtors, Nat. Mktg. Inst. (bd. govs. 1986—, v.p. 1990, pres. 1991), Ariz. Country Club. Republican. Presbyterian. Home: 3618 N 60th St Phoenix AZ 85018-6708 Office: Outdoor Sys 2502 N Black Canyon Phoenix AZ 85009

CLEMONS, BARBARA JUNE, minister, cosmetology educator; b. Balt., June 7, 1948; d. Robert and Maxine (Brook) Harcum; m. Elmer Lee Bush, Dec. 31, 1965 (div. Aug. 1978); children: Dale, Margarete, Michelle; m. Terry Clemons III, Mar. 26, 1996. Grad., Crenshaw Christian Ctr.; postgrad., Christian Heritage Coll., El Cajon, Calif.; BA in Christian Counseling, St. Stephens Ednl. Bible Coll., L.A., 1996, DLitt in Religious Humanities (hon.), 1996. Ordained minister, 1995; cert. in intermediate TV prodn. Cosmetologist, dist. sales mgr.; host Health is Prosperity KTYM AM Radio; prodr. Christian Chatter Continental Cablevision Channel 37, L.A.; host Women's Issues in the Cmty. KGER AM Radio; founder H.I.P. Ministries; resident advocate/counselor New Life Beginnings, Long Beach. Recipient Golden Star Halo award for outstanding contbn. to entertainment industry Continental Cablevision, Renaissance award for best religious program, 1992, Cert. of Appreciation Top Teens of Am.; recognized for contbns. to cmty. Jack and Jill of Am., Inc., Christian Cosmetology Internat. Assn., Sen. Teresa Hughes, 25th Dist., Congresswoman Maxine Waters, 35th Dist., numerous others. Home: 8621 Wilshire Blvd # 147 Beverly Hills CA 90211-3008

CLEMONS, STEVE ALAN, mortgage company executive, insurance company executive; b. Landstuhl, Germany, July 19, 1962; came to U.S., 1964; s. Jackson King and Beverly Ann (Douglass) C.; m. Catherine Denise Johnson, June 7, 1986 (div. June 1992); children: Barbara Simone, Rex Alan. BBA in Mgmt., Mesa Coll., 1984. Sales mgr. Western Res. Life Ins. Co., Grand Junction, Colo., 1981-86; mktg. dir. Western Res. Life Ins. Co., 1986-88; pres. Clem Corp., Grand Junction, 1988-92; mgr. Denver Mortgage Funding, 1992-95, v.p., 1995-96; CEO J.K.C. Corp., Ft. Collins, Colo., 1996—; exec. v.p. Direct Mortgage Group, Inc., Grand Junction, 1996—; co. rep. Colo. Life Cos., Denver, 1985-86; bus., fin. cons. Mostly Fish, Grand Junction, 1991-92. Mem. Home Builders Assn., C. of C., Lions. Republican.

CLEVENGER, JEFFREY GRISWOLD, mining company executive; b. Boston, Sept. 1, 1949; s. Galen William and Cynthia (Jones) C. BS in Mining Engring., N.Mex. Inst. Mining and Tech., Socorro, 1973; grad. advanced mgmt. program, Harvard U., 1996. Engr. Phelps Dodge, Tyrone, N.Mex., 1973-78, gen. mine foreman, 1979-81, mine supt., 1981-86; mine supt. Phelps Dodge, Morenci, Ariz., 1986, gen. supt., 1987; asst. gen. mgr. Chino Mines Co., Hurley, N.Mex., 1987-88; asst. gen. mgr. Phelps Dodge, Morenci, 1988-89, gen. mgr., 1989-92; pres. Phelps Dodge Morenci, Inc., 1989-92, Morenci Water & Electric Co., 1989-92; sr. v.p. Cyprus Copper Co., Tempe, 1992-93; pres. Cyprus Climax Metals Co., Tempe, 1993—; sr. v.p. Cyprus Amax Minerals Co., Littleton, Colo., 1993—. Contbr. articles to profl. jours. Bd. dirs. Valley of the Sun YMCA, Mining Hall of Fame; chmn. Copper Devel. Assn. Recipient Disting. Achievement award N.Mex. Inst. Mining & Tech., 1988. Mem. AIME (chmn. S.W. N.Mex. chpt. 1982), Soc. Mining Engrs. (Robert Peele award 1984), Mining and Metall. Soc. Am., Coppr Devel. Assn. (chmn.), Elks. Home: 4575 N Launfal Ave Phoenix AZ 85018 Office: Cyprus Climax Metals Co PO Box 22015 1501 W Fountainhead Pky Tempe AZ 85282

CLEVENGER, MARK THOMAS, communications executive, writer; b. L.A., Aug. 21, 1928; s. John Thomas Clevenger and Alice Laura (Wilburn) Gable; m. Ann Marie Kelley, Oct. 27, 1957; children: Kelley Patricia, Maura Theresa, Sean, Kate Clevenger Westerlund. BS in Agronomy, U. Calif., Davis; MA in Journalism, U. So. Calif.; PhC in Higher Edn., U. Wash. USAF, 1951-55; Pub. rels. rep. Lockheed Corp., Burbank, Calif., 1959-70; dir. pub. rels. Lockheed Shipbldg., Seattle, 1970-72; cons. Lockheed Shipbldg., 1974-82; dir. info. svcs. U. Wash., Seattle, 1972-73; instr. bus. comm. U. Wash., 1974-91; pres. Interface Comm., Kirkland, Wash., 1976—, Polychite Corp., Redmond, Wash., 1985-91. Editor various newspapers, Calif., 1955-59. Trustee Group Health Coop., Seattle, 1979-82. Various awards Calif. Newspaper Pubs. Assn.

CLIFF, RONALD LAIRD, energy company executive; b. Vancouver, B.C., Can., Mar. 13, 1929; s. Ronald Lorraine and Georgina (Laird) C.; children: Diana Maughan, Leslie Cliff Tindle, Sheila Sharp, Ronald Jr.; m. Ardelle Faith Simpson, 1983. B.Commerce, U. B.C., 1949. Chartered acct., 1954. Chmn. BC Gas Inc., Vancouver, 1972—; bd. dirs. Canfor Corp., Vancouver, Royal Bank of Can., Montreal, Westbury Can. Life Ins. Co., Toronto, Trans Mt. Pipe Line Co., Ltd., Vancouver. Fellow Inst. Chartered Accts.; mem. Royal Vancouver Yacht Club, Eldorado Country Club (Calif.), Thunderbird Country Club (Calif.). Anglican.

CLIFFORD, NATHAN JOSEPH, cardiologist; b. Denver, Apr. 19, 1929; s. Donald Francis and Anna (Karchmer) C.; m. Maryellen Baptist, June 12, 1954; 1 child, William Barnett. BS in Pharmacy, U. Colo., Boulder, 1951; MD, U. Colo., Denver, 1956. Diplomate Am. Bd. Internal Medicine. Physician USPHS Indian Hosp., Whiteriver, Ariz., 1957-58; med. officer in charge USPHS Indian Hosp., Owyhee, Nev., 1958-59; med. resident Kings County Hosp., Bklyn., 1959-61; cardiology fellow Mercy Hosp., San Diego, 1961-63; physician Buenaventura Clinic, Ventura, Calif., 1963-67, Internal Medicine and Cardiology P.C., Greeley, Colo., 1967-90; med. officer Phoenix Indian Med. Ctr., 1990—, chief of staff, 1992; clin. prof. medicine U. Colo., Denver, 1967—. Named Tchr. of Yr. No. Colo. Med. Ctr., 1974. Fellow ACP (Disting. Internist award Colo. chpt. 1988); mem. Am. Heart Assn. Roman Catholic. Home: 6302 N 73rd St Scottsdale AZ 85250-5500 Office: Phoenix Indian Med Ctr 4212 N 16th St Phoenix AZ 85016-5319

CLIFFORD, WALTER HOWARD, TV production consultant, author; b. Wausau, Wis., July 14, 1912; s. Walter and Katherine (Clarke) C.; m. Margaret Ellis, Nov. 1935 (div. 1945); 1 child, Sally Mae (Mrs. William Weber); m. Phyllis Jean Rice, Nov. 18, 1946 (div. 1961); 1 child, Karen Lynn (Mrs. Karen Doran); m. Joan Grant, Apr., 1961 (dec.); m. Henrietta Thompson, Oct. 6, 1967 (div. Mar. 1995). BBA, U. Puget Sound, 1934. Chief photographer, aviation editor Tacoma News Tribune, 1936-56; dir. advt. pub. rels. Pacific No. Airlines, Seattle, 1956-67; regional pub. rels. mgr. Western Air Lines, Seattle, 1967-77; v.p. pub. affairs Aeroamerica, Seattle, 1978; pres. Sourdough Enterprises, Seattle, 1978—; mgr. corp. communications Tour Alaska, Seattle, 1987-88; dir. corp. communications Princess Tours, Seattle, 1988-89, dir. pub. rels., 1989-92; assoc. producer MEC Prodns., Delray Beach, Fla., 1993-95. Author: Guidebook Alaska Game Fishing, 1958, Much About Totems, 1962, Skagway Story, 1975, Rails North, 1980, Doing The White Pass, 1985, Soapy Smith Skagway Uncrowned King, 1997; editor: ATPA Travel Times, 1964-69, Alaska News Rev., 1961-84, Alaska Blue Book Tour Guide, 1960-86; travel editor: Alaska Mag., 1970-72; developer first water ski safe release binding. Dir. Seattle Pub. Rels. Roundtable, 1963-64, 73-75. With USMC, 1944-46. Named to Alaska Hall of Fame, 1997. Mem. Pub. Rels. Soc. Am. (accredited), Puget Sound Sportswriters and Sportscasters (pres. 1986-88), N.W. Outdoors Writers Assn., Wash. Press Assn., Seattle-Tacoma Newspaper Guild (pres. 1955), Pacific N.W. INdsl. Editors Assn. (pres. 1970), Soc. Am. Travel Writers (chmn. Western chpt. 1980-82), Internat. Airline Ski Fedn. (pres. 1976-84), Nat. Outlaw and Lawman Assn., Nat. Assoc. for Outlaw and Lawman History. Home: 16401 3d Ave SW Normandy Park WA 98166

CLIFFORD, WALTER JESS, microbiologist, immunologist; b. Safford, Ariz., July 18, 1944; s. Walter Elijah, Jr. and Helen (Taylor) C.; m. Laura Bigler Clifford, Dec. 15, 1967; children: Jess. A., Terri L., Vera L., Jerald G., Joselh L. Rachel D., Jason C., Eva R. Student, Eastern Ariz. Coll., Thatcher, 1963, 65; BS, U. Ariz., Tucson, 1968, MS, 1975. Registered Microbiologist (Am. Acad. of Microbiology). Officer U.S. Army, 1968-72; staff microbiologist Tucson Med. Ctr., Tucson, 1972-73; tech. dir. Cochise Pathology Cons., Sierra Vista, Ariz., 1973-75; lab supr./dir. S.E. Svcs., Inc., Sierra Vista, Ariz., 1975-77, Benson Health Svc., Benson, Ariz., 1977-78; dir. of tech. svc. AID Lab., Richardson, Tex., 1978-80; v.p., tech. Bio Med Labs., N. Hollywood, Calif., 1980-83; dir. of rsch. Toxic Element Rsch. Found., Colorado Springs, Colo/, 1986-88; pres. and dir. Clifford Consulting and Rsch., Colorado Springs, Colo., 1982—; instr. Cochise Coll., Douglas, Ariz., 1977-78; UT Tech. Coll., Provo, UT, 1985-86. Author: Biomaterials Microbiology, 1980, 86, 90. Sch. Bd. Mem. Westside Union Sch. Dist., Rotary Club Mem. Rotary, Internat., Ad hoc steering com. Nat. Registry for Microbiologists. Recipient Phillip Hoekstra Memorial Lecture, Great Lakes Assn. for ALternative Medicine, Provisional Approval Materials Reactivity Testing Protocol, Internat. Acad. of Oral Medicine and Toxicology. Fellow Internat. Acad. Oral Medicine and Toxicology; mem. Am. Soc. for Microbiology, Am. Assn. for the Advancement of Sci., Am. Chemical Soc., N.Y. Acad. of Sci., Nat. Registry for Microbiologists, Am. Assn. for Clin. Chemistry. Republican. Mem LDS Ch. Office: Clifford Consulting & Rsch 2275 Waynoka Rd Ste J Colorado Springs CO 80915-1635

CLIFT, WILLIAM BROOKS, III, photographer; b. Boston, Jan. 5, 1944; s. William Brooks C. and Anne (Pearmain) Thomson; m. Vida Regina Chesnulis, Aug. 8, 1970; children: Charis, Carola, William. Free lance comml. photographer in partnership with Steve Gersh under name Helios, 1963-71; pres. William Clift Ltd., Santa Fe, 1980-85; cons. Polaroid Corp., 1965-67. Photographer one-man shows, Carl Siembab Gallery, Boston, 1969, Mus. Art, U. Oreg., Eugene, 1969, New Boston City Hall Gallery, 1970, U. Mass., Berkshire Mus., Pittsfield, Mass., William Coll., Addison Gallery of Am. Art, Wheaton Coll., Mass., Worcester Art Mus., 1971, Creative Photography Gallery, MIT, 1972, St. John's Coll. Art Gallery, Santa Fe, 1973, Wiggin Gallery, Boston Pub. Library, 1974, Australian Ctr. for Photography, Sydney, 1978, Susan Spiritus Gallery, Newport Beach, Calif., 1979, MIT Creative Photography Gallery, 1980, William Lyons Gallery, Coconut Grove, Fla., 1980, Eclipse Gallery, Boulder, Colo., 1980, Atlanta Gallery of Photography, 1980, Phoenix Art Mus., 1981, Jeb Gallery, Providence, 1981, Portfolio Gallery, 1981, Images Gallery, Cin., 1982, Boston Atheneum, 1983, Bank of Santa Fe, 1984, Susan Harder Gallery, N.Y.C., 1984, Cleve. Art Mus., 1985, Art Inst. Chgo., 1987, Amon Carter Mus., Ft. Worth, 1987, Clarence Kennedy Gallery, Cambridge, Mass., 1988, Equitable Gallery, N.Y.C., 1993, Vassar Coll. Art Mus., N.Y., 1994, Vassar Coll. Art Gallery, N.Y., 1995; exhibited in group shows Gallery 216, N.Y., N.Y. Grover Cronin Gallery, Waltham, Mass., 1964, Carl Seimbab Gallery, Boston, 1966, Lassall Jr. Coll., 1967, Hill's Gallery, Santa Fe, Tyler Mus. Art, Austin, Tex., Dupree Gallery, Dallas, 1974, Quindacqua Gallery, Washington, 1978,

Zabriskie Gallery, Paris, 1978, Am. Cultural Ctr., Paris, 1978; photographer AT&T Project-Am. Images, 1978, Seagram's Bicentennial Project, Courthouse, 1975-77, Readers Digest Assn. Project, 1984, Hudson River Project, 1985-92; author: Photography Portfolios, Old Boston City Hall, 1971, Photography Portfolios, Courthouse, 1979, Photography Portfolios, New Mexico, 1975, Certain Places, Photographs, 1987, A Hudson Landscape, Photographs, 1993. Nat. Endowment for Arts photography fellow, 1972, 79; Guggenheim fellow, 1974, 80, N.Mex. Gov.'s Excellence in The Arts award, 1987. Home and Office: PO Box 6035 Santa Fe NM 87502-6035

CLIFTON, DOROTHY I., historian, inn proprietor; b. Manilla, Iowa, Nov. 16, 1918; d. Joyce Williamina (Peterson) Hamann; children: Kinkead (dec.), Howard (dec.), Clifton (dec.), Marilyn, Janice, Daniel, Mary, Margaret Anne. Magistrate recorder Alaska ct. sys.; tchr. area schs., Valdez, Alaska; desk clk. Westmark Inn, Valdez; dir. Alaska State Housing Authority; owner Think Pink, Valdez; owner Clifton's Libr., Valdez. Bd. dirs. Salvation Army, Valdez Hist. Soc.; sec., treas. USCG Aux.; life. mem. Cook Inlet Hist. Soc. Recipient Vol. award 1st Lady, State of Alaska, Juneau. Mem. VFW, Am. Legion, Valdez Hist. Soc. (bd. dirs.), Valdez Geneal. Soc. (sec., treas.), Fraternal Order of Eagles (v.p. Valdez chpt.). Home and Office: PO Box 6 705 N Glacier Dr Valdez AK 99686

CLIFTON, MARK STEPHEN, administrator; b. San Diego, May 25, 1955; s. Paul Clifford and Dorothy Jean (Gross) C.; m. Margaret Eileen Hower, July 20, 1985; 1 child, Casey Mariah. Student, Grossmont Coll., 1973-74, San Diego City Coll., 1981. Oper. supr. San Diego Unified Sch. Dist., 1979—; owner A Home Touch Housecleaning, San Diego, 1985—; speaker in field. Author: There Goes the Neighborhood, 1993; contbr. articles to profl. jours. Mem. Ocean Beach Town Coun., San Diego, 1993—. Recipient Hon. Svc. award PTA, Point Loma High Sch., 1989. Mem. San Diego Writers and Editor's Guild, Christian Writers Guild, Adminstrs. Assn., Maranatha Surfing Assn. (founder, pres. 1983-86), Christian Surfing Assn. (co-founder 1982-83). Republican. Office: San Diego Unified Sch Dist 8460 Ruffner St San Diego CA

CLIFTON, MICHAEL EDWARD, English language educator; b. Reedley, Calif., Jan. 6, 1949; s. Edward Eugene and Helen May (Peters) C.; m. Anita May Bernardi, June 22, 1973. BA, Calif. State U., Fresno, 1971, MA with distinction, 1977; PhD, Ind. U., 1984. Tchr. English Hoover High Sch., Fresno, 1971-74; assoc. instr. Ind. U., Bloomington, 1978-80; lectr. Calif. State U., Fresno, 1982—; reader, presenter Internat. Assn. Fantastic in Arts, Ft. Lauderdale, Fla., 1988, 93, Houston, Tex., 1987, Am. Imagery Assn., San Francisco, 1986, Eaton Conf., U. Calif. Riverside, 1985. Contbr. articles to popular mags. and profl. jours. Chair Tower Dist. Design Rev. Com. Mem. MLA, AAUP. Democrat. Home: 921 N San Pablo Ave Fresno CA 93728-3627 Office: Calif State U Dept English Peters Bldg Fresno CA 93740

CLIMO, ROBERT SHIPLEY, public relations executive; b. Palo Alto, Calif., July 22, 1952; s. George Frederick and Shirley Hall (Beistle) C.; m. Mary Lou Meringo, Mar. 26, 1977; children: Theresa, Elizabeth, Tim. BA in English, U. Calif., Berkeley, 1974; MA in English, Stanford U., 1975; MBA in Mktg., Santa Clara U., 1981. Cert. adult edn. tchr., Calif.; cert. cmty. coll. tchr. Mgr. pub. programs ESL, Inc., Sunnyvale, Calif., 1979-83, mgr. divsn. pubs., 1984-87, mgr. pubs., 1988-91, mgr. adminstrv. svcs., 1991-94; mgr. public affairs TRW Sys. Integration Group, Sunnyvale, Calif., 1995—. Bd. dirs. Industry Edn. Coun. of Calif., 1996—, Jr. Achievement of Santa Clara County, 1993-95; mem. blue ribbon com. State of Calif. Reading Improvement Task Force, 1995; bd. dirs., ex-oficio mem. Workforce Silicon Valley, 1994—; chmn. public sector campaign United Way of Santa Clara County, 1994—; pres., bd. dirs. Industry Initiatives for Sci. and Math. Edn., 1993—; commr. Health and Human Svcs., Sunnyvale, 1995—. Mem. Am. Electronics Assn. (mem. edn. com.). Republican. Office: TRW 485 E Java Dr Sunnyvale CA 94089-1125

CLINARD, FRANK WELCH, JR., materials scientist, researcher; b. Winston-Salem, N.C., Aug. 4, 1933; s. Frank Welch and Hazel Helen (Hauser) C.; m. Elva Adams Hyatt, Apr. 2, 1968. BSME, N.C. State U., 1955, MSMetE, 1957; PhD, Stanford U., 1965. Staff mem. Sandia Corp., Albuquerque, N.Mex., 1957-61; research asst. Stanford U., Palo Alto, Calif., 1961-64; staff mem. Los Alamos (N.Mex.) Nat. Lab., 1964-77, sect. leader, 1977-89, lab. assoc., 1989-92, staff mem., 1992-94, guest scientist, 1995—; cons. in field, Los Alamos, 1983—; prof. materials sci. N.Mex. Inst. Mining and Tech., Socorro, 1990—. Contbr. more than 90 articles to profl. jours. Bd. dirs. County Pub. TV Orgns., Los Alamos, N.Mex., 1981-82; state chmn. Libertarian Party N.Mex., 1986-88, candidate for State Senate in Dist. 22, 1992, pub. rels. dir., 1994—. Fellow Am. Ceramic Soc.; mem. AAAS, ACLU (bd. dirs. N.Mex. chpt. 1993—), Amnesty Internat., Am. Soc. Metals (chmn. local chpt. 1969-70), Am. Nuclear Soc., Materials Rsch. Soc. (vis. scientist 1996, adv. editl. bd. jour. 1993—, bulletin subcom. 1996—), Rotary (v.p., pres. Los Alamos chpt. 1995—), Sports Car Club del. Valle Rio Grande (pres. 1967), Sigma Xi, Phi Kappa Phi, Tau Beta Pi, Pi Tau Sigma. Unitarian. Home: 2940 Arizona Ave Los Alamos NM 87544-1512 Office: Los Alamos Nat Lab Mail Stop K762 Los Alamos NM 87545

CLINCH, NICHOLAS BAYARD, III, business executive; b. Evanston, Ill., Nov. 9, 1930; s. Nicholas Bayard Jr. and Virginia Lee (Campbell) C.; m. Elizabeth Wallace Campbell, July 11, 1964; children: Virginia Lee, Alison Campbell. Student, N.Mex. Mil. Inst., Roswell, 1948-49; AB, Stanford U., 1952, LLB, 1955. Bar: Calif. 1959. Expedition leader First Ascent, Gasherbrum I (26,470 ft.), Pakistan, 1958, First Ascent, Masherbrum (25, 660 ft.), Pakistan, 1959-60; assoc. Voegelin, Barton, Harris & Callister, L.A., 1961-68; pvt. practice Washington, 1968-70; v.p., counsel Lincoln Savs. & Loan Assn., L.A., 1970-74; exec. dir. Sierra Club Found., San Francisco, 1975-81; environ. cons. Fluor Corp., Grass Valley, Calif., 1981-84; v.p., sec. CCA, Inc., Denver, 1984—; dir. Growth Stock Outlook Inc., Potomac, Md., Recreational Equipment Inc., Seattle. Author: A Walk in the Sky, 1982. Leader Am. Antarctic Mountaineering Expdn., Sentinel Range, 1966-67; co-leader Chinese Am. Ulugh Muztagh Expdn., Kun Lun Range, Xinjiang, 1985, Am. Expdns. to Kang Karpo Range, Yunnan-Tibet border, 1988, 89, 92, 93; co-founder, trustee Calif. League Conservation Voters, San Francisco, 1972—. 1st lt. USAF, 1956-57. Recipient John Oliver La Gorce medal Nat. Geog. Soc., Washington, 1967. Fellow Royal Geog. Soc., Explorers Club; mem. ABA, Am. Alpine Club (hon., pres. 1967-70), Appalachian Mountain Club (hon.), State Bar Calif., Alpine Club (London), Chinese Assn. Sci. Expdns. (hon.). Republican. Episcopalian. Home: 2001 Bryant St Palo Alto CA 94301-3714 Office: CCA Inc 4100 E Mississippi Ave Ste 1750 Denver CO 80222-3060

CLINE, BRYAN M., manufacturing manager; b. Springfield, Oreg., Mar. 18, 1959; s. Charles Frederick and Ilse Maria (Rausch) C. AAS with honors, Shoreline Community Coll., 1981; student, U. Mont., 1982; BA, U. Wash., 1984; MBA, Seattle U., 1991. Lifeguard City of Seattle, 1978-85; mfg. mgr. The Boeing Co., Seattle, 1985—. Seattle Milk Fund scholar, 1977. Mem. U.S. Postal Commemorative Soc., Beta Gamma Sigma. Democrat. Lutheran.

CLINE, CAROLYN JOAN, plastic and reconstructive surgeon; b. Boston; d. Paul S. and Elizabeth (Flom) Cline. BA, Wellesley Coll., 1962; MA, U. Cin., 1966; PhD, Washington U., 1970; diploma Washington Sch. Psychiatry, 1972; MD, U. Miami (Fla.) 1975. Diplomate Am. Bd. Plastic and Reconstructive Surgery. Rsch. asst. Harvard Dental Sch., Boston, 1962-64; rsch. asst. physiology Laser Lab., Children's Hosp. Research Found., Cin., 1964, psychology dept. U. Cin., 1964-65; intern in clin. psychology St. Elizabeth's Hosp., Washington, 1966-67; psychologist Alexandria (Va.) Community Mental Health Ctr., 1967-68; research fellow NIH, Washington, 1968-69; chief psychologist Kingsbury Ctr. for Children, Washington, 1969-73; sole practice clin. psychology, Washington, 1970-73; intern internal medicine U. Wis. Hosps., Ctr. for Health Sci., Madison, 1975-76; resident in surgery Stanford U. Med. Ctr., 1976-78; fellow microvascular surgery dept. surgery U. Calif.-San Francisco, 1978-79; resident in plastic surgery St. Francis Hosp., San Francisco, 1979-82; practice medicine, specializing in plastic and reconstructive surgery, San Francisco, 1982—. Contbr. chpt. to plastic surgery textbook, articles to profl. jours. Mem. Am. Soc. Plastic and Reconstructive Surgeons, Royal Soc. Medicine, Calif. Medicine Assn., Calif. Soc. Plastic and Reconstructive Surgeons, San Francisco Med. Soc. Office: 490 Post St Ste 735 San Francisco CA 94102-1408

CLINE, FRED ALBERT, JR., retired librarian, conservationist; b. Santa Barbara, Calif., Oct. 23, 1929; s. Fred Albert and Anna Cecelia (Haberl) C. AB in Asian Studies, U. Calif., Berkeley, 1952, MLS, 1962. Resident Internat. House, Berkeley, 1950-51; trainee, officer Bank of Am., San Francisco, Düsseldorf, Fed. Republic Germany, Kuala Lumpur, 1954-60; adminstrv. reference libr. Calif. State Libr., Sacramento, 1962-67; head libr. Asian Art Mus. San Francisco, 1967-93; ret., 1993. Contbg. author: Chinese, Korean and Japanese Sculpture in the Avery Brundage Collection, 1974; author, editor: Ruth Hill Cooke, 1985; contbr. articles and book revs. on AIDS to various publs. Bd. dirs. Tamalpais Conservation Club, 1990-94, chmn. Found., The Desert Protective Coun.; AIDS activist. Sgt. M.C., U.S. Army, 1952-54. Mem. Metaphys. Alliance (sec., bd. dirs. San Francisco chpt. 1988-91), Nature Conservancy, Sierra Club. Democrat. Home: 825 Lincoln Way San Francisco CA 94122-2369

CLINE, PLATT HERRICK, author; b. Mancos, Colo., Feb. 7, 1911; s. Gilbert T. and Jessie (Baker) C.; m. Barbara Decker, Sept. 11, 1934. Grad., N.Mex. Mil. Inst., 1930; student, Colo. U., 1930-31; LittD, No. Ariz. U., 1966, BS, 1982. Advt. solicitor Denver Post, 1931; with Civilian Conservation Corps., 1934-36; Nat. Monument ranger, 1936; pub. Norwood (Colo.) Post, 1937-38; advt. mgr. Coconino Sun, Flagstaff, Ariz., 1938-41; mng. editor Holbrook Tribune-News, 1941-45; editor Coconino Sun, 1945-46; mng. editor Ariz. Daily Sun, 1946-53, pub., 1953-69, pres., 1969-76, v.p., 1976—; rsch. assoc. Mus. No. Ariz., 1976—; adj. prof. history No. Ariz. U., 1983—. Author: They Came to the Mountain, 1976, Mountain Campus, 1983, The View From Mountain Campus, 1990, Mountain Town, Flagstaff in the 20th Century, 1994. Mem. Ariz. Commn. Indian Affairs, 1952-55, Norwood (Colo) Town Coun., 1937-38; chmn. Flagstaff Citizen of Yr. Com., 1976—; bd. dirs., past pres. Raymond Edn. Found., No. Ariz. U. Found.; bd. dirs. Transition Found; trustee Flagstaff Community Hosp., 1954-58. Recipient Ariz. Master Editor-Pub. award, 1969, El-Merito award Ariz. Hist. Soc., 1976; named Flagstaff Citizen of Yr., 1976, Disting. Citizen, No. Ariz. U. Alumni, 1983, Outstanding Flagstaff Citizen of Century award, 1994; dedicatee No. Ariz. U. Libr., 1988. Mem. Ariz. Newspapers Assn. (past pres., Golden Svc. award 1989), No. Ariz. Pioneers Hist. Soc. (trustee 1972-75), Sigma Delta Chi, Phi Alpha Theta, Phi Kappa Phi, Masons. Home: PO Box 578 Flagstaff AZ 86002-0578

CLINE, ROBERT STANLEY, air freight company executive; b. Urbana, Ill., July 17, 1937; s. Lyle Stanley and Mary Elizabeth (Prettyman) C.; m. Judith Lee Stucker, July 7, 1979; children: Lisa Andre, Nicole Lesley, Christina Elaine, Leslie Jane. BA, Dartmouth Coll., 1959. Asst. treas. Chase Manhattan Bank, N.Y.C., 1960-65; v.p. fin. Pacific Air Freight Co., Seattle, 1965-68; exec. v.p. fin. Airborne Express (formerly Airborne Freight Corp.), Seattle, 1968-78, vice chmn., CFO, dir., 1978-84, chmn., CEO, dir., 1984—; bd. dirs. Seattle-First Nat. Bank, Metricom Corp., Safeco Corp. Trustee Seattle Repertory Theatre, 1974-90, chmn. bd., 1979-83; trustee Children's Hosp. Found., 1983-91, 96—, Corp. Coun. of Arts, 1983—; bd. dirs. Washington Roundtable, 1985—, chmn. 1995-96, chmn. bd. dirs. Children's Hosp. Found., 1987-89; trustee United Way of King County, 1991-93. With U.S. Army, 1959-60. Home: 1209 39th Ave E Seattle WA 98112-4403 Office: Airborne Express PO Box 662 Seattle WA 98111-0662

CLINE, WILSON ETTASON, retired administrative law judge; b. Newkirk, Okla., Aug. 26, 1914; s. William Sherman and Etta Blanche (Roach) C.; m. G. Barbara Verne Pentecost, Nov. 1, 1939 (div. Nov. 1960); children: William, Catherine Cline MacDonald, Thomas; m. Gina Lana Ludwig, Oct. 5, 1969; children: David Ludwig, Kenneth Ludwig. Student, U. Ill., 1932-33; A.B., U. Okla., 1935, B.S. in Bus. Adminstrn., 1936; J.D., U. Calif., Berkeley, 1939; LL.M., Harvard U., 1941. Bar: Calif. 1940, U.S. Ct. Appeals (9th cir.) 1941, U.S. Dist. Ct. (no. dist.) Calif. 1943, U.S. Supreme Ct. 1953. Atty. Kaiser Richmond Shipyards, 1941-44; pvt. practice Oakland, 1945-49; prof., asst. dean, dean Eastbay Div. Lincoln U. Law Sch., Oakland, 1946-50; atty., hearing officer, asst. chief adminstrv. law judge, acting chief adminstrv. law judge Calif. Pub. Utilities Commn., San Francisco, 1949-80, ret., 1981, dir. gen. welfare Calif. State Employees Assn., 1966-67, chmn. retirement com., 1965-66, mem. member benefit com., 1980-81, mem. ret. employees div. council dist. C, 1981-82; executor estate of Warren A. Cline. Past trustee Cline Ranch Trust, various family trusts. Mem. ABA, State Bar Calif., Conf. Calif. Pub. Utility Counsel (steering com. 1967-71), Am. Judicature Soc., Boalt Hall Alumni Assn., Harvard Club of San Francisco, Commonwealth Club San Francisco, Sleepy Hollow Swim and Tennis Club (Orinda, Calif.), Masons (Orinda lodge # 494 sec. 1951-55, past Master 1949), Sirs (Peralta chpt. 12), Phi Beta Kappa (pres. No. Calif. assn. 1969-70), Beta Gamma Sigma, Delta Sigma Pi (Key award 1936), Phi Kappa Psi, Phi Delta Phi, Pi Sigma Alpha. Democrat. Mem. United Ch. Christ. Home: 110 Saint Albans Rd Kensington CA 94708-1035 Office: 3750 Harrison St Unit 304 PO Box 11120 Oakland CA 94611-0120

CLINTON, JOHN PHILIP MARTIN, communications executive; b. Sheffield, Eng., Apr. 30, 1935; came to U.S., 1967; s. John A.T. and Phyllis Mary (Fowler) C.; m. Margaret Rosemary Morgan, Aug. 26, 1961; children: Alaric, Ivan, James. BA, Oxford U., 1959, MA, 1962. Mgr. computer systems Stanford (Calif.) U., 1967-70; v.p. systems devel. Computer Curriculum Corp., Palo Alto, Calif., 1970-79; exec. v.p. Captec, Inc., Santa Clara, Calif., 1979-80; mgr. product devel. Siltec Corp., Menlo Park, Calif., 1980-82; cons. Instructive Tech., Palo Alto, 1982-83; mgr. software devel. Voicemail Internat., Inc., Santa Clara, 1983-85, v.p. engring., 1985-87, sr. v.p. engring., 1987-88; pres. In-Gate Tech., Sunnyvale, Calif., 1988—. Author: Begin Algol, 1966; editor (newsletter) Flat Tyre, 1982. Adv. com. Sunnyvale City Coun., 1994—, chmn., 1996. Hastings scholar Queens Coll., Oxford U., 1955-59. Mem. Info. Industry Assn., Modern Transit Soc., Oxford Soc. (No. Calif. com. 1993—), Ultra Marathon Cycling Assn., Western Wheelers Bicycle Club (pres. 1983), Oxford and Cambridge Club (London). Home: 2277 Bryant St Palo Alto CA 94301-3910 Office: In-Gate Tech 710 Lakeway Dr # 270 Sunnyvale CA 94086-4013

CLINTON, ROBERT EMMETT (FRITTER CLINTON), writer; b. Butte, Mont., June 7; s. Emmett Crocker and Myrtle Ione (Terpening) C.; children: Joe, Joy, Patricia. Student, Ariz. State U., 1954. Author: Pretty Petty, 1985, Chapter Forty Seven, 1990, World War Three, Hortencia, World War 3; patentee Horizontal-Vertical Apparatus, 1987, Prosthetic Apparatus, 1988. Methodist. Home: 1709 Redwood Ave Grants Pass OR 97527

CLODFELTER, RICHARD DOYLE, artist; b. Fairbanks, Alaska; s. James Kenneth Rollyn Clodfelter and Bobbie Lou McDaniel Gallentine. BFA, Pacific N.W. Coll. Art, Portland, Oreg., 1984. Artist; mem. Gallery 114, Portland. One-man shows include Woodstove Showroom, Gresham, Oreg., 1981, Portland State U., 1987, Open Loft, Portland, 1989; groups shows include Portland Art Mus., 1984, Marylhurst Coll., Lake Oswego, Oreg., 1988, First Unitarian Ch., Portland, 1995, Giant Steps Cafe, Portland, 1996, Beaverton Art Cmty. Showcase 93, 1993; author web page, 1996. Recipient Voorhis Drawing prize, 1980, 84; Mary Peterson Merit scholar., 1981. Office: Gallery 114 1100 NW Glisan Portland OR 97209

CLOSE, BEVERLY JEAN, secondary education educator; b. Portland, Oreg., July 1, 1958; d. Bertrand J. and Charlotte J. (Mollett) C. BA in Psychology, U. Oreg., 1980. Cert. English, social studies and journalism tchr., Oreg. Tchr. Glencoe High Sch., Hillsboro, Oreg., 1991, J.B. Thomas Jr. High Sch., Hillsboro, Oreg., 1991-92, Yamhill (Oreg.)-Carlton High Sch., 1992—; adv. mem. for Reflections (literary mag.), Yamhill-Carlton H.S., 1993—; adviser The Expression (newspaper) Yamhill-Carlton H.S., 1992—. Writer (newspaper) Hollywood Star, 1987-89. Mem. Jr. League of Portland, 1986—; bd. dirs. Friends of Extension, Hillsboro, 1994-95, 4-H (Washington County), Hillsboro, 1994-95. Mem. Nat. Coun. Tchrs. English. Office: Yamhill-Carlton High Sch 275 N Maple St Yamhill OR 97148-7601

CLOSE, JACK DEAN, SR., physical therapist; b. Provo, Utah, Apr. 21, 1943; s. Melvin D. Sr. and Hope (Coleman) C.; m. Gaylee King, Dec. 7, 1962; children: Jack Dean Jr., Tiffany Lee, Kristina Louise, Stephen William. BS in Zoology, Brigham Young U., 1967; MA in Phys. Therapy, U. So. Calif., 1970; postgrad., U. Nev. Las Vegas, 1978-87. Registered phys. therapist, Calif. and Nev. Staff phys. therapist Glendale (Calif.) Meml. Hosp., 1969-70; phys. and respiratory therapist So. Nev. Meml. Hosp., Las Vegas, 1970-71; pres. Phys. Therapy Svcs., Las Vegas, 1971-74, Close and Kleven, Ltd., Las Vegas, 1974-96; pres./CEO Jack D. Close and Assocs., Phys. Therapy & Rehab. Ctr., Las Vegas, 1996—; clin. instr. U. Utah, 1978-84, U. So. Calif., 1980-84, 91, U. Okla., 1980—, No. Ariz. U., 1981—, Duke U., 1988—, U. Miami, 1989—; adv. com. respiratory therapy Clark County Community Coll., 1980; adv. bd. phys. therapy U. Nev. Las Vegas, 1988—, instr. U. Nev., mem adv. bd. Phys. Therapy Asst. Program C.C. of So. Nev., 1982—; presenter various confs., profl. meetings. Contbr. articles to profl. jours. Chmn. reunions Las Vegas High Sch. Class 1961; numerous leadership positions LDS Ch.; mem. exec. com. Nev. Friendship Force; past mgr., coach Little League Baseball; past mem. profl. adv. staff Easter Seal, cons. staff Muscular Dystrophy, med. adv. bd. Multiple Sclerosis, adv. coun. and gov. bd. Health Systems Agy. adv. com. Clark County Community Devel., 1981-83; mem. Nev. State Assemblyman Dist. 15 (Las Vegas), mem. ways & means, election/procedures and ethics, and commerce coms. Allied Health Profession scholar; named one of Outstanding Young Men of Am. Brigham Young U. Alumni Assn., 1979; recipient Bachelor Commr. Sci. award Boulder Dam area coun. Boy Scouts Am., 1989, Master Commr. Sci. award, 1990, Merit award, 1991, Silver Beaver award. Mem. AACD, Am. Phys. Therapy Assn. (v.p., chmn. joint task force, trustee and exec. com. Found. Phys. Therapy 1990, pres. APT Svcs. Corp. 1989, Lucy Blair Svc. award), Nat. Athletic Trainers Assn. (assoc.), Am. Running and Fitness Assn., Nat. Strength and Conditioning Assn., Nat. Wellness Assn., Aquatic Exercise Assn., Nev. Athletic Trainers Assn. Office: Jack D Close and Assocs Phys Therapy & Rehab Ctr 4560 S Eastern Ave Ste B-18 Las Vegas NV 89119

CLOSE, SANDY, journalist; b. N.Y.C., Jan. 25, 1943. BA, U. Calif., Berkeley, 1964. Exec. dir., editor Pacific News Svc., San Francisco. MacArthur fellow, 1995. Office: Pacific News Service 450 Mission St Ste 204 San Francisco CA 94105-2505*

CLOUD, BARBARA LEE, adult education educator; b. Tulare, Calif., June 12, 1938; d. Virgil R. and Nina N. Hicks; m. Stanley Donovan Cloud, 1960. BA, Stanford U., 1960; MA, U. Oreg., 1967; PhD, U. Wash., 1979. News editor Springfield (Oreg.) News, 1961-65; info. officer Australian Nat. U., Canberra, 1968-70; pub. rels. cons. Eric White Assoc., Perth, Australia, 1970-76; asst., assoc. and prof. U. Nev., Las Vegas, 1979—. Author: The Business of Newspapers on the Western Frontier, 1992 (Nev. Humanities award); co-author: Media Law in Nevada, 1992; editor Journalism History, 1992—; contbr. articles to profl. jours. Mem. Nev. Humanities Com., 1994—. Mem. Am. Journalism Historians Assn. (pres. 1984-85), Assn. Edn. Journalism and Mass Comm. (head history divsn. 1992-93, History Svc. award 1995), Soc. Profl. Journalists, Conf. Hist. Jours., Phi Kappa Phi. Office: U Nev Hank Greenpun Sch Comm 4505 Maryland Las Vegas NV 89154-5007

CLOUD, JAMES MERLE, university and hospital administrator, learning specialist; b. Winston-Salem, N.C., Feb. 16, 1947; s. Merle Vail and Jane Crawford (Moore) C.; BA, U. N.C., 1970; PhD, Columbia Pacific U., 1979. Co-founder Wholistic Health and Nutrition Inst., Mill Valley, Calif., 1974, dir. edn., 1974-76, dir. health resource consultation, 1976-78; dir., v.p. No. Calif. Internat. Coop. Coun., 1975-77; admissions dir. Columbia Pacific U., 1978-84, sec.-treas., dir., 1978-84; v.p. Calif. U. for Advanced Studies, Novato, 1984-85; dir. Wholistic Health and Nutrition Inst., 1974-85; adminstr. Autumn Care Convalescent Hosp., 1989-90; founder Memorobics Seminars of Memory Skills for Fgn. Lang. Study, 1992, Speed Learning Systems, 1992, Learning Made Easy Study Skills Seminars. Author: The Healthscription, 1979, Directory of Active Senior Organizations and Communications Resources, 1989, The Foreign Language Memory Book, 1995, The Bible Memory Book, 1995, The Memory Game: Learning Made Easy!, 1996; (poetry) Aeolus, 1971, No One Loves with Solitude, 1970. Sec., dir. Citizens of Marin Against Crime, 1983. Columnist Ukiah Penny Pincher, 1990. Mem. Assn. Holistic Health (v.p. 1976, dir.), Airplane Owners and Pilots Assn., Am. Assn. Active Srs. (v.p. 1988-89), Internat. Friends of the Iron Horse (founder, pres. 1990—), Internat. Assn. of Body Mechanics (pres. 1991—), Mendocino County Railway Soc. (dir. 1991), Nat. Assn. of Railway Passengers, Train Riders Assn. of Calif., Pacific Internat. Trapshooters Assn. Home: 4286 Redwood Hwy San Rafael CA 94903-2610

CLOUGH, SHERYL ANNE, secondary school educator, poet; b. Spokane, Wash., Aug. 16, 1950; d. Storrs Bernard and Theresa Rosalie (Storwick) Clough; m. Bill Hommer McGeary, Dec. 31, 1994; 1 child, Theresa Christine Olson. BA, U. Wash., 1990; MFA, U. Alaska, Fairbanks, 1994. Grad. tchg. asst. U. Alaska, Fairbanks, 1991-94; instr. Della Keats Enrichment Program, Anchorage, 1995, Upward Bound Math/Sci. Program, Fairbanks, 1993—; panel mem. Filling the Northern Niche pub. conf., Fairbanks, 1994; lectr. in field. Editor: Transplants at Dock Point (poetry chapbook), 1996; contbg. author: (anthology) Alaska Passages: 20 Voices From Above the 49th Parallel, 1996, Solo: On Her Own Adventure, 1996, (poetry collection) Flights of Fancy: Alaska Birds in Verse, 1994; feature writer Heartbeat newsletter, 1995. Lit. reader Habitat for Humanity Benefit, Bellingham, 1996, Elliott Bay Books, Seattle, 1996; vis. poet in schs. Airport Heights Sch., Anchorage, 1995. Recipient Dorothy Daniels Hon. Writing award Assn. Am. Pen Women, 1992; U. Alaska-Fairbanks Travel grantee, 1993. Mem. Am. Contract Bridge League (accredited tchr.), Phi Beta Kappa.

CLOUSE, VICKIE RAE, biology and paleontology educator; b. Havre, Mont., Mar. 28, 1956; d. Olaf Raymond and Betty Lou (Reed) Nelson; m. Gregory Scott Clouse, Mar. 22, 1980; 1 child, Kristopher Nelson. BS in Secondary Sci. Edn., Mont. State U. No., Havre, 1989; postgrad., Mont. State U., Bozeman, 1991-94. Teaching asst. biology and paleontology Mont. State U.-No., Havre, 1986-90; rsch. asst. dinosaur eggs and embryos Mus. of the Rockies, Bozeman, 1992-95; instr. biology and paleontology Mont. State U.-No., Havre, 1990—. Bd. trustees H.E. Clack Mus., Havre, 1991-97, H.E. Clack Mus. Found., Havre, 1991-97, Mont. Bd. Regents of Higher Edn., Helena, 1989-90, Mont. Higher Edn. Student Fin. Assistance Corp., Helena, 1989-90; mem. Ea. Mont. Hist. Soc., 1993—. Named Young Career Woman of Yr., Bus. and Profl. Woman's Club, 1986. Mem. AAAS, Soc. Vertebrate Paleontologists, Mont. Geol. Soc. Office: Mont State U-No Hagener Sci Ctr Havre MT 59501

CLOWES, ALEXANDER WHITEHILL, surgeon, educator; b. Boston, Oct. 9, 1946; s. George H.A. Jr. and Margaret Gracey (Jackson) C.; m. Monika Meyer. AB, Harvard U., 1968, MD, 1972. Resident in surgery Case Western Reserve, Cleve., 1972-74, 76-79; rsch. fellow in pathology Harvard Med. Sch., Boston, 1974-76; fellow in vascular surgery Brigham and Womens Hosp. Harvard Med. Sch., 1979-80; asst. prof. surgery U. Wash., Seattle, 1980-85, assoc. prof., 1985-90, prof., 1990—, assoc. chmn. dept., 1989-91, acting chmn. dept., 1992-93, adj. prof. pathology, 1992, chief divsn. vascular surgery, 1995—, dept. vice chmn., 1995—. Contbr. chpts. to books; author numerous sci. papers. Trustee Marine Biol. Labs., Woods Hole, Mass., 1989—, Seattle Symphony, 1994—; bd. dirs. Seattle Chamber Music Festival, 1990. Recipient NIH Rsch. Career Devel. award, 1982-87; NIH Tng. fellow, 1974-77; Loyal Davis Traveling Surg. scholar ACS, 1987. Mem. Am. Surg. Assn., Am. Assn. Pathologists, Am. Heart Assn. (coun. on arteriosclerosis), Am. Soc. Cell Biology, Internat. Soc. Applied Cardiovasc. Biology, Seattle Surg. Soc., Soc. Vascular Surgery, Cruising Club Am., Quisset Yacht Club, Sigma Xi. Episcopalian. Home: 702 Fullerton Ave Seattle WA 98122-6432 Office: U Wash Dept Surgery Box 356410 Seattle WA 98195

CLOYD, SANDRA GOMEZ, bilingual educator; b. Phoenix, Ariz., Dec. 24, 1956; d. Alberto and Julia (Mendoza) Gomez; m. John Straton Cloyd, May 20, 1978; children: Christopher Gomez, Kimberly Maria, Gabriela Emma. BS in Elem. Edn., Grand Canyon U., 1990. Cert. elem. edn., Ariz. Pers. mgr. U.S. Army, Ft. Bragg, N.C., 1979-80; receptionist Ariz. Fed. Credit Union, Phoenix, 1983-84; adminstrv. asst. Landmark Elem. Sch., Glendale, Ariz., 1984-85; elem. sch. tchr. St. Jerome Sch., Phoenix, 1990-91; bilingual tchr. Cartwright Sch. Dist., Phoenix, 1991—. Home room mother Sine Elem. Sch., Glendale, 1986-89; vol. case worker Cmty. Action Program, Glendale, 1977; polit. activist League United Latin Am. Citizens, Phoenix, 1974-76, Movimiento Estudiantil Chicano de Aztlan, Phoenix, 1975-76. Mem. NEA, Ariz. Edn. Assn., Cartwright Edn. Assn., Westside Reading Conf., Women in Mil. Svc. for Am. Meml. Found. Democrat. Roman Catholic. Home: 7829 W Brown St Peoria AZ 85345-0701 Office: Starlight Park Sch 7960 W Osborn Rd Phoenix AZ 85033-3521

CLUCAS, RICHARD ALLEN, political science educator; b. Orange, Calif., May 31, 1958; s. Edward Leroy and Helen (Selfridge) C.; m. Elizabeth Marie Blenz, Apr. 1, 1958; children: Nathaniel Edward, Alexander Martin. BA, U. Calif., Irvine, 1980; MA, U. Calif., Santa Barbara, 1984, PhD, 1990. Mng. editor Orange County Bus. Jour., Santa Ana, Calif., 1982-83; vis. lectr. Calif. Poly. U., San Luis Obispo, 1991, U. Calif., Santa Barbara, 1990-91; asst. prof. U. Wis., Eau Claire, 1991-95; asst. prof. polit. sci. Portland (Oreg.) State U., 1995—. Author: The Speaker's Electoral Connection: Willie Brown and the California Assembly, 1995, Encylopedia of American Political Reform, 1996. Mem. Am. Polit. Sci. Assn., Midwest Polit. Sci. Assn., S.W. Polit. Sci. Assn., Western Polit. Sci. Assn., Pacific N.W. Polit. Sci. Assn. Office: Portland State U Polit Sci Dept Portland OR 97201

CLUXTON, JOANNE GENEVIEVE, elementary school educator; b. Omaha, May 2, 1936; d. Joseph Emil and Anna (Nespesny) Sabacky; m. William Wayne Cluxton, Aug. 2, 1959; 1 child, Edsel Ross. BS in Edn., U. Nebr., Omaha, 1959; postgrad., Pepperdine U., L.A., 1975-77, San Diego U., L.A., 1987-88, Evangel Coll., 1989. Cert. gen. elem. and lang. devel. specialist. Tchr. Graham Elem. Sch., L.A., 1969-83; kindergarten and resource tchr. 92d St. Sch., L.A., 1983-88; kindergarten mentor tchr. San Gabriel Ave. Sch., South Gate, Calif., 1988—; presenter insvc. workshops, L.A. Unified Sch. Dist., 1990—. Organist Bell (Calif.) Friends Ch., 1975-83; pianist 1st So. Bapt. Ch., Downey, Calif., 1983—. Mem. NEA (life), Calif. Tchrs. Assn., United Tchrs. L.A. Republican. Office: San Gabriel Ave Sch 8628 San Gabriel Ave South Gate CA 90280-3112

COACH, MARLENE EVONNE, clinical social worker; b. Chgo.; d. Charles Joseph and Geraldine Isaac; m. David Coach (div.); 1 child, Du Shun. BA, Ea. Mich. U., 1979; MSW, Wayne State U., 1981; postgrad. in Edn., U. So. Calif., 1995. Lic. social worker; lic. real estate agt., Hawaii; cert. occupl. therapist. Asst. payments worker Mich. Dept. Social Svcs., Romulus, Mich., 1979-1980; foster care worker Cath. Social Svcs., Detroit, 1981-1982; case mgr. II Cmty. Case Mgmt. Svcs., Detroit, 1982-1983; adoption worker Children's Aid Soc., Detroit, 1983-86; asst. prof. Knox Coll, Galesburg, Ill., 1986-89; clin. social worker VA, Honolulu, 1993—. Maj. U.S. Army, 1989-93. Mem. ASPA (bd. dirs. 1994—), Res. Officer's Assn., Nat. Assn. of Social Workers, Occupl. Therapy Assn., DAV. Home: PO Box 8504 Honolulu HI 96830-0504

COAD, DENNIS L., marketing executive, management consultant; b. St. Louis, Mar. 16, 1959; s. Satnley Meredith and Olga Martha (Salarano) C.; m. Linda Marie Kasmarzik, June 20, 1980 (div. May, 1982): 1 child, Jason Christopher. AA, Jefferson Coll., Pevely, Mo., 1979; BS, S.W. Mo. State U., 1988, MBA, 1990. Systems engr. Computer Task Group, St. Louis, 1981-84; owner, mng. dir. Sci. Resources Cons. Group, La Mirada, Calif., 1990—; dir. bus. devel. AGCT Inc., Irvine, Calif., 1993—. Author: Nature, 1994—, Genetic Engring News, 1993—, Biotechniques, 1996. Active United We Stand, Calif., 1992. With U.S. Army, 1984-87. Boatmen's Bank scholar, 1977. Mem. AAAS, Am. Mgmt. Assn., Smithsonian Inst., Regulatory Profl. Soc. Roman Catholic. Home: 2070 Rosemary Ct Hemet CA 92545-5614 Office: Sci Resources Cons Group PO Box 4471 Hemet CA 92546

COAKLEY, WILLIAM THOMAS, utilities executive; b. Dubuque, Iowa, Oct. 18, 1946; s. Harold Leo and Mary Margaret (Schwartz) C.; m. Deborah Dixon Leach, Nov. 25, 1971; children: Matthew David, Kenneth William. BA, Loras Coll., 1968; postgrad., Drake U., 1968-69, 71. Commd. U.S. Army, 1970, advanced through grades to capt.; co. exec. officer U.S. Army, Fort Bragg, N.C., 1971-73; brigade staff officer U.S. Army, Stuttgart, Fed. Republic of Germany, 1973-75; budget analyst U.S. Army Corps of Engrs., Frankfurt, Fed. Republic of Germany, 1975-77; budget officer U.S. Army Corps of Engrs., Riyadh, Saudi Arabia, 1977-80; resigned U.S. Army Corps of Engrs., 1980; budget and fin. officer Western Area Power Adminstrn., Billings, Mont., 1980-85, fin. mgr., 1985-95; fin. sys. mgr. Western Area Power Adminstrn., Golden, Colo., 1996—. Author, editor Fiscal Procedures and Control of Funds, 1975. Chmn. divsn. United Way Fundraiser of Yellowstone County, 1992, 93, mem. bd. dirs., 1994-96; mem. St. Patrick's Co-Cathedral Parish Coun., 1990-92, pres., 1991-92. Mem. Internat. Soc. Am. Mil. Engrs. (sec., treas. Frankfurt chpt. 1974-75), Yellowstone Country Club (bd. dirs. 1984-86, 95-96), Rotary, Pacific Northwest Golf Assn. (Mont. rep. 1995-96). Republican. Roman Catholic. Home: 2164 S Parfet Ct Lakewood CO 80227 Office: Western Area Power Adminstrn PO Box 3402 1627 Cole Blvd Golden CO 80401-3398

COATE, LESTER EDWIN, university administrator; b. Albany, Oreg., Jan. 21, 1936; s. Lester Francis and Mildred Roxana (Clarck) C.; m. Marilyn Nan Robinson (dec.); chidlren: Steven, David, Carol; m. Cheryl Diane Mizer, Dec. 20, 1973. BS, Oreg. State U., 1959; MS, San Diego State U., 1969; PhD, U.S. Internat. U., 1973; vis. scholar, U. Wash., 1985-86. Engr. Los Angeles County, L.A., 1959-61; mng. ptnr. Robinson & Coate, Valley Center, Calif., 1961-64; asst. to pres. White House, Washington, 1970-71; environ. dir. San Diego County, San Diego, 1971-73; dep. regional adminstr. U.S. EPA, Seattle, 1973-86; v.p. fin. and adminstrn. Oreg. State U., Corvallis, 1986-92; vice chancellor bus. and adminstrv. svcs. U. Calif., Santa Cruz, 1992-95; v.p. Bus. Svcs./Mira Costa Coll., 1995—. Author: Regional Environmental Management, 1974; contbr. articles to profl. jours. Bd. dirs. U. Calif. Santa Cruz Found. Fellow Am. Acad. Environ. Engrs., White House Fellows, Salzburg Fellows; mem. Nat. Assn. Coll. and Univ. Bus. Officers (chmn. fin. com., Neil Hines award for publs. 1994, Profl. Devel. award 1996), C. of C. (past v.p.), Rotary (past pres.), Phi Kappa Phi. Home: 2649 Hartford St San Diego CA 92110 Office: Mira Costa Coll 1 Barnard Dr Oceanside CA 92056

COATES, ROSS ALEXANDER, art educator; b. Hamilton, Ont., Can., Nov. 1, 1932; s. Ralph Mansfield and Dorothea (Alexander) C.; m. Agnes Dunn, 1955 (div. 1979); children: Meagan Scott, Arwyn Alexandra; m. Marilyn Kathleen Lysohir, Sept. 27, 1980. BFA, Sch. of the Art Inst. of Chgo., 1956; MA, NYU, 1960, PhD, 1972. Asst. prof. Montclair (N.J.) State Coll., 1965-68; art tutor Canon Lawrence Coll., Lira, Uganda, 1968-70; chair fine arts dept. Russell Sage Coll., Troy, N.Y., 1971-76; prof. Wash. State U., Pullman, 1976—, chair art dept., 1976-84; vis. instr. in art Kansas City (Mo.) Art Inst., 1963-64. Editor: Gods Among Us, 1990; numerous one man shows and group exhibitions; founder, editor High Ground art jour. Idaho Arts Commn. fellow, 1990. Mem. Coll. Art Assn. Office: Wash State U Fine Art Dept Pullman WA 99164

COATES, WAYNE EVAN, agricultural engineer; b. Edmonton, Alta., Can., Nov. 28, 1947; came to U.S., 1981; s. Orval Bruce Wright and Leora (Raesler) C.; m. Patricia Louise Williams, Aug. 28, 1970. BS in Agr., U. Alta., 1969, MS in Agrl. Engring., 1970; PhD in Agrl. Engring., Okla. State U., 1973. Registered profl. engr., Ariz., Sask. Forage systems engr. Agr. Can., Melfort, Sask., 1973-75; project engr., tech. advisor, asst. sta. mgr. Prairie Agrl. Machinery Inst., Humboldt, Sask., 1975-81; cattle, grain farmer pvt. practice, Humboldt, 1975-81; assoc. prof. U. Ariz., Tucson, 1981-91, prof., 1991—; prof. titular ad honorem U. Nat. de Catamarca, Argentina, 1993—; cons. Vols. in Coop. Assts. and Ptnrs. of Ams., 1991—, Paraguayan Govt. UN Devel. Program, 1987-90, Argentine Govt., univs. and pvt. industry, 1991—, govt., univ. and agrl. orgns., Mid East agrl. projects, 1986-89; spkr. at internat. confs., Australia, Paraguay, Argentina, Peru, Chile, U.S. Designer farm equipment primarily for alternative crops and tillage; patentee in field; contbr. articles to profl. jours. Pres. Sunrise Ter. Village Townhomes Homeowners Assn., Tucson, 1990-92. Grantee USDA, Washington, 1981—, Ariz. Dept. Environ. Quality, Phoenix, 1989—, U.S. Dept. of Energy, Washington, 1991—, agrl. industries western U.S., 1982—. Mem. AAAS, NSPE, Am. Soc. Agrl. Engrs. (chmn. Ariz. sect. 1984-85, vice-chmn. Pacific region 1988-89, dir. dist. 4 1991-93, rep. to AAAS Consortium of Affiliates for Internat. Programs 1992-97, internat. dir. 1994-96), Assn. for Advancement of Indsl. Crops (pres. 1994-95), Soc. Automotive Engrs., Air and Waste Mgmt. Assn., Can. Soc. Agrl. Engring., Australian Soc. for Agrl. Engring., Asian Assn. for Agrl. Engring., Asociacion Latinoamericana de Ingenieria Agricola, Sigma Xi. Office: U Ariz Office Arid Lands Studies 250 E Valencia Rd Tucson AZ 85706 6800

COBARRUVIAZ, LOUIS A., protective services official. Chief police San Jose (Calif.) Police Dept. Office: San Jose Police Dept 201 W Mission St San Jose CA 95110

COBB, LUTHER FUSON, surgeon, educator; b. Little Rock, Apr. 24, 1952; s. Lewis Latane Cobb and Eulalia Anne-Belle (Fuson) Vaughn; m. Mary Ellen Mahoney, Apr. 24, 1983; 1 child, Kathleen R.M.; 1 stepchild, David J. Haffner. BS, Mich. State U., 1974; MD, Stanford U., 1978. Diplomate Am. Bd. Surgery. Resident surgery Stanford (Calif.) U. Dept. Surgery, 1978-85, clin. asst. prof. surgery, 1985-94, clin. assoc. prof. surgery, 1994—; staff surgeon Santa Clara Valley Med. Ctr., San Jose, Calif., 1985—; dir. trauma svcs. Santa Clara Valley Med. Ctr., San Jose, 1987—. Contbr. articles to profl. jours. Recipient Nat. Rsch. Svc. award NIH, 1980; Nat. Merit scholar Merit Scholarship Bd., 1970, Alumni Disting. scholar Mich. State U., 1970. Mem. AMA, Calif. Med. Assn. (del. 1993—), Santa Clara County Med. Assn. (v.p. 1986—), Sigma Xi, Phi Kappa Phi. Democrat. Office: Santa Clara Valley Med Ctr 751 S Bascom Ave San Jose CA 95128-2604

COBB, ROY LAMPKIN, JR., computer sciences corporation executive; b. Oklahoma City, Sept. 23, 1934; s. Roy Lampkin and Alice Maxine (Ellis) C.; B.A., U. Okla., 1972; postgrad. U. Calif., Northridge, 1976-77; m. Shirley Ann Dodson, June 21, 1958; children—Kendra Leigh, Cary William, Paul Alan. Naval aviation cadet U.S. Navy, 1955, advanced through grades to comdr., 1970; ret., 1978; mktg./project staff engr. Gen. Dynamics, Pomona, Calif., 1978-80; mgr. dept. support svcs. Computer Scis. Corp., Point Mugu, Calif., 1980—. Decorated Navy Commendation medal, Air medal. Mem. Assn. Naval Aviators, Soc. Logistic Engrs. (editor Launchings 1990—). Republican. Christian. Club: Las Posas Country, Spanish Hills Country Club. Home: 2481 Brookhill Dr Camarillo CA 93010-2112 Office: Computer Scis Corp PO Box 42273 Port Hueneme CA 93044-4573

COBB, SHARON YVONNE, screenwriter; b. DeLand, Fla., Apr. 19, 1958; d. Charles William and Bonnie (Elizabeth (Lyons) C. Grad. high sch., Pierson, Fla. Owner, mgr. Sharon Cobb Advt., Jacksonville, Fla., 1978-81; fiber sculptor Key West, Fla., 1981-86; dir. Keys Advt. & Mktg., Key West, 1986-87; pub. Fla. Travel Directory, Jacksonville, 1987-89; screenwriter Neptune Beach, Fla., 1989-93; film writer, Beverly Hills, Calif., 1993—; lectr. screenwriting UCLA. Co-author: Secrets of Selling Your Script to Hollywood, Witness, 1985 (Oscar award 1996); rewriter screenplay Baja Triangle; rewriter, polisher feature film Just Write (Best of Fest award Santa Barbara Film Festival 1997). Founder, bd. dirs. Earth Ctr. Inc., Jacksonville, 1978-81. Recipient Addy award Jacksonville Advt. Fedn., 1976, 77, Golden Image award Fla. Pub. Rels. Assn., 1978, 1st place pub. rels. program award So. Pub. Rels. Fedn., 1978. Mem. Fla. Freelance Writers Assn. (award for mag. feature writing 1992), Fla. Motion Picture and TV Assn. (Crystal Reel award for best screenplay 1993).

COBB, SHIRLEY ANN, public relations specialist, journalist; b. Oklahoma City, Jan. 1, 1936; d. William Ray and Irene (Fewell) Dodson; m. Roy Lampkin Cobb, Jr., June 21, 1958; children: Kendra Leigh, Cary William, Paul Alan. BA in Journalism with distinction, U. Okla., 1958, postgrad., 1972; postgrad., Jacksonville U., 1962. Info. specialist Pacific Missle Test Ctr., Point Mugu, Calif., 1975-76; corr. Religious News Svc., N.Y.C., 1979-81; splty. editor fashion and religion Thousand Oaks (Calif.) News Chronicle, 1977-81; pub. rels. cons., Camarillo, Calif., 1977—; media mgr. pub. info City of Thousand Oaks, 1983—. Contbr. articles to profl. jours. Trustee Ocean View Sch. Bd., 1976-79; pres. Point Mugu Officers' Wives Club, 1975-76, 90—; bd. dirs. Camarillo Hospice, 1983-85; sec. Conejo Valley Hist. Soc., 1993-96; sec. Ednl. TV for Conejo, 1997—. Recipient Spot News award San Fernando Valley Press Club, 1979. Mem. Pub. Rels. Soc. Am. (L.A. chpt. liaison 1991), Calif. Assn. Pub. Info. Ofcls. (pres. 1989-90, Paul Clark Lifetime Achievement award 1993), Sigma Delta Chi, Phi Beta Kappa, Chi Omega. Republican. Clubs: Las Posas Country, Spanish Hills Country, Town Hall of Calif. Home: 2481 Brookhill Dr Camarillo CA 93010-2112 Office: 2100 E Thousand Oaks Blvd Thousand Oaks CA 91362-2903

COBBLE, STEVEN BRUCE, political consultant, strategist; b. Perrysburg, Ohio, July 7, 1951; s. Milan H. and Nancy L. (Musselman) C.; m. Molly E. Smith, July 3, 1983; children: Elizabeth A., Julia S. BS in Math., N.Mex. State U., 1974, BA in Govt., 1974. Speechwriter, spl. asst. Office of Gov., Santa Fe, N.Mex., 1982-86; nat. del. selection dir. Jesse Jackson for Pres., Chgo. and Washington, 1987, 88; exec. dir. Keep Hope Alive Polit. Action Com., Washington, 1988-90; advisor Ron Brown for Dem. Nat. Com. Chair Campaign, Washington, 1988, 89; democracy reform cons. Ctr. for New Democracy, Grinnell, Iowa, 1991-93; polit. and fin. dir. Carol Moseley-Braun for U.S. Senate Campaign, Chgo., 1992; speechwriter, policy analyst Office of Mayor, Albuquerque, 1994, 95; polit. dir. Nat. Rainbow Coalition, Washington, 1996—; pub. spkr. numerous groups, meetings, 1970-96; panelist, presenter numerous polit. forums/panels, 1970-96; adv. bd. Hotline Index, Campaign Hotline newsletter, Washington, 1995, 96. Editor Nat. Rainbow Coalition Jax Fax, 1996; contbr. articles to profl. jours.; guest appearance CNN's Inside Politics TV show, Washington, 1995. Nat. conv. del. Dem. Nat. Conv., Miami, 1972; democracy trainer Nat. Dem. Inst./African Nat. Congress, South Africa, 1991; mem. nat. rules com. Nat. Dem. Party, Washington, 1992; polit. party trainer Nat. Dem. Inst., Panama, 1993. Fellow LBJ Sch. Pub. Affairs, Austin, Tex., 1974, Inst. Politics, Harvard U., Cambridge, Mass., 1990; named Young Polit. Leader Am. Coun. Young Polit. Leaders, Washington, 1986. Methodist. Home: 520 Cedar NE Albuquerque NM 87106 Office: Nat Rainbow Coalition 1700 K St NW Ste 800 Washington DC 20006

COBIANCHI, THOMAS THEODORE, engineering and marketing executive, educator; b. Paterson, N.J., July 7, 1941; s. Thomas and Violet Emily (Bazzar) C.; m. Phyllis Linda Asch, Feb. 6, 1964; 1 child, Michael. Student, Clemson U., 1963; BS, Monmouth Coll., 1968, MBA, 1972; postgrad., U. Pa., 1987; D Bus. Adminstrn., U.S. Internat. U., 1994. Sales mgr. Westinghouse Electric Corp., Balt., 1968-74; sr. internat. sales engr. Westinghouse Electric Corp., Lima, Ohio, 1975-77; program mgr. Westinghouse Electric Corp., Pitts., 1977-78, mgr. bus. devel., 1978-82; dir. mktg. Westinghouse Electric Corp., Arlington, Va., 1982-86; acting dir., engring. mgr. General Dynamics Corp., San Diego, 1986-89; dir. bus. devel. RPV Programs Teledyne Ryan Aero., San Diego, 1989-90; pres. Cobianchi & Assocs., San Diego, 1990; v.p. strategic planning and program devel. S-Cubed div. Maxwell Labs., Inc., San Diego, 1991; v.p. corp. devel. Orincon Corp., 1995—; instr., lectr. various ednl. instns. Active various polit. and ednl. orgns.; mem. bus. adv. coun. U.S. Internat. U.; bd. dirs. Cath. Charities San Diego; vol. exec., sect. chmn. United Way San Diego. Mem. Armed Forces Communications and Electronics Assn. (acting chmn. 1988), Princeton Club of Washington, Nat. Aviation Club, General Dynamics Health Club, Delta Sigma Pi. Home: 16468 Calle Pulido San Diego CA 92128-3249

COBLE, HUGH KENNETH, engineering and construction company executive; b. Rochester, Pa., Sept. 26; s. John L. and Victoria (Neilson) C.; m. Constance Stratton, June 2, 1956; children: Keith Allen, Kimberly Ann, Jon Arthur, Scott Arnold, Neal Stewart. BSChemE, Carnegie Mellon U., 1956; postgrad., UCLA, 1966, U. Houston, 1963-65, Stanford U., 1981. Engr. Standard Oil Calif., El Segundo, 1956-61; sales mgr. Turco Products, Houston, 1961-63; sales dir. W.R. Grace, Houston, 1963-65; vice chrmn., bd. dirs. Fluor Corp., Irvine, Calif., 1966-97. Mem. bd. dirs. Beckman Instruments, Inc., 1996—; mem. bd dirs. Duriron Co., Inc., 1995—; Bd. dirs. John Henry Found., Orange, Calif., 1992-96; trustee Scripps U., Claremont, Calif., 1991-93, Fluor Found.; mem. adv. bd. Thunderbird U., Phoenix, 1992—; exec. engring. adv. com. U. Calif.-Irvine. Mem. Am. Petroleum Inst., Am. Inst. Chem. Engrs. (bd. dirs. 1983-88). Presbyterian.

COBLEY, JOHN GRIFFIN, biochemist and educator; b. London, Oct. 28, 1946; s. William Thomas and Olive Marion Cobley; m. Evelyn Rogers, Jan. 4, 1986; children: Allison Claire, Caitlin Amanda. BSc in Biochemistry, U. Bristol, U.K., 1968, PhD in Biochemistry, 1972. Postdoctoral scientist U. Calif., San Francisco, 1972-74, U. Dundee, Scotland, 1974-76; asst. prof. biochemistry U. San Francisco, 1977-84, assoc. prof., 1984-91, prof. biochemistry, 1991—, chmn. dept. chemistry, 1986 89; vis. faculty U. Utrecht, Netherlands, 1984. Contbr.: (book) Microbial Chemoautotrophy, 1984; contbr. articles to profl. jours. Recipient Disting. Rsch. award U. San Francisco, 1994. Mem. Am. Soc. Plant Physiologists, Am. Soc. Photobiology. Office: Univ of San Francisco Dept Chemistry 2130 Fulton St San Francisco CA 94117-1080

COBOS, JOSÈ MANUEL, Spanish language educator; b. Sabinas Hgo, Nuevo Leon, Mex., Feb. 13, 1957; came to U.S., 1972; s. Juan and Olga (Flores) C.; m. Susan Ojeda, Aug. 19, 1989; 1 child, Aracely Susan. BA, U. Calif., Berkeley, 1978; MA, U. Calif., Santa Barbara, 1980; JD, U. Calif., San Francisco, 1984. Spanish tchr. Vista Coll., Berkeley, 1980-82; substitute tchr. Hayward (Calif.) Unified Sch. Dist., 1984, 88-89, San Francisco Unified Sch. Dist., 1984-87; paralegal San Francisco, 1987-88; Am. govt. tchr. Merritt Coll., Oakland, Calif., 1988-90; Spanish tchr. James Logan H.S., Union City, Calif., 1990—. Vol. Pelosi for Congress, San Francisco, 1987. Summer fellow Govt. of Mex., 1979. Mem. NEA, Fgn. Lang. Assn., Calif. Tchrs. Assn., Hastings Alumni Assn. Democrat. Roman Catholic. Office: James Logan HS 1800 H St Union City CA 94587

COBURN, MARJORIE FOSTER, psychologist, educator; b. Salt Lake City, Feb. 28, 1939; d. Harlan A. and Alma (Ballinger) Polk; m. Robert Byron Coburn, July 2, 1977; children: Polly Klea Foster, Matthew Ryan Foster, Robert Scott Coburn, Kelly Anne Coburn. B.A. in Sociology, UCLA, 1960; Montessori Internat. Diploma honor grad. Washington Montessori Inst., 1968; M.A. in Psychology, U. No. Colo., 1979; Ph.D. in Counseling Psychology, U. Denver, 1983. Licensed clin. psychologist. Probation officer Alameda County (Calif.), Oakland, 1960-62, Contra Costa County (Calif.), El Cerrito, 1966, Fairfax County (Va.), Fairfax, 1967; dir. Friendship Club, Orlando, Fla., 1963-65; tchr. Va. Montessori Sch., Fairfax, 1968-70; spl. edn. tchr. Leary Sch., Falls Church, Va., 1970-72, sch. administr., 1973-76; tchr. Aseltine Sch., San Diego, 1976-77, Coburn Montessori Sch., Colorado Springs, Colo., 1977-79; pvt. practice psychotherapy, Colorado Springs, 1979-82, San Diego, 1982—; cons. spl. edn., agoraphobia, women in transition. Mem. Am. Psychol. Assn., Am. Orthopsychiat. Assn., Phobia Soc., Council Exceptional Children, Calif. Psychol. Assn., San Diego Psychological Assn., The Charter 100, Mensa. Episcopalian. Lodge: Rotary. Contbr. articles to profl. jours.; author: (with R.C. Orem) Montessori: Prescription for Children with Learning Disabilities, 1977. Office: 826 Prospect St Ste 101 La Jolla CA 92037-4206

COBURN, ROBERT JAMES, music educator, composer; b. Montebello, Calif., Oct. 29, 1949; s. Tyler Hadley and Elizabeth Coburn; m. Jeanne Nadine Ashby, May 12, 1974; 1 child, Benjamin Tyler. MusB in Theory and Composition, U. of the Pacific, 1972; MA in Music Composition, U. Calif., Berkeley, 1974; PhD in Music Composition, U. Victoria, Can., 1995. Adj. faculty Lewis and Clark Coll., Portland, Oreg., 1978-84; chair music dept. Marylhurst Coll., Portland, 1984-90; assoc. prof. music theory and composition U. of the Pacific, Conservatory of Music, Stockton, Calif., 1993—; dir. Group for New Music Portland, Oreg., 1975-81, Ctr. for Electronic Music, Lewis and Clark Coll., Portland, 1979-85; featured composer Portland (Oreg.) Composers Festival, 1985; mem. arts design team Oreg. Conv. Ctr., Portland, 1987-89. Composer, sound artist/designer in field; commd. by Bell Circles II, Oreg., 1987-90, 39 Bells for Phila., 1994-96; composer Time's Shadow for clarinet and ensemble, 1995, Shadowbox for clarinet, 1994, Luminous Shadows, 1993. Oreg. Artists fellow Oreg. Arts Commn., 1978, Grad. fellow U. Victoria, B.C., 1991-93; Composers grantee Met. Arts Commn., Portland, 1981. Mem. Internat. Soc. for the Arts, Scis. and Tech. (Leonardo rev. com. 1993—), World Forum for Acoustic Ecology (founding mem.), Internat. Computer Music Assn., Pi Kappa Lambda. Office: Univ of the Pacific Conservatory Music Stockton CA 95211

COCHRAN, CAROL LOUISE, home care manager, nurse; b. Gauhati, India, Nov. 25, 1951; came to U.S. 1968; d. George Simon and Dorothy Louise (Drotz) Johnson; m. Thomas J. Cochran; children: Matthew, Samuel, Noah. BSN, Seattle Pacific U., 1973. RN, Wash., Oreg., Idaho. Nurse emergency rm. Group Health, Seattle, 1973-74; nurse Peace Corps, Colombia, 1974-75, Vis. Nurse Soc., Phila., 1976-79, Geneva Ctr. Camp, Rochester, Ind., summers 1978-79, Greater Albany (Oreg.) Pub. Schs., 1979-84; RN dir. Home Care Network, Albany, 1984—; mem. sr. disabled svc. adv. com., Corvallis, Oreg., 1986-89. Mem. Oreg. Assn. for Home Care (bd. dirs. 1987-89, mem. reimbursement com. 1985—), Oreg. Hospice Assn. Democrat. Office: Home Care Network 1046 6th Ave SW Albany OR 97321-1916

COCHRAN, JOHN HOWARD, plastic and reconstructive surgeon; b. Muncie, Ind., Sept. 6, 1946; s. John H. and Lois M. (Woolridge) C.; m. Elizabeth M. Cochran; 1 child, Ryan K. BS cum laude, Colo. State U., 1968; MD, U. Colo. Sch. Medicine, 1973. Intern surgery U. Calif., San Diego, 1973-74; resident head and neck surgery Stanford U., Palo Alto, Calif., 1974-77; resident plastic surgery U. Wis., Madison, 1979-81; pvt. practice plastic surgery Denver, 1981-90; chief plastic surgery St. Joseph Hosp., Denver, 1987-93, Colo. Med. Group, Denver, 1990-95; chmn. dept. surgery St. Joseph Hosp., 1993—. Pres. bd. trustees Kilimanjaro Children's Hosp., Tanzania, E. Africa, 1989—. Fellow Am. Soc. Plastic and Reconstructive Surgery, Am. Coll. SUrgeons, Acad. Otolaryngology, Head and Neck Surgery; mem. Am. Assn. Plastic Surgeons. Office: 2045 Franklin St Denver CO 80205-5437

COCHRAN, VERLAN LEYERL, soil scientist; b. Declo, Idaho, Feb. 19, 1938; s. Harley Earl and Anna Helena (Christensen) C.; m. Diana Larraine Dennis, June 21, 1969; children: Dean Scott, Vincent Lee. BS in Soil Sci., Calif. Poly. U., 1966; MS in Soils, Wash. State U., 1971. Soil scientist USDA-ARS, Pullman, Wash., 1966-85; soil scientist USDA-ARS, Fairbanks, Alaska, 1985-89, supervisory soil scientist, 1989-94; supervisory soil scientist USDA-ARS, Sidney, Mont., 1994—. Contbr. chpt. to book and articles to profl. jours. Mem. Am. Soc. Agronomy, Soil Sci. Soc. Am., Am. Soc. Microbiologists (br. pres. 1989). Office: USDA-ARS No Plains Soil & Water Rsch Ctr 1500 N Central Sidney MT 59270

COCHRAN, WENDELL, science editor; b. Carthage, Mo., Nov. 29, 1929; s. Wendell Albert and Lillian Gladys (Largent) C.; m. Agnes Elizabeth Groves, Nov. 9, 1963; remarried Corinne Des Jardins, Aug. 25, 1980. A.B., U. Mo., Columbia, 1953, A.M. in Geology, 1956, B.J., 1960. Geologist ground-water br. U.S. Geol. Survey, 1956-58; reporter, copyeditor Kansas City (Mo.) Star, 1960-63; editor Geotimes and Earth Sci. mags., Geospectrum newsletter, Alexandria, Va., 1963-84; v.p. Geol. Survey Inc., Bethesda, Md., 1984-86. Co-author: Into Print: A Practical Guide to Writing, Illustrating, and Publishing, 1977; sr. editor: Geowriting: A Guide to Writing, Editing and Printing in Earth Science, 1973; contbr. articles to profl. jours. and encys. Mem. geol. socs. Washington, London, Assn. Earth Sci. Editors (award Outstanding Contbns. 1982), Dog in the Night-time. Home: 4351 SW Willow St Seattle WA 98136-1769

COCHRAN, WILLIAM MICHAEL, librarian; b. Nevada, Iowa, May 6, 1952; s. Joseph Charles and Inez (Larson) C.; m. Diane Marie Ohm, July 24, 1971. BLS, U. Iowa, 1979, MA with distinction in Libr. Sci., 1983; MA in Pub. Adminstrn., Drake U., 1989. Dir. Red Oak (Iowa) Pub. Libr., 1984; patron svcs. libr. Pub. Libr. of Des Moines, 1984-87; LSCA program coord. State Libr. of Iowa, Des Moines, 1987-88, dir. libr. devel., 1988-89, asst. state libr., 1989-90; dir. Parmly Billings Libr., 1990—. Contbr. articles to profl. jours. Bd. dirs. Billings Cmty. Cable Corp., 1994—. Mem. ALA, Mont. Libr. Assn. (bd. dirs. 1991-93, pub. libr. divsn. 1991—, chair 1991-92, legis. com. chair 1992-93, task force on lobbying chair 1992-93, ad hoc com. on Mont. Libr. edn. 1991-92), Mont. Gov.'s Blue Ribbon Telecommunications Task Force, White House Conf. on Libr. and Info. Svcs. (del.-at-large, elected mem. conf. recommendations com.), Libr. Adminstrn. and Mgmt. Assn. (govtl. affairs com. 1992-96, pub. rels. sect., govtl. advocacy skills com. 1992-94, program chair for 1994 Miami conf. 1992-94), Pub. Libr. Assn., U. Iowa Alumni Assn. (life), Rotary, Beta Phi Mu. Office: Parmly Billings Library 510 N Broadway Billings MT 59101-1156

COCKHILL, BRIAN EDWARD, historical society executive; b. Aug. 13, 1942; s. Linda Ann Moudree Cockhill, Sept. 10, 1966; 1 child, William Frederick Cockhill. Student, Mont. Sch. Mines, Butt, 1960-63; BA in History (hon.), U. Mont., Missoula, 1964; MA in Western Am. History, 1970. Metallurgical rsch. tech. Anaconda (Mont.) Co., 1964-66; teaching asst., rsch. fellow U. Mont., 1967-70; asst. archivist, 1969-70, acting archivist, 1970-71; asst. archivist Mont. Historical Soc., 1971-73; state archivist, 1973-84; program mgr. Ctrl. Svcs. Mont. Historical Soc., 1984-91; deputy dir., 1991-92, dir., 1992—; coord. Mont. Historic Records Adv. Coun., 1976-84; records adv. com. Mont. State, 1977-84; served on Mont. State Records Adv. Com., 1977-84. editor/compiler: (with Dale Johnson) Guide to Manuscripts in Montana Repositories, 1973, Not in Precious Metala ALone: A Manuscript History of Montana, 1976. Recipient Larry Dobell scholarship, 1961-62, Outstanding Am. History Student in a Montana Coll., 1962, U. Mont. Teaching Assistantships, 1967-70. Mem. Soc. Am. Archivists, Am. Hist. Assn., Phi Alpha Theta, Phi Kappa Phi. Office: Montana Historical Soc PO Box 201201 Helena MT 59620-1201

COCKRELL, FRANK BOYD, II, film production company executive; b. Redding, Calif., May 3, 1948; s. Alfred Marion Sr. and Blanch Delma (Webb) C.; children: Catherine, Francis Marion V, Ross, Sabrina, Brooke, Amanda, Richard Sears III. AA, Shasta Jr. Coll., 1968; BS, Sacramento (Calif.) State U., 1970; postgrad., U. Pacific, 1970-72. Pres., chmn. Als Towing & Storage Co., Sacramento, 1976-78, Compacts Only Rental Cars, Sacramento, 1976-78; film producer, actor, comedian Sacramento, L.A. and Las Vegas, Nev., 1976—; fin. cons., 1974—; pres., chmn. Cockrell Prodns., Inc., L.A., 1984—, Palm Spring Employment Agy., Inc., Palm Desert, Calif., 1986; chmn. Contractor's Surety and Fidelity Co., Ltd., U.S. Mining Corp., 21st Century Ins. Group, Inc.-Nev., Hollywood, Calif., 1992—, 21st Century Travel, Inc., Camarillo, Calif., 1992—; CEO, 1st Am. Contractors Bonding Assn., Inc. Author: Vietnam History, 1970. Candidate Assembly 6th Dist. Rep. Party, Sacramento, 1974; mem. Sacramento Rep. Cen. Com., 1975-76, Calif. State Cen. Rep. Com., 1974-76. Bank of Am. scholar, 1966, Shasta Coll. scholar, 1967. Lodge: Optimists (pres. Sacramento chpt. 1975-76, lt. gov. 1976-77). Office: Cockrell Prodns Inc PO Box 1731 Studio City CA 91614-0731

COCKRUM, WILLIAM MONROE, III, investment banker, consultant, educator; b. Indpls., July 18, 1937; s. William Monroe C. II and Katherine J. (Jaqua) Moore; m. Andrea Lee Deering, Mar. 8, 1975; children: Catherine Anne, William Monroe IV. AB with distinction, DePauw U., 1959; MBA with distinction, Harvard U., 1961. With A.G. Becker Paribas Inc., L.A., 1961-84, mgr. nat. corp. fin. div., 1968-71, mgr. pvt. investments, 1971-74, fin. and adminstrv. officer, 1974-80, sr. v.p., 1975-78, vice chmn., 1978-84, also bd. dirs.; prin. William M. Cockrum & Assocs., L.A., 1984—; mem. faculty Northwestern U., 1961-63; vis. lectr. grad. sch. mgmt. UCLA, 1984-88, adj. prof., 1988—. Mem. Monterey Club (Palm Desert, Calif.), Deke Club (N.Y.C.), UCLA Faculty Club, Alisal Golf Club (Solvang, Calif.), Bel-Air Country Club (L.A.), Delta Kappa Epsilon.

COCKS, J. FRASER, III, educator; b. Detroit, July 15, 1941; s. James Fraser Jr. and Lillias (Campbell) C.; m. Catherine S. Herlihy, July 17, 1965; children: Margaret Hanley, Catherine Campbell. BA, Occidental Coll., L.A., 1963; PhD, U. Mich., 1975. Field rep., asst. dir. Mich. Hist. Collection/Bentley Libr., Ann Arbor, 1965-75; head spl. collections Colby Coll., Waterville, Maine, 1975-90; curator spl. collections U. Oreg., Eugene, 1990-92; dir. Dimensions of Culture program U. Calif. San Diego, La Jolla, 1993—. Contbr. articles to profl. jours.

CODONI, FREDERICK PETER, editor; b. San Rafael, Calif., Dec. 22, 1934; s. Frederick Q. and Ruth A. (Steinkellner) C.; m. Sheila Ann Kane, Feb. 4, 1961 (div. Aug. 1986); m. Denyce Vogler, July 7, 1989; children: Frederick Jr., James, Michael, Charles. BA, U. San Francisco, 1956. Mgr. loading svcs. So. Pacific R.R., San Francisco, 1963-88; editor The Native Son, The Headlight, The Northwesterner; cons. transp., Fairfax, Calif., 1988—. Sgt. U.S. Army, 1958-60, Korea. Mem. Native Sons of Golden West (grand pres. 1994-95), Northwestern Pacific R.R. Hist. Soc. (editor 1986—), Fairfax Hist. Soc., Marin County Hist. Soc., Bay Area Electric R.R. Assn. Republican. Roman Catholic. Home and Office: 162 Porteous Ave Fairfax CA 94930-2036

CODY, FRANK JOSEPH, secondary school administrator, teacher education educator; b. Detroit, Sept. 13, 1940; s. Burns J. and Margaret (Dowley) C.; m. Shirley Black, May 16, 1992. AB, Loyola U., 1962, MA, 1966, MDiv, 1975; PhD, Ohio State U., 1980. Cert. tchr., prin., supr., Ohio, Mich. Prin. St. Ignatius H.S., Cleve., 1977-81; dir. Chapel Sch., Sao Paulo, Brazil, 1981-83, U. Detroit Ctr. Econ. Edn., 1988-91; assoc. prof., tchr. adminstrv. edn. U. Detroit, 1983-91; adminstr. Grand Rapids Cath. Secondary Schs., 1991-95; headmaster Woodside Priory Sch., Portola Valley, Calif., 1995—; trustee Wheeling Coll., 1980-82, mem. coun. entrance svcs. Coll. Bd., 1978-81; mem. Mich. Supt.'s Com. on Accreditation, 1984-88; commr. Nat. Assn. Secondary Sch. Prins./Carnegie Found. Commn. on Am. H.S., 1994-96. Author: Manual of Educational Risk Management; contbr. articles to profl. jours. Bd. trustees Trinity Sch., Manlo Park, Calif., 1996—. Mem. ASCD (assoc.), ACSA (bd. dirs. Region V 1995—), Nat. Assn. Secondary Sch. Prins. (nonpub. schs. com. 1993-96), Am. Ednl. Rsch. Assn., Nat. Cath. Edn. Assn. (regional assoc.), Bay Area Heads Assn., Portola Valley Cable TV Commn., Woodside Rotary Club (bd. dirs. 1996—). Roman Catholic. Office: Woodside Priory Sch 302 Portola Rd Portola Valley CA 94028

CODY, PATRICIA HERBERT, health educator; b. New London, Conn., Sept. 14, 1923; d. John Newman and Rosalia Bertha (Harr) Herbert; m. Fred Cody, Aug. 24, 1946 (dec. July 1983); children: Martha, Anthony, Nora, Celia. BA in Edn., State Tchrs. Coll., 1943; MA in Econs., Columbia U., 1948. Staff writer Economist Intelligence Unit, London, Eng., 1952-72; co-founder Cody's Books, Berkeley, Calif., 1956-77; program dir. DES Action, Oakland, Calif., 1978—, also bd. dirs. Author: Cody's Books: The Life and Times of a Berkeley Bookstore, 1956-77, 1992. Bd. dirs. Civil Justice Found., Washington, 1992—; mem. steering com. Nat. Women's Polit. Caucus Alameda North, Oakland, 1991-95. Recipient Meritorious Svc. award ATLA, 1987, Consumer Advocate of the Yr. award Calif. Trial Lawyers Assn., 1990. Home: 3021 Fulton St Berkeley CA 94705-1804 Office: DES Action 1615 Broadway Oakland CA 94612-2115

CODYE, CORINN, writer, editor; b. L.A., Sept. 16, 1950; d. Richard Charles and Juanita Corinne (Myers) Wahl; m. Graham G. Scott, Oct. 4, 1980 (div. Nov. 1984); children: Richard Graham, Peter William (twins). BA, U. Calif., Riverside, 1975; postgrad., UCLA, 1976. Author, editor, project mgr. Quercus Corp., 1980-86, exec. editor, 1986-87. Author: (children's books) Cairo, 1991, Queen Isabella, 1991, Luis W. Alvarez, 1991, Vilma Martinez, 1991 (Outstanding Merit award, Nat. Coun. for the Social Studies 1990), If You Are Sick, 1994, Do You Hear Music?, 1994, I Like Surprises, 1994; contbg. author, mng. editor: Raintree Illustrated Science Encyclopedia, 1991; pub. (Justin Stone books) Meditation for Healing, Justin Stone Speaks on T'ai Chi Chih, Spiritual Stories 1 and 2, T'ai Chi Chih! Joy Through Movement, 1984-91, The Body Talks...and I Can Hear It (Jeanie Lemaire), 1995, T'ai Chi Chih with Corinn Codye, 1995, T'ai Chi Qigong, 1996.

COE, ANNE ELIZABETH, artist; b. Henderson, Nev., Feb. 27, 1949; d. Percy Ellis and Mary Ernest (Jackson) Coe; m. Dennis Neal Barr, Sept. 13, 1970 (div. May 1973); 1 child, Laurye; m. Robert Patrick Horvath, Apr. 11, 1992. BA cum laude, Ariz. State U., Tempe, 1970, MFA cum laude, 1980. Artist in residence Ariz. Commn. for the Arts, Phoenix, 1982. Illustrator: (children's book) Here is the Southwestern Desert, 1995; exhibited in solo shows at Harry Wood Gallery/Ariz. State U., 1980, Elaine Horwitch Galleries, 1987, 89, 92, 94, Anne Reed Gallery, Sun Valley, Idaho, 1991, 92, Horwitch Newman Gallery, Scottsdale, 1995, 96, Moynihan Gallery, Jackson, Wyo., 1995, others; group shows include Suzanne Brown Gallery, Scottsdale, The White House, Washington, Segal Gallery, N.Y.C., Bruce Mus., Greenwich, Conn., White Tops Gallery, Palm Desert, Calif., Elaine Horwitch Galleries, Soho West, Denver, Americana Mus., El Paso, Ariz. Mus. for Youth, MARS Artspace, Phoenix, numerous others; included in collections at Eiteljorg Mus., Indpls., Centro de Arte Moderna, Guadalajara, Mex., Mus. of N.D., Grand Forks, Sky Harbor Internat. Airport, Phoenix, Smithsonian Instn., Washington, Ariz. State U., Tempe, Scottsdale Ctr. for the Arts, numerous others; subject of numerous articles. Mem. adv. bd. Ctrl. Ariz. Land Trust, 1994—; chmn. superstition area land trust Apache Junction Sch. Dsit., 1995-96; mem. Gov.'s Exec. Task Force for the Ariz. Preserve Initiative, 1995; mem. State Land Conservation Adv. Com., 1996. Home: 5776 E Forest Apache Junction AZ 85219

COE, MARGARET LOUISE SHAW, community service volunteer; b. Cody, Wyo., Dec. 25, 1917; d. Ernest Francis and Effie Victoria (Abrahamson) Shaw; m. Henry Huttleston Rogers Coe, Oct. 8, 1943 (dec. Aug. 1966); children: Anne Rogers Hayes, Henry H.R., Jr., Robert Douglas II. AA, Stephens Coll., 1937; BA, U. Wyo., 1939. Asst. to editor The Cody Enterprise, 1939-42; mem. Australian Procurement, 1942-43, War Labor Bd., 1943-44; editor The Cody Enterprise, 1968-71. Chmn. bd. trustees Buffalo Bill Hist. Ctr., Cody, 1966—, Cody Med. Found., 1964—; commr. Wyo. Centenniel Commn., Cheyenne, 1986-91. Recipient The Westerner award Old West Trails Found., 1980, Gold Medallion award Nat. Assn. Sec. of State, 1982, disting alumni award U. Wyo., 1984, exemplary alumni award, 1994, Gov.'s award for arts, 1988; inducted Nat. Cowgirl Hall of Fame, 1983. Mem. P.E.O., Delta Delta Delta. Republican. Episcopalian. Home: 1400 11th St Cody WY 82414-4206

COE, WILLIAM CHARLES, psychology educator; b. Hanford, Calif., Oct. 22, 1930; s. Bernard and Bertha (Vaughan) C.; m. Charlene L. Brown; children: Karen Ann, William Vaughan. B.S., U. Calif., Davis, 1958; post-grad., Fresno State Coll., 1960-61; Ph.D. (NSF fellow), U. Calif., Berkeley, 1964. Rsch. helper Fresno State Coll., 1960-61; rsch. asst. U. Calif., Berkeley, 1961-62, 63-64; NSF rsch. fellow U. Calif., 1963-64; clin. psychology trainee VA Hosp., San Francisco, 1962-63; staff psychologist Langley Porter Neuropsychiat. Inst., San Francisco, 1964-66; asst. clin. prof. med. psychology U. Calif. Sch. Medicine, San Francisco, 1965-66; instr. corr. div. U. Calif., Berkeley, 1967-76; asst. prof. psychology Fresno State Coll., 1966-68; assoc. prof. psychology Calif. State U., Fresno, 1968-72; prof. Calif. State U., 1972—, chmn. dept. psychology, 1979-84; instr. Calif. Sch. Profl. Psychology, Fresno, 1973, Northeastern U., Boston, 1974; research assoc. U. Calif., Santa Cruz, 1975; cons. Tulare and Kings County Mental Health Clinics, Kingsview Corp., 1966-68, Visalia Unified Sch. Dist., 1967-68; Head Start Program, Fresno, 1970-71, Fig Garden Hosp., Fresno, 1972-73, Concentrated Employment Program, Fresno, 1973-74, VA Hosp., Fresno, 1974; vis. prof.U. Queensland, Australia, 1982. Author: (with T.R. Sarbin) The Student Psychologists Handbook: A Guide to Source, 1969, Hypnosis: A Social Psychological Analysis of Influence Communication, 1972, Challenges of Personal Adjustment, 1972, (with L. Gagnon and D. Swiercinsky) instructors Manual for Challenges of Personal Adjustment, 1972, Psychology X118: Psychological Adjustment, 1973, (with T.R. Sarbin) Mastering Psychology, 1984; Contbr.: chpts. to Behavior Modification in Rehabiliation Settings, 1975, Helping People Change, 1975, 80, Encyclopedia of Clinical Assessment, 1980, Hypnosis: The Cognitive-Behavioral Perspective, 1989, Hypnosis: Current Theory, Research and Practice, 1990, Theories of Hypnosis: Current Models and Perspectives, 1991, Contemporary Hypnosis Research, 1992; contbr. articles to profl. jours. Served with USAF, 1951-55. Decorated D.F.C., Air medal with oak leaf cluster.; NSF grantee, 1967, 71. Fellow Am. Psychol. Assn. (pres. div. 30 psychol. hypnosis 1986-87), Soc. for Clin. and Exptl. Hypnosis; mem. Western Psychol Assn., Calif. Psychol Assn., San Francisco Psychol Assn. (editor San Francisco Psychologist 1966), Central Calif. Psychol. Assn. (pres. 1969, dir. 1972-73), Assn. for Advancement Behavior Therapy, Phi Beta Kappa, Sigma Xi, Phi Kappa Phi, Psi Chi. Office: Calif State U Dept Psychology Fresno CA 93740-0011*

COEN, DANA, playwright, TV and film scriptwriter; b. Leominster, Mass., Oct. 16, 1946; s. Lloyd Albert Coen and Beatrice (Furst) Pearlmutter; m. Victoria Zane Loveland, Nov. 13, 1994. BS in Broadcasting and Film, Boston U., 1969; playwriting workshop, Arthur Kopit, 1984-87; MFA in Playwriting, UCLA, 1997. Dramaturg pvt. acting coach, tchr., 1980-86. Scriptwriter, story editor for TV shows includes Room for Two, staff writer Carol & Co., The Wonder Years, Silk Stalkings Gen. Hosp., series devel. deal Walt Disney TV, 1988-90, 4 TV pilots for ABC, NBC, FOX Network and MCA; script doctor for Neuromancer, Bells; plays produced in L.A. include Speak, Tinkle Time, Act One Festival, Ali Baba, Is It You?, Bunches of Betty, Internal Bleeding, Sympathy; plays produced in N.Y.C. Sympathy, Soul of Wood; literary mgr. Theatre of Open Eye; dir. 20 plays; actor 25 plays. Mem. Actor's Equity Assn., Dramatist's Guild, Writer's Guild West, L.A. Playwrights Group. Democrat. Jewish. Home and Office: 5706 Noble Ave Van Nuys CA 91411-3230

COFER, BERDETTE HENRY, public management consulting company executive; b. Las Flores, Calif.; s. William Walter and Violet Ellen (Elam) C.; m. Ann McGarva, June 27, 1954 (dec. Feb. 20, 1990); children: Sandra Lea Cofer-Oberle, Ronald William; m. Sally Ann Shepherd, June 12, 1993. AB, Calif. State U., Chico, 1950; MA, U. Calif., Berkeley, 1960. Tchr. Westwood (Calif.) Jr.-Sr. High Sch., 1953-54, Alhambra High Sch., Martinez, Calif., 1954-59; prin. adult and summer sch. Hanford (Calif.) High Sch., 1959-60, asst. supt. bus., 1960-67; dean bus. svcs. West Hills Coll., Coalinga, 1967-76; vice chancellor Yosemite Community Coll. Dist., Modesto, 1976-88; pres. BHC Assocs., Inc., Modesto, 1988—; chmn. Valley Ins. Program Joint Powers Agy., Modesto, 1986-88. Contbr. articles to profl. publs. Pres. Coalinga Indsl. Devel. Corp., 1972-74, Assn. for Retarded Citizens, Modesto, 1985; mayor City of Coalinga, 1974-76; foreman Stanislaus County Grand Jury, Modesto, 1987-88. 1st lt. USAF, 1951-53. Recipient Outstanding Citizen award Coalinga C. of C., 1976, Walter Starr Robie Outstanding Bus. Officer award Assn. Chief Bus. Officers Calif. Community Colls., 1988. Mem. Assn. Calif. C.C. Adminstrs. (life), Commonwealth Club Calif. (San Francisco) Elks, Lions (dist. gov. 1965-66), Phi Delta Kappa (pres. Kings-Tulare chpt. 1962-63), Am. Legion, 40 and 8, Sons in Retirement. Democrat. Home and Office: 291 Leveland Ln # D Modesto CA 95350-6806

COFFELT, JANICE LITHERLAND, procurement systems analyst; b. Fargo, N.D., May 9, 1953; d. Robert Norris and Phyllis (Chilcott) Litherland; m. James Frederick Coffelt, Aug. 27, 1988; 1 child, Laura. BS in Hotel Mgmt., Moorhead State U., 1976; MS in Tech. Comm., U. Colo., Denver, 1993. Purchasing agt. VA Med. Ctr., Denver, 1983-85, Nat. Oceanic and Atmospheric Ad., Boulder, Colo., 1985-88; from chief small purchases to contract specialist U.S. Bur. Mines, Denver, 1988-96; analyst procurement sys. U.S. Geol. Survey, Denver, 1996—. Mem. Nat. Contract Mgmt. Assn. (cert. profl. contract mgr.), Fed. Acquisition Coun., Buffalo Toastmasters. Home: 2359 S Holland Ct Lakewood CO 80227 Office: US Geol Survey Denver Fed Ctr MS-204 B 53 Denver CO 80225

COFFEY, C. SHELBY, III, newspaper editor; m. Mary Lee Coffey. Ed., U. Va. With Washington Post, 1968-85, dep. mng. editor, asst. mng. editor for nat. news; editor U.S. News and World Report, 1985-86; sr. v.p., editor Dallas Times Herald, 1986; from dep. assoc. editor to exec. editor L.A. Times, 1986-89, editor, exec. v.p., 1989—. Named Editor of Yr., Nat. Press Found., 1994. Mem. Am. Soc. Newspaper Editors, Am. Press Inst., Internat. Press Inst., Coun. on Fgn. Rels., New Directions for News, Found. for Am. Comms., Assoc. Press Mng. Editors, Calif. Newspaper Pubs. Assn. Office: LA Times Times Mirror Co Times Mirror Sq Los Angeles CA 90053*

COFFILL, MARJORIE LOUISE, civic leader; b. Sonora, Calif., June 11, 1917; d. Eric J. and Pearl (Needham) Segerstrom; A.B. with distinction in Social Sci., Stanford U., 1938, M.A. in Edn., 1941; m. William Charles Coffill, Jan. 25, 1948, (dec.); children: William James, Eric John. Asst. mgr. Sonora Abstract & Title Co. (Calif.), 1938-39; mem. dean of women's staff Stanford, 1939-41; social dir. women's campus Pomona Coll., 1941-43, instr. psychology, 1941-43; asst. to field dir. ARC, Lee Moore AFB, Calif., 1944-46; partner Riverbank Water Co., Riverbank and Hughson, Calif., 1950-68. Mem. Tuolumne County Mental Health Adv. Com., 1963-70; mem. central advisory coun. Supplementary Edn. Ctr., Stockton, Calif., 1966-70; mem. advisory com. Columbia Jr. Coll., 1972-89, pres., 1980—; pres. Columbia Found., 1972-74, bd. dirs., 1974-77; mem. Tuolumne County Bicentennial Com., 1974—; active PTA, ARC. Pres., Tuolumne County Rep. Women, 1952—, assoc. mem. Calif. Rep. Central Com., 1950. Trustee Sonora Union High Sch., 1969-73, Salvation Army Tuolumne County, 1973—; bd. dirs. Lung Assn. Valley Lode Counties, 1974—, life 1986—. Recipient Pi Lambda Theta award, 1940, Outstanding Citizen award C. of C., 1974, Citizen of Yr. award, 1987; named to Columbia Coll. Hall of Fame, 1990; named Alumnus of Yr., Sonora Union High Sch., 1994. Mem. AAUW (charter mem. Tuolumne County br., pres. Sonora br. 1965-66). Episcopalian (mem. vestry 1968, 75). Home: 376 Summit Ave Sonora CA 95370-5728

COFFIN, THOMAS M., federal magistrate judge; b. St. Louis, May 30, 1945; s. Kenneth C. and Agnes M. (Ryan) C.; m. Penelope Teaff, Aug. 25, 1973; children: Kimberly, Laura, Colleen, Corey, Mary, Brendan, T.J. BA, St. Benedict's Coll., 1967; JD, Harvard, 1970. Bar: Mo. 1970, Calif. 1972, Oreg. 1982, U.S. Dist. Ct. (so. dist.) Calif. 1971, U.S. Dist. Ct. Oreg. 1980, U.S. Ct. Appeals (9th cir.) 1971. Asst. U.S. atty., chief criminal divsn. U.S. Attys. Office, San Diego, 1971-80; asst. U.S. atty., supr. asst. U.S. atty. U.S. Attys. Office, Eugene, Oreg., 1980-92; U.S. Magistrate judge U.S. Dist. Ct., Eugene, Oreg., 1992—; sr. litigation counsel U.S. Dept. Justice, 1984. Mem. Oreg. Bar Assn. Office: US Dist Ct 211 E 7th Ave Eugene OR 97401-2722*

COFFINGER, MARALIN KATHARYNE, retired air force officer, consultant; b. Ogden, Iowa, July 5, 1935; d. Cleo Russell and Katharyne Frances (McGovern) Morse. BA, Ariz. State U., 1957, MA, 1961; diploma, Armed Forces Staff Coll., 1972, Nat. War Coll., 1977; postgrad., Inst. for Higher Def. Studies, 1985. Commd. 2nd lt. USAF, 1963, advanced through grades to brig. gen., 1985; base comdr., dep. base comdr. Elmendorf AFB, Anchorage, Alaska, 1977-79; base comdr. Norton AFB, San Bernardino, Calif., 1979-82; chmn. spl. and incentive pays Office of Sec. Def., Pentagon, Washington, 1982-83; dep. dir. pers. programs USAF Hdqrs., Pentagon, Washington, 1983-85; command dir. NORAD, Combat Ops., Cheyenne Mountain Complex, Colo., 1985-86; dir. pers. plans USAF Hdqrs., Pentagon, Washington, 1986-89; ret. USAF, 1989; dir. software products ops. Walsh America, 1992-94. Keynote speaker, mem. dedication ceremonies Vietnam Meml. Com., Phoenix, 1990; mem. Phoenix Symphony Orch., 1954-63; prin. flutist Scottsdale Cmty. Orch., Scottsdale Concert Band. Decorated Air Force D.S.M., Def. Superior Svc. medal, Legion of Merit, Bronze Star.; recipient Nat. Medal of Merit. Mem. NAFE, Air Force Assn. (vet./retiree coun., pres. Sky Harbor chpt. 1990), Nat. Officers Assn., Ret. Officers Assn., Maricopa County Sheriff's Exec. Posse, Ariz. State U. Alumni Assn. (Profl. Excellence award 1981), Nat. Assn. Uniformed Svcs. Roman Catholic. Home: 8059 E Maria Dr Scottsdale AZ 85255

COFIELD, PHILIP THOMAS, educational association administrator; b. Monmouth, Ill., July 3, 1951; s. Earl Crescant and Vera (Shunick) C.; divorced; children: Calla, Megan. BA in English, St. Ambrose U., 1973. Dir. Jr. Achievment of Quad Cities, Davenport, Moline, Iowa, Ill., 1980-83; account exec. Jr. Achievment Inc., 1983-85; pres., CEO Jr. Achievment of Utah, Salt Lake City, 1985—. Established Utah Bus. Hall of Fame, 1991. Mem. Utah Coun. on Economic Edn. (bd. dirs.), Salt Lake area C. of C., Rotary Club, (com. co-chmn. Salt Lake City). Office: Jr Achievement of Utah 182 S 600 E Salt Lake City UT 84102-1909

COGAN, JOHN DENNIS, artist; b. Wichita Falls, Tex., Feb. 24, 1953; s. John Patrick and Thrasilla Barbara (Forster) C.; m. Karen Elizabeth Smith, May 15, 1976; children: Jennifer, Tiffany, Kimberly, Courtney. BS in Physics, Tex. A&M U., 1975; MA in Physics, Rice U., 1978, PhD in Physics, 1981. Geophysicist Shell Oil Co., Houston, 1980-82; artist pvt. practice, Houston, Farmington, N.Mex., 1982—. Artist: one man show San Juan Coll., Farmington, N. Mex., 1994. Recipient Landscape award of merit Nat. Park Acad. Arts, Jackson, Wyo., 1994, Collectors award, 1995.

COGAN, KAREN ELIZABETH, author, educator; b. Houston, Sept. 24, 1954; d. Hugh and Kathryn (DeGaugh) Smith; m. John Cogan, May 15, 1976; children: Jennifer, Tiffany, Kimberly, Courtney. BS in Elem. Edn., U. Houston, 1976. Kindergarten tchr. Houston Ind. Sch. Dist., 1976-79; writer Farmington, N.Mex., 1981—. Contbr. to anthology; author articles and short stories. Mem. Nat. Writers Assn. (profl. mem.), Soc. Children's Book Writers and Illustrators.

COGGIN, CHARLOTTE JOAN, cardiologist, educator; b. Takoma Park, Md., Aug. 6, 1928; d. Charles Benjamin and Nanette (McDonald) Coggin; BA, Columbia Union Coll., 1948; MD, Loma Linda U., 1952, MPH, 1987; DSc (hon.), Andrews U., 1994. Intern, L.A. County Gen. Hosp., L.A., 1952-53, resident in medicine, 1953-55; fellow in cardiology Children's Hosp., L.A., 1955-56, White Meml. Hosp., L.A., 1955-56; rsch. assoc. in cardiology, house physician Hammersmith Hosp., London, 1956-57; resident in pediatrics and pediatric cardiology Hosp. for Sick Children, Toronto, Ont., Can., 1965-67; cardiologist, co-dir. heart surgery team Loma Linda (Calif.) U., asst. prof. medicine, 1961-73, assoc. prof., 1973-91, prof. medicine, 1991—, asst. dean Sch. Medicine Internat. Programs, 1973-75, assoc. dean, 1975—, spl. asst. to univ. pres. for internat. affairs, 1991, co-dir., cardiologist heart surgery team missions to Pakistan and Asia, 1963, Greece, 67, 69, Saigon, Vietnam, 1974, 75, to Saudi Arabia, 1976-87, People's Republic China, 1984, 89-91, Hong Kong, 1985, Zimbabwe, 1988, Kenya, 1988, Nepal, 1992, 93, China, 1992, Zimbabwe, 1993, Myanmar, 1995, North Korea, 1996; mem. Pres's. Advisory Panel on Heart Disease, 1972—; hon. prof. U. Manchuria, Harbin, People's Republic China, 1989, hon. dir. 1st People's Hosp. of Mundanjiang, Heilongjiang Province, 1989. Apptd. mem. Med. Quality Rev. Com.-Dist. 12, 1976-80. Recipient award for service to people of Pakistan City of Karachi, 1963, Medallion award Evangelismos Hosp., Athens, Greece, 1967, Gold medal of health South Vietnam Ministry of Health, 1974, Charles Elliott Weinger award for excellence, 1976, Wall Street Jour. Achievement award, 1987, Disting. Univ. Svc. award Loma Linda U., 1990; named Honored Alumnus Loma Linda U. Sch. Medicine, 1973, Outstanding Women in Gen. Conf. Seventh-day Adventists, 1975, Alumnus of Yr., Columbia Union Coll., 1984. Diplomate Am. Bd. Pediatrics. Mem. Am. Coll. Cardiology, AMA (physicians adv. com. 1969—) Calif. Med. Assn. (com. on med. schs., com. on member services), San Bernardino County Med. Soc. (chmn. communications com. 1975-77, mem. communications com. 1987-88, editor bull. 1975-76, William L. Cover, M.D. Outstanding Contbn. to Medicine award 1995), Am. Heart Assn., AAUP, Med. Research Assn. Calif., Calif. Heart Assn., AAUW, Am. Acad. Pediatrics, World Affairs Council, Internat. Platform Assn., Calif. Museum Sci. and Industry MUSES (Outstanding Woman of Year in Sci. 1969), Am. Med. Women's Assn., Loma Linda Sch. Medicine Alumni Assn. (pres. 1978), Alpha Omega Alpha, Delta Omega. Author: Atrial Septal Defects, motion picture (Golden Eagle Cine award and 1st prize Venice Film Festival 1964); contbr. articles to med. jours. Democrat. Home: 11495 Benton St Loma Linda CA 92354-3682 Office: Loma Linda U Magan Hall Rm 105 11060 Anderson St Loma Linda CA 92350

COGHILL, DAVIS GAROLD, secondary school educator; b. Gallup, N.M., Mar. 25, 1948; s. Donald Garold and June Elizabeth (Davis) C.; m. Dianna H. Glick, Jan. 26, 1991 (div.); 1 child, Matthew Donald. BA in Psychology, Calif. State Univ., L.A., 1973, MA in Spl. Edn., 1975, MA in Psychology, 1981; PhD in Counseling Psychology, U. Santa Barbara, 1985; D in Chiropractic cum laude, Life Chiropractic Coll. West, 1990. Lic. marriage, family and child counselor. Instr., counselor L.A. County Office Edn., 1976—; acad. counselor Life Chiropractic Coll. West, San Lorenzo, Calif., 1987-90; instr. L.A. Unified Sch. Dist., 1973-74; pvt. practice So. and No. Calif., 1982—; oral commr. Bd. Behavioral Sci. Examiners, Calif., 1987—; counselor Montebello Unified Sch. Dist., 1993—; mem. med. team Humanitarian Med. Mission, Tabago, Trinidad, 1996; lectr. in field. Patentee in field. Mem. NEA, Am. Chiropractic Assn., Am. Counseling Assn., Am. PUb. Health Assn., Calif. Assn. Bilingual Educators, Calif. Assn. Marriage Family Child Therapists, Calif. Chiropractic Assn., Calif. Tchrs. Assn., Internat. Chiropractic Assn. Calif., Internat. Chirpractic Sports Fedn., Nat. Grief Counselors Assn., Nat. Poetry Therapy Assn., Soc. Traumatic Stress Studies. Office: 100 N Hill Ave Ste 205 Pasadena CA 91106

COGHILL, JOHN BRUCE, former state official; b. Fairbanks, Alaska, Sept. 24, 1925; s. William Alexander and Winefred (Fortune) C.; m. Frances Mae Gilbert, 1948; children: Patricia, John Jr., James, Jerald, Paula, Jeffry. Grad. high sch., Nenana, Alaska. Ptnr. Coghill's Inc., Nenana, Alaska, 1948—; owner Tortella Lodge & Apts., 1951, J.B. Coghill Oil Co., 1958-87, Nenana Fuel Co., 1960-87; mem. from senate dist. J Alaska State Legislature, Juneau, 1959-64, 85-90; chmn. resources com., chmn. majority caucus, vice chmn. transp., mem. oil and gas com., spl. joint com. on tax policy, nre revenue work group and fin. budget subcommittees on DNR, DEC and fish & game; lt. gov. State of Alaska, 1990-94; mayor City of Nenana, 1962-84; ptnr. Coghill's, Inc.; sec. Nenana Industries, Nenana Fuel Co. Mem. sch. bd., 1948-59; mem. Alaskan territorial Ho. of Reps., 1953, 57, Alaska Const. Conv., 1955; spl. asst. to gov. State of Alaska, 1967; sec. North Commn., 1968-72; chmn. Alaska Statehood Commn., 1980-83. Sgt. Alaska Command U.S. Army, 1944-46. Mem. VFW, Am. Legion, Eagle Hist. Soc., Pioneers of Alaska, Lions Club, Masons, Eagles, Moose. *

COGNATA, JOSEPH ANTHONY, football commissioner; b. Ashtabula, Ohio, Feb. 11, 1946; s. Joseph and Ella Jane (Dispense) C.; m. Betty Jean Jacobs, Dec. 17, 1978; children: Lisa Ann, Joseph Anthony Jr., Christina Ann, Gilbert Jerome. Student, Kent State U., 1964-66. Sales rep. Endicott

Buick, Pompano Beach, Fla., 1977-80; sales mgr. Fla. Chrysler Plymouth, West Palm Beach, Fla., 1980-82; owner, CEO So. States Football Club, Tequesta, Fla., 1982-85; backfield/spl. teams coach San Jose (Calif.) Bandits Minor League Football Sys., 1987-90; asst. head coach Calif. Outlaws Minor League Football Sys., Hayward, Calif., 1990-91; asst. to dir. football ops. Profl. Spring Football League, Meadowlands, N.J., 1991-92; co-founder Golden West Football League, Sacramento, 1991—; commr. West Coast Amateur Football League, Mountain View, Calif., 1992—; pres., CEO, commr. Pacific Western Football Alliance, Sacramento, 1992—; pres. CEO U.S. Amateur Football Fedn., 1994—; pres., CEO West Coast Football Conf., 1994—. Author: Complete Football Playbook, 1969. Lutheran. Home and Office: 107 S Mary Ave Apt 33 Sunnyvale CA 94086-5851

COGUT, THEODORE LOUIS, environmental specialist, meteorologist; b. Royal Oak Twp., Mich., Jan. 3, 1928; s. Louis and Mary Agnes (Evanish) C.; m. Martha Marie Nordstrom, Nov. 1, 1945; children: Leta Marie Cogut Mach, Willa Lynette Cogut Swartz, Pamela Anne Cogut Bryant. Grad. several meteorol. schs., USAF and U.S. Army; BA with honors, U. Md., 1965; MA in Teaching, Wayne State U., 1970. Weather forecaster USAF, 1948-53, 56-62; environ. analyst Climatology Ctr. USAF, Washington, 1962-64; instr. U.S. Army Arty. Meteorology Sch., Ft. Sill, Okla., 1965; grad. rsch. asst. in meteorology U. Okla., 1972-73; chief meteorologist Phelps Dodge Corp., Morenci, Ariz., 1974-79; environ. svcs. supr. Phelps Dodge Morenci, Inc., 1979-93; environ. cons. Tucson, Ariz., 1993—; mem. SKYWARN Spotter Network of Nat. Weather Svc., 1991-93; Citizen Amb. Environ. Del. to China, 1988; editor-in-chief Morenci Copper Rev., 1985—. Author: (programmed text) Ballistic Wind Plotting, 1968; author meteorol. newsletters, 1968-69; inventor computerized air quality and weather prediction system MCAPS, 1975. Pres. Greenlee County Hist. Soc., Clifton, Ariz., 1990. Chief warrant officer arty. U.S. Army, 1965-69, Vietnam. Decorated Bronze Star, Legion of Merit; Gallantry Cross (Vietnam). Mem. AIME (chmn. Morenci chpt. 1989), Am. Meteorol. Soc. (pres. So. Ariz. chpt. 1980), Nat. Weather Assn. (mem. indsl. meteorology com. 1980), Air and Waste Mgmt. Assn., Greenlee County C. of C. (pres. 1992-93), Rotary Internat. (sec. Clifton-Morenci chpt. 1979), Phi Kappa Phi (U. Md. chpt.). Home and Office: 5810 E Paseo San Valentine Tucson AZ 85750

COHAN, CHRISTOPHER, professional sports team executive; b. Salinas, Calif., 1951; s. Helen C.; m. Angela; three children. BA, Ariz. State U., 1973. With Feather River Cable TV Corp., Orinda, Calif., 1973-77; owner Sonic Comms., Alaska, 1977; owner, CEO Golden State Warriors, Calif.; bd. dirs. Calif. TV Assn. Office: Oakland Coliseum Arena 700 Coliseum Way Oakland CA 94621-1818 also: Golden State Warriors 1221 Broadway 20th Fl Oakland CA 94612-1918

COHEN, ANDREW NEAL, activist, writer, scientist; b. Boston, Dec. 21, 1954; s. Arthur I. and Florence (Goldberg) C. BA in Environ. Scis., U. Calif., Berkeley, 1985, MS in Energy and Resources, 1989, PhD in Energy and Resources, 1996. Exec. dir. Urban Creeks Coun., Berkeley, 1988-89; marine rsch. assoc. Maritime Studies/Mystic (Conn.) Seaport, 1993—; v.p. East Bay Mcpl. Utility Dist., Oakland, Calif., 1991-94; environ. scientist San Francisco Estuary Inst., Richmond, Calif., 1996—; mem. Com. for Water Policy Consensus, Sacramento, 1985-88, Tech. Adv. Com. San Francisco Estuary Project, Oakland, 1987-91, Rural Water Impact Network, Davis, Calif., 1993-95, Citizens Alliance to Restore the Estuary, Oakland, 1989-92. Author: Introduction to the Ecology of the San Francisco Estuary, 1990, Biological Invasions of the San Francisco Bay and Delta, 1995, Gateway to the Inland Coast: The Story of the Carquinez Strait, 1996; contbr. articles to profl. jours. Pres. Calif. Water Policy Group, Oakland, 1987-91; chair Buckhorn Canyon Legal Def. Fund, Oakland, 1989-90; founding mem. Pub. Ofcls. for Water and Environ. Reform, Sacramento, 1991-92. Named Pub. Ofcl. of Yr. San Francisco Bay chpt. Sierra Club, Oakland, Calif., 1994; recipient Scholarship award U. Calif. Club, Berkeley, 1989, Grad. Student Rsch. award Nat. Audubon Soc., Washington, 1989. Office: San Francisco Estuary Inst 180 Richmond Field Sta Richmond CA 94804

COHEN, ARTHUR M., education educator; b. Caldwell, N.J., June 14, 1927; s. Harry Cohen and Rae Berke; m. Florence Brawer; children: Bill, Wendy, Andrew, Nancy. BA, U. Miami, 1949, MA, 1955; PhD, Fla. State U., 1964. Prof. higher edn. UCLA, 1964—. Author: The American Community College, 1996. Office: U Calif 405 Hilgard Los Angeles CA 90024

COHEN, CHARLES ROBERT, state agency administrator; b. Irvington, N.J., Mar. 25, 1959; s. Barry and Mara Judith (Cantor) C. BA, SUNY, Binghamton, 1981; JD, Ariz. State U., 1985. Bar: Ariz. Assoc. Warner Angle Roper & Hallam, Phoenix, 1985-87; asst. atty. gen. Office Ariz. Atty. Gen., Phoenix, 1987-92; asst. dep. receiver Ariz. Dept. Ins., Phoenix, 1992-93, acting dep. dir., 1993-94, exec. asst. dir., 1994-95, dep. dir., 1995—. Mem. Ariz. State Bar Assn. Office: Arizona Dept Insurance 2910 N 44th St Phoenix AZ 85018

COHEN, CLARENCE BUDD, aerospace engineer; b. Monticello, N.Y., Feb. 7, 1925; s. Isidor and Dora Cohen; m. Beatrice Sholofsky, Jan. 1, 1947; children: William David, Deborah Ann. BAE, Rensselaer Poly. Inst., 1945, MAE, 1947; MA, Princeton U., 1952, PhD, 1954. Aerospace research scientist NASA, Cleve., 1947-56; assoc. chief spl. projects br. TRW Electronics and Def., Redondo Beach, Calif., 1957-87, head hypersonics research section, 1957-61; mgr. aerodynamics dept. TRW Electronics and Defense, Redondo Beach, Calif., 1961-63, mgr. aero scis. lab., 1966-69, dir. tech. application, 1970-80, dir. technology, 1980-87; cons. in field. Contbr. articles to profl. jours; patentee manned spacecraft with staged reentry. Trustee, vice chmn. Northrup U., 1991—; With USNR, 1943-46. Recipient Class of 1902 Rsch. Prize, Rensselaer Poly. Inst., 1945; Guggenheim fellow Princeton U., 1950-52. Fellow AIAA; mem. Licensing Execs. Soc., Research Soc. Am. (past pres.), Indsl. Research Inst. (emeritus), Sigma Xi. Club: King Harbor Yacht. Home: 332 Via El Chico Redondo Beach CA 90277-6756

COHEN, D. ASHLEY, clinical neuropsychologist; b. Omaha, Oct. 2, 1952; d. Cenek and Dorothy A. (Bilek) Hrabik; m. Donald I. Cohen, 1968 (div. 1976); m. Lyn J. Mangiameli, June 12, 1985. BA in Psychology, U. Nebr., Omaha, 1975, MA in Psychology, 1979; PhD in Clin. Psychology, Calif. Coast U., 1988. Lic. psychologist, Calif.; lic. marriage and family therapist, Nev. Family specialist Ea. Nebr. Human Svcs. Agy. Consultation & Edn., 1979-80; psychotherapist Washoe Tribe, Gardnerville, Nev., 1980; therapist Family Counseling Svc., Carson City, Nev., 1980-93; psychotherapist Alpine County Mental Health, Markleeville, Calif., 1981-89, dir., 1990-93; psychologist Golden Gate Med. Examiners, San Francisco, San Jose, Calif., 1993—; conf. presenter and spkr. in field; presenter rsch. findings 7th European Conf. Personality, Madrid, 1994, Oxford (Eng.) U. ISSID Conf., 1991; site coord. nat. standardization Kaufmann brief intelligence test A.G.S., 1988-90. Vol. EMT, Alpine County, 1983-93. Recipient Svc. to Youth award Office Edn., 1991. Mem. APA, Internat. Neuropsychol. Soc., Internat. Soc. Study Individual Differences, Am. Psychol. Soc., Nat. Acad. Neuropsychology. Office: 127 Carson Ct Sunnyvale CA 94086-5804

COHEN, DANIEL MORRIS, museum administrator, marine biology researcher; b. Chgo., July 6, 1930; s. Leonard U. and Myrtle (Gertz) C.; m. Anne Carolyn Constant, Nov. 4, 1955; children—Carolyn A., Cynthia S. BA, Stanford U., 1952, MA, 1953, PhD, 1958. Asst. prof., curator fishes U. Fla., Gainesville, 1957-58; systematic zoologist Bur. Comml. Fisheries, Washington, 1958-60; dir. systematics lab. Nat. Marine Fisheries Service, Washington, 1960-81; sr. scientist Nat. Marine Fisheries Service, Seattle, 1981-82; chief curator life scis. Los Angeles County Mus. of Natural History, 1982-93, dep. dir. rsch. and collections, 1993-95; emeritus, 1995—; adj. prof. biology U. So. Calif., 1982—. Contbr. numerous articles to profl. jours. Fellow AAAS, Calif. Acad. Sci.; mem. Am. Soc. Ichthyologists and Herpetologists (v.p. 1969, 70, pres. 1985), Biol. Soc. Washington (pres. 1971-72), Soc. Systematic Biology (mem. coun. 1976-78). Home: 3667 Greve Dr Rancho Palos Verdes CA 90275-6281 Office: LA County Mus of Nat History 900 Exposition Blvd Los Angeles CA 90007-4057

COHEN, ELLIS AVRUM, producer, writer; b. Balt., Sept. 15, 1945; s. Leonard Howard and Selma Jean (Lattin) C. *Mother Selma Jean Cohen, who died July 2, 1996, was praised by The Baltimore Sun as someone who--along with her husband, Leonard, retired business executive-- "opened her heart to ill and handicapped children and adults and succeeded in bringing smiles to their faces." The Ronald McDonald House hailed them as "ultimate volunteers." She, for 25 years, was Director of Nursing Home Bed Registry for the Maryland State Health Department. She was honored, posthumously, by the United States Congress, the Senate, the Maryland governor, and Baltimore mayor. Brother Jerry is a screenwriter-author.* AA in Comm., C.C. of Balt., 1965. Dir. pub. rels. The Camera Mart, Inc., N.Y.C., 1971-72; editor-in-chief TV/New York mag., N.Y.C., 1972-74; dir. worldwide pub. rels., advt. and mktg. William Morris Agy., N.Y.C., 1974-77; sr. publicist Solters, Roskin & Friedman, L.A., 1977-78; sr. v.p. creative affairs Don King Prodns., N.Y.C., 1978; TV-movie prodr. (staff) CBS Entertainment Prodns., Studio City, Calif., 1979-88; CEO/pres. Hennessey Entertainment, Ltd., L.A., 1983—; film cons. Assn. Film Commrs., 1987—. Author: Dangerous Evidence, 1995, Avenue of the Stars, 1991; prodr. (CBS-TV) Love, Mary, 1985 (Luminas award 1986), First Steps, 1985 (Film Adv. Bd. award 1985), Aunt Mary, 1979 (Grand prize winner MIFED film festival, Milan, Italy 1980). Polit. cons. Mayor Tom Bradley re-election campaign, L.A., 1977; mayoral appointee Com. in the Pub. Interest, N.Y.C., 1973-77; prodr., dir., cons. Dem. Nat. Conv., N.Y.C., 1975-76. With U.S. Army, 1965-67. Recipient Gov.'s award for employment of the handicapped, L.A., 1980, Christopher award, 1980, Humanities cert. Human Family Cultural & Ednl. Inst., L.A., 1986, Key-to-City mayor of Balt., 1979. Mem. AARP, Writers Guild of Am., West (nominated Outstanding TV Movie Story 1979). Democrat. Jewish.

COHEN, HENRY, historian, retired educator; b. Bklyn.; s. Sam and Lily Cohen. BA, Columbia Coll., 1955; PhD, Cornell U., 1965. Asst. prof. Calif. State Coll., Long Beach, 1964-69; from asst. prof. to prof. Loyola U., Chgo., 1969-94. Author: Business and Politics in America to the Civil War, 1971, Brutal Justice, 1981; founder, editor Criminal Justice History: An International Annual 1980-83; editor The Public Enemy, 1981. Social Sci. Rsch. Coun. fellow, 1960-62. Mem. Group for Use of Psychoanalysis in History, Internat. Soc. for Polit. Psychology.

COHEN, JOYCE E., utilities executive, former state senator, investment executive; b. McIntosh, S.D., Mar. 27, 1937; d. Joseph and Evelyn Petik; children: Julia Jo, Aaron J. Grad., Coll. Med. Tech., Minn., 1955; student, UCLA, 1957-58, Santa Ana Coll., 1957-62. Med. rsch. technician dept. surgery U. Minn., 1955-58; dept. immunology UCLA, 1958-59; dept. bacteriology U. Calif., 1959-61; med. rsch. scientist Allergan Pharms., Santa Ana, Calif., 1961-70; ptnr. Co-Fo Investments, Lake Oswego, Oreg., 1978-84; mem. Oreg. Ho. of Reps., 1979-83, Oreg. State Senate, 1983-94, Pacific Northwest Electric Power/Conservation Planning Coun., 1994—. Chmn. trade and econ. devel., govt. reorgn. and reinvention com., senate judiciary com.; mem. senate revenue and sch. fin. com.; vice-chair agr. & natural resources com., health care & bio-ethics com.; mem. bus., housing & fin. com., rules com.; co-chair joint task force on lottery oversight; mem. joint com. on asset forfeiture oversight adv.; mem. Senate Exec. Appointments; mem. joint com. on land use, alt. joint com. legis. audit; mem. Energy Policy Rev. Bd.; appointed to Oreg. Coun. Econ. Edn., Oreg. Criminal Justice Coun., adv. com. Ctr. for Rsch. on Occupational and Environ. Toxicology; mem. Jud. Br. State Energy Policy Rev. Com., 1979, Gov's. Commn. on Child Support. Woodrow Wilson Lecture series fellow, 1988. Mem. LWV, Assn. Family Conciliation Cts. (founding mem.), Oreg. Environ. Coun., Oreg. Women's Polit. Caucus. Democrat. Office: 620 SW 5th Ave Ste 1025 Portland OR 97204-1424

COHEN, MANLEY, gastroenterologist; b. Johannesburg, South Africa, May 6, 1937; came to U.S., 1963; s. Tuvia and Frieda Cohen; m. Barbara Hazel Cohen, Aug. 30, 1961; children: Darien, Ronan, Gila. MB BCh, U. Witwatersrand, Johannesburg, South Africa, 1960; MS in Medicine, U. Minn., 1972. Diplomate Am. Bd. Internal Medicine, Am. Bd. Gastroenterology. Intern Saint Bartholomew's Hosp., Rochester, Eng., 1962, Passavant Meml. Hosp., Northwestern U., Chgo., 1963; fellow in medicine and gastroenterology Mayo Clinic and Mayo Grad. Sch. Medicine, Rochester, Minn., 1963-69; chief edn. dept. medicine Long Beach (Calif.) Meml. Med. Ctr., 1969-94; clin. prof. medicine U. Calif., Irvine. Fellow ACP, Am. Coll. Gastroenterology; mem. Am. Soc. Gastrointestinal Endoscopy, So. Calif. Soc. Gastroenterology (pres.). Jewish. Home: 650 Flint Ave Long Beach CA 90814-2041 Office: 2840 N Long Beach Blvd Long Beach CA 90806-1531

COHEN, MARK JEFFREY, cartoonist agent; b. Stockton, Calif., Nov. 19, 1942; s. Samuel and Sadie (Tager) C.; m. Rose Marie McDaniel, May 31, 1990; 1 child, Eric S. Owner, broker Mark J. Cohen, Santa Rosa, Calif., 1975-95; owner Mark J. Cohen Cartoonist's Agy., Santa Rosa, 1995—; keynote spkr. Guinness Internat. Cartoon Festival, 1995. Writer for comic strips including Gasoline Alley, Popeye, and Wee Pals, 1970—; author various comic books; contbr. articles to Real Estate Today and Cartoonists Profiles. Treas., pres. No. Calif. Cert. Residential Specialists, 1980-85; past pres. Optimists Club, Santa Rosa, 1985-86; merit badge counselor Boy Scouts, Santa Rosa, 1985—. Named Disting. pres. Optimists Internat., 1986, Realtor of Yr., Sonoma County Bd. Realtors, 1988, Gallon donor Blood Bank of the Redwoods, 1989; recipient Merit award Cmty. Svc., City of Santa Rosa, 1988. Mem. Nat. Cartoonists Soc. (No. Calif. chpt. sec. 1989-94) . Office: Mark J Cohen 589 Mendocino # 5 Santa Rosa CA 95401

COHEN, SEYMOUR I., lawyer; b. N.Y.C., Apr. 15, 1931; s. Fred and Nettie (Sederer) C.; m. Rhoda Goldner, July 22, 1956; children: Cheryl Lynn, Marcy Ann, Lori Beth. BBA cum laude, CCNY, 1951; LLB, Bklyn. Law Sch., 1954, JD, 1967; MBA, NYU, 1960. Bar: N.Y. 1954, U.S. Tax. Ct. 1954, Calif. 1973, U.S. Dist. Ct. (cen. dist.) Calif. 1973, U.S. Ct. Appeals (9th cir.) 1973, U.S. Supreme Ct. 1976; CPA, Ohio, Calif. Staff acct. S.D. Leidesdorf, N.Y.C., 1958-61; mgr., acct. Rockwell, Columbus, Ohio, and L.A., 1961-69; mgr. contracts Logicon, L.A., 1970-71; mgr. internal audit Daylin, 1971-72; contr. NYSE Co., 1972-73; pvt. practice, Torrance, Calif., 1973—. Mem. AICPA, Los Angeles County Bar Assn. (appellate ct. com. 1979—, svcs. com. 1981-82), S. Bay Bar Assn. (pres. 1986-87, chmn. referral svc. 1977-81), State Bar Calif. (client trust fund commr. 1983, 84), Ohio Inst. CPAs, N.Y. Inst. CPAs, Calif. Inst. CPAs, Inst. Mgmt. Accts., L.A. Trial Lawyers Assn., N.Y. State Bar Assn., Calif. Bar Assn. Jewish. Republican. Home: 30691 Via La Cresta Palos Verdes Peninsula CA 90275-5353 Office: 18411 Crenshaw Blvd Ste 411 Torrance CA 90504-5081

COHEN, STEPHEN MITCHELL, optometrist; b. Bklyn., Sept. 24, 1956; s. Herbert William Cohen and Diana Kalifowitz Flax; m. Stephanie Helene Shapiro, Apr. 6, 1986; children: Joshua, Arielle, Zachary. BA in Sci. Edn., Ariz. State U., 1980; BS in Optical Sci., Pa. Coll. Optometry, Phila., 1983, OD, 1985. Optometrist Family Vision Care, Scottsdale, Ariz., 1985-88, Ariz. Eye and Vision Care, Scottsdale, 1988-93, Scottsdale Vision Ctr., Scottsdale, 1993—; vision cons. Kachna Country Day Sch., Scottsdale, 1987—. Pres. Scottsdale "TIPS" Bus. Group, 1986-91, Desert Foothills Cmty. Theatre, Carefree, Ariz., 1985-94; v.p. Project Prevention, Phoenix Children's Hosp., 1986-92, mem. parent adv. bd., 1993-94; mem. Valley Leadership, Phoenix, 1989-90; treas. Coun. for Jews with Spl. Needs, Phoenix, 1993-95. Named Outstanding Actor, Desert Foothills Cmty. Theater, 1988, 91. Mem. Am. Optometric Assn., Ariz. Optometric Assn. (bd. dirs., Service award 1988, membership com.), Rotary (pres. 1986-93, Outstanding Svc. award 1991). Republican. Jewish. Office: Scottsdale Vision & Achieve 10505 N 69th St Ste 1000 Scottsdale AZ 85253-1479

COHEN, WARREN, musician, writer; b. Montreal, Quebec, Canada, July 2, 1954; came to U.S., 1976; s. Philip Stanley and Olive (Harrison) C. BA, Concordia U., Montreal, Quebec, 1976; MA, U. Hawaii, 1979. Music tchr. Trafalgar Sch., Montreal, Quebec, Can., 1973-76; pianist Honolulu City Ballet, 1978-79; tchr. U. Hawaii Lab. Sch., Honolulu, 1982-95; adj. faculty Chaminade U., Honolulu, 1989-95. Author: Ethics in Thought and Action, 1994; mus. dir. Kumu Kahua Theatre, 1984-91, The Best of Am. Mus. Theatre, 1993—; artistic dir.: Music We Listened to concert series, 1990-91; condr. Diamond Head Theatre, 1995, Manoa Valley Theatre, 1989-95, Stagebrush Theatre, 1996-97, Hawaii Chamber Orch. Soc., 1994-95; condr., pianist. Morning Music Honolulu, 1980-95; composer: Sinfonia Concertante for Orch. and Piano, 1991-92, Just So Stories, 1992, Concerto Grosso string quartet and string orch., 1994, Suite for Chamber Orchestra, Innocent Songs and Dances, 1997. Music dir. So. Ariz. Symphony Orch., 1996—. Prodn. grantee State Found. for Culture and the Arts, 1991, tour grantee Hawaii Bur. of Econ. Devel., 1991; recipient Po'okela award Hawaii State Theatre Coun., 1993, 95, composition award ASCAP, 1994, 95, 96. Mem. Musician's Assn. Hawaii. Home: 3441 E Turquoise Ave Phoenix AZ 85028

COHEN, WILLIAM, construction executive; b. 1962. Graduate, Loyola U., 1974. Assoc. Monteleone & McCrory, L.A., 1974-80; v.p. Valley Crest Landscape, Inc., Calabasas, Calif., 1980—. Office: Valley Crest Landscape Inc 24121 Ventura Blvd Calabasas CA 91302-1449*

COHLBERG, JEFFREY A., biochemistry educator; b. Phila., Feb. 26, 1945; s. Raymond G. and Helen E. (Greenberg) C. AB in Chemistry, Cornell U., 1966; PhD in Biochemistry, U. Calif., 1972. Postdoctoral Inst. For Enzyme Rsch. U. Wis., 1972-75; prof. Calif. State U., Long Beach, 1975—. Contbr. articles to profl. jours. Mem. Am. Soc. Cell Biology. Office: Calif State U Dept Chemistry Biochem Long Beach CA 90840

COHN, DANIEL HOWARD, laboratory director; b. Santa Monica, Calif., Aug. 24, 1955; s. Sidney Lorber and Mynda Ellen (Zimmerman) C.; m. Ludmila Bojman, May 16, 1982; children: Zachary, Marissa, Rachel. BA, U. Calif., Santa Barbara, 1977; PhD, Scripps Inst. Oceanography, 1983. Postdoctoral fellow U. Wash., Seattle, 1983-88; 0sch. scientist, asst. prof. Cedars-Sinai Med. Ctr./UCLA, 1988-93, assoc. prof., 1993-97, prof., 1997—; mem. genetics tng. program UCLA, 1988—; reviewer various jours. and granting agys. Editorial bd. various jours.; contbr. articles to profl. jours. and books. Grants com. chair, bd. dirs. Concern Found. for Cancer Rsch., L.A., 1988—. Recipient Martin Kamen award U. Calif., San Diego, 1983, Eckhart prize Scripps Inst. Oceanography, 1983; postdoctoral award NIH, 1985-88, grantee, 1988—. Mem. AAAS, Phi Beta Kappa. Democrat. Jewish. Office: Cedars-Sinai Med Ctr 8700 Beverly Blvd Los Angeles CA 90048-1804*

COHN, DAVID LESLIE, health facility executive; b. Chgo., May 24, 1949; s. Herman and Elsa (Kahn) C.; m. Valerie Kaye Smith, June 11, 1974; children: Joshua Smith, Zachary Smith. BA in Zoology, U. Mich., 1971; MD, U. Ill., Chgo., 1975. Diplomate Am. Bd. Internal Medicine, Am. Bd. Infectious Diseases. Resident in internal medicine U. Wis., Madison, 1975-78; fellow in infectious diseases U. Colo., Denver, 1979-81; contract physician Denver Health & Hosps., 1979-81, asst. dir. disease control svc., 1981-87, dir. disease control svc., 1987—, assoc. dir. Denver Pub. Health, 1989—, dir. AIDS svcs., 1989—; temporary advisor WHO, Geneva, 1992, med. officer, 1994-95; instr. U. Colo. Health Sci. Ctr., Denver, 1981-83, asst. prof., 1983-88, assoc. prof., 1988-96, prof., 1996—. Contbr. chpts. to books, articles and revs. to profl. jours. Hon. bd. dirs. Colo. AIDS Project, Denver, 1987—; Gov.'s AIDS Coun., 1988-94; mem. Leadership Denver, 1987-88. Recipient Outstanding Sr. award Chgo. Tribune, 1967, Citation for AIDS/HIV Rsch. and Prevention, U.S. Dept. Health and Human Svcs., Denver, 1988; named Hero in the AIDS Epidemic, Colo. AIDS Project, Denver, 1992. Fellow Am. Coll. Physicians, Infectious Disease Soc. Am.; mem. Am. Thoracic Soc., Internat. AIDS Soc., Western Soc. Clin. Investigation, Internat. Union Against TB, Phi Eta Sigma. Jewish. Office: Denver Health & Hosps 605 Bannock St Denver CO 80204-4505

COHN, LAWRENCE STEVEN, physician, educator; b. Chgo., Dec. 21, 1945; s. Jerome M. and Francis C.; BS, U. Ill., 1967, MD, 1971; m. Harriett G. Rubin, Sept. 1, 1968; children: Allyson and Jennifer (twins). Intern, Mt. Zion Hosp., San Francisco, 1971-72, resident, 1972-73; resident U. Chgo., 1973-74; practice medicine specializing in internal medicine, Paramount, Calif.; pres. med. staff Charter Suburban Hosp., 1981-83; mem. staff Long Beach Meml. Hosp., Harbor Gen. Hosp; assoc. clin. prof. medicine UCLA. Maj. USAF, 1974-76. Recipient Disting. Teaching award Harbor-UCLA Med. Ctr., 1980, 90; diplomate Am. Bd. Internal Medicine. Fellow Am. Coll. Physicians; mem. A.C.P., AMA, Calif. Med. Assn., L.A. County Med. Assn., Am. Heart Assn., Soc. Air Force Physicians, Phi Beta Kappa, Phi Kappa Phi, Phi Lambda Upsilon, Phi Eta Sigma, Alpha Omega Alpha. Home: 6608 Via La Paloma Palos Verdes Peninsula CA 90275-6449 Office: 16415 Colorado Ave Ste 202 Paramount CA 90723-5054

COIT, R. KEN, financial planner; b. L.A., Aug. 26, 1943; s. Roger L. and Thelma D. C.; BS, U. Ariz., 1967; MBA, Pepperdine U., 1981; m. Donna M. Schemanske, Oct. 8, 1977; children: Kristin M., Shannon, Darren, Lauryn. Prin. Coit Fin. Group, 1981; mem. adj. faculty Coll. Fin. Planning, Denver, 1978-79; pres. Walnut Creek adv. bd. Summit Bank, 1987-95, Sequoia Equities Securities Corp., Walnut Creek, Calif.; bd. dirs. R.H. Phillips Winery; mem. adv. bd. Mt. Diablo Nat. Bank, 1996—. Mem. dean's adv. bd. Pepperdine U., 1988-91; nat. bd. advisor Coll. Pharmacy U. Ariz.; bd. dirs., chmn. investment com. East Cmty. Found., 1994—. Recipient Outstanding Alumnus award Pepperdine U. Sch. Bus. and Mgmt., 1986. Mem. Internat. Assn. Fin. Planners (chpt. pres. 1978-79), Inst. Cert. Fin. Planners, East Bay Gourmet Club, Blackhawk Country Club. Office: 1655 N Main St Bldg 270 Walnut Creek CA 94596-4610

COLACE, JOSEPH J., agricultural products company executive; b. 1955. Officer Colace Bros., El Centro, Calif., 1976-83, pres., 1983—; pres. Five Crowns, Inc., Brawley, Calif. Office: Five Crowns Inc 551 W Main St Ste 2 Brawley CA 92227-2246*

COLACE, WILLIAM M., food products executive; b. 1955. With Colace Bros., El Centro, Calif., 1980-83; v. p., treas. Five Crowns, Inc., Brawley, Calif., 1987—. Office: Five Crowns Inc 551 W Main St Ste 2 Brawley CA 92227-2246*

COLANGELO, JERRY JOHN, professional basketball team executive; b. Chicago Heights, Ill., Nov. 20, 1939; s. Larry and Sue (Drancek) C.; m. Joan E. Helmich, Jan. 20, 1961; children: Kathy, Kristen, Bryan. B.A., U. Ill., 1962. Partner House of Charles, Inc., 1962-63; assoc. D.O. Klein & Assocs., 1964-65; dir. merchandising Chgo. Bulls basketball club, 1966-68; gen. mgr. Phoenix Suns basketball club, 1968-87, now also exec. v.p., until 1987, pres., chief exec. officer, 1987—. Mem. Basketball Congress Am. (exec. v.p., dir.), Phi Kappa Psi. Republican. Baptist. Clubs: University, Phoenix Execs. Office: Phoenix Suns 201 E Jefferson St Phoenix AZ 85004-2412*

COLBERT, GEORGE CLIFFORD, college administrator; b. Cedar Rapids, Iowa, Mar. 22, 1949; s. Louis Charles and Betty Mae Colbert; m. Marion Patricia Clark, Aug. 4, 1973; children: Bridget, Dontá. AA, Kirkwood C.C., Cedar Rapids, 1972; BA in Criminal Justice and Social Work, Mt. Mercy Coll., Cedar Rapids, 1974; MEd in Leadership Edn., No. Ariz. U., 1993. Coord. continuing edn. Kirkwood C.C., Cedar Rapids, 1978-89; dir. student svcs., dir. continuing edn. Ctrl. Ariz. Coll., Apache Junction, 1989-95; student svc. assoc. Ctrl. Ariz. Coll., Coolidge, 1995—; part-time instr. Ctrl. Ariz. Coll., various locations, 1990—, chmn. enhancement of program offerings, Apache Junction, 1993—; notary public, Ariz., 1993—. Rsch. participant: (book) Profile/Status (Blk) Males in Arizona, 1992, Impace and Challenges of (Blk) Policy Makers in Arizona, 1991. Mem. commn. on excellence in edn. Mesa (Ariz.) C.C., 1993—; mem. nat. coun. instl. adminstrs. All State Cmty. Colls., Ariz., 1990—; v.p. Cedar Rapids br. NAACP, 1978-80; continuing edn. chmn. Kirkwood C.C., 1986-87; founder, chmn. higher ednl. minority scholarship, Cedar Rapids, 1978; vol. probation officer Juvenile Ct., Cedar Rapids, 1974; vol. dept. pub. safety Apache Junction Police Dept., Ariz., 1990. With USMC, 1967-69. Recipient Outstanding Cmty. Svc. award Apache Junction Unified Sch. Dist., 1989, 90, Vol. award Iowa Gov. terry Branstad, 1987. Mem. Am. Vets. Assn. (life mem. Phoenix chpt. Post 15). Home: 6228 E Covina St Mesa AZ 85205

COLBURN, GENE LEWIS, insurance and industrial consultant; b. Bismarck, N.D., July 12, 1932; s. Lewis William and Olga Alma (Feland) C.; PhD, City U. L.A., 1983. Pres., gen. mgr. Multiple Lines Ins. Agy., Auburn, Wash., 1953-79; ins. and risk mgmt. cons., Auburn, Wash., 1980—; pres. Feland Safe Deposit Corp.; bd. dirs. Century Svc. Corp. subs. Capital Savs. Bank, Olympia, Wash.; mem. exec. com. Great Repub. Life Ins. Co., Portland, Oreg., 1971-75; mem. Wash. State Ins. Commrs. Test Devel. Com., 1986-87. cons. indsl. risk mgmt. Councilperson Auburn City, 1982-85; mayor-pro tem, City of Auburn, 1984; co-incorporator, chmn. bd. SE Community Alcohol Ctr., 1971-75; mem. Wash. State Disaster Assistance Coun., 1981-82, founding mem.; pres. Valley Cities Mental Health Ctr., 1980; mem. instn. rev. com. Auburn Gen. Hosp., 1978—; prin. trustee Dr. R. B. Bramble Med. Rsch. Found., 1980-90; bd. dirs. Wash. Assn. Chs.

(Luth. Ch. in Am.), Asian Refugee Resettlement Mgmt. div., 1981-83, Columbia Luth. Home, Seattle, 1985-87, Wash. Law Enforcement Officers and Fire Fighter's Pension Disability Bd., Auburn, 1980-84. Cert. ins. counselor, 1978. Recipient Disting. Alumni award Green River Community Coll., 1982. Fellow Acad. Producer Ins. Studies (charter); mem. Internat. Platform Assn. Lodge: Auburn Lions (past pres.). Office: 720 L St SE Auburn WA 98002-6219

COLBY, BARBARA DIANE, interior designer, consultant; b. Chgo., Dec. 6, 1932; d. Raymond R. and Mertyl Shirley (Jackson) C.; 1 son, Lawrence James. Student Wright Jr. Coll., 1950, Art Inst. Chgo., UCLA. Owner, F.L.S., Los Angeles, 1971-77; ptnr. Ambiance Inc., Los Angeles, 1976-77; owner Barbara Colby, Ltd., Los Angeles, 1977-81; bus. adminstr. Internat. Soc. Interior Designers, Los Angeles, 1982—; owner Chromanetics, Glendale, Calif., 1981—; instr. Otis/Parsons Sch. Design, Los Angeles Fashion Inst. Design and Merchandising; dir. color Calif. Coll. Interior Design, Costa Mesa, Calif., 1987; also lectr. in field. Author: Color and Light Influences and Impact, 1990; contbg. editor Giftware News. Instr. L.A. County Regional Occupation Program, 1990-94; tng. cons. United Edn. Inst., 1994—. Recipient award for Best Children's Room, Chgo. Furniture Show, 1969, award Calif. Design Show '76, 1976. Mem. Am. Soc. Interior Designers (cert.), Color Mktg. Group of U.S. Author: Color and Light: Influences and Impact, 1990; contbr. articles to profl. jours. Office: Colby Handcrafted Miniatures 245 W Loraine St Ste 309 Glendale CA 91202-1849

COLBY, BILL, artist; b. Beloit, Kans., Jan. 8, 1927; s. Albert Warren and Nellie Dell (Lawson) C.; m. Gertrude Ann Bednorz, June 19, 1955; children: Andrea Lee, Sara Louise, Lisa Lorraine, Celia Dee. BA, U. Denver, 1950; MA, U. Ill., 1954. Art tchr. Portland (Oreg.) High Schs., 1950-53, 55-56; prof. art U. Puget Sound, Tacoma, 1956-89; trustee Tacoma Art Mus., 1962-94; lectr. Wash. Commn. of Humanities, Seattle, 1987-90; bd. dirs. Kittredge Gallery, Tacoma, 1958-66, 74-89. Exhibited in shows in Phila., San Francisco, N.Y.C., Pasadena, Wichita, Seattle, Portland, others; represnted in permanent collections at Tacoma Art Mus., Portland Art Mus., Henry Art Gallery at U. Wash., Seattle, Library of Congress, Washington, Wash. State Hist. Mus., Tacoma, Seattle Art Mus., Bradley U. Art Ctr., Peoria, Ill., Wichita Art Mus., First Interstate Bank, Portland, Wells Fargo Bank, Portland, Salishan Lodge, Glenden, Oreg., Weyerhaeuser Corp., Federal Way, Wash., Seafirst Bank, Seattle, others. Pres., treas., bd. dirs. Campfire, Tacoma, 1967-73; mem., rschr. City Club, Tacoma. 1986-94; mem. City Urban Waterfront Com., Tacoma, 1989-92; mem. Sister City Com., Japan, 1990-93. Served to sgt. U.S. Army, 1945-47, Germany. Recipient Civic Achievement award Allied Arts of Tacoma, 1964, others. Mem. Tacoma Arts and Crafts Assn. (pres., bd. dirs.), Puget Sound Sumi Artists (b.p., bd. dirs.), N.W. Print Coun. (bd. dirs.). Home: 3706 N Union Ave Tacoma WA 98407-6141

COLE, CHARLES EDWARD, lawyer, former state attorney general; b. Yakima, Wash., Oct. 10, 1927; married; 3 children. BA, Stanford U., 1950, LLB, 1953. Law clk. Vets. Affairs Commn. Territory of Alaska, Juneau, 1954, Territorial Atty. Gen.'s Office, Fairbanks, Alaska, 1955-56, U.S. Dist. Ct. Alaska, Fairbanks, 1955-56; city magistrate City of Fairbanks, 1957-58; pvt. practice law, 1957-90; atty. gen. State of Alaska, 1990-94; pvt. law comml. litigation, 1995—; profl. baseball player, Stockton, Calif. and Twin Falls, Idaho, summers of 1950, 51, 53. With U.S. Army, 1946-47. Mem. Calif. State Bar, Washington State Bar Assn., Alaska Bar Assn. Office: Law Dept State of Alaska Office of Atty Gen PO Box 110300 Juneau AK 99811-0300 also: Law Offices of Charles E Cole 406 Cushman St Fairbanks AK 99701-4632*

COLE, DAVID MACAULAY, editor, publisher, consultant, writer; b. Richmond, Calif., Feb. 17, 1954; s. Fredrick George and Norma Ann (Caudle) C. Attended, San Francisco State U., 1972-76. Exec. editor, gen. mgr. Feed/Back Mag., San Francisco, 1974-83; asst. editor Rolling Stone Mag., San Francisco, 1976-77; copy & news editor San Francisco Examiner, 1977-80, sys. editor, 1980-87, asst. mng. editor, 1987-89; cons. The Cole Group, San Francisco, 1989—; editor, publisher The Cole Papers, San Francisco, 1991—; contbg. editor Presstime Mag., Vienna, Va., 1994—, Newspapers & Tech., Denver, 1993-94, Asian Newspaper Focus, Hong Kong, 1995—, Seybold Report On Publishing Sys., Media, Pa. 1996—, Publish Mag., San Francisco, 1997—; fellow Seybold Foster City, Calif. Seminars. Editor: Cole's Guide to Publishing Systems, 1994—. Trustee Jr. Statesman Found., San Mateo, Calif., 1996—. Fellow Seybold Seminars; mem. Nat. Press Photographers Assn., Soc. Newspaper Design, Soc. Profl. Journalists. Office: The Cole Papers 2590 Greenwich St Ste 9 San Francisco CA 94123-3333

COLE, DERMOT MATTHEW, newspaper columnist, historian; b. Allentown, Pa., Sept. 23, 1953; s. William Patrick and Anne Cole; m. Debbie Carter, Aug. 4, 1980; children: Connor, Aileen, Anne. BA, U. Alaska, 1979. Journalist AP, Seattle, 1988-89; journalist Fairbanks (Alaska) Daily News-Miner, 1976-88, editor, columnist, 1989—. Author: Frank Barr: Bush Pilot in Alaska and the Yukon, 1986, Hard Driving: The 1908 Auto Race from New York to Paris, 1991. Fellow U. Mich., 1986-87. Roman Catholic. Office: Fairbanks Daily News-Miner 210 N Cushman St Fairbanks AK 99701-2832

COLE, GEORGE WILLIAM, foundation administrator; b. Denver, Oct. 1, 1950; s. Herbert Merril and Frances Jane (Buchanan) C. Grad. high sch., Denver. Cert. real estate investment counselor. Owner Jayhawker Investment Co., Inc., 1965--95; pres. Herb Cole Real Estate, Inc., Denver, 1969-95; bd. dirs. Cos. West Group, Inc., Denver, Jayhawker Investment Co., Denver; cons. Bus. Concepts Corp., Denver, 1981-84, Centennial Growth Equities Corp., 1981-82; pres. Co. West Group, 1982-93, exec. dir. Cole Found., 1993—. Author: Real Estate Investing for the Future, 1981, Mom: A Study in Grieving Grace, 1990; pub.: (newlsetter) Encouraging Words, 1986-92. Deacon Baptist Ch., 1987; bd. dirs. World Wide Leadership coun., Compa Food Mins., others. Grace Lay Min. Sch. fellow. Republican. Home and Office: 3270 E Virginia Ave Denver CO 80209-3523

COLE, JEAN ANNE, artist; b. Greeley, Colo., Jan. 30, 1947; d. Philip Owen and Rose Margaret (Maser) Dahl; m. Nelson Bruce Cole, June 22, 1968; children: Ashley Paige, Travis Allyn. BA in Interior Design, U. Calif., Berkeley, 1968. Interior designer K.S. Wilshire Design, L.A., 1969-70; interior designer Milton Swimmer Planning & Design, Beverly Hills, Calif., 1970-73, Denver, 1973-75; tchr. watercolor workshops, 1991—. Exhibited in numerous shows at Foothills Art Ctr., Golden, Colo., 1989, 91, 93, 94, 96, Brea (Calif.) Civic and Cultural Ctr., 1989, 90, Nevile Pub. Mus., Green Bay, Wis., 1990, 93, Nat. Watercolor Soc., 1991, Denver Mus. Natural History, 1991, Pikes Peak Ctr. Performing Arts, Colorado Springs, Colo., 1992, Colo. History Mus., 1992, 93, 94, 95, 96, Kneeland Gallery, Las Vegas, Nev., 1993, 94, 95, Salmagundi Club, N.Y.C., 1994, 97, Met. State Coll. Ctr. for Visual Arts, Denver, 1994; contbr. articles to mags.; artist greetings cards Leanin'Tree. Recipient 2d pl. watercolor award Art Zone Regional Show, 1988, 1st pl. watercolor award Colo. ARtists Convention, 1989, 1st pl., hon. mention People's Choice awards Denver Allied Artists, 1989, Best of Show award Pikes Peak Watercolor Invitational, 1992, Quaintance award Rocky Mountain Nat. Watermedia Exhibit, 1993, Paul Schwartz Meml. award Am. Watercolor Soc., 1994, Founder's award Watercolor West XXVI Ann. Nat. Transparent Watercolor Exhbn., Calif., 1994. Mem. Nat. Watercolor Soc., Colo. Watercolor Soc. (pres., treas., award of merit 1993). Republican. Home: 78 Ash St Denver CO 80220

COLE, LECIL, agricultural products company executive. With Puna (Hi.) Sugar; pres. Hawaiian Sweet, Inc., Keaau, Hi., 1991—. Office: Hawaiian Sweet Inc Milo St Keaau HI 96749*

COLE, LEE ARTHUR, new product development executive; b. Pitts., May 2, 1953; m. Loni Kay Chestor, May ll, 1985. BS, Indiana U. Pa., 1975; PhD, Dartmouth Coll., 1979. Postdoctoral fellow physics dept. Tulane U., New Orleans, 1979-8l; project mgr. Solar Energy Rsch. Inst., Dept. Energy, Golden, Colo., 198l-85; program mgr. Solid State Elec. div. Honeywell Co., Colorado Springs, Colo., 1985-87; mgr. R&D Unisys CAD-CAM, Inc., Boulder, Colo., 1987-91; v.p. rsch. and devel. Graftek, Inc., a Unisys Co., Boulder, 1991-92; dir. product devel. Hunter Douglas, Broomfield, Colo., 1992-94, dir. mkt. rsch., 1992—; founder, ptnr. Cole-Chestor & Co. Contbr. articles to profl. jours. Mem. Am. Phys. Soc. Home: 29937 Gigi Dr Evergreen CO 80439-7213 Office: Hunter Douglas Inc One Duette Way Broomfield CO 80020

COLE, LEON MONROE, retired senior government executive; b. Dallas, Apr. 4, 1933; s. Kenneth McCutchen and Cacy Ann (Robbins) C.; m. Jeannie Campbell Tudor, Apr. 1, 1961; children: Kenneth Tudor, Kevin Robbins, Susanna Ellis. BSCE magna cum laude, So. Meth. U., 1955; MSE, U. Wash., 1961; MCP, Harvard U., 1963, PhD, 1965. Asst. prof. planning and transp. Harvard U., 1965-67, assoc. prof., 1967-69; staff dir. U.S. Dept. HUD, Washington, 1967-68, div. dir., 1968-69; prof., dir. grad. program in planning U. Tex., Austin, 1969-73; sr. specialist transp. Congl. Rsch. Svc. Libr. Congress, Washington, 1973-93, chief econs. div., 1975-93, ret., 1993; chmn. group I coun. NAS, NRC, Transp. Rsch. Bd., Washington, 1978-81, chmn. various coms. on transp. policy and rsch., 1970-85. Co-author, editor: Tomorrow's Transportation: New Systems for the Urban Future, 1969; author: Economic Policymaking in U.S. Government, 1988, Transportation in the United States: Perspectives on Federal Policies, 1989, Economizing Transportation Responsibilities in the Federal Government, 1993; contbr. chpts. to books and articles to profl. jours. Commr. Tex. State Urban Devel. Commn., Austin, 1970-72; chmn. Austin City Bd. Environ. Quality, 1972-73; pres. bd. dirs. La Luz Landowners Assn., Albuquerque, 1997. Capt. USNR, ret. Recipient Meritorious Achievement award HUD, 1969, Libr. of Congress, 1993; Spl. Resolution of Commendation City of Austin, 1974; Resident fellow Harvard U., 1962-64. Mem. ASCE, Am. Econ. Assn., Am. Inst. Cert. Planners, Am. Planning Assn., Sigma Xi, Chi Epsilon, Sigma Tau. Democrat. Home: 3 Berm St NW Albuquerque NM 87120-1802

COLE, MALVIN, neurologist, educator; b. N.Y.C., Mar. 21, 1933; s. Harry and Sylvia (Firman) C.; A.B. cum laude, Amherst Coll., 1953; M.D. cum laude, Georgetown U. Med. Sch., 1957; m. Susan Kugel, June 20, 1954; children: Andrew James, Douglas Gowers. Intern, Seton Hall Coll. Medicine, Jersey City Med. Ctr., 1957-58; resident Boston City Hosps., 1958-60; practice medicine specializing in neurology, Montclair and Glen Ridge, N.J., Montville, N.J., 1963-72, Casper, Wyo., 1972—; teaching fellow Harvard Med. Sch., 1958-60; Research fellow Nat. Hosp. for Nervous Diseases, St. Thomas Hosp., London, Eng., 1960-61; instr. Georgetown U. Med. Sch., 1961-63; clin. assoc. prof. neurology N.J. Coll. Medicine, Newark, 1963-72, acting dir. neurology, 1965-72; assoc. prof. clin. neurology U. Colo. Med. Sch., 1973-88, clin. prof. 1988—; mem. staff Wyo. Med. Ctr., Casper, U. Hosp., Denver. Served to capt. M.C., AUS, 1961-63. Licensed physician, Mass., N.Y., Calif., N.J., Colo., Wyo.; diplomate Am. Bd. Psychiatry and Neurology, Nat. Bd. Med. Examiners. Fellow ACP, Am. Acad. Neurology, Royal Soc. Medicine; mem. Assn. Research Nervous and Mental Disease, Acad. Aphasia, Am. Soc. Neuroimaging, Internat. Soc. Neuropsychology, Harveian Soc. London, Epilepsy Found. Am., Am. Epilepsy Soc., Am. EEG Soc., N.Y. Acad. Sci., Osler Soc. London, Alpha Omega Alpha. Contbr. articles to profl. jours. Office: 246 S Washington St Casper WY 82601-2921

COLE, RICHARD GEORGE, public administrator; b. Irvington, N.J., Mar. 11, 1948; s. Warner W. and Laurel M. (Wilson) C. AS in Computer Sci., Control Data Inst., Anaheim, Calif., 1972; BA in Sociology with high honor, Calif. State U., Los Angeles, 1974; MA in Social Ecology, U. Calif., Irvine, 1976; postgrad., So. Oreg. State Coll., 1979. Computer operator Zee Internat., Gardena, Calif., 1971; teaching asst. U. Calif., Irvine, 1974-75; planner Herman Kimmel & Assocs., Newport Beach, Calif., 1976-78; program analyst The Job Council, Medford, Oreg., 1980-81, compliance officer, 1981-82, mgr. adminstrv. svcs., 1982—; instr. credential Calif. C.C.; chmn. bd. trustees Job Coun. Pension Trust, Medford, 1982—; mem. curriculum adv. com. Rogue C.C., Grants Pass, Oreg., 1986; mgr. computer project State of Oreg., Salem, 1983-84; mem. Oreg. Occupational Info. Coordinating Com., Salem, 1982-84. Pres. bd. trustees Vector Control Dist., Jackson County, Oreg., 1985, treas., 1986, bd. dirs., 1984-87, mem. budget com., 1988—, sec., 1988-89; cand. bd. dirs. Area Edn. Dist., Jackson County, 1981; treas. Job Svc. Employer Com., Jackson County, 1987— (Spl. Svc. award 1991); dir. fin. joint pub. venture System Devel. Project, Salem, Oreg., 1986-89; mem. adv. bd. New Jobs Planning, Medford, Oreg., 1987-88, Fin. Audit and Risk Mgmt. Task Force, 1987-91, chm., 1989-90. Fellow LaVerne Noyes, U. Calif., Irvine, 1974; Dr. Paul Doehring Found. scholar, Glendale, Calif., 1973; Computer Demonstration grantee State of Oreg., Salem, 1983; recipient Award of Fin. Reporting Achievement Govt. Fin. Officers Assn. of U.S. and Can., 1989-90, Fin. Ops. recognition Vector Control Dist., Jackson County, Oreg., 1990, Nat. 2d Pl. Chpt. award Jackson County Job Svc. Employer Com., 1989, Oreg. Job Svc. Employer Com. Stat award, 1991, Oreg. Individual Citation award Internat. Assn. Profls. in Employment Security, 1993. Mem. Soc. for Human Resources Mgmt., Assn. So. Oreg. Pub. Adminstrs., Oreg. Employment and Tng. Assn., Pacific N.W. Personnel Mgmt. Assn. (chpt. treas. 1985-87, orgnl. liaison dir. 1988-89, Appreciation award 1985), Govt. Fin. Officers Assn., Oreg. Mcpl. Fin. Officers assn., The Nature Conservancy. Home: 575 Morey Rd Talent OR 97540-9725 Office: The Job Council 673 Market St Medford OR 97504-6125

COLE, SHERRIE, communications technician; b. Medford, Oreg., Aug. 20, 1956; d. James Pettigrew and Louise McBee; m. Steven Frison, Sept. 12, 1976 (div. Dec. 1983); m. Gene Kalar, Oct. 1, 1994; children: Whitney, Sam. Grad. h.s., Portland, Oreg. Cert. elec. journeyman ltd. energy. Chmn. reflection com. PTA, 1996—. Mem. Wy'east Artisan's Guild (v.p. 1994, pres. 1995-96), Portland Bead Soc. Home: 65440 E Alpine Way Rhododendron OR 97049

COLE, TERRI LYNN, organization administrator; b. Tucson, Dec. 28, 1951; m. James R. Cole II. Student, U. N.Mex., 1975-80; cert., Inst. Orgn. Mgmt., 1985. Cert. chamber exec. With SunWest Bank, Albuquerque, 1971-74, employment adminstr., 1974-76, communications dir., 1976-78; pub. info. dir. Albuquerque C. of C., 1978-81, gen. mgr., 1981-83, pres., 1983—; pres. N.Mex. C. of C. Execs. Assn., 1986-87, bd. dirs., 1980—; bd. regents Inst. for Orgn. Mgmt., Stanford U., 1988—, vice chmn., 1990-91, chmn., 1991; bd. dirs. Hosp. Home Health, Inc. Recipient Bus. Devel. award Expn. Mgmt. Inc., 1985, Women on Move award YWCA, 1986; named one of Outstanding Women of Am., 1984. Mem. Am. C. of C. Execs. Assn. (chmn. elect bd. 1992—). Republican. Office: Greater Albuquerque C of C PO Box 25100 Albuquerque NM 87125-0100

COLE, VERLA FAYE, music educator; b. Norwood, Mo., Oct. 13, 1945; d. Floyd Leon and Edna Cled (Thompson) C. BA, Coll. of Ozark, 1967; studied with Anna Kaskas, Eastman Sch. Music, 1967. Cert. tchr. Tchr. Ava (Mo.) Pub. Sch., 1968-82, Crystal Cathedral Acad., Garden Grove, Calif., 1982-88; pvt. tchr., performer Newport Beach, Calif., 1989—; owner Tsid-Kenu Prodns., Newport Beach, 1991—. Performances in Sweden and Japan, 1988; writer, prodr., performer album Grand Hotel, 1990, video Choices, 1989. Mrs. W. Alton Jones scholar, 1967. Home: PO Box 952 Balboa CA 92661

COLE, VERNA JO, educator; b. Greeley, Colo., Sept. 13, 1933; d. Bennie Alfred and Leah June Brooks; m. Donald Kennedy Cole, Aug. 28, 1954;p 1 child, Sherryl Lynne. BA, Calif. State U., 1962, MA, 1972; EdD, U. So. Calif., L.A., 1989. Calif. state credentials adminstrv. svcs., gen. elem., jr. high, reading specialist. Tchr. Sacramento City Unified Sch. Dist., 1962-77, elem. prin., 1977-80; elem./mid. prin. San Juan Unified Sch. Dist., Sacramento, 1980-83; area III supt. Sacramento City Unified Sch. Dist., 1983-93; spl. cons. math., engring., sci. Calif. Sch. Leadership, Sacramento, 1993—; chairperson Sacramento City Coun. Edn. Task Force, 1984-89; chairperson, bd. mem. Capitol Ctr. Math., Engring., Sci., Sacramento, 1983—; facilitator Sch. Leadership Team, 1988—; bd. mem. Women in Ednl. Leadership, Sacramento, 1983-88. Coord. Mello Roos Bond, Sacramento City, 1984; vol. Christmas in April, Sacramento, 1996; bd. mem. Jr. Achievement Adv. Com., 1979; Chairperson bd. ATC Adminstrn. Tng. Ctr., 1989. Recipient Regional Merit award Calif. Sch. Leadership Acad., State of Calif., 1989, Founder's award Math., Engring. Sci., Sacramento, 1993; named Calif. Adminstr. of Yr. Calif. Assn. Ednl. Office Profls., 1993, Finalist Woman of Yr. YWCA, Sacramento, 1996. Mem. U. So. Calif. Alumnae, Calif. State U. Alumnae, Soroptimist Internat. (pres. 1991-92, 96—, Phi Delta Kappa.

COLE, WILLIAM L., lawyer; b. L.A., May 13, 1952. AB magna cum laude, U. Calif., Irvine, 1974; JD, Stanford U., 1977. Bar: Calif. 1977. Atty. Mitchell, Silberberg & Knupp, L.A., mng. ptnr., 1991—. Mem. ABA, State Bar Calif., Los Angeles County Bar Assn. (mem. exec. com. labor law sect. 1989-90), Phi Beta Kappa, Order of Coif. Office: Mitchell Silberberg & Knupp 11377 W Olympic Blvd Los Angeles CA 90064-1625

COLEMAN, ARLENE FLORENCE, nurse practitioner; b. Braham, Minn., Apr. 8, 1926; d. William and Christine (Judin) C.; m. John Dunkerken, May 30, 1987. Diploma in nursing, U. Minn., 1947, BS, 1953; MPH, Loma Linda U., 1974. RN, Calif. Operating room scrub nurse Calif. Luth. Hosp., L.A., 1947-48; indsl. staff nurse Good Samaritan Hosp., L.A., 1948-49; staff nurse Passavant Hosp., Chgo., 1950-51; student health nurse Moody Bible Inst., Chgo., 1950-51; staff nurse St. Andrews Hosp., Mpls., 1951-53; pub. health nurse Bapt. Gen. Conf. Bd. of World Missions, Ethiopia, Africa, 1954-66; staff pub. health nurse County of San Bernadino, Calif., 1966-68, sr. pub. health nurse, 1968-73, pediatric nurse practitioner, 1973—. Contbr. articles to profl. jours. Mem. bd. dist. missions Bapt. Gen. Conf., Calif., 1978-84; mem. adv. coun. Kaiser Hosp., Fontana, Calif., 1969-85, Bethel Sem. West, San Diego, 1987—; bd. dirs. Casa Verdugo Retirement Home, Hemet, Calif., 1985—; active Calvary Bapt. Ch., Redlands, Calif., 1974—; mem. S.W. Bapt. Conf. Social Ministries, 1993—. With USPHS, 1944-47. Calif. State Dept. Health grantee, 1973. Fellow Nat. Assn. Pediatric Nurse Assocs. and Practitioners; mem. Calif. Nurses Assn. (state nursing coun. 1974-76). Democrat.

COLEMAN, BARBARA MCREYNOLDS, artist; b. Omaha, May 5, 1956; d. Zachariah Aycock and Mary Barbara (McCulloh) McR.; m. Stephen Dale Dent, Mar. 12, 1983 (div. Dec. 20, 1992); children: Madeleine Barbara, Matthew Stephen; m. Ross Coleman, Oct. 16, 1993; 1 child, Marie Jeanne Coleman. Student, U. N.Mex., 1979, MA in Community and Regional Planning, 1984. Artist, 1986-92; lectr. U. N.Mex. Sch. of Architecture, Albuquerque, 1979-82, 91—; assoc. planner, urban designer City of Albuquerque Planning Div., 1982-84; city planner, urban designer City of Albuquerque, N.Mex. Redevel. Div., 1984-88; cons. City of Albuquerque Redevel. Dept., 1987-88; urban design cons. Southwest Land Rsch., Albuquerque, 1991. Columnist for "Kids and Art", 1990-92; author: Coors Corridor Plan (The Albuquerque Conservation Assn. urban design award 1984), Electric Facilities Plan, Downtown Core Revitalization Strategy and Sector Development Plan; contbg. author: Anasazi Architecture and American Design, 1994; contbr. articles to profl. publs.; exhibited in shows at Dartmouth St. Gallery, Chimayo (N.Mex.) Trade and Mercantile, JoAnne Chappel Gallery, San Francisco, Southwest Arts Festival, Albuquerque. Vol. art tchr. Chaparral Elem. Sch., Roosevelt Mid. Sch., Albuquerque, 1989-92. Recipient First Pl. for Pastels, 20th Ann. Nat. Small Painting Exhibition, N.Mex. Art League, 1991, Best of Show awards Pastel Soc. of N.Mex., 1990, Award of Merit, Pastel Soc. of S.W., 1989, TACA award for Urban Design, 1984. Mem. Pastel Soc. of Am., Pastel Soc. N.Mex. (pres. 1991-92). Democrat. Episcopalian. Office: U NMex Sch Architecture Albuquerque NM 87131

COLEMAN, DALE LYNN, electrical engineer; b. Topeka, June 17, 1958; s. Dale R. Coleman and Linda C. (Parks) Meiergerd; m. Patricia Bermudez, Nov. 20, 1982; 1 child, Athena C. AS in Electronic Engring. Tech. with honors, Cleve. Inst. Electronics, 1987, BS in Electronic Engring. Tech. summa cum laude, 1993. Cert. quality engr., 1996; regulatory affairs cert., 1996. Electronic engring. technician Litton G & CS, L.A., 1979-82; sr. electronics technician Cedars-Sinai Med. Ctr., L.A., 1982-85; svc. engr. Litton AMS, San Diego, 1985-86; elect. engr. tech. IMED Corp. R & D, San Diego, 1987-93, regulatory affairs engr., 1993—; participant Space Life Scis. mission Space Sta. Freedom, NASA; project mgr. Internat. Space Sta. Infusion Pump Project, 1995—. Co-author: The Art of Hsin Hsing Yee Ti Kenpo Kung Fu, 1991; contbr. articles to various publs. Active UN Assn., 1979—, bd. dirs., 1994—; sr. officer USCG Aux., 1980—, aviator flotilla comdr., 1994-95; USCG liaison U.S. Naval Sea Cadet Corps., NAS Miramar, 1985—. With USN, 1976-79. Recipient Outstanding Achievement Gold medal U.S. Dept. Transp; named Outstanding Citizen Exch. Club, 1989, Outstanding Grad. Cleve. Inst. Electronics, 1990. Mem. AAAS, IEEE, Am. Soc. for Quality Control, Planetary Soc., Nat. Space Soc., Regulatory Affairs Profl. Soc., Alpha Beta Kappa. Office: IMED Corp R & D 9775 Businesspark Ave San Diego CA 92131-1699

COLEMAN, DONALD GENE, education educator; b. Ft. Wayne, Ind., June 20, 1934; s. Clarence R. and Ruth F. (Wise) C.; m. Eileen E. Hoffman, Apr. 25, 1959; children: Suzanne Eileen, Jessica Ruth. BS, Ind. U., 1965; MA, St. Francis Coll., 1967; EdD, Ball State U., 1973. Tchr. Ft. Wayne (Ind.) Schs., 1965-67; asst. prof. Ind. U., Ft. Wayne, 1967-74; prof. N.E. Mo. State U., Kirksville, 1974-86, San Diego State U., 1986-88, Calif. State U., Fresno, 1988—; cons. in field. Author: Slams, 1985. With U.S. Army, 1954-56. Danforth Found. grantee, St. Louis, 1990, 91, 92. Mem. Am. Assn. Sch. Adminstrs., Nat. Coun. Profl. Edn. Adminstrs., Nat. Assn. Elem. Sch. Prins., Calif. Profl. Edn. Adminstrn., Assn. Calif. Sch. Adminstrs., Phi Delta Kappa. Office: Calif State U Sch Edn Fresno CA 93740

COLEMAN, HENRY JAMES, JR., management educator, consultant; b. Cleve., Nov. 28, 1947; s. Henry James and Kathryn Adele (Ketchum) C.; m. Sharon Ann Boothe, Sept. 12, 1971 (div. Jan. 1975). AB, Dartmouth Coll., 1969, MBA, 1970; PhD, U. Calif., Berkeley, 1978. Employment mgr. Lima (Ohio) Meml. Hosp., 1977-78; strategic planner NCR Corp., Dayton, Ohio, 1980-81; vis. asst. prof. Calif. Poly. State U., San Luis Obispo, 1983-85; dean Sch. Mgmt., Columbia Pacific U., San Rafael, Calif., 1985-92; assoc. prof. mgmt. St. Mary's Coll. Calif., Moraga, 1992—; adj. prof. Holy Names Coll., Oakland, Calif., 1987, 90-92; mgmt. cons. Orgn. Dynamics, Berkeley, 1970, Comm. Workers Am., San Francisco, 1971, Exide Corp., Reading, Pa., 1988-89, Retirement Fin. Ctrs. Am., Las Vegas, Nev., 1996. Contbr. articles to profl. jours. Nat. Def. Grad. fellow, 1971. Mem. Western Acad. Mgmt., Phi Beta Kappa. Episcopalian. Office: Saint Marys Coll Calif 1928 Saint Marys Rd Moraga CA 94575

COLEMAN, J.D., author; b. Spokane, Wash., Dec. 16, 1930; s. Thomas Coleman and Lois Leona (LeBreche) Magar; m. Madeline Y. Young, Sept. 14, 1952; children: Kathleen, Darrell, Roger, Michelle, Joseph. BA in Journalism, U. Montana, 1956; postgrad. mass comms., U. Ind., 1968. Reporter Columbia Basin News, Pasco, Wash., 1956-58; news dir. KQTE Radio, Missoula, Mont., 1958-61, WDZ Radio, Decatur, Ill., 1961-63; commd. lt. U.S. Army, 1963, advanced through grades to lt. col., retired, 1979; dir. comms. Atlanta C. of C., 1980-83; owner Creative Comms., Atlanta, 1983-86; dir. pub. affairs Ga. Dept. Pub. Safety, Atlanta, 1987-90; pub. affairs officer Flathead Nat. Forest, Kalispell, Mont., 1991-97. Author: Pleieu: The Dawn of Helicopter Warfare in Vietnam, 1987, Incursion: From America's Chokehold on North Vietnamese Lifelines to the Sacking of Cambodian Sanctuaries, 1990. Active pub. rels. and mktg. coms. numerous civic and charitable orgns., Atlanta, 1980-86; mem. Nat. Resources Com. Kalispell C. of C., Mont., 1991—. Decorated Silver Star, U.S. Army, Vietnam, 1966, Legion of Merit, 1969, 71, 79; recipient mng. editor's award, Assoc. Press, Missoula, Mont. 1959, Grand award Total Comms., Am. C. of C., Atlanta, 1981. Mem. Pub. Rels. Soc. Am. (accredited pub. rels. profl.). Office: Flathead Nat Forest 222 Lakeshore Dr Kalispell MT 59901-5759

COLEMAN, LEON HORN, real estate investor, factor; b. L.A., Jan. 29, 1931; s. Jack L. and Esther P. Coleman. BS, UCLA, 1953, JD, 1961. Writer, editor Commerce Clearing House, San Francisco, 1966-73; writer, editor Matthew Bender, Inc., San Francisco, 1973-90, author, 1990-93; pres. Leeco Investments, Beaverton, Oreg., 1975—. Author: (chpts.) California Legal Forms, 1982-90, New Jersey Tax Service, 1982-90, Texas Tax Service, 1982-90. Founder, Log Cabin of Oreg., Portland area, 1990; mem. Rep. Party Ctrl. Com., Washington, 1990—; co-founder Oreg. Rep. Mainstream Com., Portland area, 1995; mem. Bull Bridge Acad., 1993; participant Basic Rights Oreg., 1994—. Staff sgt. USAF, 1953-58. Lutheran.

COLEMAN, LEWIS WALDO, bank executive; b. San Francisco, Jan. 2, 1942; s. Lewis V. and Virginia Coleman; m. Susan G.; children: Michelle, Gregory, Nancy, Peter. B.A., Stanford U., 1965. With Bank Calif., San Francisco, 1965-73; with Wells Fargo Bank, San Francisco, 1973-86, exec. v.p., chmn. credit policy com., until 1986; vice chmn., CFO, treas. Bank Am., San Francisco, 1986-95; sr. mng. dir. Montgomery Securites, San Francisco, 1995—.

COLEMAN, ROGER DIXON, bacteriologist; b. Rockwell, Iowa, Jan. 18, 1915; s. Major C. and Hazel Ruth Coleman; A.B., UCLA, 1937; postgrad. Balliol Coll., Oxford (Eng.) U., 1944; MS, U. So. Calif., 1952, PhD, 1957; m. Lee Aden Skov, Jan. 1, 1978. Sr. laboratorian Napa (Calif.) State Hosp., 1937-42; dir. Long Beach (Calif.) Clin. Lab., 1946-86, pres., 1980-86; mem. Calif. State Clin. Lab. Commn., 1953-57. Served as officer AUS, 1942-46. Diplomate Am. Bd. Bioanalysts. Mem. Am. Assn. Bioanalysts, Am. Assn. Clin. Chemists, Am. Soc. Microbiologists, Am. Chem. Soc., Am. Venereal Disease Assn., AAAS (life), Calif. Assn. Bioanalysts (past officer), Med. Research Assn. Calif., Bacteriology Club So. Calif., Sigma Xi, Phi Sigma (past chpt. pres.). Author papers in field. Home: 7 Laguna Woods Dr Laguna Niguel CA 92677-2829 Office: PO Box 7073 Laguna Niguel CA 92607-7073

COLEMAN, RONNY JACK, fire chief; b. Tulsa, May 17, 1940; s. Clifford Harold and Elizabeth Ann (Teter) C.; m. Susan René Calvert, July 18, 1963 (div. Jan. 1971); children: Lisa René, Christopher Alan; m. Marie Katherine McCarthy, Nov. 18, 1972. AS in Fire Sci., Rancho Santiago Coll., 1971; BS in Polit. Sci., Calif. State U., Fullerton, 1974; MS in vocat. edn., Calif. State U., Long Beach, 1993. Tanker, foreman U.S. Forest Svc., Trabuco, Calif., 1960-62; ops. chief Costa Mesa (Calif.) Fire Dept., 1962-73; fire chief San Clemente (Calif.) Fire Dept., 1973-85, Fullerton (Calif.) Fire Dept., 1985-92; state fire marshal Dept of Forestry& Fire Protection, Sacramento, CA; pres. Phenix Tech., Inc., San Clemente, 1971—. Author: Management of Fire Service Operations, 1975, Fire Truck Toys for Men and Boys, Vols. I and II, 1978, Alpha to Omega: History of Fire Sprinklers, 1983; patentee firefighter helmets. Chmn. Pete Wilson's Fire Brigade, San Clemente, 1990, United Fund Dr., Costa Mesa, 1968. Cpl. USMC, 1957-60. Rayford-Worsted scholar, 1968, Moore scholar, 1961; named Polyurethane Man of Yr. Polyurethane Assn., 1988, Richard Parmalee award Am. Fire Sprinkler Assn., 1989. Mem. Internat. Assn. Fire Chiefs (pres. 1988-89, chmn. Nat. Fire Svcs. Accreditation task force 1988—, v.p. Comite Technique Internat. De Prevention et D'Extinction Du Feu (CTIF)), Nat. Fire Protection Assn., League of Calif. Cities (pres. fire chiefs dept. 1988-89), Orange County Fire Chief's Assn. (pres. 1983-84), Orange County Burn Assn. (bd. dirs. 1990). Republican. Home: 8866 Saint Anthony Ct Elk Grove CA 95624-9443 Office: Dept of Forestry & Fire Protection PO Box 944246 Sacramento CA 94244-2460

COLEMAN-LEVY, JACK ROBIN, photographic laboratory design consultant; b. Bklyn., Mar. 24, 1956; s. Paul and Eileen (Moyal) L.; m. Judith Angell Coleman, May 15, 1982; children: Angella Rose, Benjamin Herschell, Maggie Illana. Tng. mgr. Shelley's Audio, L.A., 1976-79; western regional mktg. dir. Photo Lab Fabrications, Central Islip, N.Y., 1979-88; owner Photolab Innovations, Lancaster, Calif., 1988—. Bd. dirs. Lancaster Cmty. Shelter, 1993-95; chair Beth Knesset Bamidbar Social Action Com., 1991-94; bd. dirs. Beth Knesset Bamidbar Early Childhood Ctr., 1992-94, 95—. Jewish. Office: Photolab Innovations 3328 Monte Carlo Ct Lancaster CA 93536-4844

COLE-MCCULLOUGH, DANIEL, music educator, conductor, clinician; b. Portland, Oreg., May 22, 1946; s. John Virgle and Barbara Jean (Johnson) Cole; m. Maryl Marcelite, Apr. 21, 1979; 1 child, Erika Kristine. BA in Music, Marylhurst Coll., 1984; MMus in Conducting, U. Portland, 1987; MAT, Lewis and Clark Coll., 1996. Cert. music tchr., Oreg., Wash. Music instr., orch. condr. Clark Coll., Vancouver, Wash., 1975-89; music instr. Marylhurst (Oreg.) Coll., 1985-94; prof. music, prof. bands Warner Pacific Coll., Portland, Oreg., 1993—; condr., music dir. Pacific Crest Wind Ensemble, Marylhurst, 1988—; guest condr. Pres.'s USCG Band, 1994, Mercer U. Band, 1996. Author: Mardsan Guitar Method, 1979; editor Oreg. Music Educators Assn. mag., 1994—. With USAR, 1966-73. Recipient Clark County Theater Art award, 1988, Disting. Svc. to Music Edn. award Oreg. Music Educators, 1994. Mem. Music Educators Nat. Conf., Conductors Guild, World Assn. of Symphonic Bands and Ensembles, Coll. Music Soc., Coll. Band Dirs. Nat. Assn. (sec-treas. N.W. divsn.), Assn. Concert Bands, Nat. Band Assn., Am. Legion, Oreg. Music Educators Assn., Oreg. Band Dir. Assn., Wash. Music Educators Assn., Quarter Horse Assn., Phi Mu, Tau Kappa Epsilon. Lutheran. Home: 17806 NE Edmonds Rd Vancouver WA 98682-8607 Office: Warner Pacific Coll Dept Music 2219 SE 68th Ave Portland OR 97215-4026

COLES, BRENT, mayor; m. Julie Allred; 5 children. B in Polit. Sci., Brigham Young U., 1977; MPA, Calif. State U., Long Beach, 1980. Asst. city mgr. City of Boise, city planner, mem. city coun., mayor, 1993—; mem. adv. bd. U.S. Conf. Mayors. Bd. dirs. Assn. Idaho Cities, Boise Future Found., Ada Planning Assn.; co-chair Drug Control Task Force. Address: PO Box 500 Boise ID 83701-0500

COLESSIDES, NICK JOHN, lawyer; b. Kavala, Greece, Jan. 14, 1938; came to U.S., 1958; s. John T. and Maroula (Karakas) C.; m. Sophia Simons Symeonidis, Oct. 5, 1970. BS in Polit. Sci., U. Utah, 1963, MS Polit. Sci., 1967, JD, 1970. Bar: Utah 1970, U.S. Dist. Ct. Utah 1970, U.S. Ct. Appeals (10th cir.) 1970, U.S. Dist. Ct. (so. dist.) Ohio 1975, U.S. Ct. Appeals (9th cir.) 1976. Chief deputy county atty. Salt Lake County (Utah) Atty.'s Office, 1970-74; city atty. West Jordan (Utah) City Atty.'s Office, 1971-78, Park City (Utah) Atty.'s Office, 1976-80; atty. pvt. practice, Salt Lake City, 1970—; bd. dirs. Merrill Lynch Nat. Fin., Salt Lake City Cty. Bd. trustees Greek Orthodox Ch., SaltLake City, 1976, 77, 87, 88. Mem. Assn. Trial Lawyers Am., Utah Trial Lawyers Assn., U. Utah Coll. of Law Alumni Assn. (trustee), Utah State Bar Assn., Salt Lake County Bar Assn., Am. Inn of Ct. VII (master of the bench). Greek Orthodox. Home: 32 Haxton Pl Salt Lake City UT 84102 Office: 466 S 400 E Ste 100 Salt Lake City UT 84111-3325

COLINO, RICHARD RALPH, communications consultant; b. N.Y.C., Feb. 10, 1936; s. Victor and Caroline (Pauline) C.; m. Wilma Jane Rubinstein, June 10, 1962 (div. Oct. 1991); children: Stacey Anne, Geoffrey William. BA, Amherst Coll., 1957; JD, Columbia U., 1960. Assoc. Sargoy & Stein, N.Y.C., 1960-61; atty. FCC, Washington, 1962-64, U.S. Info. Agy., Washington, 1964-65; dir. internat. affairs Communications Satellite Corp., Washington, 1965-68; dir. Europe Communications Satellite Corp., Geneva, 1968-69; asst. v.p. Communications Satellite Corp., Washington, 1969-75, v.p. and gen. mgr. internat. ops., 1975-79; pres., chief exec. officer Continental Home Theatre, Burlingame, Calif., 1979-80, DynaCom Enterprises Ltd., Chevy Chase, Md., 1980-83; dir. gen., chief exec. officer Internat. Telecommunications Satellite Orgn., Washington, 1983-86; v.p., cons. W. L. Pritchard & Co., Inc., Cons. Engrs., Bethesda, Md., 1990-92; v.p. Jackson-Richards Cons. Ltd. Telecomm. Cons., Irvine, Calif., 1992—. Contbr. to more than 30 books and articles. Bd. dirs. Washington Opera, 1986-87, Overseas Devel. Coun., 1986-87, Internat. Inst. Communication, London, 1985-86, Big Bros., Washington, 1975-77; co-chmn., chmn. Fund Raisers, Washington, 1983-89; docent The Irvine Mus., 1994—. With U.S. Army, 1961-62. Named one of top 15 people in U.S. comms. Comms. Week, 1986; recipient Adam Thompson award Amherst Coll., 1982. Home: 326 Deerfield Ave Irvine CA 92606-7606 Office: Jackson Richards Cons Ltd 14252 Culver Dr Ste A715 Irvine CA 92604-0317

COLLAMER, SONJA MAE SOREIDE, veterinary facility administrator; b. Rapid City, S.D., Sept. 3, 1937; d. Louis Severin and Mae Marie (Barber) Soreide; m. John Harry Collamer, Dec. 30, 1959; children: Debra, Michael, Kenneth, Kerry. BS in Bacteriology, Colo. State U., 1959. Practice mgr. Saratoga (Wyo.) Vet. Clinic, 1966-94, ret., 1994; sec., mem. Wyo. Bd. Medicine, 1995—. Pres., mem. Wyo. Jaycettes, 1962-70; elder, clk. session First Presbyn. Ch., Saratoga, 1966—, chair pastor nominating com.; neighborhood chmn., leader Girl Scouts Am., Saratoga, 1967-77; sec., mem. Snowy Range Cattlewomen, Carbon County, Wyo., 1967—; active bd. of edn. Sch. Dist. #9, Saratoga, 1968-72; chmn., treas. bd. edn. Sch. Dist. #2, Carbon County, 1972-81; mem. Carbon County Rep. Ctrl. Com., 1980—, Wyo. state com. woman, 1982-86; vice chair, mem. Saratoga Sr. Ctr. Bd., 1982-86; pres., mem. Snowy Range Ambs., Saratoga, 1984—; chair Region VIII Child Devel. Program, Carbon County, 1983-90; mem., fundraiser Saratoga Cmty. Choir, 1988—; mediator Wyo. Agrl. Mediation Bd., 1988—; co-chair Thomas for Congress Com., Carbon County, 1990; chair Saratoga Hist. and Cultural Assn. Bd., 1988-97; active Planning & Devel. Commn., Carbon County, 1994—. Mem. Am. Vet. Med. Assn. Auxiliary, Wyo. Vet. Med. Assn. Auxiliary (pres.), Kappa Delta. Republican. Presbyterian. Home: PO Box 485-806 Rangeview Saratoga WY 82331

COLLARD, LORRAINE FULLMER, music educator; b. Salt Lake City, Mar. 25, 1957; d. Merlin Don and Mary Suz Anne (Christensen) F.; m. Steven Robert Collard, June 26, 1981; children: Grant, Christopher, Michael, Richard. MusB, Brigham Young U., 1980; MA in Music, San Diego State U., 1986. Cert. music tchr., Calif., Utah. Instr. violin Calif., Utah, 1970—; tchr. string orch. Nebo Sch. Dist., Payson, Utah, 1980-81; substitute tchr. Poway, City Schs., Escondido Dists., San Diego, 1982-84; instr. group lessons in violin, San Diego, 1991—. Violinist San Jose State U. Chamber Orch., 1975-77, San Jose State U. Orch., 1975-77, San Diego State U. Quartet, 1976-77, Brigham Young U. Philharmonic, 1977-79, Brigham Young U. Chamber Orch., 1978-79, San Diego State U., 1982-85; concertmaster U. San Diego, 1981-82; active mem. LDS Ch.; den mother cub scouts Boy Scouts Am., San Diego, 1984-85; asst. concertmaster Palomar Orch., San Marcos, Calif., 1989-91; coord. Handel's Messiah Orch., San Diego, 1988-92; violinist, dir. Campanella Quartet, 1995—. Rudolph Giskin Meml. scholar San Jose State U., 1975, Gov. scholar State of Calif., 1975, San Jose Tchr.'s Assn. scholar, 1975, music scholar Brigham Young U., 1977-79, grad. scholar San Diego State U., 1982-83; recipient music award Bank of Am., 1975, 3d runner-up award Miss Am. County Pageant, 1975, Swimsuit Competition award, 1975. Mem. Suzuki Assn. Am., Suzuki Music Assn. Calif., Am. Family Assn., Calif. Scholastic Fedn. (life).

COLLENTINE, JOHN THOMAS, arbitrator, public art consultant; b. Madison, Wis., Dec. 14, 1920; s. Arthur Owen and Anna May (Blotz) C.; m. Mary Theresa Lavin, May 21, 1949; children: Sean, Dennis, Brian, Ann, Therese, Patrick, David. BA in Econs., U. Wis., 1943, JD, 1948; CLU, Am. Coll., 1968. Bar: Wis. Lawyer Kiel, Wis., 1948-59; city lawyer City of Kiel, 1950-59; staff lawyer Horner Agy., Madison, 1959-65; supv. advanced underwriting Northwestern Mut. Life Ins. Co., Milw., 1965-68; gen. agt. Northwestern Mut. Life Ins. Co., Sacramento, Calif., 1968-73; asst. v.p., dir. estate and bus. plans div. Pacific Mut. Life Ins. Co., Newport Beach, Calif., 1973-85; pub. art cons. Sacramento, 1986—; arbitrator Am. Arbitration Assn., Sacramento, 1986—, NASD, San Francisco, 1990—; mediator SAC Mediation Ctr., 1996—; cons., bd. dirs. Charitable Giving Spec., Inc., Sacramento, 1988—, coord. Save Outdoor Sculpture Project, Sacramento, 1992-95. Bd. dirs., pres. Solar Cookers Internat., Sacramento, 1992—. Lt. (j.g.) USNR, 1943-46, Europe TO. Mem. Internat. Sculpture Ctr., Rotary. Democrat. Roman Catholic. Home: 1431 3rd St Apt 18 Sacramento CA 95814-5305

COLLER, BETH-ANN GRISWOLD, molecular biologist, research scientist; b. Hartford, Conn., Nov. 1, 1959; d. Edward Wells and Dorothy (Allen) Griswold; m. John Coller, July 17, 1982. BS, Norwich U., 1981; diploma med. tech., U. Va., 1982; MS, U. Dayton, 1986; PhD, U. Nebr., 1993. Cert. med. tech. Am. Soc. of Clin. Pathologists. Med. tech. Va. Med. Ctr., Hampton, 1982-84; grad. tchg. asst. U. Dayton, Ohio, 1984-86; grad. rsch. asst. U. Nebr., Omaha, 1986-93; rsch. scientist Hawaii Biotech. Group, Aiea, 1993—. Contbr. articles to profl. jours. Mem. AAAS, Am. Soc. Virology, Sigma Xi (grant-in-aid of rsch. 1992, 93). Home: 98-1781 Kaahumanu St Apt C Aiea HI 96701-1818 Office: Hawaii Biotech Group Inc 99-193 Aiea Heights Dr Aiea HI 96701-3900

COLLETT, MERRILL JUDSON, management consultant; b. Winona Lake, Ind., Feb. 20, 1914; s. Charles Alfred and Dora (Jenkins) C. BA, Stanford (Calif.) U., 1934; MPA, Syracuse (N.Y.) U., 1938. Western rep. Pub. Adminstrn. Svs., Chgo., 1940-43; U.S. Bur. of Budget, 1945-46; pers. dir. Bonneville Power Adminstrn., Portland, Oreg., 1946-50; dir. pers. and mgmt. prodn., mktg. adminstrn. USDA, Washington, 1950-52; dir. wartime organizational planning Office Def. Mobilization, Washington, 1954-58; co-owner Collett and Clapp, P.R., 1958-65; founder, pres. Exec. Mgmt. Svc., Arlington, Va., 1967-82; editor-at-large The Bureaucrat, Washingt, 1981—; cons. for mgmt. Tucson Met. Ministry, 1985-88. Contbr. articles to profl. jours. Moderator Calvary Bapt. Ch., Washington, 1981-83; bd. dirs. Efforts from Ex-Convicts, Washington, 1967-83, Bacone Coll., Muskogee, Okla., 1980-86, 91—, Tucson Met. Ministry, 1989-91. Lt. USNR, 1943-46. Mem. Internat. Pers. Mgmt. Assn. (hon. life, Stockberger award), Ariz. Pers. Mgmt. Assn. (hon. life).

COLLETT, ROBERT LEE, financial company executive; b. Ardmore, Okla., July 1, 1940; s. Pat (Dowell) Conway; m. Sue Walker Healy; 1 child, Catherine April. BA in Math., Rice U., 1962; MA in Econs., Duke U., 1963. Chief actuarial asst. Am. Nat. Ins. Co., Galveston, Tex., 1963-66; actuary Milliman & Robertson, Inc., Phila., 1966-70; prin. Milliman & Robertson, Inc., Houston, 1970-89, pres., 1990; pres., CEO Milliman & Robertson, Inc., Houston and Seattle, 1991-92, Seattle, 1992—. Bd. dirs. Seattle Symphony, 1992—. Fellow Soc. Actuaries (chmn. internat. sect. 1992—); mem. Rainier Club. Episcopalian. Office: Milliman & Robertson Inc 1301 5th Ave Ste 3800 Seattle WA 98101-2646

COLLEY, JANET SCRITSMIER, investment consultant; b. Pomona, Calif., May 21, 1960; d. Jerome Lorenzo and Mildred Joan (Lloyd) Scritsmier; children: Justin Michael, Corey Gray, Cody James; m. Glenn Turner Colley, Dec. 27, 1996. Student Calif. State Poly. U., 1978-79. Vice pres. sales E.L.A. Co., Industry, Calif., 1979-84; investment cons. Cameron Properties Inc., Covina, Calif., 1980—. Asst. instr. Dale Carnegie Sales Course, 1981-82, Human Relations, 1983. Republican. Mormon. Home: 3646 Westridge Ave Covina CA 91724

COLLIAS, NICHOLAS ELIAS, zoology educator, ornithologist; b. Chicago Heights, Ill., July 19, 1914; s. Elias and Marina (Giatras) C.; m. Elsie Cole, Dec. 21, 1948; 1 child, Karen. BS, U. Chgo., 1937, PhD, 1942. Instr. biology Amherst (Mass.) Coll., 1946-47; instr. zoology U. Wis., Madison, 1947-51; postdoctoral fellow Cornell U., Ithaca, N.Y., 1953-54; prof. zoology Ill. Coll., Jacksonville, 1954-58; from asst. prof. to prof. zoology UCLA, 1958—. Author: Evolution of Nest-building in the Weaverbirds, 1964, Nest Building and Bird Behavior, 1984; editor: External Construction by Animals, 1976. 1st lt. USAAC, 1943-46. Guggenheim fellow, 1962-63; NSF grantee, 1960-80. Fellow AAAS, Am. Ornithologists Union (Elliott Coues award 1980), Animal Behavior Soc.; mem. Cooper Ornithol. Soc. (hon.). Office: U Calif Dept Biology Los Angeles CA 90095-1606

COLLIER, DAVID, political science educator; b. Chgo., Feb. 17, 1942; s. Donald and Malcolm (Carr) C.; m. Ruth Berins, Mar. 10, 1968; children: Stephen, Jennifer. BA, Harvard U., 1965; MA, U. Chgo., 1967, PhD, 1971. From instr. to assoc. prof. Ind. U., Bloomington, 1970-78; from assoc. prof. to prof. U. Calif., Berkeley, 1978—, chmn. dept. polit. sci., 1990-93; faculty fellow U. Notre Dame, 1986, 87; vis. prof. U. Chgo., 1989; chmn. Ctr. for Latin Am. Studies U. Calif., Berkeley, 1980-83; co-dir., co-founder Stanford-Berkeley Joint Ctr. for Latin Am. Studies, 1981-83. Author: Squatters and Oligarchs: Authoritarian Rule and Policy Change in Peru, 1976; co-author: Shaping the Political Arena, 1991 (Prize, Best Book on Comparative Politics Am. Polit. Scis. Assn. 1993—), editor: The New Authoritariansim in Latin America, 1979. Recipient Guggenheim fellowship, 1988-89; fellow Ctr. for Advanced Studies in Behavioral Scis., Stanford, 1994-95, pres. APSA comparative politics sect., 1997—; grantee NSF5-77, 80-83. Mem. Latin Am. Studies Assn., Am. Polit. Sci. Assn., Coun. on Fgn. Rels. Office: Univ Calif Dept Polit Sci 210 Barrows Hall Berkeley CA 94720-1951

COLLIER, DAVID HARRIS, rheumatologist; b. Fresno, Calif., June 8, 1951; s. Alan and Beatrice Emily (Raimondo) C.; m. Catherine Joyce Isom, Aug. 18, 1979; 1 child, Alison Elizabeth. BS in Chemistry, Calif. Inst. Technology, Pasadena, 1973; MD, Washington U., St. Louis, 1977. Diplomate Am. Bd. Internal Medicine, Am. Bd. Rheumatology, Diplomate Nat. Bd. Medical Examiners. Intern, resident Barnes Hosp., St. Louis, 1977-80; fellow in rheumatology U. Calif., San Francisco, 1980-83; asst. prof. medicine U. Colo., Denver, 1983-90; assoc. prof. medicine U. Colo., 1990—; chief of rheumatology Denver Health Med. Ctr., 1985—; lectr. in field. Contbr. articles to profl. jours., chpts. to books in field. Bd. dirs. Arthritis Found., Rocky Mountain Chpt., Denver, 1994—, chmn. advocacy com., 1993—; pres. Rocky Mountain Rheumatism Soc., Denver, 1994. Recipient Sidney J. Schwab Book prize, Washington U., Merck, Sharp and Dohme Sr. Rheumatology Fellow award for Rsch.; grantee Wash. U., 1974, No. Calif. Arthritis Found., 1981, 82, Rocky Mountain Arthritis Found., 1984, 87, U. Colo. Sch. Medicine, 1986, 89. Fellow Am. Coll. Rheumatology; mem. KC. Democrat. Roman Catholic. Office: Denver Health Med Ctr 777 Bannock St Denver CO 80204-4507

COLLIER, GAYDELL MAIER, library director, writer, rancher; b. Long Island, N.Y., June 28, 1935; d. Harry and Jean (Gaydell) Maier; m. Roy H. Collier, 1955; 4 children. Student, Middlebury Coll., U. Wyo. Circulation mgr. U. Wyo. Libr., Laramie, 1974; rancher Laramie and Sundance, Wyo., 1971—; bookshop mgr. Backpocket Ranch Bookshop, Sundance, Wyo., 1977—; dir. Crook County Pub. Libr. System, Wyo., 1985—. Co-author: Basic Horsemanship: English and Western, 1974, 2d edit., 1993, Basic Training for Horses: English and Western, 1979, paperback edit., 1989 (Best Non-fiction Book award 1980), Basic Horse Care, 1986, paperback edit., 1989, German translation, 1992; co-editor: Leaning Into the Wind: Women Write from the Heart of the West, 1997; book reviewer; contbr. articles to profl. jours. Bd. dirs. Albany County Pub. Libr., 1968-74, Vore Buffalo Jump Found., 1991—. Mem. Wyo. Libr. Assn. (Outstanding Dedication and Contbns. award 1974, Libr. of Yr. 1990), Western Writers Am., Women Writing the West, Wyo. Writers, Inc.(pres. 1987-88), Bear Lodge Writers. Office: Crook County Libr PO Box 910 414 Main St Sundance WY 82729

COLLIER, RICHARD BANGS, philosopher, foundation executive; b. Hastings, Nebr., Aug. 12, 1918; s. Nelson Martin and Stella (Butler) C. BA, U. Wash., 1951. Fgn. aid officer GS14, air traffic control supr. gen. & airway comms. engr., civil aviation Am. embassy, Bangkok, Thailand, 1958-63; founder, dir. Pleneurethics Society, Tacoma, 1985—; founder Inst. Ethics & Sci., Tacoma, 1988—, Pleneurethics Inst., 1995—. Carnegie fellow Inst. Pub. Affairs, Grad. Sch., U. Wash., 1950-51. Nat. adv. bd. Am. Security Council. Capt. USAF, 1965-66. Recipient Rep. Presdl. Legion of merit, Medal of Freedom, Rep. Senatorial, 1964. Mem. Assn. Supervision & Curriculum Devel., Soc. Health & Human Values, Senatorial Trust (U.S. Senatorial Medal of Freedom), Royal Inst. Philosophy (Eng.), Nat. Rep. Senatorial Inner Circle (Presdl. commn.), Rep. Nat. Com. (life, Eisenhower commn., charter mem. chmn.'s adv. bd.). Author: Pleneurethic, 20 vols., 1964-93, Pleneurethics: A Philosophical System Uniting Body, Brain and Mind, 2d edit. 1990, contrb. to Journal of Pleneurethics. Home: PO Box 1256 Tacoma WA 98401-1256

COLLIER, RUTH BERINS, political science educator; b. Hartford, Conn., June 20, 1942; d. Maurice and Esther (Meyers) Berins; m. David Collier; children: Stephen, Jennifer. AB, Smith Coll., 1964; MA, U. Chgo., 1966, PhD, 1974. Asst. prof. rsch. Ind. U., Bloomington, 1975-78; asst. to assoc. rsch. polit. scientist U. Calif., Berkeley, 1979-83, lectr., 1983-90, assoc. prof., prof., 1990—. Author: Regimes in Tropical Africa, 1982, The Contradictory Alliance: Labor Politics and the Regime Change in Mexico, 1992 (Hubert Herring award, 1993); co-author: Shaping the Political Arena: The Labor Movement, Critical Junctures, and Regime Dynamics in Latin America, 1991 (Comparative Politics Sect. award Am. Polit. Sci. Assn., 1993). Fellow Ctr. for Advanced Study in the Behavioral Scis., Stanford, 1994-95.

COLLING, CATHARINE MARY, nurse, hospital administrator; b. Broomfield, Colo., Jan. 15, 1909; d. Patrick and Margaret Mary (Ryan) Kirby; m. Anthony Joseph Colling; 1 child, Mary Helen Colling Nightingale. BA, Ursuline Coll., 1934. RN, Calif. Supr. Mary's Help Hosp., 1945-50; adminstrv. indsl. nurse Standard Oil Co. of Calif., San Francisco, 1951-62; ward conservator Bank of Am. Trust Dept., 1964-67; instr. indsl. nursing Univ. San Francisco, 1954-69; adminstr. White Sands Convalescent Hosp., Pleasant Hill, Calif., 1967-70, Hillhaven Lawton Convalescent Hosp., San Francisco, 1970-91; dir. Hillhaven, San Francisco, 1991-95; ret., 1994. Founder, chmn. Vols. Aux. for Hillhaven, San Francisco, 1994—. Recipient numerous nursing awards. Mem. Am. Coll. Nursing Home Adminstr., No. Calif. Assn. Indsl. Nurses, Western Indsl. Nurses, Calif. Nurses Assn., Mary's Help Hosp. Alumni Assn., Calif. Assn. Hosp. Facilities. Republican. Roman Catholic. Office: 1359 Pine St San Francisco CA 94109-4807

COLLING, KENNETH FRANK, hospital administrator; b. Watertown, N.Y., Apr. 17, 1945. BA, Cornell U., 1967, M Hosp. Adminstrn., 1969. Adminstrv. res. New Britain (Conn.) Gen. Hosp., 1968; asst. prof. Baylor Army program Healthcare Adminstrn., San Antonio, 1971-73; asst. adminstr. Kaiser Found. Hosp., Fontana, Calif., 1973-75, assoc. adminstr., 1979-81; asst. adminstr. Kaiser Found. Hosp., Panorama City, Calif., 1975-79; adminstr. Kaiser Found. Hosp., San Diego, 1981—, sr. v.p., area mgr. Contbr. articles to profl. jours. Mem. Calif. Hosp. Assn. (exec. com., trustee). Home: 3024 Cadencia St Carlsbad CA 92009-8307 Office: Kaiser Found Hosp 4647 Zion Ave San Diego CA 92120-2507*

COLLINGS, CELESTE LOUISE (SHORTY VASSALLI), marketing executive, professional artist; b. Highland Park, Ill., Dec. 9, 1948; d. Robert Zane Jr. and Laura (Vasaly) C.; m. John Austin Darden III, July 17, 1971 (div. July 1975); 1 child, Desiree Anne; m. John Cochran Barber, Dec. 13, 1984. BA, U. Ariz., 1970; postgrad., N.Mex. State U., 1975; completed mktg. mgr. seminar, U. Calif., Irvine, 1978; cert. of achievement, Wilson Learning Course, 1983. Art tchr. Devargas Jr. High Sch., Santa Fe, 1971; artist, pvt. tchr. Las Cruces, N.Mex., 1971-75; sales rep. Helpmates Temp. Services, Santa Ana, Calif., 1975-76; sales account mgr. Bristol-Myers Products, N.Y.C., 1976-82; sales mgr. Profl. Med. Products, Greenwood, S.C., 1982-85; mktg. mgr. med. products Paper-Pak Products, La Verne, Calif., 1985-88; owner Multi-Media West, Newport Beach, Calif., 1988—; mgmt. trainee Bristol-Myers, Kansas City, Mo., 1978; sales trainee Profl. Med. Products, Greenwood, 1983, product strategy, 1984, chmn. nat. adv. com., 1983-84; owner and pres. Accent Shoji Screens, Newport Beach, Calif., 1981—. Exhibited in one-woman shows at Nancy Dunn Studio and Gallery, San Clemente, Calif., 1980, The Collectables, San Francisco, 1980, Breeden Gallery, Orange Calif., 1992, Orange County Cen. for Contemporary Art, Santa Ana, Calif., Laguna Beach (Calif.) Festival of the Arts Art-A-Fair, 1981, Ariz. Inter-Scholastic Hon. Exhibit, 1st place award, 1962-66, Glendale Fed. Savs. Art Exhibition, 1982; numerous others; represented by Patricia Corriea Art Gallery, Santa Monica, Calif., Breeden Gallery, Orange, Calif., L.A. Artcore. Mem. Orange County Performing Arts Ctr., Colona Del Mar, Calif., 1981, Orange County Visual Artists, 1990, Orange County Ctr. for Contemporary Art, 1993; asst. dir. Orange County Satellite, Womens Caucus for Art, organizer, 1993. Recipient 10 sales awards Bristol-Meyers, 1976-82, Western Zone Sales Rep. award Profl. Med. Products, 1984, Gainers Club award, 1984; named Nat. Sales Rep. of Yr. Profl. Med. Products, 1984. Mem. Humanities Assocs., U. Ariz. Alumni Assn., Kappa Alpha Theta Alumni.

COLLINGS, CHARLES LEROY, supermarket executive; b. Wewoka, Okla., July 11, 1925; s. Roy B. and Dessie L. C.; m. Frances Jane Flake, June 28, 1947; children—Sandra Jean, Dianna Lynn. Student, So. Methodist U., 1943-44, U. Tex., 1945. Sec., contr., dir. Noble Meat Co., Madera, Calif., 1947-54; chief acct. Montgomery Ward & Co., Oakland, Calif., 1954-56; with Raleys, Sacramento, 1956—; sec. Raleys, 1958—, pres., 1970—, CEO, 1993—, also dir. Bd. dirs. Pro Athlete Outreach, Youth for Christ, Kevin Johnson's St. Hope Acad., Dave Dravecky Found. With USNR, 1943-46. Mem. Calif. Grocers Assn. (officer, past chmn. and mem. bd. dirs.), Calif Retailers Assn. (past mem. bd. dirs.). Republican. Baptist. Home: 6790 Arabella Way Sacramento CA 95831-2325 Office: Raley's PO Box 13778 Sacramento CA 95852 *My goal is to live my life in such a way that when I leave this earth those who knew me can truthfully say, "He loved his God, and loved and did good toward his fellow man.".*

COLLINS, AMY DENISE, reporter; b. Bakersfield, Calif., Sept. 8, 1968. BA in English, U. Calif., Santa Barbara, 1991. Editor-in-chief Daily Nexus, Santa Barbara, 1989-90; bus. editor Prognosis, Prague, Czechoslovakia, 1991-92; City Hall reporter The Dispatch, Gilroy, Calif., 1992-94; freelance reporter Prague, Czech Republic and Croatia, 1994-95; copy editor Daily News, L.A., 1995-96; reporter Daily News, Los Angeles, 97—.

COLLINS, CHARLES ARTHUR, III, mechanical engineer; b. Bryan, Tex., July 13, 1952; s. Charles Arthur II and Jo Ellen (Bedgood) C.; m. Janet Lee Rogers, June 4, 1977; children: Stephanie Erin, Eric Scott. BS, U. Ariz., 1974. Gen. engr. U.S. Army, Red River Army Depot, Tex., 1975-76; mech. engr. U.S. Army, Warren, Mich., 1977-78; gen. engr. U.S. Army, Blue Grass Army Depot, Ky., 1979-81; elec. engr. U.S. Army, Ft. Huachuca, Ariz., 1982—. Author: The Great Escape: The Apache Outbreak of 1881, 1994.

Mem. Coun. on Am.'s Mil. Past, Ariz. Hist. Soc. Republican. Baptist. Home: 2301 S Calle Mesa Del Oso Tucson AZ 85748

COLLINS, DANE H., marketing executive; b. Champaign, Ill., Feb. 2, 1961; s. Ronald Milton Collins and Beverly Carolyn (Brown) Patnaude; m. Leigh Ann Paulsen, Oct. 4, 1989. Student, Iowa State U., 1979-82. Acct. exec. Phoenix Pub., Inc., 1982-83, advt. mgt., 1983-85; comml. artist Jackie Awerman Assocs., Phoenix, 1983-88; acct. svcs. supr. The Lutzker Group, Phoenix, 1985-86; advt. dir. Intersouth Communications, Scottsdale, Ariz., 1986-87; mktg. dir. Ariz. Bus. & Devel., Phoenix, 1988-89; v.p. S.W. Communications, Phoenix, 1988-90, Balloon Buddies, Inc., Mesa, Ariz., 1988-90; mktg. dir. Orange-Sol, Inc., Gilbert, Ariz., 1989-91, 1993—; ptnr. Interactive Techs., Inc., 1996—; cons. Continental Am. Corp., Wichita, Kans., 1990-92, Ariz. Bus. & Devel., Phoenix, 1990-91. Illustrator: (books) Power, Influence, Sabotage: The Corporate Survivor's Coloring Book & Primer, 1986, Good Morning Mr. President, 1988; patentee decorative message display. Vol. DeNovo, Phoenix, 1984, Cystic Fibrosis Found., Scottsdale, 1985, Aid to Women's Ctr., Phoenix, 1987, Dayspring U.M.C. Missions for Homeless, Tempe, Ariz., 1990-93. Mem. Phoenix Soc. Communicating Arts. Republican. Methodist. Home: 2650 E South Fork Dr Phoenix AZ 85048-8976

COLLINS, DENNIS ARTHUR, foundation executive; b. Yakima, Wash., June 9, 1940; s. Martin Douglas and Louise Constance (Caccia) C.; m. Mary Veronica Paul, June 11, 1966; children: Jenifer Ann, Lindsey Kathleen. BA, Stanford U., 1962, MA, 1963; LHD, Mills Coll., 1994. Assoc. dean admissions Occidental Coll., Los Angeles, 1964-66, dean admissions, 1966-68, dean of students, 1968-70; headmaster Emma Willard Sch., Troy, N.Y., 1970-74; founding headmaster San Francisco U. High Sch., 1974-86; pres. James Irvine Found., San Francisco, 1986—; trustee Coll. Bd., N.Y.C., 1981-85, Ind. Ednl. Svcs., Princeton, N.J., 1981-85, Calif. Assn. Ind. Schs., L.A., 1982-86, Branson Sch., 1987-89, Aspen Inst. Nonprofit Sector rsch. Fund, 1992—; chmn. bd. So. Calif. Assn. Philanthropy, L.A., 1989-91, No. Calif. Grantmakers, 1987-90; dir. Rebuild L.A., 1992-93. Trustee Cathedral Sch. for Boys, San Francisco, 1976-82, Marin Country Day Sch., Corte Madera, Calif., 1978-84, San Francisco Exploratorium, 1984-86, Ind. Sector, Washington, 1987-95, Am. Farmland Trust, Washington, 1992—; bd. dirs., vice chmn. Children's Hosp. Found., San Francisco, 1984-86; chmn. bd. dirs. Coun. for Cmty. Based Devel., Washington, 1989-92. Mem. Council on Founds. Democrat. Episcopalian. Clubs: World Trade, University; California (L.A.). Home: 432 Golden Gate Ave Belvedere Tiburon CA 94920-2447 Office: The James Irvine Found Spear Tower 1 Market St Ste 1715 San Francisco CA 94105-1521

COLLINS, DICK, artist; b. South Pittsburg, Tenn., Feb. 16, 1930; s. William Columbus and Flora James (Lee) C.; divorced; children: Michael Charles, Deborah Marie. BA, U. Tenn., Chattanooga, 1953; MFA, Calif. State U., Fullerton, 1993. Cert. secondary tchr., Tenn. Tech. editor/writer Bechtel Power Co., Norwalk, Calif., 1972-75, Parsons Engrng., Pasadena, Calif., 1975-86; instr. life drawing Calif. State U., Fullerton, 1992-93; figurative and landscape artist, 1993—. Paintings include California Dreaming, No More Closets, Just As I Am; exhibited in group shows at Rose City Gallery, Pasadena, 1993-94, Da Gallery, Pomona, Calif., 1994-97, Orlando Gallery, Sherman Oaks, Calif., 1994-97, Art Angles Gallery, Orange, Calif., 1995, 96, Hollywood (Calif.) Bowl Art Festival, 1996, 97. Staff sgt. USAF, 1946-50, Japan. Mem. Omicron Delta Kappa. Home: 18133 Northam St La Puente CA 91744-5927

COLLINS, FUJI, mental health professional; b. Tokyo, Nov. 3, 1954; s. Boyd Leslie and Kimiko (Terayama) C.; 1 child, Lacey Nichole. BS, Ariz. State U., 1977; MS, Ea. Wash. U., 1989; MA, The Fielding Inst., 1993, PhD, 1994. Registered clin. therapist. Commd. 2d lt. U.S. Army, 1978, advanced through grades to maj., 1989, lt. platoon leader, adminstrv. officer, 1978-79; lt. bat. adjutant 509th Airborne Bat. Combat Team, 1977-80; capt., air def. fire coordination officer U.S. Army, 1981-83, capt. battery comdr., 1983-85, capt., 1985-86; clin. therapist Wash. State Patrol, 1985-95; dir. of adminstrn., Japanese Counseling Program Richmond Area Multi-Svcs., Inc., San Francisco, 1995—, dir. children and youth svcs., 1995—; coord. Wash. State Patrol Critical Incident/Peer Support Team, Wash. State Hostage Negotiator; mem. Thurston/Mason County Critical Incident Stress Debriefing Team; dir. Richmond Counseling Ctr., 1995—; vis. lectr. Georgetown U., 1996—; faculty Nat. Asian Am. Psychology Tng. Ctr., San Francisco, 1996—. Vol. Thurston/Mason County Crisis Clinic; mem. steering com. Thurston/Mason County Critical Incident Team. Mem. ACA, APA, Wash. State Psychol. Assn., Asian Am. Psychol. Assn., Soc. for Psychol. Study of Ethnic Minority Issues, Am. Critical Incident Stress Found., Wash. State Hostage Negotiation Assn., Assn. Police Planning and Rsch. Officers. Home: 3 Bayside Ct Richmond CA 94804-7441 Office: Nat Asian Am Psychology Tng Ctr San Francisco CA 94121

COLLINS, GARY SCOTT, physicist, researcher; b. Plainfield, N.J., Dec. 15, 1944; s. John Dillard and Elizabeth Woodson (Miller) C.; m. Peggy Lynn Webb, June 24, 1978; children: Daniel Robert Smithson, Emily Abigail Davis. BA in Physics, Rutgers Coll., 1966; PhD in Physics, Rutgers U., 1976. Vol. Peace Corps US, Togo, W. Africa, 1966-68; postdoctoral rsch. assoc. Clark U., Worcester, Mass., 1977-79, rsch. asst. prof., 1979-85; assoc. prof. Wash. State U., Pullman, 1985—. NSF grantee Clark U., 1980-86, Wash. State U., 1987-99. Mem. Am. Phys. Soc., Materials Rsch. Soc., Metall. Soc. Home: 1825 NW Turner Dr Pullman WA 99163-3530 Office: Wash State U Dept Physics Pullman WA 99164-2814

COLLINS, GEORGE TIMOTHY, computer software consultant; b. Connersville, Ind., Aug. 21, 1943; s. Robert Emerson and Oma (Richie) C.; m. Martha Elizabeth Holt, Apr. 30, 1966; children: Kirsten Stephanie, Eowyn Erika. BA in Math., Ind. U., 1966; MS in Computer Sci., Rensselaer Poly. Inst., 1971. Engr. program analyst Sikorsky Aircraft, Stratford, Conn., 1966-70; research mathematician Peter Eckrich, Ft. Wayne, Ind., 1970-75; sr. systems analyst Pyrotek Data Service, Ft. Walton Beach, Fla., 1975-77; sr. aerosystems engr. Gen. Dynamics, Ft. Worth, 1977-79; sr. specialist Electronic Data Systems, Las Vegas, Nev., 1979-81; sr. assoc. CACI Fed., San Diego, 1981-82; prin., gen. mgr. Structured Software Systems, Escondido, Calif., 1982-88; sr. software engr. Sci. Applications Internat. Corp., San Diego, 1988-94; pvt. practice cons. Escondido, 1994-96; prin. engr. Orbital Scis. Corp., 1996—; cons. Hi-Shear Corp., Los Angeles, 1973-75. Developer (computer model and data base) Aircraft Stores Interface, 1975, (computer model) TAC Disrupter, 1981; co-developer (computer model) Tactical Air Def., Battle Model, 1978, Tactical Air and Land Ops., 1980; prime contbr. (computer data collection and analysis sys.) Mobile Sea Range, 1988-90; contbr. (computer comm. sys.) Lightweight Deployable Comm., 1990, Joint Advanced Spl. Ops. Radio Sys., 1992, Orbital Scis. Corp.'s Maj. Constituent Analyzer Environ. Control/Life Scis. Sys. for Internat. Space Station (team received NASA Manned Flight Awareness award), Orbital Scis. Corp. Software Lead Meterology Sensor Module, 1996. Bd. dirs. Family and Children's Service, Ft. Wayne, 1974. Mem. N.Y. Acad. Scis., North County Chess Club. Unitarian. Home: 121 W 8th Ave Escondido CA 92025-5001 also: Orbital Scis Corp 2771 N Garey Ave Pomona CA 91769

COLLINS, HAROLD THEODORE, urologist; b. N.Y.C., Nov. 30, 1942; s. Harold Reeves and Atanaska (Vitonoff) C. BA in Chemistry, Kent State U., 1964; MD, Ohio State U., 1968. Intern Ohio State Hosps., Columbus, 1968-69; resident Ochsner Found., New Orleans, 1972-75; urologist North Bend Med. Ctr., Coos Bay, Oreg., 1975—. Capt. U.S. Army, 1969-71. Mem. AMA, Am. Urol. Assn. Home: 1040 E Bay Dr North Bend OR 97459-9201 Office: North Bend Med Ctr 1900 Woodland Dr Coos Bay OR 97420-2045

COLLINS, JENNI JEAN, writer; b. Arcadia, Calif., Nov. 18, 1953; d. Albert Joseph and Yolanda Vincenzina (Raymond) Secchi; divorced; 1 child, Jason Michael. Degree in liberal arts, Calif. State U., L.A., 1991. Author: (poetry) Freight Train, Vigil Press, Sepia Poetry Press, Psychopoetica; producer play, 1994. Mem. N.W. Playwright Soc.

COLLINS, MICHAEL DAVID, environmental health educator, developmental toxicologist; b. Yonkers, N.Y., Oct. 4, 1949; s. Gilbert and Millicent (Sorkness) C.; m. Karen Lynn Mitchell, May 21, 1977; children: Brock Damon, Kyna Monique. BS, U. Ill., 1971, MS, 1977; MSPH, U. Mo., 1981, PhD, 1982. Interdisciplinary Programs in Health fellow Harvard Sch. Pub. Health, Boston, 1982-84; rsch. fellow Children's Hosp. Rsch. Found., Cin., 1984-87; rsch. instr. dept. pediatrics U.Cin., 1986-88, rsch. asst. prof., 1988-93; asst. prof. environ. health scis. UCLA Sch. Pub. Health and Ctr. Occup. and Environ. Health, 1993-95, assoc. prof., 1995—; vis. scientist Freie U. Berlin, 1989-90; mem. biology faculty Raymond Walters Coll., U. Cin., 1992-93, Environ. Sci. and Engring. Program, 1994—, Ctr. Environ. Risk Reduction, 1996—. First Ind. Rsch. Support and Transition grantee NIH, 1987. Mem. Teratology Soc., The Oxygen Soc., Am. Inst. Nutrition. Home: 4044 Jim Bowie Rd Agoura Hills CA 91301-3608 Office: UCLA School Public Health 10833 Le Conte Ave Los Angeles CA 90024-1602

COLLINS, MICHAEL K., lawyer; b. Sikeston, Mo., Feb. 13, 1943. AB, Washington U., St. Louis, 1965, JD, 1969. Bar: Calif. 1970, U.S. Dist. Ct. (cen., so. and no. dists.) Calif. 1970, U.S. Ct. Appeals (9th cir.) 1970. With Greenberg, Glusker, Fields, Claman & Machtinger, L.A. Editor-in-Chief Washington U. Law Quar., 1968-69. Mem. Assn. Bus. Trial Lawyers, State Bar Calif., L.A. County Bar Assn. (exec. com. real property sect. 1981-83), Century City Bar Assn., Order of Coif, Wilshire Hunting Club. Office: Greenberg Glusker Fields Claman & Machtinger 1900 Avenue Of The Stars Fl 20 Los Angeles CA 90067-4301

COLLINS, MICHAEL PAUL, secondary school educator, earth science educator, consultant; b. Chula Vista, Calif., Jan. 2, 1959; s. William Henry and Linda Lee (Capron) C.; m. Helen Marie Wassmann, July 23, 1994; 1 child, Kyle P. Collins; children from a previous marriage: Christopher M., Matthew R. A in Gen. Studies, Clatsop Community Coll., Astoria, Oreg., 1983; BS in Sci. Edn., Oreg. State U., 1987, BS in Geology, 1987; postgrad., U. Alaska, Anchorage. Cert. tchr., Wash., Alaska. Emergency med. technician II, fireman Sitka (Alaska) Fire Dept., 1978-80; paramedic Medix Ambulance, Astoria, 1980-83; cartographer technician U.S. Geol. Survey, Grants Pass, Oreg., 1985; earth sci. tchr. Lake Oswego (Oreg.) Sch. Dist., 1987-88; sci. tchr. Gladstone (Oreg.) Sch. Dist., 1988-90; radon technician Radon Detection Systems, Portland, Oreg., 1988-90; sales and mktg. dir. Evergreen Helicopters of Alaska, Inc., Anchorage, 1990-91; sci./math tchr. Anchorage Sch. Dist., 1991—; instr. geology Alaska Jr. Coll., Anchorage, 1992-93; cons. earth sci. edn. Project ESTEEM, ctr. astrophysics Harvard U., Cambridge, Mass., 1992—; field technician Water Quality Divsn., City of Anchorage, 1993; cons. Am. Meteorol. Assn., atmospheric ednl. resource agt. Project Atmosphere, 1994—, Project MicroObservatory Ctr. for Astrophysics, Harvard U., 1995—; cons. Alaska State H.S. Scis. Olympics, co-coord., 1994; co-coord. Instr. Project DataStreme Am. Meteorol. Soc., 1996—. Co-author: Merrill Earth Science Lab Activities, 1989. With USCG, 1977-81. Mem. NEA, Am. Assn. Petroleum Geologists, Geol. Soc. Am., Nat. Sci. Tchrs. Assn., Am. Geol. Inst., Am. Meteorol. Soc., Alaska Geol. Soc. Inc., Nat. Assn. Geosci. Tchrs. (pres. N.W. sect. 1995—). Home: 9501 Morningside Loop Apt 4 Anchorage AK 99515-2187 Office: West Anchorage HS 1700 Hillcrest Dr Anchorage AK 99517-1347

COLLINS, MICHAEL SEAN, obstetrician and gynecologist, educator; b. Yankton, S.D., Sept. 8, 1951; s. Edward Daniel and Joyce (Slatky) C.; m. Judy Furman, Sept. 20, 1975; children: Lauren, Sean, Carolyn. BS, Davidson Coll., 1973; MD, Med. U. S.C., 1977. Diplomate Am. Bd. Ob-Gyn. Chief resident in ob-gyn Med. U. S.C., Charleston, 1980-81; instr. ob-gyn U. Oreg. Health Scis. Ctr., Portland, 1981—; chmn. dept. ob-gyn Good Samaritan Hosp., Portland, 1983-85; cons. Prepared Childbirth Assn., Portland, 1981—, Triplet Connection, L.A. , 1985—. Fellow ACOG (adv. coun. 1991—, chmn. Oreg. sect.); mem. AMA, Oreg. Med. Assn., Oreg. Ob-Gyn. Soc., Pacific Coast Ob-Gyn. Soc., Pacific N.W. Ob-Gyn. Soc., Am. Fertility Soc., Porsche Club Am., Oreg. Ob-Gyn. Soc. (vice-chmn. 1991-94, chmn. 1995—), Am. Assn. Gynecologic Laparoscopists, Internat. Soc. Advancement Humanistic Studies Medicine, Alpha Omega Alpha. Republican. Roman Catholic. Home: 716 NW Rapidan Ter Portland OR 97210-3129 Office: Portland Ob-Gyn Assocs 1130 NW 22nd Ave Ste 120 Portland OR 97210-2934

COLLINS, ROBERT D., lawyer, consultant; b. Eugene, Oreg., Oct. 12, 1947; s. Warren D. and Claudeen R. (Kelly) c.; m. Suzanne Lawlor, Mar. 21, 1970 (div. June 1995); children: Brooke A. Collins Vanderlyn, Bradley L. BA, Calif. State U., Sacramento, 1969; JD, UOP, 1972. Bar: Calif. 1972, U.S. Dist. Ct. (ea. dist.) Calif. 1972, U.S. Ct. Appeals (9th cir.) 1972, U.S. Ct. Claims 1992. Asst. dist. atty. Sacramento Cty. Dist. Atty.'s Office, 1976-79; assoc. Schei, Fort, Taylor & Pendergast, Sacramento, 1979-82; ptnr. Schei, Pendergast & Collins, Sacramento, 1982—; cons. title ins. cos., Calif., 1982—; gen. counsel Alta Springs Water Co., Alta, Calif., 1996. Bd. dirs. Sacramento Sci. Ctr., 1985-92, B St. Theater, Sacramento, 1996. Capt. JAG, USMC, 1973-76, Vietnam. Mem. Calif. State Bar, Calif. Land Title Assn., Sacramento Cty. Bar Assn., West Sacramento Rotary (pres. elect 1996). Republican. Home: 290 Rivertree Way Sacramento CA 95831 Office: Schei Pendergast & Collins 555 Capitol Mall Ste 200 Sacramento CA 95814

COLLINS, ROBERT WAYNE, photographer, public speaker; b. San Francisco, July 25, 1943; s. Glen Hogan and Frieda Conrad (Niebuhr) C.; m. Marcia Madelyn Nutt, Aug. 20, 1978 (div. 1991); 1 child, Brianna Leigh; children from a previous marriage: Richard Wayne, Tanya Kishla. BA, Williams Coll., 1973; PhD in Psychology and Human Relations, Brantridge Forest Sch., 1976. Analyst, asst. to v.p. pub. rels. Factfinders, Inc., San Francisco, 1965-69; med. sales rep. Mead Johnson Labs, Orange County, Calif., 1969-72; comms. cons. Pacific Telephone Co., Orange County, Calif., 1978-84; owner Bob Collins Studios, Dana Pt., Calif., 1987—; owner, pub. spkr., therapist Dr. Collins Sems., Dana Pt., Calif., 1988—. Author: Measuring the Whole Man, 1976, Major Peterson Method of Predicting Job Fitness, 1977, Testing the Whole Man, 1977. Sgt. Orange County Sheriff's Search Rescue Team, 1978—; bd. dirs. Orange Coast Cmty. Coll., Costa Mesa, Calif., 1993—. Served with U.S. Army, 1961-64. Office: PO Box 526 Dana Point CA 92629

COLLINS, WILLIAM LEROY, telecommunications engineer; b. Laurel, Miss., June 17, 1942; s. Henry L. and Christene E. (Finnegan) C. Student, La Salle U., 1969; BS in Computer Sci., U. Beverly Hills, 1984. Sr. computer operator Dept. Pub. Safety, Phoenix, 1975-78, data communications specialist, 1978-79, supr. computer ops., 1981-82; mgr. network control Valley Nat. Bank, Phoenix, 1979-81; mgr. data communications Ariz. Lottery, Phoenix, 1982-85; mgr. telecommunications Calif. Lottery, Sacramento, 1985—; Mem. Telecomm. Study Mission to Russia, Oct. 1991. Contbr. to profl. publs. Served as sgt. USAF, 1964-68. Mem. IEEE, Nat. Sys. Programmers Assn., Centrex Users Group, DMS Centrex User Group, Accunet Digital Svcs. User Group, Telecomms. Assn. (v.p. edn. Sacramento Valley chpt. 1990-94, pres. 1995, chpt. assn. dir. 1996-97, chpt. past pres. 1996), Telecom. Assn. (chmn. corp. edn. com. 1994-95, conf. com. 1994-95, co-chair conf. program com. 1996, program dir. edn. 1996, corp. dir. edn. 1996-97), SynOptics User Group, Timeplex User Group, Assn. Data Comm. Users, Soc. Mfg. Engrs., Data Processing Mgmt. Assn., Am. Mgmt. Assn., Assn. Computing Machinery, Am. Soc. for Quality Control, Bldg. Industry Cons. Svc. Internat., Assn. for Quality and Participation, KC. Roman Catholic. Home: 116 Valley Oak Dr Roseville CA 95678-4378 Office: Calif State Lottery 600 N 10th St Sacramento CA 95814-0393

COLLIS, KAY LYNN, professional beauty consultant; b. Dallas, July 15, 1958; d. Martin Edward and Norma June C. AA, Tyler Jr. Coll., 1978; BBA, Sam Houston State U., 1982. Mgr. World Fin. Corp., Bryan, Tex., 1977-81; ops. analyst Republic Bank Dallas, 1983-85; asst. v.p. MBank, Dallas, 1985-87; v.p., Murray Fed. Savs., 1987-90; owner KC Enterprises, 1990—; sr. beauty cons. Mary Kay, 1994—; advisor Collis Cons. Co., Sulphur Springs, Tex., 1983—. Columnist Contemporary Singles Lifestyles, 1993-96; contbr. articles to mags. Vol. Speaker Bur. Mem. NAFE, Fin. Women Internat. (group pres. 1989-90, Tex. mktg./pub. rels. 1990-91), Las Vegas C. of C., Toastmasters Internat. (divsn. gov. 1996—, Disting. Toastmaster). Republican. Episcopalian. Home and Office: PO Box 33579 Las Vegas NV 89133-3579

COLLMER, RUSSELL CRAVENER, data processing executive, educator; b. Guatemala, Jan. 2, 1924; s. G. Russell and Constance (Cravener) C.; BS, U. N.Mex., 1951; MS in Meteorology, Calif. Inst. Tech., 1944, MS in Math., State U. Iowa, 1955; m. Ruth Hannah Adams, Mar. 4, 1950; 1 son, Reed Alan. Staff mem. Mass. Inst. Tech., Lincoln Lab., Lexington, 1955-57; mgr. systems modeling, computer dept. Gen. Electric, Phoenix, 1957-59; mgr. ARCAS Thompson Ramo Wooldridge, Inc., Canoga Park, Cal., 1959-62; assoc. mgr. tech. dir. CCIS-70 Bunker-Ramo Corp., 1962-64; sr. assoc. Planning Rsch. Corp., Los Angeles, 1964-65; pres. R. Collmer Assocs., Benson, Ariz., 1965—; pres. Benson Econ. Enterprises Corp., 1968-69. Lectr. computer scis. Pima Community Coll., Tucson, 1970—. Served with USAAC, 1942-46, to capt. USAF, 1951-53. Mem. IEEE, Am. Meteorol. Soc., Assn. for Computing Machinery, Phi Delta Theta, Kappa Mu Epsilon. Republican. Baptist. Office: R Collmer Assocs PO Box 864 Benson AZ 85602-0864

COLMAN, RONALD WILLIAM, computer science educator; b. L.A., Sept. 13, 1930; s. William Maynard Colman and Edna Eliza (Halford) Smith. BA in Math., UCLA, 1957; PhD in Computer Sci., U. Calif., Irvine, 1976. Electronics tech. Lockheed Aircraft Corp., Burbank, Calif., 1952-53; staff specialist Western Electric Co., N.Y.C., 1957-58; assoc. math. Burroughs Corp., Pasadena, Calif., 1958-60; sr. computer analyst Beckman Instruments, Inc., Fullerton, Calif., 1960-62; mgr. L.A. dist. Digital Equipment Corp., L.A., 1962-64; chmn. computer sci. Calif. State U., Fullerton, 1964-80; prof. computer sci. Calif. State U., Northridge, 1980-89; ptnr. Windward Ventures, Venice, Calif.; chmn. session on heuristic search Internat. Joint Conf. on Artificial Intelligence, Stanford, 1973; chmn. nat. symposium on computer sci. edn. Assn. Computing Machinery, Anaheim, Calif., 1976; chmn. registration Nat. Computer Conf., Anaheim, 1978, 80. With USN, 1948-52. Home: 2800 Baywater Ave Apt 8 San Pedro CA 90731-6695

COLN, WILLIAM ALEXANDER, III, pilot; b. Los Angeles, Mar. 20, 1942; s. William Alexander and Aileen Henrietta (Shimfessel) C.; m. Lora Louise Getchel, Nov. 15, 1969 (div. July 1979); 1 child, Caryn Louise. BA in Geography, UCLA, 1966. Cert. airline transport pilot, flight engr. Commd. USN, Pensacola, Fla., 1966; pilot, officer USN, Fighter Squadron 102, 1969-71, Pt. Mugu, Calif., 1975-77; pilot, officer USNR, Port Mugu, Calif., 1971-75, advanced through grades to lt. comdr., 1978; ret. USNR, 1984; airline pilot Delta Airlines, Inc. (formerly Western Airlines Inc.), Los Angeles, 1972—. Recipient Nat. Def. medal USN, 1966. Mem. Nat. Aero. Assn., Airline Pilots Assn., Aircraft Owners and Pilots Assn., UCLA Alumni Assn., Am. Bonanza Soc., Internat. Platform Assn. Democrat. Club: Santa Barbara (Calif.) Athletic. Home: 519 W Quinto St Santa Barbara CA 93105-4829 Office: Delta Air Lines Inc LA Internat Airport Los Angeles CA 90009

COLOGNE, GORDON BENNETT, lawyer; b. Long Beach, Calif., Aug. 24, 1924; s. Knox M. Cologne; div.; children: Steven J., Ann Maureen. BS, U. So. Calif., 1948; LLB cum laude, Southwestern U. Sch. of Law, L.A., 1951. Bar: Calif. 1951, U.S. Supreme Ct. 1961. Trial atty. U.S. Dept. of Justice, Jacksonville, Fla., 1951-52; pvt. practice Indio, Calif., 1952-61; mayor Indio City Coun., 1954; mem. state assembly Calif. Legis., Sacramento, 1961-65; mem. senate Calif. State Senate, Sacramento, 1965-72; justice Ct. of Appeal, San Diego, 1972-84; govt. rels. atty. Sacramento, 1984—. With USN, 1944-46. Named one of Outstanding Young Men of Calif., Calif. Jr. C. of C., 1961; recipient Freedom Found. award, 1965.

COLTON, ROY CHARLES, management consultant; b. Phila., Feb. 26, 1941; s. Nathan Hale and Ruth Janis (Baylinson) C.; B.A., Knox Coll., 1962; M.Ed., Temple U., 1963. With Sch. Dist. of Phila., 1963-64; systems analyst Wilmington Trust Co., 1967-69; exec. recruiter Atwood Consultants Inc., Phila., 1969-71; pres. Colton Bernard Inc., San Francisco, 1971—; occasional lectr. Fashion Inst. Tech., Phila. Coll. Textiles and Scis. Served with AUS, 1964-66. Mem. San Francisco Fashion Industries, San Francisco C. of C., Calif. Exec. Recruiter Assn., Nat. Assn. Exec. Recruiters, Am. Apparel Mfrs. Assn., Am. Arbitration Assn. (panel arbitrators). Office: Colton Bernard Inc 870 Market St Ste 822 San Francisco CA 94102-2903

COLTON, STERLING DON, lawyer, business executive, missionary; b. Vernal, Utah, Apr. 28, 1929; s. Hugh Wilkins and Marguerite (Maughan) C.; m. Eleanor Ricks, Aug. 6, 1954; children: Sterling David, Carolyn, Bradley Hugh, Steven Ricks. BS in Banking and Fin., U. Utah, 1951; JD, Stanford U., 1954. Bar: Calif. 1954, Utah 1954, D.C. 1967. Ptnr., Van Cott, Bagley, Cornwall & McCarthy, Salt Lake City, 1957-66; former vice chair, sr. v.p., gen. counsel Marriott Corp., Washington, 1966-93, former bd. dirs.; sr. v.p., vice chair, gen. counsel, bd. dirs. Marriott Internat., 1993-95; pres. Can. Vancouver Mission Ch. of Jesus Christ of Latter Day Saints, 1995—, also bd. dirs.; v.p. Colton Ranch Corp., Vernal, 1987—; former bd. dirs. Megaherz Corp. and Dyncorp; former chmn. bd. dirs. Nat. Chamber Litigation Ctr. Former bd. dirs. Polynesian Cultural Ctr.; former chmn. nat. adv. coun. U. Utah, Ballet West, nat. adv. counsel; mem. adv. coun. The Nat. Conservancy.Maj. JAG, U.S. Army, 1954-57. Mem. ABA, Calif. Bar Assn., Utah Bar Assn., D.C. Bar Assn., Washington Met. Corp. Counsel Assn. (former pres., dir.), Sigma Chi. Republican. Mem. LDS Ch. Office: 8440 Williams Rd, Richmond, BC Canada V7A 1G6

COLUCCI, CHUCK ROGER, management consultant; b. Chgo., Dec. 17, 1955; s. Ralph Michael and Mary Ann (Dolfi) C. BA with honors, Calif. State U., 1980; MBA, U. Calif., Irvine, 1983. Sr. analyst Ford Motor Co., Newport Beach, Calif., 1984-89; internal cons. County of Orange, Santa Ana, Calif., 1990-91; mgmt. cons. John Goodman & Assocs., Las Vegas, 1991-94; pres. IPA, Irvine, Calif., 1994—; pres. Grad. Sch. Mgmt. Health Care Alumni Group U. Calif., Irvine, 1996—. Editor: (with others) Programmed Business Math, 1986; contbr. articles to profl. jours. Bank of Am. scholar, 1979. Mem. U. Calif. Irvine Grad. Sch. Mgmt. Alumni Network (pres. 1990-91), U. Calif. Irvine Grad. Sch. Mgmt. Alumni Network Healthcare Alumni Group (pres. 1996—), Phi Kappa Phi. Office: 6 Chardonnay Irvine CA 92614

COLVARD, D. MICHAEL, ophthalmologist, consultant, educator; b. Atlanta, Jan. 16, 1947; s. Stewart Brown and Virginia (Nelms) C.; m. Susan Marie Talty, June 19, 1976; children: Matthew, Caitlin, Megan. MD, Emory U., 1973. Diplomate Am. Bd. Opthalmology. Assoc. cons. Mayo Clinic, Rochester, Minn., 1978-79; pvt. clin. practice Ctr. Ophthalmic Surgery, Encino, Calif., 1979—; asst. clin. prof. U. So. Calif., L.A., 1981—; med. cons. Pharmacia-Upjohn, Kalamazoo, Mich., 1987—, Premier Laser, Irvine, Calif., 1992-96, Oasis Med. Corp., Glendora, Calif., 1995—. Numerous medical patents in ophthalmic surgery. Contbr. articles to profl. jours. Fellow AWAKES; mem. AMA, Am. Acad. Ophthalmology (Honor award 1994), Am. Soc. Cataract and Refractive Surgeons, Calif. Med. Assn., Calif. Assn. Ophthalmology, Phi Beta Kappa, Alpha Omega Alpha. Office: Ctr Ophthalmic Surgery 5363 Balboa Blvd # 545 Encino CA 91316

COLVIS, JOHN PARIS, aerospace engineer, mathematician, scientist; b. St. Louis, June 30, 1946; s. Louis Jack and Jacqueline Betty (Beers) C.; m. Nancy Ellen Fritz, Mar. 15, 1969 (div. Sept. 16, 1974); 1 child, Michael Scott; m. Barbara Carol Davis, Sept. 3, 1976; 1 child, Rebecca Jo; stepchildren: Bruce William John Zimmerly, Belinda Jo Zimmerly Little. Student, Meramec Community Coll., St. Louis, 1964-65, U. Mo., 1966, 72-75, Palomar Coll., San Marcos, Calif., 1968, U. Mo., Rolla, 1968-69; BS in Math., Washington U., 1977. Assoc. system safety engr. McDonnell Douglas Astronautics Co., St. Louis, 1978-81; sr. system safety engr. Martin Marietta Astronautics Group-Strategic Systems Co., Denver, 1981-87; sr. engr. Martin Marietta Astronautics Group-Space Launch Systems Co., Denver, 1987-95, Lockheed Martin Astronautics Co.-Space Launch Sys., Denver, 1995—; researcher in field. Precinct del., precinct committeeman, congl. dist. del., state del. Rep. Party. Lance cpl. USMC, 1966-68, Vietnam. Mem. VFW (post 4171), Colo. Home Educators' Assn. (pres. 1989), Khe Sahn Vet Incorp. Evangelical. Home: 4978 S Hoyt St Littleton CO 80123-1988 Office: Lockheed Martin Astronautics Group-SLS PO Box 179 Denver CO 80201-0179

COLWELL, JAMES LEE, humanities educator; b. Brush, Colo., Aug. 31, 1926; s. Francis Joseph and Alice (Bleasdale) C.; BA, U. Denver, 1949; MA, U. No. Colo., 1951; cert. Sorbonne, Paris, 1956; diploma U. Heidelberg (Ger.), 1957; A.M. (Univ. fellow), Yale U., 1959, PhD (Hale-Kilborn fellow), 1961; m. Claudia Alsleben, Dec. 27, 1957; children—John Francis, Alice Anne. Tchr. high sch., Snyder and Sterling, Colo., 1948-52; civilian edn. adviser U.S. Air Force, Japan, 1952-56; assoc. dir. Yale Fgn. Student Inst., summers 1959-60; asst. dir. European div. U. Md., Heidelberg, 1961-65; dir. Office Internat. Edn., assoc. prof. Am. lit. U. Colo., Boulder, 1965-72; prof. Am. studies, chmn. lit. U. Tex. Permian Basin, Odessa, 1977-82, dean Coll. Arts and Edn., 1972-77, 82-84, K.C. Dunagan prof. humanities, 1984-87, prof. emeritus, 1988—. Mem. nat. adv. council Inst. Internat. Edn., 1969-75. Vice pres. Ector County chpt. ARC, 1974-76; mem. Ector County Hist. Commn., 1973-75. Served with USAAF, 1945; brig. gen. USAF Res. Ret. Mem. AAUP, Am. Studies Assn., Western Social Sci. Assn. (life; pres. 1974-75), MLA, NEA (life), Orgn. Am. Historians (life), South Central MLA, Permian Basin Hist. Soc. (life; pres. 1980-81), Air Force Assn. (life), Air Force Hist. Found. (life), Res. Officers Assn. (life), Ret. Officers Assn. (life), Phi Beta Kappa. Unitarian-Universalist. Contbr. articles to learned jours. Home: 4675 Gordon Dr Boulder CO 80303-6747

COMANOR, WILLIAM S., economist, educator; b. Phila., May 11, 1937; s. Leroy and Sylvia (Bershad) C.; m. Joan Thall; children: Christine, Katherine, Gregory. Student, Williams Coll., 1955-57; BA, Haverford Coll., 1959; MA, PhD, Harvard U., 1963; postgrad., London Sch. Econs., 1963-64. Spl. econ. asst. to asst. atty. gen. Antitrust div. U.S. Dept. Justice, Washington, 1965-66; asst. prof. econs. Harvard U., Cambridge, Mass., 1966-68; assoc. prof. Stanford (Calif.) U., 1968-73; dir. bur. econs. FTC, Washington, 1978-80; prof. econs. U. Calif., Santa Barbara, 1975—, dept. chmn., 1984-87; prof. Sch. Pub. Health U. Calif., L.A., 1990—. Author: National Health Insurance in Ontario, 1980, Advertising and Market Power, 1974, Competition Policy in Europe and North America, 1990, Competition Policy in the Global Economy, 1997; contbr. articles to profl. jours. Mem. Am. Econ. Assn. Home: 621 Miramonte Dr Santa Barbara CA 93109-1428 Office: U of Calif Santa Barbara Dept Econs Santa Barbara CA 93106

COMAR, KANWAR DAVE, surgeon; b. Peshawar, India, Apr. 4, 1918; came to U.S., 1950; m. Bertha Sarmento Comar, Jan. 5, 1979; children: Dave Inder, Maadhevi C. BSc, U. Punjab, India, 1935; MD, King Edward Med. Coll., Lahore, India, 1941; postgrad., Royal Coll. Surgeons, Eng., 1948, Western Res. U., 1950. Diplomate Am. Bd. Surgery, Am. Bd. Thoracic Surgery. Intern Irwin Hosp., New Delhi, 1941-42; med. officer Japanese Internment Camp, 1942-44; med. officer tech. tng. scheme Govt. of India, 1942-46; resident, fellow West Middlesex, Guys and Hammersmith Postgrad. Hosps., London, 1946-50; fellow Huron Rd. Hosp., East Cleve., 1950-51, Cleve. Clinic, 1951-53, Hosp. of Good Samaritan and Children's Hosp., L.A., 1953-54; pvt. practice L.A., 1960—; chief surgeon So. Calif. Edison Co., 1960-75; examiner Calif. Bd. Med. License. Contbr. numerous articles, papers to profl. jours. and internat. med. confs. Chmn. L.A. County Met. Heart Assn., 1970; hospitality vol. L.A. World Affairs Coun. Recipient Internat. Pers. Rsch. Creativity award. Fellow ACS, Internat. Coll. Surgeons, Royal Soc. Medicine (Eng.), Am. Coll. Angiology; mem. Masons, Lions Club Internat. Hindu. Office: 1323 E 1st St Los Angeles CA 90033-3217

COMBS, CORA VICTORIA, chemist; b. Manila, Philippines, Oct. 10, 1950; came to U.S., 1975; d. Marcos Peña and Elisa (Ramos) Victoria; m. Albert Ronald Combs, Aug. 21, 1981. BS in Chemistry, Mapua Inst. Tech., Manila, 1972; MS in Chemistry, Western Mich. U., 1979. Chemist E.R. Squibb, Manila, 1972-73; chemist-in-charge Central Colls., Quezon City, Philippines, 1973-75; grad. asst. Western Mich. U., Kalamazoo, 1975-79; lead chemist Banner Pharmaceuticals, Chatsworth, Calif., 1979-83; sr. chemist/group leader 3M Pharmaceuticals, Northridge, Calif., 1983—; pres. Mapua Inst. Tech. Assn. of Chem. Students, Manila, 1971-72. Recipient Pres.'s Gold medal Mapua Inst. Tech., 1972; Western Mich. U. grantee, 1978. Mem. Am. Chem. Soc, Philippine Chem. Soc., 3M Club. Republican. Roman Catholic. Office: 3M Pharmaceuticals 19901 Nordhoff St Northridge CA 91324-3213

COMBS, W(ILLIAM) HENRY, III, lawyer; b. Casper, Wyo., Mar. 18, 1949; s. William Henry and Ruth M. (Wooster) C.; divorced; 1 child, J. Bradley. Student, Northwestern U., 1967-70; BS, U. Wyo., 1972, JD, 1975. Bar: Wyo. 1975, U.S. Dist. Ct. Wyo. 1975, U.S. Ct. Appeals (10th cir.) 1990, U.S. Supreme Ct. 1990. Assoc. Murane & Bostwick, Casper, 1975-77, ptnr., 1978—. Mem. com. on resolution of fee disputes, 1988-92. Mem. ABA (tort and ins. practice, law office mgmt. sects.), Natrona County Bar Assn., Def. Rsch. Inst., Am. Judicature Soc., Wyo. Trial Def. Counsel, Assn. Ski Def. Attys., Nat. Bd. Trial Advocacy (cert.), U.S. Handball Assn., Am. Water Ski Assn., Casper Boat Club, Casper Petroleum Club, Porsche Club Am., BMW Club Am., Sports Car Club Am. Republican. Episcopalian. Office: Murane & Bostwick 201 N Wolcott St Casper WY 82601-1922

COMEAUX, KATHARINE JEANNE, realtor; b. Richland, Wash., Jan. 18, 1949; d. Warren William and Ruth Irma (Remington) Gonder; m. Jack Goldwasser, May 25, 1992; 1 child, Thelma Morrow. AA, West Valley Coll., 1970; student, San Jose State U., 1970-71. Cert. realtor. Realtor Value Realty, Cupertino, Calif., 1975-79, Valley of Calif., Cupertino, 1979-81, Coldwell Banker, Cupertino, 1981-82, Fox & Carskadon, Saratoga, Calif., 1984-90. With Los Gatos-Saratoga Bd. Realtors Polit. Action, 1984-89; v.p. Hospice of Valley Svc. League, Saratoga, 1984-89; Big Sister Big Bros./Big Sisters, San Jose, Calif., 1976-90; bd. dirs. Mountain Energy Inc., United Way of Josephine County, Energia Natural, Honduras, Boys and Girls Club. Home: 4330 Fish Hatchery Rd Grants Pass OR 97527-9547

COMES, ROBERT GEORGE, research scientist; b. Bangor, Pa., July 7, 1931; s. Victor Francis and Mabel Elizabeth (Mack) C.; student U. Detroit, 1957-58, Oreg. State Coll., 1959-60, U. Nev., 1960, Regis Coll., 1961-62; m. Carol Lee Turinetti, Nov. 28, 1952; children: Pamela Jo, Robert G. II, Shawni Lee, Sheryl Lynn, Michelle Ann. Tech. liaison engr. Burroughs Corp., Detroit, 1955-60, mgr. reliability and maintainability engring., Paoli, Pa., 1962-63, Colorado Springs, Colo., 1963-67; sr. engr. Martin Marietta Corp., Denver, 1960-62; program mgr., rsch. scientist Kaman Scis. Corp., Colorado Springs, 1967-75; dir. engring. Sci. Applications, Inc., Colorado Springs, 1975-80; mgr. space def. programs Burroughs Corp., Colorado Springs, 1980-82; tech. staff Mitre Corp., Colorado Springs, 1982-85; dir. Colorado Springs opn. Beers Assoc., Inc., 1985; dir. space programs Electro Magnetic Applications, Inc., Colorado Springs, 1985-87; dir. Space Systems, Profl. Mgmt. Assocs., Inc., 1987-88; mgr. Computer Svcs., Inc., Colorado Springs, 1989—; dir. mktg. Proactive Techs., Inc., Colorado Springs, 1990—; chmn. Reliability and Maintainability Data Bank Improvement Program, Govt.-Industry Data Exch. Program, 1978-80—; cons. in field. Youth dir. Indian Guides program YMCA, 1963-64; scoutmaster Boy Scouts Am., 1972-73; chmn. bd. dirs. Pikes Peak Regional Sci. Fair, 1972-84. Served with USAF, 1951-55. Mem. AAAS, IEEE, Inst. Environ. Scis., Soc. Logistics Engrs., Am. Soc. Quality Control. Lutheran. Club: Colorado Springs Racquet. Author: Maintainability Engineering Principles and Standards, 1962. Inventor Phase Shifting aircraft power supply, 1957. Home: 4309 Tipton Ct Colorado Springs CO 80915-1034 Office: Proactive Tech Inc 4309 Tipton Ct Colorado Springs CO 80915-1034

COMFORT, CLIFTON C., management consultant; b. Dallas, June 19, 1943; s. Clifton C. and Nola B. (Harris) C.; m. Jacquelynn S. Henderson, June 27, 1964 (div. Nov. 1981); 1 child, Amy Elizabeth (Mrs. James Pratt). BBA in Acctg. with honors, U. Tex., Arlington, 1964; MBA, U. Phoenix, 1989. CPA, cert. internal auditor, cost analyst, fraud examiner, Tex. Auditor U.S. Govt., Dallas, 1964-75, fin. mgr., 1975-78, audit mgr., 1978-83; mgmt. cons. C.C. Comfort Cons., Dallas, 1983-86, 92—; dir. compliance Litton Industries, Tempe, Ariz., 1986-92; mem. Fed. Exec. Bd., Dallas, 1979-82, Intergovtl. Audit Forum, Dallas, 1979-82; co. rep. to Electronic Industries Assn., Washington, 1986-92, Machinery and Alied Products Inst., Washington, 1986-92; presenter seminars in field. Contbr. articles to profl. jours. Bd. dirs. Assn. Govt. Accts., 1983-84; res. dep. sheriff Sheriff's Dept. Dallas, 1976-83; pres. U. Tex.-Arlington Alumni Assn., 1984-85. Recipient Cert. of Merit Sheriff's Dept. Dallas, 1980, Best Tech. Article award Assn. Govt. Accts., 1979. Mem. ABA, AICPA, Soc. for Advancement of Mgmt. (bd. dirs. 1984-85), Nat. Contract Mgmt. Assn. (v.p. 1994-95), Assn. Cert. Fraud Examiners (bd. dirs. 1994-95), Inst. Mgmt. Cons. Office: CC Comfort Cons 3370 N Hayden Rd Ste 123 Scottsdale AZ 85251

COMINGS, DAVID EDWARD, physician, medical genetics scientist; b. Beacon, N.Y., Mar. 8, 1935; s. Edward Walter and Jean (Rice) C.; m. Shirley Nelson, Aug. 9, 1958; children: Mark David, Scott Edward, Karen Jean; m. Brenda Gursey, Mar. 20, 1982. Student, U. Ill., 1951-54; B.S., Northwestern U., 1955, M.D., 1958. Intern Cook County Hosp., Chgo., 1958-59; resident in internal medicine Cook County Hosp., 1959-62; fellow in med. genetics U. Wash., Seattle, 1964-66; dir. dept. med. genetics City of Hope Med. Ctr., Duarte, Calif., 1966—; mem. genetics study sect. NIH, 1974-78; mem. sci. adv. bd. Hereditary Disease Found., 1975—, Nat. Found. March of Dimes, 1978—. Author: Tourette Syndrome and Human Behavior, 1990; editor: (with others) Molecular Human Cytogenetics, 1977; mem. editorial bd.: (with others) Cytogenetics and Cell genetics, 1979—; editor in chief Am. Jour. Human Genetics, 1978-86. Served with U.S. Army, 1962-64. NIH grantee, 1967—. Mem. Assn. Am. Physicians, Am. Soc. Clin. Investigation, AAAS, Am. Soc. Human Genetics (dir. 1974-78, pres. 1988), Am. Soc. Cell Biology, Am. Fedn. Clin. Research, Western Soc. Clin. Research, Council Biology Editors. Office: City of Hope Med Ctr 1500 Duarte Rd Duarte CA 91010-3012

COMMANDER, EUGENE R., lawyer; b. Sioux City, Iowa, Jan. 10, 1953. BA in Architecture, Iowa State U., 1975; JD with distinction, U. Iowa, 1977. Bar: Iowa 1977, Colo. 1981. Mem. Hall & Evans, Denver. Mem. ABA (forum com. on constrn. industry, subcoms. on bonds, liens, ins. and contract documents, tort and ins. practice sect. coms. on fidelity, surety law, property ins.), AIA (profl. affiliate, Colo. chpt.), Am. Arbitration Assn. (panel constrn. industry arbitrators 1983—), Am. Law Firm Assn. (constrn. industry practice group), Def. Rsch. Inst. (constrn. law and fidelity and surety law coms.), Profl. Liability Underwriting Soc. Office: Hall & Evans 1200 17th St Ste 1700 Denver CO 80202-5835

COMPTON, ALLAN, psychoanalyst, researcher; b. New Brunswick, N.J., May 8, 1934; s. Luther Allan and Emily Ethel (Jones) C.; m. Dorothy Jean Morris, June 20, 1959 (div. Aug. 1974); children: Kaila M., John A., Susan Beth Compton Pelman; m. Miriam Tasini, July 4, 1977. BS, Rutgers U., 1955; MD, Cornell U., N.Y.C., 1959. Diplomate Am. Bd. Psychiatry and Neurology. Intern in surgery St. Luke's Hosp., N.Y.C., 1959-60; resident 2d surgical divsn. Bellevue Hosp., N.Y.C., 1960-61; resident in psychiatry N.Y. VA Hosp., N.Y.C., 1961, Bronx (N.Y.) Mcpl. Hosp., 1961-64; pvt. practice, N.Y.C., 19644-67, N.Y. Psychoanalytic Inst., N.Y.C., 1962-67, L.A., 1969—; founder, pres. L.A. Ctr. for Psychoanalytic Rsch., 1989—. Contbr. over 40 articles to med. jours. Comdr. M.C., USN, 1967-69. Mem. Am. Psychoanalytic Assn. (councillor-at-large 1995—). Democrat.

COMPTON, ALLEN T., state supreme court justice; b. Kansas City, Mo., Feb. 25, 1938; m. Sue Ellen Tatter; 3 children. B.A., U. Kans., 1960; LL.B., U. Colo., 1963. Pvt. practice Colorado Springs, 1963-68; staff atty. Legal Svcs. Office, Colorado Springs, 1968-69, dir., 1969-71; supervising atty. Alaska Legal Svcs., Juneau, Alaska, 1971-73; pvt. practice Juneau, 1973-76; judge Superior Ct., Alaska, 1976-80; assoc. justice Alaska Supreme Ct., Anchorage, 1980—, chief justice, 1995—. Mem. 4 bar assns. including Juneau Bar Assn. (past pres.). Office: Alaska Supreme Ct 303 K St Anchorage AK 99501-2013

COMPTON, JAMES VINCENT, retired history educator; b. Perth Amboy, N.J., July 5, 1928; s. Lewis Compton and Beatrice Camille (Vincent) Copsey. BA, Princeton U., 1950; MA, U. Chgo., 1952; postgrad., U. Munich, 1954-55; PhD, U. London, 1964. Lectr. European divsn. U. Md., 1954-60; lectr. U. London, 1961-64; lectr. U. Edinburgh, Scotland, 1964-68, chair Am. studies, 1964-68; assoc. prof. history Trinity Coll., Hartford, Conn., 1968-69; prof. history San Francisco State U., 1969-95; ret., 1995. Author: The Swastika and The Eagle, 1967, America and Origins of Cold War, 1970, (study unit) The New Deal, 1973; cons. editor: For the President: Personal Secret, 1972. Konrad Adenauer fellow German Govt., 1954-55. Mem. Orgn. Am. Historians, Brit. Assn. Am. Studies. Democrat. Roman Catholic. Home: 170 Diamond St San Francisco CA 94114-2414

COMPTON, MERLIN DAVID, Spanish language educator; b. Ogden, Utah, July 22, 1924; s. George Albert and Margaret Estella (Mattson) C.; m. Avon Allen Compton, June 17, 1950; children: Terry Ann Compton Harward, Todd Merlin, Tamara Jane Compton Hauge, Timothy George, Tina Louise. BA, Brigham Young U., 1952, MA, 1954; PhD, UCLA, 1959. Asst. prof. Adams State Coll., Alamosa, Colo., 1959-63; assoc. prof. Weber State Coll., Ogden, Utah, 1963-64; prof. Spanish Brigham Young U., Provo, Utah, 1964-89. Author: Ricardo Palma, 1982, Trayectoria de las Tradiciones de Ricardo Palma, 1989. Staff sgt. USAF, 1943-46. Mem. Phi Kappa Phi. Mem. LDS Ch. Home: 1015 S River Rd Apt 27 Saint George UT 84790-2220

COMUS, LOUIS FRANCIS, JR., lawyer; b. St. Marys, Ohio, Feb. 26, 1942. BA, Antioch Coll., 1965; JD, Vanderbilt U., 1968. Bar: N.Y. 1969, Ariz. 1973. Dir. Fennemore Craig P.C., Phoenix, 1975—. Notes editor Vanderbilt Law Rev., 1967-68. Fellow Am. Coll. Trust and Estate Counsel; mem. ABA, State Bar Ariz., Maricopa County Bar Assn., Order of Coif. Office: Fennemore Craig PC 3003 N Central Ave Ste 2600 Phoenix AZ 85012

CONANT, DAVID ARTHUR, architectural acoustician, educator, consultant; b. Biloxi, Miss., Dec. 22, 1945; s. Roger and Lillian Rose May (Lovell) C.; m. Nancy Hayes, June 17, 1972; children: Christopher, Tyler. BS in Physics, Union Coll., 1968; MA in Geology, Columbia U., 1972; BArch, Rensselaer Poly. Inst., 1975, MArch, 1975. Faculty fellow Lamont-Doherty Earth Obs., Palisades, N.Y., 1970-72; teaching asst. Rensselaer Poly. Inst., Troy, N.Y., 1973-76; asst. prof. dept. architecture Calif. State Poly. U., Pomona, 1976-78; sr. cons. Bolt Beranek Newman Inc., Canoga Park, Calif., 1977-87; prin. McKay Conant Brook, Inc., Westlake Village, Calif., 1987—; cons. IBM Bldg. Energy Rsch. Group, Marina del Rey, Calif., 1976-77, Expo '93, Taejon, Korea; prin. acoustical cons. Disneyland Paris, 1989-92, Guggenheim Mus., Bilbao, Spain, 1994-96, Hawaii Convention Ctr., Honolulu, 1995-97, Tokyo Disney Seas, 1996-97; lectr. acoustics UCLA. Co-author: (textbook) Fundamentals and Abatement of Highway Traffic Noise, 1980; author computer software. Instr., vol. Upward Bound, Schenectady, N.Y., 1967-68; overseas vol. Am. Friends Svc. Com., Yugoslavia and Denmark, 1967. With U.S. Army, 1968-70. Recipient Honor award Am. Inst. Architects, 1991. Mem. ASHRAE, Acoustical Soc. Am. (archtl. acoustics tech. com.), Nat. Coun. Acoustical Cons. (bd. dirs.), Constrn. Specifications Inst., Sigma Xi (univ. chpts. lectr. physics). Republican. Presbyterian. Home: 1504 Grissom St Thousand Oaks CA 91362-2010 Office: McKay Conant Brook Inc 5655 Lindero Canyon Rd Ste 325 Thousand Oaks CA 91362-4045

CONCEPCIÖN, DAVID ALDEN, arbitrator, educator; b. Carmel, Calif., Aug. 6, 1935; s. Don Dominador Cuales Concepciön and Elma Elizabeth Davis; m. Ann Martin Worster, Dec. 3, 1960; children: Leslie Martin Concepciön Mayns, David Worster. BA, U. Calif., Santa Barbara, 1959. Adminstrv. exec. Lawrence Berkeley Lab. U. Calif., Berkeley, 1962-70, dir. mgmt. analysis, 1970-75; assoc. dean adminstrn. Hastings Coll. Law U. Calif., San Francisco, 1975-80; pvt. practice Berkeley, 1980—; mem. adv. bd. Calif. Pub. Employee Rels. at U. Calif., Berkeley, 1978—. Contbr. articles to profl. jours. Capt. USMC, 1959-62. Mem. Nat. Acad. Arbitrators (mem. com. 1995—), Am. Arbitration Assn. (mem. No. Calif. Adv. Coun. 1980—, mem. nat. bd. dirs. 1980-86, Disting. Svc. award 1990), Soc. Profls. in Dispute Resolution, Indsl. Rels. Rsch. Assn., Soc. Fed. Labor Rel. Profls. Democrat. Mem. United Ch. Christ. Office: 65 Stevenson Ave Berkeley CA 94708-1732

CONDIE, CAROL JOY, anthropologist, research facility administrator; b. Provo, Utah, Dec. 28, 1931; d. LeRoy and Thelma (Graff) C.; m. M. Kent Stout, June 18, 1954; children: Carla Ann, Erik Roy, Paula Jane. BA in Anthropology, U. Utah, 1953; MEd in Elem. Edn., Cornell U., 1954; PhD in Anthropology, U. N.Mex., 1973; Quivira Rsch. Ctr. Edn. coordinator Maxwell Mus. Anthropology, U. N.Mex., Albuquerque, 1973, interpretation dir., 1974-77; asst. prof. anthropology U. N.Mex., 1975-77; cons. anthropologist, 1977-78; pres. Quivira Research Ctr., Albuquerque, 1978—; cons. anthropologist U.S. Congl. Office Tech. Assessment, chair Archeol. Resources Planning Adv. Com., Albuquerque, 1985-86; leader field seminars Crow Canyon Archeol. Ctr., 1986—; appointee Albuquerque dist. adv. coun., bur. land mgmt. U.S. Dept. Interior, 1989; study leader Smithsonian Instn. Tours, 1991; mem. Albuquerque Heritage Conservation Adv. Com., 1992. Author: The Nighthawk Site: A Pithouse Site on Sandia Pueblo Land, Bernalillo County, New Mexico, 1982, Five Sites on the Pecos River Road, 1985, Data Recovery at Eight Archeological Sites on the Rio Nutritas, 1992, Data Recovery at Eight Archaeological Sites on Cabresto Road Near Questa, 1992, Archeological Survey in the Rough and Ready Hills/Picacho Mountain Area, Dona Ana County, New Mexico, 1993, Archeological Survey on the Canadian River, Quay County, New Mexico, 1994, Archeological Testing at LA 103387, Nizhoni Extension, Gallup, McKinley County, New Mexico, 1995, Two Archeological Sites on San Felipe Pueblo Land, New Mexico, 1996, Four Archeological Sites at La Cienega, Santa Fe County, New Mexico, 1996; co-editor: Anthropology in the Desert West, 1986. Mem. Downtown Core Area Schs. Com., Albuquerque, 1982. Ford Found. fellow, 1953-54; recipient Am. Planning Assn. award, 1985-86, Gov.'s award, 1986. Fellow Am. Anthrop. Assn.; mem. Soc. Am. Archeology (chmn. native Am. rels. com. 1983-85), N.Mex. Archeol. Coun. (pres. 1982-83, hist. preservation award 1988), Albuquerque Archeol. Soc. (pres. 1992), Maxwell Mus. Assn. (bd. dirs. 1980-83), Las Arañas Spinners and Weavers Guild (pres. 1972), N.Mex. Heritage Preservation Alliance. Democrat. Home and Office: Quivira Research Ctr 1809 Notre Dame Dr NE Albuquerque NM 87106-1011

CONDIT, GARY A., congressman; b. Apr. 21, 1948. AA, Modesto Jr. Coll.; BA, Calif. State Coll. Councilman City of Ceres, Calif., 1972-74, mayor, 1974-76; supr. Stanislaus County, Calif., 1976-82; assemblyman State of Calif., 1982-89; mem. 101st-104th Congresses from 15th (now 18th) Calif. Dist., 1989—; ranking minority mem. Ag. subcom. on nutrition & fgn. ag., mem. govt. reform & oversight. Democrat. Office: US Ho of Reps 2444 Rayburn Washington DC 20515*

CONDIT, PHILIP MURRAY, aerospace executive, engineer; b. Berkeley, Calif., Aug. 2, 1941; s. Daniel Harrison and Bernice (Kemp) C.; m. Madeleine K. Bryant, Jan. 25, 1963 (div. June 1982); children: Nicole Lynn, Megan Anne; m. Janice Condit, Apr. 6, 1991. BS MechE, U. Calif., Berkeley, 1963; MS in Aero. Engring., Princeton U., 1965; MS in Mgmt., MIT, 1975. Engr. The Boeing Co., Seattle, 1965-72, mgr. engring., 1973-83, v.p., gen. mgr., 1983-84, v.p. sales and mktg., 1984-86, exec. v.p., 1986-89, exec. v.p., gen. mgr. 777 div., 1989-92, pres., 1992-96, chmn., CEO, 1996—; mem. adv. coun. Dept. Mech. and Aerospace Engring., Princeton (N.J.) U., 1984—; chmn. aero. adv. com. NASA Adv. Coun., 1988-92; bd. dirs. The Fluke Corp., 1987—, Nordstom, Inc., 1993—. Co-inventor Design of a Flexible Wing, 1965. Mem. Mercer Island (Wash.) Utilities Bd., 1975-78; bd. dirs. Camp Fire, Inc., 1987-92; mem. exec bd. chief Seattle coun. Boy Scouts Am., 1988-90; trustee Mus. of Flight, Seattle, 1990—. Co-recipient Laurels award Aviation Week & Space Tech. magazine, 1990; Sloan fellow MIT, Boston, 1974. Fellow AIAA (aircraft design award 1984, Edward C. Wells tech. mgmt. award 1982), Royal Aero. Soc.; mem. NAE, Soc. Sloan Fellows (bd. govs. 1985-89), Soc. Automotive Engrs. Clubs: Rainier, Columbia Tower (Seattle). Office: The Boeing Co PO Box 3707 7755 E Marginal Way S Seattle WA 98124-2207*

CONDO, JAMES ROBERT, lawyer; b. Somerville, N.J., Mar. 2, 1952; s. Ralph Vincent and Betty Louise (MacQuaide) C. BS in Bus. and Econs., Lehigh U., 1974; JD, Boston Coll., 1979. Bar: Ariz. 1979, U.S. Dist. Ct. Ariz. 1979, U.S. Ct. Appeals (9th cir.) 1982, U.S. Ct. Appeals (D.C. cir.) 1989, U.S. Ct. Appeals (10th cir.) 1989, U.S. Supreme Ct. 1983, U.S. Ct. Appeals (6th cir.) 1991, U.S. Ct. Appeals (4th cir.) 1994. Assoc. Snell & Wilmer, Phoenix, 1979-84, ptnr., 1985—. Fellow Ariz. Bar Found.; mem. ABA, State Bar Ariz., Maricopa County Bar Found., Am. Arbitration Assn., Ariz. Town Hall, Def. Rsch. Inst. Home: 2939 N Manor Dr Phoenix AZ 85014 Office: Snell & Wilmer One Arizona Ctr Phoenix AZ 85004

CONDON, DONALD STEPHEN, real estate investor and developer, broker, consultant, actor, model; b. Bklyn., Dec. 26, 1930; s. Joseph Francis and Helen (Carboy) C.; m. Cristina Maria Basarrate, Sept. 27, 1969 (div.); children: Gregg, Mark, Brian, Alexander, Kevin. Student Oberlin Coll., 1949-50; BA, Northwestern U., 1953; postgrad. U. Detroit, 1956. Mem. sales and mktg. dept. Owens-Corning Fiberglas, 1955-63; v.p., gen. mgr. Howard T. Keating Co., Birmingham, Mich., 1963-65; CEO Condon Investment & Devel. Corp., Bloomfield Hills, Mich., 1965-69; pres. Condyne, Inc., N.Y.C., 1969-74; chmn., dir. Parr, O'Mara, Condon & Assocs., Inc., N.Y.C. and Palm Beach, Fla., 1974-81; pres., CEO The Condon Corp., L.A., 1981—; lectr. Practising Law Inst., 1970-71. Actor appearing in TV and Film, 1991, also South Beach, All My Children, BL Striker, over 150 nat. commls.; spokesperson various cos.; also model, 1991—. Served with Signal Corps, U.S. Army, 1953-55. Contbr. articles to House and Home, Profl. Builder mag., Bus. week, Instn. Investor, others. Recipient Sales Builder award Owens-Corning Fiberglas, 1959, Am. Home Builders award for design, 1964, Practical Builders Top Merchandising award, 1966, Mktg. Mgr. of Yr. award Nat. Assn. Home Builders, 1967, Product of Year award Mich. C. of C., 1968, Assn. Indsl. Mgmt. award, 1972; Oberlin Coll. scholar, 1949-50, Northwestern U. scholar, 1953. Mem. SAG, AFTRA, BAC, Phi Gamma Delta. Home and Office: Condon Corp 11730 W Sunset Blvd Apt 329 Los Angeles CA 90049-2979

CONDON, STANLEY CHARLES, gastroenterologist; b. Glendale, Calif., Feb. 1, 1931; s. Charles Max and Alma Mae (Chinn) C.; m. Vaneta Marilyn Mabley, May 19, 1963; children: Lori, Brian, David. BA, La Sierra Coll., 1952; MD, Loma Linda U., 1956. Diplomate Nat. Bd. Med. Examiners, Am. Bd. Internal Medicine, Am. Bd. Gastroenterology; cert. nutrition support physician. Intern L.A. County Gen. Hosp., 1956-57, resident gen. pathology, 1959-61; resident internal medicine White Meml. Med. Ctr., L.A., 1961-63, attending staff out-patient clinic, 1963-64; active jr. attending staff L.A. County Gen. Hosp., 1964-65; dir. intern-resident tng. program Manila Sanitarium and Hosp., 1966-71, med. dir., 1971-72; chief resident internal medicine out-patient clinic Loma Linda U. Med. Ctr., 1972-74; fellow in gastroenterology Barnes Hosp./Wash. U., 1974-76; attending staff, asst. prof. medicine Loma Linda U. Med. Ctr., 1976-91, assoc. prof. medicine, 1991—, med. dir. nutritional support team, 1984—. Contbr. articles to profl. jours. Capt. U.S. Army, 1957-59. Fellow ACP; mem. AMA, Am. Soc. for Parenteral and Enteral Nutrition, Am. Gastroent. Assn., Calif. Med. Assn., So. Calif. Soc. Gastroenterology, Inland Soc. Internal Medicine, San Bernardino County Med. Soc. Republican. Seventh-day Adventist. Home: 11524 Ray Ct Loma Linda CA 92354-3630 Office: Loma Linda U Med Ctr 11370 Anderson St Loma Linda CA 92350

CONDRY, ROBERT STEWART, retired hospital administrator; b. Charleston, W.Va., Aug. 16, 1941; s. John Charles and Mary Louise (Jester) C.; m. Mary Purcell Heinzer, May 21, 1966; children: Mary-Lynch, John Stewart. BA, U. Charleston, 1963; MBA, George Washington U., 1970. Asst. hosp. dir. Med. Coll. of Va., Richmond, 1970-73, assoc. adminstr., 1973-75; assoc. hosp. dir. McGaw Hosp., Loyola U., Maywood, Ill., 1975-84, hosp. dir., 1984-93, ret., 1993; pres. Inter-Hosp. Planning Assn. of Western Suburbs, Maywood, 1983-93; bd. dirs. PentaMed, Inc., San Antonio. Bd. dirs. Met. Chgo. Healthcare Coun., 1985-93, mem. exec. com., 1989-93; bd. dirs. Cath. Hosp. Alliance, 1992, chmn. bd. dirs., 1992, mem. exec. com. 1988-94; mem. Ill. Gov.'s Adv. Bd. on Infant Mortality Reduction, 1988-93, Rev. Bd. on Emergency Medicine Svcs., 1989-93. With U.S. Army, 1964-66. Recipient preceptorship George Washington U., 1985, U. Chgo., 1984, St. Louis U., 1984, Tulane U., 1984, Yale U., 1991. Fellow Am. Coll. Healthcare Execs., Am. Acad. Med. Adminstrs.; mem. Am. Hosp. Assn., Cath. Hosp. Assn., Am. Mgmt. Assn. Republican. Roman Catholic.

CONE, LAWRENCE ARTHUR, research medicine educator; b. N.Y.C., Mar. 23, 1928; s. Max N. and Ruth (Weber) C.; m. Julia Haldy, June 6, 1947 (dec. 1956); m. Mary Elisabeth Osborne, Aug. 20, 1960; children: Lionel Alfred. AB, NYU, 1948; MD, U. Berne, Switzerland, 1954; DSc (hon.), Rocky Mountain Coll., 1993. Diplomate Am. Bd. Internal Medicine, Am. Bd. Infectious Diseases, Am. Bd. Allergy and Immunology, Am. Bd. Med. Examiners. Intern Dallas Meth. Hosp., 1954-55, resident internal medicine, 1955; resident Flower 5th Hosp., N.Y.C., 1957-59, Met. Hosp., N.Y.C., 1959-60; rsch. fellow infectious diseases and immunology NYU Med. Sch., N.Y.C., 1960-62; from asst. prof. to assoc. prof. N.Y. Med. Coll., N.Y.C., 1962-72, chief sect. immunology and infectious diseases, 1962-72; assoc. clin. prof. medicine Harbor UCLA Med. Sch., 1984—; career scientist Health Rsch. Coun. N.Y.C., 1962-68; chief sect. immunology and infectious diseases Eisenhower Med. Ctr., Rancho Mirage, Calif., 1973 , chmn. dept. medicine, 1976-78, pres. elect, pres., past pres. med. staff, 1984-90; cons. infectious disease Desert Hosp., Palm Springs, Calif., 1980-85. Contbr. articles to profl. jours. Bd. dirs. Desert Bighorn Rsch. Inst., Palm Desert, Calif., pres., bd. dirs., 1995-97; nat. adv. coun., mem., bd. trustees Rocky Mountain Coll., Billings, Mont.; mem. med. adv. staff Coll. of Desert, Palm Desert; Pres. Cir. Desert Mus., Palm Springs, Calif., Idaho Conservation League, Gilcrease

Mus., Tulsa, Sun Valley Ctr. for Arts and Humanities, Smithsonian Inst., Buffalo Bill Historic Mus., Cody, Wyo.; life mem. The Living Desert, Palm Desert. Fellow ACP, Royal Soc. Medicine, Interam. Soc. Chemotherapy, Am. Coll. Allergy, Am. Acad. Allergy and Immunology, Am. Soc. Infectious Diseases, Am. Geriatric Soc. (founding fellow we. divsn.); mem. AAAS, Internat. AIDS Soc., Am. Soc. Microbiology, Reticulocudothelial Soc., Am. Fedn. for Clin. Rsch., Faculty Soc. UCLA, Surg. Soc. N.Y. Med. Coll. (hon.), Woodstock Artists Assn., Harvey Soc., N.Y. Acad. Scis., NYU Alumni Assn., Berne Alumni Assn., Lotos Club, Tamarisk Country Club, Coachella Valley Gun and Wildlife Club, Faculty Soc. UCLA Harbor Med. Ctr., O'Donnell Golf Club, Sigma Xi. Republican. Home: 765 Via Vadera Palm Springs CA 92262-4170 Office: Probst Profl Bldg # 308 39000 Bob Hope Dr Rancho Mirage CA 92270-3221 also: Larkspur Condominiums Box 1503 Sun Valley ID 83353

CONGDON, ROGER DOUGLASS, theology educator, minister; b. Ft. Collins, Colo., Apr. 6, 1918; s. John Solon and Ellen Avery (Kellogg) C.; m. Rhoda Gwendolyn Britt, Jan. 2, 1948; children: Rachel Congdon Lidbeck, James R., R. Steven, Jon B., Philip F., Robert N., Bradford B., Ruth A. Mahner, Rebecca York Skones, Rhoda J. Miller, Marianne C. Potter, Mark Alexander. BA, Wheaton Coll., 1940; postgrad, Eastern Bapt. Sem., 1940-41; ThM, Dallas Theol. Sem., 1945; ThD, Dallas Theology Sem., 1949. Ordained to ministry Bapt. Ch., 1945. Exec. sec., dean Altanta Bible Inst., 1945-49; prof. theology Carver Bible Inst., Atlanta, 1945-49; prof. Multnomah Bible Coll., Portland, Oreg., 1950-87; pastor Emmanuel Bapt. Ch., Vancouver, Wash., 1985—; past dean of faculty, dean of edn., v.p., chmn. libr. com., chmn. achievement-award com., chmn. lectureship com., advisor grad. div. and mem. pres.'s cabinet Multnomah Bible Co.; chmn. Chil Evang. Fellowship of Greater Portland, 1978—; founder, pres. Preaching Print Inc., Portland, 1953—. Founder, speaker semi-weekly radio broadcast Bible Truth Forum, KPDQ, Portland, Oreg., 1989—; author: The Doctrine of Conscience, 1945. Chmn. Citizen's Com. Info. on Communism, Portland, 1968-75. Recipient Outstanding Educators of Am. award, 1972, Loraine Chafer award in Systematic Theology, Dallas Theol. Sem. Mem. Am. Assn. Bible Colls. (chmn. testing com. 1953-78), N.Am. Assn. Bible Colls. (N.W. rep. 1960-63), Near East Archaeol. Soc., Evang. Theol. Soc. Republican. Home: 16539 NE Halsey St Portland OR 97230-5607 Office: Emmanuel Bapt Ch 14810 NE 28th St Vancouver WA 98682-8357 *A base person's problems usually consist in selecting between overt evils. The average person chooses between the shady and the good. But the truly noble person, who follows Jesus Christ, never bothers with evils or shady acts; he ever seeks to discern the transcendent, to choose the best of all good choices.*

CONGER, JOHN D., vascular physiologist, nephrologist; b. Cottonwood, Idaho, Jan. 15, 1939; s. Earnest A. and Helen M. (Hines) C.; m. Carol A. Cherberg, May 13, 1961; children: David, James, Paul, Carolyn, Catherine. BS in Chemistry, Seattle U., 1961; MD, U. Wash., 1965. Diplomate Am. Bd. Internal Medicine. Rsch. fellow U. Calif., San Francisco, 1971-73; asst. prof. U. Colo., Denver, 1973-77, assoc. prof., 1977-87, prof., 1988—; chief of staff VA Med. Ctr., Denver, 1997—; cons. Cole Labs., Lakewood, Colo., 1974-80; mem. adv. bd. SmithKline & Beecham, Phila., 1994—; chmn. rsch. com. Am. Heart Assn. Colo., Denver, 1995—. Contbr. chpt. to book, articles to profl. jours. Chmn. minority com. U. Colo., Denver. Lt. comdr. USN, 1965-71. NIDDK/NIH grante, 1989—. Fellow ACP; mem. Am. Phys. Soc., Am. Soc. Clin. Investigation, Assn. Am. Physicians, Internat. Soc. nephrology. Office: VA Med Ctr Chief Staff 1055 Clermont St Denver CO 80220-2820

CONIGLIO, JOHN VINCENT, publishing company executive, acquisitions editor; b. East Chgo., Ind., Dec. 21, 1963; s. George and Margaret Irene (Chovanec) C.; m. Stacey Lynn Erickson, June 24, 1994. BA in journalism, U. Wis., 1986. Advt. salesman Orange Coast Mall Mags., Lake Forest, Calif., 1986-87; yellow pages acct. rep. Southwestern Bell Publs., St. Louis, 1987-89; pres., founder Burcon Financial, Inc., Brea, Calif., 1989-95; acquisitions editor Kendall/Hunt Pub. Co., Dubuque, Iowa, 1995—. Author: Rumors of Angels, 1994; appeared on numerous radio and TV talk shows including WORD Radio, Pitts., 1994, KSLR Radio, San Antonio, 1994, 21 Huntley St. and others. Office: Burcon Fin Inc 1215 W Imperial Hwy Brea CA 92821-3738

CONKLIN, HAL (HAROLD CONKLIN), mayor; b. Oakland, Calif., Dec. 11, 1945; s. Ralph Harold and Stella (Garabedian) C.; m. Barbara Elaine Lang, Mar. 25, 1972; children: Nathaniel, Joseph Lucas, Zachary. Student, Calif. State U., Hayward, 1967-71. Editor New Focus Mag., Santa Barbara, Calif., 1969-72; co-dir. Community Environ. Coun., Santa Barbara, 1972-82; pres. Santa Barbara Renaissance Fund, 1983—; mayor City of Santa Barbara, 1993—; dir. pub. affairs So. Calif., Edison, Calif. Councilman City of Santa Barbara, 1977-93; bd. dirs. Santa Barbara Redevel. Agy., 1978—, Calif. Local Govt. Commn., Sacramento, 1979—, Nat. League of Cities, 1987-89, Santa Barbara Civic Light Opera; pres. Calif. Ctr. Civic Renewal, La Casa do Maria Retreat Ctr.; v.p. Santa Barbara Romantic Design Co.; v.p. Nat. League of Cities, 1994. Mem. League of Calif. Cities (bd. dirs. 1986—, pres. 1991-92), Calif. Resource Recovery Assn. (pres. 1978-82). Methodist. Home: 214 El Monte Dr Santa Barbara CA 93109-2006

CONKLIN, THOMAS RAY, secondary education educator; b. Rockford, Ill., Oct. 3, 1962; s. Jack R. and Katherine E. (Helley) C.; m. Deborah A. Aning, Nov. 27, 1985; children: Luke, McKenzie. BS in Edn., Northwestern Coll., St. Paul, 1985; MA in Sports Medicine, Mankato (Minn.) State U., 1992; postgrad., U. Calif., Berkeley, 1987, U. Oreg., 1994-95. Cert. secondary tchr., Minn., Wash., Oreg. Tchr., coach Bridgemont H.S., San Francisco, 1986-90; part-time instr. phys. edn. Mankato State U., 1990-92; athletic dir. North Eugene (Oreg.) Sch. Dist., 1992-93; tchr., coach Springfield (Oreg.) Sch. Dist., 1993-94; tchr. computers, phys. edn. McKenzie Sch. Dist., Finn Rock, Oreg., 1994-95, Petersburg Sch. Dist., The Dalles, Oreg., 1995—. Contbr. articles to profl. pubs. Home: 903 W 23rd St The Dalles OR 97058-1219 Office: Petersburg Dist 3855 Fifteen Mile Rd The Dalles OR 97058-9638

CONLEY, ZEB BRISTOL, art gallery director; b. Andrews, N.C., Feb. 12, 1936; s. Zeb Bristol and A. Elizabeth (Faircloth) C.; student N.C. State Coll., 1954-55, Mars Hill Coll., 1955-57, Coll. William and Mary, 1957-61; m. Betty Ann Wiswall, May 25, 1974; stepchildren—Peter Wiswall Betts, Stephen Wood Betts, Frederick Beale Betts, III. Designer, Seymour Robins, Inc., N.Y.C., 1961, First Nat. Bank, Las Vegas (N.Mex.), 1964-65, Swanson's Inc., Las Vegas, 1965-73, v.p., 1969-86; dir. Jamison Galleries, Santa Fe, 1973—, guest curator Alfred Morang: A Retrospective at Mus. of S.W. Midland, Tex., 1985; sec. Marbasconi, Inc., d.b.a. Jamison Galleries, 1974-80, pres., 1980—. Republican. Office: care The Jamison Galleries 560 Montezuma Ave Ste 103 Santa Fe NM 87501-2590

CONN, RICHARD GEORGE, retired art museum curator; b. Bellingham, Wash., Oct. 28, 1928; s. Bert Grover and Mary Ann (Slack) C. BA, U. Wash., 1950, MA, 1955. Curator history Ea. Wash. State Hist. Soc., Spokane, 1959-61, dir., 1961-66; chief human history Man. (Can.) Provincial Mus., Winnipeg, 1966-70; dir. Heard Mus., Phoenix, 1970-72; curator Indian art Denver Art Mus., 1955-59, curator native art, 1972-90, chief curator, 1990-93; ret., 1993; bd. dirs. Native Am. Art Studies, 1989-93. Author: (exhbn. catalogues) Robes of White Shell and Sunrise, 1974, Circles of the World, 1982, A Persistent Vision, 1986, (collection catalogue) American Indian in the Denver Art Museum, 1979. With U.S. Army, 1951-53. Recipient Excellence in Arts award Colo. Gov.'s Office, 1993, Rosenstock Lifetime Achievement award, 1994; fellow McCloy Found., Germany, 1979. Mem. Am. Assn. Mus., An. Anthrop. Assn., Westeners (Denver Posse). Democrat. Office: Denver Art Mus 100 W 14th Ave Denver CO 80204-2713

CONNELL, ELIZABETH ANN, elementary educator; b. Portsmouth, Va., Sept. 21, 1949; d. Robert Joseph and Juanita Georgia (Harrill) C. BS in Edn., Old Dominion U., Norfolk, Va., 1971; MA in Reading Edn., U. No. Colo., Greeley, 1975; PhD in Edn., Lit. and Curriculum, U. Colo., Boulder, 1991. Cert. elem. edn. K-6, reading edn. K-12, K-12 adminstrn. Tchr. 6th grade Norfolk Pub. Schs., 1971-74; tchr. Littleton (Colo.) Pub. Schs., 1975—; tchg. assoc. U. Colo., Boulder, 1988-90; instr. U. Colo., Denver, 1994; lit. com. When Author Meets Author, Colo. Coun. of Internat. Reading Assn., Denver; judge children's writing contest Friends of the Libr., Littleton, 1992-96. Author: A Community of Learners Selecting and Developing Writing Topcs, 1991. Recipient Outstanding Tchr. award Assn. for Childhood Edn. Internat., Denver, 1992; multicultural grantee Summit CHART: Pub. Edn. Coalition, Denver, 1994. Mem. ASCD, NEA, Internat. Reading Assn., Colo. Edn. Assn., Littleton Edn. Assn., Phi Delta Kappa. Office: Littleton Pub Schs Franklin Elem Littleton CO 80209

CONNELLY, CYNTHIA DONALDSON, nursing scientist; b. Barre, Vt.; d. Dugald Campbell and Jennie Gould (Smith) Donaldson; m. Robert F. Connelly, Dec. 19, 1978. Diploma, Hartford Hosp. Sch. Nursing, 1971; BA, U. Redlands, 1977, MA, 1980; MSN, U. San Diego, 1984; PhD in Nursing, U. R.I., 1993. Postdoctoral rsch. fellow U. Wash., Seattle, 1995—. Mem. ANA, N.H. Nurses Assn., Sigma Theta Tau.

CONNELLY, JAMES P., prosecutor. U.S. atty. U.S. Dist. Ct. (ea. dist.) Wash., Spokane. Office: US Courthouse PO Box 1494 920 Riverside Ave W Spokane WA 99210-1494

CONNELLY, JOHN WILLIAM, wildlife research biologist; b. Waterbury, Conn., June 7, 1952; s. John William and Katherine Marie (McHann) C.; m. Cheryl Ann Hinman, Aug. 24, 1974; children: Jennifer, Allison. AS, Paul Smiths Coll., 1972; BS, U. Idaho, 1974; MS, Wash. State U., 1977, PhD, 1982. Rsch. asst. Wash. State U., Pullman, 1974-80; biol. technician U.S. Fish and Wildlife Svc., Missoula, Mont., 1980-82; wildlife scientist EG&G Idaho Inc., Idaho Falls, 1982-84; regional wildlife biologist Idaho Dept. Fish & Game, Salmon, 1984-85; prin. wildlife rsch. biologist Idaho Dept. Fish & Game, Pocatello, 1985—; rschr. sage and sharp-tailed grouse Idaho Dept. Fish and Game, Pocatello, 1977—; state rep. Western States Grouse Workshop, Boise, 1985—, Prairie Grouse Tech. Conf., Boise, 1991—; mem. EPA Pesticide Adv. Panel, Seattle, 1990—; cons. Oreg. and Utah Fish and Wildlife, Blackfoot, Idaho, 1988—, U.S. Forest Svc., 1996; lectr. R.O. Butler Lectures, S.D. State U., 1990-96; grad. faculty U. Idaho, Moscow, Idaho State U., Pocatello. Contbr. tech. papers to profl. jours. Soccer coach Blackfoot Youth Soccer Assn., 1992-96, Blackfoot AYSO, 1988-96; regional soccer coach AYSO, Blackfoot, 1994-95; merit badge counselor Boy Scouts Am., Blackfoot and Shelley, Idaho, 1988—. Recipient Ted Trueblood comms. award, 1991, Profl. and Tech. award Idaho Dept. Fish and Game, 1993, Tech. Rsch. award U.S. Forest Svc, 1995; rsch. grantee various funding sources, 1977—. Mem. Am. Ornithologists Union, The Wildlife Soc. (com. mem.), Idaho chpt. The Wildlife Soc. (pres. 1988-92, Wildlife Profl. of Yr. 1992), Cooper Ornithol. Soc., Soc. for Range Mgmt. (chpt. chmn. 1989), Soc. for Conservation Biology. Methodist. Office: Idaho Dept Fish and Game 1345 Barton Rd Pocatello ID 83204-1847

CONNER, LINDSAY ANDREW, screenwriter, producer; b. N.Y.C., Feb. 19, 1956; s. Michael and Miriam (Mintzer) C. BA summa cum laude, UCLA, 1976; MA, Occidental Coll., 1977; JD magna cum laude, Harvard U., 1980. Bar: Calif. 1980, U.S. Dist. Ct. (cen. dist.) Calif. 1983. Assoc. Kaplan, Livingston, Goodwin, Berkowitz & Selvin, Beverly Hills, Calif., 1980-81, Fulop & Hardee, Beverly Hills, 1982-83, Wyman, Bautzer, Kuchel & Silbert, L.A., 1983-86; ptnr., entertainment dept. head Hill Wynne Troop & Meisinger, L.A., 1986-93. Author: (with others) The Courts and Education, 1977; editor: Harvard Law Rev., 1978-80. Trustee L.A. Community Coll., 1981—, bd. pres., 1989-90; pres. Calif. Community Coll. Trustees, 1992-93. Mem. ABA, UCLA Alumni Assn. (life), Harvard-Radcliffe Club, Phi Beta Kappa. Office: 54th St Prodns Ste 2080 10880 Wilshire Blvd Los Angeles CA 90024

CONNER, NATALIE ANN, community health nurse specialist; b. Iowa City, May 6, 1962; d. Frederick Raymond and Sheila Ruth (Rapoport) Greenberg; m. Eric Lyle Conner, Sept. 12, 1987 (div. May 1995). BSN, U. Wash., 1984; MS, U. Calif., San Francisco, 1992. Cert. specialist cmty. health, pub. health nurse, State Calif., HIV counselor DHHS/ Oreg. State Health Divsn. Charge nurse Riverton Hosp. Care Unit., Seattle, 1985; community health nurse Sound Heart, Seattle, 1985-88; staff nurse Univ. Hosp., Seattle, 1986-88; nurse Portland (Oreg.) Indian Health Clinic, 1988-89; staff nurse San Francisco State U. Student Health Svc., 1989-92; clin. instr. U. California, San Francisco, 1992; rsch. nurse dept. pediatrics U. Wash., Seattle, 1992—; nurse cons. job corps program region X Dept. Labor, 1992—; sec. Grad. Nurses Student Coun., U. Calif., 1991-92, mem. commencement com., 1992; chairperson Nursing Peer Rev. Com. Student Health Svcs. San Francisco State U., 1991-92. Delegate Washington State Democratic Convention, Seattle, 1984. Mem. Am. Nurses Assn., Am. Pub. Health Assn., King County Nurses Assn. (membership com. 1986-88), Sigma Theta Tau. Democrat. Jewish.

CONNOLLY, DAVID KEVIN, healthcare executive, consultant, educator; b. Napoleon, Ohio, Feb. 20, 1948; s. Cletus Jerome and Ruth Elaine (Huse) C.; m. Diane Elizabeth Landes, June 13, 1970; children: Christopher, Carrie Ann, Jeremy, Joseph. BA, Seattle Pacific U., 1974; MPA, Evergreen State Coll., 1995. Sr. mgmt. analyst/auditor U.S. Gen. Acctg. Office, Seattle, 1974-78; mgr. HMO Devel. Kitsap Physicians Svc., Bremerton, Wash., 1978-81; dir. alt. delivery sys. Blue Cross of Wash. and Alaska, Seattle, 1981-83; asst. adminstr. planning/devel./mktg. St. Joseph Hosp., Aberdeen, Wash., 1983-86; dir. provider rels. Equicor Health Plans, Seattle, 1986-88; prin., sr. cons. Quorum Assocs., Montesano, Wash., 1988-90, 93—; dir. ops., planning and devel. Pacific Health Plans, Seattle, 1990-93; mem. exec. com., bd. dirs., pres. Grays Harbor chpt. ARC; adj. faculty Sch. Bus., Seattle Pacific U.; mem. exec. com. Harbor Health Coalition; bd. dirs. S.W. Wash. Health Sys. Agy.; pres. Grays Harbor/Pacific County Health Coun.; mem. continuing edn. faculty Grays Harbor Coll.; presenter, spkr. various seminars and confs. on mgmt., mktg. and orgnl. devel. Named Outstanding Young Man of Am., U.S. Jr. C. of C. Mem. ASPA (Nat. Tng. Conf. Student Grant award), Rotary Internat. (chair various local coms.), Toastmasters Internat. (past dist. gov., various local and dist. offices, chmn. and host for region 1 conf., Disting. Dist. Gov.), Grays Harbor C. of C. (bd. dirs., chmn. govt. affairs com.).

CONNOLLY, JOHN EARLE, surgeon, educator; b. Omaha, May 21, 1923; s. Earl A. and Gertrude (Eckerman) C.; m. Virginia Hartman, Aug. 12, 1967; children: Peter Hart. John Earle, Sarah. A.B., Harvard U., 1945, M.D., 1948. Diplomate: Am. Bd. Surgery (bd. dirs. 1976-82), Am. Bd. Thoracic and Cardiovascular Surgery, Am. Bd. Vascular Surgery. Intern. in surgery Stanford U. Hosps., San Francisco, 1948-49, surg. research fellow, 1949-50, asst. resident surgeon, 1950-52, chief resident surgeon, 1953-54, surg. pathology fellow, 1954-55, 1957-60, John and Mary Markle Scholar in med. scis., 1957-62; surg. registrar professional unit St. Bartholomew's Hosp., London, 1952-53; resident in thoracic surgery Bellevue Hosp., N.Y.C., 1955; resident in thoracic and cardiovascular surgery Columbia-Presbyn. Med. Ctr., N.Y.C., 1956; from instr. to assoc. prof. surgery Stanford U., 1957-65; prof. U. Calif., Irvine, 1965—, chmn. dept. surgery, 1965-78; attending surgeon Stanford Med. Ctr., Palo Alto, Calif., 1959-65; chmn. cardiovascular and thoracic surgery Irvine Med. Ctr. U. Calif., 1968—; attending surgeon Children's Hosp., Orange, Calif., 1968—, Anaheim (Calif.) Meml. Hosp., 1970—; vis. prof. Beijing Heart, Lung, Blood Vessel Inst., 1990, A.H. Duncan vis. prof. U. Edinburgh, 1984; Hunterian prof. Royal Coll. Surgeons Eng., 1985-86; Kinmonth lectr. Royal Coll. Surgeons, Eng., 1987; mem. adv. coun. Nat. Heart, Lung, and Blood Inst.-NIH, 1981-85; cons. Long Beach VA Hosp., Calif., 1965—. Contbr. articles to profl. jours.; editorial bd.: Jour. Cardiovascular Surgery, 1974—, chief editor, 1985—; editorial bd. Western Jour. Medicine, 1975—, Jour. Stroke, 1979—, Jour. Vascular Surgery, 1983—. Bd. dirs. Audio-Digest Found., 1974—; bd. dirs. Franklin Martin Found., 1975-80; regent Uniformed Svcs. U. of Health Scis., Bethesda, 1992—. Served with AUS, 1943-44. Recipient Cert. of Merit, Japanese Surg. Soc., 1979, 90. Fellow ACS (gov. 1964-70, regent 1973-82, vice chmn. bd. regents 1980-82, v.p. 1984-85), Royal Coll. Surgeons Eng. (hon.), Royal Coll. Surgeons Ireland (hon.), Royal Coll. Surgeons Edinburgh (hon.); mem. Am. Surg. Assn., Soc. Univ. Surgeons, Am. Assn. Thoracic Surgery (coun. 1974-78), Pacific Coast Surg. Assn. (pres. 1985-86), San Francisco Surg. Soc., L.A. Surg. Soc., Soc. Vascular Surgery, Western Surg. Assn., Internat. Cardiovascular Soc. (pres. 1977), Soc. Internat. Chirurgie, Soc. Thoracic Surgeons, Western Thoracic Surg. Soc. (pres. 1978), Orange County Surg. Soc. (pres. 1984-85), James IV Assn. Surgeons (councillor 1983—). Clubs: California (Los Angeles); San Francisco Golf, Pacific Union, Bohemian (San Francisco); Cypress Point (Pebble Beach, Calif.); Harvard (N.Y.C.); Big Canyon (Newport Beach). Home: 7 Deerwood Ln Newport Beach CA 92660-5108 Office: U Calif Dept Surgery Irvine CA 92717

CONNOLLY, PHYLLIS MARIE, nursing educator, clinical specialist; b. Summit, N.J., Oct. 24, 1942; d. William James Connolly Sr. and Margaret Elizabeth Coughlin; m. Bruno E. Zorzi, Sept. 21, 1963 (div. June 1978); children: Michael K. Zorzi, Colleen Patricia Zorzi; m. G. Michael Northrup, Aug. 16, 1980. BA magna cum laude, Georgian Ct. Coll., 1974; MS, Rutgers U., 1981; PhD, Golden Gate U., 1987. RN, Calif., N.J.; cert. clin. specialist adult psychiat./mental health nursing ANCC. Staff nurse ICU Middlesex Gen. Hosp., New Brunswick, N.J., 1963-64; staff nurse Community Meml. Hosp., Toms River, N.J., 1966-67, staff nurse coronary care unit, 1967-68, evening supr., 1968-74, insvc. instr., 1974; pub. health nurse Ocean County Health Dept., Toms River, N.J., 1974-75; nursing care coord. emergency dept., mainland div. Atlantic Mental Health Ctr., Atlantic City, N.J., 1975-76; insvc. educator mainland div. Atlantic Mental Health Ctr., Pomona, N.J., 1976-78; mental health cons. Atlantic Mental Health Ctr., Atlantic City, 1978-81, adminstrv. asst. C.I.P., 1980-81; asst. prof. Stockton State Coll., Pomona, N.J., 1981-83; assoc. prof. San Jose (Calif.) State U., 1983-90, interim dept. chair, 1990, prof., 1991—; pvt. practice, 1982—, coord. transdisciplinary collaboration project, 1993—; facilitator, trainer Moller-Wer Simultaneous Patient Family Edn., 1994—; dir. Inst. Nursing Rsch. & Practice, 1995—; instr., mentor Consortium of Calif. State U. Nursing Program, 1984-86; psych. nurse cons., Vis. Nurses' Assn., Santa Clara, Calif., 1986-89; active in acad. governance local campus and statewide Calif. State U., 1987-94, chair personnel com., 1991-93; cons., content dir. Nat. Coun. Licensure exam, CTB McGraw-Hill Psych./Mental Health Nursing, 1988, 89; coord. nurse managed ctrs., 1988-92, semester 6 chair, 1984-88, 92-94, project dir. Los Gatos CDBG, 1989-92; presenter profl meetings, local, state, nat. and internat. Contbr. articles to profl. jours. Mem. Santa Clara County Alliance for the Mentally Ill, 1986—; curriculum and tng. network Spl. Com. of Nat. Alliance for Mentally Ill, 1989—; bd. dirs. ACT for Mental Health, San Jose, 1987—; chair profl. adv. com. ACT, 1987—. Recipient NIMH Grad. Tgn. grant, Rutgers U., 1979-80, Sigma Theta Tau scholarship, 1985, 86, 87, 90, 93. Fellow Am. Orthopsychiat. Assn.; mem. ASPA, ANA (cert. clin. specialist, govt. rels. com. 1984-94), Am. Psychiat. Nurses Assn. (chair of regional and state reps. 1991-94, regional rep. Calif. 1991—, co-chair The Consumer & Family Educators spl. interest group 1994—, chair task force on spl. interest groups 1995, pres.-elect 1996), Calif. Faculty Assn., Bay Area Nursing Diagnosis Assn. (sec. 1991-92), Calif. Alliance for the Mentally Ill (co-chair task force on families and mental illness 1991-96, cons. to Bakersfield Alliance for Mentally Ill and Calif. State U. Bakersfield 1995), Sigma Theta Tau (nominating com. 1993-94). Republican. Roman Catholic. Office: San Jose U Sch Nursing San Jose CA 95192

CONNOLLY, THOMAS JOSEPH, bishop; b. Tonopah, Nev., July 18, 1922; s. John and Katherine (Hammel) C. Student, St. Joseph Coll. and St. Patrick Sem., Menlo Park, Calif., 1936-47, Catholic U. Am., 1949-51; JCD, Lateran Pontifical U., Rome, 1952; DHL (hon.), U. Portland, 1972. Ordained priest Roman Cath. Ch., 1947. Asst. St. Thomas Cathedral, Reno, 1947, asst., rector, 1953-55; asst. Little Flower Parish, Reno, 1947-48; sec. to bishop, 1949; asst. St. Albert the Gt., Reno, 1952-53; pastor St. Albert the Gt., 1960-68, St. Joseph Ch., Elko, 1955-60, St. Theresa's Ch., Carson City, Nev., 1968-71; bishop Baker, Oreg., 1971—; Tchr. Manogue High Sch., Reno, 1948-49; chaplain Serra Club, 1948-49; officialis Diocese of Reno; chmn. bldg. com., dir. Cursillo Movement; moderator Italian Cath. Fedn.; dean, mem. personnel bd. Senate of Priests; mem. Nat. Bishops Liturgy Com., 1973-76; region XII rep. to adminstrv. bd. Nat. Conf. Cath. Bishops, 1973-76, 86-89, mem. adv. com., 1974-76; bd. dirs. Cath. Communications Northwest, 1977-82. Club: K.C. (state chaplain Nev. 1970-71). Home: 63255 Overtree Rd Bend OR 97701-9759 Office: Bishop of Baker PO Box 5999 911 SE Armour Bend OR 97702*

CONNOR, GARY EDWARD, manufacturing company marketing executive; b. S.I., N.Y., Nov. 13, 1948; s. Everett M. and Josephine (Amato) C.; B.S. in Elec. Engring., U. Md., 1973; M.B.A., U. Santa Clara (Calif.), 1979. Quality assurance engr. Frankford Arsenal, 1973; quality assurance engr., field service engr. Lockheed Electronics Co., 1973-74; group leader memory test engring. sect. head bipolar product engring. Nat. Semicondr. Corp., 1975-79; internat. mktg. mgr. Am. Microsystems Inc., 1979-80; mktg. mgr. GenRad-STI, Santa Clara, 1980-82; prodn. mktg. exec. AMD, Sunnyvale, Calif., 1982-86; dept. mgr. IDT, Santa Clara, Calif., 1986—. Mem. IEEE, Electronics Internat. Adv. Panel, Am. Security Council (nat. adv. bd.), Franklin Mint Collectors Soc. Republican. Home: 5121 Kozo Ct San Jose CA 95124-5527 Office: 2670 Seely Ave San Jose CA 95134-1929

CONNOR, PAUL LYLE, medical librarian; b. San Francisco, June 1, 1954; s. Harold Leon and Greta Frances (Holliger) C.; m. Martha Emily Bowman, Aug. 30, 1980; children: Laura, Erin, Rebecca, Daniel. BA, U. Calif., Berkeley, 1976, M Libr. Info. Svcs., 1981. Med. libr. VA Med. Ctr., Fresno, Calif., 1981-89, Valley Children's Hosp., Fresno, 1989—. Mem. Acad. Health Info. Profls., Med. Libr. Assn., No. Calif. and Nev. Med. Libr. Group, Med. Libr. Group So. Calif. and Ariz. Office: Valley Children's Hosp 3151 N Millbrook Ave Fresno CA 93703-1425

CONNORS, JOHN MICHAEL, retired city official; b. Concord, Mass., Jan. 26, 1932; s. Raymond George and Helen Mary (Nee) C.; m. Margaret Johns, Dec. 10, 1966; children: Kip, Tammy, Christine. Constrn. engr. BF Petrini & Sons, Boston, 1958-59; survey party chief William Morrissey Engr., Boston, 1959-61; field engr. RCA Victor Comm., L.A., 1962-63; asst. and assoc. civil engr. City of Laguna Beach, Calif., 1963-74; devel. svcs. specialist, zoning adminstr. City of Laguna Beach, 1974-95. Ward capt. Dana Point (Calif.) Cityhood, 1974-75. Cpl. U.S. Army, 1952-55. Democrat. Avocation: reading. Home: 33922 El Encanto Dana Point CA 92629

CONOVER, FREDERIC KING, lawyer; b. Portchester, N.Y., June 4, 1933; s. Julian D. and Josephine T. Conover; m. Kathryn B. Conover, Dec. 21, 1955; children: Frederic, Elizabeth, Pamela, Margaret; m. 2d, Jacquelyn Wonder, Aug. 24, 1979. B.A., Amherst Coll., 1955; J.D., U. Mich., 1961. Bar: Colo. 1962, U.S. Dist. Ct. Colo. 1962, U.S. Ct. Appeals (10th cir.) 1962. Ptnr. Conover, McClearn & Heppenstall, P.C., Denver, 1972-88, Faegre & Benson, Devner, 1988—, ptnr. in charge dispute resolution svcs. The Faegre Group, 1993—. Trustee Mt. Airy Psychiat. Ctr.; dir. Legal Aid Soc.; chmn. citizens adv. com. Denver Regional Council Govts., bd. govs., trustee, Nat. Ctr. for Preventive Law, pannel of disting. neutrals, Ctr. for Pub. Resources; bd. dirs., Lawyers Alliance for World Security. Served to lt. USN, 1955-59. Fellow Am. Coll. Trial Lawyers, Am. Bar Found., Colo. Bar Found.; mem. ABA, Denver Bar Assn. (pres. 1983-84), Colo. Bar Assn. (pres. 1990-91), Law Club (v.p.), City Club of Denver (dir.), Denver Tennis Club. Democrat. Office: The Faegre Group 2500 Republic Plz 370 17th St Denver CO 80202

CONRAN, JAMES MICHAEL, consumer advocate, public policy consultant; b. N.Y.C., Mar. 15, 1952; s. James Adrian and Mary Ellen (McGarry) C.; m. Phyllis Jean Thompson, Aug. 1, 1984; children: Michael O., Thomas O. BA, Calif. State U., Northridge, 1975; M in Urban Studies, Occidental Coll., 1978. Mgr. regulatory rels. Pacific Bell, San Francisco, 1985-88, mgr. pub. affairs & pub. issues, 1988-91; dir. State of Calif. Dept. Consumer Affairs, Sacramento, 1991-94; founder, pres. Consumers First, 1994—; bd. dirs. Consumer Interest Rsch. Inst., Nat. Consumers League, Elec. Consumers Alliance, TRW Consumer Adv. Coun., Great Western Fin. Corp., Consumer Adv. Panel, Electric Inst. Consumer Adv. Panel; mem. Coun. Licensing Enforcement and Regulation. Contbr. articles to profl. jours. Bd. dirs. Fight Back! Found., L.A., 1991—, Disabled Children's Computer Group, Orinda, Calif., Telecomm. Edn. Trust Fund-Calif. Pub. Utilities Commn., San Francisco, 1990-91; chair adminstrv. sect. United Calif. State Employees Campaign, Sacramento; mem. Stream Preservation Commn., Orinda, 1988-91, Calif. Rep. Party Cen. Com., Orinda, 1992; del. Rep. Nat. Conv., Houston, 1992; regional chair Bush-Quayle campaign, Orinda, 1992. Fellow Coro Found., 1977, Levere Meml. Found., 1976. Mem. Coro Assocs., Calif. Agenda for Consumer Edn., Sigma Alpha Epsilon. Roman Catholic.

CONSOR, JENNETTE ESTELLE, lawyer, consultant and fundraiser; b. N.Y.C., Nov. 4, 1948; d. Hediberto and Estelle (Ortiz De Carballo) Morales Irrizary; children: Brice Nathaniel, Simone Ronit. BA, U. Houston, 1974;

JD, So. Meth. U., 1978. Bar: Tex. 1980. Law clerk., atty. Bates, Tibbals & Lee, Dallas, 1978-81; corp. atty. Hunt Oil Corp., Dallas, 1981-84; corp./bus. atty. in sole practice Dallas, 1984-89; legal svcs. mgr. Resolution Trust Corp./FDIC, Dallas, 1990-93, sr. atty. in litigation, 1993-96; legal and bus. cons. various cos. in Aspen (Colo.) Area, 1996—; cons. Women in Film/Dallas, 1985-92, Crescent Club Social Com., Dallas, 1989-92, Walt Garrison Rodeo Com. Multiple Sclerosis, Dallas, 1991-93; legal, bus. cons. to CEOs in Aspen (Colo.) Area, 1996—. Fundraiser for polit. campaigns, 1985-94; apptd. mem. Motion Picture Commn. Classification Bd., Dallas, 1983-85, Human and Health Svcs. Commn., Dallas, 1987-89, Cultural Affairs Commn., 1992-93; mem. Walt Garrison Rodeo com. Multiple Sclerosis, Dallas, 1991-93; acting exec. dir. S.W./Tradefest, 1994; chmn. vol. task force Dallas Tradefest, 1993; bd. dirs. Mexican Cultural Ctr., 1994-96, West Dallas Cmty. Ctrs., 1995, Women Issues Network, 1996—. Olympic torch bearer, 1996. Mem. State Bar Tex., Dallas Bar Assn., Dallas Women's Bar Assn., Women in Film Dallas (bd. dirs. and editor newsletter 1989-90), Hispanic C. of C. of Dallas, Dallas Women's Found., Dallas Friday Group, Dallas World Salute Young Profl. League. Home and Office: PO Box 9485 Aspen CO 81612

CONSTANT, CLINTON, chemical engineer, consultant; b. Nelson, B.C., Can., Mar. 20, 1912; came to U.S., 1936, naturalized, 1942; s. Vasile and Annie (Hunt) C.; m. Margie Robbel, Dec. 5, 1965. BSc with honors, U. Alta., 1935, postgrad., 1935-36; PhD, Western Res. U., 1939. Registered profl. engr., Calif., Wis. Devel. engr. Harshaw Chem. Co., Cleve., 1936-38, mfg. foreman, 1938-43, sr. engr. semi-works dept., 1948-50; supt. hydrofluoric acid dept. Nyotex Chems., Inc., Houston, 1943-47, chief devel. engr., 1947-48; mgr. engring. Ferro Chem. Co., Bedford, Ohio, 1950-52; tech. asst. mfg. dept. Armour Agrl. Chem. Co. (name formerly Armour Fertilizer Works), Bartow, Fla., 1952-61, mfg. research and devel. div., 1961-63; mgr. spl. projects Research div. (co. name changed to USS Agri-Chems 1968), Bartow, Fla., 1963-65, project mgr., 1965-70; chem. adviser Robert & Co. Assocs., Atlanta, 1970-79; chief engr. Almon & Assocs., Inc., Atlanta, 1979-80; project mgr. Engring. Service Assocs., Atlanta, 1980-81; v.p. engring. ACI Inc., Hesperia, Calif., 1981-83; sr. v.p., chief engr. MTI (acquisition of ACI), Hesperia, 1983-86; engring. cons. San Bernardino County APCD, Victorville, Calif., 1986-90; instr. environ. chemistry Victor Valley C.C., 1990; pvt. cons. Victorville, Calif., 1991—; cons. in engring., 1992—. Author tech. reports, sci. fiction; patentee in field. Fellow AAAS, Am. Inst. Chemists, Am. Inst. Chem. Engrs., N.Y. Acad. Scis., AIAA (assoc.); mem. Am. Chem. Soc., Am. Astron. Soc., Astron. Soc. Pacific, Royal Astron. Soc. Can., NSPE, Am. Water Works Assn., Calif. Water and Pollution Control Assn., Air Pollution Control Assn., Soc. Mfg. Engrs., Calif. Soc. Profl. Engrs.

CONSTANTINEAU, CONSTANCE JULIETTE, retired banker; b. Lowell, Mass., Feb. 18, 1937; d. Henry Goulet and Germaine (Turner) Goulet-Lamarre; m. Edward Joseph Constantineau; children: Glen Edward, Alan Henry. Student, Bank Adminstrn. Inst. and Am. Inst. Banking, 1975-87. Mortgage sec. The Cen. Savs. Bank, Lowell, 1955-57; head teller First Fed. Savs. & Loan, Lowell, 1957-59, Lowell Bank & Trust Co., Lowell, 1973-74; br. mgr. Century Bank & Trust Co., Malden, Mass., 1975-78; v.p. purchasing, mgr. support svcs. First Security Bank of N.Mex. (formerly First Nat. Bank Albuquerque), 1983-96; ret., 1996; mem. planning purchasing mgr.'s conf. Bank Adminstrn. Inst., San Antonio, Orlando, Fla., New Orleans; treas. polit. action com. First Nat. Bank, 1986. Bd. dirs., historian Indian Pueblo Cultural Ctr., Albuquerque, 1986-89. Mem. Fin. Women Internat., In-Plant Mgmt. Assn. (charter). Home: 13015 Deer Dancer Trl NE Albuquerque NM 87112-4831 Office: 1st Security Bank NMex 40 First Plaza Ctr NW Albuquerque NM 87102-3355

CONTE, JULIE VILLA, nurse, administrator; b. Manila, July 4, 1951; came to U.S., 1970; d. Gregorio Cortes and Lourdes (Villa) Dirige; m. Michael Don Conte, Jan. 22, 1983. BSN, Calif. State U., L.A., 1974; MBA, U. Phoeniz, San Diego, 1993. RN, Calif. Staff nurse Santa Monica (Calif.) Hosp., 1976-78; pub. health nurse Kaiser Found. Hosp., Panorama City, Calif., 1978-85; nursing supr. Nat. Med. Homecare, L.A., 1985-86; dir. home health Holy Cross Hosp., Mission Hills, 1986-88; dir. profl. svcs. Care Home Health, San Diego, 1988—; dir. nursing Health Prime Home Health Svcs. of San Diego, Inc., 1988-92; dir. home health svcs. Alvardado Home Health Agy., San Diego, 1993-94; expert consulting Home Health and Bus. Cons., San Diego, 1994—; dir. patient care svcs. Unlimited Care, Inc., 1995—; pub. health nurse cons. Able Home Health Care, Wilmington, Calif., 1984; bd. dirs. nursing Health Prime, Inc. Mem. NAFE, Nat. Assn. Home Care, Associational Woman's Missionary Union (dir.), San Diego So. Bapt. Assn., Alpha Delta Chi. Republican. Baptist. Home: 4444 Bancroft St San Diego CA 92116-4513

CONTI, ISABELLA, psychologist, consultant; b. Torino, Italy, Jan. 1, 1942; came to U.S., 1964; d. Giuseppe and Zaira (Melis) Ferro; m. Ugo Conti, Sept. 5, 1964; 1 child, Maurice. J.D., U. Rome, 1966; Ph.D. in Psychology, U. Calif.-Berkeley, 1975. Lic. psychologist. Sr. analyst Rsch. Inst. for Study of Man, Berkeley, Calif., 1967-68; postgrad. rsch. psychologist Personality Assessment and Rsch. Inst., U. Calif.-Berkeley, 1968-71; intern U. Calif.-Berkeley and VA Hosp., San Francisco, 1969-75; asst. prof. St. Mary's Coll., Moraga, Calif., 1978-84; cons. psychologist Conti Resources, Berkeley, Calif., 1977-85; v.p. Barnes & Conti Assocs., Inc., Berkeley, 1985-90; pres. Lisardco, El Cerrito, Calif., 1989—; bd. dirs. ElectroMagnetic Instruments, Inc., El Cerrito, Calif., 1985—. Trustee Monterey Inst. Internat. Studies, 1996—. Author: (with Alfonso Montuori) From Power to Partnership, 1993; contbr. articles on creativity and mgmt. cons. to profl. jours. Regents fellow U. Calif.-Berkeley, 1972; NIMH predoctoral rsch. fellow, 1972-73. Mem. APA. Office: Lisardco 1318 Brewster Dr El Cerrito CA 94530-2526

CONTO, ARISTIDES, advertising agency executive; b. N.Y.C., Feb. 10, 1931; s. Gus Dimitrios and Osee (Kenney) C.; BA, Champlain Coll., 1953; MS in Journalism, UCLA, 1958, certificate in indsl. rels., 1965; m. Phyllis Helen Wiley, June 22, 1957; 1 son, Jason Wiley. Reporter, City News Svc., L.A., 1958; dir. pub. rels. Galaxy Advt. Co., Los Angeles, 1959-60; news media chief Los Angeles County Heart Assn., 1960-61; pub. rels. assoc. Prudential Ins. Co., L.A., 1961-64; advt. mgr. Aerospace Controls Co., L.A., 1964-65; comml. sales promotion coord. Lockheed-Calif. Co., Burbank, 1965-73; pres. Jason Wiley Advt. Agy., L.A., 1973-92; dir. Tower Master, Inc., L.A. With U.S. Army, 1955-56. Recipient advt. awards. Mem. Nat. Soc. Published Poets, L.A. Press Club, Bus.-Profl. Advt. Assn. L.A.s, Pub. Rels. Soc. Author: The Spy Who Loved Me, 1962; The Diamond Twins, 1963, Edit Me Dead, 1992, I Marcus, 1994, A Short Life, 1995, (screenplays) Lannigan, 1973, Haunted Host, 1976, Captain Noah, 1977, Government Surplus, 1983.

CONTOS, PAUL ANTHONY, engineer, investment consultant; b. Chgo., Mar. 18, 1926; s. Anthony Dimitrios and Panagiota (Kostopoulos) C.; m. Lilian Katie Kalkines, June 19, 1955 (dec. Apr. 1985); children: Leslie, Claudia, Paula, Anthony. Student, Am. TV Inst., Chgo., 1946-48, U. Ill., 1949-52, 53-56, Ill. Inst. Tech., 1952-53, U. So. Calif., 1956-57. Engr. J.C. Deagan Co., Inc., Chgo., 1951-53, Lockheed Missile and Space Co., Inc., Sunnyvale, Calif., 1956-62; engring. supr. Lockheed Missile and Space Co., Inc., Sunnyvale, 1962-65, staff engr., 1965-88; pres. PAC Investments, Saratoga, Calif., 1984-88; pres. PAC Investments, San Jose, Calif., 1988—, also advisor, 1984—. Mem. Pres. Coun. U. Ill., 1994—. With U.S. Army, 1944-46, ETO. Decorated Purple Heart. Mem. DAV (life, commdr. Chgo. unit 1948-51), VFW (life), Pi Sigma Phi (pres. 1951-53). Republican. Greek Orthodox. Home and Office: 1009 Blossom River Way Apt 105 San Jose CA 95123-6305

CONWAY, JAMES F., writer, counselor, minister; b. Cleve., Jan. 11, 1932; m. Sally Ann Christon, June 2, 1954; children: Barbara Conway, Schneider, Brenda Conway Russell, Becki Conway Sanders. MDiv, Denver Seminary, 1957; MA in Psychology, Trinity Evangel. Divinity Sch., Ill., 1968; DMin in Theology, Fuller Theol. Seminary, Pasadena, Calif., 1979; PhD in Adult Devel., U. Ill., 1987. Ordained minister. Pastor Newton (Kans.) Bible Ch., 1958-63, Village Ch. of Carol Stream, Wheaton, Ill., 1963-69; instr. Coll. Christian Studies, Urbana, Ill., 1972-77; sr. pastor Twin City Bible Ch., Urbana, 1969-81; assoc. prof. Biola U., La Mirada, Calif., 1981-86, dir. D of Ministry Program, 1981-86; co-founder, pres. Mid-Life Dimensions, 1981—; counseling dir. Internat. Missions Convs. Urbana 76, Urbana 78; conf. and retreat leader; appearances on numerous TV and radio programs, including Focus on the Family, Mid-Morning LA, Michael Jackson Talk Radio, 700 Club, numerous CBN programs, others; adj. prof. U. Nebr., Gordon Coll., Mass., Sterling Coll., Kans., Taylor U., Ind., Spring Arbor Coll., Mich., Loma Linda (Calif.) U., Kettering Med. Sch., Ohio, Grace Bible Coll., Nebr., St. Paul Bible Coll., Minn., Columbia Sch. of the Bible, S.C., Fuller Theol. Sem., Calif., Denver Seminary, Covenant Sem., Mo. Author: Men in Mid-Life Crisis, 1978, Friendship, 1989, How to Make Real Friends in a Phony World, 1991, Adult Children of Legal or Emotional Divorce, 1990, Sexual Harassment No More, 1993; co-author: (with Sally Conway) Women in Mid-Life Crisis, 1983, Maximize Your Mid-Life, 1987, Your Marriage Can Survive Mid-Life Crisis, 1990, What God Gives When Life Takes, 1989, Moving On After He Moves Out, 1995, (with Sally Conway and Bill and Pam Farrel) Pure Pleasure, 1994, others; contbr. articles to profl. jours., books in field. Trustee Sterling (Kans.) Coll., 1984—, chmn. various coms. Recipient Disting. Parents' award Taylor U., 1980, Disting. Alumni award Sterling Coll., 1984. Mem. Phi Kappa Phi. Evangelical. Office: Mid-Life Dimensions PO Box 3790 Fullerton CA 92834-3790

CONWAY, JOHN E., federal judge; b. 1934. BS, U.S. Naval Acad., 1956; LLB magna cum laude, Washburn U., 1963. Assoc. Matias A Zamora, Santa Fe, 1963-64; ptnr. Wilkinson, Durrett & Conway, Alamogordo, N.Mex., 1964-67, Durrett, Conway & Jordon, Alamogordo, 1967-80, Montgomery & Andrews, P.A., Albuquerque, 1980-86; city atty. Alamogordo, 1966-72; mem. N.Mex. State Senate, 1970-80, minority leader, 1972-80; chief fed. judge U.S. Dist. Ct. N.Mex., Albuquerque, 1986—. 1st lt. USAF, 1956-60. Mem. Nat. Commrs. on Uniform State Laws, Fed. Judges' Assn. (bd. dirs.), 10th Cir. Dist. Judges' Assn. (pres.), N.Mex. Bar Assn., N.Mex. Jud. Coun. (vice chmn. 1973, chmn. 1973-75, disciplinary bd. of Supreme Ct. of N.Mex. vice chmn. 1980, chmn. 1981-84), Albuquerque Lawyers Club. Office: US Dist Ct PO Box 1160 Albuquerque NM 87103-1160

CONWAY, NANCY ANN, editor; b. Foxboro, Mass., Oct. 15, 1941; d. Leo T. and Alma (Goodwin) C.; children: Ana Lucia DaSilva, Kara Ann Martin. Cert. in med. tech., Carnegie Inst., 1962; BA in English, U. Mass., 1976, cert. in secondary edn., 1978. Tchr. Brazil-Am. Inst., Rio de Janeiro, 1963-68; freelance writer, editor Amherst, Mass., 1972-76; staff writer Daily Hampshire Gazette, North Hampton, Mass., 1976-77; editor Amherst Bull., 1977-80, Amherst Record, 1980-83; features editor Holyoke (Mass.) Transcript/Telegram, 1983-84; gen. mgr. Monday-Thursday Newspapers, Boca Raton, Fla., 1984-87; dir. editorial South Fla. Newspaper Network, Deerfield Beach, 1987-90; pub., editor York (Pa.) Newspapers, Inc., 1990-95; exec. editor, v.p. Alameda Newspaper Group, Pleasanton, Calif., 1995—. Bd. dirs. Math.: Opportunities in Engring., Sci. and Tech.-Pa. State, York, 1991-95. Recipient writing awards, state newspaper assns. Mem. Am. Soc. Newspaper Editors, Soc. Profl. Journalists, Pa. Newspaper Pub. Assn. Office: 66 Jack London Sq Oakland CA 94604*

CONWAY, REBECCA ANN KOPPES, lawyer; b. Colorado Springs, Colo., May 18, 1952; d. Virgil Lee and Betty J. Koppes; children: Kelley, Kathrine; m. Sean P. Conway, Nov. 26, 1994. BA, U. Colo., 1975, JD, 1978. Bar: Colo. 1978, U.S. Dist. Ct. Colo. 1978. Atty. EEOC, Denver, 1978-79, Dist. Atty.'s Office, Adams County, Brighton, Colo., 1979-80; ptnr. Gutierrez & Koppes, Greeley, Colo., 1980-92; prin. Law Office of Rebecca Koppes Conway, Greeley, 1992—; mem. Colo. Pub. Defenders Commn., 1985-95, chair, 1990-95. Chmn. Placement Alternatives Commn., Weld County, Colo., 1987-89; dir. Our Saviors Luth. Ch., Greeley, 1989-90; chmn. bd. dirs. Colo. Rural Legal Svcs., Denver, 1984-85, 94-96; vice chair Weld Child Care Network, 1988. Mem. ABA (House of Dels.), Colo. Bar Assn. (mem. various coms., mem. exec. coun. 1986-90, bd. govs. 1983-90, 94—, pres.-elect. 1996-97, chmn. young lawyers divsn. 1988-89, Outstanding Young Lawyer 1988, v.p. 1989-90), Weld County Bar Assn. (pres. 1992-93, mem. various coms.). Home: 2595 56th Ave Greeley CO 80634-4503 Office: 912 8th Ave Greeley CO 80631-1112

CONWAY, SALLY, writer, lecturer, counselor; b. Pennington County, S.D., Mar. 23, 1934; m. Jim Conway, June 2, 1954; children: Barbara Conway Schneider, Brenda Conway Russell, Becki Conway Sanders. BS in Edn. magna cum laude, U. Ill., 1974, MS in Human Devel. & Family Ecology, 1986. Co-founder, v.p. Mid-Life Dimensions, Calif., 1981—; adj. instr., coord. women's concerns Talbot Sch. Theology, Biola U., La Mirada, Calif., 1981-86; adj. instr. or lectr. U. Nebr., Gordon Coll., Mass., Sterling Coll., Kans., Taylor U., Ind., Spring Arbor Coll., Mich., Loma Linda (Calif.) U., Kettering Med. Sch., Ohio, Grace Bible Coll., Nebr., St. Paul Bible Coll., Minn., Columbia Sch. Bibl. Edn., S.C., Fuller Theol. Sem., Calif., Denver Sem., Covenant Sem., Mo., Talbot Sem., Calif.; numerous TV and radio appearances including Focus on the Family, Mid-Morning L.A., Michael Jackson Talk Radio, 700 Club, numerous CBN programs, others. Author: Your Husband's Mid-Life Crisis, 1980, Menopause, 1990, When a Mate Wants Out, 1992, (with Jim Conway) Women in Mid-Life Crisis, 1983, Maximize Your Mid-Life, 1987, Your Marriage Can Survive Mid-Life Crisis, 1987, Traits of a Lasting Marriage, 1991, Sexual Harassment No More, 1993, Traits of a Lasting Marriage, 1991, Moving On After He Moves Out, 1995, (with Jim Conway and Bill and Pam Farrel) Pure Pleasure, 1994, (with Becki Conway Sanders & Jim Conway) What God Gives When Life Takes/Trusting God in a Family Crisis, 1989; contbg. author numerous other books; contbr. articles to various jours.; author tapes. Recipient Disting. Parents award Taylor U., 1980, Disting. Alumni award Sterling Coll., 1984. Mem. Kappa Delta Pi. Address: PO Box 3790 Fullerton CA 92834-3790

CONWAY, WALLACE XAVIER, SR., retired curator; b. Washington, June 11, 1920; m. Jessie Dedeaux, June 1, 1943. B.A., Miner Tchrs. Coll., 1941; postgrad. Cath. U., Washington, 1957, 58, 61, Trenton State Coll., 1977-78, U. Paris, Sorbonne, 1977, NYU, 1987, 88, Mercer County Coll., 1975-76, MA. 1988; postgrad Venice, Italy, 1989, Art Inst. Chgo., 1990, NYU. Owner, dir. Co-Art Studios, Washington, 1950-64; graphic artist Dept. Commerce, U.S. Weather Bur., Washington, 1964-65; graphic supr. Smithsonian Inst., Washington, 1965-69; curator, chmn. exhibits bur. N.J. State Mus., Trenton, 1969-88; ret.; tech. cons. mural The Life of Martin Luther King at Martin Luther King Libr., Washington, 1984-86; cons. Pa. Council on the Arts/Minority Arts; museum cons. Mother Bethel A.M.E. Ch., nat. hist. landmark, Phila.; mem. art com. Mercer Med. Ctr.; cons. Afro-Am. Hist. Soc. Mus., Jersey City. Mem. adv. bd. Minority Arts Council, Phila. Mem. Art Students League (Colo. chpt., Best of Show award, two honorable mentions, First Place print category), Kappa Alpha Psi, Beta Kappa (charter). Lodge: Rotary Internat. Home: 2119 Olympic Dr Colorado Springs CO 80910-1262

COOK, ALBERT THOMAS THORNTON, JR., financial advisor; b. Cleve., Apr. 24, 1940; s. Albert Thomas Thornton and Tyra Esther (Morehouse) C.; m. Mary Jane Blackburn, June 1, 1963; children: Lara Keller, Thomas, Timothy. BA, Dartmouth Coll., 1962; MA, U. Chgo., 1966. Asst. sec. Dartmouth Coll., Hanover, N.H., 1972-77; exec. dir. Big Brothers, Inc., N.Y.C., 1977-78; underwriter Boettcher & Co., Denver, 1978-81; asst. v.p. Dain Bosworth Inc., Denver, 1981-82, Colo. Nat. Bank, Denver, 1982-84; pres. The Albert T.T. Cook Co., Denver, 1984—; arbitrator Nat. Assn. Securities Dealers, N.Y.C., 1985—, Mcpl. Securities Rulemaking Bd., Washington, 1987—. Pres. Etna-Hanover Ctr. Community Assn., Hanover, N.H., 1974-76; mem. Mayor's Task Force, Denver, 1984; bd. dirs. Rude Park Community Nursery, Denver, 1985-87, Willows Water Dist., Colo., 1990—, sec.; trustee The Iliff Sch. Theol., Denver, 1986-92; mem. Dartmouth Coll. Com. on Trustees, 1990-93. Mem. Dartmouth Alumni Coun. (exec. com., chmn. nominating and trustee search coms. 1987-89), University Club (admissions com. 1996—), Cactus Club (Denver), Dartmouth Club of N.Y.C., Yale Club, Lions (bd. dirs. Denver chpt. 1983-85, treas. 1986-87, pres. Denver Found. 1987-88), Delta Upsilon. Congregationalist. Home: 7099 E Hinsdale Pl Englewood CO 80112-1610 Office: One Tabor Ctr 1200 17th St Ste 1303 Denver CO 80202-5813

COOK, BEVERLY LAVONNE, medical administrator; b. Madera, Calif., Mar. 1, 1960; d. Charles Edward and Beverly Ann (Ross) Holbert; m. Steven Duane Cook, Feb. 25, 1984; children: Abigail Marie, Tyler Wayne. Diploma, Chowchilla (Calif.) Union H.S., 1978. Optometric asst. Office of Wayne A. Nishio, OD, Chowchilla, 1981-89; med. office mgr. Office of V.A. Reyes, MD, Chowchilla, 1989—; owner, operator Beverly's Billing and Mgmt. Svcs., Chowchilla, 1995—. Choir dir. Assembly of God Ch., coord. Children's Bible Clubs. Mem. Chowchilla C. of C. Republican. Home and Office: 1325 Kings Ave Chowchilla CA 93610

COOK, DIERDRE RUTH GOORMAN, school administrator, secondary education educator; b. Denver, Nov. 4, 1956; d. George Edward and Avis M. (Wilson) Goorman; m. Donald Robert Cook, Apr. 4, 1981; 1 child, Christen. BA in Theatre Arts, Colo. State U., 1980, MA in Adminstrn., MEd, 1995. Cert. secondary tchr. Tchr. Centennial High Sch., Ft. Collins, Colo., 1983-87; tchr., also dir. student activities Poudre H.S., Ft. Collins, 1987-95; asst. prin. Lesher Jr. H.S., Ft. Collins, 1995—; mem. curriculum devel. com. Poudre R-1 Sch. Dist., Ft. Collins, 1984, mem. instrnl. improvement com., 1985-94, trainer positive power leadership, 1986-87, mem. profl. devel. com. 1992-94; comm. cons. Woodward Gov. Com., Ft. Collins, 1991, 92, 95; mem. evaluation visitation team North Ctrl. Evaluation, Greeley, Colo., 1991. Campaign worker Rep. Party, Littleton, Colo., 1980, Ft. Collins, 1984, 88; mem. Colo. Juvenile Coun., Ft. Collins United Way, 1986, 88, loaned exec., 1987; bd. dirs. Youth Unltd., 1994-95; mem. Leadership Ft. Collins, 1992-93; troop leader Girl Scouts U.S., 1991-94. NEH scholar, 1992; named Disting. Tchr. 1993 Colo. Awards Coun.; recipient Tchr. Excellence award Poudre High Sch., 1992. Mem. NEA, ASCD, Colo. Edn. Assn., Poudre Edn. Assn. (rep. 1989-91), Nat. Speech Comm. Assn., Nat. Forensics League (degree for outstanding distinction 1992), Nat. Platform Soc., Kappa Kappa Gamma (pres. Epsilon Beta chpt. 1985-90, mem. corp. house bd., alumni pres. Ft. Collins 1996-97), Evangelica Free Ch. Home: 1600 Burlington Ct Fort Collins CO 80525 Office: Poudre R-1 Sch Dist 1400 Stover Rd Fort Collins CO 80524

COOK, DONALD E., pediatrician; b. Pitts., Mar. 24, 1928; s. Merriam E. and Bertha (Gwin) C.; BS, Colo. Coll., 1951; MD, U. Colo., 1955; m. Elsie Walden, Sept. 2, 1951; children: Catherine, Christopher, Brian, Jeffrey. Intern, Fresno County Gen. Hosp., Calif., 1955-56; resident in gen. practice Tulare (Calif.) County Gen. Hosp., 1956-57; resident in pediatrics U. Colo., 1957-59; practice medicine specializing in pediatrics, Aurora, Colo., 1959-64, Greeley (Colo.) Med. Clin., Greeley Sports Medicine Clin., 1964-93; med. adv. Centennial Develop. Svcs., Inc., clin. faculty U. Colo., clin. prof., 1977—; organizer, dir. Sports Medicine Px Exam Clinic for indigent Weld Co. athletes, 1990-96; mem. adv. bd. Nat. Center Health Edn., San Francisco, 1978-80; mem. adv. com. on maternal and child health programs Colo. State Health Dept., 1981-84, chmn., 1981-84; preceptor Sch. Nurse Practitioner Program U. Colo., 1978-88. Mem. Weld County Dist. 6 Sch. Bd., 1973-83, pres., 1973-74, 76-77, chmn. dist. 6 accountability com., 1972-73; mem. adv. com. dist. 6 teen pregnancy program, 1983-85; mem. Weld County Task Force on teen-aged pregnancy, 1986-89, Dream Team Weld County Task Force on sch. dropouts, 1986-92, Weld County Interagy. Screening Bd., Weld County Cmty. Ctr. Found., 1984-89, Weld County Task Force Speakers Bur. on AIDS, 1987—; mem. Weld County Task Force Adolescent Health Clinic; mem. Task Force Child Abuse, C. of C.; bd. dirs. No. Colo. Med. Ctr., 1993—, No. Colo. Med. Ctr. Found., 1994—; med. advisor Weld County Sch. Dist. VI-Nurses, 1987-97; mem. Sch. Dist. 6 Health Coalition, Task Force on access to health care; group leader neonatal group Colo. Action for Healthy People Colo. Dept. Pub. Health, 1985-86; co-founder Colorodoans for seatbelts on sch. buses, 1985-90; co-founder, v.p. Coalition of primary care physicians, Colo., 1986; mem. adv. com. Greeley Cen. Drug and Alcohol Abuse, 1984-86, Rocky Mtn. Ctr. for Health Promotion and Edn., 1984—, bd. dirs., 1984—, v.p., 1992-93, pres. 1994-95; rep. coun. on med. specialty soc., AAP, 1988-89, mem. coun. pediatric rsch., 1988-89, oversight com. fin., oversight com. communications, rep. to nat. PTA, 1990-94, mem. coun. on govt. affairs, 1989-90, rep. to coun. sects. mgmt. com., mem. search com. for new exec. dir.; med. cons. Sch. Dist. 6, 1989—; adv. com. bd. comm., adv. com. bd. membership comm., adv. com. bd. finance, adv. com. bd. dirs. AAP 1990-95, AAP com. govt. affairs, 1990; bd. dirs. N. Colo. Med. Ctr., 1993—, United Way Weld County, 1993—; founder, med. dir. Greeley Children's Clinic, 1994—; affiliate prof. nursing U. No. Colo., 1996. With USN, 1946-48. Recipient Disting. Svc. award Jr. C. of C., 1962, Disting. Citizenship award Elks, 1975-76, Svc. to Mankind award Sertoma Club, 1972, Spark Plug award U. No. Colo., 1981, Eta Sigma Gamma Svc. award, 1996; Mildred Doster award Colo. Sch. Health Coun. for sch. health contbns., 1992, Citizen of Yr. award No. Colo. Med. Ctr. Found., 1996, Humanitarian of Yr. award Weld County United Way, 1996, Alfred Winchester Humanitarian award Greeley/Weld Sr. Found., Inc., 1996. Diplomate Am. Bd. Pediatrics. Mem. Colo. Soc. Sch. Health Com. (chmn. 1967-78), Am. Acad. Pediatrics (alt. dist. chmn. 1987-93, dist. chmn. dist. VIII 1993, chmn. alt. dist. chmn. com. 1991-93, chmn. sch. health com. 1975-80, chmn. Colo. chpt. 1982-87, mem. task force on new age of pediatrics 1982-85, Ross edn. and award com. 1985-86, media spokesperson Speak Up for Children 1983—, mem. coun. sects. mgmt. 1991-92, mem. search com., exec. dir.), AMA (chmn. sch. and coll. health com. 1980-82, James E. Strain Community Svc. award 1987, 94, coun. pediatric practice), Adams Aurora Med. Soc. (pres. 1964-65), Weld County Med. Soc. (pres. 1968-69), Colo. Med. Soc. (com. on sports medicine, 1980-90, com. chmn. 1986-90, chmn. com. sch. health 1988-91, A.H. Robbins Community Svc. award 1974), Centennial Pediatric Soc. (pres. 1982-86), Rotary (bd. dirs. Greely chpt. 1988-91, mem. immunization com. 1994—, chmn. immunization campaign Weld county, 1994). Republican. Methodist. Home: 1710 21st Ave Greeley CO 80631-5143 Office: Greeley Sports Medicine Clinic 1900 16th St Greeley CO 80631-5114

COOK, DOUGLAS NEILSON, theater educator, producer, artistic director; b. Phoenix, Sept. 22, 1929; s. Neil Estes and Louise Y. (Wood) C.; m. Joan Stafford Buechner, Aug. 11, 1956; children: John Richard, Peter Neilson, Stephen Barton. Student, Phoenix Coll., 1948-49, U. Chgo., 1949-50, UCLA, 1950-51, Los Angeles Art Inst., 1948; B.F.A., U. Ariz., 1953; M.A., Stanford U., 1955; postgrad., Lester Polakov Studio Stage Design, 1966-67. Instr. San Mateo (Calif.) Coll., 1955-57, Nat. Music Camp, Interlochen, Mich., 1961; asst. prof. drama U. Calif., Riverside, 1957-66; assoc. prof., chair theatre dept. U. Calif., 1967-70; head dept. Pa. State U., University Park, 1970-88, sr. prof. theatre arts, 1988-92; prof. emeritus Pa. State U., 1992—. Actor Corral Theatre, Tucson, 1952-53, Orleans (Mass.) Arena Theatre, 1953; dir., designer Palo Alto (Calif.) Community Theatre, 1954, Peninsula Children's Theatre, 1956-57; assoc. producer Utah Shakespearean Festival, Cedar City, 1964-90, producing artistic dir., 1990—; producer Pa. State Festival Theatre, State College, 1970-85, The Nat. Wagon Train Show, 1975-76. Instl. rep. Juniata Valley council Boy Scouts Am., 1973-77; bd. dirs. Central Pa. Festival Arts, 1970-75, 84-87, v.p., 1984-86; bd. dirs. Nat. theatre Conf., 1980-90, v.p. 1983-85, pres. 1987-88. Recipient disting. alumni award U. Ariz., 1990; named to Coll. of Fellows of the Am. Theatre, 1994. Mem. AAUP, Shakespeare Theatre Assn. Am. (v.p. 1990-92, pres. 1993-94), Nat. Assn. Schs. Theatre, Am. Theatre Assn. (bd. dirs. 1977-86, exec. com. 1979-80, pres. 1984-85), U.S. Inst. Theatre Tech., Am. Soc. Theatre Rsch., Univ. Resident Theatre Assn. (bd. dirs. 1970-88, v.p. 1975-79, pres. 1979-83), Theatre Assn. Pa. (bd. dirs. 1972-76). Home: PO Box 10194 Phoenix AZ 85064-0194 Office: Utah Shakespearean Festival 351 W Center St Cedar City UT 84720-2470

COOK, GARY DENNIS, music educator, administrator; b. Jackson, Mich., Jan. 20, 1951; s. Jerome D. and Mary Jane (Read) C.; m. Kirsten M. Odmark, June 3, 1972; children: Tekla M., Tamara K. MusB, U. Mich., 1972, MusM, 1975. Instr. music La. Tech. U., Ruston, 1972-75; timpanist/prin. percussion Tucson Symphony Orch., 1976-96; asst. dir. bands U. Ariz., Tucson, 1975-77, asst. prof. music, 1975-80, assoc. prof. music, 1981-90, prof. music, 1990—, interim dir. Sch. Music and Dance, 1994-96, dir. Sch. Music and Dance, 1996—. Author: Teaching Percussion, 1988, 2d edit., 1996; co-author: The Encyclopedia for Percussion; contbr. articles to profl. jours. and ency. Charles and Irene Putnam award for excellence in teaching in the College of Fine Arts. Mem. Percussive Arts Soc., Coll. Music Soc., Music Tchrs. Nat. Assn., Am. Fedn. Musicians, Pi Kappa Lambda, Kappa Kappa Psi, Phi Mu Alpha. Office: U Ariz Sch Music and Dance Tucson AZ 85721

COOK, GLORIA JEAN, writer; b. Scott City, Kans., June 1, 1948; d. John Alfred and Norma Irene (Russell) C.; m. Billy Chris Batman, June 28, 1975 (div. Apr. 1993); 1 child, Stephanie Jo Batman. Student, U. Colo., 1966-68; BA, U. Colo., 1971, MA, 1978. Tech. writer M.D.C. Holdings, Inc., Denver, 1987-88; mgr. documentation J.D. Edwards & Co., Denver, 1988-93, sr. editor, 1993-95; freelance writer Evergreen, Colo., 1995—; elected mem. State Pers. Employees Exec. Coun., Greeley, Colo., 1983-84. Author:

numerous software manuals, 1985-96; (novel) The Shaman's Spell, 1996; contbr. articles to profl. jours. Regents' scholar U. Colo., 1966-68. Mem. Writers Connection, Women in Comm.

COOK, IAN AINSWORTH, psychiatrist, researcher, educator; b. N.Y.C., May 1, 1960; s. Charles David and Bobette Cook. BS in Engring. magna cum laude, Princeton U., 1982; MD, Yale U., 1987. Diplomate Nat. Bd. Med. Examiners. Resident in surgery U. Colo., Denver, 1987-88; resident in psychiatry Neuropsychiat. Inst. UCLA, 1991-94, chief resident in liaison psychiatry, 1993-94, instr. dept. psychiatry, 1995—, asst. dir. residency edn. dept. psychiatry, 1995-96, asst. prof psychiatry, 1996—. Mem. editl. bd. Jefferson Jour. Psychiatry, 1992-94; contbr. articles to profl. jours. Rsch. fellow Nat. Inst. Mental Health, 1993-96; recipient Young Investigator award Nat. Alliance Rsch. Schizophrenia and Depression, 1995. Mem. Am. Psychiat. Assn. (Burroughs-Wellcome fellow 1992, mem. com. of resident and fellows 1992-94, mem. steering com./practice guidelines 1994—), Nat. Eagle Scout Assn., Sigma Xi, Tau Beta Pi. Office: UCLA Neuropsychiat Inst & Hosp 760 Westwood Plz Los Angeles CA 90024-8300

COOK, LYLE EDWARDS, retired fund raising executive, consultant; b. Astoria, Oreg., Aug. 19, 1918; s. Courtney Carson and Fanchon (Edwards) C.; m. Olive Freeman, Dec. 28, 1940; children: James Michael, Ellen Anita Cook Otto, Mary Lucinda Cook Vaage, Jane Victoria. A.B. in History, Stanford U., 1940, postgrad., 1940-41. Instr. history Yuba Jr. Coll., Marysville, Calif., 1941-42; methods analyst Lockheed Aircraft Corp., 1942-45; investment broker Quincy Cass Assocs., Los Angeles, 1945-49; mem. staff Stanford U., 1949-66, asso. dean Sch. Medicine, 1958-65; sr. staff mem. Lester Gorsline Assos., Belvedere, Calif., 1966-72, v.p., 1967-70, exec. v.p., 1970-72; v.p. univ. relations U. San Francisco, 1973-75; fund-raising and planning cons., 1975; dir. fund devel. Children's Home Soc. Calif., 1976-78; exec. dir. That Man May See, Inc., San Francisco, 1978-87; co-founder, trustee, chmn. bd. The Fund Raising Sch., 1977-86; spl. cons. NIH, 1960-62. Mem. Marin County Grand Jury, 1987-88. Mem. Nat. Soc. Fund Raising Execs. (bd. dirs. 1976-88, chmn. certification bd. 1988-90, recipient first Nat. Chmn.'s award 1981, named Outstanding Fund Raising Exec. 1987), Stanford Assocs., Stanford Founding Grant Soc. (dir. 1994—), Belvedere Tennis Club, Theta Delta Chi. Democrat. Episcopalian. Home: 25 Greenwood Bay Dr Tiburon CA 94920-2252

COOK, MARCY LYNN, mathematics educator, consultant; b. Culver City, Calif., Mar. 5, 1943; d. Lloyd Everett and Theresa J. (Matusek) Rude; m. Robert Lee Cook, Aug. 26, 1968; children: Bob, Jim. BA, U. Calif., Santa Barbara, 1964; MA, Stanford U., 1968. Tchr. 5th and 6th grades Sunnyvale (Calif.) Sch. Dist., 1964-67; tchr. Thessaloniki (Greece) Internat. H.S., 1968-70; tchr. primary grades Carmel (Calif.) Unified Sch. Dist., 1970-72; faculty of edn. Calif. State U., Fullerton, 1973-80; tchr. gifted and talented Newport Mesa Unified Sch. Dist., Calif., 1980-85; math. cons. Newport Beach, Calif., 1985—; lectr. in field nationally and internationally. Author over 100 books including Act It Out, Assessing Math Understanding, Basic Games, Book A, Book B, Clues and Cues, Communicating with Tiles, Contrasting Facts, Coop Thinking, Crack The Code Book A, Book B, Do Math, Do Talk It Over, Duo Do Dominoes, Follow the Clues, I Have, Justify Your Thinking, Numbers Please! Questions Please!, Postitive Math at Home and School, I, II, Primary Today is the Day, Reason Together, Show Me and Stump Me, Talk It Over, Think in Color, Tile Awhile, many others. Stanford U. fellow, 1968. Mem. Calif. Assn. Gifted, Calif. Math. Coun., Nat. Coun. Tchrs. Math., Assn. for Advancement of Internat. Edn., Nat. Coun. Suprs. of Math. Home and Office: PO Box 5840 Newport Beach CA 92662-5840

COOK, MERRILL A., explosives industry executive; b. Phila., May 6, 1946; s. Melvin A. and Wanda (Garfield) C.; m. Camille Sanders, Oct. 24, 1969; children—Brian, Alison, Barbara Ann, David, Michelle. BA magna cum laude, U. Utah, 1969; MBA, Harvard U., 1971. Profl. staff cons. Arthur D. Little, Inc., Cambridge, Mass., 1971-73; mng. dir. Cook Assocs., Inc., Salt Lake City, 1973-78; pres. Cook Slurry Co., Salt Lake City, 1978—. Patentee in field. Del. Rep. Nat. Conv., Kansas City, Mo., 1976. Mem. Salt Lake City C. of C., Phi Kappa Phi. Mormon. Home: 2989 Sherwood Dr Salt Lake City UT 84108-2558 Office: 1800 Beneficial Life Tower Salt Lake City UT 84111-1401

COOK, PAUL M., technology company executive; b. Ridgewood, N.J.. BSChemE, MIT, 1947. With Stanford Rsch. Inst., Menlo Park, Calif., 1948-53, Sequoia Process Corp., 1953-56; with Raychem Corp., Menlo Park, Calif., 1957—, founder, former pres., CEO, until 1990, chmn., bd. dirs., until 1995; now dir.; chmn., CEO CellNet Data Sys., San Carlos, Calif., 1990-94, now chmn., bd. dirs.; chmn., bd. dirs SRI Internat., 1993—; chmn., CEO DIVA Sys. Corp., Menlo Park, Calif., 1995—. Mem. exec. com. San Francisco Bay Area Coun., 1988-94, chmn., 1990-91. Recipient Nat. Medal Tech., 1988. Mem. NAE, Am. Acad. Sci., Environ. Careers Orgn. (chmn., bd. trustees), MIT Corp. (life). Office: SRI Internat 333 Ravenswood Ave Menlo Park CA 94025-3453*

COOK, PETER GIFFORD, communications engineer; b. Corning, N.Y., Aug. 11, 1933; s. Edward Austin and Alberta Damon C.; m. Susan Merz, Oct. 8, 1955; children: Jean, Keith, Jonathan, Paul. BA in Physics, Williams coll., 1955. Product devel. engr. Corning Glass Works, Bradford, Pa., 1960-63; sys. analyst Corning Glass Works, Corning, 1963-69; software devel. mgr. Corning Glass Works, Raleigh, N.C., 1969-72; dir. software devel. Tektronix, Inc., Beaverton, Oreg., 1972-80; v.p. software Motorola, Inc., Cupertino, Calif., 1980-85; liason rep. MCC/Motorola, Austin, Tex., 1985-89; prin. mem. techstaff Motorola, Inc., Scottsdale, Ariz., 1989—. Contbr. chpts. to books, articles to profl. jours. Lt. col. USAF, 1955-60. Home: 435 E Barbarita Ave Gilbert AZ 85234

COOK, ROBERT DONALD, financial service executive; b. Chicago Heights, Ill., Nov. 1, 1929; s. Webster Warren and Gladys (Miner) C.; m. Maxine Jensen, Nov. 11, 1950; children: Carolyn Jean, Robert Donald II. B.S. in Bus, U. Md., 1956; grad. advanced mgmt. program, Harvard U., 1973. C.P.A., Md. Audit mgr. Arthur Andersen & Co. (CPAs), Washington, 1956-63; comptroller Peoples Drug Stores, Washington, 1963-68; v.p., controller Booz, Allen & Hamilton, Inc., Chgo., 1968-72; pres. Cookemper Rentals, Inc., Barrington, Ill., 1971-73; controller Esmark, Inc., Chgo., 1973-77; pres., chief operating officer Castle & Cooke, Inc., San Francisco, 1977-86; chmn. R.D. Cook Mgmt. Corp., 1986—; chmn. bd. dirs. Am. Nursery Products, Inc.; bd. dirs. Redwood Empire Bancorp, IF&GP Foods, PAFCO, Inc. Served with USNR, 1948-52. Mem. Inst. C.P.A.s, Fin. Execs. Inst., Beta Alpha Psi. Clubs: Masons (32 deg.), Shriners. Home and Office: RD Cook Mgmt Corp 75 Rolling Hills Rd Belvedere Tiburon CA 94920-1501

COOK, ROBERT P., II, business development executive; b. Balt., Nov. 23, 1931; s. Edward Damerel Cook and Emma Elizabeth (Tagmyer) Amstutz; m. Jean Lee Whittle, Mar. 31, 1951 (div. Jan. 1977); children: Robert, Susan. BS in Biochemistry, Johns Hopkins U., 1960. Pharm. rep. Borden, Inc., N.Y.C., 1954-62, mktg. mgr., 1962-71; product mgr. Syntex Labs., Inc., Palo Alto, Calif., 1971-81, group product dir., 1981-85, dir. bus. devel., 1985-88, dir. generics bus., 1988-94; pres. Cook and Co., Los Altos, Calif., 1994—; sr. v.p., founding ptnr. Scinopharm Investments, Ltd., Los Altos; seminar spkr. Inst. Internat. Rsch., 1990, 93, I.B.C., Inc., 1991, 92, Windhover Assocs., 1990. With USN, 1949-53, lt. comdr. USNR, 1953-64. Mem. Licensing Execs. Soc. Republican. Home: 60 Doud Dr Los Altos CA 94022-2326 Office: Unit 15 1901 Old Middlefield Way Mountain View CA 94043

COOK, ROBERTA LYNN, agricultural economist, educator; b. Oceanside, Calif., Feb. 27, 1954; d. Robert Merold and Wanda Eugenia (Wright) C.; m. Manuel Villarreal, Dec. 23, 1975 (div. Sept. 1983). BA, Mich. State U., 1976, MS, 1981, PhD, 1985. Grad. rsch. asst. Mich. State U., East Lansing, 1978-81, 84; cons. Banco de Mexico, Mexico City, 1981-84; ext. economist, prof. U. Calif., Davis, 1985—; bd. dirs. Calif. Kiwifruit Commn., Sacramento, 1991—, Calif. Tomato Commn., Fresno, 1993—; mem. Internat. adv. coun. Produce Mktg. Assn., Newark, Del., 1994—; cons. OECD, Colombian Govt., Trade Bur., U.S. AID, World Bank, others; chair S-222 Regional Rsch. Group on Fruits and Vegetables, 1991-93. Contbr. articles to profl. jours. Bd. dirs. Katalysis Found., Stockton, Calif., 1987-91; chair U. Calif./Legis. Task Force on Cooperatives, Davis, 1987-88. Recipient Grad. Inst./Coop. Leadership award U.S. Dept. Agr., U. Mo., Columbia, 1986, Affirmative Action award U. Calif., 1991. Mem. Food Dist. Rsch. Soc. (bd. mem. 1995—), Am. Agrl. Econs. Assn. (various coms. 1984—), Produce Mktg. Assn. (various coms. 1987—), United Fresh Fruit and Vegetable Assn. (various coms. 1987—), Internat. Soc. Hort. Sci. (v.p. econ. divsn. 1992—). Office: U Calif Davis Dept Agr and Resource Econs Davis CA 95616

COOK, SHARON EVONNE, university official; b. Pocatello, Idaho, July 16, 1941; d. Willard Robert and Marian (Bartlett) Leisy; m. John Fred Cook, June 19, 1971 (div. Nov. 1980). BEd, No. Mont. Coll., 1970; M in Secondary Edn., U. Alaska, Juneau, 1980; EdD, U. San Francisco, 1987. Cert. secondary sch. tchr., Alaska. Loan officer 1st Nat. Bank, Havre, Mont., 1964-68; adminstrv. asst. Alaska State Legis., Juneau, 1970-71; tchr. Juneau Dist. High Sch., 1971-75; instr. Juneau Dist. Community Coll., 1975-79; assoc. prof. U. Alaska, Juneau, 1979-90, dean Sch. Bus. and Pub. Adminstrn., 1986-90; assoc. dean Coll. Tech., Boise (Idaho) State U., 1990—; editor in chief office tech. McGraw Hill Book Gregg Div., N.Y.C., 1983-84; mem. exec. bd. statewide assembly U. Region V Vocat. Assn., 1978-80, del. 1982. Treas. Alaska State Vocat. Assn., 1980-82, pres.-elect, 1986, pres., 1987; pres. U. Alaska Juneau Assembly, 1978-80, v.p., 1980-82. No. Mont. Coll. scholar, Havre, 1968-70; named Outstanding Tchr., U. Alaska, 1976. Republican. Home: 2551 S Swallowtail Ln Boise ID 83706-6150 Office: Boise State U Coll Tech Office Assoc Dean 1910 University Dr Boise ID 83725-0001

COOK, STANLEY JOSEPH, English language educator, poet; b. Spicer, Minn., June 9, 1935; s. William Joseph and Lillie Esther (Feeland) C.; m. Janet Lucille Terry, Oct. 9, 1964 (div. June 1988); children: John Hildon, Laurel Erin; m. Michaela Dianne Higuera, Dec. 18, 1989; 1 step-child, Richard Scott. BA, U. Minn., 1957; MA, U. Utah, 1966, PhD (NDEA fellow), 1969. Project specialist in English, U. Wis., Madison, 1967; instr. English, U. Utah, Salt Lake City, 1968-69; prof. English and fgn. langs. Calif. State Poly. U., Pomona, 1969—; cons. communications. Served with USMCR, 1958-64. NSF grantee, 1966; Calif. State U. and Colls. grantee, 1973-74. Mem. SUBUD, AAUP, NEA, Phi Beta Kappa. Democrat. Roman Catholic. Editor: Language and Human Behavior, 1973, Man Unwept: Visions from the Inner Eye, 1974; author: (with others) The Scope of Grammar: A Study of Modern English, 1980, Cal Poly through 2001: A Continuing Commitment to Excellence, 1987; fieldworker Dictionary of Am. Regional English, 1986—. Home: 1744 N Corona Ave Ontario CA 91764-1236 Office: Calif State Poly U 3801 W Temple Ave Pomona CA 91768-2557

COOK, STEPHEN CHAMPLIN, retired shipping company executive; b. Portland, Oreg., Sept. 20, 1915; s. Frederick Stephen and Mary Louise (Boardman) C.; m. Dorothy White, Oct. 27, 1945; children: Mary H. Cook Goodson, John B., Samuel D., Robert B. (dec.). Student, U. Oreg., 1935-36. Surveyor U.S. Engrs. Corp., Portland, Oreg., 1934-35; dispatcher Pacific Motor Trucking Co., Oakland, Calif., 1937-38; manifest clk. Pacific Truck Express, Portland, 1939; exec. asst. Coastwise Line, San Francisco, 1940-41, mgr. K-Line svc., 1945-56; chartering mgr. Ocean Svc. Inc. subs. Marcona Corp., San Francisco, 1956-75, ret., 1975; cons., San Francisco, 1976-78. Author 1 charter party, 1957. Mem. steering com. Dogwood Festival, Lewiston, Idaho, 1985-92; sec. Asotin County Reps., Clarkston, Wash., 1986-88; adv. bd. Clarkston Pt. Commrs., 1989-92. Lt. USN, 1941-45, PTO. Recipient Pres.'s award Marin (Calif.) coun. Boy Scouts Am., 1977, Order of Merit, 1971, 84, Skillern award Lewis Clark coun., 1982, Silver Beaver award 1987; Lewis-Clark Valley Vol. award, 1987, Youth Corps award Nat. Assn. Svc. and Conservation Corps, 1990, Pres.'s Spl. award Clarkston C. of C., 1983. Mem. VFW, Asotin County Hist. Soc. (hon. life pres. 1982-83, bd. dirs.), Asotin C. of C. (v.p. 1994-95). Republican. Mem. Stand for United Ch. of Christ.

COOK, STEVEN DONALD, electrical engineer; b. Pendleton, Oreg., Jan. 19, 1953; s. Donald Jack and Lillian Helen (Lorenzen) C.; m. Judith Elizabeth Meermeier; children: Aaron, Lauren, Kathryn. BS in Elec. Engring., Oreg. State U., 1976. Inside sales, industry products Westinghouse Electric Corp., Seattle, 1976-77; outside sales, industry products Westinghouse Electric Corp., Salt Lake City, 1977-79; jr. engr. CH2M Hill, Inc., Portland, Oreg., 1979-82, sr. engr. elec. dept., 1982-85; mgr. elec. engring. dept. Indsl. Design Corp., A CH2M Hill Co., Portland, 1985-88, mgr. elec. engring., 1988-94, sr. project mgr., 1994—. Mem. IEEE. Republican. Roman Catholic. Office: Indsl Design Corp 2020 SW 4th Ave Portland OR 97068

COOK, TODD MCCLURE, health care executive; b. Frankfort, Ind., Nov. 3, 1962; s. Robert Eugene and Patricia (McKinney) C. Student Calif. State U., 1981-82; BA in Econs./English George Mason U., 1983; MBA in Health Care Adminstrn., Columbia Pacific U., 1990. Asst. dir./acting dir. This Way House, Alexandria, 1983-85; pvt. cons., 1985-86; bus. mgr. Falls Church (Va.) Med. Ctr., Va., 1986-88; adminstr., Neurology Svcs., Inc., Fairfax, Alexandria, Woodbridge, Va. and Washington, 1989-92; sr. ptnr. Cook & Miele Assocs., Alexandria and L.A., 1989-93; health care exec. RehabCare Corp., Rio Hondo Hosp., Downey, Calif., Valley Presbyn. Hosp., Van Nuys, Calif., Alhambra (Calif.) Hosp., St. Louis, Mo., 1993—; cons. St. Elizabeth's Hosp. Crisis Intervention Tng., Washington, 1985, Alexandria's Child Safety Day, 1984; Bd. dirs. Help in Emotional Trouble, Fresno, 1982, v.p., bd. dirs., 1983; bd. dirs. Mental Health Assn., Alexandria, 1984, v.p. bd., 1985; del. Nat. Network of Runaway and Youth Services Symposium, Bethesda, Md., 1985; v.p. Alexandria Mental Health Assn., 1983-86; active Nat. Head Injury Found., Va. Head Injury Found., Calif. Head Injury; vol. Alexandria Crisis Hot-Line. Grantee Youth Devel. Bur., 1984, 85, Alexandria City grantee, 1985. Mem. SAR, Am. Coll. Health Care Execs. (affiliate), Am. Coll. Med. Quality (affiliate), Am. Bd. Quality Assurance and Utilization Rev. Physicians (diplomate), Am. Acad. Med. Adminstrs., Am. Coll. Neuromusculoskeletal Adminstrs. Democrat. Presbyterian. Club: Entrepreneur Orgn. (Alexandria) (pres. 1985). Lodge: Demolay. Avocation: tennis.

COOKE, CHARLES MAYNARD, vineyardist, business executive; b. Honolulu, Oct. 19, 1931; s. Charles Maynard and Mary Louise (Cooper) C.; m. Judith Marguerite Flanagan, Dec., 1958 (div. Nov. 1966); m. Diane Smith, Feb., 1967 (div. Nov. 1977); children: Mary Elizabeth, Stephanie Marguerite; m. Sara Louise Peterson, July 18, 1978. BS, U.S. Naval Acad., 1953; MA in Chinese History, U. Wash., 1965. Commd. 2nd lt. USAF, 1953, advanced through grades to maj., 1969; flight line maintenance officer 43rd B Wing Armament & Electronics Squadron, Tucson, 1954-58; assoc. prof. history USAF Acad., Colorado Springs, Colo., 1960-65; pacification planner J-3 Mil. Assistance Command, Vietnam, Saigon, Vietnam, 1966; Vietnam desk officer, asst. sec. Internat. Security Affairs, Dept. of Def., Washington, 1967-69; spl. advisor for Vietnam Undersec. of State, U.S. State Dept., Washington, 1969-70; mgr. Office of Spl. Concerns HEW, Washington, 1970-73; dep. asst. sec. edn. legislation Dept. H.E.&W., Washington, 1973-74, dep. asst. sec. edn. planning, 1974-75; fed. program coord. Calif. Dept. Edn., Sacramento, 1975-83; chmn. of bd. Pacific Enterprises Group Corp., Sonoma, Calif., 1989—. Dir. Econ. Devel. Bd.-Sonoma County, Santa Rosa, 1987-91, Pvt. Industry Coun.-Sonoma County, Santa Rosa, 1987-91, Sonoma County Agrl. Preservation and Open Space Dist., 1991—, Sonoma Valley Visitors Bur., 1992-96; planning commr. Sonoma County Planning Agy., Santa Rosa, 1991—; owner, operator Cooke Zinfandel Vineyard, 1979—. Decorated Air Force Commendation medals USAF, 1958, 65, Bronze star USAF, 1967, Legion of Merit, Dept. of Def., 1969. Home and Office: Pacific Enterprises Group Corp 3060 Lovall Valley Rd Sonoma CA 95476-4813

COOKE, JUDY, artist, educator; b. Bay City, Mich., July 8, 1940; d. George Wight and Edith (Holden) Cooke; m. Robert Jackson Hanson, June 15, 1963; 1 child, Joshua Blazo. Honors Diploma in Printmaking, Sch. of Mus. of Fine Arts, Boston, 1963; BFA, Tufts U., 1965; MAT, Reed Coll., 1970. Assoc. prof. Pacific N.W. Coll. of Art, Portland, 1986—; Artist tarp Portland Art Mus., 1973, charcoal drawing Boston Mus., 1967. Exhibited works in solo shows at Ingrid Fassbender Gallery, Chgo., 1996, Elizabeth Leach Gallery, Portland, Oreg., 1987, 91, 93, 95, Linda Hodges Gallery, Seattle, 1995; group exhbns. include Esther Saks Gallery, Chgo., 1990; represented incollections at Hewlett Packard Corp., Portland, Portland Art Mus., Bank of Am., San Francisco, Physio-Control, Seattle. Edvard Munch resident Norweigan Govt., Oslo, 1994; Bonnie Bronson fellow, 1993, NEA Visual Artist fellow, 1989. Home: 2317 NW Quimby St Portland OR 97210-2625 Office: Pacific NW Coll Art 1219 SW Park Ave Portland OR 97205-2430

COOKE, THOMAS PAUL, education educator; b. Panama Canal, Oct. 12, 1948; s. Thomas Paul and Sarah Anne (Downing) C.; m. Sharon Anne Raver, Dec. 18, 1968 (div. June 1975); 1 child, James Mitchell; m. Marrianne McKinley, Apr. 14, 1990. BA, U. South Fla., 1970, MA, 1971; PhD, Vanderbilt U., 1974. Coord. spl. edn. Sonoma State U., Rohnert Park, Calif., 1982-88; prof. edn. Sonoma State U., Rohnert Park, 1983—, chmn. dept. edn., 1988-92. Author: Exceptional Children: Assessing and Modifying Social Behavior, 1976, Towards Excellence: Achievements in Residential Arrangements, 1980, Early Independence: A Curriculum System, 1981, Self Instructional Curriculum Development, 1981, A New Look at Guardianship, 1984; contbr. articles to profl. jours. Chmn. bd. Found. for Ednl. Devel., Napa, Calif., 1993-96.

COOLEN, PHYLLIS R., community health nurse; b. Monterey, Calif., Oct. 13, 1950. BSN, U. Wash., 1973, MSN, 1981. Hospice clinician Providence Med. Ctr., Seattle, 1980-86; nursing cons. adv., quality care coord. Dept. Social and Health Svc. Med. Asst. Adminstrn., Olympia, Wash., 1993-95, acting dir. divsn. utilization svcs., 1995-97; dir. divsn. health svcs. quality support Dept. Social and Health Svc. Med. Asst. Adminstrn., Olympia, 1997—; theory, clin. instr. fundamentals and advanced med.-surg. Kauai C.C., Lihue, Hawaii, 1983-85; clin. instr. advanced med.-surg. Seattle C.C., 1985-86; nursing cons. advisor. Lt. comdr. USNR, 1989-96. Mem. SEARCHIN Cmty. Health Nurse Rsch., Res. Officers Assn. (v.p. Navy), Navy Res. Assn., Wash. State Assn. for Health Care Quality. Home: 14040 Prairie Pky SW Olympia WA 98512-9267 Office: Med Assistance Adminstrn Divsn Svcs Quality Support PO Box 45510 Olympia WA 98504

COOLEY, WES, former congressman; b. L.A., Calif., Mar. 28, 1932; married; 4 children. AA, El Camino C. C.; BS in Bus., U. So. Calif., 1958. Asst. to pres. Hyland Labs. divsn. Baxter Labs. Allergan Pharmaceuticals; asst. to chmn. bd. ICN, divsn. mgr., dir. drug regulatory affairs; v.p. Virateck divsn.; founder, co-owner Rose Labs., Inc., 1981—; mem. Oregon State Senate, 1992-94; congressman 104 Congress from 2nd Oreg. dist., 1994—; mem. House Com. Agriculture, House Com. Resources, House Com. Veteran Affairs, Subcommittee Gen. Farm Commodities, Subcommittee on Livestock, Dairy and Poultry, Subcommittee on Nat. Pks., Forests and Lands, SubcommitteeWater and Power Resources. With U.S. Army, 1952-54. Home: 2550 Walker Rd Bend OR 97701 address: 25550 Walker Rd Bend OR 97701

COOMBE, GEORGE WILLIAM, JR., lawyer, retired banker; b. Kearny, N.J., Oct. 1, 1925; s. George William and Laura (Montgomery) C.; A.B., Rutgers U., 1946; LL.B., Harvard, 1949; m. Marilyn V. Ross, June 4, 1949; children—Susan, Donald William, Nancy. Bar: N.Y. 1950, Mich. 1953, Calif. 1976, U.S. Supr. Ct. Practice in N.Y.C., 1949-53, Detroit, 1953-69; atty., mem. legal-staff Gen. Motors Corp., Detroit, 1953-69, asst. gen. counsel, sec., 1969-75; exec. v.p., gen. counsel Bank of Am., San Francisco, 1975-90; ptnr. Graham and James, San Francisco, 1991-95; sr. fellow Stanford Law Sch., 1995—. Served to lt. USNR, 1942-46. Mem. Am., Mich., Calif., San Francisco, Los Angeles, N.Y.C. bar assns., Phi Beta Kappa, Phi Gamma Delta. Presbyterian. Home: 2190 Broadway St Apt 2E San Francisco CA 94115-1311 Office: Am Arbitration Assn Asia Pacific Ctr 417 Montgomery St San Francisco CA 94104-1129

COONEY, MIKE, state official; b. Washington, Sept. 3, 1954; s. Gage Rodman and Ruth (Brodie) C.; m. Dee Ann Marie Gribble; children: Ryan Patrick, Adan Cecelia, Colin Thomas. BA in Polit. Sci., U. Mont., 1979. State rep. Mont. Legislature, Helena, 1976-80; exec. asst. U.S. Sen. Max Baucus, Butte, Mont., 1979-82, Washington, 1982-85, Helena, Mont., 1985-89; sec. of state State of Mont., Helena, 1988—. Bd. dirs. YMCA; mem. adv. panel Fed. Clearinghouse. Mem. Nat. Secs. of State (pres.-elect.), Nat. Assns. Secs. of State (pres. 1997). Home: PO Box 754 Helena MT 59624-0754 Office: Office Sec of State 225 State St Helena MT 59601-5786

COONTZ, JOANNE, mayor. Mayor City of Orange (Calif.). Office: 300 E Chapman Orange CA 92666

COOPER, ANNETTE CARLESTA, entrepreneur; b. Huntington Park, Calif., Feb. 20, 1949; d. Joette Clarina (Murin) C.; Ron Stokes, Jan. 27, 1969 (div.). Massage therapist Fabulous Faces, San Francisco, 1977-80, Shiseido, Manila, Phillipines, 1980-82; mgr. Says Who?, Oakland, San Francisco, Calif., 1984-87; pvt. practice Began Annette's Sizes 14 & Up, Santa Rosa, 1987—; comml. real estate broker, 1990; pres., bd. mem. Montgomery Village Bd. Dirs., Santa Rosa, Calif., 1991-93. Columnist Ask Annette, 1991. Vol. hospice clothing drive, Santa Rosa, Calif., 1991—; pres. Sonoma County (Calif.) chpt. Nat. Women's Polit. Caucus, 1995-96. Named Merchant Ambassador of Yr., Montgomery Village Coding Enterprises, Santa Rosa, Calif., 1993. Mem. C. of C. Office: Annette's Plus Sizes 711 Village Ct Santa Rosa CA 95405-5006

COOPER, AUSTIN MORRIS, chemist, chemical engineer, consultant, researcher; b. Long Beach, Calif., Feb. 1, 1959; s. Merril Morris and Charlotte Madeline (Wittmer) C. BS in Chemistry with honors, Baylor U., 1981; BSChemE with honors, Tex. Tech U., 1983, MSChemE, 1985. Solar energy researcher U.S. Dept. Energy, Lubbock, Tex., 1983-85; advanced mfg. and process engring. mgr. McDonnell Douglas Space Systems Co., Huntington Beach, Calif., 1986-87, chem.-process line mgr., 1987-89, sr. material and process engr., 1989—. Contbr. articles to profl. jours. Mem. Am. Inst. Chem. Engrs., Am. Chem. Soc., Soc. Advancement of Materials and Process Engrs., Sigma Xi, Omega Chi Epsilon, Kappa Mu Epsilon, Beta Beta Beta.

COOPER, B. LEE, college administrator, author, history educator; b. Hammond, Ind., Oct. 4, 1942; s. Charles Albert and Kathleen Marie (Kunde) C.; m. Jill Elizabeth Cunningham, June 13, 1964; children: Michael Lee, Laura Ellen, Julie Allison. BS, Bowling Green State U., 1964; MA, Mich. State U., 1965; PhD, Ohio State U., 1971; cert. Harvard U., 1980. Assoc. prof. history Urbana (Ohio) Coll., 1965-73, dean student affairs, 1973-74, dean coll., 1974-76; v.p. acad. affairs Newberry Coll., S.C., 1976-85; v.p. acad. affairs Olivet (Mich.) Coll., 1986-93, U. Gt. Falls, Mont., 1993—. Author: Images of American Society in Popular Music (ASCAP-Deems Taylor award 1983), 1982, Popular Music Handbook, 1984, Literature of Rock, 1986, Resource Guide for Themes in Contemporary Am. Song Lyrics, 1986, Rock Music in American Popular Culture, 1995, II, 1997. Recipient Tchr. of Yr. award Urbana Coll., 1967, Outstanding Educator in Am. award, 1970, 73, 75., Mem. Am. Hist. Assn., Nat. Council Social Studies, Popular Culture Assn., Am. Culture Assn., Phi Alpha Theta (grad. scholar 1964), Omicron Delta Kappa. Office: Univ Great Falls 2301 20th St S Great Falls MT 59405-6456

COOPER, GINNIE, library director; b. Worthington, Minn., 1945; d. Lawrence D. and Ione C.; m. Richard Bauman, Dec. 1995; 1 child, Daniel Jay. Student, Coll. St. Thomas, U. Wis., Parkside; BA, S.D. State U.; MA in Libr. Sci., U. Minn. Tchr. Flandreau (S.D.) Indian Sch., 1967-68, St. Paul Pub. Schs., 1968-69; br. libr. Wash. County Libr., Lake Elmo, Minn., 1970-71, asst. dir., 1971-75; assoc. adminstr., libr. U. Minn. Med. Sch., Mpls., 1975-77; dir. Kenosha (Wis.) Pub. Libr., 1977-81; county libr. Alameda County (Calif.) Libr., 1981-90; dir. librs. Multnomah County Libr., Portland, Oreg., 1990—. Chair County Mgr. Assn.; county adminstr. Mayor's Exec. Roundtable. Mem. ALA (mem. LAMA, PLA and RASD coms., elected to coun. 1987, 91, mem. legislation com. 1986-90, mem. orgn. com. 1990—), Calif. Libr. Assn. (pres. CIL, 1985, elected to coun. 1986, pres. Calif. County Librs. 1986), Oreg. Libr. Assn., Portland Libr. Assn. (pres. 1997—). Office: Multnomah County Libr 205 NE Russell St Portland OR 97212-3708

COOPER, GREGORY M., protective services official. Chief of police Provo, Utah. Office: 48 S 300 W Provo UT 84603

COOPER, JAMES MELVIN, healthcare executive, consultant; b. Prescott, Ariz., Oct. 29, 1940; s. Audrey Louise Cooper; m. Marlene Kitay, Oct. 29, 1960; children: Jamie Lynn Hill, David Paul. BS in Adminstrn., George

Washington U., 1976, MBA, 1979. Cert. healthcare exec. Enlisted USN, 1959, advanced through grades to capt.; officer-in-charge pers. support detachment Naval Hosp., San Diego, 1979-81; dir. for ambulatory care Naval Hosp., Camp Pendleton, Calif., 1981-83; manpower analyst The Pentagon, Washington, 1983-85; dir. for adminstrn. Naval Med. Clinics, San Diego, 1985-88; exec. officer Naval Hosp., Long Beach, Calif., 1988-91; comdg. officer U.S. Naval Hosp., Naples, Italy, 1991-93; ret. USN, 1993; v.p. Capital Health Svcs., San Diego, 1994—; treas. Ramona/Julian Health Care Adv. Coun., 1996—. Bd. dirs., chmn. Ramona (Calif.) Food and Clothes Closet, 1995—. Decorated Legion of Merit, Meritorious Svc. medal (2). Fellow Am. Acad. Med. Adminstrs.; mem. Am. Coll. Healthcare Execs. (diplomate), Am. Coll. Managed Care Execs., San Diego Women in Health Adminstrn., Fed. Health Care Execs. Inst. (life), DAV (life), Assn. Med. Svc. Corps Officers (chmn. mentoring com. 1996—), Kiwanis of Ramona (pres. 1996-97), VFW (life). Home: 2148 Cook Pl Ramona CA 92065 Office: Navcare Prime Clinic 9332 Clairemont Mesa Blvd San Diego CA 92123

COOPER, JON HUGH, public television executive; b. Wynnewood, Okla., Aug. 6, 1940; s. John Hughes and Sarah Edna (Ray) C.; m. L. Ilene Batty, Dec. 16, 1961 (div. Jan. 1984); children: Jon Shelton, Geoffrey Harold; m. Patricia Carol Kyle, Jan. 28, 1989; children: Cynthia Lynne Elliott, Jennifer Jon Kyle. BA, Okla. State U., 1962; postgrad., U. Ariz., U. Denver, U. Colo., Denver. Mgmt. positions with Evening Star Broadcasting, Washington and Lynchburg, Va., 1962-67; producer, program mgr., dir. prodn. Sta. KUAT-AM-TV, Tucson, 1967-73; exec. dir. Rocky Mountain Network, Denver, 1973-77; exec. dir. Pacific Mountain Network, Denver, 1977-79, also bd. dirs.; gen. mgr. Sta. KNME-TV, Albuquerque, 1979—; lectr. speech and journalism U. Ariz., 1967-73; mem. interconnection com. PBS, 1983-92, bd. dirs., 1986-92, mem. exec. com., 1988-90, 91-92; bd. dirs. PBS Enterprises and Nat. Datacast, 1990-94; bd. dirs. Pacific Mountain Network Japan Survey Team. Bd. dirs., v.p., pres. Pueblo Los Cerros Homeowners Assn., 1987-88; bd. dirs. Samaritan Counseling Ctr., Albuquerque, 1987, N.Mex. Better Bus. Bur., 1991—; bd. advisors Pub. TV Outreach Alliance, 1992—; mem. N.Mex. Edn. Tech. Coun., 1992-94; chmn. N.Mex. Commn. Pub. Broadcasting, 1992—; mem. steering com. Western Coop. on Ednl. Telecommunications. Named Govt. Bus. Adv. of Year U.S. Hispanic C. of C. Region II, 1990. Mem. Albuquerque Rotary Club.

COOPER, LARRY S., cleaning network executive, textile consultant; b. Bklyn., June 14, 1957; s. Jack and Evelyn (Weinfeld) C.; m. Tryna Lee Giordano, Dec. 31, 1975; children: Jonathan, Jennifer, Jillian. Student, U. Colo., 1975-78. Cert. master cleaner, sr. level carpet insp. Owner Cooper's Carpet Cleaners, Boulder, Colo., 1975-79; pres. Profl. Cleaning Network, Denver, 1979—; owner Textiles Cons., Denver, 1986—. Chmn. Broomfield (Colo.) Connection, 1988-90; mayor pro-tem City of Broomfield, 1995-96, mem. city coun., 1996—. Named Cleanfax Man of Yr., Clean Fax Mag., 1990. Mem. Profl. Carpet and Upholstery Cleaners Assn. (pres. 1980-81, 84-86), Internat. Inst. of Carpet and Upholstery Cert. (v.p. 1984-85, pres. 1985-87, chmn. bd. dirs. 1988, chmn. cert. bd. 1990—, hon. dir.). Office: Profl Cleaning Network 6345 Downing St Denver CO 80216

COOPER, LYNN DALE, retired minister, retired navy chaplain; b. Aberdeen, Wash., Aug. 11, 1932; s. Lindsey Monroe and Mattie Ann (Cattron) C.; m. Doris Marlene Aydelott, June 2, 1956; children: Kevin Dale, Kathy Cooper O'Briant, Karen Doris Cooper Henthorn. Student, Gray's Harbor Coll., 1950-51; BTh, Northwest Christian Coll., 1955; MDiv, Phillips U., 1961, D Ministry, 1977. Ordained to ministry Christian Ch., 1954. Commd lt. (j.g.) USN, 1965, advanced through grades to comdr., 1988, ret., 1988; assoc. pastor First Christian Ch., Olympia, Wash., 1955-57; minister First Christian Ch., Aline, Okla., 1957-61, Sumner, Wash., 1961-66; chaplain U.S. Navy, 1966-88; minister Cen. Christian Ch., Prosser, Wash., 1988-97; bd. dirs. Jubilee Ministries, Prosser, Wash., 1988—. Recipient many Navy and Marine Corps awards and medals; decorated Bronze Star medal. Mem. Mil. Chaplains Assn. U.S.A. (life), Disciples of Christ Hist. Soc. (life), Navy League of U.S., Ret. Officers Assn. (life), Kiwanis (past pres. Prosser, Wash. chpt.), De Molay (past master councillor 1950—). Home: 1818 Benson Ave Prosser WA 99350-1547

COOPER, MINNA LOUISE MORGAN (BOBBIE COOPER), volunteer; b. Pierce County, Wash., Nov. 21, 1913; d. William Clarence and Eda (Krause) Morgan; m. Vincent Leon Cooper, Feb. 14, 1936 (div. Oct. 1979); children: Marjorie Suzanne, Nancy Jane, O. Leon. Student, Ariz. State U., Tempe, 1954-57, Grand Canyon U., 1962-63, Phoenix Coll., 1954-87. Supr. Hallmark Cards, Kansas City, Mo., 1930-41; with Iron Lung-Polio Meml. Hosp., Phoenix, 1941-49; ch. and civic vol. Telephone Rsch. & Svcs. Vol., Phoenix, 1952-60, 60—; music rschr. KOY, 1970-80. Officer Oasis Women's Club, Gen. Fedn. Women's Clubs, Phoenix, 1943-88. CEO, 21st Century Charter Schs. of Ariz., 1995—. Mem. Valley Innkeepers Assn. Republican. Baptist.

COOPER, ROBERTA, mayor; b. Mar. 18, 1937; m. Jerrel Cooper. BA, MA. Ret. secondary sch. tchr.; mem. Hayward (Calif.) City Coun., 1988-92; elected mayor City of Hayward, 1994—; former mem. Gen. Plan Revision Task Force, dir. League of Calif. Cities. Active Eden (Calif.) Youth Ctr., Literacy Plus, Hayward Edn. Assn. Democrat. Office: Office of Mayor 25151 Clawiter Rd Hayward CA 94545-2759

COOPER, STEVEN JON, health care management consultant, educator; b. Oct. 19, 1941; B.A., U. Calif., Los Angeles, 1966; M.Ed., Loyola U., 1973; PhD Union Sch., 1979; m. Sharon M. Lepack; children: Robin E., Erik S. Ednl. coordinator dept. radiology Mt. Sinai Hosp. Med. Ctr., Chgo., 1969-72; chmn. dept. radiol. scis. U. Health Scis., Chgo. Med. Sch.; VA Hosp., North Chicago, 1972-79; v.p. C&S Inc., Denver, 1980-81; pres. Healthcare Mktg. Corp., Denver, 1981-84; corp. officer, exec. v.p. Sharon Cooper Assocs. Ltd., Englewood, Colo., 1984—; cons. HEW; lectr. in field. Pres. bd. dirs. Hospice of St. John. Served with USAF, 1960-64, USAFR, 1964-66. Mem. W.K. Kellogg Found. grantee. Mem. Am. (mem. edn., curriculum review coms., task force), Ill. (chmn. annual meeting 1976, program Midwest conf., 1977) socs. radiol. tech., Coll. Radiol. Scis., Am. Hosp. Radiology Adminstrs. (mem. edn. com., treas. Midwest region, nat. v.p.), AMA (com. on allied health edn. and accreditation), Kiwanis Club of Inverness (charter, pres.), Sovereign Order of St. John of Jerusalem, Knights of Malta, Inverness Club (bd. dirs.), Sigma Xi. Author numerous publs. in field. Home: 8522 E Dry Creek Pl Englewood CO 80112-2701 Office: 9085 E Mineral Cir Ste 160 Englewood CO 80112-3418

COOPER, SUSAN, artist; b. L.A., Apr. 25, 1947; d. Morris and Zelda (Lefkowitz) C.; m. Joseph C. Anderson, July 25, 1976 (div. 1990); children: Martha Cooper, David Gaylord; m. Richard A. Cohn, Jan. 25, 1992. BA in Art and Anthropology with honors, U. Calif., Berkeley, 1968, MA, 1970. Instr. Met. State Coll., Denver, 1987-89, U. Colo., Denver, 1990-91; bd. dirs. Ctr. for Idea Art, 1985-87; guest spkr. U. Denver, 1988, 89, No. Ky. U., 1979, Met. State Coll., 1989. One-woman shows include Denver Art Mus., 1989, Henri Gallery, Washington, 1989, Inkfish Gallery, Denver, 1990, 93, Galleria Expositum, Mexico City, 1992, Foothills Art Ctr., Golden, Colo., 1996, Boulder Mus. Contemporary Art, 1996, Western Colo. Ctr. for the Arts, 1996, Sargre de Cristo Art Ctr., 1996, others; paintings represented in permanent collections at Denver Art Mus., City and County Bldg., Denver, Ea. N.Mex. State U., Sch. Am. Rsch., Santa Fe, N.Mex., St. Luke's Hosp., Denver, Denver Pub. Libr., Congress Park, Denver, City and County Bldg., Denver, 1993, others. Pres., dir. Rocky Mountain Women's Inst. U. Denver, 1977-87.

COOPER, SUSAN CAROL, environmental, safety and health professional; b. Milw., Dec. 25, 1939; d. Carroll Arthur and Edith Estelle (Hicks) Brooks; m. William Randall Cooper, June 20, 1964; children: Darin Benbrook, Carol Kimberly, Ryan Randall. BS in Biology, U. Wis., Milw., 1962; MS in Physiology, Wash. State U., 1966; PhD in Physiology, U. Idaho, 1972, MS in Geol. Engring., Hydrology, 1990. EIT. Sr. lab. technician Dept. Vet. Pathology, Wash. State U., Pullman, 1965-68; postdoctoral assoc. dept. chemistry U. Idaho, Moscow, 1972-74, vis. prof. chemistry, 1974; instr. facilitator for gifted/talented Highland Sch. Dist., Craigmont, Idaho, 1975-76; program dir. YWCA, Lewiston, Idaho, 1977-78; support asst. Exxon Nuclear Idaho Corp., Idaho Falls, 1983; engr. Exxon Nuclear Idaho Corp. and Westinghouse Idaho Nuclear Co. Inc., Idaho Falls, 1983-84; environ. engr., sr. environ. engr. Westinghouse Idaho Nuclear Co. Inc., Idaho Falls, 1984-86, mgr. environ., safety and health, SIS Project, 1986-90; mem. Environ. Compliance Office Dept. Energy Idaho Ops. Westinghouse Idaho Nuclear Co. Inc., 1989; mgr. environ. compliance, environ. permits and programs, adv. engr. Waste Isolation divsn., Westinghouse Electric Co., Carlsbad, N.Mex., 1990-92; sr. project mgr., regulatory compliance specialist S.M. Stoller Corp., Albuquerque, 1992-95; v.p. Sisneros-Cooper Environ. Coop., 1995—; artist Albuquerque, 1993—; pres. Cooper Creations-Printing, 1996—; instr. hazardous waste mgmt. N.Mex. State U., Carlsbad, 1991; instr. Clean Air Act, Sch. Environ. Excellence, Westinghouse/Dept. Energy, 1990-91; mem. speaker's bur. Idaho Nat. Engring. Lab./Westinghouse Idaho Nuclear Co. Inc., 1988-90, Waste Isolation divsn. Westinghouse Electric Co., 1990-92; bus. mgr. Cooper Creations, 1996—; presenter profl. confs. Contbr. articles to profl. jours. Mem. presenting team Marriage Encounter, 1980-90; campaign group leader United Way, 1986-87, campaigner, 1985-86; mem., historian Mayor's Com. for Employment of Handicapped and Older Workers, Idaho Falls, 1985-86; singer Idaho Falls Opera Theater, 1983-85; lay preacher, lay reader, lay Eucharistic minister Episc. Ch., Idaho and N.Mex., 1984—; mem. choir St. John's Ch., Idaho Falls, 1983-85, Grace Episc. Ch., Carlsbad, 1990-92, Holy Trinity/St. Francis Ch., Albuquerque, 1992-96, St. John's Episcopal Cathedral, 1996—, Soli Deo Gloria, 1995—; del. Dem. Conv., Boise, Idaho, 1975. NSF fellow, 1963, NDEA fellow, 1963-65, NASA trainee, 1968-70, Nat. Assn. Geology Tchrs. scholar, 1980. Mem. Pastel Soc. N.Mex. (treas. 1997), Artist Studio (treas. 1997), Toastmasters (past pres, founder 2 corp. clubs, adminstrv. v.p., Competent Toastmaster, Able Toastmaster). Home and Office: Sisneros-Cooper Environ Corp 3413 Dellwood Ct NE Albuquerque NM 87110-2203

COOPER, WILLIAM CLARK, physician; b. Manila, P.I., June 22, 1912 (father Am. citizen); s. Wibb Earl and Pearl (Herron) C.; MD, U. Va., 1934; MPH magna cum laude, Harvard U., 1958; m. Ethel Katherine Sicha, May 1, 1937; children: Jane Willoughby, William Clark, David Jeremy, Robert Lawrence. Intern, asst. resident U. Hosps., Cleve., 1934-37; commd. asst. surgeon USPHS, 1940, advanced through grades to med. dir., 1952; chief occupational health Field Hqrs., Cin., 1952-57; mem. staff div. occupational health USPHS, Washington, 1957-62, chief div. occupational health, 1962-63; ret., 1963; rsch. physician, prof. occupational health in residence Sch. Pub. Health, U. Calif.-Berkeley, 1963-72; med. cons. AEC, 1964-73; sec.-treas. Tabershaw-Cooper Asso., Inc., 1972-73, v.p., sci. dir., 1973-74; v.p. Equitable Environ. Health Inc., 1974-77; cons. occupational medicine, 1977-94. Served to 1st lt. M.C., U.S. Army, 1937-40. Diplomate Am. Bd. Internal Medicine, Am. Bd. Preventive Medicine, Am. Bd. Indsl. Hygiene. Fellow AAAS, Am. Pub. Health Assn., Am. Coll. Chest Physicians, Am. Coll. Occupational Medicine, Royal Soc. Medicine (London); mem. Internat. Commn. on Occupational Health, Western Occupational Med. Assn., Am. Indsl. Hygiene Assn., Cosmos Club. Contbr. articles to profl. jours. Home: 8315 Terrace Dr El Cerrito CA 94530-3060

COOPERMAN, OLIVER B(URTON), psychiatrist; b. Perth Amboy, N.J., Jan. 18, 1946; s. Eli Louis and Dorothy (Salinger) C.; m. Corrie Boulden, Apr. 28, 1985; 1 stepson, Jason Corder. AB, Dartmouth Coll., 1966; MD, Harvard U., 1971. Diplomate Am. Bd. Psychiatry and Neurology with added qualifications in addiction psychiatry, Am. Bd. Adolescent Psychiatry; lic. physician and surgeon, Wyo.; lic. physician and surgeon, Mont., N.Mex. Rotating internship Herrick Meml. Hosp., Berkeley, Calif., 1971-72; residency in psychiatry Mt. Zion Hosp. and Med. Ctr., San Francisco, 1972-75; rsch. assoc. dept. child devel. Inst. Edn., U. London, 1968-69; ward chief, staff psychiatrist Palo Alto (Calif.) VA Hosp., 1976, 76-77; asst. chief mental hygiene clinic San Francisco VA Hosp., 1977-78; pvt. practice adult and adolescent psychiatry San Francisco, Petaluma, Calif., 1976-88, Casper, Wyo., 1988-90, Santa Fe, 1991-93, Albuquerque, N.Mex., 1994-96; pvt. practice adult and adolescent psychiatry $D, Red Lodge, Mont., 1996—, Fowell, Wyo., 1996—; assoc. med. dir. Pinon Hills Hosp., Santa Fe, N.Mex., 1991-93; assoc. clin. dir. Yellowstone Treatment Ctrs., Billings, Mont., 1993-94; cons. psychiatrist Mental Health Ctr., Billings, Mont., 1996—, Lewistown, Mont., 1996—; clin. instr. dept. psychiatry Stanford (Calif.) U. Sch. Medicine, 1976-78, lectr. in psychiatry, 1978-81; asst. clin. prof. dept. psychiatry U. Calif. Sch. Medicine, San Francisco, 1978—; clin. faculty U. Wyo. Family Practice Residency Program, Casper, 1988-89; mem. active staff Charter-Heights Hosp., Albuquerque, 1994-96; mem. cons. staff Carbon County Meml. Hosp., Red Lodge, Deaconness Hosp., Billings, Powell (Wyo.) Hosp.; spkr. in field. Contbr. articles to profl. jours. Mem. GREX, affiliate of A. K. Rice Inst., 1975-90, bd. dirs., 1978-84, sec.-treas. bd. dirs., 1979-80, pres. bd. dirs., 1980-82; mem. Orgnl. Devel. Network. Recipient Spl. Merit Advancement award VA Ctrl. Office. Mem. Am. Psychiat. Assn., Am. Group Psychotherapy Assn., Am. Soc. Adolescent Psychiatry, Am. Assn. Psychiatrists in Alcohol and Addictions, Wyo. Med. Soc. Office: 777 Ave H Powell WY 82435

COOR, LATTIE FINCH, university president; b. Phoenix, Sept. 26, 1936; s. Lattie F. and Elnora (Witten) C.; m. Ina Fitzhenry, Jan. 18, 1964 (div. 1988); children: William Kendall, Colin Fitzhenry, Farryl MacKenna Witten; m. Elva Wingfield, Dec. 27, 1994. AB with high honors (Phelps Dodge scholar), No. Ariz. U., 1958; MA with honors (Univ. scholar, Universal Match Found. fellow, Carnegie Corp. fellow), Washington U., St. Louis, 1960, PhD, 1964; LLD (hon.), Marlboro Coll., 1977, Am. Coll. Greece, 1982, U. Vt., 1991. Adminstrv. asst. to Gov. Mich., 1961-62; asst. to chancellor Washington U., St. Louis, 1963-67, asst. dean Grad. Sch. Arts and Scis., 1967-69, dir. internat. studies, 1967-69, asst. prof. polit. sci., 1967-76, vice chancellor, 1969-74, univ. vice chancellor, 1974-76; pres. U. Vt., Burlington, 1976-89; prof. public affairs, and pres. Ariz. State U., Tempe, 1990—; cons. HEW; spl. cons. to commr. U.S. Commn. on Edn., 1971-74; chmn. Commn. on Govtl. Rels., Am. Coun. on Edn., 1976-80; dir. New Eng. Bd. Higher Edn., 1976-89; co-chmn. joint com. on health policy Assn. Am. Univs. and Nat. Assn. State Univs. and Land Grant Colls., 1976-89; mem. pres. commn. NCAA, 1984-90, chmn. div. I, 1989; mem. Ariz. State Bd. Edn., 1993—. Trustee Am. Coll. Greece. Mem. Nat. Assn. Stae Univs. and Land Grant Colls. (chmn. bd. dirs. 1991-92), New Eng. Assn. Schs. and Colls. (pres. 1981-82), Am. Coun. on Edn. (bd. dirs. 1991-93, chmn. Pacific 10 Conf. 1995-96). Office: Ariz State U Office of President Tempe AZ 85287

COORS, PETER HANSON, beverage company executive; b. Denver, Sept. 20, 1946; s. Joseph and Holly (Hanson) C.; m. Marilyn Gross, Aug. 23, 1969; children: Melissa, Christien, Carrie Ann, Ashley, Peter, David. B.S. in Idsl. Engring., Cornell U., 1969; M.B.A., U. Denver, 1970. Prodn. trainee, specialist Adolph Coors Co., Golden, Colo., 1970-71, dir. fin. planning, 1971-75, dir. market research, 1975-76, v.p. self distbn., 1976-77, v.p. sales and mktg., 1977-78, sr. v.p. sales and mktg., 1978-82, div. pres. sales, mktg. and adminstrn., 1982-85, pres. brewing div.; pres. Coors Brewing Co., Golden, Colo., 1989—, Coors Distbn. Co., 1976-82, 1976-81, chmn., from 1981, dir.; dir. Adolph Coors Co., 1973—, asst. sec.-treas., 1974-76; dir. CADCO, 1975-85; exec. v.p. Adolf Coors Co., Golden, Colo., 1991—; vice-chmn., CEO Coors Brewing Co., Golden, Colo., 1991—. Bd. dirs. Nat. Wildlife Fedn., 1978-81, Wildlife Legis. Fund, 1987—; hon. bd. dirs. Colo. Spl. Olympics Inc., 1978—; trustee Colo. Outward Bound Sch., 1978—, Adolph Coors Found., Pres.'s Leadership Com., U. Colo., 1978—; chmn. Nat. Commn. on the Future of Regis Coll., 1981-82, chmn. devel. com., 1983—, now trustee. Mem. Nat. Indls. Adv. Council, Opportunities Ctrs. of Am., Young Pres.' Orgn., Ducks Unlimited (nat. trustee 1979, sr. v.p., mem. mgmt. com., exec. com. 1982—, dir. Can. 1982—, pres. 1984-85, chmn. bd. 1986—). Club: Met. Denver Exec. (dir 1979, pres. 1981—). Office: Adolf Coors Co BC300 PO Box 4030 Golden CO 80401*

COORS, WILLIAM K., brewery executive; b. Golden, Colo., Aug. 11, 1916. BSChemE, Princeton U., 1938, grad. degree in chem. engring., 1939. Pres. Adolph Coors Co., Golden, Colo., from 1956, Chmn. bd., 1970—, also corp. pres. Office: Adolph Coors Co 16000 Table Mountain Pkwy Golden CO 80403

COPELAND, LAWRENCE R., construction company executive; b. 1947. Graduate, U. Notre Dame. With Fluor Corp., Irvine, Calif., 1969-93; now pres. Fluor Constructors Internat., Irvine, Calif., 1993—. Office: Fluor Constructors Intl 3353 Michelson Dr Irvine CA 92690*

COPELAND, PHILLIPS JEROME, former academic administrator, former air force officer; b. Oxnard, Calif., Mar. 22, 1921; s. John Charles and Marion Moffatt) C.; student U. So. Calif., 1947-49; BA, U. Denver, 1956, MA, 1958; grad. Air Command and Staff Coll., 1959, Indsl. Coll. Armed Forces, 1964; m. Alice Janette Lusby, Apr. 26, 1942; children: Janette Ann Copeland Bosserman, Nancy Jo Copeland Briner. Commd. 2d lt. USAAF, 1943, advanced through grades to col. USAF, 1964, pilot 8th Air Force, Eng., 1944-45; various flying and staff assignments, 1945-51; chief joint tng. sect. Hdqrs. Airsouth (NATO), Italy, 1952-54; asst. dir. plans and programs USAF Acad., 1955-58; assigned to joint intelligence, Washington, 1959-61; plans officer Cincpac Joint Staff, Hawaii, 1961-63; staff officer, ops. directorate, then team chief Nat. Mil. Command Center, Joint Chiefs Staff, Washington, 1964-67; dir. plans and programs USAF Adv. Group, also adviser to Vietnamese Air Force, Vietnam, 1967-68; prof. aerospace studies U. So. Calif., L.A., 1968-72, exec. asst. to pres., 1972-73, assoc. dir. office internat. programs, 1973-75, dir. adminstrv. services Coll. Continuing Edn., 1975-82, dir. employee relations, 1982-84. Decorated D.F.C., Bronze Star, Air medal with 3 clusters; Medal of Honor (Vietnam). Mem. Air Force Assn., Order of Daedalians. Home: 81 Cypress Way Palos Verdes Peninsula CA 90274-3416

COPELAND, POPPY CARLSON, psychotherapist; b. Evanson, Ill., Dec. 18, 1939; d. Frederick Winsor and Polly (Packard) C.; m. Marshall S. Johnson (div. 1979); children Erica Winsor, Lara Siree; m. Lawrence E. Carlson, June 15, 1985. BA, U. Calif., Berkeley, 1962; MA, U. Denver, 1975; ABD (hon.) in Internat. Studies, U. Colo., 1980; M in Psychology, Counseling Inst. Transpersonal, Palo Alto, Calif., 1992. Lic. profl. counselor, Colo.; lifetime tchg. credential, Calif. Tchr. Temple City (Calif.) Sch. Dist., 1965-67; chmn. sch. assistance Mitrapah Found., Bangkok, Thailand, 1969-73; rsch. assoc. edn. Commn. of States, Denver, 1976-78; rsch. assoc. Boulder County Bd. Developmental Disabilities, Boulder, Colo., 1978-79; social policy writer Boulder Camera, Denver Post, 1981-84; sr. trainer, counselor Tucker Internat., Boulder, 1984—; dir. Internat. Women's Week, U. Colo., 1981-83, Internat. Pedestrian Conf., City of Boulder, 1981-83; cons. Colo. Civil Rights Commn., 1987-89. Dir. Boulder Peace Consortium, 1983-86, Friendship City Nicaragua, Boulder, 1984-86; com. mem. World Affairs Conf., U. Colo., 1995-96, bd. dirs. Refugee Mental Health Acess Program, Colo. Mem. ACA. Home: 2541 Bluff St Boulder CO 80303 Office: Tucker International 9900 28th St Ste 200 Boulder CO 80303

COPEN, MELVYN ROBERT, management educator, university administrator; b. N.Y.C., Jan. 23, 1938; s. Samuel L. Copen and Frieda (Kroun) Zucker; m. Linda B. Kopans, Feb. 17, 1960 (div. 1991); children: Erika Beth Ellingsen, Susan Andrea Holtey; m. Beverly Joyce Stein, Sept. 7, 1991. BS in Bus., Engring Adminstrn., MIT, 1958, MS in Indsl. Mgmt., 1959; DBA in Prodn., Internat. Mgmt., Harvard U., 1967. Various positions Gen. Elec. Co., various locations, 1959-61; program assoc., rsch. fellow Harvard Bus. Sch., Boston, Ahmedabad, India, 1961-67; assoc. dean, prof., dir. grad. studies U. Houston, 1967-71; dir. office mgmt. improvement automated decision sys. U.S. Dept. Agr., Washington, 1971-74; dir. strategic planning Westinghouse Corp., Pitts., 1974-75; dir. internat. planning Gould, Inc., Rolling Meadows, Ill., 1975-77; assoc. dean, dean grad. studies coll. bus. adminstrn. Ga. State Univ., Atlanta, 1977-80; v.p. acad. affairs Babson Coll., Wellesley, Mass., 1980-87; rector Ctrl. Am. Inst. Bus. Adminstrn., Alajuela, Costa Rica, 1987-91; dean sch. internat. mgmt. Internat. Univ. Japan, Urasa, Tokyo, 1991-94; chmn., CEO Global Enterprises, Atlanta, 1991—; sr. v.p. acad. affairs, prof. internat. mgmt. Am. Grad. Sch. Internat. Mgmt., Glendale, Ariz., 1995—; membership chmn. audit com. Nat. Bank Ga.-1st Am., Atlanta, 1980-87. Co-author: International Manangement and Economic Development, 1971, Production Management, 1972; contbr. articles to profl. jours. Bd. dirs. White House Fellows Found., Washington, 1973-74, Epilepsy Found. Ga., Atlanta, 1979-80, Hemophilia Ga., Atlanta, 1978-80; chmn. Arts in Progress, Roxbury, Mass., 1985-87, Am. Coll., Atlanta, 1996—. With USAR, 1960. Recipient Command Gen. Citation, U.S. Transp. Corps., 1960; White House fellow, 1970-71. Mem. Beta Gamma Sigma, Omicron Delta Epsilon. Home: 1907 E Karen Dr Phoenix AZ 85022 Office: Am Grad Sch Internat Mgmt 15249 N 59th Ave Glendale AZ 85306-3236

COPENHAVER, BRIAN PAUL, university administrator, historian; b. Balt., Dec. 21, 1942; s. Olin Franklin and Rose Mary (Fitzptrick) C.; m. Kathleen Ann Gulick, Sept. 4, 1965; children: Gregory, Rebecca. BA, Loyola Coll., 1964; MA, Creighton U., 1966; PhD, U. Kans., 1970. Asst. prof. liberal studies Western Wash. U., Bellingham, 1971-74, assoc. prof., 1974-77, prof., assoc. dean Arts & Sci., 1977-81; prof. history, dean Arts & Sci. Oakland U., Rochester, Mich., 1981-88; prof. history and philosophy, dean Humanities & Soc. Sci. U. Calif., Riverside, 1988-93; prof. history and philosophy, provost letters and sci. UCLA, 1993—; pres. Mich. Coun. Arts and Scis. Deans, 1987. Author: Symphorien Champler and the Reception of the Occultist Tradition, 1978, Pseudomagia: A Neo-Latin Drama by William Mewe, 1979, Renaissance Philosophy, 1992, Hermetica, 1992; mem. bd. editors Annals of Sci., 1986—, Jour. of History of Philosophy, 1988—; contbr. articles to profl. jours. Bd. dirs. Haven Shelter for Abused Women and Children, 1982-88; mem. bd. dirs. planning coun. St. Joseph's Mercy Hosp., 1982-88. 1st lt. U.S. Army, 1970. Fulbright scholar Dept. State, 1968-69. Mem. Am. Hist. Assn., History of Sci. Soc., Renaissance Soc. Am., Am. Soc. Ch. History, 16th Century Studies Soc., Sigma Xi. Democrat. Roman Catholic.

COPENHAVER, LARRY JAMES, journalist; b. Independence, Iowa, Sept. 16, 1943; s. George Hugh and Winona Louise Copenhaver; m. Shirley Anne Songderoth, Dec. 24, 1986. BA, U. Ariz., 1973. Journalist Tucson Citizen Newspaper, 1985—. Recipient Unite award in Media Lincoln U., 1987, Ariz. Sch. Bd. Assn. award Flowing Well Unified Sch. Dist., 1990, award of Excellence, Ariz. Sch. Pub. Rels. Assn., 1992, 2nd Pl. award Best of Gannett, 1995, Cmty. Svc. award Ariz. Newspaper Assn., 1996, 1st Pl. award Ariz. Press Club, 1996, 3rd Pl. award Best of Gannett, 1997. Office: Tucson Citizen Newspaper 4850 S Park Ave Tucson AZ 85714-1637

COPLEY, HELEN KINNEY, newspaper publisher; b. Cedar Rapids, Iowa, Nov. 28, 1922; d. Fred Everett and Margaret (Casey) Kinney; m. James S. Copley, Aug. 16, 1965 (dec.); 1 child, David Casey. Attended, Hunter Coll., N.Y.C., 1945. Assoc. The Copley Press, Inc., 1952—, chmn. exec. com., chmn. corp., dir., 1973—, chief exec. officer, sr. mgmt. bd., 1974—; chmn. bd. Copley News Svc., San Diego, 1973—; chmn. editorial bd. Union-Tribune Pub. Co., 1976—; pub. The San Diego Union-Tribune, 1973—; bd. dirs. Fox Valley Press., Inc. Chmn. bd., trustee James S. Copley Found., 1973—; life mem. Friends of Internat. Ctr., La Jolla, Mus. Contemporary Art, San Diego, San Diego Hall of Sci., Scripps Meml. Hosp. Aux., San Diego Opera Assn., Star of India Aux., Zool. Soc. San Diego; mem. La Jolla Town Coun. Inc., San Diego Soc. Natural History, YWCA, San Diego Symphony Assn.; life patroness Makua Aux.; hon. chmn., bd. dirs. Washington Crossing Found.; hon. chmn. San Diego Coun. Literacy. Mem. Inter-Am. Press Assn., Newspaper Assn. Am., Calif. Press Assn., Am. Press Inst., Calif. Newspaper Pubs. Assn., Calif. Press Inst., San Francisco Press Club, L.A. Press Club. Republican. Roman Catholic. Clubs: Aurora (Ill.) Country, Army and Navy (D.C.), Univ. Club San Diego, La Jolla Beach and Tennis, La Jolla Country. Office: Copley Press Inc 7776 Ivanhoe Ave La Jolla CA 92037-4520*

COPLEY, JOHN DUANE, civil engineer; b. Visalia, Calif., May 25, 1938; s. John Harrington and Emma Theresa Copley; m. Jeanette Sue Nunn, July 1, 1961; children: John Kent, Kari Lynne, Kevin Michael. AA, Coll. of Sequoias, Visalia; BSCE, Stanford U. Registered profl. engr., Calif. Sr. civil engr. City of Davis (Calif.) Pub. Works Dept., 1965—. Served with U.S. Army, 1961-63. Mem. ASCE, Am. Pub. Works Assn. (pres. Sacramento chpt. 1974). Home: 2901 Catalina Dr Davis CA 95616-0105 Office: City of Davis Pub Works Dept 23 Russell Blvd Davis CA 95616-3837

COPMAN, LOUIS, radiologist; b. Phila., Jan. 17, 1934; s. Jacob and Eve (Snyder) C.; m. Avera Schuster, June 8, 1958; children: Mark, Linda. BA, U. Pa., 1955, MD, 1959. Diplomate Am. Bd. Radiology; Nat. Bd. Med. Examiners. Commd. ensign Med. Corps USN, 1958; advanced through grades to capt. M.C. USN, 1975; ret.; asst. chief radiology dept. Naval Hosp., Pensacola, Fla., 1966-69; chief radiology dept. Doctors Hosp., Phila., 1969-73; radiologist Mercer Hosp. Ctr., Trenton, N.J., 1973-75; chmn. radiology dept. Naval Hosp., Phila., 1975-84; chief. radiology dept. Naval Med. Clinic, Pearl Harbor, Hawaii, 1984-89; pvt. practice radiologist Honolulu, 1989-92; cons. Radiology Services, Wilmington, Del., 1978-84, Yardley (Pa.)

Radiology, 1979-84. Author: The Cuckold, 1974. Recipient Albert Einstein award in Medicine, U. Pa., 1959. Mem. AMA, Assn. Mil. Surgeons of the U.S., Royal Soc. Medicine, Radiol. Soc. N.Am., Am. Coll. Radiology, Photographic Soc. Am., Sherlock Holmes Soc., Phi Beta Kappa, Alpha Omega Alpha. Home: PO Box 384767 Waikoloa HI 96738-4767 Office: 68-1771 Makanahele Pl Waikoloa HI 96738-4767 *Throughout one's life, one should choose his companions wisely.*

COPPERMAN, WILLIAM H., value engineer, consultant; b. Cleve., Dec. 4, 1932; s. Jack Jason and Ruth (Rollnick) C.; m. Rena June Dorn, Dec. 26, 1954; children: Randy Lee, David Marc. BS, Duquesne U., 1954; MBA, U. So. Calif., L.A., 1962; JD, U. San Fernando, 1977. Cert. value specialist. Corp. mgr., value engr. Hughes Aircraft Co., L.A., 1957-89; pres. Copperman Assocs. in Value Engring., Inc., L.A., 1983—; bd. dirs. Miles Value Found., Washington; cert. bd. SAVE, Chgo., 1986-88. Author books, video tape series in value engring.; contbr. articles to profl. jours. Recipient Outstanding Achievement award U.S. Army, 1986, Value Engring. award Purchasing Mag., Washington, 1987, Achievement in Value Engring. U.S. Army, 1977, 78, 79, 80, 82. Mem. Soc. Am. Value Engrs. (exec. v.p. 1975—). Home and Office: Copperman Assocs Value Eng 32 Lincoln Pl Rancho Mirage CA 92270-1970

COPPERSMITH, SAM, lawyer; b. Johnstown, Pa., May 22, 1955; m. Beth Schermer, Aug. 28, 1983; children: Sarah, Benjamin, Louis. AB in Econs. magna cum laude, Harvard U., 1976; JD, Yale Law Sch., 1982. Fgn. svc. officer U.S. Dept. State, Port of Spain, Trinidad, 1977-79; law clk. to Judge William C. Canby Jr. U.S. Ct. Appeals (9th cir.), Phoenix, 1982-83; atty. Sacks, Tierney & Kasen, P.A., Phoenix, 1983-86; asst. to Mayor Terry Goddard City of Phoenix, 1984; atty. Jones, Jury, Short & Mast P.C., Phoenix, 1986-88, Bonnett, Fairbourn & Friedman P.C., Phoenix, 1988-92; mem. 103d Congress from 1st Ariz. Dist., 1993-95; atty. Coppersmith & Gordon, PLC, 1995—. Former dir., pres. Planned Parenthood Ctrl. and No. Ariz.; former chair City of Phoenix Bd. of Adjustment; former dir. Ariz. Cmty. Svc. Legal Assistance Found., 1986-89; chair Ariz. Dem. Party, 1995-97. Mem. ABA, State Bar of Ariz., State Bar of Calif., Maricopa County Bar Assn. Democrat. Office: Coppersmith & Gordon Plc 2633 E Indian School Rd Ste 300 Phoenix AZ 85016-6762

COPPOCK, RICHARD MILES, nonprofit association administrator; b. Salem, Ohio, Mar. 17, 1938; s. Guy Lamar and Helen Angeline (Johnston) C.; m. Rita Mae McArtor, June 20, 1961 (div. 1973); 1 child, Carole; m. Trelma Anne Kubacak Hafer, Nov. 21, 1973; children: James, Lori. BS, USAF Acad., 1961; MSME, U. Colo., 1969. Commd. 2d lt. USAF, 1961, advanced through grades to lt. col., 1983, ret., 1983; pres., CEO Assn. Grads. USAF Acad., Colo., 1983—; bd. dirs. Air Acad. Nat. Bank, Colo.; v.p. Nat. Assns. in Colorado Springs. Decorated DFC (4), Air medal (29); named Outstanding Alumnus Salem H.S., 1980. Mem. Colorado Springs C. of C. (mil. affairs coun. 1985-90), VFW (life), Am. Legion, Air Force Assn., Ret. Officers Assn., Elks. Republican. Methodist. Home: 2513 Mirror Lake Ct Colorado Springs CO 80919-3515 Office: USAF Acad Assn Grads 3116 Academy Dr U S A F Academy CO 80840-4475

CORAM, DAVID JAMES, marketing professional; b. San Diego, Oct. 17, 1962; s. Thomas Harry and Joan Catherine (Reuter) C.; m. Irma Elizabeth Aquino, Jan. 14, 1989 (dec. July 1991); children: Catherine May, Corinna Briann, Carston James; m. Corinna Kay Ward, May 6, 1995. AS with honors, Miramar Coll., 1989; honor grad. sheriff acad. basic tng., Southwestern Coll., 1986. Computer oper. Cubic Data Systems, San Diego, 1981-83, Electronic Data Systems, San Diego, 1983-84; ct. svc. officer San Diego County Marshal, 1985-86, deputy marshal, 1986—; pres. Coram Consulting Group, 1994—. Mediator San Diego Community Mediation Ctr., 1990—. Awarded Gold medal soccer Ariz. Police Olympics, 1990, 91, Silver medal, 1993, Marksmanship award San Diego Marshal, Outstanding Young Men Am. award, 1989; 2d pl. Mid. Weight San Diego Gold's Gym Classic, 1993, Bronze medal Bodybuilding Calif. Police Olympics, 1994. Mem. Calif. State Marshal's Assn. (dir. on state bd. 1994), San Diego County Marshal's Assn. (parliamentarian 1988, dir. 1989-91, 93-94), San Diego County Marshal's Athletic Fedn. (dir. 1993-95), Nat. Physique Com. (contest judge). Republican. Office: Coram Cons Group PO Box 0863 Temecula CA 92593-0863

CORAY, JEFFREY WARREN, assistant principal, instructor; b. Chgo., July 16, 1958; s. Warren George and Rose (Paul) C. Student, U. Calif., Berkeley, 1976-77; BA, Occidental Coll., 1980; MA, Calif. State U., San Bernardino, 1996. Instr. Damien High Sch., La Verne, Calif., 1982—, dir. student activities, 1983-87, chair social sci. dept., 1986-88, asst. prin. student activities, 1987-88, asst. prin. acad. affairs, instr. social sci., 1988—; cons. advanced placement program N.J. Coll. Bd., 1987—, exam reader, 1988—. Mem. Omicron Delta Epsilon, Phi Kappa Phi. Republican. Roman Catholic. Home: PO Box 116 La Verne CA 91750-0116 Office: Damien High Sch 2280 Damien Ave La Verne CA 91750-5210

CORBETT, ELLEN M., mayor. BS in Polit. Sci., U. Calif., Davis; JD McGeorge Law Sch., U. Pacific. Mem. San Leandro (Calif.) City Coun., 1990-94; mayor City of San Leandro, 1994—; co-chair U.S. Conf. Mayors Police Policy Bd.; bd. dirs. Alameda County Econ. Devel. Adv. Bd. Co-chair San Leandro Partnership for Youth Safety. Office: 835 E 14th St San Leandro CA 94577

CORBIN, ROSEMARY MAC GOWAN, mayor; b. Santa Cruz, Calif., Apr. 3, 1940; d. Frederick Patrick and Lorena Maude (Parr) MacGowan; m. Douglas Tenny Corbin, Apr. 6, 1968; children: Jeffrey, Diana. BA, San Francisco State U., 1961; MLS, U. Calif., Berkeley, 1966. Libr. Stanford (Calif.) U., 1966-68, Richmond (Calif.) Pub. Libr., 1968-69, Kaiser Found. Health Plan, Oakland, Calif., 1976-81, San Francisco Pub. Libr., 1981-82, U. Calif., Berkeley, 1982-83; mem. coun. City of Richmond, 1985-93, vice mayor, 1986-87, mayor, 1993—; mem. Solid Waste Mgmt. Authority, 1985—, Contra Costa Hazardous Materials Commn., Martinez, Calif., 1987—, San Francisco Bay Conservation and Devel. Commn., 1987—; mem. League of Calif. Cities Environ. Affairs Com., 1994—; mem. energy and environ. com. U.S. Conf. Mayors and Nat. League of Cities, 1993—. Contbr. articles to profl. publs. Mem. Calif. Libr. Assn., Local Govt. Commn., League Calif. Cities, Nat. League Cities, LWV, NOW, Nat. Women's Polit. Caucus. Democrat. Home: 114 Crest Ave Richmond CA 94801-4031 Office: Richmond City Hall 2600 Barrett Ave Richmond CA 94804-1654

CORBOY, JAMES MCNALLY, investment banker; b. Erie, Pa., Nov. 3, 1940; s. James Thomas and Dorothy Jane (Schluraff) C.; m. Suzanne Shaver, July 23, 1965; children: Shannon, James McNally. BA, Allegheny Coll., 1962; MBA, U. Colo., 1986. Sales staff Boettcher & Co., Denver, 1964-70; sales staff Blyth Eastman Dillon, Denver and Chgo., 1970-74, William Blair & Co., Chgo., 1974-77; mgr. corp. bond dept. Boettcher & Co., Denver, 1977-79; ptnr. in charge William Blair & Co., Denver, 1979-86; first v.p. Stifel, Nicolaus & Co., Denver, 1986-88; pres., chief exec. officer SKB Corboy Inc., Denver, 1988—. With USMC, 1962-67. Mem. Nat. Assn. Securities Dealers (bd. arbitrators), Country Club at Castle Pines, Met. Club. Republican. Presbyterian. Home: Castle Pines Village 870 Homestake Ct Castle Rock CO 80104-9022 Office: 6530 S Yosemite St Englewood CO 80111

CORCORAN, JOHN, advertising executive. Exec. v.p., COO FCB Health-care, San Francisco, Calif. Office: One Lombard St San Francisco CA 94111*

CORDES, FAUNO LANCASTER, retired nuclear medicine technologist; b. San Francisco, Nov. 3, 1927; d. Frederick Carl and Faun-Hope (Lancaster) C. AA, U. Calif. Berkeley, 1946, BA in Psychology, 1948; MA in Geography, San Francisco State U., 1991. Chief hematology rsch. technician NIH and U. Calif. Lab. of Exptl. Oncology, San Francisco, 1949-53, City of Hope Med. Ctr., Duarte, Calif., 1953-59; nuclear medicine technologist Mt. Zion Hosp., U. Calif., San Francisco, 1959-92; exec. com. Soc. Nuclear Medicine, No. Calif. Tech. Soc., San Francisco, 1968-81. Contbr. numerous articles to profl. publs. Mem. AAAS, Soc. Nuclear Medicine, Soc. Woman Geographers, Calif. Acad. Scis., Antarctican Soc., Gleeson Libr. Assocs., The Explorers Club, Sigma Xi. Home: 355 Arballo Dr San Francisco CA 94132-2156

CORDNER, TOM, advertising executive. Co-chmn. bd., creative dir. Team One Advertising, El Segundo, Calif. Office: 1960 E Grand Ave Ste 700 El Segundo CA 90245*

CORDOVA, ALEXANDER M., city clerk; b. Phoenix, June 22, 1943; s. Alexander A. and Violet (Moreno) C.; m. Joyce Hendricks, June 12, 1982. Student, Ariz. State U., 1962, Phoenix Coll., 1965. Cert. mcpl. clk. Right of way aid City of Phoenix, 1965-67, right of way agt. I, 1967-70, oper. analyst, 1970-72, election supr., 1974-80, elections and gen. svcs. adminstr., 1980-86; chief dep. city clk. City of Phoenix Mcpl. Employees Assn., 1986—. Mem. Internat. Right of Way Assn., 1975-85, Statewide Election Reform, 1987-88. With USN, 1962-64. Mem. Ariz. Mcpl. Clks., Internat. Inst. Mcpl. Clks., Am. Mgrs. Assn., Internat. Assn. County Recorders, Election Ofcls. and Treas., Ariz. Assn. Election Ofcls. and County Records, Am. Legion. Roman Catholic. Office: City of Phoenix 200 W Washington St Ste 1500 Phoenix AZ 85003-1611

CORDOVA, JEANNE ROBERT, publisher, journalist, activist; b. Bremerhaven, Germany, July 18, 1948; d. Frederick Benedict Jr. and Joan Frances (McGuinness) C.; life ptnr. Lynn Harris Ballen, Aug. 19, 1995. BA, UCLA, 1970, MSW, 1972. Pub. Lesbian Tide Mag., L.A., 1971-80; advt. exec. Cordova Promotional Systems, L.A., 1980-82; pub. Cmty. Yellow Pages, So. Calif.'s Gay and Lesbian Phone Book, L.A., 1982—; pres. Internat. Gay and Lesbian Archives, L.A., 1995—, 1995—; v.p. Connexxus Women's Ctr., L.A., 1984-88. Author: Sexism; It's A Nasty Affair, 1976, Kicking the Habit, 1990; editor: L.A. Free Press, 1973-76; contbr. articles to mags. and anthologies. Mem. Calif. Dem. Party, sec., 1980; pres. Stonewall Dem. Club, 1979-81; organizer Nat. Lesbian Conf., Calif., 1973. Office: 1604 Vista Del Mar St Los Angeles CA 90028-6420

CORDTS, PAUL ROGER, surgeon; b. Cumberland, Md., Sept. 27, 1958; s. Harold J. and Jeanne (Moore) C.; m. Patricia Ann Cordts. BA, Johns Hopkins U., 1980; MD, USUHS, 1984. Diplomate Am. Bd. Surgery, Am. Bd. Surg. Critical Care, Am. Bd. Gen. Vascular Surgery. Commd. med. officer U.S. Army, 1980; intern, resident in surgery William Beaumont Army Med. Ctr., El Paso, Tex., 1984-89; staff surgeon Munson Army Community Hosp., Ft. Leavenworth, Kans., 1989-90; fellow in vascular surgery Boston U. Med. Ctr., Boston, 1990-92; chief vascular surgery sect. Tripler Army Med. Ctr., Honolulu, 1992-93, chief gen. surgery svc., tng. dir. surg. residency program, 1993—. Fellow ACS (Hawaii chpt.); mem. AMA, Am. Med. Polit. Action Com., Uniformed Svcs. U. Health Scis. Surg. Assocs., Am. Venous Forum, Peripheral Vascular Surgery Soc., 38th Parallel Med. Soc., Soc. Critical Care Medicine, Soc. for Clin. Vascular Surgery, Assn. Mil. Surgeons U.S., Assn. for Acad. Surgery, Johns Hopkins U. Alumni Assn., Am. Legion (Farrady Post 24), Omicron Delta Kappa Nat. Leadership Soc. Home: 98-1323 Kaonohi St Aiea HI 96701-2836 Office: Tripler Army Med Ctr Gen Surgery Svc Honolulu HI 96859-5000

COREY, JO ANN, senior management analyst; b. Methuen, Mass., Jan. 26, 1965; d. Joseph Augustine and Marie Ellen (Dowe) C. BA, Calif. State U., Fullerton, 1987, MPA, 1989. Adminstrv. intern City of Brea, Calif., 1987-90; mgmt. analyst City of Mission Viejo, Calif., 1990-92, sr. mgmt. analyst, 1992—. Mem. Mcpl. Mgmt. Assts. So. Calif. (programming com. 1987—), Calif. Parks and Recreation Soc., Calif. League of Cities, Phi Alpha Theta. Democrat. Roman Catholic. Office: City of Mission Viejo 25909 Pala Mission Viejo CA 92691-2778

CORIELL, BRUCE RICHARD, clergy; b. Millington, N.J., Aug. 15, 1956; s. Richard and Kathleen Veronica (Franolich) C.; m. Eleanor Ann Sents, Aug. 19, 1978; children: Richard Bruce, Alyssa Kathleen. BA, Wheaton (Ill.) Coll., 1978; MDiv, Princeton Theol. Sem., 1981; postgrad., Vanderbilt U., 1989. Ordained to ministry Am. Bapt. Ch., 1981. Assoc. chaplain DePauw U., Greencastle, Ind., 1981-85; asst. chaplain Vanderbilt U., Nashville, 1986-88; chaplain Colo. Coll., Colorado Springs, 1988—. Mem. Martin Luther King Jr. Holiday Com., Colorado Springs, 1988—, chair, 1990; bd. dirs. Ci tizen's Project, Colorado Springs, 1994—, Gay and Lesbian Cmty. Ctr., Colorado Springs, 1992—, San Luis Valley Christian Cmty. Svcs., 1990—, United Way, others; mem. Pikes Peak Peace and Justice Commn., Colorado Springs, 1991—. Harold Vanderbilt scholar, 1985-88. Mem. Am. Acad. Religion, Nat. Assn. Coll. and Univ. Chaplains, Assn. Coll. and Univ. Religious Affairs (exec. bd., pres. 1996—). Office: Colo Coll Shove Meml Chapel Colorado Springs CO 80903

CORINBLIT, NITA GREEN, artist, educator; b. Detroit, Mar. 3, 1924; d. Leo and Gussie Green; m. Jack Corinblit, Mar. 9, 1944; children: Meryl Marshall, Barbara Graff, Nancy Montgomery. BFA, Art Inst. Chgo., 1949; MA, Calif. State U., 1971. Cert. art tchr., Calif. Art, history of art and English tchr. jr. and sr. H.S. L.A., 1963-85; arts and humanities cons. L.A. Unified Sch. Dist., 1982-86; methods tchg. crafts instr. Calif. State U., Northridge, 1969-71; humanities instr. Lee Coll. U. Judaism, L.A., 1989-91; participant NEH project, Greensboro, N.C., summer 1982. Exhibited in group shows at Libr. of Congress, Washington, nat. and local exhbns. Witness U.S. House Ways and Means com., Am. Assn. Mus., Washington, 1980; docent L.A. Mus. Contemporary Art, 1987-92; docent cord. Platt Gallery, U. Judaism, L.A., 1990-96, mem. exec. bd. fine arts coun., 1996—; mem. Women's Polit. Com., L .A., 1992—. Grantee Calif. Coun. for the Humanities, NEH, 1986, Calif. Arts Coun., 1983-84, U.S. Arts for the Aging, 1980-81. Mem. Aspen Inst. Soc. Fellows, Calif. Humanities Assn. (pres. 1986-87, newsletter editor 1988—, treas. 1978-85, Perlee award 1991), L.A. Art Assn., L.A. Printmaking Soc. Home: 5854 Hillview Park Ave Van Nuys CA 91401-4022

CORKERN, ROBERT J., agricultural products company executive; b. 1944. Graduate, U. Nev., 1966. With Klein Bros., Stockton, Calif., 1971-92; pres. Klein-BergerCo., Stockton, Calif., 1992—. With U.S. Army, 1967-70. Office: Klein-Berger Co PO Box 609mont St Stockton CA 95201-2625*

CORKERY, PAUL JEROME, author, editor; b. Everett, Mass., Nov. 5, 1946; s. James Richard and Eileen Elizabeth (Collins) C. BA, Harvard U., 1968; postgrad., Clare Hall, Cambridge, Eng., 1968-69. Reporter Boston Herald, 1969-71; asst. to dean Harvard U., Cambridge, 1970-72; editor Boston Phoenix, 1973-74, Boston Mag., 1974-76; articles editor Nat. Enquirer, Lantana, Fla., 1977-79; editl. staff L.A. Herald-Examiner, 1979-82; columnist TV Guide, 1984-85; editor Press Ready Ink, San Francisco, 1982—; script and tech. cons. various TV and movie prodns., 1981—; editor various books; host Movers and Shakers TV talk show, 1984; frequent guest various TV and radio talk shows, 1984—. Contbr. numerous articles to pubs. including Harper's, The New Republic, The New Yorker, People, Rolling Stone, TV Guide, Spy, Vanity Fair; author: Carson, 1987. Mem. Selective Svc. Bd., Everett, Mass., 1970-73; mem. Fourth St. Dem. Club, San Francisco, 1992—. Knox fellow Harvard U., 1968. Mem. Authors Guild, Cold Day Club. Office: Press Ready Inc 1072 Folsom St #306 San Francisco CA 94103

CORKRAN, JOHN ROGERSON, fundraising executive; b. Chgo., Dec. 16, 1936; s. David Hudson Jr. and Marion (Montgomery) C.; m. Carol Tonette Bender, Jan. 4, 1963; children: Carol, Susan, Timothy, Laurel. BA in History, Wesleyan U., 1958. Recreation technician U.S. Forest Svc., Estacada, Oreg., 1962-64; work supr. Job Corps U.S. Forest Svc., Roseburg, Oreg., 1964-65, asst. corpsmen supr. Job Corps, 1966; dir. ann. giving Wesleyan U., Middletown, Conn., 1966-69; dir. devel. Catlin Gabel Sch., Portland, Oreg., 1969-80, Fountain Valley Sch., Colorado Springs, Colo., 1980-86, The Bush Sch., Seattle, 1986-90; exec. dir. Bethany of N.W. Found., Everett, Wash., 1990—; chmn. dist. VIII, bd. dirs. Coun. for Advancement and Support of Edn., Washington, 1977-78. Mem. fin. com. Horn of Africa Svcs., Seattle, 1993-94; bd. dirs. Presbyn. Counselling Svc., Seattle, 1986-93, chair dirs. search com., 1991; mem. Shohomish County Estate Planned Giving Coun., 1991-94; sec. bd. dirs. Colo. Assn. Fundraisers, 1983. Recipient Robert Bell Crow award Coun. for Advancement and Support of Edn., 1984. Mem. Snohomish, Whatcom Island, Skagit County Devel. Officers (chair program com. 1993-94, pres. 1995), No.w. Devel. Officers Assn., Washington Planned Giving Coun. Democrat. Lutheran. Home: 4715 44th Ave S Seattle WA 98118-1807 Office: Bethany of NW Found 3322 Broadway Everett WA 98201-4425

CORLESS, DOROTHY ALICE, nurse educator; b. Reno, Nev., May 28, 1943; d. John Ludwig and Vera Leach (Wilson) Adams; children: James Lawrence Jr., Dorothy Adele Carroll. RN, St. Luke's Sch. Nursing, 1964. Clinician, cons., educator, author, adminstr. Fresno County Mental Health Dept., 1970-94; pvt. practice mental health nurse Fresno, 1991-94; instr. police sci. State Ctr. Tng. Facility, 1991-94; pvt. practice, mental health con., educator Florence, Oreg., 1994—. Vol. ARC, Disaster Mental Health Svcs., 1993—. Maj. USAFR, 1972-94. Mem. NAFE, Forensic Mental Health Assn. Calif., Calif. Peace Officer's Assn., Critical Incident Stress Found. Office: 1580 Kalla Kalla Ct Florence OR 97439-8963

CORMIER, EVELYN M., educator; b. Choteau, Mont., July 15, 1931; d. Wallace Elmer and Alice Maude (Dangerfield) Murdoch; children by previous marriage: Pauline, David. BS in Edn., Calif. State U., Hayward, 1966, MS in Edn., 1981. 1st grade tchr. Mowry Sch., Fremont, Calif., 1966-73; tchr. K-1, 1st, 2nd grade Brookvale Sch., Fremont, 1973-84; 2nd grade gifted class tchr. Ardenwood Sch., Fremont, 1984-88, 2nd grade tchr., 1988—; mentor Fremont Unified Sch. Dist., 1984-86; program quality rev. participant So. Alameda County Consortium, Fremont. Mem. Hayward Human Rels. Commn., 1970-80; mem. Hayward Affirmative Action Commn., 1984-91; mem., chair Hayward Libr. Commn.; mem., vice chair Fairway Park Neighborhood Task Force, Hayward, 1994-95; founding mem. South Hayward Parish, 1966-70's; vol. San Francisco Bay Don Edwards Wildlife Refuge, 1983—; sch. rep. Fremont Unified Dist. Tchrs. Assn., sec. exec. bd., 1991-95, 2nd v.p., 1995-96; mem. Hayward Area Planning Assn., circulator Save Our Open Space Initiative. Named Commn. of Yr., Hayward Vol. Dinner Commn., 1984, Grant, Monterey Bay Aquarium Tchr. Inst., Monterey, Calif., 1991, 93, Neighborhood Earth Day Environ. award City of Hayward, 1996. Mem. LWV (chair voter's study Human Rels. Commn. 1967-68), Hayward Vol. Recognition Com., Fremont Unified Dist. Tchrs. Assn., Sierra Chautauqua Coop. Recreational Cabin. Democrat. Unitarian-Universalist. Office: Ardenwood Sch 33955 Emilia Ln Fremont CA 94555-2068

CORNABY, KAY STERLING, lawyer, former state senator; b. Spanish Fork, Utah, Jan. 14, 1936; s. Sterling A. and Hilda G. C.; m. Linda Rasmussen, July 23, 1965; children: Alyse, Derek, Tara, Heather, Brandon. AB, Brigham Young U., 1960; postgrad. law Heidelberg (Ger.), 1961-63; JD, Harvard U., 1966. Bar: N.Y. 1967, Utah 1969, U.S. Patent and Trademark Office 1967. Assoc. Brumbaugh, Graves, Donahue & Raymond, N.Y.C., 1966-69; ptnr. Mallinckrodt & Cornaby, Salt Lake City, 1969-72; sole practice, Salt Lake City, 1972-85; mem. Utah State Senate, 1977-91, majority leader, 1983-84; shareholder Jones, Waldo, Holbrook & McDonough, Salt Lake City, 1985—; mem. adv. coun. Salt Lake Dist. SBA, 1984-91. Mem. Nat. Commn. on Uniform State Laws, 1988-93; mem. adv. bd. U. Mich. Ctr. For Study Youth Policy, 1990-93, Utah State Jud. Conduct Commn., 1983-91, chmn. 1984-85; bd. dirs. KUED-KUER Pub. TV and Radio, 1982-88, adv. bd. KUED, 1982—; bd. dirs. Salt Lake Conv. and Visitors Bur., 1985—. Mem. New York Bar, Utah Bar, Utah Harvard Alumni Assn. (pres. 1977-79), Harvard U. Law Sch. Alumni Assn. (pres. 1995—), Alta Club. Office: Jones Waldo Holbrook & McDonough 1500 1st Interstate Plz 170 S Main St Salt Lake City UT 84101-1605

CORNELL, KENNETH LEE, lawyer; b. Palo Alto, Calif., Feb. 23, 1945; s. Clinton Burdette and Mildred Lucy (Sheafer) C.; m. Barbara J. Smith, June 26, 1966; children: Melinda Lee, Geoffrey Mark. BBA, BA in Social Sci., Pacific Union Coll., 1966; JD, U. Wash., 1971. Bar: Wash. 1971, U.S. Dist. Ct. (we. dist.) Wash. 1971, U.S. Supreme Ct. 1974. Ptnr. Keller & Rohrback, Seattle, 1971-75, Richard, Rossano & Cornell, Seattle, 1975-77, Moren, Lageschulte (now Cornell, Hansen, Bugni & McConnell), Seattle, 1978-87, Cornell, Hansen, Bugni & McConnell PS (firm name change), 1995—; cons. atty. Town of Clyde Hill, Wash. 1980-87. Editor Wash. U. Law Rev., 1970-71. Bd. dirs. Kirkland (Wash.) Seventh Day Adventist Sch., 1972-78, Auburn (Wash.) Acad., 1974-80, Western Wash. Corp. Seventh Day Adventists, Bothell, 1974-80. Mem. ABA, Assn. Trial Lawyers Am., Wash. State Bar Assn., Wash. State Trial Lawyers Assn., Order of Coif. Democrat. Office: Cornell Hansen Bugni & McConnell PS 11320 Roosevelt Way NE Seattle WA 98125-6228

CORNETT, DONNA J., counselor, alcohol moderation administrator; b. Calif., Jan. 26, 1949; d. L.D. and Shirley A. Cornett. BA in Psychology, San Jose State U., 1972, MA in Psychology, 1973. Founder dir., Drink/Link Moderation Program, Santa Rosa, Calif., 1987—; founder, dir. The Responsible Drinking Inst. Am., Santa Rosa, 1994—; mem. Responsible Hospitality Project, San Rafael, Calif., 1993-95. Author: 7 Weeks to Safe Social Drinking: How to Effectively Moderate Your Alcohol Intake, 1996; copyrighted moderation program developer, 1987. Mem. Calif. State Psychol. Assn. Office: The Drink/Link Moderation Program PO Box 5441 Santa Rosa CA 95402

CORNFORD, ADAM FRANCIS, literature and writing educator, poet; b. Newcastle-upon-Tyne, Eng., Feb. 26, 1950; came to U.S., 1969; s. Christopher Francis and Mary Lucy (Jameson) C.; m. Marjorie Perry Gebbie, Dec. 2, 1984 (div. May 1988); m. Karen Sue Balke, Aug. 18, 1988; 1 child, Raphael Christopher. BA in English and Spanish, U. Calif., Santa Cruz, 1974; MA in English, San Francisco State U., 1979. Cert. tchr., Calif. Project dir. Horizons Unltd. Inc., San Francisco, 1977-81; poetry tchr. Berkeley (Calif.) Pub. Schs., 1981-84, classroom tchr., 1984; curriculum writer U.S. Dept. Edn., San Francisco, 1985-87; textbook editor Houghton Mifflin, San Francisco, 1985-87; freelance tech. editor, writer, 1986-87; prof. literature and writing, chair poetics program New Coll. of Calif., San Francisco, 1987—; cons. Cloverleaf Multi Media Prodns., San Francisco, 1995—. Trustee Bay Area Ctr. for Art and Tech., San Francisco, 1992-95. Nat. Endowment for Arts grantee, 1984. Mem. ACLU, PEN Am. Mem. New Party. Office: New Coll Calif Sch Humanities 766 Valencia St San Francisco CA 94110

CORNISH, LINDA SOWA YOUNG, children's books author and illustrator, educator; b. Woodburn, Oreg., May 14, 1943; d. Cecil Edward and Marian Regina (Nibler) Sowa; m. Edmund Y.W. Young, June 11, 1966 (div. July 1988); children: Laura Young Engelmann, Amy L.H. Young, Kimberly Young Brummund; m. H.T. Cornish, Oct. 6, 1991. BA, U. Portland, 1966; EdM, Temple U., 1968; postgrad., Pacific U., Forest Grove, Oreg., 1997—. Tchr. spl. edn. Phila. Sch. System, 1966-69; tchr. elem. and spl. edn. North Clackamas Dist. 12, Milwaukie, Oreg., 1974-92; author, illustrator Cornish Hen, Dahlia Pub. Co., Hillsboro, Oreg., 1994—. Author, illustrator: (juvenile) Pong's Visit, 1994, Pong's Ways, 1995. Adv. for homeless mentally ill women. Mem. AAUW, ASCD, Assn. for Childhood Edn. Internt., Oreg. Coun. Tchrs. English, Northwest Assn. Book Publishers. Democrat. Methodist. Home: 1295 SW Brookwood Ave Hillsboro OR 97123-7593

CORNOG, ROBERT ALDEN, engineering consultant; b. Portland, July 7, 1912; s. Jacob Rodenbaugh and Emma Daisy (Ripley) C.; divorced; children: Ann, David. BS in Mech. Engring., U. Iowa, 1933; MS in Physics, U. Calif., Berkeley, 1939, PhD in Nuclear Physics, 1940. Physicist, engr. various organizations, 1940—; atomic bomb devel. Los Alamos, N.Mex., 1943-45; co-discover tritium; cons. in field. Contbr. articles to profl. jours.; patentee in field. Fellow British Interplanetary Soc. (life); mem. IEEE (sr.), Tau Beta Pi, Sigma Xi. Home: 2242 20th St Apt 4 Santa Monica CA 90405-1738 Office: Pacific Infrared Systems 6914 Canby Ave Ste 109 Reseda CA 91335-4313

CORNYN, JOHN EUGENE, III, management consultant; b. Evanston, Ill., May 5, 1945; s. John Eugene and Virginia Ryder (Shannahan) C.; m. Patricia R. Benner, July 27, 1992; 1 child, Kelly. B.S. in Hotel and Restaurant Adminstrn., Okla. State U., 1968. Mgr. Indian Trail Restaurant, Winnetka, Ill., 1970-71; employee services mgr. Zenith Corp., Chgo., 1971-72; mgr. Red Lion Corp., Portland, Oreg., 1973; cons. Pannell, Kerr, Forster, Chgo., 1973-75; prin., ptnr. The Cornyn Fasano Group, Portland, 1976—; v.p. Seven Seas, Inc., Winnetka, Ill., 1978—, All Seas, Inc., Winneka, Ill., 1980—. Co-author: Noncommercial Foodservice-An Administrator's Handbook, 1994. Served to 1st lt. U.S. Army, 1968-70. Mem. Foodservice Cons. Soc.

Internat. (chmn. mgmt. cons. com. 1983—), Inst. Mgmt. Cons. Republican. Club: Portland City. Home: 3350 NE Holladay St Portland OR 97232-2533 Office: The Cornyn Fasano Group 1618 SW 1st Ave Ste 315 Portland OR 97201-5708

CORRADINI, DEEDEE, mayor. Student, Drew U., 1961-63; BS, U. Utah, 1965, MS, 1967. Adminstrv. asst. for public info. Utah State Office Rehab. Svcs., 1967-69; cons. Utah State Dept. Community Affairs, 1971-72; media dir., press sec. Wayne Owens for Congress Campaign, 1972; press sec. Rep. Wayne Owens, 1973-74; spl. asst. to N.Y. Congl. Rep. Richard Ottinger, 1975; asst. to pres., dir. community rels. Snowbird Corp., 1975-77; exec. v.p. Bonneville Assocs., Inc., Salt Lake City, 1977-80; pres. Bonneville Assocs., Inc., 1980-89, chmn., CEO, 1989-91; mayor Salt Lake City, 1992—; mem. urban con. policy com. U.S. Conf. on Mayors, mem. unfunded fed. mandates task force, mem. crime and violence task force, chmn. adv. bd.; chair Mayor's Gang Task Force; mem. interngovtl. policy adv. com. U.S. Trade Rep., 1993-94; mem. transp. and comm. com. Nat. League of Cities, 1993-94. Bd. trustees Intermountain Health Care, 1980-92; bd. dirs., exec. com. Utah Symphony, 1983-92, vice chmn., 1985-88, chmn., 1988-92; dir. Utah chpt. Nat. Conf. Christians and Jews, Inc., 1988; bd. dirs. Salt Lake Olympic Bid Com., 1989—; chmn. image com. Utah Partnership for Edn. and Econ. Devel., 1989-92; co-chair United Way Success by 6 Program; pres. Shelter of the Homeless Com.; active Sundance Inst. Utah Com., 1990-92; disting. bd. fellow So. Utah U., 1991; active numerous other civic orgns. and coms. Mem. Salt Lake Area C. of C. (bd. govs. 1979-81, chmn. City/County/Govt. com. 1976-86). Office: Office of the Mayor City & County Bldg 451 S State St Rm 306 Salt Lake City UT 84111-3104*

CORRAL, JEANIE BELEYN, journalist, school board administrator; b. Wichita, Kans., Aug. 31, 1943; d. George Rush Holloway and Helen Elizabeth (Eberly) Holloway-Jamison; m. Raymond Corral, Sept. 1, 1962; children: Camella, Nena, Cheyminne, Cwennen, Channing. AA, Palo Verde Jr. Coll., 1964; BA in History, Calif. State U., Fullerton, 1983, MA in History, 1989. Writer, cartoonist Lake Elsinore (Calif.) Sun, 1974-83; writer, columnist Lake Elsinore Sun-Tribune, 1983-85, Community News Network, Temecula, Calif., 1990-92; mem. Lake Elsinore Unified Sch. Dist., 1988—, pres., 1991-92; staff writer, columnist Sun Tribune, 1992—; presenter workshops in field. Author: If These Walls Could Speak: Elsmore Union High School 1891-1991, 1996, Scruffy 'n Me, 1993, (ch. history) Growing of a Mustard Seed, 1987; asst. editor Pacific Oral History Rev., 1984. Lay/master catechist St. Frances of Rome Parish Sch., Lake Elsinore, 1963-78; liaison Mt. San Jacinto Jr. Coll. Dist., Lake Elsinore, 1988-90; mem. Riverside Centennial Com., 1992-93; mem. parish coun. St. Frances of Rome Ch., 1987-90; mem. religious life commn. Second Synod of San Diego, 1972-76; mem. city police task force, Lake Elsinore, 1991; sec. Riverside County Dem. Cen. Com., 1988-91; mem. bilingual adv. com. Lake Elsinore Unified Sch. Dist., 1984—, mem. curriculum adv. coun., 1988—. Recipient 1st Place Environ. award Twin Counties Press Club, 1982, 2d Place Collaborative Coverage award Twin Counties Press Club, 1983, 4th Place Humor award Woman's Day mag., 1974; McNeal Pearce grantee, 1988. Mem. Calif. Fedn. Women's Club (De Anza Dist. 23 dist. history 1st place 1989, 90, 92, 2d place 1991), Lake Elsinore Women's Club (pres. 1974-76), Rotary, S.W. Oral History Assn., Phi Kappa Phi, Delta Gamma Omega, Phi Alpha Theta. Home: 16410 Lakeshore Dr Lake Elsinore CA 92530-5020

CORRICK, DAVID LAWRENCE, radio producer, editor, journalist; b. Redondo Beach, Calif., May 31, 1964; s. Lawrence Rexford Corrick and Eleanora Pizzoruss; m. Jin Lee, Apr. 10, 1995. BA in History, San Diego State U., 1986. Cert. in transp. of hazardous materials. Pub. affairs officer USAFR, Van Nuys, Calif., 1987-90; logistics officer USAF, Dover and worldwide, Del., 1990-91; traffic mgr. Applied Graphics Tech., Glendale, Calif., 1992-93; art dir. Richard N. McGulne Prodns., L.A., 1993-94; co-host cooking show Sta. KIEV, Glendale, Calif., 1994-95; prodr. radio show Paul Wallach Inc., L.A., 1995; art dir. Golden Mean Prodns., L.A., 1995-96; cons. coord. dept. film and TV, UCLA, 1997—; mem. adv. bd. bd. Hispanic Employees of Restaurants Awards, L.A., 1995—. Editor: Paul Wallach Restaurant Guide, 1995—, Dining Out with Style, 1996; food editor Hot Lava Mag., 1994-95; editor, pub.: (book) Lounge Los Angeles, 1993-96 (Magellan award); actor (comedy video short) Night Flight TV, 1991; constrn. coord. (feature film) Isle of Lesbos, 1996; contbr. articles to mags. Campaign dir. Ed Ocharocha for Sch. Bd., L.A., 1995; activist 50's Coffeeshop Preservation Group, L.A., 1991. Capt. USAFR, 1987-94. Decorated Nat. Def. Svc. medal, 1991. Mem. IATSE, VFW, Air Force Assn. (life), Nat. Hist. Trust for Archtl. Preservation, L.A. Conservancy, St. Jude Hunt and Fish Club (founder). Roman Catholic. Office: Paul Wallach Inc PO Box 41726 Los Angeles CA 90041

CORRIE, RICHARD WAYNE, lighting designer, artist, musician; b. Indpls., Aug. 28, 1956; s. Donald William Corrie and Betty Louise (Sutton) Terry; m. Florence Ann Quick-Van Epps, July 11, 1987 (div. June 1992). Ed. pub. schs. Clk. ABC Records, Indpls., 1972-75; in sales J.L. Marsh Records, North Hollywood, Calif., 1976-79; isntr. Celebrity Ctr. Internat., Hollywood, 1979-84; light designer Light Energy Studio, North Hollywood, 1985—; performing artist Celebrity Ctr., Hollywood, 1979-84; in lighting Gallery Theater, Silver Lake, Calif., 1993, Theater Theater, Hollywood, 1994; lighting/sculpture for film Eternity, Hollywood, 1990. Light designer sculpture Light Energy Cocktail Table, 1991; light designer Light Energy Murals, 1992; dir., designer Light Energy Video. Home and Office: Light Energy Studio 4819 Matilija Ave Sherman Oaks CA 91423

CORRIGAN, GERALD F., executive search consultant; b. Dublin, Ireland, Apr. 16, 1937; came to the U.S., 1959; s. Nicholas J. and Bridget (Donohue) C.; m. Virginia Tang, 1965; children: Peter, Elizabeth. AB, UCLA, 1963, MBA, 1965. Asst. dean adminstrn. and external affairs UCLA Grad. Sch. Mgmt., dean exec. edn.; mgmt. cons. Booz, Allen & Hamilton, Cresap, Inc.; exec. search cons., pres. The Corrigan Group, L.A., 1978—; bd. arbitrators NASD; pub. arbitrator Pacific Stock Exch. Mem. N.Am. bd. Michael Smurfit Grad. Sch. Bus. U. Coll. Dublin. Mem. UCLA Alumni Assn. (life), Jonathan Club. Democrat. Roman Catholic. Home: 1057 Corsica Dr Pacific Palisades CA 90272-4013 Office: The Corrigan Group 1333 Ocean Ave Santa Monica CA 90401-1023

CORRIGAN, MARY KATHRYN, theater educator; b. Mpls., July 11, 1930; d. Arthur Joseph Kolling and Hazel (Pierce) Colp; children: Michael Edward, Timothy Patrick. BA, U. Minn., Mpls., 1965, MA, 1967. Advisor, counselor Coll. Liberal Arts U. Minn., Mpls., 1964-65, instr. dept. theatre, 1966-69, asst. prof. dept. theatre, 1969-73; assoc. prof. dept. theatre Fla. State U., Tallahassee, 1973-75; assoc. prof. dept. theatre U. Calif., San Diego, 1975-89, 92-96, prof. emeritus, 1996—; assoc. dir. U. Calif. Study Ctr. U.K., Ireland, 1989-91; master tchr. Brit. Am. Drama Acad., Balliol Coll., Oxford U., Eng., summers, 1987—, chair undergrad. & intermediate programs midsummer, 1992-97. Actress nat. pub. radio Chopin, 1984, video film Ultrasonography, 1986. Mem. adv. con. United Ministeries, Mpls., 1968-73, Mpls. Sch. Bd., 1968-72; vol. KPBS Reading Svc.; vol. dir. for Actors Alliance; mediator work with juvenile offenders. Recipient Tozier Found. award, Eng., 1967, Best Actress award Globe Theatre, San Diego, 1979, NEH award Folger Shakespeare Theatre, 1992-93; grantee Rockefeller Found., 1968, McMillan grantee U. Minn., Eng., 1968, U. Calif.-San Diego, 1982-87, NEH grantee Folger Inst., Washington, 1993-94, Stanford U., summer 1994, Creativity LaJolla Conf., 1995. Mem. Am. Theatre Assn. (exec. com., v.p. performance tng. 1984-86), Voice and Speech Theater Assn. (bd. dirs. 1986-89). Democrat. Home: 2645 Gobat Ave San Diego CA 92122-3127 Office: U Calif San Diego Theatre Dept La Jolla CA 92093-0344

CORRIGAN, ROBERT ANTHONY, academic administrator; b. New London, Conn., Apr. 21, 1935; s. Anthony John and Rose Mary (Jengo) C.; m. Joyce D. Mobley, Jan. 12, 1975; children by previous marriage: Kathleen Marie, Anthony John, Robert Anthony; 1 stepdau., Erika Mobley. A.B., Brown U., 1957; M.A., U. Pa., 1959, Ph.D., 1967; LHD (hon.), 1995. Researcher Phila. Hist. Commn., 1957-59; lectr. Am. civilization U. Gothenburg, Sweden, 1959-62, Bryn Mawr Coll., 1962-63, U. Pa., 1963-64; prof. U. Iowa, 1964-73; dean U. Mo., Kansas City, 1973-74; provost U. Md., 1974-79; chancellor U. Mass., Boston, 1979-88; pres. San Francisco State U., 1988—. Author: American Fiction and Verse, 1962, 2d edit., 1970, also articles, revs.; editor: Uncle Tom's Cabin, 1968. Vice chmn. Iowa City Human Rels. Commn., 1970-72, Gov.'s Commn. on Water Quality, 1983-84; mem. Iowa City Charter Commn., 1972-73; chmn. Md. Com. Humanities, 1976-78, Assn. Urban Univs., 1988-92; mem. Howard County Commn. Arts, Md., 1976-79; bd. dirs. John F. Kennedy Libr.; trustee San Francisco Econ. Devel. Corp., 1989-92, Modern Greek Studies Found., Found. of Spain and U.S., Adv. Coun. of Calif. Acad. Scis., Bishop Desmond Tutu South African Refugee Scholarship Fund, Calif. Historical Soc., 1989-92; co-chmn., bd. dirs. Calif. Compact, 1990-93; mem. exec. com. Campus Compact, 1991—, chmn., 1995—; Mayor's Blue Ribbon Commn. on Fiscal Stability, 1994-95; chmn. Pres. Clinton's Steering Com. of Coll. Pres. for Am. Reads, 1996-97. Smith-Mundt prof., 1959-60; Fulbright lectr., 1960-62; grantee Standard Oil Co. Found., 1968, NEH, 1969-74, Ford Found., 1969, Rockefeller Found., 72-75, Dept. State, 1977; recipient Clarkson Able Collins Jr. Maritime History award, 1956, Pa. Colonial Soc. Essay award, 1958, 59, William Lloyd Garrison award Mass. Ednl. Opportunity Assn., 1987; Disting. Urban Fellow Assn. Urban U., 1992. Mem. San Francisco C. of C. (bd. dirs.), San Francisco World Affairs Coun. (bd. dirs.), Pvt. Industry Coun. (bd. dirs. 1992—), Boston World Affairs Coun. (1983-88), Greater Boston C. of C. (v.p. 1987-89), Fulbright Alumni Assn. (bd. dirs. 1978-80), Univ. Club, City Club, World Trade Club, Commonwealth Club (bd. dirs. 1995—), Phi Beta Kappa. Democrat. Office: San Francisco State U 1600 Holloway Ave San Francisco CA 94132-1722

CORRIGAN, WILFRED J., data processing and computer company executive; b. 1938. Divsn. dir. Motorola, Phoenix, 1962-68; pres. Fairchild Camera & Instrument, Sunnyvale, Calif., 1968-80; chmn. bd., CEO LSI Logic Corp., Milpitas, Calif., 1980—, also dir. Office: LSI Logic Corp 1551 Mccarthy Blvd Milpitas CA 95035-7424*

CORSER, KIRA DOROTHY CARRILLO, photographic artist; b. San Antonio, Tex., Feb. 27, 1951; d. William Franklin and Maria (McCarthy) Freeman; children: Robert William, Anna Katrina. BA in Journalism and Art, San Diego State U., 1984. dir. photography dept. KPBS TV and Radio Stas., 1979-89; lectr. in field. Co-author, prodr. (with Frances Payne Adler) Home Street Home, 1984, Struggle to be Borne, 1987, When the Bough Breaks Pregnancy and the Legacy of Addiction, 1993; photographs have appeared in numerous books and exhbns. Recipient Calif. State Senate award for artistic excellence and social collaboration, 1989; David Copley Art grantee, 1984, 87, 89, Combined Arts and Edn. grantee NEA, San Diego, 1987, Las Patronas grantee and March of Dimes Birth Defects Found. grantee, 1989, Monterey Cultural Arts Commn. grantee, 1991, Santa Clara County Arts Commn. grantee, 1992, Irvine Found. Art grantee, 1993, others. Home and Office: Art for Social Change Matriot Video Prodn 17467 Via Cielo Carmel Valley CA 93924-9169

CORSI, SANDRO, artist, educator; b. Rome, June 21, 1958; came to the U.S., 1983; s. Luigi and Adriana (De Simoni) C.; m. Elena Pascuzzi, Jan. 26, 1987. BFA, Sch. Art Inst. Chgo., 1984, MFA, 1986. Freelance illustrator Rome, 1979-83; animation intern David Alexovich Animation, Chgo., 1984-86; computer graphics cons. Northwestern U. Med. Libr., Chgo., 1987; faculty U. Wis., Oshkosh, 1987-92, Fullerton (Calif.) Coll., 1992—; speaker in field; guest lectr. Syracuse (N.Y.) U., 1989. Exhibited in numerous group shows including 1st Annual Art & Design Contest Computer Pictures Mag., No. Ill. U. Gallery, Chgo., 1992, Gallery 100, Cape Girardeau, Mo., 1992, Milw. Art Mus., 1991, U. of Arrts, Phila., 1990, Edna Carlsten Gallery U. Wis., Stevens Point, 1990, St. Louis C.C., 1989, Conn. Coll., New London, 1989, many others. Mellon fellow, 1985-86; scholar Sch. Art Inst. Chgo., 1985-86. Office: Fullerton Coll 321 E Chapman Ave Fullerton CA 92832-2011

CORSINI, RAYMOND JOSEPH, psychologist; b. Rutland, Vt., June 1, 1914; s. Joseph August and Evelyn Carolyn (Lavaggi) C.; m. Kleona Rigney, Oct. 10, 1965; 1 dau., Evelyn Anne. B.S., CCNY, 1939, M.S. in Edn, 1941; Ph.D., U. Chgo., 1955. Prison psychologist Auburn (N.Y.) Prison, 1941-45, San Quentin Prison, 1945-47, Wis. Prison System, 1947-50; research assoc. U. Chgo., 1955-57; pvt. practice indsl. psychology Alfred Adler Inst., Chgo., 1957-63; assoc. prof. Ill. Inst. Tech., 1964-65, U. Calif. at Berkeley, 1965-66; pvt. practice psychology Honolulu, 1965-89; faculty research affiliate Sch. Pub. Health, U. Hawaii, 1970—; affiliate grad. faculty dept. psychology, U. Hawaii; founder, sr. counselor Family Edn. Centers Hawaii, 1966—. Author: Methods of Group Psychotherapy, 1957, Roleplaying in Business and Industry, 1961, Roleplaying in Psychotherapy, 1966, The Family Council, 1974, The Practical Parent, 1975, Role Playing, 1980, Give In or Give Up, 1981, Individual Psychology: Theory and Practice, 1982, Effective Discipline in the Home and the School, 1989, Five Therapists and One Client, 1990, Coping with Your Teenager, 1990; editor: Critical Incidents in Psychotherapy, 1959, Adlerian Family Counseling, 1959, Critical Incidents in Teaching, 1965, Critical Incidents in School Counseling, 1972, Critical Incidents in Nursing, 1973, Current Psychotherapies, 1973, 77, 83, 89, 95, Current Personality Theories, 1978, Great Cases in Psychotherapy, 1979, Alternative Educational System, 1979, Theories of Learning, 1980, Comparative Educational Systems, 1981, Handbook of Innovative Psychotherapies, 1981, Adolescence: The Challenge, Encyclopedia of Psychology, 1984, 2d edit., 1994, Concise Encyclopedia of Psychology, 1987, 2d rev. edit. 1996, Encyclopedia of Aging, 1987. Bd. dirs. Hawaii chpt. John Howard Assn., 1966-68. Recipient James McKeen Cattell award psychology Psychol. Corp., 1944; Sertoma award, 1980. Mem. Am. Psychol. Assn. (Significant Profl. Contbn. award Hawaii chpt. 1985), N.Am. Soc. Adlerian Psychology. Club: Waikiki Yacht (Honolulu). Address: 140 Niuiki Cir Honolulu HI 96821-2349

CORSON, KIMBALL JAY, lawyer; b. Mexico City, Sept. 17, 1941; came to U.S., 1942; s. Harland Jerry and Arleen Elizabeth (Jones) C.; m. Ann Dudley Wood, May 25, 1963 (div. Apr. 1978); 1 child, Claudia Ring; m. Joy Lorann Sligh, June 16, 1979; children: Bryce Manning, Jody Darlene. BA, Wayne State U., 1966; MA, U. Chgo., 1968, JD, 1971. Bar: Ariz. 1972, U.S. Dist. Ct. 1971, U.S. Supreme Ct. 1991. Assoc. Lewis & Roca, Phoenix, 1971-74, ptnr., 1974-90; ptnr. Horne Kaplan & Bistrow, Phoenix, 1990—. Co-author: Document Control: Organization, Management and Production, 1988; contbg. author: Litigation Support Using Personal Computers, 1989. Co-founder Desert Hills Improvement Assn., Phoenix, 1988—. With U.S. Army, 1961-64. Fellow Woodrow Wilson Found., 1966, 67. Mem. ABA (civil practice and procedures com. antitrust sect. 1988—), Ariz. Bar Assn. (spkr. 1991—), Maricipa County Bar Assn., Internat. Trademark Assn. (editl. bd. The Trademark Reporter 1993-94, mem. publs. com. 1995—, INTA Speaker's award 1988), Am. Sailing Assn., Phi Beta Kappa. Home: Summit Ranch 35808 N 15th Ave Phoenix AZ 85027 Office: Horne Kaplan & Bistrow 40 N Central Ave Ste 2800 Phoenix AZ 85004-4447

CORTELYOU, ROBERT J(OHN), civil engineer; b. Taft, Calif., July 2, 1937; s. John Taylor and Mildred Louise (Kessel) C.; m. Barbara Jean Watson, May 26, 1962; children: Robert John, Jr., John Charles. BS in Mech. Engring., Calif. State Poly. Coll., 1960. Registered profl. engr., Calif. Mech., civil engr. GE, Louisville, San Jose, Calif., 1960-61; mech. engr. Calif. State Dept. of Water Resources, Sacramento, 1965-70, Sonoma County Water Agy., Santa Rosa, Calif., 1970-78; supr. design engr. Western Water Dist. Riverside (Calif.) County, 1978-80; design engring. supr. Sonoma County Water Agy., 1980—. Lt. USN, 1961-64; capt. USNR, 1965-92. Decorated Navy Commendation medal, Nat. Def. medal; recipient Welding Design Contest 1st Pl. award Lincoln Electric Co., 1960. Mem. ASME, ASCE, San Francisco Bay Area Engrs. Coun. (scholarship com.), U.S. Navy League, Model A Ford Car Club, Tau Sigma. Home: 6640 Saint Helena Rd Santa Rosa CA 95404-9694 Office: Sonoma County Water Agy 2150 W College Ave Santa Rosa CA 95401-4442

CORTEZ, EDDIE, mayor. Mayor City of Pomono, Calif. Office: City of Pomona 505 S Garey Ave Pomona CA 91766

CORTINEZ, VERONICA, literature educator; b. Santiago, Chile, Aug. 27, 1958; came to U.S. 1979; d. Carlos Cortinez and Matilde Romo. Licenciatura en Letras, U. Chile, 1979; MA, U. Ill., Champaign, Ill., 1981, Harvard U., 1983; PhD, Harvard U., 1990. Teaching asst. U. Chile, Santiago, 1977-79, U. Ill., Champaign, 1979-80; teaching fellow Harvard U., 1982-86, instr., 1986-89; assoc. prof. colonial and contemporary Latin Am. lit. UCLA, 1989—; fgn. corres. Caras, Santiago, 1987—. Editorial bd. Mester/Dept. Spanish and Portuguese of UCLA, 1989—; editor Plaza mag., 1981-89, Harvard Rev., 1983-89; contbr. articles to profl. jours. Recipient award for Tchg. Excellence Derek Bok Ctr., Harvard U., 1982, 83, 84, 85, 86, Tchg. prize Romance Lang. Dept., Harvard U., 1986; Whiting fellow. Mem. Cabot House, Phi Beta Phi. Office: UCLA Dept Spanish and Portuguese 5310 Rolfe Hall Los Angeles CA 90024

CORTLUND, JOAN MARIE, educator; b. Ponoka, Alta., Can., Aug. 22, 1947; came to U.S., 1961; d. Chester Doty and Kathleen Mary (Fowler) Cook; children: Kimberly Rae Green, David James Chesley. AA, Green River C.C., Auburn, Wash., 1981; BA in Edn., Pacific Luth. U., 1988; MEd, U. Wash., Tacoma, 1995, credentials in adminstrn., 1996. Cert. tchr., Wash. Instrnl. asst. White River Sch. Dist., Buckley, Wash., 1981-88; tchr. Sumner (Wash.) Sch. Dist., 1988-97, adminstr., 1997—. Recipient Wash. State Excellence in Edn. award State of Wash., 1994.

CORTNER, HANNA JOAN, science administrator, research scientist, educator; b. Tacoma, Wash., May 9, 1945; d. Val and E. Irene Otteson; m. Richard Carroll Cortner, Nov. 14, 1970. BA in Polit. Sci. magna cum laude with distinction, U. Wash., 1967; MA in Govt., U. Ariz., 1969, PhD in Govt., 1973. Grad. tchg. and rsch. asst. dept. govt. U. Ariz., Tucson, 1967-70, rsch. assoc. Inst. Govt. Rsch., 1974-76, rsch. assoc. forest-watershed and landscape resources divsns. Sch. Renewable Natural Resources, 1975-82, adj. assoc. prof. Sch. Renewable Natural Resources, 1983-89; exec. asst. Pima County Bd. Suprs., 1985-86; adj. assoc. prof. renewable natural resources, assoc. rsch. scientist Water Resources Rsch. Ctr. U. Ariz., Tucson, 1988-89, prof., rsch. scientist Water Resources Rsch. Ctr., 1989-90, prof., rsch. scientist, dir. Water Resources Rsch. Ctr., 1990-96, prof., rsch. scientist Sch. Renewable Resources, 1997—; program analyst USDA Forest Svc., Washington, 1979-80; vis. scholar Inst. Water Resources, Corps of Engrs., Ft. Belvoir, Va., 1986-87; com. arid lands AAAS, 1986-89; com. natural disasters NAS/NRC, 1988-91, com. on planning and remediation of irrigation-induced water quality impacts, 1994-95; rev. com. nat. forest planning Conservation Found., Washington, 1987-90; chair adv. com. renewable resources planning techs. for pub. lands Office of Tech. Assessment U.S. Congress, 1989-91; mem. policy coun. Pinchot Inst. Conservation Studies, 1991-93; co-chair working party on evaluation of forest policies Internat. Union Forestry Rsch. Orgns., 1990-95, chair working party on forest instns. and forestry adminstrn., 1996; vice chair Man and the Biosphere Program, Temperate Directorate, U.S. Dept. State, 1991-96; bd. dirs. 7th Am. Forest Congress, 1994-96; mem. sci. adv. com. Consortium for Environ. Risk Evaluation, 1996—; cons. Greeley and Hansen, Cons. Engrs., U.S. Army Corps Engrs., Ft. Belvoir, U.S. Forest Svc., Washington, Portland, Oreg., Ogden, Utah. Assoc. editor Society and Natural Resources, 1992-94; book reviewer Western Polit. Sci. Quar., Am. Polit. Quar., Perspectives, Natural Resources Jour., Climatic Change, Society and Natural Resources, Jour. of Forestry; mem. editl. bd. Jour. Forest Planning, 1995—; pub. papers and monographs; contbr. articles to profl. jours. Bd. dirs. Planned Parenthood So. Ariz., 1992-94, mem. planning com., 1992, mem. bd. devel. and evaluation com., 1994; bd. dirs. N.W. Homeowners Assn., 1982-83, v.p., 1983-84, pres., 1984; vice chmn., chmn. Pima County Bd. Adjustment Dist. 3, 1984; active Tucson Tomorrow, 1984-88; mem. water quality subcom. Pima Assn. Govts., 1983-84, mem. environ. planning adv. com., 1989-90, chmn., 1984, mem. Avra Valley task force, 1988-90; bd. dirs. So. Ariz. Water Resources Assn., 1984-86, 87-95, sec., 1987-89, mem. com. alignment and terminal storage, 1990-94, mem. CAP com., 1988-92, chairperson, 1989-90, mem. basinwide mgmt. com., 1983-86, chairperson, 1992-93; active Ariz. Interagy. Task Force on Fire and the Urban/Wildland Interface, 1990-92; mem. wastewater mgmt. adv. com. Pima County, 1988-92, mem. subcom. on effluent reuse Joint CWAC-WWAC, 1989-91, mem. citizens water adv. com. Water Resources Plan Update Subcom., 1990-91; bd. dirs. Ctrl. Ariz. Water Conservation Dist., 1985-90, mem. fin. com., 1987-88, mem. spl. studies com., 1987-88, mem. nominating com., 1987; mem. Colo. River Salinity Control, 1989-90; chairperson adv. com. Tucson Long Range Master Water Plan, 1988-89; active water adv. com. City of Tucson, 1984. Travel grantee NSF/Soc. Am. Foresters; Rsch. grantee US Geol. Survey, US Army Corps of Engrs., USDA Forest Svc., Soil Conservation Svc., Utah State U., Four Corners Regional Commn., Office of Water Rsch. & Tech.; Sci. & Engring. fellow AAAS, 1986-87; recipient Copper Letter Appreciation cert. City of Tucson, 1985, 89, SAWARA award, 1989. Mem. Am. Water Resources Assn. (mem. nat. award com. 1987-90, mem. statues and bylaws com. 1989-90, tech. co-chairperson ann. meeting 1993), Am. Forests Assn. (mem. forest policy ctr. adv. coun. 1991-95), Soc. Am. Foresters (mem. task force on sustaining long-term forest health and productivity 1991-92, mem. com. on forest policy 1994-96), Am. Polit. Sci. Assn., Western Polit. Sci. Assn. (mem. com. on constrn. and bylaws 1976-80, chairperson 1977-79, mem. exec. coun. 1980-83, mem. com. on profl. devel. 1984-85, mem. com. on status of women 1984-85), Nat. Fire Protection Assn. (mem. tech. com. on forest and rural fire protection 1990-94), Phi Beta Kappa. Democrat. Home: 1425 W Calle Tiburon Tucson AZ 85704-1023 Office: U Ariz Sch Renewable Nat Resources 325 Bio Sci E Tucson AZ 85721

CORTRIGHT, INGA ANN, accountant; b. Silver City, N.Mex., Sept. 30, 1949; d. Lester Richard and Claudia Marcella (Huckaby) Lee; m. Russell Joseph Cortright, June 25, 1987. BS in Acctg., Ariz. State U., 1976, MBA, 1978; postgrad., Walden U., 1991—. CPA, Ariz., Tex. Sole practice cert. pub. acctg. Ariz., 1981—; cons. in field. Mem. AICPA, Beta Alpha Psi. Republican. Episcopalian. Office: 9421 W Bell Rd Ste 108 Sun City AZ 85351-1361

CORY, ANGELICA JO, spiritual consultant, author; b. Marshalltown, Iowa, Feb. 28, 1950; d. Douglas Alan and Mary Lou (Brewster) Beckwith; m. Phillip Charles Cory, Feb. 24, 1971 (div. Feb. 1985); children: Shane Douglas, Sean Phillip. BS in BA, U. N.Mex., 1971. Lic. real estate broker, Ariz.; lic. pilot, Ariz. Bookkeeper Goodyear Tires, Inc., Albuquerque, 1968-71; instr., model Barbizon Sch. Modeling, Phoenix, 1972-75; cons., pilot Cory's Gasoline Sta., Inc., Mesa, Ariz., 1975-80; dir., cons. Sunshine Fuels, Mesa, 1980-83; dir. mgmt. and real estate Cimmarron Devel., Phoenix, 1984-86; owner, broker KCB Brokerage, Mesa, 1986-91; owner, dir. Ultimate Practices, Mesa, 1989-91; spiritual cons. Mesa, 1991—. Author: Reflections of the Mind, 1995, Reflections of the Heart, 1996; contbg. composer: (cassette-CD) Light of the World, 1996; contbg. author: (poetry) Morning Song, 1996, Best Poems of 1997, 1996-97; contbr. articles, poetry to profl. jours. Founder Tara-Angelica Found., 1997. Mem. Internat. Soc. Poets (Disting. Mem. 1996—).

CORY, ROLLAND WAYNE, business administrator; b. Camp Zama, Sagamihira, Japan, Feb. 7, 1957; s. Claude Charles Cory and Kyoko (Narasaki) Reibel; m. Victoria Athena Dale Plasting, Nov. 8, 1980. AS in Transp. and Bus. Adminstrn., Chaffey Coll., 1992. Crane tender Ameron Steel Producing Div., Etiwanda, Calif., 1976; structural fitter Kaiser Steel Fabricated Products Group, Fontana, Calif., 1976-81; retail camera salesman Fedco Inc., San Bernardino, Calif., 1981; elevator mechanic Exec. Elevator Co., Fontana, Calif., 1985; storekeeper TTX Co./Calpro div., Mira Loma, Calif., 1981—; pres. United Steelworkers of Am. Local Union # 8844, Mira Loma, 1982-84, safety chmn., 1983-88, rec. sec., 1985-88, legis. educator, 1985—, sec., treas., 1995-97. Mem. Nat. Geog. Soc. (cert. 1982), Calif. Turtle and Tortoise Club (treas. Inland Empire chpt. 1990-96, Plaque 1991). Democrat. Office: PR Photography PO Box 976 Fontana CA 92334-0976

CORY, WALLACE NEWELL, state official, civil engineer; b. Olympia, Wash., Mar. 10, 1937; s. Henry Newell and Gladys Evelyn (Nixon) C.; m. Roberta Ruth Matthews, July 4, 1959; children: Steven Newell, Susan Evelyn Cory Carbon. BS in Forestry, Oreg. State U., 1958, BSCE, 1964; MSCE, Stanford U., 1965. Registered profl. engr., Idaho, Oreg. Asst. projects mgr. CH2 M/Hill, Boise, Idaho, 1965-70; environ. mgr. Boise Cascade Corp., 1970-78, dir. state govt. affairs, 1978-82; dir. indsl. group JUB Engrs., Boise, 1982-84; chief engr. Anchorage Water & Wastewater, 1984-90; dir. pub. works City of Caldwell, Idaho, 1990-92; prin. engr. Montgomery Watson, Pasadena, Calif., 1992-95; adminstr. Idaho Divsn. Environ. Quality, Boise, 1995—. Precinct committeeman Idaho Rep. Com., Boise, 1968-72, region chmn., 1973-77. Capt. USAF, 1958-62. Mem. ASCE, NSPE, Idaho Soc. Profl. Engrs. (pres. 1976-77, Young Engr. of Yr. award 1971), Air Pollution Control Assn. (chmn. Pacific N.W. sect. 1977-78), Idaho Assn. Commerce and Industry (chmn. environ. com. 1974-75). Home: 7174 Cascade Dr Boise ID 83704 Office: Idaho Divsn Environ Quality 1410 N Hilton Boise ID 83706

COSGROVE, CAMERON, insurance executive; b. Arcadia, Calif., July 25, 1957; s. Joseph Patrick Jr. and Marion (Barrons) C.; (div.); children: Christopher Farley, Steven Patrick. BS in Mgmt., Calif. State U., Long Beach, 1980. Asst. v.p. Pacific Mut. Life Ins. Co., Newport Beach, 1982—. Co-author city ordnance Regulation of Ozone, Depleting Compounds, 1989-90; contbr. articles to newspaper. Fin. commr. City of Irvine, Calif., 1983-87, planning commr. 1987-88, city councilman, 1988-90; bd. dirs. Irvine Transp. Authority, 1988-90.; founding advisor Irvine Conservancy, advisor, 1986-88, Irvine Infrastructure Authority, 1988-90; founder San Joaquin Marsh Adv. Com., chair 1988-90. Recipient Sea and Sage Audubon Conservation award, 1990. Mem. Life Office Mgmt. Assn. (tech. and mgmt. com. 1990—). Republican. Office: Pacific Mut Life Ins 700 Newport Center Dr Newport Beach CA 92660-6307

COSGROVE, JAMES, artist, industrial designer; b. Phoenix; s. Donald and Evelyn (Dresden) C.; m. Madeline Matranga, Sept. 20, 1969 (div. June 1986); children: Shannon, Kenneth, Marcia, Daniel. AA in Liberal Arts, Mt. San Antonio Coll., 1974; AA in Fine Art, Sacramento City Coll., 1994, AS in Metals Tech., 1995. With Mattel Toys, L.A., 1973-78; prin. Cos Design Group, Sacramento, 1994—. Inventor, designer in field. Recipient Award of Merit, State of Calif. Works Exhibit, 1995, Award of Excellence, 1996. Mem. Artist-Blacksmith Assn. N.Am., Calif. Blacksmith Assn. Studio: 8371 Jackson Rd Sacramento CA 95826

COSMAN, MARK GOODRICH, association administrator, author; b. Hartford, Conn., May 1, 1945; s. William and Lila (Goodrich) C.; m. Susan Fuentes, Oct. 13, 1967; 1 child, Morgan. BA, N. Mex. Highlands U., 1972. Nat. dir. spl. projects Muscular Dystrophy Assn., N.Y.C., 1974-81; dir. nat. field orgn. Hugh O'Brian Youth Fedn., L.A., 1981-84; pres. Vols. Am. Internat., L.A., 1984—. Author: (book) In the Wake of Death, 1996; inventor Marco Polo awards for China, , 1987, I Remember Mama (Nat. Mother's Day Tribute), Medallion of the Nile award for Egypt, Salute to Working Kids (Nat. Tribute). Office: Vols Am Internat 3600 Wilshire Blvd Ste 1500 Los Angeles CA 90010-2619

COSSITT, HELEN, poet; b. Miles City, Mont., May 18, 1931; d. Oscar and Gladys (Venable) Cain; m. Lester A. Cossitt, Dec. 14, 1952 (dec. Feb. 1996); 1 child, Carl A. Student, Billings (Mont.) Normal Coll., 1948-50. Author: (poetry books): Trail Thoughts, 1990, Trail Thoughts II, 1996.

COST, BETTYJO (BETTYJO COST-HANSEN), art gallery executive, agent, print distributor; b. Merced, Calif., June 3, 1931; d. James Doyle Byrd and Ethel (Fondren) Root; m. James Peter Cost, Apr. 17, 1957 (div. Oct. 1989); children: Shelley Anne Cost Chaffee, Nancy Cost Loose; m. Ronald Gene Hansen, Sept. 3, 1992; 1 child, Tylor. Student, Monterey Peninsula Coll., 1964—, Calif. State U., Long Beach, 1963. Owner, mgr. James Peter Cost Gallery, Carmel, Calif., 1964-89, Cost Gallery, Carmel, 1991—; print distbr. Cost & Co., Carmel, 1970—. Fund raiser for candidate Calif. Assembly, Monterey County, 1982. Mem. Jr. League Monterey Peninsula. Republican. Christian Scientist. Office: PO Box 3638 Carmel CA 93921-3638

COST, JAMES PETER, artist; b. Phila., Mar. 3, 1923; s. Peter and Rose (Perry) C.; children: Curtis, Shelley, Janet, Nancy. B.A., U. Calif. at Los Angeles, 1950; M.S., U. So. Calif., 1959. Tchr. art Los Angeles City Sch. Dist., 14 years; lectr. art Northwood Insts., Midland, Mich., Dallas, 1971; mem. faculty of art Principia Coll., 1975. One-man shows, Northwood Inst., Midland, 1971, R.W. Norton Gallery, Shreveport, La., 1971; exhibited in group shows at, Artists Guild Gallery Am., Carmel, 1961-63, James Peter Cost Gallery, (1964), Mus. Fine Arts, Springfield, Mass., 1965, 73, Nat. Arts Club, N.Y.C., 1966; represented in permanent collection, R.W. Norton Mus., Shreveport, also numerous pvt. collections; commd. 12 paintings for golf courses, Kobe, Osaka and Tokyo, Japan, 1986-87. Pres. Carmel Bus. Assn., 1970, Republican candidate for Calif. State Assembly, 1982. Served with USCGR, 1942-45. Recipient gold medal Franklin Mint, 1973. Republican. Christian Scientist. Studio: 85 Heaaula Pl Haiku HI 96708-5903 *Briefly and in reverse order of importance, the ideas, goals and standards necessary to ones success are: an over-all plan, a time line, religion, talent, hard work, self discipline, understanding, good friends and - most - important - constant improvement in work and all other aspects of life.*

COSTA, JOHN A., newspaper editor. Exec. editor Idaho Statesman, Boise. Office: 1200 N Curtis Rd Boise ID 83707

COSTA, JOHN ANTHONY, social services administrator; b. San Francisco, Oct. 20, 1946; s. Henry Milton and Martha Florence (Seineke) C. BA, San Francisco State Univ., 1969; student, George Washington Univ., 1969-73, Univ. San Francisco, 1987-88. Cert. legal asst., Pa. Analyst internat. rels. Libr. Congress Congl. Rsch. Svc., Washington, 1969-82; coord. Family Svc. Agy. San Mateo County, Burlingame, Calif., 1984—. Pres., v.p., sec. Bentana Park Condominium, Reston, Va., 1977-81; bd. dirs. St. Dunstan Sch., Millbrae, Calif., 1991-92. Mem. Internat. Studies Assn. (chpt. sec. 1970-71), Internat. Platform Assn., Worl Affairs Coun. No. Calif., Commonwealth Club San Francisco. Home: 2250 Shelter Creek Ln San Bruno CA 94066-6076 Office: Family Svc Agy 1870 El Camino Real Ste 107 Burlingame CA 94010-3107

COSTA, VINCENZO FRANCESCO, engineer; b. Santa Cruz, Calif., Jan. 7, 1956; s. Francesco Vincenzo Costa. BSME, U. Calif., Santa Barbara, 1980, MSME, 1981. Pres. Aluminum Unltd., Santa Clara, Calif., 1974-77; rider Cobar Racing, Sacramento, 1982-87; engr. Lockheed Missiles and Space Co., Sunnyvale, Calif., 1987-89; pres. Tigra, Milpitas, Calif., 1989—; explorer Triceratops Expeditions, Africa, 1982; cons. Mitek Med., San Jose, Calif., 1994; expert witness Boccada Law Firm, San Jose, 1986. Author: Suspension Set Up, 1990, Dinosaur Safari Guide, 1994, (photographs) Images from the Past, 1993; patentee in field. Recipient Most Creative Design award AIAA, 1981; Formula 1 Champion, AFM, 1985, 86, 750 Champion, AFM, 1985. Office: Tigra 449 Glenmoor Cir Milpitas CA 95035-2948

COSTA, WALTER HENRY, architect; b. Oakland, Calif., July 2, 1924; s. Walter H.F. and Mamie R. (Dunkle) C.; m. Jane Elisabeth Ledwich, Aug. 28, 1948; 1 dau., Laura. B.A., U. Calif., Berkeley, 1948, M.A., 1949. Designer Mario Corbett (architect), San Francisco, 1947-48, Ernst Born (architect), San Francisco, 1949; draftsman Milton Pflueger, San Francisco, 1950-51; designer Skidmore, Owings & Merrill, San Francisco, 1951-57, participating assoc., then assoc. prtnr., 1957-69, gen. prtnr., 1969-89, ret., 1990. Bd. dirs. East Bay Regional Park Dist., 1977-87, pres., 1984-85; mem. city council, Lafayette, Calif., 1972-76, mayor, 1973. Served with USSNR, 1943-46. Fellow AIA. Clubs: Olympic (San Francisco), Univ. (San Francisco), Lakeview (Oakland, Calif.). Home: 1264 Redwood Ln Lafayette CA 94549-2416 Office: Skidmore Owings & Merrill 333 Bush St San Francisco CA 94104-2806

COSTANZO, PATRICK M., constuction executive. Sr. v.p., asst. sec. Granite Constrn. Inc., Watsonville, Calif. Office: Granite Construction Inc PO Box 50085 Watsonville CA 95077-5085*

COSTA-ZALESSOW, NATALIA, foreign language educator; b. Kumanovo, Macedonia, Dec. 5, 1936; came to the U.S., 1951; d. Alexander P. and Katarina (Duric) Z.; m. Gustavo Costa, June 8, 1963; 1 child, Dora. BA in Italian, U. Calif., Berkeley, 1959, MA in Italian, 1961, PhD in Romance Langs. and Lits., 1967. Tchg. asst. U. Calif., Berkeley, 1959-63; instr. Mills Coll., Oakland, Calif., 1963; asst. prof. San Francisco (Calif.) State U., 1968-74, assoc. prof., 1974-79, prof., 1979—, coord. Italian program, 1992—. Author: Scrittrici italiane dal XIII al XX secolo, Testi e critica, 1982; editor: Anima, 1997; transl.: Her Soul, 1996; contbr. articles to profl. publs. Sidney M. Ehrman scholar U. Calif., Berkeley, 1957-58, Gamma Phi Beta scholar U. Calif., Berkeley, 1958, Herbert H. Vaughan scholar U. Calif., Berkeley, 1959-60, Advanced Grad. Traveling fellow in romance lang. and lit. U. Calif., Berkeley, 1964-65. Mem. MLA, Am. Assn. Tchrs. Italian, Renaissance Soc. Am., Dante Soc. Am., Croatian Acad. Am. Roman Catholic. Office: San Francisco State U Dept Fgn Lang and Lit San Francisco CA 94132

COSTEA, ILEANA, civil engineer, educator, consultant, researcher; b. Bucuresti, Romania, May 20, 1947; came to U.S., 1973.; d. Paul and Ana (Ciumetti) Paunescu; m. Nicolas Vincent Costea, Apr. 20, 1973. MArch, Ion Mincu Inst., Bucuresti, 1972; MA in Indsl. Design, UCLA, 1974, PhD in Engring., 1982. Chief teaching asst. UCLA, 1981; scientist ground systems analysis sect. Hughes Aircraft Co., Fullerton, Calif., 1982; lectr. dept. mgmt. sci. Sch. Bus. Adminstrn. Calif. State U., Northridge, 1982-83; cons. CAE Office vehicle engring. div. Aerospace Corp., El Segundo, Calif., 1984; sr. scientist, cons. Perceptronics, Inc., Woodland Hills, Calif., 1985; asst. prof. dept. civil and indsl. engring. Calif. State U., Northridge, 1983-86; cons. Jet Propulsion Lab. Calif. Inst. Tech., Pasadena, 1986-87, assoc. prof. dept. civil and indsl. engring. and mechanics, 1986-89, prof. dept. civil and indsl. engring. and applied mech., 1989—; vis. prof. U. Calif., Davis, 1980, U. Metz, France, 1989-93, U. Claude Bernard, Lyon, France, U. Metz, U. Catholique de l'Ouest, Angers. France, Inst. Français du Petrole, France, Rueil Malmaison, France, 1989-93, Ecole Centrale de Lille, France, U. Milan, Italy, 1990-91; vis. rschr. Social Sci. Rsch. Inst., U. So. Calif., 1982. Author: Artificial Intelligence/Expert Systems/CAD/CAM and Computer Graphics; contbr. articles to profl. jours.; reviewer for NSF and IEEE Computer jours. Recipient Merit award San Fernando Valley Engrs.' Coun., 1986. Mem. AAAS, IEEE (sec. Systems, Man and Cybernetics), AAUP, AIAA, Computer Soc. of IEEE, Nat. Computer Graphics Assn., Assn. for Computing Machinery, Inst. Mgmt. Sci., Ops. Rsch. Soc. Am., Calif. Faculty Assn., Am. Inst. for Decision Scis., Women in Sci. and Engring., Am. Assn. Artificial Intelligence, European Assn. for Computer Graphics, Am. Inst. Indsl. Engrs., Computer and Automated Systems Assn., Soc. Women Engrs. Home: 3651 Terrace View Dr Encino CA 91436-4019 Office: Calif State U 18111 Nordhoff St Northridge CA 91330-0001

COSTERTON, JOHN WILLIAM FISHER, microbiologist; b. Vernon, B.C., Can., July 21, 1934; married, 1955; 4 children. BA, U. B.C., 1955, MA, 1956; PhD in Microbiology, U. Western Ont., Can., 1960. Prof. biology Baring Union Christian Coll., Punjab, India, 1960-62, dean sci., 1963-64; fellow bot. Cambridge (Eng.) U., 1965; prof. assoc. microbiology McGill U., 1966-67, asst. prof., 1968-70; assoc. prof. U. Calgary, Alta., Can., 1970-75, prof. microbiology, 1975-93, indsl. rsch. chair biofilm microbiology, 1985-93; dir. Ctr. Biofilm Engring. Mont. State U., Bozeman, 1993—. Author 2 books on biofilms; contbr. more than 750 articles to profl. jours. Recipient Sir Frederick Haultain prize, 1985, Isaac Walton Killam prize, 1990. Mem. Can. Soc. Microbiology, Am. Soc. Microbiology. Office: Montana State Univ-Bozeman Ctr Biofilm Engineering 409 Cobleigh Hall Bozeman MT 59717

COTÉ, RALPH WARREN, JR., mining engineer, nuclear engineer; b. Berkeley, Calif., Oct. 5, 1927; s. Ralph Warren and Clara Maria (Neves) C.; m. Lois Lydia Maddox, Aug. 8, 1950; children: Ralph Warren III, Michele Marie. BSME, N.Mex. Inst. Mining and Tech., 1952. Registered profl. nuclear engr., Calif. Resident engr. Am. Smelting and Refining Co., Page, Idaho, 1952-54; shift boss Bunker Hill Co., Kellogg, Idaho, 1954-57, gen. mine foreman, 1958-60; project engr. Union Carbide Nuclear Co., Grand Junction, Colo., 1957-58; shift supr. GE, Richland, Wash., 1960-63; shift supr. GE, Vallecitos, Calif., 1963-66, maintenance mgr., 1966-67; start-up shift supr. GE, San Jose, Calif., 1967-71; project start-up mgr. Bechtel Power Corp., San Francisco, 1971-89. Served to 2d lt. U.S. Army and U.S. N.G., 1946-50. Mem. Am. Nuclear Soc., VFW. Republican. Home: 14610 W Sky Hawk Dr Sun City West AZ 85375-5925 Office: Bechtel Power Corp 50 Beale St San Francisco CA 94105-1813

COTE, RICHARD JAMES, pathologist, researcher; b. L.A., May 10, 1954; s. Richard Patrick and Kathrine (Bisbas) C.; m. Anne Louise Foxen, Feb. 8, 1992; children: Nicholas Foxen, Juliet Anne. BS in Biology, U. Calif., Irvine, 1976, BA in Chemistry, 1976; MD, U. Chgo., 1980. Diplomate Am. Coll. Pathologists. Intern in surgery U. Mich. Hosp., Ann Arbor, 1980-81; rsch. fellow, immunology Meml. Sloan-Kettering Cancer Ctr., N.Y.C., 1981-83; rsch. assoc., immunology Meml. Sloan-Kettering Hosp., N.Y.C., 1983-85, fellow, pathology, 1987-88, chief fellow, pathology, 1988-90; resident, pathology Cornell U. Med. Ctr., N.Y.C., 1985-87; asst. prof., pathology U. So. Calif., L.A., 1990-95, assoc. prof., 1995—; attending pathologist Kenneth Norris Cancer Ctr., L.A., 1990—; founder, dir. Impath, Inc., N.Y.C., 1987—; scientific dir. Neoprobe Corp., Columbus, Ohio, 1992—. Author: Immunomicroscopy, 1994; contbr. scientific papers to profl. jours., book chpts. Patentee in field. Am. Cancer Soc. fellow, 1988; recipient rsch. grants, awards NIH, ACS, others, 1981—. Mem. Soc. for Basic Urologic Rsch., Internat. Soc. for Hematotherapy, Phi Beta Kappa. Office: U So Calif 1441 Eastlake Ave Los Angeles CA 90033-1048

COTHERMAN, AUDREY MATHEWS, management and policy consultant, administrator; b. St. Paul, May 20, 1930; d. Anthony Joseph and Nina Grace (Harmon) Mathews; m. Richard Louis Cotherman, Dec. 30, 1950 (div. 1973); children: Steven, Michael, Bruce, Gen Elizabeth. BA, Hamline U., 1952; MA, U. Wyo., 1973, EdD, 1977. Communications coord. Natrona Sch. Dist., Casper, Wyo., 1968-69; hostess TV program KTWO-TV, Casper, 1970-71; exec. dir. United Way, Casper, 1971-73, Wyo. Coun. Humanities, Laramie, 1973-79; dep. state supt. Wyo. Dept. Edn., Cheyenne, 1979-90; devel. officer Coll. Edn. U. Wyo., Laramie, 1990-91; pres. Connections: Mgmt. and Policy Cons., Casper, 1991—; spl. asst. U.S. Dept. Edn. Region VIII, 1996—; exec. sec. Wyo. Bd. Edn., 1979-90; dir. comty. programs HSS, Cheyenne, 1986-90; cons. Wyo. Atty. Gen., Cheyenne, 1990; dealer Profiles, Internat. Dem. precinct chair, Laramie, 1986-90. State exec. policy fellow U.S. Dept. Edn., 1985. Mem. LWV (past pres. local chpts., Wyo. chpt.), Am. Assn. Pub. Adminstrs. (pres. 1987-88), Wyo. Assn. Pub. Adminstrs. (Pub. Adminstr. of Yr. 1982), Phi Delta Kappa. Presbyterian. Home. 1250 Galapago Apt 106 Denver CO 80204

COTTER, CORNELIUS PHILIP, political scientist, educator; b. N.Y.C., Mar. 18, 1924; s. Cornelius Joseph and Charlotte F. (Keller) C.; m. Rose Marie Ackerl, 1946 (div. 1961); children: Cornelia, Lawrence, Charles, Steven; m. Beverly Blair Cook, 1966; children: Linda, C. Randall, Gary A., Scott. BA, Stanford U., 1949; MPA, Harvard U., 1951, PhD, 1953. Asst., then assoc. prof. Stanford (Calif.) U., 1953-61; asst. to chmn. (on leave from Stanford U.) Rep. Nat. Com., Washington, 1958-60; asst. dir. U.S. Commn. Civil Rights, Washington, 1960-63; prof. polit. sci. Wichita (Kans.) State U., 1963-66; prof. polit. sci. U. Wis., Milw., 1966-89, prof. emeritus, 1989—; instr. Columbia Univ., N.Y.C., 1953-54. Author: Government and Private Enterprise, 1960; co-author: Powers of President During Crises, 1960, Politics Without Power, 1964, Party Organizations in Am. Politics, 1984, others. Disting. Univ. Prof., Univ. Bologna, Fulbright Found., 1988. Mem. Am. Polit. Sci. Assn., Midwest Polit. Sci. Assn. Republican. Home: 9040 Junipero Ave Atascadero CA 93422

COTTER, JOHN CATLIN, marketing consultant; b. Monterey Park, Calif., Apr. 3, 1950; s. Frank Cotter and Duncanne (Kilday) Tyson; children: Chris, Lisa. BS in Mktg., Ariz. State U., 1972. Promotion mgr. Gillcable, San Jose, Calif., 1982-85; mktg. dir. Stas. KSJO/KHTT, San Jose, 1985-87, Heritage Cablevision, San Jose, 1987-89; owner, mgr. The Cotter Media Group, advt. agy. and cons., Citrus Heights, Calif., 1989—.

COTTER, LAWRENCE RAFFETY, management consultant; b. Albany, Calif., Aug. 13, 1933; s. Malcolm Thompson Cotter and Una Elyse Raffety. AA, U. Calif., Berkeley, 1953, BA in Astronomy, 1956; MS in Bus. Adminstrn., The George Washington U., 1967; PhD in Mgmt. Theory, UCLA, 1977. Commd. 2nd lt. USAF, 1956, advanced through grades to col., 1975, ret., 1982; orbital analyst, network controller Project Space Track USAF, Bedford, Mass., 1958-61; staff scientist Hdqs. N.Am. Air Def. Command, Colorado Springs, Colo., 1962-66, Hdqrs. USAF, Washington, 1967-70; dir. test and deployment DEF. Support program USAF, Los Angeles, 1975-76; commdr. detachment 1 Electronic Systems Div. USAF, Tehran, Iran, 1976-78; system program dir. Electronic Systems div. USAF, Bedford, Mass., 1978-79; dep. commdr. network plans and devel. AF Satellite Control Facility USAF, Sunnyvale, Calif., 1979-82; mgmt. cons. Berkeley, 1982—; adminstrv. asst. Arnold Air Soc., Washington, 1959-72. Co-author: The Arnold Air Soc. Manual, 1956; (computer program) SPACE, 1970; editor: The Arnold Air Soc. Manual 1964-72. Recipient Departmental Citation U. Calif. Berkeley, 1955, Citation of Honor, Arnold Air Soc., 1967. Mem. AF Assn., The Royal AF Club, Beta Gamma Sigma.

COTTON, BARBARA LYNN, correctional health systems management consultant; b. St. Catharines, Ont., Can., Apr. 17, 1945; d. Ivan and Dorothy Rose (Manvil) Remely; m. Robert Lee Cotton, June 21, 1971 (div. Oct. 1979). ADN, Mont. State U., 1966, BSN, 1967; M of Health Svcs. Adminstrn., St. Marys Coll. of Calif., 1986. Instr. Bishop Clarkson Sch. Nursing, Omaha, 1971-74; discharge planning cons. Vis. Nurse Assn., Modesto, Calif., 1974-76; spl. projects officer Stanislaus County Med. Soc., Modesto, 1976-79; mgr. correctional programs Calif. Med. Assn., San Francisco, 1979-85; prin. Norman & Cotton Assocs., Lafayette, Calif., 1985-89; pres., owner The Cotton Group, Lafayette, 1989—; cons. Calif. Med. Assn., San Francisco, 1985—. Co-author, editor: Guidelines for Planning and Evaluating Jail Health Svcs., 1989. Capt. U.S. Army Nurse Corps, 1966-70. Mem. Am. Jail Assn., Am. Correctional Assn. (del. assembly 1989-91), Am. Correctional Health Svcs. Assn. (bd. dirs. 1981-93, v.p. 1985-87, pres. 1989-91, Disting. Svc. award 1994). Home: 669 Sky Hy Cir Lafayette CA 94549-5228 Office: The Cotton Group PO Box 1307 Lafayette CA 94549-1307

COTTON, KATHLEEN LAURA, financial planner; b. Camas, Wash., Dec. 20, 1940; d. Charles Herschel Miller and Gladys Louise (Bundy) Miller Coffey; m. David Cotton, July 15, 1970 (div. 1979); children: Laura Suzanne Cotton Nelson, Stephen Ross Nelson, Thomas Charles; m. Leon Franssen, Mar. 25, 1989. BS with honors, City U., Bellevue, Wash., 1981; Cert. Fin. Planner, Coll. Fin. Planning, 1984. Fin. planner Painter Fin. Group, Bellevue, 1982-83; owner, fin. planner MoneyWorks, Bellevue, 1983-85; fin. cons. Old Stone Savs. & Loan, Seattle, 1985-86; adj. faculty City U., 1985—; prin. Cotton & Heffelfinger Ind. Cert. Fin. Planners, Seattle, 1988-92, Equitable Solutions, 1990—; ptnr. Cotton & Paysse, Inc., Lynnwood, Wash., 1993-96; fin. planner Cotton Fin. Advisors Inc., Lynnwood, 1996—. Author: Financial Planning for the Not Yet Wealthy, 1987, Keys to Controlling Your Financial Destiny, 1990, Spend Your Way to Wealth, 1992, Financial Planning from We to Me, 1996. Mem. Puget Sound Assn. Pre-Divorce Cons. (founder, pres. 1989-90), Internat. Assn. Fin. Planning (pres. 1988-89), Interant. Soc. Retirement Planning, Inst. Cert. Fin. Planners, Nat. Assn. Pers. Fin. Advisors. Episcopalian. Office: Cotton Fin Advisors 4232 198th St SW Ste 200 Lynnwood WA 98036-6736

COTTRELL, ROBERT CHARLES, history educator; b. Denver, Colo., Nov. 1, 1950; s. Robert and Sylvia (Light) C.; m. Susan Lou Phillips Cottrell, Aug. 12, 1989; 1 child, Jordan Alexandra. BA with honors, U. Tex., 1973; MA, U. Tex., Arlington, 1977; PhD, U. Okla., 1983; JD, Calif. No. Sch. Law, Chico, 1995. Instr. U. Okla., Norman, 1983-84; asst. prof. Calif. State U., Chico, 1984-89, assoc. prof., 1989-94, prof. History and Am. Studies, 1994—; adj. prof. of History Okla. City. C. C., 1980-84. Author: Izzy: A Biography of I.F. Stone, 1993, The Social Gospel of E. Nicholas Comfort: Founder of the Oklahoma School of Religion, 1997; contbr. articles to profl. jours., essays to books. Grantee Am. Philos. Soc., 1993, 96; recipient Muriel H. Wright award Okla. State Hist. Soc., 1984, Calif. State U. profl. achievement award, 1994, rsch. award, 1994; NEH summer stipend. Mem. Ogrn. Am. Historians, Phi Alpha Theta. Democrat. Jewish. Office: Calif State U Dept of History Chico CA 95929-0735

COUCH, JOHN CHARLES, diversified company executive; b. Bremerton, Wash., May 10, 1939; s. Richard Bailey and Frances Harriet (Gilmore) C. BS in Engring., U. Mich., 1963, MS, 1964; MBA, Stanford U., 1976. With Ingalls Shipbldg. div. Litton Industries, 1967-74; asst. to sr. v.p. engring. and marine ops. Matson Navigation Co. subs. Alexander and Baldwin., San Francisco, 1976-78; v.p. Matson Navigation Co., 1978-84; exec. v.p., chief operating officer Matson Navigation Co. subs. Alexander and Baldwin., San Francisco, 1984; pres., chief operating officer Matson Navigation Co., 1985, Alexander and Baldwin Inc., Honolulu, 1991—; pres., chief exec. officer Alexander and Baldwin, Inc., Honolulu, 1992-95, chmn., pres., CEO, 1995—; bd. dirs. A&B Devel. Co., Calif., A&B Properties, Inc., East Maui Irrigation Co., Ltd., Kahului Trucking & Storage, Inc., McBryde Sugar Co., Ltd., Ohanui Corp., WDCI Inc., Calif. and Hawaiian Sugar Co., First Hawaiian Bank, First Hawaiian Inc., Hawaiian Sugar Transp. Co., Inc., A&B Hawaii, Inc., Alexander & Baldwin, Inc., McBryde Farms, Inc., Kauai Comml. Co., Inc., Kukuiula Devel. Co., Inc., Matson Navigation Co., Inc., South Shore Community Svcs., Inc., South Shore Resources, Inc. Mem. Maui Econ. Devel. Bd., 1986—; mem. exec. bd. Aloha coun. Boy Scouts Am., 1986—; bd. dirs. Aloha United Way, 1988, campaign chmn., 1988, chmn. bd. dirs. Mem. Hawaiian Sugar Planters' Assn. (bd. dirs.), C. of C. of Hawaii (bd. dirs. 1986—), Hawaii Maritime Ctr. (vice-chmn. 1988-89, chmn. 1990—), Honolulu Club, Oahu Country Club, Plaza Club. Office: Alexander & Baldwin Inc PO Box 3440 822 Bishop St Honolulu HI 96813-3925

COUGHENOUR, JOHN CLARE, federal judge; b. Pittsburg, Kans., July 27, 1941; s. Owren M. and Margaret E. (Widner) C.; m. Gwendolyn A. Kieffaber, June 1, 1963; children: Jeffrey, Douglas, Marta. B.S., Kans. State Coll., 1963; J.D., U. Iowa, 1966. Bar: Iowa 1963, D.C. 1963, U.S. Dist. Ct. (we. dist.) Wash. 1966. Ptnr. Bogle & Gates, Seattle, 1966-81; vis. asst. prof. law U. Washington, Seattle, 1970-73; judge U.S. Dist. Ct. (we. dist.) Wash., Seattle, 1981—. Mem. Iowa State Bar Assn., Wash. State Bar Assn. Home: 2122 E Shore Ave Freeland WA 98249-9595 Office: US Dist Ct US Courthouse 1010 5th Ave Seattle WA 98104-1130*

COULTER, CHRISTOPHER HARVEY, physician, healthcare executive; b. Rahway, N.J., Feb. 23, 1952; s. Harvey Franklin and Doris Lillian (Collins) C. BA, Yale U., 1974; MD, U. Va., 1978; MPH, Johns Hopkins U., 1988. Diplomate Am. Bd. Internal Medicine, Am. Bd. Geriatrics, Am. Bd. Med. Mgmt. Intern, resident Georgetown Univ. Hosp., Washington, 1978-81; attending physician Bon Secours Hosp., Balt., 1981-87; med. dir. Schick Shadel Hosp., Santa Barbara, Calif., 1987-89, FHP, Fountain Valley, Calif., 1989-91; CEO UltraLink, Costa Mesa, Calif., 1991—; surveyor Nat. Com. for Quality Assurance, Washington, 1993—. Mem. editorial bd. Managed Care Medicine, 1994; contbr. articles to profl. jours. Fellow Am. Coll. Physician Execs. Democrat. Office: UltraLink 535 Anton Blvd Ste 900 Costa Mesa CA 92626

COULTER, DAVID A., bank executive; b. Pitts.; married;. B in Math., Carnegie-Mellon U., M in Indsl. Adminstrn. Fin. cons., then mem. world banking, treasury and corp. planning divsns., pres. BankAmerica Corp., San Francisco, 1976—, past head U.S. Corp. Group divsn., past head U.S. and Internat. Groups divsn., chmn., CEO; pres., CEO Bank of Am. NT & SA; bd. dirs. BankAmerica, Bank of Am., chmn. operating policy com., mng. com.; bd. dirs. Pacific Gas and Electric Corp., Local Initiatives Support Corp., Joint Venture Silicon Valley Netword Bd., Inst. Internat. Fin. Inc. Active U. Calif. San Diego Grad. Sch. Internat. Rels., Pacific Studies Adv. Bd., Opportunity Capital Ptnrs. II, LP Adv. Com., Bay Area Coun.; bd. dirs. San Francisco Art Inst., San Francisco Zoo. Soc., Fine Arts Muss. San Francisco, Am. Cancer Soc. Office: BankAmerica Corp 555 California St San Francisco CA 94104

COULTER, GEORGE PROTHRO, retired lawyer, real estate executive; b. El Dorado, Ark., June 8, 1930; s. Edward Herbert Sr. and Estella Martha (Prothro) C.; m. Gloria Phyllis Cohn, Dec. 28, 1952; children: Craig R., Christopher N., Cameron M. AB, UCLA, 1951; JD, George Washington U., 1957; postgrad., U. So. Calif., 1958-59. With Nat. Security Agy., Washington, 1955-57; assoc. Gordon & Weinberg, L.A., 1958-63; ptnr. Coulter & Coulter, L.A., 1963-68; prin. Coulter, Vernoff & Pearson, Pasadena, Calif., 1968-94, of counsel, 1982-94; CEO Parade Properties, Inc., L.A., 1965-84; gen. ptnr. Welsh Hill Orgn., Temecula Valley, 1980—; cons. CLE, State Bar of Calif., 1982-83;. Pres., trustee Neighborhood Improvement Assn., Altadena, Calif., 1980-82; trustee Westminster Ctr., Pasadena, 1982—, pres., 1992; bd. dirs. Altadena Heritage, 1992-95; trustee House of Rest Found., 1992-95. Lt. USN, 1951-56, Korea. Mem. Nat. Genealogical Soc., Honourable Soc. Cymmrodorion, Assn. Profl. Genealogists, Soc. Genealogists. Presbyterian. Home: 589 Cocopan Dr Altadena CA 91001-4012

COULTER, JOHN ARTHUR, academic administrator; b. Buffalo, N.Y., July 24, 1944; s. William David and Myra Elizabeth (Murray) C.; m. Ann Ahrens, July 4, 1966; children: Jennifer, Kelly, Amanda. BS, SUNY, Buffalo, 1967, MBA, 1975. Asst. to chmn. dept. physics SUNY, Buffalo, 1967-69, asst. dean Sch. of Pharmacy, 1969-73; asst. dean/adminstr./dir admissions SUNY, 1973-75; asst./assoc. dean medicine SUNY, Stony Brook, 1975-79; asst. v.p. health scis. U. Wash, Seattle, 1979-83, assoc. v.p. health scis.,

1983-92; exec. dir. health scis adminstn./assoc. v.p. for med. affairs U. Wash., Seattle, 1992—. Bd. dirs. Cmty. Health Plan of Suffolk, N.Y., 1978-79, Wash. Assn. for Biomed. Rsch., Seattle, 1988-96, Nat. Assn. for Biomed. Rsch., 1996, Poison Control Ctr., Seattle, 1994—; active United Way Leadership Tomorrow, C. of C., Seattle, 1985. Mem. Am. Assn. Med. Colls., Assn. Acad. Health Scis. Ctrs. Office: Univ Wash Health Scis Ctr Box 356355 Seattle WA 98195

COUNELIS, JAMES STEVE, education educator; b. Streator, Ill., June 26, 1927; s. Steve and Mary (Drivas) C.; m. Anna Catherine Marakas, Nov. 25, 1962; children: Steven George, George James. AA, Chgo. City Jr. Coll., 1948; AM, U. Chgo., 1951, PhD, 1961. Cert. high sch., jr. coll. tchr., pub. sch. principal, Ill. High sch. tchr. Chgo. Pub. Schs., 1951-55; asst. prof. history and social scis. Chgo. City Jr. Coll., Woodrow Wilson br., 1955-62, dir. evening program, 1962-64; asst. prof. edn. Chgo Tchrs. Coll., 1964-66; assoc. prof. edn. Pa. State U., University Park, 1966-67; sr. adminstrv. analyst U. Calif., Berkeley, 1968-70; prof. edn. U. San Francisco, 1970—, dir. instl. studies and mgmt. info. systems, 1971-75, coord. evaluation Sch. Edn., 1986-90, chmn. orgn. and leadership program, 1989-91. Author, editor: To Be A Phoenix: The Education Professoriate, 1969; author: Higher Learning and Orthodox Christianity, 1990, Inheritance and Change in Orthodox Christianity, 1995; contbr. articles, revs. and papers to profl. publs. pres., trustee Greek Orthodox Cathedral of the Ascension, Oakland, Calif., 1973; pres. Hellenic Am. Profl. Soc., San Francisco, 1974, 75; trustee tenure Hellenic Coll./Holy Cross, 1951-53, trustee, 1982-86; mem. Calif. Council on Criminal Justice, 1987; bd. dirs. Paul Wattson Lecture series, 1989. Served with Signal Corps, U.S. Army, 1946-47. Recipient Archon Chartoularius (honoris causa) award Ecumenical Patriarchate Constantinople and New Rome, 1976, Norbert Wiener award The World Orgn. Gen. Systems and Cybernetics, 1978, Scholar U. Chgo., 1951-52, 60-61, Pacific Sch. Religion, 1958; U. Calif. grantee, Berkeley, 1962; Coolidge Rsch. fellow Andover-Newton Theol. Sch., 1985, Wayne J. Doyle Rsch. award, 1986, Hellenic Coun. on Edn. award for scholarship and univ. teaching, 1991. Mem. AAAS, Am. Assn. Artificial Intelligence, Am. Assn. Higher Edn., Am. Assn. Instnl. Rsch., Am. Ednl. Rsch. Assn., Am. Ednl. Studies Assn., Internat. Soc. System Scis., Hellenic Am. Profl. Soc. (Axion award 1982), Hellenic Coun. on Edn. (award for Scholarship and University Teaching 1991), Orthodox Theol. Soc. Am., U. San Francisco Faculty Assn., Mensa, Gold Key, Phi Delta Kappa (U. San Francisco chpt. v.p. for programs 1990-91, pres. 1991-92). Office: U San Francisco Sch Edn San Francisco CA 94117-1080

COUNSELL, ANN BERNER, academic administrator; b. Chgo., Aug. 2, 1960; d. Carl Frederick and Rosemary (Davis) B.; m. Richard Clay Counsell, Sept. 7, 1992; 1 child, Alyson Rose. Student, U. London, 1981; BA, Whitman Coll., 1982; MS, U. Oreg., 1988. Chpt. cons. Kappa Alpha Theta, Indpls., 1982-83; resident counselor Kappa Alpha Theta, Providence, R.I., 1983-84; asst. to the dean of students U. Oreg., Eugene, 1984-88; acting dir. of devel. Eastside Cath. High Sch., Bellevue, Wash., 1988-89; dir. devel. Forest Ridge Sch., Bellevue, 1989-90; assoc. v.p. for devel. Whitman Coll., Walla Walla, Wash., 1990-92; dir. of devel. Villa Acad., Seattle, Wash., 1992—. Mem. PEO, Bellevue, 1981-85, Eugene, 1985-88; vol. Whitman Coll. Admissions, Redmond, Wash., 1988-90, Make-A-Wish Found., Seattle, 1991-92. Mem. Kappa Alpha Theta Seattle Alumnae Assn. (Ann D. Bern award 1984, adv. bd. 1989-90), N.W. Devel. Officers Assn. Home: 6019 143rd Ct NE Redmond WA 98052-4674 Office: Villa Acad 5001 NE 50th Seattle WA 98105

COUNSIL, WILLIAM GLENN, electric utility executive; b. Detroit, Dec. 13, 1937; s. Glenn Dempsey and Jean Beverly (Rzepecki) C.; m. Donna Elizabeth Robinson, Sept. 10, 1960; children: Glenn, Craig. Student, U. Mich., 1955-56; BS, U.S. Naval Acad., 1960; Advanced Mgmt. Program, Harvard U., 1991. Ops. supr., asst. plant supt.. sta. supt. N.E. Nuclear Energy Co., Waterford, Conn., 1967-76; project mgr., v.p. nuclear engring. and ops. N.E. Utilities, Hartford, Conn., 1976-80, sr. v.p. nuclear engring. and ops., 1980-85; exec. v.p. nuclear engring. and ops., electric-generating div. Tex. Utilities Generating Co., 1985-88; vice chmn. Tex. Utilities Electric Co., 1989-93; mng. dir. Wash. Pub. Power Supply System, Richland, 1993-96. With USN, 1956-67. Recipient Outstanding Leadership award ASME, 1986. Republican. Presbyterian. *My goal has been to improve our quality of life first through service in the United States Navy and second by ensuring an adequate and safe energy supply for our country.*

COURT, ARNOLD, climatologist; b. Seattle, June 20, 1914; s. Nathan Altshiller and Sophie (Ravitch) C.; m. Corinne H. Feibelman, May 27, 1941 (dec. Feb. 1984); children: David, Lois, Ellen; m. Mildred Futor Berry, Apr. 6, 1988. BA, U. Okla., 1934; postgrad., U. Wash., 1938, MS, 1949; PhD, U. Calif., Berkeley, 1956. Reporter and city editor Duncan (Okla.) Banner, 1935-38; observer, meteorologist U.S. Weather Bur., Albuquerque, Washington, Little Am., Los Angeles, 1938-43; chief meteorologist U.S. Antarctic Service, 1939-41; climatologist office Q.M. Gen. U.S. Army, Washington, 1946-51; research meteorologist U. Calif., Berkeley, 1951-56; meteorologist U.S. Forest Service, Berkeley, 1956-60; chief applied climatology, Cambridge Research Labs. USAF, Bedford, Mass., 1960-62; sr. scientist Lockheed-Calif. Co., Burbank, 1962-65; prof. climatology San Fernando Valley State Coll. (now Calif. State U.), Northridge, 1962-85, chmn. dept. geography, 1970-72, prof. emeritus, 1985—; part-time prof. Calif. State U., Northridge, 1986-87, UCLA, 1987-90. Editor: Eclectic Climatology, 1968; assoc. editor Jour. Applied Meteorology, 1978-88; chmn. editorial bd. Jour. Weather Modification, 1978-86; contbr. articles and revs. to profl. jours. Served to 1st lt. USAAF, 1943-46. Recipient Spl. Congl. medal, 1944. Fellow AAAS, Am. Meteorol. Soc., Royal Meteorol. Soc.; mem. Am. Geophys. Union (life), Am. Statis. Assn., Assn. Am. Geographers, Assn. Pacific Coast Geographers (pres. 1978-79), Calif. Geog. Soc., Weather Modification Assn. (trustee 1973-76), Western Snow Conf., Sigma Xi, Phi Beta Kappa. Home: 17168 Septo St Northridge CA 91325-1672 Office: Calif State U Dept Geography Northridge CA 91330

COURTNEY, MARY E., writer, editor; b. Dallas, May 3, 1955; d. John Francis and Ellen Mary (O'Connell) C.; m. Paul A. Messick, Nov. 22, 1990. BA in English, U. Tex., 1977; MEd in Internat. Edn., U. Mass., 1985; MA in English and Creative Writing, So. Meth. U., 1994. Tng. dir. Greater Dallas Coun. on Alcholism and Drug Abuse, 1988-90; asst. event coord. Shakespeare World Congress, L.A., 1995-96; tchr., trainer Futurekids, Manhattan Beach, Calif., 1997—; website prodr., L.A., 1996—; freelance editor, writer, rschr., 1987—. Curator, author exhibit catalog Visionaries and Rebels: Ameican Literature After the Atom Bomb, 1995. AIDS trainer in schs. AIDS Project L.A., 1996—; bd. dirs. Celiac Found., Studio City, Calif., 1996—. Home: 626 Santa Monica Blvd Ste 80 Santa Monica CA 90401-2538

COURTRIGHT, MORRIS, electrical engineer and educator; b. Saginaw, Mich., May 2, 1930; s. Morris Alexander and Helen Esther (Gould) C.; m. Phyllis Joanne Jones, Mar. 2, 1952 (div. Mar. 1988); children: Helen, Patricia, Pamela, Mike, Deborah, Elaine, Eileen, David, Kathy, Gregory, Brenda; m. Barbara Jean Grzeczka, Aug. 15, 1989. BSEE, U. Colo., 1963; MSEE, Columbia Pacific Coll., San Rafael, Calif., 1986, PhD, 1987. Registered profl. engr., Ariz., N.Mex. Commd. 2d lt. USAF, 1956, advanced through grades to maj., 1966; cons. engr. Phoenix, Ariz., 1970—; tchr. Gateway Cmty. Coll., Phoenix, 1983-94, Eastern Ariz. Coll., Payson, 1994-95. Author/editor Broadcast Engring., 1968-76. Rep. Ariz. State Legis., Phoenix, 1979-82. Decorated Air Force Commendation medal; recipient Dept. of Def. Commendation, 1965. Mem. Soc. Broadcast Engrs. (nat. dir.), Assn. Fed. Comms. Cons. Engrs., Nat. Assn. Elec. Inspectors, Elks (sec. 1986—), KC (state dep.). Republican. Roman Catholic. Home and Office: 612 6th Ave San Manuel AZ 85631-9701

COUSE, R. D., construction company executive; b. 1947. BSME, Wash. State U. With Bechtel Constrn. Co., San Francisco, 1969—; now pres. Bechtel Constrn. Co., Gaithersburg. Office: Bechtel Construction Co 9801 Washingtonian Blvd Gaithersburg MD 20878-5356*

COUSINEAU, PHILIP ROBERT, writer, filmmaker; b. Columbia, S.C., Nov. 26, 1952; s. Stanley Horace and Rosemary Marie (La Chance) C.; 1 child, Jack Philip Blue Beaton-Cousineau. BA cum laude, U. Detroit, 1974. Writer-in residence Shakespeare and Co. Bookstore, Paris, 1987; script judge Bay Guardian Scriptwriting Contest, 1987-89; judge Nat. Ednl. Film and Video Festival, 1990; mem. adv. bd. Joseph Campbell Archives and Libr., 1991—; documentary film judge Emmy Awards, 1992; dir. mythological tours Joseph Campbell Found., 1993-96; documentary judge San Francisco Film Festival, 1993-95. Author: Deadlines, 1991, UFOs: Manual for the Millenium, 1995, Portugese edit., 1996, German edit., 1997, Soul Moments: Marvelous Stories from the World of Synchronicity, 1997; editor; The Hero's Journey: Joseph Campbell on His Life and Work, 1990, Portuguese edit., 1995, The Soul of the World, 1993 (Quality Paperback Book Club selection 1993, Book of Yr. award Contemporary Photography 1994), Soul: An Archaeology, 1994, Chinese edit., 1997, Prayers at 3 A.M., 1995, Design Outlaws, 1997, The Book of Roads, 1997; co-dir., screenwriter documentary films The Peyote Road, 1993 (best documentary award Gt. Plains Film Festival, Bronze Telly award, silver award Chgo. Film Festival, award Mill Valley Film Festival), Ecological Design, 1994; co-writer The 1932 Ford V888, Silverado Prodns., 1986, The Presence of the Goddess, Balcorman Films, 1987, (film) Eritrea: A Portrait of the Eritrean People, 1989; co-writer video Wiping the Tears of Seven Generations, 1991 (Best Video award Am. Indian Film Festival, Silver Telly award, Gold Apple award Nat. Ednl. Film Festival; co-writer, assoc. prodr. The Hero's Journey: The World of Joseph Campbell, 1987 (Silver Apple award Ednl. Film and Video Festival); co-writer film Forever Activists: Stories from the Veterans of the Abraham Lincoln Brigade, 1990 (Acad. Award nomination, jury prize San Francisco Film Festival), also others. Trustee Native Land Found., 1993-96. Recipient award Nat. Assn. Ind. Pubs., 1991; fellow Calif. Inst. Integral Studies, 1991-95. Office: Harper San Francisco Pubs 1160 Battery San Francisco CA 94111

COUTURE, RICHARD EDMUND, tax auditor; b. Bay City, Mich., Nov. 30, 1950; s. Alfred Daniel Sr. and Florence Elaine (Beaumont) C. Student, Northeastern Sch. Commerce, 1970; BS in Acctg., Ferris State U., 1972. Acct. Victor H. Arida & Co., Tucson, 1973-75; field auditor I City of Tucson, 1975-76, field auditor II, 1976-79, field auditor III, 1979-88, prin. auditor, 1988—. Mem. Am. Coaster Enthusiasts. Home: 1710 S Kevin Dr Tucson AZ 85748-7454 Office: City of Tucson 255 W Alameda St Tucson AZ 85701-1303

COUVILLION, KENNETH PAUL, accountant; b. Baton Rouge, Jan. 2, 1943; s. Lindsey Joseph and Doneta (Deering) C.; m. Jean Ann Wood, Apr. 16, 1966; children: Karen Lynn, Mark Alan. BS, Calif. State U., Northridge, 1966; MBA, Pepperdine U., Malibu, Calif., 1976; EdD, U. So. Calif., L.A., 1995. CPA, Calif. CFO Hometown Enterprises, Stockton, Calif., 1978-84; acct. Stockton, 1976—; prof. San Joaquin Delta Coll., Stockton, 1976—; fin. advisor Sr. Citizens of Stockton, 1996. Res. police officer Stockton Police Dept., 1983-92. With U.S. Army, 1966-68. Mem. AICPA, Calif. Soc. CPAs, Aircraft Owner's and Pilot's Assn. Republican. Office: 2155 W March Ln Ste 3E Stockton CA 95207-6420

COVELL, RUTH MARIE, medical educator, medical school administrator; b. San Francisco, Aug. 12, 1936; d. John Joseph and Mary Carolyn (Coles) Collins; m. James Wachob Covell, 1963 (div. 1972); 1 child, Stephen; m. Harold Joachim Simon, Jan. 4, 1973; 1 child, David. Student, U. Vienna, Austria, 1955-56; BA, Stanford U., 1958; MD, U. Chgo., 1962. Clin. prof. and assoc. dean sch. medicine U. Calif. San Diego, La Jolla, 1969—; dir. Acad. Geriatric Resource Ctr.; bd. dirs. Calif. Coun. Geriatrics and Gerontology, Beverly Found., Pasadena, Alzheimer's Family Ctr., San Diego, San Diego Epilepsy Soc., Devel. Svcs. Inc., San y Sidro Health Ctr., NIH SBIR Stude Sect. Geriatrics; cons. Agy. Health Care Policy and Rsch. Contbr. articles on health planning and quality of med. care to profl. jours. Mem. AMA, Am. Health Svcs. Rsch., Assn. Tchrs. Preventive Medicine, Am. Pub. Health Assn., Assn. Am. Med. Colls. Group on Instl. Planning (chair 1973-74, sec. 1983-84), Phi Beta Kappa, Alpha Omega Alpha. Home: 1604 El Camino Del Teatro La Jolla CA 92037-6338 Office: U Calif San Diego Sch Medicine M-002 La Jolla CA 92093

COVINGTON, B(ATHILD) JUNE, business owner, advocate; b. Butte, Mont., June 21, 1950; d. Joe Talmage Covington Sr. and Betty Lou (Jones) Tomlinson; m. Mark Halsey Stephens, Aug. 2, 1969 (div. 1982); children: Mark Halsey Jr., Kimm Covington Stephens; m. James Bradford Hams, Feb. 20, 1987 (div. 1994); 1 stepchild, Brent Keir Mulvaney. Student, So. Utah State U., 1968-69, Indian Valley Colls., 1981-83. Advt. asst. McPhail's, Inc., San Rafael, Calif., 1973-75; mgr. Clothes Factory, San Francisco, 1976; graphic designer Press Rm. Printing, Redding, Calif., 1977; co-owner Player's Choice Retail Store, Redding, 1978-80; with advt. and in-house display dept. Indian Valley Colls. Book Store, Novato, Calif., 1981-82; advt. mgr. part-time Heritage Homes Realty, Novato, 1983-87; interior design asst., graphic designer, project coord. Ruth Livingston Interior Design, Tiburon, Calif., 1983-85, 87; project mgr., spl. needs design div. head Potter & Co. Builders, Richmond, Calif., 1987-88; owner, prin. CDT Assocs., Novato, 1988—; dir. ops. Tilia, Inc., San Francisco, 1989-92; master's candidate advisor Acad. Art Coll., San Francisco, 1989—; pvt. practice cons. sexual abuse, No. Calif., 1982—; instr. tng. seminars on social issues, internt. bus. ops. and procedures at colls., univs. and pub. agys., No. Calif., 1982—; prin. Friends Affecting Cohesive Efforts for Intervention and Treatment, Novato, 1991—; pub. rels. for Voices Unheard, San Francisco, 1994; mem. Action Against Sexual Violence, San Francisco, 1993. Co-producer video documentary Victims of Incest: The Price They Pay, 1983, Surviving Incest: A Path to the Future, 1988; producer video pilot program Straight From the Lip, 1985, We are 68, 1988; producer, editor photo essay and exhibit FACE IT, 1991—; contbr. articles to profl. jours. Mem. maj. gifts com. Novato Human Needs Ctr., 1988; foster parent Marin County Social Svcs., San Rafael, 1983-84; pub. speaker Ind. and Parents United, Calif., 1982—; sponsor Sexual Abuse Survivors, Marin County, 1988-89; mem. exec. com., adv. bd. and edn. com. Sexual Assault Prevention Agy., No. Calif., 1991—; bd. dirs. Survivorship, 1993—; co-founder Healing Kidz, Inc., San Francisco, 1992, v.p. bd. dirs.; co-producer Kicked-Up, an internat. portfolio featuring at-risk and homeless youth. Coll. of Marin Found. scholar, 1983; Marin Community Colls. grantee, 1983, 88. Mem. Hospitality Industry Assn. (co-chair philanthropy com. San Francisco chpt. 1988-89, chair, fundraiser San Francisco chpt. 1988-89), Parents United of Marin County (chair interior design com. 1987-89, bd. dirs., v.p., chair edn. com. 1989—). Democrat. Home: #D108-217 5932 W Bell Rd Glendale AZ 85308

COVINGTON, FRANCIS A., marketing executive; b. Chgo.; m. Deborah Coleman; 1 child, Devin; children from previous marriage: Francis III, Kaywanna, Shawntel. BA in Mktg., Calif. State U., Dominguez Hills, 1974; postgrad., South Bay Sch. Law, 1974-77. Cert. disaster recovery cons. and project mgr. Sr. account exec. Levi Strauss & Co., L.A., 1978-82; regional sales mgr. IBM/OZALID Corp., L.A., 1982-84, Terak Corp., L.A., 1984-85, David Jamison Carlyle Corp., L.A., 1985-86; br. mgr. Project Software & Devel., Inc., Newport Beach, Calif., 1986-88; regional sales mgr. SunGard Disaster Recovery Svcs., L.A., 1988-93; sales mgr. network solutions Boole & Babbage Software, L.A., 1993-94; v.p. sales and mktg. western region Seagate Software Storage Mgmt., L.A., 1994—; exec. bd. officer WICODA Leather Goods Co., 1993—; exec. bd. officer Home Alone Programs-Corp. Decisions, 1995—. Pres. Ingelwood (Calif.) Child Devel. Ctr. PTA, 1975; mem. Image award com. NAACP, Beverly Hills, Calif., 1991, 92, 93. Home: PO Box 7000-168 Palos Verdes CA 90274

COVINGTON, ROBERT EDWARD, mining executive, geologist; b. Waterloo, Iowa, Mar. 24, 1921; s. Rex and Jeanne Marie Stephens C. BA in Geology, U Colo., 1947. Geologist Phillips Petroleum Co., Alvin, Tex., 1947, Carter Oil Co., Vernal, Utah, 1948-49; cons. and ptnr. Caldwell & Covington, Vernal, 1949-64; sec.-treas., mgr. exploration Hiko Bell Mining & Oil Co., Vernal, 1964—. Contbr. articles to profl. jours. With USN, 1942-45. Fellow AAAS; mem. Am. Inst. Profl. Geologists, Am. Assn. Petroleum Geologists, Geol. Soc. Am., Sigma Gamma Epsilon. Office: Hiko Bell Mining & Oil Co PO Box 1845 Vernal UT 84078-5845

COWAN, GEORGE ARTHUR, chemist, bank executive, director; b. Worcester, Mass., Feb. 15, 1920; s. Louis Abraham and Anna (Listic) C.; m. Helen Dunham, Sept. 9, 1946. BS, Worcester Poly. Inst., 1941; DSc, Carnegie-Mellon U., 1950. Research asst. Princeton U., 1941-42, U. Chgo., 1942-45; mem. staff Columbia U., N.Y.C., 1945; mem. staff, dir. rsch., sr. fellow Los Alamos (N.Mex.) Sci. Lab., 1945-46, 49-88, sr. fellow emeritus, 1988—; teaching fellow Carnegie Mellon U., Pitts., 1946-49; chmn. bd. dirs. Trinity Capital Corp., Los Alamos, 1974-95; pres. Santa Fe Inst., 1984-91; mem. The White House Sci. Coun., Washington, 1982-85, cons., 1985-90, Air Force Tech. Applications Ctr., 1952-88; chmn. Los Alamos Nat. Bank, 1965-94; bd. dirs. Title Guaranty, Inc., Universal Properties, inc. Contbr. sci. articles to profl. jours. Bd. dirs. Santa Fe Opera, 1964-79; treas. N.Mex. Opera Found., Santa Fe, 1970-79; regent N.Mex. Inst. Tech. Socorro, 1972-75; bd. dirs. N.Am. Inst., Santa Fe Inst., Coalition for Quality TV, Nat. Ctr. for Genomes Resources. Recipient E.O. Lawrence award, 1965, Disting. Scientist award N.Mex. Acad. Sci., 1975, Robert H. Goddard award Worcester Poly. Inst., 1984, Enrico Fermi award, Presdl. Citation, Dept. Energy, 1990. Fellow AAAS, Am. Phys. Soc.; mem. Am. chem. Soc., N.Mex. Acad. Sci., Sigma Xi. Home: 721 42nd St Los Alamos NM 87544-1804 Office: Santa Fe Inst 1399 Hyde Park Rd Santa Fe NM 87501-8943

COWAN, JAMES CORNELIUS, security firm executive; b. Little Rock, June 28, 1929; s. George Thomas and Willie Francis (Thomas) C.; m. Elnora Aileen Mattison, Aug. 9, 1950; children: John Frederick, Evelyn Dianne, Kathryn Dianne. MS in Adminstrn., Calif. State U., Carson, 1979; PhD in Mgmt., Calif. Coast U., 1996. Cert. pvt. patrol operator, Calif. Bur. Consumer Affairs; life designated tchg. credential in security and law enforcement, Calif. Sr. materials and process engring. analyst Douglas Missile & Materials and Process Engring. Dept., Torrance, Calif., 1955-61; staff mgr. Universal Life Ins. Co., L.A., 1956-57; sr. engring. checker and parts complier Butler's Engring., Hawthorne, Calif., 1957-59; sr. engring. rsch. asst., mech. rsch. engring. lab. supr. Hughes Aerospace Divsn., Culver City, Calif., 1961-74; founder, pres. L.A. Inst. for Security Officers, 1971-73, Cowan's Security, Patrol and Investigatives Svcs., Moreno Valley, Calif., 1973—. Platoon sgt., L.A. res. dep. sheriff L.A. County Sheriff Acad., 1970; L.A. spl. police officer L.A. Bd. Police Commr., 1973-75; pilot instr., curriculum developer for security and law enforcement L.A. S.W. Coll., 1973-78; mgr. pers., payroll, EEO/AAO, ins., comm. Ark. Dept. Corrections, Pine Bluff, Ark., 1978-79; acad. asst. to pres., provisional pres. Ark. Bapt. Coll., Little Rock, 1980-81; adj. instr. Bus. and Econs. Philander Smith Coll., Little Rock, 1981; adj. prof. mktg., mgmt., bus. and econs. Nat. U., Riverside, Calif., 1996—; bd. mem. Sunnymead Ranch Homeowners Assn., Moreno Valley, 1989-90; adv. bd. mem. Calif. State U. Dominguez Hills Alumni Bd. Dirs., Carson, 1991-92; mem. alumni coun. Calif. State U. Sys., 1992; chancellor appointee Triennial Rev. of Campus Pres., Calif. State U. Sys., Long Beach, 1992. With U.S. Army, 1951-53, Korea. Democrat. Methodist. Home: 22500 Country Gate Rd Moreno Valley CA 92557-2661 Office: Cowans Mgmt and Cons PO Box 1418 Moreno Valley CA 92556

COWAN, STUART MARSHALL, lawyer; b. Irvington, N.J., Mar. 20, 1932; s. Bernard Howard and Blanche (Hertz) C.; m. Marilyn R.C. Toepfer, Apr., 1961 (div. 1968); m. Jane Alison Averill, Feb. 24, 1974 (div. 1989); children: Fran Lori, Catherine R.L., Erika R.L., Bronwen P.; m. Victoria Yi, Nov. 11, 1989. BS in Econ., U. Pa., 1952; LLB, Rutgers U., 1955. Bar: N.J. 1957, Hawaii 1962, U.S. Supreme Ct., 1966. Atty., Greenstein & Cowan, Honolulu, 1961-70, Cowan & Frey, Honolulu, 1970-89, pvt. practice, 1989—; of counsel Price Okomoto Himeno & Lum, 1993—; arbitrator Fed. Mediation & Conciliation Svc., Honolulu, 1972—, Am. Arbitation Assn., Honolulu, 1978—, Hawaii Pub. Employee Rels. Bd., 1972—. Bd. dirs. Honolulu Symphony; pres. Hawaii Epilepsy Soc., 1984-86. Lt. USN, 1955-61. Jewish. Mem. ABA, Hawaii Bar Assn., Am. Judicature Soc., Trial Lawyers Assn. of Am. (state committeeman for Hawaii 1965-69, bd. govs. 1972-75), Hawaii Trial Lawyers Assn. (v.p. 1972-78), Japan-Hawaii Lawyers Assn., Soc. Profls. in Dispute Resolution, Inter Pacific Bar Assn., Waikiki Yacht Club, Hawaii Yacht Club, San Francisco Comml. Club, Plaza Club, Honolulu Club, Hawaii Scottish Assn. (chieftain 1983-88), St. Andrews Soc., Caledonian Soc. (vice chieftain 1983-85), St. Francis Yacht Club, Honolulu Pipes and Drums (sec.-treas. 1985-90), New Zealand Police Pipe Band, Masons (York Rite, Scottish Rite, Grand Lodge Hawaii, grand orator 1992, sr. grand steward 1993, jr. grand warden 1994, sr. grand warden 1995, grand master 1997), Pearl Harbor (master 1971, chaplain 1992-96), Masada (#51 N.J.), Hawaiian Koolau, Elks, Chinese Acacia Club. Home: 47-339 Mapumapu Rd Kaneohe HI 96744-4922 Office: 707 Richards St Honolulu HI 96813-4623 also: 47-653 Kamehameha Hwy # 202 Kaneohe HI 96744-4965

COWART, BILL F(RANK), academic administrator; b. San Benito, Tex., Aug. 5, 1932; m. Janet Marie Dube, Aug. 6, 1954; 1 child, Richard. BS, Tex. A&I U., 1954; MA, Stephen F. Austin State Coll., 1959; PhD, U. Tex., 1963. Asst. mgr. Brownie Butane, Inc., McAllen, Tex., 1956-57; office mgr. Cowart Cattle Co., Henderson, Tex., 1957-59; tchr. Tivy Jr. High Sch., Kerrville, Tex., 1959-61; dir. secondary teaching Tex. A&I U., Kingsville, 1963-66, dir. project Upward Bound, 1966-69; pres. Laredo State U., Tex., 1969-84; provost Western Oreg. State Coll., Monmouth, 1984-94, pres., 1994-95; mem. exec. coun. Univ. System of South Tex., 1969-84; mem. Commrs. Adv. Com. on Bi-Lingual Edn., State of Tex., 1974. Pres. United Fund of Laredo, 1980; chmn. Laredo Coun. for the Arts, 1980-84, Borderfest Steering Com., Laredo, 1980-83. 1st lt. U.S. Army, 1954-56. Named Man of Yr., Laredo Times, 1979, Exec. of Yr., Coll. de Licenciados en Adminstrn. de Nuevo, 1981. Mem. S.W. Philosophy of Edn. Soc. (pres. 1970-71). Home: 2313 Swallow Ave Mcallen TX 78504

COWEE, JOHN WIDMER, JR., architecture company executive; b. Madison, Wis., Jan. 23, 1949; s. John Widmer Cowee, Sr. and Annette (Oetking) C.; m. Marion Emiko Hironaka, Mar. 21, 1971; 1 child, Misa Melina. AB in Architecture, U. Calif., Berkeley, 1971, MA in Architecture, 1973. Assoc. architect Kaiser Engrs., Oakland, Calif., 1974-82; prin. Lundy, Ng & Cowee, Architects, Oakland, Calif., 1975-79; project mgr. ED2 Architects, San Francisco, 1982-84; assoc. Leo A. Daly Co. Architects, San Francisco, 1984-91; prin. Tecta Assocs., San Francisco, 1986-88; prin./owner Architectural Concepts, Albany, Calif., 1991—; ptnr. Yost & Cowee, Archs., 1995—. Active El Cerrito, Calif. Redevel. Com., 1974-75, chmn. El Cerrito Design Review Bd., vice chmn. El Cerrito Planning Commn., 1975-79; mem. waterfront com. City of Albany. Mem. El Cerrito Aquatic Masters, Friends of El Cerrito Pool (co-chmn. 1992-94). Democrat.

COWELL, ERNEST SAUL, lighting designer, consultant; b. Hollywood, Calif., Jan. 27, 1927; s. Ernest S. and Bernice Michael (Waterman) C.; m. Beverly Sue Bloom, Apr. 15, 1950 (div. May 1960); children: Steven Richard, Craig Wesley, Marilyn Tobiann. BA, UCLA, 1950; student, Moorpark Coll., 1971, Cerritos Jr. Coll., 1979; MS Illuminating Engring., Penn State U. Regional mgr. Prentice Hall Inc., San Francisco, 1954-59; pvt. practice indsl. and govtl. sales L.A., 1959-70; area mgr. Philips Lighting, L.A., 1970-79; v.p. Coons & Cowell Lighting Unltd., Thousand Oaks, Calif., 1979-83; pres. Lighting Designs, L.A., 1983—; cons. City of Thousand Oaks, 1970-90; crime prevention specialist L.A. Police Dept., 1991—, adv. bd., 1994—. Mem. Rep. Presdl. Task Force, 1978—, Rep. Nat. Com., 1992—; mem. gen. plan com. City of Thousand Oaks, 1967, gen. plan rev. com., 1984, 86, 88; commdg. officer Betsy Ross divsn. U.S. Naval Sea Cadet Corps, 1994-95, dep. dir. for aviation tng., 1995—. Founding Officer Ronald Reagan Divsn., 1995, com. chair, 1996—, Sgt. U.S. Army, 1943-46, PTO; with USNR, 1950-58, 70-90. Recipient Edison award Excellence in Lighting, Gen. Electric Corp., 1985, 86. Fellow Inst. Advancement Engring.; mem. Illuminating Engring. Soc. (bd. dirs. So. Calif. sect. 1977-85, nat. chmn. schs. and colls. lighting stds. com., residential lighting stds. com., Internat. Illumination Design award 1983, 84, 85, 87, Disting. Svc. award), Internat. Assn. Lighting Designers, U.S. Nat. Com. to Internat. Commn. Illumination, Libr. Lighting Stds. (nat. chmn. 1988-90), Designers Lighting Forum (bd. dirs. 1988-95), Internat. Soc. Interior Designers (design affiliate), Navy League (pres. Hollywood/L.A. coun. 1993-94, bd. dirs. Beverly Hills coun. 1994—), Roadway Lighting Forum (bd. dirs. 1988-90), Kiwanis (pres. Westlake Village club 1977-79).

COWELL, FULLER A., publisher; m. Christmas Cowell; 1 child, Alexis. BBA, U. Alaska Fairbanks. With McClatchy Newspapers, 1981—; pub. Gavilan Newspapers, Calif., 1987-91, Anchorage Daily News, 1993—. Office: Anchorage Daily News PO Box 149001 Anchorage AK 99514-9001

COWHEY, PETER FRANCIS, international relations educator, government official, consultant; b. Chgo., Sept. 28, 1948; s. Eugene F. and Vivien (High) C.; m. Mary Pat Williams, July 1973 (div. June 1978); m. M. Margaret McKeown, June 29, 1985; 1 child, Megan. BS in Fgn. Svc., Georgetown U., 1970; MA, PhD, U. Calif., Berkeley, 1976. Lectr. U. Calif.,

Berkeley, 1975-76; from asst. to assoc. prof. polit. sci. U. Calif. San Diego, La Jolla, 1976-88, prof. polit. sci. & internat. rels., 1989—; sr. counselor internat. econ. and competition policy FCC, Washington, 1994-97, chief internat. bur., 1997—; market planner AT&T Internat., Basking Ridge, N.J., 1985-86; advisor Telemation Assocs., Washington, 1987-88; mem. telecom. adv. bd. A.T. Kearney, Chgo., 1988-91; co-dir. project on internat. and security affairs U. Calif., San Diego, 1990-94; rsch. scholar Berkeley Roundtable on the Internat. Economy, 1992-94; vis. prof. Juan March Inst., Madrid, 1992; rsch. prof. Inst. of Oriental Culture, U. Tokyo, 1993; U.S. del. G-7 Ministerial, 1995, U.S. del. Asian Pacific Econ. Cmty. Ministerial, 1995. Author: Problems of Plenty, 1985; co-author: Profit and the Pursuit of Energy, 1983, When Countries Talk, 1988, Managing the World's Economy, 1993; co-editor: Structure and Policy in Japan and the United States, 1994; mem. editl. bd. Internat. Orgn., 1989-94. Mem. adv. bd. Project Promothee, Paris, 1985-94, Ctr. on Telecom. Mgmt., Lincoln, Nebr., 1988-92; com. mem. NRC, 1992-93. Rockefeller Found. internat. affairs fellow, 1984-87. Mem. Am. Polit. Sci. Assn., Coun. Fgn. Rels. (internat. affairs fellow 1985-86), Internat. Studies Assn. Democrat. Home: 1522 40th Ave Seattle WA 98122 Office: U Calif San Diego Grad Sch Internat Rels & Pacific Studies La Jolla CA 92093 also: Internat Bur FCC 2000 M St NW 8th Fl Washington DC 20554

COWLES, WILLIAM STACEY, publisher; b. Spokane, Wash., Aug. 31, 1960; s. William Hutchinson 3rd and Allison Stacey C.; m. Anne Cannon, June 24, 1989. BA in Econs., Yale Coll., 1982; MBA in Fin., Columbia U., 1986. V.p., pub. The Spokesman Rev., Spokane, Wash. Office: Cowles Publishing Co PO Box 2160 Spokane WA 99210

COWLEY, GERALD DEAN, architect; b. Great Bend, Kans., Oct. 2, 1931; s. Stone Oden and Elizabeth (Lillich) C.; m. Lois Ester Traudt, Aug. 10, 1957 (div. 1983); children: Tara Elizabeth, Craig Stone; m. Frances Leach, Dec. 28, 1986. BArch, Kans. State U., 1960. Lic. architect, Colo. Architect James H. Johnson Architect, Lakewood, Colo., 1963-74, James H. Johnson & Assocs. Architects, Lakewood, 1963-74; architect, ptnr., prin. Johnson Hopson & Ptnrs., Denver, 1974-82, JHP Architecture Interior Design and Planning, Denver, 1982—. Prin. works include Rocky Mountain Energy Headquarters Bldg., 1983, others. Sgt. USAF, 1951-55. Mem. AIA, Constrn. Specifications Inst. Republican. Home: 645 E Yale Pl Englewood CO 80110-1673 Office: JHP Architecture 1600 Stout St Ste 600 Denver CO 80202-3106

COWLEY, PAULA JEAN, computer scientist, consultant; b. Spokane, Wash., Nov. 1, 1946; d. Harold Robert and Pauline (Morasch) Keiser; m. William L. Cowley; children: David, Brian. BA in Math. summa cum laude, Gonzaga U., Spokane, 1970; MS in Computer Sci., Wash. State U., Pullman, 1977. With Pacific N.W. Lab./Battelle Meml. Inst., Richland, Wash., 1977—, staff scientist info. mgmt. planning & consulting, 1990—, project mgr. Hanford Environ. Info. Sys., 1987-94; info. tech. recruiter, 1995—. Contbr. articles to profl. jours. Mem. Columbia Basin Concert Band, 1979-91; choir accompanist Ch. Choir, 1985—. Episcopalian. Office: Battelle NW Labs PO Box 999 MS K7-22 Richland WA 99352

COWSER, DANNY LEE, lawyer, mental health specialist; b. Peoria, Ill., July 7, 1948; s. Albert Paul Cowser and Shirley Mae (Donaldson) Chatten; m. Nancy Lynn Hatch, Nov. 11, 1976; children: Kimberly Catherine Hatch Cowser, Dustin Paul Hatch Cowser. BA, No. Ill. U., 1972, MS, 1975; JD, DePaul U., 1980. Bar: Ill. 1980, Wis. 1981, U.S. Dist. Ct. (no. dist.) Ill. 1981, U.S. Ct. Appeals (7th cir.) 1983, U.S. Dist. Ct. (ea. and we. dists.) Wis. 1984, U.S. Supreme Ct. 1984, Ariz. 1985, U.S. Ct. Appeals (9th cir.) 1987, U.S. Dist. Ct. Ariz. 1989, U.S. Tax Ct. 1990, U.S. Ct. Claims 1990. Adminstr. Ill. Dept. Mental Health, Elgin, 1972-76, psychotherapist, 1976-79; assoc. Slaby, Deda & Henderson, Phillips, Wis., 1982-83; ptnr. Slaby, Deda & Cowser, Phillips, 1983-86; asst. atty. City of Flagstaff, Ariz., 1986-88; pub. defender Coconino County, Flagstaff, 1988-89; pvt. practice Flagstaff, 1989—; atty. City Park Falls, Wis., 1983-86; spl. dep. Mohave County capital def., 1989-90; instr. speech comms. No. Ariz. U., 1992—; adminstrv. law judge Ariz. Dept. Econ. Security, 1997—. Bd. dirs. DeKalb County (Ill.) Drug Coun., 1973-75, Counseling and Personal Devel., Phillips, 1985-86, Northland YM-WYCA, 1990-91. Reginald Heber Smith fellow, 1980-81; C.J.S. legal scholar, 1979; recipient Am. Jur. award secured transactions, 1979, Am. Jr. award corps., 1979. Mem. ABA, Ill. Bar Assn., Ariz. Bar Asn., Nat. Criminal Def. Coll., Lions, State Bar of Ariz. (cert. specialist in criminal law), State Bar of Wis. Democrat. Office: PO Box 22329 612 N Beaver St Flagstaff AZ 86002

COX, CHRISTOPHER, congressman; b. St. Paul, Oct. 16, 1952; s. Charles C. and Marilyn A. (Miller) C.; m. Rebecca Gernhardt; children: Charles, Kathryn. BA, U. So. Calif., 1973; MBA, JD, Harvard U., 1977. Bar: Calif. 1978, D.C. 1980. Law clk. to judge U.S. Ct. Appeals (9th cir.), 1977-78; assoc. Latham & Watkins, Newport Beach, Calif., 1978-82; lectr. bus. adminstrn. Harvard U., 1982-83; ptnr. Latham & Watkins, Newport Beach, Calif., 1984-86; sr. assoc. counsel to the Pres. The White House, Washington, 1986-88; mem. 101st-104th Congresses from 40th (now 47th) dist. Calif., Washington, 1986-87; mem. budget com., joint econ. com., govt. ops. com. U.S. Ho. of Reps., Washington, ranking mem. subcom. on commerce, consumer & monetary affairs; mem. Bipartisan Commn. on Entitlement and Tax Reform, Washington, 1994—; chmn. Rep. policy com., mem. commerce com., 1995—; prin., founder Context Corp., St. Paul, 1984-88. Editor Harvard Law Rev., 1975-77. Roman Catholic. Office: E Tower Ste 430 4000 Macarthur Blvd Newport Beach CA 92660-2516 Office: US Ho of Reps 2402 Rayburn HOB Washington DC 20515*

COX, CLARICE R., writer; b. Helena, Mont., May 11, 1914; d. William Mont and Adelia Anne (Geier) Robinson; m. Gene H. Cox, June 11, 1938 (dec. June 1996); children: William Edward, James Laurence, Willa Margaret. BA in English, Intermountain Union, 1935; MEd in Comms., U. Hawaii, 1968. H.S. tchr. Mont., Oreg. and Hawaii schs., 1936-60; asst. base edn. adviser 408th Fighter Group USAF, Klamath Falls, Oreg., 1960-61; writer, demonstrator Maui Project NIMH, Wailuku, Hawaii, 1965-67; instr. Honolulu C.C., 1967-73, 75-79; freelance writer Roseburg, Oreg., 1995—; cons. State of Mont. Pers. Ctr., Helena, 1979-88; cons., lectr. Queen's Med. Ctr., Honolulu, 1980-89, Am. Soc. Ind. Security, Honolulu, 1981, Honolulu Police Dept., 1980-88; presenter in field. Author: Criminal Justice: Improving Police Report Writing, 1977, Instant Teaching Skills, 1995, (with Jerrold G. Brown) Report Writing for Criminal Justice Professionals, 1991; contbr. articles, poems, short stories to profl. jours. and popular mags. Mem. Oreg. Com. on Aging, 1996-97, Hawaii Com. on Aging, 1973-78; mem. panel John Jay Coll. Criminal Justice, N.Y.C., 1996, Acad. Criminal Justice Scis., Las Vegas, Nev., 1996-97; panelist Writer's Clubs 1st Ann. Conf., Nev., 1997; vol. Mercy Hosp., Roseburg, Oreg., 1995—. Mem. AAUP, Nat. Soc. Lit. and Arts, U. Hawaii Profl. Assembly. Home: 2665 Van Pelt Blvd # 45 Roseburg OR 97470

COX, GARY EVANS, aerospace company official, consultant; b. Ogden, Utah, July 4, 1937; s. Donald Evans and Maxine Louise (Altweis) C.; m. Carole Sue Brown, June 6, 1959; children: Theresa, Patrick, Colleen. BS in Indsl. Mgmt., U. Portland, 1961; MS in Pub. Adminstrn., Auburn UU., 1973. Commd. 2d lt. USAF, 1961, advanced through grades to col., 1982; pilot USAF, Europe, Korea, Vietnam, U.S., 1961-87; ret., 1987; program mgr. McDonnell Douglas Corp., Phoenix, 1987—; cons. McDonnell Douglas Corp., St. Louis, 1987. Pres. Holy Redeemer Sch. Bd., Tampa, Fla., 1976-78; scoutmaster Tampa coun. Boy Scouts Am., 1977-78; com. chmn. Hampton (Va.) Rep. Com., 1982. Decorated DFC, 20 Air medals; recipient Superior Svc. award Dept. Def., 1987. Mem. Air Force Assn., Ret. Officers Assn., Daedalian Soc. Roman Catholic. Home: 7733 W Villa Theresa Dr Glendale AZ 85308-8262 Office: McDonnell Douglas Aerospace Svcs Co PO Box 218 Litchfield Park AZ 85340-0218

COX, JIM, petroleum geologist, technical writer; b. Tulsa, May 19, 1932; s. Leland W. and Evelyn (Bell) C.; m. Marcia Ann Dick, Oct. 15, 1960; children: Galen, Karsten, Cydney. BS in Geology, Okla. State U., Stillwater, 1955. Geologist Gulf Oil Corp., Casper, Wyo., 1959-60, Mule Creek Oil Co., Billings, Mont., 1960-66; geologist Jim Cox-Petroleum Geologist, Inc., Gillette, Wyo., 1966-79, Prescott, Ariz., 1979-81, Littleton, Colo., 1981-87, Idaho Falls, Idaho, 1987—; v.p. Wulf Oil Co., Gillette, 1979-81; exploration mgr. Aberdeen Resources, Denver, 1980-81, Quantum Resources, Denver, 1981-83. Contbr. articles to profl. jours. 1st lt. USAF, 1955-58. Mem. Am. Assn. Petroleum Geologists. Home and Office: 2002 Dalmation Dr Idaho Falls ID 83402-2466

COX, JOSEPH WILLIAM, academic administrator; b. Hagerstown, Md., May 26, 1937; s. Joseph F. and Ruth E. C.; m. Regina M. Bollinger, Aug. 17, 1963; children—Andrew, Matthew, Abigail. B.A., U. Md., 1959, Ph.D., 1967; Doctor (hon.), Towson State U., 1990. Successively instr., asst. prof., assoc. prof., prof. history Towson (Md.) State U., 1964-81, dean evening and summer programs, 1972-75, acting pres., 1978-79, v.p. acad. affairs and dean of univ., 1979-81; prof. history, v.p. acad. affairs. No. Ariz. U.,, Flagstaff, 1981-87; pres. So. Oregon Coll., Ashland, 1987-94; chancellor Oreg. State Sys. Higher Edn., Eugene, 1994—. Author: Champion of Southern Federalism: Robert Goodloe Harper of South Carolina, 1972, The Early National Experience: The Army Corps of Engineers, 1783-1812, 1979; mem. bd. editors Md. Hist. Mag., 1979-89; columnist So. Oreg. Hist. Mag., 1989-94; contbr. articles to profl. jours. Bd. dirs. Oreg. Hist. Soc., Oreg. Shakespearean Festival, 1989-95, So. Oreg. Econ. Deve. Bd., 1988-94, Jackson/Josephine Co. Mem. AAUP, Am. Assn. Higher Edn., Am. Assn. State Colls. and Univs., Phi Kappa Phi, Omicron Delta Kappa. Episcopalian. Home: 2237 Spring Blvd Eugene OR 97403-1897 Office: Oreg State Sys Higher Edn Office of Chancellor PO Box 3175 Eugene OR 97403

COX, KIM CARROLL, lawyer, broadcaster; b. Chgo., Feb. 8, 1955; s. Carroll Thomas and Alice (Macqueen) C. BA, U. Ill., 1976; JD, Thomas Jefferson Sch. Law, San Diego, 1982. Bar: Calif., 1988, U.S. Supreme Ct., 1993, U.S. Ct. Appeals (7th, 9th & 10th cir.), 1993, 96, U.S. Dist. Ct. (so. dist.) Calif., 1988., U.S. Dist Ct. (so. dist.) Ill., 1996. Broadcaster KSDS-FM, San Diego, 1985—; sec. chair Calif. Electoral Coll., 1992-96; assoc. Law Offices of Floyd Morrow, San Diego, 1989-95, Law Offices of Denise Moreno Ducheny, San Diego, 1996—; mem. mediation panel San Diego County Superior Ct., 1995—. Chair Crawford County (Ill.) Young Dems., Robinson, 1974-76, San Diego County Dem. Party, 1990-95; field dir. Dukakis for Pres., San Diego, 1988; mem. exec. bd. Calif. Dem. Party, 1989-94. Mem. San Diego County Bar Assn. (alternative dispute resolution com. 1994—). Home: 2050 Emerald St Apt 3 San Diego CA 92109-3519 Office: Law Offices of Denise Ducheny 2168 Logan Ave San Diego CA 92113-2204

COX, PAT, artist; b. Pasadena, Calif., Mar. 6, 1921; d. Walter Melville and Mary Elizabeth (Frost) Boadway; m. Dale William Cox Jr., Feb. 19, 1946; children: Brian Philip, Dale William III, Gary Walter. BA, Mills Coll., 1943, MA, 1944. Graphic artist Pacific Manifolding Book Co., Emeryville, Calif., 1944-45; tchr. art to adults China Lake, Calif., 1957-63; tchr. art to children Peninsula Enrichment Program, Rancho Palos Verdes, Calif., 1965-67; graphic artist Western Magnum Corp., Hermosa Beach, Calif., 1970-80; tchr. art workshop Art at Your Fingertips, Rancho Palos Verdes, 1994-95. One woman shows include Palos Verdes Art Ctr., Rancho Palos Verdes, Calif., 1977, 79, 83, 92, Thinking Eye Gallery, L.A., 1988, Ventura (Calif.) Coll. Art Galleries, 1994, Mendenhall Gallery, Whittier (Calif.) Coll., 1995, The Gallery at Stevenson Union, So. Oreg. Coll., Ashland, 1996; two person exhibits Laguna Art Mus., Laguna Beach, Calif., 1971, Creative Arts Gallery, Burbank, Calif., 1993; group exhibits include Long Beach Mus. Art, Art Rental Gallery, 1979, L.A. County Mus. Art, Art Rental Gallery, 1979, Palm Springs Mus. Art, 1980, Laguna Art Mus., 1981, N.Mex. Fine Arts Gallery, 1981, Pacific Grove Art Ctr., 1983, Phoenix Art Mus., 1983, Brea Cultural Ctr., Calif., 1983, Riverside Art Mus., 1985, San Bernardino Art Mus., 1985, Laguna Art Mus., 1986, Zanesville Art Ctr., Ohio, 1987, The Thinking Eye Gallery, L.A., 1987, 89, Hippodrome Gallery, Long Beach, 1988, Palos Verdes Art Ctr., Calif., N.Mex. State Fine Arts Gallery, 1988, Long Beach City Coll., 1989, Newport Harbor Art Mus., 1989, Downey Mus. Art, 1990, 92, Rachele Lozzi Fine Art Gallery, L.A., 1991, Internat. Contemporary Art Fair L.A., 1986, 87, 88, 92, U. Tex. Health Sci. Ctr., 1992, Long Beach Arts, 1991, 92, 93, The Internat. Air Fair, L.A., 1992, Young Aggressive Art Mus., Santa Anna, 1993, U. Ark. Fine Arts Gallery, Fayetteville, 1994, Laura Knott Art Gallery, Bradford Coll., Mass., 1994, Bridge Street Gallery, Big Fork, Mont., 1994, St. John's Coll. Art Gallery, Santa Fe, 1995, L.A. Harbor Coll., Calif., 1995, Walker Art Collection, Garnett, Kans., 1995, San Francisco State U., 1996, Coleman Gallery, Albuquerque, 1996, Loyola Law Sch., L.A., 1996, San Bernardino County Mus., 1996, Prieto Gallery, Mills Coll., Oakland, Calif., 1996, U. So. Calif. Hillel Gallery, L.A., 1997, others. Trustee L.A. Art Assn., 1972-79; bd. dirs. Palos Verdes Art Ctr., 1966-70, 87-89, chair exhbn. com., 1982-85, co-chair Art for Fun(d)s Sake, 1966; judge Tournament of Roses Assn., Pasadena, 1975; mem. strategic planning Palos Verdes Art Ctr., 1988; mem. Pacific Pl. Planning Commn. Percent for Art, San Pedro, Calif., 1989; juror Pasadena Soc. Artists, 1973, 81, Women Painters West, 1984-85. Recipient Silver Pin award Palos Verdes Art Ctr., 1988, Calif. Gold Discovery award V.I.P. Jury Panel, L.A., 1994. Mem. Nat. Watercolor Soc. (juror 1981, 1st v.p. 1980, 4th v.p. 1984), Nat. Mus. Women in the Arts, Mus. Contemporary Art, L.A. County Mus. Art, Palos Verdes Cmty. Art Assn. (cert. appreciation 1981).

COX, PAUL ALAN, biologist, educator; b. Salt Lake City, Oct. 10, 1953; s. Leo A. and Rae (Gabbitas) C.; m. Barbara Ann Wilson, May 21, 1975; children: Emily Ann, Paul Matthew, Mary Elisabeth, Hillary Christine, Jane Margaret. BS, Brigham Young U., 1976; MSc, U. Wales, 1978; AM, Harvard U., 1978, PhD, 1981. Teaching fellow Harvard U., Cambridge, Mass., 1977-81; Miller research fellow Miller Inst. Basic Research in Sci., Berkeley, Calif., 1981-83; asst. prof. Brigham Young U., Provo, Utah, 1983-86, assoc. prof., 1986-91, prof., 1991-93, dean gen. edn. and honors, 1993—; ecologist Utah Environ. Coun., Salt Lake City, 1976; project ecologist Utah MX Coordination Office, Salt Lake City, 1981. Mem. editorial bd. Pacific Studies. Recipient Bowdoin prize, The Goldman Environ. prize, 1997;; Danforth Found. fellow, 1976-81, Fulbright fellow, 1976-77, NSF fellow, 1977-81, Melbourne Univ. fellow, 1985-86, named NSF Presdl. Young Investigator, 1985-90. Mem. AAAS, Brit. Ecol. Soc., Internat. Soc. Ethnopharmacology (pres.), Am. Soc. Naturalists, Assn. Tropical Biology, Soc. Econ. Botany (pres.), New Eng. Bot. Club. Mormon. Office: Brigham Young U General Edn and Honors 302 Maeser Bldg PO Bx 22600 Provo UT 84602

COX, WILLIAM LARRY, astrologer, educator; b. New Kensington, Pa., May 18, 1953; s. Clyde Edward Cox, Sr. and Jane Gwendolyn (Pierre) Lloyd. Grad. high sch., Albany, La. Cert. emotional support counselor, Shanti. Astrologer Tucson, Prescott, Ariz., 1978; instr. Tucson Open Univ., 1996—; counselor, Prescott, 1990-93, Shanti Found., Tucson, 1994—; owner, pres. Milagro Press Publs., Tucson, 1995—; spkr. in field. Author: a journey into Love, 1996 (award); prodr. videos. Mem. Vote No On Proposition 101, Prescott, 1992. Mem. Tucson Computer Soc., Phi Theta Kappa. Republican. Office: Tucson Open U 2030 E Broadway Ste 100 Tucson AZ 85710

COX, WILLIAM VAUGHAN, lawyer; b. Jersey City, N.J., Nov. 12, 1936; s. Walter Miles and Emily (McNenney); divorced; children: Millicent S., Jennifer V. BA, Princeton U., 1958; LLB, Yale U., 1964. Bar: Colo. 1965, Conn. 1972, N.Y. 1974. Law clk. Holland & Hart, Denver, 1963; atty. Conoco Inc., Denver, 1966-72; asst. to v.p., gen. counsel Conoco Inc., Stamford, Conn., 1972-73; v.p., gen. counsel Stromberg-Carlson Corp., Rochester, N.Y., 1974-78; mng. ptnr. Bader & Cox, Denver, 1979-86, of counsel, 1986-88; pres. William V. Cox, P.C., Denver, 1988—, also bd. dirs.; project and planning dir. Interwest Comm. Corp., 1995-97; pres., bd. dirs. New West Indies Trading Co., Denver, 1984—; pres. Coll. Football Ltd., Denver, 1990—. Sportswriter/editor: Colorado Springs (Colo.) Free Press, 1960-61. Football coach Cheyenne Mountain H.S., Colorado Springs, 1961; founder, bd. dirs., v.p., com. chmn. editor Colo. chpt. Nat. Football Found., 1992—; mem. adv. bd. Downtown Denver Dist., 1991-93; bd. dirs., com. chmn. Downtown Denver Residents, 1990-93; pres., bd. dirs. Barclay Towers Condominiums, Denver, 1990-92; dist. capt. Rep. Party, Cherry Hills, Colo., 1980-85; bd. dirs. Monroe County Humane Soc., Rochester, 1975-78. Mem. ABA, Colo. Bar Assn., Denver Bar Assn. (awards com., professionalism com.), Denver Lower Downtown Bar Assn. (v.p. 1992-94), Am. Legion, Ancient Order Hibernians, Lincoln Club, Univ. Club Denver (admissions com.), Yale Club N.Y., Genesee Valley Club (Rochester), Rocky Mountain Princeton Club (com. chmn. 1966-72), Law Club Denver (com. chmn. 1969-72), Corbey Ct., Phi Delta Phi. Roman Catholic. Office: 1625 Larimer St Ste 2707 Denver CO 80202-1538

COYLE, ROBERT EVERETT, federal judge; b. Fresno, Calif., May 6, 1930; s. Everett LaJoya and Virginia Chandler C.; m. Faye Turnbaugh, June 11, 1953; children—Robert Allen, Richard Lee, Barbara Jean. B.A., Fresno State Coll., 1953; J.D., U. Calif., 1956. Bar: Calif. Ptnr. McCormick, Barstow, Sheppard, Coyle & Wayte, 1958-82; chief judge U.S. Dist. Ct. (ea. dist.) Calif., 1982—; chair, space & security com. 9th cir. Mem. Calif. Bar Assn. (exec. com. 1974-79, bd. govs. 1979-82, v.p. 1981), Fresno County Bar Assn. (pres. 1972), 9th Cir. Dist. Conf. of Chief Dist. Judges, 9th Cir. Com. on State and Fed. Cts. Office: US Dist Ct 5116 US Courthouse 1130 O St Fresno CA 93721-2201

COZAD, LYMAN HOWARD, city manager; b. Painesville, Ohio, May 22, 1914; s. William Howard and Ethyl (Phelps) C.; m. Arliss Smith, Sept. 6, 1978; children: Bradford, Roberta, Kimberly. BSBA, Ohio State U., 1935, MS in Pub. Adminstrn., 1936; postgrad., Yale U., 1936-37, USC, 1948-57. Dir. exam City of L.A., 1939-42; personnel officer Nat. Housing Agy., Washington, 1942-43; personnel dir. UNRRA, Washington, 1944-47; So. Calif. mgr. Louis J. Kroeger & Assocs., L.A., 1947-56; city mgr. City of Colton, 1957-64; adminstrv. officer City of Beverly Hills, Calif., 1964-66; city mgr. City of Arcadia, Calif., 1966-77; So. Calif. mgr. League of Calif. Cities, 1977-84; ranger rider, 1985—; v.p., So. Calif. rep. Pub. Svc. Skills Inc., Sacramento, 1986—; instr. U. So. Calif., 1941-42, 48-58, U. Calif., Riverside, 1961-63, Calif. State U., Long Beach, 1974-77. Contbr. articles to profl. jours. With U.S. Army, 1943-44. Mem. ASPA, Internat. City Mgrs. Assn., City Mgrs. Dept. League of Calif. Cities (Sacramento pres. 1972, life), So. Calif. Pub. Pers. Assn. L.A. (pres. 1942), Rotary (Colton chpt. dir. 1961-62, Arcadia chpt. 1970-77). Home: 952 Canyon View Dr La Verne CA 91750-1811 Office: Pub Svc Skills Inc 1400 K St Sacramento CA 95814-3916

COZART, REBECCA LYDIA, medical association executive; b. Phoenix, June 1, 1953; d. Edwin L. and June R. (Bast) Laplante; m. William E. Cozart, July 28, 1978. BA in Journalism, U. Nev., 1975. Cert. assn. exec.; cert. meeting profl. Display ad coord. Gazette Jour., Reno, Nev., 1974-76; edn. and mktg. dir. Nev. Assn. Realtors, Reno, 1977-83; meeting and edn. dir. Ariz. Assn. Realtors, Phoenix, 1984-86; profl. devel. dir. Nat. Spkrs. Assn., Phoenix, 1986-87; asst. dir. Oreg. Concrete & Aggregate Prodrs. Assn., Salem, 1989-94; exec. dir. Marion-Polk County Med. Soc., Salem, 1995—. Mem. Rotary. Office: Marion-Polk Co Med Soc 1155 Mission St SE Ste 103 Salem OR 97302

COZEN, LEWIS, orthopedic surgeon; b. Montreal, Aug. 14, 1911; came to U.S. 1922; AB, U. Calif., San Francisco, 1929, MD, 1934. Diplomate Am. Bd. Orthopedic Surgery. Intern San Francisco Hosp., 1933-34; resident orthopedic surgeron U. Iowa, 1934-35; resident and fellow orthopedic surgery San Francisco County Hosp., 1935-36, Children's Hosp. and Mass. Gen. Hosp., Boston, 1936-39; pvt. practice orthopedic surgery L.A., 1939-40, 45—; clin. prof. orthopedic surgery UCLA, 1965-93; assoc. clin. prof. emeritus Loma Linda Med. Sch., 1963—; attending orthopedic surgeon, emeritus Cedars Sinai Med. Ctr., 1939—, Orthopaedic Hosp., 1939—; chief orthopedic surgery City of Hope, 1948-67; sr. attending orthopedic surgeons, emeritus Unit One L.A. County Hosp., 1950-63; vis. lectr. U. Santo Tomas, Manila, U. Madrid, Spain; Far East Sch. of Medicine, Manila, 1994, Hadassah Med. Ctr., Jerusalem, 1994, U. Brussels; lectr. in field. Author: Office Orthopedics, 1955, 4th edit. 1973, Operative Orthopedic Clinics (with Dr. Avia Brockway), 1960, Atlas of Orthopedic Surgery, 1966, Difficult Orthopedic Diagnosis, 1972, Plannings and Pitfalls in Orthopedic Surgery, Natural History of Orthopedic Disease, 1993, Supplement Book, 1996; mem. editl. bd. Resident & Staff Physician; contbr. numerous articles to profl. jours. Vol. physician Internat. Children's Program, Orthopedic Hosp., Mexicali, Mexico. Lt. col. U.S. Army, 1940-45. Fellow ACS, Internat. Coll. Surgeons, Am. Coll. Rheumatology, Royal Soc. Medicine; mem. Am. Rheumatism Assn., Internat. Orthopedic Assn., Am. Orthopaedic Assn. (sr.), Am. Acad. Orthopaedic Surgeons, So. Calif. Rheumatism Assn. (pres. 1979), Western Orthopaedic Assn., Phi Beta Kappa, Alpha Omega Alpha.

CRABBS, ROGER ALAN, publisher, consultant, small business owner, educator; b. Cedar Rapids, Iowa, May 9, 1928; s. Winfred Wesley and Faye (Woodard) C.; m. Marilyn Lee Westcott, June 30, 1951; children: William Douglas, Janet Lee Crabbs Turner, Ann Lee Crabbs Menke. B.A. in Sci., State U. Iowa, 1954; M.B.A., George Washington U., 1965, D.B.A., 1973; M.Christian Leadership, Western Conservative Bapt. Sem., 1978. Commd. 2nd lt. USAF, 1950, advanced through grades to lt. col., 1968, Ret., 1972; prof. mgmt. U. Portland, Oreg., 1972-79; prof. bus. George Fox Coll., Newberg, Oreg., 1979-83; pres. Judson Bapt. Coll., The Dalles, Oreg., 1983-85; pres., assoc. pub. Host Pubs. Inc. doing bus. as Travelhost of Oreg. and S.W. Wash., 1985—; pres., chmn. various corps., 1974-86; past chmn. nat. adv. bd. TRAVELHOST, Inc.; cons. to various orgns., corps. and agys. Author: The Infallible Foundation for Management-The Bible, 1978, The Secret of Success in Small Business Management-Is in the Short Range, 1983; co-author: The Storybook Primer on Managing, 1976. Past pres. English Speaking Union, 1994-96, bd. dirs., 1994—; bd. dirs. Christ Comty. Ch., Washington County Visitors Assn., Oakhills Townhouse Assn., v.p., 1991-95; mem. Minority Conv. Tourism Adv. Coun., Oreg. Decorated Air Force Commendation medal with oak leaf cluster, Meritorious Service medal Dept. Def.; rated Command Air Force Missileman; recipient regional, dist. and nat. awards SBA. Mem. Acad. Mgmt., Am. Arbitration Assn., Svc. Corps Ret. Execs., Air Force Assn., Portland Officers Club, Rotary (past pres.), Masons, Kiwanis, Lang Syne Soc. of Portland, Alpha Kappa Psi, Delta Epsilon Sigma, Phi Mu Alpha. Republican. Office: Host Publs Inc 822 NW Murray Blvd Ste 173 Portland OR 97229-5868 *A positive attitude, sincere interest in others and a sense of humility have been the building blocks of my personal philosophy. They have served me well through my three careers - professional military, university professor and publisher.*

CRABILL, LINDA JEAN, municipal government official; b. St. Albans, Vt., Oct. 12, 1954; d. Marvin Henry and Mildred Theresa (McKenney) Ladue; m. James Daniel Crabill, Sept. 17, 1977 (div. May 1991); 1 child, Krisanne Michele. AA, Evergreen Valley Coll., San Jose, Calif., 1985; student, San Jose State U., 1985-89. Analyst United Techs. Corp., Windsor Locks, Conn., 1973-75; cryptologic technician USN, San Vito dei Normanni, Italy, 1975-78; polit. aide to city coun. City of San Jose, Calif., 1984-89; asst. program coord. Foothill Coll., Los Altos, Calif., 1989-91; cmty. rels. coord. City of Sunnyvale, Calif., 1991—. Author, editor: Citizens Access Handbook, 1993 (3d place statewide Excellence in Comm. 1994). Co-chair coord. coun. United Way Santa Clara County (Coord. of Yr., Santa Clara County, 1993), San Jose, 1994—; state bd. dirs. Combined Health Appeal of Calif.(Person of Yr. 1995), Sacramento, 1996—; bd. mem. local affiliate Combined Health Appeal Santa Clara County, San Jose, 1993— (Outstanding Campaign coord. 1993, 94, 95); com. mem. adv. bd. Am. Cancer Soc. of Santa Clara County, 1996—; mem. Dem. Senatorial Com., Washington, 1995—; mem. Olympic Torch Relay, Santa Clara County, 1996; mem. Sunnyvale Mgmt. Cert. Program, 1993-94; bd. mem. Holy Family Ch. fin. com., San Jose, 1992-95. With USN, 1975-78, Italy. Recipient Disting. Grad. award, Evergreen Valley Coll., 1985. Mem. ASPA (bd. dirs. 1993-95, Pres.'s award 1995), Calif. Pub. Info. Officers Assn., South Bay Pub. Rels. Round Table (pres. 1994-95, v.p. 1993). Democrat. Roman Catholic. Home: 4110 Wessex Dr San Jose CA 95136-1855 Office: City of Sunnyvale Office of City Mgr 603 All America Way Sunnyvale CA 94088-3707

CRABTREE, DAVIDA FOY, minister; b. Waterbury, Conn., June 7, 1944; Alfred and Davida (Blakeslee) Foy; m. David T. Hindinger Jr., Aug. 28, 1982; stepchildren: Elizabeth Anne, David Todd. BS, Marietta Coll., 1967; MDiv, Andover Newton Theol. Sch., 1972; D of Ministry, Hartford Sem., 1989. Ordained to ministry United Ch. of Christ, 1972. Founder, exec. dir. Prudence Crandall Ctr. for Women, New Britain, Conn., 1973-76; min., dir. Greater Hartford (Conn.) Campus Ministry, 1976-80; sr. min. Colchester (Conn.) Federated Ch., 1980-91; bd. dirs. Conn. Conf. United Ch. of Christ, Hartford, 1982-90; conf. min. So. Calif. Conf., United Ch. of Christ, Pasadena, 1991-96, Conn. Conf., United Ch. of Christ, Hartford, 1996—; rsch. assoc. Harvard Div. Sch., Cambridge, Mass., 1975-76. Author: The Empowering Church, 1989 (named one of Top Ten Books of Yr. 1990); editorial advisor Alban Inst., 1990—. Bd. dirs. Hartford region YWCA, 1979-82; trustee Cragin Meml. Libr., Colchester, 1980-91, Hartford Sem., 1983-91; founder Youth Svcs. Bur., Colchester, 1984-89; pres. Creative Devel. for Colchester Inc., 1989-91; coun. Religious Leaders of L.A., 1991-96; v.p. Hope in Youth Campaign, 1992-96; trustee Sch. of Theology at

Claremont, 1993-96; dir. UCC Ins. Adv. bd., 1993—. Recipient Antoinette Brown award Gen. Synod, United Ch. of Christ, 1977, Conf. Preacher award Conn. Conf. United Ch. of Christ, 1982, Woman in Leadership award Hartford region YWCA, 1987; named one of Outstanding Conn. Women, UN Assn., 1987, Somos Uno award United Neighborhood Orgn., 1995. Mem. Nat. Coun. Chs. (bd. dirs. 1969-81), Christians for Justice Action (exec. com. 1981-91). *

CRABTREE, LOREN WILLIAM, dean, history educator; b. Aberdeen, S.D., Sept. 2, 1940; s. Benjamin Forrest and Harriet Caroline (Zempel) C.; m. Sheila Ann Volz, Aug. 25, 1961 (div. May 1987); children: Christopher, Kathryn, Paul; m. Monica Sue Christen, 1987. BA, U. Minn., 1961, MA, 1965, PhD, 1969. Instr. Bethel Coll., St. Paul, 1965-67; from instr. to prof. history Colo. State U., Ft. Collins, 1967—, dean Coll. Liberal Arts, 1991—; vis. assoc. prof. U. Colo., Boulder, 1980; vis. prof., dean semester at sea program U. Pitts., 1986, 91; faculty affiliate Nat. Faculty, Atlanta, 1988—. Author: The Lion and the Dragon, 1970; co-author: Civilizations: A Cultural Atlas, 1994; contbr. articles to profl. publs. Trustee Am. Bapt. Ch., Ft. Collins, 1970-74; bd. deacons First Christian Ch., Ft. Collins, 1984-86. NDFL Chinese Lang. fellow Harvard U., 1964. Mem. Assn. for Asian Studies (pres. western conf. 1983-84), Coun. Colls. of Arts and Scis., Phi Beta Kappa, Phi Alpha Theta. Democrat. Home: 2201 Grosvenor Ct Fort Collins CO 80526 Office: Colo State U Coll Liberal Arts Fort Collins CO 80523

CRACROFT, RICHARD HOLTON, English literature educator; b. Salt Lake City, June 28, 1936; s. Ralph and Grace Darling (White) C.; m. Janice Marie Alger, Sept. 17, 1959; children: Richard Alger, Jeffrey Ralph, Jennifer Cracroft Lewis. BA, U. Utah, 1961, MA, 1963; PhD in English and Am. Lit., U. Wis., 1969. Student instr. U. Utah, Salt Lake City, 1961-63; instr. English Brigham Young U., Provo, Utah, 1963-66; grad. instr. U. Wis., Madison, 1966-69; from asst. prof. English to assoc. prof. English Brigham Young U., Provo, 1969-74, prof. English, 1974—, dept. chair English, 1975-80, dean Coll. Humanities, 1981-86; dir. Ctr. for Study of Christian Values in Lit., Brigham Young U., Provo, 1993—; bd. judges David Evans Biography Prize, Logan, Utah, 1983—, Orton Prize for Mormon Letters, Salt Lake City, 1991—. Author: Washington Irving: The Western Works, 1974; co-editor: A Believing People: The Literature of the Latter-day Saints, 1974, 1979, 22 Young Mormon Writers, 1975, Voices From the Past: (LDS) Journals, Diaires, Autobiographies, 1980; editor: (jour.) Lit. and Belief, 1993—; founding assoc. editor: The Carpenter, 1966-70; assoc. editor: Dialogue, 1969-73, Western Am. Lit., 1973-86; mem. editl. bd.: BYU Studies, 1981-86, This People, 1996—; contbg author: Instruction and Delight, Critical Essays on Thomas Wolfe: A Literary History of the American West, Mark Twain Ency., Turning Hearts: Short Stories of Family Life, others; contbr. articles to profl. and popular jours. Bishop, stake pres., mission pres. LDS Ch. Democrat. Home: 770 E Center St Provo UT 84606 Office: Brigham Young U Dept English 3146 Jesse Knights Hum Bldg Provo UT 84604-2724

CRAFT, BRIAN THOMAS, stand-up comedian, embetterment consultant; b. Long Beach, N.Y., Aug. 20, 1957; s. Frank Henry and Geraldine (Shannon) C.; m. Kelly Jones, Nov. 25, 1989. Stand-up comedian, 1979—; owner Comedy Land Inc., Anaheim, Calif., 1988-92; embetterment cons. and CFO Comedy Lifeline Internat., Costa Mesa, Calif., 1989—. Cons. editor Hemalog, 1993—; author prose Ways and Means, 1994. Bd. dirs. and mem. golf fund-raising com. Hemophilia Found. of So. Calif., Pasadena, 1993—, chmn. pub. info. com. and v.p. bd. dirs., 1995—, v.p., 1995—, pub. rels. com., 1996—. Recipient Spl. award Nat. Hemophilia Found., 1985, Cert. of Appreciation, 1993, Pub. Info. award, 1996; recipient Svc. award Camp Fire Coun. of O.C., Tustin, Calif., 1991-92, Award of Excellence, Step into the Future Archer Found., 1991; featured on TV and radio. Mem. Network of Coaches Alliance. Ch. of Religious Sci. Home and Office: Comedy Lifeline Internat 1555 Mesa Verde Dr E Apt 11H Costa Mesa CA 92626-5112

CRAFT, ROBBIE WRIGHT, artist; b. St. Louis, Feb. 22, 1951; d. Robert Edward and Irene (Tosch) Wright; m. Joseph Walter Epply III (div. 1978); 1 child, Joseph Walter IV; m. Raymond Wood Craft II, Feb. 14, 1987. Student, Casper Jr. Coll., 1969-71. Mgr. restaurant and bar Widow Browns, Crofton, Md., 1978-84; adminstrv. asst. U.S. Dept. Def., Andrews AFB, Md., 1974-75; illustrator, supr. U.S. Dept. Def., Cheyenne, Wyo., 1985-88, EEO counselor, 1987—, chief visual info., 1988—, chief, support flt., 1996—; ind. artist Maryland, Wyo., 1974—; ind. interior designer Wyo., 1985—. Mem. visual info. bd. USAF. Lutheran. Home: 7223 Tumbleweed Dr Cheyenne WY 82009-1014 Office: Visual Info Bldg 242 Cheyenne WY 82005

CRAGUN, CALVIN, business owner; b. Salt Lake City, Nov. 14, 1940; s. Robert Wallace and Vivian (Parker) C.; m. Celestia Van Tussenbroek, Dec. 20, 1967; children: Marlayn, Caroline, David, Robert. BS, U. Utah, 1963, MS, 1966. Tchr. Utah Sch. for the Deaf, Ogden, 1966-72; from salesperson to mgmt. dept. Home Life of N.Y., Salt Lake City, 1972-82; with ins. sales dept. Standard of Oreg., Salt Lake City, 1982-84; owner Custom Benefits, Salt Lake City, 1984—, Rocky Mt. Brokerage, Salt Lake City, 1985-88, Ins. Designers, Salt Lake City, 1988—. Mem. Nat. Conf. for Autism, Salt Lake City, 1983; regional coord. Internat. Winter Spl. Olympics, Salt Lake City, 1985; mem. Utah Gov.'s Com. for Handicapped, Salt Lake City, 1983-84, Family Support Adv. Coun., 1995; vol. Jr. Achievement, 1991; tchr. Life Underwriter Tng. Coun., 1992; chmn. steering com. Adult Handicap Social Club, 1993—. Mem. Utah Coun. for Handicapped (v.p. 1982-83), After Hours (chairperson 1993—). Home and Office: 2686 Towne Dr Salt Lake City UT 84121-5146

CRAIG, CAROL MILLS, marriage, family and child counselor; b. Berkeley, Calif.. BA in Psychology with honors, U. Calif., Santa Cruz, 1974; MA in Counseling Psychology, John F. Kennedy U., 1980; doctoral student, Calif. Sch. Profl. Psychology, Berkeley, 1980-87, Columbia Pacific U., San Rafael, Calif., 1987—. Psychology intern Fed. Correction Inst., Pleasanton, Calif., 1979-81, Letterman Army Med. Ctr., San Francisco, 1980-82; psychology intern VA Mental Hygiene Clinic, Oakland, Calif., 1981-82, Martinez, Calif., 1982-83; instr. Martinez Adult Sch., 1983, Piedmont Adult Edn., Oakland, 1986; biofeedback and stress mgmt. cons. Oakland, 1986—; child counselor Buddies-A Nonprofit, Counseling Svc. for Persons in the Arts, Lafayette, Calif., 1993—; founder Chesley Sch., 1994; rsch. asst. Irvington Pubs., N.Y.C., 1979, Little, Brown and Co., Boston, 1983. Mem. Calif. Assn. Marriage and Family Therapists (clin.), Musicians Union Local 424, Calif. Scholarship Fedn. (life).

CRAIG, JAMES NORMAN, communications engineer, Internet consultant; b. San Pedro, Calif., Nov. 28, 1968; s. Russell T. and Phoebe Francis C.; m. Lisa Renee Collins. BA, U. Ariz., 1991. Promotions dir. Tucson Raceway Park, 1991-92; pub. rels. dir. Ad Dimensions, Tucson, 1992; sports corr. Albuquerque Jour., 1992-93; salesman Samon's Electrical, Albuquerque, 1993, asst. mgr., 1993-94; comm. specialist N.Mex. Educators Federal Credit Union, Albuquerque, 1994-96, comm. engr., 1996—. Vol. Greater Albuquerque Habitat for Humanity, 1996—, chair devel. com., 1995. Recipient 1st place awards Internet Mktg., 1996, Newsletter 3 colors or less, CUNA Mktg., 1995, Credit Union Exec. Soc., 1995. Democrat. Home: 511 1/2 Vassar SE Albuquerque NM 87106 Office: NM Educators Federal Credit Union 6501 Indian School Rd NE Albuquerque NM 87110-5306

CRAIG, JOAN CARMEN, secondary school educator, drama teacher; b. Sacramento, Calif., July 13, 1932; d. Frank Hurtado and Enid Pearl (Hogan) Alcalde; m. Elmer Lee Craig, Aug. 14, 1955 (dec. Jan. 1981); children: Shelley, Wendy, Cathleen, Scott. BA, San Jose State U., 1954, gen. secondary cert., 1955; postgrad. studies, various univs., 1956—. Cert. tchr. (life), Calif. Drama tchr. Willow Glen High Sch. San Jose (Calif.) Unified Sch. Dist., 1955-58, Kennedy Jr. High Sch. Cupertino (Calif.) Sch. Dist., 1968-93; cons. Cupertino Unified Sch. Dist., 1990—; coord. program activiy Growth Leadership Ctr., Mountain View, Calif., 1993; presenter Computer Use in Edn., 1990-93. Author, coord.: Drama Curriculum, 1971-93, Musical Comedy Curriculum, 1985-93, (Golden Bell, Calif. 1992). Dir. Nat. Multiple Sclerosis Soc., Santa Clara County, 1983-86. Recipient Spl. svc. award Nat. Multiple Sclerosis Soc., Santa Clara, Calif., 1986, Hon. Membership award Nat. Jr. Honor Soc., 1990, Hon. Svc. award Calif. Congress Parents, Tchrs. and Students, Inc., 1992; named Tchr. of Year, Kennedy Jr. High, Cupertino Union Sch. Dist., 1993. Mem. AAUW, NEA, Calif. Tchrs. Assn., Cupertino Edn. Assn. (rep. 1982). Home: 3381 Brower Ave Mountain View CA 94040-4512 Office: Growth Leadership Ctr 1451 Grant Rd Ste 102 Mountain View CA 94040-3250

CRAIG, LARRY EDWIN, senator; b. Council, Idaho, July 20, 1945; s. Elvin and Dorothy Craig. B.A., U. Idaho; postgrad. George Washington U. Farmer, rancher Midvale area, Idaho; mem. Idaho Senate, 1974-80, 97th-101st Congresses from 1st Dist. Idaho, 1981-90; senator 102nd Congress from Idaho, 1990-96, mem. com. agr., nutrition and forestry, com. energy and natural resources, spl. com. on aging, chmn. com. Rep. policy, vets. affairs, appropriations, chmn. subcom. on forests and pub. land mgmt., chmn. subcom. forestry conservation and rural revitalization; senator 105th Congress from Idaho, 1996—; chmn. Idaho Rep. State Senate Races, 1976-78, chmn. senate steering com.; mem. joint econ. com., com. veterans' affairs, subcom. energy R & D. Pres. Young Rep. League Idaho, 1976-77; mem. Idaho Rep. Exec. Com., 1976-78; chmn. Rep. Central Com. Washington County, 1971-72; advisor vocat. edn. in public schs. HEW, 1971-73; mem. Idaho Farm Bur., 1965-79. Served with U.S. Army N.G., 1970-74. Mem. NRA (bd. dirs. 1983—), Future Farmers of Am. (v.p. 1965). Methodist. Office: US Senate 313 Hart Bldg Washington DC 20510-0009

CRAIG, MICHAEL SCOTT, real estate executive, pharmacologist; b. Atlanta, Tex., Feb. 21, 1956; s. Hoyt Dean and Ellenda Claudia (Clements) C.; m. Angela Ruth Francisco, May 30, 1992. BS in Pharmacy, U. Tex., 1979, MBA in Real Estate/Fin., 1985. Registered pharmacist, Tex.; registered real estate broker, Calif. Pharmacist mgr. Script Shop Pharmacies, Austin, Tex., 1979-83; comml. loan credit mgr. Franklin Savs. & Loan, Austin, 1985-87; asset mgr. Continental Mgmt., Dallas, 1987-88; v.p. asset mgmt. Postal Mgmt. Svc. Corp., L.A., 1988-89; sr. v.p. asset mgmt. RRP Mgmt. Corp., L.A., 1989-96, C&S Property Svcs., L.P., L.A., 1996—; dir. Supermarket Video, Inc., L.A., 1988; cons. Assoc. U.S. Postal Svc. Lessors, L.A., 1989-93. Mem. Inst. Real Estate Mgmt., Beta Gamma Sigma.

CRAIG, SANDRA KAY, sales executive; b. Willoughby, Ohio, Nov. 21, 1962; d. Charles Soloman and Lacey Marie (Webb) Eggers; m. Robert Joseph Craig, June 28, 1986 (div. Jan. 1993); 1 child, Misty Marie Mangus; m. Robert David Del Tiempo, Feb. 14, 1995; stepchildren: Jaime Brandon, Joseph David Del Tiempo. AAB cum laude, Shawnee State U., 1985; BBA summa cum laude, Ohio U., 1987. From territory mgr. to sales mgr. ARA Cory, San Diego, 1988-90; sales rep. Rsch. Inst. Am., Menifee, Calif., 1990-92, 96—; regional sales mgr. Rsch. Inst. Am., Menifee, 1992-96, leader's coun., 1996, dist. mgr., 1996—, pres. bd. dirs., 1996-97, asst. mgr., 1997; dist. mgr. The Infortext Group (divsn. Equitrac), Torrance, Calif., 1996; cons. Video Ave., Paradise Pizza, Chillicothe, Ohio, 1987-88. Active Girl Scouts U.S., Menifee, 1988-92, Jr. All Am. Football. Mem. NAFE, NOW, PTA, Phi Kappa Phi, Phi Theta Kappa. Democrat. Home: 4888 Via de la Luna Yorba Linda CA 92886 Office: Rsch Inst Am Group 90 Fifth Ave New York NY 10011

CRAIG, STEPHEN WRIGHT, lawyer; b. N.Y.C., Aug. 28, 1932; s. Herbert Stanley and Dorothy (Simmons) C.; m. Margaret M. Baker, June 10, 1958 (div. 1984); children: Amelia Audrey, Janet Elizabeth, Peter Baker; m. Bette Piller, 1984. AB, Harvard U., 1954, JD, 1959. Bar: Maine 1959, Calif. 1960, Ariz. 1963. Reporter Daily Kennebec Jour., Augusta, Maine, 1956; with pub. rels. staff Am. Savoyards, 1957; atty. IRS, San Francisco, 1959-61; atty.-adviser U.S. Tax Ct., 1961-63; ptnr. Snell & Wilmer, Phoenix, 1963-78, Winston & Strawn (formerly Craig, Greenfield & Irwin), Phoenix, 1978-87; investment banker Myers, Craig, Vallone, Francois, 1987-89; ptnr. Brown & Bain, Phoenix and Palo Alto, Calif., 1989—; guest lectr. Amos Tuck Sch. Bus., Dartmouth U., 1962; lectr. Ariz. and N.Mex. Tax Insts., 1966-67; guest lectr. sch. law Ariz. State U., 1984, adj. prof. law, 1985-87. Chmn. Jane Wayland Child Guidance Ctr., 1968-70; mem. Maricopa County Health Planning Coun., chmn. mental health task force; bd. dirs. Combined Met. Phoenix Arts, 1968, adv. bd., 1968-69; adv. bd. Ariz. State U. Tax Insts., 1968-70; bd. dirs. Phoenix Cmty. Coun., Phoenix Cmty. Alliance. Home: 1723 E Frier Dr Phoenix AZ 85020 Office: Brown & Bain 2901 N Central Ave Ste 2000 Phoenix AZ 85012-2740

CRAIGIE, EARLE JAMES, manufacturing consultant; b. Cambridge, Mass., Feb. 5, 1944; s. James Alexander and Louisa Florence (Harwood) C.; children: Kenneth D., Wayne A. BS in Indsl. Mgmt., Northeastern U., Boston, 1973. Cert. fellow in prodn. and inventory mgmt. Line mgr. Analog Devices Inc., Norwood, Mass., 1966-80; bus. materials mgr. Digital Equipment Corp., Natick, Mass., 1980-82; promotion and tng. mgr. Digital Equipment Corp., Marlboro, Mass., 1982-84; corp. materials tng. mgr. Digital Equipment Corp., Northboro, Mass., 1984-87, materials and fin. cons., 1987-89; sr. mfg. cons. Digital Equipment Corp., Santa Clara, Calif., 1989—. Mem. Am. Prodn. and Inventory Control Soc. (past pres. Boston chpt., active mem. Santa Clara chpt., CFPIM, active mem. cert. coun.). Office: Digital Equipment Corp 2575 Augustine Dr Santa Clara CA 95054-3097

CRAIN, CHESTER RAY, statistician, consultant; b. St. Louis, Apr. 17, 1944; s. Chester Raymond and Mary Louise (Landers) C.; m. Barbara Hope Fagnan, Sept. 2, 1967; 1 child, Michelle Wigmore. AB, Knox Coll., 1965; MA, U. Calif., Riverside, 1967; PhD, U. N.Mex., 1974. Rsch. statistician Knoll Pharm. Co., Whippany, N.J., 1980; mgr. stats. McNeil Pharm., Spring House, Pa., 1980-81; sr. biostatistician Miles Pharms., West Haven, Conn., 1981-83; dir. statis. svcs. Boots Pharms., Shreveport, La., 1983-84; mgr. biometrics DuPont Co., Wilmington, Del., 1984-85, cons. dept. cen. R & D, 1985-90; dept. coord. Corp. Electronic Info. Security Com., 1987-90; sr. statistician Baxter Hyland Div., Glendale, Calif., 1990-91, Advanced Micro Devices, Sunnyvale, Calif., 1991-93; ind. cons., 1993—. Author: Scientific Computing Division's Enhanced Statistical Products Product Plan; contbr. articles to profl. jours. Mem. ASTD, Am. Soc. Quality Control (chmn-elect local sect. 1995), Am. Statis. Assn., Soc. Clin. Trials, Orgn. Devel. Network, Phi Beta Kappa, Sigma Xi. Democrat. Unitarian. Home: 1038 Sandalwood Ln Milpitas CA 95035-3232

CRALLEY, LESTER VINCENT, retired industrial hygienist, editor; b. Carmi, Ill., Mar. 27, 1911; s. John W. Cralley and Martha Jones; m. Gertrude E. Wilson, Aug. 24, 1940; 1 child, Agnes D. BS, McKendree Coll., 1933; PhD, U. Iowa, 1942. Res. officer USPHS, Bethesda, Md., 1941-45; chief indsl. hygienist Aluminum Co. of Am., Pitts., 1945-67, mgr. environ. health svcs., 1968-74; mem. Sec. of Labor's Nat. Safety Adv. Com., Washington, 1969-70. Co-editor: Theory and Rationale of Industrial Hygiene Practice, 1985, new edit., 1994, In Plant Practices for Job Related Health Hazards Control, 1989, Health and Safety Beyond the Workplace, 1990. Mem. Am. Indsl. Hygiene Assn. (hon., treas. 1953-56, pres. 1956-57, Cummings Meml. award 1971), Am. Acad. Indsl. Hygiene, Internat. Commn. on Occupational Health, Planetary Soc. Home: 1453 Banyan Dr Fallbrook CA 92028-1105

CRAM, DONALD JAMES, chemistry educator; b. Chester, Vt., Apr. 22, 1919; s. William Moffet and Joanna (Shelley) C.; m. Jane Maxwell, Nov. 25, 1969. BS, Rollins Coll., 1941; MS, U. Nebr., 1942; PhD, Harvard U., 1947; PhD (hon.), U. Uppsala, 1977; DSc (hon.), U. So. Calif., 1983, Rollins Coll., 1988, U. Nebr., 1989, U. Western Ontario, 1990, U. Sheffield, 1991. Rsch. chemist Merck & Co., 1942-45; asst. prof. chemistry UCLA, 1947-50, assoc. prof., 1950-56, prof., 1956-90, S. Winstein prof., 1985-95, univ. prof., 1988-90, univ. prof. emeritus, 1990—; chem. con. Upjohn Co., 1952-88, Union Carbide Co., 1960-81, Eastman Kodak Co., 1981-91, Technicon Co., 1984-92, Inst. Guido Donegani, Milan, 1988-91; State Dept. exch. fellow to Inst. de Quimica, Nat. U. Mex., 1956; guest prof. U. Heidelberg, Fed. Republic Germany, 1958; guest lectr. S. Africa, 1967; Centenary lectr. Chem. Soc. London, 1976. Author: From Design to Discovery, 1990, (with Pine, Hendrickson and Hammond) Organic Chemistry, 1960, 4th edit., 1980, Fundamentals of Carbanion Chemistry, 1965, (with Richards and Hammond) Elements of Organic Chemistry, 1967, (with Cram) Essence of Organic Chemistry, 1977, (with Cram) Container Molecules and Their Guests, 1994; contbr. chpts. to textbooks, articles in field of host-guest complexation chemistry, carbanions, stereochemistry, mold metabolites, large ring chemistry. Named Young Man of Yr. Calif. Jr. C. of C., 1954, Calif. Scientist of Yr., 1974, Nobel Laureate in Chemistry, 1987, UCLA medal, 1993; recipient award for creative work in synthetic organic chemistry Am. Chem. Soc., 1965, Arthur C. Cope award, 1974, Richard Tolman medal, 1985, Willard Gibbs award, 1985, Roger Adams award, 1985, Herbert Newby McCoy award, 1965, 75, Glenn Seaborg award, 1989, Nat. Medal of Science, Nat. Sci. Found., 1993; award for creative rsch. organic chemistry Synthetic Organic Chem. Mfrs. Assn., 1965; Nat. Rsch. fellow Harvard U., 1947, Am. Chem. Soc. fellow, 1947-48, Guggenheim fellow, 1954-55. Fellow Royal Soc. (hon. 1989); mem. NAS (award in chem. scis. 1992), Am. Acad. Arts and Scis., Am. Chem. Soc., Royal Soc. Chemistry, Surfers Med. Assn., San Onofre Surfing Club, Sigma Xi, Lambda Chi Alpha. Office: UCLA Dept Chemistry Los Angeles CA 90024

CRAMER, EUGENE NORMAN, nuclear power engineer, computer educator; b. Arkansas City, Kans., Apr. 26, 1932; s. Norman Charles and Hulda Margaret (Maier) C.; m. Donna Marie Gagliardi, May 18, 1957 (dec. 1984); children: Lorene, Kristine, Eileen, Carla; m. Marlene McLean, Dec. 29, 1985. B.S. in Physics, Kans. State Coll., 1955, B.S. in Math., 1955; grad. Oak Ridge Sch. Reactor Tech., 1959; M.A. in Mgmt., Claremont Grad. Sch., 1976, M.B.A., 1985. Registered profl. engr., Calif. Jr. engr. Westinghouse Bettis, Pitts., 1955-57; devel. engr. Oak Ridge Nat. Lab., 1959-69; cons. examiner AEC, 1961-73; engr. advanced energy system So. Calif. Edison, Los Angeles, 1969-88, mgr. nuclear comm., 1988-95, pres., asst. to edn. 1995—; sec. task force on nuclear safety research Electric Research Council, 1969-74; chmn. Pub. Edn. Utility Nuclear Waste Mgmt. Group, 1978-81, Pub. Edn. Calif. Radioactive Waste Mgmt. Forum, 1982—. Sect. editor Nuclear Safety jour., 1964-69. Contbr. articles to profl. jours. Mem. Capistrano Unified Sch. Dist. Edn. Found., 1994-96. Served as 1st lt. Signal Corps, U.S. Army, 1957-59. Fellow Inst. for Advancement Engrng.; mem. Am. Nuclear Soc. (bd. dirs. 1978-81, Meritorious Service award 1981, pub. info. com. 1983—), Health Physics Soc., Soc. for Risk Analysis. Republican. Roman Catholic. Club: Sierra. Home and Office: 2176 Via Teca San Clemente CA 92673-5648

CRAMER, JAMES DALE, physicist, scientific company executive; b. Canton, Ohio, Aug. 4, 1937; s. Dale and Vera Arlene (Lindower) C.; B.S., Calif. State U. at Fresno, 1960; M.S., U. Oreg., 1962; Ph.D., U. N.Mex., 1969; m. Geraldine M. Bendoski, July 20, 1957; children—Karen Lynn, Eric James. Mem. tech. staff U. Calif., Los Alamos, 1962-70; v.p., Davis-Smith Corp., San Diego, 1970-73; mem. tech. staff Sci. Applications Inc., LaJolla, Calif., 1970-73, group v.p., Albuquerque, 1973-80, dir., 1974-80; pres. Sci. & Engrng. Assocs., Inc., Albuquerque, 1980—; cons. in field. Pres. Albuquerque Mus. Found., 1981-83. Mem. Am. Phys. Soc., IEEE, Contbr. articles to profl. publs. nuclear physics. Home: PO Box 30691 Albuquerque NM 87190-0691 Office: 6100 Uptown Blvd NE Ste 700 Albuquerque NM 87110-4343*

CRAMPTON, ESTHER LARSON, sociology and political science educator; b. Plainview, Nebr., Apr. 14, 1915; d. Charles W. and Anna Margrethe (Staugaard) Larson; m. Francis Asbury Crampton, Jan. 19, 1949 (dec.); children: Jacqueline, Edith. AB, Colo. Coll. of Edn., 1935; MA, U. Wis., 1937; PhD, Am. U., 1972. Observer, writer U.S. Weather Bur., Washington, 1942-48; interpreter Portuguese RFC Rubber Devel. Corp., Manaos, Brasil, 1943; tchr. Latin Glenn County High Sch., Willows, Calif., 1954-57; tchr. Latin/German Scottsdale (Ariz.) High Sch., 1957-62; tchr. Latin Natrona County High Sch., Casper, Wyo., 1962-64; tchr. social studies Bourgade High Sch., Phoenix, 1964-65; substitute tchr. Phoenix High Sch., 1965-66; instr. supr. We. N.Mex. U. Lab. Sch., Silver City, 1966-67; prof. sociology and polit. sci. Cochise C.C., Douglas, Ariz., 1967-77. Sec., v.p., bd. dirs. Easter Seal Soc. of Santa Cruz, 1979-81; active Nat. Women's Polit. Caucus Br., Santa Cruz, 1979; tutor reading Literacy Coun., San Luis Obispo, 1988. Grantee Amazonia Rsch. Orgn. of Am. States, 1970, Am. Coun. of Learned Socs., 1941. Mem. AAUW (chair 1977-81, internat. rels. group Santa Cruz br. mem.-at-large 1981—), Am. Assn. Women in Cmty. and Jr. Colls. (charter mem.).

CRANE, STEVEN, financial company executive; b. Los Angeles, Jan. 21, 1959; s. Roger D. and Violet (Heard) C.; m. Peggy Anne Gilhooly, Apr. 25, 1987; 1 child Allison Nicole. Grad. high sch. With Mobar Inc., Torrance, Calif., 1976-78; v.p. internat. Fluid Control Internat., Marina del Rey, Calif., 1978-79; pres. Energy Devel. Internat., Torrance, 1979-85; pres., chief exec. officer Kaempen USA, Inc., Anaheim, Calif., 1985-91; founding ptnr., chmn. Western Fin. Group, Inc., Redondo Beach, Calif., 1991-95; CEO, Artist Network, Huntington Beach, Calif., 1993-95; chmn., CEO, CorpHQ Inc., Long Beach, 1995—; bd. dirs. Artist Network; chmn. bd. dirs. We. Finance Group, Inc. Mem. Office: CorpHQ-Cmty Bus Network Inc 110 Pine Ave 2d Fl Long Beach CA 90802

CRANSTON, FREDERICK PITKIN, physics educator; b. Denver, Aug. 28, 1922; s. Frederick Pitkin and Alta (Kinney) C.; m. Bonnie Louise Debe, Apr. 17, 1947 (div. Mar. 1971); children: Carol, Frederick, Rodney, claudia; m. Jerneral Warran Johnson, Mar. 21, 1971; 1 child, Lawrence Duncan Crist. BA in Physics, Colgate U., 1943; MS in Physics, Stanford U., 1950, PhD in Physics, 1959. Instr. Denver U., 1946-47; staff physicist Los Alamos (N.Mex.) Nat. Lab., 1953-62; assoc. prof. Humboldt State U., Arcata, Calif., 1962-66, prof., 1966—, dept. chair, 1971-74; cons. Lawrence Livermore (Calif.) Lab., 1964-69, Lawrence Berkeley Lab., 1970; vis. prof. U. Calif., berkeley, 1974. Pres. Los Alamos Fedn. Am. Scientists. Maj. U.S. Army, 1942-66. Mem. Am. Phys. Soc., Am. Assn. Pysics Tchrs. Democrat. Unitarian. Home: PO Box 767 Trinidad CA 95570-0767 Office: Humboldt State U Arcata CA 95521

CRANSTON, HOWARD STEPHEN, lawyer, management consultant; b. Hartford, Conn., Oct. 20, 1937; s. Howard Samuel and Agnes (Corvo) C.; m. Karen Youngman, June 16, 1962; children: Margaret, Susan. BA cum laude, Pomona Coll., 1959; LLB, Harvard U., 1962. Bar: Calif. 1963. Assoc. MacDonald & Halsted, L.A., 1964-68; ptnr. MacDonald, Halsted & Laybourne, L.A., 1968-82, of counsel, 1982-86; pres. Knapp Comm., L.A., 1982-87; pres. S.C. Cons. Corp., 1987—; bd. dirs. Boys Republic. 1st lt. U.S. Army, 1962-64. Mem. Assn. Corp. Growth, San Gabriel Country Club, Harvard Club (N.Y.). Republican. Episcopalian. Author Handbook for Creative Managers, 1987, Management Decision Mag., 1988—. Office: 1613 Chelsea Rd # 252 Pasadena CA 91108

CRAPO, MICHAEL DEAN, congressman, lawyer; b. Idaho Falls, Idaho, May 20, 1951; s. George Lavelle and Melba (Olsen) C.; m. Susan Diane Hasleton, June 22, 1974; children: Michelle, Brian, Stephanie, Lara, Paul. BA Polit. Sci. summa cum laude, Brigham Young U., 1973; postgrad., U. Utah, 1973-74; JD cum laude, Harvard U., 1977. Bar: Calif. 1977, Idaho 1979. Law clk. to Hon. James M. Carter U.S. Ct. Appeals (9th cir.), San Diego, 1977-78; assoc. atty. Gibson, Dunn & Crutcher, L.A., 1978-79; atty. Holden, Kidwell, Hahn & Crapo, Idaho Falls, 1979-92, ptnr., 1983-92; mem. Idaho State Senate from 32A Dist., 1984-93; asst. majority leader, 1987-88; pres. Pro Tempore, 1989-92; congressman U.S. House of Reps., 2d Idaho dist., Washington, 1992—; mem. commerce com., new mem. leader 103rd Congress, sophomore class leader 104th Congress, co-chair Congl. Beef Caucus, dep. whip western region U.S. House of Reps., Washington, vice chair energy and power subcom., mem. House Leadership 105th Congress; precinct committeeman Dist. 29, 1980-85; vice chmn. Legislative Dist. 29, 1984-85. Mem. Health and Welfare Com., 1985-89, Resources and Environ. Com., 1985-90, State Affairs Com., 1987-92; Rep. Pres. Task Force, 1989. Leader Boy Scouts Am., Calif., Idaho, 1977-92; mem. Bar Exam Preparation, Bar Exam Grading; chmn. Law Day.; Bonneville County chmn. Phil Batt gubernatorial campaign, 1982. Named one of Outstanding Young Men of Am., 1985; recipient Cert. of Merit Rep. Nat. Com., 1990, Guardian of Small Bus. award Nat. Fedn. of Ind. Bus., 1990, 94, Cert. of Recognition Am. Cancer Soc., 1990, Idaho Housing Agy., 1990, Idaho Lung Assn., 1985, 86, 89, Friend of Agr. award Idaho Farm Bur., 1989-90, medal of merit Rep. Presdl. Task Force, 1989, Nat. Legislator of Yr. award Nat. Rep. Legislators Assn., 1991, Golden Bulldog award Watchdogs of the Treas., 1996, Thomas Jefferson award Nat. Am. Wholesale Grocers Assn.-Ind. Food Distbrs. Assn., 1996, Spirit of Enterprise award U.S. C. of C., 1993, 94, 95, 96. Mem. ABA (antitrust law sect.), Idaho Bar Assn., Rotary. Mormon. Office: US Ho of Reps 437 Cannon HOB Washington DC 20515

CRAVEN, JAMES MICHAEL, economist, educator; b. Seattle, Mar. 10, 1946; s. Homer Henry and Mary Kathleen Craven; m. Aleyamma P. Thomas, Aug. 27, 1977; 1 child, Christina Kathleen Florindo-Craven. Student, U. Minn., 1966-68; BA in Sociology, U. Manitoba, Winnipeg, Can., 1971, BA in Econs., 1971, MA in Econs., 1974. Lic. pilot; cert. ground instr. Instr. econ. and bus. Red River C.C., Winnipeg, 1974-76; lectr. rsch. methods of stats. U. Manitoba, Winnipeg, 1977-78; instr. econ. and bus. Big Bend C.C., Moses Lake, Wash., 1980-81; planning analyst Govt. P.R., San Juan, 1984; prof. econs. and bus. Interam. U. P.R., Bayamon, 1984-85; instr. econs., lectr. history Green River C.C., Auburn, Wash., 1988-92; prof. dept. chair econs. Clark Coll., Vancouver, Wash., 1992—; adj. prof. econs. Wash. State U., 1997—; vis. prof. St. Berchman's U., Kerala, India, 1981, 83, 86, 91; instr. econs. Bellevue (Wash.) C.C., 1988-92; cons. Bellevue, 1988—, Irwin Pubs., 1995—; adj. prof. econs. Wash. State U., 1997—. Inventor in field; contbr. articles to profl. jours. Platform com. mem. Wash. State Dem., Seattle, 1992; cons. Lowry for Gov. Campaign, Seattle, 1992; mem. (assoc.) Dem. Party Nat. Com., 1994—; mem. Nat. Steering Com. for Re-election of Pres. Clinton, 1995-96; mem. Pres.'s Second Term Com., 1996—. With U.S. Army, 1963-66. Recipient pilot wings FAA, 1988-92; Govt. Can. fellow, 1973-74. Mem. AAUP, Internat. Platform Assn., Assn. Northwest Econ. Educators, Wash. Edn. Assn. Syrian Orthodox. Home: 904 NE Minnehaha St Apt C9 Vancouver WA 98665-8732 Office: Clark Coll Dept Econs 1800 E Mcloughlin Blvd Vancouver WA 98663-3509

CRAVEN, WILLIAM DONALD, internal auditor, consultant; b. Kennewick, Wash., Dec. 18, 1959; s. William Chester and Donna Marie (Wilson) C.; m. Sheri May Emery, Aug. 4, 1984; 1 child, Amanda Irene. BA in Polit. Sci., Wash. State U., 1985; BS in Acctg., Cen. Wash. U., 1987; postgrad., Wash. State U. CPA, Wash., Va.; cert. govt. fin. mgr.; cert. mgmt. acct. Photographer Tri-City Herald, Kenewick, 1976-78; mgr. ANDCO Corp., Seattle, 1983-84; auditor Def. Contract Audit Agy., Seattle, 1987-90, ops. auditor, 1990-91, sr. auditor, 1991-94; cost/price analyst Westinghouse Hanford Co., Richland, Wash., 1994-96, Fluor Daniel Hanford, Inc., Richland, 1996-97; internal auditor Bechtel Hanford, Inc., Richland, 1997—. Bd. dirs. Richland Police Citizen Adv. Bd., 1995-98, Richland Utility Adv. Bd., 1996-2002; treas. Sacajawea Elem. PTA, Richland, 1995-96; sec./treas. Deaf-Blind Svc. Ctr., Seattle, 1993-94. Mem. AICPA, Inst. Mgmt. Accts., Assn. Govt. Accts., Wash. Soc. CPAs (pres. Seattle chpt. 1992-93, dir. 1994-96, Outstanding Leadership award 1992, Chpt. Pres. of Yr. 1993), Inst. Internal Auditors, Nat. Contract Mgmt. Assn., MENSA, Kiwanis Club Three Rivers. Home: 518 Doubletree Ct Richland WA 99352 Office: Fluor Daniel Hanford Inc 2355 Stevens Dr Richland WA 99352

CRAW, NICHOLAS WESSON, motor sports association executive; b. Governor's Island, N.Y., Nov. 14, 1936; s. Demas Thurlow Craw and Mary Victoria Wesson. BA, Princeton U., 1959; MBA, Harvard U., 1982. Dir. ops. Project Hope, Washington, 1960-68; pres., CEO Scorpio Racing, Washington, 1968-80, Sports Car Club Am., Englewood, Colo., 1983—; pres. Sports Car Club Am. Found, Englewood, 1986—; chmn. Nat. Motorsports Coun., 1992—; bd. dirs. SCCA Pro Racing Ltd., SCCA Enterprises, Inc., Rsch. Sys., Inc. Dir. Manpower divsn. VISTA, Washington, 1970-72; assoc. dir. ACTION, Washington, 1972-73; dir. U.S. Peace Corps, Washington, 1973-74. Office: Sports Car Club Am 9033 E Easter Pl Englewood CO 80112-2105

CRAWFORD, CHARLOTTE JOANNE, psychologist, psychoanalyst, psychological anthropologist; b. Santiago, Chile, June 10, 1942; came to U.S., 1953; d. Randall LaVern and Florence Ahleen (Bamber) C.; m. José Maria Garcia-Diez, Dec. 28, 1969 (div. Sept. 1986); children: S. Amaya Garcia, Tamara S. Garcia. BA in Sociology, U. Wash., 1965; MA in Anthropology, Columbia U., 1969; Lic. Psychology, U. Barcelona, Spain, 1974, PhD in Psychology, 1982. From asst. prof. to assoc. prof. U. Basque Country, Bilbao, Spain, 1970-90; vis. scholar Harvard U., Cambridge, 1990-91; rsch. assoc. U. Calif., Berkeley, 1991-92; clinician Children's Health Coun., Palo Alto, Calif., 1992-95, San Jose (Calif.) Unified Sch. Dist., 1995-96; adj. faculty Wright Inst., Berkeley, 1991-93, Pacific Grad. Sch. Psychology, Palo Alto, 1991-93, Saybrook Inst., San Francisco, 1992—; pvt. practice clinician, Bilbao, 1975-90, Oakland, Calif., 1997. Author, editor: Identidad: Norma y Diversidad, 1988; author: La Psicoterapia de Inspiración Psicoanalitica, 1989, Estudio Integral de la Personalidad, 1990. Study fellow for internat. devel. Ford Found., 1966-68, grad. fellow Govt. of Spain, 1975-77; Barandiaran grantee Soc. for Basque Studies, 1981-83, rsch. grantee U. Basque Country, 1987-88, 90-91, 91-92, grantee Govt. of Spain, 1988-90, 90-91. Mem. APA, Internat. Psychoanalytical Studies Orgn. (pres. 1983-85), Soc. Psychol. Anthropology, Am. Anthropol. Assn. Democrat. Home and office: 1863 Clemens Rd Oakland CA 94602

CRAWFORD, GEORGE TRUETT, health facility executive; b. Alcorn County, Miss., Mar. 13, 1936; s. Bascrum Claude and Louise K. (Killough) C. Grad., Northwest Christian Coll., Interfaith Sem., Santa Cruz, Calif., 1997. Ordained Interfaith Min., Apr. 1997. Dir. food svcs. Food Dimensions, Inc., San Francisco, 1975-81; dir. food and nutrition Dominican Santa Cruz (Calif.) Hosp., 1981-90; pres. Diverse Mgmt. Sys., Half Moon Bay, Calif., 1990-94; dir. guest svcs. Sutter Maternity and Surgery Ctr., Santa Cruz, Calif., 1996-97; cons. Diverse Mgmt. Sys., 1987-89; bd. dirs. food tech. adv. bd. Cabrillo Coll., Santa Cruz. Contbr. articles to profl. jours. Pres. Calif. Hosp. Food Svc. Adminstrn., San Francisco, 1979. Mem. Interfaith Mins. Assn., Food Svc. Cons. Soc. Internat. Am. Soc. Hosp. Food Svc. Adminstrn. No. Calif. (sec. 1975-77, pres.-elect 1978, pres. 1979), Nat. Inst. Off Premise Catering (faculty). Republican. Interfaith. Home: 808 Balboa Ave Capitola CA 95010-2338

CRAWFORD, JAMES BARCLAY, management consultant, travel writer; b. Evanston, Ill., Sept. 12, 1949; s. John William and Margaret Gilbert (Stephens) C. BS in Polit. Sci., Mktg., Mich. State U., 1971, M of Labor - Indls. Rels., 1972. Pers. adminstr. Hewlett Packard Co., Cupertino, Calif., 1972-76; cons. Crawford Assocs., Scotts Valley, Calif., 1976-78; mgr. compensation/benefits ROLM Corp., Santa Clara, Calif., 1978-82; v.p., human resources and adminstr. Xebec Corp., San Jose, Calif., 1982-84; mgmt. cons. Pescadero, Calif., 1984—; chmn. Peninsula Compensation Assn., Palo Alto, Calif., 1981-82; founder, chmn. Santa Clara Mfg. Group Com. on Health Care, 1982-83; guest lectr. Stanford U. Grad. Sch. Bus., 1979-84, U. Santa Clara, 1980, San Jose State U., 1982-83; instr. H.R. Mgmt. Cert. Program Am. Electronics Assn., Santa Clara, 1981—. Author: Honor Camp 1979, Compensation Management, 1981, rev. edit., 1985, Corporate Benefits Mgmt., 1982, rev. edit., 1996; contbr. over 40 travel articles. Home and Office: 9649 Cabrillo Hwy Pescadero CA 94060-9712

CRAWFORD, KEVAN CHARLES, nuclear engineer, educator; b. Salt Lake City, Utah, Jan. 26, 1956; s. Paul Gibson and Norma Irene (Christiansen) C. MS, U. Utah, 1983, PhD, 1986. Lic. Sr. reactor oper. U.S. NRC. V.p. Computer Mktg. Corp., Salt Lake City, 1977-81; sr. reactor engr. U. Utah Nuclear Engring. Lab., Salt Lake City, 1981-86; mgr. reactor ops. Tex. A&M U. Nuclear Sci. Ctr., College Station, Tex., 1986-88; prof. U. Utah, Salt Lake City, 1988-92, Idaho State U., Pocatello, 1991-94; pres. Precision Engring. Corp., Salt Lake City, 1994—; cons. Envirocare of Utah, Inc., Salt Lake City, 1989, Westinghouse Idaho Nuclear, 1992-93, Belarussian Popular Front, 1996-97. Cadet Air Force Acad., 1974-75. S.S. Kisler scholar U. Utah, Salt Lake City, 1975-78; Fulbright prof. Minsk, Belarus, 1994-95. Mem. Am. Nuclear Soc., Am. Soc. Engring. Educators, Phi Kappa Phi, Alpha Nu Sigma. Mormon. Office: Precision Engring Corp 3781 S 3145 E Salt Lake City UT 84109-3744

CRAWFORD, MARCELLA, migrant bilingual resource educator; b. Durango, Colo., Sept. 25, 1958; d. Antonio José and Antonia Rosa (Montaño) Martinez; m. James DeForest Crawford, Oct. 17, 1980; stepchildren: Jessie, Rheanna; children: Jamie, Sean. BA, So. Oreg. State Coll., Ashland, 1990. Migrant bilingual resource tchr. Klamath Falls (Oreg.) City Schs., 1990—, Mills Elem., Ponderosa Jr. H.S., Klamath Falls, 1990-93, Fairview Elem. Sch., Klamath Falls, 1993-94, Fairview Elem., Mills Elem., Klamath Falls, 1994-95, Mills Elem. Sch., Klamath Falls, 1995—; mem. 2d Lang. Com., 1994—. Troop leader Girl Scouts U.S.A., Klamath Falls, Oreg., 1986-91; bilingual translator, 1996—. Home: 1903 Crest St Klamath Falls OR 97603-4700 Office: Mills Elem Sch 520 E Main St Klamath Falls OR 97601-3236

CRAWFORD, MICHAEL, city council; married. BS in Computer Sci., Wright State U., 1988; law degree, U. Ariz., 1991. Clk. Ariz. Ct. Appeals; computer software cons.; vice chmn. Ariz. Common Cause; criminal def. atty. Pima County Pub. Defenders Office, 1994—. Office: 1510 E Grant Rd Tucson AZ 85719

CRAWFORD, NATALIE WILSON, applied mathematician; b. Evansville, Ind., June 24, 1939; d. John Moore and Edna Dorothea (Huthsteiner) Wilson; BA in Math., U. Calif., L.A., 1961, postgrad., 1964-67; m. Robert Charles Crawford, Mar. 1, 1969. Programmer analyst N.Am. Aviation Corp., El Segundo, Calif., 1961-64; mem. tech. staff Rand Corp., Santa Monica, Calif., 1964—, project leader, engring. tech., theater conflict and force employment programs, 1975—; dir. Theater Forces Program, 1988-90, Theater Force Employment Program, 1990-92, Force Structure and Force Modernization Program, 1992-93, Force Modernization and Employment Program, 1993-95, assoc. dir. Project Air Force, 1995—; mem. Air Force Sci. Adv. Bd., 1988—, vice chmn., 1990-91, co-chmn., 1996—; cons., joint tech. coordinating group munition effectiveness. Named YWCA Woman of Yr., 1983. Mem. Am. Def. Preparedness Assn., USAF Assn. Republican. Home: 20940 Big Rock Dr Malibu CA 90265-5316

CRAWFORD, PHILIP STANLEY, bank executive; b. Wichita, Kans., Nov. 30, 1944; s. Carson Eugene and Elizabeth Ellen (Childs) C.; m. Carolyn Louise Stephenson, June 10, 1989. BA, Sterling Coll., 1967; MBA, Baruch Coll., 1973. Programmer, analyst City of N.Y., 1968-72; planning analyst Fed. Reserve Bank, Boston, 1972-74; cons. Index Systems, Cambridge, Mass., 1974-79; sr. cons. Ernst & Whinney, Los Angeles, 1979; v.p. Union Bank, Los Angeles, 1979—. Mem. Pres.'s Coun. Sterling Coll. Mem. Mgmt. Info. Continuing Seminar (pres. 1985), Assn. Computing Machinery. Republican. Home: 3815 Olive Ave Long Beach CA 90807-3519 Office: Union Bank 1980 Satura St Monterey Park CA 91755

CRAWFORD, SARAH CARTER (SALLY CRAWFORD), broadcast executive; b. Glen Ridge, N.J., Oct. 3, 1938; d. Raymond Hitchings and Katherine Latta (Gribbel) Carter; m. Joseph Paul Crawford III, Sept. 10, 1960 (dec. 1966). BA, Smith Coll., 1960. Media dir. Kampmann & Bright, Phila., 1961-64; sr. media buyer Foote, Cone & Belding, N.Y.C., 1964-69; assoc. media dir. Grey Advt., Los Angeles, 1969-75; account exec., research dir. Sta. KHJ-TV, Los Angeles, 1975-76; mgr. local sales Sta. KCOP-TV, Los Angeles, 1977-82; gen. sales mgr. Sta. KTVF-TV, Fairbanks, Alaska, 1982-96; nat. sales mgr. KTVF, KTVA, Fairbanks, 1996—; bd. dirs. Vista Travel, Fairbanks; mem. adv. com. Golden Valley Electric Corp., Fairbanks, 1984-86; mem. coun. UAF Tanana County Campus, 1989-96, chair mktg. com. Chmn. Fairbanks Health and Social Svc. Commn., 1986-96; vice chmn. Fairbanks North Star Borough Health and Social Svc. Commn., 1993-96; pres. Fairbanks Meml. Hosp. Aux., 1988-90, creator trust fund, chmn. fin. com., 1990-94; bd. dirs. Fairbanks Downtown Assn., 1984-87; mem. FBKS Health Ctr. Coalition; mem. search com. UAF Tanana Valley Campus dir.; bd. dirs. Interior Regional Health Corp.; mem. Tesoro (Alaska) Citizens Adv. Coun. Mem. Fairbanks Women's Softball Assn., Fairbanks Women's Hockey Assn.. Episcopalian. Office: KTVF/KTVA 401 International Airport Anchorage AK 99518

CRAWSHAW, RALPH, psychiatrist; b. N.Y.C., July 3, 1921. A.B., Middlebury (Vt.) Coll., 1943; M.D., N.Y. U., 1947. Diplomate: Nat. Bd. Med. Examiners, Am. Bd. Psychiatry and Neurology. Intern Lenox Hill Hosp., N.Y.C., 1947-48; resident Menninger Sch. Psychiatry, Topeka, 1948-50, Oreg. State Hosp., Salem, 1950-51; practice medicine specializing in psychiatry Washington, 1954; staff psychiatrist C.F. Menninger Meml. Hosp., Topeka, 1954-57; asst. chief VA Mental Hygiene Clinic, Topeka, 1957-60; staff psychiatrist Community Child Guidance Clinic, Portland, Oreg., 1960-63; founder, clinic dir. Tualatin Valley Guidance Clinic, Beaverton, Oreg., 1961-67; pvt. practice medicine, specializing in psychiatry Portland, 1960—; mem. staff Holladay Park Hosp., 1961—; lectr. dept. child psychiatry Med. Sch. U. Oreg., 1961-63, clin. prof. dept. psychiatry, 1976; lectr. Sch. Social Work, Portland State U., 1964-67; founder Banjamin Rush Found., 1968, pres., 1968—; founder Friends of Medicine, 1969, Ct. of Man, 1970, Club of Kos, 1974, Oreg. Health Decisions, 1983, Am. Health Decisions, 1989, Health Vol. Overseas, 1984; Sonian Machanic vis. prof. South African Coll. Medicine, 1993. Contbr. editor: AMA Jour. of Socio-Econs, 1972-75; Columnist: Prism mag, 1972-76, The Pharos, 1972—, Portland Physician, 1975, Western Jour. Medicine, 1980—; Contbr. articles to med. jours. Cons. Bur. Hearings and Appeals, HEW, 1964-90; cons. Albina Child Devel. Center, Portland, 1965-75, HEW Region 8 Health Planning, 1979; mem. Inst. Medicine, Nat. Acad. Sci., 1978, Oreg. Health Coordinating Council, 1979; Mem. Gov.'s Adv. Com. on Mental Health, 1966-72; ad hoc com. Nat. Leadership Conf. on Am. Health Policy, 1976, Gov.'s Adv. Com. on Med. Care to Indigent, 1976—; trustee Millicent Found., 1964-67, Multnomah Found. for Med. Care, 1977; pres. Bull Run Heritage Found., 1996; vis. scholar Center for Study Democratic Instns., 1969, Jack Murdock Charitable Trust, 1977, U.S.-USSR exchange scholar, 1973; founder Bull Run Heritage Found., 1996. Served with AUS, 1943-46; to lt., M.C. USN, 1951-54. Named Oreg. Dr./Citizen of Yr., 1978; U.S.-USSR rsch. scholar, 1973, 79; recipient I.N. Piragou medal for humanitarian Svcs., Russian Govt., 1992; Ralph Crawshaw Ann. Lectr. in Civic Medicine named in honor by Oreg. Found. for Med. Excellence, 1987. Fellow Am. Psychiat. Assn.; mem. AMA, APA, AAAS, Nat. Med. Assn., Oreg. Med. Assn. (trustee 1972—), Multnomah County Med. Soc. (pres. 1975), Royal Soc. Medicine, Inst. of Medicine of NAS, North Pacific Soc. Neurology and Psychiatry, Soc. for Psychol. Study Social Issues, Western European Assn. Aviation Psychology, Am. Med. Writers Assn., Portland Psychiatrists in Pvt. Practice (pres. 1971), Russian Acad. Natural Scis. (fgn. mem.), Alpha Omega. Address: 2525 NW Lovejoy St Ste 404 Portland OR 97210-2865

CRAYMER, LORING GODDARD, engineer; b. Oklahoma City, Feb. 17, 1950; s. Loring Gentry and Mary Frances (Morrison) C.; m. Susan Jane Eberlein, Aug. 7, 1982 (div. 1988); 1 child, Kenneth Loring. BS in Biology, Calif. Inst. Tech., 1972; PhD in Genetics, U. Wis., 1977. Rsch. fellow Calif. Inst. Tech., 1977-87; mem. tech. staff Jet Propulsion Lab., Pasadena, Calif., 1988—. Contbr. articles to profl. jours. Office: Jet Propulsion Lab 4800 Oak Grove Dr Pasadena CA 91109-8001

CREAN, JOHN C., housing and recreational vehicles manufacturing company executive; b. Bowden, N.D., 1925; married. Founder Fleetwood Enterprises, Inc., Riverside, Calif., 1950, pres., 1952-70, chmn., chief exec. officer, 1950—, also dir. Served with USN, 1942; with U.S. Mcht. Marines, 1944-45. Office: Fleetwood Enterprises Inc PO Box 7638 3125 Myers St Riverside CA 92513-7638

CREASON, PAUL JOSEPH, college administrator; b. Sierra Madre, Calif., Nov. 4, 1966; s. Stephen Gary amd Barbara Jo (Valencia) C.; m. Sandra Sue Swarts, Mar. 18, 1995; children: Anthony, Julia. AA, Cypress Coll., 1987; BA, Calif. State U., Fullerton, 1989, MA, 1995. R&D technician Cerritos Coll., Norwalk, Calif., 1988-90; rsch. ananlyst Long BEach (Calif.) City Coll., 1990-95, dir. grants, 1995—. Mem. Nat. Coun. Resource Devel., Rsch. and Planning Group, Los Serranos Golf Club. Democrat. Office: Long Beach City Coll 4901 E Carson St Long Beach CA 90808-1706

CREECH, WILBUR LYMAN, retired military officer; b. Argyle, Mo., Mar. 30, 1927; s. Paul and Marie (Maloney) C.; m. Carol Ann DiDomenico, Nov. 20, 1969; 1 son, William L. Student, U. Mo., 1946-48; B.S., U. Md., 1960; M.S., George Washington U., 1966; postgrad., Nat. War Coll., 1966. Commd. 2d lt. U.S. Air Force, 1949; advanced through grades to gen.; fighter pilot 103 combat missions USAF, North Korea, 1950-51; pilot USAF Thunderbirds, 1953-56; comdr., leader Skyblazers, Europe aerial demo team USAF, 1956-60; dir. Fighter Weapons Sch., Nellis AFB, Nev., 1960-61; advisor to comdr. Argentine Air Force, 1962; exec., aide to comdr. Tactical Air Command, 1962-65; dep. comdr. fighter wing, 177 combat missions in F-100 fighters and asst. dep. chief staff for ops. 7th Air Force, Vietnam, 1968-69; comdr. fighter wings USAF in Europe, Spain and W.Ger., 1969-71; dep. for ops. and intelligence Air Forces Europe, 1971-74; comdr. Electronic Systems Div., Hanscom AFB, Mass., 1974-77; asst. vice chief of staff HQS Air Force, Washington, 1977-78; comdr. Tactical Air Command, Langley AFB, Va., 1978-85; lectr., internat. mgmt. expert; cons. in field. Author: The Five Pillars of TQM, 1994. Decorated D.S.M. with three oak leaf clusters, Silver Star medal, Legion of Merit with two oak leaf clusters, D.F.C. with three oak leaf clusters, Air medal with 14 oak leaf clusters, Air Force Commendation medal with two oak leaf clusters, Army Commendation medal; Spanish Grand Cross. Home and Office: 20 Quail Run Rd Henderson NV 89014-2147

CREEL, DONNELL JOSEPH, research scientist, educator; b. Kansas City, Mo., June 17, 1942; m. Jalna Rose Schultz, Nov. 10, 1977; 1 child, Molly Rose. BA, U. Mo., 1964, MA, 1966; PhD, U. Utah, 1969. Rsch. assoc. VA, Kansas City, Mo., 1969-71; chief neuropsychology rsch. VA, Phoenix, 1971-76; rsch. scientist VA, Salt Lake City, 1976-78, rsch. career scientist, 1979—; rsch. prof. ophthalmology U. Utah, Salt Lake City, 1982—. Author book chpts. Decision Making in Pediatric Opthalmology, 1993, Metabolic and Molecular Basis of Inherited Disease, 1995, others; contbr. articles to profl. jours. Office: U Utah Moran Eye Ctr Salt Lake City UT 84132

CREER, JAMES READ, financial officer; b. Ogden, Utah, Oct. 26, 1942; s. Harold and Geraldine (Jacobson) C.; m. Ann L. Curran, Aug. 7, 1964 (div. Aug. 1974); children: Wendy, Kellie, Mark, Jennifer; m. Carolyn Rudd, Jan. 11, 1985. BS in Acctg., U. Utah, 1968. CPA. Staff acct. PMM & Co., L.A., 1968-71; sr. acct. PMM & Co., Salt Lake City, 1971-72, Haynie, Tebbs & Smith, Salt Lake City, 1972-73; ptnr. Roberts & Creer, Salt Lake City, 1973-74; pvt. practice Salt Lake City, 1974-81; pres., CEO Johnstone Supply, Salt Lake City, 1995—; v.p., CFO ACW Enterprises Inc., Salt Lake City, 1989—; pres. Creer Corp., 1995—; acctg. instr. Utah Tech. Coll., Stevens-Henegar Coll. Bus., 1973-76. With USMC, 1960-63. Mem. Children's Justice Ctr. (adv. bd.), Rotary (pres. so. Salt Lake City chpt. 1989-90, Paul Harris fellow 1988). Republican. Mem. LDS Ch. Office: Johnstone Supply 2940 S 300 W Salt Lake City UT 84115-3405

CREIGHTON, JOHN W., JR., forest products company executive; b. Pitts., Sept. 1, 1932; married; 3 children. BS, Ohio State U., 1954, JD, 1957; MBA, U. Miami, 1965. With Arthur Andersen and Co., 1957-59, Arvida Corp., 1959-66; exec. v.p. Mortgage Cons. Inc., 1966-70; gen. mgr. Shelter Group Weyerhaeuser Co., 1970, corp. v.p., 1970-85, exec. v.p., 1985-88, pres., dir., 1988—, pres., CEO; bd. dirs. Am. Forest and Paper Assoc., Unocal Corp., Quality Food Ctrs. Inc., Civil War Trust, Wash. Energy Co., Portland Gen. Corp., Local Initiatives Support Corp., NHP, Inc.; mem. press devel. adv. bd. U. Wash. Trustee U. Puget Sound; pres. Boy Scouts Am. With U.S. Army, 1954-56. Office: Weyerhaeuser Co 33663 Weyerhaeuser Way S Federal Way WA 98003

CREIGHTON, JOHN WALLIS, JR., consultant, author, former management educator; b. Yeung Kong, China, Apr. 7, 1916; s. John Wallis and Lois (Jameson) C.; m. Harriet Harrington, June 30, 1940; childrn: Carol (Mrs. Brian LeNeve), Joan (Mrs. Robert Nielsen). Student, Wooster Coll., 1933-36; BS in Forestry, U. Mich., 1938; AB, Hastings Coll., 1939; PhD in Wood Tech. and Indsl. Engring., U. Mich., 1954. Operator, sawmill Cayahoga Falls, Ohio, 1939-41; mem. staff U.S. Bd. Econ. Warfare, Ecuador, 1941-43; asst. gen. mgr. R.S. Bacon Veneer Co., Chgo., 1943-44; gen. mgr., v.p. Bacon Lumber Co., Sunman, Ind., 1943-45; mem. faculty Mich. State U., Lansing, 1945-54; prof. wood tech. Mich. State U., 1945-54; asst. to gen. mgr., v.p. Baker Furniture Inc., Grand Rapids, Mich., 1954-58; pres. Creighton Bldg. Co., Santa Barbara, Calif., 1958-65; prof. mgmt. Colo. State U., Fort Collins, 1965-67, U.S. Naval Postgrad. Sch., Monterey, Calif., 1967-86; emeritus prof. U.S. Naval Postgrad. Sch., 1986—, chmn. dept., 1967-71, dir. fed. exec. mgmt. program, 1974-82; cons. to govt. Assoc editor and co-founder Jour. Tech. Transfer, 1975-88; contbr. papers to field. Mem. Forestry Commn., Carmel, Calif., 1986-95. Recipient various research grants in lumber mfg., research and orgn. studies for U.S. Navy and U.S. Forest Service. Mem. Tech. Transfer Soc., Writer's Internat. Network, Calif. Writer's Club. Presbyterian. Home: 8065 Lake Pl Carmel CA 93923-9514

CREPEAU, JOHN CHRISTIAN, mechanical engineer; b. Long Beach, Calif., July 21, 1961; s. Philip Cochrane and Patricia Ann (Ryan) C.; m. Maarn Jergensen, May 14, 1963; children: Megan, Philip. Robin. BS, U. Calif., Berkeley, 1983; PhD, U. Utah, 1991. Engr. Litton Guidance and Control, Woodland Hills, Calif., 1983-84, Hercules Aerospace, Magna, Utah, 1987, Hydroflame Corp., Salt Lake City, 1988; instr., vis. asst. prof. U. Utah, Salt Lake City, 1988-92; scientist Andrulis Rsch. Corp., Salt Lake City, 1988-92; postdoctoral fellow Humboldt U., Berlin, Fed. Republic of Germany, 1992-93; asst. prof. Dept. Mech. Engring. U. Idaho, Idaho Falls, 1993—; deans coun. U. Utah, Salt Lake City, 1989-90; bd. dirs. Westmark Fed. Credit Union. Missionary LDS Ch., Guatemala, Cen. Am., 1984-86. Recipient John F. McCarthy, Jr. Meml. award Internat. Coun. Aero. Scis., 1990. Mem. AIAA (assoc., Abe M. Zarem award 1990), ASME (assoc.), Am. Phys. Soc. Office: U Idaho PO Box 50778 Idaho Falls ID 83405

CRESPI, VINCENT HENRY, physicist; b. Hinsdale, Ill., Aug. 29, 1966; s. Henry Louis and Mary Joan Crespi. BS in Physics, MIT, 1988; PhD in Physics, Univ. Calif., Berkeley, 1994. Rsch. asst. Univ. Calif., Berkeley, 1989-94, postdoctoral rschr., 1994-96; founder Number 2, Inc., 1996—; asst. prof. Pa. State U., 1997—; lectr. Univ. Calif., Berkeley, 1995-96. Author book chpt., 1993; founder Index of Physics Rsch., 1997; patentee in field; contbr. articles to profl. jours. Nat. Merit scholar, 1984; NSF fellow, 1988, Sci. and Engring. Grad. fellow Dept. Def., 1991. Mem. KQED, Am. Physical Soc., Phi Beta Kappa.

CRESWELL, DONALD CRESTON, management consultant; b. Balt.; s. Carroll Creston and Verna Moore (Taylor) C.; student Johns Hopkins U.; MBA, U. Dayton; postgrad. bus. Stanford U.; m. Terri Sue Tidwell; 1 child, Creston Lee. Cons. engr. A.D. Ring & Assocs., Washington; sales and mktg. mgr. Ampex Corp., Redwood City, Calif.; dir. mktg., magnetic products div. RCA Corp., N.Y.C.; staff v.p. sales and advt. Pan Am. World Airways, N.Y.C.; prin. mgmt. cons., dir. mktg. svcs. Stanford Rsch. Inst., Menlo Park, Calif.; v.p. and gen. mgr. Decisions Systems; dir. R & D Strategy Practice; gen. mgr. R & D Decision Quality Assoc.; with Strategic Decisions Group, Menlo Park, Calif., 1987—; bd. dirs. Rogerson Aircraft Controls, 1981-85; bd. dirs., mgmt. com. Jets Cybernetics, 1987-94; lectr. planning and mktg. mgmt. Am. Mgmt. Assn., 1968-69; program chmn. Grad. Bus. Assn., 1965; rep. to Electronics Industries Assn., 1968-71, to Internat. Air Transport Assn., 1971-74. Bd. dirs. Peninsula Youth Soccer Club, 1981-82; nat. dir. referee assessment, mem. referee com. U.S. Soccer Fedn., 1986-88; regional chief referee San Carlos Am. Youth Soccer Orgn., 1981-85; State dir. assessment Calif. Soccer Assn., 1982-85; mem. L.A. Olympics Organizing Com., 1983-84, nat. referee assessor, 1987—; ofcl. N. Am. Soccer League, 1983-84, World Cup, 1994. Mem. Am. Mktg. Assn. (exec. mem.), Am. Theatre Organ Assn. (bd. dirs. 1978-79), Nat. Intercollegiate Soccer Ofcls. Assn. (World cup video inspector, 1994), Charles Lindbergh Fund, U.S. Soccer Fedn. (cert. soccer referee, nat. assessor, USSF referee inspector), Wings Club, The Churchill Club, Stanford Jazz Com. Republican. Home: 8 Pyrola Ln San Carlos CA 94070-1532 Office: Strategic Decisions Group 2440 Sand Hill Rd Menlo Park CA 94025-6900

CRETARA, DOMENIC ANTHONY, artist, educator; b. Chelsea, Mass., Mar. 29, 1946; s. Anthony Mario and Carmella (Addivinola) C.; BFA magna cum laude, Boston U., 1968, MFA, 1970; m. Elizabeth Tarquinio, June 20, 1970; children: Jeanette, Anthony. One-man shows: Art Inst. Boston, 1976, Boston U., 1977, Camargo Found., Cassis, France, 1979, Helen Bumpus Gallery, Duxbury, Mass., 1980, Coll. William and Mary, 1980, U. Mass., 1980, Duxbury Art Complex Mus., 1982, First St. Gallery, N.Y.C., 1983, Segal Gallery, N.Y.C., 1984, 85, Koplin Gallery, L.A., 1987, Victor McNeil Gallery, N.Y.C., 1988, Alon Gallery, Brookline, Mass., 1989, 91, 95, John Thomas Gallery, Santa Monica, Calif., 1991-93, Brenda Taylor Gallery, N.Y.C., 1995-96, Mulligan Gallery, San Francisco, 1997; group shows: Fitchburg (Mass.) Art Mus., 1973, Am. Embassy, Rome, 1975, Inst. Internat. Edn., N.Y.C., 1978, Boston Cyclorama, 1980, Drawing Ctr., N.Y.C., 1983, Weatherspoon Art Gallery, Greensboro, N.C., 1983, Sherry French Gallery, N.Y.C., 1987, L.A. Internat. Arts Fair, 1975, 86, 88, 96, Riverside (Calif.) Art Mus., 1989, Triton Mus. Art, Santa Clara, Calif., 1990, 94, Gallery 84, N.Y.C., 1994, Mulligan-Shanosky Gallery, San Francisco, 1995, others; represented in permanent collections: Boston U., Art Inst. Boston, Met. Mus., Triton Art Mus., Duxbury Art Ctr. Mus., Riverside Art Mus., Calif.; represented by Brenda Taylor Gallery, N.Y., Mulligan-Shanosky Gallery, San Francisco; instr. painting DeCordova Mus. Sch., Lincoln, Mass., 1971-73, Fitchburg Art Mus., 1970-74; chmn. fine arts dept. Art Inst. Boston, 1972-78, instr. painting and drawing, 1970-83, assoc. prof. painting, 1983-86; prof. painting Calif. State U.-Long Beach, 1986—. Fulbright-Hays grantee, Italy, 1974-75; resident painter Camargo Found., Cassis, France,

1978-79; Boston-Padua Sister Cities grantee, 1984. Mem. Coll. Art Assn. Drawings and paintings reproduced in: Figure Drawing, 1976; The Art of Responsive Drawing, 1977, American Artist, 1992, Oil Highlights, 1995; Painting: Visual and Technical Fundamentals, 1979. Video: Domenic Cretara Painting Circumstantial Evidence (Best Shot Video award Bronxville, N.Y., 1997); Contbr. articles to The Artist's Mag., 1990, 91, 93, Am. Artist, 1995.

CREWS, WILLIAM ODELL, JR., seminary administrator; b. Houston, Feb. 8, 1936; s. William O. Sr. and Juanita (Pearson) C.; m. Wanda Jo Ann Cunningham; children: Ronald Wayne, Rhonda Ann Crews Bolei. BA, Hardin Simmons U., 1957, HHD, 1987; BDiv, Southwestern Bapt. Theol. Sem., 1964; DD, Calif. Bapt. Coll., 1987. Ordained to ministry Bapt. Ch., 1953. Pastor Grape Creek Bapt. Ch., San Angelo, Tex., 1952-54, Plainview Bapt. Ch., Stamford, Tex., 1955-57, 1st Bapt. Ch., Sterling City, Tex., 1957-60, 7th St. Bapt. Ch., Ballinger, Tex., 1960-65, Woodland Heights Bapt. Ch., Brownwood, Tex., 1965-67, Victory Bapt. Ch., Seattle, 1967-72, Met. Bapt. Ch., Portland, Oreg., 1972-77; dir. comm. N.W. Bapt. Conv., Portland, 1977-78; pastor Magnolia Ave Bapt. Ch., Riverside, Calif., 1978-86; pres. Golden Gate Bapt. Theol. Sem., Mill Valley, Calif., 1986—; pres. N.W. Bapt. Conv., Portland, 1974-76, So. Bapt. Gen. Conv. Calif., Fresno, 1982-84. Trustee Fgn. Mission Bd., Richmond, Va., 1973-78, Golden Gate Bapt. Theol. Sem., 1980-85, Marin Cmty. Hosp. Found., 1992-95; bd. dirs. Midway Seatac Boys Club, Des Moines, 1969-72. Mem. Marin County C. of C. (bd. dirs. 1987-95), Midway C. of C. (bd. dirs. 1968-72), Rotary (bd. dirs. San Rafael chpt. 1992—, pres. Portland club 1975-76, pres.-elect Riverside club 1984-85). Home: 157 Chapel Dr Mill Valley CA 94941-3100 Office: Golden Gate Bapt Theol Sem Strawberry Pt Mill Valley CA 94941

CRICK, FRANCIS HARRY COMPTON, science educator, researcher; b. June 8, 1916; s. Harry and Annie Elizabeth (Wilkins) C.; m. Ruth Doreen Dodd, 1940 (div. 1947); 1 son; m. Odile Speed, 1949; 2 daus. B.Sc., Univ. Coll., London; PhD, Cambridge U., Eng. Scientist Brit. Admiralty, 1940-47, Strangeways Lab., Cambridge, Eng., 1947-49; with Med. Rsch. Coun. Lab. of Molecular Biology, Cambridge, 1949-77; Kieckhefer Disting. prof. Salk Inst. Biol. Studies, San Diego, 1977—, non-resident fellow, 1962-73, pres., 1994-95; adj. prof. psychology U. Calif., San Diego; vis. lectr. Rockefeller Inst., N.Y.C., 1959; vis. prof. chemistry dept. Harvard U., 1959, vis. prof. biophysics, 1962; fellow Churchill Coll., Cambridge, 1960-61; Korkes Meml. lectr. Duke U., 1960; Henry Sidgewick Meml. lectr. Cambridge U., 1963; Graham Young lectr., Glasgow, 1963; Robert Boyle lectr. Oxford U., 1963; Vanuxem lectr. Princeton U., 1964; William T. Sedgwick Meml. lectr. MIT, 1965; Cherwell-Simon Meml. lectr. Oxford U., 1966; Shell lectr. Stanford U., 1969; Paul Lund lectr. Northwestern U., 1977; Dupont lectr. Harvard U., 1979, numerous other invited meml. lectrs. Author: Of Molecules and Men, 1966, Life Itself, 1981, What Mad Pursuit, 1988, The Astonishing Hypothesis: The Scientific Search for the Soul, 1994; contbr. papers and articles on molecular, cell biology and neurobiology to sci. jours. Recipient Prix Charles Leopold Mayer French Academies des Scis., 1961; (with J.D. Watson) Rsch. Corp. award, 1961, Warren Triennial prize, 1959, (with J.D. Watson & Maurice Wilkins) Lasker award, 1960, Nobel Prize for medicine, 1962; Gairdner Found. award, 1962, Royal Medal Royal Soc., 1972, Copley medal, 1975, Michelson-Morley award, 1981, Benjamin P. Cheney medal, 1986, Golden Plate award, 1987, Albert medal Royal Soc. Arts, London, 1987, Wright Prize VIII Harvey Mudd Coll., 1988, Joseph Priestly award Dickinson Coll., 1988, Order of Merit, 1991, Disting. Achievement award Oreg State U. Friends of Libr., 1995. Fellow AAAS, Univ. Coll. London, Royal Soc., Indian Nat. Sci. Acad., Rochester Mus., Indian Acad. Scis. (hon.), Churchill Coll. Cambridge (hon.), Royal Soc. Edinburgh (hon.), Caius Coll. Cambridge (hon.), John Muir Coll. U. Calif., San Diego (hon.), Tata Inst. Fundamental Rsch., Bombay (hon.), Inst. Biology London (hon.); mem. Acad. Arts Scis. (fgn. hon.), Am. Soc. Biol. Chemists (hon.), U.S. Nat. Acad. Scis. (fgn. assoc.), German Acad. Sci., Am. Philos. Soc. (fgn. mem.), French Acad. Scis. (assoc. fgn. mem.), Royal Irish Acad. (hon.), Hellenic Biochemical and Biophysical Soc. (hon.). Office: Salk Inst Biol Studies PO Box 85800 San Diego CA 92186-5800

CRIDER, JEFFREY JOHN, journalist; b. Fontana, Calif., Oct. 16, 1962; s. Peter Roemer Crider and Barbara Jean (Matus) Wood; m. Michelle Marissa Strickland, July 20, 1991; 1 child, Isabella Marissa. Student, St. Louis U., Madrid, Spain, 1982-83; B of Spanish and European Studies, Loyola Marymount U., L.A., 1984; M of Hispanic and Internat. Studies, Monterey Inst. Internat. Studies, 1987. Reporter Imperial Valley Press, El Centro, Calif., 1987-91; bus. reporter The Desert Sun, Palm Springs, Calif., 1991-94, The Press-Enterprise, Riverside, Calif., 1994—. Mem. Latino adv. com. Cmty. Blood Bank, Rancho Mirage, Calif., 1993. Recipient award Calif. Newspaper Pubs. Assn. Mem. Soc. Profl. Journalists (bd. dirs. Inland Profl. chpt. 1996—), Sigma Delta Pi, Alpha Mu Gamma. Democrat. Roman Catholic. Office: The Press Enterprise 27740 Jefferson Ave Ste 380 Temecula CA 92590-2698

CRILEY, RICHARD LAWRENCE, retired advocate; b. Paris, Oct. 20, 1911; came to U.S., 1913; s. Theodore Morrow and Mary Myrtle (Brotherton) C.; m. Florence Atkinson, Jan. 1942 (dec. May 1976); m. Jan Bounds Cords, Jan. 1977 (dec. Sept. 1988); 1 stepchild, Ann Edgerton-Smith; m. Jan Franklin Penney, Apr. 21, 1989; several stepchildren. Student, Stanford U., 1930-32; BA in History, U. Calif., Berkeley, 1934; postgrad., U. Calif., 1934-36. Exec. dir. Chgo. Com. to Defend the Bill of Rights, 1960-77; midwest dir. Nat. Com. to Abolish the Ho. UnAm. Activities Com., Chgo., 1960-77; No. Calif. dir. Nat. Com. Against Repressive Legis., 1975—; exec. dir. Monterey County (Calif.) chpt. ACLU, 1980—; mem. coord. com. Nat. Com. Against Repressive Legis., L.A., Washington, 1984—, adv. coun. S.W. Chgo. War on Poverty, 1973; bd. dirs. United Cmty. Coun. of S.W. Lawndale, Chgo., 1964-77, Greater Lawndale Conservation Commn. (sec. 1962-70). Author: The FBI vs. the 1st Amendment, 1991. Mem. adv. com. affirmative action program, Monterey Peninsula C.C., 1986-90; pres., mem. bd. dirs. Carmel Highlands Assn., Inc., 1983-90. Capt. U.S. Army, 1942-46, ETO. Recipient Francis Heisler award Monterey chpt. ACLU, 1984, Earl Warren award ACLU of No. Calif., 1985, Human Rights Day award Baha'i Faith of Monterey Peninsula, 1993, cert. of recognition Ill. Youth Commn., Chgo., 1963. Home: RR 1 Box 67 Carmel CA 93923-9803

CRILLY, EUGENE RICHARD, engineering consultant; b. Phila., Oct. 30, 1923; s. Eugene John and Mary Virginia (Harvey) C.; m. Alice Royal Roth, Feb. 16, 1952; ME, Stevens Inst. Tech., 1944, MS, 1949; MS, U. Pa., 1951; postgrad. UCLA, 1955-58. Sr. rsch. engr. N.Am. Aviation, L.A., 1954-57; sr. rsch. engr., Canoga Park and Downey, Calif., 1962-66; process engr. Northrop Aircraft Corp., Hawthorne, Calif., 1957-59; project engr., quality assurance mgr. HITCO, Gardena, Calif., 1959-62; sr. rsch. specialist Lockheed-Calif. Co., Burbank, 1966-74; engring. specialist N.Am. aircraft ops. Rockwell Internat., El Segundo, Calif., 1974-89. Author tech. papers. Mem. nat. com. 125th Anniversary Founding of Stevens Inst. Tech. in 1870. Served with USNR, 1943-46; comdr. Res. ret. Mem. Soc. for Advancement Material and Process Engring. (chmn. L.A. chpt. 1978-79, gen. chmn. 1981 symposium exhbn., nat. dir. 1979-86, treas. 1982-85, Award of Merit 1986), Naval Inst., ASM Internat., Naval Res. Assn., VFW, Mil. Order World Wars (adj. San Fernando Valley chpt. 1985, 2d vice comdr. 1986, commdr. 1987-89, vice comdr. West, Dept Cen. Calif., 1988-89, comdr. Cajon Valley-San Diego chpt. 1990-92, adj./ROTC chmn. region XIV 1990-91, comdr. Dept. So. Calif. 1991-93, vice comdr. region XIV, 1992-93, dep. comdr. Gen. Staff Officer region XIV 1993-94, comdr. region XIV, 1994-95, Disting. Chpt. Comdr. Region XIV 1990-91, comdr. San Diego chpt. 1997—), Former Intelligence Officers Assn. (treas. San Diego chpt. one 1990-94), Ret. Officers Assn. (treas. Silver Strand chpt. 1992—), Navy League U.S. (treas. Coronado coun. 1997), Naval Order U.S., Naval Intelligence Profls. Assn., Brit. United Svc. Club L.A., Marines' Meml. Club (San Francisco), Sigma Xi, Sigma Nu. Republican. Roman Catholic. Home and Office: 276 J Ave Coronado CA 92118-1138

CRIMINALE, WILLIAM OLIVER, JR., applied mathematics educator; b. Mobile, Ala., Nov. 29, 1933; s. William Oliver and Vivian Gertrude (Sketoe) C.; m. Ulrike Irmgard Wegner, June 7, 1962; children: Martin Oliver, Lucca. B.S., U. Ala., 1955; Ph.D., Johns Hopkins U., 1960. Asst. prof. Princeton (N.J.) U., 1962-68; asso. prof. U. Wash., Seattle, 1968-73; prof. oceanography, geophysics, applied math. U. Wash., 1973—, chmn. dept. applied math., 1976-84; cons. Aerospace Corp., 1963-65, Boeing Corp., 1968-72, AGARD, 1967-68, Lenox Hill Hosp., 1967-68, ICASE, NASA Langley, 1990—; guest prof., Can., 1965, France, 1967-68, Germany, 1973-74, Sweden, 1973-74, Scotland, 1985, 89, 91, Eng., 1990, 91, Stanford, 1990, Brazil, 1992; Nat. Acad. exch. scientist, USSR, 1969, 72. Author: Stability of Parallel Flows, 1967; Contbr. articles to profl. jours. Served with U.S. Army, 1961-62. Boris A. Bakmeteff Meml. fellow, 1957-58, NATO postdoctoral fellow, 1960-61, Alexander von Humboldt Sr. fellow, 1973-74, Royal Soc. fellow, 1990-91. Fellow Am. Phys. Soc.; mem. AAAS, Am. Geophys. Union, Fedn. Am. Scientists. Home: 1635 Peach Ct E Seattle WA 98112-3428 Office: U Wash Dept Applied Math Box 352420 Seattle WA 98195

CRINELLA, FRANCIS MICHAEL, neuropsychologist, science foundation director; b. Petaluma, Calif., Dec. 22, 1936; s. Marino Peter and Marian (Eleanor) C.; m. Terrie Kay Lynd, Sept. 19, 1959; children: Ramona, Gina, Peter, Andrew, Christina. BA, U. Notre Dame, 1958; MS, San Francisco State U., 1962; PhD, La. State U., 1969. Lic. clin. and exptl. psychologist, Calif. Psychology intern Alameda County (Calif.) Guidance Clinic, 1961-62, New Orleans, 1968-69; rsch. assoc. spl. edn. La. State U., Baton Rouge, 1966-69; staff psychologist Sonoma State Hosp., Eldridge, Calif., 1969-72, sr. psychologist, 1971-72, cons. program rev., 1972-77; research psychologist Brain Behavior Research Ctr., Eldridge, 1969-77; dir. Petaluma Hosp. Dist., 1971-76, treas., 1975; exec. dir. Fairview State Hosp., Costa Mesa, Calif., 1977-85; assoc. clin. prof. to clin. prof. psychiatry U. Calif., Irvine, 1977—, assoc. clin. prof. to clin. prof. phys. medicine, 1981—; dir. Devel. Research Insts., Costa Mesa, 1985—; pres. Rehab. Ctr. for Brain Dysfunction, Irvine, 1982—. Contbr. articles on neuropsychiatry to profl. jours. Bd. dirs. United Way Orange County, Calif., Orange County Epilepsy Soc., also pres., 1978—. Served to capt. USAF, 1962-66. Recipient Career Scientist award Rehab. Ctr. Brain Dysfunction Inc., 1983; grantee Nat. Inst. Child Health and Human Devel., 1972, Nat. Inst. Neurol. Diseases Communicative Disorders and Stroke, 1973, Nat. Inst. Aging, 1985, Nat. Inst. Mental Health, 1989. Mem. AAAS, Am. Psychol. Assn., Am. Acad. on Mental Retardation, Nat. Acad. Neuropsychologists, Western Psychol. Assn., Redwood Psychol. Assn. Republican. Roman Catholic. Club: Mesa Verde Country (Costa Mesa). Office: State Devel Rsch Insts 2501 Harbor Blvd Costa Mesa CA 92626-6143

CRIPPENS, DAVID LEE, broadcast executive; b. Nashville, Sept. 23, 1942; s. Nathaniel and Dorothy (Sharp) C.; m. Eloise Brown, Aug. 3, 1968; 1 child, Gerald Chinua. BA in Polit. Sci., Antioch U., 1964; MSW, San Diego State U., 1968. Assoc. dir. ednl. opportunities program San Diego State U., 1968-69; producer KPBS-TV, San Diego, 1969-71; staff producer, writer, newsperson WQED-TV, Pitts., 1971-73; dir. ednl. svc. KCET, L.A., 1973-77, v.p. ednl. svc., 1977-80, v.p., sta. mgr., 1980-83, v.p. nat. prodns., 1983-85, sr. v.p. ednl. enterprises, 1985—; Rufus Putnam vis. prof. Ohio U. Sch. Telecommunications, Athens, fall 1995. Exec. producer Count On Me, New American Work Force, Not the Way to Go/Get a Life, Begingin the Journey, Giving Care Taking Care, Community Under Siege, Mindworks; contbr. articles to profl. publs. Bd. dirs. Unite L.A., Inroads L.A., Cmty. Coalition for Substance Abuse Prevention and Treatment; mem. Editl. Projects in Edn. Bd.; bd. councilors Sch. Social Wk., U. So. Calif.; vol. Peace Corps, Nigeria, 1964-66. Recipient Excellence in Edn. Commendation award Calif. Poly. Black Faculty and Staff Assn., 1991, Prin.'s Orgn. award Sr. High Sch. Prins., 1991, honor Assn. Adminstrs. L.A., 1988, Calif. Coalition for Pub. Edn., 1987, Nat. Assn. Media Women, 1986, Calif. Assembly Legis. Com., 1971, San Diego State Black Student Coun., 1971, named One of Pitts.' Most Influential Blacks, Pitts. Post Gazette, 1973, Outstanding Ednl. Leadership award Phi Delta Kappa, 1992, Nat. Citation award, 1993, Positive Image award Frank D. Parent PTA, 1992, John Senett award for outstanding coverage of educational concerns Calif. Tchrs. Assn., 1993, Martin award INROADS, L.A., Inc. Home: 5252 W 64th St Inglewood CA 90302-1016 Office: KCET 4401 W Sunset Blvd Los Angeles CA 90027-6017

CRISCUOLO, WENDY LAURA, lawyer, interior design consultant; b. N.Y.C., Dec. 17, 1949; d. Joseph Andrew and Betty Jane (Jackson) C.; m. John Howard Price, Jr., Sept. 5, 1970 (div. Apr. 1981); m. Ross J. Turner, July 23, 1988. BA with honors in Design, U. Calif., Berkeley, 1973; JD, U. San Francisco, 1982. Space planner GSA, San Francisco, 1973-79; sr. interior designer E. Lew & Assocs., San Francisco, 1979-80; design dir. Beier & Gunderson, Inc., Oakland, Calif., 1980-81; sr. interior designer Environ. Planning and Rsch., San Francisco, 1981-82; interior design cons. Hillsborough, Calif., 1982—; law clk. to Judge Spencer Williams U.S. Dist. Ct., San Francisco, 1983-84; atty. Ciros Investments, Rancho Santa Fe, Calif., 1984—. Author: (with others) Guide to the Laws of Charitable Giving, 3d rev. edit., 1983; staff mem. U. San Francisco Law Rev., 1983. Bd. dirs., v.p. and treas. Marin Citizens for Energy Planning, 1986-89; bd. dirs., pres. Calif. Ctr. for Wildlife, 1987-90; trustee Cayote Point Mus. for Environ. Edn., 1990-93. Mem. ABA, State Bar Calif. Episcopalian.

CRISMAN, MARY FRANCES BORDEN, librarian; b. Tacoma, Nov. 23, 1919; d. Lindon A. and Mary Cecelia (Donnelly) Borden; m. Fredric Lee Crisman, Apr. 12, 1975 (dec. Dec. 1975). BA in History, U. Wash., 1943, BA in Librarianship, 1944. Asst. br. librarian in charge work with children Mottet br. Tacoma Pub. Libr., 1944-45, br. librarian, 1945-49, br. librarian Moore br., 1950-55, asst. dir., 1955-70, dir., 1970-74, dir. emeritus, 1975—; mgr. corp. libr. Frank Russell Co., 1985-96, retired, 1997; chmn. Wash. Community Library Council, 1970-72. Hostess program Your Library and You, Sta. KTPS-TV, 1969-71. Mem. Highland Homeowners League, Tacoma, 1980—, incorporating dir. 1980, sec. and registered agt., 1980-82. Mem. ALA (chmn. mem. com. Wash. 1957-60, mem. nat. library week com. 1965, chmn. library adminstrn. div. nominating com. 1971, mem. ins. for libraries com. 1970-74, vice chmn. library adminstrn. div. personnel adminstrn. sect. 1972-73, chmn. 1973-74, mem. com. policy implementation 1973-74, mem. library orgn. and mgmt. sect. budgeting acctg. and costs com. 1974-75), Am. Library Trustee Assn. (legis. com. 1975-78, conf. program com. 1978-80, action devel. com. 1978-80), Pacific N.W. (trustee div. nominating com 1976-77), Wash. Library Assn. (exec. bd. 1957-59, state exec., dir. Nat. Library Week 1965, treas., exec. bd. 1969-71, 71-73), Urban Libraries Council (editorial sec. Newsletter 1972-73, exec. com. 1974-75), Ladies Aux. to United Transp. Union (past pres. Tacoma), Friends Tacoma Pub. Library (registered agt. 1975-83, sec. 1975-78, pres. 1978-80, bd. dirs. 1980-83), Smithsonian Assocs., Nat. Railway Hist. Soc., U. Wash. Alumni Assn., U. Wash. Sch. Librarianship Alumni Assn. Roman Catholic. Club: Quota Internat. (sec. 1957-58, 1st v.p. 1960-61, pres. 1961-62, treas. 1975-76, pres. 1979-80) (Tacoma). Home: 6501 N Burning Tree Ln Tacoma WA 98406-2108

CRISMAN CARLSON, RUTH MARIE, writer; b. Oak Park, Ill., June 16, 1914; d. John Henry and Ruth Ethel (Stiles) Thorup; m. James Lester Crisman July 7, 1941 (dec. 1992); children: Carol Ann, James Alan; m. Lennert Carlson, Feb. 6, 1993. BA in Elem. Edn., Calif. State Coll., L.A., 1966, MA in Elem. Edn., 1971, MA, 1976. Cert. tchr. reading, elem. edn. Dental asst. Dr. Bartram, L.A., 1931-41; dental clerk, typist, libr. clerk, 1954-65; tchr. L.A. City Schs., 1966-79. Author: The Mississippi Franklin Watts, 1984, Hot Off the Press, 1991, Thomas Jefferson, a Biography, 1992, Racing the Iditarod Trail, 1993; contbr. articles to newspapers, publs. Recipient PEN award. Mem. Soc. Childrens Book Writers Illustrators, Nat. League Am. PEN Women (pres. L.A. chpt. 1994—), Calif. Fedn. Chaparral Poets, Calif. Writers Club, Pi Lambda Theta. Republican. Methodist.

CRISP, GEORGE ROBERT, pastor; b. Washington, Mar. 10, 1951; s. George Robert Sr. and Betty Margurite (Harpst) C.; m. Sandra Margaret Turner, Oct. 30, 1974 (div. Jan. 1982); m. Leona Sue Crisp, Nov. 3, 1984; stepchildren: Andrew Stough, Matthew Stough. BA, U. Redlands, 1974; MDiv, Clarement Sch. Theology, 1982, DMin, 1993. Ordained to ministry Meth. Ch., 1981. Choir dir. Colton (Calif.) First Bapt. Ch., 1972-74; dir. youth ministries St. Paul's United Meth. Ch., San Bernardino, Calif., 1975-80; founding pastor Hesperia (Calif.) United Meth. Ch., 1980-85; pastor Del Rosa United Meth. Ch., San Bernardino, 1985-90; dir. Wesley Found. Calif. Polytech. Inst., San Luis Obispo, 1990-93; sr. pastor San Luis Obispo United Meth. Ch., 1990-93; pastor Wahiawa (Hawaii) United Meth. CH., 1993—. Author numerous poems; composer musical scores. Mem. coun. on youth ministries United Meth. Ch., Pasadena, 1980-84, mem. com. on status and role of women, 1984-88; mem. conf. Commn. on Equitable Compensation, 1988-96, Conf. Coun. on Fin. and Adminstrn., 1996—; chmn. Hawaii Com. on Dist. Superintendency, 1994—; mem. Hawaii Com. on Ministry, 1995—, Wahiawa Neighboorhood Bd. (advisory to Honolulu City Coun.), 1996—. Mem. Sn Bernardino Ministerial Assn. (pres. 1987), San Luis Obispo Ministerial Assn. (v.p. San Luis Obispo chpt. 1992-93), Kiwanis (chaplain Hesperia club 1984), Order of St. Luke (west jurisdiction formation officer 1993—). Democrat. Home: 350 Iliwai Dr Wahiawa HI 96786-2309 Office: Wahiawa United Meth Ch 1445 California Ave Wahiawa HI 96786-2541

CRISPIN, JAMES HEWES, engineering and construction company executive; b. Rochester, Minn., July 23, 1915; s. Egerton Lafayette and Angela (Shipman) C.; m. Marjorie Holmes, Aug. 5, 1966. A.B. in Mech. Engring., Stanford U., 1938; M.B.A., Harvard U., 1941; grad., Army Command and Gen. Staff Sch., 1943. Registered profl. mech. engr., Calif. With C.F. Braun & Co. Alhambra, Calif., 1946-62; treas. Bechtel Corp., San Francisco, 1962-73, v.p., mem. fin. com., 1967-75, mgr. investment dept., 1973-75; retired, 1976; investment cons., Santa Barbara, Calif., 1978—. Trustee Santa Barbara Mus. Art, 1979-91, 97—, pres., 1986-88, life. hon. trustee, 1992—. Lt. col. Ordnance Corps, AUS., 1941-46. Decorated Army Commendation medal with oak leaf cluster. Mem. Mil. Order World Wars, S.R., Soc. Colonial Wars, Colonial Wars Calif., Baronial Order Magna Carta, Mil. Order Crusades, Am. Def. Preparedness Assn., World Affairs Coun. No. Calif. (trustee 1968-75), Santa Barbara Mus. Art (trustee 1979-91, 97—, pres. 1986-88, life hon. trustee 1992), Calif. Hist. Soc. (trustee 1979-86), Valley Club of Montecito (pres. 1987-90, bd. dirs. 1981-91), Calif. Club L.A., World Trade Club San Francisco (pres. 1977-78, bd. dirs. 1971-78), Santa Barbara Club (pres. 1995-96, bd. dirs. 1991-96), Pacific Union Club, San Francisco, Beta Theta Pi. Republican. Home: 1340 E Mountain Dr Santa Barbara CA 93108-1215 Office: La Arcada Bldg 1114 State St Ste 220 Santa Barbara CA 93101-2716

CRISTIANO, MARILYN JEAN, speech communication educator; b. New Haven, Jan. 10, 1954; d. Michael William Mary Rose (Porto) C. BA, Marquette U., 1975, MA, 1977; postgrad., Ariz. State U., 1977; EdD, Nova Southeastern U., 1991. Speech comm. instr. Phoenix Coll., 1977-87, Paradise Valley C.C., Phoenix, 1987—; presenter at profl. confs., workshops and seminars. Author tng. manual on pub. speaking, 1991, 92, 95, 97; contbr. articles to profl. publs. Mem. ASTD, Speech Comm. Assn., Western Speech Comm. Assn., Ariz. Comm. Assn. Office: Paradise Valley CC 18401 N 32nd St Phoenix AZ 85032-1210

CRISWELL, ELEANOR CAMP, psychologist; b. Norfolk, Va., May 12, 1938; d. Norman Harold Camp and Eleanor (Talman) David; m. Thomas L. Hanna. BA, U. Ky., 1961, MA, 1962; EdD, U. Fla., 1969. Asst. prof. edn. Calif. State Coll., Hayward, 1969; prof. psychology, chair Calif. State U., Sonoma, 1969—; faculty adviser Humanistic Psychology Inst., San Francisco, 1970-77; dir. Novato Inst. Somatic Research and Tng.; editor Somatics jour.; cons. Venturi, Inc., Autogenic Systems, Inc.; clin. dir. Biotherapeutics, Kentfield Med. Hosp., 1985-90. Founder Humanistic Psychology Inst., 1970. Co-editor: Biofeedback and Family Practice Medicine, 1983; author: How Yoga Works, 1987, Biofeedback and Somatics, 1995. Mem. APA, Biofeedback Soc. Calif. (dir.), Aerospace Med. Assn., Assn. for Transpersonal Psychology, Assn. for Humanistic Psychology (past pres.). Patentee optokinetic perceptual learning device. Office: Sonoma State U Psychology Dept 1801 E Cotati Ave Rohnert Park CA 94928-3613

CRISWELL, KIMBERLY ANN, public relations executive, dancer; b. L.A., Dec. 6, 1957; d. Robert Burton and Carolyn Joyce (Semko) C. BA with honors, U. Calif.-Santa Cruz, 1980; postgrad. Stanford U., 1993—. Instr., English Lang. Services, Oakland, Calif., 1980-81; freelance writer Verbum mag., San Diego, Gambit mag., New Orleans, 1981; instr. Tulane U., New Orleans, 1981; instr., editor Haitian-English Lang. Program, New Orleans, 1981-82; instr. Delgado Coll., New Orleans, 1982-83; instr., program coord. Vietnamese Youth Ctr., San Francisco, 1984; dancer Khadra Internat. Folk Ballet, San Francisco, 1984-89; dir. mktg. comm. Centram Systems West, Inc., Berkeley, Calif., 1984-87; comm. coord. Safeway Stores, Inc., Oakland, 1985; dir. corp. comm. TOPS, div. Sun Microsystems, Inc, 1987-88; pres. Criswell Comm., 1988—; dir. corp. comm. CyberGold, Inc., Berkeley, Calif., 1996—. Vol. coord. Friends of Haitians, 1981, editor, writer newsletter, 1981; dancer Komenka Ethnic Dance Ensemble, New Orleans, 1983; mem. Contemp. Art Ctr.'s Krewe of Clones, New Orleans, 1983, Americans for Nonsmokers Rights, Berkeley, 1985; active San Francisco Multimedia Developers Group, Artspan. Mem. Sci. Meets the Arts Soc. (founding), Oakland Mus. Assn., Mus. Soc. Democrat. Avocations: visual arts, travel, creative writing. Office: CyberGold Inc 2921 Adeline St Berkeley CA 94703

CRISWELL, MARVIN EUGENE, civil engineering educator, consultant; b. Chappell, Nebr., Oct. 31, 1942; s. Wilbur Arthur and Evelyn Lucille (Jeffries) C.; m. Lela Louise Kennedy, Sept. 5, 1965; children: Karin Lee, Glenn Alan, Dianne Marie, Melanie Anne. BSCE, U. Nebr., 1965; MSCE, U. Ill., 1966, PhD in Civil Engring., 1970. Registered profl. engr., Colo. Structural engr. Clark & Enerson, Olson, Burroughs & Thompson, Lincoln, Nebr., 1965; research structural engr. U.S. Army Corps Engrs. Waterways Experiment Station, Vicksburg, Miss., 1967-69; asst. prof. civil engring. Colo. State U., Ft. Collins, 1970-75, assoc. prof., 1975-84, prof., 1984—, acting assoc. dept. head, 1989-91, assoc. dept. head Acad. Affairs, 1991—; program visitor Accreditation Bd. Engring. and Tech., 1981-89; bd.dirs., sec. Engring. Data Mgmt., Inc., Ft. Collins, 1983-85. Co-author: Properties and Tests of Engineering Materials, 1978. Recipient Abel Faculty Tchg. award Colo. State U., 1984, 88, Disting. Faculty award Colo. State U. Alumni Assn., 1995. Mem. ASCE (past mem. com. on curricula and accredition 1984-88, past sec. adminstrn. com. on bridges 1990-92, com. on wood, safety of bldgs, design of engineered wood constrn. stds., past chmn. subcom. on reliability and wood design 1992-96, com. on curriculum and accreditation 1984-88, sec. adminstrv. com. on bridges 1990-92), ASTM, Am. Soc. Engring. Edn. (chmn. civil engring. div. 1981-82, Rocky Mountain sect. 1987-88, bd. dirs. and zone IV chmn. 1990-92, Dow Outstanding Young Faculty award 1978, Wadlin award civil engring. div. G, best paper award 1992), Am. Concrete Inst. (coms. on fiber concrete, space applications of concrete, connections in monolithic concrete, and shear and torsion, chair subcom. structural design and use 1996—, chair subcom. on structural design and uses of fiber concrete, civil engring. program evaluator accredition bd. for engring. and tech. 1981-89). Methodist. Home: 1536 Freedom Ln Fort Collins CO 80526-1707 Office: Colo State U Dept Civil Engring Fort Collins CO 80523-1372

CRITES, RICHARD RAY, international franchising company executive; b. Rapid City, S.D., Aug. 29, 1952; s. Charles Dayton and Marcia Ann (Heil) C.; m. Randel E. Golobic, Dec. 27, 1980 (div. May 1988). B of Liberal Studies, U. Okla., 1975; MS, Stanford U., 1978; cert. sr. security checker, Advanced Orgn. L.A., 1987, cert. false purpose rundown auditor, 1988. Cert. staff status II, exec. status I, Am. St. Hill Orgn., exec. dir. full hat course Celebrity Ctr. Internat., 1992; cert. in ins.: series 7 securities lic., series 63, series 24; cert. life and disability ins., Calif. Nat. sales trainer Continental Mktg. Corp., Detroit, 1975-76, regional sales mgr., 1976-80; pres., chief exec. officer Retail Packaging Specialists, Inc., San Mateo, Calif., 1982-86; owner, chief exec. officer Miracle Method of San Mateo, Inc., 1985-87, Miracle Method of Beverly Hills, Inc., L.A., 1987-90, Miracle Method of So. Calif., Inc., L.A., 1986-92, Miracle Method of No. Calif., Inc., L.A., 1988-89; v.p., treas., chmn. bd. Miracle Methods of the U.S., Inc., L.A., 1988-92; pres., chmn. bd. Internat. Miracle Method Appearance Ctrs. Pacific, Inc., L.A., 1988-92, Internat. Miracle Method Ctrs. Equip. & Supply, Inc., L.A., 1989-92; pres., chmn. bd. dirs. Miracle Method of the U.S., Inc., L.A., 1992-96; gen. mgr. Stellar Mgmt. Co., L.A., 1993-96; mng. mem. Stellar Mgmt. Co., 1996—; registered rep. WMA Securities, Inc., Norcross, Ga., 1996—; trustee New Civilization Found., 1996—. Mem. Citizen's Commn. on Human Rights, Citizens for an Alternative Tax System. Mem. Internat. Assn. Scientologists (sponsor). Republican. Scientologist. Office: Stellar Mgmt LLC 3131 Foothill Blvd Ste J La Crescenta CA 91214

CROCKER, KENNETH FRANKLIN, data processing consultant; b. Centralia, Wash., July 29, 1950; s. Earl Thomas and Mary Jane (Hamil) C.; m. Mary Louise Underwood, June 15, 1974 (div. Dec. 1987); children: Matthew A., Benjamin F., Jonathan C.; m. Sally Marlene Gammelgard, Dec. 21, 1987 (div. 1992). AS in Computer Programming and System Design, Control Data Inst., Long Beach, Calif., 1972. Programmer City of Greenville, S.C., 1973; computer operator Winn Dixie Stores, Greer, S.C., 1973-75; programmer Piedmont Industries, Greenville, S.C., 1975-78; systems engr. Micro-Systems, Greenville, 1978; sr. programmer Reeves Bros., Lyman, S.C.,

1978-80; systems analyst Cryovac div. W.R. Grace Co., Duncan, S.C., 1980-84; sr. cons. Cap Gemini Am., San Francisco, 1984-85; prin. mem. tech. staff Citibank-FSB Calif., Oakland, 1985-91; sr. software engr. Lucky Stores Inc., Dublin, Calif., 1991-94; tech. cons. Lawrence Berkeley Labs., Berkeley, Calif., 1994-95, Delta-Net, San Francisco, 1995; plan architect, DBA technician Safeway, Oakland, Calif., 1995—. Umpire Contra Costa Ofcls. Assn., 1990—. Libertarian. Baptist. Home and Office: 301 Livorna Heights Rd Alamo CA 94507-1326

CROCKETT, ROBERT YORK, architect; b. West Covina, Calif., Nov. 27, 1962; s. Bob York and Carolyn Kathleen (McLellan) C. BArch, U. So. Calif., 1985; Masters, UCLA, 1994. Registered architect, Calif., Nev., Ariz., Miss., La. Designer TNT Architecture Internat., Malibu, Calif., 1983-85, Pace Group, L.A., 1985-87; architect in pvt. practice Marina Del Rey, Calif., 1988—; bd. dirs. (P.A.C.E.) Planning Architecture Consulting Engring., Phoenix. Home and Office: 123 Catamaran St Marina Del Rey CA 90292

CROCKETT, RONALD MICHAEL, chiropractor; b. Salem, Oreg., Nov. 6, 1951; s. Donald Floyd and Valena Jean (Garver) C.; m. Christine Bernadette Kelley, Feb. 16, 1974; children: Chereen N., Jamie Lynn. BS, Oreg. Coll. Edn., 1974; DC, Western States Chiropractic, Coll./Portland, Oreg., 1979. Fellow Internat. Acad. Clin. Acupuncture. Chiropractor Bourland Chiropracti Clinic, Hillsboro, Oreg., 1979-80, Crockett Chiropractic Ctr., Salem, 1980—. Mem. Internat. Chiropractic Assn. Office: Crockett Chiropractic Ctr 862 Lancaster Dr SE Salem OR 97301-5831

CROCKETT-MAILLET, GINNY LOU, obstetrician/gynecologist nurse practitioner; b. Shelbyville, Ind., Sept. 5, 1954; d. Howard M. and Virginia (Crockett) Johnson; m. L.J. Maillet; 1 child, Jaison Rhyley. A of Nursing, Ind. U., 1979; BS in Nursing, U. Ky., 1984; postgrad., UCLA, 1989, U. No. Colo., 1994-95. RN, Ind., Ky. Nurse Ky. Sch. for the Blind, Louisville, 1979-80; obstet. nurse Humana Hosp. Audubon, Louisville, 1981-84; research coordinator Planned Parenthood of Louisville, 1984; coordinator Maternal Child Health Clinic, New Albany, Ind., 1984-87, mem. adv. council, 1986-87; maternal educator Humana Hosp. S.W., Louisville, 1987; coordinator regional edn. U. Louisville, 1987; health educator Floyd County Health Dept., New Albany, 1988-89; with NAFC Health Dept., 1988-89; educator St. Elizabeth's Home of So. Ind., 1990-91; pvt. practice lactation edn. New Albany, Ind., 1992; dir. pub. health nursing Elbert County Nursing Svcs., Kiowa, Colo., 1992-93; childbirth educator Humana Hosp., Aurora, Colo., 1992—; pub. health nurse II child health program Larimer County Health Dept., Ft. Collins, Colo., 1993-95; childbirth educator Poudre Valley Hosp., Ft. Collins, Colo., 1994-95; ob-gyn nurse practitioner program Planned Parenthood of Rocky Mountains, Denver, 1995—; women's health nurse practitioner Dist. 7 Health Dept., Idaho Falls, Idaho, 1996—; obstet. cons. Clark County Meml. Hosp., Jeffersonville, Ind., 1988—, educator, 1989-91; mem. Childbirth Educators Tng. Assn. Vol. New Albany ARC, 1988; mem. Head Start adv. bd., New Albany, 1985-87; mem. Friends of the Culbertson Mansion, New Albany. Grantee March of Dimes, Louisville, 1986-91. Fellow Ind. Council on Adolescent Pregnancy, Healthy Mothers/Healthy Babies, AIDS Coalition; mem. Ind. Perinatal Assn. (membership com. 1985-86), Nat. Assn. Nurse Practitioners Reproductive Health, Am. Acad. Nurse Practitioners. Home: 5209 Pinyon Dr Pocatello ID 83204

CROCKFORD, WILLIAM RICHARD, II, newspaper editor; b. L.A., May 2, 1952; s. William Richard and Doris Mary Ellen (Driscoll) C.; m. Deborah Suzette Westby, Aug. 17, 1974; children: Heather, Rebecca, Theresa. BA in Journalism, U. Mont., 1975. Editor Ronan (Mont.) Pioneer, 1975; assoc. news dir. KEIN Radio, Great Falls, Mont., 1976-77; writer, editor, ad layout staff Young Ideas, Great Falls, 1977-78; farm editor South Idaho Press, Burley, 1978-81, Minidoka County News, Rupert, Idaho, 1978-81; editor Shelby (Mont.) Promoter, 1982-90, Anaconda (Mont.) Leader, 1990—; dir. Mont. Newspaper Advt. Svc., 1984—; dir., sec.- treas. S.W. Mont. Fed. Credit Union, Anaconda, 1994—; pres. Soc. Profl. Journalists, Mont., 1988-90. Pres. United Way Anaconda, 1992-93; dir. Prevention Child Abuse/Family Enrichment Coun., Anaconda, 1995—. Named Conservation Writer of the Yr., Idaho Assn. Conservation Dists., 1981; recipient numerous writing awards Mont. Newspaper Assn., Helena, 1982—. Mem. Anaconda Kiwanis Club (v.p. 1996—), KC (coun. 882, fin. sec.). Roman Catholic. Home: 315 Spruce St Anaconda MT 59711 Office: Anaconda Leader 121 Main St Anaconda MT 59711

CROFT, RICHARD TODD, psychotherapist; b. Idaho Falls, Idaho, Sept. 11, 1967; s. Richard Paul and Kathy (Perkins) C.; m. Kim Andrus; 1 child, Ryan. BA in Am. Studies, Idaho State U., 1990, MA in Counseling, 1992. Lic. profl. counselor. Adolescent/pediat. program coord. Eastern Idaho Regional Behavioral Health Ctr., Idaho Falls, 1993—. Home: 807 Maplewood Dr Idaho Falls ID 83401-4014 Office: Eastern Idaho Regional Behavioral Health Ctr PO Box 2077 Idaho Falls ID 83403-2077

CROFTS, MARY AUSTIN, parks and recreation director; b. Jackson, Minn., Aug. 4, 1949; d. Leo Leslie and Rose Marie (Huschka) Austin; m. Kimberly Keith Crofts, June 20, 1987; stepchildren: Tyler, Ryan. BS, U. Kans., 1971. Prodn. mgr. Christenson, Barclay & Shaw, Kansas City, Mo., 1971-73; v.p. prodn. Barkley & Evergreen, Kansas City, 1973-79; v.p., account supr. BB&W Advt., Boise, Idaho, 1979-81; dir. mktg. Sun Valley (Idaho) Health Inst., 1981-82; mng. editor Commtek Pub., Hailey, Idaho, 1982-83; exec. dir. Blaine County Recreation Dist., Hailey, 1984—. Com. mem. City of Ketchum, Idaho, 1984—. Recipient Trails Achievement award Idaho Trails Coun., 1992, Alexander Calder Conservation award The Found., 1991. Mem. Idaho Recreation and Parks Assn. (bd. dirs., pres. 1984-96, Fellowship award 1995), Sun Valley/Ketchom C. of C. (Citizen of Yr. 1991), Hailey C. of C. Office: Blaine County Rec Dist PO Box 297 Hailey ID 83333 also: 308 N Main St Hailey ID 83333

CROFTS, RICHARD A., academic administrator. PhD in Info., Duke U. Mem. faculty U. Toledo; assoc. v.p. rsch., dean Grad. Sch. E. Tenn. State U.; dep. commr. acad. affairs Mo. Univ. Sys., Helena, 1994-96, interim commr. higher edn., 1996—. Office: Mont Univ Sys 2500 Broadway Helena MT 59624*

CROKER, ROBERT ERNEST, vocational and human resource development educator; b. East Chicago, Ind., Feb. 10, 1946; s. David Robert and Donna Lorraine (Williams) C.; m. Susan Joan Relinski, Sept. 3, 1966; children: Amy, Allison, Amanda, Adam. BS, Purdue U., 1979; MS, Ind. State U., 1980; EdD, Wash. State U., 1986. Tchr. Tech. Vocat. High Sch., Hammond, Ind., 1976-79, Edison High Sch., Lake Station, Ind., 1979-81; grad. teaching asst. Wash. State U., Pullman, 1981-83; assoc. prof. career tech., adult edn., Idaho State U. Served with USN, 1963-67. Mem. ASCD, Am. Vocat. Assn., Idaho Vocat. Assn., Idaho Lifelong Learners Assn., Mountain Plains Adult Edn., Phi Kappa Phi. Mormon. Office: Idho State Univ Campus Box 8081 Pocatello ID 83209

CROMBACH, DANITA LYNN, communications professional; b. Ventura, Calif., Dec. 12, 1962; d. Edwin Marvin and Patricia Anne (Robinson) Osborne; m. Timothy John Crombach, May 9, 1992; children: Christopher Pritchard, Brian Jeffrey, Amanda Christine. Cert. tchr. in comm. and radio tech. Police reserve officer Oxnard (Calif.) Police Dept., 1982-84; pub. safety dispatcher III Oxnard (Calif.) Police & Fire Depts., 1984-89; pub. safety comm. instr. San Jose (Calif.) Police Dept., 1989-92; dir. ops. A&R Fin. and Ins. Svcs., Agoura Hills, Calif., 1992-94; comm. mgr. Inglewood (Calif.) Police & Fire Depts., 1994—; instr. Ventura (Calif.) C.C., 1989, West Valley Coll., Saratoga, Calif., 1989-92; cons. Apple, Inc., Cupertino, Calif., 1991, Vallejo (Calif.) Police Dept., 1991. Recipient Commendation cert. State of Calif., 1987. Mem. Comm. Ops. Mgrs. Assn., Tri-Counties Comm. Assn. (founder, pres.), Assn. Pub. Safety Comm. Officers. Address: 2174 Paseo Noche Camarillo CA 93012-9335

CROMPTON, ARNOLD, minister, educator; b. Leeds, Yorkshire, Eng., Dec. 19, 1914; came to U.S., 1923; s. Harold and May Almyeria (Milward) C. BA, Case Western Res. U., 1936; MA, U. Chgo., 1939; BD, Meadville Theol. Sch., Chgo., 1939; ThD, Pacific Sch. of Religion, 1956; DD (hon.), Meadville-Lombard Theol. Sch., 1972. Ordained to ministry Unitarian Ch., 1939. Minister 1st Unitarian Ch. of Erie, Pa., 1939-45, 1st Unitarian Ch., Oakland, Calif., 1945-82; minister emeritus 1st Unitarian Ch. of Erie, Oakland, Calif., 1982—; lectr. ch. history Starr King Sch. for the Ministry, Berkeley, Calif., 1953-67; dir. Earl Morse Wilbur Library, Berkeley, 1961-67, tutor, 1990—; adj. prof. history Union Inst., Cin., 1993—; scholar-on-line Graduate Theological Union, Berkeley, 1996—; anniversary lectr. Taegu (Republic of Korea) U., 1986; Wilbur Meml. lectr. on religion on Pacific Rim, Berkeley, 1990; lectr. Free Religious Assn., Japan, 1992; bd. dirs., past pres. Oakland-Fukuoka Soc., Oakland, 1975—; pres. Rossmoor Religious Coun., Walnut Creek, Calif., 1989—; min. Rossmoor Unitarian Universalist Soc., Walnut Creek, 1993—. Author: Apostle of Liberty, 1950, Unitarianism on Pacific Coast, 1954, Aurelia H. Reinhardt, 1981; contbr. articles to profl. jours. Lectr. Ebell Soc., Oakland, 1982—; pres. Internat. Inst. of the East Bay, Oakland, 1981-82, Rossmoor Activities Coun., Walnut Creek, 1989—; chmn. Alameda County Crime Prevention Commn., Calif., 1978-80; bd. dirs. English summer sch. Bir Zeit Coll., Jordan, 1963-64, English Lang. Program-Komagane, Japan, 1967. Recipient Silver Beaver award Boy Scouts Am., 1966, citation Calif. State Assembly, 1970, Calif. State Senate, 1975, Ho. of Reps., 1990, Ohio Ho. of Reps., 1989, Disting. Alumnus award Case Western Res. U., 1989, Pub. Svc. citation U. Chgo., 1992, Thomas Starr King award Starr King Sch. for Ministry, Berkeley, 1993; named one of Outstanding Immigrants, Internat. Inst., 1976. Mem. Unitarian Universalist Ministers Assn. (pres. Pacific Coast chpt. 1970, spl. envoy to chs. of Japan 1989), Rotary (pres. Rossmoor chpt. 1986-87), Masons (grand chaplain 1979-80), Phi Alpha Theta (hon.), Phi Kappa Tau. Home: 1449 Skycrest Dr # 1 Walnut Creek CA 94595-1870 Office: 1st Unitarian Ch 685 14th St Oakland CA 94612-1242

CRONE, RICHARD ALLAN, cardiologist, educator; b. Tacoma, Nov. 26, 1947; s. Richard Irving and Alla Marguerite (Ernst) C.; m. Becky Jo Zimmerlund, Dec. 11, 1993. BA in Chemistry, U. Wash., 1969, MD, 1973. Intern Madigan Army Med. Ctr., Tacoma, 1973-74, resident in medicine, 1974-76, fellow in cardiology, 1977-79; commd. med. officer U.S. Army, Tacoma, Denver, San Francisco, 1972; advanced through grades to lt. col. U.S. Army, 1981; dir. coronary care unit Fitzsimons Army Med. Ctr., Denver, 1979-81; practice medicine specializing in cardiology Stevens Cardiology Group, Edmonds, Wash., 1981—, also dir. coronary care unit, cardiac catheter lab, 1982—; clin. assoc. prof. medicine U. Wash., Seattle, 1983—. Fellow Am. Coll. Angiology; mem. AMA, Am. Coll. Cardiology, Am. Heart Assn., Seattle Acad. Internal Medicine, Wash. State Soc. Internal Medicine, Wash. State Med. Assn. Republican. Roman Catholic. Home: 10325 66th Pl W Mukilteo WA 98275-4559 Office: 21701 76th Ave W Ste 100 Edmonds WA 98026-7536

CRONIN, LARRY V., lawyer, pro tempore judge; b. Keystone, Nebr., Aug. 19, 1937; s. William Joseph and Mary Lanora (Roper) C.; m. Carol Ann Alonzo, Feb. 15, 1992; children: Kelly Jean Vesely, Kevin Scott. BA, Hastings (Nebr.) Coll., 1959; JD, U. Mich., 1962. Bar: Ariz. 1963. Assoc. Fennemore Craig Allen & McLonnon, Phoenix, 1962-64; dep. county atty. Maricopa County, Phoenix, 1964-74; asst. city atty. City of Phoenix, 1974-77; dep. county atty. Maricopa County, Phoenix, 1977-92; judge pro tem, Scottsdale, Ariz., 1995—, Fountain Hills, Ariz., 1995—; pro tempore judge Phoenix, 1996—. Co-founder Big Brothers of Phoenix, 1964; co-founder, dir., officer Treatment Alternatives to Street Crime, Phoenix, 1978. Mem. Stone Creek Golf Club. Home: 3401 N 37th St #5 Phoenix AZ 85018

CRONIN, THOMAS EDWARD, academic administrator; b. Milton, Mass., Mar. 18, 1940; s. Joseph M. and Mary Jane Cronin; m. Tania Zaroodny, Nov. 26, 1966; 1 child, Alexander. AB, Holy Cross Coll., 1961; MA, Stanford U., 1964, PhD, 1968; LLD (hon.), Marietta Coll., 1987, Franklin Coll., 1993. Tchg. fellow Stanford (Calif.) U., 1962-64; staff mem. The White House, Washington, 1966-67; faculty mem. U. N.C., 1967-70; staff fellow Brookings Instn., 1970-72; faculty mem. Brandeis U., Waltham, Mass., 1975-77, U. Del., Newark, 1977-79; McHugh prof. of Am. instns. The Colo. Coll., Colorado Springs, 1985-93, acting pres., 1991-92; pres. Whitman Coll., Walla Walla, Wash., 1993—; moderator Aspen Inst. Exec. Seminars, 1975—; pres. CRC, Inc., 1980—, Presidency Rsch. Group, 1981-82; cons. in field; guest polit. analyst various tv programs. Author: The State of the Presidency, 1980, Direct Democracy, 1989, Colorado Politics and Government, 1993, The Paradoxes of the American Presidency, 1997; co-author: Government By the People, 1997. Dir. Nat. Civic League, Denver, Inst. for Ednl. Leadership, Washington; bd. dirs. Ctr. for Ethical Leadership. Mem. AAUP, Am. Polit. Sci. Assn. (exec. com. 1990-92), Western Polit. Sci. Assn. (pres. 1993-94), Urban League, C. of C. Office: Whitman Coll 345 Boyer Ave Walla Walla WA 99362-2067

CROOK, SEAN PAUL, aerospace systems program manager; b. Pawtucket, R.I., July 6, 1953; s. Ralph Frederick and Rosemary Rita (Dolan) C.; m. Mary Wickman, June 10, 1978; children: Kimberly Anne, Kelly Dolan, Erin Webster, Mary Katherine. BSME, U.S. Naval Acad., 1975; MBA, U. So. Calif., 1991. Commd. ensign USN, 1975, advanced through grades to lt., 1979, resigned, 1981; sr. systems engr. space div. Gen. Electric Co., Springfield, Va., 1982-84; sr. aerospace systems engr. Martin Marietta Aero. Def. Systems, Long Beach, Calif., 1984-87; sr. aerospace system engring. mgr. Martin Marietta Aero Def. Systems, Long Beach, Calif., 1987-93; chief engr. GDE Sys. Inc., A Tracer Co., San Diego, 1993-96, program mgr., 1996—; sec., bd. dirs. Guardian Minerals Inc. Commdr. USNR, 1992—. Mem. Am. Mgmt. Assn., U. So. Calif. Exec. MBA Alumni Assn. (bd. dirs.), U.S. Naval Acad. Alumni Assn. Home: 23565 Via Calzada Mission Viejo CA 92691-3625 Office: GDE Sys Inc PO Box 509008 MZ 6500E San Diego CA 92150-9008

CROOKE, STANLEY THOMAS, pharmaceutical company executive; b. Indpls., Mar. 28, 1945; m. Nancy Alder (dec.); 1 child, Evan; m. Rosanne M. Snyder. BS in Pharmacy, Butler U., 1966; PhD, Baylor Coll., 1971, MD, 1974. Asst. dir. med. rsch. Bristol Labs., N.Y.C., 1975-76, assoc. dir. med. rsch., 1976-77, assoc. dir. R&D, 1977-79, v.p. R&D, 1979-80; v.p. R&D Smith Kline & French Labs., Phila., 1980-82; pres. R&D Smith Kline Beckman, Phila., 1982-88; chmn. bd., chief exec. officer ISIS Pharms., Inc., Carlsbad, Calif., 1989; cons. Enzytech, Cambridge, Mass., 1988, Bachem Biosci., Phila., 1988, Centocor, Malvern, Pa., 1988, BCM Techs., Houston, 1988; chmn. bd. dirs. GES Pharms., Inc., Houston, 1989-91; adj. prof. Baylor Coll. Medicine, Houston, 1982, U. Pa., Phila., 1982-89; bd. dirs. GeneMedicine, Houston, Calif. Healthcare Inst., Indsl. Biotech. Assn., Washington, 1993; mem. sci. adv. bd. SIBIA, La Jolla, Calif.; adj. prof. pharmacology UCLA, 1991, U. Calif. San Diego, 1994. Editor: Anti Cancer Drug Design, 1984; mem. editl. adv. bd. Molecular Pharmacology, 1986-91, Jour. Drug Targeting, 1992; editl. bd. Antisense Rsch. and Devel., 1994; sect. editl. bd. for biologicals and immunologicals Expert Opinion on Investigational Drugs, 1995. Trustee Franklin Inst., Phila., 1987-89; bd. dirs. Mann Music Ctr., Phila., 1987-89; children's com. Children's Svcs., Inc., Phila., 1983-84; adv. com. World Affairs Coun., Phila. Recipient Disting. Prof. award U. Ky., 1986, Julius Stermer award Phila. Coll. Pharmacy and Sci., 1981, Outstanding Lectr. award Baylor Coll. Medicine, 1984. Mem. AAAS, Am. Assn. for Cancer Rsch. (state legis. com.), Am. Soc. for Microbiology, Am. Soc. Pharmacology and Exptl. Therapeutics, Am. Soc. Clin. Pharmacology and Therapeutics, Am. Soc. Clin. Oncology, Indsl. Biotech. Assn. (bd. dirs. 1992-93). Office: ISIS Pharms Inc 2292 Faraday Ave Carlsbad CA 92008-7208

CROSBY, JOHN O'HEA, conductor, opera manager; b. N.Y.C., July 12, 1926; s. Laurence Alden and Aileen Mary (O'Hea) C. Grad., Hotchkiss Sch., 1944; BA, Yale U., 1950, DFA (hon.), 1991; LittD (hon.), U. N.Mex., 1967; MusD (hon.), Coll. of Santa Fe, 1968, Cleve. Inst. Music, 1974; LHD (hon.), U. Denver, 1977. pres. Manhattan Sch. Music, 1976-86. Accompanist, opera coach, condr., N.Y.C., 1951-56, gen. dir., mem. conducting staff Santa Fe Opera, 1957—; guest condr. various opera cos. in U.S. and Can. and Europe, 1967—; condr. U.S. stage premiere Daphne, 1964; U.S. profl. premier Friedenstag, 1988; world premiere Wuthering Heights, 1958. With inf. AUS, 1944-46, ETO. Recipient Nat. Medal of Arts, 1991, Verdienstkreuz 1st klasse Bundesrepublik, Deutschland, 1992. Roman Catholic. Clubs: Metropolitan Opera (N.Y.C.), Century Assn. (N.Y.C.), University (N.Y.C.). Office: Santa Fe Opera PO Box 2408 Santa Fe NM 87504-2408

CROSS, BRUCE MICHAEL, lawyer; b. Washington, Jan. 30, 1942. AB magna cum laude, Dartmouth Coll., 1964; JD magna cum laude, Harvard U., 1967. Bar: Wash. 1967. Law clk. to Hon. Frank P. Weaver Supreme Ct. Wash., 1967-68; mem. Perkins Coie, Seattle. Office: Perkins Coie 1201 3rd Ave Fl 40 Seattle WA 98101-3099

CROSS, CHRISTOPHER S., fundraising executive; b. Lawrence, Mass., Oct. 11, 1943; s. Jerome Whitman and Margaret (Bain) C. BS, Boston U., 1967. Assoc. dir. Haney Assocs., Concord, Mass., 1969-71; nat. dir. devel. U.S. Ski Team, Denver, 1971-72; dir. mktg. Denver Merchandise Mart, 1972-76; v.p. Profl. Travel Advisors, Boulder, Colo., 1976-79, Animal Health Ins. Co., Danbury, Conn., 1985-91; nat. dir. devel. Am. Humane Assn., Denver, 1983-85; devel. officer Boulder County Hospice, Boulder, 1992—; bd. dirs. Cross Assocs., Boulder. Bd. dirs. Desiderata Sch., Berthoud, Colo., 1992—, Ednl. Films Inst., Albuquerque, 1989; hon. chair Colo. Contingent for U.S. Ski Team, Boulder, 1977; co-founder Colo. Trade Show Coun., Denver, 1975. Decorated Bronze Star, Air medal. Mem. Cmty. Shares of Colo. (bd. dirs. 1994—), Nat. Soc. Fundraising Execs., Planned Giving Roundtable, Assn. for Health Care Philanthropy. Office: Boulder County Hospice 2825 Marine St Boulder CO 80303-1027 Home: PO Box 1075 Niwot CO 80544-1075

CROSS, GLENN LABAN, engineering company executive, development planner; b. Mt. Vernon, Ill., Dec. 28, 1941; s. Kenneth Edward and Mildred Irene (Glenn) C.; m. Kim Lien Duong, Aug. 30, 1968 (div. Oct. 1975); m. Tran Tu Thach, Dec. 26, 1975; children: Cindy Sue, Cristy Luu, Crystal Tu, Cassandra Caitlynn; BA, Calif. Western U., 1981, MBA, 1982. Hosp. adminstr. pub. health div. USAID, Dept. State, Washington, 1966-68; pers. mgr. Pacific Architects and Engrs., Inc., L.A., 1968-70, contract adminstr., 1970-73, mgr. mgmt. svcs., 1973-75; contracts adminstr. Internat. Svcs. div., AVCO, Cin., 1975-77; sr. contract adminstr. Bechtel Group, Inc., San Francisco, 1977-80, Arabian Bechtel Co. Ltd.; contract adminstrv. supr. Bechtel Civil, Inc., Jubail Industrial City, Saudi Arabia, 1980-85; cons. Bechtel Western Power Corp., Jakarta, Indonesia, Pacific Engrs. and Constructors, 1985-90, prin. contract adminstr. Ralph M. Parsons Co., Pasadena, Calif., 1990-93, contract adminstr. Parsons-Brinckerhoff, Costa Mesa, Calif., 1993; project mgr. Pacific Architects and Engrs., Inc., 1993—. Author: Living With a Matrix: A Conceptual Guide to Organizational Variation, 1983. Served as sgt. 1st spl. forces group, airborne, AUS, 1962-65; Okinawa, Vietnam. Decorated Combat Infantryman's Badge. Mem. Nat. Contract Mgmt. Assn., Construction Mgmt. Assn. Am., Internat. Pers. Mgmt. Assn., Assn. Human Resource Systems Profls., Human Resource Planning Soc., Assn. MBA Execs., Am. Mgmt. Assn., Am. Arbitration Assn., Internat. Records Mgmt. Coun., Adminstrv. Mgmt. Soc. Republican. Avocations: swimming, reading. Home: 25935 Faircourt Ln Laguna Hills CA 92653-7517 Office: Pacific Architects and Engrs Inc 1111 W 6th St Los Angeles CA 90017-1800

CROSS, KATHRYN PATRICIA, education educator; b. Normal, Ill., Mar. 17, 1926; d. Clarence L. and Katherine (Dague) C. BS, Ill. State U., 1948; MA, U. Ill., 1951, PhD, 1958; LLD (hon.), SUNY, 1988; DS (hon.), Loyola U., 1980, Northeastern U., 1975; DHL (hon.), De Paul U., 1986, Open U., The Netherlands, 1989. Math. tchr. Harvard (Ill.) Community High Sch., 1948-49; rsch. asst. dept. psychology U. Ill., Urbana, 1949-53, asst. dean of women, 1953-59; dean of women then dean of students Cornell U., Ithaca, N.Y., 1959-63; dir. coll. and univ. programs Ednl. Testing Svc., Princeton, N.J., 1963-66; vis. prof. U. Nebr., 1975-76; rsch. educator Ctr. Rsch. and Devel. in Higher Edn. U. Calif., Berkeley, 1966-77; rsch. scientist, sr. rsch. psychologist, dir. univ. programs Ednl. Testing Svc., Berkeley, 1966-80; prof. edn., chair dept. adminstrn., planning & social policy Harvard U., Cambridge, Mass., 1980-88; Elizabeth and Edward Conner prof. edn. U. Calif., Berkeley, 1988-94, David Pierpont Gardner prof. higher edn., 1994—; del. to Soviet Union, Seminar on Problems in Higher Edn., 1975; vis. scholar Miami-Dade Community Coll., 1987; mem. sec. adv. com. on automated personal data systems Dept. HEW, 1972-73; speaker, cons. in field. Author: Beyond the Open Door: New Students to Higher Education, 1971, (with S. B. Gould) Explorations in Non-Traditional Study, 1972, (with J. R. Valley and Assocs.) Planning Non-Traditional Programs: An Analysis of the Issues for Postsecondary Education, 1974, Accent on Learning, 1976, Adults as Learners, 1981, (with Thomas A. Angelo) Classroom Assessment Techniques, 1993, (with Mimi Harris Steadman) Classroom Research, 1996; contbr. articles, monographs to profl. publs., chpts. to books; mem. editl. bd. to several ednl. jours.; cons. editor ednl. mag. Change, 1980—. With Nat. Acad. Edn., 1975—, Coun. for Advancement of Exptl. Learning, 1982-85; trustee Bradford Coll., Mass., 1986-88, Antioch Coll., Yellow Springs, Ohio, 1976-78; mem. nat. adv. bd. Nat. Ctr. of Study of Adult Learning, Empire State Coll.; mem. nat. adv. bd. Okla. Bd. Regents; mem. higher edn. rsch. program Pew Charitable Trusts. Mem. Am. Assn. Higher Edn. (bd. dirs. 1987—, pres. 1975, chair 1989-90), Am. Assn. Comty. and Jr. Colls. (vice chair commn. of future comty. colls.), Carnegie Found. Advancement of Tchg. (adv. com. on classification of colls. and univs.), Nat. Ctr. for Devel. Edn. (adv. bd.), New Eng. Assn. Schs. and Colls. (commn. on instns. higher edn. 1982-86), Am. Coun. Edn. (commn. on higher edn. and adult learner 1986-88). Office: U Calif Sch Edn 3531 Tolman Hall Berkeley CA 94720

CROSS, LYNDA LEE, health facility administrator, nurse; b. L.A., June 18, 1943; d. Fredrick Lewis Heyle and Bonnie Verda (Fridell) Covey; m. Jim Carl Eckler, June 7, 1963 (div. Sept. 1972); children: Barry, Dennis, Shantel, Candace; m. Douglas William Cross, Apr. 10, 1981. Diploma, Paradise Valley Sch. Nursing, 1964; BSN, Sonoma State U., 1981. RN; cert. infusion therapist, 1987. Clin. coord. urology San Diego Urological Med. Group, 1965-71; relief head nurse nursery Grossmont Hosp., La Mesa, Calif., 1971-75; relief head nurse neonatal ICU Balboa Naval Hosp., San Diego, 1976-77; coord. IV therapy St. Helena Hosp. and Health Ctr., Deer Park, Calif., 1977-79; staff nurse, IV therapist Mass. Eye and Ear Infirmary, Boston, 1982-84; pres., owner, IV clinician I.V. Lifeline, Inc., Berkley, Mass., 1984—. Developer IV homecare module, 1984 (1st Nurse award), coop. extended IV therapy in physicians setting, 1993. Fellow New Eng. Intravenous Nurses Soc. (scholarship chmn. 1985-86); mem. Intravenous Nurses Soc. Home and Office: 15861 Highway 101 S Brookings OR 97415-9560

CROSS, ROBERT LOUIS, realtor, land use planner, writer; b. Alton, Ill., Aug. 9, 1937; s. Louis William and Marion (Hanna) C.; m. Paula Sutton, June 8, 1958 (div. June 1970); children: Britomart, Christopher, Amoret; m. Carolee Sharko, May 5, 1990. BA, U. Kans., 1959, MA, 1961; grad., UCLA, 1969, Realtors Inst., L.A., 1980. Lectr. English lang. U. Kans., Lawrence, 1959-60, Washburn U., Topeka, Kans., 1960-61; editorial-mktg. rep. Prentice-Hall, Inc., Englewood Cliffs, N.J., 1962-64; dir. pub. info. Forest Lawn Meml. Pk., Glendale, Calif., 1964-68; account exec. pub. rels. J. Walter Thompson, L.A., 1968-70; sr. account exec. pub. rels. Botsford Ketchum, L.A., 1970-71, Harsh, Rotman & Druck, L.A., 1971-72; pres. Crossroads Combined Communications, L.A., 1973-80; real estate agt. Carmel (Calif.) Bd. Realtors, 1979—; gen. ptnr. Crossroads Design Ltd., Big Sur, Calif., 1990—; cons. Watts Mfg. Corp., L.A., 1970-73, U.S. Office Edn., Washington, 1971, U.S. Dept. Interior, Washington, 1972, Calif. State Coastal Commn., San Francisco, 1980-85. Author: Henry Miller: The Paris Years, 1991; assoc. editor Calif. Life Mag., 1976; contbr. IN Monterey Mag., 1977; real estate editor Monterey Life Mag., 1978. Pres., dir. Big Sur Hist. Soc., 1980-90, Coastlands Mut. Water Co., Big Sur, 1984—; co-founder Dialogue for Big Sur, 1984; dir. Big Sur Natural History Assn., 1984-86; founding docent Dept. Pks. and Recreation, Pt. Sur Historic State Park, Big Sur, 1987; With U.S. Army, 1961-63. Mem. Archeol. Inst. Am., Nat. Assn. Realtors, Am. Soc. Landscape Architects, Nat. Assn. Real Estate Appraisers (cert.), Calif. Assn. Realtors, Carmel Bd. Realtors (Multiple Listing Svc. Sales award 1980), Carmel Multiple Listing Svc., Big Sur Grange, Coast Property Owners Assn., Environ. Assesment Assn. (cert.). Home: PO Box 244 Big Sur CA 93920-0244 Office: Crossroads Design Ltd PO Box 244 Big Sur CA 93920-0244

CROUTHAMEL, DAVID WAYNE, oral and maxillofacial surgeon; b. Augsburg, Germany, May 1, 1953; (parents Am. citizens); s. George N. and Vera E. (Gilderslieve) C.; m. Janice Nolan, Aug. 28, 1976; 1 child, Joshua David. BS, Monmouth Coll., 1976; DDS, Temple U., 1982; cert. in oral and maxillofacial surgery, U. Pa., 1990. Diplomate Am. Bd. Oral and Maxillofacial Surgery. Med. technologist J.C. Blair Meml. Hosp., Huntingdon, Pa., 1976-78; gen. dentist Indian Health Svc., Sacaton, Ariz., 1982-87; oral and maxillofacial surg. resident U. Pa., 1987-90; pvt. practice, Chandler, Ariz., 1991—. Mem. ADA, Am. Assn. Oral and Maxillofacial Surgeons, Ariz. Soc. Oral and Maxillofacial Surgeons, Ariz. Dental Assn., Ctrl. Ariz.

Dental Soc., Phoenix Soc. Oral and Maxillofacial Surgeons, Rotary (bd. dirs. Chandler Horizon 1995-96). Office: 800 W Chandler Blvd Ste 3 Chandler AZ 85224-5340

CROW, KENNETH ARTHUR, pathologist; b. Boise, Idaho, July 16, 1938; s. Arthur Holbeach and Blanche Aleen (Tate) C.; m. Roberta Monroe, June 12, 1965; children: Jonathan and Jason (twins), Justin. AA, Boise Jr. Coll., 1958; BS, U. Utah, 1960; MD, U. Wis., 1964. Diplomate Am. Bd. Pathology. Rotating intern Denver Gen. Hosp., 1964-65; pathologist Albany (Oreg.) Gen. Hosp., 1973—; resident in pathology U. Colo. Med. Ctr., 1969-73; chief of pathology, clin. lab. Albany (Oreg.) Gen. Hosp., 1991—. Lt. USN, 1965-67. Fellow Am. Soc. Clin. Pathologists, Coll. Am. Pathologists; mem. AMA, Oreg. Med. Assn., Oreg. Pathologists Assn. Home: 1500 12th Ave SW Albany OR 97321-2033 Office: Albany Gen Hosp 1046 6th Ave SW Albany OR 97321-1916

CROWDER, RICHARD MORGAN, pilot; b. Wurzburg, Bavaria, Germany, July 22, 1963; (parents Am. citizens); s. Richard Thomas and Margaret Taylor (Rainey) C. BS, U. Minn., 1986; postgrad., U. Colo., 1995—. Pilot Classic Aviation, Mpls., 1985-87, Air South, Homestead, Fla., 1987, AVAir, Raleigh, N.C., 1987-88, Am. Eagle, Dallas, 1988-89, USAir, Arlington, Va., 1989-92, United Airlines, Chgo., 1992—. Republican.

CROWE, BEVERLY ANN, middle school educator; b. Kenton, Ohio, Mar. 1, 1940; d. Clayton Derwood and Kathryn Emma (Aurand) Kramer; m. R. Dale Crowe, Dec. 20, 1959; children: R. Kurt, Tawni, Kimber. BS, Bowling Green State U., 1964; MA, U. N.Mex., 1981. Nat. Bd. Cert. Tchr. Tchr. Ada (Ohio) Village Schs., 1960-62, Hardin No. Schs., Dola, Ohio, 1962-65, Chuska Boarding Sch., Tohatchi, N.Mex., 1967-79, Tohatchi Elem. Sch., 1979-88; tchr. Tohatchi Mid. Sch., 1988—, head dept. lang. arts, 1990—, head dept. social studies, 1990—; jr. varsity girls basketball coach Tohatchi H.S., 1986—; demonstration tchr. for 2d lang. methods Chuska Boarding Sch., Tohatchi, 1967-75; presenter workshops in field. Organizer, pres. PTA, Tohatchi, 1970-76; pres., treas. Tohatchi Athletic Club, 1976-85; sec., commr. Tohatchi Planning Com., 1977-81; mem. Chuska Assn. for Fighting Back, Tohatchi, 1995-96. Recipient Cmty. Svc. award Bur. Indian Affairs, 1975; named N.Mex. Asst. Coach of Yr. for Girls Basketball. Mem. Internat. Reading Assn., N.Mex. Coun. Tchrs. English, N.Mex. Coun. for the Social Studies, Geography Alliance of N.Mex. (tchr./cons.), Alpha Delta Kappa (pres., sec.), Kappa Delta Pi. Home: PO Box 121 Tohatchi NM 87325 Office: Tohatchi Middle School PO Box 322 Tohatchi NM 87325

CROWE, EDITH LOUISE, librarian; b. Buffalo, N.Y., Nov. 12, 1947; d. Harold Peter and Edith Louise (Robinson) C. BA in Art History with honors, SUNY, Buffalo, 1970; MLS, SUNY, Geneseo, 1971; MA in Humanities, Calif. State U., Dominguez Hills, 1980. Libr. San Jose (Calif.) State U., 1971-75, 77—, Calif. State U., Hayward, 1976-77; book reviewer Art Documentation, 1988—. Mem. editl. bd. Art Ref. Quar., 1992—; contbr. articles to profl. jours. Mem. ALA, Nat. Women's Studies Assn., Art Librs. Soc. (chair No. Calif. chpt. 1982-83, 93), Mythopoeic Soc., Phi Beta Kappa. Democrat. Office: San Jose State U Clark Libr 1 Washington Sq San Jose CA 95192-0028

CROWE, JOHN T., lawyer; b. Cabin Cove, Calif., Aug. 14, 1938; s. J. Thomas and Wanda (Walston) C.; m. Marina Protopapa, Dec. 28, 1968; 1 child, Erin Aleka. BA, U. Santa Clara, 1960, JD, 1962. Bar: Calif. 1962, U.S. Dist. Ct. (no. dist.) Calif. 1964, U.S. Dist. Ct. (ea. dist.) Calif. 1967. Practiced in Visalia, Calif., 1964—; ptnr. firm Crowe, Mitchell & Crowe, 1971-85; referee State Bar Ct., 1976-82; commdg. gen. 319th Transp. Brigade U.S. Army, 1990-94, commdg. gen., 311th Corps Support Command, 1995—; chmn. Army Res. Forces Policy Com., 1997—; gen. counsel Sierra Wine, 1986—; bd. dirs. World Parts Industries, 1993—. Bd. dirs. Mt. Whitney Area Coun. Boy Scouts Am., 1966-85, pres., 1971, 72; bd. dirs. Visalia Associated In-Group Donors (AID), 1973-81, pres., 1978-79; mem. Visalia Airport Commn., 1982-90. 1st lt. U.S. Army, 1962-64; major gen. Res. Decorated Legion of Merit with oak leaf cluster, Meritorious Svc. Medal with 3 oak leaf clusters, Army Commendation Medal; named Young Man of Yr., Visalia, 1973; Senator, Jr. Chamber Internat., 1970; recipient Silver Beaver award Boy Scouts Am., 1983. Mem. ABA, Tulare County Bar Assn., Nat. Assn. R.R. Trial Counsel, State Bar Calif., Visalia C. of C. (pres. 1979-80). Republican. Roman Catholic. Clubs: Rotary (pres. 1980-81). Home: 3939 W School Ave Visalia CA 93291-5514

CROWELL, SAMUEL M., JR., education educator; b. Lexington, N.C., May 8, 1949; s. Samuel Marvin and Margaret Louise (Riddle) C.; m. Deborah Jane Costolo, Jan. 1, 1987; 1 child, Chesley Carole. BA, Carson-Newman Coll., 1971; MS, Radford U., 1975; EdD, U. Va., 1992. Tchr. elem. edn. Carroll County Sch. Dist., Hillsville, Va., 1971-73; dir. career opportunities program Carroll County Schs., Hillsville, 1973-75, prin., 1975-78; dir. elem. edn., dir. ednl. adminstrn. U. Redlands, Calif., 1982-87; prof. Calif. State U., San Bernardino, 1987—; coord. elem. edn. Calif. State U., San Bernardino, 1987-89, dir. Ctr. for Rsch. in Integrative Studies, 1989—. Author: Mindshifts, 1994, Reenchantment of Learning, 1997; contbr. chpts. and articles to profl. publs. Mem. Idyllwild (Calif.) Environ. Group, 1993—, Idyllwild Poetry Readings, 1995—. Mem. ASCD, Phi Beta Delta, Phi Delta Kappa. Home: PO Box 1511 Idyllwild CA 92549

CROWLEY, DANIEL JOHN, anthropologist; b. Peoria, Ill., Nov. 27, 1921; s. Michael Bartholomew and Elsie Magdalene (Schnebelin) C.; m. Pearl Rita Ramcharan, Feb. 4, 1958; children: Peter Mahendranath, Eve Lakshmi, Magdalene Lilawati. AB, Northwestern U., 1943, PhD, 1956; MA, Bradley U., 1948. Instr. art history Bradley U., Peoria, 1948-50; tutor in anthropology U. West Indies, St. Augustine, Trinidad, 1953-56; instr. in anthropology Northwestern U., Evanston, Ill., 1956-57; asst. prof. U. Notre Dame., Ind., 1958-59; from asst. prof. to prof. U. Calif., Davis, 1961-93 ret.; vis. rsch. prof. Inst. African Studies U. Ghana, Legon, 1969-71; vis. prof. U. West Indies, 1973-74, Latrobe U., Bundoora, Australia, 1990. Author: I Could Talk Old-Story Good, 1966; editor African Folklore in the New World, 1977; contbg. editor African Arts, 1966—, Research in African Lits., 1973-90, Jour. African Studies, 1976—; translator (book) Congolese Sculpture, 1982; contbr. articles to profl. jours. Active U.S. Nat. Commn. for UNESCO, Washington, 1972-78. Served to lt. (j.g.) USN, 1942-46, PTO. Fellow Ford Found., 1959-60, Fulbright, 1978-79; grantee Indo-U.S. Commn., 1985; recipient Centennial Citation U. Calif. Santa Cruz, 1968, Archer Taylor Meml. lectr. U. Calif. Folklore Soc., 1986. Fellow Am. Folklore Soc. (life, pres. 1969-71, Stafford prize 1952), Am. Anthropol. Assn., Calif. Folklore Soc. (pres. 1980), African Studies Assn.; mem. Southwestern Anthropol. Assn. (Disting Lect. 1993), Sigma Xi. Democrat. Roman Catholic. Home: 726 Peach Pl Davis CA 95616-3218 Office: U Calif Dept Anthropology Davis CA 95616

CROWLEY, JOHN CRANE, real estate developer; b. Detroit, June 29, 1919; s. Edward John and Leah Helen (Crane) C.; m. Barbara Wenzel Gilfillan, Jan. 12, 1945; children: F. Alexander, Leonard, Philip, Eliot, Louise, Sylvia. BA, Swarthmore Coll., 1941; MS, U. Denver, 1943. Asst. dir. Mcpl. Finance Officers Assn., Chgo., 1946-48; So. Calif. mgr. League Calif. Cities, Los Angeles, 1948-53; mgr. City of Monterey Park, Calif., 1953-56; founder, exec. v.p. Nat. Med. Enterprises, L.A., 1968; pres. Ventura Towne House (Calif.), 1963-96; mem. faculty U. So. Calif. Sch. Pub. Adminstrn., 1950-53; bd. dirs. Regional Inst. of So. Calif., The L.A. Partnership 2000, Burbank-Glendale-Pasadena Airport Authority. Trustee Pacific Oaks Friends Sch. and Coll., Pasadena, 1954-57, 92—, Swarthmore Coll., 1987—; bd. dirs. Pasadena Area Liberal Arts Ctr., 1962-72, pres., 1965-68; bd. dirs. Pacificulture Found. and Asia Mus., 1971-76, pres., 1972-74; bd. dirs. Nat. Mcpl. League, 1986-92; chmn. Pasadena Cultural Heritage Commn., 1975-78; city dir. Pasadena, 1979-91; mayor City of Pasadena, 1986-88; bd. dirs. Western Justice Ctr., 1992—, v.p., 1995—, LA County Commn. on Efficiency and Economy, 1994—. Sloan Found. fellow, 1941-43. Mem. Internat. City Mgmt. Assn., Nat. Mcpl. League (nat. bd. 1980-92, Disting. Citizen award, 1984), Inst. Pub. Adminstrn. (sr. assoc.), Phi Delta Theta. Democrat. Unitarian. Home: 615 Linda Vista Ave Pasadena CA 91105-1122

CROWLEY, JOSEPH NEIL, university president, political science educator; b. Oelwein, Iowa, July 9, 1933; s. James Bernard and Nina Mary (Neil) C.; m. Johanna Lois Reitz, Sept. 9, 1961; children: Theresa, Neil, Margaret, Timothy. BA, U. Iowa, 1959; MA, Calif. State U., Fresno, 1963; PhD (Univ. fellow), U. Wash., 1967. Reporter Fresno Bee, 1961-62; asst. prof. polit. sci. U. Nev., Reno, 1966-71, asso. prof., 1971-79, prof., 1979—, chmn. dept. polit. sci., 1976-78, pres., 1978—; bd. dirs. Citibank Nev.; policy formulation officer EPA, Washington, 1973-74; dir. instl. studies Nat. Commn. on Water Quality, Washington, 1974-75. Author: Democrats, Delegates and Politics in Nevada: A Grassroots Chronicle of 1972, 1976, Notes From the President's Chair, 1988, No Equal in the World; An Interpretation of the Academic Presidency, 1994; editor: (with R. Roelofs and D. Hardesty) Environment and Society, 1973. Mem. Commn. on Colls., 1980-87; mem. adv. comn. on mining and minerals rsch. U.s. Dept. Interior, 1985-91; mem. coun. NCAA, 1987-92, mem. pres.' commn., 1991-92, pres., 1993-95; bd. dirs. Nat. Consortium for Acads. and Sports, 1992—; mem. Honda Awards Program Adv. Bd., 1994—; bd. dirs., campaign chmn. No. Nev. United Way, 1985-90. Recipient Thornton Peace Prize U. Nev., 1971, Humanitarian of Yr. award NCCJ, 1986, Alumnus of Yr. award Calif. State U., 1989, ADL Champion of Liberty award, 1993, Disting. Alumni award U. Iowa, 1994, Giant Step award Ctr. for Study of Sport in Soc., 1994; Nat. Assn. Schs. Pub. Affairs and Adminstrn. fellow, 1973-74. Roman Catholic. Home: 1265 Muir Dr Reno NV 89503-2629 Office: U Nev Office of Pres Reno NV 89557-0095

CROWTHER, RICHARD LAYTON, architect, consultant, researcher, author, lecturer; b. Newark, Dec. 16, 1910; s. William George and Grace (Layton) C.; m. Emma Jane Hubbard, 1935 (div. 1949); children: Bethe Crowther Allison, Warren Winfield, Vivian Layton; m. 2d Pearl Marie Tesch, Sept. 16, 1950. Student, Newark Sch. Fine and Indsl. Arts, 1928-31, San Diego State Coll., 1933, U. Colo., 1956. Registered architect, Colo. Prin. Crowther & Marshall, San Diego, 1946-50, Richard L. Crowther, Denver, 1951-66, Crowther, Kruse, Landin, Denver, 1966-70, Crowther, Kruse, McWilliams, Denver, 1970-75, Crowther Solar Group, Denver, 1975-82, Richard L. Crowther FAIA, Denver, 1982—; vis. critic, lectr. U. Nebr., 1981; holistic energy design process methodology energy cons. Holistic Health Ctr., 1982-83; adv. cons. interior and archtl. design class U. Colo., 1982-83, Cherry Creek, Denver redevel., 1984-88, Colo. smoking control legislation, 1985, interior solar concepts Colo. Inst. Art, 1986, Bio-Electro-Magnetics Inst., 1987-88; mentor U. Colo. Sch. Architecture, 1987-88. Author Sun/Earth, 1975 (Progressive Architecture award, 1975), rev. edit., 1983, reprint, 1995, Affordable Passive Solar Homes, 1983, reprint, 1996, Paradox of Smoking, 1983, Women/Nature/Destiny: Female/Male Equity for Global Survival, 1987, (monographs) Context in Art and Design, 1985, Existence, Design and Risk, 1986, Indoor Air: Risks and Remedies, 1986, Human Migration in Solar Homes for Seasonal Comfort and Energy Conservation, 1986, 88, Ecologic Architecture, 1992, Ecologic Digest, 1993, Ecologic Connections, 1996, others. NSF grantee, 1974-75. Fellow AIA (commr. research, edn. and environ. Colo. Central chpt. 1972-75, bd. dirs. chpt. 1973-74 AIA Research Corp. Solar Monitoring Program contract award, spkr. and pub. Colo. Ecologic Connections open forum 1996). *Inner awareness, relevancy, persistence and adaptiveness are all that we have in a world of vanity, variety and change.*

CROXTON, DOROTHY AUDREY SIMPSON, speech educator; b. Las Vegas, N.Mex., Feb. 29, 1944; d. Clyde Joseph and Audrey Shirley (Clements) Simpson; m. Gary Alan Beimer, May 13, 1972 (div. Apr. 1986); children: Laura Lea Beimer Nelson, Rose Anne Colleen; m. Ian B. Croxton, Dec. 27, 1992 (div. Oct. 1993). BA, N.Mex. Highlands U., 1965; MS, U. Utah, 1968; EdD, U. N.Mex., 1989. Cert. secondary edn., N.Mex. Tchr. West Las Vegas (N.Mex.) H.S., 1966-67, Santa Rosa (N.Mex.) H.S., 1968-71, Questa (N.Mex.) Consol. Schs., 1972-73; prof. speech comm. N.Mex. Highlands U., Las Vegas, 1975—. Author: Hovels, Haciendas, and House Calls: The Life of Carl H. Gellenthien, M.D., 1986, Speaking for Life: A Speech Communication Guide for Adults, 1990, Wreck of the Destiny Train, 1993. Active Emmanuel Bapt. Ch., Las Vegas, 1959—. Recipient Educator of Yr. award Pub. Svc. Co. of N.Mex., Albuquerque, 1990. Mem. P.E.O. Republican. Home: PO Box 778 Las Vegas NM 87701 Office: NMex Highlands Univ Communication Arts Dept Las Vegas NM 87701

CRUICKSHANK, JOHN DOUGLAS, newspaper editor; b. Toronto, Ont., Can., Apr. 7, 1953; s. Norman and Jean (McPherson) C.; m. Jennifer Hunter; children: Simone, Noah. BA with honors, U. Toronto, 1975. Reporter The Kingston (Ont., Can.) Whig-Standard, 1977-79, The Montreal Gazette, 1979-81; edn. writer The Globe & Mail, Toronto, 1981-82, Queen's Park writer, 1982-85; bur. chief The Globe & Mail, Vancouver, 1985-88; editorial writer The Globe & Mail, Toronto, 1988-90, assoc. editor, 1990-92, mng. editor, 1992—. Office: The Globe and Mail, 444 Front St W, Toronto, ON Canada M5V 2S9

CRUM, ROBERT M., business management executive. AB in English with highest honors, U. Pitts., 1950, JD, 1953; postgrad., U. Mich., 1959-60. Clk., rschr. Lewis and Drew Law Office, Pitts., 1954-55; rsch. analyst Blue Cross of Western Pa., Pitts., 1955-56, planning asst. to pres., 1956-61, asst. legal counsel, 1958-61; adminstrv. asst. to pres. Capital Blue Cross, Harrisburg, Pa., 1961-68, project coordinator for Medicare, 1966-68; mgr. pub. rels. and advt. Calif. Blue Shield, San Francisco, 1968-70, dir. corp. planning and rsch., 1970-72; exec. dir. Am. Dietetic Assn., Chgo., 1972-74; mng. dir. Nat. Parent Tchrs. Assn., Chgo., 1974-76; pres. Assn. and Soc. Mgmt., San Francisco, 1976—. Pres. Ch. Bd., Employee Credit Union. Mem. Am. Soc. Assn. Execs., No. Calif. Soc. Assn. Execs., Lions Club (bd. dirs.), Chgo. Soc. Assn. Execs., C. of C. *

CRUMB, ROBERT, cartoonist; b. Phila., Aug. 30, 1943; s. Charles Sr. C.; m. Dana Morgan (div. 1977); m. Aline Kominski, 1978. Colorist Am. Greetings Corp., 1963-67; cartoonist Fantagraphics Books, Seattle, 1967—. Creator: (comic book) Zap, 1968; founder, cartoonist: (mag.) Wierdo, 1981-89; author: The Complete Crumb Comics, (with Aline Kominski) My Troubles with Women, 1991, Wierdo Art of R. Crumb: His Early Period 1981-85, 1992, Crumb's Complete Dirty Laundry Comics, 1993; illustrator: The Monkey Wrench Gang by Edward Abbey, 1985; frequent contbr. to comic mags.; subject of documentary film: Crumb, 1994; creator cartoon character Fritz the Cat. Office: Fantagraphics Books 7563 Lake City Way NE Seattle WA 98115-4218*

CRUMBLEY, PAUL JAMES, English language educator; b. Montevideo, Uruguay, Sept. 26, 1952; came to U.S., 1956; s. T. A. and Janet (Christly) C.; m. Phebe Clare Jensen, June 14, 1986; 1 child, Nell Clare. MA, Sch. Theology at Claremont, 1976; MA in Teaching Lang. Arts, Reed Coll., 1978; MA, Bread Loaf Sch. English, Middlebury, Vt., 1986; PhD, U. N.C., 1993. Tchr. English Helen Bush Sch., Seattle, 1980-86, chair English dept., 1984-86; lectr. English U. N.C., Wilmington, 1986-87; tchg. asst. English U. N.C., Chapel Hill, 1987-93, dir. writing ctr., 1990-92; asst. prof. English Niagara U., N.Y., 1993-95, Utah State U., Logan, 1995—; faculty cons. Ednl. Testing Svc., 1992—. Author: Inflections of the Pen: Dash and Voice in Emily Dickinson, 1996, (chpt.) The Emily Dickinson Handbook, 1997. Mem. MLA, Am. Lit. Assn., Am. Studies Assn., Emily Dickinson Internat. Soc. (sec. 1995—). Office: Utah State U Dept English Logan UT 84322-3200

CRUMP, GLORIA JEAN, elementary and adult educator; b. L.A., Nov. 7, 1951; d. Robert and Florence (Spencer) C.; 1 child, Lavelle Gabrielle Alexander. BS, U. So. Calif., 1974. Tchr. Inglewood Unified Sch. Dist., L.A., 1975—, L.A. Unified Sch. Dist., 1980—. Poet: (anthology) Darkside of the Moon, 1995 (Best Poems of 1995, Internat. Poet of Merit award 1995). Mem. Internat. Soc. Poets, Delta Sigma Theta. Democrat. Presbyterian. Home: PO Box 470446 Los Angeles CA 90047-0246 Office: 401 S Inglewood Ave Inglewood CA 90303

CRUMPTON, CHARLES WHITMARSH, lawyer; b. Shreveport, La., May 29, 1946; s. Charles W. and Frances M. (McInnis) C.; m. Thu-Huong T. Cong-Huyen, Sept. 17, 1971; children: Francesca, Ian. BA, Carleton Coll., 1968; MA, U. Hawaii, 1974, JD, 1978. Bar: Hawaii 1978, U.S. Dist. Ct. Hawaii 1978, U.S. Ct. Appeals (9th cir.) 1982. Tchr. dept. edn. State of Hawaii, Honolulu, 1972-73, 75-77; Fulbright prof. U. Can Tho, Vietnam, 1973-75; assoc. John S. Edmunds, Honolulu, 1978-80, Ashford & Wriston, Honolulu, 1980-85, David W. Hall, Honolulu, 1985-88; dir. Hall & Crumpton, Honolulu, 1988-93; dir., shareholder Stanton Clay Tom Chapman & Crumpton, Honolulu, 1993—; pres./dir. Internat. Law Found., 1996—; barrister Am. Inn of Ct. IV, Honolulu, 1985-87; arbitrator Court-Annexed Arbitration program 1st Cir. Ct. State of Hawaii, 1987—; arbitrator, mediator Am. Arbitration Assn., 1988—, Arbitration Forums, 1990—, Mediation Specialists, 1994—, Dispute Prevention & Resolution, 1995—; mem. com. on lawyer professionalism Hawaii State Jud. Conf., 1988-89; arbitrator/mediator com. fee disputes Hawaii Bar Assn., 1990—, mem. com. jud. adminstrn., 1990—, mem. com. jud. performance, 1992-94, chair sect. on alternative dispute resolution, 1997—; prof. Hawaii Pacific U., 1995—; faculty/spkr. on ins. law, employment law, alternative dispute resolution, civil litigation, 1993—. Asst. dir. youth vols. Am. Cancer Soc., Honolulu, 1972-73. Fulbright grantee U.S. Dept. State, 1973-75. Mem. ATLA, ABA (torts and ins. practice sect., litigation sect., alt. dispute resolution sec.), Hawaii Bar Assn., Inter-Pacific Bar Assn. Home: 47-538 Hui Iwa St Kaneohe HI 96744-4658 Office: Stanton Clay Tom Chapman & Crumpton 345 Queen St Ste 600 Honolulu HI 96813

CRUSE, ALLAN BAIRD, mathematician, computer scientist, educator; b. Birmingham, Ala., Aug. 28, 1941; s. J. Clyde and Irma R. Cruse. AB, Emory U., 1962, PhD, 1974; postgrad. (Woodrow Wilson fellow) U. Calif., Berkeley, 1962-63, MA, 1965; tchg. fellow Dartmouth Coll., 1963-64. Instr., U. San Francisco, 1966-73, asst. prof. math., 1973-76, assoc. prof., 1976-79, prof., 1979—, chmn. math. dept. 1988-91; vis. instr. Stillman Coll., summer 1967; vis. assoc. prof. Emory U., spring 1978; prof. computer sci. Sonoma State U., 1983-85; cons. math edn. NSF fellow, 1972-73. Mem. Am. Math. Soc., Math. Am. Math. Soc., Math. Assn. Am. (chmn. No. Calif. sect. 1995-96), Assn. Computing Machinery, U. San Francisco Faculty Assn., Sigma Xi (Dissertation award 1974). Author: (with Millianne Granberg) Lectures on Freshman Calculus, 1971; research, publs. in field. Office: U San Francisco Harney Sci Ctr San Francisco CA 94117

CRUSE, DENTON W., marketing and advertising executive, consultant; b. Washington, May 21, 1944; s. Denton W. Sr. and Frances Rankin (Moore) C.; m. Susan Costello, June 11, 1988; 1 child, Thomas Moore. BS, Va. Commonwealth U., 1966; MBA, So. Ill. U., 1977. Media supr. Procter & Gamble Co., Cin., 1967-73; assoc. media dir. Ralston Purina Co., St. Louis, 1973-78; dir. advt. Armour-Dial Co., Phoenix, 1978-81; mktg. dir. Valentine Greeting Inc., Phoenix, 1981-82; dir. mktg. svcs. J. Walter Thompson/USA, L.A., 1982-83; cons. L.A., 1983-86; dir. advt. svcs. Mattel Inc., L.A., 1986-88; cons. C and O Assocs., L.A., 1988—; instr. UCLA, 1986—; spkr. internat. mktg. seminar Tech. Tng. Corp., 1993—. Editor-in-chief: Cobblestone, 1965. Marathon monitor L.A. Olympic Organizing Com., 1984; bd. dirs. Old Hometown Fair. Mem. Mktg. Club L.A., Beta Gamma Sigma, Pi Sigma Epsilon. Republican. Presbyterian.

CRUTCHFIELD, JAMES N., publishing executive; b. McKeesport, Pa., Dec. 7, 1947. BA in Journalism, Duquesne U., 1992. Pub. info. officer Pitts. Model Cities Program., 1971; reporter Pitts. Post-Gazette, 1971-76, Detroit Free Press, 1976-79; press. sec. for U.S. Sen. Carl Levin of Mich., 1979-81; chief of bur. Free Press., Lansing, Mich., 1981-83, city editor, met. editor, dep. mng. editor, 1983-89; managing editor Akron (Ohio) Beacon Journal, 1989-93; sr. v.p., exec. editor Press-Telegram, Long Beach, Calif., 1993—. Office: Press-Telegram Publs Inc 604 Pine Ave Long Beach CA 90844-0003

CSENDES, ERNEST, chemist, corporate and financial executive; b. Satu-Mare, Szatmár-Németi, Romania, Mar. 2, 1926; came to U.S., 1951, naturalized, 1955; s. Edward O. and Sidonia (Littman) C. m. Catharine Vera Tolnai, Feb. 7, 1953; children: Audrey Carol, Robert Alexander Edward. BA, Protestant Coll., Hungary, 1944; BS, U. Heidelberg (Ger.), 1948, MS, 1950, PhD summa cum laude, 1951. Rsch. asst. chemistry U. Heidelberg, 1950-51; rsch. assoc. biochemistry Tulane U., New Orleans, 1952; rsch. fellow chemistry Harvard U., 1952-53; rsch. chemist organic chems. dept. E. I. Du Pont de Nemours and Co., Wilmington, Del., 1953-56, elastomer chems. dept., 1956-61; dir. rsch. and devel. agrl. chems. div. Armour & Co., Atlanta, 1961-63; v.p. corp. devel. Occidental Petroleum Corp., L.A., 1963-64, exec. v.p. rsch., engring. and devel., mem. exec. com., 1964-68; COO, exec. v.p., dir. Occidental Rsch. and Engring. Corp., L.A., London, Moscow, 1963-68; mng. dir. Occidental Rsch. and Engring. (U.K.) Ltd., London, 1964-68; pres., CEO TRI Group, London, Amsterdam, Rome and Bermuda, 1968-84; chmn., CEO Micronic Techs., Inc., L.A., 1981-85; mng. ptnr. Inter-Consult Ltd., Pacific Palisades, Calif.; internat. cons. on tech., econ. feasibility and mgmt., 1984—; pres., chief tech. officer Gen. Grinding Corp., L.A., 1991—; chmn., CEO Eden Mgmt. Ltd., L.A. and London, 1993—. Contbr. 250 articles to profl. and trade jours., studies and books; achievements include 29 patents; rsch. in area of elastomers, rubber chemicals, adhesives, dyes and intermediates, organometallics, organic and biochemistry, high polymers, antioxidants, phosphates, plant nutrients, pesticides, process engineering, design of fertilizer plants, sulfur, potash, phosphate and iron ore mining and metallurgy, coal burning and acid rain, coal utilization, methods for aerodynamic grinding of solids, particles technology, advanced building materials, petrochemicals, biomed. engring., consumer products; also acquisitions, mergers, internat. fin. related to leasing investments and loans, trusts and ins., new Eurodollar instruments; regional indsl. devel. related to agr. and energy resources; projects in western Europe, no. Africa, Russia, Japan, Saudi Arabia, India, China and the Philippines. Recipient Pro Mundi Beneficio gold medal Brazilian Acad. Humanities, 1975; Harvard U. fellow, 1953. Fellow AAAS, Am. Inst. Chemists, Royal Soc. Chemistry (London); mem. AIAA, IEEE, SMME, AIChE, Am. Chem. Soc., German Chem. Soc., N.Y. Acad. Sci., Am. Concrete Inst., Am. Water Works Assn., AMS Internat., Acad. Polit. Sci., Am. Def. Preparedness Assn., Sigma Xi. Home: 514 N Marquette St Pacific Palisades CA 90272-3314

CUBIN, BARBARA LYNN, congresswoman, former state legislator, public relations consultant; b. Salinas, Calif., Nov. 30; d. Russell G. and Barbara Lee (Howard) Sage; m. Frederick William Cubin, Aug. 1; children: William Russell, Frederick William III. BS in Chemistry, Creighton U., 1969. Chemist Wyo. Machinery Co., Casper, Wyo., 1973-75; social worker State of Wyo.; office mgr. Casper, Wyo.; mem. Wyo. Ho. Reps., 1987-92, Wyo. Senate, 1993-94; pres. Spectrum Promotions and Mgmt., Casper, 1993-94; congresswoman, Wyo., at large U.S. House Reps., Washington, 1995—; mem. fin. & hazardous materials, health & environment, energy & mineral resources coms.; mem. com. Nat. Coun. State Legislators, San Francisco, 1987—, Lexington, Ky., 1990—. Mem. steering com. Exptl. Program to Stimulate Competitive Rsch. (EPSCOR); mem. Coun. of State Govts.; active Gov.'s Com. on Preventive Medicine, 1992; vice chmn. Cleer Bd. Energy Coun., Irving, Tex., 1993—; chmn. Wyo. Senate Rep. Conf., Casper, 1993—; mem. Wyo. Rep. Party Exec. Com., 1993; pres. Southridge Elem. Sch. PTO, Casper, Wyo. Toll fellow Coun. State Govts., 1990, Wyo. Legislator of Yr. award for energy and environ. issues Edison Electric Inst., 1994. Mem. Am. Legis. Exch. Coun., Rep. Women. Episcopalian. Office: US House Reps Office House Mem 1114 Longworth HOB Washington DC 20515

CUCCHIARA, ALFRED LOUIS, health physicist; b. Greenport, N.Y., Mar. 3, 1948; s. Mario Victor Cucchiara and Florence (Osinski) Lopez; m. Deborah Anne Horne, Jul. 14, 1989; children: Troy Adam Cucchiara, Daved Chane Cucchiara, James Horne. BS, Coll. Emporia, 1970; MS in radiation biophysics, U. Kans., 1975; cert. nuclear medicine, Wesley Medical Ctr., 1971. Cert. radiol. technician for nuclear medicine, Am. Registry Radiol. Technicians. Asst. health physicist U. Kans., Lawrence, 1971-73; environ. engr. United Nuclear Industries, Hanford, Wash., 1974-78; health physicist Los Alamos (N.Mex.) Nat. Lab., 1978-89, section leader/team leader, 1989—; mem., std. reviewer ASTM, 1994; cons., author Am. Nat. Stds. Inst., 1984—; session chmn., co-organizer Fine Particle Soc., 1984—; pres. Muscular Devel. and Rehab., LTD, Los Alamos, 1990—; profl. witness City of Santa Fe versus INS, 1996; speaker Rio Grande chpt. Health Physics Soc. ann. mtg., 1997. Contbr. over 30 articles to profl. jours. Recipient 1st place YMCA, Los Alamos Bench Press Contest, 1997. Mem. Coll. Emporia Student Body (v.p. 1969-70), Los Alamos Recreational Club 1663 (bd. dirs., vice chmn. 1982-84). Republican. Home: 972 Tsankawi St Los Alamos NM 87544-2836 Office: Los Alamos Nat Lab PO Box 1663 Los Alamos NM 87544-0600

CUCINA, VINCENT ROBERT, retired financial consultant; b. Balt., Mar. 31, 1936; s. Anthony James and Josephine (Lazzaro) C.; m. Rosemary Warrington, Apr. 24, 1965; children: Victor, Gregory, Russell. BS in Acctg. magna cum laude, Loyola Coll., Balt., 1958; MS in Fin. Mgmt., George

Washington U., 1967. CPA, Calif. Auditor Haskins & Sells, CPAs, Balt., 1958, 61-63; acctg. mgr. books and reports Chesapeake & Potomac Telephone Co. (AT&T), Cockeysville, Md., 1964-68; mgr. fin. controls ITT, N.Y.C., 1968; contr. ITT World Directories, N.Y.C., 1969-70; v.p. fin. analysis and planning Dart Industries, Inc., L.A., 1970-82; v.p. fin., chief fin. officer Epson Am., Inc., Torrance, Calif., 1984-87; cons. Westlake Village, Calif., 1988-95; lectr. planning and fin. Calif. Luth. U., 1991-95. Capt. U.S. Army, 1959-60, USAR, 61-64. Mem. AICPA, Fin. Execs. Inst. Roman Catholic. Home: 32305 Blue Rock Rdg Westlake Village CA 91361-3912

CUDDIHY, GERALDINE NORIKO, English educator; b. Pepeekeo, Hawaii, Sept. 3, 1949; m. James A. Cuddihy; 1 child, Joy S. BA in English, U. Hawaii, Hilo, 1973; M in Edn.-Curriculum and Instrn., U. Hawaii, Honolulu, 1983. Tchr. English State of Hawaii Dept. Edn., Hilo, 1980—. Mem. Historic Hawaii Found., Japanese Am. Citizens League. Mem. NEA, Hawaii State Tchrs. Assn. (grievance rep. 1980—), Johns Hopkins Alumni Assn., Hugh O'Brian Alumni Assn. Home: 1613 E Nelson Gonzales LA 70737 Office: Kau HS Box 100 Pahala HI 96777

CUELLO, JOEL L., biosystems engineer, educator; b. San Pablo City, Philippines, Nov. 20, 1962; came to U.S., 1988; s. Vicente Reyes and Gertrudis B. (Lansigan) C. BSin Agrl. and Biol. Engring., U. Philippines, 1984; MS in Agrl. and Biol. Engring., Penn State U., 1990, PhD in Agrl. and Biol. Engring., 1994. Rsch. engr. Mktg. Resources and Devel., Inc., Manila, 1984; instr. U. Philippines, Los Baños, 1984-88; grad. rsch. asst. Penn State U., University Park, 1988-93; rsch. assoc. nat. rsch. coun. NASA Kennedy Space Ctr., Cape Canaveral, Fla., 1994; asst. prof. U. Ariz., Tucson, 1995—. Mem. editor Internat. Symposium on Plant Prodn. in Closed Ecosystems, 1996; contbr. articles to profl. jours. Vol. Voluntary Action Ctr., State College, Pa., 1990-92. Rsch. grantee USDA, 1996, NASA, 1997. Mem. Am. Soc. Agrl. Engring. (sec. biol. engring. adv. com. 1995—, chmn. plant biol. engring. com. 1995, sec. Ariz. chpt. 1996—, advisor Ariz. student br. 1996—, Best Paper 1992), Inst. Biol. Engring., Am. Soc. Engring. Edn., Nat. Honor Soc. Agr., Nat. Honor Soc. Engring., Honor Soc. Agrl. and Biol. Engring. (pres. Pa. chpt. 1993). Office: U Ariz Dept Agrl and Biosystems Engring 507 Shantz Bldg Tucson AZ 85721

CULBERSON, GARY MICHAEL, hotel manager; b. Jackson, Miss., Sept. 16, 1955; s. William James and Peggy Ann (Pickett) C.; m. Mary Lee Yadron, May 8, 1986; 1 child, Ashley Victoria. Student, Miss. State U., 1973-78. Cert. hotel adminstr. Resident mgr. Kingston Plantation, Myrtle Beach, S.C.; exec. asst., mgr. Brown Palace Hotel, Denver; mng. dir. Tremont Hotel, Chgo., 1991; gen. mgr. Embassy Suites Hotel, Denver, 1996-97; hotel mgr. Casino Magic Hotel, Biloxi, Miss., 1997—. Mem. Confrerie De La Chaine Des Rotisseurs (Maitre of Table Restaurateur 1991-92), Mensa.

CULL, CHRIS ALAN, operations executive; b. Las Cruces, N.Mex., Jan. 3, 1947; s. William Roy Cull and Doris Jean (Compton) Morgan; m. DuAnne Elizabeth Diers King, July 26, 1967 (div. 1979); children: Joey Lynn, Jamie Ayn, Brandon Alan. BS, N.Mex. State U., 1976. Lab./field technician N.Mex. State U., Las Cruces, 1973-76; research soil scientist Mont. State U., Bozeman, 1976-77; reclamation supr. Western Energy Co., Colstrip, Mont., 1977-80; mgr. ops. permitting Western Energy Co., Billings, Mont., 1980-85; asst. project mgr. En Tech Inc., Butte, Mont., 1985-86; mgr. ops. Spl. Resource Mgmt. Inc., Billings, 1986-87; owner EnviroChek Inc., Billings, 1987-88; dir. environ. svcs. Western Tech. Inc., Tucson, 1988-90; dir. regulatory affairs Western Tech. Inc., Golden, Colo., 1990-91; mgr. regulatory affairs Sergent, Hauskins & Beckwith, Lakewood, Colo., 1991-92; mgr. regulatory svcs. Morrison-Maierle Environ., Billings, Mont., 1992, Morrison-Maierle Environ. Corp., Billings, 1992—; v.p. regulatory svcs., 1994—. Contbr. articles to profl. jours. Mem. Am. Indsl. Hygiene Assn., Nat. Assn. Environ. Profls., Soil Conservation Soc. Am. (chmn. surface mine reclamation com. 1978-80, mem. univ. and coll. rels. com. 1977-78, spl. task force surface mine reclamation divsn. 1977-79, pres. Mont. chpt. 1980-82), Mont. Coal Coun. (co-chmn. environ./tech. com. 1983-85), Mining and Reclamation Coun. Am. (tech. com. 1983-85), Am. Coun on Sic. and Health, SME Inc., N.W. Mining Assn., Mont. Mining Assn. Home: 3295 Granger Ave E Apt 18 Billings MT 59102-6064 Office: Morrison-Maierle Environ Corp 2020 Grand Ave Billings MT 59102-2679

CULLEN, JACK JOSEPH, lawyer; b. Sept. 20, 1951; s. Ray Brandes (stepfather) and Helen Cullen; m. Deborah L. Vick, Oct. 28, 1978; children: Cameron, Katherine. BA, Western Wash. State Coll., 1973; JD, U. Puget Sound, 1976. Bar: Wash. 1977, U.S. Dist. Ct. (we. dist.) Wash. 1977, U.S. Dist. Ct. (ea. dist.) Wash. 1977, U.S. Tax Ct. 1984, U.S. Ct. Appeals (9th cir.) 1980. Staff atty. Wash. State Bar Assn., Seattle, 1977-79; assoc. Hatch & Leslie, Seattle, 1979-85, mng. ptnr., 1985-91; ptnr. Foster Pepper & Shefelman, Seattle, 1991-96, mng. ptnr., 1996—, mem. exec. com., 1991—. Co-author: Prejedgment Attachment, 1986; speaker, panelist over 50 regional, local seminars on bankruptcy, bus. reorgn. Active Frank Lloyd Wright Bldg. Conservancy, 1989—. Mem. ABA (bus. law sect.), Am. Bankruptcy Inst., Wash. State Bar Assn. (creditor-debtor sect., chair exec. 1982-90, spl. dist. counsel 1988—, hearing officer 1990), Seattle-King County Bar Assn. (bankruptcy rules subcom. 1988-90), Vancouver-Seattle Involvency Group (charter mem. 1990—), U.S. Sport Parachuting Team (nat. and world champions 1976, instrument rated pilot), Wash. Athletic Club. Office: Foster Pepper & Shefelman 1111 3rd Ave Ste 3400 Seattle WA 98101-3299

CULLEN, ROBERT JOHN, publishing executive, financial consultant; b. York, Pa., Feb. 14, 1949; s. John Joseph and Florence Susanne (Staab) C.; m. Elizabeth Maule, Oct. 20, 1984; 1 child, Michael Joseph. BA, Winona (Minn.) State U., 1972. CFP; registered investment advisor. Editor-in-chief Overseas Life, Leimen, Fed. Republic of Germany, 1978-80; feature editor L.A. Daily Commerce, 1980-83; pres. HighTech Editorial, L.A., 1983—; fin. planner Cullen Fin. Svcs., Rancho Cucamonga, Calif., 1989—; computer editor Plaza Communications, Irvine, Calif., 1984-91. With U.S. Army, 1974-78, ETO. Mem. Internat. Assn. Fin. Planners, Calif. Advs. Nursing Home Reform.

CULLY, SUZANNE MARÍA, modern language educator; b. Albuquerque, N. Mex., Mar. 15, 1957; d. Jack Francis and Martha (Crittenden) C.; m. Rex Smith, Jr., May 10, 1986 (div. Jan. 1991); 1 child, Maria Makenna Smith. BA, U. N. Mex., 1980, MA in French Lit., 1993; Cert. des Études Politiques, U. Aix, Marseilles, France, 1981. Tchr. French U. N. Mex., Albuquerque, 1991-93; tchr. Spanish Albuquerque Pub. Schs., 1994, tchr. Spanish, French, 1994-95, tchr. French Lit., 1995-96; grant writing cons. N. Mex. Agy. on Aging, Santa Fe, 1992-93, Albuquerque Pub. Schs., 1995-96. Mem. Jr. League of Albuquerque, 1987—; bd. dirs. Nat. Coun. on Alcoholism, 1996—. Recipient Grad. fellowship U. N. Mex., Albuquerque, 1991-93; grantee for study in Cuernavaca, Mex., Ctr. for Tchg. Excellence, Portales, N. Mex., 1996. Democrat. Roman Catholic.

CULNON, SHARON DARLENE, reading specialist, special education educator; b. Balt., Apr. 20, 1947; d. Clayton Claude and Ann (McIntyre) Legg; m. Allen William Culnon, July 9, 1975. BA in Elem. Edn., U. Mich., 1972; MAT in Reading Edn., Oakland U., 1980; Learning Disabilities Cert., Ariz. State U., 1983. Cert. K-8 edn., K-12 reading specialist, K-12 learning disabilities specialist. Tchr. Mt. Morris (Mich.) Consolidated Schs., 1972-77; reading specialist Paradise Valley Schs., Phoenix, 1978-87, learning disabilities specialist, 1987-90, tchr., 1990—. Mem. Kachina Jr. Women's Club, Phoenix, 1980-83, sec., 1981-82. Recipient Learning Leader/dist. award Paradise Valley Bd. of Edn., Phoenix, 1986. Mem. Phi Delta Kappa (historian 1987-88). Presbyterian. Home: 9035 N Concho Ln Phoenix AZ 85028-5318 Office: Hidden Hills Elem Sch 1919 E Sharon Dr Phoenix AZ 85022-5057

CULP, GORDON CALVIN, retired lawyer; b. Auburn, Wash., Feb. 17, 1926; s. Norman and Cara Virl (Carter) C.; widowed, 1996. BS, U. Wash., 1950, JD, 1952. Assoc. Ferguson & Burdell, Seattle, 1952-55; pvt. practice Seattle, 1955-57; counsel subcom. on territories and insular affairs U.S. Senate, Washington, 1957-58; ptnr. Culp, Dwyer & Guterson, Seattle, 1959-60; asst. to chmn. Dem. Nat. Com., Washington, 1960-61; ptnr., of counsel Culp, Dwyer, Guterson & Grader, Seattle, 1961-91; ret., 1991; scheduling officer Henry M. Jackson for Pres. Campaign, Washington, 1972. Bd. regents U. Wash., Seattle, 1977-89, U. Wash. Med. Ctr., Seattle, 1989—. With USN, 1944-46. Mem. ABA, Seattle-King County Bar Assn. Democrat.

CULTON, PAUL MELVIN, retired counselor, educator, interpreter; b. Council Bluffs, Iowa, Feb. 12, 1932; s. Paul Roland and Hallie Ethel Emma (Paschal) C. BA, Minn. Bible Coll., 1955; BS, U. Nebr., 1965; MA, Calif. State U., Northridge, 1970; EdD, Brigham Young U., 1981. Cert. tchr., Iowa. Tchr. Iowa Sch. for Deaf, Council Bluffs, 1956-70; ednl. specialist Golden West Coll., Huntington Beach, Calif., 1970-71, dir. disabled students, 1971-82, instr., 1982-88; counselor El Camino Coll., Via Torrance, Calif., 1990-93, acting assoc. dean, 1993-94; counselor El Camino Coll., Via Torrance, Calif., 1994-97; interpreter various state and fed. cts., Iowa, Calif., 1960-90; asst. prof. Calif. State U., Northridge, Fresno & Dominguez Hills, 1973, 76, 80, 87-91; vis. prof. U. Guam, Agana, 1977; mem. allocations task force, task force on deafness, trainer handicapped students Calif. C.C.s, 1971-81. Editor: Region IX Conf. for Coordinating Rehab. and Edn. Svcs. for Deaf proceedings, 1970, Toward Rehab. Involvement by Parents of Deaf conf. proceedings, 1971; composer Carry the Light, 1986. Bd. dirs. Iowa NAACP, 1966-68, Gay and Lesbian Cmty. Svcs. Ctr., Orange County, Calif., 1975-77; founding sec. Dayle McIntosh Ctr. for Disabled, Anaheim and Garden Grove, Calif., 1974-80; active Dem. Cent. Com. Pottawattamie County, Council Bluffs, 1960-70; del. People to People N.Am. Educators Deaf Vis. Russian Schs. & Programs for Deaf, 1993. League for Innovation in Community Coll. fellow, 1974. Mem. Registry of Interpreters for Deaf, Congress Am. Instrs. Deaf, Am. Deafness and Rehab. Assn., Calif. Assn. Postsecondary Educators Disabled, Am. Fedn. Tchrs., Nat. Assn. Deaf. Mem. Am. Humanist Assn. Home: 2567 Plaza Del Amo Apt 203 Torrance CA 90503-8962

CULVER, LARRY G., medical research executive; b. 1949. MBA, U. Wis., 1977. Dir. fin. planning Marine Power Group Brunswick Corp., Fon du Lac, Wis., 1971-79; controller Eaton Corp., Milw., Salt Lake City, 1979-85; CFO Summation Inc., Kirkland, Wash., 1985-91; sr. v.p. Cellpro Inc., Bothell, Wash., 1991—. *

CUMBER, SHERRY G., psychotherapist, research consultant; b. Dallas; d. Jessie Ray and Dorothy Mae (Weeden) Wiliford; 1 child Brooke Dawn Thrash Willis. BA, U. Colo., Colorado Springs, 1993; MA, Chapman U., Colorado Springs, 1997. Cert. profo. hypnotherapist. CEO CSI, Inc., Tulsa, 1975-87; bus. cons. ind. contractor, Costa Mesa, Calif., 1987-90; rschr. U. Colo., Colorado Springs, 1990-93; bus. cons. Colorado Springs, 1993-95; psychotherapist in pvt. practice, Colorado Springs, 1995—. State legis. candidate Dem. Party, Okla., 1978, legis. and congl. campaign coord., 1978-86; lobbyist NRA, Oklahoma City, 1983. Recipient Contbn. award NRA, 1983, Participation award Okla. Pub. Sch. Sys., 1984-87. Mem. ACA, Assn. for Drug and Alcohol Addiction. Office: Acad Counseling 6170 Lehman Dr Ste # 100 Colorado Springs CO 80919

CUMELLA, STEPHEN PAUL, geologist; b. Colorado Springs, Colo., Aug. 19, 1955; s. Ronald and Claire Mabel (Person) C.; m. Cindy Kay Carothers, July 12, 1986; children: Nathan, Paul, Kimberly. BS in Geology, U. Tex., 1977, MA in Geology, 1981. cert. petroleum geologist. Geologist Chevron U.S.A., Denver, 1981-90, Chevron Overseas Petroleum, Inc., San Ramon, Colo., 1988-90; cons. geologist Cockrell Oil Corp., Grand Junction, Colo., 1990-92; project mgr. Rust Environ. & Infrastructure, Englewood, Colo., 1992—. Contbr. articles and abstracts to scientific jours. Vol. Meals-on-Wheels, Denver, 1984-88, Grand Junction, 1995-96. Mem. Am. Assn. Petroleum Geologists, Nat. Ground Water Assn., Grand Junction Geol. Soc. (pres. 1993), Uncompahgre Plateau Paleontological Soc. Home: 27395 Mountain Park Rd Evergreen CO 80439

CUMES, DAVID M., urologist; b. Johannesburg, South Africa, Aug. 12, 1944; came to U.S., 1975; s. Jack and Lillian (Beare) C.; children: Lila, Terence, Paul, Roni. M.B.B.Ch., U. Witwatersrand, Johannesburg, 1967. Diplomate Am. Bd. Urology. Intern, resident in gen. surgery Johannesburg, 1968-75; resident in urology Stanford (Calif.) Med. Sch., 1975-79, staff urologist, 1979-80; staff urologist Mason Clinic, Seattle, 1980-81; pvt. practice Santa Barbara, Calif., 1981—. Mem. Am. Urol. Assn. (western sect.), Santa Barbara Med. Soc. Office: 601 E Arrellaga St Santa Barbara CA 93103-2274

CUMMINGS, BARTON, musician; b. Newport, N.H., July 10, 1946; s. C. Barton and Ruth (Ricard) C.; m. Florecita L. Lim, July 23, 1983;. BS in Music Edn., U. N.H., 1968; MusM, Ball State U., Muncie, Ind., 1973. Dir. music Alton (N.H.) Pub. Sch., 1971-72; lectr. San Diego State U., 1974-79; instr. music Point Loma Coll., San Diego, 1976-79; instr. San Diego Community Coll. Dist., 1977-79, Delta State U., Cleveland, Miss., 1979-82; supr. Clarksdale Separate Sch. Dist., 1982-84; dir. music Walnut (Calif.) Creek Concert Band, 1985--, Richmond Unified Sch. Dist., 1988—, Golden Hills Concert Band, 1990—; condr. Devil Mountain Symphony, 1991—; tuba player Vallejo Symphony Orch., 1988—, Concord Pavilion Pops Orch., 1985—, Brassworks of San Francisco, 1985—, Solano Dixie Jubilee. Author: The Contemporary Tuba, 1984, The Tuba Guide, 1989, Teaching Techniques for Brass Instruments, 1989; composer over 6 dozen pub. compositions; recorded on Capra, Coronet and Crystal, Channel Classics, Mark labels. Mem. ASCAP, NACUSA, T.U.B.A., Am. Fedn. of Musicians, Conductor's Guild, Phi Mu Alpha Sinfonia. Home: 550 Cambridge Dr Benicia CA 94510-1316

CUMMINGS, DAROLD BERNARD, aircraft engineer; b. Batavia, N.Y., June 27, 1944; s. Bernard Laverne and Doris Helen (Klotzbach) C.; children from a previous marrage: Carla, Bret; m. Karen Jean Cacciola, Dec. 19, 1992; children: Kyle, Scott. BS in Indsl. Design, Calif. State U., Long Beach, 1967. Engr. aircraft design Rockwell Internat., L.A., 1967-82; chief engr. Boeing N.Am., Seal Beach, Calif., 1988—; chief designer advanced design Northrop Corp., Hawthorne, Calif., 1982-88; lectr. Calif. State U., Long Beach, 1969-73; pres. Matrix Design, Hawthorne, 1967—. Author: What Not to Name Your Baby, 1982; cons., actor (movie) Search for Solutions, 1979; multiple patents in field. Mem. Air Force Assn. Republican. Home: 5320 W 124th Pl Hawthorne CA 90250-4154 Office: Rockwell Internat Seal Beach CA 90740

CUMMINGS, LESLIE EDWARDS, hospitality management educator; b. Modesto, Calif., Feb. 17, 1951; d. George Robert and Mary Lou (Bomberger) Edwards; m. William Theodore Cummings Jr., Mar. 12, 1977. BS in Home Econs., Ariz. State U., 1974, MS in Agriculture, 1977, D in Pub. Adminstrn., 1990. Intern General Mills, Inc., Golden Valley, Minn., summer 1968; diet technician Mesa (Ariz.) Luth. Hosp., 1972-73; salesperson Romney Products, Inc., 1974; pharm. ins. auditor Pharm. Card Sys., Inc., 1974-76; mem. chain hdqrs. staff Fry's Supermarkets, Inc., 1977; adj. instr. foodsvc. Auburn (Ala.) U., 1978-79, from asst. mgr. to mgr. Campus Ctr. Foodsvcs., 1979-80; customer support analyst WANG Labs., Inc., 1981-83; asst. prof. U. Nev., Coll. Hotel Adminstrn., Las Vegas, 1983-87, assoc. prof., 1987-93, prof., 1993—; presenter Hotel-Motel Expo, 1985, So. Nev. Dietetics Assn. and So. Nev. Home Econs. Assn., Las Vegas, 1986, Inst. Food Technologists, Las Vegas, 1987, Universidad Madre y Maestra System, Santo Domingo, Dominican Republic, 1987, Internat. Assn. Hospitality Accts., Las Vegas, 1986, Foodsvc. and the Environment, Scottsdale, Ariz., 1990, State of Ariz. Dietetics Assn., Scottsdale, 1991, Assn. for the Study of Food and Soc., Tucson, 1991, ASPA, Las Vegas, 1991, Foodsvcs. Sys. Beyond 2000 Conf., Israel, 1992, Gaming Educator's Conf., Las Vegas, Hospitality Info. Tech. Assn., New Orleans, 1995, Environments for Tourism Conf., Las Vegas, 1996, Internat. Hospitality Tech. Conf., Nashville, 1996; panelist, spkr. in field of applied tech. and gaming trends. Author: (textbook) (with Lendal Kotschevar) Nutrition Management for Foodservices, 1989, Instructor's Manual for Nutrition Management for Foodservices, 1989; contbr. numerous articles to profl. jours. Vol. Women's Resource Network Career Event, Annual Nev. Gov.'s Conf. for Women. Recipient Nat. Assn. Schs. Pub. Adminstrn. dissertation award, 1990, Boyd Rsch. award, 1991, Ace Denken Disting. Rsch. award, 1996, 97; fellow Rotary Internat., 1978. Mem. ASPA, Am. Dietetic Assn. (treas. environ. nutrition dietetic practice group 1992-95, registered dietitian), Inst. Internal Auditors (cert.), Coun. on Hotel, Restaurant and Instnl. Edn., Phi Beta Kappa, Phi Kappa Phi, Pi Alpha Alpha. Office: WF Harrah Coll Hotel Adminstrn Food & Beverage Mgmt Dept 4505 S Maryland Pkwy Las Vegas NV 89154-9900

CUMMINGS, NICHOLAS ANDREW, psychologist; b. Salinas, Calif., July 25, 1924; s. Andrew and Urania (Sims) C.; m. Dorothy Mills, Feb. 5, 1948; children: Janet Lynn, Andrew Mark. AB, U. Calif., Berkeley, 1948; MA, Claremont Grad. Sch., 1954; PhD, Adelphi U., 1958. Chief psychologist Kaiser Permanente No. Calif., San Francisco, 1959-76; pres. Found Behavioral Health, San Francisco, 1976—; chmn., CEO Am. Biodyne, Inc., San Francisco, 1985-93, Kendron Internat., Ltd., Reno, Nev., 1992-95; chmn. Nicholas & Dorothy Cummings Found., Reno, 1994—; chmn., pres. U.K. Behavioural Health, Ltd., London, 1996—; Disting. prof. U. Nev., 1997—; co-dir. South San Francisco Health Ctr., 1959-75; pres. Calif. Sch. Profl. Psychology, L.A., San Francisco, San Diego, Fresno campuses, 1969-76; chmn. bd. Calif. Cmty. Mental Health Ctrs., Inc., L.A., San Diego, San Francisco, 1975-77; pres. Blue Psi, Inc., San Francisco, 1972-80, Inst. for Psychosocial Interaction, 1980-84; mem. mental health adv. bd. City and County San Francisco, 1968-75; bd. dirs. San Francisco Assn. Mental Health, 1965-75; pres., chmn. bd. Psycho-Social Inst., 1972-80; dir. Mental Rsch. Inst., Palo Alto, Calif., 1979-80; pres. Nat. Acads. of Practice, 1981-93. Served with U.S. Army, 1944-46. Fellow Am. Psychol. Assn. (dir. 1975-81, pres. 1979); mem. Calif. Psychol. Assn. (pres. 1968). Office: Nicholas & Dorothy Cummings Found 561 Keystone Ave Ste 212 Reno NV 89503-4331

CUMMINGS, RUSSELL MARK, aerospace engineer, educator; b. Santa Cruz, Calif., Oct. 3, 1955; s. Gilbert Warren and Anna Mae (Phillips) C. BS, Calif. Poly. State U., 1977, MS, 1985; PhD, U. So. Calif., 1988. Mem. tech. staff Hughes Aircraft Co., Canoga Park, Calif., 1979-86; rsch. assoc. Nat. Rsch. Coun. at NASA Ames Rsch. Ctr., Moffett Field, Calif., 1988-90; prof. aerospace engring. Calif. Poly. State U., San Luis Obispo, Calif., 1986—; dept. chmn. aero. engring. dept. Calif. Poly. State U., 1992-96; cons. Steiner and Assocs., San Luis Obispo, 1989-90; vis. acad. computing lab. Oxford U., 1995, 96. Contbr. chpt. to book Numerical and Physical Aspects of Aerodynamic Flows, 1990; assoc. editor Jour. Spacecraft and Rockets, 1994-97; contbr. 15 articles to profl. jours., presented 35 tech. papers at sci. confs. and meetings. Asst. scoutmaster Boy Scouts Am., San Luis Obispo, 1978-79, Eagle Scout. Hughes Engring. fellow 1980-84, Howard Hughes Doctoral fellow 1984-86; NASA grantee, 1986-96; recipient Group Achievement awards NASA, 1989, 90, AIAA Nat. Faculty Advisor award, 1994, Northrop Grumman Excellence in Teaching and Applied Rsch. award, 1995. Fellow AIAA (assoc.); mem. Am. Soc. Engring. Educators, Royal Aero. Soc., Sigma Xi, Sigma Gamma Tau. Republican. Mem. Evangelical Christian Ch. Office: Calif Poly State U Dept Aero Engring San Luis Obispo CA 93407

CUMMINGS, SHARON SUE, state extension service youth specialist; b. Trinidad, Colo., Aug. 26, 1945; d. James H. and Mima (McDonald) C. BS, Colo. State U., 1967, MEd, 1974; PhD, Ohio State U., 1991. Summer agt. Colo. State Coop. Extension, Canon City, 1966; extension home agt. Colo. State Coop. Extension, Colo. Springs, 1967-68; county dir. Leadville, 1968-70; area extension home economist San Luis Valley, 1970-74; agt., home economist Castle Rock, 1974-80; specialist 4H youth Ft. Collins, 1980-89, '91—; grad. assoc. Ohio State U. Coop. Extension, Columbus, 1989-91. Co-author: National Ambassador Handbook, 1984; (curriculum for youth) over 20 pubs.; assoc. editor (newsletter) Youthoughts, 1990, '91. Active on coms. United Meth. Ch. various Colo. locations, 1975—. Recipient Agrl. Extension scholarship Ohio State U., 1991; spotlighted alumna Dept. Human Resources Colo. State U., 1985-86; 1 of 50 in U.S chosen for Exec. Devel. Inst. USDA Extension Svc., 1987-89. Mem. Nat. Assn. Extension 4-H Youth Agts. (pres. Colo. 1981-82), Colo. Home Econs. Assn. (treas. 1983-85), Colo. State U. Extension Specialist Assn. (pres. 1982-84), CERES (assoc., chpt. advisor 1983-85), Phi Kappa Phi, Gamma Sigma Delta, Epsilon Sigma Phi (pres. Colo. 1996-97). Office: Colo State U Coop Extension 127 Aylesworth NW Fort Collins CO 80523

CUMMINS, CHARLES FITCH, JR., lawyer; b. Lansing, Mich., Aug. 19, 1939; s. Charles F. Sr. and Ruth M. Cummins; m. Anne Warner, Feb. 11, 1961; children: Michael, John, Mark. AB in Econs., U. Mich., 1961; LLB, U. Calif., Hastings, 1966. Bar: Calif. 1966, Mich. 1976. Assoc. Hall, Henry, Oliver & McReavy, San Francisco, 1966-70, ptnr., 1971-75; ptnr. Cummins & Cummins, Lansing, Mich., 1976-82, Pitto & Ubhaus, San Jose, Calif., 1982-85; prin. Law Offices Charles F. Cummins Jr., San Jose, 1985-87; ptnr. Cummins & Chandler, San Jose, 1987-92; prin. Law Offices of Charles F. Cummins, Jr., San Jose, 1992—. Bd. dirs., officer various civic orgns., chs. and pvt. shcs. Lt. (j.g.) USNR, 1961-63. Mem. Kiwanis. Office: Law Offices of Charles F Cummins Jr 4 N 2nd St Ste 1230 San Jose CA 95113-1307

CUMMINS, JOHN STEPHEN, bishop; b. Oakland, Calif., Mar. 3, 1928; s. Michael and Mary (Connolly) C. A.B., St. Patrick's Coll., 1949. Ordained priest Roman Catholic Ch., 1953; asst. pastor Mission Dolores Ch., San Francisco, 1953-57; mem. faculty Bishop O'Dowd High Sch., Oakland, 1957-62; chancellor Diocese of Oakland, 1962-71; rev. monsignor, 1962, domestic prelate, 1967; exec. dir. Calif. Cath. Conf., Sacramento, 1971-77; consecrated bishop, 1974; aux. bishop of Sacramento, 1974-77; bishop of Oakland, 1977—; Campus minister San Francisco State Coll., 1953-57, Mills Coll., Oakland, 1957-71; Trustee St. Mary's Coll., 1968-79. Home: 634 21st St Oakland CA 94612-1608 Office: Oakland Diocese 2900 Lakeshore Ave Oakland CA 94610-3614*

CUMMINS, NANCYELLEN HECKEROTH, electronics engineer; b. Long Beach, Calif., May 22, 1948; d. George and Ruth May (Anderson) Heckeroth; m. Weldon Jay Cummins, Sept. 15, 1987; children: Tracy Lynn, John Scott, Darren Elliott. Student avionics, USMC, Memphis, 1966-67. Tech. publ. engr. Missile and Space divsn. Lockheed Corp., Sunnyvale, Calif., 1973-76, engring. instr., 1977; test engr. Gen. Dynamics, Pomona, Calif., 1980-83; quality assurance test engr. Interstate Electronics Co., Anaheim, Calif., 1983-84; quality engr., certification engr. Rockwell Internat., Anaheim, 1985-86; sr. quality assurance programmer Point 4 Data, Tustin, Calif., 1986-87; software quality assurance specialist Lawrence Livermore Nat. Lab., Yucca Mountain Project, Livermore, Calif., 1987-89, software quality mgr., 1989-90; sr. constrn. insp. EG&G Rocky Flats, Inc., Golden, Colo., 1990, sr. quality assurance engr., 1991, engr. IV software quality assurance, 1991-92, instr., developer environ. law and compliance, 1992-93; software, computer cons. CRI, Dabois, Wyo., 1993—; customer engr. IBM Gen. Sys., Orange, Calif., 1979; electronics engr. Exhibits divsn. LDS Ch., Salt Lake City, 1978; electronics repair specialist Weber State Coll., 1977-78. Author: Package Area Test Set, 6 vols., 1975, Software Quality Assurance Plan, 1989. Vol., instr. San Fernando (Calif.) Search and Rescue Team, 1967-70; instr. emergency preparedness and survival, Claremont, Calif., 1982-84, Modesto, Calif., 1989; mem. Lawrence Livermore nat. Lab. Employees Emergency Vols., 1987-90, EG&G Rocky Flats Bldg. Emergency Support Team, 1990-93, Dubois Search and Rescue, 1995—. Mem. NAFE, NRA, Nat. Muzzle Loading Rifle Assn., Am. Soc. Quality Control, Job's Daus. (majority mem.). Republican. Mem. LDS Ch. Office: CRI PO Box 69 Hurricane UT 84737

CUNEO, DENNIS CLIFFORD, automotive company executive; b. Ridgway, Pa., Jan. 12, 1950; s. Clifford Francis and Erma Theresa (Nissel) C.; m. Bonnie Frances Mish, Aug. 18, 1972; children: Corinne, Kyle, James. BS, Gannon U., 1971; MBA, Kent State U., 1973; JD, Loyola U., New Orleans, 1976. Bar: D.C. 1977. Trial atty. U.S. Dept. Justice, Washington, 1976-80; assoc. Arent, Fox, Kintner, Plotkin & Kahn, Washington, 1980-84; gen. counsel New United Motor Mfg. Inc. joint venture GM-Toyota, Fremont, Calif., 1984-88, v.p. legal and govt. affairs, 1988-90, v.p. corp. planning and legal affairs, 1990-92, v.p. corp. planning and external affairs, corp. sec., 1992-96; v.p. legal and external affairs Toyota Motor Mfg. N.Am., 1996—; chmn. Calif. Workside Rsch. Com., Sacramento, 1988-96; lectr. exec. program U. Calif., Davis, 1988-95; mem. Gov. Pete Wilson Trade Mission to Asia, 1993; bd. dirs. Toyota Motor Corp. Svcs., Inc. Campaign chmn. United Way, Alameda County, 1993-95; co-chmn. Blue Ribbon com. to Save the Oakland A's, 1994; vice chmn. Alameda County Econ. Devel. Bd., Oakland, 1990-96, Team Calif., Sacramento, 1994; bd. visitors Loyola Law Sch., 1987—; mem. select com. on jud. retirement, 1993; mem. steering com. Bay Area Coun., San Francisco, 1990-95, Bay Area Dredging Coalition, San Francisco, 1991-96; mem. Statewide Pupil Assessment Rev. Panel, Sacramento, 1996—; bd. dirs. Oakland-Alameda County Coliseum, 1995—, Cin. United Way, 1997—. Mem. ABA, Calif. Mfrs. Assn. (vice chmn. 1994-96, pres. Calif. manufactures svcs. corp. 1996—), Oakland Football Mktg.

Assn. (pres. 1995—), No. Ky. C. of C. (bd. dirs. 1997—). Office: Toyota Motor Mfg NAm 25 Atlantic Ave Erlanger KY 41018

CUNNANE, PATRICIA S., medical facility administrator; b. Clinton, Iowa, Sept. 7, 1946; d. Cyril J. and Corinne Spain; m. Edward J. Cunnane, June 19, 1971. AA, Mt. St. Clare Coll., Clinton, Iowa, 1966. Mgr. Eye Med. Clinic of Santa Clara Valley, San Jose, Calif. Mem. Med. Adminstrs. Calif. Polit. Action Com., San Francisco, 1987. Mem. Med. Group Mgmt. Assn., Am. Coll. Med. Group Adminstrs. (nominee), Nat. Notary Assn., NAFE, Exec. Women Internat. (v.p. 1986-87, pres. 1987—), Profl. Secs. Internat. (sec. 1979-80), Am. Soc. Ophthalmic Adminstrs., Women Health Care Execs., Healthcare Human Resource Mgmt. Assn. Calif. Roman Catholic. Home: 232 Tolin Ct San Jose CA 95139-1445 Office: Eye Med Clinic of Santa Clara Valley 220 Meridian Ave San Jose CA 95126-2903

CUNNING, TONIA, newspaper managing editor. BS in Journalism, U. Nev. Soc. editor/feature writer-editor/asst. mng. editor Reno (Nev.) Gazette-Jour., 1971-92, mng. editor, 1992—. Office: Reno Gazette-Journal PO Box 22000 Reno NV 89520

CUNNINGHAM, ELEANOR ELIZABETH, nurse; b. Bklyn., Mar. 13, 1931; d. Arthur Christian and Alice (Brusack) Philipps; m. Joseph Lawrence Cunningham, Sept. 6, 1958; children: Michael, Kevin, Kathleen, Matthew. RN, Mt. Sinai Sch. Nursing, 1951; BA in Social Svcs., U. Nev., Las Vegas, 1981; MS in Health Adminstrn., St. Francis Coll., 1987. RN, Nev.; cert. diabetes educator, Nev. Staff nurse Mt. Sinai Hosp., N.Y.C., 1951-53, Cedars of Lebanon Hosp., L.A., 1953-55, Mt. Sinai Hosp., L.A., 1955-58; staff nurse St. Rose Dominican Hosp., Henderson, Nev., 1958-87, head nurse med./surg. unit, 1973-85, hosp. educator, 1987-92; cert. diabetes educator In-House Home Health Inc., Las Vegas, 1993-96, Nev. Regional Home Care, 1996—; cert. Diabetes Treatment Ctr. at Desert Springs Hosp.; CPR instr., Las Vegas, 1990-96; mem. ethics com. St. Rose Dominican Hosp., 1992-94; I Can Cope cancer facilitator Am. Cancer Soc., Las Vegas, 1990; cert. diabetes educator All Care Home Health, 1996. Active crisis intervention-sudden death E.A.S.E./Nathan Adelson Hospice, Las Vegas, 1992-94; mem. women's aux. Boys and Girls Club Nev., Las Vegas, 1980-88; area capt. Am. Heart Assn., Las Vegas, 1977; vol. St. Rose Dominican Hosp., 1992-95, mem. women's aux., 1960-94; vol. Nathan Adelson Hospice, 1992—. Named Nurse of Yr. March of Dimes, 1990. Mem. Am. Hosp. Assn., Clark County Health Educators (pres. 1990-91), So. Nev. Soc. Health, Edn. Tng. (sec.-treas. 1991-95), Nev. Educators Assn. for Diabetes (treas. 1995—, Phi Kappa Phi. Roman Catholic. Home: 3581 Cherokee Ave Las Vegas NV 89121

CUNNINGHAM, GEORGE, senator; m. Marjorie Fisher; children: Paul, Eve, Molly. B of Pub. Adminstrn., U. Ariz., M of Pub. Adminstrn. Spl. asst. to pres. Ariz. State Senate, Tucson, 1956; v.p. adminstrv. svcs. U. Ariz., Tucson, 1985-88; chief of staff Gov. Rose Mofford, 1988-90; with U. Ariz., Tucson, 1990-93; rep. State of Ariz., 1993-96, senator, 1996—; co-chmn. Pima County Com. on Property Tax and State Revenue Reform, 1996.

CUNNINGHAM, JOEL DEAN, lawyer; b. Seattle, Feb. 19, 1948; s. Edgar Norwood and Florence (Burgunder) C.; m. Amy Jean Radewan, Oct. 1, 1970; children: Erin Jane, Rad Norwood. BA in Econs., U. Wash., 1971, JD with high honors, 1974. Lawyer, ptnr. Williams, Kastner & Gibbs, Seattle, 1974-95; ptnr. Luvera, Barnett, Brindley, Beninger & Cunningham, Seattle, 1995—. Fellow Am. Coll. Trial Lawyers, Am. Bd. Profl. Liability Attys.; mem. Am. Bd. Trial Attys. (pres. Washington chpt. 1994), Order of Coif. Office: Luvera Barnett Brindley Beninger & Cunningham 6700 Columbia Ctr 701 Fifth Ave Seattle WA 98104-7016

CUNNINGHAM, JOHN RANDOLPH, systems analyst; b. Alexandria, La., July 17, 1954; s. John Adolphus and Zelma Audrey (Cox) C.; m. Teresa Ellen Toms, Jan. 22, 1977. BS in Computer Sci., La. Tech. U., 1976. Customer support specialist South Ctrl. Bell Tel. Co., New Orleans, 1977-81; data communication designer Weyerhaeuser, Tacoma, 1981-87, acct. rep., 1987-89, planning mgr., 1989-92, EDI project leader, 1992—; mem. adv. bd. U. Wash., Seattle, 1989-94; spkr. fin. EDI confs. Contbr. articles to profl. jours. Vol. Big Bros., Tacoma, 1989—, Wash. State First Responder, 1989—; instr. CPR, 1990—. Mem. Computer and Automated Systems Assn. (treas. 1991-95, pres. 1995—), Project Mgmt. Inst., Indsl. Computing Soc., Instrument Soc. Am., Toastmasters Internat., Upsilon Pi Epsilon. Republican. Baptist. Home: 319 SW 328th St Federal Way WA 98023-5645

CUNNINGHAM, LARRIE JOHN, retired engineering executive, arbitrator; b. Peterborough, Ont., Can., Feb. 8, 1934; came to U.S., 1959; s. Lorne Bertram and Alberta Catherine (Throop) C.; m. Judy Ann Long, Jan. 30, 1966. Diploma in archl. and bldg. tech., Ryerson Poly. Inst., Toronto, 1956. Estimator, asst. supt. Grirenthwaite Constrn. Co., Hamilton, Ont., 1956-57; asst. supt., field engr. S. Crump Mech. Ctr., Toronto, 1957-58; chief bldg. inspector, asst. city engr. Can. Dept. Mcpl. Affairs, Elliott Lake, Ont., 1958-59; exec. v.p., dir. Spencer, White & Prentis, Inc., San Francisco, 1959-89; pvt. practice as arbitrator, cons. Scottsdale, Ariz., 1989—; cons. Fleming Corp., L.A., 1990—, Marc S. Caspe Co., L.A., 1993—. Named Lecture Honorarium Dept. Civil Engring. U. Calif., 1977. Mem. Am. Arbitration Assn., U.S. Arbitration & Mediation Assn. Home: 8664 E Corrine Dr Scottsdale AZ 85260-5305

CUNNINGHAM, RANDY, congressman; b. L.A., Dec. 8, 1941; m. Nancy Jones; 3 children. BA, U. Mo., MA; MBA, Nat. U. Mem. 102nd-104th Congresses from Calif. dist. 44 (now 51), 1991—; mem. nat. security com. 102nd-103rd Congresses from Calif. dist. 44 (now 51), mem. appropriations com. Republican. Christian. Office: US Ho of Reps 2238 Rayburn HOB Washington DC 20515

CUNNINGHAM, RON, choreographer, artistic director; b. Chgo., Sept. 15, 1939; m. Carrine Binda, June 12, 1982; children: Christopher, Alexandra. Student, Allegro Ballet, 1961-65, Am. Ballet Theatre, 1968-70; studies with Merce Cunningham, N.Y.C., 1968-70; BS in Mktg., Roosevelt U., 1966. Dancer Allegro Am. Ballet Co., Chgo., 1962-66; artistic dir. Ron Cunningham Contemporary Dance Co., Chgo., 1966-68; dancer Lucas Hoving Dance Co., 1968-72, Lotte Goslar Pantomime Circus, 1968-72, Daniel Nagrin Dance Co., 1968-72; prin. dancer, resident choreographer Boston Ballet, 1972-85; artistic dir. Balt. Ballet, 1985-86; artistic assoc. Washington Ballet, 1986-87; ind. choreographer, 1987-88; artistic dir. Sacramento Ballet, 1988—; panelist various regional and state art councils, 1979—; dir. Craft of Choreography, 1985; adjudicator, master tchr. Nat. Assn. Regional Ballet, 1985—, Am. Coll. Dance Assn., 1986. Dancer, choreographer 40 original internat. ballets, 1972—, 4 ballets Nat. Choreography Plan, 1978—, Cinderella, Peoples Republic of China, 1980. Nat. Endowment Arts fellow, 1977, 86, Mass. Art Council fellow, 1984, Md. Arts Council fellow, 1988. Mem. Nat. Assn. Regional Ballet, Dance/U.S.A.

CUPERY, ROBERT RINK, manufacturing executive; b. Beaver Dam, Wis., Apr. 5, 1944; s. Rink Eli and Ruby Elizabeth (Haima) C.; m. Kathleen Gonzalez; children: Ryan Edward, Jennifer. Airframe and Powerplant, Northrop U., 1967; BSBA, U. Redlands, 1978. Aircraft mechanic Northwest Airlines, Mpls., 1968-69; corp. flight engr. Northrop Corp., Hawthorne, Calif., 1969-76, engr., 1976-79, sr. staff customer relations, 1979-82, internat. quality mgr., 1982-84; founder Aircraft Window Repairs, Torrance, Calif., 1984—; pres., chief exec. officer Cupery Corp., Torrance, Calif., 1994, North Port, Fla., 1995—; bd. advisers Northrop Rice Aviation Sch., 1992; lectr. throughout U.S. and Europe, 1986, 89, 90. Contbr. articles to profl. jours. Served as staff sgt. USAF, 1962-66. Mem. Profl. Aviation Maintenance Assn. (corp.), Can. Aviation Mech. Engring., Nat. Bus. Aircraft Assn., Aero Club So. Calif. (bd. dirs. 1992). Republican.

CURCIO, CHRISTOPHER FRANK, city official; b. Oakland, Calif., Feb. 3, 1950; s. Frank William and Virginie Theresa (Le Gris) C. BA in Speech/Drama, Calif. State U., Hayward, 1971; MBA in Arts Adminstrn., UCLA, 1974; MPA in Pub. Policy, Ariz. State U., 1982. Intern John F. Kennedy Ctr. for Arts, Washington, 1973; gen. mgr. Old Eagle Theatre, Sacramento, 1974-75; cultural arts supr. Fresno (Calif.) Parks and Recreation Dept., 1975-79; supr. cultural and spl. events Phoenix Parks, Recreation and Libr. Dept., 1979-87, budget analyst, 1987, mgmt. svcs. adminstr., 1987—; mgmt. and budget analyst City of Phoenix, 1985; grants panelist Phoenix Arts Commn., 1987, Ariz. Commn. on Arts, 1987-88; voter Zony Theatre Awards, 1991-92; freelance theater critic, 1987-89; theater critic Ariz. Republic/Phoenix Gazette, 1990—, Verv Mag., 1997—, PHX Downtown, 1997—. Active Valley Leadership Program, Phoenix, 1987—, Valley Big Bros./Big Sisters, 1980-94; chair allocation panel United Way, 1990-92; sec. Los Olivos Townhome Assn., Phoenix, 1986-92. Mem. Am. Soc. Pub. Adminstrn., Nat. Recreation and Park Assn., Am. Theatre Critics Assn., Internat. Theater Critics Assn., Ariz. Park and Recreation Assn. Republican. Office: Phoenix Parks Recreation and Libr Dept 200 W Washington St Fl 16 Phoenix AZ 85003-1611

CURD, JOHN GARY, physician, scientist; b. Grand Junction, Colo., July 2, 1945; s. H. Ronald and Edna (Hegested) C.; m. Karen Wendel, June 12, 1971; children: Alison, Jonathan, Edward, Bethany. BA, Princeton U., 1967; MD, Harvard U., 1971. Diplomate Am. Bd. Internal Medicine, Am. Bd. Rheumatology, Am. Bd. Allergy and Immunology. Rsch. assoc. NIH, Bethesda, Md., 1973-75; fellow in rheumatology U. Calif., San Diego, 1975-77; fellow in allergy-immunology Scripps Clinic, La Jolla, Calif., 1977-78, asst. mem. rsch. inst., 1978-81, mem. div. rheumatology, 1981-91, head div. rheumatology, vice chmn. dept. medicine, 1989-91; pres. med. staff Green Hosp., La Jolla, 1988-90; clin. dir. Genentech Inc., South San Francisco, Calif., 1991-96; sr. dir., head clin. sci. Genentech Inc., South San Francisco, 1996—. Author numerous. sci. papers in field. Med. dir. San Diego Scleroderma Found., 1983-91; sec. San Diego Arthritis Found., 1986-87. Lt. comdr. USPHS, 1973-75. Mem. Princeton Club No. Calif. Republican. Home: 128 Reservoir Rd Hillsborough CA 94010-6957 Office: Genentech Inc 460 Point San Bruno Blvd South San Francisco CA 94080-4918

CURL, JAMES MICHAEL, special events producer, manager; b. N.Y.C., Dec. 19, 1948; s. Joseph Nicholas and Ann Maria (Horris) C.; m. Nicole Susan Ballenger, Apr. 1, 1978 (div. Jan. 1981); m. Karen Lynn Nelson, July 22, 1984; children: Caitlin Linnea, Emily Jean. AA, Cabrillo Coll., 1973; BA, U. Calif., Santa Cruz, 1975; JD, U. Calif., Berkeley, 1978. Bar: Calif. 1979. Legal rschr. Continuing Edn. of Bar, Berkeley, 1976-77; law clk. Hon. Harry A. Ackley, Woodland, Calif., 1978-79; assoc. Weintraub, Genshlea, Giannoni & Sproul, Sacramento, 1979-80, Turner & Sullivan, Sacramento, 1980-81; pres. Endurance Sports Prodns., Davis, Calif., 1981-84, CAT Sports, Carlsbad, Calif., 1984-94, Event Media, Del Mar, Calif., 1993—; faculty, speaker Internat. Events Group, Chgo., 1992-94; founder Triathlon Fedn. U.S.A., L.A., 1982, v.p., Colorado Springs, Colo., 1984-86. Author: How to Organize a Triathlon, 1982; developer sports events NFL Quarterback Challenge, 1988—, Michelob Night Riders, 1988, Bud Light U.S. Triathlon Series, 1982-93; developer, prodr. Caribbean Sports & Spl. Events Conf., Kingston, Jamaica, 1994-95, James Bond Jamaica Festival, Ocho Rios, 1996. Chmn. Parks and Recreation Com., Encinitas, Calif., 1989-92; founder Encinitas Sister City, 1988. Recipient Spl. Achievement award Triathlete Mag., 1990. Mem. Calif. State Bar. Office: Event Media 13765 Mira Montana Dr Del Mar CA 92014-3419

CURLEY, ELMER FRANK, librarian; b. Florence, Pa., Jan. 13, 1929; s. Augustus Wolfe and Bessie (Andrews) C. BA, U. Pitts., 1961; MLS, Carnegie Mellon U., Pitts., 1962; Adv. Cert., U. Pitts., 1964. Ref. librarian U. Pitts., 1962-64; head ref. dept. SUNY-Stony Brook, 1964-67; head pub. svcs. U. Nev.-Las Vegas, 1967-76, asst. dir. libr. svcs., 1976-81, ref. bibliographer, 1981-94, ret., 1994.

CURRAN, MICHAEL HARVEY, finance executive; b. Pasadena, Calif., Mar. 5, 1948; s. James Albert and Jane Eleanor (Harvey) C.; m. Vicki Ann Rowland, Apr. 22, 1978; children: Sean, Robert. BBA, Loyola U., 1970; MBA, U. So. Calif., 1971. Cert. real estate broker Calif. V.p. Wells Fargo Bank, L.A., 1971-79; exec. v.p., CFO Real Property Resources, Torrance, Calif., 1979-90, Doric Devel., Alameda, Calif., 1990-93; CFO, treas. Continental Devel., El Segundo, Calif., 1993—; dir. Datasystems, Encino, Calif., 1986, also pres.; dir. Harbor Bay Bus. Park Assn., Alameda, 1990-93. Project dir. Jr. C. of C., L.A., 1973-79; mem. Internat. Coun. Shopping Ctrs., L.A., 1983-90. Home: 2311 John St Manhattan Beach CA 90266-2615 Office: Continental Devel Corp 2041 Rosecrans Ave El Segundo CA 90245-4707

CURRY, DANIEL ARTHUR, superior court judge; b. Phoenix, Mar. 28, 1937; s. John Joseph and Eva May (Wills) C.; m. Joy M. Shallenberger, Sept. 5, 1959; children: Elizabeth, Catherine, Peter, Jennifer, Julia , David. B.S., Loyola U., Los Angeles, 1957, LL.B., 1960; postgrad., U. So. Calif. Law Center, 1964-65; postgrad. exec. program, Grad. Sch. Bus., Stanford U., 1980. Bar: Calif. 1961, Hawaii 1972, N.Y. 1988, U.S. Dist. Ct. (cen. dist.) Calif. 1961, U.S. Ct. Appeals (9th cir.) 1961, U.S. Ct. Mil. Appeals 1963, U.S. Customs Ct. 1968, U.S. Dist. Ct. Hawaii 1972, U.S. Dist. Ct. (no. dist.) Calif. 1983 . Assoc. Wolford, Johnson, Pike & Covell, El Monte, Calif., 1964-65, Demetriou & Del Guercio, Los Angeles, 1965-67; counsel, corporate staff divisional asst. Technicolor, Inc., Hollywood, Calif., 1967-70; v.p., sec., gen. counsel Amfac, Inc., Honolulu, 1970-78; sr. v.p., gen. counsel Amfac, Inc., Honolulu and San Francisco, 1978-87; v.p., gen. counsel Times Mirror, L.A., 1987-92; judge Superior Ct. of State of Calif., 1992—, County of L.A.; bd. regents Loyola Marymount U., Chaminade U. (hon.). Served to capt. USAF, 1961-64. Mem. ABA (hon., com. corp. law depts.), L.A. Country Club, Sigma Rho, Phi Delta Phi. Office: Superior Ct 111 N Hill St Los Angeles CA 90012-3117

CURRY, JANE KATHLEEN, theater educator; b. Rock Island, Ill., Nov. 29, 1964; d. Richard Alan and Barbara Jean (Smith) C. BFA in Theater, U. Ill., 1985; MA in Theater, Brown U., 1987; PhD in Theater, CUNY, 1991. Asst. prof. theater Hunter Coll.-CUNY; asst. prof. theater and speech Mont. State U., Havre, 1993—. Author: Nineteenth-Century American Women Theater Managers, 1994. Mem. Am. Soc. Theater Rsch., Assn. for Theater in Higher Edn.

CURRY, LANDON, political science educator; b. Corpus Christi, Tex., Jan. 22, 1955; s. Landon and Connie C. (Cacciola) C. BA, U. Tex., Austin, 1976; MA, U. Calif., Berkeley, 1977, PhD, 1984. Prof. U. Calif., Berkeley, 1977-82, U. Ga., Athens, 1983-84, U. Tex., Austin, 1985-92, Southwest Tex. State U., San Marcos, 1986-91, U. Idaho, Moscow, 1992-96, U. Calif., Berkeley, 1996—; cons. in field. Author: Politics of Fiscal Stress, 1990; contbr. articles to profl. jours. Dir. State Govt. Internship Program, Austin, 1986-92, Moscow, 1992-94. Mem. Am. Polit. Sci. Assn., Southwest Polit. Sci. Assn., Pacific Northwest Polit. Sci. Assn., U.S. Handball Assn. Home: 1120 Cornell Albany CA 94706 Office: Univ Calif Inst Govtl Studies 109 Moses Berkeley CA 94720

CURRY, WILLIAM SIMS, procurement executive; b. Mt. Vernon, Washington, Feb. 6, 1938; s. Eli Herbert Curry and Winona Geraldine (Davis) Mickelson; m. Kirsten Ingeborg Arms, May 20, 1971; children: William II, Kevin, Randal, Kim Cannova, Derek. BS in Bus. Mgmt., Fla. State U., 1967; MBA, Ohio State U., 1968. Cert. profl. contracts mgr. Asst. purchasing officer Stanford (Calif.) Linear Accelerator Ctr., 1977-80; subcontract adminstr. Lockheed Missiles & Space Co., Sunnyvale, Calif., 1980-81; materials mgr. Altus Corp., San Jose, Calif., 1981-86; purchasing mgr. Litton Electron Devices, San Carlos, Calif., 1986-95, Comms. & Power Industries, Palo Alto, Calif., 1995—; bd. dirs. Industry Coun. for Small Bus. Devel., Sunnyvale, 1992—, v.p. programs, 1992-93, exec. v.p., 1994-95, pres., 1995—. Contbr. articles to profl. jours. Capt. USAF, 1955-77. Decorated Meritorious Svc. medal with one oak leaf cluster, USAF, 1977. Fellow Nat. Contract Mgmt. Assn.; mem. Am. Mensa, Ltd., Beta Gamma Sigma. Republican. Home: 8289 Del Monte Ave Newark CA 94560-2129 Office: Comm & Power Indus 811 Hansen Way PO Box 50750 Palo Alto CA 94303-0750

CURTIN, DAVID STEPHEN, newswriter; b. Kansas City, Mo., Dec. 18, 1955; s. Gerald and Nadine (Pemberton) C. BS in Journalism, U. Colo., 1978. Newswriter Littleton (Colo.) Independent, 1976-77, Boulder (Colo.) Daily Camera, 1978-79, Greeley (Colo.) Daily Tribune, 1979-84, Durango (Colo.) Herald, 1984-87, Colorado Springs (Colo.) Gazette Telegraph, 1987—; Pulitzer Prize juror, 1991-92. Recipient Pulitzer Prize for feature writing, 1990. Democrat. Methodist.

CURTIN, THOMAS LEE, ophthalmologist; b. Columbus, Ohio, Sept. 9, 1932; s. Leo Anthony and Mary Elizabeth (Burns) C.; m. Constance L. Sallman; children: Michael, Gregory, Thomas, Christopher. BS, Loyola U., L.A., 1954; MD, U. So. Calif., 1957; cert. navy flight surgeon U.S. Naval Sch. Aviation Medicine, 1959. Intern. Ohio State U. Hosp., 1957-58; resident in ophthalmology U.S. Naval Hosp., San Diego, 1961-64; practice medicine specializing in ophthalmology, Oceanside, Calif., 1967—; mem. staff Tri City, Scripps Meml. Mercy hosps.; sci. adv. bd. So. Calif. Soc. Prevention Blindness, 1973-76; bd. dirs. North Coast Surgery Ctr., Oceanside, 1987-96; cons. in field. Trustee, Carlsbad (Calif.) Unified Sch. Dist., 1975-83, pres., 1979, 82, 83; trustee Carlsbad Libr., 1990—, pres, 1993. Served as officer M.C., USN, 1958-67. Diplomate Am. Bd. Ophthalmology. Mem. Am., Calif. med. assns., San Diego County Med. Soc., Am. Acad. Ophthalmology, Aerospace Med. Assn., San Diego Acad. Ophthalmology (pres. 1979), Calif. Assn. Ophthalmology (dir.), Carlsbad Rotary, El Camino Country Club. Republican. Roman Catholic. Office: 3231 Waring Ct Ste S Oceanside CA 92056-4510

CURTIS, BRUCE FRANKLIN, geologist, consultant; b. Denver, Dec. 16, 1918; s. Francis William and Marguerite Jessie (Wenk) C.; m. Ruth Esther Bachrach, May 30, 1958. A.B., Oberlin Coll., 1941; M.A., U. Colo., 1942; Ph.D., Harvard U., 1949. Asst. geologist U.S. Geol. Survey, Denver, 1942; asst. geologist to Rocky Mountain regional geologist Conoco, Inc., Denver, 1946-57; from assoc. prof. to prof. U. Colo., Boulder, 1957-83; cons. geologist Curtis Cons., Boulder, 1983—; Author, editor books and articles. Served to 1st lt. USAAC, 1942-45; PTO. Fellow Geol. Soc. Am. (Service award 1973, chmn. various coms.); mem. Am. Assn. Petroleum Geologists (chmn. various coms.), Rocky Mountain Assn. Geologists (hon.; pres. 1956), Phi Beta Kappa, Sigma Xi. Republican.

CURTIS, GARY LYNN, accountant; b. Castro Valley, Calif., Feb. 3, 1956; s. Bill J. and Rosemary (Endsley) C. BS, Phillips U., Enid, Okla., 1980. CPA, Okla. Mgr. Ernst and Whinney, Oklahoma City, 1980-86; dir. Deloitte & Touche, Dallas and L.A., 1987—; instr. Deloitte & Touche Re-orgn. Svcs. Group and Mergers and Acquisition Group. Home: 354 White Cap Ln Newport Coast CA 92657 Office: Deloitte & Touche 695 Town Center Dr Costa Mesa CA 92626-9978

CURTIS, JOAN CORFIELD, retired college administrator; b. Tacoma, Jan. 28, 1935; d. Charles Clyde and Ethel Elvie (Heffron) C.; m. Boyd Howard Curtis, Dec. 28, 1958; 1 child, Amy Elizabeth. BS in Home Econs., U. Wash., 1957. Tchg. cert., Wash. Tchr. home econs. Bothell (Wash.) H.S., 1957-61; foods and nutrition instr. Shoreline C.C., Seattle, 1963-67; early childhood coord. Clover Park Tech. Coll., Tacoma, 1969-94; chmn. adv. bbd. Steilacoom (Wash.) H.S., 1982-95. Author, editor: Town on the Sound, 1988; author, editor Steilacoom Hist. Mus. Quar., 1972—. Mem. town coun. Town of Steilacoom, 1976-81, planning commn., 1972-76, 84-89, chair urban design com., 1987-89, chair hist. preservation com., 1995—; pres. Steilacoom Hist. Mus., 1980-82, dir., 1986-91, curator, 1980—; historian Oberlin Congl. Ch., 1985—. Recipient grant for writing workshop Am. Assn. State and Local History, Nashville, 1979, Outstanding Citizen award Town of Steilacoom, 1989. Mem. Nat. Trust for Hist. Preservation. Home: 1505 Euclid PO Box 88284 Steilacoom WA 98388

CURTIS, JOHN BARRY, archbishop; b. June 19, 1933; s. Harold Boyd and Eva B. (Saunders) C.; m. Patricia Emily Simpson, 1959; four children. BA, U. Toronto, 1955, LTh, 1958; student, Theol. Coll., Chichester, Sussex, Eng.; DD (hon.), Trinity Coll., 1985, U. Toronto, 1985. Ordained to deacon The Anglican Ch. of Can., 1958, priest, 1959. Asst. curate Holy Trinity, Pembroke, Ont., 1958-61; rector Parish of March, Kanata, Ont., 1961-65, St. Stephen's Ch., Buckingham, Que., 1965-69, All Saints (Westboro), Ottawa, Ont., 1969-78; program dir. Diocese of Ottawa, 1978-80; rector Christ Ch., Elbow Park, Calgary, Alta., 1980-83; bishop Diocese of Calgary, 1983-94; archbishop Calgary-Met. of Rupert's Land, 1994—. Mem. Ranchmen's Club (Calgary). Office: Diocese Calgary, 3015 Glencoe Rd SW, Calgary, AB Canada T2S 2L9

CURTIS, LEGRAND R., JR., lawyer; b. Ogden, Utah, Aug. 1, 1952. BA summa cum laude, Brigham Young U., 1975; JD cum laude, U. Mich., 1978. Bar: Utah 1978, U.S. Ct. Appeals (10th cir.) 1985, U.S. Ct. Claims 1986, U.S. Supreme Ct. 1987. Assoc. Manning, Curtis Bradshaw & Dednar, LLC, Salt Lake City. Mem. Utah State Bar, Salt Lake County Bar Assn. Office: Manning Curtis Bradshaw & Bednar LLC 370 E S Temple Ste 200 Salt Lake City UT 84111-5233

CURTIS, MICHAEL, food products executive; b. 1922; s. Glen C. Real estate broker Yuma, Ariz., 1950-72; with Glen Curtis, Inc., Yuma, Ariz., 1971-72. Office: Glen Curtis Inc 4400 E Us Highway 80 Yuma AZ 85365-7518*

CURTIS, NANCY NELL, publisher, rancher; b. Duncan, Okla., June 6, 1947; d. William Herbert Jr. and Edwina (Crabtree) Johnson; m. Douglas J. Curtis, July 23, 1966; 1 child, Wendy J.J. AA, Casper Coll., 1967; BA, U. Wyo., 1969; grad. in pub., U. Denver, 1986. Tchr. English, Douglas and Glendo (Wyo.) Schs., 1969-79; advt. mgr. White's Marine Ctrs., Glendo, 1984-91; rancher Glendo, 1969—; pub. High Plains Press, Glendo, 1984—. Author: Visions of Wyoming, 1994; contbr. articles to various publs.; co-editor: Leaning into the Wind, 1997. Mem., clk. Platte County (Wyo.) Sch. Dist. 1, 1980-84; bd. dirs. Wyo. Coun. on Arts, 1994-96, chmn. bd., 1996—. Recipient Wrangler award Nat. Cowboy Hall of Fame, Oklahoma City, 1991, 94. Mem. Rocky Mountain Book Pubs. Assn., Western Writers Am., Wyo. Writers (pres., treas., Emmie award 1982). Office: High Plains Press 539 Cassa Rd Glendo WY 82213-9628

CURTIS, ROBERT ORIN, research forester; b. Portland, Maine, Oct. 27, 1927; s. Walter Edson and Ruby (Whitehouse) C.; m. Helen Locke Thompson, Aug. 16, 1952; children: Stephen, Anne, Ruth. BS in Plant Sci., Yale U., 1950, MF, 1951; PhD in Silviculture and Biometrics, U. Wash., 1965. Rsch. forester Northeastern Forest Experiment Sta., U.S. Forest Svc., various locations, 1951-62; mensurationist Pacific N.W. Rsch. Sta., Portland, Oreg., 1965-78; prin. mensurationist Pacific N.W. Rsch. Sta., Olympia, Wash., 1978—; affiliate prof. Coll. Forest Resources, U. Wash., Seattle, 1988—; courtesy prof. Coll. of Forestry, Oreg. State U. Mem. editorial bd. Forest Sci., Washington, 1971-85; contbr. articles to profl. jours. Served with U.S. Army, 1946-47. Mem. Soc. Am. Foresters. Home: 2312 Killarney Ct NW Olympia WA 98502-3445 Office: Pacific NW Rsch Sta 3625 93d Ave SW Olympia WA 98512

CURTISS, A.B., writer; b. N.Y.C., Mar. 29, 1934; m. Raymond G. Curtiss, Sept. 8, 1956; children: Deane, Ford, Demming Forsythe, Sunday, Wolf. BA, U. Md.; MA in Family Counseling, San Diego State U. Author: In the Company of Bears, 1994 (Benjamin Franklin award 1995), Children of the Gods, 1995 (San Diego Book award 1996), Hallelujah, a Cat Comes Back, 1996, Legend of the Giant Panda, 1997, Time of the Wild, 1997.

CURTISS, ELDEN F., bishop; b. Baker, Oreg., June 16, 1932; s. Elden F. and Mary (Neiger) C. B.A., St. Edward Sem., Seattle, M.Div., 1958; M.A. in Ednl. Adminstrn, U. Portland, 1965; postgrad., Fordham U., U. Notre Dame. Ordained priest Roman Cath. Ch., 1958; campus chaplain, 1959-64, 65-68; supt. schs. Diocese of Baker (Oreg.), 1962-70; pastor, 1968-70; pres./rector Mt. Angel Sem., Benedict, Oreg., 1972-76; mem. bd. regents Mt. Angel Sem., Benedict, 1976-93; bishop of Diocese of Helena (Mont.), 1976-93; archbishop Diocese of Omaha, 1993—; mem. ecumenical ministries State of Oreg., 1972; mem. pastoral services com. Oreg. State Hosp., Salem, 1975-76; bishop Diocese Helena, Mont., 1976—; chmn. bd. Boys Town USA, Cath. Mut. Relief Soc. Am.; mem. Pontifical Coun. for Family (Rome); Episcopal advisor Serra Internat. Mem. Nat. Cath. Ednl. Assn. (Outstanding Educator 1972, bishops and pres's com. coll. dept.). Office: Archdiocese of Omaha 100 N 62nd St Omaha NE 68132-2702*

CUSHING, RICHARD GOLLÉ, journalist; b. N.Y.C., Apr. 30, 1917; s. Melvin Abbott and Blanche (Goll) C.; m. Nancy Heizer, Mar. 23, 1940; children: Jeffrey, Martha, Lincoln. BA, San Francisco State Coll., 1945; LLD (hon.), U. Havana, Cuba, 1955. Reporter AP, San Francisco, 1935-42; war corr. AP, PTO, 1943-45; bur. chief AP, Shanghai, 1945-46; news editor

AP, San Francisco, 1947-49; fgn. svc. officer USIA, Santiago, Chile, 1950-65, Cuba, Nairobi and Caracas, Venezuela, 1953-65; acting dir. Voice of Am., Washington, 1966-69; mem. Sr. Seminar on Fgn. Policy, Washington, 1970-71; San Francisco corr. Voice of Am. USIA, 1977—. Author: Too Pure for the Hyenas, 1976. Mem. grand jury Marin County, Calif., 1984. Mem. World Affairs Coun. (San Francisco chpt.), Commonwealth Club (San Francisco), Press Club San Francisco, Nat. Geog. Soc. Democrat. Home and Office: 389 Molino Ave Mill Valley CA 94941-3301

CUSTER, CONSTANCE M., critical care nurse, surgical nurse; b. Meadville, Pa., May 25, 1950. RN, Broward Community Coll., Coconut Creek, Fla., 1985. Cert. BCLS, ACLS, CNOR, hemodynamic monitoring. RN, surg., open heart North Ridge Med. Ctr., Ft. Lauderdale, Fla., Enloe Hosp., Chico, Calif.; agy. RN, CCU Skilled Nursing Svcs., Erie, Pa.; agy. RN telemetry and oper. rm. Nurse Care, Inc., DelRay Beach, Fla.; RN oper. rm. Travel Agys., Boca Raton and Malden, Fla./Mass.; staff RN, oper. rm. asst., staff inservice edn. preceptor Sonoma Valley Hosp.; per diem nurse Bethesda Hosp., Boynton Beach, Fla.; staff nurse oper. room St. Helena Hosp., Deer Park, Calif., 1995—. Recipient Nursing Sch. scholarship North Ridge Med. Ctr. Vols. Mem. Assn. Oper. Rm. Nurses (cert.), Beta Sigma Phi.

CUSUMANO, JAMES ANTHONY, chemical company executive, former recording artist; b. Elizabeth, N.J., Apr. 14, 1942; s. Charles Anthony and Carmella Madeline (Catalano) C.; m. Jane LaVerne Melvin, June 15, 1985; children: Doreen Ann, Polly Jean. BA, Rutgers U., 1964, PhD, 1967; grad. Exec. Mktg. Program, Stanford U., 1981, Harvard U., 1988. Mgr. catalyst rsch. Exxon Rsch. and Engring. Co., Linden, N.J., 1967-74; pres., chief exec. officer, founder Catalytica Inc., Mountain View, Calif., 1974-85, chmn., 1985—, also bd. dirs.; pres., CEO, Catalytica Fine Chems., Inc., Mountain View, Calif., 1993—; also bd. dirs.; lectr. chem. engring. Stanford U., 1978, Rutgers U., 1966-67, Charles D. Hurd lectr. Northwestern U., 1989-90; advisor Fulbright scholar progam Inst. Internat. Edn.; spkr. to chem. and physics grads., U. Wis., 1992, Mankato U., 1994; spkr. A. Einstein-Magritte Internat. Conf. on Future of Civilization, Vrije U., Brussels, 1995: mem. com. on catalysts and environ. NSF; exec. briefings with Pres. George Bush and Cabinet mems., 1990, 92, plenary lectr. in field. Author: Catalysis in Coal Conversion, 1978, (with others) Critical Materials Problems in Energy Production, 1976, Advanced Materials in Catalysis, 1977, Liquid Fuels from Coal, 1977, Kirk-Othmer Encyclopedia of Chemical Technology, 1979, Chemistry for the 21st Century, Perspectives in Catalysis, 1992, Science and Technology in Catalysis 1994, 1995; contbr. articles to profl. jours., chpts. to books; founding editor Jour. of Applied Catalysis, 1980; rec. artist with Royal Teens and Dino Take Five for ABC Paramount, Capitol and Jubilee Records, 1957-67; single records include Short Shorts, Short Shorts Twist, My Way, Hey Jude, Rosemarie, Please Say You Want Me, Lovers Never Say Goodbye; albums include The Best of the Royal Teens, Newies But Oldies; appeared in PBS TV prodn. on molecular engring., Little by Little, 1989. Recipient Surface Chemistry award Continental Oil Co., 1964; Henry Rutgers scholar, 1963, Lever Bros. fellow, 1965, Churchill Coll. fellow Cambridge Univ., 1992. Mem. AIChE, Am. Chem. Soc. (plenary lectr. to chem. educators nat. meeting 1994), Am. Phys. Soc., N.Y. Acad. Scis., Soc. Organic Chems. Mfrs. (bd. dirs. 1996), Am. Mus. Natural History, Pres.'s Assn., Smithsonian Assocs., Sigma Psi, Phi Lambda Upsilon. Republican. Roman Catholic. Home: 1644 Candace Way Los Altos CA 94024-6242 Office: Catalytica Inc 430 Ferguson Dr Ste 3 Mountain View CA 94043-5215 *Reach for a distant shining star. Celebrate life each day. Falter not your quest for basic values. And you will find a way.*

CUTINO, BERT PAUL, chef, restaurant owner; b. Carmel, Calif., Aug. 7, 1939; m. Bella Manigiapane; children: Marc, Bart. AA in Bus., Monterey Peninsula Coll., 1964; D of Culinary Arts (hon.), Johnson and Wales Coll., 1988. Various restaurant positions Monterey, Calif.; owner Sardine Factory, Monterey, 1968—; co-founder Cannery Row Co., Monterey, 1976—; comml. real estate developer, Pacific Hospitality, Inc., 1983—; protocol chmn. 1992 USA Nat. Culinary Team; formation of Western Region Culinary Team to 1988 Culinary Olympics, Frankfurt; founder Culinary Arts Program at local community coll., 1981; hospitality amb. internat. teams to Am. Culinary Classic, 1991; bd. trustees Antonin Careme Soc., 1997; spkr. and lectr. in field. Contbr. articles for hospitality industry publs. and profl. jours.; featured in TV commls. for Am. Express and Duralon. Food chmn. Calif. Wine Festival, 1977—, March of Dimes, 1985-89; chmn. Taste of Monterey, 1987-89; co-chmn. Easter Week Brunch for Alliance on Aging, March of Dimes, Monterey County, 1987-89, Jumpin Pumpkins money raiser for local pub. schs., 1984-87, African Relief Fund, 1985; v.p. Monterey Peninsula C. of C., 1984-88; mem. Sheriff's Adv. Com., Monterey County; hon. judge March of Dimes Gourmet Gala, 1985-92; dir. Found. to Support Monterey Peninsula Schs., 1984-86. With USNR, 1959-67. Recipient numerous awards including Disting. Restaurants N.Am., Mobil Guide, Nat. Restaurant News Hall of Fame, Calif. Top 10 Restaurants, Town and Country; one of 50 restaurants in Am. selected to serve at Pres. Reagan's Inauguration, 1981, 85; recipient Alumni award Calif. C.C., 1982, Antonin Careme Soc. medal Chefs Assn. of Pacific Coast, 1987, Medal of Honor, Escoffier Soc., 1986, Presdl. Medallion, Les Toques Blanches Internat., 1989, 1st Soviet-Am. Culinary Exchange Medallion, 1988, Medallion of World Trade Ctr., Moscow, 1988; named Chef of Yr., Monterey Peninsula Chefs Assn., 1983, Humanitarian of Yr., Boy Scouts Am., 1996; named to Les Toques Blanches Internat. Hall of Fame, 1993, named 1st nat. pres. U.S.A., 1994; inducted into Calif. Tourism Hall of Fame, Calif. Trade and Commerce Agy., 1997. Mem. Am. Culinary Fedn. (life, cert. exec. chef, western region v.p. 1985-89, bd. dirs. The Chef and the Child Found. 1989, nat. membership com. 1982, western regional coord. 1983, nat. accreditation team 1987, Nat. Chef of Yr. 1988, Pres.'s medal 1982, 89, Pres. Recognition award 1994), Am. Acad. Chefs (nat. chmn. 1995—), Am. Acad. of Restaurant Scis., Am. Inst. of Wine and Food (founding), Knights of Vine (master knight), Wine Inst., Soc. for Am. Cuisine (founding), Calif. Restaurant Assn. (Chef of Yr., 1984), Nat. Restaurant Assn., Guild of Sommeliers Eng., Am. Inst. Food and Wine, Les Amis d'Escoffier Soc. N.Y. (amb.-at-large), Internat. Assn. Cooking Profls., Soc. Advancement of Food Svc. Rsch., Italian Restaurant Soc., Calif. Culinary Acad. (adv. bd. 1990—), L'Ordre Mondial Des Gourmets Degustateurs (spl. medal of honor, 1991), Confrerie de la Chaine Des Rotisseurs (bailli 1995, Bronze medal, 1990), Assn. Des Maitres Conseils en Gastronomie Francaise (comdr.), Les Toques Blanches Internat. Club (founder Monterey chpt., mem. internat. bd., Presdl. Medallion), Les Toques Blanches (1st nat. pres. 1994), Calif. Travel Industry Assn. (F. Norman Clark Entrepreneur award 1992), Monterey Peninsula C. of C. (v.p.), Disting. Restaurants of N.Am. (nat. chmn. 1996). Office: Restaurants Central 765 Wave St Monterey CA 93940-1016

CUTLER, LORRAINE MASTERS, interior designer, facilities manager; b. Indpls., Oct. 19, 1943; d. James Mark and Dorothy Aileen (DeLawter) Masters; m. Albert B. Cutler III, June 3, 1965 (div.); children: Valina Dawn, Anthony Bret. BFA, Ariz. State U., 1974, BA, 1974; MA, U. Phoenix, 1989. Intern Walsh Bros., Phoenix, 1973, jr. designer, 1973-74, staff designer, 1978-80; dir. interior design Dick & Fritsche Design Group, Phoenix, 1980-84; dir. interior design and space planning HNC Inc., Phoenix, 1984-87; mgr. advanced facilities planning PCS, Inc., Scottsdale, Ariz., 1987-89; cons. Cons. Mgmt. Systems, 1989—; assoc. prof. interior design and facility mgmt. Ariz. State U., Tempe, 1991—. Participant Interior Design Efforts for Ariz. Legis., Phoenix, 1986-87; bd. dirs. Southwest Builds, 1985-88, chmn. fin. com., 1987-88. Recipient Presdl. Citation Am. Soc. Interior Designers, 1984. Mem. Internat. Interior Design Assn. (profl., acad. liaison 1991-93, pres. 1985-87, v.p. programs 1983-85, sec. 1981-83, Cert. Appreciation 1981), Internat. Facility Mgmt. Assn. (profl., treas.). Home: 4034 E Yowy St Phoenix AZ 85044-1527 Office: Ariz State U Coll Architecture and Environ Design Tempe AZ 85287-2105

CUTLER, PHILIP EDGERTON, lawyer; b. Evanston, Ill., Mar. 18, 1948; s. John A. and Catherine (Hedman) C.; m. Barbara Anne Phippen, Oct. 27, 1948; children: David, Nathanael, Andrew. AB in History, Georgetown U., 1970; JD with honors, Northwestern U., 1973. Assoc. Perkins Coie, Seattle, 1973-79; ptnr. Sax and MacIver, Seattle, 1979-85; ptnr., shareholder Sax and MacIver merged Karr Tuttle Campbell, Seattle, 1986-89; shareholder, pres. Cutler & Nylander, Seattle, 1990—, also bd. dirs.; ct.-approved arbitrator King County Superior Ct., 1982—, U.S. Dist. Ct. (we. dist.) Wash., 1992—; mediator U.S. Dist. Ct. (we. dist.) Wash., 1982—; judge pro tem King County Superior Ct., 1993—; mem. comml. arbitration panel Am. Arbitration Assn., 1992—, mediator, 1997—; lectr., program chmn. numerous continuing legal edn. programs; mem. arbitration panel Nat. Assn. Securities Dealers, 1996—. Co-founder Country Dr. Comty. Legal Clinic, Seattle, 1974—; co-pres. parents club St. Joseph Sch., Seattle, 1984-86, mem. sch. adv. bd., 1985-88; dir. St. Joseph Endowment Fund, 1986—, St. Joseph Parish Sch. Fund, 1990—, St. George Sch. Endowment Found., Seattle, 1994—, sec., 1996—; mem. sch. adv. bd. Blanchet H.S., Seattle, 1991—, mem. devel. com., 1992—; chair Georgetown Alumni Admissions Interviewing Program, 1975—; active St. Patrick Parish, Seattle, 1974-82, St. Joseph Parish, Seattle, 1982—, Cursillo Movement, 1975-85, Cath. Archdiocese of Seattle, 1979-82, YMCA Indian Guides/Indian Princesses program, 1980-84, chief of Husky Nation, 1982-84. Mem. ABA (antitrust and litigation sects., civil practice and procedure com. antitrust sect. 1980-90), FBA (chair ct. congestion/alt. dispute resolution com. 1985—, mem. spl. alt. dispute resolution task force 1994 western dist. Wash.), Wash. State Bar Assn. (consumer protection, antitrust and unfair bus. practices sect., litigation sect., alt. dispute resolution sect.), St. Thomas More Soc. Seattle (pres. 1993-95), Georgetown Alumni Assn. (bd. dirs. 1977-80, alumni sen. 1980—), King County Bar Assn. (numerous coms.), Rainier Club, Wash. Athletic Club, Georgetown Club Wash. (pres. 1980-86, mem. exec. com. 1986—). Roman Catholic. Office: Cutler & Nylander 999 3rd Ave Ste 3150 Seattle WA 98104-4007

CUTRONE, LAWRENCE GARY, school system administrator, consultant, writer; b. Washington, Pa., Oct. 7, 1947; s. Lawrence James and Ruth (Neebling) C.; m. Jean Valene Osment, Feb. 14, 1982; children: Christopher, Carly, Anthony. BA, Doane Coll., 1969; MPA, Ind. U., 1976. Editor, writer Ind. U., Bloomington, 1976-77; econ. devel. planner San Carlos (Ariz.) Apache Tribe, 1978-80; planning dir. Pascua Yaqui Tribe, Tucson, 1981-88, cons., 1988-89; asst. dep. coord. Tohono O'Odham Nation, Tucson, 1988-89; contract mgr. Tucson Unified Sch. Dist., 1990—. Contbr. articles to profl. jours. Denmaster Boy Souts Am., Tucson, 1993-95; v.p. PTA, Tucson, 1994-95. Fellow Ind. U., 1976, U. Ariz., 1981. Mem. Nat. Contract Mgmt. Assn. (cert. profl. cotnracts mgr.), Assn. Sch. Bus. Ofcls. Internat. Democrat. Home: 2550 E Edison St Tucson AZ 85716

CUTTS, JAMES ALFRED, aerospace scientist; b. Liverpool, Eng., Sept. 29, 1943; came to U.S., 1965; s. John George-Bilton and Vera (Hopkin) C.; m. Karen Daine Lemos, Apr. 22, 1967; children: Brianna Catherine, Dominique Caroline. BA in Natural Scis., Cambridge U., 1965; MS in Geophysics, Calif. Inst. Tech., 1967, PhD in Planetary Sci., 1971. Mem. tech. staff Jet Propulsion Lab., Pasadena, Calif., 1967-75; divsn. mgr. Sci. Applications Internat. Corp., San Diego, 1975-82; divsn. technologist Jet Propulsion Lab., Pasadena, Calif., 1982-89, program mgr., 1989—; mem. Viking imaging team NASA, Washington, 1975-81, chmn. sensor working group, 1987-88, mem. TOPS sci. working group, 1992-93. Pres. Pasadena Young Musicians Orch., Pasadena, 1987-88. Recipient Robert N. Goddard trophy Nat. Space Club, 1978. Mem. AAAS (Newcomb Cleve. prize 1976), AIAA, Internat. Soc. Optical Engring. Office: Jet Propulsion Lab 4800 Oak Grove Dr Pasadena CA 91109-8001

CYMERYS, MARGARET J., conservationist, environmentalist, consultant; b. Hartford, Conn., Apr. 23, 1959; d. Frederick J. and Therese M. (Ferland) C.; m. Antonio V. Valente da Silva, July 13, 1989. BS in Earth Scis., U. Calif., 1986, BA in Environ. Scis., 1986; M in Environ. Studies, Yale U., 1991. Researcher coop. parks studies unit Pinnacles Nat. Monument, Calif., 1984-85; hack site attendant Sanat Cruz (Calif.) Predatory Bird Rsch. Group, 1985-86; asst. researcher World Wildlife Fund, Manaus, Amazonas, Brazil, 1987-88; cons. Biosyss. Analysis, Tiburon, Calif., 1988-89; program mgr. wildlife Woods Hole Rsch. Ctr., Belém, Pará, Brazil, 1993-96; environ. cons. Point San Quentin, Calif., 1996—; cons. proposal negotiations Tropical Resources Inst., New Haven, Conn., 1992-93. Contbr. articles to profl. jours. Lat. Am. Studies grantee Yale U., 1990, grantee Tropical Resources Inst., 1990. Mem. Soc. Conservation Biology (exec. Yale chpt. 1990-91), N. Am. Assn. Environ. Edn. Office: Box 194 Point San Quentin CA 94964

DACKAWICH, S. JOHN, sociology educator; b. Loch Gelley, W.Va., Jan. 31, 1926; s. Samuel and Estelle (Jablonski) D.; m. Shirley Jean McVay, May 20, 1950; children—Robert John, Nancy Joan. B.A., U. Md., 1955; Ph.D., U. Colo., 1958. Instr. U. Colo., 1955-57; instr. Colo. State U., 1957-59; prof., chmn. sociology Calif. State U., Long Beach, 1959-70; prof. sociology Calif. State U., Fresno, 1970-94, chmn. dept., 1970-75, prof. sociology emeritus, 1994—; pvt. practice survey research, 1962—. Contbr. articles and rsch. papers to profl. publs. Mem. Calif. Dem. Ctrl. Com., 1960-62; co-dir. Long Beach Ctrl. Area Study, 1962-64, Citizen Participation Study, Fresno. With USMCR, 1943-46, U.S. Army, 1950-53. Mem. Am., Pacific sociol. assns. Home: 5841 W Judy Ct Visalia CA 93277-8601 Office: Calif State U Dept Sociology 5340 N Campus Dr Fresno CA 93740-8019

DACKOW, OREST TARAS, insurance company executive; b. Wynyard, Sask., Can., Sept. 17, 1936; s. Luke Dackow and Irene Stacheruk; m. Florence Dorothy Waples, Sept. 20, 1958; children: Trevor Wade, Heather Lynn, Donna Louise. B.Commerce with honors, U. Man., Winnipeg, Can., 1958; Grad. Advanced Mgmt. Program, Harvard U., 1976. Enrolled actuary. V.p. individual ops. Great-West Life Ins. Co., Winnipeg, Man., Can., 1976-78, sr. v.p. individual ops., 1978-79, sr. v.p. U.S., 1979-83; exec. v.p., chief operating officer U.S. Great-West Life Assurance Co., Denver, 1983-88; exec. v.p. corp. fin. and control Great-West Life Assurance Co., Winnipeg, 1988-90, pres., 1990-94, dir., 1992—; pres., CEO, dir. Great-West Lifeco Inc., 1992—. Bd. dirs. Met. YMCA, Winnipeg, 1971-80, pres., 1979-80; bd. dirs. Met. YMCA, Denver, 1981-84, Colo. Alliance of Bus., 1986-87, Nat. Jewish Ctr. for Immunology and Respiratory Medicine, 1985—, Health Scis. Centre Rsch. Found., 1990-94, Instrumental Diagnostics Devel. Office, 1992-94. Fellow Soc. Actuaries, Can. Inst. Actuaries; mem. Am. Acad. Actuaries.

DADO, ARNOLD EMMETT, financial and insurance consultant; b. Petaluma, Calif., Mar. 17, 1938; s. Emmett Stephen and Madeline Lenore (Ouzts) D.; m. Frances Clark, June 10, 1958 (div. June, 1970); children: Alan, Sharlyn, Melanie; m. Susan Carol Forbes, June 9, 1990. Student, U. San Francisco, 1956-61. CLU, chartered fin. cons. Sales rep. ins. industry, 1962-67; asst. mgr. Mut. of N.Y., Oakland, Calif., 1967-71; tng. asst. Mut. of N.Y., N.Y.C., 1971; mgr. Mut. of N.Y., San Rafael, Calif., 1971-73, field sales dir. western region, 1973; mgr. Mut. of N.Y., Santa Rosa, Calif., 1973-80; pvt. practice fin. planning Santa Rosa, 1980—; expert witness for Tech. Adv. Svc. for Attys., 1990—, U.S. Dept. Justice, 1991; lectr. in field. Organizer Spl. Olympics, Santa Rosa, 1975—; past bd. dirs. Petaluma Wildlife Mus., 1994—. Sgt. U.S. Army, 1960-64. Mem. Am. Soc. CLU and Chartered Fin. Cons. (past pres., chmn. continuing edn. com.), Redwood Empire Assn. Life Underwriters (chmn. ethics com., former bd. dirs.), Estate Planning Coun. (former bd. dirs.), Elks Club. Democrat. Roman Catholic. Office: 2300 Bethards Dr Ste J Santa Rosa CA 95405-9005

DAEHLING, WILLIAM A., academic administrator. Chancellor Mont. State U. No., Havre. Office: Mont State U No Office of Chancellor PO Box 7751 Havre MT 59501*

DAEMEN, JAAK JOSEPH K., mining and geotechnical engineering educator; came to the U.S., 1967; Degree in mining engring., U. Leuven, Belgium, 1967; PhD in Geol. Engring., U. Minn., 1975. Registered profl. engr., Ariz. Rsch. asst., then rsch. assoc. U. Minn., Mpls., 1967-75; rsch. engr. explosives products divsn. E.I. DuPont de Nemours & Co., Martinsburg, W.Va., 1975-76; asst.prof. mining and geol. engring. U. Ariz., Tucson, 1976-83; assoc. prof. mining and geol. engring., 1983-90; prof., dept. chair U. Nev., Reno, 1990—; acting dean Mackay Sch. Mines, 1995—. Mem. ASCE, AIME, Internat. Soc. for Rock Mechanics, Am. Underground Space Assn., Am. Geophys. Union, Internat. Soc. Explosives Engrs., Internat. Soc. for Soil Mechanics and Found. Engring., Royal Flemish Engring. Soc., Royal Belgium Assn. of Engrs. and Industrialists. Home: 2620 Pioneer Dr Reno NV 89509-7605 Office: U Nev Dept Mining Engring Reno NV 89557-0139

DAENER, PAMELA HILL, university budget officer; b. Alameda, Calif., Aug. 12, 1951; d. William Butterfield and Julia Helene (Hill) Decker; m. Neil Robert Daener, Aug. 26, 1979; children: Laura Anne, William Christian. BA, Stanford U., 1973; MBA, UCLA, 1978; PhD, U. Oreg., 1993. Bus. mgr. Am. Conservatory Theatre, San Francisco, 1976-78; fin. analyst Stanford (Calif.) U., 1979-84, Rogue Valley Med. Ctr., Medford, Oreg., 1985-88; budget officer U. Oreg., Eugene, 1988—; ind. cons. Korty Films, Inc., Mill Valley, Calif., 1978-79, San Francisco Neighborhood Arts Program; rsch. asst. Yale U. Dept. Biology, 1974-75; tchg. asst. Stanford U. Dept. Biology, 1973-74; presenter in field. Contbr. papers to profl. mtgs. Mem. AAUW, Am. Assn. Higher Edn., Am. Ednl. Rsch. Assn., Assn. Study of Higher Edn., Soc. for Coll. and Univ. Planning, Beta Gamma Sigma. Office: U Oreg Office Resource Mgmt 1242 U Oreg Eugene OR 97403-1242

DAFFORN, GEOFFREY ALAN, biochemist; b. Cunningham, Kans., Feb. 4, 1944; s. Francis Elston and Anna Elizabeth Dafforn; m. Gail McLaughlin, July 14, 1973; 1 child, Christine Elizabeth. BA cum laude, Harvard U., 1966; PhD, U. Calif., Berkeley, 1970. Postdoctoral fellow U. Calif., Berkeley, 1973; asst. prof. U. Tex., Austin, 1974; from asst. prof. to assoc. prof. Bowling Green (Ohio) State U., 1974-81; sr. chemist Syva Co., Palo Alto, Calif., 1982-87, rsch. fellow, 1987—. Author articles and abstracts; patentee in field. Grantee Army Rsch. Office, 1979-82, Am. Chem. Soc., 1975-80. Mem. AAAS, Am. Chem. Soc., Sierra Club. Office: Behring Diagnostics Inc 3403 Yerba Buena Rd San Jose CA 95135

DAFOE, DONALD CAMERON, surgeon, educator; b. Appleton, Wis., Nov. 22, 1949. BS in Zoology, U. Wis., 1971, MD, 1975. Diplomate Am. Bd. Surgery. Intern Hosp. of U. of Pa., Phila., 1975-76, resident, 1976-80, Measey rsch. fellow, 1978-80, chief resident, 1980-81, clin. fellow, Culpeper Found. fellow, 1981-82; asst. prof. surgery U. Mich., Ann Arbor, 1982-87; dir. clin. pancreas transplantation program u. Mich., Ann. Arbor, 1984-87; assoc. prof. surgery U. Mich., Ann Arbor, 1987; assoc. prof. surgery, chief divsn. transplantation Hosp. of U. of Pa., Phila., 1987-91, Stanford (Calif.) U. Med. Ctr., 1991—. Reviewer various publs.; mem. editorial bd. Transplantation Sci., 1992, The Chimera, 1993; contbr. over 100 articles to profl. jours; also numerous book chpts. Mem. ACS, Am. Surg. Assn., Am. Diabetes Assn., Am. Soc. Transplant Surgeons, Assn. for Acad. Surgery, Soc. Internat. de Chirurgie, The Transplantation Soc., Pacific Coast Surg. Assn., Ctrl. Surg. Assn., Frederick A. Coller Surg. Soc., Soc. Univ. Surgeons, Surg. Biology Club II, Ravdin-Rhoads Surg. Soc., United Network for Organ Sharing, Calif. Transplant Donor Network, Western Assn. Transplant Surgeons. Office: Dept Surgery H2104 Stanford Univ Hosp Stanford CA 94305

DAGGETT, ROBERT SHERMAN, lawyer; b. La Crosse, Wis., Sept. 16, 1930; s. Willard Manning and Vida Naomi (Sherman) D.; children: Ann Daggett McCluskey, John Sullivan; m. Helen Hosler Ackerman, July 20, 1976. AB in Polit. Sci./Journalism with honors, U. Calif., Berkeley, 1952, JD, 1955. Bar: Calif. 1955, U.S. Supreme Ct. 1967. Assoc. firm Brobeck, Phleger & Harrison, San Francisco, 1958-66, ptnr., 1966-95, of counsel, 1996—; of counsel Calif. Senate, 1972-73; adj. prof. evidence and advocacy Hastings Coll. Law, 1982-84; instr. No. Dist. Fed. Practice Program, 1982-83; demonstrator-instr. Nat. Inst. for Trial Advocacy, 1981—, Stanford and U. San Francisco Law Schs., Hastings Ctr. for Trial and Appellate Advocacy, 1981-88, mem. adv. bd., 1983-88; vol. pro tem judge San Francisco Mcpl. Ct., 1981-88, San Francisco Superior Ct., 1990—, chmn. com. ind. judiciary, 1995—; arbitrator and pvt. comml. arbitrator, 1984—; co-host Face to Face, Sta. KQED-TV; commentaries Sta. KQED-FM. Bd. editors Calif. Law Rev., 1953-55; author: Daggett's Dicta (www.brobeck.com); contbr. articles and lectures to profl. jours. Bd. dirs. San Francisco Legal Aid Soc.; bd. visitors U. Calif., Santa Cruz. 1st lt. JAGC, U.S. Army, 1958-62. Walter Perry Johnson scholar, 1953. Fellow Am. Bar Found.; mem. ABA, FBA (pres. no. dist. Calif. chpt. 1992-95), AFTRA, State Bar Calif., San Francisco Bar Assn. (past bd. dirs.), Am. Judicature Soc., Am. Law Inst., Bohemian Club, Commonwealth Club, Comml. Club (bd. dirs. 1989—, pres. 1993), Order of Golden Bear, Phi Delta Phi, Theta Xi. Republican. Office: Brobeck Phleger & Harrison Tower 1 Market Plz Spear St San Francisco CA 94105-1019

DAGGETT, VALERIE D., biophysicist, educator; b. Portland, oreg., Apr. 26, 1961; d. Frank and Lyla (Culbertson) D.; m. Ulf Patrik Edenholm; children: Garrett Daggett-Edenholm, Tess Daggett-Edenholm. BA in Chemistry, Reed Coll., 1983; PhD in Pharm. Chemistry, U. Calif., San Francisco, 1990. Rsch. asst. dept. biochemistry and microbiology Rutgers U., N.J., 1983-85, biochemistry tutor, 1984-85; tchg. asst. in phys. chemistry U. Calif., San Francisco, 1986-87, tutor in phys. chemistry, 1988; cons. Triton Bioscis., Inc., 1988-89; postdoctoral fellow dept. cell biology Stanford (Calif.) U., 1990-92, staff rsch. assoc., 1992-93; asst. prof. medicinal chemistry U. Wash., Seattle, 1993—; former profl. downhill ski instr.; writer, processor crime reports Portland Police Bur. Mem. edit. bd. Folding and Design, Protein Sci.; contbr. articles to profl. publs. Alumni rep. admissions office Reed Coll., 1985—; vol. tchr. Sci. Edn. Partnership, 1989-90; vol. escort Swedish Ctr. for Internat. Child Welfare. Recipient Young Investigator award Office of Naval Rsch.; Oreg. scholar, 1979-83, Coca Cola acad. scholar, 1979-81; Grad. Opportunity fellow U. Calif., San Francisco, 1985-86, fellow Katherine McCormick Fund for Women,Stanford U., 1990-91, 92-93, Jane Coffin Childs Found., 1990-93; rsch. grantee Grad. Student Fund U. Wash., Am. Health Assistance Found., NSF, Sandoz Found., NIH, Am. Chem. Soc. Office: U Wash Dept Medicinal Chemistry Box 357610 Seattle WA 98195-7610

DAGODAG, MELISSA KERRY, product design company executive; b. Oxnard, Calif., Nov. 28, 1968; d. Wlliam Tim and Christine Ellen (Peasley) D. AB, Stanford U., 1991, MA, 1991. Staff writer The Stanford (Calif.) Daily, 1987-91; fashion model Elite Model Mgmt., Miami, Fla., 1988-93, L.A., 1988-93; owner, chief exec. Mine Design, L.A., 1993—. Author: Murder South Beach Style, 1994; inventor in field.

DAHL, BREN BENNINGTON, photo retoucher; b. Gary, Ind., Nov. 15, 1954; d. Paul Wayland and Shirley Ann (Havard) Bennington; m. Curtis Ray Dahl; children: Austin Brooks, Darren Curtis. Student Principia Coll., Elsah, Ill., 1972-74, Sch. of Art Inst. of Chgo., 1983; BA in English with honors, U. Hawaii, 1977. Tchr. English, Peace Corps, Mbuji-Mayi, Zaire, 1977-79, Asahi Cultural Ctr., Osaka, Japan, 1981-82, Osaka Inst. Fgn. Trade, Osaka, 1981-82, Kansai U. of Fgn. Studies, Osaka, 1980-82, Matsushita Electric, Osaka, 1982; pres., owner Video Enterprises, North Palm Beach, Fla., 1983-87; prodr.'s asst. Casady Entertainment, Hollywood, Calif., 1989-91; photo retoucher Kaish-Dahl Photography. Screenwriter: Ties That Bind, 1991, The Spider Clock, 1993, Ticking Off Ryan, 1995. Mem. Temple Beth Haverim Choir, 1996, Palm Beach Opera Chorus, 1984-85; bd. dirs. First Neighborhood Homeowners Assn., 1996-97. Fred Waring Scholar, 1972. Mem. Exec. Women of Palm Beaches, Fla. Motion Picture and TV Assn., Am. Film Inst., No. Palm Beach County C. of C. (co-chmn. spl. events 1985-86), BBB Scriptwriters Network, Tourette Syndrome Assn. Republican. Jewish. Avocation: calligraphy, singing, gourmet cooking.

DAHL, CHRISTIAN ADAM, engineer; b. Salt Lake City, Feb. 8, 1954; s. Harold Arthur and Josephine Helen (Andersen) D.; m. Ann Marie Yensen, Dec. 11, 1952; children: Mark Douglas, Madelyn Marie, Patrick Andrew. BS in Chem. Engring., U. Utah, 1976, MS in Chem. Engring., 1979. Rsch. engr. Lockheed Idaho Martin Techs. Co. and predecessors, Idaho Falls, 1978—; process surveillance engr. Lockheed Idaho Techs. Co. and predecessors, Idaho Falls, 1982-84, sr. engr., 1984, mgr. process monitoring, 1984-90, mgr. process evaluation, 1990-92, acting mgr. model integration, 1992, mgr. systems modeling, 1992-94, adv. engr., 1994—. Contbr. articles to profl. jours. Office: Lockheed Idaho Techs Co PO Box 1625 MS 3114 Idaho Falls ID 83415-3114

DAHL, DONALD DOUGLAS, newswriter; b. Savage, Mont., Mar. 25, 1920; s. Alfred Kristian and Elsie (McDonell) D.; m. Helen Copeland, Oct. 6, 1946 (div. 1978); children: Christine Dahl, Karen McKenzie. BA, U. N.D., 1941; MS, Columbia U., 1950. Supr. Fed. Writers Project, Bismarck, N.D., 1941; extension editor U. N.H., Durham, 1946-49; reporter Journal Bulletin, Providence, 1950; correspondent United Press, Manila, The Philippines, 1951-53; copy editor, wire editor, news editor The Albuquerque Tribune, 1954-82. Lt. USNR, 1942-46, PTO. Mem. Beta Theta Pi. Presbyterian. Home: 1305 Girard Blvd SE Albuquerque NM 87106-2905

DAHL, RICHARD L., elementary school educator; b. Valley City, N.D., Mar. 8, 1948; s. Ordean L. and Alvina Dahl; m. Judith C. Saude, Nov. 19, 1972; children: Maraleis, Richard J. BA in Bus. Adminstrn., Minot State U., 1975; BS in Elem. Edn., U. N.D., 1979; MA in Edn. Adminstrn., U. So.

Miss., 1992. Tchr. jr. h.s. social studies St. Leo's Elem., Minot, N.D., 1980-82; tchr. 6th grade Battle Mountain (Nev.) Jr. H.S., 1982-86; tchr. 4th grade Mary S. Black Elem. Sch., Battle Mountain, 1986—. With U.S. Army, 1969-72. Home: 310 Good St Battle Mountain NV 89820-2140 Office: Mary S Black Elem Battle Mountain NV 89820

DAHLGREN, DOROTHY, museum director; b. Coeur d'Alene, Idaho; m. Robert Eagan, 1985; 1 child, Ivan. BS in Museology and History, U. Idaho, 1982; postgrad., Gonzaga U., 1997—. Dir. Mus. N. Idaho, Coeur d'Alene, 1982—; grant reviewer gen. operating support grants Inst. Mus. and Libr. Svcs., 1993—; mem. Kootenai County Historic Preservation Commn. Author: (with Simone Carbonneau Kincaid) In All the West No Place Like This; A Pictorial HIstory of the Coeur d'Alene Region, 1996. mem. Idaho Heritage Trust com. N. region. Office: Mus N Idaho PO Box 812 Coeur D Alene ID 83816-0812

DAHLIN, DENNIS JOHN, landscape architect; b. Ft. Dodge, Iowa, June 12, 1947; s. Fred E. and Arlene (Olson) D.; m. Jeanne M. Larson, Mar. 2, 1969 (div. 1990); 1 child, Lisa. BA, Iowa State U., 1970; M in Landscape Architecture, U. Calif., Berkeley, 1975. Lic. landscape architect. Assoc. planner San Luis Obispo County, Calif., 1971-73; prin. Dennis Dahlin Assocs., Modesto, Calif., 1975-90; pres. WPM Planning Team, Inc., Sacramento, 1991—; v.p. El Porvenir Found., Sacramento, Calif., 1991—. Contbg. author: The Energy Primer, 1976. Bd. dirs. Ecology Action Ednl. Inst., Modesto, 1984-85, Econ. Conversion Coun., San Diego, 1988-89; pres. San Joaquin Habitat for Humanity, Stockton, Calif., 1986-87. Ferrand fellow U. Calif., 1974, Kearney fellow Harvard U., 1975. Mem. Am. Planning Assn., Am. Soc. Landscape Architects (bd. dirs. Sierra chpt. 1993-95). Methodist. Office: PO Box 261 Sacramento CA 95812-0261

DAHLSTEN, DONALD LEE, entomology educator, university dean; b. Clay Center, Nebr., Dec. 8, 1933; s. Leonard Harold and Shirley B. (Courtright) D.; m. Reva D. Wilson, Sept. 19, 1959 (div.); children: Dia Lee, Andrea; m. Janet Clair Winner, Aug. 7, 1965; stepchildren: Karen Rae, Michael Allen. BS, U. Calif., Davis, 1956; MS, U. Calif., Berkeley, 1960, PhD, 1963. Asst. prof. Los Angeles State Coll., 1962-63; asst. entomologist U. Calif., Berkeley, 1963-65, lectr., 1965-68, asst. prof., 1968-69, assoc. prof., 1969-74, prof. entomology, 1974—, chmn. div. Biol. Control, 1980-88;, 1990-91; chmn. dept. cons. and resource studies U. Calif., Berkeley, 1989-91, dir. lab. biol. control, 1992-94; assoc. dean instrn. and student affairs Coll. Natural Resources, U. Calif., Berkeley, 1996—; vis. prof. Yale Sch. Forestry and Environ. Studies, 1980-81, Integrated Pest Mgmt. Team People's Republic China, 1980, 81.. Mem. AAAS, Am. Inst. Biol. Scis. (vis. prof., lectr. 1970-71), Entomol. Soc. Am., Entomol. Soc. Can., Soc. Am. Foresters. Office: U Calif Ctr for Biol Control 201 Wellman Hall Berkeley CA 94720-3112

DAHMER, JOAN MARIE, physician; b. Kitchener, Ont., Can., June 18, 1959; came to U.S., 1992; d. John Aloysius and Marie Genevive (McDonald) Keating; m. Scott J. Dahmer, June 14, 1980; children: Leah, Trevor. Student, U. Western Ont., London, Can., 1977-78, MD, 1982. Diplomate Am. Bd. Internal Medicine. Intern McGill U., Montreal, Can., 1982-83; resident in internal medicine Dalhousie U., Halifax, N.S., Can., 1983-86, chief resident, 1986-87, resident in hematology, 1987-88; fellow in hematology McMaster U., Hamilton, Can., 1988-89; pvt. practice Sudbury, Ont., Can., 1989-92; chief medicine Laurentian U., 1990-92; med. dir. Sudbury Regional Hemophilia Clinic, 1990-92; pvt. practice Windsor, Calif., 1992—; med. cons. Med. Scis. Lab., 1992-93; cons. physician N.E. Ont. Cancer Ctr., Sudbury; med. dir. HAVEN Program N.E. Ont., 1989-92; active staff Healdsburg Gen. Hosp.; provisional staff Santa Rosa (Calif.) Meml. Hosp.; tchg. staff Cmty. Hosp., Santa Rosa; speaker various schs. and civic orgns.; bd. dirs. HIV Caregiver Network, Blood Bank of the Redwoods; editorial advisor Charcot-Marie Tooth Newsletter, 1984-90. Contbr. articles to profl. jours. and newsletters. Fellow Royal Physicians and Surgeons Can. (cert.); mem. Calif. soc. Internal Medicine (CME com. 1993—, women in medicine com. 1993-95, HIV/AIDS com. 1993—), Sonoma County Med. Soc., Calif. Med. Assn., Amnesty Internat. (med. network 1984—), U. Western Ont. Alumni Assn., Dalhousie Med. Alumni, Sierra Club. Office: 911 Medical Center Plz Ste 22 Windsor CA 95492-7817

DAHOOD, ROGER, English literature educator; b. N.Y.C., Dec. 21, 1942; s. Michel A. and Sophie Dahood; m. Karen Jeanne Helberg, May 3, 1980; children: Gregory, Ann, Thomas Fisher. BA, Colgate U., 1964; MA, Stanford U., 1967, PhD, 1970. Asst. prof. English U. Ariz., Tucson, 1970-76, assoc. prof., 1977-84, prof., 1985—. Editor: The Avowing of King Arthur, 1984; co-editor: (with R.W. Ackerman) Arcrene Riwle: Introduction and Part One, 1984; contbr. chpt. to book, articles to profl. jours. Trustee St. Gregory Coll. Prep. Sch., Tucson, 1991-96; mem. adv. bd. Ariz. Ctr. for Medieval and Renaissance Studies, Tempe, 1994—. Mem. Medieval Acad. Am., Medieval Assn. of the Pacific, New Chaucer Soc., Internat. Arthurian Soc. Office: U Ariz Dept English Modern Lang Bldg Tucson AZ 85721

DAIGON, RUTH, editor, poet; b. Winnipeg, Manitoba, Can., Mar. 3, 1923; came to U.S., 1947; d. Nathan and Rose (Levin) Popeski; m. Arthur daigon, Apr. 11, 1952; children: Tom, Glenn. BA, U. Manitoba, 1943; Diploma in Music, Royal Conservatory of Toronto, Can., 1946. Soprano soloist Vancouver Symphony, B.C., Can., 1946-48; soloist Temple Emanuel, N.Y.C., 1949-54; soprano soloist N.Y. Pro Musica, N.Y.C., 1950-54; recording artist Columbia Records, N.Y.C., 1950-56; recital and TV artist U. Conn., Storrs, 1963-70; soloist Great Neck (N.Y.) Community Ch., 1952-63; editor Poets On: (series), Mill Valley, Calif. and, Chaplin, Conn., 1976—. Author: (poetry books) Learning Not To Kill You, 1975, A Portable Past, 1986, Between One Future And The Next, 1995; editor: (books) Poets On:, 1976—, About A Year, 1996. Organizer poetry/Hartford (Conn.) Festival of Arts, 1980, other poetry programs for PBS/Conn., 1984-86. Recipient The Eve of St. Agnes nat. award Negative Capability Press, Mobile, Ala., 1993; fellow Va. Ctr. for Arts, 1987. Mem. PEN, Poetry Soc. of Am., Poets and Writers, Acad. of Am. Writers. Home: 29 Loring Ave Mill Valley CA 94941-3409

DAILEY, DAVID KEVIN, psychiatrist; b. Jacksonville, Ill., Aug. 9, 1947; s. Paul Anthony and Margaret Ellen (Eagen) D. BA, U. Notre Dame, 1969; MEd, Boston Coll., 1975; MD, Loyola U., Chgo., 1985. Diplomate Am. Bd. Psychiatry and Neurology, Am. Bd. Geriatric Psychiatry. Intern, resident Psychiat. and Psychosomatic Inst. Michael Reese Hosp. and Med. Ctr.; staff psychiatrist VA Hosp., Seattle, 1986-87, Group Health Coop, Seattle, 1987-88; med. dir. N.W. Mental Health Svcs., Auburn, Wash., 1988-91, Mental Health North, Seattle, 1991-95; clin. asst. prof. dept. psychiatry U. Wash. Sch. Medicine, Seattle, 1986—; med. dir. Cmty. Psychiat. Clinic/Mental Health North, Seattle, 1995—. Mem. Am. Psychiat. Assn., Am. Assn. Cmty. Psychiatrists, Wash. Psychiat. Assn. (exec. com. 1993-94), Wash. Assn. Cmty. Psychiatrists (pres. 1993-94, exec. coun. 1989-95). Democrat. Office: Cmty Psychiat Clinic 4120 Stoneway N Seattle WA 98103-8014

DAILEY, DAWN ELAINE, public health service official; b. Berkeley, Calif., Feb. 2, 1965; d. Stanley Wilfred Sr. and Mercedes Anderson; m. Kenneth Lamar Dailey, Apr. 19, 1986; 1 child, Mariana. BSN, U. San Francisco, 1988; MSN, Samuel Merritt Coll., 1997. RN, Calif. Nurse Alta Bates Hosp., Berkeley, 1988-91; home health nurse Kaiser Permanente, Martinez, Calif., 1992-94; coord. Contra Costa County SIDS Program, Martinez, 1995—; pub. health nurse Contra Costa County, Martinez, 1989—; cons. Calif. SIDS Program, Fair Oaks, 1994—; mem. Calif. SIDS Adv. Coun., Sacramento, 1996—, pres. No. Calif. Regional SIDS Adv. Coun., Berkeley, 1993—; mem. Contra Costa Immunization Coalition, Martinez, 1996—, Childhood Injury Prevention Coalition, Contra Costa County, 1993—; bd. mem. Fetal and Infant Mortality Rev. Bd., Berkeley. Vol. Crisis and Suicide Intervention, Walnut Creek, Calif., 1996; bd. dirs. Child Abuse Prevention Coun. Contra Costa County. Shirley C. Titus scholarship Calif. Nurses Assn., 1995, Nursing Edn. scholarship, 1996. Mem. APHA, Assn. SIDS Program Profls., Assn. Death Edn. and Counseling, Black Nurses Assn., Calif. Pub. Health Nursing Assn., Sigma Theta Tau, Chi Eta Phi (Basileus 1997, Omicron Phi chpt.). Home: 898 Sage Dr Vacaville CA 95687

DAILEY, DIANNE K., lawyer; b. Great Falls, Mont., Oct. 10, 1950; d. Gilmore and Patricia Marie (Linnane) Halverson. BS, Portland State U., 1977; JD, Lewis & Clark Coll., 1982. Assoc. Bullivant, Houser, Bailey, et. al., Portland, Oreg., 1982-88, ptnr., 1988—. Contbr. articles to profl. jours. Mem. ABA (vice chair tort and ins. practice sect. 1995-96, chair-elect tort and ins. practice sect. 1996—, governing coun. 1992—, property ins. law com., ins. coverage litigation com., comm. com., chair task force on involvement of women 1990-93, liaison to commn. on women 1993—, chair task force CERCLA reauthorization, litigation sect., sect. natural resources energy and environment), N.W. Environ. Claims Assn., Wash. Bar Assn., Oreg. State Bar, Oreg. Assn. Def. Counsel, Multnomah Bar Assn. (bd. dirs. 1994-95), Internat. Assn. Def. Counsel, Def. Rsch. Inst., Fedn. Ins. and Corp. Counsel. Office: Bullivant Houser Bailey 300 Pioneer Tower 888 SW 5th Ave Portland OR 97204-2012

DAILEY, GARRETT CLARK, publisher, lawyer; b. Bethesda, Md., Mar. 22, 1947; s. Garrett Hobart Valentine and Margaret (Clark) Dailey; m. Carolynn Farrar, June 21, 1969; children: Patrick, Steven. AB, UCLA, 1969; MA, Ariz. State U., 1974; JD, U. Calif., Davis, 1977. Bar: Calif. 1977, U.S. Dist. Ct. (no. dist.) Calif. 1969. Assoc. Stark, Stewart, Simon & Sparrowe, Oakland, Calif., 1977-80; ptnr. Davies & Dailey, Oakland, 1980-85, owner, 1986-90; ptnr. Blum, Davies & Dailey, Oakland, 1985-86; pres., pub. Attys. Briefcase, Inc., Oakland, 1989—, pres., CEO, 1989—; lectr. U. Calif. Davis Sch. Law, 1988-90, Golden Gate U. Grad. Sch. Taxation, San Francisco, 1986—. Bd. dirs. Amigos de las Americas, San Ramon Valley, Calif., 1980-85, Rotary 517 Found., Oakland, 1985, Kid's Turn, 1993. Recipient Hall of Fame award Calif. Assn. Cert. Family Law Specialists, 1995. Fellow Am. Acad. Matrimonial Lawyers; mem. Assn. Cert. Family Law Specialists. Democrat. Congregationalist. Home: 1651 W Livorna Rd Alamo CA 94507-1018 Office: Attys Briefcase Inc 519 17th St Fl 7 Oakland CA 94612-1503

DAILEY, MICHAEL DENNIS, painter, educator; b. Des Moines, Aug. 2, 1938; s. Malcolm Nelson and Lois Marjorie (Rider) D.; children: John, Susanne. BA, U. Iowa, 1960, MFA, 1963. Prof. Sch. of Art U. Wash., Seattle, 1963—. Mem. Phi Beta Kappa. Office: Francine Seders Gallery 6701 Greenwood Ave N Seattle WA 98103-5225

DAILEY, VICTORIA KEILUS, antiquarian bookseller, writer; b. Los Angeles, Jan. 21, 1948; d. Charles Stuart and Gloria Mann Keilus; m. William Dailey, Nov. 30, 1973. B.A., UCLA, 1970. Researcher Edn. Devel. Ctr., Cambridge, Mass., 1970-72; gallery asst. Zeitlin & Ver Brugge Inc. Los Angeles, 1972-73; co-owner, operator W&V Dailey Ltd., Los Angeles, 1974-95; owner Victoria Dailey, Pub., L.A., 1995—. Editor: Henri Riviere, 1983; pub. WASP (Steve Martin), 1996; contbr. articles on art to mags. Office: Victoria Dailey Pubs PO Box 461150 Los Angeles CA 90046

DAILY, JOHN G., protective services official; b. Lafayette, Ind., June 27, 1950; s. Jewell T. and Barbara (Gunnels) D.; m. Carolyn Jean Schorr, May 31, 1975; children: Jeremy Scott, Jennifer Lynn. BSME, Purdue U., 1972; postgrad., U. Wyo., 1973, 75. Owner Jackson (Wyo.) Hole Engring., 1977-93, Jackson Hole Sci. Investigations, 1993—; dep. sheriff Teton County Sheriff's Office, Jackson, 1977-89, sgt., 1989—; mem. adj. teaching faculty U. North Fla., Jacksonville, 1982—, course devel. cons., 1982—; cons. traffic accident reconstruction Jackson Hole Sci. Investigations. Inventor new type of discarding sabot; author: Fundamentals of Traffic Accident Reconstruction, 1988; co-author: Fundamentals of Applied Physics for Traffic Accident Investigators, 1996. Chmn. J.H. chpt. ARC, Jackson, 1976—. Named Peace Officer of Yr., Teton County Peace Officer Assn., 1981. Mem. SAE, ASME, Ill. Assn. Tech. Accident Investigators, Soc. Accident Reconstructionists, J.H. Rotary Club, Elks, 4-H (ch. coun. 1980-94). Republican. Lutheran. Home: 95 Nelson Dr Box 2206 Jackson WY 83001

DALDER, EDWARD NEIL CLIFF, materials engineer; b. Bklyn., May 24, 1935; s. Edward Henry and Estelle (Cliff) D.; m. Dorothy Jeanne Crosby, Aug. 12, 1967 (div. Jan. 1978); children: Erin Jeanne, Edward Robert, Linda Megan; m. Barbara Jeanne Kennedy, Oct. 2, 1982; 1 child, Brian Henry. BS in Engring., Polytechnic U., Bklyn., 1956, MS in Engring., 1964; PhD in Engring., Ohio State U., 1973. Metallurgist Grumman Corp., Bethpage, N.Y., 1956-59, Rep. Aviation Corp., Farmingdale, N.Y., 1959-62; group leader United Aircraft Corp., East Hartford, Conn., 1962-64, U.S. Steel Corp., Monroeville, Pa., 1964-69; project adminstr. Dept. Energy, Germantown, Md., 1973-79; materials engr. Lawrence Livermore (Calif.) Labs., 1979-83, project engr., 1983—; adj. prof. U. Calif., Berkeley, 1983-88, George Washington U., Washington, 1976-79. Contbr. articles to profl. jours. Treas. Shadyside Young Rep. Club, Pitts., 1964-69. Recipient Lincoln medal Lincoln Co. Found., Cleve., 1980. Mem. Am. Soc. for Metals, The Metall. Soc., Am. Welding Soc., Am. Nuclear Soc., ASME. Office: Lawrence Livermore Lab 7000 East Ave Livermore CA 94550-9516

DALE, DANIEL R., criminology educator, college dean; b. Santa Monica, Calif., May 22, 1947; s. James Thomas and Virginia Hall (Reed) D.; m. Alison Gay Usuk, July 4, 1987. BS, Calif. State U., L.A., 1976; MA, Calif. State U., Fresno, 1991; EdD, Nova Southeastern U., 1994. Police officer L.A. Police Dept., 1969-80; tchr. Visalia (Calif.) Unified Schs., 1982-91; prof. criminology Porterville (Calif.) Coll., 1991—, dir. dept., 1991-96, dean instrn., 1996—; bd. dirs. Daleco Synergy Devel., Three Rivers, Calif. Author: P.O. Guide to Criminal Law, 1995. With USN, 1967-69, Vietnam. Home: PO Box 96 Three Rivers CA 93271-0096 Office: Porterville Coll 100 E College Ave Porterville CA 93257

DALE, JACK E., mayor; m. Deb Dale; children: Jacquelyn, Janae, Jordanne, Jason, Jarrett. Mayor City of Santee, Calif., 1992—. Mem. City Coun., Santee, 1986-92; past treas. bd. dirs. Padre Dam Mcpl. Water Dist.; Santee rep. to Automated Regional Justice Sys. Joint Powers Agy., East County Econ. Devel. Coun., San Diego Assn. Govts.; chair TransNet; grad. LEADS tng. program; former mem. Dads Against Drinking and Drugs, Burn Inst.; hon. bd. dirs. Santee Child Abuse Ctr.; past pres. ch. Address: 10765 Woodside Ave Santee CA 92071

DALESIO, WESLEY CHARLES, former aerospace educator; b. Paterson, N.J., Mar. 26, 1930; s. William James and Sarah (Sheets) Delison; m. Dorothy May Zellers, Nov. 17, 1951; children: Michael Kerry, Debra Kaye Dalesio Weber. Student, Tex. Christian U., 1950, U. Tex., Arlington, 1957. Enlisted USAF, 1948, advanced through grades to sr. master sgt., 1968; aircraft engine mech., mgmt. analyst USAF, worldwide, 1948-70; ins. agt. John Hancock Ins., Denver, 1970-71; office mgr. Comml. Builder, Denver, 1972-73; aerospace educator Sch. Dist. 50, Westminster, Colo., 1973-93; dir. aerospace edn. CAP, Denver, 1982-86, 94—. Mem. Crimestoppers, Westminster, 1988-91, Police and Citizens Teamed Against Crime, Westminster, 1992-93. Lt. col. CAP, 1981—. Mem. Nat. Assn. Ret. Mil. Instrs. (charter mem.), Westminster Edn. Assn., 7th Bomb Wing B-36 Assn., Internat. Platform Assn., Nat. Aeronautic Assn., Acad. Model Aeronautics, Arvada Associated Modelers (life). Episcopalian. Home: 2537 W 104th Cir Westminster CO 80234-3507

DALESSANDRI, KATHIE MARIE, surgeon; b. Stambaugh, Mich., May 4, 1947; d. Paris Henry and Kathryn Mary (Macuga) D. BS in Biology, Mich. Tech. U., 1969; MS in Biophysics, Purdue U., 1971; MD, U. Mich., 1976. Intern, resident Martinez (Calif.) VA Hosp., 1976-79; resident U. Calif., Davis, 1979-81; staff surgeon Martinez (Calif.) VA Med. Ctr., 1982-92, Palo Alto (Calif.) VA Med. Ctr., 1992—; asst. prof. surgery U. Calif., Davis, 1982-88, assoc. clin. prof. surgery, 1989-95; clin. assoc. prof. surgery Stanford (Calif.) U., 1993—; Diplomate Am. Bd. Surgery; chairperson mammography action com. Reviewer jours.; contbr. articles to profl. jours. Recipient 1st prize in rsch. nat. VA Surgeons, 1981. Fellow ACS; mem. East Bay Surg. Soc. (1st prize in rsch. 1981), Assn. Acad. Surgery, Internat. Coll. Surgeons, Soc. Internat. de Chirurgie, Assn. Surg. Edn. Home: PO Box 1173 Point Reyes Station CA 94956-1173 Office: Palo Alto VA Med Ctr Surgery Dept 3801 Miranda Ave Palo Alto CA 94304-1207

DALEY, RICHARD HALBERT, foundation executive; b. Centralia, Ill., Oct. 8, 1948; s. Richard Glen D.; m. Lucy W. Costen, Nov. 27, 1976. Student, Lake Forest (Ill.) Coll., 1966-67; BS, Colo. State U., 1970, MS, 1972. Instr. Colo. State U., Ft. Collins, 1972; from dir. biol. svcs. to dir. programs Mo. Bot. Garden, St. Louis, 1973-84; exec. dir. Mass. Hort. Soc., Boston, 1984-91, Denver Botanic Gardens, 1991—; instr. Environ. Ethics Denver U., 1992—. Mem. editorial com. Am. Mus. Natural History, N.Y.C., 1983-92. Bd. trustees Ctr. for Plant Conservation, 1994—. Mem. Am. Assn. Bot. Gardens (bd. trustees), Hort. Club Boston, Rotary Club Denver. Office: Denver Botanic Gardens 909 York St Denver CO 80206-3751

DALKE, JOHN DAVID, family therapist; b. Stafford, Kans., Apr. 23, 1937; s. Jacob Joseph and Katherine Elizabeth (Shaler) D.; m. Sheryl Ankerstar, Oct. 6, 1990; children: Julie, Mike, Mary Beth. BA in Psychology, Sociology, Friends U., 1959; MTh, Drew Theol. Sch., Madison, N.J., 1962; DMin, San Francisco Theol. Seminary, San Anselmo, Calif., 1977. Pastor, cons. United Meth. Ch., Pratt and Belle Plaine, Kans., 1962-70; adminstrv. asst. Kans. Children's Svc. League, Wichita, 1970-75; family therapist Wichita and Longmont, Colo., 1975—; human resources dir. Air Mid-West Airline, Wichita, 1982-84; trainer for pub. seminars Career Track, Boulder, Colo., 1988; cons. to pvt./pub. orgns., 1975—; tchr. Friends U., Wichita, 1975, Aims C.C., Greeley, Colo., 1985—. Author books and video/audio tapes in field. Recipient Disting. Svc. award Nat. C. of C., Pratt, 1968. Mem. Am. Counseling Assn., Assn. of Death Edn. Counseling, Ctr. for Dispute Resolution. Home: 1113 Hawkeye St Fort Collins CO 80525-2205 Office: 2133 Meadow St Longmont CO 80501-1254

DALLAS, SANDRA, correspondent, writer; b. Washington, June 11, 1939; d. Forrest Everett and Harriett (Mavity) Dallas; m. Robert Thomas Atchison, Apr. 20, 1963; chidlren: Dana Dallas, Povy Kendal Dallas. BA, U. Denver, 1960. Asst. editor U. Denver Mag., 1965-66; editorial asst. Bus. Week, Denver, 1961-63, 67-69, bur. chief, 1969-85, 90-91, sr. corr., 1985-90; book reviewer Denver Post, 1961—, regional book columnist, 1980—. Author: Gaslights and Gingerbread, 1965, rev. edit., 1984, Gold and Gothic, 1967, No More Than 5 in a Bed, 1967, Vail, 1969, Cherry Creek Gothic, 1971, Yesterday's Denver, 1974, Sacred Paint, 1980, Colorado Ghost Towns and Mining Camps, 1985, Colorado Homes, 1986, Buster Midnight's Cafe, 1990, The Persian Pickle Club, 1995, The Diary of Mattie Spenser, 1997; editor: The Colorado Book, 1993; contbr. articles to various mags. Bd. dirs. Vis. Nurse Assn., Denver, 1983-85, Hist. Denver, Inc., 1979-82, 84-87. Recipient Wrangler award Nat. Cowboy Hall of Fame, 1980, Lifetime Achievement award Denver Posse of Westerners, 1996; named Colo. Exceptional Chronicler of Western History by Women's Library Assn. and Denver Pub. Library Friends Found., 1986. Mem. Women's Forum Colo., Denver Woman's Press Club, Western Writers Am., Women Writing the West. Democrat. Presbyterian. Home and Office: 850 Humboldt St # 3 Denver CO 80218-3573

DALPATADU, ROHAN JAYANTHA, mathematician, educator; b. Moratuwa, Sri Lanka, May 29, 1951; came to the U.S., 1980; s. Kosmapatabendige Arthur and Nandawathie (Manawadu) D.; m. Sreeni Manohari Punchihewa, Jan. 18, 1979. BS in Math. with honors, U. Ceylon, 1974; MS, So. Ill. U., 1981, PhD, 1986. Asst. lectr. U. Sri Jayewardenepura, Nugegoda, Sri Lanka, 1975-80; teaching asst. So. Ill. U., Carbondale, 1980-85; instr. U. Nev., Las Vegas, 1985-86, asst. prof., 1986-91, assoc. prof., 1991—; dir. freshman math. U. Nev., 1993-95, assoc. chair, 1995—. Contbr. articles to profl. jours. Mem. Soc. Actuaries (assoc.), Am. Math. Soc., Math. Assn. Am., S.W. Actuarial Edn. and Rsch. Consortium (program chmn. 1993-95). Buddhist. Office: U Nev 4505 S Maryland Pky Las Vegas NV 89154-9900

DAL PORTO, DANNA S., art educator, artist; b. Longview, Wash., Dec. 29, 1944; d. Winfred L. and Margaret Kingen; m. Steve Dal Porto; 1 child. BFA, U. Puget Sound, 1966; MA, Ea. Wash. U., 1981; MFA, Ctrl. Wash. U., 1991. Cert. tchr., Wash. Art tcvhr. Medical Lake (Wash.) Schs., 1967-72, Warden (Wash.) Schs., 1972-80, Quincy (Wash.) Schs., 1992—; part time art instr. Big Bend C.C., Moses Lake, Wash., 1980-90; art and drama tchr. Soap Lake (Wash.) Schs., 1991-92; bd. dirs. Gallery 76, 1980—; mem. Gallery One, 1982—. One woman shows at Unitarian Ch. Gallery, Tacoma, 1965, 66, Wallenstein Gallery, Moses Lake, Wash., 1981, Old Hotel Gallery, Othello, Wash., 1982, 86, Yakima (Wash.) Regional Libr., 1983, Ellensburg (Wash.) C.C., 1983, Crescent Bar (Wash.) Gallery, 1984, Champs d'Brionne Gallery, George, Wash., 1985, Anzelini's Gallery, Moses Lake, 1l988, Adams East Mus. and Art Gallery, Moses Lake, 1992, Larson Gallery, Yakima Valley C.C., 1993; exhibited in numerous group shows, including Ellensburg C.C. Gallery, 1983, Larson Gallery, 1983, Wenatchee (Wash.) Valley C.C., 1984, 86, 87, 88, 92, 95, 96, Allied Arts Gallery, Richland, Wash., 1984, Doris E. Roberts Gallery, Richland, 1985, The Gallery, Coure d'Alene, Idaho, 1985, Champs d'Brione Gallery, 1985, Masonic Temple, Chelan, Wash., 1985, Doris E. Roberts Gallery, Richland, 1985, Ellensburg (Wash.) C.C., 1985, Dakota Art Gallery, Rapid City, S.D., 1985, Carnegie Ctr. Gallery, Walla Walla, Wash., 1985, Wallenstein Gallery, 1985, 88, 89, 90, Old Hotel Gallery, 1986, Bellevue Art Mus., 1986, Ellensburg Cmty. Gallery, 1988, 89, Kittredge Gallery, Tacoma, 1988, Yakima Valley C.C., 1988, 90, 91, Cheney Cowles Mus., Spokane, 1990, Larson Gallery, 1990, 93, Adam East Mus. and Art Gallery, 1991, 92, Allied Arts Gallery, Yakima, 1995, Gallery One, Ellensburg, 1996, others; represented in permanent collections at Ctrl. Wash. State U. Found., Rockwell Corp., Richland, Ctrl. Wash. State U., Larson Gallery Guild. Bd. dirs. Gallery 76, Wenatchee, 1985-89; judge art exhibits Grant County Fair, Moses Lake, 1983-96, small animal supt., 1995-96; dir. arts and crafts Grant Adams 4H Camp, Ephrata, 1988—; mem. Grant County Solid Waste Adv. Bd., 1994—. Ford Found. fellow, 1966; Recipient Purchase award Rockwell Found., 1985, Ctrl. Wash. U. Found., 1989, 91. Mem. Coll. Art Assn., Columbia Basin Allied Arts, Larson Guild. Office: Quincy HS Art Dept Quincy WA 98848

DALRYMPLE, GARY BRENT, research geologist; b. Alhambra, Calif., May 9, 1937; s. Donald Inlow and Wynona Edith (Pierce) D.; m. Sharon Ann Tramel, June 28, 1959; children: Stacie Ann, Robynne Ann Sisco, Melinda Ann Dalrymple McGurer. AB in Geology, Occidental Coll., 1959; PhD in Geology, U. Calif., Berkeley, 1963; DSc (hon.), Occidental Coll., Los Angeles, 1993. Registered geologist, Calif. Rsch. geologist U.S. Geol. Survey, Menlo Park, Calif., 1963-81, 84-94, asst. chief geologist we. region, 1981-84; dean, prof. coll. oceanic and atmospheric sci. Oregon State U., Corvallis, 1994—; vis. prof. sch. earth scis. Stanford U., 1969-72, cons. prof., 1983-85, 90-94; disting. alumni centennial spkr. Occidental Coll., 1986-87. Author: Potassium-Argon Dating, 1969, Age of Earth, 1991; contbr. chpts. to books and articles to profl. jours. Fellow NSF, 1961-63; recipient Meritorius Svc. award U.S. Dept. Interior, 1984. Fellow Am. Geophys. Union (pres.-elect 1988-90, pres. 1990-92), Am. Acad. Arts and Scis., Geol. Soc. Am.; mem. AAAS, NAS (chair geology sect. 1997—), Am. Inst. Physics (bd. govs. 1991-97), Consortium for Oceanographic Rsch. & Edn. (bd. govs. 1994—), Joint Oceanographic Inst. (bd. govs. 1994—, chair 1996—). Home: 1847 NW Hillcrest Dr Corvallis OR 97330-1859 Office: Oregon State U Coll Oceanic and Atmospheric Sci Corvallis OR 97331-5503

DALTON, JAMES EDWARD, aerospace executive, retired air force officer; b. N.Y.C., Oct. 17, 1930; s. Edward A. and Marion (Conway) D.; m. Betty Jane Irwin, Nov. 28, 1958; children: Christopher, Stephanie, Todd. B.S., U.S. Mil. Acad., 1954; M.S.E. in Instrumentation Engring, U. Mich., 1960, M.S.E. in Aero./Astronautical Engring, 1960; grad. with distinction, Air Command and Staff Coll., 1965, Indsl. Coll. Armed Forces, 1970. Commd. 2d lt. U.S. Air Force, 1954, advanced through grades to gen., 1983; served in numerous operational and research assignments, 1954-73; comdr. 39th Aerospace Rescue and Recovery Wing, Eglin AFB, Fla., 1973-75, Air Res. Personnel Center, Denver, 1975-76; dep. dir. concepts Hdqrs. USAF, Washington, 1976-77; dep. dir. Force Devel. and Strategic Plans, Plans and Policy Directorate, Office Joint Chiefs of Staff, Washington, 1977-78; vice dir. Joint Staff, 1978-80; commandant Indsl. Coll. of Armed Forces, Washington, 1980-81; dir. Joint Staff, 1981-83; chief of staff SHAPE, 1983-85; pres. Logicon RDA, corp. v.p.; bd. dirs. The Presley Cos. Decorated Def. Disting. Service medal with two oak leaf clusters, Legion of Merit with 1 oak leaf cluster, D.F.C., Bronze Star, Air medal with 5 oak leaf clusters, Meritorious Service medal with 2 oak leaf clusters, Air Force Commendation medal. Mem. Air Force Assn., Assn. Grads. U.S. Mil. Acad., Council Fgn. Relations. Roman Catholic. Home: 61 Misty Acres Rd Palos Verdes Peninsula CA 90274-5749 Office: Logicon R & D Assocs PO Box 92500 Los Angeles CA 90009*

DALTON, LINDA CATHERINE, university administrator; b. Seattle, May 5, 1945; d. Chester Carlton and Dorothy Catherine (Salladay) Little; m. Thomas Barron Fitzpatrick, June 10, 1967 (div. 1983); children: Pandora Catherine, Benjamin Lawrence; m. Thomas Carlyle Dalton, Aug. 16,

1984. AB magna cum laude, Radcliffe Coll., 1967; M.Urban Planning, U. Wash., 1974, PhD in Urban Planning, 1978. Archtl./historic preservation staff Boston Redevel. Authority, 1967-68; long-range campus planner MIT, Cambridge, Mass., 1969-71; environ. impact analyst Kelly Pittelko Fritz & Forssen Cons., Seattle, 1974-76; lectr. Seattle U., 1976-78, asst. prof., 1978-82, assoc. prof., 1982-83; asst. prof. Calif. Poly. State U., San Luis Obispo, 1983-87, prof. city and regional planning, 1987—, dept. head city and regional planning, 1989-95; interim assoc. v.p. acad. resources Calif. Poly. State U., 1995—. Contbr. articles to profl. jours. Mem. Citizen Transp. Adv. Com., San Luis Obispo, 1990-94; mem. vis. com. Coll. Arch. and Urban Planning, U. Wash., Seattle, 1982-83; mem., vice chair, chair Seattle City Planning Commn., 1979-83; mem. Planning Accreditation Bd., 1992—, chair, 1993—; v.p. Calif. Planning Found., 1995—. Am. Coun. on Edn. fellow, 1994-95; Nat. Merit scholar, 1963-67. Mem. Am. Inst. Cert. Planners (cert.), Am. Planning Assn., Assn. Collegiate Sch. of Planning (exec. com. 1990—). Office: California Poly State Univ San Luis Obispo CA 93407

DALTON, PHYLLIS IRENE, library consultant; b. Marietta, Kans., Sept. 25, 1909; d. Benjamin Reuben and Pearl (Travelute) Bull; m. Jack Mason Dalton, Feb. 13, 1950. BS, U. Nebr., 1931, MA, 1941; MA, U. Denver, 1942. Tchr. city schs., Marysville, Kans., 1931-40; reference libr. Lincoln Pub. Libr., Nebr.; libr. U. Nebr., Lincoln, 1941-48; libr. Calif. State Libr., Sacramento, 1948-57, asst. state libr., 1957-72; pvt. libr. cons., Scottsdale, Ariz., 1972—. Author: Library Services to the Deaf and Hearing Impaired Individuals, 1985, 91 (Pres.' Com. Employment of Handicapped award 1985); contbr. chpt., articles, reports to books and publs. in field. Mem. exec. bd. So. Nev. Hist. Soc., Las Vegas, 1983-84; mem. So. Nev. Com. on Employment of Handicapped, 1980-89, chairperson, 1988-89; mem. adv. com. Nat. Orgn. on Disability, 1982-94; mem., sec. resident coun. Forum Pueblo Norte Retirement Village, 1990-91, pres. resident coun., 1991-94; bd. dirs. Friends of So. Nev. Libraries; trustee Univ. Library Soc., U. Nev.-Las Vegas; mem. Allied Arts Council, Pres.' Com. on Employment of People with Disabilities, mem. emeritus 1989—, Ariz. Gov's. Com. on Employment of People with Disabilities, 1990—, Scottsdale Mayor's Com. on Employment of People with Disabilities, 1990—, chmn. 1996—; mem.Scottsdale Pub. Libr. Ams. With Disabilities Com., 1994—. Recipient Libraria Sodalitas, U. So. Calif., 1972, Alumni Achievement award U. Denver, 1977, Alumni Achievement award U. Nebr., Lincoln, 1983; named Mover and Shaker Scottsdale Mag., 1994. Mem. LWV, ALA (councilor 1963-64, exceptional svc. award 1981, award com. O.C.L.C. Humphreys Forest Press award 1994), Am. Assn. U. Women, Assn. State Librs. (pres. 1964-65), Calif. Libr. Assn. (pres. 1969), Nev. Libr. Assn. (hon.), Internat. Fedn. Libr. Assns. and Instns. (chair working group on libr. svc. to prisons, mem. standing com. Sect. Librs. Serving Disadvantaged Persons 1981-95), Nat. League Am. Pen Women (Las Vegas chpt. 1988-94, mem. com. on qualifications for Letters membership 1994—, parliamentarian Scottsdale chpt. 1989-94, v.p. 1992-94, 96—, v.p. regional chpt. 1996—), Am. Correctional Assn. (libr. svcs. instns. com. 1994—), Pilot Internat. (mem.-at-large). Republican. Presbyterian. Home: 7090 E Mescal St Apt 261 Scottsdale AZ 85254-6125

DALTON, THOMAS GEORGE, paralegal, social worker, legal consultant; b. Hoonah, Alaska, Mar. 13, 1940; s. George and Jessie K. (Starr) D.; m. Hazel Hope, Nov. 1960 (div. Sept. 1965); children: Roderick O., Rhoeda J. Garcia, Pamela Y. Masterman; m. Kathy Pelan, Sept. 1972 (div. Feb. 1980); children: Deirdra J. (dec.), Thomas L., Michael G. AAS, Shoreline Community Coll., Seattle, 1981; BA, Seattle Pacific U., 1984. Paralegal, social worker Pub. Defender's Assn., Seattle, 1983—; client advocate in criminal justice system Seattle, 1984—; legal cons., Seattle; tchr. Tlingit Culture and Lang., Northwest Indian Coll., Bellingham, Wash. Elder United Presbyn. Ch., Hoonah, 1973—; pres. Alaska Native Brotherhood, Seattle, 1984—, Nat. Am. Community Coun., Seattle, 1990—; pres. Seattle chpt. Tlinget and Haida Indians Alaska; bd. dirs. LANCE (Leading Am. Native for Excellence), 1996—. Recipient Founder's award Alaska Native Brotherhood, 1989. Democrat. Home: 7009 10th Ave NW Seattle WA 98117-5242 Office: Ctrl Bldg 8th fl 810 3rd Ave Seattle WA 98104-1614

DALY, CAROL LYNN, economic policy center executive; b. Evanston, Ill., Oct. 4, 1942; d. James Clark and Cornelia Bertha (Gore) King; m. Paul Lawrence Daly, Mar. 20, 1921; stepchildren: Janette, Jennifer, Paula, Camilla. BA, Bennington (Vt.) Coll., 1964. Field rep. U.S. Office of Econ. Opportunity, Washington, 1964-65, Kansas City and Missoula, 1965-69; co-owner, v.p. Exec. Air Corp., Spokane, Wash., 1969-77; econ. devel. specialist Mont. Dept. of Cmty. Affairs, Helena, 1978-80; exec. dir. Pvt. Industry Coun., Helena, 1980-82; co-owner, v.p. JBM Inc., Kalispell, Mont., 1983-94; adminstr., bus. asst. Mont. Dept. Commerce, Helena, 1986-88; exec. dir. Flathead Econ. Devel. Corp., Kalispell, Mont., 1988-95; pres., exec. dir. Flathead Econ. Policy Ctr., 1995—; co-owner, operator Cattle/Hay/Timber ranches, Ovando and Condon, Mont., 1969-93; bd. dirs. North Flathead Mfg. Network, Columbia Falls, Mont.; mem. leadership coun. N.W. Policy Ctr., Seattle, 1992—, chairperson, 1996—; mem. loan com. N.W. Mont. Microbus. Fin., Kalispell, 1992—, chairperson, 1996—, Mont. Cmty. Fin. Corp., Helena, 1993—. Author: Potential Uses/Coal Tax Trust, 1985, Which Way To Tomorrow?, 1992, Flathead Gauges, 1995, 2d edit., 1996. Co-chair Coop. Planning Coalition, Kalispell, 1993-94. Recipient Woman of Distinction award Whitefish Soroptomists Internat., 1992, Partnership award Glacier Nat. Park, 1994; named Citizen of Yr., Citizens for Better Flathead, 1996. Mem. Am. Soc. Quality Control. Democrat. Episcopalian. Home: 921 Columbia Ave Whitefish MT 59937-2841 Office: Flathead Econ Policy Ctr 15 Depot Park Kalispell MT 59901

DALY, PAUL SYLVESTER, mayor, retired academic administrator; b. Belmont, Mass., Jan. 8, 1934; s. Matthew Joseph and Alice Mary (Hall) D.; m. Maureen Teresa Kenny, May 25, 1957; children: Judith Mary, Paul S. Jr., Susan Marie, John Joseph, Maureen H. BS in Engring. Sci., Naval Postgrad. Sch., 1968; MBA, U. W. Fla., 1971. Commd. ensign USN, 1955; coll. dean Embry-Riddle Aero. U., Daytona Beach, Fla., 1979-81; advanced through grades to capt. Embry-Riddle Aero. U., 1979, chancellor, 1981-95; mayor City of Prescott, Ariz., 1996—; lectr. seminars, 1977-85; cons. British Aerospace, 1979-84, McDonnell Douglas, 1979-84, IBM, 1983-84; sr. faculty U. Phoenix, 1983-86. Bd. dirs. Yavapai Regional Med. Ctr., Prescott, Ariz., 1983-86, Ariz. Hosp. Fedn., Prescott C. of C., 1982-84; chmn. Ariz. State Bd. Pvt. Postsecondary Edn., Phoenix, 1982—, Interactive Health Corp.; pres. Ind. Coll. and Univs. of Ariz., Phoenix, 1982—; pres., founder West Yavapai County Am. Heart Assn. Chpt., chmn. affiliate of Am. Heart Assn./Ariz. Decorated Legion of Merit. Mem. Ariz. Airport Assn., Ret. Officers Assn., Ariz. Town Hall. Republican. Roman Catholic. Office: City of Prescott PO Box 2059 Prescott AZ 86302

DALY, TOM, mayor; m. Debra Daly; children: Anna, Ryan. BA, Harvard U., 1976. Elected mem. City Council of Anaheim, 1988, elected mayor, 1992-94, 94—. mem. bd. trustees Anaheim Union Hish Sch. Dist., 1985—; active Anaheim Library Bd., 1985—; mem. adv. bd. Anaheim Boys and Girls Club; mem. bd. dirs. cmty. support group Anaheim Meml. Hosp.; mem. bd. dirs. Orange County Transp. Authority, Urban Water Inst.; mem. El Toro Citizens Adv. Commn.; chair regional adv. planning coun. Orange County, 1992—. Office: Office of the Mayor/City Council City Hall 200 S Anaheim Blvd Ste 733 Anaheim CA 92805-3820*

DAMASCHINO, ANN TOOTHMAN, development consultant; b. Oakland, Calif., Dec. 14, 1938; d. James Wesley and Aileen Elizabeth (Cox) Toothman; m. Douglas Alan Damaschino, Aug. 12, 1961; children: Lori Damaschino Berry, Ellen Damaschino Mellies, Gerald, Anthony. BA in English Lit. with honors, Holy Names Coll., 1962; MA in Philanthropy and Devel., St. Mary's U., Minn., 1994. Reader in English/social studies Acalanes Union H.S. Dist., Lafayette, Calif., 1964-77; interior designer, ptnr. Damaschino/Thurling, Lafayette, Calif., 1973-81; tech. writer, editor Shell Oil Co., Martinez, Calif., 1981-85; dir. devel. St. Mary's Coll. H.S., Berkeley, Calif., 1985-96; cons. devel. fund-raising, Lafayette. Pres., sec., treas. Walnut Creek (Calif.) Gallery Guild, 1968-76; mem. Contra Costa County Bd. "Project Second Chance" Adult Literacy Program, 1986-88. Mem. AAUW, Coun. for Advancement and Support of Edn., East Bay Devel. Dirs., Diocese of Oakland Devel. Dirs. Democrat. Roman Catholic.

D'AMICO, MICHAEL, architect, urban planner; b. Bklyn., Sept. 11, 1936; s. Michael and Rosalie (Vinciguerra) D.; BArch, U. Okla., 1961; postgrad. So. Meth. U. Sch. Law, 1962-63, Coll. Marin, 1988-89;, San Francisco Law Sch., 1994—; m. Joan Hand, Nov. 26, 1955; children: Michael III, Dion Charles. Supr. advanced planning sect. Dallas Dept. City Planning, 1961-63; designer, planner in charge Leo A. Daly Co., San Francisco, 1963-66; project planner Whisler, Patri Assos., San Francisco, 1966-67; architect, urban planner D'Amico & Assocs., San Francisco, N.Y., Guam, 1967-73, pres. D'Amico & Assocs., Inc., Mill Valley and San Francisco, Calif., and Guam, 1973—; pres. Jericho Alpha Inc., 1979-82, pres. Alpha Internet Syss., Inc., 1996—; cons. architect, planner City of Seaside (Calif.), 1967-72, 79-81, 89—; cons. urban redevel. Eureka (Calif.), 1967-82; cons. planner, Lakewood, Calif.; redevel. cons. to Daly City (Calif.), 1975-77; redevel. adviser to Tamalpais Valley Bus. Assn., 1975-77; archtl. and hist. analyst to Calif. Dept. Transp., 1975-77; agt. for Eureka, Calif. Coastal Commn., 1977-79; devel. cons. City of Scotts Valley, 1988-95, City of Suisun, 1988-89, City of Union City, 1989-91. Mem. steering com. San Francisco Joint Com. Urban Design, 1967-72. Recipient Community Design award AIA, 1970; First prize award Port Aransas (Tex.) Master Plan Competition, 1964; Design award Karachi Mcpl. Authority, 1987, Merit award St. Vincent's/Silveira. Mem. AIA (inactive), Am. Inst. Cons. Planners, Am. Planning Assn., Calif. Assn. Planning Cons. (sec., treas. 1970-72), World Future Soc., Solar Energy Soc. Am. Office: 525 Midvale Way Mill Valley CA 94941-3705

DAMON, JAMES CHRISTIAN, communications engineer; b. Ft. Belvoir, Va., Oct. 30, 1951; s. John Charles and Alice Darlene (Hays) D. ASET, Grantham Sch. Engring., Washington, 1972. Lic. FCC 1st class radiotelephone with radar endorsement. Sr. engring. asst. Lockheed Missiles and Space, San Diego, to 1986; owner and prin. Signal Scis., Flagstaff, Ariz., 1986—; licensee, prin. KZZA-TV Channel 6, Flagstaff, Ariz., 1991—. Designer programmable channel deletion filter, designer, builder RRCS com. CATV system for Rough Rock, Ariz. Precinct committeeman, Coconino County Rep. Party, Flagstaff, 1987-89; speaker, Sunshine Rescue Mission, Flagstaff, 1988. Mem. IEEE, Soc. Cable TV Engrs., Soc. Broadcast Engrs. Republican. Home and Office: PO Box 31120 Flagstaff AZ 86003

DAMON, JAMES GRAHAM, lawyer; b. L.A., Dec. 5, 1957; s. James G. and Tessie A. Damon; m. Jennifer Amelia Martyn; children: Allison, Corinne, Jay. BA, Johns Hopkins U., 1980; JD, Loyola Law Sch. L.A., 1984. Bar: Calif. 1984, Conn. 1985. Clk. to hon. Warren Eginton U.S. Dist. Ct. Judge, Bridgeport, Conn., 1985-86; assoc. Loeb and Loeb, L.A., 1986-92; litigation ptnr. Voss Cook & Thel, Newport Beach, Calif., 1992—. Mem. Orange County Bar Assn. Office: Voss Cook & Thel 840 Newport Center Dr Ste 700 Newport Beach CA 92660-6326

DAMPHOUSSE, VINCENT, professional hockey player; b. Montreal, Ont., Can., Dec. 17, 1967. Left wing/center Edmonton (Can.) Oilers, 1991-93; left wing Montreal Canadiens, 1993—; mem. Stanley Cup championship team, 1993. Shares NHL All-Star single-game record for most goals (4), 1991. Office: Montreal Canadiens, 1260 rue de la Gauchetierre Qst, Montreal, PQ Canada H3B 5E8*

DAMSBO, ANN MARIE, psychologist; b. Cortland, N.Y., July 7, 1931; d. Jorgen Einer and Agatha Irene (Schenck) D. B.S., San Diego State Coll., 1952; M.A., U.S. Internat. U., 1974, Ph.D., 1975. Diplomat Am. Acad. Pain Mgmt., Am. Coll. Forensic Examiners. Commd. 2d lt. U.S. Army, 1952, advanced through grades to capt., 1957; staff therapist Letterman Army Hosp., San Francisco, 1953-54, 56-58, 61-62, Ft. Devers, Ft. Devens, Mass., 1955-56, Walter Reed Army Hosp., Washington, 1958-59, Tripler Army Hosp., Hawaii, 1959-61, Ft. Benning, Ga., 1962-64; chief therapist U.S. Army Hosp., Ft. McPherson, Ga., 1964-67; ret. U.S. Army, 1967; med. missionary So. Presbyterian Ch., Taiwan, 1968-70; psychology intern So. Naval Hosp., San Diego, 1975; pre-doctoral intern Naval Regional Med. Ctr., San Diego, 1975-76, postdoctoral intern, 1975-76, chief, founder pain clinic, 1977-86; chief pain clinic, 1977-86; adj. tchr. U. Calif. Med. Sch., San Diego; lectr., U.S., Can., Eng., France, Australia; cons. forensic hypnosis to law enforcement agys.; approved cons. in hypnosis. Contbr. articles to profl. publs., chpt. to book. Tchr. Sunday sch. United Meth. Ch., 1945—; Rep. Nat. Candidate Trust Presdl. adv. com., platform planning commn. at-large-del. Fellow Am. Soc. Clin. Hypnosis (psychology mem.-at-large, exec. bd. 1989-90), San Diego Soc. Clin. Hypnosis (pres. 1980); mem. AAUW, Am. Phys. Therapy Assn., Calif. Soc. Clin. and Hypnosis (bd. govs.), Am. Soc. Clin. Hypnosis Edn. Rsch. Found. (trustee 1992-94), Internat. Platform Assn., Am. Soc. Clin. Hypnosis (exec. bd.), Ret. Officers Am., Ret. Officers Assn. (rep. presdl. task force, pres. adv. com.), Toastmasters (local pres.), Job's Daus. Republican. Home and Office: 1062 W Fifth Ave Escondido CA 92025-3802 *A purpose in life is essential to happiness. Success is a matter of making the most of the talents we are given, not receiving greater talents. Time is the most important gift. We can ill afford to waste it or wish it away. All accomplishment is meaningless unless one walks in harmony and fellowship with her maker and her fellow human beings. I am grateful to my parents and teachers for their examples and for providing me the opportunity for self-actualization.*

DAMSKY, ROBERT PHILIP, communications executive; b. Boston, May 19, 1921; s. Mark and Ann (Wisser) D.; m. Rose Hollender, Jan. 18, 1955 (div. 1985); children: Marla Markley, Lori Diana. Cert., MIT, 1939, Tex. A&M U., 1944; diploma, Spartan Sch. Aero., Tulsa, 1946. Indsl. editor Spartan Aircraft Co., Tulsa, 1946-47; with Transocean Airlines, Hartford, Conn., 1947; chief pilot MIT, Beverly, Mass., 1947-48; sr. check pilot Civil Air Patrol, Beverly, 1948; airport mgr. Hartport, Inc., Bellfontaine, Ohio, 1948-49; airline pilot Slick Airlines and U.S. Overseas Airlines, Burbank, Calif. and Wildwood, N.J., 1949-55; founder Flight Edn. Assn., Santa Ana, Calif., 1955-80; pub., editor, pres. Aeromedia Nat. Syndicate, L.A., 1980—. Aviation editor: Beverly News, Mass., Gen. Aviation News. With U.S. Army Air Corps, 1940-45. Decorated Purple Heart, 1941. Mem. Airline Pilots Assn., Aircraft Owners and Pilots Assn., Silver Wings, VFW, Am. Legion, Pearl Harbor Survivors Assn. Home: PO Box 2704 Costa Mesa CA 92628-2704

DAN, BARBARA GRIFFIN, publisher, editor, author; b. Glen Ridge, N.J., Apr. 10, 1934; d. Frank L. Jr. and Marjorie McDougal Griffin; m. John Dan, May 9, 1959; children: Georgia Lee, Carrie Joyce, Michael Casey, Peter John. BA in Theatre Arts, Thomas A. Edison State Coll., Trenton, N.J., 1986; MA in Humanities, Calif. State U-Dominguez Hills, 1988. Cert. couples comms. workshop instr. Editor LionHearted Pub., Zephyr Cove, Nev., 1993-94; pub., owner Eden Pub., Newberg, Oreg., 1994—; adj. prof. George Fox U., fall 1996. Author 9 novels, (nonfiction) Survival Strategies for the Holidays, 1995; co-author: Power to Choose, 1995; writer for numerous orgns., TV prodn. co., mags., others; author articles, adventure and children's fiction. Co-founder Las Vegas Writers Workshop, 1993. Mem. Silver State Fiction Writers (chmn. Las Vegas chpt. 1992-93), Romance Writers Am. Republican. Christian. Office: 815 1/2 N Center St Newberg OR 97132

DANA, GEORGE FREDERICK (PETE DANA), consulting geologist; b. Waynesboro, Va., Oct. 23, 1929; s. George William and Madalyn (Hollar) D.; m. Phyllis Whitford, Aug. 15, 1949 (div. Sept. 1959); children: George, Debra, Sandra; m. Joan Nelson, Aug. 13, 1960; children: Donald, Karin. BS, U. Okla., 1952, MS, 1954. Registered profl. geologist, Wyo. Geologist Marathon Oil Co., Cody, Wyo., 1954-59, Husky Oil Co., Cody, 1959-60; chief ground water devel. State of Wyo.-Natural Resources Bd., Cheyenne, Wyo., 1960-63; geologist U. Wyo.-Nat. Resources Rsch. Inst., Laramie, Wyo., 1963-65; rsch. geologist U.S. Bur. Mines, Laramie, 1965-74, sr. geologist, 1974-79; mgr. geology and geochemistry US DOE-Laramie (Wyo.) Rsch. Ctr., 1979-83, Western Rsch. Inst., Laramie, 1983-85; pres., owner Dana Cons., Laramie, 1985—. Contbr. articles to profl. jours. Mem. Am. Assn. Petroleum Geologists (asst. oil shale councillor 1975-85), Elks. Lutheran. Home and Office: 2539 Overland Rd Laramie WY 82070-4855

DANA, HUGH RICHARD, internist, educator; b. Balt., May 28, 1950; s. Edward Runkle and Lilian Lorraine (Kirschner) D. BS, U. N.C., 1973; MD, U. So. Calif., 1978. Diplomate Am. Bd. Internal Medicine. Intern in medicine St. Mary's Hosp.-UCLA, Long Beach, 1978-79; rsch. in hematology Mayo Clinic, Rochester, Minn., 1979-80; resident in internal medicine U. Calif.-Irvine program VA Hosp., Long Beach, 1980-82, physician ambulatory care clinic, 1983-89; staff physician Kaiser Permanente, Bellflower, Calif., 1989-91, Family Health Plan Inc., Long Beach, Calif., 1991—; asst. clin. prof. U. Calif.-Irvine Sch. Medicine, Orange, 1989—. Mem. ACP, AMA. Home and Office: PO Box 1267 Placentia CA 92871

DANCE, FRANCIS ESBURN XAVIER, communication educator; b. Bklyn., Nov. 9, 1929; s. Clifton Louis and Catherine (Tester) D.; m. Nora Alice Rush, May 1, 1954 (div. 1974); children: Clifton Louis III, Charles Daniel, Alison Catherine, Andrea Frances, Frances Sue, Brendan Rush; m. Carol Camille Zak, July 4, 1974; children: Zachary Esburn, Gabriel Joseph, Caleb Michael, Catherine Emily. BS, Fordham U., 1951; MA, Northwestern U., 1953, PhD, 1959. Instr. speech Bklyn. Adult Labor Schs., 1951; instr. humanities, coordinator radio and TV U. Ill. at Chgo., 1953-54; instr. Univ. Coll., U. Chgo., 1958; asst. prof. St. Joseph's (Ind.) Coll., 1958-60; asst. prof., then assoc. prof. U. Kans., 1960-63; mem. faculty U. Wis., Milw., 1963-71, prof. communication, 1965-71, dir. Speech Communication Center, 1963-70; prof. U. Denver, 1971—, John Evans prof., 1995—; content expert and mem. faculty adv. bd. to Internat. U. on Knowledge Channel, 1993-95; cons. in field. Author: The Citizen Speaks, 1962, (with Harold P. Zelko) Business and Professional Speech Communication, 1965, 2d edit., 1978, Human Communication Theory, 1967, (with Carl E. Larson) Perspectives on Communication, 1970, Speech Communication: Concepts and Behavior, 1972, The Functions of Speech Communication: A Theoretical Approach, 1976, Human Communication Theory, 1982, (with Carol C. Zak-Dance) Public Speaking, 1986, Speaking Your Mind, 1994, 2d edit., 1996; editor Jour. Comm., 1962-64, Speech Tchr., 1970-72; adv. bd. Jour. Black Studies; editl. bd. Jour. Psycholinguistic Rsch; contbr. articles to profl. jours. Bd. dirs. Milw. Mental Health Assn., 1966-67. 2d lt. AUS, 1954-56. Knapp Univ. scholar in communication, 1967-68; recipient Outstanding Prof. award Standard Oil Found., 1967; Master Tchr. award U. Denver, 1985, University Lectr. award U. Denver, 1986. Fellow Internat. Communication Assn. (pres. 1967); mem. Speech Communication Assn. (pres. 1982), Psi Upsilon. Office: U Denver Dept Human Comm Studies Denver CO 80208 *Life should include a personal commitment to excellence with a corresponding humane tolerance for failure in self or in others. A belief in the progressive acquisition of autonomy can help guide both personal and professional decisions.*

DANCIGER, MATTHEW ALLEN, producer; b. Ft. Worth, Sept. 24, 1967; s. David Kendal and Emma Anne Alvis. BA, Occidental Coll., 1989; BFA, Art Ctr. Coll. Design, 1992. Pres., ceo Panoptikon, Inc., L.A., 1987-91, Loki Prodns., Venice, Calif., 1991—; prodr. Candlelight Enterprise, Pasadena, Calif., 1993-94, Purse Prodns., L.A., 1995-96; cinematographer 20th Century Fox, Culver City, Calif., 1996. Writer, dir.: (film) Incarnation, 1991, (film) Outside, 1993 (Acad. award Dir.'s Guild Student award 1993). Recipient: Student Acad. award Acad. Motion Pictures Arts and Scis., 1993, Spl. Jury award Houston World Fest, 1993. Mem. Independent Feature Project/W. Office: Loki Prodns Inc 822 Hampton Dr Venice CA 90291-3021

DANDASHI, FAYAD ALEXANDER, operations research scientist; b. Damascus, July 20, 1959; came to U.S., 1982; naturalized, 1989; s. A.K. and Ghada (Bahnasi) D.; m. Mami Tazaki, Apr. 12, 1989. BArch, U. Aleppo, 1982; BSCE, George Washington U., 1987, Applied Scientist in Gen. Ops. Rsch., 1992; MSME in Aeronautics, Astronautics and Rocket Propulsion, George Washington U. & NASA, 1989; MSc in Math., Oxford (Eng.) U., 1994. Designer, design div. George Washington U., Washington, 1985-89, head design div., 1989-91, doctoral fellow, 1992-93, applied scientist, sci. rsch. assoc., 1992-93; dir., pres., CEO, sec. FANEX USA, Inc., Irvine, Calif., 1995—; dir., pres., CEO FANEX Internat. Coll., Irvine, 1995—; dir., vice chmn., pres., CEO FANEX Australia Pty. Ltd., Brisbane, 1995—; dir., pres., CEO Internat. Coll. Queensland, Australia, 1995—; vis. scientist, rsch. scholar Kyoto (Japan) U., 1996-97. Mem. AAAS, AIAA (sr. mem.), Ops. Rsch. Soc. Am., Inst. Mgmt. Sci., Fedn. Am. Scientists, Omega Rho (v.p. 1993-94), Sigma Gamma Tau, Sigma Xi. Home: 48 W 68th St Apt 4A New York NY 10023-6015 Office: FANEX USA Inc 4255 Campus Dr Ste A255 Irvine CA 92612-2620 also: FANEX Australia Pty Ltd, 455 Upper Edward St Level 3, Spring Hill Brisbane QLD 4004, Australia

DANG, MARVIN S. C., lawyer; b. Honolulu, Feb. 11, 1954; s. Brian K.T. and Flora (Yuen) D. BA with distinction, U. Hawaii, 1974; JD, George Washington U., 1978. Bar: Hawaii 1978, U.S. Dist. Ct. Hawaii 1978, U.S. Ct. Appeals (9th cir.) 1979. Atty. Gerson, Steiner & Anderson and predecessor firms, Honolulu, 1978-81; owner, atty. Law Offices of Marvin S.C. Dang, Honolulu, 1981—; sr. v.p., bd. dirs. Rainbow Fin. Corp., Honolulu, 1984-95; bd. dirs. Foster Equipment Co. Ltd., Honolulu, Hawaii Cmty. Reinvestment Corp.; bd. dirs. Hawaii Fin. Svcs. Assn., sec., 1991, treas., 1992, v.p., 1993, pres. 1994; vice chmn. Hawaii Consumer Fin. Polit. Action Com., 1988-95; hearings officer (per diem) Adminstrv. Drivers License Revocation Office, Honolulu, 1991-95. State rep., asst. minority floor leader Hawaii State Legislature, Honolulu, 1982-84; chmn., vice chmn., mem. Manoa Neighborhood Bd., Honolulu, 1979-82, 84-87; pres., v.p., mem. Hawaii Coun. on Legal Edn. for Youth, Honolulu, 1979-86; mem. Hawaii Bicentennial Commn. of U.S. Constn., Honolulu, 1986-88;. Recipient Cert. of Appreciation award Hawaii Speech-Lang.-Hearing Assn., Honolulu, 1984; named one of Ten Outstanding Young Persons of Hawaii, Hawaii State Jaycees, 1983. Mem. ABA (coun. of fund for justice and edn. 1993—, standing com. on law and electoral process 1985-89, spl. com. on youth edn. for citizenship 1979-85, 89-92, Hawaii membership chmn. 1981-93, exec. coun. young lawyers divsn. 1986-88), Hawaii State Bar Assn. (bd. dirs. young lawyers divsn. 1990), Plaza Club Hawaii. Republican. Office: PO Box 4109 Honolulu HI 96812-4109

D'ANGELO, VICTORIA SCOTT, entrepreneur, writer; b. Phila., June 5, 1964; d. George Anthony and Antonia (Billett) D'A. BA, U. Va., 1981; MBA, Columbia U., 1986. Cert. attendance Sorbonne/Sorbonne Nouvelle, Paris, 1980, Inst. Scis. Politiques, Paris, 1980, Brit. Am. Acting Acad., London, N.Y.C., 1982. Fin. cons., broker deals, cons. on bus. negotiations healthcare project Victory Angel Enterprises, Santa Monica, Calif., 1987—, CEO, 1990—; exec. v.p. Northeastern U.S. Acad. Gymnastics, Northampton, N.H., 1995—. Dir. (documentary) Leslie Clark—Nomad Painter, 1995; prodr., actor (TV situation comedies) Dinette, 1996, The Crasher, 1996. Vol. Permanent Charities Com., Hollywood Women's Polit. Com.; fundraiser Breast Cancer Rsch. Mem. Am. Film Inst. (3d decade coun.), Hollywood Radio and TV Soc., U.S. Field Hockey Assn. (videographer), Athenaeum. Episcopalian. Home: PO Box 5132 Santa Monica CA 90409-5132

DANIEL, BARBARA ANN, elementary and secondary education educator; b. LaCrosse, Wis., Mar. 22, 1938; d. Rudolph J. and Dorothy M. (Farnham) Beranek; m. David Daniel; children: Raychelle, Clarence, Bernadette, Brenda. BS in Edn. cum laude, Midwestern U., Wichita Falls, Tex., 1967; postgrad., U. Alaska, Fairbanks, Anchorage, Juneau, U. Alaska, Bethel. Cert. tchr., Alaska. Primary tchr. Bur. Indian Affairs, Nunapitchuk and Tuntutuliak, Alaska, 1967-70; tchr., generalist, English, reading, english lang. devel. grades 6-12 Lower Kuskokwim Sch. Dist., Tuntutuliak, 1981—; English language leader grades k-12 Lower Kuskokwim Sch. Dist., Tuntutuliak, 1981—; mem. lang. arts curriculum revision task force Lower Kuskokwim Sch. Dist., 1990; mem. state bd. Academic Pentathlon, Alaska; acad. decathlon, pentathlon coach, 1980's. Rsch. video recording of elders in Alaskan village. Mem. NEA, Lower Kuskokwim Edn. Assn., Alaska Coun. Tchrs. English, Alaska Assn. Bilingual Assn. Home: 25 West Circle PO Box WTL Tuntutuliak AK 99680-9998

DANIEL, GARY WAYNE, communications and music industry executive; b. Wendall, Idaho, June 22, 1948; s. Milan Chauncey Daniel and Ila Fay (Cox) Harkins; m. Jeanne Laurane Blandford, July 1969 (div. Aug. 1972); 1 child, Kelly Jean; m. Sandra Kay Modey, July 26, 1974; 1 child, Marcus Chauncey. AA, Boise Bus. Coll., 1969; PhD in Psychology, West Brook U., 1994. Cert. master practitioner Neuro Linguistic Programming. Program dir. Sta. KSKI, Sun Valley, Idaho, 1967-68, Sta. KYME, Boise, Idaho, 1968-69; gen. mgr. Sta. KSPD, Boise, 1969-72; radio personality Sta. KBBK-FM, Boise, 1972-74; account exec. ABC-TV, Nampa, Idaho, 1974-77; nat. sales dir. Agri-Steel Corp., Boise, 1977-79; mgmt. ptnr. Agri. Devel. Corp., Caldwell, Idaho, 1979-82; owner, prin. Video Magic Amusement Co., Caldwell, 1982-85; pres., chief exec. officer Victory Media Group, Santa Rosa, Calif., 1985—; gen. mgr. Victory Record Label, 1986—, also bd. dirs.; bd. dirs. Bay City Records, San Francisco; pres. Lightforce Music Pub., Santa Rosa, 1987—; mktg. cons. Firenze Records, San Francisco, 1987—,

Capital Bus. Systems, Napa, Calif., 1986-91, Plum, Inc., Napa, 1985-86. Author: Concert Operations Manual, 1987; devel. of the Neuro Achievement System. Recipient Most Humorous TV Comml. award Boise Advt. Club, 1975, Most Creative TV Comml. award Boise Advt. Club, 1976; named Top Radio Personality Idaho State Broadcasters Assn., 1971. Mem. ASCAP, NARAS, Ind. Record Mfrs. and Distbrs., Am. Coun. Hypnotist Examiners, Hypnotist Examiners Coun. Calif., Am. Assn. Behavioral Therapists, Internat. Assn. Neuro Linguistic Programming, Time Line Therapy Assn. Office: Neuro Achievement Ctr 55 Maria Dr Ste 844 Petaluma CA 94954-3563

DANIEL, HELEN ANDERSON, secondary education educator, psychotherapist, intern; b. San Francisco, Aug. 16, 1941; d. Wallace Robert and Etta Mignon (Stanton) Anderson; m. Bernard Bell Thornquist, Aug. 29, 1960 (div. Dec. 1972); children: Ingrid Anne, Carl Robert; m. Douglas Walker Daniel, Dec. 26, 1985; stepchildren: Jennifer Lynn, Laura Lee. BA, San Jose State Coll., 1963; MA, John F. Kennedy U., 1992. Std. secondary tchg. credential. Tchr. DeAnza H.S., El Sobrante, Calif., 1964-65, Fredriksen Sch., Dublin, Calif., 1966-67, Fresno (Calif.) County Youth Authority, 1972; tchr. Livermore (Calif.) H.S., 1972—, chair English dept., 1976-82, 88—; therapist Valley Cmty. Health Ctr., Pleasanton, Calif., 1994—; com. mem. Dist. Curriculum Devel. Com., Livermore, 1988-90, Dist. Tech. Com., Livermore, 1990-92, Gifted and Talented Com., Livermore, 1990-92, Dist. Mentor Selection Com., 1994—, Dist. Student Support Svcs. for Gay, Lesbian and Bisexual Students, 1996—; mentor tchr., Livermore H.S., 1986, 87, 92, 93. Author: (booklet) Star Writer: The Empowered Student, 1992. Tech. grantee State of Calif., 1992, libr. grantee, 1995. Home: 1950 Neptune Rd Livermore CA 94550-6322 Office: Livermore HS 600 Maple St Livermore CA 94550-3242

DANIEL, RAMON, JR., psychologist, consultant, bilingual educator; b. Phoenix, Oct. 30, 1936; s. Ramon Sr. and Rosario (Lopez) D.; m. Lydia Cadriel, June 4, 1960; children: Lynda Ruth, Michael Ray, Patricia Lynn. BA in Edn., Ariz. State U., 1964, MA in Edn., 1966; PhD, U.S. Internat. U., 1990. Lic. psychologist, Calif.; cert. bilingual and math. tchr., Calif. Tchr. Phoenix Sch. Dist., 1964, Garden Grove (Calif.) Unified Sch. Dist., 1964-75, Cypress (Calif.) Coll., 1975-77; psychologist Santa Ana (Calif.) Unified Sch. Dist., 1978—; dropout prevention program specialist, student success teams coord. Santa Ana Unified Sch. Dist.; mem. adj. faculty Nat. U., Irvine, Calif., 1991—; with Mexican Consulate, Orange County (Calif.) Office Ednl. Affairs, 1991. Columnist (newspapers) La Conexion Humana, 1988. Mem. Least Restrictive Edn. Task Force, Santa Ana, 1990, Task Force on Linguistic and Cultural Differences, Santa Ana, 1990-91, Community Svc. Bd., Anaheim, Calif., 1990—. Mem. Calif. Assn. Sch. Psychologists, Coun. for Exceptional Children, Assn. Mex.-Am. Educators, Phi Delta Kappa (pres. Calif. chpt. 1988-89, 96—, Svc. Key 1989). Office: Santa Ana Unified Sch Dist 1601 E Chestnut Ave Santa Ana CA 92701-6322

DANIEL, WILEY Y., lawyer; b. Louisville, Sept. 10, 1946; m. Ida S. Daniel; children: Jennifer, Stephanie, Nicole. BA in History, Howard U., JD. Atty. Gorsuch, Kirgis, Campbell, Walker & Grover, Denver; shareholder Popham, Haik, Schnobrich & Kaufman Ltd., Denver. Trustee Iliff Sch. Theology, Denver. Mem. Colo. Bar Assn. (pres. 1992-93), Denver Bar Assn., State Bd. Architecture. Democrat. Office: US District Court of Colorado Byron White US Courthouse 1929 Stout St Denver CO 80294*

DANIELS, C. EUGENE, owner executive search company; b. Fordyce, Ark., Aug. 28, 1943; s. H. C. and Annie (Shook) D.; m. Peggy Sue Pitchford, Aug. 26, 1962; children: Janet Lynn, Troy Eugene, Greg Alan. BS, U. Ark., 1965. Mgr. human resources Gen. Foods Corp., various cities, 1967-81; v.p. human resources Leprino Foods Co., Denver, 1981-84; sr. v.p. adminstrn. Oxford Devel. Group, Toronto, Ont., Can., 1984-86; v.p. human resources and adminstrn. Apache Corp., Denver, 1987-91; dir. human resources Western Gas Resources, Inc., Denver, 1992-93; owner Sigma Group Internat., Denver, 1993—. Office: Sigma Group Internat 6551 S Revue Pky Englewood CO 80111

DANIELS, FREDERICK THOMAS, reactor engineer; b. Ontario, Oreg., Sept. 7, 1947; s. Frederick Aaron Daniels and Maxine Virginia (Harris) Marrs; m. Judy Rose Kajmowicz, Oct. 7, 1979; children: Tami Ann, Thomas Aaron, Tara Ashley. AA, Olympic Coll., 1975; BA, Western Ill. U., 1983; MS in Energy Econs., Websters U., 1986. Cert. naval nuclear engr., internat. safeguards insp. Enlisted USN, 1965, advanced through grades; ret. Gen. Physics/Engring. Diverse Svcs. Nuclear, 1977; cons. Gen. Physics/EDS Nuclear, 1977-78; sr. resident insp. U.S. Nuclear Regulatory Commn., Chgo., 1978-82; safeguards insp. IAEA, Vienna, Austria, 1982-89; sr. reactor engr., team leader U.S. Nuclear Regulatory Commn., Washington, 1989-91; dir. Dept. Energy, Washington, 1991-94, Richland, Wash., 1994—; mem. affirmative action adv. com. bd. U.S. Nuclear Regulatory Commn., Washington, 1990-91; vice chmn. staff coun. IAEA, Vienna, Austria, 1985. Author: Safeguard Practices for Research Reactors, 1987, Safeguard Practices for Critical Assemblies, 1987. Asst. dist. commr. Boy Scouts Am., Balt., 1990-94. Mem. Am. Nuclear Soc. (founder Austria local sect., pres. 1985-86, cert. of governance 1985, exec. bd. 1985-88), Am. Legion (activities chmn. 1981), Elks (outer guard 1974, 75, nat. patron 1989). Republican. Mem. LDS Ch. Home: 1111 Country Ridge Dr Richland WA 99352-9546

DANIELS, JAMES ARTHUR, electronics sales company executive; b. Indpls., Feb. 1, 1937; s. Arthur Weldon and Helen Marie (Collins) D.; m. Beverly Ann Monfreda, Aug. 25, 1956; children: Kristina, Rebecca, Kevin, Caroline, Bryan, Bret, Susan, Erica. AB in Sociology, U. Notre Dame, 1958; MBA, U. So. Calif., 1966. Engr. Ralph M. Parsons, Pasadena, Calif., 1960-61; sales engr. Dressen Barnes, Pasadena, Calif., 1961-64; sales mgr. Burton Mfg., Van Nuys, Calif., 1964-66; productmgr. Leach Relay, L.A., 1966-67; sales mgr. Bourns Trimpot Products, Riverside, Calif., 1967-74; pres. J.A. Daniels Assocs., Solana Beach, Calif., 1974—; bd. dirs. San Diego Elec. Shows & Meeting Inc., 1985-94. Mem. Elec. Rep. Assn. (pres. 1974, 75, dir. 1981-84, white pin 1983), Elec. VIPs. Roman Catholic. Home: 662 Nardo Ave Solana Beach CA 92075-2308 Office: JA Daniels Assocs PO Box 1311 Solana Beach CA 92075-7311

DANIELS, LORI S., state legislator, insurance agent; b. Burlingame, Calif., Nov. 5, 1955; d. Robert William and Sue Ann (McCowen) McCroskey; m. Stephen L. Daniels, June 19, 1976 (div. June 1980). Student, Ariz. State U., 1973-76; BA in Mgmt., U. Phoenix, 1994. CLU. Trainer Campus Crusade for Christ, San Bernadino, Calif., 1977-79; with instalment loans dept. Ariz. Bank, Mesu, 1979-80; ins. agt. State Farm Ins., Chandler, Ariz., 1980—; mem. Ariz. Ho. Reps., 1992—, majority leader 6yh dist., 1997—; bus. cons. Jr. Achievement, Mesu, 1987-92; mem. various com. including ways and means, rules, 1997—. V.p. Valley of Sun United Way, Phoenix, 1991-93, chmn. Chandler Area Reg. Coun., 1991-92. Recipient Small Bus. Person of Yr. award Gilbert C. of C., 1989. Mem. Chandler C. of C. (v.p. cmty. devel. 1991-92, v.p. membership svc., 1992-93, Pres.'s award 1990, Chamber cup 1992). Republican. Home: 941 W Detroit St Chandler AZ 85224-4453 Office: 1700 W Washington Rm 110 Phoenix AZ 85007

DANIELS, LYDIA M., health care administrator; b. Louisville, Dec. 21, 1932; d. Effort and Gladys T. (Turner) Williams; student Calif. State U., Hayward, 1967, 69-72; BA, Golden Gate U., 1992, MS, 1993; cert. Samuel Merritt Hosp. Sch. Med. Record Adminstrs., 1959; student Cen. State Coll., Ohio, 1950-52; children by previous marriage: Danny Winston, Jeffrey Bruce, Anthony Wayne. Sec. chemistry dept. Cen. State Coll., Wilberforce, Ohio, 1950-52; co-dir. Indian Workcamp, Pala Indian Reservation, Pala, Calif., 1956-58; clk.-typist Camarillo (Calif.) State Hosp., 1956-58; student med. record adminstr. Samuel Merritt Hosp., Oakland, Calif., 1958-59, asst. med. record adminstr., 1962-63, asst. chief med. record adminstr., 1965, chief med. record adminstr., 1965-72; med. record adminstr. Albany (Calif.) Hosp., 1964-65; asst. med. record adminstr. Children's Hosp., San Francisco, 1960; co-dir. interns in community svc. Am. Friends Svc. Com., San Francisco, 1960-61; med. record adminstr. Pacific Hosp., Oakland, Calif., 1963-64; med. record cons. Tahoe Forest Hosp., Truckee, Calif., 1969-73; chief med. record adminstr. Highland Gen. Hosp., Oakland, 1972-74; dir. med. record svcs. U. Calif. San Francisco Hosps. and Clinics, 1975-82; mgr. patient appointments, reception and registration Kaiser-Permanente Med. Ctr., 1982-88; dir. ambulatory adminstrv. svcs., 1988-94, asst. dir. human resources, 1994-96, dir. human resources Brookside Hosp., San Pablo, Calif., 1996—; adj. prof. mgmt., labor mgmt. rels. Golden Gate U., 1978—; pres. Daniels Consultation Svcs., 1988—. Leader Girl Scouts Am. Oakland area council, 1960-62; sunday sch. tchr. Soc. of Friends, Berkeley, Calif., 1961-63, mem. edn. com., 1965-68; mem. policy and adv. bd. Far West Lab. Demonstration Sch., Oakland, 1973-75; bd. dirs. The Californians, Oakland, 1993—, Patrons of the Arts and Humanities, Oakland, 1994—, YWCA, Berkeley, 1995—. Recipient Mgmt. Fellowship award U. Calif., San Francisco, 1979-80. Mem. Am. Med. Record Assn., Calif. Med. Record Assn. (editorial bd. 1976-77, pres. 1974-75), East Bay Med. Record Assn. (chmn. edn. com. 1971-72, pres. 1969-70), Assn. Systems Mgmt., Am. Mgmt. Assn., San Francisco Med. Records Assn. (pres.-elect 1982-83, pres. 1983-84), Am. Assn. Tng. and Devel. (Golden Gate chpt., v.p. prof. devel. 1994—). Author: Health Record Documentation: A Look at Cost, 1981; Inservice Training as a Tool in Managing the Changing Environment in the Medical Record Department, 1983; the Budget as a Management Tool, 1983. Issues editor Topics in Health Record Management, Parts I and II, 1983. Home: 545 Pierce St Apt 1105 Albany CA 94706-1048 Office: Brookside Hosp 2000 Vale Rd San Pablo CA 94806-3808

DANIELS, MARK CORNWALL, sales executive; b. Salt Lake City, Oct. 29, 1952; s. Courtney Robert and Marian Fay (Bolin) D.; m. Sabrina Marie Boyter, Aug. 29, 1975; children: Melissa Dawn, Jared Mark, Michael David. BS in Bus. Mgmt., U. Utah, 1977. Asst. contr. Samons Home Improvement, North Salt Lake, Utah, 1977-79; cash control acct. N.W. Pipeline Corp., Salt Lake City, 1979-81; sales rep. Interstate Brick Co., Salt Lake City, 1981-88, Buehner Block Co., Salt Lake City, 1989—. Mem. Salt Lake Home Builders Assn. (sec.-treas. 1995-96, assoc. v.p. 1996—), Products Coun. Mem. LDS Ch. Office: Buehner Block Co 2800 S West Temple Salt Lake City UT 84115

DANIELS, PHILIP BLISS, psychology educator; b. Annabella, Utah, Nov. 9, 1928; s. William Bliss and Lavern (Hawley) D.; m. Patsy Unger, July 3, 1951; children: Matt, Darsi, Jamie, Drew, Patrick. BS, Brigham Young U., 1954, MS, 1957; PhD, Harvard U., 1962. Prof. Brigham Young U., Provo, Utah, 1961-92; assoc. Nat. Tng. Lab., Washington, 1965-75; CEO Behavioral Sci. Resources, Provo, 1972-95; cons. pvt. practice, Provo, 1965—. Co-author: manual Management Profiling, 1975, 4 mgmt. profiling instruments, 1972, 1981, 1985, 1986. Capt. USAF, 1954-56. Recipient rsch. grant U.S. Office of Edn., 1964. Mormon. Home: 1814 N 1500 E Provo UT 84604-5750 Office: BSR PO Box 411 Provo UT 84603-0411

DANIELS, RICHARD MARTIN, public relations executive; b. Delano, Calif., Feb. 24, 1942; s. Edward Martin and Philida Rose (Peterson) D.; m. Kathryn Ellen Knight, Feb. 28, 1976; children: Robert Martin, Michael Edward. A.A., Foothill Coll., 1965; B.A., San Jose State U., 1967; M.A., U. Mo., 1971. News reporter Imperial Valley Press, El Centro, Calif., summers 1963-66, San Diego (Calif.) Evening Tribune, 1967-68, Columbia Daily Tribune (Mo.), 1969-70; nat. news copy editor Los Angeles Times, 1966-67; staff writer San Diego Union, 1971-74, real estate editor, 1974-77; v.p. pub. relations Hubbert Advt. & Pub. Relations, Costa Mesa, Calif., 1977-78; ptnr. Berkman & Daniels, San Diego, 1979-91; prin. Nuffer, Smith, Tucker, Inc., 1991-94; prin. RMD Communications, 1994—; lectr. various bus. groups and colls. Chmn. bd. dirs. March of Dimes San Diego County, 1984-87, bd. dirs. Nat. Coun. Vols., 1983—. Served with USN, 1959-62. Mem. Pub. Rels. Soc. Am., Counselors Acad. (accredited). Republican. Office: 2261 Ritter Pl Escondido CA 92029-5608

DANIELS, RONALD DALE, conductor; b. San Mateo, Calif., Aug. 19, 1943; s. Worth W. and Margurite Pearl (Chandler) D.; m. Judith Monson, July 24, 1993; 1 child, Ryan Stark. BMus, San Francisco Conservatory, 1968. Conductor, music dir. Musical Arts of Contra Costa (Calif.) County, 1968-75, U. Calif., Berkeley, 19173-75, Contra Costa Symphony, 1976-79, Reno (Nev.) Philharm., 1979—; guest conductor various orchs.; grants rev. cons. in field. With USMC, 1966. Recipient Lucien Wulsin award Baldwin Piano Co., Tanglewood Festival, 1968, Gov.'s Art award State of Nev., 1981. Office: Reno Philharm Assn 300 S Wells Ave Ste 5 Reno NV 89402

DANIELSON, CRAIG, wholesale grocery corporation executive. Chmn. United Grocers Inc., Portland, Oreg. Office: United Grocers Inc PO Box 5490 Oregon City OR 97045-8497*

DANIELSON, GORDON DOUGLAS, dentist; b. Everett, Wash., Nov. 11, 1942; s. Marvin and Elanor (Weers) D.; m. Jamie Lynn Waters, Jan. 9, 1977. BS with honors, U. Oreg., 1968; postgrad., MIT, 1968-69; MA in Molecular Biology, U. Calif., 1974, BS in Med. Sci., DDS, 1975. DDS. Pvt. practice Larkspur, Calif., 1975—; exec. v.p. Atmospheric Rsch. Tech., Sacramento, Calif., 1984-85; cons. Freeport Fin. Svcs., Denver, 1985-87; pres. Lynmar Enterprises Inc., Rno, 1987—; bd. dirs. Freeport Venture Fund. MIT fellow, 1968-69; U. Calif., Berkeley fellow, 1969-71; U. Calif., San Francisco fellow, 1973-75, pres. fellow, 1973-75. Mem. U. Calif. Dental Alumni Assn., U. Oreg. Alumni Assn., Marin County Dental Soc. (chmn. emergency care 1975-81), St. Francis Yacht Club (mem. com. 1973—), Aircraft Owners and Pilots Assn., Omicron Kappa Upsilon. Republican. Office: 5 Bon Air Rd Ste 114 Larkspur CA 94939-1127

DANIHER, JOHN M., retired engineer; b. LaJunta, Colo., Aug. 2, 1926; s. Gerald and Mary Isabelle (Manly) D.; m. Edna Erle Hoshall, Sept. 4, 1948; children: Lyn Mari, Suzanne Laurie, Patricia Gail, Jerome Matthew, Michael Kevin. AB, Western State Coll., Gunnison, Colo., 1948; postgrad. Idaho State U., 1957-74, U. Idaho, 1974-76. High sch. tchr., Grand Junction, Colo., 1948-52; salesman Century Metalcraft, Denver, 1952-53; chem. plant supr. U.S. Chem. Corps., Denver, 1953-56; sr. engr. instrument and controls Phillips Petroleum Co., Idaho Falls, 1956-76; project engr. E G & G Idaho, Idaho Falls, 1976-85, engring. specialist, 1985-91; adv. Eastern Idaho Vocat. Tech. Sch., 1975-80. Cubmaster, Boy Scouts Am., 1970-75, asst. scoutmaster, 1975-80; v.p. Bonneville Unit Am. Cancer Soc., 1994, pres., v.p., 1995—. Recipient Cub Man of Yr., Boy Scouts Am., 1973. Mem. Am. Nuclear Soc. Roman Catholic. Club: K.C. (state dep. 1979-81, Supreme council 1979-84, 94) Home: 250 12th St Idaho Falls ID 83404-5370

DANILOV, VICTOR JOSEPH, museum management program director, consultant, writer, educator; b. Farrell, Pa., Dec. 30, 1924; s. Joseph M. and Ella (Tominovich) D.; m. Toni Dewey, Sept. 6, 1980; children: Thomas J., Duane P., Denise S. BA in Journalism, Pa. State U., 1945; MS in Journalism, Northwestern U., 1946; EdD in Higher Edn., U. Colo., 1964. With Sharon Herald, Pa., 1942, Youngstown Vindicator, 1945, Pitts. Sun-Telegraph, 1946-47, Chgo. Daily News, 1947-50; instr. journalism U. Colo., 1950-51; asst. prof. journalism U. Kans., 1951-53; with Kansas City Star, 1953; mgr. pub. relations Ill. Inst. Tech. and IIT Research Inst., 1953-57; dir. univ. relations and pub. info. U. Colo., 1957-60; pres. Profile Co., Boulder, Colo., 1960-62; exec. editor, exec. v.p. Indsl. Research Inc., Beverly Shores, Ind., 1962-69; pub., exec. v.p. Indsl. Research Inc., 1969-71; dir., v.p. Mus. Sci. and Industry, Chgo., 1971-77; pres., dir. Mus. Sci. and Industry, 1978-87, pres. emeritus, 1987—; dir. mus. mgmt. program, adj. prof. U. Colo., 1987—; mem. rural industrialization adv. group Dept. Agr., 1967; mem. panel internat. transfer tech. Dept. Commerce, 1968; mem. sci. info. coun. NSF, 1969-72; chmn. Conf. on Implications Metric Change, 1972, Nat. Conf. Indsl. Rsch., 1966-70; chmn. observance Nat. Indsl. Rsch. Week, 1967-70; chmn. Midwest White House Conf. on Indsl. World Ahead, 1972, Internat. Conf. Sci. and Tech. Museums, 1976, 82; mem. task force on fin. acctg. and reporting by non bus. orgns., others. Author: Public Affairs Reporting, 1955, Starting a Science Center, 1977, Science and Technology Centers, 1982, Science Center Planning Guide, 1985, Chicago's Museums, 1987, rev. edit., 1991, America's Science Museums, 1990, Corporate Museums, Galleries, and Visitor Centers: A Directory, 1991, A Planning Guide for Corporate Museums, Galleries, and Visitors Centers, 1992, Museum Careers and Training: A Professional Guide, 1994, University and College Museums, Galleries, and Related Facilities, 1996; also articles; editor: Crucial Issues in Public Relations, 1960, Corporate Research and Profitability, 1966, Innovation and Profitability, 1967, Research Decision-Making in New Product Development, 1968, New Products--and Profits, 1969, Applying Emerging Technologies, 1970, Nuclear Power in the South, 1970, The Future of Science and Technology, 1975, Museum Accounting Guidelines, 1976, Traveling Exhibitions, 1978, Towards the Year 2000, 1981; editor profl. procs. V.p., trustee Women of the West Mus., 1991—; trustee La Rabida Childrens Hosp. and Rsch. Ctr., 1973-83; mem. U. Chgo. Citizens Bd., 1978-87. Mem. Am. Assn. Mus. (exec. com. 1976-77, bd. dirs. 1985-88, chmn. mus. studies task force 1988-89), AAAS, Assn. Sci.-Tech. Ctrs. (bd. dirs. 1973-84, sec.-treas. 1973-74, pres. 1975-76), Internat. Coun. Mus. (com. on sci. and tech. mus. 1972—, vice chmn. 1977-87, chmn. 1982-83, bd. dirs. 1985-88), Chgo. Coun. on Fine Arts (chmn. 1976-84), Ill. Arts Alliance (bd. dirs. 1983-86), Sci. Mus. Exhibit Collaborative (pres. 1983-86), Mus. Film Network (pres. 1984-86). Home: 250 Bristlecone Way Boulder CO 80304-0413 Office: Univ Colo Mus Mus Mgmt Program Campus Box 218 Boulder CO 80309-0218

DANKO, GEORGE, engineering educator; b. Budapest, Hungary, Apr. 3, 1944; came to U.S., 1986; s. Gyorgy and Ilona (Mihaly) D.; m. Eva Arvay, Dec. 14, 1976; 1 child, Reka. BSME, Tech. U. Budapest, 1968, PhD, 1976; MS in Applied Math., Eotovs U. of Scis., Budapest, 1975; PhD, Hungarian Acad. Scis., Budapest, 1985. Cert. Profl. Ski Instrs. Am. Assn. Asst. prof. Tech. U. Budapest, 1968-75, assoc. prof., 1979-86; fellow Hungarian Acad. Scis., Budapest, 1975-79; rsch. assoc. U. Nev., Reno, 1986-90, assoc. prof., 1990-95, prof. mining engring., 1995—; cons. Sierra Sci., Reno, 1990—; chmn. High-Level Radioactive Waste Mgmt. Conf., 1991, 92; portrait painter, Reno, 1987-92. Co-author: Methods for the Calculation of Pipeline Transients, 1976, Warming-up and Cooling of Electrical Machinery, 1982; contbr. articles to profl. jours. Com. rep. Truckee River Steering Com., Reno, 1993-94. Grantee U.S. Bur. Mines, 1986-97, U.S. Dept. Energy, 1991—, Clarkson Co., 1992—. Mem. ASME, ISES (internat. organizing com. 1993-94), IFAC (internat. program com. 1995—), Soc. Mining Engrs., Am. Nuclear Soc. Office: U Nev Reno Mining Engring Dept/173 Reno NV 89557

DANNENBAUM, ROBERT MARCUS, publisher, editor; b. Houston, Jan. 14, 1933; s. Henry Joseph and Adele (Blissard) D.; m. Sandra Dannenbaum (div. 1979); children: Gary, Lisa, Rebecca; m. Rosalie Irene Ray, Aug. 21, 1982. BA in Liberal Arts, Tex. A&M U., 1955. Account mgr. Goodwin-Dannenbaum Advt., Houston, 1958-64; advt. mgr. Savage labs., Bellaire, Tex., 1964-66; v.p. mktg. G.D. Littman & Wingfield, Houston, 1966-68, Internat. Dairy Queen, Mpls., 1968-72; account mgr. Campbell-Mithun, Inc., Mpls., 1972-74; pres. Meyenberg Milk, L.A., 1975-79; acct. supr. George C. May, San Francisco, 1980-82; pub. West Coast Peddler, Whittier, Calif., 1982—. Chair policy adv. com. Minn. Farmer-Labor Dem. Party, Mpls., 1972; chmn. bd. dirs. Julia C. Hester House, United Fund, Houston, 1966. 1st lt. U.S. Army, 1956-58. Recipient Silver Anvil awrd Pub. Rels. Soc. Am., 1961, Grand Prix radio Houston Ad Club, 1967. Democrat. Office: West Coast Peddler 7007 Washington Ave Ste 311 Whittier CA 90602-1484

DANNER, PAUL KRUGER, III, telecommunications executive; b. Cin., Aug. 20, 1957; s. Paul Kruger Jr. and Phyllis Jean (Speak) D.; m. Cynthia Lee Hurst, May 5, 1984; children: Catherine Hurst, Elizabeth Speak, Caroline Tyree. BS, Colo. State U., 1979; MBA, Old Dominion U., 1986. Mktg. rep. Control Data Corp., Denver, 1985-86; dist. mgr. NEC Home Electronics (U.S.A.), Inc., Denver, 1987-88; regional mgr. NEC Home Electronics, Inc. subs. NEC Corp. (Tokyo), L.A., 1988-89, v.p. NEC Techs., Inc. subs., 1989-91; v.p. sales and mktg. Command Communications, Aurora, Colo., 1991—. Lt. USN, 1979-85; comdr. USNR, 1985—. Mem. Navy League of U.S., U.S. Naval Inst., NRA, Ducks Unltd., Met. Club, Castle Pines Country Club. Republican. Home: 503 Providence Dr Castle Rock CO 80104-9018

DANOFF, DUDLEY SETH, surgeon, urologist; b. N.Y.C., June 10, 1937; s. Alfred and Ruth (Kauffman) D.; m. Hevda Amrani, July 1, 1971; children: Aurele Alfie, Doran. BA summa cum laude, Princeton U., 1959; MD, Yale U., 1963. Diplomate Am. Bd. Urology. Surg. intern Columbia-Presbyn. Med. Ctr., N.Y.C., 1963-64; resident in surgery Yale New Haven Med. Ctr., 1964-65; resident in urologic surgery Squier Urologic Clinic, Columbia-Presbyn. Med. Ctr., 1965-69; NIH trainee Francis Delafield Hosp., N.Y.C., 1969; asst. in urology Columbia U.-Columbia-Presbyn. Hosp., N.Y.C., 1969; cons., surgeon New Orleans VA Hosp., 1970; asst. surgeon Tulane U., New Orleans, 1970; pvt. practice urologic surgery L.A., 1971—; attending urologic surgeon Cedars-Sinai Med. Ctr., L.A., Midway Hosp., L.A., Century City Hosp., L.A. VA Hosp., L.A.; attending urologic surgeon, clin. faculty UCLA. Author: Superpotency, 1993, Research: Laparoscopic Urologic Procedures; contbr. articles to profl. jours. Bd. dirs. Tel-Hashomer Hosp., Israel, Christian Children's Fund, Beverly Hills Edn. Found.; trustee Anti-Defamation League; mem. prof. adv. bd. The Wellness Comty.; mem. nat. exec. bd. Gesher Found.; mem. adv. com., past pres. Med. divsn. L.A. Jewish Fedn. Coun.; mem. nat. leadership cabinet United Jewish Appeal; chmn. Am. Friends of Assaf Harofeh Med. Ctr., Israel; pres. western states region and internat. bd. govs. Am. Friends Hebrew U. Jerusalem; pres. western region Am. Commn. for Shaare Zedek Med. Ctr. Jerusalem. Fellow ACS; mem. AMA, Internat. Coll. Surgeons, Israeli Med. Assn., Am. Fertility Soc., Soc. Air Force Clin. Surgeons, Am. Urologic Assn., Societe International d'Urologie, Transplant Soc. So. Calif., Los Angeles County Med. Assn., Soc. for Minimally Invasive Surgery, Am. Technion Soc., Profl. Men's Club of L.A. (past pres.), Princeton Club So. Calif., Yale Club So. Calif., Hillcrest Country Club, Phi Beta Kappa, Sigma Xi, Alpha Omega Alpha, Phi Delta Epsilon (past pres., mem. exec. com.). Jewish. Office: Cedars-Sinai Med Ctr Towers 8631 W 3rd St Ste 915E Los Angeles CA 90048-5912

DANSE, ILENE HOMNICK RAISFELD, physician, educator, toxicologist; b. Bklyn., June 24, 1940; d. Jack and Henrietta (Poverstein) Homnick; m. James Atherton Danse, Aug. 10, 1982; children: Arthur Raisfeld, Robin Raisfeld. BS, CUNY, 1960; MD, NYU, 1964. Diplomate Nat. Bd. Med. Examiners, Am. Bd. Internal Medicine, Am. Bd. Toxicology. Assoc. prof. internal medicine SUNY, Stony Brook, 1975-83, assoc. prof. pharmacology, 1977-83, dir. clin. pharmacology and toxicology Sch. Medicine, 1978-83; acting chairperson clin. pharmacology Northport VA Hosp., L.I., N.Y., 1978-83; sr. advisor Chevron Environ. Health Ctr., San Pablo, Calif., 1982-84; prin. ENVIROMED Health Svcs., Inc., San Rafael, Calif., 1985—; ind. med. examiner toxicology and internal medicine Dept. Indsl. Rels., State of Calif., 1985—; assoc. clin. prof. dept. medicine div. occupational and environ. medicine U. Calif., San Francisco, 1986; assoc. clin. prof. dept. community and internat. health U. Calif., Davis, 1991—; cons. in fields of environ., occupational and internal medicine, toxicology and pharmacology, 1984—; mem. bd. sci. advisors Am. Coun. Sci. & Health; mem. sci. rev. panel Hazardous Substances Data Base, Nat. Libr. of Medicine. Author: Common Sense Toxics In the Workplace, 1991; contbr. articles to sci. pubis. Mem. bd. sci. advisors Am. Coun. on Sci. and Health; mem. sci. rev. panel Hazardous Substances Data Base, Nat. Libr. of Medicine. Fellow ACP, Am. Coll. Clin. Pharmacology; mem. AAAS, Am. Acad. Clin. Toxicology, Am. Chem. Soc. (environ. health and safety sect.), Am. Coll. Occupational Medicine, Am. Indsl. Hygiene Assn. (occupational medicine sect.), Am. Coll. Toxicology, Am. Soc. Pharmacology and Therapeutics, Soc. Toxicology, Western Occupational Med. Assn. Office: ENVIROMED Health Svcs Inc 18 Prof Ctr Pkwy 2d Fl San Rafael CA 94903

D'ANTONIO, JAMES JOSEPH, lawyer; b. Tucson, Jan. 13, 1959; s. Lawrence Patrick and Rosemary Catherine (Kane) D'A. Student, Tufts U., 1978-79; BA, U. Ariz., 1981, JD, 1984. Bar: Ariz. 1984, U.S. Dist. Ct. Ariz. 1984, U.S. Ct. Appeals (9th cir.) 1993. Assoc. Law Office of D'Antonio and D'Antonio, Tucson, 1984-93; pvt. practice law Law Offices of James J. D'Antonio, Tucson, 1993—. Chmn. bd. govs. U. Ariz. Coll. Law, 1983-84; mem. Pima County Teen Ct. Adv. Bd; mem. Health South Rehab. Inst., Tucson Cmty. Adv. Bd.; bd. dirs. Coyote Task Force. Named Outstanding Pro Bono Lawyer Pima County Vol. Lawyers Program, 1993. Fellow Ariz. Bar Found.; mem. ABA, Assn. Trial Lawyers Am., Ariz. Bar Assn., Ariz. Trial Lawyers Assn., Pima County Bar Assn. Office: 70 W Cushing St Tucson AZ 85701-2218

DANUPATAMPA, EKACHAI, electrical engineer; b. Bangkok, Oct. 4, 1942; s. Yok-Hoo and Uy-Ty (Ung) Dan; m. Voranart Tanehsakdi, May 26, 1973; 1 child, Irv. BEE with distinction, Featí U., Manila, 1968; MEE, Calif. State U., Long Beach, 1974; D in Elec. Engring., U. So. Calif., 1979. Project elec. engr. Carnation Co., L.A., 1974-78; elec. engr. Dept. Navy, Port Hueneme, Calif., 1978-79; project elec. engr. Rodriguez and Assocs., L.A., 1979-80; sr. instrument engr. C.F. Braun & Co., Alhambra, Calif., 1980-85; sr. facilities design specialist Rockwell Internat., El Segundo, Calif., 1985-90; prin. instrument engr. Ralph M. Parsons Co., Pasadena, Calif., 1990-92, Saudi Arabian Parsons Ltd., Dhahran, 1992—; cons. Meza Engring., Inc., South Gate, Calif., 1985—. Vol. various charitable orgns., polit. orgns.

Mem. IEEE, Instrument Soc. Am., Assn. Thai Profls. in Am. and Can. Democrat. Buddhist. Home: 1136 N Vera Cruz St Montebello CA 90640-2551

DANZIGER, LOUIS, graphic designer, educator; b. N.Y.C., Nov. 17, 1923; s. Harry and Dora (Scheck) D.; m. Dorothy Patricia Smith, Apr. 10, 1954. Student, Art Ctr. Sch., Los Angeles, 1946-47, New Sch., N.Y.C., 1947-48. Asst. art dir. War Assets Adminstrn., Los Angeles, 1946-47; designer Esquire mag., N.Y.C., 1948; freelance designer, cons. Los Angeles, 1949—; instr. graphic design Art Ctr. Coll. Design, Los Angeles, 1952-60, 86—, Chouinard Art Inst., Los Angeles, 1960-72; instr. Calif. Inst. Arts, 1972-88, head graphic design program, 1972-82; vis. prof. Harvard U., Cambridge, Mass., summers 1978-80, 83, 84, 86-88; instr. Art Ctr. Coll. Design; mem. graphic evaluation panel Fed. Design Program, Nat. Endowment Arts, 1975—; design cons. Los Angeles County Mus. Art, 1957—. Served with cav. U.S. Army, 1943-45; PTO. Recipient numerous awards and medals, art dirs. show; Disting. Achievement award Contemporary Art Council, Los Angeles County Mus. Art, 1982; Disting. Designer award NEA, 1985. Mem. Alliance Graphique Internationale, Am. Inst. Graphic Arts, Am. Ctr. for Design (hon.). Home: PO Box 660189 Arcadia CA 91066-0189

DARANY, MICHAEL ANTHONY, financial executive; b. Detroit, Sept. 10, 1946; s. Sam and Betty Darany; m. Deborah Collins; 1 child, Daniel-le. Cert. fin. planner. Debit agt. Met. Life Ins. Co., Coral Gables, Fla., 1968-71; pres. Darany, Malagon & Assocs. Ins. Agy., Miami, Fla., 1970-71; loan appraiser Mortgage Corp. Am., Miami, Fla., 1971-72; loan officer J.I. Kislak Mortgage Co., Miami, Fla., 1973-74, Midwest Mortgage Co., Miami, Fla., 1973-74; pres. Consortium Group (subs. D&R Internat.), Miami, Fla., 1974-76; staff mgr. Peninsular Life Ins. Co., Miami, Fla., 1976-78; asst. to mgr. Sun Life Can., Miami, Fla., 1978-82; pres. Consortium Group(subs. D&R Internat.), Miami, Fla., 1982—. Co-author: The Expert's Guide, 1988; contbr. articles to profl. pubs. First v.p. Unico Nat., Coral Gables, 1975-76, sec. 1978-79, pres., 1980-81. Served with USN, 1963-67, Vietnam. Recipient Man of Yr. award Sun Life Can., 1978-81. Mem. Inst. Cert. Fin. Planners, Internat. Assn. Fin. Planners, Nat. Assn. Life Underwriters, Registry Fin. Planning, Nat. Fin. Adv. Panel, Internat. Bd. Standards and Practices. Republican. Episcopalian.

DARBY, MICHAEL RUCKER, economist, educator; b. Dallas, Nov. 24, 1945; s. Joseph Jasper and Frances Adah (Rucker) D.; children: Margaret Loutrel, David Michael; Lynne Ann Zucker-Darby, 1992; stepchildren: Joshua R. Zucker, Danielle T. Zucker. AB summa cum laude, Dartmouth Coll., 1967; MA, U. Chgo., 1968, PhD, 1970. Asst. prof. econs. Ohio State U., 1970-73; vis. asst. prof. econs. UCLA, 1972-73, assoc. prof., 1973-78, prof., 1978-87, 96—, prof. Anderson Grad. Sch. Mgmt., 1987-94, Warren C. Cordner prof. money and fin. mkts., 1995—, vice chmn., 1992-93; dir. John M. Olin Ctr. for Policy, 1993—; assoc. dir. orgnl. rsch. program UCLA Inst. for Social Sci. Rsch., 1995—; assoc. dir. Ctr. for Internat. Sci., Tech., Cultural Policy Sch. Pub. Policy and Social Rsch., UCLA, 1996—; dir. John M. Olin Ctr. for Policy, 1993—; rsch. assoc. Nat. Bur. Econ. Rsch., 1976-86, 92—; asst. sec. for economic policy U.S. Dept. Treasury, Washington, 1986-89; mem. Nat. Commn. on Superconductivity, 1988-89; under sec. for econ. affairs U.S. Dept. Commerce, Washington, 1989-92; adminstr. Econs. and Stats. Adminstrn., 1990-92; v.p., dir. Paragon Industries, Inc., Dallas, 1964-83; mem. exec. com. Western Econ. Assn., 1987-90; chmn. The Dumbarton Group, 1992—; adj. scholar Am. Ent. Inst. for Pub. Policy Rsch., 1992—; economist stats. income divsn. IRS, 1992-94; mem. Regulatory Coordination Adv. Com. of the Commodity Futures Trading Commn., 1992-96. Author: Macroeconomics, 1976, Have Controls Ever Worked: The Post-War Record, 1976, Intermediate Macroeconomics, 1979, 2d edit., 1986, The Effects of Social Security on Income and the Capital Stock, 1979, The International Transmission of Inflation, 1981, Labor Force, Employment, and Productivity in Historical Perspective, 1984, Reducing Poverty in America: Views and Approaches, 1996; editor Jour. Internat. Money and Fin., 1981-86, mem. editl. bd., 1986—; mem. editl. bd. Am. Econ. Rev., 1983-86, Contemporary Policy Issues, 1990-93, Contemporary Econ. Policy, 1994—, Internat. Reports, 1992-95. Bd. dirs. The Opera Assoc., 1992—; mem. acad. adv. bd. Ctr. Regulation and Econ. Growth of the Alexis de Tocqueville Instn., 1993-96. Recipient Alexander Hamilton award U.S. Treasury Dept., 1989; sr. fellow Dartmouth Coll., 1966-67, Woodrow Wilson fellow, 1967-68, NSF grad. fellow, 1967-69, FDIC grad. fellow, 1969-70, Harry Scherman rsch. fellow Nat. Bur. Econ. Research, 1974-75, vis. fellow Hoover Instn., Stanford U., 1977-78. Mem. Acad. Polit. Sci., Am. Econ. Assn., Am. Fin. Assn., Am. Statis. Assn., Nat. Assn. Bus. Economists, Mont Pelerin Soc., Royal Econ. Soc., So. Econ. Assn., Western Econ. Assn., Capitol Hill Club (D.C.). Episcopalian. Home: 3937 Purdue Ave Dallas TX 75225-7115 Office: UCLA Anderson Grad Sch Mgmt Los Angeles CA 90095-1481

DARBY, WESLEY ANDREW, minister, educator; b. Glendale, Ariz., Sept. 19, 1928; s. Albert Leslie and Beulah E. (Lamb) D.; student Bible Inst. L.A., 1946, No. Ariz. U., 1946-47, Rockmont Coll., Denver, 1948-50, Ariz. State U., 1965, St. Anne's Coll., Oxford (Eng.) U., 1978; m. Donna Maye Bice, May 29, 1947; children: Carolyn Darby Eymann, Lorna Dale, Elizabeth Darby Larimer, Andrea Darby Perdue. Ordained to ministry Bapt. Ch., 1950; pastor Sunnyside Bapt. Ch., Flagstaff, Ariz., 1947-48, First Bapt. Ch. of Clifton, Ariz., 1950-55, West High Bapt. Ch., Phoenix, 1955-90; pastor emeritus, 1990—; dep. assessor Greenlee County, 1951-55; instr. English lit. and pastoral subjects Southwestern Conservative Bapt. Bible Coll., Phoenix, 1961-87. Chmn. bd. Conservative Bapt. Found. Ariz., 1974-83, Gospel Wings, 1960-88; v.p. Ariz. Bapt. Conf., 1976-83; pres. Ariz. Alcohol-Narcotic Edn. Assn., 1968-90. Dep. Maricopa County (Ariz.) Sheriff's Exec. Posse, 1993—; chaplain Civil Air Patrol, 1951-55. Recipient God, Family and Country award Freeman Inst., 1981. Mem. Evang. Philos. Soc., Greater Phoenix Assn. Evangelicals (pres. 1960-63, 91-96), Ariz. Breakfast Club, (chaplain 1969-96, pres. 1996—), Ariz. Militia (chaplain 1994—). Contbr. articles to profl. jours. Republican. Home: 5628 N 11th Dr Phoenix AZ 85013-1714 Office: 3301 N 19th Ave Phoenix AZ 85015-5761

DARGIS, JEAN ANTHONY, retired voluntary health agency executive; b. Mpls., Mar. 9, 1931; s. Henry Joseph and Josephine Marie (Violette) D.; m. Mary Ruth Buschman, July 2, 1956; 1 child, Melissa Jeanne Dargis Herzog. BA, St. Paul (Minn.) Sem., 1952; MusB, Universite Laval, Quebec, Can., 1954. Tchr. St. Anthony Acad., Mpls., 1954-59, Holy Childhood Sch., St. Paul, 1955-57; various positions March of Dimes Birth Defects Found., White Plains, N.Y., 1959-92; v.p., dir. nat. office of vols. March of Dimes Birth Defects Found., White Plains, 1989-92. Author: (handbook) Manual for Chapters, 1990; editor: (handbook) Volunteer Development Guide, 1991, (booklet) Basic Principles of Volunteer Developement, 1989. Mem. Diocesan Commn./Devel., San Jose, Calif., 1983-90; dir. Diocesan Choir, San Jose, 1983-90, St. Victor's Parish Choir, San Jose, 1971—. Mem. Mensa, Latin Liturgy Assn. Republican. Roman Catholic. Home: 3479 Grossmont Dr San Jose CA 95132-3120

DARKE, CHARLES BRUCE, academic administrator, dentist; b. Chgo., Sept. 22, 1937; s. Paul Olden and Annie Waulene (Tennin) D.; m. Annetta McRae-Darke, Aug. 15, 1965 (div. 1982); 1 child, Charles B. II; m. Judith Anne Chew, Dec. 15, 1990. AA, Wilson Jr. Coll., Chgo., 1960; DDS, Meharry Med. Coll., 1964; MPH, U. Calif., Berkeley, 1972. Staff dentist Children's Hosp., Oakland, Calif., 1967-68, Mt. Zion Hosp., San Francisco, 1967-71; pvt. practice in dentistry San Francisco, 1967—; dir. dental svcs. San Francisco Gen. Hosp., 1973-80; asst. adminstr. outpatient svcs. San Francisco Med. Ctr., 1980-88; ops. officer primary care network San Francisco Dept. Health, 1988-89; dir. student health Calif. State U., Fullerton, 1989—; dental cons. Dept. Labor Job Corps, Washington, 1973-88; chief examiner state dental bd. Calif. State Bd. Dental Examiners, Sacramento, 1976-89; surveyor ambulatory care Joint Commn. on Accreditation of Health, Oakbrook, Ill., 1986—; bd. dirs. Yorba Hills Med. Ctr., Yorba Linda, Calif., 1993—. Found Tooth Trip-Free Dental Care, San Francisco, 1969. Capt. USAF, 1965-67. Mem. ADA, Am. Endodontic Soc., Nat. Dental Assn., Am. Coll. Health Assn., Pacific Coast Coll. Health Assn. (bd. dirs. 1993), Nat. Dental Soc. Bay Area (past pres.).

DARLING, LYNDA KAREN, secondary education educator; b. Portland, Oreg., Oct. 25, 1949; d. Howard Wayne and Ruth Eileen (Russell) D.; m. Scott Reagen Hannigan, Feb. 14, 1975. BS, Portland State U., 1971, MS, 1976. Cert. basic integrated sci., std. extreme learning problems, std. reading. Reading tchr. Vocat. Village H.S.-Portland (Oreg.) Pub. Schs., 1972—; mem. Vocat. Village H.S. Citizen Adv. Com., Portland, 1980—; co-founder Read-Rite Assocs., Portland, 1982—. Coach Jr. Bowlers, Portland, 1993—. Recipient Outstanding Support to Spl. Needs Students award Nat. Assn. Vocat. Edn. Spl. Needs Pers., Portland, 1982; named Secondary Alternative Educator of Yr., Oreg. Assn. for Alternatives in Edn., 1990. Mem. Internat. Reading Assn., Oreg. Assn. Learning Disabilities, Portland Assn. Tchrs. (mem. legis. com. 1983-86, bd. mem. tchrs. voice in politics bd. 1984-86), Phi Kappa Phi. Office: Vocat Village HS 8020 NE Tillamook St Portland OR 97213-6655

DARLING, MARY ELIZABETH, environmental affairs consultant; b. Worcester, Mass., June 10, 1955; d. William Edward and Anne Marie (Hastings) Bacon; m. Richard Dale Darling, June 22, 1996. BS, Calif. State U., Sacramento, 1977, MS, 1981; JD, U. of the Pacific, Sacramento, 1984. Ecology technician USN, San Diego, 1975-76; fisheries technician Calif. Dept. Fish and Game, Sacramento, 1976-79; forest biologist U.S. Forest Svc., Redding, Calif., 1979-86; mgr. wildlife and fisheries program U.S. Forest Svc., Sparks, Nev., 1986-92; project mgr. WESTEC, Reno, 1992-94; cons. Elko, Nev., 1994-96; v.p. Darling Environ. Surveying Ltd., Tucson, 1996—. Mem. Am. Fisheries Soc. (sec., treas. 1989-91), Nat. Ski Patrol, Desert Fishes Coun., Trout Unltd. (regional v.p. Calif., Nev., Hawaii 1993-95, pres. 1993-94), Toastmasters Internat. Home: 3431 N Camino de Piedras Tucson AZ 85750

DARLING, SCOTT EDWARD, lawyer; b. Los Angeles, Dec. 31, 1949; s. Dick R. and Marjorie Helen (Otto) D.; m. Cynthia Diane Harrah, June 1970 (div.); 1 child, Smokie; m. Deborah Lee Cochran, Aug. 22, 1981; children: Ryan, Jacob. BA, U. Redlands, 1972; JD, U.S.C., 1975. Bar: Calif. 1976, U.S. Dist. Ct. (cen. dist.) Calif. 1976. Assoc. atty. Elver, Falsetti, Boone & Crafts, Riverside, 1976-78; ptnr. Falsetti, Crafts, Pritchard & Darling, Riverside, 1978-84; pres. Scott Edward Darling, A Profl. Corp., Riverside, 1984—; grant reviewer HHS, Washington, 1982-88; judge pro tem Riverside County Mcpl. Ct., 1980, Riverside County Superior Ct., 1987-88; bd. dirs. Tel Law Nat. Legal Pub. Info. System, Riverside, 1978-80. Author, editor: Small Law Office Computer Legal System, 1984. Bd. dirs. Youth Adv. Com. to Selective Svc., 1968-70, Am. Heart Assn. Riverside County, 1978-82, Survival Ministries, 1986-89; atty. panel Calif. Assn. Realtors, L.A., 1980—; pres. Calif. Young Reps., 1978-80; mem. GI Forum, Riverside, 1970-88; presdl. del. Nat. Rep. Party, 1980-84; asst. treas. Calif. Rep. Party, 1981-83; Rep. Congl. candidate, Riverside, 1982; treas. Riverside Sickle Cell Found., 1980-82, recipient Eddie D. Smith award; pres. Calif. Rep. Youth Caucus, 1980-82; v.p. Riverside County Red Cross, 1982-84; mem. Citizen's Univ. Com., Riverside, 1978-84, World Affairs Council, 1978-82, Urban League, Riverside, 1980-82. Calif. Scholarship Fedn. (life). Named one of Outstanding Young Men in Am., U.S. Jaycees, 1979-86. Mem. ABA, Riverside County Bar Assn., Speaker's Bur. Riverside County Bar Assn., Riverside Jaycees, Riverside C. of C. Lodge: Native Sons of Golden West. Office: 3697 Arlington Ave Riverside CA 92506-3938

DARMSTAETTER, JAY EUGENE, secondary education educator; b. Altadena, Calif., Nov. 30, 1937; s. Eugene Jamison and Virginia (Fagans) D. AA, L.A. City Coll., 1958; BA, L.A. State Coll., 1960, MA, 1962; postgrad., U. So. Calif., 1962-65. Cert. secondary edn. tchr., secondary adminstr. Tchr. L.A. Unified Schs., 1960—, athletic dir., 1965-83; tng. tchr. UCLA, Calif. State U., Whittier Coll., L.A., 1966—; master tchr. L.A. Unified Schs., 1983-84; announcer L.A. Unified Schs., 1970—, CIF/So. Section, Artesia, Calif., 1964-85, State CIF, Fullerton, Calif., 1970-85. Soloist Christian Sci. Chs., L.A., 1958—; mem. Citizens Community Planning Coun., L.A. County, 1989-96. Recipient Nat. Def. Edn. Assn. award Dept. of Edn., L.A., 1968. Mem. NEA, Calif. Tchrs. Assn., United Tchrs. L.A., Phi Mu Alpha Sinfonia. Republican. Office: Wilson High/LA Schools 4500 Multnomah St Los Angeles CA 90032-3703

DARNALL, ROBERTA MORROW, academic administrator; b. Kemmerer, Wyo., May 18, 1949; d. C. Dale and Eugenia Stayner (Christmas) Morrow; m. Leslie A. Darnall, Sept. 3, 1977; children: Kimberly Gene, Leslie Nicole. BS, U. Wyo., Laramie, 1972. Tariff sec., ins. adminstr. Wyo. Trucking Assn., Casper, 1973-75; asst. clerical supr. Wyo. Legislature, Cheyenne, 1972-77; congl. campaign press aide, 1974; pub. relations dir. in Casper, Wyo. Republican Central Com., 1976-77; asst. dir. alumni relations U. Wyo., 1977-81, dir. of alumni, 1981—; bd. dir. Ivinson Meml. Hosp. Found. Mem. St. Matthews Guild and Acolyte (coord.). Mem. Higher Edn. Assn. Rockies, Am. Soc. Assn. Execs., Laramie C. of C. (edn. com.), PEO (former courtesy com., officer), Zonta Internat. Republican. Episcopalian. Home: 15 Snowy View Ct Laramie WY 82070-5358 Office: PO Box 3137 Laramie WY 82071-3137

DARNEY, PHILIP DEMPSEY, gynecologist, educator; b. Granite, Okla., Feb. 27, 1943; s. Walter Preston and Corene (Barton) D.; m. Virginia Grant (div. 1981); children: Blair, Barton; m. Uta Landy, Oct. 13, 1984; 1 child, Undine. AB, U. Calif., Berkeley, 1964; MD, U. Calif., San Francisco, 1968; MSc, London Sch. Hygiene, 1972. Diplomate Am. Bd. Preventive Medicine, Am. Bd. Ob-Gyn. Intern USPHS Hosp., San Francisco, 1968-69; resident in ob-gyn Brigham and Women's Hosp., Boston, 1973-76; dep. dir. div. reproductive health Ctrs. Disease Control, Atlanta, 1971-73; asst. prof. ob-gyn Harvard Med. Sch., Boston, 1976-78; assoc. prof. ob-gyn Oreg. Health Scis. U., Portland, 1978-80; prof. ob-gyn U. Calif. Sch. Medicine, San Francisco, 1981--; cons. AID, Washington, 1971-74, Pathfinder Internat., Boston, 1973-83, The Population Coun., Family Health Internat., Internat. Projects Assistance Svc., Family Planning Internat. Assistance, Johns Hopkins U., 30 countries;lectr., writer in field. Author: Protocols for Office Gynecologic Surgery, 1996, Clinical Guide for Contraception, 1996; contbr. over 100 articles on contraception, abortion and sterilization to med. jours., chpts. to books; reviewer 20 med. jours. Bd. dirs. Assn. for Vol. Surg. Contraception, Planned Parenthood Fedn. Am., N.Y.C., Alan Guttmacher Inst. Named Outstanding Young Profl. Am. Pub. Health Assn., 1984. Fellow Am. Coll. Obstetricians and Gynecologists, Am. Coll. Preventive Medicine. Democrat. Office: San Francisco Gen Hosp Dept Ob-Gyn San Francisco CA 94110

DA ROZA, VICTORIA CECILIA, human resources administrator; b. East Orange, N.J., Aug. 30, 1945; d. Victor and Cynthia Helen (Krupa) Hawkins; m. Thomas Howard Kaminski, Aug. 28, 1971 (div. 1977); 1 child, Sarah Hawkins; m. Robert Anthony da Roza, Nov. 25, 1983. BA, U. Mich., 1967; MA, U. Mo., 1968. Contract compliance mgr. City of San Diego, 1972-75; v.p. personnel Bank of Calif., San Francisco, 1975-77; with human resources Lawrence Livermore (Calif.) Nat. Lab., 1978-86; pvt. cons. Victoria Kaminski-da Roza & Assocs., 1986—; lectr. in field; videotape workshop program on mid-career planning used by IEEE. Contbr. numerous articles to profl. jours. Mem. social policy com. City of Livermore, 1982. Mem. Am. Soc. Tng. and Devel., Western Gerontol. Soc. (planning com. Older Worker Track 1983), Gerontol. Soc. Am. Home and Office: 385 Borica Dr Danville CA 94526-5457

DARRABY, JESSICA L., lawyer, educator, writer; b. June 17. BA, UCLA, 1974; MA, U. Calif., 1976, JD, 1979. Bar: Calif. 1979. Gallery dir., owner Jessica Darraby Gallery, L.A., 1984-88; cons., expert witness, 1988—; adj. prof. Pepperdine Sch. Law, Malibu, Calif., 1988—; bd. dirs. Art Table, Inc., N.Y.C., treas. So. Calif. exec. com., 1992-93, lawyer, 1993—. Author: Art, Artifact and Architecture Law, 1995, 96, 97—. Fellow Can. Council Fellowship Canadian Govt., 1975. Mem. ABA (copyright, sports and entertainment forum), Am. Soc. Appraisers (affiliate), Contemporary Arts Coun., Mus. Modern Art (N.Y.C.), Exec. Women's Golf Assn. Office: Pepperdine Sch Law Malibu CA 90263

DARRINGTON, JOHN CHARLES, city administrator; b. Burley, Idaho, July 29, 1946; s. John Harry and Gladys (Tennant) D.; m. Susan Gayle Turner, Jan. 27, 1969; children: Melissa, John Scott, Spencer Bruce, Marcus Turner, Rebecca, Stephanie, Kimberly. BA, Brigham Young U., 1970, MPA, 1972; Cert., Harvard U., 1988. Manpower dir. Utah County Cmty. Action, Provo, 1972; dir. adminstrv. svcs. Mountainland Assn. of Govts., Provo, 1972-77; city adminstr. City of Soda Springs, Idaho, 1977-81; city mgr. City of Rawlins, Wyo., 1981-85; city adminstr. City of Gillette, Wyo., 1985—; mem. Environ. Quality Coun., State of Wyo., Cheyenne, 1988—, chmn., 1992-94. Author: Goal Setting-Steps To Progress, 1992. Mem. Ctrl. Wyo. Coun. Boy Scouts of Am. (pres. 1994), Rotary Internat. (pres. 1991). Republican. LDS. Home: 1310 Overdale Dr Gillette WY 82718-7545 Office: City of Gillette PO Box 3003 Gillette WY 82717

DARROW, GEORGE F., natural resources company owner, consultant; b. Osage, Wyo., Aug. 13, 1924; s. George Washington and Marjorie (Ord) D.; m. Elna Tannehill, Oct. 23, 1976; children by previous marriage: Roy Stuart, Karen Josanne, Reed Crandall, John Robin. AB in Econs., U. Mich., 1945, BS in Geology, 1949. Geologist Amerada Petroleum Corp., Billings, Mont., 1949-50; v.p. Northwest Petroleum Co., 1951-58; prin. Resource Consultants, Billings, 1959-76; pres., CEO Crossbow Corp., Billings, 1962—; v.p. Kootenai Galleries, Bigfork, Mont., 1976—; sr. ptnr. Crossbow Assocs., resource mgrs., Bigfork, 1976—; chmn. Mont. Environ. Quality Coun., Helena, 1971-73; bd. dirs. Ord Ranch Corp., Lusk, Wyo.; apptd. faculty affil. U. Mont., 1995—. Contbr. articles on resource mgmt. and econs. to various publs. Elected mem. Mont. Ho. of Reps., 1967-69, 71-73, Mont. Senate, 1973-75; bd. dirs. Bigfork Ctr. Performing Arts, 1980—; apptd. mem. Mont. Ambs., 1994—. Lt. (j.g.) USNR, 1943-46, PTO. Fellow AAAS; mem. Internat. Soc. Ecol. Econs., Am. Assn. Petroleum Geologists (past pres. Rocky Mountain sect.), Am. Inst. Profl. Geologists (charter), Mont. Geol. Soc. (founder, charter), Billings Petroleum Club. Home and Office: Crossbow Corp 2014 Beverly Hills Blvd Billings MT 59102-2014 also: Paladin Farms 924 Chapman Hill Dr Bigfork MT 59911-6215

DARROW, PAUL GARDNER, painter, printmaker, cartoonist, illustrator; b. Pasadena, Calif., Oct. 31, 1921; s. Frank Richard and Ruth Anne (Coutant) D.; m. Nadine Gunderson, June 13, 1944 (div. 1963); children: Christopher, Joan, Elizabeth, Eric; m. Suzanne Standlee Smith, June 8, 1965 (dec. Nov. 1985). AA, Pasadena Jr. Coll., 1939; student, Art Ctr. Sch. Fine Arts, Pasadena, Calif., 1940-41, Colorado Springs Fine Arts Ctr., 1944-45, Claremont Grad. Sch., 1945-49. Prof. art Otis Art Inst., L.A., 1962-68; instr. Calif. Inst. Tech., Pasadena, 1979-72; prof. art Claremont (Calif.) Grad. Sch., 1955-92; prof. Scripps Coll., Claremont, 1955-92, prof. emeritus, 1992—; artist-corr. Vietnam war on ships at sea, Japan, Okinawa, Taiwan, 1964. 35 one-man shows, including mus in Phila., Denver, Museo del Arte Moderne, Brazil, La Mus., Newport Mus., Laguna Mus., Portland Mus.; retrospective show Lang Galleries, Claremont Colls., 1992; murals executed Air France, P & O SS, Wells Fargo Bank, Monsanto; illustrator N.Y. Times, Partisan Rev., Saturdy Rev; illustrator books Academic Bestiary (Richard Armour), 1973, Concrete Jungle (Couffer), 1963, Guide for the Married Man, 1967. Grantee NEH, 1972; Ford rsch. grantee, 1978. Mem. Calif. Watercolor Soc. (v.p. 1962-63), L.A. Printmaking Soc. (co-founder). Home and Studio: 690 Cuprien Way Laguna Beach CA 92651-2563

DARVAS, ENDRE PETER, artist; b. Kisvadra, Sz-Szatmar, Hungary, July 18, 1946; came to U.S., in 1957; s. Bela and Maria (Filtczer) Darvas. BFA, U. Tex., 1969. Pres. Studio Arts and Frames, Inc., South Lake Tahoe, Calif., 1974-78; owner Darvas Studio, South Lake Tahoe, 1969—. One-man shows include Dallas, 1963, Taos, N.Mex., 1971, Carmel, Calif., 1975, San Carlos, Mex., 1987, Galerias del Pacifico, Sonora, Mex., 1989, Studio Retrospective, Lake Tahoe, 1990, Sierra Galleries, Lake Tahoe, 1991-94; represented in permanent collections Sierra Galleries, Rosequist Gallery, Tucson. Recipient numerous awards from art exhibits. Mem. Soc. Am. Impressionists, Southwestern Watercolor Soc. Office: Darvas Studio PO Box 711 South Lake Tahoe CA 96156-0711

DAS, SUBHENDU, electrical engineer; b. Burnpur, India, Nov. 17, 1944; came to U.S., 1981; s. Satya Kinkar and Chandra Bali (Mohanta) D.; m. Swarna Rani Ghish, Mar. 6, 1981; children: Tania Debbie, Pamela Renee. BSEE, Jadavpur U., India, 1967; MSEE, Indian Inst. Tech., India, 1969; PhD of Elec. Engring., Indian Inst. Tech., 1972. Lectr. Jadavpur U., Calcutta, 1972-76; asst. prof. Indian Inst. Mgmt., Calcutta, 1976-81; engring. specialist Litton Guidance and Control, Woodland Hills, Calif., 1989-92; cons. L.A. AFB, 1993—; faculty mem. Calif. State U., Northridge, Ponoma, 1983-92; nat. assoc. Govt. India, 1975-80. Patentee in field; contbr. articles to profl. jours. Home: 9732 Kessler Ave Chatsworth CA 91311-5503 Office: Amcomp Corp 3525 Lomita Blvd # 102 Torrance CA 90505-5016

DASGUPTA, AMITAVA, chemist, educator; b. Calcutta, India, May 6, 1958; came to U.S., 1980; naturalized U.S. citizen, 1996; s. Anil Kumar and Hasi Dasgupta. BS with honors, U. Calcutta, India, 1978; MS in Chemistry, U. Ga., 1981; PhD in Chemistry, Stanford U., 1986. Diplomate Am. Bd. Clin. Chemistry. Fellow in clin. chemistry U. Wash., Seattle, 1986-88; asst. dir. clin. chemistry U. Chgo., 1988-93; dir. clin. chemistry lab. U. N.Mex. Hosp., Albuquerque, 1993—; assoc. prof. pathology and biochemistry U. N.Mex., Albuquerque, 1993—; lectr in field. Reviewer jours. Clin. Chemistry, Nephron, Jour. Liquid Chromatography; contbr. articles to Clin. Chemistry, Am. Jour. Clin. Pathology, Jour. Am. Soc. Nephrology,. SYVA, 1990-91, Home Health Care, 1992-93. Fellow Nat. Acad. Clin. Biochemistry (Grannis award 1993); mem. Am. Assn. Clin. Chemistry, Acad. Clin. Labs. Physicians and Scientists. Hindu. Home: 801 Locust Pl NE # 2257 Albuquerque NM 87102 Office: U NMex Hosp Pathology Svcs Albuquerque NM 87106

DASHIELL, G. RONALD, marshal. U.S. marshal U.S. Dist. Ct. (ea. dist.) Wash., Spokane. Office: US Courthouse 920 Riverside Ave W Spokane WA 99210

DASHJIAN, MICHAEL BRYAN, lawyer; b. L.A., May 8, 1957; s. Ronald Karl and Neva Lorraine Dashjian; m. Beth Dashjian, Apr. 8, 1992. BA magna cum laude, UCLA, 1978; MA in Law and Diplomacy, Tufts U., 1980; JD, U. Calif., Berkeley, 1983. Bar: Calif. 1983, Conn. 1984, U.S. Dist. Ct. Conn. 1984, U.S. Ct. Appeals (2nd cir.) 1989, U.S. Dist. Ct. (no., ea., ctrl. and so. dists.) Calif. 1992, U.S. Ct. Appeals (9th cir.) 1992, U.S. Supreme Ct. 1993; cert. Appellate Law Specialist, Calif. Law clk. to Hon. Thomas J. Meskill U.S. Ct. Appeals (2nd cir.), N.Y.C., 1983-84; assoc. Tyler Cooper & Alcorn, Hartford, Conn., 1984-89; sr. atty. U.S. SEC, Washington, 1989-92; pvt. practice Atascadero, Calif., 1992—. Advisor FORECITE, 1994—; contbr. articles to profl. jours. mem. Mensa, Nat. Audubon Soc., Order of Coif. Mem. Armenian Apostolic Ch. Office: 7343 El Camino Real Ste 351 Atascadero CA 93422

DATSKO, TINA MICHELLE, writer, producer; b. Ann Arbor, Mich., Jan. 23, 1960; d. Joseph and Doris Mae (Ross) D.; m. Jose Sanchez H., 1994. BA magna cum laude, U. Mich., 1983, MFA in Creative Writing, 1985; MFA in Sreenwriting, U. So. Calif., 1989. Film/video cons., 1986; story analyst Too Magic, Inc., Columbia Pictures, Burbank, Calif., 1987-88; scriptwriter Women in Film Festival, 1988; writer/producer Illarij Prodns., L.A., 1990—; lectr. Film and Electronic Arts Dept. Calif. State U., Long Beach, 1989—. Films includes: I Dont Understand Grown-Ups, 1986, Rudolf Arheim: A Life in Art, 1994, La Paz, 1994; Contbr. numerous articles to profl. publs. Recipient 14 Hopwood awards, 1979-85, L.A. Arts Coun., award, 1988-89, 2 Virginia Voss awards, 1982, Mich. Ctr. artist grant, 1985, IFP, IFFM fellowship, 1996. Mem. Phi Kappa Phi. Home: 550 Orange Ave Unit 339 Long Beach CA 90802-7011 Office: Calif State U 1250 N Bellflower Blvd Long Beach CA 90840-0006

DATTA, PURNA CHANDRA, clinical psychologist, educator; b. Barisal, India, Jan. 1, 1943; came to U.S., 1980; s. Jogendra Kumar and Kanak (Ghosh) D.; m. Anita Rani, Feb. 7, 1969; children: Partha Michael, Aparna Kara. BA in Philosophy with honors, Dacca (Bangladesh) U., 1963, MA in Philosophy, 1964, MA in Psychology, 1967; PhD in Clin. Psychology, Newcastle U., NSW, Australia, 1979, M in Clin. Psychology, 1982. Lic. psychologist, Ga., Calif.; cert. eye movement desensitization reprocessing; diplomate Bd. Cert. Forensic Examiners, Am. Bd. Forensic Medicine; diplomate-fellow Prescribing Psychol. Register. Psychologist Morisset (NSW) Hosp., 1974-80, clin. psychologist, 1983-84; psychologist Fairview State Hosp., Costa Mesa, Calif., 1980-83; psychologist Ctrl. State Hosp., Milledgeville, Ga., 1985-86, sr. psychologist, 1989-90; program dir. Gladesville (NSW) Hosp., 1984-85, So. Met. Devel. Disabilities Svc., Gladesville, 1986-88; staff psychologist Stockton (Calif.) Devel. Ctr., 1990-94, O.H. Close Sch. (Calif. Youth Authority), Stockton, 1994—; lectr. psychology Dacca Coll., 1968-69, Dacca U., 1969-73; tutor, demonstrator Newcastle U., 1973-74; lectr. psychiat. nursing Newcastle Tech. Coll., 1974-80; clin. instr. psychiatry U. Calif., Irvine, 1981-83; adj. prof. psychology U.

Pacific, Stockton, 1992—; clin. psychologist mental health svcs. Perry Street Cmty. Ctr., Newcastle, 1976-77, 77; clin. psychologist pediatric unit Royal Newcastle Hosp., 1977-78; psychol. asst. Dr. F.M. Crinella, Costa Mesa. 1982-83; presenter in field. Contbr. articles to profl. jours. Talent scholar Commonwealth U. Dacca, 1960-64. Mem. APA, Calif. Psychol. Assn., Am. Assn. Clin. Hypnosis (cert. in hypnotherapy), Am. Coll. Forensic Psychology, Am. Coll. Forensic Examiners, Am. Coll. Forensic Counselors (master addiction counselor). Home: 7221 Shoreham Pl Stockton CA 95207-1224 Office: Behavior Therapy and Counseling Assocs Ste 204 1652 W Texas St Fairfield CA 94533

DAUGHADAY, DOUGLAS ROBERT, computer engineer; b. Highland Park, N.J., Mar. 13, 1954; s. Robert Owings and Mary D.; m. Ilene D. Eichel, Feb. 14, 1987; 1 child, Brian Douglas. BSEE cum laude, W.Va. Inst. Tech., 1976; MSEE, U. So. Calif., 1979. Mem. tech. staff Hughes Aircraft Co., Culver City, Calif., 1977-79; sr. engr. Litton G&CS, Woodland Hills, Calif., 1979-80; lab. engr. Garrett Airesearch, Torrance, Calif., 1980-84; mem. tech. staff The Aerospace Corp., El Segundo, Calif., 1984-87, mgr., 1987-93; project engr., 1993-96, engring. specialist, 1996—. Mem. IEEE, ACM, Soc. Am. Magicians (pres. assembly #22), Nat. Assn. Underwater Instrs. (instr.), U. S.C. Alumni Assn. (life), Eta Kappa Nu (life). Democrat. Home: 27910 Ridgebrook Ct Rancho Palos CA 90275-3300 Office: The Aerospace Corp 2350 E El Segundo Blvd El Segundo CA 90245-4609

DAUGHERTY, LEO, literature and language educator; b. Louisville, May 16, 1939; s. F.S. and Mollie Repass (Brown) D.; m. Virginia Upton; 1 child, Mollie Virginia; m. Lee Graham. AB in Fine Arts and Lit., Western Ky. U., 1961; MA in English, U. Ark., 1963; PhD in Am. Lit., East Tex. State U., 1970; postgrad., Harvard U., 1970-71. Cert. fine arts tchr. Asst. prof. lit. U. Wis., Superior, 1962-63; teaching fellow East Tex. State U., Commerce, 1963-65; asst. prof. lit. Frederick Coll., Portsmouth, Va., 1965-66, Va. State U., Norfolk, 1966-68; prof. lit. and linguistics Evergreen State Coll., Olympia, Wash., 1972—; acad. dean Evergreen State Coll., Olympia, 1975-76, dir. Ctr. Study of Sci. and Human Values, 1990—; past grant evaluator NEH. Author: The Teaching of Writing at Evergreen, 1984; contbr. short stories, articles to profl. and literary jours. Active Friends of Bodleian Libr., Oxford, Eng., 1983—; assocs. Alderman Libr., U. Va., 1996—. Recipient NEH award, 1973. Mem. MLA (life), Internat. Assn. Fantasy in Arts, Shakespeare Assn. Am., Soc. Lit. and Sci. Office: Evergreen State Coll Olympia WA 98505

DAUNER, C. DUANE, health facility administrator; b. Isabel, Kans.; m.; 2 children. Student, Pepperdine U., 1958-60; BA, Wichita State U., 1962, MA, 1964; postgrad., U. Nebr., 1964-65. Asst. prof. Washburn U., Topeka, Kans., 1965-66; dir. rsch. Kans. Health Facilities Info. Svc., Topeka, 1966-68; v.p. Kans. Hosp. Assn., Topeka, 1968-75; pres., CEO Mo. Hosp. Assn., Jefferson City, 1975-85, Calif. Assn. Hosps. and Health Systems, Sacramento, 1985—, Calif. Healthcare Assn., Sacramento, 1996—; bd. dirs. Calif. Hosps. Affiliated Ins. Svcs., Inc., Calif. Hosp. Ins. Co.; preceptor, lectr. Washington U., 1978-85, U. Mo., Columbia, 1977-85. Author: The Health Care Solution, 1995. Fellow Am. Coll. Healthcare Execs.; mem. Am. Hosp. Assn. (bd. trustees 1993-96, fed. rels. 1977-79, chmn., coun. mem. 1980-82, chmn. polit. action com. 1985-88, com. on allied hosp. assns. 1989-90), Am. Soc. Assn. Execs. Office: Calif Healthcare Assn PO Box 1100 1201 K St Ste 800 Sacramento CA 95212-1100

DAVAGNINO, JUAN V., scientist; b. Santiago, Chile, July 14, 1952; came to U.S., 1985; s. Juan A. and Vicenta (Gilabert) D.; m. Judith M. Salinas, Mar. 8, 1956; 1 child, Andres. BS in Biology, U. Chile, Santiago, 1976, MS in Biology, 1978, PhD in Biochemistry, 1985. Postdoctoral fellow Harvard Med. Sch., Boston, 1985-90, Calif. Inst. Tech., Pasadena, 1990-92; scientist IV Baxter Healthcare Co., Duarte, Calif., 1992-94, scientist V, 1994-95, group leader formulation, 1995—. Contbr. articles to profl. jours. Nat. rsch. fellow Nat. Commn. for Rsch., Santiago, 1979-81, Harvard U. fellow, 1985, Cancer Rsch. Campaign Internat. fellow, 1986, Charles A. King Trust fellow Med. Found. Boston, 1987-89. Mem. AAAS. Office: Baxter Healthcare Co Hyland Divsn 1720 Flower Ave Duarte CA 91010-2923

DAVENPORT, ALFRED LARUE, JR., manufacturing company executive; b. Upland, Calif., May 6, 1921; s. Alfred Larue and Nettie (Blocker) D.; m. Darrow Ormsbee Beazlie, May 16, 1950 (div. 1953); m. Jean Ann Given, June 21, 1957 (wid. Apr. 1990); children: Lawrence, Terisa, Lisa, Nancy; m. Inez Bothwell, Aug. 8, 1993. Student, Chaffey Jr. Coll., Ontario, Calif., 1940; BE in Indsl. Engring., U. So. Calif., 1943. Weight engring. Lockheed Aircraft, Burbank, Calif., 1940-41; ptnr. Pacific Traders, L.A., 1946-48; founder, pres. Pactra Industries, Inc., L.A., 1947-79; owner Davenport Internat., Ltd., Van Nuys, Calif., 1979—; pres., founder Trans Container, Inc., Upland, Calif., 1970-79; pres., owner Pactra Hobby, Inc., Encino, Calif., 1983—, Davenport Export-Import, Inc., Encino, Calif., 1982-93; cons. Plasti-Kote, Inc., Medina, Ohio, 1985-87; pres. Pactra Coatings Inc., Hobby Div., Upland, 1985-89; mgr. craft div. Plasti-Kote Inc., Medina, Ohio, 1989-92; bd. dirs. R.C. Dudek, Inc., Oxnard, Calif.;stockholder, v.p., mktg. dir. Enviroman Inc., 1994—; dir. mktg. Therapy Easel Products, 1996—. Lt. USN, 1943-46. Recipient Blue Key, U. So. Calif., L.A., 1942. Mem. So. Calif. Hobby Industry Assn. (sec. 1959-62), Hobby Industry Assn. Am. (dir. 1961-64), Young Pres. Orgn. (L.A. chpt.), World Bus. Coun. (bd. dirs. 1980-84), Woodland Hills Country Club (treas. 1981-83), Sigma Phi Epsilon (v.p. 1954-81, alumni bd. dirs. 1955-75, Disting. Bro. award 1979, Alumni of Yr. award 1975), Balboa Basin Yacht Club. Republican. Congregationalist. Home: 5330 Dubois Ave Woodland Hills CA 91367-6017 Office: Davenport Internat-Pactra Inc Enviroman Internat 18075 Ventura Blvd Encino CA 91316-3517

DAVENPORT, JANET LEE, real estate saleswomen, small business owner; b. Napa, Calif., Dec. 10, 1938; d. George Perry and Stella Dolores (Ramalho) Gomez; m. Bingo George Wesner, Aug. 4, 1957 (July 1978); children: Bing George, Diane Estelle; m. Marvin Eugene Davenport, Jan. 13, 1979. Student, U. Calif., Davis, 1956-57, Nat. Jud. Coll., 1975-79. Co-owner, operator Bar JB Ranch, Benicia, Calif., 1960-71, Lovelock, Nev., 1971-78; owner, mgr. Wesner Bookkeeping Svc., Lovelock, 1973-78; chief tribal judge Ct. Indian Offenses, Lovelock, 1975-79; justice of peace, coroner County of Pershing, Lovelock, 1975-79; paralegal, legal sec. Samuel S. Wardle, Carson City, Nev., 1979; dep. ct. adminstr. Reno Mcpl. Ct., Reno, 1979-81; co-owner horse farm Reno, 1979—, freelance real estate investor, 1979—; real estate saleswoman Merrill Lynch Realtors, Sparks, Nev., 1981-82; realtor, farm and ranch div. mgr. Copple and Assocs., Realtors, Sparks, 1982-91; real estate saleswoman Vail and Assocs. Realty, Reno, Nev., 1991—; co-owner, operator Lovelock (Nev.) Merc. Co., 1988—; sec. Nev. Judges Assn., 1977-78. Dir. Pershing County Drug and Alcohol Abuse Council, Lovelock, 1976-78. Mem. Reno/Sparks Bd. Realtors, Nat. Assn. Realtors, Nev. Assn. Realtors, Am. Quarter Horse Assn. Republican. Roman Catholic. Home: 4805 Sinelio Dr Reno NV 89502-9510 Office: Vail and Assocs Realty 1700 S Virginia St Reno NV 89502-2811

DAVENPORT, ROBERT RALSEY, writer; b. Brookline, Mass., Apr. 30, 1950; s. Harry Augustus and Jean Ann (Yeager) D. BA, Middlebury Coll., 1972; JD, St. John's U., N.Y.C., 1979; MBA, Harvard U., 1984. Bar: N.Y. 1980, Calif. 1988. Atty. U.S. Dept. Justice, Washington, 1979-81, Office Gen. Counsel Dept. Navy, Washington, 1981-82; creative exec. Twentieth Century-Fox Film Corp., L.A., Calif., 1983, Columbia Broadcasting System, L.A., 1984-85, Viacom Prodns., L.A., 1986-87; dir. bus. affairs New World TV, L.A., 1987-88; exec. v.p. Soaring Eagle Prodns., L.A., 1988-89; pres. The Historic Trust, L.A., 1992—. Author: The Davenport Genealogy, 1982, Hereditary Society Blue Book, 1992, 94, 95, 96, 97, Rich and Famous Baby Name Book, 1994, Pet Names of The Rich and Famous, 1995, The Celebrity Almanac, 1995, The Celebrity Birthday Book, 1996. Maj. U.S. Army. Mem. Soc. of Cincinnati (past pres. Calif. chpt.), St. George's Soc. L.A. (pres.), DAV (life), Order of Indian Wars of U.S., Aztec Club of 1847. Office: The Historic Trust PO Box 1989 Beverly Hills CA 90213

DAVENPORT, ROGER LEE, research engineer; b. Sacramento, Calif., Oct. 27, 1955, s. Lee Edwin and Ada Fern (Henderson) D.; m. Mary Rebecca Alice Youtz, Dec. 31, 1977 (div. Apr. 1992). AB Physics, U. Calif., Berkeley, 1977; MSME, U. Ariz., 1979. Assoc. engr. Solar Energy Rsch. Inst., Golden, Colo., 1979-82; cons. Darmstadt, Fed. Republic Germany, 1982-84; missionary Eastern European Sem., Vienna, Austria, 1984-87; staff researcher Sci. Applications Internat. Corp., San Diego, 1987—. Mem. Am. Solar Energy Soc., Denver Electric Coun., Sierra Club, Colo. Mountain Club, Phi Beta Kappa. Home: 19076 W 59th Dr Golden CO 80403-1057 Office: SAIC Ste 202 15000 W 6th Ave Golden CO 80401-5047

DAVENPORT, WILLIAM HAROLD, mathematics educator; b. Jackson, Tenn., Dec. 21, 1935; s. John Heron and Mary (Troutt) D.; m. Mary Janice Johnson, Mar. 18, 1960; children—Mark Edson, Amber Yvette; m. Sandra Elaine Holloway, July 30, 1973; children—William Harold II, David Carleton, Bennett John Joseph. B.S., U. Tenn., 1962; M.S., Tex. A&M U., 1966; Ph.D. in Math., U. Ala., 1971. Aerospace technologist NASA Manned Spacecraft Ctr., Houston, 1962-64; research mathematician Brown Engring. Co., Huntsville, Ala., 1966-67; teaching fellow, instr. math. U. Ala., University, 1967-71; mathematician U.S. Army Missile Command, Huntsville, 1971-72; asst. prof. math. U. Petroleum and Minerals, Dhahran, Saudi Arabia, 1972-77, Columbus Coll., Ga., 1977-81; assoc. prof. U. Ark., Little Rock, 1981-87, Northwestern State U., Natchitoches, La., 1987-88, Mesa State Coll., Grand Junction, Colo., 1988—. Served with USN, 1954-58. Mem. Am. Math. Soc., Math. Assn. Am., Sigma Pi Sigma, Phi Kappa Phi, Pi Mu Epsilon. Roman Catholic. Avocation: tennis.

DAVEY, PATRICIA AILEEN, poet, artist, writer; b. Portland, Oreg., Nov. 21, 1933; d. James Lewis and Jean K. (Dick) Watson; widowed; 1 child, Georgia Aileen Davey; m. Maurice R. Jones (div.). Student, Lewis and Clark Coll., 1951-54, U. Wash., 1964-66, Portland State U., 1966-67. Various office jobs Portland and Seattle, 1954-66; poet, artist and writer, 1968—. Exhibited in group shows at Eloise's Contemporary Gallery, many others; contbr. poems to mags. and anthologies. Mem. Astara.

DAVIAU, DONALD GEORGE, foreign language educator; b. West Medway, Mass., Sept. 30, 1927; s. George and Jenny (Burbank) D.; m. Patricia E. Mara, Aug. 20, 1950; children: Katherine Anne, Robert Laurence, Thomas George, Julie Marie. BA, Clark U., 1950; MA, U. Calif., Berkeley, 1952, PhD, 1955. From asst. prof. to prof. German U. Calif., Riverside, 1955—. Author: Hermann Bahr: The Catalyst of Modernity, 1986, The Major Figures of Austrian Literature, vol. 1, 1988, vol. 2, 1990, vol. 3, 1992, vol. 4, 1995; contbr. articles to profl. jours. With USN, 1945-46. Recipient Cross of Honor for Art and Sci. Austrian Govt., 1978. Mem. MLA, Am. Assn. Tchrs. German, Philol. Assn. the Pacific Coast, Internat. Arthur Schnitzler Assn. (pres.), Am. Coun. for the Study Austrian Lit. (pres.), Jura Soyfer Soc. Office: Univ Calif Dept Literatures Riverside CA 92521

DAVID, WARD S., bank officer, retired federal agency executive; b. Bertrand, Nebr., Nov. 29, 1934; s. Stanton S. and Helen M. (Gifford) D.; married Aug. 12, 1956; children: Kimberly, Jeri, Mickey, Stanley, Rod. BS in Agriculture, U. Nebr., 1956. Conservationist USDA, North Platte, Nebr., 1957-59; work unit conservationist USDA, Holdrege, Nebr., 1959-68; dist. conservationist USDA, Alma, Nebr., 1968-75; area conservationist USDA, Tucumcari, N.Mex., 1975-83, Escondido, Calif., 1983-86; divsn. ops. mgr. USDA, Washington, 1986-93, ret., 1993; ops. mgr. Bank of Am., Fallbrook, Calif., 1994—. Author: Ask Not for Victory, 1991; contbr. articles to various publs. Mem. sch. bd. Alma, 1971-75. With USAFR, 1956-57. Mem. Soc. Conservation Soc. Am. (charter, pres. 1967-69), Am. Assn. Ret. Persons (officer). Republican. Methodist. Home: 2321 Morro Rd Fallbrook CA 92028 Office: Bank of Am 1125 S Main Fallbrook CA 92028

DAVIDOW, SHELDON M., consulting firm and insurance executive; b. Winnipeg, Man., Can., Apr. 17, 1950; came to U.S., 1964; s. Harold C. and Corinne L. (Trester) D.; m. Carol Curinga, May 1, 1976 (div. Dec. 1993); children: Katherine C., Allison C.; m. Kathryn Kendrick, Sept. 17, 1994; stepchildren: Clancy Coakley, Betty Kay Coakley, Kendrick Coakley. BS magna cum laude, UCLA, 1974. Aid L.A. City Coun., 1974-78; dir. Hollywood C. of C., L.A., 1978-80; pres. Spectrum Resources, Inc., L.A., 1979-82; chief cons. Calif. State Senate, Sacramento, 1982-88; exec. v.p. The Doctors' Co., Napa, Calif., 1988-93; pres. Sheldon M. Davidow & Assocs., Napa, 1993—; COO Archtl. Glass Design, Inc., Napa, 1995-96; bd. dirs. Robert Plan Corp., Alistar Ins. Co., Archtl. Glass Design, Inc. Author: Guide to Auto Insurance, 1987. Pres. Napa Valley Econ. Devel. Corp., 1995—; chmn. Bus. Edn. Partnership, Napa, 1993-95; mem. Napa Valley Flood Control Corp., 1996—; mem. L.A. County Dem. Coun., 1978-80. Recipient Pub. Svc. award Prism Soc., L.A., 1977, Calif. State Senate award, 1977, 88, Calif. State Assembly award, 1988. Democrat. Jewish. Office: 46 Kreuse Canyon Rd Napa CA 94559

DAVIDSON, ALICE WARE, nurse, educator; b. Warren, Ohio, Feb. 24, 1945; d. Harold V. and Ruby Arlene (Brunson) Ware; widowed; children: Anne Claire, William John. Diploma, St. Luke's Hosp., Cleve., 1966; BSN, Case Western Res. U., 1969, MSN, 1971; PhD, U. Colo., 1988. Rsch. asst. Coll. Environ. Design U. Colo., Boulder; coord. ambulatory care Mercy Med. Ctr., Springfield, Ohio; asst. prof. Wright State U., Dayton, Ohio; rsch. educator Boulder Community Hosp., 1989-93; asst. prof. U. Colo., Denver, 1989-95; rsch. fellow Harvard Med. Sch., McLean Hosp., Boston, 1994-95; with Ware Davidson Environ. Consulting, Boulder, 1995—; cons. on environ. design, Denver. Contbr. articles to profl. publs. Home: 1045 Pine St Boulder CO 80302

DAVIDSON, BILL (WILLIAM JOHN DAVIDSON), entertainment journalist, author; b. Jersey City, Mar. 4, 1918; s. Louis J. and Gertrude (Platt) D.; m. Muriel Roberts, May 21, 1960 (dec. Sept. 1983); 1 child, Carol; m. Maralynne Beth Nitz, July 27, 1986. BA, NYU, 1939. Assoc. editor Collier's mag., N.Y.C., 1946-56; contbg. editor Look mag., N.Y.C., 1956-61; editor-at-large Saturday Evening Post, N.Y.C., 1961-69; radio commentator NBC, N.Y.C., 1968-71; TV writer Universal Studios, Universal City, Calif., 1971-76; contbg. editor TV Guide, Radnor, Pa., 1971-90, L.A. Mag., 1992-95; chmn. alumni communications com. NYU, 1959-64. Author: The Real and the Unreal, Six Brave Presidents, 1962, Indict and Convict, 1971, (with Sid Caesar) Where Have I Been?, 1982, Spencer Tracy: Tragic Idol, 1988, Jane Fonda: An Intimate Biography, 1990, (with Danny Thomas) Make Room for Daddy, 1991. Mem. N.Y. County Dem. com., N.Y.C., 1948-50. Served as sgt. U.S. Army, 1941-45, ETO. Recipient Disting. Reporting award Sigma Delta Chi, 1951, 53, Albert Lasker Med. Journalism award, 1953, Disting. Journalism award Family Service Assn. Am., 1963. Mem. Writers Guild Am. West. Democrat. Home: 13225 Morrison St Sherman Oaks CA 91423-2156

DAVIDSON, GORDON, theatrical producer, director; b. Bklyn., May 7, 1933; s. Joseph H. and Alice (Gordon) D.; m. Judith Swiller, Sept. 21, 1958; children: Adam, Rachel. B.A., Cornell U.; M.A., Case Western Res. U.; L.H.D. (hon.), Bklyn. Coll.; D. Performing Arts (hon.), Calif. Inst. Arts; D.F.A. (hon.), Claremont U. Ctr. Stage mgr. Phoenix Theatre Co., 1958-60, Am. Shakespeare Festival Theatre, 1958-60, Dallas Civic Opera, 1960-61, Martha Graham Dance Co., 1962; mng. dir. Theatre Group at UCLA, 1965-67; artistic dir., producer Center Theatre Group Mark Taper Forum, 1967—; co-founder New Theatre For Now, Mark Taper Forum, 1970; Past mem. theatre panel Nat. Endowment for Arts; past pres. Theatre Communications Group; mem. adv. council Internat. Theatre Inst.; mem. adv. com. Cornell Ctr. for Performing Arts; cons. Denver Center for the Performing Arts; bd. dirs. several arts orgns. including Am. Arts Alliance. Producer, dir. over 150 major theatrical prodns. including The Deputy, 1965, Candide, 1966, The Devils, 1967, Who's Happy Now, 1967, In the Matter of J. Robert Oppenheimer, 1968 (N.Y. Drama Desk award), Sew, Murderous Angels, 1970, Rosebloom, 1970, The Trial of the Catonsville Nine, 1971 (Obie award, Tony award nomination), Henry IV, Part I, 1972, Mass, 1973, Hamlet, 1974, Savages, 1974 (Obie award), Too Much Johnson, 1975, The Shadow Box, 1975 (Tony award, Outer Critics Circle Best Dir. award), And Where She Stops Nobody Knows, 1976, Getting Out, 1977, Black Angel, 1978, Terra Nova, 1979, Children of a Lesser God, 1979, The Lady and the Clarinet, 1980, Chekhov in Yalta, 1981, Tales from Hollywood, 1982, The American Clock, 1984, The Hands of Its Enemy, 1984, Traveler in the Dark, 1985, The Real Thing, 1986, Ghetto, 1986, A Lie of the Mind, 1988; dir. operas including Cosi Fan Tutte, Otello, Beatrice and Benedick, Carmen, La Boheme, Il Trovatore, Harriet, A Woman Called Moses, A Midsummer Night's Dream, 1988; TV film The Trial of the Catonsville Nine, 1971; exec. producer Zoot Suit, 1981; producer for TV It's the Willingness, PBS Visions Series, 1979, Who's Happy Now?, NET Theatre in Am. Series; dir. A Little Night Music, 1990. Trustee Ctr. for Music, Drama and Art; past pres. League Resident Theatres; past v.p. Am. Nat. Theatre Acad; advisor Fund for New Am. Plays. Recipient N.Y. Drama Desk award for direction, 1969; recipient Los Angeles Drama Critics Circle awards for direction, 1971, 74, 75, Margo Jones award New Theatre for Now, 1970, 76, Obie award, 1971, 77, Outer Critics Circle award, 1977, Tony award for direction, 1977, award John Harvard, award Nat. Acad. TV Arts and Scis., award Nosotros Golden Eagle, award N.Y. League for Hard of Hearing, award N.Y. Speech and Hearing Assn., award Am. Theatre Assn., award Los Angeles Human Relations Commn.; Guggenheim fellow, 1983. Mem. League Resident Theatres (past pres.), ANTA (v.p. 1975). Office: Ctr Theatre Group Mark Taper Forum 135 N Grand Ave Los Angeles CA 90012-3013

DAVIDSON, IDELLE, writer; b. L.A., Jan. 26, 1953; d. Donald and Taube (Weisbart) Wiseman; m. Peter A. Davidson; children: Benjamin, Matthew. BA in Polit. Sci., UCLA, 1974, MPA, 1975. Author: (with others) Nonfiction for the 1990s, 1990; reporter: Time Mag., 1989; contbr. articles to profl. jours. Mem. Am. Soc. Journalists and Authors (chpt. bd. mem. 1993-94), Independent Writers of So. Calif. (dir.-at-large 1992, Svc. awards 1992, 94).

DAVIDSON, JAMES MADISON, III, engineer, technical manager; b. San Antonio, Feb. 24, 1930; s. James Madison Jr. and Ella Louise (Wehmeyer) D.; m. Geneva Upchurch, Aug. 28, 1949; children: Robert John, William Allen, James Brian. BS, S.W. Tex. State U., 1951. Registered profl. engr., Wash. Engr., sr. engr. GE Co., Richland, Wash., 1951-65; mgr. fast flux test facility, materials and tech. dept. Battelle-Pacific N.W. Lab., Richland, 1965-67, sr. adviser to lab. dir., 1967-72; mgr. office nat. security tech. Battelle-Pacific N.W. Lab., 1972-89; staff mem. Los Alamos (N.Mex.) Nat. Lab., 1989-90, acting group leader, 1990-91, group leader, 1992-94; sr. advisor nonproliferation and internat. tech., 1994—; tech. adviser Coordinating Com. on Munitions, Paris, 1987—. Exec. bd. Boy Scouts Am., 1970-75. Recipient Silver Beaver award Boy Scouts Am., 1972. Home: 18 W Wildflower Dr Santa Fe NM 87501-8506

DAVIDSON, JEANNIE, costume designer; b. San Francisco, Mar. 21, 1938; d. Willis H. and Dorothy J. (Starks) Rich; children from previous marriage: David L. Schultz (dec. Jan. 1997), Mark P. Schultz, Seana Davidson, Michael Davidson (dec. 1996); m. Bryan N. St. Germain, June 14, 1980. BA, Stanford (Calif.) U., 1961, postgrad., 1965-68. Resident costume designer Oreg. Shakespearean Festival, Ashland, 1969-91; owner, designer Ravenna Fabric Studio, Inc., Medford, Oreg., 1994—; mfr. custom ch. vestments. Designer over 150 prodns. including all 37 of Shakespeare's plays. Recipient numerous awards for excellence in costume design. Mem. U.S. Inst. for Theatre Tech., Phi Beta Kappa.

DAVIDSON, JOEL, surgeon; b. Pitts., June 23, 1939; s. Jack and Clara (Locker) D.; m. Linda Lee, Sept. 2, 1984; children: Amy Kubas, Shana, Sharon. BS, Washington & Jefferson U., 1960; MD, U. Pitts., 1964. Intern Washington (Pa.) Hosp., 1964-65; resident West Penn Hosp., Pitts., 1965-69; surgeon Davidson/Rosen Chartered, Las Vegas, Nev., 1970—; vice chief of surgery Sunrise Hosp., Las Vegas, 1979-82; pres. Nev. Peer Rev. Orgn., Las Vegas, 1985. Bd. dirs. Am. Cancer Soc., Las Vegas, 1988-90. Capt. USAFR, 1969-73. Fellow ACS, AMA, Am. Bd. Surgeons, Am. Soc. for Laser Medicine and Surgery, Nev. State Med. Soc., Clark County Med. Soc. (bd. trustees 1973-84, pres. 1982-83). Jewish. Office: Davidson/Rosen Chartered 3196 S Maryland Pkwy Ste 204 Las Vegas NV 89109-2313

DAVIDSON, JOHN ROBERT (JAY), banking executive; b. L.A., Mar. 30, 1950; s. John Robert Davidson and Carolyn Rose Monson Wiederanders; m. Kristina Maria Jonson, Dec. 29, 1978; children: Joshua Kingseley, Michelle Maria. BSME, U. N.D., 1972; postgrad., AMP Corp. Leadership Coll., 1990. Engr. Dow Chem. Co., Pauls Valley, Okla., 1972-74; investor Mpls., 1974-77; account exec. AMP Inc., Boulder, Colo., 1977-83; mkt. mgr. AMP Inc., Harrisburg, Pa., 1983-86; dist. mgr. AMP Inc., Denver, 1986-90, nat. mgr., 1990-95; chmn. of bd., CEO 1st Am. State Bank of Denver, 1995—; dir./cons. Am. State Bank, Williston, N.D., 1988—, dir. funds mgmt. com., 1994—, mem. exec. com., 1996; mem. exec. com., chmn. bd. dirs. First Am. State Bank, Denver, 1995—; personal fin. cons./investor, 1988—. Supporter Jr. League of Denver; supporter, mem. bd. dirs. Kempe Children's Found.; supporter, men's guild bd. mem., mem. devel. bd. Am. Heart Assn., Arthritis Found., Children's Hosp., Vols. of Am. Heart Assn.; mem. Rep. Nat. Com.; mem. devel. bd. Am. Heart Assn.; event chairperson Arapahee House. Recipient Presdl. Legion of Merit, Colo. Rep. Party. Mem. Masons, Presdl. Legion of Merit. Home: 5780 Goldsmith Pl Greenwood Village CO 80111 Office: 1st Am State Bank 8101 E Belleview Ave Denver CO 80237

DAVIDSON, JULI, creativity consultant; b. Houston, Aug. 23, 1960; d. Martin J. Davidson and Ruth Marder. Diploma, Park Sch., Brooklandville, Md., 1978; Cert., Richmond Coll., Surrey, Eng., 1978; student, Austin Coll., U. N.Mex, others, 1978-84, Hollywood Film Inst., 1996. Cert. med. terminology and transcription, 1981. Pres. mail order co. Surrenderings, Inc., Albuquerque, 1989-93; owner, artist Juli Davidson Studio Gallery, Albuquerque, 1987-89; freelance writer, editor, photographer Albuquerque, 1985-86; pres., paper artist, writer SI: A Paperworks Gallery, Sante Fe, 1993; exec. adminstr. Albuquerque Art Bus. Assn., 1989; bd. sec. Albuquerque United Artists, 1988; media, entertainment, and multimedia creativity cons. Editor, pub. 2C3P ZN, 1995; contbr. to various publs. and subject of various art revs.; writer, pub. mail-order publs., 1995; pub. creativity products for The Creative Process; screenplay and teleplay contest critic Southwest Writers Workshop, 1996; mkt. rsch. theatrical film reviewer, Audience Response, 1995; sitcom bible and pilot writer Think Tank Ink Prods, 1995. Recipient 2d and 3d place photography awards Churches in New Mexico Exhibit, 1985, 4th place Colorfest Human Interest Category, Colo., 1986; recipient writing award Garden Writers Assn. of Am., 1993, for publishing handmade booklet on dividing and multiplying potted plants. Mem. Writers Connection. Studio: PO Box 21669-WW Albuquerque NM 87154-1669

DAVIDSON, MARK, writer, educator; b. N.Y.C., Sept. 25, 1938; m. Elizabeth Browne, May 29, 1989; 1 child, Samantha. BA in Polit. Sci., UCLA, 1958; MS in Journalism, Columbia U., 1960. Sci. writer U. So. Calif., L.A., 1980-90; prof. comm. Calif. State U., Dominguez Hills, Carson, 1985—; freelance writer; faculty adviser Soc. Profl. Journalists, 1993-96; lectr. in field; writer for Steve Allen Show, 1964, Dinah Shore Show, 1978, CBS Mag. Show with Connie Chung, 1980. Author: Thought Control, 1995, rev. edt., 1997 (Nat. Emmy for writing NATAS), Watchwords: A Dictionary of American English Usage, 1995, rev. edit., 1997. Sackett scholar Columbia U. Mem. PEN, Am. Soc. Journalists and Authors, Nat. Assn. Sci. Writers, Am. Med. Writers Assn., Authors Guild, Writers Guild Am., Calif. Faculty Assn. (v.p. Dominguez Hills chpt. 1992-96), Soc. Advancement Edn. (assoc. mass media editor 1997—). Home: 195 Malcolm Dr Pasadena CA 91105-1309 Office: Calif State U 1000 E Victoria St Carson CA 90747-0001

DAVIDSON, ROBERT LEE, III, retired lawyer, author, consultant; b. Nevada, Mo., May 10, 1923; s. Robert Lee and Nancy Helen (Manker) D.; m. Lorena Elizabeth Turner, children: Roberta Anne, Curtis Lee. BSChemE, U. Mo., 1944, MSChemE, 1947; JD, Fordham U., 1978. Bar: N.J. 1980. Editor in chief Petro/Chem. Engring., Dallas, 1964-66; mng. editor Chem. Engring., N.Y.C., 1966-75; editor-in-chief McGraw Hill Book Co., N.Y.C., 1975-80, dir. book pub. ctr., 1980-82; pvt. practice, Princeton, N.J., 1980-93; ret., 1993; editor Attys. Computer Report, 1984-85, cons. on publs., 1982—. Author: Successful Process Plant Practices, 1958. Author: Contracting Your Services, 1990; co-editor: Petroleum Processing Handbook, 1967, Handbook of Water Soluble Gums and Resins, 1980, Contracting Your Services, 1990, Small Business Incorporation Kit, 1993, Small Business Partnership Kit, 1993, Small Business Bankruptcy Kit, 1993. 1st lt. U.S. Army, 1942-46. Mem. AIChE, Sigma Xi, Tau Beta Pi. Home: 18404 N Laurel Dr Sun City AZ 85373-1755 Office: PO Box 2286 Sun City AZ 85372-2286

DAVIDSON, TERENCE MARK, surgery educator, otolaryngologist; b. Chgo., July 7, 1945. MD, UCLA, 1971. Diplomate Am. Bd. Otolaryngology. Intern UCLA, 1971-72; fellow Am. Acad. Facial Plastic and Reconstructive Surgery, Brookline, Mass., 1976; resident in surgery and otolaryngology U. Calif., San Diego, 1972-75; attending staff physician U. Calif. Med. Ctr., San Diego, 1976—, assoc. dean continuing med. edn., 1982—, asst. prof., 1976-82, assoc. prof., 1982-86, prof., 1986—, acting chief div. head and neck surgery, 1984-85; dir. Nasal Disfunction Clinic U. Calif., San Diego, 1985—; staff surgeon VA Med. Ctr., San Diego, 1976—, sect. chief head and neck surgery, 1978-90, sect. chief, 1993—; courtesy staff physician Pomerado Hosp., Poway, Calif., 1981—, cons. staff physician, 1990—; clin. researcher in smell, taste, and nasal dysfunction, 1987—. Med. TV producer, 1976—. Grantee NIH, 1991-96. Fellow ACS, Skin Cancer Found. (hon.); mem. AMA, Am. Acad. Facial Plastic and Reconstructive Surgeons (John Dickinson Tchr. of Yr. award 1985), Am. Acad. Otolaryngology-Head and Neck Surgeons, Am. Rhinologic Soc., Calif. Med. Assn. Office: U Calif Med Ctr 200 W Arbor Dr San Diego CA 92103-1911

DAVIDSON, THOMAS FERGUSON, chemical engineer; b. N.Y.C., N.Y., Jan. 5, 1930; s. Lorimer Arthur and Elizabeth (Valentine) D.; m. Nancy Lee Selecman, Nov. 10, 1951; children: Thomas Ferguson, Richard Alan, Gwyn Ann. BS in Engring., U. Md., 1951. Sr. project engr. Wright Air Devel. Ctr., Dayton, Ohio, 1951-58; dep. dir. Solid Sys. Divsn., Edwards, Calif., 1959-60; mgr. govt. ops. Thiokol Chem. Corp., Ogden, Utah, 1960-64; dir. aerospace mktg. Thiokol Chem. Corp., Bristol, Pa., 1965-67; dir. tech. mgmt. Thiokol Chem. Corp., Ogden, 1968-82; v.p. tech. Morton Thiokol Inc., Chgo., 1983-88, Thiokol Corp., Ogden, 1989-90; cons. Ogden, 1990—; mem. subcom. lubrications and wear NACA, Washington, 1955-57; chmn. Joint Army, Navy, NASA, Air Force exec. com., 1959-60. Editor: National Rocket Strategic Plan, 1990; contbr. articles to profl. jours. Chmn. bd. dirs. Wesley Acad., Ogden, 1990-94; trustee Family Counseling Svc., Ogden, 1991-97; bd. dirs. Habitat for Humanity Internat., 1991-93; mem. Am. Security Coun., Washington, 1976—, Rep. Presdl. Task Force, Washington, 1987—; vice moderator SHARED Ministry Utah, 1993-94; mem. Utah Bd. Edn., 1993-96, Utah Space Ctr. Authority Bd., 1993-95. Lt. USAF, 1951-53. Fellow AIAA (assoc., sect. chmn. 1979-80, chmn. AIAA rocket propulsion com. 1987-90, mem. AIA aerospace tech. coun. 1987-90, Wyld Propulsion award 1991); mem. Am. Newcomen Soc., Smithsonian Instn., Exch. Club, Ogden Golf and Country Club, Weber State Wildcat Club. Republican. Methodist. Home: 4755 Banbury Ln Ogden UT 84403-4484

DAVIDSON, VALERIE LAVERGNE, institute administrator; b. Chgo., Nov. 23, 1949; d. Richard W. and Jeraldine (Schliephake) D.; m. David Townsend Mason III, Aug. 16; 1 child, Yuri R. Mason. BA, Calif. State U., Northridge, 1985; MS in Health Adminstrn., Calif. State U., L.A., 1994; cert. in human performance, U. So. Calif., 1996. Supr. support svcs. St. John's Hosp., Santa Monica, Calif., 1976-81; adminstrv. dir. So. Calif. PSA Inst., Beverly Hills, Calif., 1983—; mgmt. cons. for charitable orgns., L.A., 1990—. Contbr. articles to profl. publs. Pres. Sch. Bus. Alumni Calif. State U., 1995—, adv. mem. health care mgmt. program., 1995—. Mem. ASTD, Am. Coll. Health Care Execs., Phi Kappa Phi. Home and Office: 11260 Overland Ave # 20F Culver City CA 90230

DAVIDSON-SHEPARD, GAY, secondary education educator; b. Long Beach, Calif., Dec. 15, 1951; d. Leyton Paul and Ruth Leona (Gritzmaker) Davidson; m. Daniel A. Shepard, June 24, 1983. BA, U. Calif., Irvine, 1972; MA, Columbia Pacific U., 1986. Cert. elem. and secondary edn. tchr. Tchr. mid. sch. Ocean View Sch. Dist., Huntington Beach, Calif., 1973—; team mem. Calif. learning assessment system State Dept. of Edn., Sacramento, 1987—; chief reader Orange County pentathlon and decathlon Orange County Dept. Edn., Costa Mesa, Calif., 1980—; sr. reader new standards State Dept. Edn., Sacramento, 1995—; lang. arts cons. various sch. dists., Calif., 1976—; chief reader Calif. Learning Assessment System, Sacramento, 1993—; sr. reader New Stds., 1995—. Author/cons.: Teacher's Guide for Direct Assessment Writing, 1990; test writer Acad. Pentathlon Test, 1984—, Dist. Lang. Art Proficiency Test, 1980—. Mem. NEA, AAUS, AAUW, Nat. Assn. Tchrs. of English, Calif. Reading Assn., Mensa, Calif. Tchrs. Assn., Ocean View Tchrs. Assn. Democrat. Home: 6782 Rook Dr Huntington Beach CA 92647-5641 Office: Mesa View Sch 17601 Avilla Ln Huntington Beach CA 92647-6612

DAVIES, GARRY, biology educator; b. Blackpool, Eng., Jan. 12, 1943; came to U.S., 1954; s. John Verdon and Nellie (Rowley) D.; m. Rebecca Sue Truesdell, May 13, 1973. B of Forestry, Stephen F. Austin State Coll., 1967; MSc in Forestry, Stephen F. Austin State U., 1973; PhD in Forestry, Tex. A&M U., 1981. Seasonal naturalist Nat. Pk. Svc., Yellowstone Nat. Pk., Wyo., summers 1972-85; curator of collections Nat. Pk. Svc., Anchorage, 1987-90; asst. prof. biology U. Alaska, Anchorage, 1990—. Vol. sci. tchr. Anchorage Elem. Schs., 1990—; comty. advisor Toshiba-Nat. Sci. Tchrs. Assn. Explora Vision Awards, 1996. With USN, 1967-71. Herbarium grantee Alaska Native Plant Soc., 1996. Home: 8800 Tempest Cir Anchorage AK 99507 Office: U Alaska 3211 Providence Dr Anchorage AK 99508

DAVIES, HARRIETT MARIE (LOLLY DAVIES), educator; b. Chgo., July 2, 1942; d. Howard Jack and Mamie Marie (Harriett) Cox; m. Ronald Lee Davies, Mar. 22, 1975. BS in Home Econs., So. Ill. U., 1965, MS in Edn., 1973. Tchg. cert. in home econs., bus., mktg., Coop. Office Edn., Ariz. Home econs. tchr. Hanover (Ill.) H.S., 1965; home econs., health tchr., home econ. dept. head Sholes Jr. H.S., Milw., 1965-67; vocat. home econs., consumer edn. tchr. Roxana (Ill.) H.S., 1967-78; bus. instr. Lamson Bus. Coll., Tucson, Ariz., 1981-83; legal secretarial instr. Tucson Coll. Bus., 1983-84; instr. Portable Practical Edn. Preparation, Casa Grande, Ariz., 1984-85; tchr. bus. and hotel/restaurant mgmt., travel and tourism Casa Grande Union High Sch., 1985—; conv. coord. Ill. Consumer Edn. Assn., Springfield, Ill., 1973-75, v.p., 1975; spl. consumer cons. Ill. Office Edn., Springfield, 1975-78; mem. family fin. regional coun. Ind. State U., Terre Haute, Ind., 1973-75; coord. Sch.-Within-a-Sch., 1989-90. Food coord. C. of C. Golf Tourney, Casa Grande, 1993. Mem. NEA (life), Ariz. Edn. Assn., Ariz. Vocat. Assn., Casa Grande Edn. Assn. Home: 339 E Orange Dr Casa Grande AZ 85222-4043 Office: Casa Grande Union HS 420 E Florence Blvd Casa Grande AZ 85222-4140

DAVIES, JOHN G., federal judge; b. 1929. BA, U. Mich., 1953; postgrad., U. Sydney, 1956-57; LLB, UCLA, 1959. Assoc. Hagenbaugh, Murphy & Davies, L.A., 1961-72, Rosenfeld, Meyer & Susman, Beverly Hills, Calif., 1972-86; dist. judge U.S. Dist. Ct., L.A., 1986—; L.A. Ct. Arbitrator; Inns of Ct. Winner Gold medal in swimming 1952 Olympic Games, Helsinki, Finland. Mem. ABA, Internat. Acad. Trial Lawyers,Am. COll. Trial Lawyers, Am. Bd. Trial Advocates. Office: US Dist Ct US Courthouse Rm 890 22 E Temple St Los Angeles CA 90012*

DAVIES, JOHN NORMAN, state legislator; b. Bethesda, Md., Feb. 2, 1945; s. John William and Mary Jean (Norman) D.; m. Linda Ann Schandelmeier, July 17, 1993; children: Brian, Karen, Ben; stepchildren: Lauren, Mara. BA in Physics, Reed Coll., 1967; MS in Geophysics, U. Alaska, Fairbanks, 1970, PhD, 1975. Rsch. assoc. Lamont-Doherty Geol. Obs., Palisades, N.Y., 1974-81; state seismologist Alaska Dept. Natural Resources, Fairbanks, 1981-86, Geophys. Inst., U. Alaska, Fairbanks, 1986-92; mem. Alaska State Legislature, 1992—; mem. Nat. Earthquake Prediction Evaluation Coun.; coordinating scientist Alaska Volcano Obs., Fairbanks. Mem. Fairbanks North Star Borough Assembly, 1989-92. Named Disting. Alumnus, Reed Coll.; named among 3 most effective freshman legislators Legis. Staff and Lobbyists, Juneau, 1993. Mem. AAAS (pres. Alaska chpt.), Earthquake Enging. Rsch. Inst. (dir. Alaska chpt.). Democrat. Home: PO Box 81781 Fairbanks AK 99708 Office: Alaska State Legislature 119 N Cushman St Ste 207 Fairbanks AK 99701

DAVIES, JOHN TUDOR, physicist; b. Pontypridd, Wales, Eng., May 9, 1937; s. Herbert John and Catherine Mary Davies; m. Kay Dierst, Aug. 4, 1964; children: Gwen, Ceri, Rhodri. BA, Oxford (Eng.) U., 1959, MA, 1963, DPhil, 1963. Rsch. assoc. U. Pitts., 1962-65; lectr. U. Wales, Swansea, 1965-78; tech. devel. mgr. IPC/Branson/Gasonics, San Jose, Calif., 1978-95, DD Systems, 1995—. Mem. Am. Vacuum Soc., Semicondr. Equipment and Materials Inst. Methodist.

DAVIES, KELVIN JAMES ANTHONY, research scientist, educator, consultant, author; b. London, Oct. 15, 1951; came to U.S., 1975, dual citizenship, 1993; s. Alfred B. and Phyllis (Garcia) D.; m. Joanna Davies, Sept. 14, 1980; children: Sebastian, Alexander. BEd, Liverpool/Lancaster (Eng.) U., 1974; BS summa cum laude, MS, U. Wis., 1976, 77; C.Phil., U. Calif., Berkeley, 1979, PhD, 1981; DSc (hon.), U. Moscow, Russia, 1993; MD (hon.), U. Gdansk, Poland, 1995. Instr. Beal Sch. for Boys, London, 1974-75; rsch. asst. U. Wis., Madison, 1975-77; rsch. asst. U. Calif., Berkeley, 1977-80, lectr. physiology dept. physiology and anatomy, 1980-81; rsch. assoc. dept. biochemistry, inst. toxicology U. So. Calif., L.A., 1981-82, asst. prof. biochemistry, toxicology, 1983-86, assoc. prof. biochemistry, toxicology, 1986-90, prof. biochemistry, toxicology, 1990; instr., sr. rsch. assoc. dept. physiology and biophysics med. sch. Harvard U., 1982-83; prof. biochemistry and molecular biology Albany (N.Y.) Med. Coll., 1991-96, John A. Muntz Univ. prof., 1991-96, chmn. dept. biochemistry and molecular biology, 1991-96, prof. molecular medicine dept. medicine, 1993-96; prof., assoc. dean rsch. Andrus Gerontology Ctr. U. So. Calif., L.A., 1996—; James E. Birren chair gerontology, dir. Andrus Rsch. Inst., 1996—; dir. Nat. Parkinson's Found. Lab., 1996—; founder, dir. STAR program U. So. Calif./L.A. County Schs. Dist., 1984-90; dir. grad. studies inst. toxicology U. So. Calif., 1985-90, mem. cell biology program, 1986-91, fellow inst. molecular medicine, 1988-91; hon. dist. prof. Russian State Med. U., Moscow, 1989; coun. mem. Gordon Rsch. Confs. Frontiers of Sci., 1995-96. Author: Oxidative Damage and Repair: Chemical, Biological and Medical Aspects, 1992, Oxygen '93, 1994, The Oxygen Paradox, 1995; editor in chief: (jour.) Free Radical Biology and Medicine, 1981—; mem. editl. bd. Advances in Free Radical Biology and Medicine, 1985-87, The Biochem. Jour., 1989-95, Amino Acids, 1991—, Methods in Enzymology, 1991—, Molecular Aspects of Medicine, 1993—, Jours. Gerontology, 1996—, Cell and Molecular Life Scis., 1996—; contbr. over 200 articles to profl. jours. and books. Active Arts Coun., Pasadena, Calif., 1988-90; pres. Calif. Philharm. Orch. Found., 1996—; bd. govs. The Albany Acad. for Boys, 1994-96. Recipient Chancellors award for Rsch., U. Calif., Berkeley, 1981, Young Investigator award NIH, 1984, 50th Anniversary medal U. Gdansk, 1995; rsch., program project grantee NIH, 1983—; fellow Hoffman-La Roche, 1981, Arco, 1981, Am. Heart Assn., 1982, NIH, 1983. Fellow AAAS, Russian Acad. Scis.; mem. Am. Coll. Sports Medicine, Gerontol. Soc. Am., Am. Physiol. Soc. (Harwood S. Belding award 1982), Am. Soc. for Biochemistry and Molecular Biology, Internat. Union Biochemistry and Molecular Biology (coun. mem. 1995—), Biochem. Soc., Biophys. Soc., European Soc. Free Radical Rsch., Internat. Soc. Free Radical Rsch. (coun. 1988—), Internat. Cell rsch. Orgn., N.Y. Acad. Sci., Rsch. Coun. New Zealand, The Oxygen Soc. (fellow, sec. gen. 1987-90, pres.-elect 1990-92, pres. 1992-95), Sigma Xi, Phi Beta Kappa, Kappa Delta Pi. Office: Univ So Calif Andrus Gerontology Ctr 3715 McClintock Ave Rm 306 Los Angeles CA 90089-0191 Office: Andrus Gerontology Ctr Univ So Calif 3715 McClintock Ave Rm 306 Los Angeles CA 90089-0191

DAVIES, MERTON EDWARD, planetary scientist; b. St. Paul, Sept. 13, 1917; s. Albert Daniel and Lucile (McCabe) D.; AB, Stanford, 1938, postgrad., 1938-39; m. Margaret Louise Darling, Feb. 10, 1946; children: Deidra Louise Stauff, Albert Karl, Merton Randel. Instr. math. U. Nev., 1939-40; group leader Math. Lofting, Douglas Aircraft Co., El Segundo, Calif., 1940-48; sr. staff Rand Corp., Santa Monica, Calif., 1948-59, 62—, liaison USAF, Washington, 1959-62. U.S. observer inspected stas. under terms Antarctic Treaty, 1967; TV co-investigator Mariner Mars, 1969, 71, Mariner Venus/Mercury 1973 Mission, Voyager Mission, Galileo Mission, Magellan Mission, Mars Observer Mission, Clementine Mission. Fellow AIAA (assoc.); mem. AAAS, Am. Soc. Photogrammetry. Author: (with Bruce Murray) The View from Space, 1971; (with others) Atlas of Mercury, 1978. Patentee in field. Home: 1414 San Remo Dr Pacific Palisades CA 90272-2737 Office: RAND 1700 Main St Santa Monica CA 90401-3208

DAVIES, PAUL LEWIS, JR., retired lawyer; b. San Jose, Calif., July 21, 1930; s. Paul Lewis and Faith (Crummey) D.; m. Barbara Bechtel, Dec. 22, 1955; children: Laura (Mrs. Segundo Mateo), Paul Lewis III. AB, Stanford U., 1952; JD, Harvard U., 1957. Bar: Calif. 1957. Assoc. Pillsbury, Madison & Sutro, San Francisco, 1957-63, ptnr., 1963-89; gen. counsel Chevron Corp., 1984-89; bd. dirs. FMC Corp. Hon. trustee Calif. Acad. Scis., trustee, 1970-83, chmn., 1973-80; pres. Herbert Hoover Found.; bd. overseers Hoover Instn., chmn., 1976-82, 91-93; hon. regent U. of Pacific, regent, 1959-90. Lt. U.S. Army, 1952-54. Mem. Bohemian Club, Pacific-Union Club, Villa Taverna, World Trade Club (San Francisco), Claremont Country Club, Lakeview (Oakland, Calif.), Cypress Point (Pebble Beach, Calif.), Sainte Claire (San Jose, Calif.), Collectors, Explorers, Links (N.Y.C.), Met. Club, 1925 F St. (Washington), Chgo. Club, Phi Beta Kappa, Pi Sigma Alpha. Republican. Office: 50 Fremont St Ste 3520 San Francisco CA 94105-2239

DAVIES, WILLIAM RALPH, service executive; b. Santa Barbara, Calif., Aug. 17, 1955; s. Ralph Emmett and Georgann Marie (Cordingly) D.; m. Karen L. Blake, May 12, 1984. AA in Real Estate, Am. River Coll., 1978; BS in Fin., Ins. and Real Estate, Calif. State U., Sacramento, 1980; postgrad. in Internat. Bus., Golden Gate U., 1982-84. Real estate assoc. Kiernan Realtors, Sacramento, 1975-77; co-owner real estate firm Sacramento, 1977, pvt. practice real estate cons., property mgr., 1978-80; broker assoc. MBA Bus. Brokers, Sacramento, 1980-85, pres., 1985—; pres. WRD Cons. Group, Sacramento, 1984—; bd. dirs. WRD, Inc., Sacramento. Mem. Assisted Living Fedn., Calif. Assisted Living Facilities Assn. (bd. dirs.). Republican. Office: 1555 River Park Dr Ste 206 Sacramento CA 95815-4604

DAVINCI, USHANA MARALDO, multimedia artist, environmental designer; b. Osnabruck, Fed. Republic of Germany. BFA, Mich. State U.; MA, U. Osnabruck, Fed. Republic Germany; postgrad., U. Mexico. Owner, pub. Luma Arts Pubs., Woodland Hills, Calif., 1982-87; owner, dir. Sunstar Prodns., Santa Barbara, Calif., 1981-95. Artist, photographer for 2029 MAGAZIN (internat. edit. 1991, 92), Art series: Humana, Cities of Light, Cosmic Calculus series; published in Printworld Directory of Contemporary Prints, 1988. Recipient Excellence award in Painting, Art Horizons, 1988, Excellence award in Photography, Internat. Art Competition, 1988, Excellence award Photographer's Forum Magazine, 1992. Studio: Da Vinci Prodns Ste B456 16055 Boones Ferry Rd Lake Oswego OR 97035

DAVIS, ALLEN, professional football team executive; b. Brockton, Mass., July 4, 1929; s. Louis and Rose (Kirschenbaum) D.; m. Carol Segall, July 11, 1954; 1 son, Mark. Student, Wittenberg Coll., 1947; A.B., Syracuse U., 1950. Asst. football coach Adelphi Coll., 1950-51; head football coach Ft. Belvoir, Va., 1952-53; player-personnel scout Baltimore Colts, 1954; line coach The Citadel, 1955-56, U. So. Calif., 1957-59; asst. coach San Diego Chargers, 1960-62; gen. mgr., head coach Oakland Raiders (now Los Angeles Raiders), 1963-66, owner, mng. gen. ptnr., 1966—, now pres., gen. ptnr.; former mem. mgmt. council and competition com. Nat. Football League. Served with AUS, 1952-53. Named Profl. Coach of Year A.P., Profl. Coach of Year U.P.I., Profl. Coach of Year Sporting News, Profl. Coach of Year Pro-Football Illustrated, 1963; Young Man of Yr. Oakland, 1963; only individual in history to be an asst. coach, head coach, gen. mgr., league commr. and owner. Mem. Am. Football Coaches Assn. Office: Oakland Raiders 332 Center St El Segundo CA 90245-4047*

DAVIS, ALPHONSE, health facility administrator, special education counselor; b. Shreveport, La., Aug. 5, 1958; s. M. T. and Cleo (Walker) D.; m. Rebecca Pamela Harris, May 18, 1991; 1 child, Monique. B of Sociology, N.E. La. U., 1980, MEd, 1983; MSW, La. State U., 1987; postgrad., Nova Southeastern U., 1994—, LaSalle U., Manderville, La., 1995. Counseling intern E.A. Conway Meml. Hosp., Monroe, La., 1982-83; social work intern La. Dept. Corrections, Baton Rouge, 1985-87; alcohol drug abuse social worker Joseph R. Briscoe Treatment Ctr., Lake Charles, La., 1987-88; psychiat. social worker Behavioral Med. Care, Inc., Texarkana, Tex., 1988-89; social svc. counselor Dept. Civil Svc., La., 1989-90; clin. social worker USAF, 1990-92; spl. edn. counselor Clovis (N.Mex.) Mcpl. Schs., 1992—; dir. med. social svc. Bethel Home Health Care, Duncanville, Tex., 1996—. Sr. choir program chmn. Bethlehem Bapt. Ch., Clovis, 1993-94; music coord., mem. Martin Luther King Commn., Clovis, 1993—, ednl. advisor, 1994—. Recipient music scholarship N.E. La. U., 1976-80, Army ROTC scholarship N.E. La. U., 1978-80, Outstanding Educator award Clovis Community Coll., 1993-94. Mem. NEA, Nat. Edn. Supervision and Curriculum Assn., N.E. La. U. Alumni Assn., N.Mex. Alliance Sch. Social Workers, N.Mex. Afro-Am. Social Workers Assn. Democrat. Baptist.

DAVIS, ARTHUR DAVID, psychology educator, musician; m. Gladys Lesley Joyce, Dec. 29, 1965; children: Kimaili, Mureithi, Taisha. Student, Manhattan Sch. Music, 1953-56, Juilliard Sch. Music, 1953-56; BA suma cum laude, CUNY, 1973; MA, City Coll., N.Y.C., 1976, NYU, 1976; PhD with distinction, NYU, 1982. Lic. sch. psychologist. Musician various worldwide tours, 1962—, NBC-TV Staff Orch., N.Y.C., 1962-63, Westinghouse TV Staff Orch., N.Y.C., 1964-68, CBS-TV Staff Orch., N.Y.C., 1969-71; prof. Manhattan Community Coll., N.Y.C., 1971-86, U. Bridgeport, Conn., 1978-82; psychologist Lincoln Med. and Mental Health Ctr., Bronx, 1982-85; sch. psychologist, cons. Lakeside Union Free Sch. Dist., Spring Valley, N.Y., 1985-86; psychologist, tchr. N.Y. Med. Coll., Valhalla, 1982-87; prof. Orange Coast Coll., Costa Mesa, Calif., 1987—, Calif. State U., Fullerton, 1988-90, U. Calif.-Irvine, 1993-94; psychologist Cross Cultural Ctr., San Diego, 1986-91; cons. Head Start, Bklyn., 1981-82, Orange County Minority AIDS, Santa Ana, Calif., 1987-88, Orange County Fair Housing, Costa Mesa, 1988, Sickle Cell Anemia Assn., Santa Ana, Calif., 1987-88, Human Rels. Orange County City, Costa Mesa, 1988-89, William Grant Still Mus., L.A., 1988—; musician various symphonies Radio City Music Hall Orch. Nat. Symphony, Symphony of the Air N.Y. Philharmonic, Met. Opera Orch., L.A. Philharmonic, 1995; John Coltrane, others, 1960—. Author: The Arthur Davis System for Double Bass, 1976, A Brief History of Jazz, 1995; record composer Interplay, 1980, Art Davis Reemeryance, ARKIMU, 1985, Dr. Art Davis, Live, Soulnote, 1987, Art Davis, Live, A Time Remembered, 1995. Composer, condr., mem. coun. Diaglogue, Costa Mesa, 1988; mgr. Little League of Cortlandt, N.Y., 1979-82; pack master Cub Scouts Am., Cortlandt and Croton, N.Y., 1979-80, dist. chmn., 1980-81; bd. dirs. Local 47 Musicians' Union, Hollywood, Calif., 1993—, Orange County Urban League, Inc., 1992-95; chmn. Better Advantages for Students and Soc., Corona del Mar, Calif., 1993; adv. bd. dirs. John W. Cultrane Cultural Soc., Inc. NIMH grantee, 1976-77; named World's Foremost Double Bassist IBA, 1969—; recipient Lion award Black MBA Assn., 1985, Chancellor's Disting. Lectr.'s award U. Calif., Irvine, 1991-92, Exemplary Standards in Music Edn. award Orange County Urban League, 1993; Ann. Dr. Art Davis Scholarships established in his honor Dr. Art Davis Fan Club. Mem. APA, ASCAP, Am. Soc. Music Arrangers & Composers, Chamber Music Am., N.Y. Acad. Scis., Astron. Soc. of the Pacific (charter), Orange County Psychol. Assn., Assn. of Black Psychologists, Planetary Soc. (charter), Am. Hort. Soc., Nat Trust for Hist. Preservation Soc., Rec. Musicians Assn., Stanford U. Alumni Assn., NYU Alumni Assn., CCNY Alumni Assn., Sierra Club. Office: ARKIMU 3535 E Coast Hwy Ste 50 Corona Del Mar CA 92625-2404*

DAVIS, BEATRICE, management consultant; b. Berkeley, Calif., Dec. 28, 1950; d. H. Virgil and Margie (Snowden) D. BSBA, U. Denver, 1973, MBA, 1974. Asst. adminstr. Davis Nursing Home, Inc., Denver, 1972-76; prof. Universidad De Santo Tomas, Bogota, Colombia, 1977-78; writer, translater Sintesis Economica, Bogota, 1978-79; prof. Universidad Los Andes, Bogota, 1979-80; mgr. Serviminas Ltd., Medellin and Bogota, 1978-81; prof. Eafit U., Medellin, 1982-84; pres. Performance Plus, Sacramento, Trinidad and Evergreen, Colo., 1986; mayor City of Trinidad, 1991-93; prof. Regis U., 1990—; pres. Negodianostics Ltd., Medellin, 1981-85. Adv. Colo. State Legisl. Register Health/Planning Bd., Denver, 1974-75; alt. del. Denver County Rep. Conv., 1971; del. Colo. Rep. Conv., 1990, Leadership Denver, 1975; co-chair Colo. Rural Econ. Devel. Coun., del. to Gov. Romer's Regional Confs. on Econ. Devel., 1993. Mem. Sacramento Women's Network (chair com. 1986), AAUW (pres. Trinidad chpt. 1989-90), Delta Sigma Pi (pres. 1975).

DAVIS, BETTY JEAN BOURBONIA, real estate investment executive; b. Ft. Bayard, N.Mex., Mar. 12, 1931; d. John Alexander and Ora M. (Caudill) Bourbonia; BS in Elem. Edn., U. N.Mex., 1954; children: Janice Cox Anderson, Elizabeth Ora Cox. Gen. ptnr. BJD Realty Co., Albuquerque, 1977—. Bd. dirs. Albuquerque Opera Guild, 1977-79, 81-83, 85-86, 86-87, membership co-chmn., 1977-79; mem. Friends of Art, 1978-85, Friends of Little Theatre, 1973-85, Mus. N.Mex. Found.; mem. grand exec. com. N.Mex. Internat. Order of Rainbow for Girls; mem. Hodgin Hall Preservation com. U. N.Mex. Recipient Matrix award for journalism Jr. League. Mem. Albuquerque Mus. Assn., N.M. Hist. Soc., N.Mex. Symphony Guild, Jr. League Albuquerque, Alumni Assn. U. N.Mex. (dir. 1973-76), Mus. N.Mex. Found., Alpha Chi Omega (Beta Gamma Beta chpt., adv., bldg. corp. 1962-77), Tanoan Country Club, Order Eastern Star, Order Rainbow for Girls (past grand worthy adv. N.Mex., past mother adv. Friendship Assembly 50, state exec. com. N.Mex. Order 1989, chair pub. rels. com., co-chair gen. arrangements com. 1990-97). Republican. Methodist. Home: 9505 Augusta Ave NE Albuquerque NM 87111-5820

DAVIS, BRUCE WARREN, architect; b. Chgo., Oct. 27, 1947; s. Howard Warren and Elizabeth Florence (Barber) D. BArch., U. Ill., 1970. Registered architect, N.Mex. Jr. architect Skidmore, Owings & Merrill, Chgo., 1969-73; pvt. practice, Santa Fe, Albuquerque, 1973—. Home and Office: 526 Wellesley Dr SE Albuquerque NM 87106-2318

DAVIS, CHARLES LEE, fire marshal; b. Anchorage, July 24, 1940; s. Edward V. and De Ette C. (Scholberg) D.; m. Mary Margaret Walker, Aug. 24, 1963; 1 child, Edward Charles. LLB, U. Idaho, 1966; grad. 28th Recruit Acad., Alaska Dept. Pub. Safety, 1977. Bar: Alaska 1967; cert. firefighter, Alaska, fire svc. instr., Alaska; uniform fire code cert. Internat. Conf. Bldg. Ofcls., cert. plans examiner ICBO; Nat. Fire Acad. fire/arson investigation, fire prevention specialist II; World Safety Orgn. cert. safety specialist, safety mgr., safety and security dir., level II fire extinguisher permit, Alaska. Law clk., atty. Hughes, Thorsness, Lowe, Gantz & Clark, Anchorage, 1966-68; adjustor, appraiser Gen. Adjustment Bur., Alaska, 1968-73; adjuster, damage appraiser Alaska Adjusting Co., Fairbanks, 1974-75; dep. fire marshal State of Alaska, Fairbanks, 1975—. Contbr. posters, cards and photographs to numerous publs. Mem., past vestry mem., jr. warden St. Matthew's Episcopal Ch., Fairbanks, chmn. endowment bd., 1991—. Recipient prize Joint Pubs. of Am. Jurisprudence-Bancroft Whitney Co., 1966; scholar Rocky Mountain Mineral Law Inst., 1966. Mem. NRA (Alaska No. chpt.), Internat. Conf. Bldg. Ofcls. (founder Alaska No. chpt., dir., v.p., pres.), Alaska Bar Assn., Pioneers of Alaska (life, igloo #4), Moose (life lodge 1392). Episcopalian. Home: 1359 Great View Ln Fairbanks AK 99712-2136 Office: Alaska Dept Pub Safety Divsn Fire Prevention 1979 Peger Rd Fairbanks AK 99709-5257

DAVIS, COLLEEN TERESA, elementary education educator, reading educator; b. Monroe, Wis., Aug. 28, 1946; d. Francis Benedict and Norma Irene Doherty; m. John Oswin Davis, Aug. 25, 1973; children: John Francis, Christine Elizabeth. BS in Elem. Edn., Marian Coll., Fond Du Lac, Wis., 1967; MS in Edn.-Reading, U. Wis., Whitewater, 1975; MS in Ednl. Adminstrn., Ariz. State U., Phoenix, 1994. Cert. K-12 adminstr., K-12 curriculum supr., K-12 reading specialist. Elem. tchr. Holy Trinity Sch., Kewaskum, Wis., 1967-69; reading tchr. Friendship Mid. Sch., Adams, Wis., 1970-71, Ozaukee Mid. Sch., Fredonia, Wis., 1971-73; reading tchr. Johnson Creek (Wis.) Schs., 1973-75, 78-84, reading specialist, 1978-84; adult reading tchr. Waukesha County Tech. Inst., Pewaukee, Wis., 1976-79; reading tchr.-specialist Royal Palm Mid. Sch., Phoenix, 1984-93, chpt. 1 coord./curriculum, 1993-95, tchr. gifted, 1995-96, team tchr. mid. sch., 1996—, active drug prevention program, 1994-97; presenter Wis. State Reading, Oconomowoc, 1981-82, Ariz. Reading Assn., Tucson, 1988, Washington Sch. Dist., Phoenix Mid. Sch. Conf., 1995, 6-7-8 Grade Acad., 1996; instr. reading Glendale (Ariz.) C.C., 1995—. Author: (programs) Arizona Quality Programs and Practices, 1987, WSD Promising Practices, 1988. Lit. Days vol. Phoenix West Reading Coun., 1992-93. Recipient Golden Apple award Washington Sch. Dist., 1989, Tchr. of Excellence Royal Palm, PTO, Phoenix, 1989, 92, Lit. award-Leadership in Profession, Internat. Reading Assn./Phoenix West Reading Coun., 1990, Recognition award for drug prevention program, U.S. Dept. Edn., 1995. Mem. ASCD, Internat. Reading Assn., Ariz. Reading Assn. (conf. com. 1984—), Phoenix West Reading Coun. (rec. sec., v.p., pres., membership chair), Ariz. Assn. Sch. Adminstrs. Office: Royal Palm Mid Sch 8520 N 19th Ave Phoenix AZ 85021-4201

DAVIS, DARRELL L., automotive executive; b. Sharon, Pa., Aug. 8, 1939; s. Paul Darrell and Dorothy Jane (Snyder) D.; m. Jacqueline Donna Pain, July 18, 1986; children: Paul Darrell II, Robert Tod. BS, Youngstown State U., 1963; cert. Stanford Exec. Program, Stanford U., 1987; cert. Global Leadership Program, U. Mich., 1993. Svc. rep., warranty mgr., dist. mgr., asst. zone mgr. Chrysler Motors Corp., Orlando, Fla., 1966-77; zone mgr. Chrysler Motors Corp., Omaha, 1977-78, Troy, Mich., 1978-79; nat. distbn.

mgr., regional mgr., gen. mgr. import export ops., gen. sales mgr. Chrysler Motors Corp., Detroit, 1979-88; pres., chief exec. officer Alfa Romeo Distbrs. N. Am., Orlando, 1988-91; gen. sales mgr. Chrysler Corp., Orange, Calif., 1991-93; v.p. Chrysler Internat. Corp., Detroit, 1993-95; gen. mgr. Europe Chrysler Corp., Detroit, 1993-95; pres., COO Chrysler Fin. Corp., Southfield, Mich., 1995—. Lt. U.S. Army, 1963-65. Republican.

DAVIS, DAVID RICHARD, business succession consultant; b. Indpls., July 27, 1937; s. Calvin Fred and Clara Marie (Rademacher) D.; divorced; children: Susan Marie, David R. Jr., Edward C. Student, U. Richmond, 1955-57, Am. U., Washington, 1958. CLU; ChFC; cert. family bus. specialist; ordained deacon Presbyn. Ch., 1990. Sales rep. N.Y. Life Ins. Co., Washington, 1958-66; gen. agt. Mass Mut. Life Ins. Co., Arlington, Va., 1967-72; sr. officer v.p. Mass Mut. Life Ins. Co., Springfield, Mass., 1972-75; gen. agt. Mass Mut. Life Ins. Co., Beverly Hills, Calif., 1975-79; sales rep. Mass Mut. Life Ins. Co., L.A., 1980—; advisor agts. exec. com. Mass Mut. Life Ins. Co., Springfield, 1989-91. Fund raiser and bd. dirs. Am. Cancer Soc., San Fernando Valley, Calif., 1987-91; fund raiser and vol. Coll. of the Canyons Found., Valencia, Calif., 1995-96, Big Bros. L.A., 1996. Recipient Outstanding Cmty. Svc. Citizen award City L.A., County L.A., State Assembly Calif., 1988. Mem. Assn. Advanced Life Underwriters, Am. Soc. CLU and ChFC (chpt. pres. 1966—), Nat. Assn. Life Underwriters (bd. dirs. 1958—), Nat. Estate Planning Coun., Family Firm Inst., Million Dollar Roundtable, San Fernando Valley Estate Planning Coun. (pres. 1984-85), L.A. Estate Planning Coun., L.A. Leaders (pres. 1978—). Presbyterian. Office: The Bus Succession Group 4601 Wilshire Blvd 3d Fl Los Angeles CA 90010

DAVIS, DONALD ALAN, author, news correspondent, lecturer; b. Savannah, Ga., Oct. 5, 1939; s. Oden Harry and Irma Artice (Gay) D.; m. Robin Murphy, Mar. 17, 1983; children by previous marriage—Russell Glenn, Randall Scott. B.A. in Journalism, U. Ga., 1962. Reporter Athens (Ga.) Banner-Herald, 1961-62, Savannah Morning News, 1962; with UPI, 1963-65; reporter, editor St. Petersburg (Fla.) Times, 1965-66; with UPI, 1967-83, Vietnam corr., 1971-73, New Eng. editor, 1977-80, White House corr., 1981-83; polit. reporter, columnist San Diego Union, 1983-91; pub. Pacific Rim Report newsletter, 1985-88; instr. journalism Boston U., 1979; lectr. U.S. Naval War Coll., 1983, Queen Elizabeth 2, 1991, Vistafjord, 1992; bd. dirs. Fgn. Corr. Club, Hong Kong, 1974. Author: The Milwaukee Murders, 1991, The Nanny Murder Trial, 1992, Bad Blood, 1994, Death of An Angel, 1994, Fallen Hero, 1994, Appointment with the Squire, 1995, Death Cruise, 1996, A Father's Rage, 1996, The Gris-Gris Man, 1997. Fellow Keizai Koho Ctr., Tokyo, 1985. Presbyterian. Office: 6350 Modena Ln Longmont CO 80503

DAVIS, DONALD G(LENN), lawyer; b. San Gabriel, Calif., Sept. 15, 1949; s. Maurice G. and Elinore C. (Leigh) D.; m. Alex Davis; children: Christian Glenn, Alexandra, Donald Glenn Jr., Regina Ann Rogers, Katherine Ann, Andrew Glenn. BS in Acctg., Calif. State U., Pomona, 1966; JD, U. So. Calif., 1969. Assoc. Adams, Duque & Hazeltine, L.A., 1968, Omlevny & Meyers, L.A., 1969-72; prof. of law Southwestern U. Law Sch., L.A., 1972-80; gen. counsel Republic Corp., L.A., 1973; ptnr. Danielson, St. Clair & Davis, L.A., 1974-77; mng. ptnr. Davis & Assocs., L.A., 1980—, DGD Enterprises P.V., L.A., 1980—, DGD Investment Banking, L.A., 1980—. Exec. editor Law Rev. jour., U. So. Calif., 1968-69. Vice-pres. student body, Calif. State U., Pomona, 1964-65; candidate 42nd Congl. Dist., Calif., 1988. Mem. ABA, L.A. Bar Assn. (chmn. securities cooperative seminar 1988, chmn. bus. lawyers sect. 1986-87), Order of Coif, Calif. Club, L.A. Yacht Club, Arrowhead Lake Assn. Home: Whispering Point 28776 Palisades Dr Lake Arrowhead CA 92352 also: Villa Del Mare Palos Verdes Estates CA 90274 also: Blackbeard's Castle Avalon CA 90704 Office: Davis & Assocs care Ritz Carlton Annex PO Box 12009 Marina Del Rey CA 90295 also: 2121 Ave Of Stars Fl 22 Century City CA 90067-5010 also: 4667 Macarthur Blvd Ste 422 Newport Beach CA 92660-1817 also: 833 Via Del Monte Ste 100 Palos Verdes Estates CA 90274-1613

DAVIS, E. E. (GENE DAVIS), educational administrator; b. Seward, Nebr., Oct. 31, 1938; s. Walter Ernest and Ruth Louise (Strinz) D.; m. Andrea Lee Chicoine, Dec. 28, 1960; children: Charles, Christopher, Charise. BA, Nebr. Wesleyan U., 1960; MEd, U. Nebr., 1966; EdD, U. Mont., 1977. Asst. dir. Missoula (Mont.) Tech. Ctr., Mont., 1969-72; dir. vocat. edn. Anchorage Sch. Dist., 1972-76, dir. fed. programs, 1976-77, asst. supt. programs, 1977-80, asst. supt., 1980-81, supt., 1981-89, Chesterfield (Va.) County Pub. Schs., 1987-91; dir. office profl. devel. schs., assoc. prof. ednl. adminstrn. Idaho State U., Pocatello, 1993—; bd. dirs. Northwest Regional Lab., Portland, Oreg., 1981-87. Mem. Sister Cities Commn., Anchorage, 1984—; bd. dirs. Western coun. Boy Scouts Am., Anchorage, 1982—, Alaska Boys Club, Anchorage, 1982—, Jr. Achievement of Alaska, Anchorage, 1982—. Recipient Svc. award March of Dimes, 1981; UN Assn. award AAUW, 1981; Friends of Campfire award, 1985; named one of Exec. 100, Exec. Mag., 1984. Mem. Am. Assn. Sch. Adminstrs., Assn. Supervision and Curriculum Devel. (dir. 1981-82), Nat. Sch. Bds. Assn., Coun. Ednl. Facility Planners Internat., Phi Delta Kappa. Roman Catholic. Home: PO Box 4865 Pocatello ID 83205 Office: Idaho State Univ Box 8019 Pocatello ID 83209

DAVIS, ERIC KEITH, former professional baseball player; b. L.A., May 29, 1962; m. Erica D. Baseball player Cin. Reds, 1980-91, 96, L.A. Dodgers, 1991-93, Detroit Tigers, 1993-94, Balt. Orioles, 1997—. Mem. Nat. League All-Star Team, 1987, 89, Nat. League Silver Slugger team, 1987, 89, NL Gold Glove 1987-89; named to Sporting News Nat. League. All-Star team, 1987, 89; named Nat. League Comeback Player of Yr., 1996. Office: Baltimore Orioles 333 W Camden St Baltimore MD 21201*

DAVIS, FRANK GRODAVENT FOY, database manager; b. St. Joseph, Mich., Mar. 27, 1943; s. Frank Foy and Marjorie (Fickinger) D.; m. Julianne King, Jan. 23, 1971; 1 child, Elinor Jane Foy. BS in Psychology, U. Wyo., 1967, BA in Anthropology, 1972, MA in Anthropology, 1974, MS in Computer Sci., 1989. Cert. EMT. Rsch. asst., statis. cons. dept. psychology U. Wyo., Laramie, 1966-74, rsch. aide dept. atmosphere sci., 1974-77; computer specialist U.S. Dept. Energy, Laramie, 1977-83; sr. programmer analyst Western Rsch. Inst., Laramie, 1983-85; cons. computer sci. Laramie, 1990-94; rsch. asst. Inst. for Energy Rsch., 1994-96, data base mgr., 1996-97, assoc. rsch. sci., 1997—. Contbr. articles to profl. jours. Instr. ARC, Laramie, 1964—, divsn. rep., chpt. chmn., 1979-82; nat. patroller Nat. Ski Patrol, Laramie, 1968—, patrol dir. 1979-83, sect. chief, 1983-91, ea. region winter emergency care adv. 1994-95, Rocky Mtn. divsn. outdoor emergency care adminstr. 1995-96; winter emergency care instr. trainer, 1989—, Rocky Mtn. Divsn. ea. region winter emergency care adminstr., 1994-95. Named Nat. Runner-up Outstanding Instr., Nat. Ski Patrol, 1993, Rocky Mountain Divsn. Outstanding Instr., Nat. Ski Patrol, 1993. Mem. IEEE Computer Soc., Assn. for Computing Machinery, Am. Assn. Avalanche Profls., Internat. Soc. for Computers and Their Applications. Home and Office: Box 3192 University Sta Laramie WY 82071

DAVIS, GENE, public relations professional, state legislator; b. Salt Lake City, July 2, 1945; s. John Albert and Glenna Rachel (Cameron) D.; m. Penny Lou Hansen, Mar. 9, 1971; children: James, Pamela. Cert. electronic engring., Radio Operational Engring., Burbank, Calif., 1963; LLB, LaSalle Ext. U., Chgo., 1974. Announcer KNAK Radio, Salt Lake City, 1965-75; prodn. continuity dir. KALL Radio AM/FM, Salt Lake City, 1976-86; owner G. Davis Advt., Pub. Rels., Salt Lake City, 1986-91; pub. rels. profl. Valley Mental Health, Salt Lake City, 1990—; treas. Comm. Fed. Credit Union, Salt Lake City, 1981-86. Vice chair East County Recreation Bd., Salt Lake City, 1991—; rep. Utah State Ho. Reps., Salt Lake City, 1986—, minority caucus leader, exec. appropriations com., health and human svcs., transp., health and human svcs. appropriatiions sub-com., audit com., coun. of state govt.-health capacity task force. Mem. Sugar House Rotary Club, Sugar House Cmty. Coun. (chmn. 1984-85). Democrat. Mem. LDS Ch. Home: 865 Parkway Ave Salt Lake City UT 84106-1704 Office: Valley Mental Health 5965 S 900 E Salt Lake City UT 84121-1720

DAVIS, GENEVIEVE ANNA, clinical counselor, marriage and family therapist; b. Detroit, Oct. 31, 1953; m. Thomas William Laga, May 18, 1976 (div. Jan. 1987). Student, Calif. State U., Fullerton, 1971-73; BA in Theater Edn., Prescott Coll., 1975; MA in Psychology and Counseling, Antioch U., 1986. Dir. clin. counselor, marriage and family therapist Biofeedback Clinic of Santa Fe, 1984—; clin. counselor, marriage and family therapist Women's Health Svcs., Santa Fe, 1990—; mem. clin. stds. com. N.Mex. Counseling and Therapy Practice Bd., Santa Fe, 1994—; grief intervention counselor Office of the Med. Investigator, State of N.Mex.; small group coord., advisor N.Mex. Dept. Health, Women's Wellness Project, Santa Fe, 1985—. Mem. smoking cessation group Smoke Free Santa Fe-Nat. Cancer Inst.; mem. adv. bd. N.Mex. Respiratory Therapy, 1988—; mem. N.Mex. Acupuncture Bd., Santa Fe, 1994. Mem. Assn. for Applied Psychophysiology and Biofeedback, N.Mex. Soc. Biofeedback and Behavioral Medicine (pres. 1993-94, treas. 1995-96), N.Mex. Psychol. Assn., Biofeedback Cert. Inst. Am. (cert.). Office: 546 Harkle Rd Ste C Santa Fe NM 87505-4738

DAVIS, GERALDINE SAMPSON, special education educator; b. Tacoma, Wash., Aug. 18, 1919; d. Philip and Merta M. (Thomas) Sampson; m. John Allen Davis, Nov. 26 1942 (div. 1971); children: Denise, Karin, Glen (dec.), Grant (dec.), Page, Gail (dec.). BS with distinction, U. Minn., 1941; MEd, San Francisco State U., 1971. Cert. tchr., Calif., cert. adminstr., Calif. Art and English instr. White Bear Lake (Minn.) Jr. and Sr. High Sch., 1941-43; Am. club mobile operator ARC, Eng. and Europe, 1944-45; exec. dir. Lincoln County chpt. ARC, Newport, Oreg., 1947-48; substitute tchr. Santa Cruz (Calif.) County Dept. Edn., 1964-67; learning disabled instr. Live Oak Dist. Schs., Santa Cruz, 1967-89; peer tutor developer Live Oak Schs., 1970-73, reading program mgr., 1973-76; evaluation team mem. County of Santa Cruz, 1980-84. Exhibited paintings in numerous galleries shows including Los Gatos Art Cooperative, 1961-65, Santa Cruz Art Festival, 1962, San Juan Bautista Art Fair, 1963, Santa Cruz County Fair, 1965; paintings represented in several pvt. collections. Chpt. sec. March of Dimes, Lincoln County, 1949-51, Santa Cruz County; vol. tutor Vols. of Santa Cruz, 1978-83; fundraiser Boulder Creek (Calif.) Schs., 1963; scenic and prop designer Santa Cruz County Schs., 1964, Boulder Creek Theater Group, 1965. Mem. Calif. Assn. Neurol. Handicapped Children (chair 1964-66, scholarships 1968-71), Women's Dem. Club, AAUW (com. chair for women's issues 1990—), Reproductive Rights Network, Santa Cruz Reading Assn. (sec. 1980, rep. Asilomar reading conf. bd. 1981-82, Chpt. and Internat. Reading Assns. award 1985), Calif. Ret. Tchrs. Assn. (nominating com. 1985—), Assn. Ret. Persons, Sr. Citizens Santa Cruz County, Pub. Citizens, Pub. Broadcasting Network, Conservation of Am, Amnesty, Delta Phi Delta (life, pres. Mpls. chpt. 1939-41), Pi Lambda Theta (life). Home: 319 35th Ave Santa Cruz CA 95062-5514

DAVIS, GRAY, lieutenant governor; b. N.Y.C., Dec. 26, 1942; m. Sharon Ryer, Feb. 20, 1983. BA cum laude, Stanford U., 1964; JD, Columbia U., 1967. Chief of staff to Gov. Edmund G. Brown State of Calif., 1974-81, state rep., 1982-86, state contr., 1986-94; lt. gov., 1994—; chmn. Housing and Community Devel. Com., Calif. Coun. on Criminal Justice, Franchise Tax Bd., State Lands Commn.; mem. Bd. Equalization, State Tchrs. Retirement System, Pub. Employees Retirement System, Nat. Coun. Institutional Investors. Founder Calif. Found. for the Protection of Children. Office: Office of Lieutenant Governor State Capitol Rm 1114 Sacramento CA 95814

DAVIS, J. ALAN, lawyer, producer, writer; b. N.Y.C., Nov. 7, 1961. Student, Marlborough Coll., Eng., 1979; BA with distinction, So. Meth. U., 1983; JD with honors, U. Tex., 1987. Bar: Calif. 1988. Assoc. O'Melveny & Myers, L.A., 1987-89, Rosenfeld, Meyer & Susman, Beverly Hills, Calif., 1989-90; pvt. practice L.A., 1990-94; ptnr. Davis & Benjamin, L.A., 1995—. Mem. Calif. Bar Assn., Beverly Hills Bar Assn. (entertainment law sect. exec. com.), Brit. Acad. Film and TV Arts (bd. dirs.). Office: Davis & Benjamin Ste 2520 2049 Century Park E Ste 2520 Los Angeles CA 90067-3127

DAVIS, JACK, securities dealer; b. 1938. With Harris Corp., Melbourne, Fla., 1962-86, Dataproducts Corp., Woodland Hills, Calif., 1986—; chmn. Morgan Wedbush Securities. Office: Morgan Wedbush Securities 1000 Wilshire Blvd Ste 900 Los Angeles CA 90017-2457*

DAVIS, JAMES ALLAN, gerontologist, educator; b. Portland, Oreg., May 20, 1953; s. Alfred Jack and Anne (Dickson) D.; m. Lois Carol Lindsay, Dec. 17, 1978; children: Sarah Elizabeth, Matthew Simon. BS, U. Oreg., 1975, MS, 1976, EdD, 1980. State mental health gerontologist Oreg. Mental Health Div., Salem, 1978-80; project dir. Oreg. Long Term Care Tng. Project, Salem, 1979-80; tng. specialist Nat. Assn. Area Agys. on Aging., Washington, 1981; asst. dir. for internships and vol. svc. exptl. learning programs U. Md., 1981-86, mem. rsch. and instructional faculty, 1982-86; com. adminstr. Oreg. State Human Resources Com., Salem, 1987; exec. dir. Oreg. State Coun. Sr. Citizens, Salem, 1987-90; program coord. for sr. mental health care Oreg. Sr. and Disabled Svcs. Div., Salem, 1989—; pres. James A. Davis and Assocs. Inc., Portland, 1991—; state project dir. Oreg. Assn. RSVPs; vis. asst. prof. Ctr. for Gerontology, U. Oreg., 1990-92; co-chair Audio-Visual Program, Internat. Congress Gerontology, 1985; nat. gerontology acad. adv. panel, Nat. Hosp. Satellite Network, 1983-85; presenter nat. confs. on aging, health care, exptl. edn., age stereotyping; lobbyist United Srs. Oreg., Oreg. State Coun. Sr. Citizens, 1987—, Oreg. State Denturist Assn., Oreg. State Pharmacist Assn., Oreg. Soc. Physician Assts., Oreg. Legal Techs. Assn., Oreg. Dental Lab. Assn., Wash. Denturist Assn., Nat. Denturist Assn., 1991—. Co-author: TV's Image of the Elderly, 1985; contbg. editor Retirement Life News, 1988-92; sr. issues editor Sr. News, 1989—; contbr. articles to profl. jours.; producer, host approximately 400 TV and radio programs. Founding pres. Oreg. Alliance for Progressive Policy, 1988-89; co-chair mental health com., vice chair legis. com., Gov.'s Commn. on Sr. Svcs., 1988-89; exec. coun., media chair Human Svcs. Coalition Oreg., 1988-89; bd. dirs. Oreg. Health Action Campaign, 1988-92; 2d v.p., bd. dirs. Oreg. State Coun. for Sr. Citizens, 1977-80, 90-92, Oreg. Medicaid Com., 1996—; co-chair Oreg. Medicare/Medicaid Coalition, 1995—, Oreg. Long Term Care Campaign, 1996—; mem. Gov.'s Task Force for Volunteerism, State of Md., 1983-84, State Legis. Income Tax Task Force, 1990; vice chair Oreg. State Bd. Denture Technology, 1991-96; mem. com. for assessment on needs for volunteerism, Gov.'s Vol. Coun., State of Md., 1984-86; others. Recipient Disting. Svc. award City of Salem, 1980, Spl. Human Rights award, 1981, Svc. award U. Md., 1984, Hometown U.S.A. award Community Cable TV Producers, 1988, Disting. Svc. award Oreg. State Coun. Sr. Citizens, 1991. Mem. Nat. Assn. State Mental Health Dirs. (nat. exec. com. 1978-80, vice chmn. 1979-80, mem. aging div., spl. cons. 1981-82), Gerontol. Soc. Am. (mental health task force 1982-84, co-chmn. 1983-84), Nat. Gray Panthers (nat. bd. dirs. 1984-92, nat. exec. com. 1984-87, co-chmn. nat. program com. 1984-87, nat. media chair 1985-92, program co-chmn. nat. biennial conv. 1986, nat. health task force 1981—, co-chmn. 1983-84, chmn. mental health subcom. 1981-86, editor Health Watch, 1982-84, state program developer Oreg. chpt. 1979-80, 89, lobbyist 1987—). Democrat. Office: James A Davis and Assocs Inc 1750 SW Skyline Blvd Ste 10 Portland OR 97221-2543

DAVIS, JAMES LUTHER, retired utilities executive, lawyer; b. Memphis, May 8, 1924; s. Luther and Sarah (Carter) D.; m. Natalie Young, Jan. 26, 1947; children: James Luther, Fred C., Peggy E. BBA, U. Ariz., 1946, LLB, 1949. Bar: Ariz. 1949. Sole practice Tucson, 1949-52, asst. city atty., 1952-53, city mgr., 1953-55; with Tucson Gas & Electric Co. (now Tucson Electric Power Co.), 1955-96, exec. v.p., 1958-59, pres., 1959-76, emeritus, 1989-96, chmn. bd., 1967-88; bd. dirs. El Paso br. Fed. Res. Bd., Dallas, 1974-77, chmn. 1976-77. Mem. charter rev. com. City of Tucson, 1965-71; bd. dirs. Tucson Airport Authority, 1957-62, 64-70, pres., 1965; bd. dirs. Tucson Med. Ctr., 1955-58, 59-65, pres., 1957-58; mem. Tucson Indsl. Devel. Bd., 1959-64; bd. dirs. Ariz. Town Hall, 1962-74, 78-82, Health Planning Coun. Tucson, 1964-71, Tucson Regional Plan, 1966-89, United Way, 1985-88; bd. dirs. Green Fields Sch., 1964-69, chmn. bd., 1964-66; bd. dirs. U. Ariz. Found., 1985-92, dir. emeritus, 1992-96. Home: 6781 N Altos Primero Tucson AZ 85718-2054

DAVIS, JAMES WESLEY, university program administrator, artist, writer, composer; b. L.A., Oct. 9, 1940; s. Charles Wesley and Hazel Virginia (Porter) D.; m. Linnea Sharsmith, Mar. 31, 1962 (div. 1978); children: Marc Jerome, Timothy Andrew; m. Ellen Alva Hales, Oct. 6, 1990. BA in Edn., Calif. Coll. Arts & Crafts, Oakland, 1964; BFA, Calif. Coll. Arts & Crafts, 1965; MFA, U. Colo., 1967, MA, 1970. Lectr. art dept. U. Ark., Fayetteville, 1967-96; prof. art dept. Western Ill. U., Macomb, 1969-81; instr. art dept. U. Colo., Denver, 1981; dir. performance art prodns. Denver, 1981-83; head art dept. East Tex. State U., Commerce, 1983-88; chair art dept. Ind. State U., Terre Haute, 1988-89; dir. inter-arts ctr. San Francisco State U., 1989—; bd. dirs. Paul Dresher Ensemble, San Francisco, 1994—. Exhibited in over 100 mus. exhbns. worldwide, 1984—; represented in permanent collections over 20 museums; contbr. to profl. jours.; composer over 50 musical works; performer in field. Recipient purchase awards 8 museums worldwide, 1970—, award Swarovski Internat., Belgium, 1968, award Phelan Commn., Oakland, 1975. Office: San Francisco State U Inter-Arts Ctr 1600 Holloway Ave San Francisco CA 94132-1722

DAVIS, JEFFREY ALAN, secondary school educator, coach; b. Cleve., Mar. 12, 1960; s. Samuel and Marlene (Moot) D.; m. Faith Yvonne Quisenberry, Apr. 6, 1991; children: Paige, Aleisha. BA, Calif. State U., Northridge, 1983; MA, Ohio State U., 1984; postgrad., U. So. Calif., 1997—. Sports info. dir. Oberlin (Ohio) Coll., 1985-86; tchr., coach El Camino Real High Sch., Woodland Hills, Calif., 1986-89, Canoga Park (Calif.) High Sch., 1989-93; tchr., coach Burbank (Calif.) High Sch., 1993-95, asst. prin., 1995-96; dean of students Littlerock (Calif.) High Sch., 1996—; vice-prin. Desert Winds H.S., Littlerock; assoc. prin. Leuzinger H.S., Lawndale, Calif. Recipient Vol. Svc. award L.A. City Coun. Dept. Human Rels., 1987. Mem. L.A. Coaches Assn. (v.p. 1990-91, pres. 1992-93), Nat. Coun. Tchrs. of English, Soc. Profl. Journalists, Nat. Assn. Basketball Coaches, Ohio State U. Alumni Assn., Assn. Calif. Sch. Adminstrs., Calif. State U.-Northridge Alumni Assn. Democrat. Home: PO Box 3675 Seal Beach CA 90740-7675 Office: Leuzinger High Sch 4118 W Rosecrans Ave Lawndale CA 90260

DAVIS, JEREMY MATTHEW, chemist; b. Bakersfield, Calif., Aug. 5, 1953; s. Joseph Hyman and Mary (Pavetto) D.; m. Bernadette Sobkiewicz, Aug. 28, 1976; children: Andrew Jeremy, Christopher Peter. BS in Biol. Scis., U. Calif., Irvine, 1974; M in Pub. Adminstrn., Calif. State U., Long Beach, 1983. Chemist I, II, Orange County Water Dist., Fountain Valley, Calif., 1977-84, chemist supr., 1984—. Papers in field. Adult leader Boy Scouts Am.; lay reader St. Margaret of Scotland Episcopal Ch., San Juan Capistrano, Calif. Named Lab. Person of Yr., Calif. Water Environment Assn., Santa Ana River Basin, 1984. Mem. Am. Chem. Soc., Am. Water Works Assn., Calif. Water Environment Assn. (bd. dirs. Santa Ana River Basin chpt. 1984), Toastmasters Internat. (club pres. 1996). Office: Orange County Water Dist PO Box 8300 Fountain Valley CA 92728-8300

DAVIS, JOAN, business manager, general contractor, tax preparer, vocational business educator; b. Anderson, Ind., Nov. 24, 1947; d. Harold Brewer and Alice Marie (Doll) Hall; m. L.R. Collier Sr., May 19, 1967 (div. 1980); children: Missy JoAn Collier Basham, L.R. Jr.; m. Timothy G. Davis, Oct. 10, 1982; stepchildren: Geraldine Marie, Eugene Francis. Grad. high sch., Riverside, Calif. Sec. Svc. Electric, Inc., Riverside, 1966-68; pres. Power Electric, Inc., Norco, Calif., 1972-76; office mgr. Cutter Electric, Inc., Rialto, Calif., 1976-77; exec. asst., controller, corp. sec. Home & Country, Inc., Riverside, 1977—; owner, tax preparer Davis Bus. Svc., Riverside, 1978—. Republican. Home: 6981 Pacheco Ct Riverside CA 92509-6326 Office: Aware Devel Co Inc 3733 Arlington Ave # C Riverside CA 92506

DAVIS, JOHN, mayor. Mayor City of Encinitas, Calif. Office: 505 S Vulcan Ave Encinitas CA 92024

DAVIS, JOHN ALBERT, lawyer; b. Seattle, July 29, 1940; s. Carl Lee and Helen Irene (Corner) D.; m. Judith Ann colvin, June 21, 1959 (div. 1978); children: John Albert, James Colvin, Jennifer Lynn. Student, U. Calif., Berkeley, 1957-58; postgrad., Diablo Valley Coll., 1962; JD, Golden Gate U., 1970. Bar: Calif. 1971, U.S. Dist. Ct. (no. dist.) Calif. 1971, U.S. Ct. Appeals (9th cir.) 1971, U.S. Supreme Ct. 1986. Pres. Cal-State Distbrs., Oakland, Calif., 1959-78; pvt. practice Oakland, 1978-81, San Ramon, 1985—; v.p., chief operating officer Madre Mining, Ltd., Sacramento, 1981-85; pres., bd. dirs. O'Hara Resources, Ltd., Vancouver, B.C., Can., 1989—; bd. dirs. Troy Gold Industries, Ltd., Calgary, Alta., Can. Mem. Calif. Bar Asns., Commwealth Club Calif., Sequoia Woods Country Club. Republican. Presbyterian. Office: PO Box 2096 San Ramon CA 94583

DAVIS, JOHN JEFFREY, musician; b. Chgo., Aug. 15, 1944; s. John Ross Davis and Edith Elizabeth Stephens. BA, Dallas Bapt. Coll., 1969; MMus, U. S.C., 1974. Factotum and carillonist U. Calif., Berkeley, 1983—; pres. Guild of Carillonneurs in N.Am., 1996—. Composer: Betsy Ross and the Red White and Blue, 1976, Three Liturgical Dances, 1974, Passion, 1993, Symphony for Orchestra, 1994. Pres. pastoral coun. Most Holy Redeemer Ch., San Francisco, 1989-90. Named Disting. Alumnus Nat. Music Camp, Interlochen, Mich., 1974, Berkeley medal U. Calif., 1993. Mem. Guild of Carillonneurs in N.Am., ASCAP. Home: 46 Mott Pl Oakland CA 94619-3114

DAVIS, JOHN WARREN, contract specialist; b. York, Pa., Feb. 14, 1946; s. Frank Asbury Jr. and Lillian Margaret (Billings) D. BA in Polit. Sci., Drake U., 1968; AA in Real Estate, San Diego City Coll., 1976; MS in Acquisition and Contract Mgmt., West Coast U., 1987; postgrad., Walden U., 1992—. Real estate sales staff, 1972-79; clk. GS 3 Naval Ocean Sys. Ctr., 1979-80; contract intern, contract adminstr. Office of Naval Rsch., 1980-84; contract specialist, warranted ordering officer Gen. Svc. 1102-11 Naval Weapons Sta., 1984-86; contract specialist Gen Svc. 1102-12 Navy Space Sys. Activity, 1986-88; procurement analyst Gen Svc. 102-12 COMNAVAIRPAC, 1988—; del. San Diego State U. to the Nat. Acad. Conf. for Contract Mgmt. Educators, 1991, 92, 93; profl. cons. Computer Applications, Inc., 1992; mem. tech. program com., chairperson for electronic data interchange Soc. of Logistics Engrs., 1995; mem. Golden Hill planning com. City of San Diego; adj. instr. San Diego State U., chmn. curriculum rev. com. for acquisitiion. With U.S. Army, Vietnam, 1968-72. Fellow Nat. Contract Mgmt. Assn. (cert. profl. contract mgr.); mem. ABA (mem. sub-com. pub. law sector, sub-com. on intellectual property), SAR (nat., Calif. and San Diego chpts.), Am. Arbitration Assn. (nat. panel mem.), Am. Soc. Mil. Comptrs., Soc. Govt. Meeting Planners (v.p. San Diego chpt.), Soc. Logistics Engrs., San Diego Athletic Club (immediate past pres.), San Diego Writers and Editors Guild, Author's Guild (assoc.). Episcopalian. Home: PO Box 620657 San Diego CA 92162-0657 Office: COMNAVAIRPAC (N411) PO Box 357051 San Diego CA 92135

DAVIS, KIMBERLY B., art gallery director; b. L.A., 1953. BFA, Pratt Inst., N.Y.C., 1975; postgrad., Hunter Coll., N.Y.C. Dir. Bernard Jacobson, L.A., 1979-84, N.Y.C., 1983; dir. L.A. Louver, Venice, Calif., 1985—. Office: L A Louver 45 N Venice Blvd Venice CA 90291-4127

DAVIS, LENARD EUGENE, middle school education educator; b. L.A., Jan. 28, 1953; s. Arthur Charles and Virginia Hope (Healey) D. BA in History, Principia Coll., Elsah, Ill., 1975; student, U. Calif., Irvine, 1975-77; MEd, U.S. Internat. U., San Diego, 1990. Tchr. Huntington Beach (Calif.) Union H.S. Dist., 1985-89; thcr. middle sch. journalism and history Santa Ana (Calif.) Schs., 1989—. Contbr. articles to Christian Sci. Monitor, others. Candidate for Newport-Mesa Sch. Dist., Calif., 1979. Mem. Orange County Journalism Edn. Assn. (v.p. 1991-93), Santa Ana Educators Assn., Columbia Scholastic Press Assn. (medalist/1st place award for sch. newspaper 1989-96), World Affairs Coun. of Orange Co. Home: Ten Goodwill Ct Newport Beach CA 92663 Office: MacArthur Intermediate Sch 600 W Alton Ave Santa Ana CA 92707-4073

DAVIS, LINDA ANN, anesthesiologist, physician; b. Riverside, Calif., Aug. 2, 1957. DO, Kirksville (Mo.) Coll. Osteo., 1985. Diplomate Am. Bd. Pain Mgmt., Am. Bd. Anesthesiology. Intern Phoenix Gen. Hosp., 1985-86; resident in anesthesiology and pain mgmt. Cleve. Clinic, 1987-88, U. Ariz., 1988-90; anesthesiologist Marcus Lawrence Med. Ctr., Cottonwood, Ariz., 1990—; pain mgmt. specialsit Ctr. for Back Pain and Headache, Cottonwood, Ariz., 1992—; med. dir. Cottonwood Day Surgery Ctr., 1994—. Recipient Achievement award Janet Glasgow Found., 1985. Mem. Am. Soc. Anesthesiologists, Am. Acad. Pain Mgmt., Am. Soc. Pain Practitioners, Ariz. Soc. Anesthesiologists, Ariz. Osteo. Med. Assn., Phi Beta Kappa. Office: Ctr for Back Pain and Headache 55 S 6th St Cottonwood AZ 86326-4237

DAVIS, LINDA JACOBS, municipal official; b. Miami, July 10, 1955; d. Martin Jacque and Doris Harriet (Stucker) Jacobs; m. John Joseph Mantos, Jan. 1, 1984 (dec. 1988); m. Perry Davis, June 4, 1989; children: Aaron,

Jacob. Student, U. South Fla., 1977. Mgr. Werner Erhard & Assocs., San Francisco, 1978-82, program leader, 1979-90; asst. exec. dir. The Breakthrough Found., San Francisco, 1982-88; owner Mantagaris Galleries, San Francisco, 1988-92; dir. mktg. devel. Marin Child Care Coun., San Rafael, Calif., 1992-94; dir. devel. and pub. affairs Planned Parenthood of Marin, Sonoma and Menodcino, Calif., 1994-96; ptnr. Women's Initiative for Leadership Devel., 1994-96; pres., CEO Mill Valley C. of C., 1996—; profl. fund-raiser. Vol. The Hunger Project, Fla., 1977-78; bd. dirs. Marin Child Care Coun.; appointed commr. Marin Commn. on Women, 1994-97. Recipient Outstanding Young Women Am. Mem. NOW (pres. local chpt.), Marin Women's Coalition. Democrat. Jewish. Home: 419 Karla Ct Novato CA 94949-5478 Office: Mill Valley C of C 85 Throckmorton Mill Valley CA 94941

DAVIS, LOYD EVAN, defense industry marketing professional; b. Newark, Ohio, Apr. 10, 1939; s. Paul Edwin and Eleanor Amanda (Loyd) D.; m. Delores Madeline Wells, Nov. 10, 1959 (div. 1975); children: Mark Evan, Geoffrey Scott; m. Judith Ann Lambert, Sept. 15, 1977; 1 child, James Richard. BS in Elec. Engring., Okla. State U., 1963, MS in Elec. Engring., 1968. Commd. 2d lt. USAF, 1964, advanced through grades to maj., 1974; served in various locations, then ret. U.S. Air Force, 1979; mem. sr. profl. staff Dynatrend, Inc., Arlington, Va., 1979-82; mktg. mgr. govt. systems sector Harris Corp., Alexandria, Va., 1982-87; mktg. mgr. E-Systems Melpar Div., Falls Church, Va., 1987-90; mem. sr. profl. staff Adroit Systems, Inc., Alexandria, Va., 1990-95; staff engr. L3 Comms Corp., Salt Lake City, 1996—. Mem. Assn. U.S. Army, Am. Def. Preparedness Assn., Air Force Assn., Armed Forces Communications Electronics Assn., Assn. Old Crows, Woodbridge Wireless Club (pres. 1972-73, 88-89), Davis County Amateur Radio Club (v.p. 1997), Mt. Vernon Amateur Radio Club (pres. 1987-88), Masons. Republican. Methodist. Home: 1476 S Madera Hills Dr Bountiful UT 84010-1523 Office: L3 Comms Corp Wideband Systems 640 North 2200 West Salt Lake City UT 84116-2988

DAVIS, MARK DEHLEN, military officer; b. Grand Rapids, Minn., May 9, 1958; s. John Louis Davis and Helen Fischer; m. Elida Maria Echevarria, June 15, 1991; children: Carlos F. R. Fernos, Emily L. Fernos. BA Polit. Sci., BA Oriental Studies, U. Ariz., 1986. Commd. 2d lt. U.S. Army, 1987, advanced through grades to capt., 1990; asst. brigade S-2 197th Inf. Brigade, Ft. Benning, Ga., 1990-91; bn. S-2 2-18 Inf. Bn., 24th Inf. Divsn., Ft. Benning, 1991-93; imagery officer J-2, U.S. Forces, Seoul, 1993-94; aviation brigade S-2 Aviator Brigade, 25th ID, Wheeler Army Airfield, Hawaii, 1994-95; asst. G-2 ops. G-2, 25 Inf. Divsn., Schofield Barracks, Hawaii, 1996—. Decorated Meritorious Svc. medal, Army Commendation medal (2), Army Achievement medal. Republican. Office: HHC (G-2) 25th Infantry Divsn Schofield Barracks HI 96857

DAVIS, MARVIN, petroleum company executive, entrepreneur; b. Newark, Aug. 28, 1925; s. Jack Davis; m. Barbara Davis; 5 children. BSCE, NYU, 1947. Gen. ptnr., owner Davis Oil Co., Denver; co-owner 20th Century-Fox, 1981-85. Office: Davis Oil Co 2121 Ave Of Stars Ste 2800 Los Angeles CA 90067-5010

DAVIS, MICHAEL CHASE, aerospace industry executive, consultant, retired naval officer; b. Fullerton, Calif., Oct. 12, 1931; s. Arthur Elling Davis and Mary Stafford (O'Brien) Greene; m. Edna Elisabeth Ann Gulick, Apr. 9, 1983; children by previous marriage—Michael Chase, Jr., Mark Stafford. B.S., U.S. Naval Acad., 1953; S.M., MIT, 1961, Sc.D., 1961. Commd. ensign U.S. Navy, 1953, advanced through grades to capt., 1971; design supt. Mare Island Naval Shipyard, Calif., 1966-68, systems analyst Office of Asst. Sec. of Def., Washington, 1968-70; ship design dir., Trident Submarine and Aegis Warships, Naval Sea Systems Command, Arlington, Va., 1970-75; comdg. officer David Taylor Naval Ship Research and Devel. Ctr., Bethesda, Md., 1975-77, ret., 1977; program mgr. Sci. Applications, Inc., Arlington, 1977-79; program mgr. and dir. Sea Shadow Stealth Ship and other marine programs, Lockheed Martin Missiles and Space Co., Sunnyvale, Calif., 1979-96; cons., 1996—. Recipient DAR award for seamanship, 1953, D.W. Taylor award for sci. achievement, 1963, award for sci. achievement Bur. Ships, 1963, Joint Service commendation Sec. of Def., 1970; decorated Legion of Merit, 1977. Mem. Am. Soc. Naval Engrs. (council mem. 1971-73), Soc. Naval Architects and Marine Engrs., IEEE, U.S. Naval Inst. Republican. Home: 1073 Sargent Dr Sunnyvale CA 94087-2839

DAVIS, NATHANIEL, humanities educator; b. Boston, Apr. 12, 1925; s. Harvey Nathaniel and Alice Marion (Rohde) D.; m. Elizabeth Kirkbride Creese, Nov. 24, 1956; children: Margaret Morton Davis Mainardi, Helen Miller Davis Presley, James Creese, Thomas Rohde. Grad., Phillips Exeter Acad., 1942; AB, Brown U., 1944, LLD, 1970; MA, Fletcher Sch. Law and Diplomacy, 1947, PhD, 1960; postgrad. Russian lang. and area, Columbia, Cornell U., Middlebury Coll., 1953-54, U. Central de Venezuela, 1961-62; Norwich U., 1989. Asst. history Tufts Coll., 1947; joined U.S. Fgn. Service, 1947; 3d sec. Prague, Czechoslovakia, 1947-49; vice consul Florence, Italy, 1949-52; 2d sec. Rome, Italy, 1952-53, Moscow, USSR, 1954-56; Soviet desk officer State Dept., 1956-60; 1st sec. Caracas, Venezuela, 1960-62; acting Peace Corps dir. Chile, 1962; spl. asst. to dir. Peace Corps, 1962-63, dept. asso. dir., 1963-65; U.S. minister to Bulgaria, 1965-66; sr. staff Nat. Security Council (White House), 1966-68; U.S. ambassador to Guatemala, 1968-71; to Chile, 1971-73; dir. gen. Fgn. Service, 1973-75, asst. sec. of state for African affairs, 1975; U.S. ambassador to Switzerland, 1975-77; State Dept advisor and Chester Nimitz prof. Naval War Coll., 1977-83; lectr. Naval War Coll., San Diego, 1991—; Alexander and Adelaide Hixon prof. humanities Harvey Mudd Coll., Claremont, Calif., 1983—; faculty exec. com. Harvey Mudd Coll., 1986-89, acting dean of faculty, 1990; mem. Mellon Found. Grant Inter-coll. Steering Com. for the Six Claremont Colls., establishing a Summer Lang. Inst. and coordinated lang. program; mem. Consortiumn, Task Force on the Future of the Clairmont Colleges, 1996, Fulbright scholarship, Moscow, Russia, 1996-97; lectr. U.S. history Centro Venezolano-Americano, 1961; lectr. Russian and Soviet history Howard U., 1962-65, 66-68; lectr. constnl. law and social problems Salve Regina Coll., 1981-83. Author: The Last Two Years of Salvador Allende, 1985, Equality and Equal Security in Soviet Foreign Policy, 1986, A Long Walk to Church: A Contemporary History of Russian Orthodoxy, 1995. Mem. ctrl. com. Calif. Dem. Party, 1987-90, 91—, mem. exec. bd., 1993—, mem. exec. com., bus. and profl. caucus, 1992—; mem. L.A. County Dem. Ctrl. Com., 1988-90, 92—, regional vice chmn., 1994-96; del. Dem. Nat. Conv., 1988, 92, 96; del. So. Calif. conf. United Ch. of Christ, 1986-87. Lt. (j.g.) USNR, 1944-46. Recipient Cinco Aguilas Blancas Alpinism award Venezuelan Andean Club, 1962, Disting. Pub. Svc. award U.S. Navy, 1983, Elvira Roberti award for outstanding leadership Los Angeles County Dem. Party, 1995. Mem. AAUP (pres. Claremont Coll. chpt. 1992-96, rep. so. Calif. pvt. colls., Calif. coun.), Am. Fgn. Svc. Assn. (bd. dirs., vice chmn. 1964), Coun. on Fgn. Rels., Am. Acad. Diplomacy, Nat. Book Critics Cir., Cosmos Club, Phi Beta Kappa. Home: 1783 Longwood Ave Claremont CA 91711-3129 Office: Harvey Mudd Coll 301 E 12th St Claremont CA 91711-5901

DAVIS, PAMELA ANN, women and childrens health education manager; b. Salem, Mass., Feb. 11, 1960; d. Donald Lee Gorrell and JoAnn Patricia (Hanna) Butcher; m. Joseph Patrick Davis, Aug. 3, 1964; children: Ryan, Cory. BSN, U. Calif., Chico, 1984; MPA, U. San Francisco, 1988. RN, Calif.; RN cert., cert. BLS instr.; Am. Heart Assn./Am. Acad. Pediats. neonatal resuscitation; cert. hosp. based instr. Staff nurse Sutter Meml. Hosp., Sacramento, 1984-92, exracoporeal membrame oxgenator coord., 1989-92, asst. nurse mgr. spl. care nursery, 1990-91, acting nurse mgr. spl. care nursery, 1991-92, womens and childrens health edn. mgr., 1992—; instr. grandparenting class Sutter Meml. Hosp., Sacramento, 1992—, neonatal resuscitation instr., 1992—, BLS instr., 1995—. Assoc. bd. mem. Women Escaping a Violent Environment, Sacramento, 1994—. Mem. Intern. Child Edn. Assn.

DAVIS, PAUL BRYAN, political science educator; b. L.A., June 13, 1947; s. Michael and Rebecca (Badner) D. AA in Polit. Sci., Santa Monica Coll., 1967; BA, Calif. State U., Long Beach, 1969; MA, San Diego State U., 1971; PhD, U. Utah, 1978. Instr. polit. sci. San Diego State U., 1971-73; lectr. polit. sci. U. Utah, Salt Lake City, 1974-76; prof. polit. sci. Truckee Meadows C.C., Reno, Nev., 1976—, Sierra Nevada Coll., Incline Village, Nev., 1977-79, U. Nev., Reno, 1980-93, U. Md. European divsn., 1984-85, U. Pitts., 1995; adminstrv. analyst City of San Diego, 1972; mem. nat. adv. bd. Dushkin Pub., Conn., 1990-94; lectr., rschr. in field. Co-author: Introduction to Political Terrorism, 1989; contbr. revs., articles to profl. publs.; TV and radio analyst ABC, CBS, NBC, 1981—. Campaign coord. Utah State Presl. Campaign for Senator Frank Church, 19767, Nev. State Presdl. Campaign for Senator Eugene McCarthy, 1976, Nev. State Presdl. Campaign for Congressman John Anderson, 1980; mem. Washoe County Nev. Rep. Ctrl. Com., Reno, 1996—; mem. state ctrl. com. Nev. State Rep. Party, Reno, 1996—; rschr. for Rep. Nat. Conv., San Diego, 1996; co-developer internat. seminar Nev. World Trade Coun., Reno, 1996. Grantee NEH, 1990, U.S. Inst. of Peace, 1995; Fulbright fellow, India, 1990, Israel, 1982, Egypt, 1986, NEH rsch. fellow, 1983; named Outstanding Prof. of Yr., Phi Theta Kappa, 1996; recipeint Cert. of Appreciation, City of San Diego, 1972. Mem. Am. Fedn. Tchrs., Am. Polit. Sci. Assn., Policy Studies Orgn., Internat. Polit. Sci. Assn., Western Gerontol. Soc., Presdl. Studies Assn., Animal Protection Inst. Am., Fulbright Alumni Assn., Phi Sigma Alpha. Home: PO Box 50666 Sparks NV 89435 Office: Truckee Meadows CC 7000 Dandini Blvd Reno NV 89512

DAVIS, PAUL KENSIL, strategic planner; b. Youngstown, Ohio, Dec. 20, 1943; s. Paul K. Davis and Ruth A. Gladhill; m. Joyce E. Lindstrom, Sept. 30, 1966; 1 child, Elise. BS in Chemistry, U. Mich., 1965; PhD in Chem. Physics, MIT, 1970. Postdoctoral fellow James Franck Inst., U. Chgo., 1970-71; sr. staff mem. Inst. for Def. Analysis, Alexandria, Va., 1971-75; analyst ACDA, Washington, 1975-77; analyst Office of Sec. of Def., Washington, 1977-79, sr. exec., 1979-81; program dir. Rand, Santa Monica, Calif., 1982-90, corp. rsch. mgr. for def. and tech. planning, 1990-96, strategic planner, 1996—; mem. faculty Rand Grad. Sch. Policy Studies, Santa Monica, 1982—. Author: Deterring or Coercing Opponents in Crisis: The Case of Saddam Hussein, 1991, Defense Planning in the Post Cold War Era, 1993; editor, author: New Challenges for Defense Planning, 1994. Mem. Internat. Inst. of Strategic Studies, Sigma Xi. Home: 3243 Fermi Dr Topanga CA 90290-4432 Office: Rand 1700 Main St Santa Monica CA 90401-3208

DAVIS, RANDY L., soil scientist; b. L.A., Nov. 23, 1950; s. Willie Vernon and Joyce Catherine (Manes) D. AA, Yuba Community Coll., 1972; BS in Soils and Plant Nutrition, U. Calif., Berkeley, 1976. Vol. soil scientist U.S. Peace Corps, Maseru, Lesotho, 1976-79; soil scientist Hiawatha Nat. Forest, Sault Saint Marie, Mich., 1979-86; forest soil scientist Bridger-Teton Nat. Forest, Jackson, Wyo., 1986—; detailed soil scientist Boise (Idaho) Nat. Forest, 1989, 92, Mendocino (Calif.) Nat. Forest, 1996. Editor Soil Classifiers newsletter; contbr. articles to profl. jours. Pres. Sault Community Theater, Sault Saint Marie, 1984-86. Mem. Am. Chem. Soc., Soil Sci. Soc. Am., Soil and Water Conservation Soc. (bd. dirs. 1991-92, chpt. pres. 1993-95), Am. Water Resources Assn., Internat. Soc. Soil Sci., Soc. for Range Mgmt. Methodist. Home: PO Box 7795 Jackson WY 83002-7795 Office: Bridger-Teton Nat Forest PO Box 1888 Jackson WY 83001-1888

DAVIS, RICHARD CALHOUN, dentist; b. Manhattan, Kans., Jan. 4, 1945; s. William Calhoun and Alison Rae (Wyland) D.; Danna Ruth Ritchel, June 13, 1968; 1 child, Darin Calhoun. Student, Ariz. State U., 1963-65, BA, 1978; BA, U. Ariz., 1966; DDS, U. of Pacific, 1981. Retail dept. head Walgreens, Tucson, 1965-66; mgmt. trainee Walgreens, Tucson, San Antonio, 1967-70; asst. store mgr. Walgreens, Baton Rouge, 1970-72; field rep. Am. Cancer Soc., Phoenix, 1972-74; dept. head Lucky Stores, Inc., Tempe, Ariz., 1976-78; practice dentistry specializing in gen. dentistry Tucson, 1981—; bd. dirs. Home Again, Inc. Chmn. bd. Capilla Del Sol Christian Ch., Tucson, 1984. Mem. ADA, Acad. Gen. Dentists, Am. Straight Wire Orthodontic Assn., Am. Assn. Functional Orthodontics, Sleep Disorders Dental Soc., So. Ariz. Bus. Assn., N.W. Dental Study Club, Optimists (past pres. N.W. club), Elks. Republican. Mem. Disciples of Christ Ch. Office: 2777 N Campbell Ave Tucson AZ 85719-3101

DAVIS, RICHARD ERNEST, engineer; b. San Francisco, Nov. 20, 1936; 1 child, Richard Jr.; m. Sharon L. Buss, Aug. 26, 1961; children: Dawn, Michelle. BS in Engring., Calif. State Poly. U., San Luis Obispo, 1967. Facilities engr., energy conservation engr. Naval Weapons Ctr., China Lake, Calif., 1967-77; solar program coordinator U.S. Dept. Energy, Oakland, Calif., 1977-78; program mgr. Solar Energy Research Inst., Golden, Colo., 1978-80; engring. specialist Holmes & Narver, Mercury, Nev., 1980-90; engring. specialist nuclear waste Nev./Yucca Mountain Project Raytheon Svcs., Mercury, 1990-93; constrn. engr. mgr. Fluor Daniel, Inc., 1993-96; city constrn. mgr. Fluor Daniel Telecom, 1996—. Contbr. articles to profl. jours. Served with USAF, 1954-62. Home: HC 69 Box 495 Amargosa Valley NV 89020-9801 Office: Fluor Daniel Inc 3333 Michelson Dr Irvine CA 92612

DAVIS, ROBERT H., financial executive, arbitrator, mediator, educator; b. Phila., Mar. 26, 1943; student Los Angeles Valley Coll., 1965-67, Alexander Hamilton Inst., 1965-68, Grad. Sch. of Credit and Fin. Mgmt., Stanford U., 1977-80, Pepperdine U., 1981; 1 dau., Michelle R. Cert. arbitrator, mediator, counselor Am. Arbitration Assn., Singapore Arbitration Ctr. and Inst. Internat. Negotiation and Conflict Mgmt. Asst., sr. internat. arbitratior, Korean Commercial Arbitration Commission, 1996, controller, credit mgr. Wyo. Machinery Co., Casper, 1978-83; controller/sec.-treas., dir. John E. Burns Drilling Co., Casper, 1979-82; comptroller, v.p. Philip Crosby Assocs., Inc., Winter Park, Fla., 1982-84, 84—; v.p., treas. Crosby Assocs. Internat., Inc., Winter Park, Fla.; pres., CEO Davis, Keller & Davis, New Orleans, Oreg. and Wash., 1989—; mgmt./cons. and internat. arbitrator/mediator, author, lectr. Am. Arbitration Assn., Singapore Arbitration Ctr., fin. cons. Western Energy Co., Huey's Smoked Meats, Nashville, Trans-Equip., Casper, Three Percent, Inc., Riverton, Wyo., 1979-80; mem. subcom. USA/NAFTA, Washington; arbitrator, mediator BBB of Oreg. Adv. bd. dirs. Highland Park Community Ch., 1980—. Served with USNR, 1961-63. Mem. Nat. Assn. Credit Mgmt. (state rep. 1979-82, founder, chmn. Casper Credit Group), Soc. Profls. in Dispute Resolution, Am. Soc. Internat. Law, Credit Mgrs. Assn. So. Calif. (dir. bus. re-orgn. and bankruptcy 1973-74), Credit Research Found., Am. Mgmt. Assn., Practicing Law Inst. (assoc.), Wash. Export Coun. (apptd. mem. by the sec. of commerce & U.S. Trade Rep.), La. Export Coun., U.S. Dept. Commerce Industry Consultation Program (customs com.), Stanford U. Alumni Assn., Internat. Platform Assn., Internat. Inst. Negotiation and Conflict Mgmt. (Australia); cons. U.S.A./NAFTA nat. com. mem. Alliance for GATT Pres's. Export Coun. Club: Order of Demolay (sr. award 1960). Author: Charting Your Businesses Practices-U.S. Small Business Adminstrn., Transnational Arbitration as a Means of Managing Corporate Risks, International Risk Management for U.S. Small Businesses, Leasing as a Secondary Source of Financing in the Heavy Equiptment Industry.

DAVIS, ROGER LEWIS, lawyer; b. New Orleans, Jan. 27, 1946; s. Leon and Anada A. (Russ) D.; m. Annette Vucinich; 1 child, Alexandra. BA, Tulane U., 1967; MA, UCLA, 1969; PhD, UCLA, 1971; JD, Harvard U., 1974. Bar: Calif. 1974. Assoc. Orrick, Herrington & Sutcliffe, L.L.P., San Francisco, 1974-79, ptnr., 1980—, chmn. pub. fin. dept., 1981—. Mem. Bay Area Coun., San Francisco, 1988-90. Mem. ABA (tax sect., mem. com. tax exempt financing), Nat. Assn. Bond Lawyers (mem. com. profl. responsibility and gen. tax matters). Office: Orrick Herrington & Sutcliffe LLP 400 Sansome St San Francisco CA 94111-3308

DAVIS, RON LEE, clergyman, author; b. Carroll, Iowa, Oct. 17, 1947; s. David Clarence and Elizabeth Regina (Thompson) D.; m. Shirley Louise O'Connor, Aug. 31, 1973; children: Rachael LeeAnn, Nathan Paul. BA cum laude, Tarkio (Mo.) Coll., 1969; MDiv cum laude, Dubuque (Iowa) Theol. Sem., 1971; DDiv, Bethel Theol. Sem., St. Paul, 1977. Ordained to ministry Presbyn. Ch., 1971. Chaplain Minn. Vikings, Mpls., 1975-80; assoc. pastor Hope Presbyn. Ch., Mpls., 1971-80; sr. pastor First Presbyn. Ch., Fresno, Calif., 1981-86, Community Presbyn. Ch., Danville, Calif., 1986-91; tchr. Bible Oakland (Calif.) A's, 1990-91; writer, 1983—; sr. pastor Bear Creek Cmty. Ch., Stockton, Calif., 1997—; invited speaker at gen. sessions and confs. and on TV. Author: Gold in the Making, 1983, A Forgiving God in an Unforgiving World, 1984, Healing Life's Hurts, 1986, A Time for Compassion, 1986, Courage to Begin Again, 1988, Mistreated, 1989, Becoming a Whole Person in a Broken World, 1990, Mentoring, 1990. Mem. pres.'s adv. coun. Fellowship of Christian Athletes; bd. dirs. Youth for Christ, cen. Calif., 1982-85, Fresno Pacific Coll., 1983-84. Recipient award for outstanding leadership State Bar; named to Outstanding Young Men of Am. Home: 3513 Canfield Dr Danville CA 94526-5507

DAVIS, ROSWITA BEATE, architectural engineer; b. Ranzau, Germany, Sept. 27, 1945; came to U.S., 1966; d. Heinz Otto and Erika (Waht) Neander; 1 child, Erika Neander. Archtl. Draftsperson, Trade and Tech. Coll., Unna, Westphalen, 1963. Lic. engr., Germany. Chmn. bd. Interior Design Assoc., 1978-81; sr. facilities engr. Ford Aerospace and Comm. Corp., 1981-85. Author: (poetry) Assorted Lives, 1996; (poetry anthologies) Seasons to Come, 1995 (award 1995), Beyond the Stars, 1996 (award 1996), A Tapestry of Thoughts (award 1996), Best Poems of 1996 (award 1996); (novel) Stones That Lie, 1996.

DAVIS, SCOTT MILTON, information systems professional; b. Cin., Dec. 6, 1952; s. Robert Milton and Marjorie Alma Martha (Hecker) D. BA in Sociology, U. Cin., 1978; MA in Environ. Planning, Ariz. State U., 1986. From cons. to asst. to pres. Cosanti Found., Scottsdale, Cordes Jct., Ariz., 1981-84, 89—. Co-author: Paolo Soleri's Earth Casting, 1984. Vol. Yellowstone Nat. Park, 1978. Home and Office: Cosanti Found HC Box 4136 Mayer AZ 86333

DAVIS, STANFORD EVOL, civil engineer; b. Oakland, Calif., Jan. 31, 1937; s. Stanford Leroy and Leona (Parsons) D.; m. Carole Ann McCrindle, Mar. 26, 1960; children: Glen Leroy, Linda Carole. BS in Engring., San Jose State Coll., 1960; pub. adminstrn. cert., Calif. State U., Hayward, 1974; transp. cert., Calif. State U. Registered profl. civil engr., Calif.; registered traffic engr. Jr. and asst. engr. Contra Costa County, Martinez, Calif., 1960-64; asst. city engr. City of Antioch, Calif., 1964-69, city engr., 1969-73, dir. cmty. devel., city engr., 1973-78, dir. pub. works, city engr., 1978—; chair Contra Costa County Transp. Adv. Com., 1988-91; mem. City-County Engring. Adv. Com., Contra Costa County, 1969—; mem. Mcpl. Pub. Works Officers Conf., Bay Area, 1969—. Sgt. 1st class Calif. Army N.G. Mem. ASCE, NSPE, Am. Water Works Assn., Am. Pub. Works Assn., Calif. Soc. Profl. Engrs. (chpt. officer). Democrat. Home: 1409 Saint Francis Dr Antioch CA 94509-4629 Office: City of Antioch PO Box 130 Antioch CA 94509-0504

DAVIS, STANFORD MELVIN, engineering executive, publishing consultant; b. Camden, N.J., June 12, 1941; s. Winford and Rose Marie (Rich) D.; m. Pamela Davis, Nov. 25, 1967 (div. 1980); children: Peter, Shawna; m. Laura A. Rudolph, Feb. 21, 1987. AB, BSEE, Rutgers U., 1964; postgrad., UCLA, 1967; MBA, U. Portland, 1974. Elec. engr. RCA, Van Nuys, Calif., 1966-68; project engr. Tek, Wilsonville, Oreg., 1968-79; S/W mgr. Tektronix, Wilsonville, 1979-81, mgr. mktg., 1981-83; founder, v.p. engring. Concept Technologies, Portland, 1983-86; mgr. engring. program INTEL, Hillsboro, Oreg., 1986-87; product line mgr. INTEL, Hillsboro, 1987-88; engring. mgr. Graphic Printing div. Textronix, Wilsonville, Oreg., 1989-95; pres. Straight-on Industries, Beaverton, Oreg., 1995—; with worldwide Web, Internet design firm; pres. Internet Profls. Northwest. Patentee in field. Served to capt. U.S. Army, 1964-66. Recipient Outstanding Product award Datapro, Delran, N.J., 1985. Mem. IEEE, Assn. of Computing Machinery, N.W. Assn. Internet Profls., Software Assn. Oreg., Portland City Club (Pres.'s award 1996). Home and Office: 7320 SW 103rd Ave Beaverton OR 97008-6048

DAVIS, STERLING EVAN, television executive; b. Mpls., Feb. 10, 1941; s. Lyman Eugene and Ruby Elizabeth (Larson) D.; m. Bonnie S. Taylor, Jan. 15, 1977; children: Evan, Emily, Robin. BA, Taylor U., 1963; postgrad., U. So. Calif., L.A., 1968-70. Chief engr. Metrotape, Hollywood, Calif., 1974-78; v.p. ops. The Vidtronics Co., Hollywood, 1978; chief engr. Telemation Prodns., Seattle, 1978-82; dir. ops. Sta. KTVU, Inc., Oakland, Calif., 1982—. Bd. dirs. Post Adoption Ctr. for Edn. & Rsch., Easter Seal Soc. of The Bay Area. Lt. USN, 1963-67, Vietnam. Mem. IEEE, Soc. Motion Picture & TV Engrs., Audio Engring. Soc., Soc. Broadcast Engrs. Office: KTVU PO Box 22222 Oakland CA 94623-2222

DAVIS, STEVEN ARTHUR, photographer, educator; b. July 12, 1957; s. James Robert and Ann Elizabeth (LaGrone) D.; m. Monique Anderson, Dec. 8, 1985. BS in Comms.-Photo/Film, U. Idaho, 1979, MFA, 1983. Photographer Evergreen State Coll., Olympia, Wash., 1986—, coord. photographic imaging, part-time faculty, 1987—, vis. faculty, 1993-94; vis. prof. U. Idaho, Moscow, 1989. Exhibited in one-person shows at Univ. Gallery, U. Idaho, 1978, Donnally/Hayes, Seattle, 1985, Prichard Gallery, Moscow, 1988, So. Light Gallery of Amarillo (Tex.) Coll., 1989; in group shows at Notre Dame U., 1992, Evergreen State Coll., 1993, L.A. Conv. Ctr., 1993, Pacific Luth. U., Tacoma, 1993, CyberSpace Gallery, West Hollywood, Calif., 1993, Holter Mus. Art, Helena, Mont., 1994, Krannert Mus., Champaign, Ill., 1995, Contemporary Art Ctr., New Orleans, L.A., 1996—, Ctr. on Contemporary Art, Seattle, 1996; in collections at Musee de la Photographie, Charleroi, Belgium, Bethel Sch. Dist., Pierce County, Wash., EZTV, Hollywood, Calif. Recipient Silver award Seattle Design and Advt. Show, 1981, award of merit Calif. Works, Sacramento, 1986, Award of Excellence Univ. and Coll. Designers Assn., 1990, others; artist fellowship Wash. State Arts Commn., 1989. Mem. Soc. for Photog. Edn. (chair regional conf. 1992), Coll. Art Assn., N.W. Comms. Assn. Office: Evergreen State Coll L 1302 Olympia WA 98505

DAVIS, TERRY LEE, communications and control systems engineer; b. Enid, Okla., Aug. 18, 1950; s. Walter Joseph and Bessie Lee (McDaniel) D.; m. Jennie Sue Petrik, Jan. 21, 1972; children: Mistie Rae, Brandon Scott. BSCE, Okla. State U., 1972. Registered profl. engr., Okla., Colo., Wash. Civil engr. U.S. Army C.E., Webbers Falls, Okla., 1973, Omaha, 1974; water resources engr. U.S. Bur. Reclamation, Grand Junction, Colo., 1974-75, Amarillo, Tex., 1974-75, Montrose, Colo., 1976; water resources engr. U.S. Bur. Reclamation, AID, Dubai, United Arab Emirates, 1977-78; comm. and control sys. engr. Western Area Power Adminstrn., U.S. Dept. Energy, Loveland, Colo., 1979-84; comm. and control sys. engr. Boeing, Seattle, 1984-95, sr. prin. scientist, 1995—. Mem. Issaquah (Wash.) Devel. Commn., 1986-96, chmn., 1994-96; mem. Issaquah Basin Planning Team, 1990-92; mem. Issaquah Telecom. and Cable TV Commn., 1997—; mem., chmn. Grand Ridge Devel. Commn., 1996-97. Mem. Masons (master of Myrtle Lodge #108 1995), Order Ea. Star. Republican. Office: Boeing Info & Support Svcs PO Box 3707 Seattle WA 98124-2207

DAVIS, WANDA ROSE, lawyer; b. Lampasas, Tex., Oct. 4, 1937; d. Ellis DeWitt and Julia Doris (Rose) Cockrell; m. Richard Andrew Fulcher, May 9, 1959 (div. 1969); 1 child, Greg Ellis; m. Edwin Leon Davis, Jan. 14, 1973 (div. 1985). BBA, U. Tex., 1959, JD, 1971. Bar: Tex. 1971, Colo. 1981, U.S. Dist. Ct. (no. dist.) Tex. 1972, U.S. Dist. Ct. Colo. 1981, U.S. Ct. Appeals (10th cir. 1981, U.S. Supreme Ct. 1976. Atty. Atlantic Richfield Co., Dallas, 1971; assoc. firm Crocker & Murphy, Dallas, 1971-72; prin. Wanda Davis, Atty. at Law, Dallas, 1972-73; ptnr. firm Davis & Davis Inc., Dallas, 1973-75; atty. adviser HUD, Dallas, 1974-75, Air Force Acctg. and Fin. Ctr., Denver, 1976-92; co-chmn. regional Profl. Devel. Inst., Am. Soc. Mil. Comptrollers, Colorado Springs, Colo., 1982; chmn. Lowry AFB Noontime Edn. Program, Exercise Program, Denver, 1977-83; mem. speakers bur. Colo. Women's Bar, 1995—, Lowry AFB, 1981-83; mem. fed. ct. liaison com. U.S. Dist. Ct. Colo., 1983; mem. Leaders of the Fed. Bar Assn. People to People Del. to China, USSR and Finland, 1986. Contbr. numerous articles to profl. jours. Bd. dirs. Pres.'s Coun. Met. Denver, 1981-83; mem. Lowry AFB Alcohol Abuse Exec. Com., 1981-84. Recipient Spl. Achievement award USAF, 1978; Upward Mobility award Fed. Profl. and Adminstrv. Women, Denver, 1979, Internat. Humanitarian award CARE, 1994. Mem. Fed. Bar Assn. (pres. Colo. 1982-83, mem. nat. coun. 1984—, Earl W. Kintner Disting. Svc. award 1983, 1st v.p. 10th cir. 1986-97, Internat. Humanitarian award CARE, 1994), Zach Found. for Burned Children (award 1995), Colo. Trial Lawyers Assn., Bus. and Profl. Women's Club (dist. IV East dir. 1983-84, Colo. pres. 1988-89), Am. Soc. Mil. Comptrollers (pres. 1984-85), Denver South Met. Bus. and Profl. Women's Club (pres. 1982-83), Denver Silver Spruce Am. Bus. Women's Assn. (pres. 1981-82; Woman of Yr. award 1982), Colo. Jud. Inst., Colo. Concerned Lawyers, Profl. Mgrs. Assn., Fed. Women's Program (v.p. Denver 1980), Colo. Woman News Community adv. bd., 1988—, Dallas Bar Assn., Tex. Bar Assn., Denver Bar Assn., Altrusa, Zonta, Denver Nancy Langhorn Federally Employed Women. (pres. 1979-80). Christian.

DAWDY, FAYE MARIE CATANIA, photographer, lecturer; b. San Mateo, Calif., Sept. 15, 1954; d. Frank Benjamin and Melba Rita (Arata) Catania; m. John Thomas Dawdy, May 5, 1974; children: Tracy Marie, John

Franco. AA, Coll. of San Mateo, 1979; student, San Francisco State U., 1979—. With Proctor & Gamble Distbg. Co., San Mateo, 1973-78; ptnr. Dawdy Photography, Millbrae, Calif., 1978—; dir., sec.-treas. Millbrae Stamp Co., 1980—; instr. Winona Sch. Profl. Photography, Mt. Prospect, Ill.; lectr. to high schs., various clubs, photography convs. including Goteborg, Sweden, Idaho, Oreg., Colo., Tex., Ill., Fla., Mo., Kans., Nev., Iowa, N.J., Chile, S.A. Contbr. articles to profl. jours. Area chmn. Millbrae Am. Heart Assn. Ann. Fund Dr., 1977-82; mem. fund raising and nutrition coms. San Mateo County chpt. Am. Heart Assn., 1980-88; co-chmn. Miss Millbrae Pageant, 1981, Queen Isabella Columbus Day Festival, 1981; judge arts and crafts exhbns. Millbrae Art and Wine Festival; judge photography competition Marin County Fair Photography Exhibit; vol. photographer Rotoplast, La Serena, Chile, 1994; mem. sister city com. City of Millbrae; trustee Golden Gate Sch. Profl. Photographers, 1985-90. Recipient awards No. Calif. Coun. Camera Clubs, 1979, 81, Mktg. contest award Mktg. Today mag., 1988; photograph accepted for Profl. Photographers Am. loan collection and on exhibit at Epcot Ctr., Fla., 1995. Mem. Profl. Photographers Am. (photog. craftsman degree), Profl. Photographers Greater Bay Area, Profl. Photographers No. Calif., Profl. Photographers Calif., Wedding Photographers Assn., NAFE, Millbrae C. of C. (sec. women's divsn. 1979, bd. dirs. 1991), South San Francisco C. of C., Millbrae Art Assn. (pres. 1979-80), Portola Camera Club (nature chmn. 1978—), Millbrae Hist. Assn., Friends Millbrae Libr., Italian Cath. Fedn., Calif. Women in Profl. Photography, Fedn. Ind. Bus., St. Dunstan Women's Club, Soroptimist (sec. 1981-82). Democrat. Roman Catholic. Office: 449 Broadway Millbrae CA 94030-1905

DAWES, DOUGLAS CHARLES, retired military officer; b. Detroit, Nov. 24, 1952; s. Carl Joseph and Margaret Elisabeth (Ingalls) D.; m. Theresa Neel, June 9, 1990. BBA in Mgmt., Loyola U., New Orleans, 1974; grad. with honors, Command and Gen. Staff Coll., 1987; MA in Procurement and Acquisition Mgmt., Webster U., St. Louis, 1990. Field artillery officer U.S. Army, various locations, 1974-80; asst. fin. officer U.S. Army, Ft. Sill, Okla., 1980-82; deputy fin. and acctg. officer U.S. Army, Fed. Republic of Germany, 1982-86, Ft. Carson, Colo., 1986-87; comdr. and fin. officer U.S. Army, Ft. Carson, 1987-88, budget officer, asst. div. comptr., 1988-90, div. comptr., 1990-91; chief joint pay operation Joint Svc. Software, Def. Fin. and Acctg. Svc., Denver, 1991-94; ret., 1994; payroll mgr. Neodata Svcs., Inc., Louisville, Colo., 1995—. Vol., water safety instr. trainer ARC. Mem. Disabled Am. Vets. (life), Delta Sigma Pi (life, chancellor Delta Nu chpt. 1973, 1st v.p. 1974), Am. Legion, Am. Payroll Assn. Republican. Home: 17523 E Caspian Pl Aurora CO 80013-4172

DAWES, WALLACE ERNEST, small business owner; b. Grafton, Mass., Oct. 9, 1927; s. Wallace and Marion (Storey) D.; m. Marie (Furillo) Dawes, 1950 (div. Oct. 1970); children: Jane, Nancy; m. RoseMarie (Fusillo) Dawes, June 15, 1972. BA, CUNY (Bklyn. Coll.). Salesman F.W. Anderson Co., N.Y.C., 1952-59, Blake, Moffitt & Towne, L.A., 1973-75, Kirk Paper, L.A., 1975-77, Andrews/Nelson/Whitehead, N.Y.C., 1960-72; tech. mgr., product mgr. Paper Mill & Paper Source, L.A., 1977-95; ind. cons. and seminar condr. L.A., 1995—; tchr., presenter numerous seminars on history, making and conservation of paper; guest lectr. Columbia U., N.Y.C., NYU, N.Y.C., Paper Historians Conf., Fabriano, Italy, 1976, UCLA, 1980, Internat. Conf. on Paper for Arts, Kyoto, Japan, 1983; instr. on paper Printing Industries Assn.; tchr., presenter papermaking workshop Internat. Conf. for Calligraphy, Claremont, Calif., 1985. Lt. USNR. Recipient award Printing Craftsmens Assn., 1993. Mem. Am. Inst. for Conservation, Western Assn. Art Conservation, Soc. for Calligraphy, Internat. Printing Mus., Printing House Craftman Assn. Home: 2349 Vestal Ave Los Angeles CA 90026-2057

DAWRANT, STACEY BETH, dietitian; b. Elmhurst, Ill., June 9, 1968; d. Stanley Robert and Carole Susan (Prochazka) Rachesky; m. Andrew Charles Dawrant, July 5, 1991. BS, U. Ill., 1990; MS in Human Nutrition, Hampton U., 1993; registered dietitian, Med. Coll. Va., 1994. Cardiac dietitian U. Ill., Chgo., 1994; med. sales rep. Penny Saver Med. Supply, Denver, 1994—; sales rep. Stan's Frozen Foods, Inc., 1995—; med. nutritional sales rep. Ross Products divsn. Abbott Labs., 1995. Contbr. nutrition articles to local mags. Mem. Am. Dietetic Assn. Home and Office: 4431 S Independence Trail Evergreen CO 80439

DAWSON, ADAM, private investigator, former newspaper editor; b. N.Y.C., May 4, 1950; s. Martin and Renee D.; m. Constance Jo Stewart, Oct. 21, 1950. BA, Syracuse Univ., N.Y., 1972. Lic. private investigator, Calif. Press sec. U.S. Congressman M. Blouin, Washington, 1977-78; reporter Evening News, Annapolis, Md., 1978-79, Daily News, L.A., 1979-84; L.A. bureau chief Orange County Register, Santa Ana, Calif., 1984-88; city editor Journal Tribune, Biddeford, Maine, 1988-89; owner Dawson Ryan Assocs., L.A., 1989—; sr. instr. UCLA Extension, L.A., 1981-91. Mem. sports advisory coun. City Santa Monica, Calif., 1996—. Named Best Investigative Reporting Valley Press Club, L.A., 1982, named Best Investigative Series Orange County Press Club, 1986. Office: Dawson Ryan Assocs 12021 Wilshire Blvd #846 Los Angeles CA 90025

DAWSON, DEREK, investment company executive; b. 1942. With Hendale Group, London, 1965-82; officer Southbrook and City Holdings, London, 1982-87; chmn. Southbrook Corp., Beverley Hills, Calif., 1987—. Office: Southbrook Corp 150 S El Camino Dr Beverly Hills CA 90212

DAWSON, EUGENE ELLSWORTH, university president emeritus; b. Kansas City, Mo., Jan. 23, 1917; s. Harold Lambert and Betty Ross Dawson; m. Arlene Wilburma Clark, May 7, 1935; children: Eugene Jr., Clark (dec.), LoLita, Edward, Brent, Deborah. BA, Pittsburg (Kans.) State U., 1940; STB, Harvard U., 1944; PhD, Boston U., 1949; postgrad., U. Chgo., 1953; DHL (hon.), U. Colo., 1967; HHD (hon.), Regis U., Denver, 1967; DLitt (hon.), Keuka Coll., Keuka Pk., N.Y., 1968; DD (hon.), U. Redlands, Calif., 1978; postgrad., St. Elizabeth's Hosp., Washington, 1978-79. Asst. prof. psychology Pittsburg State U., 1946-48, dean of adminstrn., prof. psychology, 1949-57; pres. Colo. Woman's Coll., Denver, 1957-70; pres. U. Redlands, 1970-78, pres. emeritus, 1978—; instr. summer sessions U. Chgo, Kent State U., U. Houston, Western Oreg. U., Iliff Sch. Theology; cons. higher edn. and human svcs., 1980—; evaluator grants to univs. and ednl. instns., 1990—. Contbr. articles to profl. jours., chpts. to books. Bd. dirs. Estes Pk. (Colo.) Med. Found., 1980—, Estes Pk. Ch. of the Air, 1980—, Qualife Wellness Cmty., Denver, 1982—, Samaritan Counseling Ctr., Denver, 1985—; sec. bd. trustees Temple Hoyne Buell Found., Englewood, Colo., 1990—; sec. bd. dirs. Buell Devel. Corp., Englewood, 1990—. Recipient Outstanding Alumni award Pittsburg State U., 1957, Meritorious Svc. award, 1977, Talmud Torah award Congregation Hebrew Edn. Alliance, Denver, 1969. Mem. Rotary Internat. (Paul Harris fellow So. Calif. divsn. 1972, pres. Denver chpt. 1964-65, dist. gov. 1967-68, Denver Rotary Found., 1985—). Baptist. Home: Longs Pk Rt 1361 Willow Ln Estes Park CO 80517 Office: TH Buell Found 2700 E Hampden Englewood CO 80110

DAWSON, FRANCES EMILY, poet, nurse; b. Augsburg, Germany, Dec. 7, 1952; d. Emmett C. Jr. and B. Louise (Boddie) D. BS in Nursing, Pa. State U., 1974. RN, D.C. Staff nurse Howard U. Med. Ctr., Washington, 1974-75, charge nurse, 1975-77. Author: Live for Today, 1986, With You in Mind, 1987, Reflections, 1988, (poetry cassette rec.) Soul Connection, 1992. Active Disabled Resource Ctr., Lupus Found. Am., Calif. Assn. Physically Handicapped; model Operation Confidence Program for the Disabled, 1985-86, head cheerleader drill team, 1985-86; mem. Long Beach Task Force for the Ams. with Disabilities Act, 1994—; active Christ 2d Baptist Ch., 1985—. Recipient Golden Poetry award, 1985-92, excellence in lit. award Pinewood Poetry, 1987-89. Mem. BMI, Walt Whitman Guild, Internat. Soc. Poets (hon. charter), Pa. State U. Alumni Assn., Detroit Black Poets Guild. Democrat. Baptist. Home: 408 Elm Ave # 303 Long Beach CA 90802-3058

DAWSON, JOHN JOSEPH, lawyer; b. Binghamton, N.Y., Mar. 9, 1947; s. Joseph John and Cecilia (O'Neill) D. BA, Siena Coll., 1968; JD, U. Notre Dame, 1971. Bar: Ariz. 1971, Nev. 1991, Calif. 1993, D.C. 1994, N.Y. 1996. Sr. bankruptcy dir. Streich Lang, P.A., Phoenix, 1971—; reporter local rules ct. U.S. Bankruptcy Ct. for Dist. Ariz.; atty. rep. U.S. Ct. Appeals (9th cir.), 1992-95. Co-author: Advanced Chapter 11 Bankruptcy, 1991. Cpl. U.S. Army, USAR, 1964-70. Fellow Ariz. Bar Found.; mem. State Bar Ariz. (chmn. bankruptcy sect. 1976-77, 80-81), Am. Bankruptcy Inst., Comml. Law League Am. Republican. Roman Catholic. Office: Streich Lang PA Renaissance One Two North Central Ave Phoenix AZ 85004-2391

DAX, BETTY JOYCE, primary education educator; b. Superior, Wis., Feb. 5, 1945; d. Everett Walter and Evelyn Linnea (Hultman) Johnson; m. Earl Edward Dax, May 27, 1967 (div. Oct. 1974); 1 child, Earl Everett. BS, Wis. State U., 1967; postgrad., U. N.Mex. Head tchr. Heights Christian Kindergarten, Albuquerque, 1967-71; tchr. Los Lunas (N.Mex.) Consol. Schs., 1972-91, Clark County Schs., Las Vegas, 1991—; tchr. Helen Herr Elem.; coord. World Children's Day Project, Twin Lakes Elem., Las Vegas, 1992. Active various polit. candidates. Recipient Excellence in Edn. award Clark County Schs., 1992, Golden Apple award Channel 8, Las Vegas, 1993, Nev. State award World Children's Day Found., 1993. Mem. NEA (N.Mex. congl. contact team 1990-91, past bldg. rep. and negotiation team Los Lunas, co-pres. 1990-91), Clark County Tchrs. Assn. (instrnl. and profl. devel. com. chmn. 1994-96), Nev. State Edn. Assn. Instrl. and Profl. Devel. Com., Phi Delta Kappa. Democrat. Home: 1350 E Flamingo Rd # 269 Las Vegas NV 89119

DAY, ANTHONY, newspaper writer; b. Miami, Fla., May 12, 1933; s. Price and Alice (Alexander) D.; m. Lynn Ward, June 25, 1960; children—John, Julia (dec.). A.B. cum laude, Harvard U., 1955, postgrad. (Nieman fellow), 1966-67; L.H.D. (hon.), Pepperdine U., 1974. Reporter Phila. Bull., 1957-60, Washington, 1960-69; chief Washington bur. Phila. Bull., 1969; chief editorial writer L.A. Times, 1969-71, editor editorial pages, 1971-89, sr. corr., 1989-95, freelance writer, 1995—. Mem. Am. Soc. Newspaper Editors, Signet Soc. Harvard, Asia Soc. Inter Am. Press Assn., Coun. Fgn. Rels., Pacific Coun. on Internat. Policy, Inst. Current World Affairs. Office: Los Angeles Times Times Mirror Sq Los Angeles CA 90053-3816*

DAY, CHARLOTTE ELLEN, education administrator; b. Milw., Nov. 5, 1946; d. Paul Christopher and Mary Bridget (McGinn) Brust; m. Peter Leonard Day, Sept. 15, 1973 (div. Feb. 1983); 1 child, Steven. BS in Polit. Sci., Santa Clara U., 1968; MS in Ednl. Leadership, Calif. State U., Hayward, 1992. Elem. tchr. Lincoln Elem., Richmond (Calif.) Unified Sch. Dist., Calif., 1969-89; vice prin. Lincoln Elem., Richmond (Calif.) Unified Sch. Dist., San Pablo, 1989-91; project asst. Richmond (Calif.) Unified Sch. Dist., 1991-94; prin. Mira Vista Elem. West Contra Costa Unified Sch. Dist., Richmond, 1994-95, bilingual LEP monitor, 1995—; mentor tchr. Richmond (Calif.) Unified Sch. Dist., 1984-85, 85-86, 87-88; new tchr. coach St. Mary's Coll., Moraga, Calif., 1993-94. mem. ASCD, Calif. Sch. Leadership Assn., Santa Clara Alumni Assn.

DAY, GERALD W., wholesale grocery company executive. With Albertson's, Heber City, Utah, 1945-72; CEO Days Markets; chmn., bd. dirs. Associated Food Stores Inc. Office: Day's Market 26 N Main Heber City UT 84032*

DAY, JANINE, marketing specialist, insurance agent; b. L.A., Nov. 12, 1966; d. Edward Golden and Geneva Jane (Batiste) D. BA, UCLA, 1989. Program coord. UCLA, 1989-94; self-employed mktg. specialist Schoolhouse Hop, Redondo Beach, Calif., 1993-95; life agt. Equitable Life, L.A., 1996—; music cons. for polit. party events Black Classics Entertainment, L.A., 1992—. Creator interlocking foam puzzles and mats for Wondermat, 1993. Mem. event planning party com. CMTO-Mayor Bradley, L.A., 1989, Diane Watson, L.A., 1992; mem. campaign planning com. Stan Sanders for Mayor of L.A., 1993; vol. Nat. Dem. Com., 1996. Recipient Encouragement award Ola Romani Found., 1992. Mem. Am. Mgmt. Assn., Nat. Assn. Security Dealers, William Grandhill Performing Arts Soc.

DAY, JOHN DENTON, retired company executive, cattle and horse rancher, trainer, wrangler, actor; b. Salt Lake City, Jan. 20, 1942; s. George W. and Grace (Denton) Jenkins; m. Susan Hansen, June 20, 1971; children: Tammy Denton Wadsworth, Jeanett B, Lloyd. Student, U. Utah, 1964-65; BA in Econs. and Bus. Adminstrn. with high honors, Westminster Coll., 1971. Riding instr., wrangler Uinta wilderness area U-Ranch, Neola, Utah, 1955-58; stock handler, driver, ruffstock rider Earl Hutchinson Rodeo Contractor, Idaho, 1959; wrangler, riding instr. YMCA Camp Rodger, Kamas, Utah; with Mil. Data Cons., Inc., L.A., 1961-62, Carlseon Credit Corp., Salt Lake City, 1962-65; sales mgr. sporting goods Western Enterprises, Salt Lake City, 1965-69; founder Rockin d Ranch, Millcreek, Utah, 1969; Western rep. PBR Co., Cleve., 1969-71; dist. sales rep. Crown Zellerbach Corp., Seattle and L.A., 1971-73; pres., founder Dapco paper, chem., instl. food and janitorial supplies, Salt Lake City, 1973-79, John D Day Greeting Cards, 1990—; owner, founder, pres. John D. Day, mfrs. reps., 1972—; dist. sales mgr. Surfonics Engrs., Inc., Woods Cross, Utah, 1976-78, Garland Co., Cleve., 1978-81; rancher Heber, Utah, 1976-90, horse tng. facility and ranch, Temecula, Calif., 1984-90, St. George, Utah, 1989—; sec. bd. Acquadyne, 1974, 75. Dir., prodr. (movies) The Big Sky, 1952, Rebel Without a Cause, 1955, Devils Brigade, 1967, Coyote Summer, 1995, (videos) Someday Soon, 1993, All For the Love of Horse, 1982-83, Stallion Management, 1985, others; contbr. articles to jours. Group chmn. Tele-Dex fund raising project Westminster Coll.; vol. Dixie Nat. Forest, 1989-94, USDA Forest Svc.; 1st U.S. wilderness ranger USDA, US Forest Svc., Dixie Nat. Forest, Pine Valley Ranger Dist., Pine Valley Mountain Wilderness, So. Utah, 1994—. With AUS, 1963-64. Recipient grand nat. award Internat. Custom Car Show, San Diego, 1962, Key to City, Louisville, 1964, Champion Bareback Riding award, 1957, Vol. award USDA Forest Svc., 1991, 92, 93, Outstanding Performance award, 1995; Dally team roping heading and heeling champion, 1982. Mem. Internat. Show Car Assn. (co-chmn. 1978-79), Am. Quarter Horse Assn. (life, high point reining champion 1981, qualified for world championship, Dodge, Toyota Fall Futurite Circuit Champion Working Cowhorse 1994-95, World Championship Show qualifier and participant Oklahoma City Sr. Cutting 1994), Intermountain Quarter Horse Assn. (sr. reining champion 1981, champion AMAT reining 1979-81), Utah Quarter Horse Assn. (champion AMAT reining 1979, 80, AMAT barrel racing 1980, working cowhorse champion 1982, trained working cowhorse and rider champion 1992, trained amateur reining horse and rider champion 1996, open cutting res. champion 1993-95, open cutting champion 1994, Menlove Dodge Toyota Fall Futurity circuit champion working cowhorse, 1994-95, open working cowhorse champion & broadmare halter champion 1995, Rose cir. working cowhorse champion 1995, Rose cir. open cutting champion 1996, bd. dirs. 1992-94), Profl. Cowhorseman's Assn. (world champion team roping, heeling 1986, 88, high point rider 1985, world champion stock horse rider 1985-86, 88, world champion working cowhorse 1985, PCA finals open cutting champion, 1985-88, PCA finals 1500 novice champion 1987, PCA finals all-around champion 1985-88, inducted into Hall of Fame 1988, first on record registered Tex. longhorn cutting contest, open champion, PCA founder, editor newsletter 1985-89, pres. 1984-88), World Rodeo Assn. Profls. (v.p. Western territory 1989—). Home and Office: PO Box 55 Saint George UT 84771-0055 also: 1876 E 2450 S Daylark Ln Saint George UT 84771

DAY, KEVIN ROSS, pomologist, researcher, consultant, farmer; b. Dinuba, Calif., Aug. 2, 1960; s. Ronald Keith and Dolores Ione (Unruh) D. AA, Reedley (Calif.) Coll., 1980; BS magna cum laude, Calif. State U., Fresno, 1983, MS with honors, 1985. Cert. tchr., Calif. Lectr. Calif. State U., Fresno, 1984-85; postgrad. rschr. U. Calif., Davis, 1985-88, rsch. assoc., 1988-91; farm advisor U. Calif., Berkeley, 1991—; mng. ptnr. Day Orchards, Dinuba, 1981—; cons. K.R. Day Hort. Cons., Dinuba, 1988—. Editor, author newsletter Orchard Notes, 1991—; contbr. chpt. to book, articles to profl. jours. Announcer Dinuba High Sch. Football and Baseball, 1988—. Calif. Agrl. Tech. Inst. fellow, 1984, U. Calif. leadership fellow, 1995. Mem. Am. Soc. for Hort. Sci., Am. Pomological Soc., Lions (bd. dirs. Dinuba club 1992—, sec. 1993-96, 3d v.p. 1996—), Kaweah Flyfishers (sec. 1994-95, v.p. 1996, pres. 1997), Phi Kappa Phi. Republican. Presbyterian. Home: 41139 Road 70 Dinuba CA 93618-9702 Office: U Calf Agrl Bldg 2500 W Burrel Visalia CA 93291-4584

DAY, L. B., management consultant; b. Walla Walla, Wash., Sept. 16, 1944; s. Frank Edmond and Geraldine Eloise (Binning) D. BS, Portland State Coll., 1966; MBA, George Washington U., 1971. Design mktg. cons. Leadership Resources Inc., Washington, 1970-71; faculty mem. USDA Grad. Sch. of Spl. Programs, Washington, 1971-74; mgr. Office of Employee Devel. Oreg. Dept. Transp., Salem, 1972-75; prin. Day-Henry Assoc. Inc., Portland, Oreg., 1975-78, Day-Floren Assocs. Inc., Portland, Oreg., 1978-95, LB Day & Co., Portland, Oreg., 1996—; cons. Allergan, U.S., Italy, Am. Bankers Assn., Arthur Andersen & Co., AMD, John Fluke Mfg. Co., U.S., The Netherlands), Intel Corp., U.S., Eng., France, Malaysia, Fujitsu, Peek, Exabyte, P.R., Sequent Computer Sys., Inc., VLSI Tech., Inc., also others; mem. faculty Am. Bankers Assn., Bank trainers Sch., 1981-84; adj. prof. Willamette U. Grad. Sch. Adminstrn., Salem, 1978, Oreg. Grad. Inst., 1994; bd. dirs. Microchip Tech., Inc. Author: The Supervisory Training Program, 1977, Performance Management, 1981, Team-Oriented Management, 1989; contbr. articles to profl. jours. With U.S. Army, 1967-70. Scottish Rite fellow George Washington U., 1970. Mem. ASTD (chmn. transp. spl. interest group 1977, cert. of appreciation). Office: L B Day & Co Inc Fl 11 806 SW Broadway Portland OR 97205-3333

DAY, LUCILLE LANG, health facility administrator, educator, author; b. Oakland, Calif., Dec. 5, 1947; d. Richard Allen and Evelyn Marietta (Hazard) Lang; m. Frank Lawrence Day, Nov. 6, 1965 (div. 1970); 1 child, Liana Sherrine; m. 2nd, Theodore Herman Fleischman, June 23, 1974 (div. 1985); 1 child, Tamarind Channah. AB, U. Calif., Berkeley, 1971, MA, 1973, PhD, 1979. Teaching asst. U. Calif., Berkeley, 1971-72, 75-76, research asst., 1975, 77-78; tchr. sci. Magic Mountain Sch., Berkeley, 1977; specialist math. and sci. Novato (Calif.) Unified Sch. Dist., 1979-81; instr. sci. Project Bridge, Laney Coll., Oakland, Calif., 1984-86; sci. writer and mgr. precollege edn. programs, Lawrence Berkeley (Calif.) Nat. Lab., 1986-90, life scis. staff coord., 1990-92; mgr. Hall of Health, Berkeley, Calif., 1992—. Author numerous poems, articles and book reviews; author: (with Joan Skolnick and Carol Langbort) How to Encourage Girls in Math and Science: Strategies for Parents and Educators, 1982, Self-Portrait with Hand Microscope (poetry collection), 1982, Fire in the Garden (poetry collection), 1997. NSF Grad. fellow, 1972-75; recipient Joseph Henry Jackson award in lit. San Francisco Found., 1982. Mem. No. Calif. Sci. Writers Assn., Nat. Assn. Sci. Writers, Math/Sci. Network, Soc. for Pub. Health Edn. (No. Calif. chpt.), Phi Beta Kappa, Iota Sigma Pi. Home: 1057 Walker Ave Oakland CA 94610-1511 Office: Hall of Health 2230 Shattuck Ave Berkeley CA 94704-1424

DAY, RICHARD SOMERS, author, editorial consultant; b. Chgo., June 14, 1928; s. Milo Frank and Ethel Mae (Somers) D.; m. Lois Patricia Beggs, July 8, 1950; children: Russell Frank, Douglas Matthew, Gail Leslie. Student, Ill. Inst. Tech., 1946, U. Miami, 1947. Promotion writer, editor Portland Cement Assn., Chgo., 1958-62, promotion writer, 1963-66; editor Am. Inst. Laundering, Joliet, Ill., 1962-63; freelance writer, Monee, Ill., 1966-69, Palomar Mountain, Calif., 1969-87; cons. editor home and shop Popular Sci. mag., N.Y.C., 1966-89; editorial cons. St. Remy Press, Montreal, Que., Can., 1987—; pres., exec. producer Vi-Day-O Prodns., Inc., Palomar Mountain, Calif., 1991—. Author numerous home improvement & repair books including: Patios and Decks, 1976, Automechanics, 1982, Do-It-Yourself Plumbing--It's Easy with Genova, 1987, Building Decks, Patios, and Fences, 1992 (Nat. Assn. Home and Workshop Writers Stanley Tools Do-It-Yourself Writing award 1992); editor: (newspaper) Powderlines, 1958; (mag.) Concrete Hwys. and Pub. Improvements, 1958-62; (mag.) Soil-Cement News, 1960-62; (mag.) Fabric Care, 1962-63; prodr. videos: How to Cure Toilet Troubles, 1994, Mountain Man Horse Packing, 1994; contbr. chpts. to books. Bd. dirs. Palomar Mountain Planning Orgn., 1984-91. Mem. Nat. Assn. Home and Workshop Writers (mng. editor newsletter 1982-96, bd. dirs. 1974—, pres. 1984-85). Home: PO Box 10 Palomar Mountain CA 92060-0010

DAY, ROBERT WINSOR, cancer research administrator; b. Framingham, Mass., Oct. 22, 1930; s. Raymond Albert and Mildred (Doty) D.; m. Jane Alice Boynton, Sept. 6, 1957 (div. Sept. 1977); m. Cynthia Taylor, Dec. 16, 1977; children: Christopher, Nathalia, Natalia, Julia. Student, Harvard U., 1949-51; MD, U. Chgo., 1956; MPH, U. Calif., Berkeley, 1958, PhD, 1962. Intern USPHS, Balt., 1956-57; resident U. Calif., Berkeley, 1958-60; research specialist Calif. Dept. Mental Hygiene, 1960-64; asst. prof. sch. medicine UCLA, 1962-64; dep. dir. Calif. Dept. Pub. Health, Berkeley, 1965-67; prof., chmn. dept. health services Sch. Pub. Health and Community Medicine, U. Wash., Seattle, 1968-72, dean, 1972-82, prof., 1982—; dir. Fred Hutchinson Cancer Rsch. Ctr., Seattle, 1981-97, pres., 1991-97; mem. Nat. Cancer Adv. Bd., 1992—, Nat. Cancer Polity Bd., 1996—; cons. in field. Served with USPHS, 1956-57. Fellow AAAS, Am. Pub. Health Assn., Am. Coll. Preventive Medicine; mem. Am. Soc. Clin. Oncology, Soc. Preventive Oncology, Am. Assn. Cancer Rsch., Assn. Schs. Pub. Health (pres. 1981-82), Am. Assn. Cancer Insts. (bd. dirs. 1983-88, v.p. 1984-85, pres. 1985-86, chmn. bd. dirs., 1986-87). Office: Fred Hutchinson Cancer Rsch Ctr 1100 Fairview Ave N LM-101 Seattle WA 98109-1024

DAY, THOMAS BRENNOCK, university president; b. N.Y.C., Mar. 7, 1932; s. Frederick and Alice (Brennock) D.; m. Anne Kohlbrenner, Sept. 5, 1953; children: Erica, Monica, Mark, Kevin, Sara, Timothy, Jonathan, Patrick, Adam. B.S., U Notre Dame, 1953; Ph.D., Cornell U., 1957. Prof. U. Md., College Park, 1964-78, vice chancellor for acad. planning and policy, 1970-77, spl. asst. to pres., 1977-78, vice chancellor for acad. affairs Baltimore County, 1977-78; pres. San Diego State U., 1978-96; cons. Bendix Corp., IBM Corp., Digital Equipment Corp.; vis. physicist Brookhaven Nat. Lab., 1963; cons. Argonne Nat. Lab., Ill., 1967; vice chair Nat. Sci. Bd., bd. dirs. Scripps Clinic and Research Found. Contbr. articles to profl. jours. Mem. Am. Phys. Soc., Sigma Xi, Phi Kappa Phi. Republican. Roman Catholic. Lodge: Rotary. Office: San Diego State U 5250 Campnile Dr San Diego CA 92182-1930 also: NSF Nat Sci Bd 4201 Wilson Blvd Rm 1225 Arlington VA 22230-0001*

DAYDAY, HENRY, mayor. Formerly alderman City of Saskatoon, Sask., elected mayor, 1988. Office: Office of Mayor, City Hall 222 3 Ave N, Saskatoon, SK Canada S7K 0J5*

DAY-GOWDER, PATRICIA JOAN, association executive, consultant; b. Lansing, Mich., Apr. 9, 1936; d. Louis A. and Johanna (Feringa) Whipple; m. Duane Lee Day, Jan. 7, 1961 (div.); children: Kevin Duane, Patricia Kimberley; m. William A. Gowder, Nov. 30, 1986. BA, Mich. State U., 1958; MA, Lindenwood (Mo.) Coll., 1979; postgrad. U. So. Calif., 1982-83. Cert. secondary tchr., Calif. Health edn. asst. YWCA, Rochester, N.Y., 1958-59; tchr. jr. high schs., Flint, Mich., 1959-61; tchr. Brookside Acad., Montclair, N.J., 1963-68; adult program dir. YMCA, Long Beach, Calif., 1968-73; community edn. dir. Paramount (Calif) Unified Sch. Dist., 1973-78; exec. dir. counseling ctr., Arcadia, Calif., 1978-80; sr. citizens program dir. City of Burbank (Calif.), 1981-83; div. dir. Am. Heart Assn., L.A., 1983-87; exec. dir. Campfire Orgn., Pasadena, 1987-89; exec. dir. greater L.A. chpt. Nat. Found. of Ileitis and Colitis, 1989-90; mgr. sr. citizens mktg. dept. Meth. Hosp. So. Calif., 1989—; cons. community edn. State Dept. Edn., Fed. Office Community Edn., L.A. County Office Edn. Bd. dirs., v.p. Children's Creative Ctr., Long Beach, Calif., 1969-73, Traveler's Aid Soc., 1969-72; vice-chmn. Cerritos YMCA, 1968-73. Mott Found. fellow, 1977-78. Mem. AAUW, Western Gerontology Assn., Nat. Assn. Female Execs., Calif. Community Edn. Assn. (sec.-treas., 1974-77), LWV. Democrat. Congregationalist. Avocations: tennis, hiking, bicycling, painting, reading. Home: 170 Oak Forest Cir Glendora CA 91741-3718 Office: Meth Hosp So Calif 300 W Huntington Dr Arcadia CA 91007-3402

DAYNES, BYRON WILFORD, political science educator; b. Salt Lake City, Oct. 26, 1937; s. Byron Woodruff and Maxine (Gaddie) D.; m. Kathryn Mickelsen, June 20, 1966; children: Austen Laurence, Elizabeth Marie, Warren Joseph. BS, Brigham Young U., 1963, MS, 1965; PhD, U. Chgo., 1971. Prof. polit. sci. De Pauw U., Greencastle, Ind., 1971-90, chair dept. polit. sci., 1979-88; prof. polit. sci. Brigham Young U., Provo, Utah, 1990—; rsch. asst. Am. Judicature Soc., Chgo., summers 1967-69; mem. rsch. staff Congressman Lee H. Hamilton (Dem.-Ind.), Washington, summer 1973; vis. instr. Butler U., Indpls., 1974; vis. prof. Brigham Young U., 1986-87; book reviewer. Co-author: Contemporary Readings in American Government, 1980, The Politics of Abortion, 1981, Presidential Power in the United States, 1984; co-editor: Social Regulatory Policy, 1988; contbr. articles to profl. jours.; presenter So. Regional Sci. Assn., New Orleans, 1973, Ind. Acad. Social Scis., Indpls., 1973, 75, Ind. Polit. Sci. Assn., Ball State U., Muncie, Ind., 1978, Acad. Criminal Justice Scis., Oklahoma City, 1980, Ind. U.-Purdue U., Ft. Wayne, 1980, Loyola U. Chgo., 1987, We. Polit. Sci. Assn., Newport Beach, Calif., 1990, Pasadena, Calif., 1993, Albuquerque, 1994, Ind. Polit. Sci. Assn., 1993, Am. Polit. Sci. Assn., Washington, 1993, So. Polit. Sci. Assn., Savannah, Ga., 1993, others. Rsch. grantee Divsn. Govtl. Studies, Wash. State U., 1989. Mem. Am. Polit. Sci. Assn., Ind.

Polit. Sci. Assn. (v.p. 1985-86, pres. 1980-81), Soc. for Sci. Study of Religion, Can. Polit. Sci. Assn., So. Polit. Sci. Assn., Western Polit. Sci. Assn. (membership com. 1993-94), Alpha Lambda Delta, Phi Eta Sigma. Democrat. Mem. LDS Ch. Office: Brigham Young U Dept Polit Sci Provo UT 84602

DAYTON, DOUGLAS EMORY, computer marketing consultant; b. Lakewood, N.J., Sept. 17, 1951; s. Samuel S. and Estelle Dayton. BA, San Diego State U., 1973; postgrad., U. Calif., San Diego, 1974-75, U. Wash., 1976. Mktg. rep. IBM, Seattle, 1981-82; mgr. original equipment mfr. sales and contract support Microsoft Corp., Seattle, 1982-85; founder, pres. Dayton Assocs., Seattle, 1985—, Client-Centered Tng., Inc., Seattle, 1991—. Author: Computer Solutions for Business, 1988, Information Technology Audit Handbook, 1997, Selling Microsoft, 1997; contbr. articles to profl. jours. Mem. Wash. State Software Assn. Office: Dayton Assocs 477 123rd Pl NE Bellevue WA 98005-4819

DAYTON, MERRIL TAYLOR, gastrointestinal surgeon; b. Salt Lake City, Feb. 16, 1948; s. Sharon Reed and Lois Whitaker (Taylor) D.; m. Susan Thompson, June 8, 1973; children: Cameron, Damian, Brandon, Adrian, Ethan. BS, Brigham Young U., 1972; MD, U. Utah, 1976. Diplomate Am. Bd. Surgery, Nat. Bd. Med. Examiners. Resident in surgery UCLA Med. Sch., 1976-82, rsch. fellow, 1982-83, adj. asst. prof., 1982-83; asst. prof. U. Iowa Med. Sch., Iowa City, 1983-86; asst. prof. U. Utah Med. Sch., Salt Lake City, 1986-91, assoc. prof., 1991—; chief gen. surgery Salt Lake City VA Med. Ctr., 1987—, acting chief surgery, 1989; asst. dean admissions U. Utah Med. Sch., Salt Lake City, 1990-96; mem. sci. adv. bd. Nat. Assn. for Ileitis and Colitis, Iowa City, 1984-86, Ostomy Found., Salt Lake City, 1987—. Editor: Essentials in General Surgery, 1988, Essentials of the Surgery Specialties, 1993 (Best Health Sci. Book award 1993), Manual of Surgical Objectives, 1988. Pres. Canyon Cove Homeowners Assn., Salt Lake City, 1990; merit badge counselor Boy Scouts Am., Salt Lake City, 1989—. Fellow Am. Coll. Surgeons; mem. Soc. Univ. Surgeons (nominating com. 1992—), Assn. for Surg. Edn. (pres. 1993—), Salt Lake Surg. Soc. (pres. 1993-94), Assn. for Acad. Surgery (chmn. com. on issues 1989—), Soc. for Surgery of Alimentary Tract. Republican. Mormon. Office: Univ Utah Sch Medicine 50 N Medical Dr Salt Lake City UT 84132-0001

DEACON, MAXINE SHIRLEY, grant writer, fundraiser; b. Aberdeen, S.D., Nov. 14, 1934; d. Albert William and Doris Bertha (Homer) Hunter; m. James Everett Deacon, Aug. 15, 1956 (div. Feb. 1984); children: Cynthia Doris, David Everett. AA, Midwestern U., Wichita Falls, Tex., 1954; student, U. Nev., 1963-87, U. N.Mex., 1968. Math. rsch. asst. U. Kans., Lawrence, 1956-57; adminstrv. asst. Centron Corp., Lawrence, 1957-60; exec. sec. Edgerton, Germeshausen and Grier, Inc., Las Vegas, 1961-65; group leader, spokesperson, vocalist Young Audiences Opera Quartet, Las Vegas, 1963-73; dir. music First Christian Ch., Las Vegas, 1962-73, 96—; asst. to dir. Desert Rsch. Inst., Las Vegas, 1961-71; storeowner Custom Leather Tack, Inc., Las Vegas, 1971-87; music tchr. Temple Beth Shalom, Las Vegas, 1987-89; asst. dir. Leisure Worlds, Las Vegas, 1989-92; grants writer, devel. dir. Nev Dance Theatre Nutcracker HOLIDAY MARKET, Las Vegas, 1993-97; owner Hunter-Elliott Distinctive Creations, 1995—; also literary agent, editor; bd. dirs. Nev. Sch. of the Arts, Las Vegas. Co-author: (slides and text) The Galapagos Islands: General Setting, Sea Lions, Birds, Iguanas and Tortoises, Baja California: Coastal Inhabitants; author: Handling Grief. Past officer, bd. dirs. Las Vegas Symphony, 1960-65, Assistance League of Las Vegas, 1980—; instr. music Salvation Army, Gene Eppley Camp; activities dir. Country Club at Valley View, Las Vegas, 1997—. Nev. State Champion equestrian, 1981-82, 93. Mem. Interior Decorator and Designer, Nat. Soc. Fund Raising Execs. Home and Office: 4790 Woodridge Rd Las Vegas NV 89121-5814

DEAL, LUISA, management consultant, trainer, speaker, former elementary school educator; b. Naples, Italy, July 15, 1943; came to U.S., 1948; d. Elaine (DeMarino) Bonomo; children: Pamela, Mark, Paula. AA, Muskegon C.C., Mich., 1967; BA, Saginaw Valley State U., 1969; MA, Cen. Mich. U., 1973; Ednl. Specialist, Mich. State U., 1982. Tchr. Saginaw (Mich.) Twp. Cmty. Schs., 1969-72, reading cons., 1972-77, reading specialist, 1977-86; mgmt. devel. trainer Automobile Club of Mich., Dearborn, 1986; assoc. mgr. ops. Gen. Physics Corp., Troy, Mich., 1987; tng. analyst Ball Systems Engring., San Diego, 1988; pres. Tng. Support Network, La Jolla, Calif., 1989—. Active Nine-Nines Internat., Detroit and San Diego, 1988—. Mem. ASTD (Detroit chpt. bd. dirs. 1987-88, San Diego chpt. EFO 1989-90, sec. 1990-91), Am. Soc. for Quality Control (chair 1996-97), Nat. Speakers Assn., Deming User Group, La Jolla Sunrise Rotary. Office: Tng Support Network PO Box 207 La Jolla CA 92038-0207

DEAL, LYNN HOFFMANN, interior designer; b. Atlantic City, N.J., Nov. 7, 1953; d. Ralph Eaton and Helen Hoffmann, Michael Stanton Hegner and Mary Clyde Brown; m. James A. Deal, Sept. 19, 1981; 1 child, Katherine M. Diploma in environ. and interior design, U. Calif., Irvine, 1989. Prin. Lynn Deal and Assocs., Newport Beach, Calif., 1982—; mem. adv. bd. U. Calif., Irvine, 1984—. Chmn. Philharm. Showcase House, 1992; mem. Orange County Philharm. Soc. Mem. Am. Soc. Interior Designers (recipient Chpt. award 1991, Pres.'s award 1992, author introductory video Orange County chpt.), Internat. Furnishings and Design Assn., Interior Educators Coun., Orange County Pharm. Soc. Republican. Episcopalian.

DEAL, TERRY DEAN, marketing executive; b. Lyons, Kans., Sept. 27, 1948; s. Willis Clifton and Geneva G. (Gamble) D.; m. Diana Kathlene Gerstner, Feb. 14, 1970; 1 child, M. Shane. BS Agricultural Bus., Ft. Hays Kans. State U., 1971. Area sales mgr. Senvita Products Inc., Seneca, Kans., 1971-73, total sales mgr., 1973-74; unit sales mgr. Agri-Distbrs. and Leasing, Abilene, Kans., 1974-75; gen. mgr. Agri-Distbrs. and Leasing, Abilene, 1975-76; terr. mgr. Owatonna (Minn.) Mfg. Co., 1976-84, regional sales mgr., 1984-87; dir. mktg. Impulse Hydraulics Inc., San Diego, 1987-90; product specialist ESCO Corp., Portland, Oreg., 1990—; pres. Agri-Distbrs. and Leasing, 1974-85. Bd. dirs. Persimmon Homeowners Assn., 1989—, Owatonna Swimming Assn., 1985-86; mem. Owatonna Little Theatre, 1984-88. Mem. NRA (presdl. transition com. 1989), Sertoma (bd. dirs. 1982-83), Elks, Tau Kappa Epsilon. Republican. Methodist. Office: ESCO Corp 2141 NW 25th Ave Portland OR 97210-2578

DEAN, WALTER EDWARD, JR., research geologist; b. Wilkes-Barre, Pa., July 12, 1939; s. Walter Edward and Marion (Cassedy) D.; m. Beverly Ann Nenstiel, Dec. 30, 1961; children: Scott Alan, Kevin Neil. AB in Geology, Syracuse U., 1961; MS in Geology, U. N.Mex., 1964, PhD in Geology, 1967. Rsch. assoc. U. Minn., Mpls., 1967-68; asst. and assoc. prof. Syracuse (N.Y.) U., 1968-75; rsch. geologist U.S. Geol. Survey, Denver, 1975—. Contbr. articles to profl. jours. Fellow Geol. Soc. Am.; mem. AAAS, Am. Assn Petroleum Geologists, Am. Geophysical Union, Am. Soc. Limnology and Oceanography, Soc. Econ. Paleontologists. Home: 30107 Carriage Loop Dr Evergreen CO 80439-8559 Office: US Geol Survey MS980 Federal Center Denver CO 80225

DEANDREA, GARY ANTHONY, neurologist; b. South Plainfield, NJ, Jan. 24, 1958; s. Joseph DeAndrea Sr. and Margaret (Battlebury) Reidy; m. Susan Ellen Pickett, Dec. 30, 1993. BS, Georgetown U., 1980, MD, 1985; MBA with concentration in info. sys., U. Wash., 1997. Diplomate Am. Bd. Psychiatry & Neurology, Am. Bd. Sleep Medicine, Am. Bd. Clin. Neurophysiology, Nat. Bd. Med. Examiners. Intern in internal medicine Providence Med. Ctr., Portland, Oreg., 1985-86; resident in neurology Georgetown U. Med. Ctr., Washington, 1986-89; instr. EEG and clin. neurophysiology U. Wash. Med. Ctr., Seattle, 1989-91, clin. asst. prof. medicine, 1992—; med. dir. EEG & clin. neurophysiology Swedish Med. Ctr. Ballard Campus, Seattle, 1991—, med. dir. Seattle Sleep Disorders Ctr., 1991—. Mem. AMA, Am. Sleep Disorders Assn., Am. Sleep Apnea Assn., Am. Acad. Neurology, Am. Epilepsy Soc., Am. Clin. Neurophysiol. Soc., Am. Coll. Physician Execs., Am. Telemedicine Assn., Wash. State Med. Assn., King County Med. Soc. Office: Seattle Sleep Disorders Ctr Swedish Med Ctr 5300 Tallman Ave NW Seattle WA 98107-3932

DEANGELIS, DAN, transportation executive; b. Stockton, Calif., July 23, 1947; m. Shari Thornton, 1973; children: Ryan, Jamie. BA in Adminstrn. Justice, Delta Coll., 1967. Lic. comml. pilot; cert. airline transport pilot. Chief pilot, flight instr. Werner's Aero Svc. Stockton Metropolitan Airport; with City of Manteca, 1974-76; airport ops. dep. Dept. Aviation County of San Joaquin, 1976-85, asst. airport ops. mgr., 1985-87, dep. airport mgr. ops., 1987-90; airport mgr. Stockton Metropolitan Airport, 1990—. Office: Stockton Met Airport 5000 S Airport Rd 202 Stockton CA 95206-3911*

DEANS, PENNY CANDACE, business educator; b. Wilson, N.C., Nov. 30, 1952; d. Lemon Calvin Jr. and Pennie Hazel (Daniel) Deans. BS, U. N.C., 1975; MEd, N.C. State U., 1979; MBA, East Carolina U., 1985; PhD, U. S.C., 1989. Tchr., chemistry Wake County Sch. System, Raleigh, N.C., 1975-83; instr., bus. East Carolina U., Greenville, N.C., 1984-85; asst. prof., bus. Wake Forest U., Winston Salem, N.C., 1989—; vis. prof. U. S.C., Columbia, 1988-89. Contbr. articles to profl. jours. Rsch. grantee, Wake Forest U., 1990, PEW Found. grantee, 1991. Mem. Internat. Acad. Info. Mgmt., Acad. Internat. Bus., Soc. Info. Mgmt., Info. Resource Mgmt. Assn., Inst. Mgmt. Sci., Decision Sci. Inst., Beta Gamma Sigma. Presbyterian. Office: Thunderbird Sch Internat Mgmt 15249 N 59th Ave Glendale AZ 85306-3236

DEAR, RONALD BRUCE, social work educator; b. Phila., Sept. 23, 1933; s. John David and Margaret (McDade) D.; 1 child, Bruce. BA, Bucknell U., 1955; honors cert., U. Aberdeen, Scotland, 1955; MSW, U. Pitts., 1957; PhD in Social Work, Columbia U., 1972. Cert. social worker, N.Y., Wash. Chief social worker Mental Hygiene Cons. Svc., Aberdeen Proving Ground, Md., 1958-60; chief Neuropsychiat. Clinic, 7th Inf. Divsn., Korea, 1960-61; residence dir. Horizon House, Inc., Phila., 1961-64; prof. U. Wash., Seattle, 1970—; vis. prof. U. Bergen, Norway, 1984, U. Trondheim, Norway, 1996; faculty lobbyist U. Wash., 1983-85, 88-91, faculty pres., 1993-95; master tchr. Coun. on Social Work Edn., 1991, 93, 94, 97; mem. adv. bd. Internat. Population and Family Assocs., 1994—; bd. dirs. Wash. Future, 1994—. Editor: Poverty in Perspective, 1973; contbr. articles to profl. jours. and encys. apptd. by gov. to income assistance adv. com., 1987-93, to adv. com. for Dept. S ocial and Health Svcs., 1980-83, Human Svcs. Policy Ctr., 1996—, adv. com. Wash. State Econ. Svcs., 1996—. 1st lt. U.S. Army, 1957-61. Mem. NASW (Social Worker of Yr. Wash. chpt. 1981, mem. staff legis. N.Y.C. chpt. 1968-69), Acad. Cert. Social Workers, Coun. on Social Work Edn. Home: 7328 16th Ave NE Seattle WA 98115-5737 Office: U Wash Sch Social Work 4101 15th Ave NE Seattle WA 98105-6250

DEATHERAGE, LEO JACKSON, JR., real estate developer, construction consultant; b. Clovis, N.Mex., May 26, 1944; s. Leo Jackson and Vendla (Smith) D.; m. Paula Edith Simpson, Dec. 7, 1963 (div. Mar. 1970); children: Leo Jackson III, Harry Blaine; m. Suzanne Marie Wilfong, July 10, 1993. Grad., Munich Am. H.S., 1961. Lic. gen. contractor, Wash. Insp. Continental Can Co., Olympia, Wash., 1964-67; pres. Deatherage Properties, Olympia, 1965—; sec., treas. Seasons Devel., Olympia, 1987—; pres. Ctrl. Svcs. Inc., Olympia, 1990-95; sec., treas. Springfield Devel., Olympia, 1993-94; pres. Springfield Devel., 1994—; cons., expert, arbitrator constrn. field, Wash., 1986—; cons. hiring and interview panels, Olympia and Tumwater, Wash., 1985—. Bd. dirs. Thurston County Econ. Devel., Olympia, 1983-87; mem. bd. appeals Thurston County Dept. Comml. Planning, 1991—; project mgr. South Sound YMCA, Olympia, 1995—, bd. dirs. 1995—; commr. Olympia Planning Commn., 1995—; auction chmn. Family Support Ctr., Olympia, 1996; minister Universal Life Ch., 1987—. Mem. Nat. Assn. Home Builders (bd. dirs. 1983-88), Bldg. Industry Assn. Wash. (bd. dirs. 1981—, Builder of Yr. 1988), Olympia Master Builders (pres. 1982, 85, Norm Paulson Meml. Svc. award 1983, Golden Hammer award 1984, 85, 87, Life Directorship 1988), Lacey Lamplighters Lions. Republican. Office: Deatherage Properties Inc PO Box 5809 Lacey WA 98509

DEAVER, PHILLIP LESTER, lawyer; b. Long Beach, Calif., July 21, 1952; s. Albert Lester and Eva Lucille (Welton) D. Student, USCG Acad., 1970-72; BA, UCLA, 1974; JD, U. So. Calif., 1977. Bar: Hawaii 1977, U.S. Dist. Ct. Hawaii 1977, U.S. Ct. Appeals (9th cir.) 1978, U.S. Supreme Ct. 1981. Assoc. Carlsmith, Wichman, Case, Mukai & Ichiki, Honolulu, 1977-83, ptnr., 1983-86; ptnr. Bays, Deaver, Hiatt, Lung & Rose, Honolulu, 1986, mng. ptnr., 1986-95. Contbr. articles to profl. jours. Dir. Parents and Children Together. Mem. ABA (forum com. on the Constrn. Industry), AIA (affiliate Hawaii chpt.), Am. Arbitration Assn. (arbitrator). Home: 2471 Pacific Heights Rd Honolulu HI 96813-1029 Office: Bays Deaver Hiatt Lung & Rose PO Box 1760 Honolulu HI 96806-1760

DEAVER, SHARON MAE, special education educator; b. Sacramento, Calif., Oct. 14, 1937; d. Lloyd C. and Beryl Goldie (Wilimzig) Estes; m. John Morris Coon, Nov. 4, 1955 (dec. Apr. 1991); children: Debra Leigh, Robert Allen, Linda Michelle, Janis Gayle; m. Roscoe Ferrell Deaver, July 30, 1994. AA, Mt. San Antonio Coll., 1971; BA with honors, Calif. State U., L.A., 1974, MA, 1981. Cert. elem. tchr., spl. educator of learning handicapped, severely handicapped, resource specialist, Calif. Classroom music specialist Pasadena (Calif.) Christian Sch., 1974-76; spl. educator East Whittier (Calif.) City Sch. Dist., 1976-81, West Covina (Calif.) Unified Sch. Dist., 1981-82; resource specialist Bassett High Sch., La Puente, Calif., 1982-83; resource specialist Light & Life Christian Schs., Duarte, Calif., 1983-87, tchr. third grade, 1986-87; resource specialist Walnut (Calif.) Valley Unified Sch. Dist., 1987-89; spl. educator El Monte (Calif.) City Sch. Dist., 1989—. Recipient Grant Calif. State, 1978-81. Mem. Coun. for Exceptional Children, Sigma Alpha Iota (chmn. scholarship com. 1970-80), Kappa Alpha Phi. Presbyterian. Home: 703 N Leaf Ave West Covina CA 91791-1048 Office: Cherrylee Sch 5025 Buffington Rd El Monte CA 91732-1499

DEBARD, ROGER, investment executive; b. Cleve., Nov. 10, 1941; d. Victor and Margaret Ann (Henderson) DeB.; m. Janet Marie Schulz, July 3, 1965; children: Eila Burns, Ryan Alexander. BS, Bowling Green State U., 1963; MBA, Case Western Res. U., 1968; MA, Claremont Grad. Sch., 1978, PhD, 1981. Asst. v.p. A.G. Becker & Co., L.A., 1972-76; sr. portfolio mgr. Scudder Stevens & Clark, L.A., 1976-81; v.p. Crocker Investment Mgmt., L.A., 1981-85; exec. v.p., CFO Hotchkis and Wiley Funds, L.A., 1985—; prin., 1992-94; gen. ptnr. Hotchkis and Wiley, L.A., 1994-95; mng. dir., mem., 1995—; adj. prof. fin. Pepperdine U., L.A., 1981-85. Mem. The Founders-Music Ctr. L.A., L.A. World Affairs Coun., 1988—, L.A. Libr. Assn., 1976—, pres. 1980-81. Recipient First Pl. Pub. award Investment Dealers Digest, 1971, Outstanding Svc. award City of L.A., 1980; grad. fellow Rand Grad. Inst., 1974-76. Mem. L.A. Bd. Bond Club (sec./dir. 1986-89), L.A. Soc. Fin. Analysts, Yosemite Assoc., Calif. Club, Bel-Air Bay Club, L.A. Country Club, Sigma Chi. Republican. Episcopalian. Home: 48 Haldeman Rd Santa Monica CA 90402-1004 also: PO Box 6926 230 Gaduate Ln Ketchum ID 83353 Office: Hotchkis and Wiley 800 W 6th St Los Angeles CA 90017-2704

DEBARTOLO, EDWARD JOHN, JR., professional football team owner, real estate developer; b. Youngstown, Ohio, Nov. 6, 1946; s. Edward J. and Marie Patricia (Montani) DeB.; m. Cynthia Ruth Papalia, Nov. 27, 1968; children: Lisa Marie, Tiffanie Lynne, Nicole Anne. Student, U. Notre Dame, 1964-68. With Edward J. DeBartolo Corp., Youngstown, Ohio, 1960—, v.p., 1971-76, exec. v.p., 1976-79, chief adminstrv. officer, 1979-94; pres., CEO, 1995—; owner San Francisco 49ers, 1977—; chmn. bd. DeBartolo Realty Corp., 1994—; chmn., CEO DeBartolo Entertainment, Inc. Trustee Youngstown State U., 1974-77; nat. adv. coun. St. Jude Children's Rsch. Hosp., 1978—, local chmn., 1979-80; chmn. local fund drive Am. Cancer Soc., 1975—; mem. Nat. Cambodia Crisis Com., 1980—; chmn. 19th Ann. Victor Warner award, 1985, City of Hope's Spirit of Life Banquet, 1986; apptd. adv. coun. Coll. Bus. Adminstrn. U. Notre Dame, 1988; adv. coun. Nat. Assn. People with AIDS, 1992; bd. dirs. Cleve. Clinic Found., 1991; lifetime mem. Italian Scholarship League. With U.S. Army, 1969. Recipient Man of Yr. award St. Jude Children's Hosp., 1979, Boy's Town of Italy in San Francisco, 1985, Sportsman of Yr. award Nat. Italian Am. Sports Hall of Fame, 1991, Cert. of Merit, Salvation Army, 1982, Warner award, 1986, Silver Cable Car award San Francisco Conv. and Visitors Bur., 1988, Nat. Football League Man of Yr. award Football News, 1989, Svc. to Youth award Cath. Youth Orgn., 1990, Hall of Fame award Cardinal Mooney High Sch., 1993. Mem. Internat. Coun. Shopping Ctrs., Italian Scholarship League (life), Tippecanoe Country Club, Fonderlac Country Club, Dapper Dan Club (dir. 1980—). Office: Edward J DeBartolo Corp PO Box 3287 Youngstown OH 44513-3287 also: care San Francisco 49ers 4949 Centennial Blvd Santa Clara CA 95054-1229 *Personal philosophy: Success in business and sporting competition relies on the same basic ingredients--hire the best qualified people and then provide them with the leadership and best resources to accomplish the task.**

DEBARTOLO, JACK, JR., architect; b. Youngstown, Ohio, May 6, 1938; s. Jack and Virginia (Sassinelli) DeB.; m. Patsy McLamore, Aug. 15, 1958; children: Ava, Gina, Jack III. B.Arch., U. Houston, 1962; M.Arch., Columbia U., 1964. Sr. v.p., dir. design Caudill Rowell Scott, 1964-73; sr. v.p. William Wilde & Assocs., Tucson, 1973; pres. Anderson DeBartolo Pan Inc., Phoenix, 1975-85; dir. design, founding prin. Anderson DeBartolo Pan Inc., Tucson, 1973-95; prin. DeBartolo Archs. Ltd., Phoenix, 1995—; Fellow Am. Inst. of Archs., bd. dirs., U. of Ariz. Found., mem. of exec. comm. of AIA Col. of Fellows. Notable works include: (award winning project), CRS Office Bldg., Houston, Joilet Jr. Coll., Ill., Pima Cmty. Coll., Tucson, West Campus & Life Sci. Bldg of Ariz. State Coll. Deacon Phoenix First Assembly Ch. Fellow AIA (past pres. Ariz., So. Ariz. chpt., chmn. jury of fellows 1987-90, chancellor Coll. of Fellows 1997); mem. Tuscon Tomorrow, City of Tuscon Pres.'s Club, U. Ariz. Found. Bd., Ariz. State U. Coll. Architecture Coun. of Design Excellence. Republican. Club: Tucson Breakfast. Office: DeBartolo Archs Ltd 4450 N 12th St Ste 120 Phoenix AZ 85014-6011

DE BEIXEDON, S(USAN) YVETTE, psychologist; b. Pasadena, Calif., Jan. 2, 1965; d. Edward Kingsland Framaux and Margaret Pauline (Rinderknecht) de B.; m. Jacques E. Mitrani, Dec. 21, 1985 (div. Oct. 22, 1992); m. Richard E. Bresnahan, May 14, 1994; children: Paul, Taylor, Hannah, Dane. BA, U. Calif., San Diego, 1985; MA, PhD, Northwestern U., 1990. Lic. psychologist, Calif., Ga., Tenn. Pvt. practice, Laguna Niguel, Calif., 1995—. Author: Lovers & Survivors, 1995. Mem. APA, South Orange County C. of C. Episcopalian. Office: Ste 109 30101 Town Center Dr Laguna Niguel CA 92677

DEBENHAM, RAY GENE, electric supply company executive; b. Salt Lake City, Oct. 1, 1935; s. Shirley R. and Lillian (Greguhn) D.; m. Rita J. Peterson, Aug. 14, 1959; children: Debra, Julie, Michael, Shaun. BS, Alaska Pacific U., 1972; OPM, Harvard U., 1987. CEO Debenham Alaska Investments, Anchorage, 1960—, Taku Enterprises, Anchorage, 1988—; pres. Kiana Investments, Anchorage, 1968-91, CEO, 1968—; chmn. bd. dirs. Profl. Botanicals, Ogden, Utah, 1979-80; bd. advisers SBA, Washington, 1983-88, Philips Lighting, 1990-92, Cuttler Hammer, 1989-90. Mem. bd. trustees Alaska Pacific U., 1992—. Mem. Nat. Assn. Elec. Distbrs. (chmn. utility com. 1981-85), Nat. Assn. Disbtrs., Am. Legion. Mormon.

DEBOCK, RONALD GENE, real estate company executive; b. Buckley, Wash., Sept. 12, 1928; m. Donna J. DeBock, Sept. 24, 1949; children: Beverly J. DeBock Satter, Gary, Janice. BA, N.W. Coll., Kirkland, Wash., 1953; MDiv., Western Evangelical Sem., Portland, Oreg., 1960; AA, Tacoma (Wash.) C.C., 1979; PhD, Calif. Grad. Sch. Theology, Glendale, 1979. Ordained minister Assemblies of God Ch., 1953-96. Commd. ensign USNR, 1957, advanced through grades to lt. comdr., 1971, chaplain, 1958-71; founder, owner Rainier Rentals, Puyallup, Wash., 1975—, Fireball Publs., Puyallup, 1993—; instr. Am. sign lang. Cmty. Ednl. Opportunity, Orting, Wash., 1995-96. Author: Practice What You Preached, 1993. Active Aloha Hotel Chapels Ministry, Honolulu, 1988-96; bd. dirs. Romanian Renewal Internat., 1993-96, v.p., 1995-96; del. Pierce County Rep. Conv.; charter mem. Rep. Presdl. Task Force. Decorated Vietnam Cross of Gallantry with palm; recipient Delta Epsilon Chi award, 1975, Paul Harris award Rotary, 1992. Mem. Wash. Assn Realtors, Inc., Puyallup C. of C., Mil. Chaplains Assn. USA, VFW, DAV. Office: Fireball Pubs 422 W Main Ave Ste P Puyallup WA 98371

DEBOER, DAVID JAMES, transportation executive; b. Kalamazoo, Apr. 11, 1938; s. James Frederick and Marion Elaine (Teal) DeB.; m. Sandra Lou Ogden, Aug. 29, 1959; children: Kathleen, James, Christopher. AB, U. Mich., 1960, MBA, 1963. Asst. dir. market rsch. N.Y. Cen. R.R., N.Y.C., 1963-69; mgr. cargo mktg. Trans World Airlines, N.Y.C., 1969-71; dir. office of policy U.S. Dept. Transp.-Fed. R.R. Adminstrn., Washington, 1971-77; office of policy Interstate Commerce Com., Washington, 1977-78; asst. v.p. So. Pacific R.R., San Francisco, 1978-84; pres. Greenbrier Intermodal, Walnut Creek, Calif., 1984—. Author: Piggyback and Containers, 1992; contbr. articles to profl. jours. Vice chair citizens adv. com. Met. Transport Com., Bay Area, 1996. Mem. Intermodal Coun. N.Am. (bd. dirs. 1991-97, chmn. 1997, Silver Kingpin award 1997), Nat. Rail Intermodal Assn. (bd. dirs. 1982-91), Univ. Club San Francisco. Office: Greenbrier Intermodal 100 Pringle Ave S-450 Walnut Creek CA 94596

DEBREU, GERARD, economics and mathematics educator; b. Calais, France, July 4, 1921; came to U.S., 1950, naturalized, 1975; s. Camille and Fernande (Decharne) D.; m. Françoise Bled, June 14, 1945; children: Chantal, Florence. Student, Ecole Normale Supérieure, Paris, 1941-44, Agrégé de l'Université, France, 1946; DSc, U. Paris, 1956; Dr. Rerum Politicarum honoris causa, U. Bonn, 1977; D. Scis. Economiques (hon.), U. Lausanne, 1980; DSc (hon.), Northwestern U., 1981; Dr. honoris causa, U. des Scis. Sociales de Toulouse, 1983, Yale U., 1987, U. Bordeaux I, 1988. Rsch. assoc. Centre Nat. De La Recherche Sci., Paris, 1946-48; Rockefeller fellow U.S., Sweden and Norway, 1948-50; rsch. assoc. Cowles Commn., U. Chgo., 1950-55; assoc. prof. econs. Cowles Found., Yale, 1955-61; fellow Ctr. Advanced Study Behavioral Scis., Stanford U., 1960-61; vis. prof. econs. Yale U., fall 1961; prof. emeritus U. Calif., Berkeley, 1962—, prof. Miller Inst. Basic Rsch. in Sci., 1973-74, prof. math., 1975—, univ. prof., 1985—; Guggenheim fellow, vis. prof. Ctr. Ops. Rsch. and Econometrics, U. Louvain, 1968-69, vis. prof., 1971, 72, 88; Erskine fellow U. Canterbury, Christchurch, New Zealand, 1969, 87, vis. prof., 1973; Overseas fellow Churchill Coll., Cambridge, Eng., 1972; Plenary address Internat. Congress Mathematicians, Vancouver, 1974; vis. prof. Cowles Found. for Rsch. in Econs., Yale U., 1976; vis. prof. U. Bonn, 1977; rsch. assoc. Cepremap, Paris, 1980; faculty rsch. lectr. U. Calif., Berkeley, 1984-85, univ. prof., 1985—, Class of 1958 Chair, 1986—; vis. prof. U. Sydney, Australia, 1987; lectr. in field. Author: Theory of Value, 1959, Mathematical Economics: Twenty Papers of Gerard Debreu, 1983; assoc. editor Internat. Econ. Rev., 1959-69; mem. editorial bd. Jours. Econ. Theory, 1972—, SIAM Jours. on Applied Math., 1976-79, Jours. of Complexity, 1985—, Games and Econ. Behavior, 1989—, Econ. Theory, 1991; mem. adv. bd. Jours. Math. Econs., 1974—; correspondent Math. Intelligencer, 1983-84. Served with French Army, 1944-45. Decorated Chevalier de la Légion d'Honneur, Commandeur de l'Ordre National du Mérite, Officer Le Légion d'Honneur; recipient Nobel Prize in Econ. Scis., 1983, Berkeley Citation, 1991; sr. U.S. Sci. awardee Alexander von Humboldt Found., 1977. Fellow AAAS, Econometric Soc. (mem. coun. 1964-72, 78-85, Fisher-Schultz lectr. 1969, exec. com. 1969-72, 80-82, pres. 1971), Am. Econ. Assn. (disting. fellow 1982, pres.-elect 1989, pres. 1990); mem. NAS (chmn. sect. econ. scis. 1982-85, com. human rights 1984-90, chair class V behavioral and social scis. 1989-92, mem. Coun. of NAS of USA 1993—), Am. Philos. Soc., French Acad. Scis. (fgn. assoc.), Berkeley Fellows. Office: U Calif Dept Econs 549 Evans Hall # 3880 Berkeley CA 94720-3880*

DE BROUX, PEGGY C., English educator, French educator, publisher; b. Skidmore, Tex., Jan. 14, 1935; d. Robert Willis and Evelyn Laura (Wooten) King; m. Bob Cole, June 4, 1954 (div. July 1964); children: Heather Kay, Michael Harold; m. Jay de Broux, July 14, 1970 (dec.). BA in Comparative Lit., U. Wash., 1967, MA in Comparative Lit., 1968; MA in French, U. B.C., 1976. Instr. comparative lit. Hiram Scott Coll., Scottsbluff, Nebr., 1970-71; instr. English and French Flagler Coll., St. Augustine, Fla., 1972-74; legal sec. Atty. Gen.'s Office, Seattle, 1989-93; instr. English and French Peninsula Coll., Port Angeles, Wash., 1993—; owner, operator Strait Pub., Port Angeles, 1994—; co-chair grad. fgn. lang. seminars 35th Fgn. Lang. Conf., U. Ky., Lexington, 1982. Pres. Olympic Unitarian-Universalist Fellowship, Port Angeles, 1995-97. Naomi Clark scholar Port Townsend (Wash.) Writers' Conf., 1995. Mem. MLA, Macintosh Users Group (sec. Port Angeles chpt.). Democrat. Home: 240 W 3d St Port Angeles WA 98362

DE BRUYCKER, LLOYD HENRY, rancher, feedlot operator; b. Great Falls, Mont., Dec. 1, 1933; s. Achiel Henry and Rose Presperine (Emperor) De B.; m. Jane Crystal, July 2, 1954; 7 children. Grad. high sch., Dutton, Mont. Grain elevator laborer, 1954-59, rancher, 1959—. Home: Box 7700

Dutton MT 59433 Office: North Mt Feeders Inc 7 Miles N Box 218 Choteau MT 59422

DEBUS, ELEANOR VIOLA, retired business management company executive; b. Buffalo, May 19, 1920; d. Arthur Adam and Viola Charlotte (Pohl) D.; student Chown Bus. Sch., 1939. Sec., Buffalo Wire Works, 1939-45; home talent producer Empire Producing Co., Kansas City, Mo., sec. Owens Corning Fiberglass, Buffalo; pub. rels. and publicity Niagara Falls Theatre, Ont., Can.; pub. rels. dir. Woman's Internat. Bowling Congress, Columbus, Ohio, 1957-59; publicist, sec. Ice Capades, Hollywood, Calif., 1961-63; sec. to contbr. Rexall Drug Co., L.A., 1963-67; bus. mgmt. acct. Samuel Berke & Co., Beverly Hills, Calif., 1967-75; Gadbois Mgmt. Co., Beverly Hills, 1975-76; sec., treas. Sasha Corp., L.A., 1976-92; former bus. mgr. Dean Martin, Debbie Reynolds, Shirley MacLaine. Mem. Am. Film Inst. Republican. Contbr. articles to various mags.

DECARLO, ANGELA ROCCO, writer, journalist; b. Chgo., Sept. 11, 1949; d. Peter J. And Della (Serritella) Rocco; m. Daniel G. DeCarlo; children: Mark, Michael, Daniel. BA in Communications and Edn., Benedictine U., 1975. Cert. K-12 tchr., Ill. Disney writer Chgo. Tribune; journalist, columnist The Bus. Traveler Las Vegas (Nev.) Rev. Jour., 1985; pres. DeCarlo Comm., Orange, Calif., 1985—. Docent, co-chair prologues Opera Pacific. Mem. Profl. Writers Orange County (bd. dirs.). Home and Office: DeCarlo Comm 2718 N Vista Knolls Rd Orange CA 92667-1750

DE CARO, MARC CLEMENT, artist, designer; b. Paris, May 28, 1920, came to U.S. 1926; s. George Louis and Fernande Marie (Ressie) Vallee de C.; m. Cleo Williams, Aug. 30, 1943; children: Marc Frederic, George Claude. Student, Cleve. Art Inst., 1947-50, Art Students League of N.Y., 1950-51. Free-lance designer and artist, Longmont, Colo. Executed murals Stewart Air Force Base, Passenger Terminal, N.Y.C., Philip Morris Inc. Hdqrs. Richmond, Va. 2nd lt. USAAF, 1941-45, ETO.

DE CECCO, JOHN PAUL, psychology and human sexuality educator, author; b. Erie, Pa., Apr. 18, 1925; s. John and Rose Marie (Lombardozzi) De C. BS, Allegheny Coll., 1946; MA, U. Pa., 1949, PhD, 1953. Tchr. Erie (Pa.) Pub. High Schs., 1946-48; faculty U. Detroit, 1953-55, Mich. State U., East Lansing, 1955-60; prof. psychology San Francisco State U., 1960—, dir. human sexuality studies, 1981-97; dir. Gay, Lesbian & Bisexual Studies, 1992—; dir. Ctr. for Rsch. and Edn. in Sexuality, 1975—. Editor: Homophobia, 1987, Gay Relationships, 1990, If You Seduce a Straight Person, 1993, Sex, Cells & Sexual Desire: Biology of Sexual Preference, 1995; editor Jour. Homosexuality, 1977—; editor-in-chief book series on gay and lesbian studies, Haworth Press, 1985—. Recipient Magnus Hirschfeld medal Germany Sociol. Soc., Berlin, 1992, Evelyn Hooker Rsch. award Gay Acad. Union, L.A., 1978; NIMH grantee, 1974-80. Fellow Internat. Acad. Sex Rsch.; mem. APA, Soc. for Scientific Study of Sex. Office: San Francisco State Univ Dept of Psychology San Francisco CA 94132

DECHARIO, TONY HOUSTON, symphony orchestra executive; b. Girard, Kans., Sept. 25, 1940; s. Tony and Enid Eulalia (Frogue) D.; m. Rachel Dennisse Kennedy, Apr. 12, 1963 (div. Dec. 1974); children: Samuel Paul, Rachel Christina, Mary Rebecca; m. Mary Gill Roby, Dec. 29, 1974; 1 child, Toni Elizabeth; stepchildren: Edmund Kidd II, Kenneth Hamilton Kidd, Todd Roby Kidd. Student, U. Wichita, 1958-61; MusB, performer's cert., Eastman Sch. Music, U. Rochester, 1962, MusM, 1963. 2d trombone Kansas City (Mo.) Philharm. Orch., 1963-64; prin. trombone Dallas Symphony Orch., 1964-65; 2d trombone Rochester (N.Y.) Philharm. Orch., 1965-75, personnel mgr., 1972-75, gen. mgr., 1975-84, exec. dir., 1984-85, pres., chief exec. officer, 1985-88. Exec. dir. Honolulu Symphony Soc., 1991-95. Mem. Am. Symphony Orch. League.

DECHERT, PETER, photographer, writer, foundation administrator; b. Phila., Dec. 17, 1924; s. Robert and Helen Hope (Wilson) D.; m. Phoebe Jane Booth; children: Sandra, Robin Booth, Caroline. BA, U. Pa., 1948, MA, 1950, PhD, 1955. Owner, Peter Dechert Assocs., Bryn Mawr, Pa., 1956-68; asst. dir. Sch. of Am. Rsch., Santa Fe, 1968-71; pres. Indian Arts Fund, Santa Fe, 1971-72; pres. S.W. Found. for Audio-Visual Resources, Santa Fe, 1973-77; self-employed writer, photographer, Santa Fe; tchr., cons. photog. comm., 1964—. Author: Canon Rangefinder Cameras, 1933-68, 1985, The Contax Connection, 1990, Olympus Pen SLR Cameras, 1989, Canon SLR Cameras, 1959-91, 1992, The Contax S Camera Family, 1991, Los Alamos Ranch Book of Rosters, 1991; former contbg. editor Shutterbug mag., other photographic periodicals; contbr. articles on history and design of miniature cameras and other photog. topics to profl. publs. Bd. dirs. St. Vincent Hosp. Found. (pres. 1981-83, v.p. 1983-84); vestry Ch. of the Holy Faith, 1994-97. With AUS, 1943-46. Mem. N.Mex. Poetry Soc. (pres. 1969-74), Am. Soc. Media Photographers, N.Mex. Jazz Workshop, Don Quixote Club, Phi Beta Kappa, Delta Psi. Address: PO Box 636 Santa Fe NM 87504-0636

DECK, RICHARD ALLEN, political scientist, consultant, writer; b. Concord, N.H., May 6, 1953; s. Herbert Heller Jr. and Eleanor DuVall (Deyo) D.; m. Jo Ann Marie Passariello, Nov. 15, 1986. Student, Ripon Coll., 1972-73, Waseda U., Japan, 1974-75; BA in Polit. Sci. and East Asian Studies summa cum laude with honors, Macalester Coll., 1977; cert. city and regional planning, Harvard U., 1978; grad. cert. British fgn. policy, Oxford (U.K.) U., 1980; MA in Econs. in Pub. Policy & Adminstrn., U. Manchester (U.K.), 1982; MCP (ABT) in City and Regional Planning, U. Calif., Berkeley, 1982; AM in Polit. Sci., Stanford U., 1985; MALS, Dartmouth Coll., 1994; PhD in Polit. Sci., Stanford U., 1997. Survey rchr. and analyst Project on Volunteerism Adelphi U., L.I., 1978; co-chair external affairs Grad. Assembly U. Calif., Berkeley, 1981-82; fellow internat. peace and security studies Social Studies Rsch. Coun. and John D. and Catherine T. MacArhtur Found., Southeast Asia, 1986-88; vis. joint fellow nat. and internat. security U. So. Calif. and UCLA, 1989; rsch. fellow and project coord. Asian Regionalization Asian Pacific Rsch. Ctr., Stanford U. and The Asia Found. San Francisco, Calif., 1991-92; v.p. Catalyst Concepts, Berkeley, 1992—; social sys. dir. and bd. dirs. U. Calif. Space Working Group, U. Calif., Berkeley, 1979-80, 81-82; grad. rep. student body pres.' coun. U. Calif., Berkeley, 1981-82; tchg. asst. Stanford (Calif.) U., 1983, 86, mem. grad. studies com., 1983-84, head tchg. asst., 1984, observer Project Peace and Coop. Asia-Pacific Region, 1984, mem. internat. rels. sr. faculty search com., 1985-86, co-instr., 1991; lectr. and participant World Affairs coun. No. Calif., San Francisco, 1985; participant Project Soviet Internat. Behavior, U. Calif., Berkeley and Stanford U., 1985-86; ofcl. observer U.S. del. Pacific Econ. Cooperation Coun., PECC Gen. Meeting/Conf., San Francisco, 1992. Author: (with others) Peace,Conflict, and Strategic Culture in the Asia-Pacific Region, 1997; mem. edtl. bd., edtl. writer, polit. corr., and polit. feature writer The Stanford Daily, 1982-83; rschr. and writing cons. The Concept of Relationship in International Politics, 1989-90; contbr. papers to various organizations; interview subject (TV) Friday Background, Current Affairs Unit, Singapore Broadcasting Corp., 1987, (newspaper) Internat. Herald Tribune, Republic of Singapore, 1987, (radio) The Michael Fay Caning Affair, The Phil Till Show, Radio Can., Vancouver, 1994. Del. candidate N.H. Pres. Preferences Primary, Dem. Nat. Conv., Keene, 1972, Calif. Pres. Primary, Stanford, 1984, Berkeley, 1992; candidate N.H. Constl. Conv., Keene, 1974; city and campus chairperson Calif. Dem. Pres. Primary Campaign, Stanford U. and Palo Alto, Calif., 1984, 92; conf. participant and del. 40th Anniversary Commemoration of the Signing of the UN Charter in San Francisco: Conf. Assessing the UN After 40 Years, UN Assn. San Francisco and World Affairs Coun. No. Calif., 1985. Airman 3d class, USAF Aux., 1966. Recipient World Affairs Coun. Staff award, 1985; Nat. Forensic League scholar Ripon Coll., 1972-73; Harry Sherman scholar MacAlester Coll., 1976-77; John W. Searle Meml. scholar MacAlester Coll., 1976-77; N.Y. State Assembly Grad. Scholar fellow, 1979; Roothbert Fund fellow U. Calif., Berkeley, 1979-80, 81-82; Inst. Internat. Edn. scholar Oxford U., 1980; Rotary Internat. Grad. fellow U. Manchester, 1980-81; Lasker scholar U. Calif., Berkeley, 1981-82; Newhouse fellow U. Calif., Berkeley, 1981-82; Eisenhower Meml. Grad. scholar Stanford U., 1982-83; AMVETS scholar Stanford U., 1982-86; Stanford U. Grad. fellow 1982-86; MALS Grad. fellow, 1984, 86; UN Assn. and World Affairs Coun. scholar, 1985; Fgn. Lang. and Area Studies grantee U.S. Dept. Edn., 1985. Mem. Internat. Studies Assn., Asian Media Info. and Comm. Ctr., Assn. Asian Studies, Acad. Polit. Sci., Am. Polit. Sci. Assn., Pi Kappa Delta, Phi Alpha Theta, Pi Sigma Alpha, Phi Kappa Beta. United Ch. of Christ. Office: Catalyst Concepts PO Box 8393 Berkeley CA 94707

DECKARD, STEVE WAYNE, science educator; b. Lawrenceville, Ill., Apr. 9, 1953; m. Mary E. Chester, May 5, 1982; 1 child, Daniel. BS, McKendree Coll., 1975; MS, U. Ill., 1980; EdD, U. Sarasota, 1986; PhD in Christian Edn., Vision Internat. U. Cert. secondary and cmty. coll. tchr., Calif. Prof. The King's Coll., Briarcliff, N.Y., 1989-92; asst. prof. Inst. Creation Rsch., Santee, Calif., 1991—. Author: Homeschooling Laws All Fifty States, (9 edits., 1985—. Office: Inst Creation Rsch 10946 Woodside Ave N Santee CA 92071-2833

DECKER, BO, artist; b. San Jose, Calif., Jan. 2, 1969; s. Jerry Alton Mattson and Gayle Louise (Decker) Van Osten. BA in Studio Art, Calif. State U., Chico, 1993; postgrad., Sch. Visual Arts, N.Y.C. Illustrator The News and Review, Chico, 1992; asst. scenic artist theatre dept. Calif. State U., Chico, 1992-93; scenic artist Forest Theatre Guild, Carmel, Calif., 1993, San Jose Repertory Co., 1994; freelance illustrator, 1995—; gallery office mgr. San Francisco, 1996—. Contbr. poetry to publs. Disc jockey Sta. KCSC, Chico, 1991-93. Mem. ISC, Cacophany Soc. Home: 5425 Nicole Way Gilroy CA 95020-6810

DECKER, CATHERINE HELEN, English language educator; b. Lower Merion, Pa., June 1, 1965; d. Leonard Edward and Harriet Anne (Shields) D.; m. Roland Curt Burgess, May 25, 1991. BA, LaSalle U., 1987; MA, U. Rochester, 1989, PhD, 1994. Instr. English U. Rochester, N.Y., 1989-92; lectr. English SUNY, Geneseo, 1990-91; instr. English Auburn (Ala.) U., 1993, San Bernardino (Calif.) Valley Coll., 1995, 97; instr. arts and humanities Chaffey Coll., Rancho Cucamonga, Calif., 1995—; instr. English Calif. State U., San Bernardino, 1995—; rschr. psychology U. Calif., Riverside, 1992—; rschr. ESTC, Riverside, Calif., 1993. Contbr. book rev. to Wordworth Cir., 1995; editl. asst.: (electronic jour.) Electric Dreams, 1994-95; webmistress: (web sites) The Regency Fashion Page, The Regency Page, The Aphra Behn Society Page. Competitive scholar La Salle U., 1983-87; Sproull fellow U. Rochester, 1987-89, fellow, 1989-90, NEH summer seminar fellow, 1995. Mem. MLA, Am. Soc. 18th-Century Studies, Aphra Behn Soc. (comm. chair 1994-95, editor newsletter 1995), Cat Lovers of Am., Freedom Valley Girl Scout Alumnae. Democrat. Unitarian Universalist. Office: U Calif Riverside Dept Psychology 1419 Life Scis Riverside CA 92521-0426

DECKER, RICHARD JEFFREY, lawyer; b. Manhasset, N.Y., Aug. 26, 1959; s. Alan B. and Shelley T. (Belkin) D.; m. Carrie Ann Gordon, Aug. 13, 1989. BA, Union Coll., Schenectady, N.Y., 1981; JD, Boston U., 1984. Bar: N.Y. 1985, Calif. 1985, Mass. 1985, U.S. Dist. Ct. (cen. dist.) Calif. 1985. Assoc. Turner, Gesterfeld, Wilk & Tigerman, Beverly Hills, Calif., 1985-86, Shapiro, Posell & Close, L.A., 1986-90, Katten, Muchin, Zavis & Weitzman, L.A., 1990-93; of counsel Ginsburg, Stephan, Oringher & Richman, L.A., 1993—. Mem. Los Angeles County Bar Assn., Beverly Hills Bar Assn., Century City Bar Assn. Office: Ginsburg Stephen Oringher & Richman 10100 Santa Monica Blvd Ste 800 Los Angeles CA 90067-4012

DECKER, RICHARD KELSEY, equipment distribution company executive; b. Monrovia, Calif., Dec. 31, 1927; s. Raymond Grant and Dorothy Irene (Heady) D.; m. Barbara Carolyn Carlson, 1956; children—Richard Brian, Carolyn Ann Decker Johnson. B.S., U. So. Calif., 1952. Cost. acct. S.W. Products Co., Monrovia, 1953-55; controller Scotsman Refrigeration Inc., Monterey Park, Calif., 1955-64; with Scotsman Distbrs. of Los Angeles, Inc., La Verne, Calif., 1964—, retired, 1991; pres., chief exec. officer, 1976—. Served with USN, 1945-47. Mem. Alpha Kappa Psi (pres.), Beta Gamma Sigma.

DECKER SLANEY, MARY TERESA, Olympic athlete; b. Bunnvale, N.J., Aug. 4, 1958; d. John and Jacqueline Decker; m. Ron Tabb (div. 1983); m. Richard Slaney, June 1, 1985; 1 child, Ashley Lynn. Student, U. Colo., 1977-78. Amateur runner, 1969—, holder several world track and field records, 1980—; winner 2 gold medals at 1500 and 3000 meters World Track and Field Championship, Helsinki, Finland, 1983; mem. U.S. Olympic teams, 1980, 84; cons. to CBS Records, Timex, Eastman Kodak. Recipient Jesse Owens Internat. Amateur Athlete award, 1982, Sullivan award AAU, 1982; named Amateur Sportswoman of the Yr., Women's Sports Found., 1982, 83, Top Sportswoman A.P. Europe, 1985. Address: 2923 Flintlock St Eugene OR 97408-4660*

DECKERT, FRANK, park administrator; m. Gloria Quick; children: Christopher, Jason, Alisa. BS in Forest Mgmt., Humboldt State Coll. With U.S. Forest Svc., Calif., 1963-66; ranger, dist. naturalist Shenandoah Nat. Park Nat. Park Svc., Va., 1967-71; dist. ranger Isle Royale Nat. Park Nat. Park Svc., Mich., 1971-73; interpretive specialist Lake Mead Nat. Recreation Area Nat. Park Svc., Ariz., Nev., 1973-75; chief park naturalist Big Bend Nat. Park Nat. Park Svc., Tex., 1975-80; regional chief of interpretation Alaska Regional Office Nat. Park Svc., Anchorage, 1980-86; supt. Petersburg Nat. Battlefield Nat. Park Svc., 1986-92, supt. Carlsbad (N.Mex.) Caverns Nat. Park, 1992—. Trustee San Vicente Common Sch. Dist. Recipient Silver Beaver award Boy Scouts of Am., 1992. Mem. Carlsbad Rotary Club (v.p./pres. elect 1997—). Office: 3225 Nat Parks Hwy Carlsbad NM 88220

DECKERT, HARLAN KENNEDY, JR., manufacturing company official; b. Evanston, Ill., May 22, 1923; s. Harlan Kennedy Sr. and Lady Otey (Hutton) D.; BS, U. Calif., Berkeley, 1949; MBA, U. So. Calif., 1962; m. Mary Emma Eldredge, Nov. 27, 1971; children: Mary Adrienne, Christine Ann, Daniel Gregory, Deborah Alice. Systems analyst Northrop Corp., Hawthorne, Calif., 1949-53, supr. engring. adminstrv. svcs., 1953-57, adminstrv. systems engr., 1957-59; with AiResearch Indsl. div. Garrett Corp., Torrance, Calif., 1959-88, systems svc. adminstr., 1962-72, mgr. adminstrv. svcs., 1972-75, adminstr. internat. ops., 1975-80, sr. staff advisor Garrett Automotive Group Allied-Signal, Inc., 1980-88, ret., 1988. Active mem. L.A. County Mus. Art, Wild Beast Soc., docent; Greater L.A. Zoo Assn.; mem. L.A. County Mus. Natural History, San Luis Obispo zoological Soc., Exotic Cat Breeding Compound, African Wildlife Found., Friends Cabrillo Marine Aquarium, Assn. Zoo & Aquarium Docents; supporting mem. Living Desert. With USAAF, 1943-46, CBI, capt. USAFR, 1946-57. Mem. Am. Assn. Zoo Keepers, Am. Zoo and Aquarium Assn., Nat. Wildlife Fedn., Oreg. Wildlife Safari, San Diego Zool. Soc. (Keeper's Club), World Wildlife Fund, Nature Conservancy, Wildlife Waystation, Jane Goodall Inst., Santa Monica Mus. Flying, Wildlife Conservation Soc., Internat. Wolf Ctr. Home: 2433 33rd St Santa Monica CA 90405-2103

DE CONCINI, DENNIS, former senator, lawyer; b. Tucson, May 8, 1937; s. Evo and Ora (Webster) DeC.; children: Denise, Christina, Patrick Evo. B.A., U. Ariz., 1959, LL.B., 1963. Bar: Ariz., D.C., 1963. Mem. firm Evo DeConcini; ptnr. DeConcini & McDonald, Tucson, 1968-73; dep. Pima County atty. Sch. Dist. 1, 1971-72, county atty., 1972-76; U.S. Senator from Ariz., 1977-95; atty. Perry-Romani Assocs., Washington, 1995—, De Concini, McDonald, Bramer, Yetwin & Lacy, Tuscon, 1995—; mem. appropriations com., U.S. Senate, chmn. subcom. on Treasury, Postal Svc. and Gen. Govt.; mem. subcom. on Def., subcom. on Energy and Water Devel., subcom. on Fgn. Ops., subcom. on Interior Related Agys.; mem. Jud. com.; chmn. subcom. on Patents, Copyrights and Trademarks; mem. subcom. on Antitrust, Monopolies and Bus. Rights, subcom. on the Constitution, com. on Rules and Adminstrn., com. on Vets. Affairs; chmn. select com. on Intelligence; chmn. Commn. on Security and Cooperation in Europe; select com. Indian Affairs; mem. Internat. Narcotics Control Caucus, West Coalition of Senators; former pres., bd. dirs. Shopping Ctrs., Inc.; bd. dirs. Fed. Home Mortgage Corp. Chmn. legis. com. Tucson Cmty. Coun., 1966-67; mem. major gifts com., devel. fund drive St. Joseph's Hosp., 1970, mem. devel. coun., 1971-73; bd. dirs. Nat. Ctr. for Missing and Exploited Children, 1995—; mem. major gifts com. Tucson Mus. and Art Ctr. Bldg. Fund, 1971; adminstr. Ariz. Drug Control Dist., 1975-76; precinct committeeman Ariz. Dem. Ctrl. Com., 1958—; mem. Pima County Dem. Ctrl. Com., 1958-67, Dem. State Exec. Com., 1958-68; state vice chmn. Ariz. Dem. Com., 1964-66, 70-72; vice chmn. Pima County Dem. Com., 1970-73. Served to 2d lt. JAG U.S. Army, 1959-60. Named Outstanding Ariz. County Atty., 1975. Mem. ABA, NAACP, Nat. Dist. Attys. Assn., Am. Judicature Soc., Ariz. Bar Assn., D.C. Bar Assn., Ariz. Sheriffs and County Attys. Assn., Ariz. Pioneer Hist. Soc., Pima County Bar Assn., U. Ariz. Alumni Assn., Pres.'s Club, Tucson Fraternal Order Police, Phi Delta Theta, Delta Sigma Rho, Phi Alpha Delta. Roman Catholic.

DE COTEAU, DENIS, music director, conductor; b. N.Y.C.. BA, MA in Music, NYU; studied, Mozarteum, Salzburg, Austria; MusD, Stanford U. Asst. condr. San Francisco Ballet, 1970-74, music dir., condr., 1974—; artistic advisor Stockton Symphony, 1994—; condr. Oakland Symphony Youth Orch., 1970-79, Aichii U. Orch., Nagoya, Japan, 1982—, Tokyo City Philarm. Orch., 1989, San Francisco Conservatory of Music; prin. guest condr. Deutches Jugendorchester, 1976, 78, 80; guest condr. Nat. Music Camp Assn. Australian Youth Orch., 1980—, Oreg. Mozart Players, 1989; assoc. condr. San Francisco Symphony, 1986; music dir., condr. Flagstaff (Ariz.) Festival of Arts, 1977-83. Guest appearances with numerous dance cos. including Kansas City Ballet, State of Ala. Ballet, San Diego Ballet, Ballet West, Honolulu Ballet, and Oakland Ballet; guest condr. BBC Scottish Symphony, St. Louis Symphony, New Orleans Philharm., Tokyo City Philharm, Radio Frei Orch. (Berlin), San Francisco Symphony, Seattle Symphony, Oakland Symphony, San Francisco Chamber Orch. and others; appeared with Yomiuri Orch., Tokyo; invited condr. (recs.) Nat. Philharm. London, (concerts) Australia's Bicentennial, World Expo, Brisbane; condr. opera premiere Song of Pegasus (Marin Theatre Playhouse). Recipient Pierre Monteux Conducting Prize, 1969, Adventuresome Programming award ASCAP, 1976. Office: Conservatory of Music Orch 1201 Ortega St San Francisco CA 94122-4411 also: San Francisco Ballet 455 Franklin St San Francisco CA 94102-4438*

DEDEAUX, PAUL J., orthodontist; b. Pass Christian, Miss., Feb. 22, 1937; s. Mack and Harriet D.; m. Janet Louise Harter, June 29, 1971; children: Michele, Kristen, Kelly. BA, Dillard U., 1959; DDS, Howard U., 1963; MS, Fairleigh Dickinson U., 1975. Pvt. practice, Washington, 1976-93, Santa Ana, Calif., 1976-93; instr. Howard U., Washington, 1967-69; dental dir. Dr. Martin Luther King Health Ctr., Bronx, N.Y., 1969-70, dentist, 1970-76; chief dentist Calipatria State Prison, Calif., 1993-96, Calif. Med. Facility, Vacaville, 1996—; instr. Howard U., Washington, 1967-69; cons. Hostos C.C., Bronx, 1971-76; mem. adv. panel Dental Econs. mag., 1976; adj. assoc. prof. Columbia U., N.Y.C., 1970-72. Contbr. articles to profl. jours. Capt. U.S. Army, 1963-67, USAR, 1975—, col., 1985—, comdr., 1994—. Mem. Am. Assn. Orthodontists, Pacific Coast Soc. Orthodontists, ADA, Calif. Dental Assn., Assn. Mil. Surgeons of U.S. Democrat. Methodist. Home: 12181 Anzio St Garden Grove CA 92840-4644 Office: Calif Med Facility PO Box 2000 1600 California Dr Vacaville CA 95696

DEDIO, PATRICIA ANN, city/county official; b. Wiesbaden, Germany, Mar. 17, 1970; came to U.S., 1974; d. John Anthony and Irmgard Elizabeth (Knab) D. BA, BS, U. Colo., 1993. Reporter/photographer Ark. Valley Pub., Leadville, Colo., 1993-95; copy/news editor Macari-Healey Pub., Littleton, Colo., 1995-96; editor/writer Harvard Bus. Sch., Denver, 1996—; editl. technician Career Svc. Authority, City/County of Denver, 1996—; part-time swim coach, waterbabies instr., water safety, lifeguard Aurora (Colo.) Pub. Schs., 1989—. Freelance writer Highlands Ranch Herald, Littleton, 1995—, Mentor for a Child, 1996—. Recipient Goethe Inst. award, 1992. Mem. Soc. Profl. Journalists, Colo. Press Assn. Home: 9725 E Harvard Ave X-373 Denver CO 80231 Office: Career Service Authority 110 16th St Denver CO 80202

DEE, ANTHONY JAMES, psychiatrist; b. Manila, Philippines, Feb. 15, 1940; s. Charles and Diana (Schmidt) D.; m. Mary Dee; children: Jocelyn Suzette, Anthony Mark. BS in Physics, U. Philippines, 1961; MD, U. of the East, Philippines, 1966; MBA, U. Hawaii, 1979. Diplomate Am. Bd. Psychiatry and Neurology. Asst. prof. Yale U., New Haven, 1970-75; dir. Diamond Head Health Ctr., Honolulu, 1975-82; chief of dept. VA Hosp., Erie, Pa., 1982-87; med. dir. West L.A. VA Hosp., 1987-89; pres. Pragma Tech., Manila, 1990—, Macani Enterprises, L.A., 1989—; assoc. prof. U. Hawaii, Honolulu, 1975-82, SUNY, Buffalo, 1982-87; assoc. clin. prof. UCLA, 1987-89; lectr. Lake Area Health Edn. Ctr., Pa., 1996—; mem. adv. coun. Fox Studios. Contbr. articles to profl. jours. Mem. allocations com. United Way, L.A., 1993—; bd. dirs. ARC, L.A., 1993—, vice chmn., Erie, 1982-87; pres. Internat. Inst., Erie, 1985-87. Capt. USN, 1987. Office: 1606 S Barrington Ave Ste 1 Los Angeles CA 90025-4041

DEERNOSE, KITTY, museum curator; b. Crow Agency, Mont., Apr. 14, 1956. AA in Mus. Studies, Crow Studies, Inst. Am. Indian Arts, Santa Fe, 1985. Mus. intern Heard Mus. Anthropology & Primitive Art, Phoenix, 1984; interpreter Little Bighorn Battlefield Nat. Monument, Crow Agency, Mont., 1985-90, mus. curator, 1990—; mus. intern Smithsonian Inst., Washington, 1988. Recipient White Glove award Nat. Park Svc., 1995. Mem. Am. Assn. Muss., Am. Assn. State and Local History, Mountain Plains Mus. Assn. Office: Little Bighorn Battlefield Nat Monument PO Box 39 Crow Agency MT 59022-0039

DEES, FRED J., protective services official. Chief police Gilbert (Ariz.) Police Dept. Office: Gilbert Police Dept 1025 S Gilbert Rd Gilbert AZ 85296

DEFAZIO, LYNETTE STEVENS, dancer, choreographer, educator, chiropractor, author, actress, musician; b. Berkeley, Calif., Sept. 29; d. Honore and Mabel J. (Estavan) Stevens; children: J.H. Panganiban, Joanna Pang. student U. Calif., Berkeley, 1950-55, San Francisco State Coll., 1950-51; D. Chiropractic, Life-West Chiropractic Coll., San Lorenzo, Calif., 1983, cert. Techniques of Teaching U. Calif., 1985, BA in Humanities, New Coll. Calif., 1986; Lic. Chiropracter, Mich. Diplomate Nat. Sci. Bd.; eminence in dance edn., Calif. Community Colls. dance specialist, standard services, childrens ctrs. credentials Calif. Dept. Edn., 1986. Contract child dancer Monogram Movie Studio, Hollywood, Calif., 1938-40; dance instr. San Francisco Ballet, 1953-64; performer San Francisco Opera Ring, 1960-67; performer, choreographer Oakland (Calif.) Civic Light Opera, 1963-70; dir. Ballet Arts Studio, Oakland, Calif., 1960; teaching specialist Oakland Unified Sch. Dist., 1965-80; fgn. exchange dance dir. Academie de Danses-Salle Pleyel, Paris, France, 1966; instr. Peralta Community Coll. Dist., Oakland, 1971—, chmn. dance dept., 1985—; cons., instr. extension courses UCLA, Dirs. and Suprs. Assn., Pittsburg Unified Sch. Dist., 1971-73, Tulare (Calif.) Sch. Dist., 1971-73; researcher Ednl. Testing Services, HEW, Berkeley, 1974; resident choreographer San Francisco Childrens Opera, 1970—, Oakland Civic Theater; ballet mistress Dimensions Dance Theater, Oakland, 1977-80; cons. Gianchetta Sch. Dance, San Francisco, Robicheau Boston Ballet, TV series Patchwork Family, CBS, N.Y.C.; choreographer Ravel's Valses Nobles et Sentimentales, 1976. Recipient Foremost Women of 20th Century, 1985, Merit award San Francisco Children's Opera, 1985, 90. Author: Basic Music Outlines for Dance Classes, 1960, rev., 1968, Teaching Techniques and Choreography for Advanced Dancers, 1965, Basic Music Outlines for Dance Classes, 1965, Goals and Objectives in Improving Physical Capabilities, 1970, A Teacher's Guide for Ballet Techniques, 1970, Principle Procedures in Basic Curriculum, 1974, Objectives and Standards of Performance for Physical Development, 1975, Techniques of the Ballet School, 1970, rev., 1974, The Opera Ballets: A Choreographic Manual Vols. I-V, 1986. Assoc. music arranger Le Ballet du Cirque, 1964; assoc. composer, lyricist The Ballet of Mother Goose, 1968; choreographer: Valses Nobles Et Sentimentales (Ravel), Transitions (Kashevaroff), 1991, The New Wizard of Oz, 1991, San Francisco Children's Opera (Gingold); Canon in D for Strings and Continuo (Pachelbel), 1979; appeared in Flower Drum Song, 1993, Gigi, 1994, Fiddler on the Roof, 1996, The Music Man, 1996; violinist Oakland Cmty. Concert Orch., 1995—. Mem. Calif. State Teacher Assn., Bay Area Chiropractic Research Soc., Profl. Dance Teacher Assn. Home and Office: 4923 Harbord Dr Oakland CA 94618-2506

DEFAZIO, PETER A., congressman; b. Needham, Mass., May 27, 1947; m. Myrnie Daut. BA in Econs. and Polit. Sci., Tufts U., 1969; postgrad., U. Oreg., 1969-71, MS in Pub. Adminstrn./Gerontology, 1977. Aide to U.S. Rep. Jim Weaver, 1977-82; sr. issues specialist, caseworker, dist. field office U.S. rep. Jim Weaver, 1977-78, legis. asst. Washington office, 1978-80, dir. constituent services, 1980-82; mem. commn. representing Springfield Lane County (Oreg.) Commn., 1982-86; mem. 100-103rd Congresses from 4th Oreg. dist., Washington, D.C., 1987—; ranking minority mem. resources com., mem. transp. and infrastructure com. Mem. Lane County Econ. Devel. com., Ingergovtl. Relations com.; bd. dirs. Eugene-Springfield Met. Partnership; Lane County Dem. precinct person, 1982—. Served with USAFR. Mem. Assn. of Oreg. Counties (legis. com.), Nat. Assn. of Counties (tax and fin. com.). Office: US Ho of Reps 2134 Rayburn Washington DC 20515

DEFFLEY, MARK GARON, environmental purchasing executive; b. Springfield, Mass., Aug. 21, 1966; s. David Garon and Anne Kathryn (Murray) D.; m. Sherry Lynn Swenson, June 12, 1993; 1 child, Garon Lane. BBA in Mktg., U. Notre Dame, 1988; MBA, U. Tex., San Antonio, 1996. Sr. contracts rep. SAIC, San Diego and San Antonio, 1988-96; purchasing mgr. Ogden Environ., San Diego, 1996—; coord. Red Cross blood dr. SAIC, San Diego, 1989-91. Mem. Nat. Assn. Purchasing Mgrs., Nat. Contract Mgmt. Assn., Notre Dame Club (coord. San Diego crew classic 1989-91, database mgr. 1992-93, summer svc. project coord. 1996—). Roman Catholic. Home: 11124 Doverhill Rd San Diego CA 92131 Office: Ogden Environ 5510 Morehouse Dr San Diego CA 92121

DE FONVILLE, PAUL BLISS, historic organization administrator; b. Oakland, Calif., Mar. 3, 1923; s. Marion Yancey and Charlotte (Bliss) de F.; m. Virginia Harpell, June 17, 1967. Student, Calif. Poly. U., 1942-44, Michael Chekhov Group, 1947-52. Founder, pres. Cowboy Meml. and Libr., Caliente, Calif., 1969—; tchr. outdoor edn. Calif. State U., Bakersfield, 1980. Life mem. Presdl. Task Force, Washington, 1984—, Rep. Senatorial inner circle, Washington, 1989—, Nat. Rep. Congl. Com., Washington, 1990—, Rep. Nat. Com., 1987—, U.S. Senatorial Club, 1988—, Rep. Senatorial Commn., 1991, Presdl. Election Registry, 1992; del. Presdl. Trust, 1992; mem. Presdl. Commn. Am. Agenda; affiliate Lake Isabella Bd. Realtors, 1993; hon. marshall Lake Isabella, Kern County Christmas Parade, 1993. Recipient Slim Pickens award Calif. State Horsemen, 1980, Marshall-Working Western award Rose Parade, Pasadena, 1980, recognition Kern County, 1984, proclamations Mayor of Bakersfield, 1984, 85, Govt. of Calif., 1984, resolution Calif. Senate, 1988, Calif. Assembly, 1990, Presdl. Order of Merit, 1991, Congl. Cert. of Merit, 1992, Rep. Presdl. Legion of Merit award, 1992, Rep. Presdl. Legion of Merit award, 1992, document Gov. of Calif., 1993, Rep. Nat. Com. Cert. Recognition, 1992, Rep. Presdl. adv. Commn. Cert. award, 1993, Congl. Cert. Appreciation, 1993, Cert. Commendation Washington Legal Found., 1993, Rep. Presdl. award, 1994, Rep. Congl. Order of Liberty, 1993, Internat. Order of Merit medal, 1993, 20th Century award for achievement, 1993, Rep. Senatorial Medal of Freedom, 1994, Ronald Reagan Eternal Flame of Freedom medal and cert., 1995, Cmty. Svc. and Profl. Achievement medal, 1995, World Lifetime achievement award ABI-USA, 1996. Mem. SAG, NRA, Calif. State Horsemen (life), Equestrian Trails (life), Forty Niners (life), Calif. Rep. Assembly, Heritage Found., Cowboy Turtles Assn. (life), Rodeo Cowboys Assn. (life), Pro Rodeo Cowboys Assn. (life), Internat. Platform Assn., Lake Isabella C. of C., Kern County C. of C. Baptist. Home: 40371 Cowboy Ln Caliente CA 93518-1405

DEFOREEST, JOANNE MARIE, educator; b. Seattle, May 28, 1961; d. Robert Gregory and Millicent (Barnes) DeF.; m. Frederick Andrew McCandless, Dec. 21, 1996; 1 stepchild, Aaron David. BA, Gonzaga U., 1985; MEd, Seattle Pacific U., 1993. Cert. tchr., Wash. Tchr. Spokane (Wash.) Diocese, 1986-89; ednl. cons. pvt. practice, Wash., 1989—; tchr. Seattle Archdiocese, 1989-94, Achieve Prep, Edmonds, Wash., 1994-95, Home Sch., Seattle, 1995—; adj. prof. Seattle Pacific U., Western Washington U., 1995—. Inventor in field. Mem. ASCD, Nat. Coun. Tchrs. English, Wash. Orgn. Reading Devel., Internat. Reading Assn., Holy Names Alumnae Assn. (pres. Alumnae Assn. bd. 1993—). Democrat. Roman Catholic. Home and Office: 7722 34th Ave NE Seattle WA 98115

DE FOREST, EDGAR LESTER, actor, poet, educator; b. Hull, Mass.; s. Edgar Leonard and Ellen Marian (Huntington) De F.; m. Beulah Mary Ingalls, Nov. 21, 1940; children: Peter, Stephen, David, Richard. Diploma, Leland Powers Sch. of Theatre, Boston, 1937; BS, Boston U., 1940; MA, U. So. Calif., 1941; EdD, Columbia U., 1954. Cert. elem. tchr., Calif. (life); cert. secondary tchr., Calif. (life); cert. sch. adminstr., Calif. Dir. reading Mich. State U. (formerly Mich. State Coll.), East Lansing, 1945-48, asst. dir. summer program, 1954-57; dir. students Suffolk U., Boston, 1948-52; assoc. survey research Columbia U., N.Y.C., 1952-53; acting dean instruction Ventura (Calif.) Coll., 1957-60; prof. Coll. Desert, Palm Desert, Calif., 1962-78, prof. emeritus, 1979—; dean of ship U. Seven Seas, Whittier, Calif., 1964-65. Author various poems; appeared in plays Man of La Mancha, 1982, Death of a Salesman, 1983, Homage to Dali, 1988, Becket, The Fantastiks, Booth Majority of One, The King and I. Mem. Mayor's cultural planning 2000 com., Palm Desert, 1985-86; pres. Friends of the Library Coll. of the Desert, Palm Desert, 1983-85. Named Ideal Citizen of the Age of Enlightenment, World Govt. for the Age of Enlightenment, 1971. Mem. Mich. Reading Assn. (founder 1956), Lambda Chi Alpha. Democrat. Home: 220 Pinyon Crest Mountain Center CA 92561-9756

DEFRAIN, DENNIS ALLEN, education director, retired army officer; b. Fairbury, Nebr., Mar. 3, 1943; s. Howard Willis and Anna Pauline (Eisenhauer) De F.; m. Carol Jean Daugherty, Nov. 21, 1964; 1 child, Darren Craig. BSc, U. Nebr., 1965; MSc, U. So. Calif., 1972; EdD, Cath. U. Am., 1983. Commd. 2d lt. U.S. Army, 1965, advanced through grades to lt. col., 1982; adminstrv. officer 2d Bn., 15th Arty., Ft. Wainwright, Alaska, 1965-66, unit comdr., 1966-67; adminstrv. officer Adv. Team 55, Rach Gia, Vietnam, 1968-69; unit comdr. 2d Bn., 59th Arty., El Paso, Tex., and Schwabach, W.Ger., 1970-71, personnel mgr., Schwabach, 1971-73; asst. prof. U. Wis.-Oshkosh, 1973-76; personnel mgr. U.S. Army Personnel Ctr., Alexandria, Va., 1976-78; faculty devel. adminstr., instructional technologist Command and Gen. Staff Coll., Ft. Leavenworth, Kans., 1979-82; prof. mil. sci. Weber State Coll., Ogden, Utah, 1982-85, dir. internat. programs, 1987-94, program dir. continuing edn., 1994—. Interim dir. David Eccles Conf. Ctr. and Peery's Egyptian Theater, 1996; dir. youth bowling Ft. Leavenworth Youth Activities, 1979-80, dir. rifle marksmanship, 1981-82; mem. adv. bd. Layton High Sch. Decorated Bronze Star medal, Army Commendation medal, Meritorious Service medal with two oak leaf clusters. Mem. Nat. Univ. Continuing Edn. Assn. (membership chmn. region VI 1991-94, past chmn. internat. div.), Am. Assn. for Adult and Continuing Edn., Layton C. of C. (bd. dirs., pres.), Alpha Gamma Rho. Home: 2762 Brinton Way Layton UT 84040-8152 Office: Weber State U Ogden UT 84408

DEFREECE, GERALD ARLINGTON, retired dentist, orthodontist; b. Thermopolis, Wyo., May 31, 1923; s. Gerald Arlington and Iva Dell (Holloway) DeF; m. Betty Jean Boles, Aug. 27, 1949; children: Robin Leslie, Bryn Kendal. Student, State U. Iowa, 1941-43, Miami U., 1943-44; DDS, Marquette U., 1947. Diplomate Am. Bd. Orthodontics. Owner Gen. Dentistry, Bell Gardens, Calif., 1948-52, Covina, Calif., 1954-63; owner Orthodontic Practice, Glendora, Calif., 1964-89, ret., 1989; cons. Citrus Coll. Dental, Glendora, 1967-87; mem. bd. councilors divsn. health scis. U. So. Calif., 1982-83; guest lectr. Mt. San Antonio C.C., Walnut, Calif., 1984-87. Contbr. articles to profl. jours. Vestryman Holy Trinity Episcopal Ch., Covina, 1957-60; bd. dirs. Blind Children's Learning Ctr. Orange County, Santa Ana, Calif., 1990-94; pres. western sect. Charles H. Tweed Internat. Found. Orthodontic Rsch., 1979-81, bd. dirs., 1982-88. 1st lt. U.S. Army, 1950-52, Korea, with U.S. Army Dental Corps., 1952-54, with U.S.N.R. Fellow Am. Coll. Dentists; mem. ADA (life), Am. Assn. Orthodontists (lic.), Coll. Diplomates, Dental Alumni Assn., Orthodontic Alumni Assn., San Gabriel Valley Dental Soc. (pres. 1976-77), Fedn. Dentaire Internat., Pierre Fauchard Soc., Century Club (life, pres. 1982-83), Lions Club (bd. dirs. 1960-63), Delta Sigma Delta (life). Rep. Home: 49 Beacon Bay Newport Beach CA 92660-7220

DEFTOS, LEONARD JOHN, medical scientist and educator, jurist; b. Brockton, Mass., 1937. B.A. cum honoribus, Brown U., 1959; M.D. cum laude, U. Vt., 1964; JD, We. State U. Coll. Law, 1994; postgrad., U. San Diego, 1995—. Diplomate: Am. Bd. Internal Medicine; subsplty. cert. endocrinology and metabolism. Intern in medicine Columbia U. Med. Ctr., N.Y.C., 1964-65; resident in medicine Columbia-Presbyn. Med. Center, N.Y.C., 1965-66; staff assoc., attending physician Clin. Center NIH, Bethesda, Md., 1966-68; instr. medicine Harvard Med. Sch., 1968-70, asst. prof., 1970-71; clin. and research fellow Mass. Gen. Hosp., Boston, 1968-70; assoc. prof. medicine U. Calif., San Diego, 1972-76; prof. U. Calif., 1976—; chief endocrine research lab. VA Med. Ctr., San Diego, 1972—; cons. U.S. Naval Hosp., San Diego, 1973—, Naval Regional Med. Ctr., Camp Pendleton, Cal., 1975—; clin. investigator VA, 1974-77; mem. study sect. NIH, 1975-79, 85-89; mem. sci. adv. bd. Osteoporosis Found., 1986—. Mem. editorial bd., reviewer, contbr. numerous articles to books and profl. jours. Served to lt. comdr. USPHS, 1966-68. Am. Cancer Soc. Research scholar, 1971. Mem. Am. Fedn. Clin. Research, Am. Soc. Clin. Investigation, Endocrine Soc., Am. Soc. Bone and Mineral Research, Western Assn. Physicians, Assn. Am. Physicians, Alpha Omega Alpha. Address: 3350 La Jolla Village Dr San Diego CA 92161-0002

DE GARCIA, LUCIA, marketing professional; b. Medellin, Colombia, June 26, 1942; came to the U.S., 1962; d. Enrique Giraldo Botero and Carolina (Vega) Estrada; m. Alvaro Garcia Osorio, July 30, 1962; children: Carolina Alexandra, Claudia Maria. BS, Nat. U., 1962. Engring. arch. designer Vorhees, Trindle & Nelson, Newport Beach, Calif., 1974-78; pres., CEO Elan Internat., Newport Beach, 1984—; speaker, lectr. on success, protocol in bus. with Latin Am., free trade agreement between U.S. and Mexico. Editor: Elan mag., 1988-90. Trustee Nat. U., Calif., 1989-93; area campaign mgr. Bush for Pres., Orange County, Calif., 1988, Christopher Cox for Congress, 1988, Pete Wilson for Gov., 1990, People to Watch, 1994; bd. dirs. ARC, 1985-90, Am. Cancer Rsch. Ctr., 1986—; active South Coast Repertory Theater, 1982—. Named Dama de Distincion U.S./Mexico Found., 1991, Hispanic Woman of Yr. LULAC, 1986, One on the 10 Most Influential Women in Orange County, Orange County Metropolitan, 1994, One of the Hispanic 100 Most Influential in the U.S., Hispanics Bus. Mag., 1994; recipient Internat. award U.S. Hispanic C. of C., 1992. Mem. U.S./Mexico Found. (trustee 1990—), Latin Bus. Assn. (bd. dirs. 1992-93), World Trade Ctr. Assn. Republican. Roman Catholic. Home: 17532 Wayne Ave Irvine CA 92614-6658 Office: Elan Internat 620 Newport Center Dr Fl 11 Newport Beach CA 92660-6420

DEGETTE, DIANA, congresswoman; b. Tachikawa, Japan, May 17, 1957; m. Lino Lipinsky; 2 children. BA, Colo. Coll., 1980; JD, NYU, 1984. Atty. in pvt. practice, 1984-92; mem. Colo. Ho. of Reps., 1993-96, 105th Congress from 1st dist. Colo., 1997—. Democrat. Office: 1404 Longworth Washington DC 20515-1408

DE GETTE, DIANA LOUISE, lawyer, state legislator; b. Tachikawa, Japan, July 29, 1957; came to U.S., 1957; d. Richard Louis and Patricia Anne (Rose) De G.; m. Lino Sigismondo Lipinsky de Orlov, Sept. 15, 1984; children: Raphaela Anne, Francesca Louise. BA magna cum laude, The Colo. Coll., 1979; JD, NYU, 1982. Bar: Colo. 1982, U.S. Dist. Ct. Colo. 1982, U.S. Ct. Appeals (10th cir.) 1984, U.S. Supreme Ct. 1989. Dep. state pub. defender Colo. State Pub. Defender, Denver, 1982-84; assoc. Coghill & Goodspeed, P.C., Denver, 1984-86; sole practice Denver, 1986-93; of counsel McDermott & Hansen, Denver, 1993-96; mem. Colo. Ho. of Reps., 1992-96, asst. minority leader, 1995-96; mem. U.S. Ho. of Reps. (Colo.), 1997—. Editor: (mag.) Trial Talk, 1989-92. Mem. Mayor's Mgmt. Rev. Com., Denver, 1983-84; resolutions chair Denver Dem. Party, 1986; bd. dirs. Root-Tilden Program, NYU Sch. Law, N.Y.C., 1986-92; bd. trustees, alumni trustee Colo. Coll., Colorado Springs, 1988-94. Recipient Root-Tilden scholar NYU Sch. Law, N.Y.C., 1979, Vanderbilt medal, 1982. Mem. Colo. Bar Assn. (bd. govs. 1989-91), Colo. Trial Lawyers Assn. (bd. dirs., exec. com. 1986-92), Colo. Women's Bar Assn., Denver Bar Assn., Phi Beta Kappa, Pi Gamma Mu. Office: McDermott & Hansen 1890 Gaylord St Denver CO 80206-1211

DEGNAN, JAMES HENRY, physicist; b. Norristown, Pa., July 18, 1947; s. James Henry and Madeleine Mary (Bennis) D.; m. Elizabeth Teresa Castillo, Aug. 8, 1970 (div. May 21, 1984); children: James Henry, Michelle Teresa; m. Rikki Layne Quintana, May 15, 1988; 1 child, Siobhan Kathleen. BS in Physics, St. Joseph's U., Phila., 1969; MS in Physics, U. Pitts., 1972, PhD in Physics, 1973. Physicist GS-13 Air Force Weapons Lab., Kirtland AFB, N.Mex., 1978-85; physicist GS-14 Phillips Lab. (formerly Air Force Weapons Lab.), Kirtland AFB, 1985-94, physicist GS-15, 1994—; adj. prof. U. N.Mex., Albuquerque, 1980-83; mem. tech. adv. group Def. Nuclear Agy., Washington, 1992-95. Contbr. 35 articles to profl. jours., over 100 abstracts to sci. confs. Capt. USAF, 1973-78, Lt. Col. USAFR, 1978—. Mem. IEEE (session chmn. 1991, 93, 95), Am. Phys. Soc. Republican. Roman Catholic. Office: Phillips Lab WSQ 3550 Aberdeen SE Kirtland AFB NM 87117-5776

DEGRASSI, LEONARD RENE, art historian, educator; b. East Orange, N.J., Mar. 2, 1928; s. Romulus-William and Anna Sophia (Sannicolo) DeG.; m. Dolores Marie Welgoss, June 24, 1961; children: Maria Christina, Paul. BA, U. So. Calif., 1950, BFA, 1951, MA, 1956; postgrad., Harvard U., 1953, Istituto Centrale del Restauro di Roma, 1959-60, U. Rome, 1959-60, UCLA, 1970-73. Tchr. art Redlands (Calif.) Jr. High Sch., 1951-53, Toll Jr. High Sch., Glendale, Calif., 1953-61, Wilson Jr. High Sch., Glendale, 1961; mem. faculty Glendale Coll., 1962—, prof. art history, 1974-92, chmn. dept., 1972, 89, prof. emeritus, 1992—. Prin. works include: (paintings) high altar at Ch. St. Mary, Cook, Minn., altar screen at Ch. St. Andrew, El Segundo, Calif., 1965-71, 14 Stas. of the Cross Ch. St. Mary, Cook, Minn., altar screen at Ch. of the Descent of the Holy Spirit, Glendale, 14 Stas. of the Cross at Ch. of St. Benedict, Duluth, Minn; also research, artwork and dramatic work for Spaceship Earth exhbn. at Disney World, Orlando, Fla., 1980. Decorated Knight Grand Cross Holy Sepluchre, 1974, knight St. John of Jerusalem, 1976, knight Order of Merit of Republic of Italy, 1973 Cross of Merit, 1984, 89; named First Disting. Faculty, 1987, Outstanding Educator of Am., 1971. Mem. Art Educators Assn., Am. Rsch. Ct. Egypt, Tau Kappa Alpha, Kappa Pi, Delta Sigma Rho. Office: 1500 N Verdugo Rd Glendale CA 91208-2809

DEGRAZIA-SANDERS, JOHN JOSEPH, headmaster; b. Hollywood, Calif., Aug. 19, 1955; s. Donald Alvin and Grace Catherine (DeGrazia) Sanders; children: Candace Brown, Chelsea, Morgaine. BA in Psychology cum laude, Pacific Luth. U., 1980; postgrad., Pacific Luth. Theol. Sem., 1980-82. Cert. tchr., Calif. Tchr. social scis., dept. chair Santa Clara H.S., Oxnard, Calif.; headmaster Cyber H.S., Oxnard. Bd. dirs. Ojai (Calif.) Shakespeare Festival, 1993-94. With U.S. Army, 1974-77. Mem. ASCD, Nat. Cath. Ednl. Assn. (tchr. assoc.). Lutheran. Home and Office: 2121 Saviers Rd Oxnard CA 93033-3824

DEHAAS, JOHN NEFF, JR., retired architecture educator; b. Phila., July 4, 1926; s. John Neff and Sadie Lavinia (Hagel) DeH.; m. C. Bernice Wallace, Dec. 27, 1950; children: Kenneth Eric, Jocelyn Hilda. BArch, Tex. A&M U., 1948, MEd, 1950. Registered architect, Mont. Instr. Tex. A&M U., College Station, 1948-50, U. Tex., Austin, 1950-51; successively instr. to prof. Mont. State U., Bozeman, 1951-80; supervisory architect Historic Am. Bldgs. Survey, summers San Francisco, 1962, Bozeman, 1963, 65, Milw., 1969; cons. Mont. Historic Preservation Office, Helena, 1977-78, mem. rev. bd., 1968-79. Author: Montana's Historic Structures, Vol. 1, 1864, Vol. 2, 1969, Historic Uptown Butte, 1977; editor quar. newsletter Mont. Ghost Town Preservation Soc., 1972—. Bd. dirs. Mont. Assn. for Blind, Butte, 1984-95. Recipient Centennial Preservation award Mont. Historic Preservation Office, 1989, Dorothy Bridgman award for Outstanding Svc. to the Blind Montana Assn. for the Blind, 1990. Fellow AIA (com. on historic resources 1974—); mem. Mont. Hist. Soc. (trustee's award 1989). Republican. Methodist. Home: 1021 S Tracy Ave Bozeman MT 59715-5329

DEHART, DOUGLAS ALAN, state agency executive; b. Portland, Oreg., Mar. 14, 1946; s. Carl Edward DeHart and Ethel Linn (Smith) Brinson; m. Michele Claudet Warner, Apr. 30, 1982; children: Marc Michael, Matthew Lee. AB, Harvard U., 1968; MS, Oreg. State U., 1974; PhD, U. Wash., 1987. Rsch. biologist Oreg. Dept. Fish and Wildlife, Corvallis, 1974-75; freshwater dir.st Oreg. Dept. Fish and Wildlife, Portland, 1989-95, fisheries dir., 1995—; environ. biologist C.E. U.S. Army, Portland, 1975-80; fishery biologist Nat. Marine Fisheries Svc., Portland, 1980-89. Fishery ops. com. N.W. Power Planning Coun., Portland, 1990-95; sci. adv. com. Am. Rivers Coun., Washington, 1992—. Mem. Am. Fisheries Soc. (cert. fisheries scientist), Willamette Sailing Club (youth dir. 1996—). Democrat. Home: 3930 NE Wistaria Dr Portland OR 97212 Office: Oreg Dept Fish & Wildlife 2501 SW First Ave Portland OR 97201

DEHAVEN, KENNETH LE MOYNE, retired physician; b. The Dalles, Oreg., Mar. 28, 1913; s. Luther John and Dora (Beeks) DeH.; m. Ledith Mary Ewing, Jan. 11, 1937; children: Marya LeMoyne DeHaven Keeth, Lisa Marguerite DeHaven Jordan, Camille Suzanne DeHaven. BS in Pharmacy, North Pacific Coll. Oreg., 1935; MD, U. Mich., 1946. Intern USPHS Hosp., St. Louis, 1947; intern Franklin Hosp., San Francisco, 1947-48, resident, 1949; clinician Dept. Pub. Health, City San Francisco, Dept. V.D., 1949-51; practice family medicine, Sunnyvale, Calif., 1955-87; mem. staff El Camino Hosp., Mt. View, Calif., San Jose (Calif.) Hosp. Pres. Los Altos Hills Assn. Served to capt., USAF, 1952-55. Fellow Am. Acad. Family Practice; mem. AMA, Ariz. Med. Assn., Calif. Med. Assn., N.Y. Acad. Scis., Santa Clara County Med. Soc., Astron. Soc. Pacific, Sunnyvale C. of C. (bd. dirs. 1955-56), Book Club (San Francisco), Masons, Alpha Kappa Kappa. Republican. Home: 9348 E Casitas Del Rio Dr Scottsdale AZ 85255-4313

DEHMELT, HANS GEORG, physicist; b. Germany, Sept. 9, 1922; came to U.S., 1952, naturalized, 1962; s. Georg Karl and Asta Ella (Klemmt) D.; 1 child from previous marriage, Gerd; m. Diana Elaine Dundore, Nov. 18, 1989. Grad., Graues Kloster, Berlin, Abitur, 1940; D Rerum Naturalium, U. Goettingen, 1950; D Rerum Naturalium (hon.), Ruprecht Karl-Universitat, Heidelberg, 1986; DSc (hon.), U. Chgo., 1987. Postdoctoral fellow U. Goettingen, Germany, 1950-52, Duke U., Durham, N.C., 1952-55; vis. asst. prof. U. Wash., Seattle, 1955; asst. prof. physics U. Wash., 1956, asso. prof., 1957-61, prof., rsch. physicist, 1961—; cons. Varian Assocs., Palo Alto, Calif., 1956-76. Contbr. articles to profl. jours. Recipient Humboldt prize, 1974, award in basic research Internat. Soc. Magnetic Resonance, 1980, Rumford prize Am. Acad. Arts and Scis., 1985, Nobel prize in Physics, 1989, Nat. Medal of Science, 1995; NSF grantee, 1958—. Fellow Am. Phys. Soc. (Davisson-Germer prize 1970); mem. Am. Acad. Arts and Scis., Am. Optical Soc., Nat. Acad. Scis., Sigma Xi. Home: 1600 43rd Ave E Seattle WA 98112-3205 Office: U Wash Physics Dept FM 15 Seattle WA 98195

DEIBEL, FARRELL LEE, aerospace engineer; b. Paris, Sept. 22, 1959; came to U.S., 1962; s. Karl Edward and Sandra Sue (Jackson) D.; m. Karlyn Marie Szabo, June 23, 1984; children: Taylor, Brent, Riley. BSME, Calif. Poly. State U., 1981; MSME, U. So. Calif., L.A., 1990. Registered profl. engr., Calif. Mem. tech. staff Hughes Aircraft Co., Torrance, Calif., 1981-85, staff engr., 1985-90, sr. staff engr., 1990-97; sr. scientist Hughes Aircraft Co., Torrance, 1997—. Co-inventor hermetic seal, 1990. Recipient Golden State award Who's Who Hist. Soc., 1991. Mem. Tau Beta Pi, Phi Kappa Phi. Office: Hughes Aircraft Co 3100 Lomita Blvd Torrance CA 90505-5104

DEIKMAN, ARTHUR J., psychiatrist; b. N.Y.C., Sept. 27, 1929. AB, Harvard Coll., 1951; MD, Harvard Med. Sch., 1955. Assoc. prof. U. Colo. Med. Ctr., Denver, 1968-71; supr. psychiatrist Bur. of Alcoholism, San Francisco, 1971-76; assoc. clin. prof. U. Calif., San Francisco, 1972-85, clin. prof., 1985—. Author: Personal Freedom, 1976, The Observing Self, 1982, The Wrong Way Home, 1990. Capt. USAF, 1956-59. Mem. Am. Psychiat. Assn. (life). Office: 10 Millwood St Mill Valley CA 94941-2066 also: 649 Irving St San Francisco CA 94122-2401

DEIOTTE, CHARLES EDWARD, computer software company executive; b. Gary, Ind., Jan. 31, 1946; s. Raymond Louis and Dorothy Jane (Paulson) D.; A.A., Skagit Valley Jr. Coll., 1966; student Wash. State U.; children—Raymond, Karl, Ronald. Programmer, Wash. State U., Pullman, 1969-70; project dir. AGT Mgmt. Systems, Renton, Wash., sr. tech. cons., sect. mgr. McDonnell-Douglas Automation, Bellevue, Wash., 1972-73; sr. engr. Boeing Computer Services, Seattle, 1973-75, computer based instrn. specialist, Tng. div., 1975-79; mgr. microprocessor design support center Boeing Aerospace Co., Kent, Wash., 1979-80; mgr. concept research Federal Express Corp., Colorado Springs, Colo., 1980-81, mgr. microprocessor support group, 1981-82; pres. Deitron Systems, Inc., Auburn, Wash., 1976-81; pres., chmn. bd. Logical Systems Inc., Colorado Springs, 1981-87; chmn., CEO Cedsys Inc., 1987-91, sr. software engr., cons. LinCom Corp., 1992-93; software systems specialist, MCI Corp., 1993—; chmn. bd. Summit Med. Systems, Inc., 1985-86 . Neighborhood commr. Chief Seattle council Boy Scouts Am., 1971-72; v.p. REACT alert, Seattle, 1974; advisor Jr. Achievement, Colorado Springs, 1980; coach Odyssey of the Mind, 1991-92. Recipient Boeing Aerospace Co. Cert. of Achievement, 1979. Mem. Assn. Computing Machinery, IEEE, AAAS, Data Processing Mgmt. Assn., Am. Mgmt. Assn., Gamma Sigma Epsilon. Home: 16955 Vollmer Rd Colorado Springs CO 80908-1622 Office: 4678 Alpine Meadows Ln Colorado Springs CO 80919-3159

DEISENROTH, CLINTON WILBUR, electrical engineer; b. Louisville, Aug. 9, 1941; s. Clifton Earl and Nell (Pierce) D.; m. Lisbeth D. Isaacs, May 10, 1974; 1 dau., Susan Michelle. BEE, Ga. Inst. Tech., 1965. With Raytheon Co., 1966-81, div. mgr. Addington Labs., Inc., solid state products div., Santa Clara, Calif., 1975-77, program mgr. electromagnetic systems div., Goleta, Calif., 1977-79, dir. surface navy electronic warfare systems, 1979-81; sr. v.p. systems div. Teledyne-MEC, 1981-84; pres. Teledyne CME, 1984-90; exec. v.p., gen. mgr. Aerospace Products div. G&H Tech., Inc., 1990-92; v.p. bus. devel. Whittaker Electronic Systems, 1992-94, v.p., gen. mgr., 1994-96, pres., 1996; pres. CWD and Assocs. Mem. IEEE, Am. Mgmt. Assn. Home: 518 Oakhampton St Thousand Oaks CA 91361-1344

DEITER, NEWTON ELLIOTT, clinical psychologist; b. N.Y.C., Dec. 12, 1931; s. Benjamin and Anna (Leibowitz) D. BS, UCLA, 1957; MS, Leland Stanford, 1960; PhD in Clin. Psychology, U. Chgo., 1965. Cert. in clin. psychology. Pvt. practice clin. psychology L.A., 1965-90; exec. dir. Nat. Family Planning Coun., L.A., 1965-76, Gay Media Task Force, L.A., 1976—; staff cons. Aaron Spelling Prodns., L.A., 1980-90, spl. cons. NBC, L.A., 1970-79, cons. broadcast standards dept. CBS, L.A., 1968-82, cons. City Coun., City of L.A., 1975-85. Columnist Bottomline Mag., 1992—, Palm Springs Presents Mag., 1996—. Mem. Dem. Ctrl. Com., L.A., 1972-76; bd. dirs. Gay Cmty. Svcs. Ctr., L.A., 1970-75, Am. Cancer Soc., L.A., 1972-77, Palm Springs Gay Tourism Coun., 1993-95, Desert Gay Tourism Guild, 1996—; commr. L.A. Probation Commn., 1977-85; bd. advisors San Francisco Sheriffs Dept., 1969-79. Lt. col. USAFR, 1950-75. Inductee Internat. Gay Travel Assn. Hall of Fame, 1994. Mem. Acad. TV and Scis., Press Club L.A., Internat. Gay Travel Assn. (bd. dirs. 1986-93, pres. 1991-92), Desert Bus. Assn. (v.p. 1993, bd. dirs. 1992), Internat. Food, Wine and Travel Writers Assn. (bd. dirs., v.p./treas. 1995-97, pres. 1997—), Air Force Assn., Am. Mensa, Masons. Home: 71426 Estellita Dr Rancho Mirage CA 92270-4215 Office: Rancho Mirage Travel 71-428 US Highway 111 Rancho Mirage CA 92270-4130

DEJARNATT, GEORGE LEE, financial executive, business owner; b. Owensboro, Ky., Feb. 22, 1948; s. Benjamin Marshall and Mildred Ernestine (Fox) D.; m. Dana Haviland Meade, Sept. 1, 1974; 1 child, Dashiell Haviland. BA, Vanderbilt U., 1971; postgrad., U. Wash., 1973-74; MBA, U. Puget Sound, 1980. CPA, Wash.; cert. mgmt. acct. Rschr. Ctr. for Health Care Rsch., Nashville, 1970-73; office mgr. Timeline, Inc., Seattle, 1976-78; acct. Callahan, Reed, Gunn & Thomas, CPAs, Seattle, 1978-82; cons., owner Dash Mgmt., Seattle, 1980—; CEO Haviland Winery, Lynnwood, Wash., 1982-87; CFO Am. Communications, Seattle, 1987-92, Watchdog, Inc., 1990-95, Steeler, Inc., Seattle, 1995—; instr. City U., Bellevue, Wash., 1988—. Vol. Boy Scouts Am., Seattle, 1988—. Mem. AICPA, Wash. Soc. CPAs, Inst. Mgmt. Accts., Inst. Cert. Mgmt. Accts., Controllers' Roundtable, Hi-Tech Roundtable. Home: 18984 Forest Park Dr NE Seattle WA 98155-2436 Office: Steeler Inc 10023 ML King Way S Seattle WA 98178

DE JONG-HAWLEY, CHERIE, reading and language arts educator; b. Boise, Idaho, Dec. 19, 1947; d. Jack McCartney Marley and Marilyn (Carlock) Cunningham; 1 child, Brienne. BS, San Diego State U., 1971; MA, U. Calif., Santa Barbara, 1979, PhD, 1989. Supr. tchr. edn. reading clinic U. Calif., Santa Barbara, 1982-88; asst. prof. Calif. State U., L.A., 1989-95, assoc. prof., 1995—, dir. Reading/Lang. Arts Clinic, 1989—. Contbr. articles to profl. jours. Bd. dirs. So. Calif. chpt., Reading is Fundamental, L.A., 1990—. Mem. ASCD, Internat. Reading Assn., Am. Ednl. Rsch. Assn., Calif. Reading Assn. (pres. Santa Barbara chpt. 1986-89), Kappa Delta Pi (counselor Iota Phi chpt. 1992—). Home: 401 Deep Hill Rd Diamond Bar CA 91765 Office: Calif State U LA Charter Sch Edn 5151 State University Dr Los Angeles CA 90032

DELACOTE, GOERY, museum director. Exec. dir. The Exploratorium, San Francisco. Office: The Exploratorium 3601 Lyon St San Francisco CA 94123-1019*

DE LA CRUZ, JENNIFER LYN, marketing and finance executive; b. Long Beach, Calif., June 3, 1960; d. Reuben and Patricia Ann (Morris) De La Cruz; m. Jeffrey Alan Upton, Dec. 29, 1981. BSChemE cum laude, U. Mich., 1981; MSChemE, Stanford U., 1984; MBA, U. Pa., 1990. Summer intern GM Corp., Warren Mich., 1980, assoc. project engr., 1981-84, project engr., 1984-86, sr. process engr., 1986-89; mktg. assoc. Rohm and Haas Co., Phila., 1989-90; bus. mgr. Protogenesis, Inc., Carlsbad, Calif., 1990-95, mgr. mktg. and fin., 1995—; mem. bus. mgmt. adv. com. Mira Costa Coll. Mem. Soc. Mfg. Engrs. Home: 826 S Rancho Santa Fe Rd Apt F San Marcos CA 92069-4668 Office: Protogenesis Inc 2722 Loker Ave W Ste E Carlsbad CA 92008-6607

DELA CRUZ, JOSE SANTOS, retired state supreme court chief justice; b. Saipan, Commonwealth No. Mariana Islands, July 18, 1948; s. Thomas Castro and Remedio Sablan (Santos) Dela C.; m. Rita Tenorio Sablan, Nov. 12, 1977; children: Roxanne, Renee, Rica Ann. BA, U. Guam, 1971; JD, U. Calif., Berkeley, 1974; cert., Nat. Jud. Coll., Reno, 1985. Bar: No. Mariana Islands, 1974, U.S. Dist. Ct. No. Mariana Islands 1978. Staff atty. Micro. Legal Svcs. Corp., Saipan, 1974-79; gen. counsel Marianas Pub. Land Corp., Saipan, 1979-81; liaison atty. CNMI Fed. Laws Commn., Saipan, 1981-83; ptnr. Borja & Dela Cruz, Saipan, 1983-85; assoc. judge Commonwealth Trial Ct., Saipan, 1985-89; chief justice Supreme Ct. No. Mariana Islands, 1989-95; retired, 1995; mem. Conf. of Chief Justices, 1989-95, Adv. Commn. on Judiciary, Saipan, 1980-82; chmn. Criminal Justice Planning Agy., Saipan, 1985-95. Mem. Coun. for Arts, Saipan, 1982-83; chmn. Bd. of Elections, Saipan, 1977-82; pres. Cath. Social Svcs., Saipan, 1982-85. Mem. No. Marianas Bar Assn. (pres. 1984-85). Roman Catholic. Office: Commonwealth Supreme Ct Civic Ctr Saipan MP 96950 *There is an inherent goodness in every person, no matter how bad that person may appear. Recognizing that goodness in each gives us hope that the future of mankind will not be destructive.*

DE LA FUENTE, LAWRENCE EDWARD, artist; b. Chgo., Sept. 29, 1947. Student, Kansas City Art Inst., 1966-68. Exhbns. include San Francisco Art Commn., 1971, 72, Berkeley (Calif.) Art Ctr., 1973, San Jose (Calif.) State U., 1973, Gallery West, Mendocino, Calif., 1973, San Francisco Mus. Art, 1973, 74, 75, 76, 78, Mendocino Art Ctr., 1977, 80, 83, 93, Wilkinson-Cobb Gallery, Mendocino, 1977, Tucson (Ariz.) Mus. Art, 1977, Nat. Coll. Fine Art, Smithsonian, Washington, 1977, 80, mus. Mill Valley, Calif., 1978, Albuquerque Mus. Art, 1978, El Paso (Tex.) Mus.. Art, 1978, Blaffer Gallery, U. Houston, 1978, Taylor Mus. Art, Colorado Springs, 1978, Everson Mus., Syracuse, N.Y., 1979, Witte Mus., San Antonio, 1979, Contemporary Arts Mus., Chgo., 1979, U. Ga., Athens, 1979, Tyler U., Phila., 1979, Palacio de Mineria, Mexico City, 1980, Internat. Sculpture Conf., Washington, 1980, Western States Fair, Pomona, Calif., 1980, Macintosh-Drysdale Gallery, Washington, 1981, Fondo del Sol Gallery, Wahsington, 1981, Alternative Mus., N.Y.C., 1982, P.S.1 Clocktower, N.Y.C., 1982, Ronald Feldman Gallery, N.Y.C., 1982, Knot Art Gallery, Mendocino, 1983, U. Houston, 1984, Cultural Arts Ctr. Santa Barbara, 1985, Pulsations, Phila., 1986, Retreti Art Ctr., Helsinki, 1987, Living Art Show, Mendocino, 1987, Philbrook Mus. Art, Tulsa, Okla., 1987, Chgo. Pub. Libr., 1988, Kohler Mus. Art, Sheboygan, Wis., 1989, Va. Mus. Fine Art, Richmond, 1989, Orlando (Fla.) Mus. Art, 1989, Tokyo Mus. Modern Art, 1990, Kyoto (Japan) Mus. Modern Art, 1990, Smithsonian Instn. Renwick Gallery, 1990, Calif. State U. Chico, 1993, Natural History Mus., L.A., 1994, Smithsonian Traveling Exhbn., 1994, others. NEA fellow 1980, 88, 95. Home: PO Box 954 Mendocino CA 95460 also: 41401 Comptche Ukiah Rd Mendocino CA 95460

DELANEY, DJ, freelance writer, clergywoman; b. Butte, Mont., Dec. 9, 1947; m. M. Ryan. BS in English/Journalism, Western Mont. State U., Dillon, 1970; MS in Comms., Moorhead (Minn.) State U., 1976; PhD in Theology/Counseling, Am. U., 1978. Ordained to ministry; lic. secondary tchr., social worker, mental health counselor. Secondary educator English, journalism, comm. Mont/Idaho, 1970-80; prof. comm., writing, comparative religion and psychology Idaho State U., Polk County C.C., Laramie County C.C./U. Wyo., PIMA Med. Inst.; minister Ministry of Salvation Ch.; psychotherapist various non-profit orgns.; supr. mental health interns U. N.Mex., Highlands U.; ret., 1994; master tchr. Moorhead State U., Idaho State U.; practitioner-lectr. Wyo. Peace Officers Assn., Albuquerque Police Acad. Publs. include 3 poetry anthologies, numerous articles in Laramie Daily, Albuquerque Tribune, Casper-Star Tribune, Idaho Fall Post-Register, others; contbr. to Albuquerque Woman, N.Mex. Woman Mags.; contbr. poetry to lit. anthologies, children's book The Adventures of the Cat with the Purple Tail. Past v.p. Mont. Young Dems.; del. Dem. Nat. Conv.; nat. rep. Nat. Coalition Against Sexual Assault; co-coord. Wyo. Coalition Against Domestic Violence and Sexual Assault. Recipient Wyo. Woman of Achievement award, Albuquerque Woman on the Move award, Outstanding Achievement award for work in social svcs., Albuquerque Human Rights award, Poetry award from Maya Angelou, others. Mem. S.W. Writers Assn., Nat. Writers' Union, Phi Kappa Delta. Democrat.

DELANEY, MARION PATRICIA, bank executive; b. Hartford, Conn., May 20, 1952; d. William Pride Delaney Jr. and Marian Patricia (Utley) Murphy. BA, Union Coll., Schenectady, N.Y., 1973. Adminstrv. asst. N.Y. State Assembly, Albany, 1973-74; account exec. Foote, Cone & Belding, N.Y.C., 1974-78; sr. account exec. Dailey & Assocs., L.A., 1978-81; pub. rels. cons. NOW, Washington, 1981-83; account supr. BBDO/West, L.A., 1983-85; v.p. Grey Advt., L.A., 1985-87, San Francisco, 1987-89; sr. v.p. McCann-Erickson, San Francisco, 1989-95; sr. v.p., dir. advt./mktg. comms. Bank of Am., San Francisco, 1995—. Del. Dem. Nat. Conv., San Francisco, 1984; bd. dirs. JED Found., Hartford, Conn., 1989—, Easter Seals Soc., Bay Area, 1995—. Mem. NOW (v.p. L.A. chpt. 1980-83, pres. 1984, advisor 1985-87). Congregationalist. Home: 11 Gary Way Fairfax CA 94930-1002

DELANEY, MATTHEW SYLVESTER, educator, academic administrator; b. Ireland, Nov. 26, 1927; s. Joseph C. and Elizabeth M. (Bergin) D.; came to U.S., 1947, naturalized, 1952; student St. John's Coll., 1947-51; BA, Immaculate Heart Coll., L.A., 1958; MS, Notre Dame U., 1960; PhD, Ohio State U., 1971. Ordained priest Roman Cath. Ch., 1951; assoc. pastor L.A. Cath. Diocese, 1951-55; instr. math., physics Pius X High Sch., Downey, Calif., 1955-58, vice prin., 1960-62; instr. math. Immaculate Heart Coll., L.A., 1962-65, asst. prof., 1965-72, assoc. prof., 1972-76, prof., 1976—; asst. acad. dean, 1973-78; dean acad. devel. Mt. St. Mary's Coll., L.A., 1978-82, acad. dean, 1978-91; prof. math., 1991—, prof. emeritus, 1996—. NSF grantee, 1959-60, 61. Achievements include: Formal recognition of the eponyms, "Delaney Sets" and "The Delaney Symbol" in the disciplines of discrete geometry and math. crystallography, 1985. Mem. Internat. Union Crystallography, Am. Math. Soc., Math. Assn. Am., N.Y. Acad. Scis.. Democrat. Contbr. articles to math. publs., profl. jours. Home: Apt 32C 13700 El Dorado Dr Seal Beach CA 90740-3843 Office: Mount Saint Mary's Coll 12001 Chalon Rd Los Angeles CA 90049-1526

DELANEY, MICHAEL BEN, marketing executive, computer applications consultant; b. Balt., July 18, 1949; s. Louis and Selma Rita (Shapiro) Shapiro; m. Elaine Plieskatt, Feb. 1968 (div. 1973); m. Sherry Ann Epley, 1989. Grad. high sch., Mechanicsburg, Pa. Systems analyst Central Bank, Oakland, Calif., 1970-71, Farm Bur. Ins., Berkeley, Calif., 1971; assoc. dir. Soker Kaseman Gallery, San Francisco, 1971-75; pres. Vaarkaart, San Francisco, 1975-83; mktg. dir., spl. asst. pres., Dahlgren Control Systems, San Francisco, 1982-84, acting dir. logo system devel. team, 1981-82; pres. Delaney Cos. formerly Delaney and Assocs., Mill Valley, Calif., 1984—; pres. CyberEdge Info. Svcs., Inc., Sausalito, Calif., 1996—; pub., editor CyberEdge Journal, 1991—; dir., producer talent TV Series Countdown, 1981-82, direct mktg. mgr. PC World mag., 1988-90. Editor newsletter Dahlgren Notes, 1982-84; pub. Marketing News, 1985-87. Charter mem. Progressive Space Forum, Fairfax, Calif., 1979-85; bd. dirs. Artists in Print, San Francisco, 1979-81, Home Bus. Group, 1985; assoc. coordinator Spaceweek 80, San Francisco, 1980; v.p. Alliance for Future, San Francisco, 1979-83. Recipient neon design 2nd place award East Bay Express, 1982. Fellow Acad. Malt Scotch Whiskey; mem. Electronic Frontier Found., Assn. Computing Machinery, Computer Press Assn., San Francisco Virtual Reality Ednl. Found. Office: CyberEdge Info Svcs Inc #1 Gate Six Rd Ste G Sausalito CA 94965

DE LA PAVA, DANIEL, plastic surgeon; b. Bogota, Colombia, Oct. 30, 1942; came to U.S., 1969; s. Daniel and Maria Mercedes (Orrego) D.; m. Vianney Perdoma, Apr. 26, 1969; 1 child, Daniel Francisco. MD, U. Nat. de Colombia, 1967. Diplomate Am. Bd. Plastic Surgery. Intern Drs. Hosp., Washington, 1969-70; resident in gen. surgery Providence Hosp., Washington, 1970-73; resident in plastic surgery Christ's Hosp., Cin., 1973-75; fellow, clin. instr. Inst. Reconstructive and Plastic Surgery, NYU Med. Ctr., N.Y.C., 1975-76; pvt. practice Augusta, Maine, 1976-77, Sun City, Ariz., 1980—; Australia rsch. fellow, clin. asst. St. Vincent's Hosp., Melbourne, 1977-78; bd. dirs. Thunderbird Samaritan Hosp. Burn Svc., 1994; asst. prof. Maricopa County Hosp. Plastic Surgery Residency Program, Ariz., 1980-87; organized micro-surgery unit, Taipei, Taiwan, 1978; spkr. in field; vol. surgery Yerevan, Armenia, 1993, Ctrl. and S.Am., 1970-90, Kuwait, 1991. Recipient Spl. Recognition award 10 yr. anny. celebration Taiwan Micro-Surgery Unit, 1988, Vol. Svc. award for Kuwait surgery, 1991. Mem. Am. Soc. Plastic Reconstructive Surgeons, Lipolysis Soc. N.Am., Ariz. Plastic Surgery Soc., U.S. Colombian Med. Assn., U.S. Mex. Soc., Maricopa County Plastic Surgeon Soc. (sec./treas. 1994—). Roman Catholic. Office: 1300 N 103rd Ave # 54 Sun City AZ 85351

DELAPLANE, SUSAN AVEN, writer, poet; b. Salt Lake City, Feb. 25, 1931; d. Horace William and Ruth (Allen) Aven; m. Stanton Hill Delaplane, Feb. 2, 1961 (dec. Apr. 1988); children: Andrea Aven, John Berry Hill. BA in English, UCLA, 1953; MA in Humanities, San Francisco State U., 1991. Reporter L.A. Examiner, 1953-54, West L.A. Ind., 1955, L.A. Times, 1956-59; staff writer Ladies' Home Jour., Phila., 1960; asst. dir. publicity Pacific Area Travel Assn., San Francisco, 1976; freelance writer Marin and Sonoma Counties, Calif., 1977—. Active campaign worker Marin County Dem., 1987-92; mem. spks. bur. Marin County Commn. Status on Women, 1992-95. Mem. Nat. Writers Union (mem. book com. local 3 San Francisco/ Oakland chpt.). Home and Office: 745 1st St W # 7 Sonoma CA 95476-7024

DE LA VEGA, DIANNE WINIFRED DEMARINIS (MRS. JORGE DE LA VEGA), government official; b. Cleve.; d. Gerald M. and Dorothy (Philp) DeMarinis; student Case Western Res. U., 1948-50, MA, 1969; BA, U. Am., 1952; PhD in Psychology, Internat. Coll., Los Angeles, 1977; MA, Goddard Coll., 1978; m. Jorge Alejandro de la Vega, July 19, 1952; children: Constance, Francisco Javier, Alexandra. Faculty, Western Res. U., Cleve., 1961-62; instr. Instituto Mexicano-Norteamericano de Relaciones Culturales, Mexico, 1967; supr. fgn. press Mexican Olympic Organizing Com., Mexico, 1968; asst. to producer Producciones Ojo, Canal 8 TV, Mexico, 1969; exec. asst. Internat. Exec. Service Corps, Mexico City, 1969-70; asst. to dir. U.S. Internat. U. Mexico, Mexico City, 1970-75; family planning evaluator for Latin Am., AID, 1976; with dept. spl. edn. region IX Nat. Ctr. on Child Abuse and Neglect, Children's Bur., Office Child Devel., HEW, Calif. State U., 1977—. Chmn. Puppet's Jr. League, Mexico City, 1967, chmn. ways and means, 1968; sec. Tlaxcala-Okla. Partner's of Alliance for Progress, 1967—; pres. acculturating hispanic and Asian refugee children Los Angeles Unified Sch. Dist.; bd. dirs. Hot Line of Mexico City; mem. Los Angeles adv. com. 1984 Olympics. Lic. marriage and family counselor; active LEARN Com., 1995—; mem. steering com. Weingart Grant, 1996—. Mem. Los Angeles chpt. Calif. Marriage and Family Therapists Assn., Flying Samaritans, Pro Salud Maternal, Transactional Analysis Assn. Club: Jr. League (Los Angeles). Home: 130 Alta Ave Apt D Santa Monica CA 90402-2737

DEL CAMPO, MARTIN BERNARDELLI, architect; b. Guadalajara, Mexico, Nov. 27, 1922; came to U.S., 1949; s. Salvador and Margarita (Bernardelli) Del C.; BA, Colegio Frances Morelos, Mexico City, 1941; Archtl. degree Escuela Nacional de Arquitectura, Mexico City, 1948; m. Laura Zaikowska, May 25, 1945; children: Felicia (dec.), Margarita, Mario. Ptnr., Del Campo & Fruiht, architects, Santa Rosa, Cal., 1955-56, Del Campo & Clark, San Francisco, 1957-63; mgr. Hotel Victoria, Oaxaca, Mexico, 1964-67; pres. Gulli-Del Campo, architects, San Francisco, 1968-70; ptnr. Del Campo Assocs., San Francisco, 1977-81. Lectr. archtl. design Coll. Environmental Design, U. Calif., Berkeley, 1973-74. Mem. AIA. Archtl. works include: Calif. Med. Facility South, Vacaville, Phillip Burton Fed. Bldg. remodeling, San Francisco, Hall of Justice, San Francisco, San Francisco Airport Internat. Terminal. Address: Del Campo & Maru Architects Inc 45 Lansing St San Francisco CA 94105-2611*

DEL CARO, ADRIAN, German language and literature educator; b. Eveleth, Minn., Dec. 29, 1952; s. Pietro and Luisa (Abbatangeli) Del C.; m. Evelyn Mulhearn, Aug. 10, 1985. BA magna cum laude, U. Minn., Duluth, 1976; MA, U. Minn., Mpls., 1977, PhD with distinction, 1979. Lectr. U. Calif., Riverside, 1979-80; asst. prof. German La. State U., Baton Rouge, 1980-83, assoc. prof., 1983-89, prof., 1989-92; prof. German, chair dept. U. Colo., Boulder, 1992—. Author: Dionysian Aesthetics, 1981, Nietzsche contra Nietzsche, 1989; Holderlin: The Poetics of Being, 1991, Hugo von Hofmannsthal: Poets and the Language of Life, 1993, Paul Celan: In the Beginning was The Word, 1997; translator: Puntigam or The Art of Forgetting (by Gerald Szyszkowitz), 1990; contbr. articles to profl. jours. With U.S. Army, 1970-72. Recipient various fellowships and grants. Mem. MLA, N.Am. Nietzsche Soc., German Studies Assn., N.Am. Heine Soc. Office: U Colo Germanic Slavic Dept McKenna 129 Boulder CO 80309

DELEAR, RICHARD HENRY, personnel consultant; b. Wichita, Kans., Dec. 19, 1927; s. Ernest C. Delear and Clara M. Boberg; m. Helen J. Clark (dec. Mar. 1994); children: Cherie, Cindy, Kimberly, Kirkland, Dianne, Michelle. Student, Hiedleburg U., Germany, 1946-47, San Jose St. U., 1959-60. Cert. hypnotherapist. Enlisted U.S. Army, 1944, advanced through grades to m/sgt., 1952, ret., 1959; entrepreneur Calif., 1960-74; human resources cons. Success Thru Humaneering, Scotts Valley, Calif., 1974—. Author: Leadership Strategies, 1988. Pres. Exchange club, Scotts Valley, 1978-79. Decorated two Bronze Stars, two Purple Hearts, Silver Star. Republican. Roman Catholic. Office: Success Thru Humaneering 202 Burlwood Dr Scotts Valley CA 95066-3704

DELEHANTY, MICHAEL PATRICK, sail designer; b. Big Rapids, Mich., Feb. 3, 1960; s. Michael John and Joan Jene (Lowden) D. Sailmaker Hood Sails, St. Clair Shores, Mich., 1978-81; ski racer Squaw Valley (Calif.) Ski Team, 1981-84; race technician Squaw Valley USA, 1985-87; founder and sail designer Gorge Sails, Underwood, Wash., 1987—. U.S. speed sailing record Winner Racing, 1993; current record holder U.S. fastest sailor at 51.2 miles per hour. Mem. U.S. Windsurfing Assn. Office: Gorge Sails 62 Office Rd Underwood WA 98651

DELFFS, DUDLEY J., writer, educator; b. Sewanee, Tenn., Nov. 27, 1964; s. Dudley Julian and Norma (Thompson) D.; m. Dorothy Kilpatrick Scruggs, May 14, 1989; children: Mary Elise, Annie Kilpatrick. BA in English, U. Tenn., 1987, MA in English, 1989; MA in Counseling, Colo. Christian U., 1992. Tech. writer, rschr. Energy, Environ. Resource Ctr., Knoxville, Tenn., 1990-91; instr. English U. Tenn., Knoxville, Tenn., 1988-91, Colo U., Lakewood, 1991-96; counseling intern Colo. Christian U., Morrison, 1993-94. Author: (novel) Forgiving August, 1993; (non-fiction) Repentant Heart, 1995, (non-fiction) Prayer Centered Life; contbr. poetry and short stories to lit. mags. Recipient Scholastic Press Poetry award Columbia U., 1986, award Fiction Editor, Mars Hill rewiew. Mem. Nat. Coun. Tchrs. English, Am. Counseling Assn., Assembly on Lit. for Adolescents, Colo. Lang. Arts Soc. Office: Colo Christian U Dept Eng 180 S Garrison St Denver CO 80226

DELGADO, ROGER RODRIGUEZ, surgeon, educator; b. El Paso, Jan. 11, 1946; s. Roger R. and Eva (West) D.; m. Linda Susan Ferguson, Dec. 27, 1968; children: Jessica Lorraine, Nathan Roger. BA, U. Tex. El Paso, 1966; MD, U. Tex. Galveston, 1970. Diplomate Am. Bd. Surgery. Intern R.E. Thomason Horst, El Paso, 1970-71; resident surgery Naval Regional Med. Ctr., Portsmouth, Va., 1971-75; staff surgeon Naval Regional Med. Ctr., Camp Pendleton, Calif., 1975-78; pvt. practice surgeon Sebastopol, Santa Rosa, Calif., 1978—; assoc. clin. prof. U. Cal. San Francisco, 1978—; chief staff Palm Dr. Hosp., Sebastopol, 1980-81, bd. trustees, 1980-83, 90-94, dir. surg. svcs., 1996—. Contbr. articles to profl. jours. Fellow ACS; mem. Soc. Clin. Vascular Surgery, Soc. Am. Gastrointestinal Endoscopic Surgeons, Beta Beta Beta. Roman Catholic. Office: Santa Rosa Sebastopol Hosp 6800 Palm Ste C-1 Sebastopol CA 95472

DELGADO, THERESA MICHELLE, middle school educator; b. Marysville, Calif., Oct. 15, 1965; d. Frank and Cynthia Lee (Navarette) D.; m. Richard Martinez; children: Ricky Delgado-Martinez, Daniel Delgado-Martinez. BA, St. Mary's Coll., 1987; tchr. credential, Fresno State U., 1991. Cert. tchr., Calif. Recreation leader City of South San Francisco (Calif.) Parks and Recreation, 1989; basketball reporter Calif. State U., Fresno, 1989-93; bilingual tchr. Tenaya Mid. Sch., Merced, Calif., 1991—; cons. Merced Coll. Tchr. Readiness Program, 1992, mentor migrant edn., 1992—; mentor tchr. MCSD; master tchr. Chapman and Nat. Univs. Adviser Club Live/Red Ribbon, Merced, 1992-93; mem. Kops for Kids, Merced, 1992; cheerleading coach Tenaya Mid. Sch., 1992-94. Mem. ASCD, Calif. Reading Assn., Merced Area Reading Assn. Democrat. Roman Catholic. Home: 165 Westmont Ct Merced CA 95348

D'ELIA, WILLIAM VINCENT, film director; b. N.Y.C., Mar. 23, 1948; s. Vincent Peter and Dorothy (McGlynn) D'E.; m. Eleanor Ann Dombrowski, Apr. 8, 1972; children: Christopher, Matthew. BS in Communication, Ithaca Coll., 1969; MA in Communication, William Paterson Coll., 1975. Film dir. D'Elia, Uricola & Platt, N.Y.C., 1979-88, Fifth Ave. Films, N.Y.C., 1989-90. Writer, prodr., dir. feature film The Feud, 1990; dir. Northern Exposure CBS-TV, 1990-94, Doogie Howser, M.D. ABC-TV, 1990-92, Civil Wars, 1991-92, Reasonable Doubt NBC-TV, 1991-93, Beverly Hills 90210 Fox-TV, 1991-93, Harts of the West CBS-TV, 1993, Picket Fences CBS-TV, 1993-94, Lois and Clark ABC-TV, 1993-94, Time Well Spent ABC-TV, 1994, The Dottie West Story CBS-TV, 1995; dir. Chicago Hope, CBS-TV, 1994-97, co-exec. prodr., 1996, exec. prodr., 1996—; dir. The Tomorrow Man CBS-TV, 1995, After Laurette Fox-TV movie, 1995; consulting prodr., dir. Courthouse CBS-TV, 1995. With U.S. Army, 1970-71. Mem. NATAS, Dirs. Guild Am., Montclair Golf Club. Roman Catholic.

DELISI, DONALD PAUL, fluid mechanician, geophysicist; b. Pitts., Nov. 15, 1944; s. Samuel P. and Jennie (Moffie) D.; m. Adele Pedicord Orr, Aug. 7, 1971; 1 child, Bergen Orr Delisi. B.S.E. magna cum laude, Princeton U., 1966; MS, U. Calif., Berkeley, 1967, PhD, 1972. Resident rsch. assoc. Geophys. Fluid Dynamics Lab./NOAA, Princeton, N.J., 1972-74; sr. rsch. scientist Flow Rsch., Inc., Kent, Wash., 1974-77; staff scientist Phys. Dynamics Inc., Bellevue, Wash., 1977-86; v.p., treas., sr. rsch. scientist N.W. Rsch. Assocs., Inc., Bellevue, 1986—. Contbr. articles to Jour. Geophys. Rsch., Jour. of the Atmospheric Scis., Pure and Applied Geophysics, AIAA Jour., Jour. of Aircraft. Mem. Am. Meteorol. Soc., Am. Geophys. Union, AIAA, Am. Inst. Physics. Office: NW Rsch Assocs Inc 300 120th Ave NE Bldg 7 Bellevue WA 98005-3020

DELK, RICHARD ALLEN, accountant, financial consultant; b. Joliet, Ill., Aug. 5, 1958; s. Franklin D. and Lois M. Delk. BA, Luther Coll., 1980; MBA, U. Phoenix, 1986; JD, U. Denver, 1994. Bar: Colo. 1994; CPA, Colo., Iowa. Asst. state auditor Office of Auditor of State of Iowa, Des Moines, 1980-81; state audit supr. Office of Auditor of State of Iowa, Ames, Iowa, 1981-84; internal auditor U.S. West, Inc., Englewood, Colo., 1984-87; gen. ledger mgr. U.S. West Info. Sys., Englewood, 1987-88; fin. analyst U.S. West Comms., Inc., Denver, 1988-93, sr. ops. cons., 1993-96; internat. bus. devel. staff U.S. West Internat., Englewood, Colo., 1996-97; sr. bus. case analyst Carrier Divsn. US West Comms., Denver, 1997—. Office: US West Comms Inc 1801 California St Ste 2350 Denver CO 80202-2658

DELL, KENNETH CHARLES, city planner and urban designer; b. Billings, Mo., Mar. 18, 1938; s. Charles Albert and Lollomary (O'Mallory) Dell; m. Sally Ann Henderson, Feb. 28, 1969; children: Tana, Tiffany. BS in Architecture, Mont. State U., 1963; postgrad., U. Colo., 1968-71, U. No. Colo., 1968-71. Cert. urban planning. Draftsman, jr. designer Harmon, O'Donnell and Henninger, Assocs., Inc., Denver, 1963-67; planner planning office divsn. neighborhood studies City of Denver, Colo., 1967; sr. planner planning dept. City of Boulder, Colo., 1967-72; planning dir. City of Longmont, Colo., 1972-77; assoc. Moberg and Assocs., Boulder, 1977-79; prin. Kenneth C. Dell and Assocs., Boulder, 1979-83; planner Rocky Mountain Cons., Inc., Longmont, 1983—. Mem. Bd. Environ. Affairs, Longmont, Colo., 1994. Mem. Am. Planning Assn. (charter mem.), Am. Inst. Cert. Planners (charter mem.), Sertoma (treas. 1987—). Home: 1107 Purdue Dr Longmont CO 80503-3634 Office: Rocky Mountain Cons 700 Florida Ave Longmont CO 80501-6452

DELLAMAS, LLOYD RICHARD, government financial consultant; b. Santa Maria, Calif., Aug. 4, 1940; s. Victor Lloyd and Delya Eleanore (Freeman) deL.; m. Caroline Ruth Cox, Nov. 12, 1967; children: Ingrid Dionne, Chelsea Denise. BS, Calif. State U., San Diego, 1963. Analyst City of San Diego, 1963-66; asst. to city mgr. City of Torrance, Calif., 1966-68; city mgr. City of Woodlake, Calif., 1968-71, City of Lawndale, Calif., 1971-76, City of Monterey Park, Calif., 1976-87; pres. Hinderliter, deLlamas and Assocs., Diamond Bar, Calif., 1987—; also dir. HdL Coren & Cone, Diamond Bar. Active L.A. Com. on Sch. Orgn., Downey, Calif., 1989—. Mem. Calif. Mcpl. Fin. Officers Assn., Urban Land Inst., San Gabriel Valley City Mgrs. Assn. (pres. 1986), Calif. Redevel. Agencies Assn. (dir. 1981-87), Internat. City Mgmt. Assn. Office: HdL Cos 1340 Valley Vista Dr Diamond Bar CA 91765-3910

DELLAS, ROBERT DENNIS, investment banker; b. Detroit, July 4, 1944; s. Eugene D. and Maxine (Rudell) D.; m. Shila L. Clement, Mar. 27, 1976; children—Emily Allison, Lindsay Michelle. B.A. in Econs., U. Mich., Ann Arbor, 1966; M.B.A., Harvard U., Cambridge, 1970. Analyst Burroughs Corp., Detroit, 1966-67, Pasadena, Calif., 1967-68; mgr. U.S. Leasing, San Francisco, 1970-76; pres., dir. Energetics Mktg. & Mgmt. Assn., San Francisco, 1978-80; sr. v.p. E.F. Hutton & Co., San Francisco, 1981-85; prin. founder Capital Exchange Internat., San Francisco, 1976-94; gen. ptnr. Kanland Assocs., Tex., 1982, Claremont Assocs., Calif., 1983, Lakeland Assocs., Ga., 1983, Americal Assocs., Calif., 1983, Chatsworth Assocs., Calif., 1983, Walnut Grove Assocs., Calif., 1983, Somerset Assocs., N.J., 1983, One San Diego Assocs., Calif., 1984, Big Top Prodns., L.P., Calif., 1994. Bd. dirs., treas. Found. San Francisco's Archtl. Heritage. Mem. U.S. Trotting Assn., Calif. Harness Horse Breeders Assn. (Breeders award for Filly of Yr. 1986, Aged Pacing Mare, 1987, 88, Colt of Yr. 1990), Calif. Golf Club San Francisco. Home: 1911 Sacramento St San Francisco CA 94109-3419 Office: Big Top Prodns 1911 Sacramento St San Francisco CA 94109

DELLUMS, RONALD V., congressman; b. Oakland, Calif., Nov. 24, 1935; m. Leola Roscoe Higgs; 3 children. A.A., Oakland City Coll., 1958; B.A., San Francisco State Coll., 1960; M.S.W., U. Calif., 1962. Psychiat. social worker Calif. Dept. Mental Hygiene, 1962-64; program dir. Bayview Community Ctr., San Francisco, 1964-65; from assoc. dir. to dir. Hunters Point Youth Opportunity Ctr., 1965-66; planning cons. Bay Area Social Planning Coun., 1966-67; dir. concentrated employment program San Francisco Econ. Opportunity Coun., 1967-68; sr. cons. Social Dynamics, Inc., 1968-70; mem. 92nd-103rd Congresses from 9th Calif. Dist., 1971—; former chmn. house com. on D.C., former mem. permanent select com. on intelligence, chmn. house armed svcs. com., 1993; lectr. San Francisco State Coll., U. Calif., Berkeley; mem. U.S. del. North Atlantic Assembly, ranking minority mem. Nat. Security Com.; former chmn. Congl. Black Caucus, Calif. Dem. Congl. Del. Author: Defense Sense: The Search For A Rational Military Policy, 1983. Mem. Berkeley City Coun., 1967-71. With USMCR, 1954-56. Democrat. Office: US Ho of Reps 2108 Rayburn Bldg Ofc Washington DC 20515-0005 also: 1301 Clay St Ste 1000 N Oakland CA 94612-5217

DELOACH, ROBERT EDGAR, corporate executive; b. Daytona Beach, Fla., Jan. 6, 1939; s. Ollie Newman and Sally Gertrude (Schrowder) DeL. Student U. Alaska-Anchorage, 1967-69, Alaska Meth. U., 1970, Pacific Luth. U., 1972. Lic. elec. engr. and adminstr., Alaska, 1979; lic. pvt. pilot, real estate broker, ins. agt. Former chmn. bd. Alaska Stagecraft, Inc., Anchorage; pres. BG Systems Co., BG Tax & Acctg., Inc., The Electric Doctor, Inc., Apollo Travel, Inc.; former pres. Coastal Electronics, Inc.; former owner-mgr. Bargain Towne, Anchorage. Active Anchorage Community Theatre, Anchorage Theater Guild. Mem. Assn. Ind. Accts., Internat. Assn. Theatrical Stage Employees and Moving Picture Machine Operators U.S. (pres. local 770), Ind. Elec. Contractors Assn., Internat. Assn. Elec. Insps. Home: 1207 W 47th Ave Anchorage AK 99503-6917 Office: 7910 King St Anchorage AK 99518-3058

DEL OLMO, FRANK, newspaper editor; b. L.A., May 18, 1948; s. Francisco and Margaret Rosalie (Mosqueda) D.; m. Karen Margaret King, Feb. 6, 1970 (div. Sept. 1982); 1 child, Valentina Marisol; m. Magdalena Beltran-Hernandez, Nov. 10, 1991; 1 child, Francisco Manuel. Student, UCLA, 1966-68; BS magna cum laude in Journalism, Calif. State U., Northridge, 1970. Reporter-intern L.A. Times, 1970-71, gen. assignment reporter, 1971-80, columnist, editorial bd., 1980-90, deputy editor, 1990—; instr. Chicano Studies, Calif. State U., 1970-71; contbg. editor Race Relations Reporter, Nashville, 1973-75; on-air host, writer "Ahora" Sta. KCET-TV, L.A., 1974; chief writer, rschr. KNBC, 1975; bd. contbrs., freelance reporter Nuestro Mag., 1976-81; program co-dir. Summer Program Minority Journalists, 1990, faculty mem. 1979, vis. faculty mem. 1978, 80-83, 85, 89; vis. profl. Dow-Jones Newspaper Fund U. So. Calif. Sch. Journalism, 1975, bd. dirs. Numerous lectrs., presentations at colls., univs. Named Senior Faculty of Summer Program Minority Journalists Inst. Journalism Edn.; recipient Emmy award, 1976, Sigma Delta Chi Achievement award, 1982, Profl. Achievement award UCLA Alumni, 1990, Pulitzer Prize, 1984; Neiman fellowship Harvard U., 1987-88. Office: Los Angeles Times 202 W 1st St Los Angeles CA 90012-4105

DELONG, JAMES CLIFFORD, air transportation executive; b. N.Y.C., Jan. 29, 1940; s. Mary (Oles) DeL.; m. Nancy L. Hill; children: Andrew Hill, Theodore James. BS, Colgate U.; MA, U. Calif. Asst. mgr. Wichita Mid-continent Airport, 1970, airport mgr., 1971-74; asst. mgr. Houston Inter-Continent Airport, 1975-77, airport mgr., 1980-85; airport mgr. Houston Hobby Airport, 1978-79; dep. dir. dept. aviation Houston Dept. Aviation, 1986-87; dir. aviation Phila. Divsn. Aviation, 1987-93, Denver Divsn. Aviation, 1993—. Bd. dirs. Phila. Conv. and Vis. Bur., 1992-93. Pilot, USAF, 1963-70. Mem. Am. Assn. Airport Execs. (bd. dirs. 1989), Internat. Civil Aviation Orgn. (helicopters panel 1985—), Airport Operators Internat. (bd. dirs. 1990, info. sys. com. 1988, chmn. tech. com. 1979), Airport Coun. Internat. (bd. dirs., chmn. 1996), Nat. Transp. Rsch. Bd. (exec. bd. dirs. 1992-95), Variety Club Internat. (bd. dirs. 1992-93). Office: Denver Internat Airport Airport Office Bldg 8500 Pana Blvd Denver CO 80249-6340

DE LONG, KATHARINE, retired secondary education educator; b. Germantown, Pa., Aug. 31, 1927; d. Melvin Clinton and Katherine Frances (Brunner) Barr; m. Alfred Alvin De Long, June 21, 1947; children: Renée, Claudia, Jane. AA, Mesa Jr. Coll., Grand Junction, Colo., 1962; BA, Western State Coll., Gunnison, Colo., 1964; MA, Colo. State U., 1972. Camp dir. Kannah Creek Girl Scout Camp, 1960-64; tchr. Mesa County Valley Sch. Dist. #51, Grand Junction, 1964-84, dept. chmn., 1970-79; ret., 1984; tour coord., escort Mesa Travel, 1990—; substitute instr. Mesa State Coll., 1986-90; student council sponsor Mesa County Valley Sch., 1976-80; bd. dirs. Am. Red Cross, mem. disaster team, 1996—. Bd. dirs. Chipeta Girl Scout Coun., Grand Junction, 1960-66; pct. committeewoman Mesa County Dem. Party; mem., vice-chmn. Profl. Rights and Responsibilities Commn. for Dist. #51 Schs., Grand Junction, 1978-84; trustee Western Colo. Ctr. for the Arts, Grand Junction, 1987-88; mem. Mesa County Hist. Soc. Mem. AAUW (pres. local chpt. 1979-81, chmn. state cultural interest) AARP (Colo. legis. com. area I, asst. state dir., transp. task force, dist. dir. dist. 1, del. to nat. conv., dir. state conv. 1991), LWV (Grand Junction Area, sec. bd. dirs. 1995—), Pub. Employees Retirement Assn. (legis. adv. com. 1990-91), Colo. Ret. Sch. Employees Assn. (v.p.), Phi Theta Kappa. Congregationalist.

DE LORCA, LUIS E., educational administrator, educator, speaker; b. L.A., Oct. 18, 1959; s. Patricia Jean Clougher Harvey; m. Lori Ann Vanzant, Mar. 23, 1991. AA, Rio Hondo Jr. Coll., Whittier, Calif., 1983; BA, Calif. State Poly. U., 1989; MA in Humanities, Calif. State U., Dominguez Hills, 1997. H.s. football coach various high schs., So. Calif., 1980; pub. rels. dir. Calif. Poly Pomona Music Dept., 1987-89; pres. Exclusive Concepts, L.A., 1987-89; lifeguard L.A. City Recreation Dept., 1980-87; tchr. English Cathedral H.S., L.A., 1989-90; tchr., rsch. specialist Whittier (Calif.) Union H.S., 1990; founder, dir. The Learning Advantage Ctr., Whittier, 1991—; elem. tchr. St. Paul of the Cross Sch., La Mirada, Calif., 1993-95; CEO New Ednl. Wave Inc., Whittier, 1994—; tchr. L.A. County Office Edn., 1995—. Active Big Bros. of Am., Fair Housing, Greenpeace. Mem. Whittier C. of C., Cousteau Soc. Democrat. Unity Ch. Home: 2010 Madonna Ln La Habra CA 90631-3344 Office: Downey Pregnant Minor Program 7320 Firestone Blvd # 113 Downey CA 90624

DELORENZO, DAVID A., food products executive; b. 1947. Colgate U.; MBA, U. Pa. With Dole Food Co., Inc., Thousand Oaks, Calif., 1970—, exec. v.p., 1990-91, 93—, pres., 1991-93; pres. Dole Food Co., Internat., 1993—. Office: Dole Food Co Inc 31365 Oak Crest Dr Westlake Village CA 91362-4633*

DELORENZO, GEORGE OLIVER, production company executive, artist, writer, publisher; b. Jersey City, Mar. 29, 1949; s. George Stanley and Francis (Amato) DeL.; m. Cheryl Lynn Pickering, Feb. 18, 1970; 1 child, Angelo. Student, Valley Coll., Van Nuys, Calif., 1968-70. Freelance writer, artist, 1970-93; CEO King Comics, Hacienda Heights, Calif., 1993—; v.p. Make Magic Prodns., Commerce, Calif., 1996—; bd. dirs. Acad. Arts & Scis.; pres. West Coast Comic Club, Orange, Calif., 1996—. Artist, writer, creator: (book-sold for film) Rimcon Rave, 1996, Justicia (Spanish film), 1996, Shining Star, 1996. Trustee Sons of Italy in Am., Long Beach, Calif., 1994—; presentor Manning award Comic Con, San Diego, 1996. Mem. AAS. Home: 2401 S Hacienda Blvd Apt 17 Hacienda Heights CA 91745-4757 Office: Make Magic Prodns 5949 Smithway St City Of Commerce CA 90040

DELOYHT-ARENDT, MARY I., artist; b. Independence, Mo., Mar. 10, 1927; d. Frank Howard and Edith Isobel Strickland; m. William Joseph Arendt; children: Tracey McKee, Tammy DeLoyht. AA, Columbia Coll., 1946; BA in Fine Arts, U. Mo., 1949. Group exhibits include Brea Art Ctr., Conejo Valley Mus., San Bernardino County Mus., West Bend Gallery, Western Colo. Ctr., Grady Gammage Auditorium, Ariz. State U., Tex. U., San Antonio, Goddard Art Ctr., Ardmore, Okla., Waldorf Astoria, N.Y.C., Utah State U., Gonzaga U., Ad Gallery, Spokane, The Casino, Avalon, Calif.; represented in pvt. collections Valley Nat. Bank, Empire Machinery, Giant Industries, First Interstate Bank, Thunderbird Bank, Ariz. Biltmore, Marriott Camelback Inn, GalleyA., Taos, N.Mex., Vaneer Roberts, Scottsdale, Sunbird Gallery, Los Altos, Calif., Waterhouse Gallery, Santa Barbara, El Presidio Gallery, Tucson. Mem. Nat. Watercolor Soc. (signature), Ariz. Watercolor Soc. (Royal mem.), Ariz. Artists Guild, Plein Air Painters Am., 22x30 Profl. Critique Group, Western Acad. Women Artists.

DEL PAPA, FRANKIE SUE, state attorney general; b. 1949. BA, U. Nev.; JD, George Washington U., 1974. Bar: Nev. 1974. Staff asst. U.S. Senator Alan Bible, Washington, 1971-74; assoc. Law Office of Leslie B. Grey, Reno, Nev., 1975-78; legis. asst. to U.S. Senator Howard Cannon, Washington, 1978-79; ptnr. Thornton & Del Papa, 1979-84; pvt. practice Reno, 1984-87; sec. of state State of Nev., Carson City, 1987-91; atty. gen. State of Nev., 1991—. Mem. Sierra Arts Found. (bd. dirs.), Trust for Pub. Land (adv. com.), Nev. Women's Fund. Democrat. Office: Office of Atty Gen Capitol Complex 100 N Carson Carson City NV 89701-4731*

DEL PURGATORIO, KAREN FRANCINE, English educator; b. Long Beach, Calif., Apr. 1, 1948; d. Bertram Paul and Beverly Jeanne (Opdyke) Sherman; m. William Del Purgatorio, Oct. 31, 1971; children: David Todd, Traci Kim. AA, Los Medanos Coll., 1988; BA in English, U. Calif., Berkeley, 1990; MA in English, U. Calif., Hayward, 1994. Cert. English tchr., Calif. Voter registration coord. Antioch, Calif., 1986-87; tchr. English Antioch Unified Sch. Dist., 1990—. Del. State Dem. Com., Calif., 1988-96; chief amb., v.p. Antioch C. of C., 1988-89; bd. dirs. Adminstrv. Appeals Bd., Antioch, 1985-93; commr. Antioch Police Commn., 1993-95. Mem. Calif. Tchrs. Assn. (state rep. 1995—, polit. action chair 1996), Calif. League of Mid. Schs., U. Calif. Alumni Assn., Assn. of Responsible Citizens, Order Sons of Italy (fin. sec. 1994—), Alpha Delta Kappa, Phi Beta Kappa, Golden Key Honor Soc. Jewish.

DELUCA, PETER, state agency administrator, lawyer; b. Binghamton, N.Y., Apr. 7, 1946; s. Frank Emelio and Harriet Eloise (Munson) DeL.; m. Susan Lorraine Thompson, June 8, 1968 (div. Jan. 1972); m. Jean Francine Szymanski, May 8, 1982; 1 child, Mario Frank. BA, Coll. of Idaho, Caldwell, 1968; JD, Willamette U., 1975. Bar: Oreg. 1975, U.S. Dist. Ct. (Oreg. dist.) 1979. Emplyee rep. Oreg. Pub. Employees Union, Salem, 1975-76; legal counsel Oreg. Pub. Employees Union, 1976-83; project analyst Oreg. Exec. Dept., Salem, 1983-84; asst. atty. gen. Oreg. Dept. Justice, Salem, 1984-87; chief labor lawyer, asst. atty. gen. Oreg. Dept. Justice, 1987-92, trial atty., asst. atty. gen., 1992-94; adminstr. labor rels. State of Oreg., Salem, 1994-96; adminstr. Oreg. OSHA, Salem, 1996—. Scoutmaster Candalaria Cub Scouts, Salem, 1990-93; area rep. South Salem Neighborhood Assn., 1994—; chair task force on employee bargaining, Gov. Oreg., Salem, 1996. Democrat. Office: Oreg OSHA 350 Winter St NE Rm 430 Salem OR 97310

DELUCCHI, GEORGE PAUL, accountant; b. Richmond, Calif., Apr. 20, 1938; s. George Carl and Rose Caroline (Golino) D. BA, San Jose State U., 1959. CPA, Calif. Ptnr. Delucchi, Swanson & Co., Santa Clara, Calif., 1968-74, Delucchi, Swanson & Sandival, Santa Clara, 1974-76, Delucchi, Sandoval & Co., Santa Clara, 1976-77, Wolf & Co., San Jose, Calif., 1977-78; v.p. Lautze & Lautze, San Jose, 1978-82, also bd. dirs.; sr. ptnr. G.P. Delucchi & Assocs. (name changed to Delucchi, Robinson, Streit & Co., San Jose, 1982—. Treas. Crippled Children's Soc., San Jose, 1967-71, San Jose Catholic Charities, 1984—, F. Schmidt Found. for Youth; bd. dirs. Serra Med. Found., Mission City Cmty. Fund, Bill Wilson Marriage and Family Counseling Ctr.; pres. Santa Clara Police Activity League, 1977-78; mem. bd. fellows Santa Clara U., 1975-94; chair pioneer dist. Santa Clara coun. Boy Scouts Am. Lt. U.S. Army, 1959-62. Mem. AICPA, Calif. Soc. CPAs (bd. dirs. 1993-95, treas. 1995-96, sec. 1996-97), Silicon Valley Capital Club, Serra Club, Elks (Santa Clara exalted ruler 1969-70), Rotary (pres. 1993-94, bd. dirs. 1986-89), Knights of Malta (invested, Knight of Magistral Grace). Republican. Roman Catholic. Home: 774 Circle Dr Santa Clara CA 95050-5927 Office: 1871 The Alameda Ste 400 San Jose CA 95126

DELUGACH, ALBERT LAWRENCE, journalist; b. Memphis, Oct. 27, 1925; s. Gilbert and Edna (Short) D.; m. Bernice Goldstein, June 11, 1950; children: Joy, David, Daniel, Sharon. B.J., U. Mo., 1951. Reporter Kansas City (Mo.) Star, 1951-60, St. Louis Globe Democrat, 1960-69, St. Louis Post Dispatch, 1969-70; investigative reporter Los Angeles Times, 1970-89. Served with USNR, 1943-46. Recipient Pultizer prize for spl. local reporting, 1969, Gerald Loeb award for disting. bus. and fin. journalism, 1984. Mem. Sigma Delta Chi. Home: 4313 Price St Los Angeles CA 90027-2815

DELUZE, JAMES ROBERT, physician; b. L.A., Sept. 14, 1948; s. James Vierea and Jean Ruth (Hanna) DeL. BA, U. Hawaii, 1974; student, Andrews U., 1980-82; DO, U. Health Scis., Kansas City, 1987. Product specialist Hanna Enterprise, Kailua, Hawaii, 1972-74; pres. Ecol. Engring., Honolulu, 1976-79; intern Kirksville (Mo.) Osteo. Med. Ctr., 1987-88; pvt. practice medicine Kailua, 1988-89; physician Mental Health Systems, San Diego, 1989-90; pvt. practice Waialua, Hawaii, 1991-95. Rep. candidate U.S. Ho. of Reps., 1992, 96, U.S. Senate, 1994; pres. Waialua Rep. Precinct, 1992; del. Rep. State Conv., Honolulu, 1992. Mem. Am. Assn. Clin. Anatomists, Am. Coll. Occupational and Environ. Medicine, Am. Osteo. Assn. (del. 1992), Hawaii Assn. Osteo. Physicians and Surgeons (v.p. 1991-92, pres. 1992-93), Nat. Space Soc., U.S. C. of C. Republican. Seventh Day Adventist. Home and Office: PO Box 541 Waialua HI 96791-0541

DEL VECCHIO, DAWN MARIE, theater manager; b. Phila., Mar. 16, 1957; d. Alfred Frederick and Edna Florence (McCoy) Del V. BS in Bus. Adminstrn., U. La Verne, Calif., 1994. Theatre mgr. Cinamerica Theatres, L.P., Encino, Calif., 1978—. Office: 650 W Huntington Dr Monrovia CA 91016-3261

DELVOYE, JACQUES VICTOR, bank executive; b. Lille, France, May 10, 1947; came to U.S., 1976; s. Victor Edouard and Jeanne Emilie (Gilleron) D.; m. Terry Davidowitz, Mar. 2, 1975; children: Eric, Stefan. BA, Ecole St. Genevieve, Versailles, France, 1966; MBA, Ecole des hautes Etudes Comml., Paris, 1969; MA, U. Paris, U. Caen, 1970; postgrad., U. Calif., San Diego, 1969-71. Trust dept. portfolio mgr. Credit Lyonnais, Paris, 1972-76; asst. v.p. Credit Lyonnais, L.A., 1976-78; v.p. Credit Lyonnais, N.Y.C., 1978-81, L.A., 1981-84; v.p., mgr. corp. banking Banque Indosuez, L.A., 1984-86; mgr. Western U.S. Banca Nazionale dell'Agricoltura, L.A., 1987-94; v.p. Bank Leumi, Beverly Hills, Calif., 1995—. Author: (internal pub.) Etude de la Conjoncture Economique a la Banque de France. Treas. Italy-Am. C. of C., L.A., 1990. Fulbright scholar U. Calif. San Diego, 1969; U. Calif. fellow, 1969. Mem. Internat. Bankers Assn. in Calif., Beverly Hills Country Club. Home: 2247 S Beverly Dr Los Angeles CA 90034-1005 Office: 8383 Wilshire Blvd Ste 400 Beverly Hills CA 90211

DEMANES, FLOYD A., lawyer, arbitrator, mediator, consultant; b. Kewanee, Ill., Nov. 20, 1921; s. James and Mary (Mikwee) D.; m. Eve Douquet, June 1, 1947 (div. July, 1985); children: David Jeffrey, Mark Scott. Student Econs., U. Ill., 1939-43, JD, 1949. Bar: Ill. 1950, Calif. 1960. Assoc. Murphy, Pearson and O'Connor, Chgo., 1950; pvt. practice Peoria, 1950-59; pub. defender Peoria County, Ill., 1956-59; chief trial counsel So. Pacific R.R. Cos., San Francisco, 1959-61; pvt. practice San Bruno, Calif., 1961-66, Burlingame, Calif., 1966—; judge pro tem San Mateo Superior Ct., 1972-91; former rating atty. for Martindale-Hubbell over 25 yrs., numerous mediations and arbitrations. Contbr. articles to profl. jours.; frequent lectr. and speaker to bar assn. meetings in U.S. and Can. Capt. U.S. Army, 1943-46 ETO. Decorated Bronze Star medal; named Lawyer of Yr. U. Ill., 1975. Mem. ABA, ATLA (aviation law com. 1970-72, chmn environ law sect 1970-72, bd. govs. 1979-80), Ill. Bar Assn., Peoria County Bar Assn. (ethics com.), Calif. Bar Assn. (com. on fed. cts. 1973, del to state bar conv. 1963-64), San Mateo County Bar Assn. (past mem. bench and bar com., ethics com.), North San Mateo County Bar Assn. (past mem., pres. ethics com.), World Jurist Assn., Lawyer Pilots Bar Assn., Am. Bd. Profl. Liability Attys., Nat. Bd. Trial Advocacy, Internat. Soc. Air Safety Investigators (life), Air Travelers' Assn. (nat. adv. bd.), Profl. Airman's Assn. (pres. 1971), Calif. Trial Lawyers Assn. (bd. govs. 1965—, chmn. aviation law sect. 1968-72, environ. problems com. 1970-72, pres. 1973-74), San Mateo County Trial Lawyers Assn. (founder, pres. 1967-68, bd. dirs. 1963-65), North San Mateo County Bar Assn. (pres.1965). Republican. Episcopalian. Office: 1800 Trousdale Dr Burlingame CA 94010-4510

DEMARCO, RALPH JOHN, real estate developer; b. N.Y.C., Mar. 22, 1924; s. Frank and Mary (Castriota) DeM.; m. Arlene Gilbert, July 1, 1945; children: Sheryl DeMarco Grahn, Stephen, Laura DeMarco Wilson. BA, Claremont Men's Coll., 1956. Assoc. John B. Kilroy Co., Riverside, Calif., 1960-64, also mgr. ops. Riverside, San Bernardino counties, 1960-64; v.p. Marcus W. Meairs Co., 1964-67; pres. Diversified Properties, Inc., Riverside, 1967-72; v.p. Downey Savs. & Loan Assn. (Calif.), 1972-75; exec. v.p. DSL Svc. Co., 1972-75; pres. Interstate Shopping Ctrs., Inc., Santa Ana, Calif., 1975-87; exec. dir. comml. devel. Lewis Homes Mgmt. Corp., Upland, Calif., 1987-89; pvt. practice, San Diego, Calif., 1989—. Mem. City of Riverside Planning Commn., 1955-59, Airport Commn., 1960-70; mem. Urban Land Inst. 1st lt. USAF, 1942-45. Mem. Internat. Coun. Shopping Ctrs. Home: 44-489 Town Center Way # D 273 Palm Desert CA 92260-2723 Office: 16236 San Dieguito Rd #1-23 Rancho Santa Fe CA 92067

DEMARCO-DENNIS, ELEANOR (POPPY DEMARCO-DENNIS), elementary education educator, community activist; b. Boston, Nov. 28, 1937; d. Alvin Randolph Sweeney and Eleanor Beatrice (Marcy) Lee; m. John R. DeMarco, Dec. 30, 1966 (div. 1974); 1 child, Cambria; m. Richard Dennis, Jan. 15, 1980 (dec.); 1 child, Eric. BA in Psychology, Biology, Math., San Francisco State U., 1960; MA in Psychology and Counseling, San Diego State U., 1970. Caseworker San Diego County Welfare Dept., 1962-64; tchr., resource specialist La Mesa (Calif.) and Spring Valley Schs., 1964—; owner Bea Sweeney Tech. Resource Ctr., La Mesa, 1990—. Mem. San Dieguito (Calif.) Citizen Planning Bd., 1972-84; legis. asst. environ. San Diego County Supr., 1974-84; mem. exec. bd. Cmty. Coalition Network, 1991—, Calif. Dem., 1992—; bd. dirs. Unitarian Svc. Com., 1976-82; mem. Nat. Jewish Dem. Com. Recipient Ted Bass Tchr. in Politics award Calif. Tchrs. Assn., 1992. Mem. AAUW, LWV, Nat. Women's Polit. Caucus, Calif. Elected Women's Assn. Edn. and Rsch. Home: 4690 North Lane Del Mar CA 92014 Office: 991 C Loma Santa Fe Solana Beach CA 92075

DEMAREE, BETTY, artist, educator; b. Denver, Oct. 19, 1918; d. Nathaniel and Margaret Elizabeth (Sanderson) Wolfson; m. Dean Clay DeMaree, Jan. 15, 1962; 1 stepchild. Student Cooper Union Sch. Art, 1938-41. Textile designer Am. Textile Co., N.Y.C., 1940-43; self-employed greeting card designer, Los Angeles, 1945-48; self-employed designer, photographer, Bolivia, 1948-53; self-employed custom ceramics designer, Denver, 1954-65; self-employed painter, tchr., Denver, 1967—; condr. numerous workshops; pvt. instr. art; judge various art shows; bd. dirs. Rocky Mtn. Nat. Watermedia Soc. ann. exhbn. Exhibited in group shows at Southwestern Watercolor Soc., Dallas, 1968-84, Am. Watercolor Soc., N.Y.C., 1976-84, San Diego Watercolor Soc. and Traveling Show, 1983, Ky. Watercolor Soc., 1984-87, Allied Artists Am., N.Y.C., 1977-87; Rocky Mtn. Nat. Watermedia Exhbn., 1975-85, Gallery A, Taos, N.Mex., The Bath House Gallery, Denver, Colo., The Stevens Gallery, Art of Denver Gallery, Paint Horse Gallery, Breckinridge, Colo. Artists Assoc. Exhbns., Scottsdale, Ariz., Catherine Lorillard Wolfe Exhibit, N.Y.C., 1984, 87 (Strathmore Paper award), Montgomery House, Boulder, Colo.; represented in permanent collections Los Alamos Nat. Lab., United Bank of Denver, Mason, Reuler and Peake, Denver, Cen. Bank and Trust, Denver, Colo. State U., Fort Collins, Rocky Mtn. Energy Corp., Broomfield, Colo., Dwight Energy Data, Natkin & Co., Englewood, Denver, James Ins. Co., Denver, Sheraton Hotel, Ft. Lauderdale, Fla., Combs-Gates Airport, Denver, Harris Bank and Trust, Scottsdale, Utah State U., Logan, Jefferson County Bank, Lakewood, Colo., Mill End Fabric Store, Aurora, Colo., Glendale Dental Group, The Bank at Cherry Creek, Denver, and others. Mem. Southwestern Watercolor Soc. (named Best of Show 1969, selected for travelling show 1969), Am. Watercolor Soc. (Emily Lowe Meml. award 1976), Allied Artists Am. (John Young-Hunter award 1977, Winsor Newton award for watercolor 1978), Audubon Artists Am., Rocky Mountain Nat. Watermedia Soc., Colo. Watercolor Soc. Denver Artists Guild, Colo. Artist Assn. (award 1981, 89, Best of Show award 1986, 1st watercolor 1987, 1992 conv., conv. award 1993), San Diego Watercolor Soc. and Travelling Show, Channel 6 Pub. TV (chosen for anniversary collection 1988-89, painting chosen for month of Dec. 1990 calendar, 1992 mktg. poster). Republican. Home and Office: Betty DeMaree Studio 4725 W Quincy Ave Denver CO 80236-3231

DEMAREE, SUZETTE ENGLISH, artist, photographer; b. Denver, June 21, 1955; d. Arlo Craig and Muriel Ann (Hosking) English; m. Scott David Demaree, Mar. 20, 1982 (div. May 1994); 1 child, Alexandra Danielle. AA in Fine Arts, Casper Coll., Wyo., 1975, AA in English, 1996. Mgr. Buccaneer Ltd., Casper, 1975-79, Graphic Arts, Casper, 1979-82; owner Wood Cellar Furniture, Casper, 1982-94; freelance artist, photographer, writer Casper, 1994—; trainer Dale Carnegie Courses, Casper, 1987-88. Editor-in-chief Casper College-Expression Mag., 1995-96, Expression, 1996; author: Your Own Best Friend, The Face in the Mirror, 1995; patentee in field; potter, sculptor, poet, photographer. Chmn. drive United Way, Casper, 1988-89, chmn. bd. dirs., 1990-91; bd. dirs. Casper Area Economic Devel. Alliance, 1992-93. Mem. Wyo. Writers Assn., Poetry Soc. Am., C. of C. (chmn. bd. dirs. 1992-93).

DE MARINO, THOMAS JOHN, lawyer; b. Greensburg, Pa., Nov. 24, 1937; s. Thomas Camille and Sue Eleanor (Nicholson) de M.; m. Elizabeth Hamilton Bardsley, Aug. 22, 1959 (div. Aug. 1978); children: Jeffrey, Lynn; m. Joyce Hobson Lee, May 18, 1979 (dec. Sept. 1995). BA, Dickinson Coll., 1959, JD, 1962. Bar: Pa. 1963, Colo. 1965, U.S. Dist. Ct. Colo. 1965, U.S. Ct. Appeals (10th cir.) 1965, U.S. Supreme Ct. 1984. Assoc. Hamilton, Darmo, Malloy, Phila., 1963; ptnr. firm Ellison, de Marino & Knapp, Denver, 1965-76, de Marino & Knapp, Denver, 1976-77, Sheldon, Bayer, McLean & Glasman, Denver, 1978; Colo. mng. atty. law dept. litigation div. Travelers Ins. Co., Denver, 1979-93; dir. Weinberger & Kanan, P.C., Denver, 1994—. Author: Colorado Workers Compensation Law and Practice, 1984; contbr. articles to legal jours. Pres. Denver Lyric Opera Co., 1973; treas. Colo. Mountain Club Found., Denver, 1984. Mem. Colo. Bar Assn. (bd. govs. 1985-90, chmn. interprofl. com., 1983, chmn. workers' compensation sect. 1983, vice chmn. litigation sect. coun. 1988), Denver Bar Assn. (pres. 1997, 1st v.p. 1988, bd. trustees 1991-94, chmn. barristers benefit ball com. 1989, Merit award 1995), Colo. Def. Lawyers Assn. (v.p. 1975, pres. 1976), Def. Rsch. Inst. (exceptional performance citation 1977). Republican. Congregationalist. Club: Colo. Mountain (bd. dirs. Denver 1974). Office: 1700 Broadway Ste 1910 Denver CO 80290-1901

DE MASSA, JESSIE G., media specialist. BJ, Temple U.; MLS, San Jose State U., 1967; postgrad., U. Okla., U. So. Calif. Tchr. Palo Alto (Calif.) Unified Sch. Dist., 1966; librarian Antelope Valley Joint Union High Sch. Dist., Lancaster, Calif., 1966-68, ABC Unified Sch. Dist., Artesia, Calif., 1968-72; dist. librarian Tehachapi (Calif.) Unified Sch. Dist., 1972-81; media specialist, free lance writer, 1981—; assoc. Chris DeMassa & Assocs., 1988—. Contbr. articles to profl. jours. Mem. Statue of Liberty Ellis Island Found., Inc.; charter supporter U.S. Holocaust Meml. Mus., Washington; supporting mem. U.S. Holocaust Meml. Coun., Washington. Named to Nat. Women's Hall of Fame, 1995. Fellow Internat. Biog. Assn.; mem. Calif. Media and Libr. Educators Assn., Calif. Assn. Sch. Librs. (exec. coun.), AAUW (bull. editor chpt., assoc. editor state bull., chmn. publicity, 1955-68), Nat. Mus. Women in Arts (charter), Hon Fellows John F. Kennedy Libr. (founding mem.), Women's Roundtable of Orange County, Nat. Writer's Assn. (so. Calif. chpt.), Calif. Retired Tchrs. Assn. (Harbor Beach divsn. 77), The Heritage Found. Home: 9951 Garrett Cir Huntington Beach CA 92646-3604

DEMELLO, AUSTIN EASTWOOD, astrophysicist, concert artist, poet, writer; b. New Bedford, Mass., Oct. 15, 1939; s. Manuel and Dora (Eastwood) De M; children: Adragon Eastwood De Mello, Brad Steven. BA in English, UCLA, 1974; MSc in Physics and Astronomy, Met. Coll. Inst., London, 1977, DSc in Theoretical Astrophysics, 1981. Engring. writer Raytheon Co., Santa Barbara, Calif., 1982; dir. research and sci. publs. Cosmosci. Research Inst., Sunnyvale, Calif., 1983—; sr. engring. writer, cons. Lockheed Martin, Sunnyvale, 1997. Author: Black Night Poetry, 1960, Tengu, 1962, (record) El Duende Flamenco, 1965, The Metagalactic System, 1969, The Four States of Man, 1971, Early Development of the Scientific Mind, 1981, Theory of Cosmodynamics, 1983, The Cosmotorsion Effect, 1984, James Bay Missionaries, 1986, The Origin and Influence of Flamenco Music on the Classics, 1992, Offenbach and the Can-Can Dance, 1993, Adragon: The Youngest Scholar, 1993, Legacy of Poetry and Philosophy, 1993, The Magic Formula, 1993, Views of Chaos, 1993, Haiku of the Sea Poet, 1997, Beware the Dragon of the Id, 1997, Evolution of an Assassin, 1997, The Scholar and the University, 1997, The Violent Life, 1997, (staged screen play) Petenera, 1997. Acad. Merit scholar UCLA, 1972-74. Mem. AIAA, AAAS, N.Y. Acad. Sci., Am. Astronautical Soc., Mensa Internat. Home: PO Box 461 Moss Landing CA 95039-0461 Office: CSR Inst 663 S Bernardo Ave Sunnyvale CA 94087-1020

DEMEREE, GLORIA See **LENNOX, GLORIA**

DEMERSMAN, JAMES RICHARD, museum director; b. Rochester, N.Y., July 31, 1957; s. Richard Oscar and Carolyn Ruth (Morse) DeM.; m. Pricilla Ann McClellan Hill, Nov. 29, 1980 (div. Dec. 1987); 1 child, Andrew Joseph; m. Richard Erland Patenaude, Oct. 9, 1993. BA in History and Bus. Adminstrn., Houghton Coll., 1980. Asst. to dir. edn. Genesee Country Mus., Mumford, N.Y., 1980; dir. edn. Hist. Speedwell Village, Morristown, N.J., 1980-83; dir. edn. Rosemount Victorian House Mus., Pueblo, Colo., 1983-85, exec. dir., 1985-87; asst. dir. Nat. Trust for Hist. Preservation, Washington, 1987-91; dir. Molly Brown House Mus., Denver, 1991-93, Hi-Desert Nature Mus., Yucca Valley, Calif., 1993—; peer reviewer Inst. Mus. Svcs., Washington, 1985—. Editor: (newsletter) Integrity of the Desert, Palm Springs, Calif., 1994—. Male co-chmn. Alliance for Lesbian and Gay Concerns, Washington, 1993—. Preservation Leadership tng. Nat. Trust for Hist. Preservation, 1993. Mem. Am. Assn. Museums (vis. cons. 1991—, mem. nat. program planning com. 1996-97), Western Mus. Assn., Calif. Assn. Museums, Calif. Preservation Found., Registrar's Coun., Nat. Trust for Hist. Preservation. Democrat. Episcopalian. Home: 504 N Tercero Cir Palm Springs CA 92262-6243 Office: Hi-Desert Nature Mus 57116 Twenty Nine Palms Hwy Yucca Valley CA 92284

DEMERY, DOROTHY JEAN, secondary school educator; b. Houston, Sept. 5, 1941; d. Floyd Hicks and Irene Elaine Burns Clay; m. Leroy W. Demery, Jan. 16, 1979; children: Steven Bradley, Rodney Bradley, Craig Bradley, Kimberly Bradley. AA, West L.A. Coll., Culver City, Calif., 1976; AS, Harbor Coll., Wilmington, Calif., 1983; BS in Pub. Adminstrn., Calif. State U., Carson, 1985; MS in Instructional Leadership, Nat. U., San Diego, 1991. Cert. real estate broker, tchr. math. and bus. edn., bilingual tchr., crosscultural lang. and acad. devel.; lang. devel. specialist. Eligibility social worker Dept. Pub. Social Svcs., L.A., 1967-74; real estate broker Dee Bradley & Assocs., Riverside, Calif., 1976—; tchr. math L.A. Unified Sch. Dist., 1985-91; math/computer sci. tchr. Pomona (Calif.) Unified Sch. Dist.,

1991—; adj. lectr. Riverside C.C., 1992-93; mem. Dist. Curriculum Coun./Report Card Task Force, Pomona, 1994—. Chairperson Human Rights Com., Pomona, 1992—, sec. steering com., 1993—, adv. bd., 1993—; mem. polit. action com. Assoc. Pomona Tchrs., 1993-94. Recipient Outstanding Svc. award Baldwin Hills Little League Assn., L.A., 1972. Mem. Nat. Bus. Assn., Nat. Coun. Tchrs. Math., Aux. Nat. Med. Assn., Alpha Kappa Alpha. Home: PO Box 2796 Riverside CA 92516-2796 Office: Simons Middle School 900 E Franklin Ave Pomona CA 91766-5362

DEMETRESCU, MIHAI CONSTANTIN, research scientist, educator, computer company executive; b. Bucharest, Romania, May 23, 1929; s. Dan and Alina (Dragosescu) D.; M.E.E., Poly. Inst. of U. Bucharest, 1954; Ph.D., Romanian Acad. Sci., 1957; m. Agnes Halas, May 25, 1969; 1 child, Stefan. Came to U.S., 1966. Prin. investigator Research Inst. Endocrinology Romanian Acad. Sci., Bucharest, 1958-66; research fellow dept. anatomy UCLA, 1966-67; faculty U. Calif.-Irvine, 1967-83, asst. prof. dept. physiology, 1971-78, assoc. researcher, 1978-79, assoc. clin. prof., 1979-83; v.p. Resonance Motors, Inc., Monrovia, Calif., 1972-85; pres. Neurometrics, Inc., Irvine, Calif., 1978-82; pres. Lasergraphics Inc., Irvine, 1982-84, chmn., chief exec. officer, 1984—. Mem. com. on hon. degrees U. Calif.-Irvine, 1970-72. Postdoctoral fellow UCLA, 1966. Mem. Internat. Platform Assn., Am. Physiol. Soc., IEEE (sr.). Republican. Contbr. articles to profl. jours. Patentee in field. Home: 20 Palmento Way Irvine CA 92612-2109 Office: 20 Ada Irvine CA 92618-2303

DEMETRIOS, MICHAEL B., wildlife theme park director. Pres. Marine World-Africa U.S.A., Vallejo, Calif. Office: Marine World-Africa USA 2001 Marine World Pky Vallejo CA 94589-4002

DEMICHELE, BARBARA JOAN, public relations executive; b. Phoenix, Sept. 28, 1953; d. Glenn Vernon and Diana Jean (Warford) Stanley; m. O. Mark DeMichele, May 22, 1982; 1 child, Angela Marie. BA, U. Ariz., 1975. Editor Tombstone (Ariz.) Epitaph, 1974-75; reporter Herald Dispatch, Sierra Vista, Ariz., 1975-76; cmty. rels. Caithness Corp., Tucson, 1976-78; writer Ariz. Pub. Svc. Co., Phoenix, 1978-79; pub. rels. officer Valley Nat. Bank, Phoenix, 1979-81, United Bank of Ariz., Phoenix, 1981-83; pres. B.J. Comms., Inc., Phoenix, 1984—. Chmn. Phoenix/Valley of the Sun Visitors and Conv. Bur., 1994-95; dir. Herberger Theater Ctr., Phoneix, 1994—; chmn. Phoenix Little Theater Co., 1985-86; bd. dirs. Phoenix Symphony, 1988-94; chmn. Symphony Ball, 1987, Herberger Headlines, 1995. Recipient Humanitarian award Multiple Sclerosis Soc., 1995, Visionary award Valley Leadership, 1996. Mem. Pub. Rels. Soc. Am., Phoenix C. of C. (vice chmn. 1994—). Republican. Episcopal. Office: BJ Comms Inc 3101 N Central Ave Ste 870 Phoenix AZ 85012-2640

DEMILLE, LESLIE BENJAMIN, artist; b. Hamilton, Ont., Can., Apr. 24, 1927; came to U.S., 1958; s. Warren Clarence and Nora Lillian (Connor) DeM.; m. H. Isobel Don, Sept. 6, 1947; children: Dianne Lynne, Leslie Dane, Malcolm Don, Richard Ian, Mark Cameron. Student, Art Students League, N.Y.C., 1945-47. Tchr. portraiture, 1960—. Portraits commd. by numerous people and orgns., including Pres. Richard M. Nixon and Pres. Ronald Reagan; bronze sculptures including "Peacemakers" presented to Pres. Reagan, 1988, now on permanent exhibit at Reagan Libr., Simi, Calif.; painter protraits of Arnold Palmer, Jack Nicklaus, others; monumental bronze sculpture of 3 Native Am. Indians, Sedona, Ariz., 1991, Sam Snead, Phoenix Open Superbowl XXX Charity Cup. Home and Studio: 50 Cathedral Ln Sedona AZ 86336

DEMING, ROBERT JACKSON, mayor; b. Turner, Mont., Jan. 29, 1930; m. Lorraine Deming; children: Richard, Gregory P., Lisa Gaye. BS in Edn., Mont. State U., 1952; MS in Edn., Utah State U., 1966. Tchr. grades 1-8 Cole Sch., Rural Blaine County, Mont., 1948-49; tchr., coach football, basketball and track Laurel (Mont.) Pub. Schs., 1955-59; counselor, coach football, basketball and track Laurel Jr. H.S., 1959-66, prin., coach basketball and track, 1966-69; prin., sch. for blind Montana Sch. for Deaf and Blind, 1969-72, prin., 1972-78, asst. supt., 1978-81, supt., 1981-92; devel. dir. U. Great Falls, Mont., 1987-92, McLaughlin Rsch., 1992; commr. City of Great Falls, 1990-92, elected mayor, 1996—; extension prof. Ea. Mont. Coll., 1973—; asst. dir. Mont. Assn. Blind summer program at Mont. State U., Bozeman, 1970; participant numerous workshops, confs., convs. and seminars in field of edn. of blind and deaf; cons. in field Tripod, Colorado Springs, E.S.E.A., Billings, Title III, Napa, Idaho, Reading Coun., Billings, Ski-Hi, Logan, Utah, Project Vision-Up, Boise, Idaho, Sch. for Deaf, Casper, Wyo. Interpreted news (TV program) Today in Montana, KRTV, Great Falls, for 6 yrs. Ch. coun. pres. Am. Luth. Ch., Laurel; pres. Parent-Tchrs.-Houseparents, Inc., Great Falls. With U.S. Army Counter-Intelligence Corps, 1952-55. Recipient Man of Yr. award, 1975, Bahai of Great Falls, Disting. Alumni award, Ea. Mont. Coll., 1984. Mem NEA, Mont. Edn. Assn., Am. Assn. Instrs. of the Blind, Am. Assn. Workers for the Blind, Conv. Am. Instrs. of the Deaf, Coun. for Exceptional Children (state pres. 1975-76), Mont. Speech, Lang. and Hearing Assn., Internat. Assn. Parents of the Deaf, Mont. Assn. Registry of Interpreters for Deaf, Great Falls C. of C., Great Falls Lions Club, Optimists, Rotary, Jaycees, Am. Legion, Great Falls Quarterbacks Club (pres. 1977-79), Phi Delta Kappa. Office: Office of Mayor PO Box 5021 Great Falls MT 59401

DEMMER, RICHARD JAMES, biologist; b. Madison, Wis., Mar. 19, 1949; s. Lawrence Frederick and Caroline Laura (Erdman) D.; m. Gay Louise Zerwer, Sept. 4, 1981. BS in Biology, U. Ctrl. Fla., 1976, MS in Biology, 1981; MS in Forest and Range Mgmt., Wash. State U., 1984. Dist. naturalist Fla. Dept. Natural Resources, Orlando, 1978-80; tech. illustrator Advanced Rsch. and Devel., Miami, Fla., 1981-82; interpretive naturalist Jewel Cave Nat. Monument Nat. Park Svc., 1982; drafter Tech. Staff Inc., Seattle, 1984-88; biologist Dept. Interior Bur. Land Mgmt., Prineville, Oreg., 1988—. Author: (poetry) Desert Light, 1995, National Library of Poetry, 1996. With U.S. Army, 1969-71. Mem. Soc. NW Vertebrate Biology, Pacific NW Amphibian and Reptile Consortium, Oreg. Natural Desert Assn., Xi Sigma Pi. Home: PO Box 388 Redmond OR 97756 Office: Bur Land Mgmt Dept Interior PO Box 550 Prineville OR 97754

DEMOFF, MARVIN ALAN, lawyer; b. L.A., Oct. 28, 1942; s. Max and Mildred (Tweer) D.; m. Patricia Caryn Abelov, June 16, 1968; children: Allison Leigh, Kevin Andrew. BA, UCLA, 1964; JD, Loyola U., L.A., 1967. Bar: Calif. 1969. Asst. pub. defender Los Angeles County, 1968-72; ptnr. Steinberg & Demoff, L.A., 1973-83, Craighill, Fentress & Demoff, L.A. and Washington, 1983-86; of counsel Mitchell, Silberberg & Knupp, L.A., 1987—. Mem. citizens adv. bd. Olympic Organizing Com., L.A., 1982-84; bd. trustees Curtis Sch., L.A., 1985-94, chmn. bd. trustees, 1988-93; sports adv. bd. Constitution Rights Found., L.A., 1986—; bd. dirs. 4A Found., 1988—. Mem. ABA (mem. forum com. on entertainment and sports), Calif. Bar Assn., UCLA Alumni Assn., Phi Delta Phi. Office: Mitchell Silberberg Knupp Los Angeles CA 90064

DEMOREST, MARGARET ORAHOOD, humanities educator; b. Burdett, Kans., May 30, 1916; d. Fred Marvin Wynett and Louisa Belle (Allen) Orahood; m. Albert Louis Demorest, Oct. 28, 1938; children: Janet Lee, David Louis. BA in English, U. Mont., 1937; MA in English, U. Wyo.; postgrad., Boston U., 1973, Princeton U., 1983. Tchr. English, music, drama Judith Gap (Mont.) H.S., 1937-39, Jackson (Wyo.)-Wilson H.S., 1943, 56-57; tchr., head English dept. Star Valley H.S., Afton, Wyo., 1947-55; instr. English, humanities, honors program Casper (Wyo.) Coll., 1959-85, cons. spl. programs, 1985-86, mem. humanities com., 1986—; cons. editor Rocky Mountain MLA, Boise, presenter, panel chairwoman, 1975-85. Author: Name in the Window, 1996; contbr. poetry and essays to popular mags. Guest mem. Salt Lake Tabernacle Choir, Salt Lake City, 1935-38; organist Chapel of Transfiguration, Moose, Wyo., 1953-57; actress John Stark's Theatre from New York, Jackson, summer 1956. Ann. Margaret Demorest Lectr. in Humanities named in her honor Casper Coll., 1986—. Episcopalian. Home: 3760 Carmel Ave Casper WY 82604

DEMPSEY, BARBARA MATTHEA, medical, surgical and critical care nurse; b. The Netherlands, July 27, 1943; d. Petrus Antonius and Hendrika Petronella (Kemp) Petersen; m. James D. Dempsey, June 13, 1981; children: Jennifer, Daniel. AA, Santa Monica (Calif.) Coll., 1970; cert. lactation educator, UCLA, 1982; BSN, Sonoma State U., 1997—. Staff nurse med./surg. Santa Monica Hosp., 1967-72; surg. intensive care nurse VA Wadsworth Hosp., L.A., 1973-77; staff nurse med./surg. Community Hosp., Santa Rosa, Calif., 1988-90; staff nurse Redwood Nurses Registry, Santa Rosa, 1990-93, Norrell Healthcare, Santa Rosa, Calif., 1990-93; charge nurse Creekside Convalescent Hosp., 1994.

DEMPSEY, DAVID A., company official, small business owner; b. Eglin AFB, Fla., Sept. 5, 1957; s. David Leroy and Marguerite (Thomas) D.; m. Debra Kay Gross, Jan. 22, 1982; children: Nakia, Elisabeth, David. AS in Restaurant Mgmt., C.C. of Air Force, Maxwell AFB, Ala., 1987, AS in Contracts Mgmt., 1989; BS in Logistics Sys. Mgmt., Colo. Tech. U., 1995. Postal asst. U.S. Postal Svc., Wilmington, Del., 1974-75; enlisted man USAF, 1975, advanced through grades to master sgt.; ret., 1995; sr. subcontract adminstr. TRW, Inc., Colorado Springs, Colo., 1995—. Pres. bldg. accountability com. Evans Elem. Sch., Colorado Springs, 1993—; coord. D-Day, Share Colo., Ctrl. United Meth. Ch., Colorado Springs, 1993—, also Sunday sch. tchr.; candidate for sch. bd. dirs. Falcon Sch. Dist.. 49, Colorado Springs, 1995, 96, mem. long range planning com., 1996—; mem. planning and design com. Sand Creek H.S., Colorado Springs, 1995—; mem. sch. fee adv. com. El Paso County Bd. Commrs., Colorado Springs, 1996—; precinct capt. El Paso County Dem. Com., 1996-97. Mem. Nat. Contract Mgmt. Assn. (publicity chmn. 1996—), Noncommd. Officers Assn. (chmn. 1995), Ret. Enlisted Assn., Toastmasters (v.p. 1994-95, pres. 1995).

DENARDO, GERALD LOUIS, academic director; b. Aug. 24, 1932. BA in Medicine, U. Calif., Berkeley, 1954; MD in Medicine, U. Calif., San Francisco, 1957. Diplomate Am. Bd. Internal Medicine, Am. Bd. Nuclear Medicine. Intern Letterman Gen. Hosp., San Francisco, 1957-58; resident in internal medicine William Beaumont Gen. Hosp., El Paso, Tex., 1958-60, chief resident, 1960-61, fellow in radioisotope-endocrinology svc., 1960-61; dir. Fitzsimmons Gen. Hosp., Denver, 1961-65, VA Hosp., Palo Alto, Calif., 1965-67; mem. staff Stanford U. Med. Ctr., 1967-70; from assoc. prof. to prof. vet. medicine U. Calif., Davis, 1970-85, mem. prof. staff, 1982-87, dir. sch. medicine, 1987—; cons. Letterman Army Med. Ctr., 1985—, HHS, FDA, 1986-89, Dept. Energy, 1987-89; v.p. Am. bd. Nuclear Medicine, 1979-80. Contbr. articles to profl. jours.; patentee in field. Mem. AAAS, AMA, Am. Fedn. Clin. Rsch., Am. Heart Assn. (coun. cardiovascular radiology), Am. Coll. Nuclear Physicians (pres. 1975-76), Nat. Soc. Nuclear Medicine (Berson Yalow award 1978, 84), Calif. Med. Assn., Western Regional Soc. Nuclear Medicine (Disting. Scientist award 1992), Soc. Nuclear Medicine (pres. 1969-71, 81-82), Soc. Biol. Therapy, Alpha Sigma Nu. Home: 1508 Alhambra Blvd # 214 Sacramento CA 95816-6510

DENAVIT, JACQUES, retired physicist; b. Paris, Oct. 1, 1930; came to U.S., 1952; s. Georges and Marie (Arnould) D.; m. Catherine Dahlinger, Aug. 6, 1954; children: George, Paul, Mary. Degree in Gen. Math./Physics, U. Paris, 1952; MSEE, Northwestern U., 1953, PhD in Mech. Engring., 1956. Asst. prof. Northwestern U., Evanston, Ill., 1958-61, assoc. prof., 1961-66, prof. mech. and nuclear engring., 1966-82; rsch. physicist plasma physics divsn. Naval Rsch. Lab., Washington, 1969-71; rsch. physicist Lawrence Livermore Nat. Lab., Livermore, Calif., 1982-93. Author: (with R.S. Hartenberg) Kinematic Synthesis of Linkages, 1964; contbr. numerous articles on plasma physics and computer simulation to profl. jours. Fellow Am. Phys. Soc. Home: 3536 Gresham Ct Pleasanton CA 94588

DENEA, MICHAEL PHILIP, lawyer, minister of music; b. Gowanda, N.Y., Apr. 15, 1964; s. Richard Arthur and Deanna Jean (Silleman) D. B in Music, Oberlin Coll., 1986; JD, Case Western Reserve U., 1989. Bar: Pa. 1990, Ariz. 1993. Gen. counsel Ariz. Automobile Dealers Assn., Phoenix, 1992—. Rep. first v.p., Dist. 15; mem. C. of C. Tax Policy Com. Mem. Am. Soc. Assn. Execs., Ariz. Assn. Industries, Ariz. Bar Assn., Phoenix Symphony Coun. Office: Ariz Auto Dealers Assn 4701 N 24th St # B-3 Phoenix AZ 85016-4851

DENG, SHENGLIANG, marketing educator; b. Wuhan, China, Aug. 1, 1954; came to U.S. 1982; s. Yaohua and Meizheng (Feng) D.; m. Huidi Wang, Feb. 15, 1991; 1 child, Arlinda Jie. BA in Fgn. Lit. with high honors, Huazhong U. Sci. and Tech., Wuhan, China, 1981; MBA, Boston U., 1983, D in Bus. Adminstrn. in Internat. Mktg., 1987. Asst. prof. mktg. and internat. bus. Coll. Bus. and Mgmt. Northeastern Ill. U., Chgo., 1986-89, chmn. mktg. dept., 1987-89; sr. lectr. mktg. and internat. bus. mktg. dept. U. Otago, Dunedin, New Zealand, 1988-89; assoc. prof. mktg. and internat. bus. Coll. Commerce U. Sask., Saskatoon, Can., 1990-93, prof. mkt. and internat. bus., 1993—; liaison, interpreter UN Mgmt. Tng. Ctr., Hubei, China, 1981; bus. cons. Clancy, Shulman & Assocs., Inc., Boston, 1984; rsch. asst. Grad. Sch. Mgmt., Boston U., 1983-86; invited guest prof. Xi'an Jiaotong U., People's Republic of China, Huazhong U. Sci. and Tech., Nankai U., People's Republic of China, Northeastern U., Ctrl. S. Univ. Tech., Hunan, China, Xian U. Sci. and Tech., People's Republic of China, Acad. Social Scis., Hunan, Yunnan Inst. Trade and Fin., Kumin, Yunnan, People's Republic of China; econ. advisor Wuhan City Govt., Benxi City Govt., Yunnan Provincial Govt., People's Republic of China; vis. prof. mktg. Sch. Mgmt., Boston U., 1996-97. Author: Information Searching and Supplier Selection in Import Purchasing from Developing Countries, 1987, Modern Comparative Management: Theory and Practices of Canada, China, United States and Japan, 1992, Modern Comparative Decision Making: Theory and Practices of Canada, China, United States and Japan, Modern Comparative Marketing: Theory and Practices of Canada, China, United States and Japan, 1992; co-author (with S. Xu and G. Zhang) Strategic Marketing Management, 1994, (with N. Li) A Dictionary of Marketing Science, 1994, (with Wei Tung) Principles of Marketing, 1995, (with Yuan Li) Competitive Strategies for Enterprises in Economic Transition, 1997, Marketing Management: Theory and Strategies, 1997; mem. editl. bd. Jour. Applied Mgmt. Studies, Jour. Small Bus. and Entrepreneurship, Jour. Chinese Mgmt. Issues, (in Chinese) Book Series of Bus. Mgmt., Book Series of Basic Econs. and Mgmt., Coll. Textbook Series on Econs. and Mgmt.; paper referee Jour. Internat. Consumer Mktg., Jour. Small Bus. and Entrepreneurship, Internat. Execs., Bus. Jour.; also monographs in field; contbr. articles, book revs. to profl. jours., chpts. to books. Mem. adv. bd. State Coun. People's Republic of China. Rsch. grantee Northeastern Ill. U., 1987, 88, U. Otago, New Zealand, 1989, U. Sask., 1990-95, Can. Ministry External Affairs, 1990, Social Scis. Humanities Rsch. Coun. Can., 1991, 93, China Young Scientists' Found., 1992, Can. Coun. Small Bus. and Entrepreneurship, 1992, Can. Internat. Devel. Agy., 1992, 93, 94, 95, Hong Kong Bank of Can., 1993, 94, 95, 96, UN Devel. Program, 1994, 95. Fellow Chinese Economists Soc., USA (v.p. 1993-96, paper reviewer, paper discussant, conf. divsn. chair 1993); mem. Acad. Mktg. Scis., Acad. Internat. Bus. (conf. paper reviewer 1990), Am. Decision Sci. Inst., Assn. Global Bus. (conf. paper reviewer 1993, discussant 1991, 94), Assn. Overseas Chinese Profs., USA, Chinese Cultural Soc. Sask., Overseas Chinese Scholars' Soc. Office: Univ Saskatchewan, 25 Campus Drive, Saskatoon, SK Canada S7N 5A7

DENHAM, RENA BELLE, lawyer, educator; b. Salina, Kans., Oct. 1956; d. Charles Morris and Alice Jane (Quandt) D. BA in Philosophy with honors, Mills Coll., Oakland, Calif., 1977; MA in Philosophy, U. Pa., 1979; JD, U. San Francisco, 1982. Bar: Calif. 1982, U.S. Dist. Ct. (No. Dist.) Calif. 1983, U.S. Ct. Appeals (9th cir.). Assoc. Burnhill, Morehouse, Burford, Schofield & Blunden, Walnut Creek, Calif., 1984-85, Daniel B. Schick, Walnut Creek, Calif., 1985-90; pvt. practice civil litigation Concord, Calif., 1991-92; ptnr. Mullin & Denham, Concord, Calif., 1992-93; pvt. practice Oakland, Calif., 1993-95; instr. legal asst. studies Truckee Meadows C.C., Reno, Nev., 1995—; part-time instr. paralegal studies Calif. State U., Hayward, 1985-95; instr. bus. law Diablo Valley Coll., Pleasant Hill, Calif., 1984-85. Mem. Univ. and Cmty. Coll. Sys. of Nev. (mem. Status of Women com.), Sierra Nev. Celtic Soc. Office: Truckee Meadows CC 700 Dandini Blvd M-75 Reno NV 89512

DENIOUS, JON PARKS, publishing executive; b. Buffalo, Apr. 5, 1939; s. Wilbur Franklin Jr. and Nancy (Parks) D.; m. Sharon Marie Fee, June 17, 1963; children: Timothy, Elizabeth. Owner Durango (Colo.) Printing and Graphics, 1985-90; publ. Silverton Standard and The Miner, Colo., 1990—. Mem. Nat. Newspaper Assn., Colo. Press Assn. Office: The Silverton Standard The Miner 1257 Greene St Silverton CO 81433

DENIOUS, SHARON MARIE, publisher; b. Rulo, Nebr., Jan. 27, 1941; d. Thomas Wayne and Alma (Murphy) Fee; m. Jon Parks Denious, June 17, 1963; children: Timothy Scot, Elizabeth Denious Cessna. Grad. high sch. Operator N.W. Pipeline co., Ignacio, Colo., 1975-90; pub. The Silverton Standard & The Miner, Colo., 1990—. Mem. Colo. Press Assn., Nat. Newspaper Assn. Office: The Silverton Standard The Miner 1257 Greene St Silverton CO 81433

DENISON, MICHAEL STEVEN, education educator; b. Shirley, Mass., Dec. 8, 1954; s. Alan Everet and Alma Rose D.; m. Grace Lynn Bedoian, Aug. 30, 1991. AA with hons., County Coll. of Morris, 1975; MS in Marine Biology magna cum laude, St. Francis Coll., 1977; MS in Animal Physiology, Miss. State U., 1980; PhD in Environ. Toxicology, Cornell U., 1983. Asst. prof. dept. biochemistry Mich. State U., East Lansing, 1988-92; asst. prof. dept. environ. toxicology U. Calif., Davis, 1992-94, assoc. prof. environ. toxicology, 1994—; adj. asst. prof. Pesticide Rsch. Ctr. Mich. State U., 1990-93, dept. biochemistry; postdoct. rsch. Hosp. for sick Children, Toronto, 1983-85, Stanford (Calif.) U., 1985-88; numerous faculty coms.; participant scientific rev. panel, Washington, 1992; invited lectr. seminars in field. Editorial bd. mem. Molecular Toxicology jour., 1991, Biochem. Toxicology, 1991—, European Jour. of Pharmacology, 1991—; referee numerous jours. in field; contbr. articles to profl. jours. Mem. Am. Soc. Biochemistry and Molecular Biology, Soc. Toxicology, Internat. Soc. Study of Xenobiotics, Am. Soc. Microbiology. Office: Univ Calif Dept Environ Toxicology Meyer Hall Davis CA 95616

DENISON, WILLIAM CLARK, mycologist, educator; b. Rochester, N.Y., June 1, 1928; s. Glenn M. and Rhoda T. (Torrance) D.; m. Margaret R. Mellinger, Sept. 11, 1948; children: Robert Ford, Thomas C., Glenn T., Rebecca S. Denison Johnston. BA, Oberlin (Ohio) Coll., 1950, MA, 1952; PhD, Cornell U., 1956. Apprentice millwright Eastman Kodak Co., Rochester, 1944-46; co-dir. Kanawauke Regional Mus., Bear Mtn. (N.Y.) Park, summer 1947; preparator Dept. Preserved Materials Gen. Biol. Supply House, Chgo., 1948-49; teaching asst. Dept. of Botany Oberlin Coll., 1950-52; teaching asst. Dept. of Plant Pathology Cornell U., 1952-55; asst. prof. Dept. of Biology Swarthmore (Pa.) Coll., 1955-66; assoc. prof. Dept. of Botany & Plant Pathology Oreg. State U., Corvallis, 1966-93, curator, 1966-93, assoc. prof. emeritus, 1993—; vis. asst. prof. Dept. of Botany U. N.C., Chapel Hill, 1958-59; pres., sr. scientist Northwest Mycological Cons., Inc., Corvallis, 1985—; rsch. in field. Contbr. articles to numerous profl. jours. Co-organizer, counselor Corvallis Draft Info. Ctr., 1968-72; chmn. North Benton County Citizen's Adv. Com., 1974-78; charter mem., firefighter Adair Rural Fire Protection Dept., Adair Village, Oreg., 1975-83; foster parent Children's Svcs. Div. Oreg. Dept. HHS, 1976-79; citizen mem. representing Benton County Benton Govt. Com., 1978-80; pres. Friends of Benton County, 1978-88; founding mem. First Alternative Coop., Corvallis; bd. dirs. Willamette Inst. Biol. Control. Grantee NSF, Am. Philos. Assn. Mem. Internat. Lichenological Assn., AAUP, AAAS, Mycological Soc. Am., Oreg. Natural Resources Coun., Oreg. Pub. Employee Union (assoc.). Home: 37043 Beldon Creek Rd Corvallis OR 97330-9358 Office: Oreg State Univ Dept Botany Corvallis OR 97331

DENKE, PAUL HERMAN, aircraft engineer; b. San Francisco, Feb. 7, 1916; s. Edmund Herman and Ella Hermine (Riehl) D.; m. Beryl Ann Lincoln, Feb. 10, 1940; children: Karen Denke Mottaz, Claudia Denke Tesche, Marilyn Denke Dunn. BCE, U. Calif.-Berkeley, 1937, MCE, 1939. Registered profl. engr., Calif. Stress engr. Douglas Aircraft Co., Santa Monica, Calif., 1940-62, mgr. structural mechanics Long Beach, Calif., 1962-65, chief sci. computing, 1965-71, chief structures engr. methods and devel., 1972-78, chief scientist structural mechanics, 1979-84, staff mgr. MDC fellow, 1985—; mem. faculty dept. engring. UCLA, 1941-50. Assoc. fellow AIAA; mem. Soc. Automotive Engrs. (Arch T. Colwell Merit award 1966, IAE Outstanding Engr. Merit award 1985), Sigma Xi, Chi Epsilon, Tau Beta Pi. Democrat. Pioneered and developed finite element method of structural analysis; author numerous technical papers. Home: 1800 Via Estudillo Palos Verdes Peninsula CA 90274-1908

DENKLER, KEITH ALAN, surgeon; b. Alton, Ill., Dec. 25, 1954. MD, Baylor U., 1979. Intern St. Joseph Hosp., Houston, 1979-80, surgeon, 1981-84, plastic surgeon, 1985-87; hand surgeon U. Calif., San Francisco, 1984-85; cranial surgeon Dr. Paul Tessier, Paris, 1987-88; now surgeon Marin Gen. Hosp., Greenbrae, Calif. Office: 275 Magnolia Ave Larkspur CA 94939*

DENNERY, PHYLLIS ARMELLE, pediatrician, educator; b. Port au Prince, Haiti, June 5, 1958; came to U.S., 1980; d. Jean-Maurice and Mona (Leroy) D.; m. Gregory Lyman Mundy, Aug. 8, 1987; children: Ariana Lillian, Miles Alexander. BS in Biology, McGill U., Montreal, Quebec, Can., 1980; MD, Howard U., 1984. Diplomate Am. Bd. Pediatrics with subspecialty in neonatology. Resident in pediatrics Children's Hosp., Washington, 1984-87; postdoctoral fellowship Case Western Reserve U., Cleve., 1987-90; asst. prof. pediatrics Stanford U., Palo Alto, Calif., 1990—. Author: (book chpt.) Workbook of Practical Neonatology, 1992, Neonatal Management of Hemolytic Hyperbilirubinemia in Diseases of the Fetus and Newborn: Genetics, Pathology, Imaging & Management, 1994. Health adv. bd. NAACP, Santa Clara chpt., 1994. Recipient Michael Oliver Dumas prize Alpha Omega Alpha, 1984, Janet Glascow award AMA, 1984, Drew-Syphax prize in Surgery, Howard U., 1984; Andrew W. Mellon fellow Mellon Found., 1992, 93. Mem. Am. Thoracic Soc. (membership com. 1990—, sci. com. 1993—, nominating com. 1994, chair membership com. 1995), Nat. Med. Assn., Western Soc. for Pediatric Rsch. (Ross Young Investigator award 1997), Soc. for Perinatal Rsch., Oxygen Soc., Alpha Omega Alpha. Roman Catholic. Office: Stanford U Sch of Medicine 750 Welch Rd Ste 315 Palo Alto CA 94304-1510

DENNEY, DORIS ELAINE, pharmacist; b. Norwalk, Conn., Sept. 5, 1940; d. Harry Taylor and Mary Matilda (Lobeda) D. BS in Pharmacy, U. Conn., 1962; MBA, Boise State U., 1990. Registered pharmacist, Conn., Idaho, Mass. Retail pharmacist Gilbert Pharmacy, Noroton Heights, Conn., 1963-64; sr. pharmacist Children's Hosp. Med. Ctr., Boston, 1964-68; pharmacist Project Hope, Colombia, 1968-70; adminstrv. intern Denver Gen. Hosp., 1972; dir. pharmacy svcs. Terry Reilly Health Svcs., Nampa, Idaho, 1973—; cons. (Bolivia) Mgmt. Scis. for Health, Cambridge, Mass., 1976. Bd. dirs. Payada drug abuse orgn., Boise, 1983-88, Arts for Idaho, 1995—, v.p., 1996-97; mem. health adv. com. Idaho State U., Boise, 1988-89; bd. dirs., mem. Boise Master Chorale, pres., 1992-94. Named Preceptor of Yr. Syntex Labs., 1987; recipient McKesson Leadership award McKesson-Robbins, 1987, Pharmacy Leadership award Nat. Assn. Retail Druggists, 1987. Mem. Idaho State Pharm. Assn. (pres. 1987-88), Am. Pharm. Assn., Am. Pub. Health Assn. (cons. 1978), Am. Soc. of Hosp. Pharmacists, Boise City Arts Commn., Lambda Kappa Sigma. Democrat. Lutheran. Home: 1519 N 19th St Boise ID 83702-0702 Office: Terry Reilly Health Svcs 223 16th Ave N Nampa ID 83687-4058

DENNIE, JANICE LYNN See REED, JANICE LYNN

DENNING, MICHAEL MARION, computer company executive; b. Durant, Okla., Dec. 22, 1943; s. Samuel M. and Lula Mae (Waitman) D.; m. Suzette Karin Wallance, Aug. 10, 1968 (div. 1979); children: Lila Monique, Tanya Kerstin, Charlton Derek; m. Donna Jean Hamel, Sept. 28, 1985; children: Caitlin Shannon, Meghan O'Donnell. Student, USAF Acad., 1963; BS, U. Tex., 1966, Fairleigh Dickinson U., 1971; MS, Columbia U., 1973. Mgr. systems IBM, White Plains, N.Y., 1978-79; mgr. svc. and mktg. IBM, San Jose, Calif., 1979-81; nat. market support mgr. Memorex Corp., Santa Clara, Calif., 1979-81, v.p. mktg., 1981-82; v.p. mktg. and sales Icot Corp., Mountain View, Calif., 1982-83; exec. v.p. Phase Info. Machines Corp., Scottsdale, Ariz., 1983-84, Tricom Automotive Dealer Systems Inc., Hayward, Calif., 1985-87; pres. ADS Computer Svcs., Inc., Toronto, Ont., Can., 1985-87, Denning Investments, Inc., Palo Alto, Calif., 1987—, Pers. Solutions Group, Inc., Menlo Park, Calif., 1990—. With USAF, 1962-66; Vietnam. Mem. Rotary, English Speaking Union, Phi Beta Kappa, Lambda Chi Alpha (pres. 1965-66). Republican. Methodist. Home and Office: 9144 N 69th St Paradise Valley AZ 85253 Office: Denning Investments Inc 222 Front St Fl 7 San Francisco CA 94111-4403

DENNIS, DAVID TAPPEN, epidemiologist; b. Portland, Oreg., Mar. 31, 1939; s. Walter James and Louise Aline (Labbe) D.; m. Elizabeth Alison Jones, Dec. 27, 1969; 1 child, Sutinah Louise. AB, Whitman Coll., 1961; MD, Cornell U., 1965; Diploma Clin. Medicine of Tropics, U. London, 1970; MPH, Harvard U., 1974. Diplomate Am. Coll. Preventive Medicine.

Fellow infectious diseases N.Y. Hosp., Cornell U., N.Y.C., 1969-70; commd. 2d lt. USN, 1970, advanced through grades to capt., 1979; med. officer in charge provincial health assistance team USN, Quang Tri, Vietnam, 1970-71; med. officer in charge US Naval Med. Rsch. Detachment USN, Addis Ababa, Ethiopia, 1971-73; officer in charge US Naval Med. Rsch. Unit USN, Jakarta, Indonesia, 1974-79; ret. USN, 1979; head rsch. and tng. team in tropical diseases Fed. Ctrs. for Disease Control & Prevention, Kuala Lumpur, Malaysia, 1979-83; state epidemiologist, chief bur. disease control Fed. Ctrs. for Disease Control & Prevention, Concord, N.H., 1983-87; med. epidemiologist Fed. Ctrs. for Disease Control & Prevention, Harrisburg, Pa., 1987-90; chief bacterial zoonosis branch Fed. Ctrs for Disease Control and Prevention, Fort Collins, Colo., 1990—; cons. WHO, Geneva, India, Brazil, 1985-92, CDC, Bahrain, 1985, Sudan, 1985, United Arab Emirates, Saudia Arabia, 1986-87, India, 1994. Contbr. over 70 articles to profl. jours., chpts. to books. Office: Ctrs for Disease Control PO Box 2087 Fort Collins CO 80522-2087

DENNIS, KAREN MARIE, plastic surgeon; b. Cleve., Dec. 23, 1948; d. Chester and Adele (Wesley) D.; m. Miles Auslander, June 21, 1974; 1 child, Kristin. BS, Ohio State U., 1971, MD, 1974. Diplomate Am. Bd. Plastic Surgery, Am. Bd. Otolaryngology. Intern Kaiser Permanente, L.A., 1974-75; resident in otolaryngology Roosevelt Hosp., N.Y.C., 1976-79; resident in plastic surgery Ohio State Univ. Hosps., Columbus, 1979-81; pvt. practice Beverly Hills, Calif., 1981—. Mem. Am. Soc. Reconstructive and Plastic Surgeons, Calif. County Med. Assn., L.A. County med. Assn., L.A. Soc. Plastic Srugeons (sec. 1993-94), Phi Beta Kappa. Office: 433 N Camden Dr Beverly Hills CA 90210-4426

DENNISON, GEORGE MARSHEL, academic administrator; b. Buffalo, Ill., Aug. 11, 1935; s. Earl Fredrick and Irene Gladys (McWhorter) D.; m. Jane Irene Schroeder, Dec. 26, 1954; children: Robert Gene, Rick Steven. AA, Custer County (Mont.) Jr. Coll., 1960; BA, U. Mont., 1962, MA, 1963; PhD, U. Wash., 1967. Asst. prof. U. Ark., Fayetteville, 1967-68; vis. asst. prof. U. Wash., Seattle, 1968-69; asst. prof. Colo. State U., Fort Collins, 1969-73, assoc. prof., 1973-77, assoc. dean Coll. Arts, Humanities and Social Sci., 1976-80, prof., 1977-87, acting acad. v.p., 1980-82, acting assoc. acad. v.p., 1982-86, assoc. acad. v.p., 1987; provost, v.p. acad. affairs Western Mich. U., Kalamazoo, 1987-90; pres. U. Mont., Missoula, 1990—; cons. U.S. Dept. Justice, 1976-84; bd. Community Med. Ctr, Missoula, 1st Bank, Missoula, Inst. Medicine and Humanities, Missoula. Author: The Dorr War, 1976; contbr. articles to jours. in field. Bd. dirs. Kalamazoo Ctr. for Med. Studies, 1989-90. With USN, 1953-57. ABA grantee, 1969-70; Colo. State U. grantee, 1970-75, Nat. Trust for Hist. Preservation grantee, 1976-78; U.S. Agy. for Internat. Devel. grantee, 1979—; Colo. Commn. on Higher Edn. devel. grantee, 1985. Mem. Am. Hist. Assn., Orgn. Am. Historians, Am. Assn. Higher Edn., Am. Soc. for Legal History. Office: U Montana Office of The Pres Univ Hall Rm 109 Missoula MT 59812*

DENNISON, JOHN ROBERT, physicist, educator; b. Madison, Wis., Oct. 22, 1957; s. John Manley Dennison and Wilma Kay Bailey; m. Marian Roberta Campbell, June 21, 1986; children: James Arlo, Sarah Samantha. BS in Physics, Appalachian State U., 1979; MS in Physics, Va. Tech., 1983, PhD in Physics, 1985. Teaching asst. to rsch. asst. Va. Tech. U., Blacksburg, 1980-85; rsch. assoc. U. Mo., Columbia, 1985-88; asst. prof. Utah State U., Logan, 1988-94, assoc. prof., 1994—; rsch. collaborator Brookhaven Nat. Lab., Upton, N.Y., 1985—; cons. Varian/Elamar, Salt Lake City, 1988-89, Thiohol Corp., Brigham City, Utah, 1991-92, Mathsoft, Inc., Cambridge, Mass., 1995—, K'Nex, Inc., Boston, 1995-96. Grantee Petroleum Rsch. Fund, 1991-93, NSF, 1991, NASA, 1995—, Dept. of Energy, 1995, Dept. Edn., 1995-96, AFOSR, 1995-96, Utah Higher Edn. Technology Initiative, 1995-97. Mem. Am. Assn. Physics Tchrs., Am. Physical Soc., Soc. Physics Students, Sigma Pi Sigma, Phi Kappa Phi. Presbyn. Office: Utah State U Physics Dept Logan UT 84322-4415

DENNISON, RONALD WALTON, engineer; b. San Francisco, Oct. 23, 1944; s. S. Mason and Elizabeth Louise (Hatcher) D.; children: Ronald, Frederick. BS in Physics and Math., San Jose State U., 1970, MS in Physics, 1972. Physicist, Memorex, Santa Clara, Calif., 1970-71; sr. engr. AVCO, San Jose, Calif., 1972-73; advanced devel. engr. Perkin Elmer, Palo Alto, Calif., 1973-75; staff engr. Hewlett-Packard, Santa Rosa, Calif., 1975-79; program gen. mgr. Burroughs, Westlake Village, Calif., 1979-82; dir. engring., founder EIKON, Simi Valley, Calif., 1982-85; sr. staff technologist Maxtor Corp., San Jose, 1987-90; dir. engring. Toshiba Am. Info. Systems, 1990-93, cons. engr., 1994—; materials. Author tech. publs. Served to sgt. USAF, 1963-67. Mem. IEEE, Am. Vacuum Soc., Internat. Soc. Hybrid Microelectronics, Internat. Disk Drive Equipment and Materials Assn. Republican. Methodist. Mem. Aircraft Owners and Pilots Assn., Internat. Comanche Soc. Home: 2217 Yosemite Dr Milpitas CA 95035-6649

DENNISTON, DOUGLAS, artist, educator; b. Cornwall-on-Hudson, N.Y., Nov. 19, 1921; s. Jesse and Edith (Buchenberger) D.; Patricia Davidson, Oct. 29, 1945; children: Denise, Abigail, Joshua. Two-year cert. Richmond Profl. Inst., Coll. William and Mary, 1942; BFA, U. N.Mex., 1945, MA, 1948. Instr. U. N.Mex., 1947-48, Tex. Western Coll., El Paso, summer 1949, Colo. Women's Coll., Denver, 1948-59; prof. U. Ariz., Tucson, 1959-83, prof. emeritus, 1983—; instr. U. Nev., Reno, summer 1967. Illustrator: Edward Hopper: an Appreciation, 1963, Calendar: A Cycle of Poems (Richard Shelton), 1972; one-man shows include N.Mex. State Mus., Santa Fe, 1946, Acad. Arts, Flint, Mich., 1953, Denver Art Mus., 1954, La Galeria Escondida, Taos, N.Mex., 1954, 55, Johnson Art Gallery, Albuquerque, 1954, Ajo, Ariz., 1958, Colo. Women's Coll., Denver, 1959, Tucson Art Ctr., 1963, Dakota Art Gallery, Rapid City, S.D., 1977, Internat. Mus., McAllen, Tex., 1977, Coll. William and Mary, Williamsburg, Va., 1976, Fine Arts Ctr., Prescott, Ariz., 1986, Local 803 Gallery, Tucson, Ariz., 1995, others; group exhbns. include Va. Mus. Fine Arts, Richmond, 1943, N.Mex. State Fair, Albuquerque, 1944-47 (various prizes), Met. Mus. Art, N.Y.C., 1952, MOMA, N.Y.C., 1953, Denver Arts Mus., 1950, 52 (purchase prize), Denver Art Mus., 1951, 52, 54, 55, 56, 58, 61, 71, Joslyn Art Mus., Omaha, 1952, 54, Butler Art Inst., Youngstown, Ohio, 1954, San Francisco Art Mus., 1954, Tucson Art Ctr., 1961 (award), 66 (purchase), 67, 68, 69, 71, 72, 74, Mus. Fine Arts, Sante Fe, 1962, 76, Phoenix Art Mus., 1962, 69, 70, 73, Wollheim's Rosequist Galleries, Tucson, 1973, Ctrl. Art Collective, 1991, numerous others; represented in permanent collections Va. Mus. Fine Arts, Denver Art Mus., Gilpin County Arts Assn., Ctrl. City, Colo., Jonson Gallery, Albuquerque, Yuma Art Ctr., U. Ariz. Mus. Art, Tucson Airport. Home: 1844 N Vine Ave Tucson AZ 85719

DENNISTON, MARTHA KENT, business owner, author; b. Phila., Feb. 8, 1920; d. Samuel Leonard and Elizabeth (Cryer) Kent; m. Edward Shippen Willing, May 14, 1942 (div. 1972); children: Peter, Matthew, Thomas, Stephen; m. George C. Denniston, July 5, 1974. BA, Bryn Mawr (Pa.) Coll., 1941; MA, U. Wash., Seattle, 1965. Clinic dir. Population Dynamics, Seattle, 1973-84; pvt. practice investor, 1950—; resort owner Ecologic Pl., Port Townsend, Wash., 1972—; sec. bd. dirs. Population Inst., Washington, 1980-83, Ctr. for Population Communications, N.Y.C., 1983-86. Author: Beyond Conception, Our Children's Children, 1971, (poems) The Bladed Quiet, 1994. Bd. dirs. Population Action Coun., Washington, 1977-80. Mem. Nat. Soc. Colonial Dames Am., Am. Farmlands Trust, Sigma Xi. Home: 13030 12th Ave NW Seattle WA 98177-4109

DENNY, JAMES CLIFTON, tree farm administrator, forestry consultant; b. Palo Alto, Calif., Aug. 3, 1922; s. James Milton and Alma May (Siler) D.; m. Ann Elliott, Oct. 31, 1948; children: Christine, Stuart, James, Matthew, Katharine. BS, U. Calif., Berkeley, 1948. Registered profl. forester, Calif. Forest fire dispatcher Calif. Div. Forestry, Redding, 1948-50, asst. forest technician, 1950-53, forest technician, 1953-59, sr. forest techinician, 1959-62; asst. dep. state forester Calif. Div. Forestry, Sacramento, 1962-71, Santa Rosa, Calif., 1971-75; chief resource mgmt. Calif. Dept. Forestry, Sacramento, 1975-80; forestry cons., 1980—; bd. dirs., sec. Forest Landowners of Calif., Sacramento, 1989-96. 1st lt. USAF, 1942-46, ETO. Mem. Soc. Am. Foresters. Republican. Presbyterian. Home and Office: 8996 Ritts Mill Rd Shingletown CA 96088-9556

DENNY, JOHN LEIGHTON, JR., mathematics educator; b. Birmingham, Ala., Oct. 11, 1931; s. John Leighton and Miriam Marie (Starr) D.; m. Anne Temple Hood, Sept. 5, 1953. BA, Stanford U., 1953; PhD, U. Calif., 1962. Asst. prof. math. Ind. U., Bloomington, 1962-65, U. Calif., Riverside, 1965-67; assoc. prof. math. U. Ariz., Tucson, 1967-72, prof. math., 1972-93, head statistics dept., 1985-90, prof. math. emeritus, prof. radiology emeritus, 1994—. Editor: Section on Ergodic Theory and Probability, 1990-93; contbr. articles to profl. jours. With U.S. Army, 1954-56, Korea. Mem. Am. Statistical Assn. (vis. lectr. 1978-82), Optical Soc. Am.

DENT, ERNEST DUBOSE, JR., pathologist; b. Columbia, S.C., May 3, 1927; s. E. Dubose and Grace (Lee) D.; m. Dorothy McCalman, June 16, 1949; children: Christopher, Pamela; m. 2d, Karin Frehse, Sept. 6, 1970. Student, Presbyn. Coll., 1944-45; M.D., Med. Coll. S.C., 1949. Diplomate clin. pathology and pathology anatomy Am. Bd. Pathology. Intern U.S. Naval Hosp., Phila., 1949-50; resident pathology USPHS Hosp., Balt., 1950-54; chief pathology USPHS Hosp., Norfolk, Va., 1954-56; assoc. pathology Columbia (S.C.) Hosp., 1956-59; pathologist, dir. labs. Columbia Hosp., S.C. Baptist Hosp., 1958-69; with Straus Clin. Labs., L.A., 1969-72; staff pathologist Hollywood (Calif.) Community Hosp, St. Joseph Hosp., Burbank, Calif., 1969-72; dir. labs. Glendale Meml. Hosp. and Health Ctr., 1972-94; ret.; bd. dirs. Glendale Meml. Hosp. and Health Ctr. Author papers nat. med. jours. Mem. Am. Cancer Soc., AMA, L.A. County Med. Assn. (pres. Glendale dist. 1980-81), Calif. Med. Assn. (councillor 1984-90), Am. Soc. Clin. Pathology, Coll. Am. Pathologists (assemblyman S.C. 1965-67; mem. publs. com. bull. 1968-70), L.A. Soc. Pathologists (trustee 1984-87), L.A. Acad. Medicine, S.C. Soc. Pathologists (pres. 1967-69). Lutheran. Home: 1605 La Plaza Dr San Marcos CA 92069-4841 Office: S Central and Los Feliz Aves Glendale CA 91225-7036

DENTON, MICHAEL JOHN, research economist, electric utility expert, consultant; b. Kokomo, Ind., July 31, 1955; s. John Louis and Marguerite (Layden) D. BSE in Interdisciplinary Engring., Purdue U., 1977; MBA in Fin. and Internat. Bus., U. Chgo., 1981; MA in Econs., U. Ariz., 1994, PhD, 1997. Registered profl. engr., Ind. Mech. engr. Sargent & Lundy, Engrs., Chgo., 1977-80; field project engr. Amoco Oil Co., Chgo., 1980-83; sr. assoc. Theodore Barry & Assocs., L.A., 1983-85; mng. assoc. Metzler & Assocs., Deerfield, Ill., 1986-92; lectr., electric markets rschr. Econ. Sci. Lab. U. Ariz., Tucson, 1992-95; dir. econ. and tech. analysis Utilities Internat., Inc., Chgo., Ill., 1994—; exec. dir. M. Denton & Co., Tucson, 1992-95, prin. Power Procurement Group, 1997—; expert witness Pa. Pub. Utilities Commn., Phila., 1989. Bd. dirs. Cystic Fibrosis Found., Chgo., 1990-94. Mem. Nat. Assn. Bus. Economists, Am. Economists Assn., Acad. Mgmt., Econ. Sci. Assn. Home: 2216 E 5th St Tucson AZ 85719 Office: U Ariz Dept Econs McClelland Hall Rm 401 Tucson AZ 85721

DENTON, PATRY REDDING, artist, educator; b. Scottsbluff, Nev., July 20, 1943; d. Dale and Louise (Covington) Redding; m. Lawrence Edward Denton, Aug. 23, 1964; children: Robert, Christopher Lance, Heather Redding. Cert. in Art, Art Instr. Sch., Mpls., 1968; vocat. cert., Colo. State U., Ft. Collins, 1994. Instr. Colo. Inst. Art, Denver, 1983-86, Arapahoe C.C., Colo., 1994—. Contbr. articles to Best of Colored Pencil II, 1994, Creative Colored Pencil, 1995, other profl. jours. Numerous awards to include San Diego Internat. Watercolor award, Rocky Mountain Nat. watermedia award, Poudre Valley Nat. Meritorious award N.E. Watercolor Soc. Nat. Excellence award, 1992, Parkersburg Art Ctr. award, Spl. award, Tubac Ctr. for Arts, Nat. Smallworks Tech. Excellence award, 1993. Mem. Nat. Watercolor Soc. (Festival of Arts Laguna Beach award), Foothills Art Ctr. Home: 2948 Pierson Way Lakewood CO 80215-7136

DENVER, THOMAS H.R., lawyer; b. N.Y.C., Oct. 29, 1944; s. Thomas H. Rorke and Eileen Ann Boland; m. Barbara Ann Denver, Dec. 19, 1987; children: Rorke, Nate. BS, Syracruse U., 1966; MS, U. Wash., 1967; J.D., U. Calif., San Francisco, 1973. Bar: Calif. 1973, U.S. Dist. Ct. (no. dist.) Calif. 1973. From assoc. to mng. ptnr. Hoge, Fenton, Jones & Apple, Inc., San Jose, Calif., 1973—; judge pro tem Santa Clara County Superior Ct., San Jose, 1980—; instr. Stanford U. Law Sch. Advocacy Program; mem. faculty Hastings Coll. of Advocacy; mediator, arbitrator. Contbr. articles to profl. jours. Fellow Am. Coll. Trial Lawyers; mem. Assn. Def. Counsel (bd. dirs. No. Calif. chpt. 1991-92), Am. Bd. Trial Advocates, Santa Clara County Civil Litigation Com., Santa Clara County Bar Assn. (chmn. fast track com.). Office: Hoge Fenton Jones & Appel 60 S Market St San Jose CA 95113

DEPALO, WILLIAM ANTHONY, JR., Latin American studies educator; b. N.Y.C., July 17, 1941; s. William Anthony and Elsie Elizabeth (Reighton) DeP.; m. Deborah Jean Borgmann, Dec. 30, 1983; children: Brian William, Katherine Elizabeth. BS in Microbiology, N.Mex. State U., 1963; MA in History, U. Okla., 1971; student, Interam. Def. Coll., Ft. McNair, Washington, 1985-86; PhD in Latin Am. Studies, U. N.Mex., 1994. Commd. 2d lt. U.S. Army, 1963, advanced through grades to col., 1985; comdr. 1st Bn., 10th Infantry, Ft. Carson, Colo., 1983-85, 4th Psychol. Ops. Group, Ft. Bragg, N.C., 1986-89, U.S. Army Sch. of the Ams., Ft. Benning, Ga., 1989-91; vis. scholar U. N.Mex., Albuquerque, 1995—. Author: The Mexican National Army, 1997; contbr. Encyclopedia of the Mexican War, 1997. Decorated Silver Star, Bronze Star for Valor, Purple Heart (2), Legion of Merit (3). Mem. Am. Hist. Assn. Republican. Roman Catholic. Home: 4009 Shenandoah Pl NE Albuquerque NM 87111 Office: U NMex Latin Am Inst Albuquerque NM 87131

DEPAOLIS, POTITO UMBERTO, food company executive; b. Mignano, Italy, Aug. 28, 1925; s. Giuseppe A. and Filomena (Macchiaverna) deP.; Vet. Dr., U. Naples, 1948; Libera Docenza, Ministero Pubblica Istruzione (Rome, Italy), 1955; m. Marie A. Caronna, Apr. 10, 1965. Came to U.S., 1966, naturalized, 1970. Prof. food service Vet. Sch., U. Naples, Italy, 1948-66; retired, 1966; asst. prof. A titre Benevole Ecole Veterinaire Alfort, Paris, France, 1956; vet. inspector U.S. Dept. Agr., Omaha, 1966-67; sr. research chemist Grain Processing Corp., Muscatine, Iowa, 1967-68; v.p., dir. product devel. Reddi Wip, Inc., Los Angeles, 1968-72; with Kubro Foods, Los Angeles, 1972-73, Shade Foods, Inc., 1975—; pres. Vegetable Protein Co., Riverside, Calif., 1973—, Tima Brand Food Co., 1975—, Dr. Tima Natural Foods, 1977—. Fulbright scholar Cornell U., Ithaca, N.Y., 1954; British Council scholar, U. Reading, Eng., 1959-60; postdoctoral research fellow NIH, Cornell U., 1963-64. Mem. Inst. Food Technologists, Italian Assn. Advancement Sci., AAAS, Vet. Med. Assn., Biol. Sci. Assn. Italy, Italian Press Assn., Greater Los Angeles Press Club. Contbr. articles in field to prol. jours. Patentee in field. Home: Bel Air 131 Groverton Pl Los Angeles CA 90077-3732 Office: 8570 Wilshire Blvd Beverly Hills CA 90211-3133 also: 6878 Beck Ave North Hollywood CA 91605-6205

DE PASSE, SUZANNE, record company executive; m. Paul Le Mat. Student, Manhattan Community Coll. Former talent coordinator Cheetah Disco, N.Y.C.; creative asst. to pres. Motown Prodns., Los Angeles, 1968-81, pres., from 1981; now c.e.o. de Passe Entertainment, L.A. Acts signed and developed for Motown include The Commodores, The Jackson Five, Frankie Valli and the Four Seasons, Lionel Richie, Thelma Houston, Billy Preston, Teena Marie, Rick James, Stephanie Mills; co-author screenplay for film Lady Sings the Blues (Acad. award nomination); exec. producer: (TV miniseries) Lonesome Dove, (TV series) Motown on Showtime, Nightlife starring David Brenner, Motown Revue starring Smokey Robinson, Motown Returns to the Apollo (Emmy award, NAACP Image award), (TV spl.) Motown 25: Yesterday, Today, Forever (Emmy award, NAACP Image award); writer: (TV spls.) Happy Endings, Jackson 5 Goin' Back to Indiana, Diana; creative cons: Git on Broadway-Diana Ross & The Supremes & Temptations, TCB-Diana Ross & The Supremes & Temptations. Office: de Passe Entertainment 5750 Wilshire Blvd Ste 640 Los Angeles CA 90036-3697*

DEPEW, MARIE KATHRYN, retired secondary school educator; b. Sterling, Colo., Dec. 1, 1928; d. Amos Carl and Dorothy Emelyn (Whiteley) Mehl; m. Emil Carlton DePew, Aug. 30, 1952 (dec. 1973). BA, U. Colo., 1950, MA, 1953. Post grad. Harvard U., Cambridge, Mass., 1962; tchr. Jefferson County Pub. Schs., Arvada, 1953-73; mgr. Colo. Accountability Program, Denver, 1973-83; sr. cons. Colo. Dept. Edn., Denver, 1973-85, ret., 1985. Author: (pamphlet) History of Hammil, Georgetown, Colorado, 1967; contbr. articles to profl. jours. Chmn. Colo. State Accountability Com., Denver, 1971-75. Fellow IDEA Programs, 1976-77, 79-81. Mem. Colo. Hist. Assn., Jefferson County Edn. Assn. (pres. 1963-64), Colo. Edn. Assn. (bd. dirs. 1965-70), Ky. Colonels (hon. mem.), Phi Beta Kappa. Republican. Methodist. Home: 920 Pennsylvania St Denver CO 80203-3157

DEPIES, LISA J., physicist; b. Cleve., Aug. 5, 1961; d. Charles Wendorff and Johanna Paulette (Sluger) Foye; m. Steven Robert Depies, July 21, 1990. BS Physics, Valparaiso U., 1983; MS Med. Physics, U. Health Scis./Chgo. Med., Sch., 1985. Bd. eligible Am. Bd. Radiology. Radiol. physicist Greenville (S.C.) Hosp. System, 1985-89; cons. radiol. physicist Radiol. Physics Svcs., Phoenix, 1989—, v.p., 1996—, also bd. dirs. Mem. Am. Assn. Physicists in Medicine (com. mem. 1983—). Home: 12412 South 37th Ct Phoenix AZ 85044 Office: Radiol Physics Svcs Inc 12412 S 37th Ct Phoenix AZ 85044-3811

DEPLOIS, MOLLY, library director; b. Coos Bay, Oreg., July 12, 1956; d. John A. and Violette E. (Carrillo) Barrett; m. Jacques Philippe DePlois, Aug. 2, 1992; children: Emmeline Cosette Adele, Madeline Marie Violette. Libr. asst. Coquille (Oreg.) Pub. Libr., 1976-85, asst. libr., 1985-86, libr. dir., 1986—. Adv. coun. Southwestern Oreg. Cmty. Coll., Coos Bay, 1990-94; bd. dirs. Sawdust Theatre, Coquille, 1987-92, pres., 1991-92. Mem. ALA, LWV, Oreb. Libr. Assn. Democrat. Roman Catholic. Home: 577 N Dean St Coquille OR 97423-1671

DEPPISCH, PAUL VINCENT, data communications executive; b. Madison, Wis., Dec. 15, 1950; s. Vincent Francis and Evelyn Catherine (Eichmeier) D. Cable splicing foreman GTE Calif., Santa Monica, 1968-73; gen. foreman DataCom Inc., Santa Monica, 1973-78; sr. project mgr. A.I.D.C.O., North Hollywood, Calif., 1978-84; cons. Systex Group Ltd., Phoenix, 1984-90; pres. Ambient Data Tech. Inc., Upland, Calif., 1990—; founder, dir. Boogere Prodns. Internat., Santa Monica, 1973—; bd. dirs. Systex Group Ltd. Min. Universal Life Ch., Modesto, Calif. Mem. Bldg. Industry Cons. Svc., Inc., C. of C. Home: PO Box 1712 Santa Monica CA 90406 Office: Ambient Data Tech Inc 517 N Mountain Ave # 101 Upland CA 91786

DEPREIST, JAMES ANDERSON, conductor; b. Phila., Nov. 21, 1936; s. James Henry and Ethel (Anderson) De P.; m. Betty Louise Childress, Aug. 10, 1963; children: Tracy Elisabeth, Jennifer Anne; m. Ginette Grenier, July 19, 1980. Student, Phila. Conservatory Music, 1959-61; BS, U. Pa., 1958, MA, 1961, LHD (hon.), 1976; LHD (hon.), Reed Coll., 1990, Portland State U., 1993; MusD (hon.), Laval U., Quebec City, Can., 1980, Linfield Coll., 1986, Juilliard, 1993; DFA (hon.), U. Portland, 1983, Pacific U., 1985, Willamette U., 1987, Drexel U., 1989, Oreg. State U., 1990; Doctor of Arts and Letters (hon.), St. Mary's Coll., Moraga, Calif., 1985; HHD (hon.), Lewis and Clark U., 1986. Am. specialist music for State Dept., 1962-63; condr.-in-residence Bangkok, 1963-64; condr. various symphonies and orchs., 1964—. Condr.: Am. debut with N.Y. Philharm., 1964, asst. condr. to Leonard Bernstein, N.Y. Philharm. Orch., 1965-66, prin. guest condr. Symphony of New World, 1968-70, European debut with Rotterdam Philharm., 1969; Helsinki Philharm., 1993; assoc. condr. Nat. Symphony Orch., Washington, 1971-75, prin. guest condr. Nat. Symphony Orch., 1975-76; music dir. L'Orchestre Symphonique de Que., 1976-83, Oreg. Symphony, 1980—, prin. guest condr. Helsinki Philharmonic, 1993, Mus. Dir. Monte Carlo Philharm., 1994; appeared with Phila. Orch., 1972, 76, 84, 85, 87, 90, 92, 93, 94, Chgo. Symphony, 1973, 90, 92, 94, Boston Symphony, 1973, Cleve. Orch., 1974; condr.: Am. premiere of Dvorak's First Symphony, N.Y. Philharm., 1972; chief condr. Malmö Symphony, 1991-94; author: (poems) This Precipice Garden, 1987, The Distant Siren, 1989. Trustee Lewis and Clark Coll., 1983—. Recipient 1st prize gold medal Dimitri Mitropoulos Internat. Music Competition for Condrs., 1964, Merit citation City of Phila., 1969, medal of City of Que., 1983; grantee Martha Baird Rockefeller Fund for Music, 1969, Insignia of Comdr. of Order of Lion of Finland, 1992. Fellow Am. Acad. Arts and Scis.; mem. Royal Swedish Acad. Music. Office: Oreg Symphony Orch 711 SW Alder St Ste 200 Portland OR 97205

DEPREZ, DANIEL ROBERT, writer; b. Portland, Oreg., June 20, 1954; s. Robert Newton and Alice (Stellges) DeP. AA in Radio Prodn., Mt. Hood C.C., Gresham, Oreg., 1975; BA, Evergreen State Coll., Olympia, Wash., 1976. Freelance writer, disc jockey Portland, 1976-78; standup comedian, 1983-91; features writer Willamette Week, Portland, 1991—; columnist Exotic Mag., Portland, 1995—; cons. in pub. rels. and spl. event planning for non-profits, 1992—. Author: 31 Days At A Time, 1993; author/performer recording: Love and Denial, 1992. Office: Daymare Prodns 12311 NE Glisan St # 150 Portland OR 97230-2118

DERDENGER, PATRICK, lawyer; b. L.A., June 29, 1946; s. Charles Patrick and Drucilla Marguerite (Lange) D.; m. Jo Lynn Dickins, Aug. 24, 1968; children: Kristin Lynn, Bryan Patrick, Timothy Patrick. BA, Loyola U., L.A., 1968; MBA, U. So. Calif., 1971, JD, 1974; LLM in Taxation, George Washington U., 1977. Bar: Calif. 1974, U.S. Ct. Claims 1975, Ariz. 1979, U.S. Ct. Appeals (9th cir.) 1979, U.S. Dist. Ct. Ariz. 1979, U.S. Tax Ct. 1979, U.S. Supreme Ct. 1979; cert. specialist in tax law. Trial atty. honors program U.S. Dept. Justice, Washington, 1974-78; ptnr. Lewis and Roca, Phoenix, 1978—; adj. prof. taxation Golden Gate U., Phoenix, 1983-87; mem. Ariz. State Tax Ct. Legis. Study Commn. Author: Arizona State and Local Taxation, Cases and Materials, 1983, Arizona Sales and Use Tax Guide, 1990, Advanced Arizona Sales and Use Tax, 1987-96, Arizona State and Local Taxation, 1989, 93, 96, Arizona Sales and Use Tax, 1988-96, Arizona Property Taxation, 1993-96, ABA Sales and Use Tax Deskbook, Property Tax Deskbook. Past pres., bd. dirs. North Scottsdale Little League. Served to capt. USAF, 1968-71. Recipient U.S. Law Week award Bur. Nat. Affairs, 1974. Mem. ABA (taxation sect., various coms.), Ariz. Bar Assn. (taxation sect., various coms., chair sect. taxation, former treas., chmn. state and local tax com., chmn. continuing legal edn. com., tax adv. com.), Maricopa County Bar Assn., Inst. Sales Taxation, Nat. Tax Assn., Inst. Property Taxation Met. C. of C., Ariz. C. of C. (chair tax com.), U. So. Calif. Alumni Club (past pres., bd. dirs.), Phi Delta Phi. Home: 10040 E Happy Valley Rd # 478 Scottsdale AZ 85255 Office: Lewis and Roca 2 Renaissance Plz 40 N Central Ave Phoenix AZ 85004-4429

DERGRIGORIAN, RONALD, water microbiologist; b. Shiraz, Fars, Iran, Dec. 18, 1960; came to U.S., 1979; s. Arnold and Elma (Dror) D.; m. Ida Avanessian, Sept. 6, 1986; 1 child, Tara. BA in Biology and Microbiology, Calif. State U., 1983, MS in Microbiology with distinction, 1989. Instr. Calif. State U., Northridge, 1983-86; from lab. technician I to water biologist Hyperion Treatment Plant, L.A., 1986-91; water microbiologist Dept. Water & Power, L.A., 1991—; hazardous materials mgmt. staff Dept. Water & Power, L.A., 1982—, emergency response team capt., 1993—, total quality mgmt. team, 1993-95. Co-author: Microbiology Laboratory Training Manual, 1989-90. Fund raising com. Armenian Gen. Benevolent Union, L.A., 1988, 94. Scholastic Achievement grantee Calif. State U., 1988-89. Mem. ASM, Am. Soc. Microbiology. Armenian Apostolic. Office: Dept Water and Power Rm 1F49 8501 Arleta Ave Sun Valley CA 91352

DERICKSON, STANLEY LEWIS, minister, writer; b. Lexington, Nebr., Feb. 19, 1940; s. George Henry and Mary LeOra Derickson; m. Faith Louann Diefenbach, Feb. 28, 1964; children: Stanley L. II, Laurie Lynn, Timothy James. BA, Denver Bapt. Bible Coll., 1973; ThB, Western Bapt. Bible Coll., Salem, Oreg., 1978; ThM, Trinity Theol. Sem., Newburgh, Ind., 1980; PhD, Trinity Theol. Sem., 1981. Ordained to ministry Berean Ch., 1976. Missionary WEF Ministries, 1982-87; tchr. Frontier Sch. of Bible, LaGrange, Wyo., 1987-91; interim pastor Immanuel Bapt. Ch., Salem, Oreg., 1996—. Author: Mr. D.'s Notes on Theology, 1993; contbr. articles to Bapt. Bulletin, Voice mag. With USN, 1958-62.

DERN, CHRISTOPHER M., construction executive; b. 1956. Grad., U. Wash., 1979. With Arthur Anderson, Seattle, 1979-82, Peat Marwick, Seattle, 1982-89, Fletcher Challenge Industries USA Ltd., Bothell, 1989—. Office: Fletcher Chllnge Inds USA LTD 19515N Creek Pky Ste 312 Bothell WA 98011*

DE ROEST, JAN M., mental health counselor; b. Seattle, Wash., Oct. 9, 1965; d. Stanley Robert and Glenna Muriel (Bennett) Hagedorn; m. Gary Eugene De Roest, Apr. 26, 1987. BS in Microbiology, Oreg. State U., 1987; MA in Counseling Psychology, Lewis and Clark Coll., 1996. Cert. nursing asst. Med. asst. Met. Clinic, Portland, Oreg., 1987-89; rsch. asst. Oreg.

Health Sci. U., Portland, 1989-90; med. asst. Portland Clinic, 1991-92; rsch. asst. VA Med. Ctr., Portland, 1992-93; med. asst. Neighborhood Health Clinic, Portland, 1995-96, master's intern, 1995-96; master's intern Delaunay Family of Svcs., Portland, 1995-96. Mem. Am. Counseling Assn., Am. Aging and Devel. Assn., Am. Mental Health Counseling Assn., Lewis and Clark Alumni Assn. Democrat. Roman Catholic.

DE ROO, REMI JOSEPH, bishop; b. Swan Lake, Man., Can., Feb. 24, 1924; s. Raymond and Josephine (De Pape) De R. Student, St. Boniface (Man.) Coll.; STD, Angelicum U., Rome, Italy.; LLD (hon.), U. Antigonish, N.S., 1983, U. Brandon, Man., 1987; DD (hon.), U. Winnipeg, Man., 1990; LLD (hon.), U. Victoria, B.C., 1991. Ordained priest Roman Cath. Ch., 1950. Curate Holy Cross Parish, St. Boniface, 1952-53; sec. to archbishop of St. Boniface, 1954-56; diocesan dir. Cath. action Archdiocese St. Boniface, 1953-54; exec. sec. Man. Cath. Con., 1958; pastor Holy Cross Parish, 1960-62; bishop of Victoria, B.C., Can., 1962—; Can. Episcopal rep. Internat. Secretariat Apostleship See, 1964-78, Pontifical Commn. Culture, 1984-87; chairperson Human Rights Commn. B.C., 1974-77; mem. social affairs commn. Can. Conf. Cath. Bishops, 1973-87, 91-95, mem. theology commn., 1987-91; pres. Western Cath. Conf. Bishops, 1984-88; hon. pres. World Conf. for Religion and Peace for Can., 1994—. Hon. fellow Ryerson Poly. Inst., 1987. Address: 4044 Nelthorpe St # 1, Victoria, BC Canada V8X 2A1

DEROSA, FRANCIS DOMINIC, chemical company executive; b. Seneca Falls, N.Y., Feb. 26, 1936; s. Frank and Frances (Bruno) DeR.; m. Vivian DeRosa, Oct. 24, 1959; children: Kevin, Marc, Terri. Student, Rochester Inst. Tech., 1959-61; BS, Chadwick U., MBA; PhD, City U. L.A. Cert. med. photographer. CEO Advance Paper & Equipment Supply Inc., Mesa, Ariz., 1974—, Pottery Plus Ltd., Mesa, 1984—, Advance Tool Supply Inc., Mesa, 1989-94. Vice chmn. bd. adjustments City of Mesa, 1983-89, bd. dirs. dept. parks and recreation, 1983-86; pres. Christ the King Mens Club, 1983-84; bd. dirs. Mesa C. of C., 1983-88. Mem. Ariz. Sanitary Supply Assn. (pres. 1983-84), Internat. Sanitary Supply Assn. (coord. Ariz. chpt. 1994-96, sec. bd. 1994-96), Gilbert, Ariz. C. of C. (bd. dirs., v.p. 1992-96, pres. 1996-97, sec. internat. bd. 1994-96), Gilbert Heights Owners Assn. (pres. 1992-93), Mesa Country Club, Santa Monica (Calif.) Yacht Club, Rotary (pres. Mesa Sunrise chpt. 1987-88, Paul Harris fellow 1988), Masons (32 degree, pres. 1973), Sons of Italy (pres. 1983-84), Shriners. Home: 513 E Horseshoe Ave Gilbert AZ 85296-1705 Office: Advance Paper & Maintenance Supply Inc 33 W Broadway Mesa AZ 85210-1505

DEROUIN, JAMES G., lawyer; b. Eau Claire, Wis., July 11, 1944. BA cum laude, U. Wis., 1967, JD, 1968. Bar: Wis. 1968, Ariz. 1986. Mem. Steptoe & Johnson LLC, Phoenix, Ariz. Chair PCB chair., Wis. Dept. Natural Resources, 1976-78, Phoenix Environ. Qoualty Com., 1989-92; mem. spl. com. on solid waste mgmt., Wis. Legis. Coun., 1976-79, ad hoc com. on hazardous wast mgmt., 1980-82, spl. com. on groundwater mgmt.; Wis. Dept.Nat. Resources Metallic Mining Coun., 1978-85; chair Phoenix Environ.Quality Commissim, 1986; Ariz. Govs. Regulatory Review Coun. 1986—. Chair. State Bar Ariz. (environ. and nat. resources law sect. 1989-90). Office: Steptoe & Johnson LLC 40 N Central Ave Ste 2400 Phoenix AZ 85004

DEROUX, DANIEL GRADY, artist; b. Juneau, Alaska, Oct. 25, 1951; s. Harold Edward DeRoux and Mary Elizabeth (Rice) Quist; m. JoAnn Marie Grady, Aug. 16, 1992; children: Eric, Katie. Curator of exhibits Alaska State Mus., Juneau, 1978-79; set designer Perseverance Theatre, Douglas, Alaska, 1988-91; owner Gallery Still Russian and Alaskan Contemporary Art, Juneau, 1991-92; artist, 1971—. Sole exhibns. include Natsoulas/Novelozo Gallery, Davis, Calif., 1989, Czar's Summer Palace, St. Petersberg, Russia, 1992, Somar Gallery, San Francisco, 1992, Mercer-Hood Gallery, Seattle, 1994, Ft. Mason Ctr., San Francisco, 1995. Recipient Gold medal for most accomplished artist, Bronze medal in Mixed Media, L.A. Internat. Art Competition, 1984, Third Place award N.Y. Internat. Art Competition, 1988; named Best of Show, Calgene West Coast Art Competition, Calif., 1988. Home and Studio: 19191 Randall Rd Juneau AK 99801-8209

DERR, JOHN SEBRING, geophysicist, seismologist; b. Boston, Nov. 12, 1941; s. Thomas Sieger and Mary Ferguson (Sebring) D.; children: Alex, Mary, Nathan. BA, Amherst Coll., 1963; MA, U. Calif., Berkeley, 1965, PhD, 1968. Geophysicist Pan Am. Petroleum Corp., Midland, Tex., 1964; research assoc. MIT, Cambridge, 1968-70; research scientist Martin-Marietta Aerospace Corp., Denver, 1970-74; chief ops. Nat. Earthquake Info. Service U.S. Geol. Survey, Golden, Colo., 1974-79; chief tech. reports U.S. Geol. Survey, Menlo Park, Calif., 1980-83; chief spl. seismol. analysis project U.S. Geol. Survey, Golden, Colo., 1983-89; global seismological network chief U.S. Geol. Survey, Albuquerque, N.Mex., 1989—. Contbr. articles to profl. jours. Mem. AAAS, Am. Geophys. Union, Seismol. Soc. Am., Soc. Sci. Exploration (councilor 1986-93), Sigma Xi. Office: US Geol Survey Albuquerque Seismologi Albuquerque NM 87115

DERR, KENNETH T., oil company executive; b. 1936; m. Donna Mettler, Sept. 12, 1959; 3 children. BME, Cornell U., 1959, MBA, 1960. With Chevron Corp. (formerly Standard Oil Co. of Calif.), San Francisco, 1960—, v.p., 1972-85; pres. Chevron U.S.A., Inc. subs. Chevron Corp., San Francisco, 1978-84; head merger program Chevron Corp. and Gulf Oil Corp., San Francisco, 1984-85; vice-chmn. Chevron Corp., San Francisco, 1985-88, chmn., chief exec. officer, 1989—, also bd. dirs.; bd. dirs. AT&T, Citicorp, Potlatch Corp. Trustee emeritus Cornell U. Mem. The Bus. Coun., Calif. Bus. Roundtable, Am. Petroleum Inst. (bd. dirs.), Nat. Petroleum Coun., Bus. Roundtable, San Francisco Golf Club, Orinda Country Club, Pacific Union Club. Office: Chevron Corp PO Box 7643 575 Market St San Francisco CA 94105

DERUCHER, KENNETH NOEL, university dean; b. Messina, N.Y., Jan. 24, 1949; s. Kenneth John and Vienna May (MacDougall) D.; m. Barbara Eileen Frick, Apr. 15, 1978; children: Kenneth James, Robert Vincent. AA, Erie County Tech. Coll., Buffalo, 1969; BCE, Tri-State U., Angola, Ind., 1971; MS, U. N.D., 1973; PhD, Va. Poly. Inst., 1977. Asst. prof. civil engrng. U. Md., Coll. Park, 1976-79; rsch. cons. Civil Design Corp., Laurel, Md., 1979-80; assoc. prof. Stevens Inst. Tech., Hoboken, N.J., 1980-82, head dept. civil engrng., 1982-89, prof., 1985-89, dean grad. sch., 1989-91, dean acad. intrastructure devel., 1991-94; dean Coll. Engrng., Computer Sci. and Tech. Calif. State U., Chico, 1994—; rsch. cons. various govt. orgns.; cons. engr. 1983. Author: Structural Analysis and Design, 1980, Materials for Civil and Highway Engineering, 1981, 3d rev. edit., 1993, Bridge Maintenance Evaluation, 2d edit., 1992, others; contbr. numerous articles to profl. jours. Pres. Marcel Lake Property Owners Assn., 1986-89. Fellow ASCE (bd. dirs. N.J. sect. 1981-82, awards chmn. N.J. br. 1980-83, v.p. 1981-82, pres. 1983-84, Educator of Yr. award 1981); mem. Sigma Xi (sec. Md. chpt. 1977-79, pres. Stevens chpt. 1989-92).

DERY, GABRIEL, optometrist; b. Rabat, Morocco, July 7, 1938; came to U.S., 1966; s. Albert and Renee Sultana D.; m. Marina A. Déry; children: Mark Alain, Kenneth Jacques. OD (valedictorian), Superior Sch. Optometry, 1964; OD, U. Montreal, 1965; OD, So. Calif. Coll. Optometry, 1975. Pres., optometrist Gabriel Dery OD, Inc., L.A., 1975—; mem. med. staff Cedars-Sinai Med. Center; mem. faculty Pa. Coll. Optometry, Ind. Coll. Optometry; cons. spl. visual effects dept. 20th Century Fox; clin. investigator contact lenses, solutions. Bd. dirs. EM Habanim, Tifereth Israel temples. Recipient Bronze medal for svcs. rendered to sci. French Govt., 1978. Fellow Am. Acad. Optometry; mem. Am. Optometric Assn., Calif. Optometric Assn., San Fernando Valley Optometric Assn., Coll. Optometrists Vision Devel., Council of 1000 at So. Calif. Coll. Optometry (cons. sport vision), Grand Prix Humanitaire de France, West Hollywood, Beverly Hills C. of C., Omega Epsilon Phi. Democrat. Contbr. articles to Optometric Mgmt. Jour. Home: 34331 Violet Lantern Dana Point CA 92629 Office: Gabriel Dery OD Inc 8500 Melrose Ave Ste 107 West Hollywood CA 90069-5145

DE SÁ E SILVA, ELIZABETH ANNE, secondary school educator; b. Edmonds, Wash., Mar. 17, 1931; d. Sven Yngve and Anna Laura Elizabeth (Dahlin) Erlandson; m. Claudio de Sá e Silva, Sept. 12, 1955 (div. July 1977); children: Lydia, Marco, Nelson. BA, U. Oreg., 1953; postgrad., Columbia U., 1954-56, Calif. State U., Fresno, 1990, U. No. Iowa, 1993; MEd, Mont. State U., 1978. Cert. tchr., Oreg., Mont. Med. sec., 1947-49; sec. Merced (Calif.) Sch. Dist., 1950-51; sec., asst. Simon and Schuster, Inc., N.Y.C., 1954-56; tchr. Casa Roosevelt-União Cultural, São Paulo, Brazil, 1957-59, Coquille (Oreg.) Sch. Dist., 1978-96; tchr. piano, 1967-78; instr. Spanish, Southwestern Oreg. C.C., Coos Bay, 1991-94; pianist/organist Faith Luth. Ch., North Bend, Oreg., 1995—, vocal soloist, 1996—, voice tchr., 1997—. Chmn. publicity Music in Our Schs. Month, Oreg. Dist. VII, 1980-85; sec. Newcomer's Club, Bozeman, Mont., 1971. Quincentennial fellow U. Minn. and Found. José Ortega y Gasset, Madrid, 1991. Mem. AAUW (sec., scholarship chmn., co-pres., pres., treas.), Nat. Trust Hist. Preservation, Am. Coun. on Tchg. Fgn. Langs., Am. Assn. Tchrs. Spanish and Portuguese, Nat. Coun. Tchrs. English, Music Educators Nat. Conf., Oreg. Music Educators Assn., Oreg. Coun. Tchrs. English, Confedn. Oreg. Fgn. Lang. Tchrs., VoiceCare Network. Republican. Home: 3486 Spruce St North Bend OR 97459-1130

DESAI, ASHA, allergist; b. Surat, India, 1950. MD, Gujarat U., Surat, India, 1973. Intern Phila. Gen. Hosp., 1974-75; pediatrician Mercy Cath. Med. Ctr., Phila., 1975-76, Coll. Medicine & Dentistry, Newark, 1976-77; allergist and immunologist Mt. Sinai Med. Sch., N.Y.C., 1981-83; now allergist Mercy Gen. Hosp., Sacramento. Office: 1600 Creekside Dr Ste 2700 Folsom CA 95630-3447*

DE SANTIS, MARK EDWARD, anatomist, neuroscientist and educator; b. Vineland, N.J., May 9, 1942; s. Orazio James and Ellice Cecelia De S.; m. Gail Chambers, July 5, 1968; 1 child, Michael Kevin. BS, Villanova (Pa.) U., 1963; MS, Creighton U., 1966; PhD, UCLA, 1970. Rsch. assoc. Naval Aerospace Med. Rsch. Lab., Pensacola, Fla., 1970-71; instr. to assoc. prof. Georgetown U., Washington, 1971-78; assoc. prof. to prof. anatomy and neurosci. U. Idaho, Moscow, 1978—; cons. in neurobiology Dr. E.N. Albert, George Washington U., 1973-78; guest lectr. Walter Reed Army Med. Ctr., Washington, 1972-78, Madigan Army Med. Hosp., Tacoma, Wash., 1979-82, Chulalongkorn U. Sch. Dentistry, Bangkok, Thailand, 1996; textbook reviewer Scott Foresman Little Brown & Co., Chgo., 1987-88. Contbr. articles to profl. jours. Scoutmaster Troop 344, Boy Scouts Am., Moscow, 1982-85. Recipient Golden Apple Teaching award Med. Class of 1980, Georgetown U., 1977, Excellence in Teaching award Med. Class of 1997, WAMI Program, 1994; NIH rsch. grantee, 1974-76, 89-92; NSF Rsch. grantee, 1984-85; Fulbright scholar, Egypt, 1994-95; NASA rsch. grantee, 1994—. Mem. Soc. for Neurosci., Am. Assn. Anatomists, Microscopy Soc. Am., Sigma Xi (chpt. pres. 1985), Phi Sigma (faculty advisor 1987-93, 95—). Office: Univ of Idaho Dept Biol Scis WAMI Program Moscow ID 83844-3051

DESCHNER, JANE WAGGONER, collage artist, public relations consultant; b. Bellefont, Pa., Feb. 9, 1948; d. George Ruble and Helen Louise (Talbert) Waggoner; m. William Henry Deschner, July 26, 1969 (div. Dec. 1987); children: John William, Elisabeth Anne. BA in Geography, U. Kans., 1969; BA in Art, Mont. State U., Billings, 1987. Economist Mid-Am. Regional Coun., Kansas City, Mo., 1970-73; ptnr., owner Castle Art Gallery, Billings, Mont., 1982-88; asst. dir. client svcs. Mont. Inst. of Arts Found., Billings, 1988-89; account exec., artist, writer Exclamation Point Advt., Billings, 1989-94; artist Billings, 1981—, cons. pub. rels./graphic design, 1994—; pers. rep. Fred. J. Urbaska Investments, Billings. Exhibited at Toucan Gallery, Billings, U. Mont., Missoula, Mont., Art Mus. Missoula, Mont. State U., Billings, Holter Mus. Art, Helena, Mont., Broken Diamond Gallery, Billings, Mont. State U., Bozeman, Deering Galleries, Taos, N.Mex. Bd. dirs. Billings Mental Health Assn., 1988-92, v.p., 1989, 90; gallery dir., bd. dirs. The Women's Ctr., St. Vincent Hosp. and Health Ctr., Billings, 1991—; mem. Youth Ct. Conf. Com. 13th Jud. Dist. Mont., Billings, 1992—. Recipient 1st pl. award in non-comml. art Billings Advt. and Mktg. Assn., 1992, 93. Mem. Yellowstone Print Club (bd. dirs., pres. acquisitions chair), Yellowstone Art Ctr. (Auction Artist 1989—). Unitarian. Studio: 1313 Granite Ave Billings MT 59102-0869

DE SHAZO, BILLY W., physician, plastic surgeon; b. Ashford, Ala., Jan. 10, 1931; s. Neal C. and Woodie Lee (Harrison) De S.; m. Charlotte Jean McKay, Aug. 21, 1954; children: Jean, William, Edwin, John, Thomas. BS, So. Meth. U., 1952; MD, Southwestern Med. Sch., 1956. Diplomate Am. Bd. Plastic Surgery. Resident gen. surgery Calif. Hosp., L.A., 1959-62; resident plastic surgery U. Wis., Madison, 1962-64; chief plastic surgery Good Samaritan Hosp., St. Vincent's Hosp. Office: 1245 Wilshire Blvd Los Angeles CA 90017-4810

DE SIO, ANTHONY WILLIAM, communications executive; b. N.Y.C., Feb. 2, 1930; s. Oresto Joseph and Concetta (Curci) D.; children: Douglas, Darcy. BSEE, U. Conn., 1958; BA, U. Santa Clara, 1970. Mgr. Lockheed Missile and Space Co., Sunnyvale, Calif., 1958-71; staff asst. Exec. Office of the Pres., Washington, 1971-72; mgr. Gen. Electric Co., King of Prussia, Pa., 1972-74; dep. v.p. Western Union Space Commn., Upper Saddle River, N.J., 1974-77; dir. Linkabit Corp., San Diego, 1977-78; chief exec. officer, vice chmn. Mail Boxes Etc., San Diego, 1979—; bd. dirs. Mail Boxes Etc., San Diego, Global Imaging Corp., Solana Beach, Calif. Advisor Interfaith Shelter Network, San Diego, 1988—, Brother Benn's Kitchen, Oceanside, Calif., 1988—. Recipient Outstanding Achievement award Pres. Nixon, 1972. Mem. Pres. Exec. Interchange Assn., Pres. Round Table, Nat. Assn. of Corp. Dirs. Lodge: Rotary. Office: Mail Boxes Etc 6060 Cornerstone Ct W San Diego CA 92121*

DE SMIDT, FRANK JOSEPH, communications executive; b. San Francisco, Sept. 4, 1941; s. Paul Jerome and Mary Elizabeth (Ahern) D.; m. Deborah Kay Yoakum, Sept. 4, 1984; children: Michael Joseph, Jonathan Paul. Student, Peralta Coll., 1961-63. Gen. mgr. Sta. KPEN FM, Los Altos, Calif., 1978-82; pres. Los Altos Broadcasting, Inc., 1978-84, L.D.S. Enterprises, Inc., Milpitas, Calif., 1971—. Del. White House Conf. on Small Bus.; mem. Milpitas Community Task Force, 1982-83; Dem. committeeman Calif., 1983-85. Mem. Milpitas C. of C. (pres. 1972-73, chmn. govt. affairs com. 1980—, cert. of appreciation 1977, 95, Disting. Svc. award 1973, 78, President's award 1981, Bus. Person of Yr. award 1990, Cert. Appreciation 1994-95), Rotary (bd. dirs. Milpitas 1987, sec. 1988-89, v.p. 1989-90, pres.-elect 1990-91, pres. 1991-92), KC (Milpitas Citizen of Yr. award 1993). Republican. Roman Catholic. Office: LDS Enterprises Inc 16 Corning Ave Ste 160 Milpitas CA 95035-5343

DESMOND, LEIF, writer; b. Inglewood, Calif., Mar. 2, 1920; s. Guy Marion and Elma Agusta (Miller) Smith; m. Soledad Saenz, July 9, 1945 (div. Apr. 1982); children: Judith, Virginia, Marilyn Susan, Theresa, Loretta, Lawrence, Glenn; m. Yolanda Rambo, June 21, 1982. Student, Iowa State Coll., 1939-40, 42, San Fernando State Coll., 1959-65, U. Calif. Ext., 1961; AA in Bus. Adminstrn., Ventura (Calif.) Coll., 1959. Author: In the June of Summer, 1986, The Sparrow Safari, 1995, In Old October, 1996. Home: 2178 Javelina Ave Yuma AZ 85364

DESOTO, LEWIS DAMIEN, art educator; b. San Bernardino, Calif., Jan. 3, 1954; s. Lewis Dan and Albertina (Quiroz) DeS. BA, U. Calif., Riverside, 1978; MFA, Claremont Grad. Sch., 1981. Tchr. Otis Parsons, L.A., 1982-85; chmn. art dept. Cornish Coll. of Arts, Seattle, 1985-88; assoc. prof. art San Francisco State U., 1988—; dir. grad. studies Calif. Coll. Arts and Crafts, Oakland, 1993-95. Exhibited at New Mus., N.Y.C., 1992, Centro Cultural De La Raza, San Diego, 1993, Moderna Museet, Stockholm, Sweden, 1993, Christopher Grimes Gallery, Santa Monica, Calif., 1994, Denver Art Mus., 1994, Columbus Mus. Art, 1994, Des Moines Art Ctr., 1995, Fundacao Serralves, 1995, Oporto, Portugal, 1995. Mem. photo coun. Seattle Art Mus., 1987-88. Recipient New Genres award Calif. Arts Coun., 1992. Mem. L.A. Ctr. for Photographic Studies (bd. dirs. 1983-85), CameraWork (exec. bd. dirs. 1991-93), Ctr. for Arts (adv. bd. 1993—), Friends of Photography (peer award bd. 1991—). Office: San Francisco State U Art Dept 1600 Holloway Ave San Francisco CA 94132-1722

DESROCHERS, JERI KILZER, artist; b. Lincoln, Nebr., Sept. 24, 1957. BS in Bus. Adminstrn., Colo. State U., 1985. Gallery mgr. Evergreen Gallery, 1995-96. Works exhibited Greeley Stampede Art Show, 1992, NPVAG Nat. Juried Art Show, 1993, Boulder Open Juried Show, 1994, Glenwood Springs Fall Arts Festival, 1991, 92, 93, 94, Evergreen Fine Arts Fair, 1992, 93, 94, Phi Theta Kappa Six-State Art Competitive, 1993, Thompson Valley Regional Art Show, 1993, Colo. Watercolor Soc. Statewide Exhbn., 1993, 94, 95, Gilpin County Arts Exhbn., 1996. Mem. Signature Colo. Watercolor Soc., Evergreen Artists Assn. (membership dir., publs. coord., sec. 1989-97), Colorado Springs Art Guild, Foothills Art Ctr. Office: Studio Jeri Desrochers 27222 Hilltop Dr Evergreen CO 80439-9217

DESROCHES, BRIAN, psychotherapist, organizational systems consultant; b. Windsor, Ont., Can., Aug. 22, 1946; came to U.S., 1971; s. Henry and Mary (Zola) DesR.; m. Mara Pauli, June 9, 1971 (div. May 1978); m. Patricia I. DesRoches, Dec. 30, 1987; children: David Joseph, Christine Carmen. B in Comm. (hon.), U. Windsor, 1969; MHA, U. Ottawa, 1973; MS in Counseling, Ea. Mont. Coll., 1976; MBA, U. Puget Sound, 1980; PhD, N.W. Theol. Union, 1993. Mgr. computer ops. Henry Ford Hosp., Detroit, 1967-69; project mgr. NNE Regional Med. Program, Burlington, Vt., 1971; assoc. adminstr. Billings (Mont.) Deaconess Hosp., 1973-77; asst. adminstr. Providence Med. Ctr., Seattle, 1977-80; v.p. planning and devel.-health and hosp. svcs. Sister of St. Joseph, Bellevue, Wash., 1977-80; mgmt. cons. Seattle, 1981-83; exec. dir. Faulkner Treatment Ctr., Austin, Tex., 1983-84; psychotherapist, cons. Seattle, 1985—. Author: Reclaiming Yourself, 1990, Faces of Recovery, 1991, Your Boss Is Not Your Mother, 1995; contbg. author: Talk, Trust, Feel, 1992. Mem. bd. Mad-Jac Econ. Devel. Coun., Seattle, 1980-81, Cath. Community Svcs., Seattle, 1981. Mem. Am. Assn. Marriage and Family Therapists (clin.). Office: 2800 E Madison St # 302 Seattle WA 98112-4859

DESROSIER, JAMES NORMAN, marketing executive; b. West Lafayette, Ind., Jan. 31, 1955; s. Norman Wilfred and Anne Colwell (O'Brien) D.; m. Christine Lepez, Aug. 24, 1985. BA in Philosophy, Kenyon Coll., 1977. Freelance copy editor AVI Pub. Co., Inc., Westport, Conn., 1977; mgr. editorial svcs. Matthew Bender & Co., Inc., N.Y.C., 1978-82; account supr. Grey Advt., Inc., N.Y.C., 1982-85, Saatchi & Saatchi-Compton, Inc., N.Y.C., 1985; v.p., mgmt. supr. HDM/N.Y., N.Y.C., 1986-90; v.p. advt. MasterCard Internat. Inc., N.Y.C., 1990-93, v.p. mktg. and product mgmt. debit divsn., 1994-95; sr. v.p. global brand mktg. MasterCard Internat. Inc., Purchase, N.Y., 1995-96; chief mktg. officer Infoseek Corp., Santa Clara, Calif., 1996—. Co-author: Technology of Food Preservation, 4th edit., 1977. Recipient Effie award Am. Mktg. Assn., 1988-91, 93-94, Spire award, 1991, Forty Under Forty award Crain's N.Y. Bus., N.Y.C., 1993. Home: 610 Park View Dr Santa Clara CA 95054-3572 Office: Infoseek Corp 2620 Augustine Dr Santa Clara CA 95054-2903

DES SAGETTES, CHRISTIANE GUILLERMIN, pharmacist, biologist; b. Rodez, France, Dec. 17, 1932; came to the U.S., 1985; d. Charles Christian Loretz and Madeleine Causse; m. Ishan Dodan, Sept. 2, 1955 (dec. 1980); children: Inci, Ayben, Nihal; m. Baron Jean Claude Guillermin des Sagettes, Nov. 20, 1981. Diploma of pharmacist, Pharmacy Sch., Paris, 1961; serology cert., Faculty Medicine Paris, 1961; microbiology cert., Inst. Pasteur, 1962. Pharmacist in charge Hosp. Melun, France, 1969-75; owner dir., Med Ctr Arpajon, France, 1976-85; intern pharmacist Midwest Pharmacy, L.A.; owner French low calorie restaurant Baroness & Daughters, Santa Monica, Calif., 1986-87; intern pharmacist Pharmacare, Inglewood, Calif., 1989, Santa Maria Hosp., L.A., 1990; pharmacist in charge Million Dollars Pharmacy, L.A., 1991-95. Author: Femmes Sans Frontieres-Women Without Borders, 1981, Book of Nutrition: Dietetics, He Is An Homeless I'll Love You Forever, 1989. Roman Catholic. Home: 1433 N Harper Ave Apt 3 West Hollywood CA 90046-3765

DESTLER, DAVE M., publisher, editor, journalist; b. Buffalo, Sept. 14, 1954. BA, Calif. State U., Northridge, 1979. Owner 2D Studio, Canoga Park, Calif., 1978-85, 2D Publishing, Canoga Park, 1985—. Publisher, editor (mags.) British Car Mag., 1985-96, Jr. League Baseball, 1996—. Office: 2D Pub PO Box 9099 Canoga Park CA 91309-0099

DE TOMASO, ERNEST PAT, general building contractor, developer; b. Pescara, Italy, July 27, 1915; s. Anthony and Frances Mary (Tarsa) DeT.; m. Lida Janet Sherlock, June 30, 1940; children: Ernest Patrick, John Anthony. *Pescara 1860-1927, by Raffaele Colapietra, gives detailed accounts of various members of the Di Tommaso (the European spelling was later changed to De Tomaso) family. The De Tomaso's were prominent in social, political, and professional activities in the community and province. The Progressive Men of the State of Wyoming, by A. W. Bowen, and Women of Wyoming, by S. E. Boyer, both feature extensive accounts of the pioneer Sherlock family, whose members were prominent in society, mercantile enterprise, and cattle and sheep ranching. Son Ernest P., married Sharleen Shaffer in 1995. Son John A., married Carla Stewart in 1967. Three grandsons, three grandaughters, and one great-grandson have blessed the union of Ernest P. De Tomaso and Lida Janet Sherlock.* Student, San Bernardino Coll., 1961, Shabbarazzi Sch. Music, Rochester, N.Y., 1932. Musician Pat Thomas and His Orch., Rochester, 1931-37; baker Thrifty Drug Stores, L.A., 1938-46; ptnr. Anthony and Ernest P. DeTomaso Bldg. Contractors, Fontana, Calif., 1946-50; bldg. contractor Ernest P. DeTomaso Bldg. Contractor-Developer, Fontana, 1950-79; owner, lessor Towne Plaza Shopping Ctr., Fontana, 1987—; bd. dirs., v.p. Marybold Mut. Water Co., Bloomington, Calif. Mem. Greater Fontana United Fund, 1966-73, pres., 1973; mem. Planning Commn., Fontana, 1968-80, pres., 1970-71; founder, bd. dirs. Fontana Polit. Action Coalition, 1993—; trustee Eastern Star Homes of Calif., 1989-92. Recipient Devoted and Invaluable Svcs. award C. of C., Fontana, 1980, Outstanding Achievment award Greater Fontana United Fund, 1980, Svcs. Rendered award City of Fontana, 1981. Mem. Masons, Rotary, Order Eastern Star (worthy patron, grand officer, Exceptional Svc. award 1985). Republican. Home: 17155 Manzanita Dr Fontana CA 92335

DETTERMAN, ROBERT LINWOOD, financial planner; b. Norfolk, Va., May 1, 1931; s. George William and Jeanneille (Watson) D.; m. Virginia Armstrong; children: Janine, Patricia, William Arthur. BS in Engring., Va. Poly. Inst., 1953; PhD in Nuclear Engring., Oak Ridge Sch. Reactor Tech., 1954, postgrad., 1954; cert. in fin. planning, Coll. Fin. Planning, Denver, 1986. Registered investment advisor, Calif. Engrng. test dir. Foster Wheeler Co., N.Y.C., 1954-59; sr. research engr. Atomics Internat. Co., Canoga Park, Calif., 1959-62; chief project engr. Rockwell Internat. Co., Canoga Park, Calif., 1962-68, dir. bus. devel., 1968-84, mgr. internat. program, 1984-87; pres. Bo-Gin Fin., Inc., Thousand Oaks, Calif., 1987—; owner Bo-Gin Arabians, Thousand Oaks, 1963—; nuclear cons. Danish Govt., 1960, Lawrence Livermore Lab., Calif., 1959. Trustee, mem. exec. com. Morris Animal Found., Denver, 1984—, chmn., 1984-88, now trustee emeritus; treas., trustee Arabian Horse Trust, Denver, 1979-94, now trustee emeritus; pres. Rolling Oaks Homes Assn., Thousand Oaks, Calif., 1980-82; chmn. Cal Bred Futurity. Mem. Nat. Assn. Personal Fin. Advisers, Internat. Assn. Fin. Planners, Inst. Cert. Fin. Planners, Am. Nuclear Soc., Acad. Magical Arts, Am. Horse Shows Assn., Am. Horse Coun., Magic Castle Club, Internat. Arabian Horse Assn. Club, Tau Beta Phi, Eta Kappa Nu, Phi Kappa Phi. Republican. Office: Bo-Gin Fin Inc Ste 220 3625 E Thousand Oaks Blvd Thousand Oaks CA 91362-3626

DETTON, DAVID K., lawyer; b. Rupert, Idaho, Sept. 20, 1949. BA cum laude, Brigham Young U., 1973, JD magna cum laude, 1976. Bar: Utah, 1976. Law clk. to Hon. David T. Lewis U.S. Ct. Appeals (10th cir.), 1976-77; mem. Holme Roberts & Owen, LLP, Salt Lake City; part time faculty Oil and Gas Law Brigham Young U., 1979—. Comment and Case Note editor Brigham Young U. Law Review, 1975-76. J. Clark Reuben scholar. Mem. Utah State Bar, Phi Kappa Phi. Office: Holme Roberts & Owen LLC 111 E Broadway Ste 1100 Salt Lake City UT 84111-5233

DETWEILER, ROBERT CHESTER, university president, historian; b. French Camp, Calif., Dec. 8, 1938; s. Chester and Alice Mae (Gallagher) D.; m. Susan Jan Krudwig, Nov. 22, 1978; 1 dau., Lara Anne. B.A., Humboldt State U., 1960; M.A., San Francisco State U., 1965; Ph.D., U. Wash., 1968. Asst. prof. history San Diego State U., 1968-71, assoc. prof., 1971-74, prof., 1974-78, chmn. dept. history, 1977-78, assoc. dean Coll. Arts and Letters, 1978-80, dean coll., 1980-85; v.p. Calif. State U., San Bernardino, 1985-89; pres. Calif. State U., Dominguez Hills, 1989—; now pres./chancellor. Author: Richard Bland and the Origins of the Virginia Revolt, 1982; editor: Environmental Decay in Its Historial Context, 1973, Race, Prejudice and the Origins of Salvery in America, 1975, Liberation in the Americas,, 1978. Served to col. USMCR, 1960-89. Mem. Orgn. Am. Historians, Am. Hist. Assn., USMCR Officers Assn. (pres. chpt. 1977-79). Home: 1500 E Roosevelt Rd Long Beach CA 90807-3723 Office: Calif State U Dominiguez Hills Office of President 1000 E Victoria St Carson CA 90747-0005

DETWILER, PETER MURRAY, legislative consultant, educator; b. Visalia, Calif., Nov. 5, 1949; s. Donald M. and Mary Alice (Murray) D.; m. Caroline Margaret Cain, Sept. 2, 1972; children: Stephen C., Eric J. BA in Govt., St. Mary's Coll. Calif., 1971; MA in Pub. Policy and Adminstrn., U. Wis., 1972. Asst. exec. officer Local Agy. Formation Commn., San Diego, 1972-75; dir. local govt. unit Gov.'s Office Planning and Rsch., Sacramento, 1975-81; staff dir. Senate Local Govt. Com., Sacramento, 1982-95; dir. staff Senate Housing and Land Use Com., Sacramento, 1995—; instr. Calif. State U., Sacramento, 1991—. Author: (chpt.) Calif. Environ. Law, 1989, State & Regional Initiatives for Managing Development, 1992; mem. bd. exec. editors, contbr. articles Land Use & Environment Forum, 1991-96. Leader Boy Scouts Am., Sacramento, 1984—. Democrat. Roman Catholic. Office: Senate Housing and Land Use State Capitol Rm 407 Sacramento CA 95814-4906

DEUBLE, JOHN L., JR., environmental science and engineering services consultant; b. N.Y.C., Oct. 2, 1932; s. John Lewis and Lucille (Klotzbach) D.; m. Thelma C. Honeychurch, Aug. 28, 1955; children: Deborah, Steven. AA, AS in Phys. Sci., Stockton Coll., 1957; BA, BS in Chemistry, U. Pacific, 1959. Cert. profl. chemist, profl. engr., environ. inspector; registered environ. profl., registered environ. assessor. Sr. chemist Aero-Gen Corp., Sacramento, Calif., 1959-67; asst. dir. rsch. Lockheed Propulsion Co., Redlands, Calif., 1968-73; asst. div. mgr. Systems, Sci. and Software, La Jolla, Calif., 1974-79; gen. mgr. Wright Energy Nev. Corp., Reno, Nev., 1980-81; v.p. Energy Resources Co., La Jolla, 1982-83; dir. hazardous waste Aerovironment Inc., Monrovia, Calif., 1984-85; sr. program mgr. Ogden Environ. and Energy Svcs., San Diego, 1989-96; environ. cons. Encinitas, Calif., 1986-88, 97—. Contbr. articles profl. jours. With USAF, 1951-54. Recipient Tech. award Am. Ordnance Assn., 1969, Cert. of Achievement Am. Men and Women of Sci., 1986, Envrion. Registry, 1992. Fellow Am. Inst. Chemists; mem. ASTM, Am. Chem. Soc., AM. Inst. Chem. Engrs., Am. Meteorol. Soc., Am. Nuclear Soc., Am. Def. Preparedness Assn., Air and Waste Mgmt. Assn., Calif. Inst. Chemists, Hazardous Materials Control Rsch. Inst., N.Y. Acad. Scis., Environ. Assessors Assn. Republican. Lutheran. Home and Office: Planning Asssocs 369 Cerro St Encinitas CA 92024-4805

DE URIOSTE, GEORGE ADOLFO, IV, software company executive; b. San Francisco, June 25, 1955; s. George Adolfo Sr. and Janet Germaine (Bruzzone) de U. BS, U. So. Calif., L.A., 1978; MBA, U. Calif., Berkeley, 1980. CPA, Calif. Auditor, cons. Deloitte Haskins & Sells, San Francisco, 1980-83; sr. fin. analyst Genstar Corp., San Francisco, 1983-85, Rolm Mil-Spec Computers, Inc., San Jose, Calif., 1986-88; mgr. fin. planning and analysis Ask Computer Systems, Inc., Mountain View, Calif., 1988-90; CFO TeamOne Systems, Inc., Sunnyvale, Calif., 1990-92; v.p. of fin. Remedy Corp., Mountain View, Calif., 1992—. Pres. U. So. Calif. Commerce Assocs., San Francisco, 1988-89. Mem. AICPA, Calif. Soc. CPAs, Churchill Club (bd. dirs., vice chmn. Palo Alto, Calif. 1989-94). Home: 282 Walker Dr Mountain View CA 94043-2108 Office: Remedy Corp 1505 Salado Dr Mountain View CA 94043-1110

DEUTSCH, BARRY JOSEPH, management development company executive; b. Gary, Ind., Aug. 10, 1941; s. Jack Elias and Helen Louise (La Rue) D.; B.S., U. So. Calif., 1969, M.B.A. magna cum laude, 1970; m. Gina Krispinsky, Feb. 20, 1972. Lectr. mgmt. U. So. Calif., L.A., 1967-70; pres., founder The Deutsch Group, Inc., mgmt. cons. co. tng. upper and middle mgmt., L.A., 1970—, chmn. bd., 1975—; founder, chief exec. officer, chmn. bd. Investment Planning Network, Inc., 1988—; dir. Red Carpet Corp. Am., 1975-77, United Fin. Planners, 1984-86. Chmn. bd. govs. Am. Hist. Ctr., 1980—. With M.I., U.S. Army, 1964-66. Mem. Am. Mgmt. Assn., Am. Soc. Bus. and Mgmt. Cons.'s, Am. Soc. Tng. and Devel., Internat. Mgmt. by Objectives Inst. Author: Leadership Techniques, 1969, Recruiting Techniques, 1970, The Art of Selling, 1973, Professional Real Estate Management, 1975, Strategic Planning, 1976, Employer/Employee: Making the Transition, 1978, Managing by Objectives, 1980, Conducting Effective Performance Appraisal, 1982, Advanced Supervisory Development, 1984, Managing A Successful Financial Planning Business, 1988, How to Franchise Your Business, 1991. Home: 4509 Candleberry Ave Seal Beach CA 90740-3026

DEUTSCH, GARY MICHAEL, internist; b. Chgo., Sept. 26, 1951; s. Sidney Deutsch and Olivia Sellinger; m. Debra Melshenker, May 2, 1976; children: Gordon, Adam, Ryan, Tyler. AB in Biology, Washington U., 1973; MD, Rush U., 1977. Diplomate Am. Bd. Internal Medicine. Resident in internal medicine U. Calif., San Francisco, 1980; pvt. practice Santa Paula, Calif., 1980—; asst. clin. prof. Ventura (Calif.) County Med. Ctr. UCLA Sch. Medicine, 1980—; qualified med. evaluator Calif. Indsl. Bd., Sacramento, 1994—. Bd. dirs., safety dir. Am. Youth Soccer Orgn., Ventura, 1994—. Mem. Calif. Med. Soc., Ventura County Med. Soc., Phi Beta Kappa, Alpha Omega Alpha. Office: 243 March St Santa Paula CA 93060-2511

DEVANEY, DONALD EVERETT, law enforcement official; b. Providence, Nov. 21, 1936; s. William Francis and Elizabeth Florence (Hill) D.; m. Tokiko Yoshida, May 19, 1960; 1 child, George Y. AA in Edn., El Paso Community Coll., 1973; BA, SUNY, Albany, 1979. Cert. healthcare protection adminstr. Internat. Healthcare Safety and Security Found. Sgt. maj. U.S. Army, 1954-83; customs inspector U.S. Customs Svc., Honolulu, 1983-84; provost marshal Tripler Army Med. Ctr., Honolulu, 1984—; regional chair Europe and Asia, 1989-93; Pacific rep. Chief of Staff Retiree Coun.; past dir. Kalihi-Palama Immigrant Svc. Ctr.; extraordinary min. of the eucharist Tripler Catholic Cmty. Cmty. mem. cmty. based ednl. coun. Webling Elem. Sch.; bd. dirs. USO, 1996, Coalition for a Drug Free Hawaii, 1996. Decorated Legion of Merit; recipient Disting Svc. award Hawaii Joint Police, 1977, 86, George Washington Honor medal Freedom's Found., 1973, Order Mil. Med. Merit, 1996. Mem. Hawaii Joint Police Assn. (pres. 1985), U.S. Army CID Command (assoc.), Nat. Assn. for Uniformed Svcs. (v.p. Hawaii chpt., nat. bd. dirs. 1996—), U.S. Army Retiree Coun. (U.S. Army Pacific rep., vice chmn.), Hawaii Law Enforcement and Pvt. Security (chmn. awards com.), Hawaii Joint Police Assn. (past pres.), Internat. Assn. for Healthcare Security and Safety (sec. Hawaii chpt.), Hawaii Coun. Police and Pvt. Security (bd. dirs. 1996—), Noncommd. Officer Assn. (life), Ret. Enlisted Assn. (life), DAV (life chpt. 3), Friend Med. Regt., Rotary (pres. Pearl Harbor chpt. 1991-92, dir. cmty. svc. dist. 5000, 1992-93), KC. Roman Catholic. Home: 98-911 Ainanui Loop Aiea HI 96701-2766 Office: Office Provost Marshal Tripler Army Med Ctr Honolulu HI 96859

DEVENOT, DAVID CHARLES, human resource executive; b. Indpls., May 27, 1939; s. Charles Joseph and Pearl (Geodfry) D.; children: Daniel, Mark. BBA, U. Hawaii, 1962. Dir. indsl. rels. USP Corp subs. Consol. Foods, Sara Lee, San Jose, Calif., 1964-70; sr. human resource cons. Hawaii Employers Coun., Honolulu, 1970—. Bd. dirs. Hawn Humane Soc., Honolulu, 1975—, Lanikila Rehab. Ctr., Honolulu, 1985—, Am. Cancer Soc., 1989, pres. Pacific divsn. Mem. Santa Clara Valley Pers. Assn. (pres. 1968-69), Soc. Human Resource Mgmt., Indsl. Rels. Rsch. Assn. Home: 46-141 Nahiku St Kaneohe HI 96744-3629 Office: Hawaii Employers Coun 2682 Waiwai Loop Honolulu HI 96819-1938

DEVILBISS, JONATHAN FREDERICK, aircraft sales engineer; b. Saiburi, Pattani, Thailand, July 23, 1961; s. Frederick Henry and Iva Marie (Weidner) D.; m. Laura Anne Carr, June 4, 1994. BS in Aero. Engring., Purdue U., 1984; BA in Liberal Arts, Wheaton (Ill.) Coll., 1984. Sales engr. Brit. Aerospace Inc., Herndon, Va., 1985-88, tech. sales engr., 1988-89, sr. tech. sales engr., 1989-91, sr. product engr., 1991-92; mgr. product mktg. Jetstream Aircraft subs. Brit. Aerospace, Sterling, Va., 1993-94. Mem. AIAA, SAE (assoc.). Republican. Evangelical Christian. Home: 1651 S Riverstone Ln Apt 305 Boise ID 83706

DEVIN, JERRY PRESTON, orthodontist; b. Dubuque, Iowa, Nov. 9, 1939; s. James Howard ad Edna May (Waltemeyer) D.; m. Irene Kathryn Duvall, June 7, 1964; children: Lance, Shelley, Clint. DDS, U. Iowa, 1963; MS in Dentistry, U. Minn., 1969. Pvt. practice, Laramie, Wyo., 1969—; chmn. bd. Delta Dental Wyo., Cheyenne, 1990-92. Lt. USN, 1964-66. Mem. Pierre Fauchard Acad., Rocky Mountain Soc. Orthodontists (pres. 1992-93), Rotary (pres. Laramie 1989-90). Republican. Lutheran. Home: 3601 Grays Gable Rd Laramie WY 82070 Office: 502 S 4th St Laramie WY 82070-3704

DEVIN, RICHARD, film industry executive; b. Rochester, N.Y., Oct. 30, 1963; s. Patsy and Antoinette (Perrone) LaFica. AA, Monroe Coll., Rochester, 1983; BA, Cornell U., 1986. Actor N.Y.C., 1986-91; dir. project devel. Entertainment Mktg., Universal City, Calif., 1991-95; media advisor Simco & Assocs., L.A., 1995-96; exec. casting dir. Am. Film, L.A., 1996—; producing dir. Light Opera of L.A., 1996—. Author: Actors' resumes, 1994, Do You Want to be an Actor?, 1996; playwright: My Mother's Coming, 1990 (Gypsy award 1995), Deceptive Peace, 1990. Recipient Vital Arts award Found. for Vital Arts, 1990. Office: Entertainment Mktg Co PO Box 8559 Universal City CA 91618

DEVINCINTIS, LANI, adult educator. Recipient Regional Person of Yr. award, 1993, State Cmty. Educator of Yr. award, 1996. Office: Glendale Community Coll 1500 N Verdugo Rd Glendale CA 91208-2809

DEVINE, MICHAEL J., history center director, history educator; b. Aurora, Ill., Jan. 5, 1945; s. Richard J. and Elayne Marie (Esser) D.; m. Maija Rhee, Nov. 7, 1970; children: Bret, Christopher, Mia, Lisa, T. Brian. BA, Loras Coll., Dubuque, Iowa, 1967; MA, Ohio State U., 1968, PhD, 1974; LHD (hon.), Lincoln (Ill.) Coll., 1988. Vol. Peace Corps, 1969-70; from instr. to asst. prof. history Ohio U., Athens, 1972-74; program adminstr. Ohio Hist. Soc., Columbus, 1974-77, asst. dir., 1977-79; exec. dir. Cin. Consortium Colls., 1979-82; dep. dir. Hist. St. Mary's (Md.) City, 1982-85; dir. State of Ill. Hist. Preservation Agy. and Hist. Soc., Springfield, 1985-91; rsch. ctr. dir. Am. Heritage Ctr., Univ. Wyo., Laramie, 1991—; adj. lectr. history Xavier U., Cin., 1979-82; sr. lectr. Fulbright Commn., Argentina, 1983; apptd. Wyo. Commn. Parks and Cultural Affairs, 1994. Author: John W. Foster, 1981; editor: (with others) Ohio: The Next 25 Years, 1978. Mem. St. Mary's County Libr. Planning Commn., 1984-85; sec. Abraham Lincoln Assn., Springfield, 1985-91; trustee Cin. Fire Mus., 1980-82; appointed Ill., Mich. Canal Nat. Heritage Corridor Commn., 1988-91; elected Wyo. Coun. Humanities, 1996. Am. Philos. Soc. grantee, 1978, NEH fellow, 1980. Mem. Am. Hist. Assn., Am. Assn. State and Local History, Nat. Coun. Pub. History (bd. dirs. 1993). Home: 3707 Reynolds St Laramie WY 82070-5069 Office: U Wyo Am Heritage Ctr Laramie WY 82070

DEVITT, JOHN LAWRENCE, consulting engineer; b. Denver, Sept. 27, 1925; s. Oliver Hinkley and Ellen Elizabeth (McPherson) D.; children: Jane, David, Ellen. BSEE, U. Colo., 1945, MS, 1949. Registered profl. engr., Colo. Engr. U.S. Bureau of Reclamation, Denver, 1947-50; plant mgr. AMF Corp., Colorado Springs, Colo., 1951-55; v.p., gen. mgr. Whittaker Corp. Power Sources div., Denver, 1955-61; chief engr. Metron Instrument Co., Denver, 1962-65; mgr. of electrochemistry Gates Corp., Denver, 1965-71; pvt. practice as a consulting engr. Denver, 1971—; profl. jazz musician (saxophone), Denver, 1946—. Co-inventor sealed lead-acid and lead-chloride batteries. Lt. USNR, 1943-52, PTO. Recipient Battery Research award, The Electrochem. Soc., 1986. Mem. The Electrochem. Soc., Am. Chem. Soc., Inst. Elect. and Electronic Engrs., Colo. Mountain Club (pres. 1975), Am. Alpine Club, New York. Office: Consulting Engr 985 S Jersey St Denver CO 80224-1418

DEVITT-GRASSO, PAULINE VIRGINIA, civic volunteer, nurse; b. Salem, Mass., May 13, 1930; d. John M. and Mary Elizabeth (Cologey) Devitt; m. Frank Anthony Grasso, Oct. 26, 1968; 1 stepson, Christopher Anthony. BSN, Boston Coll., 1952; student, Boston U., 1954-55, Boston State Tchrs. Coll., 1953-54. RN. Staff nurse J.P. Kennedy Jr. Meml. Hosp., Brighton, Mass., 1952-53; head nurse, day supr. J.P. Kennedy Jr. Meml. Hosp., Brighton, 1953-54, day supr., 1955, clin. instr., 1955-58, adminstrv. asst., 1968, dir. nursing edn., 1958-68; vis. instr. Boston Coll., Mass. State Coll., Meml. Hosp. Sch. Nursing, Newton, Mass. Meml. Hosp. Sch. Nursing, 1955-68, CUA S of N, 1990; bd. dirs. Behavioral Health Svcs. Inc., treas., 1996. Pres. Project H.O.P.E., Manhattan Beach, Calif., 1982; pres. adv. coun. Meals on Wheels, Salvation Army, 1989, 90, 91, bd. dirs. Redondo Beach, 1992—, sec. bd. dirs., 1994; cons. Manhattan Beach Housing Found., 1986—, Manhattan Beach Case Mgr., 1982—; mem. adv. coun. South Bay Sr. Svcs., Torrance, Calif., 1986—, pres., 1994, pres. adv. bd. 1995—; sr. advocate City of Manhattan Beach, 1982; bd. dirs. Ret. Sr. Vol. Program, Torrance, 1986-90; bd. dirs. Behavioral Health Svcs., 1992—, treas. 1996, hosp. com., fin. com., exec. com., devel. com.; neighborhood chair Girl Scouts U.S.; mem. Beach City Coun. on Aging, 1983-91; mem. Salvation Army Ladies Aux.; mem. adv. bd. Salvation Army Corps, Redondo Beach. Recipient Cert. of Appreciation, County of L.A., 1988, Vol. of the Yr. award City of Manhattan Beach, 1988, Award of Honor County of L.A., 1989, State of Calif. Senate Rules Com. Resolution Commendation, 1988; named Outstanding Vol. Cath. Daus. of Am., 1986, Vol. of Yr. City Manhattan Beach, 1986-87; Rose and Scroll award Manhattan Beach C. of C., 1989, Art Michel Meml. Community Svc. award Manhattan Beach Rotary Club, 1989, Cert. of Appreciation KC's Queen of Martyrs Coun., 1989, Redondo Beach Lila Bell award Salvation Army, 1989, others, Manhattan Beach Vol. Appreciation award, 1982, 83, 84, 85, 86, 88, 90, 91, 92, 93, cert. South Bay Centinela Credit Union, 1990; nominated for Pres's. Vol. Action award Project H.O.P.E., 1987. Mem. AARP, South Bay Geneal. Soc., New Eng. Hist. and Geneal. Soc., Polish Genal. Soc. So. Calif., Am. Martyrs Altar Soc. (pres. 1983, coun. mem.-at-large 1992), Cath. U. Am. Nat. Alumni Assn. (hon.), Cath. U. Am. Sch. Nursing Alumni Assn. (hon.), Boston Coll. Alumni Assn., Manhattan Beach Sr. Citizens Club (pres. 1985-86, 88-89), Lions (Citizen of Yr. award Manhattan Beach club 1986), DAV (comdr.'s club 1990, 91, 92), Lady in Equestrian Order of Holy Sepulchre of Jerusalem. Democrat. Roman Catholic. Home: 329 3rd St Manhattan Beach CA 90266-6410

DEVLIN, DAVID STUART, biology educator; b. Greensboro, N.C., Dec. 12, 1957; s. Joseph Stuart and Margaret Joan (Wright) D.; m. Marguerite Cochrane, Aug. 1, 1981 (div. July 1989); 1 child, Joshua Ryan; m. Sandra Escobar, June 21, 1991; stepchildren: Stephanie Grijalva, Crystal Grijalva, Kathleen Grijalva, Levi Grijalva, Victoria Grijalva. BA, Luther Coll., 1980; MA in Tchg., Western N.Mex. U., 1993. Cert. secondary sci. and biology tchr. H.s. sci. tchr. Deming (N.Mex.) Pub. Schs., 1983-84; jr. h.s. sci. tchr. Cobre Pub. Schs., Bayard, N.Mex., 1984-93, dept. chair, 1989-93; field supr. for edn. Western N.Mex. U., Silver City, 1993; h.s. biology tchr. Apollo H.S., Glendale, Ariz., 1993—. Editor of jr. div. papers N.Mex. Jour. of Sci., 1993. Mem. NEA (local pres.), AAAS, Nat. Sci. Tchrs. Assn., N.Mex. Acad. of Sci. (state dir. of jr. acad. of sci. 1992-93, bd. dirs. 1992-93), N.Mex. Sci. Tchrs. Assn. Democrat. Office: Apollo H S 8045 N 47th Ave Glendale AZ 85302-6402

DEVLIN, PATRICIA, lawyer; b. Vallejo, Calif., July 25, 1945. BA magna cum laude, U. Wash., 1968; JD, U. Calif., 1977. Bar: Calif. 1977, Hawaii 1978, U.S. Dist. Ct. Hawaii 1978. With Carlsmith Ball Wichman Case & Ichiki, Honolulu. Mem. ABA, State Bar Calif., Hawaii Soc. Corp. Planners (pres. 1992-93), Phi Beta Kappa. Office: Carlsmith Ball Wichman Case & Ichiki 1001 Bishop St Honolulu HI 96813-3429

DEVOE, KENNETH NICKOLAS, food service executive, mayor; b. Mineola, N.Y., Sept. 13, 1944; s. Kenneth Pettit and Wykiena (Bos) D.; m. Linda Faye Mizer, May 7, 1965; children: Andrea W., Christina L., Kenneth C., Paula A. Student, Merced Coll., 1970-75. Police sgt. Merced (Calif.) Police Dept., 1966-75; sheriff sgt. Mariposa (Calif.) County Sheriff, 1975-81; pk. mgr. Am. Campgrounds Inc., Bellevue, Wash., 1981-83; owner DeVoe Enterprises, Atwater, Calif., 1983—. Chmn. Merced County Assn. Govts., 1990—, Atwater 4th of July Com., 1983—; asst. mayor City of Atwater, 1987-94, mayor, 1994—. With USAF, 1962-66. Mem. Atwater C. of C. (dir. 1991, dir.-at-large 1983-86, Citizen of Yr. 1987), Merced Trade Club (dir. 1991—), Castle Air Force Base Cols. Club., Kiwanis, Masons. Republican. Home: 3302 Sextant Dr Atwater CA 95301-4725 Office: Devoe Enterprises 1898 Bellevue Rd Atwater CA 95301-2668

DEVON, GARY ALBERT, newspaper editor; b. Ellensburg, Wash., Apr. 9, 1961; s. Larry D. and Judith A. (Connot) DeV.; m. Anne F. Ringwood, Sept. 24, 1994; children: Segornae, Morgan. BA in Comm. and Journalism, Gonzaga U., 1983. Reporter, photographer Post Falls (Idaho) Tribune, 1982-83; freelaance journalist and photographer, Seattle, 1983-87; mng. editor Okanogan Valley Gazette-Tribune, weekly, Oroville, Wash., 1987—. Recipient 1st place award for comprehensive coverage of story and for news photograph Wash. Newspaper Pubs. Assn., 1990, 1st place award for news photograph and 2d place award for best article, 1991, 2d place award for best news article, 1992, 1st place award for best editorial, 1993. Mem. Soc. Profl. Journalists. Democrat. Roman Catholic. Home: PO Box 1144 Oroville WA 98844-1144 Office: Okanogan Valley Gazette- Tribune 813 Central Ave Oroville WA 98844

DEVORE, MARILYN RUTH, education educator, consultant; b. Torrance, Calif., Mar. 6, 1947; d. Floyd Raymond and MaryEllen (Jordon) DeVore; numerous foster children. BA in Edn., Ariz. State U., 1968; MA in Adminstrn., Columbia Pacific U., 1979, PhD in Curriculum Devel., 1981. Cert. elem. tchr., math., tchr., adminstr., Calif. Tchr. Ocean View Sch. Dist., Huntington Beach, Calif., 1968-77; tchr. San Juan Ridge Union Sch. Dist., North San Juan, Calif., 1977-79, prin./supt., 1979-83, hmesch. program devel., 1979-83; program dir. Butte County Office Edn., Oroville, Calif., 1983-88; tchr. homesch. program Marysville (Calif.) Joint Unified Sch. Dist., 1988—; man contbr./cons. Idea & Co., North San Juan, 1982-89; alternative edn. cons. Calif. State Dept. Edn., Sacramento, 1981—; feasibility and needs specialist to numerous pvt. and pub. schs.; presenter in field. Author: The Home School Parent Manual, 1985; co-author: books, manuals, and curricula. Officer, mem. PTA, Huntington Beach, 1968-77; bd. dirs. San Juan Vol. Fire Dept. North San Juan, 1978-82; treas. Forbestown (Calif.) Adv. Coun., 1990—; mem., pres. Yuba Feather Hist. Assn. and Mus., Forbestown, 1989—; adult edn. and continuation tchr., Forbestown, 1989—. Recipient Tchr. of Yr. award San Juan Tchrs. Assn., 1981. Mem. NEA (nat. del. 1970-76), Calif. Tchrs. Assn. (rep., Golden Apple awrd 1975), Ocean View Tchrs. Assn. (pres. 1975-77), Marysville Unified Tchrs. Assn., Learning Alternatives Resources Network, Nat. Assn. Investors, Habitat for Humanity. Democrat. Christian. Office: Abraham Lincoln Sch 1919 B St Marysville CA 95901-3731

DEVORE, PAUL CAMERON, lawyer; b. Great Falls, Mont., Apr. 25, 1932; s. Paul Theodore and Maxine (Cameron) DeV.; m. Roberta Humphrey, Feb. 3, 1962; children: Jennifer Ross, Andrew Cameron, Christopher Humphrey. BA, Yale U., 1954; MA, Cambridge U., 1956; JD, Harvard U., 1961. Bar: Wash. 1961. Assoc. Wright, Innis, Simon & Todd, Seattle, 1961-66; ptnr. Davis Wright Tremaine, Seattle, 1967—, chmn. exec. com., 1983-95; bd. dirs. Seattle Times Co., 1976-94; mem. adv. bd. BNA Media Law Reporter, 1978—. Chmn. Seattle C.C., 1967-68; pres. A Contemporary Theatre, Seattle, 1972-74, Bush Sch., Seattle, 1976-79, Virginia Mason Med. Found., 1984-85; sec. Seattle Art Mus., 1973—; chmn. Virginia Mason Rsch. Ctr., 1983-84, Seattle Found., 1985-87, Children's Hosp. Found., 1988—, chmn., 1993-95; trustee Lakeside Sch., 1995—; chmn. bd. visitors U. Wash. Sch. Comm., 1989—. Mem. ABA (chmn. forum on comm. law 1981-84), Wash. State Bar Assn. (chmn. sect. corp. bus. and banking law 1981-82, bench, bar, press com. 1984-90), Seattle-King County Bar Assn. (trustee 1975-76), Seattle Tennis Club, Univ. Club, Phi Beta Kappa, Beta Theta Phi. Home: 1516 E Howe St Seattle WA 98112-2824 Office: Davis Wright Tremaine 2600 Century Sq 1501 4th Ave Seattle WA 98101-1662

DE VRIES, KENNETH LAWRENCE, mechanical engineer, educator; b. Ogden, Utah, Oct. 27, 1933; s. Sam and Fern (Slater) DeV.; m. Kay M. McGee, Mar. 1, 1959; children: Kenneth, Susan. AS in Civil Engring., Weber State Coll., 1953; BSME, U. Utah, 1959, PhD in Physics, Mech. Engring., 1962. Registered profl. engr., Utah. Rsch. engr. hydraulic group Convair Aircraft Corp., Fort Worth, 1957-58; prof. dept. mech. engring. U. Utah, Salt Lake City, 1969-75, mem. faculty, 1969—; prof. dept. mech. engring., 1976—; Disting. prof. U. Utah, Salt Lake City, 1991—, chmn. dept., 1970-81, sr. assoc. dean Coll. Engring., 1983-97, acting dean Coll. Engring., 1997—; program dir. div. materials rsch. NSF, Washington, 1975-76; materials cons. Browning, Morgan, Utah, 1972—; cons. 3M Co., Mpls., 1985—; tech. adv. bd. Emerson Electric, St. Louis, 1978—; mem. Utah Coun. Sci. and Tech., 1973-77; trustee Gordon Rsch. Conf., 1989—, chair, 1992-93. Co-author: Analysis and Testing of Adhesive Bonds, 1978; contbr. chpts. to numerous books, articles and abstracts to profl. publs. Fellow ASME, Am. Phys. Soc.; mem. Am. Chem. Soc. (polymer div.), Soc. Engring. Scis. (nat. officer), Adhesion Soc. (nat. officer). Mem. LDS Ch. Office: U Utah Coll Engring 2220 Merrill Engring Bldg Salt Lake City UT 84112

DEW, WILLIAM WALDO, JR., bishop; b. Newport, Ky., Dec. 14, 1935; s. William Waldo and Thelma (Dittus) D.; m. Mae Marie Eggers, Jan. 5, 1958; children: Linda Dew-Hiersoux, William, Marilyn. BA, Union Coll., Barbourville, Ky., 1957; MDiv, Drew Theol. Sch., 1961; PhD (hon.), Rust Coll., 1991, Union Coll., 1992. Ordained to ministry United Meth. Ch. as deacon, 1958, as elder, 1963. Pastor Springville (Calif.) United Meth. Ch., 1961-64, Lindsay (Calif.) United Meth. Ch., 1964-67, Meml. United Meth. Ch., Clovis, Calif., 1967-72, Epworth United Meth. Ch., Berkeley, Calif., 1972-79; dist. supt. Cen. Dist. Calif.-Nev. Annual Conf., Modesto, Calif., 1979-84; pastor San Ramon Valley United Meth. Ch., Alamo, Calif., 1984-88; bishop United Meth. Ch., Portland, Oreg., 1988-96, United Meth. Ch. Desert S.W. Conf., Phoenix, 1996—; lectr. Pacific Sch. Religion, Berkeley, 1976-79. Trustee Willamette U., Salem, Oreg., 1988-96, Alaska Pacific U., Anchorage, 1988-96, Claremont Sch. Theology, 1996—. Paul Harris fellow Rotary Internat., 1988. Democrat. Office: United Meth Desert Southwest Conf 1550 E Meadowbrook # 200 Phoenix AZ 85014-4040

DEWALL-OWENS, KAREN MARIE, marketing consultant; b. Phoenix, May 31, 1943; d. Merle C. and Agnes M. (Larson) Feller; m. Charles E. DeWall, Sept. 3, 1963 (div. Feb. 1988); 1 child, Leslie Karen; m. John Dailor Owens, Apr. 16, 1995. AA, Phoenix Coll., 1969. Media buyer Wade Advt., Sacramento, 1964-66; media dir., Harwood Advt., Phoenix, 1967-71; co-owner, account exec. DeWall & Assocs. Advt. Co., 1971-87; dir. advt. Auto Media, Inc./Automotive Investment Group, Phoenix, 1987-93; owner Karen & Co. Advt., Phoenix, 1993—. Bd. dirs. Bosom Buddies-Breast Cancer Orgn., Sunday on Ctrl. Festivals; sustaining mem. Jr. League of Phoenix; mem. Heritage Sq. Commn., City of Phoenix. Named Ad-2 Advt. Person of Yr., Phoenix, 1984. Mem. Am. Women in Radio and TV (achievement award 1986), Phoenix Union Alumni Assn. Republican. Home: 10847 N 11th St Phoenix AZ 85020-5836 Office: Karen & Co Advt 10847 N 11th St Phoenix AZ 85020-5836

DEWEY, DONALD WILLIAM, magazine publisher, editor, writer; b. Honolulu, Sept. 30, 1933; s. Donald William and Theckla Jean (Engeborg) D.; m. Sally Rae Ryan, Aug. 7, 1961; children: Michael Kevin, Wendy Ann. Student, Pomona Coll., 1953-55. With Pascoe Steel Corp., Pomona, Calif., 1955-56, div. Reynolds Aluminum Co., Los Angeles, 1956-58, Switzer Panel Corp., Pasadena, Calif., 1958-60; sales and gen. mgr. Western Pre-Cast Concrete Corp., Ontario, Calif., 1960-62; editor, pub. R/C Modeler Mag., Sierra Madre, Calif., 1963—, Freshwater and Marine Aquarium Mag., Sierra Madre, 1978—; pres., chmn. bd. R/C Modeler Corp., Sierra Madre, 1963—. Author: Radio Control From the Ground Up, 1970, Flight Training Course, 1973, For What It's Worth, Vol. 1, 1973, Vol. 2, 1975; contbr. articles to profl. jours. Sustaining mem. Rep. Nat. Com., 1981—; charter mem. Nat. Congl. Club, 1981—; mem. Rep. Presdl. Task Force, 1981—, U.S. Senatorial Club, 1983—, 1984 Presdl. Trust, Conservative Caucus, Nat. Tax Limitation Com., Nat. Conservative Polit. Action Com., Ronald Reagan Presdl. Libr. Served with Hosp. Corps, USN, 1951-53. Mem. Acad. Model Aeronautics, Nat. Aeronautic Assn., Sport Flyers Assn., Exp. Aircraft Assn., Nat. Amateur Radio Assn., Am. Radio Relay League, APS Writers Unit 30, Am. First Day Cover Soc., Am. Philatelic Soc., Am. Tropical Assn., Am. Revenue Assn., Am. Air-Mail Soc., United Postal Stationery Soc., Confederate Stamp Alliance, Bur. Issues Assn., Precancel Stamp Soc., Pitcairn Island Study Group, Am. Ctr. Law & Justice; Claremont Inst., Found. Endowment, Rutherford Inst., Heritage Found, Calif. State Sheriff's Assn., Am. Dedn. Police, Ven Order Michael the Archangel (hon. knight.). Republican. Lutheran. Home: 410 W Montecito Ave Sierra Madre CA 91024-1716 Office: 144 W Sierra Madre Blvd Sierra Madre CA 91024-2435

DEWEY, RICHARD RYDER, retired internist, educator; b. Westfield, N.J., Feb. 7, 1929; s. Benjamin Harold and Julia (Donlan) D.; m. June Louise Schoknecht, June 2, 1956; children: Richard R. Jr., Valerie Margaret. BA, St. Vincent Coll., 1951; MD, Washington U., St. Louis, 1955. Diplomate Am. Bd. Internal Medicine. Intern Barnes Hosp., St. Louis, 1955-56, asst. resident, 1956-57, fellow in medicine, 1957-58; sr. assoc. resident Strong Meml. Hosp., Rochester, N.Y., 1958-59; clin. instr. Stanford Med. Ctr., Palo Alto, Calif., 1956-64, clin. asst. prof., 1964-74, clin. assoc. prof., 1974-84, clin. prof. Medicine, 1984-94; emeritus clin. prof. medicine, 1994—; pres.

Welch Rd. Internal Med. Orgn., Palo Alto, 1985-94. Dir. health commn. Santa Clara County, San Jose, Calif., 1975-76. Sgt. U.S. Army, 1946-48, Korea. Mem. Am. Soc. Internal Medicine. Republican. Roman Catholic. Home: 38 Wishram Tr PO Box 529 Graeagle CA 96103

DEWHURST, TIMOTHY ANDREW, clinical cardiologist, researcher; b. Farnborough, Kent, Eng., Dec. 24, 1961; arrived in Can., 1969; arrived in U.S., 1986; s. William George and Margaret (Dransfield) D.; m. Rebecca Dana Fox, Aug. 21, 1988. BSc in Chem. and Biology with honors, Stanford U., 1982; MD in Rsch. with honors, U. Alberta, Edmonton, Alberta, Can., 1986. Diplomate Am. Bd. Internal Medicine, Am. Bd. Cardiovascular Diseases. Resident internal medicine Emory U. Affiliated Hosps., Atlanta, 1986-89; cardiology fellow U. Washington, Seattle, 1989-91, chief cardiology fellow, 1991-92, interventional cardiology fellow, 1992-93; acting instr. U. Washington Med. Ctr., Seattle, 1992—; staff physician U. Washington Med. Ctr., Seattle VA Med. Ctr., 1992-94; cardiologist The Polyclinic, Seattle, 1994—. Author: (with others) The Practice of Interventional Cardiology, 1993, Nuclear Cardiology: State of the Art and Future Directions, 1993, Nuclear Cardiology, 1994; contbr. to profl. jours. Am. Heart Assn. grantee, 1992-93. Fellow Am. Coll. Cardiology; mem. Am. Heart Assn., Am. Coll. Physicians, Alpha Omega Alpha. Office: The Polyclinic 1145 Broadway Seattle WA 98122-4201

DEWHURST, WILLIAM GEORGE, psychiatrist, educator, research director; b. Frosterley, Durham, Eng., Nov. 21, 1926; came to Can., 1969; s. William and Elspeth Leslie (Begg) D.; m. Margaret Dransfield, Sept. 17, 1960; children—Timothy Andrew, Susan Jane. B.A., Oxford U., Eng., 1947, B.M., B.Ch., 1950; MA, Oxford U., 1961; D.P.M. with distinction, London U., 1961. House physician, surgeon London Hosp., 1950-52, jr. registrar, registrar, 1954-58; registrar, sr. registrar Maudsley Hosp., London, 1958-62, cons. physician, 1965-69; lectr. Inst. Psychiatry, London, 1962-64, sr. lectr., 1965-69; assoc. prof. psychiatry U. Alta., Edmonton, Can., 1969-72, prof., 1972-92, prof. emeritus, 1992—, Hon. prof. pharmacy and pharm. scis., 1979—, chmn. dept. psychiatry, 1975-90, dir. emeritus neurochem. rsch. unit, 1990—, hon. prof. oncology, 1983—, chmn. med. staff adv. bd., 1988-90; mem. Atty. Gen. Alta. Bd. Rev., 1991, N.W.T. Bd. Rev., 1992, 95 Yukon Bd. Rev., 1994—; pres.'s coun. U. Alta. Hosps., 1988-90, quality improvement coun., 1988-90, ethics consultative com., 1984-88, planning com. Vision 2000, 1985-87, hosps.' planning com. and joint conf. com., 1971, 80, 87-90; cons. psychiatrist Royal Alexandra Hosp., Edmonton, Edmonton Gen. Hosp., Alberta Hosp., Ponoka, Ponoka Gen. Hosp.; chmn. med. coun. Can. Test Com., 1977-79, Royal Coll. Text Com. in Psychiatry, 1971-80, examiner, 1975-83. Co-editor: Neurobiology of Trace Amines, 1984, Pharmacotherapy of Affective Disorders, 1985; also conf. procs. Referee Nature, Can. Psychiat. Assn. Jour., Brit. Jour. Psychiatry; mem. editorial bd. Neuropsychobiology, Psychiat. Jour. U. Ottawa. Contbr. over 100 articles to profl. jours. Chmn. Edmonton Psychiat. Svcs. Steering Com., 1977-80; chmn. Edmonton Psychiat. Svcs. Planning Com., 1985-90; mem. Provincial Mental Health Adv. Coun., 1973-79, Mental Health Rsch. Com., 1973, Edmonton Bd. Health, 1974-76; Can. Psychiat. Rsch. Found., 1985— (also bd. dirs.); bd. dirs. Friends of Schizophrenics, 1980—, Alta., 1988; grant referee Health & Welfare Can., Med. Rsch. Coun. Can., Ont. Mental Health Found., Man. Health Rsch. Coun., B.C. Health Rsch. Found. Capt. Royal Army M.C., 1952-54. Fellow Can. Coll. Neuropsychopharmacology (pres. 1982-84, Coll. medal 1993), Am. Psychopathol. Assn., Am. Coll. Psychiatrists, Am. Psychiat. Assn., Royal Coll. Psychiatrist; mem. AAAS, Alta. Psychiat. Assn. (pres. 1973-74), Can. Psychiat. Assn. (pres. 1983-84), Alta Coll. Physicians and Surgeons (nominating coun. 1992-93, health issues coun. 1994—, co-chmn. task force on drug info., 1996—), Alta. Med. Assn., Child and Adolescent Assn. (bd. dirs., v.p. 1992, pres. 1994—), Assn. for Acad. Psychiatry, Brit. Med. Assn., Faculty Club. Anglican. Office: U Alta Dept Psychiatry, 1E1 01 Mackenzie Ctr, Edmonton, AB Canada T6G 2B7

DEWITT, BARBARA JANE, journalist; b. Glendale, Calif., Aug. 5, 1947; d. Clarence James and Irene Brezina; m. Don DeWitt, Apr. 21, 1974; children: Lisa, Scarlett. BA in Journalism, Calif. State U., Northridge, 1971. Features editor The Daily Ind. Newspaper, Ridgecrest, Calif., 1971-84; fashion editor The Daily Breeze, Torrance, Calif., 1984-89; freelance fashion reporter The Seattle Times, 1990; fashion editor, columnist The Los Angeles Daily News, L.A., 1990—; instr. fashion writing UCLA, 1988, Am. Coll. Applied Arts, L.A., 1996—. Dir. Miss Indian Wells Valley Scholarship Pageant, 1980-84. Recipient 1st Pl. Best Youth Page, Calif. Newspaper Pubs. Assn., 1980, 1st Pl. Best Fashion, Wash. Press Assn., 1989, The Aldo award for fashion journalism, 1995. Republican. Lutheran. Office: The Daily News 21221 Oxnard St Woodland Hills CA 91367-5015

DEWITT, CHARLES NEIL, educational administrator; b. Holbrook, Ariz., Nov. 7, 1949; s. Malcolm Reeves and Martha (Turley) DeW; m. Barbara Jean Pender, July 25, 1969; children: Chas., Brandi Jo DeWitt Hanchett, Cody. Student, Ea. N. Mex. U., 1967-68, Ea. Ariz. Coll., 1968-69; BS in Edn., No. Ariz. U., MA in Edn., 1975. Cert. elem., secondary tchr., prin., supt., ESL tchr., Ariz. Tchr., coach Thatcher (Ariz.) H.S., 1971-74, Show Low (Ariz.) H.S., 1974-75; prin., coach Joseph City (Ariz.) H.S., 1975-79, 80-84; asst. prin. Winslow (Ariz.) H.S., 1979-80; prin. Holbrook (Ariz.) H.S., 1984-92, Pima (Ariz.) H.S., 1992—. Pres. Holbrook Rotary Club, 1990-91; v.p. Holbrook Kiwanis Club, 1991-92. All Star Head Wrestling Coach Ariz. Coaches Assn., Phoenix, 1976, 78, 80, Coach of Yr., 1977, 78; head coach Nat. Jr. Team U.S.A. Wrestling Assn., 1979; inductee Nat. Wrestling Hall of Fame, Stillwater, Okla. Mem. Ariz. Sch. Administrators (secondary exec. bd. 1993—), Ariz. Interscholastic Assn. (bd. dirs. 1996—). Republican. LDS Ch. Home: 6973 N Bryce-Eden Rd Pima AZ 85543 Office: Pima High Sch 131 S Main St Pima AZ 85543

DEWOLFE, FRED STANLEY, social science educator, consultant; b. Seattle, Jan. 7, 1928; s. Tom E. and Mary (Chamberlain) DeW.; m. Brigitte Stolwitzer, Feb. 10, 1955; children: Andrew, Christopher. BA, Lewis & Clark Coll., 1954; MA, Portland U., 1960, Reed Coll., 1963. Mgr. speakers bur. Southwestern Oreg. Community Coll., Coos Bay, Oreg., 1962-63; chmn. faculty assn. Clackamas Community Coll., Oregon City, Oreg., 1968-70; film lectr., N.W. Film Studies Ctr. Clackamas Community Coll., Oregon City, 1970's, chmn. social sci. dept., 1967—; cons., discussant on war and architecture on various TV stas., Portland, 1970—; staff writer N.W. Examiner, Portland. Author: Impressions of Portland, 1970, Old Portland, 1973, Portland West, 1976, Portland Tradition Buildings and People, 1980, Heritage Lost: Two Portlaand Mansions through the Lens of Minorwhite, 1995; contbr. articles to profl. jours. Dir. S.W. Hills Residential League, 1989; mem. Oreg. Cultural Heritage Commn. With U.S. Army, 1951. Decorated Purple Heart. Mem. Oreg. Hist. Soc., Multnomah, Athletic Club. Home: 2752 SW Roswell Ave Portland OR 97201-1664 Office: Clackamas Community Coll 19600 S Molalla Ave Oregon City OR 97045-8980

DEXTER, DALLAS-LEE, education administrator; b. Rockville Center, N.Y., Nov. 30, 1950; d. David D. and Jane (Nesbitt) D.; m. Leonard Eugene Carter, Nov. 6, 1975 (div. 1982). Student numerous dance courses; BS, Mills Coll., 1972; MA, Tchrs. Coll. Columbia U., 1974; postgrad., Nat. U. Mex., 1974, Lesley Coll., 1974, Fgn. Service Inst., 1977, Johns Hopkins Sch. Advanced Internat. Studies, 1982, Middle East Inst., 1982-83, U. N.C., 1972, Bank St. Coll., 1989-92, Bklyn. Coll., 1989-90, U. Alaska, Fairbanks, 1994-96. Cert. sch. adminstr., sch. supr., sch. dist. adminstr., N.Y. Tchr. Am. Sch., Hawalli, Kuwait, 1975-76, Copenhagen (Denmark) Internat. Sch., 1978-80, Rygaards (Denmark) Internat. Sch., Denmark, 1980-82; mktg. contractor Nat. Right to Work Com., Springfield, Va., 1986-87, 21st Century Telemedial Mktg. Services, Inc., Roslyn, Va., 1986; sales mgr. Best Programs, Inc., Arlington, Va., 1987-88; cons. Success, Inc., Palm Beach, Fla., 1985-86, Resources Planning Sys., 1983-86, Mgmt. Engring. Affiliates, Calabasa, Calif., 1984, Aerojet Gen., Washington, 1983; ednl. cons. Mayors Program Summer Youth Employment, Washington, 1986; lectr. troop info. program USMC Hdqrs., Arlington, Va., 1983-84; sales rep. 1st Investors Corp., Arlington, 1983-86; assoc. Potomac Ins. and Fin. Planning Group, Rockville, Md., 1984-89; Am. adminstr., tchr. Kingdom Saudi Arabia, Islamic Saudi acad., Washington, 1986-87; mgr. telesales divsn. Best Programs, Inc., Arlington, 1987-88; dancer Twyla Tharp Dance Co., 1969-70, James Cunningham Co., 1970, others; dir. Head Start programs the Children's Aid Soc., N.Y.C., 1991-94; cons. to child devel. assoc. Nat. Credentialing Coun., Washington, 1994—; coord. Early Intervention/Infant Learning/Respite Programs, North Slope Borough, 1994—; trainer Indian Health Svcs. Physicians; mem. health & social svcs. staff on human growth & devel. Fibromyalgia, CFIDS, 1995—; founder, leader Healing and Support Group for Phys. Pain, 1996—; spkr., trainer numerous univ. presentations on pers. issues, edn. and social svcs. topics. Testified before Mayor's Commn. on Early Childhood and Child Care Programs, N.Y.C., 1991; charter mem., sponsor assn. for Friends of Art Mus. Ams.; bd. dirs. Tchrs. Coll., Columbia U., 1989-91, Kid Pac, 1996—; mem. Family Network Support. Mem. ASCD, NAFE (network dir. 1985-87), Mid. East Inst., Nat. Acad. TV Arts and Scis., Am. Def. Preparedness Assn., Nat. Assn. Edn. Young Children, Family Network Support, Coun. for Exceptional Children (v.p. Alaska divsn. for early childhood 1995—, pres.- elect), Alaska Hist. Soc., Rotary, Columbia U. Club, Phi Delta Kappa (bd. dirs.). Unitarian.

DEY, CAROL RUTH, secondary education educator; b. N.Y., Mar. 9, 1943; d. Robert Lewis Adelson and Anne Millman; m. John Peter Dey, Feb. 9, 1968 (div. Feb. 1978). AA, San Bernardino Valley Coll., 1965; BA, Calif. State U., Sacramento, 1969; MBA, Calif. State U., San Bernardino, 1983, postgrad., 1994—. Sec. U.S. Dept of Interior, USAF, Retail Industry, San Bernardino, Sacramento, Calif., 1960-80; logistics mgr. USAF, San Bernardino, 1980-94; substitute tchr. San Bernardino Unified Sch. Dist., 1994—. Dancer Coppélia, San Bernardino, Calif., 1984; mem. St. Anne's Ch., San Bernardino, 1978—. Mem. Am. Bus. Women's Assn. (Calif. State Coll. scholar), Smithsonian Inst., AF Assn., Alumni Assn. Calif. State U. San Bernardino. Republican. Roman Catholic.

DEYO, RICHARD ALDEN, medical educator; b. New Orleans, May 26, 1949; s. Henry Alden and Jane Morse (Cushman) D.; m. Christina D. Chavez, Oct. 28, 1978 (div. Apr. 1995); children: Andrew, Elizabeth. BA, Grinnell Coll., 1971; MD, Pa. State U., 1975; MPH, U. Wash., 1981. Resident U. Tex. Health Sci. Ctr., San Antonio, 1975-79, asst. prof. medicine, 1982-86; assoc. prof. medicine & health scis. U. Wash., Seattle, 1986-92, prof. medicine & health sci., 1992—; dir. health svcs. rsch. & devel. program Seattle VA Med. Ctr., 1986-92; chair adv. com. on rsch. Que. Workers Compensation Agy., Montreal, Can., 1991-93. Data modeling task force Wash. State Dept. Health, Olympia, 1994-95. Treatment Effectiveness grantee Agy. Health Care Policy & Rsch., 1989—; Robert Wood Johnson Clinical scholar U. Wash., 1979-81. Fellow Am. Coll. Physicians; mem. Am. Soc. Clin. Investigation, Am. Pub. Health Assn., Western Assn. Physicians, Soc. Gen. Internal Medicine (coun. mem.), Assn. Health Svcs. Rsch.

DEZURICK, PAUL A., lawyer; b. Portland, Oreg., 1942. BS, U. San Francisco, 1963, JD, 1968. Bar: Calif. 1968. Law clk. U.S. Dist. Ct. (no. dist.) Calif., 1968-69; ptnr. Graham & James, San Francisco, 1969-93, Dezurick, Edginton & Harrington, Emeryville, Calif., 1993—. Chmn. Emeryville Brownfields Task Force, 1996-97; sec., dir. Alameda County Cmty. Action Program, 1997; sec., dir. Allied Housing, Inc., 1997. Mem. Emeryville Industries Assn. (pres., dir. 1997), West Oakland Commerce Assn. (co-chair bus. resources com. 1996-97). Office: Dezurick Edginton et al 6400 Hollis St Ste 9 Emeryville CA 94608-1052

DEZZANI, DAVID JOHN, lawyer; b. Oakland, Calif., July 31, 1936; s. Maurice Joseph and Henryetta Esther (Greene) D.; m. Rochelle Lee Renner, Nov. 17, 1967; children—Scott, John, Michael, Douglas. Student, U. Vienna, 1960; B.A., U. Calif.-Berkeley, 1961, J.D., 1965; postgrad. U. Tuebingen, Fed. Republic Germany, 1962-63. Bar: Calif. 1965, Hawaii 1966, U.S. Supreme Ct. 1975. Assoc. Goodsill Anderson Quinn & Stifel, Honolulu, 1965-70, ptnr., 1970—. Rotary Found. fellow, 1962; Ford Found. grantee, 1964. Fellow Am. Coll. Trial Lawyers; mem. ABA, Hawaii State Bar Assn. (bd. dirs. 1992-93, 96—), Calif. State Bar Assn., Am. Bd. Trial Advs. (adv.). Office: PO Box 3196 Honolulu HI 96801-3196

D'HEILLY, LOUIS PAUL, marketing executive; b. San Diego, Oct. 22, 1937; s. Andrie Paul and Nellie Mae (Persons) d'H.; m. Maelyn M. Deane McKinley, Apr. 30, 1958 (div. Jan. 1977); children: Daniel, David, Janice, Douglas; m. Jeanne Hesler, Oct. 17, 1997. AA, San Bernardino Valley Coll., 1963; BA, U. Calif., Riverside, 1965. Sr. sales exec. Xerox Corp., San Diego, 1966-76; pres. Mktg. Assocs., Bellevue, Wash., 1977-84; mktg./sales mgr. Triple-L Devel., Escondido, Calif., 1984-85; pres. PdH Internat. Mktg., Seattle, San Diego, 1985—, $D, Del Mar, Calif., 1992—; stock broker, v.p. First Wall St., La Jolla, Calif., 1989-92; pres. Paul d'Heilly Internat. Mktg. and subs., Del Mar, Calif., 1992—; bus. cons. PdH Internat. Mktg., San Diego, pres.; pres., PdH Internat. Telecom., Del Mar; internat. v.p. mktg. Solin Internat., Montreal, Que., Can. Campaign chair Assemblyman Election, Anchorage, 1974; bd. mem. com. Child Abuse Prevention Internat., San Diego, 1987; vice chair LaJolla Latchkey Com., 1990; mem. LEAD San Diego, 1991. Mem. Kiwanis (pres. 1990).

DHUEY, MICHAEL JOSEPH, computer engineer; b. Milw., July 20, 1958; s. Joseph Norbert and Anne King (Neinuber) D.; 1 child, Erica. BSEE, U. Wis., 1980. Computer programmer Morthwest Mutal Life, Milw., 1974-80; computer engr. Apple Computer, Cupertino, Calif., 1980—. Designer Macintosh II Computer, 1987. Mem. IEEE, ACM. Office: Apple Computer 1 Infinite Loop Cupertino CA 95014-2083

DIAMA, BENJAMIN, retired educator, artist, composer, writer; b. Hilo, Hawaii, Sept. 23, 1933; s. Agapito and Catalina (Buscas) D. BFA, Sch. Art Inst. Chgo., 1956. Cert. tchr., Hawaii. Tchr. art, basketball coach Waimea (Kauai, Hawaii) High Sch., 1963-67; tchr. music and art Campbell High Sch., Honolulu, 1967-68; tchr. math. and art Waipahu High Sch., Honolulu, 1968-69; tchr. art and music Palisades Elem. Sch., Honolulu, 1969-70; tchr. typing, history, art and music Honokaa (Hawaii) High Sch., 1970-73; tchr. music Kealakehe Sch., Kailua, 1973-74; ret., 1974. Author, writer, composer: Hawaii, 1983; author: Poems of Faith, 1983-88, School One vs. School Two On The Same School Campus, 1983, The Calendar-Clock Theory of the Universe with Faith -- Above and Beyond, 1984-90; contbr. author to book: Benjamin Diama -- The Calendar Clock Theory of the Universe, 1991, 92; producer, composer (Cassette) Hawaii I Love You, 1986; inventor universal clock, double floater boat. Recipient achievement award Waimea Dept. Edn., purchase award State Found. Arts on Culture and the Arts, 1984, State Found. Arts and Culture Acquisition Painting Art award State of Hawaii Govt. Art Collection. Mem. NEA, Hawaii Tchrs. Assn., Hawaii Edn. Assn., AAAS, Nat. Geog. Soc., Smithsonian Assocs., ASCAP, N.Y. Acad. Scis., Nat. Libr. Poetry (assoc.), Internat. Soc. Poets. Mem. Salvation Army. Home: PO Box 2997 Kailua Kona HI 96745-2997

DIAMANT, JOEL CHARLES, internist; b. N.Y.C., Oct. 11, 1963; s. Bernard and Alice Susan (Ruskin) D.; m. Caroline Ruth Taliaferro, Oct. 9, 1994. AB, U. Calif., Berkeley, 1985; MD with honors, U. Ill., 1990. Diplomate Am. Bd. Internal Medicine. Intern Scripps Clinic/Green Hosp., 1990-91; resident in internal medicine Scripps Clinic, La Jolla, Calif., 1991-93, chief resident in internal medicine, 1993-94, staff physician, 1994—; assoc. dir. internal medicine residency Scripps Clinic/Green Hosp., 1996—. James scholar U. Ill. Coll. Medicine, 1990. Office: Scripps Clinic 10666 N Torrey Pines Rd La Jolla CA 92037-1027

DIAMOND, JOSEF, lawyer; b. L.A., Mar. 6, 1907; s. Michael and Ruby (Shifrin) D.; m. Violett Diamond, Apr. 2, 1933 (dec. 1979); children: Joel, Diane Foreman; m. Ann Dulien, Jan. 12, 1981 (dec. 1984); m. Muriel Bach, 1986. B.B.A., U. Wash., 1929, J.D., 1931. Bar: Wash. 1931, U.S. Dist. Ct. (we. dist.) Wash. 1932, U.S. Ct. Appeals (9th cir.) 1934, U.S. Supreme Ct. 1944. Assoc. Caldwell & Lycette, Seattle, 1931-35; ptnr. Caldwell, Lycette & Diamond, 1935-45; ptnr. Lycette, Diamond & Sylvester, 1945-80, Diamond & Sylvester, 1980-82, of counsel, 1982-88; of counsel Short, Cressman & Burgess, 1988—; chmn. bd. Diamond Parking Inc., Seattle, 1945-70; cons. various businesses. Bd. dirs. Am. Heart Assn., 1960; chmn. Wash. Heart Assn., 1962. Col. JAGC U.S. Army, World War II. Decorated Legion of Merit. Mem. Assn. Trial Lawyers Wash., Wash. Bar Assn., Seattle Bar Assn., The Beavers, Mil. Engrs. Soc., Wash. Athletic Club, Bellevue Athletic Club, Harbor Club, Seattle Yacht Club, Rainier Club. Office: 3000 First Interstate Ctr 999 3rd Ave Seattle WA 98104-4001

DIAMOND, MILTON, anatomy and reproductive biology educator; b. N.Y.C., Mar. 6, 1934; s. Aaron and Jennie (Arbor) D.; m. Grace H. Whitney, Dec. 18, 1955 (dec. Sept. 1989); children: Hinda Louise, Irene Wanda, Sara Elizabeth, Leah Naiomi. BS, CCNY, 1955; PhD, U. Kans., 1962. Instr., asst. prof. anatomy U. Louisville, 1962-67; assoc. prof. anatomy U. Hawaii, 1967-71, prof. anatomy and reproductive biology, 1971—; rsch. prof. psychiatry SUNY, Stony Brook, 1976-78; dir. Pacific Ctr. for Sex and Soc., 1985—; dept. edn. State of Hawaii, 1971-88, NSF/NIH, 1973-88, others; prin. investigator various studies on abortion, contraception, sex, and sexual devel. Author: Abortion Politics, 1976, Sexual Decision, 1980, Sex Watching, 1984, 2d edit., 1992, AIDS: Love, Sex, Disease, 1989; editor: Perspectives in Reproduction and Sexual Behavior, 1967; mem. editl. bd. Archives Sexual Behavior, Jour. Psychology and Human Sexuality, others. Chair Hawaii AIDS Task Group, 1985-92. 1st lt. U.S. Army, 1955-58. Fellow Soc. for Scientific Study of Sex (pres. western region 1987); mem. Am. Assn. Sex Educators, Counselors and Therapists (cert. educator, therapist), Animal Behavior Soc. (charter), Harry Benjamin Internat. Soc. for Gender Dysphoria, Internat. Acad. Sex Rsch. (charter), Soc. for Devel. Psychobiology, Soc. for Study of Reproduction (charter), Assn. Sexologists (charter), Polish Acad. Sexological Sci. (hon., Sodalem honoris causa). Office: U Hawaii Sch Medicine 1951 E West Rd Honolulu HI 96822-2321

DIAMOND, RICHARD, secondary education educator; b. N.Y.C., June 23, 1936; s. Oscar and Frieda (Rosenfeld) D.; m. Donna Jean Berkshire Wilson, June 14, 1961 (div. June 1974); m. Betty Ruth Jane Foster, Nov. 17, 1975; children: Thomas, Laura, Rick, Jeff. BA, U. Calif., Berkeley, 1958. Cert. tchr., Calif. Tchr. Riverside (Calif.) Unified Schs., 1959-67, 73—, coord. social studies, 1967-69, program dir. compensatory edn., 1969-72, attendance officer, 1972-73; author curriculum programs Afro-Am. history and Chicano studies, 1968; developer law and youth H.S. course, 1978. Contbr. articles and photographs to profl. and popular publs. Co-creator nationally recognized h.s. vol. program, h.s. svc. learning coord., 1995—; mem. Riverside County Hist. Commn., 1997—; Dem. Party worker, 1964-72; Rep. Party worker, 1992—. Named Social Studies Tchr. of Yr., Inland Empire Social Studies Assn., 1980, Tchr. of Yr., Arlington H.S., Riverside, 1992; recipient hon. svc. award Dist. Coun. PTA, Riverside, 1993. Mem. NEA, Calif. Tchrs. Assn., Riverside County Tchrs. Assn. Presbyterian. Office: Arlington HS 2951 Jackson St Riverside CA 92503-5732

DIAMOND, ROCHELLE ANNE, biologist; b. Phoenix, Aug. 9, 1951; d. Harold and Helen (Garfinkle) D.; m. Clifford L. Sailor Jr., July 6, 1976 (div. 1985). BA in Molecular Biology, U. Calif., Santa Barbara, 1974. Technician U. So. Calif., L.A., 1974-77; rsch. technician City of Hope Nat. Med. Ctr., Duarte, Calif., 1978-81; assoc. biologist UCLA, 1981-82; rsch. biologist Calif. Inst. Tech., Pasadena, 1982-91, chief opr., tech. applications specialist cell sorting facility, 1984—, profl. staff, 1991—. Guest editor Methods, 1991; mem. editl. bd. Immunology, RG Landes Biosci.; contbr. articles to profl. jours. Com. mem. AIDS Project L.A. Med. Adv. Com., 1985-87; bd. dirs., v.p. Lesbian and Gay Health and Health Policy Found., 1994—. Recipient LACE award L.A. Gay and Lesbian Ctr., 1997. Mem. AAAS, Am. Chem. Soc., Nat. Orgn. Gay and Lesbian Scientists and Tech. Profls. (chair 1985—), N.Y. Acad. Sci., L.A. Gay and Lesbian Scientists (co-chair 1984-96), Internat. Soc. Analytical Cytology, Athenaeum. Democrat.

DIAMOND, SARA ROSE, writer, sociologist, lecturer; b. 1958. BA in Spanish, U. Calif., Irvine, 1979; MA in Sociology, U. Calif., Berkeley, 1988, PhD in Sociology, 1993. Lectr. U. Calif., Santa Cruz, 1988, 91, 94, U. Calif., Berkeley, 1994, Calif. State U. Hayward, 1995—. Author: Spiritual Warfare: The Politics of the Christian Right, 1989, Roads to Dominion: Right-Wing Movements and Political Power in the United States, 1995, Facing the Wrath: Confronting the Right in Dangerous Times, 1996. Home: PO Box 2439 Berkeley CA 94702

DIAMOND, STANLEY JAY, lawyer; b. Los Angeles, Nov. 27, 1927; s. Philip Alfred and Florence (Fadem) D.; m. Lois Jane Broida, June 22, 1969; children: Caryn Elaine, Diana Beth. B.A., UCLA, 1949; J.D., U. So. Calif., 1952. Bar: Calif. 1953. Practiced law Los Angeles, 1953—; dep. Office of Calif. Atty. Gen., Los Angeles, 1953; ptnr. Diamond & Tilem, Los Angeles, 1957-60, Diamond, Tilem & Colden, Los Angeles, 1960-79, Diamond & Wilson, Los Angeles, 1979—; lectr. music and entertainment law UCLA; Mem. nat. panel arbitrators Am. Arbitration Assn. Bd. dirs. Los Angeles Suicide Prevention Center, 1971-76. Served with 349th Engr. Constrn. Bn. AUS, 1945-47. Mem. ABA, Calif. Bar Assn., Los Angeles County Bar Assn., Beverly Hills Bar Assn., Am. Judicature Soc., Calif. Copyright Conf., Nat. Acad. Rec. Arts and Scis., Zeta Beta Tau, Nu Beta Epsilon. Office: 3d Fl 12304 Santa Monica Blvd Los Angeles CA 90025-2551

DIAMOND, STEPHEN EARLE MICHAEL, investor, consultant, inventor; b. San Francisco, Dec. 2, 1944; s. Earl Conrad and Sally (Gonzales) D. Pvt. study music and drama, 1956-65; grad., Ft. Sam Houston Army Med. Sch., 1964; Cert. computer sci. programmer, Elkins Coll. Nat. Career Inst., 1969; PhD, World Acad. Assn., 1994; DMS, London Inst. Applied Rsch., 1994, LLD (hon.), 1995. Exec. dir. Gondia Corp., San Francisco, 1973-76, exec. chmn., 1976-78; chief exec. officer G.C.I. C'ies, San Francisco, 1978-80, chief adminstrv. officer, 1980-85; owner S.E. Diamond Founds., San Francisco, 1985-86, S.E. Diamond Assn., San Francisco, 1986—, The Dover Rd. Inn Group, 1990—; prof. neurophysics, life fellow Australian Inst. Coordinated Rsch., 1994. Discoverer in field, inventor; patentee in field; contbr articles to profl. jours.; assoc. prodr. Nat. Empowerment TV, 1992; author: Architeture Engineering, 1976—, Treatise on Cures and Treatments, 70 vols., 1971—; creator/designer monetary invention, others; originator, orator, writer The Actual 2,000,000 Words Vocabulary 1970-96. Leader 5th Congl. dist. Strategic Def. Initiative, chmn. high frontier def. com. 5th-8th Congl. dists. west region, 1989; active Am. Inst. Cancer Rsch., 1981—; charter founder Ronald Reagan Rep. Ctr., Washington, 1987; state advisor U.S. Congl. adv. bd., Washington and San Francisco, 1983-86; hon. charter mem. St. Mary's Hosp., San Francisco, 1988; friend San Francisco Symphony Orch., 1980—; founding mem. Am. Space Frontier Com., Falls Church, 1984-86, Challenger Space Ctr., 1987—, Am. Air Mus., Duxbury, Eng., 1994—; sponsor, prodr. Concerned Women for Am., 1984—; mem. world planning coun. WWII Victory 50th Anniversary Events, 1992—; charter mem. Citizens Against Govt. Waste, 1991—; charter mem. Rep. Nat. Commn. on Am. Agenda; founding charter mem. Normandy D-Day Mus., Caen, France, 1990—; charter founding mem. USN Meml. U.S.A. Washington Dist., 1989; charter founder mem. Nat. Com. to Preserve Social Security; mem. nat. gov. bd. U.S. Olympic Com. Shooting Team, 1994. Recipient merit award Rep. Nat. Com., 1984, merit award Rep. Party, 1985, Achievement award United Inventors and Scientists, L.A., 1975, Editor's Choice award Nat. Poetry Contest, 1995, 96; decorated Knight Comdr. Lofsensic Ursinius Orden, Knight Grand Cross Order of Saints Peter & Paul, 1996, Knight Templar, 1996; titled Count San Ciriaco, Italy, Lord Camster Burn Estate, Argylshire, Scotland, Baron Royal Order of Boheme; Capt. Legion de le Aisle de le Mer, The Netherlands, 1995. Mem. Nat. Small Bus. Assn., Nat. Taxpayers Union, Statue of Liberty and Ellis Island Found. (charter), Presdl. Task Force (charter), Clan Morrison Soc. (life active), North Shore Animal League, Internat. Affairs Inst. Paris, Internat. Cult. Corr. Inst. India, Academie Maison, Internat. Soc. Poets, Internat. Des Intellectueles, M.I.D.I., A.M.U., Munich, Germany, 1994. Republican. Office: PO Box 246 South Lake Tahoe CA 96156-0246

DIAZ, MICHAEL ANTHONY, electrical engineer, software engineer; b. West Point, N.Y., Aug. 26, 1957; s. Antonio and Gloria (Torado) D.; m. Yvonne Marie Martinez, Apr. 20, 1991; children: David, Jonathan. BSEE, MS in Computer Engring., Boston U., 1991. Softwre programmer IBM, Poughkeepsie, N.Y., 1978, Sandia Labs., Albuquerque, 1979, 80, Hewlett Packard, Cupertino, Calif., 1981; chief software engr. Motorola GSTG, Scottsdale, Ariz., 1982-96; dir. quality Motorola ISD, 1996—. Contbr. articles to symposia. With USN, 1975-76. Recipient Outstanding Software award Dept. Def., Nat. Security Agy., 1993. Mem. IEEE, Assn. for Computing Machinery, Motorola Sci., Adv. bd. Assn. Home: 8244 E Appaloosa Trl Scottsdale AZ 85258-1305 Office: Motorola GSTG 8201 E Mcdowell Rd Scottsdale AZ 85257-3812

DIAZ, RAMON VALERO, retired judge; b. Manila, Oct. 13, 1918; came to Guam, 1951; s. Vicente and Bibiana (Valero) D.; m. Josefina Dela Concepcion, July 3, 1945; children: Marilu, Mariles, Maribel, Marilen, Maryann, Anthony, Vincent, Ramon, Maricar. PhB, U. St. Tomas, Manila, 1940, LLB, 1941; grad. U.S. Army J.A.G. Sch., 1945; Diploma Jud. Skills, Am. Acad. Jud. Edn., 1984. Bar: Philippines 1941, Guam 1956, U.S. Ct. Appeals (9th cir.) 1966, High Ct. of Trust Territories 1977, No. Marianas 1985.

Assoc. Diokno Law Office, Manila, 1943-44; pvt. practice, Guam, 1960-80; judge Superior Ct. of Guam, Agana, 1980-94; ret. 1994; mem. U.S. Selective Service Bd. Appeals, Guam, 1950-62. Permanent deacon Roman Catholic Ch. Judge Adv. Gen.'s Svc., Philippine Army, 1941-51. Mem. Am. Judges Assn., Nat. Council Juvenile and Family Ct. Judges, VFW II and POW. Survivor Bataan Death March, 1942. Home: 114 Mangga Ct Dededo GU 96912-1451 also: PO Box 22978 GMF Barrigada GU 96921-2978

DIAZ-FLORES, HEBERT DE JESUS, scientist, engineer, consultant, manager; b. Merida, Yucatan, Mexico, Jan. 11, 1960; came to U.S., 1982; s. Hebert De Jesus Diaz-Vazquez and Gloria (Flores-Cervera) Flores-Diaz; m. Suzanne Marie Britz, June 30, 1984; 1 child, Gloria Patricia. BS in Engring., Merida (Mex.) Inst. Tech., 1981; MS in Engring., Purdue U., 1984; PhD in Engring., U. Calif., Davis, 1991. Prof., rschr. Veracruz (Mex.) Inst. Tech., 1984-86, grad. coord., 1985-86; grad. rsch. asst. Calif. Energy Commn., Sacramento, 1986-89, energy analyst, 1989, assoc. energy specialist, 1989-92, energy commn. specialist, 1992; sr. engr., scientist Radian Corp., Sacramento, 1992-95; energy planning cons. Telos Corp., Sacramento, 1994-95; sr. rsch. mgr. Calif. Energy Commn., Sacramento, 1995—. Contbr. articles to profl. jours.; editor (newsletter) Mex. Student Assn., U. Calif., Davis, 1988-90. V.p. Mex. Student Assn., U. Calif., Davis, 1988-89;. Recipient scholarship Coun. of Sci. and Tech., Mex., 1986; named nat. rschr. Coun. of Sci and Tech., Mex., 1984. Mem. IEEE, Soc. Automotive Engrs., Air and Waste Mgmt. Assn., Assn. Computer Machinery, Sacramento Foxpro Users Group. Home: 1811 Rushmore Lane Davis CA 95616 Office: Calif Energy Commn 1516 9th St Sacramento CA 95814-5504

DIAZ-ZUBIETA, AGUSTIN, nuclear engineer, executive; b. Madrid, Spain, Mar. 24, 1936; came to U.S., 1953; s. Emilio Diaz Cabeza and Maria Teresa Zubieta Atucha; m. Beth Lee Fortune, Sept. 6, 1958; children: Walter Agustin, Michael Joel, Anthony John. B, U. Madrid, 1953; BSc in Physics, U. Tenn., 1958; MSc in Mech. Engring., Duke U., 1960; PhD in Nuclear Engring., U. Md., 1981. Nuclear engr. Combustion Engring., Tenn., 1954-58; instr. engring. Duke U., Durham, N.C., 1958-60; nuclear physicist Allis Chalmers Co., Washington, 1960-64; country mgr. South Africa Allis Chalmers Co., 1964-66; mgr. internat. power generation projects GE, N.Y.C., 1966-69, mgr. Europe and Middle East strategic planning, 1969-71; dir. internat. constrn. planning GE, Westport, Conn., 1971-75, dir. constrn., 1975-83; chief exec. officer GE Affiliate, Westport, 1983-87; v.p. internat. sales, devel. Internat. Tech. Corp., L.A., 1987-94; mng. dir. IT Italia S.P.A., IT Spain, S.A. Author: Measurement of Subcriticality of Nuclear Reactors by Stocastic Processes, 1981. Pres. Fairfield (Conn.) Assn. Condo Owners, 1983-87. Named Astronomer of Yr. Barnard Astronomical Soc., Chattanooga, 1957; fgn. exchange scholar U.S. Govt., 1953-58; grantee, NSF, 1958-60, U.S. Office of Ordinance Rsch. U.S. Army, 1958-60. Mem. Am. Nuclear Soc., Am. Soc. Mech. Engrs., Am. Soc. Profl. Engrs., Sigma Xi. Republican. Roman Catholic. Home: 47 Country Meadow Rd Rolling Hills Estates CA 90274-5774

DIBB, CHARLES ROBERT, physician, educator; b. Downey, Calif., July 21, 1959; s. Alfred Wallace and Betty Ann (Dayton) D.; m. Sandra Louise Hammons, Apr. 26, 1986; children: William Kenneth, James Thomas, Alexander Joseph. BS, U. Calif., Davis, 1981; MD, U. Health Sci. Chgo. Med. Sch., 1985. Diplomate Am. Bd. Internal Medicine, Am. Bd. Med. Oncology. Intern, resident U. Tex. Health Sci. Ctr., Houston, 1985-88; fellow U. Mich., Ann Arbor, 1989-92, lectr., 1992; staff physician Medford (Oreg.) Clinic, 1992—; med. dir. Rogue Valley Med. Ctr. Hospice, 1992—; investigator Nat. Sci. Adj. Breast and Bowel Project, 1992—. Author: (book chpt.) Head & Neck Cancer: Basic & Clinical Aspects, 1995. Fellow Am. Coll. Physicians; mem. Assn. Hospice Physicians, Oreg. Med. Assn., Jackson County Med. Soc., Medford Clinic Found. (v.p.). Episcopalian. Home: 428 Silverado Cir Medford OR 97504-8167 Office: Medford Clinic PC 555 Black Oak Dr Medford OR 97504-8311

DIBELL, MARTA LEE, foreign language educator; b. Santa Barbara, Calif., July 3, 1964; d. David Lawrence Dibell and Helen Marie Smith. BA in German, Fla. State U., 1986. Rschr. Prentice Hall, Tallahassee, 1986-88; customer svc. rep. Prentice Hall, Santa Ana, Calif., 1988-90; tchr. Walnut (Calif.) Valley Unified Sch. Dist., 1991—. Mem. Am. Assn. Tchrs. German, U.S. Parachute Assn. (Falcon Relative Work award 1996), Fgn. Lang. Assn. Orange County. Home: 2734 Quail Ridge Cir Fullerton CA 92835 Office: Walnut H S 400 N Pierre Rd Walnut CA 91789

DIBLE, ROSE HARPE MCFEE, special education educator; b. Phoenix, Apr. 28, 1927; d. Ambrose Jefferson and Laurel Mabel (Harpe) McFee; m. James Henry Dible, June 23, 1951 (div. Jan. 1965); 1 child, Michael James. BA in Speech Edn., Ariz. State U., Tempe, 1949; MA in Speech and Drama, U. So. Calif., L.A., 1950; fellow, Calif. State U., Fullerton, 1967. Cert. secondary tchr., spl. edn. tchr. English and drama tchr. Lynwood (Calif.) Sr. High Sch., 1950-51, Montebello (Calif.) Sr. High Sch., 1952-58; tchr. English and Social Studies Pioneer High Sch., Whittier, Calif., 1964-65; spl. edn. tchr. Bell Gardens (Calif.) High Sch., 1967-85, spl. edn. cons., 1985-90. Mem. DAR, Daus. Am. Colonists, Whittier Christian Woman Assn., La Habra Womans Club, Eastern Star Lodge, Kappa Delts, Phi Delta Gamma. Republican. Presbyterian. Home: 1201 Russell St La Habra CA 90631-2530 Office: Montebello Unified Sch Dist 123 Montebello Blvd Montebello CA 90640

DICK, HENRY HENRY, minister; b. Russia, June 1, 1922; s. Henry Henry and Mary (Unger) D.; m. Erica Penner, May 25, 1946; children—Janet (Mrs. Arthur Enns), Judith (Mrs. Ron Brown), James, Henry. Th.B., Mennonite Brethren Bible Coll., 1950. Ordained to ministry Mennonite Brethren Ch., 1950; pastor in Orillia, Ont., Can., 1950-54, Lodi, Calif., 1954-57, Shafter, Calif., 1958-69; faculty Tabor Coll., 1954-55; gen. sec. Mennonite Brethren Conf. of U.S.A., 1969-72; pres. Mennonite Brethren Bibl. Sem., Fresno, Calif., 1972-76; vice moderator Gen Conf. Mennonite Brethren Ch., 1975-78, moderator, 1979-84; pastor Reedley Mennonite Brethren Ch., 1976-88; ret., 1989; dir. ch. and constituency relations Mennonite Brethren Biblical Sem., 1987-89; moderator Pacific Dist. Conf., 1959-60, 61-63, 75-77; mem. exec. com. Mennonite Central Com. Internat., 1967-75, mem. bd. reference and counsel, 1966-69, 72-75, mem. bd. missions and services, 1969-72; exec. sec. Bd. Edn. Mennonite Brethren, 1969-72; chmn. Bd. Missions and Services, 1985-91; pastor emeritus Reedley Mennonite Brethren Ch., 1987. Columnist bi-weekly publ. Christian Leader, 1969-75. Bd. dirs. Bob Wilson Meml. Hosp., Ulysses, Kans., 1969-72; dist. minister Pacific Dist. Conf. Mennonite Brethren, 1989—. Recipient Humanitarian award Shafter C. of C., 1969, Citation bd. dirs. Bibl. Sem. Clubs: Kiwanis, Reedley Rotary. Home: 783 W Carpenter Ave Reedley CA 93654-3903 Office: 1632 L St Reedley CA 93654-3340

DICK, TESSA BUSBY, English educator; b. Culver City, Calif., June 20, 1954; m. Philip Kindred Dick, Apr. 18, 1973. AA, Fullerton (Calif.) Coll., 1979; BA, Chapman U., Orange, Calif., 1982, MA, 1990. Prof. English Chapman U., Orange, 1991—. Editor various pamphlets; contbr. articles to profl. jours. Mem. AAUP. Home: PO Box 486 Fullerton CA 92836

DICKAU, KEITH MICHAEL (MIKE DICKAU), artist, secondary school educator; b. Monterey Park, Calif., Apr. 20, 1944; s. Keith Robert and Beaula May (Chamness) D.; m. Ramona Sue Wilson, May 6, 1967; children: Robert Michael, Ian Christopher; m. Carolyn Gloria Isaak, Dec. 22, 1973. BA in Zoology, U. Calif., Davis, 1966. Cert. secondary tchr., Calif. Tchr. math. L.A. City Sch. Dist., 1967-70; tchr. sci. and math. Grant Joint Union H.S. Dist., Sacramento and Rio Linda, Calif., 1970—. Exhibited in numerous shows including Candy Store Gallery, Folsom, Calif., Artists' Collaborative Gallery, Sacramento, Fla. State U., Tallahassee, Crocker Art Mus. Sculpture Park, Sacramento, Whittier (Calif.) Mus., Gallery 25, Fresno, Calif., L.A. Artist Equity Assn., Sacramento Fine Arts Ctr., Mercer Gallery, Rochester, N.Y., The Artery, Davis, Archivio Artistico, Ravenna, Italy, Antic Ajuntament, Terragona, Spain, Santa Barbara (Calif.) Mus., SFAC Gallery, Carmichael, Calif., 1996, Ecole de Nuces, Valady, France, M.J.C., Saint-Cere, France, 1996, Seulement pour les Fous, Troyes, France, 1996, New Artworks Fine Arts Gallery, Fair Oaks, Calif., 1996, Bur. de Poste, Joigny, France, 1996, The Ink People Ctr. for the Arts, Eureka, Calif., 1996, Mercer Gallery, Monroe C.C., Rochester, N.Y., 1996, L'Inst. Superieur des Arts Appliques, Rennes, France, Ulrike-Ulrike, Antwerp, Belgium, 1997, The Living Room, Santa Monica, Calif., 1997, Kawaguchi-Shi, Japan, 1997; contbr. poetry and art to mags. Recipient Hon. Sci. award Bausch and Lomb, 1962, Sculpture award Calif. Art League, 1987, Artist of Month award No. Calif. Artists, numerous other awards; NSF grantee, 1972. Mem. NEA, Calif. Tchrs. Assn., Grant Dist. Edn. Assn., No. Calif. Artists, Inc. Democrat. Methodist.

DICKERSON, COLLEEN BERNICE PATTON, artist, educator; b. Cleburne, Tex., Sept. 17, 1922; d. Jennings Bryan and Alma Bernice (Clark) Patton; m. Arthur F. Dickerson; children: Sherry M., Chrystal Charmine. BA, Calif. State U., Northridge, 1980; studied with John Pike. presenter demonstrations Cayucos Art Assn., Morro Bay Art Assn., El Camino Real Art Assn. One-woman shows include Morro Bay Cmty. Bldg., Amandas Interiors, Arroyo Grande, Calif., 1996, Gt. Western Savs., San Luis Obispo, Calif.; exhibited in group shows; represented in permanent collections, including Polk Ins. Co., San Luis Obispo, Med. Ctr. MDM Ins. Co., L.A. Mem. Ctrl. Coast Watercolor Soc. (pres. 1986-87), Art Ctr., Oil Acrylic Pastel Group (chmn., co-chmn. 1989—), Morro Bay Art Assn., San Luis Obispo Art Ctr., Mus. Women in Arts (assoc.). Home and Studio: 245 Hacienda Ave San Luis Obispo CA 93401-7967

DICKERSON, CYNTHIA ROWE, marketing firm executive, consultant; b. Cin., Apr. 14, 1956; d. Richard Emmett and Frances Jeanette (Ellwanger) Rowe; m. Mark Alan Dickerson, Oct. 24, 1981; children: Shannon Gayle, Meredith Lynne. BSBA, U. So. Calif., 1979. Mgmt. asst. Computer Scis. Corp., Pasadena, Calif., 1974-78; rsch. asst. Dailey & Assocs., L.A., 1978-79; account exec. Young & Rubicam, L.A., 1979-81, Rowley & Linder Advt., Wichita, Kans., 1981-82, Chiat/Day Inc. Advt., San Francisco, 1983-85; product mgr. Sun-Diamond Growers of Calif., Pleasanton, 1985-88; mktg. cons. San Francisco, 1988-90; sr. bus. mgr. Del Monte Foods, San Francisco, 1990-93; dir. mktg. Yorkshire Dried Fruit & Nuts, Inc., San Francisco, 1993-94, Potlatch Corp., 1995—. Named Outstanding Youth Women of Am., Jr. C. of C., 1985. Mem. Am. Mktg. Assn., Soc. Consumer Affairs Profls., Am. Rose Soc., Heritage Rose Group. Republican.

DICKERSON, EUGENIE ANN, writer, journalist; b. Chgo., Oct. 4, 1946; d. Hubert Eugene and Theresa Veronica (Tallarico) King; m. Brian W. Dickerson, Feb. 4, 1967. BA in History, U. Ill., 1968. Newsletter editor Sammamish Aero Modelers Soc., Redmond, Wash., 1976-79; freelance writer, 1977—, illustrator, 1981—, photographer, 1991—; speech writer for cmty. figures, 1992—; restaurant reviewer Seattle Times and others; columnist Bellevue (Wash.) Weekly News, 1990; book editor, cons. to various authors, 1988—. Contbr. chpt. to Developing Arguments, 1990, The Writer's Handbook, 1993. Recipient 3d place for editorial Nat. Fedn. Press Women, 1989. Mem. Washington Press Assn. (1st place for editorial 1989), Soc. Profl. Journalists. Office: 1212 146th Ave SE Bellevue WA 98007-5651

DICKERSON, JOE BERNARD, principal, educator; b. Marburg, Hesse, Germany, Mar. 24, 1951; came to U.S., 1954; s. Joseph Bernard and Eva Maria (Heitmann) D.; m. Joylyne Barbara Ginter, June 11, 1972; children: Alia Dawn, Aaron Mitchell. BSc in Edn., Valparaiso (Ind.) U., 1978; MSc in Edn., U. Mich., Dearborn, 1989; EdD, Nova Southeastern U., Ft. Lauderdale, Fla., 1996. Tchr. St. Joseph Sch., Adelaide, South Australia, 1972-74, St. John Bosco Sch., Adelaide, South Australia, 1974-76; prin. Zion Luth. Sch., Detroit, 1978-80, 86-91; tchr. Point Pearce (South Australia) Aboriginal Sch., 1980; prin. Trinity Luth. Sch., Southport, Queensland, Australia, 1980-82, Ceduna (South Australia) Luth. Sch., 1982-86; prof. of writing Purdue U., Ft. Wayne, Ind., 1992—; prin. Ctrl. Luth. Sch., New Haven, Ind., 1991-95; supt. Luth. Sch. Foothills, La Crescenta, Calif., 1995-96; prin. Pilgrim Luth. Sch., Santa Monica, Calif., 1996—. Editor: QBD Theatre mag., 1974; author monograph: Into the 80's - Lutheran Education in Australia, 1982. Mem. ASCD, Nat. Assn. Luth. Prins., Nat. Assn. Elem. Prins., Nat. Assn. Tchrs. Math., Nat. Assn. Luth. Dirs. of Devel., Ind. Luth. Prins. Assn. Lutheran. Home: 7741 Apperson St Tujunga CA 91042-2110 Office: Pilgrim Luth Sch 1730 Wilshire Blvd Santa Monica CA 90403-5510

DICKERSON, WILLIAM ROY, lawyer; b. Uniontown, Ky., Feb. 15, 1928; s. Banjamin Franklin and Honor Mae (Staples) D. BA in Acctg., Calif. State U., 1952; JD, UCLA, 1958. Bar: Calif. 1959. Dep. atty., ex-officio city prosecutor City of Glendale, Calif., 1959-62; assoc. James Brewer, Los Angeles, 1962-68, LaFollette, Johnson, Schroeter & DeHaas, Los Angeles, 1968-73; sole practice, Los Angeles, 1973—; arbitrator Los Angeles Superior Ct.; judge pro tem Los Angeles Mcpl. Ct., judge pro tem Los Angeles Superior Ct., Small Claims Ct., Traffic Ct.; lectr. and speaker in field. Bd. dirs. LosFeliz Improvement Assn., 1986-88, Zoning Commn.; co-chmn. Streets and Hwys. Commn. Mem. ABA, Calif. Bar Assn., Los Angeles County Bar Assn., Soc. Calif. Accts., Fed. Bar Assn., Am. Film Inst., Internat. Platform Assn. Home and Office: 813 N Doheny Dr Beverly Hills CA 90210-3528

DICKEY, GARY ALAN, minister; b. Santa Monica, Calif., Jan. 25, 1946; s. Charles Harry and Audrey W. (White) D.; m. Tamara Jean Kimble, Jan. 11, 1976. BA, UCLA, 1968; MDiv, Fuller Theol. Sem., Pasadena, 1972; DMin, Sch. Theology, Claremont, Calif., 1974; PhD, Trinity Theol. Seminary, 1996. Assoc. pastor Magnolia Pk. United Meth. Ch., Burbank, Calif., 1974-78; sr. pastor St. James United Meth. Ch., Pasadena, 1978-90, First United Meth. Ch. of Canoga Park, 1990—; exec. com. mem. Calif.-Pacific Ann. Conf. Bd. of Ordained Ministry, 1980-88; chmn. Pasadena Dist. Com. on Ordained Ministry, 1978-90; supervising pastor Bd. Higher Edn., Nashville, 1978—. Recipient Polonia Restituta, 1990. Mem. Soc. Colonial Wars (mem. gentlemen of coun. 1993—), Soc. War of 1812 (chaplian 1989—, Calif. state pres.), Soc. of Sons of Am. Revolution (chaplain 1988—, pres. 1994, 95, Outstanding Citizenship award 1990, Meritorious Svc. award 1995, Silver Good Citizenship award 1996, Patriot medal 1997), Soc. of Sons of the Revolution, Descendants of Soldiers of Valley Forge, Soc. Sons Am. Colonists, Soc. Sons. Vets. Civil War, Vet. Corps Artillery State N.Y., United Empire Loyalists Assn. (Can.), Royal Soc. St. George (Eng.), Rotary (pres. 1989-90, Paul Harris fellow 1986), Am. Coll. Genealogists (accredited genealogist). Republican. Methodist. Home: 22167 Bryant St Canoga Park CA 91304-2306 Office: First United Meth Ch 22700 Sherman Way Canoga Park CA 91307-2332

DICKEY, ROBERT MARVIN (RICK DICKEY), property manager; b. Charleston, S.C., Dec. 3, 1950; s. John Lincoln II and Ruth (Marvin) D.; m. Teresa Ann Curry, Dec. 19, 1969 (div. 1979); 1 child, Gena Lynette. A of Computer Sci., USMC Degree Program, Washington, 1975. Cert. apt. property supr. Nat. Apt. Assn., Wash., occupancy specialist Nat. Ctr.for Housing Mgmt., Wash. Enlisted USMC, 1968, advanced through grades to staff sgt., 1968-78; shop mgr., bookkeeper Amalgamated Plant Co., Las Vegas, Nev., 1978-79; supr. constrn. Joseph Yousem Co., Las Vegas, 1979-80; apt. mgr. Robert A. McNeil Corp., Las Vegas, 1980, comml. bldg. mgr., leasing agt., 1980-82; asst. v.p., regional property mgr. Westminster Co., Las Vegas, 1982-87, Weyerhaeuser Mortgage Co., Las Vegas, 1988-89; pres., ptnr. Equinox Devel., Inc., Las Vegas, 1989-91; dir. residental properties R.W. Robideaux & Co., Spokane, Wash., 1992—. Contbr. articles to profl. jours. Mem. Nat. Assn. Realtors, Wash. Assn. Realtors, Spokane Assn. Realtors, Inst. Real Estate Mgmt. (accredited residential mgr., legis. chmn. 1987-88, Accredited Residential Mgr. award 1985, 86, 90), Nev. Apt. Assn. (v.p. 1985, pres. 1988—, bd. dirs.), So. Nev. Homebuilders Assn., Las Vegas Bd. Realtors (mgmt. legis. com. 1988).

DICKEY, ROBERT PRESTON, author, educator, poet; b. Flat River, Mo., Sept. 24, 1936; s. Delno Miren D. and Naomi Valentine (Jackson) D.; children: Georgia Rae, Shannon Ezra, Rain Dancer. BA, U. Mo., 1968, MA, 1969; PhD, Walden U., 1975. Instr. U. Mo., 1967-69; asst. prof. English and creative writing U. So. Colo., 1969-73; assoc. mem. faculty Pima Coll., Tucson, 1975-78. Author: (with Donald Justice, Thomas McAfee, Donald Drummond) poetry Four Poets, 1967, Running Lucky, 1969, Acting Immortal, 1970; Concise Dictionary of Lead River, Mo., 1972, The Basic Stuff of Poetry, 1972, Life Cycle of Seven Songs, 1972, McCabe Wants Chimes, 1973, Admitting Complicity, 1973; opera librettos Minnequa, 1976, The Witch of Tucson, 1976; Jimmie Cotton!, 1979, Way Out West, 1979, The Poetica Erotica of R.P. Dickey, 1989, The Little Book on Racism and Politics, 1990, The Way of Eternal Recurrence, 1994, Ode on Liberty, 1996; contbr. poetry to popular mags., Poetry, Saturday Rev., Commonwealth, Prairie Schooner; founder, editor: The Poetry Bag quar., 1966-71; poetry editor: So. Colo. Std., 1973-74. With USAF, 1955-57. Recipient Mahan award for poetry U. Mo., 1965-66. Home: PO Box 87 Ranchos De Taos NM 87557

DICKINSON, ELEANOR CREEKMORE, artist, educator; b. Knoxville, Tenn., Feb. 7, 1931; d. Robert Elmond and Evelyn Louise (Van Gilder) C.; m. Ben Wade Oakes Dickinson, June 12, 1952; children: Mark Wade, Katherine Van Gilder, Peter Somers. BA, U. Tenn., 1952; postgrad., San Francisco Art Inst., 1961-63, Academie de la Grande Chaumière, Paris, 1971; M.F.A., Calif. Coll. Arts and Crafts, 1982, Golden Gate U., 1984. Escrow officer Security Nat. Bank, Santa Monica, Calif., 1953-54; mem. faculty Calif. Coll. Arts and Crafts, Oakland, Calif., 1971—, assoc. prof. art, 1974-84, prof., 1984—, dir. galleries, 1975-85; artist-in-residence U. Tenn., 1969, Ark. State U., 1993; mem. faculty U. Calif., 1967-70; lectr. in field. Co-author, illustrator: Revival, 1974, That Old Time Religion, 1975; also mus. catalogs; illustrator: The Complete Fruit Cookbook, 1972, Human Sexuality: A Search for Understanding, 1984, Days Journey, 1985; commissions: University of San Francisco, 1990-92; one-person exhbns. include Corcoran Gallery Art, Washington, 1970, 74, San Francisco Mus. Modern Art, 1965, 68, Fine Arts Mus. San Francisco, 1969, 75, U. Tenn., Michael Himovitz Gallery, Sacramento, Calif., 1988, 89, 91, 93, 97; touring exhbns. include Smithsonian Inst., 1975-81, Oakland Mus., 1979, Interart Ctr., N.Y., 1980, Tenn. State Mus., 1981-82, Galeria de Arte y Libros, Monterrey, Mex., 1978, Hatley Martin Gallery, San Francisco, 1986, 89, Gallery 10, Washington, 1989, Diverse Works, Houston, 1990, Ewing Gallery, U. Tenn., 1991, G.T.U. Gallery, U. Calif., Berkeley, 1991, Mus. Contemporary Religious Art, St. Louis, 1995; represented in permanent collections Nat. Collection Fine Arts, Corcoran Gallery Art, Libr. of Congress, Smithsonian Instn., San Francisco Mus. Modern Art, Butler Inst. Art, Oakland Mus., Santa Barbara Mus.; prodr. (TV program) The Art of the Matter-Professional Practices in Fine Arts, 1986—. Bd. dirs. Calif. Confedn. of the Arts, 1983-88; bd. dirs., v.p. Calif. Lawyers for the Arts, 1986—; mem. coun. bd. San Francisco Art Inst., 1966-91, trustee, 1964-67; sec., bd. dirs. YWCA, 1955-62; treas., bd. Westminster Ctr., 1955-59; bd. dirs. Children's Theater Assn., 1958-60, 93-94, Internat. Child Art Ctr., 1958-68. Recipient Disting. Alumni award San Francisco Art Inst., 1983, Master Drawing award Nat. Soc. Arts and Letters, 1983, Cert. of Recognition, El Consejo Mundial de Artistas Plasticos 2d Internat. Conf., 1993, Pres.'s award Nat. Womens Caucus for Art, 1995; grantee Zellerbach Family Fund, 1975, Calif. Coll. Arts and Crafts, 1994, NEH, 1978, 80, 82-85, Thomas F. Stanley Found., 1985, Bay Area Video Coalition, 1988-92, PAS Graphics, 1988, San Francisco Cmty. TV Corp., 1990, Skaggs Found., 1991. Mem. Coalition of Women's Art Orgns. (dir., v.p. 1978-80), Coll. Art Assn., AAUP, Calif. Confederation of Arts (bd. dirs. 1983-89), Calif. Lawyers for Arts (v.p. 1986—), San Francisco Art Assn. (sec., dir. 1964-67), NOW, Artists Equity Assn. (nat. v.p., dir. 1978-92), Arts Advocates, Women's Caucus for Art (nat. Affirmative Action officer 1978-80). Democrat. Episcopalian. Office: Calif Coll Arts and Crafts 5212 Broadway Oakland CA 94618-1426

DICKINSON, JAMES GORDON, editor; b. Melbourne, Australia, Nov. 13, 1940; came to U.S., 1974, naturalized, 1983; s. David Rushbrook and Lorna Aida (Anderson) D.; m. Carol Rosslyn McBurnie, Sept. 7, 1963; children: Craig, Peter (dec.), Samantha; m. Sheila Laraine Ferguson McManus, Aug. 20, 1982. Student Melbourne U., 1960-63. Cadet reporter Hobart Mercury, 1957-59, Melbourne Age, 1959-63; reporter Melbourne Herald, 1963-64, TV Channel O, Melbourne, 1964-66; cons. Internat. Public Relations Pty. Ltd., 1966-68; editor, pub. Australian Jour. Pharmacy, 1968-74; asst. exec. dir. Am. Pharm. Assn., Washington, 1975; sr. editor FDC Reports Inc., Washington, 1975-78; founder, editor Washington Drugwire, 1978-79; Washington bur. chief Drug Topics, Med. Econs. Co., 1978-83; Washington corr. Scrip, Clinica World Med. Device News, Animal Pharm World Vet. News (U.K.), 1978-85, Pharm. Tech., Pharm. Exec., 1977-89, N.Z. Pharmacy, Brit. Pharm. Jour., Drug News & Perspectives mag. (Spain), Med. Device and Diagnostic Industry mag., Med. Mktg. & Media, 1990—; pres., chief exec. officer Ferdic Inc., 1982—; editor, pub. Dickinson's FDA and Dickinson's PSAO industry newsletters, 1985-93, VixeNews, 1989-90, Dickinson's Pharmacy newsletter, 1989-96, Dickinson's FDA Inspection newsletter, 1992-93, Dickinson's FDA Review, 1994—, Dickinson's FDA Update by Fax Weekly; columnist syndicated all state pharm. jours., 1986-94; cons. to drug industry; pres. Australian Monthly Newspapers and Periodicals Assn., 1972-74; founding sec. Melbourne Press Club, 1971-74. Editor: Weekly Pharmacy Reports, 1975-78. Mem. Australian Liberal Party, 1971-74; pres. Lee Forest Civic Assn., 1977-79. Mem. Periodical Corrs. Assn., Am. Pub. Health Assn. Club: Nat. Press (Washington). Office: PO Box 367 Las Cruces NM 88004-0367

DICKINSON, JANET MAE WEBSTER, relocation consulting executive; b. Cleve., Oct. 2, 1929; d. Richard and Gizella (Keplinger) Fisher; m. Rodney Earl Dickinson, June 18, 1965 (div. 1976); 1 child, Kimberly Cae. Grad., Larson Coll. for Women, New Haven; student, Portland State Coll. Lic. broker, Oreg. Pub. rels./promotion dir. KPTV-Channel 27, Portland, Oreg., 1951-54; exec. dir. Exposition-Recreation Commn., Portland, 1954-58; v.p. Art Lutz & Co., Realtors, Portland, 1975-79, Lutz Relocation Mgmt., Portland, 1977-79; corp. relocation mgr. Ga. Pacific Corp., Portland, 1979-82; pres., broker Ga. Pacific Fin. Co., Portland, 1980-82; pres., chief exec. officer The Dickinson Cons. Group, Portland, 1982—; pres. Wheatherstone Press, Lake Oswego, Oreg., 1983—, The Relocation Ctr., Portland, 1984—; cons. in field; lectr. in field; conductor workshops/seminars in field. Author: The Complete Guide to Family Relocation, The International Move, Building Your Dream House, Obtaining the Highest Price for Your Home, Have a Successful Garage Sale, Moving with Children, My Moving Coloring Book, The Group Move, Counseling the Transferee, Games to Play in the Car, Portland (Oreg.) Facts Book, Welcome to the United States, many others; contbr. articles to profl. jours. Mem. Pres.'s Com. to Employ Physically Handicapped, Oreg. Prison Assn.; established Women's Aux. for Waverly Baby Home; bd. dirs. Columbia River coun. Girl Scouts U.S.A., Salvation Army; active various polit. orgns.; chmn. ways and means com. Oreg. Symphony Soc., Portland Art Mus., Assistance League, Portland Jr. Symphony, March of Dimes, others. Mem. Employee Relocation Coun., City Club, Multnomah Athletic Club, Tualatin Valley Econ. Devel. Assn. (dir. 1988—). Republican. Episcopalian. Home: 901 SW King Ave Apt 12H Portland OR 97205-1316 Office: The Dickinson Cons Group Lincoln Ctr 10250 SW Greenburg Rd Ste 125 Portland OR 97223-5460

DICKINSON, ROBERT EARL, atmospheric scientist, educator; b. Millersburg, Ohio, Mar. 26, 1940; s. Leonard Earl and Carmen L. (Ostby) D.; m. Nancy Mary Mielinis, Jan. 5, 1974. AB in Chemistry and Physics, Harvard U., 1961; MS in Meteorology, MIT, 1962, PhD in Meteorology, 1966. Rsch. assoc. MIT, Cambridge, 1966-68; scientist Nat. Ctr. Atmospheric Rsch., Boulder, Colo., 1968-73, sr. scientist, 1973-90, head climate sect., 1975-81, dep. dir. A.A.P. div., 1981-86, acting dir., 1986-87; prof. atmospheric physics U. Ariz., 1990-93; regents prof., 1993—; mem. climate rsch. com. NRC, Washington, 1985-90, chmn., 1987-90, com. earth sci., 1985-88, global change com., 1985-92; mem. WCRP sci. steering group GEWEX, 1988-92; UNU steering com. Climatic, Biotic and Human Interactions in Humid Tropics, 1984-88, steering com. Internat. Satellite Land Surface Climatology project, 1984-89. Editor: The Geophysiology of Amazonia, 1986; contbr. articles to profl. jours. Recipient G. Unger Vetlesen prize, 1996. Fellow AAAS, Am. Meteorol. Soc. (chmn. com. biometeorol. and aerobiol. 1987-89, Meisinger award 1973, Editors award 1976, Jule Charney award 1989, Walter Orr Roberts lectr. in interdisciplinary sci. 1995, Carl-Gustaf Rossby award 1997), Am. Geophys. Union (com. earth as a sys. 1986-88, pres.-elect 1988-90, pres. 1990-92, Revelle medal 1996); mem. NAS, Internat. Assn. Meteorol. and Atmospheric Physics (sec. climate commn. 1983-87). Democrat. Home: 9290 N Yorkshire Ct Tucson AZ 85741-9357 Office: U Ariz Inst Atmospheric Physics Tucson AZ 85721

DICKINSON, SCOTT WARD, printing company executive; b. Hartford, Conn., Sept. 20, 1960; s. Robert Carl and Sheila Vance (Lee) D.; m. Robin Lou Karras, Oct. 19, 1985; children: Katie Lee, Daniel Robert. Student, Harvard U., 1977, Rochester Inst. Tech., 1982-84. Butcher's apprentice Ye Olde Butcher Shoppe, Acton, Mass., 1976-78; estimator Polaris Printing, Las Vegas, Nev., 1978-82; mgr. The Print Shop, Las Vegas, 1984-86; v.p., gen. mgr. Dickinson Printers, Las Vegas, 1986-95; info. sys. mgr. Constrn. Notebook News, Las Vegas, 1996—. Founder, editor: (newspaper) The Nev. Rep., 1990-91. Counselor Code Hotline, Acton, 1974-78; lobbyist Nev. Assoc. and Ind. Business, Carson City, Nev., 1991, 93, 95; mem. state cen. com. Nev. Rep. Party, Carson City, 1992-94; mem. county exec. bd. Clark

County Rep. Party, Las Vegas, 1988-94; vice chmn. state party Ind. Am. Party of Nev., 1994-95; mem. Leadership Las Vegas, 1994-95. Recipient Pres.'s Legion of Merit, Rep. Nat. Com., Washington, 1993-94. Mem. Nat. Assn. Printers and Lithographers, Nev. Assn. Ind. Bus. (bd. trustees 1990-94, v.p. 1995, pres. 1996), So. Nev. Graphic Arts Assn. (sec. 1992—), Printing Industries of Am., Las Vegas C. of C. (com. chair 1992—), Las Vegas S.W. Rotary, Las Vegas Fremont Rotary (bull. editor 1986-91), Citizens for Responsible Govt., Nev. Concerned Citizens (lobbyist, bd. dirs. 1994-95, 96—), Phi Kappa Tau (sgt. at arms Gamma Nu chpt. 1982), Gamma Epsilon Tau (hon.). Home: 3616 Fortune Ave Las Vegas NV 89107-2174 Office: Constrn Notebook News 3131 Meade Ave Las Vegas NV 89102-7809

DICKS, NORMAN DE VALOIS, congressman; b. Bremerton, Wash., Dec. 16, 1940; s. Horace D. and Eileen Cora D.; m. Suzanne Callison, Aug. 25, 1967; children: David, Ryan. BA, U. Wash., 1963, JD, 1968; LLD (hon.), Gonzaga U., 1987. Bars: Wash. 1968, D.C., 1978. Salesman, Boise Cascade Corp., Seattle, 1963; labor negotiator Kaiser Gypsum Co., Seattle, 1964; legis. asst. to Senator Warren Magnuson of Wash., 1968-73, adminstrv. asst., 1973-76; mem. 95th-104th Congress from 6th Wash. Dist., Washington, 1977—. Mem. U. Wash. Alumni Assn., Sigma Nu. Democrat. Lutheran. Office: US Ho Reps 2467 Rayburn House Office Bldg Washington DC 20515

DICKSON, DAVID DOUGLAS, humanities educator; b. Ogden, Utah, Sept. 2, 1939; s. Forde and Elma B. (Whitesides) D.; m. Eleanor Taylor Ridges, Aug. 31, 1964; children: Catherine Marie Dickson Sutherland, Johnathan David. AA, Weber Coll., 1959; BA, Weber State, 1964; MA, Brigham Young U., 1966; postgrad., U. Calif., Davis, 1988—. Laborer Reed Constrn. Co., Morgan, Utah, 1958-59; missionary, min. LDS Ch., various locations, Germany, 1959-63; documents-libr. asst. U. Utah, Salt Lake City, 1963-64; landscapist, gardener Portand Cement Co., Devils Slide, Utah, 1964-66; teaching asst. Brigham Young U., Provo, Utah, 1965-66; prof. fine arts Sierra Coll., Rocklin, Calif., 1966—; cons. for German Geneal. Socs., Calif., 1986-93; chair Libr. Learning Resources Ctr. com. Sierra Coll., 1992-96. Author: Great Germans, 3 vols., 1972, 84, 96, Adolf Clarenbach, The Reformer, 1987, (with others) Philo Hodge, 1756-1842, 1992; co-author: Life Story of Elma B. Whitesides, 1987; author, prodr. (video and book) Berlin, 1986. Bishop Auburn ward LDS Ch., 1970-73, Auburn 2d ward, 1973-75; chair varsity scouts Boy Scouts Am., greater Auburn area, 1986-89; tour leader Greater Sacto Cultural Exch. Club, Europe, 1967—; club leader 4-H, Meadow Vista, Calif., 1979-89; coach Am. Fedn. Soccer Clubs, greater Auburn area, 1983-85; coord. name extraction Auburn Calif. LDS Stake, Grass Valley, Nevada City, others, 1986-93. Mem. Nat. Coun. Tchrs. English, Am. Assn. Tchrs. German, Modern Lang. Assn., Sierra Coll. Faculty Assn. Home: 800 Cole Rd Meadow Vista CA 95722-9566 Office: Sierra Coll 5000 Rocklin Rd Rocklin CA 95677-3337

DICOCCO, MARC, air force officer, flight test engineer; b. Lackland AFB, Tex., Aug. 17, 1962; s. Severino and Anne Marie (Bopp) DiC. BS in Aerospace Engring., Va. Poly. Inst., 1985; MS in Aerospace Engring., U. Dayton, 1990. Cert. acquisition officer in program mgmt., test and evaluation and systems engring. Commd. 2d lt. USAF, 1985; advanced through ranks to capt., 1989; technician Prophet 21 Systems Inc., Yardley, Pa., 1984-85; advance concepts design engr. USAF Aeronautical Systems Divsn., Wright-Patterson AFB, Ohio, 1985-88, acquisition officer in tng., 1985-88, test project mgr., 1988-90; F-15E flight test engr. USAF Weapons and Tactics Ctr., Nellis AFB, Nev., 1990-94; chief upper stages divsn. Titan 4 Launch Vehicle Program, Space and Missile Ctr., L.A. AFB, 1994—; pres. aeronautic systems divsn. company grade officers adv. coun. Wright-Patterson AFB, 1989-90. Min. to youth club Our Lady of Peace Cath. Ch., Wright-Patterson AFB, 1987-90; altar server trainer Lady of the Skies Cath. Ch., Nellis AFB, 1993-94. Decorated Air Force Commendation medal (2), Air Force Achievement medal (2). Mem. AIAA, Aircraft Owners & Pilots Assn., Air Force Assn. (life), Planetary Soc.

DICOCHEA, ALFRED QUIJADA, municipal executive; b. Tucson, Aug. 23, 1944; s. Luis Miranda and Frances (Quijada) D.; m. Mary Ann Gutierrez, Oct. 5, 1968; children: Alfred Jr., Elizabeth Ann, Catherine Ann. BA, U. Ariz., 1968, MPA, 1975. Asst. town mgr. Town of South Tucson, 1968-70; program mgr. Com. for Econ. Opportunity, Tucson, 1970-72; citizen participation adminstr. City of Tucson, 1972-74; interim dir. Tucson-Pima Drug Abuse Clinic, 1974; urban programs adminstr. City of Tucson, 1974-78, departmental adminstrv. mgr., 1978—; urban transp. internship Carnegie-Mellon U., Pitts., 1977. Mem. Town of South Tucson Health Community Retirement Assn., 1968-70, Mex.-Am. Forum, 1969-74, Liaison in Neighborhood Knowledge, 1969-70, Awareness House, 1971-72, Policy Bd. of Model Cities, 1971-72, Mex.-Am. Scholarship Found., 1973-80, Ctr. Econ. Devel., 1974, Accion 80's, 1982-85; chmn. leadership com. San Xavier dist. Boy Scouts Am., 1969-70, Model Cities, Unit 10, 1972; past pres. Mex.-Am. Unity Coun., 1971; alt. to Study Group Coun. of Model Cities, 1972; del. to Transp. Task Force, 1972; pres. IMAGE de Tucson, 1977-78; mem. Spanish speaking coun. Diocese of Tucson, 1978-81; dir. region IX Nat. IMAGE Inc., 1979-81; mem. govt. rels. com. United Way, 1989-90; bd. dirs. Pio Decimo Ctr., 1971-73, Local Alcoholism Reception Ctr., 1973-75, Nosotros, Inc., 1978-93, El Pueblo Clinic, 1996—. With Ariz. Army N.G., 1967-73. Recipient Image of Tucson Community award Hispanic Image Chpt., 1978, Hispanic Recognition award Hispanic Community, 1992. Mem. Am. Mgmt. Assn., Am. Pub. Works Assn., Nat. Hispanic Assn. Inc. (bd. dirs. 1981-86), League United Latin Am. Citizens (chpt. # 1046), Ariz. Mcpl. Mgmt. Asst. Assn., Internat. Personnal Mgmt. Assn. Democrat. Roman Catholic. Office: City of Tucson Dept Transp PO Box 27210 Tucson AZ 85726-7210

DIEDERICH, J(OHN) WILLIAM, financial consultant; b. Ladysmith, Wis., Aug. 30, 1929; s. Joseph Charles and Alice Florence (Yost) D.; m. Mary Theresa Klein, Nov. 25, 1950; children: Mary Theresa Diederich Evans, Robert Douglas, Charles Stuart, Michael Mark, Patricia Anne Diederich Irelan, Donna Maureen (dec.), Denise Brendan, Carol Lynn Diederich Weaver, Barbara Gail, Brian Donald, Tracy Maureen Jorgensen, Theodora Bernadette Diederich Davidson, Tamara Alice, Lorraine Angela. PhB, Marquette U., Milw., 1951; MBA with distinction, Harvard U., 1955. With Landmark Comm., Inc., Norfolk, Va., 1955-90, v.p., treas., 1965-73, exec. v.p. fin., 1973-78, exec. v.p. community newspapers, 1978-82, exec. v.p., CFO, 1982-90, fin. cons., 1990—; chmn. bd. dirs. Landmark Cmty. Newspapers, Inc., 1977-88; pres. Exec. Productivity Sys., Inc., 1982-88, LCI Credit Corp., 1991-93, Landmark TV Inc., 1991—, LTM Investments, Inc., 1991—; v.p., treas., KLAS, Inc., 1994-95; v.p. Internet Express, Inc., 1994—; pres., bd. dirs. Wide World Web Internat., 1995—, TWC Holdings, Inc., 1996—; instr. Boston U., 1954, Old Dominion U., 1955-59. Lt. col. USMC, 1951-53, USMCR, 1953-71. Baker scholar Harvard U., 1955. Mem. SAR, Nat. Assn. Accts., Am. Numismatic Assn., Nat. Geneal. Soc., Wis. Geneal. Soc., Pa. Geneal. Soc., Sigma Delta Chi. Roman Catholic. Home and Office: PO Box 7677 1466 Glarus Ct Incline Village NV 89452-7677

DIEDRICK, GERALDINE ROSE, retired nurse; b. Chgo.; d. Milton Edward and Rose Agnes (Michalski) Goodman; R.N., Mt. San Antonio Coll., Walnut, Calif., 1963; BS, Calif. State U., L.A., 1966; MS, UCLA, 1968; divorced; 1 son, Scott Wesley. Nurse, State of Calif., 1960-83, dir. nursing Met. State Hosp., Norwalk, 1977-83; cons. in mental health, devel. disabilities. Recipient Letter of Commendation, State of Calif., 1974-77. Mem. Am. Nurses Assn., Nat. League Nursing, Am. Assn. Devel. Disabilities, Calif. Nurses Assn. (svc. awards), Am. Hosp. Assn., World Future Soc., Town Hall Calif. Lutheran. Contbr. to profl. jours.

DIEHR, DAVID BRUCE, social service administrator; b. Toledo, Ohio, June 4, 1939; s. Harlan E. and Lillis R. (Consaul) D.; m. Kathryn D. Welsh, Apr. 2, 1966; 1 child, Erik W. AB, Coll. William and Mary, 1961; postgrad., George Williams Coll., Chgo., 1961-63. Phys. dir. YMCA of Xenia-Greene County, Xenia, Ohio, 1964-68, YMCA of Joliet, Ill., 1968-74; exec. dir. N.W. YMCA of San Antonio, Tex., 1974-77; gen. dir. YMCA of Ctrl. Tex., Waco, 1977-86; group v.p. YMCA of Tucson, 1987-95; nat. field cons. YMCA of the USA-West, San Mateo, Calif., 1995—; treas., bd. dirs. Calif. Collaboration for Youth, Sacramento, 1995—. Mem. Assn. Profl. Dirs. (chpt. prs. 1980-83, dist. v.p. 1983-86), U.S. Power Squadron, Omicron Delta Kappa. Republican. Presbyterian. Office: YMCA of the USA 1650 S Amphlett Blvd Ste 314 San Mateo CA 94402

DIEKMANN, BARBARA BRANDENBURG, computer systems researcher and practitioner; b. Chgo., Aug. 11, 1946; d. Warner Otto and Anne (Storm) Brandenburg; m. Jeffrey Craig Fowler; children: Megan Anne, Molly Jean; m. James Edward Diekmann; stepchildren: Joshua, Jessica, Jacob. BA in Philosophy, Colo. State U., 1968; MA in Linguistics, U. Colo., 1990, Cert. in Cognitive Sci., 1993, PhD, 1996. Eng. tchr. U.S. Peace Corps, Tamil Nadu, India, 1968-69; planning and scheduling engr. Bechtel Corp., San Francisco, and Edmonton, Alberta, Can., 1970-75; software documentation editor, sys. analyst IBM, Boulder, Colo., 1985-87; program analyst, staff asst., cons. Nuc. Ops. Pub. Svc. Co., Denver and Platteville, Colo., 1987-89; mem. human interface design and rsch. group U.S. West Advanced Techs., Boulder, 1992-95; cons., 1984—. Editl. bd. Colo. Rsch. in Lingustics, 1992-94. Mem. Inst. Cognitive Sci., Linguistic Soc. Am., Cognitive Sci. Soc., Computer Human Interaction, Assn. Computing Machinery. Home: 11797 Flatiron Dr Lafayette CO 80026

DIELI, MARY ADELAIDE, software engineer consultant. BA in Am. Studies, SUNY, Binghamton, 1977; PhD in Rhetoric, Carnegie Mellon U., 1986. Rsch. asst. Comm. Design Ctr., Carnegie Mellon U., Pitts., 1981-82; product trainer Apple Computer, Inc., 1982, project supr., cons., 1983-84; sr. document designer AT&T, 1984-85; document design cons. Lasselle-Ramsay, Inc., 1986-88; usability mgr. Microsoft Corp., Redmond, Wash., 1988-93; user interface design, usability cons. Seattle, 1994—; tchg. asst. SUNY-Binghamton, 1978-79, instr., 1979, 80; instr. Broome C.C., Binghamton, 1980, Carnegie Mellon, 1980-81, Jefferson C.C., Watertown, N.Y., 1986; vis. asst. prof. dept. English Santa Clara U., 1986-87; tech. publs. mgr. Adobe Sys., Inc., Mountain View, Calif., 1987-88; affiliate asst. prof. tech. comm. dept. U. Wash., Seattle, 1991-93; mem. usability adv. bd. PC/Computing, 1993—; presenter in field. Contbr. articles to profl. jours. Mem. IEEE (Profl. Comm. Soc.), Wash. Software Assn., Soc. for Tech. Comm., Nat. Coun. Tchrs. English, Human Factors Soc. (spl. interest groups on computer sys., personality and individual differences in human performance, test and evaluation, visual performance), Assn. Computing Machinery (spl. interest groups on computer human interaction and documentation), Internet Soc. Home: 120 W Highland Dr # 421 Seattle WA 98119-3565 Office: 1509 Queen Anne Ave N # 270 Seattle WA 98109-5730

DIEMER, WILLIAM DAVID, retired engineer, research analyst; b. Cleve., May 19, 1924; s. Clarence Peter and Eleanor Marie (Champion) D.; m. Doris Grover Mudgett, June 11, 1960; children: Diane Beatrice, Karen Lisa. BS in Civil Engring., Case Inst. Tech., 1945; AM in Edn., U. Chgo., 1952. Structural engr. Am. Rolling Mill Co., Middletown, Ohio, 1945-46; cadastral engr. F.A. Pease Engring. Co., Cleve., 1946-48; admissions counselor Case Inst. Tech., Cleve., 1948-50; structural engr. Chgo., 1952-53; instr. mechanics Ill. Inst. Tech., Chgo., 1953-59; structural engr. Bertrand Goldberg Assocs., Chgo., 1959-60; rsch. project dir. Coll. Engring., UCLA, 1960-67; simulation programmer McDonnell-Douglas Corp., Santa Monica, Calif., 1968-70; dir. Acad. Census Data Ctr., Pacific Palisades, Calif., 1971; programmer Jet Propulsion Lab., Pasadena, 1972-73; rsch. analyst City of L.A., 1973-86, liaison 1990 census, 1987-90; editor, pub. Nat. Housing Register, Davis, Calif., 1991—. Author: Los Angeles Street Address Directory, 1989-93, Catalog I: Academic Census Data Center, 1971; author, pub.: Davis Almanac, 1997. Bd. dirs., pres. Consumers Co-op, Santa Monica, 1965-70, Unitarian Soc. L.A. West, 1962-66; bd. dirs. UN Assn. U.S.A., Davis, Calif., 1992-95, Davis Cmty. Network, 1993—; mem. Transp. Adv. Com. Yolo County, 1995—, chair, 1996—. Recipient Commendation/Plaque/Cert., City of L.A., 1990. Mem. Urban and Regional Info. Systems Assn., Internat. Assn. Assessing Officers. Democrat. Unitarian. Home: 27239 Meadowbrook Dr Davis CA 95616-5049 Office: Nat Housing Register 1403 5th St Davis CA 95616

DIENER, ROYCE, corporate director, retired healthcare services company executive; b. Balt., Mar. 27, 1918; s. Louis and Lillian (Goodman) D.; m. Jennifer S. Flinton; children: Robert, Joan, Michael. BA, Harvard U.; LLD, Pepperdine U. Comml. lending officer, investment banker various locations to 1972; pres. Am. Med. Internat., Inc., Beverly Hills, Calif., 1972-75, pres., chief exec. officer, 1975-78, chmn., chief exec. officer, 1978-85, chmn. bd., 1986-88, chmn. exec. com., 1986-89; bd. dirs. Calif. Econ. Devel. Corp., Acuson, Inc., Advanced Tech. Venture Funds, Am. Health Properties, AMI Health Svcs., plc., Consortium 2000. Author: Financing a Growing Business, 1966, 4th edit., 1995. Bd. visitors Grad. Sch. Mgmt., UCLA; mem. governing bd., UCLA Med. Ctr.; mem. vis. com. Med. Sch. and Sch. Dental Medicine, Harvard U.; bd. dirs. L.A. Philharm. Assn., L.A. chpt. ARC, Heritage Sq. Mus., Santa Monica. Served to capt. USAF, 1942-46, PTO. Decorated D.F.C. with oak leaf cluster. Mem. L.A. C. of C. (bd. dirs.), Calif. C. of C. (bd. dirs.), Calif. Bus. Round Table (bd. dirs.), Harvard Club, Regency Club, Calif. Yacht Club, Riviera Country Club (L.A.), Marks Club (London).

DIEPHOLZ, DANIEL RAY, real estate consultant, accountant; b. Hemet, Calif., Aug. 25, 1964; s. Eugene L. and Ruby J. (Forsch) D. BSBA in Acctg., Valparaiso U., 1985; MS in Real Estate with acad. honors, NYU, 1990. CPA, Calif.; lic. real estate broker, Calif. Auditor Blue Cross Calif., Woodland Hills, 1986-87; corp. fin. assoc., v.p. Bateman Eichler, Hill Richards Inc., L.A., N.Y.C., 1987-89; real estate cons. Price Waterhouse, L.A., 1990-96; founder Diepholz & Co., Indian Wells, Calif., 1996—; chmn. bd. Taos Palms Inc., L.A., 1990—. Mem. Nat. Assn. Accts. (bd. dirs. 1990-95). Republican. Mem. LDS Ch. Home: 270 N Canon Dr # 1140 Beverly Hills CA 90210-5323 Office: Diepholz & Co 45-220 Vista Santa Rosa Indian Wells CA 92210-9164

DIESTELKAMP, DAWN LEA, systems analyst; b. Fresno, Calif., Apr. 23, 1954; d. Don and Joy LaVaughn (Davis) Diestelkamp. BS in Microbiology, Calif. State U.-Fresno, 1976, MS in Pub. Adminstrn., 1983, MBA, 1995, cert. in tng. design & mgmt., 1992. Lic. clin. lab. technologist, Calif.; cert. clin. lab. dir. Clin. lab. technologist Valley Med. Ctr., Fresno, 1977-82, info. systems coord., 1983-84, quality control coord. Valley Med. Ctr., Fresno, 1984-90, systems & procedures analyst, 1990-91; systems & procedures analyst Fresno County Cts., 1991—; instr. Fresno City Coll. Tng. Inst., 1993—; cons., instr. in field. Mem. ASTD, AAUW, Calif. Ct. Clks. Assn. (dir.), Fresno Women's Network (chair newsletter com., bd. dirs.), Fresno Met. Mus. Soc. Democrat. Office: 1100 Van Ness Ave Rm 200 Fresno CA 93724

DIETRICH, WILLIAM ALAN, reporter; b. Tacoma, Sept. 29, 1951; s. William Richard and Janice Lenore (Pooler) D.; m. Holly Susan Roberts, Dec. 19, 1970; children: Lisa, Heidi. BA, Western Wash. U., 1973. Reporter Bellingham (Wash.) Herald, 1973-76, Gannet News Svc., Washington, 1976-78, Vancouver (Wash.) Columbian, 1978-82, Seattle Times, 1982—. Author: The Final Forest, 1992, Northwest Passage, 1995. Recipient Paul Tobenkin award Columbia U., 1986, Pulitzer prize for nat. reporting, 1990; Nieman fellow Harvard U., 1987-88. Office: Seattle Times PO Box 70 Seattle WA 98111-0070

DIETTERT, GERALD ALLEN, cardiologist; b. Moscow, Idaho, Sept. 25, 1927; s. Reuben Arthur and Charlotte (Thompson) D.; m. Ethel P. Caras, June 12, 1949; children: Craig, Carol, Scott, Bruce. Student, U. Mont., 1945-46, 48-50, BA, 1984, MA, 1990; MD, Washington U., St. Louis, 1954. Diplomate Am. Bd. Internal Medicine. Intern medicine Barnes Hosp., St. Louis, 1954-55; resident in medicine Barnes Hosp., 1955-56; fellow in cardiology Washington U., St. Louis, 1956-58; internist, cardiologist Western Mont. Clinic, Missoula, 1960-90; assoc. prof. U. Wash., Seattle and Missoula, 1970-85; pres. med. staff St. Patrick Hosp., Missoula, 1976, governing bd., 1976-82; pres. bldg. corp. Western Mont. Clinic, Missoula, 1970-80; pres. Mont. Heart Assn., Great Falls, 1963-64. Author: Grinnell's Glacier, 1992; contbr. articles to profl. jours. Mem. bd. edn. Sch. Dist. #5, Missoula, 1960-66, Missoula County H.S., 1962-66, Sch. Dist. #1, Missoula, 1966-72. With U.S. Army, 1946-48. Mem. Missoula Exch. Club (pres. 1961, Man of Yr. 1970, 80). Republican. Congregationalist. Home and Office: 9505 Nevada Trl Missoula MT 59802-9335

DIETZ, JANIS CAMILLE, sales executive; b. Washington, May 26, 1950; d. Albert and Joan Mildred (MacMullen) Weinstein; m. John William Dietz, Apr. 10, 1981. BA, U. R.I., 1971; MBA, Calif. Poly. U., Pomona, 1984; PhD Claremont Grad. Sch., 1997. Customer svc. trainer People's Bank, Providence, 1974-76; salesman, food broker Bradshaw Co., L.A., 1976-78; salesman Johnson & Johnson, L.A., 1978-79, GE Co., L.A., 1979-82; regional sales mgr. Leviton Co., L.A., 1982-85; nat. sales mgr. Jensen Gen. div. Nortek Co., L.A., 1985-86; retail sales mgr. Norris div. Masco, L.A., 1986-88; nat. sales mgr. Thermador Waste King div. Masco, L.A., 1988-91; nat. accts. mgr. Universal Flooring div. Masco, 1991-92; western regional mgr. Peerless Faucet div. Masco, 1992-95; performance devel. cons., Delta Faucet, div. Masco, 1995—; asst. prof. bus. adminstrn. U. LaVerne, 1995—; sales trainer, Upland, Calif., 1985—; instr. Calif. Poly. U., 1988—; lectr. Whittier Coll., 1994. Dir. pub. rels. Jr. Achievement, Providence, 1975-76; bd. trustees Nat. Multiple Sclerosis Soc., So. Calif. chpt. Recipient Sector Svc. award GE Co., Fairfield, Conn., 1980, Outstanding Achievement award, 1988. Mem. NAFE, Sales Profls. L.A. (v.p. 1984-86), Toastmasters (adminstrv. v.p. 1985). Unitarian.

DIETZ, PATRICIA ANN, engineering administrator; b. L.A., Nov. 30, 1958; m. Frank Raymond Dietz, July 1, 1978; children: Lindy K., Frank R. Jr. BA in Polit. Sci., U. Colo., 1983; MA in Psychology, Pepperdine U., 1993; Paralegal Cert., U. San Diego, 1988. Investment broker 1st Investors Corp., Colorado Springs, Colo., 1986-88; paralegal Law Offices of Ben Williams, Santa Monica, Calif., 1988-89; mgmt. analyst Bur. of Engring., City of L.A., 1989—; camp commandant Operation Safe Harbor-Haitian Humanitarian Relief Effort, 1992. Mem. Parent Tchr. Student Assn., Rosamond, Calif., 1992. With U.S. Army, 1983-86, capt. USAR, 1986—. Nat. Urban fellow, 1991. Mem. Civil Affairs Assn., Res. Officers Assn., Engrs. and Architects Assn. Republican.

DIETZ, RUSSELL SCOTT, communications company executive; b. Freeport, N.Y., Mar. 1, 1963; s. Russell N. and Mary E. (Sattler) D.; m. Carla R. Cadwell, June 4, 1983. BS in Computer Sci., SUNY, Stony Brook, 1985. Computer system mgr. Shoreham Wading River Schs., Shoreham, N.Y., 1979-81; sr. computer programming RMS Data Svcs., Hicksville, N.Y., 1981-83; bd. dirs. Technically Elite Concepts Inc., Hermosa Beach, Calif.; sr. systems programmer/analyst Bendix Field Engring. Corp., St. Inigoes, Md., 1983-84; system implementation specialist Magnavox Electronic Systems Co., Ashburn, Va., 1984-87; prin. software specialist Digital Equipment Corp., Landover, Md., 1987-88; v.p. systems devel. Technically Elite Concepts Inc., Hermosa Beach, Calif., 1988-95; v.p. engring., chief tech. officer Technically Elite, Inc., Campbell, Calif., 1995—, chief tech. officer, 1995—; cons. Cedars-Sinai Med. Ctr., L.A., 1988-90. Contbr. articles to profl. jours. Mem. Digital Equipment Corp. User Soc., DC VAX Local Users Group (chmn. 1985-87). Republican. Lutheran. Office: Technically Elite Inc 6330 San Ignacio Ave San Jose CA 95119-1209

DIGGS, BRADLEY C., lawyer; b. Missoula, Mont., Sept. 18, 1948. BA magna cum laude, Amherst Coll., 1970; JD cum laude, Harvard U., 1973. Bar: Wash. 1973. Mng. ptnr. Davis Wright Tremaine, Seattle. Mem. ABA, Phi Beta Kappa. Office: Davis Wright Tremaine 2600 Century Sq 1501 4th Ave Seattle WA 98101-1662

DIGHTON, STEPHEN DORIAN, writer, retired nurse; b. Phoenix, Aug. 21, 1944; s. Ralph Maurice Jr. and Neelia Matilde (Jonkmans) D.; m. Kathy Ellen Livermore, Jan. 31, 1969. BA, Chapman Coll., 1966; AA, Golden West Coll., 1971. RN, Calif., Oreg. Correctional nurse, various positions Orange County, Santa Ana, Calif., 1966-90; mental health nurse Mercy Med. Ctr., Roseburg, Oreg., 1990-94; cons., reviewer Am. Jour. Nursing, N.Y.C., 1984-88; resource cons. Bahá'í Forum-Am. Online, 1993—. Author: (book) Locked In, 1996, (booklet) His New Name, 1994; editor: (newsletter) The Oreg. Bahá'í, 1995-96. Bahá'í Faith.

DI GIACINTO, SHARON, artist, educator; b. Chula Vista, Calif., Apr. 13, 1960; d. Vendal J. and Virginia J. Di G.; m. Richard K. Hillis, Aug. 1983; children: Tiffany Di Giacinto, Nikos Di Giacinto-Hillis, Gino Di Giacinto-Hillis. BFA, Ohio U., 1981; MFA, Tex. Woman's U., 1983. Teaching asst. art Stephen F. Austin State U., Nacogdoches, Tex., 1981, Tex. Woman's U., Denton, 1982-83; art instr. Phoenix Coll., 1983-84, Glendale (Ariz.) C.C., 1985-88; ind. artist Peoria, Ariz. Solo exhbns. include Glendale C.C. Art Gallery, 1984, Phoenix Coll. Art Gallery, Scottsdale (Ariz.) C.C., 1989, Sun Cities Art Mus., 1989, Phoenix Visual Arts Gallery, 1990, Madison House, Sun City West, 1990; group exhbns. include 2-person exhbn. Chandler (Ariz.) Ctr. for Arts, 1991, Peoria (Ariz.) City Hall, 1995, Narthex Art Exhibit, Phoenix, 1996, Udinotti Gallery, Scotsdale, 1986, Casa Grande (Ariz.) Art Mus., 1997. Co-chair Peoria Arts Commn., 1988-91. Mem. Coll. Art Assn. Am., Phoenix Art Mus., Phoenix Zoo. Democrat. Roman Catholic. Home: 6741 W Cholla St Peoria AZ 85345-5818

DI GIROLAMO, ROSINA E., education educator; b. Monterey, Calif., Aug. 3, 1945; d. Anthony and Frances (Lucido) DiG. AA, Monterey Peninsula Coll., 1965; BA, Calif. State U., Hayward, 1967; MA, Calif. Polytech., San Luis Obispo, 1975. Tchr. Monterey (Calif.) Pub. Unified Sch. Dist., 1968—. Polit. action chairperson Monterey Bay Tchrs. Assn., 1993-94; mem. City's Youth Task Force, 1997. Nominee for Outstanding Tchr., Lori Flagg Found., Monterey, 1991-92. Mem. Calif. Reading Assn., Calif. Tchrs. of English, Nat. Tchrs. of English, ASCD, Internat. Reading Assn., Calif. Leadership Team. Democrat. Roman Catholic. Home: 77 Via Chualar Monterey CA 93940-2528 Office: Walter Colton Mid Sch 100 Toda Vis Monterey CA 93940-4237

DIGNAN, MARY, lawyer; b. Dallas, Oct. 14, 1954; d. David Paul and Elizabeth Louise (Jennings) D.; m. Andy Rosten, Ocy. 6, 1984. Student, St. Mary's Coll. Calif., 1972-74; BA, Santa Clara U., 1976; JD with hons., McGeorge, U. Pacific, 1994. News reporter Visalia (Calif.) Times-Delta, 1976-79; congl. aide U.S. Ho. Reps., Washington, 1979-82; com. cons. Calif. Assembly Agr., Sacramento, 1982-83; adminstrv. asst. Kern County Water Agy., Bakersfield, Calif., 1983-85; water issues cons., Sacramento, 1985-91; law clk. DeCuir & Somach, Sacramento, 1991-94; assoc. Kronick, Moskovitz, Tiedemann & Girard, Sacramento, 1994—. Mem. adv. com. to persons with disabilities Sacramento County Bd. Suprs. Rocky Mountain Mineral Law Found. scholar, 1993-94, Nat. Fedn. for Blind scholar, 1993. Mem. Traynor Honor Soc., Alpha Sigma Nu. Office: Kronick Moskovitz Tiedemann Girard 400 Capitol Mall Fl 27 Sacramento CA 95814-4417

DIKE, KENNETH P., elementary school educator, principal; b. Chgo., Nov. 22, 1954; s. Burton L. and G. Joan (Damon) K.; m. L. Cindy Taylor, Oct. 1, 1977; children: Amie, Christian. BS, George Williams Coll., 1976, MS, 1979. Dir. Catalina Island Camps, L.A., 1981-83, Camp Forbing, Shreveport, La., 1983-85, Alta Sierra Camps, Dunlap, Calif., 1979-81, 85-87; prin., tchr. Miramonte (Calif.) Elem. Sch., 1987—; cons. R. Howard Walker Found., Long Beach, Calif., 1984—; curriculum cons. Kings Canyon Unified Sch. Dist., Reedley, Calif., 1992—. Author: Teaching Outdoor Education, 1996. Mem. ASCD, Ctrl. Sierra C. of C. Home and Office: PO Box 106 Miramonte CA 93641-0106

DILBECK, CHARLES STEVENS, JR., real estate company executive; b. Dallas, Dec. 2, 1944; s. Charles Stevens Sr. and Betty Doris (Owens) D.; 1 child, Stephen Douglas; m. Carolyn Jane DeBoer, Sept. 4, 1994. BS, Wichita State U., 1968; MS, Stanford U., 1969, postgrad., 1970-71. Engr. United Tech. Ctr., Sunnyvale, Calif., 1971-72; cons. Diversicom, Inc., Santa Clara, Calif., 1972-73; engr. Anamet Labs., San Carlos, Calif., 1973-75; cons. real estate investment Cert. Capital Corp., San Jose, Calif., 1975-82; pvt. practice in real estate, San Jose, 1981—; prin. Am. Equity Investments, San Jose, 1982—; mem. Los Gatos (Calif.) Rent Adv. Com., 1988. Mem. Nat. Apt. Assn., San Jose Real Estate Bd., Tri-County Apt. Assn., Gold Key Club, Tau Beta Pi (pres. 1968), Sigma Gamma Tau. Republican. Home: 301 Alta Loma Ln Santa Cruz CA 95062-4620 Office: Am Equity Investments 301 Alta Loma Ln Santa Cruz CA 95062-4620

DILL, KENNETH AUSTIN, pharmaceutical chemistry educator; b. Oklahoma City, Dec. 11, 1947; s. Austin Glenn and Margaret (Blocker) D. S.B., Mass. Inst. Tech., 1971, S.M., 1971; Ph.D., U. Calif.-San Diego, 1978. Fellow Damon Runyon-Walter Winchell Stanford (Calif.) U., 1978-81; asst. prof. chemistry U. Fla., Gainesville, 1981-82; asst. prof. pharm. chemistry and pharmacy U. Calif., San Francisco, 1982-85, assoc. prof.,

1985-89, prof., 1989—; adj. prof. pharmaceutics U. Utah, 1989—. PEW Found. scholar. Contbr. numerous sci. articles to profl. publs.; patentee in field. Fellow Am. Phys. Soc., AAAS; mem. Am. Chem. Soc., Biophys. Soc. (Nat. lectr. 1996, pres.-elect 1997). Office: Univ Calif Pharm Chemistry Dept San Francisco CA 94143

DILL, LADDIE JOHN, artist; b. Long Beach, Calif., Sept. 14, 1943; s. James Melvin and Virginia (Crane) D.; children: Ariel, Jackson Caldwell. BFA, Chouinard Art Inst., 1968. Chmn. of visual arts The Studio Sch., Santa Monica, Calif.; lectr. painting and drawing UCLA, 1975-88. Exhbns. include: San Francisco Mus. Modern Art, 1977-78, Albright Knox Mus., Buffalo, 1978-79, Charles Cowles Gallery, N.Y.C., 1983-85, The First Show, Los Angeles; represented in permanent collections: Mus. Modern Art, N.Y.C., Laguna Mus. Art, Los Angeles County Mus., Mus. Contemporary Art, Los Angeles, Santa Barbara Mus., San Francisco Mus. Modern Art, Seattle Mus., Newport Harbor Art Mus., Oakland Mus., Smithsonian Instn., IBM, Nat. Mus., Seoul, Republic of Korea, San Diego Mus. Art, La. Mus., Denmark, Am. Embassy, Helsinki, Finland, Corcoran Gallery Art, Washington, Chgo Art Inst., Greenville County (S.C.) Mus., Palm Springs Desert Mus., Phoenix Art Mus., William Rockhill Nelsen Mus., Kansas City, Phillips Collection. Nat. Endowment Arts grantee, 1975, 82; Guggenheim Found. fellow, 1979-80; Calif. Arts Council Commn. grantee, 1983-84.

DILLARD, JOHN MARTIN, lawyer, pilot; b. Long Beach, Calif., Dec. 25, 1945; s. John Warren and Clara Leora (Livermore) D.; student U. Calif., Berkeley, 1963-67; BA, UCLA, 1968; JD, Pepperdine U., 1976; m. Patricia Anne Yeager, Aug. 10, 1968; children: Jason Robert, Jennifer Lee. Instr. pilot Norton AFB, Calif., 1973-77. Bar: Calif., 1976. Assoc. Magana, Cathcart & McCarthy, L.A., 1977-80, Lord, Bissell & Brook, L.A., 1980-85; of counsel Finley, Kumble, Wagner, 1985-86, Schell & Delamer, 1986-94, Law Offices of John M. Dillard, 1986—, v.p., gen. counsel, dir. Resort Aviation Svcs, Inc., Calif., 1988-93; mng. ptnr. Natkin & Weisbach, So. Calif., 1988-89. Active Am. Cancer Soc.; bd. dirs. Placentia-Yorba Linda Ednl. Found., Inc. Capt. USAF, 1968-73, Vietnam. Mem. ATLA (aviation litigation com.), Am. Bar Assn. (aviation com.), Orange County Bar Assn., Fed. Bar Assn., L.A. County Bar Assn. (aviation com.), Century City Bar Assn., Internat. Platform Assn., Res. Officers Assn., Orange County Com. of 100, Sigma Nu. Home: 19621 Verona Ln Yorba Linda CA 92886-2858 Office: 313 N Birch St Santa Ana CA 92701-5263

DILLARD, MARILYN DIANNE, property manager; b. Norfolk, Va., July 7, 1940; d. Thomas Ortman and Sally Ruth (Wallerich) D.; m. James Conner Coons, Nov. 6, 1965 (div. June 1988); 1 child, Adrienne Alexandra Dillard Coons (dec.). Studied with Russian prima ballerina, Alexandra Danilova, 1940's; student with honors at entrance, UCLA, 1958-59; BA in Bus. Adminstrn. with honors, U. Wash., 1962. Modeling-print work Harry Conover, N.Y.C., 1945; ballet instr. Ivan Novikoff Sch. Russian Ballet, 1955; model Elizabeth Leonard Agy., Seattle, 1955-68; mem. fashion bd., retail worker Frederick & Nelson, Seattle, 1962; retail worker I. Magnin & Co., Seattle, 1963-64; property mgr. Seattle, 1961—; antique and interior designer John J. Cunningham Antiques, Seattle, 1968-73; owner, interior designer Marilyn Dianne Dillard Interiors, 1973—; mem. rsch. bd. advisors Am. Biog. Inst., Inc., 1990—. Author: (poetry) Flutterby, 1951, Spring Flowers, 1951; contbr., asst. chmn. (with Jr. League of Seattle) Seattle Classic Cookbook, 1980-83. Charter mem., pres. Children's Med. Ctr., Maude Fox Guild, Seattle, 1965—, Jr. Women's Symphony Assn., 1967-73, Va. Mason Med. Ctr. Soc., 1990—, Nat. Mus. of the Am. Indian, Smithsonian Instn., Washington, 1992; mem. Seattle Jr. Club, 1962-65; bd. dirs. Patrons N.W. Civic, Cultural and Charitable Orgns. (chmn. various coms.), Seattle, 1976—, prodn. chmn., 1977-78, 84-85, auction party chmn., 1983-84, exec. com., 1984-85, chmn. bd. vols., 1990-91, adv. coun., 1991—; mem. U. Wash. Arboretum Found. Unit, 1966-73, pres., 1969; bd. dirs. Coun. for Prevention Child Abuse and Neglect, Seattle, 1974-75; mem. bd. dirs., v.p., mem. various coms. Seattle Children's Theatre, 1984-90, asst. in lighting main stage plays, 1987-93, mem. adv. coun., 1993—; asst. in lighting main stage plays Bathhouse Theatre, 1987-90; adv. bd. N.W. Asian Am. Theatre, 1987—, Co-Motion Dance Co., 1991—; organizer teen groups Episcopal Ch. of the Epiphany, 1965-67; provisional class pres. Jr. League Seattle, 1971-72, next to new shop asst. chmn., 1972-73, bd. dirs. admissions chmn., 1976-77, exec. v.p., exec. com., bd. dirs., 1978-79, sustaining mem., 1984—; charter mem. Jr. Women's Symphony Assn., 1967-73; mem. Seattle Art Mus., 1975-90, Landmark, 1990—, Corp. Coun. for the Arts, 1991—; founding dir. Adrienne Coons Meml. Fund, 1985, v.p., 1985-92, 95—, pres. 1992-95; mem. steering com. Heart Ball Am. Heart Assn., 1986, 87, auction chmn., 1986; mem. steering com. Bellevue Sch. Dist. Children's Theatre, 1983-85, pub. rels. chair, 1984, asst. stage mgr., 1985. Named Miss Greater Seattle, 1964. Mem. AFTRA, Am. Biographical Inst., U. Wash. Alumnae Assn. (life), Pacific N.W. Ballet Assn. (charter), Progressive Animal Welfare Soc., Associated Women (student coun. U. Wash. 1962), Profl. Rodeo Cowboys Assn. (assoc.), Seattle Tennis Club. Republican. Episcopalian. Home and Office: 2053 Minor Ave E Seattle WA 98102-3513

DILLARD, MICHAEL L., food products company executive; b. 1942. BS in Acctg., Miss. Coll., 1964. Various acctg. positions Chrysler Corp., Cape Canaveral, Fla., 1964-66; divsn. acct. Blue Goose Growers, Vero Beach, Fla., 1966-76; CFO Pure Gold, Redlands, Calif., 1976-85, Saticoy Lemon Assocs., Inc., Santa Paula, Calif., 1985—. Office: Saticoy Lemon Assoc Inc PO Box 46 Santa Paula CA 93061-3013*

DILLON, FRANCIS PATRICK, human resources executive, management and personnel sales consultant; b. Long Beach, Calif., Mar. 15, 1937; s. Wallace Myron and Mary Elizabeth (Land) D., B.A., U. Va., 1959; M.S., Def. Fgn. Affairs Sch., 1962; M.B.A., Pepperdine U., 1976; m. Vicki Lee Dillon, Oct. 1980; children: Cary Randolph, Francis Patrick Jr., Randee, Rick. Traffic mgr., mgr. pers. svcs. Pacific Telephone Co., Sacramento and Lakeport, Calif., 1966-69; asst. mgr. manpower planning and devel. Pan-Am. World Airways, N.Y.C., 1969-71; mgr. pers. and orgn. devel. Continental Airlines, L.A., 1971-74; dir. human resources Bourns, Inc., Riverside, Calif., 1974-80; v.p. employee and cmty. relations MSI Data Corp., 1980-83; pres. Pavi Enterprises, 1983—; cons. mgmt. Pers. Outplacement Counseling/Sales/Mgmt., fin. svcs. and estate planning/mortgage reductions 1983—; pres., CEO Pers. Products & Svcs., Inc., 1984-91; v.p. Exec. Horizons, Inc., 1988-94; sr. profl. svcs. cons. Right Assocs., 1994—; pres. Meditrans Inc.; v.p. Princeton Masters Internat., 1997—. Bd. dirs. Health Svcs. Maintenance Orgn., Inc., Youth Svcs. Ctr., Inc.; vol. precinct worker. Served to lt. comdr. USN, 1959-66; asst. naval attaché, Brazil, 1963-65. Recipient Disting. Svc. award Jaycees, 1969; Jack Cates Meml. Vol. of Year award Youth Svc. Ctr., 1977. Mem. Assn. Internal Mgmt. Cons.'s, Am. Soc. Personnel Adminstrn., Personnel Indsl. Rels. Assn., Am. Soc. Tng. and Devel., Am. Electronics Assn. (human resources com., chmn. human resources symposium), Lake Mission Viejo Assn. (sec., bd. dirs. 1990-94). Republican. Episcopalian. Clubs: Mission Viejo Sailing, YMCA Bike, Mission Viejo Ski, Caving, Toastmasters (pres. 1966-67), Have Dirt Will Travel, Capo Valley 4 Wheelers. Office: Pavi Enterprises 27331 Via Amistoso Mission Viejo CA 92692-2410

DILLON, ROBERT MORTON, retired association executive, architectural consultant; b. Seattle, Oct. 27, 1923; s. James Richard and Lucille (Morton) D.; m. Mary Charlotte Beeson, Jan. 6, 1943; children: Robert Thomas, Colleen Marie Dillon Brown, Patrick Morton. Student, U. Ill., 1946-47; BArch., U. Wash., 1949; MA in Architecture, U. Fla., 1954. Registered architect, Fla. Designer-draftsman Williams and Longstreet (Architects), Greenville, S.C., 1949-50, William G. Lyles, Bissett, Carlisle & Wolff (Architects), Columbia, S.C., 1949-50, Robert M. Dillon and Wm. B. Eaton (Architects), Gainesville, Fla., 1952-55; staff architect Bldg. Rsch. Adv. Bd., Nat. Acad. Scis.-NRC, Washington, 1955-56, project dir., 1956-58, exec. dir., 1958-77; exec. sec. U.S. nat. com. for Conseil Internat. du Batiment, 1962-74; Sec. U.S. Planning Com. 2d Internat. Conf. on Permafrost, Yakutsk, USSR, 1972-74; exec. asst. to pres. Nat. Inst. Bldg. Scis., Washington, 1978-81, v.p., 1982-84, acting contr., 1983-84; exec. v.p. Am. Coun. Constrn. Edn., Washington, 1984-89, cons., 1989—; asst. prof. arch. Clemson Coll., 1949-50; instr., asst. prof. arch. U. Fla., 1950-55; lectr. structural theory and design Cath. U. Am., 1956-62; guest lectr. Air Force Inst. Tech., Wright-Patterson AFB, 1964-65; disting. faculty Acad. Code Adminstrn. and Enforcement U. Ill., 1972, professorial lectr. George Washington U., 1973-77, 81-82; vis. prof. Coll. Environ. Design U. Okla., 1984, adj. assoc. prof. bldg. sci., 1985-89, grad. sch. arch. Univ. Utah, 1978. Author: (with S.W. Crawley) Steel Buildings: Analysis and Design, 1970, 4th edit., 1993 (also 3d edit. pub. in Spanish 1992); contbg. author: Funk and Wagnall's New Ency., 1972, Ency. of Architecture, 1989; editor-in-chief: Guide to the Use of NEHRP Provisions in Earthquake Resistant Design of Buildings, 1987, Building Seismic Safety Coun., Nat. Inst. Bldg. Scis. Cons. Ednl. Facilities Labs., N.Y.C., 1958-71; mem. adv. com. low-income housing demonstration program HUD, Washington, 1964-67; mem. working groups U.S.-USSR Agreement on Housing and Other Constrn., 1975-85; mem. sub-panel housing White House Panel on Civilian Tech., Washington, 1961-62; mem. advs. to F. Stuart Fitzpatrick Meml. Award Trustee, 1969-84, chmn., 1974-78; mem. adv. panel Basic Homes Program OEO and HUD, 1972-77; mem. Nat. Adv. Coun. Rsch. Energy Conservation, 1975-78; mem. adv. com. Coun. Am. Bldg. Ofcls., 1976-86; mem. tech. coun. on bldg. codes and stds.; sec. Home and Land Owners Assn., Angel Fire, N.Mex., 1991-95; co-chmn., sec. initial bd. dirs. Assn. Angel Fire Property Owners, 1995-96; mem. Angel Fire Planning and Zoning Commn., 1997—. Mem. AIA (com. rsch. for architecture 1962-67, chmn. 1969, chmn. com. archtl. barriers 1967-68, nat. housing com. 1970-72, 84-85, mem. emeritus 1990—), ASCE (life, task com. cold regions 1977-79, tech. coun. cold regions engring., exec. com. 1976-84, chmn. 1981, standards com. 1987-94,), DAV (life), Nat. Acad. Code Adminstrn. (trustee 1976-80, exec. com. 1978-82, new bd. dirs. 1980-82, 83-84, sec.-treas. 1982-82, life), Am. Inst. Steel Constrn., Am. Inst. Constructors, Am. Coun. Constrn. Edn. (trustee 1990-96), N.Mex. Soc. Architects, Nat. Inst. Bldg. Scis. (cons. coun. 1984-93, honor award 1997). Home and Office: PO Box 193 Angel Fire NM 87710

DILORENZO, FRANCIS X., bishop; b. Philadelphia, PA, Apr. 15, 1942. ordained priest May 18, 1968. Titular bishop of Tigia, 1988; aux. bishop Diocese of Scranton, 1988; apostolic admin. Diocese of Honolulu, 1993-94, bishop, 1994—. Office: Chancery Office 1184 Bishop St Honolulu HI 96813-2838*

DILUIGI, RONALD RICHARD, health care agency executive; b. Vineland, N.J., Aug. 26, 1946; s. Dominick and Anna (Alzerano) DiL.; m. Paula Louise Pletcher, July 8, 1967; children: Jason Ronald, Marisa Nicole, Adrienne Christine. BA, Calif. State U., Fullerton, 1972, MPA, 1974; grad. exec. program, U. Calif., Irvine, 1984. Cert. community coll. instr., Calif. Adminstrv. intern City of Huntington Beach (Calif.) City Mgrs. Office, 1972-73; adminstrv. aide City of Huntington Beach Dept. of Fin., 1973-74; adminstrv. analyst Orange County Adminstrv. Office, Santa Ana, Calif., 1974-76; asst. chief mgmt., budget and legis. Orange County Adminstrv. Office, Santa Ana, 1976-82; dir. agy. adminstrn. Orange County Health Care Agy., Santa Ana, 1982-86, asst. agy. dir., 1986—; bd. dirs. Maternal Outreach Mgmt. Sys., Santa Ana, 1992—, St. Jude Med. Ctr. Meml. Found., 1989-93, St. Jude Heritage Health Found., Fullerton, Calif., 1994—; exec. coun. Am. Soc. Pub. Adminstrn., County of Orange, Calif., 1981-83; bd. trustees St. Jude Hosp., Yorba Linda, 1984-89; bd. trustees St. Jude Medical Ctr., 1993—. Chair planning commn. City of Yorba Linda, 1983—, mem. parks and recreation commn., 1983-89, mem. housing and cmty. devel. coun., 1983-89; mem. care for poor fund allocation com. St. Joseph Health Sys., Orange, Calif., 1991—. With USNR, 1966-68. Mem. Calif. State Fullerton Alumni Assn. Home: 20780 Paseo De La Rambla Yorba Linda CA 92887-2420 Office: Orange County Health Care 515 N Sycamore St Santa Ana CA 92701-4637

DIMAIO, VIRGINIA SUE, gallery owner; b. Houston, July 6, 1921; d. Jesse Lee and Gabriella Sue (Norris) Chambers; AB, U. Redlands, 1943; student U. So. Calif., 1943-45, Scripps Coll., 1943, Pomona Coll., 1945; m. James V. DiMaio, 1955 (div. 1968); children: Victoria, James V. Owner, dir. Galeria Capistrano, San Juan Capistrano and Santa Fe, N.Mex., 1979—; founder Mus. Women in Arts, Washington; cons., appraiser Southwestern and Am. Indian Handcrafts; lectr. Calif. State U., Long Beach; established ann. Helen Hardin Meml. scholarship for woman artist grad. Inst. Am. Indian Art, Santa Fe, also ann. Helen Hardin award for outstanding artist at Indian Market, S.W. Assn. on Indian Affairs, Santa Fe; bd. dirs. Mus. of Man, San Diego, 1989, Am. Diabetes Assn. Santa Fe, 1996—, Appraisals, Etc., 1996—; mem. Intertribal Coun. U. Calif., Irvine, 1990; founder Inst. Am. Indian Art, Santa Fe, 1993, bd. dirs., 1992—, chmn. devel. com., 1996—; mem. task force San Juan Capistrano City, 1995; bd. dirs. Futures for Children, 1996. Author: (forward to Mus. of Man exhibit catalogue) Paths Beyond Tradition. Recipient Bronze Plaque Recognition award Navajo Tribal Mus., 1977. Mem. Indian Arts and Crafts Assn., S.W. Assn. Indian Affairs, Heard Mus., San Juan Capistrano C. of C. Republican. Roman Catholic. Office: PO Box 22868 Santa Fe NM 87502-2868

DI MARTINI, STACY JEAN, elementary education educator; b. Denver, June 8, 1955; d. John and Caroljeanne (Veigel) Priola; m. John Thomas DiMartini, Apr. 17, 1982. BA in Edn. cum laude, Regis Coll., Denver, 1977; MA in Edn.-Reading Instrn., U. Colo., 1984. Cert. reading specialist. Tchr. Jefferson County (Colo.) Pub. Schs., 1977—; tchr. 1st through 4th grades Warder Elem Sch., 1981-90; tchr. K-2d grades Betty Adams Elem. Sch., 1990—; tchr. 1st through 3d grades Fremont Elem. Sch., Peiffer Elem. Sch., Juchem Elem. Sch., 1977-81; course cons. Regis Coll., Denver, 1990—; nat. trainer Wright Group Intergrated Learning Program; pvt. tutor, Arvada, Colo., 1988—; cons. Dist. 1 schs. Valley View Elem., Western Hills Elem., Denver, 1990; lectr. various confs. Author: Teaching Reading Through Mother Goose, 1987, 88; co-editor: Literacy Resource Directory, 1989. Recipient Outstanding Reading Educator award Colo. Coun. Internat. Reading Assn., 1992. Mem. Internat. Reading Assn., Colo. Coun. Internat. Reading Assn. (mem. conv. planning com. Preconv. Insts. 1989), Jefferson County Coun. Internat. Reading Assn. (mem. young writers planning com. 1989-90, sec. 1990—), Jefferson County Edn. Assn. Home: 3255 E 128th Pl Denver CO 80241-2142 Office: Betty Adams Elem 6450 W 95th Pl Broomfield CO 80021-6421

DIMATTIO, TERRY, historic site administrator. Park supt. Cabrillo National Monument, San Diego, Calif. Office: Cabrillo Nat Monument 1800 Cabrillo Memorial Dr San Diego CA 92166-0670*

DIMITRIADIS, ANDRE C., health care executive; b. Istanbul, Turkey, Sept. 29, 1940; s. Constantine N. and Terry D. BS, Robert Coll., Istanbul, 1964; MS, Princeton U., 1965; MBA, NYU, 1967, PhD, 1970. Analyst Mobil Oil Internat., N.Y.C., 1965-67; mgr. TWA, N.Y.C., 1967-73; dir. Pan Am. Airways, N.Y.C., 1973-76; asst. treas. Pan Am. Airways, 1976-79; v.p., chief fin. officer Air Calif., Newport Beach, 1979-82; exec. v.p. fin. and adminstrn., chief fin. officer Western Airlines, Los Angeles, 1982-85; dir. Western Airlines; sr. v.p. (fin) Am. Med. Internat., from 1985, chief fin. officer, 1985-89, exec. v.p., 1988-89; dir., exec. v.p. fin., chief fin. officer Beverly Enterprises Inc., Ft. Smith, Ark., 1989-92; chmn., CEO LTC Properties, Inc., 1992—; bd. dirs. Magellan Health Svc., Health Mgmt. Inc., Assisted Living Concepts, Inc. Democrat. Greek Orthodox. Home: 4470 Vista Del Preseas Malibu CA 90265-2540 Office: Ltc Properties Inc 300 E Esplanade Dr Ste 1860 Oxnard CA 93030-1250

DIMMICK, CAROLYN REABER, federal judge; b. Seattle, Oct. 24, 1929; d. Maurice C. and Margaret T. (Taylor) Reaber; m. Cyrus Allen Dimmick, Sept. 10, 1955; children: Taylor, Dana. BA, U. Wash., 1951, JD, 1963; LLD, Gonzaga U., 1982, CUNY, 1987. Bar: Wash. Asst. atty. gen. State of Wash., Seattle, 1953-55; pros. atty. King County, Wash., 1955-59, 60-62; sole practice Seattle, 1959-60, 62-65; judge N.E. Dist. Ct. Wash., 1965-75, King County Superior Ct., 1976-80; justice Wash. Supreme Ct., 1981-85; judge U.S. Dist. Ct. (we. dist.) Wash., Seattle, 1985-94, chief judge, 1994—; chmn. Jud. Resources Com., 1991-95, active, 1987-95. Recipient Matrix Table award, 1981, World Plan Execs. Council award, 1981, others. Mem. ABA, Am. Judges Assn. (gov.), Nat. Assn. Women Judges, World Assn. Judges, Wash. Bar Assn., Am. Judicature Soc., Order of Coif (Wash. chpt.), Wash. Athletic Club, Wingpoint Golf and Country Club, Harbor Club. Office: US Dist Ct 911 US Courthouse 1010 5th Ave Seattle WA 98104-1130

DINEL, RICHARD HENRY, lawyer; b. L.A., Sept. 16, 1942; s. Edward Price and Edith Elizabeth (Rheinstein) D.; m. Joyce Ann Korsmeyer, Dec. 26, 1970; children: Edward, Alison. BA, Pomona Coll., 1964; JD, Stanford U., 1967. Bar: Calif. Owner Richard H. Dinel, A Profl. Law Corp., L.A., 1971-79; ptnr. Richards, Watson & Gershon, L.A., 1979-92, of counsel, 1992-93; pres. R. H. Dinel Investment Counsel, Inc., 1992—; bd. dirs. The Price Co., 1990-92. Chmn. bd. Pomona Coll. Assocs., 1987-89; ex-officio trustee Pomona Coll., 1987-89; arbitrator Chgo. Bd. Options Exch., 1978—, Pacific Stock Exch., 1979—; bd. govs. Western Los Angeles County Coun. Boys Scouts Am., 1993—. Mem. Securities Ind. Assn. (speaker compliance and legal div. 1978-92), Pomona Coll. Alumni Assn. (chmn. alumni fund and continuing edn. com. 1972-73), Nat. Assn. Securities Dealers (mem. nat. bd. arbitrators 1978-90), City Club on Bunker Hill, Bond Club L.A. Office: Ste 400 11661 San Vicente Blvd Los Angeles CA 90049-5112

DING, MAE LON, employee compensation consultant; b. Norwalk, Calif., May 7, 1954; d. Lock Gee and Ruth (Tang) D.; m. Stephen M. Batcheller, Nov. 30, 1985 (div. Mar. 1992); m. David J. Mashaw, July 2, 1995. BA, UCLA, 1976; MBA, U. So. Calif., 1979. Cons. Forum Corp., Boston, 1978, Wyatt Co., Boston, 1978-81; sr. cons. R. A. Smith & Assoc., Mission Viejo, Calif., 1981-83; mgr. compensation Allergan Pharms., Irvine, Calif., 1983-85; pres. Pers. Systems Assoc., Tustin, Calif., 1985—; instr. U. Calif., Irvine, 1988-89, Calif. State U., Long Beach, 1988-90, Calif. State Coll., Pomona, 1987-88, Chapman Coll., Orange, Calif., 1991; speaker in field. Author: Survey Sources, 1991, 4th rev. edit., 1997; contbr. articles to profl publs. Mem. Assn. Profl. Cons. (bd. dirs. 1989—, pres. 1993-94, 94-95), Am. Compensation Assn. (instr. 1984—), Orange County Compensation Assn., Orange County Forensic Cons. Assn. (bd. dirs. 1994, 95, 96, 97), Forum Corp. Dirs. Office: Pers Systems Assoc 2282 Aspen St Tustin CA 92782-8341

DINI, JOSEPH EDWARD, JR., state legislator; b. Yerington, Nev., Mar. 28, 1929; s. Giuseppe and Elvira (Castellani) D.; m. Mouryne Landing; children: Joseph, George, David, Michael. BSBA, U. Nev., Reno, 1951. Mem. Nev. State Assembly, Carson City, 1967-98; majority leader Nev. State Assembly, 1975; speaker Nev. State Assembly, Carson City, 1977, 87, 89, 91, 93, 97; minority leader Nev. State Assembly, 1985; interim fin. com. mem., 1985-95, speaker pro tem, 1973; co-spkr. Nev. State Assembly, Carson City, 1995; chmn. water policy com. Western Legis. Conf., 1993-94, 96-97; pres. Dini's Lucky Club Casino, Yerington, Nev., 1972—; mem. legis. com. Nev. State Assembly, 1971-77, 91, 93, 95, 97, vice chmn., 1981-82, chmn., 1982-83, 93-94. Recipient Outstanding Citizen award Nev. Edn. Assn., 1973, Friend of Edn. award Nev. State Edn. Assn., 1986, Citizen of Yr. award Nev. Judges Assn., 1987, Dedicated and Valued Leadership award Nat. Conf. State Legislatures, 1989, Excellence in Pub. Svc. award Nev. Trial Lawyers Assn., 1990, Silver Plow award Nev. Farm Bur., 1991, Skill, Integrith, Responsibility award Assoc. Gen. Contractors, 1994, Guardian of Small Bus. award Nat. Fedn. Ind. Bus., 1996; named Conservation Legislator of Yr. Nev. Wildlife Fedn., 1991. Mem. Mason Valley C. of C. (pres.), Rotary (pres. Yerington 1989), Lions (pres. Yerington chpt. 1975), Masons, Shriners, Gamma Sigma Delta, Phi Sigma Kappa (Disting. Alumna award 1993). Home: 104 N Mountain View St Yerington NV 89447-2239 Office: Dini's Lucky Club Inc 45 N Main St Yerington NV 89447-2230

DINKEL, JOHN GEORGE, magazine editor; b. Bklyn., Aug. 1, 1944; s. Charles Ernest and Loretta Gertrude D.; m. Leslie Hawkins, Oct. 25, 1969; children: Meredith Anne, Kevin Carter. BS in Mech. Engring, U. Mich., 1967, MS in Mech. Engring, 1969. Staff engr. Chrysler Corp., Highland Park, Mich., 1967-69; engring. editor Car Life Mag., Newport Beach, Calif., 1969-70; engring. editor Road & Track Mag., Newport Beach, 1972-79, editor, 1979-88, editor in chief, 1988-91, editor at large, 1991-92; dir. product communications Hill-Holliday, 1991-92; pres. John Dinkel & Assocs., 1991—; editor-at-large Sports Car Internat., 1992—; v.p. editl. ops. Calcar, 1995—; organizer, chmn. sessions on fuel economy and small cars SAE, 1978-79; commencement speaker U. Mich., Dearborn, 1987; hon. judge Meadow Brook Hall Concourse D'Elegance, 1985-86, Hillsborough Concourse D'Elegance, 1989, Palo Alto Concours D'Elegance, 1990; v.p. editl. ops., Calcar, 1994—; spkr. Direct Mktg. Club So. Calif., 1992. Author: Road & Track Auto Dictionary, 1977; co-author: RX-7: Mazda's Legendary Sports Car, 1991; co-host daily radio show Auto Report, 1986-88; host weekly radio show Drive Time, 1996—; contbr. articles to profl. jours. Nat. chmn. U. Mich. Ann. Fund, 1988—; commr. Irvine (Calif.) Baseball Assn.; sec. Irvine Pony Baseball-Softball, 1995—; organizer clothing drive victims of Armenia earthquake, 1988; soccer coach AYSO, 1984-90, Irvine Soccer Club, 1991—; baseball coach Northwood Little League, 1994—; basketball coach Irvine Boys and Girls Club, 1993—. Honored by Colden Ctr. for the Performing Arts, Queens Coll., N.Y.C., 1990. Mem. Soc. Automotive Engrs. (panelist conf. on impacts of intelligent vehicle hwy. systems 1990), Am. Racing Press Assn., Internat. Motor Press Assn., Sports Car Club Am., Internat. Motor Sports Assn., Motor Press Guild (pres. 1991), Pi Tau Sigma. Office: Calcar 122 S El Camino Real # 139 San Clemente CA 92672

DINKELSPIEL, PAUL GAINES, investment banking and public financial consultant; b. San Francisco, Feb. 12, 1935; s. Edward Gaines and Pauline (Watson) D. A.B., U. Calif., Berkeley, 1959. Gen. ptnr. Stone & Youngberg, San Francisco, 1961-71; 1st v.p. Shearson Lehman Hutton and predecessor firms, San Francisco, 1971-79; pres., chmn. bd. dirs. Dinkelspiel, Belmont & Co., Inc., San Francisco; investment banking and pub. fin. cons., 1979—; bd. dirs. Gemstone Investors Assurance Corp., N.Y.C. With AUS, 1959-60. Mem. Govt. Fin. Officers Assn., Am. Water Works Assn., San Francisco Mcpl. Forum, Calif. Pub. Securities Assn. (public fin. com.), San Francisco Comml. Club, Commonwealth Club of Calif., Mcpl. Bond Club, N.Y. World Trade Club, Calif. Waterfowl Assn., Ducks Unltd., Sigma Chi. Home: PO Box 727 Stinson Beach CA 94970-0727 Office: 101 California St Fl 37 San Francisco CA 94111-5802

DINNER, MARIE BERNICE, social services program administrator; b. Bolton, Eng., Mar. 3, 1947; came to U.S., 1958; d. Philip and Sarah (Reich) Myers; m. Bruce Jon Dinner, June 18, 1967; children: Alec W., Tara Lee. BA, U. Denver, 1971, MA, 1973; PhD, U. Colo., 1981. Audiologist Rose Med. Ctr., Denver, 1973-76; clin. supr. U. Colo. Comm. Disorders Clinic, Denver and Boulder, Colo., 1977-81; audiologist Pfenninger Inst., Wheat Ridge, Colo., 1982-84; dir. of cochlear implants Childrens Deafness Found., Denver, 1984-88, exec. dir., 1987-88; founder, pres. Hear Now, Denver, 1988—. Bd. dirs. Allied Jewish Fedn., Denver, 1990-94; pres. Beth Joseph Congregation, Denver, 1989-91. Mem. Sales Profls. Internat., Am. Speech, Hearing, Lang. Assn. (cert. clin. competence-audiology), Acad. of Audiology, Cochlear Implant Club Internat. (adv. bd. 1990-92, bd. dirs. 1992-96). Democrat. Office: Hear Now 9745 E Hampden Ave Ste 300 Denver CO 80231-4923

DINSMORE, PHILIP WADE, architect; b. Gilroy, Calif., Nov. 4, 1942; s. Wilbur Allen and Elizabeth Eleanor (Hill) D.; m. Mary Kathryn Mead; children: Robert Allen, Kerry Philip. B.Arch., U. Ariz., 1965. Registered arch., Ariz., Calif., Nev., N.C., Wyo. Nat. Coun. Archtl. Registration Bds. Designer, William L. Pereira & Assocs., L.A., 1965-67; assoc. CNWC Archs., Tucson, 1967-69; prin., ptnr. Architecture One Ltd., Tucson, 1970-90; pres. Durrant Architects Ariz., Phoenix and Tucson, 1995, bd. dir. Durrant Group, 1992—. Mem., chmn. Archtl. Approval Bd., City of Tucson, 1974-75, 77; bd. dir. Tucson Met. YMCA, 1993—; trustee AIA Benefit Ins. Trust, 1997—. Fellow AIA (nat. bd. dirs. 1981-84, nat. sec. 1984-88, Ariz. Archs. medal 1985, Western Mountain Region Citation award 1973, 76, 78, Award of Honor 1983, Silver medal 1992); mem. Am. Archtl. Found. (bd. regents 1988-92), Constrn. Specifications Inst., Ariz Soc. Archs. (citation 1977-80, 89). Recipient Tucker award Bldg. Stone Inst., 1986. Fellow AIA (regional fellows rep. 1990-96, trustee benefit ins. trust 1997—). Republican. Presbyterian. Office: Durrant Roberts/Dinsmore Assoc 450 W Paseo Redondo Ste 130 Tucson AZ 85701-8275

DIORIO, ROBERT JOSEPH, psychotherapist, consultant; b. Chgo., Dec. 21, 1945; s. Joseph and Mary Jane (Christopher) DiO.; m. Diane Rose Belcastro, Sept. 30, 1967; children: Jason, Adam. BA, St. Mary's Coll., Winona, Minn., 1967; MA in Biology, Edn., U. Chgo., 1969; PhD in Clin. Psychology, U. for Humanistic Studies, Las Vegas, Nev., 1984. Supervising probation officer 18th Jud. Cir. Ct., Wheaton, Ill., 1970-78; cons., adminstr. Nat. Med. Svc., Las Vegas, 1978-82; out-patient dir. Western Counseling Assn., Las Vegas, 1982-84; adminstr., psychotherapist Assn. Counselors of So. Nev., Las Vegas, 1984—; bd. dirs. Ctr. for Independent Living, Las Vegas, Las Vegas Exec.'s Assn.; mem. adv. bd. Compassionate Friends, Las Vegas, 1996—. Fellow Am. Bd. Med. Psychotherapists (diplomate), Am. Bd. Cert. Managed Care Providers; mem. ACA, Las Vegas Exec.'s Assn.

(pres. 1990-91), Am. Coun. Hypnotist Examiners (hypnotherapist), Nat. Assn. Drug and Alcohol Counselors (master addiction counselor 1995—), Thought Field Therapy. Office: Health Care Cons Inc 2860 E Flamingo Rd Ste H Las Vegas NV 89121-5270

DI PALMA, JOSEPH ALPHONSE, airline company executive, lawyer; b. N.Y.C., Jan. 17, 1931; s. Gaetano and Michela May (Ambrosio) Di P.; m. Joycelyn Ann Engle, Apr. 18, 1970; children: Joycelyn Joan, Julianne Michelle. BA, Columbia U., 1952; JD, Fordham U., 1958; LLM in Taxation, NYU, 1959. Bar: N.Y. 1959. Tax atty. CBS, N.Y.C., 1960-64; v.p. tax dept. TWA, N.Y.C., 1964-74; pvt. practice law N.Y.C., 1974-87; investor, exec. dir. Di Palma Family Holdings, Las Vegas and N.Y.C., 1987—; cons. in field; head study group Comprehensive Gaming Study, N.Y.C. and Washington, 1990—; think tank exec. dir. Di Palma Position Papers; founder Di Palma Forum, U. Nev., Las Vegas. Contbr. articles to profl. jours.; author: Di Palma Postion Papers. Bd. dirs. Friends of the Henry St. Settlement, N.Y.C., 1961-63, Outdoor Cleanliness Assn., N.Y.C., 1961-65; chmn. Air Transport Assn. Taxation Com., 1974. With U.S. Army, 1953-54. Recipient Disting. Svc. and Valuable Counsel commendation award Air Transport Assn., 1974. Mem. Internat. Platform Assn., N.Y. State Bar Assn., N.Y. Athletic Club. Roman Catholic. Home: 3111 Bel Air Dr Apt 21B Las Vegas NV 89109-1506 Office: PO Box 72158 Las Vegas NV 89170-2158 also: 930 Fifth Ave 4-J&H New York NY 10021

DIPAOLO, PATRICIA ANN, reading specialist; b. Indpls., Nov. 24, 1946; d. George F. and Lauretta Wilkins; m. Beverly G. Hughes, Nov. 30, 1968 (div. Apr. 1983); m. Julio S. DiPaolo, Aug. 17, 1991; stepchildren: Leah, Rob, Ed, Russell. BA in Sociology, U. La Verne, Calif., 1968, MA in Ednl. Reading, 1981. Cert. tchr., Ryan reading specialist, Miller-Unruh reading specialist. Tchr. Chino (Calif.) Unified Schs., 1968-76, reading specialist, 1976-95, lit. fellow, 1995-96; early literacy program specialist San Bernardino (Calif.) Schs., 1996—. Pres. PTA, Glenmeade, Calif., 1974; pres. Boys Repubic Aux., 1995—. Mem. Calif. Tchrs. Assn., Reading Recovery Coun., Delta Kappa Gamma (v.p. 1996—). Office: San Bernardino Supt Schs Office 601 E St San Bernardino CA 92410

DIRKS, JERALD FREDERICK, psychotherapist; b. Newton, Kans., Dec. 28, 1949; s. Fred and Hazel Marie (Mickelson) D.; m. Debra Lea Stucky, Sept. 14, 1969; 1 child, Sean. BA in Philosophy, Harvard U., 1971, MDiv, 1974; MA in Child Clin. Psychology, U. Denver, 1976, PsyD in Clin. Psychology, 1978. Chief clin. psychology Nat. Jewish Hosp., Denver, 1978-82; asst. prof. psychiatry U. Colo. Sch. Medicine, Denver, 1980-83; psychotherapist Nelson F. Jones & Assocs., Denver, 1978—; adj. asst. prof. U. Denver, 1978-82; dir., ptnr. Psychometric Designs, Denver, 1990—; ptnr. Nelson F. Jones & Assocs., Denver, 1978—; cons. Colo. Rehab. Inst., Denver, 1986—, Centennial Rehab. Assocs., Denver, 1982—. Contbr. numerous articles to profl. jours. Mem. adv. bd. Sch. Profl. Psychology, U. Denver, 1976, Bethesda Comty. Mental Health Ctr., Denver, 1976-77, Colo. Multiple Sclerosis Soc., Denver, 1981-82. Hollis scholar Harvard U., 1968. Fellow Am. Bd. Med. Psychotherapists (diplomate); mem. Am. Psychosomatic Soc., Soc. for Personality Assessment, Internat. Psychosomatic Inst., N.Y. Acad. Sci., Arabian Horse Historians Assn. (founding mem., sec.-treas. 1992-93). Islam. Office: Nelson F Jones & Assocs 2343 E Evans Ave Denver CO 80210-4709

DIRUSCIO, LAWRENCE WILLIAM, advertising executive; b. Buffalo, Jan. 2, 1941; s. Guido Carmen and Mabel Ella (Bach) DiR.; m. Gloria J. Edney, Aug. 19, 1972; children: Lawrence M., Lorie P., Darryl C., Teresa M., Jack D. With various broadcast stas. and instr., adminstr. Bill Wade Sch. Radio and TV, San Diego, San Francisco, Los Angeles, 1961-69; account exec. Sta. KGB Radio, San Diego, 1969, gen. sales mgr., 1970-72; pres. Free Apple Advt., San Diego, 1972-94, Fin. Mgmt. Assocs., Inc., San Diego, 1979-84, Self-Pub. Ptnrs., San Diego, 1981—, Media Mix Assocs. Enterprises, Inc., 1984-86; pres. Press-Courier Pub. Co., Inc., 1985-86; pres. Media Mix Advt. and Pub. Relations, 1985—, Taking Care of Bus. Pub. Co., 1990—; pres. Formula Mktg. Co., 1993. Chmn. bd. Quicksilver Enterprises, Inc., A Public Corp., 1992-93; lectr., writer on problems of small bus. survival. Served with USN, 1958-60. Five Emmy nominations for T.V. commercial writing and prodn. Mem. Nat. Acad. TV Arts and Scis. Democrat. Roman Catholic. Office: Media Mix Advt and Pub Rels 726 W Kalmia St San Diego CA 92101-1311

DISALLE, MICHAEL DANNY, secondary education educator; b. Denver, May 16, 1945; s. Michael and Agnes Marie (Kulik) DiS.; m. Marikaye Lucas, June 22, 1968; children: Katharine Marie, Kristin Jean, Michael Charles, Matthew Gregory. BA, Regis Coll., 1967; MEd, Lesley Coll., 1992. Cert. tchr., Colo. Tchr. Assumption Sch., Welby, Colo., 1968-74, Cherry Creek High Sch., Englewood, Colo., 1974-95; poet, writer, 1995—. Author: (computer program/tchr.'s guide) Adventures of Tom Sawyer, 1983, One Day in the Life of Ivan Denisovich, 1984. Asst. den leader Boy Scouts Am., Aurora, Colo., 1988-89. Mem. ASCD, Nat. Coun. Tchrs. of English, Nat. Scholastic Press Assn., Journalism Edn. Assn., Colo. Lang. Arts Soc., Colo. State High Sch. Press Assn., Columbia Scholastic Press Assn.

DISICK, RENÉE, real estate broker, real estate securities broker; b. Bklyn., Apr. 22, 1941; d. Morris and Mary (Lubin) Sherrow; m. David Martin Disick, Aug. 15, 1971. BSBA summa cum laude, Ohio State U., 1962; MAT, Stanford U., 1967. Tchr. French Mayfield (Ohio) Schs., 1962-66, Valley Stream (N.Y.) Schs., 1967-75; pvt. practice photography N.Y.C., 1975-80; real estate broker South Village Realty, Warren, Vt., 1980-89; broker-dealer Hotel Condominium Investments, Warren, 1987-89; real estate broker Charles H. Greenthal Residential Sales, N.Y.C., 1989-92, The Corcoran Group Real Estate, N.Y.C., 1993-96; broker Franz Klammer Lodge, Telluride, Colo., 1996—; speaker Resort Seminars, Inc., Warren, 1987-89. Author: Individualizing Foreign Language Instruction, 1974, (with others) Performance Objectives and Individualization, 1971; contbr. numerous articles various publs. Mem. Phi Beta Kappa.

DISNEY, MICHAEL GEORGE, financial services executive; b. Harvey, Ill., Nov. 30, 1955. Grad. h.s., Harvey; grad., Life Underwriters Tng. Coun. Sales mgr. Met. Life Ins. Co., Naperville, Ill., 1979-84; regional dir. Firemens Fund Ins. Co., San Diego, 1984-85; owner, mgr. Disney Fin., Inc., San Diego, 1985—; pres., founding mem. Grossmont Letip, 1992—. Founding mem., pres. Grossmont Letip, 1993-94. Mem. Nat. Assn. Life Underwriters, Life Underwriters Tng. Coun. (moderator-cons. 1986-87), Million Dollar Round Table (coord., chmn. San Diego chpt. 1987-89), La Mesa (Calif.) C. of C., San Diego C. of C., El Cajon C. of C., Toastmasters. Grossmont Letip (founder, pres. 1994-96). Home: 3910 Dorsie Ln La Mesa CA 91941-7335 Office: Ste 123 2815 Camino Del Rio S San Diego CA 92108

DISNEY, ROY EDWARD, broadcasting company executive; b. Los Angeles, Jan. 10, 1930; s. Roy Oliver and Edna (Francis) D.; m. Patricia Ann Dailey, Sept. 17, 1955; children: Roy Patrick, Susan Margaret, Abigail Edna, Timothy John. B.A., Pomona Coll., 1951. Guest relations exec. NBC, Hollywood, Calif., 1952; apprentice film editor Mark VII Prodns., Hollywood, 1942; asst. film editor, cameraman prodn. asst., writer, producer Walt Disney Prodns., Burbank, Calif., 1954-77, dir., 1967—; pres. Roy E. Disney Prodns. Inc., Burbank, 1978—; chmn. bd. dir. Shamrock Broadcasting Co., Hollywood, 1979—; chmn. bd. dir., founder Shamrock Holdings Inc., Burbank, 1980—; trustee Calif. Inst. Arts, Valencia, 1967—; vice chmn. Walt Disney Co., Burbank. Author: novelized adaptation of Perri; producer (film) Pacific High, Mysteries of the Deep (TV show) Walt Disney's Wonderful World of Color, others; exec. producer Cheetah; writer, dir., producer numerous TV prodns. Bd. dirs. Big Bros. of Greater Los Angeles; mem. adv. bd. dirs. St. Joseph Med. Ctr., Burbank; mem. U.S. Naval Acad. Sailing Squadron, Annapolis, Md.; fellow U. Ky. Recipient Acad. award nomination for Mysteries of the Deep. Mem. Dirs. Guild Am. West, Writers Guild Am. Republican. Clubs: 100, Confrerie des Chevaliers du Tastevin, St. Francis Yacht, Calif. Yacht, San Diego Yacht, Transpacific Yacht, Los Angeles Yacht. Office: Walt Disney Co 500 S Buena Vista St Burbank CA 91521-0001*

DISRUD, CAROL ANN, interior designer; b. Rolla, N.D., Apr. 7, 1946; d. Oral Desmond and Vera Cecelia (Bisom) D.; m. James Kormier, June 28, 1990. BS in Interior Design, N.D. State U., 1968. Mgr. furniture showrooms AB Bacos and Berg, Halmstad, 1968-73; mgr. small shopping ctr. The Farm, Bruchuelbach, Germany, 1973-74; interior designer Design Collaborative/VVKR Architects, Alexandria, Va., 1970-79; v.p. Gensler and Assocs. Architects, San Francisco, 1980-92; owner, pres. Carol Disrud & Assocs., Healdsburg, Calif., 1992—; speaker in field. Recipient outstanding alumni award N.D. State U., 1993. Fellow Internat. Interior Design Assn. (nat. v.p. 1985-87, no. Calif. chpt. pres. 1982-85, disting. merit award 1991, Best Of competition award IBD/Interior Design mag. 1989, Top Ten award 1991, Interior Design award 1993); mem. Healdsburg C. of C. (bus. and econ. devel. com. 1991—, bd. dirs. 1997—). Democrat. Office: Carol Disrud & Assocs 1207 Vine St Healdsburg CA 95448-4824

DISTECHE, CHRISTINE M., geneticist; b. Liege, Belgium, July 22, 1949. PhD, U. Liege, Belgium, 1976. Genetics fellow Harvard U., Boston, 1977-80; now med. geneticist U. Wash. Hosp., Seattle; prof. pathology U. Wash., Seattle. Office: U Wash Hosp Dept Pathology PO Box 357470 Seattle WA 98195-7470*

DITMANSON, DENNIS L., national monument administrator; b. Webster, S.D., June 17, 1947; s. Arnold H. and Evelyn (Burns) D.; m. Barbara Jean Buekhart, Aug. 15, 1970; children: Ethan James, Rebecca Jean, Kevin Jon. BS in Edn., U. S.D., 1972. Seasonal ranger Custer Battlefield Nat. Monument, Crow Agency, Mont., 1971, 72, supt., 1987—; ranger Lyndon B. Johnson N.H.S., Johnson City, Tex., 1973, Sanjuan Island N.H.P., Ferry Harbor, Wash., 1973-75; chief Fort Clark Nat. Monument, Asbrig, Oreg., 1975-77, Bent's Old Fort N.H.S., La Junta, Wyo., 1977-81; mgr. Jewel Cave Nat. Monument, Custer, S.D., 1981-86. Leader Cub Scouts Am., Custer, 1985-86, Odessy of the Mind, Custer, 1985-86; com. mem. Hardin Area C. of C. and Agrl., Hardin, Mont., 1987—. Mem. Assn. Nat. Park Rangers (bd. dirs.), Nat. Park Service Employees and Alumni Assn., Council on Am. Military Past., Rotary, Kiwanis, Elks. Office: Custer Battlefield Nat Monument PO Box 39 Crow Agency MT 59022-0039

DITOMMASO, KARL JOSEPH, business executive; b. L.A., Jan. 12, 1969; s. Nina Brambila DiT.; 1 adopted child, Ciprian. AA in Bus. Adminstrn., Southbay Coll., Baldwin, Calif., 1989; BA in Bus. Fin. and Mgmt., Calif. State Poly. U., 1991. V.p. sales and financing B&B Assocs., Rancho Cucamonga, Calif.; chmn. and CEO Merc. Nominees, Ltd., San Bernardino, Calif. Mem. BBB, U.S. C. of C. Office: Merc Nominees Ltd 9089 Baseline Rd Ste 100 Rancho Cucamonga CA 91730

DITTMAN, DEBORAH RUTH, real estate broker; b. Sacramento, Apr. 15, 1932; d. Charles Harwood and Ruth (Potter) Kinsley; m. John Alvin Cardoza, Sept. 1950 (div. 1964); children: Harold Cardoza, Nancy Jongeward, John Allan Cardoza, Gregory Cardoza, Janice Boswell; m. Edgar Marshall Dittman, Jan. 22, 1967 (dec. Jan. 6 1982); m. Philip George Vrieling, July 7, 1990. Student Humprey's Coll., Stockton, Calif., 1966; grad. real estate sales Anthony Schs., 1978; cert. in real estate San Joaquin Delta Coll., 1977. Lic. real estate broker, Calif., 1978, real estate sales assoc., 1974-78; cert. residential specialist. Sec. Calif. Dept. Water Resources, Patterson and Tracy, 1966-72; hostess Welcome Wagon, Tracy, 1973-74; assoc. realtor Reeve Assocs., Tracy, 1975-80; broker Allied Brokers, Tracy, 1980-83; ptnr. real estate Putt, Fallavena, Willbanks & Dittman, Tracy, 1983—; mem. adv. bd. Tracy Fed. Bank(formerly Tracy Savings & Loan), 1989—, Women's Coun. Realtors, 1990—. Mem. Residential Sales Coun., 1989, Women's Coun. Realtors, 1990. Mem. Tracy Bd. Realtors (pres. 1981, 85, dir. 1976, 77, 80-83, 85-86), Calif. Assn. Realtors (dir. 1980-81, 85), Cert. Real Estate Specialists (v.p. no. Calif. chpt. 1990, pres. 1991), Nat. Assn. Realtors, Cen. Valley Assn. Realtors, So. Alameda Assn. Realtors, Tracy C. of C. (bd. dirs. 1988-90). Home: 12134 Midway Dr Tracy CA 95376-9113 Office: 1045 Tracy Blvd Tracy CA 95376-3726

DITTMAN, WILLIAM ALBERT, SR., hematologist; b. La Crosse, Wis., July 31, 1926; s. Albert L. and Kathleen (Kennedy) D.; m. Catherine Harris, Dec. 19, 1950; children: William A. Jr., John C., Andrew H. BA, U. Wis., 1949, MD, 1953. Diplomate Am. Bd. Internal Medicine, Am. Bd. Hematology. Intern Salt Lake County Gen. Hosp., Salt Lake City, 1953-54; resident in internal medicine U. Utah, Salt Lake City, 1954-56, fellow in hematology, 1956-58; staff physician VA Hosp., Albuquerque, 1958-59; pvt. practice, Spokane, Wash., 1959-77; dir. hematology Sacred Heart Med. Ctr., Spokane, 1961-95; chmn. Inland N.W. Blood Ctr., 1992-93. Sgt. U.S. Army. Fellow ACP; mem. Am. Soc. Hematology. Office: Sacred Heart Med Ctr 101 W 8th Ave Spokane WA 99204-2307

DITZLER, ANN MARIE, nutritionist benefit contract analyst; b. Flint, Mich., June 4, 1947; d. James Alfred and Elsie (McDowell) Herrick; m. Thomas F. Ditzler, Feb. 20, 1971; children: Benjamin T.E., Nathan J.M. BS, Mich. State U., 1969; MS, Case Western Res. U., 1971. Registered dietitian. Chief/clin. dietitian Flint (Mich.) Osteo. Hosp., 1971-79; clin. dietitian Honolulu Area Hosps., 1979-83; supr., staff asst. Hawaii Med. Svc. Assn., Honolulu, 1983-91, trainer, analyst long range system planning, 1992-95. Chair Windward subarea coun. State Health Planning and Devel. Agy., Honolulu, 1990-95; chair troop com. Aloha coun. Boy Scouts Am., Honolulu, 1993—; mem. chair Aloha Coun., 1995-97; mem. Gov.'s Conf. on Health Care in the 1990s, Honolulu, 1985-86; loaned exec. Aloha Pacesetter campaign United Way, 1995. Recipient Borden award Mich. State U., 1969, DuBois award, 1969. Mem. Am. Dietetic Assn. (Recognized Young Dietitian 1977), Jr. League of Honolulu (sustaining mem.), Profl. Women's Network, Internat. Baseball Goodwill Assn. of Hawaii (v.p. 1991-95). Home: 112 Puwa Pl Kailua HI 96734-1742

DIVELY, DWIGHT DOUGLAS, finance director; b. Spokane, Wash., Sept. 24, 1958; s. Richard Lorraine and Marie Eleanor (Barnes) D.; m. Susan Lorraine Soderstrom, June 13, 1987; children: Nathan Douglas, Natalie Lorraine. BSChemE, Rose-Hulman Inst. Tech., 1980; MPA of Pub. Affairs, Princeton U., 1982; PhC in Civil Engring., U. Wash., 1986. Rsch. scientist Battelle, Seattle, 1982-84; policy analyst, staff dir. Wash. High Tech. Coord. Bd., Seattle, 1984-86; cons. Bellevue, Wash., 1986-87; legis. analyst Seattle City Coun., 1987-90, supervising analyst, 1990-92, staff dir., 1992-94; dir. Seattle Fin. Dept., 1994—; cons. We. Interstate Commn. on Higher Edn., Boulder, Colo., 1986-91; affiliate prof. U. Wash., 1989—; instr. South Seattle C.C., 1992—; mem. faculty Cascade Ctr., Seattle, 1992—. Co-author: Benefit-Cost Analysis in Theory and Practice, 1994. Chmn. interview panel Truman Scholarship Found., Washington, 1989—. Recipient Elmer B. Staats award Truman Scholarship Found., 1994. Mem. Govt. Fin. Officers Assn. Lutheran. Office: Fin Dept Rm 103 600 4th Ave Ste 103 Seattle WA 98104-1826

DIVINE, THEODORE EMRY, electrical engineer; b. Hailey, Idaho, May 27, 1943; s. Theodore Clyde and Muriel Juanita (Kirtley) D.; BSEE, U. Wash., Seattle, 1966, MBA, 1970; m. Roberta Louise Erickson, Mar. 19, 1966; children: Timothy Shannon, Brianna Kristine, Rachel Melissa. Engr., Gen. Telephone Co. of N.W., 1968-69; mem. tech. staff NW ops. Computer Scis. Corp., 1970-72; research engr. Battelle Pacific N.W. Labs., Richland, Wash., 1973—, research sect. mgr., 1978, staff engr., def. programs, 1980-89; program mgr., special programs Idaho Nat. Engr. Lab., Idaho Falls, 1989—, mgr. Nat. Security Programs Office, 1992-93, spl. programs mgr., 1993-96; staff scientist Battelle Pacific Northwest Labs., Richland, Wash., 1996—. Pres. Mid-Columbia Sci. Fair Assn., 1975-76, product line mgr. spl. programs, 1997—; ruling elder First Presbyn. Ch., Prosser, Wash., 1982-84. Served as officer Signal Corps, USAR, 1966-84; Vietnam, 1967. Decorated Bronze Star. Mem. IEEE, Am. Def. Preparedness Assn., Assn. of U.S. Army, Am. Soc. Agrl. Engrs. (com. chmn. 1977-78, 82-83, chmn. nat. conf. on electronics in agr. 1983), Beta Gamma Sigma. Mem. editorial adv. bd. Internat. Jours. Computers & Electronics in Agr., Elsevier, The Netherlands, 1983—.

DIX, GARY ERROL, engineering executive; b. Bieber, Calif., Jan. 10, 1942; s. Errol Alvin and Evelyn Nadine (Miller) D.; m. Lanaya Diane Easley, Jan. 4, 1964. BS in Mech. Engring., U. Calif., Berkeley, 1963, MS in Mech. Engring., 1965, PhD in Mech. Engring., 1971. Engr. Gen. Electric Nuclear, San Jose, Calif., 1965 71; mgr. thermal devel. Gen. Electric Nuclear, San Jose, 1971-75, mgr. safety and hydraulics, 1975-82, mgr. core methods, 1982-85, mgr. automation sys., 1985-89, mgr. quality assurance and automation, 1989-94, mgr. devel. programs, 1994-97; code rev. group cons. Nuclear Regulatory Comm., Washington, 1976-85; cons. in field, 1997—. Contbr. articles to profl. jours.; patentee in field. Fellow Am. Nuclear Soc. (exec. com. Thermal Hydraulics divsn. 1981-91, chmn. 1986-87); mem. ASME. Office: Gen Electric Nuclear Energy 175 Curtner Ave San Jose CA 95125-1014

DIXIT, VIVEK, biomedical scientist, medical educator; b. Mumbai, India, Nov. 7, 1954; came to U.S., 1988; s. Mahesh Chandra and Kaushal (Tiwari) Dikshit; m. Neeta Awasthi, Dec. 27, 1987; children: Vineet Aditya, Ram Anand. BSc in Biology magna cum laude, Concordia U., Montreal, Que., Can., 1978; MSc in Physiology, McGill U., Montreal, 1980, PhD in Physiology, 1986. Postdoctoral fellow Sunnybrook Med. Ctr./U. Toronto, Can., 1986-88; vis. asst. rschr. UCLA, 1988-91, asst. rschr., 1991-93, assoc. prof. medicine, 1993—; dir. rsch., liver bio-support, hepatitis rsch. lab., 1990—, co-dir. basic sci. tng. program divsn. digestive diseases, 1993-95; liver disease program steering com. mem. Sunnybrook Med. Ctr., Toronto, 1986-87; mem. sci. program com. 3rd Internet World Congress on Biomed. Scis., Symposium on Tissue Engring. and Bioartificial Organs, 1996; lectr. and presenter in field. Manuscript reviewer Artificial Organs, ASAIO Jour., Cell Transplantation, Digestive Disease and Sci., Jour. Infectious Diseases, Gastroenterology, Hepatology, Jour. of Artificial Cells, Blood Substitutes and Immobilization Biotech., Jour. Hepatology, and Liver Transplantation and Surgery. Sunnybrook Fund fellow U. Toronto, 1987, McGill U. fellow, 1981, 85, Ministry Edn. Que. fellow, 1981-83, 86-87; grantee UCLA, 1994, 96, Oppenheimer Found., 1995, United Liver Assn., 1988, 90-92, 95, Physicians Svcs. Inc. Found., 1987-89. Mem. Internat. Soc. Artificial Organs, Internat. Soc. for Artificial Cells, Blood Substitutes and Immobilization Biotech. (mem. internat. program com., editl. bd. jour.), Internat. Assn. Study of Liver, Am. Soc. for Artifical Internal Organs (mem. sci. program com., editl. bd. jour.), Cell Transplant Soc. (editl. bd. jours.), Gastroenterology Rsch. Group, Am. Gastroenterol. Assn., Am. Assn. for Study Liver Diseases. Hindu. Home: 5522 Babcock Ave North Hollywood CA 91607-1531 Office: UCLA Sch Medicine 675 Circle Dr S # 1240 Los Angeles CA 90024-8322

DIXON, ANN RENEE, librarian, writer; b. Richland, Wash., Feb. 26, 1954; d. David Sherman and Barbara Mae (Cook) Dixon; m. Walter Raymond Pudwill, May 30, 1982; children: Linnea Clare, Noranna Noel. BA in Swedish Lang. and Lit., U. Wash., 1976. Libr. Willow (Alaska) Pub. Libr., 1987—. Author: (children's books) How Raven Brought Light to People, 1991, The Sleeping Lady, 1994, Merry Birthday, Nora Noel, 1996. Mem. Soc. Children's Book Writers and Illustrators, Alaska Libr. Assn.

DIXON, DANNY ANDRÉ, secondary education educator, minister; b. San Angelo, Tex., May 24, 1959; s. Leonard Isaiah David and Pearl Ellen (King) D. BA, Abilene Christian U., 1981, MA, 1984. Cert. secondary tchr., Tex.; life-time provisional tchr., Tex. Univ. minister Ch. of Christ, Blacksburg, Va., 1985-86, Culver-Palms Ch. of Christ, L.A., 1987-90; interim evangelist McCamey (Tex.) Ch. of Christ, 1991-92; sch. tchr. Crosbyton (Tex.) Consol. Sch. Dist., 1992-94, Lubbock (Tex.) Ind. Sch. Dist., 1994-95; youth minister Christ's Ch. in the City, L.A., 1995-96; sec. English tchr., J.V. track coach Ft. Stockton (Tex.) Indep. Sch. Dist, 1996—; interim pulpit min. Oakey Blvd. Ch. of Christ, Las Vegas, summer 1987; asst. dormitory dir. Abilene Christian U., 1984, 87. Author: Discipling Ministries, 1987, Essential Christian Baptism, 1990, Standing to Change/Changing to Stand, 1993, Baptism: Which One Did You Receive?, 1996. Intake asst. Covenant House, Hollywood, Calif., 1989-90. Republican. Home: PO Box 1263 Fort Stockton TX 79735-1263 Office: Fort Stockton High Sch Fort Stockton TX 79735-1263

DIXON, DIANE BROOKS, communications executive; b. Evanston, Ill., Nov. 11, 1951; d. James Read and Helen (Green) Brooks; m. Patrick Richard Dixon, Sept. 6, 1975; 1 child, Colleen Brooks. BA in Polit. Sci. with honors, U. So. Calif., 1973, postgrad. Asst. mgr. govt. rels. L.A. Area C. of C., 1973-77; mgr. govtl. affairs programs GTE-Calif., Thousand Oaks, 1977-79; account exec. Deaver & Hannaford, Inc., L.A., 1979-81; princ. Diane Dixon and Assocs., L.A., 1981-82; dir. corp. comm. Avery Dennison Corp., Pasadena, Calif., 1982-85; v.p. corp. comm. Avery Dennison Corp., Pasadena, 1985—. Past chair L.A. Pub. Affairs Officers' Assn.; dir. Five Acres Children's Agy., trustee Polytechnic Sch., Pasadena; co-founder Women in Pub. Affairs, L.A. Mem. Nat. Investor Rels. Inst., Pub. Rels. Soc. Am., Pasadena C. of C. (dir.), Calif. Bus. Roundtable (dep.), Pasadena C. of C. (dir.). Office: Avery Dennison Corp 150 N Orange Grove Blvd Pasadena CA 91103-3534*

DIXON, JULIAN CAREY, congressman; b. Washington, Aug. 8, 1934; m. Bettye Lee; 1 child, Cary Gordon. BS, Calif. State U., L.A., 1962; LLB, Southwestern U., L.A., 1967. Mem. Calif. State Assembly, 1972-78; mem. 96th-105th Congresses from Calif. 28th (now 32nd) Dist., mem. House Appropriations Com. 96th-105nd Congresses from Calif. 32d Dist.; mem. subcom. on D.C.; mem. subcom. Commerce, Justice, State and Judiciary; mem. select com. on intelligence, mem. subcom. on nat. security; bd. dirs. CBC Found., Inc., pres., 1986-90. With U.S. Army, 1957-60. Mem. NAACP, Urban League, Calif. Arts Commn. Democrat. Office: House of Representatives 2252 Rayburn Washington DC 20515

DIXON, KATHLEEN B., mayor. Diploma in nursing, Wesley Sch. Nursing, Wichita, Kans., 1976; BSW, U. Wyo., 1985, JD, 1988. RN, Wyo. Various nursing positions Kans., 1976-82; dir. emergency nursing, chief flight nurse air rescue Wyo. Med. Ctr., Casper, 1982-85; assoc. atty. Murane and Bostwick, Casper, 1988-92, ptnr., 1993—; mem. Casper City Coun., 1995—; vice mayor City of Casper, 1996, mayor, 1997—. Contbr. articles to profl. jours.; lectr. in field. Bd. dirs. Wyo. Symphony Orch., 1988—, United Way, 1994—, admissions and allocations com., 1995—. Mem. LWV (bd. dirs. 1985-94), ABA, Wyo. Bar Assn., Natrona County Bar Assn., The Am. Assn. Nurse Attys., Am. and Wyo. Nurses Assn., Casper Area C. of C. (bd. dirs. 1996—), Soroptimists Internat., Rotary Internat. Home: 201 N Wolcott Casper WY 82609

DIXON, KATIE LOOSLE, county official; b. Clarkston, Utah, Oct. 10, 1929; d. Reuben O. and Sylvia (Griffiths) Loosle; divorced; children: Jerry, Michael, Keven Todd, Darcy. BS, Utah State U., 1945; LDH, Salt Lake C.C., 1993. Recorder Salt Lake County, Salt Lake City, 1975-94; trainer, facilitator workshops and seminars; mem. panel to evaluate U.S. std. lics. and certs. Nat. Ctr. Stats., USPHS, 1984-85; mem. State of Utah adv. bd. Nat. Hist. Publs. and Records Commn., 1979-91, chmn. local govt. records task force, 1983-84. Contbr. articles to profl. pubs. Bd. dirs., mem. strategic planning com. Leadership Am., Fairfax, Va., 1991—; mem. Concord Coalition Adv. Bd., 1993—; mem. alumni recognition adv. com. Utah State U., 1991; nat. adv. bd. U. Utah Children's Dance Theater, Salt Lake City, 1990-91; adv. bd. Utah Women's Arts Project, Salt Lake City, 1989—; mem. Salt Lake C.C. Devel. Bd., Salt Lake City, 1989-91; chmn. Utah Columbus Quincentenary Commn., 1988-92; mem. celebrity roast com. Am. Lung Assn. of Utah, 1988; bd. dirs. Women's Fedn. Utah Reps., 1968-69; active Salt Lake County Rep. Party, 1960-89, Utah State Rep. Party, 1966-84; campaign co-mgr. Sherman P. Lloyd Congl. campaigns, 1964, 66, 68, 70; mem. adv. bd. Utah Citizens for Arts, 1981-89, Utah Assn. Retarded Citizens, 1982-89; mem. Utah com. Fifty States Project on Discrimination Against Women in the Law, 1982-83; mem. art adv. bd. Salt Lake County, 1982, mem. bicentennial community com. on U.S. Constitution, 1986-87; mem. funding study com. Utah State Bd. Edn., 1984; mem. adv. com. Utah Women's Conf., 1984—; chmn. child care task force Salt Lake County, 1985; mem. dean's adv. coun. Coll. Bus. Utah State U., Logan, 1986-89; chair membership com., chair govt. com. Utah Women's Forum, Salt Lake City, 1987; bd. dirs. Utah Opera Guild, Salt Lake City, 1987-94, Westminster Coll. Found., Salt Lake City, 1987-89; mem. adv. bd. U. Utah Grad. Sch. Social Work, 1987-93, vice chair, 1989, chair, 1990-93; mem. policy coun. on strengthening the family Nat. Policy Form, Washington, 1994; mem. Salt Lake City Futures Commn., 1995-96, Futurist Commn. Spl. Olympics 2002, 1997; bd. fellows So. U. of Ut., Cedar City, 1994—; bd. dirs. Trauma Awarness and Treatment Ctr., 1994—; mem. Salt Lake Futures Comm., 1995—; Vol. instr. Presidential Classroom, Wash., D.C., 1996-97. Katie Dixon scholar, 1993, scholar Nat. Dem. and Rep. Coms., 1986; recipient Cert. of Honor, Soroptimist Internat. of Salt Lake, 1990, Alumnus of Yr. award Utah State U., 1978, Disting. Svc. award Utah Tech. Coll., 1979, Susa Young Gates award Utah Women's Polit. Caucus, 1980; named Hon. Chmn. Ann. Banquet, NAACP, 1977. Mem. ASPA (chmn. state conf. 1977), Nat. Assn. Counties (bd. dirs. 1980-81, 83-5, 87—, mem. various coms., mem. NACoNet 1992-93, chmn. bd. event 1991, Salt Lake County com. for ann.

conf. 1991), Nat. Assn. County Recorders and Clks. (bd. dirs. 1976-78, 79—, sec./treas. 1979-80, chmn. convention com. 1976-77, v.p. 1982-83, pres. 1983-84, mem. various coms.), Women Ofcls. of Nat. Assn. Counties (v.p. 1979-80, pres. 1980-81), Inst. for Land Info. (1st v.p. 1986, 87, pres. 1988-90), Utah Women's Internat. Connection, Internat. Women's Forum, Utah Assn. Counties (bd. dirs. 1976-77), Salt Lake Area C. of C. (civic responsibility com. 1987, state legis. action com. 1987—, WIBCO program planning com. 1987), Utah Key Rep. Club (bd. dirs. 1985—), Pi Alpha Alpha. Mem. LDS Ch. Home: 3781 Lois Ln Salt Lake City UT 84124-2309 Office: Salt Lake County Recorder 2001 S State St # 1600 Salt Lake City UT 84190-0001

DIXON, ROBERT GENE, manufacturing engineering educator, mechanical engineering company executive; b. Clatskanie, Oreg., Feb. 15, 1934; s. Hobart Jay and Doris Marie D.; m. Janice Lee Taylor, Sept. 19, 1954; children: Linda Dixon Johnson, Jeffrey, David. AS in Indsl. Tech., Chemeketa C.C., 1978, related spl. courses, 1978-80. Cert. welder, Oreg., trainer Devel. Dimension Internat. interaction mgmt., master trainer techniques for empowered workforce; cert. trainer for total quality transformation, trainer customer svc. Journeyman machinist to asst. mgr. AB McLauchlan Co., Inc., 1956-69; supt. design, rsch., devel. engring. and prodn. Stevens Equipment Co., 1969-70; co-owner, operator Pioneer Machinery, 1970-72; supt. constrn. and repair Stayton Canning Co., 1972-73; mgr. Machinery div. Power Transmission, 1973-75; owner, operator Dixon Engring., Salem, Oreg., 1975—, ret., 1996; instr., program chair mfg. engring. tech. Chemeketa C.C., 1975-92, tech. project coord. to Oreg. Advanced Tech. Ctr., 1992-95; apptd. tech. project coord. Oreg. Advanced Tech. Consortium., 1995-96, self employed cons. tng., Dixon Engring., 1997— with U.S. Navy, 1952-56, Mgr., of the Devel. Dimensions Internat. Resource Ctr., Named Tchr. of Yr., Chemeketa Deaf Program, 1978, Outstanding Instr. of Yr., Am. Tech. Edn. Assn., 1983. Mem. ASTD, Am. Prodn. and Inventory Control Soc., Am. Vocat. Assn. (Outstanding Tchr. award 1981), Oreg. Vocat. Assn. (Instr. of Yr. 1980; pres. 1984), Oreg. Vocat. Trade Tech. Assn. (Instr. of Yr. 1979; pres. 1981; Pres.'s Plaque 1982), Soc. Mfg. Engrs. (cert., sr., chmn. Oreg. sect. 1988—, internat. dir. nominating com. 1992, 95, Outstanding Internat. Faculty adv., 1989, 91), Am. Welding Soc., Am. Soc. Metals, Chemeketa Edn. Assn. (pres. 1979), Am Soc. Quality Control, Computer Automated Systems Assn., Phi Theta Kappa. Author: Benchwork, 1980, Procedure Manual for Team Approach for Vocational Education Special Needs Students, 1980, Smart Cam CNC/CAM Curriculum for Point Control Company; tech. reviewer textbook pubs., 1978—; designer, patentee fruit and berry stem remover. Home: 4242 Indigo St NE Salem OR 97305-2134

DI XX MIGLIA, GABRIELLA, artist, conservationist; b. Genoa, Italy, June 10, 1949; d. Walter and Maria Giovanna (Lupo) Repetto Carboneschi di Ventimiglia; m. Fredi Chiappelli Zdekauer, June 10, 1980 (dec. Mar. 1990). Student, Acad. Ligustica of Art, Genoa, 1970, Acad. Ligustica of Art, Genoa, 1974-77. Owner G. Di XX Miglia Painting, L.A., 1980—; conservationist/restorationist paintings L.A., 1979-85, China, 1985-91; cons. in art conservation, 1990—. One woman shows include La Piccola Gallery, Esther Robles Gallery, L.A., City art Mus., Florence, UCLA Faculty Ctr.; group shows include L.A. Art Orgn., 1990-93, What's Women Got to do With It, SCLA, 1993, Gallery 825, West Hollywood, Calif., 1996, others. Recipient Gold medal for best drawing Genoa, 1972, Cert. of Commendation County of L.A. Bd. Suprs., 1991. Mem. Westwood Art Assn. (bd. dirs. 1983-84), AFEA (bd. dirs. 1983-86), L.A. Art Assn. Galleries (bd. dirs. 1990—), WCLA Medieval and Renaissance ctr. (hon.), Nat. Art Assn., Robinson Gardens. Roman Catholic. Office: 600 N Kenter Ave Los Angeles CA 90049

DJAO, ANGELA WEI, sociology educator; b. Shanghai, China. BA, U. Toronto, 1970, MA, 1971, PhD in Sociology, 1976. Rsch. asst. Clarke Inst. Psychiatry, Toronto, Ont., Can., 1970; vis. scholar U. Hong Kong, 1973-74; asst. prof. U. Lethbridge (Alta., Can.), 1975-78; assoc. prof. U. Sask., Saskatoon, Can., 1978-86, U. Regina (Sask), Sask. Indian Federated Coll., 1980-84; sr. lectr. Lingnan Coll., Hong Kong, 1986-87; prof. Calif. State U., Hayward, 1987-88, De Anza Coll., Cupertino, Calif., 1989-90; prof. Can. studies U. Wash., Seattle, 1991—; permanent instr. North Seattle Coll., 1992—. Author: Inequality and Social Policy, 1983; co-author: Choices and Chances, 1990. Office: North Seattle Cmty Coll Asian Studies/Social Scis 9600 College Way N Seattle WA 98103-3514

DJAWAD, SAID TAYEB See **JAWAD, SAID TAYEB**

DJUJICH, DAVID B., computer software company executive; b. Redondo Beach, Calif., Jan. 14, 1964; s. Bosko and Mirjana Djujich. BS in Info. and Computer Sci., U. Calif., Irvine, 1987. Programmer Lakeshore Toys, Carson, Calif., 1987-88; mng. cons., head of programming Prounis Cons. Group, N.Y.C., 1989-92; pres. Info. Mgmt. Solutions, Torrance, Calif., 1992-95; dir. product mgmt. Elite Info. Systems, L.A., 1995—. Mem. IEEE Computer Soc., Assn. for Computing Machinery, Young Execs. of Am. Office: Elite Info Systems Ste 500 3415 S Sepulveda Blvd Los Angeles CA 90034

D'LUZANSKY, JAMES JOSEPH, urologist, nephrologist; b. Patton, Pa., Aug. 22, 1929; s. George S. and Mary (Simko) D'L.. BA in Chemistry, St. Vincent Coll., 1950; MD, Hahnemann U., 1954. Diplomate Am. Bd. Urology. Intern Altoona (Pa.) Hosp., 1954; resident in urology Ind. U., Indpls., 1957-61; chief urology U.S. VA Hosp., Altoona Hosp., 1961-80. Lt. comdr. USNR, 1957-77. Fellow Am. Coll. Surgeons; mem. Soc. for Pediat. Urology, Ariz. Urologic Soc. Home and Office: Southwest Ctrl Urology 7617 E Minnezona Ave Scottsdale AZ 85251

DO, TAI HUU, mechanical engineer; b. Quang Binh, Vietnam, May 31, 1942; came to U.S., 1975; s. Mau Do and Thi Hai Nguyen; 1 child, Frederick Quan. BSME, U. Paris, 1970, MS, 1971. Rsch. engr. Soc. Automobile Engrs., Paris, 1970-71; test engr. Yanmar Diesel Co., Ltd., Osaka, Japan, 1971-72; prodn. mgr. Vietnam Products Co., Ltd., Saigon, Vietnam, 1972-75; chief engr. European Parts Exchange, Irvine, Calif., 1975-77; project mgr. Fairchild Aerospace Div., Santa Ana, Calif., 1977—. Co-author: Literary Dissident Movement in Vietnam; editor: Khai Phong Mag.; patentee in field; contbr. articles to profl. jours. Mem. Soc. Automotive Engrs., Soc. Mfg. Engrs. Buddhist. Office: Fairchild Aerospace Div 3130 W Harvard St Santa Ana CA 92704-3937

DOAK, ROBERT A., JR., geologist; b. Canyon, Tex., Feb. 5, 1928; s. R.A. and Thelma C. (Crawford) D.; m. Frances L. Doak. BS in Geology, U. Oreg., 1952, MS in Geology, 1953. Geologist Texaco, Wichita Falls, Tex., 1953-55, Vandyke Oil Co., Wichita Falls, Tex., 1955-57, Denver, 1958-79; pres. Mountains West Exploration, Inc., Albuquerque, 1979—. Served to sgt., U.S. Army, 1946-48. Mem. Am. Assn. Petroleum Geologists. Office: Mountains West Exploration 616 Central Ave SE Ste 213 Albuquerque NM 87102-3656

DOBBEL, RODGER FRANCIS, interior designer; b. Hayward, Calif., Mar. 11, 1934; s. John Leo and Edna Frances (Young) D.; m. Joyce Elaine Schnoor, Aug. 1, 1959; 1 child, Carrie Lynn. Student, San Jose State U., 1952-55, Chouinard Art Inst., L.A., 1955-57. Asst. designer Monroe Interiors, Oakland, Calif., 1957-66; owner, designer Rodger Dobbel Interiors, Piedmont, Calif., 1966—. Pub. in Showcase of Interior Design, Pacific edit., 1992, 100 Designers' Favorite Rooms, 1993, 2d edit., 1994; contbr. articles to mags. and newspapers. Decorations chmn. Trans Pacific Ctr. Bldg. Opening, benefit Oakland Ballet, various other benefits and openings, 1982—; chmn. Symphonic Magic, Lake Marritt Plaza, Opening of Oakland Symphony Orch. Season and various others, 1985—; cons. An Evening of Magic, Oakland Hilton Hotel, benefit Providence Hosp. Found., bd. dirs., 1991; auction chmn. County Meals on Wheels, 1994, 95; prodn. chmn. Nutcracker Ball, benefit Oakland Ballet, 1995; mem. bd. regents Holy Names Coll., 1997—. Recipient Cert. of Svc., Nat. Soc. Interior Designers, 1972, 74; recipient Outstanding Contbn. award, Oakland Symphony, 1986, Nat. Philanthropy Day Disting. Vol. award, 1991. Mem. Nat. Soc. Interior Designers (profl. mem. 1960-75, v.p. Calif. chpt. 1965, edn. found. mem. 1966—, nat. conf. chmn. 1966), Am. Soc. Interior Designers , Claremont Country, Diabetic Youth Found. Democrat. Roman Catholic.

DOBBS, GREGORY ALLAN, journalist; b. San Francisco, Oct. 9, 1946; s. Harold Stanley and Annette Rae (Lehrer) D.; m. Carol Lynn Walker, Nov. 25, 1973; children: Jason Walker, Alexander Adair. B.A., U. Calif., Berkeley, 1968; M.S.J., Northwestern U., 1969. Assignment editor, reporter Sta. KGO-TV, San Francisco, 1966-68; news dir. San Francisco Tourist Info. Program Service, 1968; editor ABC Radio, Chgo., 1969-71; producer ABC News, Chgo., 1971-73; corr. ABC News, 1973-77, London, 1977-82, Paris, 1982-86, Denver, 1986-92; host The Greg Dobbs Show/Sta. KOA Radio, 1992—; lectr. Northwestern U. Sch. Journalism, 1975, 76; prof. U. Colo. Sch. Journalism, 1996—. Recipient Sigma Delta Chi Disting. Svc. award for TV reporting Soc. Profl. Journalists, 1980, Emmy award for outstanding documentary, 1989, award of excellence Colo. Broadcasters Assn., 1993, 94, award for best talk show Colo. Soc. Profl. Journalists, 1994; Lippmann fellow Ford Found., 1975. Office: 1380 Lawrence St Denver CO 80204-2054

DOBEL, J. PATRICK, dean, educator; b. Kansas City, Mo., Sept. 15, 1948; s. Jerome Patrick Jr. and Joan (Woehler) D.; m. Lea Vaughn, June 12, 1978; children: Hilary Vaughn, Matthew Patrick. AB in Polit. Sci., Boston Coll., 1970; PhD, Princeton U., 1976. Lectr. Univ. Mich., Dearborn, 1974-76, asst. prof., 1976-80, assoc. prof., 1980-84; assoc. prof. Univ. Wash., Seattle, 1984—; dir., grad. studies, Sch. Pub. Affairs, Univ. Wash., Seattle, 1988-92, assoc. dean, 1996—. Author: Compromise and Political Action: Political Morality in Liberal and Democratic Life, 1991; contbr. articles to profl. jours. Chair Seattle Overflight Com., 1985-86, King County (Wash.) Ethics Bd., 1987-95, cons. on leadership, mgmt., ethics. With USAR, 1970-76. Recipient Nat. Endowment of Humanities fellowship to Inst., Chgo., Nat. Endowment of Humanities fellowship for Coll. Tchrs., Washington. Mem. Am. Polit. Sci. Assn., Am. Soc. Pub. Adminstrn., Assn. for Policy Analysis and Mgmt., Soc. for Legal and Polit. Philosophy. Roman Catholic. Office: Univ Wash Grad Sch Pub Affairs PO Box 353055 Seattle WA 98195

DOBELIS, GEORGE, manufacturing company executive; b. July 31, 1940; s. John and Dorothy Dobelis; m. Dolores Ann Nagle, Dec. 2, 1972; children: Sally Ann Berg, Christian Eric Berg, Kurt Conrad Berg. AA in Engring., Santa Monica Coll., 1963; student, Control Data Inst., 1970. Engring. Masterite Ind., Torrance, Calif., 1969-70; engring. mgr. Elco Corp., El Segundo, Calif., 1964-76, mgr. new products, 1976-77; pres. Connector Tech. Inc., Anaheim, Calif., 1977—. Patentee in field; contbr. articles to profl. jours. Served as sgt. N.G., 1963-69. Mem. IEEE. Republican.

DOBLER, DAVID LEE, pastor; b. Yankton, S.D., Sept. 30, 1949; s. Walter Emmanuel and Pauline Marie (Schillereff) D.; m. Laura Mary Ellithorpe, Sept. 15, 1979; 1 child, Isaac Emmanuel; children from previous marriage: Catherine Therese, David Christian. Student, Reed Coll., 1969-71; MDiv, San Francisco Theol. Sem., 1980; DD (hon.), U. Dubuque Theol. Sem., 1994. Ordained pastor Presbyn. Ch. Buyer, mgr. Wood Bros. Lumber Co., Tucson, Ariz., 1972-77; pastor Yakutat (Alaska) Presbyn. Ch., 1980-85, Jewel Lake Parish, Anchorage, 1985-95; exec. presbyter Yukon Presbytery PC (USA), Anchorage, 1995—; moderator 205th gen. assembly Presbyn. Ch. USA, Louisville, Ky., 1993-94. Bd. dirs. Alaska Refugee Outreach, Anchorage, 1989-95, United Campus Ministry, Anchorage, 1991-95; trustee Sheldon Jackson Coll., Sitka, Alaska, 1995—, Anchorage Cmty. Found., 1996—. Home: 2930 Lexington Cr Anchorage AK 99502 Office: Presbytery of Yukon 616 W 10th Ave Anchorage AK 99501-3426

DOBRONSKI, MARK WILLIAM, state government official; b. Detroit, Oct. 8, 1957; s. Clarence Robert and Jean (Shotey) D.; m. Susan Kay Roach, Sept. 12, 1980; children: Clarence Robert III, Juli E. AS, Henry Ford C.C., 1980; Bachelor's degree, Shaw Coll., Detroit, 1983. Cert. engr. Nat. Assn. Radio and Telecomm. Engrs. V.p. Mobilfone, Inc., Dearborn, Mich., 1977-79; asst. v.p. RAM Broadcasting Corp., N.Y.C., 1979-86; adminstr. State of Ariz., Phoenix, 1986-88, 89—; divsn. comdr. City of Peoria (Ariz.) Police Dept., 1991; cons., expert witness Teletech, Inc., Dearborn, 1980—. Mem., bd. dirs. Congl. Ch. of the Valley, United Ch. of Christ, Scottsdale, Ariz., 1994-96. Republican. Office: PO Box 4221 Scottsdale AZ 85261-4221

DOBROTKA, DAVID A., protective services official; m.; 2 children. BS, MPA. With Minn. Police Dept., Mpls., 1976-94; chief Glendale (Ariz.) Police Dept., 1994—. Office: Glendale Police Dept 6835 N 57th Dr Glendale AZ 85301

DOBSON, MARGARET VELMA, experimental psychologist, educator; b. Burbank, Calif., June 8, 1948; d. Joel Gerald and Margaret Velma (Biggs) D.; m. Patrick Maurice Burke, June 3, 1975; children: Andrew G. Burke, Margaret K. Burke. BA, Fla. State U., 1970; ScM, Brown U., 1973, PhD, 1975. Rsch. scientist Med. Sch. Tufts U., 1974-75; postdoctoral fellow U. Wash., Seattle, 1975-78, rsch. asst. prof. psychology, 1978-82, rsch. assoc. prof., 1982-84; assoc. prof. psychiatry and psychology U. Pitts., Seattle, 1984-94; rsch. prof. ophthalmology and psychology U. Ariz., Tucson, 1994—. Contbr. articles to profl. jours. Leader troop Girl Scouts Am., Pitts., 1987-92. Woodrow Wilson fellow, 1970; rsch. grantee Nat. Eye Inst. NIH, 1978—. Mem. Assn. for Rsch. in Vision and Opthalmology, Internat. Soc. for Infant Studie, Phi Beta Kappa. Office: U Ariz Dept Ophthalmology 1801 N Campbell Tucson AZ 85719

DOBY, KAREN ELAINE, data processing company executive; b. Amarillo, Tex., Nov. 1, 1955; d. Laurance Lee and Helen Marie (Davis) D. AS, Belleville (Ill.) Area Coll., 1976; BS, So. Ill. U., Edwardsville, Ill., 1977; MS, Georgetown U., 1978; MBA, Loyola U., New Orleans, 1984. Ops. researcher Dept. of Energy, Washington, 1977-78; geophysicist Naval Oceanographic Office, Bay St. Louis, Miss., 1978-82; engring. analyst Middle S. Utilities System, New Orleans, 1982; sr. systems analyst, mgr. Exploration and Devel. Systems CNG Producing Co., New Orleans, 1982-88; mgr. network security Sun Micro Systems, Inc., Mountain View, Calif., 1992-96; dir. enterprise network svcs. Sun Microsystems, Inc., Mountain View, Ca., 1996—; cons. Macrobiotic Inst., New Orleans, 1987—. Mem. Nat. Computer Graphics Assn., IEEE Computer Soc., Am. Assn. Petroleum Geologists. Democrat. Home: 4546 B-10 El Camino Real # 321 Los Altos CA 94022-1041

DOBYNS, ZIPPORAH POTTENGER, minister, educator, writer; b. Chgo., Aug. 26, 1921; d. William Albert and Martha Cobb (Livingston) Pottenger; m. Henry F. Dobyns (div. Aug. 1958); children: Rique, William, Maritha, Mark. BA in anthropology, U. Chgo., 1944; MA in psychology, U. Ariz., 1966, PhD in psychology, 1969. Minister and dir. psychology svcs. L.A. Cmty. Ch. of Religious Sci., 1969—. Author: God's World, 1957, Expanding Astrology's Universe, 1983, Progressions, Dirs. and Rect., 1974, (with William Wrobel) Paths to Understanding, 1987, Finding the Person in the Horoscope, 1973, (with Maritha Pottenger) Planets in the Move, 1994, The Book of Saturn, 1997; contbr. articles to profl. jours. Recipient Outstanding Contb. award Profl. Astrologers Inc., 1975, Regulas award United Astrology Congress, 1992, Svc. to Astrology award Aquarius Workshops, 1992, So. Cross award Fed. Australian Astrologers, 1995. Mem. Am. Psychological Assn., Assn. Humanistic Psychology, Transpersonal Psychological Assn., Internat. Soc. Astrological Rsch. (dir. 1969-95), Nat. Coun. Geocasmic Rsch. (adv. bd. 1975—), Assn. for Astrological Networking (adv. bd. 1986—). Home: PO Box 1132 Jamul CA 91935-7506

DOCKSTADER, JACK LEE, retired electronics executive; b. Los Angeles, Dec. 14, 1936; s. George Earl and Grace Orine (Travers) D.;m. Kerry Jo King, Oct. 24, 1987; children: Travis Adam Mayer, Bridget Olivia Mayer. student UCLA, 1960-70. Rate analyst Rate Bur., So. Pacific Co., Los Angeles, 1954-57; traffic analyst traffic dept. Hughes Aircraft Co., Fullerton, Calif., 1957-58, Culver City, Calif., 1958-59, traffic mgr. Hughes Research Labs., Malibu, Calif., 1959-70, material mgr., 1970-75; material mgr. Hughes Aircraft Co., Culver City, 1975-80, prodn. material mgr. Electro-Optical and Data Systems Group, El Segundo, Calif., 1980-84, mgr. material total quality 1984-85, mgr. cen. material ops. and property mgmt. 1987-88, mgr. group property mgmt., 1988-93, mgr. electro optical systems, property mgmt., aerospace and def. sector, 1993; ret., 1993. Mem. adv. council transp. mgmt. profl. designation program UCLA, 1966-80, mem. Design for Sharing Com., 1977-82; adv. com. transp. program Los Angeles Trade Tech. Coll., 1970-80. Served with USNR, 1954-96, ret. 1996. Mem. Nat. Property Mgmt. Assn. (pres. L.A. chpt. 1992, 93), UCLA Alumni Assn., Nat. Contracts Mgmt. Assn., Naval Enlisted Res. Assn., Hughes Aircraft Co. Mgmt. Club, Hughes Aircraft Retirees Assn., Delta Nu Alpha (pres. San Fernando Valley chpt. 1965-66, v.p. Pacific S.W. region 1969-71, region man of year 1971). Presbyterian. Home: PO Box 3156 Redondo Beach CA 90277-1156

DODD, DEBORAH JANE, military contracting officer; b. Longmont, Colo., Oct. 11, 1947; d. John Jerome and Margaret Cora (Slee) D. BA, U. Colo., 1969; cert. teaching, Keane Coll., 1971; MS, San Jose State U., 1975. Vista vol. Palatka, Fla., 1969-70; tchr. N.J. Urban Edn. Corp., Newark, 1971-72, English Conversation Circle, Tokyo, Japan, 1972-73; camp dir. Baker Beach Golden Gate Nat. Recreation Area, San Francisco, 1975; recreation therapist Casa Grande (Ariz.) Rehab. Ctr., 1975-76; office mgr., counselor Tucson Rape Crisis Ctr., 1976-78; customs inspector U.S. Customs Service, Nogales, Ariz., 1978-81; elem. edn. tchr. Salome Show-Low Schs., Ariz., 1981-82; contract negotiator and contracting officer USAF, McClellan AFB, Calif., 1982—; gen. ptnr. Wymer and Assocs. Biol. Cons., Citrus Heights, Calif., 1986—. Mem. Calif. Native Plant Soc., McClellan Mgmt. Soc., Nat. Contract Mgmt. Assn., Federally Employed Women, Phi Beta Kappa. Democrat.

DODD, JOE DAVID, safety engineer, consultant, administrator; b. Walnut Grove, Mo., Jan. 22, 1920; s. Marshall Hill and Pearl (Combs) D.; m. Nona Bell Junkins, Sept. 17, 1939; 1 dau. Linda Kay Dodd Craig. Student S.W. Mo. State U., 1937-39, Wash. U., 1947-55. Cert. profl. safety engr. Calif. Office asst. retail credit co., Kansas City, Mo., 1939-42; bus driver City of Springfield (Mo.), 1945-47; ops., engring., and personnel positions Shell Oil Co., Wood River (Ill.) Refinery, 1947-66; health and safety dept. mgr. Martinez Mfg. Complex, Calif., 1966-83, retired 1983; exec. dir. Fire Protection Tng. Acad., U. Nev.-Reno; rep. Shell Oil Co., Western Oil and Gas Assn., 1970-81. Mem. Republican Presdl. Task Force. Served with USMC, 1942-45. Decorated Presdl. Citation. Mem. Western Oil and Gas Assn. (Hose Handler award 1972-81, Outstanding mem. award), Am. Soc. Safety Engrs., Veterans Safety, State and County Fire Chiefs Assn., Peace Officers Assn., Nat. Fire Protection Assn. Presbyterian (elder). Established Fire Protection Tng. Acad., U. Nev.-Reno, Stead Campus.

DODDS, DALE IRVIN, chemicals executive; b. Los Angeles, May 3, 1915; s. Nathan Thomas and Mary Amanda (Latham) D.; m. Phyllis Doreen Kirchmayer, Dec. 20, 1941; children: Nathan E., Allan I., Dale I. Jr., Charles A. AB in Chemistry, Stanford U., 1937. Chem. engr. trainee The Texas Co., Long Beach, Calif., 1937-39; chemist Standard Oil of Calif., Richmond, 1939-41; chief chemist Scriver and Quinn Interchem., L.A., 1941-46; salesman E.B. Taylor and Co. Mfg. Rep., L.A., 1947-53, Burbank (Calif.) Chem. Co., 1953-57, Chem. Mfg. Co./ICI, L.A., 1957-68; pres., gen. mgr. J.J. Mauget Co., L.A., 1969—. Inventor: Systemic Fungicide, 1976; patentee in field; contributed to devel. Microinjection for Trees. Fellow Am. Inst. Chemists; mem. Am. Chem. Soc., L.A. Athletic Club, Sigma Alpha Epsilon Alumni (pres. Pasadena, Calif. chpt. 1973, 90). Republican. Christian Scientist. Office: JJ Mauget Co 5435 Peck Rd Arcadia CA 91006

DODDS, MICHAEL BRUCE, lawyer; b. Spokane, Wash., June 27, 1952; s. Bruce Alison and Janet Lorraine (Swanbeck) D.; m. Karen Lynn Sifford, Jan. 5, 1972; children: Jennifer Ann, Stephanie Marie, Alexander Michael, Matthew Tyler. BA, Gonzaga U., 1974, JD, 1979. Bar: Wash. 1980, U.S. Dist. Ct. (ea. dist.) Wash. 1983, U.S. Dist. Ct. (we. dist.) Wash. 1987, U.S. Ct. Appeals (9th cir.) 1994, U.S. Supreme Ct. 1987. Dep. prosecutor Okanogan (Wash.) County, 1980-87, Clark (Wash.) County, 1987—. Served to 2d lt. U.S. Army, 1974-76. Recipient Excellence in Performance award Clark County, 1995. Mem. Clark County Bar Assn., Wash. State Bar Assn., Nat. Dist. Attys. Assn., Phi Alpha Delta. Republican. Lodge: Eagles, Moose. Home: 2104 NE Cranbrook Dr Vancouver WA 98664-2960 Office: Clark County Prosecuter's Office PO Box 5000 Vancouver WA 98666-5000

DODGE, DOUGLAS STUART, federal agency administrator; b. Van Nuys, Calif., May 26, 1951; s. John Marvin and Barbara Jean (McMillan) D.; m. Leslie Ann Condron, Apr. 24, 1982; children: Sarah Elizabeth, Gwendolyn Marie. BA in History, U. Calif., Davis, 1975. Outdoor recreation planner Bur. Land Mgmt., U.S. Dept. Interior, Yuma, Ariz., 1976-80, Salt Lake City, 1980-83; dist. archeologist Bur. Land Mgmt., U.S. Dept. Interior, Salt Lake City, Utah, 1983-88; supervisory resource mgmt. specialist Bur. Land Mgmt., U.S. Dept. Interior, Bishop, Calif., 1989—. Softball umpire Am. Softball Assn., U.S. Slow-pitch Softball Assn., So. Calif., Mcpl. Athletic Fedn., Calif., Ariz., Utah, 1976—. Mem. Utah Profl. Archeologist Coun., Roundalab Internat. Tchrs. Assn. (edn1. com. 1987-88), Utah Round Dance Assn. (pres. 1988-89), Utah Round Dance Tchrs. Assn. (chmn. 1983-85), Lions. Home: 131 Mountain Rd Big Pine CA 93513-2005 Office: Bur Land Mgmt 785 N Main St Ste E Bishop CA 93514-2471

DODGE, PETER HAMPTON, architect; b. Pasadena, Calif., July 1, 1929; s. Irving C. and Edna D. (Allison) D.; m. Janice Coor-Pender, Aug. 30, 1952; children: Susan Julia, Sarah Caroline. Student, Art Center Sch., Calif., 1947-49; A.B. with honors in Architecture, U. Calif., Berkeley, 1956. Cert. architect, Calif., Hawaii, Nev., Idaho, Colo., The Nat. Coun. of Archtl. Registration Bds., (NCARB). Apprentice Alvin Lustig (designer), Los Angeles, 1949-50; draftsman Joseph Esherick (AIA), 1956, architect, 1959-63; asso. architect Joseph Esherick and Assos. (architects), San Francisco, 1963-72; prin. Esherick, Homsey, Dodge and Davis (architects and planners, P.C.), San Francisco, 1972—; pres. Esherick, Homsey, Dodge and Davis (architects and planners, P.C.), 1979-85; lectr. dept. architecture U. Calif., Berkeley, 1961-64, 71; vis. lectr. dept. design San Francisco Art Inst., 1965. Prin. archtl. works include grad. residence facility U. Calif.-Davis, 1970, Shortstop Inc. markets, office and warehouse, Benicia, Calif., 1976, Ekahi Village (297 condominium units) Wailea, Hawaii, 1976, TWA and Western Airlines at San Francisco Internat. Airport, 1977, Citizens Utility Ctr., Susanville, Calif., 1983, various projects Golden Gate U., San Francisco, 1984—, additions and renovation Forest Hill Mcpl. R.R. Sta., San Francisco, 1985, Life Sci. Bldg. Mills Coll., Oakland, Calif., 1986, showroom R.A.B. Motors Mercedes-Benz , San Rafael, Calif., 1986, U.S. Embassy, La Paz, Bolivia, 1979-87, boarding area "B" expansion San Francisco Internat. Airport, 1987, additions and renovations Mills. Coll. Art Ctr., Oakland, 1987, F.W. Olin Libr. Mills Coll., Oakland, 1989, Calif. State U. at Bakersfield Walter Stiern Libr., 1993, Mills Hall restoration, Olney Hall rehab. Mills Coll., 1994 ; mem. editorial bd. Architecture Calif. mag., 1984-88, chmn. bd., 1985-88, Landscape mag., 1986—. Mem. Rockridge Community Planning Council, Oakland, Calif., 1971. Served with C.E., U.S. Army, 1957-58. Firm recipient of highest nat. honor for archtl. firm. AIA, 1986. Fellow AIA (dir. Calif. council 1979-81, dir. San Francisco chpt. 1977-78, sec. 1979, v.p. 1980, pres. San Francisco chpt. 1981, Honor award 1970, Bartlett award 1970); mem. U. Calif. at Berkeley Coll. Environ. Design Alumni Assn. (mem. founding steering com., pres. 1990-91). Office: c/o Esherick Homsey Dodge & Davis 2789 25th St San Francisco CA 94110-3516*

DODS, WALTER ARTHUR, JR., bank executive; b. Honolulu, May 26, 1941; s. Walter Arthur Sr. and Mildred (Phillips) D.; m. Diane Lauren Nosse, Sept. 18, 1971; children: Walter A. III, Christopher L., Peter D., Lauren S. BBA, U. Hawaii, 1967. Mktg. officer 1st Hawaiian Bank, Honolulu, 1969, asst. v.p. mktg. div., 1969-71, v.p., chmn. mktg. and rsch. group, 1971-73, sr. v.p. mktg. and rsch. group, 1973-76, exec. v.p. retail banking group, 1976-78, exec. v.p. gen. banking group, 1978-84, pres., 1984-89, chmn., ceo, 1989—; chmn., pres., CEO First Hawaiian, Inc., 1989-90, chmn., CEO, 1989—; chmn., CEO First Hawaiian Creditcorp., 1989-92; bd. dirs. First Hawaiian Inc., 1st Hawaiian Bank, First Hawaiian Creditcorp Inc., First Hawaiian Leading, Inc., Alexander & Baldwin Inc., A&B-Hawaii Inc., Duty Free Shoppers Adv. Bd., Matson Navigation Co. Inc., 1st Ins. Co. Hawaii Ltd., GTE Calif., GTE Hawaiian Telephone Co., GTE Northwest, Grace Pacific Corp., Oceanic Cablevision Inc., Pacific Guardian Life Ins. Co., Princeville Adv. Group, RHP, Inc., Restaurant Suntory USA, Inc., Suntory Resorts, Inc. Bd. dirs. Ahahui Koa Anuenue, East-West Ctr. Found.; past sec., treas. The Rehab. Hosp. of the Pacific; exec. bd. mem. Aloha Coun., Boy Scouts Am.; trustee, past chmn., trustee Blood Bank Hawaii; past chmn. bd. Aloha United Way; past chmn. Bd. Water Supply; bd. govs., v.p. fin. Ctr. for Internat. Comml. Dispute Resolution; bd. dirs., treas. Coalition for Drug-Free Hawaii; trustee Contemporary Mus. co-chmn. corp. campaign com.; mem. Duty Free Shoppers Adv. Bd.; past chmn. Gubernatorial Inauguration, 1974, 82; bd. govs. Hawaii Employers Coun.; trustee Hawaii Maritime Ctr; mem. Gov.'s Adv. Bd. Geothermal/Inter-Island Cable Project, Gov.'s Blue Ribbon Panel on the Future of Healthcare in

Hawaii; dir., past chmn. Hawaii Visitors Bur.; exec. com. Hawaiian Open; past spl. dir. Homeless Kokua Week; bd. gov. Honolulu Country Club, Japanese Cultural Ctr. Hawaii, Pacific Peace Found.; trustee Japan-Am. Inst. Mgmt. Sci., The Nature Conservancy Hawaii, Punahou Sch.; Hawaii chmn. Japan-Hawaii Econ. Coun.; chmn., dir. Pacific Internat. Ctr. for High Tech. Rsch.; past co-chmn., chmn. bldg. fund St. Louis High Sch.; treas. The 200 Club; dir. World Cup Honolulu 1994. Named Outstanding Jaycee in Nation, 1963, Outstanding Young Man Am. from Hawaii, 1972, Marketer of Yr., Am. Mktg. Assn., 1987; recipient Riley Allen Individual Devel. award, 1964, Hawaii State Jaycees 3 Outstanding Young Men award, 1971, Am. Advt. Fedn. Silver medal, 1977, St. Louis High Sch.'s Outstanding Alumnus award, 1980. Mem. Am. Bankers Assn., Bank Mktg. Assn., Hawaii Bankers Assn., Hawaii Bus. Roundtable, C. of C. of Hawaii, Honolulu Press Club. Office: 1st Hawaiian Bank PO Box 3200 Honolulu HI 96847*

DOEBLER, BETTIE ANNE, language educator, researcher, writer; b. Atlantic City, N.J.; d. Willloughby Foster and Ann Bailey (Ratledge) Young; m. John W. Doebler, Sept. 1, 1954 (dec. Aug. 26, 1994); 1 child, Mark B. BA, Duke U., 1953, MA, 1955; PhD, U. Wis., 1961. From instr. to assoc. prof. Dickinson Coll., Carlisle, Pa., 1961-70; assoc. prof. Ariz. State U., Tempe, 1971, prof., 1975, prof. emeritus, 1994—, dir. interdisciplinary humanities program, 1989-94. Author: The Quickening Seed: Death in the Sermons of John Donne, 1974, Rooted Sorrow: Dying in Early Modern England, 1994; contbr. essays to English Literary History, Shakespeare Studies, Studies in English Literature, poems to The New Eng. Rev., Monuments and Cantos, Passages North. Angier B. Duke Grad. fellow Duke U., 1954; recipient Faculty Rsch. award Ariz. State U., 1984. Episcopalian. Office: Ariz State U Dept English Tempe AZ 85287

DOELGER, NANCY MICKLICH, geologist, minerals environmental specialist; b. Lawrence, Kans., Oct. 11, 1949; d. John Robert and Katherine Louise (Ewing) Micklich; m. Mark Jonathan Doelger, July 2, 1978; children: Peter Jonathan, Gwendolyn Marie. BS in Geology and Chemistry, No. Ariz. U., 1972; MS in Geology, U. Wyo., 1981. Registered profl. geologist, Wyo. Geol. engr. Shell Oil Co., Midland/Houston, 1972-74; coal geologist U.S. Geol. Survey, Casper, Wyo., 1974-78; exploration geologist Gulf Oil Corp., Casper, Wyo., 1980-83; consulting geologist Clark and George, Casper, Wyo., 1983-86; geologist, engr., environ. specialist, resource advisor Bur. of Land Mgmt., Casper, Wyo., 1987—; pres. Wyo. State Geol. Survey Bd., Laramie, 1993, sec., 1994. Mem. Am. Assn. Petroleum Geologists, Rocky Mtn. Assn. Geologists, Wyo. Geol. Assn. (sec. 1983, 1st v.p. 1984, pres. 1992, Frank Morgan award 1987), Five Trails Rotary (sec. 1997). Home: 3331 Carmel Dr Casper WY 82604-4992

DOERPER, JOHN ERWIN, publisher, editor; b. Wuerzburg, Fed. Republic of Germany, Sept. 17, 1943; came to U.S., 1963, permanent resident, 1973; s. Werner and Theresia (Wolf) D.; m. Victoria McCulloch, Dec. 2, 1970. BA, Calif. State U., Fullerton, 1968; MA/ABD, U. Calif., Davis, 1972. Writer/author Seattle, 1984—; food columnist Washington, Seattle, 1985-88, Seattle Times, 1985-88; food editor Wash.-The Evergreen State Mag., Seattle, 1989-94, Pacific Northwest mag., 1989-94, Seattle Home and Garden, 1989-91; pub., editor, founder Pacific Epicure, Quarterly Jour. Gastronomy, Bellingham, Wash., 1988—; dir. Annual N.W. Invitational Chef's Symposium. Author: Eating Well: A Guide to Foods of the Pacific Northwest, 1984, The Eating Well Cookbook, 1984, Shellfish Cookery: Absolutely Delicious Recipes from the West Coast, 1985; author, illustrator: The Blue Carp, 1994, Wine Country: California's Napa and Sonoma Valleys, 1996; contbr. articles to profl. jours., intro. and chpts. to books; co-author: Washington: A Compass Guide, 1995. Recipient Silver medal, White award for city and regional mags. William Allen White Sch. Journalism, U. Kans. Mem. Oxford Symposium Food and Cookery (speaker 26th Ann. Pacific Northwest Writer's Conf. 1982, 92). Home: 610 Donovan Ave Bellingham WA 98225-7315

DOERR, PATRICIA MARIAN, elementary and special education educator; b. Rochford, Essex, Eng., Mar. 14, 1947; came to U.S., 1976; d. Edward Earnest and Winifred May (Daniels) Earl; m. Hans Joachim Doerr, Dec. 17, 1983; children: Daniel, Nicholas, Carla. Cert. of Edn., Sussex U., 1968; Diploma in Edn. of Handicapped, London U., 1974; MS, Calif. Luth. U., 1986. Tchr. Long Road Jr. Sch., Canvey Island, Eng., 1968-70; tchr. scale 1 Belvedere (Kent, Eng.) Jr. Sch., 1970-71; tchr. scale 2 Bostal (Kent, Eng.) Manor Jr. Sch., 1971-73; tchr. scale 3, head remedial Warren Wood Boys Comprehensive Sch., Rochester, Kent, 1974-76; ednl. therapist Westvalley Ctr. for Ednl. Therapy, Canoga Park, Calif., 1977-79; tchr. K-2 Sundance Sch., Simi Valley, Calif., 1977-78; spl. tchr. Conejo Valley Unified Sch. Dist., Thousand Oaks, Calif., 1979-94; elem. tchr. Meadows Elem. Sch., Thousand Oaks, Calif., 1994—; ednl. cons. Scwrip & Independent, Ventura County, Calif., 1988—; mem. London Panel of Art Tutors, ILEA Evening Inst., 1969-73; mentor spl. edn. and lang. arts Conejo Valley Unified Sch. Dist., 1988-95. Recipient Award of Tchr. Excellence, AMGEN, 1996; Scwrip fellow Santa Barbara U., 1988. Mem. Calif. Assn. Mediated Learning (bd. dirs. 1991-95). Episcopalian. Home: 1933 Tamarack St Westlake Village CA 91361

DOGLIONE, ARTHUR GEORGE, data processing executive; b. Bklyn., May 24, 1938; s. Francis and Georgia (Smith) D.; m. Maryann Laurette Bonfanti, Sept. 3, 1960; children: Dana Ann, Arthur Todd, Lora Michele. AA, Scottsdale (Ariz.) Community, 1978; AAS, Maricopa Tech. Coll., Phoenix, 1984; BS, Ariz. State U., 1985. Salesman Columbus Realty Co., Trenton, N.J., 1962-65; appraiser J.H. Martin Appraisal Co., Trenton, 1965-68; office mgr. Mcpl. Revaluations, Avon-by-the-Sea, N.J., 1968-69; pres., broker Area Real Estate Agy., Wall, N.J., 1969-76; property appraiser Ariz. Dept. Revenue, Phoenix, 1976-78; investment appraiser Continental Bank, Phoenix, 1978-79; appraisal systems specialist Ariz. Dept. Revenue, Phoenix, 1979-80; project dir. Ariz. Dept. Adminstrn., 1980-83; pres. Logical Models, Scottsdale, Ariz., 1983-95; founder Genus Tech., Scottsdale, 1989—; tax assessor Upper Freehold Twp., N.J., 1974-75, Borough of Bradley Beach, N.J., 1975; lectr. in field. Author various software. Counselor SCORE, SBA, Mesa, Ariz., 1986-90. Mem. Phi Theta Kappa. Republican. Roman Catholic. Office: GENUS Technology PO Box 725 Scottsdale AZ 85252-0725

DOHM, RODGER MATTHEW, painter, sculptor; b. La Jolla, Calif., June 2, 1967; s. Francis Leon and Susan Elizabeth (McWilliams) D. BA in Math. and Art Edn., Brigham Young U., 1995. Cert. tchr. K-12. Painter and sculptor Provo, Utah, 1991-94, Poway, Calif., 1991-94. Group shows include Springville Art Museum, 1994; prin. works include Bringham Young U., Provo, Utah, 1994. Recipient merit award for Excellence in Arts Bringham Young U., 1993. Mem. Nat. Art Edn. Assn. (co-pres. 1992-93). Home: 12437 Robins Blvd Poway CA 92064

DOHRER, GARY RAY, English language educator; b. Wichita, Kans., Dec. 27, 1951; s. M.R. and Julia Teresa (Garlick) D.; m. Kim Debra Hanner, Feb. 17, 1978. BA in English, Wichita State U., 1974; MA in Edn., St. Louis U., 1979; PhD in English, Lang. Arts Edn., U. Tex., 1989. Tchr. Bishop Carroll High Sch., Wichita, Kans., 1974-76, Wichita High Sch. East, 1976-79; tchr. Wichita High Sch. Metro (Alternative), 1979-85, English dept. chair, 1981-85; instr. computers in the classroom Wichita State U., 1984-85; student teaching supr. U. Tex., Austin, 1987-89; assoc. prof. English Weber State U., Ogden, Utah, 1989—. Contbr. articles to profl. jours. Mem. Phi Delta Kappa, Pi Lambda Theta, Kappa Delta Pi. Home: 3519 E 3100 N Eden UT 84310-9754 Office: Weber State U Dept English Ogden UT 84408-1201

DOHRING, DOUG, marketing executive. Chmn. Dohring Co., Calif. Office: Dohring Co 550 N Brand Ave Glendale CA 91203*

DOHRING, LAURIE, marketing executive. CEO Dohring Co., Glendale, Calif. Office: Dohring Co 550 N Brand Ave Glendale CA 91203*

DOI, LOIS, psychiatric social worker; b. Honolulu, Oct. 24, 1951; d. James Masato and Thelma Kimiko Miyamoto; m. Brian Doi, May 26, 1972; children: Michael, Lorian. BS, U. Hawaii, 1974, MSW, 1978. Lic. clin. social worker, Calif. Psychiat. social worker, child specialist Desert Community Mental Health Ctr., Indio, Calif., 1979-92, coordinator children's day treatment program, 1982-91; pvt. practice psychiat. social worker 1-2-1 Counseling, Palm Springs, Calif., 1992—; owner, ptnr. 1-2-1 Counseling, Rancho Mirage, Calif.; psychiat. social worker, adult case mgr. Desert Community Mental Health Ctr., Palm Springs, Calif., 1992-93; expert examiner, Bd. of Behavioral Sci. Examiners, 1987—. Vol. advisor Community Recreation Ctr. Youth Group, Hawaii, 1967-69; vol. interviewer ARC Food Stamp Program, Hawaii, 1973; vol. asst. YWCA Programs Young Mothers and Teens, Hawaii, 1973; vol. group leader YWCA Juvenile Delinquent Program, Hawaii, 1973; placement counselor Vols. In Service to Am., L.A., 1975; VISTA counselor L.A. Urban League, 1975-76. Mem. Nat. Assn. Social Workers. Office: 1-2-1 Counseling # 409 42-600 Bob Hope Dr Rancho Mirage CA 92270

DOIG, BEVERLY IRENE, systems specialist; b. Bozeman, Mont., Oct. 21, 1936; d. James Stuart Doig and Elsie Florence (Andes) Doig Townsend. AA, Graceland Coll., 1956; BA, U. Kans., 1958; MS, U. Wis., 1970; cert. in Interior Design, UCLA, 1993, tng. classes Windows 96 oper. sys., 1996. Aerodynamic technician II Ames Labs.-NACA, Moffett Field, Calif., 1957; real time systems specialist Dept. of Army, White Sands Missile Range, N.Mex., 1958-66; large systems specialist computing ctr. U. Wis., Madison, 1966-70; sr. systems analyst Burroughs, Ltd., Canberra, Australia, 1970-72; systems specialist Tech. Info. Office Burroughs Corp., Detroit, 1973-78; sr. systems specialist Burroughs Gmbh, Munich, 1978-79, Burroughs AB, Stockholm, 1979-80; networking cons. Midland Bank, Ltd., Sheffield, Eng., 1980-83; networking specialist Burroughs Corp. (now UNISYS), Mission Viejo, Calif., 1983—; teaching asst. Canberra (Australia) Coll., 1972; tchr. Wayne State U. Ext., Detroit, 1976-77; freelance interior designer, 1992—. Vol. youth groups and camps Reorganized LDS Ch., N.Mex., Wis., Australia, Mich., Calif., Germany, U.K.; inner youth worker, Detroit; mentor Saddleback H.S. Scholar Mitchell Math., 1956-58, Watkins Residential, 1956-58. Mem. Assn. Computing Machinery (local chpt. chmn. membership 1969), Lambda Delta Sigma. Republican. Office: UNISYS 25725 Jeronimo Rd Mission Viejo CA 92691-2711

DOLAN, ANDREW KEVIN, lawyer; b. Chgo., Dec. 7, 1945; s. Andrew O. and Elsie (Grafner) D.; children: Andrew, Francesca, Melinda. BA, U. Ill., Chgo., 1967; JD, Columbia U., 1970, MPH, 1976, DPH, 1980. Bar: Wash. 1980. Asst. prof. law Rutgers-Camden Law Sch., N.J., 1970-72; assoc. prof. law U. So. Calif., L.A., 1972-75; assoc. prof. pub. health U. Wash., Seattle, 1977-81; ptnr. Bogle & Gates, Seattle, 1988-93; pvt. practice law, 1993—. Commr. Civil Svc. Commn., Lake Forest Park, Wash., 1981; mcpl. judge City of Lake Forest Park, 1982—. Russell Sage fellow, 1975. Mem. Order of Coif, Washington Athletic Club. Office: 5800 Columbia Ctr 701 5th Ave Seattle WA 98104-7016

DOLAN, BRIAN THOMAS, lawyer; b. Springfield, Ill., Dec. 27, 1940; s. William Stanley and Dorotha Caroline (Battles) D.; m. Kathleen Lois Smith, Sept. 14, 1963; children: Elizabeth Beaumont, Leslie Caroline. AB, Stanford U., 1963, JD, 1965. Bar: Calif. 1966, Colo. 1966, D.C. 1980. Capt. USAF, 1966-70; ptnr. Davis, Graham & Stubbs LLP, Denver, Washington, 1970—. Office: Davis Graham & Stubbs LLP 370 17th St #4700 Denver CO 80202

DOLAN, JAMES WILSON, sculptor; b. L.A., Apr. 10, 1948; s. James Wilson and Alice Jean (Addleman) D.; m. Jean Kathleen Drummond, June 25, 1974 (dec. Sept. 1991); children: Jamie M., Jacob D.; m. Vicki Ann Crook, Feb. 14, 1992; children: Jason L., Matthew A. BS, Mont. Stae U., 1970, MS, 1971. Prin. works include 10 lifesize geese of welded steel (Art in Airports award FAA 1979). Bd. dirs. Creative Inst. of Montana, Emigrant, 1989—, Big Sky (Mont.) Inst. of ARts, 1985—; soup kitchen vol. Found. for Life Action, L.A., 1994. Recipient Melvin C. Jones award Lions Club Internat., 1988, Soc. Centennial Alumni award Mont. State U., 1993. Home and Studio: 3501 Airport Rd Belgrade MT 59714

DOLAN, JUNE ANN, health facility administrator; b. Oakland, Calif., June 24, 1942; d. Edward Joseph and Pauline (McCune) D. AA, Orange Coast Coll., 1969; B of Religion and Philosophy, Loyola-Mary Mount U., Orange, Calif., 1965. MICN, ACLS. Asst. head nurse med./surg, ICU and neuro surg. ICU Riverside (Calif.) Gen. Hosp., head nurse med./surg. ICU, asst. dir. of nurses; care provider handicapped, 1987—. Vol. Spl. Olympics, 1987-91; mem. Inland AIDS project; adult advisory mem. Ability Counts Sheltered Workshop; Sister at St. Joseph of Orange, 1960-65. Mem. RGH Aux., Nursing Mgmt. Coun.

DOLAN, MARY ANNE, journalist, columnist; b. Washington, May 1, 1947; d. William David and Christine (Shea) D.; BA, Marymount Coll., Tarrytown, N.Y., 1968, HHD (hon.), 1984; student Queen Mary, Royal Holloway colls. U. London, London Sch. Econs., also Kings Coll., Cambridge U., 1966-68. Reporter, editor Washington Star, 1969-77, asst. mng. editor, 1976-77; mng. editor Los Angeles Herald Examiner, 1978-81, editor, 1981—; speaker Internat. Soc. Appraisers conv., San Francisco. Author: Commonsense Collecting, 1991. Recipient Golden Flame award Calif. Press Women, 1980, Woman Achiever award Calif. Fed. Bus. and Profl. Women's Clubs, 1981; bd. selectors for Neiman Fellows Harvard U.; mem. Pulitzer Prize Journalism Jury, 1981, 82. Mem. Am. Soc. Newspaper Editors, NOW. Office: MAD Inc. 1033 Gayley Ave Ste 205 Los Angeles CA 90024-3417

DOLAN, MARYANNE MCLORN, small business owner, writer, educator, lecturer; b. N.Y.C., July 14, 1924; d. Frederick Joseph and Kathryn Cecilia (Carroll) McLorn; m. John Francis Dolan, Oct. 6, 1951 (dec.); children: John Carroll, James Francis McLorn, William Brennan. B.A., San Francisco State U., 1978, M.A., 1981. Tchr. classes and seminars in antiques and collectibles U. Calif., Berkeley, Davis, Santa Cruz, Coll. of Marin, Kentfield, Calif., Mills Coll., Oakland, St. Mary's Coll., Moraga, 1969-90, Solano C.C., 1990—; tch. writing Dolan Sch., 1969-90; owner antique shop, Benicia, Calif., 1970—; lectr. Nat. Assn. Jewelry Appraisers Symposium, Tucson; lectr. Vintage Fashion Expo., Oakland, Calif. for Appraisers, Placentia, Calif. Author: Vintage Clothing, 1880-1980, 3d edit., 1983, Collecting Rhinestone Jewelry, 3d edit., 1984, Old Lace and Linens, 1989, Commonsense Collecting, 1991, 300 Years of American Sterling Silver Flatware, 1992; weekly columnist The Collector, 1979-88; contbr. articles to profl. jours. Mem. Antique Appraisal Assn. Am. Inc., Costume Soc. Am., New Eng. Appraisers Assn., Questers, Women's Nat. Book Assn. Inc., Nat. Assn. Jewelry Appraisers, Internat. Soc. Appraisers (lectr. ann. meeting), Internat. Platform Assn. Republican. Roman Catholic. Home and Office: 138 Belle Ave Pleasant Hill CA 94523-4640

DOLAN, PATRICK THOMAS, English educator; b. Evanston, Ill., Apr. 17, 1948; s. Patrick Thomas and Mary Agnes (Dobyns) D.; m. Bonnie Katherine Longworth, Dec. 20, 1976; children: Sydney Alison Webster, Anna Foster. BA in English, Met. State Coll., Denver, 1971; MA in English, Colo. State U., 1972. Lectr. in English Arapahoe Cmty. Coll., Littleton, Colo., 1973-75; mem. dept. English Arapahoe Cmty. Coll., 1975—; dir. honors program Arapahoe Cmty. Coll., 1996—. Mem. Colo. Right to Life Com., Denver, 1994—. Mem. SAR, AAUP (state steering com., pres. chpt. 1979-82), Nat. Assn. Scholars (stae exec. com. 1990—), Colo. Edn. Assn. (chpt. exec. com. 1976-78), Christian Leadership Ministries, Colo. C.S. Lewis Soc. (bd. dirs. 1980—), Rocky Mountain G.K. Chesterton Soc. (bd. dirs. 1993—). Republican. Evangelical Lutheran. Office: Arapahoe Cmty Coll 2500 W College Dr Littleton CO 80160

DOLCOURT, JOYCE LINDA, social service administrator; b. Denver, Sept. 24, 1949; d. David I. and Rose (Kraut) Papper; m. John Lawrence Dolcourt, Sept. 3, 1972; children: Bram Austin, Cameron Grant. BA, Temple Buell, 1971; MA, U. Denver, 1974. Dir. Freeman-Sheldon Parent Support Group, Salt Lake City, 1981—; Consumer Mountain States Regional Genetic Svcs. Network, 1987—. Mem. adv. bd. Jewish Reconstructionist Fedn., 1994—, Leadership Legis. Coalition for People with Disabilities, 1994—; mem. Utah Health Policy Commn. Long Term Care Tech. Adv. Group, 1996—. Mem. Nat. Orgn. for Rare Disorders, Alliance of Genetic Support Groups. Office: Freeman-Sheldon Parent Support Group 509 Northmont Way Salt Lake City UT 84103-3324

DOLENCE, MICHAEL G., writer, consultant, educator; b. Oct. 18, 1950; m. Maryann Merena, Sept. 24, 1983. BA in Biology, Russel Sage Coll., 1977; postgrad. in Edn. Adminstrn., SUNY, Albany, 1977-79. Founder/CEO Survival One, St. Johnsville, N.Y., 1971-76; co-founder S&D Computer Tech., Albany, 1977-79; dir. rsch. planning The Commn. on Ind. Colls. and Univs., Albany, 1979-85; strategic planning adminstr. Calif. State U., L.A., 1985-94; pres. Michael G. Dolence & Assocs., Claremont, Calif., 1994—; pres. Sch. Improvement Program, Altadena, Calif., 1989-91. Author: The Survival One Manual of Survival, 1973, Strategic Enrollment Management: A Primer for Campus Administrators, 1993, Transforming Higher Education, 1995, Strategic Enrollment Management: Cases From the Field, 1996, Working Towards Strategic Change: A Step by Step Guide to the Planning Process, 1996, Strategic Change in Colleges and Universities, 1996; syndicated columnist nat. newspapers A Matter of Romance, 1990—; contbr. over 135 articles to profl. jours. Pres. Nine Block Sq. Neighborhood Assn., 1979-83, Baseline Assn. Neighborhoods, Claremont, 1994; chair edn. com. Am. Cancer Soc., Albany, 1980-82; pres. sch. site coun. Elliot Mid. Sch., Altadena, 1989-91. Mem. So. Calif. Planning Forum (v.p. membership, programs, mktg., pres.-elect), Soc. for Coll. and Univ. Planning (seminar faculty 1985—), Am. Assn. Collegiate Registrars and Admissions Officers (seminar faculty 1989—), Poets, Essayists, Novelists, Phi Beta Delta. Office: 848 Decatur Cir Claremont CA 91711-2206

DOLGOW, ALLAN BENTLEY, consulting company executive; b. N.Y.C.; BIE, NYU, 1959, MBA, 1972; postgrad. Hunter Coll., 1976, U. Calif., 1991; m. Nina Kim; children: Nicole, Marc, Ginger, Kimbie. with, Republic Aviation Corp., Farmingdale, N.Y., 1959-60; mgr. Internat. Paper Co., N.Y.C., 1960-73; project mgr. J.C. Penney Co. Inc., N.Y.C., 1973-76; dir. mfg. and planning Morse Electro Products, N.Y.C., 1976-77, exec. mgr. Morse Electrophonic Hong Kong Ltd., 1976-77; internat. project mgr. Revlon Inc., Edison, N.J., 1977-79; cons. SRI Internat., Menlo Park, Calif., 1979-90, Dolgow Cons. Group, Menlo Park, 1996—. With U.S. Army, 1954-56, Germany. Office: 2407 Sharon Rd Menlo Park CA 94025-6800

DOLIBER, DARREL LEE, design engineer, consultant, laboratory manager; b. Mpls., June 19, 1940; s. Russell Clifford Doliber and Helen Carol (Homa) Price; m. Ethel Lorraine Dzivi, June 17, 1962; children: Wendy Lorraine, Heather Leigh; m. Helga Renate Miggo, Oct. 31, 1986. AA, Palomar Coll., 1973. Prodn. engr. Hughes Aircraft Co., Carlsbad, Calif., 1969-74; sr. engr. I.T.T., Roanoke, Va., 1974-77; dir. mfg. Gainsboro Elec. Mfg. Co., Inc., Roanoke, Va., 1977-78; mfg. engr. Litton Industries, Tempe, Ariz., 1978-82; sr. engr. Datagraphix, Inc., San Diego, 1982-84; lab. mgr. S.A.I.C., San Diego, 1984—; proprietor Victoria Rock Bed and Breakfast, 1995—. Contbr. articles in field; patentee in field. Mem. Soc. Photo-Optical and Instrumentation Engrs. Roman Catholic. Home: 2952 N Victoria Dr Alpine CA 91901-3673 Office: Sci Applications Internat Corp 4161 Campus Point Ct San Diego CA 92121-1513

DOLICH, ANDREW BRUCE, sports marketing executive; b. Bklyn., Feb. 18, 1947; s. Mac and Yetta (Weiselter) D.; m. Ellen Andrea Fass, June 11, 1972; children: Lindsey, Caryn, Cory. BA, Am. U., 1969; MEd, Ohio U., 1971. Adminstrv. asst. to gen. mgr. Phila. 76ers, NBA, 1971-74; v.p. Md. Arrows Lacrosse, Landover, 1974-76; mktg. dir. Washington Capitals, NHL, Landover, 1976-78; exec. v.p., gen. mgr. Washington Diplomats Soccer, 1978-80; v.p. bus. ops. Oakland A's Baseball, Calif., 1980-92, exec. v.p., 1993-95; pres., COO Golden State Warriors NBA, Oakland, Calif., 1995-96; pres. Dolich & Assoc. Sports Mktg., Alameda, Calif., 1996—; nat. fundraising chmn. sports adminstrs. program Ohio U., Athens, dir., 1978-82; lectr. sports mktg. U. Calif. Ext. Bd. dirs. Bay Area Sports Hall of Fame, 1982—, Celebrate Oakland Com., Internat. Sports Mktg. Coun., Oakland Zoo Adv. Coun. Recipient Alumni of Yr. award Ohio U. Sports Adminstrs. Program, Athens, 1982; recipient Clio award Am. Advt. Fedn., 1982.

DOLL, LINDA A., artist, educator; b. Bklyn., May 5, 1942; d. William James Harrington and Ann B. (Casey) Cook; m. William John Doll, Feb. 4, 1962; children: Patricia, William Jr. AA, Palomar Coll., 1974; BA, San Diego State U., 1976. chairperson Arts Adv. Com. to Congressman Jim Bates, 1983-84; U.S. Coast Guard Artist, 1985—. Exhibited in group shows with Am. Watercolor Soc., 1985-91 (selected for one yr. nat. travel show, Elsie and David Ject-key award 1988) N.Y.C., 1986, 87, 88, Canton, Ohio, 1985, Nat. Watercolor Soc., Brea, Calif., 1984-89, Watercolor West Annual, Riverside, Calif., 1982, 84-88 (E. Gene Crain Purchase Selection award 1985, Second Place Jurors award 1982), Rocky Mountain Nat., Golden, Colo., 1984-85, Midwest Annual, Davenport, Iowa, 1983, 85, Nat. Watercolor Soc., Riverside, 1985 (selected for one yr. nat. travel show) 88, Canton Ohio, 1985, Watercolor Internat., San Diego, 1978-79, 82-88 (selected for one yr. nat. travel show 1983-84), Watercolor Okla., 1982-84 (Harry Hulett Jr. award 1984), Pa. Soc. Watercolor Painters, Harrisburg, 1988, 1982 (hon. mention); represented in permanent collections including E. Gene Crain Collection, Scripps Hosp., La Jolla, Calif., Redlands Community Hosp., Riverside, Campbell River Community Art Council, Can., Simpact Assocs. Inc., San Diego. Mem. San Diego Watercolor Soc. (past pres., life), Nat. Watercolor Soc. (past pres., life), Knickerbocker Artists, Am. Watercolors Soc. (past juror, bd. dirs.). Office: 17490 Matinal Dr San Diego CA 92127

DOLLINGER, MALIN ROY, physician, author; b. San Francisco, Oct. 7, 1935; s. Mel King and Marilyn Hinda (Rosenbloom) D.; m. Lenore Carole Levy, June 5, 1960; children: Jeffrey, Marc, Deborah, Cynthia. AB in Biology, Stanford U., 1956; MD, Yale U., 1960. Diplomate Am. Bd. Internal Medicine, Am. Bd. Med. Oncology, Am. Bd. Quality Assurance and Utilization Rev. Physicians, Am. Bd. Forensic Examiners, Am. Bd. Forensic Medicine. Intern UCLA, 1960; resident in internal medicine U. Calif. Hosps., San Francisco, 1961, 63-65; USPHS fellow in oncology Meml./Sloan Kettering Inst., N.Y.C., 1965-68; clin. asst. physician Meml. Hosp., N.Y.C., 1969; assoc. Pasadena (Calif.) Tumor Inst., 1970-71; dir. oncology svc. UCLA-Harbor Med. Ctr., Torrance, Calif., 1971-72; ptnr. Cancer Care Assocs., Torrance, 1972-95; v.p. for med. affairs John Wayne Cancer Inst., Santa Monica, Calif., 1995—; Mellor vis. scholar Meml. Hosp., N.Y.C., 1973; clin. prof. medicine U. So. Calif., L.A., 1991—; pres. Smart Tactics Programs, Inc. Author: Everyone's Guide to Cancer Therapy, 1991; assoc. editor poetry Mediphors, 1992—. Poet-at-large L.A. County Med. Assn., 1993—. Lt. USN, 1961-63. Fellow ACP, Am. Coll. Clin. Pharmacology; mem. Am. Cancer Soc. (pres. 1990-93, Achievement awards 1975-94). Home: 700 Via Somonte Palos Verdes Estates CA 90274-1629 Office: John Wayne Cancer Inst 2200 Santa Monica Blvd Santa Monica CA 90404-2301

DOLLIVER, JAMES MORGAN, state supreme court justice; b. Ft. Dodge, Iowa, Oct. 13, 1924; s. James Isaac and Margaret Elizabeth (Morgan) D.; m. Barbara Babcock, Dec. 18, 1948; children: Elizabeth, James, Peter, Keith, Jennifer, Nancy. BA in Polit. Sci. with high honors, Swarthmore Coll., 1949; LLB, U. Wash., 1952; D in Liberal Arts (hon.), U. Puget Sound, 1981. Bar: Wash. 1952. Clk. to presiding justice Wash. Supreme Ct., 1952-53; sole practice Port Angeles, Wash., 1953-54, Everett, Wash., 1961-64; adminstrv. asst. to Congressman Jack Westland, 1955-61, Gov. Daniel J. Evans, 1965-76; justice Supreme Ct. State of Wash., 1976—, chief justice, 1985-87; adj. prof. U. Puget Sound Sch. Law, 1988-92. Chmn. United Way Campaign Thurston County, 1975; chmn. Wash. chpt. Nature Conservancy, 1981-83; pres. exec. bd. Tumwater Area coun. Boy Scouts Am., 1972-73, Wash. State Capital Hist. Assn., 1976-80, 85—, also trustee, 1983-84; trustee Deaconess Children's Home, Everett, 1963-65, U. Puget Sound, 1969—, chair exec. com., 1990-93, Wash. 4-H Found., 1977-93, Claremont (Calif.) Theol. Sem., assoc. mem., Community Mental Health Ctr., 1977-84; bd. mgrs. Swarthmore Coll., 1980-84; bd. dirs. Thurston Mason Community Health Ctr., 1977-84, Thurston Youth Svcs. Soc., 1969-84, also pres., 1983, mem. exec com. 1970-84, Wash. Women's Employment and Edn., 1982-84; mem. jud. coun. United Meth. Ch., 1984-92, gen. cong., 1970-72, 80—, gen. bd. ch. and soc., 1976-84; adv. coun. Ret. Sr. Vol. program, 1979-83; pres. Wash. Ctr. Law-related Edn., 1987-89, bd. dirs. 1987-95; bd. dirs. World Assn. for Children and Parents, 1987-93; trustee U. Wash. Law Sch. Found., 1982-90, Olympic Park Inst., 1988-94; mem. bd. visitors U. Wash. Sch. Social Work, 1987-93; chair bd. visitors U. Puget Sound Sch. Law, 1988-90, bd. visitors, 1988-93; chmn. bd. dirs. Pub. Lands Employee Recognition Fund, 1994—; mem. bd. dirs. St. Peter Hosp. Med. Rehab. Community Adv. Bd., 1993—. With USN, 1943-45; ensign USCG, 1945-46. Recipient award Nat. Council Japanese Am. Citizens League, 1976; Silver Beaver award, 1971; Silver Antelope award, 1976. Mem. ABA, Wash. Bar Assn., Am. Judges Assn., Am. Judicature Soc., Pub. Broadcast Found. (bd. dirs. 1982-95), Masons, Rotary, Phi Delta Theta, Delta Theta Phi. Office: Wash Supreme Ct PO Box 40929 Temple of Justice (AV-11) Olympia WA 98504

DOLSEN, DAVID HORTON, mortician; b. Durango, Colo., Feb. 27, 1940; s. Donald B. and Florence I. (Maxey) D.; BA, Southwestern Coll., 1962; Mortuary Sci. Degree, Dallas-Jones Coll. Mortuary Sci., 1963; m. Jo Patricia Johnson, Dec. 23, 1962; children: Wendy, Douglas. Apprentice, Davis Mortuary, Pueblo, Colo., 1963-64; bus. mgr. George F. McCarty Funeral Home, Pueblo, 1964-65; owner Dolsen Mortuary, Lamar, Colo., 1965-72; pres., gen. mgr., dir. Almont, Inc., Pueblo, 1972-92; sec. Dolsen, Inc., 1967—; pres. Wilson Funeral Dirs. Inc., 1972-92, Carlson Travel Network/Let's Talk Travel, Inc., Pueblo/Denver. Mem. Lamar City Council, 1969-73; mayor City of Lamar, 1971-73. Bd. dirs. Lamar Community Coll., 1967-73, Prowers County Hist. Soc., 1966—, San De Cristo Arts and Conf. Center, 1979-85; bd. dirs., sec. Pueblo Met. Mus. Assn., 1975-79; chmn. council on fin. and adminstrn. Rocky Mountain Conf. United Meth. Ch., 1976-94, del. Gen. Conf., 1980, 84, 88, 92, dir. adminstrv. svcs., treas., 1994—; mem. Pres.'s Council Nat. Meth. Found., 1978-90, Iliff Sch. Theology, 1986-88; trustee, mem. exec. com. Southwestern Coll., Winfield, Kans., 1979—; dist. chmn. Boy Scouts Am., 1981-88; treas., mem. exec. com. Girl Scouts USA, 1981-88; mem. council on fin. and adminstrn. Western Jurisdiction, United Meth. Ch., 1980-88; trustee, gen. council on fin. and adminstrn. United Meth. Ch., 1980-88, gen. coun. on mininstries, mem. gen. bd. of higher edn. and ministries; trustee Meth. Corp., 1988—, United Meth. Ch. Ins. Trust, 1982-88, Iliff Sch. Theology, 1992—; mem. Assn. United Meth. Conf. Pension and Benefit Officers, 1994—, Assn. United Meth. Treas., 1994—; mem. World Service Commn., Meth. Episcopal Ch., 1980-88; mem. gen. council on adminstrn., bd. adminstrn. Ch. of United Brethren in Christ, 1980-88; trustee Sunny Acres Retirement Community, 1986, bd. dirs.; trustee Africa U., Mutare, Zimbabwe. Mem. Am. Soc. Travel Assn. Execs., Nat. Funeral Dirs. Assn., Nat. Selected Morticians, Cremation Assn. Am., Monument Builders N.Am., Colo. Funeral Dirs. Assn., Internat. Assn. Travel Agts., Masons, Shriners, Elks, Rotary (bd. dirs., pres. 1990—, Paul Harris fellow), Pi Sigma Eta, Pi Kappa Delta, Pi Gamma Mu. Home: 1511 S Krameria Denver CO 80224 Office: 2200 S University Blvd Denver CO 80210-4708

DOMAN, MARGARET HORN, land use planning consultant, civic official; b. Portland, Oreg., July 28, 1946; d. Richard Carl and Dorothy May (Teepe) Horn; m. Steve Hamilton Doman, July 12, 1969; children: Jennifer, Kristina, Kathryn. BA, Willamette U., 1968; postgrad., U. Wash., 1968-69, 72. Cert. tchr. Tchr. jr. high Bellevue (Wash.) Sch. Dist., 1969-70, subs. tchr., 1990-91; tchr. jr. high University City (Mo.) Sch. Dist., 1970-71; employment counselor Wash. State Dept. Employment Security, Seattle, 1971; planning commn. mem. City of Redmond, Wash., 1980-83, chmn., 1982-83; city coun. mem. City of Redmond, 1983-91, pres., 1990-91; exec. dir. Eastside Human Svcs. Coun., Redmond, Wash., 1992; employment specialist Wash. State Dept. Employment Security, 1993; cons. land use planning & govt. process Redmond, 1993—; Redmond rep. Puget Sound. Coun. of Govt., Seattle, 1984-91, vice chmn., 1988, 90, chmn. transp., 1986-88, exec. bd., 1987, mem. standing com. on transp., 1986-91; bd. dirs., pres. Eastside Human Svcs. Coun., Bellevue, 1983-91, pres., 1990. Bd. dirs. Redmond YMCA, 1985-86; mem. state exec. com. Nat. History Day, Olympia, Wash., 1986; vol. Bellevue Sch. Dist., 1977-96; bd. dirs. Eastside br. Camp Fire, Bellevue, 1992-94. Mem. Redmond C. of C. (land use and transp. com. 1994—), Bellevue Rotary. Republican. Unitarian. Home: 2104 180th Ct NE Redmond WA 98052-6032

DOMENICI, PETE (VICHI DOMENICI), senator; b. Albuquerque, May 7, 1932; s. Cherubino and Alda (Vichi) D.; m. Nancy Burk, Jan. 15, 1958; children: Lisa, Peter, Nella, Clare, David, Nanette, Helen, Paula. Student, U. Albuquerque, 1950-52; BS, U. N.Mex., 1954, LLD (hon.); LLB, Denver U., 1958; LLD (hon.), Georgetown U. Sch. Medicine; HHD (hon.), N.Mex. State U. Bar: N.Mex. 1958. Tchr. math. pub. schs. Albuquerque, 1954-55; ptnr. firm Domenici & Bonham, Albuquerque, 1958-72; chmn., ex-officio mayor Albuquerque, 1967; mem. U.S. Senate from N.Mex., 1972—; city commr. Albuquerque, 1966-68; mem. appropriations com., energy and natural resources com., chmn. subcom. on energy rsch. and devel.; mem. com. on environ. and pub. works, mem. govtl. affairs com.; chmn. budget com., com. on Indian affairs; mem. Presl. Adv. Com. on Federalism. Mem. Gov.'s Policy Bd. for Law Enforcement, 1967-68; chmn. Model Cities Joint Adv. Com., 1967-68. Recipient Nat. League of Cities award Outstanding Performance in Congress; Disting. Svc. award Tax Found., 1986, Legislator of Yr. award Nat. Mental Health Assn., 1987, public sector leadership award, 1996. Mem. Nat. League Cities, Middle Rio Grande Council Govts. Office: US Senate 328 Hart Senate Office Bldg Washington DC 20510-0001

DOMENICO, FRANCES ANN, school counselor; b. Detroit, Jan. 18, 1945; d. Humphrey Joseph and Melva Mary (Lynch) Desmond; m. Benedict Albert Domenico, Mar. 29, 1969; children: Daniel Desmond, Anna Nicole, John Patrick. BA, U. Mich., 1966; MA with distinction, U. Colo., 1970. Cert. tchr., sch. counselor, Colo. Pub. rels. clk. U-M TV Ctr., Ann Arbor, Mich., 1964-66; tchr. Denver Pub. Schs., 1966-68, Jeffco (Colo.) Pub. Schs., 1968-72; tchr. Boulder (Colo.) Pub. Schs., 1976-91, counselor, 1991—. Sec. Homeowner Soc., Boulder, 1983; county and state del. Dem. Party, Boulder, 1992. Regents alumni scholar U. Mich., 1962-66, Colo. Tchrs. scholar U. Colo., 1967-68. Mem. NEA, Colo. Edn. Assn., Am. Sch. Counselors Assn., Colo. Sch. Counselors Assn. (regional rep. 1996—). Roman Catholic. Home: 2489 Briarwood Dr Boulder CO 80303 Office: Baseline Mid Sch 700 20th St Boulder CO 80302

DOMEÑO, EUGENE TIMOTHY, elementary education educator, principal; b. L.A., Oct. 22, 1938; s. Digno and Aurora Mary (Roldan) D. AA, Santa Monica (Calif.) City Coll., 1958; BA, Calif. State U., 1960, MA, 1966. Cert. elem. tchr., gen. sch svcs, special secondary tchr. Elem. tchr. L.A. Unified Sch. Dist., 1960-70; asst. prin. Pomona (Calif.) Unified Sch. Dist., 1970-71, prin., 1971—; cons. testing and evaluation Pomona Unified Sch. Dist., 1990—. With USNR, 1957-65. Recipient PTA Hon. Svc. award Granada Elem. PTA, Granada Hills, Calif., 1960, Armstrong Sch. PTA, Diamond Bar, Calif., 1990, Calif. Disting. Sch. Calif. Dept. Edn., 1989, Nat. Blue Ribbon Sch. U.S. Dept. Edn., Washington, 1990, Prin. and Leadership award, 1990. Mem. ASCD, Nat. Assn. Elem. Sch. Prins. (Prin. of Leadership award with Nat. Safety Com., 1991), Nat. Assn. Year Round Sch., Assn. Calif. Sch. Administrs., Pomona Elem. Prin.'s Assn., Diamond Bar C. of C. (edn. com.). Office: Neil Armstrong Elem Sch 22750 Beaverhead Dr Diamond Bar CA 91765-1566

DOMHOFF, GEORGE WILLIAM, psychology and sociology educator; b. Youngstown, Ohio, Aug. 6, 1936; s. George William and Helen Susanne (Cornett) D.; m. Judith Clare Boman, Aug. 20, 1961 (div. July 1975); children: Lynne Starr, Lori Susanne, William Packard, Joel James. BA, Duke U., 1958; MA, Kent State U., 1959; PhD, U. Miami, 1962. Asst. prof. psychology L.A. State U., 1962-65; from asst. prof. to prof. psychology and sociology U. Calif., Santa Cruz, 1965—. Author: Who Rules America?, 1967, The Higher Circles, 1970, Fat Cats and Democrats, 1972, The Bohemian Grove and Other Retreats, 1974, Who Really Rules in New Haven?, 1978, The Powers That Be, 1979, Who Rules America Now?, 1983, The Mystique Dreams, 1985, The Power Elite and the State, 1990, State Autonomy or Class Dominance, 1996, Finding Meaning in Dreams: A Quantitative Approach, 1996; co-author: Jews in the Protestant Establishment, 1982, Blacks in the White Establishment, 1991. Harbor commr. Santa Cruz Port Dist., 1977-78. Office: U Calif Dept Psychology Santa Cruz CA 95064

DOMINGUEZ, EDDIE, artist; b. Tucumcari, N.Mex., Oct. 17, 1957. BFA, Cleve. Inst. Art, 1981; MFA, Alfred U., 1983. Grad. asst., ceramics and visual design courses Alfred (N.Y.) U., 1981-83; artist-in-residence, lectr. Ohio State U., Columbus, 1984; artist-in-edn. N.Mex. Arts Divsn., Santa Fe, 1985-86; artist-in-residence Cleve. Inst. Art, 1986; artist-in-residence, lectr. U. Mont., Missoula, 1988; Lectr., presenter workshops, mem. panels Ill. Arts Coun., Chgo., 1994, NEA, Washington, 1994, Ariz. Commn. on the Arts, 1994, Concordia U., Montreal, Que., Can., 1994, Mass. Coll. Art, Boston, 1994, Bennington (Vt.) Coll., 1994, 95, 96, Peters Valley, Layton, N.J., 1994, Firehouse Art Ctr., Norman, Okla., 1994, Haystack Mountain Sch. Arts & Crafts, Deer Isle, Maine, 1994, Ghost Ranch, Abiquiu, N.Mex., 1995, We. States Arts Fedn., Santa Fe, 1995, Colo. Coun. on the Arts, Boulder, 1995, Durango (Colo.) Art Ctr., 1995, Tamarind Inst., Albuquerque, 1995, 96, Kansas City (Mo.) Ar Inst., 1995, Hallmark Cards, Kansas City, 1996, Wichita (Kans.) Ctr. Arts, 1996, La. State U., Baton Rouge, 1996, Idaho State Arts Coun. Grants, Boise, 1996, Mattie Rhodes Counseling and Art Ctr., Kansas City, 1996, Southwest Ctr. Crafts, San Antonio, 1997, Very Spl. Arts, Albuquerque, 197, Topeka (Kans.) and Shawnee County Pub. Libr., 1997, numerous others. Solo exhbns. include Pro Art Gallery, St. Louis, 1990, Mobilia Gallery, Cambridge, Mass., 1990, Munson Gallery, Santa Fe, 1990, 92, 94, 95, 97, Mariposa Gallery, Albuquerque, 1990, Joanne Rapp Gallery, Scottsdale, Ariz., 1991, 93, 95, Felicita Found., Escondido, Calif., 1991, Tucumcari (N.Mex.) Area Vocat. Sch., 1992, Manchester Art Ctr., Pitts., 1993, Wetsman Collection, Detroit, 1993, Clovis (N.Mex.) C.C., 1993, Firehouse Art Ctr., 1994, Kavesh Gallery, Sun Valley, Idaho, 1995, Jan Weiner Gallery, Kansas City, 1995, 96, numerous others; group exhbns. include Fred Jones Mus. Art, U. Okla., Norman, 1995, Roswell (N.Mex.) Mus. & Art Ctr., 1995, Nancy Margolis Gallery, N.Y.C., 1995, Sharadin Art Gallery, Kutztown (Pa.) U., 1995, Richard Kavesh Gallery, 1995, Jan Weiner Gallery, 1995, Ariz. State U. Art Mus., Tempe, 1995, Islip (N.Y.) Mus., 1995, Bruce Kapson Gallery, Santa Monica, Calif., 1996, Site Sante Fe Gallery, 1996, Johnston County C.C., Overland Parks, Kans., 1996, Jane Haslem Gallery, Washington, 196, Karen Ruhlen Gallery, Santa Fe, 1996, Margo Jacobson Gallery, Portland, Oreg., 1996, Very Spl. Arts Gallery, Albuquerque, 1997, Joanne Rapp Gallery, 1997, numerous others; pub. art project include, among others, murals at Great Brook Valley Health Ctr., Worcester, Mass., 1994, Mass. Gen. Hosp., 1996; represented in many permanent collections, including Cooper-Hewitt, N.Y.C., Mus. Fine Arts, Santa Fe, Cleve. Inst. Art, Fed. Reserve Bank, Dallas, Roswell Mus. and Art Ctr., Albuquerque Mus. Fine Arts, City of Tucson (Ariz.), Phoenix Airport, pvt. collections. Recipient numerous grants, including NEA fellowships, 1986, 88, Kohler Arts-in-Industry grant, Sheboygan, Wis., 1988, Percent for Art Project grant, Phoenix Arts Coun., 1990, 1992; recipient various prizes, including Clay, Fiber and Wood Best in Show, Albuquerque, 1984, Clay in '87 1st place award, Albuquerque St. Fair Exhbn., 1987. Home: 37 Laughing Raven Rd Santa Fe NM 87505

DOMINO, KAREN BARBARA, anesthesiology educator; b. Chgo., Oct. 21, 1951; d. Edward F. and Antoinette (Kaczorowski) D.; m. Gene L. Brenowitz, June 7, 1975; children: Willa Domino Brenowitz, Noah Domino Brenowitz. BA, Vassar Coll., 1973; MA in Psychology, U. N.Mex., 1974; MD, U. Mich., 1978. Diplomate Am. Bd. Anesthesiology. Asst. prof. anesthesiology U. Pa., Phila., 1982-83, U. Pitts., 1983-86; asst. prof. anesthesiology U. Wash., Seattle, 1986-91, assoc. prof. anesthesiology, 1991—; adj. assoc. prof. neurologic surgery U. Wash., Seattle, 1991—; assoc. examiner Am. Bd. Anesthesiology, 1995—. Contbr. articles to med. jours.; editl. bd. Am. Jour. Anesthesiology, 1994—, Jour. Cardiothoracic Vascular Anesthesiology, 1995—. Recipient B.B. Sankey Anesthesia Advancement award, 1990, Clin. Investigator award Nat. Heart, Lung, and Blood Inst., 1990-95. Mem. Internat. Anesthesia Rsch. Soc., Soc. Neurosurg. Anesthesia and Critical Care, Assn. Univ. Anesthesiologists (councillor-at-large), Am. Soc. Anesthesiologists (respiration subcom., com. on sci. papers), Phi Beta Kappa, Alpha Omega Alpha. Office: Univ of Wash Sch of Medicine Box 356540 Seattle WA 98195

DOMIZIO, DAN, physician assistant, consultant; b. N.Y.C., Nov. 5, 1944; s. Joseph and Harriet (Zarmon) DiDomizio; m. Honorah Christina Phillips, Sept. 13, 1973; children: Jude, Zoë. BS, CCNY, 1966; B of Health Sci., Duke U., 1975; MPH, U. N.C., 1982. Cert. physician asst., Hawaii; cert. ACLS, PALS. Health generalist Peace Corps, Satawal, Micronesia, 1966-69; cross cultural trainer Peace Corps, Saipan, Micronesia, 1970; med. officer Peace Corps/Ministry of Health, Barbuda, West Indies, 1976-78; clin. coord./clin. assoc., P.A. program Duke U. Med. Ctr., Durham, N.C., 1978-82; field program dir. Project Concern Internat., Belize, Ctrl. Am., 1982-85; physician asst./cmty. health coord. Project Concern Internat., Chilchinbeto, Ariz., 1985-86; physician asst./clinic mgr. Indian Health Svc. Clinic, Supai, Ariz., 1986; cmty. health educator U. N.C. Family Medicine Residency Program, Chapel Hill, 1986-87; program dir./physician asst. Chilchinbeto Health Program, 1988-91; physician asst./emergency rm. staff Waianae (Hawaii) Coast Comprehensive Health Ctr., 1991-95; dir., pres., cons. Calumet Devel. Svcs. Inc., Pahoa, Hawaii, 1987—; dir. physician asst. program devel. U. Hawaii, Hilo, 1995—; physician asst./med. staff Pahoa (Hawaii) Family Health Ctr., 1995—; cons. Essex C.C., Balt., 1987, Peace Corps, Papua New Guinea, 1987, Chilchinbeto Health and Devel. Corp., 1988-91, physican asst. tng. program U. Hawaii, 1994—; clin. preceptor N.C. Student Rural Health Coalition, summers 1979, 80, 81; chmn. Gov.'s Subcom. Studying Safety and Efficiency of Out of Hosp. Childbirth and Midwifery Practice in N.C., 1981-83; co-organizer Hawaii Health Team's ann. visits to Yap State, Micronesia, Aug. 91, 92, 93, 94; participant Sugarloaf Inst. for New Physicians Assts. Program Dirs., 1994; chmn. Hawaii State Primary Care Roundtable, 1994—. Author: (chpt.) The Unfinished Health Agenda, 1994. Recipient grant Robert Wood Johnson Found., 1989, grant The Queen's Health Sys., 1994. Mem. APHA, Am. Acad. Physician Assts., Hawaii Acad. Physician Assts. (pres. elect.), Hawaii Pub. Health Assn., Nat. Coun. for Internat. Health. Home: 12-4592 Kalapana Rd Pahoa HI 96778

DOMMISSE, JOHN VLOK, nutritional, metabolic physician, psychiatrist; b. Worcester, South Africa, Oct. 19, 1940; arrived in Can., 1967; came to U.S., 1976; s. John Herbert and Louise Adriana (Vlok) D.; m. Marion Linsingen, Apr. 2, 1965 (div. Feb. 1972); m. Bettina Dignas, Oct. 21, 1972; children: Liesl Angelique, Janneke Andria. MBChB, U. Capetown Med. Sch., 1965. Rotating intern in medicine, pediat., obstetrics, gynecology, psychiatry, emergency medicine # 2 Mil. Hosp., CapeTown, South Africa, 1966; gen. practice resident Bridgeport (Conn.) Hosp., 1967; clin. med. officer of health Worcester, South Africa, 1971-73; sr. med. officer Eben Donges Gen. Hosp., Worcester, 1974; demonstrator in psychiatry U. Toronto, 1975-76; dir. out-patient svcs. Maryview Psychiat. Hosp., Cmty. Mental Health Ctr., Portsmouth, Va., 1976-78; pvt. practice psychiatry and nutritional medicine Portsmouth, 1978-94, pvt. practice metabolic medicine, 1988-94; pvt. practice metabolic medicine Tucson, 1994—; pvt. gen. practice, Worcester, 1967, Toronto, 1971. Contbr. articles to profl. jours. Recipient Benjamin Rush award Benjamin Rush Soc., 1985, Book award Coalition Against Racism & Apartheid, 1985. Fellow Royal Coll. Physicians of Can. (cert. in psychiatry); mem. Can. Psychiat. Assn., Physicians for Nat. Health Program, African Nat. Congress of South Africa (health dept. 1978—), Com. Health in So. Africa, Nat./Va./Portsmouth Alliance for the Mentally Ill, Tidewater Acad. Psychiatry, Portsmouth Acad. Medicine, Tidewater Nutrition Coun., Complementary Med. Assn., Am. Preventive Med. Assn. Democrat. Unitarian. Office: Nutrnl-Mtblc & Psych Med 1840 E River Rd Ste 210 Tucson AZ 85718-5892

DOMONDON, OSCAR, dentist; b. Cebu City, Philippines, July 4, 1924; Came to U.S., 1954, naturalized, 1956.; s. Antero B. and Ursula (Maglasang) D. ; m. Vicky Domondon. children—Reinelda, Carolyn, Catherine, Oscar. DMD, Philippine Dental Coll., 1951; DDS, Loma Linda U., 1964. Dentist Manila Sanitarium and Hosp., 1952, U.S. Embassy, Manila, 1952-54; pvt. practice dentistry Long Beach, Calif., 1964—; Dentist, Children's Dental Health Center, Long Beach, part-time, 1964-68; past mem. Calif. State Bd. Dental Examiners. Past pres., Filipino Community Action Services, Inc. With AUS, 1946-49, U.S. Army, 1954-60. Fellow Acad. Dentistry Internat., Acad. Gen. Dentistry, Internat. Inst. Community Svc., Acad. Internat. Dental Studies, Internat. Coll. Dentists, Am. Coll. Dentists (life), Acad. Continuing Edn.; mem. ADA (life), Am. Soc. Dentistry Children, Am. Acad. Oral Radiology (award 1964), Internat. Acad. Orthodontists, Am. Soc. Clin. Hypnosis, Am. Endodontic Soc., Western Conf. Dental Examiners and Dental Sch. Deans, Fedn. of Assns. of Health Regulatory Bds., Calif. Assn. Fgn. Dental Grads. (past pres.), Filipino Dental Soc. (past pres.), Philippine Tech. and Profl. Soc. (v.p.), Am. Acad. Dentistry for Handicapped, Am. Assn. Dental Examiners (life), Nat. Assn. Filipino Dentists in Am. (past pres.), Pierre Fauchard Acad., Knights of Rizal (comdr.), Lions (past pres.), Elks (past chmn. rangers), Masons, Shrine Noble, Am. Legion (comdr. Post 688), Disabled Am. Vets. (comdr. dist. 7, comdr. chpt. 17), VFW (comdr. post 875). Republican. Home: 3570 Aster St Seal Beach CA 90740-2801 Office: 3714 Atlantic Ave Long Beach CA 90807-3409

DONAHOE, PETER ALOYSIUS, lawyer. BA in Polit. Sci., U. Wash., Seattle, 1957; JD, Harvard U., 1960. Bar: Hawaii 1961. Assoc. Carlsmith, Carlsmith, Wichman & Case, Hilo, Hawaii, 1960-63; staff Senate Majority Hawaii State Senate, Honolulu, 1963; dep. Atty. Gen. anti-trust divsn. State of Hawaii, Honolulu, 1963-65; asst. U.S. Atty. U.S. Dept. Justice, Honolulu, 1965-67; ptnr. Robertson, Castle & Anthony, Honolulu, 1967-71; pvt. practice Honolulu, 1973-91; dir. Atty.'s and Judge's Assistance Program Supreme Ct. for State of Hawaii, Honolulu, 1993—; vis. prof. polit. sci. Am. Coll. Switzerland, Leysan, 1971-73; chmn. liquor commn., City and County of Honolulu, 1969; lectr. Hawaii Inst. CLE. Contbr. articles to profl. jours. Mem. Hawaii State Bar Assn. Home: 55 S Kukui St Apt 3115 Honolulu HI 96813

DONAHOO, STANLEY ELLSWORTH, orthopaedic surgeon; b. St. Joseph, Mo., Dec. 3, 1933; s. Charles Ellsworth and Opal (Cole) D.; m. Cheryl R. Donahoo; children: Shan Maureen, Brian Patrick, Mary Kathleen, Jane Eileen; stepchildren: Trina Person, Kevin. MD, U. Wash., 1963. Resident, Duke U., Durham, N.C., 1967-68, U.S. Naval Hosp., Oakland, Calif., 1963-67; commd. lt., U.S. Navy, 1963 advanced through grades to lt. comdr. (orthopaedic surgeon), 1971; practice medicine, specializing in orthopaedic surgery, Roseburg, Oreg., 1971—; chief surgery Mercy Hosp., Roseburg, 1973-74; chief surgery Douglas Community Hosp., Roseburg, 1973, chief of staff, 1974—; cons. Guam Meml. Hosp., co-dir. rehab. unit, 1970-71; cons. orthopaedic surgery VA Hosp., Roseburg, 1971—; chmn. Douglas County (Oreg.) Emergency Med. Services Com., 1973-74. Trustee Douglas Community Hosp., 1975. Served with AUS, 1952-55. Diplomate Am. Bd. Orthopaedic Surgery. Fellow Am. Acad. Orthopaedic Surgeons (admissions com. region 14), North Pacific Orthopaedic Soc. (v.p. 1984-85, trustee 1991-95, pres.-elect 1996—); mem. Piedmont Orthopaedic Soc., Western Orthopedic Assn. (pres. Oreg. chpt. 1996—), Oreg. Med. Assn. (mem. sports medicine com., med. rev. com. 1981), Guam Med. Soc. (pres. 1970), Am. Trauma Soc. (founding mem.), Roseburg C. of C. (bd. govs. 1978—). Home: 173 Songbird Ct Roseburg OR 97470-9400 Office: 1813 W Harvard Blvd Ste 201 Roseburg OR 97470-2790

DONAHUE, PHILIP RICHARD, artist, educator; b. Detroit, Apr. 1, 1943; s. Theodore R. and Margaret M. (Schneider) D. BA, St. Peter's Coll., Jersey City, 1969; MA, Spring Hill Coll., Mobil, Ala., 1974, Jesuit Sch. Theology, Berkeley, Calif., 1977; PhD, U. Calif., Berkeley, 1985. Joined S.J., Roman Cath. Ch., 1964, ordained priest, 1976. Artist, educator, adminstr., priest S.J., Rome, 1964-82; v.p. Link Art Internat., San Francisco, 1982-86; owner, adminstr., educator, artist Donahue Studios, Oakland, Calif., 1986—. Author: Visual Hermeneutics, 1985, Meaning in Visual Art, 1992; exhibited in groups shows at AT Gallery, Tokyo, 1982-91, Hunger Project, San Francisco, 1982-85, Farralon Co., San Francisco, 1991-94, Link Art Internat. Ltd., San Francisco, 1982-94, others; represented in permanent collections including City Hall, Jersey City, Gov.'s Mansion, Birmingham, St. Peter's Coll., Jersey City, Farralon Co., San Francisco, Grace Cathedral, San Francisco. Recipient award U.S. dir. fine arts Hakuhodo, Tokyo, 1991-83, Oscar d'Italia Acad. Italia, Calvatone, 1985. Mem. Internat. Soc. Artists (bd. dirs. No. Hemisphere 1977—). Studio: 3700 Virden Ave Oakland CA 94619-1537

DONAHUE, RICHARD KING, athletic apparel executive, lawyer; b. Lowell, Mass., July 20, 1927; s. Joseph P. and Dorothy F. (Riordan) D.; m. Nancy Lawson, Sept. 19, 1953; children: Gail M., Timothy J., Michael R., Nancy C., Richard K., Daniel J., Alicia A., Stephen J., Christopher P., Tara E., Philip A. A.B., Dartmouth Coll., 1948; J.D., Boston U., 1951. Bar: Mass. 1951. Ptnr. Donahue & Donahue, Attys., P.C., Lowell, Mass., 1951-60, 63-90; v.p., chmn. bd., Nike, Inc., 1990— ; asst. to Pres. Kennedy, Washington, 1960-63. Served with USNR. Recipient Herbert Harley award Am. Judicature Soc., 1981. Mem. Am. Bd. Trial Advs., ABA (gov., ho. of dels. 1972—), Am. Coll. Trial Lawyers, Mass. Bar Assn. (past pres., Gold medal 1979), New Eng. Bar Assn. (past pres.). Clubs: Union League (Boston); Vesper Country (Tyngsboro, Mass.); Fed. City (Washington); Yorick (Lowell). Office: Nike Inc 1 Bowerman Dr Beaverton OR 97005-0979*

DONALDSON, GEORGE BURNEY, chemical company executive; b. Oakland, Calif., Mar. 16, 1945; s. George T. and L.M. (Burney) D.; m. Jennifer L. Bishop, Feb. 16, 1974; children: Dawn Marie, Matthew George. AS in Criminology, Porterville Coll., 1972. Registered environ. assessor, Calif.; cert. transp. specialist. Police officer City of Lindsay (Calif.), 1966-67; distbn. mgr. Ortho div. Chevron Chem. Co., Lindsay, 1967-73; safety specialist Wilbur-Ellis Co. Fresno, Calif., 1973-77, safety dir., 1977-79, dir. corporate regulatory affairs, 1979—; industry rep. to White House Inter-Govtl. Sci. Engrng., and Tech. Adv. Panel, Task Force on Transp. of Non-Nuclear Hazardous Materials, 1980; industry rep. Transp. Rsch. Bd.'s Nat. Strategies Conf. on Transp. of Hazardous Materials and Wastes in the 1980's, NAS, 1981, Hazardous Materials Transp. Conf., Nat. Conf. of State Legislatures, 1982. speaker and moderator in field; dir. Western Fertilizer and Pesticide Safety seminar, Sacramento, 1979; speaker Southeastern Agrl. Chem. Safety seminar, Winston-Salem, N.C., 1986. Chmn. industry/govt. task force for unique on-site hazardous waste recycling, devel. task force for computerized regulatory software and data base system, devel. task force modifying high expansion foam tech. for fire suppression; hazardous materials adviser, motor carrier rating com. Calif. Hwy. Patrol, 1978-79. With U.S. Army, 1962-65. Mem. Western Agrl. Chems. Assn. (past chmn. transp., distbn. and safety com., outstanding mem. of year 1981, govtl. affairs com., regulatory affairs com., trustee polit. action com.), Nat. Agrl. Chems. Assn. (past chmn. transp. and distbn. com., occupational safety and health com., environ. mgmt. com., state affairs com., moderator spring conf. 1989), Am. Soc. Safety Engrs., Calif. Fertilizer Assn. (transp. and distbn. com., environ. com.), Fresno Agri. Round Table, Fresno City and County C. of C. (agrl. steering com., govt. affairs com.), Calif. C. of C. (environ. policy com.), Am. Legion, Elks. Republican. Office: 191 W Shaw Ave Ste 107 Fresno CA 93704-2826

DONALDSON, MARY KENDRICK, nurse; b. Tifton, Ga., June 25, 1937; d. Howard Story and Trudy (Donalson) Marlin; m. Harvey Kendrick Sr., Apr. 13, 1953 (dec. 1965); children: Jerome, Micheal, Harvey Jr., Merry, Sheila, Larry; m. Isaac Hargett, Feb. 16, 1985. AA, Compton (Calif.) Coll., 1969; BS, Pepperdine U., 1972, MA, 1976; diploma in nursing, SW Coll., Los Angeles, 1984. Staff nurse St. Francis Hosp., Lynwood, Calif., 1965-67; pvt. duty nurse Profl. Nurse's Registry, L.A., 1967-82; elem. tchr. Compton Sch. Dist., Calif., 1975-80; caseworker, clk. L.A. County Probation Dept., 1980-90, dep. probation officer, 1990—; pediatric nurse companion Personal Care Health Service, Torrance, Calif., 1984—; home economist Dept. Welfare, Compton, 1970-72; asst. dir. Century Plaza Hotel, Century City, Calif., 1971-72. Chairperson Com. To Elect Garland Hardeman For Councilman, Inglewood, Calif., 1987. Exec. Housekeeping scholarship Century Plaza Hotel, Los Angeles, 1971. Mem. Fellow Am. Home Econs. Assn., Pepperdine Alumni Assn., Pepperdine's Kappa-Kappa Sorority, Am. Nurse's Assn. Democrat. Home: 4730 Falcon Ave Long Beach CA 90807-1204 Office: L A County Probation Dept 1601 Eastlake Ave Los Angeles CA 90033-1009

DONALDSON, WILBURN LESTER, property management corporation executive; b. St. Augustine, Fla., Mar. 2, 1938; s. Chester Campbell and Dovie (Pratt) D.; m. Patricia Lilias Babcock, Sept. 11, 1956; children: John Randolph, David Chester, James Robert. BA, San Francisco State U., 1968, MBA, 1971. Transp. clk. Armour Food Co., San Francisco, 1958-60, transp. mgr., 1960-65, product mgr., 1965-70; So. Calif. sales mgr. Armour Food Co., L.A., 1970-73; tng. mgr. Armour Food Co., Phoenix, 1973-77, nat. mktg. mgr., 1977-80; region sales mgr. Armour Food Co., Pitts., 1980-83; nat. tng. mgr. Armour Food Co., Phoenix, 1983-84; pres. Allied Investment Mgrs., Inc., Phoenix, 1984—. Author: How To Use Psychological Leverage, 1978, Conversational Magic, 1978, Behavioral Supervision, 1980, Human Resource Development, 1986. Republican. Home: 350 E Deepdale Rd Phoenix AZ 85022-4229 Office: Allied Investment Inc 718 E Bethany Home Rd Phoenix AZ 85014-2104

DONDER, PAULINE VERONICA, legal secretary, library page; b. Torrington, Conn., Apr. 2, 1951; d. Charles Hansen and Veronica Donder Pavek; m. Manuel Angel Guillen, July 17, 1976 (div. Sept. 10, 1983); children: Veronica, Juliana. Grad., Wykeham Rise, Washington, Conn., 1969; student, Ithaca Coll., 1969-70, Denver U., 1970-71. With Vagabond Ranch, Granby, Colo., 1951-74. Author: Crisis Paper for Colorado Parents, 1993; co-author: Youth on the Edge, 1994. Mem. juvenile justice subcom. Safe City Summit, Denver, 1994, Homeless and Runaway Youth Adv. Group, Denver, 1994, homeless youth subcom. Colo. Children's Code Recodification, 1995; mentor Denver Kids, Inc., 1996. Home: 4180 Wolff St Denver CO 80212

DONE, ROBERT STACY, criminal investigation specialist, consultant; b. Tucson, Apr. 7, 1965; s. Richard Avon Done and Nancy Jane (Meeks) Burks; m. Michele Renae Barwick, May 17, 1987 (div. Mar. 1990); m. Elizabeth Evans Robinson, Feb. 20, 1993. AS in Law Enforcement, Mo. So. State Coll., 1987, BS in Criminal Justice Adminstrn., 1987; MPA, U. Ariz., 1992. Lic. realtor, Ariz., pvt. investigator, Ariz. Criminal investigator Pima County, Tucson, 1988—; pres. Data Methods Corp., Tucson, 1984—. Mem. Am. Evaluation Assn., Acad. Mgmt. Republican. Home: PO Box 64967 Tucson AZ 85728-4967 Office: Pima County Pub Defender 2337 E Ajo Way Tucson AZ 85713-6215

DONEGAN, ELIZABETH ANN, anesthesiologist; b. Springfield, Mo., Dec. 6, 1946; d. George Joseph and Elizabeth (Shepard) D. BS in Biology, Webster Coll., 1968; MS in Microbiology, U. Mo., 1972, MD, 1975. Diplomate Am. Bd. Anatomic and Clinical Pathology. Intern in medicine U.S. Pub. Health Hosp., San Francisco, 1975-76; resident lab. medicine, anatomic pathology U. Calif., San Francisco, 1976-80; asst. rsch. physician, adj. lectr. U. Calif., 1980-81, asst. clin. prof., 1981-89, assoc. prof., 1989-93, resident in anesthesia, 1993-96; pathologist Good Samaritan Hosp., San Jose, Calif., 1981-82, Naval Hosp., Oakland, Calif., 1982-85; med. dir. blood bank Moffitt-Long Hosps., chief blood bank and donor ctr., U. Calif., San Francisco, 1985-91. Comdr. USNR, 1985-95. Office: 5400 Golden Gate Oakland CA 94618

DONELSON, KENNETH LAVERN, English language educator; b. Holdrege, Nebr., June 16, 1927; s. Lester Homer Irving and Minnie Irene (Lyons) D.; m. Virginia Juanita Watts (div. 1970); children: Sheryl Lynette George, Kurt Allen; m. Annette Whetton (div. 1983); m. Marie Elizabeth Smith, May 30, 1983; 1 child, Jeanette, 1 stepchild, Jenny. BA, U. Iowa, 1950, MA, 1951, PhD, 1963. English tchr. Glidden (Iowa) High Sch., 1951-56, Thomas Jefferson High Sch., Cedar Rapids, Iowa, 1956-63; asst. prof. English Edn. Kans. State U., Manhattan, 1963-65; asst. prof. English Ariz. State U., Tempe, 1965-67, assoc. prof. English, 1967-71, prof. English, 1971—. Co-author: Literature for Today's Young Adults, 1980, 5th edit., 1997, Inspiring Literacy, 1993; author: The Student's Right to Read, 1972. With USN, 1945-46. Mem. Nat. Coun. Tchrs. English (chmn. conf. on English edn. 1974-76, Award for Outstanding Contbn. to the Field of Adolescent Lit. 1983, pres. adolescent lit. assembly 1980-81, co-editor English Jour. 1980-87). Democrat. Episcopalian.

DONER, JOHN ROLAND, hospital administrator; b. Ontario, Oreg., May 6, 1949; s. L. L. and Majorie R. (Robinson) D.; m. Kathleen M. Lang, Mar. 6, 1970; children: J. R., Erica C. BA in Bus. Adminstrn., Boise (Idaho) State U., 1971. Lic. nursing home adminstr., Idaho. Disability claims adjucator Idaho Disability Determinators Unit, Boise, 1972-74, quality assurance specialist, 1974-76, unit mgr., 1976-78; mgmt. and fin. cons. Idaho Dept. Health & Welfare, Boise, 1978-81; asst. adminstr. Idaho State Sch. & Hosp., Nampa, 1981-92, adminstrv. dir., 1993—. Sec., treas. bd. dirs. Idaho Spl. Olympics, Boise, 1985-92; vice chmn. Nampa Cmty. Work Release Ctr. Bd., 1987—; mem. adv. bd. Bogus Basin Recreation Assn. Inc., Boise, 1987—; mem., pres., bd. dirs. Archie B. Teater Fund for Hanidcapped, Inc., 1991—. Mem. Profl. Ski Instrs. Am. (cert.). Home: 10341 Shiloh Dr Boise ID 83704-2736 Office: Idaho State Sch & Hosp 3100 11th Ave N Ext Nampa ID 83687-3188

DONGES, SAMUEL ARNOLD, process control engineer; b. Ashland, Ohio, Oct. 9, 1958; s. George H. and Cathleen (Vanosdal) D. BSEE, Metro State Coll., 1971. Quality control Martin Co., Denver, 1960-61; water commr. City of Frisco (Colo.), 1961-65; contract adminstr. MSI of Tenn., Huntsville, Ala., 1966-68; svc. mgr. BCS Assocs., Orlando, Fla., 1968-69; prodn. supr. Honeywell, Denver, 1969-70; process control engr. Autometrics, Boulder, Colo., 1970—. Designer several process control sys. for So. Peru Copper, Indpls. Light & Power, CODELCO, Chile. With USN, 1956-60. Mem. Instrument Soc. Am., Elks, Masons, Scotish Rite, York Rite.

DONICA, CHERYL MARIE, elementary education educator; b. Greensburg, Ind., Aug. 26, 1953; d. Thurman Lloyd and Kathryn Lucille (Chadwell) D. BS in Edn., Ind. U., 1975, MS in Edn., 1979. Tchr. Decatur County Schs., Greensburg, Ind., 1975-81, Escola Americana de Brasilia, Brazil, 1981-85, Fontana (Calif.) Unified Schs., 1986—; mentor tchr. Fontana Unified Schs., 1989-92, 93-94, program specialist, 1990-92, 96—, reading recovery tchr., 1993—. Reading and Literacy Merit award Arrowhead Reading Coun., San Bernardino, Calif., 1989. Mem. NEA, Calif. Tchrs. Assn., Internat. Reading Assn., Assn. Childhood Edn. Internat. Calif. Kindergarten Assn., Nat. Assn. Edn. of Young Children. Republican. Methodist. Home: 1965 Coulston St Apt 6 Loma Linda CA 92354-1741 Office: Tokay Elem 7846 Tokay Ave Fontana CA 92336-1827

DONLEY, DENNIS LEE, school librarian; b. Port Hueneme, Calif., July 19, 1950; s. Mickey Holt and Joan Elizabeth (Smith) D.; m. Ruth Ann Shank, June 10, 1972; children: Eric Holt, Evan Scott. AA, Ventura Coll., 1970; BA with honors, U. Calif., Santa Barbara, 1973; MLS, San Jose State U., 1976. Cert. secondary tchr., Calif. Libr. media tchr. San Diego Unified Sch. Dist., 1975—; lectr. Calif. State U., L.A., 1987-89; libr. cons. San Diego C.C. Dist., 1990; chmn. sch. adv. com. Point Loma H.S., San Diego, 1986-87; coop. book rev. bd. San Diego County, 1984-86; creator adult sch. curriculum, 1984-86. Mem. ALA, Calif. Libr. Media Educators Assn. Office: Hoover HS 4474 El Cajon Blvd San Diego CA 92115-4312

DONLON, TIMOTHY A., cytogeneticist; b. Pasadena, Calif., Apr. 16, 1952. PhD, U. Oreg., 1984. Med. genetics fellow Children's Hosp., Boston, 1984-86; chief molecular clin. cytogenetics Kapiolani Med. Ctr., Honolulu, 1992—, dir., 1995; assoc. prof. U. Hawaii Burns Sch. Medicine, Honolulu, 1992—. Office: Kapiolani Med Ctr Dept Molecular & Clin Cytogenetics 1946 Young St Ste 400 Honolulu HI 96826-2150*

DONLON, WILLIAM CHRISTOPHER, maxillofacial surgeon, educator, author, editor; b. N.Y.C., Oct. 17, 1952; s. William Aloyisius and Margaret Mary (O'Donovan) D.; m. Marianne Patricia Truta, May 28, 1983; 1 child, Sean Liam Riobard. BA, Hofstra U., 1974, MA, 1975; DMD, Tufts U., 1979. Diplomate Am. Bd. Oral Maxillofacial Surgery (examining com. 1993—). Resident Mt. Sinai Med. Ctr., N.Y.C., 1979-81, chief resident, 1981-82; asst. clin. prof. U. Pacific, San Francisco, 1982-88, assoc. clin. prof., 1988—; prin. surgeon Peninsula Maxillofacial Surgery, South San Francisco, Calif., 1982—, Burlingame, Calif., 1988—, Redwood City, Calif., 1990-95, Menlo Park, Calif., 1990-95, San Carlos, Calif., 1995—; dir. Facial Pain Rsch. Ctr., San Francisco, 1986-93; lectr. in field; vis. faculty dept. maxillofacial surgery U. Mich., 1994—; vis. prof. dept. maxillofacial, head, neck and facial plastic surgery U. Chile and Cath. U. of Chile, 1993—; mem. hosp. staff Mills-Peninsula Hosps., 1984—, chief svc., 1992-96; mem. hosp. staff Sequoia Hosp., 1990—, San Mateo County Gen. Hosp., 1992—; mem. courtesy staff Seton Med. Ctr., 1984—, Kaiser Hosps., San Francisco and Redwood City, 1984—. Editor: Headache and Facial Pain, 1990; reviewer Cleft Craniofacial jour.; contbr. articles to profl. jours. Fellow Am. Dental Soc. Anesthesiology, Am. Assn. Oral Maxillofacial Surgeons (chmn. com. on hosp. affairs 1992-95, chmn. reference com. House of Dels. 1992—, Committeeman of Yr. 1994, vice-chmn. clin. interest group on temparamandibular disorders 1994-96, chmn., 1996—), Am. Coll. Oral Maxillofacial Surgeons, Am. Coll. Dentists, Internat. Coll. Dentists, Pierre Fauchard Acad.; mem. AMA, ADA, Am. Soc. TMJ Surgeons, Am. Cleft Palate-Craniofacial Assn., N.Am. Skull Base Soc., Western Soc. Oral Maxillofacial Surgeons (bd. dirs. 1993—), European Assn. Craniomaxillofacial Surgery, Internat. Assn. Maxillofacial Surgery, Calif. Dental Assn., No. Calif. Oral Maxillofacial Surgeons (bd. dirs. 1986-88, sec.-treas. 1990-91, pres. 1992-93), Calif. Assn. Oral Maxillofacial Surgeons (bd. dirs. 1991-94, pres.-elect 1993-94, pres. 1994-95), Soc. of Med. Friends Wine, Tufts Dental Alumni Assn. (v.p. Calif. chpt. 1984-86, pres. 1984-96). Office: Peninsula Maxillofacial Surgery 1860 El Camino Real Ste 300 Burlingame CA 94010-3114

DONNALLY, PATRICK ANDREW, quality management consultant; b. South Charleston, W Va., Sept. 7, 1932; s. Charles Lewis and Gladys Olean (Bright) D.; m. Bonnie Lou Blosser, Nov. 29, 1963; children: Shea Lynn, Melissa Ann, Kevin Patrick. BS in Indsl. Engring., W.Va. U., 1959, MS in Indsl. Engring., 1963; MBA, Rollins Coll., 1985. Registered profl. engr., Calif. Quality systems cons. Gen. Systems Co., Pittsfield, Mass., 1976-79; dir. corp. quality Storage Tech. Corp., Louisville, Colo., 1979-81, MagneTek, Inc., L.A., 1990-92; v.p. Stromberg Carlson, Lake Mary, Fla., 1981-84; sr. v.p. Philip Crosby Assocs., Winter Park, Fla., 1984-89; sr. cons. Ernst & Young, San Jose, Calif., 1989-90; pres., CEO Jones Reilly, Milpitas, Calif., 1992-93, Patrick Donnally Assocs., San Ramon, Calif., 1993—; speaker in field; pres., CEO Coun. for Continuous Improvement, 1996. Mem. patient care com. San Jose Med. Ctr., 1987-90. With U.S. Army, 1953-55. Mem. Am. Soc. Quality Control (sr.), Alpha Pi Mu. Democrat. Baptist. Office: Patrick Donnally Assocs PO Box 3159 Danville CA 94526

DONNALLY, ROBERT ANDREW, lawyer; b. Washington, July 10, 1953; s. Reaumur Stearnes and Katherine Ann (Sutliff) D.; m. Patricia Kane Broderick, Dec. 30, 1977; 1 child, Danielle Christine. BA in Psychology, U. Md., 1976; JD, U. Balt., 1980; cert., Stanford Grad. Sch. Bus., Palo Alto, Calif., 1996. Bar: Md. 1980, Calif. 1986. Pvt. practice Oxen Hill, Md., 1980-81; rsch. contract staff officer Dept. Def., Ft. Meade, Md., 1981-85; with legal and contractual ops. ARGOSystems, Inc., Sunnyvale, Calif., 1985-90; asst. dir. Inst. Def. Analyses, San Diego, 1990-91; dep. chief counsel ARGOSystems, Inc., 1991-93, chief counsel, corp. sec., 1993—. Editor-in-chief The Forum, 1979-80. Active The Pillars Soc./United Way, 1991—. Waxter Legal scholar U. Baltimore, 1978. Mem. Am. Corp. Counsel, Nat. Contract Mgmt. Assn., Md. Bar Assn., Calif. Bar Assn., Tae Kwon Do Assn. (Black Belt). Office: ARGOSystems Inc 324 N Mary Ave Sunnyvale CA 94086

DONNICI, PETER JOSEPH, lawyer, law educator, consultant; b. Kansas City, Mo., Sept. 5, 1939; s. Albert H. and Jennie (Danubio) D.; m. Diane DuPlantier, July 27, 1985; children—JuliaAnn Donnici Clifford, Joseph A., Joann Donnici Powers. B.A., U. Mo.-Kansas City, 1959, J.D., 1962; LL.M., Yale U., 1963. Bar: Mo. 1963, U.S. Supreme Ct. 1966, Calif. 1969. Asst. prof. law U. San Francisco, 1963-65, assoc. prof., 1965-68, prof., 1968-91, prof. emeritus, 1992—; assoc. Law Offices Joseph L. Alioto, San Francisco, 1967-72; sole practice, San Francisco, 1974—; ptnr. Donnici & LuPo, San Francisco, 1982-92, Donnici, Kerwin, Phillips & Donnici, San Francisco, 1993—; asst. prosecutor Jackson County Prosecutor's Office, Mo., 1963; cons. to Office of Mayor of San Francisco, 1968-72; No. Calif. bd. dirs. Coun. on Legal Ednl. Opportunity, San Francisco, 1969-70; conciliator for housing discrimination cases HUD, San Francisco, 1976; cons. Calif. Consumer Affairs' Task Force on Electronic Funds Transfer, Sacramento, 1978-79; bd. dirs. Air Micronesia, Inc., DHL Internat., Ltd, Bermuda, Continental Micronesia; spl. counsel and del. to internat. confs. Commonwealth of No. Mariana Islands, 1983-84; faculty adviser U. San Francisco Law Rev., 1966-91; bd. counselors U. San Francisco, 1993—. Editor in chief U. Mo.-Kansas City Law Rev., 1961-62; contbr. articles to profl. jours., 1964—. Lawyers' Com. for Urban Affairs, San Francisco, 1965-68. Wilson scholar U. Mo.-Kansas City, 1956-62; Sterling fellow Law Sch., Yale U., 1962-63. Mem. Bench and Robe, Phi Delta Phi. Democrat. Roman Catholic. Home: 190 Cresta Vista Dr San Francisco CA 94127-1635 Office: One Post St Ste 2450 San Francisco CA 94104

D'ONOFRIO, MARY ANN, medical transcription company executive; b. Detroit, Jan. 24, 1933; d. Charles Henry and Cecilia Rose (Levan) Clifford; m. Dominic Armando D'Onofrio, Apr. 19, 1958; children: Margaret Clement, Anthony, Elizabeth, Maria Spurgeon. BA, Marygrove Coll., 1954; MLS, U. Mich., 1955. Cert. med. transcriptionist. Reader's advisor Detroit Pub. Libr., 1955-58; cataloger Willow Run (Mich.) Pub. Libr., 1959-61, St. Thomas Grade and High Sch., Ann Arbor, Mich., 1968-72; med. record analyst Chelsea (Mich.) Community Hosp., 1972-79; pres. Meditranscript Svc., Ann Arbor, 1979-81; asst. office mgr. Dr. Maxfield, D.O., Tucson, 1981-82; quality assurance analyst, utilization rev. Tucson (Ariz.) Gen. Hosp., 1983-86; exec. asst. Dr. McEldoon M.D., Tucson, 1986-88; pres. Meditranscript Svc., Tucson, 1986-88; co-owner Med-Comm Assocs., Tucson, 1989—; co-owner, assoc. designer EMA of Tucson custom apparel and jewelry design co. Co-author: Psychiatric Words & Phrases, 1990, 2d edit., 1997; contbr. articles to profl. jours; co-developer Cross-Search. Block leader Infantile Paralysis Assn., Ann Arbor, 1975-80, Easter Seal Assn., Tucson, 1983-86, Am. Heart Assn., 1994, Am. Cancer Soc., 1992, 96. Mem. Am. Assn. for Med. Transcription (parliamentarian Sonora Desert chpt. 1984-86, 90-93, 95, bylaws com. 1996-97, compiler/editor AAMI Annotated Bibliography 1981, Named Disting. Mem. 1984, treas. Sonora Desert chpt. 1987, jour. columnist 1982-86, by-laws com. 1995-97, policies & procedures panelist 1997), Ednl. Honor Soc., Pi Lambda Theta (life).

DONOGHUE, JOHN CHARLES, software management consultant; b. Oswego, N.Y., Sept. 19, 1950; s. James Charles and Marion Louise (Farrell) D.; m. Ann Marie Perry, Dec. 20, 1969; children: John Charles II, Kelly Anne. BS in Electronic Tech., Chapman Coll., 1981; student, U. Calif., Irvine, 1981-82; MA, U. Redlands, 1987; postgrad., Western State U. Coll., 1988-89, Azusa Pacific U., 1991-93. Enlisted USAF, 1969, advanced through grades to staff sgt., 1977, resigned, 1979; mgr. Lockheed Aircraft, Ontario, Calif., 1979-85; project engr. Northrop Corp., Pico Rivera, Calif., 1985—; cons., Fontana, Calif., 1981—; mem. software coun. Northrop Corp., Hawthorne, Calif., 1987—, software improvement network U. Calif., Irvine, 1988—, capability maturity model corr. group Software Engring. Inst., Pitts., 1993—, L.A. software improvement network U. So. Calif., 1994—; charter mem. Software Inspection and Rev. Orgn., Sunnyvale, Calif., 1981—. Vol. cons. S.W. Anthropol. Assn. Calif. State U., L.A., 1996—, Resource Conservation Dist., Rancho Cucamonga, Calif., 1996—. Mem. IEEE, Northrop Gruman Mgmt. Club, N.Y. Acad. Scis., Nat. Space Soc. Office: Northrop Gruman Corp Mil Aircraft Sys Divsn 8900 Washington Blvd Pico Rivera CA 90660-3765

DONOHUE, CHRISTOPHER A., banker; b. Lincoln, Nebr., May 21, 1956; s. Robert Francis and Grace Josephine (Huster) D.; m. Dana Lea Gauld, Oct. 10, 1981; children: Ryan Patrick, Colleen Marie. BS in BA, Calif. State U., Fresno, 1979. Mgmt. trainee, ops. officer, consumer credit loan officer Security Pacific Nat. Bank, various locations, Calif., 1979-88; constrn. mgr. Old Stone of Calif., Sacramento, 1988-89; v.p., constrn. mgr. Pacific First Bank, Las Vegas, Nev., 1989-92, InterWest Mortgage, Las Vegas, 1992—. Founder Stockton (Calif.) Unified Sch. Dist. Hearing Impaired Parents Group, 1987; chmn. Ruby Thomas Elem. Parents Group Hearing Impaired Program, Las Vegas, 1991-94; mem. spl. edn. adv. com. Clark County Sch. Dist., Las Vegas, 1993-94, spl. edn. com., 1993-94; bd. dirs. Sign Design Theatre Co., Las Vegas, 1992-94, exec. dir., 1993-94; chmn. hearing impaired program adv. com. Clark County Sch. Dist., 1993—; mem. Gov.'s Task Force on Am. Sign Lang., Las Vegas, 1991—, chmn. subocm. on lic. and cert., 1996; coach green Valley Bobysox Softball, Las Vegas, 1995, Silver State Girls Soccer League, Las Vegas, 1995—. Mem. So. Nev. Home Bldrs. Assn., Sertoma (1st v.p. 1996—). Democrat. Lutheran. Office: InterWest Mortgage 2670 Chandler #3 Las Vegas NV 89120

DONOHUE, STACEY LEE, English language educator; b. Patchogue, N.Y., Dec. 1, 1963; d. Harold E. and Janice C. (Devine) Mahneke; m. Steven B. Huddleston, Dec. 15, 1996. BA in English, SUNY, Binghamton, 1985; PhD in English, CUNY, 1995. Instr. English Borough Manhattan C.C., N.Y.C., 1988-95; asst. prof. English Cen. Oreg. C.C., Bend, 1995—; adj. instr. NYU, 1990-93. Editor: (newspaper) The Lookout, Bend, 1995-96. Bd. dirs. Cen. Oreg. Forest Issues Com., Bend, 1995-96; mem. Friends of the Libr., Bend, 1996-97. Mem. MLA, Pacific N.W. Am. Studies Assn., Multi Ethnic Lit. of the U.S. Office: Cen Oreg C C Humanities Dept 2600 NW College Way Bend OR 97701

DONOHUGH, DONALD LEE, physician; b. Los Angeles, Apr. 12, 1924; s. William Noble and Florence Virginia (Shelton) D.; m. Virginia Eskew McGregor, Sept. 12, 1950 (div. 1971); children: Ruth, Laurel, Marilee, Carol, Greg; m. Beatrice Ivany Redick, Dec. 3, 1976; stepchildren: Leslie Ann, Andrea Jean. BS, U.S. Naval Acad., 1946; MD, U. Calif., San Francisco, 1956; MPH and Tropical Medicine, Tulane U., 1961. Diplomate AM. Bd. Internal Medicine. Intern U. Hosp., San Diego, 1956-57; resident Monterey County Hosp., 1957-58; dir. of med. svcs. U.S. Depart. Interior, Am. Samoa, 1958-60; instr. Tulane U. Med. Sch., New Orleans, 1960-63; resident Tulane Svcs. V.A. and Charity Hosp., New Orleans, 1961-63; cons. Internat. Ctr. for Rsch and Tng., Costa Rica, 1961-63; asst. prof. medicine & preventive medicine La. State U. Sch. Medicine, 1962-63; assoc. prof., 1963-65; vis. prof. U. Costa Rica, 1963-65; faculty advisor, head of Agy. Internat. Devel. program U. Costa Rica Med. Sch., 1965-67; dir. med. svcs. Med. Ctr. U. Calif. (formerly Orange County Hosp.), Irvine, 1967-69; assoc. clin. prof. U. Calif., Irvine, 1967-79, clin. prof., 1980-85; pvt. practice Tustin, Calif., 1970-80; with Joint Commn. on Accreditation of Hosps., 1981; cons. Kauai, Hawaii, 1981—. Author: The Middle Years, 1981, Practice Management, 1986, Kauai, 1988, 3d edit., 1990; co-translator; Rashomon (Ryonosuke Akutagawa), 1950; also numerous articles. Lt. USN, 1946-52, capt. USNR, 1966-84. Fellow Am. Coll. Physicians (life); mem. Delta Omega. Republican. Episcopalian. Home: 4890 Lawai Beach Rd Koloa HI 96756-9675

DONOVAN, DENNIS, agricultural products executive; b. 1951. With family farm, Salinas, Calif., 1972-76, Pismo-Ocenao (Calif.) Vegetable Exch., 1976—. Office: Pismo-Oce^ao Vegetable Exch 1731 Railroad St Oceano CA 93445-9510*

DONOVAN, LESLIE ANN, honors division educator, consultant; b. Kansas City, Mo., July 9, 1957; d. Richard Wayne and Marilyn (Lovelady) D. BA in English, U. N.Mex., 1982, MA in English, 1986; diploma with honors, U. Coll., Dublin, Ireland, 1987; PhD in English, U. Wash., 1993. Tchg. asst. dept. English U. Wash., Seattle, 1989-90; asst. dir. English computer-integrated courses, Seattle, 1990-92; instr. Albuquerque TV-I, 1993-96; instr. dept Women Studies U. N.Mex., Albuquerque, 1994-96; instr. English U. N.Mex., 1994-96, instr. gen. honors program, 1995-96, asst. prof. gen. honors divsn., 1996—; Legacy Curriculum, U. N.Mex., 1993, chair com. gen. honors, 1996—, mem. coun. women studies, 1995-96; freelance editor, proofreader, Albuquerque, 1987—. Contbr. articles, poetry to jours. in field. ITT Internat. fellow Internat. Exch., 1986. Mem. AAUW, MLA, Soc. for Advancement of Scandinavian Studies, Rocky Mountain Modern Lang. Assn. (chair Old English 1996—). Office: U NMex Gen Honors Program Humanities Bldg Albuquerque NM 87131

DONOVAN, WILLARD PATRICK, retired elementary education educator; b. Grand Rapids, Mich., Sept. 1, 1930; s. Willard Andrew and Thelma Alfreda (Davis) D.; m. Dorothy Jane Nester, Nov. 27, 1954 (dec. May 1981); children: Cindy Jane, Kimberly Sue. BS, Ea. Mich. U., 1965, MA, 1969. Cert. grades K-8, Mich. Enlisted U.S. Army, 1947, advanced through grades to master sgt., 1953, platoon sgt. Korean War, ret., 1964; pharm. sales Nat. Drug Co., Detroit, 1964-66; tchr. Cromie Elem. Sch. Warren (Mich.) Consol. Schs., 1966—, ret., 1995; reading textbook and curriculum devel. com. Warren (Mich.) Consol. Schs., 1969-73, sci. com., 1970-95; curriculum and textbook com. Macomb County Christian Schs., Warren, 1982-95. Decorated Combat Infantry badge U.S. Army, Korea, 1950, Purple heart with three clusters U.S. Army, Korea, 1950-51, Korea-Japan Svc. medal, 1951, Presdl. citation, 1951, Korean medal with three campaign clusters, 1951, Nat. Def. Svc. medal, 1951, Bronze star, Silver star. Mem. NRA, Am. Quarterhouse Assn., Assn. U.S. Army, Detroit Area Coun. Tchrs. Math., Met. Detroit Sci. Tchrs. Assn., The Chosin Few, Nat. Edn. Assn., Mich. Edn. Assn., Warren (Mich.) Edn. Assn. Home: PO Box 563 8440 Mission Hills Arizona City AZ 85223

DONOVAN-JOHNSON, D. J., artist, educator; b. Thayer, Kans., June 14, 1940; d. Lawrence R. and Pauline Rosilind (Shearer) Hague; m. John Thomas Donovan, June 4, 1960 (dec. 1969); 1 child, Erik; m. Gregory B. Johnson, Dec. 29, 1972; children: Ruthie, Julie. BS, Western Mich. U., 1962; MA, Wash. State U., 1965. Instr. pub. schs., Mont., Mich. and Wash.; juror for art shows; workshop instr. One woman and group shows include Salmagundi Club, State of the Art, N.Y.C., Water Media U.S., Open, Facet, Taos, N.Mex., Gallery of Interior, Washington, House Gallery, Oklahoma City, Jewish Cmty. Ctr., Art Mart, U. Denver, Colorado Springs Art Ctr., Coyote Woman Gallery, Harbor Springs, Mich., Art Expo/Calif., L.A., Miriam Pearlman Gallery, Chgo. Bd. dirs., founding pres. Flatirons Ctr. for Arts, Boulder, 1986-89;ch. sch. tchr. First Presbyn. Ch., Boulder, 1980—. Recipient Best of Boulder, Artist Choice award Daily Camera, 1992, Wash. State W.S. award, 1994, Kans. State W.S. award, 1994, Red River W.S. Silver medal award, 1994. Mem. Nat. Painters in Casein and Acrylic, Nat. League Am. Pen Women, Studio Six Artists Coop. (founding mem.). Home and Studio: 225 Bristlecone Way Boulder CO 80304-0467

DONTIGNY, RICHARD LOUIS, physical therapist; b. Havre, Mont., Aug. 9, 1931; s. Theodore Emil and Helen Estelle (Halverson) D.; m. Josephine Virginia Faltrino, June 15, 1957; children: Debra Jo, Laura Jean, Richard Emil, Julie Ann. BS, Mont. State Coll., 1954; cert. in phys. therapy, U. Iowa, 1958. Staff therapist St. Francis Hosp., Colorado Springs, Colo., 1958-60, chief therapist, 1960-61; staff therapist No. Pacific Beneficial Assn., Missoula, Mont., 1961-63; chief therapist Sacred Heart Hosp., Havre, Mont., 1963-74, Deaconess Hosp., Havre, 1963-74, No. Mont. Hosp., Havre, 1974-83; staff therapist Havre Clinic, 1983-86; pvt. practice DonTigny Phys. Therapy, Havre, 1986-96, retired, 1996; mem. Mont. Bd. Phys. Therapy Examiners, 1984-87; book, manuscript reviewer Jours. Phys. Therapy, Arlington, Va., 1978—. Contbr. articles to profl. publs., chpt. to book. With U.S. Army, 1954-56. Mem. Am. Phys. Therapy Assn. (pres. Mont. chpt. 1970-74, subject matter expert orthopedic specialty coun. 1987). Home: 66 15th St W Havre MT 59501-5274

DONZE, JERRY LYNN, electrical engineer; b. Wauneta, Nebr., June 12, 1943; s. John Henry and Virgina May (Francis) D.; m. Marilyn Grace Bascue, Feb. 22, 1964 (div. May. 1980); children: Scott. L., Michele A.; m. Sandra Kay Morris, July 25, 1981. Cert. technician, Denver Inst. Tech., 1964; BSEE, U. Colo., 1972; postgrad., Advanced Metaphysics Inst. Religios Sci., 1986. Electronic technician A.B.M. Co., Lakewood, Colo., 1964-71; computer programmer Nat. Bur. Standards, Boulder, Colo., 1971-72; electronic engr. Autometrics Co., Boulder, Colo., 1972-76, Gates Research and Devel., Denver, 1976-77; devel. engr. Emerson Electric Co., Lakewood, 1977; engring. mgr. Storage Tech., Louisville, Colo., 1977—; cons. Sun Co., Arvada, Colo., 1974-75. Patentee in field. Mem. IEEE Student Soc. (treas. 1971-72), Eta Kappa Nu. Republican. Religious Scientist. Home: 12021 W 54th Ave Arvada CO 80002-1907 Office: Storage Tech 2270 S 88th St Louisville CO 80028-0001

DOOLEY, CALVIN MILLARD, congressman; b. Visalia, Calif., Jan. 11, 1954. BS, U. Calif., Davis; MA, Stanford U. Mem. 102nd-104th Congresses from Calif. Dist. 17 (now 20th), 1991—; mem. agriculture com., mem. natural resources com. Democrat. Methodist. Office: House of Representatives 1227 Longworth Bldg Washington DC 20515-0004*

DOOLIN, JAMES LAWRENCE, artist, educator; b. Hartford, Conn., June 28, 1932; s. Lawrence J. and Ruth Jennie (Blodgett) D.; m. Leslie E. Edwards, June 28, 1962 (div. Mar. 1984); children: Matthew James, Paul Lawrence; m. Lauren J. Richardson, Mar. 30, 1985; 1 child, Eve Eleanor. BFA, Phila. U. of Arts, 1954; MFA, UCLA, 1971. Instr. adult edn. Union Carbide Corp., N.Y.C., 1964-65; lectr. Prahran Coll. Advanced Edn., Melbourne, Australia, 1965-66; lectr. dept. art UCLA, 1972-80; instr. Otis Art Inst., L.A., 1977, 79-80, Cerro Coso Coll., Ridgecrest, Calif., 1982-83, Santa Monica (Calif.) Coll., 1984-86, Art Inst. So. Calif., Laguna Beach, 1992, 93; vis. artist Victorian Coll. of Arts, Melbourne, 1978, Claremont (Calif.) Grad. Sch., 1985, 87, U. Nev., Las Vegas, 1988; artist L.A. County Transp. Authority, 1993, 94, lead artist, 1994-96. One man shows include Gallery A, Melbourne, 1966, Ctrl. St. Gallery, Sydney, Australia, 1967, 70, Boise (Idaho) State U., 1974, L.A. Mcpl. Gallery, 1977, Victorian Coll. of Arts, Australia, 1978-79, Cerro Coso Coll., 1982, Koplin Gallery, Santa Monica, Calif., 1984, 86, 92, U. So. Calif. Atelier Gallery, Santa Monica, 1985, U. Wis., Oshkosh, 1993; exhibited in group shows at Victorian Nat. Gallery, Melbourne, Australia, 1968, Art Gallery N.S.W., Sydney, Australia, 1968, Long Beach (Calif.) Mus. Art, 1971, Palos Verdes (Calif.) Mus. Art, 1972, DeYoung Mus. Downtown Ctr., San Francisco, 1977, Australian Nat. Gallery, Canberra, 1983, Acad. Fine Arts, N.Y.C., 1986, Laguna Art Mus., Laguna Beach, Calif., 1986, Power Gallery Contemporary Art, Sydney, 1987, San Diego Mus. Art, 1991, Santa Barbara Contemporary Arts Forum, 1991, L.A. Mcpl. Art Gallery, 1991, El Camino Coll., Torrance, Calif., 1991, Security Pacific Gallery, San Francisco, 1991, Oakland (Calif.) Mus., 1992, Nev. Mus. Art, Reno, 1992, Fresno (Calif.) Met. Mus., 1992, Stremmel Gallery, Reno, Nev., 1993, Riverside (Calif.) Art Mus., 1993, Contemporary Realist Gallery, San Francisco, 1994, Occidental Coll., L.A., 1994, Nev. Inst. Contemporary Art, Las Vegas, 1995, L.A. Mcpl. Gallery, 1995, Art Ctr. Coll. of Design, Pasadena, Calif., 1996, Tatistscheff/Rogers Gallery, Santa Monica, Calif., 1996; represented in permanent collections Art Gallery N.S.W., Sydney, Australian Nat. Gallery, Canberra, Australian Nat. U., Canberra, Bank of Am., L.A., Contemporary Art Mus., Honolulu, Homart Devel. Co., L.A., Jonathan Club, L.A., Long Beach Mus. Art, Loyola Law Sch., L.A., Mus. Contemporary Art, Sydney, Nat. Gallery Victoria,

Melbourne, Nestle U.S.A., Inc., Glendale, Calif., Newcastle Art Mus., N.S.W., State Gallery Queensland, Brisbane, Australia, U. Vt., Burlington. With U.S. Army, 1955-57. Painting fellow Guggenheim Found., 1980, Nat. Endowment for Arts, 1981, 85, 91. Home: 2619 Cardiff Ave Los Angeles CA 90034-1842

DOOLITTLE, JOHN TAYLOR, congressman; b. Glendale, Calif., Oct. 30, 1950; s. Merrill T. and Dorothy Doolittle; B.A. in History with honors, U. Calif., Santa Cruz, 1972; J.D., McGeorge Sch. Law, U. Pacific, 1978; m. Julia Harlow, Feb. 17, 1979; children: John Taylor Jr., Courtney A. Bar: Calif. 1978. Mem. Calif. State Senate, 1980-90; mem. 102nd-103rd Congresses from Calif. 4th dist., 1991—; mem. agriculture com., chair water and power resources subcom. Republican. Mem. LDS Ch. Office: House of Representatives 1526 Longworth Bldg Washington DC 20515-0004*

DOOLITTLE, ROBERT FREDERICK, II, high energy astrophysicist; b. Chgo., Dec. 21, 1925; s. Arthur K. and Dortha (Bailey) D.; m. Mary Agnes Parker, Apr. 30, 1955 (dec. Dec. 1972); children: Robert Arthur, Nancy Elizabeth; m. Karen M. Kruse, Dec. 28, 1976. AB, Oberlin Coll., 1948; MS, U. Mich., 1950, PhD, 1958. Asst. prof. physics San Diego State U., 1958-60; sr. scientist TRW Space and Def., Redondo Beach, Calif., 1960-83; various computer programming positions, 1983—; cons. Space Tech. Labs., L.A., 1959, 3D Graphics, Pacific Palisades, Calif., 1993, Magnesys, Santa Clara, Calif., 1987. Lt. comdr. USNR, 1944-46, 52-54. Mem. Am. Astron. Soc., Assn. for Computing Machinery. Home: 1290 Monument St Pacific Palisades CA 90272-2541

DOPPS, CAROLA FROUKINA SOPHIA, advertising media consultant; b. Nuenen, Netherlands, Feb. 7, 1971; came to U.S., Sept. 1989; d. Peter Antonius and Gonnie FFH (Vanden Wildenberg) Jaspers; m. Stan Walter Dopps, May 12, 1993. AA in Arts and Science, Columbia Basin Coll., Pasco, Wash., 1993; BA in Social Sciences, Wash. State U., 1994; MEd in Counseling, Heritage Coll., 1996. Cert. school counselor, Wash. Mental health counselor Carondelet Psychiat. Care Ctr., Richland, Wash., 1994-95; advt. media cons. Tri-City Herald, Kennewick, Wash., 1994—; cmty. counselor AYUSA Internat., Tri-Cities, Wash.; family therapist Cath. Cmty. Svcs., Tacoma, Wash. Mem. Tri-City Counselor Assn., Am. Counseling Assn., Am. Mental Health Assn., Am. Sch. Counseling Assn., Wash. State Counseling Assn., Kennewick C. of C (ambassador). Home: 23417 SE 242nd St Maple Valley WA 98038-8298 Office: 1 Post St 7th Fl San Francisco CA 94104

DORAN, CARTER, academic administrator; b. Galveston, Tex., May 5, 1938; s. Philip Chester and Frances Elizabeth (Carter) D.; m. Constance John Mohr, June 21, 1963; children: Elisabeth Mohr, Meredith Christine. AB, Yale U., 1960; MDiv, Fuller Theol. Sem., Pasadena, 1963; MA, Occidental Coll., L.A., 1966; PhD, U. So. Calif., L.A., 1980. Dean students L.A. Pacific Coll., 1964-65; drama/speech instr. Mt. San Antonio Coll., Walnut, Calif., 1966-68; dir. theatre Mt. San Antonio Coll., 1968-77, dean humanities, 1977-83, dean humanities and social scis., 1983-86; vice chancellor acad. affairs Rancho Santiago Coll., Santa Ana, Calif., 1986-92; asst. supt./v.p. instruction and student svcs. Coll. of the Canyons, Santa Clarita, Calif., 1992—. Named Outstanding Educator, Mt. San Antonio Friends of the Coll., 1985; Occidental Coll. grad. fellow, 1965-66. Mem. Calif. C.C. Chief Instrn. Officers (pres. 1990-91), Ednl. Leadership Colloquia (facilitator 1987-91). Home: 7917 E Timberland Ave Orange CA 92869-5634 Office: Coll of the Canyons 26455 Rockwell Canyon Rd Santa Clarita CA 91355-1803

DORAN, VINCENT JAMES, steel fabricating company consultant; b. Ephrata, Wash., June 13, 1917; s. Samuel Vincent and Sarah Anastasia (Fitzpatrick) D.; B. Phil., Gonzaga U., Spokane, 1946; m. Jean Arlene Birrer, Jan. 15, 1949; children: Vincent James, Mollie Jean, Michele Lee, Patrick Michael. Mgr., Flying Service, Coulee Dam, Wash., 1947-48; mgr. constrn. Morrison-Knudsen Co., Wash. and Alaska, 1953-60; co-owner C.R. Foss Inc., constrn., Anchorage, 1961-64; mgr. Steel Fabricators, Anchorage, 1965-86. Inventor method of reducing and dewatering sewage sludge. Active Boy Scouts Am.; co-founder, pres. Chugach Rehab. Assn., 1962; mem. Alaska Gov.'s Rehab. Adv. Bd., 1962-63; mem. CAP. Served with USAAF, 1943-45, USAF, 1949-50. Decorated Air medal with 4 clusters. Mem. Welding Inst. Alaska (co-organizer, dir. 1977-78), 34th Bomb Group Assn. Roman Catholic. Club: Toastmasters. Compiler, pub. home owners' and builders' guide to sun's positions in N.Am. during solstices and equinoxes, designer packaged water, sewage treatment plants and water collection systems Arctic communities. Home: 3811 Knik Ave Anchorage AK 99517-1061 Office: 3243 Commercial Dr Anchorage AK 99501-3020

DORATO, PETER, electrical and computer engineering educator; b. N.Y.C., Dec. 17, 1932; s. Fioretto and Rosina (Lachello) D.; m. Marie Madeleine Turlan, June 2, 1956; children: Christopher, Alexander, Sylvia, Veronica. BEE, CCNY, 1955; MSEE, Columbia U., 1956; DEE, Poly. Inst. N.Y., 1961. Registered profl. engr., Colo. Lectr. elec. engring. dept. CCNY, 1956-57; instr. elec. engring. Poly. Inst. N.Y., Bklyn., 1957-61, prof., 1961-72; prof. elec. engring., dir. Resource System Analysis U. Colo., Colorado Springs, 1972-76; prof. elec. and computer engring. U. N.Mex., Albuquerque, 1984—, chmn. dept., 1976-84; hon. chaired prof. Nanjing Aero. Inst., 1989; vis. prof. Politecnico di Torino, Italy, 1991-92. Co-author Linear Quadratic Control, 1995, Robust Control for Unstructured Perturbations, 1992; editor: Robust Control, Recent Results in Robust Control and Advances in Adaptive Control, reprint vols., 1987, 90, 91, IEEE Press Reprint Vol. Series, 1989-90; assoc. editor Automatica Jour., 1969-83, 89-92, editor rapid publs., 1994—; assoc. editor IEEE Trans on Edn., 1989-91; contbr. articles on control systems theory to profl. jours. Fellow IEEE; mem. Am. Soc. for Engring. Edn., IEEE Control Systems Soc. (Disting. Mem. award). Democrat. Home: 1514 Roma Ave NE Albuquerque NM 87106-4513 Office: U NMex Dept Elec Computer Eng Albuquerque NM 87131

DORFMAN, PAUL MICHAEL, bank executive; b. Chgo., Mar. 16, 1939; s. Isaiah Sol. and Lillian M. D.; m. Janet Ruth, June 18, 1961; children: Judith A. Mendelsohn, Jeffrey H., Eric M., Benjamin K. BA in Econs., Princeton Univ., 1961; JD, Yale Univ., 1964. Bar: Ill. 1964. Attorney Mayer, Brown and Platt, Chgo., 1964-69; v.p. Continental Ill. Venture Corp., Chgo., 1969-71; exec. v.p. JMB Realty Corp., Chgo., 1971-73; v.p. transportation sect., client info. svcs., others Bank Am., San Francisco, 1973-79, v.p. strategic planning world banking divsn., 1979-80; group v.p., head credit adminstrn. Europe Middle East Divsn Bank Am., London, 1980-82; sr. v.p. Asia divsn. Bank Am., Tokyo, 1982-85; sr. v.p. world banking divsn. Bank Am., San Francisco, 1985-86, sr. v.p. credit policy, 1986-90, exec. v.p. credit risk mgmt., 1990—; vice chmn. credit policy com. Bank Am., 1986; dir., office Robert Morris Assocs., 1993—. Contbr. articles to profl. jours. Mem. bd. dirs. San Francisco Chpt. Am. Jewish Com., 1987—; dir. Japan Soc. No. Calif., 1996—. Mem. Phi Beta Kappa. Office: Bank Am 555 California St San Francisco CA 94104-1502

DORFMAN, STEVEN DAVID, electronics company executive; b. Bklyn., Sept. 26, 1935; s. Murray Dorfman and Eleanor Judith (Blitzer) Pisani; m. Georgina Breckenridge (divorced): 1 child, Jennifer; m. Beverly Joan Pain, Dec. 28, 1965; children: Lorraine, Gene, Lynn. BSEE, U. Fla., 1957; MSEE, U. So. Calif., 1959. With Hughes Cos., 1957—; mgr. adv. programs Hughes Aircraft Co., El Segundo, Calif., 1967-72, mgr. Pioneer Venus, 1972-78, assoc. mgr. NASA Systems Div., 1978-82, mgr. NASA Systems Div., 1983; pres., chief exec. officer Hughes Communications Inc. subs. Hughes Aircraft Co., L.A., 1983-86; corp. v.p., pres. space and communications group, mem. policy bd. Hughes Aircraft Co., L.A., 1986-92; pres., CEO Hughes Space & Comm. Co., L.A., 1992-93; pres. telecomms. and space, sr. v.p., mem. office of chmn. GM Hughes Electronics Corp., L.A., 1993—; chmn. comml. space transp. adv. com. (COMSTAC) Washington Dept. Transp., 1987—; mem. space systems tech. adv. com. NASA, Washington, 1982—; mem. U.S. Info. Agy. TV/Telecom Adv. Coun., Washington, 1985-90; mem. Nat. Rsch. Coun. Aeronautics and Space Engring. Bd., 1992—. Contbr. articles to profl. jours.; patentee in field. State Senate scholar, Fla., 1955-56; recipient Disting. Pub. Svc. medal NASA, 1980. Mem. NEA, Nat. Rsch. Coun. Home: 517 Veteran Ave Los Angeles CA 90024-1915 Office: Hughes Telecommunication Co PO Box 80028 Los Angeles CA 90080-0028*

DORIA, ROBIN GALIAN, financial consultant; b. L.I., N.Y., Oct. 29, 1946; s. Oswald and Helen E. (Moss) D.; m. Deborah A. Martin, June 19, 1970; children: Stacey L., Kable M., Kasy R. BS in Bus. Econs., Okla. State U., 1970; MA in Internat. Rels., Troy (Ala.) State U., 1980. Commd. 2nd lt. USAF, 1970, advanced through grades to lt. col., 1991; pilot front line fighter aircraft, F-4s and F-15s Tactical Air Command, USAF, U.S. and Germany, 1975-89; chief safety 17,000 person indsl. complex McClellan AFB, Sacramento, Calif., 1989-91; fin. cons. Merrill Lynch, Sacramento, 1991—, coord., mgr. profl. devel. program, 1995—; charter pres. LeTip of Roseville-Granite Bay, 1991-93, bd. dirs., 1991—. Decorated DFC with 4 oak leaf clusters, meritorious svc. medal with 3 oak leaf clusters. Mem. Woodcreek Oaks Golf Course, Granite Bay Tennis Club. Republican. Office: Merrill Lynch 1435 River Park Dr Ste 100 Sacramento CA 95815-4510

DORIUS, KERMIT PARRISH, architect; b. Salt Lake City, Aug. 2, 1926; s. Raymond E. and Claire Ford (Parrish) D.; m. Mary Jo Singleton, Jan. 28, 1954; children: Lynn, Kristin, Mark. Student, U. Utah, 1943-44; B.Arch., U. Calif., Berkeley, 1950. Project architect Frederick Hodgdon (AIA), Newport Beach, Calif., 1954-57; prin. Brownell & Dorius, Corona Del Mar, Calif., 1957-59; pres., now chmn. bd. Kermit Dorius & Assocs., Corona Del Mar, 1960—. Recipient numerous awards Nat. Assn. Homebuilders/Pacific Coast Builders Conf., Orange County chpt. AIA, Better Homes & Gardens, 1975—. Fellow AIA (pres. Orange County chpt. 1966, v.p. Calif. coun. 1976-77); mem. Architects, Designers, Planners for Social Responsibility (chair Orange County chpt. 1987—), Orange County Bldg. Industry Assn. (HomeAid exec. com. 1991—). Office: JBZ Dorius 2415 Campus Dr Ste 200 Irvine CA 92612-1527*

DORLAND, FRANK NORTON, art conservator, educator; b. Peru, Nebr., Oct. 11, 1914; s. Frank Norton and Marion Hope (Abbot) D.; m. Mabel Vyvyan Jolliffe, July 29, 1938 (dec. Mar. 1991); m. Vandria Rayner, Apr. 7, 1995. Student Calif. Christian Coll., 1931-33; San Diego State Coll., 1933-38. Artist preliminary design engring. Convair Co., San Diego, Calif., 1938-49; pvt. practice as art conservator, La Jolla, Calif., 1949-59, San Francisco, 1959-63, Mill Valley, Calif., 1963-73, Santa Barbara, Calif., 1973-85; head art dept. The Quaderia Inst., San Luis Obispo, Calif., 1994—; formerly engaged in authentication and classification art objects; cons. art assns. galleries, mus., collectors, chs. Author: Holy Ice: The Story of Electronic Quartz Crystal, 1992; authenticated original Our Lady of Kazan (The Black Virgin of Kazan) Russian Icon, 1963. Mem. Internat. Inst. for Conservation, Internat. Coun. Museums, Am. Mus. Assn. Pioneer in use of spl. waxes in painting; inventor oil and water mix wax mediums, first scientifically compounded fine arts wax; engaged in research and devel. waxes and resins and properties and usage of electronic quartz crystals, also pioneer biocrystallographer, researcher on crystals, the human mind and the evolution of human consciousness. Home: PO Box 6233 Los Osos CA 93412-6233

DORMAN, N.B., writer; b. Iowa, 1927; divorced; 2 children. BA, Calif. State U., Chico, 1963. Various clerical and sales positions, asst. county libr., free-lance typesetter and copy editor, writer, 1972—. Author: (juvenile) Laughter in the Background, Elsevier/Nelson, 1980, (juvenile) Petey and Miss Magic, Linnet/Shoe String, 1993; contbr. stories to mags. Vol. in alcohol recovery programs. Address: PO Box 775 Chico CA 95927-0775

DORMAN, THOMAS ALFRED, internist, orthopaedist; b. Nairobi, Kenya, Nov. 16, 1936; came to U.S., 1977; s. Charles and Elizabeth D.; m. Allison Margaret Millar, Oct. 24, 1970; children: Jill, Michael, Andrew, Erin. Student, Liverpool U., 1959-62; MB, BChir, Edinburgh U., 1965. Diplomate Am. Bd. Internal Medicine. Staff gen. surgery Leith Hosp., Edinburgh, 1965-66; staff gen. medicine Western Gen. Hosp., Edinburgh, 1966; staff Elsie Inglis Maternity Hosp., Edinburgh, 1966-67, Norway House Hosp., Northern Manitoba, 1967; resident in medicine Union Meml. Hosp., Balt., 1967; staff anaesthetics dept. Sir Patrick Duns Hosp., Dublin, 1967-68; staff gen. surgery Naas Hosp., Ireland, 1968; staff pediat. neurology Royal Hosp. Sick Children, Edinburgh, 1968-69; registrar cardiology, gen. medicine Western Gen. Hosp., Edinburgh, 1969-71; staff internal medicine and cardiology Ft. Frances Clinic, Ontario, 1971-77; resident in internal medicine Winnipeg Gen. Hosp./U. Manitoba, 1972-73; pvt. practice San Luis Obispo, Calif., 1977—; staff Sierra Vista Hosp., San Luis Obispo, French Hosp., San Luis Obispo, San Luis Obispo Gen. Hosp. Editor, columnist Jour. Orthop. Medicine; contbr. articles to profl. jours. Fellow Royal Coll. Physicians; mem. Assn. Am. Physicians and Surgeons, Am. Back Soc. (bd. dirs.), British Med. Assn., British Inst. Manual Medicine, Am. Assn. Orthop. Medicine (charter mem., bd. dirs., chmn. rsch. com., newsletter editor), Cyriax Found., N.Am. Spine Soc., Assn. Musculoskeletal Medicine, Coll. Physicians and Surgeons Ontario, Calif. Med. Assn., San Luis Obispo County Med. Soc.. Office: 515 W Harrison St Ste 200 Kent WA 98032-4403

DORN, EDWARD MERTON, poet, educator; b. Villa Grove, Ill., Apr. 2, 1929. Student, U. Ill., Black Mountain Coll. Vis. prof. Am. lit., Fulbright lectr. U. Essex, 1965-68; vis. poet U. Kans., 1968-69; mem. faculty Idaho State U., Northeastern Ill. U., U. Colo., 1977—; sr. editor Rolling Stock mag., Boulder, Colo., 1981—. Author: What I See in the Maximus Poems, 1960, The Newly Fallen: Poems, 1961, Hands Up!, 1964, From Gloucester Out, 1964, (with M. Rumaker and W. Tallman) Prose I, 1964, The Rites of Passage: A Brief History, 1965, rev. edit. as By the Sound, 1971, Idaho Out, 1965, Geography, 1965, The Shoshoneans: The People of the Basin-Plateau, 1966, North Atlantic Turbine, 1967, Gunslinger Book I, 1968, Gunslinger Book II, 1969, Twenty Four Love Songs, 1969, The Midwest is That Space Between the Buffalo Statler and the Lawrence Eldridge, 1969, The Cosmology of Finding Your Spot, 1969, Songs: Set Two, A Short Count, 1970, Spectrum Breakdown: A Microbook, 1971, A Poem Called Alexander Hamilton, 1971, The Cycle, 1971, Some Business Recently Transacted in the White World, 1971, The Hamadryas Baboon at the Lincoln Park Zoo, 1972, Gunslinger Book II: The Winterbook Prologue to the Great Book IV Kornerstone, 1972, Recollections of Gran Apacheria, 1973, Gunslinger, Books I, II, III, IV, 1975, Collected Poems of Edward Dorn, 1975, 1984, Hello, La Jolla, 1978, Views, Interviews, 1978, Selected Poems, 1978, Yellow Lola, 1981, Captain Jack's Chaps, 1983, Abhorrences, 1990; By the Sound, 1991, Way West, 1993, The Denver Landing, 1994, Edward Dorn Sampler, 1996; translator Image of the New World, 1979, (with G. Brotherston) Tree Between the Two Walls, 1969, Our World: Guerilla Poems from Latin America, 1968, Selected Poems by Vallejo, 1976, (with Jennifer Dunbar) Manchester Square, 1975. Nat. Endowment for Arts grantee, 1966, 68; D.H. Lawrence fellow, 1969. Office: U Colo Campus Box 226 Boulder CO 80309

DORN, JAMES MARTIN, school safety coordinator; b. Poughkeepsie, N.Y., May 30, 1961; s. William Henry Sr. and Anne E. Elizabeth (Mooney) D.; m. Irene Nemec, Sept. 17, 1983; children: Cristina Elizabeth, Katherine Marie. AAS, Albuquerque Tech. Vocat. Inst., 1990; BA in Polit. Sci., U. N.Mex., 1992, MPA, 1995. Police officer Albuquerque Pub. Sch. Police Dept., 1982-83, police sgt., 1985-96; police officer Rio Rancho (N.Mex.) Police Dept., 1983-85; safety and security coord. Rio Rancho Pub. Schs., 1996—; mem. bd. dirs. So. Sandoval County Arroyo Flood Control Authority, 1995—. Mem., vice chair Rio Rancho Parks and Recreation Commn., 1993-96; Middle Rio Grande Coun. Govts., 1996—. Donald C. Rider Meml. scholar N.Mex. Mcpl. League, 1993, 94; U.S. Army ROTC scholar, 1979. Mem. Nat. Assn. Sch. Safety and Law Enforcement Officers, Nat. Rifle Assn. Republican. Roman Catholic. Office: 500 Laser Rd NE Rio Rancho NM 87124

DORN, MARIAN MARGARET, educator, sports management administrator; b. North Chicago, Ill., Sept. 25, 1931; d. John and Marian (Petkovsek) Jelovsek; m. Eugene G. Dorn, Aug. 2, 1952 (div. 1975); 1 child, Bradford Jay. BS, U. Ill., 1953; MS, U. So. Calif., 1961. Tchr., North Chicago Cmty. H.S., 1954-56; tchr., advisor activities, high sch., Pico-Rivera, Calif., 1956-62; tchr., coach Calif. H.S., Whittier, 1962-65; prof. phys. edn., chmn. dept., coach, asst. chmn. div. women's athletic dir. Cypress (Calif.) Coll., 1966—; men's, women's golf coach; mgr. Billie Jean King Tennis Ctr., Long Beach, Calif., 1982-86; founder King-Dorn Golf Schs., Long Beach, 1984; pres. So. Calif. Athletic Conf., 1981; curriculum cons. Calif. Dept. Edn., 1989-92; spkr. Citizen Amb. Program China Conf. women, 1995. Mem. del. to China Citizens Ambassador Program, 1995. Recipient cert. of merit Cypress Elem. Sch. Dist., 1976; Outstanding Service award Cypress Coll., 1986; named Women's Coach of Yr. Orgn. Empire Conf., 1995, Master Profl., 1996; nominated Coach of Yr., L.P.G.A. Western Sect., 1991-96. Mem. Calif. (v.p. So. dist.), San Gabriel Valley (pres.) Assns. Health, Phys. Edn. and Recreation, So. Calif. C.C. Athletic Coun. (sec., dir. pub. rels.), NEA, Calif. Tchrs. Assn., AAHPERD, Ladies Profl. Golf Assn. Conglist. Author: Bowling Manual, 1974. Office: 9200 Valley View St Cypress CA 90630-5805

DORN, VIRGINIA ALICE, art gallery director; b. Mpls., June 22, 1916; d. Raymond Edwin and Ruth Virginia (Nylander) Henneman; m. John Emil Dorn, Feb. 22, 1937 (dec. Sept. 1971); children: John Robert, Michael Raymond. BS, U. Minn., 1937. Mgr. med. lab. Orinda, Calif., 1955-61; instr. art Orinda Civic Ctr., 1980-81; mgr., tchr. San Francisco Women Artists Gallery, 1984—. One woman shows include Lucien LaBaudt Gallery, San Francisco, 1975, St. Paul's Towers, Oakland, Calif., 1976, Contemporary Arts, Berkeley, Calif., 1977, 80, Trinity Gallery, Berkeley, 1982, Valley Arts Gallery, Walnut Creek, Calif., 1982, Univ. Club, San Francisco, 1983, Holy Names Coll. Gallery, Oakland, 1987, Wellness Cmty. Gallery, Walnut Creek, 1991, Vincent's Ear Gallery, Orinda, Calif., 1994, also many juried and invitational shows in Calif. Recipient Lifetime Achievement award Women's Caucus for Art, 1996. Mem. San Francisco Women Artists (bd. dirs., fund raiser, mgr., instr., coord.), Oakland Art Assn., Valley Art Assn., Ctr. for the Visual Arts, Berkeley Art Ctr., East Bay Women Artists. Home: 95 Evergreen Dr Orinda CA 94563-3114

DORNAN, ROBERT KENNETH, former congressman; b. N.Y.C., Apr. 3, 1933; s. Harry Joseph and Gertrude Consuelo (McFadden) D.; m. Sallie Hansen, Apr. 16, 1955; children: Robin Marie, Robert Kenneth II, Theresa Ann, Mark Douglas, Kathleen Regina. Student, Loyola U., Westchester, Calif., 1950-53. Nat. spokesman Citizens for Decency Through Law, 1973-76; mem. 95th-97th Congresses from 27th Calif. dist., 1977-83, 99th-103rd Congresses from 38th Calif. dist., 1985-93, 103rd Congress and 104th Congress from 46th Calif. dist., 1993—; chmn. Nat. Sec. Subcom. on Military Personnel, chmn. Tech. and Tactical Intelligence. Host TV polit. talk shows in Los Angeles, 1965-73; host, producer: Robert K. Dornan Show, Los Angeles, 1970-73; combat photographer/broadcast journalist assigned 8 times to Laos-Cambodia-Vietnam, 1965-74; originator POW/MIA bracelet. Served to capt., fighter pilot USAF, 1953-58, fighter pilot, amphibian rescue pilot and intelligence officer USAFR, 1958-75. Mem. Am. Legion, Navy League, Air Force Assn., Res. Officers Assn., AMVET, Assn. Former Intelligence Officers, Am. Helicopter Soc. Special Forces Assn., AFTRA. Republican. Roman Catholic. Lodge: K.C. address: PO Box 3460 Garden Grove CA 92643*

DORNEMAN, ROBERT WAYNE, manufacturing engineer; b. Oaklawn, Ill., Nov. 13, 1949; s. Robert John and Julia (Vorchenia) D.; m. Katrina Holland, July 30, 1977; children: Tamara, Tiana. BA in Biol. Sci., Calif. State U., Fullerton, 1974. Mfg. engr. Gen. Telephone Co., Anaheim, Calif., 1974-77, Xerox/Century Data, Anaheim, 1977-80; advance mfg. engr. MSI Data, Costa Mesa, Calif., 1980-83; sr. mfg. engr. Parker Hannifin, Irvine, Calif., 1983-86; sr. advanced mfr. engr. Western Digital, Irvine, 1986-89, mgr. advanced mfg. engring., 1989-91; mfg. engr. Pairgain Tech., Cerritos, Calif., 1991-93, mgr. mfg. engring., 1993-94; mgr. engring. svcs. Pairgain Tech., Tustin, Calif., 1994—; specialist automated assembly of circuits; cons. Base 2, Fullerton, 1980; developer surface mount tech. for computer mfg. industry; set up computer assemble plants internat. Devel. and implimented environ. safe mfg. process for computer bd. industry; contbr. articles in 3M-Alert to profl. jours. Mem. Nat. Assn. Realtors (broker), N. Orange County Bd. Realtors (broker), Calif. Assn. Realtors, Aventura Yacht Club, Internat. Soc. Hybrid Mfg., Tau Kappa Epsilon. Republican. Home: 21 Fair Elms Laguna Niguel CA 92677-5908 Office: Pairgain Tech 14402 Franklin Ave Tustin CA 92780-7013

DORNETTE, RALPH MEREDITH, church organization executive, educator, minister; b. Cin., Aug. 31, 1927; s. Paul A. and Lillian (Bauer) D.; m. Betty Jean Pierce, May 11, 1948; 1 child, Cynthia Anne Dornette Orndorff. AB, Cin. Bible Coll., 1948; DD (hon.), Pacific Christian Coll., 1994. Ordained to ministry Christian Ch., 1947. Min. Indian Creek Christian Ch., Cynthiana, Ky., 1946-51; assoc. prof. Cin. Bible Coll., 1948-51; sr. min. First Christian Ch., Muskogee, Okla., 1951-57; founding min. Bellaire Christian Ch., Tulsa, 1957-59; exec. dir. So. Calif. Evangelistic Assn., Torrance, Calif., 1959-62, 68-77; sr. min. Eastside Christian Ch., Fullerton, Calif., 1962-68; dir. devel., prof. ministries Cin. Bible Coll. & Sem., 1977-79; exec. dir. Ch. Devel. Fund, Inc., Fullerton, 1968-77, CEO, 1979-94; sr. preaching minister 1st Christian Ch., Downey, Calif., 1971, 91; preaching minister Hemet (Calif.) Valley Christian Ch., 1992—; pres. So. Calif. Christian Mins. Assn., Fullerton, 1975. Author: Bible Answers to Popular Questions, 1954, Walking With Our Wonderful Lord, 1955, Bible Answers to Popular Questions II, 1964. Pres. Homeowners Assn., Anaheim, Calif., 1980-81. Named Churchman of Yr. Pacific Christian Coll., Fullerton, 1973; recipient Disting. Alumni award Cin. Bible Coll. and Seminary, 1994. Mem. N.Am. Christian Conv. (conv. com. Cin. chpt. 1963, chair nat. registration 1963, v.p. 1972, exec. com. 1963, 70-72, 80-82).

DORRA, HENRI, art historian, educator; b. Alexandria, Egypt, 1924; came to U.S., 1947, naturalized, 1953; s. Clement and Aimee (Castro) D.; m. Mary Lawrence Tonetti, 1965; children: Amy Lawrence, Helen Hyde. B.Sc. (Eng.), U. London, 1944; S.M., A.M., Harvard, 1950, Ph.D., 1953. Asst. dir. Corcoran Gallery Art, 1954-61, Phila. Mus. Art, 1961-62; exec. v.p. Art Assn. Indpls., 1962-63; faculty UCLA, 1963-65; prof. U. Calif., Santa Barbara, 1965-94, prof. emeritus, 1994—. Author: (with John Rewald) Georges Seurat, 1959, The American Muse, 1961, Art in Perspective, 1973, Symbolist Art Theories, 1994; also articles. Trustee Santa Barbara Mus. Art. Recipient Bowdoin prize Harvard, 1948; student fellow Met. Mus. Art, 1951-52, Guggenheim fellow, 1978-79. Office: U Calif Santa Barbara Dept Art History Santa Barbara CA 93106

DORRANCE, DEBRA ANN, secondary school educator; b. N.Y.C., Oct. 13, 1961; d. William Joseph and Dorothy Patricia (Anderson) Clark; m. Paul Dorrance, Dec. 30, 1986. BA in English and Lit., SUNY, Binghamton, 1983; postgrad., Carroll Coll., Helena, Mont., 1985; BS in Libr. Sci., U. Utah, 1987; MA in Edn., Lesley Coll., Boston, 1996; postgrad., Seattle Pacific U., 1996—. Tchr. english Helena H.S., 1986, Broadwater H.S., Townsend, Mont., 1987; tchr. English and writing Headmaster Distance Learning, Helena, 1988-92; tchr. English Capital H.S., Helena, 1993—. Mem. Nat. Coun. Tchrs. English, Arts Plus. Home: 150 Horse Shoe Bend Helena MT 59602-7417 Office: Capital High School 100 Valley Dr Helena MT 59601

DORSET, PHYLLIS FLANDERS, technical writer, editor; b. Tacoma, Wash., Sept. 10, 1924; d. William Winchell and Rhea Louise (MacDougall) Flanders; m. Donald Edward Dorset, Apr. 20, 1963. BA, U. Wash., 1948, MA, 1949; postgrad., U. N.Mex., 1949-50. Tech. writer Sandia Corp., Albuquerque, 1952-56; tech. writer/editor SRI Internat. (formerly Stanford Rsch. Inst.), Menlo Park, Calif., 1956—. Author: Historic Ships Afloat, 1967, The New Eldorado, 1970; editor: Fluid Dynamics; contbr. articles to profl. jours. Mem. Arts Commn., Menlo Park, 1970-73. Mem. Authors Guild. Home: 460 Sherwood Way Menlo Park CA 94025-3716

DORWARD, DAVID WILLIAM, microbiologist, consultant; b. Columbus, Ohio, June 5, 1956; s. Donald Lyle and Helen Ruth (Birkett) D.; m. Margaret Lynn Brockhaus, Apr. 23, 1983 (div. Sept. 1987); 1 child, Lori Marie Dorward; m. Renae Leilani Jensen, Feb. 14, 1997. BS in Botany, Miami U., Oxford, Ohio, 1979; MS in Botany, Miami U., 1981; PhD in Microbiology, U. Mont., 1987. Instr. Botany dept. U. Mont., Missoula, 1985, 88; instr. Microbiology dept. U. Mont., 1987; staff fellow NIH Rocky Mt. Labs., Hamilton, Mont., 1988-92; sr. staff fellow NIH Rocky Mt. Labs., Hamilton, 1992-96, microbiologist, 1996—; owner Infectious Disease Consulting, Hamilton, 1991—. Contbr. articles, editorials, rsch. proceedings to profl. jours. Patentee in field. Vol. Nat. Ski Patrol, Missoula, 1981-85, Sci.-by-Mail, 1995—. Recipient Diatome award for microtomy, 1996; Sigma Xi Rsch. grantee Miami U., 1980; NIH fellow award for rsch. excellence, 1995; Bertha Morton scholar, 1987. Mem. AAAS, Am. Soc. for Microbiology, Microscopy Soc. Am. (award for biol. sci. 1996). Home: PO Box 1623 Hamilton MT 59840-1623 Office: NIH Rocky Mt Labs 903 S 4th St Hamilton MT 59840-2999

DOSCHER, RICHARD JOHN, protective services official; b. Livermore, Calif., Aug. 31, 1952; s. Henry John and Violet Mary (Sutton) D.; m. Kathryn Laura Vierria, May 5, 1979; children: Cameron, Shannon. AS in Adminstrn. Justice, Yuba C.C., Marysville, Calif., 1987; BPA, U. San Francisco, 1991, MPA, 1993. From police officer to sgt. Yuba City (Calif.) Police Dept., 1977-85, sgt., watch commander, 1985-86, lt., divsn. commdr., 1986-89, lt., divsn. cmmdr. tech. svcs. and support, 1989-91, capt., divsn. cmmdr. field ops, 2d in commd agy., 1991-93, capt., divsn. cmmdr. investigation, 2d in commd. agy., chief of police, 1995—. Bd. dirs. Yuba/Sutter Easter Seal Soc., 1988—; vol. Calif. Prune Festival, 1988—, Spl. Olympics, 1987—, Bok Kai Chinese Cultural Festival, 1993—, Yuba City Cmty. Theater, 1992—; adv. com. Adminstrn. of Justice Yuba Coll., 1993—; eucharistic min. St. Isidore's Cath. Ch., 1984—. With USAF, 1972-76. Mem. Am. Soc. for Pub. Adminstrn., Calif. Assn. Police Tng. Officers, Calif. Police Chiefs Assn., Calif. Peace Officers Assn., Peace Officers' Rsch. Assn. Calif., Yuba City Police Officers Assn. (past officer 1978-80), Kiwanis Club (bd. dirs., 2d v.p. Yuba City), Yuba City Health and Racquet Club. Office: Yuba City Police Dept 1545 Poole Blvd Yuba City CA 95993-2615

DOSS, JAMES DANIEL, electrical engineer, writer; b. Reading, Pa., Mar. 9, 1939. BS in Maths., Ky. Wesleyan Coll., 1964; MSEE, U. N.Mex., Albuquerque, 1969. Mem. staff Los Alamos (N.Mex.) Nat. Lab., 1964—; adj. instr. in radiology and surgery U. N.Mex. Sch. of Medicine. Author: Engineer's Guide to High Temperature Superconductivity, 1989, (novels) The Shaman Sings, 1993, The Shaman Laughs, 1995, The Shaman's Bones, 1997; contbr. numerous articles to profl. jours. Mem. Mystery Writers Am. Episcopalian. Office: Los Alamos Nat Lab AOT-5 MS-H827 Los Alamos NM 87545

DOSSETT, LAWRENCE SHERMAN, professional services company official; b. Santa Ana, Calif., May 11, 1936; s. Wheeler Sherman and Eunice Elizabeth (Bright) D.; student U. Ariz., 1957-58, U. Calif., Irvine, 1973-75, Loyola Marymount Coll., 1974; m. Joanne Kallisch; children: Todd Sherman, Garrick Robert (dec.), Dana Shelene, Ryan William. Engring. draftsman Hughes Aircraft Co., Tucson, 1955-57, John J. Foster Mfg. Co., Costa Mesa, Calif., 1958, Standard Elec. Products, Costa Mesa, 1959; engring. mgr. Electronic Engring. Co., Santa Ana, 1959-79; product quality mgr. Farwest Data Systems, Irvine, Calif., 1979-82; dist. mgr. profl. svcs., nat. cons. mgr., sr. industry cons. Comserv/MSA/DBSoftware, L.A., 1982-92, sr. manufacturing industry cons., 1992-93; mfg. cons. Marcam Corp., Irvine, Calif., 1993-94; sr. industry cons. Cincom Sys., Inc., Irvine, Calif., 1994—. Mem. Western Electronic Mfrs. Assn., Am. Prodn. and Inventory Control Soc., Computer Mfrs. Conf., Cert. in mgmt. Am. Mgmt. Assn. Author: MRPXXI Asset/Liability Management System, 1993; co-author patent reel spindle, 1972.

DOSSEY, DONNA MARIE, state official; b. Lorain, Ohio, Oct. 17, 1948; d. Donald Richard and June (Trifiletti) Jenkins; m. Steven Monroe Dossey, Sept. 23, 1978; 1 child, Alexandria Marie. BA in Psychology, Auburn U., 1969; MA in Mgmt., U. Phoenix, Santa Fe, N.Mex., 1994. Lead instr. Troup City Tng. Ctr., LaGrange, Ga., 1972-78; program coord. New Vistas, Santa fe, 1981-89; program mgr. N.Mex. dept. Health, Santa fe, 1989-96; bur. chief N.Mex. Hwy. and Transp. Dept./Traffic Safety Bur., Santa fe, 1996—. Recipient Svc. award State and territorial Injury Prevention Dirs. Assn., 1995. Office: New Mexico State Hwy and Transp Dept Traffic Safety Bur 604 W San Mateo Rd Santa Fe NM 87501

DOSTOURIAN, DICK, computer systems executive; b. L.A., Oct. 30, 1948; s. John and Elizabeth (Cholakian) D.; m. Jeanette Adrienne Torigian; children: Leslie Ann, Christopher Scott. AA in Engring., East L.A. Coll., 1968; BS in Math., Calif. State U., L.A., 1970, MS in Math., 1972. Computer engr. McDonnell Douglas, L.A., 1973-76, prin. computing specialist, 1976-80, sect. mgr. engring. sys., 1980-83, mgr. product definition sys., 1983-89, mgr. info. tech., 1989-94; sr. mgr. software devel. Keane, Inc., L.A., 1994-95; software devel. mgr. Home Savings Am., Irwindale, Calif., 1995—. Mem. St. James Armenian Ch., L.A., 1989-94. Mem. IEEE, Assn. for Computing Machinery, Nat. Computer Graphics Soc., Data Processing Mgmt. Assn., Calif. State U. Alumni Assn. Home: 10781 Via Jacara Stanton CA 90680-1926 Office: Home Savings Am 4900 Rivergrade Rd Irwindale CA 91706

DOTO, IRENE LOUISE, statistician; b. Wilmington, Del., May 7, 1922; d. Antonio and Teresa (Tabasso) D. BA, U. Pa., 1943; MA, Temple U., 1948, Columbia U., 1954. Engring. asst. RCA-Victor, 1943-44; research asst. U. Pa., 1944; actuarial clk. Penn Mut. Life Ins. Co., 1944-46; instr. math. Temple U., 1946-53; commd. lt. health services officer USPHS, 1954, advanced through grades to capt., 1963; statistician Communicable Disease Ctr., Atlanta, 1954-55, Kansas City, Kans., 1955-67; chief statis. and publ. services, ecol. investigations program Ctr. for Disease Control, Kansas City, 1967-73, chief statis. services, div. hepatitis and viral enteritis, Phoenix, 1973-83; statis. cons., 1984—; mem. adj. faculty Phoenix Ctr., Ottawa U., 1982—. Mem. Am. Statis. Assn., Biometrics Soc., Am. Pub. Health Assn., Ariz. Pub. Health Assn., Ariz. Council Engring. and Sci. Assn. (officer 1982-90, pres. 1988-89), Primate Found. Ariz. (mem. animal care and use com. 1986—), Bus. and Profl. Women's Club Phoenix, The Retired Officers Assn. (state sec.-treas. 1995-96), Sigma Xi, Pi Mu Epsilon. Office: PO Box 22197 Phoenix AZ 85028-0197

DOTSON, GERALD RICHARD, biology educator; b. Brownsville, Tex., Sept. 8, 1937; s. Jasper William and Mary Agnes (Courtney) D.; m. Rose Delores Gonzales; children: Roberta Ana, Deborah, Matthew. BS, Coll. Santa Fe (N.Mex.), 1960; MS, U. Miss., 1966; PhD, U. Colo., 1974; postgrad., U. Tex., El Paso, 1960-61, Loyola U., New Orleans, 1962-63. Sci. tchr. Cathedral High Sch., El Paso, Tex., 1959-61; sci./math./music tchr. St. Paul's High Sch., Covington, La., 1961-62; sci./math./Spanish tchr. Christian Bros. Sch., New Orleans, 1962-63; sci. tchr., chmn. Hanson High Sch., Franklin, La., 1963-67; biology instr. Coll. Santa Fe (N.Mex.), 1967-69, U. Colo., Boulder, 1969-70, Community Coll. Denver, 1970-77; prof. biology and chmn. sci. Front Range Community Coll., Westminster, Colo., 1977—; mem. com. for tchg. excellence FRCC in Westminster, 1988—, mem. curriculum devel. com., 1970—, mem. acad. stds. com., 1980—, mem. student assessment com., student retention com., 1997—. Reviewer biology textbooks, media software, 1970—; contbr. articles to profl. jours. Mem. recreation dept. City of Westminster, 1971—. Mem. Am. Microscopical Soc., Am. Soc. Limnology and Oceanography, Nat. Assn. Biology Tchrs., Nat. Sci. Tchrs. Assn. (regional sec. 1965), Human Anatomy and Physiology Soc., Eagles, KC (3rd and 4th deg.), Elks, Sigma Xi, Phi Sigma. Roman Catholic. Home: 8469 Otis Dr Arvada CO 80003-1241 Office: Front Range Community Coll 3645 W 112th Ave Westminster CO 80030-2105

DOTY, EVERETT, food products executive; b. 1929. With Inland Fruit & Produce Co., Wapato, Wash., 1964—, v.p., 1992—. Office: Inland Fruit & Produce Co Frontage Rd Wapato WA 98951*

DOTY, HORACE JAY, JR., theater administrator, arts consultant; b. St. Petersburg, Fla., May 25, 1924; s. Horace Herndon and Mabel (Bruce) D.; student Sherwood Music Sch., Chgo., 1942-43; BA in Music, Pomona Coll., 1950; cert. La Verne Coll., 1969; MA in Edn., Claremont Grad. Sch., 1972; cert. in Bus. Adminstrn., 1984; m. Wanda L. Flory, Dec. 27, 1947; 1 child, Janet. Propr. Jay Doty's Inc., Claremont, 1960-68; concert mgr. Claremont Colls., 1968-73, supr. Garrison Theater, U. Ctr. Box Office, dir. Auditorium, theater events, coordinator programs, 1973-79, 81-90; exec. dir. Flint Ctr. for Performing Arts, Cupertino, Calif., 1979-81. Mem. blue ribbon com. Fox Theater Restoration, Pomona, Calif., 1982; mem. Claremont Bicentennial Com. for Performing Arts, 1975-76; mem. touring adv. panel, cons. and site visitor Calif. Arts Council; mem. exec. bd., Calif. Presenters. Served with inf. AUS, 1943-46. NEA fellow, 1986. Mem. Assn. Coll., Univ. and Community Arts Adminstrs. (dir. 1983-86), Western Alliance Arts Adminstrs. (pres. 1975-77), Internat. Assn. Auditorium Mgrs., Claremont C. of C. (pres. 1965-66). Office: Jay Doty Arts Cons 4145 Oak Hollow Rd Claremont CA 91711-2329

DOUGHERTY, MICHAEL, writer, filmmaker; b. Hammond, Ind., Dec. 28, 1924; s. Edward Daniel and Mary Estelle (Race) D.; divorced; 1 child, Race. BS, U. So. Calif., 1950. From press agt. to dir. spl. projects CBS TV, 1950-60; motion picture prodr. in South and S.E. Asia U.S. Fgn. Svc., Pakistan and India, 1961-62; media dir. Dem. Party, Hawaii, 1962-70; electronic media cons. U.S. Dept. State, Washington, 1967; freelance writer, ind. documentary film producer, 1963—; exec. sec. Gov.'s Constl. Conv. Com., 1968. Author: To Steal A Kingdom, 1994; writer/dir. (films) Colette, A Bridge to Space, Building the New Hawaii, No Free Lunch, Cross Roads, No Best Culture, Our Children's Children, The Big Island, Da Kine Sandbox, Rivers of Fire, Count Down to Gridlock, and others. Served with USMC, 1942-45, PTO. Hawaii State Found. of Culture and Arts grantee, 1978. Home: 41-020 Alaihi St Waimanalo HI 96795-1601

DOUGHERTY, MICHAEL JOSEPH, oil company executive; b. Olympia, Wash., May 17, 1949; s. Joseph John and Thelma Christine (Holthusen) D.; m. Paula Marie Fournier, June 26, 1971; children: Ronald C., Brian A., Jennifer A. BS in Chemistry, Oreg. State U., 1971; MS in Environ. Sci., Calif. State U., Fullerton, 1977; postgrad., Harvard U., 1989. Rsch. chemist Union Oil, Brea, Calif., 1971-77; coord. environ. control Union Oil, L.A., 1977-80, mgr. environ. control, 1980-86; mgr. state govt. rels. Unocal, L.A., 1986—. Chmn. petroleum com. Air Pollution Control Assn., Pitts., 1978-81; chmn. air pollution rsch. adv. com. Coord. Rsch. Coun., Atlanta, 1985-86; leader Boy Scouts Am., Placentia, Calif., 1989—; mem. Orange (Calif.) Diocese Cath. Com. on Scouting. 1990—. Mem. Am. Petroleum Inst., Western States Petroleum Assn., Calif. Mfrs. Assn. (bd. dirs. 1995—). Republican. Roman Catholic. Home: 668 Highlander Ave Placentia CA 92870-3229 Office: Unocal/76 Products 555 Anton Blvd Costa Mesa CA 92626-1461

DOUGHERTY, (MARY) PATRICIA, history educator; b. Monterey, Calif., Dec. 7, 1944; d. John Francis Dougherty and Clotilde (Quarelli) Hoefle. BA, Dominican Coll., 1967; MA, Georgetown U., 1979, PhD, 1984. Tchr. grades 4-8, 1967-77; teaching asst. dept. history Georgetown U., Washington, 1978-81, 82-83; chmn. dept. history Dominican Coll., San Rafael, Calif., 1984—. Contbr. articles and revs. to profl. jours. Fulbright fellow, Paris, 1981-82, Georgetown U. fellow, Washington, 1978-81, 82-83; grantee NEH, summer 1992. Mem. Am. Hist. Assn., Am. Cath. Hist. Assn., Soc. French Hist. Studies, Western Soc. French History (gov. coun. 1995—). Office: Dominican Coll 50 Acacia Ave San Rafael CA 94901-2298

DOUGHERTY, PATRICK, editor. Mng. editor Anchorage Daily News. Office: Anchorage Daily News 1001 Northway Dr Anchorage AK 99514-9001

DOUGHERTY, RAE ANN, semiconductor manufacturing company executive; b. Palo Alto, Calif., Feb. 26, 1955; d. Russell A. and Ilse D. (Dittman) Eversole; m. Richard Edward Dougherty, Aug. 24, 1979. BS in Environ. Sci., Rutgers U., 1977; MS in Engring., Colo. State U., 1979; MBA in Engring. Mgmt., U. Dallas, 1993. Rsch. asst. Colo. State U., Ft. Collins, 1977; meteorologist NOAA, Environ. Rsch. Lab., Boulder, Colo., 1979; project engr. TRC Environ. Cons., Denver, 1979-81; conservation engr. to dir. safety, health, environ. svcs. Arco Oil and Gas Co., Dallas, 1981-93; worldwide mgr. environ., health and safety Intel Corp., Rio Rancho, N. Mex., 1993—. Contbr. articles to profl. jours. Active Girl Scouts U.S.A., 1973—, bd. dirs. Tejas coun. 1992-94, Chapparell coun., 1994—, World Assn. Girl Guides and Girl Scouts Com., 1994—. Recipient Tejas Continuing Svcs. award Tejas Girl Scout Coun., Inc., 1989, Green Angel award, 1988. Mem. Am. Soc. Quality Control, Soc. Petroleum Engrs., Soc. Women Engrs., Am. Meteorol. Soc. (sec. 1979-81, Howard H. Hanks Jr. award 1979), Bus. and Profl. Womans Club (1st v.p. 1989-92), Leadership Tex., DAR, Zonta (Amelia Earhart fellow 1977-79). Home: 10405 Prestwick NE Albuquerque NM 87111-6554 Office: Intel Corp 4100 Sara Rd SE # F954 Tr Rio Rancho NM 87124-1025

DOUGHERTY, RALEIGH GORDON, manufacturer's representative; b. Saginaw, Mich., Aug. 19, 1928; s. Raleigh Gordon and Helen Jean (McCrum) D.; 1 child, Karen Kealani. Salesman, H.D. Hudson Mfg. Co., Chgo., 1946-48; field sales rep. Jensen Mfg. Co., Chgo., 1948-50; field sales mgr. Regency Idea, Indpls., 1950-54; mgr. Brenna & Browne, Honolulu, 1954-56; owner, pres. Dougherty Enterprises, Honolulu, 1956—. With U.S. Army, 1950-52. Mem. Hawaii Hotel Assn., Internat. Home Furnishings Reps. Assn., Air Force Assn., DAV (life), Navy League U.S., Am. Legion, Hawaii Restaurant Assn., Nat. Fedn. Ind. Bus., Korean Vet. Small Bus. of Hawaii, Historic Hawaii Found., Elks (past trustee Hawaii), Kani Ka Pila Golf Club. Republican. Methodist. Home and Office: 1326 Lunalilo Home Rd Honolulu HI 96825-3216

DOUGHTY, JOHN ROBERT, mechanical engineer, college president; b. Clarksburg, W.Va., July 30, 1936; s. Merrill Newton and Margaret Clara (Watson) D.; m. Betty Jeanette Smith, June 5, 1970; children: Donna, Marc, John, Denise, James, Dawn. BSME, U. N.Mex., 1958; PhD, U. Ariz., 1971. Registered profl. engr., Calif. Commd. 2d lt. USAF, 1958, advanced through grades to lt. col., 1975; sect. head Air Force Weapons Lab., Kirtland AFB, N.Mex., 1970-75; div. chief Air Force Space Div., L.A. Air Force Sta., 1975-79; ret., 1979; mem. tech. staff Gen. Rsch. Corp., El Segundo, Calif., 1979-80; sect. head space and tech. group TRW, Redondo Beach, Calif., 1980-85; vis. lectr., researcher Ben Gurion U., Beersheva, Israel, 1985-86; cons. engr. Doughty Rsch. Engring., Huntington Beach, Calif., 1986-88, Albuquerque, 1988-94; adj. prof. Embry-Riddle Aero. U., Kirtland AFB Ext., 1990-94. Contbr. articles to profl. jours. Mem. exec. com. Am. Assocs. Ben Gurion U., Orange County, Calif., 1984-88; sec. Christian Missionary Pilots, Newport Beach, Calif., 1983-85; v.p. Albuquerque Bible Coll., 1989-91, pres., 1991—; sec.-treas. Creation Sci. Fellowship N.Mex., Albuquerque, 1990—; pilot N.Mex. Wing, CAP, 1991—. Mem. AIAA, ASME. Republican. Home: 532 Calle De Los Hijos NW Albuquerque NM 87114-2039

DOUGLAS, DIANE MIRIAM, museum director; b. Harrisburg, Pa., Mar. 25, 1957; d. David C. and Anna (Barron) D.; m. Steve I. Perlmutter, Jan. 23, 1983; 1 child, David Simon. BA, Brown U., 1979; MA, U. Del., 1982. Oral history editor Former Members of Congress, Washington, 1979-80; assoc. curator exhibitions John Michael Kohler Arts Ctr., Sheboygan, Wis., 1982-83; dir. arts ctr. Lill Street Gallery, Chgo., 1984-88; exec. dir. David Adler Cultural Ctr., Libertyville, Ill., 1988-91; dir. Bellevue (Wash.) Art Mus., 1992—; program chair, exec. bd. nat. Coun. for Edn. in Ceramic Arts, Bandon, Oreg., 1990-93; nat. adv. bd. Friends of Fiber Art, 1992; artists adv. com. Pilchuck Glass Sch., 1993—; mem. bd. dirs. Archie Bray Found., Helena, Mont., 1995—. Office: Bellevue Art Mus 301 Bellevue Sq Bellevue WA 98004-5000

DOUGLAS, DONALD WILLS, JR., energy executive; b. Washington, July 3, 1917; s. Donald Wills and Charlotte Marguerita (Ogg) D.; m. Molly McIntosh, May 1, 1939 (dec.); children: Victoria Thoreson, Holly Douglas Adams (dec.); m. Jean Cooper, Aug. 17, 1950 (dec.); m. Linda Alstead, Nov. 16, 1986. Student, Stanford U., 1934-38, Curtiss-Wright Tech. Inst., Glendale, Calif., 1939. With engring. Douglas Aircraft Co., 1939-43, dir. testing divsn., 1943-51, dir. contract adminstrn., 1948-51, dir. rsch. labs., 1949-51, v.p., 1951-57, pres., 1957-67, also bd. dirs.; corp. v.p. adminstrn. McDonnell Douglas Corp., 1967-71, corp. sr. v.p. adminstrn., 1971-72, pres. Douglas Devel. Corp., 1972-74; sr. ptnr. Ptnrs. Real Estate, Inc., 1978-80; pres. Douglas Energy Co., Placentia, Calif., 1981—, chmn., CEO, 1986-92; Chmn. Group IX Aerospace Systems, 1984—; chmn. Douglas Internat. Group, 1989—; mem. Nat. Export Expansion Coun., U.S. Dept. Commerce, 1964-73, exec. com., 1965-73, com. econ. devel., 1970-73, coun. fgn. rels., 1970-73; sr. cons. McDonnell Douglas Corp., 1974-75; bus. cons., 1974-75; sr. cons. market devel. Biphase Energy Systems, joint venture Rsch.-Cottrell and Transamerica Delaval, 1981-82, Biphase Energy Systems, subs. Transamerica Delaval, 1982-86; chmn., CEO DCOR Ptnrs., Inc., 1979-80; dir., chmn. bd. Aerotech Cons., Inc., 1982-84; dir. Reno Airline; chmn. Douglas Pvt. Jets. Mem. Pres. Com. on Youth Fitness, 1958-59; coun. v.p. fin. Boy Scouts Am., 1981-86, chmn. adv. com. Gt. Western Coun., 1978-80, hon. pres., 1968, bd. mem. St. Louis area coun., 1970-72; hon. pres. Crescent Bay Coun., 1967, pres., 1955-67, mem.-at-large nat. coun., 1951—; chmn. trustees Donald Douglas Mus. & Libr., 1975-89, Mus. of Flying, 1989—. Recipient Officiale of Order of Merit Republic of Italy, 1962, Chevalier, French Legion of Honor award, 1961, Silver Antelope award Boy Scouts Am., western region, 1983. Assoc. fellow AIAA; mem. Aerospace Industries Assn. (chmn. bd. govs. 1964), Air Force Assn., Air Force Mus. Assn., Assn. U.S. Army (adv. bd. 1966-67), Conquistadores del Cielo (pres. 1965-66, chmn. bd. 1966-67, sports chmn. 1965—, sec.-treas. 1971—), Nat. Def. Transp. Assn. (life, nat. v.p. 1958-63, gen. chmn. 22nd Forum La. 1967), Naval Aviation Mus. Assn., Inc. (dir. 1971-90), Navy League U.S. (life), Transpacific Yacht Club, Rancheros Visitadores, Phi Gamma Delta. Home: Skycrest Farm 38851 Avenida La Cresta Murrieta CA 92562 Office: Douglas Energy Co 181 W Orangethorpe Ave Ste D Placentia CA 92870-6931 also: Douglas Pvt Jets/Douglas Internat Group Ste HH 41690 Enterprise Cir N Temecula CA 92590

DOUGLAS, EVERETT LAWRENCE, physicist, environmental engineer; b. St. Louis, May 24, 1939; s. Curtis Albert and Alice Rose (Elsie) D. BA in Zoology, U. Mo., 1961; PhD in Marine Biology/Animal Physiology, U. Calif. San Diego, 1967. Prof. U. Mo., Columbia, 1967-73; postdoctoral assoc. Case We. Res. U., Cleve., 1974-75; physicist U.S. Navy, San Diego, 1977—; br. head Aircraft Environ. Support Office, USN, San Diego, 1991—. Contbr. articles to profl. jours. Lectr. on preservation of wilderness areas San Diego City Schs., 1965—. Recipient Antarctica Svc. medal U.S. Govt., 1965-74; Sverdrup fellow Scripps Instn. Oceanography, 1962-67. Mem. Soc. Aerospace Engrs. (vice chair E-31 com.), Phi Beta Kappa, Sigma Xi. Home: 4310 Piedmont Dr San Diego CA 92107-4135

DOUGLAS, JOEL BRUCE, lawyer; b. L.A., Jan. 25, 1948. BA magna cum laude, Calif. State U., Northridge, 1970; postgrad., East L.A. Coll.; JD, Loyola U., L.A., 1973. Bar: Calif. 1973, U.S. Dist. Ct. (ctrl. dist.) Calif. 1974, U.S. Ct. Appeals (9th cir.) 1978, U.S. Supreme Ct. 1979. Ptnr. Bonne, Bridges, Mueller, O'Keefe & Nichols P.C., L.A.; adj. prof. sch. law Pepperdine U., Malibu, Calif., 1981-84; judge pro tempore L.A. Mcpl. Ct., 1980—, L.A. Superior Ct., 1988—. Assoc. editor Loyola U. L.A. Law Rev., 1972-73. Mem. ABA (litigation sect., tort and ins. practice sect.), State Bar Calif., L.A. County Bar Assn. (mem. legal-med. com. 1979-83, staff atty. med.-legal hot line 1979-82), Am. Bd. Trial Advocates, St. Thomas Moore Law Honor Soc., Phi Alpha Delta. Office: Bonne Bridges Mueller O'Keefe & Nichols PC 3699 Wilshire Blvd Fl 10 Los Angeles CA 90010-2719

DOUGLAS, MARION JOAN, proofreader, editor, labor negotiator; b. Jersey City, May 29, 1940; d. Walter Stanley and Sophie Frances (Zysk) Binaski; children: Jane Dee, Alex Jay. BA, Mich. State U., 1962; MSW, Sacramento State Coll., 1971; MPA, Calif. State U.-Sacramento, 1981. Owner, mgr. Linkletter-Totten Dance Studios, Sacramento, 1962-68, Young World of Discovery, Sacramento, 1965-68; welfare worker Sacramento County, 1964-67, welfare supr., 1968-72, child welfare supr., 1972-75, sr. personnel analyst, 1976-78, personnel program mgr., 1978-81, labor relations rep., 1981-89; cons. State Dept. Health, Sacramento, 1975-76; cons. in field. Author/editor: (newsletter) Thursday's Child, 1972-74. Presiding officer Cmty. Resource Orgn., Fair Oaks, Calif., 1970-72; exec. bd. Foster Parent's Assn., Sacramento, 1972-75; organizer Foster Care Sch. Dist. liaison programs, 1973-75; active Am. Lung Assn., 1983-87, 93-94; rep. Calif. Welfare Dirs. Assn., 1975-76; county staff advisor Joint Powers Authority, Sacramento, 1978-81; mem. Mgmt. Devel. Com., Sacramento, 1979-80; vol., auctioneer sta. KVIE Pub. TV, Sacramento, 1970-84, 88-90; adv. bd. Job and Info. Resource Ctr., 1976-77; spl. adv. task force coordinator Sacramento Employment and Tng. Adv. Council, 1980-81; vol. leader Am. Lung Assn., Sacramento, 1983-86, 94—, Calif. Dept. Social Welfare ednl. stipend, 1967-68, County of Sacramento ednl. stipend, 1969-70. Recipient Achievement award Nat. Assn. Counties, 1981. Mem. Mgmt. Women's Forum, Indsl. Relations Assn. No. Calif., Indsl. Relations Research Assn., Nat. Assn. Female Execs., Mensa. Republican. Avocations: real estate, nutrition. Home: 7812 Palmyra Dr Fair Oaks CA 95628-3423

DOUGLAS, MICHAEL, publishing executive; b. Corpus Christi, Tex., Nov. 19, 1955; s. Phyllis Marie (Blackshear) Fusillier; children: Kenneth Muhammad, Michelle Muhammad, Gabrielle Muhammad, Phenix Muhammad, Aaron Muhammad. Student, Ariz. State U., 1979-82. Pres. Mecca Publs., Phoenix, 1986—; owner Re-Creation Enterprises, Phoenix, 1990—. Author: Brotherhood, War, Revolution, 1986, Jabril—God, Man, Angel, 1990, Apocalypse Now 1997-2007, 1995. Pres. Neighborhood Agrl. Program, Phoenix, 1988; with operation paintbrush City of Phoenix, 1988; head of unknown writer's workshop Mecca Publ., Phoenix, 1994—; homeless counselor Prodigal Son, Phoenix, 1995. With U.S. Army, 1972-74. Muslim. Office: Mecca Publs PO Box 28238 Tempe AZ 85285-8238

DOUGLAS, ROBERT OWEN, writer; b. Aberdeen, S.D., Feb. 18, 1940; s. James Garrison and Lorene Augusta (Soper) D. BA, Claremont McKenna Coll., 1962. Maritime editor San Pedro (Calif.) News Pilot, 1968-70; freelance photographer Nat. Geog. Mag., Washington, 1969; pvt. practice writer Tacoma, 1977—. Author: The Seven Seals, 1997; lyricist Bravo, You're High Voltage, 1996, The Vacation Song, 1996; inventor Douglas Tower Turbine, 1996. Lt. USN, 1963-68. Recipient Song of the Month award Chapel Rec. Co., Wollaston, Mass., 1996. Office: Golden Dawn PO Box 1513 Tacoma WA 98401-1513

DOUGLASS, AMY ANITA, museum director; b. Rio de Janeiro, Feb. 9, 1955; d. Ralph Julius and Juanita Ruth (Walls) D.; m. Bradley Nelson Lichtenstein, July 17, 1993. BA, Wellesley (Mass.) Coll., 1976; MA, Syracuse (N.Y.) U., 1980; PhD, Ariz. State U., 1987. Curatorial asst. Mus. of the Am. Indian, Heye Found., N.Y.C., 1976-78; crew chief archaeology Ariz. State U., Tempe, 1983, U. N.Mex., Albuquerque, 1983-84; exhibit coord. Ariz. State U., Tempe, 1987; pub. liaison Northland Rsch. Inc., Tempe, 1987; mus. dir. Tempe Hist. Mus., Tempe, 1988—. Author: Prehistoric Exchange and Sociopolitical Development, 1991. Mem. Soc. for Am. Archaeology (pub. edn. com.), Ariz. Archaeol. Coun. (archeology educators com.), Mus. Assn. of Ariz. (meeting co-chair), Ctrl. Ariz. Mus. Assn., Phi Kappa Phi, Phi Beta Kappa.

DOUGLASS, DONALD ROBERT, banker; b. Evanston, Ill., Oct. 7, 1934; s. Robert William and Dorothy (Gibson) D.; m. Susan Douglass. BBA, U. N.Mex., 1959, MBA, 1966. With Security Pacific Nat. Bank, Los Angeles, 1961—, mgmt. trainee, 1962-63, asst. mgr. Vernon (Calif.) br., 1963-64, asst. mgr. Whittier (Calif.), 1964, asst. v.p., 1965, asst. v.p., credit officer regional adminstrn., Los Angeles, 1966-69, v.p., San Francisco, 1969-74, mgr. corp. accounts credit adminstrn. No. Calif. Corp. Banking, 1974-77; group v.p. Annco Properties, Burlingame, Calif., 1977-79; v.p., sr. loan officer Borel Bank and Trust Co., San Mateo, Calif., 1979-83, sr. v.p., 1983-84, exec. v.p. mortgage banking div. comml. property sales, Los Altos, 1984-87 ; ptnr. Key Equities, Inc., San Mateo, 1987—; ptnr., broker Centre Fin. Group, Inc., San Mateo, 1987—, Centre Fin. Group South Inc., Menlo Park, 1987—; pres. ServiCtr. Mortgage, Inc., 1996—; instr. Am. Inst. Banking, 1963, Coll. San Mateo, 1982—. Served with AUS, 1954-56. Mem. U. N.Mex. Alumni Assn., Sigma Alpha Epsilon, Delta Sigma Phi. Republican. Presbyterian. Home: 745 Celestial Ln San Mateo CA 94404-2771

DOUGLASS, ENID HART, educational program director; b. L.A., Oct. 23, 1926; d. Frank Roland and Enid Yandell (Lewis) Hart; m. Malcolm P. Douglass, Aug. 28, 1948; children: Malcolm Paul Jr., John Aubrey, Susan Enid. BA, Pomona Coll., 1948; MA, Claremont (Calif.) Grad. Sch., 1959. Research asst. World Book Ency., Palo Alto, Calif., 1953-54; exec. sec., asst. dir. oral history program Claremont Grad. Sch., 1963-71, dir. oral history program, 1971—, history lectr., 1977—; mem. Calif. Heritage Preservation Commn., 1977-85, chmn. 1983-85. Contbr. articles to hist. jours. Mayor pro tem City of Claremont, 1980-82, mayor, 1982-86; mem. planning and rsch. adv. coun. State of Calif.; mem. city coun. City of Claremont, 1978-86; founder Claremont Heritage, Inc., 1977-80; bd. dirs., 1986-95; bd. dirs. Pilgrim Pla., Claremont; founder, steering com., founding bd. Claremont Cmty. Found., 1989-95, pres., 1990-94. Mem. Oral History Assn. (pres. 1979-80), Southwest Oral History Assn. (founding steering com. 1981, J.V. Mink award 1984), Nat. Council Pub. History, LWV (bd. dirs. 1957-59, Outstanding Svc. to Community award, 1986). Democrat. Home: 1195 N Berkeley Ave Claremont CA 91711-3842 Office: Claremont Grad Sch Oral History Program 710 N College Ave Claremont CA 91711-3921

DOUGLASS, JOHN MICHAEL, internist; b. Takoma Park, Md., Apr. 13, 1939; s. Jones All and Helen Louise D.; BA, Columbia Union Coll., Takoma Park, 1959; MD (Salutatorian), U. So. Calif., 1964; DPH Pacific West U., 1986; PhD Clayton U., 1987. m. Sue Nan Peters, May 15, 1962; children: Dina Lynn, Lisa Michele. Rotating intern Los Angeles County, U. So. Calif. Med. Ctr., 1964-65, resident internal medicine, 1965-67, home care physician, 1965-68; practice medicine specializing in internal medicine, Cin., 1968-70, L.A., 1970-91; physician Pasadena Emergency Ctr., 1965-68, Deaconess

Hosp., 1968-70; postdoctoral fellow automobile safety and trauma rsch. UCLA, 1967-68, med. cons. Emergency Med. Svcs. Project, 1970-71; commd. officer USPHS, 1968, advanced through grades to comdr., sr. surgeon USPHS Res. 1982—, asst. sci. adviser injury control program ECA, Cin., 1968-69, med. specialities cons. Office Product Safety, FDA, 1969-70; internal medicine cons. East End Neighborhood Community Health Ctr. Cin., 1968-70, Hollywood Sunset Free Clinic, 1971-72; sr. med. cons. multidisciplinary hwy. accident investigation unit U. So. Calif., 1971-73; staff internist, coordinator health improvement service Kaiser Found. Hosp., L.A., 1970-92; instr. biomedical engring. course UCLA, 1968, sr. med. cons., assoc. sci. advisors, 1970—, instr. internal medicine, 1971-74; instr. internal medicine U. Cin. Sch. Medicine, 1968-70; instr. kinesthesiology, traumatic anatomy and head injury U. So. Calif., 1971-74, instr. foodstyle and lifestyle, 1977—; mem. med. adv. bd. Dominican Sisters of Sick Poor, 1969; traffic safety cons. Countywide Conf. on Emergency Med. Svcs., 1972; mem. nutrition council Las Virgenes Sch. Dist., 1977; coord. K-PMG Health Svc.; CFO Prepared Gormet, Inc.; engring. biomed. cons; tchr. anatomy and physiology. Active mgmt. devel. program Boy Scouts Am. Execs., 1966; bd. dirs. Calif. Assn. Pvt. Schs. and Colls., 1967, Coronary Club (adult jogging program), 1967-68; co-organizer Oriental rug exhibit Pacificulture Mus., Pasadena, Calif., 1973; v.p. L.A. Med. Milk Commn. Diplomate Nat. Bd. Med. Examiners, Am. Bd. Internal Medicine. Fellow ACP; mem. AMA, Am. Acad. Body Sculpting, Calif. Med. Assn., L.A. County Med. Assn., Am. Soc. Internal Medicine, Calif. Soc. Internal Medicine, L.A. Soc. Internal Medicine, Am. Assn. Automotive Medicine (exec. com. Western chpt. 1977-82), Am. Cancer Soc. (profl. edn. com., nutrition subcom.), Internat. Hajji Baba Soc., Decorative Arts Council, L.A. Mus. Art, Sierra Club, Phi Delta Epsilon, Alpha Omega Alpha, Phi Kappa Phi. Author: The Lost Language; contbr. over 100 articles to profl. jours.

DOVE, DONALD AUGUSTINE, city planner, educator; b. Waco, Tex., Aug. 7, 1930; s. Sebert Constantine and Amy Delmena (Stern) D.; m. Cecelia Mae White, Feb. 9, 1957; children: Angela Dove Gaddy, Donald, Monica Gilstrap, Celine, Austin, Cathlyn Howze, Dianna, Jennifer. BA, Calif. State U.-L.A., 1951; MA in Pub. Adminstrn., U. So. Calif., 1966. Planning and devel. cons. D. Dove Assocs., L.A., 1959-60; supr. demographic rsch. Calif. Dept. Pub. Works, L.A., 1960-66, environ. coordinator, Sacramento, 1971-75; dir. transp. employment project State of Calif., L.A., 1966-71, chief Los Angeles Region transp. study, 1975-84; chief environ. planning Calif. Dept. Transp., L.A., 1972-75; dir. U. So. Calif. Praetors, L.A., 1984-87; panelist, advisor Pres. Conf. on Aging, Washington, 1970—, Internat. Conf. on Energy Use Mgmt., 1981; guest lectr. univs. western U.S., 1969—. Author: Preserving Urban Environment, 1976; Small Area Population Forecasts, 1966. Chmn. Lynwood City Planning Commn., Calif., 1982—; pres. Area Pastoral Coun., L.A., 1982-83; mem., del. Archdiocesan Pastoral Council, L.A., 1979-86, Compton Community Devel. Bd., Calif., 1967-71; pres. Neighborhood Esteem/Enrichment Techniques Inst., 1992-93. Served to cpl. U.S. Army, 1952-54. Mem. Am. Planning Assn., Am. Inst. Planners (transp. chmn. 1972-73), Calif. Assn. of Mgmt. (pres. 1987-88), Am. Inst. Cert. Planners, Assn. Environ. Profls. (co-founder 1973), Optimists (sec. 1978-79). Democrat. Roman Catholic. Home and Office: 11356 Ernestine Ave Lynwood CA 90262-3711

DOVE, MICHAEL ROGER, anthropology researcher; b. Dec. 26, 1949; m. Carol Carpenter. BA, Northwestern U., 1971; MA, Stanford U., 1972, PhD, 1981. Postdoctoral fellow, rsch. fellow Rockefeller Found., Java, 1979-83; project coord. East-West Ctr. Ford Found., Java, 1984-85; sr. project anthropologist Winrock Internat. Inst. Agr. Devel., Pakistan, 1985-89; fellow East-West Ctr., 1989-91; sr. fellow East-West Ctr., mem. grad. faculty anthropology U. Hawaii, Honolulu, 1991—, program dir. East-West Ctr., 1997—; tchg. asst. Stanford U., 1972, instr., 1978; vis. prof. Gadjah Mada U., 1979-85; vis. fellow Yale U., 1991-92; cons., lectr. in field. Author: Nelayan dan Kemiskinan, 1984, Swidden Agriculture in Indonesia, 1985, The Real and Imagined Role of Culture in Development, 1988, The Sociology of Natural Resources in Pakistan, 1992; contbr. chpts. to books and articles to profl. jours. Fellow Borneo Rsch. Coun.; mem. Am. Anthropol. Assn., Am. Ethnological Soc., Assn. Asian Studies, Wash. Assn. Profl. Antrhopologists, Royal Asiatic Soc., Koninklijk Inst. voor Taal-Land en Volkenkunde, Soc. Applied Anthropology, Soc. Econ. Botany. Office: East West Ctr (ENV) 1601 East-West Rd Honolulu HI 96848-1601

DOW, MARY ALEXIS, auditor; b. South Amboy, N.J., Feb. 19, 1949; d. Alexander and Elizabeth Anne (Reilly) Pawlowski; m. Russell Alfred Dow, June 19, 1971. BS with honors, U. R.I., 1971. CPA, Oreg. Staff acct. Deloitte & Touche, Boston, 1971-74; sr. acct. Price Waterhouse, Portland, Oreg., 1974-77, mgr., 1977-81, sr. mgr., 1981-84; CFO Copeland Lumber Yards Inc., Portland, 1984-86; ind. cons. in field, 1986-94; elected auditor Metro, Portland, 1995—; bd. dirs. Longview Fibre Co. Bd. dirs., exec. com., past treas. Oreg. Mus. Sci. and Industry; past chmn. bd., mem. exec. com. Oreg. Trails chpt. N.W. Regional Blood Svcs. ARC. Mem. AICPA, Pacific N.W. Intergovtl. Audit Forum (exec. com.), Am. Woman's Soc. CPAs, Oreg. Soc. CPAs (bd. dirs. ednl. found.), Fin. Execs. Inst. (past bd. dirs., past pres. Portland chpt.). Roman Catholic. Clubs: City (bd. govs.), Multnomah Athletic. Contbr. articles to profl. publs. Office: Office of Auditor Metro 600 NE Grand Ave Portland OR 97232-2736

DOWDEN, ANNE OPHELIA, botanical illustrator, writer; b. Denver, Sept. 17, 1907; d. James Campbell and Edith Belinda (Brownfield) Todd; m. Raymond Baxter Dowden, Apr. 1, 1934 (dec. Jan. 1982). BA, Carnegie Inst. Tech., Pitts., 1930; student, Art Students League, N.Y.C., 1930-32; DFA (hon.), Moore Coll. of Art, Phila., 1988. Instr. art Pratt Inst., Bklyn., 1930-33; freelance textile designer N.Y.C., 1935-52; head art dept. Manhattanville Coll., N.Y.C., 1932-53; bot. illustrator, author N.Y.C., 1952-90, Boulder, Colo., 1990—. Author-illustrator: The Secret Life of the Flowers, 1964, Roses, 1965, Look at a Flower, 1963, Wild Green Things in the City: A Book of Weeds, 1972, The Blossom on the Bough: A Book of Trees, 1975, State Flowers, 1977, From Flower to Fruit, 1984, This Noble Harvest: A Chronicle of Herbs, 1979, The Clover and the Bee: A Book of Pollination, 1990, Poisons in Our Path, 1994; illustrator Shakespeare's Flowers, 1969, The Golden Circle, 1977, Wildflowers and the Stories Behind Their Names, 1977, The Lore and Legends of Flowers, 1982, Consider the Lilies, 1986, Plants of Christmas, 1987; contbr. numerous articles to mags. Recipient Am. Inst. Graphic Arts, Children's Book Show award, 1973, ALA, Notable Children's Books, 1963, 75, 77, 82, Children's Book Coun., Showcase Selection, Sch. Library Jour., Best Books award, Nat. Sci. Tchrs. Assn., Outstanding Sci. Books for Children awards; recipient fellowship, Tiffany Found., L.I., N.Y., 1929, 30, 31, award for excellence in svc. to bot. art Am. Soc. Bot. Art, 1996, Hort. Arts award Garden Club Am., Zone XII, 1996. Mem. Bklyn. Botanic Garden, N.Y. Bot. Garden, Denver Botanic Garden. Home: 350 Ponca Pl Boulder CO 80303-3802

DOWDLE, PATRICK DENNIS, lawyer; b. Denver, Dec. 8, 1948; s. William Robert and Helen (Schraeder) D.; m. Eleanor Pryor, Mar. 8, 1975; children: Jeffery William, Andrew Peter. BA, Cornell Coll., Mt. Vernon, Iowa, 1971; JD, Boston U., 1975. Bar: Colo. 1975, U.S. Dist. Ct. Colo. 1975, U.S. Ct. Appeals (10th cir.) 1976, U.S. Supreme Ct. 1978. Acad. dir. in Japan Sch. Internat. Tng., Putney, Vt., 1974; assoc. Decker & Miller, Denver, 1975-77; ptnr. Miller, Makkai & Dowdle, Denver, 1977—; designated counsel criminal appeals Colo. Atty. Gens. Office, Denver, 1980-81; guardian ad litem Adams County Dist. Ct., Brighton, Colo., 1980-83; affiliated counsel ACLU, Denver, 1980—. Mem. Colo. Bar Assn., Denver Bar Assn. (various coms.), Porsche Club of Am. Home: 3254 Tabor Ct Wheat Ridge CO 80033-5367 Office: Miller Makkai & Dowdle 2325 W 72nd Ave Denver CO 80221-3101

DOWLIN, JANICE MARIE, science administrator; b. Hugo, Colo., June 11, 1940; d. James W. and Helen Ann (Brandt) Simmons; m. Kenneth Everett Dowlin, Mar. 11, 1961; children: Kevin E., Kristopher E. BS in Med. Tech., U. Colo., 1962. Nat. cert. lab. dir.; lic. med. technologist, Calif.; nat. cert. assn. Clin. Lab. Scientists, Med. Technologists, Am. Soc. Clin. Pathologists. Intern in med. tech. U. Colo., Denver, 1962; chief med. technologist Physicians-Surgeons Med. Lab., Denver, 1962-64; med. technologist Natrona County Meml. Hosp., Casper, Wyo., 1969-71; sr. biochem. technologist Meml. Hosp., Colorado Springs, Colo., 1977-82; med. technologist Nat. Health Labs., Colorado Springs, 1984-87; lab. mgr. Physicians Med. Clinic Labs., Daly City, Calif., 1987—; clin. labs. improvement amendments insp. Health Care Fin. Adminstrn. Fed. Govt., San Francisco, 1994-96; mem. adv. panel Med. Lab. Observer, 1990—. Mem. Calif. Assn. Med. Lab. Tech., Clin. Lab. Mgmt. Assn. Home: 359 Melrose Ave San Francisco CA 94127-2344 Office: PMC Labs 901 Campus Dr # 103 Daly City CA 94015

DOWLIN, KENNETH EVERETT, librarian; b. Wray, Colo., Mar. 11, 1941; s. Ross Everett and Fern Mae (Peterson) D.; m. Janice Marie Simmons, Mar. 11, 1961; children: Kevin Everett, Kristopher Everett. BA, U. Colo., 1963, MPA, 1981; MA, U. Denver, 1966. Bookmobile libr., libr. asst. Adams County Public Libr., Westminster, Colo., 1961-63; libr. asst. II Denver Pub. Libr., 1962-64; head libr. Arvada Public Libr., Colo., 1964-68; adminstrv. asst. Jefferson County Pub. Libr., Colo., 1969; dir. Natrona County Pub. Libr., Casper, Wyo., 1969-75, Pikes Peak Regional Libr. Dist., Colorado Springs, Colo., 1975-87; city libr. San Francisco Pub. Libr., 1987—; instr. Casper Coll., 1971-73; chmn. Colo. Librs. in Coop., 1975-76, Colo. Ad-hoc Com. Networking, 1976; libr. City of San Francisco, 1987; mem. Western Interstate Commn. Higher Edn. Libr. Network Task Force; past trustee Wyo. Dept. Libr., Archives and History; mem. Libr. of Congress Commn. on Book of Future; bd. dirs. Satellite Libr. Info. Network; bd. mem. Libr. Found. of San Francisco, 1987—, Friends of the Libr., 1987—, Bay Area Book Festival, 1988-90; mem. Calif. State Libr. Task Force on Networking, 1988—, Calif. State Libr. of Tomorrow Task Force, 1995; founding mem. Greater Bay Area Libr. Coun., 1994—; vis. instr. U. Denver, 1980, 81; vis. faculty U. Calif., Berkeley, 1993; cons. in cable TV. Editorial bd. Microcomputers for Info. Mgmt., Libr. Hi Tech., Elec. Libr. Mem. adv. bd. for series on tech. WNET, N.Y.C., 1981-83; active San Francisco Mayor's com. on Juveniles in Detention; bd. dirs. Citizens Goals for Colorado Springs, 1981-85; bd. govs. Colo. Tech. Coll., 1982-85. With USMCR, 1959-65. Recipient Disting. Alumni award U. Denver Grad. Sch. for Libr. and Info. Mgmt. Mem. ALA (coun. mem. 1985-89, commn. on equality and freedom access to info. 1984-85, chmn. awards com. 1985-86, pres.'s com. on preservation 1990—, ad hoc com. on MARC licensing, chair local arrangements com. for 1992, 1989-92, pres.'s com. on preservation policy 1989-90, Hammond Inc. Libr. Award Jury 1968), ALA Libr. and Info. Tech. Assn. (long range planning com. 1981-82, pres. 1983-84, com. mem. Gaylord Awards), Mountain Plains Libr. Assn., Calif. Libr. Assn. (fin. com., coun. mem. 1989—), Colo. Libr. Assn. (pres. 1968-69), Denver Coun. Govts. (chmn. librs. com. 1966), Colo. Mcpl. League (chmn. librs. sect. 1967), Bibliog. Ctr. Rocky Mountains (pres. 1972-74), Pikes Peak Area C. of C. (chmn. cultural affairs com. 1976-77). Office: San Francisco Pub Libr Civic Ctr San Francisco CA 94102

DOWNEY, DANIEL LEE, plastic surgeon; b. Sacramento, 1956. MD, U. Wash., 1983. Intern Virginia Mason Hosp., Seattle, 1983-84, surgeon, 1984-88, now plastic surgeon; plastic surgeon U. Rochester, N.Y., 1988-90. Office: Virginia Mason Hosp 1100 9th Ave # X-11 Seattle WA 98101-2756

DOWNEY, HEATHER ANNE, property manager; b. Belfast, Northern Ireland, May 2, 1961; d. T. J. and M. N. (Hutchman) D. BA, Antioch U., 1991. Exec. asst., asst. mktg. mgr. Pike Pl. Market Preservation & Devel. Authority, Seattle, 1985-88, daystall mgr., 1988-92, residential property mgr., 1993—; asst. property mgr. Wright Runstad & Co., Seattle, 1997—. Author: (with others) 500 Great Books by Women, 1992. Vol. Chicken Soup Brigade, Seattle, 1993—. Mem. Wash. State Affordable Housing Mgmt. Assn. (bd. dirs. 1994—). Democrat. Office: Wright Runstad and Co 85 Pike St # 500 Seattle WA 98104

DOWNEY, JAMES EDGAR, manufacturing executive; b. Spartanburg, S.C., Sept. 29, 1950; s. Vernon P. and Lu Vera (McGraw) D.; m. Jean Lucille Gallo, May 24, 1980; 1 child, Jeana Marie. BBA, U. Phoenix, 1987; MBA, Golden Gate U., 1997. Draftsman Pacific Rolling Door Co., San Lorenzo, Calif., 1970-74; prodn. mgr. Pacific Rolling Door Co., San Lorenzo, 1975-87, v.p. mfr., 1988—; cons. Innovative Bus. Resources, Vacaville, Calif., 1996—. Instr. ARC, Hayward, Calif., 1968-80, bd. dirs., 1983-87, vice chmn. disaster svcs., Solano County, Calif., 1980-90. With USAFR, 1970-91. Republican. Presbyterian. Office: Pacific Rolling Door Co 15900 Worthley Dr San Lorenzo CA 94580-1844

DOWNEY, MICHAEL DEAN, interactive distance education coordinator; b. Sidney, Nebr., Feb. 16, 1951. AA, SUNY, Albany, 1973; BSW, U.Nev., Las Vegas, 1979; MPA, U. Nev., Las Vegas, 1981; PhD, Columbia Pacific U., San Rafael, Calif., 1987. Instr. polit. sci. and history Western Nev. C.C., Carson City; health planner, statistician State of Nev., Carson City; social worker State of Nev., Las Vegas; health resources analyst State of Nev., Carson City; ops. mgr. Carson Access TV Ctr., Carson City, Nev. With USN, 1972-78. Mem. ASPA, NASW, Am. Statis. Assn., Nat. Assn. Health Data Orgns. (founder), Alliance for Cmty. Media. Home: 610 E Proctor St Apt 5 Carson City NV 89701-4282 Office: Western Nev Cmty Coll 2201 W College Pkwy Carson City NV 89703-3103

DOWNEY, PAUL SCOTT, social services administrator; b. San Diego, May 1, 1959; s. Albert Russell and Joan H. (Scott) D.; m. Mary Curran, Jan. 14, 1982; children: Colin, Jonathan. BA in Journalism, San Diego State U., 1981. Reporter Radio Sta. KSDO, San Diego, 1978-82; mng. editor Copley Videotex, San Diego, 1982-84; editl. mgr. Times Mirror Videotex, Santa Ana, 1984-86; press sec. Office of the Mayor, San Diego, 1986-92; exec. dir. Indsl. Environ. Assoc., San Diego, 1993-94; asst. CEO Pvt. Industry Coun., San Diego, 1994-95; pres., CEO Sr. Cmty. Ctr., San Diego, 1995—. Nation chief YMCA Indian Guides, San Diego, 1994—; mgr. Little League, San Diego, 1994—. Recipient Regional Comm. award Toastmasters, 1993. Democrat. Office: Sr Cmty Ctr 928 Broadway San Diego CA 92101-5514

DOWNEY, WILLIAM J., III, lawyer; b. Newton, Mass., July 27, 1947, s. William J. and Marie Louise (Dupuis) D.; m. Leslie Ann Shields, Oct. 7, 1975 (div. 1979); 1 dau., Jessica Ann; m. 2d, Sherrill R. Gould, Aug. 15, 1982 (div. 1987); 1 dau., Julie Samantha; m. Lisa G. Russell, Feb. 14, 1992. Student Grinnell (Iowa) Coll., 1965; BS magna cum laude, Northeastern U., Boston, 1983; JD cum laude, Suffolk U. Law Sch., 1988. Bar: Calif. 1988, U.S. Dist. Ct. (ctrl. and so. dists.) Calif. 1992, U.S. Dist. Ct. (no. dist.) Calif. 1995. Atty. Baum, Hedlund, Aristei, Guilford & Downey and predecessor firm Kananack, Murgatroyd, Baum & Hedlund, 1988—, shareholder, 1993—. Mem. plaintiff's steering com. in re Eli Lilly & Co./Prozac Products Liability, Perris Valley Air Crash, Northridge Earthquake Litigation, in re Fialuridine Products Liability. Recipient Am. Jurisprudence award, 1987. Mem. Phi Delta Kappa, Phi Delta Phi. Office: Baum Hedlund Aristei Guilford & Downey 12100 Wilshire Blvd Ste 950 Los Angeles CA 90025-7114

DOWNIE, PAMELA, psychologist; b. Chester, Calif., Dec. 1, 1954; d. William John and June (De La Mont) D. BA, Widener U., 1980; MS, Villanova U., 1985; PhD, U. So. Calif., 1995. Counselor, trainer Del. County C.C., Media, Pa., 1985-87; counselor, instr. New Beginnings, Media, Pa., 1986-87; tchg. asst. U. So. Calif., 1989-91, instr. practicum, 1991, psychol. intern. Student Counseling Ctr., 1991-93; staff psychologist U. San Diego, 1994-95; lectr. Calif. State U., Fullerton, 1995-96, asst. prof., 1996—. Mem. APA (student), NAFE, AACD, Am. Mental Health Coun. Assn., Assn. for Multicultural Counseling, Pa. Counselors Assn., Assn. for Specialists in Group Work, Assn. for Coun. Edn. and Supervision. Home: PO Box 660582 Arcadia CA 91066-0582 Office: Calif State U Fullerton Dept Counseling EC-105 Fullerton CA 91066

DOWNING, DAVID CHARLES, minister; b. South Gate, Calif., June 24, 1938; s. Kenneth Oliver and Edna Yesobel (Casaday) D.; m. Tommye Catherine Tew, July 11, 1959 (dec. Dec. 11, 1985); children: Sheri Lynn, Teresa Kay, Carla Jeane, Michael David. BA, N.W. Christian Coll., 1961; B in Divinity, Tex. Christian U., 1966, M in Theology, 1973; DMin, San Francisco Theol. Sem., 1987. Ordained to ministry Christian Ch., 1961. Min. Marcola (Oreg.) Ch. of Christ, 1958-59; assoc. min. First Christian Ch., Lebanon, Oreg., 1960-63; min. First Christian Ch., Ranger, Tex., 1963-65, Knox City, Tex., 1966-68, Fredonia, Kans., 1968-74; min. Ctrl. Christian Ch., Huntington, Ind., 1974-77; regional min., pres. Christian Ch. Greater Kansas City, Mo., 1978-94; sr. minister Univ. Christian Ch., San Diego, 1994—; trustee Phillips Grad. Sem., Enid, Okla., 1988-94; bd. dirs. Ch. Fin. Coun., Indpls., Midwest Career Devel. Svc., Chgo.; v.p. bd. dirs. Midwest Christian Counseling Ctr., Kansas City. Author: A Contrast and Comparison of Pastoral Counseling in Rural and Urban Christian Churches, 1972, A Design for Enabling Urban Congregations to Cope with Their Fear of Displacement When Faced with Communities in Transition, 1987. Pres. Kansas City Interfaith Peace Alliance, 1980-82. Democrat. Home: 4460 Caminito Fuente San Diego CA 92116-1003 Office: Univ Christian Ch 3900 Cleveland Ave San Diego CA 92103*

DOWNING, DOUGLAS ALLAN, economics educator, writer; b. Seattle, Oct. 11, 1957; s. Robert Allan and Marguerite Louise (Hayland) D.; m. Lori Rosenau, 1994. BS, Yale U., 1979, MPhil, 1982, PhD in Econs., 1987. Acting instr. Yale U., New Haven, Conn., 1981-83; asst. prof. Seattle Pacific U., 1983-91, assoc. prof., 1991—, undergrad. dir. sch. bus. and econs., 1995—. Author: Calculus the Easy Way, 1982, Algebra the Easy Way, 1983, Trigonometry the Easy Way, 1984; co-author: Dictionary of Computer Terms, 1986, and 9 others. Mem. State Com. on Teenage Parents, Olympia, Wash., 1986-88; witness Wash. State Legis., Olympia, 1991-94. Austin Howard grad. fellow Yale U., 1979. Mem. Am. Econ. Assn., Seattle Economist Club, Yale Assn. Western Wash. (treas. 1987-95), Phi Beta Kappa. Presbyterian. Home: 18539 NE 184th St Woodinville WA 98072-8228 Office: Seattle Pacific U McKenna Hall Seattle WA 98119

DOWNS, FLOYD L., mathematics educator; b. Winchester, Mass., Jan. 21, 1931; s. Floyd L. and Emma M. (Noyes) D.; m. Elizabeth Lenci, Dec. 29, 1955; children: Karla C., John N. AB, Harvard U., 1952; MA, Columbia U., 1955. Lic. math. tchr. Math. tchr. East High Sch., Denver, 1955-60, Kent (Conn.) Sch., 1960-62, Newton High Sch., Newtonville, Mass., 1962-63; math. tchr., dept. chair Hillsdale High Sch., San Mateo, Calif., 1964-89; lectr. Ariz. State U., Tempe, 1988—; math. scis. adv. com. The Coll. Bd., N.Y., 1979-85; mem. U.S. nat. com. 2d Internat. Math. Study, 1979-86; Golden state math. com. Calif. State Dept. Edn., Sacramento, 1985-91; exec. dir. Ariz. Math. Coalition, 1991-96. Co-author: Geometry, 1964, 91. With U.S. Army, 1952-54, Korea. Mem. Nat. Coun. Tchrs. Math., Nat. Coun. Suprs. Math., Math. Assn. Am., Calif. Math. Coun., Ariz. Assn. Tchrs. Math., Phi Delta Kappa. Home: 7753 E Bisbee Rd Scottsdale AZ 85258-3421 Office: Ariz State U Math Dept Tempe AZ 85287-1804

DOWNS, KATHLEEN JOAN, purchasing supervisor; b. Chgo., Aug. 16, 1950; d. Joseph C. and Joan Ida (Godfrey) D.; div.; 1 child, Marsha Leigh Hill. BBA, Nat. U., 1987, MBA in Fin., 1989. Buyer Rush-Presbyn. St. Luke's Med. Ctr., Chgo., 1972-74, Loyola U. Med. Ctr., Maywood, Ill., 1979-85; adminstrv. asst. U. Calif. San Diego Med. Ctr., 1986-91; purchasing supr. San Diego C.C. Dist., 1991—. Bd. dirs. Loyola U. Employees' Fed. Credit Union, Maywood, 1983-85. Mem. Parents Without Ptnrs. (1st v.p. San Diego chpt. 1989, pres. 1990), San Diego Writers/Editors Guild (editor 1995-97). Unitarian. Office: San Diego CC Dist 3375 Camino Del Rio S San Diego CA 92108-3807

DOWNS, KEITH DAVID, county official; b. Hollywood, Calif., June 25, 1944; s. Vern and Ella (Davidson) D.; m. Linda Lou Dilday, Aug. 22, 1981; 1 son, Erik. B.A., Calif. State U.-Los Angeles, 1967; postgrad. U. Calif.-Riverside, 1975; M.A., Calif. State U.-San Diego, 1977. Intern planner Port Authority, San Diego, 1972; planner II, Riverside County, Calif., 1973-74; assoc. planner Planning Dept., Riverside, Calif., 1974-79, supervising planner, 1979-81, dep. dir., 1981-89, asst. dir., 1990-92, interim dir., 1993, aviation dir., 1994; project mgr. Joint Environ. Document Wind Energy, Riverside, 1981-82; county project mgr. Habitat Conservation Plan, Coachella Valley, Calif., 1983-86. Bd. dirs., officer Riverside County Employees Credit Union, 1978—, chmn. 1986-88. Served with U.S. Army, 1967-69. Decorated Bronze Star. Mem. Am. Assn. Geography, Am. Planning Assn. (dir.), Am. Assn. Airport Execs. Republican. Office: Riverside County Planning Dept Box 1409 4080 Lemon St 9th Fl Riverside CA 92502-1409

DOYEL, DAVID ELMOND, archaeologist, museum director; b. Lindsay, Calif., Aug. 24, 1946; s. Lester Levi Doyel and Jewell Mae (Hill) Burney; m. Sharon S. Debowski, Apr. 23, 1983. BA, Calif. State U., Chico, 1969, secondary teaching credential, 1971, MA, 1972; PhD, U. Ariz., 1977. Archaeologist Ariz. State Mus., Tucson, 1972-79; dir. Archaeology and Mus. Div., Window Rock, Ariz., 1979-82; mgr. Soil Systems, Inc., Phoenix, 1982-83; dir. Pueblo Grande Mus., City of Phoenix, 1984-89; cons. Estrella Cultural Rsch., Phoenix, 1990—; dir., cons. rsch. projects for govt. agys., Indian tribes, others; with Archaeol. Consulting Svcs., Ltd., 1994—. Contbr. articles to profl. publs. Bd. dirs. San Juan County Mus., Farmington, N.Mex., 1993. Named Outstanding Supr., Navajo Nation, Window Rock, 1980. Mem. Soc. Am. Archaeology, Ariz. Archaeol. and Hist. Soc. (exec. coun. 1976), Mus. Assn. Ariz., Planetary Soc., Ariz. Archaeol. Coun. (pres. 1982), Sigma Xi. Office: PO Box 60474 Phoenix AZ 85082-0474

DOYLE, ALFREDA CARROL, publisher, writer; b. Houston, Feb. 1, 1953; d. Spencer A. and Ruby L. (Tatum) D. Pres., founder Update Publicare Co., Denver, 1982—; pres., CEO Story Time Stories That Rhyme, Denver, 1989—. Author: Fish Convention, 1994, (newsletter) Stories That Rhyme Every Time Kids Pages, 1992, (cassette tape) Story Time Stories That Rhyme, 1993. Mem. Internat. Reading Assn., Internat. Platform Assn. Office: Story Time Stories That Rhyme PO Box 416 Denver CO 80201-0416

DOYLE, MICHAEL JAMES, educator, organist; b. Bell, Calif., Aug. 24, 1939; s. Joseph Edward and Irma Louise (Smith) D.; m. Mina Katherine Martensen, Feb. 8, 1964; children: Michael James II, Mary Katherine, Matthew John. BA, Whittier Coll., 1961, MEd, 1971. Tchr. El Rancho Unified Sch. Dist., Pico Rivera, Calif., 1961-79, dept. chmn., 1967-74, acting prin., 1979; tchr., asst. prin. Alta Loma (Calif.) Sch. Dist., 1979-86, summer sch. prin., 1985, prin., 1986-95; assoc. faculty Nat. U., Riverside, Calif., 1995—; adj. prof. Calif. State U., San Bernardino, 1995—; organist, dir. various Luth. chs. in So. Calif., 1955-86; organist St. Paul's Luth. Ch., Pomona, Calif., 1986—; mem. Calif. State Program Rev., 1982-83; assoc. mem. Calif. Sch. Leadership Acad., Ontario, 1986—; v.p. So. Calif. Luth. Music Clinic, 1978-81. Clk. Zion Luth. Sch. Bd. Edn., Maywood, Calif., 1962-64, chmn., 1966-67; mem. Downey (Calif.) City Water Bd., 1977-78; mem. Luth. High Personnel Commn., La Verne, Calif., 1988-92. Named Outstanding Tchr. of Yr., Burke Jr. High Sch. PTA, Pico Rivera, 1973; recipient hon. svc. award Jasper Sch. PTA, Alta Loma, 1983, continuing svc. award, 1988, Golden Oak Svc. award, 1996; employee recognition award Alta Loma Sch. Dist., 1985. Mem. Assn. Calif. Sch. Adminstrs., Assn. West End Sch. Adminstrs., Calif. Tchrs. Assn., Am. Guild Organists, Downey Hist. Soc., Cucamonga Hist. Soc., Casa de Rancho (Cucamonga, Calif.), Phi Delta Kappa (pres. Mt. Baldy chpt. 1993-97, advisor 1997—, found. chmn. 1991-93). Democrat. Lutheran. Home: 2085 N Palm Ave Upland CA 91784-1476 Office: Nat U 4183 Fairgrounds St Riverside CA 92501-1746

DOYLE, MICHAEL JOSEPH, mining executive; b. Eveleth, Minn., Nov. 15, 1928; s. Matthew James and Lucile (McNany) D.; m. Virginia Ethel Britt, Aug. 22, 1953; children: Patricia, Matthew, Michael, Mary Anne, Thomas, Molly, Peter, Robert. BA, U. Minn., Duluth, 1952; JD, U. Minn., Mpls., 1958. Bar: Minn., U.S. Supreme Ct. Labor counsel Pickands Mather & Co., Duluth, 1959-64; asst. dir. labor Hanna Mining Co., Cleve., 1964-69, dir. environ. affairs, 1970-74, dir. govt. affairs, 1975-85; dep. dir. Ariz. Dept. Environ. Quality, Phoenix, 1987-90; pres. Nev. Mining Assn., Reno, 1990—; bus. cons. Doyle & Assocs., Chagrin Falls, 1985-87; Ariz. rep. mine waste task force EPA, Denver, 1988-90. Mem. Nev. Natural Resource Adv. Bd., Carson City, 1993—; mem. bus. and mining schs. adv. bd. U. Nev., Reno, 1992—; Nev. rep. Grand Canyon Visibility Transport Commn., Denver, 1993-96. Mem. Carlton Club (Washington). Home: 1527 Kestrel Ct Reno NV 89509

DOYLE, WILFRED EMMETT, retired bishop; b. Calgary, Alta., Can., Feb. 18, 1913; s. John Joseph and Mary (O'Neill) D. B.A., U. Alta, 1935; D.C.L., U. Ottawa, Ont., Can., 1949. Ordained priest Roman Cath. Ch., 1938; chancellor Archdiocese Edmonton, Alta., Can., 1949-58; bishop Nelson, B.C., Can., 1958-89, bishop emeritus, 1989—; Chmn. bd. govs. Notre Dame U., Nelson, 1963-74. Address: 10661-82 Ave, Edmonton, AB Canada T6E 2A6*

DOYLE, WILLIAM THOMAS, retired newspaper editor; b. Oakland, Calif., May 22, 1925; s. Albert Norman and Catherine (Stein) D.; m. Claire Louise Wogan, Sept. 1, 1946 (dec. Nov. 10, 1984); children: Patrick,

Lawrence, Brian, Carrie; m. Mary M. Doren, May 3, 1986. B.Journalism, U. Nev., 1950. Reporter Richmond (Calif.) Independent, 1950-53; reporter Oakland Tribune, 1953-62, asst. state editor, 1962-64, telegraph editor, 1964-67, fin. editor, 1967-79; editor San Francisco Bus. Jour., 1979-81; news dir. Fireman's Fund Ins. Cos., Novato, Calif., 1981-84; mng. editor West County Times, Pinole, Calif., 1984-88. Mem. editorial adv. bd.: Catholic Voice. Pres. Richmond Jr. C. of C., 1957-58; bd. dirs. Cath. Social Svc. Contra Costa County, Calif., 1959-62, Bay Area Coop. Edn. Clearing House, 1977-88, Contra Costa Coll. Found., 1984-88, Richmond Unified Edn. Fund, 1984, Am. Cancer Soc.—West Contra Costa, 1986-96; mem. Richmond Schs. Citizens Adv. Com., 1969. With USAAF, 1943-45. Recipient award for best financial sect. daily newspaper Calif., Calif. Newspaper Pubs. Assn., 1968, 70, 72, 74, Knowland award for outstanding performance, 1972, Gen. Excellence award Nat. Newspaper Assn., 1987, Outstanding Editorial Writing award Suburban Newspapers Assn., 1989, 90, 1st Place award for editorial writing Nat. Newspaper Assn., 1992; Hughes fellow Rutgers U., 1969. Mem. Soc. Am. Bus. Writers, Marine Exchange San Francisco Bay Area, Sigma Delta Chi. Clubs: Contra Costa (Calif.); Press (Best News Story award 1965) (pres. 1956), Serra of West Contra Costa. Home: 2727 Del Monte Ave El Cerrito CA 94530-1507 Office: West County Times 4301 Lakeside Dr Richmond CA 94806-5281

DOZIER, FLORA GRACE, civil and human rights activist, entrepreneur; b. Pineland, Tex., Apr. 5, 1937; d. Whitto G. and Agatha (Price) Grace; m. Robert Alan Dozier, Dec. 16, 1962 (div. Jan. 1967); 1 child, Martine Denise. AA in Real Estate, 1979; BA in Polit. Sci., Calif. State U., 1985; cert., Golden Gate U., 1993. Various positions Fed. Civil Svc., 1964-84; real estate saleswoman, 1971-77. Author: (poetry) Biscuits for My Man, 1997, Handwriting on the Wall, 1997. Mem. Merritt Coll. Community Ctr. Literacy Task Force; bd. dirs. Black Cowboys Assn.; advisory bd. Nat. Youth Sports Program; mem. legis. advocacy com. Alameda County Commn. on Aging. Recipient Parade Trophy Black Cowboy Assn., 1992, Golden Poet award, 1993, Golden Poet award World of Poetry, 1992, Franam Scholarship for Black Women San Francisco State U., 1992-93, Presidl. award Ctr. Black Concerns, 1994, Troy G. Grove Recognition award, cert. of recognition Calif. State Senate. Mem. NAACP, NAFE, NCNW, IPA, NCNW (life), Internat. Black Writers Assn., Ctr. for Black Concerns, Internat. Platform Assn., Oakland Black Writers Guild, Black United Front for Edn. Reform, Nat. Assn. of Black Reading and Lang. Educators (membership sec. Bay Area chpt.), Bay Area Black Journalists Assn., Help Abolish Legal Tyranny. Baptist. Address: 484 Lake Park #442 Oakland CA 94610

DRACHNIK, CATHERINE MELDYN, art therapist, artist; b. Kansas City, Mo., June 7, 1924; d. Gerald Willis and Edith (Gray) Weston; m. Joseph Brennan Drachnik, Oct. 6, 1946; children: Denise Elaine, Kenneth John. BS, U. Md., 1945; MA, Calif. State U., Sacramento, 1975. Lic. family and child counselor; registered art therapist. Art therapist Vincent Hall Retirement Home, McLean, Va., Fairfax Mental Health Day Treatment Ctr., McLean, Arlington (Va.) Mental Health Day Treatment Ctr., 1971-72, Hope for Retarded, San Jose, Calif., Sequoia Hosp., Redwood City, Calif., 1972-73; supervising tchr. adult edn. Sacramento Soc. Blind, 1975-77; ptnr. Sacramento Div. Mediation Svcs., 1981-82; instr. Calif. State U., Sacramento, 1975-82, 92-93, Coll. Notre Dame, Belmont, Calif., 1975—; art therapist, mental health counselor Psych West Counseling Ctr. (formerly Eskaton Am. River Mental Health Clinic), Carmichael, Calif., 1975-93; instr. U. Utah, Salt Lake City, 1988-92; lectr. in field. Author: Interpreting Metaphors in Children's Drawings, 1995; one woman shows throughout Calif., East Coast and abroad; group juried shows in Calif. and Orient. Active various charitable orgns. Mem. Art Therapy Assn. (hon. life, pres. 1987-89), No. Calif. Art Therapy Assn. (hon. life), Calif. Coalition Rehab. Therapists, Nat. Art Edn. Assn., Am. Assn. Marriage and Family Therapists, Kappa Kappa Gamma Alumnae Assn. (pres. Sacramento Valley chpt. 1991-92), Alpha Psi Omega, Omicron Nu. Republican. Home and Office: 4124 American River Dr Sacramento CA 95864-6025

DRAGER, SHARON B., vascular surgeon; b. N.Y.C., June 23, 1946; d. Marvin and Lenore (Schwam) D.; children: Troy, Brooke. AB, Brown U., 1966; MD, NYU, 1970. Cert. Am. Bd. Surgery. Resident/fellow in surgery NYU, N.Y.C., 1970-78; pvt. practice San Pablo, Calif., 1978—; attending physician Brookside Hosp., San Pablo, 1978—, chief of staff, 1988; attending physician Doctors' Hosp. of Pinole, Calif., 1978—, chief of staff, 1994; attending physician Alta Bates Hosp., Berkeley, Calif., 1978—; asst. clin. prof. surgery U. Calif., San Francisco, 1981—. Fellow ACS; mem. Am. Med. Women's Assn., Assn. Women Surgeons, No. Calif. Vascular Soc., Internat. Soc. for Cardiovascular Surgery, East Bay Surg. Soc., Alameda Contra Costa Med. Soc., Alpha Omega Alpha. Office: 2089 Vale Rd San Pablo CA 94806-3847

DRAGO, JACK, mayor. Mayor City of South San Francisco, Calif. Office: City of South San Francisco 400 Grand Ave South San Francisco CA 94080

DRAKE, E. MAYLON, academic administrator; b. Nampa, Idaho, Feb. 8, 1920; s. Austin Henry and Daisy Naomi (Smith) D.; m. Lois Elloise Noble, Oct. 12, 1940; children: E. Christopher, Cameron Lee. BS, U. So. Calif., Los Angeles, 1951, MS, 1954, EdD, 1963. Mgr. Frederick Post Co., San Francisco, 1943-47; asst. supt. Baldwin Park (Calif.) Schs., 1947-51; supt. Duarte (Calif.) Schs., 1951-64, Alhambra (Calif.) City Schs., 1964-70; dep. supt. Los Angeles County Schs., 1970-78; dir. Acad. Ednl. Mgmt., Los Angeles, 1978-80; pres. L.A. Coll. Chiropractic, Whittier, 1980-90, chancellor, 1990-93, chancellor emeritus, 1993—; adj. prof. U. So. Calif., 1964-90, bd. councilors, 1991—. Author Attaining Accountability in Schools, 1972; contbr. articles to profl. jours. Pres. Industry-Ednl. Council So. Calif., 1978; dir. United Way 1970; dir. Greater Los Angeles Zoo Bd., 1970; dir. Planned Parenthood of Pasadena, Calif., 1996; trustee L.A. Coll. Chiropractic Whittier, Calif., 1996. Recipient Am. Educator's medal Freedom Found.; named Educator of Yr. Los Angeles Chiropractic Soc., 1981. Mem. Coun. on Chiropractic Edn. (pres. 1988-90), Rotary (pres. Duarte 1954-56, bd. dirs. Alhambra 1964-70). Republican. Presbyterian. Home: Casa de Ville 206 445 S Los Robles Ave Pasadena CA 91101-3273 Office: LA Coll Chiropractic 16200 E Amber Valley Dr Box 1166 Whittier CA 90609-1166

DRAKE, JESSICA, dialect and speech coach; b. L.A., Apr. 25, 1956; d. Kenneth and Sylvie D. BA, Julliard Sch. Drama, 1981. Accent reduction/speech and dialect coach UCLA, 1988—; faculty, dialect coach L.A. City Coll., 1988-90; faculty, speech/dialect Am. Acad. Dramatic Art, Pasadena, Calif., 1986-88, Calif. inst. for Arts, Valencia, 1989-90. Dialect coach: (films) Courage Under Fire, 1996, L.A. Confidential, 1996, Don Juan de Marco, 1995, I'll Do Anything, 1994, Forrest Gump, 1994, Ed Wood, 1994, What's Love Got To Do With It, 1993, Bram Stoker's Dracula, 1992, Ruby, 1992, Hot Shots, 1991, Indian Runner, 1991, Shattered, 1991, (TV shows) Wallace, 1997, Truman, 1995, A Woman of Independent Means, 1995, A Streetcar Named Desire, 1995, Return to Lonesome Dove, 1993, Murder Between Friends, 1993, Brooklyn Bridge, 1991-93, An Inconvenient Woman, 1991, The Broken Chain, 1993; actress: (TV shows) General Hospital, 1996, A Woman of Independent Means, 1995, Return to Lonesome Dove, 1993, thirtysomething, 1989, Highway to Heaven, 1988, 87, Return of Dennis the Menace, 1987, others; extensive stage work in regional theatre. Recipient Edith Skinner Speech award Julliard Sch. Drama, N.Y.C., 1979.

DRAKE, LUCIUS CHARLES, JR., school administrator, university consultant, educator; b. Tacloban, The Philippines, June 29, 1946; s. Lucius Charles and Victoria (Badiles) D. BA, Fisk U., 1968; EdM, Temple U., 1970; EdD, U. No. Colo., 1995. Cert. sch. adminstr.; cert. guidance counselor. Math. tchr. Sch. Dist. of Phila., 1968-70, Gary (Ind.) City Schs., 1970-72, Dept. Defense Dependents Sch., Fed. Republic Germany and Okinawa, 1972-77; elemtary tchr. Dept. Defense Dependents Sch., Philippines, 1977-79; guidance counselor Dept. Defense Dependents Sch., Japan and Korea, 1979-83; asst. prin. Dept. Defense Dependents Sch., Seoul and Taegu, Korea, 1983-86; univ. cons. U. No. Colo., 1988 89; employment counselor Ft. Collins, Colo., 1989-90; asst. prin. Misawa, Japan, 1990-91, Philippines, 1991-92; chmn. math dept. Sayre Jr. High Sch., Phila., 1969-70; math. curriculum rev. com., Dept. Defense Dependents Schs., Karlsruhe, Fed. Republic Germany, 1972-73; dir. Far East Basketball Tourney, Taegu, Korea, 1984-86; mem. regional mgmt. council, Dept. Defense Dependents Schs., Okinawa, 1985-86. Chairperson human rels. commn. Ft. Collins City Coun., 1990. Recipient Disting. Educator award IDEA Acad. Fellows, Denver, 1985. Fellow Am. Bd. Master Educators (disting.); mem. ASCD, Assn. Am. Sch. Adminstrs., Nat. Assn. Secondary Sch. Prins., Nat. Assn. Elem. Sch. Prins., Internat. Educator's Inst., Phi Delta Kappa, Alpha Phi Alpha (edn. sec. Seoul chpt. 1984-85). Democrat. Baptist. Home: 3318 Hickok Dr Unit B Fort Collins CO 80526-2502 Office: U N Colo Tchr Edn Ctr McKee Hall Greeley CO 80639

DRAKE, ROB, mayor. Mayor Beaverton, Oreg. Address: PO Box 4755 Beaverton OR 97006

DRANT, SANDRA ELIZABETH, court reporter, educator; b. L.A., July 18, 1939; d. Archie Delbert and Clara Mae (Sether) DeLane; m. Richard David Drant, Sept. 5, 1959 (div. 1965); m. Feb. 3, 1966 (dec. 1996); children: Stacey Allada, Ryan David. AA, Cypress Coll., 1989; BA in English, Chapman U., 1992; MA in Edn., Pepperdine U., 1995. Cert. shorthand reporter, cert. reporting instr. Freelance reporter Long Beach, Calif., 1960-65; state hearing reporter Calif. Unemployment Ins. Appeals Bd., Long Beach, Workers' Compensation Appeals Bd., Bell Gardens, 1972-82; cert. reporting instr. Cerritos Coll., Norwalk, Calif., 1990—; faculty advisor Ct. Reporting Club, 1995-97. Vol. chaperone Mammoth Mountain Ski Edn. Found., Mammoth Lakes, Calif., 1982-84; co-chair Grad-Night com. Mammoth High Sch., Mammoth Lakes, 1988; vol. archaeologist Cypress Coll., 1989—. Recipient Cert. of Recognition Calif. Legis. Assembly, 1993; named Parent of Yr., Mammoth Mountain Ski Edn. Found., 1983-84, Outstanding Curricular Advisor, 1995-96. Mem. AAUW, Nat. Ct. Reporters Assn., Calif. Ct. Reporters Assn., Faculty Assn. Calif. C.C.s, Pacific Coast Archaeol. Soc., Stanford Univ. Mothers Club (vol. contbr. 1988—). Home: 4109 Avenida Sevilla Cypress CA 90630-3413 Office: Cerritos Coll 11110 Alondra Blvd Norwalk CA 90650-6203

DRAPER, RICHARD N., banker; b. Washington, July 29, 1959; s. Theron N. and Patricia A. (Rawson) D.; m. Laurel A. Halversen, June 22, 1985; children: R. Nathan, Natalie N., T. Cole. BS in Fin., Brigham Young U., 1985; MBA with honors, U. Utah, 1989. Loan officer First Security Bank of Utah, Salt Lake City, 1985-88; sr. cons. Ernst & Young, Salt Lake City, 1989-91; supervised loans mgr. First Nat. Bank of Layton, Utah, 1991-97, mgr. constrn. dept., 1993-97; area constrn. mgr. First Security Bank, Ogden, Utah, 1997—; pvt. practice cons., fin. advisor, Wasatch Front, Utah, 1994—; real estate advisor Simplified Real Estate, Davis County, Utah, 1996—. Mem. No. Wasatch Home Builder Assn. (chmn. Table Top fund raisers 1996-96), Kaysville C. of C., Beta Gamma Sigma. Republican. Mem. LDS Ch. Office: First Security Bank 2404 Washington Blvd Ogden UT 84401

DRAZNIN, JULES NATHAN, journalism and public relations educator, consultant; b. Chgo., May 14, 1923; s. Charles G. and Goldie (Malach) D.; m. Shirley Bernstein, Apr. 9, 1950; children: Dean, Jody, Michael. Student, Wright City Coll., Chgo., 1941; BA in Journalism, Calif. State U., Northridge, 1978, MA in Higher Edn., 1984. Various journalism positions City News Bur., Chgo., 1941; promotions and publicity Balaban & Katz Theaters, Chgo., 1942-43; asst. dir pub. rels. Combined Jewish Appeal, Chgo., 1944; prin. J.N. Draznin Assocs., Chgo., 1945-50; account supr. Olian & Bronner Advt. Agy., Chgo., 1951-53; dir. advt. Chgo. Defender Robert S. Abbott Pub. Co., 1953-55; freelance cons. Chgo., 1955-60; v.p. pub. rels. Harshe-Rotman, Chgo., 1956; pub. rels. dir. Abel and Lamensdorf Properties, Chgo., 1960-62; editor-in-chief, assoc. pub. Indsl. News Bender Publs., Calif., 1962-64; labor editor, spl. features writer Valley News, Calif., 1964; ind. ins. agt. Calif., 1965-74; tch. pub. rels. UCLA and Calif. State U., L.A.; prof. journalism and pub. rels. L.A. Trade Tech. Coll., 1975-95, chmn. lang. arts dept., 1984-90; ret., 1995; prof. journalism and pub. rels. L.A. City Coll., L.A. Pierce Coll., L.A. Southwest Coll., East L.A. Coll., L.A. Mission Coll.; guest lectr. Calif. State U., Northridge. Coord. Mass Media AARP/Vote Vols., 1996—; mem. L.A. County Commn. on Aging, 1997—. Mem. Assn. for Edn. in Journalism and Mass Communication, Soc. Profl. Journalists. *Until I retired from teaching journalism, I was a voyeuristic/activist. Now I'm a participating activist without journalistic "objectivity."*

DRECHSEL, EDWIN JARED, retired magazine editor; b. Bremen, Germany, Apr. 17, 1914; came to U.S., 1924, naturalized, 1935; s. William A. and Estelle Laura D.; m. Ilona Bolya, Aug. 12, 1972; children: John M., Barbara A. Grad., Dartmouth Coll., Amos Tuck Sch. Bus. Adminstrn., 1936. With Standard Oil Co., N.J., 1936-43; with U.S. News and World Report, 1943-79; regional editor, editorial ombudsman U.S. News and World Report, San Francisco, 1976-79. Author shipping company histories and fleet lists, catalogs of ship mail postal markings, including A Century of German Ship Posts, 1886-1986, 1987, Norddeutscher Lloyd, Bremen 1857-1970, vol. 1, 1994, vol. 2, 1995. Former chmn. Reed Sch. Bd., Marin County, Calif.; lay reader, former vestryman St. Stephen's Episcopal Ch., Belvedere, Calif., former mayor, City of Belvedere. Club: San Francisco Press. Home: 170 Hillcrest Rd Berkeley CA 94705-2846

DREES, ELAINE HNATH, artist and educator; b. Orange, N.J., Aug. 20, 1929; d. John Anthony and Helen Louise (Godlesky) Hnath; m. Thomas Clayton Drees, Feb. 9, 1952; children: Danette, Clayton, Barry, Nancy. A.Comml. Art, Parsons Sch. Design, N.Y.C. Colorist and designer Hesse Wallpaper, N.Y.C., 1950-51; designer Lanz Wallpaper, N.Y.C., 1951-52; gallery asst. Longpre Gallery, La Canada, Calif., 1976-78; pvt. art tchr. La Canada, Calif., 1985—; pres. Elly's Originals, La Canada, 1980—. One-woman shows include La Canada, Calif., 1984, Barbara's Gallery, Agoura, Calif., 1989, Pasadena Livery Gallery, 1996; group shows include Hasenbein Gallery, Glendale, Calif., 1978, White's Gallery, Montrose, Calif., 1980, Graphic Showcase Gallery, Pas, Calif., 1985, Artistic Endeavors Gallery, Simi Valley, Calif., 1987, Mission West Gallery, South Pasadena, Calif., 1991; commns. include paintings for Alpha Therapeutic, Pasadena, 1980, Shannon Interiors, Pasadena, 1988-92; contbr. reproductions to Cal. Art Rev. 1989. Recipient Cert. of Honor, Centre Internat. D'Art Contemporain, Paris, 1984. Mem. Verdugo Hills Art Assn. (awards 1988-94). Republican. Roman Catholic. Home and Studio: 784 Saint Katherine Dr La Canada Flintridge CA 91011-4119

DREHER, NICHOLAS C., lawyer; b. Michigan City, Ind., Nov. 15, 1948. AB magna cum laude, Harvard U., 1970; JD, Stanford U., 1973. Bar: Hawaii 1973. Mem. Cades Schutte Fleming & Wright, Honolulu; vice-chmn. local rules com. U.S. Bankruptcy Ct. Mem. ABA (mem. com. foreclosure and related remedies sect. real property, probate and trust law 1991—), Am. Bankruptcy Inst. (chmn. Hawaii membership com. 1989—, mem. adv. com. bankruptcy rules 1990—), Hawaii State Bar Assn. (v.p. bankruptcy law sect. 1990-91, pres. 1991—, bd. dirs. 1990—). Office: Cades Schutte Fleming & Wright PO Box 939 1000 Bishop St Honolulu HI 96813-4212

DREIBELBIS, ELLEN ROBERTS, artist; b. Cleve., Dec. 18, 1946; d. Stanly Vincent and Lylian (Geller) Roberts; m. Walter William Dreibelbis, Nov. 29, 1970 (dec. Feb. 1987). BA in Art Edn., Ohio State U., 1970. Reference asst. Cleveland Heights (Ohio) Pub. Libr., 1971-74; asst. collection devel., interlibr. loan State Libr. Ohio, Columbus, 1974-78; libr. technician U.S. Forest Svc., Berkeley, Calif., 1979-88; tech. info. specialist U.S. Forest Svc., Albany, Calif., 1988-93; artist, illustrator Citibank, Stamford, Conn., 1993-94. One person shows include Strybing Arboreteum, San Francisco, 1995, Tantrums, Santa Rosa, Calif., 1991, Potrero Hill Pub. Libr., San Francisco, 1990; exhibited at group shows at Ashtabula (Ohio) Arts Ctr., 1975, East Bay Open Studio, Oakland, Calif., 1990-93, Stanford U., Palo Alto, Calif., 1985, San Francisco Women Artist's Gallery, 1987, Am. Mus. Quilts, San Jose, Calif., 1987, Met. Mus., Miami, Fla., 1988, ArtWork Gallery, San Francisco, 1995, 96, Rainbow Gallery, Wemme, Oreg., 1978, Green Apple Books, Cleve., 1980, Southern Exposure Gallery, San Francisco, 1986, 87, 88, 89, 90, 91, Bay Area Textile Designers Christmas Show, Oakland, 1986, Fort Mason Art Ctr., San Francisco, 1986, 87, 88, 89, 90, Pro Arts Gallery, Oakland, 1991, 92, 93, O'Brien's Art Emporium, Scottsdale, Ariz., 1996, Somar Gallery, San Francisco, 1996; rep. in permanent collections at Citibank, N.Y.C., Mr. and Mrs. Stanley Roberts, Cleve., Dr. and Mrs. Henry Channan, Sanibel Island, Fla., Mr. Paul McClain, San Francisco, Mr. Eli Giladi, Tel Aviv, Israel, Dr. Timothy F. Whiteside, N.Y.C., Dr. Don F. Fenn, Oakland; prin. works include Citibank, N.A. and Citicorp Mortgage, Inc., 1993-94, Rod Enterprises, Pasadena, Calif., 1995, USDA Forest Svc., Albany, 1994, Cricket Mag., Peru, Ill., Internal Heritage Tradition, San Francisco, 1997, Cosco Publs., Singapore, 1997; creator, marketer Native Peoples Series, giclee prints of watercolors of Native Americans, South Americans and Asians. Mem. We. Acad. Women Artists. Home and Studio: 454 9th Ave #5 San Francisco CA 94118

DREIER, DAVID TIMOTHY, congressman; b. Kansas City, Mo., July 5, 1952; s. H. Edward and Joyce (Yeomans) D. BA cum laude, Claremont McKenna Coll., 1975; MA in Am. Govt., Claremont Grad. Sch., 1976. Dir. corp. rels. Claremont McKenna Coll., 1975-78; dir. mktg. and govt. rels. Indsl. Hydro, San Dimas, Calif., 1978-80; mem 97th-103rd Congresses from 35th (now 28th) Calif. dist., 1980—; v.p. Dreier Devel. Co., Kansas City, Mo., 1985—; vice chmn. rules com., 1995—, chmn. rules of the house subcom.; chmn. Speaker's Task Force on Calif., chmn. task force on com. rev.; mem. spl. task force on the devel. of parliamentary instns.; mem. U.S.-Mex. Interparliamentary Caucus; bd. dirs. Internat. Rep. Inst.; mem. task force on fed. mandates; mem. spkrs. steering com. Recipient Golden Bulldog award Watchdogs of the Treasury, 1981-96, Taxpayers Friends award Nat. Taxpayers Union, 1981-95, Clean Air Champion award Sierra Club, 1988. Office: 237 Cannon HOB Washington DC 20515

DREIER, PETER, politics and public policy educator, journalist; b. Plainfield, N.J., July 12, 1948; s. Theodore and Beatrice (Braveman) D.; m. Catherine Theresa Meng, July 5, 1992. BA, Syracuse U., 1970; MA, U. Chgo., 1972, PhD, 1977. Asst. prof. sociology Tufts U., Medford, Mass., 1977-83; dir. housing Boston Redevel. Authority, 1984-92; E.P. Clapp Disting. prof. politics Occidental Coll., L.A., 1992—, dir. pub. policy program, 1994—; bd. dirs. Nat. Housing Inst., Orange, N.J., Nat. Low-Income Housing Coalition, Washington, So. Calif. Assn. Non-Profit Housing, Liberty Hill Found.; cons. MacArthur Found., Chgo., 1992, U.S. Dept. HUD, Washington, 1993—; mem. adv. bd. Resolution Trust Corp., Washington, 1993-96, Right-to-Know Project, Washington, 1995—. Editor: Jewish Radicalism, 1973; contbr. articles to numerous publs.; mem. editorial bd. Urban Affairs Quar., 1992—, Housing Studies, 1994—. Founder Mass. Tenants Orgn., Boston, 1981. Pub. Svc. Sci. resident NSF, 1981-82; rsch. grantee U.S. Dept. HUD, 1993, Social Sci. Rsch. grantee, 1993, Haynes Found., 1994. Sr. fellow Internat. and Pub. Affairs Ctr.; mem. Am. Sociol. Assn. (chair Spivack program on applied pub. policy), Am. Planning Assn. Democrat. Jewish. Office: Occidental Coll Internat and Pub Affairs Ctr Los Angeles CA 90041

DREIFUSS-KATTAN, ESTHER, psychoanalyst, art therapy educator; b. Zurich, Switzerland, June 3, 1949; came to U.S., 1989; d. Max and Suzanne (Levy) Dreifuss; m. Shlomo Kattan, Dec. 29, 1983; children: Sarit Jolanda, Gabriela Caroline. Diploma in fashion design, Fashion Sch., Zurich; MA in Art Therapy, Goddart Coll., 1976; PhD in Art Therapy, Union Grad. Inst., 1990; PhD in Rsch. Psychoanalysis, So. Calif. Psychoanalytic Inst, 1994. Art therapist C. Jung Clinic & Rsch. Ctr., Zurich, 1972-74; art therapist, dir. Chestnut Lodge Hosp., Rockville, Md., 1974-78; art therapy cons., psychooncologist Univ. Hosp. Dept. Internal Medicine, Zurich, 1978-83; psychooncologist, cons. Tel-Hashomer U., Tel Aviv, 1983-86; lectr. art therapy U. Tel Aviv, 1984-89; lectr. art history, art therapy and health scis. UCLA Extension, L.A., 1990—; pvt. practice psychoanalysis, art therapy Beverly Hills, Calif., 1992—. Author: Clinical Introduction to Art Therapy, 1986, Cancer Stories, Creativity and Self Repair, 1989, 94; contbr. numerous sci. articles to med. jours., chpts. to books. Mem. APA (divsn. psychoanalysis), Am. Psychoanalytic Assn., Am. Art Therapy Assn. (registered). Jewish. Office: 9437 Santa Monica Blvd Beverly Hills CA 90210-4604

DREISBACH, JOHN GUSTAVE, investment banker; b. Paterson, N.J., Apr. 24, 1939; s. Gustave John and Rose Catherine (Koehler) D.; m. Janice Lynn Petitjean; children: John Gustave Jr., Cassandra Michelle, Niklas Philip, Christopher Erik. BA, NYU, 1963. With Dreyfus & Co., 1959-62, with Shields & Co., Inc., 1965-68, Model, Roland & Co., Inc., N.Y.C., 1968-72, F. Eberstadt & Co., Inc., N.Y.C., 1972-74; v.p. Bessemer Trust Co., 1974-78; pres. Community Housing Capital, Inc., 1978-80; chmn., pres. John G. Dreisbach, Inc., Santa Fe, 1980—, JGD Housing Corp., 1982—, JGD Mgmt. Corp., 1996—; gen. ptnr. numerous real estate ltd. partnerships; bd. dirs., pres. The Santa Fe Investment Conf., 1986—; assoc. Sta. KNME-TV. Mem. Santa Fe Community Devel. Commn. Served with USAFR, 1964. Mem. Internat. Assn. for Fin. Planning, Nat. Assn. Securities Dealers, Inc., NYU Alumni Assn., N.Mex. First, Friends of Vieilles Maisons Francaises Inc., Mensa, Santa Fe C. of C., Augustan Soc. Republican. Mem. Episcopalian Ch. and Lutheran Ch. Clubs: St. Bartholomew's Community, Essex, Hartford, Amigos del Alcalde. Avocations: travel, art, arch-design appreciation, classical music, Shotokan karate. Home: 730 Camino Cabra Santa Fe NM 87501-5924

DRENNAN, MICHAEL ELDON, banker; b. Yakima, Wash., June 24, 1946; s. George Eldon and Jane (Nilsson) D.; m. Alice Marie Seabolt, May 13, 1972; children: Brian, David. BS in Fin., U. Oreg., 1968; grad., Pacific Coast Banking Sch. U. Wash., 1981. Ops. officer First State Bank, Aloha, Oreg., 1972-73; ops., loan officer First State Bank, Portland, Oreg., 1973-74; asst. mgr. First State Bank, Milwaukie, Oreg., 1974-76; asst. v.p. Citizens Bank, Corvallis, Oreg., 1976-80, v.p., 1980-81; pres., chief exec. officer Bank of Corvallis, 1981-87; v.p. dist. mgr. U.S. Bank, Corvallis, Oreg., 1987; sr. v.p. market area mgr. U.S. Bank, Bend, Oreg., 1988-94; sr. v.p., dist. mgr. U.S. Bank, Eugene, Oreg., 1994—; bd. dirs. Cascades W. Fin. Svcs. Bd. dirs. United Way Benton County, 1984-88; trustee Good Samaritan Hosp. Found., 1984-88; bd. dirs. Jr. Achievement of Benton County, 1983-85, treas, 1984-85, mem. exec. bd., 1984-85; mem. budget comm. Corvallis Sch. Dist., 1987; bd. dirs. Benton County Family YMCA, 1978-80, sec. 1979, mem. fin. com., 1978-80, mem. pers. com., 1979, active sustaining membership dr.; bd. dirs. Cmty. Club, 1978-83, pres., 1978, treas., 1979-80; active Corvallis Ambs., 1976-88; mem. mgmt. com. Corvallis Conf. and Visitors Bur., 1982-85; fund raising chmn. Com. City Improvement Levy, 1980; mem. exec. com. Pack 17 Boy Scouts Am., 1984-87, treas., 1984-87; mem. adv. bd. Ctrl. Oreg. Econ. Devel. Corp., 1988-90, bd. dirs., exec. bd., treas., 1991-93, v.p., 1993, pres., 1994—; bd. dirs. Regional Arts Coun. of Ctrl. Oreg., treas., 1989-92; bd. dirs. Ctrl. Oreg. Air Svc. Task Force, 1989-94, chmn. airline rels. com., 1990; mem. Bend Bus. Assistance Team, 1989-90, United Way Deschutes County, chmn. loaned exec. recruitment, 1992; mem. planning com. St. Charles Med. Ctr. Found., 1993, dir. adminstrn. capital fund drive, 1993; mem. adv. bd. Deschutes County Fair, 1993-94; bd. dirs. Birth to Three, Eugene, 1994—, treas., 1995-96, pres.-elect., 1996-97; bd. dirs. Lane Arts Coun., 1995—, treas. exec. bd., 1996—; bd. dirs. Conv. and Visitors Assn. Lane County, 1995—; bd. dirs. Eugene-Springfield Metro Partnership, 1995—; chmn. maj. firms campaign cabinet United Way of Lane County, 1996. Lt. USN, 1968-71. Named Jr. First Citizen, Corvallis, 1980. Mem. Bend C. of C. (chmn. mem. dir. task force 1988, chmn. mem. svcs. coun. 1989, chmn. chamber forums com. 1990, Outstanding Leadership award 1989), Corvallis C. of C. (v.p. fin. 1980-83, pres. 1985-86, chmn. bd. dirs. 1986-87, Econ. Devel. award 1978, Chmn. of Bd. award 1979, George award 1980-81, Devel. award 1983), Am. Inst. Banking (cert.), Rotary (bd. dirs. Corvallis club 1981-87, Bend 1988-94, Eugene, 1994—), Eugene Execs. Assn., Chi Phi, Alpha Kappa Psi, Beta Gamma Sigma. Home: 2574 W 28th Ave Eugene OR 97405-1456 Office: US Bank PO Box 10308 Eugene OR 97440-2308

DRESP, DONALD FRANCIS, retired library director; b. Omaha, Feb. 17, 1936; s. John Joseph and Helen Marjorie (Babbitt) D.; m. Winifred Adams, Jan. 24, 1970; children: David Joseph, Jeanne Angela. AB in Philosophy and History, Immaculate Conception Coll., 1958; postgrad., Creighton U., 1958-60; MA in LS, U. Denver, 1965; postgrad., Ariz. State U., 1970. Libr. Loveland (Colo.) H.S., 1962-65; edn. libr. Ariz. State U., Tempe, 1965-67; asst. libr. dir. Scottsdale (Ariz.) Pub. Libr., 1967-71; libr. dir. Thomas Branigan Meml. Libr., Las Cruces, N.Mex., 1971-96; host weekly radio program KOBE-1450 AM, 1988-91; del. to White House Conf. on Librs. and Info. Scis., Washington, 1991; col. aide-de-camp Staff of Gov. of N.Mex., 1974. Bd. dirs. ARC, 1977-83, Dona Ana Arts Coun., 1976-81, Head Start, Dona Ana County, 1973-75, Las Cruces Meml. Med. Ctr. Found., 1990 ; pres. Las Cruces Crime and Drug Commn., 1980—, pres., 1983-84; campaign divsn. dir. United Way, 1972, 83, 84, exec. bd., 1985-87; City of Las Cruces rep. to Cmty. Action Agy. of Dona Ana County, 1972-80. Recipient Libr. of Yr. award Border Regional Libr. Assn., 1975, Regular Guy award Las Cruces Cable TV, 1986; named Employee of Yr., City of Las Cruces, 1987. Mem. ALA, N.Mex. Libr. Assn. (v.p. 1972-73, pres. 1973-74, pres. pub. libr. divsn. 1984-85, libr. devel. com. 1974-77, 82-84, Libr. of Yr. 1991), N.Mex. Mcpl. Librs. (pres. 1976-77, 86-87), Dona Ana County Hist. Soc., Rotary (Paul Harris fellow 1992, bd. dirs. 1987-89). Roman Catholic. Home: 1845 Las Tunas Dr Las Cruces NM 88011-4956

DRESSER, JACK WILLIAM, research psychologist; b. Fullerton, Calif., June 1, 1936; s. Jack William and Florence Ruth (Chaffee) D.; children: Jon A., Tascha L., Tobin B., Lara V. BA, Pomona Coll., 1958; MA, La. State U., 1962, PhD, 1966. Sales agt. Streitfeld Realty, L.A., 1954-58; child psychologist Kennedy Child Study Ctr., Santa Monica, Calif., 1966-72; pvt. practice Affiliated Psychol. Cons., Downey, Calif., 1972-80; program dir. Open Door Clinics, Alhambra, Calif., 1981-86; prevention cons. Alhambra Sch. Dist., 1987-88; sr. rsch. scientist Integrated Rsch. Svcs., Eugene, Oreg., 1988—. Contbg. editor (newsletter) Prevention Rschr., 1994; contbr. articles to profl. publs.; artist (cartoons) Internat. Gymnast, 1984. UN cons. drug demand reduction Asia-Pacific region, 1987; cons. sch. and cmty. prevention locations including San Mateo County, Calif., Linn, Benton, Douglas and Deschutes counties, Oreg., 1989—. Recipient stipend USPHS, La. State U., 1959; rsch. grantee Nat. Hwy. Traffic Safety Adminstrsn., N.Y. and Minn., 1992, 93, U.S. Dept. Edn., Oreg. and Calif., (5), 1989-95, Nat. Inst. on Alcohol Abuse and Alcoholism, 1995-2000. Mem. APA (health psychology divsn., cmty. psychology divsn.), Lane County Psychol. Assn. Office: Integrated Rsch Svcs 66 Club Rd Ste 370 Eugene OR 97401-2459

DRESSLER, ALAN MICHAEL, astronomer; b. Cin., Mar. 23, 1948; s. Charles and Gay (Stein) Dressler. BA in Physics, U. Calif., Berkeley, 1970; PhD in Astronomy, U. Calif., Santa Cruz, 1976. Carnegie Instn. of Washington fellow Hale Obs., Pasadena, Calif., 1976-78, Las Campanas fellow, 1978-81; sci. staff Carnegie Obs. (formerly Mt. Wilson and Las Campanas Obs., formerly Hale Obs.), Pasadena, 1981—, acting assoc. dir., 1988-89. Contbr. to sci. jours. Fellow Am. Acad. Arts and Scis.; mem. NAS, Am. Astron. Soc. (councilor 1989-91, Pierce prize 1983), Internat. Astron. Union. Office: Carnegie Obs 813 Santa Barbara St Pasadena CA 91101-1232

DREVER, MARK, food products executive; b. 1956. BA, U. the Pacific; JD, Loyola U. Atty. Fresh Express Inc., Salinas, Calif., 1988—, pres. Office: Fresh Express Inc PO Box 580599 1020 Merrill St Salinas CA 93912-4409*

DREW, CHARLES MILTON, chemist; b. McKinney, Tex., Feb. 13, 1921; s. Andrew Everett and Lutie Lella (Weger) D.; divorced; children: Darrell Everett, Donna Lee, Lynn Milton, Carl Allen. BS, U. N. Tex., 1943. Supr. chemist Columbia Southern, Corpus Christi, Tex., 1943-47; research scientist Naval Weapons Ctr., China Lake, Calif., 1947-70; cons. U. Ariz., Tucson, 1980—. Author: Principles of Gas Chromatography, 1959; contbr. articles to profl. jours.; patentee in field. Mem. Rsch. Soc. Am., Soaring Soc. Am., Colo. West Soaring Club, Glider Club (pres. China Lake, Calif. chpt. 1967-70), Rockhounds Club (pres. local chpt. 1949-50), Sigma Xi. Home: 1420 Walker View Rd Wellington NV 89444-9326

DREW, JODY LYNNE, secondary education educator; b. L.A., Apr. 12, 1959; d. Marvin Wayne and Patricia Ann (Dozier) D. BA in English, Whitworth Coll., 1981; MA in English, U. Washington, 1990. Cert. tchr., Wash. Tchr. Eastside Catholic H.S., Bellevue, Wash., 1982-87, B.E.S.T. Alternative Sch., Kirkland, Wash., 1987-88, White River H.S., Buckley, Wash., 1989-92; tchr. Issaquah (Wash.) H.S., 1992-96, restructuring chair, 1992; tchr. Roosevelt H.S., Seattle, 1996—. Officer precinct com. Wash. State Dem. Com., Seattle, 1988—, mem. McDonnell Project, U. Wash. Mem. ASCD, Nat. Coun. Tchrs. English, Wash. Edn. Assn. (pulse rep. 1992), Issaquah Edn. Assn. (bldg. rep. 1992—, exec. bd. mem., 1994—, sr. project coord., 1996—), Wash. SANE/Freeze, Act Up, So. Poverty Law Ctr. (tchg. project, leadership conf.). Democrat. Office: Roosevelt HS 1410 NE 66th Seattle WA 98115

DREW, SHARON LEE, sociologist; b. L.A., Aug. 11, 1946; d. Hal Bernard and Helen Elizabeth (Hammond) D.; children: Keith, Charmagne. BA, Calif. State U., Long Beach, 1983; postgrad., Calif. State U., Dominguez Hills, 1988—. Clerical support Compton (Calif.) Unified Sch. Dist., 1967-78; case worker L.A. County Dept. Pub. Social Svcs., 1978—. Den mother Boy Scouts Am., Compton, 1971-72; employee vol. Dominguez Sr. H.S., Compton, 1972-73; project coord. Calif. Tomorrow's Parent Edn. Leadership Devel. Project, 1990; mem. L.A. Caregiver's Network, 1993-94; vol. Calif. State U., Dominguez Hill's Older Adult Ctr., 1994. Recipient cert. Calif. Tomorrow-Parent Edn. Leadership Devel. Project, 1990. Mem. Am. Statis. Assn. (So. Calif. chpt.), Internat. Soc. Exploration of Tchg. Alternatives, Calif. Sociol. Assn. (1st gov. at large grad. student 1990-91), Dominguez Hills Gerontology Assn. (chairperson 1990-91), Sociology of Edn. Assn., Alpha Kappa Delta (Xi chpt. treas. 1992-95). Home: 927 N Chester Ave Compton CA 90221-2105

DREXLER, CLYDE, professional basketball player; b. New Orleans, June 22, 1962. Student, U. Houston, 1980-83. Basketball player Portland Trail-blazers, 1983-94, Houston Rockets, 1994—; mem. U.S. Olympic Basketball Team (received Gold medal), 1992. Mem. NBA All-Star Team, 1986, 88-93; mem. all-NBA first team, 1992; mem. All-NBA second team, 1988, 91; mem. All-NBA third team, 1990. Office: Houston Rockets The Summit Two Greenway Plz Ste 400 Houston TX 77046*

DREXLER, KENNETH, lawyer; b. San Francisco, Aug. 2, 1941; s. Fred and Martha Jane (Cunningham) D.; BA, Stanford U., 1963; JD, UCLA, 1969. Bar: Calif. 1970. Assoc., David S. Smith, Beverly Hills, Calif., 1970, McCutchen, Doyle, Brown and Enersen, San Francisco, 1970-77; assoc. Chickering & Gregory, San Francisco, 1977-80, ptnr., 1980-82; ptnr. Drexler & Leach, San Rafael, Calif., 1982—. Served with AUS, 1964-66. Mem. Calif. State Bar (resolutions com. conf. of dels. 1979-83, chmn. 1982-83, adminstrn. justice com. 1983-89, chmn. 1987-88, adv. mem. 1990—), Marin County Bar Assn. (bd. dirs. 1985-87), Bar Assn. San Francisco (dir. 1980-81), San Francisco Barristers Club (pres. 1976, dir. 1975-76), Marin Conservation League (bd. dirs. 1985-97). Office: 1330 Lincoln Ave Ste 300 San Rafael CA 94901-2143

DREXLER, KIM ERIC, researcher, author; b. Oakland, Calif., Apr. 25, 1955; s. Allan Barry and Hazel Edna (Gassmann) D.; m. Christine Louise Peterson, June 18, 1981. BS in Interdisciplinary Sci., MIT, 1977, MS in Engring., 1979, PhD in Molecular Nanotech., 1991. Researcher, author, lectr., inventor Cambridge, Mass., 1980-85; researcher, author, lectr., cons. Palo Alto, Calif., 1985—; rsch. affiliate MIT Space Lab, Cambridge, 1980-86, MIT Artificial Intelligence Lab, Cambridge, 1986-87; sr. rsch. fellow Inst. for Molecular Mfg., 1991—; vis. scholar Stanford (Calif.) U. Computer Sci. Dept., 1986-92; bd. dirs., chmn. The Foresight Inst., Palo Alto, 1986—. Author: Engines of Creation, 1986, Nanosystems, 1992 (Assn. Am. Pubs. Best Computer Science Book, 1992); co-author: Unbounding the Future, 1991; contbr. articles to profl. jours.; inventor high performance solar sail, method for processing and fabricating metals in space. Sec. bd. dirs. L5 Soc., Tucson, 1981, bd. dirs., 1979-86, advisor, 1979-86, co-editor jour., 1983-84; bd. dirs. Nat. Space Soc., 1986-96. Grad. fellow NSF, MIT, 1977; recipient Space Pioneer award for Scientist/Engr., Nat. Space Soc., 1991, Kilby Young Innovator award Kilby Found., Dallas, 1993. Mem. AAAS, Am. Vacuum Soc., Am. Chemistry Soc. Office: The Foresight Inst PO Box 61058 Palo Alto CA 94306-6058

DREXLER, MILLARD S., retail executive; b. 1944; married. Exec. v.p. merchandising, pres. Gap Stores div. Gap Inc., San Bruno, Calif., from 1983; now pres., bd. dirs. The Gap Inc., San Bruno; pres., chief exec. officer Ann Taylor Co. Office: The Gap Inc 1 Harrison St San Francisco CA 94105-1602*

DREYER, THOMAS MORGAN, plastic surgeon; b. Phoenix, 1947. MD, U. Ill., 1972. Resident Duke U. Med. Ctr., Durham, N.C., 1972-74; otolaryngologist U. Iowa, Iowa City, 1975-79; plastic surgeon U. N.C., Chapel Hill, 1979-81; now plastic surgeon Sacred Heart Gen. Hosp., Eugene, Oreg. Office: 1180 Paterson St Ste 1A Eugene OR 97401-1886*

DREYFUSS, JOHN ALAN, journalist; b. N.Y.C., Dec. 1, 1933; s. Henry and Doris (Marks) D.; m. Katharine Elizabeth Rich, June 28, 1958; children: Karen Elizabeth, James Henry, Kimberly Anne, Katharine Marks. BS in Biology, Boston U., 1959. Tchr. schs. in Montclair, Pebble Beach and Los Olivos, Calif., 1959-63; reporter, editor San Luis Obispo (Calif.) Telegram Tribune, 1963-64; advt. salesman Ventura County (Calif.) Star-Free Press, 1964-66; gen. assignment writer L.A. Times, 1966-69, higher edn. writer, 1969-72, environment writer, 1972-73, architecture and design critic, 1975-84, feature writer View sect., 1984-87, graphics editor View sect., 1987-89, asst. to assoc. editor, 1989-93; v.p., CFO, sec. J. Dreyfuss & Assocs., Santa Monica, Calif., 1993-94; newswriter Sta. KTLA-TV, L.A., 1994-95; pub. info. officer Jonsson Comprehensive Cancer Ctr./UCLA, 1995, dir. for comm., 1996—. With U.S. Army, 1953-55. Office: UCLA Jonsson Comprehensive Cancer Ctr 8-684 Factor Bldg Los Angeles CA 90095-1781

DRINKARD, TERRELL DEWAYNE, aeronautical engineer; b. Mobile, Ala., Apr. 7, 1957; s. William Woodrow and Susan Drinkard. BS in Aero. Engring., Calif. Poly. State U., 1991. Numerically controlled mill operator Mainland Machine, San Luis Obispo, Calif., 1987-88; computer tester Tandon Computers, San Luis Obispo, 1988-89; liaison engr. Boeing Comml. Airplane Group, Seattle, 1990-91, 96—, configuration analyst, 1992-95; mktg. product analyst Boeing Comml. Airplane Group, 1995; pvt. practice computer cons., San Luis Obispo, 1987-90. Inventor in field. Conv. del. King County (Wash.) Dems., 1992. Sgt. U.S. Army, 1975-81. Mem. AIAA (young mems. com. Pacific N.W. chpt. 1990-92, facilities dir. 1992-93, dir. pub. rels. 1994-95). Home: 8543 Midvale Ave N Seattle WA 98103-4031 Office: Boeing Comml Airplane Group PO Box 3707 Seattle WA 98124-2207

DRINKWATER, DAVIS CLAPP, JR., surgeon, educator; b. Boston. BA, Harvard U., 1969; MD, U. Vt., 1976; MSc, McGill U., 1980. Diplomate Province of Que. Certification Gen. Surgery; diplomate Am. Bd. Surgery, Am. Bd. Thoracic Surgery. Chief cardiothoracic surgery Wadsworth VA Hosp., West Los Angeles, 1984-95; asst. prof. surgery UCLA Sch. Medicine, 1984-90, assoc. prof. surgery, 1990-96, prof. surgery, 1996—; chmn. dept. cardiothoracic surgery Vanderbilt Med. Sch., Nashville, 1997—; dir. UCLA Pediat. Cardiac Transplant Program, L.A., 1993; assoc. med. dir. UCLA Perfusion and Assist Device Svc., L.A., 1995. Fellow Royal Coll. Physicians and Surgeons; mem. AMA, ACS, Am. Coll. Cardiology, Am. Assn. for Thoracic Surgery, Am. Heart Assn., Internat. Soc. for Heart and Lung Transplantation, N.Y. Acad. Scis., Physicians for Social Responsibility, Soc. Thoracic Surgeons, So. Calif. Transplant Soc., The Longmire Surg. Soc., Western Thoracic Surg. Assn. Office: UCLA Sch Medicine Cardiothoracic Surgery 10833 Le Conte Ave Los Angeles CA 90024-1602 also: Vanderbilt Med Sch 2896 Vanderbilt Clinic Nashville TN 37232-5734

DRISCOLL, CHARLES F., physics educator; b. Tucson, Feb. 28, 1950; s. John Raymond Gozzi and Barbara Jean (Hamilton) Driscoll; m. Susan C. Bain, Dec. 30, 1972; children: Thomas A., Robert A. BA in Physics summa cum laude, Cornell U., 1969; MS, U. Calif. San Diego, La Jolla, 1972, PhD, 1976. Staff scientist Gen. Atomics, San Diego, 1969; rsch. asst. U. Calif. San Diego, La Jolla, 1971-76, rsch. physicist, sr. lectr., 1976-96, prof. physics, 1996—; prof. Molecular Biosystems, Inc., San Diego, 1996—, staff physicist, cons., 1981-82; assoc. dir. Inst. for Pure and Applied Scis., La Jolla, 1991—; cons. Sci. Applications, Inc., 1980-81. Editor: Non-Neutral Plasma Physics, 1988; contbr. numerous articles to sci. jours. Fellow NSF, 1969-71. Fellow Am. Phys. Soc. (Excellence in Plasma Physics Rsch. award 1991); mem. AAAS, Math. Assn. Am., Phi Beta Kappa. Office: U Calif San Diego Dept Physics 0319 9500 Gilman Dr La Jolla CA 92093-5003

DRISCOLL, MICHAEL P., bishop; b. Long Beach, Calif., Aug. 8, 1939. Student, St. John's Sem., Camarillo, Calif.; MSW, U. So. Calif., 1975. Ordained priest Roman Cath. Ch., 1965, titular bishop of Massita. Aux. bishop Orange, Calif., 1990—. Office: Chancery Office 2811 E Villa Real Dr Orange CA 92867-1932

DRISCOLL, RICHARD STARK, land use planner; b. Denver, Sept. 16, 1928; s. Myron William and Edith Helene (Stark) D.; m. Joyce Lynn Yarbrough, Jan. 9, 1954; children: Vicki Lynn Driscoll Kiefe, Kelly Sue. BS, Colo. A&M, 1951; MS, Colo. State U., 1957; PhD, Oreg. State U., 1962. Range scientist USDA Forest Svc., Portland, Oreg., 1952-56; rsch. project leader USDA Forest Svc., Portland, 1956-62, Washington, 1962-65, Ft. Collins, Colo., 1965-77; R & D program mgr. USDA Forest Svc., Ft. Collins, 1977-83; cons. FMA Internat., Inc., Gardnerville, Nev., 1983-91; land-use expert UN-FAO, Rome, 1983-89; land use cons. Fust (Föderung von Umweltstudien), Achenkirch/Tyrol, Austria, 1993. Author, editor: Photo Interpretation for Ranges and Range Management, 1997; contbg. author Range Resources: Inventory, Evaluation, Monitoring, 1975; contbr. articles to profl. jours. Dist. chmn. Bend (Oreg.) area Boy Scouts Am., 1962, com. chair troop 26, Ft. Collins, Colo., 1989; mem., chair various coms. Westminster Presbyn. Ch. and Timnath Presbyn. Ch., Ft. Collins, 1972—; mem. com. on ministry Plains and Peaks Presbytery Presbyn. Ch. U.S.A., 1991—. Recipient presdl. citation for meritorious svc. Am. Soc. Photogrammetry and Remote Sensing, 1978, 86. Mem. Am. Inst. Biol. Scis., Soc. Range Mgmt. (chair, com. mem., Outstanding Achievement award 1983), Xi Sigma Pi, Beta Beta Beta, Sigma Xi. Home and Office: 2217 Sheffield Dr Fort Collins CO 80526-1640

DRISKILL, JAMES LAWRENCE, minister; b. Rustburg, Va., Aug. 18, 1920; s. Elijah Hudson and Annie Pharr (Carwile) D.; m. Ethel Lillian Cassel, May 29, 1949; children: Edward Lawrence, Mary Lillian. BA, Pa. State U., 1946; BD, San Francisco Theol. Sem., 1949; ThM, Princeton Sem., 1957; S.T.D., San Francisco Theol. Sem., 1969. Ordained minister in Presbyn. Ch., 1949. Missionary Presbyn. Ch. USA, Japan, 1949-72; stated supply pastor Madison Square Presbyn. Ch., San Antonio, 1973; minister Highland Presbyn. Ch., Maryville, Tenn., 1973-82; supply pastor of Japanese-Am. chs. Presbyn. Ch. USA, Long Beach, Calif., Hollywood, Calif., Altadena, Calif., 1984—; vis. prof. religion dept. Trinity U., 1972-73. Author: Adventures in Senior Living, 1997; contbr. articles to profl. jours. Mem. Sierra Club, Calif., 1988—, Nat. Parks and Conservation Assn., 1989—, Am. Farmland Trust, 1989—; trustee Osaka (Japan) Girls Sch., 1952-65, Seikyo Gakuen Christian Sch., Japan, 1953-92. With USN, 1943-46. Mem. Am. Acad. Religion, Presbyn. Writers Guild. Democrat. Home and Office: 1420 Santo Domingo Ave Duarte CA 91010-2632 *Experience has taught me that, ultimately, the meaning and value of a person's life is determined by the quality of one's personal relationships, especially by the quality of one's relationship to God.*

DRMANAC, RADOJE, molecular biologist; b. Raska, Yugoslavia, Jan. 2, 1958; arrived in U.S., 1991; s. Tomislav and Jevtimija (Nikic) D.; m. Snezana Culumovic, Oct. 23, 1983; children: Dragoljub, Martina. BS in molecular biology, U. Belgrade, Belgrade, Yugoslavia, 1981, MS in molecular biology, 1985, PhD in molecular biology, 1988. Scientific staff Galenika Pharmaceutical Industry, Belgrade, 1982-85; rsch. fellow Inst. Molecular Genetics & Genetic Engring., Belgrade, 1986-88, Imperial Cancer Rsch. Fund, London, 1989-90; group leader Argonne (Ill.) Nat. Lab., 1991-94; sr. v.p. rsch. Hyseq, Inc., Sunnyvale, Calif., 1994—; editor: Internat. Jour. Genome Rsch., 1992-94; grant reviewer Dept. Energy, Washington, 1992-94. Author: Automated DNA Sequencing, 1994, Identification of Transcribed Sequences, 1994; contbr. articles to profl. jours. Recipient DNA Sequencing grant Dept. Energy, 1988, Genome grant, 1991, ATP Diagnostics grant Nat. Inst. Stds. & Tech., 1994. Mem. Human Genome Orgn. Office: Hyseq Inc 670 Almanor Ave Sunnyvale CA 94086-3513

DROOYAN, JOHN NEAL, visual artist, photographer, fine artist; b. Glendale, Ariz., Sept. 29, 1952; s. Irving and Gertrude (Sommers) D. BS in Biology, Stanford U., 1974; MFA in Photography, San Francisco Art Inst., 1988. Photographer, asst. editor Dellen Pub. Co., San Francisco, 1978-84; freelance photographer San Francisco and L.A., 1984—; photographer United Photog. Industries, Galion, Ohio, 1996—, Event Photography Internat., Miami, Fla., 1996—; tchr. color photography A.S.U.C. Studio, U. Calif., Berkeley, 1982-86, San Francisco Art Inst., 1987-90. Solo exhbns. include Union Gallery/U. Calif., Davis, San Jose State U. Union Gallery, San Francisco Mus. Modern Rental Gallery, Sierra Arts Found., Reno, Nev., Brand Art Gallery, Glendale, Calif.; exhibited in group shows at Spectrum Gallery, San Francisco, Ventura Coll. New Media Gallery, Downey Mus. Art, numerous others. Recipient Gold award for mixed-media art Art of Calif. Mag., 1992. Mem. L.A. Ctr. for Exhbns., Santa Monica Mus. Art, Richmond Art Ctr., Mus. Contemporary Art, L.A. Artcore.

DROWN, EUGENE ARDENT, federal agency administrator; b. Ellenburg, N.Y., Apr. 25, 1915; s. Frank Arthur and Jessie Kate D.; BS, Utah State U., 1938; postgrad. Mont. State U., 1939-40; PhD in Pub. Adminstrn., U. Beverly Hills, 1979; m. Florence Marian Munroe, Mar. 5, 1938; children: Linda Harriett Oneto, Margaret Ruth Lunn. Park ranger Nat. Park Svc., Yosemite Nat. Park, 1940-47; forest ranger U.S. Forest Svc., Calif. Region, 1948-56; forest mgr. and devel. specialist U.S. Bur. Land Mgmt., Calif., 1956—; forest engring. cons., 1970—; R&D coord. U.S. Army at U. Calif., Davis., 1961-65. Mem. adv. bd. Sierra Coll., Rocklin, Calif., 1962—; active Boy Scouts Am.; instr. ARC, 1954—. With AUS, 1941-45. Decorated Bronze Star, Silver Star; registered profl. engr., profl. land surveyor, profl. forester, Calif. Recipient Nat. Svc. medal ARC, 1964. Mem. Nat. Soc. Profl. Engrs., Soc. Am. Foresters, Am. Inst. Biol. Scientists, Ecol. Soc. Am., Res. Officers Assn. U.S., NRA, Internat. Rescue and First Aid Assn., Internat. Platform Assn., Bulldog Sentinels of Superior Calif., Masons, Shriners. Methodist. Home: 5624 Bonniemae Way Sacramento CA 95824-1402

DROZD, LEON FRANK, JR., lawyer; b. Victoria, Tex., Sept. 11, 1948; s. Leon Frank and Dorothy Lucille (Smith) D.; BBA, Tex. A&M U., 1971; J.D., U. Denver, 1979. Bar: Colo., Calif., U.S. Dist. Ct. Colo. U.S. Dist. Ct. (no. dist.) Calif., U.S. Ct. Appeals (9th and 10th cirs.). Legis. asst. U.S. Ho. of Reps., also Dem. Caucus, Washington, 1971-74, chief clk. com. on sci. and tech., 1974-75; asst. to dean for devel. Coll. Law, U. Denver, 1975-79; v.p. Braddock Publs., Inc., Washington, 1975-79; land and legal counsel Chevron Shale Oil Co., Chevron Resources Co., 1980-87, ins. div., 1987-88; sr. counsel Chevron Corp. Law Dept. 1987—, Chevron Overseas Petroleum and White Nile Petroleum Co. Ltd. (Sudan), 1983, Colo. elector Anderson/Lucey Nat. Unity Campaign, 1980. Mem. ABA, Colo. Bar. Assn., San Francisco Bar Assn., Fed. Bar Assn., Am. Trial Lawyers Assn., Denver C. of C. (steering com. 1981-82). Office: Chevron Corp Law Dept PO Box 7141 555 Market St San Francisco CA 94105-2801

DRUCKMAN, JEFFREY JULIUS, lawyer; b. Pasadena, Calif., June 14, 1954. BA with honors, Stanford U., 1976; JD cum laude, Boston U., 1979. Bar: Oreg. 1979. Ptnr. Miller, Nash, Wiener, Hager & Carlsen. articles editor Boston U. Law Review, 1978-79. Mem. ABA (com. on employment and labor rels. litigation). Address: Miller Nash Wiener Hager & Carlsen 111 SW 5th Ave Portland OR 97204-3604

DRUFFEL, ANN BERNICE, researcher, writer; b. Riverside, Calif., Aug. 12, 1926; d. William and Aileen (Walsh) McElroy; m. Charles K. Druffel, Jan. 24, 1953; children: Ellen, Diana, Carolyn, Charlotte, Allis Ann. BA in Sociology, Immaculate Heart Coll.; postgrad., Cath. U. Registered social case worker, Calif. Family and child welfare worker Cath. Welfare Bur., L.A. and Long Beach, Calif., 1948-53; researcher Nat. Investigations Com. for Aerial Phenomena, Washington, 1957-73, Ctr. for UFO Studies, Chgo., 1975—; investigator Mut. UFO Network, Seguin, Tex., 1973—; asst. researcher, cons. Mobius Soc., L.A., 1986-92; pub. spkr. on psychic phenomena, UFO's, Native Am. sacred sites at sci. confs., symposia, acad. and civic groups. Co-author: (with D. Scott Rogo) The Tujunga Canyon Contracts, 1980, paperback edit., 1989, The Psychic and the Detective, 1983, 2d edit., 1995, (with Armand Marcote) Past Lives: Future Growth, 1986, 2d edit., 1994; contbr. to Ency. of UFOs; (anthology) UFO Abductions, Psychic Pets and Spiritual Animals; contbr. numerous articles to profl. publs.; cons. Flying Saucer Rev., London, 1980—; assoc. editor Mufon UFO Jour., 1978-84; author, rschr. (filmscript) Dixie North; (TV) Psychic Detectives, 1989, Report from Unknown, 1990. Recipient cert. of appreciation AIAA-IEEE/ Harvard-Radcliffe Club, 1989.

DRUMMER, DONALD RAYMOND, financial services executive; b. Binghamton, N.Y., Oct. 10, 1941; s. Donald Joseph and Louise Frances (Campbell) D.; AS, Broome C.C., 1962; BS, U. Colo., 1972; MBA, Regis U., 1981; m. Rita Kovac, May 22, 1965; children: Shelley Rita, Adam Donn. With, Lincoln First Bank, Binghamton, N.Y., 1962-69; asst. comptr. Adams & Horne, Denver, 1969; with Colo. State Bank, Denver, 1969-87, v.p., 1972-81, comptr., 1972-87, sr. v.p., 1981-87; sr. v.p., CFO Wyo. Nat. Bancorp. (formerly Affiliated Bank Corp. of Wyo.), Casper, 1987-91; v.p., contr. Crop Hail Mgmt., Kalispell, Mont., 1991-92, sr. v.p., CFO, 1992; treas. Rural Cmty. Ins, 1992; sr. v.p., CFO Wyo. Nat. Bank, Casper, Cheyenne, 1987-91; bd. dirs. Wyo. Nat. Bank, Lovell and Kemmerer, 1987-88; corp. sec. Wyo. Nat. Bancorp. (formerly Affiliated Bank Corp. of Wyo.), 1987-91; sr. v.p. finance Am. Nat. Bank, Cheyenne, 1993-95; v.p. Cmty. First Bancorp, Inc., 1994-95, cons. 95—; bd. dirs. Wheatland Ins. Agency, 1989-91; CFO, exec. com. Am. Bankers Assn., 1989-91; adj. faculty Regis U., mem. grad. edn. task force, 1986-87. Editor: Chronicle, 1980-81. Bd. dirs. Girl's Club of Casper, 1988. Mem. Inst. Mgmt. Accts. (dir. 1975-79, v.p. 1977-79), Am. Acctg. Assn., Am. Taxation Assn., Denver Sertoma Club (past pres.), City Club (v.p., dir. 1979-83). Office: 16422 Jefferson St Omaha NE 68135

DRUMMOND, MARSHALL EDWARD, business educator, university administrator; b. Stanford, Calif., Sept. 14, 1941; s. Kirk Isaac and Fern Venice (McDeritt) D. BS, San Jose State U., 1964, MBA, 1969; EdD, U. San Francisco, 1979. Adj. prof. bus. and edn. U. San Francisco, 1975-81; adj. prof. bus. and info. systems San Francisco State U., 1981-82; prof. MIS, Ea. Wash. U., Cheney, 1985—, exec. dir. info. resources, 1988, assoc. v.p. adminstrv. svcs., chief info. officer, 1988-89, v.p. adminstrv. svcs., 1989-90, exec. v.p., 1990, pres., 1990—; cons. Sch. Bus., Harvard Coll., U. Ariz. Contbg. editor Diebold Series; contbr. articles to profl. jours. Democrat. Home: 428 W 21st Ave Spokane WA 99203-1943 Office: Ea Wash U Mail Stop 130 Cheney WA 99004

DRURY, DORIS MARIE, economics educator, consultant, researcher; b. Louisville, Nov. 18, 1926; d. Coleman F. and Ursula P. (Darst) D. B.S., U. Louisville, 1955, M.B.A., 1957; M.A., Ind. U., Bloomington, 1962, Ph.D., 1964; postgrad., U. Denver Coll. Law, 1973-74. Asst. prof. econs. U. Wyo., Laramie, 1962-63; assoc. prof. La. State U., 1963-65; prof. econs. U. Denver, 1965-90, chmn. div. research, 1968-71, chmn. econs., 1972-79; John Sullivan prof., exec. dir. MBA programs Regis U., 1990—; dir. Fed. Res. Bank, Kansas City, 1980-84, chmn. bd., 1985, chmn. audit, 1980-83; dir., chmn. audit com. Pub. Service Co., Denver, 1979—; dir., founder Women's Bank, Denver, 1977-78; dir. Colo. Nat. Bankshares, Equitable of Iowa; pres., chief exec. officer Ctr. for Bus. and Econ. Forecasting, Inc. Author: Accidents in Coal Producing Countries, 1964, Phase II Economic Controls, 1972, Key Public Economic Issues, 1971, Construction Industry in Colorado, 1969, 83—; editor quarterly rev. Colo. economy and econs. perspective. Mem. Gov.'s Blue Ribbon Panel on Econ. Planning, Colo., 1979-81; bd. dirs. YWCA, Denver, 1979-81. Recipient Disting. Teaching Specialist Commendation, U. Denver, 1973; Resources of the Future, Inc. fellow, 1961-62. Mem. Nat. Assn. Bus. Economists, Am. Econ. Assn., Denver C. of C. Home: 10879 E Powers Dr Englewood CO 80111-3959 Office: Regis U 3333 Regis Blvd Denver CO 80221-1154

DRUTCHAS, GERRICK GILBERT, investigator; b. Detroit, Sept. 23, 1953; s. Gilbert Henry and Elaine Marie (Rutkowski) D.; 1 child, Gilbert Henry II. BA, Mich. State U., 1975; postgrad., U. Redlands, 1983-85. Pres. Argentum Publs., L.A., 1986—; dir. Le Baron Investigations, Pasadena. Dir. Childrens Welfare Found. Sgt. USAR, 1981-85. Named Baron, Royal House of Alabona-Ostrogojsk, 1992. Mem. Order of the Swan (chevalier), Order of St. Angilbert (chevalier), K. of P. (past chancellor 1983, 84), Delta Sigma Phi. Unitarian. Home: 601 E California Blvd Pasadena CA 91106-3852 Office: Le Baron Investigations Pasadena CA 91106

DRYDEN, ROBERT EUGENE, lawyer; b. Chanute, Kans., Aug. 20, 1927; s. Calvin William and Mary Alfreda (Foley) D.; m. Jetta Rae Burger, Dec. 19, 1953; children: Lynn Marie, Thomas Calvin. AA, City Coll., San Francisco, 1947; BS, U. San Francisco, 1951, JD, 1954. Bar: Calif. 1955; diplomate Am. Bd. Trial Advocates. Assoc. Barfield, Dryden & Ruane (and predecessor firm), San Francisco, 1954-60, jr. ptnr., 1960-65, gen. ptnr., 1965-89; sr. ptnr. Dryden, Margoles, Schimaneck, Hartman & Kelly, San Francisco, 1989—; lectr. continuing edn. of the bar, 1971-77; evaluator U.S. Dist. Ct. (no. dist.) Calif. Early Neutral Evaluation Program; master atty. San Francisco Am. Inn of Ct. Mem. bd. counsellors U. San Francisco, 1993—. With USMCR, 1945-46. Fellow Am. Coll. Trial Lawyers, Am. Bar Found., Internat. Acad. Trial Lawyers; mem. ABA (mem. product liability adv. coun.), San Francisco Bar Assn., Assn. Def. Counsel (bd. dirs. 1968-71),

Def. Rsch. Inst., Internat. Assn. Ins. Counsel, Fedn. Ins. Counsel, Am. Arbitration Assn., U. San Francisco Law Soc. (mem. exec. com. 1970-72), U. San Francisco Alumni Assn. (mem. bd. govs. 1977), Phi Alpha Delta. Home: 1320 Lasuen Dr Millbrae CA 94030-2846 Office: Dryden Margoles Schimaneck & Kelly 1 California St Ste 3100 San Francisco CA 94111-5432

D'SILVA, AECIO MOURA, aquaculture scientist; b. Belo Jardim, Brazil, Jan. 30, 1951; came to U.S., 1989; s. Francisco Frade and Clotildes Moura (Brasil) D'S.; m. Marilene da Fonseca, Apr. 4, 1970. Degree aquaculture engr., U. Fed. Rural of PE, Recife-Pernambuco, 1974; MS, Okla. State U., 1983; PhD, U. Ariz., 1993, postdoctorate, 1993—. Extension agt. Brazilian Extension Svc., Florianopolis, S.C., 1975; head of fishery affairs office Ministry of Agriculture, Brasilia, 1976-79; sr. adviser Prodecor-Ministry-Agriculture, Brasilia, 1980-83; cons. CODEVASF Ministry-Interior, Brasilia, 1983-84; pvt. cons. various cos., Brazil, USA, Can., 1985-87; head Brazilian Fishery Inst., Brazilia, 1987-88; exec. head State EPA, Joao Pessoa, 1989; prof. UN-FAO, Brazil, 1987-89; rschr. U. Ariz., Tucson, 1990—; cons. Concept. Can., Quebec, 1987, Sunwest Internat., Tucson, 1991—, World Bank, 1992—; software co. exec. NID Technologies, Tucson, 1991—. Author: Fishing Project Methodology, 1976, Mercury in the Environment, 1988, Environment Impact Assessment, 1989; inventor neurocomputing integration design software technology. Del. Internat. Labor Orgn., Geneva, 1988. Mem. World Aquaculture Soc., Am. Fishery Soc., Aquacultural Engring. Soc. Office: U Ariz 104 Bioeast Ct Tucson AZ 85721

D'SOUZA, EDWARD JOHN, educational administrator; b. Rangoon, Burma, Apr. 30, 1962; came to U.S., 1979; s. Manuel Edwin and Eva Maria D'Souza. BA in Physics, Grinnell Coll., 1984; MA in Computers, Azusa Pacific U., 1987; postgrad., Claremont Grad. Sch. Adminstrv. credential; tchg. cert. in math. and phys. sci. Tchr. math. and phys. sci. Kolb Mid. Sch., Rialto, Calif., 1984-86; tchr. math. and physics Eisenhower H.S., Rialto, 1986-90, dean of students, 1990-93; asst. prin. Kucera Mid. Sch., Rialto, 1993-95; math./sci. coord. Riverside (Calif.) County Office of Edn., 1995—; advisor Inland Area Sci. Project, Riverside, 1995; mentor tchr. Rialto Unified Sch. Dist. Ch. pianist St. Anthony's, San Bernardino, Calif., 1992-94. Tandy Tech. scholar Eisenhower H.S., 1992. Mem. ASCD, Nat. Coun. Tchrs. Math., Calif. Sci. Tchrs. Assn., Calif. Assn. of Gifted. Roman Catholic. Home: 1749 N Verde Ave Rialto CA 92376-2750 Office: Riverside County Office of Edn 3939 13th St Riverside CA 92501-3505

DUBESA, ELAINE J., biotechnology company executive; b. Alton, Ill., July 26, 1943; m. Michael Dubesa, Oct. 28, 1967. BS in Med. Tech., Loyola U., New Orleans, 1966. Rsch. assoc. pesticides project U. Hawaii, Honolulu, 1968-69; field rep., pesticides project La. State U., New Orleans, 1970-71; lab. supr. Beaufort (S.C.) County Meml. Hosp., 1971-72; asst. supr. hematology Mayo Clinic, Rochester, Minn., 1973-75; edn. coord. Sherman Hosp., Elgin, Ill., 1975-78; sect. chief PCL (now Corning Clin. Labs.), Portland, Oreg., 1978-80; quality control supr. PCL-RIA, Inc., Portland, 1980-82; quality control mgr. Am. Bioclinical Inc., Portland, 1982-87; quality assurance mgr., regulatory affairs mgr. Epitope, Inc., Beaverton, Oreg., 1987-91, v.p. regulatory affairs, 1991-95, v.p. govt. affairs, 1995-97. Active Troutdale (Oreg.) Hist. Soc. Mem. Am. Soc. Quality Control, Regulatory Affairs Profl. Soc., Am. Soc. Clinical Pathologists, Beta Epsilon Upsilon.

DUBLIN, STEPHEN LOUIS, secondary school educator, singer, musician; b. L.A., Aug. 17, 1948; s. Thomas Newton and Carole Louise Dublin. BM, Chapman U., 1970; M in Sch. Adminstrn., U. LaVerne, 1988. Vocal music and English tchr. Leland Stanford Jr. H.S., 1973-74; vocal music and gen. music tchr. Walter B. Hill Jr. H.S., 1974-77, 80-88, Woodrow Wilson H.S., 1977-80; govt. and econs. tchr., mem. various sch. coms., mentor tchr., chmn. history dept. Robert A. Millikan H.S., Long Beach, Calif., 1988—. Mem. campaign com. Harriet Williams Bd. Edn., Long Beach, 1988, 90; Calif. tchr. liason Senate Ralph Dells, Long Beach, 1988-92. Recipient scholarship Chapman U., 1966-70; named Tchr. of Yr. Milton High Sch., 1993. Mem. Calif. Assn. Econs. (charter), Social Studies Coun., Choral Conductors Guild, So. Calif. Vocal Assn., Constnl. Rights Found. (premier tchr.), Phi Delta Kappa. Home: 12562 Dale St Apt 49 Garden Grove CA 92841-4567

DUBOFSKY, JEAN EBERHART, lawyer, retired state supreme court justice; b. 1942; B.A., Stanford U., 1964; LL.B., Harvard U., 1967; m. Frank N. Dubofsky; children: Joshua, Matthew. Admitted to Colo. bar, 1967; legis. asst. to U.S. Senator Walter F. Mondale, 1967-69; atty. Colo. Rural Legal Services, Boulder, 1969-72, Legal Aid Soc. Met. Denver, 1972-73; ptnr. Kelly, Dubofsky, Haglund & Garnsey, Denver, 1973-75; dep. atty. gen. Colo., 1975-77; counsel Kelly, Haglund, Garnsey & Kahn, 1977-79, 88-90, Williams, Trine, Greenstein & Griffith, Boulder, Colo., 1990—; justice Colo. Supreme Ct., Denver, 1979-87; vis. prof. U. Colo. Law Sch., Boulder, 1987-88. Office: Williams Trine Greenstein & Griffith 1881 9th St # 210 Boulder CO 80302-5148

DU BOIS, DAVID D., plastic surgeon; b. Story City, Iowa, 1940. MD, U. Iowa, 1965. Instr. Phila. Gen. Hosp., 1965-66; resident surgeon Mayo Clinic, Rochester, N.Y., 1968-72, plastic surgeon, 1972-74; now plastic surgeon Penrose Hosp., Colorado Springs, Colo. Office: 2727 N Tejon St Colorado Springs CO 80907-6231*

DUBOIS, PATRICIA LAVONNE, retail mobile electronics company executive; b. Spokane, Wash., July 20, 1963; d. Richard Allen and Charlotte LaVerne (Kleweno) DuBois. BA, Gonzaga U., 1985. Exec. asst. N.W. Sound, Inc., Seattle, 1985-87; office mgr. N.W. Yeshiva High Sch., Seattle, 1987-88; exec. asst. Car Toys, Seattle, 1988-90, corp. ops. mgr., 1990-92, gen. mgr., 1992-96, v.p. ops., 1997—; cons., sec.-treas., COO Omniscient Prodn., Seattle, 1993—. Vol. Oil Spill Clean Up, State of Wash., Ocean Shores, 1989. Roman Catholic. Office: Car Toys 307 Broad St Seattle WA 98121

DUBOSE, FRANCIS MARQUIS, clergyman; b. Elba, Ala., Feb. 27, 1922; s. Hansford Arthur and Mayde Frances (Owen) DuB.; BA cum laude, Baylor U., 1947; MA, U. Houston, 1958; BD, Southwestern Bapt. Sem., 1957, ThD, 1961; postgrad. Oxford (Eng.) U., 1972; m. Dorothy Anne Sessums, Aug. 28, 1940; children: Elizabeth Anne Parnell, Frances Jeannine Huffman, Jonathan Michael, Celia Danielle. Pastor Bapt. chs., Tex., Ark., 1939-61; supt. missions. So. Bapt. Conv., Detroit, 1961-66; prof. missions Golden Gate Bapt. Sem., 1966—, dir. World Mission Ctr., 1979—, sr. prof., 1992; lectr., cons. in 115 cities outside U.S., 1969-82; v.p. Conf. City Mission Supts., So. Bapt. Conv., 1964-66; trustee Mich. Bapt. Inst., 1963-66; mem. San Francisco Inter-Faith Task Force on Homelessness. Mem. Internat. Assn. Mission Study, Am. Soc. Missiology, Assn. Mission Profs. Co-editor: The Mission of the Church in the Racially Changing Community, 1969; author: How Churches Grow in an Urban World, 1978, Classics of Christian Missions, 1979, God Who Sends: A Fresh Quest for Biblical Mission, 1983, Home Cell Groups and House Churches, 1987, Mystic on Main Street, 1994; contbr. to Toward Creative Urban Strategy; Vol. III Ency. of So. Baptists, also articles to profl. jours. Home: 2 Carpenter Ct San Francisco CA 94124-4429 Office: Golden Gate Bapt Sem Mill Valley CA 94941

DUBOW, SUSAN DIANE, financial consultant; b. Phila., June 13, 1948; d. Milton and Esther (Kalish) D. BArch with distinction, U. Ariz., 1974-78, postgrad., 1988--. Architect in tng. Macneil Riedel Architects,, Tucson, 1977-79; constrn. coordinator Empire West Cos., Tucson, 1979-81; investment broker A.G. Edwards, Tucson, 1982-85, Merrill Lynch, Tucson, 1985-86, Rauscher Pierce Refsnes, Inc., Tucson, 1986-94, Smith Barney Inc., Tucson, 1994—; owner Sparky's Tailwaggers, Pet Products for Pet Lovers, 1991-95; nat. speaker on investment planning, 1989—; investment broker Women's Investment Network, Tucson, 1982-89, Red Herring, Tucson, 1986-88, Health Investment Profile, Tucson, 1987-89, Great Expectations, Tucson, 1988. Mem. Tucson Women's Commn., 1983-84; coord. Cigna/Michael Landon Celebrity Tennis Classic, Tucson, 1987-88; bd. dirs. Comstock Children's Found., 1985-88; steering com., chair speakers bd. Tucson First, 1987-89; vol. Primavera Found., 1990—, bd. dirs., 1991-93, So. Ariz. Women's Fund, 1993—, chairwoman, 1995-97. Mem. Nat. Assn. Security Dealers, Women in Tax and Fin. (founder, pres. 1995-96), Pres.'s Club of Rauscher Pierce Refsnes, Inc. Democrat. Office: Smith Barney 5285 E Williams Cir Ste 5500 Tucson AZ 85711-7411

DUBROFF, HENRY ALLEN, newspaper editor; b. Neptune, N.J., Nov. 28, 1950; s. Sol and Gilda (Burdman) D.; married, 1980 (div. 1986). AB in History and Lit., Lafayette Coll., 1972; MS in Journalism, Columbia U., 1982. Staff writer Dept. Health and Human Svcs., Washington, 1972-73; tchr. English Holyoke (Mass.) St. Sch., 1974-78; employment & tng. program mgr. Knoxville (Tenn.)-Knox CY Community Action, 1978-81; bus. writer, columnist Springfield (Mass.) Newspapers, 1982-85; bus. writer, columnist The Denver Post, 1985-88, bus. editor, 1988-95; editor Denver Bus. Jour., 1995—; contbg. writer CFO Mag., Boston, 1985-90. Contbr. articles to N.Y. Times, 1982-89. Vol. Russian Resettlement Program Jewish Family & Children's Svcs., Denver, 1989-90. Recipient N.Y. Fin. Writers Assn. scholarship, 1982, Morton Margolin prize U. Denver, 1988, Bus. Story of Yr. award AP, 1989. Mem. Soc. Am. Bus. Editors and Writers (v.p.). Office: Denver Bus Jour 1700 Broadway Ste 515 Denver CO 80290-1700*

DUCA, FRANK ANTHONY, software engineer, researcher; b. Tulsa, Sept. 9, 1956; s. Joe W. and Joyce Ann (Moore) D. BSin Elec. Engring, Physics, Rice U., 1978; MS in Computer Sci., U. Colo., 1996. Devel. engr. Storage Tech. Corp., Louisville, 1978-80; geophys. sys. devel. mgr. Occidental Oil and Gas, Tulsa, 1980-86; tech. mktg. cons. Unisys Corp., St. Louis, 1986-90; adv. engr. Storage Tech. Corp., Boulder, Colo., 1990-95; instr. U. Colo., 1995—; principle cons. Network Solutions Inc., Houston, 1989-90. Recipient Tech. Excellence award Storage Tech. Corp., 1992, 94. Mem. Assn. for Computing Machinery, IEEE Computer Soc., Soc. Indsl. and Applied Math., Am. Math. Soc. Home: 2795 Darley Ave Boulder CO 80303-6305 Office: U Colo Dept Computer Sci & Engring 1200 Larimer St Denver CO 80204-5310

DUCKWORTH, GUY, musician, educator; b. L.A., Dec. 19, 1923; s. Glenn M. and Laura (Lysle) D.; m. Ballerina Maria Farra, May 23, 1948. BA, UCLA, 1951; MusM, Columbia U., 1953, PhD, 1969. Piano soloist Metro Goldwyn Mayer Studios, 1936-41, Warner Bros. Studios, 1936-41, Sta. KFI, L.A., 1938, Sta. KNX, L.A., 1939, Sta. KHJ, L.A., 1940; artist Columbia Artists, 1942-49; asst. prof. music. U. Minn., Mpls., 1955-60, assoc. prof., 1960-62; prof. piano, fellow Northwestern U., Evanston, Ill., 1962-70; chmn. dept. preparatory piano Northwestern U., 1962-70; prof. music U. Colo., Boulder, 1970-88; prof. emeritus U. Colo., 1988, originator, coordinator masters and doctoral programs in mus. arts; piano concert tours in U.S., Can., Mexico, 1947-49; condr. various music festivals, U.S., 1956—; dir. Walker Art Children's Concerts, Mpls., 1957-62; nat. piano chmn. Music Educators Nat. Conf., 1965-71; vis. lectr., scholar 96 univs., colls. and conservatories, U.S. and Can., 1964—; cons. to Ill. State Dept. Program Devel. for Gifted Children, 1968-69; vis. prof. U. Colo., 1988-90. Author: Keyboard Explorer, 1963, Keyboard Discoverer, 1963, Keyboard Builder, 1964, Keyboard Musician, 1964, Keyboard Performer, 1966, Keyboard Musicianship, 1970, Guy Duckworth Piano Library, 1974, Guy Duckworth Musicianship Series, 1975, Keyboard Musician: The Symmetrical Keyboard, 2 vols., 1987-88, Keyboard Musician: The Symmetrical Keyboard, 1988, rev. edit., 1990; contbr. to over 6 books, 23 articles on pedagogy of music to various jours.; producer, performer video tapes on piano teaching; producer, writer (film) The Person First: A Different Kind of Teaching, 1984. Nominator Irving S. Gilmore Internat. Keyboard Festival, Gilmore Artist and Young Artist Awards. With U.S. Army, 1943-46. Recipient All-Univ. Teaching award for excellence, U. Colo., 1981, Pedagogy Honors award Nat. Conf. Piano Pedagogy, Chgo., 1994; named Pioneer Pedagogue Nat. Corp. Piano Pedagogy, Princeton U. Retrospective, 1992. Mem. Music Tchrs. Nat. Assn., Colo. State Music Tchrs. Assn., Coll. Music Soc., Music Educators Nat. Conf., Music Teachers Assn. Calif., Phi Mu Alpha, Pi Kappa Lambda. Home: 6522 Ambrosia Dr # 5108 San Diego CA 92124 Office: U Colo Coll of Music Boulder CO 80302

DUCKWORTH, TARA ANN, insurance company executive; b. Seattle, June 7, 1956; d. Leonard Douglas and Audrey Lee (Limbeck) Hill; m. Mark L. Duckworth, May 16, 1981; children: Harrison Lee III, Andrew James, Kathryn Anne. AAS, Highline C.C., Seattle, 1976. From acctg. clk. to info. sys. supr. SAFECO Ins. Co., Seattle, 1977-90; rate sys. mgr. SAFECO Mut. Funds, SAFECO Credit, PNMR, Seattle, 1990-94, sys. mgr., 1994-97, mgr., 1997—; mem. tech adv. com. for the computer info. svcs. program North Seattle Community Coll., 1984-96, chairperson tech. adv. com., 1988-90. Mem. Star Lake Improvement Club, 1988-94; mem. fellowship com. St. Lukes Luth. Ch., 1986—; mem. Boy Scouts Am., 1996—. Mem. NAFE, Nat. Assn. for Ins. Women, Soc. for State Filers, Nat. PTA. Office: SAFECO Ins Co SAFECO Plz Seattle WA 98185

DUCKWORTH, WALTER DONALD, museum executive, entomologist; b. Athens, Tenn., July 19, 1935; s. James Clifford and Vesta Katherine (Walker) D.; m. Sandra Lee Smith, June 17, 1955; children: Clifford Monroe, Laura Lee, Brent Cullen. Student, U. Tenn., 1953-55; BS, Middle Tenn. State U., 1955-57; MS, N.C. State U., 1957-60, PhD, 1962. Entomology intern Nat. Mus. Nat. History, Washington, 1960-62, asst. curator, 1962-64, assoc. curator, 1964-75, entomology curator, 1975-78, spl.asst. to dir., 1975-78; spl. asst. to asst. sec. Smithsonian Inst., Washington, 1978-84; dir. Bishop Mus., Honolulu, 1984-86, pres., dir., 1986—; pres., CEO Hawaii Maritime Ctr. subs. Bishop Mus.; trustee Sci. Mus. Va., Richmond, 1982-86, bd. dirs., 1982-84, Hawaii Maritine Mus., Honolulu, 1984-95; mem. Sci. Manpower Commn., Washington, 1982-84. Co-editor: Amazonian Ecosystems, 1973; Am. editor: Dictionary of Butterflies and Moths, 1976; author, co-author numerous monographs and jour. articles in systematic biology. Pres. Social Ctr. for Psychosocial Rehab., Fairfax, Va., 1975. N.C. State U. research fellow, 1957-62; recipient numerous grants NSF, Am. Philos. Soc., Smithsonian Research Found. Assn., Exceptional Service awards Smithsonian Inst., 1973, 77, 80, 82, 84, Disting. Alumnus award Middle Tenn. State U., 1984. Mem. Am. Inst. Biol. Scis (pres. 1985-86, sec.-treas. 1978-84), Entomol. Soc. Am. (pres. 1982-83, governing bd. 1976-85, Disting. Svc. award 1981), Assn. Tropical Biology (exec. dir. 1971-84, sec.-treas. 1976-81), Hawaii Acad. Sci. (coun. 1985—), Arts Coun. Hawaii (legis. com. 1986-87), Assn. Sci. Mus. Dirs., Social Sci. Assn., Assn. Systematic Collections (v.p. 1988-89, pres. 1990-91, Disting. Svc. award 1992), Pacific Sci. Assn. (pres. 1987-91, pres. Pacific Sci. Congress, Honolulu 1991). Democrat. Presbyterian. Lodges: Rotary, Masons, Order Eastern Star. Office: Bishop Mus 1525 Bernice St Honolulu HI 96817-0916*

DUDA, LUTHER, food products executive; b. 1939. Sec. Gene Jackson Farms Inc., Oxnard, Calif. Office: Gene Jackson Farms Inc 195 Victoria Ave Oxnard CA 93030-8796*

DUDEK, F. EDWARD, educator; b. Columbus, Nebr., Sept. 12, 1947; m. Kay Dudek; children: Sara, Amanda. BS in Biol. Sci., U. Calif., Irvine, 1969, PhD in Physiology, 1973. Trainee dept. ophthalmology rsch. Columbia U., Coll. Physicians, N.Y.C., 1973-74; rsch. assoc. dept. psychobiology U. Calif., Irvine, 1974; rsch. assoc. biomed. inst. dept. physiology & biophysics U. Tex. Med. Br., Galveston, 1974-75; asst. prof. dept. zoology U. Toronto (Ont., Can.), 1975-80; assoc. prof. dept. physiology Tulane U. Sch. Medicine, New Orleans, 1980-84, prof., 1984-87; prof. mental retardation rsch. ctr. U. Calif, L.A., 1987-92, assoc. dir., 1989-91; prof., chmn. dept. anatomy and neurobiology Colo. State U., Ft. Collins, 1992—. Contbr. chpts. to books and articles to profl. jours. Isaac and Clara Jacobs scholar, 1969-70, Brython Davis scholar, 1969-70; NSF Undergrad. Rsch. fellow, 1968; recipient NIH Javits Neurosci. Investigator award, 1987-94, Behavioral and Neurisci. Study sect. award, 1985-88, Tulane Owl Club Teaching award, 1984Edward Steinhaus Outstanding Teaching award, 1972. Mem. AAAS, Am. Physiological Soc., Am. Epilepsy Soc., Soc. Neurosci. Office: Colo State U Dept Anatomy & Neurobiology Fort Collins CO 80523

DUDENHOEFFER, FRANCES TOMLIN, physical education educator; b. San Antonio, Aug. 8, 1943; d. Arthur Reader and Annie Beatrice (Everett) Tomlin; m. Arthur Wood Dudenhoeffer, July 17, 1976. BS in Edn., S.W. Tex. State U., San Marcos, 1965; MS in Phys. Edn., U. N.C., Greensboro, 1967; PhD, U. Tex., 1977. Cert. recreational sports specialist; cert. tchr., Tex. Grad. asst. U. N.C., Greensboro, 1965-66; instr. U. Okla., Norman, 1966-70, asst. prof., 1970-72; recreational sports specialist U. Tex., Austin, 1971-72, grad. asst., 1973-74; lectr., women's intramural dir. U. North Tex., Denton, 1974-76; intramural dir. N.Mex. State U., Las Cruces, 1976-97; mem. intramural task force Las Cruces Pub. Schs., 1987-89; content rev. panel N.Mex. Dept. Edn., Santa Fe, 1984; expert witness Lea County Atty., Lovington, N.Mex., 1988. Author: (manual) Intramural Staff Handbook, 1992; editl. com.: Navigating the Tides of Change, 1994; editor/author: (pamphlet) Guidelines for Intramural Programs, 1992; contbr. articles to profl. jours. Bd. dirs. Los Amigos de Krwg, Las Cruces, 1994-97. Recipient Excellence in Programming Nat. Intramural Sports Coun., Reston, Va., 1989, Disting. Alumnus in Phys. Edn. award S.W. State U., San Marcos, Tex., 1990, Disting. Svc. award Nat. Assn. Sports and Phys. Edn., Reston, Va., 1993, Ft. Bliss Fed. Credit Union Svc. award for N.Mex. State U. Profl. Staff, 1996. Mem. AAHPERD (pres. S.W. dist. 1992-93, Honor award 1994), Nat. Intramural Recreational Sports Assn. (state dir. 1994-96, editl. bd. NIRSA Jour. 1996—), N.Mex. Assn. Health, Phys. Edn., Recreation and Dance (pres. 1988-89, Honor award 1989), Kappa Delta Pi (chpt. counselor 1987-97), Phi Delta Kappa. Home: 1760 Pomona Dr Las Cruces NM 88011-4920 Office: PO Box 30001 Las Cruces NM 88003-8001

DUELL, PAUL BARTON, internist, endocrinologist, educator; b. May 22, 1956. BS cum laude, Willamette U., Salem, Oreg., 1978; MD, Oreg. Health Scis. U., 1983. Diplomate Am. Bd. Internal Medicine, Am. Bd. Endocrinology, Metabolism and Nutrition; lic. physicia, Oreg., Wash. Intern U. Chgo., 1983-84; resident in medicine Oreg. Health Scis. U., Portland, 1984-86; fellow in endocrinology, metabolism U. Wash., Seattle, 1986-89, acting instr., 1989-90; asst. prof. medicine Oreg. Health Scis. U., Portland, 1990—, attending physician, 1990—; attending physician Portland VA Hosp., 1990—; med. scientist; lectr. in field; dir. Metabolic Disorders Clinic, 1996—. Contbr. articles to profl. jours., chpts. to books. Named Disting. Citizen, State of Wash., 1988; Tartar Trust Rsch. fellow, 1980, Oreg. Heart Assn. rsch. fellow, 1980; Oreg. scholar, 1974, Mary L. Collins scholar, 1976, 77. Fellow Arteriosclerosis Coun. Am. Heart Assn.; mem. ACP, Am. Fedn. for Clin. Rsch., Am. Inst. Nutrition, Am. Soc. for Clin. Nutrition, Am. Diabetes Assn., Juvenile Diabetes Found. Internat., Phi Eta Sigma, Alpha Kappa Nu, Mortar Bd. (v.p. 1977). Office: Oreg Health Scis Univ Divsn of Endocrinology Diabetes/Nutrition L465 Portland OR 97201-3098

DUERKSEN, NICK ALAN, public administrator; b. Wasco, Calif., Oct. 26, 1963; s. Charles John and Freda Ann (Allen) D.; m. Andrea Bingham, Sept. 19, 1986; children: Sara Ann, Caroline Elizabeth, Abby Lynn. BS in Polit. Sci., Utah State U., 1991. Cmty. devel. planner Five County Assn. of Govts., St. George, Utah, 1991-93; asst. dir. Sandy (Utah) City Corp., 1993—; mem. Utah Wastewater Bd., Salt Lake City, 1992-93. Mem. ASPA. Home: 1270 West 8830 South West Jordan UT 84088 Office: Sandy City Corp 10000 Centennial Pky Sandy UT 84070

DUERNBERGER, PAUL M., computer services director, computer and electrical engineering educator. BS in Meteorology and Oceanography, SUNY, 1968; postgrad., U. Miami, 1975-76, Armes Forces Staff Coll., 1982; MS in Applied Sci., Naval Postgrad. Sch., 1986. With U.S. Dept. Commerce, NOAA, 1968-89; cons. King County Superior Ct., Seattle, 1989-90; dir. computer svcs. Found. Ednl. Achievement, San Diego, 1990—; prof. computer sci. and elec. engring. Henry Cogswell Coll., Everett, Wash., 1990—. Pres. Boradview Community Coun., Seattle, 1991-92. Mem. IEEE, Am. Cetecean Soc. (bd. dirs. Pacific Northwest chpt.), Wash. Software Assn., Assn. Computing Machinery, Soc. Am. Mil. Engrs., Digital Equipment Corp. User's Soc., Lions. Office: Henry Cogswell Coll Everett WA 98206

DUERR, ALFRED, mayor. Formerly alderman City of Calgary, Alta., Can., elected mayor, 1989. Office: City of Calgary, PO Box 2100 Stn M, Calgary, AB Canada T2P 2M5

DUESTER, KAREN CHRISTENSEN, nutritionist, food industry executive; b. Minden, Nebr., June 7, 1958; d. Edwin LeRoy and Maxine Carol (Sorensen) Christensen; m. Gregg Lee Duester, Sept. 21, 1992. BS, U. Nebr., 1980; MS, Tex. Woman's U., 1981. Registered dietitian. Intern Houston VA Med. Ctr., 1980-81; clin. dietitian Iowa Meth. Med. Ctr., Des Moines, 1982-83; chief clin. nutritionist Cleveland Meml. Hosp., Shelby, N.C., 1983-85; regional sales mgr. Practorcare, Inc., Denver, 1985-88, sales mgr. western divsn., 1988-92; v.p. healthcare Practorcare, Inc., San Diego, 1992-93; owner The Food Cons. Co., San Diego, 1993—; cons. in field, 1983—; speaker profl. confs., 1982—. Contbr. articles to profl. jours., reviewer jours. Mem. Am. Dietetic Assn. (Recognized Young Dietitian of Yr. award 1987), Inst. Food Technologists, Internat. Assn. Culinary Profls., Dietitians in Bus. and Comm., Nutrition Entrepreneurs. Office: The Food Consulting Co Ste 142 12966 Carmel Creek Rd San Diego CA 92130-2131

DUFFY, ANDREW ENDA, language educator; b. Roscommon, Ireland, Nov. 30, 1960; came to U.S., 1981; s. Andrew and Mary (McDermott) D.; m. Maurizia Boscagli, July 23, 1988. BEd, Nat. U. Ireland, Dublin, 1981; MA, Rutgers U., 1984; PhD, Harvard U., 1990. Asst. prof. Reed Coll., Portland, Oreg., 1990-91, Wesleyan U., Middletown, Conn., 1991-93; faculty fellow Humanities Ctr., 1993; Asst. prof. U. Calif., Santa Barbara, 1993-95, assoc. prof., 1995—. Author: The Subaltern Ulysses, 1994; contbr. articles to literary jours., short stories to Irish publs. Whiting fellow Whiting Found., 1989. Mem. Am. Conf. in Irish Studies, MLA, James Joyce Found. Office: U Calif English South Hall Santa Barbara CA 93106

DUFFY, BARBARA JEAN, county official, librarian, education consultant, publisher; b. Colorado Springs, Colo., Dec. 13, 1938; d. Eugene Hagaman and Ruth Mae (Sills) Vannest; m. William M. Campbell (div.); children: Holli Denise Campbell Dowell, Heidi Campbell Schmidt; m. Donald D. Duffy (div.). BS, Cen. State U., Edmond, Okla., 1972; MEd, U. Okla., 1974, EdD, 1983. Clk. acctg. dept. Continental Oil Co., Ponca City, Okla., 1959-65; sec. Apco Oil Co, Oklahoma City, 1966-70; libr. media specialist Putnam City West High Sch., Oklahoma City, 1973-80; curriculum coord. Okla. State Dept. Edn., Oklahoma City, 1980-89; cons./publisher Bayview Assocs., San Mateo, Calif., 1989-90; grants dir., profl. svcs. assoc. Assn. Calif. Sch. Adminstrs., Burlingame, Calif., 1992; program dir. edn. info. resources and svcs. Sonoma County Office Edn., Santa Rosa, Calif, 1992—; ind. cons., advisor, 1992—. Editor: One of a Kind, 1983, 86; author, producer: video Magical Mix, 1985. Mem. Edmond Women's Polit. Caucus, 1980; chair Gov.'s Speak-out on Librs. 1977; chair North Bay Video Consortium, 1994-95; adv. com. v.p. KQED; pres. Gateway Reading Coun.; treas. Sonoma County Nat. Women's Polit. Caucus, 1996; chair Sonoma County Ednl. Telecomm. Consortium, 1995-96. Mem. Ednl. Media Assn. (sec. 1995), ASCD (dir. clearinghouse on learning teaching styles and brain behavior 1986-90), Assn. for Edn. Communications and Tech. (pres. divsn. ednl. media mgmt. 1990-91, chair long-range planning com. 1986-88), Internat. Visual Literacy Assn. (bd. dirs. 1987-89), Okla. Libr. Assn. (chair libr. devel. com. 1975-76), Ednl. Media Applications (chair elect 1995-96). Democrat. Mem. Ch. of Religious Sci. Home: 261 Candlelight Dr Santa Rosa CA 95403-8007 Office: Sonoma County Office Edn 5340 Skylane Blvd Santa Rosa CA 95403-1082

DUFFY, BERNARD KARL, educator; b. Bremen, Fed. Republic Germany, Apr. 27, 1948; came to U.S., 1953; s. Bernard E. and Elfriede G. (Loennecker) D.; m. Susan Jacobelli, Aug. 14, 1976; 1 child, Elizabeth. BA with great distinction, San Jose State Coll., 1970, MA, 1971; PhD, U. Pitts., 1976. Asst. prof. Hiram (Ohio) Coll., 1976-79; asst. prof. Clemson (S.C.) U., 1979-84, assoc. prof., 1984-87, prof., 1987-88; prof. Calif. Poly. State U., San Luis Obispo, 1988—, dept. chair, 1988-91. Author: (with Martin Jacobi) The Politics of Rhetoric: Richard M. Weaver and the Conservative Tradition, 1993, (with Ronald Carpenter) Douglas MacArthur: Warrior as Wordsmith, 1997; editor: (with Halford Ryan) American Orators of the Twentieth Century, 1987, American Orators Before 1900, 1987; series advisor Great American Orators, 1989—; contbr. articles to profl. jours. NEH Summer Seminar grantee, 1981, 84. Mem. Speech Communication Assn., Western Speech Communication Assn., Phi Kappa Phi. Democrat. Episcopalian. Office: Calif Poly State U Speech Communication Dept San Luis Obispo CA 93407

DUFFY, IRENE KAREN, artist; b. Chgo., Mar. 10, 1942; d. Andrew Earl and Irene Margaret Kane (Barthley) James; m. James Ora Duffy, Jan. 24, 1963 (div. Oct. 20, 1993); children: Dawn Ann, James Sean, Maureen Marie. BA, Wash. State U., 1985, MFA, 1989. Juried invitational exhbns. include Gallery X "Out of the Box", Art Inst. Chgo., 1995, Wash. State U./U. Ill., 1994, Virginia Inn, Seattle, 1993, Chase Gallery, Spokane, 1992, Union Gallery, Pullman, 1991, Acad. Arts, Riga, Latvia, 1990, Galeria 5, Caracas, Venezuela, 1989; collections include Johanna Bur. for the Handicapped, Chgo., Gordon Gilkey Collection, Portland Art Mus., Modern Art Gallery, Leningrad, Russia, Neill Pub. Libr. Bd. dirs. Pullman/Moscow Regional Airport, 1981-84. Recipient Civic Appreciation award City of

Pullman (Mayor Pete Butkus), 1984. Mem. Palouse Folklore Soc., Lions (v.p. Garfield Club 1996-97). Home: E 525 Church PO Box 215 Palouse WA 99161 Studio: Artspace 114 E 525 Church PO Box 215 Palouse WA 99161-0215

DUFFY, LAWRENCE KEVIN, biochemist, educator; b. Bklyn., Feb. 1, 1948; s. Michael and Anne (Browne) D.; m. Geraldine Antoinette Sheridan, Nov. 10, 1972; children: Anne Marie, Kevin Michael, Ryan Sheridan. BS, Fordham U., 1969; MS, U. Alaska, 1972, PhD, 1977. Teaching asst. dept. chemistry U. Alaska, 1969-71, rsch. asst. Inst. Arctic Biology, 1974-77; postdoctoral fellow Boston U., 1977-78, Roche Inst. Molecular Biology, 1978-80; rsch. asst. prof. U. Tex. Med. Br., Galveston, 1980-82; asst. prof. neurology (biol. chemistry) Med. Sch. Harvard U., Boston, Mass., 1982-87, adv. biochemistry instr. Med. Sch., 1983-87; instr. gen. and organic chemistry Roxbury Community Coll., Boston, 1984-87; prof. chemistry and biochem. U. Alaska, Fairbanks, 1992—, head dept. chemistry and biochemistry, 1994—; coord. program biochemistry and molecular biology for summer undergrad. rsch., 1987-96. Pres., bd. dirs. Alzheimer Disease Assn. of Alaska, 1994-95; mem. instnl. rev. bd. Fairbanks Meml. Hosp., 1990. Lt. USNR, 1971-73. NSF trainee, 1971; J.W. McLaughlin fellow, 1981; W.F. Milton scholar, 1983; recipient Alzheimers Disease and Related Disorders Assoc. Faculty Scholar award, 1987; Carol Fiest Outstanding Advisor award, 1994, NIDCD Cert. of Merit for mentoring, 1996. Mem. Am. Soc. Neurochemists, Am. Soc. Biol. Chemists, N.Y. Acad. Scis., Am. Chem. Soc. (Analytical Chemistry award 1969), Internat. Soc. Toxinologists, Sigma Xi (prs. 1991 Alaska club), Phi Lambda Upsilon. Roman Catholic. Office: U Alaska Fairbanks Inst Arctic Biology Fairbanks AK 99775

DUFRESNE, ARMAND FREDERICK, management and engineering consultant; b. Manila, Aug. 10, 1917; s. Ernest Faustine and Maude (McClellan) DuF.; m. Theo Rutledge Schaefer, Aug. 24, 1940 (dec. Oct. 1986); children: Lorna DuFresne Turnier, Peter, m. Lois Burrell Klosterman, Feb. 21, 1987. BS, Calif. Inst. Tech., 1938. Dir. quality control, chief product engr. Consol. Electrodynamics Corp., Pasadena, Calif., 1945-61; pres., dir. DUPACO, Inc., Arcadia, Calif., 1961-68; v.p., dir. ORMCO Corp., Glendora, Calif., 1966-68; mgmt., engring. cons., Duarte and Cambria, Calif., 1968—; dir., v.p., sec. Tavis Corp., Mariposa, Calif., 1968-79; dir. Denram Corp., Monrovia, Calif., 1968-70, interim pres., 1970; dir., chmn. bd. RCV Corp., El Monte, Calif., 1968-70; owner DUFCO, Cambria, 1971-82; pres. DUFCO Electronics, Inc., Cambria, Calif., 1982-86, chmn. bd. 1982-92; pres. Freedom Designs, Inc., Simi Valley, Calif., 1982-86, chmn. bd. dirs., 1982-97; owner DuFresne Consulting, 1992—; chmn. bd., pres. DUMEDCO,Inc., 1993-95. Patentee in field. Bd. dirs. Arcadia Bus. Assn., 1965-69; bd. dirs. Cambria Community Services Dist., 1976, pres., 1977-80; mem., chmn. San Luis Obispo County Airport Land Use Commn., 1972-75. Served to capt. Signal Corps, AUS, 1942-45. Decorated Bronze Star. Mem. Instrument Soc. Am. (life), Arcadia (dir. 1965-69), Cambria (dir. 1974-75) C. of C., Tau Beta Pi. Home: 901 Iva Ct Cambria CA 93428-2913

DUGAN, MARIANNE GUENEVERE, lawyer; b. N.Y.C., Nov. 20, 1959; d. Kieran T.R. and Sheila M. (Johnson) D.; m. Michael S. Fields, July 14, 1984; 1 child, Selena Dugan-Fields. BA, U. Colo., 1980; JD, U. Oreg., 1993. Bar: Oreg. 1993, U.S. Dist. Ct. Oreg. 1993, U.S. Ct. Appeals (2d cir.) 1993, (9th cir.) 1994. Housing coord. Karok Tribe of Calif., Happy Camp, 1980-81; shipping clk. Feminist Press, Old Westbury, N.Y., 1981-83; delivery subcontractor Product Devel. Corp., Portland, Oreg., 1983-86; sr. coord. Gleaning Network, Medford, Oreg., 1987-88; patients accounts mgr. Ashland (Oreg.) Cmty. Hosp., 1988-90; staff atty. Western Environ. Law Ctr., Eugene, Oreg., 1993—; assoc. dir., 1995—; freelance writer N.Y.C., 1986-95; grantwriter, sec. So. Oreg. Gleaning Network, Central Point, Oreg., 1988-90; peer reviewer Tech. Studies, Lethbridge, Can., 1994; treas. The Seamless Web, Eugene, 1992-93. Editor, writer (newsletter) Report on So. Oreg. Economy, So. Oreg. Fair Share, 1987-89; mem. editl. bd. Jour. Environ. Law and Litigation, 1992-93; contbr. articles to profl. jours. Mem. steering com. So. Oreg. Women's History Month, Ashland, 1988, 89. Recipient Am. Jurisprudence award, Lawyer's Coop. Pub., 1993. Mem. Nat. Lawyers Guild, Oreg. Trial Lawyers Assn., Oreg. Women Lawyers, Oreg. State Bar Assn., Lane County Bar Assn., Order of Coif. Democrat. Office: Western Environ Law Ctr 1216 Lincoln St Eugene OR 97401-3467

DUGGAN, EDWARD MARTIN, science and mathematics educator; b. Tacoma, Wash., Sept. 23, 1953; s. John and Catherine Patricia (Fitzgerald) D.; children: Rory Emmett, Orlaith Catherine Mary. BS in Psychology, U. Wash., 1979, BA in Zoology, 1979, BS in Botany, 1980, MEd in Sci. Edn., 1982. Cert. tchr., Wash., police commr., Wash., EMT. Tchr., coach cross country, track and gymnastics Federal Way (Wash.) Pub. Schs., 1982—; police officer Wash., 1996—. Mem. Nat. Sci. Tchrs. Assn., Audubon Soc., Nat. Wildlife Fedn. Roman Catholic. Home: 2729 SW 349th Pl Federal Way WA 98023

DUH, QUAN-YANG, surgeon; b. Taipei, Taiwan, Dec. 21, 1954; came to U.S., 1970; s. Dong Liang and Lee Shiow (lee) D.; m. Ann Marie Comer, May 8, 1983; children: Katherine Lenna, Emily Ann. BS summa cum laude, Yale U., 1977; MD, U. Calif., San Francisco, 1981. Diplomate Am. Bd. Surgery. Intern U. Calif., San Francisco, 1981-82, resident in gen. surgery, 1982-88; attending surgeon surg. scv. Vet. Affairs Med. Ctr., San Francisco, 1988—, asst. chief surg. svc., 1991—; asst. prof. dept. surgery U. Calif., San Francisco, 1988-94, assoc. prof. dept. surgery, 1994—. Inventor laparoscopic tube placement; contbr. articles to profl. jours. Recipient Nusz award for outstanding rsch. U. Calif. Dept. Surgery, 1988, Student award for excellence in teaching, 1991. Fellow ACS. Democrat. Office: VA Med Ctr 4150 Clement St San Francisco CA 94121-1545

DUHART, LAWRENCE ALBERT, auralist; b. Columbus, Ohio, Dec. 20, 1957; s. Willie and Marcella D.; m. Debbie Miller, Feb. 14, 1985 (div. Feb. 1989; 1 child, Lauren. BA in Music, Howard U., 1977; BS in Elec. Tech., Grantham Tech. Sch., 1979; MBA, Pepperdine U., 1980. Music copyist Roger Farris Music, L.A., 1975-76; music arranger H.B. Barnum Music, L.A., 1976-82; rec. engr. Herbie Hancock Prodns., Beverly Hills, Calif., 1983-88; record prodr. Columbia Records/Island Records, L.A., 1985-90; auralist, pres. Aurally Yours, Inc., Hollywood, Calif., 1975—; pres. Tayo Industries, Hollywood, 1992—; music prodn. cons. MCA Records/John Klemmer, L.A., 1989-90; digital restoration prodr. Dick Clark Prodns., Burbank, Calif., 1985-89. Inventor audio processor, programs in field. Recipient Gold Record award RIAA, 1983, Gold and Platinum Video award RIAA, 1985. Mem. NARAS (Grammy award 1984), ASCAP, Broadcast Music Inc., Internat. Multimedia Assn. Office: Tayo Industries/Aurally Yours Inc 7510 Sunset Blvd # 537 Hollywood CA 90046

DUHNKE, ROBERT EMMET, JR., retired aerospace engineer; b. Manitowoc, Wis., Jan. 28, 1935; s. Robert Emmet and Vivian Dorothy (Abel) D.; m. Patricia R. Ebben, 1956 (div. 1972); children: Kim Marie, Lori Ann, Dawn Diane, Robert III, Mary Lynn; m. Judy Anne Lind, Feb. 14, 1978. BS in Aero. Engring., Purdue U., 1957. Assoc. engr. Convair/Aerodynes. Group, Pomona, Calif., 1957-58; assoc. engr., instr. Boeing Co., Seattle, 1964-66, instr. maintenance tng., 1972-83, navigation sys. analyst, 1983-90, sr. specialist engr., instr. comml. maintenance tng. ctr., 1990-95; flight navigator Flying Tigers, San Francisco, 1966-68; salesman various real estate and ins. cos., Seattle, 1968-72; shuttler Hertz, Seattle, 1996-97; reservation sales agt. Alaska Airlines, Phoenix, 1997—; contract aerospace engr. Superior Design Co., Inc., Kirkland, Wash., 1996—. Author poems in English, German and Spanish. Sponsor World Vision, Pasadena, Calif.; mem. Citizens Against Govt. Waste. Capt. USAF, 1958-64. Recipient Hon. Freedom Fighter award Afghan Mercy Fund, 1987. Mem. Inst. Navigation, Air Force Assn. Home: 1219 30th St NE Auburn WA 98002-2471 also: 30 W Carter Dr Tempe AZ 85282-6743

DUKE, DONALD NORMAN, publisher; b. L.A., Apr. 1, 1929; s. Roger V. and Mabel (Weineger) D. BA in Ednl. Psychology, Colo. Coll., 1951. Comml. photographer Colorado Springs, Colo., 1951-53; pub. rels. Gen. Petroleum, L.A., 1954-55; agt. Gen. S.S. Corp., Ltd., 1956-57; asst. mgr. retail advt., sales promotion Mobil Oil Co., 1958-63; pub. Golden West Books, Alhambra, Calif., 1964—; dir. Pacific R.R. Publs., Inc., Athletic Press; pub. relations cons. Santa Fe Ry., 1960-70. Author: The Pacific Electric: A History of Southern California Railroading, 1958, Southern Pacific Steam Locomotives, 1962, Santa Fe...Steel Rails to California, 1963, Night Train, 1961, American Narrow Gauge, 1978, RDC: the Budd Rail Diesel Car, 1989, The Brown Derby, 1990, Camp Cajon, 1991, Fred Harvey: Civilizer of the American West, 1994, Volume One, Volume Two, 1997; editor: Water Trails West, 1977, Branding Iron, 1988-91, Santa Fe...The Railroad Gateway to the American West, Vol. 1, 1995, Vol. 2, 1997. Recipient Spur award for Trails of the Iron Horse Western Writers Am., 1975. Mem. Ry. and Locomotive Hist. Soc. (dir. 1944—), Western History Assn., Newcomen Soc., Lexington Group of Transp. History, Western Writers Am., P.E.N. Internat. (v.p. 1975-77), Authors Guild Am., Book Pubs. Assn. So. Calif. (dir. 1968-77), Cal. Writers Guild (dir. 1976-77), Calif. Book Pubs. Assn. (dir. 1976-77), Westerners Internat. (hon., editor Branding Iron 1971-80, 88-91), Hist. Soc. So. Calif. (dir. 1972-75), Henry E./Arabella Huntington Soc., Kappa Sigma (lit. editor Caduceus 1968-80). Home: PO Box 80250 San Marino CA 91118-8250 Office: Golden West Books 525 N Electric Ave Alhambra CA 91801-2032

DUKE, PAMELA RUTH, reading specialist; b. Salt Lake City, Feb. 14, 1945; d. Carson Bailey Duke and Ruth (Jones) Stafford. BA, Calif. State U., Chico, 1966; MA, Chapman U., 1973. Tchr. Murray Sch. Dist., Dublin, Calif., 1967-69; tchr. Lompoc (Calif.) Unified Schs., 1969-72, math specialist, 1972-86, reading specialist, 1986—; math fellow Tri-County Math. Project, Santa Barbara, 1985; fellow Impact II, Santa Barbara, 1987—. Grantee Impact II Santa Barbara, 1988, 90; scholar Calif. PTA, L.A., 1966—. Mem. Calif. Tchrs. Assn., Reading Specialists Calif., Internat. Reading Assn., Calif. Reading Assn., Santa Maria Kennel Club. Office: Fillmore Elementary School 1211 E Pine Ave Lompoc CA 93436-4238

DUKE, WILLIAM EDWARD, public affairs executive; b. Bklyn., July 18, 1932; m. Leilani Kamp Lattin. BS, Fordham U., 1954. City editor Middletown (N.Y.) Record, 1956-60; asst. state editor Washington Star, 1961-63; exec. asst. to U.S. Senator from N.Y. State, Jacob K. Javits, Washington, 1963-69; dir. pub. affairs Corp. Pub. Broadcasting, Washington, 1969-72; dir. fed. govt. rels. Atlantic Richfield Co., Washington, 1973-78, mgr. pub. affairs, L.A., 1978-91; mgr. external affairs We. States Petroleum Assn., 1993-95; coun. Pacific Visions Comm., 1995—; lectr. U. So. Calif. Grad. Sch. Journalism, 1988—; cons. in field. Fellow Pub. Rels. Soc. Am., Nat. Press Club, Capitol Hill Club, L.A. Athletic Club. Office: Pacific Visions Com 9000 W Sunset Blvd Los Angeles CA 90069-5801

DUKE DE LEONEDES See SANCHEZ, LEONEDES MONARRIZE WORTHINGTON

DU LAC, LOIS ARLINE, writer; b. Cleve., July 17, 1920; d. Carl Walter and T. Henrietta (Lyon) Stein; m. Leo Joseph Du Lac, Apr. 20, 1941; children: Arline Du Lac Gerard, Linda Du Lac Jennings, Glen, Carl, Ralph. BA cum laude, UCLA, 1942, MA, 1962; JD, Western State U., Fullerton, Calif., 1982. Tchr. Cornelia Connelly H.S., Anaheim, Calif., 1962-63, Montebello (Calif.) Sch. Dist., 1963, Excelsior/Norwalk (Calif.) Sch. Dist., 1963-64, Garden Grove (Calif.) Unified Sch. Dist., 1964-69. Creative editor, contbg. author: Constitutional Law, 1981; contbg. author: Murder California Style, 1987, Mord in Kalifornie, 1988. Vol. law clk. Cmty. Law Ctr., Santa Ana, Calif., 1982. Mem. Mystery Writers Am. (contbg. author Edgar Ann. 1990, 92), Cath. Press Assn., Phi Beta Kappa, Alpha Mu Gamma. Office: PO Box 403301 Hesperia CA 92340-3301 *Lois Du Lac earned an MA and University Recommended Teaching Credential from UCLA, with nearly a straight A average. She received a lifetime certification from California to teach college through sophomore year. She taught Latin to Naval Commander and astronaut, David Leestma, named academic best in his freshman Annapolis class. She became poetry editor for Mythril Literary Magazine. While earning her JD, she wrote a humorous poetry column, Crimes in Rhymes. She contributed What's Cooking? Murder? to a St. Martin's Press anthology and an article, also a poem to MWA Edgar Annuals. She has won many awards and prizes for her poems, articles, and short stories.*

DULANEY, MARY ELAINA, public relations executive; b. Akron, Ohio, Aug. 10, 1968; d. William S. and Dorothy I. (Erion) Holland; m. Stephen Alan Dulaney, Oct. 3, 1992. BA in Pub. Rels., Pacific Luth. U., 1990. Corp. comm. asst. INTERLINQ Software Corp., Kirkland, Wash., 1990-91; pub. rels. coord., specialist Traveling Software, Bothell, Wash., 1991-94; sr. account exec. Waggener Edstrom, Bellevue, Wash., 1994—; chair comm. arts adv. coun. Pacific Luth. U., Seattle, 1992-94. Inst. Asian Studies scholar, 1988-89. Mem. Pub. Rels. Soc. Am. (co-chair high tech. com., bd. dirs. Puget Sound chpt. 1997). Baptist. Home: 8017 NE 125th St Kirkland WA 98034-2769 Office: Waggener Edstrom 11400 SE 8th St Ste 250 Bellevue WA 98004

DULBECCO, RENATO, biologist, educator; b. Catanzaro, Italy, Feb. 22, 1914; came to U.S., 1947, naturalized, 1953; s. Leonardo and Maria (Virdia) D.; m. Gulseppina Salvo, June 1, 1940 (div. 1963); children: Peter Leonard (dec.), Maria Vittoria; m. Maureen Rutherford Muir; 1 child, Fiona Linsey. M.D., U. Torino, Italy, 1936; D.Sc. (hon.), Yale U., 1968, Vrije Universiteit, Brussels, 1978; LL.D., U. Glasgow, Scotland, 1970. Asst. U. Torino, 1940-47; research asso. Ind. U., 1947-49; sr. research fellow Calif. Inst. Tech., 1949-52, asso. prof., then prof. biology, 1952-63; sr. fellow Salk Inst. Biol. Studies, San Diego, 1963-71; asst. dir. research Imperial Cancer Research Fund, London, 1971-74; dep. dir. research Imperial Cancer Research Fund, 1974-77; disting. research prof. Salk Inst., La Jolla, Calif., 1977—, pres., 1989-92; pres. emeritus Salk Inst., La Jolla, 1993—; prof. pathology and medicine U. Calif. at San Diego Med. Sch., La Jolla, 1977-81, mem. Cancer Ctr.,; vis. prof. Royal Soc. G.B., 1963-64, Leeuwenhoek lectr., 1974; Clowes Meml. lectr. Atlantic City, 1961; Harvey lectr. Harvey Soc., 1967; Dunham lectr. Harvard U., 1972; 11th Marjory Stephenson Meml. lectr., London, 1973, Harden lectr., Wye, Eng., 1973, Am. Soc. for Microbiology lectr., L.A., 1979; mem. Calif. Cancr Adv. Coun., 1963-67; mem. vis. com. Case Western Res. Sch. Medicine; adv. bd. Roche Inst., 1968-71, Inst. Immunology, Basel, Switzerland, others; esperto Italian Nat. Rsch. Coun.; trustee Am.-Italian Fedn. for Cancer Rsch.; mem. bd. dirs. Scientific Counselors Dept. Etiology NCI; cons. Nat. Rsch. Coun. ESPERTO, 1994—. Trustee La Jolla Country Day Sch., Am.-Italian Fedn. for Cancer Rsch.; bd. mem. sci. counselors dept. etiology NCI. Recipient John Scott award City Phila., 1958, Kimball award Conf. Pub. Health Lab. Dirs., 1959, Albert and Mary Lasker Basic Med. Rsch. award, 1964, Howard Taylor Ricketts award, 1965, Paul Ehrlich-Ludwig Darmstaedter prize, 1967, Horwitz prize Columbia U., 1973, (with David Baltimore and Howard Martin Temin) Nobel prize in medicine, 1975, Targa d'oro Villa San Giovanni, 1978, Mandel Gold medal Czechoslovak Acad. Scis., 1982, Via de Condotti prize, 1990, Cavaliere di Gran Croce Italian Rep., 1991, Natale Di Roma prize, 1993, Columbus prize, 1993; named Man of Yr., London, 1975, Italian Am. of Yr., San Diego County, 1978; hon. citizen City of Imperia (Italy), 1983, City of Arezzo, City of Sommariva Perno, City of Catanzaro, City of Torino; Guggenheim and Fulbright fellow, 1957-58; decorated grand officiale Italian Republic, 1981; hon. founder Hebrew U., 1981. Mem. NAS (Selman A. Waksman award 1974, com. on human rights), Am. Assn. Cancer Rsch., Internat. Physicians for Prevention Nuclear War, Am. Philos. Assn., Academia Nazionale del Lincel (fgn.), Academia Ligure di Scienze e Lettre (hon.), Royal Soc. (fgn.), Fedn. Am. Scientists, Am. Acad. Arts and Scis., Comitato di Collaborazione Culturale (hon. mem.), Alpha Omega Alpha. Home: 7525 Hillside Dr La Jolla CA 92037-3941*

DULEY, CHARLOTTE DUDLEY, vocational counselor; b. Lincoln, Nebr., Oct. 2, 1920; d. Millard Eugene and Inez Kathryn (Miller) Dudley; student U. Nebr., 1938-41; M.A. in Guidance Counseling, U. Idaho, 1977; B.S., Lewis and Clark State Coll., 1973; m. Phillip D. Duley, Mar. 28, 1942; (dec. Sept. 1984); children: Michael Dudley (dec.), Patricia Kaye; m. P. Fredrik Nordgaard, Sep.1, 1990. Tchr., Nebr. schs., 1951-56; with Dept. of Employment, Lewiston, Idaho, 1958-81, local office counselor handling fed. tng. programs, 1958-81; ind. job cons.; counselor; rep. Avon, Lewiston; part-time counselor, tester, 1981—. Pres., bd. dirs. Civic Arts, Inc., 1972-81; mem. women's svc. league Wash.-Idaho Symphony Orch., 1972-96; bd. dirs. YWCA, 1980-88, treas., 1981-88; mem. adv. bd. Salvation Army, 1980-94; dir. artist series Lewis and Clark State Coll., 1984-90. Recipient Altrusa Woman of Achievement award, 1984. Mem. Am., Idaho pers. guidance Assns., Idaho State Employees Assn., Internat. Assn. Employees in Employment Security, Am. Assn. Counseling & Devel., Idaho State Employment Counselors Assn. (pres. 1979-80), Stateline Guidance and Counseling Assn. (sec.-treas. 1964, 76-77), Lewiston Cmty. Concert Assn. (bd. dirs., 1980-96, pres. 1980-94), Greater Lewiston C. of C. (chmn. conv. and tourism com. 1984-95), Altrusa (bd. dirs.), Elks (pres. 1986-87, exec. bd. 1985-88, election bd. chmn. 1986-94, 1st v.p., 1993-95, ladies of elks pres. 1987-89, 95-96, bd. dirs. 1996—). Baptist. Home: 1819 Ridgeway Dr Lewiston ID 83501-3890

DULING, JEAN M. HART, clinical social worker; b. Bellingham, Wash.; d. Murry Donald and Pearl N. (McLeod) Macaulay; m. Richard D. Hart, Feb. 3, 1940 (dec. Mar. 1973); children: Margaret Hart Morrison, Pamela Hart Horton, Patricia L. Hart-Jewell; m. Lawrence Duling, Jan. 20, 1979 (dec. May 1992); children: Lenora Daniel, Larry, Jayne Munch. BA, Wash. State U., 1938; MSW, U. So. Calif., 1961. Lic. clin. social worker, Calif.; accredited counselor, Wash. Social worker Los Angeles County, 1957-58; children's svc. worker Dept. Children's Svcs., L.A., 1958-59; program developer homemakers svcs. project Calif. Dept. Children's Svcs., L.A., 1962-64; developer homemaker cons. position State of Calif., L.A., 1964-66; supr. protective svcs. Dept. Children's Svcs., L.A., 1966-67; dep. regional svc. adminstrn. Dept. Los Angeles County Children's Svcs., 1967-76; adminstr. Melton Home for Developmental Disability, 1985-86; therapist various pro bono cases. Mem. Portals Com., L.A., 1974, Travelers Aid Bd., Long Beach, Calif. 1969. Recipient Nat. award work in cmty., spl. award for work with emotionally disturbed Com. for Los Angeles, 1974. Mem. AAUW, NASW, Acad. Cert. Social Workers, Wing Point Golf and Country Club (Bainbridge Island, Wash.). Republican. Congregationalist. Office: 7300 Quill Dr Downey CA 90242-2031

DUMAINE, R. PIERRE, bishop; b. Paducah, Ky., Aug. 2, 1931; student St. Joseph Coll., Mountain View, Calif., 1945-51, St. Patrick Sem., Menlo Park, Calif., 1951-57; Ph.D., Cath. U. Am., 1962. Ordained priest Roman Cath. Ch., 1957; asst. pastor Immaculate Heart Ch., Belmont, Calif., 1957-58; mem. faculty dept. edn. Cath. U. Am., 1961-63; tchr. Serra High Sch., San Mateo, Calif., 1963-65; asst. supt. Cath. schs., Archdiocese of San Francisco, 1965-74, supt., 1974-78; ordained bishop, 1978, bishop of San Jose, Santa Clara, Calif., 1981—; dir. Archdiocesan Ednl. TV Ctr., Menlo Park, Calif., 1968-81. Mem. Pres.'s Nat. Adv. Council on Edn. of Disadvantaged Children, 1970-72; bd. dirs. Cath. TV Network, 1968-81, pres., 1975-77; bd. dirs. Pub. Service Satellite Consortium, 1975-81. Mem. Nat. Cath. Edn. Assn., Assn. Cath. Broadcasters and Allied Communicators, Internat. Inst. Communications, Assn. Calif. Sch. Adminstrs. Office: Diocese of San Jose 900 Lafayette St Ste 301 Santa Clara CA 95050-4966

DUMARS, KENNETH W., medical geneticist educator, pediatrician; b. Denver, Sept. 28, 1921; s. Kenneth W. Sr. and Annie (Wright) D.; m. Barbara Lou Belcher Dumars, Sept. 17, 1942 (dec. Sept. 1967); children: Stephen Craig, David Bruce, Peter Kent, Janet Rae, Leslie Marie; m. Gayle E. Fialko Dumars, Jan. 17, 1976. BA in Zoology, U. Denver, 1942; MD, U. Colo. Sch. Medicine, 1945. Diplomate Am. Bd. Pediatrics, Am. Bd. Med. Genetics in Clin. Genetics and Clin. Cytogenetics. Intern Mpls. Gen. Hosp., 1945-46; residency U. Colo. Sch. Medicine Pediatrics, 1948-50; pvt. practice Gt. Falls, Mont., 1950-51, Colo. Springs, 1951-61; attending physician Neurology Clinic U. Colo. Med. Ctr., 1955-61; med. dir. Cardinal Hill Convalescent Hosp., Lexington, Ky., 1961-62; dir. Chromosome Laboratory Penrose Cancer Hosp., Colo. Springs, Colo., 1963-65; pediatrician Rancho Los Amigos Hosp., Downey, Calif., 1965-68; attending physician White Meml. Hosp. Med. Ctr., L.A., 1965-68, L.A. County Gen. Hosp., 1965-68, Children Hosp. Orange County, 1965-95; attending physician (emeritus) U. Calif. Irvine Med. Ctr., 1968—; clin. instr. pediatrics U. Colo. Med. Ctr., 1955-61; asst. prof. pediatrics U. Ky. Sch. Medicine, 1961-62, U. Colo. Med. Ctr., 1962-63; asst. clin. prof. pediatrics U. Colo. Med. Ctr., 1963-65; assoc. prof. pediatrics U. Calif. Irvine Coll. Medicine, 1971-79; vis. prof. Dept. Child Health Welsh Nat. Sch. Medicine, Cardiff, Wales, 1976-77; prof. pediatrics U. Calif. Irvine Coll. Medicine, 1979-91; prof. obstetrics and gynecology, U. Calif. Irvine Coll. Medicine, 1982-91; prof. pediatrics emeritus U. Calif. Irvine Coll. Medicine, 1991—; cons. Colo. State Health Dept. for Traveling Epilepsy Clinic State of Colo., 1958-65, Fort Carson Hosp., Colo., 1958-65, Penrose Cancer Hosp., Colo. Springs, Colo., 1958-65, Divsn. of Adoptions Orange County Dept. Pub. Welfare, 1968-82, Easter Seal Rehabilitation Ctr. Orange County, 1968-71, Genetic Disease Branch Calif. State Health Dept., Berkeley, 1974-92 (numerous grants), Adminstrn. Devel. Disabilities, Sacramento, Calif., 1972-88, Washington, 1978-84 (numerous grants), Nat. Fdn. March of Dimes, Orange County, Calif., 1974-89 (numerous grants, disting. svc. award, 1976, 79, 89, med. adv. com. Orange chpt. 1974-89, exec. com. Orange chpt. 1987-89), Nat. Tuberous Sclerosis Assn., Landover, Md., 1983-91 (commendation and award 1986, med. adv. bd. 1983-91, med. rsch. com. 1983-91), Huntington Disease Fdn., L.A. chpt., 1988— (med. advisor 1988—); med. dir. Med. Genetics Fountain Valley a MediGene Facility, 1991-93; dir. Southeast Asian Genetic Program, 1984-91, U. Calif. Irvine U. Affiliated Program, 1972-86, Cytogenetics Laboratory Dept. Pediatrics, 1965-86, Divsn. of Clin. Genetics and Devel. Disabilities Dept. Pediatrics, 1972-86; dir. cytogenetic laboratory U. Calif. Irvine Coll. Medicine, 1965-86; mem. Coun. Regional Network for Genetic Diseases, Atlanta, 1988— (chair thalassemia com. 1988—, mem. sickle cell, thalassemia, other hemoglobin variants com., 1988—) and numerous others. Contbr. articles to profl. jours.; speaker in field. Cons. Rehabilitation Inst. Orange, Orange County, Calif., 1968-71, Navajo Nation, Gallup, N.M., 1980-82. Capt. AUS, 1946-48. Continuing Edn. award AMA, 1982, 90, 93, Continuing Edn. award Calif. Med. Assn., 1986-88, 89-92. Founding Fellow Am. Coll. Med. Genetics, fellow Am Bd. Paediatrics, Am. Bd. Med. Genetics; mem. AAAS, Am. Soc. Human Genetics, Am. Assn. Mental Deficiency, Am. Eugenics Soc., Environmental Mutagen Soc., Western Soc. Paediatric Rsch., European Soc. for Human Genetics, Royal Photographic Soc. of Great Britain Med. Section. Office: U Calif Irvine Med Ctr 101 The City Dr S Orange CA 92868-3201*

DUMAS, BOB ALAN, marketing executive; b. Oklahoma City, Mar. 5, 1960; s. Leo Vern Dumas and Lucille Therese (Berdel) Lamb; m. Gloria Dumas Ang, July 3, 1989; 1 child, Siena Dumas Ang. BS, U. Wash., 1981; Cert. Philosophy, U. Calif., Berkeley, 1984, PhD, 1991. Mathematician Naval Undersea Warfare Engring. Sta., Keyport, Wash., 1981-83; lectr. math. U. Calif., Davis, 1989-91; vis. asst. prof. U. Calif., Berkeley, 1991-92; mktg. mgr. Golden Grain Co., San Leandro, Calif., 1992-94; pres. Customer Mktg. Group, Inc., Redmond, Calif., 1994—. Mem. Sahalee Country Club, Phi Beta Kappa. Home and Office: 3234 264th Ave NE Redmond WA 98053

DUMAS, WILLIAM JOSEPH, filmmaker; b. Landstuhl, Fed. Republic of Germany, July 24, 1956; came to U.S., 1959; s. William Fred and Erika (Besslich) D. AA, Mohegan C.C., 1976; BA, Calif. State U., Long Beach, 1978; MFA, Am. Film Inst., 1992. Owner, exec. prodr. Vinyl Siding Records, Jewett City, Conn., 1982-90; sr. configuration mgmt. analyst Gen. Dynamics, Groton, Conn., 1982-90; intern Paramount Pictures/Marvin Worth Prodns., Propaganda Films, Hollywood, Calif., 1990-91; dir. devel. SPI Entertainment, L.A., 1991-94; vis. instr. film. Conn. Coll., 1995-96. Writer, prodr., dir. Boston Film and Video Found., 1987-90, Bill Dumas Prodns., L.A., 1992-94, (film) Through the Walls, 1993 (finalist USA Film Festival 1993-94); writer, dir. (feature film) Unto Others; co-prodr. Pacifica Films (feature film) The Barrow Gang (The Visit); exec. prodr. (feature film) Together & Alone; film series coord. Hygienic Art Show, New London, Conn., 1994-97; camera operator, sound engr. AFI Women's Directing Program, L.A., 1991. Mem. Am. Film Inst. Alumni Assn. Home: 375 Taylor Hill Rd Jewett City CT 06351-2514 Office: Bill Dumas Prodns 1973 N Van Ness Ave Los Angeles CA 90068-3624

DUMITRESCU, DOMNITA, Spanish language educator, researcher; b. Bucharest, Romania; came to U.S., 1984; d. Ion and Angela (Barzotescu) D. Diploma, U. Bucharest, 1966; MA, U. So. Calif., 1987, PhD, 1990. Asst. prof. U. Bucharest, 1966-74, assoc. prof., 1974-84; asst. prof. Spanish, U. So. Calif., 1985-89; assoc. prof. Calif. State U., L.A., 1990-94, prof., 1995—. Author: Gramatica Limbii Spaniole, 1976, Indreptar Pentru Traducerea Din Limba Romana in Limba Spaniola, 1980; translator from Spanish lit. to Romanian; assoc. editor: Hispania, 1996-98; contbr. articles to profl. jours. Fulbright scholar, 1993—. Mem. MLA, Am.-Romanian Acad. Arts and Scis., Linguistic Soc. Am., Internat. Assn. Hispanists, Assn. Linguistics and Philology L.Am., Am. Assn. Tchrs. Spanish and Portuguese (past pres. So. Calif. chpt.). Office: Calif State U 5151 State University Dr Los Angeles CA 90032-4221

DUMKE, NICOLETTE MARIE, author, food allergy consultant; b. Denver, Sept. 27, 1953; d. Eugene and Mary (Capraro) Jiannetti; m. Mark Frederick Dumke, June 12, 1976; children: Joel Michael, John Daniel. BS in Microbiology, U. Wyo., 1974; BS in Med. Tech., U. Colo., Denver, 1975. Cert. med. technologist, Am. Soc. Clin. Pathologists. Med. technologist Colo. Gen. Hosp., Denver, 1975-76, Glendale (Calif.) Adventist Hosp., 1976-79; microbiologist Hyland Diagnostics, Glendale, 1979-82; pres. Allergy Adapt, Inc., Louisville, Colo., 1988—. Author: Allergy Cooking With Ease, 1992, Easy Breadmaking for Special Diets, 1996, The Food Allergy Survival Guide, 1997. Home and Office: Allergy Adapt Inc 1877 Polk Ave Louisville CO 80027

DUMOND, MARK DOUGLAS, film and television producer; b. Chadron, Nebr., Apr. 26, 1954; s. Lewis William and Ruth Lillian (Lemons) DuM.; m. Nancy Eleanor Bodwell, May 10, 1986; children: Dan, Jessica, Alex. Student, Calif. State U., Fullerton, 1972, Orange Coast Coll., 1973-74. Transp. mgr. Freedom Newspapers, Santa Ana, Calif., 1973-77; circulation mgr. Anchorage Times, 1977-84; prodn. mgr. Sta. KTUU-TV, Anchorage, 1984-88, Sta. KOBI-TV/COBI Digital, Medford, Oreg., 1988—; dir. Rogue Studios, Ashland, Oreg., 1996-97. Author: (screenplays) Full Count, 1995, Lake of Fire, 1996; writer, prodr.: (TV documentaries) Sentenced to Life, 1990 (Emmy award 1990), Russian Roulette, 1992. Mem. So. Oreg. Film and Video Assn. (pres. 1997). Home: 329 S Grape St Medford OR 97501 Office: COBI Digital 125 S Fir St Medford OR 97501

DUMONT, JAMES KELTON, JR., actor, producer; b. Chgo., Aug. 12, 1965; s. James Kelton and Judith Katherine (Johnson) DuM.; m. Wendell Faith Hall, Dec. 14, 1968. Student, Boston U., 1983-85. Pres., CEO DuMont Entertainment Group, Hollywood, Calif., 1994—; mem. Ensemble Studio Theatre, N.Y.C., 1989—; co-artistic dir. Ensemble Studio Theatre-The L.A. Project, 1994-96; producer Winterfests 1994-96—, First Look L.A., 1996. Appeared in Broadway play Six Degrees of Separation, 1990-93, (off-Broadway play) Tony & Tina's Wedding, 1989-90; films Speed, 1993, Combination Platter, 1993, Bombshell, 1996, The Peacemaker, 1996, Primary Colors, 1997, Legal Tender, 1997; television series NYPD Blue, 1995, Lois & Clark, 1996, Chgo. Sons, 1996, Track Takes on 1995, Fallen Angels, 1995, The Client, 1995, Sweet Justice, 1995, Can't Hurry Love, 1995; producer, actor: (film) The Confession, 1996. Democrat. Buddhist. Office: Ensemble Studio Theatre 137 N Larchmont Blvd # 134 Los Angeles CA 90004

DUMOULIN, DIANA CRISTAUDO, marketing professional; b. Washington, Jan. 5, 1939; d. Emanuel A. and Angela E. (Cogliano) Cristaudo; m. Philip DuMoulin, May 30, 1964; children: Joanmarie Patricia, John Philip. MA, U. Wis., 1967; BA, Rosary Coll., 1961. Project mgr. IDC Cons. Group, Framingham, Mass., 1982-84; sr. market analyst Cullinet, Inc., Westwood, Mass., 1984-86; prof. assoc. Ledgeway Group, Lexington, Mass., 1987-89; prin. Customer Mktg. Specialist, Brookline, Mass., 1989-93; pres. Customer Solutions Int., Phoenix, 1994—; adj. faculty Ulster Count Community Coll., Stone Ridge, N.Y., 1967-74, Mass. Bay Community Coll., Wellesley Hills, Mass., 1983; lectr. Boston Coll., Chestnut Hill, Mass., 1976. Contbr. articles to profl. jours. Pres. League Women Voters, Kingston, N.Y., 1973-74. Recipient Svc. to Young Adults award 70001 Career Assn., 1977, Honorable Mention awrd Writers Digest Writing Competition, 1996; faculty fellow U. Wis., 1964-66. Mem. Am. Field Svc. Mgrs. Internat. (software support spl. interest group, chmn. minuteman chpt. 1991-92), Nat. Assn. Women Bus. Owners. Office: Customer Solutions Internat 8441 N 1st Dr Phoenix AZ 85021-5515

DUNAWAY, MARGARET ANN (MAGGIE DUNAWAY), state agency administrator, consultant; b. Fresno, Calif., Feb. 10, 1943; d. Joseph John and Anna Frances (Dice) Cumero; children from previous marriage: Christian Anthony Freitag, Erika Lynn Bullard; m. Michael Earl Babcoke, Oct. 6, 1990; 1 stepchild, Jason Ethan Babcoke. Student, U. Calif., Davis, 1960-62, U. Calif., Berkeley, 1962-63. Supr. Gov's Office, Sacramento, 1969-72; office mgr. State Health and Welfare Agy., Sacramento, 1972-73; analyst regulations devel. Calif. State Depts. Health and Social Svcs., Sacramento, 1974-84, cons. adult and children's svcs., 1984-90, rep. adult svcs., 1984-90, with food drive com., 1987-88, rep. ind. living program com., 1989-90; community program specialist Calif. State Dept. Devel. Svcs., Sacramento, 1990—; project coord. SDSS study L.A. County Children's Svcs. Caseload, 1989-90. Active Southpark Homeowner's Assn., Sacramento, 1974-78; presenter Adult Svcs. Ann. Asilomar Conf., 1987. Office: Calif Dept Devel Svcs 1600 9th St Rm 320 Sacramento CA 95814-6404

DUNAWAY, SAMANTHA JO, secondary school educator; b. Cin., Apr. 28, 1971; d. Joseph A. and Patricia A. (Lindsley) D.; m. Mark A. Gillespie, dec. 31, 1993. BS, Morehead (Ky.) State U., 1993. Substitute tchr. Kodiak Island (Alaska) Borough Sch. Dist., 1993-94, spl. edn. tchr.'s aide, 1994, spl. edn. tchr., 1994-95; libr. A. Holmes Johnson Meml. Libr., Kodiak, 1994-95; receptionist/sec.. Kodiak Island Borough Mental Health Ctr., 1995; tchr. Kenny Lake Sch., Copper Center, Alaska, 1995-96; tchr. Nome (Alaska) Pub. Schs., 1996—, chmn. dept. English, 1996—. Author book rev. col.: Life and Lit in Bering strait Record, 1996; author essays and poetry. Choir mem. Nome Cmty. Chorus, 1996, Kodiak Cmty. Chorus, 1993-94; flutist Cmty. Band, Kodiak, 1993-95. Mem. Nome Edn. assn. (publicity officer 1996—), Nome Reading Cir., Phi Kappa Phi, Kappa Delta Pi. Democrat. Unitarian Universalist. Home: PO Box 1822 Nome AK 99762 Office: Nome-Beltz High School Box 131 Nome AK 99762

DUNBAR, MAURICE VICTOR, English language educator; b. Banner, Okla., May 24, 1928; s. Moyer Haywood and Louise Edna (Curry) D.; m. Carol Ann Cline, July 28, 1948 (div. 1963); children: Kurt, Karl, Karla, Karen, Kristen. AA, Compton Jr. Coll., 1948; BA, U. Calif., Berkeley, 1952; MA, Calif. State U., Sacramento, 1965. Tchr. elem. sch. Lone Tree Sch., Beale AFB, Calif., 1962-64; tchr. jr. high sch. Anna McKenney, Marysville, Calif., 1964-66; tchr. high sch. Yuba City (Calif.) High Sch., 1966-67; instr. jr. coll. Foothill Coll., Los Altos Hills, Calif., 1967-82; prof. English De Anza Coll., Cupertino, Calif., 1982—. Author: Fundamentals of Book Collecting, 1976, Books and Collectors, 1980, Collecting Steinbeck, 1983, Hooked on Books, 1997; contbr. articles to profl. jours. With U.S. Army, 1948-58, PTO. Mem. Masons, Shriners (orator, librarian San Jose Scottish Rite Temple, 1982—), K.C.C.H., Scottish Rite, B'nai B'rith. Office: De Anza Coll English Dept De Anza Coll Cupertino CA 95014-5797

DUNBAR, R. ALLAN, college administrator, clergyman; b. Calgary, Alta., Can., Nov. 24, 1939; s. Marvel Dale and Marie Alma (Gonyea) D.; m. Judy Ann Johnson, Sept. 10, 1960; children: Daren Kirk, Jill Dione. BTh, Alta. Bible Coll., Calgary, 1961; MA, Lincoln (Ill.) Christian Sem., 1968; DDiv, Pacific Christian Coll., Fullerton, Calif., 1996. Ordained to ministry Christian Ch., 1961. Sr. min. Hanna (Alta.) Ch. of Christ, 1961-64; assoc. min. Southside Christian Ch., Hammond, Ind., 1964-68; sr. min. First Christian Ch., Florence, Oreg., 1968-73; sr. pastor Bow Valley Christian Ch., Calgary, 1973-95; dir., host TV ministry To You. . .With Love, Calgary, 1973-95; pres. Puget Sound Christian Coll., Edmonds, Wash., 1995—; pres. N.Am. Christian Conv., Louisville, 1989; founding pres. Western Can. Christian Conv., Calgary, 1992-93. Recipient Shalom award State of Israel, 1987, Outstanding Svc. award Lincoln Christian Coll., 1990. Mem. Rotary Club (pres. 1972). Office: Puget Sound Christian Coll 410 4th Ave N Edmonds WA 98020

DUNBAR, RICHARD PAUL, sales manager; b. Watertown, S.D., Aug. 28, 1951; s. Earl Paul and Leona Matilda (Clausen) D. Student, S.D. State U., 1969-71; BSBA, U. Ariz., 1981. Account mgr. bus. forms and supplies div. Nat. Cash Register, Phoenix, 1981-83; sales cons. Compugraphic Corp., Phoenix, 1983-84; sales rep. constrn. products div. W.R. Grace and Co., Phoenix and Tucson, 1985-87; sales rep. constrn. products div. for Ariz., so. Nev., N.Mex., El Paso (Tex.) region Pleko SW, Inc., Tempe, Ariz., 1987-92, S.W. regional sales mgr., 1992—. Mem. Jaycees (treas. 1977-78, recipient Outstanding Jaycee award, Pres.'s award, Jaycee of Month award), Constrn. Specifications Inst. (constrn. documents technologist, chmn. tech. documents com. Tucson chpt. 1987, program chmn. Phoenix chpt. 1988-89, Chpt. Pres.' Cert. award 1988, 90-92, dir. Phoenix chpt. 1989-90, Outstanding Indsl. award 1989, editor monthly newsletter Phoenix chpt. 1990-91, Inst. Publs. Commendation award 1990-91, Gem award 1990, 1st v.p. Phoenix chpt. 1991, rep. Ariz. Constrn. Industries Coalition 1991-93, chmn. S.W. region publs. 1992, pres.-elect Phoenix chpt. 1992, chmn. nominating com. 1992, CCPR inst. rev. com. 1992, past pres. Phoenix chpt. 1994, planning chmn. 1994, S.W. region membership chmn. 1994, mem. inst. awards com. 1994, inst. dir.-elect S.W. region 1994, inst. dir. 1995—, region dir. citation 1992, S.W. region cert. thanks 1992, pres. Phoenix chpt., 1993, Individual Appreciation award 1991, Inst. Cert. Appreciation 1993, 94, Region Publ. award S.W. region 1994, Pres.'s citation Phoenix chpt. 1994, cert. thanks S.W. region 1994, ad hoc internat. task force 1996, Cert. of Appreciation 1996, S.W. region cert. of appreciation 1997, Inst. region boundary task team 1997), Constrn. Products Mfrs. Coun. (treas. 1986), Alpha Mu Alpha. Republican. Congregational. Office: Pleko SW Inc 1824 E 6th St Tempe AZ 85281-2950

DUNCAN, DORIS GOTTSCHALK, information systems educator; b. Seattle, Nov. 19, 1944; d. Raymond Robert and Marian (Onstad) D.; m. Robert George Gottschalk, Sept. 12, 1971 (div. Dec. 1983). BA, U. Wash., Seattle, 1967, MBA, 1968; PhD, Golden Gate U., 1978. Cert. data processor, systems profl., computer profl., data educator. Comm. cons. Pacific NW Bell Telephone Co., Seattle, 1968-71; mktg. supr. AT&T, San Francisco, 1971-73; sr. cons., project leader Quantum Sci. Corp., Palo Alto, Calif., 1973-75; dir. co. analysis program Input Inc., Palo Alto, 1975-76; dir. info. sci. dept. Golden Gate U., San Francisco, 1982-83, mem. info. systems adv. bd., 1983-85; lectr. acctg. and info. systems Calif. State U., Hayward, 1976-78, assoc. prof., 1978-85, prof., 1985—, coord. computer info. sys., 1994—; cons. pvt. cos., 1975—; speaker profl. groups and confs. Author: Computers and Remote Computing Services, 1983; contbr. articles to profl. jours. Loaned exec. United Good Neighbors, Seattle, 1969; nat. committee woman, bd. dirs. Young Reps., Wash., 1970-71; adv. Jr. Achievement, San Francisco, 1971-72; mem. nat. bd. Inst. for Certification of Computer Profls. Edn. Found., 1990-93; mem. Editorial Rev. bd. Journal Info. Systems Edn., 1992—; bd. dirs. Computer Repair Svcs., 1992-94. Mem. Data Processing Mgmt. Assn. (Meritorious Svc. award, Bronze award 1984, Silver award 1986, Gold Award 1988, Emerald award 1992, Diamond award 1994), Nat. grantee, 1984. dir., edn. chmn. San Francisco chpt. 1984-85, sec. and v.p. 1985, pres. 1986, assn. dir. 1987, by-laws chmn. 1987, chair awards com., 1992-95, nat. bd. dirs. spl. interest group in edn. 1985-87), Am. Inst. Decision Scis., 1982-83, Western Assn. Schs. and Colls. (accreditation evaluation team, 1984-85), Assn. Computing Machinery, Junior Club of Seattle (Beautiful Home award Foster City 1994, 95, winner Tournament of Christmas Lights 1996), Bus. Honor Soc., Beta Gamma Sigma. Subspecialties: Information systems (information science). Current work: curriculum development, professionalism in data processing field, professional certification, industry standards, computer literacy and user education, sys. analysis and design, design of data bases and data banks. Office: Calif State U Sch of Bus and Econs Hayward CA 94542

DUNCAN, ELMORE EDWARD, psychiatrist; b. Chehalis, Wash., May 2, 1932; s. Lewis Edward and Mildred Lucille (Tucker) D.; m. Elizabeth Sylvia Wassenaar, June 20, 1958; children: Steven Lewis, Susan Mae, Kathleen Joan. BS, Pacific Luth. U., 1954; MD, U. Wash., 1958. Intern USN, Great Lakes, Ill., 1958-59; resident Monterey County Hosp., Salinas, Calif., 1962-63; family practitioner Carlisle Med. Group, El Cajon, Calif., 1963-68; resident psychiatry U. Oreg. Health Sci. Ctr., Portland, 1968-71; med. dir. Delaunay Inst., Portland, 1971-73, Woodland Park Health Unit, Portland, 1973-75; acting med. dir. St. Vincent Psychiatric Unit, Portland, 1983-84; med. dir. Caremark Behavioral Health Svcs., Portland, 1993-94; assoc. bd. dirs. Portland Access Mental Health Inc., 1995—; asst. clin. prof. U. Oreg. Health Scis. Ctr., 1972—. Lt. USN, 1957-62. Mem. AMA, Am., Psychiat. Assn., Oreg. Psychiat. Assn. (pres. 1994-95), Oreg. Med. Assn., Mult County Med. Soc., Christian Med.-Dental Soc. Baptist. Office: Northwest Resource Group 700 NE Multnomah St Ste 560 Portland OR 97232-4105

DUNCAN, GLORIA CELESTINE, elementary educator; b. Columbia, S.C., May 31, 1944; d. John DuBois and Fannie Ruby Batiste; m. (div. Dec. 1975); 1 child, Jason Ira. AA, City Coll. San Francisco, 1965; BA, U. Bridgeport, 1968; MA, U. San Francisco, 1984. Presenter Calif. State Dept., Long Beach, 1990; mentor tchr. Alum Rock Sch. Dist., San Jose, 1990-94, educator, 1972—; adv. bd. San Jose Writing Project, 1993-96; assoc. dir. San Jose State U., 1993-96. Mem. youth adv. bd. Am. Cancer Soc., Santa Clara County, 1995—, vol., 1985—; mem. edn. com. Kids Voting U.S.A., Silicon Valley, 1994—; sr. warden St. Philip's Episcopal Ch., San Jose, Calif., 1988. Mem. Delta Kappa Gamma (co-pres. 1996—), Phi Delta Kappa (historian 1995-96, treas. 1996—), Beta Pi Sigma (Soror of Yr. 1996). Office: Mildred Goss Elem Sch 2475 Van Winkle Ln San Jose CA 95116-3758

DUNCAN, H(OWARD) DANIELS, social welfare administrator; b. Coshocton, Ohio, Oct. 26, 1950; s. Howard Daniels and Evelyn (Kennedy) D.; m. Wanda Lee Kay, Nov. 29, 1986; 1 child, Scott Braydon. BS, U. Nebr., Omaha, 1973; MSW, Ariz. State U., 1975. Exec. dir. Cmty. Food Bank, Tucson, 1975-77, Info. and Referrel, Tucson, 1977-79; v.p. United Way Greater Tucson, 1979-86; dir. ops. Gunster, Yoakley, P.A., West Palm Beach, Fla., 1986-88; dir. adminstrn. Taub & Williams P.A., Tampa, Fla., 1988-90; exec. v.p. Mesa (Ariz.) United Way, 1990-91, pres., 1991—; exec. v.p. Tri-City Cmty. Svc. Ctr., Inc., Mesa, 1991—; mem. nat. profl. coun. United Way Am., Alexandria, Va., 1994—; adj. prof. Ariz. State U., Tempe, 1995—. Mem. Govs. Com. on Sys. Integration, Ariz. State Gov., Phoenix, 1996. Mem. Mesa Rotary, Mesa C. of C. (bd. mem. 1994—). Office: Mesa United Way 225 E Main St Ste 301 Mesa AZ 85201-7434

DUNCAN, JAMES HERBERT CAVANAUGH, SR., banker; b. Madison, Wis., June 13, 1925; s. Dorman L. and Marie (Cavanaugh) D.; m. Colleen Patricia Cloney, Sept. 14, 1946; children—James H., John P., Gary T., Phillip K., Katherine M., Thomas M., Mark J. Duncan. Student, Western Mich. U., 1950, LLD (hon.), 1982; grad. in fin. pub. relations, Northwestern U., 1954; grad. in banking, U. Wis., 1962; L.H.D. (hon.), Nazareth Coll., Kalamazoo, Mich., 1988. Assoc. with First Nat. Bank & Trust Co., Kalamazoo, 1950-64; sr. v.p. First Nat. Bank & Trust Co., 1964-65, exec. v.p., 1965-69, pres., 1969-76, chmn. bd., 1976-79; pres., chief exec. officer 1st Nat. Fin. Corp., Kalamazoo, 1971-78; chmn., chief exec. officer First of Am. Bank Corp., 1978-85, chmn. exec. com., dir., 1985-90; former mem. nat. adv. coun. Conf. State Bank Suprs., 1977-80. Author articles in field. Gen. campaign chmn. Kalamazoo Community Chest, 1958, pres., 1964; mem. exec. com. Operation Action Upper Peninsula, 1975-88; pres. Constance Brown Hearing Center, Kalamazoo, 1960; chmn. Kalamazoo chpt. ARC, 1967; mem., chmn. pres.'s council Nazareth Coll., Kalamazoo, 1966-71; trustee, pres. Lift Found., 1967-70; trustee Citizens Research Council Mich., 1980-86, W.E. Upjohn Inst., 1971—, sec. treas. 1982-96; trustee Borgess Med. Center, 1979-86, Kalamazoo Coll., 1985-96, trustee emeritus, 1996—; trustee Western Mich. U. Found., pres., 1982-95, dir., N. Mex. Mus. Natural History and Scis., 1992-95; bd. dirs. Jobs for Mich. Grads.; chair Santa Fe Cmty. Found., 1995-96, bd. dirs., 1993—. Served to 2d lt., inf. AUS, World War II. Decorated Bronze Star with oak leaf cluster, Purple Heart with oak leaf cluster, Combat Inf. badge; recipient Disting. Alumni award Western Mich. U., 1984. Mem. Am. Bankers Assn. (governing council 1975-79, Mich. v.p. 1976-77, dir. 1977-79, mem. edn. policy and devel. council 1975-79, chmn. 1977-79), Mich. Bankers Assn. (pres. 1972-73), Charge Account Bankers Assn. (pres. 1957), Nat. Alliance Businessmen (chmn. Southeastern Mich. metro 1975-76). Clubs: Kiwanis (pres. Kalamazoo 1964), Park (Kalamazoo) (pres. 1970). Home: 25 Tano Alto Santa Fe NM 87501-7503

DUNCAN, JAMES RICHARD, systems administrator; b. Little Rock, June 3, 1948; s. James Richard and Mary (Bond) D. BA in Geography, U. Calif., Berkeley, 1969; postgrad. in mass comms., Denver U., 1970. Cons. self-employed San Jose, Calif., 1972-90; broadcast engr. Nationwide Comms., San Jose, Calif., 1985-90; corp. engr. Kool Comms., San Jose, Calif., 1990-95; network adminstr. United Broadcasting, San Jose, 1995-96; v.p. info. systems U.S. Estate and Tax Planning Coun., 1996—; cons. Ohlone C.C., Fremont, Calif., 1990—. Mem. Soc. Broadcast Engrs. (cert.), Am. Coun. for Arts, Ariel Dance Co., Santa Clara Ballet. Office: US Estate and Tax Planning Coun 62B San Benancio Canyon Rd Salinas CA 93908

DUNCAN, JOHN WILEY, mathematics and computer educator, retired air force officer; b. San Francisco, Aug. 8, 1947; s. Vernon Alexander and Nellie May (Shaw) D.; m. Trudy Rae Hirsch, Feb. 25, 1967; children: Amber Rose, John Anthony. BS in Math. and Physics, N.W. Mo. State U., 1969; MBA, So. Ill. U., 1973; MS in Computer Sci., U. Tex., San Antonio, 1982. Tchr. Savannah (Mo.) High Sch., 1969; enlisted USAF, 1969, advanced through grades to maj.; aeromed. officer 9AES USAF, Clark Air Base, The Philippines, 1978-80; student UTSA, San Antonio, 1981-82; systems implementation team leader Sch. of Health Care Scis., Sheppard AFB, Tex., 1982-83; asst. chief med. systems Hdqrs. Air Tng. Command, Randolph AFB, Tex., 1983-86; chief med. systems Hdqrs. Pacific AF, Hickham AFB, Hawaii, 1986-89, 15 Med. Group, Hickham AFB, Hawaii, 1989; instr. Kapiolani C.C., Honolulu, 1989-94; sys. mgr. Hawaii Correctional Industries, Aiea, 1994-96, Sci. Applications Internat. Corp., Ft. Shafter, Hawaii, 1996—; computer cons., 1983—; instr. Midwestern U., Wichita Falls, 1982-83, Tex. Luth. Coll., Sequin, 1984-86, Hawaii Pacific Coll., Honolulu, 1987-89, Leeward C.C., 1989—. Cons. Ronald McDonald House, San Antonio, 1986. Presbyterian. Home: 2114 Aluka Loop Pearl City HI 96782-1317

DUNCAN, RALPH MILLER, contract management specialist; b. Springfield, Mass., Dec. 20, 1947; s. C.H. and L.I. (Rothe) D. BA, Iowa Wesleyan U., 1969; MA, Creighton U., 1971; postgrad., Ottawa U., 1972-75, San Diego C.C., 1983-84, 89-91. Cert. govt. contract mgmt. Contract mgr. Govt. Proposal Svcs., San Diego, 1983—, N.W. Publs. Svcs., Seattle, 1995-97; adj. faculty mem. Calif. C.C., San Diego C.C., National U.; cons. gen. Dynamics Land Sys., Tallahassee, Fla., 1996, Ruff, Inc., Chula Vista, Calif., 1994-95, Verle A. Williams & Assoc., San Diego, 1994, Abre Enterprises, Chula Vista, 1992, Dean's Security, Bellflower, Calif., 1992; cost/price estimator Newby Security Patrol, Long Beach, Calif., 1993; dir. contracts RHP, Inc., Laguna Hills, Calif., 1991-96; proposal writer, San diego, 1993;. Author: (manuals) Business Development Manual, 1997, ISO 9000 Software Quality Assurance, 1997; editor various proposals; writer grants in field. Vol. Home Start, Inc., San Diego, 1983-84, La Jolla (Calif.) Hist. Soc., 1982. With USNG, 1969-75. Recipient Cert. of Appreciation Home Start, Inc., 1984. Mem. Assn. Proposal Mgmt. Profls., Nat. Contract Mgmt. Assn. Home: 2425 Cranston Dr Escondido CA 92025-7061 Office: PO Box 2393 Escondido CA 92025-2393

DUNCAN, RICHARD FREDRICK, JR., secondary education educator, travel consultant; b. Millry, Ala., July 12, 1947; s. Richard F. and Claire Louise (Wood) D.; m. Rebecca Susan Davis, July 14, 1973. AA, Okaloosa-Walton Jr. Coll., 1967; BS, Fla. State U., 1969, MS, 1971; postgrad., Ore. State U., 1981-82. Tchr. Gadsden County Sch. Bd., Quincy, Fla., 1970-71, Leon County Sch. Bd., Tallahassee, Fla., 1972-73, Beaverton (Oreg.) Sch. Dist. No. 48, 1973—; microbiologist Washington County, Hillsboro, Ore., 1971-72; cons. on sci. edn. Northwest Regional Ednl. Lab., Portland, Ore., 1978-79; cons. on marine edn. Ore. Dept. Edn., Salem, 1980-81. Recipient award for excellence in sci. teaching Ore. Mus. Sci. and Industry, Portland, 1984, Psdl. award, 1984. Mem. Assn. Presdl. Awardees in Sci. Teaching (nat. pres. 1987-88), Nat. Assn.Biology Tchrs. (Ore. Biology Tchr. of Year award 1981), Nat. Sci. Tchrs. Assn. (Presdl. award for excellence in sci. teaching, 1983), Oreg. Sci. Tchrs. Assn. (pres. 1980-81, Oreg. Jr. High Tchr. of Yr. award 1982), North Assn. Marine Educators (state dir. 1978-80), Masons, Shriners. Democrat. Home: 13240 SW Juanita Pl Beaverton OR 97008-6831 Office: Beaverton Sch Dist # 48 PO Box 200 Beaverton OR 97075-0200

DUNCKER, MICHAEL CHARLES, dentist; b. Montebello, Calif., Dec. 30, 1950; s. Charles Montiel and Helen (Hunick) D.; m. Marie DeLeon, 1975 (div. 1985); 1 child, Vanessa Leann. BA, U. So. Calif., 1976; DDS, UCLA, 1980. Sr. staff dentist Community Health Found., East L.A., 1980-86; dentist/owner Cali Family Dental Ctr., Huntington Park, Calif., 1986—; pvt. practice Downey, Calif., 1993—. With U.S. Army, 1970-72. Mem. Latin Am. Dental Assn. (pres. 1991-92), Kiwanis (bd. dirs. 1991-92). Office: 11411 Brookshire Ave Ste 405 Downey CA 90241-5006

DUNDAS, DENNIS FRANKLIN, plastic surgeon; b. L.A., Oct. 12, 1942; s. John Arthur and Wanda (Yoakum) D.; m. Zoe Lynn Anderson, Feb. 9, 1969; children: Gregory, Denise. BA, Johns Hopkins U., 1964; MD, U. So. Calif., 1968. Diplomate Am. Bd Plastic Surgery. Pvt. practice Kirkland, Wash., 1978—. Lt. comdr. USN, 1978—. Fellow ACS; mem. Am. Soc. Plastic Surgeons. Office: 13114 120th Ave NE Kirkland WA 98034-3014

DUNHAM, ANNE, educational institute director. Exec. dir. Youth Sci. Inst., L.A., 1995—. Office: Youth Sci Inst 296 Garden Hill Dr Los Angeles CA 95030

DUNHAM, BANDHU SCOTT, glass artist, author; b. Dayton, Ohio, Sept. 25, 1959; s. Richard S. and Janet (Boehmer) D. Student, Princeton U., Pilchuck Glass Sch. Owner Salusa Glassworks, Prescott, Ariz., 1990—; Author: Contemporary Lampworking, 1995; editor, author mag. Attitude Problem, 1988-95; exhibited in numerous shows; work represented in permanent collection of Corning Mus. of Glass. Mem. Glass Art Soc., Ariz. Designer Craftsmen, Internat. Guild Glass Artists. Office: Salusa Glassworks Po Box 2354 Prescott AZ 86302-2354

DUNHAM, JOHN H., II, real estate developer and broker; b. Chgo., Sept. 29, 1925; s. John H. and Lee (Yerger) D.; divorced; children: John H. III, James U. BS, Purdue U., 1950. Salesman Workman Mfg., Chgo., 1950-58, Wallace Press, Chgo., 1958-66; exec. v.p. tech. sales Datafold Inc., Chgo., 1967-79; co-founder, owner Datafold Inc. (merger Am. Brands), 1979; owner, CEO, founder Span, Inc., Vail, Colo., 1980—; real estate developer and broker, 1980—; internat. chair R&D, Computer Supplies Industry Worldwide, 19770-79. Developer of test equipment; patentee in field. Active for more than 50 yrs. Boy Scouts Am., dir. transp. for 2 nat. jamborees and 1 world jamboree, 1995; bd. dirs. Bravo Guild/Music Festival of Vail, 1994—. With USN, WWII. Recipient Vigil, Scouters Key, Scout Masters Key, Dist. award of Merit, Silver Beaver award and Silver Antelope award Boy Scouts Am., 1956—. Home: PO Box 1875 Vail CO 81658 Office: Span Inc PO Drawer 5830 Avon CO 81620

DUNIGAN, PAUL FRANCIS XAVIER, JR., federal agency administrator; b. Richland, Wash., June 22, 1948; s. Paul Frances Xavier Sr. and Eva Lucille (Reckley) D.; m. Elizabeth Anne Henricks, Apr. 8, 1978; children: Katherine Anne, Theresa Anne. BS in Biology, Gonzaga U., 1970; MS in Environ. Sci., Washington State U., 1973. Tech. program mgr. ERDA, AEC, Richland, 1972-75; environ. biologist U.S. Dept. Energy, ERDA, Richland, 1975-81; waste mgmt. engr. U.S. Dept. Energy Waste Mgmt., Richland, 1981-84; civilian program mgr. Surplus Facilities Mgmt. Program U.S. Dept. Energy, Richland, 1984-87, environ. biologist, 1987—; also compliance officer Nat. Environ. Policy Act; leader environ. policy team and adminstr. Hanford Fed. Facility Agreement, Dept. of Energy, 1995-96, leader NEPA compliance team, 1996—. Contbr. articles to profl. jours. Mem. AAAS, Water Pollution Control Fedn., Pacific Northwest Pollution Control Fedn. Roman Catholic. Home: 1612 Judson Ave Richland WA 99352-2944 Office: US Dept Energy PO Box 550 Richland WA 99352-0550

DUNIPACE, IAN DOUGLAS, lawyer; b. Tucson, Dec. 18, 1939; s. William Smith and Esther Morvyth (McGeorge) D.; m. Janet Mae Dailey, June 9, 1963; children: Kenneth Mark, Leslie Amanda. BA magna cum laude, U. Ariz., 1961, JD cum laude, 1966 Bar: Ariz. 1966, U.S. Supreme Ct. 1972, Nev. 1994. Reporter, critic Long Branch (N.J.) Daily Record, 1963; assoc. firm Jennings, Strouss, Salmon & Trask, Phoenix, 1966-69; assoc. Jennings, Strouss & Salmon, PLC, Phoenix, 1969-70, ptnr., 1971-93, mem., 1993—. Reporter Phoenix Forward Edn. Com., 1969-70; mem. Phoenix Arts Commn., 1990-93, chmn., 1992-93; bd. mgmt. Downtown Phoenix YMCA, 1973-80, chmn., 1977-78; bd. dirs. Phoenix Met. YMCA, 1976-87, 88—, chmn., 1984-85; bd. mgmt. Paradise Valley YMCA, 1979-82, chmn., 1980-81; bd. mgmt. Scottsdale/Paradise Valley YMCA, 1983, mem. legal affairs com. Pacific Region YMCA, 1978-81; chmn. YMCA Ariz. State Youth and Govt. Com., 1989—; bd. dirs. The Schoolhouse Found., 1990-96, pres., 1990-94, Kids Voting, 1990-94, Beaver Valley Improvement Assn., 1977-79, Pi Kappa Alpha Holding Corp., 1968 72, The Heard Mus. 1993-94, Ariz. Bar Found., 1996—; trustee Paradise Valley Unified Sch. Dist. Employee Benefit Trust, 1980-93, chmn., 1987-93, Sch. Theology, Claremont, Calif., 1994—; trustee First Meth. Found. of Phoenix, 1984-93; mem. Greater Paradise Valley Cmty. Coun., 1985-87; bd. dirs. Heard Mus. Coun., 1990-95, pres. 1993-94; mem. Ariz. Venture Capital Conf. Planning Com., 1994—, Assn. for Corp. Growth, 1995-96, Ariz. Bus. Leadership Assn., 1996—. Capt.

AUS, 1961-63. Mem. State Bar Ariz. (securities regulation sect. 1970—, chmn., 1991-92, mem. com. unauthorized practice of law 1972-84, chmn. 1975-83, mem. bus. law sect. 1981—, chmn., 1984-85), State Bar Nev., State Bar Colo., Am., Fed. (pres. Ariz. chpt. 1980-81), Maricopa County Bar Assns. (bd. dirs. Corp. Coun. Divsn. 1996—), Ariz. Zool. Soc., U. Ariz. Law Coll. Assn. (bd. dirs. 1983-90, pres. 1985-86), Smithsonian Assn., U. Ariz. Alumni Assn. (bd. dirs. 1985-86), Phi Beta Kappa, Phi Kappa Phi, Phi Delta Phi, Phi Alpha Theta, Sigma Delta Pi, Phi Eta Sigma, Pi Kappa Alpha (nat. counsel 1968-72). Democrat. Methodist (mem. met. Phoenix commn. 1968-71, lay leader 1975-78, trustee 1979-81, pres. 1981; mem. Pacific S.W. ann. conf. 1969-79, lawyer commn. 1980-85, chancellor Desert S.W. ann. conf. 1985—). Clubs: Arizona, Renaissance, Orange Tree. Lodges: Masons, Kiwanis (pres. Phoenix 1984-85, disting. lt. gov. 1986-87, SW dist. cmty. svc. chmn. 1987-88, dist. activity com. coord. 1988-89, dist. laws and regulation chmn. 1989-90, 92-93, 95-96, asst. to dist. gov. for club svcs. 1990-91, field dir. 1991-92, dist. conv. chmn., 1993-94, pub. rels. chmn. 1996—, mem. internat. com. on Project 39, 1988-89, internat. com. On to Anaheim 1990-91, internat. com. on leadership tng. and devel. 1991-92, 93-94, trustee SW dist. found. 1987-92, 1st v.p. 1990-92). Comments editor Ariz. Law Rev., 1965-66. Home: 4147 E Desert Cove Ave Phoenix AZ 85028-3514 Office: Jennings Strouss & Salmon PLC 2 N Central Ave Phoenix AZ 85004-2322

DUNKEL, PETER CARL, university administrator; b. New Britain, Conn., Aug. 12, 1962; s. William Carl and Dorothy Signe (Peterson) D.; m. Kristina, Dec. 14, 1985; children: Peter Wesley, Stephen Christopher, Elizabeth Samantha. BA, Wesleyan U., Middletown, Conn., 1984; MA, Fuller Theol. Sem., Pasadena, Calif., 1988; postgrad., UCLA. Corp. fin. analyst Merrill Lynch Capital Markets, N.Y.C., 1984-86; dir. capital programs Biola U., La Mirada, Calif., 1989-91; dir. capital programs Calif. Luth. U., Thousand Oaks, 1992-93, dir. devel., 1994—; sec.-treas. bd dirs. China Ministry Internat., Pasadena, 1993—. Vol. L.A. Mission, 1991—. Mem. Nat. Soc. Fundraising Execs., Coun. for Advancement and Support of Edn. Republican. Evangelical. Home: 2321 Goldsmith Ave Thousand Oaks CA 91360-3131 Office: Calif Luth U 60 Olsen Rd Thousand Oaks CA 91360-2700

DUNKLE, WILLIAM EARL, pilot, airline executive, retired; b. Seattle, Aug. 30, 1917; s. Wesley Earl and Florence (Hull) D.; m. Joan maxine Martinson, Aug. 1, 1949; children: Julie Anne, William M. BA in Airline Ops., Boeing Sch. Aero., Oakland, 1938. Cert. fed. aviation adminstr., airline transport pilot. Pilot Nicholson Air Transport, Anchorage, 1938-40, United Airlines, Seattle, San Francisco, 1940-69; sr. v.p. flight ops. Airline Ops. Cons. A.T.A., Chgo., 1969-76, pres., 1976-90. Author: A Bird's Eye View, 1991, A Trial In San Serra, 1996. Mem. Las Posas Country Club. Recipient Cert. Appreciation, NASA, 1975, FBI, 1975, Disting. Svc. award FAA, 1976, Tribute from U.S. Congress, 1976. Republican. Home: 670 Camino Concordia Camarillo CA 93010-8419

DUNLAP, F. THOMAS, JR., electronics company executive, engineer, lawyer; b. Pitts., Feb. 7, 1951; s. Francis Thomas and Margaret (Hubert) D.; married; children: Bridgette, Katie. B.S.E.E., U. Cin., 1974; J.D., U. Santa Clara, Calif., 1979. Bar: Calif., 1979, U.S. Dist. Ct. (no. dist.) Calif. 1979. Mgr. engring. Intel Corp, Santa Clara, Calif., 1974-78, adminstr. tech. exchange, 1978-80, European counsel, 1980-81, sr. atty., 1981-83, gen. counsel, sec., 1983-87, v.p., gen. counsel, sec., 1987—. drafter, lobbyist Semiconductor Chip Protection Act, 1984. Republican. Roman Catholic. Office: Intel Corp 2200 Mission College Blvd # 4 Santa Clara CA 95054-1537

DUNLAP, JAMES RILEY, SR., former financial executive, credit manager; b. Portland, Oreg., May 21, 1925; s. William Gates and Laura (Riley) D.; m. Betty Towe; children: James R. Jr., Brian Jay, William David. BSBA, U. Oreg., 1950; postgrad., Portland State Coll., 1963-65. Sales rep. Hyster Co., Portland, 1950-61; br. asst. mgr. Reynolds Metals Co., Portland, 1961-71; corp. credit mgr. Burns Bros. Inc., Portland, 1971-79, sec.-treas., 1979-89. Contbr. articles on credit and fin. mgmt. to profl. jours. With USAAF, 1943-46. Melvin Jones fellow. Mem. Nat. Assn. Credit Mgmt. (past pres., bd. dirs.), Internat. Assn. Credit Mgmt. (past pres., bd. dirs., Disting. Svc. award 1985, Herb Barnes Meml. award 1987), Portland Retail Credit Assn. (past pres., bd. dirs.), Oreg. State Cons. Credit Assn. (past pres., lifetime bd. dirs.), Portland Jaycees, Oreg. Motor Supply Credit Assn. (past pres., bd. dirs.), Consumer Counseling Svc. Oreg. (exec. com. 1979—), Am. Contract Bridge League (past pres. Portland chpt., gold life master), Lions (past pres. host club), Masons (life), Elks, Delta Tau Delta Alumni Assn. (past pres.).

DUNLAP, JOHN DANIEL, III, state agency administrator; b. Cass City, Mich., Feb. 5, 1959; s. John Daniel Dunlap Jr. and Karen Louise (Matthews) Kleba; m. Jane Margaret Austin, June 6, 1981; children: John IV, Kathryn, Claire. BA in Polit. Sci., U. Redlands, 1981; M of Pub. Policy in Environ. Policy, Claremont Grad. Sch., 1982. Planner, policy analyst Computer Transp. Svc., Inc., L.A., 1981-83; planner, program mgr. South Coast Air Quality Mgmt. Dist., El Monte, Calif., 1983-89, pub. advisor, 1989-93; chief dep. dir. Dept. Toxic Substances Control, Sacramento, 1993-94; chair Calif. Air Resources Bd., Sacramento, 1994—. Mem. staff to Congressman Jerry Lewis, Redlands, 1980; chmn. troop com. Boy Scouts Am., Alta Loma and Auburn, Calif., 1994—; chmn. Environ. Mgmt. Com., Rancho Cucamonga, Calif., 1990-94; mem. alumni coun. Claremont Grad. Sch., 1992-96; mem. adv. coun. Chaffey C.C., 1992-96. Recipient Alumni Career Achievement award U. Redlands, 1995. Republican. Mem. LDS Ch. Office: Calif Air Resources Bd 2020 L St PO Box 2815 Sacramento CA 95812

DUNLAP, RILEY EUGENE, sociologist; b. Wynne, Ark., Oct. 25, 1943; s. Riley W. Dunlap Jr. and F. Eugenia (Jones) Anderson; m. Lonnie Jean Brown, Aug. 25, 1966; children: Sara Jean, Christopher Eugene. MS, U. Oreg., 1969, PhD, 1973. From asst. prof. to prof. sociology Wash. State U., Pullman, 1972-85, 85-96, Boeing Disting. prof. environ. sociology, 1996—; mem. socioeconomic peer review panel Office of Exploratory Rsch., U.S. EPA, 1991; mem. panel on aesthetic attributes in water resources planning NRC/Nat. Acad. Scis., 1982; Gallup fellow in environment George H. Gallup Internat. Inst., 1992—. Editor, author: (jour. symposium) Am. Behavioral Scientist, 1990; editor book: American Environmentalism: The U.S. Environmental Movement, 1970-90, 92, Pub. Reactions to Nuclear Waste, 1993. Mem. AAAS (rural sociol. soc. rep. to sect. K 1986-89), Internat. Sociol. Assn. (pres., rsch. com. on environ. and soc. 1994—), Am. Sociol. Assn. (chmn. sect. on environ. sociology 1981-83, disting. contbn. award 1986), Rural Sociol. Soc. (chmn. natural resources rsch. group 1978-79, award of merit 1985), Soc. for Study of Social Problems (chmn. environ. problems divsn. 1973-75). Office: Washington State Univ Dept Sociology Pullman WA 99164

DUNN, DAVID CAMERON, entrepreneur, business executive; b. Juneau, Alaska, Dec. 8, 1941; s. Robert Charles and Kay (Watson) D.; m. Karen Ann Leonard, Jan. 17, 1970 (div. 1990); children: David Cameron Jr., Paige. BA, Stanford U., 1963; MBA, U. Pa., 1968. Account exec. J. Walter Thompson, N.Y.C., 1968-70; product mgr. Gen. Foods, White Plains, N.Y., 1970-73; dir. mktg. Heublein, San Francisco, 1973-77; exec. v.p. Perelli-Minetti Winery, San Francisco, 1977-79; sr. v.p., bd. dirs. Valchris Farms, Modesto, Calif., 1980-84, DFS Advt., San Francisco, 1984-87; pres. Thomas-Rahm Advt., Oakland, Calif., 1987-89, Mktg. Comms. Assocs., Oakland, 1990—; co-founder Re-Con Systems (OTC) 1968; bd. dirs. PC Guardian, San Rafael, Calif. Trustee Oakland Symphony, 1989-90, Orinda (Calif.) Edn. Found., 1986-87. 1st lt. U.S. Army, 1964-66, Germany. Mem. Lakeview Club, Oakland Athletic Club, Oakland C. of C. (Small Bus. of Yr. 1991), Commonwealth Club. Republican. Roman Catholic. Office: Mktg Communs Assocs 299 3d St Oakland CA 94607

DUNN, DENNIS STEVEN, artist, illustrator; b. San Diego, Apr. 30, 1951; s. Dean Stanley and Phyllis Marie (Pratt) D.; m. Donna Rae Krogh, Dec. 29, 1973; 1 child, Claire Estelle. BA with distinction, San Diego State U., 1973. Master printer, intaglio Orr's Gallery, San Diego, 1973-74, instr. intaglio, 1974; graphic artist NARF/North Island Naval Air Sta., Coronado, Calif., 1974-76; illustrator NETSCPAC/Naval Tng. Ctr., San Diego, 1976-81, Fleet Combat Tng. Ctr., Point Loma, Calif., 1981-82, FASO Det/Miramar Naval Air Sta., San Diego, 1982-86, FCDSWA/Kirtland AFB, Albuquerque, 1986—; life drawing instr. U. N.Mex., Albuquerque, 1986-87. Group exhibits include Traveling Exhbn. to Turkey and Greece, 1975, San Diego Print Club, 1984, Spectrum Gallery, San Diego, 1986, Stables Art Gallery, Taos, N.Mex., 1986, The Wedge Gallery, Rochester, N.Y., 1988, Print Club of Albany, N.Y., 1989, Clary Minor Gallery, Buffalo, 1990, U. Anchorage, 1990, Bradley U., Peoria, Ill., 1991, Artlink Gallery, Ft. Wayne, Ind., 1991, Garret Gallery, St. Louis, 1993; works included in various mags. Recipient Letter of Commendation USN, 1985. Mem. Albuquerque United Artists (bd. dirs. 1987-88), SIGGRAPH. Home: 6209 Arvilla Ave NE Albuquerque NM 87110

DUNN, JEFFREY EDWARD, neurologist; b. Shaker Heights, Ohio, Nov. 27, 1960; s. John Kenneth and Mary Margaret (O'Neill) D.; m. Sandra Lee Judy, Feb. 3, 1990; children: Caitlin Irene, Bronwyn Leigh, Colin John Donald. BA in French Lit., Haverford (Pa.) Coll., 1983; MD, Temple U., 1989. Diplomate Am. Bd. Psychiatry and Neurology. Molecular immunologist Fox Chase Cancer Ctr., Phila., 1984-85; intern Ea. Va. Grad. Sch., Norfolk, 1989-90; resident in neurology U. Wash., Seattle, 1990-93; attending physician Neurol. Assocs. of Wash., Bellevue, 1993—; clin. asst. prof. neurology U. Wash., Seattle, 1993—; founder, med. dir. Overlake Multiple Sclerosis Ctr., Bellevue, Wash., 1996—. Guest physician TV: MS Update, Denver, 1994, ALS Update, Seattle, 1995. Recipient Cert. of Excellence in MS Rx, Prodigy Online Com., 1995; named to Outstanding Young Men of Am., 1996. Mem. Am. Acad. Neurology, Am. Neurol. Assn., World Congress Neurology, North Pacific Soc. of Psychiatry and Neurology. Office: Neurol Assocs of Wash 1600 116th Ave NE Ste 302 Bellevue WA 98004-3098

DUNN, JENNIFER BLACKBURN, congresswoman; b. Seattle, Wash., July 29, 1941; d. John Charles and Helen (Gorton) Blackburn; div.; children: Bryant, Reagan. Student, U. Wash., 1960-62; BA, Stanford U., 1963. Former chmn. Rep. Party State of Wash.; now mem. 103rd Congress from 8th Wash. dist., Washington, D.C., 1993—; mem. house oversight com., mem. Ways and Means Com. Del. Rep. Nat. Conv., 1980, 84, 88; presdl. apptd. adv. coun. Historic Preservation; presdl. apptd. adv. coun. volunteerism SBA. Mem. Gamma Phi Beta. Office: US House of Reps 432 Cannon Washington DC 20515-4708*

DUNN, KIMBERLY ANN, state agency administrator, archaeologist; b. Salem, Oreg., Nov. 25, 1947; d. Forrest Reid and Doris Wynona (Gubser) Gish; m. Robert Lee Shaw, Feb. 11, 1967 (div. June 1974); 1 child, Megan Alyson. BA, U. Oreg., 1973, postgrad., 1974; postgrad., U. Wis., 1974-75. Intern in archaeology Bonneville Power Adminstrn., Portland, Oreg., 1973; planner S.W. Wis. Cmty. Action Program, Dodgeville, 1977-80; regional housing cooord. Wis. Rural Housing Found., Madison, 1980-82; econ. devel. dir. S.W. Wis. Community Action Program, Dodgeville, 1982-84; planner Mid Willamette Jobs Coun., Salem, Oreg., 1985-88; grants coord., marketer State Job Tng. Partnership Act Adminstrn., Salem, 1988-91; grants coord. State Hist. Preservation Office, Salem, 1991—; nat. mem. Bus. Enterprise Devel. Corp., Denver, 1982-84; mem. Oreg. Occupl./Info. Adv. Com., Salem, 1985-88. Co-author: Field Guide to Archaeology, 1973, Guide to Archaeology for Managers, 1973, Evaluation of Housing Programs in Midwest, 1982, Guide to Older Worker Programs, 1983. Active Oreg. Ocean Policy Adv. Coun., Portland, 1993—. Mem. Hist. Preservation League Oreg., Assn. Oreg. Archaeologists. Home: 4505 E Portland Rd Newberg OR 97132-6963 Office: State Hist Preservation Office 1115 Commercial St NE Salem OR 97310-1000

DUNN, MARY PRICE, religious foundation executive; b. Albuquerque, Oct. 17, 1952; d. Linden Harrison and Norma (Davies) Price; m. Leo Kevin Dunn, Nov. 21, 1973; children: Molly Jo, Michael Kevin. BS in Edn., U. N.Mex., 1974, MBA, 1990. Educator Archdiocese of Santa Fe, Albuquerque, 1974-75; paralegal Sutin, Thayer & Browne, P.C., Albuquerque, 1975-83; mgmt. cons. Dunn Consulting Group, Albuquerque, 1991-93. Contbr. articles to profl. jours. Selected mem. Leadership Albuquerque, 1992-93; v.p., dir. Peppertree/Royal Oak Residents Assn., Albuquerque, 1991-93; bd. dirs., mem. exec. com. Shared Vision, 1991-94. Office: The Catholic Found 4000 Saint Josephs Pl NW Albuquerque NM 87120-1714

DUNN, ROBERT PAUL, English language educator; b. Rockford, Ill., Nov. 18, 1941; s. Marion Francis and Catherine Helene (Silvers) D.; m. Kathleen Elisabeth Kelpien, Aug. 6, 1963; children: Deborah Dunn Ferreira, Clark Robert. BA, Pacific Union Coll., 1963; PhD, U. Wis., 1970; M Religion, Sch. Theology, Claremont, Calif., 1977. Asst. prof. English La Sierra U., Riverside, Calif., 1970-73, assoc. prof. English, 1973-79, prof. English, 1979—, chair dept. English, 1977-81, 87-90, assoc. dean Coll. Arts and Scis., 1990-94, chair dept. English and comms., 1995—. Mem. Studia Mystica (editorial bd. 1986—). Home: 5566 Peacock Ln Riverside CA 92505-3168

DUNNE, KEVIN JOSEPH, lawyer; b. Pitts., Sept. 22, 1941; s. Matthew S. and Marjorie (Whelan) D.; m. Heather Wright Dunne, Sept. 27, 1963; children: Erin, Kevin Jr., Patrick, Sean. BA, U. Conn., 1963; JD, Georgetown U., 1966. Bar: Calif. 1967, U.S. Dist. Ct. (no. dist.) Calif., 1967, U.S. Dist. Ct. (ea. dist.) Calif. 1969, U.S. Dist. Ct. (ctrl. dist.) Calif. 1971, U.S. Ct. Appeals (9th cir.) 1971. Assoc. Sedgwick, Detert, Moran & Arnold, San Francisco, 1968-75, ptnr., 1975—; adj. prof. U. San Francisco Sch. Law, 1980-86; bd. editorial advisors Bender's Drug Product Liability Reporter, 1988-92. Author: Dunne on Depositions, 1995; editor Defense Counsel Training Manual, 1989; contbr. articles to profl. jours. Capt. U.S. Army, 1966-68, Vietnam. Recipient Bronze Star, Army Commendation medal; recipient Exceptional Performance award Def. Rsch. Inst., 1988. Fellow Internat. Acad. Trial Lawyers, Am. Coll. Trial Lawyers; mem. No. Calif. Assn. Def. Counsel (pres. 1987-88), Internat. Assn. Def. Counsel (pres. elect 1994-95), Am. Bd. Trial Advocates. Roman Catholic. Office: Sedgwick Detert Moran & Arnold 1 Embarcadero Ctr Ste 1600 San Francisco CA 94111-3704

DUNNE, THOMAS, geology educator; b. Prestbury, U.K., Apr. 21, 1943, came to U.S., 1964; s. Thomas and Monica Mary (Whitter) D. BA with honors, Cambridge (Eng.) U., 1964; PhD, Johns Hopkins U., 1969. Research assoc. USDA-Agrl. Research Service, Danville, Vt., 1966-68; research hydrologist U.S. Geol. Survey, Washington, 1969; asst. prof. McGill U., Montreal, Que., Can., 1969-73; from asst. prof. to prof. U. Wash., Seattle, 1973-95, chmn. dept., 1984-89; prof. sch. environ. scis. & mgmt. U. Calif., Santa Barbara, 1995—; vis. prof. U. Nairobi, Kenya, 1969-71; cons. in field, 1970—. Author (with L.B. Leopold) Water in Environmental Planning; (with L.M. Reid) Rapid Evaluation of Sediment Budgets, 1996. Fulbright scholar 1984; grantee NSF, NASA, Rockefeller Found., 1969—; named to NAS. 1988, Guggenheim fellow, 1989-90. Fellow Am. Geophys. Union (Robert E. Horton ward 1987), Am. Acad. Arts and Scis., Calif. Acad. Scis.; mem. AAAS, NAS, Geol. Soc. Am., Sigma Xi. Office: U Calif Sch Environ Scis & Mgmt 4670 Physical Sciences N Santa Barbara CA 93106

DUNNETT, DENNIS GEORGE, state official; b. Auburn, Calif., Aug. 5, 1939; s. George DeHaven and Elizabeth Grace (Sullivan) D. AA in Elec. Engring., Sierra Coll., 1959; AB in Econs., Sacramento State Coll., 1966. Engring. technician State of Calif., Marysville, 1961-62; data processing technician State of Calif., Sacramento, 1962-67, EDP programmer and analyst, 1967-74, staff services mgr. and contract adminstr., 1974-76, hardware acquisition mgr., 1976-86, support services br. mgr., information security officer, 1986-90, chief Office Security and Operational Recovery, 1990-92, spl. projects mgr., 1992-93, customer support ctr. mgr., 1994, procurement mgr., 1994—. Mem. AARP, IEEE Computer Soc., Data Processing Mgmt. Assn., Assn. Inst. Cert. of Computers Profls. (certs.), Intergovtl. Coun. on Tech. of Info. Processing, Calif. State Mgrs. Assn., The Mus. Soc., Crocker Art Mus., San Francisco Opera Guild. Home: 729 Blackmer Cir Sacramento CA 95825-4704 Office: Teale Data Ctr 2005 Evergreen St Sacramento CA 95815-3831

DUNNIGAN, MARY ANN, former educational administrator; b. St. Maries, Idaho, Sept. 7, 1915; d. William Henry and Mary Ellen (Kelly) D.; BA, Holy Names Coll., Spokane, 1942; MA, Gonzaga U., Spokane, 1957; postgrad. U. Idaho, UCLA. Tchr. rural schs. Bonner County, 1936-41, elem. schs., 1941, 45-59, high sch., 1942, 45, coordinator elem. edn., 1959-78; prin. kindergarten Sch. Dist. 271, Coeur d'Alene, Idaho, 1978-81; tchr. extension classes U. Idaho; curriculum chmn. Gov.'s Conf. on Edn.; adv. council Head Start. Mem. adv. coun. Com. for Aging; mem. N. Idaho Mus., Community Council, Community Concerts, Community Theater, N. Idaho Booster Club, Mayor's Com. on Handicapped; mem. task force and diocesan bd. Cath. Edn. of Idaho, 1969-74; mem. Coeur d'Alene U.S. Constn. Bicentennial Com., 1986-91. Bd. dirs. Coeur d'Alene Tchrs. Credit Union, 1958-87, pres., treas., 1976-89; hist. chmn. Coeur d'Alene Centennial, 1986-89, chmn. hist. com., 1988, mem. state centennial com. for Koetenai county, 1990; parliamentarian Idaho Coun. Catholic Women State Conv., 1993, Idaho Cath. Daus. of Am. State Conv., 1994, sterring com. New Holy Famliy Cath. Sch. in Koatenai County Idaho, 1994, Parliomentation fo Idaho Coun. of Cath. Women, 1992. Named Citizen of Yr. N. Idaho Coll., 1974, Idaho Cath. Dau. of Year, 1968; named to Idaho Retired Tchr.'s Hall of Fame, 1987; recipient Hon. Alumnus award N. Idaho Coll., 1987, Nat. Community Svc. award AARP/NRTA, 1989. Mem. Idaho Edn. Assn., NEA, Idaho Ret. Tchrs. Assn. (state chmn. pre-retirement 1985-92), Kootenai County Ret. Tchrs. Assn. (pres. 1983-87), Delta Kappa Gamma (charter, past pres Zeta chpt 1947-92). Club: Cath. Daus. Am. (state regent 1956-62). Home: 720 N 9th St Coeur D Alene ID 83814-4259

DUNNING, KENNETH LAVERNE, research physicist; b. Yale, Iowa, Sept. 24, 1914; s. Howard Grant and Gertrude Estelle (Dygert) D.; m. Ruth Ellen Pyle, Sept. 2, 1941; children: David M., Jane B., John K., Marion Leigh. BEE, U. Minn., 1938; MS in Physics, U. Md., 1950; PhD in Physics, Cath. U. Am., 1968. Engr. Western Union, N.Y.C., 1938-41; physicist U.S. Naval Research Lab., Washington, 1945-80; cons. Port Ludlow, Wash., 1981—. Contbr. articles to profl. jours. Pres. Highland Greens Condominium Assn., Port Ludlow, 1983-84, v.p. 1984-85. Served to maj. U.S. Army, 1941-45. Recipient Research Pub. award Naval Research Lab., 1971. Mem. IEEE, Am. Phys. Soc., Sigma Xi, Tau Beta Pi, Eta Kappa Nu. Home and Office: 10 Foster Ln Port Ludlow WA 98365-9611

DUNNING, KENNETH OWEN, mental health counselor; b. Portland, Oreg., June 26, 1950; s. David Dale and Ellen Natalie (Ecklund) D.; m. Virginia Evens, Dec. 10, 1970 (div. 1977); m. Yang Ja Ju, Dec. 10, 1979 (div. July 1987); 1 child, David Kee-Young Samuel; m. Riitta Hannele Ylinen, Dec. 12, 1988; children: Hanna Emilia, Tomas Mikael. Assoc. Gen. Studies, Centralia (Wash.) C.C., 1976; BA, Eastern Wash. State Coll., Cheney, 1977; MS, Western Oreg. State Coll., Monmouth, 1989. Cert. mental health counselor, Wash.; nat. cert counselor. Counselor J Bar D Boy's Ranch, Ione, Wash., 1983-84; child care worker Secret Harbor Sch., Anacortes, Wash., 1988-90; therapist Skagit Mental Health, Mt. Vernon, Wash., 1989-95; team leader Cath. Cmty. Svcs., Bellingham, Wash., 1995-96; pvt. practice Mt. Vernon, Wash., 1995—; mem. adv. bd. Fetal Alcohol Syndrome Family Resource Inst., Lynnwood, Wash., 1993—. Collaborator: (directory) Residential Child Care in America, 1990. Named Very Important Prevention Person, Skagit County Substance Abuse Coalition, 1995. Mem. ACA.

DUNNING, WILLIAM VANCE, fine arts educator; b. Glendale, Calif., Oct. 29, 1933; s. Judge B. and Billy Jolly Dunning; m. Sandra Jane Springer, Apr. 6, 1963; children: Stacy Rain, Amy Snow, Judge Blue. AA in Arch., El Camino C.C., 1954; BFA, U. So. Calif., L.A., 1958, MFA in Sculpture, 1961; MFA in Painting, U. Ill., 1964. Art instr. Imperial Valley Coll., Imperial, Calif., 1957-59, Phoenix (Ariz.) Coll., 1960-62; sr. preceptor Parsons Coll., Fairfield, Iowa, 1966-67; prof. fine arts Cen. Wash. U., Ellensburg, 1964—. Author: Changing Images of Pictorial Space: A History of Spatial Illusion in Painting, 1992 (One of Outstanding Acad. Books Choice mag. 1992), Roots of Postmodernism, 1994; contbr. articles to prof. jours. including Jour. Aesthetics and Art Criticism, Brit. Jour. Aesthetics, also books; exhibited sculpture and paintings throughout Midwest and Western U.S. Home: 806 W 15th Ave Ellensburg WA 98926-9467 Office: Cen Wash U Dept Fine Arts Ellensburg WA 98926-7564

DUNSTAN, LARRY KENNETH, insurance company executive; b. Payson, Utah, May 26, 1948; s. Kenneth Leroy Dunstan and Verna Matilda (Carter) Taylor; m. Betty K. Limb, Sept. 23, 1966 (div. June 1975); children: Tamara, Thane; m. Jacqueline Lee Darron, Oct. 7, 1975; children: Tessa, Matthew, Bennett, Spencer, Adam. CLU, CPCU, chartered fin. cons., registered health underwriter, life underwriter tng. council fellow. Mgr. Diamond Bar Inn Ranch, Jackson, Mont., 1972-73; agt. Prudential Ins. Co., Missoula, Mont., 1973-77; devel. mgr. Prudential Ins. Co., Billings, Mont., 1977-78; div. mgr. Prudential Ins. Co., Gt. Falls, Mont., 1978-83; pres. Multi-Tech Ins. Services, Inc., West Linn, Oreg., 1983—; agy. mgr. Beneficial Life Ins. Co., Portland, Oreg., 1983-88. Mem. planning commn. City of West Linn, Oreg., 1968; mem. bishopric Ch. Jesus Christ of Latter Day Sts., West Linn, 1984-86, exec. sec. Lake Oswego Oreg. Stake, 1987-89; scouting coord. Boy Scouts Am., West Linn, 1984-86, scoutmaster various troops; pres. West Linn Youth Baskeetball Assn., 1991-97, West Linn/Wilsonville Youth Track Club, 1993-96. Named Eagle Scout Boy Scouts Am., 1965, recipient Heroism award 1965. Fellow Life Underwriter Tng. Coun. (bd. dirs. 1980-81); mem. Gen. Agts. and Mgrs. Assn. (bd. dirs. 1981-82), Am. Soc. CLU (pres. 1982-83). Republican. Home: 19443 Wilderness Dr West Linn OR 97068-2005 Office: Multi-Tech Ins Svcs 19125 Willamette Dr West Linn OR 97068-2019

DUONG, NGHIEM DUC, estate planner; b. Saigon, Vietnam, Dec. 2, 1946; came to the U.S., 1975; s. Trac Duc and Thom Thi (Nguyen) D.; m. Vuong Thi; children: Hong-Thy, Thuy-Tien, Phoi-Thien. BA in Oriental Philosophy, Saigon U., 1974. Cert. estate planner. Pres., CEO Unipoint Corp., Costa Mesa, Calif., 1985—; ins. agt., broker, mgr. Metlife Ins. Co., Torrance, Calif., 1979—; registered rep. Metlife Securities, Inc., Del., 1985—. Promoter, fundraiser for lepers in Vietnam, 1991-92. Fellow Life Underwriter Tng. Coun., 1985. Home: 28401 Via Alfonse Laguna Niguel CA 92677-7061

DU PEN, EVERETT GEORGE, sculptor, educator; b. San Francisco, June 12, 1912; s. George E. and Novelle (Freeman) DuP.; m. Charlotte Canada Nicks, July 1, 1939; children: Stuart, Destia, Novelle, William, Ninia, Marguerite. Student, U. So. Calif., 1931-33, Chouinard Art Sch., Los Angeles, summer 1932, Harvard Sch. Architecture, summer 1933; B.F.A. (scholar), Yale, 1937; B.F.A. European traveling fellow, 1937-38. Teaching fellow Carnegie Inst. Tech. Sch. Art, 1939-39; teaching asst. sculpture Washington U. Sch. Art, St. Louis, 1939-42; marine draftsman and loftsman Sausalito Shipbldg. Corp., Calif., 1942-45; instr. sculpture U. Wash. Sch. Art, Seattle, 1945-47; asst. prof. U. Wash. Sch. Art, 1947-54, asso. prof. sculpture, 1954-60, prof. art, 1960-82, prof. emeritus, 1982—, chmn. sculpture div. One-man shows include Seattle Art Mus., 1950, Bon Marche Nat. Gallery, Seattle, 1970, Fred Cole Gallery, Seattle, 1973, Pacific Luth. U., Tacoma, 1975, Wash. Mut. Savs. Bank, Seattle, 1979-80, Frye Art Mus., Seattle, Martin and Zambito Gallery, Seattle; exhibited Prix de Rome Exhbn., Grand Central Gallery, N.Y.C., 1935-37, 39, St. Louis Mus. Ann., 1939-42, Nat. Acad. Design, N.Y.C., 1943, 49, 53-55, 57-58, Seattle Art Mus. Ann., 1945-59, Pa. Acad. Art, Phila., 1950-52, 55-58, Ecclesiastical Sculpture competition, 1950, Sculpture Ctr., N.Y.C., 1951, 53, 54, Pa. Acad. Fine Arts, 1954-58, Detroit Mus. Art, 1958, N.W. Inst. Sculpture, San Francisco Art Assn., 1959, Mainstreams, 1972, Marietta Coll., 1972, Holt Galleries, Olympia, Wash., 1980, Martin & Zambotti Gallery, Seattle, 1991-92, Freemont Art Gallery, Seattle, 1991-92, Ellensburg, Wash. Community Art Gallery, 1988, Bellevue, Wash. Invitational, Bellevue Art Mus., 1988, NAD, 1989, Wash. State Art Centennial Exhbn., Tacoma Art Mus., 1990; retrospective exhibits at Martin & Zambet Gallery, Seattle, 1994, Firye Art Mus., Seattle, 1994; represented in permanent collections Wash. Mut. Savs. Bank, Seattle, Bell Telephone Co., Seattle, Nat. Acad. Design, N.Y.C. (Saltus medal 1954), Seattle Art Mus., Safeco Ins. Co., U. Wash., also sculptures in pvt. collections; creator garden figures and portrait heads, small bronze, terra cotta, hardwood sculptures, archtl. medallions, sculpture panels for comml. bldgs. and theatres, figures and wood carvings various chs., relief panels U. Wash. campus, 1946, 83, bronze fountain Wash. State Library, Olympia, 1959, Du Pen Fountain, bronze fountain Coliseum Century 21, Seattle World's Fair, 2 walnut screens Mcpl. Bldg., Seattle, 8 large sculpture commns. Seattle chs., 1957-64, wood carving Risen Christ, St. Pius X Cath. Ch., Montlake Terrace, Wash., 1983, 3-foot wood carving St. Joseph and Mary, 1985, 6-foot wood carving Ascension, St. Elizabeth Seton Ch., Bothell, Wash., 1986, Elizabeth and Mary, 5-foot mahogany for Visitation Ctr., Fed. Way, Wash., 1990, 2-figure group for Dallas, 1982, bronze figure Edmonds, Wash., 1983-84, bronze sculpture of Charles Odegaard, pres. U. Wash., 1973, pvt. commns. Mem. U. Wash. Senate, 1952-55, exec. com., 1954-55; v.p. Allied Arts Movement for Seattle; mem. Seattle Municipal Art Commn., 1958-63. Recipient Saltus gold medal NAD, 1954, 1st prize for sculpture Bellevue (Washington) Arts and Crafts Fair, 1957; U. Wash. research grantee for creative sculpture, 1953-54. Fellow Nat. Sculpture Soc. (hon. mention Henry Herring competition); mem. Artists Equity Assn. (bd. Seattle chpt.), Nat. Acad. Design, Puget Sound N.W. Painters Group (bd.), N.W. Inst. Sculpture (pres. 1957), Allied Artists Am., U. Wash. Research Soc., Northwest Stone Sculptors, Seattle (bd. dirs. 1989—). Home: 1231 20th Ave E Seattle WA 98112-3530

DUPLESSIS, AUDREY JOSEPH, school system administrator; b. New Orleans, June 23, 1920; d. Louis Joseph and Sidonie Josephine (DeLaRose) Boyer; m. Norwood Jerome Duplessis, Sr., June 27, 1984. B in Vocat. Edn., So. U., Baton Rouge, 1942; BA, Calif. State U., 1959, MA, 1966. Tchr., dir. Tri State Coll., New Orleans, 1948-50; from elem. tchr. to dir. Magnet Sch. L.A. Unified Schs., 1954—; playground L.A. Unified Schs., 1956-59, reading resource tchr., 1965-70, curriculum coord., 1972-78; reading tchr. Calif. Lutheran Coll., Thousand Oaks, 1968-70. Mem. United Tchrs. PAC, L.A., 1980-88. Recipient svc. award Congress of Parents, L.A., 1988, spl. recognition U.S. Congress, 1988. Mem. Internat. Assn. Childhood Edn. (state pres. 1987-89, appreciation award 1989), St. Brigid Edn. Com., Delta Sigma Theta. Democrat. Roman Catholic.

DUPRAT, JO ANN, pediatric rehabilitation nurse, consultant; b. Vallejo, Calif., May 21, 1948; d. Albert John Chester Jr. and Dorothy Marie (Anderson) Smith; m. Dennis Albert Duprat, May 14, 1966; children: Dana Marie, Daniel Gordon. ASN, Contra Costa Coll., San Pablo, Calif., 1982; BS in Health and Human Svcs., Columbia Pacific U., San Rafael, Calif., 1991, MS in Health and Human Svcs., 1992, postgrad., 1994—. RN, Calif.; CRRN, cert. rehab. nursing, UR/QA/discharge planning/risk mgmt. Learning Tree Univ. Staff nurse, adolescent Children's Hosp., Oakland, Calif., 1982-83, staff nurse med./surg. pediatric, 1983-84, pediatric rehab. nurse specialist, case mgr., 1984—; nursing supr. Adult Care Svcs., Walnut Creek, Calif., 1992-93; nurse cons. Regional Ctr. of East Bay, Emeryville, Calif., 1985—; panel nurse Calif. Children's Svcs., Sacramento, 1985—; clin. coord. Calif. Children's Svcs. Med. Therapy Unit, Del Norte and Humboldt Counties, 1996—. Author: Spina Bifida, Current Trends, 1991; Historical Perspectives and Attitudes Towards Women, Sexuality, Childbirth and Parenting, 1993. Supporting mem. San Pablo Little League, 1991-92. Mem. Spina Bifida of Calif., Assn. Rehab. Nurses, Children's Orthotics/Prosthetics Clinics, Nat. Neurofibramatosis Soc., Assn. for Syringomyelia, Simon Found., Alpha Gamma Sigma. Office: Children's Hosp 747 52nd St Oakland CA 94609-1809

DUPREE, MARSHA ANNE, academic administrator; b. Miami Beach, Fla., Oct. 19, 1951; d. James Thomas Taylor and Daisy Mae (Comer) Wallace; m. Kenneth Ray Dupree, Aug. 14, 1976; children: Kenneth R. II, Anita R., Marcus A. BA in Sociology, Calif. State U., Long Beach, 1973; MA in Counseling, U. Nev., 1994. Personnel asst. So. Calif. Air Pollution Control, L.A., 1976; tchr. gen. music Reno (Nev.) Jr. Acad., 1978-79; office mgr. Reno Seventh Day Adventist Ch., 1978-82; adminstrv. aid II, mgmt. asst. I Sch. of Home Econs. U. Nev., Reno, 1983-85, mgmt. asst. II Affirmative Action Office, 1985-87, mgmt. asst. III, 1987-88, outreach coord., 1988-90, admission and recruitment coord., 1990-94, acting dir. affirmative action, 1994-95, fin. aid counselor, 1995—; mentor Project Call/Community Action Leaders' Liasion, U. Nev., 1993-96. Bd. dirs. No. Nev. Black Cultural Awareness Soc., Reno, 1989—, Reno Jr. Acad., 1990-94; mem. Nev. Women's Fund Allocation Com., Reno, 1993, Washoe-at-Risk Taskforce, Reno, 1993—; co-facilitator 12-Step Recovery Group Program, Sparks (Nev.) Seventh Day Adventist Ch., 1994-95; mem. Nev.-Utah Conf. Seventh Day Adventist Assn. Bd., 1992-95; mem. Heavenbound Prison Ministry, Carson City, Nev., 1989—, Reno-Sparks Interfaith Gospel Choir, 1977—. Named Outstanding Faculty Mem., Black Student Orgn., U. Nev., 1993. Mem. Am. Counseling Assn., Assn. for Multicultural Counseling and Devel., Nev. Assn. for Counseling and Devel., We. Assn. of Student Fin. Aid Adminstrs., UNS Alliance of Racial Minorities (pres. 1993-94, sec. 1985-88), Nat. Assn. Student Fin. Aid Adminstrs. Democrat. Home: 95 El Molino Dr Sparks NV 89436-9246 Office: U Nev 9th and Center St Reno NV 89557

DUQUETTE, DIANE RHEA, library director; b. Springfield, Mass., Dec. 15, 1951; d. Gerard Lawrence and Helen Yvette (St. Marie) Morneau; m. Thomas Frederick Duquette Jr., Mar. 17, 1973. BS in Sociology, Springfield Coll., 1975; MLS, Simmons Coll., 1978. Libr. asst. Springfield City Libr., 1975-78; reference libr. U. Mass., Amherst, 1978-81; head libr. Hopkins Acad., Hadley, Mass., 1980; instr. Colo. Mountain Coll., Steamboat Springs, 1981-83; libr. dir. East Routt Libr. Dist., Steamboat Springs, 1981-84; agy. head Solono County Libr., Vallejo, Calif., 1984; dir. libr. svcs. Shasta County Libr., Redding, Calif., 1984-87; dir. librs. Kern County Libr., Bakersfield, Calif., 1987—; chmn. San Joaquin Valley Libr. System, 1988. Contbr. articles to profl. jours. Recipient John Cotton Dana Spl. Pub. Rels. award, H.W. Wilson and ALA, 1989. Mem. ALA, Calif. Libr. Assn. (mem. coun. 1987—), Calif. County Librs. Assn. (pres. 1990). Democrat. Roman Catholic. Home: Pine Mountain Club PO Box 6595 Frazier Park CA 93222 Office: Kern County Libr 701 Truxtun Ave Bakersfield CA 93301-4816

DURAN, MARGARET ADELAIDE PROCTOR, librarian; b. Kalispell, Mont., July 5, 1929; d. Ellery Clarence and Adelaide (Durfee) Proctor; m. David Stephen Duran, June 14, 1952; children: Lita Duran Feeney, Margaret Duran Roughan, Stephen David, Nancy Anne. BA, L.A. State U., 1951; postgrad., Immaculate Heart Coll., L.A., 1966-79. Tchr. L.A. County Schs., 1951-52, San Diego Schs., 1952-53; libr. asst. City Sierra Madre, Calif., 1966-80; assoc. libr. City Sierra Madre, 1980—; tchr. reference courses Sierra Madre Libr., others; lectr. travelogues and book revs. Columnist Sierra Madre News, 1993-96; contbr. articles to profl. jours. Hist. St. Rita's Guild, Sierra Madre, 1992-95; cashier Sierra Madre Art Fair, 1980-96; lector St. Rita's Ch., Sierra Madre, 1991-96. Home: PO Box 314 Sierra Madre CA 91025-0314 Office: Sierra Madre Pub Libr 440 W Sierra Madre Blvd Sierra Madre CA 91024-2314

DURAN, MICHAEL CARL, bank executive; b. Colorado Springs, Colo., Aug. 27, 1953; s. Lawrence Herman and Jacqueline Carol (Ward) D. BS magna cum laude, Ariz. State U., 1980. With Valley Nat. Bank (name now Bank One, Ariz., N.A.), Phoenix, 1976—; corp. credit trainee Bank One Ariz. (formerly Valley Nat. Bank Ariz.), Phoenix, 1984-85; comml. loan officer Valley Nat. Bank Ariz. (name now Bank One Ariz.), Phoenix, 1985-86; br. mgr., asst. v.p. Valley Nat. Bank Ariz. (name now Bankone, Ariz.), Phoenix, 1986-90, comml. banking officer, asst. v.p., 1990-93, credit mgr., v.p., 1993—; cons. various schs. and orgns., 1986—; incorporator Avondale Neighborhood Housing Svcs., 1988. Mem. Cen. Bus. Dist. Revitalization Com., Avondale, Ariz., 1987-88, Ad-Hoc Econ. Devel. Com., 1988; coord. Avondale Litter Lifters, 1987-88; vol. United Way, Phoenix, 1984; bd. dirs. Jr. Achievement, Yuma, Ariz., 1989-91, vol., Phoenix, 1993—; yokefellow 1st So. Bapt. Ch. of Yuma, 1990-91. Recipient Outstanding Community Svc. award City of Avondale, 1988. Mem. Robert Morris Assocs., Ariz. State U. Alumni Assn. (life), Toastmasters, Kiwanis (local bd. dirs. 1986-88), Beta Gamma Sigma, Phi Kappa Phi, Phi Theta Kappa, Sigma Iota Epsilon. Democrat. Baptist. Home: 925 N Quartz St Gilbert AZ 85234-3661

DURANT, PENNY LYNNE RAIFE, author, educator; b. Albuquerque, May 22, 1951; d. John Carl and Patricia Fay (Bremermann) Raife; m. Omar Duane Durant, Jan. 2, 1971; children: Geoffrey Alan (dec.), Adam Omar. Student, Lawrence U., Appleton, Wis., 1969-70; BS, U. N.Mex., 1973, MA, 1980. Mem. adv. bd. Soc. Children's Book Writers and Illustrators/N.Mex., Albuquerque, 1996—. Author: Make a Splash!, 1991, Prizewinning Science Fair Projects, 1991, When Heroes Die, 1993 (Lambda Lit. award 1993, 1st prize juvenile novel Nat. League Am. Pen Women 1993, award of excellence N.Mex. Press Women 1993), Bubblemania!, 1995, Exploring the World of Plants, 1995, Exploring the World of Animals, 1995; conbr. articles to Parents Mag., Durango Mag., Working Parents, The Luth. Sec. bd. dirs. Albuquerque Children's Theatre, 1995—. Mem. Nat. League Am. Pen Women (v.p. Albuquerque br. 1990, sec. 1996, state letters chair 1996), S.W. Writers Workshop, Soc. Children's Book Writers and Illustrators. Democrat. Lutheran. Home: 305 Quincy NE Albuquerque NM 87108

DURAY, JOHN R., physicist; b. East Chicago, Ind., Jan. 28, 1940; s. John S. and Margaret A. D.; m. Elizabeth A. Meyer, Nov. 19, 1986; children: Sam, Vince, Mike. BS, Benedictine U., 1962; PhD, U. Notre Dame, 1968. Postdoctoral fellow Ohio State Univ., Columbus, 1968-70; instr. Princeton (N.J.) Univ., 1970-75; asst. prof. Ind. Univ. N.W., Gary, 1975; mgr. subsurface sys. Bendix Field Engring., Grand Junction, Colo., 1975-86; mgr. tech. programs Rust Geotech, Grand Junction, 1986-96; prin. scientist Sensible Environ. Solutions, Grand Junction, 1996—. Home: 2137 Banff Ct Grand Junction CO 81503 Office: Sensible Environ Solutions 454 Main Ste 1 Grand Junction CO 81501

DURHAM, BARBARA, state supreme court justice; b. 1942. BSBA, Georgetown U.; JD, Stanford U. Bar: Wash. 1968. Former judge Wash. Superior Ct., King County; judge Wash. Ct. Appeals; assoc. justice Wash. Supreme Ct., 1985—, chief justice, 1995—. Office: Wash Supreme Ct Temple of Justice PO Box 40929 Olympia WA 98504-0929

DURHAM, CHRISTINE MEADERS, state supreme court justice; b. L.A., Aug. 3, 1945; d. William Anderson and Louise (Christensen) Meaders; m. George Homer Durham II, Dec. 29, 1966; children: Jennifer, Meghan, Troy, Melinda, Isaac. A.B., Wellesley Coll., 1967; J.D., Duke U., 1971. Bar: N.C. 1971, Utah 1974. Sole practice law Durham, N.C., 1971-73; instr. legal medicine Duke U., Durham, 1971-73; adj. prof. law Brigham Young U., Provo, Utah, 1973-78; ptnr. Johnson, Durham & Moxley, Salt Lake City, 1974-78; judge Utah Dist. Ct., 1978-82; assoc. justice Utah Supreme Ct., 1982—. Pres. Women Judges Fund for Justice, 1987-88. Fellow Am. Bar Found.; mem. ABA (edn. com. appellate judges' conf.), Nat. Assn. Women Judges (pres. 1986-87), Utah Bar Assn., Am. Law Inst. (coun. mem.), Nat. Ctr. State Courts (bd. dirs.). Home: 1702 Yale Ave Salt Lake City UT 84108-1836 Office: Utah Supreme Ct 332 State Capitol Building Salt Lake City UT 84114-1202*

DURHAM, FLETA EVELYN, educator, community volunteer; b. Nara Visa, N.Mex., May 24, 1919; d. Isaac Oren and Nellie Raye (Etheridge) D.; children: Mary Evelyn Price, Jo Beth Johnson. BA in Edn., Eastern N.Mex. U., 1953, postgrad. Elem. sch. tchr. Carlsbad (N.Mex.) Schs., 1953-75, team tchr. art, music and social studies, 1970-74; choir dir. Hillcrest Meth. Ch., Carlsbad, 1957; drama/puppet plays Meth. Chs., Carlsbad, 1978; vol. Connection Ctrs. Internat., Carlsbad, 1987-90, Hearts, Living Histories (Internat.) McDowell Pl., Phoenix, 1996. Originator, coord. children's drama, stories, 1960; composer children's songs, hymns, anthems, 1990-95; contbr. to World of Poetry, 1984. Founder Yokefellow divsn. Red Cross, Carlsbad, 1978-88; local coord. AARP Health Advocacy, 1990, AARP Vote, 1989. Named Tchr. of Yr. Carlsbad City Schs., 1975. Home: 2635 N 20th Ave Phoenix AZ 85009

DURHAM, HARRY BLAINE, III, lawyer; b. Denver, Sept. 16, 1946; s. Harry Blaine and Mary Frances (Oliver) D.; m. Lynda L. Durham, Aug. 4, 1973; children: Christopher B., Laurel A. BA cum laude, Colo. Coll., 1969; JD, U. Colo., 1973. Bar: Wyo. 1973, U.S. Tax Ct. 1974, U.S. Ct. Appeals (10th cir.) 1976. Assoc., Brown, Drew, Apostolos, Massey & Sullivan, Casper, Wyo., 1973-77; ptnr. Brown & Drew, 1977—. Permanent class pres. Class of 1969, Colo. Coll., Nat. Alumni Coun. Colo. Coll., 1995—; bd. dirs. Casper Amateur Hockey Club, 1970-77, sec. 1974-77; bd. dirs. Casper Symphony Assn., 1974-88, v.p., 1979-82, pres., 1983-87; bd. dirs., sec. Wyo. Amateur Hockey Assn., 1974-85, pres., 1985-88; bd. dirs. Natrona County United Way, 1974-76, pres., 1975-76; mem. City of Casper Parks and Recreation Commn., 1985-94, vice chmn., 1987-94, Nat. Alumni Coun. of The Colo. Coll., 1995—. Mem. ABA, Wyo. Bar Assn., Natrona County Bar Assn., Nat. Assn. Railroad Trial Counsel, Phi Beta Kappa. Republican. Articles editor U. Colo. Law Rev., 1972-73. Home: 3101 Hawthorne Ave Casper WY 82604-4975 Office: 123 W 1st St Ste 800 Casper WY 82601-2486

DURHAM, ROBERT DONALD, JR., judge; b. Lynnwood, Calif., May 10, 1947; s. Robert Donald Durham and Rosemary Constance (Brennan) McKelvey; m. Linda Jo Rollins, Aug. 29, 1970; children: Melissa Brennan, Amy Elizabeth. BA, Whittier Coll., 1969; JD, U. Santa Clara, 1972. Bar: Oreg. 1972, Calif. 1973, U.S. Dist. Ct. Oreg. 1974, U.S. Ct. Appeals (9th cir.) 1980, U.S. Supreme Ct. 1987. Law clk. Oreg. Supreme Ct., Salem, 1972-74; ptnr. Bennett & Durham, Portland, Oreg., 1974-91; assoc. judge Oreg. Ct. Appeals, Salem, 1991-93; assoc. justice Oreg. Supreme Ct., Salem, 1994—; mem. adv. com. to Joint Interim Judiciary Com., 1984-86; chair Oreg. Commn. on Adminstrv. Hearings, 1988-89; faculty Nat. Jud. Coll., Reno, Nev., 1992; mem. Case Disposition Benchmarkes Com., 1992-93, Coun. on Ct. Procedures, 1992-93. Mem. ACLU Lawyer's Com., Eugene and Portland, Oreg., 1978-91. Recipient award for civil rights litigation ACLU of Oreg., 1988, Ed Elliott Human Rights award Oreg. Edn. Assn., Portland, 1990. Mem. Am. Acad. Appellate Lawyers (ninth cir. screening com. 1991—, rules com. 1994, co-chair appellate cts. liaison com. 1994), Oreg. Appellate Judges Assn. (pres. 1996-97), Oreg. State Bar (chair labor law sect. 1983-84, adminstrv. law com. ovt. law sect. 1986), Calif. State Bar, Willamette Valley Inns of Ct. (master of bench, team leader 1994-96). Office: Oreg Supreme Ct 1163 State St Salem OR 97310-1331

DURINGER, JACOB CLYDE, project engineer, researcher; b. Calexico, Calif., Oct. 18, 1956; s. Jacob Clyde Sr. and Stella Marie (Pippin) D.; m. Catherine Ann Grecich, Sept. 20, 1986 (div. Feb. 1988); 1 child, Irena Mauve; m. Mary Helen Montes, May 27, 1989; 1 child, Trint Jacob. AA in Electronics, Electronic Tech. Inst., 1978. Staff engr. Mitsubishi Electronics, Santa Ana, Calif., 1978-81; sr. technician Efratom, Irvine, Calif., 1981-82, MCT Electronics, Carpinteria, Calif., 1982-83; project engr. Parker Bertea Aerospace, Irvine, 1985—. Inventor monolithic two dimensional keyboard; prodr. (compact disc) The Duringer Expeditions Vol. 1, 1995. Mem. Nat. Assn. Music Mchts. Mem. Christian Ch. Home: Box 4 127 24331 Muirlands Blvd Lake Forest CA 92630

DURYEE, DAVID ANTHONY, management consultant; b. Tacoma, Wash., July 29, 1938; s. Schuyler L. and Edna R. (Muzzy) D.; m. Anne Getchell Peterson, Nov. 26, 1966; children: Tracy Anne, Tricia Marie. BA in Bus., U. Wash., 1961, MBA, 1969; diploma, Pacific Coast Banking Schs., Seattle, 1973. Cert. fin. planner. Lending officer Seattle 1st Nat. Bank, 1964-68, v.p., trust officer, 1970-80; cons., chmn. Mgmt. Adv. Svcs., Inc., Seattle, 1980-93; mng. prin. Mgmt. Adv. Svcs. divsn. Moss Adams, 1994—; bd. dirs. Lafromboise Newspapers, Inc., Seattle; lectr. in field; expert witness Wash., N.Y., Md., Calif., Mass., Ind., Fla. Author: The Business Owners Guide to Achieving Financial Success, 1994; contbr. articles to profl. jours. Capt. U.S. Army, 1962-64. Mem. Am. Soc. Appraisers, Internat. Assn. Fin. Planners, Inst. for Cert. Planners, Inst. Bus. Appraisers (speaker), Am. Bankers Assn., Nat. Retail Jewelers, Nat. Moving and Storage assn., Pacific N.W. Bankers Assn., Internat. Assn. for Fin. Planning, Estate Planning Coun. Seattle, Washington Bar Assn., Wash. State Trial Lawyers Assn., Wash. State Automobile Dealers Assn., Ky./Mo. Auto Dealers Assn., Motor Dealers Assn. B.C., Nat. Office Products Assn., Mayflower Warehousemen's Assn., Can. Movers Assn., Fedn. of Automobile Dealer Assns. of Can., Seattle Tennis Club, Seattle Yacht Club, Rotary. Home: 3305 E John St Seattle WA 98112-4938 Office: Mgmt Adv Svcs 1001 4th Ave Ste 2700 Seattle WA 98154-1101

DUSARD, JAY, photographer; b. St. Louis, Feb. 18, 1937; s. Justin Rime and Dorothy Mildred (May) D.; m. Katherine Elizabeth Kraetz, Oct. 9, 1965. BArch, U. Fla., 1961. Cowboy, Slaughter Ranch, Douglas, Ariz., 1963; designer, draftsman Ellery C. Green, Architect, Tucson, 1964; cartographic draftsman water resources divsn. U.S. Geol. Survey, Tucson, 1965-66; designer, lithographer Northland Press, Flagstaff, Ariz., 1966-68; asst. prof. light graphics Prescott (Ariz.) Coll., 1968-75; engring. tech. VA, Prescott, 1975-81; freelance photographer Prescott, 1981—; cons. Malpai Borderlands Group, Douglas, 1994—; amateur jazz musician. Author, photographer: The North American Cowboy: A Portrait, 1983, Open Country, 1994 (Third Place award Photography Book of Yr. Competition, 1994); photographer: La Frontera: the United States Border with Mexico, 1986 (Four Corners Book award, 1988), Beyond the Rangeland Conflict: Toward a West That Works, 1995 (Pulitzer Prize nominee, 1996). Mem. bd. advisors Ctr. for Photographic Art, Carmel, Calif. With U.S. Army, 1961-63. County of Dade Archs. travelling scholar, 1960; photography fellow Guggenheim Meml. Found., 1981. Mem. Santa Maria Mountains Group. Home and Office: 2221 View Dr Prescott AZ 86301

DUSCHA, JULIUS CARL, journalist; b. St. Paul, Nov. 4, 1924; s. Julius William and Anna (Perlowski) D.; m. Priscilla Ann McBride, Aug. 17, 1946 (dec. Sept. 1992); children: Fred C., Steve D., Suzanne, Sally Jean. Student, U. Minn., 1943-47; AB, Am. U., 1951; postgrad., Harvard Coll., 1955-56. Reporter St. Paul Pioneer Press, 1943-47; publicist Dem. Nat. Com., 1948, 52; writer Labor's League for Polit. Edn., AFL, 1949-52, Internat. Assn. Machinist, 1952-53; editorial writer Lindsay-Schaub Newspapers, Ill., 1954-58; nat. affairs reporter Washington Post, 1958-66; assoc. dir. profl. journalism fellowships program Stanford (Calif.) U., 1966-68; dir. Washington Journalism Ctr., 1968-90; columnist, freelance journalist, West Coast corr. Presstime mag., San Francisco, 1990—. Author: Taxpayer's Hayride: The Farm Problem from the New Deal to the Billie Sol Estes Case, 1964, Arms, Money and Politics, 1965, The Campus Press, 1973; editor: Defense Conversion Advisory; contbr. articles to mags., including Washingtonian, N.Y. Times Mag., Changing Times. Recipient award for distinguished Washington corr. Sigma Delta Chi, 1961. Mem. Cosmos Club (Washington), Kappa Sigma. Home: 2200 Pacific Ave Apt 7D San Francisco CA 94115-1412

DUSHANE, PHYLLIS MILLER, nurse; b. Portland, Oreg., June 3, 1924; d. Joseph Anton and Josephine Florence (Eicholtz) Miller; m. Frank Maurice Jacobson, Mar. 13, 1945 (dec. 1975); children: Karl, Kathleen, Kraig, Kirk, Karen, Kent, Krista, Kandis, Kris, Karlyn; m. Donald McLelland DuShane, July 21, 1979 (dec. 1989); stepchildren: Diane DuShane Bishop, Donald III. BS in Biology, U. Oreg., 1948; BS in Nursing, Oreg. Health Scis. U., 1968. R.N., Oreg. Pub. health nurse Marion County Health Dept., Salem, Oreg., 1968-77; pediatric nurse practitioner Marion County Health Dept., Salem, 1977-91, Allergy Assocs., Eugene, Oreg., 1979-89; mem. allied profl. staff Sacred Heart Gen. Hosp., Eugene, 1979—. Named Oreg. Pediatric Nurse Practitioner of Yr., 1991. Mem. P.E.O., P.E.O. Sisterhood, Oreg. Pediatric Nurse Practioners Assn. (v.p. Salem chpt. 1977-78), Am. Nurses Assn., Oreg. Nurses Assn., Nat. Assn. Pediatric Nurse Assocs. and Practitoners, Am. Acad. Nurse Practitioners, Nurse Practitioners Spl. Interest Group, Salem Med. Aux. (sec. 1968), Oreg. Republican Women, Delta Gamma Alumni (v.p. 1979). Presbyterian. Home: 965 E 23rd Ave Eugene OR 97405-3074 Office: Oakway Pediatrics P C 465 Oakway Rd Eugene OR 97401-5405 also: Eugene Pediatric Assocs 1680 Chambers St Eugene OR 97402-3655

DUSSERRE-FARRELL, MICHELLE, dietitian, gymnastics coach; b. Long Beach, Calif., Dec. 26, 1968; d. Martin Burdette and Kerry Elizabeth (Eckholdt) D.; m. Matt Farrell. BS, Ariz. State U., 1992; postgrad., Colo. U., 1996. Asst. coach women's gymnastics Ariz. State U., Tempe, 1987-92; sports rschr. Olympic Games NBC TV, Barcelona, Spain, summer 1992; dietetic intern Calif. State U., Long Beach, 1992-93; gymnastics coach Aerials Gymnastics, Colorado Springs; sports rschr. Olympic Games NBC TV, Atlanta, 1996; mem. U.S. Olympic Com. Athletes Coun., Colorado Springs, 1994—. Full acad. scholar Ariz. State Women's Gymnastics Coach, 1987-91; Fitch Craig scholardept. home econs. Ariz. State U., 1991; 5-time Nat. Team, mem. 1984 Olympic Gymnastics Team. Mem. Am. Dietetic Assn., USA Gymnastics (mem. athletes coun. 1990-94, mem. women's selection com. ad hoc com. 1992-94, mem. exec. com. 1992-94.

DUTT, BIRENDRA, research specialist; b. 1950. Cons. L.A.; with R & DLabs., Culver City, Calif., 1983—, now pres. Office: Research & Development Labs 5800 Uplander Way Culver City CA 90230-6608*

DUTTON, ANGELA LOIS, trucking industry executive; b. Kailua, Oahu, Hawaii, Sept. 17, 1969; d. Larry Dennis Harrison and Lois Ann (Hinson) Benson; m. Todd Alan Dutton, Jan. 15, 1994. Adminstrv. asst. Supply Ctr., Costa Mesa, Calif., 1990-91; sales mgr. Allen Gorson Prodns., Sherman Oaks, Calif., 1991; purchasing agt. Precision Airparts, Garden Grove, Calif., 1992-95; owner, operator American Red Ball, Anaheim, Calif., 1995—, Indpls., 1995—; cons. Allen Gorson Prodns., Sherman Oaks, 1991; bus. mgr. Todd Dutton Trucking, Anaheim, 1995—. Recipient Editor's Choice award Nat. Libr. Poetry, 1995. Mem. Buick Grand Nat. Racing Assn.

DUTTON, JO SARGENT, education educator, researcher, consultant; b. L.A., Calif., Oct. 26, 1940; d. Paul and Jayne (O'Toole) Sargent; m. Ted W. Dutton, Nov. 15, 1979; children: Brooks, Berndan, Mark; step-children: Robert, William, Jeanne, Jerry. BS, U. So. Calif., 1962, MS, 1966; PhD, U. Calif. Riverside, 1996. Cert. elem. tchr., Calif.; corp. paralegal cert.; preliminary adminstrv. svcs. credential. Elem. sch. tchr. 6th grade Lawndale Unified Sch. Dist., 1963-64; reading instr. Culver City (Calif.) Unified Sch. Dist., 1964; prof. edn. U. So. Calif., 1964-65; remedial reading instr. Santa Monica (Calif.) Unified Sch. Dist., 1965-66; dist. remedial reading instr. San Marino Unified Sch. Dist., 1967-70; real estate broker Calif., 1972-96; adj. prof. English Chaffey C. C., Rancho Cucamonga, Calif., 1991-93; rsch. fellowCalif. Ednl. Rsch. Coop. U. Calif., Riverside, 1993-95; Co-owner GPE. Contbr. articles to profl. jours. Mem. exec. com. Inland Empire Cultural Found., 1980-83, Sister Cities Internat., Ontario, Calif., 1980-82; chair steering com. San Bernardino County Arts League, 1983-84; commr. San Bernardino County Mus.; mem. bd. Inland Empire Symphony; survey and assessment conductor Calif. Arts Coun. Mem. Am. Ednl. Rsch. Assn., Chaffey Cmty. Arts Assn., Calif. Ednl. Rsch. Assn. Home: PO Box 2960 Blue Jay CA 92317-2960 Office: U Calif Riverside Sch of Edn Calif Ednl Rsch Coop Riverside CA 92502-9874

DUTTON, PAULINE MAE, fine arts librarian; b. Detroit, July 15; d. Thoralf Andreas and Esther Ruth (Clyde) Tandberg; 1 child, Nancy Katherine; B.A. in Art, Calif. State U., Fullerton, 1967; M.S. in Library Sci., U. So. Calif., 1971; m. Richard Hawkins Dutton, June 21, 1969. Elem. tchr., Anaheim, Calif., 1967-68, Corona, Calif., 1968-69; fine arts librarian Pasadena (Calif.) Public Library, 1971-80; art cons., researcher, 1981—. Mem. Pasadena Librarians Assn. (sec. 1978, treas. 1979-80), Calif. Library Assn., Calif. Soc. Librarians, Art Librarians N.Am., Nat. Assn. Female Execs., Am. Film Inst., Am. Entrepreneurs Assn., Gilbert and Sullivan Soc., Alpha Sigma Phi. Club: Toastmistress (local pres. 1974).

DUUS, PETER, history educator; b. Wilmington, Del., Dec. 27, 1933; s. Hans Christian and Mary Anita (Pennypacker) D.; m. Masayo Umezawa, Nov. 25, 1964; 1 child, Erik. AB magna cum laude, Harvard U., 1955, PhD, 1965; MA, U. Mich., 1959. Asst. prof. history Washington U., St. Louis, 1964-66, Harvard U., Cambridge, Mass., 1966-70; assoc. prof. history Claremont (Calif.) Grad. Sch., 1970-73; assoc. prof. history Stanford (Calif.) U., 1973-78, prof., 1978—. Author: Party Rivalry and Political Change in Taishō Japan, 1968, Feudalism in Japan, 1969, The Rise of Modern Japan, 1976, The Cambridge History of Japan, Vol. 6: The Twentieth Century, 1989, The Japanese Informal Empire in China, 1989, The Abacus and the Sword: The Japanese Penetration of Korea, 1995, The Japanese Discovery of America, 1996. Exec. sec. Inter-Univ. for Japanese Lang. Studies, Tokyo, 1974-90; bd. dirs. Com. for Internat. Exchange of Scholars, Washington, 1987-91. Served with U.S. Army, 1955-57. NEH sr. fellow, 1972-73, Japan Found. postdoctoral fellow, 1976-77, Fulbright rsch. fellow, 1981-82, 94-95, Japan Found. rsch. fellow, 1986-87. Fellow AAAS, mem. Assn. for Asian Studies (bd. dirs. 1972-75, nominating com. 1983), Am. Hist. Assn. (bd. editors 1984-87). Home: 818 Esplanada Way Palo Alto CA 94305-1015 Office: Stanford U Dept of History Stanford CA 94305

DUYCK, KATHLEEN MARIE, poet, musician, retired social worker; b. Portland, Oreg., July 21, 1933; d. Anthony Joseph Dwyer and Edna Elisabeth Hayes; m. Robert Duyck, Feb. 3, 1962; children: Mary Kay Boeyen, Robert Patrick, Anthony Joseph. BS, Oreg. State U., 1954; MSW, U. Wash., 1956. Cert. NASW, Oreg. Adoption worker Cath. Svcs., Portland, 1956-61, Cath. Welfare, San Antonio, 1962; musician Tucson Symphony, 1963-65; prin. cellist Phoenix (Ariz.) Coll. Orch., 1968-78, Scottsdale (Ariz.) Symphony, 1974-80; poet, 1993—. Author: (poetry cassettes) Visions, 1993 (Contemporary Series Poet 1993), Visions II, 1996 (Contemporary Series Poet 1996); contbr. to 6 Natatonal Library of Poetry Anthologies. Rep. worker Maricopa County Reps., Phoenix, 1974; mem. Scottsdale Cultural Coun.; NASW bd. Cath. Charities Rep., Portland, 1959-61. Recipient Golden Poet award World of Poetry, 1991, 92, Editor's Choice awards Nat. Libr. Poetry, 1993—, Sec. gift Phoenix Exec. Bd., 1976. Recognition award Archbishop Howard, 1961, 5-Yr. Kathleen Duyck award Cello Congress V, 1996. Mem. Internat. Poetry Hall Fame, Ariz. Cello Soc., Nat. Libr. Poetry, Internat. Soc. Poets, Phoenix Symphony Guild (exec. bd. 1970-80). Republican. Roman Catholic. Home: 4545 E Palomino Rd Phoenix AZ 85018

DÜZGÜNES, NEJAT A., biophysicist, microbiologist; b. N.Y.C., Feb. 28, 1950; s. Orhan and Zeliha Duzgunes. BS, Mid. East Tech. U., Ankara, Turkey, 1972; PhD, SUNY, Buffalo, 1978. Postdoctoral fellow U. Calif., San Francisco, 1978-81, asst. rsch. biochemist, 1981-87, asst. adj. prof., 1985-87, assoc. rsch. biochemist, 1987-91, assoc. adj. prof., 1987-97; assoc. prof., chmn. dept. microbiology U. Pacific, San Francisco, 1990-95, prof., chmn. dept. microbiology, 1995—; vis. prof. dept. biophysics Kyoto (Japan) U., 1988. Editor: Membrane Fusion in Fertilization Cellular Transport and Viral Infection, 1988, Mechanisms and Specificity of HIV Entry into Host Cells, 1991, Membrane Fusion Techniques, Methods in Enzymology, Vols. 220 & 221, 1993; co-editor Trafficking of Intracellular Membranes, 1995. Vol. AFS Internat. Intercultural Programs, N.Y.C., 1969-86. Co-recipient Orgn. award U.S.-Japan Binat. Seminar on Membrane Fusion, NSF, 1992; Japan Soc. Promotion of Sci. fellow, 1988; grantee Am. Heart Assn., 1983-87, Calif. Univ. Wide AIDS Rsch. Program, 1986-90, 92-93, NIAID/NIH, 1988—. Mem. Am. Soc. Cell Biology, Am. Soc. Microbiology, Internat. Soc. Antiviral Rsch., Internat. AIDS Soc., Am. Assn. Dental Schs., Am. Assn. Dental Rsch., Biophys. Soc., Am. Soc. Virology. Office: U Pacific Dept Microbiology 2155 Webster St San Francisco CA 94115-2333

DUZY, MERRILYN JEANNE, artist, educator; b. L.A., Mar. 29, 1946; d. Berton John and Marva Lorinne (Barrow) D.; m. Howard Bentkower, Sept. 28, 1974. BA, Calif. State U., Northridge, 1974; MFA, Otis Art Inst., L.A., 1988. Tchr. L.A. H.S. for Arts, 1988-90; freelance comml. artist, West Hills, Calif., 1988—; pvt. tchr., lectr., West Hills, 1991-93; creator slide lecture Walking Through History: Women Artists Past and Present, 1982—; curator Autobiographies, 1977, Erotica '88, 1988, Angeles, Ancestors and Spirit Guides, 1994, Closure invitational Artspace Gallery, 1994, Quarks to Quasars, 1997. Founder Artists Networking, Woodland Hills, Calif., 1992-93. Mem. Coll. Art Assn., Women's Caucus for Art (pres. So. Calif. chpt. 1980-82, founder, pres. Fla. West Coast chpt. 1983-84, mem. nat. adv. bd.), Artists Alliance. Home and Studio: 8356 Capistrano Ave West Hills CA 91304-3319

DVORAK, RAY P., insurance company official; b. Center, N.D., Sept. 24, 1931; s. Stanley Joseph and Katherine (Schimpf) D.; m. Deanna Ellen Kern, June 1961 (div. 1974); children: Mitchell Scott, Lara Suzanne; m. Delores Marie Davis, Mar. 12, 1975 (dec. Jan. 1990). BS, U. Oreg., 1953; LLB, LaSalle Extension U., Chgo., 1964. CLU; CPCU; charter fin. cons. Claim rep. State Farm Ins. Co., Salem, Oreg., 1957-67; claim supt. State Farm Ins. Co., Medford, Oreg., 1967—. With USAF, 1953-55, lt. col. Res. ret. Mem. Soc. CPCU, Am. Soc. CLU's. Republican. Methodist. Home: PO Box 188 840 S Oregon St Jacksonville OR 97530 Office: State Farm Ins Co PO Box 790 Medford OR 97501-0055

DWORKIN, MICHAEL LEONARD, lawyer; b. Bridgeport Ct., Oct. 10, 1947; s. Samuel and Frances (Stein) Dworkin; m. Christina Lyn Hildreth, Sept. 25, 1977; children: Jennifer Hildreth, Amanda Hildreth. BA in Gov. with honors, Clark U., 1969; JD with honors, George Washington U., 1973. Bar: D.C. 1973, Calif. 1975, U.S. Ct. Appeals (9th cir.) 1982, U.S. Supreme Ct. 1978, U.S. Claims Ct. 1983. Atty. FAA, Washington, Los Angeles, 1973-77, United Airlines, San Francisco, 1977-81; sole practice, San Francisco, 1981-95, San Mateo, Calif., 1995—; instr. Embry Riddle Aeronautical U., San Francisco, 1980-81; dir. Poplar Ctr., San Mateo, Calif., 1979-86. Jonas Clark scholar Clark U., 1966-69. Mem. ABA, Lawyer Pilot's Bar Assn., Nat. Transp. Safety Bd. Bar Assn. (regional v.p. 1986-87, 90—, chmn. rules com. 1985-96), Aircraft Owners and Pilots Assn., Soaring Soc. Am., Internat. Soc. Air Safety Investigators (bd. dirs. San Francisco regional chpt. 1988-89), State Bar Calif., D.C. Bar Assn., Regional Airline Assn., Commonwealth Club of Calif. Jewish. Office: 155 Bovet Rd Ste 455 San Mateo CA 94402-3112

DWORZANSKI, JACEK PAWEL, analytical biochemist, researcher; b. Wloclawek, Poland, Jan. 5, 1952; came to U.S., 1987; s. Augustyn Franciszek and Cecylia (Piasecka) D.; m. Maria Teresa Siedlecka, June 12, 1987. MS, Silesian Med. Acad., Katowice, Poland, 1976; PhD, Jagiellonian U., Cracow, Poland, 1981. Instr., teaching fellow Silesian Med. Acad., Katowice, 1976-82, asst. prof., 1982-87; postdoctoral fellow U. Utah, Salt Lake City, 1987, Johns Hopkins U., Balt., 1987-88; rsch. assoc. U. Utah, Salt Lake City, 1989-93, asst. dir. micro analysis and reaction chemistry, 1995—; vis. prof. U. Utah, 1993—. Co-author: (with H.L.C. Meuzelaar) Modern Techniques for Rapid Microbiological Analysis, 1991; contbr. articles to profl. jours. Recipient Internat. Fogarty fellowship NIH, 1987. Mem. AAAS, Am. Soc. Mass Spectrometry, Am. Chem. Soc., Polish Inst. Arts and Scis. Am., N.Y. Acad. Scis. Roman Catholic. Office: U Utah Ctr Micro Analysis Reaction Chemistry Emrl Bldg 61 Rm 214 Salt Lake City UT 84112

DWYER, DORIS DAWN, adult education educator; b. Cin., Feb. 19, 1948; d. James Daniel and Marjorie Elaine (Fisher) D. ABin Social Sci., Ea. Ky. U., 1970, MA in History, 1971; PhD, Miami U., Oxford, Ohio, 1979. Instr. social sci. Ea. Ky. U., Richmond, 1971-74; postdoctoral fellow Miami U., Oxford, 1974-78; asst. prof. social sci. Coll. Ganado (Ariz.), 1979-80; prof. history Western Nev. C.C., Fallon, 1980—; bd. dirs. Nev. Humanities Com., Reno, 1983-89, mem. chautauqua performance, Nev. and Calif., 1994—. Author: A Century of City-Building, 1983. Mem. World History Assn., Western History Assn., Nev. Hist. Soc., Nev. Women's History Project; mem. women's archives bd. Reno Libr., U. Nev., 1995—; vice-chmn. bd. dirs. Nev. State Mus. and History, Carson City, 1994—; bd. dirs. Nev. Hist. Preservation, Carson City, 1990-94; chmn. bd. trustees Churchill County Libr., Fallon, Nev., 1989-96. Named Cmty. Woman of the Yr. Fallon Bus. and Profl. Women, 1992. Democrat. Roman Catholic. Office: Western Nev C C 160 Campus Way Fallon NV 89406

DWYER, WILLIAM L., federal judge; b. Olympia, Wash., Mar. 26, 1929; s. William E. and Ila (Williams) D.; m. Vasiliki Asimakopulos, Oct. 5, 1952; chldren: Joanna, Anthony, Charles. BS in Law, U. Wash., 1951; JD, NYU, 1953; LLD (hon.), Gonzaga U., 1994. Bar: Wash. 1953, U.S. Ct. Appeals (9th cir.) 1959, U.S. Supreme Ct. 1968. Law clk. Supreme Ct. Wash., Olympia, 1957; ptnr. Culp, Dwyer, Guterson & Grader, Seattle, 1957-87; judge U.S. Dist. Ct. (we. dist.) Wash., Seattle, 1987—. Author: The Goldmark Case, 1984 (Gavel award ABA 1985, Gov.'s award Wash. 1985). 1st lt. U.S. Army, 1953-56. Recipient Outstanding Svc. award U. Wash. Law Rev., 1985, Helen Geisness disting. Svc. award Seattle-King County Bar Assn., 1985, Disting. Alumnus award U. Wash. Sch. of Law, 1994, W.G. Magnuson award King County Mcpl. League, 1994, Judge of Yr. Wash. State Trial Lawyers, 1994. Fellow Am. Coll. Trial Lawyers, Am. Bar Found., Hon. Order of Coif; mem. ABA, Inter-Am. Bar Assn., Am. Judicature Soc., Supreme Ct. Hist. Soc., 9th Cir. Hist. Assn. Office: US Dist Ct 502 US Courthouse 1010 5th Ave Seattle WA 98104-1130

DWYRE, WILLIAM PATRICK, journalist, public speaker; b. Sheboygan, Wis., Apr. 7, 1944; s. George Leo and Mary Veronica (O'Brien) D.; m. Jill Ethlyn Jarvis, July 30, 1966; children—Amy, Patrick. B.A., U. Notre Dame, Ind. Sports copy editor Des Moines Register, 1966-68; sports writer, asst. sports editor, sports editor Milw. Jour., 1968-81; asst. sports editor, sports editor Los Angeles Times, 1981—; speaker Mark Reede's Sportstars, Los Angeles, 1986; columnist Referee Mag., 1977—; voting mem., bd. dirs. Amateur Athletic Found. Nat. Sports Hall of Fame, 1981—. Named Sportswriter of Yr., Wis. Nat. Sportscasters, Sportswriters Assn., 1980; Nat. Editor of Yr., Nat. Press Found., 1985; recipient award for Sustained Excellence by Individual, L.A. Times, 1985, Red Smith award AP sports Editors, 1996. Mem. Assoc. Press Sports Editors (pres. 1989), Nat. Baseball, Pro Basketball and Football Writers Assn. Club: Milw. Pen and Mike. Office: Los Angeles Times Times Mirror Sq Los Angeles CA 90012

DYBOWSKI, DOUGLAS EUGENE, education educator, economist; b. Wiesbaden Air Base, Germany, Dec. 7, 1946; s. Eugene L. and Margaret Alma (Hart) D.; m. Deborah Jane Dalpiaz, Dec. 27, 1986; children: Noelle C., Eric W. BA in Govt. and Politics, U. Md., College Park, 1969; grad. edn. econ., Trinity U., San Antonio, 1971; Calif. teaching credential, Calif. State U., San Bernardino, 1975; AS in Computer Sci., San Bernardino Valley Coll., 1982. Stockman J.C. Pennys, 1965; advtg. asst. Sears & Roebuck, Washington, D.C., 1966; air conditioning and heating helper J&W Contractors, McLean, Va., 1967; legis. aide to hon. Michael Feighan U.S. Congress, Washington, 1969; asst. mgr. Mr M Food Store, San Antonio, Tex., 1970-71; econ. Bur. Labor Statistics Dept. Labor, Dallas, 1971-73; fine jewelry salesman May Co., San Bernardino, Calif., 1974-78; tchr. Rialto and San Bernardino Sch. Dists., 1973-85; realtor Gallery of Homes, San Bernardino, Calif., 1979; tchr. Diocese of San Bernardino, Calif., 1985-87; instr. computer sci. San Bernardino Valley Coll., Calif., 1983-84; tchr. Colton (Calif.) Joint Unified Sch. Dist., 1987—; art ctr. San Bernardino, Calif., 1989-95. Artist (painting) San Bernardino County Mus., 1994. Recipient Lounsbury Svc. award San Bernardino Valley Coll., 1982. Mem. Sigma Chi. Republican, Presbyterian. Office: Colton Joint Unified Sch Dist 1212 Valencia Dr Colton CA 92324-1731

DYCK, ANDREW ROY, philologist, educator; b. Chgo., May 24, 1947; s. Roy H. and Elizabeth (Beck) D.; m. Janis Mieko Fukuhara, Aug. 20, 1978. BA, U. Wisc., 1969; PhD, U. Chgo., 1975. Sessional lectr. U. Alta., Edmonton, Can., 1975-76; asst. prof. U. Minn., Mpls., 1977-78; vis. asst. prof. philology UCLA, 1976-77, asst. prof., 1978-82, assoc. prof., 1982-87, prof., 1987—, chmn. dept. classics, 1988-91. Author: A Commentary on Cicero, De Officiis, 1996; editor: Epimerismi Homerici, 2 vols., 1983, 95, Essays on Euripides and George of Pisidia and on Helidorus and Achilles Tatius (Michael Psellus), 1986. Alexander von Humboldt-Stiftung fellow, Bonn, Fed. Republic of Germany, 1980-89; NEH fellow, 1991-92. Mem. Am. Philol. Assn., Calif. Classical Assn., Byzantine Studies Conf., U.S. Nat. Com. on Byzantine Studies. Office: UCLA Classics Dept 405 Hilgard Ave Los Angeles CA 90095-1417

DYER, ALICE MILDRED, psychotherapist; b. San Diego, July 4, 1929; d. William Silas Cann and Louise Lair (Addenbrooke) Vaile; divorced; children: Alexis Dyer Guagnano, Bryan, Christine Dyer Morales; m. James Vawter, Dec. 26, 1972. BA, Calif. State U., Fullerton, 1965, MA, 1967; PhD, U.S. Internat. U., 1980. Coord., counselor Brea (Calif.)-Olinda High Sch., 1968-72; sch. psychologist Cypress (Calif.) Sch. Dist., 1972-86; instr. North Orange County Community Coll., Fullerton, 1975-77; pvt. practice ednl. psychology Long Beach and Fountain Valley, Calif., 1978—; pvt. practice marriage and family therapy Fullerton and Brea, Calif., 1979—; psychologist, cons. Multiple Sclerosis Soc. Orange County, 1986-95; facilitator adult mental health La Habra (Calif.) Comty. Hosp., 1988-89. Bd. dirs., officer, pres. Friends of Fullerton Arboretum, 1974-95; pres., bd. dirs. Fullerton Beautiful, 1987-88, Brea Ednl. Found., 1988-89; therapist Orange County Juvenile Connection Project, 1988—. Recipient Appreciation award Gary Ctr., La Habra, 1975, Multiple Sclerosis Soc. Orange County, 1987. Mem. Calif. Assn. Marriage and Family Therapists, Assn. for Children and Adults with Learning Disabilities (cons. 1970—, bd. dirs., facilitator), AAUW, Am. Bus. Women's Assn., Soroptomists (health chmn. Brea chpt. 1987-88). Republican. Unitarian. Office: Brea Mental Health Assocs PO Box 1688 Brea CA 92822-1688

DYER, CHARLES ARNOLD, lawyer; b. Blairstown, Mo., Aug. 29, 1940; s. Arnold and Mary Charlotte (West) D.; children: Kristine, Erin, Kathleen, Kerry. BJ, U. Mo., 1962; JD, U. Calif., 1970. Bar: Calif. 1971, U.S. Sup. Ct. 1976. Ptnr., Dyer & White, Menlo Park, Calif.; judge Pro Tem Mcpl. and Superior Ct., San Mateo County, Pro Tem Superior Ct. Santa Clara County, arbitrator and mediator; lectr. in field. Bd. dirs. Boys Club of San Mateo, 1971-83, pres., 1975; mem. exec. council Boys Clubs of the Bay Area, 1977-83; mem. Democratic Nat. Fin. Com., 1978. Capt. USNR, 1963-93, ret. Mem. Calif. Bar Assn., San Mateo County Bar Assn., Santa Clara County Bar Assn., Palo Alto Bar Assn., Assn. Trial Lawyers Am., Consumer Attys. Calif., Consumer Attys. San Mateo County, Assn. Atty. Mediators, Trial Lawyers Pub. Justice, Am. Bd. Trial Advs., Nat. Bd. Trial Advocacy, Am. Arbitration Assn. Roman Catholic. Office: Dyer & White 800 Oak Grove Ave Menlo Park CA 94025-4477

DYER, KECIA CAROLE, interior designer; b. Dallas, Mar. 27, 1965; d. Eldon Royce and Carole Lynn (Wade) D. BS in Interior Design, U. Tex., 1989. Cert. interior designer. Designer Reese Design, Austin, Tex., 1989-90; project designer Space Designs, Inc., Mountainview, Calif., 1990-95; assoc. Reel Grobman and Assocs., Interior Architecture, San Jose, Calif., 1995-96; interior designer Archtl. Planning & Interior Design, Santa Clara, Calif., 1997—. Vol. Design Response, bd. dirs.; task force mem. Palo Alto (Calif.) Task Force for Disability Awareness, 1993-94. Recipient C.J. Davidson scholarship U. Tex., Austin, 1989. Mem. Internat. Interior Design Assn. (bd. dirs. No. Calif. chpt. 1993-96). Republican. Office: Archtl Planning & Interior Design Inc 3945 Freedom Cir Ste 108 Santa Clara CA 95054

DYER-RAFFLER, JOY ANN, special education diagnostician, educator; b. Stiltner, W.Va., Aug. 10, 1935; d. Ralph William and Hazel (Terry) Dyer; m. John William Raffler, Sr., Jan. 1, 1993; 1 child from a previous marriage, Keith Brian DeArmond. BA, U. N.C., 1969; MEd in Secondary Edn., U. Ariz., 1974, MEd in Spl. Edn., 1976. Cert. spl. edn.-learning disabilities, art edn., spl. edn.-emotionally handicapped. Art educator Tucson Unified Sch. Dist., Tucson, 1970-75, spl. edn. educator, 1975-89, spl. edn. diagnostician, 1989—. Den mother Cub Scouts Am., Raleigh, N.C., 1968-69. Recipient grant Tucson Unified Sch. Dist., 1977. Mem. NEA, Tucson Edn. Assn., Learning Disabilities Assn., Coun. Exceptional Children, Coun. Ednl. Diagnostic Svcs. Home: 4081 N Kolb Rd Tucson AZ 85750-6127 Office: AJO Svc Ctr 2201 W 44th St Tucson AZ 85713-4575

DYKSTRA, DAVID CHARLES, management executive, accountant, consultant, author, educator; b. Des Moines, July 10, 1941; s. Orville Linden and Ermina (Dunn) D.; m. Ello Paimre, Nov. 20, 1971; children: Suzanne, Karin, David S. BSChemE, U. Calif., Berkeley, 1963; MBA, Harvard U., 1966. CPA, Calif. Corp. contr. Recreation Environs., Newport Beach, Calif., 1970-71, Hydro Conduit Corp., Newport Beach., 1971-78; v.p. fin. and adminstrn. Tree-Sweet Products, Santa Ana, Calif., 1978-80; pres., owner Dykstra Cons., Irvine, Calif., 1980-88; pres. Easy Data Corp., 1981-88; pub. Easy Data Computer Comparisons, 1982-87; sr. mgr. Deloitte & Touche, Costa Mesa, Calif., 1988-90; prof. mgmt. info. systems Nat. U., Irvine, 1984-90; pub. Dykstra's Computer Digest, 1984-90; pres., owner Golden West Pers., Long Beach, 1992-93; exec. v.p. Tegris Corp., Bellevue, Wash., 1994—. Author: Manager's Guide to Business Computer Terms, 1981, Computers for Profit, 1983; contbr. articles to profl. jours. Chmn. 40th Congl. Dist. Tax Reform Immediately, 1977-80; mem. nat. com. Rep. Com.; vice-chmn. Orange County Calif. Rep. Assembly, 1979-80; bd. dir. Corona Del Mar Rep. Assembly, 1980-94, v.p., 1980-87, pres. 1987-89. Mem. AICPA, Am. Mgmt. Assn., Calif. Soc. CPA's, Data Processing Mgmt. Assn., Am. Prodn. and Inventory Control Soc., Ind. Computer Cons. Assn., Internat. Platform Assn., Data Processing Mgmt. Assn., Orange County C. of C., Newport Beach C. of C., Harvard U. Bus. Sch. Assn. Orange County (bd. dir. 1984-90, v.p 1984-86, 87-88, pres. 1986-87, 91-92, chmn. 1993-94), Harvard U. Bus. Sch. Assn. So. Calif. (bd. dirs. 1986-87, 91-92, v.p. 1992-93), Harvard U. Bus. Sch. Assn. Puget Sound, Town Hall, John Wayne Tennis Club, Lido Sailing Club, Rotary (bd. dirs. 1984-86). Home: 2805 75th Pl SE Apt 44 Mercer Island WA 98040-2746 Office: 600 108th Ave NE Bellevue WA 98004-5110

DYM, CLIVE LIONEL, engineering educator; b. Leeds, Eng., July 15, 1942; came to U.S., 1949, naturalized, 1954; s. Isaac and Anna (Hochmann) D.; children: Jordana, Miriam. BCE, Cooper Union, 1962; MS, Poly. Inst. Bklyn., 1964; PhD, Stanford U., 1967. Asst. prof. SUNY, Buffalo, 1966-69; assoc. professorial lectr. George Washington U., Washington, 1969; research staff Inst. Def. Analyses, Arlington, Va., 1969-70; assoc. prof. Carnegie-Mellon U., Pitts., 1970-74; vis. assoc. prof. TECHNION, Israel, 1971; sr. scientist Bolt Beranek and Newman, Inc., Cambridge, Mass., 1974-77; prof. U. Mass., Amherst, 1977-91, head dept. civil engring., 1977-85; Fletcher Jones prof. engring. design, dir. Ctr. Design Edn. Harvey Mudd Coll., Claremont, Calif., 1991—; vis. sr. rsch. fellow Inst. Sound and Vibration Rsch., U. Southampton, Eng., 1973; vis. scientist Xerox PARC, 1983-84; vis. prof. civil engring. Stanford U., 1983-84, Carnegie Mellon U., 1990; cons. Bell Aerospace Co., 1967-69, Dravo Corp., 1970-71, Salem Corp., 1972, Gen. Analytics Inc., 1972, ORI, Inc., 1979, BBN Inc., 1979, Avco, 1981-83, 85-86, TASC, 1985-86; vice chmn. adv. bd. Amerinex Artificial Intelligence, 1986-88. Author: (with I.H. Shames) Solid Mechanics: A Variational Approach, 1973, Introduction to the Theory of Shells, rev. edit. 1990, Stability Theory and Its Applications to Structural Mechanics, 1974, (with E.S. Ivey) Principles of Mathematical Modeling, 1980, (with I.H. Shames) Energy and Finite Element Methods in Structural Mechanics, 1985, (with R.E. Levitt) Knowledge-Based Systems in Engineering, 1990, Engineering Design: A Synthesis of Views, 1994, Structural Modeling and Analysis, 1997; editor: (with A. Kalnins) Vibration: Beams, Plates, and Shells, 1977, Applications of Knowledge-Based Systems to Engineering Analysis and Design, 1985, Artificial Intelligence for Engring. Design Analysis and Mfg., 1986—; contbr. articles and tech. reports to profl. publs. NATO sr. fellow in sci., 1973. Fellow Acoustical Soc. Am., ASME, ASCE (Walter L. Huber research prize 1980); mem. AAAS, Am. Assn. for Artificial Intelligence, Computer Soc. of IEEE, ASEE (Western Electric Fund award 1983). Jewish. Office: Harvey Mudd Coll Engring Dept 301 E 12th St Claremont CA 91711-5901

DYMAN, JENNI L., author; b. Oklahoma City, Aug. 10, 1941; d. Ernest F. Hiser and Jennie M. (Bick) Hiser Moore; m. James E. Caldwell, Jan. 26, 1962 (div. Sept. 1967); m. Thaddeus S. Dyman, Apr. 11, 1987; 1 child, Ken C. BA, U. Denver, 1963; MA, U. Okla., 1968; PhD, U. Colo., 1990. Tchr. Arapahoe C.C., Littleton, Colo., 1969-96, dept. chmn., 1980-82, 91-96. Author: Lurking Feminism: The Ghost Stories of Edith Wharton, 1996. English-Speaking Union scholar, 1979. Mem. MLA, Edith Wharton Soc., Edith Wharton Restoration Soc. Democrat. Unitarian. Home: 524 S Ogden Denver CO 80209

DYRNESS, WILLIAM ARTHUR, religion educator, dean; b. Geneva, Ill., Jan. 23, 1943; s. Enock Christian and Grace (Williams) D.; m. Grace Strachan Roberts, Mar. 16, 1968; children: Michelle Lynn, Andrea Elisabeth, Jonathan Roberts. BA, Wheaton (Ill.) Coll., 1965; BD, Fuller Theol. Sem., Pasadena, Calif., 1968; ThD, U. Strasbourg, France, 1970; Doctorandus, Free U., Amsterdam, The Netherlands, 1975. Prof. theology Asian Theol. Sem., Manila, 1974-82; prof. theology New Coll. Berkeley, Calif., 1982-90, pres., 1982-86; dean, prof. theology and culture Fuller Theol. Sem., 1990—. Author: Themes in Old Testament Theology, 1979, Christian Apologetics in a World Community, 1983, How Does America Hear the Gospel?, 1989, Learning About Theology from the Third World, 1990. Democrat. Presbyterian. Office: Fuller Theol Sem 135 N Oakland Ave Pasadena CA 91182-0001

DZIEWANOWSKA, ZOFIA ELIZABETH, neuropsychiatrist, pharmaceutical executive, researcher, educator; b. Warsaw, Poland, Nov. 17, 1939; came to U.S., 1972; d. Stanislaw Kazimierz Dziewanowski and Zofia Danuta (Mieczkowska) Rudowska; m. Krzysztof A. Kunert, Sept. 1, 1961 (div. 1971); 1 child, Martin. MD, U. Warsaw, 1963; PhD, Polish Acad. Sci., 1970. MD recert. U.K., 1972, U.S., 1973. Asst. prof. of psychiatry U. Warsaw Med. Sch., 1969-71; sr. house officer St. George's Hosp., U. London, 1971-72; assoc. dir. Merck Sharp & Dohme, Rahway, N.J., 1972-76; vis. assoc. physician Rockefeller U. Hosp., N.Y.C., 1975-76; adj. asst. prof. of psychiatry Cornell U. Med. Ctr., N.Y.C., 1978—; v.p., global med. dir. Hoffmann-La Roche, Inc., Nutley, N.J., 1976-94; sr. v.p. and dir. global med. affairs Genta Inc., San Diego, 1994—; lectr. in field U.S. and internat. confs. Contbr. articles to profl. publs. Bd. dirs Royal Soc. Medicine Found.; mem. alumni coun. Cornell U. Med. Ctr. Recipient TWIN Honoree award for Outstanding Women in Mgmt., Ridgewood (N.J.) YWCA, 1984. Mem. AMA, AAAS, Am. Soc. Pharmacology and Therapeutics, Am. Coll. Neuropsychopharmacology, N.Y. Acad. Scis., PhRMA. (vice chmn. steering com. med. sect., chmn. internat. med. affairs com., head biotech. working group), Royal Soc. Medicine (U.K.), Drug Info. Assn. (Woman of Yr. award 1994), Am. Assn. Pharm. Physicians. Roman Catholic. Office: Genta Inc 3550 General Atomics Ct San Diego CA 92121-1122

DZYALOSHINSKII, IGOR EKHIELIEVICH, physicist; b. Moscow, Feb. 1, 1931; s. Ekhiel Moiseevich and Maria Semionovna (Aseeva) D.; m. Elena Aronovna Lebedeva, Dec. 2, 1960; 1 child, Elena. MA in Physics, Moscow State U., 1953; PhD in Physics, Inst. for Phys. Problems, Moscow, 1957, DSc in Physics, 1962. Sr. rschr. Inst. for Phys. Problems, Moscow, 1957-65; head dept. magnetism Landau Inst. for Theoretical Physics, Moscow, 1965-91; prof. physics U. Calif., Irvine, 1992—. Author: Methods of Quantum Field, Theory in Statistical Physics (in Russian, English, Japanese and Chinese), 1962, 3d edit., 1975. Decorated Order of Red Banner of Labour, Order of Honor, Medal of Vet. of Labour, Govt. of Russia; recipient State prize Govt. USSR, 1984. Fellow Am. Phys. Soc.; mem. Russian Acad. Scis. (Lomonosov prize 1962, Landau prize 1989), Am. Acad. Art and Scis. (hon. fgn. mem.). Office: Univ Calif Dept Physics Irvine CA 92697

EADIE, MARGARET L., educational and career consultant. BA, Miami U., Oxford, Ohio; MA, Chapman U., Orange, Calif.; Advanced MEd, U. So. Calif. Master tchr. Tustin (Calif.) H.S.; lectr., continuing edn. program coord. Calif. State U., Fullerton; edn. and career cons. Pacific Grove, Calif. Recipient 2 Panhellenic awards. Mem. APA, Speech Comm. Assn., Hon. Assn. of Women in Edn., Delta Delta Delta (nat. networking cons., alumnae chpt. pres.), Philanthropic and Edn. Orgn. (chpt. pres.). Office: 1000 Sage Pl Pacific Grove CA 93950-5007

EADINGTON, WILLIAM RICHARD, economist, educator; b. Fullerton, Calif., Jan. 1, 1946; s. Thomas James and Mary Elizabeth (Bastanchury) E.; m. Margaret Ann Dean, Feb. 3, 1968; children: Diana, Michael. BS, Santa Clara U., 1967; MA, Claremont Grad. Sch., 1970, PhD, 1973. Asst. prof. econs. U. Nev., Reno, 1969-74, assoc. prof., 1974-81, prof. econs., 1981—, U. Nev. Reno Found. prof., 1990-91; dir. Inst. for Study of Gambling and Comml. Gaming, Reno, 1989—; vis. prof. U. Utah, Germany, 1977-78, U. Salford, 1995—; vis. prof. Ctr. Addiction Studies, Harvard U., Cambridge, Mass., 1989-90, lectr. Kennedy Sch. Govt., 1990; acad. visitor London Sch. Econs., 1978, 87. Editor: Gambling and Society, 1976, Annals Am. Acad. Soc. and Polit. Sci., 1984, Gambling Resarch, 1988, Indian Gaming and the Law, 1990, Gambling and Public Policy, 1991, Gambling and Commercial Gaming, 1992, Tourism Alternatives, 1992, Gambling Behavior and Problem Gambling, 1993, Jour. Gambling Studies, 1989; assoc. editor Annals Tourism Rsch., 1983-89. Named Outstanding Rschr./Educator Nat. Coun. Compulsive Gambling, 1989. Fellow Internat. Acad. Study of Tourism; mem. Am. Econ. Assn. Republican. Roman Catholic. Home: 25 Somers Loop Crystal Bay NV 89402 Office: U Nev Dept Econs Reno NV 89557

EAKIN, MARGARETTA MORGAN, lawyer; b. Ft. Smith, Ark., Aug. 27, 1941; d. Ariel Thomas and Oma (Thomas) Morgan; m. Harry D. Eakin, June 7, 1959; 1 dau., Margaretta E. B.A. with honors, U. Oreg., 1969, J.D., 1971. Bar: Oreg. 1971, U.S. Dist. Ct. Oreg. 1973, U.S. Ct. Appeals (9th cir.) 1977. Law clk. to chief justice Oreg. Supreme Ct., 1971-72; Reginald Heber Smith Law Reform fellow, 1972-73; house counsel Hyster Co., 1973-75; assoc. N. Robert Stoll, 1975-77; mem. firm Margaretta Eakin, P.C., Portland, Oreg., 1977—; tchr. bus. law Portland State U., 1979-80; speaker; mem. state bd. profl. responsibility Oreg. State Bar, 1979-82. Mem. bd. visitors U. Oreg. Sch. of Law, 1986-93, vice chair, 1989-91, chair, 1992-93; mem. ann. fund com. Oreg. Episc. Sch., 1981, chmn. subcom. country fair, 1981; sec. Parent Club Bd., St. Mary's Acad., 1987; mem. Oreg. State. Bar Com. on Uniform State Laws, 1989-93; vol. lawyer Fed. Emergency Mgmt. Assn., 1996—. Paul Patterson fellow. Mem. ABA, Assn. Trial Lawyers Am., Oreg. Trial Lawyers Assn., Oreg. Bar Assn., Multnomah County Bar Assn. (jud. selection com. 1992-94), 1000 Friends of Oreg., City Club. Office: 30th Fl Pacwest Ctr 1211 SW 5th Ave Portland OR 97204-3713

EAKLE, ARLENE HASLAM, genealogist; b. Salt Lake City, July 19, 1936; d. Thomas E. and margaret (Mitchell) Haslam; m. Alma D. Eakle, Jr., Feb. 8, 1957; children: JoAnn, Richard, Linda, John. ADN, Weber State U.; MA in English history, U. Utah, PhD of English history. Co-author: (with Vincent L. Jones and Mildred Christensen) Family History for Fun and Profit, 1972, (with Johni Cerny) The Source: A Guidebook for American Genealogy, 1984, (with Johni Cerny) Ancestry's Guide to Research, 1985; editor: Research News, Immigration Digest; editor: Virginia Notebooks, N.Y. Rsch. Fellow Utah Geneal. Assn., 1987; recipient Award of Merit Fedn. Geneal. Soc., 1984. Mem. Am. Family Records Assn. (bd. dirs.), Assn. Profl. Genealogists (pres. 1980-82, Grahame Thomas Smallwood Jr. Award of Merit 1984), Md. Geneal. Soc., Utah Geneal. Assn., West Fla. Geneal. Soc. Home: 875 N 300 E Tremonton UT 84337-1010 Office: Genealogical Inst PO Box 22045 Salt Lake City UT 84122-1045

EARLY, DANIEL KEEFE, anthropologist, sociologist, educator; b. Ann Arbor, Mich., May 25, 1943; s. Raymond Robert and Mary Margaret E.; m. Julia Lagunes Capistrán, Mar. 4, 1978; 1 child, Michelle Maria. BA, U. Calif., Berkeley, 1966; MA, Cath. U., 1973, PhD, 1978. Rschr. Inst. Mex. Cafe, Mexico City, 1975-76; instr. Montgomery Coll., Rockville, Md., 1977-78; assoc. prof. Ctrl. Oreg. C.C., Bend, Pa., 1978—; rschr. Rodale Rsch.,

Emmaus, Pa., 1979, U. Nat., Cozco, Peru, 1985-86; lectr. Oreg. State U., Bend, 1982-83, Linfield Coll., Bend, 1995; expert witness Cultural Access, Bend, 1993—. Author: Café: Dependencia y Efectos, 1982. Mem. U.S. Radio Sport Team., Khabarovsk, Russia, 1995. Grantee Assn. Fulbright Internat. Exch. Scholars, 1984-85, Earthwatch, 1991. Office: Ctrl Oreg Cmty Coll 2600 NW Awbrey Bend OR 97701

EARLY, ROBERT JOSEPH, magazine editor; b. Indpls., Sept. 22, 1936; s. Robert Paul and Helen Theresa (Schluttenhofer) E.; m. Gail Louise Horvath, Sept. 6, 1958; children: Mary Jane, Joseph Robert, Jill Ann. BA, U. Notre Dame, 1958. Reporter Indpls. Star, 1958-61; reporter The Ariz. Republic, Phoenix, 1961-66, asst. city editor, 1966-69, city editor, 1969-77, asst. mng. editor, 1977-78, mng. editor, 1978-82; pres. Telesource Communication Svcs. Inc., Phoenix, 1982-90; editor Phoenix Mag., 1985-89, Ariz. Hwys., Phoenix, 1990—; lectr. Ariz. State U., 1992, 94; editor in residence No. Ariz. U., 1992, 93, 94.. Chmn. Victims Bill of Rights Task Force, Phoenix, 1989. Recipient Virg Hill Newsman of Yr. award Ariz. Press Club, 1976. Mem. Soc. Profl. Journalists. Republican. Roman Catholic. Office: Ariz Hwys 2039 W Lewis Ave Phoenix AZ 85009-2819

EASLEY, GEORGE WASHINGTON, construction executive; b. Williamson, W.Va., Mar. 14, 1933; s. George Washington and Isabel Ritchie (Saville) E.; student U. Richmond, 1952-56; children: Bridget Bland, Kathy Clark, Saville Woodson, Marie Alexis, Isabell Roxanne, George Washington, Laura Dean, Dorothy Elizabeth, Isabel Louiza. m. Bettyrae Fedje Hanner, Sep. 15, 1990. Hwy. engr. Va. Dept. Hwys., Richmond, 1956-62; dep. city mgr. City of Anchorage, 1962-68; prin. assoc. Wilbur Smith & Assos., Los Angeles, 1969-70; commr. pub. works State of Alaska, Juneau, 1971-74; exec. v.p. Burgess Internat. Constrn. Co., Anchorage, 1974, pres., 1975; pres., chmn. bd. George W. Easley Co., Anchorage, 1976-86 ; pres. Alaska Aggregate Corp., Fairbanks Sand & Gravel Co., 1986-90; constrn. mgr. Alaska Pipeline Svc. Co., 1990-96; ind. cons., 1996—; bd. dirs. Totem Ocean Trailer Express, Inc. Recipient commendations City of Anchorage, 1966, Greater Anchorage, Inc., 1969, Ketchikan C. of C., 1973, Alaska State Legis., 1974, Gov. of Alaska, 1974; named one of Outstanding Young Men, Anchorage Jaycees, 1964. Registered profl. engr., Calif. Mem. U.S. C. of C., Alaska C. of C. (dir. 1978—, chmn. 1982-83), Anchorage C. of C. (sec.-treas. 1976, v.p. 1977, pres.-elect 1978, pres. 1979-80, dir. 1982-88, Gold Pan award 1969, 77), Hwy. Users Fedn. Alaska (dir. 1972—, treas. 1974—), Orgn. Mgmt. of Alaska's Resources (past dir.), Am. Pub. Works Assn., Anchorage Transp. Commn. (past chmn.), Associated Gen. Contractors (dir. Alaska chpt. 1978—, chpt. treas. 1980-81, sec. 1981, pres. 1984, nat. com. labor relations, Hard Hat award, 1985), Am. Mil. Engrs. (v.p. Alaska chpt. 1978), Alaska Trucking Assn. (bd. dirs. 1986-90), Inst. Mcpl. Engrs., Inst. Traffic Engrs., Internat. Orgn. Masters, Mates and Pilots (hon.), Common Sense for Alaska (past pres.), Commonwealth North (charter). Democrat. Presbyterian. Club: San Francisco Tennis. Lodge: Rotary. Home and Office: 4921 Sportsman Dr Anchorage AK 99502-4193

EASLEY, LOYCE ANNA, painter; b. Weatherford, Okla., June 28, 1918; d. Thomas Webster and Anna Laura (Sanders) Rogers; m. Mack Easley, Nov. 17, 1939; children: June Elizabeth, Roger. BFA, U. Okla., 1943; postgrad., 1947-49; student, Art Students League, N.Y.C., 1977; postgrad., Santa Fe Inst. Fine Arts, 1985. Tchr. Pub. Sch., Okmulgee, Okla., 1946-47, Hobbs, N.Mex., 1947-49; tchr. painting N.Mex. Jr. Coll., Hobbs, 1965-80; tchr. Art Workshops in N.Mex., Okla., Wyoming. Numerous one-woman shows and group exhbns. in mus., univs. and galleries, including Gov.'s Gallery, Santa Fe, Selected Artists, N.Y.C., Roswell (N.Mex.) Mus., N.Mex. State U., Las Cruces, West Tex. Mus., Tex. Tech U., Lubbock; represented in permanent collections USAF Acad., Colorado Springs, Colo., Roswell Mus., Carlsbad (N.Mex.) Mus., Coll. Santa Fe, N.Mex. Supreme Ct, also other pvt. and pub. collections; featured in S.W. Art and Santa Fe mag., 1981, 82. Named Disting. Former Student, U. Okla. Art Sch., 1963; nominated for Gov's. award in Art, N.Mex., 1988. Mem. N.Mex. Artists Equity (lifetime mem. 1963). Democrat. Presbyterian. Home: 10909 Country Club Dr NE Albuquerque NM 87111-6548

EASTAUGH, ROBERT L., judge. Assoc. justice Alaska Supreme Ct., 1994—. Office: Alaska Supreme Court 303 K St Anchorage AK 99501-2013

EASTHAM, THOMAS, foundation administrator; b. Attelboro, Mass., Aug. 21, 1923; s. John M. and Margaret (Marsden) E.; m. Berenice J. Hirsch, Oct. 12, 1946; children: Scott Thomas, Todd Robert. Student English, Northwestern U., 1946-52. With Chgo. American, 1945-56, asst. Sunday editor, 1953-54, feature writer, 1954-56; news editor San Francisco Call Bull., 1956-62, exec. editor, 1962-65; exec. editor, then D.C. bur. chief San Francisco Examiner, 1965-82; dir. pub. info,press sec. to mayor of San Francisco, 1982-88; v.p., western dir. William Randolph Hearst Founds., 1988—. Active Nat. Trust Historic Preservation. Served with USMC, 1941-45. Pulitzer prize nominee, 1955. Mem. Am. Soc. Newspaper Editors, Inter-Am. Press Assn., Am., Internat. press insts., White House Corrs. Assn., Nat. Press Club, Ind. Sector, Coun. on Foundations, Commonwealth Club, Sigma Delta Chi. Home: 1473 Bernal Ave Burlingame CA 94010-5559 Office: Hearst Found 90 New Montgomery St Ste 1212 San Francisco CA 94105-4504

EASTMAN, FRANCESCA MARLENE, volunteer, art historian; b. Jamaica Plain, Mass., Jan. 26, 1952; d. Therald Carlton and Martha Jane (Welch) E.; m. Edward Charles Goodstein, Aug. 27, 1989. AB in Art History, Manhattanville Coll., 1972; MA in Art History, Clark Art Inst./Williams Coll., 1974; postgrad., Stanford U., 1976-80. Intern Mus. of Fine Arts, Boston, summers 1971-73; lectr. in art Regis Coll., Weston, Mass., 1974-76; sr. house assoc. Stanford (Calif.) U., 1977-80, tchg. fellow, 1978-79; student svcs. intern Menlo Coll., Atherton, Calif., 1980-81; now freelance editor. Bd. sec. Trinity Episcopal Sch., Menlo Park, Calif., 1992-96, bd. chair, 1996—; trustee David B. and Edward C. Goodstein Found., L.A., 1995—; vol. scholarship com. Peninsula Cmty. Found., San Mateo, Calif., 1995—; grad. Leadership Redwood City, Calif., 1995—; arts commr. Town of Atherton, Calif., 1996—; mem. steering com. Peninsula Episcopal H.S. Project, Foster City, Calif., 1996—. Mem. Cornell Club (N.Y.C.), Williams Club (N.Y.C.). Democrat. Roman Catholic.

EASTMAN, MICHAEL PAUL, chemistry educator; b. Wis., Apr. 14, 1941; s. Leroy Irons and Virginia Marie (Anderson) E.; m. Frances Lyle, Oct. 23, 1963 (div. Jan. 1976); children: Nathan, Eli; m. Carol Kennedy, Aug. 23, 1980. BA, Carleton Coll., 1963; PhD, Cornell U., 1968. Postdoctoral Los Alamos (N.Mex.) Nat. Lab., 1968-70; asst. prof. chemistry U. Tex., El Paso, 1970-74, assoc. prof. chemistry, 1974-80, prof. chemistry, 1980-88, asst. dean of sci., 1981-84, asst. v.p. acad. affairs, 1984-85; prof. chemistry No. Ariz. U., Flagstaff, 1988—, chmn. dept. chemistry, 1988—, interim dir. environ. sci., 1990-91; elected mem. Assn. Western Univs., Utah, 1990-93; com. chmn. Edn. and Rsch. Coun., 1993; mem. com. on lab. sci. admission requirements Ariz. Bd. Regents, Flagstaff, 1992. Contbr. articles to profl. jours. mem. environ. task force Flagstaff C. of C., 1992—, chmn., 1993. Mem. Sigma Xi, Phi Beta Kappa. Home: 853 Parker Dr Flagstaff AZ 86001-8958 Office: No Ariz U Dept Chemistry PO Box 5698 Flagstaff AZ 86011

EASTMOND, DAVID ALBERT, environmental toxicology educator; b. Logan, Utah, Mar. 23, 1956; s. Jefferson Nicholls and Alberta (Van Wagoner) E.; m. Elizabeth Sessions, Aug. 11, 1989; stepchildren: C. Chad Anselmo, Matthew J. Anselmo, Barbara T. Anselmo, Peter R. Anselmo. BS in Zoology, Brigham Young U., 1980, MS in Entomology, 1983; PhD in Environ. Health Scis., U. Calif., Berkeley, 1987. Field technician Brigham Young U., Raft River, Idaho, 1978; field supr. Utah State U., Delta, 1979; rsch. asst. in environ. toxicology Brigham Young U., Provo, 1979-83; intern with Environ. Effects Br., Office Toxic Substances EPA, Washington, 1983; rsch. asst. biochem. toxicology U. Calif., Berkeley, 1983-87; Alexander Hollaender Disting. postdoctoral fellow Livermore Nat. Lab., Livermore, 1987-89; asst. rsch. toxicologist biomed. and environ. health scis. U. Calif., Berkeley, 1989; asst. then assoc. prof. environ. toxicology dept. entomology U. Calif., Riverside, 1990—; participant internat. program on chem. safety task group WHO, Carshalton Surrey, Eng., 1993; manuscript reviewer Environ. and Molecular Mutagenesis, Mutation Rsch., Mutagenesis, Toxicology and Applied Pharmacology, Chemico-Biol. Interactions, Internat. Jour. Radiation Biology, Cytometry, Cancer Rsch., Am. Jour. Human Genetics, 1987—; cons. on projects assessing potential of projects assessing the potential from human exposure to solvents and groundwater contaminants, 1985—. Contbr. articles to profl. jours.;, chpts. for conf. proceedings; mem. editl. bd. Mutation Rsch., 1994—. Recipient outstanding postdoctoral rsch. presentation award Genetic and Environ. Toxicology Assn. No. Calif., 1988; Alvin S. Barrett scholar Brigham Young U., 1974-75, 77-80. Mem. AAAS, Am. Chem. Soc., Soc. Toxicology (new investigator 1987), Environ. Mutagen Soc., Sigma Xi, Phi Kappa Phi. Office: U Calif Dept Entomology Riverside CA 92521

EASTON, ROBERT (OLNEY), author, environmentalist; b. July 4, 1915; s. Robert Eastman and Ethel (Olney) E.; m. Jane Faust, Sept. 24, 1940; children: Joan Easton Lentz, Katherine Easton Renga (dec.), Ellen Easton Brumfiel, Jane. Student, Stanford U., 1933-34, postgrad., 1938-39; BS, Harvard U., 1938; MA, U. Calif., Santa Barbara, 1960. Ranch hand, day laborer, mag. editor, 1939-42; co-pub., editor Lampasas (Tex.) Dispatch, 1946-50; instr. English Santa Barbara City Coll., 1959-65; writing and pub. cons. U.S. Naval Civil Engring. Lab., Port Hueneme, Calif., 1961-69. Author: The Happy Man, 1943, (with Mackenzie Brown) Lord of Beasts, 1961, (with Jay Monaghan and others) The Book of the American West, 1963, The Hearing, 1964, (with Dick Smith) California Condor: Vanishing American, 1964, Max Brand: The Big Westerner, 1970, Black Tide: The Santa Barbara Oil Spill and Its Consequences, 1972, Guns, Gold and Caravans, 1978, China Caravans: An American Adventurer in Old China, 1982, This Promised Land, 1982, Life and Work, 1988, Power and Glory, 1989, (with Jane Faust Easton) Love and War, 1991; editor: Max Brand's Best Stories, 1967, (with Mackenzie Brown) Bullying the Moqui, 1968, (with Jane Faust Easton) Max Brand's Best Poems, 1992, (with Jane Faust Easton) Max Brand: Collected Stories, 1994; contbr. to numerous mags. including Atlantic and N.Y. Times mag.; also anthologies including Great Tales of the American West. Co-chmn. Com. for Santa Barbara, 1973-81; trustee Santa Barbara Mus. Natural History, 1975-78, rsch. assoc., 1980-83; trustee Santa Barbara Community Environ. Coun., 1974-79; co-founder Sisquoc Sanctuary for Calif. Condor, 1937, also first wilderness area established under Nat. Wilderness Act, Los Padres Nat. Forest, Calif., 1968. Served to 1st lt. inf. U.S. Army, World War II. Recipient Honor award Calif. Conservation Coun., 1975. Home: 2222 Las Canoas Rd Santa Barbara CA 93105-2113

EASTON, ROGER DAVID, art history educator; b. Douglaston, N.Y., Jan. 4, 1923; s. Spencer Garnet and Ruth Natalie (Albright) E.; m. June Marcella Healy, Dec. 21, 1953. BS, SUNY, 1949; MA, State U. Iowa, 1951; EdD, U. Denver, 1958; postgrad., U. Rochester, Fogg Mus., Harvard U. Cert. tchr., N.Y., Colo. Fellow U. Iowa, Iowa City, 1950-51; instr. to assoc. prof. SUNY, Cortland, 1951-58; prof. Ball State U., Muncie, Ind., 1958-85, ret., 1985. One-man shows include S.W. Savs. and Loan, Green Valley, Ariz., 1989; exhibited in group shows at Smithsonian Instn. Crafts Invitational Nat. Traveling Exhibit, 1960-62, Ball State U. Art Gallery, 1977-80, 80-81, Sheldon Swope Art Gallery, Terre Haute, Ind., 1979-80, 83, Ft. Wayne Mus. Art, 1981-82, Tubac Ctr. of the Arts, 1989, 90, Santa Cruz Valley Art Assn., Tubac, Ariz., 1990, 93-95, Kessel-Long Gallery, Scottsdale, Ariz., 1990, So. Ariz. Watercolor Guild, 1991, 92-95, Ariz. Aqueous, 1992, 95, 97, So. Ariz. Art Guild, 1993, 95, 96, 97, Canoa Ctr. Exhbns., 1994-95, 96, Ariz. Watercolor Assn. Phoenix Exhbn., 1990-91, 94-95, 96, and numerous others; contbr. articles to profl. jours. Mem. Nat. Watercolor Soc., So. Ariz. Watercolor Guild, Santa Cruz Valley Art Assn., Ariz. Watercolor Assn., Nat. Art Edn. Assn., Ariz. Art Edn. Assn. Home: 3371 Placita Esconces Green Valley AZ 85614

EASTWOOD, SUSAN, medical scientific editor; b. Glens Falls, N.Y., Jan. 2, 1943; d. John J. and Della Eastwood; m. Raymond A. Berry. BA, U. Colo., 1964. Diplomate Bd. Editors in Life Scis. Adminstr. rsch. assoc. Depts. Psychol., Psychiat., Stanford (Calif.) U., 1965-68; prin., tchr. Colegio Capitan Correa, Arecibo, P.R., 1968-70; sr. editor dept. lab. medicine U. Calif., San Francisco, 1971-77, prin. analyst sci. publs. dept. neurol. surgery and Brain Tumor Rsch. Ctr., 1977—; cons. March of Dimes Calif. Birth Defects Monitoring Program, Emeryville, 1988—; mem. CONSORT group, QUOROM group and coord. Asilomar Working Group on recommendations for reporting clinical trials and meta-analysis, 1993-97. Collaborating editor: Current Neurosurgical Practice, 1984-91, Brain tumor biology and therapy, 1984; editor: Brain Tumors: A Guide, 1992; author: Guidelines on Research Data and Manuscripts, 1989. Recipient Pres. award Am. Med. Writers Assn., Bethesda, Md., 1989, Chancellors Outstanding Achievement award U. Calif., San Francisco, 1989, 94, Cert. of award Nat. Brain Tumor Found., 1992, Am. Soc. Journalists and Authors, 1992. Fellow Am. Med. Writers Assn.; mem. European Assn. Sci. Editors, Internat. Fedn. Sci. Editors, N.Y. Acad. Scis., Coun. Biology Editors (v.p. 1995-96, pres. 1996-97). Office: U Calif Dept Neurosurgery M-787 Box 0112 505 Parnassus Ave San Francisco CA 94143-0112

EATON, DAVID E., city administrator; b. Laconia, N.H., July 15, 1959; s. David Elwell and Doris Aileen (VanBlaricum) E.; m. Judy Kuen Toy, Nov. 21, 1980; children; Meagan Mei-Lai, Nathaniel David. BA, Sangamon State U., 1982; MA, Claremont Coll., 1986. Ordained priest Soto-Zen Buddhist Ch.; lic. real estate broker, Calif. Cmty. outreach worker, caseworker Salvation Army and United Meth. Ministries, Chgo., 1977-82; youth edn. dir. Presbyn. Ch. USA, L.A., 1983-87; mil. intelligence specialist U.S. Dept. Def., 1987; mktg. rep. Anheuser Busch & Adolph Coors, L.A., 1988-90; acctg. tech. Fed. Civil Svc., DOD, L.A., 1990-93; priest, psychotherapist Shoshinkai Fellowship, Phoenix, 1993; job developer, caseworker II dislocated workers program dept. human svcs. City of Phoenix, 1994—; early head start site mgr. S.W. Human Devel. Corp., City of Phoenix, 1996—; chaplain, addictions counselor Chandler (Ariz.) Valley Hope Drug & Alcohol Treatment Ctr. Contbr. articles to profl. jours. Active Chinatown 10K Com., L.A., 1992, Chinese-Am. Citizens' League, Phoenix, 1993-94, Japan-Am. Citizens League, Phoenix, 1993; cons. child protective svcs. field investigations of child abuse. Recipient Citizens Svc. to Local Cmty. award Castelar Elem. Sch., 1991. Mem. ACA, Am. Mental-Health Counseling Assn., Nat. Employment Counselor Assn., Nat. Employment and Tng. Profl. Assn., Constructive Living Assn. Democrat. Home: 18836 N 15th St Phoenix AZ 85024-8200 Office: S W Human Devel Corp Dislocated Workers Program 202 E Earll Dr Ste 140 Phoenix AZ 85012-2636

EATON, EDGAR EUGENE, educator, writer; b. Kline, Colo., Nov. 9, 1934; s. Randy Biggs Eaton and Merle Lamar (Behrmann) Mathews; m. Clayta Bernice Hathaway, Dec. 3, 1954; children: Steven, Elizabeth, Robert, Jennifer. BS, Ricks Coll., 1956; MA, U. Wash., 1964, So. Ill. U., 1970. Reporter Standard-Jour., Rexburg, Idaho, 1956; sports editor Evening Observer, LaGrande, Oreg., 1956, Post-Register, Idaho Falls, Idaho, 1957; tchr. Sugar-Salem H.S., Sugar City, Idaho, 1957-59, Centralia (Wash.) Coll., 1960-65, Green River C.C., Auburn, Wash., 1965-97; reporter, editor Valley Daily News, Kent, Wash., summers 1965-85. Author: Linemen Don't Score Touchdowns, 1984, Strike Two, 1994; playwright (one-act plays) Kissing Bandit Plus Four, 1996, (three-act play) Ginny, Kate, and Lady Di. Chair Auburn Planning Commn., 1996—. Mormon. Home: 1313 F St SE Auburn WA 98002 Office: Green River CC 12401 SE 320th St Auburn WA 98092-3622

EATON, GARETH RICHARD, chemistry educator, university dean; b. Lockport, N.Y., Nov. 3, 1940; s. Mark Dutcher and Ruth Emma (Ruston) E.; m. Sandra Shaw, Mar. 29, 1969. BA, Harvard U., 1962; PhD, MIT, 1972. Asst. prof. chemistry U. Denver, 1972-76, assoc. prof., 1976-80, prof., 1980—, dean natural scis., 1984-88, vice provost for rsch., 1988-89; organizer annual Internat. Electron-Paramagnetic Resonance Symposium. Author, editor 2 books; mem. editorial bd. 4 jours.; contbr. articles to profl. jours. Served to lt. USN, 1962-67. Mem. AAAS, Am. Chem. Soc., Royal Soc. Chemistry (London), Internat. Soc. Magnetic Resonance, Soc. Applied Spectroscopy, Am. Phys. Soc., Internat. Electron Paramagnetic Resonance Soc. Office: U Denver Dept Chemistry Denver CO 80208

EATON, GEORGE WESLEY, JR., petroleum engineer, oil company executive; b. Searcy, Ark., Aug. 3, 1924; s. George Wesley and Inez (Roberson) E.; m. Adriana Amin, Oct. 28, 1971; 1 child, Andrew. BS in Petroleum Engring., U. Okla., 1948. Registered profl. engr. Tex., N.Mex. Petroleum engr. Amoco, Longview, Ft. Worth, Tex., 1948-54; engring. supr. Amoco, Roswell, N.Mex., 1954-59; dist. engr. Amoco, Farmington, N.Mex., 1959-70; constrn. mgr. Amoco Egypt Oil Co., Cairo, 1970-81; ops. mgr. Amoco Norway Oil Co., Stavanger, 1981-84; petroleum cons. G.W. Eaton Cons., Albuquerque, 1984-94; adj. prof. San Juan Coll., Farmington, 1968-70. Bd. dirs. Paradise Hills Civic Assn., Albuquerque, 1986-89; elder Rio Grande Presbyn. Ch., Albuquerque, 1987-90; mem. Rep. Nat. Com., Washington, 1986-92. Mem. N.Mex. Soc. Profl. Engrs. (bd. dirs. 1967-70), Soc. Petroleum Engr. (sr.), Egyptian Soc. Petroleum Engrs. (chmn. 1980-81). Home: 5116 Russell Dr NW Albuquerque NM 87114-4325

EATON, MARYBETH BRENDON, interior designer; b. Landstuhl, Germany, Aug. 29, 1953; came to U.S., 1954; d. Robert Kendall and Mary Elizabeth (O'Connell) Garrabrant; m. Glenn K. Eaton, Aug. 29, 1975. AA, Truckee Meadows C.C., 1991; BS, U. Nev., 1993. Interior designer Mildred Reis Interiors, Sacramento, 1994-95, Habitats Design Studio, Cameron Park, Calif., 1995—, Eaton Design Concepts, Placerville, Calif., 1995—. Mem. Am. Soc. Interior Design, Nat. Trust History Preservation, Golden Key Honor Soc. Home: 5015 Thunderhead Court Placerville CA 95667

EATON, PAULINE, artist; b. Neptune, N.J., Mar. 20, 1935; d. Paul A. and Florence Elizabeth (Rogers) Friedrich; m. Charles Adams Eaton, June 15, 1957; children: Gregory, Eric, Paul, Joy. BA, Dickinson Coll., 1957; MA, Northwestern U., 1958. Lic. instr., Calif. Instr., Mira Costa Coll., Oceanside, Calif., 1980-82, Idyllwild Sch. Music and Arts, Calif., 1983—; juror, demonstrator numerous art socs. Recipient award Haywood (Calif.) Area Forum for the Arts, 1986. Exhibited one-woman shows Nat. Arts Club, N.Y.C., 1977, Designs Recycled Gallery, Fullerton, Calif., 1978, 80, 84, San Diego Art Inst., 1980, Spectrum Gallery, San Diego, 1981, San Diego Jung Ctr., 1983, Marin Civic Ctr. Gallery, 1984, R. Mondavi Winery, 1987; group shows include Am. Watercolor Soc., 1975, 77, Butler Inst. Am. Art, Youngstown, Ohio, 1977, 78, 79, 81, NAD, 1978, N.Mex. Arts and Crafts Fair, (Best in Show award) 1994, Corrales Bosque Gallery; represented in permanent collections including Butler Inst. Am. Art, St. Mary's Coll., Md., Mercy Hosp., San Diego, Sharp Hosp., San Diego, Redlands Hosp., Riverside, 1986; work featured in books: Watercolor, The Creative Experience, 1978, Creative Seascape Painting, 1980, Painting the Spirit in Nature, 1984, Exploring Painting (Gerald Brommer); author: Crawling to the Light, An Artist in Transition, 1987. Trustee San Diego Art Inst., 1977-78, San Diego Mus. Art, 1982-83. Recipient Best of Show award N.Mex. Arts and Crafts Fair, 1994, Grumbacher award Conf. 96 Hill Country Art Ctr. Mem. Nat. Watercolor Soc. (exhibited traveling shows 1978, 79, 83, 85), Rocky Mountain Watermedia Soc. (Golden award 1979, Mustard Seed award 1983), Nat. Soc. Painters in Acrylic and Casein (hon.), Watercolor West (Strathmore award 1979, Purchase award 1986), Soc. Experimental Artists (pres. 1989-92, Nautilus Merit award 1992), Marin Arts Guild (instr. 1984-87), San Diego Watercolor Soc. (pres. 1976-77, workshop dir. 1977-80), Artists Equity (v.p. San Diego 1979-81), San Diego Artists Guild (pres. 1982-83), N.Mes. Watercolor Soc. (Grumbacher award), Western Fedn. Watercolor Socs. (chmn. 1983, 3d prize 1982, Grumbacher Gold medal 1983), West Coast Watercolor Soc. (exhbns. chmn. 1983-86, pres. 1989-92), Eastbay Watercolor Soc. (v.p. 1988-90), Soc. Layerists in Multi-Media (bd. dirs. 1992—), Corrales Bosque Gallery (charter mem., pres. 1996). Democrat. Home: 68 Hop Tree Trl Corrales NM 87048-9613

EATON, RICHARD MAXWELL, history educator; b. Grand Rapids, Mich., Dec. 8, 1940; s. Robert Menzo and Miriam (Adams) E. BA, Coll. Wooster, 1962; MA, U. Va., 1967, U. Wis., 1968; PhD, U. Wis., 1972. Asst. prof. history U. Ariz., Tucson, 1972-78, assoc. prof., 1978-94, prof., 1994—. Author: Sufis of Bijapur, 1978, The Rise of Islam and The Bengal Frontier, 1993. Mem. Assn. Asian Studies, Mid. East Studies Assn. Office: Univ Ariz Dept History Tucson AZ 85721

EAVES, SALLY ANN, logistics specialist, research administrator; b. Salt Lake City, Feb. 25, 1945; d. Frank C. and Magdalene (Buller) Winslow; m. Stephen Douglas Eaves, Apr. 27, 1974; children: Trevor Bernard, Lindsay Douglas, Christrian Francis. BA in English, Gonzaga U., 1967; postgrad., Utah State U., 1980, U. So. Calif., 1985. Individual mobilization asst. to dir. of logistics U.S. Forces Korea, 1983-87; individual mobilization asst. to chief of transp., dir. distbn., dir. commodities Ogden (Utah) Air Logistics Ctr., 1987-93; individual mobilization asst. to dir. logistics N.Am. Aerospace Def. Command and U.S. Space Command, Peterson AFB, Colo., 1993-95; mobilization asst. to commdr. Okla. Air Logistics Ctr., Oklahoma City, 1995—; v.p. N.W. Rsch. Inst., Las Vegas, 1996—. V.p., bd. dirs. The Pond Homeowners Assn., Arvada, Colo., 1992-95; ednl./comty. vol. Jeffco Pub. Schs., 1992-95; ch. vol. Spirit of Christ Cath. Ch., Arvada, 1989—; career devel. counselor Adams County Sch. Dist. 50, Westminster, Colo., 1989—. Col. USAFR, 1967—. Decorated Def. Meritorious Svc. medal, Meritorious Svc. medal, Air Force Achievement medal with 1 oak leaf cluster. Mem. Nat. Def. Transp. Assn., Soc. Logistics Engrs., Air Force Assn., Res. Officers Assn. (v.p. Okla. chpt. 1996—). Home: 8708 Independence Way Arvada CO 80005

EAVES, STEPHEN DOUGLAS, educator, vocational administrator; b. Honolulu, Aug. 30, 1944; s. Alfred Aldee and Phyllis Clarissa (Esty) E.; m. Sally Ann Winslow, Apr. 27, 1974; children: Trevor Bernard, Lindsay Douglas, Christian Francis. BA in Polit. Sci., U. Hawaii, 1967; MS in Bus. Mgmt., U. Ark., 1974; PhD in Edn. Adminstrn., Colo. State U., 1997. Cert. secondary tchr., prin., vocat. dir., post secondary bus. tchr., Colo. Commd. 2d lt. USAF, 1967, advanced through grades to lt. col., ret., 1989; aerospace sci. tchr. Adams County Sch. Dist. 50, Westminster, Colo., 1989-94, vocat. dir./asst. prin., 1994—; cons. Dept. of Edn., Colo., 1993—. Eucharistic min. Spirit of Christ Cath. Ch., Arvada, Colo., 1989—. Decorated Silver Star, DFC, Air medals, Commendation medals, Air Force Achievement medal; named Outstanding Tchr. Focus on Excellence Program, 1992, Outstanding Nat. Aerospace Sci. Tchr., 1994. Mem. ASCD, Coun. for Exceptional Children, Am. Vocat. Assn., Colo. Vocat. Assn., Colo. Assn. Vocat. Adminstrs., Colo. Assn. Sch. Execs., Am. Nat. Rose Soc., Royal Nat. Rose Soc., Lions (sec. Adams Centennial chpt. 1991-92, Lion of Yr. 1992), Elks, Phi Delta Kappa, Omicron Tau Delta. Home: 8708 Independence Way Arvada CO 80005-1247 Office: Career Enrichment Park 7300 Lowell Blvd Westminster CO 80030-4821

EBBINGA, CRYSTALLE YVONNE, social services administrator; b. Wall, S.D., Jan. 23, 1936; d. Earl Benjamin and Josie Amanda (Lee) Adamson; m. Gerald Richard Ebbinga, June 3, 1961; children: Kurtis Herm, Spencer Kirk, Brittanee Leigh. MusB, MacPhail Coll. Music, Mpls., 1960. Tchr. elem. music Boyceville (Wis.) Consol., 1960-61; tchr. and music supr. St. Louis Park (Minn.) Elem. Sch., 1961-63, St. Croix Consol. Sch. Dist., Hammond and Roberts, Wis., 1963-66; substitute tchr. Prince Albert (Sask., Can.) Pub. Schs., 1979-80; parish asst. First Luth. Ch., Pomona, Calif., 1981-86; adminstrv. asst. LaVerne (Calif.) U., 1986-87; asst. to gen. dir. YMCA, Pomona, 1988-89; dir. Hill and Dale Child Devel. Ctr., Las Vegas, Nev., 1989-90; pres., CEO St. Thomas Child and Family Ctr., Great Falls, Mont., 1990—. Editor The Supporter newsletter, 1992-96. Chmn. agy. dirs. United Way, Great Falls, Mont., 1992-95; bd. dirs. Families Count, Great Falls, 1992-95; adv. bd. Families Self-Sufficiency (Great Falls Housing Authority). 1993—; lobbyist Mont. Child Care Assn., Helena, 1992; asst. chmn. Great Falls Community Needs Assessment Com., 1993-95; mem. steering com. Dept. Family Svcs. Project; mem. Leadership Great Falls, 1991. Mem. NAFE, Soc. for Non-Profit Orgn., Nat. Parent Aide, Mont. Coun. for Families, Healthy Mothers Healthy Babies, Great Falls Advt. Club. Home: 6 Meadowlark Rdg Great Falls MT 59405-5532 Office: Saint Thomas Child & Family Ct 416 23rd St N Great Falls MT 59401-2847

EBEL, DAVID M., federal judge; b. 1940. BA, Northwestern U., 1962; JD, U. Mich., 1965. Law clk. assoc. justice Byron White U.S. Supreme Ct., 1965-66; pvt. practice Davis, Graham & Stubbs, Denver, 1966-88; judge U.S. Ct. Appeals (10th cir.), Denver, 1988—; adj. prof. law U. Denver Law Sch., 1987-89; sr. lectr. fellow Duke U. Sch. Law, 1992-94. Mem. Am. Coll. Trial Lawyers, Colo. Bar Assn. (v.p. 1982), Jud. Conf. U.S. (com. on codes of conduct 1991—, co-chair 10th cir. gender bias task force 1994—). Office: US Ct Appeals 1823 Stout St Rm 109L Denver CO 80257-1823

EBER, KEVIN, science writer; b. Cleve., Aug. 14, 1958; s. Julius Louis and Winifred Ann (Hanf) E. BSChemE, Case Western Res. U., 1980; MA in Journalism, U. Colo., Boulder, 1990. Engr. Westinghouse Naval Reactors Facility/Idaho Nat. Engring Lab., Idaho Falls, 1980-82, Northeast Utilities, Berlin, Conn., 1982-87; tech. writer Stoller Corp., Boulder, 1988-89; sci. writer Brookhaven Nat. Lab., Upton, N.Y., 1989; journalism intern Boulder Daily Camera, 1990; sci. writer Nat. Renewable Energy Lab., Golden, Colo.,

1991—. Asst. editor: Advances in Solar Energy, vol. 7, 1992; author, project leader various brochures on energy sources. Mem. Nat. Assn. Sci. Writers. Office: Nat Renewable Energy Lab 1617 Cole Blvd Golden CO 80401-3305

EBER, MARILYN LOUISE, real estate investor; b. Denver, Colo.; d. Sam and Rose (Kaminsky) Rollnick; m. Fred Silverberg (dec.) children: Judie, Sam; m. Alan Eber (div.); 1 child, Jennifer. BA, Denver U. Docent Denver Art Mus., Mus. Natural Hist.; Native arts specialist and advisor for 30 years; real estate investor, 1962—; study group adviser Denver Mus. of Natural History. Pres. Project Madison; trustee Mizel Mus. Judaica, 1991—. Named Scholar of Yr. Denver Art Mus., 1991. Mem. LWV, Douglas Soc. (pres.). Democrat. Jewish. Home and Office: 432 Madison St Denver CO 80206

EBERHART, DAVID L., state legislator. Mem., majority whip dist. 19 Ariz. Ho. of Reps., Phoenix, 1994—; mem. environment, govt. ops., and rules coms. Republican. Office: Ariz Ho of Reps 1700 W Washington Phoenix AZ 85002

EBERHART, ERIKA LEE, government agency official; b. St. Louis, July 14, 1970; d. Ralph Edward and Karen Sue (Gies) E. BS in Mktg., Clemson U., 1992. Contract specialist Air Force Office Sci. Rsch., Washington, 1993-96, NH. Guard Bur. Environ. Orgn., Falls Church, Va., 1996; contracting officer Hickam AFB, Hawaii, 1996—; owner Penguin Parade, Arlington, Va., 1994-96. Mem. Nat. Contract Mgmt. Assn., Beta Gamma Sigma. Home: 425 South St # 3102 Honolulu HI 96813

EBERL, PATRICIA JO, professional society administrator, editor; b. Cleve., May 26, 1947; d. David Reidinger and Peggy L. (Laughlin) Buschman; m. Dennis D. Eberl, Mar. 7, 1970; children: Karuna Sky, Lucas Elliot. Student, Conn. Coll. for Women, 1965-67; BA, Case Western Reserve U., 1970; postgrad., U. Colo., Denver, 1983, U. Colo., Boulder, 1993-94. ESL tchr. Jefferson County Sch. Dist., Evergreen, Lakewood, Colo., 1983-85; free lance editor Evergreen, 1986-89; mgr./editor Clay Minerals Soc., Boulder, Colo., 1989—; editl. intern Human Rights Info. Ctr. of Coun. of Europe, Strasbourg, France, 1992. Editor: The Third Sector, 1982-83, The Hardware's Mountain Handbook, 1989, (quar. publ.) CMS News, 1989—. County coord. fgn. langs. in elem. schs., Jefferson County Schs., Lakewood, 1982-85; with edn./publicity divsn. Global Response, Boulder, 1991-93; prodn. editor, advocate Boulder Action for Soviet Jewry, 1991—; vol. Am. Indian Sci. & Engring. Soc., Boulder, 1993; mem./sponsor Colo. Friends of Tibet; mem. Native Am. Rights Fund. Office: Clay Minerals Soc PO Box 4416 Boulder CO 80306

EBERLE, MICHAEL LEE, air force officer; b. Evanston, Ill., Sept. 24, 1955; s. Marcus Herbert and E. Louise (Wilkins) E.; m. Karen Ann Straight, Aug. 12, 1978; children: Ernest James, Matthew Jonathan, Janet Christine. BS in Aero. Engring., USAF Acad., 1977; MS in Aero. and Astronautics, U. Wash., 1978. Registered profl. engr., Va.; lic. single and multi engine comml. pilot. Commd. 2d lt. USAF, 1977—, advanced through grades to lt. col., 1993; student pilot 82d Flying Tng. Wing, Williams AFB, Ariz., 1978-79, T-38 instr. pilot/acad. instr., 1979-82; instructional program developer 3305 Sch. Squadron, Randolph AFB, Tex., 1982-84; asst. prof. dept. mechanics U.S. Mil. Acad., West Point, N.Y., 1984-87; flight comdr./chief acads. 47th Flying Tng. Wing, Laughlin AFB, Tex., 1987-89; comdr. companion trainer program detachment 43d Air Refueling Wing, Malmstrom, Mont., 1989-92; chief companion trainer program sect. 15th Air Force, Travis AFB, Calif., 1992-95, chief operational support airlift/aeromed. evaluation sect., 1995—. Contbr. articles to profl. jours. Coach N.E. Youth Soccer Assn., San Antonio, 1983; referee Laughlin-Del Rio Soccer Assn., 1987-88; mem. Civairs, Great Falls, Mont., 1989-92. NSF fellow, 1977-78. Mem. AIAA (sr.), Air Force Assn., USAF Acad. Assn. Grads., Order of Daedalians. Home: 114 Bradley Blvd Travis AFB CA 94535-1341

EBERSOLE, PRISCILLA PIER, mental health nurse, geriatrics nurse; b. Salem, Oreg., Aug. 17, 1928; d. Joseph H. and Miriam E. (Holder) Pierre; m. Raymond V. Ebersole, May 14, 1948; children: Lorraine, Raymond, Randolph, Elisabeth. AA, Coll. San Mateo, 1965; BS, San Francisco State U., 1971; MS, U. Calif., San Francisco, 1973; PhD, Columbia Pacific U., 1986. RN, Calif.; BRN; VSC. Instr. Chabot Coll., Hayward, Calif., 1973, U. So. Calif., L.A., 1977-80; prof. nursing San Francisco State U., 1973-95; vis. prof. Cellar Endowed Chair in Gerontology Case Western Res. U., Cleve. 1988. Editor Geriatric Nursing Jour. Named Alumni of Yr. San Francisco State U., 1987. Mem. ANA, ASA, GSA, AGHE, WIN. Home: 2790 Rollingwood Dr San Bruno CA 94066-2610

EBERWEIN, BARTON DOUGLAS, construction company executive, consultant; b. Balt., Aug. 19, 1951; s. Bruce George and Thelma Joyce (Cox) E. BS, U. Oreg., 1974, MBA, 1988. Sales mgr. Teleprompter of Oreg., Eugene, 1974-75; pres., owner Oreg. Images, Eugene, 1975-80; mktg. mgr. Clearwater Prodns., Eugene, 1980-82; sales mgr. Western Wood Structures, Portland, Oreg., 1982-84, mktg. coordinator, 1984-85, mktg. dir., 1985-89; dir. bus. devel. Hoffman Constrn. Co., Portland, 1989-93, v.p., 1993—. Bd. dirs. N.W. Youth Corps, Eugene, 1984—, Police Activity League, 1991, Portland Arts and Lectrs., 1994—; vol. bd. dirs. Goodwill, Oreg. Symphony. Mem. Soc. Mktg. Profl. Svcs., Am. Mktg. Assn., Univ. Club, Founders Club, Riverplace Athletic Club. Democrat. Presbyterian. Home: 5639 SW Menefee Dr Portland OR 97201-2781 Office: Hoffman Constrn Co 1300 SW 6th Ave Portland OR 97201-3464

EBI, KRISTIE LEE, epidemiologist, consultant; b. Detroit, Nov. 17, 1950; d. Albert R. and Dorothy (Wicen) Ebi; 1 child, Katherine M. Kryston. MS, MIT, 1977; MPH, U. Mich., 1983, PhD, 1985. Biochem. rsch. asst. Upjohn Co., Kalamazoo, 1973-74; toxicologist Equitable Environ. Health, Inc., Rockville, Md., 1977-78; indsl. toxicologist GM, Detroit, 1978-81; rsch. fellow London Sch. Hygiene and Tropical Medicine, 1985-87; rsch. asst. Med. Coll. of St. Bartholomew's Hosp., London, 1988-90; sr. scientist Failure Analysis Assocs., Inc., Menlo Park, Calif., 1990-93; mgr. Electric Power Rsch. Inst., Palo Alto, Calif., 1993—. Contbr. articles to sci. jours. Mem. Am. Coll. Epidemiology, Soc. for Epidemiologic Rsch., Internat. Epidemiologic Assn., Soc. Toxicology (assoc.), Mortar Bd. Office: EMF Health Studies Program Electric Power Rsch Inst 3412 Hillview Ave Palo Alto CA 94304-1395

EBY, MICHAEL JOHN, marketing research and technology consultant; b. South Bend, Ind., Aug. 3, 1949; s. Robert T. and Eileen Patricia (Holmes) E.; m. Judith Alyson Gaskell, May 17, 1980; children: Elizabeth, Katherine. Student, Harvey Mudd Coll., 1969-70; BS in Biochemistry with high honors, U. Md., 1972, MS in Chemistry, 1977; postgrad., IMEDE, Lausanne, Switzerland, 1984. Product mgr. LKB Instruments Inc., Rockville, Md., 1976-79; mktg. mgr. LKB-Produkter AB, Bromma, Sweden, 1979-87; strategic planning mgr. Pharmacia LKB Biotech. AB, Bromma, 1987-88; dir. mktg. Am. Bionetics, Hayward, Calif., 1988-89; pres. PhorTech Internat., San Carlos, Calif., 1989—. Author: The Electrophoresis Explosion, 1988, Electrophoresis in the Nineties, 1990, DNA Amplification, 1993, DNA Sequencing, 1993, Blotting and Hybridization, 1993, Densitometers and Image Analysis, 1993, Capillary Electrophoresis, 1993, HPLC in the Life Sciences, 1994, Molecular Biology Reagent Systems, 1994, Global Laboratory Product Usage, 1994, 96, Microplate Equipment, 1995, Synthetic Oligonucleotides, 1995, Electrophoretic Gel Media, 1995, Visualization Reagents, 1995, U.S. Laboratory Product Usage, 1996, Cell Biology Reagent Systems, 1996, Centrifugation, 1996, Worldwide Directory of Life Science Distributors, 1997, DNA Diagnostics, 1997; contbr. articles to profl. jours. Mem. AAAS, European Soc. Opinion and Mktg. Rsch., Am. Chem. Soc., Am. Soc. Cell Biology, The Electrophoresis Soc., Internat. Electrophoresis Soc., Spirit of LKB Internat. Assn., U. Md. Alumni Assn., Am. Mensa Ltd., Calif. Separation Sci. Soc., N.Y. Acad. Sci. Episcopalian. Office: PhorTech Internat 238 Crestview Dr San Carlos CA 94070-1503

ECCLES, MATTHEW ALAN, golf course and landscape architect; b. Ft. Dodge, Iowa, Apr. 19, 1956; s. Guy Eldon Jr. and Mary Ellen (Baldwin) E.; m. Debra Kay Sorenson, Mar. 19, 1983; children: Stephanie Ann, Jason Alan. BS in Landscape Architecture, Iowa State U., 1978. Registered landscape architect, Kans., Minn. From project mgr. to dir. golf course design THK Assocs., Inc., Greenwood Village, Colo., 1980-94; pres. Eccles Design Inc., Englewood, Colo., 1994—. Mem. Am. Soc. Landscape Architects, U.S. Golf Assn., Golf Course Supts. Assn. Am., Nat. Golf Found., Nat. Ski Patrol, Tau Sigma Delta. Home: 8120 S Monaco Cir Englewood CO 80112-3022 Office: Eccles Design Inc 8120 S Monaco Cir Englewood CO 80112-3022

ECCLES, SPENCER FOX, banker; b. Ogden, Utah, Aug. 24, 1934; s. Spencer Stoddard and Hope (Fox) E.; m. Cleone Emily Peterson, July 21, 1958; children: Clista Hope, Lisa Ellen, Katherine Ann, Spencer Peterson. B.S., U. Utah, 1956; M.A., Columbia U., 1959; degree in Bus. (hon.), So. Utah State Coll., 1982; LLB (hon.), Westminster Coll., Salt Lake City, 1986. Trainee First Nat. City Bank, N.Y.C., 1959-60; with First Security Bank of Utah, Salt Lake City, 1960-61, First Security Bank of Idaho, Boise, 1961-70; exec. v.p. First Security Corp. Salt Lake City, 1970-75, pres., 1975-86, chief operating officer, 1980-82, chmn. bd. dirs., chief exec. officer, 1982—; dir. Union Pacific Corp., Anderson Lumber Co., Zions Corp., Merc. Instn.; mem. adv. council U. Utah Bus. Coll. Served to 1st lt. U.S. Army. Recipient Pres.'s Circle award Presdl. Commn., 1984, Minuteman award Utah N.G., 1988; Named Disting. Alumni U. Utah, 1988. Mem. Am. Bankers Assn., Bankers Roundtable, Salt Lake Country Club, Alta Club. Office: 1st Security Corp PO Box 30006 79 S Main St Salt Lake City UT 84130

ECKARD, ROY CONRAD (CONNIE ECKARD), communications consultant, writer, editor; b. Fulton, N.Y., Dec. 25, 1933; s. Frank Brewer and Rachel Hester (Warner) E.; m. Betty Joyce Deaux, May 29, 1957 (div. 1974); children: Andrea Lea, Charles Kevin, Steven Deaux; m. Patricia Herold Brown, Apr. 21, 1975 (div. 1986); m. Donna Irene Wolf, Aug. 8, 1988; children: Shirley Ann Wolf, Debra Sue Wolf. BA in English and Journalism, A&M Coll. Tex., 1957; postgrad., Tex. A&M U., 1968-70; PhD in Comm. Mgmt., Pacific Western U., L.A., 1985; PhD (hon.), Clayton U., 1983; LLD (hon.), Pacific States U., 1986. Advt. staff Seguim Enterprise, Tex., 1957, Arlington Citizen Journal, Tex., 1958-59; sports editor Pasadena Citzen, Tex., 1959-60, Houston Post, Tex., 1960-63; internal comm. mgr. Tex. Instruments Inc., Dallas, 1963-68; dir. publs. Assn. Former Students, College Station, Tex., 1968-71; publs. coord. Skelly Oil Co., Tulsa, 1971-77; publs. editor Getty Refining and Mktg. Co., Tulsa, 1977-80; spl. comm. mgr. Atlantic Richfield Co., L.A., 1980-84; exec. prin. The Communicationist, L.A., 1984-85; employee comm. specialist Aircraft divsn. Northrop Corp., Hawthorne, Calif., 1985-86; sr. mgmt. systems analyst Electro-Mech. divsn. Northrop Corp., Anaheim, Calif., 1986-88; mgr. employee comm. LTV Corp., Dallas, 1988-91; v.p. Editorial Svcs., Dallas, 1991-92; mgmt. comm. specialist Westinghouse Hanford Co., Richland, Wash., 1992-93; sr. staff asst. ICF Kaiser Hanford Co., Richland, 1993-96; mgr. internal/external commn. DynCorp Tri-Cities Svcs., Inc., Richland, 1996-97; mng. editor Homesick Texan, 1991-93. Editor-in-residence Ball State U., Muncie, 1979; contbr. articles to profl. publs.; contbg. editor Comm. Illustrated, 1984-86. Mem. pub. rels. com. Hanford 50th Anniversary, Richland, 1993-94; mem. corps. devel. coun. Tex. A&M U., College Station, 1989—; chair ROTC adv. coun. Calif. State U.-Long Beach, 1986-88; mem. admissions adv. panel USAF Acad., Colorado Springs, 1984-87; singer gospel, recovery No Half Measures, Richland, 1993—; performer Richard Players, 1994—; softball player Columbia Basin A&M Club, Richland, 1992—; allocation rev. team Tri-Cities Corp. Coun. for Arts, Richland, 1995—; mem. Congl. Mil. Acad. Selection Com., 1995—. Col. USAFR, 1957-89. Named Nat. Admissions Liaison Officer of Yr., USAF Acad./Air Force ROTC, Colorado Springs, 1987, Calif. Air Force Res. Officer of Yr., 1987; recipient Dist. Tech. Comm. award Soc. Tech. Comm., Dallas, 1992, Matrix award Women in Comm., Inc., Dallas, 1992. Mem. Internat. Assn. Bus. Communicators (accredited, v.p. fin. 1973-75, dist.-at-large rep. 1994-96, Gold Quill award 1972, 75, 79, 81, 82, Chmn.'s award 1990), Tulsa/Dallas chpt. Internat. Assn. Bus. Communicators (life, treas. Dallas 1966, pres. Tulsa 1979, numerous awards 1965-93), Soc. Profl. Journalists (chair various coms. 1967, 83, 96), Women in Comm., Inc. (pres. Mid-Columbia chpt. 1996—), Air Force Assn. (life, v.p. edn. L.A. chpt. 1984-88, Merit award 1985), Res. Officers Assn. (life, v.p. Air Force Tulsa 1979-80). Republican. Mem. Christian Ch. Home: 1321 Perkins Ave Richland WA 99352-3106 Office: DynCorp Tri-Cities Svcs Inc PO Box 1400 Richland WA 99352-1400

ECKELMAN, RICHARD JOEL, engineering specialist; b. Bklyn., Mar. 25, 1951; s. Leon and Muriel (Brietbart) E.; m. Janet Louise Fenton, Mar. 21, 1978; children: Christie, Melanie, Erin Leigh. Student, Ariz. State U., 1988—. Sr. engr., group leader nondestructive testing Engring. Fluor Corp., Irvine, Calif., 1979-83; sr. engr. nondestructive testing McDonnell Douglas Helicopter Co., Mesa, Ariz., 1983-91; engring. specialist Convair div. Gen. Dynamics, San Diego, 1991-94; sr. tech. specialist McDonnell Douglas Techs., Inc., San Diego, 1994-96; engr. McDonnell-Douglas, Mesa, Ariz., 1996—. Mem. Am. Soc. Nondestructive Testing (nat. aerospace com. 1987—, sec. Ariz. chpt. 1987-88, treas. 1988—, sect. chmn. 1989—, sect. bd. dirs. 1990-91), Am. Soc. Quality Control, Soc. Mfg. Engrs., Porsche Owners Club Am., Lindbergh Yacht Club. Home: 11604 N 110th Pl Scottsdale AZ 85259

ECKERSLEY, DENNIS LEE, professional baseball player; b. Oakland, Calif., Oct. 3, 1954; m. Nancy O'Neill; 1 child, Mandee. Baseball player Cleve. Indians, 1972-78, Boston Red Sox, 1978-84, Chgo. Cubs, 1984-87, Oakland A's, 1987-95, St. Louis Cardinals, 1996—. Recipient Cy Young award Baseball Writers Assn. Am., 1992, named MVP, 1992; mem. Am. League All-Star Team, 1977, 82, 88, 90-92; named A.L. Fireman of Yr. The Sporting News, 1988, 91, 92, Am. League Rookie Pitcher of Yr., 1975; pitched no-hit game, 1977. Office: St Louis Cardinals 250 Stadium Plz Saint Louis MO 63102

ECKERSLEY, NORMAN CHADWICK, banker; b. Glasgow, Scotland, June 18, 1924; came to U.S., 1969; s. James Norman and Beatrice (Chadwick) E.; m. Rosemary J. Peters, May 23, 1986, 1 child, Anne. D Laws Strathclyde U., Scotland. With Chartered Bank, London and Manchester, 1947-48; acct., Bombay, 1948-52, Singapore, 1952-54, Sarawak, 1954-56, Pakistan, 1956-58, Calcutta, 1958-59, Hong Kong, 1959-60, asst. mgr. Hamburg, 1960-62, mgr. Calcutta, 1962-67, Thailand, 1967-69; pres. Chartered Bank London, San Francisco, 1964-74, chmn., chief exec., 1974-79; chmn. Standard Chartered Bancorp, 1978-81; dep. chmn. Union Bank, L.A., 1979-82; chmn., CEO The Pacific Bank, San Francisco, 1982-93, chmn. emeritus, 1993; chmn. Diners Club (Asia), 1967-69, Devel. Bank Thailand, 1967-69, Scottish Am. Investment Com., U. Strathclyde Found.; chmn., CEO Balmoral Capital Corp., 1994—; chmn. Balmoral Fin. Corp., 1995—. With RAF, 1940-46. Decorated D.F.C.; Comdr. Order Brit. Empire. Mem. Overseas Banks Assn. Calif. (chmn. 1972-74), Calif. Coun. Internat. Trade, San Francisco C. of C., World Trade Assn., Royal and Ancient Club, Royal Troon Golf Club (Scotland), World Trade Club, San Francisco Golf Club, Pacific Union Club (San Francisco). Mem. Ch. of Scotland. Home: 401 El Cerrito Ave Hillsborough CA 94010-6819 Office: 345 California St Fl 7 San Francisco CA 94104-2635

ECKERT, GERALDINE GONZALES, language professional, educator, entrepreneur; b. N.Y.C., Aug. 5, 1948; d. Albert and Mercedes (Martinez) Gonzales; m. Robert Alan Eckert, Apr. 1, 1972; children: Lauren Elaine, Alison Elizabeth. BA, Ladycliff Coll., Highland Falls, N.Y., 1970; student, U. Valencia, Spain, 1968; MA, N.Y.U., 1971; student, Instituto de Cultura Hispanica, Madrid, 1970-71. Tchr. Spanish Clarkstown High Sch. N. (N.Y.), 1971-73, Rambam Torah Inst., Beverly Hills, Calif., 1973-75; translator City of Beverly Hills, 1976-83; edn. cons. Los Angeles County of Calif. Dept. Forestry, Capistrano Beach, 1982-84; lang. services and protocol Los Angeles Olympic Organizing Com., 1983-84; pension adminstr. Pension Architects, Inc., Los Angeles, 1984-87; instr. El Camino Coll., Torrance, Calif., 1987-88, Santa Monica (Calif.) Coll., 1975—; owner, pres. Bilingual Pension Cons., L.A., 1987-89; bd. dirs. Institute for Hispanic Cultural Studies, Los Angeles; spl. asst. to Internat. Olympic Com., Lausanne, Switzerland, 1983—. V.p. Notre Dame Acad. Assoc., West L. A., 1987—; mem. L.A. March of Dimes Ambassadors Group, 1987; co-founder, pres. Blind Cleaning Express, L.A., 1989—; bd. dirs. Inst. Hispanic Cultural Studies, L.A., 1984-89; spl. asst. to pres. Internat. Olympic Com. Lausanne, Switzerland, 1983—. Democrat. Roman Catholic. Clubs: Five Ring, Los Angeles, Friends of Sport, Amateur Athletic Found., Los Angeles. Office: 8885 Venice Blvd Ste 103 Los Angeles CA 90034-3242

ECKERT, STEVEN PAUL, social services administrator; b. Boston, July 4, 1955; s. Arthur Frederick John and Audrey (Hill) E.; m. Janaki Elizabeth Tompkins, Aug. 30, 1987 (div. 1992). BA in Psychology, Lynchburg Coll., 1978; MSW, San Francisco State U., 1984. Lic. clin. social worker, Calif. Program specialist Youth Family Assistance, Redwood City, Calif., 1980-82; counseling intern Family Svc. Agy. San Francisco, 1983-84; family therapist North Peninsula Family Alternatives, South San Francisco, Calif., 1984—, JSO program coord., 1988-90, clin. coord., 1990-92, dir., 1992—; pvt. practice, San Bruno, Calif., 1988—; cons. San Quentin Prison, San Francisco, 1990-94; traffic violators instr. Pacific Seminars, 1986-88. Mem. NASW, Calif. Assn. Marriage and Family Therapists. Democrat. Office: 883 Sneath Ln # 117 San Bruno CA 94066-2412

ECKLES, PAUL DAVID, city manager; b. Whittier, Calif., Aug. 19, 1940; s. Paul Newton and Loretta May (Madison) E.; m. Donna Maria Arrigone, July 24, 1966; children: Paul Madison, Janice Marie. BA in Econs., Stanford U., 1962; MPA, Ill. Inst. Tech., 1970. Adminstrv. trainee Calif. Dept. Employment, Sacramento, 1963; adminstrv. analyst Calif. Dept. Gen. Svcs., Sacramento, 1964-66; mgmt. cons. Pub. Adminstrn. Svc., Chgo., 1966-73; asst. city mgr. City of Inglewood, Calif., 1973-75; city mgr. City of Inglewood, 1975-97; cons. L.A., 1997—. Bd. dirs. Cities in Schs., Inglewood, 1988—, St. Mary's Acad., Inglewood, 1989—; pres. Centinela Valley YMCA, Inglewood, 1984-85. Mem. Internat. City Mgmt. Assn.

ECKLUND, CARL DAVID, security services executive; b. La Mesa, Calif., Feb. 10, 1962; s. Carl and Joan Marie (Lewis) E.; m. Kathryn Yvonne Mellish, July 15, 1989. BS in Psychobiology, UCLA, 1985; MDiv, Biola U., 1990, ThM, 1992. Cmty. svc. officer UCLA Police Dept., 1980-85; field supr. Biola U. Security, La Mirada, Calif., 1986-93; police officer Cheney (Wash.) Police Dept., 1994, Sherwood (Oreg.) Police Dept., 1994-95; dir. security George Fox U., Newberg, Oreg., 1996—. Named to Nat. Police Officer's Hall of Fame, Fla., 1993. Mem. Internat. Assn. Campus Law Enforcement Adminstrs., Oreg. Peace Officers Assn. Republican. Quaker. Office: George Fox Univ 414 N Meridian Newberg OR 97132

ECKLUND, JUDITH LOUISE, academic administrator; b. Baton Rouge, June 14, 1946; d. Norman Carl and Laverne (Borg) E. BA, U. Calif., Davis, 1968; MA, Cornell U., 1971, PhD, 1977. Adminstr. U. Calif., Berkeley, 1971-72, Cornell U., Ithaca, N.Y., 1976-78; adminstr. Tulane U., New Orleans, 1980-90, v.p. devel. & alumni affairs, 1984-87, co-dir. internat. devel. ctr., 1987-90; dir. devel. The Carter Ctr., Atlanta, 1990-92; dir. internat. devel. UCLA, L.A., 1992—; mem. adv. coun. Cornell U., 1991—. Fellow Am. Anthropology Assn.; mem. Assn. Asian Studies. Office: UCLA Devel Office Ste 1400 10920 Wilshire Blvd Los Angeles CA 90024-6502

EDDLEMAN, JANIE ANN, nurse; b. Vincennes, Ind., Nov. 30, 1945; d. Bub and Mary Elizabeth (Halter) Holscher; m. James Lewis Eddleman, June 25, 1966 (dec. Oct. 1996); children: Lisa, Lynda, Daniel. Diploma in nursing, St. Mary's Sch. Nursing, 1966. RN, Calif. Staff nurse critical care Valley Meml. Hosp., Livermore, Calif., 1970-74, nurse computer analyst, 1985-90; recreation specialist Livermore Area Park & Recreation Dist., 1973-77; tchr., dir. Wee Care Nursery Sch., Livermore, 1977-85, owner, 1977—; cancer care coord. Valley Health Sys., Livermore, 1990—. Bd. dirs. Hope Hospice, Dublin, Calif., 1991-94, pres., 1995—. Mem. Oncology Nursing Soc. (editor patient edn. spl. interest group 1995—, pres. Calif. East Bay chpt. 1994-95). Roman Catholic. Home: 2155 Westbrook Ln Livermore CA 94550-6428 Office: Valley Care Health Libr # 120 5575 W Las Positas Blvd Pleasanton CA 94588-5800

EDDY, DAVID MAXON, health policy and management administrator. BA, Stanford (Calif.) U., 1964, PhD with great distinction, 1978; MD, U. Va., 1968. Intern in gen. surgery Stanford U. Med. Ctr., 1968-69, resident, postdoct. fellow cardiovascular surgery, 1969-71, acting asst. prof., 1976-78; dir. program for the analysis of clin. policies Dept. Engring.-Econ. Systems, Stanford U., 1978-81, assoc. prof., 1978-80, prof., 1980-81; dir. Ctr. for Health Policy Rsch. and Edn., Duke U., 1981-88; J. Alexander McMahon prof. health policy and mgmt. Duke U., 1986-90, prof. health policy and mgmt., 1990-95; dir. WHO Collaborating Ctr. for Rsch. in Cancer Policy, 1984-95; sr. advisor health policy mgmt. Kaiser Permanente So. Calif. Region, 1991—; columnist Jour. of the AMA, 1990—; spl. govt. employee Hillary Rodham Clinton's Health Care Task Force, 1993; assoc. prof. by courtesy Sch. of Medicine, Stanford U., 1978-81; expert adv. panel on cancer WHO, 1981-96; adv. coun. World Orgn. for Sci. and Health, 1985-96; mem. internat. commn. Centre Oncologique et Biologique de Recherche Appliquee, 1987-96; cons. numerous cos., orgns. and assns. Author: A Manual for Assessing Health Practices and Designing Practice Policies, 1992, FAST*PRO: Software for Meta-Analysis by the Confidence Profile Method, 1992, The Synthesis of Statistical Evidence: meta-Analysis by the Confidence Profile Method, 1992, Common Screening Tests, 1991, Screening for Cancer: Theory, Analysis and Design, 1980, (Lanchester Prize, 1981), Clinical Decision Making: From Theory to Practice, 1996; mem. editl. bd. Jour. Ctr. for the Future of Children, 1990-95, Report Med. Guidelines and Outcomes Rsch., 1990—; contbr. articles to profl. jours. Fellowship NIH, 1970-71, Bay Area Heart Assn., 1969-70; rsch. Scientific and Technol. Achievement award EPA, 1993, FHP Prize Internat. Soc. of Tech. Assessment in Health Care, 1991. Mem. Inst. of Medicine, Nat. Acad. Scis.

EDELHERTZ, HERBERT, criminologist, policy analyst; b. N.Y., Jan. 7, 1922; s. Isidore and Bessie (Shabman) E.; m. Ruth Weiss; children: Jean, Paul. AB, U. Mich., 1943; JD, Harvard Law Sch., 1948. Lawyer Tompkins, Lauren & Edelhertz, N.Y., 1949-58, ptnr., 1958-62; chief and deputy chief fraud sec. crim. divsn. U.S. Dept. Justice, Washington, 1962-69; acting ctr. chief Nat. Inst. Justice, Washington, 1969-71; ctr. dir. and staff scientist Battelle Meml. Inst., Seattle, 1971-84; counsel Appel & Glueck, Seattle, 1984-92; pres. Northwest Policy Studies Ctr., Kirkland, Wash., 1984—. Coauthor: Public Compensation to Victims of Crime, 1974, The White-Collar Challenge to Nuclear Safeguards, 1978, A National Strategy for Containing White-Collar Crime, 1980, White-Collar Crime: An Agenda for Research, 1982, The Containment of Organized Crime, 1983, The Business of Organized Crime, 1993. Recipient Spl. Commendation award U.S. Dept. Justice, Washington, 1968, Superior Performance award, 1965. Home and Office: 4509-102nd Ln NE Kirkland WA 98033

EDELMAN, GERALD MAURICE, biochemist, educator; b. N.Y.C., N.Y., July 1, 1929; s. Edward and Anna (Freedman) E.; m. Maxine Morrison, June 11, 1950; children: Eric, David, Judith. B.S., Ursinus Coll., 1950, Sc.D., 1974; M.D., U. Pa., 1954, D.Sc., 1973; Ph.D., Rockefeller U., 1960; M.D. (hon.), U. Siena, Italy, 1974; DSc (hon.), Gustavus Adolphus Coll., 1975, Williams Coll., 1976; DSc Honoris Causa, U. Paris, 1989; LSc Honoris Causa, U. Cagliari, 1989; DSc, Georgetown U., 1989; DSc Honoris Causa, U. degli Studi di Napoli, 1990, Tulane U., 1991, U. Miami, 1995, Adelphi U., 1995. Med. house officer Mass. Gen. Hosp., 1954-55; asst. physician hosp. of Rockefeller U., 1957-60, mem. faculty, 1960-92, assoc. dean grad. studies, 1963-66, prof., 1966-74, Vincent Astor disting. prof., 1974-92; mem. faculty and chmn. dept. neurobiology Scripps Rsch. Inst., La Jolla, Calif., 1992—; mem. biophysics and biophys. chemistry study sect. NIH, 1964-67; mem. Sci. Council, Ctr. for Theoretical Studies, 1970-72; assoc., sci. chmn. Neurosciences Research Program, 1980—, dir. Neurosci. Inst., 1981—; mem. adv. bd. Basel Inst. Immunology, 1970-77, chmn., 1975-77; non-resident fellow, trustee Salk Inst., 1973-85; bd. overseers Faculty Arts and Scis., U. Pa., 1976-83; trustee, mem. adv. com. Carnegie Inst., Washington, 1980-87; bd. govs. Weizman Inst. Sci., 1971-87, mem. emeritus; researcher structure of antibodies, molecular and devel. biology. Author: Neural Darwinism, 1987, Topobiology, 1988, The Remembered Present, 1989, Bright Air, Brilliant Fire, 1992. Trustee Rockefeller Bros. Fund., 1972-82. Served to capt. M.C. AUS, 1955-57. Recipient Spencer Morris award U. Pa., 1954, Ann. Alumni award Ursinus Coll., 1969, Nobel prize for physiology or medicine, 1972, Albert Einstein Commemorative award Yeshiva U., 1974, Buchman Meml. award Calif. Inst. Tech., 1975, Rabbi Shai Shacknai meml. prize Hebrew U.-Hadassah Med. Sch., Jerusalem, 1977, Regents medal Excellence, N.Y. State, 1984, Hans Neurath prize, U. Washington, 1986, Sesquicentennial Commemorative award Nat. Libr. Medicine, 1986, Cécile and Oskar Vogt award U. Dusseldorf, 1988, Disting. Grad. award U. Pa., 1990, Personnalité de l'année, Paris, 1990, Warren Triennial Prize award Mass. Gen. Hosp., 1992. Fellow AAAS, N.Y. Acad. Scis., N.Y. Acad. Medicine; mem. Am. Philos. Soc., Am. Soc. Biol. Chemists, Am. Assn.

Immunologists, Genetics Soc. Am., Harvey Soc. (pres. 1975-76, Am. Chem. Soc., Eli Lilly award biol. chemistry 1965), Am. Acad. Arts and Scis., Nat. Acad. Sci., Am. Soc. Cell Biology, Acad. Scis. of Inst. France (fgn.), Japanese Biochem. Soc. (hon.), Pharm. Soc. Japan (hon.), Soc. Developmental Biology, Council Fgn. Relations, Sigma Xi, Alpha Omega Alpha. Office: Scripps Rsch Inst Dept Neurobiol SBR-14 10550 N Torrey Pines Rd La Jolla CA 92037-1027

EDELSTEIN, ROSE MARIE, nurse educator, medical-legal consultant; b. Drake, N.D., Mar. 3, 1935; d. Francis Jerome and Myrtle Josephine (Merbach) Hublou; m. Harry George Edelstein, June 22, 1957 (div.); children: Julie, Lori, Lynn, Toni Anne. BSN, St. Teresa of Avila Coll., Winona, Minn., 1956; MA in Edn., Holy Names Coll., Oakland, Calif., 1977; EdD, U. San Francisco, 1982, postgrad., 1987; postgrad. in pub. health U. Ariz., 1985—; cert. pub. health nurse U. Calif., Berkeley, 1972. Dir., clin. supr. San Francisco Sch. for Health Professions, 1971-74, Rancho Arroyo Sch. of Vocat. Nursing, Sacramento, 1974-75; intensive care nurse Kaiser-Permanente Hosp., San Rafael, Calif., 1976-77; dir. inservice edn. Ross Hosp., Calif., 1977-78; assoc. dir. nursing, nursing edn. St. Francis Meml. Hosp., San Francisco, 1978-85; med.-legal nursing cons., med.-surg. staff nurse met. hosps., San Francisco, 1985-90, St. Luke's Hosp., Duluth, Minn., 1990-91, St. Charles Hosp., New Orleans, 1992, UTMB, Galveston, Tex. 1992-94, staff RN family medicine faculty practice, 1994-95; med.-surg. nurse St. Anthony of Padua Hosp., Oklahoma City, Okla., 1995; medical medicare experience, RN medics and treatments Northgate Conv. Hosp., San Rafael, Calif., 1995—; RN, night charge nurse Creekside Conv. Hosp., Santa Rosa, Calif., 1996; RN, charge nurse medications, treatment and alzheimers unit, Fallon Conv. Ctr., Nev., 1996; RN charge medicare unit White Pine Conv. Ctr., Ely, Nev., 1997—; invited mem. People to People Nursing Edn. and Adminstrn., candidate to East Asia, Philosophy, 1985; postgrad. candidate U. Zurich, Switzerland, 1988. Candidate U.S. Senate Inner Circle, 1988, 89. Lt. col. USAR Med. Res. Mem. Calif. Nurses Assn., Am. Heart Assn., Sigma Theta Tau. Roman Catholic. Author: (with Jane F. Lee) Acupuncture Atlas, 1974; The Influence of Motivator and Hygiene Factors in Job Changes by Graduate Registered Nurses, 1977; Effects of Two Educational Methods Upon Retention of Knowledge in Pharmacology, 1981. Address: PO Box 545 Ely NV 89301-0545

EDEN, EDWARD FRANK, probation officer; b. Grass Valley, Calif., Apr. 16, 1935; s. William Charles and Evelyn Florence (Ducotey) E.; m. Sheila Thordis Carpenter, Nov. 19, 1960; children: Andrew, Karen Eden Hennessy. AA, Yuba Coll., 1955; BA, San Jose State U., 1957; MPA, U. So. Calif., 1975. Pers. analyst Calif. Youth Authority, Sacramento, 1958-59; dep. probation officer County of Yolo, Woodland, Calif., 1959-60; probation divsn. dir. County of Ventura, Calif., 1960-75; chief probation officer County of Sutter, Yuba City, Calif., 1975-91; advisor Ventura County Criminal Justice, 1965-76, Sutter County Juvenile Justic e Commn., Yuba City, 1975-91. Vice chair Alliance for the Mnetally Ill, 1990—; pres. Friends of the Libr., 1980—, Hist. Soc., 1980—; co-chair Calif. PTA, 1968-70; v.p. Habitat for Humanity, 1990—; mem. com. Yuba-Sutter Prune Festival, 1996—; v.p. Bou Scouts Am., Ventura, 1961-76, scoutmaster, Marysville, Calif., 1995—; pres.-elect Am. Cancer Soc., Marysville, 1995—; elder St. andrew Presbyn. Ch., Yuba City, 1987-90, 92-95; pres. bd. dirs. Yuba-Sutter United Way, Marysville, 1976—. With U.S. Army, 1957-63. Recipient Silver Beaver award Boy Scouts Am., 1984, Petro award United Way, 1993, Rodger Kunde award Sutter County Juvenile Justice, 1986; named Olympic Torch Bearer Yuba-Sutter Cmty. Hero Selection Bd., 1996. Mem. Calif. Probation Officers Calif. (sec., regional chair 1976-91), Calif. Probation, Parole and Correctional Assn. (regional chair, mem. various coms. 1959-91). Home: 428 Littlejohn Rd Yuba City CA 95993

EDENFIELD, T(HOMAS) KEEN, JR., music publishing and real estate investor; b. Chattanooga, May 8, 1943; s. Thomas Keen Sr. and Francis (Love) E.; m. Ann Louise Goodney, Jan. 24, 1976; children: Thomas Keen III, Andrew Ward, Stuart Douglas, Curtis Arthur. BS in Econs., Emory U., 1967; MS, Oxford Sch. Econs., London, 1969. Capt. Saudi Arabian Airlines, 1976-78, Air Jamaica, 1978-80; owner, pres. Mountain Hospitality, Inc., Albuquerque, 1982-86, Lamb Realty & Investment, Albuquerque, 1980-84; pres. Seeganex Internat. Ltd., London, 1986—; chmn. Seeganex N.Am., Albuquerque; defense contractor, pres. Advanced Tech. Corp., Santa Fe, 1993—; CIA aviation operative, Washington, 1974-85. Contbr. articles to profl. jours. Decorated Turkish Civilian Wings award, 1976; recipient Jamaican Disting. Citizen Humanitarian award, 1978, Nicaraguan Civilian Humanitarian award, 1984. Mem. Albuquerque Country Club, Wings Club of Arabia (pres. 1978-79), Sigma Chi. Office: Advanced Tech Corp PO Box 26026 Albuquerque NM 87125-6026

EDENS, GARY DENTON, broadcasting executive; b. Asheville, N.C., Jan. 6, 1942; s. James Edwin and Pauline Amanda (New) E.; m. Hannah Suellen Walter, Aug. 21, 1965; children: Ashley Elizabeth, Emily Blair. BS, U. N.C., 1964. Account exec. PAMS Prodns., Dallas, 1965-67; account exec. Sta. WKIX, Raleigh, N.C., 1967-69; gen. mgr. Sta. KOY, Phoenix, 1970-81; sr. v.p. Harte-Hanks Radio, Inc., Phoenix, 1978-81, pres., chief exec. officer, 1981-84; chmn., chief exec. officer Edens Broadcasting, Inc., 1984—; dir. Gt. Western Bank & Trust Ariz., 1975-86, Citibank Ariz., 1986—, Inter-Tel, Inc., 1994—; chmn. The Hanover Cos., Inc., 1995—. Bd. dirs. Valley Big Bros., 1972-80, Ariz. State U. Found., 1979—, COMPAS, 1979—, Men's Arts Coun., 1975-78. Named One of Three Outstanding Young Men, Phoenix Jaycees, 1973; entrepreneurial fellow U. Ariz., 1989. Mem. Phoenix Execs. Club (pres. 1976), Nat. Radio Broadcasters Assn. (dir. 1981-86), Radio Advt. Bur. (dir. 1981—), Young Pres. Orgn. (chmn. Ariz. chpt. 1989-90), Chief Execs. Orgn., Ariz. Pres. Orgn. Republican. Methodist. Office: Ste 1400 2400 E Arizona Biltmore Cir Phoenix AZ 85016-2107

EDGAR, HERMAN BURTON, aerospace engineer, managment and tax consultant; b. Memphis, Tex., Dec. 27, 1928; s. Everett Burton and Willie Mae (Loftin) E.; m. Eura Dell Clark, Nov. 5, 1957 (div. May 1970); children: Stephany, John, George; m. Rose Iva Chatman, Nov. 21, 1970; children: Keith, Jacques, Herman Burton, Marlene. BSME in Machine Design, Healds Coll., 1955; BSEE in Feedback Control Systems, West Coast U., 1967, MSSE in Systems Mgmt., 1969; postgrad., U.S. Internat. U., San Diego, 1981-88. Engr. Rockwell Internat. (N.R.) Corp., Downey, Calif., 1955-89; mgr., owner Burton's Profl. Svcs., Altadena, Calif., 1971—; systems design engr. Apollo, GAM 77, N.Am./Rockwell Internat., Downey and Seal Bech, Calif., 1964-72; supr. hydraulics analysis and test Space Shuttle, Rockwell Internat., Downey, 1973-78, mgr. hydraulics system, 1979-84, project mgr. mech. fluid systems, 1985-89. Co-Author: WCU Systems Anal Jour., 1969, Servo Control VLVS Design, 1959. Cons. engr. Altadena Town Coun., 1992—; deacon, pres. long-range planning com. Lincoln Ave Bapt. Ch., Pasadena, 1974. Served with U.S. Army, 1950-52, Korea. Selected to 1st flight team Apollo, NASA-Johnson Space Ctr., Clearlake, Tex., 1969; recipient Excellence in Leadership award NASA-Johnson Space Ctr. and Rockwell Internat. Corp., Clearlake, 1980, Group Achievement award for first space shuttle flight Johnson Space Ctr., 1983; Cert. of Honor, Glorious Praise Christian Acad., Pasadena, Calif., 1992. Fellow Rockwell Mgmt. Club; mem. Altadena Srs. Golf Club (pres. 1992—), Altadena Optimist Club (v.p. 1993). Democrat. Home: 1701 Skyview Dr Altadena CA 91001-2143

EDGAR, JAMES MACMILLAN, JR., management consultant; b. N.Y.C., Nov. 7, 1936; s. James Macmillan Edgar and Lilyan (McCann) E.; B in Chem. Engring., Cornell U., 1959, MBA with distinction, 1960; m. Judith Frances Storey, June 28, 1958; children: Suzanne Lynn, James Macmillan, Gordon Stuart. New product rep. E.I. duPont Nemours, Wilmington, Del., 1960-63, mktg. services rep., 1963-64; with Touche Ross & Co., 1964-78, mgr., Detroit, 1966-68, ptnr., 1968-71, ptnr. in charge, mgmt. services ops. for No. Calif. and Hawaii, San Francisco, 1971-78, ptnr. Western regional mgmt. services, 1978; sr. ptnr. Edgar, Dunn & Co., San Francisco, 1978—; bd. dirs. Associated Oreg. Industries Svcs. Corp., 1991—; dir. Harding Lawson Assocs. Group, 1996—. Active San Francisco Mayor's Fin. Adv. Com., 1976—, mem. exec. com., 1978—, Blue Ribbon com. for Bus., 1987-88, Alumnae Resources adv. bd., 1986-94, San Francisco Planning and Urban Rsch. Bd., 1986-89, mem. adv. bd., 1989-93, mem. program adv. com., 1996—; mem. alumni exec. council Johnson Grad. Sch. Mgmt. Cornell U., Cornell Coun., 1970-73; mem. steering com. Bay Area Coun., 1989-93, mem. program adv. com., 1996—; chmn. San Francisco Libr. Found., 1989-96; bd. dirs. Rosenberg Found., 1995—, dirs., Harding Lawson Assoc Group, 1996—. Recipient Award of Merit for outstanding pub. svc. City and County of San Francisco, 1978; Honor award for outstanding contbns. to profl. mgmt. Johnson Grad. Sch. Mgmt., Cornell U., 1978. CPA, cert. mgmt. cons. Mem. Assn. Corp. Growth (v.p. membership San Francisco chpt. 1979-81, v.p. programs 1981-82, pres. 1982-83, nat. bd. dirs. 1983-86), AICPA, Calif. Soc. CPAs, Inst. Mgmt. Cons. (regional v.p. 1973-80, dir. 1975-77, bd. v.p. 1977-80), Profl. Services Mgmt. Assn., San Francisco C. of C. (bd. dirs. 1987-89, 91—, mem. exec. com. 1988-89, 91-95, chmn. mktg. San Francisco program 1991-92, membership devel. 1993, chmn. bd. dirs. 1994, dir. emeritus 1995—), Tau Beta Pi. Clubs: Pacific Union, Commonwealth of San Francisco, Marin Rod and Gun. Patentee nonwoven fabrics. Home: 10 Buckeye Way San Rafael CA 94904-2602 Office: Edgar Dunn & Co Inc 847 Sansome St San Francisco CA 94111-1529

EDGAR, MARILYN RUTH, counselor; b. Springfield, Mo., Oct. 2, 1948; d. Donald LaVerne Sr. and Ruth Elenor (McClellan) Wilson; m. Robert Stephen Edgar, June 23, 1979; stepchildren: Terri, John, Shawna. BA in Psychology, Calif. State U., Sacramento, 1983, MS in Counseling, 1987. Lic. marriage, family, and child counselor, Calif. Counselor Sacramento Life Ctr., 1983-91; marriage and family therapist New Horizons Counseling Ctr., Carmichael, Calif., 1987—, exec. dir., supr. intern counselors, 1993—. Guest profl. therapist Faith in Crisis Group, Sacramento; mem. Warehouse Ministries of Sacramento, 1978—; mem. Arthritis Found., 1996. Mem. Calif. Assn. Marriage and Family Therapists (Valley chpt. 1992—), Capital City Motorcycle Club (pub. rels. officer 1994, sec., bd. mem. 1996-97). Republican. Office: New Horizons Counseling Ctr 3300 Walnut Ave Carmichael CA 95608-3240

EDGE, JAMES EDWARD, health care administrator; b. Anacortes, Wash., Apr. 29, 1948; s. Edward and Carol Marie (Lian) E.; m. Nellie Ruth Horton, Mar. 21, 1970; children: Elissa Marie, Gina Dawn. BS in Pharmacy, U. Wash., 1971; MPH, U. Hawaii, 1979. Registered pharmacist. Commd. USPHS, 1969—, advanced through grades to capt.; staff pharmacist USPHS Indian Hosp., Albuquerque, 1971-73; chief pharmacy, lab/x-ray S.W. Indian Poly. Inst., Albuquerque, 1972-73, Neah Bay Indian Health Ctr., Wash., 1973-75; svc. unit dir. Neah Bay Svc. Unit, Indian Health Svc., 1975-78, Western Oreg. Service Unit, Indian Health Svc., Salem, 1980—; cons. in field. Active Combined Fed. Campaign, Salem, 1985—. John Quick Pharmacy scholar, U. Wash., 1967, Health Professions scholar, 1969. Mem. APHA, Am. Coll. Healthcare Adminstrs., Am. Acad. Med. Adminstrs., Assn. Mil. Surgeons U.S., Mensa, Res. Officers Assn., Commd. Officer USPHS, Wash. Pharm. Assn., nat. Coun. Svc. Unit Dirs. (chmn. 1986-88). Office: PHS Indian Health Ctr 3750 Chemawa Rd NE Salem OR 97305-1119

EDGEMAN, RICK LEE, statistics educator, consultant; b. Pueblo, Colo., Nov. 28, 1954; s. Howard Curtis and Eunice Marie (Stucker) E.; m. Lisa Anne Allen, Aug. 12, 1978; children: Emily, Grant, Stephen. BS in Exptl. Psychology, U. So. Colo., 1977; MS in Rsch. and Statis. Methodology, U. No. Colo., 1979; PhD in Stats., U. Wyo., 1983. Lectr. in stats. U. Wyo., Laramie, 1981-83; asst. prof. bus. Bradley U., Peoria, Ill., 1983-85; study design and analysis mgr. Bausch and Lomb, Rochester, N.Y., 1985; asst. prof. stats. Rochester (N.Y.) Inst. Tech., 1985-86; asst. prof. mgmt. sci. U. North Tex., Denton, 1986-88; assoc. prof. computer info. sys. Colo. State U., Ft. Collins, 1988-93, prof. computer ino. sys., 1993—, dir. Ctr. for Quality and Productivity Improvement, 1988—; statis. cons. Eastman-Kodak, Rochester, 1985-86, Mobil Chem., Macedon, N.Y., 1985-86, Hewlett-Packard, Ft. Collins, 1988-89, Colo. Dept. Social Svcs., Denver. Contbr. some 70 articles to profl. jours. Pres. Colo. Citizens for Decency, Ft. Collins, 1989-91; dir. Jesus Video Project Ft. Collins (Colo.), Campus Crusade for Christ, 1993-94. Caterpillar Tractor Co. Rsch. fellow Caterpiller Rsch. Found., Peoria, 1983-84. Mem. IEEE (mem. reliability soc., higher edn. com.), Am. Soc. for Quality Control (editor Quality Progress 1991-94), Am. Statis. Assn. (pres. Rochester N.Y. chpt. 1985-86), Sigma Xi. Republican. Home: 4010 Highlands West Dr Fort Collins CO 80526-5394 Office: Colo State U Computer Info Sys Dept C115 Clark Bldg Coll Bus Fort Collins CO 80523

EDGERTON, BRADFORD WHEATLY, plastic surgeon; b. Phila., May 8, 1947; s. Milton Thomas and Patricia Jane (Jones) E.; children: Bradford Wheatly Jr., Lauren Harrington. BA in Chemistry, Vanderbilt U., 1969, MD, 1973. Diplomate Am. Bd. Plastic Surgery, Am. Bd. Hand Surgery. Intern in surgery U. Calif., San Francisco, 1973-74; resident U. Va., Charlottesville, 1974-78; resident in plastic surgery Columbia-Presbyn., N.Y., 1979-81; fellow in hand surgery NYU, 1981-82, clin. instr. plastic surgery, 1981-89; ptnr. So. Calif. Permanente Med. Group, L.A., 1989—; assoc. prof. clin. plastic surgery U. So. Calif., L.A., 1989—. v.p., trustee W. Alton Jones Found., Charlottesville, Va., 1978—. Mem. Am. Assn. Hand Surgery, Am. Soc. Plastic and Reconstructive Surgery, Am. Soc. Surgery of Hand, L.A. Tennis Club. Republican. Episcopal. Home: 248 S Clark Dr Beverly Hills CA 90211 Office: 6041 Cadillac Ave Los Angeles CA 90034-1702

EDMISTON, JOSEPH TASKER, state official; b. Monterey Park, Calif., Oct. 27, 1948; s. Tasker Lee and Beula Viola (Bates) E.; m. Pepper Salter Abrams, 1985; children: William Tasker, Charles Henry. AA, East L.A. Coll., 1968; AB, U. So. Calif., 1970. Mgr. of ct. process Roy Rottner & Associates, Hollywood, Calif., 1970-73; So. Calif Coastal coord. Sierra Club, L.A., 1973-76, energy coord., Sacramento, Calif., 1976-77; dir. State of Calif. Santa Monica Mountains Land Acquisition Program, 1979-80; exec. dir. Santa Monica Mountains Comprehensive Planning Commn., L.A., 1977-79; exec. dir. Santa Monica Mountains Conservancy, State of Calif., 1980—; regents lectr. Coll. Environ. Design U. Calif., Berkeley, 1995—. Pres. Associated Students, East L.A. Coll., 1968. Recipient Weldon Heald Conservation award Sierra Club, 1970; Hollywood Heritage, Inc. (bd. dirs.). Mem. Marine Tech. Soc. (dir. L.A. region sect. 1975-77), Coastal Soc., Am. Planning Assn. (vice dir. policy L.A. Sect. 1989-90), Phi Rho Pi, Delta Sigma Rho, Tau Kappa Alpha. Democrat. Office: 5810 Ramirez Canyon Rd Malibu CA 90265-4421

EDMONDS, CHARLES HENRY, publisher; b. Lakewood, Ohio, Sept. 4, 1919; s. Howard H. and Mary Frances (Galena) E.; student Woodbury Bus. Coll., 1939-40; m. Ruth Audrey Windfelder, Nov. 4, 1938; children: Joan Dickey, Charles Henry, Carolyn Anne, Dianne Marie. Owner, Shoreline Transp. Co., L.A., 1946-58; mgr. transp. Purity Food Stores, Burlingame, Calif., 1958-61; supr. Calif. Motor Express, San Jose, 1961-64; account exec. Don Wright Assos., Oakland, Calif., 1964-65; sales mgr. Western U.S., Shippers Guide Co., Chgo., 1965-70; pub. No. Calif. Retailer, San Jose, 1970-83; v.p. Kasmar Publs., 1983-88; pub. Retail Observer, 1990—. Recipient journalism awards various orgns. Republican. Roman Catholic. Contbr. articles to profl. jours. Home: 1442 Sierra Creek Way San Jose CA 95132-3618

EDMONDS, HARVEY LAWRENCE, neurologist; b. Cleve., Aug. 1, 1946; s. Albert Rosen and Doris (Rubinow) E.; m. Christine Patricia, June 1973 (div. 1982); children: Zachary, Oliver; m. Irma Corral, Mar. 27, 1988; children: Alexandra, Max. BS, U. Calif. Berkely, 1968; MD, UCLA Sch. Medicine, 1972. Diplomate Am. Bd. Psychiatry & Neurology. Intern Harbor Gen. Hosp., Torrence, Calif., 1972-73; residency V.A. Hosp. Wadsworth, L.A., 1976-78; neurologist Fresno (Calif.) Neurol. Assocs. Med. Group, 1978—. Mem. Am. Acad. Neurology, Am. Soc. Neuroimaging, Alpha Omega Alpha. Office: Fresno Neurol Assocs 6113 N Fresno St Ste 101 Fresno CA 93710-5207

EDMONDS, IVY GORDON, writer; b. Frost, Tex., Feb. 15, 1917; s. Ivy Gordon and Delia Louella (Shumate) E.; student pub. schs.; m. Reiko Mimura, July 12, 1956; 1 dau., Annette. Freelance writer; author books including: Solomon In Kimono, 1957; Ooka the Wise, 1961; The Bounty's Boy, 1963; Hollywood RIP, 1963; Joel of the Hanging Gardens, 1966; Trickster Tales, 1966; Taiwan—the Other China, 1971; The Possible Impossibles of Ikkyo The Wise, 1971; The Magic Man, 1972; Mao's Long March, 1973; Motorcycling for Beginners, 1973; Micronesia, 1974; Pakistan, Land of Mystery, Tragedy and Courage, 1974; Automotive Tuneups for Beginners, 1974; Ethiopia, 1975; The Magic Makers, 1976; The Shah of Iran, 1976; Allah's Oil: Mid-East Petroleum, 1976; Second Sight, 1977; Motorcycle Racing for Beginners, 1977; Islam, 1977; Buddhism, 1978; The Mysteries of Troy, 1977; Big U Universal in the Silent Days, 1977; D.D. Home, 1978; Bicycle Motocross, 1979; Hinduism, 1979; Girls Who Talked to Ghosts, 1979; The Magic Brothers, 1979; (with William H. Gebhardt) Broadcasting for Beginners, 1980; (with Reiko Mimura) The Oscar Directors, 1980; The Mysteries of Homer's Greeks, 1981; The Kings of Black Magic, 1981; Funny Car Racing for Beginners, 1982; The Magic Dog, 1982; author textbooks: (with Ronald Gonzales) Understanding Your Car, 1975, Introduction to Welding, 1975; also author pulp and soft cover fiction and nonfiction under names of Gene Cross and Gary Gordon and publishers house names; pub. relations mgr. Northrop Corp., Anaheim, Calif., 1968-79, indsl. editor, Hawthorne, Calif., 1979-86. Served with USAAF, 1940-45, USAF, 1946-63. Decorated D.F.C., Air medals, Bronze Star. Home: 5801 Shirl St Cypress CA 90630-3326

EDMONDS, ROBERT LESLIE, forestry educator; b. Sydney, NSW, Australia, May 6, 1943; came to the U.S., 1966; s. Harold M. and Elizabeth (Osborne) E.; m. Victory C. Lesher, Apr. 25, 1969; children: Nicole T., Stephen R. BS, Sydney (Australia) U., 1964; MS, U. Wash., 1968, PhD, 1971. Rsch. forestry officer Forest Rsch. Inst., Canberra, Australia, 1964-65; rsch. asst. dept. forestry Australian Nat. U., Canberra, 1965-66; rsch. asst. Coll. for Rsch. U. Wash., Seattle, 1966-70, rsch. asst. prof., 1973-76, asst. prof., 1976-79, assoc. prof., 1979-82, prof., 1982—, chair ecosystem sci. and conservation divsn., 1993—; program coord. to dir. U.S.-internat. biol. program aerobiology program botany dept. U. Mich., Ann Arbor, 1971-73. Author, editor: Aerobiology: The Ecological System Approach, 1979, Analysis of Coniferous Forest Ecosystems in the Western United States, 1982; assoc. editor: Northwest Sci. Jour.; contbr. articles to profl. jours. Mem. U.S. Nat. Com. for the Internat. Biol. Program, NRC, Washington, 1973-74, chmn. aerobiology com., 1976-80; mem. mayor's com. Secondary Use Com. for the Cedar River Watershed, Seattle, 1987-88. Rsch. grantee NSF. Mem. Am. Phytopathol. Soc., Internat. Assn. for Aerobiology, Soil Sci. Soc. Am., Soc. Am. Foresters, Ecol. Soc. Am. Office: Univ Wash Coll Forest Resources Seattle WA 98195

EDMUNDS, HOLLY BROOK, market research consultant; b. Lansing, Mich., May 27, 1960; d. Gary Lee Twichell and Heather Kay Powell; m. David James Edmunds, Sept. 25, 1988; children: James Easley IV, Rebecca Lynn. BA in Econs. and Mgmt. and French, Albion Coll., 1982; postgrad., Ea. Mich. U., 1984-87. Internat. mem. svc. rep. FTD, Southfield, Mich., 1982-83, rsch. analyst, 1983-84; rsch. coord. FTD, Southfield, 1984-88; sr. project mgr. Market Trends Rsch., Bellevue, Wash., 1988-90; R&D devel. officer Puget Sound Bancorp, Tacoma, 1990-92; pres. Edmunds Rsch. Svcs., Redmond, Wash., 1991—; instr. U. Wash. Ext., Seattle, 1991. Contbr. articles to profl. jours. Bd. dirs. Puget Sound Rsch. Forum; mem. mktg. com., cons. Bathhouse Theatre, 1993-94; mem. steering com. Mesa Arts Ctr., 1996—. Mem. Am. Mktg. Assn., U. Wash. Speakers' Bur., Greater Seattle C. of C. Home and Office: Edmunds Rsch Svcs 1120 E Bishop Dr Tempe AZ 85282

EDMUNDS, KRISTINE ANN, public administrator; b. Chula Vista, Calif., July 4, 1964; d. James Marshall and Marjorie (Burgraff) E. BA, Willamette U., 1986; MPA with distinction, Monterey Inst. Intl. Studies, 1993. Tchr. English U.S. Peace Corps, Lolodorf, Cameroon, 1986-88; legis. asst. Congressman Jim Bates, Washington, 1989-90, legis. dir., 1990-91; dir. edn. & fund devel. Ctr. Cmty. Advocacy, Salinas, Calif., 1994—; tech. trainer U.S. Peace Corps, Cameroon, summers 1987, 88; coord. Amnesty Internat., Ecuador, 1994—. Vol., precinct. worker Bill Monning for Congress, Monterey, Calif., 1992, for Assembly, 1994; precinct worker United Dem. Campaign, 1996. Mem. Devel. Execs. Network.

EDSON, WILLIAM ALDEN, electrical engineer; b. Burchard, Nebr., Oct. 30, 1912; s. William Henry and Pearl (Montgomery) E.; m. Saralou Peterson, Aug. 23, 1942; children: Judith Lynne, Margaret Jane, Carolyn Louise. B.S. (Summerfield scholar), U. Kans., 1934, M.S., 1935; D.Sc. (Gordon McKay scholar), Harvard U., 1937. Mem. tech. staff Bell Telephone Labs., Inc., N.Y.C., 1937-41; supr. Bell Telephone Labs., Inc., 1943-45; asst. prof. elec. engring. Ill. Inst. Tech., Chgo., 1941-43; prof. physics Ga. Inst. Tech., Atlanta, 1945-46; prof. elec. engring. Ga. Inst. Tech., 1946-51, dir. sch. elec. engring., 1951-52; vis. prof., research asso. Stanford U., 1952-56, cons. prof., 1956; mgr. Klystron sub-sect. Gen. Electric Microwave Lab., Palo Alto, Calif., 1955-61; v.p., dir. research Electromagnetic Tech. Corp., Palo Alto, 1961-62; pres. Electromagnetic Tech. Corp., 1962-70; sr. scientist Vidar Corp., Mountain View, Calif., 1970—71; asst. dir. Radio Physics Lab., SRI Internat., Menlo Park, Calif., 1971-77; sr. prin. engr. Geosci. and Engring. Ctr., SRI Internat., 1977—; cons. high frequency sect. Nat. Bur. Standards, 1951-64; dir. Western Electronic Show and Conv., 1975-79. Author: (with Robert I. Sarbacher) Hyper and Ultra-High Frequency Engineering, 1943, Vacuum-Tube Oscillators, 1953. Life fellow IEEE (chmn. San Francisco sect. 1963-64, com. standards piezoelectricity 1950-67); mem. Am. Phys. Soc., Sigma Xi, Tau Beta Pi, Sigma Tau, Phi Kappa Phi, Eta Kappa Nu, Pi Mu Epsilon. Home: 23350 Sereno Ct Unit 29 Cupertino CA 95014-6543 Office: SRI Internat 333 Ravenswood Ave Menlo Park CA 94025-3453

EDSTROM, PAM, public relations executive; b. 1954. Pvt. practice, 1968-74; with Fred Meyer Savings and Loan, Portland, Oreg., 1974-77, Tektronix, Inc., Beaverton, Oreg., 1977-81, Micro Soft, Redmond, Wash., 1981-83; sr. v.p. Waggener Edstrom, Inc., Portland, 1983—. Office: Waggener Edstrom Inc 550 SW Macadam Ave Ste 200 Portland OR 97219-2398*

EDWARDS, ANDREW, arts administrator; b. N.Y.C., Sept. 19, 1952; s. Jack Edwards and Lois Rea; m. Valarie Lynn Grudier, Sept. 15, 1979; children: Pierce Andrew Carl, Caitlin Rea. BA, Dickinson Coll., 1974; MFA, U. Portland, 1981. Theatre mgr. Lake Oswego (Oreg.) Cmty. Theatre, 1977-79; exec. dir. Lakewood Theatre Co., Lake Oswego, 1979—, Lakewood Ctr. for Arts, Lake Oswego, 1980—; bd. dirs. Portland (Oreg.) Area Theatre Alliance, 1987-90, pres., 1990-92, active, 1987—. Recipient Vocat. Svc. award Lake Oswego Rotary, 1994. Mem. Lake Oswego C. of C., Lake Oswego Rotary Club (pres. 1988-89). Roman Catholic. Office: Lakewood Ctr for Arts 368 S State St Lake Oswego OR 97034-3936

EDWARDS, ARDIS LAVONNE QUAM, retired elementary education educator; b. Sioux Falls, S.D., July 30, 1930; d. Norman and Dorothy (Cade) Quam; m. Paul Edwards, Apr. 18, 1953 (dec. Sept. 1988); children: Kevin (dec. 1980), Kendall, Erin, Sally, Kristin, Keely. Teaching credentials, Augustana Luth. Coll., Sioux Falls, 1949; provisional teaching credentials, San Jose State Coll., 1953. Lic. pvt. pilot, FAA, 1984. Mgr. The Cottage Restaurant, Sioux Falls, 1943-50; one-room sch. tchr. Whaley Sch., Colman, S.D., 1949-50, East Sioux Sch., Sioux Falls, 1950-51; recreation dir. City of Albany, Calif., 1951-52; first grade tchr. Decoto (Calif.) Sch. Dist., 1952-58. Author Health Instrn. Unit Study Packet for Tchrs. Bible sch. tchr. East Side Luth. Ch., Sioux Falls, S.D., 1945-51, Sunday sch. tchr., 1945-51; charter mem. Our Savior Luth. Ch., Fremont, Calif., 1964—, mem. choir; Christian Week Day Sch. tchr., 1970, 87, ch. historian, 1986—, other offices; treas. PTA, Hayward, Calif., 1959; pres. Luth. Women's Missionary League, 1976; chmn. OSLC Blood Bank, 1968—; edn. officer, fraternal communicator, respecteen officer Luth. Brotherhood. Recipient Spl. Svc. award Girl Scouts U.S., 1971, Arthritis Found., Fremont, 1974, 75, Spl. Commendation March Fong Eu, 1954. Mem. NAFE, AARP, Republic Airlines Ret. Pilots Assn., Ret. Airline Pilots Assn., N.W. Airlines Ret. Pilots Assn., Aircraft Owners and Pilots Assn., S.W. Airways Pilots Wives Assn., Concerned Women for Am., Am. Heart Assn., Am. Cancer Soc., Arthritis Found., March of Dimes, World Affairs Coun. Republican.

EDWARDS, BRUCE GEORGE, ophthalmologist, naval officer; b. Idaho Springs, Colo., Apr. 6, 1942; s. Bruce Norwood and Evelyn Alice (Kohut) Edwards. BA, U. Colo., 1964; MD, U. Colo., Denver, 1968. Diplomate Am. Acad. Ophthalmology. Commd. ensign USN, 1964; advanced through grades to capt. U.S. Naval Hosp., 1980; intern U.S. Naval Hosp., San Diego, 1968-69; USN med. officer USS Long Beach (CGN-9), 1969-70; gen. med. officer U.S. Naval Hosp., Taipei, Taiwan, 1970-72, U.S. Naval Dispensary Treasure Island, San Francisco, 1972-73; resident in ophthalmology U.S. Naval Hosp., Oakland, Calif., 1973-76, U. Calif., San Francisco, 1973-76; mem. opthalmologist staff Naval Hosp., Camp Pendleton, Calif., 1976-83; ophthalmologist, chief of med. staff Naval Hosp., Naples, Italy, 1983-85; ophthalmology head Camp Pendleton Naval Hosp., 1985-97, dir. surg. svcs., 1990-92, dir. physician advisor quality assurance, 1985-86; vol. Internat. Eye Found., Harar, Ethiopia, 1975. Fellow Am. Acad. Ophthalmology; mem.

AMA, Calif. Med. Assn., Calif. Assn. Ophthalmologists, Am. Soc. Contemporary Ophthalmologists, Assn. U.S. Mil. Surgeons, Pan Am. Assn. Ophthalmology, Order of DeMolay (Colo. DeMolay of Yr. 1961, Idaho Springs Chevalier, Colo. State sec. 1961-62). Republican. Methodist. Office: US Naval Hosp Ophthalmology Dept Camp Pendleton CA 92055

EDWARDS, CHARLES GARLAND, minister, counselor, health educator; b. Muncie, Ind., Sept. 25, 1926; s. Lowell Adelbert and Josephine Thelma (Cunnington) E.; m. June Elizabeth Day, Aug. 4, 1946; children: James Joseph, Robert Jan. BA, Andrews U., 1946; MS in Pub. Health, Loma Linda (Calif.) U., 1975; PhD, Newport (Calif.) U., 1981. Pastor, evangelist Ind. Conf. of Seventh Day Adventists, 1946-54, Ky., Tenn. Seventh Day Adventists, 1954-63, So. New England Seventh Day Adventists, 1963-64; evnagelist, youth and public rels. dir. Upper Columbia Seventh Day Adventists, Spokane, Wash., 1964-68; youth dir. Northern Calif. Seventh Day Adventists, Oakland, 1968-71; health and pub. rels. Northern Calif. Seventh Day Adventists, Pleasant Hills, 1971-85; pastor Upper Columbia Seventh Day Adventists, Wentachee, Wash., 1985—. Author: A Bold One for God., 1978, Stress, 1980, Wacifundo and the Whirlwind, 1994, One Pilgrim's Progress Through the Twentieth Century, 1996. Bd. mem. Friendship Ctr., Wenatchee, 1985—, Habitat for Humanity, 1992—; pres. Cooperating Christian Chs. of the Wenatchee Valley, 1990-94. Mem. Riverview Kiwanis (pres. 1971-72, award 1972). Home and Office: 1245 5th St NE East Wenatchee WA 98802-4925

EDWARDS, CHARLES RICHARD, retired printing equipment and supplies company executive; b. South Bend, Ind., July 16, 1931; s. Bernard Stuart and Mary Irene (Chamberlaine) E.; student pub. schs.; m. Joanne Wood, Dec. 15, 1950; children: Timothy Stuart, Terry Lynne, David Bryan. Pressman, Toastmasters Internat., Santa Ana, Calif., 1954-60; with 3M Co., 1960-69, Salesman, Western U.S. tech. service and nat. market mgr., St. Paul, 1966-69; CEO, sec., CFO, co-owner Graphic Arts Supplies, Inc., Orange, Calif., 1969-86; owner, operator Edwards Bus. Svcs., 1987-91; bus. and trade cons., 1986-91; instr., cons. in field. Bd. dirs., treas. #1 Network, Inc., Chgo., 1982-86. Served with USAF, 1950-54; Korea. Mem. Nat. Assn. Lithographic Clubs (chpt. co-founder, officer, dir.), Nat. Assn. Printing House Craftsmen (past chpt. pres., regional officer), Toastmasters, Hobo Golf Assn. (pres. 1985—). Republican. Home: 7221 Judson Ave Westminster CA 92683-6163

EDWARDS, CLARENCE JEROME, environmental services administrator; b. Evansville, Ind., Sept. 5, 1948; m. Sheila Edwards; children: Jaye, Kevin, Sheva. AA, Compton Coll., 1969, L.A. S.W. Coll., 1979. Dir. environ. scis. Crothall Am., L.A., 1986-87, United Health Svc., Pomona, Calif., 1987-90, Marriott Internat., Pomona, Calif., 1990-92, ServiceMaster Co., Pomona, Calif., 1992-95, Marriott Internat., Pomona, Calif., 1995—. Author: Trojan Horses: Psychic Secrets Revealed, 1996; author poems. Mem. steering com. Youth Motivation Task Force, L.A., 1988-92. With U.S. Army, 1970-72. Recipient Employer of Yr. award Project Industry, 1994, Employer of Yr. award l.A. Urban League Tng., Employment, Counseling, 1995; named to Internat. Poetry Hall of Fame, 1996. Mem. Internat. Soc. Poets (Internat. Poet of Merit 1996).

EDWARDS, DALE LEON, library director; b. Nampa, Idaho; s. Wayne Martin and Thelma Lucile Edwards; m. Julie Ann Rosa, Aug. 19, 1975; children: David, Corey, Stephen, Lisa, Russell. BA, Brigham Young U., 1980, M of Libr. and Info. Sci., 1990. Program dir., announcer Sta. KSUB, Cedar City, Utah, 1977-80; news dir. Sta. KRPX, Price, Utah, 1980-84; news writer Sun Advocate Newspaper, Price, 1984-86; dir. Learning Resource Ctr., Price Libr., Price, 1986-90; dir. libr. svcs. Treasure Valley Community Coll., Ontario, Oreg., 1990—; legis. com. mem. Utah Libr. Assn., Salt Lake City, 1986-90. Recipient Excellence in Reporting award Utah Sch. Bds. Assn., 1985. Mem. ALA, Oreg. Libr. Assn., Oreg. C.C. Libr. Assn. (pres. 1993-94), Oreg. Edn. Assn. (legis. com. 1990—), Pacific N.W. Libr. Assn., Treasure Valley Chorale (pres. 1991-93), Beta Phi Mu. Mormon. Office: Treasure Valley CC Libr 650 College Blvd Ontario OR 97914-3423

EDWARDS, DANIEL WALDEN, lawyer; b. Vancouver, Wash., Aug. 7, 1950; s. Chester W. Edwards and Marilyn E. Russell; m. Joan S. Heller, Oct. 18, 1987; children: Nathaniel, Matthew, Stephen, Alexander. BA in Psychology magna cum laude, Met. State Coll., Denver, 1973, BA in Philosophy, 1974; JD, U. Colo., 1976. Bar: Colo. 1977, U.S. Dist. Ct. Colo. 1977. Dep. pub. defender State of Colo., Denver, 1977-79, Littleton, 1979-81, Pueblo, 1981-86; head office pub. defender State of Colo., Brighton, 1987-89; mem. jud. faculty State of Colo., 1988-91; sole practitioner Denver, 1991-93; magistrate Denver Juvenile Ct., 1993—; instr. sch. of law U. Denver, 1988-91, adj. prof., 1991—, coach appellate advocacy team, 1991—; adv. coun. Colo. Legal Svcs., 1989—; adj. mem. Colo. Supreme Ct. Grievance Com., 1991—. Author: Basic Trial Practice: An Introduction to Persuasive Trial Techniques, 1995. Mem. visual arts com. City Arts III, 1989-90, com. chmn., mem. adv. coun., 1991; bd. dirs. Metropolitan State Coll. Alumni Assn., 1991-92; vol. lectr. CSE Thursday Night Bar Pro Se Divorce Clinic, 1991—. Named Pub. Defender of Yr. Colo. State Pub. Defender's Office, 1985, Outstanding Colo. Criminal Def. Atty., 1989. Mem. ABA, Assn. Trial Lawyers Am., Colo. Bar Assn., Adams County Bar Asss., Denver Bar Assn., Met. State Coll. Alumni Assn. (bd. dirs. 1991—). Home: 2335 Clermont St Denver CO 80207-3134 Office: Denver Juvenile Ct Divsn 6 City and County Bldg Denver CO 80202

EDWARDS, DARREL, psychologist; b. San Francisco, July 9, 1943; s. Darrus and Rose Pearl (Sannar) E.; children: Alexander Hugh, Peter David, James Royce. BS in Psychology and Philosophy, Brigham Young U., 1965, MS in Psychology and Philosophy, 1967, PhD in Clin. Psychology and Philosophy, 1968. Diplomate Am. Bd. Profl. Psychology. Postdoctoral fellow in psycholinguistics Pa. State U., 1969; commd. lt. (j.g.) USN, 1970, advanced through grades to lt. comdr., 1978; dir. psychologist Tri Community Svc. Systems, San Diego, 1973-78; prof. Calif. Sch. Profl. Psychology, San Diego, 1971-78; dir. Grid Rsch., San Diego, 1978-83; pres. The Edwards Assoc., San Diego, 1983—; pres. Strategic Vision, 1987—; cons. strategist for govt. and pvt. sector, U.S. and Eng., 1978—. Co-inventor in field; contbr. articles to profl. jours. Polit. cons. U.S., U.K., Italy, Republic of China, 1986—. Mem. Am. Psychol. Assn. Office: The Edwards Assocs PO Box 420429 San Diego CA 92142-0429

EDWARDS, F(LOYD) KENNETH, journalist, educator, management consultant, marketing executive; b. Salina, Kans., Sept. 29, 1917; s. Floyd Altamus and Grace Frances (Miller) E.; AB, Fort Hays State U., 1940; MS, 1970; m. Virginia Marie Lewark, Sept. 10, 1970; children: Elaine Patricia, Diana, Kenneth, John Michael, Melody, Daniel J. Ins. sales exec., Denver, 1947-50; reporter Sterling (Colo.) Daily Jour., 1950, editor, 1950-52; editor Waverly (Iowa) Newspapers, 1953-55; editor, pub. Edina (Minn.) Courier Newspapers, 1955-56; v.p., editor Mpls. Suburban Newspapers, Hopkins, Minn., 1956-65; editor, gen. mgr. Valley of the Sun Newspapers, Tempe, Ariz., 1968; instr. Mankato (Minn.) State U., 1970-72, asst. prof., 1972-73; assoc. prof. U. Ala., 1973-80, prof., 1980, prof. emeritus, 1981—; vis. prof. communications U. Portland (Oreg.), 1981-83, Western Wash. U., 1987-88; mktg. and sales dir. C.C. Publs., Tualatin, Oreg., 1983-86; pres. GoodLife Publs., Bellingham, Wash., 1988-93; cons. on newspaper mgmt., mktg., pub. rels. Pres. Calhoun-Harriet Home Owners Assn., Mpls., 1958-60; bd. dirs. Hennepin County Assn. for Mental Health, 1959-60, S.W. Activities Council, 1960-61, S.W. High Sch. PTA, Mpls., 1960-61; asst. dir. Wash. State AARP, 1990-92. With USN, World War II. Grantee Ford Found., 1976, U. Ala., 1977. Recipient awards for community svc. and editorial writing. Mem. VFW, Nat. Conf. of Editorial Writers. Republican. Contbr. articles to profl. jours., chpts. to books; author newspaper profit planning and management manual and mktg. primer for small bus. owners. Home: 123 Devil's Kitchen Dr Sedona AZ 86351 Address: PO Box 20155 Sedona AZ 86341 *So live that your words and actions make every place you leave better than you found it.*

EDWARDS, GERALD ELMO, botany educator; b. Mt. Airy, Va., Sept. 17, 1942; s. Thomas George and Ruth (Inge) E.; m.Sandra Ann Gee, July 3, 1969; children: Christopher, Sara. BS in Agrl. Edn., Va. Poly. Inst., 1965; MS in Agronomy, U. Ill., 1966; PhD in Plant Sci./Plant Physiology, U. Calif., Riverside, 1969. NIH postdoctoral fellow biochemistry dept. U. Ga., Athens, 1969-71; asst. prof. horticulture dept. U. Wis., Madison, 1971-75, assoc. prof., 1975-78, prof., 1978-81; prof., chmn. botany dept. Wash. State U., Pullman, 1981-86, fellow Inst. Biol. Chemistry, 1983—, prof. botany dept., 1986—; cons. Calgene, Inc., Davis, Calif., 1984-85, Phytogen, Inc., Pasadena, Calif., 1985, 89-91. Co-author: C3, C4: Photosynthesis, 1984; assoc. editor Photosynthesis Rsch., 1988—; mem. editorial bd. Archives of Biochemistry and Biophysics, 1985—; past mem. editorial bd. Plant Physiology, Plant and Cell Physiology; contbr. articles to profl. jours., chpts. to books. Guggenheim fellow Simon Guggenheim Found., Eng., 1977-78, Fulbright fellow Fulbright Found., Eng., 1992-93; grantee USDA, NSF, EPA, others. Mem. AAAS, Am. Soc. Plant Physiologists, Japanese Soc. Plant Physiologists, Sigma Xi (pres. Wash. State U. chpt. 1995—), Alpha Zeta, Phi Kappa Phi. Democrat. Methodist. Office: Wash State U Botany Dept Pullman WA 99164-4238

EDWARDS, H. BOYD, air transportation executive; b. 1956. Grad., Western State Coll., 1979. Prin. Aspen (Colo.) Aviation, 1980-84; v.p. Aspen (Colo.) Base Ops., Inc., 1984—. Office: Aspen Base Ops Inc 69 E Airport Rd Aspen CO 81611-3532*

EDWARDS, JOHN DAVID, artist; b. Pitts., Aug. 15, 1952; s. John Rex and Winifred (Beattie) E.; m. Brenda L. Duchemin, Jan. 12, 1974 (div. Feb. 1981); 1 child, John David Duchemin; m. Eunice Ying Zhou, June 10, 1987. AA in Fine Art, City Coll. San Francisco, 1976; BA in Studio Art and Art History, U. Calif., Berkeley, 1979. Ellen Battell Stoeckel fellow Summer Sch. Music and Art Yale U., New Haven, 1978; asst. in mural painting U. Calif., 1977-79; instr. color etching Associated Students of Univ. of Calif. Studio, Berkeley, 1981-82; master printer Vorpal Gallery, San Francisco, 1985—; workshop mgr. Kala Inst., Berkeley, 1988—. Exhibited in group shows at Yale Summer Sch. of Music and Art, 1978, Crocker Art Mus., Sacramento, 1982, 93, San Francisco Arts Festival, 1984, Bannam Pl., San Francisco, 1985, 86, Weir Gallery, Berkeley, 1987, 93, Rolando Castellon Art Gallery, San Francisco, 1987, Kala Inst., Berkeley, Calif., 1988, 90, 92, Juniper Gallery, Napa, Calif., 1991, Pyramid Atlantic, Washington, 1992, L.A. Printmaking Soc., 1992, Manhattan Graphics, N.Y., 1993, Crocker Art Mus., 1993, Pacific Print Competition, 1994, Triton Mus. Competition, 1995, others. Mem. L.A. Printmaking Soc., Kala Inst. Roman Catholic. Office: PO Box 621 Berkeley CA 94701-0621

EDWARDS, JOHN WESLEY, JR., urologist; b. Ferndale, Mich., Apr. 9, 1933; s. John W. and Josephine (Wood) E.; m. Ella Marie Law, Dec. 25, 1954; children: Joella, John III. Student, Alma Coll., 1949-50; BS, U. Mich., 1954; postgrad., Wayne State U., 1954-56; MD, Howard U., 1960. Internship Walter Reed Gen. Hosp., 1960-61, surg. resident, 1962-63, urol. resident, 1963-66; asst. chief urology Tripler Army Med. Ctr., 1966-69; comdr. 4th Med. Battalion, 4th Infantry Div., Vietnam, 1969; chief profl. svcs., urology 91st Evacuation Hosp., Vietnam, 1969-70; urologist Straub Clinic, Inc., 1970-74; pvt. practice, 1974—; v.p. med. staff. svcs. Queen's Med. Ctr., Honolulu, 1993-94; v.p. physician rels. Queen's Health Sys., Honolulu, 1994-96; acting administr. Diagnostic Lab. Svcs., Inc., Honolulu, 1995-96, pres., 1996—; chief Dept. Surgery, Straub Clinic and Hosp., 1973; asst. chief Dept. Surgery Queen's Med. Ctr., 1977-79, chief, 1989-93; cons. in urology; chief Dept. Clin. Svcs., Kapiolani Women's and Children's Med. Ctr., 1981-83; clin. assoc. prof. U. Hawaii Sch. of Medicine; chmn. task force on phys. hosp. collaboration The Queens Health System, 1993—. Contbr. articles to profl. jours. Bd. dirs. Am. Cancer Soc., Honolulu unit, 1977-79, Hawaii Med. Svc. Assn., 1979-85, Hawaii Heart Assn., 1977-79, Hawaii Assn. for Physician's Indemnification, 1980-86; commr. City and County of Honolulu, 1990-91; mem. med. adv. bd. Nat. Kindey Found., Hawaii, 1994—; mem. adv. bd. MADD, Hawaii, 1992-96, bd. dirs., 1996—; bd. dirs. Neighborhood Justice Ctr., 1995—. Recipient Howard O. Gray award for Professionalism, 1988, Leaders of Hawaii award, 1983; named Hawaii African-Am. Humanitarian of the Yr. by Hawaii chpt. Links, Inc., 1991. Fellow ACS (sec.-treas. Hawaii chpt. 1980-81, gov.-at-large 1986-92); mem. AMA, NAACP, Am. Urol. Assn. (alt. del. Western sect. 1991-92, gen. chmn. Western sect. 56th ann. meeting 1980, exec. com. 1983-84, del. dist. 1 1985-86, gen. chmn. 63d ann. meeting 1987, pres. 1989-90, nom. com. 1990-93, chmn. nom. 1992-93), Am. Coll. Physician Execs., Nat. Med. Assn., Hawaii Urol. Assn., Hawaii Med. Assn., Surgicare of Hawaii (v.p. 1983-86), Alpha Phi Alpha, Chi Delta Mu, Alpha Omega Alpha. Office: Diagnostic Lab Svcs & Accupath 770 Kapiolani Blvd Ste 100 Honolulu HI 96813-5254

EDWARDS, JULIE DIANE, maternity and staff nurse; b. Lewiston, Idaho, Jan. 4, 1958; d. William and Shirley Hinkley; adopted by Karl Frank and Margaret Esther (Carver) Stoehr, 1965; m. Raymond LeRoy Murphy, Jr., Mar. 19, 1977 (div. Mar. 1982); 1 child, Raymond LeRoy Murphy III; m. Monte Russell Edwards, Dec. 22, 1984; 1 child, Bryan James. AS with honors, Highline Cmty. Coll., Des Moines, Wash., 1982; AAS with honors, Mt. Hood Cmty. Coll., Gresham, Oreg., 1993. RN, Oreg.; cert. Neonatal Resuscitation Program. Staff nurse, maternity Woodland Pk. Hosp., Portland, Oreg., 1993—; staff on call nurse, maternity Providence Milwaukie Hosp., Milwaukie, Oreg., 1994-95. Mem. adv. bd. Adult Basic Edn., Pocatello, Idaho, 1982-85; VISTA vol., 1984-85; vol. Crisis Pregnancy Ctr., Portland, Oreg., 1990—; tchr. aide Good Shepherd Sch., 1992—; Sunday sch. tchr. Good Shepherd Cmty. Ch., 1984-91, 94—. With U.S. Army, 1976-79. Republican. Christian. Home: 304 NE 188th Ave Portland OR 97230-7612 Office: Woodland Park Hospital 10300 NE Hancock St Portland OR 97220-3831

EDWARDS, KENNETH NEIL, chemist, consultant; b. Hollywood, Calif., June 8, 1932; s. Arthur Carl and Ann Vera (Gomez) E.; children: Neil James, Peter Graham, John Evan. BA in Chemistry, Occidental Coll., 1954; MS in Chem. and Metall. Engring., U. Mich., 1955. Prin. chemist Battelle Meml. Inst., Columbus, Ohio, 1955-58; dir. new products rsch. and devel. Dunn-Edwards Corp., L.A., 1958-72; sr. lectr. organic coatings and pigments dept. chem. engring. U. So. Calif., L.A., 1976-80; bd. dirs. Dunn-Edwards Corp., L.A.; cons. Coatings & Plastics Tech., L.A., 1972—. Contbr. articles to sci. jours. Mem. Am. Chem. Soc. (chmn. divisional activities 1988-89, exec. com. divsn. polymeric materials sci. and engring. 1963-96, chair divsn. 1970, mem. devel. adv. com. 1996—, Disting. Svc. award 1996), Alpha Chi Sigma (chmn. L.A. profl. chpt. 1962, counselor Pacific dist. 1967-70, grand profl. alchemist nat. v.p. 1970-76, grand master alchemist nat. pres. 1976-78, nat. adv. com. 1978—). Home: Bottle Bay Rd Sagle ID 83860 also: 2926 Graceland Way Glendale CA 91206-1331 Office: Dunn Edwards Corp 4885 E 52nd Pl Los Angeles CA 90040-2828

EDWARDS, KIRK LEWIS, real estate company executive; b. Berkeley, Calif., July 30, 1950; s. Austin Lewis and Betty (Drury) E.; m. Barbara Lee Preston, Oct. 21, 1983; children: Elliott Tyler, Jonathan Bentley. BA in Rhetoric and Pub. Address, U. Wash., Seattle, 1972; postgrad., Shoreline Coll., 1976. Cert. bus. broker. From salesperson to mgr. Rede Realty, Lynnwood, Wash., 1973-77; br. mgr. Century 21/North Homes Realty, Lynnwood, Wash., 1977-79, Snohomish, Wash., 1979-81; pres., owner Century 21/Champion Realty, Everett, Wash., 1981-82, Champion Computers, Walker/Edwards Investments, Everett, 1981-82; br. mgr. Advance Properties, Everett, 1982-87; exec. v.p. Bruch & Vedrich Better Homes & Garden, Everett, 1987-88, dir. career devel., 1988-90; pres., chief exec. officer Century 21/Champion Realty, Everett, 1991-95; pres., CEO KR Bus. Brokers, Lynnwood, Wash., 1995—. Named Top Business Broker In Washington Investment Brokers Assn., 1994, 95. Mem. Snohomish County Camano Bd. Realtors (chmn. 1987-88), Snohomish County C. of C., Hidden Harbor Yacht Club. Republican. Office: KR Business Brokers 4208 198th St SW # 104 Lynnwood WA 98036

EDWARDS, LISA SIMONE, technical college educator; b. Memphis, July 30, 1963; d. Cas Edwards and Marcelle Cohen. BA in Edn., Western Wash. U., 1987; MEd, U. Puget Sound, 1992. Cert. tchr., Wash. Instr. Puyallup (Wash.) Sch. Dist., 1987-92; health educator Virginia Mason Med. Ctr., Seattle, 1992-93; instr. ARC, Tacoma, 1992—, Bates Tech. Coll., Tacoma, 1992—; fundraising trainer United Way, Tacoma, 1993-94. Vol. ARC, Tacoma, 1993-95. NSF Tchr. Trainer grantee, 1992. Mem. U.S. Tennis Assn. Office: Bates Tech Coll 1101 S Yakima Ave Tacoma WA 98405-4831

EDWARDS, LYDIA JUSTICE, state official; b. Carter County, Ky., July 9, 1937; d. Chead and Velva (Kinney) Justice; m. Frank B. Edwards, 1968; children: Mark, Alexandra, Margot. Student, San Francisco State U. Began career as acct., then Idaho state rep., 1982-86; treas. State of Idaho, 1987—; legis. asst. to Gov. Hickel, Alaska, 1967; conf. planner Rep. Gov.'s Assn., 1970-73; mem. Rep. Nat. Commn., 1972, del. to nat. conv., 1980. Mem. Rep. Womens Fedn. Congregationalist. Office: State Treas Office PO Box 83720 Boise ID 83720-0002*

EDWARDS, MARGARET H., English as second language instructor; b. Falkirk, Scotland, Jan. 28, 1940; came to U.S., 1967; d. John Hobbs and J. Catherine Muir (Rankine) Erskine; m. W. Peter Edwards, Dec. 24, 1964; 1 child, Gemma Rhiain. Diploma, U. Grenoble, France, 1960, U. Santander, Spain, 1962; BA, U. Durham, Eng., 1961, MA; MA, U. Wash., 1970; grad. diploma in edn., U. Leicester, 1962. Head dept. French Chester-le-Street H.S., England, 1962-64; tchr. English, French, Spanish Maple Ridge Sr. H.S., Haney, B.C., Can., 1964-66; tchg. asst. U. Wash., Seattle, 1968-69; instr. Sullivan lang. sch. Behavioral Rsch. Labs., Palo Alto, Calif., 1970-71; field researcher DIME Project, Denver, 1971-72; instr. French Evergreen State Coll., Olympia, Wash., 1986-91; ESL, French, Spanish instr. No. Thurston H.S., Lacey, Wash., 1976—. Mem. Wash. Assn. Educators of Spkrs. of Other Langs. Office: No Thurston HS 600 Sleater Kinney Rd NE Lacey WA 98506-5241

EDWARDS, MARIE BABARE, psychologist; b. Tacoma; d. Nick and Mary (Mardesich) Babare; B.A., Stanford, 1948, M.A., 1949; m. Tilden Hampton Edwards (div.); 1 son, Tilden Hampton Edwards Jr. Counselor guidance center U. So. Calif., Los Angeles, 1950-52; project coordinator So. Calif. Soc. Mental Hygiene, 1952-54; pub. speaker Welfare Fedn. Los Angeles, 1953-57; field rep. Los Angeles County Assn. Mental Health, 1957-58; intern psychologist UCLA, 1958-60; pvt. practice, human rels. tng., counselor tng. Mem. Calif., Am., Western, Los Angeles psychol. assns., AAAS, So. Calif. Soc. Clin. Hypnosis. Author: (with Eleanor Hoover) The Challenge of Being Single, 1974, paperback edit., 1975. Office: 6100 Buckingham Pky Culver City CA 90230-7237

EDWARDS, PATRICIA BURR, small business owner, counselor, consultant; b. Oakland, Calif., Feb. 19, 1918; d. Myron Carlos and Claire Idelle (Laingor) Burr; m. Jackson Edwards, Nov. 14, 1942; children: Jill Forman-Young, Jan Kurzweil. AB, U. So. Calif., 1939, MSEd, 1981. Prin. Constructive Leisure, L.A., 1968—; speaker, lectr. in field; writer, prodr. counseling materials for career, leisure and life planning including computer software, audio cassettes and assessment surveys. Author: You've Got to Find Happiness: It Won't Find You, 1971, Leisure Counseling Techniques: Individual and Group Counseling Step-by-Step, 1975, 3d edit., 1980; (computer software) Leisure PREF, 1986, Over 50: Needs, Values, Attitudes, 1988, Adapting to Change: The NVAB Program, 1997; contbr. articles to profl. jours., mags. and books. Chmn. L.A. County Foster Families 50th Anniversary, 1962-64, Hollywood Bowl Vols., L.A., 1952—. Mem. Am. Counseling Assn., Calif. Assn. for Counseling and Devel., Nat. Recreation and Park Assn., Assn. for Adult Devel. and Aging, Trojan League, Travellers Aid Soc. L.A., Jr. League L.A., First Century Families of L.A., Delta Gamma. Republican. Episcopalian.

EDWARDS, PETER JOHN, secondary education educator, historic preservation consultant, coach; b. Seattle, Oct. 16, 1965; s. Harry Brad Edwards and Linda Ottmar. BA in History, Internat. Affairs, Lewis and Clark Coll., Portland, Oreg., 1988; MA in Social Studies, Lewis and Clark Coll., 1992. Archeol. technician USDI Bur. Land Mgmt., Oreg., 1988; social studies tchr. Beaverton (Oreg.) H.S., 1993—; head rowing coach Lewis and Clark Coll., Portland, Oreg., 1988-94; historic resources cons. Columbia Hist. Rsch., Portland, Oreg., 1990—. Contbr. articles to profl. jours. dir. Lewis and Clark Alumni Assn., Portland, Oreg., 1989-91. Mem. Hist. Preservation League of Oreg., 1000 Friends of Oreg., Nat. Trust for Hist. Preservation, Nat. Coun. for Pub. History, U.S. Rowing Assn., Station L Rowing Club (pres.). Democrat. Home and Office: 6128 SW Corbett Ave Portland OR 97201-3602

EDWARDS, PRISCILLA ANN, litigation support business owner; b. Orlando, Fla., Sept. 28, 1947; d. William Granville and Bernice Royster. Paralegal cert., U. Calif., Berkeley, 1994. Paralegal Charles R. Garry Esquire, San Francisco, Calif., 1989-90, Marvin Cahn Esquire, San Francisco, 1990-91; owner, mgr. Fed. Legal Resources, San Francisco, 1991—; speaker Sonoma State U., Santa Rosa, Calif., 1993. Publisher: (book) Zero Weather, 1981. Recipient Wiley W. Manuel award for pro bono legal svcs. Bd. Govs. State Bar of Calif., 1994, 95, 96, 97. Mem. ATLA, Bar Assn. San Francisco. Episcopalian. Office: Fed Legal Resources 345 Franklin St San Francisco CA 94102-4427

EDWARDS, RALPH M., librarian; b. Shelley, Idaho, Apr. 17, 1933; s. Edward William and Maude Estella (Munsee) E.; m. Winifred Wylie, Dec. 25, 1969; children: Dylan, Nathan, Stephen. B.A., U. Wash., 1957, M.Library, 1960; D.L.S., U. Calif.-Berkeley, 1971. Libr. N.Y. Pub. Libr., N.Y.C., 1960-61; catalog libr. U. Ill. Libr., Urbana, 1961-62; br. libr. Multnomah County Libr., Portland, Oreg., 1964-67; asst. prof. Western Mich. U., Kalamazoo, 1970-74; chief of the Central Libr. Dallas Pub. Libr., 1975-81; city librarian Phoenix Pub. Libr., 1981-95, ret., 1996—. Author: Role of the Beginning Librarian in University Libraries, 1975. U. Calif. doctoral fellow, 1967-70; library mgmt. internship Council on Library Resources, 1974-75. Mem. ALA, Pub. Library Assn. Democrat. Home: 2884 Spring Blvd Eugene OR 97403

EDWARDS, RICHARD ALAN, lawyer; b. Portland, Oreg., June 28, 1938; s. Howard A. and Kay E. (Sheldon) E.; m. Renee Rosier, June 18, 1960; children: Teri Edwards Obye, Lisa Edwards Smith, Steve. BS, Oreg. State U., 1960; JD summa cum laude, Willamette U., 1968. Bar: Oreg. 1968, U.S. Dist. Ct. Oreg. 1968, U.S. Ct. Appeals (9th cir.) 1969. Various positions 1st Interstate Bank of Oreg., Portland, 1960-65; assoc. Miller, Nash, Wiener, Hager & Carlsen, Portland, 1968-74, ptnr., 1974—, mng. ptnr., 1991-96. Editor Willamette Law Jour., 1967-68. Mem. ABA (litigation sect. 1972), Oreg. State Bar (chairperson debtor-creditor sect. 1981-82, mem. various coms.). Republican. Presbyterian. Office: Miller Nash Wiener Hager & Carlsen 111 SW 5th Ave Portland OR 97204-3604

EDWARDS, SHERI RAE, elementary education educator; b. Bismarck, N.D., Feb. 24, 1950; d. Charles Jefferson and Ruth Emma (McIntosh) E.; m. Robert Erwin Fischer, May 21, 1971 (div. June 1981); children: Gregory Robert, Jacob Steven; m. Scott Warren Hunter, Oct. 11, 1986. AA, Bismarck Jr. Coll., 1971; BA in Edn., Ea. Wash. U., 1985, MA in Curriculum and Instruction, 1992. First grade tchr. Nespelem (Wash.) Sch., 1985-88, sixth grade tchr., 1988-96, gifted & talented tchr., 1986-96, eighth grade tchr., 1996—; presentor Svc. Learning Conf., Wash., 1994, Oreg., 1994, Wash. Indian Edn. Assn., 1991; trainer in field. Contbr. chpt. to book: How to Create a Community of Caring School, 1991. Advisor Parent Edn. Com., Nespelem, 1986—; com. mem. strategic planning Grand Coulee Sch. Dist., Coulee Dam, Wash., 1991. Recipient Excellence award North Ctrl. Ednl. Svc. Dist., Wash., 1996; named Tchr. of Yr., Wash. Assn. Edn. of Talented & Gifted, 1995. Mem. Assn. for Supervision and Curriculum Devel., Nat. Coun. of Tchrs. of English, Internat. Reading Assn., Nespelem Edn. Assn. (legis. rep. 1994-96), Phi Kappa Phi. Office: Nespelem Sch Dist PO Box 291 School Loop Rd Nespelem WA 99155

EDWARDS, VICKI ANN, elementary school assistant principal; b. Fremont, Nebr., Dec. 19, 1947; d. Howard Carl and Donna Marie (Earleywine) Schneider; m. Charles Douglas Edwards, May 27, 1977; 1 child, Janci. BS in Edn., Midland Luth. Coll., Fremont, 1972; MA in Edn., Ariz. State U., 1979, No. Ariz. U., 1986; EdD in Curriculum and Instrn., No. Ariz. U., 1988. Lang. arts tchr. Arlington (Nebr.) Pub. Schs., 1972-76, Glendale (Ariz.) Elem. Sch. Dist., 1977-80; reading specialist Deer Valley Sch. Dist., Phoenix, 1980-92, asst. prin., 1992—. Recipient award of achievement U.S. West Comm., Ariz., 1992. Mem. Internat. Reading Assn., Assn. for Supervision and Curriculum Devel. Nat. Coun. Tchrs. English, Phi Kappa Phi, Phi Delta Kappa. Democrat. Home: 2336 W Laurel Lane Phoenix AZ 85029 Office: Mountain Shadows Elem Sch 19602 N 45th Ave Glendale AZ 85308-7339

EDWARDS, WAYNE A., school administrator, religious studies educator; b. Putnam, Conn., Dec. 26, 1934; s. Dorian Arthur and Celia Evangeline (Gallup) E.; m. Esther Sylvia Balwit, June 4, 1955; children: Valerie, Kevin, Karen, Lynette. BA in Psychology and Sociology, Ea. Nazarene Coll., 1959;

MEd in Edn. and Reading, Holy Names Coll., 1974; postgrad., Western Evang. Sem., 1995—. Teaching asst. Ea. Nazarene Coll., Wollaston, Mass., 1957-59; educator Oakland (Calif.) Pub. Schs., 1959-76; cons. NEA, Burlingamee, Calif., 1976-77; exec. v.p. Ednl. Svcs., Inc., Oakland, 1965-72; owner, adminstr. Wayne Edwards Learning Ctrs., Walnut Creek, Calif., 1972-92; Bibl. counselor trainer McMinnville, 1992—; adminstr. Valley Christian Sch., McMinnville, 1995—; vice chmn. retirement com. Calif. Tchrs. Assn., Oakland, 1975-77; ednl. cons., 1993—. Author: (seminar program) Learning for Keeps, 1987. Dir. West Contra Costa PTA Coun., Richmond, Calif., 1968-72; dir., v.p., pres. Pinole (Calif.) C. of C., 1977-85; founding dir., counselor, educator Shepherd's Way Drug Rehab., San Pablo, Calif., 1989-91. Scholar Calif. Assn. Neurologically Handicapped Children, 1974. Mem. Nat. Released Time Edn. Assn. (western dir. 1988—, pres. 1993-94), Calif. Released Time Edn. Assn. (founding pres. 1982-89, bd. dirs., tchr. trainer 1989-92), Coun. Exceptional Children, El Sobrante C. of C., Gideons Internat. (various offices 1960-67). Home: 531 Westvale St Mcminnville OR 97128-7123 Office: Biblical Counseling Tng PO Box 456 Mcminnville OR 97128-0456

EDWARDS, WILLIAM H., SR., retired hotel corporation executive; b. Muskegon, Mich., May 25, 1917; s. William H. and Ruby A. (Tipson) E.; m. Ruth Ann Nolan, May 16, 1942; children: William H. Jr., Bradley N. Sr. BA, U. Mich., 1939; LLD, Northwood U., Midland, Mich., 1982. Cert. hotel adminstr. V.p., mng. dir. Palmer House Hilton, Chgo., 1966-68; v.p. Chgo. div. Hilton Hotels Corp., Chgo., 1968-70, sr. v.p., 1970-71, exec. v.p. ops., 1971-78; pres. Hilton Hotel div. Hilton Hotels Corp., Beverly Hills, Calif., 1978-89, vice chmn., 1985-89, bd. dirs., mem. exec. com., 1971-89, vice chmn. and dir. emeritus, 1989—; bd. dirs. Conrad Hilton Found., L.A., 1989—; bd. dirs. Travel and Tourism adv. bd. Dept. Commerce, Washington, 1983-88. Trustee Radiol. Soc. N.Am./Rsch. and Edn. Fund, Oak Brook, Ill., 1988-93, treas. 1988-89; trustee, v.p. So. Calif. chpt. Nat. Multiple Sclerosis Soc., 1984—. Recipient Cmty. Svc. award Brandeis U., 1975, Am. Tourism award New Sch. for Social Rsch., 1983, Amb. of Hospitality award Nat. Restaurant Assn. Ednl. Found., 1990, Convention Liaison Coun.-Hall of Leaders award, 1985. Mem. Am. Hotel Motel Assn. (pres. 1986, chmn. 1987), Travel Industry Assn. Am. (nat. chmn. 1982-84, bd. dirs. 1978—), L.A. Country Club. Republican. Roman Catholic. Home: 10350 Wilshire Blvd Los Angeles CA 90024-4700

EDWARDS, WILLIAM JOSEPH, lawyer, educator; b. Balt., May 18, 1962; s. Ronald and Kathleen (Marshall) E. BA, Loyola Coll., Balt., 1985; JD, Western State U., San Diego, 1991. Bar: U.S. Dist. Ct. (no. dist.) Calif. 1994. Intern Office of The Pub. Defender, Annapolis, Md., 1984-85; law clerk Goldberg, Frant & Hall, San Diego, 1987-88, Pfeffer and Turner, San Diego, 1988-89, Office of Pub. Defender, San Diego, 1989-90, Sheela and Sheela, San Diego, 1990-91; law clk. Office of Pub. Defender, San Bernardino, Calif., 1990-91; atty., law clk. Riverside County, Calif., 1991-95; dep. pub. defender Office of Pub. Defender, Riverside, Calif., 1995—; instr. Phillips Coll., Riverside, Calif., 1993-94, U. Calif., Irvine, 1994—; cons. in field. Law rev. staff writer, 1989, notes editor, 1990, asst. exec. editor, 1991; contbr. publs. to profl. jours. Bd. dirs. Assn. Retarded Citizens, Calif. Loyola Coll. Senatorial scholar, 1981; Joyce Yoshioka scholar Calif. Attys. for Crimal Justice, 1994-95; named Profl. of Yr., Assn. Retarded Citizens of Calif., 1995. Mem. ABA (criminal law sect., planning bd. human and civil rights and criminal and juvenile justice com.) Nat. Assn. Criminal Def. Lawyers (drunk driving advocacy com., death penalty commn., NLADA, death penalty litigation sect., criminal justice task force for persons with devel. disabilities, chair criminal justice process com.), Calif. Attys. for Criminal Justice, Calif. Pub. Defenders Assn., Calif. State Bar Assn. (criminal law sect.). Home: 73552 Silver Moon Trl Palm Desert CA 92260-6114 Office: Office of Public Defender 46209 Oasis St Ste 314 Indio CA 92201-5963

EEN, MIRIAM BLACKHAM, dietitian; b. Murray, Utah, May 23, 1963; d. VerNon T. and Lorene (Burton) Blackham; m. Kim Perry Een, June 30, 1990; children: Aria, Alayna. BS in Med. Dietetics, Brigham Young U., 1985; MS in Nutrition, U. Calif., Berkeley, 1991. Registered dietitian. Lab. asst. Benson Inst. Lab., Provo, Utah, 1983-85; therapeutic dietitian Valley Hosp., Las Vegas, Nev., 1985-86; cons. dietitian Beverly Manor, Las Vegas, 1985-86; nutrition cons. Sunnyvale (Calif.) Med. Clinic, 1987-88; rsch./tchg. asst. in nutrition sci. U. Calif., Berkeley, 1988-90; dietary svc. cons. Horizon Healthcare Corp., Las Vegas, 1990-93; asst. prof. U. Nev. Sch. Medicine, Las Vegas, 1991—; adj. faculty mem. U. Nev., Las Vegas, 1990-91, C.C. So. Nev., Las Vegas, 1994—. Contbr. rsch. papers, abstracts to profl. jours. Recipient Hope of Am. award Kiwanis, 1975; selected Recognized Young Dietitian of Yr., 1995. Mem. Am. Dietetic Assn. (mem. abstract rev. team 1994—), So. Nev. Dietetic Assn. (chair nominating com. 1990-94), Nev. Dietetic Assn. (pres.-elect, pres. 1994-96), Nutrition Educators of Health Profls., Soc. Tchrs. Family Medicine, Omicron Nu, Alpha Zeta. Republican. Mem. LDS Ch. Office: U Nev Sch Medicine 2040 W Charleston Blvd Ste 200 Las Vegas NV 89102-2206

EFFORD, MICHAEL ROBERT, police administrator, educator; b. L.A., July 22, 1950; s. Robert Victor and Mary (Athens) E.; m. Jolene Lynn Buttner, Mar. 20, 1976 (dec. Jan. 1980); m. Patricia Ann Jones, Feb. 2, 1985; children: Stacy Anne, Ashley Elizabeth. AA in Criminal Justice, Western Nev. Community Coll., 1976; BA in Bus., Calif. Coast U., 1993, MBA, 1996. Trooper Nev. Hwy. Patrol, Las Vegas, 1976-80; law instr. Western Nev. Community Coll., Carson City, 1980-94; adminstrv. lt. Carson City Sheriff's Dept., 1972—, in charge of planning & tng., 1993—; sheriff Carson City, 1980-94; chief of police Sonora (Calif.) Police Dept., 1994—; instr. Reno Police Acad., 1980-94, Nev. Hwy Patrol Acad., Carson City, 1980-94, Nev. Peace Officer Stds. and Tng. Acad. Editor Carson City Sheriff's Supervisory Assn. newsletter, 1989—. Pres. Carson City Labor Coalition, 1992—, planning commr. Regional Planning Commn., Carson City, 1989—; mem. Mainstreet/Redevel. Authority Carson City, 1991-94; mem. Nev. Day com., Carson City, 1985-94, 4th of July com., 1985-94, Gov.'s Ball com., 1985-94; apptd. to criminal justice tech. skills com. Western Nev. C.C., 1994. Sgt. U.S. Army, 1970-73. Recipient Svc. award Carson City Bd. Suprs., 1984. Mem. AFL-CIO Police Assn. (pres. 1989—), Kiwanis. Republican. Roman Catholic. Home: 100 S Green St Sonora CA 95370-4643

EGAN, KATHRYN SMOOT, communications educator; b. Salt Lake City, Mar. 11, 1942; d. Reed and Stella (Madsen) S.; m. David Edward Caldwell, Aug. 7, 1971 (div.); children: Jason Reed, Sherilyn Kathryn; m. Kenneth Wayne Egan, June 18, 1988. BS, U. Utah, Salt Lake City, 1964; MS, Northwestern U., 1965; PhD, U. So. Calif., 1972. Comm. coord. regional med. program UCLA, 1970-72; dir. instrl. design VA Experiments in Health Care, Denver, 1972-79; co-owner radio stas. KBLF-AM, KSNR, KNXN, Red Bluff, Quincy, Calif., 1981-85; rsch. coord. Bonneville Internat. Corp., Salt Lake City, 1985-87; prof. comm. Brigham Young U., Provo, Utah, 1987—; Rsch. cons. Salt Lake Tribune, Salt Lake City, 1994-95, Geneva Steel, Provo, 1994-95; guest lectr. UN Devel. Program, Lodz, Poland, 1995. Author: (books) Chandelle, Self-Propelled, 1993 (Utah Writers Competition award 1993), Spaces Between the Rocks, 1995 (2d place Utah Writers Competition 1995); columnist Salt Lake Tribune, 1992-95, Network Mag., Salt Lake City, 1995—; contbr. articles to jours. Mem. Am. Women in Radio and TV (v.p. programming 1991-92), Women in Comm. Mem. LDS Ch. Home: 5565 Hunt Rd Salt Lake City UT 84117 Office: Brigham Young U E 509 Harris Fine Arts Ctr Provo UT 84602

EGAN, SUSAN CHAN, security analyst; b. Manila, Feb. 11, 1946; came to U.S., 1969; d. Mariano Sui Ming and Rita Patricia (Quejong) Chan; m. Ronald Christopher Egan, Mar. 22, 1971; 1 child, Louisa. BA in Chinese Lang. and Lit., U. Wash., 1970; MBA, Boston U., 1981; MA in Comparative Lit., U. Wash., 1971. Chartered Fin. Analyst. Bus. counselor Local Devel. Corp. of South End, Boston, 1973-74; cons. Boston, 1974-76; dir. edn. and tng. Mass. Dept. Commerce and Devel., Boston, 1976-79, program devel. cons., 1979-81; trust investment officer State St. Bank and Trust Co., Boston, 1981-83, sr. trust investment officer, 1983-86, v.p., 1986-87; v.p. Scudder, Stevens & Clark, L.A., 1987—. Author: Coping With Utility Bills and Other Enegry Costs, 1971, How to Do Business with the State, 1980, New Business, 1981, A Latterday Confucian, 1987, Hung Yeh Chuan, 1992, An Introduction to Securities Markets, 1997. Mem. Assn. for Investment Mgmt. and Rsch., L.A. Soc. Fin. Analysts. Home: 921 W Campus Ln Santa Barbara CA 93117-4341 Office: 333 S Hope St Los Angeles CA 90071-1406

EGER, DENISE LEESE, rabbi; b. New Kensington, Pa., Mar. 14, 1960; d. Bernard D. and Estelle (Leese) E. BA in Religion, U. So. Calif., 1982; MA in Hebrew Letters, Hebrew Union Coll., L.A., 1985; Rabbi, Hebrew Union Coll., N.Y.C., 1988. Ordained rabbi, 1988. Rabbi Temple Beth Ora, Edmonton, Alta., Can., 1983-85; chaplain Isabella Geriatric Ctr., N.Y.C., 1986-88, Rabbi Beth Chayim Chadashim, L.A., 1988-92; founding rabbi Congregation Kol Ami, West Hollywood, Calif., 1992—. Columnist Edge mag., Lesbian News, Rainbow Ally; contbr. articles to religious publs., chpts. to anthologies. Bd. dirs. So. Calif. Bd. of Rabbis; vice chmn., spiritual adv. com. AIDS project L.A.; cmty. adv. bd. Shanti Found.; pres. Lesbian & Gay Interfaith Clergy Assn; treas. Women Rabbinic Network; clergy chair Freedom to Marry Coalition. Recipient Rainbow Key award City West Hollywood. Mem. Cen. Conf. Am. Rabbis. Office: Congregation Kol Ami Ste 100 9056 Santa Monica Blvd West Hollywood CA 90069 *I have found that in my work with the lesbian and gay community, as well as persons with AIDS, a unique resourcefulness, wellsprings of spirit and hope, in the face of death and oppression. These are truly inspirational and gifts to be shared with all humanity.*

EGER, MARILYN RAE, artist; b. Offett AFB, Nebr., Jan. 2, 1953; d. John W. and Joyce Faye (Carpenter) Shaver, stepmother Myrle I. MAsoner; m. Darrell W. Masoner, Feb. 28, 1971 (div. Sept. 1977); children: William Matthew, Melissa Rae; m. Gerard J. Eger, Jan. 30, 1982. BA, Calif. State U., Turlock, 1987. Cert. art tchr. 1990, Calif., lang. devel. specialist, 1993. Freelance artist oil painting Gibson Greetings Inc., Cin.; tchr. art, A.P. art, advanced art Bear Creek High Sch., Stockton, Calif.; tchr. art privately. One-woman shows include Stockton Fine Arts Gallery, 1984-88, Accurate Art Gallery, Sacramento, 1989-90, Sharon Gile Gallery, Isleton, Calif., 1988-91, Le Galerie, Stockton, 1989-91, Masterpiece Gallery, Carmel, Calif., 1991-95, Alan Short Gallery, Stockton, 1991; represented by Iona's Gallery, Stockton, 1995-96, Heart of the Arts Gallery, Stockton, 1996—, C's Floral Gallery, Stockton, 1995—, Lodi Art Ctr., 1997; represented in permanent collections Gulf Oil Chems., Kaiser Permanente, Masterpiece Gallery; prints pub. in Mus. Edits. West. Bd. dirs. Lodi Art Ctr., 1988-91, chmn. 1989. Recipient Award of Excellence Unitarian Fall Art Festival, 1990, Award of Excellence in Oils, 1992, Ben Day Meml. award, 1993, Bank Stockton award and H.M. Haggin Mus., 1989, U.S. Nat. Collegiate Art Merit award, 1988, Lodi 31st Ann., 1st Oils, 1988, Award of Excellence in Pastel Haggin Mus., 1992, 1st Oils and Don Morrell Meml. award CCAL Gallo Show, 1993, Art of Calif. Bronze Discovery award, 1993, 1st pastel Lodi Art Ann., 1995, award of merit Haggin Mus., 1997, numerous others; Mellon grantee, 1994. Mem. C.A.E.A., Stockton Art League, Nat. League Am. Pen. Women, West Coast Pastel Soc., Calif. Art League, Ctrl. Calif. Art League. Republican. Methodist. Home: 1295 E Peltier Rd Acampo CA 95220-9652 Studio: 1295 1/2 E Peltier Rd Acampo CA 95220

EGERTER, JOHN, information services executive; b. Wilmington, Del.; s. George and Harumi Egerter. BS in Computer Sci., U. Wash., 1989. Database cons. King County Med. Examiner, Seattle, 1988-89; client svcs. cons. SoundTel, Inc., Woodinville, Wash., 1990-96; dir. info. svcs. Matrix Comm., Portland, Oreg., 1996—. Home: 712 NE 148th Ave Vancouver WA 98684 Office: Matrix Comm Ste C 4243 SE International Way Portland OR 97222

EGGAN, PETER CORNELIUS, mathematician; b. Eugene, Oreg., Mar. 19, 1958; s. Lawrence Carl Eggan and Janet Francis (Windecker) Glubrecht; m. Madeline Faith Greenberg, Sept. 14, 1986; children: Elliott Reuben, Pierce Samuel. BA in Math. and Physics, U. Ill., 1981; MA in Math., UCLA, 1983, PhD of Math., 1985. Staff engr. Hughes Aircraft Co., El Segundo, Calif., 1985-90; sr. mem. tech. staff Aerospace Corp., El Segundo, Calif., 1990-96, dir. info. tech. dept., 1996—. Contbr. articles to profl. jours. Office: Aerospace Corp PO Box 92957 Los Angeles CA 90009-2957

EGGEBROTEN, ANNE MARIE, literature educator; b. Boulder, Aug. 19, 1948; d. Kermit Kenneth and Evelyn Frances (Gustafson) E.; m. John MacDonald Arthur, June 3, 1972; children: Rosamond Arthur, Ellen A.E., Marie A.E. BA, Stanford U., 1970; MA, U. Calif., Berkeley, 1973, PhD, 1979. Instr. Calif. State U., San Bernardino, Calif., 1981-82, City Coll. San Francisco, 1982-85; instr. Whittier (Calif.) Coll., 1987-89, Long Beach, 1990-91; assoc. prof. English, coord. women's studies program Mt. St. Mary's Coll., L.A., 1991—. Editor: Abortion: My Choice, God's Grace, Christian Women Tell Their Stories, 1994. Troop leader Girl Scouts U.S., Costa Mesa, Calif., 1989-90; elder Presbyn. Ch., Daly City, Calif., 1980-86. Mem. MLA (nat. steering com. 1975-78), NOW, Nat. Women's Studies Assn., Evangelical and Ecumenical Women's Caucus, Med. Acad. Am., Religious Coalition for Reproductive Choice. Episcopalian. Office: Mount Saint Marys Coll 12001 Chalon Rd Los Angeles CA 90049-1526

EGGER, ERNEST ALOIS, urban planner; b. San Diego, Dec. 21, 1956; s. Ivo and Ernestine Gertrude (Stockalper) E.; m. Corinne Mary Chavez, Mar. 12, 1983; children: Ryan Alfred, Hollyann Corinne. BS, Calif. State Poly. U., Pomona, 1979. Registered environ. assessor, Calif. Asst. planner City of Brea, Calif., 1979-80; assoc. planner County of Riverside, Calif., 1980-81; prin. planner Willdan Assocs., Industry, Calif., 1981-89; dir. planning Trans-Pacific Cons., Temecula, Calif., 1989-93; prin./v.p. Urban Logic Cons., Temecula, 1993—; pres. Urban logic Svcs., Temecula, 1994—. Dir. Hillcrest Carden Sch., Temecula, 1993—, Cherry Festival Assn., Beaumont, Calif., 1994-96. Mem. Am. Planning Assn. (vice dir. profl. devel. 1991-93, newsletter editor 1989-91, Meritorious Planning award 1990), Am. Inst. Cert. Planners, Beaumont C. of C. Republican. Roman Catholic. Office: Urban Logic Consultants 43517 Ridge Park Dr Ste 200 Temecula CA 92590-3602

EGGERT, ROBERT JOHN, SR., economist; b. Little Rock, Dec. 11, 1913; s. John and Eleanora (Fritz) Lapp; m. Elizabeth Bauer, Nov. 28, 1935 (dec. Dec. 1991); children: Robert John, Richard F., James E.; m. Annamarie Hayes, Mar. 19, 1994. BS, U. Ill., 1935, MS, 1936; candidate in philosophy, U. Minn., 1938; LHD (hon.), Ariz. State U., 1988. Research analyst Bur. Agrl. Econs., U.S. Dept. Agr., Urbana, Ill., 1935; prin. marketing specialist War Meat Bd., Chgo., 1943; research analyst U. Ill., 1935-36; rsch. analyst U. Minn., 1936-38; asst. prof. econs. Kans. State Coll., 1938-41; asst. dir. marketing Am. Meat Inst., Chgo., 1941-43; economist, assoc. dir. Am. Meat Inst., 1943-50; mgr. dept. marketing research Ford div. Ford Motor Co., Dearborn, Mich., 1951-53; mgr. program planning Ford div. Ford Motor Co., 1953-54, mgr. bus. research, 1954-57, mgr. marketing research marketing staff, 1957-61; mgr. marketing research Ford div. Ford Motor Co. (Ford div.), 1961-64, mgr. internat. marketing research marketing staff, 1964-65, mgr. overseas marketing research planning, 1965-66; mgr. marketing research Ford div. Ford Motor Co. (Lincoln-Mercury div.), 1966-67; dir. agribus. programs Mich. State U., 1967-68; staff v.p. econ. and marketing research RCA Corp., N.Y.C., 1968-76; pres., chief economist Eggert Econ. Enterprises, Inc., Sedona, Ariz., 1976—; lectr. mktg. U. Chgo., 1947-49; adj. prof. bus. forecasting No. Ariz., 1976-79; mem. econ. adv. bd. U.S. Dept. Commerce, 1969-71, mem. census adv. com., 1975-78; mem. panel econ. advisers Congl. Budget Office, 1975-76; interim dir. Econ. Outlook Ctr. Coll. Bus. Adminstrn. Ariz. State U., Tempe, 1985-86, cons., 1985—; mem. Econ. Estimates Commn. Ariz., 1979—; apptd. Ariz. Gov.'s Commn. Econ. Devel., 1991—. Investment Adv. Coun. Ariz. State Retirement System, 1993—; trustee Marcus J. Lawrence Med. Ctr. Found., 1992-96, vice-chmn., 1996—; co-chmn. Gov.'s Strategic Partnership for Econ. Devel., Sr. Living Cluster, Dec. 1995—. Contbr. articles to profl. lit.; founder, editor emeritus: monthly Blue Chip Econ. Indicators, 1976—; exec. editor Ariz. Blue Chip, 1984—, Western Blue Chip Econ. Forecast, 1986—, Blue Chip Job Growth Update, 1990—, Mexico Consensus Econ. Forecast, 1993—. Elder Ch. of Red Rocks. Recipient Econ. Forecast award Chgo. chpt. Am. Statis. Assn., 1950, 60, 68; Seer of Yr. award Harvard Bus. Sch. Indsl. Econs., 1973. Fellow Am. Statis. Assn. (chmn. bus. and econ. stats sect. 1957—, pres. Chgo. chpt. 1948-49), Nat. Assn. Bus. Economists (coun. 1969-72); mem. Coun. Internat. Mktg. Rsch. and Planning Dirs. (chmn. 1965-66), Am. Mktg. Assn. (dir., v.p. mktg. mgmt. divsn. 1972-73, nat. pres. 1974-75), Fed. Stats. Users Conf. (chmn. trustees 1960-61), Conf. Bus. Economists (chmn. 1972-74), Am. Quarter Horse Assn. (dir. 1966-73), Ariz. Econ. Roundtable, Am. Econs. Assn., Phoenix Econ. Club (hon.), Ariz. C. of C. (bd. dirs. 1991-95), Alpha Zeta. Republican. Office: Eggert Econ Enterprises Inc PO Box 2243 Sedona AZ 86339-2243 *I have always strived to be a person of greater value. My modest success has resulted largely from the manifold contribution of others. In fact, the only true measure of my accomplishments will unfold in the future. What the future will be is difficult to foretell, but it always has been a challenge to maximize productivity and to look ahead, and to dream of things that never were and say—why not? My motto is "Aiming for Excellence in Economic Forecasting".*

EGUCHI, YASU, artist; b. Japan, Nov. 30, 1938; came to U.S., 1967; s. Chihaku and Kiku (Koga) E.; m. Anita Phillips, Feb. 24, 1968. Student, Horie Art Acad., Japan, 1958-65. Exhibited exhbns., Tokyo Mus. Art, 1963, 66, Santa Barbara Mus. Art, Calif., 1972, 73, 74, 85, Everson Mus. Art, Syracuse, N.Y., 1980, Nat. Acad. Design, N.Y.C., 1980—, one-man shows, Austin Gallery, Scottsdale, Ariz., 1968-87, Joy Tash Gallery, Scottsdale, 1989—, Greyston Galleries, Cambria, Calif., 1969, 70, 72, Copenhagen Galleries, Calif., 1970-78, Charles and Emma Frye Art Mus., Seattle, 1974, 84, Hammer Galleries, N.Y.C., 1977, 79, 81, 93, City of Heidenheim, W. Ger., 1980, Artique Ltd., Anchorage, 1981—; pub. and pvt. collections, Voith Gmbh, W. Ger., City of Giengen and City of Heidenheim, Fed. Republic Germany, represented, Deer Valley, Utah, Hunter Resources, Santa Barbara, Am. Embassy, Paris, Charles and Emma Frye Art Mus., Seattle, Nat. Acad. Design, N.Y.C.; author: Der Brenz Entlang, 1980; contbr. to jours in field. Active Guide Dogs for the Blind, San Raphael, Calif., 1976; active City of Santa Barbara Arts Council, 1979, The Eye Bank for Sight Restoration, N.Y., 1981, Anchorage Arts Council, 1981, Santa Barbara Mus. Natural History, 1989. Recipient Selective artist award Yokohama Citizen Gallery, 1965; recipient Artist of Yr. award Santa Barbara Arts Council, 1979, Hon. Citizen award City of Heidenheim, 1980, The Adolph and Clara Obrig prize NAD, 1983, Cert. of Merit NAD, 1985, 87. Home: PO Box 30206 Santa Barbara CA 93130-0206

EHNES, JACK, state insurance commissioner. BS, Cornell U., 1973; MA, Vanderbilt U., 1975. Pers. rsch. psychologist State of Tenn., 1981-83; pers. specialist Colo. Dept. Pers., 1983-86, mgmt. analyst, 1986-87; mgr. employee benefits Colo. Dept. Adminstrn. Dept. Pers., Denver, 1987-91; dir. fin. and benefits divsn. Colo. Dept. Pers., Denver, 1991-92; dep. commr. ins. Colo. Divsn. Ins., Denver, 1992-94, commr. of ins., 1994—; chmn. Nat. Assn. Ins. Commr.'s spl. com. on Blue Cross, vice-chair accident and health com.; bd. dirs. Colo. State Employees Credit Union. Trustee Pub. Employees Retirement Assn. Office: Divsn of Ins 1560 Broadway Ste 850 Denver CO 80202

EHRET, CHRISTOPHER PAUL, history and linguistics educator; b. San Francisco, July 27, 1941; s. Robert Ashworth and Margaret (Scott) Fish; m. Patricia Louise Clemmer; children: Susannah Marie, Seth John, Allan Thomas Gulledge, Jana Chrystene Gulledge. BA, U. Redlands, 1963; MA, Northwestern U., 1966, PhD, 1968. Asst. prof. UCLA, 1968-72, assoc. prof., 1972-78, prof., 1978-94, disting. (step VI) prof., 1994—, assoc. dir. James S. Coleman African Studies Ctr., 1995-96; chair undergrad. program in African studies UCLA, 1976—; lectr. in field. Author: Southern Nilotic History: Linguistic Approaches to Study of the Past, 1971, The Historical Reconstruction of Southern Cushitic Phonology and Vocabulary, 1980, Reconstructing Proto-Afroasiatic: Vowels, Tone, Consonants and Vocabulary, 1995; author, editor: The Archaeological and Linguistic Reconstruction of African History, 1982; editl. bd. Sprache und Geschichte in Africa, 1975—; contbr. articles to profl. jours. Coach Am. Youth Soccer, Calif., 1983-90. Grantee Ford Found., U.S., Kenya, Tanzania, 1971-76; Nat. Merit scholar Caltech, U. Redlands, 1959-63; Fgn. Area fellow Social Sci. Rsch. Coun., Kenya, Tanzania, Uganda, 1966-68; Fulbright Rsch. fellow, Somalia, 1982. Mem. African Studies Assn. (life). Office: Univ Calif Dept History Los Angeles CA 90024

EHRET, JOSEPHINE MARY, microbiologist, researcher; b. Roswell, N.Mex., Feb. 26, 1934; d. Edward and Glenna (Memmer) E. BS, U. N.Mex., 1955. Med. technologist U. Colo. Health Scis. Ctr., Denver, 1956-75, rsch. microbiologist, 1956—; rsch. microbiologist Denver Dept. Health and Hosps., 1980—; instr. sch. medicine U. Colo., 1985—. Contbr. articles to profl. publs. Mem. Am. Soc. for Microbiology, Am. Soc. Med. Technologists (cert.), Am. Venereal Disease Assn., Calif. Assn. Continuing Med. Lab. Edn. Democrat. Home: 1344 S Eudora St Denver CO 80222 Office: Denver Pub Health Dept 605 Bannock St Denver CO 80204-4505

EHRHORN, THOMAS FREDERICK, software quality assurance engineer; b. Lebanon, Pa., Nov. 12, 1946; s. Frederick William and Evelyn Matilda (Daullary) E.; m. Elaine Mae Thernlund, Feb. 16, 1974; 1 child, Susan Marie. BA in Computer Sci., SUNY, Albany, 1981; AS in Tng. Devices Technology, C.C. of the Air Force, Maxwell AFB, Ala., 1986; MA in Edn., Chapman U., 1992. Cert. tchr. computer sci., Calif. Enlisted USAF, 1966, advanced through ranks to chief master sgt.; electronics tech. USAF, various, 1966-86; ret. USAF, 1986; electronics tech. Systems Rsch. Labs, Castle AFB, Calif., 1986-89; computer sci. USAF, Castle AFB, 1989-93; electronics engr. USAF, Kirtland AFB, N.Mex., 1994-95; software quality assurance engr. Intera Environ. Svcs., Albuquerque, N. Mex., 1995—. Registrar Atwater (Calif.) Youth Soccer League, 1990-93; mem./pres. Winton (Calif.) Sch. Bd., 1987-91; exec. bd. Yosemite Area Coun., Boy Scouts Am., modesto, Calif., 1985-87; chmn. Fresno (Calif.) Diocese Youth Ministry Bd., 1985-86. Mem. KC, Am. Soc. Quality Control, Mensa. Democrat. Roman Catholic. Office: Intera Albuquerque 1650 University Blvd NE Albuquerque NM 87102-1726

EHRSAM, ELDON EDWARD, operations research analyst, real estate broker; b. Bern, Kans., July 8, 1936; s. Loyd and Elma Elizabeth (Bauman) E.; m. Clara Louise Schwartz, Nov. 20, 1957; children: Elizabeth Sue, Jeffrey Edward, John Eldon, Brian Loyd. BS, Washburn U., Topeka, 1962; MS, U. So. Calif., 1969; cert. computer tech., U. Calif., Santa Barbara, 1972. Lic. real estate broker, Calif. Physicist Naval Ordnance Lab., Corona, Calif., 1962-65; electronic engr. Hdqs. Space and Missile Test Ctr., Vandenberg AFB, 1968-73, telemetry sys. mgr., 1973-76, ops. rsch. analyst, 1976—; broker assoc. Real Properties Investments, Solvang, Calif., 1981-89; securities rep. Vestcap Securities Corp., Solvang, 1982-89; broker Hunter Prudential Realty, Lompoc, Calif., 1990—. Co-contbr. articles to profl. jours. Asst. scoutmaster Boy Scouts Am. Mem. AIAA, Internat. Platform Assn., Nat. Assn. Securities Dealers, Nat. Assn. Realtors, Real Estate Securities and Syndication Inst., Sigma Pi Sigma, Masons, Elks. Office: Space and Missile Sys Ctr Detachment 9 Vandenberg AFB CA 93437-5320

EHST, ERIC RICHARD, aerospace engineer; b. Washington, Nov. 20, 1951; s. Richard Paul and Eileen Marjorie (Kohout) E.; m. Vickie Anita Bentley, Jan. 6, 1977; children: Nicholas Eric, Spencer Alexander. BS in Aerospace Engrng., U. Md., 1973. Devel. engr. Flight Systems, Inc., Arlington, Va., 1977-78; sr. exptl. engr. Pratt & Whitney Aircraft, West Palm Beach, Fla., 1978-83; sr. devel. specialist Allied Signal Aerospace, Phoenix, 1983—. Asst. scoutmaster Boy Scouts Am., Bethesda, Md., 1969-72, scoutmaster, 1973; pres. S.W. Outdoor Club, Tempe, Ariz., 1993; chmn. Ariz. Dist. 24 Dems., Phoenix, 1995-96; vice chmn. Ariz. Dem. Party, 1997—. Served with USAF, 1973-77. Home: 14409 N 43d St Phoenix AZ 85032 Office: Allied Signal Engines MS 301-226 111 S 34th St Phoenix AZ 85034-2802

EICHINGER, MARILYNNE H., museum administrator; m. Martin Eichinger; children: Ryan, Kara, Julia, Jessica, Talik. BA in Anthropology and Sociology magna cum laude, Boston U., 1965; MA, Mich. State U., 1971. With emergency and outpatient staff Ingham County Mental Health Ctr., 1972; founder, pres., exec. dir. Impression 5 Sci. and Art Mus., Lansing, Mich., 1973-85; pres. Oreg. Mus. Sci. and Industry, Portland, 1985-95; bd. dirs. Portland Visitors Assn., 1985-95; pres. Informal Edn. Products Ltd., 1995—, Portland, 1995—; bd. dirs. Portland Visitors Assn., 1994—, NW Regional Edn. Labs., 1991—; instr. Lansing (Mich.) C.C., 1978; ptnr. Eyrie Studio, 1982-85; bd. dirs. Assn. Sci. Tech. Ctrs., 1980-84, 88-93; mem. adv. bd. Portland State U.; condr. numerous workshops in interactive exhibit design, adminstrn. and fund devel. for schs., orgns., profl. socs. Author: (with Jane Mack) Lexington Montessori School Survey, 1969, Manual on the Five Senses, 1974; pub. Mich. edit. Boing mag. Founder Cambridge Montessori Sch., 1964; bd. dirs. Lexington Montessori Sch., 1969, Mid-Mich. South Health Sys. Agy., 1978-81, Cmty. Referral Ctr., 1981-85, Sta. WKAR-Radio, 1981-85; active Lansing "Riverfest" Lighted Boat Parade, 1980; mem. state Health Coordinating Coun., 1980-82; mem. pres.'s adv. coun. Portland State U., 1986—; mem. pres.' adv. bd. Portland State U., 1987-91. Recipient Diana Cert. Leadership, YWCA, 1976-77, Woman of Achievement award, 1991, Community Svc. award Portland State U., 1992. Mem. Am. Assn.

Mus., Oreg. Mus. Assn., Assn. Sci. and Tech. Ctrs., Zonta Lodge (founder, bd. dirs. East Lansing club 1978), Internat. Women's Forum, City Club Portland, Portland C. of C. Office: Informal Edn Products Ltd 2520 SW Sherwood Dr Portland OR 97201-1615

EICHMAN, PATRICIA, interior designer; b. Detroit, Mich., Dec. 12, 1938; d. Stanley Z. Pasierbek and Annette T. (Rogusz) Spindler; m. Richard R. Bourassa, 1957 (div. 1978); children: Robert, Jeffrey, Lori; m. John W. Eichman Jr., 1983 (div. 1992); m. John Walters, 1995. Grad. H.S., Detroit. Cert. interior designer, Calif. Sales designer Ethan Allen Store, Phoenix, 1974-79; interior designer Lou Regester Furniture, Phoenix, 1979-84, VJ Lloyds Furniture, San Diego, 1985-94; pvt. practice San Diego, 1994—. Treas. Friends of Downtown San Diego, 1993, bd. dirs., 1993-94, 97, co-chair charities, 1994, 97, 2d v.p., 1995, 97, bd. dirs. Design Alliance to Combat Areas, San Diego, 1990-91. Recipient Sam award Bldg. Industry Assn., San Diego, 1993, Grand Orchid award Orchid & Onions, San Diego, 1993, Best Master Bedroom Suite award Street of Dreams, San Diego, 1991; featured in ASID Kitchen and Bath Showcase and San Diego Home & Garden Mag., 1995. Mem. Internat. Soc. Interior Designers (pres. San Diego chpt. 1992, treas. 1987-89, bd. dirs. 1989-93), Am. Soc. Interior Designers, Internat. Interior Design Assn. Home and Office: 843 Wulff St San Marcos CA 92069

EIDE, JOEL S., museum director. Dir. No. Ariz. U. Art Mus. and Galleries. Office: No Ariz U Art Mus and Galleries PO Box 6021 Flagstaff AZ 86011

EIFLER, CARL FREDERICK, retired psychologist; b. Los Angeles, June 27, 1906; s. Carl Frederick and Pauline (Engelbert) E.; m. Margaret Christine Aaberg, June 30, 1963; 1 son, Carl Henry; 1 adopted son, Byron Hisey. BD, Jackson Coll., 1956; Ph.D., Ill. Inst. Tech., 1962. Insp. U.S. Bur. Customs, 1928-35, chief insp., 1936-37, dep. collector, 1937-56; bus. mgr. Jackson Coll., Honolulu, 1954-56, instr., 1955-56; grad. asst. instr., research asst. Ill. Inst. Tech., Chgo., 1959-62; psychologist Monterey County Mental Health Services, Salinas, Calif., 1964-73; ret., 1973. Contbg. author Psychon. Sci., vol. 20, 1970; co-author: The Deadliest Colonel; author, pub.: Jesus Said. Served with U.S. Army, 1922-23, 40-47; col. ret. Decorated Combat Infantryman's Badge, Legion of Merit with 2 oak leaf clusters, Bronze Star medal, Air medal, Purple Heart; named to Military Intelligence Corps Hall of Fame, 1988; recipient Albert Gallatin award U.S. Treas. Dept., 1963, Gen. William J. Donovan award, 1993. Mem. AAUP, Am. Psychol. Assn., Western States Psychol. Assn., Calif. Psychol. Assn., Res. Officers Assn. (Hawaii pres. 1947), Assn. Former Intelligence Officers (bd. govs., Western coord.), Pearl Harbor Survivors, 101 Assn., Assn. U.S. Army Vets. of OSS (past bd. govs., Western coord., v.p.), Ret. Officers Assn., Masons, KT, Shriners, Elks, Nat. Sojourners, Psi Chi. Home: 22700 Picador Dr Salinas CA 93908-1116

EIGLER, DONALD MARK, physicist; b. L.A., Mar. 23, 1953; s. Irving Baer and Evelin Muriel (Baker) E.; m. Roslyn Winifred Rubesin, Nov. 2, 1986. BA, U. Calif., San Diego, 1975, PhD in Physics, 1984. Rsch. assoc. U. Köln (Fed. Republic Germany), 1975-76; rsch. assoc. U. Calif., San Diego, 1977-84, postdoctoral rsch. assoc., 1984, assoc. rsch. physicist dept. physics, 1986; postdoctoral mem. tech. staff AT&T Bell Labs., Murray Hill, N.J., 1984-86; rsch. staff mem. IBM, San Jose, Calif., 1986-93, IBM fellow, 1993—; Alexander M. Cruickshank lectr. in phys. sci. (Gordon Rsch. Confs.), 1994. Co-winner 1993-94 Newcomb Cleveland prize AAAS; recipient Dannie Heineman prize Göttingen Acad. Scis., 1995. Fellow Am. Physical Soc. Office: IBM Almaden Rsch Ctr 650 Harry Rd San Jose CA 95120-6099

EIGSTI, ROGER HARRY, insurance company executive; b. Vancouver, Wash., Apr. 17, 1942; s. Harry A. and Alice E. (Huber) E.; m. Mary Lou Nelson, June 8, 1963; children: Gregory, Ann. BS, Linfield Coll., 1964. CPA, Oreg., Wash. Staff CPA Touche Ross and Co., Portland, Oreg., 1964-72; asst. to controller Safeco Corp., Seattle, 1972-78, controller, 1980; controller Safeco Life Ins. Co., Seattle, 1978-80; pres. Safeco Credit Co., Seattle, 1980-81, Safeco Life Ins. Co., Seattle, 1981-85; exec. v.p., CFO Safeco Corp., Seattle, 1985—, chmn., pres., CEO, chmn. CEO. bd. dirs. Ind. Colls. of Wash., Seattle, 1981-87, bus. dir. Seattle Repertory Theatre, 1981—, bd. dirs. 1981—. Mem. Am. Inst. CPA's, Life Office Mgmt. Assn. (bd. dirs. 1983—), Seattle C. of C. (chmn. metro budget rev. com. 1984—). Republican. Clubs: Mercer Island (Wash.) Country (treas., bd. dirs. 1981-84); Central Park Tennis. Home: 11701 NE 36th Pl Bellevue WA 98005-1234*

EIKENBERRY, ARTHUR RAYMOND, writer, service executive, researcher; b. Sebring, Fla., June 5, 1920; s. Leroy Albertus and Vernie Cordelia (Griffin) E.; m. Carol Jean Parrott, June 10, 1955; children: Robin Rene, Shari LaVon, Jan Rochelle, Karyn LaRae, Kelli Yvette. Student, Pasadena (Calif.) Jr. Coll., 1939, Kunming U., China, 1944-45. MSgt. Army Air Corps, 1941-45, re-enlisted in grade of TSgt., 1947; advanced through grades to SMSgt. USAF; ret., 1973, mgmt., pers., adminstrv. and security insp.; mgr. property control, real estate agent TR Devel. Co., Englewood, Colo., 1973-74; real estate agt. The Pinery, Parker, Colo., 1974-75; mgr., patient acctg. dept. Univ. Colo. Health Scis. Ctr., Denver, 1975-89. Author: Investment Strategies for the Clever Investor, 1989, LOTTO GURU (Omni-Personal Selection Systems & Strategies), 1989. Charter mem. U.S. Congl. Adv. Bd. Fellow Internat. Biog. Ctr. (hon. life patron, dep. dir. gen.); mem. Am. Biog. Inst. (life, dep. gov., nat. adviser), World Inst. of Achievement (disting.), Masons, Eastern Star, Royal Order of the Amaranth. Address: The Lakes 8524 W Sahara Ave # 174 Las Vegas NV 89117-1818

EILBER, FREDERICK RICHARD, surgeon; b. Detroit, Aug. 17, 1940; s. Frederick Benjamin and Margaret (Patterson) E.; m. Harriet Harris Comstock, Dec. 2, 1964; children: Frederick C., Gregory K., Timothy B., Matthew C. MD, U. Mich., 1965. Intern U. Md., 1965-66; surg. resident U. Md., Balt., 1965-72; clin. assoc. NIH Surgery, Bethesda, Md., 1967-71; sr. fellow M.D. Anderson, Houston, 1972-73; asst. prof. dept. surgery UCLA, 1973-75, assoc. prof., 1975-79, prof., 1979-91, prof., chief surgery/oncology, 1991—. Recipient Disting. Alumni award M.D. Anderson, 1985. Fellow ACS, Am. Surg. Assn., Soc. Univ. Surgeons, Soc. Head and Neck Surgeons, Soc. Surg. Oncology (James Ewing Resident award 1970); mem. Am. Radium Soc. (pres. 1986). Office: UCLA Divsn Surg Oncology 54-140 CHS 10833 Le Conte Ave Los Angeles CA 90024-1602

EILENBERG, LAWRENCE IRA, theater educator, artistic director; b. Bklyn., May 26, 1947; s. Jerome and Dorothy Vera (Natleson) E.; m. Diane Marie Eliasof, Nov. 25, 1973 (dec. Dec. 1984); children: David Joseph, Benjamin Alan; m. Judith Heiner, Nov. 10, 1990 (dec. Nov. 1994). BA, Cornell U., 1968; MPhil, Yale U., 1971, PhD, 1975. Jr. fellow Davenport Coll., Yale U., New Haven, 1971-72; asst. prof. theatre dept. Cornell U., Ithaca, N.Y., 1972-75; vis. asst. prof. in theatre U. Mich., Ann Arbor, 1975-77; asst. prof., then assoc. prof. U. Denver, 1977-82, 83; prof. San Francisco State U., 1983—, chmn. theatre arts dept., 1984-92; artistic dir. Magic Theatre, San Francisco, 1992-93, dramaturg, 1997—; theatre corr. Sta. KCFR (NPR), Denver, 1979-82; literary mgr. Denver Ctr. Theatre Co., 1981-83; artistic dir. San Francisco New Vaudeville Festival, 1985-89; dramaturg One Act Theatre Co., San Francisco, 1986-88; bd. dirs. Theatre Bay Area, San Francisco, 1985-90, pres., 1987-89; co-dir. Congress of Clowns, 1994; speaker, lectr. in field. Editor Stage/Space mag., 1981-83; contbr. articles, book and theater revs. to profl. publs. U.S. del. Podium Festival of USSR, Moscow, 1989. Grantee Lilly Found., 1981, Idaho Humanities Assn., 1983, 84, 85, NEA, 1986, 92, Calif. Arts Coun., 1987, 88, 92; recipient Best Broadcast award Colo. Broadcasters Assn., 1982. Mem. Literary Mgrs. and Dramaturgs Am. (v.p. 1989-90), Nat. Assn. Schs. of Theatre (bd. accreditation, 1990-91, evaluator 1986—). Home: 1059 Union St Apt N San Francisco CA 94133-2575 Office: San Francisco State U Theatre Arts Dept 1600 Holloway Ave San Francisco CA 94132-1722

EINSTEIN, CLIFFORD JAY, advertising executive; b. L.A., May 4, 1939; s. Harry and Thelma (Bernstein) E.; m. Madeline Mandel, Jan. 28, 1962; children: Harold Jay, Karen Holly. BA in English, UCLA, 1961. Writer Norman, Craig and Kummel, N.Y.C., 1961-62, Foote, Cone and Belding, L.A., 1962-64; ptnr. Silverman and Einstein, L.A., 1965-67; pres., creative dir. Dailey and Assos., L.A., 1968-93, chmn., CEO, 1994—, also bd dirs.; dir. Campaign '80, advt. agy. Reagan for Pres., 1980; lectr. various colls.; founder, bd. dirs. First Coastal Bank. Contbr. articles to Advertising Age; prodr.: (play) Whatever Happened to Georgie Tapps, L.A. and San Francisco, 1980; film appearances include Real Life, Modern Romance, Defending Your Life, Face/Off, 1997; T.V. appearance in Bizarre, Super Dave Show. Bd. dirs. Rape Treatment Ctr., Santa Monica Med. Ctr.; trustee Mus. Contemporary Art, L.A., 1994—. With U.S. Army, 1957. Recipient Am. Advt. award, 1968, 73, 79, Clio award, 1973, Internat. Broadcast Pub. Svc. award, 1970, 85, Nat. Addy award, 1979, Gov.'s award, 1987; named Creative Dir. of the West, Adweek Poll, 1982, Exec. of West, 1986, Western States Assn. Advt. Agys. Leader of Yr., 1992. Mem. AFTRA, ASCAP, SAG, Dirs. Guild Am., Beverly Hills Tennis Club, Calif. Club. Office: Dailey & Assocs 3055 Wilshire Blvd Los Angeles CA 90010-1108

EINSTEIN, STEPHEN JAN, rabbi; b. L.A., Nov. 15, 1945; s. Syd C. and Selma (Rothenberg) E.; m. Robin Susan Kessler, Sept. 9, 1967; children: Rebecca Yael, Jennifer Melissa, Heath Isaac, Zachary Shane. AB, UCLA, 1967; BHL, Hebrew Union Coll., L.A., 1968, DHL, 1995; MAHL, Hebrew Union Coll., Cin., 1971; DD (hon.), Hebrew Union Coll., 1996. Ordained rabbi. Rabbi Temple Beth Am, Parsippany, N.J., 1971-74; rabbi Temple Beth David, Westminster, Calif., 1974-76, Congregation B'nai Tzedek, Fountain Valley, Calif., 1976—. Co-author: Every Person's Guide to Judaism, 1989; co-editor: Introduction to Judaism, 1983. Pres., trustee Fountain Valley (Calif.) Sch. Bd., 1984-90; mem. Personnel Commn. Fountain Valley Sch. Dist., 1991—; chaplain Fountain Valley Police Dept. Honored for Maj. Contributions to Jewish Learning, Orange County (Calif.) Bur. Jewish Edn., 1986; recipient Micah Award for Interfaith Activities, Am. Jewish Com., 1988. Mem. Ctrl. Conf. Am. Rabbis (mem. exec. bd. 1989-91, mem. ethics com. 1993—), Pacific Assn. Reform Rabbis (mem. exec. bd. 1987-91, 97—), Orange County Bd. Rabbis (pres. 1976-79, 97—), Jewish Educators Assn. Orange County (pres. 1979-81), Orange County Bur. Jewish Edn. (v.p. 1982-84, 92-94, pres. 1994-97), Am. Cancer Soc. (v.p. West Orange County dist. 1994—), Phi Beta Kappa. Democrat. Office: Congregation Bnai Tzedek 9669 Talbert Ave Fountain Vly CA 92708-5146

EIS, JOEL DAVID, scenic and lighting designer; b. Washington; s. Morton Lion and Edith (Cohen) E.; m. Carol Nelson, Sept. 1, 1972 (div. Sept. 1976); 1 child, Chelsea; stepchildren: Debra, Brian; m. Toni Paullette Laboni, May 1997. B in Acting/Directing, U. Calif., Santa Barbara, 1968; M in Directing/Design, Humboldt State U., Arcata, Calif., 1978; MFA, San Francisco Art Inst., 1997. Instr. Lassen C.C., Susanville, Calif., 1973-76, Calif. State Penitentiary, Susanville, 1974-75, Chapman Coll., L.A., 1979-81; artist in residence San Francisco Sch. of Arts, 1982-90; arts resident scenic/lighting design Mercy H.S., Riordan H.S., San Francisco, 1994-96; tchg. asst. San Francisco Art Inst., 1996; guest lighting designer Ohlone Coll., Fremont, Calif., 1992; guest scenic designer San Francisco City Coll., 1993. Author: State Crafts: A Complete Basic Training Manual for Performing Arts Technologies, 1st edit., 1986; dir. several dozen plays, dramatic readings, spl. events; scenic and lighting designer over 125 designs for profl. theatre, dance, trade, fashion and music events; tech. dir. over 15 profl. theatre and dance cos.; contbr. articles to profl. jours.; playwright: Are We Turned On?, 1975, A Short Vacation, 1976, Ubu Roi, 1977, Just Another One Night Stand, 1981, The Village and the Dragon, 1984, Ceremonies, 1992, Blood of Lions, 1993, Ubu! A Thrash Rock Musical, 1994, Way Out West, 1994, Men of Steel, 1994, Like Trains in the Night, 1995, All the Right Moves, 1995, Hamlet or the Great Mechanical, 1996, Fire in My Hands/Dream of Motion, 1997, others. Recipient Drama Critic's Circle award City of L.A., 1970, 71, San Francisco BAy Area Critics Circle award, 1980, Dramalogue award State of Calif., 1981; grantee Koret Found. Vocat. Minority Tng., San Francisco Sch. of Arts, 1986, Getty Found. Team, 1989.

EISEMANN, KURT, director computer center, mathematics educator; b. Nuremberg, Germany, June 22, 1923; came to U.S., 1948; s. Lazarus and Lina (Bacharach) E.; m. Marlene K. Cross, June 22, 1969 (div. Oct. 1988); children: Jamin, Caroline. BA in Math., Yeshiva U., 1950; MS in Applied Math., MIT, 1952; PhD in Applied Math., Harvard U., 1962. Sr. mathematician IBM, N.Y.C., 1952-56; rsch. mathematician IBM, 1956-61; mgr. math. rsch. Univac Div. Sperry Rand Corp., Washington, 1961-63; dir. computer ctr., assoc. prof. Sch. Engring. Cath. U. Am., Washington, 1963-66; tech. dir. Comput. Usage Devel. Corp., Boston, 1966-68; dir. acad. computer svc., prof. computer sci. Northeastern U., Boston, 1968-74; dir. computer svc., prof. math and computer sci. U. Mo. Kansas City, Kansas City, 1974-82; dir. univ. computer ctr., prof. math. scis. San Diego State U., 1982-92, prof. emeritus, 1992—; lectr. Yeshiva U., 1953-55, Cath. U. Am., 1962-63. Office: San Diego State U Math Dept San Diego CA 92182

EISENBERG, RONALD LEE, radiologist; b. Phila., July 11, 1945; s. Milton and Betty (Klein) E.; m. Zina Leah Schiff; 2 children. AB, U. Pa., 1965, MD, 1965, JD, 1996. Diplomate Am. Bd. Radiology; bar: Calif. Staff radiologist VA Med. Ctr., San Francisco, 1975-80; prof. and chmn. dept. radiology La. State U., Shreveport, 1980-91; chmn. dept. radiology Highland Hosp., Oakland, Calif., 1991—. Author: Gastrointestinal Radiology, 1982, 3d edit., 1996, Diagnostic Imaging in Internal Medicine, 1985, Diagnostic Imaging in Surgery, 1986, Clinical Imaging: An Atlas of Differential Diagnosis, 1987, ed edit., 1997, Atlas of Differential Diagnoses, 1988, Radiology: An Illustrated History, 1992, others; co-author: (newspaper column) Doctor/Doctor; contbr. numerous articles to profl. jours. Maj. U.S. Army, 1971-73. Named Man of the Yr., Am. Physicians Fellowship, Boston, 1987. Fellow Am. Coll. Radiology; mem. Radiol. Soc. N.Am., Am. Roentgen Ray Soc., Assn. of Univ. Radiologists, Soc. for Gastrointestinal Radiology, So. Med. Assn., Am. Coll. Radiology, Ark-La-Tex Radiol. Soc. Office: Highland Hosp Dept Radiology 1411 E 31st St Oakland CA 94602-1018

EISENMAN, ATHENA JOYCE, association administrator; b. Birmingham, Ala., July 3, 1948; d. George Frank and Lillian (Crawford) Taylor; m. Alva George Eisenman, Mar. 24, 1973; children: Aaron, Adrianne. BA in Comm., Met. State Coll., Denver, 1975; MA in Orgnl. Mgmt., U. Phoenix, 1994. Social scis. instr. C.C. of Denver, 1977; pub. rels. dir. Denver Walking Tours, 1977-78; legis. aide and analyst Hon. Wm. R. Roberts, Denver City Coun., 1978-79; mem. telemktg./sales staff MCI, Denver, 1980-81; mgmt. cons. AJE Consulting Group, Denver, 1983-96; exec. dir. Colo. Sickle Cell Assn., Denver, 1995—; bd. dirs., comm. chair Speakers Bureau Tng., Nat. Voluntary Health Agencies, Denver, 1995—. Bd. dirs., sec. Adult Care Mgmt. Inc., Denver, 1993-96; pres. Montbello United Neighbors, Denver, 1993-95; mem. black edn. adv. coun. Denver Pub. Schs., 1992-95; adult edn. instr. All Nations GED Ctr., Aurora, Colo., 1996—; del. Nat. Rep. Conv., 1st Congl., Denver, 1996; named to Rep. Leadership Program, Colo. State Reps., Denver, 1989-90. Mem. Metro Denver Black Rep. Forum (bd. dirs. 1995—, pres. 1996—), Colo. Lincoln Club, Colo. H.S. Assn. (forensic judge), Nat. Forensic League (forensic judge). Republican. Home: 5180 Deephaven Ct Denver CO 80239 Office: Colo Sickel Cell Assn Inc 4280 Hale Pkwy Denver CO 80220

EISENSTAT, BENJAMIN, artist; b. Phila., June 4, 1915; s. Philip and Rose (Muskett) E.; m. Jane Sperry, Aug. 23, 1940; children: Kathryn Krall, Alice Amanda Carter. Student, Fleisher Art Meml., Phila., 1932-36, Pa. Acad. Fine Art, 1936-37, Albert Barnes Found., 1937-38. Prof. emeritus U. of the Arts, Phila., 1946-84; tchr. Fleisher Art Meml., 1946-50, Phila. Mus. Art, 1962-66, Parson's Sch. of Design, 1976-81, Acad. of Art, San Francisco, 1986; vis. prof. Cambridge (Eng.) Coll. of Art, 1976, Syracuse U., 1981; lectr. Royal Coll. Art, London, N.Y. Hist. Soc., Montclair (N.J.) State Coll., others. Group shows include Met. Mus., Nat. Acad., Pa. Acad. Fine Arts, N.Y. Soc. Illustrators, Phila. Mus. Art, Norfolk Mus., Rutgers U.; represented in collections Phila. Mus. Art, Woodmere Mus., Phila., Jefferson Hosp. U., Ford Motor Co., Mich., New Britain Mus. Am. Art, Colo., Mus. U.S. Army, Washington; murals commissioned by Heritage Trust Co., N.J., Oreland Bapt. Ch., Pa., Burlington County Bank and Trust, N.J., Abraham Strause Co. Dept. Store, others; contbr. drawings, paintings and articles to popular and profl. mags. Cpl. U.S. Army, 1943-46, ETO. Recipient Harrison Morris prize (3) Pa. Acad. Fine Art Fellowship Anns., Thornton Oakely prize Phila. Watercolor Club, Medal of Achievement, Phila. Watercolor Club, 1st prize Phila. Art Dir.'s Ann., 1st prize Watercolor USA, Springfield Mus. Fellow Pa. Acad. Fine Art; mem. Am. Watercolor Soc., Phila. Watercolor Soc. Home: 3639 Bryant St Palo Alto CA 94306-4209

EISNER, MICHAEL DAMMANN, entertainment company executive; b. Mt. Kisco, N.Y., Mar. 7, 1942; s. Lester and Margaret (Dammann) E.; m. Jane Breckenridge; children: Breck, Eric, Anders. BA, Denison U., 1964. Began career in programming dept. CBS; asst. to nat. programming dir. ABC, 1966-68, mgr. spls. and talent, dir. program devel.-East Coast, 1968-71, v.p. daytime programming, 1971-75, v.p. program planning and devel., 1975-76, sr. v.p. prime time prodn. and devel., 1976; pres., chief operating officer Paramount Pictures, 1976-84; chmn., chief exec. officer Walt Disney Co., Burbank, Calif., 1984—; governor Mighty Ducks of Anaheim, 1993. Bd. trustees Denison U., Calif. Inst. Arts; bd. dirs. Am. Hosp. of Paris Found., Conservative Internat., UCLA Exec. Bd. for Med. Sci. Office: Walt Disney Co 500 S Buena Vista St Burbank CA 91521-0001*

EISSLER, FREDERICK, environmentalist, retired educator; b. Phila., May 19, 1922; s. Frederick and Anne (Stonesifer) E.; m. Anne Parker, Apr. 14, 1952; children: Margaret, Christine. BA in Lit., U. N.C., 1943. Cert. elem.-secondary tchr., Calif. Primary, secondary tchr. Santa Barbara (Calif.) Sch. Dist., 1958-81; exec. dir. Scenic Shoreline Preservation Conf., Santa Barbara, 1968—; exec. dir. Scenic Shoreline Def. Fund., Santa Barbara, 1981—. Mem. nat. bd. dirs. Sierra Club, San Francisco, 1963-69, sec., 1969. Civilian pub. svc. with Am. Friends Svc. Com., 1942-46. Mem. Phi Beta Kappa. Home: 4623 More Mesa Dr Santa Barbara CA 93110-2028

EISSMANN, WALTER JAMES, consulting company executive; b. Newark, N.J., Apr. 20, 1939; s. Walter Curt Eissmann and Alice Delice (Irving) Clark; m. Dorothea Ann Donaldson, June 1, 1963; children: Patricia Helene Ridenhour, Walter William. B.S. in Indsl. Engring., Rutgers U., 1962. Account mgr. Gen. Electric, Englewood Cliffs, N.J., 1962-67; regional sales mgr. Tymshare, Englewood Cliffs, 1968-71, Buffalo, N.Y., 1971-73, Washington, 1973-74, v.p. mktg. service div., Cupertino, Calif., 1974-79, div. v.p., Cupertino, 1980-84; sr. v.p. McDonnell Douglas Corp., Cupertino, 1984-86; gen. ptnr. Archer Assocs., 1985-92; pres., chmn. bd. Walter J. Eissmann, Inc., Saratoga, 1989—; bd. dirs. NSF Corp., Nutri/System Franchisee Corp., 1986-90; chmn. bd. Businesswise, Inc., 1992-93; mng. gen. ptnr. Grand Tyme Partnership, 1992—. Bd. dirs. Saratoga Little League, Calif., 1976-81, Saratoga Boosters, 1981-84; active Vienna Theatre Players, Va., 1973; mem. Church Men's Choir, Saratoga, 1980-82. Named to President's Club Tymshare, Golden Circle, Nutri/System Master of the Keys. Mem. Pi Tau Sigma. Republican.

EITELBERG, MARK JAN, public administration educator, consultant; b. Jan. 5, 1948; s. Alfred Jack and Olga Barbara (Lipski) E.; m. Deborah Jean Brant, July 20, 1982; children: Matthew Jan, Andrew James. AB in Govt., Franklin and Marshall Coll., 1970; MPA, NYU, 1973, PhD, 1979. Pers. analyst State of N.J., 1975; mem., contbg. author mil. svc. working group Atlantic Coun. U.S., Washington, 1980-81; assoc. staff fgn. policies studies program Brookings Instn., Washington, 1980-82; rsch. asst. Human Resources Rsch. Orgn., Alexandria, Va., 1975—, rsch. assoc., 1975-76, rsch. scientist, 1976-79, sr. scientist, 1979-82; adj. rsch. prof. pub. adminstrn. U.S. Naval Postgrad. Sch., Monterey, Calif., 1982-89, assoc. prof. pub. adminstrn., 1989—; assoc. chmn. dept. sys. mgmt. U.S. Naval Postgrad. Sch., 1995—, dir. def. force mgmt. and analysis curriculum, 1996—; mem. tech. coop. program, Dept. Def., Washington, 1990—; cons. global demographic trends group, Pres.'s Commn. on Integrated Long-Term Strategy, Nat. Def. U., Washington, 1987-88, Nat. Commn. on Testing and Pub. Policy, U. Calif., Berkeley, 1988-89; presenter papers in field. Author: Military Representation, 1979, Blacks and the Military, 1982, Screening for Service, 1984, Manpower for Military Occupations, 1988, Becoming Brass, 1991, Marching Toward the 21st Century, 1994, America's All-Volunteer Force, 1995; contbr. articles to profl. jours. and govt. docs., book chpt., tech. reports. With U.S. Army Res. and N.G., 1970-76. Fellow Inter-Univ. Seminar on Armed Forces and Soc. (assoc. chmn.); mem. APA, ASPA, Internat. Mil. Testing Assn., Am. Ednl. Rsch. Assn. Office: US Naval Postgrad Sch Dept Sys Mgmt Monterey CA 93943

EIZENBERG, JULIE, architect. BArch, U. Melbourne, Australia, 1978; MArch II, UCLA, 1981. Lic. architect, Calif., reg. architect, Australia. Principal, architect Koning Eizenberg Architecture, Santa Monica, Calif., 1981—; instr. various courses UCLA, MIT, Harvard U.; lectr. in field; jury member P/A awards. Exhbns. incl. Koning Eizenberg Architecture 3A Garage, San Francisco, 1996, "House Rules" Wexner Ctr., 1994, "The Architect's Dream: Houses for the Next Millenium" The Contemporary Arts Ctr., 1993, "Angels & Franciscans" Gagosian Gallery, 1992, Santa Monica Mus. Art, 1993, "Broadening the Discourse" Calif. Women in Environmental Design, 1992, "Conceptional Drawings by Architects" Bannatyne Gallery, 1991, Exhbn. Koning Eizenberg Projects Grad. Sch. Architecture & Urban Planning UCLA, 1990; prin. works include Digital Domain Renovation and Screening Room, Santa Monica, Lightstorm Entertainment Office Renovation and Screening Room, Santa Monica, Gilmore Bank Addition and Remodel, L.A., 1548-1550 Studios, Santa Monica, (with RTA) Materials Rsch. Lab. at U. Calif., Santa Barbara, Ken Edwards Ctr. Cmty. Svcs., Santa Monica, Peck Park Cmty. Ctr. Gymnasium, San Pedro, Calif., Sepulveda Recreation Ctr., L.A. (Design award AIA San Fernando Valley 1995, Nat. Concrete and Masonry award 1996, AIA Calif. Coun. Honor award 1996, L.A. Bus. Coun. Beautification award 1996), PS # 1 Elem. Sch., Santa Monica, Farmers Market, L.A. Additions and Master Plan (Westside Urban Forum prize 1991), Stage Deli, L.A., Simone Hotel, L.A. (Nat. Honor award AIA 1994), Boyd Hotel, L.A., Cmty. Corp. Santa Monica Housing Projects, 5th St. Family Housing, Santa Monica, St. John's Hosp. Replacement Housing Program, Santa Monica, Liffman Ho., Santa Monica, (with Glenn Erikson) Electric Artblock, Venice (Beautification award L.A. Bus. Coun. 1993), 6th St. Condominiums, Santa Monica, Hollywood Duplex, Hollywood Hills (Record Houses Archtl. Record 1988), California Ave. Duplex, Santa Monica, Tarzana Ho. (Award of Merit L.A. chpt. AIA 1992, Sunset Western home Awards citation 1993-94), 909 Ho., Santa Monica (Award of Merit L.A. chpt. AIA 1991), 31st St. Ho., Santa Monica (Honor award AIACC 1994, Nat. AIA Honor award 1996), others. Recipient 1st award Progressive Architecture, 1987; named one of Domino's Top 30 Architects, 1989. Mem. L.A. County Mus. Art, Westside Urban Forum, Urban Land Inst., Architects and Designers for Social Responsibility, Mus. Contemporary Art, The Nature Conservancy, Sierra Club. Office: Koning Eizenberg Architecture 1548 18th St Santa Monica CA 90404-3404

EKDALE, ALLAN ANTON, geology educator, paleontology researcher; b. Burlington, Iowa, Aug. 30, 1946; s. Warren E. and Marian L. (Nielsen) E.; m. Susan Faust Rostberg, July 5, 1969; children: Joan Diane, Eric Gregory. BA, Augustana Coll., Rock Island, Ill., 1968; MA, Rice U., 1973, PhD, 1974. Prof. geology U. Utah, Salt Lake City, 1974—. Fellow AAAS; mem. Geol. Soc. Am., Nat. Assn. Geology Tchrs., Paleontol. Soc., Soc. Econ. Paleontologists and Mineralogists. Office: U Utah Dept Geology and Geophysics Salt Lake City UT 84112

EKEY, CARRIE RAE, elementary education educator; b. North Platte, Nebr., July 6, 1947; d. Chester O. and Alice A. (Johnson) Florom; m. Glenn W. Ekey, Mar. 22, 1970; children: Brian, Todd. BA in Elem. Edn. and Math., U. No. Colo., 1969; MA in Curriculum and Instrn., U. Colo., Denver, 1990. Cert. elem. tchr., Colo. 3d grade tchr. Jefferson County, Lakewood, Colo., 1969-73; 4th-6th grade tchr. Jefferson County, Wheatridge, Colo., 1981-85; 1st-2d grade tchr. Jefferson County, Arvada, Westminster, Colo., 1985—; staff developer Jefferson County, Lakewood, Colo., 1992-93; instr. Regis U., Denver, 1989—, curriculum coord. Masters in Whole Learning program, 1994—; cons. various sch. dists., Colo., 1989—. Mem. Nat. Coun. Tchrs. English, Nat. Coun. Tchrs. Math., Internat. Reading Assn., Assn. for Supervision and Curriculum Devel., Colo. Coun. Tchrs. English, Colo. Reading Assn. Office: Lukas Elementary Sch 9650 W 97th Ave Broomfield CO 80021-4282

EKLUND, CARL ANDREW, lawyer; b. Denver, Aug. 12, 1943; s. John M. and Zara (Zerbst) E.; m. Nancy Jane Griggs, Sept. 7, 1968; children: Kristin, Jessica, Peter. BA, U. Colo., 1967, JD, 1971. Bar: Colo. 1971, U.S. Dist. Ct. Colo. 1971, U.S. Ct. Appeals (9th cir.) 1975, U.S. Ct. Appeals (10th cir.) 1978, U.S. Supreme Ct. 1978. Dep. dist. atty. Denver Dist. Attys. Office, 1971-73; ptnr. DiManna, Eklund, Ciancio & Jackson, Denver, 1975-81, Smart, DeFurio, Brooks & Eklund, Denver, 1982-84, Roath & Brega, P.C., Denver, 1984-88, Faegre & Benson, Denver, 1988-94, LeBoeuf, Lamb, Greene & MacRae L.L.P., Denver, 1994—; local rules com. Bankruptcy Ct. D.C., 1979-80; reporter Nat. Bankruptcy Conf., 1981-82; lectr. ann. spring meeting Am. Bankruptcy Inst., Rocky Mountain Bankruptcy Conf., Continuing Legal Edn. Colo., Inc., Colo. Practice Inst., Colo. Bar Assn., Nat. Ctr. Continuing Legal Edn., Inc., Profl. Edn. Systems, Inc., Comml. Law Inst. Am., Law Edn. Inst., Inc., Bur. Nat. Affairs, Inc., Practising Law Inst., So. Meth. U. Sch. Law, Continuing Edn. Svcs., Lorman Bus. Ctr., Inc. Contbg. author: Collier's Bankruptcy Practice Guide, Representing Debtors in Bankruptcy, Letters Formbook and Legal Opinion, Advanced Chapter 11 Bankruptcy Practice, Wiley Law Pubs.; mem. adv. bd. ABI Law Rev., 1993—. Fellow Am. Coll. Bankruptcy; mem. ABA (bus. law and corp. banking sect. 1977—, bus. bankruptcy com. 1982—, subcom. on rules 1981—), Colo. Bar Assn. (bd. govs. 1980-82, corp. banking and bus. law sect. 1977—, ethics com. 1981-82, subcom. bankruptcy cts.), Am. Bankruptcy Inst. (dir. SW Bankruptcy Conf., Rocky Mountain Bankruptcy Conf.), Denver Bar Assn. (trustee 1983-86). Office: LeBoeuf Lamb Greene & MacRae LLP 633 17th St Ste 2000 Denver CO 80202-3660

ELAINE, KAREN, musician, educator; b. San Jose, Calif., Nov. 6, 1965; d. Gaston Ortega and Alice Lee (Ray) Sanders, III. Diploma in music, Curtis Inst. of Music, Phila., 1987; studies with Karen Tuttle, Michael Tree, Curtis Inst. Music, 1987; studies with Louis Kievman, L.A., 1988-90. Solo viola New Am. Chamber Orch., Detroit, 1986-87; prin. viola San Diego Symphony Orch., 1987-90; string specialist Sch. Creative & Performing Arts, San Diego, 1987-90; pvt. instr. Studio of Karen Elaine, San Diego, 1987—; viola prof. Chanterelle Music Festival, Pouidoux, Switzerland, 1989—; violin and viola prof. Utah Chamber Music Festival, 1994—; solo and prin. viola Sun Valley Summer Symphony, 1991—; viola sect. Hollywood Film and Record Industry, 1993—; asst. prin., solo viola Pro Musica Chamber Orch., Santa Fe, 1994—; vol. lectr., recitalist spl. edn. dept. Morse H.S., 1987—; adj. prof. viola San Diego State U., 1989—; featured on TV program Reflections in Music, San Diego, El Cajon, Calif., 1990; solo viola Delos Internat. Records, Paraiba Symphony Orch., Brazil, 1988, Laurel Records, London Symphony Orch., 1990, Harmonia Mundi, City of London Sinfonia, 1990; guest soloist and lectr. 19th and 25th Internat. Viola Congress, 1991, 97, solo recitalist throughout U.S.; guest speaker Sta. KFSD-FM, Sta. KPBS-FM; solo concert tour under sponsorship of Australian Broadcast Co. and Australian Arts Coun., 1994. Commissions include Concert Piece for Viola and Orch., David Baker, 1989, Cinnabar Concerto for Viola and Strings, David Ward-Steinman, 1991, Concerto for Viola and Orch., Gordon Kerry, 1993, Hetep: Tranquility #2, Ismail Wadada Leo Smith, Li'l Phrygian Rondo for Karen, Katrina Wreede, 1992; contbg. writer to The Lyre that Sings Truth: Classics in Opera; contbr. articles to Jour. of Internat. Viola Soc. Donor World Wildlife Fund, Washington, 1989—. Recipient 1st Pl. award Bruno Giurana Internat. Viola Competition, Brazil, 1988; winner numerous solo competitions Musical Merit of San Diego, 1988, 89, Rio Hondo Symphony Young Artists' Solo Competition, 1989, S.E. L.A. Young Artists Solo Competition, 1990, Nat. Assn. Negro Musicians Young Artists Solo Competition, 1992. Mem. Am. Viola Soc., Rec. Musicians Assn., Musicians Union Locals 325 (San Diego) and 47 (L.A.). Democrat. Home: 208 Welling Way San Diego CA 92114-5947

EL-BAYOUMY, LOTFI E., engineering executive; b. Fayoum, Arab Republic of Egypt, Jan. 18, 1942; came to U.S., 1966; s. El-Sayed Ibrahim and Nageyya F. (El-Zainy) El-B.; m. Shahira A. El-Masry, Aug. 17, 1973; children: Sharif, Khalid, Dena. BS with honors, Cairo U., 1964, MS, 1966; PhD with honors, NYU, 1970. Asst. prof. NYU, 1969-70; prin. engr. Dathar Corp., Ramsey, N.J., 1970-72; advanced vibrations analyst Pratt & Whitney, East Hartford, Conn., 1972-74; group engr. Sundstrand Corp., Rockford, Ill., 1975-80; mgr. engring. tech. Western Gear Corp. (now Geared Systems Inc.), Park City, Utah, 1980-96; tech. staff Moog Aircraft Group, Torrance, Calif., 1996—; engring. cons. NASA Lewis, Cleve., 1981-94; assoc. prof. mech. engring. Calif. State U., Long Beach, 1981-93, No. Ill. U., Dekalb, 1979-80. Contbr. articles to profl. jours. Mem. Am. Acad. Mechanics (founding), AIAA (sr.), ASME (Power Transmission and Gearing com. 1983—), Assn. Egyptian-Am. Scholars, Nat. Mgmt. Assn., Soc. Automotive Engrs. (G-5 com. 1984—). Home: 5105 Vista Montana Yorba Linda CA 92686-4505 Office: Moog Aircraft 20263 Western Ave Torrance CA 90501

ELDENBURG, MARY JO CORLISS, mathematics educator; b. Tacoma, Wash., Mar. 5, 1942; d. John Ronald and Mary Margaret (Slater) Corliss; m. Paul Garth Eldenburg, Aug. 31, 1963; 1 child, Anthony Corliss. BA with honors, Wash. State U., 1964; MS, SUNY, Buffalo, 1971. Cert. secondary math. tchr. Tchr. math. Colton (Wash.) High Sch., 1964-65, Bellevue (Wash.) Jr. High Sch., 1965-68, Issaquah (Wash.) Jr. High Sch., 1968-75, Issaquah High Sch., 1975-77; tchr. math., dept. chair Liberty High Sch., Issaquah, 1977-93, Holy Names Acad., Seattle, 1994—. Co-editor books: Cartesian Cartoons, 1980, Cartesian Cartoons, Holiday, 1990, Lil Gridders, 1977. Treas. Sch. Bd., Kirkland, Wash., 1987-90; pres. Bridle Trails/South Rose Hill Neighborhood Assn., Kirkland, 1987-93; precinct committee woman Issaquah Precinct, 1980-84. Mem. Issaquah Edn. Assn. (sec., negotiator 1969-75, 74-86), Wash. Edn. Assn. (dir. 1970-74), Math. Assn. Am., Oreg. State Coun. Tchrs. Math., Wash. State Coun. Tchrs. Math., Nat. Coun. Tchrs. Math., Phi Kappa Phi. Democrat. Roman Catholic. Office: Holy Names Acad 728 21st Ave E Seattle WA 98112-4022

ELDREDGE, GARTH MELVIN, rehabilitation counseling educator; b. Idaho Falls, Idaho, Oct. 1, 1935; s. Melvin A. and Eva L. (Bowles) E.; m. Ann Smith, Aug. 5, 1960; children: Merri L. Gillespie, Julianne Bond, Pamela Gosch. BS, U. Utah, 1959, MS, 1963, PhD, 1965. Cert. rehab. counselor; nat. cert. counselor. Tchr. Granite Dist. Schs., Salt Lake City, 1959-61; counselor Salt Lake C.C., 1963-66; prof. vocat. rehab. counseling U. No. Colo., Greeley, 1966-90, Utah State U., Logan, 1990—. Contbr. articles to profl. jours. Tng. grantee U.S. Office of Edn., Utah, 1991, 94, 95, Devel. Distance Edn. grantee U.S. Office of Edn., Utah, 1993. Mem. Nat. Coun. on Rehab. Edn. (adminstrv. sec. 1991-96). Mem. LDS Ch. Office: Dept Spl Edn and Rehab Utah State Univ Logan UT 84322-2865

ELDREDGE, JEFFREY ROBERT CARLETON, librarian; b. St. Albans, Vt., Jan. 17, 1951; s. Carleton and Faith E. BA, U. N.H., 1973; MLS, U. R.I., 1982. Libr. asst. U. N.H., Durham, 1973-83; libr. Hawaii State Pub. Libr. System, Honolulu, 1984-90, 96—; dist. adminstr. Hawaii State Pub. Libr. System, Lihue, 1990-92, Pearl City, 1993-95. Adv. bd. Retired Srs. Vol. Program, Lihue, 1990-92; mem. Friends of the Libr. of Hawaii, Honolulu, 1991—. Mem. ALA, Hawaii Libr. Assn. (treas. 1988-90), Kauai Libr. Assn. (v.p. 1991-92). Republican. Office: Kaimuki Pub Libr 1041 Koko Head Ave Honolulu HI 96816

ELDRIDGE, ROGER GILBERT, JR., education educator; b. Middleborough, Mass., Apr. 19, 1946; s. Roger G. and Carolyn M. (Nason) E.; m. Polly G. Sherman, June 24, 1967 (div. Sept. 1980); children: Jeffrey, Jana, Myles; m. Patricia A. Heino. BA, U. Mass., 1969; PhD, U. Wis., 1981. Cert. elem. tchr., reading specialist. Elem. tchr. Mattapoisett (Mass.) Schs., 1969-73; reading specialist Barnstable (Mass.) Schs., 1973-78; rsch. asst., reading lectr. U. Wis., Madison, 1978-81; asst. prof., assoc. prof. East Carolina U., Greenville, N.C., 1981-89; assoc. prof., prof. U. No. Colo., Greeley, 1989—; presenter in field. Contbr. chpts. in books and articles to profl. jours. Office: Univ No Colo Greeley CO 80639

ELDRIDGE, TERRANCE FOY, avionics engineer; b. Phoenix, Nov. 28, 1957; s. Robert Vincent Sr. and Ruth Loretta (Foy) E.; m. Kristen Marie Marut, July 19, 1985; children: Katelyn Marie, Erin Lindsey. BS in Physics, Harvey Mudd Coll., 1980; PhD in Physics, MIT, 1985. Rsch. asst. Los Alamos (N.Mex.) Nat. Labs., 1980, Livermore (Calif.) Nat. Lab., 1981, MIT, Cambridge, Mass., 1981-85; software engr. Hughes Aircraft Co., El Segundo, Calif., 1985-87; avionics engr. McDonnell Douglas, Mesa, Ariz., 1987—; rsch. scientist Ariz. State U., Tempe, 1994—. Contbr. articles to profl. jours. Mem. IEEE, Am. Phys. Soc. Home: 5940 E Fountain Cir Mesa AZ 85205-5513 Office: McDonnell Douglas 5000 E Mcdowell Rd Mesa AZ 85215-9707

ELECCION, MARCELINO, marketing executive, editor, writer, lecturer, artist; b. N.Y.C., Aug. 22, 1936; s. Marcelino G. and Margaret J. (Krcha) E.; m. Marcia L. Smith, June 6, 1962; 1 child, Mark Eaton; m. Naomi E. Kor, Jan. 5, 1978; 1 child, Jordan Kai. BA, NYU, 1961; postgrad. Courant Inst. Math. Scis., 1962-64; AS, Coll. San Mateo, 1988; postgrad. San Jose State U., 1988-91. Electromech. draftsman Sch. Engring., NYU, Bronx, 1954-57, chief designer dept. elec. engring., 1957-60, tech. editor lab. for electrosci. research, 1960-62, editor publs. Sch. Engring. and Scis., 1962-67; asst. editor IEEE Spectrum, N.Y.C., 1967-69, assoc. editor, 1969-70, staff writer, 1970-76, contbg. editor, 1976—; dir. adminstrn. Internat. Bur. Protection and Investigation, Ltd., N.Y.C., 1976-78; account exec. Paul Purdom & Co., pub. relations, San Francisco, 1978-81, creative dir., 1981-83; dir. mktg. communications Am. Info. Systems, Palo Alto, 1983-85; dir. engring. Tech. Cons., Palo Alto, 1986—; cons. tech. artist, 1953—; music orchestration cons., 1956-70; cons. Ency. Britannica, 1969-70, Time-Life Books, 1973; spl. guest lectr. Napa Coll., 1979—. Aux. police officer, N.Y.C. Police Dept., 1964-70, aux. sgt., 1970-73, aux. lt., 1973-76, aux. capt., 1976-78. Recipient Mayor's commendation award N.Y.C., 1971. Mem. IEEE (sr.), N.Y. Acad. Scis., Am. Math. Soc., AAAS, Optical Soc. Am., Smithsonian Assocs., Am. Numis. Assn., Nat. Geog. Soc., U.S. Judo Fedn., Athletic Congress, AAU. Fedn. Home: 3790 El Camino Real # 2004 Palo Alto CA 94306-3314

ELFMAN, ERIC, writer; b. Boston, Jan. 29, 1958; s. Robert S. and Estelle (Berman) E.; m. January K. Silverstrom; 1 child, Robert J. Student, UCLA, 1975-78, Calif. State U., Long Beach, 1978-79. Freelance writer, 1980-82; books and film reviews Santa Monica Free Weekly, 1983-84; writer English lang. dialogue for dubbing fgn. film/cartoons Intersound Prodn., 1985-88; writer English language films for dubbing foreign films and cartoons Saban Prodn., 1989-90; program analyst CBS TV, 1990; freelance writer, 1991-92; study guide writer Mark Taper Forum, L.A., 1993-95; writer James Stanfield Prodns., Santa Barbara, 1994-96; cons. Galef Inst., L.A., 1992, 93. Author: Three Minute Thrillers, 1994, The Very Scary Almanac, 1994, More Three Minute Thrillers, 1995, Almanac of the Gross Disgusting and Totally Repulsive, 1995 (ALA award 1995), Our town: AN X-Files Novel, 1997.

ELGIN, RON ALAN, advertising executive; b. Milw., Sept. 15, 1941; s. Carl John and Vivian Elaine (Phillips) E.; m. Bonnie Kay Visintainer, Dec. 3, 1968; 1 child, Alison. BA in Advt., U. Wash., 1965. With Cole & Weber, Seattle, 1965-81; pres. Elgin Syferd, Seattle, 1981-89; chmn. Elgin Syferd/Drake, Boise, Idaho, 1987—; pres., CEO Elgin DDB, 1989—; pres. DDB Needham Retail, 1990-93; chmn. Hornall Anderson Design Works, Seattle, 1982-91; ptnr. Christiansen & Fritsch Direct, Seattle, 1988-96; bd. dirs. Hart Crowser, Trust Co. of Wash. Bd. dirs. Ronald McDonald House, Seattle, 1984—, Big Bros., Seattle, 1986—, Spl. Olympics, Seattle, 1987-90, Pacific N.W. Ballet, Seattle, 1988—, Poncho, Seattle, 1991—, Odyssey, 1993—, Swedish Hosp., 1995—; mem. adv. bd. U. Wash., Wash. State U. Lt. U.S. Army, 1965-69. Mem. Am. Assn. Advt. Agencies, Am. Mktg. Assn., Mktg. Comm. Execs. Internat. Office: Elgin DDB 1008 Western Ave Seattle WA 98104-1032

ELIA, JOHN PATRICK, health education and psychology educator; b. Burlingame, Calif., Apr. 2, 1963; s. John Kenneth and Barbara Jean (DeStefano) E. BA in Phys. Edn. and History cum laude, San Francisco State U., 1986, MA in History, 1989; PhD in Edn., U. Calif., Davis, 1997. Tchr. adult edn. divsn. South San Francisco Unified (Calif.) Sch. Dist., 1986-91; lectr. health edn., human sexuality and psychology San Francisco State U., 1987—. Author: Human Sexuality-Instructor's Manual, 1992, If You Seduce a Straight Person Can You Make Them Gay: Issues in Social Constructionism vs. Biological Essentialism in Gay and Lesbian Identities, 1993. Mem. NEA, Am. Hist. Assn., Philosophy of Edn. soc., Soc. for the Sci. Study of Sexuality, Calif. Assn. for Philosophy of Edn., Calif. Hist. Soc. Democrat. Roman Catholic. Home: 299 Canterbury Ave Daly City CA 94015-4439 Office: San Francisco State Univ Psychology Dept 1600 Holloway Ave San Francisco CA 94132-1722

ELIASSEN, MEREDITH MORGAN, librarian, archivist, writer; b. Berkeley, Calif., May 7, 1965; d. John Weld and Constance Jean (DeFeo) E. AA, Santa Rosa (Calif.) Jr. Coll., 1985; BA in Broadcasting and Electronic Comm., San Francisco State U., 1988; MLS, Simmons Coll., 1991. Libr. technician North Bay Coop. Libr. Sys., Santa Rosa, 1986-87; intern bur. consumer affairs KGO Radio, San Francisco, 1988; libr. asst. III archives/spl. collections San Francisco State U., J. Paul Leonard Libr., 1989-90, 91—; with film and video resource ctr. WGBH Ednl. Found., Boston, 1991; libr. program asst. II Mus. Fine Arts, William Morris Hunt Meml. Libr., Boston, 1990-91; cataloger San Francisco State U. Found., Inc., 1991-92, 93-94; vol. planning group Commn. on Univ. Strategic Planning, San Francisco State U., 1995-96, staff rep. libr. edn. com., 1995-97; spkr. in field. Author: A Guide to Emmy Award-Winning Programs, 1974-86, 1990; prodr., performer: Printing with the Handpress at Wellesley Coll., 1991; designer: (exhibit) Introducing the Marguerite Archer Collection of Historic Children's Books, 1993-96; contbr. chpts. to books, jours. Mem. San Francisco Edn. Fund Adv. Bd. for Libr. Power, San Francisco, 1994, Marion Wright Edelman Inst. for Study of Children, Youth and Family, 1996-97; historian Univ. Women's Assn. San Francisco State U., 1996-97; vol. Calif. Pacific Med. Ctr. Planetree Libr., 1992-93; mediator KGO Radio Consumer Affairs Bur., San Francisco, 1988; prodr. dept. pub. affairs KFTY TV50, Santa Rosa, 1985-86. Scholar Spl. Libr. Assn., San Antonio, 1991-92; recipient art award Bank of Am., 1983. Mem. Am. Libr. Assn., Pacific Ctr. for Book Arts, Soc. Children's Book Writers and Illustrators. Office: J Paul Leonard Libr Spl Collections 1630 Holloway Ave San Francisco CA 94132

ELIKANN, LAWRENCE S. (LARRY ELIKANN), television and film director; b. N.Y.C., July 4, 1923; s. Harry and Sadye (Trause) E.; m. Corinne Schuman; Dec. 6, 1947; children—JoAnne Jarrin, Jill Barad. B.A., Bklyn. Coll., 1943; E.E., Walter Harvey Coll., 1948. Tech. dir. NBC-TV, N.Y.C., 1948-64; comml. dir. VPI-TV, N.Y.C., 1964-66, Filmex-TV, N.Y.C., 1966-68, Plus two TV, N.Y.C., 1968-70. Dir. mini-series Last Flight Out, The Great L.A. Earthquake, The Big One, The Inconvenient Woman, Fever, Story Lady, One Against the Wind, Bonds of Love, I Know My First Name is Steven, Hands of a Stranger, Kiss of a Killer, God Bless the Child, Out of Darkness, Menendez—A Killing in Beverly Hills, Tecumseh—The Last Warrior, A Mother's Prayer, Blue River, "Unexpected Family", Lies He Told. Mem. Mus. Contemporary Art of L.A., L.A. County Mus.; mem. rsch. coun. Scripps Clinic and Rsch. Found. With Signal Corps, U.S. Army, 1943-46. Recipient Emmy award, 1978-79, 89, Golden Globe award, 1989, 91, Christopher award 1973-76, 77, 78-79, 91, Chgo. Internat. Film Festival award 1977, Internat. Film and TV Festival of N.Y. award, 1977, Dir. of Yr. award Am. Ctrs. for Children, 1978; Humanitas prize, 1988, 94, 96. Mem. NATAS (gov. 1961-63), Dirs. Guild Am., Am. film Inst., Nat. Hist. Preservation Soc., Smithsonian Inst., Scripps Inst. (bd. dirs.), Acad. TV Arts and Scis.

ELINSON, HENRY DAVID, artist, language educator; b. Leningrad, USSR, Dec. 14, 1935; came to U.S., 1973; s. David Moses and Fraida Zelma (Ufa) E.; m. Ludmila Nicholas Tepina, Oct. 7, 1955; 1 child, Maria Henry. Student, Herzen State Pedagogical U., Leningrad, 1954-57; BA, Pedagogical Inst., Novgorod, USSR, 1958; MA, Pedagogical Inst., Moscow, 1963. Cert. educator. Spl. edn. tchr. Leningrad Sch. Spl. Edn., 1961-64; supr. dept. speech therapy Psychoneurological Dispensary, Leningrad, 1964-73; instr. Russian lang. Yale U., New Haven, Conn., 1975-76, Def. Lang. Inst., Presidio of Monterey, Calif., 1976-94. One-man shows include The Light and Motion Transmutation Galleries, N.Y.C., 1974, Thor Gallery, Louisville, 1974, Monterey (Calif.) Peninsula Art Mus., 1977, U. Calif. Nelson Gallery, Davis, 1978, Nahamkin Gallery, N.Y.C., 1978, Nahamkin Fine Arts, N.Y.C., 1980, Gallery Paule Anglim, 1981, 85, 87, Gallery Paule Anglim, San Francisco, 1991, 93, 96, Dostoevsky's Mus., St. Petersburg, Russia, 1992, Mus. Art Santa Cruz, Calif., 1994, Duke U. Mus. Art, 1996; exhibited in group shows at Bklyn. Coll. Art Ctr., 1974, CUNY, 1974, Galleria II Punto, Genoa, Italy, 1975, New Art From the Soviet Union, Washington, 1977, Gallery Hardy, Paris, 1978, Mus. of Fine Art, San Francisco, 1979, Santa Cruz Mus. Fine Arts, 1994, V. Morlan Gallery Transylvania U., Lexington, Ky., 1995, numerous others; represented in permanent collections Mus. Fine Arts, San Francisco, Yale U. Art Gallery, Monterey Mus. Art, U. Calif. Art Mus., Berkeley, Bochum Mus., Germany, Check Point Charlie Mus., Berlin, State Russian Mus., Leningrad, Zimmerly Art Mus., Rutgers U., N.J., Duke U Mus. Art, 1996. Mem. Underground Anti-Soviet Govt. Students' Orgn., 1957. Recipient Gold medal Art Achievement City of Milan, 1975. Home: 997 Benito Ct Pacific Grove CA 93950-5333

ELIOT, THEODORE LYMAN, JR., international consultant; b. N.Y.C., Apr. 14, 1951; m. Patricia F. Peters. B.A., Harvard U., 1948, M.P.A., 1956; LL.D., U. Nebr., Omaha, 1975. With U.S. Fgn. Svc., 1949-78; spl. asst. to under sec. of state, to sec. treasury; country dir. for Iran Dept. State; exec. sec. State Dept.; also spl. asst. to sec. of state Dept. State; ambassador to Afghanistan; insp. gen. Dept. State., Washington; dean Fletcher Sch. Law and Diplomacy, Tufts U., 1979-85; exec. dir. Ctr. for Asian Pacific Affairs Asia Found., San Francisco, 1985-87; bd. dirs. Raytheon Co., Neurobiol. Tech., Fiberstars. Trustee Asia Found. Mem. Am. Acad. Diplomacy, Somerset Club, Univ. Club (San Francisco).

ELISARA, CHERYL DENISE, educator; b. Lamar, Colo., Feb. 25, 1959; d. Robert Leslie Taylor and Marcella (Helwig) Brittain; m. Mataio Pita Elisara, June 19, 1982; children: Travis Matthew, Cameron Taylor. BA, Wash. State U., 1982. Cert. tchr. Wash., 1996. Sec. Wash. State U., Pullman, 1982-84, adminstrv. asst., 1984-86, student recruiter, 1986-87; consumer svc. rep. Nintendo of Am., Redmond, Wash., 1989-90; sec., clk. Spokane (Wash.) Pub. Schs., 1991-95, substitute tchr., 1996; tchr. Clover Park Sch. Dist., Lakewood, Wash., 1996—. Chmn. Lincoln Hts. Cmty. Devel., Spokane, 1993-94, sec., 1991-93; chmn. Lincoln Hts. Task Force, 1993-94; pres., v.p. Adams PTSA, Spokane, 1991-92. Presbyterian. Home: 8404 82d St SW #201 Lakewood WA 98498 Office: Mann Mid Sch 11509 Holden Rd SW Lakewood WA 98499

ELKAN, CHARLES PETER, engineer educator; b. Wellington, New Zealand, Mar. 17, 1963; came to U.S., 1984; s. Peter Gabriel and Anne Mildred (Marsh) E. BA, U. Cambridge, Eng., 1984; PhD, Cornell U., 1990. Postdoctoral assoc. U. Toronto, Ont., Can., 1989-90; asst. prof. U. Calif., San Diego, 1990—. Contbr. articles to profl. jours. Mem. IEEE Computer Soc., Am. Assn. Artificial Intelligence. Office: U Calif Dept Computer Sci & Engring La Jolla CA 92109-0114

ELKINGTON, SANDRA LOUISE, writer; b. San Francisco, Dec. 3, 1944; d. Leon Stanton and Alice Kathryn (Begert) Erickson; m. William Brice Elkinton, Oct. 17, 1987 (dec. Nov. 1995); children: Jamie, Mark, Tammy Caudy. Grad. in secretarial sci., U. Alaska, Anchorage, 1970. Trapper, dogsledder, legal sec., Chulitha and Eagle, Alaska, 1963-77; adminstrv. asst. BP Petroleum Co., Anchorage, 1977-85; disc jockey, comml. writer, broadcaster Wta. KBYR, Anchorage, 1987-91; sec., loan processor FNBA, Anchorage, 1985-92; freelance and mag. writer, Quito, Ecuador, 1993-96, Tucson, 1995—. Author: This Distant Land, 1985, Caverns of Ecuador, 1994, Trapped, 1995. Home: 9950 N Stratton Saddle Tucson AZ 85742

ELKINS, CARL, food products executive; b. 1932. Attended, Taft Coll., 1955-57. Potato broker Higby & Sons, Bakersfield, Calif., 1957-60; office mgr. Sycamore Farms, Arvin, Calif., 1960-63; salesman, office and packing house mgr. Miller & Lux Corp., Bakersfield, 1963-72; pvt. practice, 1972-74; salesman Demont Packing Co., Victor, Calif., 1974-76; various positions Delta Packing Co., Lodi, Calif., 1976—, now pres. With USAF, 1951-55. Office: Delta Packing Co 5950 E Kettleman Ln Lodi CA 95240-6410*

ELKINS, HOLLIS, secondary education educator; b. Watertown, S.D., May 28, 1945. BA in English, Augustana Coll., 1967; MA in English, N.Mex. State U., 1970; PhD in Am. Studies, U. N.Mex., 1977. Cert. secondary tchr., N.Mex. Tchr. Rio Grande H.S., Albuquerque, 1981—; instr. U. N.Mex., Albuquerque, 1977-80, Albuquerque Tech.-Vocat. Inst., 1988—. Recipient Tchr. Yr. award Albuquerque C. of C., 1994, 95, 96. Mem. Nat. Coun. Tchrs. English, N.Mex. Coun. Tchrs. English. Office: Rio Grande H S 2300 Arenal SW Albuquerque NM 87105

ELKUS, JONATHAN BRITTON, music publisher, music educator; b. San Francisco, Aug. 8, 1931; m. Marilyn McCormick, July 30, 1966; 1 child, Ian. BA, U. Calif., Berkeley, 1953; MA, Stanford U., 1954. Prof. music Lehigh U., Bethlehem, Pa., 1957-73; dir. music Cape Cod Acad., Osterville, Mass., 1979-85, chmn. dept. humanities, 1985-89; founder J.B. Elkus & Son, Music Publs., Laureate Music Press, Overland Music Distbrs., East Bay Books, Albany, Calif., 1984—; chmn. dept. history Stuart Hall, Staunton, Va., 1989-92; lectr. music U. Calif., Davis, 1992—; editorial assoc. Charles Ives Soc., N.Y.C., 1977—. Composer: (opera) The Mandarin, 1968, (plays) Tom Sawyer, 1952, Act Your Age, 1983; contbr. profl. mags. and jours. Ford Found. fellow, 1962. Mem. ASCAP. Office: Overland Music Distbrs 555 Pierce St #409 Albany CA 94706-1002

ELLEBY, GAIL, management consultant; b. Seattle, Sept. 15, 1949; d. William Lee and Marie (Davis) E.; 1 child, Courtney Champion. BA, U. Wash., 1973, MPA, 1975; M in Sports Adminstrn., Ohio U., 1980. Adminstrn. specialist Mayor's Office, City of Seattle, 1986-87; adminstrv. asst. Seattle 1990 Goodwill Games, 1987-88; adminstr. Met. Enrichment Ctr., San Francisco, 1988-90; assoc. v.p. United Way of the Bay Area, San Francisco, 1990-93; cons., pres. Gail Elleby & Assocs., Daly City, Calif., 1993—; developer various orgnl., cmty. devel., collaboration tng., non-profit founds., corp. programs. Mem. BBB, Sam Mateo County, Calif., 1995—; bd. dirs. Boys and Girls Club of San Mateo County, South San Francisco, Calif., 1993—; mem. San Mateo County Child Care Coun., 1992—; mem. San Mateo County Commn. on Status of Women, 1994—; mem. Bay Area Blacks in Philanthropy, 1992—. Mem. SAMCEDA, Cons. Group (founder). Mem. Ch. of Christ. Home: 64 Camelot Ct Daly City CA 94015

ELLENSOHN, KAROL KAYE, psychotherapist; b. Dubuque, Iowa, Sept. 14, 1942; d. Walter Alden and Winifred Mae (Putney) Roe; m. James Henry Mitchell, June 8, 1963 (div. 1984); 1 child, Jennifer Kaye; m. Edgar Ulrich Ellensohn, Sept. 27, 1989. AAS, William Rainey Harper Coll., Palatine, Ill., 1977; BS, U. San Francisco, 1982; MS, U. La Verne, 1984; postgrad., Fielding Inst., Santa Barbara, Calif., 1984-86. RN, Calif., Ill.; MFCC; cert. comty. coll. tchr. Pers. dir. Mercy Hosp., Cedar Rapids, Iowa, 1963-64; pers. dir., exec. sec. to adminstr. Meml. Hosp., Colorado Springs, 1964-67; primary care and charge nurse oncology-hematology unit Evanston (Ill.) Hosp., 1977-78; adminstrv. asst. to interior designer Westlake Village, Calif., 1978-79; oncology nurse Vis. Nurses Assn., Ventura, Calif., 1979-81; contract therapist Caostal Radiation Oncology Med. Svcs., Inc., 1984—; art dealer, 1986—; contract chem. dependency therapy, 1983-84; pvt. practice as nurse therapist, Ventura County, Calif., 1979-83; quality assurance coord. Oxnard (Calif.) Cmty. Hosp., 1982, acting dir. nurses, 1982; part-time clin. instr. in psychology and neurology Ventura Coll., 1981-82; cons. in quality assurance Simi Valley (Calif.) Cmty. Hosp.; cons. Wellness Cmty., Westlake Village, 1988—, Palm Desert (Calif.) Art Assn., 1988—. Contbr. articles to local newspapers. Mem. lectr. staff Camarillo Women's Day.; vol., contbr. Bighorn Inst., Palm Desert, 1989—, AIDS Assistance Program, Palm Springs, 1993; contbr. McCallum Theatre for the Performing Arts, Palm Desert, 1993, Hospice of Valley, Scottsdale, 1996; vol. Phoenix Art Mus. Home Tour, 1996; counselor, developer Nat. Disting. Svc. Registry, 1989-90. Recipient award Danforth Found., 1956. Mem. AACD, Calif. Assn. Marriage and Family Therapists, Ill. Nurses Assn., ABA, Calif. Nurses Assn., So. Calif. Hospice Assn., Ventura County Hospice Assn. (lectr.), Ventura County Discharge Planners Assn., Nat. Assn. Quality Assurance Profls., Am. Cancer Soc. (vol. svc. and rehab. com., speaker's bur., facilitator coping with cancer therapy groups, co-facilitator understanding cancer course, bd. dirs., Midge Wilson award 1980, Order Golden Sword 1981, Outstanding Svc. 1983), Art Dealers Assn. Home: 55-801 Congressional La Quinta CA 92253-4754 Office: Le KAE Galleries 7175 E Main St Scottsdale AZ 85251

ELLER, THOMAS JULIAN, computer company executive, astronautical engineer; b. Pelham, Ga., Oct. 19, 1937; s. Eugene Robert and Frances Elizabeth (Greer) E.; m. Beverly Anne Lafitte, June 7, 1963; children: Julie Anne Eller Schake, Elizabeth Jean, Robert Lafitte. Student, Furman U., 1955-57; BS in Engring. Scis., USAF Acad., 1961; MS in Aero. and Astronautics, Purdue U., 1969; PhD in Aerospace Engring., U. Tex., 1974. Commd. 2nd lt. USAF, 1961, advanced through grades to col., 1981, pilot, 1961-69; prof., asst. dean faculty USAF Acad., Colorado Springs, Colo., 1969-78, comdr. 2nd group, 1978-79, prof., head dept. astronautics and computer sci., 1979-81; ret. USAF, 1981; program mgr. Internat. Tng. & Ed. Co., Boston, 1981-82; chief contracts requirements Martin Marietta Aerospace, Denver, 1982-85; bus. devel. mgr. Kaman Scis. Corp., Colorado Springs, 1985-86, space applications and astrodynamics mgr., 1986-94; tech. ctr. dir. Titan Client/Server Technologies, Colorado Springs, 1994-95; program mgr. digital secure TV system Titan Broadband Comm., San Diego, 1995—; chmn. Mil. Space Doctrine Symposium USAF Acad., 1981; mem. space adv. com. Colo. 5th U.S. Congl. Dist., 1987—, chmn. 1992—; assoc. fellow AIAA (chmn.-elect astrodynamics tech. com. 1991-92, chmn. 1992-94, astrodynamics standards com. 1991-96). Contbr. articles on astronautics to profl. jours. Trustee Colorado Springs Fine Arts Ctr., 1986-92; bd. dirs. The Falcon Found., Colorado Springs, 1983—, Acad. Rsch. and Devel. Inst., Colorado Springs, 1986—; founder, pres. Colo. Vietnam Vets. Leadership Program, Denver, 1983-84. Mem. Accreditation Bd. Engring. and Tech. (engring. visitor 1981—), Assn. Grads. of USAF Acad. (v.p. 1975-79, bd. dirs. 1969-75, pres., chmn. 1979-83); mem. Am. Astron. Soc. (spaceflight mechanics com. 1995—). Republican. Presbyterian. Office: Titan Client/ Server Technologies 1115 Elkton Dr Colorado Springs CO 80907-3535

ELLINGBOE, BRADLEY ROSS, musician, educator; b. Farmington, Min., Apr. 16, 1958; s. Oscar Glenn and Veola Yvonne (Soberg) E.; m. Karen Lee Hersey, July 18, 1981; children: Peter, Alexander, Kristen. BA, Saint Olaf Coll., 1980; M in Music, Eastman Sch. Music, 1983. Assoc. prof. music U. N.Mex., Albuquerque, 1985—; bass soloist with numerous orchestras U.S., Germany, Scandinavia, Japan, Korea, Mex., 1980—. Editor: A Grieg Song Anthology, 1990, 45 Songs Edvard Grieg, 1988; composer choral music; contbr. articles to profl. jours. Recipient Medal of St. Olav, King Harald of Norway, 1994. Lutheran. Office: U New Mex Dept of Music Albuquerque NM 87131

ELLINGS, RICHARD JAMES, political and economic research institution executive; b. Santa Barbara, Calif., Jan. 7, 1950; s. George MacMachan and Barbara Marie (Kollin) E.; m. Marta Anna Korduba; children: Katherine Nicole, John William, Julia Victoria, Ruric George. AB, U. Calif., Berkeley, 1973; MA, U. Wash., 1976, PhD, 1983. Lectr. Calif. Poly. State U., San Luis Obispo, 1980-81; lectr. U. Wash., Seattle, 1982-83, assoc. dir. Henry M. Jackson Sch. Internat. Studies, 1986-89; legis. asst. U.S. Senate, Washington, 1984-85; exec. dir. Nat. Bur. Asian Rsch., Seattle, 1989—; also bd. dirs.; participant Continuing N.W. Regional Colloquim on Internat. Security, 1982—; dir. George E. Taylor Fgn. Affairs Inst., Seattle, 1986-89; lectr. USIA, 1992; cons. in field. Author: Embargoes and World Power, 1985; co-author: Private Property and National Security, 1991, (monograph) Asia's Challenge to American Strategy, 1992; editor: Americans Speak to APEC: Building a New Order with Asia, 1993, MFN Status, Human Rights and U.S.-China Relations, 1994, Access Asia: A Guide to Specialists and Current Research, 1994—, NBR Analysis, 1990—, Southeast Asian Security in the New Millenium, 1996. Del. Rep. Party State Conv., Tacoma, 1988. Grantee Dept. Def., 1990-95, Dept. State, 1994, Henry M. Jackson Found., 1989—, Japan Found. Ctr. for Global Partnership, 1995—. Mem. Am. Polit. Sci. Assn., Western Polit. Sci. Assn., Internat. Studies Assn., Pacific Coun. on Internat. Policy. Home: 644 NW 114th Pl Seattle WA 98177 Office: Nat Bur Asian Rsch 715 Safeco Plz Seattle WA 98185

ELLINGTON, JAMES WILLARD, mechanical design engineer, retired; b. Richmond, Ind., May 26, 1927; s. Oscar Willard and Leola Lenora (Sanderson) E.; m. Sondra Elaine Darnell, Dec. 6, 1952 (dec. Jan. 1997); children: Ronald, Roxanna. BSME summa cum laude, West Coast U., L.A., 1978. Designer NATCO, Richmond, Ind., 1954-67; design engr. Burgmaster, Gardena, Calif., 1967-69; sr. mfg. engr. Xerox Co., El Segundo, Calif., 1969-84; cons. mem. engring. staff Xerox Co., Monrovia, 1984-87; staff engr. Photonic Automation, Santa Ana, Calif., 1987-88; sr. mech. engr. Optical Radiation Co., Azusa, Calif., 1988; sr. staff engr. Omnichrome, Chino, Calif., 1988-96, ret., 1996. With USN, 1945-52. Mem. Soc. Mfg. Engrs. (sec. 1984), West Coast U. Alumni Assn. (bd. dirs. 1988—, v.p. budget and fin.). Republican. Baptist.

ELLINGTON, WILL BOYD, forester, consultant; b. Palo Alto, Calif., Dec. 10, 1930; s. Will Boyd and Elsie Vivian (Prosser) E.; m. Janet Anne Chipman, June 9, 1956; children: Mark William, Lynn Rose Ellington Reese. BS, U. Calif., Berkeley, 1952. Registered profl. forester, Calif. Summer forestry aide Castle Creek Lumber Co., Castella, Calif., 1948-51; engr. officer U.S. Army, Korea, 1952-54; main logging road engr. Wildwood (Calif.) Lumber Co., 1955-58; operation forester Ralph L. Smith Lumber Co., Castella, 1958-61; forestry & logging mgr. Ralph L. Smith Lumber Co., Mt. Shasta, Calif., 1961-67; field forestry rep. Western Wood Products Assn., 1967-71; chief forester Associated Oreg. Loggers, 1971-73; project forestry cons. H.C. Mason & Assocs., 1973-77; pres. Lava Nursery, Inc., Parkdale, Oreg., 1977-93, chmn. bd. dirs., 1993—. 1st lt. U.S. Army Corps of Engrs., 1952-54. Mem. Soc. Am. Foresters, Assn. Consulting Foresters, Calif. Lic. Foresters Assn., Oreg. Small Woodlands Assn. Republican. Home: 1161 Sunningdale Rd Lake Oswego OR 97034-1736

ELLIOTT, CORINNE ADELAIDE, retired copywriter; b. Chgo., Nov. 20, 1927; d. Bertram Otto and Lylia Arletta (Mansfield) Briscoe; m. William S. Elliott, June 18, 1947 (div. Nov. 1985); children: Patricia Frances, Christine Grace, Annie Lou. Cert., Famous Artists Schs., Conn., 1959; BA in English maxima cum laude, Carroll Coll., 1975. Advt. writer Sandy McPherson, Realtor, Helena, Mont., 1975-79; advt. copywriter KCAP Radio, Helena, 1979-83; Helena corr. Great Falls (Mont.) Tribune, 1981-83; radio copywriter Sta. KMTX-AM-FM, Helena, 1986-93; writer in field, 1994—; pres., owner The Funding Edge, Helena, 1991-95, Elliott Impress Silk Screen Works, Whitefish, Mont., 1960-70, Lotus Light Designs, Helena, 1988—; contbr. Salem Press, Pasadena, Calif. One-person show at Mont. Hist. Soc., 1956-59, Deer Lodge, Mont., 1994; exhibited in group shows at Electrum Fine Arts Show (Merit award), Hockaday Art Gallery, Kalispell, Mont., Ball State U., Mont. Inst. Arts, 1992, Art Chateau, Butte, Mont., 1992, New Eng. Fine Arts Inst., Boston, 1993, Mont. Interpretations, Butte, 1994 (Honorable mention); 5 paintings in Autumn Arts Walk, 1996-97, works represented in permanent collections Cason Gallery, Helena, also Utick and Grosfled Collection, Helena; contbr. articles to mags. and ref. books; ongoing contbr. Convergence Mag., Concord, N.H. Leader 5-8th grades Girl Scouts U.S., Stanford, Mont., 1955-59; tchr. Happy Medium Art Group, Whitefish, 1959-68; violinist Waukegan Philharm., 1945-47, Billings Symphony, 1951-55; donated art works for benefit auctions to Hockaday Gallery, 1970, Kalispell, 1971, Mont. Food Bank, 1991, 92, 93, Aids Found., 1990, Helena Area Habitat for Humanity, 1993. Co-recipient prize for radio program of yr. Mont. Advt. Coun., 1992. Mem. Mont. Inst. Arts, Mont. Watercolor Soc. (bd. mem. 1983), Nat. Writers Club.

ELLIOTT, DENI, ethics educator; b. Nanticoke, Pa., Nov. 16, 1953; d. Francis J. and Lottie (Peitrovich) Nitkowski; m. James P. Cramer; 1 child, James Wesley. BA, U. Md., 1974; MA, Wayne State U., 1982; DEd, Harvard U., 1984. Cert. secondary tchr., Mich. Journalism and English tchr. Plymouth (Mich.) Canton High Sch., 1979-81; assoc. prof. comms. Utah State U., Logan, 1985-88; rsch. assoc. prof. edn., adj. assoc. prof. dept. philosophy Dartmouth Coll., Hanover, N.H., 1988-92, dir. Ethics Inst., 1988-92; Mansfield prof. ethics U. Mont., Missoula, 1992-96, dir. Practical Ethics Ctr., prof. ethics, 1996—, prof. philosophy, 1996—, adj. prof. Sch. Journalism, 1996—; reporter, ethics coach Sta. WCSH-TV, Portland, 1988, Louisville Courier-Jour., 1987, Phila. Inquirer, Phila., 1985. Author, editor: Responsible Journalism, 1986, The Ethics of Asking, 1995, A Coursebook for Research Ethics, 1997, A Guidebook for Faculty, 1997; co-prodr. video documentary A Case of Need, 1989 (Silver Apple 1991), Buying Time, 1991 (Bronze Apple 1992), Burden of Knowledge: Moral Dilemnas in Prenatal Testing; columnist FineLine Mag., Louisville, 1989-91; contbr. articles to profl. jours., chpts. to books. Recipient Bronze Plaque Columbus Internat. Film Festival, 1990; Marion and Jasper Whiting Found. fellow Harvard U., 1983, Rockefeller fellow Dartmouth Coll., 1987. Mem. Soc. of Profl. Journalists, Am. Philosophical Assn., Assn. for Edn. in Journalism and Mass Communication, Assn. for Practical and Profl. Ethics (governing bd.). Home: PO Box 846 Lolo MT 59847-0846 Office: U Mont Dept Philosophy Missoula MT 59812

ELLIOTT, GLADDEN V., retired radologist; b. Cabool, Mo., Jan. 25, 1922; s. Gaylord V. and Mary Iola (Gladden) E.; m. Peggy Pile, Sept. 25, 1943; children: Nancy Gay Elliott Manchee, Sarah Jane Elliott McCarthy. AB, Ctrl. Meth. Coll., Fayette, Mo., 1942; MD, Washington U., St. Louis, 1946. Instr. Washington U. Med. Sch., St. Louis, 1949-52, asst. prof. radiology, 1952-55, assoc. prof. radiology, 1957-58; assoc. radiologist Grossmont Hosp., La Mesa, Calif., 1958-92; retired, 1993; bd. trustees Calif. Blue Shield, San Francisco, 1987-96; commr. Calif. Med. Assistance Commn., Sacramento, 1993-96. Trustee Hall of Sci., San Diego, 1977-83. Capt. USAF, 1955-57. Named Physician Citzen of Yr., San Diego, 1985; recipient Disting. Alumni citation Ctrl. Meth. Coll., Fayette, Mo., 1986, Alumni Achievement award Washington U. Med. Ctr. Alumni Assn., St. Louis, 1996. Mem. Calif. Med. Assn. (spkr. 1977-84, exec. com. 1977-88, pres. 1986-87), Am. Med. Polit. Action Com. (trustee 1988-92). Republican. Presbyterian. Home: 3535 1st Ave Apt 9C San Diego CA 92103-4845

ELLIOTT, GORDON JEFFERSON, English language educator; b. Aberdeen, Wash., Nov. 13, 1928; s. Harry Cecil and Helga May (Kennedy) E.; m. Suzanne Tsugiko Urakawa, Apr. 2, 1957; children: Meiko Ann, Kenneth Gordon, Nancy Lee, Matthew Kennedy. AA, Grays Harbor Coll., 1948; BA, U. Wash., 1950; Cert. Russian, Army Lang. Sch., Monterey, Calif., 1952; MA, U. Hawaii, 1968. Lifetime credential, Calif. Community Coll. System. English prof. Buddhist U., Ministry of Cults, The Asia Found., Phnom Penh, Cambodia, 1956-62; English instr. U. Hawaii, Honolulu, 1962-68; dir., orientation English Coll. Petroleum and Minerals, Dhahran, Saudi Arabia, 1968-70; asst. prof., English/linguistics U. Guam, Mangilao, 1970-76; tchr., French/English Medford (Oreg.) Mid High Sch., 1976-77; instr., English Merced (Calif.) Coll., 1977—; cons. on Buddhist Edn., The Asia Found., San Francisco, Phnom Penh, Cambodia, 1956-62; cons. on English Edn., Hawaii State Adult Edn. Dept., Honolulu, 1966-68; conf. on English Edn. in Middle East, Am. U., Cairo, Egypt, 1969; vis. prof. of English, Shandong Tchrs. U., Jinan, China, 1984-85. Co-author: (textbooks, bilingual Cambodian-English) English Composition, 1962, Writing English, 1966, (test) Standard English Recognition Test, 1976; contbr. articles to profl. jours. Mem. Statue of Liberty Centennial Commn., Washington, 1980-86, Heritage Found., Washington, Lincoln Inst., Am. Near East Refugee Aid, Washington, Sgt. U.S. Army Security Agy., 1951-55. Tchr. Fellowship, U. Mich., Ann Arbor, 1956; recipient summer seminar stipend, Nat. Endowment For Humanities, U. Wash., Seattle, 1976, travel grants, People's Rep. of China, Beijing, 1984-85. Mem. NRA, Collegiate Press (editorial adv. bd.), Merced Coll. Found., Am. Assn. Woodturners, Elks. Republican. Home: 680 Dennis Ct Merced CA 95340-2410 Office: Merced Coll 3600 M St Merced CA 95348-2806

ELLIOTT, JAMES HEYER, retired university art museum curator, fine arts consultant; b. Medford, Oreg., Feb. 19, 1924; s. Bert R. and Marguerite E. (Heyer) E.; m. Judith Ann Algar, Apr. 23, 1966 (div.); children: Arabel Joan, Jakob Maxwell. BA, Willamette U., Salem, Oreg., 1947, DFA (hon.), 1978; AM, Harvard U., 1949; DFA (hon.), San Francisco Art Inst., 1991. James Rogers Rich fellow Harvard U., 1949-50; Fulbright grantee Paris, 1951-52; art critic European edit. N.Y. Herald-Tribune, 1952-53; curator, acting dir. Walker Art Center, Mpls., 1953-56; asst. chief curator, curator modern art Los Angeles County Mus. Art, 1956-63, chief curator, 1964-66; dir. Wadsworth Atheneum, Hartford, Conn., 1966-76; dir. Univ. Art Mus., Berkeley, Calif., 1976-88, chancellor's curator, 1989-90, dir. emeritus, 1990—; adj. prof. Hunter Coll., N.Y.C., 1968, U. Calif., Berkeley, 1976-90; commr. Conn. Commn. Arts, 1970-76; fellow Trumbull Coll., Yale U., 1971-75; mem. mus. arts panel Nat. Endowment Arts, 1974-77; bd. dirs. San Francisco Art Inst., 1980-90; art adv. com. Exploratorium, 1982-91; adv. com. Artists TV Access, 1987-90. Author: Bonnard and His Environment, 1964, James Lee Byars: Notes Towards a Biography, 1990. Trustee Marcia Simon Weisman Found., 1991—, 23 FIVE Found., San Francisco, 1993—, di Rosa Preserve, Napa, Calif., 1996—; mem. adv. bd. Artspace San Francisco, 1989—. With USNR, 1943-46. Mem. Internat. Coun. Mus., Am. Assn. Mus., Coll. Art Assn., Artists Space N.Y. (bd. dirs. 1980-84), Arts Club (Berkeley). Home: 13 Yellow Ferry Hbr Sausalito CA 94965-1327

ELLIOTT, JEANNE BATE, retired English educator, writer; b. Kearney, Nebr., May 20, 1924; d. William and Vera Grace (Clark) Bate; m. Clarence V. Lawson, Aug. 3, 1943 (div. June 1952); 1 child, Pamela; m. Stewart P. Elliott, June 20, 1969. BA in English, U. Calif., Berkeley, 1945, MA in English, 1949, PhD, 1956. Tchg. asst. dept. English U. Calif., Berkeley, 1951-54, lectr., 1956-57; instr. U. Nev., Reno, 1954-56; asst. prof. San Jose (Calif.) State U., 1957-62, assoc. prof., 1962-70, prof., 1970-91. Contbr. poetry to various publs.; editor Reed Mag., San Jose, 1962-65. Postdoctoral fellow AAUW, 1956-57. Mem. MLA, AAUP, Philological Assn. of Pacific Coast, Victorian Studies Assn. Democrat. Episcopalian. Home: 1211 Via Vicam Green Valley AZ 85614

ELLIOTT, JEANNE MARIE KORELTZ, transportation executive; b. Virginia, Minn., Mar. 9, 1943; d. John Andrew and Johanna Mae (Tehovnik) Koreltz; m. David Michael Elliott, Apr. 30, 1983. Student, Ariz. State U., 1967, U. So. Calif. Cert. aviation safety inspector. Tech. asst. Ariz. State U., Tempe, 1966-68; from supr. to mgr. inflight tng./in-svc. programs Northwest Airlines Inc. (formerly Republic Airlines, Hughes Airwest, Air West Inc.), Seattle, 1968—; air carrier cabin safety specialist Flight Standards Service, FAA, Washington, 1975-76; cons. Interaction Research Corp., Olympia, Wash., 1982—. Contbg. editor Cabin Crew Safety Bull., Flight Safety Found., 1978—. Recipient Annual Air Safety award Air Line Pilots Assn., Washington, 1971, Annual Safety award Ariz. Safety Council, Phoenix, 1972; first female to hold FAA cabin safety inspector's credential, 1976. Mem. Soc. Air Safety Investigators Internat., Survival and Flight Equipment Assn., Assn. Flight Attendants (tech. chmn. 1968-85), Soc. Automotive Engrs. (chmn. cabin safety provisions com. 1971—), Teamsters Local 2000 (chair nat. safety and health), So. Calif. Safety Inst. (exec. com., bd. dirs.). Republican. Roman Catholic. Home: 16215 SE 31st St Bellevue WA 98008-5704 Office: NW Airlines Inc Inflight Svcs Dept Seattle-Tacoma Internat Airport Seattle WA 98158

ELLIOTT, JOHN GREGORY, aerospace design engineer; b. Surabaya, Dutch East Indies, Nov. 9, 1948; came to U.S., 1956; s. Frans Jan and Charlotte Clara (Rosel) E.; m. Jennifer Lee Austin, May 7, 1988. AA, Cerritos Coll., 1974; BS, Calif. State U., Long Beach, 1978. Design engr. Douglas Aircraft Co., Long Beach, 1978-82, lead engr., 1983-89, sect. mgr. elect. installations group, 1989—. With USN, 1969-73. Mem. So. Calif. Profl. Engring. Assn., Douglas Aircraft Co. Tennis Club, Douglas Aircraft Co. Surf Club, Douglas Aircraft Co. Mgmt. Club. Republican. Presbyterian. Office: Douglas Aircraft Co Internal Mail Code 800-53 3855 N Lakewood Blvd Long Beach CA 90846-0003

ELLIOTT, JON FREDERICK, environmental consultant, educator, lawyer; b. Atlanta, Sept. 30, 1956; m. Elizabeth Lees Taggart; children: Martin Alexander, Madeleine Joy. BSE in Mech. Engring., Princeton U., 1977; M of Pub. Policy, U. Calif., Berkeley, 1980, JD, 1981. Bar: Calif.; registered environ. assesor, Calif. Advisor to pres. Calif. Pub. Utility Commn., San Francisco, 1981-83; staff atty. Toward Utility Rate Normalization, San Francisco, 1983-87; program mgr., regulatory info. Exceltech, Inc., Fremont, Calif., 1987-89; prin., v.p. EPICS Internat., Oakland, Calif., 1989-92; pres. Touchstone Environ., Inc., Oakland, 1992—; mem. exec. com. Environ. Law sect. State Bar Calif., San Francisco, 1992-96, chair legis. com., 1993-96; bd. dirs. Santa Fe Coun. for Environ. Excellence, 1991—. Prin. author: Hazardous Materials Program Commentary, 1988; contbg. editor: The Complete Guide to Hazardous Materials Enforcement and Liability, 1990, Environmental Compliance--A Simplified National Guide, 1992, Directors and Officers Liability, 1995, others. Mem. adv. com. No. Calif. Bus. Environ. Assistance Ctr., Santa Clara, 1994—. Democrat. Office: Touchstone Environ Inc 449 15th St Ste 301 Oakland CA 94612-2821

ELLIOTT, ROSS COX, insurance company executive; b. Orem, Utah, June 9, 1948; s. Grant Hansen and Pauline (Cox) E.; m. Mynon Hayes, Apr. 23, 1970; children: Edgar M., James W., Rosann. BS in Bus. Mgmt., Brigham Young U., 1972. Regional sales mgr. ADP Dealer Svcs., Denver, 1975-76, regional customer svc. mgr., 1976-78; dir. tng. Automatic Data Processing-Dealer Svcs., Portland, Oreg., 1979-85; dir. ins. svcs. Larry H. Miller Group, Murray, Utah, 1986—; gen. mgr. Landcar Life Ins. Co., Murray, 1986—, Landcar Agy., Murray, 1986—, Landcar Casualty Co., Murray, 1990—. Chmn. Murray City Gang Task Force, 1992-93. Mem. Ins. Acctg. and Systems Adminstrn., Utah Life and Disability Ins. Guaranty Assn. (bd. dirs. 1990—, sec.-treas. 1996—, v.p. Utah Life conv. 1996—), Murray City C. of C. (bd. dirs. 1992). Republican. Mem. LDS Ch. Home: 5865 Holstein Way Murray UT 84107-6541 Office: Landcar Insurance Svcs 5650 S State St Salt Lake City UT 84107-6131

ELLIOTT, SCOTT, lawyer; b. San Jose, July 26, 1957; s. Roland Meredith and Sandra Gale (Deem) E.; m. Nancy Marie Oller, Apr. 6, 1979; children: Tristan Robin, Jordan Brook, Robin Sage, Forest Dream. BA in Drama magna cum laude, Calif. State Univ. Stanislaus, Turlock, 1979; JD, U. Oreg., 1987. Bar: Oreg. 1987, U.S. Ct. Appeals (9th cir.) 1992, U.S. Dist. Ct. Oreg. 1988. Assoc. Larry O. Gildea, Eugene, Oreg., 1987-88, Thorp, Dennet, Purdy & Golden, Springfield, Oreg., 1988; law clk. U.S. Dist. Ct., Las Vegas, Nev., 1988-89; ptnr. Green & Elliott, Lincoln City, Oreg., 1989-95; assoc. Thorp, Purdy, Jewett, Urness & Wilkinson, Springfield, Oreg., 1995-96, Wine, Weller, Ehrlich and Green, Lincoln City, Oreg., 1996—. Precinct com. Lincoln County Dems., Newport, 1990-94; mem. choir Congl. Ch., 1997—, youth athletic coach, 1990-94, 97—. U. Oreg. Theatre grad. teaching fellow, 1979-80. Mem. Lincoln County Bar. Office: Wine Weller Ehrlich and Green Ste B 2137 NW Hwy 101 Lincoln City OR 97367

ELLIS, ELDON EUGENE, surgeon; b. Washington, Ind., July 2, 1922; s. Osman Polson and Ina Lucretia (Cochran) E.; BA, U. Rochester, 1946, MD, 1949; m. Irene Clay, June 26, 1948 (dec. 1968); m. Priscilla Dean Strong, Sept. 20, 1969 (dec. Feb. 1990); children: Paul Addison, Kathe Lynn, Jonathan Clay, Sharon Anne, Eldon Eugene, Rebecca Deborah; m. Virginia Michael Ellis, Aug. 22, 1992. Intern in surgery Stanford U. Hosp., San Francisco, 1949-50, resident and fellow in surgery, 1950-52, 55; Schilling fellow in pathology San Francisco Gen. Hosp., 1955; ptnr. Redwood Med. Clinic, Redwood City, Calif., 1955-87, med. dir., 1984-87; semi-ret. physician, 1987—; med. dir. Peninsula Occupl. Health Assocs. (now Peninsula Indsl. Med. Clinic), San Carlos, Calif., 1991-94, physician, 1995—; dir. Sequoia Hosp., Redwood City, 1974-82; asst. clin. prof. surgery Stanford U., 1970-80. Pres. Sequoia Hosp. Found., 1983-92, bd. dirs.; pres., chmn. bd. dirs. Bay Chamber Symphony Orch., San Mateo, Calif., 1988-91; mem. Nat. Bd. of Benevolence Evang. Covenant Ch., Chgo., 1988-93; mem. mgmt. com. The Samarkand Retirement Cmty., Santa Barbara, Calif.; past pres. Project Hope Nat. Alumni Assn., 1992-94, bd. dirs., 1994—; med. advisor Project Hope, Russia Commonwealth Ind. States, 1992. Served with USNR, 1942-46, 50-52. Named Outstanding Citizen of Yr., Redwood City, 1987. Mem. San Mateo County (pres. 1961-63), Calif. (pres. 1965-66), Am. (v.p. 1974-75) heart assns., San Mateo Med. Soc. (pres. 1969-70), San Mateo County Comprehensive Health Planning Coun. (v.p. 1969-70), Calif., Am. med. assns., San Mateo Individual Practice Assn. (treas. 1984—), San Mateo, Stanford surg. socs., Am. Coll. Chest Physicians, Calif. Thoracic Soc., Cardiovascular Coun. Republican. Mem. Peninsula Covenant Ch. Club: Commonwealth. Home: 3621 Farm Hill Blvd Redwood City CA 94061-1230 Office: Peninsula Indsl Med Clinic 1581 Industrial Rd San Carlos CA 94070-4111

ELLIS, EMORY LEON, retired biochemist; b. Grayville, Ill., Oct. 29, 1906; s. Walter Leon and Bertha May (Forman) W.; m. Marion Louise Faulkner, Sept. 17, 1930 (dec. Aug. 1993). BS, CalTech, 1930, MS in Chemistry, 1932, PhD of Biochemistry, 1934. Registered profl. engr., Calif. Chemist U.S. FDA, L.A., 1934-35; rsch. assoc. CalTech, Pasadena, 1935-43; dept. head U.S. Navy Ordnance Test Sta., China Lake, Calif., 1943-54; dir. ordnance plan Rheem Ordnance Lab, Downey, Calif., 1954-57; project leader Inst. for Def. Analysis, Washington, 1957-63; cons. U.S. Navy Weapons Ctr., China Lake, 1966-68; ptnr. Devcom, La Habra, Calif., 1965-68. Contbr. chpt. in books and articles to profl. jours. Paul Harris fellow Rotary Internat., 1993. Mem. AAAS, Am. Chem. Soc., Tau Beta Pi, Sigma Xi. Home: 1407 Via Beliz Santa Maria CA 93454-2601

ELLIS, EUGENE JOSEPH, cardiologist; b. Rochester, N.Y., Feb. 23, 1919; s. Eugene Joseph and Violet (Anderson) E.; m. Ruth Nugent, July 31, 1943; children: Eugene J., Susan Ellis Renwick, Amy Ellis Miller. AB, U. So. Calif., L.A., 1941; MD, U. So. Calif., 1944; MS in medicine, U. Minn., 1950. Diplomate Am. Bd. Internal Medicine and Cardiovascular Diseases. Intern L.A. County Hosp., 1944, resident, 1946; fellowship Mayo Clinic, Rochester, Minn., 1947-51; dir. dept. cardiology St. Vincent's Hosp., L.A., 1953-55; dir. dept. cardiology Good Samaritan Hosp., L.A., 1955-84; ret., ret., 1984; prof. emeritus medicine U. So. Calif., 1984—; Mem. Med. Bd. of Calif., 1984-91; pres., 1988; pres. Div. of Med. Quality, State of Calif., 1985-89; exec. com. trustees U. Redlands, 1976-86. Lt. USN, 1944-46. Contbr. articles to profl. jours. Bd. dirs. Cancer Found. Santa Barbara, Casa Dorinda Retirement Facility, Alcohol Coun. Santa Barbara. Lt. USN, 1944-46. Mem. L.A. Country Club, Pauma Valley Country Club (bd. dirs. 1980-83), Birnam Wood Golf Club (bd. dirs. 1994-95), Valley Club of Montecito. Republican. Home: 450 Eastgate Ln Santa Barbara CA 93108-2248

ELLIS, GEORGE EDWIN, JR., chemical engineer; b. Beaumont, Tex., Apr. 14, 1921; s. George Edwin and Julia (Ryan) E.; B.S. in Chem. Engring., U. Tex., 1948; M.S., U. So. Calif., 1958, M.B.A., 1965, M.S. in Mech. Engring., 1968, M.S. in Mgmt. Sci., 1971, Engr. in Indsl. and Systems Engring., 1979. Research chem. engr. Tex. Co., Port Arthur, Tex., 1948-51, Long Beach, Calif., Houston, 1952-53, Space and Information div. N.Am. Aviation Co., Downey, Calif., 1959-61, Magna Corp., Anaheim, Calif., 1961-62; chem. process engr. AiResearch Mfg. Co., Los Angeles, 1953-57, 57-59; chem. engr. Petroleum Combustion & Engring. Co., Santa Monica, Calif., 1957, Jacobs Engring. Co., Pasadena, Calif., 1957, Sesler & Assos., Los Angeles, 1959; research specialist Marquardt Corp., Van Nuys, Calif., 1962-67; sr. project engr. Conductron Corp., Northridge, 1967-68; information systems asst. Los Angeles Dept. Water and Power, 1969-92. Instr. thermodynamics U. So. Calif., Los Angeles, 1957. Served with USAAF, 1943-45. Mem. ASTM, ASME, Nat. Assn. Purchasing Mgmt., Nat. Contract Mgmt. Assn., Am. Inst. Profl. Bookkeepers, Am. Soc. Safety Engrs., Am. Chem. Soc., Am. Soc. Materials, Am. Electroplaters and Surface Finishers Soc., Am. Inst. Chem. Engrs., Inst. Indsl. Engrs., Am. Prodn. and Inventory Control Soc., Am. Soc. Quality Control, Assn. Facilities Engrs., Am. Indsl. Hygenists Assn., Steel Structure Painting Coun., Inst. Mgmt. Accts., Soc. Mfg. Engrs., L.A. Soc. Coating Tech., Assn. Finishing Processes, Pi Tau Sigma, Phi Lambda Upsilon, Alpha Pi Mu. Home: 1344 W 20th St San Pedro CA 90732-4408

ELLIS, GEORGE RICHARD, museum administrator; b. Birmingham, Ala., Dec. 9, 1937; s. Richard Paul and Dorsie (Gibbs) E.; m. Sherroll Edwards, June 20, 1961 (dec. 1973); m. Nancy Enderson, Aug. 27, 1975; 1 son, Joshua. BA, U. Chgo., 1959, MFA, 1961; postgrad., UCLA, 1971. Art supr. Jefferson County Schs., Birmingham, 1962-64; asst. dir. Birmingham Mus. Art, 1964-66; asst. dir. UCLA Mus. Cultural History, 1971-81, assoc. dir., 1981-82; dir. Honolulu Acad. Arts, 1981—. Author various works on non-western art, 1971—. Bd. dirs. Children's Lit. Hawaii, 1996—. Recipient Ralph Altman award UCLA, 1968; recipient Outstanding Achievement award UCLA, 1980; fellow Kress Found., 1971. Mem. Pacific Arts Assn. (v.p. 1985-89, exec. bd. 1989—), Hawaii Mus. Assn. (v.p. 1986-87, pres. 1987-88, pres. 1996-97), Assn. Art Mus. Dirs., Am. Assn. Mus., L.A. Ethnic Arts Coun. (hon.), Friends of Iolani Palace (bd. dirs. 1989—), Pacific Club. Office: Honolulu Academy of Arts 900 S Beretania St Honolulu HI 96814-1429

ELLIS, HARRIETTE ROTHSTEIN, editor, writer; b. Memphis, Feb. 29, 1924; d. Samuel and Edith (Brodsky) Rothstein; m. Manuel J. Kaplan, June 1, 1944 (div. 1970); children: Deborah Elise Kaplan-Wyckoff, Claire Naomi Kaplan, Amelia Stephanie Kaplan; m. Theodore J. Ellis, Aug. 22, 1971 (div. Jan. 1992). Student, Memphis State U., 1941-42, Memphis Art Acad., 1940-43, BA, U. Ala., Tuscaloosa, 1944; postgrad., UCLA, 1949-50, Chouinard Art Inst., L.A., 1948. Advt. art/copy retail industry, New Orleans, Albuquerque, L.A., 1944-49; writer, graphic artist for newspapers and mags., L.A., 1944-49; editor Jewish Fedn. News, Long Beach, Calif., 1969-81; editor, writer Calif. Fashion Publs., L.A., 1982-86; editor Valley Mag., Granada Hills, Calif., 1987; pub. rels. Joan Luther & Assocs., Beverly Hills, Calif., 1988-90; editor Jewish Cmty. Chronicle, Long Beach, 1990—; dir. corp. comms. Startel Corp., Irvine, Calif., 1991-92. Active on com. to help implement infusion of fluoridated water in city water sys., mem. comty. interfaith com., Long Beach; bd. dirs. Hillel, 1994—, Camp Komaroff, 1994—, Jewish Comty. Ctr., Long Beach. Named Woman of Yr., Temple Israel, Long Beach, Pioneer Women; recipient newspaper awards Calif. Press Women, Nat. Fedn. Press Women, Coun. of Jewish Fedns. Mem. Calif. Press Women (bd. dirs., treas., v.p., pres. 1997—), Nat. Fedn. Press Women, Women of Reform Judaism (regional and nat. bd. dirs.). Office: 3801 E Willow St Long Beach CA 90815-1734

ELLIS, JOHN W., professional baseball team executive, utility company executive; b. Seattle, Sept. 14, 1928; s. Floyd E. and Hazel (Reed) R.; m. Doris Stearns, Sept. 1, 1953; children: Thomas R., John, Barbara, Jim. B.S., U. Wash., 1952, J.D., 1953. Bar: Wash. State bar 1953. Ptnr. Perkins, Coie, Stone, Olsen & Williams, Seattle, 1953-70; with Puget Sound Power & Light Co., Bellevue, Wash., 1970—, exec. v.p., 1973-76, pres., CEO, 1976-87, also dir., chmn., CEO, 1987-92, chmn. bd., 1992—; dir., chmn. Seattle br. Fed. Res. Bank of San Francisco, 1982-88; chief exec. officer Seattle Mariners, 1992—; mem. Wash. Gov.'s Spl. Com. Energy Curtailment, 1973-74; mem. Wash. Gov.'s Coun. on Edn., 1991—; chmn. Pacific N.W. Utilities Coordinating Com., 1976-82; bd. dirs. Wash. Mut. Savs. Bank, Seattle, SAFECO Corp., Nat. Energy Found., 1985-87, FlowMole Corp., Assoc. Electric & Gas Ins. Svcs. Ltd.; chmn. Electric Power Rsch. Inst., 1984—; chmn., CEO, The Baseball Club of Seattle, L.P.; regent Wash. State U., 1992—. Pres. Bellevue Boys and Girls Club, 1969-71, Seattle/King County Econ. Devel. Council, 1984—; mem. exec. dirs. Seattle/King County Boys and Girls Club, 1972-75; bd. dirs. Overlake Hosp., Bellevue, 1974—, United Way King County, 1977—, Seattle Sci. Found., 1977—, Seattle Sailing Found., Evergreen Safety Council, 1981, Assn. Wash. Bus., 1980-81, Govs. Adv. Council on Econ. Devel., 1984—; chmn. bd. Wash. State Bus. Round Table, 1983; pres. United for Washington; adv. bd. Grad. Sch. Bus. Adminstrn. U. Wash., 1982—, Wash. State Econ. Ptnrship., 1984—; chmn. Seattle Regional Panel White Ho. Fellows, 1985—; trustee Seattle U., 1986—. Mem. ABA, Wash. Bar Assn., King County Bar Assn., Nat. Assn. Elec. Cos. (dir. 1977-79), Edison Electric Inst. (dir. 1978-80, exec. com. 1982, 2d vice chmn. 1987, 1st vice chmn. 1988, now chmn.), Assn. Edison Illuminating Cos. (exec. com. 1979-81), Seattle C. of C. (dir. 1980—, 1st vice chmn. 1987-88, chmn. 1988—), Phi Gamma Delta, Phi Delta Phi. Clubs: Rainier (Seattle) (sec. 1972, v.p. 1984, pres. 1985), Seattle Yacht (Seattle), Corinthian Yacht (Seattle); Meydenbauer Bay Yacht (Bellevue), Bellevue Athletic. Lodge: Rotary (Seattle). Home: 901 Shoreland Dr SE Bellevue WA 98004-6738 Office: Seattle Mariners PO Box 4100 83 King St Seattle WA 98104-2860 also: Puget Sound Power & Light Co PO Box 97034 Bldg Bellevue WA 98009-9734*

ELLIS, LARENE RICHINS, real estate agent, interior decorator; b. Coalville, Utah, Jan. 17, 1951; d. Fay Edwin and Clyda (Bair) Richins; m. Marvin O. Ellis, June 12, 1970; children: Marvin Todd, Chad Richins, Jana Lee, Kay Dee, Benjamin Bair, Clyda Ann. Restaurant owner Blimpie Sub & Salads, Bountiful-Layton, Utah, 1990-93; interior decorator Utah, 1982—; real estate agt. Prudential Advantage, Bountiful-Ogden, Utah, 1995—; developer properties, Park City, Utah, 1990-96. Creator, author Self Decorating Kit, 1995. Home: PO Box 762 Farmington UT 84025

ELLIS, LEE, publisher, editor; b. Medford, Mass., Mar. 12, 1924; s. Lewis Leeds and Charlotte Frances Ellis; m. Sharon Kay Barnhouse, Aug. 19, 1972. Child actor, dancer, stage, radio, movies, Keith-Albee Cir., Ea. U.S., 1927-37; announcer, producer, writer, various radio stas. and CBS, Boston, N.Y.C., and Miami, Fla., 1946-50; TV dir. ABC; mem. TV faculty Sch. Journalism U. Mo., Columbia, 1950-55; mgr. Sta. KFSD/KFSD-TV, San Diego, 1955-60, GM Imperial Broadcasting System, 1960-62; v.p., dir. advt., Media-Agencies-Clients, Los Angeles, 1962-66; v.p., dir. newspaper relations Family Weekly (name now USA Weekend), N.Y.C., 1966-89; pres., owner, editor Sharlee Publs., 1989—; voice of Nat. Date Festival, 1990-93; lectr. gen. semantics and communications Idaho State U., Utah State U., San Diego State U. Served with USN, 1941-44, PTO. Mem. San Diego Press Club, Indio C. of C. Republican. Methodist. Home and Office: 47-800 Madison St Unit 53 Indio CA 92201-6673

ELLIS, ROBERT HARRY, retired television executive, university administrator; b. Cleve., Mar. 2, 1928; s. John George Ellis and Grace Bernice (Lewis) Ellis Kline; m. Frankie Jo Lanter, Aug. 7, 1954; children: Robert Harry Jr., Kimberley Kay Ellis Murphy, Shana Lee. BA, Ariz. State U., 1953; MA, Case Western Res. U., 1962. Newswriter, announcer Sta. KOY, Phoenix, 1953-55, continuity dir., 1955-61; dir., radio ops. Ariz. State U., Tempe, 1959-61; gen. mgr. Sta. KAET-TV, Tempe, 1961-87; assoc. v.p. Ariz. State U., Tempe, 1986-90; exec. com. bd. dirs. Pub. Broadcasting Svc., Washington, 1972-77, 80-86; founder Pacific Mountain Network, Denver, 1972, pres., 1973-75; mem. ednl. telecomm. com. Nat. Assn. Ednl. Broadcasters, Washington, 1973-77, 80-86. Mem. Sister City, Tempe, Tempe Ctr. For the Handicapped, East Valley Mental Health Alliance, Mesa, Ariz., Ariz. Acad., State Ariz. Behavior Health Bd. of Examiners, 1991-92. Bd. Govs. award Pacific Mountain Network, 1987. Mem. Nat. Assn. TV Arts and Scis. (life, v.p., bd. trustees 1969-70, bd. dirs. Phoenix chpt. 1986, silver circle award 1992), Nat. Assn. Pub. TV Stas. (bd. dirs. 1988-94), Tempe C. of C. (diplomate, bd. dirs. 1987-90), Sundome Performing Arts Assn. (bd. dirs. 1986-90), Ariz. Zool. Soc. (bd. dirs., sec. 1984-90), Ariz. State U. Alumni Assn. (life), Ariz. State U. Retirees Assn. (founder, pres. 1991-92), Tempe Conv. and Visitors Bur. (founder, sec./treas. 1988-93), Tempe Sports Authority (founder 1989-95), ASU Faculty Emeritus Orgn. (pres. 1992-93). Methodist.

ELLIS, SALLY STRAND See STRAND, SALLY LEE

ELLIS, SARAH ELIZABETH, librarian; b. Vancouver, Can., May 19, 1952; d. Joseph Walter and Ruth Elizabeth (Steabner) E. BA, U. B.C., Vancouver, 1973, MLS, 1975; MA, Simmons Coll., 1980. Children's librarian Vancouver Pub. Libr., 1976-81, North Vancouver Dist. Libr., 1981—; lectr. U. B.C., 1982—. Author: The Baby Project, 1986, Next-Door Neighbors, 1989, Putting Up with Mitchell, 1989, Pick-up Sticks, 1991, Out of the Blue, 1994, Back of Beyond, 1996. Mem. Writers Union Can., Can. Soc. Children's Authors, Illustrators and Performers, PEN. Home: 4432 Walden St, Vancouver, BC Canada V5V 3S3 Office: North Vancouver Dist Libr, 1280 E 27th St, North Vancouver, BC Canada V7J 1S1

ELLIS-OGBORN, FRANCESCA ANGELA, mental health counselor and clinic administrator; b. N.Y.C., June 23, 1939; d. Antonio and Jeannette Marie (Thomas) Naveja; m. David H. Ellis, Oct. 21, 1957; children: Theresa Fae Ann Zendejas, David Cary Ellis. AA with Honors, Allan Hancock Coll., 1985; BS, Columbia Pacific U., 1988; MA, U. San Francisco, 1989. Adminstr. Community Ministry Ctr., Chino, Calif., 1977-79; bus. mgr. Humanistic Mental Health, Santa Maria, Calif., 1984-85; med. sec. A. Edward Hoctor, MD., Santa Maria, 1985; bus. mgr. Affiliated Psychotherapist, Santa Maria, 1985-87; founder, exec. dir., psychotherapist, C.E.O. AP Inst., Inc. Community Counseling Ctr., Santa Maria, 1988-95; program dir. Safe Interventions, Santa Maria, Case Mgmt. and Consulting Assocs., Santa Maria; mem. adj. faculty Columbia Pacific U., Sierra U.; founder, dir. Trias Inst., Santa Maria, 1984-95, AP Inst., Santa Maria, 1986-87, AP Inst. Valley Counseling Ctr., 1986-95; bd. dirs. Friends of Ruth Women's Shelter, Santa Maria, 1985; cons. St. Joseph's High Sch., 1990, Ctrl. Coast Cons. Assocs., 1991—. Editor, author quar. newsletter Pride, 1990—. Vol. Dem. Women's Caucus 1986; mem. Women's Network, Santa Maria, 1986-89; mental health adv. coun. Santa Barbara County, 1990, with Domestic violence Edn./Elimination Svcs., 1992-95. Mem. Am. Mental Health Counseling Assn., Assn. Christian Therapists (regional coord., 1988-90), Calif. Assn. Marriage Family Therapists, Cen. Coast Jung Soc., Western Assn. Spiritual Dirs., Cen. Coast Hypnosis Soc. Mem. Am. Assn. Prof. Hypnotherapists. Office: Lovelock Mental Health PO Box 1046 Lovelock NV 89419

ELLISON, CYRIL LEE, literary agent, publisher; b. N.Y.C., Dec. 11, 1916; s. John and Rose (Ellison) E.; m. Anne N. Nottonson, June 4, 1942. With Watson-Guptill Publs., 1939-69, v.p., advt. dir., 1939-69, assoc. pub. Am. Artist mag.; exec. v.p. Communication Channels, Inc., N.Y.C., 1969-88; pub. emeritus Fence Industry, Access Control, Pension World, Trusts & Estates, Nat. Real Estate Investor, Shopping Center World; pres. Lee Comms., 1980—; assoc. Kids Countrywide, Inc.; literary agent, 1994—; pub. cons., book rep., advt. and mktg. cons.; cons. Mark Clements Rsch. N.Y., Inc., 1994—; pub. cons. Mag. Rsch. Mktg. Co., 1994—. Pres. Westbury Hebrew Congregation, 1954, chmn. bd. trustees, 1955. Served with USAAF, 1942-46, PTO. Named Gray-Russo Advt. Man of Year Ad Men's Post Am. Legion, 1954; recipient Hall of Fame award Internat. Fence Industry Assn., 1985. Mem. Am. Legion (life, comdr. advt. men's post 1954, 64). Home: 6839 N 29th Ave Phoenix AZ 85017-1213 Office: Lee Communications 5060 N 19th Ave Phoenix AZ 85015-3210

ELLISON, LAWRENCE J., computer software company executive; b. 1944. BS. With Amdahl, Inc., Santa Clara, Calif., 1967-71; systems architect Amdahl, Inc.; pres. systems div. Omex Corp., 1972-77; with Oracle Corp., Redwood, Calif., 1977—, pres., chief exec. officer, 1978—, also bd. dirs. Office: Oracle Corp 500 Oracle Pky Redwood City CA 94065-1600*

ELLIS-VANT, KAREN MCGEE, elementary and special education educator, consultant; b. La Grande, Oreg., May 10, 1950; d. Ellis Eddington and Gladys Vera (Smith) McGee; m. Lynn F. Ellis, June 14, 1975 (div. Sept. 1983); children: Megan Marie, Matthew David; m. Jack Scott Vant, Sept. 6, 1986; children: Kathleen Erin, Kelli Christine (dec.). BA in Elem. Edn., Boise State U., 1972, MA in Spl. Edn., 1979; postgrad. studies in curriculum and instruction, U. Minn., 1985—. Tchr. learning disabilities resource room New Plymouth Joint Sch. Dist., 1972-73, Payette Joint Sch. Dist., 1973, diagnostician project SELECT, 1974-75; cons. tchr. in spl. edn. Boise Sch. Dist., 1975-90; tchr. 1-2 combination, 1990-91, team tchr. 1st grade, 1991-92, 95—, chpt. 1 program cons., 1992-95; mem. profl. Standards Commn., 1983-86. Bd. dirs. Hotline, Inc., 1979-82; mem. Idaho Coop. Manpower Commn., 1984-85. Recipient Disting. Young Woman of Yr. award Boise Jaycettes, 1982, Idaho Jaycettes, 1983; Coffman Alumni scholar U. Minn., 1985-86. Mem. NEA (mem. civil rights com. 1983-85, state contact for peace caucus 1981-85, del. assembly rep., 1981-85), NSTA, ASCD, Internat. Reading Assn. (v.p. Boise chpt. 1996—), NCTE, Internat. Coop. Learning Assn., Idaho Edn. Assn. (bd. dirs. region VII 1981-85, pres. region VII 1981-82), Boise Edn. Assn. (v.p. 1981-82, 84-85, pres. 1982-83), Nat. Council Urban Edn. Assn., World Future Soc., Council for Exceptional Children (pres. chpt. 1978-79), Nat. Coun. Tchrs. English, Minn. Coun. for Social Studies, Calif. Assn. for Gifted, Assn. for Grad. Edn. Students, Phi Delta Kappa. Contbr. articles to profl. jours.; editor, author ednl. texts and communiques; conductor of workshops, leadership tng. coop. learning. and frameworks. Office: Highlands Elem 3434 Bogus Basin Rd Boise ID 83702-1507

ELLNER, MICHAEL WILLIAM, art educator; b. N.Y.C., Apr. 1, 1938; s. Charles and Sylvia May (Golub) E.; m. Josephine Helene Bilello, Aug. 24, 1957; children: Eileen Lorraine, Deborah Lynn, Laurence Steven. AA in Engring., San Jose City Coll., 1963, AA in Art, 1966, BA, Coll. Notre Dame, 1970; MA, San Jose State U., 1971, postgrad., 1973-74; postgrad., U. Calif., Santa Cruz, 1980. Cert. secondary art tchr., c.c. art tchr., Calif. Chair art dept. John Muir Jr. High Sch., San Jose, Calif., 1973-80; assoc. prof. art San Jose State U., 1974; chair art dept. Willow Glen Edn. Park, San Jose, 1980-91; visual arts coord. A. Lincoln AVPA Magnet High Sch., San Jose, 1991-96; cons. Coll. Bd., San Jose, 1989—, San Jose Unified Sch. Dist., Saturday Acad., San Jose, 1996—, San Jose City Coll. Painting Program, 1996—; advisor Nat. Art Honor Soc., San Jose, 1991—; intern advisor Casa Program, San Jose, 1991—; co-convenor Lincoln HS Magnet Curriculum Coun., San Jose, 1991-96; mentor tchr. San Jose Unified Sch. Dist., 1985-94. Paintings included in numerous pub. collections including San Jose Mus. Art, Calif., De Saisset Mus., Santa Clara, Calif., Foot Mus., Long Beach, Calif., Coll. Notre Dame, Belmont, Calif.; curator Egyptian Mus. Art Gallery, San Jose, Calif., New World Gallery, San Jose, Calif., San Jose Art League, Calif.; guest curator Macla Gallery, San Jose, Calif., Genesis Gallery, San Jose, Calif., 1970—; exhibited in more than 100 group and one-person shows; created 15 cmty. murals. Recipient Art grant City of San Jose, 1994, Mural grant Rose Garden Assn., San Jose, 1996, grant Nat. League Am. Pen Women, 1996; named Tchr. of Yr., Willow Glen Edn. Park PTA, 1985, San Jose Shrine, 1986. Mem. Calif. Tchrs. Assn., NEA, San Jose Tchrs. Assn., San Jose Inst. Contemporary Art, Nat. Art Edn. Assn., Artists Alliance Calif., Cmty. Partnership Santa Clara County, Phi Kappa Phi. Home: 1429 Scossa Ave San Jose CA 95118-2456

ELLSAESSER, HUGH WALTER, retired atmospheric scientist; b. Chillicothe, Mo., June 1, 1920; s. Charles Theobald and Louise Minerva (Bancroft) E.; m. Lois Merle McCaw, June 21, 1946; children: Corbin Donald, Adrienne Sue. AA, Bakersfield (Calif.) Jr. Coll., 1941; SB, U. Chgo., 1943, PhD, 1964; MA, UCLA, 1947. Commd. 2d lt. USAF, 1943, advanced through grades to lt. col., 1960; weather officer USAF, Washington, Fla., Eng., 1942-63; ret., 1963; physicist Lawrence Livermore (Calif.) Nat. Lab., 1963-86, guest scientist, 1986-97. Editor: Global 2000 Revisited, 1992; contbr. numerous articles to profl. jours. Mem. Am. Meteorol. Soc., Am. Geophysics Union. Republican. Presbyterian. Home and Office: 4293 Stanford Way Livermore CA 94550-3463

ELLSWORTH, RICHARD GERMAN, psychologist; b. Provo, Utah, June 23, 1950; s. Richard Grant and Betty Lola (Midgley) E.; BS, Brigham Young U., 1974, MA, 1975; PhD, U. Rochester (N.Y.), 1979; postgrad. UCLA, 1980-84; PhD, Internat. Coll., 1983; m. Carol Emily Osborne, May 23, 1970; children: Rebecca Ruth, Spencer German, Rachel Priscilla, Melanie Star, Richard Grant, David Jedediah. Cert. Am. Bd. Med. Psychotherapy, (fellow), Am. Bd. Sexology. Instr. U. Rochester, 1976-77; asst. prof. Chapman U., 1995—; rsch. assoc. Nat. Tech. Inst. for Deaf, Rochester, 1977; instr. West Valley Coll., Saratoga, Calif., 1979-80, San Jose (Calif.) City Coll., 1980; psycholinquist UCLA, 1980-81; rsch. assoc. UCLA, 1982-85; psychologist Daniel Freeman Meml. Hosp., Inglewood, Calif., 1981-84, Broderick, Langlois & Assocs., San Gabriel, Calif., 1982-86, Beck Psychiat. Med. Group, Lancaster, Calif., 1984-87, Angeles Counseling Ctr., Arcadia, Calif., 1986-89, Assoc. Med. Psychotherapists, Palmdale, Calif., 1988—; cons. LDS Social Svcs. Calif. Agy., 1981—, Antelope Valley Hosp. Med. Ctr., 1984—, Palmdale Hosp. Med. Ctr., 1984-96, Treatment Ctrs. of Am. Psychiat. Hosps., 1985-86, Hollywood Cmty. Hosp., 1994—, Lancaster Cmty. Hosp., 1996—. Scoutmaster, Boy Scouts Am., 1976-79. UCLA Med. Sch. fellow in psychiatry, 1980-81. Mem. Am. Psychol. Assn., Am. Assn. Sex Educators, Am. Psychol. Assn., Counselors and Therapists, Assn. Mormon Counselors and Psychotherapists, Am. Soc. Clin. Hypnosis, Psi Chi. Contbr. articles to profl. jours. Office: 1220 East Ave S Ste A Palmdale CA 93550

ELMORE, JAMES WALTER, architect, retired university dean; b. Lincoln, Nebr., Sept. 5, 1917; s. Harry Douglas and Marie Clare (Minor) E.; m. Mary Ann Davidson, Sept. 6, 1947; children: James Davidson, Margaret Kay. A.B., U. Nebr., 1938; M.S. in Architecture, Columbia U., 1948. Mem. faculty Ariz. State U., 1949-86, prof. architecture, 1959-86, founding dean Coll. of Architecture, 1964-74; cons. architect, 1956—. Trustee Heard Museum, Phoenix, 1968-79; bd. dirs. Valley Forward Assn., 1969-89, pres., 1985; bd. dirs. Central Ariz. chpt. Ariz. Hist. Soc., 1973-89; bd. dirs. Ariz. Architects Found., 1978-86, Rio Salado Devel. Dist., 1980-87. Served to col., C.E. U.S. Army, 1940-46. Decorated Bronze Star. Fellow AIA; mem. Ariz. Acad. Home: 6229 N 29th Pl Phoenix AZ 85016-2251

EL-MOSLIMANY, ANN PAXTON, paleoecologist, educator, writer; b. Fullerton, Calif., Aug. 2, 1937; d. Donald Dorn and Sarah Frances (Turman) Paxton; m. Mohammed Ahmad El-Moslimany, May 31, 1962; children: Samia, Ramsey, Rasheed. BS, N.Mex. State U., 1959; MS, Am. U., Beirut, 1961; PhD, U. Wash., 1983. Tchr. various schs., 1959-83, Kuwait U., 1984-86, Seattle Ctrl. C.C., 1986-90; prin., tchr. Islamic Sch. Seattle, 1989—; paleoecological rschr. Palynological Consultants, 1987—. Author: Zaki's Ramadan Fast, 1994; contbr. articles to sci. jours.; mem. adv. bd. Muslim Kaleidescope mag., Sisters mag. Mem. Amnesty Internat., Am. Quaternary Assn., Nat. Coun. Tchrs. Math., Geog. Alliance of Wash., Seattle Islamic Sisterhood. Home: PO Box 367 Seahurst WA 98062 Office: Islamic Sch Seattle PO Box 22956 Seattle WA 98122

ELMSTROM, GEORGE P., optometrist, writer; b. Salem, Mass., Dec. 11, 1925; s. George and Emily Irene (Wedgwood) E.; grad. So. Calif. Coll. Optometry, 1951; m. Nancy DePaul, Apr. 29, 1973; children—Pamela, Beverly, Robert. Pvt. practice optometry, El Segundo, Calif., 1951—; mem. staff So. Calif. Coll. Optometry, 1951—; book cons. Med. Econs. Books, 1970—; instrument and forensic editor Jour. Am. Optical Assn.; comml. airplane and balloon pilot, 1968—. Served with U.S. Army, World War II. Decorated Silver Star; named Writer of Year, Calif. Optometric Assn., 1957, Man of Year, El Segundo, 1956; recipient spl. citation Nat. Eye Found., 1955. Fellow Am. Acad. Optometry, AAAS, Southwest Contact Lens Soc., Disting. Service Found. of Optometry, Internat. Acad. Preventive Medicine; mem. Am. Optometric Assn., Assn. for Research in Vision, Am. Soc. Ultrasonography, Am. Pub. Health Assn., Optometric Editors Assn., Assn. Research in Vision, Internat. Soc. Ophthalmic Ultrasound, Profl. Airshow Pilots Assn., Flying Optometrists Assn. Am., Beta Sigma Kappa, So. Calif. Coll. Optometry Alumni (pres. 1955-56). Author: Optometric Practice Management, 1963; Legal Aspects of Contact Lens Practice, 1966; Advanced Management for Optometrists, 1974; Modernized Management, 1982; mgmt. editor Optometric Monthly, 1973. Home: 484B Washington St Monterey CA 93940-3030 Office: PO Box S-3061 Carmel CA 93921-3061

ELRICK, BILLY LEE, English language educator; b. Jackson, Miss., May 21, 1941; d. William Robert and Wesley James (Hall) Chambers; m. Donald Lee Elrick, June 29, 1965; children: Laura Katherine, John William. BA, Millsaps Coll., 1963; MA in Edn., U. Phoenix, 1992. Tchr. lang. arts North Arvada (Colo.) Jr. High, 1963-92, dept. chair, 1984-92; dean Wheat Ridge (Colo.) High Sch., 1993; tchr. English Arvada (Colo.) H.S., 1993-94, 95—, asst. prin., 1994-95; asst. prin. Chatfield Sr. H.S., 1995—; mentor tchr. Jefferson Cnty Schs.-North; workshop presenter in field. Mem. ASCD, Nat. Assn. Secondary Sch. Prins., Phi Delta Kappa, Delta Kappa Gamma (sec. 1990-94, 2d v.p. 1994—), Sigma Lambda, Kappa Delta Epsilon. Democrat. Methodist. Home: 10615 Irving Ct Westminster CO 80030-2238 Office: Chatfield Sr H S 7227 So Simms Littleton CO 80127

ELSBERRY, SUSAN DAVISE, computer-aided manufacturing engineer; b. Lincoln, Nebr., Oct. 27, 1953; d. Leo Herbert and Genevieve (Richards) Bischof; m. Terence Ray Elsbberry, Aug. 9, 1986; 1 child, Colin Ray. BS, Brigham Young U., 1985, MS, 1992. Computer-aided mfg. engr. Northrop, Hawthorne, Calif., 1986-91; owner, tng. instr. mine safety Safety First, 1993—; ptnr. Elsberry Enterprises, 1994—; software trainer ExecuTrain, 1994—. Mem. Westec Adv. Com., 1987-90. named Whirlpool Corp. fellow, 1984-86. Fellow Inst. for Advancement of Engring.; mem. Soc. Mfg. Engrs. (officer chpt. 106 1993-94). Democrat. Roman Catholic.

ELSBREE, LANGDON, English language educator; b. Trenton, N.J., June 23, 1929; s. Wayland Hoyt and Miriam (Jenkins) E.; m. Aimee Desiree Wildman, June 9, 1952; 1 child, Anita. BA, Earlham Coll., 1952; MA, Cornell U., 1954; PhD, Claremont Grad. Sch., 1963. Instr. in English Miami U., Oxford, Ohio, 1954-57, Harvey Mudd Coll., Claremont, Calif., 1958-59; instr. humanities Scripps Coll., Claremont, Calif., 1959-60; instr., prof. Claremont McKenna Coll., 1960-94, prof. emeritus, 1994—; mem. grad. faculty Claremont Grad. Sch., 1965—; part-time lectr. Calif. State U., L.A., 1968-70; vis. prof. Carleton Coll., 1987. Author: The Rituals of Life, 1982, Ritual Passages and Narrative Structures, 1991; co-author: Heath College Handbook, 6th-12th edits., 1967-90; guest editor D.H. Lawrence Rev., 1975, 87. Bd. dirs. Claremont Civic Assn., 1964-66; mem. founding com. Quaker Studies in Human Betterment, Greensboro, N.C., 1987. Fulbright Commn. lectr., 1966-67; grantee NEH, 1975, Claremont McKenna Coll., 1980, 82, 87. Mem. AAUP, MLA, Friends Assn. Higher Edn., D.H. Lawrence Soc. (exec. bd. 1990), Virginia Woolf Soc., Coll. English Assn., Sci. Fiction Rsch. Assn., Phi Beta Kappa. Democrat. Mem. Soc. of Friends. Office: Claremont McKenna Coll Bauer Ctr 890 Columbia Ave Claremont CA 91711-3901

ELSBURY, MICHELLE LYNN, elementary educator; b. Litchfield, Ill., Oct. 13, 1965; d. Robert F. Elsbury and Sue Ellen (Starcevich) LeRoy. BA in Elem. Edn., Blackburn U., 1989. Cert. elem. tchr., Hawaii, Ill. Kindergarten tchr. Hokulani Elem., Honolulu, 1989-90; tchr. 4th grade Kaneohe (Hawaii) Elem., 1990-91; tchr. grades 4-6 Lanikai Elem., Kailua, Hawaii, 1991-93, tchr. 3rd grade, 1994—. Mem. Hawaii State Tchrs. Assn., Alliance Française de Hawaii, Kailua Canoe Club, Kanaka Ikaika Poai Puni Series. Home: PO Box 1711 Kailua HI 96734-8711

ELSER, DANNY RAY, financial planner; b. Butte, Mont., June 22, 1953; s. Duane Donald and Edith N.H. (Tam) E.; m. Janet L. Bottom, Dec. 1, 1974; children: Sara E., Katie V., Andrew J., Patrick M. BS, Colo. St. U., 1976. CLU. Mgr. Coll. Life, Bloomington, Ind., 1976-82, Prin. Fin. Group, Bloomington, 1982-86; prin. Fin. Strategies Corp., Bloomington, 1986-88; mgr. No. Colo. Prin. Fin. Group, 1988-89, Prin. Fin. Group, Billings, Mont., 1989—. Bd. dirs. Cmty. Svc. Coun., Bloomington, 1982-85; mem. Young Reps., Bloomington, 1982-86; mission chmn. Evang. Cmty. Ch., Bloomington, 1985-86, missions com. Faith Evang. Ch., Ft. Collins, Colo., 1987-88, 91—, mem. ch. coun., 1991—; ch. lay leader, coun. mem., missions com. Faith Evang. Ch., Billings; bd. dirs. working com. Mont. Found. Consumer Ins. Edn. Bd.; bd. dirs., coach Little Guy Football, 1993—; coach Little League, 1991—, Amateur Athletics Wrestling, 1990—; Fellowship of Christian Athletes state dir., 1995—. Mem. Nat. Assn. Life Underwriters (Nat. Quality and Sales Achievement award 1980-88, Outstanding Young Man of Am., 1983-85), Ind. State Assn. Life Underwriters (Bloomington chpt. bd. dirs. 1980-84, state bd. dirs. 1985-86), S.E. Mont. Assn. Life Underwriters (sec., prog. chmn., v.p. 1989-92, pres. 1992-93), Internat. Assn. Fin. Planning, Nat. Assn. Security Dealers (registered rep.), So. Ind. Estate Planning Forum, Million Dollar Round Table, Bloomington C. of C. (chmn. leadership Bloomington 1982-86), Ft. Collins C. of C. (bus. excellence com.), No. Rocky Mountain Chpt. CLU (sec., treas. 1988, bd. dirs. chartered fin. cons. 1988), Mont. Gen. Agts.-Mgrs. Assn. (bd. dirs. 1989—, Nat. Mgmt. award 1989, 90, 91, 92, 93, 94, 95, pres. 1992-94, past pres. 1991-92), Mont. Soc. CLU and Chartered Fin. Cons., Bloomington Jaycees (pres. 1982-86), ECC Club (mission chmn. 1985-86). Republican. Office: Prin Fin Group 401 N 31st St Ste 950 Billings MT 59101-1200

EL SHAMI, PATRICIA ANN, elementary school tutor; b. Brockport, N.Y., June 17, 1950; d. Myron Earl and Dorothy Elizabeth (Nichols) Williams; m. Ahmed Said El Shami, May 26, 1973; children: Omar, Amir. AA, Stephens Coll., Columbia, Mo., 1970, BA, 1972. Cert. tchr., Calif. Pvt. tutor Diagnostic Ctr. Calif. Luth. U., Thousand Oaks, 1990-94; pvt. tutor Camarillo, Calif., 1994—. Rep. Santa Rosa Homeowners Assn., Camarilla, 1992—, mem. Camelot Estate Arch. Com., 1995—. Recipient Disting. Svc. award Las Virgenes Unified Sch. Dist. Agoura Hills, Calif., 1989. Mem. Nat. Coun. Tchrs. Math., Internat. Reading Assn., Ventura County Reading Assn. Home: 11016 Red Barn Rd Camarillo CA 93012-9268

ELSTON, WOLFGANG EUGENE, geology educator, researcher; b. Berlin, Germany, Aug. 13, 1928; came to U.S., 1945; s. Frederick Gustave and Anny (Halpert) E.; m. Lorraine Hind, Dec. 26, 1952; children: Stephen, Richard. BS, CCNY, 1949; MA, PhD, Columbia U., 1953. Geologist N.Mex. Bur. Mines, Socorro, summers 1950-64; asst. prof. Tex. Technol. Coll., Lubbock, 1955-57; asst. prof. U. N.Mex., Albuquerque, 1957-63, assoc. prof., 1963-67, prof. geology, 1967—, acting chmn. dept. geology, 1982, dir. volcanology program, 1991—, sr. rsch. prof., 1992—; lectr. Columbia U., N.Y.C., 1951-52; cons. Govt. Agys. Industry, Albuquerque, 1957—; prin. investigator NASA, 1964-91, NSF, 1978—, U.S. Geol. Survey, 1975-81, N.Mex. Energy Inst., 1975-81; Univ. Found. visitor U. Auckland, N.Z., 1985-86; exchange scientist NSF, 1979, 85-86. Author, editor: Volcanism in Southwest New Mexico, 1976; co-editor: Cauldrons and Ore Deposits, 1978, Ash-Flow Tuffs, 1979; prin. editor, lead author: Volcanic Centers as Guides to Mineral Exploration, 1994; contbr. articles to profl. jours. Served with U.S. Army, 1953-55. Rsch. fellow Royal Soc. Great Britain, 1986. Fellow AAAS, Geol. Soc. Am. (v.p. Rocky Mountain sect. 1990-91); mem. Nat. Assn. Geology Tchrs. (pres. S.W. sect. 75-76), Am. Inst. Profl. Geologists (cert., pres. N.Mex. sect. 1982, 90) Internat. Assn. Volcanology and Chemistry of Earth's Interior (sec. working group on explosive volcanism 1983-86), N.Mex. Geol. Soc. (hon. life). Home: 1023 Columbia Dr NE Albuquerque NM 87106-2626 Office: U NMex Dept Earth/Planetary Scis Albuquerque NM 87131

ELTON, KIM STEVEN, state legislator, pollster; b. Havre, Mont., Apr. 9, 1948; s. Claude Reginald and Shirley May (Hammer) E.; m. Mary Lou Cooper, Nov. 9, 1989. Reporter, editor Fairbanks (Alaska) Daily News-Miner, 1973-76; editor Juneau (Alaska) Empire, 1976-78; comml. fisherman Alaska, 1978-79; policy dir. Lt. Gov. Terry Miller, Juneau, 1979-82; contract writer, mem. legis. staff Lt. Gov. Terry Miller, 1983-89; from mem. staff to exec. dir. Alaska Seafood Mktg. Inst., Juneau, 1989-94; mem. Alaska Ho. of Reps., Juneau, 1994—; ptnr. Infomatrix, Juneau, 1994—. With U.S. Army, 1969-71, Vietnam. Democrat. Office: Alaska Ho of Reps Capitol Juneau AK 99811

ELTRINGHAM, THOMAS JAMES GYGER, telecommunications professional; b. Riverside, Calif., Nov. 4, 1943; s. Thomas Lamar and May Katharyn (Gyger) E.; m. Hana Libuse Strachen, Jan. 21, 1966 (Feb. 1978); m. Lydia Rose Boss, Oct. 4, 1980; children: Glenn Alexander, Eric Douglas. HSST, Hubbard Coll., Copenhagen, 1969. Ordained to ministry. Minister Ch. of Scientology, L.A. and Clearwater, Fla., 1961-83; installations mgrs. Am. Sun, Inc., Commerce, Calif., 1984-86; v.p. ops. Power Ins. Inc., Santa Fe Springs, Calif., 1986-90; dir. L.D. Svcs., Inc., Santa Fe Springs, Calif., 1990—; CEO GCC Telecomm. Inc., 1991—. Contbr. articles to profl.

jours.; developer drug rehab. program, L.A., 1966. Mem. Internat. Assn. Scientologists. Republican.

ELWAY, JOHN ALBERT, professional football player; b. Port Angeles, Wash., June 28, 1960; s. Jack Elway; m. Janet Elway; 2 daughters: Jessica Gwen, Jordan Marie. BA in Econs., Stanford U., 1983. Quarterback Denver Broncos, 1983—. Mem. Mayor's Council on Phys. Fitness, City of Denver; chmn. Rocky Mountain region Nat. Kidney Found. Played Super Bowl XXI, 1986, XXII, 1987, XXIV, 1989; named to Sporting News Coll. All-Am. team, 1980, 82, Sporting News NFL All-Pro team, 1987, Pro Bowl team, 1986, 87, 89, 91, 93, 94. Office: Denver Broncos 13655 Broncos Pky Englewood CO 80112-4150*

ELY, MARICA MCCANN, interior designer; b. Pachuca, Mex., May 2, 1907 (parents Am. citizens); d. Warner and Mary Evans (Cook) McCann; m. Northcutt Ely, Dec. 2, 1931; children: Michael and Craig (twins), Parry Haines. B.A., U. Calif.-Berkeley, 1929; diploma Pratt Inst. of Art, N.Y.C., 1931. Free-lance interior designer, Washington and Redlands, Calif., 1931—; lectr. on flower arranging and fgn. travel, 1931—; prof. Sogetsu Ikebana Sch., Tokyo, 1972. Art editor (calendar) Nat. Capital Garden Club League, 1957-58. Pres. Kenwood Garden Club, Md.; bd. dirs. Nat. Libr. Blind, Washington; mem. adv. bd. George C. Marshall Internat. Ctr. at Dodona Manor, Leesburg, Va.; v.p. bd. dirs. Washington Hearing and Speech Soc., 1969; co-founder Delta Gamma Found. Pre-Sch. Blind Children, Order of Delta Gamma Rose. Finalist Nat. Silver Bowl Competition, Jackson-Perkins Co., 1966; garden shown on nat. tour Am. Hort. Soc., 1985. Mem. Calif. Arboretum Found., Redlands Hort. and Improvement Soc. (bd. dirs. 1982-94), Redlands Panhellenic Soc., Redlands Country Club, Chevy Chase Club (D.C.), Delta Gamma.

ELY, NORTHCUTT, lawyer; b. Phoenix, Sept. 14, 1903; s. Sims and Elizabeth (Northcutt) E.; m. Marica McCann, Dec. 2, 1931; children: Michael and Craig (twins), Parry Haines. A.B., Stanford U., 1924, J.D., 1926. Bar: Calif. 1926, N.Y. 1928, D.C. 1932, U.S. Supreme Ct. 1930. Practice law N.Y., 1926-29, D.C. and Calif., 1933—; exec. asst. to Sec. Interior, Washington, 1929-33; chmn. tech. adv. com. Fed. Oil Cons. Bd., Washington, 1931-33; represented Sec. Interior in negotiation of Hoover Dam power and water contracts, 1930-33; counsel to Gov. of Okla. in negotiating Interstate Oil Compact, 1934-35; co-executor of estate of ex-Pres. Herbert Hoover, 1964-68; spl. counsel Colo. River Bd. of Calif., 1946-76 and various Calif. water and power agys.; spl. Asst. Atty. Gen. State of Calif., 1953-64 in Ariz. v. Calif.; mem. nat. Petroleum Council, 1968-76; counsel in 7 U.S. Supreme Ct cases involving rights in Colo., Columbia, Cowlitz, Niagara Rivers and fed. natural resource statutes; legal advisor to Ruler of Sharjah in boundary disputes with Iran, Umm al Qawain, and internat. arbitration of boundary with Dubai; counsel to Swaziland in internat. river dispute with Republic of South Africa and to Mekong Commn. (U.N.) in settling principles for devel. of Mekong Basin; counsel to govts. and cos. in determination of seabed boundaries in Gulf of Thailand, Mediterranean, East China, South China, Caribbean seas, Persian Gulf; represented U.S. Mining cos. in enactment of Deepsea Hard Minerals Act, & subsequent reciprocal internat. recognition of mining leases; gen. counsel Am. Pub. Power Assn., 1941-81; counsel L.A., So. Calif. Edison Co. in renewal of Hoover Power contracts, 1980—; counsel from time to time to Govts. of Saudi Arabia, Turkey, China, Algeria, Malagasy Republic, Ethiopia, Grenada, Thailand on mining and petroleum legis.; mem. U.S. del. to UN Conf. on application of Sci. and Tech. for Benefit Less Developed Areas, 1963, UN Conf. on mineral legislation, Manila, 1969, Bangkok, 1973; mem. bd. overseers Hoover Instn.; trustee Herbert Hoover Found., Hoover Presdl. Libr. Assn. Author: Summary of Mining & Petroleum Laws of the World, Oil Conservation Through Interstate Agreement, The Hoover Dam Documents; co-author Law of International Drainage Basins, Economics of the Mineral Industries. Mem. adv. bd. Ctr. Ocean Lawys Policy, U. Va. Fellow Am. Bar Found. (life); mem. ABA (chmn. natural resource sect. 1973-74, ho. dels. 1974-80, regulatory reform com.), Calif. State Bar Assn., D.C. Bar Assn., Am. Law Inst. (life), Internat. Law Assn. (chmn. Am. br. com. on deep sea mineral resources 1970-79), Internat. Bar Assn., Sigma Nu, Phi Delta Phi, Sigma Delta Chi. Republican. Clubs: Bohemian (San Francisco); California (L.A.); Metropolitan, Chevy Chase, University (Washington); Fortnightly (Redlands, pres. 1989); Redlands Country. Home: 222 Escondido Dr Redlands CA 92373-7215 Office: 300 E State St Redlands CA 92373-5235

ELY-CHAITLIN, MARC ERIC, government official; b. Santa Monica, Calif., Apr. 18, 1959; s. Mel and Shirley Louvella (Ely) C. LLD (hon.), RUE, Dana Point, Calif. CEO FTEC, Dana Point, 1975—; exec. pres. MRMF, Inc., Dana Point, 1989; regent Nation of Am., Dana Point, 1993-94, CEO, 1994—. Author: TheConstitution Papers, 1987, Banned in America, 1996. Organizer homeless shelters Mildred Rose Meml. Found., Inc., Orange County, Calif., 1991-95. Mem. Universal Life Ch. Office: Nation of America 27036 Azul Dr Capo Beach CA 92624-1648

EMBLETON, TOM WILLIAM, horticultural science educator; b. Guthrie, Okla., Jan. 3, 1918; s. Harry and Katherine (Smith) E.; m. Lorraine Marie Davidson, Jan. 22, 1943; children: Harry Raymond (dec.), Gary Thomas, Wayne Allen, Terry Scott, Paul Henry. BS, U. Ariz., 1941; PhD, Cornell U., 1949; Diploma de Honor al Ingeniero Agronomo, Coll. Engring. Agronomy, Santiago, Chile, 1991. Jr. sci. aide Bureau Plant Industry USDA, Indio, Calif., 1942, horticulturist Bureau Plant Industry, 1942, 1946; asst. horticulturist Wash. State Coll., Prosser, 1949-50; asst. horticulturist to prof. hort. sci. U. Calif., Riverside, 1950-86, prof. hort. sci. emeritus, 1987—; cons. in field, 1973—. Contbr. numerous articles to profl. jours. Scoutmaster, coun. committeeman, pack com. Riverside Boy Scouts of Am., 1952-74. Recipient Citrograph rsch. award Citrograph mag., 1965, Chancellor's Founders' award U. Calif., 1990. Fellow AAAS, Am. Soc. Hort. Sci. (Wilson Popenoe award 1985, chmn. western region 1958-59); mem. Internat. Soc. Horticultural Sci., Internat. Soc. Citriculture (hon., exec. bd. 1984-96), Am. Soc. Agronomy (honor award 1993), Soil Sci. Soc. Am., Western Soc. Soil Sci., Calif. Avocado Soc. (life, honor award 1987), Coun. Soil Testing and Plant Analysis, Coun. Agrl. Sci. and Tech., Lemon Men's Club (Honor award 1987, life), U. Calif. Riverside Faculty Club (pres. 1958), Sigma Xi (pres. Riverside chpt. 1981-82), others. Home: 796 Spruce St Riverside CA 92507-3039 Office: U Calif Dept Botany Plant Scis Riverside CA 92521-0124

EMENHISER, JEDON ALLEN, political science educator, academic administrator; b. Clovis, N.Mex., May 19, 1933; s. Glen Allen and Mary Opal (Sasser); m. Patricia Ellen Burke, Jan. 27, 1954; 1 child, Melissa Mary Emenhiser Westerfield. Student, Am. U., 1954; BA, U. Redlands, 1955; PhD, U. Minn., 1962. Cert. community coll. adminstr., Calif. Instr. to prof. polit. sci. Utah State U., Logan, 1960-77, acting dean, 1973-74; prof. Humboldt State U., Arcata, Calif., 1977—, dean, 1977-86; acting v.p. Humboldt State U., Arcata, 1984; chair Social Sci. Rsch. and Instrnl. Coun. Calif. State U., 1994-95; prof. Jr. Statesmen Summer Sch., Stanford U., 1989—; vis. instr. U. Redlands, Calif., 1959-60; vis. prof. U. Saigon, Vietnam, 1964-65; asst. dean Colgate U., Hamilton, N.Y., 1972-73; staff dir. Utah Legislature, Salt Lake City, 1967, cons., 1968-77; dir. Bur. Govt. and Opinion Rsch., Logan, 1965-70; cons. USCG, McKinleyville, Calif., 1982; v.p. Exch. Bank, New Franklin, Mo., 1970-76; reader advanced placement exam. U.S. Govt. Coll. Bd., 1990—; vis. fellow govt. divsn. Congl. Rsch. Svc. Libr. of Congress, 1996. Author: Utah's Governments, 1964, Freedom and Power in California, 1987; editor, contbr. Dragon on the Hill, 1970, Rocky Mountain Urban Politics, 1971; producer, dir. TV broadcasts The Hawks and the Doves, 1965-66; contbr. articles to profl. jours. Sec. Cache County Dem. Party, Logan, 1962-63; chmn. Mayor's Commn. on Govt. Orgn., Logan, 1973-74; campaign mgr. various candidates and issues, Logan, 1965-75; bd. dirs. Humboldt Connections, Eureka, Calif., 1986-96, pres., 1989-92; elder Presbyn. ch. Sr. Fulbright-Hays lectr. Com. Internat. Exch. of Persons, Vietnam, 1964-65; Adminstrv. fellow Am. Coun. Edn., Colgate U., 1972-73; Paul Harris fellow Rotary Internat. Mem. Am. Polit. Sci. Assn., Western Polit. Sci. Assn., Am. Studies Assn., Phi Beta Kappa, Omicron Delta Kappa. Presbyterian. Home: PO Box 250 Bayside CA 95524-0250 Office: Humboldt State U Dept Polit Sci Arcata CA 95521

EMERICK, ROBERT EARL, sociologist, educator; b. Cleve., Mar. 17, 1942; s. Merl Lowell and Virginia Melissa (Newmyer) E.; m. Carol Ann Carter, Nov.24, 1963; children: Laura Lee, Lynn Lee Emerick Hall. BA, U. Calif., Santa Barbara, 1964; PhD, Northwestern U., 1971. Prof. sociology San Diego State U., 1968—. Contbr. numerous articles to profl. jours. Home: 3829 Albatross St San Diego CA 92103 Office: San Diego State U Dept Sociology San Diego CA 92182

EMERINE, STEPHEN EDWARD, communications executive; b. Scottsbluff, Nebr., May 4, 1935; s. Edward and Mary Lou (Stephenson) E. BA, U. Idaho, 1956; postgrad., U. Ariz., 1973. Reporter, editor Twin Falls Times-News, Idaho, 1956-57; info. officer USAF, Little Rock and Omaha, 1957-60; reporter, editor Tucson Daily Citizen, 1960-67; asst. prof. journalism Univ. Ariz., 1967-70; pres., editor, pub. The Green Valley News, Ariz., 1967-71; pres. Steve Emerine & Assocs., Tucson, 1971-73; county assessor Pima County, Tucson, 1973-80; editor, columnist The Ariz. Daily Star, Tucson, 1980-87; assoc. dir. pub. info. The U. Ariz., 1987-94; owner Steve Emerine Pub. Rels., Tucson, 1994—. Co-author, editor: (book) Jack Sheaffer's Tucson, 1985. Vice chmn. Tucson Commn. Human Rels., 1968-71; bd. dirs. Ariz. Families Children, Tucson, 1986—; pres. Tucson Jazz Soc., 1993-95; bd. dirs. So. Ariz. Sports Devel. Corp., 1994—. Named Newspaper Reporter of the Year Tucson Press Club 1967. Mem. Pub. Rels. Soc. Am. (accredited; mem. Counselors Acad.), Tucson Press Club (pres. 1965). Democrat. Home: 4973 E Silver St Tucson AZ 85712-5726 Office: PO Box 41824 Tucson AZ 85717-1824

EMERSON, ALTON CALVIN, physical therapist; b. Webster, N.Y., Sept. 29, 1934; s. Homer Douglas and Pluma (Babcock) E.; m. Nancy Ann Poarch, Dec. 20, 1955 (div. 1972); children: Marcia Ann, Mark Alton; m. Barbara Irene Stewart, Oct. 6, 1972. BS in Vertibrate Zoology, U. Utah, 1957; cert. phys. therapy, U. So. Calif., 1959. Staff phys. therapist Los Angeles County Crippled Children's Services, 1958-65; pvt. practice phys. therapy Los Angeles, 1966—; cons. City of Hope, Duarte, Calif., 1962-72; trustee Wolcott Found. Inc., St. Louis, 1972-86, chmn. bd. trustees, 1980-85. Recipient Cert. of Achievement, George Washington U., Washington, 1986. Mem. Aston Martin Owners Club, Masons (pres. Temple City High Twelve Club 1971, master Carmellia 1973, pres. Calif. Assn. High Twelve Clubs 1986, internat. pres. High Twelve 1990-91, mem. High Twelve Internat., Pasadena Scottish Rite Bodies, KCCH, Legion Merit), Royal Order Scotland, Al Malaikah Tmeple, Ancient Arabic order Nobles Mystic Shrine, DeMolay Legion of Honor, Order of DeMolay (hon. internat. supreme coun.), Conejo-Westlake Shrine Club (pres. 1996). Home and Office: 287 W Avenida De Las Flores Thousand Oaks CA 91360-1808

EMERSON, BRENDA ANN, radiology and emergency nurse; b. Kerrville, Tex., June 5, 1958; d. Ralph Wallace and Anna Frances (Hagelstein) E.; m. Robert Lewis Steinmetz, Jan. 8, 1982; children: Whitney Emerson Steinmetz, Alexandra Marie Steinmetz. LPN, Howard Coll., 1979; ADN, Ea. N.Mex. State U., Roswell, 1983; BSN with honors, N.Mex. State U., 1994. Cert. CEN, TNCC. Staff nurse Angelo Comty. Hosp., San Angelo, Tex., 1979-80; staff nurse, asst. head nurse ICU Lincoln County Med. Ctr., Ruidoso, N.Mex., 1980-86; staff nurse emergency dept. Meml. Med. Ctr., Las Cruces, N.Mex., 1987-95; staff nurse Imaging Svcs. Meml. Med. Ctr., 1996—; guest speaker Internat. Nursing conf. Accident and Emergency Assn. of Nursing, Wollongong, NSW, Australia, 1993. Mem. choir Calvary Bapt. Ch. Crimson scholar N.Mex. State U., 1993, acad. scholar Meml. Med. Ctr. Aux., 1994. Mem. ANA, Emergency Nurses Assn. (chpt. pres. 1992), Nursing Honor Soc. at N.Mex. State U. Home: 2031 Old Farm Rd Las Cruces NM 88005-3884

EMERSON, (VIRGIL) LEON, retired judge; b. Atwood, Okla., Apr. 14, 1925; s. William Harry and Ella Rea (Pegg) E.; m. Lee Kessler Emerson, Apr. 5, 1975; children: Donald Leon, David Paul, Julia Ellen; stepchildren: Darylle Lynn Goodfield, Randall Ryan Bruno. AA, Compton C.C., 1948; JD, Southwestern U., 1951. Judge Downey Mcpl. Ct., 1961-85; judge by assignment, arbitrator; bd. mem. So. Calif. Coun. Alcohol and Drugs, Downey, 1972-74, Downey Area Counseling Ctr., 1968-71, Mcpl. Judges Comty. Conf., Downey, 1967. Scoutmaster Troop 807, Downey, 1963-70. Named Man of Yr., Downey Coord. Coun. and N.Am. Mgmt. ASsn. Mem. Masons, Kiwanis, S.E. Bar Assn., L.A. Trial Lawyers Assn., L.A. Bar Assn., Calif. State Bar Assn., Calif. Trial Lawyers. Home: 7607 Yankey St Downey CA 90242-2237

EMERSON, R. CLARK, priest, business administrator; b. L.A., Mar. 9, 1945; s. George Heins and Irma Furney (Sorter) E.; m. Katharine Ann Lawrence, June 27, 1980; children: Cynthia, Holly, Angela, William, Richard. BA, San Jose State U., 1966; MDiv, Ch. Div. Sch. of Pacific, 1972. Ordained deacon Episcopal Ch., 1972, ordained priest, 1973; cert. secondary tchr., Calif. Comml. tchr. Middletown (Calif.) High Sch., 1967-69; asst. to rector St. Francis Ch., Palos Verdes, Calif., 1972-76; adminstr. Power Transistor Co., Torrance, Calif., 1977-85; priest assoc. St. John's Ch., L.A., 1976-85; adminstr. Richard B. Belli Accountancy, San Jose, Calif., 1988-96; priest assoc. St. Luke's Ch., Los Gatos, Calif., 1985—. Contr. St. John's Well Child Ctr., L.A., 1985. Republican. Episcopalian.

EMERSON, SHIRLEY, counseling educator; b. Houston, Dec. 29, 1930; d. Riley C. and Neola (Pinckney) Armstrong; m. David W. Emerson, Sept. 4, 1954; children: Richard, Eric, Ellen. BA, Rice U., 1953; MA, U. Mich., 1966, PhD, 1977. Lic. marriage and family therapist, Nev. Prof. counseling U. Nev., Las Vegas, 1984—. Contbr. articles to profl. jours. Pres. Nev. State Bd. Marriage and Family Therapist Examiners, 1989—. Mem. Am. Assn. Marriage and Family Therapists (clin. mem., approved supr.). Home: 4240 Woodcrest Rd Las Vegas NV 89121-4942 Office: Univ Nev Las Vegas 4505 S Maryland Pkwy Las Vegas NV 89154-9900

EMERT, GEORGE HENRY, biochemist, academic administrator; b. Tenn., Dec. 15, 1938; s. Victor K. Emert and Hazel G. (Shultz) Ridley; m. Billie M. Bush, June 10, 1967; children: Debra Lea Lipp, Ann Lanie Taylor, Laurie Elizabeth, Jamie Marie. BA, U. Colo., 1962; MA, Colo. State U., 1970; PhD, Va. Tech. U., 1973. Registered profl. chem. engr. Microbiologist Colo. Dept. Pub. Health, Denver, 1967-70; post doctoral fellow U. Colo., Boulder, 1973-74; dir. biochem. tech. Gulf Oil Corp., Merriam, Kans., 1974-79; prof. biochemistry, dir. biomass rsch. ctr. U. Ark., Fayetteville, 1979-84; exec. v.p. Auburn (Ala.) U., 1984-92; pres. Utah State U., Logan, 1992—; adj. prof. microbiology U. Kans., Lawrence, 1975-79. Editor, author: Fuels from Biomass and Wastes, 1981; author book chpt.; contbr. articles to profl. jours.; poet. Mem. So. Tech. Coun., Raleigh, N.C., 1985-92; dir. Ala. Supercomputer Authority, Montgomery, 1987-92, Blue Cross Blue Shield Utah, 1996—, Utah Partnership Econ. Devel.; trustee, adv. bd. First Security Bank. Capt. U.S. Army, 1963-66, Vietnam. Named to Educators Hall of Fame, Lincoln Meml. U., 1988. Fellow Am. Inst. Chemists; mem. Rotary (Paul Harris fellow, pres., v.p. 1989-90), Phi Kappa Phi, Sigma Xi. Republican. Office: Utah State U Old Main Logan UT 84322-1400

EMIGH, MIKE, agricultural products company executive; b. 1948. BA in Acctg., U. Nev., 1973. Plant contr. Johns Manville, Fresno, Calif., 1973-79; asst. contr. Sun Maid Growers of Calif., Inc., Kingsburg, Calif., 1979-84; sec., v.p., treas. Valley Fig Growers, Inc., Fresno, Calif., 1984—. Office: Valley Fig Growers Inc 2028 S 3rd St Fresno CA 93702-4156*

EMIGH, ROGER ALAN, materials scientist; b. Pullman, Wash., May 24, 1961; s. Stuart Grant and Carla Evelyn (Troeh) E.; m. Rachelle Marie Farman, June 25, 1983; children: Paul, Will. BS in Materials Sci., Wash. State U., 1983; MS in Materials Sci., U. Calif., Berkeley, 1985, PhD in Materials Sci., 1990. Metallurgist Precision Castparts, Portland, Oreg., 1990-93; rsch. mgr. electronic packaging rsch. Johnson Matthey, Spokane, Wash., 1993—. Mem. Am. Soc. Metals (chmn. Inland Empire chpt. 1993-94), The Minerals, Metals and Materials Soc. Home: 6051 Frazier St Post Falls ID 83854-8897

EMLEN, WARREN METZ, electronics engineer, consultant; b. Elizabeth, N.J., Oct. 12, 1932; s. Andrew Arnberg and Dorothy Emma (Metz) E.; m. Carol Ringold Taylor, Sept. 28, 1958; children: Deborah Emlen Baker, David Taylor, Anne Emlen Donohue. BS in Forestry, U. Calif., Berkeley, 1955; BSEE, Pa. State U., 1963; MS in Systems Mgmt., U. So. Calif., 1973; MA in Pub. Adminstrn., U. N.Mex., 1980. Jr. forester U.S. Forest Service, Klamath, Calif., 1955-56; electronic engr. USAF, Griffiss AFB, N.Y., 1967-87; cons. forester, ptnr. L&E Environ. Cons., Rome, N.Y., 1965-87; v.p., adminstrv. asst. BPLW Architects & Engrs., Inc., Albuquerque, 1988-94; adminstrv. asst. Lovelace Health Systems, 1994-95; adminstrv. coord. Molzen-Corbin & Assocs. P.A., 1995-96; cons. in field; trustee DEDANE Trust, ANDOREM Trust; co-chmn. Industry Looks at Rome Air Devel. Ctr., Griffiss AFB, 1981; sec. Def. Intelligence Tech. forum, Washington, 1981-86; automated data processing cons., 1987-88, 96—; adminstrv. asst., v.p. BPLW Architects& Engrs., Inc., Albuquerque, 1988-94; adminstrv. coord. Molzen-Corbin & Assocs., P.A., 1995-96. Contbr. numerous articles to profl. jours. Served to capt. USAF, 1956-67. Mem. ASPA, IEEE (sr., chmn. engring. mgmt. group Mohawk Valley sect. 1975-76), Armed Forces Comm. and Electronics Assn. Republican. Methodist. Home and Office: 1509 Monte Largo Dr NE Albuquerque NM 87112-6304

EMMANOUILIDES, GEORGE CHRISTOS, physician, educator; b. Drama, Greece, Dec. 17, 1926; came to U.S., 1955; s. Christos Nicholas and Vassiliki (Jordanopoulos) E.; married; children: Nicholas, Elizabeth, Christopher, Martha, Sophia. MD, Aristotelion U., 1951; MS in Physiology, UCLA, 1963. Diplomate Am. Bd. Pediatrics (pediatric cardiology and neonatal-perinatal medicine). Asst. prof. UCLA, 1963-69, assoc. prof., 1969-73, prof., 1973-95, prof. emeritus, 1995—; chief divsn. pediatric cardiology Harbor UCLA Med. Ctr., Torrance, Calif., 1963-69. Co-author: Practical Pediatric Electrocardiography, 1973; co-editor: Heart Disease in Infants, Children and Adolescents, 2d edit., 1977, Moss' Heart Disease in Infants, Children and Adolescents, 3d edit., 1983, 4th edit., 1989, 5th edit., 1995, Neonatal Cardiopulmonary Distress, 1988; contbr. more than 70 articles in field to profl. jours. Served as 2d lt. M.C., Greek Army, 1953-55. Recipient Sherman Mellincoff award UCLA Sch. Medicine, 1982, several rsch. awards Am. Heart Assn., 1965-83. Fellow Am. Acad. Pediatrics (cardiology sect., chmn. 1978-80, Founders award 1996), Am. Coll. Cardiology; mem. Am. Pediatric Soc., Soc. for Pediatric Rsch., Hellenic-Am. Med. Soc. (pres.), Acad. of Athens (corr. mem.). Democrat. Greek Orthodox. Clubs: Hellenic Univ. (Los Angeles) (bd. dirs.). Home: 4619 Browndeer Ln Rllng Hls Est CA 90275-3911 Office: Harbor-UCLA Med Ctr 1000 W Carson St Torrance CA 90502-2004

EMMANUEL, JORGE AGUSTIN, chemical engineer, environmental consultant; b. Manila, Aug. 28, 1954; came to U.S., 1970; s. Benjamin Elmido and Lourdes (Orozco) E.; 1 child, Andres Layanglawin. BS in Chemistry, N.C. State U., 1976, MSChemE, 1978; PhD in Chem. Engring., U. Mich., 1988. Registered profl. engr., Calif., environ. profl.; cert. hazardous materials mgr. Process engr. Perry Electronics, Raleigh, N.C., 1973-74; rsch. asst. N.C. State U., Raleigh, 1977-78; rsch. chem. engr. GE Corp. R & D Ctr., Schenectady, N.Y., 1978-81; Amoco rsch. fellow U. Mich., Ann Arbor, 1981-84; sr. environ. analyst TEM Assocs., Inc., Emeryville, Calif., 1988-91; pres. Environ. & Engring. Rsch. Group, Hercules, Calif., 1991—; environ. cons. to the Philippines, UN Devel. Program, 1992, 94; rsch. assoc. U. Calif., Berkeley, 1988-90. Contbr. articles to profl. jours. Mem. Assn. for Asian Studies, Ann Arbor, 1982-88; sec. Alliance for Philippine Concerns, L.A., 1983-91; assoc. Philippine Resource Ctr., Berkeley, 1988-92; bd. dirs. ARC-Ecology, San Francisco, 1990—, Asia Pacific Ctr., Washington, 1995—; bd. advisors Urban Habitat, 1995—. N.C. State U. grantee, 1976, Phoenix grantee U. Mich., 1982. Mem. NSPE, AAAS, Air and Waste Mgmt. Assn., Calif. Acad. Scis., N.Y. Acad. Sci., Filipino-Am. Soc. Architects and Engrs. (exec. sec. 1989-90, Svc. award 1990). Office: The Environ & Engring Rsch Group PO Box 5544 Hercules CA 94547-5544

EMMELUTH, BRUCE PALMER, investment banker, venture capitalist; b. Los Angeles, Nov. 30, 1940; s. William J. and Elizabeth L. (Palmer) E.; children: William J. II (dec.), Bruce Palmer Jr., Carrie E.; m. Canda E. Samuels, Mar. 29, 1987. Sr. investment analyst, corp. fin. dept. Prudential Ins. Co. Am., L.A., 1965-70; with Seidler Amdec Securities, Inc., 1970-90, sr. v.p., mgr. corp. fin. dept., 1974-90, also bd. dirs.; pres., bd. dirs. SAS Capital Corp., venture capital subs. Seidler Amdec Securities, 1977-90; mng. dir. corp. fin., mgr. corp. fin. dept., mem. exec. com. Van Kasper & Co., L.A., 1990—; bd. advisors Entrepreneurial Studies Program, Grad. Sch. Mgmt. UCLA, 1985—, past. bd. dirs. With Army NG, 1965-71. Home: 17146 Palisades Cir Pacific Palisades CA 90272-2141 Office: Van Kasper & Co Ste 1700 10877 Wilshire Blvd Los Angeles CA 90024-5115

EMMET, THOMAS ADDIS, JR., college administrator, consultant; b. Detroit, July 26, 1930; s. Thomas Addis and Leona Marguerete (Schneider) E.; m. Anne Marie Baker, Mar. 3, 1972; children: Lynn, Anthony, William Novitsky. PhB, U. Detroit, 1952, ME, 1954; EdS, EdD, U. Mich., 1963. Asst. dean U. Detroit, 1953-57, dean men, 1957-64, dean evening coll. arts and scis., 1964-66, asst. prof. higher edn., 1964-67; asst. exec. v.p. Marquette U., 1966-67, adj. prof. higher edn. Wayne State U., Detroit, 1968-70; spl. asst. to pres., prof. edn. Regis U., Denver, 1972-91; pres. higher edn. exec. assocs., 1967-72, 84-86, 89—; chmn. bd. Higher Edn. Group, 1986-89; pres. Thomas A. Emmet & Assos., 1972-84. Cons. collective negotiations in higher edn. Edn. Commn. of States, 1971-84; cons. higher edn. Opinion Research Corp.; dir. leadership seminars, sr. adviser Am. Council on Edn., 1979-85. Staff dir. Mich. State Senate Student Unrest Com., 1968-69; exec. sec. Conf. Jesuit Student Personnel Adminstrs., 1956-64; sec. Council Student Personnel Assns. in Higher Edn., 1966-69. Recipient Bernard Webster Reed award, 1963, John P. McNichols award U. Detroit, 1986. Mem. Adult Student Personnel Assn. (v.p. 1961-64), Nat. Assn. Student Personnel Adminstrs. (editor Jour. 1962-63), Phi Kappa Phi, Alpha Sigma Nu, Alpha Sigma Lambda, Phi Delta Kappa, Phi Eta Sigma. Editor: The Academic Department and Division Chairman, 1972; Collective Bargaining in Postsecondary Institutions: The Impact on the Campus and the State, 1974; asso. editor Coll. and Univ. Bus., 1969-71; pub. The Department Advisor, 1985-92. Home: 8852 Burning Ridge Ct Franktown CO 80116 Office: Regis U New Ventures 50th St and Lowell Blvd 3333 Regis Blvd Denver CO 80221

EMMONS, ROBERT JOHN, corporate executive; b. Trenton, N.J., Sept. 18, 1934; s. Charles Glunk and Ruth Marie (Heilhecker) E.; m. Christine Young Bebb, July 13, 1980; children: Bradley Thomas, Cathy Lynne, Christopher Robert, Ryan Hunter. A.B. in Econs, U. Mich., 1956, M.B.A., 1960, J.D., 1964. V.p. Baskin-Robbins Co., Burbank, Calif., 1964-68; pres. United Rent-All, Los Angeles, 1968-69, Master Host Internat., Los Angeles, 1969-71; prof. Grad. Sch. Bus., U. So. Calif., 1971-82; pres. LTI Corp., Monterey, Calif., 1982-84; chmn., chief exec. officer, dir. Casino USA/SFI Corp., from 1984; chmn. Casino USA/Smart & Final Inc., Santa Barbara, Calif. Author: The American Franchise Revolution, 1970, The American Marketing Revolution, 1980; poetry Other Places, Other Times, 1974, Love and Other Minor Tragedies, 1980. Mem. AAUP, Am. Mktg. Assn., European Mktg. Assn., Am. Econ. Assn., Calif. Yacht Club (L.A.), Hawaii Yacht Club (Honolulu), The Valley Club of Montecito (Calif.), Useppa Island Club (Fla.), The Calif. Club, Beta Gamma Sigma, Pi Kappa Alpha. Office: Casino USA/Smart & Final Inc 524 Chapala St Santa Barbara CA 93101-3412

EMPEY, DONALD WARNE, educational administrator; b. McMinnville, Oreg., Feb. 8, 1932; s. Earnest Warne and Anna May (Alsman) E.; m. Mary Catherine Reeh, July 14, 1956; children: Elizabeth, Margaret, Jennifer. BA, Willamette U., 1954; MA, Stanford U., 1955; EdD, U. Oreg., 1964. Tchr. history South Salem High Sch., Salem, Oreg., 1955-58; asst. prin. Bend Sr. High Sch., Oreg., 1958-61; prin. Bend Sr. High Sch., 1961-63; grad. asst. U. Oreg., Eugene, 1963-64; dir. instrn. Arcadia Sch. Dist., Calif., 1964-68; dep. supt. Lake Washington Sch. Dist., Kirkland, Wash., 1968-69; supt. Lake Washington Sch. Dist., 1969-76; dep. supt. Glendale Unified Sch. Dist., Calif., 1976—; vis. lectr. Claremont (Calif.) Grad. Sch., 1966-68, Calif. State U., Northridge, 1986—; mem. adv. com. on profl. growth Calif. Commn. on Tchr. Credentialing, 1985. Contbr. articles to profl. jours. Co-chmn. Glendale Youth Leadership Conf., 1986—; mem. exec. bd. Glendale Child Care Council, 1987-89; pres. Glendale Community Coordinating Council, 1987; vice chmn. Glendale Mayors Com. on Drug Free Glendale, 1991; mem. Glendale Task Force on Performing Arts Ctr., 1991. Recipient Golden Acorn award Lake Washington PTA Coun., 1975, hon. svc. award Glendale PTA Coun., 1980, spl. recognition award L.A. County Schs., 1991, Willamette U. Alumni Citation award, 1991, Outstanding Pub. Svc. award Calif. Farm Bur., 1993; Danforth Found. fellow, 1975; named Educator of Yr. Crescent Valley C. of C., 1994. Mem. Assn. Supervision and Curriculum Devel., Am. Assn. Sch. Adminstrs., Kiwanis (v.p. Glendale 1990—), Phi Delta Kappa. Republican. Presbyterian. Home: 5334 Ramsdell Ave La Crescenta CA 91214-1923 Office: Glendale Unified Sch Dist 223 N Jackson St Glendale CA 91206-4334

EMPEY, GENE F., real estate executive; b. Hood River, Oreg., July 13, 1923; BS in Animal Husbandry, Oreg. State U., 1949; M. of Tech. Journalism Iowa State U., 1950; m. Janet Halladay, Dec. 27, 1950; children: Stephen Bruce, Michael Guy. Publs. dir. U. Nev., Reno, 1950-55; mgr. Zephyr Cove Lodge Hotel, Lake Tahoe, Nev., 1955-65; owner Empey Co., real estate agy., Carson City and Tahoe, Nev., 1964—; land developer, owner investment and brokerage firm. Mem. Nev. Planning Bd., 1959-72, chmn., 1961-66; mem. Nev. Tax Commn., 1982—; selected mem. Citizens to Citizens Program mission to China, 1996. Capt., inf. U.S. Army, 1943-47; PTO. Grad. Realtors Inst. Mem. Nat. Assn. Realtors, (cert. comml. investment mem.; pres. Nev. chpt. 3 terms), Tahoe Douglas C. of C. (pres. 1962, dir.), Carson City C. of C., Carson-Tahoe-Douglas Bd. Realtors, Capital City Club, Rotary, Heavenly Valley Ski (pres. 1968) Club, The Prospector's Club. Republican. Home: PO Box 707 Zephyr Cove NV 89448-0707 Office: 512 S Curry St Carson City NV 89703-4614

ENDICOTT, WILLIAM F., journalist; b. Harrodsburg, Ky., Aug. 26, 1935; s. William O. and Evelyn E.; m. Mary Frances Thomas, Dec. 27, 1956; children: Gene, Fran, Greg. Student, Am. U., 1955; B.A. in Polit. Sci., Transylvania U., 1957. With Lexington (Ky.) Leader, 1957; sports writer Louisville Courier-Jour., 1958-62; reporter Tulare (Calif.) Advance-Register, 1963; reporter, city editor Modesto (Calif.) Bee, 1963-66; city editor Sacramento Union, 1966-67; with Los Angeles Times, 1968-85; Capitol bur. chief Sacramento Bee, 1985-95, asst. mng. editor, 1995—; Hearst vis. profl. U. Tex., 1993. Served with USMCR, 1957-58. Recipient various journalism awards Disting. Alumnus award Transylvania U., 1980. Episcopalian. Office: 925 L St Ste 1404 Sacramento CA 95814-3704

ENFIELD, D(ONALD) MICHAEL, insurance executive; b. L.A., Jan. 24, 1945; s. Fred Donald Jr. and Suzanne Arden (Hinkle) E.; m. Roseanne Burke, Dec. 29, 1978; children: Susan Ann, Michael David, Peter Christian. BA in Polit. Sci., U. San Francisco, 1967. Mgmt. trainee Marsh & McLennan, Inc., San Francisco, 1967-70, acct. exec., 1970-77, asst. v.p., 1977-79, v.p., 1979-81, sr. v.p., 1981-82, mng. dir., 1982-89; chmn., CEO Frank B. Hall & Co. of No. Calif., San Francisco, 1989-92; founder, chmn., CEO Metro/Risk, Inc., San Francisco, 1992—; cons. in field. Contbr. articles to profl. publs. Bd. dirs. Ronald McDonald House, San Francisco, 1989-92; chmn. bd. dirs. Midsummer Mozart Festival, San Francisco, 1985-90; trustee Lamplighters Music Theater, 1996—. Mem. San Francisco C. of C. (dir. bus./arts coun. 1987-93), Soc. Calif. Pioneers (county v.p. 1974—), Lotos Club of N.Y., City Club of San Francisco, Olympic Club of San Francisco. Office: Metro/Risk Inc 505 Montgomery St Ste 1600 San Francisco CA 94111-2552

ENG, JOAN LOUISE, special education educator; b. Yakima, Wash., July 29, 1934; d. Vernon Ross and Vivian Thelma (Rust) Dent; children: Andrew, Jane, William, June, Vern, Eric, Fred. BEd in English and Social Studies, Seattle U., 1961; MEd in Exceptional Children, Cen. Wash. U., 1965; postgrad., U. Wash., 1962, LeVerne U., 1972-73, Ea. Wash. U., 1975-76, Seattle Pacific U., 1976, Yakima Valley Coll., 1977. Cert. tchr., elem. prin., Wash. Tchr. English Selah (Wash.) High Sch., 1962-65, Yakima Valley Coll., 1965-66; tchr. Adams Elem. Sch., Yakima, 1966-71, McKinley Elem. Sch., Yakima, 1971-72, Stanton Elem. Sch., Yakima, 1972-77, Franklin Jr. High Sch., Yakima, 1977-82, John F. Kennedy High Sch., Seattle, 1984-85, Artz-Fox Elem. Sch., Mabton, Wash., 1988—; supt. St. Timothy's Episcopal Ch. Sch., Yakima, St. Michael's Episcopal Ch. Sch., Yakima; cons. Tonnemaker Corp., Seattle, Sister-Community of the Paraclete. Asst. min., guardian superior St. Stephen's Priory, Seattle; mentor House-in Formation, Yakima, Wash., 1994-97. Mem. NEA, Mabton Edn. Assn., Wash. Edn. Assn. Home: 802 N 40th Ave Unit 16 Yakima WA 98908-2455

ENG, ROGER STEVEN CHOI, dentist, educator; b. Seattle; m. Sylvia Diane Chow; four children. BS in Chemistry, U. Wash., 1958; DDS, U. Calif., San Francisco, 1966. Analytical chemist The Dow Chem. Co., 1959-62; dental staff San Francisco (Calif.) County Pub. Health Dept., 1966, Santa Clara (Calif.) County Pub. Health Dept., 1968-73; pvt. practice dentistry Calif., 1966—; asst. clin. prof. U. Calif. Sch. Dentistry, San Francisco, 1990—; coun. mem. Nat. Adv. Dental Rsch. Coun., Nat. Inst. Dental Rsch., 1990-94. Bd. dirs. Sunnyvale (Calif.) chpt. United Way, 1979-95, El Camino br. YMCA, 1996—, Orgn. Chinese Ams.-Silican Valley chpt., 1991—; councilman City of Los Altos, Calif., 1980-88, mayor pro tem, 1980, 85, mayor, 1983 and 86, mem. former mayors com., 1988—, chmn. mayor's blue ribbon com. for affordable housing, 1992; ; v.p. mktg., Pacific Skyline Coun.; mem. exec. cou. Boy Scouts Am., 1991—; v.p. Shih Lin subcom. Los Altos Sister Cities, Inc., 1992-95; mem. planning and allocations coun. United Way, Santa Clara County, 1979-87; del. Assn. Bay Area Govts., 1982-87; mem. Santa Clara County intercity coun., 1980-87, transp. commn., 1985-87, Intergovtl. Coun., 1981, planning policy com., 1974, social concerns subcom., 1974, airport land use com., 1972-73, drug abuse coun., 1983; mem. nat. adv. coun. East Asian and Pacific Affairs, 1979; chmn. Santa Clara County Dentists for Bush, 1988; mem. North Santa Clara County Solid Waste Mgmt. Authority, 1980-84; mem. planning commn. City of Los Altos, 1972-80, chmn., 1976-77, mem. bd. adjustments, 1972-80, chmn., 1974, 79, mem. beautification com., 1972-73; bd. dirs. Sunnyvale Cmty. Svcs., 1978-82; pres. Peninsula Lodge Chinese-Am. Citizens Alliance, 1976-77, grand lodge rep., 1978-79, auditor, bd. dirs., 1989—; treas. Troop #30 Boy Scouts Am., 1979-84, mem. parents com., 1979-84; bd. dirs. Asian Bus. League Silicon Valley, 1988-91; mem. Calif. State Rep. Ctrl. Com., 1982-89. Recipient Profile in Excellence award Peninsula Chinese Am. Club/Stanford Area Chinese Am. Club, 1986; fellow Internat. Coll. Craniomandibular Orthopedics, 1986, Paul Harris fellow The Rotary Found. Rotary Internat. Mem. ADA, Calif. Dental Assn., Mid-Peninsula Dental Assn., Santa Clara County Dental Soc. (pres. 1991, legis. com. 1982-89, sec. 1989), Univ. Calif. Dental Alumni Assn., U. Wash. Alumni Assn. (life), Stanford Area Chinese Club, Palo Alto Masons, Chinese-Am. C. of C. of Santa Clara County (bd. dirs., organizer, chmn. bd. 1988-89, pres. 1990—), Los Altos Rotary Club, Sunnyvale Met. Lions Club. Office: Wrightmont Profl Ctr 990 W Fremont Ave Ste Q Sunnyvale CA 94087-3021

ENG, SHERRI LYNN, newspaper reporter; b. San Francisco, Mar. 5, 1969; d. Howard and Helen (Hom) E.; m. Rohan Miles Lane, June 22, 1996. BSBA, U. Calif., Berkeley, 1991; MS in Journalism, Northwestern U., Evanston, Ill., 1993. Bd. dirs. Stevenson House, Palo Alto, Calif., 1996—. Mem. Soc. Profl. Journalists, Soc. Am. Bus. Editors and Writers, Asian Am. Journalists Assn. Office: San Jose Mercury News 750 Ridder Pk Dr San Jose CA 95190

ENGAR, RICHARD CHARLES, insurance executive, dentist, educator; b. Salt Lake City, Apr. 2, 1953; s. Keith Maurice and Amy Kathryn (Lyman) E.; m. Elizabeth Ann Willardson, June 21, 1977; children: Robert Keith, Thomas William, Julia Elizabeth. BA in Psychology, U. Utah, 1976; DDS, U. Wash., 1980. Resident gen. practice Sinai Hosp., Detroit, 1980-81; pvt. practice Salt Lake City, 1981-91; cons. Profl. Ins. Exch., Salt Lake City, 1990-91, atty.-in-fact, 1991—; clin. instr. dept. pathology, dental gen. practice residency program U. Utah Med. Ctr., Salt Lake City, 1988—. Author: Dental Treatment of the Sensory Impaired Patient, 1977; (with others) General Dentistry, 1996; contbr. articles to profl. jours. Dist. trainer Spring Creek Dist., Great Salt Lake coun. Boy Scouts Am., 1989-92. Fellow Acad. Gen. Dentistry (regional dir. 1991—, regional dir. chmn. 1995—), Pierre Fauchard Acad., Utah Acad. Gen. Dentistry (pres. 1987); mem. ADA, Salt Lake Dist. Dental Soc. (treas. 1986-88), Utah Dental Assn. (editor 1985-88), Acad. of Dentistry Internat., Utah Scale Modelers Assn. (v.p. 1992, 94, 97), Phi Beta Kappa, Phi Kappa Phi. Mem. LDS Ch. Home: 1806 Glenbrook Cir Salt Lake City UT 84121-1213 Office: 445 E 4500 S Salt Lake City UT 84107-3101

ENGEL, JEROME, JR., neurologist, neuroscientist, educator; b. Albany, N.Y., May 11, 1938; s. Jerome and Pauline (Feder) E.; m. Catherine Margaret Lambourne, Feb. 26, 1967; children: Sean, Jesse, Anasuya. BA, Cornell U., 1960; MD, Stanford U., 1965, PhD in Physiology, 1966. Diplomate Nat. Bd. Med. Examiners, Am. Bd. Qualification in EEG, Nat. Bd. Psychiatry and Neurology. Intern in medicine Ind. U., Indpls., 1966-67; resident in neurology Albert Einstein Coll. Medicine, Bronx, N.Y., 1967-68, 70-72; resident in EEG Nat. Hosp. Nervous and Mental Disease Queen Sq., London, 1971, Maudsley Hosp., London, 1972; attending neurologist, dir. electroencephalography labs. Bronx Mcpl. Hosp. Ctr., Hosp. Albert Einstein Coll. Medicine, 1972-76; attending neurologist, chief of epilepsy, clin. neurophysiology UCLA Hosp. and Clinics, 1976—; assoc. investigator lab. nuclear medicine of Lab. Biomed. and Environ. Scis. UCLA Med. Ctr., 1981—; dir. UCLA Seizure Disorder Ctr., 1994—; staff assoc. NINDS NIH Lab. Perinatal Physiology, San Juan, P.R.; vis. asst. prof. dept. physiology and biophysics U. P.R. Sch. Medicine, 1968-69, Lab. Neural Control, Bethesda, Md., 1969-70; asst. prof. neurology Albert Einstein Coll. Medicine, Bronx, 1972-76, asst. prof. neurosci., 1974-76; assoc. prof. neurology UCLA Sch. Medicine, 1976-80, assoc. prof. anatomy, 1977-80, prof. neurology, neurobiology (formerly anatomy and cell biology), 1980—; assoc. investigator Lab. Nuclear Medicine, Lab. Biomed. and Environ. Scis., 1981—; chmn. internat. and coop. projects study sect. NIH, 1989-90, mem. biomed. scis. study sect., 1985-89, chmn., 1988-89; vis. prof. dept. anatomy Sydney U., 1984. Author: Epilepsy and Positron CT, Clinical Relevance for Diagnosis of Epilepsy, 1985, Surgical Treatment of the Epilepsies, 1987, Seizures and Epilepsy, 1989, Surgical Treatment of Epilepsies, 1993, (with others) Neurotransmitters, Seizures and Epilepsy II, 1984, Neurotransmitters, Seizures and Epilepsy II, 1984, Neurotransmitters, Seizures and Epilepsy III, 1986, The Epileptic Focus, 1987, Fundamental Mechanisms of Human Brain Function, 1987, Clinical Use of Emission Tomography in Focal Epilepsy, Current Problems in Epilepsy, Vol. 7, 1990, Neurotransmitters in Epilepsy, 1992, Molecular Neurobiology and Epilepsy, 1992, The Progressive Nature of Epilepsy, 1996, Epilepsy: a Comprehensive Textbook, 1997; chief editor: Advances in Neurobiology of Epilepsy, 1989-91; assoc. editor: Jour. Clin. Neurophysiology, 1983—, Epilepsy Rsch., 1985—, Epilepsy Advances, 1985-87, Brain Topography, 1990—, Epilepsia, 1994—; contbr. more than 100 chpts. to books including Functional Brain Imaging, 1988, Anatomy of Epileptogenesis, 1989, EEG Handbook, rev. series vol. 4, 1990, Comprehensive Epileptology, 1990, Generalized Epilepsy, 1990, Neurotransmitters in Epilepsy, Epilepsy Research (Supplement), 1992, Molecular Neurobiology and Epilepsy; contbr. numerous articles to profl. jours. including New Issues in Neurosci., Neurology, Jour. Neurosurg., Jour. Epilepsy, Epilepsia, Can. Jour. Neurol. Sci., Radiology, Jour. Cerebral Blood Flow Metabolism, Acta Neurochirugica, Jour. Clin. Psychiatry. Active profl. adv. bd. Epilepsy Internat. League Against Epilepsy, 1988—. Recipient N.Y. State Regents scholarship, 1956-60, NIH traineeship, summer 1962, predoctoral fellowship, 1964, postdoctoral fellowship, 1965-66, career devel. award 1972-76, Epilepsy Found. Am. award, 1963, Stiftung Michael prize, 1982; named Fulbright scholar, 1971-72, fellow in neurology Sch. Medicine Stanford U., 1965-66, Lab. Applied Neuophysiology, C.N.R.S., Marseilles, France, 1966, Dagan Lectr. Winter Conf. on Brain Rsch., 1981, John Guggenheim fellow, 1983-84, Hanna lectr. Case-Western Reserve, 1983, First Aird lectr. U. Calif. San Francisco, 1985, First Cox lectr. Albert Einstein Coll. Medicine, 1985, First Vaajasalo lectr. and award, Kuopio, Finland, 1987, Aring lectr. U. Cin. Med. Ctr., 1987, First Hans Berger lectr. Internat. Congress of EEG and Clin. Neurophysiology, 1990; Covy Williams lectr. Cleve Clinic, 1992; Hans Berger lectr. Med. Coll. Va., 1993. Fellow Am. Acad. Neurology (self assessment epilepsy task force chair 1990—); mem. AAAS, Am. EEG Soc. (councillor 1984-87, chmn. rsch. fellowship com. 1988-91, pres. elect 1991-92, pres. 1992-93), Am. Epilepsy Soc. (sec. 1979-82, 2nd v.p. 1982-83, 1st v.p. 1983-84, pres. 1984-85, councillor 1985-86, v.p. to Internat. League Against Epilepsy 1990—, William G. Lennox lectr. 1990, Clin. Investigator award 1996), Am. Neurol. Assn. (mem. program com. 1987-90), Am. Physiol. Soc., Internat. Brain Rsch. Orgn., Internat. Fedn. EEG and Clin. Neurophysiology Socs. (program com. 1988-90, chmn. com. on guidelines for long-term monitoring for epilepsy 1989—), Internat. League Against Epilepsy (program com. 1986-88, commn. on epilepsy surgery 1989-93, chmn. commn. on neurobiology of epilepsy 1989-93, amb. for epilepsy award 1991, treas. 1994-97, pres. 1997—), Internat. Soc. Cerebral Blood Flow and Metabolism, Ea. Assn. Electroencephalographers (Kershman lectr. 1994), Nat. Assn. Epilepsy Ctrs. (bd. dirs. 1988—, treas. 1990-94), Soc. for Neurosci. (neurobiology of disease workshop organizing com 1989—), Australian Assn. Neurologists (hon.), Western Electroencephalography Soc., Can. Soc. Clin. Neurophysiologists (hon.), Turkish Epilepsy Soc. (hon.). Home: 791 Radcliffe Ave Pacific Palisades CA 90272-4334 Office: UCLA Sch Medicine Reed Neurol Rsch Ctr # 1250 710 Westwood Plz Los Angeles CA 90024-8300

ENGEL, LINDA JEANNE, mining executive; b. Denver, Aug. 24, 1949; d. Thomas Mintor and Irene Evelyn (Esbenson) Kelley; m. William Stephen Engel, May 6, 1972; children: Kacey, Ryan. BA in Polit. Sci., U. Colo., 1975. Statis. researcher Martin Marietta, Waterton, Colo., 1971; asst. dir. Fed. Drug Abuse Program, Denver, 1972-74; corp. sec./treas. Grayhill Exploration Co., Arvada, Colo., 1981-84; controller Western Internat. Gold-Silver, Westminster, Colo., 1985-86; investor rels. dir. and corp. sec. Canyon Resources Corp., Golden, Colo., 1986-94. Dem. campaign mgr., Mayor of Boulder, Colo., 1970. Mem. NAFE, Am. Soc. Corp. Secs., Nat. Investor Rels. Inst., Fellowship Christian Athletes, Delta Delta Delta. Republican.

ENGEL, THOMAS P., airport executive. Dir. Sacramento Met. Airport, Calif.; dir. of airports Sacramento County Dept. of Airports, Calif. Office: Sacramento County Calif Dept of Airports 6900 Airport Blvd Sacramento CA 95837-1109*

ENGELBACH, DAVID CHARLES, scriptwriter, television producer; b. Phila., Sept. 20, 1946; s. Charles David and Perle (Dogole) E.; m. Kathryn Joan Beatie, Oct. 21, 1983 (div. Aug. 1987); m. Annalisa Marta Fields, Oct. 13, 1990. BS, Fairleigh Dickinson U., L.A., 1968; postgrad., U. So. Calif., 1968-70. Motion picture scriptwriter Write Ink-Direct, Inc., L.A., 1983—, motion picture dir., 1985—; TV producer Orion Prodns., L.A., 1984-85. Writer/dir.: (motion picture) America 3000, 1986; scriptwriter (motion pictures) Over the Top, 1987, Death Wish II, 1981; creator: (TV series) Lottery, 1982. Bd. dirs. Valley Village (Calif.) Assn., 1992-94. Mem. Dirs. Guild of Am., Writers Guild of Am./West. Office: care Above the Line 9200 W Sunset Blvd Ste 401 Los Angeles CA 90069-3506

ENGLE, CINDY, medical transcriptionist; b. Denver, Aug. 12, 1958; d. Wallace Clyde and Mary Margaret (Ingram) E. AA, Arapahoe C.C., 1979; BA in Kinesiology, U. No. Colo., 1992. Cert. paralegal; former cert. paramedic, Colo. EMT/paramedic Ambulance Svc. Co., Denver, 1978-80; pers. asst. payroll Burns Security Svc., Denver, 1980-82; part-time asst. mgr. Tokoyo Bowl Restaurant, Denver, 1982-85; paramedic Platte Valley Ambulance, 1982-85; part-time flight paramedic for Air Life North Colo. Med. Ctr., Greeley, Colo., 1986-91; paramedic Weld County Ambulance, Greeley, 1985-92; intern exercise svcs. Greeley (Colo.) Med. Clinic, 1992, med. transcriptionist, 1993-94; med. transcriptionist North Colo. Med. Ctr., Greeley, 1994—; part-time EMS/criminal justice instr. Aims C.C., Greeley, 1987-96; founder The Human Factor, 1992—. Author ednl. game: The Reality Game, 1993. Office: The Human Factor 2626 23rd Ave Greeley CO 80631-7918

ENGLE, ROBERT IRWIN, music educator, musician, composer, writer; b. New Kensington, Pa., Feb. 11, 1945; s. Dale Clair Engle and Rosalyn Imogene (Timblin) Erickson. BS in Music Edn., U. Cin., 1967; postgrad., Stanford U., 1967-68, Ind. U., 1969, U. So. Calif., 1969-71; MA in Music, U. Hawaii, 1973, cert. in Samoan, 1986; PhD in Music, U. Wash., 1994. Cert. tchr. music grades K-12, Calif., Wash. Choral instr. Terminal Island Prison, San Pedro, Calif., 1969-71; choral music tchr. Palos Verdes (Calif.) High Sch., 1968-72; dir. music Makiki Christian Ch., Honolulu, 1978-84, 1st United Meth. Ch., Honolulu, 1986-88; tchr. music and French Redemption Acad., Kailua, Hawaii, 1988-91; dir. music Kapiolani Community Coll., Honolulu, 1975—; dir. choral activities U. Hawaii, Hilo, 1995-96; asst. dir. music Hilo First Samoan Assembly of God, 1995-96; cons. Performing Arts Abroad, Kalamazoo, 1979—, Pacific Basin Choral Festival in Hawaii, Berkeley, Calif., 1989—; tchr. music theory, piano S. Seattle C.C., 1993-94; choral music tchr. Inglemoor H.S., Bothell, Wash., 1994; prof. Polynesian music and dance U. Pitts., summer 1997; spkr. Internat. Soc. Music Edn. Convention, Tampa, Fla., 1994; spkr. nat. conf. Soc. Ethnomusicology, L.A., 1995, Music Educators Nat. Conf., Kansas City, 1996; spkr. in field.; coord. Tahitian drumming and dance workshop Papeete, 1997; accompanist Honolulu Bay Choir, 1996—. Author: Taking Note of Music, 1988, Piano Is My Forte, 1989; editor Pacific Island Choral Series, 1995—; composer: Talalo A Le Alii, 1984 (3d place state competition); composer, rec. artist Pese Pa'ia, 1988; profl. rec. Christmas Aloha; contbr. articles to profl. jours. Founder E Himeni Kakou Colls. Choral Festival, Honolulu, 1976—; founder, dir. Maile Aloha Singers, Honolulu, 1973-92, Carols at the Center-stage Festival, Honolulu, 1989—, Lokahi Choral Festival, Honolulu, 1989—, Aloha, America! Invitational Choral Festival, Honolulu, 1995—. Dir. mus. group representing Hawaii, Cultural Office for Territorial Activity, Papeete, Tahiti, 1982, World U. Games, 1983, Casa De La Cultura, Southeastern Mex., 1984, La. World EXPO, 1984, EXPO '86, Vancouver, Hawaiian Airlines, 1987, Goodwill Tour Am. Samoa, 1989, Artists in the Schs. Auckland, N.Z., 1991; dir. mus. group representing U.S.A., U.S. Dept. State, EXPO '85, Tsukuba, Japan, 1985; Dir. award 2d pl. group Collegiate Showcase, Chgo., 1988, Dir. award 1st place Choral Groups All Am. Festival, Orlando, Fla., 1994. Mem. AAUP, Am. Choral Dirs. Assn. (Hawaii chpt. 1978—, editor newsletter 1987-89, state pres. 1989-91), U. Hawaii Profl. Assembly, Samoa Fealofani Club, Delta Tau Delta (life). Republican. Mem. Pentecostal Ch. Home: 2901 Numana Rd Honolulu HI 96819-2904 Office: Kapiolani CC 4303 Diamond Head Rd Honolulu HI 96816-4421

ENGLISH, DONALD MARVIN, loss control representative; b. Raleigh, N.C., July 31, 1951; s. Marvin Lee and Lois (Woodard) E.; m. Rebecca Pritchard, Sept. 3, 1970 (div. 1977); m. Kathryn A. Sumner, July 3, 1993. Student, Miami U., Oxford, Ohio, 1969-70, 73-74, U. Cin., 1977-78, Calif. State U., Fresno, 1980—; AA, Fresno City Coll., 1991. Cert. safety profl. Bd. Cert. Safety Profls. Ins. inspector Comml. Services, Cin., 1974-78, Ohio Casualty Ins. Co., Fresno, 1978-93; owner Loss Control Systems, Renton, Wash., 1993; sr. loss control specialist Scott Wetzel Svcs., Inc., Federal Way, Wash., 1993-96; asst. regional loss control mgr. Am. States Ins. Co. Seattle, 1996—. Served with U.S. Army, 1970-73. Mem. Am. Soc. Safety Engrs., Soc. CPCU (cert.), Ins. Inst. Am. (assoc. in loss control mgmt. 1990), East Fresno Exch. Club (pres. 1984-85). Home: 16116 SE 175th St Renton WA 98058-9113 Office: 6021 244th St SW Mountlake Terrace WA 98043

ENGLISH, PHILIP STEPHEN, sales executive; b. Accrington, Eng., Feb. 21, 1946; s. Arthur and Anne (Hargreaves) E.; m. Victoria Kucyn English, May 12, 1979. BS in Physics, London U., 1967; MS in Math., Cambridge U., Eng., 1968; PhD in Physics, U. Waterloo, Can., 1972; MBA in Internat. Bus., U. Miami, 1993. Asst. prof. St. Francis Xavier U., Antigonish, Can., 1973-79; gen. mgr. Chocolate Cove Players, Deer Island, Can., 1979-84; acct. exec. Satellite Comm., Ft. Lauderdale, Fla., 1984-86; acct. exec. Executone Inc., Miami, Fla., 1986-87, sales mgr., 1987-88; acct. exec. AT&T, Miami, Fla., 1988-90, sys. cons., 1990-92, acct. mgr., 1992-93; nat. acct. mgr. AT&T, Phoenix, 1993—; mem. AT&T Leaders Coun., 1995. Contbr. articles to profl. jours. Chmn. Kinsmen Club, Antigonish, Can., 1977; vol. chmn. The Phoenix Zoo. Named Valedictorian MBA Class U. Miami, Fla., 1993. Mem. Phoenix Jaycees. Office: AT&T 2800 N Central Ave Ste 1000 Phoenix AZ 85004-1007

ENGLISH, STEPHEN F., lawyer; b. Portland, Oreg., Jan. 17, 1948. BA with honors, U. Oreg., 1970; JD, U. Calif., San Francisco, 1973. Bar: Oreg. 1973; U.S. Dist. Ct. Oreg. 1973; U.S. Ct. Appeals (9th cir.) Oreg. 1980; U.S. Supreme Ct. 1982. Ptnr. Bullivant, Houser, Bailey, Pendergrass & Hoffman, Portland, Oreg. Mem. ABA (vice-chair, 1987-88, self-insureds com., tort and insurance practice sect), Multnomah County Bar Assn., Oreg. State Bar Assn. (chair elect, 1989-90, exec. com., 1986—, litigation sect.), Am. Bd. of Trial Adv., Oreg. Assn. of Defense Counsel, Defense Rsch. and Trial Lawyers Assn. Office: Bullivant Houser Bailey Pendergrasss & Hoffman 300 Pioneer Tower 888 SW 5th Ave Portland OR 97204-2012

ENGRAV, LOREN HENRY, plastic surgeon; b. LaCrosse, Wis., Oct. 24, 1941; s. Henry Johannes and Ruby Martha (Olsen) E.; m. Candace Joan Gowan, July 24, 1965; children: Peter, Rebecca. BS, U. Calif., Davis, 1965; MD, UCLA, L.A., 1969. Resident in surgery St. Paul(Minn.)-Ramsey, 1975; resident plastic surgery U. Kans., Kansas City, 1977; faculty divsn. plastic surgery U. Wash. Sch. Medicine, Seattle, 1977—. Author: (book) Surgical Management of the Burn Wound, 1984; contbr. articles to profl. jours. Recipient Burn Rehab. Model System Grant Nat. Inst. on Disability & Rehab. Rsch., Washington, 1993. Fellow: Am. Assn. Plastic Surgeons, Am. Burn Assn., Am. Coll. Surgeons, Am. Soc. Plastic & Reconstructive Surgeons, Plastic Surgery Rsch. Coun.; mem. Alpha Omega Alpha. Office: Harborview Med Ctr 325 9th Ave # 359796 Seattle WA 98104-2420

ENGSTROM, ERIKA JULIE, communications educator; b. Tokyo, Japan, Sept. 20, 1964; d. Alex Joseph and Margaret Mary (Mizukami) E. BA in Radio/TV, U. Ctrl. Fla., 1984, MA in Comm., 1986; PhD in Mass. Comm., U. Fla., 1991. News anchor, producer, asst. news dir. WUCF-FM, Orlando, Fla., 1984-85; tv newswriter WCPX-TV, Orlando, 1985; news anchor, producer WUFT-FM, Gainesville, Fla., 1987; grad. tchg. asst. U. Fla., Gainesville, 1986-91; asst. prof. U. Nev., Las Vegas, 1991—. Mem. Assn. for Edn. in Journalism and Mass Comm., Internat. Comm. Assn., Speech Comm. Assn., Broadcast Edn. Assn., Las Vegas Women in Comm. Home: 1851 N Green Valley Pkwy 2323 Henderson NV 89014 Office: Univ Nev 4505 S Maryland Pkwy Las Vegas NV 89154-5007

ENNIS, KENT TAYLOR, economist; b. Dallas, June 27, 1953; s. Donald Taylor and Geneva Lee (Carpenter) E.; m. Terry Suzanne Shelby, Aug. 10, 1975 (div. Dec. 1984); m. Muriel Irma Dreyfus, Mar. 10, 1985. BA in Econ., U. Tex., 1975; MSC in Econ., London Sch. Econ., 1977. Banking officer, asst. v.p. Capital Bank, Houston, 1978-79; asst. v.p. Mercantile Nat. Bank, Dallas, 1979, v.p., 1980-85; v.p. Banque Paribas, Dallas, 1985-86; economist Comptroller of Pub. Accts., Austin, Tex., 1986-89; sr. economist Joint Budget Com, Phoenix, 1989—; lectr. Ariz. State U., 1996—. Republican. Home: 233 W Colt Rd Tempe AZ 85284 Office: 1716 W Adams St Phoenix AZ 85007-2602

ENNIS, THOMAS MICHAEL, management consultant; b. Morgantown, W.Va., Mar. 7, 1931; s. Thomas Edson and Violet Ruth (Nugent) E.; m. Julia Marie Dorety, June 30, 1956; children: Thomas John, Robert Griswold (dec.). Student, W.Va. U., 1949-52; AB, George Washington U., 1954; JD, Georgetown U., 1960. With Gov. Employees Ins. Co., Washington, 1956, 59, Air Transport Assn. Am., Washington, 1959-60; dir. ann. support program George Washington U., 1960-63; nat. dir. devel. Project HOPE, People to People Health Found., Inc., Washington, 1963-66; nat. exec. dir. Epilepsy Found. Am., Washington, 1966-74; exec. dir. Clinton, Eaton, Ingham Community Mental Health Bd., Lansing, Mich., 1974-83; nat. exec. dir. Alzheimer's Disease and Related Disorders Assn., Inc., Chgo., 1983-86; exec. dir., pres. French Found. for Alzheimer Rsch., L.A., 1986-96; pres. emeritus The John Douglas French Alzheimers Found., L.A., 1996—; clin. instr. dept. cmty. medicine and internat. health Georgetown U., 1967-74; adj. assoc. prof. dept. psychiatry Mich. State U., 1975-84; lectr. Univ. Ctr. for Internat. Rehab., 1977; cons. health and med. founds., related orgns.; cons. Am. Health Found., 1967-69, Reston, Va.-Georgetown U. Health Planning Project, 1967-70. Mem. adv. bd. Nat. Center for the Law and the Handicapped, 1971-74; advisor Nat. Reye's Syndrome Found.; mem. Nat. Com. for Research in Neurol. Disorders, 1967-72; mem. nat. adv. bd. Developmental Disabilities/Tech. Assistance System, U. N.C., 1971-78; nat. trustee Nat. Kidney Found., 1970-74, mem. exec. com. and bd. Nat. Capitol Area chpt., pres., 1972-74; bd. dirs. Nat. Assn. Pvt. Residential Facilities for Mentally Retarded, 1970-74; bd. dirs., mem. exec. com. Epilepsy Found. Am., 1977-84, Epilepsy Center Mich., 1974-83; nat. bd. dirs. Western Inst. on Epilepsy, 1969-72; bd. dirs., pres. Mich. Mid-South Health Systems Agy., 1975-78; sec. gen. Internat. Fedn. Alzheimer's Disease and Related Disorders, 1984-86; mem. panel mem. Alzheimer's Disease Edn. and Referral Ctr., 1990—. World Rehab. Fund fellow Norway, 1980. Mem. Nat. Epilepsy League (bd. dirs. 1977-78), Mich. Assn. Cmty. Mental Health (pres. 1977-79), Nat. Coalition Rsch. Neurol. Disorders (dir. at-large 1991—), Scan Health Plan (bd. govs.), Phi Alpha Theta, Phi Kappa Psi.

ENNIS, WILLIAM LEE, physics educator; b. Houston, Aug. 10, 1949; s. Arthur Lee and Helen Ennis; m. Constance Elizabeth Livsey, July 20, 1991. BS, Auburn (Ala.) U., 1974, BA, 1978. Rsch. tech. Nat. Tillage Lab., Auburn, Ala., 1974-76; tchr. Stanford Jr. H.S., Hillsborough, N.C., 1979-81; physics tchr., chmn. sci. dept. East H.S., Anchorage, 1981—; chair Anchorage Sch. Dist. Physics Tchrs.; curriculum devel. sci. cons. Copper River Schs., Anchorage, 1991. Named Tandy Tech. Outstanding Tchr., 1989-90, Tchr. of Excellence Brit. Petroleum, 1996, British Petroleum Tchr. of Yr., 1996; Fermi Lab. scholar U.S. Dept. Energy, 1991; Disting. Tchr., White House Commn. on Presdl. Scholars, Brit. Petroleum Tchr. of the Yr., Alaska. Fellow N.Y. Acad. Scis.; mem. AAAS, Am. Assn. Physics Tchrs., Am. Phys. Soc., Nat. Sci. Tchrs. Assn., Alaska Sci. Tchrs. (life), Am.

Mountain Guides Assn., Am. Alpine Club. Office: East HS 4025 E Northern Lights Blvd Anchorage AK 99508-3588

ENNISS, LEONARD FRANKLIN, religious educator; b. Kankakee, Ill., Oct. 30, 1955; s. Leonard Franklin and Elsie Irene (Lamb) E.; m. Sharon Diane Stanfield, July 17, 1976; 1 child, Clairessa Mary Fern. ThB, Western Evang. Sch. Theology, Phoenix, 1980, MEd, 1981, PhD, 1984; BA in Religion cum laude, Ottawa U., Phoenix, 1992; MA in Theology magna cum laude, U. San Francisco, 1995. Pres. Western Evang. Sch. Theology, Phoenix, 1981-90; provost and master regent S.W. Christian U., Phoenix, 1990-94; tchr. religious studies Mesa (Ariz.) C.C., 1994—; assoc. Nat. Inst. for Certification of Engring. Tech., Alexandria, Va., 1986—. Contbr. articles to profl. jours. Mem. Soc. of Christian Philosophers. Libertarian. Mem. Charismatic Episcopal Ch. Home: 4202 E Cactus Rd # 6107 Phoenix AZ 85032 Office: Mesa CC Dept Philosophy and Religion 13833 W Southern Ave Mesa AZ 85022

ENOCH, JAY MARTIN, vision scientist, educator; b. N.Y.C., Apr. 20, 1929; s. Jerome Dee and Stella Sarah (Nathan) E.; m. Rebekah Ann Feiss, June 24, 1951; children: Harold Owen, Barbara Diane, Ann Allison. BS in Optics and Optometry, Columbia U., 1950; postgrad., Inst. Optics U. Rochester, 1953; Ph.D. in Physiol. Optics, Ohio State U., 1956; DSc honoris causa, SUNY, 1993. Asst. prof. physiol. optics Ohio State U., Columbus, 1956-58; assoc. supr. Ohio State U. (Mapping and Charting Rsch. Lab.), 1957-58; fellow Nat. Phys. Lab., Teddington, Eng., 1959-60; rsch. instr. dept. ophthalmology Washington U. Sch. Medicine, St. Louis, 1958-59, rsch. asst. prof., 1959-64, rsch. assoc. prof., 1965-70, rsch. prof., 1970-74; fellow Barnes Hosp., St. Louis, 1960-64, cons. ophthalmology, 1964-74; rsch. prof. dept. psychology Washington U., St. Louis, 1970-74; grad. rsch. prof. ophthalmology and psychology Coll. Medicine U. Fla., Gainesville, 1974-80, grad. rsch. prof. physics, 1979-80; dir. Ctr. for Sensory Studies, 1976-80; dean Sch. Optometry, chmn. Grad. Group in Vision Sci. U. Calif., Berkeley, 1980-92, prof. optometry and vision sci., 1980-94, prof. of Grad. Sch., 1994—; prof. physiol. optics in ophthalmology U. Calif., San Francisco, 1980—; chmn. subcom. contact lens stds. Am. Nat. Stds. Inst., 1970-77; mem. nat. adv. eye coun. Nat. Eye Inst., NIH, 1975-77, 80-84; exec. com., com. on vision NAS-NRC, 1973-76; mem. U.S. Nat. Com. Internat. Commn. Optics, 1976-79; health scis. com. systemwide adminstrn. U. Calif., 1989-93, co-chmn. subcom. on immigrant health in Calif., 1993-94; mem. sci. adv. bd. Fight-for-Sight, 1988-92, Allergan Corp., 1991-93; mem. Lighthouse for Blind, N.Y., 1989-96, chair, 1995, Pisart award com. Contbr. numerous chpts. and articles on visual sci., receptor optics, perimetry, contact lenses and infant vision to sci. jours.; contbr. chpts. in field to med. books; assoc. editor: Investigative Ophthamology, 1965-75, 83-88, Sight-Saving Rev., 1974-84, Sensory Processes, 1974-80; mem. editl. bd. Vision Rsch., 1974-80, Internat. Ophthamology, 1977-93, Binocular Vision, 1984—, Clin. Vision Sci., 1986-93, Biomed. Optics, 1988-90; mem. editl. bd. optical scis Springer-Verlag, Heidelberg, 1978-87, biomed. scis., 1988-95. Mem. nat. sci. adv. bd. Retinitis Pigmentosa Found., 1977-95; U.S. rep. Internat. Perimetric Soc., 1974-90, also exec. com., chmn. Rsch. Group Standards; bd. dirs. Friends of Eye Rsch., 1977-88; trustee Illuminating Engring. Rsch. Inst., 1977-81; bd. dirs. Lighting Rsch. Bd., 1988-95. 2d lt. U.S. Army, 1951-52. Recipient Career Devel. award NIH, 1963-73, Everett Kinsey award Contact Lens Assn. Ophthalmologists, 1991, Berkeley citation, Festschrift U. Calif. Berkeley, 1996. Fellow AAAS, Am. Acad. Optometry (Glenn A. Fry award 1972, Charles F. Prentice medal award 1974), Optical Soc. Am. (chmn. vision tech. sect. 1974-76, mem. book pub. com. 1996—), Am. Acad. Ophthalmology (honor award 1985); mem. Assn. for Rsch. in Vision and Ophthalmology (trustee 1967-73, pres. 1972-73, Francis I. Proctor medal 1977), Concilium Ophthalmologicum Universale (chmn. visual functions com. 1982-86), Am. Optometric Assn. (low vision sect., Vision Care award 1987), Ocular Heritage Soc. (medal 1997), Sigma Xi. Home: 54 Shuey Dr Moraga CA 94556-2621 Office: U Calif Sch of Optometry Berkeley CA 94720-2020

ENOS, THERESA, English educator, editor; b. Arlington, Tex.; d. Russell Hascal Jarnagin and Edna Leta (Blackburn) King; m. Arthur G. Enos, June 25, 1964 (div. Aug. 1987); children: Mark Young, Michele Rayburn, Brennan. BA, Tex. Christian U., 1973, PhD, 1980; MA, Baylor U., 1975. Asst. prof. So. Meth. U., Dallas, 1980-87; assoc. prof. U. Ariz., Tucson, 1987—. Editor: (book) Sourcebook for Basic Writing Teachers, 1987, Defining the New Rhetorics, 1992, Professing the New Rhetorics, 1993, Encyclopedia of Rhetoric and Composition, 1996, Gender Roles and Faculty Lives in Rhetoric and Composition, 1996; founder, editor Rhetoric Rev., 1982— (Best Jour. Design award 1985). Grantee So. Meth. U., 1983, Exxon Edn., 1986, Coun. Writing Program Adminstrn., 1991, U. Ariz., 1990. Mem. Nat. Coun. Tchrs. English (coll. sect. officer 1993-97, rep. Conf. Coll. Composition and Comm. 1993-97), Conf. Coll. Composition and Comm. (exec. com. 1990-93), Coun. Writing Program Adminstrn. (bd. dirs. 1992-95, publicity chair 1992-95, bd. cons./evaluators 1989—, pres. 1997—), Rhetoric Soc. Am. Episcopalian. Home: 7621 E La Cienega Dr Tucson AZ 85715-3528 Office: Univ of Arizona Dept of English Tucson AZ 85721

ENRIGHT, CYNTHIA LEE, illustrator; b. Denver, July 6, 1950; d. Darrel Lee and Iris Arlene (Flodquist) E. BA in Elem. Edn., U. No. Colo., 1972; student, Minn. Sch. Art and Design, Mpls., 1975-76. Tchr. 3d grade Littleton (Colo.) Sch. Dist., 1972-75; graphics artist Sta. KCNC TV, Denver, 1978-79; illustrator No Coast Graphics, Denver, 1979-87; editorial artist The Denver Post, 1987—. Illustrator (mag.) Sesame St., 1984, 85; illustrator, editor "Tiny Tales" The Denver Post, 1991-94. Recipient Print mag. Regional Design Ann. awards, 1984, 85, 87, Phoenix Art Mus. Biannual award, 1979. Mem. Mensa. Democrat. Home: 1210 Ivanhoe St Denver CO 80220-2640 Office: The Denver Post 1560 Broadway Denver CO 80202-6000

ENRIQUEZ, CAROLA RUPERT, museum director; b. Washington, Jan. 2, 1954; d. Jack Burns and Shirley Ann (Orcutt) Rupert; m. John Enriquez, Jr., Dec. 30, 1989. BA in history cum laude, Bryn Mawr Coll., 1976; MA, U. Del., 1978, cert. in mus. studies, 1978. Personnel mgmt. trainee Naval Material Command, Arlington, Va., 1972-76; teaching asst. dept. history, U. Del., Newark, 1976-77; asst. curator/exhibit specialist Hist. Soc. Del., Wilmington, 1977-78; dir. Macon County Mus. Complex, Decatur, Ill., 1978-81; dir. Kern County Mus., Bakersfield, Calif., 1981—; pres. Kern County Mus. Found., 1991—; advisor Kern County Heritage Commn., 1981-88; chmn. Historic Records Commn., 1981-88; sec.-treas. Arts Council of Kern, 1984-86, pres. 1986-88; county co-chmn. United Way, 1981, 82; chmn. steering com. Calif. State Bakersfield Co-op Program, 1982-83; mem. Community Adv. Bd. Calif. State Bakersfield, Anthrop. Soc., 1986-88; bd. dirs. Mgmt. Council, 1983-86, v.p., 1987, pres. 1988; bd. dirs. Calif. Council for Promotion of History, 1984-86, v.p., 1987-88. pres., 1988-90; mem. community adv. bd. Calif. State U.-Bakersfield Sociology Dept., 1986-88; mem. women's adv. com. Girl Scouts U.S., 1989-91; bd. dirs. Greater Bakersfield Conv. and Visitors Bur., 1993-95; co-chair 34th St. Neighborhood Partnership, 1994—. Hagley fellow Eleutherian Mills-Hagley Found., 1977-78; Bryn Mawr alumnae regional scholar, 1972-76. Mem. Calif. Assn. Mus. (regional rep. 1991—, v.p. legis. affairs 1992—), Am. Assn. for State and Local History (chair awards com. Calif. chpt. 1990—), Exces. Assn. Kern County. Presbyterian. Office: Kern County Museum 3801 Chester Ave Bakersfield CA 93301-1345

ENSANA, JOEL ANTHONY, writer; b. New Brunswick, N.J., Feb. 25, 1930; s. Anthony and Rose (Fenkel) E. BA in Creative Writing, San Francisco State U., postgrad. dir. writer's workshop Jewish Cmty. Ctr., San Francisco. Contbr. plays to The Best Short Plays, Nebr. Lit. Rev., Evergreen Chronicles, Stonewall; author plays: Assassin, Ready for Teddy (Nat. Media award for Best Entertainment on Non-Commercial Television), No Flowers (1st prize Norman Corwin Playwriting Contest), At The End, The Cut!, 1982, Winchester House, 1984, The Sacred Dance of Yellow Thunder, 1984, That Guggenheim Summer, 1986 (Hon. Mention Perkins Playwriting Contest, 1984, Hats Fanchon, 1986, Class, 1987. With USAF, 1952-54. Home: 816 Fandas de la Sierra Santa Fe NM 87501

ENSIGN, DONALD DALE, art director; b. Bellingham, Wash., May 26, 1948; s. William Russell and Lucille Winifred (Holden) E. BA in Art, Western Wash. U., 1970. Assoc. art dir. Campus Crusade for Christ Internat., San Bernardino, Calif., 1976-80, art dir., 1980-82; art dir. Narramore Christian Found., Rosemead, Calif., 1982—; chmn. bd. dirs. Christian Comic Arts Soc., South Pasadena, Calif., 1984-94; founder Good Name Enterprises, 1994. Editor: (newsletter) Valiant, 1984; pub. (book) Emerald Light, 1995; pub. New Creation newsletter, 1996—. Campaign worker John Paul Stark for Congress, San Bernardino, 1978, 80, 82, Reagan for Pres., San Bernardino, 1976, Bill Hoge for State Assembly, Pasadena, Calif., 1992. Mem. New Eng. Hist. Genealogical Soc., British Isle Family History Soc. L.A., San Gabriel Valley MacIntosh Users Group, Alpha Omega (founder 1985). Republican. Congregationalist. Home: 5926 Camellia Ave Apt E Temple City CA 91780-1708 Office: Narramore Christian Found 250 W Colorado Blvd Ste 200 Arcadia CA 91007

ENSIGN, DONALD H., landscape architect; b. Salt Lake City, Sept. 5, 1936; s. C. Wesley and Mildred (Harker) E.; m. Kay Bateman, Sept. 9, 1959 (div. 1970); m. Nancy Ensign; children: Philip Wesley, Craig Allen, Michael Donald. B in Landscape Architecture, Utah State U., 1963; M in Landscape Architecture, U. Mich., 1968. Registered landscape architect, Mich., N.C. Landscape architect Frehner and Assocs., Salt Lake City, 1961-62; planner Roswell/Ensign and Assocs., Salt Lake City, 1962-66; instr. dept. landscape architecture and environ. planning Utah State U., Logan, 1963-66; planner Richard B. Wilkinson and Assocs., Ann Arbor, Mich., 1966-68; prin. Design Workshop, Inc., Aspen, Colo., 1970—; assoc. prof. sch. design N.C. State U., 1968-74, dir. basic design program, 1971-73. Prin. works include Aspen Inst., Grand Valley High Sch., Marolt Ranch, U. Mich., Utah State U., Estrella Lake Parks, Goodyear, Ariz., Fox River, Geneva, Ill., Lauder Residence, Aspen, Resort at Squaw Creek, Squaw Valley, Calif., 700 East Main, Aspen, Snowmass (Colo.) Club, Blackcomb Resort, Whistler, British Columbia, Early Winters Resort, Mazama, Wash., Grand Champions Resort, Aspen, many others. Office: Design Workshop 120 E Main St Aspen CO 81611-1714*

ENSIGN, JOHN E., congressman; b. Roseville, Calif., Mar. 25, 1958; s. Mike and Sharon E.; m. Darlene Sciarretta Ensign; 1 child, Trevor. Student, UNLV; B in Gen. Sci., Oreg. State U., 1981; D of Veterinary Medicine, Colo. State U., 1985. Owner animal hosp., Las Vegas; gen. mgr. Gold Strike Hotel & Casino, 1991, Nev. Landing Hotel & Casino, 1992; mem. U.S. Ho. of Reps., Washington, 1994—; mem. Com. Ways & Means, subcom. Health, subcom. Human Resources U.S. Ho. of Reps.; mem. Com. on Resources, 1995—. Office: US House Reps 414 Cannon House Office Bldg Washington DC 20515-2801 also: Las Vegas Office 1000 E Sahava Ave Ste D Las Vegas NV 89104 also: Henderson Office 223 Lead St Rm 100 Henderson NV 89105

ENSIGN, PAULETTE, entrepreneur; b. Trenton, N.J., Sept. 22, 1947; d. Bernard Robert and Edith (Karlin) Garvis; divorced. B Mus Edn., Hartt Sch. of Music, Hartford, Conn., 1971; MSEd, U. Bridgeport, 1973. Tchr. string instruments Pub. Sch. System, Mamaroneck, N.Y., Norwalk, Conn.; pres. Organizing Solutions, Inc., Bedford Hills, N.Y. Author: (booklet) 110 Ideas for Organizing Your Business Life, 1991, (books) How To Write and Market Booklets, 1993, Professional Organizing Industry Source Report, 1989, (audio tape) 101 Ideas to Organize Your Business Life, 1993; (videos) The Organized Office, 1995, How to Write and Market Booklets, 1996. Named Outstanding Tchr., N.Y. State PTA, 1971. Mem. Nat. Assn. Profl. Organizers (com. chmn. 1992-95, chpt. pres. 1986-89, dir. 1992-95, pres. 1995, Pres.'s award 1993). Democrat. Jewish. Address: # 179 12675 Camino Mira Del Mar San Diego CA 92130-2557

ENSLOW, MEL DENNIS, fire chief; b. St. Joseph, Mo., Oct. 7, 1941; s. Earl Ernest and Daisy Evelyn (Lanning) E.; m. Valerie J. Maclean, Mar. 2, 1962; children: Katherine, Karen, Kenneth. Cert. tchr. fire tactics and strategy, arson investigation. Millwright Kaiser Steel Plant, Fontana, Calif., 1960-63; firefighter Fontana Fire Dept., 1963-68, engr., 1968-73, capt., 1973-78; battalion chief/fire marshall San Bernardino County, Fontana, 1978-86, asst. fire chief, 1986-88, dep. fire chief, 1988-91; fire chief Redlands (Calif.) Fire Dept., 1991—; pres. San Bernardino (Calif.) County Arson Investigator, 1975-76; chmn. Confire Joint Powers Authority, San Bernardino County, 1991—. Author: (working program) Citation Program for Fire Inspectors, 1974, Cost Recovery of Fire Suppression, 1993, Civic Leader Tour of Working Fire Stations, 1994; co-author: (working program) Juvenile Firesetter Counseling Program, 1979. Bd. dirs. Redlands Cmty. Music Assn., 1995. Mem. Rotary. Office: Redlands Fire Dept 2 Cajon St Redlands CA 92373-4710

ENTRIKEN, ROBERT KERSEY, management educator; b. McPherson, Kans., Jan. 15, 1913; s. Frederick Kersey and Opal (Birch) E.; m. Elizabeth Freeman, May 26, 1940 (div. Nov. 1951); children—Robert Kersey, Jr., Edward Livingston Freeman, Richard Davis; m. Jean Finch, June 5, 1954; 1 child, Birch Nelson. B.A., U. Kans. 1934; M.B.A., Golden Gate U., 1961; postgrad. City Univ. Grad. Bus. Sch., London, 1971-73. C.P.C.U. Ins. broker, Houston, Tex. and McPherson, Kans., 1935-39; asst. mgr. Cravens, Dargan & Co., Houston, 1939-42; br. mgr. Nat. Surety Corp., Memphis and San Francisco, 1942-54; v.p. Fireman's Fund Ins. Co., San Francisco. 1954-73; adj. prof. Golden Gate U., San Francisco, 1953-73, prof. mgmt., 1974-89; resident dean Asia Programs, Singapore, 1987-88; prof. emeritus 1989—, underwriting mem. Lloyd's of London, 1985—. Contbr. articles to trade and profl. jours. Bd. dirs., sec., treas. Northstar Property Owners Assn., Calif., 1982-86. Served to capt. USNR, 1944-73, ret., 1973. Mem. Ins. Forum San Francisco (pres. 1965, trustee 1975-78, 84-88), Surety Underwriters Assn. No. Calif. (pres. 1956), CPCU Soc. (pres. No. Calif. chpt. 1957, Ins. Profl. of Yr., San Francisco chpt. 1981, bd. dirs., 1989-93), Chartered Ins. Inst., Ins. Inst. London, Musicians' Union Local No. 6 (life), U.S. Naval Inst., Assn. Naval Aviation, Phi Delta Theta. Episcopalian. Clubs: University, Marines' Meml. (San Francisco); Commonwealth. Lodge: Naval Order U.S. Office: 109 Minna St Ste 525 San Francisco CA 94105-3728

ENZI, MICHAEL BRADLEY, senator, accountant; b. Bremerton, Wash., Feb. 1, 1944; s. Elmer Jacob and Dorothy (Bradley) E.; m. Diana Buckley, June 7, 1969; children: Amy, Bradley, Emily. BBA, George Wash. U., 1966; MBA, Denver U., 1968. Cert. profl. human resources, 1994. Pres. NZ Shoes, Inc., Gillette, Wyo., 1969-95, NZ Shoes of Sheridan, Inc., Wyo., 1983-96; acctg. mgr. Dunbar Well Svc., Inc., Gillette, 1985-97; mem. Wyo. Ho. of Reps., Cheyenne, 1987-91, Wyo. State Senate, Cheyenne, 1991-96, U.S. Senate, 1997—; chmn. bd. dirs. 1st Wyo. Bank, Gillette, 1978-88; chmn. Senate Revenue Com., 1992-96. Mayor City of Gillette, 1975-82; pres. Wyo. Assn. Mcpls., Cheyenne, 1980-82. Sgt. Wyo. Air NG, 1967-73. Mem. Wyo. Order of DeMolay (state master councilor 1963-64), Wyo. Jaycees (state pres. 1973-74), Masons (Sheridan and Gillette lodges), Scottish Rite, Shriners, Lions, Sigma Chi. Republican. Presbyterian. Home: 431 Circle Dr Gillette WY 82716 Office: US Capitol Washington DC 20510

EPCAR, RICHARD MICHAEL, actor, writer, director; b. Denver, Apr. 29, 1955; s. George Buck and Shirley (Learner) E.; m. Ellyn Jane Stern, Aug. 15, 1982; children: Jonathan Alexander, Jacqueline Elizabeth. BFA in Performing Arts, U. Ariz., 1978; postgrad., U. So. Calif., L.A., 1980, U. Calif., L.A., 1981, Am. Film Inst., 1982. Pres. Trouble Shooter Prodns., L.A., 1986—. Actor (films) including Memoirs of an Invisible Man, D.C. Collins, Incident of War, Street Hawk, Escape to Love, Not of This World, (TV series) Diagnosis Murder Columbo, Beverly Hills 90210, Cheers, General Hospital, Guns of Paradise, Matlock, Who's the Boss?, Sonny Spoons, Moonlighting, Highway to Heaven, Amazing Stories, Fast Times, Crazy Like a Fox, Hell Town, Stir Crazy, Santa Barbara, Days of our Lives, (animated series) Teknoman 2 Lead Voices; author 7 episodes, co-dir. Robotech, Honey Dee Hutch, X-Men; co-dir., co-author, lead voice Eagle Riders; (on state) Why a Hero, Dracula, An Evening with Lincoln, Real Inspector Hound, Richard II; actor, writer (play) (on stage) Take My Wife...Please!, 1980; wrote and directed English adaptation of Acad. award winning Cinema Paradisco, Belle Epoque (Acad. Award winner), Women on the Verge of a Nervous Breakdown (Acad. Award nomination), Eat Drink Man Woman (Acad. Award nominated), Fencing Master (Acad. Award nominated); dir. (for TV) A Cowboy Christmas. Mem. L.A. Zoo Assn., 1983-90, 91, 94, Natural History Mus., L.A., 1989-91, Earth Save, L.A., 1990, L.A. Mus. Art, 1991; host fall festival Sta. KCET-Pub. TV, L.A., 1980; active Am. Cancer Soc. Recipient Haldeman Found. scholarship, U. Ariz., 1973-78; named Nat. Best Actor of Yr., Nat. Players, 1977, CPC Repertory Group, 1980; recipient Irene Ryan Soloist award, 1978. Office: Trouble Shooter Prodns PO Box 5429 North Hollywood CA 91616-5429

EPLEY, THELMA MAE CHILDERS, retired gifted and talented education educator; b. Ft. Wayne, Ind., Dec. 28, 1918; d. Harley Ellsworth and Bessie Mae (Corathers) Childers; m. Joseph Mendel Epley, Sept. 14, 1946. BS, Ind. U., 1941; MA, Calif. State U., Northridge, 1958; postgrad., U. So. Calif., 1964-65. Cert. elem., secondary tchr., adminstr., Calif. Tchr. Ft. Wayne Pub. Schs., 1941-42, 43-46; tchr., counselor Muncie (Ind.) Pub. Schs., 1942-43; tchr. L.A. Unified Sch. Dist., 1948-56, reserve tchr., 1955-57, specialist gifted program, 1958-70, tchr. adult edn., 1964-69, instrnl. adviser, 1970-75; instr. Occidental Coll., Eagle Rock, Calif., 1952-61, Calif. State U., 1958; newspaper edn. coord. Copley LA Newspapers, Santa Monica, Calif., 1978-93; ret.; mem. adv. bd. gifted parents groups, L.A., 1958-75; ednl. cons. state bds. edn., 1975-86; project affiliate Nat. and State Leadership Tng. Inst. for Gifted and Talented, 1976-87. Author: Annotated Bibliography on Gifted, 1958, Models For Thinking, 1982, Futuristics, 1985, Promoting Productive Thinking, 1988; contbr. articles to profl. jours. Active Nat. Rep. Com., Washington, 1982-93, Citizen Amb. Program, Washington, 1990-93. Mem. Nat. Assn. for Gifted (Achievement award 1958-75), World Coun. on Gifted, World Future Soc., Calif. Ret. Tchrs. Assn., Calif. Coords. of Newspaper in Edn., Assoc. Adminstrs. of L.A. Unified Sch. Dist., Delta Kappa Gamma (pres. Gamma Lambda chpt. 1963-65, Woman of Yr. award 1990). Republican. Home: 10201 Oro Vista Ave Sunland CA 91040-3239

EPPELE, DAVID LOUIS, columnist, author; b. Jersey City, Apr. 4, 1939; s. Joseph Anton and Lena Marie (Tadlock) E.; m. Gladys Emily Padilla (div. 1975); children: David D., Joseph E.; m. Geneva Mae Kirsch, July 7, 1977. Student, N.Mex. State U., 1958, U. N.Mex., 1966, U. Portland, 1972. Field botanist SW Deserts and Mex., 1947-96, N.Mex. Cactus Rsch., Belen, 1953-62; dir. Ariz. Cactus and Succulent Rsch., Bisbee, 1984—; editor Ariz. Cactus News, 1984—; columnist Western Newspapers, 1987—. Author (newspaper column) On the Desert, 1986—; author: On the Desert, 1991; editor: Index of Cactus Illustrations, 1990, Desert in Bloom, 1989. Mem. Mule Mountain Dem. Party, Bisbee, 1978—. With USN, 1958-59. Mem. AAAS, Cactus and Succulent Soc. Am., N.Mex. Acad. Sci., Bisbee C. of C. Home and Office: Ariz Cactus 8 Cactus Ln Bisbee AZ 85603-6306

EPPERSON, ERIC ROBERT, financial executive, film producer; b. Oregon City, Oreg., Dec. 10, 1949; s. Robert Max and Margaret Joan (Crawford) E.; m. Lyla Gene Harris, Aug. 21, 1969; 1 child, Marcie. B.S., Brigham Young U., 1973, M.Acctg., 1974; M.B.A., Golden Gate U., 1977, J.D., 1981. Instr. acctg. Brigham Young U., Provo, Utah, 1973-74; supr. domestic taxation Bechtel Corp., San Francisco, 1974-78; supr. internat. taxation Bechtel Power Corp., San Francisco, 1978-80; mgr. internat. tax planning Del Monte Corp., San Francisco, 1980-82, mgr. internat. taxes, 1982-85; internat. tax specialist Touche Ross & Co., San Francisco, 1985-87; dir. internat. tax Coopers & Lybrand, Portland, 1987-89; exec. v.p., chief fin. officer Epperson Dayton Sorenson Prodns., Inc., Salt Lake City, 1989-90, Epperson Prodns., 1990-92; exec. dir. The Oreg. Trail Found., Inc., Oregon City, 1992-93; pres. MFD Ltd., Portland, Oreg., 1993—. Author: (with T. Gilbert) Interfacing of the Secruties and Exchange Commission with the Accounting Profession: 1968 to 1973, 1974; producer (motion picture) Without Evidence, 1995; exec. producer (motion picture) Dream Machine, 1989. Scoutmaster, Boy Scouts Am., Provo, 1971-73, troop committeeman, 1973-74, 83—; mem. IRS Vol. Income Tax Assistance Program, 1972-75; pres. Mut. Improvement Assn., Ch. Jesus Christ of Latter-day Saints, 1972-74, pres. Sunday sch., 1977-79, tchr., 1974-80, ward clk., 1980-83, bishopric, 1983-87; bd. dirs. Oreg. Art Inst. Film Ctr., Oreg. Trail Coordinating Coun., Hist. Preservation League of Oreg.; vice chmn. ranch devel. com. Boy Scouts Am., Butte Creek. Mem. World Affairs Coun., Japan/Am. Soc., Internat. Tax Planning Assn., Internat. Fiscal Assn., Oreg. Trail Coordinating Coun. (exec. bd.), Oreg. Hist. Soc., U.S. Rowing Assn., Oreg. Calif. Trail Assn., Commonwealth Club. Republican. Office: 25-6 NW 23rd Ave # 180 Portland OR 97210-3518

EPPERSON, STELLA MARIE, artist; b. Oakland, Calif., Nov. 6, 1920; d. Walter Peter and Martha Josephine (Schmitt) Ross; m. John Cray Epperson, May 10, 1941; children: Therese, John, Peter. Student, Calif. Coll. Arts & Crafts, 1939, 40-41, 56, Art Inst., San Miguel d'Allende, Mex., 1972. Portrait artist Oakland Art Assn., 1956—, San Francisco Women Artists, 1962—, Marin Soc. Artists, Ross, Calif., 1971—; art docent Oakland Mus., 1969-71, mem. women's bd., 1971—, art chmn. fund raiser, 1971-89, art guild chmn., 1965-69, chmn. artists in Brazil, chmn. for honoring artist Xavier Martinez, event honoring Neil Armstrong. One-woman shows include Oakland Mus. Auction, 1993, Univ. Club, San Francisco, 1994. Recipient San Francisco Women Artists award, 1989, Oakland Art Assn. award, 1991, Marin Soc. Artists award, 1992. Mem. U. Calif. Berkeley Faculty Club, Orinda Country Club. Republican. Roman Catholic. Home: 31 Valley View Rd Orinda CA 94563-1432

EPSTEIN, ERVIN HAROLD, JR., dermatologist, educator, researcher; b. Oakland, Calif., Mar. 6, 1941; s. Ervin Harold Sr. and Selma E.; m. Sally Ann Fain, Aug. 11, 1963; children: Adam, Stephanie, Emily. AB, Harvard Coll., 1962; MD, U. Calif., San Francisco, 1966. Diplomate Am. Bd. Dermatology. Intern Barnes Hosp., Washington U., St. Louis, 1966-67; resident in dermatology Harvard U., Cambridge, Mass., 1967-68; clin. assoc. dermatol. br. NIH, Bethesda, Md., 1968-70, resident fellow in biochemistry, 1970-71; resident in dermatology NYU Med. Sch., 1971-72; asst. to clin. prof. dept. dermatology U. Calif. Med. Sch., San Francisco, 1972—, asst. to rsch. dermatologist, 1972—; prin. investigator various rsch. grants NIH Bethesda, 1971—; mem. gen. medicine study sect. 1987-91, mem. adv. coun. Nat. Inst. Arthritis, Musculoskeletal and Skin Diseases, 1993-96. Co-editor: Skin Surgery, 1977, 3rd edit., 1988; editor: Progress in Dermatology, 1982-87; assoc. editor: (audio tape) Dialogues in Dermatology, 1977-84; author numerous rsch. papers, 1966—. Lt. USPHS, 1968-70. Mem. Soc. Investigative Dermatology (sec.-treas. 1984-89, prs.-elect 1990-91, pres. 1991-92), Dermatology Found. (trustee 1981-83, 84-91), Am. Dermatol. Assn. (treas. 1992-96), Harvard Club San Francisco (v.p.). Jewish. Office: San Francisco Gen Hosp 1001 Potrero Ave Rm 269 San Francisco CA 94110-3518

EPSTEIN, JONATHAN STONE, engineering executive; b. White Plains, N.Y., May 11, 1957; s. Gerald Samual Epstein and Mary Holt (Griffen) Wilson. BS in ME, Colo. State U., Ft. Collins, 1980; PhD, Va. Poly. Inst., Blacksburg, 1983. Postdoctoral fellow Oxford (Eng.) U., 1984; engring. specialist EG&G Idaho, Inc., Idaho Falls, 1984-88, sr. engring. specialist, 1990—; asst. prof. Ga. Inst. Tech., Atlanta, 1988-90; adv. engr. LMITCO, Idaho Falls, 1990—; cons. Rockwell Missile Div., Atlanta, 1988-90, EG&G Idaho, Inc., 1988-90; reviewer U.S. Dept. Energy, Washington, 1984-90; cons. in field. Editor: Experimental Technique in Fracture, 1990, Optics and Lasers in Engineering, 1990; mem. editorial bd. Experimental Mechanics, 1990; contbr. articles to profl. jours. Mem. ASME, Soc. Engring. Sci., Soc. Exptl. Mechanics, Sigma Chi. Office: EG&G Idaho Inc PO Box 1625 Idaho Falls ID 83415-0001

EPSTEIN, MELVIN, engineering educator; b. N.Y.C., July 17, 1930; s. Paul and Rose Diana (Korenman) E.; m. Marie Wallner, Dec. 22, 1951 (div. 1974); children: David Sidney, Nancy Epstein; m. Joyce Brenner, Apr. 29, 1979 (div. 1984); m. Golda Freedman, July 17, 1990 (div. 1996). BS, NYU, 1951; MS, MIT, 1953; PhD, Poly. Inst. Bklyn., 1959. Sr. aerodynamicist Rep. Aviation Corp., Farmingdale, N.Y., 1955-56; rsch. scientist Gen. Applied Sci. Labs., Hempstead, N.Y., 1956-59, U. So. Calif., L.A., 1959-61; sr. staff scientist Aerospace Corp., El Segundo, Calif., 1961-81; prof. Calif. State U., Northridge, 1981—; dir. Video Graphics Lab., 1985—; chair Pen-X Com., Washington, 1963; mem. adv. com. Instnl. Media Ctr., Northridge, 1985-92. Prodr., dir. documentary film The Spark, 1975. 1st lt. USAF, 1953-55. Fellow AIAA (assoc.); mem. Internat. Interactive Comms. Soc., Am. Phys. Soc. Office: Calif State U 18111 Nordhoff St Northridge CA 91330-0001

EPSTEIN, NORMAN RICHARD, internist; b. N.Y.C., May 2, 1947; s. Benjamin and Ann (Stevens) E.; m. Margaret Mary Ann Pope, Sept. 23, 1980; 1 child, Evan David. BA, N.Y.U., 1968; MD, SUNY Downstate Med Ctr., Bklyn., 1972. cert. Internal Medicine. Internist El Rio Neighborhood Health Ctr., Tucson, 1975-89; med. dir. CIGNA Healthcare of Ariz., Tucson, 1980-87, v.p., 1984-87, internist, 1980—. Bd. dirs. Tucson Loan Chest, 1992-95. Recipient Physicians Recognition award AMA, 1979, 82, 87, 90, 93, 96. Mem. Am. Coll. Physicians, Am. Coll. Physician Execs., Am. Soc. Clin. Hypnosis, Physicians for Social Responsibility, Sierra Club, Nature Conservancy. Office: CIGNA Healthcare of Ariz 535 N Wilmot Rd Tucson AZ 85711-2604

EPTON, GREGG, performing company executive. Prodn. and tour. mgr. Alberta Ballet, Calgary, Can., 1987, gen. mgr., 1989, exec. dir., 1991—; co-founder Alberta Ballet Sch., 1991. Mem. Can. Assn. Profl. Dance Orgns. (corp. sec. 1992-94). Office: Alberta Ballet, 141-18 Ave SW, Calgary, AB Canada T25 0B8*

ERB, RICHARD LOUIS LUNDIN, resort and hotel executive; b. Chgo., Dec. 23, 1929; s. Louis Henry and Miriam (Lundin) E.; m. Jean Elizabeth Easton, Mar. 14, 1959; children: John Richard, Elizabeth Anne, James Easton, Richard Louis II. BA, U. Calif., Berkeley, 1951, postgrad., 1952; student, San Francisco Art Inst., 1956. Cert. hotel adminstr. Asst. gen. mgr. Grand Teton Lodge Co., Jackson Hole, Wyo., 1954-62; mgr. Mauna Kea Beach Hotel, Hawaii, 1964-66; v.p., gen. mgr. Caneel Bay Plantation, Inc., St. John, V.I., 1966-75; gen. mgr. Williamsburg (Va.) Inn, 1975-78; exec. v.p., gen. mgr. Seabrook Island Co., Johns Island, S.C., 1978-80; v.p., dir. hotels Sands Hotel and Casino, Inc., Atlantic City, 1980-81; v.p., gen. mgr. Disneyland Hotel, Anaheim, Calif., 1981-82; COO Grand Traverse Resort, Grand Traverse Village, Mich., 1982-93; gen. mgr. Stein Eriksen Lodge, Deer Valley, Utah, 1993-96; pres. The Erb Group, 1996—; pres. Spruce-Park Mgmt. Co., 1989; mem. adv. bd. travel and tourism Mich. State U., 1992-96; vice-chmn. Charleston (S.C.) Tourism Coun., 1979-81; bd. dirs. Anaheim Visitors and Conv. Bur., 1981-82, Grand Traverse Conv. and Visitors Bur., 1985-90, U.S. 131 Area Devel. Assn., 1983-93; sr. cons. Cayuga Hosp. Advisors, 1996—. Contbr. articles to trade jours. Vice-pres. V.I. Montessori Sch., 1969-71, bd. dirs., 1968-76; bd. dirs. Coll. of V.I., 1976-79; adv. bd. U. S.C., 1978-82, Calif. State Poly. Inst., 1981-82, Orange Coast C.C., 1981-82, Northwestern Mich. Coll., 1983-93; adv. bd. hospitality mgmt. program Ea. Mich. U., 1989-93; trustee Munson Med. Ctr., Traverse City, 1985-93; bd. dirs. Traverse Symphony Orch., 1984-88, N.A. Vasa, 1987-89; adv. panel Mich. Communities of Econ. Excellence Program, 1984-88; mem. hospitality adv. bd. Utah Valley State Coll., 1994—. Lt. arty. U.S. Army, 1952-54. Named hon. prof. Mich. State U. Hotel Sch., 1992—. Fellow Edn. Inst.; mem. Am. Hotel and Motel Assn. (dir. 1975-77, , 90-94, exec. bd. 1991-94, Service Merit award 1976, Lawson Odde award 1993, Gold Medalist Membership award 1993, trustee Ednl. Inst. 1977-83, mktg. com., exec. com. 1978-83, chmn. projects and programs com. 1982-83, AH&MA resort com. 1986-96, AH&MA condominium com. 1985-96, chmn. ratings com. 1988-96, Ambassador award 1986, Blue Ribbon task force 1988-89, Resort Exec. of Yr. 1988), Caribbean Hotel Assn. (1st v.p. 1972-74, dir. 1970-76, hon. life mem., Extraordinary Service Merit award 1974), V.I. Hotel Assn. (pres. chmn. bd. 1971-76, Merit award 1973), Calif. Hotel Assn. (dir. 1981-82), Caribbean Travel Assn. (dir. 1972-74), Internat. Hotel Assn. (dir. 1971-73), S.C. Hotel Assn. (dir. 1978-82), Am. Hotel Assn. Edn. Inst., (Lamp of Knowledge award 1988), Va. Hotel Assn., Williamsburg Hotel Assn. (bd. dirs. 1975-78), Atlantic City Hotel Assn. (v.p. 1981-82), Atlantic City Casino Assn. (dir. 1981-82), Cornell Soc. Hotelmen, Mich. Travel and Tourist Assn. (bd. dirs. 1983-94, treas. 1986, sec. 1987, v.p. 1988, mktg. com. 1986-93, govtl. affairs com. 1986-93, chmn. edn. com. 1983-84, chmn. bd. 1989-90, Mich. Hotelier of Yr. 1991), Mich. Restaurant Assn. (bd. dirs. 1989-91, chmn. adminstrv. com. 1989-90), Mich. Gov.'s Task Force on Tourism, 1986-87, Grand Island Adv. Commn., Grand Traverse C. of C. (bd. dirs. 1984-89), Nat. Restaurant Assn., Utah Hotel and Motel Assn. (bd. dirs. 1994-96, treas. 1996), Leadership Grand Traverse (exec. com. 1984-92, fellow 1992), Park City Lodging Assn. (bd. dirs. 1993-96), Park City C. of C. (bd. dirs. 1994—), Tavern Club, Golden Horseshoe Club, Greate Bay Club, Seabrook Island Club, Kiawah Island Club, Grand Traverse Resort Club, Rotary (Paul Harris fellow 1990), Beta Theta Pi. Congregationalist.

ERCK, WALTER W., air force officer; b. Joliet, Ill., Aug. 3, 1957; s. Walter Sr. and Joan (Haas) E. BA, William Patterson Coll., Wayne, N.J., 1979; MA, Chapman U., Orange, Calif., 1982; MBA, Golden Gate U., San Francisco, 1988. Commd. 2d lt. USAF, 1979, advanced through grades to maj., 1991; chief MWR Inspection Br., Langley AFB, Va., 1989-91, 49th MWR and Svcs. Squadron, Holloman AFB, N.Mex., 1991-93, Svcs. Inspection Br., Kirtland AFB, N.Mex., 1993—. Mem. cmty. bd. dirs. Boy Scouts Am., Big Bros. and Big Sisters, ARC, Youth Reintegration Ctr. Decorated Air Force Commendation medal with 2 oak leaf clusters. Lutheran. Home: 7213 Sorate Alto Ct NW Albuquerque NM 87120

ERDMAN, TERRI SUE, pediatric and neonatal nurse, consultant; b. Casper, Wyo., June 27, 1954; d. Frederick Robert and Gretchen May (McCabe) Braunschweig; m. Steven H. Erdman, Oct. 2, 1982; 1 child, Samuel Cody. BS, U. Wyo., 1976; MS, U. Utah, 1981. RN, Calif.; cert. neonatal nurse practitioner. Staff nurse, charge nurse, transport nurse U. Utah Med. Ctr., Salt Lake City, 1976-80; neonatal nurse practitioner Primary Children's Med. Ctr., Salt Lake City, 1981-85; program coord. U. Utah Coll. Nursing, Salt Lake City, 1981-85; unit dir. med. transport svcs. dept. U. Nebr., Omaha, 1985-88, program dir. SKYMED, 1985-88; asst. prof. nursing, clin. instr. pediatrics Loma Linda (Calif.) U., 1988-90, acad. coord., 1988-90; cons. Tucson, Ariz., 1990—. Editl. cons., mem. rev. bd. Neonatal Network, 1985—, home study course reviewer, 1991—. Bd. dirs. Tucson Cmty. Sch., 1994-95, bd. trustees, 1995—, pres. bd. trustees, 1996—. Mem. Nat. Assn. Neonatal Nurses (v.p. spl. interest group for advanced practice 1984-88, pres. 1989-91, bd. dirs. 1989-91, chair econ. task force 1992-95), Nat. Alliance Nurse Practitioners (bd. dirs., sec. 1992-95), Sigma Theta Tau Internat., Phi Kappa Phi. Democrat.

ERDMANN, JOACHIM CHRISTIAN, physicist; b. Danzig, June 5, 1928; s. Franz Werner and Maria Magdalena (Schreiber) E.; doctorate Tech. U. Braunschweig (Germany), 1958; m. Ursula Maria Wedemeyer, Aug. 24, 1957; children—Michael Andreas, Thomas Christian, Maria Martha Dorothea. Physicist, Osram Labs., Augsburg, Germany, 1954-60; sr. research scientist Boeing Sci. Research Labs., Seattle, 1960-72; sr. research scientist Boeing Aerospace Co., Seattle, 1972-73; prin. engr. Boeing Comml. Airplane Co., Seattle, 1973-81, sr. prin. engr., 1981-84; sr. prin. engr. Boeing Aerospace, Seattle, 1984-90; tech. cons., 1990—; vis. prof. Max Planck Inst. for Metals Research, Stuttgart, Germany, 1968-69; lectr. Tech. U. Stuttgart, 1968-69; pres. Optologics Inc., Seattle, 1973-94 . Mem. Am. Phys. Soc., Optical Soc. Am., Soc. Photo Optical Instrumentation Engrs. Author: Heat Conduction in Crystals, 1969. Contbr. articles to profl. jours. Research in cryogenics, statis. physics and opto electronics. Home: 14300 Trillium Blvd SE Apt 8 Bothell WA 98012-1313 Office: Boeing Def and Space Group PO Box 3999 Seattle WA 98124-2499

ERICKSEN, KENNETH JERROLD, English literature educator; b. Everett, Wash., June 7, 1939; s. Frank Ludwig and Evelyn Elvera (Carlson) E.; m. Donna Gayle Clodfelter, Jan. 1, 1976; children: Richard Harland, Douglas Craig, Hillary Janette, Adam Jerrold. BA, Pacific Luth. U., Tacoma, 1961; MA, Rice U., 1963, PhD, 1967. Prof. English Linfield Coll., McMinnville, Oreg., 1965—. Mem. MLA, Jane Austen Soc. N.Am., Am. Soc. for Eighteenth Century Studies, N.W. Soc. for Eighteenth Century Studies (pres. 1992-93, co-editor Transactions 1991-93). Lutheran. Home: 3321 Lavina Dr Forest Grove OR 97116-1041 Office: Linfield Coll Mcminnville OR 97128

ERICKSON, DENNIS, professional football coach, former university football coach; b. Everett, Wash., Mar. 24, 1947; m. Marilyn, children: Bryce, Ryan. BS Phys. Educ., Montana State U. Grad. asst. coach Montana State U., 1969, Washington State U., 1970; head football coach Billings Central H.S., Billings, Mont., 1970; backfield coach Montana State U., 1971-73; offensive coordinator, head coach U. Idaho, 1974-75, 1982-85; offensive coordinator Fresno State U., 1976-78, San Jose State U., 1979-81; head coach U. Wyoming, 1986, Washington State U., 1987-88, U. Miami Hurricanes, 1989-95, Seattle Seahawks, 1995—. Office: Seattle Seahawks 11220 NE 53rd St Kirkland WA 98033-7505*

ERICKSON, ERIC DOUGLAS, chemist; b. Astoria, Oreg., July 31, 1955; s. Douglas Leon and Patricia (Thiebes) E.; m. Barbara Marie Davenport, Sept. 3, 1977; children: Ivy Marie, Benjamin Clark. BS in Chemistry, Oreg. State U., 1977; Cert. of Proficiency Indsl. Hygiene, San Diego City Coll., 1980; PhD in Chemistry, Mich. State U., 1989. Chemist AMTECH Labs., San Diego, 1977-80, Naval Weapons Ctr., China Lake, Calif., 1980-84; teaching/rsch. asst. Mich. State U., East Lansing, 1984-89; chemist Naval Weapons Ctr., China Lake, 1989-92; chemist weapons div. Naval Air Warfare Ctr., China Lake, 1992—. Contbr. articles to profl. jours. Scout leader Cub Scouts/Boy Scouts Am., Ridgecrest, Calif., 1990-93, sci. explorer, post advisor, 1992-96. Mem. Am. Chem. Soc. (treas. Mojave Desert sect. 1990-92, chair-elect Mojave Desert sect. 1996, chmn. Mojave Desert sect. 1997), Sigma Xi (v.p. China Lake chpt. 1990, pres. China Lake chpt. 1991). Office: Naval Air Warfare Ctr Mail Stop 218D Weapons Divsn Code 4B2300D China Lake CA 93555

ERICKSON, GARY MICHAEL, business and management educator; b. Anacortes, Wash., July 7, 1945; s. Leroy Alexander and Ruby Lucille Erstrom; m. Jane Abad Sabado, June 29, 1968; children: Alvaro Sabado, Aurora Abad. BS, U. Wash., 1967; MBA, Stanford U., 1973, PhD, 1978. Asst. prof. Bus. and Mgmt. U. Pa., Phila., 1978-80; asst. prof. Bus. and Mgmt. U. Wash., Seattle, 1980-86, assoc. prof. Bus. and Mgmt., 1986-94, prof. Bus. and Mgmt., 1994—. With U.S. Army, 1969-71. Mem. Am. Mktg. Assn., INFORMS (assoc. editor Management Science 1987—). Office: U Wash Dept Mktg & Internat Bus Box 353200 Seattle WA 98195-3200

ERICKSON, MERLYN K., anesthesia nurse; b. Mankato, Minn., Mar. 15, 1936; s. Kindahl and Evelyn Erickson; m. Carolina Erickson, Feb. 18, 1989; children: Emilio, Carolina, Heidi, Kara. BSN, U. N.Mex., 1963; diploma, Walter Reed Army Anesthesiology, Washington, 1968; student, George Washington U. Cert. nurse anesthetist, ACLS, BCLS. Commd. nurse officer USPHS, advanced through grades to dir.; nurse anesthetist U.S. Army, Vietnam; staff anesthetist, clin. instr. Greater S.E. Community Hosp., Washington; staff anesthetist USPHS Alaska Native Med. Ctr., Anchorage, chief nurse anesthetist; ret.; staff anesthetist Alaska Surgery Ctr. Capt. USPHS. Decorated Bronze Star, Nat. Svc. medal, Vietnam Svc. medal. Mem. Alaska Assn. Nurse Anesthetists (pres. 1984-86). Home: 13001 Elmore St Anchorage AK 99516-2907

ERICKSON, PAMELA SUE, state agency administrator; b. Corpus Christi, Tex., Mar. 19, 1945; d. Walter Frederick Erickson and Barbara Jean (Roth) Carrigan; m. Kenneth Robert Gervais, Mar. 26, 1968 (div. Dec. 1990); 1 child, Lise Catherine Gervais; m. Gary William Domstrand Jr., Feb. 14, 1994. BA in Polit. Sci., Portland State U., 1967; MA in Govt., Georgetown U., 1974. Dep. adminstr. wage and hour divsn. Bur. Labor & Industries, Portland, Oreg., 1981-84; asst. adminstr. Oreg. Employment Divsn., Salem, 1984-91; project mgr. Metro, Portland, 1991-96; adminstr. Oreg. Liquor Control Commn., Milwaukie, 1996—. Mem. faculty Nat. Jud Coll., Reno, 1986, 87. Mem. Am. Soc. Pub. Adminstrs. (pres. Oreg. chpt. 1983, 91, mem. nat. coun. 1984-86), Oreg. Women in Pub. Svc. (founder, pres. 1990-93). Democrat. Mem. Unity Ch. Office: Oreg Liquor Control Commn 9079 SE McLoughlin Blvd Portland OR 97222

ERICKSON, RICHARD ALAN, biologist; b. Oakland, Calif., Sept. 27, 1953. BA, Humboldt State U., 1975; MS, Calif. State U., Hayward, 1985. Rsch. asst. U. Calif., Berkeley, Calif. State U., Hayward, 1976-78; cons. biologist Calif., 1978-90; project mgr. LSA Assocs., Inc., Irvine, Calif., 1990—; tchr. vertebrate biology Coll. Redwoods, Crescent City, Calif., 1981-82; wildlife biologist Redwood Nat. Park, Crescent City, 1981-82. Author: Birds of the East Bay Region of California, 1982, 2d edit., 1990, Birds of Redwood National Park, 1984, 2d edit., 1997; co-author: Birds of Northern California, 1979, 2d edit., 1988; contbr. book chpt. The Berkeley Almanac, 1976; editl. bd. mem. Western Birds, Euphonia, 1978—; regional co-editor Am. Birds, The Sandpiper, 1970-92; reviewer, contbr. articles to profl. jours. Mem. Am. Ornithologists' Union, Soc. Conservation Biology, Wilson Ornithol. Soc., We. Field Ornithologists (Calif. Bird Rec. com. 1976—, chmn. 1997—), Cooper Ornithol. Soc., Oreg. Field Ornithologists. Home: PO Box 1706 Laguna Beach CA 92652 Office: LSA Assocs Inc One Park Plz Ste 500 Irvine CA 92614

ERICKSON, RICHARD BEAU, life insurance company executive; b. Chgo., May 14, 1952; s. Charles Arthur and Carole Annette (Beaumont) E. BS, U. Ky., 1974, MBA, 1975. CLU. Sales rep. Met. Life and affiliated cos., Chgo. Hgts., Ill., 1975-78; sales mgr. Met. Life and affiliated cos., Flossmoor, Ill., 1978-80; mktg. specialist Met. Life and affiliated cos., Aurora, Ill., 1980-81; branch mgr. Met. Life and affiliated cos., Orland Park, Ill., 1981-84; corp. dir. Met. Life Gen. Ins. Agy. Inc., N.Y.C., 1984-86; regional sales mgr. Met. Life Gen. Ins. Agy. Inc., L.A., 1986-89, agy. v.p., sr. mktg. and sales exec., 1989—, agy. v.p., 1989-95, regional v.p., 1996—; rep. (Midwest) Sales Mgr. Adv., N.Y.C., 1979; dir. South Cook County Assn. Life Underwriters, Chgo., 1983. Author: Met. Manpower Development, 1981, Met. Manpower Development: A Guideline for Success, 1986. Sponsor UCLA Soccer, 1986—. Mem. NRA, Nat. Assn. Securities Dealers, Life Underwriters Tng. Counsel, Chartered Life Underwriters, U. Ky. Alumni Assn., Nat. Assn. Life Underwriters, Gen. Agts. & Mgrs. Assn., Sierra Club, Sigma Nu. Office: Met Life Ste 2240 15260 Ventura Blvd Sherman Oaks CA 91403-0003

ERICKSON, ROBERT PORTER, genetics researcher, educator, clinician; b. Portland, Oreg., June 27, 1939; s. Harold M. and Marjorie S. (Porter) E.; m. Sandra De'Ath, June 20, 1964; children: Andrew Ian, Colin De'Ath, Tanya Nadene, Tracy Lynn, Michelle Lee, Christof Phillipe. BA, Reed Coll., 1960; MD, Stanford U., 1965. Diplomate Am. Bd. Pediat., Am. Coll. Med. Genetics. Asst. prof. pediatrics U. Calif.-San Francisco Med. Sch., 1970-75; vis. scientist Institut Pasteur, Paris, 1975-76; assoc. prof. human genetics and pediat. U. Mich., Ann Arbor, 1976-80, prof., 1980—, dir. divsn. pediat. genetics, 1985—; vis. scientist Imperial Cancer Rsch. Fund, London, 1983-84; Holsclaw Family prof. human genetics and inherited diseases dept. pediat. U. Ariz., 1990—; vis fellow Hughes Hall, U. Cambridge, 1996-97. Mem. editl. bd. Jour. Reproductive Immunology, 1978—, Molecular Reprodn. and Devel., 1989—, Antisense R & D, 1992—, Jour. Rare Diseases, 1995—, Dictionary of Lab. Tech., 1983. Contbr. articles to sci. jours. With USPHS, 1967-69. Guggenheim fellow, Paris, 1975, Eleanor Roosevelt fellow, London, 1983; Fogarty Sr. Internat. fellow, 1996, Burroughs Wellcome travel fellow, 1996; Fulbright grantee, London, 1983, NIH grantee, 1971—. Mem. Am. Soc. Human Genetics, Soc. Pediat. Rsch., Am. Pediat. Soc. Avocations: skiing; backpacking. Home: 5200 N Camino Real Tucson AZ 85718-5029 Office: U Ariz Phoenix AZ 85724-5073

ERICKSON, RUSSELL JOHN, pediatrician; b. Sauk Center, Minn.; s. Russell John and Valerie Jeanette (Rose) E.; m. Patricia Ann Parker, June 22, 1958; children: Karen Michelle, Kevin David, Keith Lawrence. AB in Chemistry cum laude, Occidental Coll., 1957; MD, U. Calif., San Francisco, 1961; cert. in acupuncture, UCLA, 1990. Intern, resident and fellow in Pediatrics U. Calif., San Francisco, 1961-63; resident and fellow U. Wash., Seattle, 1963-65; pediatrician, asst. chief pediatrics Kaiser-Permanente, Oakland, Calif., 1965-66, 68-72; chief pediatrics Kaiser-Permanente, Richmond, Calif., 1972-88, chief quality assurance, 1978-84, chief med. edn., 1980-82, sr. cons., 1988-96; pvt. practice specializing in acupuncture Berkeley, Calif., 1996; rschr. in acupuncture, 1996—; clin. instr. U. Calif. Med. Sch., San Francisco, 1965-66, 68-72; chair manpower com. No. Calif. Acad. Pediatrics, 1976-78; mem. State Pediatric Healthplan Com., Calif., 1979. Contbr. articles to med. jours.; editor Am. Found. Med. Acupuncture Lit. Rev., 1996—. Founder, bd. dirs. Moraga (Calif.) Park and Recreation Dept., 1968-76; bd. dirs. Moraga Community Assn., 1970-74; pres. Saddleridge Homeowners, Pleasant Hill, Calif., 1990-93, 97—, treas.; sec. Sunrise Hills II Homeowners, Calif., 1993-96; trustee Am. Found. Med. Acupuncture, 1993—. Capt. U.S. Army, 1966-68. Fellow Am. Acad. Pediatrics; mem. Am. Acad. Med. Acupuncture, Sierra Club (life).

ERICKSON, VIRGINIA BEMMELS, chemical engineer; b. Sleepy Eye, Minn., June 19, 1948; d. Gordon Boothe and Marion Mae (Rieke) Bemmels; m. Larry Douglas Erickson, Sept. 6, 1969; children: Kirsten Danielle, Dean Michael. Diploma in Nursing, Swedish Hosp. Sch. Nursing, 1969; BSChemE, U. Wash., 1983, MChemE, 1985. RN. Asst. head nurse N. Meml. Hosp., Mpls., 1970-73; intensive care RN Swedish Med. Ctr., Seattle, 1973-83; research asst. U. Wash., Seattle, 1983-85; instrumentation and control engr. CH2M Hill, Bellevue, Wash., 1985—, mgr. dept., 1988-93, mgr. info. mgmr., 1994—, v.p., 1995—; cons. instrumentation and control engr. Mem. editorial adv. bd. Control. Leader Girl Scouts U.S., Seattle, 1985; supt. Seattle Ch. Sch., 1983; rep. United Way, 1986—. Recipient Cert. Achievement, Soc. Women Engrs., 1983, Teenfeed, 1990. Mem. AAUW, Instrument Soc. Am., Tau Beta Pi. Democrat. Mem. United Methodist Ch. Home: 6026 24th Ave NE Seattle WA 98115-7009 Office: CH2M Hill PO Box 91500 777 108th Ave NE Bellevue WA 98009-2050

ERICKSON, WILLIAM HURT, retired state supreme court justice; b. Denver, May 11, 1924; s. Arthur Xavier and Virginia (Hurt) E.; m. Doris Rogers, Dec. 24, 1953; children: Barbara Ann, Virginia Lee, Stephen Arthur, William Taylor. Degree in petroleum engring., Colo. Sch. Mines, 1947; student, U. Mich., 1949; LLB, U. Va., 1950. Bar: Colo. 1951. Pvt. practice Denver; justice Colo. Supreme Ct., 1971-96, chief justice, 1983-86; faculty NYU Appellate Judges Sch., 1972-85; mem. exec. Commn. on Accreditation of Law Enforcement Agys., 1980-83; chmn. Pres.'s Nat. Commn. for Rev. of Fed. and State Laws Relating to Wiretapping and Electronic Surveillance, 1976. With USAAF, 1943. Recipient Disting. Achievement medal Colo. Sch. Mines, 1990. Fellow Internat. Acad. Trial Lawyers (former sec.), Am. Coll. Trial Lawyers, Am. Bar Found. (chmn. 1985), Internat. Soc. Barristers (pres. 1971); mem. ABA, (bd. govs. 1975-79, former chmn. com. on standards criminal justice, former chmn. coun. criminal law sect., former chmn. com. to implement standards criminal justice, mem. long-range planning com., action com. to reduce ct. cost and delay), Colo. Bar Assn. (award of merit 1989), Denver Bar Assn. (past pres., trustee), Am. Law Inst. (coun.), Practising Law Inst. (nat. adv. coun., bd. govs. Colo.), Freedoms Found. at Valley Forge (nat. coun. trustees, 1986—), Order of Coif, Scribes (pres. 1978). Home: 10 Martin Ln Englewood CO 80110-4820

ERICSON, MARK FREDERICK, investment analyst; b. Colorado Springs, Colo., June 28, 1957; s. Frederick Walter and Eleanor Joan (Juraska) E. BS in Civil Engring., U. Colo., 1979, MBA, 1986. Registered profl. engr., Colo. Project mgr. JR Engring. Ltd., Englewood, Colo., 1982-86; cons. Kirkham Michael & Assocs., Greenwood Village, Colo., 1988-89, Merrick & Co., Aurora, Colo., 1989—; pres. Ericson Investors, Aurora, 1986—. Author: Follow the Crowd and Be Contrary, 1991, You Can Have Eternal Life for Certain, 1994; contbr. (book) Salvador Dali-A Retrospective of Master Prints, 1992; co-producer God's News Behind the News, 1994. Elder, lay pastor Calvary Temple, Disciple of Jesus Christ Evangelism Explosion Trainer. Mem. ASCE, Am. Assn. Individual Investors, Chi Epsilon. Office: 2068 S Pitkin St Aurora CO 80013-1263

ERIE, STEVEN PHILIP, political science educator; b. Bakersfield, Calif., Jan. 28, 1946; s. Harlan Eugene Erie (dec.) and Carmen Joyce (O'Brien) Barr; m. Vanessa Wilds Cunningham, June 15, 1989 (div. Aug. 1992). BA, UCLA, 1967, MA, 1969, PhD, 1975. Asst. prof. pub. adminstrn. U. So. Calif., L.A., 1975-78; asst. prof. polit. sci. SUNY, Albany, 1978-80; policy analyst U.S. Dept. Health and Human Svcs., Washington, 1980-81; asst. prof. U. Calif. San Diego, La Jolla, 1981-89, assoc. prof. polit. sci., adj. prof. history, 1989—; cons. L.A. Pub. Commn. on County Govt., 1975-76, Ednl. Testing Svc., Princeton, N.J., 1989-91; faculty, cons. Inst. for Ct. Mgmt., Denver, 1978-80. Author: Rainbow's End, 1988 (Best Book on Urban Politics, Am. Polit. Sci. Assn. 1989); contbg. editor Metro Investment Report, 1994—; mem. editl. adv. bd. U. Press of Va., Charlottesville, 1993—. Active Citizens Charter Reform Com., San Diego, 1993, San Diego Dialogue, 1995—, Citizens Coordinate for Century Three, San Diego, 1996; bd. dirs. Water and Power Assocs., L.A., 1994—. Charles F. Scott Meml. fellow UCLA, 1972-73; Faculty fellow Nat. Assn. Schs. of Pub. Affairs and Adminstrn., Washington, 1980-81; Faculty Rsch. grantee Calif. Policy Seminar, Berkeley, 1990, 94. Mem. Am. Polit. Sci. Assn. (exec. coun. urban politics sect. 1989-91, chair book prize com. 1991), Western Polit. Sci. Assn., Orgn. Am. Historians, Calif. Hist. Soc. Office: Univ Calif San Diego Dept Polit Sci La Jolla CA 92093

ERIKSEN, KENT ROGER, author, inventor; b. Redwood City, Calif., Mar. 22, 1954; s. Elwin Jesse and Dotothy H. (Jacobsen) E. Student in Journalism, Can. Coll., Redwood City, Calif., 1972-74; student, Columbia Sch. of Broadcasting, 1981; Cert. travel agt., Aszumano Travel Sch., 1993-94. Disc jockey various FM stas., San Francisco, 1981-86; counselor Columbia Sch. of Broadcasting, San Jose, Calif., 1983-85; stage mgr., song writer Hotrok Rec. Studio, San Jose, 1984-88; author Salem, Oreg., 1991—. Author, pub.: The Baby Band Book, 1987 (Bay Area Musician's award, 1988); author Lottery Games, 1994, My Summer Vacation, 1995; inventor tomato cage. Home and Office: 685 Valleywood Dr SE Salem OR 97306-1638

ERISMAN, FRANK, lawyer; b. Lackawanna, N.Y., Mar. 6, 1943; s. Henry S. and Mary Lorraine (Conlin) E.; m. Judith A. Milano, Feb. 18, 1984; children: Porter, Melanie, Lindsay, Jacob. Degree in metall. engring., Colo. Sch. Mines, 1965; JD, U. Denver, 1968. Bar: Colo., 1968. Law clk. U.S. Ct. Appeals (5th cir.), Jacksonville, Fla., 1968-69; ptnr. Holme Roberts & Owen, L.L.P., Denver, 1969—. Mem. editorial bd. American Law of Mining, 2d edit., 1984; chmn. editorial bd. (periodical) The Public Land Resources Law Digest, 1985-88. Trustee Colo. Sch. Mines, Golden; chmn. Colo. Sch. Mines Ann. Fund, 1990-91, Colo. Sch. Mines Pres.'s Coun., 1991-93; trustee Western Mus. of Mining & Industry, Colorado Springs, 1991-93. Recipient Disting. Achievement medal Colo. Sch. Mines, 1993. Mem. ABA (chmn. sect. of natural resources, energy and environ. law 1993-94), Colo. Bar Assn. (chmn. mineral law sect. 1991-92), Colo. Mining Assn. (bd. dirs. 1990-92), Rocky Mountain Mineral Law Found. (trustee, exec. bd. dirs. 1986-93, v.p. 1996—) Mining and Metallurgical Soc. Am. Office: Holme Roberts & Owen LLP 1700 Lincoln St Ste 4100 Denver CO 80203-4541

ERLICH, REESE WILLIAM, journalist; b. L.A., July 5, 1947; s. Israel Erlich; m. Elizabeth Erlich, Jan. 20, 1972; 1 child, Jason. BA, U. Calif., Berkeley, 1970. Staff writer Ramparts mag., San Francisco, 1967-69; freelance journalist Calif., 1969—, Christian Sci. Monitor, Boston, 1983—, Monitor Radio/Nat. Pub. Radio, 1986—; lectr. in mass comm. Calif. State U., Hayward, 1988—. Prodr.: (TV documentary) Prison Labor/Prison Blues, 1995; contbr. articles to profl. jours. Recipient Silver Hugo, Chgo. Internat. Film Festival, 1996. Mem. Soc. Profl. Journalists, Nat. Writers Union, Assn. Ind. in Radio, Calif. Faculty Assn. (Hayward chpt. v.p. 1993-95). Office: PO Box 19261 Oakland CA 94619

ERNEST, DOROTHETTA P., health facility administrator, critical care nurse; b. San Angelo, Tex., Aug. 20, 1939; d. Japson and Dorothy Naomi (McWilliams) Pettit; m. Henry Mason Ernest, Aug. 9, 1958; children: Robert Henry, Mason Luin, Margret Ruth, James Benjamin. Diploma, Meth. Hosp., Lubbock, Tex., 1960; AS, Cypress (Calif.) Jr. Coll., 1976; BSN, Mesa State Coll., 1989. Cert. CPR/First Aid instr. Head nurse Cerritos Gardens Hosp., Hawiian Gardens, Calif., 1972-73; dir. of nursing svc. Citrus Care Convalescent Hosp., Fontana, Calif., 1981-82; staff/head nurse, spl. care unit Orange Grove Community Hosp., Pomona, Calif., 1983-85; staff nurse, ICCU Southwest Meml. Hosp., Cortez, Colo., 1985-93; staff nurse ICU Lincoln County Med. Ctr., Ruidsoso, N.Mex., 1994-95; quality assurance/edn. specialist Chaves County Home Health Agy., Roswell, N.Mex., 1995—. Mem. ADA, N.Mex. Nurses Assn., Home Health Nurses Assn. Home: PO Box 4825 108 Paradise Canyon Dr Ruidoso NM 88345

ERNEST, DOUGLAS JEROME, librarian; b. Billings, Mont., Mar. 31, 1947; s. Clarence Henry and Ruth (Imhof) E. BA in History, U. Colo., 1969, MA in History, 1975; MA in Libr. Sci., U. Denver, 1970. Reference libr. Florence (S.C.) County Libr., 1970-73, Mo. Western State Coll., St. Joseph, 1975-81; social scis. , humanities libr. Colo. State U., Ft. Collins., 1981—. Author: (book) Agricultural Frontier to Electronic Frontier, 1996; also articles. Recipient Lit. award Colo. Libr. Assn., 1996. Mem. Sierra Club, Wilderness Soc., Nature Conservancy, Phi Beta Kappa, Beta Phi Mu. Democrat. Unitarian. Home: 1625 W Elizabeth St J-1 Fort Collins CO 80521 Office: Colo State U Morgan Libr Fort Collins CO 80523

ERNST, DONALD WILLIAM, producer; b. L.A., Jan. 25, 1934; s. William McKinley and Dorothy Elizabeth (Hast) E.; m. Janice Elaine Barber, Apr. 16, 1966; children: Stacey Dawn, Darci Lynn. BS in Civil Engring., UCLA, 1956. Apprentice editor Telemat, L.A., 1956-61; asst. editor Columbia Pictures, L.A., 1961-62, Metro-Goldwyn-Mayer, Culver City, Calif., 1962-64, film editor CBS, Studio City, Calif., 1964-72, Bakshi Prodns., L.A., 1972-79; sound editor Echo Films, L.A., 1979-82, Horta Editorial, Burbank, Calif., 1982-88; film editor Walt Disney Pictures, Glendale, Calif., 1988-89; prodr. Walt Disney Pictures, Glendale, 1989—. Prodr.: (animated film) Roller Coaster Rabbit, 1990; co-prodr.: (animated film) Aladdin, 1992; exec. prodr.: (live action film) Homeward Bound: The Incredible Journey, 1993.

Recipient Emmy awards TV Acad. Arts and Scis., 1977, 82. Mem. Am. Cinema Editors, Acad. Motion Picture Arts and Scis. Home: 26026 Trana Cir Calabasas CA 91302-1054 Office: Walt Disney Feature Animation 500 S Buena Vista Burbank CA 91505

ERNST, JOHN ALLAN, clinical neuropsychologist; b. Seattle, June 27, 1955; s. Gene Allan and Maxine Joan (Weedon) E. BA magna cum laude, U. Calif., San Diego, 1977; MS, San Diego State U., 1979; PhD, U. Mont., 1983. Diplomate Am. Bd. Clin. Neuropsychology, Am. Bd. Profl. Psychology; lic. psychologist, Calif., Wash., Queensland, Australia. Postdoctoral fellow U. Wash., Seattle, 1983-84; psychologist Western State Hosp., Lakewood, Wash., 1984-85; postdoctoral rsch. fellow Univ. Queensland, Brisbane, Australia, 1985-87; neuropsychologist St. Joseph Med. Ctr., Tacoma, Wash., 1987—; mem. Wash. State Examining Bd. of Psychology, 1995—. Contbr. articles to Behavioral Assessment, Psychology and Aging, others; mem. editl. bd. Rehab. Psychology, 1991—, SCI Psychosocial Process, 1994—. Mem. Am. Psychol. Assn. (cert. of appreciation rehab. divsn. 1991, 93), Am. Acad. of Clin. Neuropsychol., Nat. Register Health Svc. Providers in Psychology, Internat. Neuropsychol. Soc., Nat. Acad. Neuropsychology, Pacific N.W. Neuropsychol. Soc., many others. Office: St Joseph Med Ctr Dept Psychology PO Box 2197 Tacoma WA 98401

ERSKINE, JOHN MORSE, surgeon; b. San Francisco, Sept. 10, 1920; s. Morse and Dorothy (Ward) E. BS, Harvard U., 1942, MD, 1945. Diplomate Am. Bd. Surgery. Surg. intern U. Calif. Hosp., San Francisco, 1945-46; surg. researcher Mass. Gen. Hosp., Boston, 1948; resident in surgery Peter Bent Brigham Hosp., Boston, 1948-53; George Gorham Peters fellow St. Mary's Hosp., London, 1952; pvt. practice in medicine specializing in surgery San Francisco, 1954—; asst. clin. prof. Stanford Med. Sch., San Francisco, 1956-59; asst., assoc. clin. prof. U. Calif. Med. Sch., San Francisco, 1959—; surg. cons. San Francisco Vets. Hosp., 1959-73. Contbr. articles to profl. jours., chpts. to books. Founder No. Calif. Artery Bank, 1954-58, Irwin Meml. Blood Bank, San Francisco, commr., pres., 1969-74; bd. dirs. People for Open Space-Greenbelt Alliance, 1984—; chmn. adv. coun. Dorothy Erskine Open Space Fund. Capt. with U.S. Army, 1946-48. Fellow ACS; mem. San Francisco Med. Soc. (bd. dirs. 1968-72), San Francisco Surg. Soc. (v.p. 1984), Pacific Coast Surg. Soc., Am. Cancer Soc. (bd. dirs. San Francisco br. 1965-75), Calif. Med. Assn., Olympic Club, Sierra Club. Democrat. Unitarian. Home: 233 Chestnut St San Francisco CA 94133-2452

ERVIN, PATRICK FRANKLIN, nuclear engineer; b. Kansas City, Kans., Aug. 4, 1946; s. James Franklin and Irma Lee (Arnett) E.; m. Rita Jeanne Kimsey, Aug. 12, 1967; children: James, Kevin, Amber. BS in Nuclear Engring., Kans. State U., 1969, MS in Nuclear Engring., 1971; postgrad., Northeastern U., 1988. Registered profl. engr., Ill., Colo., Calif., Idaho, Wash.; cert. paleontology paraprofl., Colo. Reactor health physicist Dept. Nuclear Engring. Kans. State U., Manhattan, 1968-69, rsch. asst. Dept. Nuclear Engring., 1969-72, sr. reactor operator, temp. facility dir. Dept. Nuclear Engring., 1970-72; system test engr. Commonwealth Edison Co., Zion, Ill., 1972-73, 73-74; shift foreman Commonwealth Edison Co., Zion, 1973, shift foreman with sr. reactor operator lic., 1974-76, prin. engr., 1976-77, acting operating engr., 1977; tech. staff supr. Commonwealth Edison Co., Byron, Ill., 1977-81; lead test engr. Stone & Webster Engring. Corp., Denver, 1982-83, project mgr., 1982-95, ops. svcs. supr., 1982-86, asst. engring. mgr., 1986-89, cons. engr., 1989-94; sr. cons., 1994-96; program mgr. Rocky Flats Closure project Kaiser-Hill Co., Denver, 1996—. Contbr. articles to profl. jours. Served with U.S. Army N.G., 1971-77. Mem. Am. Nuclear Soc. (Nat. and Colo. chpts.), Am. Nat. Standards Inst. (working group on containment leakage testing). Independent. Roman Catholic. Home: 2978 S Bahama St Aurora CO 80013-2340 Office: Kaiser Hill Co PO Box 464 Golden CO 80402-0464

ERVING, CLAUDE MOORE, JR., military career officer, pilot; b. St. John's, N.F., Can., Sept. 10, 1952; s. Claude Moore Sr. and Ingeborg (Mauss) E.; m. Donna Lee Mathis, June 17, 1978; children: Zachary C., Allyson B., Michael J. M. BS in Geography, USAF Acad., 1975. Commd. 2d lt. USAF, 1975, advanced through grades to lt. col., 1979; check pilot, instr. 85th Flying Tng. Squadron, Laughlin AFB, Tex., 1976-80; flight examiner, instr. pilot, flight comdr. 460th Fighter Interceptor Tng. Squadron, Peterson AFB, Colo., 1980-82; flight comdr. 49th Fighter Interceptor Squadron, Griffiss AFB, N.Y., 1982-85; chief of tng. 18th Tactical Fighter Squadron, Eielson AFB, Alasaka, 1985-86; chief of flight safety, asst. chief of safety 343d Tactical Fighter Wing, Eielson AFB, Alasaka, 1986-88; chief ops. plans div. and exec. officer to dep. comdr. ops. for 11th Air Force and Alaskan NORAD region Hdqrs. Alaskan Air Command, Elmendorf AFB, 1988-92; comdr. 94th airmanship tng. squadron USAF Acad., Colo., 1992-94, dep. dir. pub. affairs, 1994-96; ret., 1996; aircraft accident investigator USAF, worldwide, 1986-96; pilot Fed. Express Corp. Mem. CAP (flight comdr. 1990-93). Republican. Home: 1049 Golden Pine Ln Monument CO 80132-9345

ERWIN, DONALD CARROLL, plant pathology educator; b. Concord, Nebr., Nov. 24, 1920; s. Robert James and Carol (Sexson) E.; m. Veora Marie Endres, Aug. 15, 1948; children: Daniel Erwin, Myriam Erwin Casey. Student, Wayne State (Nebr.) Tchrs.Coll, 1938-39; BSc, U. Nebr., 1949, MA, 1950; PhD, U. Calif.-Davis, 1953. Jr. plant pathologist U. Calif., Riverside, 1953-54; asst. plant pathologist U. Calif., 1954-60, assoc. plant pathologist, 1960-66, prof. plant pathology, 1966—, emeritus prof., 1991. Sr. author: Phytophthora Diseases Worldwide, 1996; editor: Phytphthora: Its Biology, Taxonomy, Ecology and Pathology, 1983; contbr. articles to profl. jours. With U.S. Army, 1942-46; ETO. Nathan Gold fellow, 1949, Guggenheim fellow, 1959. Fellow Am. Phytopathol. Soc., Sigma Xi. Democrat. Roman Catholic. Office: U Calif Dept Plant Pathology Riverside CA 92521

ERWIN, FRANCES SUZANNE, artist; b. Stockton, Calif., Nov. 24, 1924; d. Frederick Bedford and Clara Jackquiline (Seale) Davis; widow; 9 children. Student, Thomas Leighton Sch. Fine Arts, San Francisco, 1964-70, Sergie Bongart Sch., Rexburg, Idaho, 1972-73, various master artists, various cities, 1972—. Portrait painting instr. Roy Johnson Sch., Castro Valley, Calif., 1993-95, San Lorenzo (Calif.) Sch., 1995—; lectr. on visual arts, various San Francisco Bay area locations, 1987—. Portrait painter numerous pvt. commns.; commns. include Alameda County Ct. House, 1990, recreation facilities in Castro Valley and Hayward, 1991-92, Moreau H.S., Hayward, 1993, San Francisco World Trade Club, 1994, Eden Hosp., Castro Valley, 1994, Sakura Corp. Mus., Osaka, Japan, 1996; designed Sakura Corp. oil pastel container. Judge various county fairs and open art shows, Alameda County, Contra Costa County, and Santa Clara County (all in Calif.), 1988—. Recipient Best of Show award Alameda County Fair, Pleasanton, Calif., 1989, Best of Class, 1990; recipient Purchase and Founders awards Pastel Soc. Fla., 1996. Mem. Pastel Soc. of Am., Pastel Soc. of the West Coast (co-founder, bd. dirs., events chair 1985-87, v.p. 1987-88, pres. 1988-89, adv. bd. mem. 1989—, Plaques 1988, 89, Art of the West award 1994), Knickerbocker Artists USA. Republican. Roman Catholic. Home and Studio: The Studio 22125 Orange Ave Castro Valley CA 94546-6937

ERWIN, JOAN LENORE, artist, educator; b. Berkeley, Calif., Feb. 12, 1932; d. Ralph Albert and Dorothy Christine (Wuhrman) Potter; m. Byron W. Crider, Jan. 28, 1956 (div. May 1975); children: Susan Lynne Crider Adams, Gayle Leann Crider; m. Joseph G. Erwin Jr., May 28, 1976; children: Terry, Ray, Steve, Tim. BS, U. So. Calif., 1954; MS in Sch. Adminstrn., Pepperdine U., 1975. Cert. tchr., Calif.; registered occupational therapist, Calif. Occupational therapist Calif. State Hosp., Camarillo, 1955-56, Harlan Shoemaker Sch., San Pedro, Calif., 1956-57; tchr. Norwalk (Calif.) Sch. Dist., 1957-59, Tustin (Calif.) Sch. Dist., 1966-68, Garden Grove (Calif.) Sch. Dist., 1968-92; freelance artist Phelan, Calif., 1976—; comml. artist Morningstar Creations, Fullerton, Calif., 1982-92; substitute tchr. Snowline Sch. Dist., Phelan, Calif., 1994—; artist Y.U.G.O., Los Aiamitos, 1977-87. Pet portrait artist, U.S. and Eng., 1978-85; author, artist Biblical coloring books, 1985-90. Calif. Elks scholar, 1952-53; grantee Ford Found., 1957-58, Mentor Tchr. Program, 1986. Republican. Baptist. Home: 10080 Monte Vista Phelan CA 92371

ESCHENBACH, RICHARD COREY, mechanical engineer; b. Williamsport, Pa., Apr. 9, 1927; s. A. Edgar and C. Vivian (Corey) E.; m. Mary Margaret Graham, Dec. 24, 1948 (div. Aug. 1965); children: Theodore G., Sherry E.; m. Julia Faulkner Hull, Dec. 27, 1966; 1 child, Allen Edgar. BS in Physics, Carnegie-Mellon U., 1948, MS in Physics, 1949; PhD in Mech. Engring., Purdue U., 1957. Rsch. engr. Union Carbide Corp., Tonawanda, N.Y., 1948-54; supr. Union Carbide Corp., Speedway, Ind., 1954-69; mgr. adminstrn. and svcs. Union Carbide Corp., Tarrytown, N.Y., 1969-83; tech. mgr. Retech Inc., Ukiah, Calif., 1983—; mem. evaluation com. NCEE, NSF, Washington, 1988. Author: (with others) Metallurgical Applications of Plasma Technology, 1987; patentee (13) in field. Chmn. parks and recreation Town of Somers, N.Y., 1973-83; dir. choir Good Shepherd Episcopal Ch., Granite Springs, N.Y., 1975-83. George Westinghouse scholar, 1944; Shell Oil Co. fellow, 1957. Mem. AAAS (life), Am. Contract Bridge League, Mining Met. and Materials Soc. Republican. Lutheran. Home: 2181 Fawn Pl Ukiah CA 95482-3623 Office: Retech Inc divsn M4 Environ PO Box 997 100 Henry Station Rd Ukiah CA 95482-9601

ESFORMES, JOSEPH, agricultural products company executive; b. 1934. Graduate, U. Miami, 1957. V.p. Jack Esformes Corp., Miami, Fla., 1950—, Triple E Produces Corp., Tracy, Calif., 1965—; with Esformes Properties, Tracy, Calif., 1985—. Office: Triple E Produces Corp 8690 W Linne Rd Tracy CA 95376-9137*

ESFORMES, NATHAN, food products executive; b. 1936. BS, U. Miami, 1953. Pres. Jack Esformes Corp., 1950—, Triple E Produce Corp., 1953—. Office: Triple E Produce Corp 8690 W Linne Rd Tracy CA 95376-9137*

ESHELMAN, WILLIAM ROBERT, librarian, editor; b. Oklahoma City, Aug. 23, 1921; s. Cyrus Lenhert and Fern (Reed) E.; m. Mimi Blau, July 3, 1952 (div. Aug. 1956); m. Eve Kendall, June 21, 1957 (div. Apr. 1975); children: Ann, Benjamin, Zachary; m. Pat Rom, Dec. 29, 1977. BA, Chapman Coll., L.A., 1943; MA, UCLA, 1950; BLS, U. Calif. at Berkeley, 1951. Conscripted in civilian pub. service Waldport, Oreg., 1943-46; asst. dir., 1944-45; ptnr. Untide Press, Pasadena, Calif., 1946-65; teaching asst. UCLA, 1949-50, library asst., 1950; faculty Los Angeles State Coll., 1951-65, asst. librarian, 1954-59, coll. librarian, 1959-65; librarian, prof. bibliography Bucknell U., 1965-68; editor Wilson Library Bull., 1968-78; pres. Scarecrow Press, Metuchen, N.J., 1979-86; proprietor The Press at the Camperdown Elm, Wooster, Ohio, 1987-93. Editor: Take Hold Upon the Future: Letters on Writers and Writing by William Everson and Lawrence Clark Powell, 1938-1946, 1994; author: No Silence! A Library Life, 1997; contbg. author: Perspectives on William Everson, 1992; mem. editl. bd. Choice, 1966-71. Bd. dirs. Grolier Edn. Corp., 1979-86; mem. adv. council edn. for librarianship U. Calif., 1961-64; mem. acad. senate Calif. State Colls., 1964-65. Mem. AAUP (v.p. L.A. State Coll. 1958-59, pres. 1964-65), ALA (winner Libr. Periodicals award 1960, editorial com. 1964-66, mem. coun. 1972-76, com. accreditation 1977-79), Calif. Libr. Assn. (chmn. intellectual freedom com., pres. so. dist. 1965, editor Calif. Libr. jour. 1960-63), Assn. Coll. and Rsch. Librs. (publs. com.), Assn. Calif. State Coll. Profs., ACLU, Friends Com. Legis., N.J. Libr. Assn. (hon.), Rounce and Coffin Club (L.A.; sec.-treas. 1953-56), Typophiles CLub (N.Y.C.). Home and Office: 950 SW 21st Ave Apt 912 Portland OR 97205-1518

ESHLEMAN, DAVID, mayor. Mayor City of Fontana, Calif. Office: 8353 Sierra Ave Fontana CA 92335

ESHOO, ANNA GEORGES, congresswoman; b. New Britain, Conn., Dec. 13, 1942; d. Fred and Alice Alexandre Georges; children: Karen Elizabeth, Paul Frederick. AA with honors, Canada Coll., 1975. Chmn. San Mateo County Dem. Ctrl. Com., Calif., 1978-82; chair Human Rels. Com., 79-82; mem. Congress from 14th Dist. Calif., 1993—; at-large minority whip 5; chief of staff Calif. Assembly Spkr. Leo McCarthy, 1981; regional majority whip No. Calif., 1993-94. Co-founder Women's Hall of Fame; chair San Mateo County (Calif.) Dem. Party, 1980; active San Mateo County Bd. Suprs., 1982-92, pres., 1986; pres. Bay Area Air Quality Mgmt. Dist., 1982-92; mem. San Francisco Bay Conservation Devel. Commn., 1982-92; chair San Mateo County Gen. Hosp. Bd. Dirs. Roman Catholic. Office: US Ho of Reps Office Of House Mems Washington DC 20515

ESKIN, BARRY SANFORD, court investigator; b. Pitts., Mar. 6, 1943; s. Saul and Dorothy (Zaron) E.; m. M. Joyce Rosnald, Sept. 12, 1965; 1 child, David. AA, Los Angeles City Coll., 1963; BA, Calif. State U., Los Angeles, 1965; JD, Citrus Belt Law Sch., 1976. Bar: Calif. 1976. Social service worker San Bernardino (Calif.) Dept. Pub. Social Services, 1965-77; assoc. Law Office of Lawrence Novack, San Bernardino, 1978; ct. investigator San Bernardino Superior Ct., 1978, supervising investigator, 1978—; pro bono atty. Mex. Am. Commn., 1977-78. Mem. ARC Svc. Ctr. Advising Bd., San Bernardino, 1980-82; bd. dirs. Golden Valley Civ. Assn., San Bernardino, 1978-81, Congregation Emanuel, San Bernardino, 1984-87, bd. dirs. 1994-96. Mem. ABA, Calif. Assn. of Superior Ct. Investigators (pres. 1980-81, treas. 1984-85, bd. dirs.), San Bernardino County Bar Assn., Alpha Phi Omega. Democrat. Jewish. Office: San Bernardino Superior Ct 351 N Arrowhead Ave Rm 200 San Bernardino CA 92401-1605

ESLER, JOHN KENNETH, artist; b. Pilot Mound, Man., Can., Jan. 11, 1933; s. William John and Jennie Mae (Thompson) E.; m. Annemarie Schmid, June 26, 1964; children—William Sean, John Derek. B.F.A., U. Man., B.Ed., 1962. Mem. faculty dept. art Alta. Coll. Art, 1964-68; mem. faculty U. Calgary, Alta., Can., 1968-80; chmn. Print and Drawing Council Can., 1976-78. One-man exhbn., Gallery Moos, Toronto, Ont., 1978, Past and Present: One-Man Exhbn. Painting, Triangle Gallery, Calgary, Alberta, 1994, Retrospective/35 Years Printmaking, U. of C. Nickle Arts Mus., Calgary, Travelling exhbn., Sept. 1994; represented in permanent collections, Victoria and Albert Mus., London, Eng., Albright Knox Gallery, Buffalo, N.Y., Mus. Modern Art, N.Y.C., Nat. Gallery Can., Ottawa, Ont.; Author: Printing in Alberta. Life mem. Print and Drawing Coun. Can. Address: Box 2 Site 7, SS 1, Calgary, AB Canada T2M 4N3*

ESPARZA, RICHARD R., museum director; b. Washington; m. Lauraine Brekke, Oct. 24, 1992; 4 children. BA in Philosophy, Calif. State U., Hayward, 1969; student, Met. State Coll., 1972-73. Asst. curator Colo. State Mus. Colo. State Hist. Soc., Denver, 1972-73; exec. dir. South Park City Mus., Fairplay, Colo., 1973-74, Ventura (Calif.) County Mus. History and Art, 1974-80, San Diego Hist. Soc., 1980-87, Santa Barbara (Calif.) Hist. Museums, 1987-89, Nev. Mus. Art, Reno, 1991-95; dir. Riverside (Calif.) Mcpl. Mus., 1995—; faculty U. Calif. Santa Barbara Inst. Local History, 1981, Small Mus. Adminstrn. UCLA ext., 1981, Williamsburg Seminar for Historic Adminstrn., 1984. Mem. Riverside Downtown Assn. (bd. dirs.), Mission Inn Found. (bd. dirs.), Calif. Assn. Museums (bd. dirs.). Office: Riverside Mcpl Mus 3580 Mission Inn Ave Riverside CA 92501

ESPENLAUB, MARGO LINN, women's studies educator; b. Decorah, Iowa, May 1, 1944; d. Lloyd Wilson and Margaret Mary (Seegmiller) Ruid; m. Alan Ludwig Espenlaub, Aug. 8, 1988; children: Arn R. Johnson, Cara C. Johnson. BA in Philosophy, U. Colo., 1983, M in Humanities, 1985; PhD in Women's Studies, The Union Inst. Grad. Sch., 1995. Adj. prof. women's studies Met. State Coll., Denver, 1987—; adj. prof. U. Denver, The Women's Coll., 1996—; colloqium coord. Front Range Feminist Scholars, Denver, 1991—. Co-author: Women's Studies: Thinking Women, 1993. Mem. biomed. ethics com. Kaiser Permanente, Denver, 1986-96. Mem. MLA (women's caucus), Nat. Women's Studies Assn., Colo. Women's Studies Assn., Colo. Women's Agenda, Women's Caucus for Art (nat. and Colo. chpts.). Democrat. Office: Met State Coll Denver Inst for Womens Studies CB 36 PO Box 173362 Denver CO 80217-3362

ESPEY, WILLIAM MALLONEÉ, psychiatrist; b. Trinidad, Colo, June 3, 1938; s. James Gill Jr. and Virginia (Mallonee) E. BA, U. Colo., 1960, MD, 1964. Diplomate Am. Bd. Psychiatry and Neurology. Resident in psychiatry U. Colo. Sch. Medicine, 1968-72; staff psychiatrist Colo. State Hosp., 1970-71, teaching fellow, 1971-72; pvt. practice Denver, 1972-96; asst. clin. instr. psychiatry U. Colo., Denver, 1972-80, asst. clin. prof. psychiatry, 1980—; staff psychiatrist Denver VA Hosp., 1972-77, 90—; cons. United Airlines, 1989-90; therapist HIV support group Denver Nursing Project in Human Caring, 1990-96; mem. mental health clinic staff VA Hosp., 1972-77, 90—; cons. to dept. pastoral counseling Presbyn. Med. Ctr., 1976-80; mem. partial hospitalization com. Mount Airy Psychiat. Hosp., 1975-79, chmn., 1977-78, med. exec. com., 1981-82; mem. med. necessities com. Bethesda Psychiat. Hosp., 1977-81, 85-86, adolescent adv. com., 1978-80, patient care evaluation com., 1981-84, med. records com., 1987-90; staff psychiatrist Fitzsimmons Army Hosp., 1990-92. Mem. Gov.'s AIDS Coun., 1992-96, vice chairperson, 1993-96, chairperson HIV testing issues policy com. Fellow Am. Psychiat. Assn.; mem. Colo. Psychiat. Soc. (program com. 1986-87, AIDS edn. com. 1988—, exec. coun. 1989-91, sr. trustee area VII 1990-91), Colo. Med. Soc., Denver Med. Soc. Office: Denver VA Hosp 1055 Clermont Denver CO 80220

ESQUIVEL, JOE G., food products executive; b. 1938. With Hanson Farms, Salinas, Calif., 1967-83; pres. Adobe Packing Co., Salinas, Calif., 1983—. Office: Adobe Packing Co PO Box 4940t St Salinas CA 93912-1423*

ESQUIVEL, MARY, agricultural products company executive; b. 1945. Homemaker, 1976; ct. interpreter State of Calif., Salinas, 1976-83; sec., treas. Adobe Packing Co., Salinas, 1983—. Office: Adobe Packing Co P O Box 490 Salinas CA 93912-1423*

ESSA, LISA BETH, elementary education educator; b. Modesto, Calif., Nov. 19, 1955; d. Mark Newyia and Elizabeth (Warda) E. BA, U. Pacific-Stockton, 1977, MA in Curriculum and Instrn. Reading, 1980. Cert. tchr. elem., multiple subject and reading specialist, Calif. Tchr. primary grades Delhi (Calif.) Elem. Sch. Dist., 1978-80; reading clinic tutor San Joaquin Delta Community Coll., Stockton, Calif., 1980; tchr. primary grades Hayward (Calif.) Unified Sch. Dist., Supr., San Francisco host com. Dem. Nat. Conv., 1984. Femmes Club scholar, 1973; U. Calif. Optometry Alumni Assn. scholar, 1973; Jobs Daughters scholar, 1974. Mem. Internat. Reading Assn., Calif. Tchrs. Assn., Hayward Unified Tchrs. Assn., San Francisco Jr. C. of C., Jr. League San Francisco. Democrat. Episcopalian. Home: 1960 Clay St Apt 109 San Francisco CA 94109-3435

ESSIG, CHRISTINE CAY, paralegal; b. Ottumwa, Iowa, June 20, 1966; d. Aubrey Dean and Laurel Beth (Shoemaker) Nichols; m. Tracy S. Essig, Jan. 21, 1995. Student, Phoenix Coll., 1997. Cert. paralegal, Pa. Legal sec./paralegal Phoenix, 1984-87; legal sec. Udall, Shumway, Mesa, Ariz., 1987-89, Warner, Angle, Phoenix, 1989-92; paralegal Horne, Kaplan & Bistrow, Phoenix, 1992—. Edn. dir. Orpheum Theatre, Phoenix, 1994-97; mem. Tempe (Ariz.) Little Theater, 1987, 95—; sec. Nosy Neighbors Block Watch, Phoenix, 1995—; mem. Best Friends Animal Sanctuary, Kanab, Utah, 1994—. Named Best New Character, Lord Mayor, Ariz. Renaissance Festival, 1992. Mem. Nat. Notary Assn., Ariz. Paralegal Assn., Phi Theta Kappa. Democrat.

ESSMAN, ROBERT NORVEL, artist, graphic designer; b. St. Louis, Feb. 6, 1937; s. Paul M. and Rose (Solinsky) E. BFA, State U. of Iowa, 1959. Artist Simplicity Pattern Co., N.Y.C., 1961-62; artist Life Mag., N.Y.C., 1962-68, art dir., 1969; art dir. Show Mag., N.Y.C., 1969-70, Bus. Week Mag., N.Y.C., 1970-74; logo designer, creative dir. N.Y.C. Bicentennial Commn., N.Y.C., 1974-76; art dir. People Weekly Mag., N.Y.C., 1974-82; art dir., pres. Bob Essman: Design, The Cricket Press, N.Y.C., 1982—. Pubr./design dir.: Revival: Theatrical History Revisited, 1992-94. Bd. dirs. League for the Hard of Hearing, 1977—, recording sec. 1987-95; bd. dirs. Hampton-Booth Theatre Libr., 1993-94, sec., 1994. Recipient Vol. of Yr. award League for the Hard of Hearing, 1990, Excellence of Design award, Advt. Club of N.Y., 1977, Art Dirs. Club of N.Y., 1978, Gen. Excellence Nat. Mag. award Am. Soc. Mag. Editors, 1973. Mem. Am. Inst. Graphic Arts (Excellence of Design award 1980), Soc. Pub. Designers (bd. dirs. 1972-79, pres. 1976-79, Excellence of Design award 1972, 73, 75, 76, 78), Overseas Press Club (Designer Dateline 1991-92, New Club Logo 1994), The Players Club (bd. dirs. 1979-85), Dutch Treat Club (medal 1989-96, compiled membership history The Whole Who, 1995). Home and Office: The Cricket Press Box 130414 43173 Sunset Dr Big Bear Lake CA 92315

ESTEBAN, MANUEL ANTONIO, university administrator, educator; b. Barcelona, Spain, June 20, 1940; came to U.S., 1970; s. Manuel and Julia Esteban; m. Gloria Ribas, July 7, 1962; 1 child, Jacqueline. BA with 1st class honors in French, U. Calgary, Can., 1969, MA in Romance Studies, 1970; PhD in French, U. Calif., Santa Barbara, 1976. From asst. prof. to prof. French and Spanish langs. and lit. U. Mich., Dearborn, 1973-87, assoc. dean, 1984-86, acting dean coll. arts, scis., and letters, 1986-87; dean arts and scis. Calif. State U., Bakersfield, 1987-90; provost, v.p. acad. affairs Humboldt State U., Arcata, Calif., 1990-93; pres., prof. French and Spanish Calif. State U., Chico, 1993—; bd. dirs. Calif. Joint Policy Coun. on Agr. and Edn., 1995—. Author: Georges Feydeau, 1983; contbr. books revs. and articles to profl. publs. Woodrow Wilson fellow, 1969, doctoral fellow U. Calif., Santa Barbara, 1970-73, Can. Coun doctoral fellow, Govt. Can., 1970-73; Rackham grantee U. Mich., 1979, fellow, 1982-83. Mem. Am. Coun. Edn., Am. Assn. State Colls. and Univs., Greater Chico C. of C., Calif. State U. Inst. Tech. and Learning, U.S. Distance Learning Assn. Office: Calif State Univ Off of Pres Chico CA 95929-0150

ESTEP, ARTHUR LEE, lawyer; b. Forsyth, Mo., Dec. 4, 1932; s. Raymond B. and Nancy Mabel (Melton) E.; m. Joan Marie Hayes, June 16, 1956; 1 child, Sallie Ann Estep Warren. BS, U. Mo., 1954; JD, U. Ariz., 1959, honors grad., 1989. Bar: Ariz. 1959, Calif. 1959. Trust officer 1st Nat. Bank, San Diego, 1959-60; dep. city atty. City of San Diego, 1960-71; pvt. practice San Diego, 1961—. Bd. visitors U. Ariz., Tucson, 1986-96. 1st lt. USMC, 1950-56, Korea. Recipient Outstanding Svc. to Legal Profession award San Diego Bar Assn., 1986. Diplomate Am. Bd. Trial Advs. (pres. San Diego chpt. 1991, mem. nat. bd. dirs. 1990-96). Office: Estep & Warren 2257 Front St San Diego CA 92101-1909

ESTES, ANGELA M., English language educator; b. Washington, Dec. 12, 1950; d. John Douglas and Jane A. Estes. BS in Psychology, Washington State U., 1972, BA in English, 1973; MA in English, U. Ore., 1978, PhD in English, 1985. Asst. prof. dept. English Calif. Poly. State U., San Luis Obispo, 1987-92; assoc. prof. Calif. Poly. State U., 1992—; writing cons. Office Pers. Mgmt. Western Regional Tng. Ctr. U.S. Govt., 1983-84; faculty-artist-in-residence Calif. State U. Faculty Arts Inst., Kirkwood, Calif., 1989. Author: Boarding Pass, 1990, The Uses of Passion, 1995; contbr. articles, poems to profl. jours. Calif. Coun. Arts fellow, 1993, Children's Lit. Assn. rsch. fellow, 1992, Wesleyan Writers Conf. fellow, 1996; Woodrow Wilson grantee, 1983; winner Peregrine Smith Poetry Competition, 1994. Mem. MLA, Philological Assn. Pacific Coast, Rocky Mountain MLA, Phi Beta Kappa, Phi Kappa Phi, Alpha Lambda Delta. Office: Calif Poly State U English Dept. San Luis Obispo CA 93407

ESTRADA, SHARON KAY, state senator; b. Seattle, Jan. 18, 1944; d. Esquiel Marrio and Demple Caroline (Belcher) Estrada; m. Wallace bruce McLean, Dec. 31, 1985; 1 child, Peter Edward Van Haren IV. Notary public, Mont. Senator State of Mont., Helena. Campaign mgr. U.S. Congress, Billings, Mont., 1996; v.p. Am. Cancer Soc. Republican. Roman Catholic. Home: 528 Clark St Billings MT 59101 Office: Montana State Senate District 7 Helena MT 59620

ETCHART, MIKE, agricultural products company executive; b. 1961. V.p., pres. Everkrisp Vegetables, Inc., Tolleson, Ariz. Office: Everkrisp Vegetables Inc PO Box 25 Tolleson AZ 85353*

ETHRIDGE, FRANK GULDE, geology educator, consultant; b. Meridian, Miss., Dec. 21, 1938. BS, Miss. State U., 1960; MS, La. State U., 1966; PhD, Tex. A&M U., 1970. Prodn. geologist Chevron Oil Co., New Orleans, 1965-67; asst. prof. So. Ill. U., Carbondale, 1970-74, assoc. prof., 1974-75; assoc. prof. Colo. State U., Ft. Collins, 1975-81, prof., 1981—, acting head dept. earth resources, 1989, 95; cons. in field, Ft. Collins, 1977—. Co-editor: Recent and Ancient Nonmarine Depositional Environments: Medals for Exploration, 1981, Fluvial Sedimentology, 1987. 1st Lt. U.S. Army, 1960-63. Fellow Tex. A&M U., 1967, 68, grad. fellow 1970, Halbouty scholar, 1969; faculty devel. grantee Colo. State U., 1986; recipient Achievement award for outstanding performance in grad. edn. Burlington No., 1993, Jour. of Sedimentary Rsch. award for outstanding paper, 1996. Mem. Internat. Assn. Sedimentologists, Am. Assn. Petroleum Geologists (assoc. editor 1983-94), Soc. Sedimentary Geologists (Rocky Mtn. sect. sec. 1977-78, v.p. 1978-

79, pres. 1983-84), Rocky Mtn. Assn. Geologists, Sigma Xi. Roman Catholic. Office: Colo State U Dept Earth Resources Fort Collins CO 80523

ETT, ALAN PAUL, composer; b. Detroit, Mar. 2, 1952; s. Seymour and Florence (Lesan) E. BA in Psychology, U. N.C., 1972; MM, New Eng. Conservatory, 1978. Faculty Berklee Coll. Music, Boston, 1976-79; internat. concert performer W. Europe, North Am., 1979-83; composer, producer various groups, L.A., 1983—; musical dir. in field; master classes W. German Kulturamt, 1979-83. Composer music for TV shows including 227, Who's the Boss, 1987-89, Unsolved Mysteries, 1989-91, Wild & Crazy Kids, 1992, How'd They Do That, 1993, Movie Maguc, 1993-97, Sightings, 1995-97, Seatek, 1996, A&E Biography, 1996, Behind the Scenes with Joan Lunden, 1994-96, Behind Closed Doors with Joan Lunden, 1994-97; films including Fourth War, Cold Feet, Mob Boss, Madhouse, 1988-90, Pacific Heights, Thelma & Louise, Madonna-Truth or Dare; videos including Kareem-Reflections, 1989 (Golden Globe award); advt. campaigns including MCI, GM, Mazda, MCA Universal. Mem. Broadcast Music Inc., Am. Fedn. Musicians. Home: 11542 Decente Dr Studio City CA 91604-3868 Office: Alan Ett Music 3500 W Olive Ave Ste 560 Burbank CA 91505-4628

ETTENBERG, FRANK JOSEPH, artist; b. Bklyn., May 7, 1945; s. Manuel David and Rose (Edelman) E.; m. Silvia Stenitzer, Dec. 16, 1990. BS in Design, U. Mich., 1966; MA in Painting, U. N.Mex., 1971. Cert. in graphoanalysis Internat. Graphoanalysis Soc., Chgo., 1977. Gallery preparator Hills Gallery, Santa Fe, 1975-77; slipcaster Animals and Co., La Cienega, N.Mex., 1982-84; picture framer Gavin Collier & Co., Santa Fe, 1990-91; handwriting analyst pvt. practice, Santa Fe, 1972—; art restorer Santa Fe, 1995—. Exhbns. include Edith Lambert, Santa Fe, Galerie Rondula, Vienna, Austria, Fisher Gallery, Albuquerque, 1995, Highlands Gallery, Brenckenridge, Colo., 1995. Steering com. Advocates for Contemporary Art, Santa Fe, 1974-76, 77-78. Recipient Artists-in-Residence scholarship Tamarind Inst., Albuquerque, 1987; Artist-in-Residence grantee Roswell Mus. and Art Ctr., 1971-72.

EU, MARCH FONG, ambassador, former California state official; b. Oakdale, Calif., Mar. 29, 1929; d. Yuen and Shiu (Shee) Kong; children by previous marriage: Matthew Kipling Fong, Marchesa Suyin Fong; m. Henry Eu, Aug. 31, 1973; stepchildren: Henry, Adeline, Yvonne, Conroy, Alaric. Student, Salinas Jr. Coll.; BS, U. Calif.-Berkeley, 1943; MEd, Mills Coll., 1947; EdD, Stanford U., 1956; postgrad., Columbia U., Calif. State Coll.-Hayward; LLD, Lincoln U., 1984; LLB (hon.), Western U., 1985, Pepperdine U., 1993. Chmn. divsn. dental hygiene U. Calif. Med. Center, San Francisco, 1948-56; dental hygienist Oakland (Calif.) Pub. Schs., 1948-56; supr. dental health edn. Alameda County (Calif.) Schs.; lectr. health edn. Mills Coll., Oakland; mem. Calif. Legislature, 1966-74, chmn. select com. on agr., foods and nutrition, 1973-74; mem. com. natural resources and conservation, com. commerce and pub. utilities, select com. med. malpractice; chief of protocol State of Calif., 1975-83, sec. of state, 1975-94; Ambassador to Federated States of Micronesia U.S. Dept. of State, Washington, 1994—; chmn. Calif. State World Trade Commn., 1983-87; ex officio mem. Calif. State World Trade Commn., 1987—; spl. cons. Bur. Intergroup Relations, Calif. Dept. Edn.; ednl., legis. cons. Sausalito (Calif.) Pub. Schs., Santa Clara County Office Edn., Jefferson Elementary Union Sch. Dist., Santa Clara High Sch. Dist., Santa Clara Elementary Sch. Dist., Live Oak Union High Sch. Dist.; mem. Alameda County Bd. Edn., 1956-66, pres., 1961-62, legis. adv., 1963, Assembly Retirment Com., Assembly Com. on Govtl. Quality Com., Assembly Com. on Pub. Health; pres. Alameda County Sch. Bds. Assn., others. Mem. budget panel Bay Area United Fund Crusade; mem. Oakland Econ. Devel. Coun.; mem. tourism devel. com. Calif. Econ. Devel. Commn.; mem. citizens com. on housing Coun. Social Planning; mem. Calif. Interagy. Coun. Family Planning; edn. chmn., mem. coun. social planning, dir. Oakland Area Baymont Dist. Cmty. Coun.; charter pres., hon. life mem. Howard Elem. Sch. PTA; charter pres. Chinese Young Ladies Soc., Oakland; mem., vice chmn. adv. com. Youth Study Ctrs. and Ford Found. Interagy. Project, 1962-63; chmn. Alameda County Mothers' March, 1971-72; bd. councillors U. So. Calif. Sch. Dentistry, 1976; mem. exec. com. Calif. Dem. Ctrl. Com., mem. ctrl. com., 1963-70, asst. sec.; del. Dem. Nat. Conv., 1968; dir. 8th Congl. Dist. Dem. Coun., 1963; v.p. Dems. of 8th Congl. Dist., 1963; dir. Key Women for Kennedy, 1963; women's vice chmn. No. Calif. Johnson for Pres., 1964; bd. dirs. Oakland YWCA, 1965; mem. nat. vice-chmn. Clinton/Gore Reelection Campaign Com., 1996. Recipient Citizen of Yr. award Chinese-Am. United for Self Employment, 1996. Mem. Navy League (life), Am. Dental Hygienists Assn. (pres. 1956-57), No. Calif. Dental Hygienists Assn., Oakland LWV, AAUW (area rep. in edn. Oakland br.), Calif. Tchrs. Assn., Calif. Agrl. Aircraft Assn. (hon.), Calif. Sch. Bd. Assn., Alameda County Sch. Bd. Assn. (pres. 1965), Alameda County Mental Health Assn., Calif. Pub. Health Assn. Northern Divsn. (hon.), So. Calif. Dental Assn. (hon.), Bus. and Profl. Women's Club, Soroptimist (hon.), Hadassah (life), Ebell Club (L.A.), Chinese Retail Food Markets Assn. (hon.), Delta Kappa Gamma, Phi Alpha Delta (hon.), Phi Delta Gamma (hon.), others. Office: American Embassy PO Box 1286 Pohnpei FM 96941

EVANEGA, GEORGE RONALD, medical company executive; b. Cementon, Pa., Feb. 6, 1936; s. George and Helen A. (Cesanek) E.; m. Janet K. Roark, June 16, 1992; children: George C., Veronica A. BS in Engring., Lehigh U., 1957; MS, Yale U., 1958, PhD in Organic Chemistry, 1960. Rsch. scientist Union Carbide, Tarrytown, N.Y., 1962-69; mgr. Pfizer Cen. Rsch., Groton, Conn., 1969-75; dir. Biodynamics, Indpls., 1975-78; Hauptabteilungsleiter Boehringer Mannheim, Tutzing, Fed. Republic Germany, Germany, 1978-79; v.p. product devel. Boehringer Mannheim Diagnostics, Indpls., 1979-81, v.p. mktg. sales, 1981-84, v.p. tech., 1984-88; v.p., chief adminstrv. officer Miles Inc., Elkhart, Ind., 1988-91; pres., COO, Oncor Inc., Gaithersburg, Md., 1991-95; CEO, pres. Gull Labs., Inc., Salt Lake City, 1995—. NIH fellow, 1961. Mem. Am. Assn. Clin. Chemists, Am. Chem. Soc., N.Y. Acad. Sci. Home: 177 E Ensign Vista Dr Salt Lake City UT 84103

EVANGELISTA, ALLAN, clergy member, medical researcher; b. Quezon City, Manila, The Philippines, June 23, 1970; arrived in U.S., 1990.; s. Go Guan and Ana Evangelista. BA in Biology, U. La Verne, Calif., 1991; MDiv in Family, Pastoral Care and Counseling, Fuller Theological Seminary, Calif., 1996; postgrad., Loma Linda U., Calif., 1997—. Ordained and lic. Evangelical minister. Supr., administrv. asst. D. G. Engering. Works, Butuan City, The Philippines, 1988-90; host, server, cashier Coco's Bakery & Family Restaurant, Pomona, Calif., 1991-92; tchg. asst. U. La Verne, Calif., 1991; project supr., computer graphic designer Interior Corner, Monterey Park, Calif., 1992-93; inter library loan processor Fuller Seminary Libr., Pasadena, Calif., 1995-96; assoc. pastor New Life Christian Ctr., El Monte, Calif., 1992—; rsch. assoc. USC Cardiovascular Lab, L.A., Calif., 1993—; fin. investment analyst, San Gabriel, Calif., 1993—; fin. trustee New Life Christian Ctr., El Monte, Calif., 1994—, pastoral care/marriage counselor First Assembly of God Ch., El Monte, Calif., 1994—. Contbr. to professional medical jours. Vol. San Gabriel Valley Med. Ctr., Calif., 1992; med. outreach coord. First Assembly of God Ch., El Monte, Calif., 1994—; youth pastoring/bible tchr. Christian Reform Ch., West Covina, Calif., 1995—; chaplain UCLA Med. Ctr., Westwood, Calif., 1996. Recipient Ednl. Excellence award Alpha Kappa Alpha, Chgo., 1995; Harding Found. scholar, 1995-96, Fuller Theological Seminary scholar, 1995-96. Mem. Am. Fedn. Med. Rsch. (trainee investigator award 1994), Am. Assn. Adv. Sci., Am. Counseling Assn., Am. Mental Health Counselors Assn., Internat. Assn. Marriage & Family Counselors, Am. Assn. Christian Counselors. Home: 5039 Bartlett Ave San Gabriel CA 91776

EVANKOVICH, GEORGE JOSEPH, labor union administrator; b. Butte, Mont., Jan. 27, 1930; s. Joseph and Lubja (Broze) E.; m. Nevada Murray, Aug. 16, 1969; children: Karen, Lucy, Joseph, Janna. Student, U. Mont., 1954-57; BA, U. San Francisco, 1958. Miner Anaconda Co., Butte, 1946-50, Ind. Lease Mining, Helena, Mont., 1957-60; sec., treas. local 261 Laborers Internat. Union, San Francisco, 1960-68, bus. mgr., 1968-87, pres., 1987—; mem. bd. govs. dept. indsl. rels. Occupational Safety and Health Standards Bd. State of Calif., Sacramento, 1990—; pres. calif. region Pub. Employee Coun. AFL-CIO, 1973—; pres. No. Dist. Coun. of Laborers, 1977—; bd. dirs., trustee Laborer's Trust Funds, Inc., San Francisco; mem. adv. bd. NET, 1994, Lincoln Inst. Dir. labor studies program San Francisco City Coll., 1978—; chmn. San Francisco Housing Authority, 1972-76; advisor various senatorial, congl. and mayoral campaigns, 1966—; sustained mem. Rep. Nat. Com., 1980—. With inf. U.S. Army, 1951-54, Korea. Mem. Laborers Polit. Action Com. (bd. dirs.), Heritage Found., Commonwealth Club of San Francisco. Roman Catholic. Office: Laborers Union Local #261 3271 18th St San Francisco CA 94110-1920

EVANOFF, MARK EVAN, advocate; b. San Diego, Nov. 19, 1955; s. Evan and Louise Alda (Wire) E. AA, Citrus Coll., 1974; BA, Sonoma State U., 1976; MPA, Calif. State U., Hayward, 1977. Organizer, writer Abalone Alliance, San Francisco, 1978-81; writer Friends of the Earth, San Francisco, 1981-84; field dir. Greenbelt Alliance, San Francisco, 1984-94; policy asst. Assembly Mem. Michael Sweeney, 1994—; rsch. historian Calif. Pub. Utilities Com., San Francisco, 1985-86. Author various newspaper articles. founder Bay Area Ridge Trail Coun., 1986, dir., 1992—; organizer Measure AA East Bay Regional Dist., 1988, Ridelands Agreement, Pleasanton, 1993, East County Area Plan, Livermore Valley, 1994. Recipient Pioneer award Bay Area Ridge Trail Coun., San Francisco, 1990. Mem. Earth Island Inst., Sierra Club. Home: 29851 Clearbrook Cir Apt 85 Hayward CA 94544-6847 Office: Assemblymember Michael Sweeney 22320 Foothill Blvd Ste 130 Hayward CA 94541-2700

EVANS, ANTHONY HOWARD, university president; b. Clay County, Ark., Sept. 24, 1936; s. William Raymond and Thelma Fay (Crews) E.; m. Lois Fay Kirkham, Aug. 29, 1959. BA, East Tex. Bapt. Coll., Marshall, 1959; MA, U. Hawaii, 1961; PhD, U. Calif.-Berkeley, 1966. Program officer Peace Corps, Seoul, Korea, 1970-72; chief program planning Peace Corps, Washington, 1972-73, dir. planning office, 1973-75; asst. to pres. Eastern Mich. U., Ypsilanti, 1975-76, exec. v.p., 1976-79, acting pres., 1978-79, provost, v.p. acad. affairs, 1979-82; pres. Calif. State U., San Bernardino, 1982—. Mem. Orgn. Am. Historians, Phi Kappa Phi. Home: 664 E Parkdale Dr San Bernardino CA 92404-1731

EVANS, ARTHUR HAINES, JR., educational and organizational consultant; b. Mount Holly, N.J., Apr. 25, 1940; s. Arthur Haines and Betty Ogden (Dougherty) E.; m. Gay Dell Goodwin, Aug. 13, 1967; children: Kristna Jan, Ross Neil. AB cum laude, Princeton U., 1962; MBA, Stanford U., 1964; PhD in Higher Edn., U. Calif., Berkeley, 1970. Cert. cmty. supt., adminstr. and tchr., Calif. Bus. instr. City Coll. San Francisco, 1964-70; assoc. dean instrn. West Hills Coll., Coalinga, Calif., 1970-74; assoc. project dir. Pima C.C., Tucson, 1974-75, asst. to dean, 1975-79, asst. to pres., 1979-91; field faculty No. Ariz. U., Tucson, 1991—; pres. Evans and Assocs., Tucson, 1991—; rsch. cons. Pima County Interfaith Coun., Tucson, 1991—. Bd. mem. Soc. for Coll. and Univ. Planning, 1977-79, United Way Greater Tucson, 1987-90; pres. Tucson Trade Bur., 1987-90, Tucson Almaty Sister Cities, 1990-92; founding pres. United Way of Ariz., 1989-90; mem. Common Govt. Rels. Coun. for Advancement of Edn., 1990-92. Kellogg fellow U. Calif., Berkeley, 1969. Methodist. Office: Evans and Assocs PO Box 43693 Tucson AZ 85733-3693

EVANS, BERNARD WILLIAM, geologist, educator; b. London, July 16, 1934; came to U.S., 1961, naturalized, 1977; s. Albert Edward and Marjorie (Jordan) E.; m. Sheila Campbell Nolan, Nov. 19, 1962. B.Sc., U. London, 1955; D.Phil., Oxford U., 1959. Asst. U. Glasgow, Scotland, 1958-59; departmental demonstrator U. Oxford, 1959-61; asst. research prof. U. Calif., Berkeley, 1961-65; asst. prof. U. Calif., 1965-66, assoc. prof., 1966-69; prof. geology U. Wash., Seattle, 1969—; chmn. dept. geol. scis. U. Wash., 1974-79. Contbr. articles to profl. jours. Recipient U.S. Sr. Scientist award Humboldt Found., Fed. Republic Germany, 1988-89; Fulbright fellow, 1995-96. Fellow Geol. Soc. Am., Mineral Soc. Am. (pres. 1993-94, award 1970), Geochem. Soc., Geol. Soc. London, Mineral. Soc. Gt. Britain, Swiss Mineral. Soc. Home: 8001 Sand Point Way NE Apt 55C Seattle WA 98115-6399 Office: U Wash Dept Geol Scis Box 351310 Seattle WA 98195

EVANS, BERNE, III, food products company executive; b. 1936. Student, 1968. With Ernst & Ernst, Denver, 1972-75; sec., treas. Exeter (Calif.) Packers, Inc., Consolidated Growers, Inc., 1986—. With U.S. armed forces, 1968-72. Office: 7th Standard Ranch Co 33374 Lerdo Hwy Bakersfield CA 93308-9782*

EVANS, CASWELL ALVES, JR., dentist. BA, Franklin & Marshall Coll., 1965; DDS, Columbia U., 1970; MPH, U. Mich., 1972. Asst. prof. dentistry dept. dental ecology Sch. Dentistry, U. N.C., 1973-74; chief dental svc. and dir. rsch. and evaluation Healthco, Inc., 1973-74; clin. asst. prof. epidemiology and internat. health Sch. Pub. Health and Cmty. Med., Sch. Dentistry, U. Wash., 1974-85; asst. dir. health svc., dir. pub. health svc. L.A. County Dept. Health Svc., 1985-96, dir. Office of Pub. Health Initiatives, 1996—; assoc. prof. cmty. medicine Charles R. Drew U. Med. and Sci., 1986—; chief dental svc. Seattle-King County Dept. Pub. Health, 1974-85, dir. ops., 1979; dir. King County Health Svc. Divsn., 1980-85; prin. investigator grant Nat. Cancer Inst.-NIH, 1986-91; co-prin. investigator, 1989-94; adj. prof. Sch. Dentistry, U. Calif., L.A., 1987—, Sch. Pub. Health, 1988—. Mem. APHA (pres. 1995), Inst. Medicine-NAS, Am. Assn. Pub. Health Dentistry. Office: LA County Dept Health Svcs 5555 Ferguson Dr Ste 100-65 Commerce CA 90022

EVANS, DEBORAH LYNNE, private investigator, writer; b. Alhambra, Calif., Oct. 6, 1956; d. Richard Alan and Dianne (Herring) Evans; m. Eric Roger Warkentien, Nov. 20, 1993; children: Hunter Evan, Cole Evan. Student, Coastline Jr. Coll., 1977-80, Saddleback Coll., Mission Viejo, Calif., 1982-86. Lic. pvt. investigator, Calif. Investigator Block Investigations, Newport Beach, Calif., 1976-85; owner The Information Source, Newport Beach, 1985—; founder Rancho Viejo Sch. Montessori presch., 1996—; co-founder Aliso Acad. for Deaf and Hard of Hearing; cons. Block Investigations, Newport Beach, 1985—. Contbr. articles to profl. jours. Mem. Newport Beach Bus. Club (v.p. 1986-92), DAR. Republican.

EVANS, HANDEL E., marketing professional; b. 1935. Exec. v.p. IMS Internat. Inc., 1965-81; mng. dir., co-founder SMS Internat., 1981-86; pres., CEO Walsh Internat., Inc., 1988—; chmn. bd. Pharm. Mktg. Svcs., Inc., Phoenix. Office: Walsh Internat 2394 E Camelback Rd Phoenix AZ 85016-3429*

EVANS, JAMES HANDEL, university administrator, architect, educator; b. Bolton, Eng., June 14, 1938; came to U.S., 1965.; s. Arthur Handel and Ellen Bowen (Ramsden) E.; m. Carol L. Mulligan, Sept. 10, 1966; children: Jonathan, Sarah. Diploma of Architecture, U. Manchester, Eng., 1965; MArch., U. Oreg., 1967; postgrad., Cambridge (Eng.) U., 1969-70. Registered architect, Calif., U.K.; cert. NCARB. Assoc. dean. prof. architecture Calif. Poly. State U., San Luis Obispo, 1967-78; prof. art and design San Jose (Calif.) State U., 1979—, assoc. exec. v.p., 1978-81, interim exec. v.p., 1981-82, exec. v.p., 1982-91, interim pres., 1991-92, pres., 1992-95; vice chancellor Calif. State U System, Long Beach, CA, 1995-96; planning pres. Calif. State U. Channel Islands, Ventura; cons. Ibiza Nueva, Ibiza, Spain, 1977-80; vis. prof. Ciudad Universitaria, Madrid, 1977; vis. lectr. Herriott Watt U., Edinburgh, 1970; mem. adv. com. Army Command Staff Coll., Ft. Leavenworth, Kans., 1988. Trustee Good Samaritan Hosp., San Jose, 1987-90; bd. dirs. San Jose Shelter, 1988-90; dir. San Jose C. of C., 1991-94. Sci. Rsch. Coun. fellow Cambridge U., 1969-70. Fellow AIA; mem. Royal Inst. Brit. Architects, Assn. Univ. Architects. Office: Calif State Univ Channel Is 2151 Alessandro Dr Ste 290 Ventura CA 93001-3782

EVANS, JANET, Olympic swimmer; b. Aug. 28, 1971. 3 time Gold medalist, 400m Freestyle, 800m Individual Medley Seoul Olympic Games, 1988; Gold medalist, 800m Freestyle Barcelona Olympic Games, 1992, Silver medalist, 400m Freestyle, 1992; wubber 40th nat. title-400m Freestyle Phillips 66 Nat. Swimming Championships, Indpls., 1994; competed Atlanta Olympic Games, 1996. Named U.S. Swimmer of Yr., 1987. Office: US Swimming Inc One Olympic Plaza Colorado Springs CO 80909-5724*

EVANS, JOHN JOSEPH, management consultant; b. St. Louis, Mar. 1, 1940; s. Roy Joseph and Henrietta Frances (Schweizer) E.; BA, Centenary Coll., 1962; postgrad. Syracuse U., 1969, U. Wis., 1971, Harvard Bus. Sch., 1971-73; MBA, Pepperdine U., 1972; children—Todd, Karlyn, Jane, Mark. Pres. Evans & Co., 1966—; adj. prof. Centenary Coll. Bd. dirs. ARC, Mental Health Assn.; trustee Grad. Sch. Sales Mgmt. and Mktg.; pres. La. Real Estate Investment Trust; pres. N. La. Mental Health Hosp. Bd. Recipient awards United Way, 1965-69, ITVA awards, 1987-88. Mem. Nat. Beer Wholesalers Assn. (adv. dir.), Sales and Mktg. Execs. of Shreveport (pres.), S.W. Sales and Mktg. Execs. Council (pres.), Young Pres. Orgn., Conf. Bd., Aspen Inst., Sales and Mktg. Execs. Internat., Am. Soc. Tng. and Devel., Am. Soc. Personnel Adminstrn., Syracuse U. Grad. Sch. Sales Mgmt. and Mktg. Alumni Assn. (past pres., past trustee), Westlake Village C. of C. (past v.p., bd. dirs.), Personnel and Indsl. Relations Assn. (vice chmn., bd. dirs.), Harvard Club of San Diego. Home and Office: 9974 Scripps Ranch Blvd # 175 San Diego CA 92131-1825

EVANS, LAWRENCE JACK, JR., lawyer; b. Oakland, Calif., Apr. 4, 1921; s. Lawrence Jack and Eva May (Dickinson) E.; m. Marjorie Hisken, Dec. 23, 1944; children: Daryl S. Kleweno, Richard L., Shirley J. Coursey, Donald B. Diplomate Near East Sch. Theology, Beirut, 1951; MA, Am. U. Beirut, 1951; grad. Command and Gen. Staff Coll., 1960; PhD, Brantridge Forest Sch., Sussex, Eng., 1968; JD, Ariz. State U., 1971; grad. Nat. Jud. Coll., 1974. Bar: Ariz. 1971, U.S. Dist. Ct. Ariz. 1971, U.S. Ct. Claims 1972, U.S. Customs Ct., 1972, U.S. Tax Ct. 1972, U.S. Ct. Customs and Patent Appeals 1972, U.S. Ct. Appeals (9th cir.) 1972, U.S. Supreme Ct. 1975. Enlisted U.S. Navy, 1938-41, U.S. Army, 1942-44, commd. 2d lt. U.S. Army, 1944, advanced through ranks to lt. col., 1962; war plans officer, G-3 Seventh Army, 1960-62, chief, field ops. and tactics divsn., U.S. Army Spl. Forces, 1963, chief spl. techniques divsn., U.S. Army Spl. Forces, 1964, unconventional warfare monitor, U.S. Army Spl. Forces, 1964-65; ops. staff officer J-3 USEUCOM, 1965-68; mem. Airborne Command Post Study Group, Joint Chiefs of Staff, 1967; ret., 1968; mem. faculty Ariz. State U., 1968; sole practice law, cons. on Near and Middle Eastern affairs, Tempe, Ariz., 1971-72, 76—; v.p., dir. Trojan Investment & Devel. Co., Inc., 1972-75; active Ariz. Tax Conf., 1971-75; mem. adminstrv. law com., labor mgmt. rels. com., unauthorized practice of law com. Ariz. State Bar. Author: Legal Aspects of Land Tenure in the Republic of Lebanon, 1951, International Constitutional Law, (with Helen Miller Davis) Electoral Laws and Treaties of the Near and Middle East, 1951; contbr. articles to mags., chpts. to books. Chmn. legal and legis. com. Phoenix Mayor's Com. To Employ Handicapped, 1971-75; active Tempe Leadership Conf., 1971-75; chmn. Citizens Against Corruption in Govt., 1976-95; mem. Princeton Coun. on Fgn. and Internat. Studies, 1968; comdr. Ranger Area-Ariz., Ranger Region-West, 1993—. Decorated Silver Star, Legion of Merit, Bronze Star, Purple Heart, Combat Infantryman badge, Master Parachutist badge, Aircrewman badge; named Outstanding Adminstrv. Law Judge for State Service for U.S., 1974; named to U.S. Army Ranger Hall of Fame, 1981. Fellow Coll. of Rites of U.S.A.; mem. Ranger Bns. Assn. World War II (life), Tempe Rep. Mens Club (v.p., bd. dirs. 1971-72), U.S. Army Airborne Ranger Assn. (life), Mil. Order Purple Heart (life), NRA (official referee, life), Masonic Order of the Bath, The Philatethes Soc., Ye Antient and Old Order of Corks, Order of the Secret Monitor, BL (twice past master Thunderbird Lodge # 48 Phoenix, past master Ariz. Rsch. Lodge # 1), Order Ky. Colonels, Sovereign Mil. Order of Temple of Jerusalem (grand avocat pro tem 1993, grand officier 1993), Knight Commdr. Grace Sovereign Mil. Order St. John Jerusalem (Knights Hospitallers), Grand Chpt. Royal Arch Masons Ariz. (grand lectr.), Fraternal Order of Medieval Knighthood, Internat. (sovereign venerable master Ariz. Coll. 1988-93, supreme sovereign grand master 1991), YR (past high priest, past thrice illustrious master, twice eminent past comdr., Knight Templar Cross of Honor, 1988, Orator Order of High Priesthood, Grand Chpt. YRM 1989, pres. Grand Coun. Holy Order of High Priesthood of Ariz. 1996-97, York Rite Mason of Decade, Scottsdale YRB 1989), SR (32, ritual dir.), Chief Adept Ariz. Coll. Socs. Rosicruceana In Civitatibus Foederatis IX Degree, Grand Commandery of Knights Templar of Ariz. (grand insp. gen. 1990-91), Grand Royal Arch Masons Ariz. (grand lectr. 1995-96), Masons (knight U.S.A., Chevalier and Ami du Patriarchate, KCM Ordo Sancti Constantini Magni), Order of Secret Monitor, So. Calif. Rsch. Lodge, Royal Order of Scotland, Comdr. Ranger Area-Ariz. (Ranger Region- West Red 1993), Mil. Order of World Wars (historian, archivist), The Nat. Sojourners Inc., United Assn. (life, local #469 Phoenix), Phi Delta Phi, Delta Theta Phi. Episcopalian. Home: 539 E Erie Dr Tempe AZ 85282-3712

EVANS, LOUISE, psychologist, philanthropist; b. San Antonio; d. Henry Daniel and Adela (Pariser) E.; m. Thomas Ross Gambrell, Feb. 23, 1960. BS, Northwestern U., 1949; MS in Clin. Psychology, Purdue U., 1952, PhD in Clin. Psychology, 1955. Lic. Marriage, Family and Child Counselor Calif., Nat. Register of Health Svc. Providers in Psychology; lic. psychologist N.Y. (inactive), Calif.; diplomate Clin. Psychology, Am. Bd. Profl. Psychology (fellow), Am. Bd. Clin. Psychology. Intern clin. psychology Menninger Found.-Topeka (Kans.) State Hosp., 1952-53, USPHS-Menninger Found. postdoctoral fellow clin. child psychology, 1955-56; staff psychologist Kankakee (Ill.) State Hosp., 1954; head staff psychologist child guidance clinic Kings County Hosp., Bklyn., 1957-58; dir. psychology clinic Barnes-Renard Hosp., instr. med. psychology Washington U. Sch. Medicine, 1959; clin. rsch. cons. Episc. City Diocese, St. Louis, 1959; pvt. practice clin. psychology, 1960-92; fellow Internat. Coun. Sex Edn. and Parenthood, 1984; psychol. cons. Fullerton (Calif.) Community Hosp., 1961-81; staff cons. clin. psychology Martin Luther Hosp., Anaheim, Calif., 1963-70; nat., internat. lectr. clin. psychology schs. and profl. groups, 1950—; chairperson, participant psychol. symposiums, 1956—; guest speaker clin. psychology civic and cmty. orgns., 1950—. Elected to Hall of Fame, Central H.S., Evansville, Ind., 1966; recipient Svc. award Yuma County Head Start Program, 1972, Statue of Victory Personality of the Yr. award Centro Studi E. Ricerche Delle Nazioni, Italy, 1985, Alumni Merit award Northwestern U. Coll. Arts and Scis., 1997; named Miss Heritage, Heritage Publs., 1965. Fellow APA (clin. divsn., psychology of women divsn., divsn. psychotherapy, cons. divsn., dir. exec. bd. 1976-79), Acad. Clin. Psychology, Am. Assn. Applied and Preventative Psychology (charter), Royal Soc. Health England (emeritus), Internat. Council of Psychologists (dir. 1977-79, sec. 1962-64, 73-76), AAAS (emeritus), Am. Orthopsychiat. Assn. (life), World Wide Acad. of Scholars of N.Z. (life), Am. Psychol. Soc. (charter); mem. AAUP (emeritus)L.A. Soc. Clin. Psychologists (exec. bd. 1966-67), Calif. State Psychol. Assn. (life, ins. com. 1961-65), L.A. County Psychol. Assn. (emeritus), Orange County Psychol. Assn. (charter founding mem., exec. bd. 1961-62), Orange County Soc. Clin. Psychologists (founder, exec. bd. 1963-65, pres. 1964-65), Am. Public Health Assn. (emeritus), Internat. Platform Assn., N.Y. Acad. Scis. (emeritus), Purdue U. Alumni Assn. (life, mem. pres. coun., dean's club pacesetters, Citizenship award 1975, Disting. Alumni award 1993, Old Master 1993), Merit award Coll. Arts and Scis. Northwestern U., 1997. Center for Study of Presidency, Soc. Jewelry Historians USA (charter), Alumni Assn. Menninger Sch. Psychiatry, Soc. Sigma Xi Nat. Rsch. Hon. (emeritus), Pi Sigma Pi (pres. 1947-48, sec. 1946-47). Contbr. articles on clin. psychology to profl. publs. Achievements include development of innovative theories and techniques of clinical practice; acknowledged pioneer in devel. psychology as sci. and profession both nat. and internat., and pioneer in marital and family therapy, and in consulting to hospitals and clinics. Office: PO Box 6067 Beverly Hills CA 90212-1067

EVANS, MARSHA JOHNSON, naval officer; b. Springfield, Ill., Aug. 12, 1947; d. Walter Edward Johnson and Alice Anne (Field) Staffansson; m. Gerard Riendeau Evans, June 30, 1979. AB, Occidental Coll., 1968; MA, Fletcher Sch., 1977, MA in Law & Diplomacy, 1977; postgrad., Nat. War Coll., 1988-89. Commd. ensign USN, 1968, advanced through grades to real admiral, 1993; mideast policy officer Commander-in-Chief, U.S. Naval Forces, Europe, London, 1977-79; spl. asst. to sec. treasury U.S. Treasury Dept., Washington, 1979-80; staff analyst Office of Chief Naval Ops., Washington, 1980-81; dep. dir. Pres. Commn. on White House Fellowships, Washington, 1981-82; exec. officer Recruit Tng. Command, San Diego, 1982-84; commanding officer Naval Tech. Tng. Ctr., San Francisco, 1984-86; battalion officer, sr. lectr. polit. sci. U.S. Naval Acad., Annapolis, Md., 1986-88; chief of staff San Fransisco Naval Base, 1989-91, Naval Acad., Annapolis, Md., 1991-92; exec. dir. of the standing com. on mil. and civilian women Dept. of the Navy, 1992-93; comdr. Navy Recruiting Command, Washington, 1993-95; supt. Naval Postgrad. Sch., Monterey, CA, 1995—; interim dir. George C. Marshall European Ctr. Security Studies, Garmisch Partenkirchen, Germany, 1996—. White House fellow, 1979; Chief Naval Ops. scholar, 1976. Mem. Mortar Bd., Phi Beta Kappa.

EVANS, PAUL VERNON, lawyer; b. Colorado Springs, Colo., June 19, 1926; s. Fred Harrison and Emma Hooper (Austin) E.; m. Patricia Gwyn Davis, July 27, 1964; children—Bruce, Paula, Mike, Mark, Paul. B.A. cum laude, Colo. Coll., 1953; J.D., Duke U., 1956. Bar: Colo. 1956, U.S. Dist. Ct. Colo. 1956, U.S. Supreme Ct. 1971, U.S. Ct. Appeals (10th cir.) 1974. Field mgr. Keystone Readers Service, Dallas, 1946-50; sole practice, Colorado Springs, 1956-60; ptnr. Goodbar, Evans & Goodbar, 1960-63; sr. ptnr. Evans & Briggs Attys., Colorado Springs, 1963-95 ; city atty. City of Fountain, Colo., 1958-62, City of Woodland Park, Colo., 1962-78; atty. Rock Creek Mesa Water Dist., Colorado Springs, 1963—. Author instruction materials. Precinct com. man Republican Com., Colorado Springs, 1956-72. Served with USNR, 1944-46, PTO. Recipient Jr. C. of C. Outstanding Achievement award, 1957. Mem. Colo. Mining Assn., Am. Jud. Soc., ABA, Colo. Bar Assn. (com. chmn. 1966-67, 84), El Paso County Bar Assn. (com. chmn. 1956—), Assn. Trial Lawyers Am., Colo. and Local Trial Lawyers, Tau Kappa Alpha (pres.), Phi Beta Kappa. Republican. Club: Optimist (pres. 1966-67). Home: 244 Cobblestone Dr Colorado Springs CO 80906-7624 Office: 227 E Costilla St Colorado Springs CO 80903-2103

EVANS, RICHARD LLOYD, financial services company executive; b. Seattle, Oct. 16, 1935; s. Lloyd Herman and Dorleska L. (Rotta) E.; m. Judith Anne Sahlberg, Dec. 20, 1958; children: Dallas J., Douglas L., Daniel A., Marjorie A., Rebecca M. BA in Bus. Adminstrn., U. Wash., 1957. CLU; chartered fin. cons. Agt. Phoenix Mut. Life Ins. Co., Seattle, 1960-69; chmn. R.L. Evans Co. Inc., Seattle, 1969—; mng. prin. Evans Capital Mgmt. Assocs., Seattle; speaker on ins. and fin. planning to numerous orgns., 1975—. Mem. exec. bd. Chief Seattle coun. Boy Scouts Am., 1976—; chmn. N.W. Theol. Union, Seattle, 1984-88. Lt. USN, 1957-59. Recipient award of merit Chief Seattle coun. Boy Scouts Am., 1984. Mem. Am. Soc. CLU, Am. Soc. Chartered Fin. Cons., Nat. Assn. Life Underwriters, Wash. State Assn. Life Underwriters (bd. dirs. 1973-79, pres. 1977-78), Seattle Assn. Life Underwriters (v.p. 1972-73), Assn. Advanced Underwriting, Million Dollar Round Table, Estate Planning Coun. Seattle, Rainier Club, Masons, Rotary (dir.). Republican. Presbyterian. Home: HC 1 Box 37 Olga WA 98279-9702 Office: 1210 Plz 600 Bldg Seattle WA 98101

EVANS, ROBERT VINCENT, engineering executive; b. Mobile, Ala., Sept. 21, 1958; s. William Alexander Evans and Katherine Barbara (Doerr) Davidson; m. Debra Marie Winters, July 27, 1984; children: James Vernon, Chelsea Marie. BS in Computer Info. Systems, Regis U., Denver, 1987, BS in Tech. Mgmt., 1987; postgrad. in Mgmt., U. Wash., 1995. Electrician Climax (Colo.) Molybdenum Co., 1978-82; applications engr. Honeywell, Inc., Englewood, Colo., 1982-83, sales engr., 1983-87; systems engr. Apple Computer, Inc., Seattle, 1987-88; regional systems engring. mgr. Apple Computer, Inc., Portland, Oreg., 1988—. Author: Anthology of American Poets, 1981. Dir. Operation Lookout, Seattle, 1989; mem. Rep. Nat. Com.; commr. dist. com. Boy Scouts Am. Recipient USMC Blues award, Marine Corps Assn. Leatheanger award, 1977, Denver Post Outstanding Svc. award, 1983, N.Y. Zool. Soc. Hon. medal, James West fellowship award, Paul Harris fellowship award. Mem. Am. Mgmt. Assn., Am. Platform Assn., Mensa, Rotary, Kiwanis. Republican. Mem. Northwest Cmty. Ch. Office: Apple Computer Inc 10210 NE Points Dr Ste 310 Kirkland WA 98033-7872

EVANS, RONALD ALLEN, lodging chain executive; b. Louisville, Apr. 5, 1940; s. William Francis and Helen Maxine (Hart) E.; m. Lynne Anne Ingraham, Aug. 25, 1979; children: Nicole Louise, Michele Lynne, Christopher Hart. B.S. in Mgmt., Ariz. State U., 1963. Vice pres. Electronic Data Systems, Dallas, 1969-73; vice pres. First Fed. Savs., Phoenix, 1973-77, Community Fin. Corp., Scottsdale, Ariz., 1977-78; pres. Evans Mgmt. Services, Inc., Phoenix, 1978-84; pres., CEO Best Western Internat., Inc., Phoenix, 1979—. Served to lt. USNR, 1963-66. Decorated Bronze Star. Republican. Episcopalian. Lodges: Masons (32 deg.), KT, Shriner. Office: Best Western Internat Inc PO Box 10203 Phoenix AZ 85064-0203

EVANS, THOMAS EDGAR, JR., title insurance agency executive; b. Toronto, Ohio, Apr. 17, 1940; s. Thomas Edgar and Sarah Ellen (Bauer) E.; BA, Mt. Union Coll., 1963; m. Cynthia Lee Johnson, Feb. 23; children: Thomas Edgar, Douglas, Melinda, Jennifer. Tchr. Lodi, Ohio, 1963-64; salesman Simpson-Evans Realty, Steubenville, Ohio, 1964-65, Shadron Realty, Tucson, 1965-67; real estate broker, co-owner Double E Realty, Tucson, 1967-69; escrow officer, br. mgr., asst. county mgr., v.p. Ariz. Title Ins., Tucson, 1969-80; pres. Commonwealth Land Title Agy., Tucson, 1980-82, also dir.; pres. Fidelity Nat. Title Agy., 1982-90; bd. govs. Calif. Land Title Assn., 1990—; exec. v.p. Fidelity Nat. Title Ins. Co., 1990-92; v.p. Inland Empire Divsn. Fidelity Nat. Title, 1991-93, pres. Orange County Divsn., 1995—; bd. dirs. Western Fin. Trust Co., Fidelity Nat. Fin. Inc., Fidelity Nat. Title Ins. Co., Fidelity Nat. Title Agy. Pinal, The Griffin Co., Computer Market Place, Inc.; bd. dirs., chmn. bd. Cochise Title Agy., TIPCO; v.p., dir. A.P.C. Corp. Named Boss of Year, El Chaparral chpt. Am. Bus. Women's Assn., 1977. Mem. Calif. Land Title Assn. (pres. 1995-96), So. Ariz. Escrow Assn., So. Ariz. Mortgage Bankers Assn. (bd. dirs. 1982-85), Ariz. Mktg. Bankers Assn., Old Pueblo Businessmen's Assn. Tucson, Tucson Bd. Realtors, Ariz. Assn. Real Estate Exchangors (bd. dirs. 1968-69), Land Title Assn. Ariz. (pres. 1984), So. Ariz. Homebuilders Assn., Blue Key, Sigma Nu. Republican. Methodist. Clubs: Pacific, Ctr., Old Pueblo Courthouse, La Paloma, Ventana Country, Centre Court, Coto de Casa Country, Elks, Pima Jaycees (dir. 1966), Sertoma (charter pres., chmn. bd. Midtown sect. 1968-70); Tucson Real Estate Exchangors (pres. 1968); Sunrise Rotary; Old Pueblo, South Coast Repertory (bd. trustees 1996—), Pacific, Ctr. Home: 28861 Glen Rdg Mission Viejo CA 92692-4301 Office: 17592 E 17th St Ste 200 Tustin CA 92680

EVANS, WILLIAM THOMAS, physician; b. Denver, Aug. 21, 1941; s. Alfred Lincoln and Marian Audrey (Biggs) E.; m. Lucy Fales. BA, U. Colo., 1963; MD, Baylor U., 1967; grad., Chinese Coll. U.K.; Licentiate Acupuncture, Oxford, Eng., 1976. Intern Mary Fletcher Hosp., Burlington, Vt., 1967; physician Villages of Kodiak Island and Lake Iliamna, 1968-70; founder, dir. emergency dept. St. Elizabeth Hosp., Yakima, Wash., 1970-75; practice medicine specializing prevention and conservative treatment of spine injuries Denver; founder, dir. Colo. Back Sch., Denver, 1979-89; assoc. med. dir. Ctr. for Spine Rehab., 1989-96; founder Health Resilience Paradigm, Roaring Fork Valley; mem. ednl. coun. Colo. Neurol. Inst. Contbr. articles on prevention and edn. mgmt. of low back pain. Dir. Colo. Think First Program for Prevention of Head and Spinal Cord Injuries; Friends of Earth del. Limits to Medicine Congress, 1975; initiator Colo. Sun Day, 1978. Lt. comdr. Indian Health Svc., USPHS, 1968-70. Mem. AMA, Rocky Mountain Traumatological Soc. (pres.), Arapahoe County Med. Soc., Colo. Med. Soc. (workmen's compensation com.), N.Am. Spine Soc. (mem. ednl. coun.), Am. Coll. Occupational Medicine Asns., Rocky Mountain Acad. Occupational Medicine (pres.), Am. Coll. Sports Medicine, Traditional Acupuncture Soc. Home: PO Box 174 Littleton CO 80160-0174 Office: 415 E Hyman Ste 301 Aspen CO 81611

EVEN, RANDOLPH M., lawyer; b. 1943. BS, U. Calif.; JD, Calif. Western Sch. Law. Bar: Calif. 1969. Atty. Even, Crandall, Wade, Lowe & Gates and predecessor firm Genson, Even, Crandall & Wade, P.C., Woodland Hills, Calif. Mem. Am. Bd. Trial Advocates, Assn. So. Calif. Def. Counsel (bd. dirs. 1978-80, 93—). Office: Even Crandall Wade Lowe & Gates 21031 Ventura Blvd Ste 801 Woodland Hills CA 91364-2203

EVENSEN, JAY DOUGLAS, newspaper editor; b. DeKalb, Ill., Apr. 17, 1959; s. Glenn Stivers and Anne Berit (Strand) E.; m. Kirsti Elisabet Haneberg, July 16, 1982; children: Daniel, Linnea, Nils, Anders. BA, Brigham Young U., 1983. Reporter/intern UPI, N.Y.C., 1982; sports editor Clinton (Okla.) Daily News, 1983; reporter Deseret News, Salt Lake City, 1986-94, Las Vegas (Nev.) Review Jour., 1983-86; editl. writer Deseret News, Salt Lake City, 1994-96, editl. page editor, 1996—; adj. instr. journalism Weber State U., Ogden, Utah, 1988-92. Recipient 3d pl. editl. writing award Assoc. Press, 1994. Mem. Soc. Profl. Journalists (1st pl. feature writing award 1989, 2d pl. column writing award 1995), Nat. Conf. Editl. Writers. Mem. LDS Ch. Home: 9679 S Paisley Cir South Jordan UT 84095 Office: Deseret News 135 S Regent St Salt Lake City UT 84111

EVERETT, HOBART RAY, JR., engineer, naval officer, consultant, researcher, inventor; b. Charleston, S.C., Nov. 29, 1949; s. Hobart Ray and Ruth (Humphreys) E.; m. Rachael Patricia Lewis, Dec. 30, 1971 (div. Dec. 1995); children: Todd Ashley, Rebecca Nicole. BEE, Ga. Inst. Tech., 1973; MS in Mech. Engring., Naval Postgrad. Sch., 1982. Commd. ensign U.S. Navy, 1973, advanced through grades to comdr., 1988; asst. engr. USS Nitro, 1975-77; engring. recruiter for naval officer programs, Montgomery, Ala., 1977-80; robotics coordinator Naval Sea Systems Command, Washington, 1983-84, dir. Office of Robotics and Autonomous Systems, 1984-86; autonomous systems project officer Naval Ocean Systems Ctr., San Diego, 1986-88, chief engr. USMC teleoperated vehicle program, 1988-89, assoc. div. head advanced systems div., 1988-93; cons. to Computer Scis. Corp., Falls Church, Va., 1993-94; assoc. divsn. head robotics Naval Command, Control and Ocean Surveillance Ctr., San Diego, 1994—; founder DoD Robotics and Artificial Intelligence Database, 1983; Navy rep. to tri-svc. Joint Tech. Panel for Robotics, 1984-86; guest lectr. in robotics U. Md., U. Pa., 1983-86, U. Calif., San Diego, 1988; robotics researcher Naval Ocean Systems Ctr., prin. tech. cons. U.S. Army Mobile Detection Assessment and Response System interior program, 1990-93; tech. dir. Joint Army-Navy Mobile Detection Assessment and Response System interior and exterior program, 1993—. Author: Sensors for Mobile Robots, 1995, (with Borenstein and Feng) Sensors and Techniques for Mobile Robot Positioning, 1996; contbg. author Robotics Age mag., 1982-86, Sensors mag., 1987—; mem. editorial bd., contbg. author Robotics and Autonomous Systems mag.; contbr. 70 tech. publs.; inventor 1st autonomous sentry robot; patentee in field. Decorated Navy Commendation,1981, 86; recipient Naval Sea Systems Command award for Acad. Excellence, 1982, Woelful award for Acad. Excellence, Naval Sea Systems Command, 1983, Gen. Dynamics award for Acad. and Mil. Accomplishment, 1973. Mem. IEEE, Soc. Mfg. Engrs. (sr.), Robotics Inst. Am., Nat. Svc. Robot Assn. (bd. dirs. 1991—), Sigma Xi. Office: Naval Command Control & Ocean Surveillance Ctr RDT & E Divsn Code D3701 53406 Woodward Rd San Diego CA 92152-7383

EVERETT, JAMES JOSEPH, lawyer; b. San Antonio, May 7, 1955. BA, St. Mary's U., San Antonio, 1976; JD, Tex. So. U., 1980. Bar: U.S. Dist. Ct. Ariz. 1987, U.S. Tax Ct. 1980, U.S. Ct. Appeals (9th cir.) 1988. Sr. trial atty. IRS, Phoenix, 1980-87; ptnr. Brnilovich & Everett, Phoenix, 1987-89; of counsel Broadbent, Walker & Wales, 1991-95; pvt. practice Law Offices of James J. Everett, Phoenix, 1994—. Mem. ATLA, ABA (bus. and tax sects.), Fed. Bar Assn., Tex. Bar Assn., Ariz. Bar Assn., State Bar Ariz. (cert. tax specialist), Maricopa County Bar Assn., Ariz. Tax Controversy Group, Valley Estate Planners (Phoenix), Ctrl. Ariz. Estate Planners, Ariz. Soc. Boutiques. Office: 3101 N Central Ave Ste 510 Phoenix AZ 85012-2639

EVERETT, PAMELA IRENE, legal management company executive, educator; b. L.A., Dec. 31, 1947; d. Richard Weldon and Alta Irene (Tuttle) Bunnell; m. James E. Everett, Sept. 2, 1967 (div. 1973); 1 child, Richard Earl. Cert. Paralegal, Rancho Santago Coll., Santa Ana, Calif., 1977; BA, Calif. State U.-Long Beach, 1985; MA, U. Redlands, 1988. Owner, mgr. Orange County Paralegal Svc., Santa Ana, 1979-85; pres. Gem Legal Mgmt. Inc., Fullerton, Calif., 1986—; co-owner Bunnell Publs., Fullerton, Calif., 1992-96, The Millennium Network, 1997; instr. Rancho Santiago Coll., 1979—, chmn. adv. bd., 1980-85; instr. Fullerton Coll., 1989—, Rio Hondo Coll., Whittier, Calif., 1992-94; advisor Nat. Paralegal Assn., 1982—, Saddleback Coll., 1985—, North Orange County Regional Occupational Program, Fullerton, 1986—, Fullerton Coll. So. Calif. Coll. Bus. and Law; bd. dirs. Nat. Profl. Legal Assts. Inc., editor PLA News. Author: Legal Secretary Federal Litigation, 1986, Bankruptcy Courts and Procedure, 1987, Going Independent--Business Planning Guide, Fundamentals of Law Office Management, 1994. Republican. Office: 406 N Adams Ave Fullerton CA 92832-1605

EVERETTE, MABLE LOUISE, nutrition educator; b. Morrilton, Ark., Feb. 6, 1947; d. James Arthur and Mable (Brown) E. BS, Tuskegee U., 1969; MPH, U. Mich., 1971. Registered dietitian. Nutritionist City of Houston Health Dept., 1971-75, State of Calif. Health Dept., Sacramento, 1975-78; cons. sr. nutrition programs L.A., Orange and Ventura counties, 1978-91; dir. nutrition programs Charles Drew U., L.A., 1991—; mem. adv. bd. African-Am. nutrition programs Nat. Coun. Negro Women, 1991—. Editor: (video) Careers in Dietetics, 1991. Recipient Outstanding Svc. award Am. Dietetic Assn., 1988, Vol. Svc. award Eternal Promise Bapt. Ch., 1992, Continuing Svc. award Am. Heart Assn., 1991. Mem. Calif. Dietetic Assn. (chair, legis. com. 1993—, Legis. Contact award L.A. dist. 1990-91). Office: Charles Drew U MP # 22 1621 E 120th St Los Angeles CA 90059-3025

EVERHART, LEON EUGENE, retired air force officer; b. Abilene, Kans., Jan. 14, 1928; s. Charles Francis and Florence Etta (Amess) E. BS with distinction, Ariz. State U., 1957; postgrad., U. Tenn., 1965. Commd. 2d lt. USAF, 1952, advanced through grades to col., 1970, ops. officer Berlin Air Safety Ctr., 1961-63; project officer Missile Devel. Ctr. USAF, Holloman AFB, N.Mex., 1963-65, chief spl. projects div. Missile Devel. Ctr., 1965-66; tactical fighter pilot, flight commander USAF, South Vietnam, 1967-68; system program dir. Aero. Systems Div. USAF, Wright Patterson AFB, Ohio, 1968-72; dir. test engring. Devel. and Test Ctr. USAF, Eglin AFB, Fla., 1973-78; comdr. Air Force Western Test Range USAF, Vandenberg AFB, Calif., 1978-82; ret. USAF, 1982; cons. in field. Speaker on big-game hunting in Africa and wildlife conservation for various civic and ednl. orgns. Mem. Amateur Trapshooting Assn. Ohio, NRA. Home: 1285 Oak Knolls Rd Santa Maria CA 93455-4302

EVERHART, THOMAS EUGENE, academic administrator, engineering educator; b. Kansas City, Mo., Feb. 15, 1932; s. William Elliott and Elizabeth Ann (West) E.; m. Doris Arleen Wentz, June 21, 1953; children—Janet Sue, Nancy Jean, David William, John Thomas. A.B. in Physics magna cum laude, Harvard, 1953; M.Sc., UCLA, 1955; Ph.D. in Engring., Cambridge U., Eng., 1958. Mem. tech. staff Hughes Research Labs., Culver City, Calif., 1953-55; mem. faculty U. Calif., Berkeley, 1958-78, prof. elec. engring. and computer scis., 1967-78, Miller research prof., 1969-70, chmn. dept., 1972-77; prof. elec. engring., Joseph Silbert dean engring. Cornell U., Ithaca, N.Y., 1979-84; prof. elec. and computer engring., chancellor U. Ill., Urbana-Champaign, 1984-87; prof. elec. engring. and applied physics, pres. Calif. Inst. Tech., Pasadena, 1987—; fellow scientist Westinghouse Rsch. Labs., Pitts., 1962-63; guest prof. Inst. Applied Physics, U. Tuebingen, Germany, 1966-67, Waseda U., Tokyo, Osaka U., 1974; vis. fellow Clare Hall, Cambridge, U., 1975; chmn. Electron, Ion and Photon Beam Symposium, 1977; cons. in field; mem. sci. and ednl. adv. com. Lawrence Berkeley Lab., 1978-85, chmn., 1980-85; mem. sci. adv. com. GM, 1980-89, chmn., 1984-89, bd. dirs., 1989—; bd. dirs. Hewlett Packard Corp., Saint-Gobain Corp., Reveo, Inc.; tech. adv. com. R.R. Donnelly & Sons, 1981-89. Chmn. Sec. of Energy Adv. Bd., 1990-93; bd. dirs. KCET, 1989—, Corp. for Nat. Rsch. Initiatives, 1990—. NSF sr. fellow, 1966-67, Guggenheim fellow, 1974-75. Fellow IEEE, AAAS, ASEE, Royal Acad. Engring.; mem. NAE (ednl. adv. bd. 1984-88, mem. com. 1984-89, chmn. 1988, coun. 1988-94, 96—), Microbeam Analysis Soc. Am., Electron Microscopy Soc. Am. (coun. 1970-72, pres. 1977), Coun. on Competitiveness (vice-chmn. 1990-96), Assn. Marshall Scholars and Alumni (pres. 1965-68), Athenaeum Club, Sigma Xi, Eta Kappa Nu. Home: 415 S Hill Ave Pasadena CA 91106-3407 Office: Calif Inst Tech Office of Pres 1201 E California Blvd Pasadena CA 91125-0001

EVERINGHAM, HARRY TOWNER, editor, publisher; b. Memphis, Aug. 14, 1908; s. William Kirby and Ida Pauline (Towner) E.; m. Margaret Sophia Johnson; 3 children. Student, Northwestern U., Evanston, Ill., 1936-39, U. Chgo., 1940. Writer, dir. weekly radio drama WREC, Memphis; radio writer, producer Miles Lab., Chgo., Wade Advt. Agy., Chgo., 1934-35; v.p. Sehl Advt. Agy., Chgo., 1936-41; broadcasting Henry C. Lytton & Co., Chgo.; film producer, lectr. Employers Assn., Chgo., 1942; editor, pub. The Fact Finder, 1942—; pub. rels. dir. Ingalls-Shepard Div. Wyman Gordon Co., Harvey, Ill.; editor Forging Ahead Mag., 1942-46. Editor, pub. U.S.A.-Beyond the Crossroads, Chgo., The Am. Patriot, 1959-94; syndicated newspaper columnist, 1960-63. V.p. Greater Chgo. Churchmen, 1946-47; founder Pub. Club Chgo., 1942. Mem. Ariz. Breakfast Club (founder, pres.). Republican.

EVERS, LAWRENCE JOSEPH, English language educator; b. Grand Island, Nebr., Aug. 15, 1946; s. Lawrence C. and Lois (Schwenk) E.; m. Barbara Zion Grygutis, Dec. 20, 1982; children: Noah Zion, Elly. BA, U. Nebr., 1968, MA, 1969, PhD, 1972. Asst. prof. English U. Ariz., Tucson, 1974-80, assoc. prof., 1981-86, prof., 1987—, head dept., 1995—. Co-author: Yaqui Deer Songs, 1987; editor: The South Corner of Time, 1980, Home Places, 1995; producer (video series) Words and Place, 1979. Bd. dirs. El Presidio Hist. Dist. Adv. Bd., Tucson, 1986—. Recipient 1st prize Chgo. Folklore prize U. Chgo., 1988; U. Chgo. postdoctoral fellow, 1972-73. Mem. MLA, Assn. Study Am. Indian Lit. Office: U Ariz Dept English Tucson AZ 85721

EVERSLEY, FREDERICK JOHN, sculptor, engineer; b. Bklyn., Aug. 28, 1941; s. Frederick William and Beatrice Agnes (Syphax) E. B.S.E.E., Carnegie-Mellon U., 1963. One-man shows include Whitney Mus. Am. Art, N.Y.C., 1970, Nat. Acad. Sci., Washington, 1976, 81, L.A. Inst. Contemporary Art, 1976, Santa Barbara Mus., 1976, Newport Harbor Art Mus., 1976, Oakland Mus. Art, 1977, Palm Springs (Calif.) Desert Mus., 1978, AIA, 1981, Va. Mus., 1981, Bacardi Art Gallery, Miami, 1984, Laband Art Gallery, 1985, Loyola Marymount U., L.A., Hokin Gallery, Palm Beach, Fla., 1988, Juda Gallery, London, 1988, Eva Cohen Gallery, Chgo., 1991, Lorenzelli Arte, Milan, 1992, Pavilion of Saudi Arabia, Expo 92, Seville, Spain, 1992; represented in permanent collections Smithsonian Instn., Washington, IRS Nat. Hdqtrs., New Carrollton, Md., Calif. State Coll., L.A., Oakland (Calif.) Art Mus., Milw. Art Center, Whitney Mus. Am. Art, N.Y.C., John Marin Meml. Collection, N.Y.C., U., Kans. Art Gallery, Lawrence, Long Beach (Calif.) Mus. Art, Currier Gallery Art, Manchester, N.H., Taft Mus. Art, Cin., Cranbrook Art Gallery, Bloomfield Hills, Mich., Nat. Acad. Sci., Washington, Nat. Collection Fine Arts, Washington, MIT, Cambridge, Neuberger Mus. Art, Purchase, N.Y., Newport Harbor Art Mus., Newport Beach, Calif., Guggenheim Mus., N.Y.C., Smith Coll. Mus. Art, Northhampton, Mass., Nat. Air and Space Mus., Mus. Contemporary Art, L.A., Palm Springs Desert Mus., Rose Mus. of Art, Brandis U., Boston, Sammlung Goetz, Munich Germany, IRS hdqs., New Carrollton, Md., 1996; artist in residence Nat. Air and Space Mus., Washington, 1977-80. Nat. Endowment Arts grantee, 1972. Mem. L.A. Inst. Contemporary Art, Artworkers Coalition. Address: 1110 Abbot Kinney Blvd Venice CA 90291-3314

EVERSOLE, WALTER ROBERT, funeral director; b. Ukiah, Calif., May 25, 1923; s. Edward Anthony and Bess Lea (Gwartney) E.; m. Barbara Louise Ballou, Dec. 16, 1945; children: Ronald Edward, Richard Walter. BMS, San Francisco Coll. Mortuary, 1943. Lic. funeral dir., Calif. Funeral dir. Eversole Mortuary, Ukiah, 1946—; commd. flight officer USAF, 1944, advanced through grades to capt., 1958, ret., 1960; dir. Savs. Bank of Mendo County, Ukiah. Mem. Planning Commn. of Ukiah, 1954, Airport Commn., Ukiah, 1956. Recipient Silver Beaver award Boy Scouts Am., 1968, Outstanding Citizen award Ukiah C. of C., 1987. Mem. VFW, Am. Legion, Calif Funderal Dirs. Assn. (pres. 1947, 85), Redwood Empire Funeral Dirs. Assn., Masons, Elks (exalted ruler 1951), Rotary (pres. 1950-51), 20-30 Club (pres. 1946-48). Republican. Home: 180 Barbara St Ukiah CA 95482 Office: Eversole Mortuary 141 Low Gap Rd Ukiah CA 95482

EVRENSEL, ARTHUR, lawyer; b. July 2, 1958; m. Marissa Janantuono, May 14, 1995. BA with honors, McGill U., Montreal, 1981, B.C.L., LLB, 1985. Assoc. Heenan Blaikie, Montreal, 1986-91; ptnr. Heenan Blaikie, Vancouver, B.C., 1991—; lectr. faculty of mgmt. McGill U., Montreal, 1987-90; guest lectr. law U. B.C., Vancouver, 1991-92; mem. Vancouver Bd. of Trade Task Force on British Columbia Film and Entertainment Industry; apptd. B.C. Film Commns. Cmty Mktg. Group. Mem. Trade Forum adv. bd. Vancouver Internat. Film Festival, 1991; dir., founder Motion Picture Found. of B.C., 1992. Mem. Law Soc. B.C., Law Soc. Upper Can., Que. Bar Assn., British Columbia Motion Picture Assn. (co-chair govt. rels. com., bd. dirs.), Can. Bar Assn. (practice adv. panel for entertainment law).

EVRIGENIS, JOHN BASIL, obstetrician-gynecologist; b. Athens, Greece, Feb. 23, 1929; came to U.S., 1951; s. Basil I. and Maria (Soteriou) E.; m. Sophia M. Goritsan, June 22, 1952; children: Maryellen, E. Debbie, W. Gregory, John Jr. BA, U. Athens, 1947, MD, 1951. Diplomate Am. Bd. Ob-Gyn. Intern Providence Hosp., Portland, Oreg., 1951-52, resident in gen. practice medicine, 1952-53; resident in ob-gyn Emanuel Hosp. and U. Oreg. Med. Sch., Portland, 1953-56; pvt. practice specializing in ob-gyn Sacramento, 1956—; assoc. clin. prof. ob-gyn Med. Sch., U. Calif., Davis, 1975—; chief ob-gyn dept. Mercy Hosp., Sacramento, 1972-73. Mem. AMA, Am. Fertility Soc., Pan-Am. Med. Soc., Royal Soc. Medicine, Royal Soc. Health, Sacramento County Med. Soc., Calif. Med. Assn., So. Calif. Ob-Gyn. Assembly, Am. Soc. Gynecol. Laproscopists, Am. Soc. Abdominal Surgeons, No. Calif. Ob-Gyn. Soc. (pres. 1975-76), Dynamis Club, Ahepa, Del Paso Country Club, Northridge Country Club, Sutter Club, Sacramento Club, Lions, Elks, Masons, Rotary Club. Eastern Orthodox. Home: 3615 Winding Creek Rd Sacramento CA 95864-1530 Office: 3939 J St Ste 360 Sacramento CA 95819-3631

EWELL, A. BEN, JR., lawyer, businessman; b. Elyria, Ohio, Sept. 10, 1941; s. Austin Bert and Mary Rebecca (Thompson) E.; m. Suzanne E.; children: Austin Bert III, Brice Ballantyne. BA, Miami U., Oxford, Ohio, 1963; JD, Hasting Coll. Law, U. Calif.-San Francisco, 1966. Bar: Calif. 1966, U.S. Dist. Ct. (ea. dist.) Calif. 1967, U.S. Supreme Ct. 1982, U.S. Ct. Appeals (9th cir.) 1967. Pres. A. B. Ewell, Jr., A. Profl. Corp., Fresno, 1984—; formerly gen. counsel to various water dists. and assn.; gen. counsel, chmn. San Joaquin River Flood Control Assn., 1984-88; CEO Millerton New Town Devel. Co., 1988-94, chmn., 1994—; pres. Brighton Crest Country Club Inc., 1989—; mem. task force on prosecution, cts. and law reform Calif. Coun. Criminal Justice, 1971-74; mem. Fresno Bulldog Found., Calif. State U.; mem. San Joaquin Valley Agrl. Water commn., 1979-88; co-chmn. nat. adv. coun. SBA, 1981, 82, mem. 1981-87; bd. dirs. Fresno East Cmty. Ctr., 1971-73; mem. Fresno County Water Adv. Com., 1989, Fresno Cmty. Coun., 1972-73; chmn. various area polit. campaigns and orgns., including Reagan/Bush, 1984, Deukmejian for Gov., 1986; mem. adv. com. St. Agnes Med. Ctr. Found., 1983-89; trustee U. Calif. Med. Edn. Found., 1989-90, Fresno Met. Mus. Art, History and Sci., active, 1989—, mem. adv. coun., 1993—; bd. dirs. Citizens for Cmty. Enrichment, Fresno, 1990—, Police Activities League, 1995—; past mem. Hist. Preservation Commn., City of Fresno. Mem. Phi Alpha Delta, Sigma Nu. Congregationalist. Office: 516 W Shaw Ave Ste 200 Fresno CA 93704-2515

EWELL, MIRANDA JUAN, journalist; b. Beijing, Apr. 25, 1948; d. Vei-Chow and Hsien-fang Yolanda (Sun) J.; m. John Woodruff Ewell Jr., Feb. 20, 1971; children: Emily, David, Jonah. BA summa cum laude, Smith Coll., 1969; postgrad., Princeton U., 1971, U. Calif., Berkeley, 1981-82. Staff writer The Montclarion, Oakland, Calif., 1982-83; with San Jose (Calif.) Mercury News, 1984—, staff writer; now correspondent San Jose (Calif.) Mercury News, San Francisco Bureau, 1990-95; correspondent in bus. San Jose Mercury News, 1997—. Recipient Elsa Knight Thompson award Media Alliance, San Francisco, 1984, George Polk award L.I. U., N.Y., 1989, Heywood Brown award Newspaper Guild, Washington, 1989; Knight fellow Stanford U., 1995. Mem. Asian-Am. Journalists Assn.

EWELL, P. LAMONT, fire department chief. Fire chief Oakland (Calif.) Fire Dept., 1996; asst. to city mgr. City Mgr. Office, Oakland, 1996—. Office: City Mgrs Office 1 City Hall Plaza Oakland CA 94612*

EWING, DENNIS D., county clerk, realtor; b. Murray, Utah, Mar. 17, 1941; s. Deane James and Margaret (Rigby) E.; m. Zelda Marie Schorzman, Jan. 25, 1963 (div. Jan. 1988); children: Dennis Deane, Denise Marie, Deborah Ann, DeDee Kae; m. Carma Burr, Sept. 23, 1989; stepchildren: R. Brad Shafter, Sandy Shafter, Carolyn Andreasen, Marcy Andreasen, Wendy Andreasen. Student, Yuba State Coll., 1962, Weber State Coll., 1971-73. Cert. pub. ofcl. Patrolman Tooele (Utah) City Police Dept., 1966-68; dep. sheriff Tooele County Sheriff Dept., 1968-73; county clk. Tooele County Corp., 1973—; co-host summer workshops; mem. tech. publs. com. Nat. Assn. Govt. Archives and Records Adminstrs., 1990-91. Past mem. adv. bd. KUED-TV and KUER-FM Radio; mem. Tooele Vol. Fire Dept., 1970—, past fire insp.; neighborhood chair Easter Seals Fund Raiser. Served with USAF, 1961-65. Mem. Utah Assn. Counties (pres. 1992-94, intergovtl. rels. steering com., legis. com., rep. to state retirement adv. coun., rep. to Salt Lake City Olympic bid com. bd. trustees, bd. dirs. Ins. Mut., bd. dirs., chmn. by-laws com. 1993), Nat. Assn. Counties (bd. dirs. 1991-92), Nat. Assn. County Recorders and Clks. (resolutions and budget coms., pres. 1990-91, past chair elections com., chair com. future, past parliamentarian, bd. dirs.), Utah Assn. County Clks. and Auditors (past pres.), Eagles. Democrat. Mem. LDS Ch. Home: 620 Kingston Dr Tooele UT 84074-2833 Office: Tooele County Corp 47 S Main St Tooele UT 84074-2131

EWING, EDGAR LOUIS, artist, educator; b. Hartington, Nebr., Jan. 17, 1913; s. David E. and Laura (Buckendorf) E.; m. Suzanna Peter Giovan, Feb. 12, 1941. Grad., Art Inst. Chgo., 1935; studied, in France, Eng., Italy, 1935-37. Mem. faculty Art Inst. Chgo., 1937-43, U. Mich., Ann Arbor, 1946; asst. prof. fine arts U. So. Calif., 1946-54, assoc. prof., 1954-59, prof., 1959-78, Disting. prof. emeritus, 1978—; Mellon prof. Carnegie-Mellon U., Pitts., 1968-69. One-man shows M.H. DeYoung Meml. Mus. Art, San Francisco, 1948,, Long Beach Mus. Art, 1955, Dalzell Hatfield Galleries, Los Angeles, 1954, 56, 58, 61, 63, 65, Hewlett Gallery-Carnegie Mellon U., Pitts., 1969, Nat. Gallery, Athens, Greece, 1973, Los Angeles Mcpl. Art Gallery, 1974, Palm Springs (Calif.) Desert Mus., 1976-77, Fisher Gallery U. So. Calif., 1978; group exhbns. Cin Art Mus., Corcoran Gallery Art, Washington, Denver Art Mus., Dallas Mus. Fine Arts, Fort Worth Art Ctr., Met. Mus., N.Y.C.; represented: San Francisco Mus. Art, Dallas Mus. Fine Arts, Ft. Worth Art Ctr., Met. Mus., N.Y.C., Sao Paulo (Brazil) Mus. Art, Wichita Art Mus., Fisher Gallery, U. So. Calif., 1994. Served with C.E., U.S. Army, 1943-46, PTO. Recipient Aberle Florscheim Meml. prize for Oil Painting, Art Inst. Chgo., 1943, Purchase award for oil painting Los Angeles County Mus. Art, 1952, Samuel Goldwyn award, 1957, Ahmanson Purchase award City of Los Angeles Exhbn., 1962, Disting. Prof. Emeritus award U. So. Calif., 1987; Edward L. Ryerson fellow, 1935; Louis Comfort Tiffany grantee, 1948-49, Jose Drudis Fund grantee, Greece, 1967; named one of 100 Artists-100 Yrs., Art Inst. Chgo., 1980. Mem. AAUP, Nat. Watercolor Soc. (v.p. 1952, pres. 1953). Democrat. Home: 4226 Sea View Ln Los Angeles CA 90065-3350

EWING, JACK ROBERT, accountant; b. San Francisco, Feb. 14, 1947; s. Robert Maxwell and Blanche Julia (Diak) E.; m. Joan Marie Coughlin Ewing, Nov. 25, 1967; children: Theresa Marie Ewing, Christina Ann Ewing. BS, U. Mo., 1969. CPA. Staff acct. Fox & Co., St. Louis, 1969-70; radio station opr. USAF, Mountain Home, Idaho, 1970-72; internal auditor Air Force Audit Agy., Warren, Wyo., 1972-74; supr. auditor Fox & Co., St. Louis, 1974-79; audit mgr. Erickson, Hunt & Spillman, P.C., Ft. Collins, Colo., 1979-82; stockholder, owner Hunt, Spillman & Ewing, P.C., Ft. Collins, Colo., 1982-93; owner Jack R. Ewing, CPA, 1993—. Mem., pres. Parent Adv. Bd., Beattie Elem. Sch., 1982-83, 86-87; mem. Entrepreneur of Yr. Selection Com., Ft. Collins, Colo., 1989-92, Suicide Resource Ctr. of Larimer County, Ft. Collins, Colo., 1992—, bd. dirs.; mem. Leadership Ft. Collins-Class of 1992, State of Colo. Mental Health Planning Coun., 1993—; dir. treas. One West Contemporary Art Ctr., 1989—, Ctr. for Diversity in Work Place, 1991—; pres., adv. bd. Larimer County Mental Health Ctr., 1992—; v.p. Colo. Behavioral Healthcare Coun. Mem. Am. Inst. CPAs, Colo. Soc. CPAs. Office: 3112 Meadowlark Ave Fort Collins CO 80526-2843

EXLIN, GLORIA, mayor. Mayor City of Vallejo, Calif. Office: City of Vallejo 555 Santa Clara St Vallejo CA 94590

EXNER, ADAM, archbishop; b. Killaly, Sask., Can., Dec. 24, 1928. Ordained priest Roman Catholic Ch., 1957, consecrated bishop, 1974. Bishop of Kamloops B.C., Can., 1974-82; archbishop of Winnipeg Man., Can., 1982-91; archbishop of Vancouver B.C., Can., 1991—. Office: Archdiocese of Vancouver, 150 Robson St, Vancouver, BC Canada V6B 2A7*

EXTON, INEZ PAULINE, writer, apparel designer; b. Vienna, Austria, July 2, 1905; came to U.S., 1938; d. Josef and Francisca (Jung) Kraus; m. Ernst Lakenbacher (dec.); m. Harry Exton, Apr. 20, 1940 (dec. 1966). Student, Wiener Werkstatte, Austria, 1923-26. Fashion journalist Wiener Allgemeine, Vienna, Austria, 1931-34, Moderne Welt, Vienna, Austria, 1932-34; owner, haute couture salon Inez, Vienna, Austria, 1935-38; owner, designer, haute couture salon Inez, N.Y.C., 1939-73. Designed haute couture for Mrs Winthrop Rockefeller, Mrs. David Rockefeller, Rene Dupont, Ingrid Bergmann and Eartha Kitt; Author: Alphabet for Positive Living, 1987, Children of Nowhere, 1991. Founder Foundation for Visually Handicapped Writers. Democrat.

EZAKI-YAMAGUCHI, JOYCE YAYOI, renal dietitian; b. Kingsburg, Calif., Mar. 18, 1947; d. Toshikatsu and Aiko (Ogata) Ezaki; m. Kent Takao Yamaguchi, Oct. 28, 1972; children: Kent Takao, Jr., Toshia Ann. AA, Reedley Coll., 1967; BS in Foods and Nutrition, U. Calif., Davis, 1969. Dietetic intern Henry Ford Hosp., Detroit, 1969-70, staff dietitian, 1970-71; renal dietitian Sutter Meml. Hosp., Sacramento, 1971-72; therapeutic dietitian Mt. Sinai Hosp., Beverly Hills, Calif., 1972-73; clin. dietitian Pacific Hosp., Long Beach, Calif., 1973-77; consulting dietitian Doctor's Hosp., Lakewood, Calif., 1976-77; clin. dietitian Mass. Gen. Hosp., Boston, 1977-78, Winona Meml. Hosp., Indpls., 1978-80; renal dietitian Fresno (Calif.) Community Hosp., 1980—. Author: (computer program) Dialysis Tracker, 1987; author: (with others) Cultural Foods and Renal Diets for the Dietitian, 1988, Standards of Practice Guidlines for the Practice of Clinical Dietetics, 1991. Mem. Nat. Kidney Found. (exec. com. coun. renal nutrition 1992—, region V rep. 1992-93, chair elect 1994-95, chair 1995-96, immediate past chair 1996—, Disting. Svc. award 1996), Am. Dietetic Assn. (bd. cert. renal nutrition specialist, renal practice group 1993—), No. Calif/No. Nev. chpt. Nat. Kidney Found. (disting. achievement award coun. on renal nutrition 1993, co-chair-elect 1993-94, co-chair 1994-95, co-past chair 1995-96, treas., corr. sec.). Buddhist. Office: Cmty Hosps Ctrl Calif Fresno & R Sts Fresno CA 93715-2094

EZRA, DAVID A., federal judge; b. 1947. BBA magna cum laude, St. Mary's U., 1969, JD, 1972. Law clk. Office of Corp. Counsel City and County Honolulu, 1972; mem. firm Greenstein, Cowen & Frey, 1972-73, Anthony, Hoddick, Reinwald & O'Connor, 1973-80, Ezra, O'Connor, Moon & Tam, 1980-88; dist. judge U.S. Dist. Ct., Hawaii, 1988—; adj. prof. law Wm. S. Richardson Sch. Law, 1978—. Co-editor, author: Hwaii Construction Law - What to Do and When, 1987; editor: Hawaii Collection Practices Manual. 1st lt. USAR 1971-77. Daugherty Fund scholar, 1971, San Antonio Bar Assn. Aux. scholar, 1972. Mem. ABA, Hawaii State Bar, Am. Arbitration Assn., Delta Epsilon Sigma, Phi Delta Phi. Office: US Dist Ct PO Box 50128 Honolulu HI 96850*

FABE, DANA ANDERSON, judge; b. Cin., Mar. 29, 1951; d. George and Mary Lawrence (Van Antwerp) F.; m. Randall Gene Simpson, Jan. 1, 1983; 1 child, Amelia Fabe Simpson. B.A., Cornell U., 1973; J.D., Northeastern U., 1976. Bar: Alaska 1977, U.S. Supreme Ct. 1981. Law clk. to justice Alaska Supreme Ct., 1976-77; staff atty. pub. defenders State of Alaska, 1977-81; dir. Alaska Pub. Defender Agy., Anchorage, from 1981; now judge Superior Ct., Anchorage . Named Alumna of Yr., Northeastern Sch. Law, 1983. Mem. Alaska Bar Assn., Anchorage Assn. Women Attys. Office: Pub Defender 900 W 5th Ave Ste 200 Anchorage AK 99501-2029

FABER, PHYLLIS MAVIS, biologist, consultant; b. Pitts., Oct. 31, 1927; d. Paul Mitchell and Sandra Kydd; m. Edward T. Faber, Jan. 3, 1953; children: E. Mitchell, Charles Donaldson, Carolyn Lindsay. BA, Mt. Holyoke Coll., 1949; MA, Calif. State U., San Francisco, 1968; postgrad., Yale U., 1967-69. Cert. tchr., Calif. Research assoc. Rockefeller U., N.Y.C., 1949-53, Yale U., New Haven, 1967-68; instr. Coll. Marin, Kentfield, Calif., 1972-82; ptnr. Madrone Assocs., San Rafael, Calif., 1971-76; editor Fremontia Calif. Native Plant Soc., Mill Valley, 1983—; cons., Mill Valley, 1976—. Author: Common Wetland Plants, 1982, (AEP award 1983), Riparian Habitat of Southern Calif., 1986, Common Riparian Plants of California, 1989; contbr. articles to profl. jours. Commr. Calif. Coastal Commn., San Francisco, 1973-80; bd. dirs. Marin Agrl. Land Trust, Point Reyes Sta., Calif., 1980—, founder. Recipient Outstanding Environ. Document award Assn. Environ. Profls., 1982, Coastal and Ocean Mgmt. award ASCE, 1983, Marin Green award Marin Conservation League, 1990; named Enviromentalist of Yr. Marin Environ. Alliance, 1990; nawmed to Marin County Women's Hall of Fame, 1995. Mem. Assn. Wetland Scientists, Marin Discoveries (chmn. bd. dirs. 1985-89), Calif. Native Plant Soc. (v.p. publs. 1990—). Home and Office: 212 Del Casa Dr Mill Valley CA 94941-1308

FACELLI, JULIO CESAR, physics researcher, university administrator; b. Buenos Aires, Feb. 9, 1953; came to U.S., 1983; s. Julio César and Elva Nelida (Morato) F.; m. Ana Maria Elena Ferreyro, Oct. 18, 1980; children: Julie Anna, Maria Elizabeth. Licenciado in Physics, U. Buenos Aires, 1977, PhD, 1981. Undergrad. asst. dept. physics U. Buenos Aires, 1976, grad. asst. dept. physics, 1977-82; dir. Instituto de Fisica de la Atmósfera Servicio Meteorologico Nacional, Buenos Aires, 1979; rsch. assoc. dept. chemistry U. Ariz., Tucson, 1983; rsch. assoc. dept. chemistry U. Utah, Salt Lake City, 1984-86, rsch. asst. prof. dept. chemistry, 1986-90, assoc. dir. acad. supercomputing Utah Supercomputing Inst., 1989-95, acting dir. Utah Supercomputing Inst., 1992-95, dir. Ctr. for High Performance Computing, 1995—, adj. prof. chemistry, 1996—; assoc. prof. ad honorem dept. physics, U. Buenos Aires, 1987—, vis. prof., 1992; adj. assoc. prof. dept. chemistry, U. Utah, Salt Lake City, 1990-96; reviewer Jour. Am. Chem. Soc., Jour. Phys. Chemistry, Chem. Revs., Jour. Computational Chemistry, Theoretica Chimica Acta, Magnetic Resonance in Chemistry (mem. editl. bd. Computer Applications in Engring. Edn.); invited spkr. various univs., rsch. ctrs. and confs.; steering com. Supercomputing by Univ. People for Edn. and Rsch., 1989-92, chmn., 1990-91; insts. and confs. adv. bd. U. Utah, 1991—; smart node adv. bd. Cornell Nat. Supercomputing Facility, 1991—, steering com. SUP'EUR European user's group, 1990-91; libr. and data comm. com., Utah Edn. Network, 1993—. Contbr. numerous articles in sci. jours. 1st lt. Argentinian Air Force, 1978-80. Mem. Am. Chem. Soc., IEEE (Computer Soc.). Roman Catholic. Home: 1847 S 2600 E Salt Lake City UT 84108-3369 Office: Ctr for High Performance Computing Univ Utah 85 SSB Salt Lake City UT 84112

FADELEY, EDWARD NORMAN, state supreme court justice; b. Williamsville, Mo., Dec. 13, 1929; m. Nancie Peacocke, June 11, 1953; children: Charles, Shira; m. Darian Cyr, Sept. 12, 1992. A.B., U. Mo., 1951; J.D. cum laude, U. Oreg., 1957. Bar: Oreg. 1957, U.S. Supreme Ct. 1968. Practice law Eugene, Oreg., 1957-88; mem. Oreg. Ho. of Reps., 1961-63; mem. Oreg. Senate, 1963-87, pres., 1983-85; justice Oregon Supreme Ct., 1989—; mem. jud. working group Internat. Water Tribunal, Amsterdam, The Netherlands; invitee Rio Environ. Conf., 1992, Indigenous Peoples of World Conf., New Zealand, 1993; adj. prof. law U. Oreg. Chmn. Oreg. Dem. party, 1966-68; chmn. law and justice com. Nat. Conf. Legislators, 1977-78; adv. com. to State and Local Law Ctr., Washington; participants com. Washington Pub. Power Supply System, 1984-88; candidate for nomination for gov., 1986; bd. dirs. Wayne Morse Hist. Park. Lt. USNR, 1951-54. Recipient First Pioneer award U. Oreg., 1980, Assn. Oreg. Counties award for leadership in the reform of state ct. system, 1982. Mem. ABA (internat. law, pub. utility law, jud. adminstrn., bus. law), Oreg. State Bar Assn. (chmn. uniform laws com. 1962-64), Order of Coif, Alpha Pi Zeta, Phi Alpha Delta. Democrat. Methodist. Office: Oreg Supreme Ct Supreme Ct Bldg Salem OR 97310

FAGAN, FREDERIC, neurosurgeon; b. Bklyn., Oct. 18, 1935; s. Jack and Sophie (Altschuler) F.;m. Donna Fagan, Mar. 1, 1969; children: Gabrielle, Samantha. BA, Ohio State U., 1958. Intern Santa Monica (Calif.) Hosp., N.Y.C., 1959; resident N.Y. Hosp., N.Y.C., Calif., 1960; cons. AMA, L.A., 1980—. Dir. Smithsonian Assocs., Washington, 1995, U.s. Holocaust Meml. Mus., Washington, 1995. Named Surgeon of Yr. MacMillan Industries, Santa Clara, Calif., 1989. Mem. N.Y. Acad. Scis., NRA (dir. 1995). Home: 10488 Santa Clara St Cypress CA 90630-4232 Office: Woodruff Hosp 3800 Woodruff Ave Long Beach CA 90808-2125

FAGERBERG, DIXON, JR., retired accountant, weather observer; b. Prescott, Ariz., Mar. 20, 1909; s. Dixon and Amy (Nelson) F.; m. Mary Jergens, June 21, 1933 (div. Aug. 1980); children: Dick, Mary, Nelson; m. Lorraine Brenn, Sept. 22, 1980. AB in Econs. summa cum laude, Stanford U., 1931. CPA, Ariz. Valuation engr. Calif. R.R. Commn., San Francisco, 1931-32; acct. Harmon Audit Co., Prescott, 1933-34; owner, mgr. Dixon Fagerberg, Jr., CPA, Flagstaff, Kingman, Phoenix, Ariz., 1935-57; ptnr.-in-charge Peat, Marwick, Mitchell & Co., Phoenix, 1957-71; ret., 1971; vol. cons. Internat. Exec. Svc. Corps, Guatemala City, Guatemala, 1975. Co-author: 108 Sedona Westerner Trail Walks, 1979; author: Boyhood Recollections of Prescott, Arizona, 1983, Dix's Almanac of Weather and Climate, 1989; columnist Practitioner's Forum, 1954-56. Bd. dirs. Phoenix Libr., 1960-65; mem. Coconino County Planning and Zoning Commn., Flagstaff, 1973-76; councilman City of Sedona, 1988. Lt. USNR, 1944-46. Recipient medal of merit U. Ariz., 1960, Outstanding CPA award Mountain States Acctg. Conf., 1966. Mem. AICPA (nat. v.p. 1955-56), Ariz. Soc. CPA's (pres. 1938-39, columnist The Oasis 1972—), Am. Soc. Mining Engrs., Assn. Am. Weather Observers, Sedona Westerners (trail boss 1973-74), Pinewood Country Club, Masons.

FAHEY-CAMERON, ROBIN, artist, photographer; b. Bangor, Maine, Mar. 7, 1943; d. Oswald R. and Georgina Marie (Barbin) Fahey; m. Gordon W. vogel, June 27, 1966 (dec. 1973); 1 child, Darren Taggert. BA in Studio Art, U. Minn., 1968; student, LaJolla Acad. Advt. Arts, Calif., 1984. Tech. dir. The Peppermint Tent, Mpls., 1968; costume designer St. Joseph (Minn.) Coll., 1968-69; copywriter, graphic artist Western Word and Picture Co., Sausalito, Calif., 1984-86; creative dir. 20/20 Catalogue, San Francisco, 1986-89. Author: The Inner Door, 1996, Games of Deception, 1989; recent one-woman exhibits include Images of the Land, photography exhbiit, Alpine, Calif., 1988, The Ancient Land (photography exhibit), Alpine, 1989; represented in group exhibitions Fine Crafts Invitational, Durango, 1991, Photography Invitational, Durango, Colo., 1991, Artists' Invitational, Durango, 1991, Dorango Arts Ctr., 1992, 94, Drawing and Sculpture Show, Durango, 1992, Exhibit Com. Show, Durango, 1993, Heartland, the Art Room, Durango, 1994, Gallery Walk Exhibit, Landscapes, the Art Room, Durango, 1995, Points of View, Four Woman Show, Durango, 1995; mem. exhbn. com. Durango Arts Ctr., 1990-93. Mem. Exhbn. com. Durango (Colo.) Arts Ctr., 1990-93. Mem. Quill and Scroll. Democrat.

FAHL, CHARLES BYRON, college dean; b. Warsaw, N.Y., Dec. 16, 1939; s. James C. and Dorothy S. (Jarchow) F.; m. Patricia A. Killbear, Aug. 1, 1966 (dec. Oct. 1994); children: James H., Charles B. II. BS, Antioch Coll., Yellow Springs, Ohio, 1963; MS, U. Alaska, 1969, PhD, 1973. Meteorologist Dames & Moore Cons., Anchorage, 1973-80; dir. air quality svcs. Ertec NW Cons., Seattle, 1980-81; v.p. Variance Corp., Anchorage, 1981-82; faculty mem. Alaska Pacific U., Anchorage, 1982-94, dean faculty, acad. dean, 1994—. Mem. Am. Meteorol. Soc., Coun. Ind. Colls. Acad. Dean Assn.. Democrat. Episcopalian. Office: Alaska Pacific U 4101 University Dr Anchorage AK 99508-4625

FAIN, GORDON LEE, physiology educator; b. Washington, Nov. 24, 1946; s. Robert Forbes and Margaret (Smith) F.; m. Margery Jones, June 22, 1968; 2 children. Student, U. Chgo., 1964-65; BA in Biology, Stanford U., 1968; PhD in Biophysics, Johns Hopkins U., 1973. NIH predoctoral fellow Johns Hopkins U., Balt., 1968-73; NIH postdoctoral fellow Biol. Labs. Harvard U., Cambridge, Mass., 1973-74; Grass fellow Marine Biol. Labs., Woods Hole, Mass., 1974; exchange fellow Harvard U. Med. Sch. and Inst. Nat. de la Sante et de la Recherche Med., Lab. de Neurobiologie, Paris, 1974-75; asst. prof. ophthalmology UCLA Sch. Medicine, Jules Stein Eye Inst., 1975-78, assoc. prof., 1978-82, prof. ophthalmology, 1982-94, assoc. dir., 1985-94, prof. physiol. sci., 1991—, vice chmn. dept., 1991-94; spkr. in field. Contbr. numerous articles to profl. jours. Recipient NIH Merit award, 1989—, Guggenheim Fellowship award, 1997-98; NIH grantee, 1980-85, 84-88, 85—, 88—, NSF travel grantee, 1985-87. Mem. Assn. for Rsch. in Vision and Ophthalmology, Biophys. Soc., Soc. Neurosci., Am. Physiological Soc., English Physiological Soc. (fgn. mem.), Phi Beta Kappa. Office: UCLA Physiol Sci Dept Life Scis Bldg 3836 Los Angeles CA 90095-1527

FAIN, KAREN KELLOGG, retired history and geography educator; b. Pueblo, Colo., Oct. 10, 1940; d. Howard Davis and Mary Lucille (Cole) Kellogg; m. Sept. 1, 1961; divorced; 1 child, Kristopher. *Son Kristopher Kellogg Fain earned a BA Magna Cum Laude in International Relations from Brown University, in 1986, and he received an MIM from American Graduate School of International Management (Thunderbird), in 1993. He is currently employed by Tetra Pak, a Swedish corporation that handles 75% of the global market of liquid food packaging (juice, milk, etc.). He is based in Chicago. In 1984, he married Lena Pettersson of Stockholm, after spending his junior year at the Stockholm International Graduate School. They have 3 bilingual sons: Magnus, 6; Erik, 2, and Nils, 5 months. They live in Naperville, Illinois, where Magnus plays ice hockey and Kris is his part-time soccer coach.* Student, U. Ariz., 1958-61; BA, U. So. Colo., 1967; MA, U. No. Colo., 1977; postgrad., U. Denver, 1968, 72-93, Colo. State U., 1975, 91, Chadron State Coll., 1975, U. No. Ill., 1977, 83, Ft. Hayes State Coll., 1979, U. Colo., 1979, 86-87, 92, Ind. U., 1988. Cert. secondary tchr., Colo. Tchr. history and geography Denver Pub. Schs., 1967-96; tchr. West H.S., Denver, 1992-96; area adminstr., tchr. coord. Close Up program, Washington, 1982-84; reviewer, cons. for book Geography, Our Changing World, 1990. Vol., chmn. young profls. Inst. Internat. Edn. and World Affairs Coun., Denver, 1980—; mem. state selection com. U.S. Senate and Japan Scholarship Com., Denver, 1981-89, Youth for Understanding, Denver; mem. Denver Art Mus., 1970—; vol. Denver Mus. Natural History, 1989—, Am. Cancer Soc. "Jail and Bail", 1996, "Climb the Mountain", 1996, Denver Conv. Bur., 1997; bd. overseas Dept. Def. Dependents Sch., Guantanamo Bay, Cuba, 1990-91; screening panelist Tchr. to Japan Program Rocky Mtn. Regional Fulbright Meml. Fund, 1997. Fulbright scholar Chadron State Coll., Pakistan, 1975; Geog. Soc. grantee U. Colo., 1986; recipient award for Project Prince, Colo. U./Denver Pub. Schs./Denver Police Dept., 1992. Mem. AAUW, Colo. Coun. Social Studies (sec. 1984-86), Nat. Coun. Social Studies (del. 1984), World History Assn., Fulbright Assn., Am. Forum for Global Edn., Rocky Mountain Regional World History Assn. (steering com. 1984-87), Colo. Geographic Alliance (steering com. 1986), Gamma Phi Beta, Kappa Kappa Iota. Democrat. Episcopalian. Home: 12643 E Bates Cir Aurora CO 80014-3315

FAIR, ANNIE MAY, geological computer specialist; b. Coolidge, Ariz., Sept. 21, 1939; d. Jack C. and Birdie Geneva (Strickland) Cullins; m. Charles Leroy Fair, Sept. 12, 1964; children: Rex Lee Myers, Kathleen Ann, Rebecca Elizabeth. Student, Wichita State U., 1979-81, U. Colo., 1982-84, 94—, Met. State U., Denver, 1983-84. Cert. geol. engr. Pres., bd. dirs. Fresnal Minerals, Inc., Tucson, 1975-80; geol. technician Foxfire Exploration, Inc., Wichita, Kans., 1980-81, Coastal Oil & Gas Corp., Denver, 1981-93; stat. analyst fluid minerals Bur. Land Mgmt., Canon City, Colo., 1993—; applications adminstr. Colo. State U.; geol. cons. C.L. Fair & Assocs., Littleton, Colo., 1984-93. Active adv. bd. Masonic-Rainbow Girls-Grand Cross of Color, Denver, 1983-84; vol.- helper United Way Campaign, Denver, 1990, 91; vol. Am. Cancer Soc., Littleton, 1991, 92; art judge Reflections Nat. Art Contest, Denver, 1992, 93, Skyline Elem. Sch., Canon City, 1993. Recipient Grand Cross of Color, Masons-Order Rainbow/Girls, 1957; Music scholar U. No. Ariz., 1957. Mem. Am. Assn. Petroleum Geologists, Geol. Soc. Am., Rocky Mountain Assn. Geologists, Computer Oriented Geol. Soc., Alpha Lambda Delta. Home: 2853 Melvina Canon City CO 81212

FAIR, MARCIA JEANNE HIXSON, retired educational administrator; b. Scobey, Mont.; d. Edward Goodell and Olga Marie (Fredrickson) Hixson; m. Donald Harry Mahaffey (div. Aug. 1976); 1 child, Marcia Anne (dec.); m. George Justin Fair, Mar. 26, 1997. BA in English, U. Wash.; MA in Secondary Edn., U. Hawaii, 1967. Cert. secondary and elem. tchr. and adminstr. Tchr. San Lorenzo (Calif.) Sch. Dist., 1958-59; tchr. Castro Valley (Calif.) Sch. Dist., 1959-63, vice prin., 1963-67; vice prin. Sequoia Union High Sch. Dist., Redwood City, Calif., 1967-77, asst. prin., 1977-91, ret., 1991; tchr. trainer Project Impact Sequoia Union Sch. Dist., Redwood City, 1986-91; mem. supr.'s task force for dropout prevention, 1987-91, Sequoia Dist. Goals Commn. (chair subcom. staff devel. 1988); mentor tchr. selection com., 1987-91; mem. Stanford Program Devel. Ctr. Com., 1987-91; chairperson gifted and talented Castro Valley Sch. Dist.; mem. family svcs. bd., San Leandro, Calif. Vol. Am. Cancer Soc., San Mateo, Calif., 1967, Castro Valley, 1965; Sunday sch. tchr. Hope Luth. Ch., San Mateo, 1970-76; chair Carlmont H.S. Site Coun., Belmont, Calif., 1977-91; mem. Nat. Trust for Hist. Preservation. Recipient Life Mem. award Parent, Tchr., Student Assn., Belmont, 1984, Svc. award, 1989, Exemplary Svc award Carlmont High Sch., 1989; named Woman of the Week, Castro Valley, 1967, Outstanding Task Force Chair Adopt A Sch. Program San Mateo (Calif.) County, 1990. Mem. ASCD, AAUW, DAR, Assn. Calif. Sch. Adminstrs. (Project Leadership plaque 1985), Sequoia Dist. Mgmt.Assn. (pres. 1975, treas. 1984-85), Met. Mus. Art, Smithsonian Instn., Libr. of Congress Assocs. (charter), Am. Heritage - The Soc. of Am. Historians, Internat. Platform Assn., Animal Welfare Advocacy, Woodrow Wilson Internat. Ctr. Scholars, Nat. Geographic Soc., Am. Mus. Natural History (charter mem.), Bridle Trails Cmty. Club, Delta Kappa Gamma, Alpha Xi Delta (Order of Rose award). *Personal philosophy: Life is short, so make haste to be kind to one another.*

FAIR, RODNEY DALE, optometrist; b. San Antonio, Apr. 12, 1956; s. Ron G. and Patricia Ann (Shenkle) F.; m. Ella Monica Leyba, Sept. 19, 1992; 1 child, Katrina Noel. BA in Biology, Hastings Coll., 1978; BS in Visual Sci., So. Calif. Coll. Optometry, 1982, OD, 1982. Resident in pediatric eye care SUNY, N.Y.C., 1983; pvt. practice optometry Brighton (Colo.) Vision Clinic, 1983—; adj. clin. prof. optometry U. Houston, 1986-87; bd. dirs. Colo. Optometric Ctr., Denver, 1987-93; bd. dirs. Platte Valley Med. Ctr. Found., 1988—; lectr. in field. Contbr. articles to profl. publs. Precinct capt., state conv. del., 1988—; vol. Denver Rescue Mission, 1988—; bd. fine arts at cultural arts orgns., Brighton, 1991-93. Fellow Am. Acad. Optometry; mem. Am. Optometric Assn. (Optometric Continuing Edn. Recognition award 1988—), Colo. Optometric Assn. (med. adv. coun. 1992—, dist. rep. bd. trustees 1990-92, pres. 1994-95, chmn. legis. com. 1994—, Young Optometrist of Yr. 1987, Colo. Optometrist of Yr. 1995, Disting. Svc. award 1996), Brighton C. of C. (bd. dirs. 1985-87, treas. 1988), Hastings Coll. Alumni Assn. (sec. treas. Denver chpt. 1989-90), Kiwanis (pres. Brighton club 1985-86, Disting. Svc. award 1990), Toastmasters Club. Republican. Presbyterian. Home: 238 S 21st Ave Brighton CO 80601-2524 Office: Brighton Vision Clinic 105 Bridge St Brighton CO 80601

FAIRBANK, JANE DAVENPORT, editor, civic worker; b. Seattle, Aug. 21, 1918; d. Harold Edwin and Mildred (Foster) Davenport; AB magna cum laude, Whitman Coll., 1939; postgrad. U. Wash., 1940-42; m. William Martin Fairbank, Aug. 16, 1941; children: William Martin, Robert Harold, Richard Dana. Sci. staff mem. Radiation Lab., Mass. Inst. Tech., Cambridge, 1942-45. Chmn. Second Careers for Women, Stanford, Calif., 1970-75; chmn. annual continuing edn. program Whitman Coll. Sr. Alumni Coll., 1986-96; founding mem. Bay Area Consortium on Ednl. Needs of Women. 1971; mem. Canada Coll. Citizens Adv. Com. for Community Edn., 1968; mem. organizing com. for conf. on frontiers of physics Stanford U., 1982. Fellow U. Wash., 1940-42. Mem. Whitman Coll. Alumni Assn. (bd. dirs. 1986-96), Calif. Congress Parents and Tchrs. (hon. life), Mortar Bd., Phi Beta Kappa. Alpha Chi Omega. Mem. United Ch. of Christ. Mem. Stanford Faculty Women's (pres. 1975-76). Editor: Radar Maintenance Manual (2 vols.), 1945; co-editor Near Zero: New Frontiers of Physics, 1988; Second Careers for Women: A View from the San Francisco Peninsula, 1971; Second Careers for Women, vol. II: A View of Seven Fields from the San Francisco Bay Area, 1975. Office: 141 E Floresta Way Menlo Park CA 94028-7530

FAIRBANKS, MARY KATHLEEN, data analyst, researcher; b. Manhattan, Kans., June 4, 1948; d. Everitt Edsel and Mary Catherine (Moran) F. BS, St. Norbert Coll., 1970; postgrad., Calif. Family Study Ctr., 1981-82. Neuropsychology researcher U.S. VA Hosp., Sepulveda, Calif., 1970-76; mgr. print shop Charisma In Missions, City of Industry, Calif., 1976-77; neuropsychology researcher L.A. County Women's Hosp., 1977-79; mem. tech. staff Computer Scis. Corp., Ridgecrest, Calif., 1979-81; systems programmer Calif. State U., Northridge, 1982-84; bus. systems analyst World Vision, Monrovia, Calif., 1984-86; configuration analyst Teledyne System Co., Northridge, 1986-87; applications system analyst Internat. Telephone and Telegraph/Fed. Electric Corp., Altadena, Calif., 1987-88; supr. data analysts OAO Corp., Altadena, 1988—. Co-author, contbr.: Serotonin and Behavior, 1973, Advances in Sleep Research, vol. 1, 1974. Mem. OAO Mgmt. Assn., So. Calif. Application System Users Group, Digital Equipment Computer Users Soc. Roman Catholic. Home: 37607 Lasker Ave Palmdale CA 93550-7721 Office: OAO Corp 787 W Woodbury Rd Ste 2 Altadena CA 91001-5368

FAIRCHILD, JAMES LEROY, systems engineer; b. Fort Wayne, Ind., June 18, 1953; s. Robert Eugene, Sr. and Vera Grace (Auld) F.; m. Merri Kay jinnings, Aug. 18, 1973; children: Jennifer Ann, Jeffrey Matthew. BSEE, Ind. Inst. Tech., 1976; MS in Secondary Edn., Ind. U., Ft. Wayne, 1994. Fin. officer Herules Machinery Corp., Ft. Wayne, 1982-84; human factors engr. Magnavox, Ft. Wayne, 1984-91, sys. engr., 1991-95; sr. sys. engr. Magnavox, Denver, 1995—. Served from 2d lt. to lt. col. USAR, 1976—. Home: 8062D W Ken Caryl Circle Littleton CO 80123 Office: Hughes Def Comms 1313 Production Rd Fort Wayne IN 46808

FAIRCHILD, RICHARD PALMER, dental technician; b. Lindsay, Calif., Feb. 9, 1924; s. Ernest Clive and Rosella (Harrison) F.; m. Juda Gae Hattick, June 21, 1947; children: Cynthia, Marsha, Lynette, Richard A. Dental technician Valley Med. Ctr., Fresno, Calif., 1982—. With USAF, 1943-46, PTO. Home: 2465 N Knoll Ave Fresno CA 93822

FAIRECHILD, DIANA, airline passenger activist, writer, speaker; b. Bklyn., Feb. 6, 1944; d. Franklin and Pearl (Kaufman) Elias; m. J.G. Ruggles, 1969 (div. 1977); m. JG Alfer, 1981 (div. 1983). BA in French Lit., Boston U., 1965. Internat. flight attendant Pan Am World Airways, Miami, L.A., San Francisco, Honolulu, 1966-86, United Airlines, Honolulu, 1986-87; writer, pub., lectr. Kauai, Hawaii, 1992—; dir. Fair Air; syndicated columnist. Author, pub.: Jet Smart, 1992; author Healthy Flying, a cyberspace column on Internet. Office: Flyana Rhyme Inc PO Box 1177 Kilauea HI 96754

FAIRFULL, THOMAS MCDONALD, museum director; b. Greensburg, Pa., Nov. 28, 1942; s. Tom and Margaret Jane (Heasley) F.; m. Frances Allen White, Aug. 9, 1963; div. 1984; children—Timothy, Jennifer. B.A., U. Pitts., 1964; M.A., Duke U., 1972. Dir. 82d Airborne Div. Mus., Fort Bragg, N.C., 1975-78; instr. Campbell U., Buies Creek, N.C., 1976-78; dir. U.S. Army Mus. Hawaii, Honolulu, 1978—. Co-author: (with William R. Porter) History of the 3d Brigade 82d Airborne Div. 1969. Served to capt. U.S. Army, 1965-74; Vietnam. Serving as maj. USAR. Recipient Bronze Star with oak leaf cluster, USA. Mem. Am. Mil. Inst., Hawaii Mus. Assn., Council Am.'s Mil. Past. Home: 2575 Kuhio Ave Apt 1301 Honolulu HI 96815-3919 Office: US Army Museum of Hawaii Museum Division, DPTMSEC, USAGHI, Schofield Barracks HI 96857-5000*

FAIRHURST, JEFFREY THOMAS, software consultant; b. Tacoma, Wash., May 10, 1955; s. Cyrel Jackson and Evelyn Marie Fairhurst; m. Irene Johanna Moser, Sept. 22, 1976 (div. Dec. 1982); children: Johanna Evelyn, Jeffrey Jackson. Student, Ctrl. Tex. Coll. Analyst Barclay's Bank, San Jose, Calif., 1984; ind. cons. San Jose, 1984-85; analyst GE Nuclear Energy Bus., San Jose, 1985; software developer CSC, San Diego, 1986-87; analyst Lorimar, Culver City, Calif., 1987-88, Decom Sys. Inc., San Marcos, Calif., 1988, Profl. Computer Resources, Inc., Cypress, Calif., 1989, Psicor Inc., San Diego, 1990; ind. cons. Carlsbad, Calif., 1990-92, Midcom Corp., Cypress, 1992-93, Logicorp Inc., Bingham Farms, Mich., 1994; cons. Air Touch, Irvine, Calif.; cons. Found. Health Corp., 1996. With U.S. Army, 1973-84. Home: 3990 Scott Dr Carlsbad CA 92008-3625

FAIRLEY RANEY, REBECCA, journalist; b. Columbia, Mo., Sept. 7, 1965; d. James Lewis Raney and Phyllis Gail Fairley. BJ magna cum laude, U. Mo., 1987. Intern San Bernardino (Calif.) County Sun, summer 1987, reporter/computer-assisted projects, 1990—; reporter The Hemet (Calif.) News, 1987-88; gen. assignment reporter Inland Valley Daily Bulletin, Ontario, Calif., 1988-90. Contbr. articles to profl. jours. First violinist The Claremont (Calif.) Symphony Orchestra, 1988—; classroom vol. Citrus Elem. Sch., Upland, Calif., 1991-92. Recipient Celebrate Literacy award Arrowhead Reading Coun., San Bernardino, 1993, 1st pl. award Calif. Newspaper Pubs. Assn., 1993, various awards Gannett; recipient various univ. scholarships, 1st pl. award investigative reporting Best of Gannett, 1994, 1st pl. award Calif. Newspaper Pub. Assn. Pub. Svc., 1994, finalist for Livingston award. Mem. Investigative Reporters and Editors, Press Club of So. Calif. (former bd. dirs., 1st pl. investigative reporting, 1993, others 1988—), Soc. Profl. Journalists (1st pl. awards in health, polit. and minority affairs writing 1988—), Scholarship Soc., Kappa Tau Alpha. Office: San Bernardino County Sun 399 N D St San Bernardino CA 92401-1518

FAIRMAN, DAN S., internist; b. Toledo, Jan. 23, 1955; s. Ralph Charles and Ursula Annelisa (Sieber) F.; m. Melynda Kim Standlee, Mar. 5, 1986; children: Abigail, Connor. BA cum laude, Dartmouth Coll., 1977; MD, St. Louis U., 1982. Diplomate Am. Bd. Internal Medicine. Resident internal medicine U. Kans., 1985; staff physician USPHS, Glenns Ferry, Idaho, 1985-88; internist Wenatchee (Wash.) Valley Clinic, 1988-90, Assocs. in Medicine, Sun Valley, Idaho, 1990-93; emergency room physician St. Benedict Hosp., Jerome, Idaho, 1993—. Office: Wood River Med Ctr PO Box 86 Sun Valley ID 83353

FAIRWEATHER, EDWIN ARTHUR, electronics company executive; b. London, July 21, 1916; came to U.S., 1967; s. Arthur Henry and Elizabeth (Dawson) F.; m. Joan Barbara Branson, Sept. 14, 1946; children: David Martin, Janet Elizabeth Fairweather Nelson. BSME, London Poly., 1940. Quality engr. Lucas-Rotex, Toronto (Ont., Can.) and Birmingham (Eng.), 1951-58; mfg. engr. Flight Refuelling Co., Dorset, Eng., 1958-62, Spar Aerospace, Toronto, 1962-67, Sperry Flight Systems, Phoenix, 1967-71; engr. research and devel. Ford Aerospace Co., Palo Alto, Calif., 1971-85; founder, pres., chief engr. Fairweather & Co., Sunnyvale, Calif., 1980—. Patentee in field. Served with RAF, 1940-46. Home and Office: 1442 S Wolfe Rd Sunnyvale CA 94087-3669

FALCON, PATRICIA, nursing educator; b. Ness City, Kans., Apr. 6, 1963; d. Antonio and Dora (Murillo) F.; m. Michael D. Worley, Mar. 17, 1990. BSN, Ft. Hays State U., 1984; MSN, U. Ariz., 1992; postgrad. in counseling psychology, U. No. Colo., 1993—. RN, Kans., Colo., Ariz., Calif., Wash.; cert. oncology nurse. Case mgr. home care Tucson Hosp. Home Care, 1984-86; dir. oncology svcs. Redding (Calif.) Med. Ctr., 1986-89; field supr. home care Home Care of So. Ariz., Tucson, 1989-91; nurse clinician bone marrow transplants U. Ariz. Med. Ctr., Tucson, 1991-92; travel nurse acute care Flying Nurses, Dallas, 1992-93; case mgr. home care LHS Home and Cmty. Care, Greeley, Colo., 1993-95; adj. faculty U. No. Colo., Greeley, 1995—; cons. Access Tech., San Francisco, 1987-89, Tucson Gen. Hosp., 1990-93, Twilight Manor, Greeley, 1995-96, Gary and Loretta's Bd. and Care, Greeley, 1993-96. Mentor McNair scholar program U. No. Colo., 1995-96. Mem. APA, Am. Counseling Assn., Oncology Nursing Soc. Home: 2761-A 28th Ave Greeley CO 80631

FALEY, ROBERT LAWRENCE, instruments company executive; b. Bklyn., Oct. 13, 1927; s. Eric Lawrence and Anna (Makahon) F.; B.S. cum laude in Chemistry, St. Mary's U., San Antonio, 1956; postgrad. U. Del., 1958-59; m. Mary Virginia Mumme, May 12, 1950; children: Robert Wayne, Nancy Diane. Chemist, E.I. Dupont de Nemours & Co., Inc., Wilmington, Del., 1956-60; sales mgr. F&M Sci., Houston, 1960-62; pres. Faley Assos., Houston, 1962-65; sales mgr. Tech. Inc., Dayton, Ohio, 1965-70; biomed. mkt. mgr. Perkin-Elmer Co., Norwalk, Conn., 1967-69; mktg. dir. Cahn Instruments, Los Angeles, 1970-72; pres. Faley Internat., El Toro, Calif., 1972-93; pres. Status Internat., San Antonio, Tex., 1993—; speaker in field; dir. Whatman Lab. Products Inc., 1981-82, Status Instrument Corp., 1985-87; tech. mktg. cons. Whatman Ltd., Abbott Labs., OCG Tech., Inc., Pacific Biochem., Baker Commodities, Bausch & Lomb Co., Motorola Inc., Whatman Inc., Filtration Scis. Corp., PMC Industries, UVP, Inc., Ericomp, Inc., Data I/O. Mem. adv. com. on Sci., tech., energy and water U.S. 43d Congl. Dist., 1985-87. With USMS, 1944-47, 1st lt. USAF, 1948-53. Charter mem. Aviation Hall Fame. Fellow Am. Inst. Chemists, AAAS; mem. ASTM, Am. Chem. Soc. (sr.), Instrument Soc. Am. (sr.), Inst. Environ. Scis. (sr.), Aircraft Owners and Pilots Assn., U.S. Power Squadrons, VFW (life), Silver Wings Fraternity, Masons, Delta Epsilon Sigma. Contbr. articles on technique of gas chromatography to profl. jours. Home: 27850 Espinoza San Juan Capistrano CA 92692-2156 Office: 1201 Austin Hwy Ste 131 San Antonio TX 78209

FALGIANO, VICTOR JOSEPH, electrical engineer, consultant; b. San Francisco, Nov. 25, 1957; s. Victor Anthony and Frances Mary Falgiano; m. Linda Maxine Owens, July 24, 1982; children: Gregory Joseph, Nicholas Rexford. BS in Elec. Engring. Tech. magna cum laude, Cogswell Coll., 1989, BS in Computer Engring. magna cum laude, 1989. Sr. design engr. Amdahl Corp., Sunnyvale, Calif., 1978-93; prin. system devel. engr. Nat. Semiconductor Corp., Santa Clara, Calif., 1993—; mem. steering com. System Design and Integration Conf., Santa Clara, Calif.; mem. acad. adv. com. Cogswell Coll., Cupertino, Calif., 1991; evaluator Accrediting Bd. Engring. and Tech., 1995—. Contbr. articles to profl. publs. Advisor to high sch. students Jr. Achievement. Mem. IEEE (sr.), Assn. Computing Machinery, Internat. Microelectronics and Packaging Soc. Office: Nat Semicondr Notebook Bus Unit/Pers Sys Group PO Box 58090 M/S A2-575 2900 Semiconductor Dr Santa Clara CA 95052

FALGOUT, MARSHALL, mathematician, educator; b. South Gate, Calif., Sept. 13, 1946; s. Marshall Sr. and Claudia Agnes (Stump) G.; m. Mona Dawn Stafford, Mar. 15, 1986; children: Eric, Mark, Amy, Dan, Michael, Mandi. BA, Humboldt State U., 1968; M, U. San Francisco, 1984. Cert. secondary tchg., Calif. Tchr. Deep Valley Christian Sch., Redwood Valley, Calif., 1974-77, Potter Valley (Calif.) H.S., 1977-87, Ukiah (Calif.) H.S., 1987—. Co-author: (textbook) Power Algebra I, 1991. Capt. USMC, 1970-73. Democrat. Home: 380 Sherry Dr Ukiah CA 95482 Office: Ukiah HS 1000 Low Gap Rd Ukiah CA 95482

FALICK, ABRAHAM JOHNSON, printing company executive; b. Chgo., Oct. 11, 1920; s. Simon Falick and Ellen Martina (Johnson) Sherwood; m. Carolyn Weber, Dec. 11, 1947; 1 child, Leslie Carol Falick Koplof. BA, Ind. U., 1947; MBA, U. Chgo., 1951; MA, UCLA, 1967, PhD, 1970. Cert. pub. planner. Commd. ensign USNR, 1941, advanced through grades to lt. comdr., 1941-46, ret., 1967; mgr. sales/mktg. Webb-Linn Printing Co., Chgo., 1948-56; pres., chief exec. officer Murray and Gee, Inc., Culver City, Calif., 1956-60; planning economist City of Los Angeles, 1967-75; pres., chief exec. officer AJ Falick Assocs., Los Angeles, 1960-67, Navigator Press, Inc., Los Angeles, 1975—. Contbr. transp. research articles to profl. jours. Chmn. Coalition Rapid Transit, L.A., 1978—, Friends of Geography UCLA, 1989—; v.p. Westwood Dem. Club, 1988—; chair L.A. Bus./Profl. Dem. Club, 1992—. Mem. Am. Econ. Assn., Am. Planning Assn., Am. Inst. Cert. Planners (counselor 1972-74), Nat. Assn. Bus. Economists (pres. L.A. chpt. 1996—). Democrat. Jewish. Office: Navigator Press Inc 516 N Fair Oaks Ave Pasadena CA 91103-3304

FALK, BRADLEY DAVIS, information services executive; b. St. Louis, Apr. 16, 1966; m. Claudia Taake, Apr. 16, 1992. AA, Santa Monica Coll., 1994. Rschr. Field Rsch., San Francisco, 1986-87; database design mgr. Daniel Reynold's Photographics, Hayward, Calif., 1987-89; mgr. computer tech. support UCI Cons., Venice, Calif., 1990-92; asst. dir. Albert Hofmann Found., Beverly Hills, 1992-93; asst. stockbroker Prudential Securities, Beverly Hills, 1993-94; ptnr. Luna Info. Svcs., L.A., 1994-96; margin analyst mgr. J.B. Oxford & Co. Brokerage, Beverly Hills, 1996—. Recipient Cert. of Appreciation, NASA Tech. Briefs, 1992-93, Presdl. Sports award Pres.' Coun. Phys. Fitness, 1993. Mem. Albert Hofmann Found., Citizen Com. on Right to Bear Arms, Nat. Assn. to Protect Individual Rights. Libertarian. Erisian. Office: JB Oxford & Co Ste 300 9665 Wilshire Blvd Beverly Hills CA 90212

FALK, CANDACE SERENA, historian, biographer, documentary editor; b. N.Y.C., July 30, 1947; m. Lowell Stewart Finley, Oct. 23, 1977; two children. BA, U. Chgo., 1969, MA, 1971; PhD, U. Calif., Santa Cruz, 1984. Mem. faculty Stockton State Coll., 1972-76; editor Southeast Asia Chronicle, 1976-80; editor/dir. The Emma Goldman Papers U. Calif., Berkeley, 1980—. Author: (biography) Love, Anarchy and Emma Goldman, 1984; editor: (documentary, microfilm edit.) The Emma Goldman Papers, 1991, (source book) Emma Goldman: A Guide to Her Life and Documentary Sources, 1995 (Kanner prize for Best Bibliographic work in women and gender history 1995). Woodrow Wilson Women's Studies grantee, 1979; grantee Nat. Hist. Publ. Records Commn., 1980-96, Nat. Endowment for Humanities, Ford Found., The Rockefeller Found., Am. Coun. Learned Socs. Mem. Orgn. of Am. Historians (com. on archives and historians), Am. Hist. Assn. (com. on Joan Kelly prize in feminist history 1991), Assn. Documentary Editors, Western Assn. Women Historians (com. on Kanner prize in bibliographic work). Democrat. Jewish. Office: Emma Goldman Papers Univ Calif/Berkeley 2372 Ellsworth St Berkeley CA 94704-1550

FALK, HEINRICH RICHARD, theater and humanities educator; b. Frankfurt, Germany, May 3, 1939; came to U.S., 1947; s. Heinrich Wilhelm Karl and Janet Elizabeth (Prentice) F.; m. Joyce Duncan, Aug. 14, 1965. BA, Wittenberg U., 1960; PhD, U. So. Calif., 1970. Instr. mgmt. tng. div. Union Bank, L.A., 1963-64; lectr. U. So. Calif., L.A., 1964-67; instr. Chapman Coll., Orange, Calif., 1966-67; prof. Calif. State U., Northridge, 1967—; resident dir. Calif. State U., Madrid, 1986-87; vis. prof. Shanghai Theatre Acad., China, 1993. Editor: Theatre Jour. (book review sect.), 1981-83. Spl. cons. and project writer, Fine Arts and Humanities Framework com., State of Calif., 1967-72. Recipient post-doctoral scholar U. Calif., 1970-72; Younger Humanist fellow, Nat. Endowment Humanities, Madrid, Barcelona, 1972-73, Del Amo Found., Madrid, 1977-78, Asian Cultural Coun., China, 1993, Aston Magma Acad. Nat. Endowment for the Humanities, 1995; grantee Nat. Endowment for the Humanities, 1982. Mem. Internat. Soc. for Eighteenth-Century Studies, Internat. Fed.for Theatre Rsch., Am. Soc. for Theatre Rsch., Am. Soc. Eighteenth-Century Studies, Instituto Feijoo de Estudios del Siglo XVIII, Sociedad Espanola de Estudios del Siglo XVIII. Home: 2726 Cuesta Rd Santa Barbara CA 93105-3708 Office: Calif State U Dept Theatre Northridge CA 91330-8320

FALK, MARVIN WILLIAM, historian, bibliographer; b. Wichita, Kans., Jan. 29, 1943; s. Melvin Leroy and Martha Louise (Crew) F.; m. Helen Amanda Widman, June 7, 1969 (div. May 1985); children: Karl, Adelia, Stuart. BA, U. Minn., 1965; MA, U. Mass., 1966; PhD, U. Iowa, 1976. Arctic bibliographer U. Alaska, Fairbanks, 1975-81, curator rare books, 1981—. Author: Alaska, 1995, (series) Rasmusson Translation Series, 10 vols., 1985—; compiler: Alaskan Maps, 1983. Pres. Fairbanks Sch. Bd., 1985-86. Mem. Alaska Hist. Soc. (pres. 1978-80). Home: 1913 Southern St Fairbanks AK 99709 Office: U Alaska Fairbanks PO Box 756808 Fairbanks AK 99775

FALKENBERG, WILLIAM STEVENS, architect, contractor; b. Kansas City, Mo., July 21, 1927; s. John Joseph and Maraba Elizabeth (Stevens) F.; m. Janis Patton Hubner, Apr. 13, 1951; children: Ruth Elizabeth, Christopher Joseph, Charles Stevens. BS in Archtl. Engring., U. Colo., 1949. Pres. Falkenberg Constrn. Co., Denver, 1951-71, 74-84, devel. cons., 1984—; broker Hogan & Stevenson Realty, Denver, 1971-74. Chmn. constrn. Archdiocesan Housing Com., Inc.; chmn. restoration 9th Street Hist. Park; chmn. bldg. comm. Four Mile House Hist. Park; chmn. Housing Trust Coun., Denver, 1986-90; chmn. Rocky Mountain Better Bus. Bur., 1965-67; pres. Denver Friends Folk Music, 1966. Lt. (j.g.) USNR, 1945-51. Mem. AIA (bd. dirs. Denver chpt. 1978-81, treas. 1981), Home Builder Assn. Met. Denver, Colo. Hist. Soc. Found. (trustee, sec. 1987—), Serra Internat. (pres. 1971, dist. gov. 1973), Nat. Assn. Atomic Vets., Colo. Archeol. Soc., Denver Athletic Club, Equestrian Order of Holy Sepulchre, Cactus Club (pres. 1995—). Home and Office: 430 Marion St Denver CO 80218-3930

FALKNER, JAMES GEORGE, foundation executive; b. Spokane, Wash., Dec. 24, 1952; s. Albert Andrew and Amanda Rosalia (Reisinger) F.; m. Joleen Rae Ann Brown, June 22, 1974; children: James Jr., Jayson, Jerin, Jarret. BS in Acctg., U. Wash., 1975. CPA, Wash. CPA LeMaster & Daniels, Spokane, 1975-80; treas. Dominican Sisters Spokane, 1980-95; pres. Dominican Outreach Found., Spokane, 1995—; bd. dirs. Dominican Network, Spokane, Dominican Health Svcs., Providence Svcs., Spokane; mem. Bishop's Fin. Coun. Spokane Diocese, 1990-96. Bd. dirs. sch. bd. St. Mary's Ch., Veradale, Wash., 1986-89, 90, sch. found., 1987—; active acctg. adv. com. Spokane Falls Community Coll., 1989—. Mem. Healthcare Fin. Mgmt. Assn. (bd. dirs. 1982-85), AICPA, Wash. State Soc. CPAs (Spokane Wash. bd. dirs.), Nat. Notary Assn. Office: Dominican Outreach Found 3102 W Fort George Wright Dr Spokane WA 99224-5203

FALLETTA, JO ANN, musician; b. N.Y.C., Feb. 27, 1954; d. John Edward and Mary Lucy (Racioppo) F.; m. Robert Alemany, Aug. 24, 1986. BA in Music, Mannes Coll. Music, N.Y.C., 1976; MA in Music, Juilliard Sch., N.Y.C., 1982; PhD in Musical Arts, Juilliard Sch., 1989; Honorary Doctorate, Marian Coll., Wis., 1988. Music dir. Queens Philharmonic, N.Y.C., 1978-91, Den. Chamber Orch., Colo., 1983-92; assoc. condr. Milw. Symphony, Wis., 1985-88; music dir. Women's Philharmonic, San Francisco, 1986—, Long Beach Symphony, Calif., 1989—, Va. Symphony, Norfolk, 1991—. Stokowski Conducting Competition, Toscanini Conducting award. Office: ICM Artists LTD 40 W 57th St New York NY 10019-4001

FALLON, ROBERT KYLE, university administrator; b. Springfield, Mass., May 31, 1950; s. Richard A. and Jean H. (King) F.; m. Susan Moore; children—Jennifer, Kyle. A.A., Onondaga Community Coll., 1973; B.S., Eastern N.Mex. U., 1973, M.A., 1974; doctoral candidate U. No. Colo., 1981-83. Hall dir. Eastern N.Mex. U., Portales, 1974-75; dir. student activities South Plains Coll., Levelland, Tex., 1975-80; hall dir. U. No. Colo., Greeley, 1980-83, adv. residence hall assoc., 1983; asst. dir. residential life U. Minn.-Morris, 1983-86. Avocations: running, swimming, golf. Home: 3408 S Halfmoon Dr Bakersfield CA 93309 Office: Calif State U 9051 Stockdale Hwy Bakersfield CA 93311-1003

FALTIN, BRUCE CHARLES, hotel executive; b. Cin., Mar. 7, 1947; s. Charles F. and Meryl (Gunther) F.; m. H. Ann Walker; children: Sharon, Laura, John. BS, Cornell U., 1969. Mgr. Winegardner & Hammons Inc., Cin., 1969-78; ptnr. Idahotels Ltd., Boise, Idaho, 1978—; pres. Mountain States Mgmt. Inc., Boise, 1978—, also bd. dirs; trustee Rodeway Inns Advt. Fund, Phoenix, 1985-94; chmn. Rodeway Inns Owner's Coun., Phoenix, 1986-88. Co-founder, dir., pres. Idaho Hospitality Edn. Found., 1990-91. Mem. Am. Hotel and Motel Assn. (state dir. 1983-84), Nat. Restaurant Assn., Idaho Innkeepers Assn. (bd. dirs. 1974-86, 88-94, pres. 1979, treas. 1988-91), Greater Boise C. of C. (bd. dirs. 1987), Choice Hotels Brands Adv. Coun., Idaho Hospitality Edn. Found. (pres. 1990-91), Idaho Hospitality and Travel Assn. (pres. 1994-95). Home: 2423 Hillway Dr Boise ID 83702-0933 Office: Rodeway Inn of Boise 1115 N Curtis Rd Boise ID 83706-1233

FALUDI, SUSAN C., journalist, scholarly writer. Formerly with West Mag., San Jose, Calif., Mercury News; with San Francisco Bur., Wall St. Jour.; spkr. in field. Author: Backlash: The Undeclared War Against American Women, 1991 (National Book Critics Circle award for general nonfiction 1992); contbr. articles to mags. Recipient Pulitzer Prize for explanatory journalism, 1991. Office: care Sandra Dijkstra Literary Agy 1155 Camino Del Mar Ste 515 Del Mar CA 92014-2605*

FAN, LEE SIU, business executive and vocational training program administrator; b. Hong Kong, Aug. 5, 1948; came to U.S., 1974; s. Kwok-Kam and Po-Hang (Law) F. *Father Dr. Kwok-Kam Fan was a famous Chinese doctor who saved thousands of lives during his 50 years of medical practice. He was well respected. He established the well-known Ching Wah Chinese Medical Institute in 1953. Under the leadership of his eldest son, Dr. Siu-Tsun Fan, Ching Wah Institute became one of the most prestigious oriental medical institutes in Hong Kong. Mother Po-Hang bore ten children. In addition to taking care of all the children, she was able to manage her husband's busy clinic.* BSc in Bus. Mgmt. and Mktg., U. Wis., Superior, 1975; MSc in Spl. Edn., Portland State U., 1989; DBA in Bus. Mgmt., Pacific Western U., 1997. Cert. foodsvcs. mgmt. profl. Prodn. and sales mng. coord. Castle Peak Garment Factory Co., Ltd., Hong Kong, 1969-70; mng. exec. Wilson Garment Mfg. Co. Ltd., Hong Kong, 1970-74; ops. mgr. Portland State U., 1975-92; CEO Handily Enterprises (U.S.A.) Inc., Portland, 1991—, Happy Heart Foods Inc., Portland, 1992—, Lok Hop, Inc., Portland, 1996—; vocat. tng. programs coord. Portland Pub. Schs., Lake Oswego Sch. Dist., Clackamas County Employment Tng. and Bus. Svcs., Oreg. Comm. for the Blind, Westside Youth Ctr., 1986-92; adv. bd. Unicorn Fisheries Ltd., Hong Kong, 1990—. Cmty. svc. provider Loaves & Fishes Sr. Cmty. Ctr., Portland, 1991—; coord. Oreg. Gov.'s Ann. Food Dr., Salem, 1991; mem. diversity commn. Portland State U., 1992; mem. delegation on learning disabilities Citizen Ambassador of People to People Internat., Spokane, Wash., 1994. Recipient Exemplary Svc. award Portland State U., 1985, Extraordinary Svc. award, 1987, various svc. awards, 1972-92. Mem. Coun. for Exceptional Children (Beyond the Call of Duty Svc. award 1992), Nat. Assn. of Coll. and Univ. Food Svcs. (Leadership Program rep. 1986-92, named Food Svc. Mgmt. Profl. 1992), Nike Portland Running Club (2d master runner of yr. 1988, 89), Oreg. Rd. Runners Club (Inspirational Runner of Yr. 1990). Democrat. Home: 3723 SE Steele St Portland OR 97202-4260 Office: Handily Enterprises (USA) 6335 SE 82nd Ave Portland OR 97266-5607

FANCHER, MICHAEL REILLY, newspaper editor, newspaper publishing executive; b. Long Beach, Calif., July 13, 1946; s. Eugene Arthur and Ruth Leone (Dickson) F.; m. Nancy Helen Edens, Nov. 3, 1967 (div. 1982); children: Jason Michael, Patrick Reilly; m. 2d Carolyn Elaine Bowers, Mar. 25, 1983; Katherine Claire, Elizabeth Lynn. BA, U. Oreg., 1968; MS, Kans. State U., 1971; MBA, U. Wash., 1986. Reporter, asst. city editor Kansas City Star, Mo., 1970-76, city editor, 1976-78; reporter Seattle Times, 1978-79, night city editor, 1979-80, asst. mng. editor, 1980-81, mng. editor, 1981-86, exec. editor, 1986—, now vice pres., exec. editor, 1989-95; sr. v.p., 1995—; bd. dirs. Walla Walla Union-Bulletin, Yakima Herald Rep. Ruhl fellow U. Oreg., 1983. Mem. Am. Soc. Newspaper Editors. 1985-91), Soc. Profl. Journalists, Nat. Press Photographers Assn. (Editor of Yr. 1986). Office: Seattle Times Fairview Ave N & John St PO Box 70 Seattle WA 98111-0070*

FANGOR, VOY, painter; b. Warsaw, Poland, Nov. 15, 1922; came to U.S., 1966; s. Konrad and Wanda Fangor; m. Magdalena Shummer. MFA, Acad. of Fine Arts, Warsaw, 1946. Asst. prof. Warsaw Acad. Art, 1953-61; tchr. Fairleigh Dickinson U., Madison, N.J., 1966-83; participant internat. artist seminar Fairleigh Dickinson U., Madison, 1965; vis. lectr. Bath Acad. Art Corsham, Wiltshire, Eng., 1965-66; vis. critic arch. Grad. Sch. Design, Harvard U., Cambridge, Mass., 1967-68; set designer Martha Graham Dance Co., 1970. One-man shows include Inst. Contemporary Art, Washington, 1962, Galerie Lambert, Paris, 1963, Galerie Falazik, Bochum, Germany, 1964, Dom Galerie, Cologne, Germany, 1966, Galerie Chalette, N.Y.C., 1967, 69, 70, Solomon R. Guggenheim Mus., N.Y.C., 1970, Univ. Art Mus., Berkeley, Calif., 1971, Fort Worth Art Mus., Tex., 1971, Hokin Gallery, Chgo., 1974, Walter Kelly Gallery, Chgo., 1978, Bodley Gallery, N.Y.C., 1983, Zacheta Gallery, Warsaw, 1990, Mitchell Algus Gallery, N.Y.C., 1993; group shows include Stedlijk Mus., Amsterdam, 1959, Mus. Modern Art, N.Y.C., 1961, 65, Guggenheim Mus., N.Y.C., 1964, 67, 80, Riverside Mus., N.Y.C., 1965, Carnegie Inst., Pitts., 1967, 70, Newark Mus., 1969, Cin. Art Mus., 1969, Thorp Gallery, N.Y.C., 1980, Harm Bouckaert Gallery, N.Y.C., 1984, Gallery 53, Cooperstown, N.Y., 1988; represented in permanent collections Guggenheim Mus., N.Y.C., Mus. Modern Art, N.Y.C., San Antonio Mus. Art, Phillips Collection, Washington, Newark Mus., State Mus., Trenton, N.J., Aldrich Mus. Contemporary Art, Ridgefield, Conn., Rose Art Mus., Waltham, Mass., Carnegie Mus. Art, Pitts., Hirshhorn Mus., Smithsonian Inst., Washington, Power Gallery Art, Sidney, Australia, Muzeum Sztuki, Lodz, Poland, Muzeum Narodowe, Poznan and Warsaw, Poland, Stedelijk Mus., Amsterdam, Schloss Morsbroich Mus., Leverkusen, Germany, Mus. des XX Jahrhunderts, Berlin, Aachen (Germany) Mus. Art, Mus. Art, Munich, Milw. Mus. Art, Harlem Mus., N.Y.C. Recipient Alfred Jurzykowski Found. award, 1978; fellow Inst. Contemporary Art, 1962; Ford Found. grantee, 1964-65. Home: 2006 Conejo Dr Santa Fe NM 87505-6109

FANN, JAMES ILIN, cardiothoracic surgeon; b. Taipei, Taiwan, May 4, 1961; came to U.S., 1968; s. Charles C.P. and Nancy C.L. (Lee) F.; m. Andrea Hutchinson. BS, Northwestern U., 1983, MD with distinction, 1985. Diplomate Am. Bd. Surgery. Resident Stanford (Calif.) U. Med. Ctr., 1985-92; rsch. fellow Stanford U., 1987-89; vascular surgery fellow Stanford U. Med. Ctr., 1992-93, cardiothoracic surgery fellow, 1993-96; clin. asst. prof. cardiothoracic surgery Stanford U. Med. Schs., 1996—; staff cardiovascular surgeon VA, Palo Alto, Calif., 1996—; rsch. asst. Northwestern U., Chgo., 1982-84. Contbr. articles to profl. jours. Nat. Merit scholar, 1979; Carl and Leah McConnell Cardiovascular Rsch. fellow, 1987-89. Mem. AMA, Am. Heart Assn., Am. Coll. Cardiology, Calif. Med. Assn., Alpha Omega Alpha. Roman Catholic. Home: 1098 S Springer Rd Los Altos CA 94024-4930 Office: Stanford U Med Ctr 300 Pasteur Dr Palo Alto CA 94304-2203

FANNING, DON BRIAN, poet, computer services consultant; b. Burbank, Calif., Feb. 10, 1957; s. Donald Floyd and Lorraine Gwendolyn (Smith) F. BS in Physics cum laude, UCLA, 1979. With Hughes Aircraft Co., El Segundo, Calif., 1981-84; programmer UCLA, Westwood, 1985-86; computer svcs. cons. L.A., 1986-94, 96—; multimedia dept. mgr. Price Waterhouse, L.A., 1994-96; founder, facilitator Iguana Poets' Circle, North Hollywood, Calif., 1989-92, Barnsdall Arts Park Poets' Circle, Hollywood, Calif., 1992-97, elder steward, 1997—; dir. poet "lariat" Iguanaland Poetry Reading, North Hollywood, 1989-92. Author/co-author: Spaghetti and Rice, 1990, Woodlands and Waterways, 1994; editor: Tail of the Iguana, 1991, Of the People, 1994—. Outreach person Out Loud Poets Calendar, L.A., 1990-92, Poetry Flash, L.A., 1992-94; non-violent protestor Nev. Nuclear Weapons Test Site, Las Vegas, 1990-96, Desert Storm/Gulf War, L.A., 1991. Mem.

Algonquin Tribe Men's Group, Sigma Pi Sigma. Office: Uncle Don B Fanning PO Box 7667 Van Nuys CA 91409-7667

FARAGO, CLAIRE J., art historian, educator; b. Washington, Apr. 12, 1948; d. John and Kathleen (Kárpáti) F.; m. Ken Iwamasa, Dec. 19, 1990; 1 child, Mia Chunling. BA, Wellesley U., 1970; MA, Brown U., 1980; PhD, U. Va., 1988. Asst. prof. U. Colo., Boulder, 1988-95, assoc. prof. fine arts, 1995—. Author: Leonardo da Vinci's Parafone, 1992 (Best Faculty Book award); prin. author: Leonardio da Vinci: Codex Leicester, 1996; editor, contbr.: Reframing the Renaissance: Visual Culture in Europe and Latin America, 1450 to 1650, 1995. Mem. Coll. Art Assn., Renaissance Soc. Am., Sixteenth-Century Studies Assn. Office: U Colo Sibelle-Wolle Bldg Dept Fine Arts CB 318 Boulder CO 80309

FARAH, TAWFIC ELIAS, political scientist, educator; b. Nazareth, Palestine, Aug. 12, 1946; s. Elias Tawfic and Itaf Fahim F.; BA, Calif. State U., Fresno, 1970, MA, 1971; PhD, U. Nebr., 1975; m. Linda Maxwell, Apr. 24, 1969; children—Omar Lee, Aliya Jane. With Xerox Corp., Lincoln, Nebr., 1974-75; asst. prof. polit. sci. Kuwait U., 1975-79; pres. polit. risk analysis Mid. East Rsch. Group Analityca, 1979—, nat. dir. internat. edn., 1989; vis. assoc. prof. UCLA, summers 1978-83, fellow Center for Internat. and Strategic Affairs, 1980-81, Ctr. for Near Eastern Studies, 1986; Fulbright scholar, 1983. Toyota Found. grantee, 1985. Mem. Am. Polit. Sci. Assn. Author: Reinventing Palestinian Politics: A New Order in the Middle East, 1995; co-author: Research Methods in the Social Sciences, 1977, A Dictionary of Social Analysis, 1980; author: Aspects of Modernization and Consociationalism: Lebanon as an Exploratory Test Case, 1975, 77; co-editor: Palestinians Without Palestine: Socialization of Palestinian Children, 1979, Learning to Become Palestinians, 1985; editor Political Behavior in the Arab States, 1983, Pan Arabism and Arab Nationalism: The Continuing Debate, 1986, Political Socialization in the Arab States, 1987, Survey Research in the Arab World, 1987; editor Jour. Arab Affairs, 1981-95.

FARANDA, JOHN PAUL, college administrator; b. Orange, Calif., Feb. 21, 1957; s. Paul L. and Kay S. (Wilson) F. BA cum laude, Claremont McKenna Coll., 1979. Staff liaison L.A. County Bar Assn., 1979-80; spl. programs adminstr. L.A. County Med. Assn., 1980-85; dir. corp. rels. Claremont (Calif.) McKenna Coll., 1985-87, dir. campaign and devel. svcs., 1987-89, dir. devel., 1989-96, assoc. v.p. devel., 1996—. Contbr. articles to profl. jours. Campaign chmn. United Way, Mt. Baldy Region, Ontario, Calif., 1987-90; bd. govs. Faculty Ho. of the Claremont Colls., pres. 1993-95; bd. dirs. Recording for the Blind and Dyslexic, Community Friends of Internat. Students. Recipient Gold award Mt. Baldy United Way, 1988, 91. Mem. L.A. County Bar Assn. (com. on arbitration), Coun. for Advancement and Support of Edn. (USX award 1986), Athletic Club L.A. Office: Claremont McKenna Coll Bauer Ctr #320 500 E 9th St Claremont CA 91711-6400

FARBER, BERNARD, sociologist, educator; b. Chgo., Feb. 11, 1922; s. Benjamin and Esther (Axelrod) F.; m. Annette Ruth Shugan, Dec. 21, 1947 (div. 1970); children—Daniel, Michael, Lisa, Jacqueline; m. Rosanna Bodanis, June 10, 1971 (dec. June 1988); 1 dau., Tanya. A.B., Roosevelt U., Chgo., 1943; A.M., U. Chgo., 1949, Ph.D., 1953. Research asso. U. Chgo., 1951-53; asst. prof. Henderson State Tchr. Coll., Arkadelphia, Ark., 1953-54; mem. faculty U. I., 1954-71, prof. sociology, 1964-71; asso. dir. Inst. Research Exceptional Children, 1967-69; prof. Ariz. State U., 1971-92, prof. emeritus, 1992—, chmn. dept. sociology, 1971-75, 90-92; vis. prof. U. Tex., Austin, 1974-75, U. Ill., Chgo., 1988—; cons. in field, 1957—. Author: Family: Organization and Interaction, 1964, Mental Retardation: Its Social Context and Social Consequences, 1968, Kinship and Class, 1971, Guardians of Virtue, 1972, Family and Kinship in Modern Society, 1973, Conceptions of Kinship, 1981; editor Sociol. Perspectives, 1985-89; co-editor: Sociological Inquiry, 1997—. Mem. mental retardation research com. Nat. Inst. Child Health and Human Devel., 1971-75. Served with AUS, 1943-46. Recipient E.W. Burgess award Nat. Council on Family Relations, 1975; Disting. Research award Ariz. State U., 1980. Mem. Am. Sociol. Assn. (coun. mem. family sect. 1966-69), Ill. Sociol. Assn. (founding pres. 1965-66), Pacific Sociol. Assn. (pres. 1986-87). Jewish. Home: 7949 E Montebello Ave Scottsdale AZ 85250-6108 Office: Ariz State U Dept Sociology Tempe AZ 85287

FARBER, GERALDINE OSSMAN, civic worker; b. Salt Lake City, May 4, 1929; d. Lawrence N. and Janet (Perkins) Ossman; m. John Val Browning, July 19, 1949 (div. June 1964); 1 child, John Allen; m. Seymour M. Farber, June 5, 1973. Student, Vassar Coll., 1947-49, U. Liege (Belgium), 1951-53, U. Utah, 1955. Tchrs. aid spl. programs elem. schs., Ogden, Utah, Los Altos and Woodside, Calif., 1962-70; cons. Glasrock Products, Inc., 1979-80. Editor: Teilhard de chardin: In Quest of the Perfection of Man, 1973. Bd. dirs. Am. Field Service, Ogden, 1960-64, Utah Ballet, Ogden, 1963-64, Christmas Bur., Palo Alto and Los Altos, 1964-66, Jr. League Palo Alto, 1966-69. Community Com. for Internat. Students, Stanford, 1965-67; dir. Ednl. TV Fgn. Student Series, Ogden, 1963-64; bd. dirs. Vol. Bur. No. Santa Clara County (Calif.), 1965-68, exec. v.p., 1967-68; vol. parentis in locus, tubercular refugee children Caritas Catholique, Liege, 1952-55; ways and means chmn. San Francisco Ballet Assn. Aux., 1970, pres., 1974-75, trustee assn., 1974-75; co-founder, pres. bd. dirs. Archives for Performing Arts, 1975-76; bd. dirs. Am. Conservatory Theater, 1975-81; mem. Calif. Public Broadcasting Commn., 1975-85 ; vol., asst. media buyer campaign Supt. Public Instrn. Calif., 1970; mem. exec. planning com. and nat. adv. bd. John Muir Med. Film Festival, 1979-91; program com. mem. Kauai Found. Continuing Edn. and Hawaii Med. Assn., 1979-85. Recipient awards of Merit City and County San Francisco, Vol. Bur. No. Santa Clara County. Mem. San Francisco Peninsula Vassar Alumnae Club (pres. 1968-70). Home and Office: 26303 Esperanza Dr Los Altos CA 94022-2601

FARHAT, CAROL S., motion picture company executive; b. Santa Monica, Calif.; d. Annis Abraham Farhat; divorced; 1 child, Michael. Student, Santa Monica Coll., 1967; Assoc. degree, Inst. Audio Rsch., 1976-78; student, Otis Parsons Inst., 1980-84, UCLA, 1984-90; BA in Bus., Music, Antioch U., 1992. Recording studio mgr. The Village Recorder, L.A., 1972-78; audio engr. The Village Recorder Studio, L.A., 1978-79; music adminstr. 20th Century Fox Film Corp., Beverly Hills, Calif., 1980-82, music supr., 1983-86, music dir., 1986-92; supr. internat. music 20th Century Fox Film Corp., Tokyo, 1993; music prodr. Scopus Films, England, 1987-89; songwriter Music Experts Ltd., Santa Monica, Calif., 1989-90; v.p. music 20th Century Fox Film Corp., 1994-95; v.p. TV music and feature Am. Fedn. Musicians advisor 20th Century Fox Music, 1995-96. Author: China Diary, 1992; composer (music book) Children's Songbook, 1991; songwriter (for film) Rockin' Reindeer, 1990. Mem. BMI, NATAs, NARAS, Women in Film, Am. Film Inst., Pacific Composers Forum, Entertainment Industry Counsel. Office: 20th Century Fox Film Corp PO Box 900 Beverly Hills CA 90213-0900

FARISS, LAURENCE ALAN, air force officer, pilot; b. Medford, Oreg., Dec. 30, 1952; s. Darrell Laverne and Nita Mae (Junge) F.; m. Michelle Licia May, May 1, 1976; children: Jonathan, Matthew, Michael. BS, U.S. Air Force Acad., 1975; MS, Abilene Christian U., 1982. Cert. command pilot. Commd. 2d lt. USAF, 1975, advanced through grades to col., 1995; pers. officer Air Force Manpower/Pers., Randolph AFB, Tex., 1985-88; squadron ops. 773d Airlift Squadron, Dyess AFB, Tex., 1989-92; squadron comdr. 50th Airlife Squadron, Little Rock AFB, Ark., 1992-93; chief readiness and tng. U.S. Pacific Command, Camp Smith, Hawaii, 1994-96; asst. athletic dir. USAF Acad., 1997—. Named to So. Oreg. Sports Hall of Fame, 1985. Mem. Air Force Acad. Assn. Grads., Air Force Acad. Athletic Assn., Daedalions, Air Force Assn. Republican. Methodist. Home: Gen Delivery U S A F Academy CO 80840 Office: Dept Athletics U S A F Academy CO 80840

FARKAS, ABRAHAM KRAKAUER, urban developer, educator; b. Dunkirk, N.Y., Oct. 31, 1947; s. Louis Ari and Hedy (Krakauer) F.; m. Pamela Ann Price, June 15, 1970; children: Madeleine, Uri, Jacob. BA in Polit. Sci., Purdue U., 1969, MA in Am. Studies, 1971; PhD in Am. Studies, U. Minn., 1976. Asst. prof. housing and pub. policy U. Tenn., Knoxville, 1976-80; dir. community devel. and planning City of Ft. Wayne, Ind., 1980-83; mgr. econ. devel. City of Seattle, 1983-85; exec. dir. planning and devel. City of Eugene, Oreg., 1985—; mem. bd. advisors for housing and mktg. Oreg. State U., Corvallis, 1990-94. Editor Housing and Society, 1980; contbr. articles to profl. jours. Bd. dirs. Temple Beth Israel, Eugene, 1990-91, Networking for Youth, Inc., 1993—, Eugene YMCA, 1993—, Jewish Fedn. Lane County, 1995—. Lilly fellow, 1979; Tenn. Endowment for Humanities grantee, 1978. Mem. Urban Land Inst., Nat. Community Devel. Assn. (bd. dirs. 1982), Coun. for Urban Econ. Devel. (treas. N.W. chpt. 1986-87, nat. bd. dirs. 1995—). Jewish. Office: City of Eugene 99 W 10th Ave Eugene OR 97401

FARKAS, JUDI G., film studio executive; b. N.Y.C.; d. Robin Lewis and Carol Garner Farkas. BA, Wellesley Coll.; MBA, Columbia U. Dir. product devel. L'Oreal/Lancome, N.Y.C., 1984-86; v.p. creative affairs MGM/UA, N.Y.C., 1992-96; dir. devel. Universal Pictures, L.A., 1996—.

FARLEY, BILL THOMAS, entertainment industry executive; b. Yonkers, N.Y., July 11, 1944; s. William Thomas and Flora May (Rae) F. BA, Cornell U., 1966. Reporter White Plains (N.Y.) Reporter Dispatch, 1966-67; news dir. WVOX-AM/FM, New Rochelle, N.Y., 1967-69; writer/publicist Am. Broadcasting Cos., N.Y.C. and L.A., 1969-79; creative dir. BGPR Agy., L.A., 1979-83; info. mgr. 1984 Summer Olympic Games, L.A., 1984; pub. rels. mgr. Playboy Enterprises, Inc., L.A., 1985-87, dir. comm., 1987-89, nat. dir. comm., 1989—; pres. WordSmith Comm., Hollywood, Calif., 1985—. Author/editor: Apollo II: Man's Greatest Adventure, 1969; author: My Other Car Is A Porsche, 1994; author mag. Unofficial Guide to the 1984 Lia Games, 1984. Libertarian. Office: Playboy Enterprises Inc 9242 Beverly Blvd Beverly Hills CA 90210-3710

FARLEY, ROBERT DAY, metropolitan planning official; b. Jackson, Mich., Feb. 15, 1936. AA, Jackson C.C., 1956; BA in Polit. Sci., Mich. State U., 1958; MPA, U. Colo., 1981. Asst. city assessor City of East Lansing (Mich.), 1958; city mgr. Corunna, Mich., 1958-59, Hudson, Mich., 1959-62; asst. dir. Suprs. for Inter-County Com., Detroit, 1962-66; dir. intergovtl. rels. Met. Fund, Inc., Detroit, 1966-68; dep. exec. dir. S.E. Mich. Coun. of Govts., Detroit, 1968-70; exec. dir. Denver Regional Coun. Govts., 1970—, mem. transp. com., 1977—; disting. pub. exec. in residence, U. Denver, 1978; vis. lectr. U. Tex., Austin, 1978; mem. adv. coun. Grad. Sch. Pub. Affairs, U. Colo., 1978-81; mem. intergovernmental adv. com. State of Colo., 1977-81. Ex-officio mem. Denver Olympic Com. Planning Bd., 1971-72; mem. capital improvements adv. com. Denver Water Bd., 1973; mem. solid waste adv. com. Nat. League of Cities and U.S. Conf. Mayors, 1973; mem. mayor's com. on the Platte Valley, City and County of Denver, 1971-73, mayor's com. on youth problems, 1973, mayor's manpower com., 1971-73; mem. policy com. Regional Emergency Med. Care, 1973; mem. Mayor's Com. to Keep Denver a Great City, 1975-76; mem. adv. com. dept. social planning Mile High United Way, 1971-73, sect. leader campaign, 1981, 92; mem. met. community svc. bd. Colo. Coun. Chs., 1973-79, vice chmn., mem. exec. com., 1974-76, 78-79; mem. adv. panel on urban impacts Charles F. Kettering Found., Dayton, Ohio, 1980; mem. community adv. com. Jr. League Denver., 1979-84. mem. policy bd. Urban Obs. Denver, 1971-83; bd. govs. Metro Denver Urban Coalition, 1971-79, chair nominating com. 1973, exec. com., 1976; mem. adv. com. Denver Met. Area leadership Devel. and Advocacy Program, Mex. Am. Legal Def. and Edn. Fund, 1982; bd. dirs. Colo. Assn. Regional Couns., 1977—; mem. Adv. Com. Hispanic Agenda, Latin Am. Rsch. and Svc. Agy., 1988-92; chmn. transp. and parking task team. Mayor's Denver Downtown Agenda, 1992-93. Recipient Outstanding Contbn. in Meeting Urban Problems award, Denver Fed. Exec. Bd., 1987, Walter A. Scheiber Regional Leadership award Nat. Assn. Regional Coun., 1978, L.P. Cookingham award for Career Devel. Internat. City Mgmt. Assn., 1978, award Commn. on Cmty. Rels., 1976. Mem. ASPA, Nat. Assn. Regional Coun. (bd. dirs. 1972-75, 93—, exec. dirs. adv. com. 1972-79, 81-85, 88—, chmn. 1995-6, coord. U.S. presentations at 5th Internat. Conf. on regionalism 1982, mem. tng. adv. com. 1978, chmn. ann. dir.'s conf. planning com. 1977, among others), Internat. City Mgmt. Assn. (COG adv. com. 1973-80, com. on regionalism policy 1973-74, com. on growth mgmt. 1973-76, conf. planning com. 1973, 77, 83, acad. for profl. devel. 1976, metro city mgrs. assn. 1982—). Office: 2480 W 26th Ave Ste 200-b Denver CO 80211-5309

FARLEY, THOMAS T., lawyer; b. Pueblo, Colo., Nov. 10, 1934; s. John Baron and Mary (Tancred) F.; m. Kathleen Maybelle Murphy, May 14, 1960; children: John, Michael, Kelly, Anne. BS, U. Santa Clara, 1956; LLB, U. Colo., 1959. Bar: Colo. 1959, U.S. Dist. Ct. Colo. 1959, U.S. Ct. Appeals (10th cir.) 1988. Dep. dist. atty. County of Pueblo, 1960-62; pvt. practice Pueblo, 1963-69; ptnr. Phelps, Fonda & Hays, Pueblo, 1970-75, Petersen & Fonda, P.C., Pueblo, 1975—; bd. dirs. Pub. Svc. Co. Colo., Denver, Norwest Pueblo, Norwest Sunset, Found. Health Systems, Inc. Minority leader Colo. Ho. of Reps., 1967-75; chmn. Colo. Wildlife Commn., 1975-79, Colo. Bd. Agr., 1979-87; bd. regents Santa Clara U., 1987—; commr. Colo. State Fair; trustee Cath. Found. Diocese of Pueblo, Great Outdoors Colo. Trust Fund. Recipient Disting. Svc. award U. So. Colo., 1987, 93, Bd. of Regents, U. Colo., 1993. Mem. ABA, Colo. Bar Assn., Pueblo C. of C. (bd. dirs. 1991-93), Rotary. Democrat. Roman Catholic. Office: Petersen & Fonda PC 650 Thatcher Bldg Pueblo CO 81003

FARMER, GEORGE THOMAS, JR., environmental scientist, consultant; b. Pulaski, Va., May 26, 1937; s. George Thomas and Eulalia Helen Farmer. BA, U. Va., 1958, MS, 1960; PhD, U. Cin., 1968. Assoc. prof. geology James Madison U., Harrisonburg, Va., 1965-79; sr. hydrogeologist JRB/SAIC, McLean, Va., 1979-82; sr. hydrogeologist, chief geologist Versar, Inc., Springfield, Va., 1982-84; sr. hydrogeologist Uranium Mill Tailings Remedial Action Project, Albuquerque, 1984-86; sr. hydrogeologist, prin. Ecology and Environment, Inc., L.A., 1986-87; sr. hydrogeologist, quality assurance officer Brown and Caldwell Engrs. and Geologists, Pasadena, Calif., 1987-89; regional office mgr. Applied Geosys., Inc., Culver City, Calif., 1989-90; programmatic project leader Los Alamos (N.Mex.) Nat. Lab., 1990—; cons. hydrogeologist, Kleinfelder, Compton, Calif., 1986. Co-author: Earth Materials: Earth Processes, 1992. Mem. Am. Geol. Inst., Am. Assn. Profl. Geologists (cert.), Sigma Xi, Sigma Gamma Epsilon. Home: 8 Los Arboles Dr Los Alamos NM 87544-3081 Office: Los Alamos Nat Lab ER Program MS M 992 Los Alamos NM 87545

FARMER, JANENE ELIZABETH, artist, educator; b. Albuquerque, Oct. 16, 1946; d. Charles John Watt and Regina M. (Brown) Kruger; m. Michael Hugh Bolton, Apr. 1965 (div.); m. Frank Urban Farmer, May, 1972 (div.). BA in Art, San Diego State U., 1969. Owner, operator Iron Walrus Pottery, 1972-79; designer ceramic and fabric murals, Coronado, Calif., 1979-82; executed commns. for clients in U.S.A., Can., Japan and Mex., 1972—; designer fabric murals and bldg. interiors; painter rare and endangered animals, Coronado and La Jolla, Calif., 1982—; tchr. Catholic schs., San Diego, 1982-87, Ramona Unified Sch. Dist., 1988—, mentor tchr.; instr. U. Calif., San Diego, 1979-83, 92. Mem. Coronado Arts and Humanities Coun., 1979-81. Grantee Calif. Arts Coun., 1980-81, resident artist U. Calif., San Diego; U. San Diego grad. fellow dept. edn., 1984; tchr. environ. art San Diego Natural History Mus., summer 1996, 97 and San Diego Wild Animal Park, summer, 1996. Mem. edn. adv. com. La Jolla (Calif.) Playhouse, 1996. Mem. Am. Soc. Interior Designers (affiliate). Roman Catholic. Home: 4435 Nobel Dr Apt 35 San Diego CA 92122-1559

FARMER, TERRY D(WAYNE), lawyer; b. Oklahoma City, May 1, 1949; s. Gayle V. and Allene (Edsall) F.; m. Lynn J. Dively, June 30, 1979; children: Grant L., Tyler M. BA, U. Okla., 1971, JD, 1974. Bar: Okla. 1974, N.Mex. 1975, U.S. Dist. Ct. N.Mex. 1976, U.S. Ct. Claims 1975, U.S. Ct. Appeals (10th cir.) 1977, U.S. Supreme Ct. 1980. Asst. trust officer First Nat. Bank of Albuquerque, 1974-75; assoc. Nordhaus, Moses & Dunn, Albuquerque, 1975-78, ptnr., 1978-80; dir. Moses, Dunn, Farmer & Tuthill, P.C., Albuquerque, 1980—; pres. Albuquerque Lawyers Club, N. Mex., 1982-83. Fellow N.Mex. Bar Assn. (pres. Young Lawyers div., 1978-79); mem. Okla. Bar Assn., N.Mex. Trial Lawyers. Office: Moses Dunn Farmer & Tuthill PC PO Box 27047 Albuquerque NM 87125

FARMER, WESLEY STEVEN, police officer; b. Albuquerque, Dec. 1, 1950; s. Dewey B. Farmer and Bernice (Willie) Maloch; m. Wendy L. Phillips, Sept. 22, 1992; children: Erica, Alisha, Tara. BA, Calif. Bapt. Coll., 1972; MPA, Calif. State U., San Bernardino, 1989. Police officer San Bernardino (Calif.) Police, 1973-79, police detective, 1979-84, police sgt., 1984-89, police lt., 1989—; adj. faculty Riverside (Calif.) C.C., 1989, 92. Contbr. articles to profl. jours. Mem. Rotary, San Bernardino, 1983-84; bd. dirs. Family Svc. Am., Milw., 1995—, bd. chair western region, 1995—, bd. chair San Bernardino chpt., 1986-96. Mem. ASPA (bd. dirs. 1992-96), Family Svc. Agy. (bd. chair 1993-96, Svc. award 1995). Republican. Office: San Bernardino Police PO Box 1559 San Bernardino CA 92401

FARNHAM, MARY GLADE SIEMER, artist; b. Ross, Calif., Nov. 1, 1924; d. Albert Henry and Mabel Meta (Jones) Siemer; children: Thomas Ross, Evan Neil, Gwen Marie, William Blair, Hugh Porter. *Mary Farnham is a fourth generation San Franciscan. Her great grandfather, Thomas Daniel Jones, visited San Francisco in 1844, when he was seventeen. He completed his education at Cambridge and returned to San Francisco in 1848. He met his future wife, Anne Porter, dockside to tell her of the death of his friend, and her fiancé, on the voyage out. Thomas and Anne had five surviving children: Thomas, Will (grandfather of Mary Farnham), Ottiwell, Mattie, and Hubert.* Student Marin Jr. Coll., 1942-43, Goucher Coll., 1943-44; BA, U. Calif.-Berkeley, 1947. Profl. athlete, Curry Co., Yosemite, Calif., 1945; advt. prodn. mgr. City of Paris/Hale's, San Francisco, 1947; advt. artist Lipman Wolfe, Portland, Oreg., 1947-48; advt. layout artist Meier & Frank, Portland, 1948; art dir. Olds & King, Portland, 1948-50; free lance comml. artist, Portland, 1950-56; pres. Marin County Devel. Co., San Anselmo, Calif., 1963-78; pres., designer Mary Farnham Designs, Inc., Portland, 1983-89. Exhibited in 14 one woman shows and numerous group shows, U.S. & abroad. Mem. pub. art selection panel II, Met. Arts Commn., Portland, 1982-83; bd. dirs. N.W. Artists Workshop, Portland, 1977-78; sec. Artist Membership, Portland Art Assn., 1973-74. Episcopalian. Club: Multnomah Athletic. Avocations: swimming, diving, cooking. *Mary Farnham has exhibited her work in juried or invitational shows world-wide, though her work has mainly been shown in West Coast museums, university galleries, and alternative spaces.*

FARNUM, NANCY ALYSON, communications executive; b. Birmingham, Ala., Mar. 2, 1949; d. Leon Vernon and Martha Reeves (McGahee) F. BA, Rockford Coll., 1971; MSLS, Case We. Reserve U., 1972. cert. health information profl. Information specialist Merrell-Nat. Lab. Pharm. Co., Cin., 1973-78; dir. and comptroller U.S. ops. Applied Human Cybernetics, London, 1975-78; asst. prof. and online search analyst Coll. Medicine E. Tenn. State U., Johnson City, Tenn., 1982-84; assoc. dir. N.W. Area Health Edn. Ctr., Salisbury, N.C., 1984-88; asst. prof. Bowman Gray Sch. Medicine, Winston Salem, 1984-88; coord. multimedia svcs. U. Ala., Birmingham, 1989-92; cons. MRM Communications, Claremont, Calif., 1988—; cons. St. George's (Grenada) U. Sch. Medicine, 1989; chmn. K-12 devel. U. of the World, La Jolla, Calif., 1989—; mem. Gov.'s Tech. Task Force on Edn. Reform, Montgomery, Ala., 1993—. Coord. Global Awareness Seminar Birmingham Pub. Schs., 1988-93, World Peace Day Friends of the City of Birmingham, 1988—. Recipient Grad. endowment Nat. Inst. Health, Bethesda, Md., 1971-72; scholarship Sch. Theology at Claremont (Calif.), 1993, Fuller Theol. Sem., Pasadena, Calif., 1996-97. Mem. NAFE, Med. Libr. Assn., Network Birmingham, Acad. Health Info. Profls. Mem. Reformed Ch. Am. Office: Health Scis Comms Assn 750 W 8th Ave Claremont CA 91711

FARON, FAY CHERYL, private investigator, writer; b. Kansas City, Mo., Feb. 27, 1949; d. Albert David and Geraldine Fay (Morgan) F. Student, Glendale (Ariz.) C.C., 1967-68, Ariz. State U., 1968-71, U. Ariz., 1971-72. Lic. pvt. investigator, Calif. Owner Monogramation, San Francisco, 1976-80; assoc. prodr. Sta. KGO-TV, San Francisco, 1980-81, Power/Rector, San Francisco, 1982-83; owner Office in the City, San Francisco, 1982-83, The Rat Dog Dick Detective Agy., San Francisco, 1983—; lectr., guest spkr. San Francisco U., 1984—, S.F.A.L.A. (Paralegals), San Francisco, 1984—, Calif. Collectors Coun., San Francisco, 1992—. Author: A Private Eye's Guide to Collecting a Bad Debt, 1991, Missing Persons, 1997; author/editor: The Instant National Locator Guide, 1991, 2nd edit., 1993, 3rd edit, 1996; columnist Ask Rat Dog, 1993—. Founder Elder Angels. Mem. Nat. Assn. Investigative Specialists, Nat. Assn. Bunco Investigators (asst.), Profls. Against Confidence Crimes (asst.). Office: The Rat Dog Dick Detective Agy PO Box 470862 San Francisco CA 94147

FAROUDJA, PHILIPPE YVES, television director; b. San Jose, Calif., Feb. 17, 1968; s. Yves Charles and Isabell Emily (O'Brien) F. BA, Wesleyan U., Middletown, Conn., 1990; MFA, UCLA, 1994. Devel. asst. Hanna-Barbera Cartoons, 1994-95, prodr. The Real Adventures of Jonny Quest, 1995—; assoc. prodr. What a Cartoon! Cartoon Network, 1996—; Cons. artist Lumysis Corp., Sunnyvale, Calif., 1996. Patentee in field. Mem. Soc. Motion Picture and TV Engrs., Phi Beta Kappa.

FARQUHARSON, WALTER HENRY, minister, church official; b. Zealandia, Sask., Can., May 30, 1936; s. James and Jessie Ann (Muirhead) F.; m. Patricia Joan Casswell, Sept. 16, 1958; children: Scott, Michael, Catherine, Stephen. BA, U. Sask., Saskatoon, 1957, Diploma in Edn., 1969; BD, St. Andrew's Coll., Saskatoon, 1961, DD (hon.), 1975. Ordained to ministry United Ch. of Can., 1961. Min. Saltcoats-Bredenbury-Churchbridge Pastoral Charge, Sask., 1961—; moderator United Ch. of Can., 1990-92; exec. gen. coun., pres. Sask. Conf. Contbr. numerous hymns and religious songs; retreat leader. Recipient Commemorative medal 125th anniversary Confedn. Can. Home: PO Box 126, Saltcoats, SK Canada S0A 3R0 Office: United Ch of Can, PO Box 58, Saltcoats, SK Canada S0A 3R0*

FARR, DAVID DONALD, musician, educator, administrator; b. Coquille, Oreg., Feb. 28, 1942; s. Donald Haines and Emma Frances (Mulkey) F.; m. Kathleen McIntosh, June 19, 1968 (div. 1975). BA, U. Oreg., 1965, MusM, 1966; PhD in Theology and the Arts, Grad. Theol. Union, 1986; ed. various mus. seminars. Tchg. asst. U. Oreg., Eugene, 1965-66; fellow Coll. Ch. Musicians, Wash. Nat. Cathedral, 1968; choirmaster/organist St. Mark's Episcopal Ch., Berkeley, Calif., 1968-72; music master Coll. Prep. Sch., Oakland, Calif., 1970-72; choirmaster/organist All Sts. Episcopal Ch., Pasadena, Calif., 1972-78, St. Mary Magdalen Ch., Berkeley, 1979-85; dir. music, liturgical cons. to campus ministry St. Mary's Coll., Moraga, Calif., 1981-83; mus. dir. St. Luke's Episcopal Ch., San Francisco, 1986-94; exec. dir. San Anselmo (Calif.) Organ Festival, 1992—; pvt. instr. organ, piano and voice, 1960—; organist St. Ignatius Ch., U. San Francisco, 1994—; condr. seminars in field; mus. dir. Jr. Bach Festival Assn., Inc., Berkeley, 1983-85; founder 1st Am. br. Royal Sch. Ch. Music, 1977; cons. mem. Standing Commn. on Ch. Music of Episcopal Ch., 1977-79; cons. design of liturgical space/acoustical and mus. parameters St. Andrew's Newman Student Ctr., Riverside, Calif., 1985-89; cons. organ selection, design, installation All Soul's Episcopal Ch., San Diego, 1978-86. Author: A Guide to Anthems for the Lectionary, 1994; co-contbr. chpt. to: Clergy and Church Musicians, 1980; contbr. articles to profl. publs. Choral clinician to conf. on liturgy and music Diocese Miss; chmn. commn. on liturgy and ch. music Episcopal Diocese L.A., 1976-78; planner ann. conf. Chmn. of Diocesan Liturgical Commns., Santa Barbara, Calif., 1976, Albuquerque, 1979; mem. liturgical renewal commn. Diocese Calif. Mem. Am. Musicological Soc., Assn. Anglican Musicians (pres. 1974-75, chmn. membership com. 1976-77, chmn. profl. standards, status and compensation com. 1977-79, planner conf. 1975), Am. Guild Organists (dean San Francisco chpt. 1988-92, planner mid-winter conclave 1976, cons. to Western Regional Conv. 1993), Organ Hist. Soc. Democrat. Home: 500 Plymouth Ave San Francisco CA 94112-2914 Office: San Anselmo Organ Festival 2 Kensington Rd San Anselmo CA 94960-2905

FARR, DONALD EUGENE, engineering scientist; b. Clinton, Iowa, July 1, 1933; s. Kenneth Elroy and Nellie Irene (Bailey) F.; m. Sally Joyce Brauer, Mar. 8, 1954; children: Erika Lyn Farr Leventis, Jolene Karyn Farr Walters. BA in Engring. Psychology, San Diego State U., 1961; MT with honors, Nat. U., 1974; postgrad., Calif. Pacific U., 1976-80. Human factors specialist Bunker Ramo Corp., Canoga Park, Calif., Germany, 1964-69; sr. design specialist Gen. Dynamics, San Diego, 1955-63, 69-76; tech. staff Sandia Nat. Labs., Albuquerque, 1977-80; group supr., sr. tech. advisor The Babcock and Wilcox Co., Lynchburg, Va., 1980-82; dir. human factors sys. Sci. Applications, Inc., Lynchburg, 1982-83; human engring. scientist Lockheed Calif. Co., Burbank, 1983-91; MANPRINT mgr. Teledyne Electronic Sys., Northridge, Calif., 1991-94; human engring. scientist, program mgr. Symvionics, Inc., Pasadena, Calif., 1994—; ergonomics safety cons. govt., industry and academia, 1977—. Contbr. articles to profl. jours. Precinct capt., voter registration vol. Rep. Party, 1963—; lectr., support group Am. Diabetes Assn., L.A., 1993—. With USN, 1952-53. Scholarship USN, 1953; recipient Admiral's award NSIA, 1963. Mem. Human Factors and Ergonomics Soc. (pres. San Diego, L.A. chpt.), Internat. Numismatic Soc. (pres. 1973-75), Am. Nuclear Soc. (human factors chair 1980-82), Am. Legion, NRA Golden Eagles (honor role). Lutheran. Home: 20054 Avenue Of The Oaks Newhall CA 91321-1361 Office: Symvionics Inc 3280 E Foothill Blvd Ste 200 Pasadena CA 91107-3103

FARR, G(ARDNER) NEIL, lawyer; b. L.A., Jan. 9, 1932; s. Gardner and Elsie M. (Schuster) F.; m. Lorna Jean, Oct. 26, 1957; children: Marshall Clay, Jennifer T., Thomas M. BA, U. Calif., Berkeley, 1957, JD, U. Calif., San Francisco, 1960. Bar: Calif. 1961, U.S. Supreme Ct. 1977. Cert specialist family law Calif. Bd. Specialization, 1980. Dep. dist. atty. Solano County, 1961-66; recreation commr. City of Fairfield, 1964-66; dep. dist. atty. Kern County, 1966-69; ptnr. Young, Wooldridge, Paulden, Self, Farr & Hugie (now Law Offices of Young Wooldridge), Bakersfield, Calif., 1969—; dir. Cen. Calif. Appellate Program, Inc.; judge protem Kern County Superior Ct. Chmn. Kern County Juvenile Justice Commn. With USNR, 1949-53. Mem. ABA, Calif. Bar Assn., Kern County Bar Assn. (pres. 1984, past pres. family law sect.), Calif. Trial Lawyers Assn. Office: Young Wooldridge 1800 30th St Fl 4 Bakersfield CA 93301

FARR, JOHN KEVIN, social sciences educator; b. Riverside, Calif., Apr. 30, 1957; s. Conrad Landis and Mary Jean (Reilly) F.; m. Jane Margaret Petrilli, July 25, 1981; children: Kevin Landis, Margaret Elizabeth, William Conrad. BA in History and European Studies, U. San Diego, 1979; MA in Edn., San Diego State U., 1984. Cert. tchr. and adminstr., Calif. Tchr. jr. h.s. and h.s. Damascus (Syria) Cmty. Sch., 1988-89; tchr. h.s. Corona-Norco Unified Schs., Corona, Calif., 1984-88, tchr. jr. h.s., 1989—; presenter Near East South Asia Ednl. Conf., Athens, Greece, 1988, Calif. Assn. for Gifted, Long Beach, 1991. Co-author: Corona: Citrus, Races and More. . ., 1993. Bd. dirs., past pres. Corona Hist. Preservation Soc., 1991—; pres. sch. bd. St. Edward Sch., Corona, 1992—; chmn. Riverside County Libertarian Party, 1991, 92; active Riverside County Hist. Commn., 1993-96, Mission Inn Found., 1984—; mem., pres. Corona Civic Concert Band, 1993-94; trustee Corona Pub. Libr. Bd., 1996—. Recipient Spl. award for rescuing drowning child City of Corona, 1970. Mem. NEA, Calif. Tchrs. Assn. (site rep. 1990, 91), Cath. League for Religious and Civil Rights. Office: Corona Fundamental Intermediate Schs 1230 S Main St Corona CA 91720-4464

FARR, LEE EDWARD, physician; b. Albuquerque, Oct. 13, 1907; s. Edward and Mabel (Heyn) F.; m. Anne Ritter, Dec. 28, 1936 (dec.); children: Charles E., Susan A., Frances A.; m. Miriam Kirk, Jan. 12, 1985. BS, Yale U., 1929, MD, 1933. Asst. pediatrics Sch. Medicine, Yale U., 1933-34; asst. medicine Hosp. of Rockefeller Inst. Med. Rsch., 1934-37, assoc. medicine, 1937-40; dir. research Alfred I. duPont Inst. of Nemours Found., Wilmington, Del., 1940-49; vis. assoc. prof. pediatrics Sch. Medicine, U. Pa., 1940-49; med. dir. Brookhaven Nat. Lab., 1948-62; prof. nuclear medicine U. Tex. Postgrad. Med. Sch., 1962-64, prof. nuclear and environ. medicine Grad. Sch. Bio-Med. Scis., U. Tex. at Houston, 1965-68; chief sect. nuc. medicine U. Tex.-M.D. Anderson Hosp. and Tumor Inst., 1962-67, prof. environ. health U. Tex. Sch. Pub. Health, Houston, 1967-68; head disaster health svcs. Calif. Dept. Health, 1968, chief emergency health svcs. unit, 1968-70, 1st chief bur. emergency med. services, 1970-73; Lippitt lectr. Marquette U., 1941; Sommers Meml. lectr. U. Oreg. Sch. Med., Portland, 1960; Gordon Wilson lectr. Am. Clin. and Climatol. Assn., 1956; Sigma Xi nat. lectr., 1952-53; guest scientist Institut fur Medizinder Kernforschungsanlage, Julich, Germany, 1966; Brookhaven Nat. Lab. lectr., 1990. Mem. NRC adv. com. Naval Med. Res., 1953-68; chmn. NRC adv. com. Atomic Bomb Casualty Commn., 1953-68; mem. adv. com. Naval Res. to Sec. of Navy and CNO, 1966-72; NRC adv. com. on medicine and surgery, 1965-66, exec. com., 1962-65; Naval Research Mission to Formosa, 1953; tech. adviser U.S. delegation to Geneva Internat. Conf. for Peaceful Uses Atomic Energy, 1955; mem. N.Y. Adv. Com. Atomic Energy, 1956-59; mem. cholera commn. SEATO Conf., Bangkok, 1960; mem. AMA Com. Nuclear Medicine, 1963-66; mem. com. med. isotopes NASA Manned Spacecraft Ctr., 1966-68; mem. expert adv. panel radiation WHO, 1957-79; mem. Calif. Gov.'s Ad Hoc Com. Emergency Health Service, 1968-69; mem. sci. adv. bd. Gorgas Meml. Inst., 1967-72; numerous other sci. adv. bds., panels; cons. TRW Systems, Inc., 1966-70, Consol. Petroleum Co., Beverly Hills, Calif., 1946-70. Mem. alumni bd. Yale, 1962-65, mem. alumni fund, 1966-76, agent alumni fund 1994-96; with 1929 class coun. 1994-96. With USNR, 1942-46; capt. (M.C.) USNR, ret. Recipient Mead Johnson award for pediatric research, 1940, Gold Cross Order of Phoenix, Greece, 1960, Verdienstkreuz 1st class Fed. Republic Germany, 1963; named Community Leader in Am., 1969, Disting. Alumni Yale U. Med. Sch., 1989. Diplomate Nat. Bd. Med. Examiners, Am. Bd. Pediatrics. Fellow AAAS, Royal Soc. Arts, Am. Acad. Pediatrics, N.Y. Acad. Scis., Royal Soc. Health, Am. Coll. Nuclear Medicine (disting. fellow); mem. Soc. Pediatric Research, Soc. Exptl. Biology, Harvey Soc., Am. Pediatric Soc., Soc. Exptl. Pathology, Am. Soc. Clin. Investigation, Radiation Research Soc., AMA (mem. council on sci. assembly 1960-70, chmn. 1968-70), Med. Soc. Athens (hon. mem.), Alameda County Med. Assn., Sigma Xi, Alpha Omega Alpha, Phi Sigma Kappa, Nu Sigma Nu, Alpha Chi Sigma. Club: Commonwealth (San Francisco). Author articles on nuclear medicine, protein metabolism, emergency med. services, radioactive and chem. environ. contaminants, environ. noise. Home: 2502 Saklan Indian Dr Apt 2 Walnut Creek CA 94595-3001

FARR, LEONARD ALFRED, hospital administrator; b. Pleasant Hill, La., Mar. 19, 1947. BA, La. State U., 1969; MA, Washington U., 1974. Adminstr. resident HCA Wesley Med. Ctr., Wichita, Kans., 1973-74, night adminstr., 1974-75; asst. adminstr. Physicians & Surgeons Hosp., Shreveport, La., 1975, exec. v.p., 1975-76; adminstr. Colo. Springs. (Colo.) Community Hosp., 1976-78; pres., CEO St. Francis Hosp. Systems, Colo. Springs, Colo., 1978-87; COO Penrose-St. Francis Hosp., Colo. Springs, 1987-91, pres., CEO, 1991—; s.r. v.p. United HealthCare, Mpls., 1997; pres. divsn. united Am. Assn. Ret. Persons, Mpls., 1997—. Mem. Am. Hosp. Assn. (alternate del., del.), Colo. Hosp. Assn. (chmn. bd.). Office: United Health Care Mail Stop MN008 EZ10 PO Box 1459 Minneapolis MN 55440*

FARR, SAM, congressman; b. Calif., July 4, 1941; m. Shary Baldwin; 1 child, Jessica. BSc Biology, Willamette U., 1963; student, Monterey Inst. Internat. Studies, U. Santa Clara. Vol. Peace Corps, 1963-65; budget analyst, cons. Assembly com. Constl. Amendments; bd. suprs. Monterey (Calif.) County; rep. Calif. State Assembly, 1980-93; mem., regional whip 103d U.S. Congress from 17th Calif. dist., 1993—; mem. agr. com., mem. resources com. 103d U.S. Congress. Named Legislator of Yr. Calif. 9 times. Democrat. Office: House of Representatives 1117 Longworth House Office Bl Washington DC 20515

FARRAR, ELAINE WILLARDSON, artist; b. L.A.; d. Eldon and Gladys Elsie (Larsen) Willardson; BA, Ariz. State U., 1967, MA, 1969, PhD, 1990; children: Steve, Mark, Gregory, JanLeslie, Monty, Susan. Tchr., Camelback Desert Sch., Paradise Valley, Ariz., 1966-69; mem. faculty Yavapai Coll., Prescott, Ariz., 1970-92, chmn. dept. art, 1973-78, instr. art in watercolor and oil and acrylic painting, intaglio, relief and monoprints, 1971-92; grad. advisor Prescott Coll. Master of Arts Program, 1993-97. One-man shows include: R.P. Moffat's, Scottsdale, Ariz., 1969, Art Center, Battle Creek, Mich., 1969, The Woodpeddler, Costa Mesa, Calif., 1979; group show Prescott (Ariz.) Fine Arts Assn., 1982, 84, 86, 89, 90-95, 96, N.Y. Nat. Am. Watercolorists, 1982; Ariz. State U. Women Images Now, 1986, 87, 89, 90-92; works rep. local and state exhibits, pvt. nat. & internat. collections. Mem., curator Prescott Fine Arts Visual Arts com., 1992-97, mem. exec. com. 1996—; bd. dirs. Prescott Fine Arts Assn., 1995—, Friends Y.C. Art Gallery Bd., 1992-97. Mem. Mountain Artists Guild (past pres.), Ariz. Art Edn. Assn., Ariz. Women's Caucus for Art, Women's Nat. Mus. (charter Washington chpt.), Kappa Delta Pi, Phi Delta Kappa (Yavapai chpt. v.p. mem., 1994-95; Ariz State U. chpt.). *Through the visual arts many ideas and feelings are expressed that would otherwise be lost to the communication of these thoughts to others—a vital link to understanding.*

FARRAR, JAMES PAUL, electronics company official; b. Albuquerque, May 29, 1937; s. Clyde William and Lina Mae (Hudson) F.; m. Marilyn Austa Johnson, June 21, 1958; children: Paul Frederick, Jamie Austa, Kimberly Sue. BSEE, U. N.Mex., 1960; MBA, Pepperdine U., 1981; DBA, Nova U., 1991. Design engr. E.G. & G., Inc., Las Vegas, 1960-63; design, test engr. Govt. Electronics Group Motorola, Inc., Scottsdale, Ariz., 1963-66; quality assurance ops. mgr. Govt. Electronics Group, Scottsdale, Ariz., 1984-93; quality assurance mgr. Unitech Industries, Scottsdale, 1994-95; acad. affairs mgr. U. Phoenix, 1995—; engring. mgr. Collins Radio Co., Dallas, 1966-68; NIH spl. research fellow U. Tex. Med. Sch., 1968-70; program mgr. TRW Colo. Elecronics Co., Colorado Springs, 1970-74; automatic test equipment program mgr. Ford Aerospace & Communications Co., Colorado Spirngs, 1974-76, system integration mgr., Palo Alto, Calif., 1976-79; dir. prodn. support GenRad, Ind., Phoenix, 1979-84; mem. adj. facutly dept. fin., mgmt. and quantatative methods, acad. affairs mgr. U. Phoenix, 1981—; bus. cons., Phoenix, 1983—. Mem. Maricopa County Tech. Adv. Council, 1982-84. With U.S. Army, 1955-63. Mem. Am. Electronics Assn., Acad. Mgmt. Republican. Roman Catholic. Home: 16045 S 38th Pl Phoenix AZ 85044-7378 Office: 8201 E Mcdowell Rd Scottsdale AZ 85257-3812

FARRAR, LUCY ELLEN, real estate broker; b. Knoxville, Tenn., Oct. 5, 1936; d. Raymond Leon and Mable Glen (Crass) Hatmaker; m. Robert David Proffitt, Oct. 5, 1956 (div. Aug. 1974); children: Robert David Jr., Karen Lelia, Stephen Keith, Kevin Scott; m. Charles Richard Farrar, Sr., Oct. 19, 1983. BA, U. Tenn., 1963, MA, 1967. Lic. real estate broker, Colo. Instr. Maryville (Tenn.) Coll., 1967-72; prodr./hostess talk show WSJK TV (PBS), Knoxville, Tenn., 1972-74; dir. devel. Barter Found., Abingdon, Va., 1974-78; tng. coord. gas ops. Aramco, Abqaiq, Saudi Arabia, 1979-83; planning analyst fin. and acctg. Aramco, Dhahran, Saudi Arabia, 1984-85; broker, owner Pinnacle Properties, Monument, Colo., 1989-93; broker, ptnr. Tri-Lakes Realty, Inc., Monument, 1993—; dir. Realtor Svc. Corp., Colorado Springs, 1993—, pres. 1995-96; bd. dirs. Pikes Peak Assn. of Realtors, 1994—. Recipient nat. awards Operation Healthy Babies March of Dimes/Nat. Coun. Women's Club, Chgo., 1963, Project Concern/Jim Turpin, Nashville, 1964. Mem. Women's Coun. Realtors, Pikes Peak Assn. Realtors (chmn. tech. rev. and adv. 1992—, dir. 1995—), Tri-Lakes C. of C., Woodmoor Country Club (dir., sec., registered agt. 1988-90), Pi Beta Phi Alumni Club. Home: PO Box 9 Monument CO 80132-0009

FARRELL, DENNIS, sports association executive; b. Orange, Calif., Feb. 23, 1951; s. Fred Bernard and Janet Louise (Crawford) F.; m. Charlene Louise Cassingham, Jan. 11, 1975; Timothy William, Michael Ted. AA in Liberal Arts, Santa Ana Coll., 1971; BA in Journalism, San Diego State U., 1973. Sports editor Saddleback Valley News, Mission Viejo, Calif., 1974-77; sports info. dir. Saddleback Coll., Mission Viejo, Calif., 1977-80; asst. commr. Pacific Coast Athletic Assn., Santa Ana, Calif., 1980-88; assoc. commr. Big West Conf., Santa Ana, Calif., 1988-92; commr. Big West Conf., Irvine, Calif., 1992—. Mem. Collegiate Commrs. Assn. Office: Big West Conf 2 Corporate Park Ste 206 Irvine CA 92714*

FARRELL, EDWARD JOSEPH, retired mathematics educator; b. San Francisco, Mar. 28, 1917; s. Christopher Patrick and Ethel Ann (Chesterman) F.; m. Pearl Philomena Rongone, Aug. 21, 1954; children: Paul, Paula. B.Sc., U. San Francisco, 1939; M.A., Stanford U., 1942. Mem. faculty U. San Francisco, 1941—, prof. math., 1968-82, prof. emeritus, lectr., 1982-93; cons. math. text publs., mem. adv. panels NSF, 1966-75, dir. summer and in-svc. insts., 1960-75, dir. confs. geometry, 1967, 68, 70-75; mem. rev. panel Sci. Books. Author math. reports; editor studies teaching contemporary geometry. Served with AUS, 1944-46. NSF faculty fellow, 1956-57. Mem. AAAS, Am. Assn. Physics Tchrs., Nat. Coun. Tchrs. Math. (guest lectr. regional and nat. meetings 1966, 67, 69), Sch. Sci. and Math. Assn. Republican. Roman Catholic. Home: 2526 Gough St San Francisco CA 94123-5013

FARRELL, FRANCINE ANNETTE, psychotherapist, educator, author; b. Long Beach, Calif., Mar. 26, 1948; d. Thomas and Evelyn Marie (Lucente) F.; m. James Thomas Hanley, Dec. 5, 1968 (div. Dec. 1988); children: Melinda Lee Hanley, James Thomas Hanley Jr.; m. Robert Erich Haesche, June 3, 1995. BA in Psychology with honors, Calif. State U., Sacramento, 1985, MS in Counseling, 1986. Lic. marriage, family and child counselor, Calif.; nat. cert. addiction counselor. Marriage, family and child counselor intern Fulton Ct. Counseling, Sacramento, 1987-88; pvt. practice psychotherapist Sacramento, 1988—; instr. chem. dependency studies program, Calif. State U., Sacramento, 1985-94, acad. coord. chem. dependency studies program, 1988-90; trainee Sobriety Brings a Change, Sacramento, 1986-87; assoc. investigator, curriculum coord. Project S.A.F.E., Sacramento, 1990-91; presenter Sacramento Conf., ACA, 1986, 88, 89, 91, 92, Ann. Symposium on Chem. Dependency, 1993. Presenter (cable TV series) Trouble in River City: Charting a Course for Change, 1991. Mem. Nat. Coun. on Alcoholism, Calif. Assn. Marriage and Family Therapists, Calif. Assn. Alcoholism and Drug Abuse Counselors (bd. dirs. region 5, 1988-90), Phi Kappa Phi. Roman Catholic. Office: 2740 Fulton Ave # 100 Sacramento CA 95821-5108

FARRELL, THOMAS JOSEPH, insurance company executive, consultant; b. Butte, Mont., June 10, 1926; s. Bartholomew J. and Lavina H. (Collins) F.; m. Evelyn Irene Southam, July 29, 1951; children: Brien J., Susan M., Leslie A., Jerome T. Student U. San Francisco, 1949. CLU. Ptnr. Affiliated-Gen. Ins. Adjusters, Santa Rosa, Calif., 1949-54; agt. Lincoln Nat. Life Ins. Co., Santa Rosa, 1954-57, supr., 1957-59, gen. agt., 1959-74; pres. Thomas J. Farrell & Assos., 1974-76, 7 Flags Ins. Mktg. Corp., 1976-81, Farrell-Dranginis & Assocs., 1981-88, 1988-90, consultant, 1990, Specialist Dept. of developmental services, Calif.; pres., bd. dirs. Lincoln Nat. Bank, Santa Rosa, San Rafael. Pres. Redwood Empire Estate Planning Council, 1981-82, Sonoma County Council for Retarded Children, 1956-59, Sonoma County Assn. for Retarded Citizens, City Santa Rosa Traffic and Parking Commn., 1963; specialist State of Calif. Dept. Devel. Svcs., 1990—. del. Calif. State Conf. Small Bus., 1980; mem. Santa Rosa City Schs. Compensatory Edn. Adv. Bd.; bd. dirs. Santa Rosa City Schs. Consumer Edn. Adv. Bd.; pres., nat. dir. United Cerebral Palsy Assn., 1954-55; nat. coord. C. of C.-Rotary Symposia on Employment of People with Disabilities, 1985-87; v.p. Vigil Light, Inc.; chmn. bd. dirs. Nat. Barrier Awareness for People with Disabilities Found., Inc.; pres. Commn. on Emoloyment of People with Disabilities, 1986-92; mem. Pres.'s Com. on Mental Retardation, 1982-86; chmn. Santa Rosa Community Relations Com., 1973-76; pres. Sonoma County Young Reps., 1953; past bd. dirs. Sonoma County Fair and Expn., Inc.; bd. dirs. Sonoma County Family Service Agy., Eldridge Found., North Bay Regional Ctr. for Developmentally Disabled; trustee Sonoma State Hosp. for Mentally Retarded. Recipient cert. Nat. Assn. Retarded Children, 1962, Region 9 U.S. HHS Community Service award, 1985, Sonoma County Vendor's Human Service award, 1986, Individual Achievement award Community Affirmative Action Forum of Sonoma County, 1986. Mem. Nat. Assn. Life Underwriters, Redwood Empire Assn. CLU's (pres. 1974-75), Japanese-Am. Citizens League, Jaycees (Outstanding Young Man of Year 1961, v.p. 1955), Santa Rosa C. of C. (bd. dirs. 1974-75), Calif. PTA (hon. life). Svc. Club: Rotary (Svc. Above Self award 1996). Home: 963 Wyoming Dr Santa Rosa CA 95405-7342

FARRELL, WILLIAM EDGAR, sales executive, infosystems specialist, management consultant; b. Jeanette, Pa., Mar. 13, 1937; s. Arthur Richard and Lelia (Ryder) F.; m. Sara Lynnette Swing, Aug. 20, 1960; children: Wendy J., Tracy L., Rebecca J. BS in Edn., Pa. State U., 1959. Location mgr. IBM Corp., Dover, Del., 1969-72; corp. lobbyist IBM Corp., Washington, 1972-74, planning cons., 1974-78, nat. mktg. mgr., 1978-80, exec. asst., 1980-81; account exec. IBM Corp., Denver, 1981-87, policy exec., 1987-91; pres., CEO Weatherall Co., Inc., Englewood, Colo., 1993—, bd. dirs., 1994—; CFO, Wide Horizon, Inc., Denver, 1987-92, chmn. bd. trustees, 1989-92; pres. Exec. Mgmt. Cons., 1987—; sec.-treas., bd. dirs. Electronic Shoe Enterprises Inc., 1991-94; mem. Colo. Info. Mgmt. Commn., 1992-95; bd. dirs. Energaire Corp. Founding mem. River Falls Community Assn., Potomac, Md., 1975; first reader First Ch. of Christ Scientist, Chevy Chase, Md., 1976-80; chmn. Amigo's De Ser; bd. dirs. Rocky Mountain Ser, 1991-92. Recipient Outstanding Contbn. award IBM Corp., 1968. Republican.

FARRER, CLAIRE ANNE RAFFERTY, anthropologist, folklorist, educator; b. N.Y.C., Dec. 26, 1936; d. Francis Michael and Clara Anna (Guerra) Rafferty; 1 child, Suzanne Claire. BA in Anthropology, U. Calif., Berkeley, 1970; MA in Anthropology and Folklore, U. Tex., 1974, PhD in Anthropology and Folklore, 1977. Various positions, 1953-73; fellow Whitney M. Young Jr. Meml. Found., N.Y.C., 1974-75; arts specialist, grant adminstr. Nat. Endowment for Arts, Washington, 1976-77; Weatherhead resident fellow Sch. Am. Research, Santa Fe, 1977-78; asst. prof. anthropology U. Ill., Urbana, 1978-85; assoc. prof., coord. applied anthropology Calif. State U., Chico, 1985-89, prof., 1989—; dir. Multicultural and Gender Studies, 1994; cons. in field, 1974—; mem. film and video adv. panel Ill. Arts Coun., 1980-82; mem. Ill. Humanities Coun., 1980-82; vis. prof. U. Ghent, Belgium, spring 1990; named to Hulbert Endowed Chair, Hulbert Ctr. for S.W. Studies, Colo. Coll., Colorado Springs, 1997—. Author: Play and Inter-Ethnic Communication, 1990, Living Life's Circle: Mescalero Apache Cosmovision, 1991, Thunder Rides a Black Horse: Mescalero Apaches and the Mythic Present, 1994, 96; co-founder, co-editor Folklore Women's Commn., 1972; editor spl. issue Jour. Am. Folklore, 1975, 1st rev. edit., 1986; co-editor: Forms of Play of Native North Americans, 1979, Earth and Sky: Visions of the Cosmos in Native North American Folklore, 1992; contbr. numerous articles to profl. jours., mags. and newspapers, chpts. to books. Recipient numerous awards, fellowships and grants. Fellow Am. Anthrop. Assn., Royal Anthrop. Inst. (U.K.), Am. Astronomy Assn. (history divsn.); mem. Authors Guild, Am. Ethnol. Soc., Am. Folklore Soc., Am. Soc. Ethnohistory. Mem. Soc. of Friends. Office: Calif State U Dept Anthropology Butte 311 Chico CA 95929-0400

FARRIS, JEROME, federal judge; b. Birmingham, Ala., Mar. 4, 1930; s. William J. and Elizabeth (White) F.; widower; children: Juli Elizabeth, Janelle Marie. B.S., Morehouse Coll., 1951, LL.D., 1978; M.S.W., Atlanta U., 1955; J.D., U. Wash., 1958. Bar: Wash. 1958. Mem. firm Weyer, Roderick, Schroeter and Sterne, Seattle, 1958-59; ptnr. Weyer, Schroeter, Sterne & Farris and successor firms, Seattle, 1959-61, Schroeter & Farris, Seattle, 1961-63, Schroeter, Farris, Bangs & Horowitz, Seattle, 1963-65, Farris, Bangs & Horowitz, Seattle, 1965-69; judge Wash. State Ct. of Appeals, Seattle, 1969-79, U.S. Ct. of Appeals (9th cir.), Seattle, 1979—; lectr. U. Wash. Law Sch. and Sch. of Social Work, 1976—; mem. faculty Nat. Coll. State Judiciary, U. Nev., 1973; adv. bd. Nat. Ctr. for State Cts. Appellate Justice Project, 1978-81; founder First Union Nat. Bank, Seattle, 1965, dir., 1965-69. Del. The White House Conf. on Children and Youth, 1970; mem. King County (Wash.) Youth Commn., 1969-70; vis. com. U. Wash. Sch. Social Work, 1977-90; mem. King County Mental Health-Mental Retardation Bd., 1967-69; past bd. dirs. Seattle United Way; mem. Tyee Bd. Advisers, U. Wash., 1984—, bd. regents, 1985—, pres., 1990-91; trustee U. Law Sch. Found., 1978-84. With Signal Corps, U.S. Army, 1952-53. Recipient Disting. Service award Seattle Jaycees, 1965, Clayton Frost award, 1966. Fellow Am. Bar Found.; mem. ABA (exec. com. appellate judges conf. 1978-84, 87—, chmn. conf. 1982-83, del. jud. adminstrn. coun. 1987-88), Wash. Council on Crime and Delinquency (chmn. 1970-72), Am. Bar Found. (bd. dirs. 1987, exec. com. 1989—), State-Fed. Jud. Council of State of Wash. (vice chmn. 1977-78, chmn. 1983-87), Order of Coif (mem. law rev.), U. Wash. Law Sch. Office: US Ct Appeals 9th Cir 1030 US Courthouse 1010 5th Ave Seattle WA 98104-1130*

FARRIS, MARTIN THEODORE, economist, educator; b. Spokane, Wash., Nov. 5, 1925; s. Jacob B. and Edith S. (Gunderson) F.; m. Rhoda H. Harrington, Aug. 20, 1948 (dec. 1992); m. Marian B. Bolton, July 2, 1994; children: Christine A. Farris Zenobi, Diana Lynn, Elizabeth, M. Theodore II. BA, U. Mont., 1949, MA, 1950; PhD, Ohio State U., 1957. Grad. asst. U. Mont., 1949-50; asst. in econs. Ohio State U., Columbus, 1950-51, asst. instr., 1953-55, instr., 1955-57; asst. prof. Ariz. State U., Tempe, 1957-59, assoc. prof., 1959-62, chmn. dept. econs., 1967-69, prof. transp. and pub. utility econs., 1962-72, prof. transp., 1972-88, Regents' prof., 1988-92, prof. emeritus, 1992—; vis. prof. U. Hawaii, 1969-70, vis. scholar, 1979. Author: (with Roy Sampson and David Shrock) Domestic Transportation: Practice, Theory and Policy, 6th edit., 1990; (with Roy Sampson) Public Utilities: Regulation, Management and Ownership, 1973; (with Paul McElhiney) Modern Transportation, 2nd edit., 1973; (with Grant Davis and Jack Holder) Management of Transportation Carriers, 1975; (with Forrest Harding) Passenger Transportation, 1976; (with Dave Bess) U.S. Maritime: History and Prospects, 1981, (with Stephen Happel) Modern Managerial Economics, 1987; contbr. articles to profl. jours. With Signal Corps, U.S. Army, 1944-46, PTO. Decorated Philippine Liberation medal with bronze star; recipient Outstanding Faculty Achievement award Ariz. State U. Alumni Assn., 1978, Outstanding Faculty Researcher award Coll. Bus. Ariz. State U., 1982, Transp. and Logistics Educator of Yr. award Colo. Transp. Forum, 1991. Mem. Am. Econ. Assn. (Outstanding Contbn. to Transp. and Pub. Utilities award 1984), Western Econ. Assn. (bd. dirs. 1966-67), Assn. Transp. Practitioners, Transp. Rsch. Forum (Disting. Transp. Rschr. of Yr. award, 1994), Am. Soc. Transp. and Logistics (chief examiner 1961-73, Joseph C. Schleen award 1988), Coun. Logistics Mgmt., Traffic Clubs Internat., Traffic Club Phoenix (pres. 1960, Ariz. Transp. Man of Yr. 1992), Phi Kappa Phi, Omicron Delta Epsilon, Sigma Phi Epsilon, Delta Nu Alpha (Transp. Man of Yr. 1972), Beta Gamma Sigma. Episcopalian. Club: Traffic (Phoenix) (pres. 1960). Office: Ariz State U 9475 N 115th Pl Scottsdale AZ 85259-5855

FARVER, ED, vintner; b. 1947. Engr. RCA, Cherry Hill, N.J., 1968-70; with Touche Ross, San Francisco, 1970-77; various positions Domaine Chandon, Inc., Yountville, Calif., 1977-92, pres., 1992—, now chief operator officer, 1996. Office: Domaine Chandon Inc 1 California Dr Yountville CA 94599*

FARWELL, HERMON WALDO, JR., parliamentarian, educator, former speech communication educator; b. Englewood, N.J., Oct. 24, 1918; s. Hermon Waldo and Elizabeth (Whitcomb) F.; A.B., Columbia, 1940; M.A., Pa. State U., 1964; m. Martha Carey Matthews, Jan. 3, 1942; children—Gardner Whitcomb, Linda Margaret (Mrs. Richard Hammer). Commd. USAF, 1940, advanced through grades to maj., various positions, 1940-66, ret., 1966; instr. aerial photography Escola Tecnica de Aviação, Brazil, 1946-48; faculty U. So. Colo., Pueblo, 1966-84, prof. emeritus speech communication, 1984—; cons., tchr. parliamentary procedure. Author: The Majority Rules-A Manual of Procedure for Most Groups: Parliamentary Motions: Majority Motions; editor The Parliamentary Jour., 1981-87, 91-93; contbr. articles to profl. jours. Mem. Am. Inst. Parliamentarians (nat. dir. 1977-87), Commn. on Am. Parliamentary Practice (chmn. 1976), Ret. Officers Assn., Nat. Assn. Parliamentarians, Am. Legion, VFW, Air Force Assn. Home and Office: 65 MacAlester Rd Pueblo CO 81001-2052

FASEL, HERMANN F., aerospace and mechanical engineering educator; b. Schwaebisch Gmuend, Germany, Sept. 8, 1943; s. Karl N. and Maria (Rupp) Fa.; m. Janet L. Fox, June 2, 1972; children: Michael H., Lars B. BS, U. Stuttgart, Germany, 1966, PhD, 1974; MS, U. Kans., 1967. Asst. prof. U. Stuttgart, 1974-78, Heisenberg fellow, 1978-82; vis. assoc. prof. U. Ariz., Tucson, 1982-84, prof. aerospace and mech. engring., 1984—. Office: U Ariz Dept Aerospace & Mech Engr Tucson AZ 85718

FASI, FRANK FRANCIS, state senator; b. East Hartford, Conn., Aug. 27, 1920. B.S., Trinity Coll., Hartford, 1942. Mem. Hawaii Senate, 1959—; Dem. mayor City and County of Honolulu, 1969-81, Rep. mayor, 1985-94; resigned, 1994; owner Property & Bus., Honolulu, 1995. Mem. Dem. Nat. Com. for Hawaii, 1952-56; del. 2d Constl. Conv., 1968; mem.-at-large Honolulu City Coun., 1965-69. Served to capt. USMCR. Mem. Pacific-Asian Congress Municipalities (founder, past pres., exec. dir.), VFW (former comdr. Hawaii dept.), AFTRA (past v.p.). Office: 401 Waia Kamilo Rm 201 Honolulu HI 96817-4709 *Personal philosophy: My vision of a well-managed city is one where compassion and concern for the "little guy" can endure as realistic priorities, where "getting the job done" means minimizing red tape and approaching problems in a business-like manner.**

FASSEL, DIANE MARY, organizational consultant; b. San Antonio, Sept. 12, 1945; d. Robert Alois and Mary Jane (Stokman) F. BA, Webster U., 1968; MA, Harvard U., 1974; PhD, Union Inst., 1987. Chair English dept. Loretto H.S., Kansas City, Mo., 1968-72; cmty. life coord. Loretto Cmty., Denver, 1974-78; pvt. practice orgnl. cons. Denver, 1978-92, Boulder, Colo., 1994—; v.p. Wilson Schaef Assoc., Boulder, 1992-94; advisor Am. Arbitration Assn., Denver, 1978-84. Author: The Addictive Organization, 1988, Working Ourselves to Death, 1990, Growing Up Divorced, 1991, Organizational Capabilities, 1996. Bd. dirs. St. Mary's Acad., Denver, 1978-86; mem. exec. com. Loretto Cmty., Denver, 1978-82; mediator CDR Assoc., Boulder, 1984. Democrat. Roman Catholic.

FATEMAN, RICHARD J., computer science educator, researcher; b. N.Y.C., Nov. 4, 1946; s. Sol C. and Adelaide (Lapidus) F.; m. Martha A. Nelson, June 15, 1968; children: Abigail, Johanna. BS in Physics, Union Coll., 1966; PhD in Applied Math., Harvard U., 1971. Instr., lectr. math. dept. MIT, Cambridge, Mass., 1971-74; scientist Lawrence Livermore/Berkeley (Calif.) Lab., summer 1974, 78; prof. U. Calif., Berkeley, 1974—, chair, prof., 1987-90; bd. dirs. Computing Rsch. Assn. Inc., Washington, Franz, Inc., Berkeley; bd. dirs., treas. Internat. Computer Sci. Inst., Berkeley, 1987-90. Contbr. numerous articles to profl. jours. Bd. dirs. Claremont/Elmwood Neighborhood Assn., Berkeley, 1990—. NSF grantee, and many others. Mem. Assn. for Computing Machinery (chair SIGSAM, 1983-85), Soc. for Indsl. and Applied Math. Home: 2965 Magnolia St Berkeley CA 94705-2329 Office: U Calif Computer Sci Divsn # 1776 EECS Dept/Soda Hall Berkeley CA 94720-1776

FATHAUER, THEODORE FREDERICK, meteorologist; b. Oak Park, Ill., June 5, 1946; s. Arthur Theodore and Helen Ann (Mashek) F.; m. Mary Ann Neesan, Aug. 8, 1981. BA, U. Chgo., 1968. Cert. cons. meteorologist. Rsch. aide USDA No. Dev. Labs., Peoria, Ill., 1966, Cloud Physics Lab., Chgo., 1967; meteorologist Sta. WLW Radio/TV, Cin., 1967-68, Nat. Meteorol. Ctr., Washington, 1968-70, Nat. Weather Svc., Anchorage, 1970-80; meteorologist-in-charge Nat. Weather Svc., Fairbanks, Alaska, 1980—; instr. U. Alaska, Fairbanks, 1975-76, USCG Aux., Fairbanks and Anchorage, 1974—; specialist in Alaska meteorology. Contbr. articles to weather mags. and jours. Bd. dirs. Fairbanks Concert Assn., 1988—; bd. dirs., campaign chmn. No. Alaska Combined Fed. Campaign, 1996—; bd. dirs. Friends U. Alaska Mus., 1993—, pres., 1993-95, sec. 1997—; bd. visitors U. Alaska Fairbanks, 1995—; bd. dirs., sec. Fairbanks Symphony Assn., 1994—; bd. trustees U. Alaska Found., 1997—. Recipient Outstanding Performance award Nat. Weather Service, 1972, 76, 83, 85, 86, 89, Fed. Employee of Yr. award, Fed. Exec. Assn., Anchorage, 1978. Fellow Am. Meteorol. Soc. (TV and radio seals of approval), Royal Meteorol. Soc.; mem. AAAS, Am. Geophys. Union, Western Snow Conf., Arctic Inst. N.Am., Oceanography Soc. (coll. fellow U. Alaska 1993—, exec. com. 1997—), Can. Meteorol. and Oceanographic Soc., Am. Sailing Assn. Republican. Lutheran. Home: 1738 Chena Ridge Rd Fairbanks AK 99709-2612 Office: Nat Weather Svc Forecast Office 101 12th Ave Fairbanks AK 99701-6236

FATZINGER, JAMES A. S., construction educator, estimator; b. Bethlehem, Pa., Jan. 27, 1926; s. James Andrew and Cora Ellen (Steigerwalt) F.; m. Mary Lois Beckman, June 10, 1972. Student, Pa. State Coll., 1943-44, Moravian Coll., 1957-58, Fullerton Jr. Coll., 1972-73. Journeyman various cos., 1951-72; supr. 3M Co., Montpelier, Ohio, 1966-67; journeyman Endicott Brass Co., Montpelier, 1967; substation operator Pub. Svc. Elec. and Gas Co., Newark, 1959-65; constrn. estimator various cos., 1972—; contractor Calif. and Ariz., 1980-85; constrn. instr. Mesa (Ariz.) C.C., Rio Salado C.C., Mesa, 1974-78, C.C. of So. Nev., Las Vegas, 1978—, U. Nev., Las Vegas, 1992—; pres., owner Basic Estimating Ltd., Las Vegas, 1978—. Author: Basic Estimating for Construction, 1996, Blueprint Reading for Construction, 1997. Trustee Tech. Sch., Fullerton Jr. Coll., 1986-92; scoutmaster Boy Scouts Am., Bethlehem, 1950-60, commr., Huntington Beach, Calif., 1976-77. 1st sgt. U.S. Army, 1944-46, ETO. Mem. Am. Soc. Profl. Estimators (cert., emeritus mem.), Constrn. Specifications Inst. Republican.

FAULHABER, CHARLES BAILEY, Spanish language educator, librarian; b. East Cleveland, Ohio, Sept. 18, 1941; s. Kenneth Frederick and Lois Marie (Bailey) F.; m. Jamy Sue O'Banion, June 5, 1971. BA, Yale U., 1963, MPhil, PhD, 1969; MA, U. Wis., 1966. Acting instr. Yale U., 1968-69; asst. prof. Spanish U. Calif., Berkeley, 1969-75, assoc. prof., 1975-80, prof., 1980—, chmn. dept., 1989-94; dir. The Bancroft Libr., 1995—. Author: Latin Rhetorical Theory in Thirteenth and Fourteenth Century Castile, 1972, Medieval Manuscripts in the Library of the Hispanic Society of America, 1983-93, Libros y bibliotecas en la España medieval, 1987; co-author: Bibliography of Old Spanish texts, 1984, Archivo Digital de Manuscritos y Textos Españoles, 1992-93. Fulbright fellow, 1967-68, 91, Guggenheim fellow, 1982-83; NEH fellow, 1976, grantee, 1978-80, 89-93, 94-95. Mem. MLA, Medieval Acad. Am., Assn. for Computers and Humanities, Asociación Internacional de Hispanistas, Am. Assn. Tchrs. Spanish and Portuguese, Hispanic Soc. Am., Grolier Club. Office: U Calif The Bancroft Libr Berkeley CA 94720-6000

FAULK, BETTY PRICE, elementary school educator; b. Whiteville, N.C., Oct. 23, 1954; d. Ralph Lee and Velma Mae (Williams) Price; m. Stanley Cecil Faulk, Jr., Mar. 18, 1977; children: Eric Michael, Jason Matthew. BS in Bus. Adminstrn., U. N.C., Wilmington, 1976; MEd, Chapman Coll., 1991. Cert. elem. tchr. Substitute tchr. Nassau Sch. Dist., Hilliard, Fla., 1984-86, Palmdale (Calif.) Sch. Dist., 1986-88; tchr. Cactus Sch., 1988—, chair student study team, coun. rep., 1991-95; chair site com. Cactus Sch., 1992-93. Home: 39902 Golfers Dr Palmdale CA 93551-2994 Office: Palmdale Sch Dist 38060 20th St E Palmdale CA 93550-4903

FAULKNER, SEWELL FORD, real estate executive; b. Keene, N.H., Sept. 25, 1924; s. John Charles and Hazel Helen (Ford) F.; AB, Harvard, 1949; MBA, 1951; m. June Dayton Finn, Jan. 10, 1951 (div.); children: Patricia Anne, Bradford William, Sandra Ford, Jonathan Dayton, Winthrop Sewell; m. Constance Mae Durvin, Mar. 15, 1969 (div.); children: Sarah Elizabeth, Elizabeth Jane. Product mgr. Congoleum Nairn, Inc., Kearny, N.J., 1951-55; salesman, broker, chmn., pres. Jack White Co. real estate, Anchorage, 1956-86; chmn. Faulkner, Inc.; chmn. Mem. Anchorage City Council, 1962-65, Greater Anchorage Area Borough Assembly, 1964-65, Anchorage Area Charter Commn., 1969-70. Pres., Alaska World Affairs Council, 1967-68; treas. Alyeska Property Owners, Inc., 1973-75, pres., 1977-78; pres. Downtown Anchorage Assn., 1974-75; mem. Girdwood Bd. Suprs. Served with USAAF, 1943-45. Mem. Anchorage Area C. of C. (dir. 1973-74), Alaska Notch Club. Office: Faulkner Real Estate 604 K St Anchorage AK 99501-3329

FAUSCH, KURT DANIEL, fisheries ecology educator; b. Crookston, Minn., Jan. 17, 1955; s. Homer David and Guinevere Jean (Smythe) F.; m. Deborah Anne Eisenhauer, Dec. 20, 1975; children: Emily Rebecca, Benjamin Thomas. BS in Zoology, U. Minn., Duluth, 1976; MS in Fisheries and Wildlife, Mich. State U., 1978, PhD in Fisheries and Wildlife, 1981; postgrad., Colo. State U., 1995—. Postdoctoral fellow U. Ill., Champaign, 1981-82; asst. prof. fisheries biology Colo. State U., Ft. Collins, 1982-87, assoc. prof., 1987-92; prof. Colo. State U., 1992—, chmn. fishery biology major, 1991-93, 95-97; vis. assoc. prof. U. B.C., 1990; vis. rsch. fellow Japanese Soc. for Promotion of Sci., 1994; vis. prof. U. Otago, New Zealand, 1997. Contbr. articles to profl. jours. Mem. AAAS, Am. Fisheries Soc. (assoc. editor 1988-90, Albert S. Hazzard award 1982), Ecol. Soc. Am., Soc. Conservation Biology, Am. Soc. Ichthyologists and Herpetologists, Japanese Soc. Ichthyology (jour. adv. bd. 1996—), Sigma Xi, Gamma Sigma Delta. Office: Colo State U Dept Fishery & Wildlife Biology Fort Collins CO 80523

FAVELL, EUGENE HUNTER, museum director; b. May 2, 1926; s. Eugene George and Ruth (Bernard) F.; m. Winifred Carol Lamm, June 19, 1949; children: Alice, Janet, Doug, Carol, Ann, Mark. BA in Econs., Stanford U.; postgrad., U. Ore. Owner Favell Mus. of Western Art & Indian Artifacts, Klamath Falls, Ore., 1972—. Co-founder Little League Baseball, Klamath Falls, pres. 1958-59; trustee Freedo s Found.; bd. dirs. Ore. Advocates for the Arts, 1988-89. Served in U.S. Navy, 1944-47. Recipient disting. svc. award, young man of yr. award Klamath Falls Jr. C. of C., 1960, Klamath County Retailer of Yr. Klamath Falls C. of C., 1990. Mem. Kiwanis Internat. (club pres. 1960, lt. gov. 1962, dist. com. chmn., gov. Pacific Northwest Dist. 1966, chmn. Internat. com. on resolutions 1967, internat. trustee 1967, internat. found. trustee 1969-71, 73-77), Elks, Masons, Shriners. Office: Favell Mus 125 W Main St Klamath Falls OR 97601-4287

FAVERTY, PATRICK WILLIAM, principal; b. Gary, Ind., Jan. 20, 1949; s. Marion W. and Margaret (Bailey) F.; children: Scott, Andra, Shannon. BA in Secondary Edn., Utah State U., 1971; MEd in Counseling, U. Calif., Santa Barbara, 1990; EdD in Orgnl. Mgmt., U. LaVerne, 1995. From tchr. to headmaster Ojai (Calif.) Valley Sch., 1972-80; owner, dir. Potrero Canyon Sch., Camp Carmel, Calif., 1980-88; dir. Alumni Vacation Ctr. U. Calif. Santa Barbara, 1989-90; dist. counselor Saugus Union Sch. Dist., Santa Clarita, Calif., 1990-92; prin. Bennett Valley Union Sch. Dist., Santa Rosa, Calif., 1992-93; prin. McDowell Sch. Petaluma (Calif.) City Schs., 1993—; cons. Shandra Corp., Santa Barbara, 1986—; cons./workshop presenter. Author (poetry) Contemporary American Poets, 1987, Hon. Mention, 1987. Pres. bd. dirs. Ptnrs. Adoption Agy. Mem. Am. Assn. Sch. Counselors, Calif. Assn. Sch. Counselors, Assn. Calif. Sch. Adminstrs.

FAVRE, JUNE MARIE, actress, singer; b. Clay County, Kans., June 14, 1937; d. Riley Otto and Edythe May (Constable) Woellhof; m. Joseph Jean Favre, Jan. 16, 1957 (dec. Jan. 1988). Cert. respiratory therapist. Owner N.Y. Connection, Denver, 1979-92; event coord. Colo. Contemporary Dance, Denver, 1993; exec. dir. Joey Favre Humanities Ctr., Denver, 1988—; guest artist Met. State Coll., Denver, 1977, N.Mex. State Theatre, Raton, 1974; founder, actor The Third Eye Theatre, Denver, 1966-78; cons. First Night Colo., Denver, 1994; publicist Gypsy Prodns., Denver, 1992, 93. Author (children's theatre) A Christmas Carol, 1994. Recipient Writing award Fla. Citrus Dept., 1991, Rocky Mountain Women's Inst. Associateship award, 1995, Mayor's Award for Excellence in the Arts, 1996. Mem. AFTRA, The Friday Club.

FAW, DUANE LESLIE, retired military officer, law educator, lay worker, author; b. Loraine, Tex., July 7, 1920; s. Alfred Leslie and Noma Leigh (Elliott) F.; m. Lucile Elizabeth Craps, Feb. 20, 1943; children: Cheryl Leigh, Bruce Duane, Debra Leoma, Melanie Loraine. Student, N. Tex. State Coll., 1937-41; J.D., Columbia U., 1947. Bar: Tex. 1948, D.C. 1969, U.S. Supreme Ct. 1969. Commd. 2d lt. USMC, 1942, advanced through grades to brig. gen., 1969, bn. comdr., 1959-61, staff judge adv., 1961-64, policy analyst Marine Hdqrs., 1964-67, dep. chief of staff III Marine Amphibious Force, 1967-68, judge Navy Ct. Mil. Rev., 1968-69; dir. Judge Ad. Div. Marine Hdqrs. USMC, Washington, 1969-71; ret. USMC, 1971; prof. law Pepperdine U. Sch. Law, Malibu, Calif., 1971-85; Bible tchr. So. Presbyn. Ch., Denton, Tex., 1948-50, Camp Pendleton, N.C., 1959-61, Quantico, Va., 1962-63, United Meth. Ch., Arlington, Va., 1963-71; Bible tchr., elder Presbyn. Ch., Van Horn, Tex., 1950-52; lay spkr., Bible tchr. United Meth. Ch., Tustin, Malibu and Laguna Hills, Calif., 1972—, lay mem. ann. conf., 1974-81, 91, 95, 96, 97. Author: The Paramony, 1986, The Joy of Spiritual Discovery, 1995; co-author: The Military in American Society, 1978. Gen. councilor URANTIA Brotherhood, 1979-88, gen. councilor of FELLOWSHIP, 1991-94; bd. dirs. Jesusonian Found., Boulder, 1988—, Touch for Health Found., Pasadena, Calif., 1988-94. Decorated Air medal with gold star, Navy Commendation medal with gold star, Legion of Merit with combat V with gold star; UN Cross of Gallantry with gold star; VN Honor medal 1st class. Mem. ABA (adv. com. mil. justice 1969-71, adv. com. lawyers in Armed Forces 1969-71), Fed. Bar Assn. (council), Judge Advs. Assn., Am. Acad. Religion, Soc. Bibl. Lit. Club: Masons. Home: 2399 Via Mariposa W Laguna Hills CA 92653-2052 *People are placed upon this planet for a purpose greater than self-maintenance and self-indulgence. True success and happiness require a personal discovery of, and commitment to, a system of values which furthers the implementation of the Divine plan.*

FAWCETT, JOHN SCOTT, real estate developer; b. Pitts., Nov. 5, 1937; s. William Hagen and Mary Jane (Wise) F.; m. Anne Elizabeth Mitchell, Dec. 30, 161; children: Holly Anne, John Scott II (dec.). BS, Ohio State U., 1959. Dist. dealer rep. Shell Oil Co., San Diego, 1962-66; dist. real estate rep. Shell Oil, Phoenix, 1967-69; region real estate rep. Shell Oil, San Francisco, 1970-71; head office land investments rep. Shell Oil, Houston, 1972-75; pres., CEO Marinita Devel. Co., Newport Beach, Calif., 1976—; lectr. in land devel. related fields. With U.S. Army, 1960-61. Named Ky. Col., Gov. Ky., 1996. Mem. Internat. Platform Assn., Internat. Coun. Shopping Ctrs., Internat. Right of Way Assn., Internat. Inst. Valuers, Inst. Bus. Appraisers, Nat. Assn. Rev. Appraisers and Mortgage Underwriters, Am. Assn. Cert. Appraisers, Urban Land Inst., Nat. Assn. Real Estate Execs. (pres. L.A. chpt. 1975), Calif. Lic. Contractors Assn., Bldg. Industry Assn., U.S. C. of C., Town Hall of Calif., Ohio State U. Alumni Assn., Toastmasters (pres. Scottsdale Ariz. club 1968, pres. Hospitality T club 1964), U. Athletic Club, Phi Kappa Tau. Republican. Roman Catholic. Home: 8739 Hudson River Cir Fountain Valley CA 92708 Office: Marinita Devel Co 3835 Birch St Newport Beach CA 92660

FAY, ABBOTT EASTMAN, history educator; b. Scottsbluff, Nebr., July 19, 1926; s. Abbott Eastman and Ethel (Lambert) F.; m. Joan D. Richardson, Nov. 26, 1953; children: Rand, Diana, Collin. BA, Colo. State Coll., 1949, MA, 1953; postgrad., U. Denver, 1961-63; cert. advanced study, Western State U., 1963. Tchr. Leadville (Colo.) Pub. Schs., 1950-52, elem. prin., 1952-54; prin. Leadville Jr. H.S., 1954-55; pub. info. dir., instr. history Mesa Coll., Grand Junction, Colo., 1955-64; asst. prof. history Western State Coll., Gunnison, Colo., 1964-76, assoc. prof. history, 1976-82, assoc. prof. emeritus, 1982—; adj. faculty Adams State Coll., Alamosa, Colo., Mesa State Coll., Grand Junction, Colo., 1989—; propr. Mountaintop Books, Paonia, Colo.; bd. dirs. Colo. Assoc. Univ. Press; dir. hist. tours; columnist Valley Chronicle, Paonia, Best Years Beacon, Grand Junction, Guide Lines, Denver, The Historian, Fruita, Colo., Grand Mesa Byway News, Delta, Colo.; staff welcome ctr. State of Colo., Fruita; profl. speaker in field; cons. Colo. Welcome Ctr., 1997—. Author: Mountain Academia, 1968, Writing Good History Research Papers, 1980, Ski Tracks in the Rockies, 1984, Famous Coloradans, 1990, I Never Knew That About Colorado, 1993; playwright: Thunder Mountain Lives Tonight!; contbr. articles to profl. jours.; freelance writer popular mags. Founder, coord. Nat. Energy Conservation Challenge; travel cons. Colo. State Welcome Ctr., 1997—; project reviewer NEH, Colo. Hist. Soc.; steering com. West Elk Scenic & Historic Byway, Colo., 1994—; founder Leadville (Colo.) Assembly, pres., 1953-54; mem. Advs. of Lifelong Learning, 1994—. Named Top Prof. Western State Coll., 1969, 70, 71; fellow Hamline U. Inst. Asian Studies, 1975, 79. Mem. Western Writers Am., Rocky Mountain Social Sci. Assn. (sec. 1961-63), Am. Hist. Assn., Assn. Asian Studies, Western History Assn., Western State Coll. Alumni Assn. (pres. 1971-73), Internat. Platform Assn. Profl. Guides Assn. Am. (cert.), Rocky Mountain Guides Assn., Colo. Antiquarian Booksellers Assn., Am. Legion (Outstanding Historian award 1981), Advs. of Lifelong Learning, Phi Alpha Theta, Phi Kappa Delta, Delta Kappa Pi. Home: 1156 Bookcliff Ave #4 Grand Junction CO 81501

FAY, HELYN, college counselor; b. Fontana, Calif., Sept. 9, 1950; d. James R. Sammon and Patricia J. (Burton) Murarik; m. Ronald E. Fay, Sept. 4, 1971; children: Emily, Timothy. BA in English cum laude, Pasadena Coll., 1972; MS in Counseling with distinction, Calif. Poly. State U., 1991. Tchr. elem. sch. Hickman Mills Sch. Dist., Kansas City, Mo., 1972-75; tchr. asst. Cuesta C.C., San Luis Obispo, Calif., 1984-88; sch. counselor San Luis Coastal Unified Dist., San Luis Obispo, 1990-95; marriage, family and child counselor intern in pvt. practice Barry Martin, Los Osos, Calif., 1992-95; counselor Pt. Loma Nazarene Coll., San Diego, 1995—; mem. human devel. adv. com. Cuesta Coll., San Luis Obispo, 1993-95; chair eating behavior profl team Pt. Loma Nazarene Coll., San Diego, 1995—. Mem. Am. Assn. of Christian Counselors, Am. Coll. Counselors Assn., Am. Counseling Assn., Calif. Assn. of Marriage & Family Therapists (Clinton E. Phillips scholar 1990), Phi Delta Lambda. Office: Pt Loma Nazarene Coll 3900 Lomaland Dr San Diego CA 92106-2810

FAY, RICHARD JAMES, mechanical engineer, executive, educator; b. St. Joseph, Mo., Apr. 26, 1935; s. Frank James and Marie Jewell (Senger) F.; m. Marilyn Louise Kelsey, Dec. 22, 1962; BSME, U. Denver, 1959, MSME, 1970. Registered profl. engr., Colo., Nebr. Design engr. Denver Fire Clay Co., 1957-60; design, project engr. Silver Engring. Works, 1960-63; research engr., lectr. mech. engring. U. Denver, 1963-74, asst. prof. Colo. Sch. of Mines, 1974-75, founder, pres. Fay Engring. Corp., 1971—. Served with Colo. N.G., 1962. Mem. Soc. Automotive Engrs. (past chmn. Colo. sect.), ASME (past chmn. Colo. sect., past regional v.p.), La Societe des Ingenieurs de L'Automobile (France). Contbr. articles to profl. jours.; patentee in field. Office: 5201 E 48th Ave Denver CO 80216-5316

FAYAD, MIKE SAMIH, financial analyst; b. Sidon, Lebanon, Feb. 7, 1953; came to U.S., 1974; s. Samih Ali and Samia Fayad; m. Zeina Takieddine, Nov. 4, 1996. B of Elec. Engring., Am. U., 1974; M of Elec. Engring., U. So. Calif., 1976, MBA, 1984. Bus. adminstrn. trainee Elec. Constrn. Co., Wolver Hampton, England, 1973; trainer Westinghouse Corp., Jubail, Saudi Arabia, 1977; systems analyst IBM Corp., Riyadh, Saudi Arabia, 1978-81; product mktg. engr. Intel Corp., Santa Clara, Calif., 1983; mktg. mgr. SEAM Internat., Palos Verdes, Calif., 1985-86; coord. data entry dept. Webster Coll., L.A., 1988-89; mainframe specialist Andrew Corp., Torrance, 1990; sr. fin. analyst City of Hope, Duarte, 1990—; adj. faculty Nat. U., L.A., 1993-94; fin. cons. LifeCare Corp., Whittier, Calif., 1987; dir. Trader's Internat., L.A., 1991. Author of poems. Mem. Internat. Bus. Assn., L.A., 1982; v.p. Gen. Knowledge Com., Beirut, 1974, HopeMasters/Pres., Duarte, Calif., 1995-96. Mem. HBOC Users Group (speaker). Office: City of Hope 1500 Duarte Rd Duarte CA 91010-3012

FAY-SCHMIDT, PATRICIA ANN, paralegal; b. Waukegan, Ill., Dec. 25, 1941; d. John William and Agnes Alice (Semerad) Fay; m. Dennis A. Schmidt, Nov. 3, 1962 (div. Dec. 1987); children: Kristin Fay Schmidt, John Andrew Schmidt. Student, L.A. Pierce Coll., 1959-60, U. San Jose, 1960-62, Western State U. of Law, Fullerton, Calif., 1991-92. Cert. legal asst., Calif. Paralegal Rasner & Rasner, Costa Mesa, Calif., 1979-82; paralegal, adminstr. Law Offices of Manuel Ortega, Santa Ana, Calif., 1982-92; sabbatical, 1992-94; mem. editorial adv. bd. James Pub. Co., Costa Mesa, 1984-88. Contbg. author: Journal of the Citizen Ambassador Paralegal Delegation to the Soviet Union, 1990. Treas., Republican Women, Tustin, Calif., 1990-91; past regent, 1st vice regent, 2d vice regent NSDAR, Tustin, 1967—; docent Richard M. Nixon Libr. and Birthplace, 1993—, bd. dirs. Docent Guild, 1994—; docent Orange County Courthouse Mus., 1992-94. Mem. Orange County Paralegal Assn. (hospitality chair 1985-87). Roman Catholic. Home: 13571 Hewes Ave Santa Ana CA 92705-2215

FAZIO, VIC, congressman; b. Winchester, Mass., Oct. 11, 1942; m. Judy Kern; children: Dana Fazio, Anne Fazio (dec.), Kevin Kern, Kristie Kern. BA, Union Coll., Schenectady, 1965; postgrad., Calif. State U., Sacramento. Journalist, founder Calif. Jour.; congl. and legis. cons., 1966-75; mem. Calif. State Assembly, 1975-78; mem. 96th -103rd Congresses from Calif. 3rd Dist., 1979—; former chmn. Dem. Congl. Campaign Com.; chmn. Dem. caucus, house steering policy com.; mem. legis. br. appropriations subcom., ranking mem. appropriations subcom. energy and water; majority whip-at-large 96th-103rd Congress; also co-chmn. Fed. Govt. Svcs. Task Force 96th-101st Congresses, former chmn. bipartisan com. on ethics; former mem. Sacramento County Charter and Planning Commns. Bd. dirs. Asthma Allergy Found., Jr. Statesman, Nat. Italian-Am. Found. Coro Found. fellow; named Solar Congressman of Yr. Mem. Air Force Assn. Office: 2113 Rayburn Washington DC 20515

FEAR, DAVID LANE, employee benefit consultant; b. Casa Grande, Ariz., Nov. 7, 1954; s. Robert George and Evelyn Blanche (Stevens) F.; m. April Denise Pezley, Nov. 3, 1978 (div. Dec. 1993); children: Angela Christine, Kara Lynn, David Lane Jr., Michael Robert, Steven Aaron; m. Kathleen De Gruccio, Aug. 4, 1994; children: Cira, Vincent. Grad. H.S., San Andreas, Calif. Agt. Great West Life, Fresno and Denver, 1978-80; cons. Employee Benefit Specialists, Denver, 1980-83; v.p., gen. mgr. Smith Adminstrs., Houston, 1983-87; mgr. product devel. Humana, Inc., Louisville, 1987-88; v.p. Jordan Jones & Assocs., Sacramento, 1988-90; ptnr. Flexible Benefit Assocs., Sacramento, 1990-94; v.p. Health Alliance Mgmt. Svcs., Inc., Sacramento, 1994-96; employee benefits cons. Orangevale, Calif., 1996—; dir. Tex. Assn. TPA's, Austin, Tex., 1985-88; adv. bd. mem. U. Calif. Davis Sch. Mgmt., 1994-96; health reform activist Calif. Dept. Ins., Sacramento, 1996. Scoutmaster Boy Scouts Am., Citrus Heights, Calif., 1993; advisor U. Calif. Davis Sch. Mgmt., 1994. Mem. Nat. Assn. Health Underwriters (vice chair state affairs 1991-93), Calif. Assn. Health Underwriters (v.p. legislation 1993-96, Bd. Mem. of Yr. 1995), Sacramento Assn. Health Underwriters (bd. sec. 1990-94), Leading Prodrs. Roundtable. Republican. Mem. LDS Ch. Office: PO Box 751 Sacramento CA 95662

FEARN, HEIDI, physicist, educator; b. Sutton-in-Ashfield, Eng., Aug. 21, 1965; came to U.S., 1989; d. Lawrence Leonard and Erika Hanna Elfrede (Kröger) F. BS in Theol. Physics with honors, Essex U., Colchester, Eng., 1986, PhD in Theol. Quantum Optics, 1989. Grad. lab. demonstrator Essex U., 1986-89; postdoctoral rsch. asst. Max Planck Inst. Quantum Optics, Garching, Germany, 1989; rsch. assoc. U. N.Mex., Albuquerque, 1989-91; lectr. physics Calif. State U., Fullerton, 1991-92, asst. prof. physics, 1992-95, assoc. prof. physics, 1995—; vis. scholar U. Ariz., Tucson, 1989-91; cons. Los Alamos (N.Mex.) Nat. Lab., 1994—. Mem. AAAS, Am. Phys. Soc. Office: Calif State U Physics Dept 800 N State College Blvd Fullerton CA 92631-3547

FEARON, LEE CHARLES, chemist; b. Tulsa, Nov. 22, 1938; s. Robert Earl and Ruth Belle (Strothers) F.; m. Wanda Sue Williams, Nov. 30, 1971. Student, Rensselaer Polytech. Inst., 1957-59; BS in Physics, Okla. State U., Stillwater, 1961, BA in Chemistry, 1962, MS in Analytical Chemistry, 1969. Rsch. chemist Houston process lab. Shell Oil Co., Deer Park, Tex., 1968-70; chief chemist Pollution Engring. Internat., Inc., Houston, 1970-76; rsch. chemist M-I Drilling Fluids Co., Houston, 1976-83; cons. chemist Profl. Engr. Assocs., Inc., Tulsa, 1983-84; chemist Anacon, Inc., Houston, 1984-85; scientist III Bionetics Corp., Rockville, Md., 1985-86; sr. chemist L.A. County Sanitation Dist., Whittier, Calif., 1986; chemist Quanterra-Sacramento, West Sacramento, Calif., 1986-87; cons. chemist Branham Industries, Inc., Conroe, Tex., 1987-89; adv. laboratorian EILS, QA sect. Wash. State Dept. Ecology, Manchester, 1989—; cons. chemist Terra-Kleen, Okmulgee, Okla., 1988-94, Excel Pacific, Inc., Camarillo, Calif., 1993-96. Patentee for environ. soil remediation tech., 1994. With U.S. Army, 1962-65. Fellow Am. Inst. Chemists; mem. AAAS, Am. Chem. Soc. Home: PO Box 514 Manchester WA 98353-0514 Office: PO Box 488 Manchester WA 98353-0488

FEAVER, GEORGE A., political science educator; b. Hamilton, Ont., Canada, May 12, 1937; came to U.S., July 4, 1967; s. Harold Lorne and Doris Davies (Senior) F.; m. Nancy Alice Poynter, June 12, 1963 (div. 1978); m. Ruth Helene Tubbesing, Mar. 8, 1986 (div. 1991); children: Catherine Fergusson, Noah George. B.A. with Honors, U. B.C., 1959; Ph.D., London Sch. of Econs., 1962. Asst. prof. Mt. Holyoke Coll., South Hadley, Mass., 1962-65; lectr., research assoc. London Sch. Econs. and Univ. Coll., London, 1965-67; assoc. prof. Georgetown U., Washington, 1967-68, Emory U., Atlanta, 1968-71; assoc. prof. U.B.C., Vancouver, B.C., Canada, 1971-74, prof., 1974—; vis. fellow Australian Nat. U., Canberra, 1987. Author: From Status to Contract, 1969; editor: Beatrice Webb's Our Partnership, 1975; editor: The Webbs in Asia: The 1911-12 Travel Diary, 1992; co-editor: Lives, Liberties and the Public Good, 1987; contbr. articles to profl. jours., books. Fellow Canada Council, 1970-71, 74-75, Am. Council Learned Socs., 1974-75, Social Scis. and Humanities Research Council of Canada, 1981-82, 86-91. Mem. Can. Polit. Sci. Assn., Am. Polit. Sci. Assn., Am. Soc. for Polit. and Legal Philosophy, Conf. for Study of Polit. Thought, Inst. Internat. de philosophie politique. Club: Travellers' (London). Home: 4776 W 7th Ave, Vancouver, BC Canada V6T 1C6 Office: Univ British Columbia, Dept Polit Sci, Vancouver, BC Canada V6T 1Z1

FEDAK, BARBARA KINGRY, technical center administrator; b. Hazleton, Pa., Feb. 7, 1939; d. Marvin Frederick and Ruth Anna (Wheeler) Siebel; m. Raymond F. Fedak, Mar. 27, 1993; children: Sean M., James Goldey. BA, Trenton State Coll., 1961; MEd, Lesley Coll., Cambridge, Mass., 1986. Registered respiratory therapist. Dept. dir. North Platte (Nebr.) Community Hosp., 1974-75; newborn coord. Children's Hosp., Denver, 1975-79; edn. coord. Rose Med. Ctr., Denver, 1979-81; program dir. respiratory tech. program Pickens Tech., Aurora, Colo., 1981-86; mktg. rep. Foster Med. Corp., Denver, 1986-87; staff therapist Porter Meml. Hosp., Denver, 1987-88; dir., br. mgr. Pediatric Svcs. Am., Denver, 1988-90; dir. clin. edn. Pickens Tech., Aurora, Colo., 1991—, divsn. chair health occupations, 1991—; site evaluator Joint Rev. Com. for Respiratory Therapy Edn., Euless, Tex. Met. coun. mem. Am. Lung Assn., 1987-91. Mem. Am. Assn. Respiratory Care (edn. sect. program com. 1992—, abstract rev. com. 1993—, alt. del. AARC Ho. Dels., 1997—), Colo. Soc. Respiratory Care (dir. at large 1983-86, 90-92, sec. 1980-81, program com. 1982-92), Colo. Assn. Respiratory Educators (chair 1991-96), Lambda Beta (faculty). Methodist. Home: 11478 S Marlborough Dr Parker CO 80134-7318 Office: Pickens Tech 500 Airport Blvd Aurora CO 80011-9307

FEDORS, PAUL EDWARD, architectural lighting designer; b. Pasadena, Calif., Mar. 21. BA in Comm., Visual Arts, U. Calif., San Diego, 1991. With Innovative Lighting, L.A. Mem. Designers Lighting Forum, Bldg. Owners and Mgrs. Assn. (com. for San Gabriel Valley), Delta Tau Delta

Alumni Assn. Republican. Office: Innovative Lighting 10800 Richland Ave Los Angeles CA 90064

FEDRICK, C. RICHARD, food products executive; b. 1925. Chmn. Fedrick CR, Inc., Novato, Calif., 1960—; vice chmn. Synatt Corp., Tucson, Ariz., 1980—. Office: Fedrick CR inc PO Box 688 Novato CA 94948*

FEE, WILLARD EDWARD, JR., otolaryngologist; b. Portchester, N.Y., June 10, 1943; s. Willard E. and Jane Frances (Cromwell) F.; m. Caroline Fee, June 13, 1965; children: Heather, Adam. BS cum laude, U. San Francisco, 1965; MD magna cum laude, U. Colo., 1969. Intern Harbor Gen. Hosp., Torrance, Calif., 1969-70; resident in gen. surgery Wadsworth VA Hosp., L.A., 1970-71; resident in head and neck surgery UCLA Sch. Medicine, 1971-74; asst. prof. Stanford (Calif.) U. Med. Ctr., 1974-80, assoc. prof., chmn., 1980-86, prof., chmn. in otolaryngology, 1986—, Edward C. & Amy H. Sewall prof., 1996—; dir. Am. Bd. of Otolaryngology, Houston, 1985—; chmn. med. sch. faculty senate Stanford U., 1992-94. Editl. bd. Archives in Otolaryngology, Chgo., 1984-95; contbr. numerous articles to profl. jours. Mem. Collegium ORLAS-US (chmn. 1995—), Paul H. Ward Soc., Inc. (pres. 1988-89), Am. Soc. Head and Neck Surgery (pres. 1989-90), Am. Acad. Otolaryngology and Head and Neck Surgery, Calif. Soc. Otolaryngology (pres. 1995—), Alpha Omega Alpha. Home: 27299 Ursula Ln Los Altos CA 94022-3222 Office: Stanford Univ Med Ctr Divn Otolaryngology Edwards R135 300 Pasteur Stanford CA 94305-5328

FEES, NANCY FARDELIUS, special education educator; b. Santa Monica, Calif., Mar. 25, 1950; d. Carl August and Dodi Emma (Hedenschau) Fardelius; m. Paul Rodger Fees, June 4, 1971; children: Evelyn Wyoming, Nelson August. BS, Mills Coll., 1971; MA in Edn., Idaho State U., 1975. Cert. tchr., Calif., Idaho, Wyo., R.I. Specialist curriculum mgmt. Barrington (R.I.) High Sch., 1975-81; coordinator learning skills ctr. Northwest Community Coll., Powell, Wyo., 1982-84, instr., 1985—; pres. Children's Resource Ctr., 1985-89, bd. dirs., 1983-89, 91—. Editor (with others) The Great Entertainer, 1984. Vol. Buffalo Bill Hist. Ctr., Cody, Wyo., 1981—; mem. Centennial Com., Cody, 1983; mem. parent's adv. com. Livingston Sch., 1989-92, chmn., 1991-92; dir. Christian Edn. Christ Episcopal Ch., 1995—. Mem. Council Exceptional Children, Assn. Children with Learning Disabilities, Council Adminstrs. of Spl. Edn. Democrat. Episcopalian. Home: 1718 Wyoming Ave Cody WY 82414-3320

FEHR, J. WILL, newspaper editor; b. Long Beach, Calif., Mar. 8, 1926; s. John and Evelyn (James) F.; m. Cynthia Moore, Sept. 4, 1951; children—Michael John, Martha Ann. B.A. in English, U. Utah, 1951. City editor Salt Lake City Tribune, 1964-80, mng. editor, 1980-81, editor, 1981-91. Served to 1st lt. USAF, 1951-53. Mem. Am. Soc. Newpaper Editors, Sigma Chi. Clubs: Hidden Valley, Fort Douglas (Salt Lake City). Home: 468 13th Ave Salt Lake City UT 84103-3229 Office: Salt Lake City Tribune 143 S Main St Salt Lake City UT 84111-1917

FEIL, LINDA MAE, tax preparer; b. Dallas, Oreg., Apr. 9, 1948; d. Fred Henry and Ruth Irene (Hoffman) F. AA, West Valley Community Coll., 1975; student, Golden Gate U. Ctr. for Tax Studies, 1975, Menlo Coll. Sch. Bus. Adminstrn., 1978. Enrolled agt. IRS; cert. in fed. taxation. Income tax preparer, office mgr. H & R Block, Inc., Santa Clara, Calif., 1972-74, asst. area mgr., 1974-76; propr. L.M. Feil Tax Service, Santa Clara, 1976-80; ptnr. Tennyson Tax Service, Santa Clara, 1980-81; owner McKeany-Feil Tax Service, San Jose, Calif., 1981-83; owner Feil Tax Service, San Jose, 1983-90, Richmond, Calif., 1990-96, Vallejo, Calif., 1996—. Mem. Nat. Soc. Pub. Accts., Nat. Assn. Enrolled Agts. (chpt. sec. 1981-83, chpt. v.p. 1983-84), Mission Soc. Enrolled Agts. (pres. 1984-85, Enrolled Agt. of Yr. 1985), Calif. Soc. Enrolled Agts. (bd. dirs. 1985-86). Office: Feil Tax Svc 824 Foothill Dr Vallejo CA 94591

FEIN, WILLIAM, ophthalmologist; b. N.Y.C., Nov. 27, 1933; s. Samuel and Beatrice (Lipschitz) F.; m. Bonnie Fern Aaronson, Dec. 15, 1963; children: Stephanie Paula, Adam Irving, Gregory Andrew. BS, CCNY, 1954; MD, U. Calif., Irvine, 1962. Diplomate Am. Bd. Ophthalmology. Intern L.A. County Gen. Hosp., 1962-63, resident in ophthalmology, 1963-66; instr. U. Calif. Med. Sch., Irvine, 1966-69; mem. faculty U. So. Calif. Med. Sch., 1969—, assoc. clin. prof. ophthalmology, 1979—; attending physician Cedars-Sinai Med. Ctr., L.A., 1966—, chief ophthalmology clinic svc., 1979-81, chmn. div. ophthalmology, 1981-85; attending physician Los Angeles County-U. So. Calif. Med. Ctr., 1969—; chmn. dept. ophthalmology Midway Hosp., 1975-78; dir. Ellis Eye Ctr., L.A., 1984—. Mem. editorial bd. CATARACT, Internat. Jour. of Cataract and Ocular Surgery, 1992—; contbr. articles to med. publs. Chmn. ophthalmology adv. com. Jewish Home for Aging of Greater L.A., 1993—. Fellow Internat. Coll. Surgeons, Am. Coll. Surgeons; mem. Am. Acad. Ophthalmology, Am. Soc. Ophthalmic Plastic and Reconstructive Surgery, Royal Soc. Medicine, AMA, Calif. Med. Assn., L.A. Med. Assn. Home: 718 N Camden Dr Beverly Hills CA 90210-3205 Office: 415 N Crescent Dr Beverly Hills CA 90210-4860 also: 8635 W 3rd St Ste 390W Los Angeles CA 90048-6101

FEINBERG, DAVID ALLEN, computer software executive; b. Seattle, Feb. 17, 1947; s. Herman Stanford and Zelda (Hindin) F.; m. Lynne Brechner, Jan. 21, 1978; children: Kerri Jeanne, Todd Breck, Jamie Leigh, Megan Dawn, Eric Anthony. BS, Stanford U., 1968; MS in Adminstrn., George Washington U., 1972. Cert. data processor. Systems programmer Stanford (Calif.) Computer Ctr., 1966-68, NCR Corp., Los Angeles, 1968-69; systems analyst System Devel. Corp., Washington, 1971-75; mgr. Boeing Co., Seattle, 1975-87; tech. dir. Spacelabs, Inc., Redmond, 1987-90; dir. R&D Revelation Techs. Inc., Bellevue, Wash., 1990-91; founder, mng. prin. M.T. Writings. Co., Seattle, 1983—; mgr. networking and interfacing PHAMIS Inc., Seattle, 1992—; voting mem. Health Level Seven Stds. Orgn., 1994—, Accredited Stds. Com. X12, 1994—; lectr. various orgs., Seattle, 1983—. Contbr. articles to profl. jours. Pres. Rainier Beach High Sch. PTSA, Seattle, 1981; advisor Seattle Recreation Dept., 1983—; official Seattle Metro League, 1980—, Seattle Recreation Dept., 1990—; tournament umpire Pony Baseball, 1990—; referee Seattle Ofcl.'s Women's Basketball, 1995—; founder, treas. Montgomery Savoyards, Rockville, Md., 1973-75. Served to 1st. lt. Signal Corps, U.S. Army, 1969-71. Mem. Computer Soc. IEEE (affiliate), Data Processing Mgmt. Assn., Assn. Computing Machinery, Am. Arbitration Assn. (arbitrator, panelist). Home: 3662 SW Othello St Seattle WA 98126-3246 Office: PHAMIS Inc Ste 1500 1001 4th Ave Plaza Seattle WA 98154-1144

FEINHANDLER, EDWARD SANFORD, writer, photographer, art dealer, sports mentor, consultant, educator; b. Elko, Nev., Jan. 13, 1948; s. Samuel and Sylvia (Manus) F. BA, U. Nev., Reno, 1972. Supr. underpriveledged Washoe County Extension Program, Reno, 1970-71; sports editor, writer Sagebrush Campus newspaper, Reno, 1971-72; internal salesman, mgr. Trigon Corp., Sparks, Nev., 1975-88; owner, operator Art Internat. Gallery Extraordinaire, Reno, 1981—; tennis dir. City of Sparks, 1991-93, Cmty. Edn. Program, Sparks, 1994, Sparks YMCA, 1995—; with nat. news Top Ten radio interviews, U.S. and Can., 1978-79; freelance writer and photographer; pre. NNHS Tennis Assn., 1996. Contbr. articles to newspapers; extra in various movies; TV interviewee AM Chgo., AM L.A., 1979, Afternoon Exchange, Cleve., 1979, To Tell the Truth, 1975, Reno Tonight TV show, 1989, Fox Across America TV show, 1989, Wheel of Fortune, 1995. Player, coach Summer Volleyball League, Reno, 1982-85; tennis coach Cmty. Svc. Ctr., Reno, 1986-88, 94; founder softball event Make-A-Wish Found., Reno, 1985-96; active U. Nev. Journalism Dept., 1985-93, UNR Children's Svcs., Reno, 1986-88; coach Cath. Basketball, 1987-89 (2d pl.); head coach girls varsity tennis team Bishop Manogue H.S., 1989-91; coach boys varsity tennis Sparks H.S., 1993-96, spl. olympics, 1989, girls jr. varsity basketball, 1989; active Ptnrs. in Edn., 1988-90, Jr. Achievement, 1989-94, Animal Welfare Inst., Statue of Liberty Found., 1984-96, No. Nev. Cancer Coun., United Blood Svcs., Arthritis Found., Cancer Soc., Sta. KNPB, Ret. Sr. Citizens, Reno Fire Dept. Christmas Basket Delivery, 1991-96, Sierra Arts Found. Sgt. U.S. Army, 1968-69, Vietnam. Winner Ugly Man contest U. Reno, 1967, 70-72, No. Nev. Bone Marrow Program, 1991-96, ind. category Ugly Bartender contest Multiple Sclerosis, 1989-90; Sparks Tennis Club singles, doubles, and mixed doublas Champion B/C divsn., 1994, STC Singles B Champion, Mixed B Doubles Champion, 1995, STC Ladder B Singles Men's Champion, 1996, 3rd Ann. STC B Doubles Champion, 1996; recipient numerous tennis, billiards, volleyball and bowling awards including 1st pl. C divsn. NNCC Tennis Tournament, 1991, RTC C Mixed Doubles Champion, 1992, Sparks Recreation Open Doubles Champion, 1993; world record holder nosedarts and squint, 1972—; recipient Cmty. Svc. award United Blood Svcs., 1995, Svc. Above Self award Rotary Internat., 1995; winner on TV program Wheel of Fortune, 1995. Mem. DAV, Orthodox Jewish Union. Democrat. Office: Art Internat Gallery Extraordinaire PO Box 13405 Reno NV 89507-3405

FEINLAND, MARSHA, municipal official; b. N.Y., 1950; married; 1 child, Ian. BA in History, Bryn Mawr Coll., 1969; MA in Edn., Hayward State U., 1979. Tchr. Phila., 1969-73, Oakland (Calif.) Children's Ctrs., 1973-80; dir. Hoopa Tribal Day Care Ctr., 1981-82; tchr. Alameda, Calif., 1983—; mem. Berkeley (Calif.) Rent Stabilization Bd., 1994—. Active Children's Ctr. Employees Union; building rep. Alameda Edn. Assn.; candidate Berkeley Sch. Bd., 1986; candidate for 12th assembly dist. Peace and Freedom Party, 1990, 92; elected mem. Berkeley Rent Stabilization Bd., 1994; mem. Berkeley Tenants Union, Progressive Alliance of Alameda County, Bay Area Coalition for Our Reproductive Rights; north state chair Peace & Freedom Party, 1992-94, 96—, state chair, 1994-96, presdl. candidate, 1996. Home: 1801-A Cedar St Berkeley CA 94703

FEINSTEIN, BEVERLY, psychiatrist, psychoanalyst; b. N.Y.C., Dec. 11, 1943. BA, Barnard Coll., 1964; MD, NYU, 1968; PhD in Psychoanalysis, So.Calif. Psychoanalytic Inst., 1988. Diplomate in psychiatry Am. Bd. Psychiatry and Neurology; lic. physician, Calif. Intern Bellevue Hosp, N.Y.C., 1968-69; resident in psychiatry UCLA Neuropsychiat. Inst., 1969-72, asst. clin. prof., 1995—; fellow UCLA Brain Rsch. Inst., 1971-72; staff psychiatrist, biofeedback and insomnia rsch. Sepulveda (Calif.) VA Hosp., 1972-76; asst. clin. prof. UCLA, 1972—; assoc. staff St. John's Hosp., Santa Monica, Calif., 1976-95, Westwood Hosp., L.A., 1976-93. Contbr. articles to profl. jours.; presenter in field. Co-originator, co-dir. UCLA Methadone Maintenance Clinic, 1970-72; cons. Am. Inst. Family Resl., 1977-78, Jewish Family Svc., 1984-85. So. Calif. Psychoanalytic Soc. grantee to lecture in Israel, 1983. Mem. Am. Psychiat. Assn., Am. Psychoanalytic Assn., So. Calif. Psychoanalytic Inst. and Soc. (chmn. ethics com. 1991-92), So. Calif. Psychiat. Soc. (councillor 1990-92, sec. 1992-93, pres. 1995-96). Office: 586 E Channel Rd Santa Monica CA 90402-1344

FEINSTEIN, DIANNE, senator; b. San Francisco, June 22, 1933; d. Leon and Betty (Rosenburg) Goldman; m. Bertram Feinstein, Nov. 11, 1962 (dec.); 1 child, Katherine Anne; m. Richard C. Blum, Jan. 20, 1980. BA History, Stanford U., 1955; LLB (hon.), Golden Gate U., 1977; D Pub. Adminstrn. (hon.), U. Manila, 1981; D Pub. Service (hon.), U. Santa Clara, 1981; JD (hon.), Antioch U., 1983, Mills Coll., 1985; LHD (hon.), U. San Francisco, 1988. Fellow Coro Found., San Francisco, 1955-56; with Calif. Women's Bd. Terms and Parole, 1960-66; mem. Mayor's com. on crime, chmn. adv. com. Adult Detention, 1967-69; mem. Bd. of Suprs., San Francisco, 1970-78, pres., 1970-71, 74-75, 78; mayor of San Francisco, 1978-88, U.S. senator from Calif., 1992—; mem. exec. com. U.S. Conf. of Mayors, 1983-88; Dem. nominee for Gov. of Calif., 1990; mem. Nat. Com. on U.S.-China Rels., mem. Judiciary Comm., Rukes & Adminstrn,, Senate Dem. Policy Com. Mem. Bay Area Conservation and Devel. Commn., 1973-78; mem. Senate Fgn. Rels. Com. Recipient Woman of Achievement award Bus. and Profl. Women's Clubs San Francisco, 1970, Disting. Woman award San Francisco Examiner, 1970, Coro Found. award, 1979, Coro Leadership award, 1988, Pres. medal U. Calif., San Francisco, 1988, Scopus award Am. Friends Hebrew U., 1981, Brotherhood/Sisterhood award NCCJ, 1986, Comdr.'s award U.S. Army, 1986, French Legion of Honor, 1984, Disting. Civilian award USN, 1987; named Number One Mayor All-Pro City Mgmt. Team City and State Mag., 1987. Mem. Trilateral Commn., Japan Soc. of No. Calif. (pres. 1988-89), Inter-Am. Dialogue, Nat. Com. on U.S.-China Rels. Office: US Senate 331 Senate Hart Office Bldg Washington DC 20510

FEISS, GEORGE JAMES, III, financial services company executive; b. Cleve., June 24, 1950; s. George James Jr. and Bettie (Kalish) F.; m. Susan Margaret Cassel, May 30, 1981; children: Kalish Ilana Cassel-Feiss, Nika Catherine Cassel-Feiss. BA in Social Studies, Antioch Coll., 1973; MBA in Internat. Fin., Am. Grad. Sch. Internat. Mgmt., Phoenix, 1975. Registered investment advisor, Wash.; CFP Coll. Fin. Planning, Denver. Ptnr. Health-care Cons., Seattle, 1976-80; pres. M2 Inc., Seattle, 1980—; CFO, bd. dirs. Vivid Image Co., San Diego, Calif., 1994—; cons. Sta. KRAB, Seattle, 1988-89, Zion Christian Acad., Seattle, 1990—. Author: Mind Therapies/Body Therapies, 1979, Hope & Death in Exile - The Economics and Politics of Cancer in the United States, 1981. Bd. dirs. B'nai Brith, Seattle, 1988-91; mem. fin. com. Univ. Child Devel. Sch., Seattle, 1989—; mem. social action com. Am. Jewish Com., Seattle, 1992. Mem. Eastside Estate Planning Coun., Inst. for CFPs, Social Investment Forum, Social Venture Network. Home: 603 38th Ave Seattle WA 98122-6423 Office: M2 Inc 1932 1st Ave Ste 614 Seattle WA 98101

FEIST, EDWARD JOSEPH, secondary education educator; b. Denver, June 8, 1947; s. Edward J. and Jean (Nielsen) F.; m. Ricki Lynn Hetts, Aug. 15, 1970; children: Trevor, Trent. BA in Speech Arts, Colo. State U., 1970; MA in Theater Arts, Univ. No. Colo., 1972; EdD, Univ. Colo., 1987. Tchr. Estes Park (Colo.) Jr./Sr. H.S., 1970-72, Littleton (Colo.) H.S., 1972—. Coach soccer Littleton Soccer Assn., 1980-83, Cherry Creek Soccer Assn., 1983-90. Home: 7358 S Spruce St Englewood CO 80112-1752 Office: Littleton High Sch 199 E Littleton Blvd Littleton CO 80121-1106

FEISTHAMEL, JUDY, language educator, interpreter, translator; b. Prague, Czechoslovakia, Oct. 25, 1944; came to U.S., Feb. 1959; d. Ladislav Kratky and Jitka Kalder Elton; m. John Feisthamel, May 27, 1972; children: Mark, Matthew. BA with honors, UCLA, 1966, MA, 1967, PhD, 1972; MA in Edn., Calif. State U., San Jose, 1993. Cert. ct. interpreter, Calif. Asst. prof. U. Hawaii, 1970-73; instr. Defense Lang. Inst., Monterey, Calif., 1974-76; ESL cons. Pacific Grove (Calif.) Sch. Dist., 1980-82; bilingual resource tchr. Salinas (Calif.) Sch. Dist., 1982—; instr. Monterey (Calif.) Peninsula Coll., 1982—; interpreter, translator Cortes Translation, Carmel, Calif., 1982—; faculty liaison Calif. State U., Monterey Bay, 1995—. Author: Spanish Basic Course, 1976, Mil Maravillas Workbook, 1986, Campanitas de Oro, 1987. Tchg. fellow UCLA, 1968-70. Mem. Am. Assn. Tchrs. of Spanish, Am. Translators Assn., Calif. Ct. Interpreters Assn. (sec. 1980), Calif. Assn. Bilingual Edn., Modern Lang. Assn. Home: 8325 E Camino Estrada Carmel CA 93923

FEJES, CLAIRE, artist, writer; b. N.Y.C., Dec. 14, 1920; d. Sam and Dora Specht; m. Joseph Fejes, Dec. 21, 1945; children: Mark, Yolande. Grad. H.S., N.Y.C.; HHD (hon.), U. Alaska, 1985. Author, illustrator: People of the Noatak, 1965, Enuk, My Son, 1969, Villagers, 1981; author: Cold Starry Night, 1996; illustrator: Eskimo Story Teller, 1975; one-woman shows include U. Alaska, Fairbanks, 1973, Larcada Gallery, N.Y.C., 1974, Yad Le Banim, Tel Aviv, 1976, Bear Gallery, Fairbanks, 1978, Collector's Gallery, Anchorage, 1981, 89, Artique Gallery, Anchorage, 1986, others; group exhibits include Coe Kerr Gallery, N.Y., 1975, Smithsonian Exhibit-Contemporary Art for Alaska, 1978, Cork Gallery-Lincoln Ctr., N.Y., 1981, N.I.K.A. Exhibit, Tokyo Met. Mus., 1982-88, Gt. Am. Artists/Cin. Mus., 1996others; represented in permanent collections U. Alaska Mus., Laurence Blodell Estates, Mass., Gov.'s Manion, Juneau, Alaska, Ben-Zion, N.Y., Tanana Valley Clinic, Fairbanks, Frye Art Mus., Seattle, Wien Meml. Libr., Fairbanks, Anchorage Mus. Permanent Collection, Anchorage, Alaska State Mus., Juneau, Sheldon Jackson Libr., Sitka, Alaska, Anchorage Treatment Ctr., Christian Chapel, Nagoya, Japan, Nippon Chem. Sales, Tokyo, Marilyn Horne Collection, James Michener Collection-Archer M. Huntington Mus., Tex., other pvt. collections. Fellow Explorers Club. Home: 924 Kellum St Fairbanks AK 99701-4372 also: 4719 Agora Way Oceanside CA 92056

FELDE, KRISTIN LINN, primary education educator; b. Spokane, Wash., Aug. 21, 1959; d. Dale Edward and Loraine Elenor (Olsen) Hundeby; m. F. Richard Felde, Feb. 14, 1993. AA, Clark Coll., 1980; BS, Portland State U., 1989; MEd, Wash. State U., 1993. Dental hygienist Dr. Nevin/Dr. Sakai, Camas and Vancouver, Wash., 1982-89; tchr., edn. tech. coord. Battle Ground Pub. Sch., Vancouver, 1989—, tchr. rep. program delivery coun., 1994-95; tech. rep. Ednl. Tech., Battle Ground, Wash., 1991-93; co-chair Young Author's Com., Battle Ground, 1991-96. Contbr. chpt. to book. Recipient Nat. Educator award Milken Family Found., 1996; named Tchr. of the Yr. BattlegroundSch. Dist., 1994; Implementing Dreams for Ednl. Achievements grantee S.W. Wash. Cmty. Trust, Vancouver, 1993, 94, 96. Mem. Unified Doll Fedn. Home: 20006 NE 189th St Brush Prairie WA 98606-9754 Office: Pleasant Valley Primary 14320 NE 50th Ave Vancouver WA 98686-1644

FELDMAN, ALLAN JAY, financial planner, stockbroker; b. Bklyn., Mar. 19, 1936; s. William and Pearl (Stolzer) F.; m. Barbara Klein, June 24, 1956; children: Donna, Jill, Mark. Student, U. Conn., 1954-55, U. Bridgeport, 1955-58. CFP. Bus. cons., 1958-75; v.p. Amb. Internat., 1975-80; pres. Total Svcs. Investments, Scottsdale, Ariz., 1980-91; v.p. Paine Webber, Sun City, Ariz., 1991—. Author: Winning the Financial Game, 1987. Pres. Jewish Cmty. Ctr., Scottsdale, 1988-91. Mem. Internat. Assn. Fin. Planners (v.p. Phoenix 1985-86), Inst. CFP's Phoenix (pres. 1990-91), Registry CFP Lic. Practitioners, C. of C. Greater Phoenix (pres. 1991). Democrat. Home: 12538 E Poinsettia Dr Scottsdale AZ 85259-3442 Office: Paine Webber 10699 W Bell Rd Sun City AZ 85351-1175

FELDMAN, GERALD DONALD, history educator; b. N.Y.C., Apr. 24, 1937; s. Isadore and Lillian (Cohen) F.; m. Philippa Blume, June 22, 1958 (div. Feb. 31, 1982); children: Deborah, Aaron; m. Norma von Ragenfeld, Nov. 30, 1983. BA in History, Columbia U., 1958; MA in History, Harvard U., 1959, PhD in History, 1964. Asst. prof. U. Calif., Berkeley, 1963-68, assoc. prof., 1968-70, prof. history, 1970—; dir. Ctr. for German and European Studies, U. Calif., Berkeley, 1994—. Author: Army Industry and Labor in Germany, 1914-1918, 1966, Iron and Steel in the German Inflation, 1916-1923, 1977, Von Weltkrieg zur Weltwirtschaftskrise, 1985, The Great Disorder: Politics, Economics and Society in the German Inflation, 1914-1924, 1993. Guggenheim fellow, 1973-74, German Marshall Fund fellow, 1981-82, fellow Historisches Kolleg, Munich, 1982-83, fellow Inst. for Advanced Study, Berlin, 1987-88, Woodrow Wilson fellow, 1991-92. Office: U of Calif Dept of History Berkeley CA 94720

FELDMAN, ROGER LAWRENCE, artist, educator; b. Spokane, Wash., Nov. 19, 1949; s. Marvin Lawrence and Mary Elizabeth (Shafer) F.; m. Astrid Lunde, Dec. 16, 1972; children: Kirsten B., Kyle Lawrence. BA in Art Edn., U. Wash., 1972; postgrad., Fuller Theol. Sem., Pasadena, Calif., 1972-73, Regent Coll., Vancouver, B.C., 1974; MFA in Sculpture, Claremont Grad. Sch., 1977. Teaching asst. Claremont (Calif.) Grad. Sch.; assoc. prof. art Biola U., La Mirada, Calif., 1989—; adj. instr. Seattle Pacific U., 1979, 80, 82, 83, Linfield Coll., 1978, Edmonds C.C., 1978-80, Shoreline C.C., 1978; one person shows include Art Ctr. Gallery of Seattle Pacific U., 1977, 83, 84, Linfield Coll., McMinnville, Oreg., 1979, Blackfish Gallery, Portland, 1982, Lynn McAllister Gallery, Seattle, 1986, Biola U., 1989, Coll. Gallery, La. Coll., Pineville, 1990, Gallery W., Sacramento, 1991, Aughinbaugh Gallery, Grantham, Pa., 1992, Biola U., 1993, Riverside Art Mus., 1994, Azusa Pacific U., 1995, Cornerstone '96, Bushnell, Ill., 1996, Gallery W, Sacramento; guest artist and lectr. Group shows include Pasadena Artist's Concern Gallery, 1976, Libra Gallery, Claremont, 1977, Renshaw Gallery, McMinnville, 1978, Cheney Cowles Mus., Spokane, 1979, 80, 83, Lynn McAllister Gallery, Seattle, 1985, Bumbershoot, Seattle, 1985, 86, West Bend (Wis.) Gallery, 1992, L.A. Mcpl. Satellite Gallery, 1993, Greenbelt 93, Northamptonshire, Eng., 1993, Claremont Sch. Theology, 1994, Queens Coll. Cambridge U., Eng., 1994, Jr. Arts Ctr. Gallery, Barnsdall Park, L.A., 1994, Bade Mus. Pacific Sch. of Religion, Berkeley, Calif., 1995, Cen. Arts Collective, Tucson, 1995, L.A. Mcpl. Gallery Barnsdall Art Park, 1996, Reconstructive Gallery Santa Ana, Ct., 1997, Guggenheim Gallery, Chapman U., Orange, Calif., 1997; comms. include Renton Vocat. Tech. Inst., 1987-89, East Hill Cmty. Ctr., Gresham, Oreg., 1979; contbr. articles to profl. jours. Recipient King County Arts Commn. Individual Artist Project award, Seattle, 1988, David Gaiser award for sculpture Cheney Cowles Mus., 1980, Disting. Award for Harborview Med. Ctr. "Viewpoint", Assn. for Tech. Comm., 1987, Design award for "Seafirst News", Internat. Assn. Bus. Comm., 1987, Pace Setter award, 1987, others; individual artist sculpture grantee Nat. Endowment for Arts, 1986, Connemara Sculpture grante, 1990, Biola U., 1991. Office: Biola Univ 13800 Biola Ave La Mirada CA 90639-0002

FELDMAN, STANLEY GEORGE, state supreme court justice; b. N.Y.C., N.Y., Mar. 9, 1933; s. Meyer and Esther Betty (Golden) F.; m. Norma Arambula; 1 dau., Elizabeth L. Student, U. Calif., Los Angeles, 1950-51; LL.B., U. Ariz., 1956. Bar: Ariz. 1956. Practiced in Tucson, 1956-81; ptnr. Miller, Pitt & Feldman, 1968-81; justice Ariz. Supreme Ct., Phoenix, 1982, 1992-96; lectr. Coll. Law, U. Ariz., 1965-76, adj. prof., 1976-81. Bd. dirs. Tucson Jewish Community Council. Mem. ABA, Am. Bd. Trial Advocates (past pres. So. Ariz. chpt.), Ariz. Bar Assn. (pres. 1974-75, bd. govs. 1967-76), Pima County Bar Assn. (past pres.), Am. Trial Lawyers Assn. (dir. chpt. 1967-76). Democrat. Jewish. Office: Ariz Supreme Ct 1501 W Washington St Phoenix AZ 85007-3231*

FELDMAN, STEPHEN, university president; b. N.Y.C., Sept. 11, 1944; s. Harry and Mae (Morris) F.; m. Constance M. Lerudis, June 1, 1969; children—Jennifer Dawn, Timothy Richard. BBA, CCNY, 1966, MBA, 1968, PhD (fellow), 1971. Chmn. dept. banking, fin. and investments Hofstra U., Hempstead, N.Y., 1969-77, assoc. prof., 1974-77; dean Ancell Sch. of bus. Western Conn. State U., Danbury, 1977-81, univ. pres., 1981-92; pres. Nova Southeastern U., Ft. Lauderdale, Fla., 1992-94; v.p. real estate Ethan Allen Inc., Danbury, 1995-96; v.p. univ. rels., devel. Calif. State U., Long Beach, 1996—; bd. dirs. Ethan Allen Inc., Sci. Horizons Inc.; cons. IBM, N.Y. Telephone Co. Editor: Credit Unions, 1974, Handbook of Wealth Management, 1977, Smarter Money, 1985; contbr. articles to profl. publs. Trustee Danbury Hosp., United Way. Mem. Am. Assn. State Colls. and Univs. (chmn. corp. coll. rels.), Greater Ft. Lauderdale C. of C. Office: Calif State U 1250 Bellflower Blvd Long Beach CA 90840

FELISKY, BARBARA ROSBE, artist; b. Chgo., Mar. 24, 1938; d. Robert Lee and Margaret (Black) Rosbe; m. Timothy Felisky, Oct. 6, 1962; children: Kendra, Marc, Kyra. BA in Edn., U. Mich., 1960. Tchr. Peekskill (N.Y.) Sch. Dist., 1960-61; asst. to edn. dir. Simplicity Pattern Co., N.Y.C.; tchr. Anaheim (Calif.) Sch. Dist. Contbr. articles to mags. Bd. guilds Orange County Performing Arts Ctr., Costa Mesa, Calif., 1983-85. Mem. Laguna Beach Art Mus., L.A. County Mus. Art, Gamma Phi Beta. Home and Studio: 2942 E Lake Hill Dr Orange CA 92867-1910

FELL, JAMES F., lawyer; b. Toledo, Ohio, Nov. 18, 1944; s. George H. Fell and Bibianne C. (Hebert) Franklin; children from a previous marriage: Jennifer A., Brian F.; m. Betty L. Wenzel, May 23, 1981. BA, U. Notre Dame, 1966; JD, Ohio State U., 1969. Bar: N.Y. 1970, Calif. 1972, Idaho 1978, Wash. 1981, Oreg. 1984, U.S. Ct. Appeals (9th cir.) 1983, U.S. Dist. Ct. Idaho 1978. Assoc. Breed, Abbott & Morgan, N.Y.C., 1969-72; ptnr. McKenna & Fitting, L.A., 1972-78; atty. Office Atty. Gen., State of Idaho, Boise, 1978-79; dir. policy and adminstrn. Idaho Pub. Utilities Commn., Boise, 1979-81; gen. counsel, dep. dir. Northwest Power Planning Coun., Portland, Oreg., 1981-84; ptnr. Stoel Rives LLP, Portland, 1984—. Mem. ABA (pub. utility law sect.), Oreg. State Bar (exec. com. pub. utility law sect.). Office: Stoel Rives LLP 900 SW 5th Ave Ste 2300 Portland OR 97204-1232

FELLER, DANIEL M., history educator; b. Washington, Oct. 19, 1950; s. David E. and Gilda (Halpern) F.; m. Claudia Dean, Aug. 29, 1992; 1 child, Deborah Elizabeth. BA, Reed Coll., 1972; MA, U. Wis., 1974, PhD, 1981. Asst. prof. Northland Coll., Ashland, Wis., 1980-83; asst. editor The Papers of Andrew Jackson, Nashville, 1983-86; asst. prof. U. N.Mex., Albuquerque, 1986-91, assoc. prof., 1991—. Author: The Public Lands in Jacksonian Politics, 1984, The Jacksonian Promise, 1995; co-editor: The Papers of Andrew Jackson, 1987; contbr. chpt. to book, articles to profl. jours. Mem. So. Hist. Assn., Orgn. Am. Historians, Assn. Documentary Editing (membership chair 1987-89), Soc. Historians of Early Am. Republic (edtl. bd. 1990-94, conv. coord. 1990-96). Democrat. Office: U NMex Dept History Albuquerque NM 87131-1181

FELLER, DAVID E., arbitrator; b. 1916. AB, Harvard U., 1938, LLB, 1941. Bar: Mass. 1941, D.C. 1942. Lectr. law and econs. U. Chgo., 1941-42; atty. U.S. Dept. Justice, Washington, 1946-48; law clk. U.S. Supreme Ct., 1948-49; assoc. gen. counsel CIO, Washington, 1949-53, United Steelworkers, Washington, 1949-60; gen. counsel ind. union dept. AFL-CIO, Washington, 1961-66, United Steelworkers, 1961-65; ptnr. Goldberg Feller &

Bredhoff, Washington, 1955-60, Feller, Bredhoff & Anker, 1961-65, Feller & Anker, 1965-67; John H. Boalt prof. emeritus U. Calif.-Berkeley Sch. Law. Editor Harvard Law Rev. Bd. dirs. NAACP Legal Def. and Edn. Fund, 1960—; pres. Council Univ. Calif. Faculty Assns., 1973-89. Mem. Nat. Acad. Arbitrators (v.p. 1985-87, pres. 1992-93), Fed. Mediation and Conciliation Service Roster of Arbitrators, ABA (sec. labor law sect. 1972-73), Phi Beta Kappa. Home: 728 Santa Barbara Rd Berkeley CA 94707-2005 Office: U Calif Sch of Law 225 Boalt Hall Berkeley CA 94720-7201

FELLER, WILFORD CARTER, jewelry retailer, manufacturing company executive; b. St. George, Utah, June 9, 1953; s. George Russell and Mary Luella (Carter) F.; m. Deborah Lee Oxspring, Aug. 26, 1977; children: Tate, Trevor, Chelan, Christin. AA with honors, Dixie Coll., St. George, 1975; BA magna cum laude, Brigham Young U., 1977. Owner, mgr. WD Ltd., Provo, Utah, 1975—; ptnr. Amgold Corp. (doing bus. as Goldsmith Co. Jewelers), Provo, 1980-92, owner, mgr., 1992—; ptnr. John Beesley Goldsmith Co., Provo, 1979-80. Former neighborhood chmn. City of Provo; mem. Downtown Action Com. Mem. Jewelers Am. (Gemological Inst. Am. scholar), Ind. Jewelers Orgn., Intermountain Jewelers Am., Provo-Orem C. of C. (past bd. dirs.), Downtown Mchts. Assn. (past pres.). Republican. Mem. LDS Ch. Home: 1179 E 40 N Orem UT 84057-8224 Office: Goldsmith Co Jewelers 100 N University Ave Provo UT 84601-2820

FELLIN, OCTAVIA ANTOINETTE, retired librarian; b. Santa Monica, Calif.; d. Otto P. and Librada (Montoya) F. Student U. N.Mex., 1937-39; BA, U. Denver, 1941; BA in L.S., Rosary Coll., 1942. Asst. libr., instr. libr. sci. St. Mary-of-Woods Coll., Terre Haute, Ind., 1942-44; libr. U.S. Army, Bruns Gen. Hosp., Santa Fe, 1944-46, Gallup (N.Mex.) Pub. Libr., 1947-90; post libr. Camp McQuaide, Calif., 1947; freelance writer mags., newspapers, 1950—; libr. cons.; N.Mex. del. White House Pre-Conf. on Librs. & Info. Svcs., 1978; dir. Nat. Libr. Week for N.Mex., 1959. Chmn. Red Mesa Art Ctr., 1984-88; pres. Gallup Area Arts Coun., 1988; mem. Western Health Found. Century Com., 1988, Gallup Multi-Model Cultural Com., 1988-95; v.p., publicity dir. Gallup Cmty. Concerts Assn., 1957-78, 85-95; organizer Gt. Decision Discussion groups, 1963-85; co-organizer, v.p. chair fund raising com. Gallup Pub. Radio Com., 1989-95; mem. McKinley County Recycling Com., 1990—; mem. local art selection com. N.Mex. Art Dirs., 1990; mem. Gallup St. Naming Com., 1958-59, Aging Com., 1964-68; chmn. Gallup Mus. Indian Arts and Crafts, 1964-78; mem. Eccles. Conciliation and Arbitration Bd., Province of Santa Fe, 1974; mem. publicity com. Gallup Inter-Tribal Indian Ceremonial Assn., 1966-68; mem. Gov's. Com. 100 on Aging, 1967-70; mem. U. N.Mex.-Gallup Campus Cmty. Edn. Adv. Coun., 1981-82; N.Mex. organizing chmn. Rehoboth McKinley Christian Hosp. Aux., pres., 1983, chmn. aux. scholarship com., 1989—, chmn. cmty. edn. loan selection com., 1990—, bd. dirs., corr. sec., 1991-94; mem. N.Mex. Libr. Adv. Coun., 1971-75, vice chmn., 1974-75; chmn. adv. com. Gallup Sr. Citizens, 1971-73; mem. steering com. Gallup Diocese Bicentennial, 1975-78, chmn. hist. com., 1975; chmn. Trick or Treat for UNICEF, Gallup, 1972-77, Artists Coop, 1985-89; chmn. pledge campaign Rancho del Nino San Huberto, Empalme, Mex., 1975-80; active Nat. Cath. Social Justice Lobby; bd. dirs. Gallup Opera Guild, 1970-74; bd. dirs., sec., organizer Gallup Area Arts Council, 1970-78; mem. N.Mex. Humanities Council, 1979, Gallup Centennial Com., 1980-81; mem. Cathedral Parish Council, 1980-83, v.p., 1981, century com. Western Health Found., 1988-89; active N.Mex. Diamond Jubilee/U.S. Constn. Bicentennial Gallup Com., 1986-87, N.Mex. Gallup Campus 25 Silver Anniversary Com., 1994. Recipient Dorothy Canfield Fisher $1,000 Libr. award, 1961, Outstanding Community Service award for mus. service Gallup C. of C., 1969, 70, Outstanding Citizen award, 1974, Benemerenti medal Pope Paul VI, 1977, Celebrate Literary award Gallup Internat. Reading 8 Assn., 1983-84, Woman of Distinction award Soroptimists, 1985, N.Mex. Disting. Pub. Svc. award, 1987, finalist Gov's award Outstanding N.Mex. Women, 1988, Edgar L. Hewett award Hist. Soc. N.Mex., 1992; Octavia Fellin Pub. Libr. named in her honor, 1990. Mem. ALA, N.Mex. Library Assn. (hon. life, v.p., sec., chmn. hist. materials com. 1964-66, salary and tenure com., nat. coordinator N.Mex. legislative com., chmn. com. to extend library services 1969-73, Librar. of Yr. award 1975, chmn. local and regional history roundtable 1978, Community Achievement award 1983, Membership award 1994), AAUW (v.p., co-organizer Gallup br., N.Mex. nominating com. 1967-68, chmn. fellowships and centennial fund Gallup br., chmn. com. on women), Plateau Scis. Soc., N.Mex. Folklore Soc. (v.p. 1964-65, pres. 1965-66), N.Mex. Hist. Soc. (dir. 1979-85), Gallup Hist. Soc., Gallup Film Soc. (co-organizer, v.p. 1950-58), LWV (v.p. 1953-56), NAACP, Pax Christi U.S.A., Women's Ordination Conf. Network, Gallup C. of C. (organizing chmn. women's div. 1972, v.p. 1972-73), N.Mex. Women's Polit. Caucus, N.Mex. Mcpl. League (pres. libr.'s div. 1979), Alpha Delta Kappa (hon.). Roman Catholic (Cathedral Guild, Confraternity Christian Doctrine Bd. 1962-64, Cursillo in Christianity Movement, mem. of U.S. Cath. Bishop's Adv. Council 1969-74; corr. sec. Latin Am. Mission Program 1972-75, sec. Diocese of Gallup Pastoral Council 1972-73, corr. sec. liturgical comm. Diocese of Gallup 1977). Author: Yahweh the Voice that Beautifies the Land, A Chronicle of Mileposts A Brief History of the University of New Mexico, Gallup Campus. Home and Office: 513 E Mesa Ave Gallup NM 87301-6021

FELLMAN, JOHN KEEGAN, physiology educator, biochemist; b. St. Louis, Nov. 26, 1952; m. Harriet L. Hughes, Oct. 16, 1976; children: Mary Alice, John Murray. BS, Clemson (S.C.) U., 1974; PhD, U. Idaho, 1982. Postdoctoral fellow U. Idaho, Moscow, 1981-82, 1983; postdoctoral fellow Wash. State U., Pullman, 1983-86; rsch. chemist USDA/ARS, Wenatchee, Wash., 1987-88; asst. prof. U. Idaho, Moscow, 1988-93, assoc. prof., 1993-95; assoc. prof. Wash. State U., 1995—; pvt. practice post-harvest biochemist cons., pacific n.w., 1988—. Contbr. articles to profl. jours. Mem. AAAS, Am. Soc. Plant Physiologists, Am. Soc.for Horticultural Sci., Internat. Dwarf Fruit Tree Assn., Am. Chem. Soc., Sigma Xi (v.p. 1989-90, pres. 1990-92, U. Idaho chpt.). Office: Wash State Univ Dept Hovt/LA Pullman WA 99164-6414

FELLOW, ANTHONY RAYMOND, communications educator; b. Bridgeport, Conn.; s. Raymond J. and Mary Jo (Anziano) F.; m. Clara Potes, Mar. 23, 1989. BA, Calif. State U., L.A., 1971; MA in Comm., Calif. State Univ., Fullerton, 1976; MA in Comm. Mgmt., U. So. Calif., 1982, PhD in Comm. Theory and Rsch., 1984. Cert. tchr., Calif. Editor, reporter San Gabriel Valley Tribune, West Covina, Calif., 1971-80; prof. Calif. State U., L.A., 1983-85, Fullerton, 1985—. Author: Copyeditors' Handbook for Newspapers, 1997; contbr. articles to profl. publs. Bd. dirs. Met. Water Dist., L.A., 1983—, Upper Dist. Mcpl. Water Dist., El Monte, Calif., 1991—; councilman City of El Monte, 1996—. Mem. Assn. Edn. Mass Comm., Soc. Profl. Journalists, Elks. Democrat. Roman Catholic. Home: 11296 Vista Ln El Monte CA 91731 Office: Calif State U Fullerton Dept Communications Fullerton CA 92634

FELLOWS, ALICE COMBS, artist; b. Atlanta, Sept. 14, 1935; d. Andrew Grafton III and Wilhelmina Drummond (Jackson) Combs; m. Robert Ellis Fellows Jr., Aug. 20, 1957 (div. 1978); children: Ariadne Elisabeth Fellows-Mannion, Kara Suzanne. BFA, Syracuse U., 1957; M in Clin. Psychology, Antioch U., 1992. guest artist Yaddo, Saratoga Springs, N.Y., 1991; artist-in-residence Dorland Colony, Temecula, Calif., 1983; guest lectr. psychology seminar UCLA, 1990; cons. for artists and writers, specializing in creative block and dreamwork. Exhibited works in numerous group and one-woman shows including The Armory Ctr. at Pasadena, 1996, Hunsaker-Schlesinger Gallery, 1996, Barnsdall Mcpl. Gallery, 1995, Claremont Grad. Sch. Gallery, 1991, Saxon-Lee Gallery, L.A., 1989, Santa Monica Coll. Gallery Art, 1988, J. Rosenthal Gallery, Chgo., 1986, The Biennial at the Hirshhorn Mus. and Sculpture Garden, Washington, 1986, Kirk de Gooyer Gallery, L.A., 1984, 85, many others; works represented in numerous collections including The Norton, Santa Monica, Broad Found., Santa Monica, Mint Mus., Charlotte N.C., N.C. Mus. Raleigh, N.C., Security Pacific Corp., L.A., others. Arts commr. City of Santa Monica Arts Commn., 1995; bd. dirs. and artist ops. dir. Duganne Ateliers, Santa Monica, 1996. Nat. Endowment for Arts Painting fellow, 1991, Getty Trust Painting fellow, 1990, Western States Arts Fedn./NEA Painting fellow, 1990; grantee Dale Chihuly grant for Srs. Making Art workshops, 1996. Home and Studio: 656 Copeland Ct Santa Monica CA 90405-4416

FELT, PAUL SCHENK, lawyer; b. Salt Lake City, Aug. 16, 1947; s. Spencer P. and Barbara F.; m. Janet Hugie Smith; children: Elizabeth, Matthew. BS, U. Utah, 1969; JD, U. Mich., 1972. Bar: Utah 1972, U.S. Dist. Ct. (ctrl. dist.) Utah 1972. Ptnr. Ray, Quinney & Nebeker, Salt Lake City, 1972—; jury instruction review State of Utah. Mem. Utah State Bar (mem. exec. com. 1984-85), Def. Rsch. Inst. (pres. 1986-87), Am. Coll. Trial Lawyers. Office: Ray Quinney & Nebeker 79 S Main St Ste 400 PO Box 45385 Salt Lake City UT 84145-0385

FELTER, EDWIN LESTER, JR., lawyer, agency administrator; b. Washington, Aug. 11, 1941; s. Edwin L. Felter and Bertha (Peters) Brekke; m. Yoko Yamauchi-Koito, Dec. 26, 1969. B.A., U. Tex., 1964; J.D., Cath. U. of Am., 1967. Bar: Colo. 1970, U.S. Dist. Ct. Colo. 1970, U.S. Ct. Appeals (10th cir.) 1971, U.S. Supreme Ct. 1973, U.S. Tax Ct. 1979, U.S. Ct. Claims 1979, U.S. Ct. Internat. Trade 1979; Dep. pub. defender State of Colo., Ft. Collins, 1971-75; asst. atty. gen. Office of the Atty. Gen., Denver, 1975-80; state adminstrv. law judge Colo. Div. of Adminstrv. Hearings, Denver, 1980-83, chief adminstrv. law judge, dir., 1983—; disciplinary prosecutor Supreme Ct. Grievance Com., 1975-78. Contbg. editor Internat. Franchising, 1970. Mem. Colo. State Mgmt. Cert. Steering com., 1983-86; No. Colo. Criminal Justice Planning council, Ft. Collins, 1973-75; bd. dirs., vice chmn. The Point Community Crisis Ctr., Ft. Collins, 1971-73; mem. Denver County Dem. Party Steering Com., 1978-79; chmn. 12th legis. dist., 1978-79, bd. dirs., pres. Denver Internat. Program, 1989-90. Mem. ABA, Nat. Conf. Adminstrv. Law Judges (mem. exec. com.), Colo. Bar Assn. (chmn. grievance policy com. 1991-94, interprofl. com. 1995—), Arapahoe County Bar Assn., Nat. Assn. of Adminstrv. Law Judges (pres. Colo. chpt. 1982-84, Nat. Fellowship winner 1994). Office: Colo Divsn Adminstrv Hearings 1120 Lincoln St Ste 1400 Denver CO 80203-2140

FELTER, JUNE MARIE, artist; b. Oakland, Calif., Oct. 19, 1919; m. Richard Henry Felter, Feb. 7, 1943; children: Susan, Tom. Student, San Francisco Art Inst., 1960, 61, Oakland Art Inst., 1937-40. Instr. San Francisco Mus. Art, 1965-78, San Francisco State U., 1970-78, U. Calif., 1979-80, Santa Rosa (Calif.) Jr. Coll., 1981, Elaine Badgley-Arnoux Sch. Art, San Francisco, 1982, 83, U. Calif., San Francisco, 1979-80, 84-85. One-woman shows include Gumps Gallery, San Francisco, 1965-66, Linda Ferris Gallery, Seattle, 1971, Richmond Art Gallery, 1971-74, Dana Reich Gallery, San Francisco, 1978, 80-81, 871 Fine Arts Gallery, San Francisco, 1987, 89, 90, 92; exhibited in group shows at San Francisco Mus. Art., 1960-79, Civic Arts Gallery, Walnut Creek, Calif., 1983, U.S. Art, San Francisco, 1990, Oakland Art Mus., 1991, Wiegand Gallery, 1992, Jack London Square Oakland, 1993, U.S. Embassy, Vienna, Austria, 1995, numerous others. Home and Office: 1046 Amito Dr Berkeley CA 94705-1502

FELTON, SAMUEL PAGE, biochemist; b. Petersburg, Va., Sept. 7, 1919; s. Samuel S. and Pearl (Williams) F.; m. Helen Florence Martin, Dec. 31, 1955; 1 child, Samuel Page. Degree in pharmacy, U.S. Army, San Francisco, 1942; BS in Chemistry, U. Wash., 1951, postgrad., 1954. Chief technician U. Wash., Seattle, 1952-59, research assoc., 1959-62, sr. research assoc., 1976—, dir. cen. facilities lab. anesthesiology, 1969-73, dir. water quality lab., 1976-83, dir. biochem. lab. sch. of Fisheries, 1983-85; emeritus, nutrition and disease rsch. in fish Sch. Fisheries, U. Wash., Seattle, 1985—; asst. mem., asst. to dir. div. biochemistry Scripps Clinic and Research Found., La Jolla, Calif., 1962-66; asst. biochemist Children's Orthopedic Hosp., Seattle, 1966-68; vis. scientist Va. Inst. Marine Scis. at Coll. William and Mary, Williamsburg, 1985. Mem. bd. of adjustments City of Edmonds, Wash. Served to sgt. MC, U.S. Army 1941-45. Fellow Am. Inst. Chemists; mem. Am. Chem. Soc., Am. Inst. Fishery Research Biologists, N.Y. Acad. of Scis., Soc. Exptl. Biology and Medicine. Office: U Wash Fisheries Rsch & Teaching Box 355100 Seattle WA 98195

FENG, JOSEPH SHAO-YING, physicist, electrical engineer; b. Peiping, China, June 21, 1948; came to U.S., 1950; s. Paul Yen Hsiung and Mary (Pai) F. BS in Physics, Calif. Inst. Tech., Pasadena, 1969; MS in Physics, Northwestern U., 1970, MSEE, 1971; PhD in Elec. Engring., Calif. Inst. Tech., 1975. Mem. rsch. staff T. J. Watson Rsch. Lab. IBM, Yorktown Heights, N.Y., 1974-77; scientist, engr. IBM Gen. Products Div., San Jose, Calif., 1977—. Inventor in field; contbr. articles to profl. jours. Incorporation chmn. Banner Run, San Jose, 1989. Mem. ASCIT (treas. Pasadena, Calif. chpt. 1968-69), IEEE, Am. Phys. Soc., Mediaeval Acad. of Am., Greenburgh (N.Y.) Karate Club (treas. 1977), Chi Ski (officer 1980-84), Nisei Ski (officer 1986-88, 95-96).

FENNEL, PETER J., SR., retired anesthesiologist; b. Alexandria, La., Nov. 28, 1928; s. Lawrence Sr. and Ruth (Carnahan) F.; m. Ruth Kettenring, Dec. 31, 1965; children: Peter J. Jr., Tracy E. BA, Bowdoin Coll., 1948; MD, Cornell U., 1952. Diplomate Am. Bd. Anesthesiology. Intern Maine Med. Ctr., 1952-53, resident, 1953-54; resident Meml. Ctr. for Cancer, 1956-57; staff Meml. Hosp., N.Y.C., 1956-57, Touro Infirmary, New Orleans, 1959-65, Lafayette (La.) Gen. Hosp., 1966-68, Sunrise Hosp., Las Vegas, 1968—. Lt. comdr. USN, 1954-56. Mem. Am. Soc. Anesthesia. Republican. Home: 1820 Dolce Dr Las Vegas NV 89134-6150

FENNELL, DIANE MARIE, marketing executive, process engineer; b. Panama, Iowa, Dec. 11, 1944; d. Urban William and Marcella Mae (Leytham) Schechinger; m. Leonard E. Fennell, Aug. 19, 1967; children: David, Denise, Mark. BS, Creighton U., Omaha, 1966. Process engr. Tex. Instruments, Richardson, 1974-79; sr. process engr. Signetics Corp., Santa Clara, Calif., 1979-82; demo lab. mgr. Airco Temescal, Berkeley, Calif., 1982-84; field process engr. Applied Materials, Santa Clara, 1984-87; mgr. product mktg. Lam Rsch., Fremont, Calif., 1987-90; dir. sales and mktg. Ion & Plasma Equipment, Fremont, Calif., 1990-91; pres. FAI, Half Moon Bay, Calif., 1990-96; v.p. mktg. Tegal Corp., Half Moon Bay, Calif., 1997—; founder, coord. chmn. Plasma Etch User's Group, Santa Clara, 1984-87; tchr. computer course Adult Edn., Half Moon Bay, Calif., 1982-83. Founder, bd. dirs. Birth to Three program Mental Retardation Ctr., Denison, Tex., 1974-75; fund raiser local sch. band, Half Moon Bay, 1981-89; community rep. local sch. bd., Half Moon Bay, 1982-83. Mem. Am. Vacuum Soc., Soc. Photo Instrumnentation Engrs., Soc. Women Engrs., Material Rsch. Soc. Home: 441 Alameda Ave Half Moon Bay CA 94019-5337

FENSTERMACHER, CATHLEEN IRENE FIELD, art dealer, secondary education educator; b. Marysville, Calif., Aug. 17, 1950; d. Thomas David and Frances Emily (Heney) Field; m. Robert Lynn Fenstermacher, Feb. 20, 1983; children: Bradley, Elizabeth. Nursing diploma, L.A. County/U. So. Calif., 1971; BA, U. Oreg., 1985. Charge nures L.A. County/U. So. Calif. Med. Ctr., L.A., 1971-75; prenatal educator Sacred Heart Hosp., Eugene, Oreg., 1978-82; mentorship coord. Roosevelt Mid. Sch., Eugene, 1989-94; co-dir. career ctr. South Eugene H.S., Eugene, 1991-94; mgr., buyer Opus 5 Gallery, Eugene, 1994—; chair site coun. Roosevelt Mid. Sch., Eugene, 1986-89, mem., 1990-94; dir. devel. found. St. Paul Sch., 1995-96; bd. dirs. St. Paul Sch. Bd., Eugene. Bd. dirs. Eugene Symphony Guild, 1978-84; sec., bd. dirs. U. of Oreg. Mus. of Art, Eugene, 1984-86; mem. racial/ethnic task force South Eugene H.S., 1993-94. Mem. Eugene C. of C., Eugene Country Club, Downtown Athletic Club. Roman Catholic. Home: 3505 Spring Blvd Eugene OR 97405-4446 Office: 136 E Broadway Eugene OR 97401

FENTON, DONALD MASON, retired oil company executive; b. L.A., May 23, 1929; s. Charles Youdan and Dorothy (Mason) F.; m. Margaret M. Keehler, Apr. 24, 1953; children: James Michael, Douglas Charles. BS, U. Calif., L.A., 1952, PhD, 1958. Chemist Rohm and Haas Co., Phila., 1958-61; sr. rsch. chemist Union Oil Co., Brea, Calif., 1962-67, rsch. assoc., 1967-72, sr. rsch. assoc., 1972-82, mgr. planning and devel., 1982-85; mgr. new tech. devel. Unocal, Brea, 1985-92; cons. AMSCO, 1967-73; co-founder, 1st chmn. Petroleum Environ. Rsch. Forum; chmn. bd. dirs. Calif. Engring. Found., 1991-92. With U.S. Army, 1953-55. Inventor in field. Fellow Am. Inst. Chemists, Alpha Chi Sigma; mem. Am. Chem. Soc. Home: 2861 E Alden Pl Anaheim CA 92806-4401

FENWICK, JAMES H(ENRY), editor; b. South Shields, Eng., Mar. 17, 1937; came to U.S., 1965; s. James Henry and Ellen (Tinmouth) F.; m. Suzanne Helene Hatch, Jan. 27, 1968. BA, Oxford U., Eng., 1960. Freelance lectr., writer, 1960-65; assoc. editor Playboy mag., Chgo., 1965-71; planning and features editor Radio Times, BBC, London, 1971-77; U.S. rep. Radio Times, BBC, N.Y.C., 1978-87; sr. editor Modern Maturity mag., Lakewood, Calif., 1987-90, exec. editor, 1990-91, editor, 1991—. Office: Am Assn Ret Persons 601 E St NW Washington DC 20049

FERBER, NORMAN ALAN, retail executive; b. N.Y.C., Aug. 25, 1948; m. Rosine Ferber; children: Robert, Lauren, Richard. Student, L.I. U. Buyer, mdse. mgr. Atherton Industries, N.Y.C., 1976-79; v.p., mdse. mgr. Raxton Corp., N.Y.C., 1979-82; v.p. Fashion World, N.Y.C., 1982; v.p merchandising, mktg. and distbn. Ross Stores Inc., Newark, Calif., 1982-87, pres., chief operating officer, 1987-88, pres., chief exec. officer, 1988—. Home: 1455 Edgewood Dr Palo Alto CA 94301-3118 Office: Ross Stores Inc PO Box 728 8333 Central Ave Newark CA 94560*

FERBER, ROBERT RUDOLF, physics researcher, educator; b. New Eagle, Pa., June 11, 1935; s. Rudolf F. and Elizabeth J. (Robertson) F.; m. Eileen Merhaut, July 25, 1964; children: Robert Rudolf, Lynne C. BSEE, U. Pitts., 1958; MSEE, Carnegie-Mellon U., 1966, Ph.D. in Semiconductor Physics, 1967. Registered profl. engr., Pa. Mgr. engring. dept. WRS Motion Picture Labs., Pitts., 1954-58, sec., 1959-76, v.p., 1976-79; sr. engr. Westinghouse Rsch. Labs., Pitts., 1956-67; mgr. nuclear effects group Westinghouse Elec. Corp., Pitts., 1967-71, mgr. adv. engr. energy projects, East Pittsburgh, 1971-77; photovoltaic materials and collector rsch. mgr. Jet Propulsion Lab., Pasadena, Calif. 1977-85, SP100 Project contract tech. mgr., 1985-90, asst. project mgr. Spaceborne Imaging Radar, 1990-95, Earth Observing System microwave limb sounder radiometer devl. mgr., 1995—; v.p. Executaire Inc., Pitts., 1960-64; pres. Tele-Cam Inc., Pitts., 1960-78. Editor: Transactions of the 9th World Energy Conf. 1974, Digest of the 9th World Energy Conf., 1974. Contbr. articles to profl. jours. Patentee in field. Mem. Franklin Regional Sch. Dist. Bd., Murrysville, Pa., 1975-77. Fellow Buhl Found., 1965-66, NDEA, 1976-77. Mem. IEEE (sr.), ASME (chmn. 1986 Solar Energy Div. Conf.). Republican. Lutheran. Home: 5314 Alta Canyada Rd La Canada Flintridge CA 91011-1606 Office: Jet Propulsion Lab 4800 Oak Grove Dr Pasadena CA 91109-8001

FERGASON, JAMES L., optical company executive; b. Wakenda, Mo., Jan. 12, 1934; s. Joshua E. and Sarah Margret (Cary) F.; m. Dora Delaine Barlish, June 10, 1956; children: Teresa Neal, Jeffrey, John, Susan. BS in Physics, U. Mo., 1956. Sr. engr. Westinghouse Electric, 1956-66; assoc. dir. Liquid Crystal Inst. Kent State (Ohio) U., 1966-70; pres. Internat. Liquid Xtal Co., Cleve., 1970-75, Am. Liquid Xtal, Kent, Ohio, 1975-83; pvt. cons. Menlo Park, Calif., 1983-86; pres., CEO, chief scientist Optical Shields, Inc., Menlo Park, Calif., 1987—. Contbr. articles to Sci. Am., Applied Optics, Phys. Rev. Letters, Molecular Crystals and Liquid Crystals, SID Internat. Symposium Digest of Tech. Papers. Recipient IR 100 award Indsl. Rsch. mag., 1965, Laurels award Aviation Week and Space Tech., 1989; named Disting. Inventor of Yr., Intellectual Property Owners, 1989. Mem. IEEE (com. on intellectual property 1989, mem. bd. IPO), Am. Phys. Soc. (dir. for info.), Soc. Info. Display (Francis Rice Darne Meml. award 1986), N.Y. Acad. Scis. (Quiet Hero award application design 1990), Assn. Old Crows (Gold Cert. of Merit 1994), Assn. U.S. Army. Home: 158 Almendral Ave Atherton CA 94027-4057 Office: Optical Shields Inc 1390 Willow Rd Menlo Park CA 94025-1516

FERGUS, GARY SCOTT, lawyer; b. Racine, Wis., Apr. 20, 1954; s. Russell Malcolm and Phyl Rose (Muratore) F.; m. Isabelle Sabina Beekman, Sept. 28, 1985; children: Mary Marckwald Beekman Fergus, Kirkpatrick Russell Beekman Fergus. SB, Stanford U., 1976; JD, U. Wis., 1979; LLM, NYU, 1981. Bar: Wis. 1979, Calif. 1980. Assoc. Brobeck, Phleger & Harrison, San Francisco, 1980-86, ptnr., 1986—; mgr. Product Liability Insurance Coverage Environment and Anti-Trust Litigation Group., 1996—; mgr. products liability, ins. coverage Environ. and Anti-Trust Litigation Group, 1996—. Mem. ABA. Home: 3024 Washington St San Francisco CA 94115-1618 Office: Brobeck Phleger & Harrison 1 Market Plz San Francisco CA 94105-1019

FERGUSON, BRITT TATMAN, educator; b. Sacramento, Sept. 12, 1950; d. Paul Werner and Lena Marie (Giovacchini) Tatman; m. Alexander Robert Vasquez, May 20, 1972 (div. Feb. 1975); m. Jack Edward Ferguson, Feb. 17, 1992; 1 child, Anne Alyce. BA, Sacramento State U., 1972; MA, Calif. State U., Sacramento, 1980; PhD, U. Minn., 1989. Cert. tchr., Calif.; lic. marriage, family and child counselor, Calif. Resource specialist Spl. Edn. Resource Network, Sacramento, 1982-86; grad. rsch. asst. U. Minn., Mpls., 1986-89; dir. TEAMS project San Francisco Sch. Vols., 1989-92; dir. Cmty. Counseling Ctr. Calif. State U., Sacramento, 1992-95; asst. prof. edn. Chapman U., Fairfield, Calif., 1995—; owner Sierra Children's Coll., Roseville, Calif., 1982—; counselor Child Sexual Abuse Treatment Program, Sacramento, 1980-86, 92-93; tchr. Sacramento County Office of Edn., 1981-82, Folsom Cordova Unified Sch. Dist., Rancho Cordova, Calif., 1977-81. Author: (tng. manual) Teams Project, 1992, (with others) Instructional Psychology, 1995. Coord. Rainbows for All God's Children, Citrus Heights, Calif., 1994—. Mem. APA, ASCD, Profl. Assn. of Childhood Educators, Roseville C. of C., Phi delta Kappa. Democrat. Roman Catholic. Office: Sierra Childrens College 9560 Sierra College Blvd Roseville CA 95661-5921

FERGUSON, E. ROBERT, construction and engineering company executive; b. Phila., Mar. 26, 1932; s. John Harold and Vivian (Livingston) F.; m. Patricia Ann Heckman, Feb. 5, 1955; children: Robin, Sandra, Erin. BSCE, U. Mich., 1955. V.p. Dillingham Corp. & Gordon H. Ball Inc., Danville, Calif., 1958-75, Pacific Constrn. Co., Honolulu, 1975-76; mgr. ops. Rigging Internat., Oakland, Calif., 1976-81; sr. v.p. ASI Bldg. Systems Inc., Dallas, 1982-85; pres., chmn. bd. dirs., CEO, COO Kasler Corp., San Bernardino, Calif., 1985-92; pres. North Pacific Morrison Knudsen, Honolulu, 1992; v.p. internat. ops. Morrison Knudsen, Boise, 1993-95; v.p. civil maj. projects Brown & Root, Houston, 1995—. Served as 1st lt. USMC, 1955-58. Office: Brown & Root PO Box 3 Houston TX 77001

FERGUSON, GARY L., public relations executive; b. Okarche, Okla., Sept. 17, 1949; s. Jack J. Ferguson and Joan C. (Hauser) Long; m. Georgia A. Keller, Jan. 20, 1975 (div. Nov. 1994); 1 child, Laura J. Newell. BA in English, Met. State Coll., Denver, 1980; MA in Comm., U. No. Colo., 1992. Dir. pub. rels. Assoc. Builders and Contrs., Denver, 1981-83; pres. Ferguson Comm., Inc., Littleton, Colo., 1983-88; mng. editor MacGuide Mag., Lakewood, Colo., 1988-89; sr. adminstr. pub. affairs Ball Aerospace and Technologies, Broomfield, Colo., 1989-94; journalism instr. Colo. State U., Ft. Collins, 1994-95; pub. rels. rep. Storage Tech. Corp., Louisville, Colo., 1995—. Author: (book of poetry) Excavating Camelot, 1979. Mem. Pub. Rels. Soc. Am. (exec. com. employee comm. sect. 1996—, Gold Pick for feature/news writing 1991, Gold Pick Award of Merit for feature writing 1992, Silver Pick award for feature writing 1993, Silver Pick award for mag./periodicals 1994), Soc. Profl. Journalists (pres. 1992-93, 94-95, dir.-at-large 1993-94, 96-97, v.p. membership 1991-92, sec. 1990-91, Circle of Excellence award), Denver Press Club. Office: Storage Technology Corp 2280 88th St Louisville CO 80028-4310

FERGUSON, JACK LEE, retired lawyer; b. Richmond, Kans., Sept. 24, 1931; s. Oliver Lee and Mary Marjorie (Knittles) F.; m. Brent Anne Berry, Dec. 16, 1951 (div. June 1969); children: Seana Dawnelle, Robin Leigh, Valerie Lynn, Scott Wesley, Grant Angus; m. Madeleine Ruth Cash, May 19, 1976. Student, Calif. State U., 1950-52; JD, LaSalle U., 1957. Ins. investigator Equifax, Sacramento, Calif., 1954-59; right of way agt. Caltrans, Fresno, Calif., 1959-62; pvt. practice law, Napa, Calif., 1962-94; ret., 1994. Supervisor County of Napa, 1965-69, asst. dist. atty., 1963-64, vice chmn. bd. edn., 1956-59. Cpl. USMCR, 1948-52. Named oustanding young man of Am. Jaycees, 1966; recipient Man-Boy award Boys & Girls Clubs of Am., 1969. Mem. Napa County Bar Assn. (chmn. fee arbitration com. 1980-95), 25th Dist. Agrl. Assn. (dir. 1985-93), Am. Legion, Masons, Shriners, Elks, U.S. Navy League (v.p. Napa chtp. 1994), Sons of Italy in Am.

FERGUSON, JACKSON ROBERT, JR., astronautical engineer; b. Neptune, N.J., Aug. 18, 1942; s. Jackson Robert and Charlotte Carter (Rudewick) F.; m. Christina Mary Staley, Aug. 24, 1968; children: Jack Christopher, Joy Heather. BS in Engring. Sci., USAF Acad., 1965; MS in Astronautics, Air Force Inst. Tech., Dayton, Ohio, 1971; PhD in Aerospace Engring., U. Tex., 1983. Registered profl. engr., Tex. Astronautical engr. NORAD, Colorado Springs, Colo., 1972-76; asst. prof. USAF Acad., Colorado Springs, Colo., 1976-80, assoc. prof., 1982-84;, 1991-93; chief scientist European Office of Aerospace Rsch. & Devel., London, 1984-86;

program mgr. Software Engring. Inst. Air Force Systems Command, Boston, 1986-88; detachment comdr. Air Force Systems Command, Colorado Springs, 1988-91; sr. mem. tech. staff Software Engring. Inst. Carnegie-Mellon U., Pitts., 1993—; ind. rev. team mem. USAF Data System Modernization Program, Washington, 1988; head ind. rev. team USAF System 1 Software Devel. Program, 1992; vis. prof. USAF Acad., 1991-93; program mgr. software acquisition Software Engring. Inst., Carnegie Mellon U. Author: Software Acquisition Capability Maturity Model, 1996; contbr. to reference book: Handbook of Engineering Fundamentals, 1984. Parish coun. pres. Our Lady of the Pines Cath. Ch., Black Forest, Colo., 1989. Col. USAF, 1965-91. Recipient USAF Rsch. and Devel. award, 1980. Mem. IEEE. Roman Catholic. Office: Carnegie-Mellon U Software Engring Inst Colorado Springs CO 80920

FERGUSON, JOHN FRANKLIN, music educator; b. Council Bluffs, Iowa, Jan. 18, 1942; s. Ora Franklin and Francis Elizabeth (Sprague) F.; m. Cynthia Claire Hauge, June 21, 1969; children: Klaus, Erik, Scott. Student, Western Oreg. State Coll., 1960-62, Tchr. Tng. Inst., 1963-64; MusB, U. Oreg., 1966; MusM, U. Idaho, 1969. Dir. high sch. and elem. band Riddle (Oreg.) Sch. Dist., 1966-67; dir. concert band U. Idaho, Moscow, 1967-68, supr. undergrad. directed studies in music edn., 1967-68; music specialist elem. sch. Sutherlin (Oreg.) Sch. Dist., 1968-78; salesman Ricketts Music Store, Roseburg, Oreg., 1978-87; music specialist elem. sch. Roseburg Sch. Dist., 1987—. Dir. Roseburg Barbershop Chorus, 1973-77, Roseburg German Band, 1981—; mem. Ch. Choir, Roseburg, 1970—, Vintage Singers, Roseburg, 1991-93. Mem. Music Educators Nat. Conf., Masons. Republican. Presbyterian. Home: 128 W Bodie St Roseburg OR 97470-2308

FERGUSON, LLOYD ELBERT, manufacturing engineer; b. Denver, Mar. 5, 1942; s. Lloyd Elbert Ferguson and Ellen Jane (Schneider) Romero; m. Patricia Valine Hughes, May 25, 1963; children: Theresa Renee, Edwin Bateman. BS in Engring., Nova Internat. Coll., 1983. Cert. hypnotherapist, geometric tolerance instr. Crew leader FTS Corp., Denver, 1968-72; program engr. Sundstrand Corp., Denver, 1972-87, sr. assoc. project engr., 1987-90, sr. liaison engr., 1990-93, sr. planning engr., 1993—; v.p. Valine Corp. Lic. practitioner of religious sci. United Ch. of Religious Sci., L.A.; team capt. March of Dimes Team Walk, Danver, 1987; mem. AT&T Telephone Pioneer Clowns for Charity. Recipient recognition award AT&T Telephone Pioneers, 1990. Mem. Soc. Mfg. Engrs. (chmn. local chpt. 1988, zone chmn. 1989, achievement award 1984, 86, recognition award 1986, 90, appreciation award 1988), Nat. Mgmt. Assn. (cert., program instr. 1982—, honor award 1987, 90), Am. Indian Sci. and Engring. Soc., Colo. Clowns. Mem. United Ch. of Religious Sci. Home: 10983 W 76th Dr Arvada CO 80005-3481 Office: Sundstrand Corp 2480 W 70th Ave Denver CO 80221-2501

FERGUSON, MAXEL JARREL, education educator; b. Lesage, W.Va., June 27, 1935; s. Okie W. and Ruby F.; m. Jeanie Peregrine, Dec. 18, 1960; 1 child, Brenda. BS in Elem. Edn., Marshall U., 1969, MA in Ednl. Adminstrn., 1978; EdD in Curriculum and Instrn., Va. Poly. Inst. and State U., 1984. Cert. sch. supt., Alaska. Sch. prin., village adminstr. Bur. Indian Affairs, 1969-71; tchr. math., journalism Guam, 1971-73; math. resource coord. Cabell County Pub. Schs., W.Va., 1973-74; tchr., adminstr. Bur. Indian Affairs Schs., N.Mex., Ariz., Alaska, 1974-77; adminstrv. asst. to dean, instr. math. Marshall U. Coll. Edn., Huntington, W.Va., 1978-79; vis. prof., grant writer div. curriculum and instrn. Va. Poly. Inst. and State U. Coll. Edn., Blacksburg, 1979-84, instr. dept. math., 1981-84; assoc. prof. edn., head elem. block cons. So. Utah U., Cedar City, 1984—; cons. Nev. Humanities Coun., Las Vegas, 1980-91; nationwide splty. lectr. in field and broad-based cons. activities; dir. Multicultural Confs. Author: The Legacy: Our Native American Heritage, 1990, 2d edit., 1997, Education in Rural America, 1997, Multicultural Education in the Rural Southwest: Research and Recommendations, 1997; contbr. articles to profl. publs.; textbook reviewer for various pubs. With U.S. Army, 1957-60. Recipient various grants including Utah Humanities Coun., Nev. Humanities Coun., NEA, U.S. West Comms., Multicultural Original Rsch., So. Utah U. Faculty Devel. Mem. ASCD, NEA, Nat. Coun. Tchrs. Math., Phi Delta Kappa (pres.), Kappa Delta Pi (counselor advisor to student edn.). Home: 2427 W Old Meadow Ln Cedar City UT 84720-5520 Office: So Utah U 351 W Center St Cedar City UT 84720-2470

FERGUSON, MICHAEL GERARD, career officer; b. Queens, N.Y., Sept. 26, 1967; s. Joseph Peter and Mary Ann (Geraghty) F.; m. Dena Rae James, Apr. 16, 1994; 1 child, Brendan Patrick. BA in Polit. Sci., Villanova U., 1989. Commd. USMC, 1989, advanced through grades to capt., 1994. Roman Catholic.

FERGUSON, MICHAEL ROGER, newspaper executive; b. Dayton, Ohio, Oct. 15, 1951; s. Earl Roger and Betty Louise (Spahr) F.; m. Kathryn Louise Davis, July 22, 1972; children—Kellie, Stacie, Jacob. AA, Mt. San Antonio Coll., 1971; BA with honors, Calif. State Poly. U., 1973. With Progress Bull. newspaper, Pomona, Calif., 1968-82, bus. mgr. 1973-80, sales mgr., 1980-82; bus. Daily Report newspaper, Ontario, Calif., 1973-78; advt. dir. Vallejo Times-Herald (Calif.), 1982-83; gen. mgr. Woodland Daily Democrat, 1983—. Mem. Calif. Newspapers Pubs. Assn., Woodland C. of C. (dir.). Republican. Methodist. Lodge: Rotary. Home: 1080 Deborah St Upland CA 91784-1206 Office: Inland Valley Daily Bulletin 2041 E 4th St PO Box 4000 Ontario CA 91764-2605*

FERGUSON-HUNTINGTON, KATHLEEN ELIZABETH, artist, educator; b. Chgo., Jan. 31, 1945; d. Paul and Catherine A. (Graham) Wurtz; m. Stuart Ferguson, Sept. 26, 1964 (div. 1968); m. Hugh H. Huntington, Oct. 10, 1992. BFA with honors, Layton Sch. Art, 1969; MFA, RISD, 1971. Exhibit coord. Smithsonian Instn., Washington, 1973; asst. prof. L.I. U., Greenvale, N.Y., 1973-75, Nassau C.C., Garden City, N.Y., 1976; lectr. Gallery Passport, N.Y.C., 1978; vis. artist Conn. Coll., New London, 1979, U. Ky., Lexington, 1980-82, Transylvania U., Lexington, 1985; dir. Art Acumen Ednl. Systems, N.Mex., 1983—; creativity cons. K.F.C. Corp., Louisville, 1986, GE Co., Daytona Beach, Fla., 1987, E.I. DuPont deNemours, Wilmington, Del., 1988, Honeywell Corp., Mpls., 1994—; lectr. in field. One women shows at Smithsonian Instn., 1972, Conn. Coll., 1975, U. R.I., Kingston, 1975, Nobe Gallery, N.Y.C., 1977, 79, Jan Cicero Gallery, Chgo., 1979, 84, R. H. Oosterom Gallery, N.Y.C., 1980, Ctr. for Contemporary Art, U. Ky., 1980, U. Cin., 1982, Graham Modern, N.Y.C., 1985, High Mus. Art, Atlanta, 1986, Southeastern Ctr. for Contemporary Art, Winston-Salem, N.C., 1987, J.B. Speed Mus., Louisville, 1987, Sun Cities (Ariz.) Art Mus., Angels Gate Art Ctr., L.A., others; group exhbns. include Hundred Acres Gallery, N.Y.C., 1971, 73, Virginia Mus., Richmond, 1973, 112 Green St., N.Y.C., 1975, Artists Space, N.Y.C., 1975, Whitney Mus., N.Y.C., 1975, Mus. Modern Art, N.Y.C., 1976, Ginza Nissan Gallery, Tokyo, 1976, Queens Mus., Flushing, N.Y., 1978, 55 Mercer Gallery, N.Y.C., 1978, Washington Sq. Gallery, N.Y.C., 1979, Betty Parsons Gallery, N.Y.C., 1979, R. H. Oosterom Gallery, N.Y.C., 1979, Indpls. Mus. Art, 1980, Jan Cicero Gallery, Chgo., 1980, Jacksonville (Fla.) Mus. Arts, 1983, McNay Art Inst., San Antonio, 1984, Owensboro (Ky.) Mus., 1987, 88, Gallery for Contemporary Art, Raleigh, N.C., 1987, Mus. N.Mex., 1993, others; contbr. articles to profl. publs.; sculpture Honeywell Corp. Fellow Provincetown Fine Arts Work Ctr., 1971, MacDowell Colony, 1973, Helene Wurlitzer Found., 1985, 89; grantee Ky. Found. for Women, 1985, Ky. Arts Coun./Nat. Endowment for Arts, 1985, Gloval Village, N.Y.C., 1975, travel grantee Provincetown Fine Arts Work Ctr., 1971-72; named to Hon. Order of Ky. Cols., 1986—. Mem. Nat. Artists Equity Assn., Permacultural Drylands (mem. ecology teaching team 1992-94), Taos Art Assn., Angels Gate Cultural Ctr. Home and Studio: PO Box 316 Arroyo Hondo NM 87513-0316

FERGUSSON, ROBERT GEORGE, retired army officer; b. Chgo., May 20, 1911; s. Archibald Campbell and Anne (Sheehan) F.; m. Charlotte Lawrence, Nov. 18, 1937; 1 son, Robert Lawrence (dec.). Student, Beloit Coll., 1929-32; BS, U.S. Mil. Acad., 1936; MA in Internat. Rels., Boston U., 1959. Commd. 2d lt. U.S. Army, 1936, advanced through grades to maj. gen., 1962; comdg. officer 14th Inf. Regt., Hawaii, 1955-57; chief army adv. group Naval War Coll., Newport, R.I., 1957-61; asst. divsn. comdr. 24th Inf. Divsn., Augsburg, Ger., 1961-62; chief staff Hdqrs. Central Army Group (NATO), Heidelberg, Ger., 1962-65; comdg. gen. U.S. Army Tng. Center, Inf., Ft. Ord, 1965-67; comdr. U.S. Forces, Berlin, 1967-70; ret., 1970; corp. group v.p. manpower planning Dart Industries, Inc., Los Angeles, 1970-78; cons., 1978-82, ret., 1982. Decorated D.S.M., Legion of Merit with oak leaf cluster, Bronze Star with 3 oak leaf clusters, Purple Heart (U.S.); knight comdr. Cross with badge and star Order of Merit (W.Ger.); officer Legion of Honor (France). Mem. Clan Fergusson Soc. (Scotland), Beta Theta Pi. Clubs: Cypress Point (Pebble Beach); Old Capitol (Monterey, Calif.). Home: PO Box 1515 Pebble Beach CA 93953-1515

FERIA, KENNETH PETER, mortgage banker; b. Hollywood, Calif., Sept. 6, 1970; s. Peter Feria and Lisa (Bischoff) Mogisian. BA in Polit. Sci., UCLA, 1994. Staff appraiser Master Appraisal, North Hollywood, 1987-89; owner Crest Real Estate Svc., Canoga Park, Calif., 1989-91; ops. officer Ctrl. Capital Corp., Encino, Calif., 1991-95; CEO Magik Mortgage Corp., Encino, Calif., 1995—; dir. Trident Devel. Corp., Tarzana, Calif., 1994—. Vol. ARC, Van Nuys, Calif., 1994-95; mem., vol. Calif. Rep. Party, Burbank, 1993-96; grade sch. spkr. Jr. Achievement, L.A., 1990. Mem. L.A. World Affairs Coun., Masons (master, jr. deacon), Order of Demolay (chpt. chmn. 1994-95). Office: Magik Mortgage Corp 17000 Ventura Blvd Encino CA 91316-4126

FERINI, ROBERT PAT, agricultural products company executive; b. 1963. With Betteravia Farms, Santa Maria, Calif.; now ptnr. Office: Betteravia Farms PO Box 5845 Santa Maria CA 93456-5845*

FERNANDES, DIONISIO A., physician; b. Goa, India, Oct. 3, 1945; s. Joao Andre and Carmina F.; m. Fiola C. Rebello, May 28, 1976; children: Chris, Jason, Melissa. BS with honors, St. Xaviers Coll., Bombay, 1963; MD, Armed Forces Med., India, 1969. cert. Calif. Med. Bd. Intern pediatrics Jewish Hosp., Bklyn., 1970-71; resident pediatrics Baylor Coll. Medicine, Houston, 1971-72; chief pediatrician J.N. Health Ctr., Buffalo, N.Y., 1972-74, C.S.Y. Project, Dayton, Ohio, 1974-75; fellow allergy & immunology La. State U., New Orleans, 1977—; pvt. practice Castro Valley, Calif., 1977—; asst. clin. prof. U. Calif., San Francisco, 1982-96, assoc. clin. prof., 1996—. Fellow Am. Acad. Pediatrics, Am. Acad. Allergy, Am. Coll Allergy, Am. Coll. Chest Physicians; mem. Calif. Med. Assn., No. Calif. Allergy Soc. Roman Catholic. Office: 20055 Lake Chabot Rd Castro Valley CA 94546-5331

FERNANDEZ, CLEMENTE GUAJARDO, environmental specialist; b. Devine, Tex., Nov. 5, 1940; m. Carmen Sanchez, Jan. 23, 1966; children: David A., Adria L. AAS in Police Sci., C.C. USAF, 1984; A in Gen. Studies, Pima C.C., 1987; BS in Mgmt., Park Coll., 1989. Enlisted USAF, 1960, advanced through grades to sr. master sgt., retired, 1987; air quality enforcement officer Dept. environ. Quality, Tucson, Ariz., 1987-90, environ. specialist, 1990—; asbestos bldg. insp. Dept. Environ. Quality, Tucson, 1990—, asbestos contract supr., 1990—, visible emissions evaluator, 1987—; hostage negotiator USAF, 1981-87. Author: (dept. manuals) Field Service Training Manual, 1993, Field Inspection Protocol, 1994, Inspection Safety Manual, 1994, Respiratory Protection Program, 1994. Admission rep. Park Coll., Davis-Monthan AFB, Ariz., 1994—; v.p. parish coun. Christ the King Cath. Ch., Davis-Monthan AFB, 1982-83, fund coun. mem., 1982-87. Decorated Meritorious Svc. medals (3), Commendation Svc. medals (4). Democrat. Office: Pima County Dept Environn Quality 130 W Congress St Tucson AZ 85701-1332

FERNANDEZ, DENNIS SUNGA, lawyer, electrical engineer, entrepreneur; b. Manila, June 3, 1961; came to U.S., 1972; s. Gil Conui and Imelda Sunga (Miller) F.; m. Irene Y. Hu, Aug. 26, 1989; 1 child, Megan H. Fernandez. BSEE, Northwestern U., 1983; JD, Suffolk U., 1989. Bar: Mass. 1989, U.S. Dist. Ct. Mass. 1989, D.C. 1990, U.S. Ct. Appeals (Fed. cir.) 1990, Calif. 1991. Engr. NCR, Ft. Collins, Colo., 1983-84; product mgr. Digital Equipment Corp., Hudson, Mass., 1984-86; program mgr. Raytheon, Andover, Mass., 1986-88; engr. Racal, Westford, Mass., 1988-89; assoc. Nutter, McClennen & Fish, Boston, 1989-91, Fenwick & West, Palo Alto, Calif., 1991-94; v.p. Walden Internat. Investment Group, San Francisco, 1995-96, Singapore Techs./Vertex Mgmt., 1996—. Contbr. articles to profl. jours. Mem. IEEE, Sci. and Tech. Adv. Coun. (dir.).

FERNANDEZ, FERDINAND FRANCIS, federal judge; b. 1937. BS, U. So. Calif., 1958, JD, 1963; LLM, Harvard U., 1963. Bar: Calif. 1963, U.S. Dist. Ct. (cen. dist.) Calif. 1963, U.S. Ct. Appeals (9th cir.) 1963, U.S. Supreme Ct. 1967. Elec. engr. Hughes Aircraft Co., Culver City, Calif., 1958-62; law clk. to dist. judge U.S. Dist. Ct. (cen. dist.) Calif., 1963-64; pvt. practice law Allard, Shelton & O'Connor, Pomona, Calif., 1964-80; judge Calif. Superior Ct. San Bernardino County, Calif., 1980-85, U.S. Dist. Ct. (cen. dist.) Calif., L.A., 1985-89, U.S. Ct. Appeals (9th cir.), L.A., 1989—; Lester Roth lectr. U. So. Calif. Law Sch., 1992. Contbr. articles to profl. jours. Vice chmn. City of La Verne Commn. on Environ. Quality, 1971-73; chmn. City of Claremont Environ. Quality Bd., 1972-73; bd. trustees Pomona Coll., 1990—. Fellow Am. Coll. Trust and Estate Counsel; mem. ABA, State Bar of Calif. (fed. cts. com. 1966-69, ad hoc com. on attachments 1971-85, chmn. com. on adminstrn. of justice 1976-77, exec. com. taxation sect. 1977-80, spl. com. on mandatory fee arbitration 1978-79), Calif. Judges Assn. (chmn. juvenile cts. com. 1983-84, faculty mem. Calif. Jud. Coll. 1982-83, faculty mem. jurisprudence and humanities course 1983-85), Hispanic Nat. Bar Assn., L.A. County Bar Assn. (bull. com. 1974-75), San Bernardino County Bar Assn. (co-editor Newsletter 1970-72, trustee 1971-78, sec.-treas. 1973-74, 2d v.p. 1974-75, 1st v.p. 1975-76, pres. 1976-77), Estate Planning Coun. Pomona Valley (sec. 1966-76), Order of Coif, Phi Kappa Phi, Tau Beta Pi. Office: US Ct Appeals 9th Cir 125 S Grand Ave Ste 602 Pasadena CA 91105-1621

FERNANDEZ, FERNANDO LAWRENCE, research company executive, aeronautical engineer; b. N.Y.C., Dec. 31, 1938; s. Fernando and Luz Esther (Fortuno) F.; m. Carmen Dorothy Mays, Aug. 26, 1962; children: Lisa Marie, Christopher John. BSME, Stevens Inst. Tech., 1960, MS in Applied Mechanics, 1961; PhD in Aeronautics, Calif. Inst. Tech., 1969. Engr. Lockheed Missiles & Space Co., Sunnyvale, Calif., 1961-63; div. mgr. The Aerospace Corp., El Segundo, Calif., 1963-72; program mgr. R & D Assocs., Santa Monica, Calif., 1972-75; v.p. Phys. Dynamics, Inc., San Diego, 1975-76; pres. Arete Assocs., San Diego, 1976-93, AETC Inc., San Diego, 1994—; mem. Chief Naval Ops. Exec. Panel, Washington, 1983—. Editor Jour. AIAA, 1970; contbr. articles to Fluid Mechanics. Office: AETC Inc 8910 Univ Ctr Ln San Diego CA 92122

FERRAIUOLO, PERUCCI DIANDREA, journalist; b. Denver, Nov. 20, 1946; s. Francesco and Carolyn (Andrew) F.; m. Barbara Nesland, Mar. 21, 1992; children: Lisa, Megan, Benjamin. AA, Saddleback Coll., 1972; BS, Calif. State Coll., 1974. Reporter, columnist Capo Valley News, San Juan Capistrano, Calif., 1981-82; editor, syndicated writer Lifestyle Mag., Orange County, Calif., 1982-84; syndicated interviewer Intro Mag., L.A., 1983-84; syndicated feature writer O.C. Mag., Orange County, 1984-86; nat. syndicated columnist N.W. Christian Jour., Seattle, 1983—; reporter N.Y. Times Syndicated/Religious News Svc., 1980-95, Daily Jour. Am., 1995—; biography writer Sparrow Records, Nashville, 1993—, StarSong Records, Nashville, 1993—, Benson Records, Nashville, 1993—, Broken Records, Nashville, 1993—; scriptwriter Parade Pictures Corp., Hollywood, Calif., 1973-80. Author: Laughing Your Way to God, 1995, Disney of the Bible, 1996; frequent guest radio talk shows. With USMC, 1965-71. Decorated Purple Heart (2). Mem. Soc. Profl. Journalists, Investigative Reporters and Editors. Home: 7310-B NE 142d Pl Bothell WA 98011

FERRANTE, JOHN ANTHONY, engineering consultant; b. Maple Heights, Ohio, Nov. 23, 1932; s. John and Mary Louise (Feast) F.; m. Doris Ann Kniley, Mar. 19, 1955; children: John, Traci Ann, William. BS in Metall. Engring., Lafayette Coll., 1954; MS in Physics, St. Mary's Coll., 1967. Registered profl. engr., Minn. Metall. engr. Nat. Screw & Mfg., Cleve., L.A., 1954-59, Perry Kislby, Inc., L.A., 1959-60; sales engr. Wallingford Steel, Burbank, Calif., 1960-61; from metall. engr. to disk quality engr. IBM, various locations, 1961-92; ind. contractor Nashua Computer Products, Stor Media Corp., Santa Clara, Calif., 1992-96; sr. staff mfg. engr. Seagate Tech., 1996—. Holder patent in field. Fellow Am. Soc. Quality Control (treas. San Francisco sect. 1991-93); mem. Am. Soc. Metals (chair Minn. chpt. 1968), Soc. Mfg. Engrs. (chair region 13 1993-94). Home and Office: 194 French Ct San Jose CA 95139-1418

FERRARI, DAVID GUY, auditor; b. Scottsbluff, Nebr., Jan. 12, 1944; s. Guy C. and Waunita E. (Bailey) F.; m. Kay Cooper, May 29, 1966; children: Brian S., Justin D. BSBA, U. Wyo., 1966, MS in Bus. Adminstrn., 1971. Fin. dir. Wyo. Dept. Edn., Cheyenne, 1967-71; budget analyst State of Wyo., Cheyenne, 1971-73, state budge dir., 1973-75, dep. state auditor, 1975-87; cons. Cheyenne, 1987-90; state auditor State of Wyo., Cheyenne, 1991—. Author, cons.: Wyoming 1988-A Study of Revenues and Expenditures, 1988, A Study in State Government Efficiency, 1989, Accountability and Efficiency in State Government, 1990, The Final Report on Accountability and Efficiency in State Government, 1991. Elected state ofcl. Rep. Party, Cheyenne, 1991—. Mem. Rotary (hon.). Office: State Auditors Office Rm 114 Capitol Bldg Cheyenne WY 82002

FERRARO, DOUGLAS GENE, executive; b. Cleve., Jan. 13, 1949. BA, St John's Coll., 1970, MA, 1970; PHD, St Anselmo Coll., 1986. Office: LA Jr Chamber of Commerce 350 S Bixel St Los Angeles CA 90017-1420

FERRARO, JOSEPH JAMES, architect; b. Albany, N.Y., June 10, 1949; s. Joseph James and Eleanor R. Ferraro; m. Nadine Jac Stern, Jan. 6, 1987; children: Aubrey A. Hawk, Amber T. Olson. BFA, Pratt Inst., Bklyn., 1971; postgrad., U. Hawaii, 1983-87. Registered architect, Hawaii. Interior designer Interior Design Assocs., N.Y.C., 1971-72; draftsman Marvin Hammerman, Inc., N.Y.C, 1972-76; interior designer McDonald Assocs., Architects, Whitestone, N.Y., 1976-77, Sheridan Assocs. Ltd., N.Y.C., 1977-82; architect/interior designer C.J.S. Group Architects, Honolulu, 1982-88; architect Ferraro Choi and Assocs., Honolulu, 1988—. Prin. works include Crary Lab. McMurdo Sta. Nat. Sci. Found., Amundsen-Scott South Pole Replacement Sta. Antarctica. Recipient Design award of merit AIA, 1992, 94, 95. Mem. NCARB, Nat. Trust for Hist. Preservation, Malama o Manoa (design com. 1993—), Rotary Club of Honolulu Sunrise (bd. dirs. 1991—). Office: Ferraro Choi & Assocs Ltd 707 Richards St Honolulu HI 96813-4623

FERRARO, ROBERT, museum president. Pres. Boulder City (Nev.) Mus./Hoover Dam Mus., 1980—. Office: Boulder City Mus/Hoover Dam Mus 444 Hotel Plz Boulder City NV 89005 also: PO Box 60516 Boulder City NV 89006-0516

FERREE, JOHN NEWTON, JR., fundraising specialist, consultant; b. Wadesboro, N.C., Nov. 21, 1946; s. John Newton and Mary Cleo (Tice) F.; m. Ginger Ann Rogers, June 6, 1969 (div. 1991); m. Patricia Gayle Kruger, Nov. 19, 1994. AA, Bluefield (Va.) Coll., 1966; BA, Baylor U., 1968; JD, Samford U., 1975. Bar: Ala. Contr. Aetna Life Ins. Co., Seattle, 1972; atty. Ferree & Armstrong, Alabaster, Ala., 1975-82; exec. dir. Northwest Bapt. Found., Portland, Oreg., 1982-84; asst. v.p. Harris Trust Co. of Ariz., Scottsdale, 1984; v.p. Bapt. Found. of Ariz., Phoenix, 1985-89; dir. planned giving Phoenix Children's Hosp., 1989-91; pres. Scottsdale (Ariz.) Meml. Health Found., 1991—; bd. dirs. Nat. Com. Planned Giving, Charitable Accord, v.p., 1996—; instr. Cannon Sch. Found. Mgmt., 1995—; cons. in field. Mem. Nat. Soc. Fund Raising Execs. (pres. 1990), Planned Giving Roundtable of Ariz. (pres. 1992, 97), Nat. Assn. Hosp. Devel., Rotary. Republican. Baptist. Office: Scottsdale Meml Health Foun 7400 E Osborn Rd Scottsdale AZ 85251-6432

FERREIRA, ARMANDO THOMAS, sculptor, educator; b. Charleston, W.Va., Jan. 8, 1932; s. Maximiliano and Placeres (Sanchez) F.; children—Lisa, Teresa. Student, Chouinard Art Inst., 1949-50, Long Beach City Coll., 1950-53; B.A., UCLA, 1954, M.A., 1956. Asst. prof. art Mt. St. Mary's Coll., 1956-57; mem. faculty dept. art Calif. State U., Long Beach, 1957—, prof., 1967—, chmn. dept. art, 1971-77, assoc. dean Sch. Fine Arts, acting dean Coll. Arts; lectr., cons. on art adminstrn. to art schs. and universities, Brazilian Ministry Edn. One man shows include, Pasadena Mus., 1959, Long Beach Mus., 1959, 69, Eccles Mus., 1967, Clay and Fiber Gallery, Taos, 1972, group shows include, Los Angeles County Art Mus., 1958, 66, Wichita Art Mus., 1959, Everson Mus., 1960, 66, San Diego Mus. Fine Arts, 1969, 73, Fairtree Gallery, N.Y.C., 1971, 74, Los Angeles Inst. Contemporary Art, 1977, Utah Art Mus., 1978, Bowers Mus., Santa Ana, Calif., 1980, No. Ill. U., 1986, Beckstrand Gallery, Palos Verdes (Calif.) Art Ctr., 1987, U. Madrid, 1993; permanent collections include Utah Mus. Art, Wichita Art Mus., State of Calif. Collection; vis. artist, U. N.D., 1974, exhibited widely abroad including, Poland, Portugal, Morocco, Spain, France. Fulbright lectr. Brazil, 1981. Fellow Nat. Assn. Schs. Art and Design (dir.); mem. Internat. Video Network (dir.), Assn. Calif. State Univ. Profs. *I suppose much of my own life has been shaped by my experience as a first generation American. What modest success I may have had in my work is considerably due to that sense of ambition with which immigrant parents imbue their children. My vision as an artist is also shaped by the strong sense of Spanish culture that was part of my upbringing.*

FERREIRA, JAY MICHAEL, mechanical engineer; b. Allentown, Pa., July 21, 1967; s. Jacob and Margaret Louise (Frey) F. BSME, Drexel U., 1990; MSME, Ariz. State U., 1992, postgrad., 1992—. Cert. engr.-in-tng. Draftsman Siebert Ferreira Assocs., Allentown, 1985-86; with nuclear licensing dept. coop. Pa. Power and Light Co., Allentown, nuclear lic. engring. asst. coop.; nuclear maintenance engring. asst. coop.; rsch. engr. Ariz. State U., Tempe, 1992—; presenter in field. Contbr. articles to Composites Engring., Computers and Math with Applications, Mathematical and Computer Modeling. Contbr. Statue of Liberty Ellis Island Found., 1985. Capt. Ordnance U.S. Army, 1990—. Named Eagle Scout. Mem. ASME (assoc.), AIAA, Am. Helicopter Soc., Pi Tau Sigma. Republican. Roman Catholic. Home: 1649 Washington Ave Northampton PA 18067-1553 Office: Ariz State U Tempe AZ 85287

FERRELL, MARK STEPHEN, flight nurse; b. Fayetteville, Ark., Nov. 24, 1968; s. Vance Harold and Cherie Camille (Eller) F. ASN, Motlow Coll., Tullahoma, Tenn., 1989; EMT, Valencia Coll., Orlando, Fla., 1991. RN, Tenn., Calif.; CCRN; CEN; cert. flight RN, ACLS instr., pediatric advanced life support instr., neonatal resuscitation program instr., trauma nursing core course, emergency nursing pediatric course, BLS, advanced burn life support; lic. paramedic, Calif. Staff nurse ICU Fla. Hosp., Orlando, 1989-91; staff nurse emergency dept. Orlando (Fla.) Regional Med. Ctr., 1991-92; flight nurse Travelor Rapid City (S.D.) Regional Hosp. Life Flight, 1992; staff nurse Travelor U. Calif.-Davis Med. Ctr., Sacramento, 1992-93; flight nurse St. Joseph's Care Flight, Lexington, Ky., 1993-94, Stanford (Calif.) U. Hosp., 1994—; mem. protocol com. sTanford Life Flight, 1994—. Mem. AACN, Emergency Nurses Assn., Nat. Flight Nurse Assn. Seventh-Day Adventist. Home: 325M Sharon Pk Dr # 604 Menlo Park CA 94025 Office: Stanford Life Flight 300 Pasteur Dr Palo Alto CA 94304-2203

FERRERI, MICHAEL VICTOR, optometrist; b. Park Ridge, Ill., May 15, 1967; s. Samuel Joseph and Dolores Jean (Liebich) F.; m. Celaine Berenda Ward, Apr. 2, 1994; children: Christopher, Anthony. BS in Biol. Scis., U. Calif., Irvine, 1989; OD, So. Calif. Coll. Optometry, 1993. Cert. therapeutic optometrist, Calif., Tex. Extern Ctr. for the Partially Sighted, Santa Monica, Calif., 1992-93; pvt. practice Long Beach, Calif., 1993—; assoc. optometrist Antelope Mall Vision Ctr., Palmdale, Calif., 1995; color vision analysis cons. Dept. Health and Human Svcs., Long Beach, 1994-97; participating doctor Vision USA, Long Beach, 1995-97. Contbr. articles to profl. jours. Mem. Rep. Nat. Com., 1991-96; elder Grace Luth. Ch., Long Beach, 1996-97, v.p. congregation. Recipient Corning Low Vision award Corning Optics, Anaheim, Calif., 1993, Vision Therapy Enhancement cert. So. Calif. Coll. Optometry, Fullerton, 1993, Appreciation cert. for Outstanding Contbns. to Save Your Vision Week, U.S. Senate, 1997. Mem. Am. Optometric Assn. (contact lens sect.), Calif. Optometric Assn., Rio Hondo Optometric Soc. (treas.), Fellowship of Christian Optometrists, Optometric Ext. Program (clin. assoc.). Office: Los Altos Med Ctr Ste 109 1777 Bellflower Blvd Long Beach CA 90815

FERRIS, EVELYN SCOTT, lawyer; b. Detroit, d. Ross Ansel and Irene Mabel (Bowser) Nafus; m. Roy Shorey Ferris, May 21, 1969 (div. Sept. 1982); children: Judith Ilene, Roy Sidney, Lorene Marjorie. J.D., Willamette U., 1961. Bar: Oreg. 1962, U.S. Dist. Ct. Oreg. 1962. Law clk. Oreg. Tax Ct., Salem, 1961-62; dep. dist. atty. Marion County, Salem, 1962-65; judge Mcpl. Ct., Stayton, Oreg., 1965-76; ptnr. Brand, Lee, Ferris & Embick, Salem, 1965-82; chmn. Oreg. Workers' Compensation Bd., Salem, 1982-89. Bd. dirs. Friends of Deepwood, Salem, 1979-82, Salem City Club, 1972-75, Marion County Civil Svc. Commn., 1970-75; com. mem. Polk County Hist. Commn.,

Dallas, Oreg., 1976-79; mem. Oreg. legis. com. Bus. Climate, 1967-69, Govs. Task Force on Liability, 1986. Recipient Outstanding Hist. Restoration of Comml. Property award Marion County Hist. Soc., 1982. Mem. Oreg. Mcpl. Judges Assn. (pres. 1967-69), Altrusa, Internat., Mary Leonard Law Soc., Western Assn. Workers Compensation Bds. (pres. 1987-89), Capitol Club (pres. 1977-79), Internat. Assn. Indsl. Accident Bds. and Commns. (pres. 1992-93), Phi Delta Delta. Republican. Episcopalian. Home: 747 Church St SE Salem OR 97301-3715

FERRIS, RUSSELL JAMES, II, freelance writer; b. Rochester, N.Y., June 11, 1938; s. Russell James and Phyllis Helen (Breheny) F.; m. Ilma Maria dos Santos, June 29, 1968. Student, St. Bonaventure U., 1956-59; BS, U. Rochester, 1967; MS, Emerson Coll., 1989; PhD, Universal Life Ch., 1983. Cert. social worker. Film inspector City of Rochester, 1962-67; social worker Tulare County, Visalia, Calif., 1967-69, Alameda County, Oakland, Calif., 1969-71; ghostwriter self-employed, San Francisco, 1971—. Author: Crescendo, 1972 and 9 other novels. With USAR, 1956-68. Recipient Botany fellowship Emerson Coll., 1989. Mem. Assn. U.S. Army, Air Force Assn., Navy League U.S., Ret. Officers Assn. (life), Res. Officers Assn. (life), Internat. Platform Assn., Am. Mensa Inc. Libertarian. Roman Catholic. Home and Office: 202 Font Blvd San Francisco CA 94132-2404

FERRO, ROBERT JOSEPH, electronics engineer, researcher; b. Middle Village, N.Y., May 15, 1952; s. Ernest Edward and Zita Ann (Parsons) F. BSEE, U. Notre Dame, 1974; MSEE, U. Vt., 1977, PhD, 1985. Assoc. engr. IBM, Essex Junction, Vt., 1977-86; engr. Hughes Rsch. Labs., Malibu, Calif., 1986-91, Aerospace Corp., L.A., 1991—. Contbr. articles to profl. jours. Mem. IEEE, Sigma Xi (chpt. v.p. 1990), Tau Beta Pi, Eta Kappa Nu. Republican. Roman Catholic. Office: Aerospace Corp Mail Sta M4 991 PO Box 92957 Los Angeles CA 90009-2957

FERRUA, PIETRO MICHELE STEFANO, foreign language educator, writer; b. San Remo, Italy, Sept. 18, 1930; came to U.S., 1969; s. Libero and Anita Libera (Taggiasco) F.; m. Diana Jane Lobo Filho, June 24, 1957; children: Anna Piera, Franco Dorian. MA, U. Geneva, Switzerland, 1957, Cath. Pentifical U., Rio de Janeiro, 1966; postgrad., U. Fed., Rio de Janeiro, 1969; PhD, U. Oreg., 1973. Prof. Italian Ecole Internat., Geneva, 1958-62; prof. French Alliance Française, Rio de Janeiro, 1964-69; asst. prof. French Pontificia U. Cath., Rio de Janeiro, 1966-68; lectr. Italian U. Gâmafilho, Rio de Janeiro, 1968-69; asst. prof. Portuguese Portland (Oreg.) State U., 1970-73; prof. French Lewis and Clark Coll., Portland, 1970-87; prof. emeritus Lewis and Clark Coll., 1987—; cons. Nat. Endowment for the Humanities; chmn. Luso-Brazilian sect. 24th Pacific N.W. Conf. on Fgn. Lang; sec. workshop 8th INternat. Congress Comparative Lit., Budapest, 1976. Author: Gli Anarchici nella Rivoluzione Messicana: Praxedis G. Guerrero, 1976, Eros Chez Thanatos, 1979, Avanguardia Cinematografica Lettrista, 1984, Appunti Sul Cinema Nero Americano, 1987, Italo Calvino A San Remo, 1992, INI Art USA, Individual Expressions within the International Group, Espressioni individuali in sene al gruppe internazionale, 1996. Founder Ctr. Internat. de Rsch. sur L'Anarchisme, Ctr. Brasileiro de Estudos Internats. Recipient Cittadino Benemerito, Municipality of San Remo, Italy, 1984; Chmn. grantee Oreg. Com. for the Humanities, Portland, 1983, Travel grantee Am. Coun. Learned Socs., 1979. Mem. Am. Assn. Tchrs. of French, Am. Assn. Tchrs. of Italian, Am. Assn. Tchrs. of Spanish and Portuguese, Internat. Assn. Comparative Lit., Romanian Study Group, Latin Am. Studies Assn. Office: Lewis and Clark Coll Palatine Hill Rd Portland OR 97219

FERRY, MILES YEOMAN, state official; b. Brigham City, Utah, Sept. 22, 1932; s. John Yeoman and Alta (Cheney) F.; m. Suzanne Call, May 19, 1952; children: John, Jane Ferry Stewart, Ben, Helen, Sue Ferry Thorpe. BS, Utah State U., 1954. Rancher Corinne, Utah, 1952; gen. mgr. J.Y. Ferry & Son, Inc.; mem. Utah Ho. of Reps., 1965-66; mem. Utah Senate, 1967-84, minority whip, 1975-76, minority leader, 1977-78, pres. senate, 1979-84; mem. presdl. advisor commn. on intergovtl. affairs, 1984; mem. governing bd. Council State Govts., 1983-84; v.p. Legis./Exec. Consulting Firm, 1994—; chmn. Corinne Cemetery Dist., 1989—. Pres. Brigham Jr. C. of C., 1956-61, Nat. Conf. of State Legislators, 1984, v.p., 1982, pres.-elect, 1983, pres., 1984; v.p. Utah Jr. C. of C., 1960-61; nat. dir. Utah Jaycees, 1961-62; pres. Farm Bur. Box Elder County, 1958-59; commr., bd. dirs., mem. council com. Lake Bonneville council Boy Scouts Am.; food and agr. commr. USDA, commr. agr. State of Utah, 1985-93. Recipient award of merit Boy Scouts Am., 1976, Alumnusi of Yr. award Utah State U., 1981, award of merit Utah Vocat. Assn., 1981, Friend of Agr. award Utah Farm Bur., 1988, Cert. Appreciation USDA, 1988, Contbn. to Agr. award Utah-Idaho Farmers Union, 1989, Disting. Svc. award Utah State U., 1993, 94; named Outstanding Young Man of Yr., Brigham City Jr. C. of C., 1957, Outstanding Nat. Dir. U.S. Jaycees, 1963, Outstanding Young Man in Utah, Utah Jr. C. of C., 1961, Outstanding Young Farmer, 1958, One of 3 Outstanding Young Men of Utah, 1962, Rep. Legislator of Yr., 1984, One of 10 Outstanding Legislators of Yr., 1984. Mem. SAR, Sons Utah Pioneers, Gov.'s Cabinet, Utah Commn. Agr., Fed. Rsch. Com., Nat. Assn. State Depts. Agr. (bd. dirs. 1989), Western Assn. of State Depts. of Agr. (v.p. 1990-91, pres. 1991-92), Western U.S. Agr. Trade Assn. (sec. treas- elect 1987-88, pres. 1989-90), Utah Cattlemen's Assn., Nat. Golden Spike Assn. (dir. 1958—), Phi Kappa Phi, Pi Kappa Alpha. Republican. Address: 815 N 6800 W Corinne UT 84307-9737

FERRY, RICHARD MICHAEL, executive search firm executive; b. Ravenna, Ohio, Sept. 26, 1937; s. John D. and Margaret M. (Jeney) F.; m. Maude M. Hillman, Apr. 14, 1956; children: Richard A., Margaret L., Charles Michael, David W., Dianne E., Ann Marie. BS, Kent State U., 1959. CPA. Cons. staff Peat, Marwick, Mitchell, Los Angeles, 1965-69, ptnr., 1969; chmn., co-founder Korn/Ferry Internat., Los Angeles, 1969—; bd. dirs. 1st Bus. Bank, L.A., Avery Dennison, Pasadena, Calif., Dole Food Co., Calif., Pacific Mut. Life Ins. Co., Newport Beach, Calif. Trustee Calif. Inst. Tech., L.A., St. John's Hosp., Santa Monica, Calif.; bd. dirs. Cath. Charities, L.A., Calif. Cmty. Found. Republican. Roman Catholic. Office: Korn/Ferry Internat 1800 Century Park E Ste 900 Los Angeles CA 90067-1512

FERTÉ, THOMAS LEE, literature and writing educator, poet, editor; b. Columbus, Ohio, Dec. 5, 1936; s. Albert Joseph and Ruth Awa (Withrow) F.; m. Marjorie Jean McDougal, May 17, 1971; children: Sabrina Dian, Jason Andrew, Adrienne Lee (dec.), Stefan James, Deven Elizabeth. BS in Humanities, So. Oreg. State Coll., 1961; MA in English, Ariz. State U., 1962. Instr. English Portland (Oreg.) State U., 1963-66; chair humanities dept. Sheridan (Wyo.) Coll., 1966-68; prof. English Western Oreg. U., Monmouth, 1968—. Contbr. poetry to Portlander (Choice Poet award 1992) and anthology The Prescott Street Reader; editor, publisher: The Long Sigh the Wind Makes, Poems by William Stafford, 1991; editor, pub. (lit. ann.) Calapooya Collage, 1983—. Bd. dirs. Portland Poetry Festival, 1992-94. With U.S. Army, 1955-57. Carnegie fellow, Idaho State U., Pocatello, 1974; recipient Stewart Holbrook award Lit. Arts, Inc., Portland, 1995. Mem. Nat. Coun. Tchrs. English (chair Oreg. achievement awards 1968-73), Assn. Lit. Scholars and Critics. Office: Western Oreg Univ Monmouth OR 97361

FERY, JOHN BRUCE, forest products company executive; b. Bellingham, Wash., Feb. 16, 1930; s. Carl Salvatore and Margaret Emily (Hauck) F.; m. Delores Lorraine Carlo, Aug. 22, 1953; children: John Brent, Bruce Todd, Michael Nicholas. BA, U. Wash., 1953; MBA, Stanford U., 1955; D of Law (hon.), Gonzaga U., 1982; D of Nat. Resources (hon.), U. Idaho, 1983. Asst. to pres. Western Kraft Corp., 1955-56; prodn. mgr., 1956-57; with Boise Cascade Corp., Idaho, 1957-94, pres., CEO, 1972-78, chmn. bd., CEO, 1978-94; chmn. Boise Cascade Corp., Boise, Idaho, 1994-95; bd. dirs. Albertsons, Inc., Hewlett-Packard Co., US Bancorp, The Boeing Co.; active mem. Bus. Coun. Chmn. bd. Idaho Community Found. With USN, 1950-51. Named Most Outstanding Chief Exec. Officer Fin. World, 1977, 78, 79, 80. Mem. Am. Forest and Paper Assn. (exec. com., bd. dirs.), Arid Club, Hillcrest Country Club, Arlington Club. Office: F&C Corp PO Box 15407 Boise ID 83715

FESTON, EDATH ANNE, artist; b. Vancouver, Wash., Aug. 4, 1955; d. Herbert Leslie and Ottilie Gertha (Matthiesen) Walker; m. Scott Michael Feston, Oct. 21, 1978; children: David E., Joshua M., Thomas J. Diploma, Hudson Bay H.S., Vancouver, 1973. Data entry operator ADP Dealer Svcs., Portland, Oreg., 1976-77, Old Nat. Bank, Spokane, 1977-78, Poorman-Douglas Corp., Portland, 1978-80, Pacific Telecom Inc., Vancouver, 1985-93. Home: 107 Kester Dr Woodland WA 98674

FETTER, WILLIAM ALLAN, computer graphics executive; b. Independence, Mo., Mar. 14, 1928; s. William Herbert and Edna Katherine (Werner) F.; m. Darlene Glea Wyss, Aug. 20, 1950 (div. 1962); 1 child, William Arnold (dec.); m. Barbara Ann Shaffer, Dec. 21, 1963; children: Brant Shaffer, Elena Katherine (twins). Student, Kansas City Jr. Coll., 1945-46, Kansas City U., 1948-49; BFA, U. Ill., 1952. Supr. computer graphics The Boeing Co., Seattle and Wichita, Kans., 1959-69; v.p. Graphcomp. Scis., Newport, Calif., 1969-70; chair design dept., lectr. So. Ill. U., Carbondale, 1970-77; pres. So. Ill. Research and Corp. Office (SIROCO), Carbondale, Bellevue and Redmond, 1977—; also bd. dirs. So. Ill. Research Ops. and Corp. Office, Bellevue, Wash.; owner Office for Research In Graphics and Indsl. Design (ORIGIN), Bellevue, Redmond, 1982—; speaker in field. Author: (book monograph) Human figures for Designers by Computer, 1983, Computer Graphics in Communication, 1964; author (TV program) Computer Graphics, The Accurate Eye, 1975; shows include Mus. Modern Art, N.Y.C., 1976; patentee in field. Bd. dirs. Com. on Handicapped, Park Forest, Ill., 1957-58, Master Resources Council Internat., Seattle, 1980—; mem. UNESCO Tact Task Force, Washington, 1975-85. Served with U.S. Army, 1946-48. Recipient Cert. Merit Internat. Graphic Design, 1967, Letter Commendation USAF, Boeing Airplane Co., 1962, Bronze Medal Nat. Soc. Art Dirs., 1963. Fellow AIAA (assoc.); mem. Internat. Design Conf. (presenter 1976, 78), Soc. Info. Display, Indsl. Designers Soc. Am., N.W. Human Factors Soc., Mus. Modern Art Club, Sports Car Club Am., Am. Lancia Club, Alfa Romeo Owner's Club.

FETTERS, DORIS ANN, retired secondary education educator; b. N.Y.C.; d. John Joseph and Loreta Gertrude (Stratford) F. BA, Calif. State Coll., L.A., 1952. Cert. gen. secondary tchr. Tchr. Temple City (Calif.) H.S., 1954-55, L.A. City Schs., 1955-56; vice consul 3d sec. of embassy Dept. of State, Washington, 1957-60; tchr. U. Rafael Landivar, Guatemala, 1960-63, L.A. Unified Schs., 1964-90. Mem. Am. Fedn. Tchrs., United Tchrs. L.A. Democrat. Roman Catholic.

FIBIGER, JOHN ANDREW, life insurance company executive; b. Copenhagen, Apr. 27, 1932; came to U.S., 1934, naturalized, 1953; s. Borge Rottboll and Ruth Elizabeth (Wadmond) F.; m. Barbara Mae Stuart, June 22, 1956; children: Karen Ruth McCarthy, Katherine Louise. B.A., U. Minn., 1953, M.A., 1954; postgrad., U. Wis. With Lincoln Nat. Life Ins. Co., Ft. Wayne, Ind., 1956-57; with Bankers Life Ins. Co. Nebr., Lincoln, 1959-73; sr. v.p. group Bankers Life Ins. Co. Nebr., 1972-73; with New Eng. Mut. Life Ins. Co., Boston, 1973-89; vice chmn., pres., chief operating officer New Eng. Mut. Life Ins. Co., 1981-89; with Transam Life Cos., 1991-94; exec. v.p., CFO, then pres. Transamerica Occidental Life Ins. Co., L.A., 1994-95, chmn., 1995—; past vice chmn. Actuarial Bd. for Counseling and Discipline. Life trustee, past chmn. Mus. Sci., Boston, 1989-91; trustee New Eng. Med. Ctr.; bd. dirs. Menninger Found.; chmn. Menninger Fund; bd. dirs. U. So. Calif. Sch. Gerontology; pres. West Coast Bus. Inst. on Aging; past trustee Calif. Mus. Sci. and Industry. Fellow Soc. Actuaries (past bd. dirs.); mem. Nat. Acad. Social Ins. (founding mem.), Am. Acad. Actuaries (past pres.), Assn. Calif. Life Cos. (bd. chmn.).

FIEDLER, BOBBI, community agency director, former congresswoman; b. Santa Monica, Calif., Apr. 22, 1937; d. Jack and Sylvia (Levin) Horowitz; m. Paul Clarke, Feb. 15, 1987; children: Lisa, Randy. LLD (hon.), West Coast Coll. Law, 1978. Gen. office duties Miller & Co., 1955-60; owner, ptnr. 2 pharmacies, 1969-77; founder, exec. dir. BUSTOP, 1976-77; mem., chmn. com. of whole, chmn. bus. ops. com., bldg. com. L.A. Bd. of Edn., 1977-81; mem., house budget com., joint econ. com. U.S. Congress, 1981-87; bd. dirs., chmn. nominations com., vice chmn. audit com. United Edn. and Software, 1987-93; bd. commrs. L.A. Comty. Redevel. Agy., 1993—; lottery commn. Calif., 1993-94; advt. artist; 1955-60, interior decorater, 1957-60; polit. commentator Sta. KABC-TV, 1986-87; bd. commrs. Calif. State Lottery, 1993-94; cons. in pub. rels. and govt., 1987—. Vol. various comty. activities; mem. notification com. Reagan and Bush nominations, 1984; co-chair Wilson for Gov., San Fernando Valley, 1990, 94; Calif. vice-chair Bush for Pres., 1992; Calif. co-chair Bush for Pres., 1988; Calif. del. Rep. Nat. Conv., 1980, 84, 88, 92; mem. L.A. Citizen's Com. on Transit Solutions, 1987, Calif. Space and Def. Coun., 1981-87, Hadassah; statewide spokesperson Proposition 13, 1978, Proposition 1 & 4, 1979. Recipient Golden Bulldog award Watchdogs of the Treasury, 1981-87, Guardian of Small Bus. award Nat. Fedn. Ind. Bus., 1981-87, Golden Age award Nat. Alliance of Sr. Citizens, 1981-87, numerous commendations from city couns.; named Newsmaker of Yr., L.A. Daily News, 1977, 80, 84, one of Outstanding Women of So. Calif., L.A. Herald Examiner, 1978, Legislator of Yr., VFW, 1985, Outstanding Legislator, L.A. Jewish Fedn. Coun., 1982. Mem. Bus. and Profl. Women's Assn. (Woman of Yr.), Nat. Sch. Bds. Assn., Calif. State Soc. (bd. dirs.), San Fernando Valley Bus. & Profl. Assn., B'nai Brith Youth Orgn. (sponsor's bd., Anita S. Perlman award 1982).

FIEDLER, JOHN AMBERG, marketing scientist; b. Evanston, Ill., Nov. 14, 1941; s. George and Agnes Zoe (Amberg) F.; m. Frances Eudora Murphy, June 18, 1966 (div. 1983); children: Margaret, Neil; m. Lesley A. Bahner, Dec. 28, 1986. BA, U. Wis., 1965; MBA, U. Chgo., 1969. V.p. Leo Burnett Co., Inc., Chgo., 1969-72, 74-79; mgr. decision systems Market Facts, Inc., Chgo., 1972-73; exec. v.p. Ted Bates Co., Inc., N.Y.C., 1980-84; prin., founder, chief exec. officer POPULUS, Inc., Boise, Idaho, 1985—. Coauthor: (book) Psychological Effects of Advertising, 1985; contbr. articles to profl. jours. and confs.; inventor Ballot Box (TM) communication assessment system, 1985. Rsch. dir. Reagan-Bush '84, Wash., 1984, bd. dirs. Childreach, U.S.A., 1986—, mem. exec. com. Mem. Am. Mktg. Assn. Republican. Roman Catholic. Office: POPULUS Inc HC 33 Box 3270 Boise ID 83706-9701

FIELD, CAROL HART, writer, journalist, foreign correspondent; b. San Francisco, Mar. 27, 1940; d. James D. and Ruth (Arnstein) Hart; m. John L. Field, July 23, 1961; children: Matthew, Alison. BA, Wellesley Coll., 1961. Contbg. editor, assoc. editor, asst. editor City Mag., San Francisco, 1974-76; contbg. editor New West/Calif. Mag., San Francisco, L.A., 1975-80, San Francisco Mag., 1980-82; fgn. corr. La Gola, Milan, Italy, 1990—; lectr. Smithsonian Inst., Washington, 1991, 95, Schlesinger Libr., Radcliffe Coll., 1995; TV appearance with Julia Child, 1995; bd. dirs. Lyra Corp., Bay Package Prodns. Author: The Hill Towns of Italy, 1983 (Commonwealth Club award 1984), new edit., 1997, The Italian Baker, 1985 (Internat. Assn. Culinary Profls. award 1986), Celebrating Italy, 1990 (Commonwealth Club award Internat. Assn. Culinary Profls. award 1991), Italy in Small Bites, 1994 (James Beard award), Focaccia: Simple Breads from the Italian Oven, 1994, In Nonna's Kitchen: Traditional Recipes and Culture from Italian Grandmothers, 1997 (main selection Good Food Club, Book of the Month Club); contbr. articles to profl. jours. Mem. lit. jury Commonwealth Club Calif., San Francisco, 1987, 88, 92; bd. dirs. Women's Forum West, San Francisco, 1990-92, Bancroft Libr. U. Calif., Berkeley, 1991—, Headlands Inst., San Francisco, 1992-93; bd. dirs. Mechanics' Inst., San Francisco, 1987-92, pres., 1990-92. Recipient Internat. Journalism prize Maria Luigia Duchessa di Parma, Italy, 1987, Barbi Colombini prize Tuscany, 1991; named Alumna of Yr. Head Royce Sch, Oakland, Calif., 1991. Mem. Accademia Italia della Cucina, Authors Guild, Am. Inst. Wine and Food, Les Dames d'Escoffier, Internat. Assn. Culinary Profls. Home and Office: 2561 Washington St San Francisco CA 94115-1818

FIELD, CHARLES WILLIAM, metallurgical engineer, small business owner, consultant; b. Kankakee, Ill., Feb. 4, 1934; s. Euell Charles and Genevieve Thelma (Fletcher) F.; m. Barbara Sue Bird, Sept. 20, 1957; children: Charles Scott, Lynda Lois. BS in Metall. Engring., U. Ariz., 1960. Lic. real estate broker, Ariz. Research metallurgist Titanium Metals Corp. Am., Henderson, Nev., 1960-62; mgr. tech. service Titanium Metals Corp. Am., N.Y.C., 1962-67; with materials dept. for supersonic transport engine Large Jet Engine div. Gen. Electric Co., Cin., 1967-69; sr. engr. specialist, advanced tech. dept. Garrett Corp., Phoenix, 1969-76; real estate broker, prin. C.W. Field & Co., Scottsdale, 1985—; cons. titanium alloy applications, failure analysis; cons. to NASA, USAF, Secret Svc. Contbr. articles to profl. jours. Recipient commendation from U.S. Govt., 1964, Pres.'s Round Table award Phoneix Bd. Realtors, 1981, 84. Mem. American Institute of Aeronautics and Astronautics, Am. Soc. Metals, Nat. Assn. Corrosion Engrs., Space Age Materials and Process Engrs., Scottsdale Realtors (Million Dollar Club), Rotary (bd. dirs. Scottsdale), Camelback Country Club.

FIELD, EARL LYLE, dean, education educator; b. Memphis, June 20, 1943; s. Earl Lyle and Bonnie Thelma (McMahan) F.; m. Barbara Elaine Tatham, Aug. 26, 1965; children: Bonnie Elaine, Brenda Eileen. BA, Biola Coll., La Mirada, Calif., 1966, MA, 1978; PhD, Grace Grad. Sch., Long Beach, Calif., 1984. Cert. tchr., Calif. Tchr. Whittier (Calif.) Christian Schs., 1973-77; tchr., adminstr. Pomona (Calif.) 1st Bapt. Sch., 1978-82; prof. edn., chmn. dept., dean Ariz. Coll. of Bible, Phoenix, 1982-96; adj. prof. Columbia (S.C.) Bible Coll., 1987-90, Ottawa U., 1990-96, Grand Canyon U., 1993-96; ednl. cons. various sch. dists., Ariz., Calif., 1984-96; seminar and conf. speaker, Ariz.; bd. dirs. Rutherford Inst. Am. Author: Christian Schools in Alien World, 1982, Audio Visual for Teachers, 1989; contbg. editor Coll. Press; contbr. articles to various publs. Chmn. USS Arizona Mast Com., 1989-91. Mem. ASCD, Assn. Christian Schs. Internat. (accreditation commn.), Ariz. Assn. for Supervision and Curriculum Devel., Christian Educators Assn., Western History Assn., Civil War Reenactment Assn. Republican. Baptist. Home: 5437 W Dahlia Dr Glendale AZ 85304-1935

FIELD, EDWARD C., research executive; b. 1936. BS, Lehigh U., 1958, MS in Physics, 1960; PhD in Physics, UCLA, 1964. Rsch. analyst Rand Corp, Santa Monica, Calif., 1960-72; with Pacific Sierra Rsch. Corp., Santa Monica, Calif., 1972—, now pres. Office: Pacific Sierra Research Corp 2901 28th St Ste 300 Santa Monica CA 90405-2938*

FIELD, JEFFREY FREDERIC, designer; b. Los Angeles, July 6, 1954; s. Norman and Gertrude Clara (Ellman) F.; m. Susan Marie Merrin, Jan. 8, 1978. BA in Art, Calif. State U., Northridge, 1977, MA in Art, 1980. Cert. indsl. plastics tchr., Calif. Designer Fundamental Products Co., N. Hollywood, Calif., 1972-82; designer/model maker The Stansbury Co., Beverly Hills, Calif., 1982-84; mech. engr. Vector Electronic Co., Sylmar, Calif., 1984-87; pres., prin. Jeffrey Field Design Assocs., Sepulveda, Calif., 1987—; cons. MiniMed Techs., Sylmar, 1987—, Best Time Inc., Leander, Tex., 1987—, Spectrum Design, Granada Hills, Calif., 1987—, Raycom Systems Inc., Boulder, Colo., 1988-89, Alfred E. Mann Found. for Sci. Rsch., Sylmar, 1988—, Atomic Elements, L.A., E-O Products, Laguna Hills, Calif., Autogenics, Newbury Park, Calif., 1990—, Pacesetter Systems, Sylmar, 1990—, Baxter Healthcare Corp., Pharmaseal Div., Valencia, Calif., 1990—, Surgidev Corp., Goleta, Calif., 1990—, Indsl. Strength Eyewear/Grafix Mktg. Group, Manhattan Beach & Campbell, Calif., 1991—. Democrat. Jewish. Home and Office: 16715 Vincennes St Sepulveda CA 91343-2711

FIELD, JOHN LOUIS, architect; b. Mpls., Jan. 18, 1930; s. Harold David and Gladys Ruth (Jacobs) F.; m. Carol Helen Hart, July 23, 1961; children: Matthew Hart, Alison Ellen. B.A., Yale, 1952; M. Arch., 1955. Individual practice architecture San Francisco, 1959-68; v.p. firm Bull, Field, Volkmann, Stockwell, Architects, San Francisco, 1968-83; ptnr. Field/Gruzen, Architects, San Francisco, 1983-86, Field Paoli Architects, San Francisco, 1986—; guest lectr. Stanford, 1970; chmn. archtl. council San Francisco Mus. Art, 1969-71; mem. San Francisco Bay Conservation and Devel. Commn., Design Rev. Bd., 1980-84; founding chmn. San Francisco Bay Architects Review, 1977-80. Co-author, producer, dir.: film Cities for People (Broadcast Media award 1975, Golden Gate award San Francisco Internat. Film Festival 1975, Ohio State award 1976); film The Urban Preserve (Calif. Council AIA Commendation of excellence 1982); co-design architect: design for New Alaska Capital City (winner design competition). Recipient Archtl. Record award, 1961, 1972; AIA, Sunset mag. awards, 1962, 64, 69; No. Calif. AIA awards, 1967, 82; Calif. Council AIA award, 1982; certificate excellence Calif. Gov.'s Design awards, 1966; Homes for Better Living awards, 1962, 66, 69, 71, 77; Albert J. Evers award, 1974, Best Bldg. award Napa (Calif.) C. of C., 1987, Design award Internat. Council Shopping Ctrs., 1988, Stores of Excellence award Nat. Mall Monitor, 1989, 92, 93, Pacific Coast Builders Gold Nugget award, 1989, 91, Urban Design award Calif. Coun. AIA, 1991, 93. Fellow AIA (com. on design); mem. Nat. Coun. Archtl. Registration Bds., Urban Land Inst. (Design award 1995), Yale Club, Lambda Alpha. Address: Field Paoli Architects 57 Post St San Francisco CA 94104-5003

FIELD, MORTON RICHARD, lawyer; b. Chgo., July 28, 1923; s. Leo and Minnie (Rubin) F.; m. Gloria M. Krause, July 15, 1951; children: Bradley, Cathleen. BA, U. Ill., 1946; LLB, DePaul U., 1948. Bar: Ill. 1948, Calif. 1951, U.S. Ct. Mil. Appeals 1956, D.C. 1957, U.S. Supreme Ct., 1957. Atty.-advisor SEC, Chgo., 1948-50, L.A., 1950-52; ptnr. Wallenstein and Field, L.A., 1952-73, Jackson & Goodstein, L.A., 1973-79, Alschuler Grossman & Pines, L.A., 1979-88, Spensley Horn Jubas & Lubitz, L.A., 1988-95, Loeb & Loeb, 1995-96; bd. dirs. Frederick's of Hollywood, Inc., L.A. Author: (audiocassette) Going Public, 1991. Capt. U.S. Army, 1942-54. Home: 306 Bronwood Ave Los Angeles CA 90049-3106

FIELD, RAY ARVID, animal science educator; b. Ogden, Utah, Dec. 15, 1933; s. Vern James F.; children: Jim, Linda, David, Daniel, Mike. BS, Brigham Young U., 1958; MS, U. Ky., 1961, PhD, 1963. Prof. U. Wyo., Laramie, 1962—, dept. head animal sci., 1989-96. Author: Sheep and Wool-Science, Production, Management, 1988. Recipient Good Tchg. award AMOCO Found., Inc., 1983, Sr. Fellowship award Nat. Rsch. Adv. Coun. New Zealand, 1983, Pres.'s award Wyo. Meat Processors, 1986, Albany County Stockgrowers and Cowbelles Friend of Agr. award, 1986, Achievement award For Efforts to Aid the Wyo. Economy, 1989, Burlington No. Found. Faculty Achievement award, 1990. Fellow Am. Soc. of Animal Sci. (mem. editl. bd. 1970-72, 77-79, 85-87, pres. western sect. 1992-93, dir. 1991-93, award in meat rsch. 1975, Dist. Svc. award western sect. 1996); mem. Am. Meat Sci. Assn. (bd. dirs., pres.-elect, pres. 1978-81, Disting. Meat Rsch. award 1983, Signal Svc. award 1984), Inst. Food Techs., Alpha Zeta (Outstanding Faculty award 1973), Gamma Sigma Delta (Sr. Faculty award of merit 1977, Faculty award of merit 1985), Sigma Xi, Phi Kappa Phi. Republican. Mormon. Home: 1625 Howe Rd Laramie WY 82070-6889 Office: Univ Wyo Animal Sci Dept Box 3684 Laramie WY 82071

FIELD, RICHARD JEFFREY, chemistry educator; b. Attleboro, Mass., Oct. 26, 1941; s. Jeffrey Hazard and Edna Catherine (Hawkins) F.; m. Judith Lauchaire, Sept. 5, 1966; children: Elijah, Sara. BS, U. Mass., 1963; MS, Holy Cross Coll., 1964; PhD, U. R.I., 1968. Rsch. assoc., vis. asst. prof. U. Oreg., Eugene, 1968-74; sr. rsch. chemist Carnegie-Mellon U., Pitts., 1974-75; asst. prof., then assoc. prof. dept. chemistry U. Mont., Missoula, 1975-83, prof. chemistry, 1984—, chmn. dept. chemistry, 1990-95; vis. prof. U. Notre Dame, Ind., 1980, U. Würzburg, Germany, 1985-86; vis. scientist, Nat. Ctr. Atmospheric Rsch., 1995-96; referee various jours., granting agys., 1970—; mem. NSF panel on grad. fellowships, Washington, 1980-83; asst. dir. EPSCOR program in Mont., NSF, 1990—. Editor: Oscillations and Traveling Waves in Chemical Systems, 1985, Chaos in Chemistry and Biochemistry, 1993; contbr. rsch. articles to profl. publs. Grantee NSF, 1978—; recipient Burlington No. award for scholarship, 1990. Mem. Am. Chem. Soc. (tour spkr 1983, 85, 89, 91, 92, 94, 95, chair Mont. sect. 1979, editl. adv. bd. Jour. Phys. Chemistry 1988-94, Internat. Jour. Chem. Kin. 1995—). Roman Catholic. Home: 317 Livingston Ave Missoula MT 59801-8007 Office: U Mont Dept Chemistry Missoula MT 59812

FIELD, SUSAN LEE, English educator; b. Rochester, N.Y.; d. Charles F. and Nancy J. (Pecsok) Merwin; m. Tom Field, Dec. 24, 1975; children: Sam, Sarah. BA in English, U. N.Mex., 1975, MA, 1990, PhD, 1994; MLS, Peabody Coll., Nashville, 1977. Libr. Albuquerque Pub. Libr., 1978-79; mgr. Trespassors William Bookstore, Albuquerque, 1979-86; instr., rschr. U. N.Mex., Albuquerque, 1988-94; instr. dept. English U. N.Mex., Los Lunas, 1995—. Author: The Romance of Desire: Emerson's Commitment to Incompletion, 1997. Recipient Buchanan Arms award U. N.Mex., 1992. Mem. MLA, Nat. Coun. Tchrs. English, Phi Beta Kappa, Phi Kappa Phi, Phi Sigma Tau. Office: Univ of New Mexico-Valencia Campus 280 La Entrada Los Lunas NM 87031

FIELDEN, C. FRANKLIN, III, early childhood education consultant; b. Gulfport, Miss., Aug. 4, 1946; s. C. Franklin and Georgia (Freeman) F.; children: Christopher Michaux (dec.), Robert Michaux, Jonathan Dutton. Student, Claremont Men's Coll., 1964-65; AB, Colo. Coll., 1970; MS,

George Peabody Coll. Tchrs., 1976, EdS, 1979. Tutor Proyecto El Guacio, San Sebastian, P.R., 1967-68; asst. tchr. GET-SET Project, Colorado Springs, Colo., 1969-70, co-tchr., 1970-75, asst. dir., 1972-75; tutor Early Childhood Edn. Project, Nashville, 1975-76; pub. policy intern Donner-Belmont Child Care Ctr., Nashville, 1976-77; asst. to urban min. Nashville Presbytery, 1977; intern to prin. Steele Elem. Sch., Colorado Springs, 1977-78, tchr., 1978-86; resource person Office Gifted and Talented Edn. Colorado Springs Pub. Schs., 1986-87; tchr. Columbia Elem. Sch., Colorado Springs, 1987-92; tchr., pre-sch. team coord. Helen Hunt Elem. Sch., Colorado Springs, 1992-93; validator Nat. Acad. Early Childhood Programs, 1992—, mentor, 1994—, commr., 1996—; cons. Colo. Dept. Edn., Denver, 1993-96, sr. cons., 1996—; lectr. Arapahoe C.C., Littleton, Colo., 1981-82; instr. Met. State Coll., Denver, 1981; cons. Jubail Human Resources Devel. Inst., Saudi Arabia, 1982; mem. governing bd. GET-SET Project, 1969-79, 91-93. Mem. ad hoc bd. trustees Tenn. United Meth. Agy. on Children and Youth, 1976-77; mem. So. Regional Edn. Bd. Task Force on Parent-Caregiver Relationships, 1976-77; mem. day care com. Colo. Commn. Children and Their Families, 1981-82; mem. Nashville Children's Issues Task Force, 1976-77, Tenn. United Meth. Task Force on Children and Youth, 1976-77, Citizens' Goals Leadership Tng., 1986-87, Child Abuse Task Force, 4th Jud. Dist., 1986-87, FIRST IMPRESSIONS (Colo. Govs. Early Childhood Initiative) Task Force, 1987-88; mem. El Paso County Placement Alternatives Commn., 1990-96; mem. proposal rev. team Colo. Dept. Edn., 1992—; co-chair City/County Child Care Task Force, 1991-92; charter mem. City/County Early Childhood Care and Edn. Commn., 1993-96; mem. bd. dirs. Colo. Office of Resource and Referral Agys., 1996—; mem. soccer com. Colo. H.S. Activities Assn., 1996—. Recipient Arts/Bus./Edn. award, 1983, Innovative Tchg. award, 1984; fellow NIMH, 1976. Mem. ASCD, Nat. Assn. Edn. Young Children (founding mem. primary caucus 1992—, co-chair Western States Leadership Network 1993, Membership Action Group grantee 1993, mem. panel profl. ethics in early childhood edn. 1993-97), Colo. Assn. Edn. Young Children (legis. com. 1979-84, governing bd. 1980-84, 85-86, 89-95, exec. com. 1980-84, 93, sec. 1980-84, rsch. conf. chmn. 1982, tuition awards com. 1983-86, chmn. tuition awards com. 1985-86, pub. policy com. 1989-96, treas. 1993, primary grades conf. chmn. 1994), Pikes Peak Assn. Edn. Young Children, Am. Film Inst., Colorado Springs Fine Arts Ctr., Huguenot Soc. Great Britain and Ireland, Nat. Trust Hist. Preservation, Country Club Colo., Phi Delta Kappa. Presbyterian. Home: PO Box 7766 Colorado Springs CO 80933-7766 Office: 201 E Colfax Ave Denver CO 80203-1704

FIELDING, HAROLD PRESTON, bank executive; b. Roaring Springs, Tex., Oct. 18, 1930; s. Rennon Preston and Merle (Woods) F.; m. Ingrid Margarete Eva Ziegler, May 4, 1962; children: Terry Stephen, Harold Preston Jr., Rennon Preston II, Marcel Preston, Noël Preston. AA, Fresno City Coll., 1972; BA, Calif. State U., 1976. Enlisted U.S. Army, 1950, command sgt. major, 1950-72, retired, 1972; br. mgr. Bank of Am., Stockton, Calif., 1972-78; exec. v.p. Bank of Oreg., Woodburn, 1978-84; pres., chief exec. officer Calif. Valley Bank, Fresno, 1984-86; pres., chief exec. officer Am. Samoa Bank, Pago Pago, Am. Samoa, 1986—, bd. dirs. Bd. dirs. Am. Samoa Econ. Devel. Authority, Pago Pago, 1990, C. of C. of Am. Samoa, Pago Pago, 1987, Goodwill Industries of Am. Samoa, Pago Pago, 1988, Tony Solaita Scholarship Trust Fund, Pago Pago, 1990; treas. S. Pacific Mini-Games for 1997. Mem. Am. Bankers Assn., Western Ind. Bankers Assn., Calif. Bankers Assn., Oreg. Bankers Assn. Democrat. Roman Catholic.

FIELDS, ANTHONY LINDSAY AUSTIN, health facility administrator, oncologist, educator; b. St. Michael, Barbados, Oct. 21, 1943; arrived in Can., 1968; s. Vernon Bruce and Marjorie (Pilgrim) F.; m. Patricia Jane Stewart, Aug. 5, 1967. MA, U. Cambridge, 1969; MD, U. Alta., 1974. Diplomate Am. Bd. Internal Medicine. Sr. specialist Cross Cancer Inst., Edmonton, Alta., Can., 1980-85, dir. dept. medicine, 1985-88, dir., 1988—; asst. prof. medicine U. Alta., Edmonton, 1980-84, assoc. prof., 1984—, dir. divsn. med. oncology, 1985-89, dir. divsn. oncology, 1988-93. Fellow ACP, Royal Coll. Physicians and Surgeons Can. (specialist cert. med. oncology, internal medicine); mem. Can. Assn. Med. Oncologists (pres. 1994-96), Am. Soc. Clin. Oncology, Am. Fedn. Clin. Rsch., Can. Soc. for Clin. Investigation, Can. Med. Assn. Office: Cross Cancer Inst, 11560 University Ave, Edmonton, AB Canada T6G 1Z2

FIERO, PETRA SCHUG, language professional educator; b. Oberwinkling, Bavaria, Germany, June 4, 1962; came to U.S., 1985; d. Alfred and Edda (Baarmann) Schug; m. David Brian Fiero, May 25, 1989. BA, U. Regensburg, Germany, 1984; MA, U. Nebr., 1989, PhD, 1994. Tchg. asst., lectr. U. Nebr., Lincoln, 1985-94; asst. prof. German and Spanish Western Wash. U., Bellingham, 1995—. Author: Schreiben gegen Schweigen: Grenzerfahrungen in Jean Amérys autobiographischem Werk, 1997. Mem. Am. Assn. Tchrs. Germans, Modern Lang. Assn., Pacific NW Coun. Fgn. Langs., Wash. Assn. Fgn. Lang. Tchrs., Delta Phi Alpha. Home: 655 W Horton Way #140 Bellingham WA 98226 Office: Western Washington Univ HU 241 Dept Fgn Lang Bellingham WA 98225

FIFE, DENNIS JENSEN, military officer, chemistry educator; b. Brigham City, Utah, Feb. 10, 1945; s. Glen Shumway and June (Jenson) F.; m. Metta Marie Gunther, June 22, 1972; children: Kimball, Kellie, Keith, Kurt, Katie, Kenton. BS in Chemistry, Weber State U., Ogden, Utah, 1969; MBA, Inter-Am. U., San German, P.R., 1973; MS in Chemistry, Utah State U., 1978, PhD in Phsy. Chemistry, 1983. Assoc. chemist Thiokol Chem. Corp., Brigham City, 1969; commd. 2d lt. USAF, 1969, advanced through grades to lt. col.; pilot, instr., flight examiner Hurricane Hunters, Ramey AFB, P.R. and Keesler AFB, Miss., 1971-76; test project pilot 6514th Test Squadron, Ogden, Utah, 1979-81; instr. chemistry USAF Acad., Colorado Springs, Colo., 1977-79, asst. prof., 1983-85, assoc. prof., 1985-90; prof. USAF Acad., 1990; pres. Select Pubs., Inc., Colorado Springs, 1985-90, also chmn. bd. dirs., 1990; mgr. analytical labs. dept. Thiokol Corp., Brigham City, Utah, 1990—. Author: How to Form a Colorado Corporation, 1986; contbr. articles to profl. jours. Active Boy Scouts Am., 1981—, sustaining mem. Rep. Nat. Com., Washington, 1983—. Decorated Air medal with oak leaf cluster; NSF research grantee, 1967-68. Mem. Internat. Union Pure and Applied Chemistry (affiliate), Am. Chem. Soc., Phi Kappa Phi. Republican. Mormon. Office: Thiokol Corp PO Box 707 M/S 245 Brigham City UT 84302-0707

FIFE, TERRY D., neurologist; b. Ft. Wayne, Ind., Oct. 23, 1959. BS, U. Ariz., 1982; MD, Tex. A&M U., 1986. Resident U. Calif. Davis Med. Ctr., Sacramento, 1986-89; resident UCLA, L.A., 1989-92, clin. instr., 1992-93; cons. Barrow Neurol. Inst., Phoenix, 1993—, dir. balance ctr., 1994—; asst. clin. prof. neurology U. Ariz., Tucson, 1996—. Contbr. articles to profl. jours., chpts. to books. Recipient NIH Nat. Rsch. Svc. award, 1992. Mem. Am. Acad. Neurology, Am. Coll. Physicians. Office: Barrow Neurol Inst 222 W Thomas Rd Rm 110 Phoenix AZ 85013-4423

FIFER, LINDA SUE, speech pathologist, interior designer; b. Mansfield, Ohio, Nov. 7, 1952; d. Joseph Stanley and Martha Eleanor (Weatherhead) F.; m. Raymond Lee Prill, Jan. 12, 1980 (div. Aug. 1987). BA, Kent State U., 1974, MS, 1975; cert., Sheffield Sch. Interior Design, 1993. Cert. clin. competence, Am. Speech Hearing Assn., speech and lang. pathologist, Mont. Teaching asst. Kent (Ohio) State U., 1974-75; speech/lang. pathologist Mont. Easter Seal Soc., Great Falls, 1975-79, Hellgate H.S., Missoula, Mont., 1980, Cmty. Med. Ctr., Missoula, Mont., 1980—; dir., founder Paws Abilities, Missoula, 1990-92; dir. speech/lang. dept. Cmty. Med. Ctr., Missoula, 1982-86; pres. Apple Hearth Interiors, Missoula, 1993—. Writer, lyricist (musical play) Eaton Street, 1986. Pres. Missoula chpt. Pilot Club, 1987-88; bd. dirs. Missoula chpt. Am. Cancer Soc., 1986-87. U.S. Dept. Edn. grantee, 1990-93.

FIGLIN, ROBERT ALAN, physician, hematologist, oncologist; b. Phila., June 22, 1949; s. Jack and Helen Figlin; 1 child, Jonathan B. BA in Chemistry, Temple U., 1970, postgrad., 1972; MD, Med. Coll. Pa., 1976. Diplomate Am. Bd. Internal Medicine, sub-bd. Med. Oncology; diplomate Nat. Bd. Med. Examiners; lic. physician, Calif. Med. intern, resident in medicine Cedars-Sinai Med. Ctr., L.A., 1976-79, chief resident in medicine, 1979-80; fellow in hematology-oncology UCLA, 1980-82; asst. prof. medicine UCLA Sch. Medicine, 1982-88, assoc. prof., 1988-94, prof. of medicine, 1994—; dir. Bowyer Oncology Ctr., dir. outpatient clin. rsch. unit Jonsson Comprehensive Cancer Ctr., 1990-92, dir. clin. rsch. unit, 1993—; prof. medicine, 1994—; med. dir. thoracic oncology program Johnson Comprehensive Cancer Ctr., 1994—, genito uninary program, 1994—, solid tumor program, 1997—; prin. investigator UCLA S.W. Oncology Group, 1992—; scientific founder UroGeneSys, 1996—. Editor Interferons in Cytokines, 1988-90, Kidney Cancer Jour., 1993-94; affiliate editor Current Clin. Trials, 1992-96; mem. editorial bd. UCLA Cancer Trials Newsletter, 1990-96, Seminars on Oncology-Kidney Cancer, 1995; author articles and revs. Mem. med. adv. bd. Nat. Kidney Cancer Assn., 1993—; FDA cons., 1990-92. Recipient numerous awards. Fellow ACP; mem. Am. Soc. Clin. Oncology, Am. Fedn. Clin. Rsch., Am. Assn. for Cancer Rsch., Soc. for Biologic Therapy, S.W. Oncology Group. Office: UCLA Ste 2333 10945 Le Conte Ave Los Angeles CA 90095

FIGUEIREDO, HUBERT FERNANDES, aerospace engineer; b. Elizabeth, N.J., Nov. 21, 1958; s. Fernando and Maria Alexandria F.; 1 child, Christine Alexis. BS in Aerospace Engring., Polytech. Inst. N.Y., 1980; postgrad. in systems mgmt., U. So. Calif., 1986—. Prodn. inspector Amax, Inc., Carteret, N.J., 1978; analytical engr. Pratt and Whitney Aircraft Corp., East Hartford, Conn., 1979; space shuttle mech. systems test engr. Rockwell Internat. Space Div., Palmdale, Calif., 1980-84, pub. rels. speaker, 1981-84; space shuttle mechanisms/structures engr. Lockheed Space Ops. Co., Vandenberg AFB, Calif. and Kennedy Space Ctr., Fla., 1984-87; with B-2 div. Northrop Grumman Corp., Palmdale, Calif., 1987-89; engring. specialist, lead structures design engr. Northrop-Grumman Corp., Palmdale, Calif., 1990-91, group lead engr. B-2 structures design, 1990-94, engring. specialist B-2 flight line and delivery ops., 1994—; interviewed on progress of space shuttle Challenger on the Spanish Internat. Network, 1983. Mem. rsch. bd. adv. Am. Biog. Inst. Recipient Superior Achievement award Rockwell Internat. Space Div. Mem. AIAA, Northrop Grumman Mgmt. Club. Republican. Roman Catholic. Address: 2557 Garnet Ln Lancaster CA 93535-5643

FILLEY, CHRISTOPHER MARK, neurologist; b. Saranac Lake, N.Y., July 31, 1951; s. Giles Franklin and Mary Brown (Klinefelter) F. BA, Williams Coll., 1973; MD, Johns Hopkins U., 1979. Diplomate Am. Bd. Psychiatry and Neurology. Intern U. Conn., Farmington, 1979-80; resident in neurology U. Colo., Denver, 1980-83; behavioral neurology fellow Boston U., 1983-84; from instr. to asst. prof. neurology U. Colo. Sch. Medicine, Denver, 1984-91, assoc. prof. neurology, 1991-97, prof. neurology, 1997—; prin. investigator studies in Alzheimers Disease NIH, Bethesda, Md., 1991-94. Author: Neurobehavioral Anatomy, 1995; contbr. articles to profl. jours. Health com. Denver Found., 1995—. Mem. Am. Acad. Neurology, Am. Neurol. Assn., Internat. Neuropsychol. Soc., Behavioral Neurology Soc., Colo. Soc. Clin. Neurologists. Office: Univ Colo Behavioral Neurology Sect 4200 E 9th Ave Denver CO 80262

FILNER, BOB, congressman; b. 1942; m. Jane Merrill; children: Erin, Adam. BA in Chemistry, Cornell U.; MA in History, U. Del.; PhD in History, Cornell U. Prof. history San Diego State U., 1970-92; legis. asst. Senator Hubert Humphrey, 1974, Congressman Don Fraser, 1975; spl. asst. Congressman Jim Bates, 1984; city councilman 8th dist. City of San Diego, 1987-92, dep. mayor, 1992; mem. 103rd Congress from 50th Calif. dist., 1993—. Pres. San Diego Bd. Edn., 1982, mem.-elect 1979-83; chmn. San Diego Schs. of the Future Commn., 1986-87. Democrat. Office: US Ho of Reps 330 Cannon HOB Washington DC 20515-0003

FILOSA, GARY FAIRMONT RANDOLPH V., II, multimedia executive, financier; b. Wilder, Vt., Feb. 22, 1931; s. Gary F.R. de Marco de Viana and Rosaline M. (Falzarano) Filosa; m. Catherine Moray Stewart (dec.); children: Marc Christian Bazire de Villadon III, Gary Fairmont Randolph de Viana III. Grad., Mt. Hermon Sch., 1950; PhB, U. Chgo., 1954; BA, U. Americas, Mex., 1967; MA, Calif. Western U., 1968; PhD, U.S. Internat. U., 1970. Sports reporter Claremont Daily Eagle, Rutland Herald, Vt. Informer, 1947-52; pub. The Chicagoan, 1952-54; account exec., editor house publs. Robertson, Buckley & Gotsch, Inc., Chgo., 1953-54; account exec. Fuller, Smith & Ross, Inc., N.Y.C., 1955; prodr./host Weekend KCET Channel 13, N.Y.C., 1955-67; editor Apparel Arts mag. (now Gentlemen's Quar.), Esquire, Inc., N.Y.C., 1955-56; pub. Teenage, Rustic Rhythm, Teen Life, Mystery Digest, Top Talent, Rock & Roll Roundup, Celebrities, Stardust, Personalities, Campus monthly mags., N.Y.C., 1955-61; pres., chmn. bd. Filosa Publs. Internat., N.Y.C., 1956-61, L.A., 1974-83, Palm Beach, Fla., 1983-88; pres., chmn. bd. Teenarama Records, Inc., N.Y.C., 1956-62; chmn. bd., pres. Produciones Mexicanes Internationales (S.A.), Mexico City, 1957-68; assoc. pub. Laundromatic Age, N.Y.C., 1958-59; ptnr. of Warner LeRoy purchase of Broadway plays for Hollywood films, N.Y.C., 1958-61; pres. Montclair Sch., 1958-60, Pacific Registry, Inc., L.A., 1959-61; exec. prodr. Desilu Studios, Inc., Hollywood, Calif., 1959-61; exec. asst. to Benjamin A. Javits, 1961-62; dean adminstrn. Postgrad. Ctr. for Mental Health, N.Y.C., 1962-64; chmn. bd., CEO Filosa Films Internat., Beverly Hills, Calif., 1962-83, 90-92; chmn. bd., pres. Filosa Films Internat., Palm Beach, Fla., 1984-93, Miami Beach, Fla., 1993-96, Honolulu, 1996—; pres. Amateur Athletes Internat., Iowa City, Iowa, 1996—, Banana Chip Corp. Am., N.Y.C., 1964-67; chmn. bd., pres. Cinematografica Americana Internationale (S.A.), Mexico City, 1964-74; pres. Casa Filosa Corp., Palm Beach, Fla., 1982-87; dir. Community Savings, North Palm Beach, Fla., 1982-87; v.p. acad. affairs World Acad., San Francisco, 1967-68; asst. to provost Calif. Western U., San Diego, 1968-69; assoc. prof. philosophy Art Coll., San Francisoc, 1969-70; v.p. acad. affairs, dean of faculty Internat. Inst., Phoenix, 1968-73; chmn. bd. dirs., pres. Universite Universelle, 1970-73; bd. dirs., v.p. acad. affairs, dean Summer Sch., Internat. C.C., L.A., 1970-72; chmn. bd., pres. Social Directory Calif., 1967-75, Am. Assn. Social Registries, L.A., 1970-76; pres. Social Directory U.S., N.Y.C., 1974-76; pres. Herbert Hoover Iowa Forum, Iowa City, 1996—; chmn. bd. dirs. Internat. Soc. Social Registers, Paris, 1974 ; surfing coach U. Calif. at Irvine, 1975-77; instr. history Coastline C.C., Fountain Valley, Calif., 1976-77; v.p. Xerox-Systemic, 1979-80; CEO Internat. Surfing League, Palm Beach, 1987-95; pres., CEO Filosa Harrop Internat., Phoenix, 1987-89; pres. Amateur Athletes Internat., Iowa City, 1996—. Editor: Sci. Digest, 1961-62; composer: (lyrics) The Night Discovers Love, 1952,That Certain Something, 1953, Bolero of Love, 1956; author: (stage play) Let McCall Ethel, 1955, Technology Enters 21st Century, 1966, (mus.) Feather Light, 1966, No Public Funds for Nonpublic Schools, 1968, Creative Funciton of the College President, 1969, The Surfers Almanac, 1977, The Filosa Newsletter, 1986-92, The Sexual Continuum, 1990, Traveltalk, 1991, God's Own Prince, 1995, Holy Hawaii, 1996, (biography) A Plague on Paradise, 1994; (TV series) Danny thomas Show, 1963, Surfing USA, 1977, Payne of Florida, 1985, Honolulu, 1991, The Gym, 1992, Sales Pitch, 1992, 810 OceanAvenue, 1992, One Feather, 1992, Conversations with America, 1989, All American Beach Party, 1989; contbr. numerous articles to profl. jours. and encys., including Life, Look, Sci. Digest, Ency. of Sports, World Book Ency. Trustee Univ. of the Ams., Pueblo, Mex., 1986—; candidate for L.A. City Coun., 1959; chmn. Educators for Re-election of Ivy Baker Pirest, 1970; mem. So. Calif. Com. for Olympic Games, 1077-84. With AUS, 1954-55. Recipient DAR Citizenship award, 1959, Silver Conquistador award Am. Assn. Social Registes, 1970, Ambassador's Cup U. Ams., 1967, resolution Calif. State Legislature, 1977, Duke Kahanamoku Classic surfing trophy, 1977, gold pendant Japan Surfing Assn., 1978, Father of Olympic Surfing award Internat. Athletic Union, 1995, Father of Surfing trophy Amateur Athletes Internat., 1997. Mem. NAACP, NCAA (bd. dels. 1977-82), AAU (gov. 1978-82), Am. Acad. Motion Picture Arts and Scis., Am. Surfing Assn. (founder, pres. 1960-92), Internat. Surfing Com. (refounder, pres. 1960-95, 96—), U.S. Surfing Com. (founder, pres. 1960—), Internat. Surfing League (founder, pres. 1988-95, 96—), Am. Walking Soc. (founder, pres. 1980-92), Internat. Waling Soc. (founder, pres. 1987-93), Am. Assn. UN, Authors League, Authors Guild, Alumni Assn. U. Ams. (pres. 1967-70), Surf Club of the Palm Beaches (pres. 1983-94), Sierra Club, Surfing Hui of Hawaii, Internat. Soc. Bibliotherapists (Paris, pres. 1997—), Sigma Omicron Lambda (founder, pres. 1965-92). Republican. Episcopalian. Home: Box 1207 Iowa City IA 52244-1207 Office: Box 299 Beverly Hills CA 90213-0299

FINCH, THOMAS WESLEY, corrosion engineer; b. Alhambra, Calif., Dec. 17, 1946; s. Charles Phillip and Marian Louisa (Bushey) F.; m. Jinx L. Heath, Apr. 1979. Student Colo. Sch. Mines, 1964-68. Assayer, prospector Raymond P. Heon, Inc., Idaho Springs, Colo., 1968; corrosion engr. Cathodic Protection Service, Denver, 1973-80, area mgr., Lafayette, La., 1980-81; area mgr. Corrintec/USA, Farmington, N.Mex., 1981-83; dist. mgr. Cathodic Protection Services Co., Farmington, 1983—. Served with C.E., U.S. Army, 1968-72. Mem. Nat. Assn. Corrosion Engrs., Soc. Am. Mil. Engrs., U.S. Ski Assn., Am. Security Council (nat. adv. bd. 1978—), Kappa Sigma. Republican. Lutheran. Home: 2404 N Municipal Dr Farmington NM 87401 Office: PO Box 388 Farmington NM 87499-0388

FINE, CYNTHIA MIZER, producer interactive media; b. Vermillion, S.D., Dec. 7, 1958; d. Walter George and Shirlee Lynn (Perry) Mizer; m. Mark Jeremy Fine, Sept. 7, 1991; 1 child, Nicholas Walter. BA, U. Calif., Santa Barbara, 1981. Dir. promotions and advt. Harcourt, Brace, Jovanovich, San Diego, 1982-87; dir. video and computer software Holt, Rinehart, Winston, Austin, Tex., 1987-90; prodr. Philips Media, L.A., 1990-91; exec. prodr. AT&T, N.Y.C., 1991-92; v.p. product devel. Paramount Interactive, Palo Alto, Calif., 1992-94; exec. prodr. Viacom New Media, N.Y.C., 1995-96, Boxtop, L.A., 1996—; exec. prodr. Boxtop Interactive; cons. Simon & Schuster, N.Y.C., 1991, Warner Home Video, L.A., 1991, Columbia Home Video, 1991. Prodr.: (video series) Elements of Literature, 1988 (Nat. Coun. Tchrs. English award 1989), Religions of the World, 1989 (Nat. Coun. Social Studies award 1990); v.p. prodn.: (CD-ROM game) Busy Town, 1994 (award Nat. Parenting Publs. 1995); exec. prodr.: (CD-ROM game) Indian in the Cupboard, 1995 (award Nat. Parenting Publs. 1995). Home: 1101 Las Pulgas Pl Pacific Palisades CA 90272

FINEGAN, COLE, lawyer; b. Tulsa, Oct. 1, 1956; s. Philip Cole and Margaret (Hudson) F.; m. Robin Fudge, Dec. 29, 1984; children: Jordan Nicole, Ryan Andrew. BA in English, U. Notre Dame, Ind., 1978; JD, Georgetown U., 1987. Legis. asst., adminstrv. asst. Ctrl. Dist.-1st Dist. Okla., Tulsa and Washington, 1978-87; assoc. Brownstein Hyatt Farber & Strickland, Denver, 1987-91, shareholder, 1993—; dir. Office Policy and Initiatives Gov. State of Colo., Denver, 1991-93. Staff mem. The Tax Lawyer, 1984-86. Bd. mem. Greater Denver Corp., 1993-96; bd. trustees State Colls. Colo., 1993—; bd. mem. Auvaria Higher Edn. Commn., 1993-95. Democrat. Roman Catholic. Home: 1934 Forest Pky Denver CO 80220 Office: Brownstein Hyatt Farber & Strickland 410 17th St Fl 22 Denver CO 80202-4402

FINEMAN, JO ANN BOOZE, psychiatrist, psychoanalyst; b. Bloomington, Ind.; d. Herbert Henry and Nira Verne (Secrest) Booze; children: James Cameron Wilson, Neira Rebecca Fineman. Degree in Zoology, Ind. U. Lic. psychiatrist, Ind., Mass., Ariz., Calif., N.Mex. Intern New Eng. Hosp., Boston; resident in psychiatry Worcester (Mass.) State Hosp., Boston U. Med. Ctr.; fellow in child psychiatry Judge Baker Guidance Ctr. and Children's Hosp. Med. Ctr., Boston; asst. in psychiatry Harvard U. Med. Sch., Boston; pvt. practice child, adolescent and adult psychiatry, psychoanalysis Boston, 1960-83, Tucson, 1983-86, Santa Fe, Albuquerque, 1988—; mem. faculty, clin. staff Harbor-UCLA Med. Ctr., Torrance, Calif., 1986-88; asst. clin. prof. child psychiatry Boston U. Med. Sch., 1962-68, assoc. clin. prof. child psychiatry, 1968-78; assoc. clin. prof. psychiatry Tufts U. Med. Sch., Tufts New Eng. Med. Ctr., Boston, 1978-83; clin. assoc. prof. psychiatry and pediat. U. Ariz., Tucson, 1983; asst. clin. prof. Step III dept. psychiatry UCLA, 1987; lectr. psychiatry Harvard U. Med. Faculty, Boston, 1981-83; sr. lectr. psychiatry dept. psychiatry U. Ariz., 1988; assoc. attending psychiatry McLean Hosp., Belmont, Mass., 1970, assoc. attending child psychiatrist, 1977-80, assoc. child psychiatrist, 1978-83, dir. outpatient svcs. children's ctr., 1982-83; vis. staff dept. pediat. Boston City Hosp., 1972-78, dept. psychiatry Univ. Hosp., Boston, 1972-78; staff psychiatrist Union Hosp., Lynn, Mass., 1979-83, Tuscon, 1984; mem. faculty, staff U. Ariz. Health Scis. Ctr., Tucson, 1982; clin. dir. child and adolescent psychiatry divsn. Harbor-UCLA Med. Ctr., Torrance, Calif., 1986-88, mem. med. staff, 1987; cons. in field; spkr., lectr., presenter, panelist, coord. numerous confs., meetings, symposia, workshops. Contbr. articles to profl. jours. Grantee U. Ariz. Med. Ctr., Dept. Edn., State of Ariz., 1985-86, 86-87. Fellow Am. Orthopsychiat. Assn.; mem. Am. Psychoanalytic Assn., Ariz. Psychoanalytic Study Group, Boston Psychoanalytic Soc. and Inst., New Eng. Coun. for Child Psychiatry, Am. Acad. Child Psychiatry, Assn. for Child Psychoanalysis, Am. Psychiat. Assn., Psychoanalytic Ctr. Calif., So. Calif. Psychoanalytic Inst., So. Calif. Psychoanalytic Soc., N.Mex. Psychiat. Soc.

FINERAN, DIANA LOU, association administrator; b. Rice Lake, Wis., Dec. 25, 1945; d. Earl Orin and Leona May (Steltzner) Frommader; m. John James Fineran, III, Apr. 28, 1979. Grad. high sch., Rice Lake. Tel. operator Wis. Tel. Co., Rice Lake, 1964-69; svc. rep. Gen. Tel. Co., Rice Lake, 1969-79, Dallas, Tex., 1979-80; founder, sec., treas. The Traditional Cat Assn. Inc., Jonesborough, Tenn., 1987-92, Alpharetta, Ga., 1992-96, Battle Ground, Wash., 1996—. Contbr. articles to mags. Leader 4-H, Jonesborough, 1990. Lutheran. Home and Office: Traditional Cat Assn Inc 18509 NE 279th St Battle Ground WA 98604-9717

FINESILVER, SHERMAN GLENN, retired federal judge; b. Denver, Oct. 1, 1927; s. Harry M. and Rebecca M. (Balaban) F.; m. Annette Warren, July 23, 1954; children: Jay Mark, Steven Brad, Susan Saunders. BA, U. Colo., 1949; LLB, U. Denver, 1952; cert., Northwestern U. Traffic Inst., 1956; LLD (hon.), Gallaudet Coll., Washington, 1970, Met. State Coll., Denver, 1981, N.Y. Law Sch., N.Y.C., 1983, U. Colo., 1988. Bar: Colo. 1952, U.S. Ct. of Appeals (10th cir.) 1952, U.S. Supreme Ct. 1952. Legal asst. Denver City Atty.'s Office, 1949-52; asst. Denver city atty., 1952-55; judge Denver County Ct., 1955-62; judge Denver Dist. Ct., 2d Jud. Dist., 1962-71, presiding judge domestic relations div., 1963, 67, 68; judge U.S. Dist. Ct., Denver, from 1971, elevated to chief judge, 1982-94; ret., 1995—; spl. counsel Popham Haik Schnobrich & Kaufman, Attys. at Law, Denver, 1995—; adj. prof. U. Denver Coll. Law and Arts and Sci. Sch., 1955—, Met. State Coll., 1989—; mem. faculty Nat. Coll. Judiciary, Reno, 1967-84, Atty. Gen.'s Advocacy Inst., Washington, 1974—, seminars for new fed. judges, 1974—; elected to Jud. Conf. U.S., 1985-88; mem. Jud. Conf. Com. on Rules for Admission to Practice in Fed. Cts., 1976-79, Com. on Adminstrn. Probation System, 1983-87, Adv. Com. on Criminal Rules, 1984-87, Com. on Bicentennial of Constn., 1985-87, Com. on Criminal Law and Probation Adminstrn., 1988—. Contbr. chpt. to Epilepsy Rehabilitation, 1974; contbr. articles and publs. on law, medicine, legal rights of deaf, aging, physically impaired and many others, 1974-94. Mem. task force White House Conf. on Aging, 1972, presdl. commn., 1980-84; mem. Probation Com., U.S. Cts., 1985-88, Nat. Com. to Study Qualifications to Practice in Fed. Cts., 1976-82, bd. visitors Brigham Young U., 1977-80, Nat. Commn. Against Drunk Driving, 1982-86. Decorated Inspector Gen. 33d degree; recipient numerous awards including medallion for outstanding service by a non-handicapped person to physically disabled Nat. Paraplegia Found., 1972, cert. of commendation Sec. Transp., 1974, Norlin award for outstanding alumni U. Colo., 1988, numerous others. Fellow Am. Coll. Legal Medicine (Chgo., hon. fellow); mem. ABA (nat. chmn. Am. citizenship com. 1968, award of merit Law Day 1968), Colo. Bar Assn. (chmn. Law Day 1964, chmn. Am. citizenship com. 1963, bd. govs. 1982-94), Denver Bar Assn. (chmn. Law Day 1964), Am. Judicature Soc., Am. Amateur Radio, B'nai B'rith, Masons, Shriners, Phi Sigma Delta (trustee 1960-66, Nat. Man of Yr. Zeta Beta Tau chpt. 1989). •

FINK, JAMES BREWSTER, geophysicist, consultant; b. Los Angeles, Jan. 12, 1943; s. Odra J. and Gertrude (Sloot) F.; m. Georgeanne Emmerich, Aug. 24, 1970; 1 child, Jody Lynn. BS in Geophysics and Geochemistry, U. Ariz., 1969; MS in Geophysics cum laude, U. Witwatersrand, Johannesburg, Transvaal, Republic of South Africa, 1980; PhD in Geol. Engring., Geohydrology, U. Ariz, 1989. Registered profl. engr., Ariz., N.Mex.; registered land surveyor, Ariz.; registered profl. geologist, Wyo.; cert. environ. inspector. Geophysicist Geo-Comp Exploration, Inc., Tucson, 1969-70; geophys. cons. IFEX-Geotechnica, S.A., Hermosillo, Sonora, Mex., 1970; chief geophysicist Mining Geophys. Surveys, Tucson, 1971-72; research asst. U. Ariz., Tucson, 1973; cons. geophysics Tucson, 1974-76; sr. minerals geophysicist Esso Minerals Africa, Inc., Johannesburg, 1976-79; sr. research geophysicist Exxon Prodn. Research Co., Houston, 1979-80; pres. Geophynque Internat., Tucson, 1980-90, hydroGeophysics, Inc., Tucson, 1990—; cons. on NSF research U. Ariz., 1984-85, adj. lectr. geol. engring., 1985-86, assoc. instr. geophysics, 1986-87, supr. geophysicist, geohydrologist, 1986-88, bd. dirs. Lab. Advanced Subsurface Imaging, 1986—; v.p. R&D Alternative Energy Engring., Inc., Tucson, 1992—, also bd. dirs.; v.p. Reclamation Svcs., Inc., 1995—, also bd. dirs.; v.p. Catalina Marble Inc., 1996—; lectr. South African Atomic Energy Bd., Pelindaba, 1979; cons. Argonne Nat. Lab., 1992-93, Los Alamos Nat. Lab., 1987—; v.p. Rincon Stock Yard, 1997—. Contbr. articles to profl. jours. Served as sgt. U.S. Air NG, 1965-70. Named Airman of Yr., U.S. Air NG, 1967. Mem. Soc.

Exploration Geophysicists (co-chair internat. meetings 1980, 81, 92, sr. editor monograph 1990, reviewer), Am. Geophys. Union (reviewer), European Assn. Exploration Geophysicists, Assn. Ground Water Scientists, Nat. Water Well Assn. (reviewer), Mineral and Geotech. Explorationists, Ariz. Geol. Soc., Ariz. Water Well Assn., Environ. and Engring. Geophys. Soc., Pres.'s Club U. Ariz. Republican. Home and Office: Hydrogeophysics Inc 5865 S Old Spanish Trl Tucson AZ 85747-9487

FINK, ROBERT RUSSELL, music theorist, former university dean; b. Belding, Mich., Jan. 31, 1933; s. Russell Foster and Frances (Thornton) F.; m. Ruth Joan Bauerle, June 19, 1955; children: Denise Lyn, Daniel Robert. B.Mus., Mich. State U., 1955, M.Mus., 1956, Ph.D., 1965. Instr. music SUNY, Fredonia, 1956-57; instr. Western Mich. U., Kalamazoo, 1957-62, asst. prof., 1962-66, assoc. prof., 1966-71, prof., 1971-78, chmn. dept. music, 1972-78; dean Coll. Music U. Colo., Boulder, 1978-93; retired, 1994; prin. horn Kalamazoo Symphony Orch., 1957-67; accreditation examiner Nat. Assn. Schs. Music, Reston, Va., 1973-92, grad. commr., 1981-89, chmn. grad. commn., 1987-89, assoc. chmn. accreditation commn., 1990-91, chmn., 1992. Author: Directory of Michigan Composers, 1972, The Language of 20th Century Music, 1975; composer: Modal Suite, 1959, Four Modes for Winds, 1967, Songs for High School Chorus, 1967; contbr. articles to profl. jours. Bd. dirs. Kalamazoo Symnphony Orch., 1974-78, Boulder Bach Festival, 1983-90. Mem. Coll. Music Soc., Soc. Music Theory, Mich. Orch. Assn. (pres.), Phi Mu Alpha Sinfonia (province gov.), Pi Kappa Lambda. Home: 643 Furman Way Boulder CO 80303-5614

FINKELSTEIN, JAMES ARTHUR, management consultant; b. N.Y.C., Dec. 6, 1952; s. Harold Nathan and Lilyan (Crystal) F.; m. Lynn Marie Gould, Mar. 24, 1984; children: Matthew, Brett. BA, Trinity Coll., Hartford, Conn., 1974; MBA, U. Pa., 1976. Cons. Towers, Perrin, Forster & Crosby, Boston, 1976-78; mgr. compensation Pepsi-Cola Co., Purchase, N.Y., 1978-80; mgr. employee info. systems Am. Can. Co., Greenwich, Conn., 1980; mgr. bus. analysis Emery Airfreight, Wilton, Conn., 1980-81; v.p. Meidinger, Inc., Balt., 1981-83; prin. The Wyatt Co., San Diego, 1983-88; pres., chief exec. officer W. F. Corroon, San Francisco, 1988-95; chmn., CEO FutureSense, Inc., Larkspur, Calif., 1995—; founder TallyUp Software, 1996—; dir. En Wisen, Inc., 1996—; mem. regional adv. bd. Mchts. and Mfrs. Assn., San Diego, 1986-88; instr. U. Calif., San Diego, 1984-88. Mem. camp com. State YMCA of Mass. and R.I., Framingham, 1982-86; pres. Torrey Pines Child Care Consortium, La Jolla, Calif., 1987-88; vice chmn. La Jolla YMCA, 1986-88; chmn. fin. com. YMCA, San Francisco, 1992-95, vice chmn., 1993-95, chmn., 1995—; bd. dirs. San Domenico Sch., 1994—. Home: 17 Bracken Ct San Rafael CA 94901-1587 Office: FutureSense Inc 101 Larkspur Landing Cir Larkspur CA 94939-1749

FINLAY, AUDREY JOY, environmental educator, consultant, naturalist; b. Davidson, Sask., Can., Sept. 18, 1932; d. Leonard Noel and Vilhemine Marie (Rossander) Barton; m. James Campbell Finlay, June 18, 1955; children: Barton Brett, Warren Hugh, Rhonda Marie. BA, U. Man., Can., 1954; profl. diploma in edn., U. Alta., 1974, MEd, 1978. Social worker Children's Aid, Brandon, Man., 1954-55; foster home worker Social Services Province of Sask., Regina, 1955-56, City of Edmonton, Alta., 1956-59; naturalist City of Edmonton, 1965-74; tchr., cons., adminstr. Edmonton Pub. Bd., 1974-88; cons. edn., interpretation numerous projects, 1965—. Author: Winter Here and Now, 1982; co-author: Parks in Alberta, 1987, Ocean to Alpine, A British Columbia Nature Guide, 1992; contbr. nature articles to profl. jours. Chmn., chief exec. officer Wildlife '87: Canadian Centennial Wildlife Conservation, 1985-87. Named Ms. Chatelaine, Chatelaine mag., 1975; recipient Order of Bighorn award Alta Gov., Ralph D. Bird award, 1987, Can. Park Svc. Heritage award Environ. Can., 1990, Order of Can. award, 1990, Reeve's award of Distinction County of Strath, 1991, Douglas Pimlot award Can. Nat. Fedn., 1991. Fellow Alta. Tchrs. Assn. , Environ. Outdoor Coun. (founder, 1st pres., disting. mem.); mem. Canadian Nature Fedn. (v.p. 1984-90), Edmonton Natural History Soc. (Loran Goulden award 1980), Am. Nature Study Soc. (bd. dirs. 1984-91, pres. 1991-94), N.Am. Environ. Edn. Assn. (bd. dirs. 1983-89), Fedn. Alta Naturalists (bd. dirs. 1970s). Home and Office: 270 Trevlac Pl, Victoria, BC Canada V8X 3X1

FINLAY, JAMES CAMPBELL, retired museum director; b. Russell, Man., Can., June 12, 1931; s. William Hugh and Grace Muriel F.; m. Audrey Joy Barton, June 18, 1955; children: Barton Brett, Warren Hugh, Rhonda Marie. BSc, Brandon U., 1952; MSc in Zoology, U. Alta., 1968. Geophysicist Frontier Geophys. Ltd., Alta., 1952-53; geologist, then dist. geologist Shell Can., Ltd., 1954-64; chief park naturalist and biologist Elk Island (Can.) Nat. Park, 1965-67; dir. hist. devel. and archives, dir. hist. and sci. service, dir. Nature Center, dir. interpretation and recreation City of Edmonton, Alta., 1967-92; founder Fedn. Alta. Naturalists, 1969. Author: A Nature Guide to Alberta, Bird Finding Guide to Canada; (with Joy Finlay) Ocean to Alpine-A British Columbia Nature Guide, A Guide to Alberta Parks. Recipient Order of the Bighorn, Govt. of Atla., 1987, Heritage award Environment Can., 1990, Loran Goulden award Fedn. Alta Naturalists, 1991, Can. 125th Anniversary award, 1993; named to Edmonton Hist. Hall of Fame, 1976. Mem. Can. Mus. Assn. (pres. 1976-78), Alta. Mus. Assn. (founding mem., past pres.), Am. Mus. Assn. (past council), Am. Ornithol. Union. Home: 270 Trevlac Pl, RR 3, Victoria, BC Canada V8X 3X1 *I will walk but once on this earth. In this short time I hope to help my fellow man come to a greater awareness, appreciation and understanding of the world environment of which we are very much a part. I am trying to ensure that our descendants have a fit planet on which to live.*

FINLEY, JAMES DANIEL, physics educator; b. Louisville, Aug. 2, 1941; s. James Daniel and Lucile (Carter) F.; m. Judith Bernstein; children: Ian Brendan, Moira Lynn. BA in Math., BS in Physics, U. Tex., 1963; PhD in Physics, U. Calif., Berkeley, 1968. Rsch. scientist Tracor Inc., Austin, Tex., 1962-63; teaching/rsch. asst. U. Calif., Berkeley, 1963-68; asst. prof. physics U. N.Mex., Albuquerque, 1968-73; assoc. prof. physics U. N.Mex., 1973-78, prof. physics, 1978—, chmn. dept. physics, 1985-92; vis. prof. Centro de Inv. y Est. Avanz. del IPN, Mexico City, 1975, 82; vis. prof. U. Canterbury, Christchurch, New Zealand, 1990. Contbr. articles to profl. jours., chpts. to books. Mem. Am. Phys. Soc., Soc. for Gen. Rel. and Gravitation, Cactus and Succulent Soc. Am., Phi Beta Kappa, Sigma Xi. Office: U NMex Dept Physics and Astronomy Albuquerque NM 87131

FINLEY, MITCHEL BRENT, writer; b. LaGrande, Oreg., Dec. 17, 1945; s. Ralph M. and Marjorie (Klinghammer) F.; m. Kathleen M. Hickey, Mar. 9, 1974; children: Sean, Patrick, Kevin. BA in Religious Studies, Santa Clara U., 1973; MA in Theology, Marquette U., 1976. Dir. Family Life Office, Cath. Diocese of Spokane, Wash., 1977-82; freelance writer Spokane, 1982—. Author: Christian Families in The Real World, 1984 (Thomas More Medal award 1984), Catholic Spiritual Classics, 1987, Your Family in Focus, 1993, Everybody Has a Guardian Angel, 1993 (Cath. Press Assn. Book award 1994), Catholic Is Wonderful!, 1994, Heavenly Helpers: St. Anthony and St. Jude, 1994, The Gospel Truth, 1995, Whispers of Love, 1995, Building Christian Families, 1996, The Joy of Being Catholic, 1996, 101 Ways to Nourish Your Soul, 1996, Surprising Mary, 1997, The Seeker's Guide to Being Catholic, 1997. Recipient Silver Medal award Coun. for Advancement & Support Edn., 1991. Mem. Am. Soc. Journalists & Authors (Excellence in Writing award 1992), Cath. Press Assn. U.S. and Can. Roman Catholic.

FINNBERG, ELAINE AGNES, psychologist, editor; b. Bklyn., Mar. 2, 1948; d. Benjamin and Agnes Montgomery (Evans) F.; m. Rodney Lee Herndon, Mar. 1, 1981; 1 child, Andrew Marshal. BA in Psychology, L.I. U., 1969; MA in Psychology, New Sch. for Social Rsch., 1973; PhD in Psychology, Calif. Sch. Profl. Psychology, 1981. Diplomate Am. Bd. Forensic Examiners, Am. Bd. Forensic Medicine, Am. Bd. Med. Psychotherapists and Psychodiagnosticians, Am. Bd. Disability Analysts; lic. psychologist, Calif. Rsch. asst. in med. sociology Med. Coll. Cornell U., N.Y.C., 1969-70; med. abstractor USV Pharm. Corp., Tuckahoe, N.Y., 1970-71, Coun. for Tobacco Rsch., N.Y.C., 1971-77; editor, writer Found. of Thanatology Columbia U., N.Y.C., 1971-76, cons. family studies program cancer ctr. Coll. Physicians &Surgeons, 1973-74; dir. grief psychology and bereavement counseling San Francisco Coll. Mortuary Scis., 1977-81; rsch. assoc. dept. epidemiology and internat. health U. Calif., San Francisco, 1979-81, asst. clin. prof. dept. family and community medicine, 1985-93, assoc. clin. prof., dept. family and community medicine, 1993—; active med. staff Natividad Med. Ctr., Salinas, Calif., 1984—, chief psychologist, 1984-96; profl. adv. coun. Am. Bd. Disability Analysts; asst. chief psychiatry svc. Natividad Med. Ctr., 1985-96, acting chief psychiatry, 1988-89, vice-chair medicine dept., 1991-93, sec.-treas. med. staff, 1992-94; cons. med. staff Salinas Valley Meml. Hosp., 1991—, Mee Meml. Hosp., 1996—; dir. tng. Monterey Psychiat. Health Facility, 1996—, chief clin. staff, 1996—. Editor: The California Psychologist, 1988-95; editor Jour. of Thanatology, 1972-76, Cathexis, 1976-81. Mem. govs. adv. bd. Agnews Devel. Ctr., San Jose, Calif., 1988-96, chair, 1989-91, 94-95. Fellow Am. Bd. Med. Psychotherapists and Psychodiagnosticians (diplomate); mem. APA, Nat. Register Health Svc. Providers in Psychology, Calif. Psychol. Assn. (Disting. Svc. award 1989), Soc. Behavioral Medicine, Mid-Coast Psychol. Assn. (sec. 1985, treas. 1986, pres. 1987, Disting. Svc. to Psychology award 1993). Office: Monterey Psychiat Health 5 Via Joaquin Monterey CA 93940-1611

FINNEGAN, DANIEL, statistician; b. Cleve., Mar. 23, 1949; s. Edward Francis and Mary Gail (Sheppard) F.; m. Patricia Ann Wright, Feb. 19, 1972 (div.); 1 child, Carolyn Beth; m. Judith Watson, Apr. 26, 1997. BA, U. Calif., Berkeley, 1974, MA, 1976, PhD, 1978. Cert. fraud examiner. Instr. U. Calif., Berkeley, 1978-80; divsn. dir. Applied Mgmt. Scis., Washington, 1980-84; pres. Quality Planning, Oakland, Calif., 1984—; sr. staff mem. U.S. Senate, Washington, 1989; founder Qestrel Claims Mgmt.; cons. Office of Pres., U.S. Senate, Depts. of Commerce, Dept. Agr., Dept. Edn., NSF, Washington, 1980—. Author: Statistical Sampling for Non Statisticians, 1982, Statistics and Data Analysis, 1982. Cons. to Disability Rights Edn. and Def. Fund, Berkeley, 1984-90. Mem. Am. Statis. Assn. Office: Quality Planning 350 California St Ste 1760 San Francisco CA 94104-1430

FINNEY, HENRY CHRISTOPHER, artist, educator, writer; b. Springfield, Mass., Sept. 30, 1936; s. Ross Lee and Gretchen L. (Ludke) F.; m. Helen Elizabeth Sherman, June 30, 1961; children: Catherine Deanna, Christopher Anson. BA in Anthropology, U. Mich., 1959, MA in Sociology, 1961; PhD in Sociology, U. Calif., Berkeley, 1967; MFA, Pratt Inst., 1994. Asst. prof. sociology U. Wis., Madison, 1967-73, staff mem. Inst. Rsch. Poverty, 1970-73; assoc. prof. sociology U. Vt., Burlington, 1973-94, acting chmn. sociology dept., 1977; adj. prof. sociology Brigham Young U., Provo, Utah, 1979-80; lectr. MIT, Cambridge, 1990. One-man shows include U. Vt., Burlington, 1981, 1988, Chaffee Art Ctr., Rutland, Vt., 1989, 95, Beside Myself Gallery, Arlington, Vt., 1990, Vt. Coun. on the Arts, Montpelier, 1994, Sante Fe Contemporary Art, 1996; exhibited in juried group shows at Wood Art Gallery, Montpelier, 1988, 89, 90, Stratton (Vt.) Mountain Arts Festival, 1988, Vt. Studio Ctr., 1988, Vt. Women's Caucus for Art, 1989-90, SUNY Mus., Plattsubrg, 1991, Pratt Inst., N.Y.C., 1991, Vt. Coll., Montpelier, 1991, Gallery 128, East Village, N.Y., 1994, Nat. Arts Club, N.Y.C., 1988, Coll. of Santa Fe, 1996, others. NIMH fellow, 1961-65; grantee Wis. Alumni Rsch. Found., 1970-73, Inst. Rsch. Poverty Rsch., 1970-73, U. Vt. faculty, 1974, 90-91, Am. Sociol. Assn., 1975, 78-79. Mem. Am. Sociol. Assn., Coll. Art Assn. Am., Japan Soc. Vt. (bd. dirs. 1984-86), Internat. Sociol. Assn., No. Vt. Artists Assn. (pres., bd. dirs. 1981-85), Soc. for Sci. Study of Religion, Zen Mountain Monastery (bd. dirs. 1984-86, co-founder, bd. dirs. Burlington chpt. 1985-95), Hidden Mount Zen Ctr, Albuquerque, N.Mex., Phi Eta Sigma. Democrat. Buddhist. Unitarian. Home: 35 Barranca Rd Los Alamos NM 87544 Studio: 23 Bank St New York NY 10014-5201

FINNIE, C(LARENCE) HERBERT (HERB FINNIE), aerospace company executive; b. San Marcos, Tex., Feb. 22, 1930; s. Clarence Herbert and Robbie Mary (Hinkle) F.; B.S., S.W. Tex. State U., 1951; M.A., U. Calif.-Berkeley, 1955; M.B.A., U. Santa Clara, 1968; m. Bruna Rebecchi, June 28, 1955; children: Elisa Gene, John Herbert, Mary Lea, Ann Catherine. Bur. chief, disk jockey KCNY, 1950; with Lockheed Missiles & Space Co., Inc., Sunnyvale, Calif., 1958—, supr. computer programming, systems analyst, mgr. software design and devel., advanced systems staff engr. sr; free-lance writer, photographer; pres. Creative Imagineering, Sunnyvale, 1984—; cons. in field. Scriptwriter, announcer, narrator (submarine theater) Aquarena, San Marcos, Tex., 1950-51. Served to Capt. USAF, 1951-58. Mem. Assn. Computing Machinery, Nat. Mgmt. Assn., Pentagon Players (charter), Photog. Soc. Am., Air Force Assn., Nat. Assn. Prok Twangers, Assn. Old Crows, Marquis Club, Alpha Chi, Beta Gamma Sigma, Phi Mu Alpha Sinfonia. Roman Catholic. Designed and developed first generally used compiler prepared for a digital electronic computer (Univac I), computer game package and a universally used tng. system, 1952; original documentation and reference materials deeded to the Smithsonian Institution. Home: 1582 Lewiston Dr Sunnyvale CA 94087-4148 Office: 1111 Lockheed Way Sunnyvale CA 94087-4148

FINNIGAN, DENNIS MICHAEL, management consultant; b. Buffalo, Aug. 10, 1928; s. Charles Marcellus and Marie Florence (Jacobs) F; m. Barbara Ann Pfeiffer, June 16, 1951; children: Cecilia, Eileen, Dennis Jr., Kathy, Margaret, Teresa, Timothy, Kevin, Marie. BA, Stanford U., 1953, postgrad., 1953-54. With IBM Corp., Buffalo, 1949; dept. mgr. Sunsweet Growers, San Jose, Calif., 1949-51; systems analyst Stanford U., Palo Alto, Calif., 1951-53; v.p. SRI Internat., Menlo Park, Calif., 1953-81; pres. D.M. Finnigan Assocs., Los Altos, Calif., 1981—; chmn. bd. dirs. ABB Flakt, Inc., Atlanta, Blenheim, N.V., Rotterdam, The Netherlands. Bd. dirs. Serene Lakes (Calif.) Property Assn., 1980-84. Staff sgt. USAF, 1946-49. Awarded Royal Order of North Star by His Majesty the King of Sweden, 1983. Mem. Swedish-Am. C. of C. (chmn. San Francisco chpt. 1986-88). Republican. Roman Catholic.

FINSTAD, SUZANNE ELAINE, author, producer, lawyer; b. Mpls., Sept. 14, 1955; d. Harold Martin and Elaine Lois (Strom) F. Student, U. Tex., 1973-74; BA in French, U. Houston, 1976, JD, 1980; postgrad., London Sch. Econs., 1980, U. Grenoble, France, 1979. Bar: Tex. 1981. Legal asst. Butler & Binion, Houston, 1976-78, law clerk, 1978-81, assoc., 1982; spl. counsel Ad Litem in the Estate of Howard Hughes Jr., Houston, 1981; mng. ptnr. Finstad & Assoc., Houston, 1990—. Author: Heir Not Apparent, 1984 (Frank Wardlaw award 1984), Ulterior Motives, 1987, Sleeping With the Devil, 1991; Child Bride, 1997; Collaborator: Queen Noor Biography; co-producer: Sleeping With the Devil, CBS, 1997. Recipient Am. Jurisprudence award in criminal law U. Houston, 1979, named to Order of Barons, Bates Coll. Law, 1979-80. Democrat. Office: Joel Gotler Renaissance Agy 8523 W Sunset Blvd West Hollywood CA 90069-2309

FINTON, KENNETH HARPER, writer, producer, publishing executive, literary agent; b. Cleve., Sept. 21, 1942; s. William Kenneth and Doris Maxine (Harper) F.; m. Chaya Thompson, Sept. 22, 1986; stepchildren: Robert, Tasha. Grad., Bus. Sch. for Brokers, Denver, 1983. Staff writer Big Seven Music, N.Y.C., 1970-73; prodr. Atlantic & Roulette Records, N.Y.C., 1970-73; owner Heliotrope Music, Arvada, Co., 1978—, HT Records, 1980—, Heliotrope Comm., 1993—. Author: From Tribes to Nations, 1992; editor, writer, pub. mag. The Plantagenet Connection, 1993—; pub. William Whitley Newsletter, 1992—; prodr. Ghost Towns of Colo., 1991. Mem. Broadcast Music, Inc. Office: Heliotrope Comm PO Box 1401 Arvada CO 80001

FIOCK, SHARI LEE, event planner, design entrepreneur, researcher; b. Weed, Calif., Oct. 25, 1941; d. Webster Bruce and Olevia May (Pruett) F.; m. June 6, 1966 (div. 1974); children—Webster Clinton Pfingsten, Sterling Curtis. Cert. Art Instrn. Sch., Mpls., 1964; pvt. student. Copywriter Darron Assocs., Eugene, Oreg., 1964-66; staff artist Oreg. Holidays, Springfield, 1966-69, part-time 1971; co-owner, designer Artre Enterprises, Eugene, 1969-74; design entrepreneur Shari & Assocs., Yreka, Calif., 1974— (retained as cons., devel. sec. Cascade World Four Season Resort, Siskiyou County, Calif., 1980-86); part time administrv. asst., coord. of regional catalog Great Northern Corp./U.S. Dept. Commerce and Econ. Devel., 1994-96; cons., pres. Reunions, Family, Yreka, 1984—. Designer 5 ton chain saw sculpture, Oreg. Beaver, 1967; author: Goose Gabble, 1992; illustrator: Holiday Fun Book, 1978; author, illustrator Blue Goose Legend, 1995; co-creator Klamath Nat. Forest Interpretive Mus., 1979-91; owner Coyote Pub. Author, illustrator Family Reunions and Clan Gatherings, 1991. Residential capt. United Way, Eugene, 1972; researcher Beaver Ofcl. State Animal, Eugene, 1965-71; counselor Boy Scouts, 1983-91. Mem. Nat. Writers Assn. (founder, pres. Siskiyou chpt., past v.p. State of Jefferson chpt., N.W. rep.). Avocations: family activities; outdoor recreation; travel; theater; music. Home: 406 Walters Ln # 1854 Yreka CA 96097-9704

FIORINO, JOHN WAYNE, podiatrist; b. Charleroi, Pa., Sept. 30, 1946; s. Anthony Raymond and Mary Louise (Caramela) F.; m. Susan K. Bonnett, May 2, 1984; children—Jennifer, Jessica, Lauren, Michael. Student Nassau Coll., 1969-70; B.A. in Biology, U. Buffalo, 1972; Dr. Podiatric Medicine, Ohio Coll. Podiatric Medicine, 1978. Salesman, E. J. Korvettes, Carle Place, N.Y., 1962-65; orderly Nassau Hosp., Mineola, N.Y., 1965-66; operating room technician-trainee heart-lung machine L.I. Jewish-Hillside Med. Center, New Hyde Park, N.Y., 1967-69; pharmacy technician Feinmel's Pharmacy, Roslyn Heights, N.Y., 1969-70; mgr., asst. buyer Fortunoffs, Westbury, N.Y., 1972-73; bd. certified perfusionist L.I. Jewish-Hillside Med. Center, New Hyde Park, N.Y., 1973-74; clin. instr. cardiopulmonary tech. Stony Brook (N.Y.) Univ., 1973-74; operating room technician Cleve. Met. Hosp., 1975; lab. technician Univ. Hosp., Cleve., 1976-78; surg. resident Mesa Gen. Hosp., 1978-79; staff podiatrist, 1979—; pvt. practice podiatry, Mesa, 1979—; staff podiatrist Sacaton (Ariz.) Hosp., 1979—, Mesa Gen. Hosp., 1979, Valley Luth. Hosp., Mesa, 1985, Chandler Community Hosp., 1985, Desert Samaritan Hosp., Mesa, 1986, podiatrist U.S. Govt. Nat. Inst., Sacaton, 1980-87, Indian Health Services, Sacaton, 1980-87; cons. staff Phoenix Indian Med. Ctr., 1985. Served with USN, 1966-67. Mem. Am. Podiatry Assn., Ariz. Podiatry Assn. (treas. 1984-86), Acad. Ambulatory Foot Surgery, Am. Coll. Foot Surgeons (assoc.), Mut. Assn. Profls., Am. Acad. Pain Mgmt. (cert.), Pi Delta, Alpha Gamma Kappa. Home: 2624 W Upland Dr Chandler AZ 85224-7870 Office: 5520 E Main St Mesa AZ 85205-8793

FIRSTENBERG, JEAN PICKER, film institute executive; b. N.Y.C., Mar. 13, 1936; d. Eugene and Sylvia (Moses) Picker; m. Paul Firstenberg, Aug. 9, 1956 (div. July 1980); children—Debra, Douglas. BS summa cum laude, Boston U., 1958. Asst. producer Altman Prodns., Washington, 1965-66; media advisor J. Walter Thompson, N.Y.C., 1969-72; asst. for spl. projects Princeton (N.J.) U., 1972-74, dir. publs., 1974-76; program officer Markle Found., N.Y.C., 1976-80; dir. Am. Film Inst., L.A., Washington, 1980—; mem. com. L.A. Task Force on Arts; former chmn. nat. adv. bd. Peabody Broadcasting Awards; bd. dirs. Trans-Lux Corp. Former trustee Boston U.; mem. adv. bd. Will Rogers Inst., N.Y.C., Big Sisters of Los Angeles; bd. dirs. Variety Club of Calif., Los Angeles; chmn., bd. advisors Film Dept. N.C. Sch. of Arts. Recipient Alumni award for disting. service to profession Boston U., 1982; seminar and prodn. chairs at directing workshop for women named in her honor Am. Film Inst., 1986. Mem. Women in Film (Los Angeles and Washington, Crystal award 1990), Trusteeship for Betterment of Women, Acad. Motion Picture Arts and Scis. Office: Am Film Inst 2021 N Western Ave PO Box 27999 Los Angeles CA 90027 also: Am Film Inst Kennedy Ctr Performing Washington DC 20056

FISCHER, DALE SUSAN, lawyer; b. East Orange, N.J., Oct. 17, 1951; d. Edward L. and Audrey (Tenner) F. Student Dickinson Coll., 1969-70; BA magna cum laude, U. So. Fla., 1977; JD, Harvard U., 1980. Bar: Calif. 1980. Assoc. Kindel & Anderson, L.L.P., L.A., 1980-96, Heller Ehrman White & McAuliffe, L.A., 1996-97; judge L.A. Mcpl. Ct., 1997—; faculty Nat. Inst. Trial Advocacy; lawyer in classroom Constl. Rights Found.; moderator, panelist How to Win Your Case with Depositions. Mem. ABA, Am. Arbitration Assn. (panel arbitrators), Los Angeles County Bar Assn., L.A. Complex Litigation Inn of Ct. (pres.-elect, sec.-treas.). Office: L A Mcpl Ct 110 N Grand Ave Los Angeles CA 90012

FISCHER, EDMOND HENRI, biochemistry educator; b. Shanghai, Republic of China, Apr. 6, 1920; came to U.S., 1953; s. Oscar and Renée (Tapernoux) F.; m. Beverley B. Bullock. Lic. es Sciences Chimiques et Biologiques, U. Geneva, 1943, Diplome d'Ingenieur Chimiste, 1944, PhD, 1947; D (hon.), U. Montpellier, France, 1985, U. Basel, Switzerland, 1988, Med. Coll. of Ohio, 1993, Ind. U., 1993, U. Bochum, Germany, 1994. Pvt. docent biochemistry U. Geneva, 1950-53; research assoc. biology Calif. Inst. Tech., Pasadena, 1953; asst. prof. biochemistry U. Wash., Seattle, 1953-56, assoc. prof., 1956-61, prof., 1961-90, prof. emeritus, 1990—; mem. exec. com. Pacific Slope Biochem. Conf., 1958-59, pres., 1975; mem. biochemistry study sect. NIH, 1959-64, symposium co-chmn. Battelle Seattle Rsch. Ctr., 1970, 73, 78; mem. sci. adv. bd. Biozentrum, U. Basel, Switzerland, 1982-86; mem. sci. adv. bd. Friedrich Miescher Inst., Ciba-Geigy, Basel, 1976-84, chmn., 1981-84; mem. bd. sci. govs. Scripps Rsch. Inst., La Jolla, Calif., 1987—, Basil Inst. for Immunology, 1996—. Contbr. numerous articles to sci. jours. Mem. sci. council on basic sci. Am. Heart Assn., 1977-80, sci. adv. com. Muscular Dystrophy Assn., 1980-88. Recipient Lederle Med. Faculty award, 1956-59, Guggenheim Found. award, 1963-64, Disting. Lectr. award U. Wash., 1983, Laureate Passano Found. award, 1988, Steven C. Beering award, 1991, Nobel prize in Physiology or Medicine, 1992. Fellow Am. Acad. Arts and Scis.; mem. NAS, AAAS, AAUP, Am. Soc. Biol. Chemists (coun. 1989-93), Am. Chem. Soc. (adv. bd. biochemistry divsn. 1962, exec. com. divsn. biology 1969-72, monograph adv. bd. 1971-73, editl. adv. bd. Biochemistry, 1961-66, assoc. editor 1966-91), Swiss Chem. Soc. (Werner medal), Spanish Royal Acad. Scis. (fgn. assoc.), Venice Inst. Sci., Arts and Letters (fgn. assoc.), Japanese Biochem. Soc. (hon.). Office: U Washington Med Sch Box 357350 Seattle WA 98195-7350

FISCHER, FRED WALTER, physicist, engineer, educator; b. Zwickau, Germany, June 26, 1922; s. Fritz and Louiska (Richter) F.; B.S. in Mech. Engring., Columbia U., 1949, M.S., 1950; M.S. in Physics, U. Wash., 1957; Dr.Engr. in Elec. Engring., Tech. U. Munich, 1966; m. Yongja Kim, Oct. 1, 1970. Analyst, Boeing Co., Seattle, Munich, Bonn, W. Ger., 1950-84; cons. Boeing Co., 1984-88; owner Fischer Cons.; instr. physics, math., and engring. North Seattle Community Coll., 1973-93. Author: Analysis for Physics and Engineering, 1982, Renaissance Mathematics, 1992. 1st v.p. Wedgwood Cmty. Coun.; mem. Wedgwood Elem. Sch. Site Coun.; bd. mem. Seattle sect. Mercedes Benz Club Am. Served with AUS, 1943-46. Boeing scholar, Max Planck Inst. Plasma Physics, Munich, 1964-65. Mem. N.Y. Acad. Scis., Sigma Xi (life). Office: North Seattle CC 9600 College Way N Seattle WA 98103-3599

FISCHER, JOEL, social work educator; b. Chgo., Apr. 22, 1939; s. Sam and Ruth (Feiges) F.; m. Renee H. Furuyama; children: Lisa, Nicole. BS, U. Ill., 1961, MSW, 1964; D in Social Welfare, U. Calif., Berkeley, 1970. Prof. sch. social work U. Hawaii, Honolulu, 1970—; vis. prof. George Warren Brown Sch. Social Work, Washington U., St. Louis, 1977, U. Wis. Sch. Social Welfare, Milw., 1978-79, U. Natal, South Africa, 1982, U. Hong Kong, 1986; cons. various orgns. and univs. Author: (with Harvey L. Gochros) Planned Behavior Change: Behavior Modification in Social Work, 1973, Handbook of Behavior Therapy with Sexual Problems, vol. I, 1977, vol. II, 1977, Analyzing Research, 1975, Interpersonal Helping: Emerging Approaches for Social Work Practice, 1973, The Effectiveness of Social Casework, 1976, (with D. Sanders and O. Kurrem) Fundamentals of Social Work Practice, 1982, Effective Casework Practice: An Eclectic Approach, 1978, (with H. Gochros) Treat Yourself to a Better Sex Life, 1980, (with H. Gochros and J. Gochros) Helping the Sexually Oppressed, 1985, (with Martin Bloom) Evaluating Practice: Guidlines for the Helping Professional, 1982, (with Kevin Corcoran) Measures for Clinical Practice, 1987, (with Daniel Sanders) Visions for the Future: Social Work and Pacific-Asian Perspectives, 1988, (with Martin Bloom and John Orme) Evaluating Practice, 2nd edit., 1995, (with Kevin Corcoran) Measures for Clinical Practice, 2nd edit., vol. 1, 1994, Families, Children, vol. 2, 1994, Adults, 1994, East-West Connections: Social Work Practice Traditions and Change, 1992; mem. editl. bd. 12 profl. jours.; contbr. over 150 articles, revs., chpts. and papers to profl. jours. With U.S. Army, 1958. Mem. Hawaii Com. for Africa, Nat. Assn. Social Workers, Coun. Social Work Edn., Acad. Cert. Social Workers, Nat. Conf. Social Welfare, AAUP, Unity Organizing Com., Hawaii People's Legis. Coalition, Bertha Reynold Soc. Democrat. Home: 1371-4 Hunakai St Honolulu HI 96816 Office: U Hawaii 2500 Campus Rd Honolulu HI 96822-2217

FISCHER, MARY E., special education educator; b. Kansas City, Mo., July 7, 1948; d. Tom Earl and Sue Turner (Fitts) Walker; m. Timothy Montgomery Fischer, Sept. 4, 1971; children: Ethan David, Elizabeth Louise. AB, U. Mo., 1971; MSE, Cen. Mo. State U., Warrensburg, 1981; PhD, U. Wash., 1997. Occupational therapy asst. Children's Therapy Ctr., 1971-73, tchr., 1976-78, psychometrist, 1978-79; program coord. United Cerebral Palsy, Camp Wonderland, Lake of the Ozarks, Mo., 1983; developmental presch. tchr. Children's Therapy Ctr., 1979-84, 75-76; project assoc. Early Childhood Follow Along Study, U. Wash., 1985-87; rsch. assoc. U. Wash., 1987-88; project assoc. Rsch. and Evaluation Network, U. Wash.,

1989; project mgr. ChildFind project, Child Devel./Mental Retardation Ctr., Seattle, 1989-90; project coord. N.W. Insvc. Coop. for Transdisciplinary Teams U. Wash., Seattle, 1990-93; project coord. Choices, 1992-95; regional dir. Ctr. for Supportive Edn., Seattle, 1994—; sys. change coord. Wash. Statewide Sys. Change project, 1993-94. Contbr. articles to profl. jours. Mem. ASCD, Nat. Assn. Edn. Young Children, Coun. for Exceptional Children, The Assn. for Persons with Severe Handicaps, Wash. Assn. for Persons with Severe Handicaps, Wash. State Staff Devel. Assn., Phi Kappa Phi, Pi Lambda Theta (named Outstanding mem. 1990). Home: 3539 NE 113th St Seattle WA 98125-5739

FISCHER, MICHAEL LUDWIG, environmental executive; b. Dubuque, Iowa, May 29, 1940; s. Carl Michael and Therese Marie (Stadler) F.; m. Jane Pughe Rogers; children: Christina Marie, Steven Michael. BA in Polit. Sci., Santa Clara U., 1964; M in City and Regional Planning, U. Calif., Berkeley, 1967; grad. exec. program in environ. mgmt., Harvard U., 1980. Planner City of Mountain View, Calif., 1960-65; assoc. Bay Area Govts., 1966-67; planner County of San Mateo, Calif., 1967-69; assoc. dir. San Francisco Planning and Urban Rsch. Assn., nonprofit civc orgn., 1969-73; exec. dir. North Cen. region Calif. Coastal Zone Conservation Commn., San Rafael, 1973-76; chief dep. dir. Gov.'s Office Planning and Rsch., Sacramento, 1976-78; exec. dir. Calif. Coastal Commn., San Francisco, 1978-85; sr. assoc. Sedway Cooke Assocs., environ. cons., San Francisco, 1985-87; exec. dir. Sierra Club, San Francisco, 1987-93; resident fellow John F. Kennedy Sch. Govt., Inst. Politics, Harvard U., Cambridge, Mass., 1993; sr. cons. Natural Resources Def. Coun., San Francisco, 1993—; exec. officer Calif. Coastal Conservancy, Oakland, 1994—; lectr. dept. city and regional planning U. Calif., Berkeley, 1984; chairperson environ. com. adv. coun. Calvert Social Investment Fund, 1989—; mem. Harvard Commn. Global Change Info. Policy, 1993—; pres., chmn. bd. dirs. Yosemite Restoration Trust, 1994—, chairperson adv. coun., 1991-94; mem. com. on impact of maritime facility devel. NAS/NRC, 1975-78; founding bd. dirs. EDGE, 1991-93. Co-author Calif. state plan, An Urban Strategy for Calif., 1978, Building a New Municipal Railway, 1973, Oral History, Coastal Commn. Yrs., 1973-85, Oral History, Sierra Club Yrs., 1987-93; author intro. Ansel Adams: Yosemite, 1995; contbr. papers to profl. publs. Recipient Life Achievement award Assn. Environ. Profls., 1986, Disting. Leadership award. Am. Soc. Pub. Adminstrn., 1987, Outstanding Nat. Leadership award Coastal States Orgn., 1990. Mem. Nat. Resources Def. Coun., 1000 Friends of Fla., Calif. Planning and Conservation League (bd. dirs. 1970-76), The Oceanic Soc. (bd. dirs. 1983-88), Sierra Club, Friends of the Earth (bd. dirs. 1988-94), League for Coastal Protection, Save San Francisco Bay Assn., Am. Youth Hostels, Inc. (bd. dirs. 1985-87), Lambda Alpha. Office: Calif Coastal Conservancy 1100 1330 Broadway Oakland CA 94612-2503

FISCHER, ROBERT EDWARD, meteorologist; b. Bethlehem, Pa., Aug. 4, 1943; s. Frederic Philip and Muriel Winifred (Johnson) F. BS cum laude, U. Utah, 1966; MS, Colo. State U., 1969. Meteorologist Nat. Weather Svc., Fairbanks, Alaska, 1973—. Contbr. articles to profl. jours. Vol. classical music program prodr. Sta. KUAC-FM, Fairbanks. Recipient Nat. Oceanic and Atmospheric Adminstrn. Unit citation, 1989. Fellow Royal Meteorol. Soc.; mem. Am. Meteorol. Soc. (Charles L. Mitchell award 1985), Nat. Weather Assn. (Outstanding Operational Performance award 1987), Assn. Lunar and Planetary Observers, Am. Assn. Variable Star Observers, Royal Astron. Soc. Can., Sigma Xi, Phi Kappa Phi. Home: PO Box 82210 Fairbanks AK 99708-2210 Office: Nat Weather Service Forecast Office 101 12th Ave Ste 12 Fairbanks AK 99701-6236

FISCHER, ZOE ANN, real estate and property marketing company executive, real estate consultant; b. L.A., Aug. 26, 1939; d. George and Marguerite (Carrasco) Routsos; m. Douglas Clare Fischer, Aug. 6, 1960 (div. 1970); children: Brent Sean Cecil, Tahlia Georgienne Marguerite Bianca. BFA in Design, UCLA, 1964. Pres. Zoe Antiques, Beverly Hills, Calif., 1973—; v.p. Harleigh Sandler Real Estate Corp. (now Prudential-Jon Douglas), 1980-81; exec. v.p. Coast to Coast Real Estate & Land Devel. Corp., Century City, Calif., 1981-83; pres. New Market Devel., Inc., Beverly Hills, 1983—; dir. mktg. Mirabella, L.A., 1983, Autumn Pointe, L.A., 1983-84, Desert Hills, Antelope Valley, Calif., 1984-85; cons. Lowe Corp., L.A., 1985. Designer interior and exterior archtl. enhancements and remodelling; designed album cover for Clare Fischer Orch. (Grammy award nomination 1962). Soprano Roger Wagner Choir, UCLA, 1963-64. Mem. UCLA Alumni Assn. Democrat. Roman Catholic. Avocations: skiing, designing jewelry, interior, landscape and new home design, antique collecting.

FISCHLE, DANIEL KARL, school system administrator; b. North Tonawanda, N.Y., May 24, 1944; s. Edward Karl and Jane (Kendall) F.; m. Linda Reh Owen, June 12, 1981 (dec.); children: Gretchen Danielle, Rebecca Reh. BA in History and Polit. Sci., Calif. State U.-Stanislaus, Turlock, 1966, MA in History, 1972. Cert. tchr., ednl. adminstr., Calif. Tchr. Turlock Union H.S. Dist., 1967-69; tchr. Selma (Calif.) Unified Sch. Dist., 1971-73, asst. H.S. prin., 1973-80; adminstrv. cons. Fresno (Calif.) County Office Edn., 1980-81; prin. Kerman (Calif.) Union H.S., 1981-83; asst. supt. Kerman Unified Sch. Dist., 1983-87, dep. supt., 1987—; bd. dirs. Ednl. Employees Credit Union, 1995—, vice chair, 1996—; mem. supervisory com., 1988-95, chair, 1992-95. Photographer: (book) Sentenial, 1966. Pres. Peace Luth. Ch., Fresno, 1982-85; bd. dirs. Calif. Assn. Dirs. of Activities, 1974-76, Fresno County Adminstrs. Assn., 1980-84, Region IX Assn. Calif. Adminstrs., 1988-93. Mem. Am.-Hellenic Edn. Progressive Assn., Kiwanis (pres. 1985-86). Republican. Office: Kerman Unified Sch Dist 151 S 1st St Kerman CA 93630-1029

FISETTE, SCOTT MICHAEL, golf course designer; b. Orange, Tex., May 17, 1963; s. Roderick John and Addie Faye (Byrnes) F.; divorced; 1 child, Shane Roderick. BS in Landscape Architecture, Tex. A&M U., 1985. Registered landscape architect, Tex., Hawaii, Commonwealth of No. Mariana Islands. Project architect Dick Nugent Assocs., Long Grove, Ill., 1985-90; prin., pres. Fisette Golf Designs, Kaneohe, Hawaii, 1991—. Mem. Golf Course Supts. Assn. Am., Am. Soc. Landscape Architects, Nat. Golf Found., Hawaii Turf Grass Assn. (bd. dirs. 1991—), Donald Ross Soc. Office: Fisette Golf Designs PO Box 1433 Kaneohe HI 96744-1433

FISH, BARBARA JOAN, investor, small business owner; b. Seattle, June 12, 1936; d. George Francis Linehan and Maureece Shirley (Frederick) McCullough; m. Ralph Edwin Fish, July 14, 1956 (dec. Nov. 1986). Grad. high sch., Portland, Oreg. Owner Sea and Sand R.V. Park, Depoe Bay, Oreg., 1977—; real estate investor State of Oreg. Active St. Augustine's Ch. Mem. Lincoln City C. of C., Depoe Bay C. of C. Republican. Roman Catholic. Home and Office: Sea and Sand RV Park 4985 N Highway 101 Depoe Bay OR 97341-9740

FISH, RUBY MAE BERTRAM (MRS. FREDERICK GOODRICH FISH), civic worker; b. Sheridan, Wyo., July 24, 1918; d. Ryan Lawrence and Ruby (Beckwith) Bertram; R.N., St. Luke's Hosp., 1936; postgrad. Washington U., St. Louis, 1941; m. Frederick Goodrich Fish, Apr. 12, 1942; children: Bertram Frederick, Lisbeth Ann Fish Kalstein. Staff nurse Huntington Meml. Hosp., Pasadena, Calif., 1941-42; dr.'s office nurse, Denver, 1943-44; travel cons. Buckingham Travel Agy., Aurora, Colo., 1976—. Bd. dirs. Jefferson County Easter Seal Soc., 1949—, pres., 1952-53, 56-57, 66-67; pres. Colo. Easter Seal Soc., 1960-61; bd. dirs. Nat. Easter Seal Soc., 1968-69, sec. ho. of dels., 1976-77; bd. dirs. Assistance League Denver, 1968-70, 75-76, People to People for Handicapped, 1981— (Vol. of Yr. award 1991); mem. Pres.'s Com. on Employing Handicapped, 1976—; active Rehab. Internat. of U.S.A., 1972—, Rehab. Internat., 1960—. Mem. Dau. Nile-El Mejedel. Home: 6900 W Stetson Pl # 3 Littleton CO 80123-1331 Office: 13741 E Mississippi Ave Aurora CO 80012-3628

FISHBACK, PRICE VANMETER, economics educator; b. Louisville, July 8, 1955; s. William Vanmeter and Frances Henry (Taylor) F.; m Pamela Elaine Slaten, June 9, 1989. BA, Butler U., 1977; MA, U. Washington, 1979, PhD, 1983. Econ. cons. Weyerhaeuser Co., Federal Way, Wash., 1980-81; asst. prof. U. Ga., Athens, 1982-86, assoc. prof., 1987-90; assoc. prof. U. Ariz., Tucson, 1990-93; prof. U. Ariz., 1993—; rsch. assoc. Nat. Bur. Econ. Rsch., 1994—; vis. prof. U. Tex., Austin, 1987-89. Author: Soft Coal, Hard Choices: The Economic Welfare of Bituminous Coal Miners, 1890-1930, 1992; contbr. articles to profl. jours. Rsch. grantee U. Ga. Found., 1985, Earhart Found., 1988, 92, 96, Bradley Found., 1989, NSF, 1993-95. Office: U Ariz Econs Dept Tucson AZ 85721

FISHER, ALAN STEPHEN, physicist; b. Toronto, Ont., Can., Aug. 13, 1953; s. Ralph and Edith Molly (Kruger) F.; m. Barbara Rose Sommer, June 10, 1979. SB in Physics, MIT, 1974, SB in Elec. Engring., 1974, PhD in Physics, 1983. Research assoc. MIT, Cambridge, 1983; sr. scientist research div. Raytheon Corp., Lexington, Mass., 1983-84; research assoc. elec. engring. dept. Stanford (Calif.) U., 1985-89; assoc. physicist Brookhaven Nat. Lab., Upton, N.Y., 1989-94; physicist Stanford (Calif.) Linear Accelerator Ctr., Stanford U., 1994—. Contbr. articles to profl. jours. Mem. AAAS, IEEE, Am. Phys. Soc., Phi Beta Kappa, Sigma Xi. Office: Stanford Linear Accelerator Ctr PO Box 4349 Mail Stop 17 Stanford CA 94309

FISHER, ANN L., pro tem judge; b. Reading, Pa., Mar. 31, 1948; d. William E. and Florence (Makowiecki) Lewis; m. Donald E. Fisher, Dec. 27, 1965 (div. July 1986); children: Caroline E., Catherine E.; m. David H. DeBlasio, May 28, 1988; 1 child, Michael Joseph DeBlasio. BS in Liberal Studies, Oreg. State U., 1975; JD, Willamette U., 1983. Bar: Oreg. 1984, U.S. Dist. Ct. Oreg. 1984, U.S. Ct. Appeals (9th cir.) 1984, Wash. 1987, U.S. Dist. Ct. (we. dist.) Wash. 1987, U.S. Dist. Ct. (ea. dist.) Wash. 1996, U.S. Ct. Appeals (fed. cir.) 1996. Atty. Spears, Lubersky, Portland, Oreg., 1983-85, Greene & Markley, Portland, Oreg., 1985-89; asst. gen. counsel Portland GE, 1989-94; atty. Schwabe, Williamson & Wyatt, Portland, 1994-96; founder Ann L. Fisher Legal Consulting Svcs., Portland, 1996—; protem judge Multnomah County Ct., Portland, 1995—. Contbg. author: (treatise) ABA Year in Review, 1994, 95. Mem. ABA, Wash. State Bar Assn., Oreg. State Bar Assn. (ins. and bar sponsored program com. 1985-87, sec. 1986-87, chmn. 1987-88, MCLE bd. 1991-94, sec. 1992-93, chmn. 1993-94, Disciplinary Bd. Region 5 1991-96, chair 1996), Multnomah Bar Assn. (membership com. 1987-91, The Multnomah Lawyer publ. com. 1994-96, chair 1995-96), Fed. Energy Bar Assn. (electric utility regulation com. 1996—), Fed. Bar Assn., Sect. of Natural Resources, Energy and Environ. Law (vice chair electric power com., vice chair gas pipelines com., spkr. corporate ethics 1993-95), Gus Solomon Inns of Ct.

FISHER, BARRY ALAN JOEL, protective services official; b. N.Y.C., Sept. 11, 1944; s. George and Pearl (Newman) F.; m. Susan Joan Saperstein, Dec. 29, 1968; children: David, Michael. BS, CCNY, 1966; MS, Purdue U., 1969; MBA, Calif. State U., Northridge, 1973. With criminalistics lab. L.A. County Sheriff's Dept., 1969-79, chief sheriff's criminalistics lab., 1979-86, dir. Sci. Svcs. Bur., 1986—; lectr. U. Calif., L.A.; adj. lectr. Calif. State U., 1996. Fellow Am Acad. Forensic Scis. (co-chmn. local arrangements com. 1981, chmn., sec. criminalistics sect. program 1981-82, sec.t chmn. 1982-83, chmn. local arrangements com. 1991, chmn. sect. 1995—, pres. elect 1997—); mem. Am. Soc. Crime Lab. Dirs. (chmn. foresnsic sci. ops. and program com. 1982-86, bd. dirs. 1986-89, pres. elect 1987-88, pres. 1988-89, editor newsletter 1989-90), Forensic Sci. Found. (bd. dirs. 1985—, sec. 1988—), Forensic Sci. Soc., Internat. Assn. of Identification, Internat. Assn. of Chiefs of Police, Internat. Assn. Forensic Scis. (pres. 1996—). Republican. Jewish. Office: LA County Sheriffs Crime Lab 2020 Beverly Blvd Los Angeles CA 90057-2404

FISHER, BRUCE DAVID, elementary school educator; b. Long Beach, Calif., Dec. 24, 1949; s. Oran Wilfred and Irene (May) F.; m. Mindi Beth Evans, Aug. 15, 1976; 1 child, Jenny Allison Viola. BA, Humboldt State U., 1975, standard elem. credential, 1976, learning handicapped credential, 1977. Instrnl. svcs. specialist Blue Lake (Calif.) Elem. Sch.; resource specialist Fortuna (Calif.) Union Sch. Dist., tchr. 3d grade, tchr. 5th grade, 1988—; prof. Humbold State U., 1996—; sci. cons. Pitsco, 1995; cons. Newton's Apple, 1995-97, NASA, 1995; site leader tchr., curriculum writer Calif. Sci. Internet, 1995-97; mem. J.P.L./NASA/Johns Hopkins U. Core Curriculum Devel. Team Project KidSat and CASOE. Vice chmn. Tchrs. Edn. and Cmty. Helpers, Arcata, Calif., 1990—; v.p. Sequoia Pk. Zool. Soc., Eureka, 1989-90, chmn. Whale Fair, 1989—; mem. selection com. Christa McAuliffe Fellowship; bd. dirs. Redwood Environ. Edn. Fair, Eureka, 1990—, Family Wellness Project, 1991; apptd. to Calif. Curriculum and Supplemental Materials Commn.; commr. Calif. Curriculum Commn., 1992-95; chairperson math. assessment Calif. Dept. Edn., 1995; cons. PITSCO Sci., 1995, NASA/JPL, 1995-97; mem. NASA/JPL and Johns Hopkins U. CORE Curriculum Devel. Team, 1995-96; lead tchr. KidSat and CASDE projects Calif. Sci. Internat. Site. Named Calif. Tchr. of Yr. Dept. Edn., 1991, Favorite Tchrs. ABC-TV, 1991, Humboldt County Tchr. of Yr., 1991; recipient Leadership Excellence award Calif. Assn. Sci. Specialists, 1990, Masonic Meritorious Svc. award for Pub. Edn., 1991, Profl. Best Leadership award Learning Mag., Oldsmobile Corp., and Mich. State U., 1991, Nat. Educator award Miliken Found. Calif. State Dept. Edn., 1991, NASA/NSTA Newest award, 1993, Newton's Apple Multimedia Inst., 1995, Lifetime Achievement award Humboldt County Bd. Edn., 1996. Mem. Calif. Tchrs. Assn., Calif. Sci. Tchrs. Assn., Calif. Assn. Health, Phys. Edn., Recreation, and Dance. Democrat. Home: 4810 14th St Arcata CA 95521-9778 Office: Fortuna Elem Sch 843 L St Fortuna CA 95540-1921

FISHER, DANIEL RUSSELL, banker, lawyer; b. Red Bank, N.J., Feb. 16, 1960; s. Clarkson and Mae (Hoffmann) F. BA cum laude, Villanova U., 1982; JD, Seton Hall U., 1991. Asst. dir. circulation Ziff-Davis Pub. Co., N.Y.C., 1982-83; mng. editor Spencer Publs., Spring Lake, N.J., 1983-86; trust officer J.P. Morgan & Co., N.Y.c., 1985-89; asst. treas. Chem. Bank, N.Y.C., 1989; v.p., sales mgr. Chase Manhattan Bank, N.Y.C. and Beverly Hills, Calif., 1989-95, Bank One Corp., Phoenix, 1995—. Author: (screenplays) American Standard, Facing Mecca, 1994; contbr. articles to newspaper. Vol. ARC, Santa Monica, Calif., 1994, Starlight Found., N.Y.C., 1992—; bd. dirs. Literacy Vols. of Maricopa County, Ariz., 1996. Mem. Am. Bankers Assn., SAG, AFTRA. Democrat. Roman Catholic. Home: 6763 E Evans Dr Scottsdale AZ 85254 Office: Bank One 201 N Central Ave Phoenix AZ 85073

FISHER, DAVID CARL, telecommunications company executive; b. Odessa, Tex., Aug. 10, 1963; s. Dale Jackson and Clarice (Gulley) F.; life partner Marc Allen Sobul, June 30, 1990. BS in Microbiology, Tex. Tech. U., 1985, BA in Psychology, 1986, MBA, 1989. Spl. asst. to v.p. fin. Tex. Tech. U., Lubbock, 1988-89; mgmt. devel. assoc. GTE, Stamford, Conn., 1989-91; area adminstr. cmty. devel. GTE, Thousand Oaks, Calif., regional mgr. cmty. econ. devel., regional mgr. local govt. and cmty. affairs. Bd. dirs. L.A. County Econ. Devel. Corp., Think Earth, L.A., L.A. Gay and Lesbian Ctr.; bd. dirs., comm. chair So. Calif. Telecom. Partnership, L.A.; bd. govs. Human Rights Campaign, Washington, dinner chair, 1995, 96; mem. West Hollywood (Calif.) Adv. Coun. Named to Outstanding Young Men in Am., 1988. Mem. Am. Econ. Devel. Coun., Calif. Assn. Local Econ. Devel. Democrat.

FISHER, DELBERT ARTHUR, physician, educator; b. Placerville, Calif., Aug. 12, 1928; s. Arthur Lloyd and Thelma (Johnson) F.; m. Beverly Carne Fisher, Jan. 28, 1951; children: David Arthur, Thomas Martin, Mary Kathryn. BA, U. Calif., Berkeley, 1950; MD, U. Calif., San Francisco, 1953. Diplomate Am. Bd. Pediatrics. Intern, resident in pediatrics U. Calif. Med. Center, San Francisco, 1953-55; resident in pediatrics U. Oreg. Hosp., Portland, 1957-58; from asst. prof. to assoc. prof. pediatrics Med. Sch. U. Ark., Little Rock, 1960-67, prof. pediatrics, 1967-68; prof. pediatrics UCLA, 1968-73; prof. pediatrics and medicine Med. Sch., UCLA, 1973-91, prof. emeritus, 1991—; chief, pediatric endocrinology Harbor-UCLA Med. Ctr., 1968-73, rsch. prof. devel. and perinatal biology, 1975-85, chmn. pediatrics, 1985-89, sr. scientist Rsch. and Edn. Inst., 1991—; dir. Walter Martin Rsch. Ctr., 1986-91; pres. Nichols Inst. Reference Labs, 1991-93, pres. Acad. Assocs., chief sci. officer; pres. acad. assocs., chief sci. officer Quest Diagnostics-Nichols Inst., 1997—; cons. genetic disease sect. Calif. Dept. Health Svcs., 1978—; mem. organizing com. Internat. Conf. Newborn Thyroid Screening, 1977-88; examiner Am. Bd. Pediatrics, 1971-80, mem. subcom. on pediatric endocrinology, 1976-79. Co-editor: Pediatric Thyroidology, 1985, five other books; editor-in-chief Jour. Clin. Endocrinology and Metabolism, 1978-83, Pediatric Rsch., 1984-89; contbr. chpts. to numerous books; contbr. over 400 articles to profl. jours. Capt. M.C., USAF, 1955-57. Recipient Career Devel. award NIH, 1964-68. Mem. Inst. Medicine NAS, Am. Acad. Pediatrics (Borden award 1981), Soc. Pediatric Rsch. (v.p. 1973-74), Am. Pediatric Soc. (pres. 1992-93), Endocrine Soc. (pres. 1983-84), Am. Thyroid Assn. (pres. 1988-89), Am. Soc. Clin. Investigation, Assn. Am. Physicians, Lawson Wilkins Pediatric Endocrine Soc. (pres. 1982-83), Western Soc. Pediatric Rsch. (pres. 1983-84), Phi Beta Kappa, Alpha Omega Alpha. Home: 24582 Santa Clara Ave Dana Point CA 92629-3031 Office: Quest Diagnostics-Nichols Inst 33608 Ortega Hwy San Juan Capistrano CA 92675-2042

FISHER, DONALD G., casual apparel chain stores executive; b. 1928; married. B.S., U. Calif., 1950. With M. Fisher & Son, 1950-57; former ptnr. Fisher Property Investment Co.; co-founder, pres. The Gap Stores Inc., San Bruno, Calif., dir., now chmn., CEO. Office: The Gap Stores 1 Harrison St San Francisco CA 94105-1602*

FISHER, EARL MONTY, utilities executive; b. Chgo., June 26, 1938; s. Harry George and Fannie (Feinberg) F.; m. Joyce Leah Bender, Mar. 14, 1959 (div. Dec. 1978); children: Jan Carol, Wendy Robin; m. Teri Jean Janssen, Jan. 27, 1979. Student, La. Trade Tech. Coll., 1961. Apprentice and journeyman Comfort Air Refrigeration Corp., L.A., 1955-64; contractor Bonanza Air Conditioning and Refrigeration Corp., Van Nuys, Calif., 1964—. Bd. dirs. Hidden Hills (Calif.) Homeowners Assn., 1982-84, vice chmn., v.p., 1990; chmn. Hidden Hills Rds. Com., 1984-85, Hidden Hills Gate Ops. Commn., 1988-91; commr. emergency svcs. City of Hidden Hills, 1986—; pres. Hidden Hills Cmty. Assn., 1991-93; mem. Hidden Hills City Coun., 1994; mayor, Hidden Hills, 1996. Mem. Air Conditioning Sheet Metal Assn. (vice chmn. 1994-96, dir. 1996—). Democrat. Office: Bonanza Air Conditioning Heating & Refrigeration Corp 7653 Burnet Ave Van Nuys CA 91405-1006

FISHER, FREDERICK HENDRICK, retired oceanographer; b. Aberdeen, Wash., Dec. 30, 1926; s. Sam (Sverre) and Astrid K. Fisher; m. Julie Gay Saund, June 17, 1955 (dec. 1993); children: Bruce Allen, Mark Edward, Keith Russell, Glen Michael; m. Shirley Mercedes Lippert, Oct. 10, 1994. BS, U. Wash., 1949, PhD, 1957. Rsch. asst. UCLA, 1954-55; rsch. fellow acoustics Harvard, 1957-58; rsch. physicist, rsch. oceanographer Marine Phys. Lab., Scripps Instn. Oceanography, La Jolla, Calif., 1958-91, assoc. dir., 1975-87, dep. dir., 1987-93, acting assoc. dir., 1993-94; ret., 1994; dir. rsch. Havens Industries, San Diego, 1963-64; prof., chmn. dept. physics U. R.I., Kingston, 1970-71; mem. governing bd. Am. Inst. Physics, 1984-90. Editor IEEE Jour. Oceanic Engring., 1988-91. Mem. San Diego County Dem. Cen. Com., 1956-57, 60-62. NCAA nat. tennis doubles champion, 1949; named to U. Wash. Athletic Hall of Fame, 1989; recipient Disting. Svc. award IEEE Oceanic Enging. Soc., 1991, Disting. Tech. Achievement award, 1996. Midshipman U.S. Naval Acad., 1945-47; with USNR, 1945. Fellow Acoustical Soc. Am. (assoc. editor jour. 1969-76, v.p. 1980-81, pres. 1983-84, Am.'s Finest Acousticians award San Diego chpt. 1997); mem. IEEE (sr., editor Jour. of Oceanic Engring. 1988-91), Marine Tech. Soc., Am. Geophys. Union, The Oceanographic Soc., Seattle Tennis Club. Codesigner ocean research platform FLIP, 355' long manned spar buoy with 300' draft in vertical position, 1960-62. Home: 5034 Park West Ave San Diego CA 92117-1046

FISHER, JOSEPH STEWART, management consultant; b. Athens, Pa., Mar. 3, 1933; s. Samuel Royer and Agnes Corinne (Smith) F.; m. Anita Ann Coyle, May 15, 1954; 1 child, Samuel Royer. BS in Tech. Mgmt., Regis U., 1981; postgrad., U. Colo., 1986-87, Iliff Sch. Theology, 1988-89. Field engr. IBM Corp., Syracuse, N.Y., 1956-60; quality analyst, engr. IBM Corp., Endicott, N.Y., 1960-68; systems support adminstr. IBM Corp., Boulder, Colo., 1968-72, field support adminstr., 1972-78, systems assurance adminstr., 1978-79, security adminstr., 1979-87; sec. cons. Fisher Enterprises, Boulder, 1975—; bd. dirs. Vervcraft Inc., Loveland, Colo., Lexicon Med. Tech., Inc., 1993-95. Leadership devel. Boy Scouts Am., 1975—, chmn. long range planning, 1982-86, chaplain, 1991—; bd. dirs. Longs Peak Coun., 1983-87, Colo. Crime Stoppers, 1983-88; exec. dir. Caring About People, Inc., Colo., 1990—; v.p. Helplink, Inc., Boulder, 1991—. With USN, 1952-56, Korea. Recipient Silver Beaver award Boy Scouts Am., Boulder, 1978, God and Svc. award Boy Scouts Am. and United Meth. Ch., 1991, OES Rose award 1994. Mem. Am. Soc. Indsl. Security (cert. CPP 1984, treas. 1985), Colo. Crime Prevention Assn. (cert. CPS), Mason (treas. Columbia lodge #14 1969-85, 90—), Royal Arch. Masons and Commandery Knights Templar of York Rite. Republican. Methodist. Home and Office: 4645 Bedford Ct Boulder CO 80301-4017

FISHER, KURT ANDREW, real estate broker; b. Buffalo, Aug. 24, 1965; s. Kenneth A. and Carol Ann (Panek) F. BS in English/Writing, Denison U., 1988. Lic. real estate assoc. broker, Wash. Investment real estate sales agt. Marcus & Millichap, Inc., Seattle, 1989-93; sales agt., loan broker, constrn. mgr. and developer Westlake Assocs., Inc., Seattle, 1993—. Pub., editor, writer Seattle Met. Apt. Report, 1994—. Cert. Comml. Investment Mem. scholar, 1994. Republican. Office: Westlake Assocs 2810 Eastlake Ave E Seattle WA 98102

FISHER, MARK JAY, neurologist, neuroscientist, educator; b. Bklyn., Aug. 23, 1949; s. Ralph Aaron and Dorothy Ann (Weissman) F.; m. Janeth Godeau, Aug. 5, 1994. BA in Polit. Sci., UCLA, 1970; MA in Polit. Sci., U. S.D., 1972, BS in Medicine, 1973; MD, U. Cin., 1975. Diplomate Am. Bd. Psychiatry and Neurology. Intern UCLA Sepulveda VA Hosp., 1975-76; resident UCLA Wadsworth VA Med. Ctr., 1976-79, chief resident, 1979-80; faculty mem., dir. stroke rsch. program U. So. Calif. Sch. of Medicine, L.A., 1980—, prof. neurology, 1995—; dir. residency tng. program U. So. Calif. Sch. Medicine, L.A., 1992-96; prof. neurology, dir. stroke rsch. program U. So. Calif. Sch. Medicine, 1995—. Editor: Medical Therapy of Acute Stroke, 1989. Recipient Tchr. Investigator award NIH, Bethesda, Md., 1984-89, Program Project grantee, 1994—. Mem. Am. Acad. Neurology, Am. Neurol. Assn., Am. Heart Assn. (stroke coun.), Nat. Stroke Assn., Internat. Soc. for Thrombosis and Haemostasis. Office: U So Calif Sch Medicine Dept of Neurology 1333 San Pablo St MCH 246 Los Angeles CA 90033

FISHER, NANCY LOUISE, pediatrician, medical geneticist, former nurse; b. Cleve., July 4, 1944; d. Nelson Leopold and Catherine (Harris) F.; m. Larry William Larson, May 30, 1976; 1 child, Jonathan Raymond. Student, Notre Dame Coll., Cleve., 1962-64; BSN, Wayne State U., 1967; postgrad., Calif. State U., Hayward, 1971-72; MD, Baylor Coll. of Medicine, 1976; M in Pub. Health, U. Wash., 1982, certificate in ethics, 1993. Diplomate Am. Bd. Pediatrics, Am. Bd. Med. Genetics. RN coronary care unit and med. intensive care unit Highland Gen. Hosp., Oakland, Calif., 1970-72; RN coronary care unit Alameda (Calif.) Hosp., 1972-73; intern in pediatrics Baylor Coll. of Medicine, Houston, 1976-77, resident in pediatrics, 1977-78; attending physician, pediatric clinic Harborview Med. Ctr., Seattle, 1980-81; staff physician children and adolescent health care clinic Columbia Health Ctr., Seattle, 1981-87, founder, dir. of med. genetics clinic, 1984-89; maternal child health policy cons. King County div. Seattle King County Dept Pub. Health, 1983-85; dir. genetic svcs. Va. Mason Clinic, 1986-89; dir. med. genetic svcs. Swedish Hosp., 1989-94; pvt. practice Seattle, 1994-97; med. cons. supr. office of managed care Wash. State Dept. Social and Health Svcs., Olympia, 1996—; nurses aide psychiatry Sinai Hosp., Detroit, 1966-67; charge nurse Women's Hosp., Cleve., 1967; research asst. to Dr. Shelly Liss, 1976; with Baylor Housestaff Assn., Baylor Coll. Medicine, 1980-81; clin. asst. prof. grad. sch. nursing, U. Wash., Seattle, 1981-85, clin. asst. prof. dept. pediatrics, 1982—; com. appointments include Seattle CCS Cleft Palate Panel, 1984—; bd. dirs., first v.p. King County Assn. Sickle Cell Disease 1985-86, acting pres. 1986, pres. 1986-87; hosp. affiliation include Childrens Orthopedic Hosp. and Med. Ctr., Seattle, 1981-89, Virginia Mason Hosp., Seattle, 1985—, Harborview Hosp., Seattle, 1986—. Contbr. articles to profl. jours. Active Seattle Urban League, 1982—, 101 Black Women, 1986—; bd. dirs. Seattle Sickle Cell Affected Family Assn., 1984-85; mem. People to People Citizen Ambassador Group. Served to lt. USN Nurse Corps, 1966-70. Fellow Am. Coll. Medicine Genetics (founder); mem. Am. Acad. Physician Execs., Student Governing Body and Graduating Policy Com. Baylor Coll. Medicine (founding mem. 1973-76), Loans and Scholarship Com. Baylor Coll. Medicine (voting mem. 1973-76), Am. Med. Student Assn., Student Nat. Med. Assn., Admission Com. Baylor Coll. Medicine (voting mem. 1974-76), AMA, Am. Med. Women's Assn., Am. Acad. Pediatrics, Am. Pub. Health Assn. (co-chmn. genetic subsect. Mat. Child Health), Am. Soc. Human Genetics, Nat. Speakers Assn., Birth Defects and Clin. Genetics Soc., Wash. State Assn. Black Providers of Health Care, Northwest Chpt. Soc. Adolescent Medicine, Wash. State Soc. Pediatrics, Seattle C. of C. (mem. Leadership Tomorrow 1988—), Sigma Gamma Rho,

Phi Delta Epsilon. Office: Mail Stop 45506 805 Plum St SE Olympia WA 98501-1528

FISHER, PHILIP CHAPIN, physicist; b. Rochester, N.Y., Aug. 3, 1926; s. Raymond Castle and Alice Chapin (Coggins) F.; m. Virginia Ruffner Ball, Aug. 18, 1948; 1 child, Christine Chapin Fisher Latham. BS in Physics, U. Rochester, 1947; MS in Physics, U. Ill., 1948, PhD in Physics, 1953. Staff mem. Los Alamos (N.Mex.) Sci. Lab., 1953-59; cons. scientist phys. sci. lab. Lockheed Missiles & Space Co., Palo Alto, Calif., 1959-74; physicist Ruffner Assocs., Menlo Park, Calif., 1975-77, 82-94; sr. physicist Rasor Assocs., Mountain View, Calif., 1976-77; sensor engrng. mgr. Gas Tech, Inc., Newark, Calif., 1977-91; physicist Ruffner Assocs., Inc., Santa Fe, 1995—; cons. Los Alamos Sci. Lab., 1959-64. Contbr. numerous articles to profl. jours. Mem. Am. Geophys. Union, Am. Phys. Soc., Am. Astron. Soc., Internat. Astron. Union, Inst. Elec. and Electronics Engrs., Soc. Photo-Optical Instrumentation Engrs., Sigma Xi. Office: Ruffner Assocs Inc PO Box 1867 Santa Fe NM 87504-1867

FISHER, RAYMOND CORLEY, lawyer; b. Oakland, Calif., July 12, 1939; s. Raymond Henry and Mary Elizabeth (Corley) F.; m. Nancy Leigh Fairchilds, Jan. 22, 1961; children: Jeffrey Scott, Amy Fisher Ahlers. BA, U. Calif., Santa Barbara, 1961; LLB, Stanford U., 1966. Bar: Calif. 1967, U.S. Ct. Appeals (9th cir.) 1967, U.S. Dist. Ct. (no. and cen. dists.) Calif. 1967, U.S. Ct. Claims 1967, U.S. Supreme Ct. 1967. Law clk. to Hon. J. Skelly Wright U.S. Ct. Appeals (D.C. cir.), Washington, 1966-67; law clk. to Hon. William J. Brennan U.S. Supreme Ct., Washington, 1967-68; ptnr. Tuttle & Taylor, L.A., L.A., 1968-88; sr. litigation ptnr. Heller, Ehrman, White & McAuliffe, L.A., 1988—; exec. com. 9th Cir. Jud. Conf., 1989-91; mem. Am. Law Inst., So. Calif. ADR Panel, CPR Inst. for Dispute Resolution. Pres. Stanford Law Rev., 1965-66. Spl. asst. to Gov. of Calif., Sacramento and L.A., 1978—; dir. Constl. Rights Found., L.A., 1978—, pres., 1983-87; pres. L.A. City Bd. Civil Svc. Commn., 1987-88; dep. gen. counsel Christopher Commn., L.A., 1991-92; pres. L.A. City Bd. Police Commrs., 1996—. With USAR, 1957. Fellow Am. Coll. Trial Lawyers, Am. Bar Found.; mem. ABA, Fed. Bar Assn. (exec. com. 1990-96), Calif. State Bar, L.A. County Bar Assn., Chancery Club, Order of Coif. Office: Heller Ehrman White & McAuliffe 601 S Figueroa St Fl 40 Los Angeles CA 90017-5704

FISHER, ROBERT JOHN, business educator; b. North Battleford, Sask., Can., June 15, 1957; came to U.S., 1987; s. John Ingram and Shirley Anne (Aitken) F.; m. Fiona Ann Hare; children: Jane Ann, John Arthur, Amy Johnston. B Commerce, U. Sask., 1979; MBA, York U., Toronto, Ont., Can., 1984; PhD, U. Colo., 1990. Terr. mgr. Can. Packers, Edmonton, Alta., Can., 1979-81; rsch. analyst SGI, Regina, Sask., 1981-83; mktg. mgr. Beline Mfg., Kindersley, Sask., 1984-87; vis. asst. prof. U. Colo., Boulder, 1990-91; mem. faculty Sch. Bus. U. So. Calif., L.A., 1991—. Contbr. articles to profl. jours. Soccer coach Am. Youth Soccer Orgn., Hacienda Heights, Calif., 1994. Social Scis. and Humanities Rsch. Coun. grantee, 1989, 90; Gerald Hart fellow, 1988, doctoral consortium fellow U. Colo., 1989. Mem. Am. Mktg. Assn. (faculty advisor 1993-94), Assn. for Consumer Rsch. Home: 1536 Drumhill Dr Hacienda Hgts CA 91745-3353 Office: U So Calif Sch Bus Los Angeles CA 90089-1421

FISHER, ROBERT LLOYD, retired marine geologist and oceanographer; b. Alhambra, Calif., Aug. 19, 1925; s. Howard Bassett and Clara Elizabeth (Michalek) F.; m. Shirley Ann Chapman, Aug. 6, 1948 (div. 1968); 1 child, Carlos Andrew; m. Sarah Elizabeth Coburn, July 18, 1986. BS in Sci., Calif. Inst. Tech., 1949; MS in Marine Geology, UCLA, La Jolla, 1953, PhD in Oceanography, 1957. Geologist U.S. Geol. Survey, St. Lawrence Island, Alaska, 1949; rsch. geologist Scripps Inst. Oceanography, U. Calif.-San Diego, La Jolla, 1950-91, rsch. geologist emeritus, 1991—, assoc. dir., 1974-80, leader deep-sea oceanographic expdns., 1951-84; expert, adviser, mem., chmn. U.S. and fgn. sci. panels and coms. UNESCO, Paris, Monaco, Washington, 1959-96. Contbr. over 100 articles to sci. jours.; editor expdn. reports Jour. Geophys. Rsch., various other jours. With USN, 1944-46, PTO. Rsch. grantee NSF, Office Naval Rsch., 1954-88. Fellow Am. Geophys. Union, Geol. Soc. Am., Explorers Club; mem. Oceanography Soc., Sigma Xi. Office: Scripps Inst Oceanography Geosci Rsch Divsn La Jolla CA 92093-0215

FISHER, ROBERT M., foundation administrator, university administrator; b. St. Paul, Minn., Oct. 15, 1938; s. S.S. and Jean Fisher; m. Elinor C. Schectman, June 19, 1960; children: Laurie, Jonathan. AB magna cum laude, Harvard Coll., 1960; JD, Harvard U., 1963; PhD, London Sch. Econs, Polit. Sci., 1967; LLD, West Coast U., L.A., 1981; DHL, Profl. Sch. Psychology, San Francisco, 1986; DPS, John F. Kennedy U., Orinda, Calif., 1988. Rsch. assoc. Mass. Mental Health Ctr., Cambridge, 1957-62; rsch. asst. Ctr. Study Juvenile Delinquency, Cambridge, 1961-63; spl. asst. to chief psychologist British Prison Dept. Home Office, London, 1963-67; prof. Sch. Criminology U. Calif., Berkeley, 1965-71; profl. race car driver, 1972-77; pres. John F. Kennedy U., Orinda, Calif., 1974-85; exec. dir. 92d St. YMHA, N.Y.C., 1984-85; dir., CEO The San Francisco Found., 1987—; mayor, councilman Lafayette, Calif., 1968-76; mem. Minn. and Calif. Bar Specialty: charitable gift planning. Scholar-in-residence Rockefeller Found., Bellagio, 1994; Polit. Sci. vis. fellow London Sch. Econs. and Polit. Sci., 1994; named Outstanding Fundraising Exec. Nat. Soc. Fund Raising Execs. Home and Office: 85 Southwood Dr Orinda CA 94563-3026

FISHER, TERRI LYNN, intensive care nurse; b. Ames, Iowa, Apr. 7, 1970; d. Steven Carl and Paula Ann (Mayernick) F. BSN, Humboldt State U., Arcata, Calif., 1992; postgrad., Calif. State U., Sacramento, 1995—. RN, Calif.; cert. BLS, ACLS, PALS. Staff nurse shock-trauma ICU Mercy Med. Ctr., Redding, Calif., 1993-96; ICU nurse Nursefinders, San Jose, Calif., 1996—. Republican. Christian. Office: Nursefinders 4880 Stevens Creek Blvd 103 San Jose CA 95129

FISHER, WESTON JOSEPH, economist; b. Glendale, Calif., Aug. 29; s. Edward Weston and Rosalie Eloise (Bailey) F. BS, U. So. Calif., 1962, MA, 1965, MS, 1971, PhD, 1989. Sr. mgr. Naval Undersea Ctr., Pasadena, Calif., 1964-69; chief exec. officer, prin. Ventura County, Ventura, Calif., 1969-73; So. Calif. dir. County Suprs. Assn., L.A., 1974-75; coord. govtl. rels. So. Calif. Assn. Govts., L.A., 1975-78; devel. dir. Walter H. Leimert Co., L.A., 1979-90; bd. dirs. Gray Energy Corp., L.A., Mission Inn Group, Riverside, Calif., Coun. of Leaders and Specialists - UN, Peterson Oil and Gas. Mem. Gov.'s Adv. Coun. for Econ. growth, Channel Islands Conservancy. Mem. Medieval Acad. Am., El Dorado Country Club, Univ. Club, South Coast Yacht Club, Cave Creek Club, Lambda Alpha. Republican. Home: 28261 Westover Way Sun City CA 92586-2525

FISHER, WILLIAM G.E., nursing home owner and operator, state senator; b. Artesia, Calif., Mar. 24, 1936; m. Darlene F. Fisher; children: William G.E., Darryl E., Rhonda M. BA in Bibl. Langs., Walla Walla Coll., 1965; postgrad., Andrews U., Berrien Springs, Mich., 1966-67, Eastern Wash. Staet Coll., Cheney, 1968. Owner, operator Rosehaven Nursing Home, Roseburg, Oreg.; mem. Oreg. Ho. of Reps., 1992-96, Oreg. Senate, 1996—; chmn. Health and Human Svcs. Com., Oreg. Senate, 1997—, vice chmn. Agr. and Natural Resources Com., 1997—, mem. Trade and Econ. Devel. Com., Water and Land Use Com. Bd. dirs. Riverside Ctr., 1996—, Douglas County Coun. on Alcoholism, 1971-76; mem. Douglas County Pers. Rev. Bd., 1973; bd. dirs. Roseburg Jr. Acad., 1986-89, chmn. bd., 1987-88; mem. Western States Legis. Forestry Task Force, 1993-95; mem. Gov.'s Commn. on Sr. Svcs., 1995-97; mem. Oreg. Health Policy Inst., 1995—; Douglas County Precinct Committeeman, 1990, 92, 94, 96; sec. Douglas County Rep. Exec. com., 1990-93. Served with U.S. Army, 1958-60, also Res. Fellow Am. Coll. Health Care Adminstrs.; mem. Am. Health Care Assn., Oreg. Health Care Assn. (bd. dirs. 1971-73, v.p. 1974-89), Am. Legion, Douglas Timber Operators, Oreg. Farm Bur., Kiwanis Club Roseburg (bd. dirs. 1981—), NRA (life), Oreg. State Shooting Assn (life), Oreg. Hunters Assn., Roseburg Rod and Gun Club, Am. Assn. Ret. Persons, Sr. Citizens Inc., Aircraft Owners and Pilots Assn., Oreg. Pilots Assn., Exptl. Aircraft Assn., Antique Aircraft Assn., Stearman Restorers Assn., Nat. Biplane Assn., others. Seventh-day Adventist. Office: Oreg State Capitol S-204 Salem OR 97310 also: Profl Bus Ctr 1012 Oak St Ste 224 Roseburg OR 97470

FISHMAN, ARNIE, marketing executive, consultant, film producer; b. Bklyn., 1965; married; 3 children. BS, CUNY, 1965, postgrad. in Pschology, 1966. Rsch. asst. Liberman Rsch, N.Y.C., 1966, v.p., 1971; founder Lieberman Rsch. Worldwide, L.A., 1973—, also chmn. bd. dirs.; founder, chmn. bd. dirs. Interviewing Svc. Am., 1982—; expert witness Fed. Trade Commn.; spkr. in field; cons. in field. Office: Lieberman Rsch Worldwide 1900 Ave of the Stars Los Angeles CA 90067*

FISHMAN, ROBERT ALLEN, neurologist, educator; b. N.Y.C., May 30, 1924; s. Samuel Benjamin and Miriam (Brinkin) F.; m. Margery Ann Satz, Jan. 29, 1956 (dec. May 29, 1980); children: Mary Beth, Alice Ellen, Elizabeth Ann.; m. Mary Craig Wilson, Jan. 7, 1983. A.B., Columbia U., 1944; M.D., U. Pa., 1947. Mem. faculty Columbia Coll. Physicians and Surgeons, 1954-66, asso. prof. neurology, 1962-66; asst. attending neurologist N.Y. State Psychiat. Inst., 1955-66; asst. attending neurologist Neurol. Inst. Presbyn. Hosp., N.Y.C., 1955-61, asso., 1961-66; co-dir. Neurol. Clin. Research Center, Neurol. Inst., Columbia-Presbyn. Med. Ctr., 1961-66; prof. neurology U. Calif. Med. Ctr., San Francisco, 1966-94, chmn. dept. neurology, 1966-92, prof. emeritus, 1994—; cons. neurologist San Francisco Gen. Hosp., San Francisco VA Hosp., Letterman Gen. Hosp.; dir. Am. Bd. Psychiatry and Neurology, 1981-88, v.p., 1986, pres., 1987. Author: Cerebrospinal Fluid in Diseases of the Nervous System, 1992; chief editor Annals of Neurology, 1993-97; contbr. articles to profl. jours. Nat. Multiple Sclerosis Soc. fellow, 1956-57; John and Mary R. Markle scholar in med. sci., 1960-65. Mem. Am. Neurol. Assn. (pres. 1983-84), Am. Fedn. for Clin. Research, Assn. for Research in Nervous and Mental Diseases, Am. Acad. Neurology (v.p. 1971-73, pres. 1975-77), Am. Assn. Physicians, Am. Soc. for Neurochemistry, Soc. for Neurosci., N.Y. Neurol. Soc., Am. Assn. Univ. Profs. Neurology (pres. 1972-73), AAAS, Am. Epilepsy Soc., N.Y. Acad. Scis., AMA (sec. sect. on nervous and mental diseases 1964-67, v.p. 1967-68, pres. 1968-69), Alpha Omega Alpha (hon. faculty mem.). Home: 50 Summit Ave Mill Valley CA 94941-1819 Office: U Calif Med Ctr 794 Herbert C Moffitt Hosp San Francisco CA 94143

FISHMAN, STANLEY JEROME (JERRY FISHMAN), retired English language educator; b. Bklyn., Oct. 31, 1933; s. Samuel Ben Fishman and Anne Oxfeld; m. Sylvia Eunice Salter, May 13, 1961; children: Wendell Samuel, Darwin Ben. BS in Chemistry, New Eng. Coll., 1956; MA in English, U. Calif., Berkeley, 1965. Lifetime jr. coll. tchg. credential. Tchr. English Sacramento City Coll., 1965-95; chair critical thinking group Western Coll. Read Assn., 1986-87, 87-88; founder comm. based English class Sacramento City Coll., 1994. Editor comty. archive newsletter, 1995, critical thinking newsletter, 1986-90. Mem., bd. dirs. Longview Sch., Davis, Calif., 1967-69; mem. Civic Arts Commn., Davis, 1980-86. With U.S. Army, 1959-60. Recipient Proclamation for civic work Civic Arts Commn., 1986, Plaque, Nat. Edn. Ctr., 1995. Mem. Los Rios Fedn. Tchrs./Am. Fedn. of Tchrs. (rep. 1992). Home: 910 Pennsylvania Pl Davis CA 95616

FISHMAN, WILLIAM HAROLD, cancer research foundation executive, biochemist; b. Winnipeg, Man., Can., Mar. 2, 1914; s. Abraham and Goldie (Chmelnitsky) F.; m. Lillian Waterman, Aug. 6, 1939; children—Joel, Nina, Daniel. B.S., U. Sask., Can., Saskatoon, 1935; Ph.D., U. Toronto, Ont., Can., 1939; MDhc U. Umea, Sweden, 1983; Dir. cancer rsch. New Eng. Med. Ctr. Hosp., Boston, 1958-72; rsch. prof. pathology Tufts U. Sch. Medicine, 1961-70, prof. pathology, 1970-77, dir. Tufts Cancer Rsch. Ctr., 1972-76; pres. La Jolla Cancer Rsch. Found., Calif., 1976-89, pres. emeritus, 1989—; mem. basic sci. programs merit rev. bd. com. VA, 1971-75; mem. pathobiol. chemistry sect. NIH, Bethesda, Md., 1977-81. Author in field. Rsch. Career award NIH, 1962-77; Royal Soc. Can. rsch. fellow, 1939, 17th Internat. Physiol. Congress-U.K. Fedn. fellow, 1947. Fellow AIC, AAAS; mem. Am. Assn. Cancer Rsch., Am. Soc. Biol. Chemists, Am. Soc. Cell Biology, Am. Soc. Exptl. Pathology, Histochem. Soc. (pres. 1983-84), Internat. Soc. Clin. Enzymology (hon.), Internat. Soc. Oncodevel. Biology and Medicine (hon., Abbott award 1993), Univ. Club (San Diego). Jewish. Current work: Basic rsch. on expression of placental genes by cancer cells; monoclonal antibodies; oncodevelopmental markers; immunocytochemistry. Home: 715 Muirlands Vista Way La Jolla CA 92037-6202 Office: The Burnham Institute 10901 N Torrey Pines Rd La Jolla CA 92037-1005

FISK, EDWARD RAY, retired civil engineer, author, educator; b. Oshkosh, Wis., July 19, 1924; s. Ray Edward and Grace O. (Meyer) Barnes; married, Oct. 28, 1950; children: Jacqueline Mary, Edward Ray II, William John, Robert Paul. BCE Marquette U., 1949; student Fresno (Calif.) State Coll., 1954, UCLA, 1957-58; BS, MBA, Calif.-Western U.. Engr., Calif. Div. Hwys., 1952-55; engr. Bechtel Corp., Vernon, Calif., 1955-59; project mgr. Toups Engrng Co., Santa Ana, Calif., 1959-61; dept. head Perliter & Soring, Los Angeles, 1961-64; Western rep. Wire Reinforcement Inst., Washington, 1964-65; cons. engr., Anaheim, Calif., 1965; assoc. engr. Met. Water Dist. So. Calif., 1966-68; chief specification engr. Koebig & Koebig, Inc., Los Angeles, 1968-71; mgr. constrn. services VTN Consol., Inc., Irvine, Calif., 1971-78; pres. E.R. Fisk Constrn., Orange, Calif., 1978-81; corp. dir. constrn. mgmt. James M. Montgomery Cons. Engrs., Inc., Pasadena, Calif., 1981-83; v.p. Lawrance, Fisk & McFarland, Inc., Santa Barbara and Orange, 1983—; pres. E.R. Fisk & Assocs., Orange, 1983—, Gleason, Peacock & Fisk, Inc., 1987-92; v.p. constrn. svcs. Wilsey & Ham, Foster City, Calif., 1993-94; adj. prof. engrng., constrn. Calif. State U., Long Beach, 1987-90, Orange Coast Coll., Costa Mesa, Calif., 1957-78, Calif. Poly. State U., Pomona, 1974; Instr. U. Calif., Berkeley, Inst. Transportation Studies, 1978—, engrng. prof. programs U. Wash., 1994—, internationally for ASCE Continuing Edn.; former mem. Calif. Bd. Registered Constrn. Insps. Served with USN, 1942-43, USAF, 1951-52. Registered profl. engr., Ariz., Calif., Colo., Fla., Idaho, Ky., La., Mont., Nev., Oreg., Utah, Wash., Wyo.; lic. land surveyor, Oreg., Idaho; lic. gen. engrng. contractor, Calif.; cert. abritator Calif. Constrn. Contract Arbitration Com. Fellow ASCE (life fellow, past chmn. exec. com. constrn. div., former chmn. nat. com. inspection 1978—), Nat. Acad. Forensic Engrs. (diplomate); mem. Orange County Engrng. Council (former pres.), Calif. Soc. Profl. Engrs. (past pres. Orange County), Structural Engrs. Assn. Calif. (engrs. joint contracts documents com. 1993-95), Am. Arbitration Assn. (nat. panel), U.S. Com. Large Dams, Order Founders and Patriots Am. (past gov. Calif.), Soc. Colonial Wars (dep. gov. gen. Calif. chpt.), S.R. (past dir.), Engrng. Edn. Found. (trustee), Tau Beta Pi. Republican. Author: Machine Methods of Survey Computing, 1958, Construction Project Administration, 1978, 82, 88, 92, 97, Construction Engineers Complete Handbook of Forms, 1981, 92, Resident Engineers Field Manual, 1992; co-author: Contractor's Project Guide, 1988, Contracts and Specifications for Public Works Projects, 1992. Home: 1792 N Ridgewood Orange CA 92865

FISK, IRWIN WESLEY, financial investigator; b. Byers, Kans., Nov. 20, 1938; s. Walter Raleigh Fisk and Mae Pearl Irwin; m. Susie Bea Walters, Sept. 9, 1973; children: Mark Christopher, Paul Steven. Student, L.A. City Coll., 1958-60, Calif. State U., L.A., 1960-64, Pasadena C.C., 1987-88. Lic. pvt. investigator, Calif. Asst. exec. dir. Stores Protective Assn., L.A., 1962-66; sr. spl. investigator Calif. Dept. Corps., L.A., 1966-83, chief investigator, 1983-94; pres. Bus. and Fin. Investigations, Inc., Pasadena, 1994—; mem. Multi-State Law Enforcement Task Force of Fraudulent Telemarketing, L.A., 1987-94. Contbr. articles to profl. publs. Mem. U.S. Chess Fedn. (life), Am. Radio Relay League (DXCC award 1993), Authors Guild, So. Calif. Fraud Investigators Assn., Masons. Republican. Home: 374 Malcolm Dr Pasadena CA 91105-1452 Office: Bus and Fin Investigations Inc 115 W California Blvd # 240 Pasadena CA 91105-3005

FISKIN, JUDITH ANNE, artist, educator; b. Chgo., Apr. 1, 1945; d. Fred Albert and Cecile (Citron) Bartman; m. Jeffrey Allen Fiskin, Jan. 1, 1967 (div. Apr. 1975); m. Jonathan Marc Wiener, Jan. 17, 1987. BA, Pomona Coll., 1966; postgrad., U. Calif., Berkeley, 1966-67; MA, UCLA, 1969. Assoc. dean sch. art Calif. Inst. of Arts, Valencia, 1977-84, art faculty, 1977—. One-woman shows include Castelli Graphics, N.Y.C., 1976, Asher-Faure, L.A., 1991, Mus. Contemporary Art, L.A., 1992, Curt Marcus Gallery, N.Y.C., 1994, Patricia Faure Gallery, Sant Monica, Calif., 1994; exhibited in group shows at Luasanne, Switzerland, Vancouver, B.C., Internat. Ctr. for Photography, N.Y.C., San Francisco Mus. Modern Art, Corcoran Gallery Art, Washington, LaJolla (Calif.) Mus. Art and mus. in Richmond, Va., Miami, Fla., Chgo., Akron, Ohio. Cmty. funding bd. mem. Liberty Hill Found., L.A., 1994. Recipient Lifetime Achievement award in photography L.A. Ctr. for Photographic Studies, 1995; grantee Nat. Endowment for Arts, 1979, 90, Logan, 1986. Office: Calif Inst of Arts McBean Pkwy Valencia CA 91355

FISTELL, IRA J., newspaper editor, radio and television personality; b. Chgo., Mar. 31, 1941; s. Harry and Marian L. (Wolfe) F.; m. Tonda R. Sloane, Aug. 20, 1978; children: Kelly, Christopher, Katherine, Mary Ellen, Sara, Andrea. AB with honors, U. Chgo., 1962, JD, 1964; MA in U.S. History, U. Wis., 1967. Bar: Ill. 1964. Radio personality Sta. WKOW-AM, Madison, Wis., 1968-71, Sta. WEMP-AM, Milw., 1971-77, Sta. KABC-AM, L.A., 1977-95; nat. radio personality ABC Talkradio Network, L.A., 1982-88; TV personality USA & ESPN Cable Networks, 1980-84; editor L.A. Jewish Times, 1995—. Author: America By Train, 1982, Oddball America, 1986. Recipient Golden Spike award for svc. to rail passengers, NARRP, Anaheim, Calif., 1987. Mem. AFTRA, SAG, Milw. Press Club.

FITCH, BILL, professional basketball coach; children: Lisa, MarcyAnn, Tammy. Coach Coe College, 1958; head coach N.D., Bowling Green, Minn., Cleve. Cavaliers, 1970-79, Boston Celtics, 1979-83, Houston Rockets, 1983-88, N.J. Nets, 1989-92, L.A. Clippers, 1994—. Named Coach of Yr., 1980. Office: LA Clippers 3939 S Figueroa St Los Angeles CA 90037

FITCH, JACK, association executive. Grad. high sch., Barry, Ill. Exec. dir. Civilian Congress, San Francisco, 1964—. Editor: (directory) Civilian Congress Annual, 1964—. Mem. Japan Soc. No. Calif., Commonwealth Club of Calif., Internat. Diplomacy Coun. of Northern Calif. Office: Civilian Congress 2361 Mission St Rm 238 San Francisco CA 94110-1813

FITCH, NOEL RILEY, writer, educator; b. New Haven, Dec. 24, 1937; d. John Eckel and Dorcas (Tarr) Riley; m. Philip A. Fitch, May 29, 1958 (div. May 1986); 1 child, Gailyn R.; m. Albert Sonnenfeld, Aug. 23, 1987. BA in English, N.W. Nazarene Coll., 1959; MA in Lit., Wash. State U., 1965, PhD in Lit., 1969. Jr. and sr. high sch. tchr. Moscow (Idaho) Pub. Schs., 1959-63; teaching asst. Wash. State U., Pullman, 1963-66, 67-68; asst. prof. Eastern Nazarene Coll., Quincy, Mass., 1966-67, 68-71; from asst. to assoc. to full prof. Point Loma Coll., San Diego, 1971-87; dept. chair lit. and fgn. langs. Point Loman Coll., San Diego, 1982-85; inst. masters of profl. writing U. So. Calif., L.A., 1990—; vis. instr. English, U. So. Calif., L.A., 1987-90; prof. Am. U., Paris, 1987-97; cons., actor Ishtar Prodns., Hollywood, 1990-92. Author: Sylvia Beach and the Lost Generation, 1983, Hemingway in Paris, 1990, Literary Cafes of Paris, 1989, Anais: The Erotic Life of Anais Nin, 1983, Appetite for Life: Biography of Julia Child, 1997; editor: Current, 1984-86; contbr. articles to profl. jours. Campus chair United Way, San Diego, 1974-77. Fellow Nat. Endowment for the Humanities, 1980-81; rsch. grantee NEH, 1976, 78-79, Am. Philos. Soc., 1982, Am. Coun. Learned Socs., 1984. Mem. MLA, The Authors Guild, Pen Center West. Home: 11829 Mayfield Ave Los Angeles CA 90049-5764 Office: care Kristine Dahl ICM 40 W 57th St New York NY 10019

FITZGERALD, BETTY JO, artist, educator; b. Colusa, Calif., Jan. 10, 1942; d. Richard Corwith and Wanda Eloise (Jones) Summerbell; m. James Edward Fitzgerald, Jan. 15, 1966; children: Molly Fitzgerald Keogh, Brant Edward. BS magna cum laude, U. No. Calif., 1963; MS in Botany, U. Wash., 1966. Tchg. asst. U. Wash., Seattle, 1963-66; instr. botany Seattle U., 1967-70; guest lectr. ecology Evergreen State Coll., Olympia, Wash., 1973, guest lectr. art, 1996; artist Olympia, 1980—; juror, workshop tchr. art regional arts workshops, Puget Sound area, Wash., 1990-97; chmn. S.W. Wash. Exhbn., Wash. State Capital Mus., Olympia, 1986-90. Contbr. articles to profl. publs. Fellow Wash. Native Plant Soc. (hon., life, exec. sec., bd. dirs. 1976-86); mem. Nat. Collage Soc. (signature), N.W. Watercolor Soc. (signature, exhbn. chmn. 1995-97), N.W. Collage Soc. (bd. dirs. 1987-97), Women Painters Wash. (elected mem., pres. 1992-93). Republican. Studio: 3327 Windolph Ln NW Olympia WA 98502

FITZGERALD, JOHN CHARLES, JR., investment banker; b. Sacramento, May 23, 1941; s. John Charles and Geraldine Edith (McNabb) F.; BS, Calif. State U. at Sacramento, 1964; MBA, Cornell U., 1966; m. Mildred Ann Kilpatrick, June 26, 1965; children—Geraldine Kathrine, Erec John. Dir. corp. planning Bekins Co., L.A., 1966-73; mgr. corp. planning Ridder Publs., Inc., L.A., 1973-75; chief fin. officer City of Inglewood (Calif.), 1975-77; treas./contr. Inglewood Redevel. Agy., 1975-77, Inglewood Housing Authority, 1975-77; v.p. mcpl. fin. White, Weld & Co., Inc., L.A., 1977-78; v.p. pub. fin. Paine Webber Jackson & Curtis, L.A., 1978-79; v.p. and mgr. for Western region, mcpl. fin. dept. Merrill Lynch Capital Markets, L.A., 1979-82, mng. dir. Western region, mcpl. fin. dept., 1982-86; mng. dir. Seidler-Fitzgerald Pub. Fin., L.A., 1986—; sr. v.p. The Seidler Cos., Inc., L.A., 1986—, also bd. dirs., mem. exec. com.; instr. fin./adminstrn. El Camino Coll., Torrance, Calif., 1977-80; bd. dirs., mem. exec. com. The Seidler Cos., Inc. Chmn. bd. dirs., exec. com., treas., chmn. fund raising com. L.A. chpt. Am. Heart Assn., 1977—; bd. dirs. Daniel Freeman Hosps. Inc., Corondelet Health Care Corp.; trustee Mt. St. Mary's Coll., L.A., 1992—; bd. dirs. Tau Kappa Epsilon Ednl. Found., Indpls., 1995—; alumni coun. mem. Johnson Grad. Sch. of Mgmt. Cornell U., real estate council. Mem. Fin. Execs. Inst., Mcpl. Fin. Officers Assn., Calif. Soc. Mcpl. Fin. Officers, League Calif. Cities, So. Calif. Corp. Planners Assn. (past pres.), L.A. Bond, Beta Gamma Sigma. Republican. Clubs: Jonathan, The Calif., Lake Arrowhead Country. Lodge: Rotary.

FITZGERALD, JOHN EDWARD, III, lawyer; b. Cambridge, Mass., Jan. 12, 1945; s. John Edward Jr. and Kathleen (Sullivan) FitzG.; m. Nancy Balik. BCE, U.S. Mil. Acad., West Point, N.Y., 1969; JD, M in Pub. Policy Analysis, U. Pa., 1975. Bar: Pa. 1975, N.Y. 1978, Calif. 1983, U.S. Supreme Ct. 1991. Commd. 2d lt. U.S. Army, 1969, advanced through grades to capt., 1971, resigned, 1972; assoc. Saul Ewing Remick & Saul, Phila., 1975-77, Shearman & Sterling, N.Y.C., 1977-78; atty. Pepsico, Inc., Purchase, N.Y., 1978-82; sr. v.p., dept. head Security Pacific Corp., Los Angeles, 1982-83; ptnr. Schlesinger, FitzGerald & Johnson, Palm Springs, Calif., 1983-87; mng. ptnr. FitzGerald & Assocs., Palm Springs, 1987—; adj. prof. law U. Pa., Temple U., U. Redlands: judge pro tem Desert Jud. Dist.; lectr. Calif. Continuing Edn. of the Bar; trustee Nat. Coun. Freedom Found., Valley Forge, Pa.; lectr. Calif. Employment Lawyers Assn. Bd. dirs., vice chmn. Desert Hosp. Found.; bd. dirs., pres. Palm Sprngs Boys and Girls Club, Pathfinder Ranch, Desert Youth Found., United Way. Mem. ABA, Calif. Bar Assn., Desert Bar Assn. (bd. trustees), Riverside County Bar Assn., Orange County Bar Assn., Assn. Trial Lawyers Am., Calif. Trial Lawyers Assn. (lectr.), Am. Arbitration Assn. (arbitrator), Palm Springs Polo Club, O'Donnell Golf Club (Palm Springs), Com. of 25 (Palm Springs), Monarch Bay Club, Desert Roundtable, World Affairs Coun. Office: Ste 105 3001 Tahquitz Canyon Way Palm Springs CA 92262-6790

FITZGERALD, ROBERT LYNN, small business owner; b. Indiana, Pa., Oct. 1, 1939; s. Joseph and Jean (Smith) F.; m. Tomi Higuchi, May 30, 1991; 1 child, Robert Lynn Jr. Student, Orange Coast Coll., 1985-86; BA, U. Redlands, 1990; MA, U.S. Internat. U., 1993, D in Psychology, 1997. Dist. mgr. Napco Sci., Portland, Oreg., 1981-88; prin., pub. Fitzgerald's Real Estate Yellow Pages, Santa Ana, Calif., 1987—; psychol. sales cons., 1990—. Hospice vol. Orange County (Calif.), Vis. Nurses Assn., 1980; founder Orange County HELP chpt., Santa Ana, 1982. Home: 2700 W Segerstrom Ave # D Santa Ana CA 92704-6547 Office: Fitzgerald's Real Estate Yellow Pages 3941 S Bristol St Ste 335 Santa Ana CA 92704-7400

FITZGERALD, TIKHON (LEE R. H. FITZGERALD), bishop; b. Detroit, Nov. 14, 1932; s. LeRoy and Dorothy Kaeding (Higgins) F. AB, Wayne State U., 1958. Ordained deacon, 1971, priest, 1978, bishop Eastern Orthodox, 1987. Enlisted U.S. Army, 1954-57; commd. 2 lt. USAF, 1960, advanced through grades to capt., 1971; air staff, 1966-71, released, 1971; protodeacon Holy Virgin Mary Russian Orthodox Cathedral, L.A., 1972-78, rector, archpriest, 1979-87; bishop of San Francisco Orthodox Ch. in Am., L.A., 1987—. Recipient Order of St. Vladimir II Class, Patriarch Aleksy of Moscow, 1993. Democrat. Home: 649 Robinson St Los Angeles CA 90026 3612 Office: Orthodox Ch Am Diocese of the West 650 Micheltorena St Los Angeles CA 90026-3623*

FITZGERALD, TIM K., writer; b. San Jose, Calif., Jan. 3, 1946; s. Ralph George and Bernice Christine (Huston) F. *Tim is single, the oldest of three brothers. His grandfather Fitzgerald found his fortune as a baker in Nome,*

Alaska, during the Klondike gold rush. His mother's family date themselves to the Battle of King's Mountain in the American Revolution and further back to the early founding of Jamestown, Virginia. Tim himself pioneered first ascents in Yosemite Valley in its golden era of the sixties. BA, San Jose State Coll., 1971, San Jose State U., 1980; MA, San Jose State U., 1985, San Jose State U., 1997. Treas. Associated Students San Jose State Coll., 1969-70; camp bus. mgr. Boy Scouts Am., Sonora, Calif., 1973; co. budget analyst Allstate Equity Investments, San Jose, 1980; adminstrv. asst. Summer Employment of Youth program CETA, San Jose, 1981; pres. Corp. for Shared Responsibility, San Jose, 1983-84; owner/operator Raccoon Pubs., San Jose, 1991-92; freelance writer San Jose, 1986—, researcher, 1992-96; sec. Discovery, Inc., San Jose, 1991-93; adminstrv. trustee Inst. for Social Orgnl. Rsch., San Jose, 1992-94. Author: Essays in Capitalism, 1986, Civic Community, 1992, Inner City, 1993, Twilight in the Afternoon, 1997, (narrative) Trail to Black Mountain, 1978, (poetry) Impressions from Idle Rock, 1981. Mgr., candidate for State Assembly, San Jose, 1994, for San Jose City Coun., 1982; co-coord. State Green Party Platform, Calif., 1993, State Green Party campaigns and candidates, Calif., 1995—; elected mem. Green Party County Coun., Santa Clara County, Calif., 1992-94; vol. Cmty. Companions, Inc., San Jose, 1990-91; commr. City of San Jose Disability Advisement, 1993-97; mem. task force on poverty Santa Clara County, 1995—. Advanced cadet U.S. Army ROTC, 1966-67. Mem. Internat. Soc. Poets, Fellowship of Reconciliation, Commonwealth Club, Sierra Club (Loma Preita chpt.), Tau Delta Phi. Office: PO Box 720594 San Jose CA 95172 *Tim has been a civic leader in his community since his undergraduate days in the mid-sixties. He was first elected to office on a ticket with a militant black civil rights spokesperson in a campus party of ethnic pluralism. His first writings were published as letters in the campus daily. He has since been a frequent contributer to the San Jose Mercury "Letters" page since 1978. His serious writing career was begun to supplement an unsuccessful profession in teaching.*

FITZGERALD, WAVERLY, publishing executive; b. Burbank, Calif., Sept. 4, 1951; d. Earl Edward and Marie Ann (Wittak) F.; 1 child, Shaw. MA, Calif. State U., Northridge, 1981. Pvt. instr. Seattle, 1982—; publ. Priestess of Swords Press, Seattle, 1989—; editor The Beltane Papers, Seattle, 1994—. Mem. Seattle Geneaol. Soc. Office: 1463 E Republican St # 187 Seattle WA 98112-4539

FITZPATRICK, AL W., educator; b. Widby Island, Wash., Jan. 14, 1962; s. Robert Warren and Merna (Bess) F. BS in Polit. Sci., So. Oreg. State Coll., 1974, MS in Social Sci., 1975. Tchr. Mazama High Sch., Klamath Falls (Oreg.) City Schs., 1975-78; govt. and law tchr. Newport (Oreg.) High Sch., 1978—; presenter in field. Del. Republican Nat. Conv., New Orleans, 1988, Houston, 1992, San Diego, 1996; advisor YMCA Youth & Govt., Salem, Oreg., 1989-1991; selected for German marshall insvc. Nat. Coun. Social Studies, 1991; mem. Nat. Coun. Social Studies Textbook Com., 1990-1995, Nat. St. Law Conv., Washington, 1996. Recipient Leavey award Freedom Found., 1991, Levey award of Excellence in private Enterprise Edn. 1992, Arrid Tchr. Recognition award Carter-Wallace, Inc., 1992, Golden Apple award; Keizai Koho fellow Japanese C. of C., Tokyo, 1990; grantee law studies Oreg. Law Related Edn. Project, 1990; James Madison Meml. fellowship, 1992. Mem. Oreg. Theatre Arts Assn. (treas. 1985), Oreg. Speech Tchrs. Assn. (workshop presenter), Oreg. Thespians Conf. (workshop presenter), Optimists Club (dir. youth activities). Home: 1080 NE 7th Dr Newport OR 97365-2518 Office: Newport High Sch 322 NE Eads St Newport OR 97365-2819

FITZPATRICK, LOIS ANN, library administrator; b. Yonkers, N.Y., Mar. 27, 1952; d. Thomas Joseph and Dorothy Ann (Nealy) Sullivan; m. William George Fitzpatrick, Jr., Dec. 1, 1973; children: Jennifer Ann, Amy Ann. BS in Sociology, Mercy Coll., 1974; MLS, Pratt Inst., 1975. Clk. Yonkers (N.Y.) Pub. Library, 1970-73, librarian trainee, 1973-75, librarian I, 1975-76; reference librarian Carroll Coll. Library, Helena, Mont., 1976-79, acting dir., 1979, asst. prof., 1979-89, dir., 1980—, assoc. prof., 1989—; chmn. arrangements Mont. Gov.'s Pre White House Conf. on Libraries, Helena, 1977-78; mem. steering com. Reference Point coop. program for librs., 1991; mem. adv. com. Helena Coll. of Tech. Libr., 1994—; adv. coun. Mont. Libr. Svcs., 1996—. Pres. elect Helena Area Health Sci. Libraries Cons., 1979-84, pres., 1984-88; bd. dirs. Mont. FAXNET; co-chmn. interest group OCLC; chmn. local arrangements Mont. Gov.'s Pre White House Conf.; mem. adv. bd. Helena Coll. of Tech. Mem. Mont. Library Assn. (task force for White House conf. 1991, chair govt. affairs com. 1996—); chmn. EdLINK-MT, 1997—. Democrat. Roman Catholic. Club: Soroptimist Internat. of Helena (2d v.p. 1984-85, pres. 1986-87). Home: 1308 Shirley Rd Helena MT 59602-6635 Office: Carroll Coll Jack and Sallie Corette Libr Helena MT 59625-0099

FITZSIMMONS, (LOWELL) COTTON, professional basketball executive, broadcaster, former coach; b. Hannibal, Mo., Oct. 7, 1931; s. Clancy and Zelda Curry (Gibbs) F.; m. JoAnn D'Andrea, Sept. 2, 1978 (div.); 1 child, Gary. B.S., Midwestern Univ., Wichita Falls, Tex., M.A. Head coach, athletic dir. Moberly Jr. Coll, Moberly, Mo., 1958-67; head coach Kans. State U., Manhattan, 1967-70; head coach NBA Phoenix Suns, 1970-72, 1988-92, dir. player personnel, 1987-88; head coach NBA Atlanta Hawks, 1972-76; dir. player personnel NBA Golden State Warriors, Oakland, Calif., 1976-77; head coach NBA Buffalo Braves, 1977-78, NBA Kansas City Kings, Mo., 1978-84, NBA San Antonio Spurs, 1984-87; sr. exec. v.p. Phoenix Suns, 1992—, now head coach; coach Schick Rookies, 45th ann. All Star Game, America West Arena. Recipient Coach of the Yr. award Nat. Jr. Coll. Athletic Assn., 1966, 67, Coach of the Yr. award Big 8 Conf., 1970, Coach of the Yr. award NBA, 1979, 89, Coach of the Yr. award Sporting News, St. Louis, 1979, 89; inducted into Mo. Sports Hall of Fame, Jefferson City, 1981, Nat. Jr. Coll. Basketball Hall of Fame, Hutchinson, 1985. Fellow Nat. Assn. Basketball Coaches. Office: Phoenix Suns 201 E Jefferson St Phoenix AZ 85004-2412*

FITZSIMMONS, JEFFREY LYNN, astronautical engineer, military officer; b. Alexandria, Va., Jan. 14, 1958; s. John Wayne and Joan (Straight) F. BS in Astronautical Engr., USAF Acad., 1980; MS in Aero. and Astronautical Engr., MIT, 1984; MBA in Mgmt., Wright State U., 1991. Commd. 2d lt. USAF, 1980, advanced through grades to maj., 1992; chief integrated scheduling 6555th Aerospace Test Group, Cape Canaveral AFB, Fla., 1980-82; project officer, developmental engr. Plans & Advanced Programs, Ballistic Missile Office, Norton AFB, Calif., 1984-88; space sys. engr. Fgn. Tech. Divsn., Wright-Patterson AFB, Ohio, 1988-92; chief future upper stages Space and Missile Sys. Ctr., L.A., 1992-94, chief syss. engring. branch directorate program mgmt., 1994—. Contbr. articles to profl. jours. Decorated Air Force Commendation medals USAF, 1982, 92, Air Force Meritorious Svc. medal USAF, 1988; recipient Silver Medal award Colo. Engring. Coun., 1980. Mem. AIAA (assoc.; session chmn. space programs and tech. conf. 1993—), Am. Astronautical Soc. (space sta. tech. com. 1994-95), Nat. Space Soc., Brit. Interplanetary Soc. Home: 1313 Mount Rainier Rd Rancho Palos CA 90275-1913 Office: SMC/SDES 160 Skynet St Los Angeles CA 90245

FIX, TOBIE LYNN, special education educator; b. L.A., Aug. 25, 1961; d. Howard Jacob and Pearl (Bram) Berger; m. Thomas Fix, Aug. 25, 1985. AA, Nat. U., L.A., 1992, student, 1992—. Substitute tchr. asst. of trainable mentally handicapped Los Angeles County, Calif., 1980-85, tchr. asst. trainable mentally handicapped, 1985—; substitute preschool tchr. Los Angeles County, Los Angeles County, Calif., 1996—; coaching asst. Spl. Olympic State Games, Los Angeles County. Recipient Vol. awards in spl. edn. Mem. Mus. of Tolerance, Huntington Libr./Gardens, L.A. Zool. Found. Democrat. Jewish. Home: 1628 Carlson Ln Redondo Beach CA 90278-4711

FIX, WILBUR JAMES, department store executive; b. Velva, N.D., Aug. 14, 1927; s. Jack J. and Beatrice D. (Wasson) F.; m. Beverly A. Corcoran, Sept. 20, 1953; children: Kathleen M., Michael B., Jenifer L. BA, U. Wash., 1950. Credit mgr. Bon Marche, Yakima, Wash., 1951-54; controller, ops. mgr. Bon Marche, Boise, Idaho, 1954-58; sr. v.p. Bon Marche, Seattle, 1970-76; exec. v.p. Bon Marche, 1976-77, pres., chief exec. officer, 1978-87; chmn., chief exec. officer, sr. v.p. Allied Stores Corp., 1987-93; chmn. Fix Mgmt. Group, 1993—; chmn. Wash. Retail Coun., 1983-84; bd. dirs., vice chmn. Wash. Telecomm. Corp.; bd. dirs. BMC West Corp., Vans, Inc., Swirland Apparel Ventures, Inc. Mem. pres.'s adv. com. Allied Stores Corp., N.Y., 1968-72; mem. citizens adv. com. Seattle Pub. Schs., 1970-71; v.p. Citizens Council Against Crime; chmn. Seattle King County Conv. & Visitors Bur., 1990. With AUS, 1946-47. Mem. Nat. Retail Mchts. Assn., Controllers Congress, Seattle Retail Controllers Group (past pres.), Fin. Execs. Inst., Western States Regional Controllers Congress (past pres.), Seattle C. of C. (exec. com., bd. dirs.), Assn. Wash. Bus. (fin. adv.), Downtown Seattle Devel. Assn. (exec. com., trustee), Wash. Round Table, Wash. Athletic Club, Mission Hills Country Club (Rancho Mirage, Calif.), Elks, Pi Kappa Alpha, Alpha Kappa Psi, Phi Theta Kappa. Episcopalian. Home: 5403 W Mercer Way Mercer Island WA 98040-4635 Office: The Bon Marché 3rd and Pine St Seattle WA 98181

FLAGG, NORMAN LEE, retired advertising executive; b. Detroit, Jan. 21, 1932; s. Frank and Harriet (Brown) F.; m. Carolanne Flagg; children: James, Suzanne. BFA, U. Miami, Miami, Fla., 1958. Advt. supr. Smithkline Beckman, Phila., 1970-75, creative dir., 1975-80; owner Illusions Restaurants, Bryn Mawr, Pa., 1979-87, Illusions Restaurant, Tucson, Ariz., 1984-88. Author: Shooting Blanks, 1994. With USMC, 1954-56. Recipient Diana awards Whlse Druggest Assn. 1977, Aesculapius award Modern Medicine 1978. Mem. Acad. Magical Arts.

FLAGG, ROBERT FINCH, research aerospace engineer; b. Somerville, Mass., Mar. 6, 1933; s. Donald Fairbanks and Helen Constance (Finch) F.; m. Lois-Ann Davis Laughton, June 14, 1958 (div. 1975); children: Scott, Susan, Marc. BS in Aero. Engring., MIT, 1959, MS in Aero. and Astronautical Engring., 1960; PhD in Engring. Physics, U. Toronto, Ont., Can., 1967. Teaching asst. MIT, Cambridge, 1959; rsch. assoc. U. Toronto, 1964-67; program mgr. Physics Internat. Co., San Leandro, Calif., 1967-68; dir. rsch. Holex Inc., Hollister, Calif., 1968-71; v.p. tech. ops. X-Demex Corp., Dublin, Calif., 1972-79; program mgr. Artec Assocs., Hayward, Calif., 1979-80; mgr. ordnance engring. Tracor Aerospace, San Ramon, Calif., 1980-84; tech. dir. Tracor Aerospace, Camden, Ark., 1986-90; dir. IR countermeasures Bermite div. Whittaker Corp., Saugus, Calif., 1984-85; R & D scientist Lockheed Advanced Aeros., Valencia, Calif., 1985-86; sr. engring. specialist Aerojet Ordnance, Downey, Calif., 1991-94; sr. engr. Hi-Shear Tech. Corp., Torrance, Calif., 1994—. Contbr. numerous articles to sci. and tech. jours. Staff sgt. USAF, 1950-54. Staff scholar MIT, 1954-59, N. Stewart Robinson scholar U. Toronto, 1964-67; U. Toronto Inst. Aerospace Studies scholar, rsch. fellow, Presdl. fellow U. Calif. Lawrence Berkeley Lab., 1971-72. Mem. AIAA, Am. Def. Preparedness Assn., Soc. Explosives Engrs., Internat. Pyrotechnic Soc., Sigma Gamma Tau. Republican. Home: 1564 Mulberry Ave Upland CA 91786-2247 Office: Hi-Shear Tech 24255 Garnier St Torrance CA 90505

FLAHAVIN, MARIAN JOAN, artist; b. Colton, Wash., Nov. 19, 1937; d. Herbert Joseph and Margaret Thersa (McGinn) Druffel; m. G. Thomas Flahavin, Aug. 6, 1960; 1 child, John Thomas. BA in Art, Holy Names Coll., 1959; studied with, John Howard and Daniel Green. With pub. rels. Holy Names Coll., Spokane, Wash., 1959-70; artist-in-residence Spokane, 1974—; tchr. and speaker in field. Prin. work represented in galleries and shows, nation wide; prin. work includes collectible plate series, prints for benefit of children, garden sculptures of children. Mem. Pastel Soc. Am., Northwest Pastel Soc., Women Artists of Am. West, Pastel Soc. West Coast. Roman Catholic. Home and Office: RR 7 Spokane WA 99206-9801

FLAMMANG, SUSANN, author, publisher; b. Kenosha, Wis., June 2, 1950; d. Leslie James and Beatrice (Woodward) Flammang Sampe. Pres. The Family of God, Las Vegas, 1984—, World Harvest, 1985—, pub., editor The Family of God Newsletter, Poets for Africa, 1986—; pres. World Harvest, 1986—; producer, broadcaster Heart-to-Heart, Sta. KUNV-TV, Las Vegas; v.p. Art Affair. Author of 30 books, numerous works of poetry. Recipient numerous poetry awards including Calif. Fedn. of Poets award, 1983, Humanitarian award Clark County, 1986, Woman of Achievement award, 1987, Gov's Art award, 1985, 86. Mem. Internat. Women's Writing Guild, Internat. PEN Assn., Acad. Am. Poets. Office: The Family of God/World Harvest PO Box 34716 Las Vegas NV 89133

FLANAGAN, JOHN MICHAEL, editor, publisher; b. Bangor, Maine, Mar. 8, 1946; s. Joseph F. and Dorothy Elizabeth (Albert) F.; m. Mary Katherine Fastenau, June 22, 1990. Student, U. Notre Dame, 1963-65; BJ, U. Mo., 1970. With The News-Jour. papers, Wilmington, Del., 1970-84, mng. editor, 1982-84; editor Marin Ind. Jour., San Rafael, Calif., 1984-87; exec. editor Honolulu Star-Bulletin, 1987-93; editor, pub. Honolulu Star-Bull., 1993—. With U.S. Army, 1965-68. Office: Honolulu Star Bull PO Box 3080 Honolulu HI 96802-3080

FLANAGAN, LATHAM, JR., surgeon; b. Pitts., Dec. 2, 1936; s. Latham and Elizabeth Lansing (Bunting) Kimbrough; m. Elizabeth Ruth Losaw, June 26, 1961 (dec. May 1971); 1 child, Jennifer Ruth; m. Mary Jane Flanagan, Mar. 28, 1975; children: Sahale Ann, David Nooroa. MD, Duke U., 1961, student, 1957, MD, 1961. Diplomate Am. Bd. Surgery. Intern U. Calif., San Francisco, 1961-62, resident in surgery, 1962-66, chief resident in surgery, 1965-66; pvt. practice surgery Sacred Heart Hosp., Eugene, Oreg., 1968-84, 85—; clin. sr. instr. in surgery Oreg. Health Scis. U., Portland, 1968-84; assoc. prof. surgery U. Otago, Dunedin (New Zealand) Pub. Hosp., 1984-85; nat. surgeon Cook Islands, 1985; founder Oreg. Ctr. for Bariatric Surgery, Eugene, 1993—. Contbr. articles to profl. jours. Founder White Bird Clinic, Eugene, 1969-71; mem. adv. com. Planned Parenthood of Lane County, 1979-84, Lt. comdr. USNR, 1966-68, Vietnam. Fellow ACS (pres. Oreg. chpt. 1991-92); mem. AMA, Oreg. Med. Assn., Lane County med. Soc. (com. chair 1970s), Am. Soc. Bariatric Surgery (chair ins. com. 1991-94, councillor 1994-96, sec.-treas. 1996—), North Pacific Surg. Soc., Eugene Surg. Soc. (pres. 1981). Republican. Home: 31033 Foxridge Ln Eugene OR 97405-9589 Office: 655 E 11th Ave Ste 8 Eugene OR 97401-3621 *Honesty, sincerity and hard work gets you there. Not forgetting how to play - adventure -makes the journey worthwhile. Be not afraid to be different...to walk the less travelled path.*

FLANIGAN, JAMES J(OSEPH), journalist; b. N.Y.C., June 6, 1936; s. James and Jane (Whyte) F.; m. Anne Fitzmaurice, Jan. 9, 1965 (dec. Oct. 1992); children: Michael, Siobhan Jane. BA, Manhattan Coll., 1961. Fin. writer N.Y. Herald Tribune, 1957-66; bur. chief, asst. mng. editor Forbes Mag., 1966-86; bus. columnist, sr. econs. editor L.A. Times, 1986—. Office: LA Times Times Mirror Sq Los Angeles CA 90053

FLANNELLY, KEVIN J., psychologist, research analyst; b. Jersey City, Nov. 26, 1949; s. John J. and Mary C. (Walsh) F.; m. Laura T. Adams, Jan. 10, 1981. BA in Psychology, Jersey City State Coll., 1972; MS in Psychology, Rutgers U., 1975; PhD in Psychology, U. Hawaii, 1983. Rsch. asst. dept. psychology U. Ill., Champaign, 1972-73; rsch. intern Alcohol Behavior Rsch. Lab. Rutgers U., New Brunswick, N.J., 1973-75; rsch. scientist Edward R. Johnstone Tng. and Rsch. Ctr., Bordentown, N.J., 1975-78; teaching asst. dept. psychology U. Hawaii, Honolulu, 1980-81, rsch. asst. Pacific Biomed. Rsch. Ctr., 1981-83, asst. prof. Bekesy Lab. Neurobiology, 1983-85; rsch. statistician, statewide transp. planning office Hawaii Dept. Transportation, Honolulu, 1986-89; researcher Office of Lt. Gov., Honolulu, 1989-93; legis. dir., policy analyst energy and environ. protection com. State House of Reps., 1994; planning and policy analyst Gov.'s Office of State Planning, Honolulu, 1994-96; with office of planning Hawaii Dept. Bus., Econ. Devel. and Tourism, Honolulu, 1996—; statis cons. U. Hawaii Sch. Nursing, Honolulu, 1986, Hawaii Dept. Health, Honolulu, 1986; staff mem. gov's. subcabinet on early childhood edn. and childcare, 1989, Hawaii task force on ednl. governance, 1991-92; mem. Gov's. Office State Planning, environ. scanning project, 1992-94; v.p., rsch. dir. Ctr. Psychosocial Rsch., Honolulu, 1987—; instr. dept. social scis. Honolulu Community Coll., 1981; ptnr. Flannelly Cons., 1991—; rsch. dir. Mktg. Rsch. Inst., 1992—; mem. State Ridesharing Task Force, 1987. Editor: Biological Perspective on Aggression, 1984, Introduction to Psychology, 1987; reviewer 8 sci. and profl. jours., 1978—; grant reviewer NSF, 1984-92; contbr. numerous articles to profl. jours. Polit. survey cons., Honolulu, 1988—; transp. cons., Honolulu, 1989—; mktg. cons., Honolulu, 1990—. Grantee NIH, 1984, Fed. Hwy. Adminstrn., 1987; N.J. State scholar N.J. Dept. Higher Edn., 1968-72. Fellow Internat. Soc. Rsch. on Aggression; mem. AAAS, Am. Psychol. Soc., Am. Statis. Assn., Internat. Soc. Comparative Psychology, N.Y. Acad. Scis., Pacific and Asian Affairs Coun., Psychonomic Soc., Sigma Xi. Home: 445 Kaiolu St Apt 1006 Honolulu HI 96815-2239 Office: Office of Gov Hawaii State Capitol Honolulu HI 96813

FLANNELLY, LAURA T., mental health nurse, nursing educator, researcher; b. Bklyn., Nov. 7, 1952; d. George A. Adams and Eleanor (Barragry) Mulhearn; m. Kevin J. Flannelly, Jan. 10, 1981. BS in Nursing, Hunter Coll., 1974; MSN, U. Hawaii, 1984, PhD in Ednl. Psychology, 1996. RN, N.Y., Hawaii. Psychiat. nurse Bellevue Hosp., N.Y.C., 1975, asst. head nurse, 1975-77; psychiat. nurse White Plains (N.Y.) Med. Ctr., 1978-79; community mental health nurse South Beach Psychiat. Ctr., N.Y.C., 1979-81; psychiat. nurse The Queen's Med. Ctr., Honolulu, 1981-83; crisis worker Crisis Response Systems Project, Honolulu, 1983-86; instr. nursing U. Hawaii, Honolulu, 1985-92, asst. prof., 1992—; adj. instr. nursing Hawaii Loa Coll., Honolulu, 1988, Am. Samoa Community Coll., Honolulu, 1987, 89, 90; mem. adv. bd., planning com. Psychiat. Day Hosp. of The Queen's Med. Ctr., Honolulu, 1981-82; program coord. Premenstrual Tension Syndrome Conf., Honolulu, 1984; dir. Ctr. Psychosocial Rsch., Honolulu, 1987—; program moderator 1st U.S-Japan Health Behavioral Conf., Honolulu, 1988; faculty Ctr. for Asia-Pacific Exch., Internat. Conf. on Transcultural Nursing, Honolulu, 1990; mem. bd. dirs. U. Hawaii Profl. Assembly, 1994—. Contbr. articles to profl. jours. N.Y. State Bd. Regents scholar, 1970-74; NIH nursing trainee, 1983-84; grantee U. Hawaii, 1986, 91, Hawaii Dept. Health, 1990. Fellow Internat. Soc. Rsch. on Aggression; mem. AAAS, Am. Ednl. Rsch. Assn., Am. Psychol. Soc., Am. Statis. Assn., Nat. League for Nursing, N.Y. Acad. Scis., Pacific and Asian Affairs Coun., Sigma Theta Tau. Home: 445 Kaiolu St Apt 1006 Honolulu HI 96815-2239 Office: U Hawaii Sch Nursing Webster Hall Honolulu HI 96822

FLATTÉ, STANLEY MARTIN, physicist, educator; b. Los Angeles, Dec. 2, 1940; s. Samuel and Henrietta (Edelstein) F.; m. Renelde Marie Demeure, June 26, 1966; children: Michael, Anne. B.S., Calif. Inst. Tech., 1962; student, NYU, 1960-61; Ph.D., U. Calif.-Berkeley, 1966. Research particle physicist Lawrence Berkeley Lab., Calif., 1966-71; asst. prof. physics U. Calif.-Santa Cruz, 1971-73, assoc. prof., 1973-78, prof., 1978—; dir. Ctr. for Studies of Nonlinear Dynamics La Jolla Inst., 1982-86, dept. chmn., 1986-89; cons. phys. oceanography and underwater sound U.S. Govt.; vis. researcher, Cern, Geneva, 1975, Scripps Inst. Oceanography, 1980, Cambridge U., Eng., 1981. Author: (with others) Sound Transmission Through a Fluctuating Ocean, 1979; contbr. (with others) articles profl. jours. Woodrow Wilson fellow, 1962; NSF fellow, 1962-66; Guggenheim Found. fellow, 1975. Fellow AAAS, Acoustical Soc. Am., Optical Soc. Am.; mem. Am. Phys. Soc., Am. Geophys. Union, Seismol. Soc. Am., Sigma Xi. Office: Univ Calif Physics Dept Santa Cruz CA 95064 *An understanding of science requires two elements: significant, individual research accomplishment, and a knowledge of the historical development of one's discipline. Both are essential. I have tried to balance them in research, and in teaching.*

FLATTERY, THOMAS LONG, lawyer, legal administrator; b. Detroit, Nov. 14, 1922; s. Thomas J. and Rosemary (Long) F.; m. Gloria M. Hughes, June 10, 1947 (dec.); children: Constance Marie, Carol Dianne Lee, Michael Patrick, Thomas Hughes, Dennis Jerome, Betsy Ann Sprecher; m. Barbara J. Balfour, Oct. 4, 1986. BS, U.S. Mil. Acad., 1947; JD, UCLA, 1955; LLM, U. So. Calif., 1965. Bar: Calif. 1955, U.S. Patent and Trademark Office 1957, U.S. Customs Ct. 1968, U.S. Supreme Ct. 1974, Conn. 1983, N.Y. 1984. With Motor Products Corp., Detroit, 1950, Equitable Life Assurance Soc., Detroit, 1951; With Bohn Aluminum & Brass Co., Hamtramck, Mich., 1952; legal staff, asst. contract adminstr. Radioplane Co. (divsn. Northrop Corp.), Van Nuys, Calif., 1955-57; successively corp. counsel, gen. counsel, asst. sec. McCulloch Corp., L.A., 1957-64; sec., corp. counsel Technicolor, Inc., Hollywood, Calif., 1964-70; successively corp. counsel, asst. sec., v.p., sec. and gen. counsel Amcord, Inc., Newport Beach, Calif., 1970-72; v.p., sec., gen. counsel Schick Inc., L.A., 1972-75; counsel, asst. sec. C.F. Braun & Co., Alhambra, Calif., 1975-76; sr. v.p., sec., gen. counsel Automation Industries, Inc. (now PCC Tech. Industries Inc. a unit of Penn Cen. Corp.), Greenwich, Conn., 1976-86; v.p., gen. counsel G&H Tech., Inc. (a unit of Penn Cen. Corp.), Santa Monica, Calif., 1986-93; temp. judge Mcpl. Ct. Calif. L.A. Jud. Dist., 1987—; settlement officer L.A. Superior and Mcpl. Cts., 1991—; panelist Am. Arbitration Assn., 1991—; jud. arbitrator and mediator Alternative Dispute Resolution Programs L.A. Superior and Mcpl. Cts, 1993—. Contbr. articles to various legal jours. Served to 1st lt. AUS, 1942-50. Mem. ABA, State Bar Calif. (co-chmn. corp. law dept. com. 1978-79, lectr. continuing legal edn. program), L.A. County Bar Assn. (chmn. corp. law dept. com. 1966-67), Century City Bar Assn. (chmn. corp. law dept. com. 1979-80), Conn. Bar Assn., N.Y. State Bar Assn., Am. Soc. Corp. Secs. (L.A. regional group pres. 1973-74), L.A. Intellectual Property Law Assn., Am. Ednl. League (trustee 1988—), West Point Alumni Assn., Army Athletic Assn., Friendly Sons St. Patrick, Jonathan Club, Braemar Country Club, Phi Alpha Delta. Roman Catholic. Home and Office: 439 Via De La Paz Pacific Palisades CA 90272-4633

FLECK, JADE CARLSON, literature educator, nurse; b. Duluth, Minn., Dec. 4, 1948; d. Carl Adolph Carlson and Joyce Marie (Richeson) Beldin; m. Paul Douglas Fleck, June 25, 1983. AB in English Lit., U. Calif., Berkeley, 1974, PhD in English Lit., 1990; BA in Biblical Studies, Patten Coll., 1978. RN, Minn. Tchr. Patten Acad., Oakland, Calif., 1977-78; tchg. asst. dept. English U. Calif., Berkeley, 1980-81; adj. prof. New Coll., Berkeley, 1992—; com. on spirituality New Coll., Berkeley, 1993—, post-doctoral tutor, 1994; freelance copyeditor, 1994. Author: (chpt.) Reform and Counterreform, 1994. Pres. On Belay, 1991-92. U. Calif. Regents fellow, 1979-80. Mem. Am. Acad. Religion, Conf. on Christianity and Lit., Internat. Thomas Merton Soc., Soc. Study of Christian Spirituality, Phi Beta Kappa. Presbyterian.

FLECK, RICHARD FRANCIS, English language educator, writer; b. Phila., Aug. 24, 1937; s. J. Keene and Anne M. (DeLeon) F.; m. Maura B. McMahon, June 29, 1963; children: Richard Sean, Michelle Marie, Ann Maureen. BA, Rutgers U., 1959; MA, Colo. State U., 1962; PhD, U. N.Mex., 1970. Park ranger naturalist Rocky Mountain Nat. Pk., Colo., 1959; instr. English North Adams (Mass.) State Coll., 1963-65; prof. of English U. Wyo., Laramie, 1965-90; prof. intercultural studies, dir. humanities div. Teikyo Loretto Heights U., Denver, 1990-93, dir. humanities div., 1991-93; exch. prof. Osaka (Japan) U., 1981-82; vis. prof. SUNY, Cortland, 1988-89; dean arts and humanities C.C. Denver, 1993—. Author: Thoreau and Muir Among the Indians, 1985, Earthen Wayfarer, 1988, Critical Perspectives on Native American Fiction, 1993, (with others) John Muir: His Life and Works, 1993, (with others) World Without Violence: Essays in Honor of the 125th Anniversary of Gandhi's Birth, 1993, (with others) Stories and Stone: Writing the Anasazi Homeland, 1996, Where Land is Mostly Sky: Essays on The American West, 1997; asst. editor Sage U. Wyo., 1965-67; editor Thoreau Jour. Quar., 1975-77; contbg. editor Paintbrush, 1986—. Dem. precinct committeman, Laramie, 1968. With USN, 1961-63. Grantee U. Wyo., 1967, 71, Wyo. State Hist. Soc., 1973, Wyo. Humanities Coun., 1979, 80, Colo. Coun. Arts, 1995. Mem. Thoreau Soc., Appalachian Mountain Club, Sierra Club. Roman Catholic. Office: CC Denver Office of Dean Arts & Humanities 1111 W Colfax Ave Denver CO 80204-2026

FLECK, STEPHEN HARLAN, French language educator; b. Balt., Oct. 16, 1948; s. Stephen and Louise H. (Harlan) F.; m. Maria I. Lajmanovich, Oct. 22, 1989; 1 child, Benjamin H. BA in Linguistics, U. Mich., 1971; BA in Music, Sonoma State U., Rohnert Park, Calif., 1986; PhD, U. Calif., Davis, 1993. Asst. prof. French Calif. State U., Long Beach, 1992—. Author: (book) Music, Dance and Laughter: Comic Creation in Moliere's Comedy-Ballets. Mem. Pacific Ancient and Modern Lang. Assn., Am. Assn. Tchrs. of French, Soc. des Profs. Francais et Francophones d'Amerique. N. Am. Soc. for Study of Seventeenth Century French Literature.

FLEISCHMANN, ERNEST MARTIN, music administrator; b. Frankfurt, Germany, Dec. 7, 1924; came to U.S., 1969; s. Gustav and Antonia (Koch) F.; children: Stephanie, Martin, Jessica. B of Commerce, U. Cape Town, South Africa, 1950, MusB, 1954; postgrad., South African Coll. Music, 1954-56; MusD (hon.), Cleve. Inst. Music, 1987. Gen mgr. London Symphony Orch., 1959-67; dir. Europe CBS Masterworks, 1967-69; exec. dir. L.A. Philharm. Assn. and Hollywood Bowl, 1969-88, exec. v.p., mng dir., 1988—; mem. French Govt. Commn. Reform of Paris Opera, 1967-68; steering com. U.S. nat. commn. UNESCO Conf. Future of Arts, 1975. Debut as cond. Johannesburg (Republic of South Africa) Symphony Orch., 1942; asst.

condr. South African Nat. Opera, 1948-51, Cape Town U. Opera, 1950-54; condr. South African Coll. Music Choir, 1950-52, Labia Grand Opera Co., Cape Town, 1953-55; music organizer Van Riebeeck Festival Cape Town, 1952; dir. music and drama Johannesburg Festival, 1956; contbr. to music publs. Recipient Award of Merit, L.A. Jr. C. of C., John Steinway award, Friends of Music award, Disting. Arts Leadership award U. So. Calif., 1989, L.A. Honors award L.A. Arts Coun., 1989, Live Music award Am. Fedn. Musicians Local 47, 1991, Disting. Authors/Artists award U. Judaism, 1994, Treasures of L.A. award, Ctrl. City Assn. L.A., 1996, Los Amigos de Los Angeles award, L.A. Conv. and Vis. Bur., 1996, Comdr.'s Cross Order of Merit Federal Republic Germany, 1997. Mem. Assn. Calif. Symphony Orchs., Major Orch. Mgrs. Conf., Am. Symphony Orch. League, L.A. Philharm. Assn. (bd. dirs. 1984—), L.A. Arts Leaders (exec. com.), Nat. Endowment for the Arts (panelist combined arts panel 1977). Office: Los Angeles Philharm Orch 135 N Grand Ave Los Angeles CA 90012-3013 *Progress in the arts involves taking risks. Safety and blandness go hand in hand and should be banished from the artistic experience: better to stick your neck out and fail than to err on the side of correctness and caution.*

FLEISCHMANN, NANCY NORTON, medical research technician, educator; b. Marianna, Ark., Apr. 11, 1929; d. Howard Monroe and Lois (Pedersen) Norton; m. Hartly Fleischmann, Mar. 24, 1961 (div. July 1984); children: Sarah, Anne, Samuel Joseph. BA, Stanford U., Calif., 1951. Type A assessor Harold Brunn Inst., San Francisco, 1960-61, Type A assessor, tchr., 1977-83; Type A assessor, tchr. Meyer Friedman Inst., San Francisco, 1983—; Type A assessor U.S. Army War Coll., Phys. Fitness Rsch. Inst., Carlisle, Pa., 1985-93. Contbr. articles to profl. jours. Office: Meyer Friedman Inst 1515 Scott St San Francisco CA 94115-3511

FLEISHER, STEVEN M., lawyer; b. Chgo., Feb. 5, 1945; s. Max M. and Meta J. (Shifris) F.; m. Marilyn J. Eto, Sept. 2, 1984. AB cum laude, Yale U., 1966; JD cum laude, Harvard U., 1969. Bar: Calif. 1970, U.S. Ct. Appeals (9th cir.) 1970, U.S. Dist. Ct. (no. dist.) Calif. 1970, D.C. 1973, U.S. Ct. Appeals (D.C. cir.) 1973, U.S. Supreme Ct. 1973. Law clk. U.S. Dist. Ct., San Francisco, 1969-70; atty. Calif. Rural Legal Assistance, Gilroy, 1970-72; gen. counsel Food Advocates, Davis, Calif., 1973-74; dir. Drew Health Rights Project, San Francisco, 1974-76; counsel Calif. Dept. Consumer Affairs, Sacramento, 1976-78; ptnr. Fleisher & Neckritz, Oakland, Calif., 1978-82; shareholder Burnhill, Morehouse, Burford, Schofied & Schiller, Walnut Creek, Calif., 1982-87; ptnr. McNichols, McCann & Inderbitzen, Pleasanton, Calif., 1987-91, Hallgrimson, McNichols, McCann & Inderbitzen, Pleasonton, Calif., 1991-95; assoc. gen. counsel Calif. Med. Assn., San Francisco, 1995—; cons. Western Consortium for Health Edn., San Francisco, 1974-78; bd. dirs. Nat. Health Law Program, L.A., 1988-94; arbitrator U.S. Dist. Ct., San Francisco, 1984-91; judge protem Contra Costa County Superior Ct., Martinez, Calif., 1984-88. Contbg. author Advising California Partnerships, 1988, California Sole Proprietorships & Partnerships, 1992; contbg. editor Calif. Ltd. Liability Cos. Reginald H. Smith fellow Office Legal Svcs., Washington, 1970-72. Mem. ABA (bus. law sect. partnership and unicorp. assns. com. 1991—, vice chair corp. counsel com. Torts & Ins. Practice Sect. 1996—), Calif. State Bar (del. com. to confer with CMA 1983-86), D.C. Bar Assn., Calif. State Bar Partnership (com. 1989-94, exec. com. bus. law sect. 1993-96, nonprofits orgn. com. bus. law sect. 1996—). Office: Calif Med Assn 221 Main St PO Box 7690 San Francisco CA 94105

FLEISHMAN, ALAN MICHAEL, marketing consultant; b. Berwick, Pa., June 28, 1939; s. Benjamin Bennet and Ruth (Sadock) F.; m. Ann Arrasmith, Aug. 3, 1963; children: Elizabeth, Gregory, Keith. BA, Dickinson Coll., 1961; postgrad., Xavier U., 1966-67, Calif. State U., Fullerton, 1968-69. Sales and mktg. planning Procter & Gamble, Cin., 1963-67; sr. product mgr. Baxter Internat., Costa Mesa, Calif., 1967-70; dir. mkgt. Allergan, Inc., Irvine, Calif., 1970-76; exec. v.p. Hudson Vitamins, West Caldwell, N.J., 1976-77; v.p. mktg. and sales Cooper Vision, Inc., Mountain View, Calif., 1977-80; pres. Alan M. Fleishman, Mktg. Cons., San Carlos, Calif., 1980—; instr. U. Calif., Berkeley, 1990—. With U.S. Army, 1961-63. Mem. Am. Mktg. Assn., Med. Mktg. Assn. Democrat. Jewish. Home and Office: 3 Bluebell Ln San Carlos CA 94070-1526

FLEMING, DAVID A., mayor. Mayor City of Vacaville, Calif. Office: City of Vacaville 650 Merchants St Vacaville CA 95688

FLEMING, JANE WILLIAMS, retired educator, author; b. Bethlehem, Pa., May 26, 1926; d. James Robert and Marion Pauline (Melloy) Groman; m. George Elliott Williams, July 2, 1955 (div. July 1965); children: Rhett Dorman, Santee Stuart, Timothy Cooper; m. Jérome Thomas Fleming, Sept. 25, 1980. BS, UCLA, 1951; MA, Calif. State U., Long Beach, 1969. Tchr. San Diego Unified Sch Dist., 1951-55, Costa Mesa (Calif.) Sch. Dist., 1955-56, Long Beach (Calif.) Sch. Dist., 1956-58, 62-87, 1990-92; ret. Author: Why Janey Can't Teach, 1996. Fellow Phi Kappa Phi; mem. Ret. Tchrs. Assn., UCLA Alumni Assn., Planetary Soc. (charter).

FLEMING, JUNE HELENA, city manager; b. Little Rock, June 24, 1931; d. Herman Leroy and Ethel Lucille (Thompson) Dwellingham; m. Silas W. Cullins, June 5, 1956 (div.); m. Roscoe Lee Fleming Jr., Mar. 11, 1966; children: Ethel Lucille, Roscoe Lee III. BA, Talladega Coll., 1953; MLS, Drexel U., 1954. Br. libr. Bklyn. Pub. Libr., 1954-55; high sch. libr. Little Rock Pub. Schs., 1955-56; assoc. prof. Philander Smith Coll., Little Rock, 1960-66; dir. librs. City of Palo Alto, Calif., 1968-79, asst. city mgr., 1980-92, city mgr., 1992—. Mem. adv. bd. YWCA, Palo Alto, 1984—; pres. search com. Foothill Coll., Los Altos Hills, Calif., 1994; mem. allocation com. Santa Clara United Way, San Jose, Calif., 1991-93. Mem. Internat. City Mgrs. Assn., Links, Inc., Rotary (bd. dirs.), Delta Sigma Theta (corr. sec. 1993). Methodist. Home: 1101 Hamilton Ave Palo Alto CA 94301-2217 Office: City of Palo Alto 250 Hamilton Ave Palo Alto CA 94301-2531

FLEMING, MACKLIN, judge, author; b. Chgo., Sept. 6, 1911; s. Ingram Macklin Stainback and Hazel (Caldwell) Fleming; m. Polly Naething, May 17, 1941; children: Penelope, Frances, Ingram. BA, Yale U., 1934, LLB, 1937; LLD, Pepperdine U., 1968. Bar: N.Y. 1938, Calif. 1946. Assoc. Sullivan & Cromwell, N.Y.C., 1937-39; atty. Bituminous Coal divsn. U.S. Govt., Washington, 1939-41; pvt. practice San Francisco, 1946-49; spl. asst., asst. U.S. atty. U.S. Atty.'s Office, San Francisco, 1949-53; assoc. Mitchell, Silberberg & Knupp, L.A., 1954-59; judge Superior Ct., L.A., 1959-64; justice Calif. Ct. Appeals, L.A., 1964-81; of counsel Troy and Gould, L.A., 1981-91; judge Superior Ct., L.A., 1992—. Author: The Price of Perfect Justice, 1974, Of Crimes and Rights, 1978. Chmn. Far Eastern Art Coun., L.A. County Mus., 1967-69; v.p. Ctr. Theater Group, L.A., 1970. Capt. U.S. Army, 1941-46. Fellow Am. Bar Found.; mem. ABA, L.A. County Bar Assn., Bar of City of N.Y., Inst. of Jud. Adminstrn., Selden Soc., Fgn. Policy Assn., Internat. Commn. of Jurists. Democrat. Episcopalian. Home: 331 N Carmelina Ave Los Angeles CA 90049-2701 Office: 1801 Century Park E Ste 1600 Los Angeles CA 90067-2318

FLEMMING, STANLEY LALIT KUMAR, family practice physician, mayor, state legislator; b. Rosebud, S.D., Mar. 30, 1953; s. Homer W. and Evelyn C. (Misra) F.; m. Martha Susan Light, July 2, 1977; children: Emily Drisana, Drew Anil, Claire Elizabeth Misra. AAS, Ft. Steilacoom Coll., 1973; BS in Zoology, U. Wash., 1976; MA in Social Psychology, Pacific Luth. U., 1979; DO, Western U., 1985. Diplomate Am. Coll. Family Practice; cert. ATLS. Intern Pacific Hosp. Long Beach (Calif.), 1985-86; resident in family practice Pacific Hosp. Long Beach, 1986-88; fellow in adolescent medicine Children's Hosp. L.A., 1988-90; clin. preceptor Family Practice Residency Program Calif. Med. Ctr., U. So. Calif., L.A., 1989—; clin. instr. Sch. Medicine U. So. Calif., L.A., 1989-90; clin. instr. Coll. Osteopathic Medicine Pacific, Pomona, Calif., 1989-90; clin. asst. prof. Family Medicine Coll. Osteopathic Medicine Pacific, Pomona, 1987—; exam. commr., expert examiner Calif. Osteo. Med. Bd., 1987-89; med. dir. Community Health Care Delivery System Pierce County, Tacoma, Wash., 1990—; mayor City of University Place, Wash.; clin. instr. U. Wash. Sch. Medicine, 1990—; bd. dirs. Calif. State Bd. Osteo. Physicians Examiners, 1989—, cons., 1989. Mayor, City of University Place, Wash. Col. M.C., U.S. Army, 1976—. Named Outstanding Young Man Am., 1983, 85, Intern of Yr. Western U. Health Sci. Coll. Osteo. Medicine of Pacific, 1986, Resident of Yr., 1988, Alumnus of Yr., 1993, Physician of Yr., 1993; recipient Pumerantz-Weiss award, 1985. Mem. Fedn. State Bds. Licensing, Am. Osteopathic Assn., Am. Acad. Family Practice, Soc. Adolescent Medicine, Assn. Military Surgeons U.S., Assn. U.S. Army (chpt. pres.), Soc. Am. Military Engrs. (chpt. v.p.), Calif. Med. Assn., Wash. Osteopathic Med. Assn., Calif. Family Practice Soc., Long Beach Med. Assn. (com. mem.), N.Y. Acad. Sci., Calif. Med. Review Inc., Sigma Sigma Phi, Am. Legion. Episcopalian. Home: 7619 Chambers Creek Rd W University Pl WA 98467-2015 Office: Family Health Ctr Olympia WA 98504

FLETCHER, BETTY B., federal judge; b. Tacoma, Mar. 29, 1923. B.A., Stanford U., 1943; LL.B., U. Wash., 1956. Bar: Wash. 1956. Mem. firm Preston, Thorgrimson, Ellis, Holman & Fletcher, Seattle, 1956-1979; judge U.S. Ct. Appeals (9th cir.), Seattle., 1979—. Mem. ABA (Margaret Brent award 1992), Wash. State Bar Assn., Am. Law Inst., Fed. Judges Assn. (past pres.), Order of Coif, Phi Beta Kappa. Office: US Ct Appeals 9th Cir 1010 5th Ave Seattle WA 98104-1130

FLETCHER, CHARLES R., public affairs specialist; b. Gadsden, Ala., Nov. 18, 1950. B in Journalism and Mass Comm., N.Mex. State U., 1973. With USDA Forest Svc., Ft. Collins, Colo. Editor, author: (newsletter) Rocky Mountain Update, 1970-95; (quarterly mag.) Forestry Research West, 1973— (Blue Pencil award 1981). Office: USDA Forest Svc 240 W Prospect Rd Fort Collins CO 80526

FLETCHER, DONALD WARREN, microbiologist, educator; b. Phoenix, Ariz., June 8, 1929; s. Donald Warren and Ruth Marie Fletcher; children: Lisa, Timothy. BS, Oreg. State U., 1951, MS, 1953; PhD, Wash. State U., 1956. Cert. community coll. tchr., Calif. Instr. Wash. State U., Pullman, 1956-59; asst. prof. San Francisco State U., 1959-62, assoc. prof., 1962-66, prof., 1966-88, prof. emeritus, 1988—; dean coll. liberal arts U. Bridgeport, Conn., 1969-70; assoc. state univ. dean Calif. State U., Long Beach, 1975-88; exec. dir. Ctr. for Advanced Med. Tech., San Francisco, 1966-69, Commn. on Adult Edn. Calif. State U., 1987-88. Author: Microbiology, 1980; contbr. articles to profl. jours. Vice foreman grand jury, 1990-91. Fulbright fellow, 1966, 67; grantee several orgns. Fellow Calif. Acad. Sci., AAAS; mem. Am. Soc. Microbiology, Soc. for Gen. Microbiology, Sigma Xi. Home: 2070 High Mesa Dr Henderson NV 89012

FLETCHER, DOUGLAS GERALD, research scientist; b. Burlington, Vt., Nov. 15, 1957; s. John Grover Jr. and Marylin Preston (Hinsdale) F.; m. Melissa Lynn Gough, June 4, 1988. BS in Engring., U. Vt., 1979; MSME, U. Va., 1984, PhD in Mech. and Aerospace Engring., 1989. Engr. Vt. Wood Energy Corp., Stowe, 1979-80, Vt. Ski Safety Equipment Corp., Underhill, 1980-81; grad. rsch. asst. dept. mech. and aero. engring. U. Va., 1982-88; rsch. assoc. Aerospace Rsch. Lab. U. Va., Charlottesville, 1988-89; rsch. scientist NASA Ames Rsch. Ctr., Moffett Field, Calif., 1989—; lectr. dept. mech. engring. Stanford (Calif.) U., 1995—; reviewer Optics Letters AIAA, Jour., 1990—. Contbr. articles to profl. publs. Mem. AIAA, Optical Soc. Am. Mem. Green Party. Office: NASA Ames Rsch Ctr MS 230-2 Moffett Field CA 94035-1000

FLETCHER, HOMER LEE, librarian; b. Salem, Ind., May 11, 1928; s. Floyd M. and Hazel (Barnett) F.; m. Jacquelyn Ann Blanton, Feb. 7, 1950; children—Deborah Lynn, Randall Brian, David Lee. B.A., Ind. U., 1953; M.S. in L.S, U. Ill., 1954. Librarian Milw. Pub. Library, 1954-56; head librarian Ashland (Ohio) Pub. Library, 1956-59; city librarian Arcadia (Cal.) Pub. Library, 1959-65, Vallejo (Calif.) Pub. Library, 1965-70; city librarian San Jose, Calif., 1970-90, ret., 1990. Contbr. articles to profl. jours. Pres. S. Solano chpt. Calif. Assn. Neurol. Handicapped Children, 1968-69. Served with USAF, 1946-49. Mem. ALA (intellectual freedom com. 1967-72), Calif. Library Assn. (pres. pub. libraries sect. 1967), Phi Beta Kappa. Democrat. Presbyterian. Home: 7921 Belknap Dr Cupertino CA 95014-4973 *Standing up for what I believe regardless of the consequences. Accepting all human beings as important regardless of their circumstances. Emphasizing honest and forthright behavior in personal and professional life. Retaining a sense of humility and thankfulness.*

FLETCHER, J. SUE, health educator; b. Hollister, Calif., Aug. 9, 1946; d. James R. and Lois Frances (Fletcher) Prewitt; 1 child, Jeffery W. Cook. BSN, Calif. State U., Fresno, 1968, MS in Nursing, 1971; EdD, U. San Francisco, 1980. Instr., chmn. div. Modesto (Calif.) Jr. Coll., 1973-83; staff nurse Scenic Gen. Hosp., Modesto, 1983-90; prof. Calif. State U., Stanislaus, Turlock, 1983—. Co-Author: Essentials in Mental Health Nursing, 3d edit. Pres. Mercer City Sch. Dist. Bd. Edn., 1996-97; pres. Merced County Sch. Bds. Assn., 1995-96. Mem. Calif. Nurses Assn. (pres. region 8 1992-94).

FLETCHER, JAMES ALLEN, video company executive; b. Toledo, Sept. 18, 1947; s. Allen Rae and Ruth Helen (Scharf) F.; m. Kathy Jane Barrett, Jan. 25, 1975. AS, West Coast U., 1977, BSEE, 1979. Electronic technician Hughes Aircraft Co., El Segundo, Calif., 1970-72; engring. technician Altec Corp., Anaheim, Calif., 1972-75, Magna Corp., Santa Fe Springs, Calif., 1975-76; engring. technician Odetics Inc., Anaheim, 1976-79, electronic engr., 1979-86; pres., founder F & B Technologies, Orange, Calif., 1986—. Served as sgt. U.S. Army, 1967-69. Mem. Soc. Motion Picture and TV Engrs., Soc. Cable TV Engrs., Mensa. Libertarian. Office: F & B Technologies 630 N Tustin St Ste 1516 Orange CA 92867-7127

FLETCHER, LELAND VERNON, artist; b. Cumberland, Md., Sept. 18, 1946; s. Kenneth L. and Marjorie L. (Benecke) F.; m. Janis Traub, July 19, 1978; children: Nathan Fletcher, Joshua Traub. BS, U. Minn., 1972. One man shows include U. Minn. Exptl. Gallery, 1972, La Mamelle Art Ctr., San Francisco, 1976, San Jose State U. Union Gallery, 1978, Place des Nations, Maubeuge, France, 1987, Univ. Art Gallery, Calif. State U., Hayward, 1989, McHenry County Coll. Art Gallery, Crystal Lake, Ill., 1991, Lake County Mus., Calif., 1995; group exhbns. include Mus. Contemporary Art, Sao Paulo, Brazil, 1977, Urbanart '77, Vancouver, Can., 1977, L.A. Inst. Contemporary Art, 1978, Inst. Modern Art, Brisbane, 1978, Hansen Gallery, N.Y.C., 1978, Fendrick Gallery, Washington, 1979, 8th Internat. Print Bienale, Cracow, Poland, 1980, Cooper-Hewitt Mus., N.Y.C., 1980, Sch. Art Inst. Chgo., 1981, Metronome Gallery, Barcelona, 1981, 16th Bienal de Sao Paulo, 1981, Neue galerie der Stadt Linz, 1982, Bienal de Pontevedra, Spain, 1983, Lyng by Kunstbibliotek, Denmark, 1984, Otis Art Inst./Parsons Sch. Design, Los Angeles, 1984, 10th Internat. Print Bienale, Cracow, Poland, 1984, Mus. Arte da Univ. Fed. de Mato Grosso, Brazil, 1984, 11th Biennal Internat., Mus. Art Contemporani d'Eivissa, Spain, 1984, Intergrafik '84 Triennale, Berlin, Fiatel Muveszek Klubja Budapest, 1985, Intersection Gallery, San Francisco, 1985, Mus. Petit Format, Couvin, Belgium, 1985, 9th British Internat. Print Biennale, Bradford, Eng., 1986, Victoria and Albert Mus., London, 1986, Sculpt 87/3, Maubeuge, 1987, Fundacio la Caixa, Valencia, Spain, 1987, Acad. Belles Arts Sabadell, Barcelona, 1987, Taliesin Ctr. for Arts, Swansea, Eng., 1987, Worcester (Eng.) City Art Gallery, 1987, Symposium Sculpture en Plein Air, Maubeuge, France, 1987, Richards Gallery, Northeastern U., Boston, 1987, Montserrat Coll. Art, Beverly, Mass., 1987, 11 Internat. Print Biennale, Krakow, 1986, Skulptur Biennale '88 Royal Gardens, Copenhagen, Internat. Biennale Palais des Roi de Majorque, Peripignan, France, 1988, Fine Art Mus., Budapest, Hungary, 1988, Works gallery, San Jose Calif., 1988, Palthehuis Mus., Oldenzaal, The Netherlands, 1989, Budapest Galeria, Hungary, 1989, Stedelijk Hoger Institut, Cultural Ctr., Genk, Belgium, 1989, Inst. Contemporary Art, Clocktower Gallery, N.Y.C., 1989, Corporacion GOG, Pontevedra, Spain, 1989, Ea. Washington U., Spokane Ctr. Gallery, 1989, Munson-Williams-Proctor Inst., Sch. Art Gallery, Utica, N.Y., 1989, 44th Salon des Realities Nouvelles, Grand Palais, Paris, 1990, Buda Castle Palace, Budapest, 1990, Pensacola (Fla.) Mus. Art, 1990, Anchorage (Alaska) Mus. Art, 1990, Fundacao Democrito Rocha, Fortaleza, Brazil, 1991, Miejski Osrodek Kultury, Chelm, Poland, 1991, Bharat Bhavan, Bhopal, India, 1991, Chabot Coll., Hayward, Calif., 1992, Lake County Arts Coun., Lakeport, Calif., 1992, Artisans Gallery, Mill Valley, Calif., 1992, Greenville Mus. Art, N.C., Centro Civico Social, Alcorcon, Madrid, 1994, Lake Co. Mus., 1995, numerous others; represented in permanent collection at Mus. Contemporary Art, Sao Paulo, Mpls. Inst. Arts, Art Mus. of Calif. State U., Long Beach, deSaisset Mus., U. Santa Clara (Calif.), Art Inst. Chgo., Victoria and Albert Mus., London, Museen der Stadt Koln, Ludwig Mus., Cologne, Mus. Plantin-Moretus, Antwerp, Mus. de Arte Moderno, Barcelona, Bradford Mus., Eng., Kunsthalle, Hamburg, Galleria D'Arte Moderna, Trieste, Ecole des Beaux-Arts, Mus. Maubeuge, Musee de la Sculpture en plein Air, Maubeuge, Musee de Maubeuge, FMK Galeria, Budapest, Bur. for Artistic Exhibitions, Cracow, Poland, Kunsthalle Bremen, West Germany, Museu de Arte da Universidad Federal de Mato Grosso, Brazil, others. Address: 3288 Konocti Ln Kelseyville CA 95451-9131

FLICK, GERVASE MEAD, surgeon; b. Boston, Feb. 21, 1936; s. Gervase Charles and Sarah Germain (Mead) F.; m. Anne Rene LaVasseur; children: Michelle, Lisa, Heather, Buff. AB, Colgate U., 1955, MA, 1956; DO, Kirksville Coll. Osteo. Surg., 1960; MD, U. Calif., Irvine, 1962; JD, McGeorge Law Coll., 1972; MPH, U. Hawaii, 1976. Diplomate Am. Bd. Forensic Medicine, Am. Bd. Forensic Examiners, Am. Bd. Legal Medicine, Am. Bd. Experts in Traumatic Stress. Chief of staff South Gate Cmty. Hosp., Sacramento, 1970-72; pvt. practice Sacramento, 1970-72; emergency physician Kona (Hawaii) Hosp., 1972-74; chief of emergency dept. 5th Ave Hosp., Seattle, 1975; pvt. practice law and medicine Honolulu, 1976-80; chief physician Trans Alaska Pipeline Constrn. Co., Prudo Bay, 1976; pvt. practice law Sacramento, 1976-80; ship's surgeon U.S. Merchant Marine, 1980-88; emergency and occupl. medicine physician Kaiser Found. Hosp., Honolulu, 1989-92; occupl. medical physician, med./legal cons. Physorney Cons., Tacoma and Seattle, 1992—, v.p. Author: Premedical Education, 1966, Medical Malpractice in Emergency Medicine, 1992; co-author: Hawaiian Calories, 1994, Head and Spinal Injury Problems, 1996, Contracting for Different Medical Positions, 1997; inventor/patentee safety medication container. Mem. Boy's Town; v.p. Hawaii Osteo. Med. Assn., Honolulu, 1988, pres., 1989. Capt. USAF (flight surgeon), 1962-68. Fellow Am. Coll. Legal Medicine, Am. Coll. Forensic Medicine, Am. Coll. Forensic Examiners, Am. Acad. of Experts in Traumatic Stress. Office: PO Box 1954 Tacoma WA 98401-1954

FLICK, WILLIAM FREDRICK, surgeon; b. Lancaster, Pa., Aug. 18, 1940; s. William Joseph and Anna (Volkl) F.; m. Jacqueline Denise Phaneuf, May 21, 1966; children: William J., Karen E., Christopher R., Derrick W., Brian A. BS, Georgetown U., 1962, MD, 1966; MBA, U. Colo., 1990. Cert. Am. Bd. Surgeons, 1976. Self employed surgeon Cheyenne, Wyo., 1973-84; pres., surgeon Cheyenne Surgical Assocs., 1984-94; med. dir. Blue Cross Blue Shield of Wyo., Cheyenne, 1994—. Trustee Laramie County Sch. Dist. #1, Cheyenne, 1988-92. Maj., chief of surgery USAF, 1971-73. Fellow ACS; mem. Am. Coll. Physician Execs., Nat. Assn. Managed Care. Republican. Roman Catholic. Office: Blue Cross Blue Shield Wyo 400 House Ave Cheyenne WY 82007-1468

FLINN, JANICE CECILIA, secondary school educator, administrator; b. Holywood, N. Ireland, UK, Nov. 22, 1950; d. John and Renee (Finlay) F. BSc magna cum laude, Coleraine, No. Ireland, 1972; Cert. in Field Methods Archaeology, UCLA, 1981. Student counselor Youth with a Mission, Kalua-Kona, Hawaii, 1972-76; internat. travling rep. Corrie Ten Boom Ministry, Orange, Calif., 1974; tchr. Laurel Hall Sch., N. Hollywood, Calif., 1976-83; translator, editor Evangelishe Marien Schwesternschaft, Darmstadt, Germany, 1984; adminstr. Victoria Coll., Belfast, No. Ireland, 1984-89, Found. for His Ministry, Baja, Calif., Mexico, 1989-92, Apple Valley (Calif.) Christian Sch., 1993—; bd. dirs. Found. for His Ministry, Baja, Calif., Mex., 1982-92, Apple Valley Christian Sch., 1994-96; bd. dirs., chmn. Crossfire Trust, Darkley, Northern Ireland, 1986-92; dir. Christian Ireland Ministries, Belfast, No. Ireland, 1981-93; coursework moderator, examiner Northern Ireland Schs. Examination Coun., Belfast, 1988-91; workshop leader UN, Eng., 1970. Mem. Vision 2000, Apple Valley, 1996. Mem. ASCD, Assn. Christian Schs. Internat. Republican. Baptist. Home: 11643 Ash St Apple Valley CA 92308 Office: Apple Valley Christian Sch 22434 Nisqually Rd Apple Valley CA 92308-6577

FLINN, ROBERTA JEANNE, management and computer applications consultant; b. Twin Falls, Idaho, Dec. 19, 1947; d. Richard H. and Ruth (Johnson) F. Student Colo. State U., 1966-67. Cert. Novell netware engr. Ptnr., Aqua-Star Pools & Spas, Boise, Idaho, 1978—, mng. ptnr., 1981-83; ops. mgr. Polly Pools, Inc., Canby, Oreg., 1983-84, br. mgr. Polly Pools, Inc., A-One Distributing, 1984-85; comptr., Beaverton Printing, Inc., 1986-89; mng. ptnr. Invisible Ink, Canby, Oreg., 1989—. Mem. NAFE, Nat. Appaloosa Horse Club, Oreg. Dressage Soc. (pres. North Willamette Valley chpt.). Home: 24687 S Central Point Rd Canby OR 97013-9743

FLINT, LOU JEAN, state education official; b. Ogden, Utah, July 11, 1934; d. Elmer Blood and Ella D. (Adams) F.; children: Dirk Kershaw Brown, Kristie Susan Brown Felix, Flint Kershaw Brown. B.S., Weber State Coll., 1968; M.Ed., U. Utah, 1974, Ed.S, 1981. Cert. early childhood and elem. edn., Utah Bd. Edn., 1968, edn. adminstrn., 1981. Master tchr. Muir Elem., Davis Sch. Dist., Farmington, Utah, 1968-77; edn. specialist Dist. I, Dept. Def., Eng., Scotland, Norway, Denmark, Holland, Belgium, 1977-79; ednl. cons. Office Higher Edn. State of Utah, Utah System Approach to Individualized Learning, Tex., S.C., Fla., Utah, 1979-81; acad. affairs officer Commn. Higher Edn. Office State of Utah, Salt Lake City, 1982—; mem. Women's Politics Caucus; adv. bd. Women and Bus. Conf.; mem. MHCS Centennial Com., 1995-96, demonstration project State of Utah, 1992-96, foster care citizen review pilot project State of Utah. Named Exemplary Tchr., Utah State Bd. Edn., 1970-77, Outstanding Educator, London Central High Sch., 1979; recipient Appreciation award, Gov. of Utah, 1983-85, 93, Woman of Achievement award Utah Bus. and Profl. Women, 1985, Pathfinder award C. of C., 1988, Outstanding Educator award YWCA, 1989, Silver Apple award Utah State U., 1992, award for svcs. Utah Mental Health Assn., 1996. Mem. AAUW (Edn. Found. award given in her honor, 1986, named Woman Who Makes History, 1994), Nat. Assn. Women's Work/Women's Worth (Disting. Woman award 1987), Women's Polit. Caucus (Susa Young Gates award 1987), Nat. Assn. Edn. Young Children, Utah Assn. Edn. Young Children (past pres.), Women Concerned About Nuclear War, Utah Jaycee Aux. (past pres. Centerville), Crones Coun., Math Sci. Network. Mormon. Author: The Comprehensive Community College, 1980; others. Office: State of Utah Office Commr Higher Edn 355 W North Temple # 3 Triad Salt Lake City UT 84180-1114

FLINT, WILLIS WOLFSCHMIDT (WILLI WOLFSCHMIDT), artist; b. Kenton, Ohio, Dec. 27, 1936; s. Wilbur Henry and Ilo Edna (Obenour) F. Student, Art Career Sch., N.Y.C., 1957-60, Ins. Allende, San Miguel Allende, Mexico, 1961. Artist trainee Kossack Advt., Tucson, 1961; gen. boardman Mithoff Advt., El Paso, 1962-63; tech. illustrator Volt Tech. Corp., N.Y.C., 1967; gen. illustrator Salesvertising Advt., Denver, 1968; gen. boardman/cons. Burr-Brown Rsch. Corp., Tucson, 1969-71; musician, actor Paul Barons Harmonica Rascals, Bklyn., 1965-85; musician The Wild Ones, Tucson, 1982-83; muralist, San Diego, Tucson, N.Y.C., 1976-80; artist, Tucson, 1985—; originator Fantasy-Expressionism, 1984; pvt. tchr. art, Tucson, 1981-85; cons. muralist Yaqui Indian-Pascua Ctr., Tucson, 1989; freelance muralist and graphic artist Wolfschmidt & Washburn, 1994-96. Poetry included in: Best-Loved Contemporary Poems, 1979, Famous Poems of Today, 1995, A Delicate Balance, 1996, three edits. of Poetic Voices of America, 1996, Best Poems of the '90s, 1996, Best Poems of the 20th Century, 1996, Best Famous Poems of '96, 1997, Best Poems of '97, 1997; paintings exhibited in group shows at United Way Fund Drive Exhibit, Tucson, United Servicemen's Orgn. Exhibit, Mobile, Ala., Student Union Exhibit U. Ariz., Tucson, La Galeria Instituto, San Miguel de Allende, Margarita De Mena Gallery, N.Y.C.; represented in permanent collection So. Ariz. Hist. Soc., Tombstone, also pvt. collections. With USN, 1954-57, 1979-81. Recipient scholarship Latham Found., 1958, award of merit Latham Found., 1958, letter commendation U. Ariz. Family Practice, Tucson, 1978, letter commendation Dept. Navy, San Diego, 1979. Mem. The Maverick Artists, Internat. Soc. Poets. Home: 707 W Calle Progreso Tucson AZ 85705

FLOCK, ROBERT ASHBY, retired entomologist; b. Kellogg, Idaho, July 16, 1914; s. Abraham Lincoln and Florence Louise (Ashby) F.; m. Elsie Marie Ronken, Apr. 8, 1950; children: Karen Marie, Anne Louise Checkai. BS, U. Ariz., 1938, MS, 1941; PhD, U. Calif., Berkeley, 1951. Inspector Ariz. Commn. Agriculture and Horticulture, Phoenix, 1938-41, asst. entomologist, 1941-46; lab. tech. U. Calif., Riverside, 1947-52, asst. entomologist, 1952-63; entomologist Imperial County Dept. Agriculture, El Centro, Calif., 1963-85, part-time entomologist, 1985—. Contbr. articles to profl. jours. Mem. Entomol. Soc. Am., Am. Phytopathol. Soc., Pan-Pacific Entomol. Soc., AAAS, Ctr. for Process Studies, Kiwanis (pres. Imperial Valley chpt. 1984-86, Man of Yr. 1986), Sigma Xi. Republican. Methodist. Home:

667 Wensley Ave PO Box 995 El Centro CA 92244 Office: Imperial County Dept Agricu 150 S 9th St El Centro CA 92243-2801

FLOM, ROBERT MICHAEL, interior designer; b. Grand Forks, N.D., Oct. 27, 1952; s. John Nicholai and Irene Magdaline (Miller) F.; m. Holly Suzanne Schue, July 20, 1975 (div. June 1986); m. Margaret Elizabeth Moon, Oct. 15, 1988; children: Amy Michelle Moon, Jamie Bryant Moon. Student, Western Tech., 1970-71, U. N.D., 1980-83, LaSalle U., 1994-95, Century U., 1996—. Asst. food and beverage mgr. Holiday Inn/Topeka Inns, Denver, 1970-71; interior designer, fl. mgr. Crossroads Furniture, Grand Forks, 1972-85; store mgr. Greenbaums, Tacoma, 1986-88, interior designer, 1986-95; interior designer Westbay Interiors, Gig Harbor, Wash., 1996—; tng. advisor Greenbaums, Bellevue, Wash., 1988-85. Mem. Am. Soc. Interior Designers (allied mem.), Autism Soc. Tacoma-Pierce County (treas. 1991—). Home: 6816 47th St W University Place WA 98466-4912 Office: Westbay Interiors 5790 Soundview Dr Gig Harbor WA 98335

FLOOD, JAMES TYRRELL, broadcasting executive, public relations consultant; b. Los Angeles, Oct. 5, 1934; s. James Joseph and Teresa (Rielly) F.; m. Bonnie Carolyn Lutz, Mar. 25, 1966; children: Hilary C., Sean L. BA in Liberal Arts, U. Calif., Santa Barbara, 1956; MA in Communications, Calif. State U., Chico, 1981. Publicist Rogers & Cowan, 1959-60, Jim Mahoney & Assocs., 1960-61, ABC-TV, San Francisco and Hollywood, Calif., 1961-64; cons. pub. relations, Beverly Hills, Calif., 1964-72; pub. relations, advt. dir. Jerry Lewis Films, 1964-72; dir. pub. rels. MTM Prodns., 1970-72; pub. relations cons. Medic Alert Found. Internat., 1976-83; owner, mgr. Sta. KRIJ-FM, Paradise, 1983-88; instr. Calif. State U. Sch. Communications, Chico, 1982-89; gen. mgr. KIXE-TV (PBS), Redding-Chico, Calif., 1991-92; media cons., 1993—. represented numerous artists including Pearl Bailey, Gary Owens, Ruth Buzzi, Allen Ludden, Betty White, Celeste Holm, Jose Feliciano, Tom Kennedy, Shirley Jones, David Cassidy, others. Pub. rels. dir. Mary Tyler Moore Prodns., 1971. Calif. media cons. Carter/Mondale campaign, 1976; mem. Calif. Dem. Fin. Com., 1982-83. Served with USNR, 1956-58. Mem. Calif. Broadcasters Assn. (bd. dirs. 1986-88).

FLOOD, SHEILA THERESA, physical therapist; b. Spokane, Wash., Jan. 23, 1958; d. Seymour Allen and Vera Rose (Peck) F.; m. Scott Lewis Kerber, Apr. 20, 1991. BS, U. Puget Sound, 1982. Phys. therapy aide Pk. Rose Care Ctr., Tacoma, 1982-83; phys. therapist Desert Hosp., Palm Springs, Calif., 1983-85, sr. phys. therapist, 1986-94; ind. contractor home health Cathedral City, Calif., 1994—; mktg. com. for rehab. svcs. Desert Hosp., Palm Springs, 1991-93, pre-operative teaching, 1991—. Named Employee of Month, Desert Hosp., 1987. Mem. AAUW (treas. 1984-89, v.p. membership 1989-91, rec. sec. 1996-97). Methodist. Home: 68-555 Los Gatos Rd Cathedral City CA 92234-8101

FLOR, LOY LORENZ, chemist, corrosion engineer, consultant; b. Luther, Okla., Apr. 25, 1919; s. Alfred Charles and Nellie M. (Wilkinson) F.; BA in Chemistry, San Diego State Coll., 1941; m. Virginia Louise Pace, Oct. 1, 1946; children: Charles R., Scott R., Gerald C., Donna Jeanne, Cynthia Gail. With Helix Water Dist., La Mesa, Calif., 1947-84, chief chemist, 1963—, supr. water quality, 1963—, supr. corrosion control dept., 1956—. 1st. lt. USAAF, 1941-45. Registered profl. engr., Calif. Mem. Am. Chem. Soc. (chmn. San Diego sect. 1965—), Am. Water Works Assn. (chmn. water quality div. Calif. sect. 1965—), Nat. Assn. Corrosion Engrs. (chmn. western region 1970), Masons. Republican. Presbyterian.

FLORA, MARY ELLEN, bishop; b. Martinsville, Va., Sept. 19, 1944; d. Paul Haden and Vivian Aston (Riggle) F.; m. Charles Richard Eckel, June 1966 (div. 1976); m. F. Slusher, Mar. 3, 1977. BA in Sociology, Queens Coll., 1966; postgrad., Oreg. State U., 1969-70. Ordained to ministry, Ch. of Divine Man, 1976. Youth program coord. Mission Dist. YMCA, San Francisco, 1966-68; pre-kindergarten tchr. Oakland (Calif.) Sch. Sys., 1968-69; jr. and sr. H.S. tchr. Singapore-Am., 1971-72; real estate speculator Oakland, Calif., 1973-76; min., bishop, tchr. Ch. of Divine Man, Everett, Wash., 1976—; co-founder Ch. of Divine Man, Seattle, Everett, Tacoma, Spokane, Bellingham, Wash., Portland, Oreg., Vancouver, B.C., Can.; vice chmn. bd. dirs., Ch. of Divine Man, 1977—. Author: Meditation: Key to Spiritual Awakening, 1991, Healing: Key to Spiritual Balance, 1992, Claivoyance: Key to Spiritual Perspective, 1992, Chakras: Key to Spiritual Opening, 1993, Cosmic Energy: The Creative Power, 1995, Earth Energy: The Spiritual Frontier, 1996. Del. YMCA World Youth Conf. Va. YMCA, Hilversom, Holland, 1960; scholarship Queens Coll., 1964-65, DANA scholar, 1966. Office: Ch of Divine Man 2402 Summit Ave Everett WA 98201-3256

FLORENCE, KENNETH JAMES, lawyer; b. Hanford, Calif., July 31, 1943; s. Ivy Owen and Louella (Dobson) F.; m. Verena Magdalena Demuth, Dec. 10, 1967. BA, Whittier Coll., 1965; JD, Hastings Coll. Law, U. Calif.-San Francisco, 1974. Bar: Calif. 1974, U.S. Dist. Ct. (cen. dist.) Calif. 1974, U.S. Dist. Ct. (ea. and so. dists.) Calif., 1976, U.S. Dist. Ct. (no. dist.) Calif. 1980, U.S. Ct. Appeals (9th cir.) 1975, U.S. Supreme Ct. 1984. Dist. mgr. Pacific T&T, Calif., 1969-71; assoc. Parker, Milliken, et al, Los Angeles, 1974-78; ptnr. Dern, Mason, et al, 1978-84, Swerdlow, Florence & Sanchez, A Law Corp., Beverly Hills, 1984—; pres. Westside Legal Services, Inc., Santa Monica, Calif., 1982-83. Served to lt. USNR, 1966-69, Vietnam. Col. J.G. Boswell scholar, 1961. Mem. ABA (co-chmn. state labor law com. 1988-91). Democrat. Home: 1063 Stradella Rd Los Angeles CA 90077-2607 Office: Swerdlow Florence & Sanchez 9401 Wilshire Blvd Ste 828 Beverly Hills CA 90212-2921

FLORENCE, VERENA MAGDALENA, business and computer consultant; b. Interlaken, Switzerland, Nov. 4, 1946; came to U.S., 1967; d. Paul Robert and Marie (Raess) Demuth; m. Kenneth James Florence, Dec. 10, 1967. BA, U. Calif., Berkeley, 1974; MS, UCLA, 1979, PhD, 1982. Research scientist Procter & Gamble, Cin., 1983; adminstr. Swerdlow & Florence, Beverly Hills, Calif., 1984-89; pres., chief exec. officer, chmn. of bd. Böl Designs, Inc., L.A., 1989—. Contbr. articles to profl. jours. Mem. L.A. Computer Soc. (SIG leader). Democrat. Home and Office: 1063 Stradella Rd Los Angeles CA 90077-2607

FLORES, DAN LOUIE, history educator; b. Vivian, La., Oct. 19, 1948; s. Willie Clyde Jr. and Margaret Kathryn (Hale) F. BA, Northwestern State U., Natchitoches, La., 1971; MA, Northwestern State U., 1972; PhD, Tex. A&M U., 1978. Instr., history Northwestern State U., 1971-72; teaching asst. Tex. A&M U., College Station, 1974-78; vis. asst. prof. Tex. Tech. U., Lubbock, 1978-80, asst. prof., 1980-84, assoc. prof., 1984-90, prof., history, 1990-92; vis. prof. U. Wyo., Laramie, 1986; A.B. Hammond chair in western history U. Mont., Missoula, 1992—. Author: Jefferson and Southwestern Exploration, 1984 (Best Book on the West, Westerners' Internat., Best Book on Tex., Tex. State Hist. Assn.), Journal of an Indian Trader, 1985, Canyon Visions, 1989, Caprock Canyon Lands, 1990, The Mississippi Kite, 1993. Recipient NEH summer rsch. grant, 1983, Eugene Barker prize (for an article) U.Tex.-Arlington, 1978. Fellow Tex. State Hist. Assn. (Tullis prize for best article 1985); mem. Am. Assn. for Environ. History, Western History Assn. (Ray A. Billington prize for best article 1985), Ethnohistory Assn. Office: Dept History U Montana Missoula MT 59812

FLORES, FERNANDO E., diplomat, publisher; b. San José, Costa Rica, July 14, 1908; came to U.S., 1923; s. Enrique Flores-Vargas Machuca and Berta (Yglesias) Ross; m. Gloria Emelie Mazick; 1 child, Rima Maria. BBA, Heald Coll., 1925; postgrad. in Polit. Sci., U. Calif., Berkeley, 1929; HHD (hon.), Antonomous U. Guadalajara, Mex., 1990. Vice consul Govt. Costa Rica, San Francisco, 1930-42, consul gen., 1939-48; consul gen. Los Angeles, Calif., 1942-48, 82-86; amb. to UN Govt. Costa Rica, San Francisco, 1945, N.Y., 1948-49; consul gen. Govt. Costa Rica, L.A., 1982-86; consul gen. emeritus L.A. Consular Corps., 1951—; advisor pres. Costa Rica, San José, 1944-48; amb. extraordinary Spain, the Vatican, Eng., 1967; vice chmn. U.S. Costa Rica Presdl. Com., 1996—; diplomat several missions, Ctrl. Am.; founding father UN, San Francisco, 1945. Author: The Fisherman's Industrial Guide, 1960; editor (mag.) Pesca Marina, 1961, Petroleum, 1961, Aviation, 1961. Col. Costa Rican mil., 1939-45. Hons. and decorations: Kt Comm. Order of Isanbel la Catolica (Spain), Grand Cross of Italy, Presidential medal of Nicaragua, others. Mem. Union Club, Soverign Order Hosp. St. John of Jerusalem (grand master emeritus). Mem. Unidad Party. Home: 527 N Las Palmas Ave Los Angeles CA 90004

FLORES, WILLIAM VINCENT, Latin American studies educator; b. San Diego, Jan. 10, 1948; s. William J. and Velia (Aldrete) F.; m. Carole Mary Dische, July 3, 1973 (div. Jan 1986); children: Antonio Ramon, Diana Maria. BA, UCLA, 1970; MA in Polit. Sci., Stanford U., 1971, PhD in Social Theory/Pub. Policy, 1987. Teaching & rsch. fellow Stanford (Calif.) U., 1971-72; lectr. in polit. sci. Calif. State U., Hayward, 1972-75; program coord. Project Intercept, San Jose, Calif., 1976-78; assoc. dir. Gardner Cmty. Health Ctr., San Jose, 1979-84; lectr. U. Santa Clara, Calif., 1985-87; asst. dir. Inter-Univ. Program for Latino Rsch., Stanford, 1987-88; chair dept. Chicano/Latin Am. studies Calif. State U., Fresno, 1988-92, assoc. dean Sch. of Social Scis., 1992-94; dean Coll. Soc. and Behavioral Scis. Calif. State U., Northridge, 1996—; v.p., bd. trustees Arte Americas, 1995-96. Mem. exec. com. Chicano/Latino Faculty Assn. Calif. State Univ. Sys., 1994-95; chair Com. for Hispanic Ednl. Equity, Fresno, 1990-92; mem. nat. adv. bd. U.S. Students Assn., Washington, 1991-93; v.p. Latino Agenda Coalition Calif., L.A., 1984-86. Chicano Fellows Program fellow Stanford U., 1971-72; Ford Found. fellow Stanford U., 1970-74; Compton-Danforth fellow Stanford U., 1984-85.; Rockefeller Humanities fellow, 1993-94; Am. Coun. on Edn. fellow, 1993-94. Mem. Am. Anthropol. Assn., Am. Studies Assn., Nat. Assn. Chicano Studies (co-chair polit. action com. 1986), Internat. Platform Assn. Democrat. Office: Coll Social/Behav Scis 18111 Nordhoff St Northridge CA 91330-8256

FLORES, YOLANDA, literature educator; b. Bakersfield, Calif., Mar. 2, 1962; d. Simon and Micaela Flores. BA, U. Calif., Berkeley, 1987; MA, U. Chgo., 1989; PhD, Cornell U., 1995. Lectr. Cornell U., Ithaca, N.Y., 1994-95; prof. Chapman U., Orange, Calif., 1995—. Contbr. articles to profl. pubs. Mem. MLA, L.Am. Studies Assn., Am. Soc. for Theater Rsch., Rocky Mountain Modern Lang. Assn., Feministas Unidas. Democrat. Roman Catholic. Home: 1855 S Rose Ave Apt 14B Orange CA 92867 Office: Chapman U 333 N Glassell Orange CA 92666

FLOREY, JERRY JAY, management consultant; b. Geddes, S.D., Apr. 3, 1932; s. Henry Clifford and Lizzie M. Florey; m. Mary E. Richey, Sept. 17, 1955; children: Glen David, Janet Renee. BSChemE, Oreg. State U., 1955. Cert. in electronics. From research engr. to engring. supr. Rockwell Internat., Canoga Park, Calif., 1955-66; sr. project engr. Rockwell Internat., Downey, Calif., 1966-67; successively engring. mgr., engring. dir., chief engr. Rockwell Internat., Seal Beach, Calif., 1967-85, dir. advanced systems, rsch. and tech., 1985-89; sr. staff mgr. strategic planning and market analysis McDonnell Douglas Space Co., Huntington Beach, Calif., 1989-95; cons. McDonnell Douglas, 1995-96; mgmt. cons., 1996—; participant on several industry workshop panels which advised USAF regarding its mil. space systems tech. planning activities. Scoutmaster Boy Scouts Am., Costa Mesa, Calif., 1970; mem. Republican Presdl. Task Force; del. at large Rep. Platform planning com. Recipient NASA Cert. Appreciation Marshall Space Flight Ctr., Huntsville, Ala., 1972, Astronaut Person Achievement award NASA, 1969, Skylab Achievement award NASA, 1973, AIAA and USAF Recognition of Svc. certs. AFSTC, 1985. Fellow AIAA (assoc., bd. dirs., nat. space and missile systems tech. activities com., fin. and internat. membership coms.); mem. Nat. Mgmt. Assn., Nat. Mktg. Soc. Am., U.S. Space Found. Home: 2085 Goldeneye Pl Costa Mesa CA 92626-4770

FLOSS, HEINZ G., chemistry educator, scientist; b. Berlin, Aug. 28, 1934; s. Friedrich and Annemarie F.; m. Inge Sauberlich, July 17, 1956; children: Christine, Peter, Helmut, Hanna. B.S. in Chemistry, Technische Universitat, Berlin, 1956, M.S. in Organic Chemistry, 1959; Dr. rer. nat. in Organic Chemistry, Technische Hochschule, Munich, W. Ger., 1961, Dr. habil. in Biochemistry, 1966; D.Sc. (hon.), Purdue U., 1986. Hilfsassistent Technische Universitat, Berlin, 1958-59; hilfsassistent Technische Hochschule, Munich, 1959-61; wissenschaftlicher asst. and dozent Technische Hochschule, 1961-66; on leave of absence at dept. biochemistry and biophysics U. Calif.-Davis, 1964-65; assoc. prof. Purdue U., 1966-69, prof., 1969-77, Lilly Disting. prof., 1977-82, head dept. medicinal chemistry, 1968-69, 74-79; prof. chemistry Ohio State U., Columbus, 1982-87, chmn. dept. chemistry, 1982-86; prof. chemistry U. Wash., Seattle, 1987—, adj. prof. biochemistry medicinal chemistry and microbiology, 1988—; vis. scientist ETH Zurich, 1970; vis. prof. Tech. U. Munich, 1980, 86, 95; mem. bio-organic and natural products study sect. NIH, 1989-93. Mem. editorial bd. Lloydia-Jour. Natural Products, 1971—, BBP-Biochemie und Physiologie der Pflanzen, 1971-84, Applied and Environ. Microbiology, 1974-84, Planta Medica, 1978-83, Jour. Medicinal Chemistry, 1979-83, Applied Microbiology and Biotech., 1984-88, Jour. Basic Microbiology, 1989—. Recipient Lederle faculty award, 1967, Mead Johnson Undergrad. Rsch. award, 1968, rsch. career and devel. award USPHS, 1969-74, Volwiler award, 1979, Humboldt sr. scientist, 1980, Newby-McCoy award 1981, award in microbial chemistry Kitasato Inst. and Kitasato U., 1988, White Magnolia Commemoration award and medal, Shanghai, 1995. Fellow Acad. Pharm. Scis. (Research Achievement award in natural products 1976), AAAS; mem. Am. Chem. Soc., Am. Soc. Biol. Chemistry and Molecular Biology, Am. Soc. Microbiology, Am. Soc. Pharmacognosy (Rsch. award 1988), Phytochem. Soc. N.Am., Sigma Xi (Faculty Research award 1976). Home: 5609 145th Ave SE Bellevue WA 98006-4381 Office: Univ Wash Dept Chemistry Box 351700 Seattle WA 98195-1700

FLOWER, RENÉE BEVILLE, artist; b. Chgo., Oct. 22, 1950; d. Milton Oliver and Doris Lea (Beville) F.; m. Victor Allan Spiegel, June 22, 1975 (div. June 1981); m. James Anderson MacKenzie, July 31, 1982. BA in Studio Art, U. Calif., Santa Cruz, 1979. lectr. in field. Ilustrator: (books) The Complete Sylvie & Bruno, 1991, City Noise, 1994, School Supplies, 1996; one-woman shows include Eloise Pickard Smith Gallery, 1993; exhibited in group shows at Ste 311, Pacific Grove, 1985, Zaner Gallery, Rochester, N.Y., 1986, San Francisco Mus. Modern Art Rental Gallery, 1987, The Art Mus. Santa Cruz County, 1988, Christopher Grimes Gallery, Carmel, 1989, Susan Cummins Gallery, Mill Valley, Calif., 1990, One Market Plaza, San Francisco, 1991, Gallery 500, Elkins Park, Pa., 1992, and others.

FLOYD, BARBARA IRENE, newspaper editor-in-chief; b. Breckenridge, Minn., Sept. 17, 1939; d. Harry Jesse and Eugenia Elizabeth (Kirschner) Wheeler; m. Robert D. Floyd, Dec. 26, 1962; children: Brenda Swanson, Barbra-Jean Skaleberg, Bobbi-Jo, Brook. AS, N.D. State Sch. Sci., 1959; BS, Moorhead State Coll., 1961. Tchr. Columbia Heights (Minn.) H.S., 1961-63, Prescott (Ariz.) Jr. H.S., 1963-65; owner The Country Goose, Phoenix, 1983-89; editor, owner The Country Register, Phoenix, 1988-94; owner The Country Register Cafe & Tea Rm., Kennewick, Wa., 1994—; owner, tchr. B&B Ceramic Studio, Prescott, 1963-65; owner Gooseberries Tea Room, Phoenix, 1989-91. Author, editor: The Country Register Collections Cookbook, 1993. Troop leader Girl Scouts U.S., Phoenix, 1970-73; ways and means chmn. Lookout Mountain Sch. PTA, Phoenix, 1976-77. Office: The Country Register PO Box 84345 Phoenix AZ 85071-4345

FLOYD, BRETT ALDEN, mortgage banker; b. Las Vegas, Nev., Nov. 12, 1963. Branch mgr. Transamerica Fin., West Covina, Calif., 1984-89, Assocs. Fin., San Gabriel, Calif., 1989; area sales mgr. Long Beach Bank, F.S.B., Woodland Hills, Calif., 1989-94; divsn. mgr. Royal Thrift & Loan Co., L.A., 1994-96; v.p. Royal MortgageBanc, Orange, Calif., 1996—. Assoc. Ctl. Com., L.A., 1992. Republican. Home: 2747 Belden Dr Hollywood Hills CA 90068 Office: Royal MortgageBanc 701 S Parker St # 2000 Orange CA 92668

FLUKE, LYLA SCHRAM (MRS. JOHN M. FLUKE), publisher; b. Maddock, N.D.; d. Olaf John and Anne Marie (Rodberg) Schram; m. John M. Fluke, June 5, 1937; children: Virginia Fluke Gabelein, John M. Jr., David Lynd. BS in Zoology and Physiology, U. Wash., Seattle, 1934, diploma teaching, 1935. High sch. tchr., 1935-37; tutor Seattle schs., 1974-75; pub. Portage Quar. mag., Hist. Soc. Seattle and King County, 1980-84. Author articles on history. Founder N.W. chpt. Myasthenia Gravis Found., 1953, pres., 60-66; obtained N.W. artifacts for destroyer Tender Puget Sound, 1966; mem. Seattle Mayor's Com. for Seattle Beautiful, 1968-69; sponsor Seattle World's Fair, 1962; charter mem. Seattle Youth Symphony Aux., 1974; bd. dirs. Cascade Symphony, Salvation Army, 1985-87; benefactor U. Wash., 1982-88, nat. chmn. ann. giving campaign, 1983-84; benefactor Sterling Circle Stanford U., MIT, 1984, Wash. State Hist. Soc., Pacific Arts Ctr.; mem. condr.'s club Seattle Symphony, 1978—. Fellow Seattle Pacific U., 1972—; mem. Wash. Trust for Hist. Preservation, Nat. Trust for Hist. Preservation, N.W. Ornamental Hort. Soc. (benefactor, life, hon.), Nat. Assn. Parliamentarians (charter mem., pres. N.W. unit 1961), Wash. Parliamentarians Assn. (charter), IEEE Aux. (chpt. charter mem., pres. 1970-73), Seattle C. of C. (women's div.), Seattle Symphony Women's Assn. (life, sec. 1982-84, pres. 1985-87), Hist. Soc. Seattle and King County (exec. com. 1975-78, pres. women's mus. league 1975-78, pres. Moritz Thomsen Guild of Hist. Soc., 1978-80, 84-87), Highlands Orthopedic Guild (life), Wash. State Hist. Soc, Antiquarian Soc. (v.p. 1986-88, pres. 1988-90, hon. mem. John Fluke Mfg. Co. 20 Year club, 1987—), Rainier Club, Seattle Golf Club, Seattle Tennis Club, U. Wash. Pres.'s Club. Republican. Lutheran. Address: 1206 NW Culbertson Dr Seattle WA 98177-3942 also: Vendovi Island PO Box 703 Anacortes WA 98221-0703

FLYGARE, KATHLEEN TIFFENI, elementary education educator, piano educator; b. Ogden, Utah, Apr. 7, 1951; d. Jay Golwyn and Norene Sylvia (Carter) Page; m. Mark E. Flygare, Feb. 15, 1974; children: Christopher Mark, Jeremy Page. BS, Weber State U., 1976. Cert. spl. edn., resource tchr., Utah. Intern tchr. WSU Tchr. Corp., Ogden, 1974-76; dir. YWCA Presch., Salt Lake City, 1978-87; tchr. 1st grade Davis County Sch. Dist., Farmington, Utah, 1987-90, tchr. 2d grade, 1990—; chmn. joint staff study com. Monte Vista Sch., Farmington, 1988-90, reading implementor, 1990-92, self-esteem implementor, 1992-93, music implementor, 1993—. Composer/dir. Utah State Centennial Musical for Monte Vista Sch., 1996; mem. Celebration Chamber Ensemble, 1994-96. Mem. gov.'s adv. com. Utah Sch. for Deaf and Blind, Salt Lake City, 1982-84, mem. instnl. coun., 1984-90, chmn. instnl. coun., 1990-92. Mem. ASCD, Assn. for Childhood Edn. Internat., Internat. Reading Assn., Phi Delta Kappa. Republican. Mem. LDS Ch. Home: 1142 S Little Valley Rd Farmington UT 84025 Office: Monte Vista Sch 100 S 200 E Farmington UT 84025-2316

FLYNN, RALPH MELVIN, JR., sales executive, marketing consultant; b. Winchester, Mass., May 2, 1944; s. Ralph Melvin and Mary Agnus (Giuliani) F.; m. Rose Marie Petrock (div. 1988); children: John Patrick, Marc Jeffery; m. Carolyn F. Lee; 1 child, Sean Michael. Engr. Bell Tel. Labs., Holmdel, N.J., 1966-68; tech. coord. Expts. in Art and Tech., N.Y.C., 1968-69; exec. v.p. Bestline Products, San Jose, Calif., 1969-73; pres. Internat. Inst. for Personal Achievement, Palo Alto, Calif., 1975-76, Diamite Corp., Milpitas, Calif., 1977-84; dir. mktg. IMMI, Campbell, Calif., 1973-77; v.p. internat. Neo-Life Co., Fremont, Calif., 1984—; pres. Ultra Promotions, Los Gatos, Calif., 1988-89, Score Publishing, Saratoga, Calif., 1987—; tech. cons. Robert Rauschenberg, N.Y.C., 1968; cons. Std. Oil Co., San Francisco, 1975, I.B.C., Geneva, 1984-88, 1st Interstate Bank, L.A., 1985, Ray Rossi, Design Environs., Los Altos Hills, Calif., 1995; lectr. in field. Author: The Only Variable, 1985, Navigating towards Success, 1986; contbr. articles to profl. publs. Named adm. State of Nebr., 1987; Joseph Kaplan Trust scholar, 1961. Mem. Direct Selling Assn., Coffee Soc. (founder 1988), Rolls Royce Owners Club. Republican. Office: Coffee Soc 21265 Stevens Creek Blvd Cupertino CA 95014-5715

FOCH, NINA, actress, creative consultant, educator, director; b. Leyden, The Netherlands, Apr. 20, 1924; came to U.S. 1927; d. Dirk and Consuelo (Flowerton) F.; m. James Lipton, June 6, 1954; m. Dennis de Brito, Nov. 27, 1959; 1 child, Dirk de Brito; m. Michael Dewell, Oct. 31, 1967 (div.). Grad., Lincoln Sch., 1939; studies with Stella Adler. Adj. prof. drama U. So. Calif., 1966-68, 78-80, adj. prof. film, 1987—; creative cons. to dirs., writers, prodrs. of all media; artist-in-residence U. N.C., 1966, Ohio State U., 1967, Calif. Inst. Tech., 1969-70; mem. sr. faculty Am. Film Inst., 1974-77; founder, tchr. Nina Foch Studio, Hollywood, Calif., 1973—; founder, actress Los Angeles Theatre Group, 1960-65; bd. dirs. Nat. Repertory Theatre, 1967-75. Motion picture appearances include Nine Girls, 1944, Return of the Vampire, 1944, Shadows in the Night, 1944, Cry of the Werewolf, 1944, Escape in the Fog, 1945, A Song to Remember, 1945, My Name Is Julia Ross, 1945, I Love a Mystery, 1945, Johnny O'Clock, 1947, The Guilt of Janet Ames, 1947, The Dark Past, 1948, The Undercover Man, 1949, Johnny Allegro, 1949, An American in Paris, 1951, Scaramouche, 1952, Young Man with Ideas, 1952, Sombrero, 1953, Fast Company, 1953, Executive Suite, 1954 (Oscar award nominee), Four Guns to the Border, 1954, You're Never Too Young, 1955, Illegal, 1955, The Ten Commandments, 1956, Three Brave Men, 1957, Cash McCall, 1959, Spartacus, 1960, Such Good Friends, 1971, Salty, 1973, Mahogany, 1976, Jennifer, 1978, Rich and Famous, 1981, Skin Deep, 1988, Sliver, 1993, Morning Glory, 1993, 'Til There Was You, 1996, Kilronan, 1997, Reasonable Doubt, 1997; appeared in Broadway plays including John Loves Mary, 1947, Twelfth Night, 1949, A Phoenix Too Frequent, 1950, King Lear, 1950, Second String, 1960; appeared with Am. Shakespeare Festival in Taming of the Shrew, Measure for Measure, 1956, San Francisco Ballet and Opera in The Seven Deadly Sins, 1966; also many regional theater appearances including Seattle Repertory Theatre (All Over, 1972 and The Seagull, 1973); actress on TV, 1947—, including Playhouse 90, Studio One, Pulitzer Playhouse, Playwrights 56, Producers Showcase, Lou Grant (Emmy nominee 1980), Mike Hammer; series star: Shadow Chasers, 1985, War and Remembrance, 1988, LA Law, 1990, Hunter, 1990, Dear John, 1990, 91, Tales of the City, 1993; many other series, network spls. and TV films; TV panelist and guest on The Dinah Shore Show, Merv Griffin Show, The Today Show, Dick Cavett, The Tonight Show; TV moderator: Let's Take Sides, 1957-59; assoc. dir. (film) The Diary of Anne Frank, 1959; dir. (nat. tour and on-Broadway) Tonight at 8:30, 1966-67, Family Blessings, 1997; assoc. producer re-opening of Ford's Theatre, Washington, 1968. Hon. chmn. Los Angeles chpt. Am. Cancer Soc., 1970. Recipient Film Daily award, 1949, 53. Mem. AAUP, Acad. Motion Picture Arts and Scis. (co-chair exec. com. fgn. film award, membership com.), Hollywood Acad. TV Arts and Scis. (bd. govs. 1976-77). Office: PO Box 1884 Beverly Hills CA 90213-1884

FOCHT, MICHAEL HARRISON, health care industry executive; b. Reading, Pa., Sept. 16, 1942; s. Benjamin Harrison and Mary (Hannahoe) F.; m. Sandra Lee Scholwin, May 14, 1964; 1 child, Michael Harrison. Archtl. estimator Caloric Corp., Topton, Pa., 1964-65, cost acct., 1965-66, indsl. engr., 1966-68, mgr. wage rates and standards, 1968-70; indsl. engr. Am. Medicorp. Inc., Fort Lauderdale, Fla., 1970-71; exec. dir. midwest region Am. Medicorp. Inc., Chgo., 1977-78; asst. adminstr. Cypress Community Hosp., Pompano Beach, Fla., 1971-73, adminstr., 1975-77; adminstr. Doctor's Hosp. Hollywood, Fla., 1973-75; v.p. Medfield Corp., St. Petersburg, Fla., 1978-79; v.p. ops. hosp. group Nat. Med. Enterprises, Inc., Los Angeles, 1979-81; regional sr. v.p. hosp. group Nat. Med. Enterprises, Inc., Tampa, Fla., 1981-83; pres., chief exec. officer internat. group Nat. Med. Enterprises, Inc., Los Angeles, 1983-86, pres. chief exec. officer hosp. group, 1986-91; sr. exec. v.p., dir. ops. Nat. Med. Enterprises, Inc., 1991-93, pres., 1993-95; pres., COO Tenet Healthcare Corp., Santa Barbara, 1995—. Mem. Fedn. Am. Hosps. (bd. govs. 1983—), Fla. League Hosps. (bd. dirs. 1982-83). Republican. Roman Catholic. Home: PO Box 703 Santa Ynez CA 93460-0703 Office: Tenet Healthcare Corp 3820 State St Santa Barbara CA 93105-3112

FOESCH, GLORIA BOGART, elementary school educator; b. Albuquerque, July 21, 1945; d. Orel Ward and Dolores (Gurule) Bogart; m. Tom Ceburne Whithead, Oct. 22, 1967 (div. July 1975); 1 child, Melissa Miglionico; m. James A. Foesch, Aug. 14, 1976; children: Pamela Garland, Daniel, Laura. BA, U. N.Mex., 1971, MS, 1977. Cert. elem. tchr., N.Mex., Nat. Bd. Profl. Tchg. Standards Certification. Tchr. Albuquerque Pub. Schs., 1971-79, 84-94, Martin Luther King Jr. Elem. Sch., Rio Rancho, N.Mex., 1994—; mem. sci. adv. bd. Sandia Nat. Labs., Albuquerque, 1993-95; founding dir. Shepherd of the Valley Presch., Albuquerque, 1981-83; mem. Strengthening Quality in Schs. Team., 1995—. Mem. Intel/Join-A-Sch. Bd., Rio Rancho, N.Mex., 1987-89; leader Girl Scouts U.S., Rio Rancho, 1986-92; mem. Troop 741 com. Boy Scouts Am., Rio Rancho, 1989-91. Named World Class Tchr., N.Mex. World Class Tchr. Project, 1996; recipient Quality of Edn. award 3d place N.Mex. Quality of Edn. Program, 1991, Christa McAuliffe fellowship, 1997. Mem. ASCD, Rio Rancho Sch. Employees Union (exec. bd. 1994—), Alpha Delta Kappa. Republican. Presbyterian. Office: Martin Luther King Jr Elementary School 1301 27th St SE Rio Rancho NM 87124-3501

FOGARTY, THOMAS JAMES, surgery educator; b. Cin., Feb. 25, 1934; s. William Henry and Anna Isabella (Ruthemeyer) F.; m. Rosalee Mae Brennan, Aug. 28, 1965; children: Thomas James Jr., Heather Brennan, Patrick Erin, Jonathan David. BS in Biology, Xavier U., 1956; MD, U.

Cin., 1960; D (hon.), Xavier U., 1987. Intern U. Oreg. Med. Sch., Portland, 1960-61, resident, 1962-65, instr. surgery, 1967-68; chief resident, instr. surgery divsn. cardiovascular surgery Stanford (Calif.) U. Med. Ctr., 1969-70, asst. prof. surgery, 1970-71, asst. clin. prof. surgery, 1971-73; cardiovascular surgeon pvt. practice, Stanford, 1973-78; pres. med. staff Stanford U. Med. Ctr., 1977-79; cardiovascular surgeon pvt. practice, Redwood City, Calif., 1978-93; dir. cardiovascular surgery Sequoia Hosp., Redwood City, Calif., 1980-93; prof. surgery Stanford U. Med. Ctr., 1993—; bd. dirs. Satellite Dialysis Ctrs., Inc.; co-founder, bd. dirs. AneuRx, Inc., Biopsys Med., Inc., Cardiac Pathways, Inc., Gen. Surg. Innovations, Inc., LocalMed, Inc., Vital Insite, Inc., Raytel Med. Corp., Cardiovascular Imaging Sys., Inc., Devices for Vascular Intervention, Inc., Hancock Labs., Imagyn Med., Inc., Physiometrix, Inc., Ventritex, Inc., Xenotech; mem. scientific adv. bd. Autogenics, BioLink Corp., Cardio Thoracic Sys., Inc., bd. dirs.; pres., founder Fogarty Engring., Inc.; co-founder, sr. ptnr. Three Arch Ptnrs.. Contbr. articles to profl. jours.; patentee in field. Fellow U. Cin. Coll. Medicine, Good Samaritan Hosp., 1961-62, Nat. Heart Inst. Surgery br., Bethesda, Md., 1965-67, rsch. fellow divsn. cardiovascular surgery Stanford Med. Ctr., 1968-69; recipient AstroLobe award Roger Bacon High Sch., 1974, Disting. Alumnus award U. Cin. Med. Sch., 1989; named Inventor of Yr., San Francisco Patent and Trademark Assn., 1980. Mem. AMA, Am. Assn. Thoracic Surgery, Am. Bd. Thoracic Surgery, Am. Coll. Physician Inventors, Am. Coll. Surgeons, Am. Heart Assn. (grantee), Am. Inst. Med. and Biol. Engring., Am. Med. Polit. Action Com., Am. Surg. Assn., Internat. Soc. Endovascular Surgery, Western Thoracic Surg. Soc., Calif. Med. Soc., Pacific Coast Surg. Assn., San Francisco Surg. Soc., San Mateo County Med. Assn., Santa Clara County Med. Assn. (Achievement award in medicine), Internat. Soc. Cardiovascular Surg. (N.Am. chpt.), Soc. Clin. Vascular Surgery, Soc. Vascular Tech., Soc. Thoracic Surgeons, Soc. Vascular Surgery (past pres. 1995), Copco Lake Sportsmen Assn., Santa Cruz Mountain Winegrowers Assn., South Skyline Assn., Sports Car Club Am., Rapley Trail Improvement Assn., Soc. Med. Friends of Wine. Republican. Office: 3270 Alpine Rd Portola Valley CA 94028

FOGELSON, DAVID LESLIE, psychiatrist, educator; b. Santa Monica, Calif., June 22, 1951. BA, U. Calif., Santa Cruz, 1972; MD, Harvard U., Boston, 1977. Diplomate Am. Bd. Psychiatry and Neurology. Internal medicine intern Faulkner Hosp., Jamaica Plain, Mass., 1977-78; resident in psychiatry Tufts/New Eng. Med. Ctr., Boston, 1978-79, UCLA, Belmont, Mass., 1979-81; pvt. practice, Santa Monica, 1982—; dir. Anxiety Disorders Clinic, UCLA, 1982-87, assoc. clin. prof. psychiatry, 1992—; pres. Pacific Psychopharmacology Rsch. Inst., Santa Monica, 1987—; bd. dirs. Obsessive Compulsive Disorders Found., New Haven, 1987-91. Contbr. articles to med. jours. Fellow Am. Psychiat. Assn.; mem. AMA. Office: 2730 Wilshire Blvd Ste 325 Santa Monica CA 90403-4747

FOK, AGNES KWAN, cell biologist, educator; b. Hong Kong, Dec. 11, 1940; came to U.S., 1962; d. Sun and Yau (Ng) Kwan; m. Fok, June 8, 1965; children: Licie Chiu-Jane, Edna Chiu-Joan. BA in Chemistry, U. Great Falls, 1965; MS in Plant Nutrition and Biochemistry, Utah State U., 1966; PhD in Biochemistry, U. Tex., Austin, 1971. Asst. rsch. prof. pathology U. Hawaii, Honolulu, 1973-74, Ford Found. postdoctoral fellow, anatomy dept., 1975, asst. rsch. prof., 1975-82, assoc. rsch. prof., 1982-88, rsch. prof. Pacific Biomed. Rsch. Ctr., 1988-96, grad. faculty, dept. microbiology, 1977—, dir. biology program, 1994—. Contbr. articles to profl. jours. Mem. Am. Soc. for Cell Biology, Soc. for Protozoologists, Sigma Xi (treas. Hawaii chpt. 1979—). Office: U Hawaii Biology Program Honolulu HI 96822

FOLDEN, NORMAN C. (SKIP FOLDEN), information systems executive, consultant; b. San Francisco, July 28, 1933. BS in Math./English/Engring., U.S. Mil. Acad., 1956. With IBM, various locations, 1966-83; U.S. program mgr. I/S tech. IBM, Sommers, N.Y., 1983-86; owner Folden Mgmt. (Paladin Advocacy), Westchester, N.Y., 1986-91, Folden Mgmt., Las Vegas, 1991—. Author: Drug Criminalization: Organized Crime Cash Cow, Prime Cause of U.S. Victim Crime and Threat to National Sovereignty, 1996, Delegation of Legislative Authority, 1997. Mem. Internat. Platform Assn., Assn. Grads. U.S. Mil. Acad., The Federalist Soc., Little Big Horn Assocs. (life), Calif. Scholarship Fedn. (life). Home and Office: 4329 Silvercrest Ct North Las Vegas NV 89030-0116

FOLEY, DANIEL EDMUND, real estate development executive; b. St. Paul, Mar. 1, 1926; s. Edward and Gerry (Fitzgarld) F.; student U. Minn., 1941-43; m. Paula Evans, Apr. 1, 1946. Chmn. bd. Realty Ptnrs. Ltd., Los Angeles; pres. Alpha Property Mgmt. Served with AUS, 1943-46.

FOLEY, JOHN V., water company executive. Chmn. Met. Water Dist. of So. Calif., L.A. Office: Office of the Bd of Dirs 350 S Grand Ave Los Angeles CA 90071

FOLEY, LOUISE MUNRO, writer; b. Toronto, ON, Can., Oct. 22, 1933; d. William Angus and Mary Rita (Nicholls) Munro; m. Donald James Foley, Aug. 9, 1957 (div. Aug. 1976); children: Donald James Munro Foley, William Andrew Munro Foley. BA in English with honors, Calif. State U., Sacramento, 1976. lectr. Sacramento City Coll., 1975-76, Calif. State U. Ext. Program, Sacramento, 1976-84, The Learning Exch., 1987—; guest lectr. Sierra Coll., Rocklin, Calif., Am. River Coll., Sacramento, Amador Unified Sch. Dist., Sacramento City Unified Dist., San Juan Unified Dist., North Sacramento Unified Dist. Author: The Caper Club, 1969, Somebody Stole Second, 1972, A Job for Joey, 1974, Sammy's Sister, 1974, No Talking, 1974, Tackle 22, 1978, The Train of Terror, 1982, The Sinister Studios of KESP-TV, 1983, The Lost Tribe, 1983, The Mystery of the Highland Crest, 1985, The Mystery of Echo Lodge, 1985, Danger at Anchor Mine, 1985, Forest of Fear, 1986, The Mardi Gras Mystery, 1987, The Mystery of the Sacred Stones, 1988, Australia! Find the Flying Foxes, 1988, The Cobra Connection, 1990, Ghost Train, 1992, Thief! said the Cat, 1992, Blood! said the Cat, 1992, Poison! said the Cat, 1992, In Search of the Hidden Statue, 1993, Moving Target, 1993, Stolen Affections, 1995, Running Into Trouble, 1996, My Substitute Teacher's Gone Batty, 1996, The Bird-Brained Fiasco, 1996, The Phoney-Baloney Professor, 1996, The Catnap Cat-astrophe, 1997; edtl. cons.: Gatekeepers of the Profession (Edwina Leon), 1976, Managing Human Services, 1979, Social Work and Health Care Policy, 1982; editor: Stand Close to the Door, 1976 (Gold Biennial award), Women in Skilled Labor: Problems and Issues, 1979, The Melting Pot Fable (Edwina Leon), 1981; wrote various greeting cards; contbr. verses and articles various mags. Participant Sacramento Reads!, 1993, 96, San Francisco Bay Area Book Coun., 1995, 96; mem. Friends Sacramento Pub. Libr., 1985—; guest lectr. Sacramento Met. Arts Commn., 1996. Recipient Lit. Achievement award Sacramento Regional Arts Coun., 1974, Excellence in Advt. award Sacramento Advt. and Mktg. Execs. Assn., 1972. Mem. Authors Guild, Nat. League Am. Pen Women, Soc. Children's Book Writers and Illustrators, Novelists, Inc., Calif. Writers Club. Republican. Presbyterian. Home and Office: 5010 Jennings Way Sacramento CA 95819

FOLEY, MARY KATHLEEN, theater arts educator; b. Chgo., Aug. 31, 1947; d. Charles Joseph and Jane Eleanor (Considine) F.; m. Roy Mendelssohn, July 2, 1979; children: Nathan Samuel, Dierdre Jane. BA, Rosemont (Pa.) Coll., 1969; Ma, U. Mass., 1975; PhD, U. Hawaii, 1979; Fulbright cert., U. Bochum, West Germany, 1970. Vis. prof. U. Hawaii, Honolulu, 1984; asst. prof. theatre arts bd. U. Calif., Santa Cruz, 1979-87, assoc. prof., 1987-92, prof., 1992—; provost Porter Coll., U. Calif., 1989—; dalang (puppeteer) U. Calif. Indonesian Arts Troupe, Santa Cruz, 1979—. Editor: Essays on Southeast Asian Performing Arts, 1992; S.E. Asia editor Asian Theatre Jour., 1984—; contbr. articles to profl. jours. Adv. com. Festival of Indonesia, N.Y., Jakarata, 1989-92; convener Coun. of Provosts, U. Calif., Santa Cruz, 1993—; artist SPECTA, Santa Cruz, 1980—, Honolulu Artists-in-Schs. program, 1975-78; bd. dirs. Vols. in Asia, Stanford, Calif., 1988-90. Fulbright grantee Fulbright Commn., 1969-70, East-West Ctr. grantee, 1975-79, Asian Cultural Coun. grantee Asian Cultural Coun., 1988, Nat. Endowment for Humanities, 1981, 93.

FOLEY, PETER WILHELM CHRISTIAN, humanities educator, researcher, translator; b. Rinteln, Germany, Nov. 11, 1961; came to U.S., 1990; s. Hervey Michael and Waltraud Gisela (Rothe) F.; m. Pia Francesca Cuneo, Aug. 4, 1990. BA, U. Keele, Staffordshire, Eng., 1985; MA, Northwestern U., 1986; DrPhil, U. Vienna, Austria, 1990. Asst. tchr. Ulrich-von-Hutten H.S., Schluechtern, Germany, 1983-84; tchg. asst. German dept. Northwestern U., Evanston, Ill., 1985-86; lectr. U. Econs., Vienna, 1986-90; vis. lectr. dept. German, U. Ariz., Tucson, 1992, lectr. humanities program, 1992-97, asst. prof., 1997—. Author: Heinrich Von Kleist and Adam Mueller, 1990; editor-in-chief Concourse newspaper, 1981-82; contbr. articles to profl. jours. Recipient tchg. award Fund for Advancement U. Econs., 1988, 89, 90; co-recipient tchg. award U. Ariz. Provost, 1994; grantee German Acad. Exch. Svc., 1983, Austrian Fgn. Study Svc., 1987-90, U. Ariz. Tchg. Tech., 1996, 97. Mem. MLA, N.Am. Kant Soc., Fichte Soc., Nat. Liberal Club (Eng.), Am. Soc. 18th Century Studies. Mem. Liberal Democrat Party (Eng.). Roman Catholic. Office: U Ariz Humanities Program Harvill Bldg Rm 347 Tucson AZ 85721-0076

FOLEY, THOMAS STEPHEN, lawyer, former speaker House of Representatives; b. Spokane, Wash., Mar. 6, 1929; s. Ralph E. and Helen Marie (Higgins) F.; m. Heather Strachan, Dec. 1968. B.A., U. Wash., 1951, LL.B., 1957. Bar: Wash. Partner Higgins & Foley, 1957-58; dep. pros. atty. Spokane County, Spokane, 1958-60; asst. atty. gen. State of Wash., Olympia, 1960-61; spl. counsel interior and insular affairs com. U.S. Senate, Washington, 1961-64; mem. 89th-103rd Congresses from 5th Wash. dist., Washington, D.C., 1965-94; House majority whip, 1981-86, House majority leader, 1987-89; speaker U.S. Ho. of Reps., 1989-94; ptnr. Akin, Gump, Strauss, Hauer & Feld, Washington, D.C., 1995—; instr. law Gonzaga U., 1958-60; mem. bd. advisors Ctr. Strategic and Internat. Studies; mem. adv. council Am. Ditchley Found. Bd. overseers Whitman Coll.; bd. advisors Yale U. council; bd. dirs. Council on Fgn. Relations. Mem. Phi Delta Phi. Democrat. Office: Akin Gump Strauss Hauer & Feld 1333 New Hampshire Ave NW Washington DC 20036

FOLGER, WILLIAM MONTRAVILLE, actor, journalist; b. Lockport, N.Y., May 13, 1916; s. Wayne Harrison and MayBelle Alzina (Upson) F.; widowed; children: Valerie Ely, W. Earl Folger (dec.). BS in gen. bus., U. Ill., 1938; MA in pol. sci., Syracuse U., 1975. News writer, reporter, editor National Broadcasting Co., Washington, 1944-46; news writer, newscaster Washington Post, Washington, 1946-48; news commentator Radio Station WISH, Indpls., 1950-51; pub. rels. dir. Coe Coll., Cedar Rapids, Iowa, 1952-53; trans. writer, columnist Courier-Express, Buffalo, N.Y., 1955, religion writer, columnist, 1959-73; journalism lectr. Syracuse (N.Y.) U., 1973-75; journalism prof. U. Northern Colo., Greeley, 1975-81; freelance actor Denver, 1981—. Precinet chmn. Dem. Party, Greeley, 1975-77, state conv. del., 1988; spokesman Am. Civil Liberties Union, Greeley, 1978-80; editor Colo. Environ. Coalition, 1990—. Recipient Fine Reporting award Newspaper Guild, Buffalo, 1960, Interpretive Reporting award, 1961-62, Best Theatre Ensemble award Westword, Denver, 1988, Am. Scene award Am. Fedn. TV and Radio Artists, Denver, 1988; named to Colo. Journalism Hall of Fame, 1995. Mem. Soc. Profl. Journalists (Colo. chpt. pres. 1977-78), Colo. Audubon Soc. (sec. 1985-88), Colo. Environ. Coalition (sec. 1983-85, editor 1990—), Religion Writers' Assn. of U.S. and Can. (pres. 1970-74). Presbyterian. Home and Office: 172 Newport St Denver CO 80220

FOLKERSON, R., commissioner. State bank commr. Denver. Office: 1560 Broadway Ste 1175 Denver CO 80202

FOLKERTH, THEODORE LEON, cardiovascular surgeon, educator; b. Darke County, Ohio, Nov. 24, 1937; s. L.D. and Abigail Lenore (Carpenter) F.; m. Lenora Wallace, Dec. 22, 1962 (div. 1981); children: Theodore Wesley, Elizabeth Anne, Geoffrey Wallace; m. Jean. BA in Chemistry, Earlham Coll., 1959; MS in Biochemistry, Ind. U., Indpls., 1962, MD, 1965. Commd. officer USN, 1964, advanced through grades to comdr.; staff thoracic and cardiovasc. surgeon Naval Regional Med. Ctr., San Diego, 1973-77; ret., 1978; staff cardiovasc. surgeon Good Samaritan Hosp., San Jose, Calif., 1978-81; head cardiovasc. surgery Santa Rosa (Calif.) Meml. Hosp., 1981-87; pvt. practice, Oceanside, Calif., 1987—; chmn. div. cardiovasc. surgery Tri-City Med. Ctr., Oceanside, 1987—; asst. clin. prof. U. Calif., San Diego, 1975-77, assoc. clin. prof., 1987—; program dir. seminar Current Controversies in Cardiac Surgery, 1993. Fellow ACS, Soc. Thoracic Surgeons; mem. Western Thoracic Surg. Assn. Office: 3998 Vista Way Ste C204 Oceanside CA 92056-3752

FOLLETT, CAROLYN BROWN, poet, artist; b. N.Y.C., Jan. 31, 1936; d. Lorne William and Helen Rudd (Swayze) Brown; m. Alan Lee Follett; children: Jeffrey Tredwell, Paul Seward, Lorne Hillary. BA in English, Smith Coll., 1958. Copy editor, proofreader dept. publs. Stanford U., Internat. Bus. Rels., San Francisco, McCann Erickson, San Francisco, Cunningham and Walsh; designer, creator, owner, bus. mgr. The Peaceable Kingdom; art bd. dirs. Sight and Insight, Mill Valley, Calif.; bd. dirs. Marin Poetry Ctr., Marin County, Calif., de Young Mus. Art Sch., San Francisco, Art Apprentice Program, San Francisco; leader workshops Internat. Women Writers Guild; numerous poetry readings. Author: The Latitudes of Their Going, 1993, Gathering the Mountains, 1995, Beside the Sleeping Maiden: Poets of Marin, 1997; editor: Beside the Sleeping Maiden, Poets of Marin, 1997; contbr. poetry to numerous jours.; two-person shows include O'Hanlon Gallery, Mill Valley, Calif., 1994; exhibited in group shows at Artisans Gallery, Mill Valley, 1989, Signature Gallery, San Diego, 1990, 1994, O'Hanlon Gallery, Mill Valley, 1990, 91, 92, 93, 94, Perception Gallery, Ft. Mason, San Francisco, 1991. Founding trustee San Francisco U. H.S., 1973-82; trustee, bd. chmn. Urban H.S., San Francisco, 1982-88; art vol. San Francisco Edn. Aux. Recipient numerous poetry awards; Marin Arts Coun. grant for poetry, 1995. Office: Studio C 469 Coloma Sausalito CA 94965

FOLLICK, EDWIN DUANE, law educator, chiropractic physician; b. Glendale, Calif., Feb. 4, 1935; s. Edwin Fulfford and Esther Agnes (Catherwood) F.; m. Marilyn K. Sherk, Mar. 24, 1986. BA, Calif. State U., L.A., 1956, MA, 1961; MA, Pepperdine U., 1957, MPA, 1977; PhD, DTheol St. Andrews Theol. Coll., Sem. of Free Prot. Episc. Ch., London, 1958; MS in Libr. Sci., U. So. Calif., 1963, MEd in Instructional Materials, 1964, AdvMEd in Edn. Adminstrn., 1969; student, Calif. Coll. Law, 1965; LLB, Blackstone Law Sch., 1966, JD, 1967; DC, Cleve. Chiropractic Coll., L.A., 1972; PhD, Academia Theatina, Pescara, 1978; MA in Organizational Mgmt., Antioch U., L.A., 1990. Tchr., libr. adminstr. L.A. City Schs., 1957-68; law librarian Glendale U. Coll. Law, 1968-69; coll. librarian Cleve. Chiropractic Coll., L.A., 1969-74, dir. edn. and admissions, 1974-84, prof. jurisprudence, 1975—, dean student affairs, 1976-92, chaplain, 1985—, dean of edn., 1989—; assoc. prof. Newport U., 1982; extern prof. St. Andrews Theol. Coll., London, 1961; dir. West Valley Chiropractic Health Ctr., 1972—. Contbr. articles to profl. jours. Chaplain's asst. U.S. Army, 1958-60. Decorated cavaliere Internat. Order Legion of Honor of Immaculata (Italy); Knight of Malta, Sovereign Order of St. John of Jerusalem; knight Order of Signum Fidei; comdr. chevalier Byzantine Imperial Order of Constantine the Gt.; comdr. ritter Order St. Gereon, numerous others. Mem. ALA, NEA, Am. Assn. Sch. Librarians, L.A. Sch. Libr. Assn., Calif. Sch. Libr. Assn., Assn. Coll. and Rsch. Librarians, Am. Assn. Law Librarians, Am. Chiropractic Assn., Internat. Chiropractors Assn., Nat. Geog. Soc., Internat. Platform Assn., Phi Delta Kappa, Sigma Chi Psi, Delta Tau Alpha. Democrat. Episcopalian. Home: 6435 Jumilla Ave Woodland Hills CA 91367-2833 Office: 590 N Vermont Ave Los Angeles CA 90004-2115 also: 7022 Owensmouth Ave Canoga Park CA 91303-2005

FONG, MATTHEW KIPLING, state official; b. Oakland, Calif., Nov. 20, 1953; s. Chester and March Fong; m. Paula Fong, May 28, 1978; children: Matthew II, Jade. Grad., U.S. Air Force Acad., 1975; MBA, Pepperdine U., 1982; JD, Southwestern Law. Sch., 1985. Former vice chmn. State Bd. Equalization; treas. State Calif. Regent Pepperdine U., Children's Hosp. L.A.; Rep. nominee State Controller, 1990. Lt. col. Air Force Res. Office: State Treasurer PO Box 942809 Sacramento CA 94209-0001

FONTAINE, DEBORAH ANN, geriatrics nurse practitioner; b. Passaiac, N.J., Dec. 5, 1956; d. Daniel and Dorothy Elizabeth (Reif) Olasin; m. Laurence Roger Fontaine, Oct. 10, 1992. BSN, Cedar Crest Coll., 1979; MS in Gerontology, Boston U., 1983. RN, Pa., Mass., Calif. Staff nurse Hosp. U. Pa., Phila., 1979-81; evening supervisor Sherrill House, Inc., Boston, 1982-83; gerontol. nurse practitioner Sherrill House, Inc., 1983-91; neurol. rsch. U. Calif., San Diego, 1991—; coord. clin. drug trials for Alzheimers and Parkinson's Disease U. Calif., San Diego, 1992—; lectr. Alzheimers Assn., San Diego, 1992—. Mem. Calif. Nurses Assn., Calif. Coalition Nurse Practitioners, Gerontol. Soc. Am., Sigma Theta Tau. Episcopal. Office: U Calif Alzheimers Rsch Ctr 9500 Gilman Dr La Jolla CA 92093-5003

FONTANA, BERNARD LEE, retired anthropologist, writer, consultant; b. Oakland, Calif., Jan. 7, 1931; s. Bernard Campion and Hope Mary (Smith) F.; m. Hazel Ann McFeely, June 27, 1954; children: Geoffrey Earl Francis, Nicholas Anthony, Francesca Ann. BA, U. Calif., Berkeley, 1953; PhD, U. Ariz., 1960. Field historian U. Ariz., Tucson, 1960-62, 78-92; ethnologist Ariz. State Mus., Tucson, 1962-78; writer, cons. Tucson, 1992—; lectr. anthropology dept. U. Ariz., 1962-78; expert witness Papago Tribe of Ariz., Sells, 1962-64; pres. Ariz.-Sonora desert Mus., Tucson, 1983-85; cons. San Xavier Dist. ToHono O'Odham Nation, Tucson, 1992-93, KUAT-TV, Tucson, 1996. Author: Tarahumara: Where Night Is The Day Of The Moon, 1979 (Border Regional Libr. Assn. award 1979), Of Earth and Little Rain: The Papago Indians, 1981 (Border Regional Libr. Assn. award 1981), Entrada: The Legacy of Spain and Mexico in the United States, 1994; editor: Before Rebellion, 1996. Active western regional adv. com. Nat. Pk. Svc., San Francisco, 1974-76; sheriff Tucson Corral of the Westerners, 1976; sec. Patronato San Xavier, Tucson, 1989—. Calif. Alumni scholar U. Calif. Alumni Assn., Berkeley, 1948; pre-doctoral fellow Wenner Gren Found. for Anthrop. Rsch., 1959; recipient Ben Avery award Ariz. Clean and Beautiful, 1994, Ariz. Gov. Hist. Preservation award Ariz. Heritage Found., 1995. Fellow Ariz. Nev. Acad. Sci.; mem. Soc. For Hist. Arch. (life, pres. 1970, J. C. Harrington medal 1992), Ariz. Arch. and Hist. Soc. (pres. 1960-61, editor 1958-60), Am. Soc. for Ethnohistory (pres. 1965, editor 1969-72), S.W. Pks. and Monuments Assn. (life, vice chmn. 1988, Edward Danson award 1989, Emil Haury award 1991). Home and Office: 7710 S Mission Rd Tucson AZ 85746

FONTANA, SHARON MARIE, early childhood education educator; b. Pitts., Feb. 3, 1951; d. Tony and Thelma (Pereira) Simarro; m. Ernest J. Fontana, Aug. 26, 1973; children: Alison, Santino. BS, Calif. State U., Chico, 1973. Cert. secondary tchr., Calif., vocat. tchr., Wash. Home econs. tchr. Antioch (Calif.) Unified Schs., 1973-78, Lodi (Calif.) Unified Schs., 1989-92; early childhood edn. tchr. Kennewick (Wash.) Sch. Dist., 1992—; mem. GATE adv. bd. Lodi Unified Schs., 1986-92; cons. Home and Family Life Adv. Com., Kennewick, Wash., 1992-94. Master food preserver Coop. Extension, Davis, Calif., 1988-92; mem. Triaeyc, PTA. Mem. ASCD, Wash. Vocat. Assn., Nat. Assn. Edn. of Young Children. Democrat. Roman Catholic. Home: 205 Pacific Ct Richland WA 99352-8700 Office: Tri Tech Skills Ctr 5929 W Meta Line Kennewick WA 99336

FONTENOT, MARSHALL WAYNE, literary agent, author; b. Lafayette, La., July 22, 1959; s. Percy Fontenot and Mae Siemann; m. Kathy McPherson, May 16, 1980; children: Tony, Mickey. BA in English, Auburn U., 1992. Cert. literary agt. Author, screenwriter Magnolia Pub., Baton Rouge, 1985-94, manuscript supr., 1985-88, asst. editor, 1988-91, editor, 1991-93; literary agt. Frustrated Writer's, Phoenix, 1994—; Author, screenwriter: Unlike My Father, 1992; author: Tendor in the Heart, 1993, Thorns of a Rose, 1994. Speech writer Mayor's Race, Baton Rouge, 1991; mem., pub. spkr. Big Bros./Big Sisters Assn., Baton Rouge, 1992, Mothers/Fathers Against Drunk Drivers, Phoenix, 1995, Muscular Dystrophy Found., 1996—; pub. spkr. Christian Athlete's Assn., Phoenix, 1996. Recipient Acad. Scholarship award Auburn U., Montgomery, Ala., 1989; named Nat. Collegiate Athletic Assn. Soccerplayer of Yr., Auburn U., Montgomery, 1990. Mem. Nat. Screenwriters Assn. (screenwriter 1993), Nat. Leukemia Found. (pub. announcer 1995—). Democrat. Home: 5420 E Karen Dr Scottsdale AZ 85254 Office: Frustrated Writers Ltd Literary Agy PO Box 31160 Phoenix AZ 85254

FONTENOTE-JAMERSON, BELINDA, museum director. Pres. Mus. African Am. Art, L.A. Office: Mus African Am Art 4005 Crenshaw Blvd 3d Fl Los Angeles CA 90008

FONZENO, GREGORY MICHAEL, principal; b. Oakland, Calif., Mar. 1, 1955; s. Anthony Michael and Joy Ingrid (Haugan) F.; m. Christine Micheli, Dec. 17, 1983; 1 child, Nicole Elaine. BA, Holy Names Coll., 1977; MS, Calif. State U., 1991. Cert. in adminstrv. svcs. Tchr. Bishop O'Dowd High Sch., Oakland, 1977-78; tchr. St. Joseph Notre Dame High Sch., Alameda, Calif., 1978-95, vice prin., 1985-95; prin. St. Philip Neri Elem. Sch., Alameda, 1995—. Alumni bd. dirs. Holy Names Coll., Oakland, 1992-94. Mem. ASCD, Nat. Cath. Ednl. Assn., Assn. Calif. Sch. Adminstrs. Office: St Philip Neri Sch 1335 High St Alameda CA 94501

FOOTMAN, GORDON ELLIOTT, educational administrator; b. L.A., Oct. 10, 1927; s. Arthur Leland and Meta Fay (Neal) F.; m. Virginia Rose Footman, Aug. 7, 1954; children: Virginia, Patricia, John. BA, Occidental Coll., 1951, MA, 1954; EdD, U. So. Calif., 1972. Tchr., Arcadia, Calif., 1952, Glendale, Calif., 1956; psychologist Burbank (Calif.) Schs., 1956-64, supr., 1964-70, dir. pupil personnel svcs., 1970-72; dir. div. ednl. support svcs. L.A. County Office Edn., Downey, Calif., 1972-91; cons. ednl. adminstrn., counseling and pscyhol. svcs., 1991—; pres. Calif. Assn. Adult Devel. and Aging, 1994-95; lectr. ednl. psychology U. So. Calif., 1972-75, asst. prof. ednl. psychology, 1976-85. Pres. Coun. for Exceptional Children, 1969-70; pres. Burbank Coordinating Coun., 1969-70; mem. Burbank Family Svc. Bd., 1971-72. Served with AUS, 1945-47. Mem. Am. Edn. Rsch. Assn., Am. Assn. for Counseling and Devel. (senator 1983-86, gov. coun., 1989-93, exec. com. 1990-93, parliamentarian 1991-92, western region br. assembly publs. editor 1985-87, chair 1988-89, chair bylaws com. 1995-96), Am. Assn. for Humanistic Edn. and Devel. (bd. dirs., treas. 1996—), Calif. Personnel and Guidance Assn. (pres. 1981-82, exec. coun. 1996—), Calif. Assn. Sch. Psychologists and Psychometrists, Nat., Calif. (monograph editor 1977-80), Assns. Pupil Personnel Adminstrs., Calif. Assn. Counselor Educators and Suprs. (trustee), Calif. Assn. Sch. Adminstrs., Calif. Soc. Ednl. Program Auditors and Evaluators (sec. 1975-76, v.p. 1976-77, pres.), Calif. Assn. Measurement and Evaluation in Counseling and Devel. (sec. 1976, pres. 1979-80, 96-97, pres.-elect 1995—, cons. ednl. and pupil svcs. adminstrn. 1991—), Calif. Inst. Tech. Assocs., Assn. Humanities Ed. and Devel. (bd. dirs. 1996—, treas. 1996—), Harmington Libr. Soc. Fellows, Coun. Exceptional Children (pres. Foothill chpt. 1969-70), Phi Beta Kappa, Phi Alpha Theta, Psi Chi. Republican. Presbyn. Home and Office: 1259 Sherwood Rd San Marino CA 91108-1816

FORAN, KEVIN RICHARD, television station executive; b. Tucson, Apr. 6, 1972; s. Richard Charles and Mary Ann (Corella) F. BA in Media Arts, U. Ariz., 1995. Prodn. operator Sta. KUAT-TV, PBS, Tucson, 1994-95, Sta. KOLD-TV, CBS, Tucson, 1995; assoc. dir. Sta. KGUN-TV, ABC, Tucson, 1995—. asst. prodr. TV program Beat the Pro, 1996; prodr. TV program 1996 U. Ariz. Wildcat Football Preview, 1996. Office: Sta KGUN-TV 7820 E Rosewood St Tucson AZ 85710

FORBES, DAVID CRAIG, musician; b. Seattle, Feb. 12, 1938; s. Douglas James and Ruby A. (Niles) F.; m. Sylvia Sterling, Aug. 29, 1965 (div. Apr. 1973); 1 child, Angela Rose. Grad., USN Sch. Music, 1957; student, Western Wash. U., 1960-64. Prin. horn La Jolla (Calif.) Civic Orch., 1958-60, Seattle Worlds Fair Band, 1962, Seattle Opera Co., 1964—, Pacific Northwest Ballet, Seattle, 1964—; asst. prin. horn Seattle Symphony Orch., 1964—; prin. horn Pacific Northwest Wagner Fest., Seattle, 1975—; instr. horn Western Wash. State U., 1969-81, Cornish Inst., Seattle, 1964-78. Served with USN, 1956-60. Mem. NARAS, Internat. Horn Soc. Home: 9050 15th Ave NW # 2 Seattle WA 98117-3429

FORBES, KENNETH ALBERT FAUCHER, urological surgeon; b. Waterford, N.Y., Apr. 28, 1922; s. Joseph Frederick and Adelle Frances (Robitaille) F.; m. Eileen Ruth Gibbons, Aug. 4, 1956; children: Michael, Diane, Kenneth E., Thomas, Maureen, Daniel. BS cum laude, U. Notre Dame, 1943; MD, St. Louis U., 1947. Diplomate Am. Bd. Urology. Intern St. Louis U. Hosp., 1947-48; resident in urol. surgery Barnes Hosp., VA Hosp., Washington U., St. Louis. U. schs. medicine, St. Louis, 1948-52; asst. chief urology Letterman Army Hosp., San Francisco, 1952-54; fellow West Roxbury (Harvard) VA Hosp., Boston, 1955; asst. chief urology VA Hosp., East Orange, N.J., 1955-58; practice medicine specializing in urology Green Bay, Wis., 1958-78, Long Beach, Calif., 1978-85; mem. cons. staff Fairview State Hosp. U. Calif. Med. Ctr., Irvine, VA Hosp., Long Beach; asst. clin. prof. surgery U. Calif., Irvine, 1978-85; cons. Vols. in Tech. Assistance, 1986—. Contbr. articles to profl. jours. Served with USNR, 1944-46; capt.

U.S. Army, 1952-54. Named Outstanding Faculty Mem. by students, 1981. Fellow ACS, Royal Soc. Medicine, Internat. Coll. Surgeons; mem. AMA, AAAS, Calif. Med. Assn., Am. Urol. Assn. (exec. com. North Ctrl. sect. 1972-75, Western sect. 1980—), N.Y. Acad. Scis., Surg. Alumni Assn. U. Calif.-Irvine, Justin J. Cordonnier Soc. Washington U., Urologists Corr. Club, Notre Dame Club (Man of Yr. award 1965), Union League Club of Chgo., Phi Beta Pi. Republican. Roman Catholic. Home and Office: 14425 W Via Tercero Sun City West AZ 85375

FORBES, LEONARD, engineering educator; b. Grande Prairie, Alta., Can., Feb. 21, 1940; came to U.S., 1966; s. Frank and Katie (Tschetter) F.; B.Sc. with distinction in Engring. Physics, U. Alta., 1962; M.S. in E.E., U. Ill., 1963, Ph.D., 1970. Staff engr. IBM, Fishkill, N.Y. and Manassas, Va., 1970-72; IBM vis. prof. Howard U., Washington, 1972; asst. prof. U. Ark., Fayetteville, 1972-75; assoc. prof. U. Calif.-Davis, 1976-82; prof. Oreg. State U., Corvallis, 1983—; with Hewlett-Packard Labs., Palo Alto, Calif., 1978; cons. to Telex Computer Products, D.H. Baldwin, Hewlett-Packard, Santa Rosa, Fairchild, United Epitaxial Tech., Naval Ocean Systems Ctr., Hewlett-Packard Corvallis, Micron Tech. Boise; organizer Portland Internat. Conf. and Exposition on Silicon Materials and Tech., 1985-87. Served with Royal Can. Air Force, 1963-66. Mem. IEEE. Contbr. articles to profl. jours. Home: 965 NW Highland Ter Corvallis OR 97330-9706 Office: Oreg State U Dept Elec Engring Corvallis OR 97331

FORBIS, RICHARD GEORGE, archaeologist; b. Missoula, Mont., July 30, 1924; s. Clarence Jenks and Josephine Marie (Hunt) F.; m. Marjorie Helen Wilkinson, Nov. 12, 1960; children: Michael, David, Amanda. B.A., U. Mont., 1949, M.A., 1950; Ph.D., Columbia U., 1955. Sr. archeologist Pacific N.W. Pipeline Corp., Western U.S., 1955-56; archeologist Glenbow Found., Calgary, Alta., Can., 1957-63; mem. faculty U. Calgary, 1963—, prof. archaeology, 1968-88, prof. emeritus, 1988—, interim chmn. dept., Killam Meml. fellow, 1977; chmn. Alta. Public Adv. Com. Hist. and Archeol. Resources, 1971-74; mem. Alta. Historic Sites Bd., 1974-78; vis. scientist Can. Nat. Museum Man, 1970. Author: Cluny: An Ancient Fortified Village in Alberta, 1977; co-author: An Introduction to the Archaeology of Alberta, Canada, 1965. Served with AUS, 1943-46. Mem. AAAS, Soc. Am. Archaeology, Can. Archaeol. Assn. (Smith-Wintemberg award 1984), Am. Anthrop. Assn., Plains Anthrop. Conf., Champlain Soc., Sigma Chi. Office: U Calgary Dept Archeology, 2500 University Dr NW, Calgary, AB Canada T2N 1N4

FORCEY, STEPHEN EUGENE, controller, systems analyst; b. Washington, June 2, 1955; s. Herschel Eugene and Martha Ann (McLendon) F.; m. Margaret Olene Chambers, June 2, 1979; children: Jason Clark, Calvin Darby, Dwight Vernon, Charis Abigail. BS, LeTourneau U., Longview, Tex., 1977; ThM, Dallas Theol. Sem., 1981; MS, U. Colo., Denver, 1994. Pastor various chs. Tex., Okla., Wyo., 1981-85; sys. mgr. Nat. Profl. Mgmt. Corp., Englewood, Colo., 1987-95; contr. Am. Soc. Surgery of the Hand, Englewood, 1987—; owner Diamond Express Health Claims, Aurora, Colo., 1995—. Bd. dirs. Grace bible Chapel, Aurora, 1988-95. Mem. Aurora C. of C., Dallas Theol. Sem. Colo. Alumni Assn. (treas. 1993). Home: 4045 S Pitkin Way Aurora CO 80013 Office: National Profl Mgmt Corp Ste 100 6060 Greenwood Plaza Blvd Englewood CO 80111-4801

FORD, ALICE HAVENS, primary school educator; b. Phila., May 12, 1951; d. Robert James and Martha Suffern (Shepard) Vernlund; m. Lenard Wayne Ford, Dec. 1, 1980; 1 child, Jessica Erin. BS in Edn., Wheelock Coll., Boston, 1973; MEd, Univ. Mont., 1993. Cert. elem. sch. tchr., administr., Mont. Tchr. Fisher Elem. Sch., Arlington, Vt., 1973-77; spl. edn. aide Flathead County Spl. Edn. Coop., Kalispell, Mont., 1980-81; tchr. Olney (Mont.) Sch., 1982-83, Bissell Sch., Whitefish, Mont., 1983-89, Sch. Dist. # 5, Kalispell, 1990—; cons. Kendall Hunt Publ. Co., Dubuque, Iowa, 1994-96; presenter in field. Leader, Student Environ. Awareness Club, Kalispell, 1994. Mont. Coun. Tchrs. Math. scholar, 1994. Mem. ASCD, Phi Delta Kappa. Office: Russell Sch Dist # 5 227 W Nevada St Kalispell MT 59901-3634

FORD, ALYSON, accountant; b. L.A., Jan. 22, 1965; d. Alfred Ray III and Marie Claudian (Finks) Smith. AA, L.A. City Coll., 1985; BSBA, U. Phoenix, Lawndale, Calif., 1995. Bookkeeper Lowe Enterprises, Inc., L.A., 1984-88; staff acct. J.H. Snyder Co., L.A., 1988-94; project/staff acct. Highridge Ptnrs., El Segundo, Calif., 1994—; cons. Alyson Ford Consulting, Hawthorne, Calif., 1993—. Vol. Brotherhood Crusade, L.A., 1988-91; leader Angeles Girl Scout Coun., 1991-94, trainer, 1993—; election precinct coord. L.A. County Registrar/Recorder's Office, Norwalk, Calif., 1992—; mem. Recycling Black Dollars, L.A., 1996. Named Outstanding Vol. and Leader, Angeles Girl Scout Coun., 1993. Office: Alyson Ford Consulting PO Box 1701 Hawthorne CA 90251

FORD, BETTY BLOOMER (ELIZABETH FORD), health facility executive, wife of former President of United States; b. Chgo., Apr. 8, 1918; d. William Stephenson and Hortence (Neahr) Bloomer; m. Gerald R. Ford (38th Pres. U.S.), Oct. 15, 1948; children: Michael Gerald, John Gardner, Steven Meigs, Susan Elizabeth. Student, Sch. Dance Bennington Coll., 1936, 37; LL.D. (hon.), U. Mich., 1976. Dancer Martha Graham Concert Group, N.Y.C., 1939-41; fashion dir. Herpolscheimer's Dept. Store, Grand Rapids, Mich., 1943-48; dance instr. Grand Rapids, 1932-48; chmn. bd. dirs. The Betty Ford Ctr., Rancho Mirage, Calif. Author: autobiography The Times of My Life, 1979, Betty: A Glad Awakening, 1987. Bd. dirs. Nat. Arthritis Found. (hon.); trustee Martha Graham Dance Ctr., Eisenhower Med. Ctr., Rancho Mirage; hon. chmn. Palm Springs Desert Mus.; nat. trustee Nat. Symphony Orch.; bd. dirs. The Lambs, Libertyville, Ill. Episcopalian. Home: PO Box 927 Rancho Mirage CA 92270-0927*

FORD, BYRON MILTON, computer consultant; b. Hayden, Colo., Feb. 24, 1939; s. William Howard and Myrtle Oretta (Chistian) F.; BS, U. Colo., 1964; MS in Mgmt. Sci., Johns Hopkins U., 1971; m. Shirley Ann Edwards, Sept. 4, 1958; children: Gregory Scott, Barry Matthew. Sr. mathematician Applied Physics Lab., Johns Hopkins U., Laurel, Md., 1964-79; computer cons., Laurel, 1979-95, Longmont, 1996—. Mem. Ops. Rsch. Soc. Am., Nat. Assn. Self-Employed. Address: 13545 Weld County Rd 13 Longmont CO 80504

FORD, GERALD RUDOLPH, JR., former President of United States; b. Omaha, July 14, 1913; s. Gerald R. and Dorothy (Gardner) F.; m. Elizabeth Bloomer, Oct. 15, 1948; children: Michael, John, Steven, Susan. A.B., U. Mich., 1935; LL.B., Yale U., 1941; LL.D., Mich. State U., Albion Coll., Aquinas Coll., Spring Arbor Coll. Bar: Mich. 1941. Practiced law at Grand Rapids, 1941-49; mem. law firm Buchen and Ford; mem. 81st-93d Congresses from 5th Mich. Dist., 1949-74, elected minority leader, 1965; v.p. U.S., 1973-74, pres., 1974-77; del. Interparliamentary Union, Warsaw, Poland, 1959, Belgium, 1961, Bilderberg Group Conf., 1962; dir. The Travelers, Inc., Alexander & Alexander; adv. dir. Tex. Commerce Bancshares, Inc., Am. Express Co.; mem. internat. adv. coun. Inst. Internat. Studies. Served as lt. comdr. USNR, 1942-46. Recipient Grand Rapids Jr. C. of C. Distinguished Service award, 1948; Distinguished Service Award as one of ten outstanding young men in U.S. by U.S. Jr. C. of C., 1950; Silver Anniversary All-Am. Sports Illustrated, 1959; Distinguished Congressional Service award Am. Polit. Sci. Assn., 1961. Mem. Am., Mich. State, Grand Rapids bar assns., Delta Kappa Epsilon, Phi Delta Phi. Republican. Episcopalian. Clubs: University (Kent County), Peninsular (Kent County). Lodge: Masons. Home: PO Box 927 Rancho Mirage CA 92270-0927*

FORD, JAMES CARLTON, human resources executive; b. Portland, Mar. 10, 1937; s. John Bernard and Margaret (Reynolds) F.; m. Carolyn Tadina, Aug. 22, 1959; children: Scott, Michele, Mark, Brigitte, Deidre, John. BA in History, U. Portland, 1960; MS in Edn., Troy State U., 1969; MPA, U. Puget Sound, 1976. Cert. sen. profl. in human resources. Commd. 2d lt. USAF, 1960, advanced through grades to lt. col., 1976, adminstr., tng. officer, 1960-70, personnel mgmt. officer, 1971-76; dep. inspector gen. U.S. Air Force Acad., Colorado Springs, Colo., 1977-80; ret. U.S. Air Force Acad., 1980; employment mgr. Western Fed. Savs. (name changed to Bank Western), Denver, 1980-82, v.p. human resources, 1982-88, sr. v.p. mgmt. svcs., 1988-92; dir. career mgmt. AIM Exec., Inc., Cons. Svcs., 1992-95; owner Orgn./Individual Strategies, Inc., Cons., 1995—; bd. dirs. Rocky Mountain chpt. Am. Inst. Banking, Denver, 1988-92; adj. prof. U. Colo., Colorado Springs, 1978-79, USAF Acad., Colorado Springs, 1978-80; adv. bd. U. Colo. Contemporary Mgmt. Program, Regis Coll. Career Svcs.; mem. faculty U. Phoenix, Colo., 1995—; mediator Pikes Peak Better Bus. Bur., 1995—. Mediator Neighborhood Justice Ctr., Colorado Springs, 1980; vol. allocations com. Pikes Peak United Way, Colorado Springs, 1978-79; vol. campaign exec. Mile Hi United Way, Denver, 1986-89; vol. mgmt. cons. Tech. Assistance Svc., Denver, 1991. Mem. Assn. for Mgmt. of Orgn. Design, Soc. for Human Resource Mgmt. (state dir. certification 1996—). Republican. Roman Catholic. Office: Orgn/Individual Strategies, Inc 975 Tari Dr Colorado Springs CO 80921

FORD, JOHN T., JR., art, film and video educator; b. Rotan, Tex., Feb. 17, 1953; s. John T. and Lala Fern (Shipley) F.; m. Betty Jean Crawford; children: Casey, Craig, Kirk. BA, U. Redlands, 1975. Cert. tchr., Calif. Tchr. art, film, video Yucaipa (Calif.) Joint Unified Sch. Dist., 1976-88; tchr. art and crafts Vacaville (Calif.) Unified Sch. Dist., 1990-92, tchr. video prodn., 1992—; cons. Dist. Fine Arts Insvc., Yucaipa, 1987; co-sponsor Art Club, Will C. Wood High Sch., Vacaville, sponsor Video Club. Creator, coord. (conceptual art) Whole School Environments, Caves, Tubes and Streamers, Forest Edge, 1980-84; creator (comml. art prints) Toy Horse Series, 1982-83; prodr. ann. sr. video, 1994—. Mem. Yeoman Svc. Orgn., U. Redlands, 1972, Vacaville Sch. Dist. Tech. Com., Dist. Fine Arts Task Force, Yucaipa, 1984-87, Dist. Task Force for Vocat. Edn., 1992; interim dir. Hosanna House, Redlands, Calif., 1975; liaison Sch. Cmty. Svc./San Bernardino County (Calif.) Fire Dept., 1980-81. Recipient Golden Bell award Calif. Sch. Bd. Rsch. Found., 1987, Ednl. Svc. award Mason's, 1987-88; named one of Outstanding Young Men of Am., 1987, Tchr. of Yr. Calif. Continuation Edn. Assn., 1987-88; grantee Calif. Tchrs. Instructional Improvement Program, 1985; scholar U. Redlands, 1975. Mem. Am. Film Inst. Office: Will C Wood High Sch 998 Marshall Rd Vacaville CA 95687-5735

FORD, MICHAEL Q., not-for-profit association administrator; b. Washington, Dec. 12, 1949; s. Milton Q. and Jeanne Louise (Goltman) F.; m. Christine Ann Davies, Apr. 24, 1971 (div. June 1980); m. Elizabeth Julia Ginsberg, June 1, 1984; 1 child, Jennifer. BS in Journalism, Ohio U., 1971. Writer, reporter TV Digest, Washington, 1971-72; staff writer Coun. Better Bus. Burs., Washington, 1972-74; staff assoc. Ctr. for Study of Responsive Law, Washington, 1974; exec. dir. Coalition for Health Funding, Washington, 1975-77; dir. Office of Pub. Policy Nat. Coun. on Alcoholism, Washington, 1977-80; pres. Nat. Assn. Addiction Treatment Providers, Irvine, Calif., 1980-93; exec. dir. Nat. Nutritional Foods Assn., Newport Beach, Calif., 1994—; trustee Commn. on Accreditation of Rehab. Facilities, Tucson, 1985-91. Chmn. legis. com. Nat. Coalition for Adequate Alcoholism Programs, Washington, 1978-80, chmn., 1981. Fellow Am. Coll. of Addiction Treatment Adminstrs. Jewish. Home: 3013 Nestall Rd Laguna Beach CA 92651-2026 Office: Nat Nutritional Foods Assn 3931 Macarthur Blvd Ste 101 Newport Beach CA 92660-3013

FORD, ORAL IVAN (VAN FORD), engineering consultant; b. Ind., Mar. 21, 1925; s. Arnold Saris and Zetta May F.; m. Betty Joyce Taulman, Feb. 5, 1947; children: Joellen, Deanne, Charalyn. BSME, Purdue U., 1949; MS in Engring., Calif. Coast U., 1977, PhD, 1978. Aircraft engine design and devel. engr. AAerojet Gen. Corp., Sacramento, Calif., 1951-60; engring. mgr. Aerojet Gen. Corp., Sacramento, 1961-72; rsch. dir. Norris Industries, L.A., 1972-74; engring. mgr. Communications Tech., L.A., 1974-76; engring. cons. O.I. Ford Engring., Canuga Park, Calif., 1976-77, 89—; researcher GE Co., San Jose, Calif., 1977-89. Author: Low Emission G.T. Combuster, 1972, Rubbing Contact Wear in Water Handling Equipment, 1976; inventor in field. Cons. 1989—, With USNR, 1943-45. Decorated Air medal with 2 stars, DFC.

FORD, VICTORIA, public relations executive; b. Carroll, Iowa, Nov. 1, 1946; d. Victor Sargent and Gertrude Francis (Headlee) F.; m. John K. Frans, July 4, 1965 (div. Aug. 1975); m. David W. Keller, May 2, 1981 (div. Nov. 1985); m. Jerry W. Lambert, Mar. 30, 1991. AA, Iowa Lakes Community Coll., 1973; BA summa cum laude, Buena Vista Coll., 1974; MA in Journalism, U. Nev., Reno, 1988. Juvenile parole officer Iowa Dept. Social Services, Sioux City, 1974-78; staff reporter Feather Pub. Co., Quincy, Calif., 1978-80; tng. counselor CETA, Quincy, 1980; library pub. info. officer U. Nev., Reno, 1982-84; pub. relations exec. Brodeur/Martin Pub. Relations, Reno, 1984-87; pub. relations dir. Internat. Winter Spl. Olympics, Lake Tahoe (Calif.) and Reno, 1987-89; owner Ford Factor Pub. Rels. cons. firm, Reno, 1989—. Author: Making Their Mark: Reno-Sparks YWCA History, 1997, (with R.T. King and Ken Adams) War Stories, 1995; contbr. articles to profl. jours. Mem. adv. bd. Reno Philharm., 1985-87, Reno-Sparks Conv. and Visitors Authority, 1985-93; bd. dirs. Truckee Meadows Habitat for Humanity, 1992-93, half-time exec. dir., 1994; mem. Gov.'s Com. on Fire Prevention, 1991-92; mem. U. Nev. Reno Oral History Program, 1994; bd. dirs. Nev. Women's Archives, 1996; mem. Nev. Women's History Project, com. Nev. Writers Hall of Fame, 1993-96; bd. dirs. Friends of the U. Nev. at Reno Libr., 1995—. Mem. NOW, Pub. Rels. Soc. Am. (charter v.p. Sierra Nev. chpt. 1986-87, pres. 1987-88), Southwest Oral History Assn., Sigma Delta Chi. Democrat. Home: PO Box 6715 Reno NV 89513-6715 Office: The Ford Factor PO Box 6715 Reno NV 89513-6715

FORD, VICTORIA, author, educator; b. South Bend, Ind., Dec. 29, 1952; d. G. Burt and Charlotte Ann (Kupferer) F. BA, Ohio Wesleyan U., 1975; MA, Ind. U., 1978. Design team mem. Morningside Acad., Seattle, 1995—; adj. faculty Seattle Ctrl. C.C., 1990—, Antioch U., Seattle, 1995—. Author: Following the Swan, 1988, Rain Psalm, 1996.

FORDEMWALT, JAMES NEWTON, microelectronics engineering educator, consultant; b. Parsons, Kans., Oct. 18, 1932; s. Fred and Zenia (Chambers) F.; m. Suzan Lynn Hopkins, Aug. 26, 1958 (div. June 1961), m. Elizabeth Anna Hoare, Dec. 29, 1963; children: John William, James Frederick. BS, U. Ariz., 1955, MS, 1956; PhD, U. Iowa, 1960. Sr. engr. GE Co., Evandale, Ohio, 1959-60, U.S. Semcor, Inc., Phoenix, 1960-61; sect. mgr. Motorola Semiconductor Products Div., Phoenix, 1961-66; dept. mgr. Philco-Ford Microelectronics Div., Santa Clara, Calif., 1966-68; assoc. dir. R & D Am. Microsystems Inc., Santa Clara, 1968-71; assoc. rsch. prof. U. Utah, Salt Lake City, 1972-76; dir. microelectronics lab. U. Ariz., Tucson, 1976-87; assoc. prof., lab. mgr. Ariz. State U., Tempe, 1987—, assoc. chair microelectronics, 1992—, asst. chair dept. electronic and computer tech., 1993—; cons. Integrated Cirs. Engring., Scottsdale, Ariz., 1976—, Western Design Ctr., Mesa, Ariz., 1980—; mem. semiconductor com. United Techs. Corp., Hartford, Conn., 1978-87. Author: Silicon Wafer Processing Technology, 1979; editor: Integrated Circuits, 1965; contbr.: MOS Integrated Circuits, 1972. Mem. IEEE, Internat. Soc. for Hybrid Microelectronics (chpt. pres. 1982-83), Electrochem. Soc. Home: 613 W Summit Pl Chandler AZ 85224-1556

FORDHAM, MARILYN MONROE, fraternal organization administrator; b. Salem, Oreg., Dec. 12, 1935; d. James Edwin and Bernice (Becker) Monroe; m. Robert Irving Fordham, Feb. 7, 1959; children: James Irving, Barbara Jean. BSBA, U. Idaho, 1957. Exec. sec., acct. Morrison-Knudsen Co. Inc., Hells Canyon, Cambridge, Idaho, 1957-59; adminstrv. asst. Boise (Idaho) Cascade Corp., 1959-60; acct. Lincoln G. Kelly Co., Boise, 1960-61; exec. sec. Idaho First Nat. Bank, Boise, 1961-68; piano tchr. Boise, 1968—; internat. pres. Delta Gamma Fraternity, Boise and Columbus, Ohio, 1990-94; dir.-at-large Fraternity Housing Corp., Boise and Columbus, 1994—; dir. of housing Delta Gamma Fraternity, U.S., Can., 1983-85, internat. v.p. fin., 1986-90; bd. dirs. Fraternity Housing Corp., U.S., Can.; ednl. devel. chair Nat. Panhellenic Conf., Indpls., 1994—. Co-author (ednl. program series) NPC Links, 1995—; contbr. numerous articles to profl. jours. Mem. Jr. League of Boise (pres. 1975-76), Nat. Guild of Piano Tchrs. (treas. 1978-79), Delta Gamma Alumnae (pres. 1973-74), Performing Arts Ctr. Guild (vol. usher 1985-96). Republican. Presbyterian. Home: 6702 Morton Dr Boise ID 83704 Office: Delta Gamma Fraternity Housing Corp 3250 Riverside Dr Columbus OH 43221-1725

FORE, ANN, counselor, educator, country dance instructor; b. Artesia, N.Mex., July 16, 1948; d. Stanley William and Jackie (Hightower) Blocker; divorced; 1 child Richard Todd. *Great grandparents, David and Sophia Blocker, were county pioneers instrumental in establishing the small New Mexico town of Carlsbad, of which they became long-time residents. Carlsbad is noted for the magnificent Carlsbad Caverns, one of nature's many wonders! Sons of David and Sophia, Charles Ray Blocker and Stanley W. Blocker (father of Ann Fore), took a struggling newspaper called the Artesia Advocate, in the small nearby town of Artesia, and made it into a strong and reputable newspaper. The Artesia Advocate later merged with the Artesia Daily Press making it the Artesia Daily Press today.* BS, Eastern N.Mex. U., Portales, 1971, MA, 1976. Instr. sociology Eastern N.Mex. U., Clovis, 1974; counselor, instr. So. Plains Jr. Coll., Plainview, Tex., 1975-76; drug and alcohol counselor U.S. Dept. Army, Ft. Hood, Tex., 1976-77; group leader Forest Svc., USDA, Estacada, Oreg., 1980-81; owner Koda Kountry Prodns., Salem, Oreg., 1990—, Women's Issues Counseling Svcs., Salem, 1985—; tchr. country western ptnr. dancing and line dancing various ednl. settings, Salem, Oreg., Portland C.C., Salem Keizer Schs. Author: Silent Cry, 1993; choreographer 2 line dances; founder, adminstr. award-winning, nationally televised country dance team Koda Kountry Drifters. U. N.Mex. Rsch. Dept. grantee, 1972. Mem. APGA, Willamette Writers Assn., Nat. Tchrs. Assn. for Country/Western Dance Instrs., Internat. Platform Assn. Republican. Christian. Home and Office: PO Box 13851 Salem OR 97309-1851

FOREST, EVA BROWN, nurse, supervisor and paralegal; b. Ontario, Va., July 7, 1941; d. William Butler and Ruth Pauline (Simpson) Brown; m. Willie J. Forest Jr., Sept. 16, 1961; children: Geraid, Darryl, Angela. AA, Bismarck (N.D.) State Coll., 1981; BSN, U. Mary, Bismarck, 1984. RN, Colo. Charge nurse St. Alexius Med. Ctr., Bismarck, 1984-85, Cedars Health Care Ctr., Lakewood, Colo., 1989-90; staff devel. coord. Park Avenue Bapt. Home, Denver, 1990-91; supr., charge nurse Cedars Health Care Ctr., Lakewood, Colo., 1991—; charge nurse Villa Manor Health Ctr., Lakewood, Colo., 1991-93; supr., charge nurse Stovall Care Ctr., Denver, 1995-96. Vol. for cultural exch. lang., culture and fashions YWCA, Kano, Nigeria; vocalist gospel music workshop, N.D.; pianist adult and children's choir, N.D.; mem. MADD, Habitat for Humanity Internat., HALT, Vols. of Am. Mem. Nat. Multiple Sclerosis Soc., Internat. Platform Assn., DAV Commdrs. Club.

FORESTER, JOHN, cycling transportation engineer; b. London, Oct. 7, 1929; came to the U.S., 1940; s. Cecil Scott and Kathleen (Belcher) F. AB, U. Calif., Berkeley, 1951; MS, Calif. State U., Long Beach, 1964. Registered industrial engr., Calif. Cycling transporation engr. Sunnyvale, Calif., 1972—. Author: Statistical Selections of Business Strategies, 1968, Effective Cycling, 1976, 6th edit., 1993, Bicycle Transportation, 1977, 4th edit., 1994. Rsch. bd. bicycling com. transporation Nat. Acad. Scis., 1977-83. pres. Calif. Assn. Bicycling Orgns., 1973-76, League Am. Bicyclists, 1979-80, dir., 1976-83. Home and Office: 726 Madrone Ave Sunnyvale CA 94086-3041

FORGAN, DAVID WALLER, retired air force officer; b. Chgo., Sept. 28, 1933; s. Harold Nye and Ruth Ada (Waller) F.; m. Shirley Dobbins, Oct. 18, 1958; children—Bruce Dobbins, Todd Macmillan. B.S. in Mktg., U. Colo., 1955; M.S. in Mgmt., George Washington U., 1966. Commd. 2d lt. U.S. Air Force, 1956, advanced through grades to maj. gen., 1985, various positions worldwide, 1956-77; dir. programs hdgrs. tactical air command U.S. Air Force, Langley AFB, Va., 1977-79; dir. force devel. U.S. Air Force, Washington, 1979-80; dep. comdr. spl. ops. command U.S. Air Force, Fort Bragg, N.C., 1980-82; asst. chief staff ops. Allied Forces Central Europe, Brunssum, The Netherlands, 1982-85; dep. chief staff ops. U.S. Air Force Europe, Ramstein Air Base, Fed. Republic Germany, 1985-87; comdr. Sheppard Tech. Tng. Ctr. Sheppard AFB, Tex., 1987-89; ret., 1989. Decorated Silver Star, D.F.C. (3), Legion of Merit, Air medal, Def. Disting. Svc. medal, Def. Superior Svc. medal; Aero Cross of Merit (Spain). Mem. Delta Tau Delta. Republican. Home: 4935 Newstead Pl Colorado Springs CO 80906-5978

FORGANG, DAVID M., museum curator; b. N.Y.C., Mar. 26, 1947; s. Joseph Hyman and Clarice (Ishbia) F.; m. Joyce Enid Blumenthal, June 15, 1968 (div. May 1979); children: Adam, Bradley. B in Anthropology, U. Ariz., 1968, M in Anthropology, 1971. Mus. curator So. Ariz. Group Nat. Pk. Svc., Phoenix, 1971-77; regional curator we. region Nat. Pk. Svc., San Francisco, 1977-82; chief curator Yosemite (Calif.) Mus. Nat. Pk. Svc., 1982—; pres. Yosemite Renaissance Art Competition, 1983-94; dir. Yosemite Artist in Residence Program, 1985—. Mariposa County advisor El Portal (Calif.) Town Planning Adv. Bd., 1984-94. Recipient Unit Award citation USDI, 1974. Democrat. Jewish. Office: Nat Pk Svc PO Box 577 Yosemite National Park CA 95389-0577

FORGIA, KEN, mayor. Treas., chmn. Regional Pub. Transp. Authority, Peoria, Ariz.; various positions to Lt. Col. Ariz. Dept. Pub. Safety; ret., 1983; elected (at large) mayor City of Peoria, 1991-93, re-elected, 1993, 95; former mem. City of Peoria Pers. Bd.; voting mem. Maricopa County Assn. Govts.; pres. Ariz. Mcpl. Water Users Assn. Office: Mayor's Office 8401 W Monroe St Peoria AZ 85345

FORGUE, KERRY JO, artist, educator; b. McMinnville, Oreg., Sept. 10, 1963; d. Tyrone Yoshikazu and Sandra Joan (Gilbert) Kuhns; m. David Mumm Forgue, Dec. 31, 1987; 1 child, Shawnie Jo. Student, Linfield Coll., McMinnville, 1981-82; BS, Western Oreg. State Coll., Monmouth, 1995. Artist/painter Phoenix, 1985-92, Salem, Oreg., 1993-94; artist, instr. Bush Barn Art Ctr. and pvt. lessons, Salem, 1994—; co-owner Forgue's Painting, Phoenix, 1985-92, Salem, 1993—; art demonstrator/instr. Salem Art Assn. Art Fair and Festival, 1994-96. One person shows include Presidents Gallery, Western Oreg. State Coll., Monmouth, 1994, Concourse Gallery, Werner Coll. Ctr., Western Oreg. State Coll., 1994, 95, Majestic Theater, Corvallis, Oreg., 1996, Timberhill Athletic Club, Corvallis, 1996, Illahe Hills Country Club, Salem, Oreg., 1996-97; exhibited in group shows at Bush Barn Art Ctr., Salem, 1997, Oreg. Soc. Artist Gallery, Portland, 1997, Celebration of the Arts, Portland, 1995, 97, New Orleans XVIII Nat. Exhbn. at the World Trade Ctr. Contbg. artist to Northwest Passages jour. Recipient numerous awards for art, including New Orleans World Trade Ctr. and Art Experience '96 award for excellence in drawing. Mem. Nat. Colored Pencil Soc. Am., Colored Pencil Soc. Am. (dist. chpt. 210), Salem Art Assn., Corvallis Fine Arts Guild, Arts in Oreg. Coun., Mid-Valley Arts Coun., Oreg. Coast Coun. for the Arts. Baptist. Home: 5270 Parker Ct S Salem OR 97306

FORMAN, JOEL JON, numismatic appraiser; b. Bklyn., July 4, 1938; s. Eugene and Esther (Kushel) F.; m. Linda Joy Karel, July 5, 1964; children: Debra Ann, David Alon. BA in Math., San Diego State U., 1966; M in Computer Sci., West Coast U., 1975; M in Valuation Sci., Lindenwood Coll., 1993. Software engr. various def. contractors, San Diego, L.A., 1962-77, Hughes Aircraft Co., El Segundo, Calif., 1978-93; cert. numismatic appraiser Culver City, Calif., 1988—; importer/exporter Culver City, 1991—; numismatic advisor, cons. Simon Wiesenthal Ctr., L.A., 1979—. Contbr. articles to profl. jours. With USMC, 1958-61. Mem. Am. Soc. of Appraisers (internat. bd. examiners 1992—), Toastmasters Internat. (officer, many awards), B'nai B'rith Lodge (pres. 1971-72). Jewish. Home and Office: 11260 Overland Ave Ste 9G Culver City CA 90230-5532

FORMAN, JUDITH AVIS, educator; b. Chgo., Oct. 12, 1937; d. Bernard L. and Bettie (Bluhm) Becker; m. Larry S. Forman, Aug. 23, 1959; children: Mark, Kenneth, James. BA, U. Mich., 1959; MEd, Calif. Luth. U., Thousand Oaks, 1979. Life tchg. credential. Tchr. Redford Twp. (Mich.) Jr. H.S., 1959-60, Santa Maria (Calif.) H.S., 1960-61, Monte Vista Intermediate Sch., Camarillo, Calif., 1971-90, Oak Park H.S., Agoura, Calif., 1990—; fellow Nat. Writing Project, U. Calif. Santa Barbara, 1987, returning fellow, 1995; Tech. in Classroom fellow U. Calif. Santa Barbara, 1985; mentor tchr. Pleasant Valley Sch. Dist., Camarillo, 1983-86, Oak Park Sch. Dist., Agoura, 1995. Author, editor: The American Experience, 1995; contbr. articles to profl. jours. Grantee Calif. Ednl. Initiative Fund, 1992, creative ideas grantee Oak Park, 1994-95. Mem. Nat. Coun. Tchrs. English, Assn. Secondary Curriculum Devel., Calif. Assn. Tchrs. English, Smithsonian, Oak Park Tchrs. Assn. Office: Oak Park HS 899 Kanan Rd Agoura CA 91301-3904

FORMBY, BENT CLARK, immunologist; b. Copenhagen, Apr. 3, 1940; naturalized, 1991; s. John K. and Gudrun A. (Dinesen) F.; m. Irene Menck-Thygesen, June 28, 1963 (div. May 1980); children: Rasmus, Mikkel; m. Florence G. Schmid, June 28, 1980. BA in Philosophy summa cum laude, U. Copenhagen, 1959, PhD in Biochemistry, 1968, DSc, 1976. Asst. prof. U. Copenhagen, 1969-73, assoc. prof., 1973-79, prof., 1979-83; vis. prof. U. Calif., San Francisco, 1979-84; sr. scientist, dir. lab. of immunology Sansum Med. Rsch. Found., Santa Barbara, Calif., 1984—; cons. Cell Tech., Inc.,

Boulder, Colo., 1989—, Immunex Corp., Seattle, 1989—; med. adv. bd. Biocellular Rsch. Orgn., Ltd., London, Childrens Hosp. of Orange County, Lautenburg Ctr. for Gen. and Tumor Immunology, Hebrew U., Hadassah Med. Sch., Jerusalem, 1993—, Loran Med. Sys., Inc. Editor: Fetal Islet Transplantation, 1988, 2d edit. 1995; contbr. articles to profl. jours.; patentee on non-invasive blood glucose measurement. Grantee Juvenile Diabetes Found., 1987, 88, E.L. Wiegand Found., 1993, Santa Barbara Cottage Hosp. Rsch., 1993-94, Breast Cancer Rsch. U. Calif., 1995-96, 96-97. Mem. N.Y. Acad. Scis., Am. Diabetes Assn. (grantee 1985, 86, 89, pres. Santa Barbara chpt. 1995), Am. Fedn. Clin. Rsch., European Assn. for the Study of Diabetes. Office: Sansum Med Rsch Found 2219 Bath St Santa Barbara CA 93105-4321

FORREST, KENTON HARVEY, science educator, historian; b. Fort Lauderdale, Fla., Oct. 3, 1944; s. Harvey William and Marjorie A. (Boxrud) F. BA, Colo. State Coll., 1968; MA, U. No. Colo., 1981. Science tchr. Dunstan Middle Sch., Jefferson County Pub. Schs., Lakewood, Colo., 1968—, dept. chmn., 1994—; pres. Tramway Press, Inc., 1983—. Author: Denver's Railroads, 1981; (with William C. Jones) Denver-A Pictorial History, 1973; (with others) The Moffat Tunnel, 1978; Rio Grande Ski Train, 1984, History of the Public Schools of Denver, 1989, Route 3 Englewood, 1990, The Railroads of Coors Field, 1995. Trustee Colo. Railroad Hist. Found., Golden, 1975—, pres. 1994-95; mem., 1st pres. Lakewood Hist. Soc. (Colo.), 1976; office Jeffco Credit Union. Mem. NEA (life) Colo. Assn. Sci. Tchrs., Nat. Railway Hist. Soc. (Intermountain chpt. pres. 1980-83, chmn. hist. plaque commn.), Mobile Post Office Soc. Home: PO Box 15607 Lakewood CO 80215-0007 Office: Dunstan Middle Sch 1855 S Wright St Lakewood CO 80228-3963

FORRESTER, JAMES STUART, cardiologist, medical educator; b. Phila., July 13, 1937; s. James S. and Mildred W. (Smith) F.; m. Deborah MacAdam, 1963 (div. 1974); children: Jeffrey Lance, Brent Worth; m. Barbara Ann Bick, May 27, 1975; 1 child, Justin Bick. BA, Swarthmore Coll., 1959; MD, U. Pa., 1963. Diplomate Am. Bd. Internal Medicine; bd. cert. cardiovascular disease. Intern U. Pa. Hosp.; resident Harbor Gen. Hosp.; fellow Peter Bent Brigham Hosp.; prof. medicine UCLA, 1986—; dir. divsn. cardiology Cedars-Sinai Med. Ctr., L.A., 1989-95, dir. cardiovascular rsch. inst., 1993—; George Burns and Gracie Allen prof. cardiology Cedars-Sinai Med. Ctr., L.A., 1989—. Recipient Goldman award for laser rsch. SPIE, 1990, Kellerman award for prevention cardiology rsch. Internat. Soc. Heart Failure, 1996; named Best Doctors in Am., 1994, 95, 96, 97, Best Heart Doctors in Am., Good Housekeeping, 1996. Mem. Am. Coll. Cardiology (bd. trustees 1993—), Am. Heart Assn. (bd. dirs. 1993—, Disting. Sci. Achievement award 1990). Office: Cedars Sinai Med Ctr 8700 Beverly Blvd Los Angeles CA 90048-1804

FORSBERG, CHARLES ALTON, computer, infosystems engineer; b. Wilmette, Ill., May 6, 1944; s. Delbert Alton and Margery (McCleary) F. Student, Rensselaer Poly. Inst.; BSEE, U. Wis., 1966, MSEE, 1968; postgrad., various univs. and colls. From design engr. to project leader Tektronix, Portland, Oreg., 1968-74; mgr. R&D Sidereal, Portland, 1974-80; chief engr. Computer Devel. Inc., Portland, 1980-84; pres. Omen Tech. Inc., Portland, 1984—. Developer YMODEM and ZMODEM Protocols for worldwide data transfer. Recognized for outstanding contbn. to field IBM-PC Users Group, Madison, Wis., 1988, Alamo PC Orgn., San Antonio, 1988. Home and Office: 10255 NW Old Cornelius Pass Rd Portland OR 97231-2515

FORSDALE, (CHALMERS) LOUIS, education and communication educator; b. Greeley, Colo., Mar. 8, 1922; s. John Aaron and Wilhelmina (Thorkildsen) F.; m. Elinor Wulfekuhler, Aug. 22, 1947 (dec. 1963); children: Lynn, John; m. Joan Ida Rosengren, May 28, 1964 (div. 1966). B.A., Colo. State Coll., 1942; M.A., Columbia U. Tchrs. Coll., 1947; Ed.D., Columbia U., 1951. Instr. English Tchrs. Coll., Columbia U., N.Y.C., 1947-51; asst. prof. Tchrs. Coll., Columbia U., 1951-55, assoc. prof., 1955-58, prof. communication and edn., 1958-87, prof. emeritus, 1987; vis. assoc. prof. edn. U. So. Calif., Los Angeles, 1957; cons. in communication various businesses, industries and schs., 1965—; vis. scholar Iran Communication and Devel. Inst., Tehran, 1977. Author: Nonverbal Communication, 1974, Perspectives on Communication, 1981; Editor: (with others) Communication in General Education, 1961, 8MM Sound Film and Education, 1962. Served to 1st lt. USAAF, 1943-45. Recipient Tchrs. Coll. Disting. Alumni award Merit, 1989. Democrat. Home: 330 Otero St Santa Fe NM 87501-1906

FORSTER, BRUCE ALEXANDER, dean; b. Toronto, Ont., Can., Sept. 23, 1948; m. Margaret Jane Mackay, Dec. 28, 1968, (div. Dec. 1979); 1 child, Kelli Elissa; m. Valerie Dale Pendock, Dec. 8, 1979; children: Jeremy Bruce, Jessica Dale. BA in Math., Econs., U. Guelph, Ont., 1970; PhD in Econs., Australian Nat. U., Canberra, 1974. Asst. prof. U. Guelph, 1973-77, assoc. prof., 1977-83, prof. econs., 1983-88; vis. assoc. prof. U. B.C., Vancouver, 1979; vis. fellow U. Wyoming, 1979-80, vis. prof., 1983-84, 87; prof. econs., 1987—, dean Coll. Bus., 1991—; vis. prof. Profl. Tng. Ctr., Ministry of Econ. Affairs, Taiwan, 1990-95; acad. assoc. The Atlantic Coun. of the U.S., cons. in field. Author: The Acid Rain Debate: Science and Special Interest in Policy Formation, 1993; co-author: Economics in Canadian Society, 1986; assoc. editor Jour. Applied Bus. Rsch., 1987, editorial adv. bd., 1987—; editorial coun. Jour. Environ. Econs. and Mgmt., 1989, assoc. editor, 1989-91; contbr. articles to profl. jours. Trustee Wyo. Retirement Sys., 1995—, Laramie Sr. Housing, Inc., 1995-96. Jayes-Qantas Vis. scholar U. Newcastle, Australia, 1983. Mem. Am. Econ. Assn., Assn. Environ. and Resource Economists, Mid-West Assn. Bus. Deans and Divsn. Heads (pres. 1995-96), Am. Assembly Collegiate Schs. Bus. (mem. bus. accreditation com. 1995-98), Faculty Club U. Guelph (treas. 1981-82, v.p. 1982-83, 85- 86, pres. 1986-87). Avocations: weight lifting, swimming, skiing, scuba diving. Home: 3001 Sage Dr Laramie WY 82070-5751 Office: U Wyo Coll Bus Laramie WY 82071

FORSTOT, S. LANCE, ophthalmologist; b. N.Y.C., Aug. 19, 1943; s. Shepard and Edith Forstot; m. Lynne Rochelle Bitton, June 15, 1945; children: Michele, Jordan. AB, Princeton U., 1965; MD, Johns Hopkins U., 1969. Diplomate Am. Bd. Ophthalmology. Ophthalmologist Corneal Cons. of Colo., Denver, 1982—; ophthalmologist U. Colo. Sch. of Medicine, Denver, 1976-82, clin. prof., 1982—. Contbr. articles to profl. jours. Recipient Honor award Am. Acad. Ophthalmology. Mem. Contact Lens Assn. of Ophthalmology (bd. dirs. 1985-87), Internat. Soc. Refractive Surgery (bd. dirs. 1995-96). Office: Corneal Cons of Colo 8381 Southpark Ln Littleton CO 80120

FORSYTH, BEN RALPH, academic administrator, medical educator; b. N.Y.C., Mar. 8, 1934; s. Martin and Eva (Lazansky) F.; m. Elizabeth Held, Aug. 19, 1962; children: Jennifer, Beverly, Jonathan. Attended, Cornell U., 1950-53; MD, NYU, 1957. Diplomate Am. Bd. Internal Medicine. Intern, then resident Yale Hosp., New Haven, 1957-60; postdoctoral fellow Harvard U. Med. Shc., Boston, 1960-61; rsch. assoc. NIH, Bethesda, Md., 1963-66; assoc. prof. med. microbiology, prof. med. coll. U. Vt., Burlington, 1966-90, assoc. dean div. health scis., 1971-85, assoc. v.p. acad. affairs, 1977-78, v.p. adminstrn., 1978-85, sr. v.p., 1985-90; sr. exec. asst. to pres. Ariz. State U., Tempe, 1990—, prof. health adminstrn. and policy, 1991—, interim v.p. adminstrv. svcs., 1991-93; interim provost Ariz. State U. West, Phoenix, 1992-93, 1992-93, provost, v.p., 1993-96; sr. cons. Univ. Health Ctr., Burlington, 1986-90. Contbr. articles to profl. jours. V.p., chmn. United Way Planning Com., Burlington, 1974-75, Ops. Com., 1975-76, bd. dirs., officer, 1977-89; bd. trustees U. Vt., Burlington, 1996—; mem. New England Bd. Higher Edn. Com., Burlington, 1985-89; chmn. U. Vt. China Project Adv. Bd., Burlington, 1989-90. Lt. comdr. USN, 1962-63. Sinsheimer Found. faculty fellow, 1966-71. Fellow ACP, Infectious Diseases Soc. Am.; mem. Phi Beta Kappa, Alpha Omega Alpha. Office: Arizona State Univ PO Box 872203 4701 W Thunderbird Rd Tempe AZ 85287-2203

FORSYTH, RAYMOND ARTHUR, civil engineer; b. Reno, Mar. 13, 1928; s. Harold Raymond and Fay Exona (Highfill) F.; BS, Calif. State U., San Jose, 1952; M.C.E., Auburn U., 1958; m. Mary Ellen Wagner, July 9, 1950; children: Lynne, Gail, Alison, Ellen. Jr. engr., asst. engr. Calif. Div. Hwys., San Francisco, 1952-54; assoc. engr., sr. supervising, prin. engr. Calif. Dept. Transp., Sacramento, 1961-83, chief geotech. br., 1972-79, chief soil mechanics and pavement br., 1979-83, chief Transp. Lab., 1983-89; cons., lectr. in field. Served with USAF, 1954-56. Fellow ASCE (pres. Sacramento sect., chmn. Calif. council 1980-81); mem. Transp. Research Bd. (chmn. embankments and earth slopes com. 1976-82, chmn. soil mechanics sect. 1982-88, chmn. group 2 council 1988-91), ASTM. Contbr. articles to profl. publs. Home: 5017 Pasadena Ave Sacramento CA 95841-4149

FORTH, KEVIN BERNARD, beverage distributing industry consultant; b. Adams, Mass., Dec. 4, 1949; s. Michael Charles and Catherine Cecilia (McAndrews) F.; children: Melissa, Brian. AB, Holy Cross Coll., 1971; MBA with distinction, NYU, 1973. Div. rep. Anheuser-Busch, Inc., Boston, 1973-74, dist. sales mgr., L.A., 1974-76, asst. to v.p. mktg. staff, St. Louis, 1976-77; v.p. Straub Distbg. Co., Ltd., Orange, Calif., 1977-81, pres., 1981-93, chmn., CEO, 1986-93, also bd. dirs. Commr. Orange County Sheriff's Adv. Coun., 1988—; mem. adv. bd. Rancho Santiago C.C. Coll. Dist. 1978-80; bd. dirs. Children's Hosp. of Orange County Padrinos Found., 1983-85, St. Joseph's Hosp. Found., Orange County Sports Hall of Fame, 1980-89; exec. com., bd. dirs. Nat. Coun. on Alcoholism, 1980-83; mem. pres. coun. Holy Cross Coll., 1987-91; bd. dirs., pres. Calif. State Fullerton Titan Athletic Found., 1983-85, 89-90 (vol. of yr., 1991),mem. Calif. Beer Wholesalers Assn., dir., 1978-85, v.p., 1984, chmn, 1985,; bd. dirs. Freedom Bowl, 1984-93, v.p., 1984-85, pres., 1986, chmn., 1986-87, Anaheim Vis. and Conv. Bur., 1989-93; bd. dirs. Orangewood Children's Found., 1988-93; mem. Calif. Rep. State Cen. Com., 1988-93, Orange County Probation Dept. Cmty. Involvement Bd., 1992-93. Benjamin Levy fellow NYU, 1971-73; recipient Founders award Freedom Bowl, 1993. Mem. Industry Environ. Coun., Holy Cross Alumni Assn., NYU Alumni Assn., Nat. Assn. Stock Car Auto Racing, Calif. Beer & Wine Wholesalers Assn. (bd dirs. 1982-89, v.p. 1984, chmn. 1985), Sports Car Club Am. (Ariz. state champion 1982), Beta Gamma Sigma. Roman Catholic. Club: Holy Cross (So. Calif.), Nat. Beer Wholesalers Assn. (bd. dir. 1986-93, asst. sec. 1989-90, sec. 1989-91, vice-chmn. 1992, chmn. 1993). Home: 27750 Tamara Dr Yorba Linda CA 92887

FORTIER, DANA SUZANNE, psychotherapist; b. Fresno, Calif., Jan. 15, 1952; d. Dan and Louise (Metkovich) Ninkovich; m. Timothy Fortier, Jan. 29, 1994. BA in Journalism summa cum laude, Calif. State U., Fresno, 1974; BSN, Calif. State U., 1979, MSW with distinction, 1986. Registered nurse, Calif; lic. social worker, Calif. Staff nurse Valley Med. Ctr., Fresno, 1980-81; pub. health nurse Fresno County Health Dept., 1981-83; therapist II Sierra Community Hosp., Fresno, 1986-87; women's svcs. coord. Turning Point Youth Svcs., Visalia, Calif., 1987-89; psychotherapist and cons. in pvt. practice Visalia, 1989—; instr. San Joaquin Valley Coll., 1994—; clins. cons. in field. Contbr. articles to profl. jours. Mem. Task Force on Pregnant Mothers, 1990—. Mem. Calif. Women's Commn. on Drugs and Alcohol, Calif. Advocacy for Pregnent Women, Soc. for Clin. Social Wk., Nat. Assn. Social Workers, Visalia Bus. and Profl. Women's Clubs. Republican. Office: 304 S Johnson St Visalia CA 93291-6136

FORTIER, KEN, police chief; married; 3 children. B in Criminal Justice Adminstrn., San Diego State U., MPA. Asst. chief of police City of Riverside, Calif.; chief of police City of Riverside, 1993—. Address: 4102 Orange St Riverside CA 92501

FORTNA, VALERIÉ ANNETTE, dance and performing company owner, instructor; b. Denver, May 25, 1974; d. Russell Lloyd and Barbara F. Cert. dance educator. Dance instr., dancer Rock-Out to the Future, Denver, 1990-94; owner, dir. Dance Explosion, Littleton, Colo., 1993—, Protégé Performing Co., Littleton, 1993—; dance instr. Spring Break Jam, Ft. Lauderdle, Fla., 1994, Western Dance Expo, Laramie, Wyo., 1994; comml. actress Coor Brewing Co., Golden, Colo., 1993. Author: Guide to Student Engligh, 1993; choreographer Creative Expressions, Denver, 1993. Vol. fitness Charity 1993, Cherry Creek, Colo., 1993, Dance Explosion, Littleton, 1994. Recipient Miss Royale award Denver, 1992, Top Choreography award Kar Prodns., Denver, 1994, Top Studio award, 1995. Mem. Assn. Mktg. Students (cons., sec. 1992-93, vehicles and petroleum knowledge award 1992), Creative Expressions. Democrat. Home: 16890 E 116th Ct Denver CO 80022 Office: Dance Explosion 3625 W Bowles Ave Littleton CO 80123-7922

FORTNER, HUESTON GILMORE, lawyer, writer, composer; b. Tacoma, Nov. 1, 1959; s. Hueston Turner Jr. and Deborah Hewes (Berry) F. BS, Tulane U., 1981; JD, U. Miss., 1985. Bar: Miss. 1986, La. 1987, U.S. Dist. Ct. (no. and so. dists.) Miss. 1986, U.S. Dist. Ct. (ea., mid. and we. dists.) La., 1987, U.S. Ct. Appeals (5th cir.) 1986, Calif. 1989, U.S. Dist. Ct. (cen. dist.) Calif. 1989. Clk. Farrer and Co., London, Miss., 1985; assoc. Cliff Finch & Assocs., Batesville, Miss., 1986; pvt. practice New Orleans, 1987-88; atty. Parker, Milliken, Clark, O'Hara & Samuelian, L.A., 1989-90; pvt. prctice L.A., 1990—; vis. lectr. Anhui U., Hefei, People's Rep. of China, Bejing Inst. of Petrochem. Tech., 1994, Bangkok Coll. Bus. Adminstrn., 1996; participanted in Leicester vs. Leicester Rugby Union, House of Lords, Eng., 1985; assisted Queen's Counsel in Yussuf Islam (Cat Stevens) vs. Bank of Westminster P.L.C. royalties litigation 1985, Newton vs. NBC, 1988; temporary judge L.A. County mcpl. Ct., 1991—; ind. film producer. Performing musician; composer numerous mus. works; contbg. photographer Flix mag., 1993—; contbr. editor Rental, 1987-89. Recipient Space Devel. Strategies award NASA/U. Houston Advanced Rsch. Ctr., 1995; grantee NSF, 1976. Mem. Miss. Bar Assn., La. Bar Assn., State Bar Calif., Assn. Telecommunications Attys., Broadcast Music Internat., Nat. Acad. Songwriters, Los Angeles County Bar Assn., Phi Alpha Delta. Presbyterian.

FORTNEY, THOMAS KENT, cost and petroleum engineer, management consultant; b. Douglas, Ariz., June 22, 1947; s. Thomas Hayes Fortney and Edna (Cosper) Randall. BA, No. Ariz. U., 1970, MA, 1973; M Internat. Mgmt., Am. Grad. Sch. Internat. Mgmt., Glendale, Ariz., 1980; BS in Petroleum Engring., U. Okla., 1990. Cert. cost engr. Internat. Cost Engring. Coun. Mgmt. cons. Lorer and Assocs., Orange, Calif., 1981-84; cons. to Stockmar Corp., Fortney Cons., Long Beach, Calif., 1984-85; prodn. analyst E.F. Brady Constrn., L.A., 1985-87; cons. Santa Fe Drilling, London, 1990-91; mgmt. and engring. cons. Fortney Cons., Flagstaff, Ariz., 1990-91; oil well fire fighter and driller Santa Fe Drilling, Kuwait, 1991-92; cost and mgmt. cons. Fortney Cons., Mesa, Ariz., 1992-96; cons. Santa Fe North Sea Brit. Gas, Shell Oil, Brit. Petroleum, 1996; inventory control supr. Sphere Supply, Houston, 1997—; advisor Western Leisure Travel, Salt Lake City; drilling cons. Nigus Corp., Lagos, Nigeria, 1990; cons. Santa Fe-North Sea in Cost Eng., Drilling Eng., Organizational Behavior, Aberdeen, Scotland, 1996; turnkey estimator, Santa Fe, Venezuela. Vol. St. Vincent DePaul Shelters. Mem. Am. Assn. Cost Engrs. (cert., bd. dirs. Gulfcoast chpt.), Soc. Petroleum Engrs. Democrat. Baptist. Home: Apt 207 8455 Will Clayton Pky Humble TX 77338

FORTSON, JUDITH LEE, library administrator; b. Summerville, S.C., Jan. 6, 1943; d. Julien Fulton and Mary Josephine (Thronton) F.; m. Hardy Eugene Jones, Aug. 15, 1965 (div. 1979); 1 child, Hardy Ryan; m. Frederick Irwin Dretske, May 14, 1988. BA, Baylor U., 1965; MA, U. Wisc., 1968. Instr. English Concordia Coll., Austin, Tex., 1972-76; conservation specialist Nebr. State Hist. Soc., 1977-83; head libr. western langs. collection, preservation svcs. Hoover Instn., Stanford, Calif., 1983-91; cons. Nat. Assn. Govt. Archives and Records Adminstrs. Preservation Planning Project, 1989-90, Libr. of Congress, 1989, Libr. of U. Oreg., 1988, Soc. Am. ARchivists Conservation Survey Program, 1982-83, Sioux Falls Coll., 1982; instr. Western Archives Inst., L.A., 1989-, 90, Stanford U., 1985, U. Tex., Austin, 1983; guest instr. history dept. U. Nebr., 1982-83; supr. intern program experiental edn. U. Nebr., 1982; grant reviewer Dept. Edn., 1993, NEH, 1986, 90, 92, Nat. Hist. Publs. and Records Commn., Inst. Mus. Svcs. Author: Disaster Planning and Recovery: A How-To-Do-It Manual dor Librarians and Archivists, 1992; author numerous articles to profl. jours. and reviews in field; presenter in field, 1980—. Mem. ALA, Soc. Am. Archivists (chair nominating com. 1992, mem. task force on standards 1989-90, standards bd. 1990-93, vice-chair conservation sect. 1988-90, mem. adv. com. for revision of SAA basic glossary 1988-89, mem. interim bd. on cert. 1989, program com. 1984, instr., adv. bd. mem. preservation mgmt. tng. program 1992-94, instr. numerous programs 1981-86), Spl. Librs. Assn. Office: Hoover Inst Stanford U Serra and Galvez Stanford CA 94305-6010

FORTUNA, ANTHONY FRANK, educator, consultant; b. Thomas, W.Va., Apr. 8, 1914; s. Anton and Rose (Secna) F.; m. Ann Marie Barthel, Sept. 27, 1938; children: Richard, Eugene. Student, L.A. Trade Tech. Coll., Pierce Coll., Valley Coll.; grad. Warren Sch. Astronautics, L.A. Coll.; student, U.S. Aviation Cadets. Registered profl. engr., Calif. Leadman Vultee Aircraft, Downy, Calif., 1939-40; gen. supr. Hindustan Aircraft, Bangalore, India, 1942-44; supr., inspector U.S. Air Corp., Long Beach, Calif., 1945-46; tng. supr. Douglas Aircraft Co., El Segundo, Calif., 1946-55; mgr. Northrop Ventura Div., Newberry Park, Calif., 1955-79; devel. engr. Hughes Space, El Segundo, 1981-86; dir. Talley Corp., Newberry, 1980-81; tchr., instr. Pierce Coll., Woodland Hills, Calif., 1962—; source engr. BQS, Inc., 1982—; cons. in field. Mem. Am. Inst. Astronautic/Aeronautic. Republican. Mormon. Home and Office: 3415 Loadstone Dr Sherman Oaks CA 91403-4513

FORTUNATO, JOANNE ALBA, athletic director; b. Phila.; d. Frank and MaryAnn (Vasquez) Torcaso. BS, Temple U., 1957, MS, 1959; PhD, U. So. Calif., L.A., 1973, Northwestern U., Chgo., 1986. Tchr. Phila. Pub. Sch. System, 1957-64; asst. prof. Trenton (N.J.) Coll., 1964-68, Cen. Conn. State Coll., New Britain, 1968-69; teaching asst. U. So. Calif., L.A., 1970-71; asst. prof. CUNY, Bklyn., 1971-75; assoc. athletic dir. and prof. Northwestern U., Chgo., 1975-80; athletic dir. Keene (N.H.) State Coll., 1981-93; commr. athletics New Eng. Collegiate Conf., 1990-93, Calif. C.C.'s, 1995—; commr. New Eng. Collegiate Conf., 1990-93; chair infraction com. Ea. Collegiate Athletic Conf., Centerville, Mass., 1984-89; regional chair W soccer Nat. Collegiate Athletic Assn., 1987-90; commr. Div. I champ, AIAW, Washington, 1983-86. Recipient Instl. Svc. award Italian Olympic Com., Rome, 1965, Ann. Leadership award Internat. Orgn. Women Execs., 1978, Citation of Recognition USVBA, 1972. Mem. AAHPERD, Nat. Assn. Coll. Women Athletic Adminstrs., Nat. Assn. Coll. Dirs. of Athletics. Home: 3090 Sierra Blvd Sacramento CA 95864-4931 Office: CCLC/COA 2017 O St Sacramento CA 95814-5211

FORTUNE, JAMES MICHAEL, marketing executive; b. Providence, Sept. 6, 1947; s. Thomas Henry and Olive Elizabeth (Duby) F.; m. G. Suzanne Hein, July 14, 1973. Student, Pikes Peak Community Coll., Colorado Springs, Colo., 1981-83; BSBA, BS in Computer Info. Systems, Regis Coll., 1991. Owner Fortune Fin. Svcs., Colorado Springs, Colo., 1975-79; ptnr. Robert James and Assocs., Colorado Springs, 1979-81; pres. Fortune & Co., Colorado Springs, 1981-88; sr. v.p. mktg. and editorial Phoenix Communications Group, Ltd., Colorado Springs, 1988—, also bd. dirs.; also bd. dirs.; bd. dirs. Colorado Springs Computer Systems, Am. Discount Svcs., Inc., Investor's Bookshelf, Inc., N.Am. Internet, LLC; talk show host Sta. KRCC, fin. commentator Wall Street Report, Sta. KKHT, 1983-84. Editor Fortune newsletter, 1981-85, The Can. Market News, 1981-83; editor, pub. Penny Fortune newsletter, 1981—, The Low Priced Investment newsletter, 1986-87, Women's Investment Newsletter, 1987—, Can. Market Confidential, 1988—, Spl. Option Situations, 1988—; pub. Internal Revenue Strategies, 1990, Tax and Investment Planning Strategies for Medical Professionals, 1991; contbr. articles to profl. jours. Cons. Jr. Achievement bus. project, Colorado Springs, 1985. Sgt. U.S. Army, 1968-70, Vietnam. Mem. Direct Mktg. Assn., Elks. Office: 1837 S Nevada Ave Ste 223 Colorado Springs CO 80906-2516

FOSSLAND, JOEANN JONES, professional speaker, personal coach; b. Balt., Mar. 21, 1948; d. Milton Francis and Clementine (Bowen) Jones; m. Richard E. Yellott III, 1966 (div. 1970); children: Richard E. IV, Dawn Joeann; m. Robert Gerard Fossland Jr., Nov. 25, 1982. Student, Johns Hopkins U., 1966-67; cert. in real estate, Hogan's Sch. Real Estate, 1982. GRI. Owner Kobble Shop, Indiatlantic, Fla., 1968-70, Downstairs, Atlanta, 1971; seamstress Aspen (Colo.) Leather, 1972-75; owner Backporch Feather & Leather, Aspen and Tucson, 1975-81; area mgr. Welcome Wagon, Tucson, 1982; realtor assoc. Tucson Realty & Trust, 1983-85; mgr. Home Illustrated mag., Tucson, 1985-87; asst. pub., gen. mgr. Phoenix, Scottsdale, Albuquerque, Tricities Tucson Homes Illustrated, 1990-93; pres. Advantage Solutions Group, Cortaro, Ariz., 1993—; power leader Darryl Davis Seminars Power Program, 1995—; personal and profl. coach. Designer leather goods (Tucson Mus. Art award 1978, Crested Butte Art Fair Best of Show award 1980); author: Personal and Professional Coaching: Coach University, Certified Training Program, 1996. Voter registrar Recorder's Office City of Tucson, 1985-91; bd. dirs. Hearth Found., Tucson, 1987-96, pres., 1994; bd. dirs. Ariz. Integrated Residential & Ednl. Svcs., Inc., 1989-95, pres. 1994-95). Mem. NAFE, Women's Coun. Realtors (leadership tng. grad. designation, pres. Tucson chpt. 1995, Ariz. state gov. 1997, Tucson Affiliate of Yr. award 1991), Tucson Assn. Realtors (Affiliate of Yr. award 1988). Democrat. Presbyterian. Office: Advantage Solutions Group PO Box 133 Cortaro AZ 85652-0133

FOSSUM, ROBERT H(EYERDAHL), retired English literature educator; b. Beloit, Wis., Mar. 19, 1923; s. Hans Martinius and Talma Irene (Heyerdahl) F.; m. Terry O'Brien Barker, Sept. 12, 1945 (div. Feb. 1951); m. Virginia Adelaide Hammond, June 7, 1952; children: Kristin, Robert Paul, Elizabeth. BA, Beloit Coll., 1948; MA, U. So. Calif., 1950; PhD, Claremont Grad. Sch., 1963. Tchg. asst., lectr. dept. English, U. So. Calif., L.A., 1948-50; instr., asst. prof., then assoc. prof. Beloit Coll., 1950-62; assoc. prof., prof. Calif. State U., L.A., 1962-63; assoc. prof., then prof. Claremont (Calif.) McKenna Coll., 1963-87, Josephine Olp Weeks prof. lit., 1972-87, prof. emeritus, 1987—; Fulbright prof. Am. lit. U. Vienna and U. Graz, Austria, 1969-70, 76-77. Author: William Styron, 1968, Hawthorne's Inviolable Circle, 1972; co-author: Facing Mirrors, 1980, The American Dream, 1981; co-editor: American Ground, 1988. With inf. U.S. Army, 1943. Fellow Lilly Found., 1959-60, Shell Found., 1960-61. Mem. MLA, Phi Beta Kappa. Home: 403 University Cir Claremont CA 91711

FOSTER, CHRIS B., otolaryngologist; b. Glasgow, Ky., Nov. 8, 1932; s. Chris Benton Foster and Pearl (Poynter) Shannon; m. Kathleen Delores Goen, Apr. 30, 1957; children: Chris, Scott. MD, U. Louisville, 1957. Diplomate Am. Bd. Otolaryngology. Capt. USAF, Riverside, Calif., 1961-63; pvt. practice Glasgow, Ky., 1963-69, San Diego, 1969—; assoc. prof. dept. otolaryngology U. Calif. San Diego, 1975—; dir. Neurotology Lab., San Diego, 1970-95. Fellow Am. Coll. Surgeons, Am. Acad. Otolaryngology; mem. La Jolla Profl. Men's Soc., AMA. Republican. Disciples of Christ. Office: 8950 Genesee Ave Ste 650 La Jolla CA 92037

FOSTER, DAVID RAMSEY, soap company executive; b. London, May 24, 1920; (parents Am. citizens); s. Robert Bagley and Josephine (Ramsey) F.; m. Anne Firth, Aug. 2, 1957 (dec. June 1994); children:Sarah, Victoria. Student in econs., Gonville and Caius Coll., Cambridge (Eng.) U., 1938. With Colgate-Palmolive Co. and affiliates, 1946-79, v.p., gen. mgr. Europe, Colgate-Palmolive Internat., 1961-65, v.p., gen. mgr. household products div. parent co., N.Y.C., 1965-68, exec. v.p., 1968-70, pres., 1970-75, chief exec. officer, 1971-79, chmn., 1975-79. Author: Wings Over the Sea, 1990. Trustee, Woman's Sport Found. Served to lt. comdr. Royal Naval Vol. Res., 1940-46. Decorated Disting. Service Order, D.S.C. with bar, Mentioned in Despatches (2); recipient Victor award City of Hope, 1974, Herbert Hoover Meml. award, 1976, Adam award, 1977, Harriman award Boys Club N.Y., 1977, Charter award St. Francis Coll., 1978, Walter Hagen award, 1978, Patty Berg award, 1986, Commr.'s award LPGA, 1995. Mem. Soc. Mayflower Descs. Clubs: Hawks (Cambridge U.); Royal Ancient Golf (St. Andrews, Scotland); Royal Cinque Ports Golf (life), Sunningdale Golf, Swinley Forest Golf (U.K.); Sankaty Head Golf; Racquet and Tennis (N.Y.C.); Mission Hills Country, Bally Bunion Golf. Home: 540 Desert West Dr Rancho Mirage CA 92270-1310

FOSTER, DAVID WILLIAM, minister; b. Idaho Falls, Idaho, Aug. 25, 1961; s. Robert Earl Foster and Alice (Crowder) Foster-Trumblee; m. June Ann Porter, Mar. 30, 1984; children: Brandon Allen, Brittany Ann. AS, N.W. Bible Coll., Kirkland, Wash., 1981; BA, N.W. Bible Coll., 1983. Ordained to ministry Bapt. Ch., 1987. Youth intern Idaho Falls Assembly of God, 1978-82; assoc. pastor youth Neighborhood Assembly, Lake Stevens, Wash., 1983-87; min. youth Bothel (Wash.) First Bapt., 1987—; asst. dir. ACTS Drama Ministry, Kirkland, 1981-83; camp counselman Cedar Springs Com., Kirkland, 1983-87; camp dir. Cedar Springs, Lake Stevens, 1985-87; dir. mins. Mt. Pillchuck Mins. Fellowship, Lake Stevens, 1984-87; youth coord. Puget Sound Bapt. Assn., Federal Way, Wash., 1988-91; bd. dirs. Hilltop Ministries, Lake Stevens, 1990—, CYM Ministries; seminar speaker, 1990. Composer religious musicals, 1982, 85; contbr. articles to profl. jours. Co-dir. Intransit Communications, Lake Stevens, 1985-87; distributor Everett (Wash.) Rep. Party, 1986. Future Religious Leader grantee Eastern Star,

1979, 80. Mem. Nat. Right to Life Com. (presdl. commendation 1986). Office: Bothell First Bapt Ch 19527 104th Ave NE Bothell WA 98011-2401

FOSTER, DUDLEY EDWARDS, JR., musician, educator; b. Orange, N.J., Oct. 5, 1935; s. Dudley Edwards and Margaret (DePoy) F. Student Occidental Coll., 1953-56; AB, UCLA, 1957, MA, 1958; postgrad. U. So. Calif., 1961-73. Lectr. music Immaculate Heart Coll., L.A., 1960-63; dir. music Holy Faith Episcopal Ch., Inglewood, Calif., 1964-67; lectr. music Calif. State U., L.A., 1968-71; assoc. prof. music L.A. Mission Coll., 1975-83, prof., 1983—, also chmn. dept. music, 1977—; mem. dist. acad. senate L.A. Community Colls., 1991-92; mem. acad. senate L.A. Mission Coll., 1993—; dir. music 1st Luth. Ch., L.A., 1968-72. Organist, pianist, harpsichordist; numerous recitals; composer O Sacrum Convivium for Trumpet and Organ, 1973, Passacaglia for Brass Instruments, 1969, Introduction, Arioso & Fugue for Cello and Piano, 1974. Fellow Trinity Coll. Music, London, 1960. Recipient Associated Students Faculty award, 1988. Mem. Am. Guild Organists, Am. Musicol. Soc., Nat. Assn. of Scholars, Acad. Senate, Town Hall Calif., L.A. Coll. Tchrs. Assn. (pres. Mission Coll. chpt. 1976-77, v.p., exec. com. 1982-84), Mediaeval Acad. Am. Republican. Anglican. Office: LA Mission Coll Dept Music 13356 Eldridge Ave Sylmar CA 91342-3200

FOSTER, JUDITH CHRISTINE, lawyer, writer; b. Columbus, Ohio, Nov. 25, 1952; d. Paul Marvel and Jean Harper (Uhland) F.; m. Sabah Amin Wali, Dec. 28, 1973; children: Samed Michel, Russeen Paul. BS in Natural Sci. and BA in Linguistics, Pa. State U., 1973; JD, Coll. William & Mary, 1979. Bar: Va. 1979, U.S. Ct. Appeals (4th cir.) 1979, U.S. Ct. Appeals (9th cir.) 1996, U.S. Supreme Ct. 1984. Pvt. practice Fairfax, Va., 1980-90, Encino, Calif., 1991—; mem. counsel U.S. Justice Found., Escondido, Calif., 1982-90; judge Internat. Moot Ct. Competition Assn. of Student Internat. Law Soc., 1984, 86. Author: (with Erich Pratt) Sanctuary: A People's Primer, 1986. Del. Va. Reps., Fairfax, 1981, 85. Mem. Am. Immigration Lawyers Assn. (legis. com. 1985, D.C. chpt. 1980-90, L.A. chpt. 1992—).

FOSTER, LAWRENCE, concert and opera conductor; b. Los Angeles, 1941. Student, Bayreuth Festival Masterclasses; studied with, Fritz Zweig. Debut as condr., Young Musicians' Found., Debut Orch., 1960; condr., mus. dir., 1960-64, condr., San Francisco Ballet, 1961-65, asst. condr., Los Angeles Philharmonic Orch., 1965-68, chief guest condr., Royal Philharmonic Orch., Eng., 1969-75, guest condr., Houston Symphony, 1970-71, condr. in chief, 1971-72, music dir., 1972-78, Orch. Philharmonique of Monte Carlo, 1979, gen. music dir., Duisburg & Dusseldorf Opera (Ger.), 1982-86, former music dir. Lausanne Chamber Orch., 1991-96, music dir. Aspen (Colo.) Music Festival and Sch.; currently music dir. Orquestra Ciutat de Barcelona; guest condr. orchs. in, U.S., Europe, Australia and Japan. (Recipient Koussevitsky Meml. Conducting prize 1966, Eleanor R. Crane Meml. prize Berkshire Festival, Tanglewood, Mass. 1966); condr. Jerusalem Symphony Orch., 1990. Address: ICM Artists Ltd c/o Jenny Vogel 8942 Wilshire Blvd Beverly Hills CA 90211

FOSTER, LAWRENCE HUNT, JR., physician, plastic surgeon; b. Bakersfield, Calif., Dec. 22, 1934; s. Lawrence Hunt and Edna (Knittle) F.; m. Patricia Ann Hunt, June 4, 1956 (div. Feb. 1976); children: Mark, Martin, Linda Lauren, Bill. AA, Bakersfiels Coll., 1954; BA, U. Calif., Berkeley, 1956; MD, U Calif., San Francisco, 1959. Diplomate Am. Bd. Plastic and Reconstructive Surgery, Am. Bd. Bariatric Physicians. Intern Valley Forge (Pa.) Army Hosp., 1959-60; gen. surgery resident William Beaumont Army Hosp., El Paso, Tex., 1960-63; Mobile Army Surg. Hosp., Korea, 1963-64, Brooke Burn Unit, San Antonio, 1964-66; plastic surgery resident U. Calif. Hosp., San Francisco, 1966-68; pvt. practice San Francisco, 1968—; owner Tahoe Clinic, South Lake Tahoe, Calif., 1976—; active staff St. Francis Meml. Hosp., San Francisco, 1968-75, Mary's Help Hosp., Daly City, Calif., 1968-77, courtesy staff, 1968-75, Barton Meml. Hosp., South Lake Tahoe, Calif., 1975-84, 94-96; courtesy staff French Hosp., San Francisco, 1968-75, Mt. Zion Hosp., 1968-75, Carson Tahoe Hosp., Carson City Nev., 1981-85. Am. Bd. Cosmetic Surgery fellow, 1989—. Fellow ACS, Internat. Coll. Surgeons; mem. AMA, Am. Soc. Plastic Surgeons, Am. Soc. Plastic and Reconstructive Surgeons, Am. Soc. Bariatric Physicians, Internat. Soc. Clin. Plastic Surgeons, Internat. Soc. Aesthetic Plastic Surgeons. Republican.

FOSTER, MARK EDWARD, lawyer, consultant, international lobbyist; b. Detroit, May 12, 1948; s. Herbert Edward and Joyce Mary (Campbell) F.; m. Miyoko Katabami, Apr. 20, 1974; children: Lorissa Chieko. B.A., Alma Coll., 1970; M.A., U. Calif.-Berkeley, 1972, Japanese lang. cert., 1982, J.D., 1981; postgrad. Stanford Ctr., Tokyo, 1983. Bar: Calif. 1981, Oregon 1989. Grantee, Rockefeller Found. Presbyn. Ch., Geneva and Tokyo, 1972-74; law clk. U.S. Dist. Ct., San Francisco, 1980-81; atty. Hetland & Hansen, Berkeley, Calif., 1981-82; atty. Braun Moriya Hoashi, Tokyo, 1982-84; spl. counsel U.S. Embassy, Tokyo, 1984-85; Japan counsel U.S. Electronic Industries Assn., 1985-86; mng. ptnr. Law Offices Mark E. Foster, Portland, Tokyo, 1988—; lectr., cons. on internat. law and tech. standards, tech. transfer, product compliance, engring. to Internat. Standards Orgn., Geneva, Ministry of Internt. Trade and Industry of Japan, U.S. Dept. Commerce, IBEAR conf. U. So. Calif., World Trade Inst.; mem. tech. standards com. for Optoelectronics, Japanese Ministry of Posts and Telecom., 1984-86, tech. standards com. for Intelligent Office Systems, Japanese Patent Office, Japanese Ministry of Internat. Trade and Industry, 1984-86. Author articles, books in internat. law and tech. Mem. ABA, Am. Soc. Quality Control, Internat. Bar Assn., Calif. Bar Assn., Oreg. Bar Assn., Am. C. of C. in Japan, Portland World Trade (bd. advisors), World Affairs Council. Presbyterian. Office: 227 SW Pine St Ste 220 Portland OR 97204-2700

FOSTER, MARY FRAZER (MARY FRAZER LECRON), anthropologist; b. Des Moines, Feb. 1, 1914; d. James and Helen (Cowles) LeCron; BA, Northwestern U., 1936; Ph.D., U. Calif., Berkeley, 1965; m. George McClelland Foster, Jan. 6, 1938; children—Jeremy, Melissa Foster Bowerman. Research asso. dept. anthropology U. Calif., Berkeley, 1955-57, 75—; lectr. in anthropology Calif. State U., Hayward, 1966-75; mem. faculty Fromm Inst. Lifelong Learning, U. San Francisco, 1980. Fellow AAAS, Am. Anthropol. Assn.; mem. Linguistic Soc. Am., Internat. Linguistic Assn., Southwestern Anthrop. Assn., Soc. Woman Geographers. Democrat. Author: (with George M. Foster) Sierra Popoluca Speech, 1948; The Tarascan Language, 1969; editor: (with Stanley H. Brandes) Symbol As Sense: New Approaches to the Analysis of Meaning, 1980, (with Robert A. Rubinstein) Peace and War: Cross-Cultural Perspectives, 1986, (with Robert A. Rubinstein) The Social Dynamics of Peace, 1988 (with Lucy J. Botscharow) The Life of Symbols, 1990. Home: 790 San Luis Rd Berkeley CA 94707-2030

FOSTER, MICHAEL LEWIS, hospital administration, state senator; b. Townsend, Mont., Mar. 5, 1955; s. Roger Lewis and Barbara Ruth (Spencer) F.; m. Mary Louise Johns, June 9, 1979; children: Lacey, Brad, Sean. BS, Western Mont. Coll., 1977; BA, Carroll Coll., 1982; MA, U. Mont., 1993. Tchr. Townsend Schs., 1977-80; utility rate analyst Pub. Svc. Commn., Helena, Mont., 1982-91; asst. dir. Mont. Hosps. Rate Rev. Sys., Helena, 1991-95, exec. dir., 1995—. Mem. Mont. Ho. of Reps., Helena, 1991-95, Mont. Senate, 1995—. Republican. Methodist. Office: Montana Hosps Rate Rev System 2033 11th Ave Helena MT 59644

FOSTER, MICHAEL WILLIAM, librarian; b. Astoria, Oreg., June 29, 1940; s. William Michael and Margaret Vivian (Carlson) F. BA in History, Willamette U., 1962; MA, U. Oreg., 1965; postgrad., So. Oreg. Coll., 1976. Tchr. Astoria High Sch., 1963-66, librarian, 1970-96; tchr. Am. Internat. Sch. of Kabul (Afghanistan), 1966-70; bd. dirs. Astoria H.S. Scholarships, Inc., AG-BAG Internat. Ltd., Astoria Pacific Industries, Inc., Asta Ltd. Mem. Oreg. Arts Commn., Salem, 1983-91; commr. Oreg. Coun. Humanities, 1994—, chmn., 1995—; commr. Oreg. Advs. for the Arts, 1994—; bd. dirs. Am. Cancer Soc., Clatsop County, Oreg., 1980-87, Luth. Family Svcs., 1994—, Oreg. Arts Advocates Found., 1994—, Columbia Meml. Hosp. Found., 1992—, Edward Hall Scholarship Bd., pres. Clatsop C.C. Found.; bd. dirs. U. Oreg. Art Mus. Coun., 1991—, pres., 1993-95; bd. dirs., treas. Astoria Cmty. Concert Assn., 1964-88, pres., 1989—; bd. dirs., treas. Ed and Eda Ross Scholarship Trust; mem. Oreg. Econ. Devel. Dept. Task Force, 1995—; mem. adv. bd. Oreg. Symphony, 1992—. Mem. NEA, Oreg. Edn. Assn., Oreg. Edn. Media Assn., Clatsop County Hist. Soc. (bd. dirs., pres. 1983-87), Ft. Clatsop Hist. Assn. (treas. 1974-91, pres. 1991—, bd. dirs.), Astoria C. of C. (bd. dirs. 1982-88, George award 1985, pres. 1987), Lewis and Clark Trails Heritage Found., League of Historic Am. Theaters, Rotary (pres. Astoria Club 1986), Astoria Golf and Country Club, Beta Theta Pi. Republican. Roman Catholic. Home: 1636 Irving Ave Astoria OR 97103-3621

FOSTER, RUTH MARY, dental association administrator; b. Little Rock, Jan. 11, 1927; d. William Crosby and Frances Louise (Doering) Shaw; m. Luther A. Foster, Sept. 8, 1946 (dec. Dec. 1980); children: William Lee, Robert Lynn. Grad. high sch., Long Beach, Calif. Sr. hostess Mon's Food Host of Coast, Long Beach, 1945-46; dental asst., office mgr. Dr. Wilfred H. Allen, Opportunity, Wash., 1946-47; dental asst., bus. asst. Dr. H. Erdahl, Long Beach, 1948-50; office mgr. Dr. B.B. Blough, Spokane, Wash., 1950-52; bus. mgr. Henry G. Kolsrud, D.D.S., P.S., Spokane, 1958—, Garland Dental Bldg., Spokane, 1958—. Sustaining mem. Spokane Symphony Orch. Mem. Nat. Assn. Dental Assts., DAV Aux., DAV Comdrs. Club, Wash. State Fedn. Bus. and Profl. Women (dir. dist. 6), Spokane's Lilac City Bus. and Profl. Women (past pres.), Nat. Alliance Mentally Ill, Wash. Alliance Mentally Ill, Internat. Platform Assn., Spokane Club, Credit Women's Breakfast Club, Dir.'s Club, Inland N.W. Zool. Soc., Pioneer Circle of Women Helping Women. Democrat. Mem. First Christian Ch. Office: Henry G Kolsrud DDS PS 3718 N Monroe St Spokane WA 99205-2850 *Keep the joy of accomplishment in your chosen profession with fresh ideas and zeal! Always remember to lend a helping hand to people in need that will let them work towards this joy. Vision and focus!.*

FOSTER, STANLEY KENNETH, adult education educator, real estate appraiser; b. Battle Creek, Mich., May 15, 1942; s. S. K. and Alene S. (Smith) F.; m. Diane M. Stone, June 20, 1982; children: Genelle, David. BA, Calif. State U., San Bernardino, 1977, MBA, 1979. Lic. real estate appraiser, Calif. Faculty mem. Victor Valley Coll., Victorville, Calif., 1972-77, work exerience coord., 1977-79; dean occupl. edn. Palo Verde Coll., Blythe, Calif., 1979-81; 1981-89 Sacramento City Coll., faculty mem., 1989—. Vice chair cmty. planning adv. coun. Cosumnes area, Sacramento County, 1995—; vol. Golden Retriever Rescue, Sacramento, 1996—. Office: Sacramento City Coll 3835 Freeport Blvd Sacramento CA 95822

FOSTER VARGAS, KATHLEEN DIANE, legal administrator; b. Boston, Feb. 22, 1951; d. Joseph Ernest and Barbara Shirley (Dundas) Emge; children: Christian Andrew Fabian, Michelle Diane; m. Howard Vargas, 1995. BA in Anthropology/Archaeology, Pacific Luth. U., 1984, MA in Anthropology/Archaeology, 1984; JD, Am. Coll. of Law, 1989. Tchr. English Castillo Escuela, Guadalajara, Mexico, 1972-74; rsch. asst. U. Calif., Irvine, 1978-80; rsch. assoc. Hoko River Archaeol. Project, Pullman, Wash., 1981-84; law clk., investigator Law Offices of Leonard Moen, Tacoma, 1984-86; law clk. Law Offices of Thomas Moga, Upland, Calif., 1986-90; hearing rep. Law Offices of Grant Lynd, Westminster, Calif., 1990—; disc jockey, music dir. Sta. KUCI Radio, Calif., 1978-80, Sta. KPLU Radio, 1981-82. Asst. (film) Battered Women/Convicted Killers, 1981. Asst. leader Brownies/Girl Scouts, Puyallup, Wash., 1981-85. Recipient Am. Jurisprudence award for appellate advocacy Lawyers Coop/Bancroft Whitney Pub., 1988, Am. Jurisprudence award for uniform comm. code, 1988. Mem. Bus. and Profl. Women's Assn., Nat. Notary Assn. Democrat. Office: Law Offices of Grant A Lynd 14340 Bolsa Chica Rd Ste B Westminster CA 92683-4868

FOTSCH, DAN ROBERT, elementary education educator; b. St. Louis, May 17, 1947; s. Robert Jarrel and Margaret Louise (Zimmermann) F.; m. Jacquelyn Sue Rotter, June 12, 1971; children: Kyla Michelle, Jeffrey Scott, Michael David. BS in Edn. cum laude, U. Mo., 1970; MS in Edn., Colo. State U., 1973. Cert. K-12 phys. edn. and health tchr. Mo., Colo. Tchr. phys. edn., coach North Callaway Schs., Auxvasse, Mo., 1970-71; grad. teaching asst., asst. track coach Colo. State U., Ft. Collins, 1971-73; tchr. elem. phys. edn., coach Poudre R-1 Sch. Dist., Ft. Collins, 1973—; tchr. on spl. assignment Elem. Phys. Edn. Resource, 1990; adminstrv. asst. Moore Sch., 1990—; co-dir. Colo. State U. Handicapped Clinic, Ft. Collins, 1973-93; dir. Moore Elem. Lab. Sch., Ft. Collins, 1979—; dir. Colo. State U. Super Day Camp, 1979—; presenter for conf. in field. Contbr. articles to profl. jours. State dir. Jump Rope for Heart Project, Denver, 1981. Recipient Scott Key Acad. award, Sigma Phi Epsilon, 1969, Honor Alumni award, Coll. of Profl. Studies of Colo. State U., 1983; grantee Colo. Heart Assn., 1985; recipient Coaching Excellence award Ft. Collins Soccer Club, 1991-92. Mem. NEA, AAHPERD (exec. bd. mem. coun. on phys. edn. for children 1983-86, reviewer Jour. Phys. Edn., Recreation and Dance 1984—, fitness chairperson, conv. planner 1986), ASCD, Poudre Edn. Assn., Colo. Edn. Assn., Colo. Assn. Health, Phys. Edn., Recreation and Dance (pres. 1979-82, Tchr. award 1977, Honor award 1985), Internat. Platform Assn., Ctrl. Dist. Alliance for Health, Phys. Edn., Recreation and Dance (elem. divsn. chairperson for phys. edn. 1989—), Phi Delta Kappa (found. rep. 1985), Phi Epsilon Kappa (v.p. 1969, pres. 1970). Republican. Home: 5312 Elderberry Ct Fort Collins CO 80525-5529 Office: Moore Elem Sch 1905 Orchard Pl Fort Collins CO 80521-3210

FOTT, DAVID SAMUEL, political science educator; b. Clarksville, Tenn., Mar. 31, 1961; s. Solie Isaac and Mary Ready (Gilreath) F. BA, Vanderbilt U., 1983; AM, Harvard U., 1986, PhD, 1993. Asst. prof. polit. sci. U. Nev., Las Vegas, 1992—. Grad. fellow NSF, 1983-86; scholar Harry S. Truman Found., 1981. Mem. Am. Polit. Sci. Assn.

FOULK, DAVID WINGERD, retired military civilian executive; b. Lindsborg, Kans., Oct. 25, 1939; s. Earl Oliver and Verda Arlene (Wingerd) F.; m. Anita Amelia Ferrer, June 29, 1963; children: Deborah, Anthony. BA in Math., Park Coll., 1961; postgrad., U. So. Colo., 1966, U. So. Calif. extension, 1967; MS in Systems Mgmt., Fla. Inst. Tech., 1977. Claims examiner HEW, Kansas City, 1961-62; various positions in ammunition and chemical surveillance Dept. of Army, 1962-72; course mgr. Ammunition Sch. Dept. of Army, Savanna, Ill., 1972-76, dept. chief, 1976-78; sr. ammunition surveillance mgr Hdqrs. Army Material Command, Alexandria, Va., 1978-86; chief Pacific Theater Surveillance Office Ctrl. Ammo Mgmt. Office-Pacific, Ft. Shafter, Hawaii, 1986-90; chief Ammunition Sch. Army Def. Ammo Ctr. and Sch., Savanna, 1990-93, sr. project mgr., 1993-95; ret. Ammunition Sch. Ammunition Ctr., Savanna, 1995. Ordained elder Presbyn. Ch., Savanna, 1973. Mem. Am. Def. Preparedness Assn., AASR, Masons, Shriners. Republican. Presbyterian.

FOURNIER, DONALD FREDERICK, dentist; b. Phoenix, Oct. 16, 1934; s. Dudley Thomas and Margaret Mary (Conway) F.; m. Sheila Ann Templeton, Aug. 5, 1957 (div. 1972); children: Julia Marguerite, Donald Frederick, John Robert, Anne Marie Selin, James Alexander; m. Nancy Colleen Hamm, July 10, 1976; children: Catharine Jacinthe, Jacques Edouard. Student, Stanford U., 1952, U. So. Calif., L.A., 1952-54; BSc, U. Nebr., 1958, DDS, 1958. Pvt. practice restorative dentistry Phoenix, 1958—; pres. Hope Mining and Milling Co., Phoenix, 1970—; chief dental staff St. Joseph's Hosp., Phoenix, 1968; vis. prof. periodontology Coll. Dentistry U. Nebr., 1985; faculty Phoenix Coll. Dental Hygiene Sch., 1968-71; investigator Ariz. State Bd. Dental Examiners, 1978-89; mem. Meml. Dental Clinic Staff, 1968-70; dir. Canadian Am. Inst. Cariology, 1986—. Contbr. articles to profl. jours. Pres. bd. trustees Osborn Sch. Dist., Phoenix, 1976; dir. Lukesmen, Phoenix, 1978-81; patrolman Nat. Ski Patrol, Phoenix, 1974-79; pres. Longview PTA, 1969; mem. adv. bd. Phoenix Crime Commn., 1969-71, Phoenix Coll. Dean's Adv. Bd., 1968-75; mem. The Phoenix House Am. Indian Rehab., 1985-86. Lt. col. (retired) Ariz. Army Res. N.G., 1958—. USPHS fellow, 1956-57, 57-58. Fellow Am. Coll. Dentists, Internat. Coll. Dentists; mem. ADA, Ariz. State Dental Assn., Pacific Coast Soc. Prosthodontists, Am. Acad. Restorative Dentistry (pres. 1991-92), Am. Acad. Gold Foil Operators, Craniomandibular Inst. (dir.), Internat. Assn. Dental Rsch., Acad. Operative Dentistry (charter), U.S. Croquet Assn., Ariz. Croquet Club, Downtown Croquet Club (pres. 1993—), Phoenix Country Club, Am. Acad. Orofacial Pain (pres. 1988-89), Phi Delta Theta, Xi Psi Phi. Republican. Roman Catholic. Home: 86 E Country Club Dr Phoenix AZ 85014-5435 Office: 207 E Monterey Way Phoenix AZ 85012-2619 also: 26450 N Alma School Pkwy Scottsdale AZ 85255

FOUTS, GORDON PHILIP, real estate consultant; b. Walla Walla, Wash., Jan. 4, 1940; s. Joseph Leon and Carol Ina (Moore) F.; children: Kelly Jo, Kyle Lee. BA, Ctrl. Wash. State U., 1967; MPA, U. Wash., 1972. Real estate cons. Colliers Internat., Seattle; pres. Comml. Investment Coun., Seattle, 1983—. Bd. dirs. Ronald McDonald House, 1992-96, Forgotten Children Fund, 1976-96, Vols. of Am., 1995-96. Sgt. USMC, 1961-67. Mem. Wash. Athletic Club (bd. govs. 1991-97), Seafair (pres. commodores 1986-96). Republican. Presbyterian. Office: Colliers Internat 601 Union St Ste 5300 Seattle WA 98101-2327

FOWLER, GLENN W., pediatric neurologist; b. New Orleans, Feb. 8, 1934; s. John W. and Roxie L. (Breland) F.; m. Jane Meltzer, Aug. 15, 1965; children: Leslie, Joanna. BS, Tulane U., 1954; MD, La. State U., 1964. Diplomate Am. Bd. Psychiatry & Neurology. Instr. pediatrics, neurology Northwestern U., Chgo., 1969; prof. neurology and pediatrics U. Calif., Irvine, 1970—. Capt. U.S. Navy, 1954-59, Korea. Fellow Am. Acad. Neurology, Am. Acad. Pediatrics; mem. Child Neurology Soc., Orange County Neurology Soc. (pres.). Office: Children's Hosp 455 S Main St Orange CA 92868-3835

FOWLER, JOHN ROBERT, airline executive; b. Flushing, N.Y., Dec. 12, 1947; s. James Edward and Helen Katherine (D'Elosua) F.; m. Diana L. Diekroger, May 16, 1981; children from previous marriage: Thomas J., John R., Jeanne M., James E., William A. Student, Adelphi U., 1965-67; MBA, Pepperdine U., 1995. Cert. comml. and instrument rated pilot; FAA Airframe and powerplant cert.; FCC advanced radio lic. Cleaner Pan Am. World Airways, Jamaica, N.Y., 1967-68, mech., 1968-71, supr., 1971-82, tech. coord. avionics, 1982-83, mgr. avionics svcs., 1983-86, dir. aircraft appearance, 1986-88, mng. dir. maintenance planning, 1988-89, v.p. maintenance and engring., 1989-91; v.p. maintenance and engring. Alaska Airlines, Seattle, 1991-97, sr. v.p. tech. ops., 1997—; bd. dirs. ATN Syss., Inc., sr. adv. com. Air Transport Assn. Am. Republican. Lutheran. Office: Alaska Airlines PO Box 68900 Seattle WA 98168-0900

FOX, ANDREW P., mayor; m. Phebe Fox; children: Susan, Andrew, Cassie. Mayor Thousand Oaks, Calif., 1996; capt. L.A. Fire Dept.; Mem. fin. adv. com. City Thousand Oaks, 1995, pub. safety adv. com., 1995, housing issues com., 1995, Ventura Coun. Govts., 1995, Consortium for Advanced Tech. Edn., 1995, Conejo Open Space Conservation Agy., 1995; legis. liaison City Thousand Oaks; Mayor Pro team City Thousand Oaks, 1995; 46th Dist. Rep. So. Calif. Assn. Govs., 1996; pres. United Firefighters L.A. City Local 112 AFL-CIO; commr. Thousand Oaks Planning Commn., 1990-92; elected City Coun. Thousand Oaks, 1994. Hon. chair Conejo Valley Youth Employment, 1995, Boy Scouts Am. Fundraiser, 1995; trail boss COSTAC Ann. Trail Day. Mem. St. Pascal Catholic Ch. Mens Club. Address: 2100 Thousand Oaks Blvd Thousand Oaks CA 91362

FOX, FRANCES JUANICE, retired librarian, educator; b. Vicksburg, Miss., Aug. 17, 1916; d. Willie Amercy Thaxton and Fannye Lou (Spell) Hepfer; m. Leonard John Fox, Feb. 25, 1937; children: Frances Juanice, L. John Jr., Kenneth L., Robert T., William E., Elizabeth Jean. AA, Phoenix Coll., 1959; BS in Edn., Ariz. State U., 1963, MS in Edn., Libr., 1972. Cert. kindergarten, primary, and elem. tchr., cert. libr., cert. religious edn. Diocese of Phoenix. Substitute tchr. Escambia County Sch. Dist., Pensacola, Fla., 1936-38; kindergarten tchr. Lollipop Ln. Sch., Phoenix, 1960-61, 1st United Meth. Day Sch., Phoenix, 1961-62; tchr. grade 3 Wilson Elem. Sch., Phoenix, 1962-63; summer libr. R.E. Simpson Elem. Sch., Phoenix, 1964, 65; preschool tchr. Jewish Community Ctr., Phoenix, 1967-68; libr. Audio Visual Ctr. Sts. Simon and Judge Elem. Sch., Phoenix, 1969-82; cataloger First Untied Meth. Ch. Libr., Phoenix, 1963, Baker Ctr. Ariz. State Univ. Meth. and Hillel Students Libr., Tempe, 1969; tchr. ch. sch., 1942-69, ret., 1969. Contbr. poetry to varius publs., including Nat. Libr. Poetry, 1995, Poetic Voices of Am., 1990, 95, World Book of Poetry. 1990; co-compiler: (libr. manual) Diocese of Phoenix, 1980-81. Organizer, leader Girl Scouts USA, Birmingham, Ala., 1951, 52, Phoenix, 1976-83; leader cub scouts Boy Scouts Am., Birmingham, 1950-52, Phoenix, 1952-55; swim instr. ARC, Fla., Ariz., 1933, 34, 53, 54; dance instr. Circle Game and Beginning Dance, Wesley Cmty. Ctr., Phoenix, 1966, 67; sch. tchr. Meth. Ch., 1939-69. Scholar Phoenix Coll., Ariz. State Coll., 1959; recipient Gold Poet award World Book of Poetry, 1990, Honorable Mention Poetic Voices of Am., 1990, Internat. Twentieth Century Achievement award Cambridge Edn., 1994. Mem. ALA, Ariz. State Libr. Assn. (com. on continuing edn. 1979-81), Gold Star Wives of Am. Inc. (pres. 1993-94, nat. parlementarian 1990-91), DAV Aux. (life), Ariz. PTA (life mem., organizer, v.p.), Phi Theta Kappa, Iota Sigma Alpha Honor Soc. Methodist. Home: 2225 W Montebello Ave Phoenix AZ 85015-2327

FOX, GWEN, artist, educator; b. Jefferson City, Tenn., Jan. 25, 1943; d. Arthur Crowell and Margaret Fox; children: Mary, John. Student, Carson Newman Coll., Jefferson City, 1962-63. Tchr. art Belstead House, Ipswich, Eng., 1978-80, Barton Mills (Eng.) Edn., 1979-80, Bemis Art Ctr., Colorado Springs, Colo., 1992--94; tchr. art adult edn., Panama City, Fla., 1981-82; tchr. art Cheyenne Mountain Heritage Ctr., Colorado Springs, 1995—. One-woman shows, Honolulu, 1971, Mildenhall, Eng., 1977, Panama City, Fla., 1982, Monument, Colo., 1986, 87, Colorado Springs, Colo., 1995, 97; exhibited in group shows Poudre Valley Art League, 1993, N.W. Watercolor Soc., 1993, Fine Arts Ctr. and Taylor Mus., Colorado Springs, 1995 (MCI award 1995), Tex. Watercolor Soc., 1995, Colo. Watercolor Soc., 1995, U. Colo., 1997; represented in numerous pub. collections including Ctr. for Creative Leadership, also numerous pvt. collections; represented in Flowers in Watercolor, 1996. Recipient Best of Show award Colorado Springs Nat., 1994, Golden award Rocky Mountain Nat., 1994, award Catherine Lorillard Wolfe, 1996. Mem. NOW, Colo. Watercolor Soc. (signature), Ala. Watercolor Soc., Pikes Peak Watercolor Soc. (pres. 1991-93). Home: 2017 Brookwood Dr Colorado Springs CO 80918-1135

FOX, JACK, financial service executive; b. Bklyn., Mar. 8, 1940; s. Benjamin and Rebecca (Shure) F.; m. Carole Olafson, July 8, 1987; children: Neal, Stuart. BBA, CCNY, 1961; MBA, CUNY, 1969. Sales specialist Am. Can Corp., N.Y.C., 1962-63; talent agt. Gen. Artists Corp., N.Y.C., 1963-66; bus. specialist N.Y. Times, 1966-70; pres. Ednl. Learning Systems, Inc., Washington, 1971-78; budget dir. Nat. Alliance of Bus., Washington, 1979-80; pres. Computerized Fin. Services, Rockville, Md., 1980-87; regional v.p. Govt. Funding Corp., L.A., 1987-90; owner, mgr. Jack Fox Assocs., Ventura, Calif., 1986; founder Acctg. Resources Group, Ventura, 1993—; adj. prof. Am. U., Washington, 1983-85; tchr. fin. Montgomery Coll., Rockville, 1978-86. Author: How to Obtain Your Own SBA Loan, 1983, Starting and Building Your Own Accounting Business, 1984, 2d rev. edit. 1991, Accounting and Record Keeping Made Easy for the Self Employed, 1994. Mem. Internat. Platform Assn. Democrat. Jewish. Office: 6568 Beachview Dr Ste 303 Rancho Palos Verdes CA 90275

FOX, JOEL DAVID, political association executive; b. Boston, Apr. 22, 1949; s. Harry L. and Freda (Berry) F.; m. Cydney M. Finkel, May 19, 1974; children: Zachary Daniel, Eric Maxwell. BA, U. Mass., 1971; MA, U. Denver, 1974. Pub. rels. staff L.A. Bicentennial Com., 1976; aide and exec. dir. Howard Jarvis Taxpayers Assn., L.A., 1979-86, pres., 1986—; internat. speaker taxes and initiative process. Contbr. articles to profl. jours. and newspapers; author Calif. ballot initiatives. Gubernatorial appointee Calif. Citizen's Commn. on Ballot Initiatives, 1993; trustee LEARN-L.A. Sch. Reform, 1991—; mem. Calif. Commn. on Transp. Investment, 1995; mem. L.A. County Blue Ribbon Budget Task Force, 1996; gubernatorial appointee Calif. Constitution Revision Commn., 1996. Office: Howard Jarvis Taxpayers Asn 621 S Westmoreland Ave Ste 202 Los Angeles CA 90005-3981

FOX, KENNETH L., retired newspaper editor, writer; b. Kansas City, Mo., Mar. 18, 1917; s. Henry Hudson and Margaret Patience (Kiely) F.; m. Mary Harbord Manville, June 20, 1975. A.B., Washington U., St. Louis, 1938; student, U. Kansas City, 1939-40. With Kansas City Star, 1938-78, asso. editor, 1966-78; news analyst Sta. WDAF, Kansas City, 1948-53; war corr., Vietnam and Laos, 1964, corr., No. Ireland, 1973. Served to col. AUS, 1940-46. Decorated Bronze Star, Commendation medals with Oak Leaf Cluster; recipient 1st place editl. div. nat. aviation writing contest, 1957, 58, 59, 60, 67; named Aviation Man of Yr. for Kansas City, 1959. Mem. Am. Legion, 40 and 8, Res. Officers Assn., Ret. Officers Assn., Mil. Order World Wars, Phi Beta Kappa, Beta Theta Pi, Pi Sigma Alpha, Sigma Delta Chi. Clubs: Kansas City Press; Ariz. Home: 9796 E Ironwood Dr Scottsdale AZ 85258-4728*

FOX, L. ROBERT, transportation and management consultant; b. Salt Lake City, June 14, 1942; s. Lewis M. and Margaret (Cox) F.; m. Ann Schlofman, Dec. 15, 1972; children: Robert, William, Thomas. BS, Brigham Young U., 1967, MS, 1969; PhD, U. Utah, 1973. Sr. legis. analyst State of Utah, Salt Lake City, 1969-72; asst. v.p. U. Utah, Salt Lake City, 1972-84; investment banker A. G. Edwards & Sons, Inc., Phoenix, 1984-93; transp. and mgmt. cons. Utah Dept. Transp., 1993—; cons. U. Utah, 1984. Author: Fiscal Management Systems in State Government, 1972, The Politics/Administration Dictionary,1 969. Bd. dirs. Utah Opera Co., Salt Lake City, 1983-85; mem. Econ. Devel. Bd., State of Utah, 1967-69; chmn. Nat. Legis. Conf., Salt Lake City, 1968. Mem. Am. Assn. Pub. Adminstrs., Assn. Ariz. Cities and Counties, Calif. Hosp. Assn., Assn. Community Colls. of Am., Phi Kappa Phi, Gamma Theta Epsilon, Ft. Douglas Country Club. Republican. Mem. Ch. of Jesus Christ of Latter Day Saints. Home: 650 S Woodbriar Way North Salt Lake UT 84054 Office: AG Edwards & Sons Inc 77 W 200 S Salt Lake City UT 84101-1609

FOX, LORRAINE SUSAN, marketing professional; b. L.A., Feb. 8, 1956; d. Robert Lazar and Valerie Joan (Barker) Fox; m. Clark Byron Siegel, July 19, 1981 (div. Nov. 1989). AB with distinction, Stanford U., 1979; MBA, U. Chgo., 1983. Sr. fin. analyst MacIntosh div., Apple Computer, Cupertino, Calif., 1983-84; sr. fin. analyst Sun Microsystems Inc., Mountain View, Calif., 1984-85, mgr. fin. planning and analysis, 1985-86, project mgr., 1986-88, mgr. project mgmt., 1988-90, sr. product mktg. mgr., 1990-93, mgr. mktg. strategy, 1993-95; dir. multimedia product mktg. new media divsn. Oracle Corp., Redwood Shores, Calif., 1995, sr. dir. product mktg. Sun Products divsn., 1995-96; v.p. mktg. Centerview Software, Inc., San Francisco, 1996; sr. dir., bus. strategy Apple Computer, Inc., Cupertino, Calif., 1997—. Vol. fundraiser Stanford (Calif.) U., 1983-88; vol. Sun Microsystems Cmty. Vols., Mountain View, 1989—; alumni rep. undergrad. commn. on edn. Stanford U. Mem. Commonwealth Club, Stanford Profl. Women's Club, Churchill Club. Home: 707 Bryant St Palo Alto CA 94301-2554 Office: Apple Computer Inc 1 Infinite Loop Cupertino CA 95014

FOX, MICHAEL J., museum director. Dir., CEO Mus. of No. Ariz., Flagstaff. Office: Mus of No Ariz 3101 N Fort Valley Rd Flagstaff AZ 86001

FOX, RICHARD LORAIN, political science educator; b. Toledo, Ohio, Sept. 1, 1946; s. Jack Robert and Pauline Marie (Staschke) F.; m. Sylvia Anna Romero, Dec. 19, 1970; 1 child, Miles C.A. Student, U. Iowa, 1965-66; BA, U. N.Mex., 1975, MA, 1979. Legis. analyst City of Albuquerque City Coun., 1975-77; exec. asst. to pres. Monterey (Calif.) Inst. Internat. Studies, 1977-78; mgmt. analyst State of N.Mex. Fin. Dept., Santa Fe, 1980-88; adj. lectr. Gen. Honors Program, polit. sci. U. N.Mex., Albuquerque, 1981—; instr. Albuquerque Tech.-Vocat. Inst., 1987—; free-lance cons. to govts. and mgmt., Albuquerque, 1988—. Contbr. articles to Century Mag., 1980-83, N.Mex. Mag., 1987. Named Young Dem. of Yr., Bernalillo County Young Dems., Albuquerque, 1972; hon. fellow John F. Kennedy Libr. Found. Mem. Acad. Polit. Sci., Trout Unltd. Democrat.

FOX, STUART IRA, physiologist; b. Bklyn., June 21, 1945; s. Sam and Bess F.; m. Ellen Diane Berley; 1 child, Laura Elizabeth. BA, UCLA, 1967; MA, Calif. State U., L.A., 1969; postgrad., U. Calif., Santa Barbara, 1969; PhD, U. So. Calif., 1978. Rsch. assoc. Children's Hosp., L.A., 1972; prof. physiology L.A. City Coll., 1972-85, Calif. State U., Northridge, 1979-84, Pierce Coll., 1986—; cons. William C. Brown Co. Pubs., 1976—. Author: Computer-Assisted Instruction in Human Physiology, 1979, Laboratory Guide to Human Physiology, 2d edit., 1980, 7th edit., 1996, Textbook of Human Physiology, 1986, 5th edit., 1996, Human Anatomy and Physiology, 1986, 4th edit., 1995, Perspectives on Human Biology, 1991, Laboratory Manual for Anatomy and Physiology, 1986, 4th edit., 1996; contbg. author: Biology, 4th edit., 1995, Synopsis of Anatomy and Physiology, 1997. Mem. AAAS, So. Calif. Acad. Sci., Am. Physiol. Soc., Sigma Xi. Home: 5556 Forest Cove Ln Agoura Hills CA 91301-4047 Office: Pierce Coll 6201 Winnetka Ave Woodland Hills CA 91371-0001

FOXLEY, CECELIA HARRISON, commissioner. BA in English, Utah State U., 1964; MA in English, U. Utah, 1965, PhD in Ednl. Psychology, 1968. English tchr. Olympus H.S., Salt Lake City, 1965-66; asst. prof. edn., assoc. dir. student activities U. Minn., Mpls., 1968-71; from asst. prof. to assoc. prof., asst. dean Coll. Edn. U. Iowa, Iowa City, 1971-81; prof. psychology Utah State U., Logan, 1981-85, from asst. v.p. student svcs. to assoc. v.p. for student svcs. and acad. affairs, 1981-85; assoc. commr. for acad. affairs Utah State Bd. Regents, Salt Lake City, 1985-93, commr., 1993—; Utah rep. Am. Coun. on Edn. Office Women in Higher Edn., 1982-92; mem. nat. adv. coun. on nurse tng. U.S. Dept. Health and Human Svcs., 1987-91; mem. nat. adv. bd. S.W. Regional Ctr. for Drug Free Schs., 1988-93; mem. edn. bd. Utah Alliance for Edn. and Humanities, 1989-93; mem. prevention subcom. Utah Substance Abuse Coordinating Coun., 1991-93; mem. exec. bd. U.S. West Comm., 1995—; mem. adv. bd. Salt Lake Buzz, 1995—; active Consortium for Women in Higher Edn. Bd., 1981-85, Utah State Libr. Bd., 1990-93, Compact for Faculty Diversity, 1994—; presenter in field; cons. in field. Author: Recruiting Women and Minority Faculty, 1972, Locating, Recruiting, and Employing Women, 1976, Non-Sexist Counseling: Helping Women and Men Redefine Their Roles, 1979; co-author: The Human Relations Experience, 1982; editor: Applying Management Techniques, 1980; co-editor: Multicultural Nonsexist Education, 1979; author chpts. to books; contbr. articles to profl. jours. Grantee Utah State Dept. Social Svcs., 1984-85, 85-86; recipient Pres. Leadership award Assn. Utah Women Edn. Adminstrs., 1990, Disting. Alumni award Utah State U., 1991. Mem. APA, Am. Assn. Counseling and Devel., Am. Coll. Pers. Assn., Nat. Forum Sys. Chief Acad. Officers, State Higher Edn. Exec. Officers (mem. exec. com. 1994—), Western Interstate Cooperative Higher Edn. (mem. exec. com. 1994—). Office: Utah State Bd Regents 3 Triad Ctr Ste 550 355 W North Temple Salt Lake City UT 84180-1114*

FOXLEY, WILLIAM COLEMAN, cattleman; b. St. Paul, Jan. 7, 1935; s. William Joseph and Eileen (Conroy) F. BA, U. Notre Dame, 1957. Pres., chmn. bd. Foxley Cattle Co., Omaha, 1960—. Chmn. bd. Mus. Western Art, Denver. Served with USMCR, 1957-60. Republican. Roman Catholic. Office: Foxley Cattle Co 7480 La Jolla Blvd La Jolla CA 92037-5029*

FRACCHIA, CHARLES ANTHONY, investment advisor, educator; b. San Francisco, Aug. 10, 1937; s. Charles Bartholomew and Josephine (Giacosa) F.; m. Ann Escobosa, Feb. 10, 1962 (div. 1971); children: Laura E., Carla A., Charles A. Jr., Francesca S.; m. Elizabeth Ann Feaster, Aug. 15, 1987. AB in History, U. San Francisco, 1960, postgrad., 1959-61; MLS, U. Calif., Berkeley, 1976; MA in History, San Francisco State U., 1979; MA in Theology, Grad. Theol. Union, Berkeley, 1981. Stockbroker Paine Webber, San Francisco, 1961-65, J. Barth, San Francisco, 1965-70; v.p. mktg. Brennan Fin. Group, San Francisco, 1970-71; gen. mgr., analyst Walker's Manual div. Hambrecht & Quist, San Francisco, 1971-73; fin. advisor Planned Investments Inc. (now IFG Network Securities, Inc.), 1981-96; pres. Fracchia Capital Mgmt. Co.; instr. City Coll. San Francisco, 1980—. Author: Converted Into Houses, 1976, So This is Where You Work, 1980, Second Spring, 1980, Living Together Alone, 1979, How to Be Single Creatively, 1979, Fire & Gold: The San Francisco Story. Trustee Calif. Hist. Soc., San Francisco, 1966-76, 90-96; mem. San Francisco Hist. Landmarks Adv. Bd., 1968-72; pres. San Francisco Hist. Soc., 1988—. Mem. Concordia-Argonaut Club. Democrat. Roman Catholic. Home: 2881 Jackson St San Francisco CA 94115-1145 Office: Fracchia Capital Mgmt Co PO Box 420569 San Francisco CA 94142-0569

FRADIS, ANATOLY ADOLF, film producer; b. Odessa, USSR, Aug. 26, 1948; came to U.S., 1980; s. Adolf Fradis; m. Marlene Gerdts, Dec. 17, 1983 (div. Dec. 1993); 1 child, Olga. Fim dir. Mosflim Studios, Moscow, 1973-80; pres. Afra-Film Enterprises, L.A., 1980—; film commr. Russian Film Commn., L.A., 1991—. Prodr. films: Haunted Symphony, 1993, Beyond Forgiveness, 1994, Burial of the Rats, 1995, Marquis DeSade, 1996, Business for Pleasure, 1996, Termination Man, 1996, others. Mem. Union of Russian Filmmakers (hon.). Republican. Jewish. Office: Afra-Film Enterprises Inc 137 S Roberison Blvd #254 Beverly Hills CA 90211

FRAGOLA, ALBERT THOMAS, retired army officer; b. Pelham, N.Y., Dec. 31, 1942; s. Albert and Dorothy (Erlich) F.; m. Ardy Anderson; children: Kirsten Fragola Poteet, Deidre. BA in Social Sci., Tex. Christian U., 1974, MLA, 1976; diploma, U.S. Army Command & Gen. Staff Coll., 1983, U.S. Naval War Coll., 1994. Cert. comml. pilot FAA. Commd. warrant officer U.S. Army, 1966, advanced through grades to lt. col., 1992, aviator, 1966-71; sales support mgr. Tracor-Westronics, Ft. Worth, 1971-74; assoc. prof. mgmt. Tarrant County Jr. Coll., Hurst, Tex., 1975-85; aviation office 77th U.S. ARCOM U.S. Army, Ft. Totten, N.Y., 1985-88; exec. officer 244th aviation group U.S. Army, Glenview NAS, Ill., 1988-91; sec. to gen. staff 124th US ARCOM U.S. Army, Ft. Lawton, Wash., 1991-95; ret. U.S. Army, 1995. Recipient Legion of Merit, DFC, Bronze Star, Meritorious Svc. medal with 2 oak leaf clusters, Air medal with 17 oak leaf clusters, Army Commendation medal. Home: 1846 Polnell Rd Oak Harbor WA 98277-2027

FRAITAG, LEONARD ALAN, project and manufacturing engineer; b. N.Y.C., Dec. 23, 1961; s. David and Lucille Reneé (Jay) F.; children: Shoshana Elizabeth, Aaron Joseph. BSME, San Diego State U., 1987; AA, Grossmont Coll., 1983. Design engr. Restaurant Concepts, San Diego, 1987; mech. engr. Vantage Assocs., Inc., San Diego, 1988-89; design engr. Mainstream Engring. Co., Inc., San Diego, 1989; project engr. Pilkington Barnes Hind, San Diego, 1989-96, Advanced Structures, Inc., Escondido, 1996—. Inventor safe product moving device for contact lens. Mem. Shriners (Al Bahr shrine), Masons (past master), Pi Tau Sigma. Office: Advanced Structures Inc 2181 Meyers Ave Escondido CA 92029

FRAKER, MARK ARNOTT, environmental scientist; b. Columbus, Ind., Dec. 13, 1944; s. Ralph Waldo and Carol (Arnott) F.; m. Pamela Norton, May 27, 1967 (div. Feb. 1985); 1 child, Russell; m. Donice Horton, Aug. 23, 1986. BA with honors, Ind. U., 1967, MA, 1969. Biologist, project mgr. F.F. Slaney and Co., Vancouver, Can., 1972-78; biologist, project dir. LGL Ltd., Sidney, B.C., Can., 1978-82; sr. environ. scientist BP Exploration (Alaska) Inc., Anchorage, 1982-91; wildlife, restoration program mgr. divsn. oil spill impact assessment & restoration Alaska Dept. Fish and Game, Anchorage, 1991-93; prin., cons. biologist Terra Mar Environ. Rsch., Sidney, B.C., Can., 1993—; broadcaster CBC, Vancouver, 1970-72; mem. sci. com. Internat. Whaling Com., Cambridge, Eng., 1982-91; adj. prof. U. Alaska, Anchorage, 1985-89; mem. panel NAS, 1987-92; mem. rescue team Barrow Gray Whale Rescue, 1988; mem. adv. com. on polar programs NSF, 1988-90; mem. Pacific Sci. Rev. Group for Marine Mammal Stock Assessments, 1994—; mem. Ballard Locks Pinniped-Fishery Interaction Task Force, 1994—. Author: Balaena mysticetus, 1984; also articles; mem. editorial bd. Biol. Papers of the U. of Alaska. Amb. to Peru, Anchorage Olympic Organizing Com., 1986-89. Woodrow Wilson fellow, Princeton, N.J., 1967. Mem. AAAS, Am. Soc. Mammalogists, Arctic Inst. N.Am., Ottawa Field Naturalists' Club, Can. Soc. Zoologists, Soc. for Marine Mammalogy, The Wildlife Soc., Sigma Xi.

FRAME, JOHN TIMOTHY, retired bishop; b. Toronto, Dec. 8, 1930; s. Duncan McClymont and Sarah Aitken (Halliday) F.; m. Barbara Alida Butters, Sept. 8, 1956; children: Alida Grace, Bronwyn Ruth, Monica Mary (dec.). BA, Trinity Coll., Toronto, 1953, LTh, 1957, STB, 1961, DD (hon.), 1968. Ordained deacon, priest Anglican Ch. Can., 1957; minister Mission to Lakes Dist., Burns Lake, B.C., 1957-67; canon Diocese of Caledonia, 1965-67; bishop of Yukon, 1967-80; sr. bishop Province of B.C., 1971-80; acting metropolitan, 1973-75; dean of Columbia and rector Christ Ch. Cathedral, Victoria, B.C., 1980-95.

FRAME, TED RONALD, lawyer; b. Milw., June 27, 1929; s. Morris and Jean (Lee) F.; student UCLA, 1946-49; AB, Stanford U., 1950, LLB, 1952; m. Lois Elaine Pilgrim, Aug. 15, 1954; children: Kent, Lori, Nancy, Owen. Bar: Calif. 1953. Gen. agri-bus. practice, Coalinga, Calif., 1953—; sr. ptnr. Frame & Matsumoto, 1965—. Trustee, Baker Mus.; dir. West Hills Coll. Found. Mem. ABA, Calif. Bar Assn., Fresno County Bar Assn., Coalinga C. of C. (past pres.), Masons, Shriners, Elks. Home: 1222 Nevada St Coalinga CA 93210-1239 Office: 201 Washington St Coalinga CA 93210-1645

FRANCES, HARRIETTE (HARRIETTE SHERANA), painter, printmaker, consultant; b. San Francisco; d. Anton and Mary (Panos) Vatsakis; divorced; children: Mitchell, Stephanie. Student, Calif. Sch. Fine Arts, San Francisco, 1942-45, San Francisco Art Inst., 1964-66, Tamarind Lithography Inst., Albuquerque, N.Mex., 1989, 91, 92; also studied with James Weeks, Wm. H. Brown. Dir., founder Artist's Proof Graphics Workshop, Larkspur, Calif., 1974-90; former faculty Coll. of Marin, Kentfield, Calif., 1976-93; part-time workshop tchr. Artist's Proof Graphics Workshop, Larkspur, 1974-85. Solo and group shows include Calif. Palace of Legion of Honor Mus., San Francisco, 1968, Blanden Art Gallery, Ft. Dodge, Iowa, 1969, Hastings Coll. Gallery Art, Hastings, Nebr., 1970, San Francisco Mus. Modern Art, 1976, San Marco Gallery, San Rafael, Calif., 1981, Stanford U., 1991, Claudia Chapline Gallery, Stinson Beach, Calif., Bradford Gallery, San Anselmo, Calif., 1995-96, Inst. Franco-Am., Rennes, France, 1997, N.Am. Printmaking, 1997, Brandts-Klaenfabrik Mus., Funen, Denmark, 1989; numerous nat. and internat. exhbns.; work represented in pub. and corp. collections; also traveling shows. Recipient over 60 awards including James D. Phelan award in painting, 1965. Mem. Mus. Modern Art San Francisco, Calif. Soc. Printmakers, Marin Arts Coun. Home: 105 Rice Ln Larkspur CA 94939-2054 Studio: 469-A Magnolia Larkspur CA 94939

FRANCESCHI, ERNEST JOSEPH, JR., lawyer; b. L.A., Feb. 1, 1957; s. Ernest Joseph and Doris Cecilia (Beluche) F. BS, U. So. Calif., 1978; JD, Southwestern U., L.A., 1980. Bar: Calif. 1984, U.S. Dist. Ct. (cen. dist.) Calif. 1984, U.S. Dist. Ct. (ea. dist.) Calif. 1986, U.S. Dist. Ct. (no. and so. dists.) Calif. 1987, U.S. Ct. Appeals (9th cir.) 1984, U.S. Supreme Ct. 1989. Pvt. practice law L.A., 1984—. Mem. Assn. Trial Lawyers Am., Calif. Trial Lawyers Assn., L.A. Trial Lawyers Assn., Trial Lawyers for Pub. Justice, Fed. Bar Assn. Office: 445 S Figueroa St Ste 2600 Los Angeles CA 90071-1630

FRANCHINI, GENE EDWARD, state supreme court chief justice; b. Albuquerque, May 19, 1935; s. Mario and Lena (Vaio) F.; m. Glynn Hatchell, Mar. 22, 1969; children: Pamela, Lori (dec.), Gina, Joseph James, Nancy. BBA, Loyola U., 1955; degree in adminstrn., U. N.Mex., 1957; JD, Georgetown U., 1960; LLM, U. Va., 1995. Bar: N.Mex. 1960, U.S. Dist. Ct. N.Mex. 1961, U.S. Ct. Appeals (10th cir.) 1970, U.S. Supreme Ct. 1973. Ptnr. Matteucci, Gutierrez & Franchini, Albuquerque, 1960-70, Matteucci, Franchini & Calkins, Albuquerque, 1970-75; judge State of N.Mex. 2d Jud. Dist., Albuquerque, 1975-81; atty.-at-large Franchini, Wagner, Oliver, Franchini & Curtis, Albuquerque, 1982-90; justice N.Mex. Supreme Ct., Santa Fe, 1990—. Chmn. Albuquerque Pers. Bd., 1972, Albuquerque Labor Rels. Bd., 1972, Albuquerque Interim Bd. Ethics, 1972. Capt. USAF, 1960-66. Mem. Am. Bd. Trial Advocates, N.Mex. Trial Lawyers (pres. 1967-68), N.Mex. Bar Assn. (bd. dirs. 1976-78), Albuquerque Bar Assn. (bd. dirs. 1976-78). Democrat. Roman Catholic. Home: PO Box 75327 Albuquerque NM 87194-0327 Office: NMex Supreme Ct PO Box 848 Santa Fe NM 87504-0848

FRANCIS, CAROLYN RAE, music educator, musician, author, publisher; b. Seattle, July 25, 1940; d. James Douglas and Bessie Caroline (Smith) F; m. Barclay Underwood Stuart, July 5, 1971. BA in Edn., U. Wash., 1962. Cert. tchr., Wash. Tchr. Highline Pub. Schs., Seattle, 1962-64; musician Olympic Hotel, Seattle, 1962-72; 1st violin Cascade Symphony Orch., 1965-78; tchr. Bellevue (Wash.) Pub. Schs., 1965-92; founder/pres. Innovative Learning Designs, Mercer Island, Wash., 1984—; profl. violinist for TV, recs., mus. shows, 1962-85; violist Eastside Chamber Orch., 1984-86; pvt. tchr. string instruments, 1959—; spkr. in-svc. workshops, convs., music educators numerous cities, 1984—, adjudicator music festivals; instr. MIDI applications for educators, 1992—. Author-pub. Music Reading and Theory Skills (curriculum series), Levels 1, 2, 1986, Level 3, 1984; contbr. articles to profl. jours., 1984—. Mem. Snohomish Indian Tribe. Bellevue Schs. Found. grantee, 1985-86, 86-87, 89-90. Mem. NEA, Am. String Tchrs. Assn. (regional mem. chmn. 1992-94), Music Educators Nat. Conf., Music Industry Coun. Office: Innovative Learning Designs 7811 SE 27th St Ste 104 Mercer Island WA 98040-2979

FRANCIS, MARK EDWIN, literature educator; b. St. Clair, Mich., Feb. 22, 1956; s. Cecil A. and Patricia A. (Kelly) F.; m. Sing-Chen Lydia Chiang, May 13, 1989. BA in China Area Studies, U. Wash., 1978, MA in Comparative Lit., 1989; MA in Chinese, Stanford U., 1991, PhD in Chinese, 1996. Lectr. in comparative lit. U. Wash., Seattle, 1994-96; tchg. fellow U. Wash. Ctr for the Humanities, 1996; lect. in Asian lang. and lit. U. Auckland, 1997—. Editor Two Lines: The Stanford Translation Jour., 1994-96; contbr. poetry to various publs. Stanford U. doctoral fellow, 1989-93, Fgn. Lang. and Area Studies award fellow, U.S. Dept. Edn., 1993-94. Mem. Am. Assn. of Chinese Comparative Lit., Assn. for Asian Studies, Phi Beta Kappa. Home: 12620 NE 75th St Kirkland WA 98033

FRANCIS, TIMOTHY DUANE, chiropractor; b. Chgo., Mar. 1, 1956; s. Joseph Duane and Barbara Jane (Sigwalt) F. Student, U. Nev., 1974-80, We. Nev. C.C., 1978; BS, L.A. Coll. Chiropractic, 1982, Dr. of Chiropractic magna cum laude, 1984; postgrad., Clark County C.C., 1986—; MS in Bio/Nutrition, U. Bridgeport, 1990. Diplomate Internat. Coll. Applied Kinesiology, Am. Acad. Pain Mgmt., Am. Naturopathic Med. Bd.; cert. kinesiologist, applied kinesiology tchr.; lic. chiropractor, Calif., Nev. Instr. dept. recreation and phys. edn. U. Nev., Reno, 1976-80; from tchng. asst. to lead instr. dept. principles & practice L.A. Coll. Chiropractic, 1983-85; pvt. practice Las Vegas, 1985—; asst. instr. Internat. Coll. Applied Kinesiology, 1990, chmn. exam review com., 1993, chmn. syllabus review com., 1994; adj. faculty The Union Inst. Coll. of Undergrad. Studies, 1993; joint study participant Nat. Olympic Tng. Ctr., Beijing, China, 1990. Mem. editl. rev. bd. Alternative Medicine Rev., 1996; contbr. articles to profl. jours. including Internat. Coll. Applied Kinesiology. Charles F. Cutts scholar, 1980. Fellow Internat. Acad. Clin. Acupuncture, British Inst. Homeopathy (homeopathy diploma 1993); mem. Am. Chiropractic Assn. (couns. on sports injuries, mutrition, roentgenology, technic, and mental health), Nev. State Chiropractic Assn., Nat. Strength and Conditioning Assn., Gonsted Clin. Studies Soc., Found. for Chiropractic Edn. and Rsch., Internat. Chiropractors Assn., Internat. Coll. Applied Kinesiology, Internat. Fedn. Practitioners Natural Therapeutics, Nat. Inst. Chiropractic Rsch., Nat. Strength and Conditioning Assn., Am. Naturopathic Med. Assn., Nat. Acad. Rsch. Biochemists, Phi Beta Kappa, Phi Kappa Phi (v.p. 1979-80, Scholar of the Yr. award, 1980), Delta Sigma. Republican. Roman Catholic. Home: 3750 S Jones Blvd Las Vegas NV 89103-2283

FRANCISCO, WAYNE M(ARKLAND), automotive executive; b. Cin., June 14, 1943; s. George Lewis and Helen M. (Markland) F. Student, Ohio State U., 1962-63; BS in Mktg. and Acctg., U. Cin., 1967; m. Susan Francisco; children: Diana Lynn, W. Michael. Unit sales mgr. Procter & Gamble, Cin., 1967-69; mktg. mgr. Nat. Mktg. Inc., Cin., 1969-70; pres. Retail Petroleum Marketers, Inc., Cin., 1970-72, chmn. bd., chief exec. officer, Phoenix, 1972-85; chmn. bd., chief exec. officer DMC Industries, Inc., 1985—; pres., chief exec. officer Cassia Petroleum Corp., Vancouver, B.C., Can., 1980-84; bd. dirs. P.F.K. Enterprises, F.I.C. Inc., Internat. Investment and Fin. Enterprises, Inc., Alpha Realty, Inc. Class agt. 62G Culver Mil. Acad., 1987-91. Mem. Culver Legion (bd. trustees 1990—), Eugene C. Eppley Club, Phoenix Bd. Appeals, 1978-80; v.p. Cuernavaca Homeowners Assn., 1982, pres., 1983-86. Recipient Image Maker award Shell Oil Co., 1979; Top Performer award Phoenix dist. Shell Oil Co., 1979, 80. Mem. Petroleum Retailers Ariz. (pres. 1977-79), Nat. Congress Petroleum Retailers (adv. bd.), Automotive Svc. Excellence (cert.), Culver Legion (life), Studebaker Drivers Club (zone coord. Pacific S.W. 1983, nat. v.p. 1986, 87, 88, nat. pres. 1989-90, Grand Canyon chpt. pres. 1986), Avanti Owners Assn. (nat. bd. dirs. 1975-96, internat. pres. 1986-89). Republican. Lodge: Optimists (bd. dirs. Paradise Valley club 1984, sec.-treas. 1984). Office: 915 W Hatcher Rd Phoenix AZ 85021-2101

FRANCKE, UTA, medical geneticist, genetics researcher, educator; b. Wiesbaden, Germany, Sept. 9, 1942; came to U.S., 1969; d. Kurt and Gertrud Müller; m. Bertold Richard Francke, May 27, 1967 (div. 1982); m. Heinz Furthmayr, July 27, 1986. MD, U. Munich, Fed. Republic Germany, 1967; MS, Yale U., 1985. Diplomate Am. Bd. Pediatrics, Am. Bd. Med. Genetics (bd. dirs. 1981-84). Asst. prof. U. Calif., San Diego, 1973-78; assoc. prof. Yale U., New Haven, 1978-85, prof., 1985-88; prof. Stanford (Calif.) U., 1989—; investigator Howard Hughes Med. Inst., Stanford, 1989—, mem. sci. rev. bd., Bethesda, Md., 1986-88; mem. mammalian genetics study sect. NIH, Bethesda, 1990—; bd. dirs. Am. Soc. Human Genetics, Rockville, Md., 1981-84. Profl. advisor March of Dimes Birth Defects Found., White Plains, N.Y., 1990, Marfan Assn., Port Washington, N.Y., 1991. Mem. Inst. Medicine of NAS (fgn. assoc.), Human Genome Orgn., Soc. for Pediatric Rsch., Soc. for Inherited Metabolic Disorders. Office: Stanford U Med Sch Howard Hughes Med Inst Beckman Ctr Stanford CA 94305-5428*

FRANDEN, BLANCHE M., nursing educator; b. N.Y.C., June 9, 1923; d. Samuel and Rebekah (Stern) Randall; m. Robert Jacob Franden, Aug. 20, 1950; children: Richard Jules, Peter Herb, Daniel Ethan. Grad. Mass. Meml. Hosp. Sch. Nursing (now Boston U. Hosp.), 1945; B. in Vocat. Edn., Calif. State U., L.A., 1980. RN, Calif. dir. student health Mass. Meml. Hosp., Boston, 1947-49; staff nurse various hosps., N.Y., Calif., 1949-91; instr., coord. hosp. related occupations East San Gabriel Valley Regional Occupational Program, 1973-90, instr., coord., EMT 1, 1986—; program dir., instr., EMT 1 La Puente Valley Regional Occupl. Program, 1985-93; CPR instr.-trainer; mem. CPR com., local governing bd. Am. Heart Assn; mem. L.A. County Com. to Revise Curriculum for EMT1 recertification, 1992-95. Author student manual. Rec. sec. Pathways to Hope chpt. City of Hope. Mem. AAUW, VFW Women's Aux., Calif. Assn. Regional Occupl. Ctrs./Programs, Am. Vocat. Assn., Nat. Assn. EMS Educators, Calif. Assn. Health Career Educators, So. Calif. Assn. EMT Instrs. and Coords., Nat. Assn. of EMS Educators. Democrat. Jewish. Office: E San Gabriel Valley Regional Occupl Program 1501 W Del Norte West Covina CA 91790

FRANEY, PHILIP DAVID, county treasurer, tax collector; b. Bakersfield, Calif., Feb. 5, 1948; s. James T. and Dorothy (Ross) F.; m. Dina Cepeda, Jan. 24, 1976; children: Shelly, Dina. AA, Bakersfield Coll., 1968; BSBA, Calif. State U., Bakersfield, 1973. Supervising acct.ech. Bakersfield (Calif.) City Sch. Dist., 1973-76; systems acct., auditor, controller County of Kern, Bakersfield, 1976-81; asst. treas. County of Kern, 1981-87, treas., tax collector, 1987—; bd. dirs., Kern County Employees' Retirement Assn., Bakersfield, 1987—, Kern Flex Adv. Com., 1987—; adminstr., Kern County Deferred Compensation Plan, 1987—; panelist Asset Allocation Symposium, Carmel, 1989, Calif. Assn. County Treas.-Tax Collectors, Rohnert, 1990. Chmn. Kern County Employees' United Way, Bakersfield, 1988, Kern County Employees' Savings Bonds, 1989; mem. Kern County Speakers Bureau, 1988—, CSUB Alumni Speakers Assn., 1989—. With U.S. Army, 1968-73. Mem. Am. Soc. Pub. Adminstrs., Nat. Assn. Treas.-Fin. Officers, Calif. Assn. Pub. Retirement Systems, Calif. Assn. Co. Treas. & Tax Collectors (pres. 1996-97), State Assn. County Retirement Systems, Kern County Mgmt. Coun. (treas. 1981—), Kern County Speakers Bureau, Bakersfield Coll. Found., Calif. State U. Alumni, Bakersfield East Rotary (bd. dirs. 1988-89, Paul Harris fellow 1985, 85). Republican. Office: Kern County Treas 1115 Truxtun Ave Bakersfield CA 93301-4639

FRANK, ALAN, retired psychiatry educator; b. N.Y.C., May 16, 1922; s. Lawrence Kelso and Alice Vermandoir (Bryant) F.; m. Louise Thompson, 1956 (dec. 1964); children: Alexandra, Margaret, Lucia; m. Anita Magnus, May, 1969; 1 child, Loren. BA, Columbia U., 1944, MD, 1949. Diplomate Am. Bd. Med. Examiners; cert. Am. Bd. Psychiatry and Neurology. Head psychiat. div. Student Health Service U. Colo., Boulder, 1956-67; psychiatrist Health Service Pa. State U., State College, 1967-68; asst. prof. psychiatry U. N.Mex., Albuquerque, 1968-92, prof. emeritus, 1992—; cons. in field, 1969—. Fellow Am. Psychiat. Assn. (life), Am. Orthopsychiat. Assn., AAAS, ACP; mem. N.Y. Acad. Scis. Office: 8602 Aztec Rd NE Albuquerque NM 87111-4506

FRANK, CHRISTOPHER LYND, mechanical engineer; b. Chesterton, Ind., Dec. 26, 1949; s. Clarence Edward and Marie Caroline (Saylor) F.; m. Deborah Lynn Tanner, July 3, 1971; chileren: Erin Marie, Christopher David. BS in Engring., Calif. State U., Sacramento, 1983; cert. injection molding, U. Lowell, 1986. Plant mgr. Redelco Plastics, Clovis, Calif., 1975-79; owner, designer The Energy Factory, Fresno, Calif., 1977-79, Solar Utility Network, Yuba City, Calif., 1979-81; engr., designer Houston Fearless 76, Carson, Calif., 1983-86; engr., designer Air Force Advanced Composites Program, Sacramento, 1986—, head thermoplastics devel. Contbr. articles to profl. jours. Served as sgt. USAF, 1970-74. Recipient

Logistics Civilian Engr. of the year award U.S. Air Force. Mem. Soc. Automotive Engrs., ASME, Soc. Mfg. Engrs., Soc. Plastics Engrs. Office: SM-ALC/TIEC Bldg 243-e Mcclellan AFB CA 95652

FRANK, DONALD HERBERT, minister; b. Rochester, N.Y., May 12, 1931; s. Oscar Edward and Mary Charlotte (Morgan) F.; m. Anne Sadlon, Aug. 27, 1955; children: Donna Lynn Frank Bertsch, John Edward, James David. BA, Bloomfield (N.J.) Coll., 1954; MDiv, McCormick Theol. Sem., 1957, MA, 1966; DD, Coll. of Idaho, 1980. Ordained to ministry Presbyn. Ch., 1957. Asst. pastor Hamburg (N.Y.) Presbyn. Ch., 1957-60; min. Christian edn. 1st Presbyn. Ch., Pompano Beach, Fla., 1960-63, First Presbyn. Ch., Santa Ana, Calif., 1966-69, Northminister Presbyn. Ch., Evanston, Ill., 1963-66; assoc. pastor Bellflower (Calif.) Presbyn. Ch., 1969-74; pastor Boone Meml. Presbyn. Ch., Caldwell, Idaho, 1974-87; organizing pastor Covenant Presbyn. Ch., Reno, Nev., 1987-96, retired, 1997; commr. Synod of Pacific, Petaluma, Calif., 1977-81, 89-94, moderator, 1994. Bd. dirs. Metro Ministry Interfaith Agy., Reno, 1988, Washoe at Risk Task Force on Pub. Edn., Reno, 1988; mem. law enforcement chaplancy Truckee Meadows, 1996. With USNR, 1948-53. Mem. Rotary (Paul Harris fellow 1994). Democrat.

FRANK, GERALD WENDEL, civic leader,journalist; b. Portland, Oreg., Sept. 21, 1923; s. Aaron Meier and Ruth (Rosenfeld) F. Student, Stanford U., 1941-43, Loyola U., L.A., 1946-47; BA with honors, Cambridge U., 1948, MA, 1953; D Bus. Adminstrn. (hon.), Greenville (Ill.) Coll., 1971; LLD (hon.), Pacific U., 1983. Mgr. Meier & Frank Co., Salem, Oreg., 1948-65; v.p. Meier & Frank Co., Ltd., 1965—; also bd. dirs.; pres. Gerry's Frankly Speaking, 1965—; co-owner Gerry Frank's Konditorei, 1982—; bd. dirs. Oreg. Baking Co., 1995—, Std. Ins. Co. (chmn. nominating com., 1990-93), U.S. Bancorp, World Masters Games 1998, Inc., 1996—. Author: Where to Find It, Buy It, Eat It in New York, 1980, Our Little Black Book of Shopping Secrets, Friday Surprise, 1995; sr. corres. Northwest Reports, commentator/reporter Morning news shows KPTV, Portland. Trustee Lorene Sails Higgins Charitable Trust, 1993—; chief of staff to Sen. Mark O. Hatfield, 1973-92; gen. chmn. Mark Hatfield for U.S. Sen., 1966, 72, 78, 84, 90; mem. Culver Commn. on Reorganization of U.S. Senate, 1975-76; mem. mgmt. com. U.S. Senate, 1978; active Nat. Found. Infantile Paralysis, Arthritis and Rheumatism Found., Portland C. of C., Salem Area C. of C., Sunshine Divsn., Portland Police Res., Portand Area Coun., Cascade Area Coun., Cascade Pacific Coun., Nat. Coun., Boys Scouts Am., Portland Rose Festival Assn., Jr. Achievement, Travelers Aid Soc. Portland, Nat. Mcpl. League, Salem Pub. Libr. Found., Portland United Fund, Marion-Polk Counties United Good Neighbors, Salem Gen. Hosp., Nat. Retail Merchants Assn., Citizens' Conf. for Govtl. Coop., Gov.'s Econ. Devel. Commn., Oreg. Retail Distributors' Inst., Am. Heart Soc., Oreg. Rsch. Assn., Salem 4-H Club, Willamette River Days, Salem YWCA, Willamette U. bd. trustees, League Women Voters, Oreg. Grad. Inst. Sci. & Tech., Portland Met. Futures Unltd., Inc., Marion-Salem Bldg. Study Com., Oreg. Symphony Soc., Am. Legion, Oreg. Coast Aquarium, exec. com., UNICEF, Oreg. High Desert Mus., Salvation Army, Salem Art Assn., Parry Ctr. for Children, St. Vincent Hosp. & Med. Ctr., Oreg. Health Scis. U., OMSI, chair, dir., 1996-97, Oreg. Tourism Coun., chair, 1996—, Oreg. Ind. Colls. Found., AAA of Oreg., Oreg. Assn. Nurserymen, Oreg. State Bar Ho. Dels., Miss Oreg. Scholarship Program. Recipient numerous awards including Silver Beaver Boy Scouts Am., 1963, Reginald H. Vincent trophy United Good Neighbor of Yr., 1980, Brotherhood Nat. Conf. Christians and Jews, Portland, 1984, Glenn Jackson leadership Willamette U., 1984, Tom Lawson McCall fellowship Pacific U., 1987. Mem. Am. Legion, Elks, Rotary (Paul Harris fellow 1986). Home: 3250 Crestview Dr Salem OR 97302 Office: Gerrys Frankly Speaking Inc. 475 Cottage St NE Salem OR 97301

FRANK, JOE EUGENE, city planner; b. Urbana, Ill., Dec. 29, 1949. BA in design, Southern Ill. U., 1973; M in urban planning, U. Ill., 1976. City planner City of Naperville, Naperville, Ill., 1976-78, City of Ft. Collins, Ft. Collins, Colo., 1978—; exec. bd. Local Devel. Co., Inc., Ft. Collins, 1990—, Colo. Coun. of Energy Officials, Arvada, Colo., 1978-82, Historic Ft. Collins Devel. Corp., 1994—. Developed Land Devel. Guidance System, 1981, Solar Energy Policy, 1984. Recipient Ford Found. finalist, 1987, 1988. Mem. Am. Planning Assn. (Outstanding Planning award, 1982), Am. Inst. Cert. Planners, Nat. Trust For Historic Preservation. Office: City of Ft Collins 281 N College Ave Fort Collins CO 80524-2404 Home: 2945 Brumbaugh Dr Fort Collins CO 80526-6231

FRANK, JUDITH ANN (JANN FRANK), entrepreneur, small business owner; b. Fresno, Calif., Feb. 10, 1938; d. Walter R. Frank and Ethel Joan (Klomburg) Brinkerhoff; m. David Rogers, Oct. 1956 (div. June 1973). BA, Calif. State U., Fullerton, 1989, postgrad., 1990-91; postgrad., Chapman U., 1991-93. Vault teller, new accounts, comml. Bank of Am., Fresno, 1956-64; new accounts and note teller Security First Nat. Bank, Fresno, 1965-68; br. bookkeeper, supr. Wells Fargo Bank, Santa Clara and San Jose, Calif., 1968-78; student asst. Fullerton Coll. Career Planning and Placement Ctr., 1982-83; founder, owner Distant Drums Native Arts, 1994—, Jann Frank Enterprises, Placentia, Calif., 1996—. Phys. and occupl. intern transitional tng. program for brain injured adults and impaired sr. citizens Rehab. Inst. So. Calif., Orange, 1978-80, vol., 1993; vol. Sr. Citizens Transp., Lunch and Counseling Program, Fullerton, 1981-82; vol. City Wide Disaster Drill, Whittier, Calif., 1987; vol. grad. Evolution of Psychotherapy Conf., Anaheim, Calif., 1990; bd. dirs. Native Am. Inst.; amb. Placentia (Calif.) C. of C. Recipient Commendation for Vol. Svc. Orange County Coun. Women in C. of C., 1980, Woman of Distinction in Social Scis. award, 1984, Disting. Svc. award Rehab. Inst. So. Calif., Orange, 1993; tuition scholarship grantee Chapman U., Orange, 1991. Mem. Smithsonian Instn., Mus. Am. Indian, Assn. Humanistic Psychology, Am. Biog. Inst. Rsch. Assn. (lifetime dep. gov.), Calif. Indian Art Assn., Order of Internat. Fellowship, Golden Key, Alpha Gamma Sigma (Disting. Leadership award 1996, Internat. Cultural diploma of honor 1996, Twentieth Century Achievement award 1996). Office: Distant Drums Ste C 119 N Bradford Ave Ste C Placentia CA 92870

FRANK, PETER SOLOMON, art critic, curator; b. N.Y.C., July 3, 1950; s. Reuven and Bernice (Kaplow) F. B.A., Columbia U., 1972, M.A., 1974. Critic SoHo Weekly News, N.Y.C., 1973-76, Village Voice, N.Y.C., 1977-79, L.A. Weekly, 1988—; critic Long Beach Press-Telegram, 1993-96; L.A. corr. Contemporanea, 1989-91; curatorial assoc. Ind. Curators Inc., N.Y.C. and Washington, 1974—; co-curator Documenta VI, Kassel, W. Ger., 1976-77; assoc. editor Nat. Arts Guide, Chgo., 1979-81, Art Express, N.Y.C., 1980-81; curator Exxon Nat. Exhbn. of Am. Artists, Guggenheim Mus., N.Y.C., 1980-81; art critic Diversion mag., 1983-90; mem. faculty New Sch. for Social Rsch., 1974, Pratt Inst., 1975-76, Columbia U. Sch. Arts, 1978, Claremont Grad. Sch., 1989, 92-94, 95-97, U. Calif., Irvine, 1988-90, Calif. State U., Fullerton, 1990-91, U. Calif., Santa Barbara, 1994; Am. curatorial advisor Documenta 8, 1986-87. Author: The Travelogues, 1982, Something Else Press: An Annotated Bibliography, 1983; co-author: New, Used and Improved: Art in the '80s, 1987; contbr. articles to art periodicals; assoc. editor Tracks mag., 1974-76; editor Re Dact, 1983-85, Visions, 1990—; contbg. editor Art Economist, 1981-84. Nat. Endowment for Arts art critics travel fellow, 1978; critics project fellow, 1981; Royal Norwegian Ministry of Fgn. Affairs Fluxus rsch. fellow, 1987. Mem. Internat. Assn. Art Critics, Coll. Art Assn., Internationale Künstlers Gremium. Home: PO Box 24a36 Los Angeles CA 90024-1036 Office: Visions Art Quar PO Box 24589 Los Angeles CA 90024-0589

FRANK, STEPHEN RICHARD, lawyer; b. Portland, Oreg., Dec. 13, 1942; s. Richard Sigmund Frank and Paula Anne (Latz) Lewis; divorced; children: Richard Sigmund II, Theresa Anne; m. Patricia Lynn Graves, Aug. 20, 1988; stepchildren: Brian Kinney, Mathew Kinney. AB in Econs., U. Calif., Berkeley, 1964; JD, Willamette U., 1967. Bar: Oreg., U.S. Ct. Appeals (9th cir.), U.S. Supreme Ct. Assoc. Tooze, Duden, Creamer, Frank and Hutchison, Portland, 1967-72; ptnr. Tooze, Shenker, Duden, Creamer, Frank and Hutchison, Portland, 1972—; mem. audit com. Seligman & Latz NYSE, 1981-85, bd. dirs. 1976-85. Editor Willamette Law Jour., 1967. Trustee, sec. Oreg. High Desert Mus., 1977-86; sec., bd. dirs. Palatine Hill Water Dist., 1973-77; bd. dirs. Emanuel Hosp. Found., 1980-83, Portland Ctr. for Visual Arts, 1977-82. Mem. ABA, Assn. Trial Lawyers Am., Oreg. Trial Lawyers Assn., Oreg. State Bar Assn. (dir., sec. minority scholarship program 1981—, sec.-chmn. com. worker's compensation 1974-77), Oreg. Assn. Ins. Def. Counsel, Oreg. Assn. Workers Compensation Def. Counsel. Clubs: Multnomah Athletic; City (Portland). Home: 3103 SW Cascade Dr Portland OR 97201-1813 Office: Tooze Shenker Duden Creamer Frank & Hutchison 333 SW Taylor St Portland OR 97204-2413

FRANK, THOMAS, design, construction and management executive; b. Salt Lake City, Nov. 23, 1937; s. Simon and Suzanne (Seller) F. BFA, U. Utah, 1963. Lic. contractor, Utah. Owner Thomas Frank Designers & Specifiers, Salt Lake City, 1962—; owner, pres. OmmiComputer West, Salt Lake City; bd. dirs. Silver Eagle Refining, Inc.; pres. Nova Devel. Corp.; cons. in field; instr. design, textiles and drafting LDS Jr. Coll., Salt Lake City, 1963-86; lectr. on interior design for jr. and high schs. Bus. & Industry Coop. Edn. Program; profl. adviser interior design curriculum devel. program U. Utah; mem. inter-profl. adv. coun. Utah State Bldg. Bd.; lectr., presenter seminars in field. Contbr. articles to profl. publs. Exec. v.p. Salt Lake Art Ctr., 1977-80; spl. advisor Children's Ctr.; co-chmn. spl. events Utah divsn. Am. Cancer Soc., 1978. Recipient awards U. Utah, 1962, Utah Designers Craftsman Guild, 1962, State Fair Fine Arts, 1962. Fellow Am. Soc. Interior Designers; mem. N.Am. Autocadd Users Group, Nat. Kitchen and Bath Assn. (pres. mountain states chpt. west 1991-92), Am. Soc. Interior Designers (nat. long-range planning com. 1985-87, nat. comms. area coord. 1985, nat. membership devel. com. 1986-87, nat. regional dir. 1991-92, nat. edn. com. 1981, nat. chmn. energy conservation 1980-82, nat. chpt. pres.' orientation task force 1980, nat. bd. dirs. 1977-82, chmn. regional indsl. rels. 1977-78, numerous other offices, numerous awards), AID (sec. Utah 1969-71, bd. govs. 1970-74, Utah pres. 1973-75). Home: 2360 Oakhill Dr Salt Lake City UT 84121-1520 Office: Thomas Frank Designers 3369 Highland Dr Salt Lake City UT 84106-3356

FRANK, VICTOR ROBERT, electrical engineer; b. Grand Rapids, Mich., Dec. 21, 1937; s. Victor Lambert Leo and Lillian Lorraine (Krueger) F.; m. Katsuko Miyazato, May, 1963; children: Mary, Arthur. AS, Weber Jr. Coll., Ogden, Utah, 1957; student, Stanford Univ., 1960-63; BSEE, Utah State Univ., 1959, MSEE, 1960. Electronic technician Douglas Aircraft, Santa Monica, Calif., 1957, Hughes Aircraft, Culver City, Calif., 1958; physicist Nat. Bur. Standards, Boulder, 1959-60; rsch. assoc. Stanford (Calif.) Univ., 1960-70; sr. rsch. engr. SRI Internat., Menlo Park, Calif., 1970—. With Calif. Army Res. Nat. Guard, 1968. Republican. Lutheran. Home: 12450 Skyline Blvd Woodside CA 94062-4541

FRANKE, ADRIAN AMADEUS HARALD, natural products chemist, researcher; b. Kirchzarten, Germany, Apr. 26, 1956; s. Walter Wilhelm and Lotte F. Cert. chemistry, pharmaceutical, U. Freiburg, 1980, PhD in Chemistry, 1985, post doctoral studies, 1985-87. Cons. Health Dept., Bangkok, Thailand, 1987; post doctoral fellow Dept. Sci. and Indsl. Rsch., Wellington, New Zealand, 1987-89, Univ. Hawaii chemistry dept., Honolulu, 1989, U. Hawaii zoology dept., Honolulu, 1990; post doctoral fellow U. Hawaii Cancer Rsch. Ctr., Honolulu, 1991-92, asst. specialist, 1992-94, asst. rschr., 1994—, assoc. rsch. (specialist), 1996—. Contbr. numerous articles to profl. jours. Recipient Rsch. fellowship German Rsch. Soc., New Zealand, 1987-89; grantee U. Hawaii, 1991, 92, Am. Cancer Soc., 1992-94, U.S. C. of C., 1994-95. Mem. Am. Chem. Soc., Am. Assn. for Cancer Rsch., European Soc. of Herbal Medicine, German Pharm. Soc. Office: Cancer Rsch Ctr 1236 Lauhala St Honolulu HI 96813-2424

FRANKEL, CHARLES EDWARD, retired newspaperman, journalism educator; b. Chgo., Nov. 16, 1927; s. David Jay and Raina Gertrude (Goodfriend) F.; m. Helga Wolpert, Aug. 25, 1962; 1 child, David Kimo. BS in Journalism, Northwestern U., 1950. Reporter Plymouth (Ind.) Pilot News, 1950-52, AP, Columbus, Cin., Cleve., 1952-56; sub-editor Reuters, London, 1956-58; copy reader Chgo. Tribune, 1958-60; asst. editor editorial page Honolulu Star-Bull., 1960-88; fgn. expert China Daily, Beijing, 1988-89; lectr. U. Hawaii at Manoa, Honolulu, 1976-85, 89—. Editor: Thrum's Hawaiian Almank, 1967, 68. Trustee Hawaiian Hist. Soc., Honolulu, 1992-96; del. Hawaii Dem. Conv., 1996. With USN, 1945-46. Mem. Soc. Profl. Journalists (pres. Honolulu), Hawaii Newspaper Guild (exec. com. 1962-64). Jewish. Home: 1638-A Mikahala Way Honolulu HI 96816

FRANKEL, FREDERICK DAVID, psychologist; b. N.Y.C., Feb. 26, 1946; s. Jack Jacob and Beatrice (Trus) F.; m. Lucinda K. McLaughlin, Jan. 3, 1981; 1 child, Seth Joseph. BA, SUNY Stony Brook, 1967; PhD, U. Calif. Irvine, 1971. Lic. psychologist. Psychologist UCLA, 1973—. Author: Good Friends Are Hard to Find, 1996; contbr. articles to profl. jours. Office: UCLA 300 UCLA Med Plz Los Angeles CA 90024

FRANKISH, BRIAN EDWARD, film producer, director; b. Columbus, Ohio, July 28, 1943; s. John (Jack) Fletcher Frankish and Barbara Aileen (Tondro) Gray; m. Tannis Rae Benedict, Oct. 13, 1985; children: Merlin L. Reed III, Michelle Lynn Reed. AA, Chaffey Coll., 1964; BA, San Francisco State U., 1967. Freelance producer L.A.; prin. Frankish-Benedict Entertainment, L.A. Prodr. (film) Vice Squad, 1981, (TV series) Max Headroom, 1987; assoc. prodr.: (films) Elephant Parts, 1981, Strange Brew, 1982, The Boy Who Could Fly, 1985, In the Mood, 1986; exec. prodr., unit prodn. mgr. (film) Field of Dreams, 1989, Flight of the Intruder, 1990, American Me, 1991; prodr. visual effects for film Turbulence, 1996; prodr., dir. (theatrical play) Timing is Everything, 1991; 1st asst. dir.: (TV shows) Big Shamus, 1979, Skag, 1979, Why Me?, 1983, Making Out, 1984, Berrengers, 1984, (films) Strange Brew, 1982, Uncle Joe Shannon, 1978, Savage Harvest, 1980, Dead and Buried, 1980, Spring Break, 1982, Brainstorm, 1982-83, The Last Starfighter, 1983, The New Kids, 1983, Aloha Summer, 1984, The Best of Times, 1985, Odd Jobs, 1985, The Fugitive, 1993, Demolition Man, 1993, Roswell, 1994; unit prodn. mgr. Second Serve, 1986, The Net, 1995; distbr.'s rep. and completion bond rep. Made in Heaven, 1986; prodn. mgr.: The Net, 1995; other prodn. credits include: Play it Again, Sam, 1971, Everything You Always Wanted to Know About Sex..., 1972, Time to Run, 1972, Haunts, 1975, Mahogany (Montage), 1975, King Kong, 1976, The Betsy, 1977. Mem. Dirs. Guild Am., Calif. Yacht Club.

FRANKLIN, ALBERT BRENT, financial consultant; b. Austin, Tex., Feb. 11, 1952; s. "AB" and Florine Louise (Hallmon) F.; m. Joleen Ann Franklin, Nov. 20, 1976 (div. Feb. 1980); children: Nicole, Monique, Lawrence, Andre. AA, Cañada Coll., Redwood City, Calif., 1980. Pres., fin. cons. ESSENECO, 1984—. Author: (biography) New York State Historical Association, 1992, (rsch.) University of Florida, 1993. Organizer Com. to Elect Bill Royer to Congress, Burlingame, Calif., 1978, Com. to Elect Ronald Reagan for Pres., Redwood City, 1984; mem. Assn. Wash. Cities, 1976-77, Rep. Presdl. Task Force, 1988—. Mem. John Birch Soc., Hollywood Script Writers. Essene. Home: PO Box 365 San Carlos CA 94070-1365

FRANKLIN, CHERYL JEAN, engineer, author; b. Pasadena, Calif., Sept. 11, 1955; d. Peter Gordon and B. Joyce (Jette) F. BS in Math., U. Redlands, 1975; postgrad studies engring., U. Calif., Irvine, 1975-76, Calif. State U., Fullerton, 1980-81. Tech. staff mem. Boeing, Anaheim, Calif., 1976—; mem. Creative Writing adv. bd. Calif. State U., Fullerton, 1996. Author: (books) Fire Get, 1987, Fire Lord, 1989, Fire Crossing, 1991, Inquisitor (et al), 1992. Mem. Authors Guild, Sci. Fiction and Fantasy Writers of Am. Episcopalian. Home: 19502 Old Ranch Rd Yorba Linda CA 92886-4307 Office: Boeing DF07 3370 Miraloma Ave Anaheim CA 92803

FRANKLIN, DOLORES ROBERTS, elementary education educator; b. Commerce, Tex.; d. David Roberts and Earnestine (Massey) Ivory; children: Ronald Tyrone Franklin, Angela Franklin, Jocelyn Franklin. BS in Elem. Edn., Tex. Coll., 1956; MS in Elem. Edn., Portland (Oreg.) State U., 1978. Elem. tchr. Commerce Ind. Sch. Dist., 1960-61, Portland Pub. Sch. Dist., 1972—. Author sch. dist. curriculum. Impact II disseminator grantee Portland Pub. Schs., 1992. Mem. NEA, Oreg. Edn. Assn., Oreg. Sci. Tchrs. Assn., Portland Assn. Tchrs. (rep. 1989—, Impact II disseminator grantee 1992). Home: 3961 NE 19th Ave Portland OR 97212-1410

FRANKLIN, JON DANIEL, writer, journalist, educator; b. Enid, Okla., Jan. 12, 1942; s. Benjamin Max and Wilma Irene (Winburn) F.; m. Nancy Sue Creevan, Dec. 12, 1959 (div. 1976, dec. 1987); children: Teresa June, Catherine Cay; m. Lynn Irene Scheidhauer, May 20, 1988. B.S. with high honors, U. Md., 1970; LHD (hon.), U. Md., Balt. County, 1981, Coll. Notre Dame, Balt., 1982. With USN, 1959-67; reporter/editor Prince Georges (Md.) Post, 1967-70; sci. and feature writer Balt. Evening Sun, 1970-85; assoc. prof. U. Md. Coll. Journalism, 1985-88, prof., 1988-89; prof., chmn. dept. journalism Oreg. State U., Corvallis, 1989-91; prof. creative writing U. Oreg., Eugene, 1991—. Author: Shocktrauma, 1980, Not Quite a Miracle, 1983, Guinea Pig Doctors, 1984, Writing for Story, 1986, The Molecules of the Mind, 1987. pub.: *Bylines*, WriterL. Recipient James T. Grady medal Am. Chem. Soc., 1975, Pulitzer prize for feature writing, 1979, Pulitzer prize for explanatory journalism, 1985, Carringer award Nat. Mental Health Assn., 1984, Penney-Mo. Spl. award for health reporting, 1985; named to Newspaper Hall of Fame, Md.-Del.-D.C. Press Assn. Mem. Nat. Assn. Sci. Writers, Soc Profl. Journalists, The Writers Guild, Investigative Reporters and Editors. Office: U Oreg Creative Writing Program Eugene OR 97403-1299

FRANKLIN, ROBERT BLAIR, cardiologist; b. Buffalo, Dec. 18, 1919; s. Wilson Gale and Frances Eunice (Sullivan) F.; m. Anne W., Jan. 16, 1969; children: Virginia, Richard, Victor, George, Robert, Kathleen. BA, Canisius Coll., Buffalo, 1940; MD, U. St. Louis, 1943. Diplomate Am. Bd. Internal Medicine, Am. Bd. Cardiovascular Diseases. Commd. U.S. Army, advanced through grades to col.; chief med. svc. 130th Sta. Hosp. U.S. Army, Heidelberg, Germany, 1955-58, comdg. officer 5th Surg. Hosp., 1958-59; chief gen. med. svc. Fitzsimons Gen. Hosp. U.S. Army, Denver, 1959-60, chief cardiology svc., 1962-65; comdg. officer 121st Evacuation Hosp. U.S. Army, Seoul, Korea, 1965-66; chief cardiology svc. Letterman Gen. Hosp. U.S. Army, San Francisco, 1966-68; chief cardiology dept. Kaiser Permanente Med. Group, Santa Clara, Calif., 1968-79; dep. comdg. officer 130th Sta. Hosp. U.S. Army, Heidelberg/Seoul/Vicenza, Italy, 1979-89; asst. clin. prof. Med. Coll. Ga., Augusta, 1953-54, U. Colo., Denver, 1963-65, Seoul Nat. U., 1965-66; guest lectr. Phy Yonsei U., Seoul, 1965-66; asst. clin. prof. U. Calif. Med. Sch., San Francisco, 1966-68, 74-79, 89—. Contbr. 35 articles to profl. jours. Decorated Legion of Merit with 3 oak leaf clusters. Roman Catholic. Home: 20 Palomino Cir Novato CA 94947-3619

FRANKLIN, ROBERT CHARLES, probation officer; b. Falls City, Nebr., Feb. 27, 1941; s. Robert Benjamin and Grace Evelyn (Riden) F.; m. Jeanette Ilene Kritnet, Aug. 28, 1964; children: Heather T., Cynthia D. BA in Sociology, U. Nebr., 1967; MS in Psychology/Counseling, Calif. State U., Hayward, 1972. Juvenile group supr. San Mateo County Probation Dept., San Mateo, Calif., 1968-75; dep. probation officer San Mateo County Probation Dept., Redwood City, Calif., 1975-91, supervising probation officer, 1991—; pres. State Coaliton of Probation Orgns., Sacramento, 1990-91. Columnist Pres.'s Corner, Calif. Probation News, 1990-91; contbr articles to profl. jours. Served with USAF, 1959-63, Japan. Mem. Calif. Probation, Parole and Correctional Assn. (state del. chair 1990-91, bd. dirs. 1990—, state conf. chair 1994—, Chpt. Mem. of Yr. 1990, 94, Pres.'s award 1989), Toastmasters (v.p. publicity 1991—). Office: San Mateo County Adult Probation 401 Marshall St Redwood City CA 94063-1636

FRANKS, THOMAS ALLEN, editorial cartoonist; b. Mpls., Aug. 10, 1948; s. John Joseph and Edna Harriet (Johnson) F.; m. Janet Shekleton, Aug. 12, 1972 (dec. Jan. 1989); 1 child, Molly Claire; m. Lauriette C. Nielson, June 25, 1994. BA in Philosophy, St. Mary's Coll., 1970; MA in Early Childhood/Visual Handicapped, Columbia U., 1973. Vol. Peace Corps, Morocco, 1970-72; edn. cons. State of Va., Richmond, 1974-75; tchr. spl. edn. Coquille (Oreg.) Sch. Dist., 1976-79; composer, guitarist, singer Electric Bill & The Killer Watts, Portland, Oreg., 1983-84; editl. cartoonist self-syndicated, Portland, 1985—. Peace activist, Forest Grove, Oreg., 1980-94; draft councilor N.W. Draft Counciling Ctr., Portland, 1980-83; social activist Coalition for Human Dignity, Washington County, 1993. Home: 3236 NW Vaughn St Portland OR 97210-1243

FRANSON, C(ARL) IRVIN, aerospace material and process engineer, educator; b. Hibbing, Minn., Oct. 17, 1934; s. Gunnar Theodore and Ina Selena (Kamb) F.; m. Adele Esther Haselton, June 29, 1968 (div. 1969). BSChemE, Purdue U., 1956; MBA, Santa Clara U., 1963. Cert. secondary tchr., Calif. Process engr. Wyandotte (Mich.) Chem. Corp., 1956-59; materials and process engr. Lockheed Missiles and Space Co., Sunnyvale, Calif., 1959-62, staff engr., 1963-68; devel. engr. Raychem Corp., Menlo Park, Calif., 1962-63; project engr. McCormick Selph, A Teledyne Co., Hollister, Calif., 1968-69; sr. devel. engr. Johnson Controls-Globe Union, Milw., 1969-70; sr. chem. engr. Gen. Telephone-Lenkurt, San Carlos, Calif., 1970-71; sr. materials engr. Ford Aerospace (Loral), Palo Alto, Calif., 1971-91; prin., entrepreneur Sigmaform Corp., Menlo Park, 1963-66; educator Golden Gate U., San Francisco, 1973, Chabot Coll., Hayward, Calif., 1970. Contbg. author: International Encyclopedia of Composites, 1990. Treas. Valley League-San Francisco Symphony, 1987-97; docent San Francisco Symphony, 1993-97. Mem. Soc. for Advancement of Material and Process Engring. (exhibits chmn. 1986 nat. symposium, historian 1974, co-founder No. Calif. chpt. 1960), Internat. Exec. Svc. Corps. (registered), No. Calif. Golf Assn. Home: 8162 Park Villa Cir Cupertino CA 95014-4009

FRANSON, PAUL OSCAR, III, public relations executive; b. Tampa, Fla., Jan. 22, 1941; s. Paul O. and Kathleen (Collins) F.; m. Theodora L. Nelson, Dec. 29, 1959 (div. 1986); children: Chris Soden, Wendy; m. Susan Cain, Nov. 17, 1990; stepchildren: Becky, Jeremy, David, Alison. BS, Davidson Coll., 1961. Editor 73 Mag., Peterborough, N.H., 1964-67; pub. rels. dir. Motorola, Phoenix, 1966-69, Teradyne, Boston, 1970; field editor Electronics mag., Dallas, L.A., 1970-75, EDN mag., San Jose, Calif., 1975-77; editor Electronic Bus. mag., Boston, 1977-80; pres. Franson & Assocs., Inc., San Jose, 1980-90, Franson, Hagerty, 1990-92; chmn., CEO Franson, Hagerty and Assoc. Inc., 1992—. Author: The Marketing Edge, 1990; contbr. articles to profl. jours. Address: 3422 San Pablo Ave San Jose CA 95127*

FRANTZEN, JOHN JOSEPH, chemical engineer, scientist, inventor; b. St. Paul, Apr. 11, 1931; s. John Matthew and Lillian Jean (Janilla) F.; m. Marcia Marie Westergren, Sept. 24, 1949; children: John T., Stephan R., Cheryl Heywood, Alan M., Mark D. Self educated. Supr. dividing and ruling dept., prodn., engring., devel. Buckbee Mears Co., Minn., 1958-64, mgr. R&D, production, 1964-67, corporate v.p. R&D, 1967-69; corp. v.p. internat. Buckbee Mears Co., 1969-78; cons. pvt. practice, Mpls., 1978-80; mgr. engring. Koltron Corp., Sunnyvale, Calif., 1980-83; v.p. engring. Koltron Corp., Sunnyvale, 1983-86, v.p., 1986-88; engring. mgr. Elcon Inc., San Jose, Calif., 1988-90; prin., cons. Clarity Plus, Copperopolis, Calif., 1990—; cons. in field. Recipient award NASA Appollo Missions. Home and Office: 424 Poker Flat Rd Copperopolis CA 95228-9616

FRANZEN, DON ERIK, lawyer; b. Whittier, Calif., Dec. 8, 1949; s. Erik and Helen Franzen; m. Dale Seligman, Nov. 14, 1952; children: Alexandra, Olivia. BA in Philosophy, U. So. Calif., 1972, JD, 1975. Bar: Calif. 1975, U.S. Dist. Ct. (ctrl. dist.) Calif. 1976, U.S. Ct. Appeals (9th cir.) 1976, U.S. Dist. Ct. (so. and ea. dists.) Calif. 1978, U.S. Ct. Appeals (D.C. and 5th cirs.) 1978, U.S. Supreme Ct. 1979. Assoc. Law Offices of Harrison W. Hertzberg, 1975-81, Franzen & Assocs., 1981-85; assoc. Rubin Eagan & Feder, 1985-91, atty., 1991-93; ptnr. Funsten & Franzen, Beverly Hills, Calif., 1993—. Contbr. articles to profl. jours. Vol. counsel Advocate for the Arts, L.A., 1976-78, Artists for Econ. Action, 1977; bd. dirs. Music Ctr. Opera Assn., L.A., 1985—; legal advisor Reason Found., L.A., 1987—. Mem. ABA. Office: Funsten & Franzen 9595 Wilshire Blvd Ste 305 Beverly Hills CA 90212-2503

FRAPPIA, LINDA ANN, management executive; b. St. Paul, May 14, 1946; d. Orville Keith Ferguson and Marilyn Ardis (Morris) Bidwell; 1 child, Jennifer. Grad. high sch., Seattle. Cert. claims adminstr. Claims rep. Fireman's Fund Ins., L.A., 1965-68; adminstrv. asst. to v.p. Employee Benefits Ins., Santa Ana, Calif., 1969-72; claims specialist Indsl. Indemnity Ins., Orange, Calif., 1972-83; claims supr. CNA Ins., Brea, Calif., 1983-85; claims mgr. EBI Ins. Svcs., Tustin, Calif., 1985; v.p. United Med. Specialists, Santa Ana, Calif., 1985-91; chief exec. officer United Ind. Specialists, Santa Ana, 1990—; chief executive officer United Chiropractic Specialists, Santa Ana, 1987—; instr. Ins. Edn. Assn., Brea, 1988—; speaker Western Ins. Info. Svc., Orange, 1976-83. Mem. Calif. Mfrs. Assn., Pub. Agencies Risk Mgmt. Assn., Calif. Self-Insured Assn., Toastmasters Internat. (v.p. Orange chpt. 1978). Republican.

FRARY, RICHARD SPENCER, international consulting company executive; b. Greybull, Wyo., Jan. 29, 1924; s. Frederick Spencer and Margaret Lee Ellen (Chalfant) F.; m. Eros Hunsaker, July 19, 1946; children: Richard

Jr., Lorraine, John, James. BSEE, U. Colo., 1949; postgrad., N.Mex. A&M U., 1954-55, So. Meth. U., 1956-57, U. Pa., 1958. Mgr. engring. RCA, Cherry Hill, N.J., 1952-62; v.p. Ultronic Systems Corp., Pennsauken, N.J., 1962-67; v.p. govt. systems Sperry Univac, various locations, 1967-80; v.p. research and engring. A.B. Dick Co., Niles, Ill., 1980-83; with Arthur D. Little Inc., Washington, 1983-90; pvt. practice cons. RSF Assocs., 1990—. With USMC, 1943-45, 50-51. Mem. IEEE, Sons of Utah Pioneers (pres.). Republican. Mormon. Home and Office: RSF Assocs 2898 Juniper Way Salt Lake City UT 84117-7159

FRARY, TIMOTHY NEIL, physician assistant; b. Omaha, Oct. 23, 1947; s. Vincent T. and Jacqueline M. (Hamilton) F.; m. Sue M. Frary, Dec. 5, 1969 (div. Apr. 1995); 1 child, Amy M.; m. Jennifer G. Frary, July 6, 1996. BS with high distinction, U. Nebr., 1975. Cert. physician asst. Instr. physician asst. edn. U. Nebr. Med. Ctr., Omaha, 1976-81; physician asst. rural Cedar Hills Family Practice, Newcastle, Wyo., 1981-87; physician asst. primary care McLoughlin Family Practice, Vancouver, Wash., 1987-90; physician asst. in emergency medicine Emergency Med. Physicians P.C., Casper, Wyo., 1990-93; physician asst., clinic mgr. Wyo. Med. Ctr., Casper, 1993—; mem. clin. skills com. Nat. Commn. on Cert. Physician Assts., Atlanta, 1985-87. Chmn. editl. bd. Jour. Am. Acad. Physician Assts., 1988-93; contbr. articles to profl. jours., chpt. to book. Staff sgt. USAF, 1968-72. Recipient Cert. of Appreciation Jour. Am. Acad. Physician Assts., 1992. Fellow Am. Acad. Physician Assts. (chmn. profl. practice coun. 1994—, Nat. Physician Asst. of Yr. 1986), Wyo. Assn. Physician Assts. (chief del. bd. dirs. 1990-95, Disting. Svc. award 1987). Office: Wyo Med Ctr 2233 E 2nd St Casper WY 82609-2050

FRASCH, BRIAN BERNARD, lawyer; b. San Francisco, Apr. 13, 1956; s. Norman Albert Frasch and Elizabeth Louise (Michelfelder) Milsten. BA magna cum laude, U. Calif., Santa Barbara, 1978; JD, U. Calif., Berkeley, 1982. Bar: Calif. 1982, U.S. Dist. Ct. (no. dist.) Calif. 1982, U.S. Dist. Ct. (so. dist.) Calif. 1983. Law clk. to chief judge U.S. Dist. Ct. (so. dist.) Calif., 1983-84; assoc. Graham & James, San Francisco, 1984-86, Lillick & McHose, San Diego, 1986-90; ptnr. Stephenson Prairie & Frasch, San Diego, 1990-96, Hillyer & Irwin, San Diego, 1996—. Assoc. editor: California Law Rev., 1981-82. Mem. ABA (litigation sect.), Calif. Bar Assn. (litigation sect.), San Diego County Bar Assn., San Diego Bldg. Owners and Mgrs. Assn. (bd. dirs. 1990—, gen. counsel 1995—), Westside Athletic Club. Office: Hillyer & Irwin 550 W "C" St ste 1600 San Diego CA 92101-8214

FRASER, BRUCE DOUGLAS, JR., architect, artist; b. Corvallis, Oreg., Dec. 1, 1948; s. Bruce Douglas and Betty Adele (Lively) F.; m. Laura Jane Wells, June 18, 1972. BArch, Calif. Poly. State U., 1972. Registered architect, Calif. Artist, illustrator Hopkins Assocs., San Luis Obispo, Calif., 1972-73; planner U.S. Peace Corps, Mashhad, Iran, 1973-75; mem. archtl. staff Meyer-Merriam Assocs., San Luis Obispo, 1975-77; prin. MDW Assocs., San Luis Obispo, 1977-85, Merriam-Fraser Architecture and Planning, San Luis Obispo, 1985-87, Archtl. Office Bruce Fraser, San Luis Obispo, 1987—. Chair Bldg. Appeals Bd., Pismo Beach, Calif., 1990, Planning Commn., Pismo Beach, 1991-92, vice chair, 1990. Recipient various design awards Obispo Beautiful Assn., 1977—, Downtown Assn., 1990—. Mem. AIA (v.p. Calif. Ctrl. Coast chpt. 1985, pres. 1986). Office: Archtl Off of Bruce Fraser AIA 971 Osos St San Luis Obispo CA 93401*

FRASER, CATHERINE ANNE, Canadian chief justice; b. Campbellton, N.B., Can., Aug. 4, 1947; d. Antoine Albert and Anne (Slevinski) Elias; m. Richard C. Fraser, Aug. 17, 1968; children: Andrea Claire, Jonathan James. BA, U. Alta., Can., 1969, LLB, 1970; ML, U. London, 1972. Assoc., ptnr. Lucas, Bishop & Fraser, Edmonton, Alta., 1972-89; justice Ct. Queen's Bench Alta., Edmonton, 1989-91; justice Ct. Appeal Alta., Edmonton, 1991-92, chief justice Alta. and NW Ter., 1992—; dir. Can. Inst. Adminstrn. Justice, 1991-95. Recipient Tribute to Women award YWCA, 1987. Mem. Can. Bar Assn., Edmonton Bar Assn., Law Soc. Alta. Office: Ct Appeal Alta, Law Courts Bldg, Edmonton, AB Canada T5J OR2

FRASER, FREDERICK EWART, art educator; b. Berkeley, Calif., Dec. 10, 1939; s. James Ewart Fraser and Sally V. (Jensen) Attwoll; m. Mary Louise Washburn Fraser, Aug. 8, 1965; children: Carol Louise, Paul Frederick. AA, Boise Jr. Coll., 1960; BS in Edn., U. Idaho, 1967; MS, U. Oreg., 1970. Elem. tchr. Emmett (Idaho) Pub. Schs., 1961-62, Nampa (Idaho) Pub. Schs., 1962-66, Boise (Idaho) Pub. Schs., 1967-69; elem. art tchr. Eugene (Oreg.) Pub. Schs., 1969-70; elem. art specialist Richland (Wash.) Pub. Schs., 1970—, chmn. art dept., 1983-84; adj. prof. Ea. Wash. State U., Cheney, 1980-83. Prin. works include 2-D sculpture American Me, 1994; contbr. numerous prints in private collection, 1970-94. Campaign worker Richland Dem. Com., 1972. Grantee Ednl. Dist. Svc. No. 123, Pasco, 1978, computer graphics in elem. art grantee Richland Pub. Schs., 1991. Mem. NEA, Nat. Art Edn. Assn. (workshop presenter 1997), Wash. Art Edn. Assn. (chmn. Pasco 1972, state elem. art educator of yr. award 1995), Columbia Basin Model A Ford Club, Three Rivers Model T Ford Club. Methodist. Home: 628 Birch Ave Richland WA 99352-3674 Office: Jason Lee School 1702 Van Giesen St Richland WA 99352-2833

FRASER, GRANT ADAM, mathematics educator; b. N.Y.C., Dec. 14, 1943; s. Theodore Harold and Catherine Evelyn (Adam) F.; m. Caryn Edmunds, Aug. 20, 1977 (div. Dec. 1995); children: Adam, Juliet. BA Math./Philosophy with highest honors, UCLA, 1964, MA in Math., 1969, PhD in Math., 1970. Cert. rsch. psychoanalyst, Calif. Asst. prof. U. San Francisco, 1971-72; asst. prof. U. Santa Clara, Calif., 1972-77, assoc. prof., 1977-82; assoc. prof. Calif. State U., L.A., 1982-84, prof., 1984—. Contbr. rsch. articles to profl. jours. NSF fellow UCLA, 1965-69. Mem. Am. Psychoanalytic Assn. (assoc.), Phi Beta Kappa, Pi Mu Epsilon. Office: Calif State U 5151 State University Dr Los Angeles CA 90032-8204

FRASER, LAURA JANE, journalist; b. Denver, Feb. 9, 1961; d. Charles Hugh and Virginia (Hart) F.; m. Jay Rorty, Sept. 9, 1995. BA, Wesleyan U., 1982. Freelance writer San Francisco, 1982-94; columnist San Francisco Bay Guardian, 1988-91; contbg. editor San Francisco Weekly, 1991-93, Health mag., San Francisco, 1992—. Author: Losing It: America's Obsession with Weight and the Industry that Feeds on It, 1997; contbr. articles to profl. jours. Named Outstanding Young Journalist, No. Calif. Soc. Profl. Journalists, 1989.

FRASER, MAC ROBERT (ROB FRASER), livestock auction owner, auctioneer; b. Mont., Mar. 3, 1958; s. William Sidney III and Catherine Lee (Arneson) F.; m. Cynthia Jo Leland, Nov. 4, 1989; 1 child, Kelsey. Student, Mont. State U., 1981. Ptnr. Valley Ranch and Feedlot Supply, Billings, Mont., 1984-89; auctioneer Billings Livestock Commn., 1988-94; ptnr. Mont. Video Contract Auction, 1991—; owner Miles City (Mont.) Livestock Commn. Co., 1991—. Active Miles City Club, 1995—. Mem. Nat. Cattlemen's Beef Assn. (mem. internat. mktg. com. 1997), Mont. Stockgrowers (mem. mktg. com. 1997), Mont. Assn. Livestock Auction Markets, Miles City C. of C. Office: Miles City Livestock Commn Co W Main St Miles City MT 59301

FRASER, RENEE, advertising executive; b. Columbus, Ohio, June 15, 1954; d. William Burval and Ruth White; m. Scott C. Fraser, Dec. 10, 1977; children: Nicole, Caneel Skye. BA, U. So. Calif., 1973, MA, 1978, PhD, 1981. Prof., lectr. U. So. Calif., L.A., 1975-76; prin. Plog Rsch., Reseda, Calif., 1977-80; v.p., dir. rsch. Young and Rubican, L.A., 1980-84; sr. v.p. Kenyon & Eckhardt, L.A., 1984-89; exec. v.p., gen. mgr. Bozell & Jacobs, L.A., 1989-91; pres., CEO Fraser & Assocs. Advtg., L.A., 1991-95; pres. Fraser Young, Santa Monica, Calif., 1995—; bd. dirs. Western States Ad Agy. Assn., Minority Advtg. Tng. Program, Calif. Ad Alliance. Author: Marketing and Creating Healthcare Systems in 3rd World Countries, 1978, Leveraging Media Dollars: The Advertiser, 1995; contbr. articles to profl. jours. V.p. bd. dirs. Vols. of Am.; bd. dirs. L.A. Youth Programs. Office: Fraser/Young 100 Wilshire Blvd Ste 440 Santa Monica CA 90401-1111

FRASSINELLI, GUIDO JOSEPH, retired aerospace engineer; b. Summit Hill, Pa., Dec. 4, 1927; s. Joseph and Maria (Grosso) F.; m. Antoinette Pauline Clemente, Sept. 26, 1953; children: Lisa, Erica, Laura, Joanne, Mark. BS, MS, MIT, 1949; MBA, Harvard U., 1956. Treas. AviDyne Rsch., Inc., Burlington, Mass., 1958-64; asst. gen. mgr. Kaman AviDyne div. Kaman Scis., Burlington, 1964-66; asst. dir. strategic planning N. Am. ACFT OPNS, Rockwell Internat., L.A., 1966-69; mgr. program planning Rockwell Space Systems Div., Downey, Calif., 1970-76; project leader R&D Rockwell Space Systems Div., Downey, 1976-79, chief analyst bus. planning, 1980-85, project mgr. advanced programs, 1986-94. Mem. Town Hall of Calif., L.A., 1970—; treas. Ecology Devel. and Implementation Commitment Team Found., Huntington Beach, Calif., 1971-75; founding com. mem. St. John Fisher Parish Coun., Rancho Palos Verdes, Calif., 1978-85. Recipient Tech. Utilization award, NASA, 1971, Astronaut Personal Achievement award, 1985. Fellow AIAA (assoc.; tech. com. on econs. 1983-87, exec. com. L.A. sect. 1987-91), Inst. for Advancement of Engring.; mem. Sigma Xi, Tau Beta Pi. Roman Catholic. Home: 29521 Quailwood Dr Palos Verdes Peninsula CA 90275-4930

FRATT, DOROTHY, artist; b. Washington, Aug. 10, 1923; d. Hugh and Martha (Holt) Miller; m. Nicholas Diller Fratt, Sept. 4, 1943 (div. 1965); children: Nicholas, Hugh, Gregory, Peter; m. Curtis Calvin Cooper, Nov. 3, 1972. Studied with Nicolai Cikovsky, 1940; student, Mt. Vernon Coll., 1940-42, Am. U., 1942-43, Phillips Collection Art Sch., 1942-43; studied with Karl Knaths, 1943. mem. commissioning panel for NEA grant, Scottsdale, Ariz., 1971; mem. adv. bd. U. Art Mus. Ariz. State U., Tempe, 1989-95. Exhibited at UN Club Gallery, 1948, Desert Art Gallery, Scottsdale, Ariz., 1959, Tucson Art Ctr., 1964, Phoenix Art Mus., 1964, 75, Riva Yares Gallery, Scottsdale, 1965, 82, 89, 94, 95, Calif. Legion Honor, San Francisco, 1965, Mickelson Gallery, Washington, 1967, State-Wide Touring Exhibit, 1974, Scottsdale Ctr. for Arts, 1980, Carson-Sapiro Gallery, Denver, 1981, Thomas Beabor Gallery, La Jolla, Calif., 1985, U. Ariz. Gallery, Tucson, 1986; represented in pub. collections at Phoenix Art Mus., Tucson Mus., Ariz. State Mus., Tempe; represented in various corp. collections. Mem. Fine Arts Commn., Phoenix, 1965-71; mem. Sotheby Symposium Quality in Art, N.Y.C., 1990. Home: 6010 E Cholla Ln Scottsdale AZ 85253-6902

FRAUENFELDER, HANS, physicist, educator; b. Neuhausen, Switzerland, July 28, 1922; came to U.S., 1952, naturalized, 1958; s. Otto and Emma (Ziegler) F.; m. Verena Anna Hassler, May 16, 1950; children: Ulrich Hans, Kätterli Anne, Anne Verena. Diploma, Swiss Fed. Inst. Tech., 1947, Ph.D. in Physics, 1950. Asst. Swiss Fed. Inst. Tech., 1946-52; asst. prof. physics U. Ill. at Urbana, 1952-56, asso. prof., 1956-58, prof., 1958-92, prof. emeritus, 1992—; mem. staff Los Alamos (N.Mex.) Nat. Labs., 1992—; Guggenheim fellow, 1958-59, 73; vis. scientist CERN, Geneva, Switzerland, 1958-59, 63, 73. Author: The Mossbauer Effect, 1962, (with E.M. Henley) Subatomic Physics, 1974, 2d edit., 1991, Nuclear and Particle Physics, 1975; contbr. articles to profl. jours. Recipient Humboldt award, 1987-88. Fellow AAAS, Am. Phys. Soc. (Biol. Physics prize 1992), N.Y. Acad. Sci.; mem. NAS, Am. Inst. Physics (chmn. governing bd. 1986-93), Am. Acad. Arts and Sci., Am. Philos. Soc., Acad. Leopoldina.

FRAZEE, JOHN PATRIC, academic administrator, English educator; b. Colorado Springs, Colo., Sept. 21, 1948; s. Walter M. and Eileen M. (Earthman) F.; m. Dana J. Berry, June 5, 1969; children: Olivia, Samantha, Caroline. BA in English, U. Colo., 1970; MA in English, U. Calif., Berkeley, 1974, PhD in English, 1979. Asst. prof. English U. Tex., Odessa, 1979-84, assoc. prof. English, 1984-90, dir. divsn. humanities and fine arts, 1986-91, prof. English, 1990-91; prof. English, dean Sch. of Arts and Letters Adams State Coll., Alamosa, Colo., 1991—; bd. dirs. Colo. Endowment for Humanities. Contbr. articles to profl. jours. Recipient Summer Seminar fellowship NEH, 1984. Mem. Soc. for Study of Narrative Lit., Dickens Soc. Am., Phi Beta Kappa. Democrat. Unitarian. Home: 2 Alamosa Ave Alamosa CO 81101 Office: Adams State Coll Alamosa CO 81102

FRAZER, LANCE WILLIAM, writer; b. Ann Arbor, Mich., Aug. 19, 1954; s. William James and Helen Marie (Kennedy) F.; m. Celia Marie Burki, July 24, 1976; 1 child, Logan Donovan. BA, U. Santa Clara, 1976; student, Sonoma State Coll., 1982, Santa Rosa Jr. Coll., 1987. Corr. Space World Mag., 1988-89; staff writer The Inter-City Express, 1988-91; corr. Ad Astra Mag., 1989-92. contbr. articles to Trials Digest Mag., Napa-Solano Bus. Jour., Santa Rosa Bus. Jour., Environ. Health Perspectives Mag., USAIR Mag., Air & Space, New Physician. Recipient First award for Excellence in Mag. Journalism Soc. Nat. Assn. Publs., 1989. Mem. Am. Soc. Journalists and Authors (Outstanding Article award 1993), Nat. Writers Assn. (profl. divsn.). Home and Office: 209 Gareffa Way Santa Rosa CA 95401

FRECH, HARRY EDWARD, III, economics educator, consultant; b. St. Louis, Nov. 11, 1946; s. Harry Edward Jr. and Margaret Byrne (O'Reilly) F.; m. Carol Ann Vouga, June 8, 1968 (div. Aug. 1980); children: Jon Clayton, Justin Tyler; m. Elizabeth Chen, Apr. 9, 1983; 1 child, Michael Anthony. BS in Indsl. Engring., U. Mo., 1968; MA in Econs., UCLA, 1970, PhD in Econs., 1974. Economist HEW, Rockville, Md., 1970-72; asst. prof. econs. U. Calif., Santa Barbara, 1973-77, assoc. prof. econs., 1977-81, prof., 1981—, chmn. dept., 1993-94; vis. asst. prof. econs. Harvard U., Cambridge, Mass., 1976-77; vis. prof. U. Chgo., 1982; econs. cons. FTC, Washington, 1977—, HHS, Washington, 1973-78; expert witness U.S. Dept. Justice, Washington, 1984; adj. scholar Am. Enterprise Inst. Pub. Policy Rsch. Author: Competition and Monopoly in Medical Care, 1996; co-author: Public Insurance in Private Medical Markets, 1978, Taxing Energy: Oil Severance Taxation and The Economy, 1990; assoc. editor Econ. Inquiry, 1975-78; editor: Health Care in America: The Political Economy of Hospitals and Health Insurance, 1988, Regulating Doctor's Fees, 1991; co-editor Health Economics Worldwide, 1992; N.Am. editor Internat. Jour. Econs. of Bus., 1992—; mem. editl. bd. Am. Econ. Rev., 1980-82, Econ. Inquiry, 1991—; series editor Health Econs. and Pub. Policy; contbr. articles to profl. jours. Bd. dirs. Christ Luth. Ch., Goleta, Calif., 1978; co-organizer 2d World Congress on Health Econs., Zurich, Switzerland, 1990. Research grantee HEW, 1976, Found. for Research in Econs. and Edn., 1974. Mem. Am. Econ. Assn., So. Econ. Assn., Western Econ. Assn.. Republican. Home: 438 Pitzer Ct Santa Barbara CA 93117-4013 Office: U Calif Econs Dept Santa Barbara CA 93106

FREDERIC, BRAD, engineering company executive; b. 1939. BA in Math., Calif. Poly Inst., 1959; postgrad., U. Calif., 1962-67. Program mgr. Gen. Rsch. Corp., 1963-73; pres. Tecolate Rsch. Inc., Santa Barbara, Calif., 1973—. Office: Tecolote Rsch Inc 5290 Overpass Rd Ste D Santa Barbara CA 93111-2081*

FREDERICK, SHERMAN, publishing executive. Pub. Las Vegas (Nev.) Rev.-Jour. Office: Las Vegas Rev-Journal 1111 W Bonanza Las Vegas NV 89125-0070

FREDERICKS, PATRICIA ANN, real estate executive; b. Durand, Mich., June 5, 1941; d. Willis Edward and Dorothy (Plowman) Sexton; m. Ward Arthur Fredericks, June 12, 1960; children: Corrine Ellen, Lorraine Lee, Ward Arthur II. BA, Mich. State U., 1962. Cert. Grad. Real Estate Inst., residential broker, residential salesperson; cert. real estate broker. Assoc. Stand Brough, Des Moines, 1976-80; broker Denton, Tuscon, 1980-83; broker-trainer Coldwell Banker, Westlake Village, Calif., 1984-90; broker, br. mgr. Brown, Newbury Park, Calif., 1990-94; dir. tng. Brown Real Estate, Westlake Village, Calif., 1994—; gen. mgr., dir. mktg. Coldwell Banker Town & Country Real Estate, Newbury Park, Calif., 1994—; dir. mktg. Coldwell Banker Town and Country, 1995—; bd. sec. Mixtec Corp., Thousand Oaks, 1984—. Contbr. articles to profl. jours. Pres. Inner Wheel, Thousand Oaks, 1991, 96-97; bd. dirs. Community Leaders Club, Thousand Oaks, 1991, Conejo Future Found., Thousand Oaks, 1989-92, Wellness Community Ventura Valley, 1994—. Mem. Calif. Assn. Realtors (dir. 1988-95 regional chairperson 1995, vice chairperson expn. 1997), Conejo Valley Assn. Realtors (sec., v.p., pres.-elect 1989-92, pres. 1993, Realtor of Yr. 1991), Pres.'s Club Mich. State U., Com. 100, Cmty. Concerts Assn., Alliance for the Arts, Conejo Valley Symphony Guild, Wellness Cmty., Indian Wells Country Club, North Ranch Country Club. Office: 2229 Michael Dr Newbury Park CA 91320

FREDERICKS, WARD ARTHUR, venture capitalist, food industry consultant; b. Tarrytown, N.Y., Dec. 24, 1939; s. Arthur George and Evelyn (Smith) F.; BS cum laude, Mich. State U., 1962, MBA, 1963, PhD. m. Patricia A. Sexton, June 12, 1960; children: Corrine E., Lorrine L., Ward A. Assoc. dir. Technics Group, Grand Rapids, Mich., 1964-68; gen. mgr. logistics systems Massey-Ferguson Inc., Toronto, 1968-69, v.p. mgmt. svcs., comptr., 1969-73, sr. v.p. fin., dir. fin. Americas, 1975—; comptr. Massey-Ferguson Ltd., Toronto, Ont., Can., 1973-75; cons. W.B. Saunders & Co., Washington, 1962—; sr. v.p. mktg. Massey/Ferguson, Inc., 1975-78, also sr. v.p., gen. mgr. Tractor div., 1978-80; gen. mgr. Rockwell Graphic Sys., 1980-82; pres. Goss Co.; v.p. ops., Rockwell Internat., Pitts., 1980-84; v.p. Fed. MOG., 1983-84; chmn. MIXTEC Corp., 1984—, also dir., chmn.; principal Venture Assocs., 1993—. dir. Polyfet RF, Inc., Venture Assocs., Badger Northland Inc., MST, Inc., Calif., Tech-Mark Group Inc., Spectra Tech., Inc., Mixtec Group-Venture Capital, Inc., Unicorn Corp., Mixtec-Las Vegas, Mixtec Food Group Calif., Mixtec Signal Tech., Harry Ferguson Inc., M.F. Credit Corp., M.F. Credit Co. Can. Ltd. Bd. dirs., mem. exec. com. Des Moines Symphony, 1975-79; exec. com. Conejo Symphony, pres. 1988-90, pres. Westlake Village Cultural Found., 1991; mem. exec. com. Alliance for Arts.; pres. Conejo Valley Indsl. Assn., 1990, 93; mem. Constn. Bicentennial Com., 1987-88, Ventura County Airport Commn., 1995—, LaQuinta Arts Found.; bd. dirs. Ventura County Bus. Incubator, 1996—; v.p. Com. Leaders Club, 1988, pres., 1989-90, pres. Westlake Cultural Found, 1991; vice chair Alliance for the Arts; regent Calif. Lutheran U., 1990— (exec. com. 1993—, chmn. acad. affairs 1993—), exec. com. 1992—, chmn. acad. affairs, 1992—. Fellow Am. Transp. Assn., 1962-63, Ramlose, 1962-63. Mem. AAAS, IEEE, SAR, Am. Mktg. Assn., Nat. Council Phys. Distbn. Mgmt. (exec. com. 1974), Produce Mktg. Assn., Soc. Automotive Engrs., U.S. Strategic Inst., Tech. Execs. Forum (Tech. Corridor 100 award, 1989), Internat. Food Mfg. Assn., Produce Mktg. Assn., Toronto Bd. Trade, Westlake Village C. of C. (chmn. 1990), Cochella Valley Community Concerts Assn. (bd. dirs. 1992-95), Old Crows, Assn. for Advanced Tech. Edn., Air Force Assn., Aerospace Soc., Experimental Aircraft Assn., Mil. Order World Wars, Conf. Air Force (col.), Westlake Village C. of C. (chmn. bd. 1990-91), Republican Ctrl. Com., State of Calif., 1993—, Aviation Country Club, Community Leaders Club, Pres.'s Club Mich. State U., North Ranch Country Club, Indian Wells Country Club, Rotary, Flying Rotarians, Beta Gamma Sigma. Author: (with Edward W. Smykay) Physical Distribution Management, 1974, Management Vision, 1988, Competitive Advantage in Technology Organizations, 1996; contbr. articles to profl. jours. Lutheran. Home: 1640 Aspenwall Rd Westlake Vlg CA 91361-1704 also: 48143 Vista Cielo La Quinta CA 92253-2256 Office: 31255 Cedar Valley Westlake Village CA 91362

FREDERICKSEN, WALTER MAILAND, behavioral and ocean sciences educator emeritus; b. Kansas City, Mo., Dec. 30, 1934; s. Walter Mailand Sr. and Aurelia Helene (Christensen) F.; m. Demaris Lou Nebgen, Aug. 11, 1957; children: Erik Mailand, Kirsten Demaris. BA, U. Kans., 1960; MA, U. Copenhagen, 1961; postgrad., U. Oreg., 1961-63. Master USCG; lic. archaeologist, Hawaii. Teaching fellow U. Oreg., Eugene, 1961-63; head counselor Lahainaluna H.S., Lahaina, Maui, Hawaii, 1965-66; prof. U. Hawaii Maui, Kahului, 1967-95; prof. emeritus U. Hawaii, 1995—; scientist, co-dir. Xamanek Rschs., Pukalani, Maui, Hawaii, 1964—; Tsunami surveyor JIMAR, U. Hawaii, Honolulu, 1975—; capt. rsch. vessel Glass Slipper II, Lahaina, 1964—; speaker in field. Author: An Introduction to Sailing, Cruising, Navigation, 1977; author more than 100 reports Sci. Archives, State of Hawaii, 1965—. Mem., chair Marine Adv. Coun., Lahainam 1975—. Sgt. USMC, 1953-56, Korea. Mem. numerous profl. orgns. Home: PO Box 131 Pukalani HI 96788 Office: Xamanek Rschs PO Box 131 Pukalani HI 96788

FREDMAN, FAIYA RUBENSTEIN, artist; b. Columbus, Ohio, Sept. 8, 1925; d. David and Henrietta Baum (Hassel) Rubenstein; m. Milton Fredman, Feb. 14, 1947; children: Stephen Albert, Teri Lynn. BA in Visual Arts, UCLA, 1948. One-woman shows include La Jolla (Calif.) Mus. Contemporary Art, 1968, 74, 81, U. Calif.-Riverside, Irvine, 1984, U. Calif.-San Diego, 1984, Ruth Bachofner Gallery, L.A., 1985, 88, Santa Monica, 1990, Zach/Shuster Gallery, Boca Raton, Fla., 1989, Boehm Gallery, Palomar Coll., San Marcos, Calif., 1990, Southwestern Coll., Chula Vista, Calif., 1995, Porter Troupe Gallery, San Diego, 1996; group shows include La Jolla Mus. Contemporary Arts, 1973, 78, 79, 81, 86, U. Sao Paulo (Brazil) Mus. Contemporary Art, 1980, Mus. Photog. Arts, San Deigo, 1987; represented in permanent collections Mus. Photog. Arts, Oakland (Calif.) Mus., La Jolla Mus. Contemporary Arts, Ariz. State U., Tempe; artist book collections: Getty Mus., San Francisco Mus. Contemporary Art, Mus. Modern Art N.Y.C., Chgo. Art Inst., UCLA, Nat. Mus. Women in the Arts, Washington. Recipient 1st prize juried show San Diego Pub. TV, 1978. Home and Studio: PO Box 2735 La Jolla CA 92038-2735

FREDMANN, MARTIN, ballet artistic director, educator, choreographer; b. Balt., Feb. 3, 1943; s. Martin Joseph and Hilda Adele (Miller) F.; m. Kaleriya Fedicheva, Jan. 2, 1973 (div.); m. Patricia Renzetti, June 12, 1980. Student, Nat. Ballet Sch., Washington, 1962-64, Vaganova Sch., Leningrad, 1972. Prin. dancer The Md. Ballet, Balt., 1961-64; dancer The Pa. Ballet, Phila., 1964-65, Ballet of the Met. Opera Co., N.Y.C., 1965-66; prin. dancer Dortmund (Fed. Republic Germany) Ballet, 1973-75, Scapino Ballet, Amsterdam, Holland, 1975-76; tchr. German Opera Ballet, West Berlin, Fed. Republic Germany, 1979, Netherlands Dance Theater, 1979, Royal Swedish Ballet, 1980, San Francisco Ballet, 1981; tchr., coach Australian Ballet, 1982; tchr. Tokyo City Ballet, Hong Kong Ballet, 1985, 86, 87, London Festival Ballet, 1981-83; dir. ballet Teatro Comunale, Florence, Italy, 1984-85; artistic dir. Tampa (Fla.) Ballet, 1984-90; artistic dir. in alliance with The Tampa Ballet Colo. Ballet, Denver, 1987-90; artistic dir. Colo. Ballet, 1987—; tchr. German Opera Ballet, 1982, Ballet Rambert, London, Bat Dor summer course, Israel, 1983, Cullberg Ballet, Sweden, 1983, Hong Kong Acad. For Performing Arts, 1985, 86, 87, 89, 91, Tokyo City Ballet, 1985, 86, 87, 89, 90, Ballet West, 1990, Nat. Ballet Korea, 1991, Dance Divsn. Tsoying High Sch., Kaohsiung, Taiwan, R.O.C., 1992; guest lectr., tchr. Cen. Ballet China, Beijing Dancing Acad., P.L.A. Arts Coll., Beijing, 1990; tchr. Legat Sch., 1978, examiner, 1980; tchr. Eglevsky Sch., N.Y.C., 1980; asst. dir., ballet master Niavaron Cultural ctr., Tehran, Iran, 1978; tchr. Ballet Arts Sch. Carnegie Hall, N.Y.C., 1979-81, choreographer Estonia Nat. Theatre, USSR, 1991; dir. Marin Ballet, Calif., 1981. Choreographer Romeo and Juliet, 1983, Sachertorte, 1984, A Little Love, 1984, Ricordanza, 1986, Cinderella, 1986, Coppelia, 1987, The Nutcracker, 1987, Beauty and the Beast, 1988, Masquerade Suite, 1989, Silent Woods, 1989, The Last Songs, 1991, Centenial Suite, 1994. Mem. Am. Guild Mus. Artists, Fla. State Dance Assn., Nat. Assn. Regional Ballet. Home: 836 E 17th Ave Apt 3A Denver CO 80218-1449 Office: Colo Ballet 1278 Lincoln St Denver CO 80203-2114

FREDRICKS, SHIRLEY JEAN, foundation director, consultant; b. Dallas; m. Robert Emmett Fredricks; children: Laura, Robert, David, Jonathan, Lisa. BS, Marquette U. Rschr., writer USIA, Washington; nonprofit cons.; exec. dir., pres. Lawrence Welk Found., Santa Monica, Calif., 1980—; bd. dirs. L.A. Urban Funders; mem. Coun. on Founds.; adv. com. Family Philanthropy, vice chair Family Philanthropy Com.; chmn. Nat. Family Found. Conf., 1991; charter mem. L.A. Women's Movement, Santa Monica. Named Corp. Woman of Yr., Battered Women's Movement, Santa Monica, 1990; recipient Humanitarian award Nat. Conf. Christians and Jews, Santa Monica, 1993, and numerous other nonprofit awards. Mem. Soc. Calif. Assn. for Philanthropy (comms. com.). Office: Lawrence Welk Found 1299 Ocean Ave Ste 800 Santa Monica CA 90401-1040

FREEBERG, ERIC O., lawyer, real estate developer; b. L.A., Dec. 14, 1951; s. George F. and Inga M. Jonsdottir; m. Sandra L. Durrett, Aug. 19, 1972; children: Larisa, Kristina, Jon. BA in History, U. Calif., Santa Cruz; JD, U. Calif., Berkeley. Ptnr. Luce, Forward, Hamilton & Scripps, San Diego, 1979-92; pvt. practice Rancho Santa Fe, 1992—; real estate developer, 1982—; pres., chmn. various cos. U.S., 1984—; mediator Calif., 1993—; chmn., counsel E/Risk Info. Svcs., Santa Clara, Calif., 1996—. pro bono counsel, mem. Bethlehem Luth. Ch., Encinitas, Calif., 1982—; mem. fin. com. various Rep. candidates. Mem. Calif. Bar Assn., San Diego County Bar Assn., San Diego Dispute Resolution Forum, Calif. Dispute Resolution Forum, La Jolla Golden Triangle Rotary Club (chmn. world cmty. dist. 5340 San Diego County 1995—). Republican. Lutheran. Home: PO Box 8884 Rancho Santa Fe CA 92067 Office: PO Box 9440 Rancho Santa Fe CA 92067

FREED, CURT RICHARD, pharmacology educator; b. Seattle, Jan. 14, 1943; m. Nancy F. Freed. BA, Harvard U., 1965, MD, 1969. Lic. physician, Colo. Intern then resident Harbor Gen. Hosp., Torrance, Calif., 1969-71; resident Mass. Gen. Hosp., Boston, 1971-72; postdoctoral fellow U. Calif. Med. Ctr., San Francisco, 1972-75; asst. prof. medicine and pharmacology U. Colo. Sch. Medicine, Denver, 1975-81, assoc. prof. medicine and pharmacology, 1981-87, prof. medicine and pharmacology, 1987—, prof., head clin. pharm. divsn., 1993—, dir. neural transplantation program for Parkinson's disease, 1988—, dir. neurosci. ctr., 1997—. Contbg. author 3 revs. and books; contbr. 185 abstracts and 86 articles to profl. jours. Mem. rsch. com. Colo. Heart Assn., 1980-86, dir. rsch. com., 1981-84. Recipient Pharm. Mfrs. Assn. Found. faculty devel. award, 1976-79; scholar Harvard U., 1961; grantee NIH, 1978—. Mem. Assn. of Am. Physicians, Am. Soc. Clin. Investigation, Am. Soc. Clin. Pharm. and Therapeutics, Am. Soc. Pharmacology and Exptl. Therapeutics, Am. Soc. Neural Transplantation, Internat. Peptide Soc., Western Assn. Physicians, Internat. Soc. Devel. Neurosci., Am. Fedn. Clin. Rsch., Soc. for Neurosci., Sigma Xi. Office: U Colo Sch Medicine 4200 E 9th Ave # C 237 Denver CO 80220-3706

FREED, PETER QUENTIN, amusement park executive; b. Salt Lake City, Jan. 8, 1921; s. Lester David and Jasmine (Young) F.; B.A. with honors, U. Utah, 1947; children—David Wicker, Michael Stahle, Howard Eldred, Anne, Kristen, Jennifer. Pres., Freed Corp., 1952-74; v.p., sec., Freed Co., 1952-74; exec. v.p. Amusement Service, Salt Lake City, 1947—; v.p. Terrace Co., Salt Lake City, from 1952; exec. v.p. Patio Gardens, Farmington, Utah, from 1956; v.p. Westworld Corp., Salt Lake City, from 1974, Pioneer Village Campground, Farmington, from 1975; dir. Pioneer Village, Farmington; pres. Lagoon Corp., Salt Lake City, 1974—. Mem. Union Sta. Theatre Bd. Served with USNR, 1942-45. Mem. Nat. Assn. Amusement Parks, Utah Mus. Assn. Republican. Christian Scientist. Clubs: Salt Lake Tennis, New Yorker. Home: 642 Aloha Rd Salt Lake City UT 84103-3329 Office: Box N Farmington UT 84025

FREEDMAN, BART JOSEPH, lawyer; b. New Haven, Sept. 27, 1955; s. Lawrence Zelic and Dorothy (Robinson) F.; m. Esme Detweiler, Sept. 28, 1985; children: Luke Edward, Samuel Meade, Benjamin Zelic. BA, Carleton Coll., 1977; JD, U. Pa., 1982. Bar: Wash. 1984, U.S. Dist. Ct. (we. dist.) Wash. 1984, U.S. Ct. Appeals (9th cir.) 1985, U.S. Dist. Ct. (ea. dist.) Wash. 1988. Law clk. to chief justice Samuel Roberts Supreme Ct. Pa., Erie, 1982-83; asst. city solicitor City of Phila., 1984; assoc. Perkins Coie, Seattle, 1984-90; ptnr. Preston Gates & Ellis, Seattle, 1990—. Editor: Natural Resource Damages, 1993. Bd. dirs. Seattle Metrocenter YMCA, 1988—, chmn. 1993-97; bd. dirs. Leadership Tomorrow, 1996-97; chair Sierra Club Inner City Outings Program, Seattle, 1986-90; chair bd. advisors Earth Svc. Corps/YMCA, Seattle, 1990—. Mem. ABA (com. on corp. counsel 1985—), Wash. State Bar Assn., Seattle-King County Bar Assn. (participant neighborhood legal clinics 1985-94). Office: Preston Gates & Ellis 701 5th Ave Ste 5000 Seattle WA 98104-7016

FREEDMAN, DAVID NOEL, religion educator; b. N.Y.C., May 12, 1922; s. David and Beatrice (Goodman) F.; m. Cornelia Anne Pryor, May 16, 1944; children: Meredith Anne, Nadezhda, David Micaiah, Jonathan Pryor. Student, CCNY, 1935-38; AB, UCLA, 1939; BTh, Princeton Theol. Sem., 1944; PhD, Johns Hopkins U., 1948; LittD, U. Pacific, 1973; ScD, Davis and Elkins Coll., 1974. Ordained to ministry Presbyn. Ch., 1944; supply pastor in Acme and Deming, Wash., 1944-45; tchg. fellow, then asst. instr. Johns Hopkins U., 1946-48; asst. prof., then prof. Hebrew and Old Testament lit. Western Theol. Sem., Pitts., 1948-60; prof. Pitts. Theol. Sem., 1960-61, James A. Kelso prof., 1961-64; prof. Old Testament San Francisco Theol. Sem., 1964-70, Gray prof. Hebrew exegesis, 1970-71, dean of faculty, 1966-70, acting dean of sem., 1970-71; prof. Old Testament Grad. Theol. Union, Berkeley, Calif., 1964-71; prof. dept. Nr. Ea. studies U. Mich., Ann Arbor, 1971-92, Thurnau prof. Bibl. studies, 1984-92, dir. program on studies in religion, 1971-91; prof., endowed chair in Hebrew Bibl. studies U. Calif., San Diego, 1987—; coord. religious studies program U. Calif., 1989—; Danforth vis. prof. Internat. Christian U., Tokyo, 1967; vis. prof. Hebrew U., Jerusalem, 1977, Macquarie U., N.S.W., Australia, 1980, U. Queensland (Australia), 1982, 84, U. Calif., San Diego, 1985-87; Green vis. prof. Tex. Christian U., Ft. Worth, 1981; dir. Albright Inst. Archeol. Rsch., 1969-70, dir., 1976-77; centennial lectr. Johns Hopkins U., 1976; Dahood lectr. Loyola U., 1983; Soc. Bibl. Lit. meml. lectr., 1983, Smithsonian lectr., 1984; prin. bibl. cons. Reader's Digest, 1984, 88, 89, 90, 94; disting. faculty lectr. Univ. Mich., 1988; Stone lectr. Princeton Theol. Sem., 1989; Mowinckel lectr., Oslo U., 1991; lectr. Uppsala U., Sweden, 1991; vis. lectr. Brigham Young Ctr. Near Eastern Studies, Jerusalem, 1993. Co-author: (with J.D. Smart) God Has Spoken, 1949, (with F.M. Cross, Jr.) Early Hebrew Orthography, 1952, (with John M. Allegro) The People of the Dead Sea Scrolls, 1958, (with R.M. Grant) The Secret Sayings of Jesus, 1960, (with F.M. Cross, Jr.) Ancient Yahwistic Poetry, 1964, rev. edit., 1975, 95, (with M. Dothan) Ashdod I, 1967, The Published Works of W.F. Albright, 1975, (with L.G. Running) William F. Albright: Twentieth Century Genius, 1975, 2d edit., 1991, (with B. Mazar, G. Cornfeld) The Mountain of the Lord, 1975, (with W. Phillips) An Explorer's Life of Jesus, 1975, (with G. Cornfeld) Archaeology of the Bible: Book by Book, 1976, Pottery, Poetry and Prophecy, 1980, (with K.A. Mathews) The Paleo-Hebrew Leviticus Scroll, 1985, The Unity of the Hebrew Bible, 1991, (with D. Forbes and F. Andersen) Studies in Hebrew and Aramaic Orthography, 1992,(with Sara Mandell) The Relationship between Herodotus' History and Primary History, 1993; co-author, editor: (with F. Andersen) Anchor Bible Series Hosea, 1980, Anchor Bible Series Amos, 1989; editor: (with G.E. Wright) The Biblical Archaeologist, Reader I, 1961, (with E.F. Campbell, Jr.) The Biblical Archaeologist, Reader 2, 1964, Reader 3, 1970, Reader 4, 1983, (with W.F. Albright) The Anchor Bible, 1964—, including, Genesis, 1964, James, Peter and Jude, 1964, Jeremiah, 1965, Job, 1965, 2d edit., 1973, Proverbs and Ecclesiastes, 1965, I Chronicles, II Chronicles, Ezra-Nehemiah, 1965, Psalms I, 1966, John I, 1966, Acts of the Apostles, 1967, II Isaiah, 1968, Psalms II, 1968, John II, 1970, Psalms III, 1970, Esther, 1971, Matthew, 1971, Lamentations, 1972, 2d edit., 1992, To the Hebrews, 1972, Ephesians 1-3, 4-6, 1974, I and II Esdras, 1974, Judges, 1975, Revelation, 1975, Ruth, 1975, I Maccabees, 1976, I Corinthians, 1976, Additions, 1977, Song of Songs, 1977, Daniel, 1978, Wisdom of Solomon, 1979, I Samuel, 1980, Hosea, 1980, Luke I, 1981, Joshua, 1982, Epistles of John, 1983, II Maccabees, 1983, II Samuel, 1984, II Corinthians, 1984, Luke II, 1985, Judith, 1985, Mark, 1986, Haggai-Zechariah 1-8, 1987, Ecclesiasticus, 1987, 2 Kings, 1988, Amos, 1989, Titus, 1990, Jonah, 1990, Leviticus I, 1991, Deuteronomy I, 1991, Numbers 1-20, 1993, Romans, 1993, Jude and 2 Peter, 1993, Zechariah 9-14, 1993, Zephaniah, 1994, Colossians, 1995, Joel, 1995, James, 1995, Obadiah, 1996, Tobit, 1996; editor Anchor Bible Ref. Libr., Jesus Within Judaism, 1988, Archeology of the Land of the Bible, 1990, The Tree of Life, 1990, A Marginal Jew Vol. 1, 1991, The Pentateuch, 1991, The Rise of Jewish Nationalism, 1992, History and Prophecy, 1993, Jesus and the Dead Sea Scrolls, 1993, The Birth of the Messiah, 1993, The Death of the Messiah, 2 vols., 1994, Introduction to Rabbinical Literature, 1994, A Marginal Jew, vol. 2, 1994, The Scepter and the Star, 1995, (with J. Greenfield) New Directions in Biblical Archaeology, 1969, (with J.A. Baird) The Computer Bible, 1971, A Critical Concordance to the Synoptic Gospels, 1971, An Analytic Linguistic Concordance to the Book of Isaiah, 1971, I, II, III John: Forward and Reverse Concordance and Index, 1971, A Critical Concordance to Hosea, Amos, Micah, 1972, A Critical Concordance of Haggai, Zechariah, Malachi, 1973, A Critical Concordance to the Gospel of John, 1974, A Synoptic Concordance of Aramaic Inscriptions, 1975, A Linguistic Concordance of Ruth and Jonah, 1976, A Linguistic Concordance of Jeremiah, 1978, Syntactical and Critical Concordance of Jeremiah, 1978, Synoptic Abstract, 1978, I and II Corinthians, 1979, Zechariah, 1979, Galatians, 1980, Ephesians, 1981, Philippians, 1982, Colossians, 1983, Pastoral Epistles, 1984, 1 & 2 Thessalaians, 1985, Density Plots in Ezekiel, 1986, Exodus, 1987, Hebrews, 1988, Ruth, 1989, James, 1991, 1 & 2 Peter, 1991, 1, 2 & 3 John and Jude, 1991, Psalms, Job and Proverbs, 1992, Apocalypse, 1993, The Pentateuch, 1995, Aramaic Inscriptions, 1975, (with T. Kachel) Religion and the Academic Scene, 1975, Am. Schs. Oriental Research publs; co-editor: Scrolls from Qumran Cave I, 1972, Jesus: The Four Gospels, 1973, Pomegranates and Golden Bells, 1995; Reader's Digest editor: Atlas of the Bible, 1981, Family Guide to the Bible, 1984, Mysteries of the Bible, 1988, Who's Who in the Bible, 1994, The Bible Through the Ages, 1996; assoc. editor Jour. Bible Lit., 1952-54, editor, 1955-59; cons. editor Interpreter's Dictionary of the Bible, 1957-60, Theologisches Wörterbuch des Alten Testaments, 1970-92, English Translation Theological Word-Book of the Old Testament, 1975—; editor in chief The Anchor Bible Dictionary, 6 vols., 1992; co-editor (with W.H. Propp and Baruch Halpern) The Hebrew Bible and Its Interpreters, 1990; contbr. numerous articles to profl. jours. Recipient prize in New Testament exegesis Princeton Theol. Sem., 1943, Carey-Thomas award for Anchor Bible, 1965, Layman's Nat. Bible Com. award, 1978, 3 awards for Anchor Bible Bibl. Archaeol. Soc., 1993; William H. Green fellow in Old Testament, 1944, William S. Rayner fellow Johns Hopkins U., 1946, 47, Guggenheim fellow, 1959, Am. Assn. Theol. Schs. fellow, 1963; Am. Coun. Learned Socs. grantee-in-aid, 1967, 76. Fellow U. Mich. Soc. Fellows (sr., chmn. 1980-82); mem. Soc. Bibl. Lit. (pres. 1975-76), Am. Oriental Soc., Am. Schs. Oriental Rsch. (v.p. 1970-82, editor bull. 1974-78, editor Bibl. Archeologist 1976-82, dir. publs. 1974-82), Archaeol. Inst. Am., Am. Acad. Religion, Bibl. Colloquium (sec.-treas. 1960-90). Office: U Calif San Diego Dept History 0104 9500 Gilman Dr La Jolla CA 92093-5003

FREEDMAN, GAIL, financial analyst; b. Oyster Bay, N.Y., Dec. 26, 1963; d. Noble Aubrey and Dorothy Ann Langille; m. Jonathan Eric Freedman, Oct. 23, 1993. BA in Polit. Sci., Bethany (W.Va.) Coll., 1986; MBA in Mktg. and Fin., U. So. Calif., 1992; student, UCLA, 1996—. Cert. in healthcare mgmt. Legis. intern legis. affairs Dept. Treasury, Washington, 1985, adminstrv. asst. adminstrn., 1986, rsch. asst. legis. affairs, 1986-88; spl. asst. Congressman Thomas McMillen, Washington, 1988; sr. legal asst. Pepper, Hamilton & Scheetz, Washington, 1988-90; cons. L.A. County Dept. Transp., 1990-91; licensing intern Applause Co., Woodland Hills, Calif., 1991; mgr. rsch. unit Tobacco Control Program, L.A., 1992-93; fin. analyst L.A. County Dept. Health Svcs., PHP Fin. Mgmt., 1993-95, PacifiCare of Calif, Cypress, 1995—; mentor to students U. So. Calif. Grad. Sch. Bus., L.A., 1991—. Author: (poetry) Fortnight, 1981, The Harbinger, 1985; author commentary newspaper The Tower, 1985-86. Founder, singer Sunday Sound, L.A., 1993—. Mem. U. So. Calif. Commerce Assn., Healthcare Fin. Mgmt. Assn., Kappa Delta Konnection. Home: 512 S Ogden Dr Los Angeles CA 90036-3231 Office: PacifiCare of Calif 5701 Katella Ave Cypress CA 90630-5019

FREEDMAN, GREGG, real estate appraisal company executive; b. Burbank, Calif., Feb. 1, 1957; s. Morton Ira and Charlotte (Chernick) F.; m. Laura Jean Anderson, May 20, 1989; 1 child, Hillary Anne. Student, U. So. Calif., Calif. State U., L.A. Cert. gen. real estate appraiser Calif.; cert. rev. appraiser, sr. cert. prof. appraiser, cert. comml. property appraiser, cert. real estate owned appraiser, cert. appraiser. Appraiser, mgr. Freedman and Freedman Cons., Monrovia, Calif., 1984-88; pres. Gregg Freedman and Assocs., Inc., Pasadena, Calif., 1988—; Tchr. real estate appraisal classes Monrovia H.S. Adult Edn.; bd. dirs. Pacific Commerce Fed. Credit Union. Prodr. Music Theater of So. Calif. Former commr. City of Duarte Econ. Devel. Coun.; bd. dirs. Meth. Hosp. Arcadia Found. Fellow Coll. Real Estate Appraisers; mem. Appraisal Inst. (assoc.), U. So. Calif. Alumni Assn. Home: 195 S Canon Ave Sierra Madre CA 91024-2601 Office: G Freedman & Assocs 468N Rosemead Bl Ste 103 Pasadena CA 91107

FREEDMAN, JONATHAN BORWICK, journalist, author, lecturer; b. Rochester, N.Y., Apr. 11, 1950; s. Marshall Arthur and Betty (Borwick) F.; m. Maggie Locke, May 4, 1979; children: Madigan, Nicholas. AB in Lit. cum laude, Columbia Coll., N.Y.C., 1972. Reporter AP of Brazil, Sao Paulo and Rio de Janeiro, 1974-75; editorial writer The Tribune, San Diego, 1981-90; syndicated columnist Copley News Service, San Diego, 1987-89; freelance opinion writer L.A. Times, 1990—; free-lance editorial writer N.Y. Times, 1990-91; dist. vis. lectr. and adj. faculty San Diego State U., 1990—; mem. U.S.-Japan Journalists Exch. Program, Internat. Press Inst., 1985. Author, illustrator: The Man Who'd Bounce the World, 1979; author: The Editorials and Essays of Jonathan Freedman, 1988; contbg. author: Best Newspaper Writing, From Contemporary Culture, 1991, (nonfiction) From Cradle to Grave: The Human Face of Poverty in America, 1993; freelance columnist, 1979-81; contbr. articles to N.Y. Times, Chgo. Tribune, San Francisco Examiner, Oakland Tribune, others. Moderator PBS, San Diego, 1988; bd. dirs. Schs. of the Future Commn., San Diego, 1987. Recipient Copley Ring of Truth award, 1983, Sigma Delta Chi award, 1983, San Diego Press Club award, 1984, Spl. citation Columbia Grad. Sch. Journalism, 1985, Disting. Writing award Am. Soc. Newspaper Editors, 1986, Pulitzer prize in Disting. Editorial Writing, 1987; Cornell Woolrich Writing fellow Columbia U., 1972, Eugene C. Pullian Editorial Writing fellow Sigma Delta Chi Found., 1986, Media fellow Hoover Instn., Stanford, Calif., 1991, Kaiser Media fellow, 1995. Mem. Soc. Profl. Journalists (Disting. Svc. award 1985, Casey medal for meritorious journalism 1994), Nat. Conf. Editl. Writers, Authors Guild, Phi Beta Kappa. Jewish. Office: 4506 Adair St San Diego CA 92107-3804

FREEDMAN, ROBERT ALLEN, arts executive; m. Leslie Thompson; 1 child, Leigh Karen. BA in Dramatic Art, Rutgers Univ.; postgrad., Bklyn. Coll. Exec. dir. Clemens Ctr., Elmira, N.Y., 1980-83; mgr. Ohio Theater, Columbus, 1983-84; exec. dir. Zeiterion Theatre, Mass., 1984-90; dir. Portland (Oreg.) Ctr. Performing Arts, 1990-94; v.p. performing arts Calif. Ctr. for the Arts., Escondido, 1994-97; acting CEO, pres. Calif. Ctr. for the Arts, Escondido, 1997—; guest lectr., instr. Drexel U., Elmira Coll., Kean Coll., Bklyn. Coll.; bd. dirs. Internat. Soc. of Performing Arts Administrs., First Night, San Diego Performing Arts League, Escondido Downtown Bus. Assn.; Nat. Endowment for the Arts Site visitor, 1983-84. Author: The Clemens Center Story-Finger Lakes Living, 1981; prodr. theater, N.Y., Phila., Mass.; chaired various com. orgns.; spkr., presenter, panelist, moderator numerous confs. Mem. facilities task force Portland's Arts Plan 2000; bd. dirs. First Night Escondido, San Diego Performing Arts League. Mem. Internat. Soc. Performing Arts, Assn. Performing Arts Presenters, Internat. Assn. Assembly Mgrs. Office: Calif Ctr Arts Escondido 340 N Escondido Blvd Escondido CA 92025

FREELAND, DARRYL CREIGHTON, psychologist, educator; b. Omaha, Feb. 22, 1939; s. Elverson Lafayette and Lauretta Joyce (Coffelt) F.; m. Tina Anne Richmond, July 21, 1979; children—Adam Daniel, Noah Nathan, Sarah Eileen. B.S., U. Nebr., 1961; S.T.B., Fuller Theol. Sem., 1965; M.A., Calif. State U.-Fullerton, 1966; Ph.D., U. So. Calif., 1972. Lic. psychologist, Calif. Tchr. elem. schs., Calif., 1961-66; instr. Glendale Community Coll., Calif., 1966-67, Citrus Community Coll., Glendora, Calif., 1967-79; pvt. practice psychology, Laguna Niguel, Calif., 1969—; field faculty and vis. prof. Calif. State U.-Los Angeles, 1970, San Marino Community Presbyterian Ch., 1972, Calif. Sch. Profl. Psychology, Los Angeles, 1972-73, U. Calif.-Riverside, 1973, Humanistic Psychology Inst., San Francisco, 1976-79, U. Humanistic Studies, San Diego, 1983; assoc. prof. psychology and family U.S. Internat. U., 1986—; asst. dir. clin. psychology tng. Marriage and Family Therapy Tng., 1986-89; pvt. post-secondary com. for qualitative rev. and assessment of licensure Calif. Dept. Edn., 1989-97. Finisher, Newport Beach-Irvine Marathon, 1981, San Francisco Marathon, 1982, Long Beach Marathon, 1988. Office: 30131 Town Center Dr Ste 298 Laguna Niguel CA 92677-2040

FREELAND, ROBERT FREDERICK, retired librarian; b. Flint, Mich., Dec. 20, 1919; s. Ralph V. and Susan Barbara (Goetz) F.; m. June Voshel, June 18, 1948; children: Susan Beth Visser, Kent Richard. BS, Eastern Mich. U., 1942; postgrad., Washington & Lee U., 1945; MS, U. So. Calif., 1948, postgrad., 1949; postgrad., U. Mich., 1950-52, Calif. State U., 1956-58, UCLA, 1960; LittD (hon.), Linda Vista Bible Coll., 1973. Music supr. Consol. Schs. Warren, Mich., 1946-47; music dir. Carson City (Mich.) Pub. Schs., 1948-49; librarian, audio-visual coord. Ford Found., Edison Inst., Greenfield Village, Dearborn, Mich., 1950-52, Helix High Sch. Library, 1952-77; librarian, prof. library sci. Linda Vista Bible Coll., 1976—; reference libr. San Diego Pub. Libr. System, 1967—; cons. edn., libr. and multimedia. Editor book and audio-visual aids review, Sch. Musician, Dir. and Teacher, 1950-75. Former deacon and elder Christian Reform Ch., libr., 1969-72, Classis archivist, 1991—; pub. affairs officer, sr. program officer, moral leadership officer Sq. 57 GP III, Calif. wing CAP. With USAAF, 1942-46. Named Scholar Freedoms Found., Valley Forge, Pa., 1976-80. Mem. NEA (life), ALA, Calif. Tchrs. Assn., Music Libr. Assn. So. Calif. (adviser exec. bd.), Calif. Libr. Assn. (pres. Palomar chpt. 1972-73), Sch. Libr. Assn. Calif. (treas. 1956-73), Calif. Media and Libr. Educators (charter mem.), Am. Legion (Americanism chmn. 22d dist. San Diego County, chmn. oratorical contest com. La Mesa post), Ret. Officers Assn., San Diego Aero Space Mus., San Diego Mus. Art. Home: 4800 Williamsburg Ln Apt 223 La Mesa CA 91941-4651

FREEMAN, DAVID M., educator; b. Glendive, Mont., Jan. 29, 1939; s. Simon Peter and Helen Luella (Adkins) F.; m. Sandra Kay Bradford, Aug. 30, 1960; children: Brent Simon, Bradford Russell, Bryan James, Rebecca Joyce. BA, Rocky Mountain Coll., 1961; MPIA, U. Pitts., 1965; PhD, U. Denver, 1968. Prof., chmn. Dept. Sociology Colo. State U., Ft. Collins, 1967—. Author: Technology and Society, 1974, Local Organization for Social Development, 1989, Choice Against Choice, 1992. Mem. AAAS, Am. Sociol. Assn., Am. Polit. Sci. Assn., Policy Studies Assn. Office: Colo State U Dept Sociology Fort Collins CO 80523

FREEMAN, FILLMORE, chemist, educator. BS magna cum laude, Ctrl. State U., Wilberforce, Ohio, 1957; PhD, Mich. State U., 1962. Rsch. chemist Calif. Rsch. Corp., Richmond, 1962-64; asst. prof., assoc. prof. chemistry Calif. State Univ., Long Beach, 1965-73; assoc. prof. chemistry Univ. Calif., Irvine, 1973-75, prof. chemistry, 1975—; vis. prof. Univ. Paris, 1971-72, Max-PlanckúInst., Göttingen, Germany, 1977, 78, Inst. Chimie Substances Naturelles, Gif-sur-Yvette, France, 1982, 85; assoc. dean sch. physical scis., Univ. Calif., Irvine, 1974, vice chair chemistry dept., 1987-89, acting chair, 1988, vis. scholar, ULCA, 1991, 93, 94; adj. prof. chemistry Univ. Ill., Chgo., 1976; vis. scientist, program dir. organic and macromolecular chemistry NSF, Washington, 1989-90; mem. review panel undergraduate rsch. participation program, NSF, 1976, pre-coll. tchr. devel. in sci., 1978; mem. adv. panel postdoctoral fellowship NSF NATO, 1980, 95, rsch. experiences for undergraduates, NSF, 1989; mem. site visit team minority biol. rsch. support NIH, 1986; mem. adv. com. minority biol. rsch. support Calif. State Univ., Long Beach, 1988-95, joint rsch. Howard Univ., 1990; mem. rsch. improvement in minority inst. panel NSF, 1988, 89, 90; mem. rsch. careers for minority scholars panel NSF, 1991, 92, 95; mem. minority grad. fellowship orogram NRC-NAS-NSF, 1991, 1991, 92; mem. young investigators panel NSF, 1993; mem. RFA CA-94-030 panel NIH, 1995. NIH fellow, 1964-65, Alexander von Humboldt Found. fellow, 1977, 78; Fulbright-Hays sr. rsch. scholar, 1977; inducted into Ctrl. State Univ. Hall of Fame, 1992. Fellow Chem. Soc. (Disting. Mil. Grad.), Am. Inst. Chemists.; mem. AAAS, Am. Chem. Soc., Nat. Congress Black Faculty, Calif. Assn. Chemistry Tchrs., Calif. Black Faculty Staff Assn., Chem. Soc., London, Mich. State Chemists Assn., Nat. Orgn. Black Chemists Chem. Engrs., Coblentz Soc., Wash. Orgn. Black Scis., Yale Chemists Assn., N.Y. Acad. Scis., Beta Kappa Chi, Sigma Xi, Alpha Kappa Mu. Office: Dept Chemistry Univ Calif Irvine CA 92697-2025

FREEMAN, ION CHALMERS, health provider; b. Boston, Apr. 25, 1968; s. Mark Phillips and Helen (Millin) F. BA, Rutgers U., 1989; postgrad., U. Wash., 1992-95. Asst. mgr. Cooper Grant Campus Gen. Store, Camden, N.J., 1987-89; tchr. U.S. Peace Corps, Kisii, Kenya, 1989-91; sci. explainer Pacific Sci. Ctr., Seattle, 1992-94; rsch. asst. U. Wash., Seattle, 1992-95; program asst. Group Health Coop., Seattle, 1995-96. Coord. 25th anniversary Cascade Bicycle Club, Seattle, 1995. Presbyterian. Home: 1400 Hubbell Pl # 601 Seattle WA 98101

FREEMAN, JOHN FRANCIS, foundation executive; b. London, Feb. 18, 1940; came to U.S., 1940; BA in History, Antioch Coll., 1963; MA in European History, U. Mich., 1964, PhD in Early Modern Europe, 1969. Asst. prof. Calif. Poly., Pomona, 1966-69, Calif. State U., Northridge, 1969-71; dean West Wyoming Community Coll., Rock Springs, Wyo., 1971-74; asst. dean arts and sci. U. Wyo., Laramie, 1974-86; exec. dir. Wyo. Vol. Assistance Corp., Laramie, 1986-89; pres. Wyo. Community Found., Laramie, 1989—. Co-author: Citizens & Clergy of Grasse, 1988; contbr. articles to profl. jours. Mem. Wyo. Arts Coun., 1973-85, chmn., 1983-85. Woodrow Wilson fellow, 1963-64, Univ. fellow U. Mich., 1964-65. Mem. Agrl. Hist. Soc., French Hist. Studies, Rotary. Office: Wyo Community Found PO Box 4008 Laramie WY 82071-4008

FREEMAN, LESLIE JEAN, neuropsychologist, researcher; b. San Diego, Feb. 17, 1965; d. Richard Joseph and Jean Doris (Weber) Currier; m. Drue Scott Freeman, Sept. 6, 1986. BA, U. Calif., Irvine, 1989; MA in Clin. Psychology, Antioch U., L.A., 1992; postgrad., Calif. Sch. Profl. Psychology, Fresno, 1993—. Marriage, family and child counselor intern So. Calif. Counseling Ctr., L.A., 1990-93; marriage, family, child counselor intern/psychology intern Bakersfield (Calif.) Med. Hosp., 1993-94; intern, resident in neuropsychology pvt. practice and Drs. Hosp., Modesto, Calif., 1994—; guest lectr. in field. Contbr. articles to profl. jours. Mem. APA, Nat. Acad. Neuropsychology, Internat. Neuropsychol. Soc., Am. Neuropsychiat. Assn., Calif. Assn. Marriage and Family Therapy, Calif. Assn. Psychology Providers. Home: 2079 Flintcrest Dr San Jose CA 95148-1229 Office: The Darrell Bldg Ste 440 1601 I St Modesto CA 95354

FREEMAN, NEIL, accounting and computer consulting firm executive; b. Reading, Pa., Dec. 27, 1948; s. Leroy Harold and Audrey Todd (Dornhecker) F.; m. Janice Lum, Nov. 20, 1981. BS, Albright Coll., 1979; MS, Kennedy-Western U., 1987, PhD, 1988. Cert. systems profl., data processing specialist, info. system security profl. Acct. Jack W. Long & Co., Mt. Penn, Pa., 1977-78; comptroller G.P.C., Inc., Bowmansville, Pa., 1978-79; owner Neil Freeman Cons., Bowmansville, 1980-81; program mgr., systems cons. Application Systems, Honolulu, 1981-82; instr. Chaminade U., Honolulu, 1983-96; owner Neil Freeman Cons., Kaneohe, Hawaii, 1982-96, Grand Junction, Colo., 1996—. Author: (computer software) NFC Property Management, 1984, NFC Mailing List, 1984; (book) Learning Dibol, 1984. Served with USN, 1966-68, Vietnam. Mem. Nat. Assn. Accts., Am. Inst. Cert. Computer Profls., Assn. Systems Mgmt. Office: PO Box 60070 Grand Junction CO 81506

FREEMAN, PATRICIA ELIZABETH, library and education specialist; b. El Dorado, Ark., Nov. 30, 1924; d. Herbert A. and M. Elizabeth (Pryor) Harper; m. Jack Freeman, June 15, 1949; 3 children. BA, Centenary Coll., 1943; postgrad., Fine Arts Ctr., 1942-46, Art Students League, 1944-45; BSLS, La. State U., 1946; postgrad., Calif. State U., 1959-61, U. N.Mex., 1964-74, EdS, Peabody Coll., Vanderbilt U., 1975. Libr. U. Calif., Berkeley, 1946-47; libr. Albuquerque Pub. Schs., 1964-67, ind. sch. libr. media ctr. cons., 1967—. Painter lithographer; one-person show La. State Exhibit Bldg., 1948; author: Pathfinder: An Operational Guide for the School Librarian, 1975, Southeast Heights Neighborhoods of Albuquerque, 1993; compiler, editor: Elizabeth Pryor Harper's Twenty-One Southern Families, 1985; editor: SEHNA Gazette, 1988-93. Mem. task force Goals for Dallas-Environ., 1977-82; pres. Friends of Sch. Librs., Dallas, 1979-83; v.p., editor Southeast Heights Neighborhood Assn., 1988-93. With USAF, 1948-49. Honoree AAUW Ednl. Found., 1979; vol. award for outstanding service Dallas Ind. Sch. Dist., 1978; AAUW Pub. Service grantee 1980. Mem. ALA, AAUW (dir. Dallas 1976-82, Albuquerque 1983-85), LWV (sec. Dallas 1982-83, editor Albuquerque 1984-88), Nat. Trust Historic Preservation, Friends of Pub. Libr., N.Mex. Symphony Guild, Alpha Xi Delta. Home: 3016 Santa Clara Ave SE Albuquerque NM 87106-2350

FREEMAN, RICHARD J., medical products financial executive; b. Boston, Mar. 5, 1950; s. Richard T. and Helen E. (Leary) F.; m. Nancy Anne White, July 28, 1973; children: Adrienne M., Richard A. BA, Ohio Wesleyan U., 1973; MBA, Boston U., 1975. CPA, Ohio. Acct. Continental Ins. Co., Columbus, Ohio, 1975-76; sr. acct. Babcock and Wilcox, Lancaster, Ohio, 1976-79; accting. mgr. Babcock and Wilcox, Irvine, Calif., 1979-83; dir. accting. McCormick and Co./SETCO, Anaheim, Calif., 1983-87; v.p. fin. Sunrise Med./Quickie Designs, Fresno, Calif., 1987—. Auditor PTA, Fresno, 1989-91. Mem. Inst. Mgmt. Accts. (pres. Fresno chpt. 1991-92). Home: 3211 W La Costa Ave Fresno CA 93711-0227 Office: Sunrise Med/Quickie Designs 2842 N Business Park Ave Fresno CA 93727-1328

FREEMAN, VAL LEROY, geologist; b. Long Beach, Calif., June 25, 1926; s. Cecil LeRoy and Marjorie (Austin) F.; BS, U. Calif., Berkeley, 1949, MS, 1952; m. June Ione Ashlock, Sept. 26, 1959 (div. June 1962); 1 child, Jill Annette Freeman Michener; m. Elizabeth Joann Sabia, Sept. 4, 1964 (div. Oct. 1972); 1 child, Rebecca Sue Freeman Shepard; 1 stepchild, Frank J. Sabia; m. Betty M. Avey, Oct. 9, 1993. Geologist, U.S. Geol. Survey, 1949-85, Fairbanks, Alaska, 1955-57, Denver, 1957-70, 74-85, Flagstaff, Ariz., 1970-74, dep. chief coal resources br., until 1985. With USNR, 1943-45. Fellow Geol. Soc. Am. Contbr. articles to profl. jours. Home: 26 S Indiana Pl Golden CO 80401-5082

FREEMAN, WILLIAM ROSEMAN, ophthalmologist; b. N.Y.C., Aug. 21, 1953; m. Karen Fleischer; children: Elana Sarah, Samuel Robert. BA, Columbia U., 1975; student, MD, 1979. Diplomate Am. Bd. Ophthalmology; lic. physician and surgeon, Calif., N.Y. Intern Cedars Sinai

Med. Ctr./U. Calif., L.A., 1979-80; resident in ophthalmology Lenox Hill Hosp., N.Y.C., 1980-83; prof. ophthalmology U. Calif. Sch. Medicine, San Diego, 1994—; chief retina svc. dept. ophthalmology U. Calif., San Diego, dir. ophthalmic photography, resident supr. dept. ophthalmology, 1985-86, adminstrv. dir. retina svcs., 1988—, dir. vitreoretinal fellowship program, 1987—, attending physician vitreo-retinal surgeon dept. ophthalmology, 1986—; staff physician ophthalmology sect. Alhambra (Calif.) Cmty. Hosp., 1984-86, Huntington Meml. Hosp., Pasadena, Calif., 1984-86; staff physician dept. ophthalmology U. So. Calif. Med. Ctr., L.A., 1985-86; staff physician Doheny Eye Hosp., L.A., 1985—; mem. fellowship rev. panel Fight for Sight Rsch. Divsn. Nat. Soc. Prevent Blindness, 1993—; lectr. and presenter in field. Sci. reviewer Am. Jour. Ophthalmology, Archives of Ophthalmology, Critical Revs. in Immunology, Exptl. Eye Rsch., Investigative Ophthalmology and Visual Sci., Jour. AMA, Ophthalmology, Retina, Survey of Ophthalmology; editl. bd. Retina, Ophthalmology; contbr. articles to profl. jours. Francis I. Proctor Found. fellow U. Calif., 1983-84, Estelle Doheny Eye Found. fellow U. So. Calif., 1984-86. Fellow Am. Acad. Ophthalmology (Honor award 1991); mem. AMA, Am. Uveitis Soc., Aspen Retinal Detachment Soc., Assn. for Rsch. in Vision and Ophthalmology, Assn. Proctor Fellows, Fight for Sight Rsch. Div. the Nat. Soc. to Prevent Blindness, Macula Soc., Ophthalmic Microbiology and Immunology Group, Pacific Coast Oto-Ophthalmol. Soc., Retina Soc., Western Assn. for Vitreo-Retinal Edn. (founding mem.), Alpha Omega Alpha. Office: Univ Calif Shiley Eye Ctr 0946 9415 Campus Point Dr La Jolla CA 92093-0946

FREIBERG, ROBERT JERRY, physicist, engineer, technology administrator; b. Chgo., Mar. 26, 1939; s. Jerry and Mildred (Lukes) F.; m. Deanna Corrine Qualls, July 8, 1968; children: Joseph, Sean, Jamison. BS in Physics, Rensselear Poly. Inst., 1961; MS in Physics, U. Ill., 1963, PhD, 1966. Postgrad. rsch. assoc. U. Ill., Urbana, 1966-67; rsch. scientist Hughes Rsch. Labs., Malibu, Calif., 1967-69; group mgr. United Tech. Rsch. Labs., East Hartford, Conn., 1969-75; gen. mgr. United Tech., West Palm Beach, Fla., 1975-79; bus. mgr. optics TRW, Redondo Beach, Calif., 1979-83; program dir. Baxter Healthcare, Inc., Irvine, Calif., 1983-86; dir. engring. and mfg. ops. Pfizer Laser Sys., Irvine, 1986-92; dir. engring. Lumonics, Inc., Camarillo, Calif., 1992-94; sr. v.p. engring. and program mgmt. View Engring., Inc., Simi Valley, Calif., 1994-97; v.p. engring. Indsl. Electronic Engrs. Inc., Van Nuys, Calif., 1997—; mem. tech. adv. bd. Premier Laser Sys., Irvine, 1992—; numerous presentations in field. Contbr. numerous articles to Procs. IEEE, Laser Focus, Applied Optics, IEEE Jour. Quantum Electronics, Jour. Applied Physics, Phys. Rev., Applied Physics Letters, Bull. Am. Phys. Soc. Asst. scoutmaster Boy Scouts Am., Mission Viejo, Calif., 1989-92, varsity scoutmaster, Newbury Park, Calif., 1994—. Fellow NSF, 1962-66. Fellow Internat. Soc. for Optical Engring. (mem. membership com. 1994—, chmn. 1994-96); mem. IEEE, Am. Electronics Assn., Optical Soc. Am., Am. Soc. for Laser Surgery and Medicine, Nat. Ctr. Mfg. Scis. (Strategic Initiative Group com. 1995-97), Sigma Xi. Home: 325 Fox Ridge Dr Thousand Oaks CA 91361-1328 Office: Indsl Electronics Engrs 7740 Lemona Ave Van Nuys CA 91409-9234

FREIBOTT, GEORGE AUGUST, physician, chemist, priest; b. Bridgeport, Conn., Oct. 6, 1954; s. George August and Barbara Mary (Schreiber) F.; m. Jennifer Noble, July 12, 1980 (div.); children: Jessica, Heather, George; m. Arlene Ann Steiner, Aug. 1, 1982. BD, Am. Bible Coll., Pineland, Fla., 1977; BS, Nat. Coll. NHA, International Falls, Minn., 1978; ThM, Clarksville (Tenn.) Sch. Theology, 1979; MD, Western U., Phoenix, 1982; ND, Am. Coll., 1979; MsT, Fla. Sch. Massage, 1977. Diplomate Nat. Bd. Naturopathic Examiners; ordained priest Ea. Orthodox Ch., 1983. Chief mfg. cons. in oxidative chemistry Am. Soc. Med. Missionaries, Priest River, Idaho, 1976-88; mfg. cons. Oxidation Products Internat. div. ASMM, Priest River, 1974—; chemist/oxidative chemistry Internat. Assn. Oxygen Therapy, Priest River, 1985—; oxidative chemist, scientist, priest A.S. Med. Missionaries, Priest River, 1982—; massage therapist Fla. Dept. Profl. Registration, Tallahassee, 1977-91; cons. Benedict Lust Sch. Naturopathy; lectr. in field. Author: Nicola Tesla and the Implementation of His Discoveries in Modern Science, 1984, Warburg, Blass and Koch: Men With a Message, 1990, Free Radicals and Their Relationship to Complex Oxidative Compounds, 1991, Complex Oxidative Molecules: Their Implication in the Rejuvenation of the Human Cell, 1994, History of Naturopathy or Pseudomedicalism: Naturopathy's Demise?, 1990, 95; contbr. articles to profl. jours. Recipient Tesla medal of Scientific Merit, Benedict Lust Sch. Natural Scis., 1992. Mem. Am. Chem. Soc., Tesla Meml. Soc., Tesla Coil Builder's Assn., Internat. Bio-Oxidative Med. Found. (Disting. Spkr. award 1994), Brit. Guild Drugless Practitioners, Internat. Assn. for Colon Therapy, Am. Massage Therapy Assn., Am. Naturopathic Med. Assn., Am. Soc. Med. Missionaries, Am. Coll. Clinic Adminstrs., Nat. Assn. Naturopathic Physicians, Am. Psychotherapy Assn., Am. Soc. Metals, Am. Naturopathic Assn. (trustee, pres.), Internat. Traders. Home and Office: PO Box 1360 Priest River ID 83856-1360

FREIHEIT, CLAYTON FREDRIC, zoo director; b. Buffalo, Jan. 29, 1938; s. Clayton John and Ruth (Miller) F. Student, U. Buffalo, 1960; DHL (hon.), U. Denver, 1996. Caretaker Living Mus., Buffalo Mus. Sci., 1955-60; curator Buffalo Zool. Gardens, 1960-70; dir. Denver Zool. Gardens, 1970—. Contbr. articles to profl. jours. Named Outstanding Citizen Buffalo Evening News, 1967. Mem. Internat. Union Dirs. Zool. Gardens, Am. Assn. Zool. Parks and Aquariums (pres. 1967-68 Outstanding Service award). Home: 3855 S Monaco Pky Denver CO 80237-1271 Office: Denver Zool Gardens City Park Denver CO 80205

FREILICHER, MELVYN STANLEY, writer, educator; b. N.Y.C., Nov. 8, 1946; s. Jack and Frances (Altman) F. BA in Psychology, Brandeis U., 1968; postgrad., U. Calif., San Diego, 1972. Mem. faculty writing program lit. dept. U. Calif.-San Diego, La Jolla, 1979—; vis. faculty lit. dept. San Diego State U., 1979—. Editor mag. Crawl Out Your Window, 1975-89; book reviewer San Diego Union, 1990-92, Jour. L.A. Inst. Contemporary Arts, San Diego Mag., N.Y. Times, L.A. Times, San Diego Reader, others; contbg. guest editor Fiction Internat., 1992; contbr. fiction and essays to numerous profl. publs. Pres. United Artists Coalition, San Diego, 1977-81; v.p. bd. dirs. Sushi Performance Space, 1979-82; pres. bd. dirs. Found. for New Lit., San Diego, 1983-89; mem. adv. bd. Inst. for Cultural Democracy, Ukiah, Calif., 1987—; coord. arts festival, San Diego Lesbian and Gay Ctr., 1979, tchr. workshop, 1994. Recipient award Nat. Endowment for Arts, Calif. Arts Coun. Lit., San Diego City Commn. on Arts and Culture. Home: 3945 Normal St Apt 5 San Diego CA 92103-3420 Office: U Calif San Diego Lit Dept 9500 Gilman Dr La Jolla CA 92093-5003

FREIMARK, ROBERT (BOB FREIMARK), artist; b. Doster, Mich., Jan. 27, 1922; s. Alvin O. and Nora (Shinaver) F.; m. Mary Carvin (dec.); 1 son, Matisse Jon; m. Lillian Tihlarik; 1 child, Christine Gay. B.E., U. Toledo, 1950; M.F.A., Cranbrook Acad. Art, 1951. Prof. art emeritus San Jose State U., 1964-86; W.I.C.H.E. prof. Soledad State Prison, 1967; established artist in residence program Yosemite Nat. Park,1984-85. Guest artist Harvard U., 1972-73; first Am. to make tapestries in Art Protis technique at Atelier Vlnena, Brno, Czechoslovakia.; contbr. to profl. publs.; Numerous solo shows including, Minn. Inst. Arts, Toledo Mus. Art, Salpeter Gallery, Morris Gallery, N.Y.C., Des Moines Art Center, Santa Barbara Mus., Moravska Mus., Czechoslovakia, Brunel U., London, Amerika Haus, Munich, Stuttgart, Regensburg, Joslyn Ctr. for Arts, Torrance, Calif, Stanford U., San Jose (Calif.) Mus. Art, Triton Mus., Santa Clara, Calif., Guatemalteco, Guatemala City, Dum Umeni Brno, CSFR, Strahov Closter, Prague, 1990, Walter Bischoff Gallery, Stuttgart, 1990, Kunstler aus den USA, Kunsthaus Ostbayern and Amerika Haus, Stuttgart, 1991, Max Planck Inst., Munich, The Gag Theatre, Prague, 1992, Haus Wiegand, Munich, 1993, San Jose State U., 1994, Viva!, Tokyo, 1994, Gallery Q, Sacramento, 1997, Parish Gallery, Wash. D.C., 1997, Barton Gallery, Sacramento, Calif., 1997; exhibited in group shows, Art Inst. Chgo., 1952, Pa. Acad. Fine Arts, 1953 (Lambert Fund prize), Detroit Inst. Arts, 1956, Mich. State U., 1956, N.A.D., 1956, Boston Print Symposium, 1997, Internat. Print Exibition Art Mus., 1997, Bklyn. Mus., Mus. Modern Art, Michael Stone Collection, D.C., Contempo Collection, Tokyo, others, L.A., Boston, San Francisco, Omaha, Oklahoma City, Des Moines, Dallas, Phoenix, San Jose, Havana, Tokyo, Manila, Rio de Janeiro, Mexico City, Sao Paulo, Prague, exhbn. 50 States toured, European Mus., 1970-71, represented in collections, Pa. Acad. Fine Art, Boston Mus. Fine Arts, Fogg Mus., Butler Inst. Am. Art, Ford Motor Co., South Bend Art Assn., Joslyn Art Mus., Seattle Art Mus., Ga. Mus., Huntington Gallery, Des Moines Art Center, Smithsonian Instn., Libr. Congress, L.A. County Art Inst., Brit. Mus., Nat. Gallery, Prague, Birmingham (Eng.) Mus., Moravske Mus., Brno, Czechoslovakia, Bibliotheque Nationale, Paris, Harn Mus., Gainsville, Fla., Portland Mus. Art (complete prints), Nat. Mus., Washington, others; numerous tapestries in pub. and pvt. collections, created tapestry representing U.S. for Olympic Games, Moscow, 1980; produced film El Día Tarasco, 1982; guest artist, Joslyn Meml. Mus., 1961, instr. painting and drawing, Ohio U., 1955-59, artist in residence, Des Moines Art Center, 1959-63, dir., Crystal Lake Art Center, Frankfort, Mich., (1955-57), guest lectr., one man show, Columbia U., 1963, cultural exchange exhibit, Northamerican Cultural Inst., Mexico City, 1963; guest artist, Riverside Art Center, 1964, Agora Vienna, Austria, 1994; curated exhibit Stuttgart, 1993; founder Bob & Lil Freimark Collection Portland Art Mus.; contbr. to craft and fibre publs. Served with USNR, 1939-46. Recipient 2d award for oil Northwest Territorial exhibit, 1954, Roulet medal Toledo Mus. Art, 1957, 1st award Print Exhbn., 1958, purchase award Midwest Biennial and Northwest Printmakers, Jurors award Berkeley Art Ctr, 1996; Calif. State Coll. Sys. spl. creative leave edit. serigraphs; elected to New Talent in U.S.A., 1957; Ohio U. rsch. grantee, 1958-59, Ford Found. grantee, 1965; Western Interstate Commn. for Higher Edn. grantee, 1967, San Jose State Coll. Found. grantee, 1966, 67, 68, 69, 70, 71, 85; designated ofcl. U.S. Bicentennial Exhbn. Amerika Hausen, Fed. Republic Germany, 1976; donated Bob & Lil Freimark Collection, Mexican Arts & Crafts, Gavilan Coll., Gilroy, Calif., 1996; represented by Parish Gallery, Washington, Triad Gallery, Seal Rock, Oreg., Takara Gall., Houston, Haus Wiegand, Munich, Konfese, Brno, Czech Republic, Gall. Q, Sacramento. Home: 539A Dougherty Ave Morgan Hill CA 95037-9241 Office: Grass Valley Studios Morgan Hill CA 95037

FREIMUTH, WILLIAM RICHARD, architect; b. Crawford, Nebr., Nov. 26, 1949; s. Frank Francis and Freda (Miller) F.; m. Ann Agnes Hume, Aug. 11, 1984. BS in Arch. Studies, U. Nebr., 1979. Registered architect, N.Mex. Draftsman Clark Enersen Ptnrs. A&E, Lincoln, Nebr., 1974-79; architect intern Lescher & Mahoney A&E, Farmington, N.Mex., 1979-82; architect, ptnr. Johnson Freimuth Arch., P.C., Farmington, 1982-89; architect, CEO William Freimuth Arch. P.C., Farmington, 1989—. Prin works include Piñon Hills Mcpl. Golf Course, Anasazi Amphitheatre, Farmington Aquatic Ctr., Farmington and Bloomfield Post Office, San Juan County Adminstrn. Bldg., 4-Corners Vietnam Vets. Meml. Pres. River Reach Found., Farmington, 1988. Mem. AIA (Farmington chpt. pres. 1986, 93, N.Mex. chpt. pres. 1989, 95). Republican. Roman Catholic. Home and Office: 316 N Behrend Ave Farmington NM 87401-5843

FREISER, HELEN, editor; b. Bklyn., Apr. 13, 1928; d. Jacob and Lillian (Reiss) Hammer; m. Leonard H. Freiser, Dec. 13, 1950; children: Leslie, Erik. BA, Bklyn. Coll., 1950; MLS, Columbia U., 1955. Sr. editor adult books BookList, ALA, Chgo., 1973-79; assoc. editor Hewitt Assocs., Lincolnshire, Ill., 1980-82; buyer trade books Sunshine Books, Phila., 1982-84; assoc. editor The H.W. Wilson Co., Cambridge, Mass., 1984-85; mng. editor Jour. of Shaw Hist. Libr., Klamath Falls, Oreg., 1986—. Editor: Guardhouse, Gallows and Graves, 1988. Home: 1215 SE 16th Ave Portland OR 97214-3707

FREITAG, PETER ROY, transportation specialist; b. L.A., Dec. 19, 1943; s. Victor Hugo and Helen Veronica (Burnes) F. Student, U. Fla., 1961-63, George Washington U., 1964-65. Chief supr. Eastern Airlines, L.A., 1965-77; tariff analyst, instr. United Airlines, San Francisco, 1977-84; mng. ptnr. Bentdahl, Freitag & Assoc., San Francisco, 1984-86; v.p. ops. PAD Travel, Inc., Mountain View, Calif., 1985-86; travel mgr. Loral Aerospace Corp, San Jose, Calif., 1986-95; pres. Capital Fin. Ptnrs. Corp., San Francisco, 1995—. Co-editor: (textbook) International Air Tariff and Ticketing, 1983. Vol. San Francisco Bay chpt. Oceanic Soc., 1984-95. Mem. Silicon Valley Bus. Travel Assn., Bay Area Bus. Travel Assn. Episcopalian.

FREITAS, ANTOINETTE JUNI, insurance company executive; b. Kansas City, Mo., Feb. 14, 1944; d. Anthony P. and Mariam L. Freitas; BA, Calif. State U.-Long Beach, 1966; MA, U. So. Calif., 1974; m. Stephen R. Krajcar, July 4, 1980. Chartered life underwriter, chartered fin. cons. Counselor, U. So. Calif., 1967-70, assoc. dir. fin. aid, 1970-75; sales agt. Equitable Life Assurance Co., 1975-79, dist. mgr., San Francisco, 1979-84; pres. Group Mktg. Services, Inc., field dir. Northwestern Mut. Life, San Francisco, 1984-86; pres. Peninsula Fin. Group, Inc., 1986—; mktg. mgr. Home Life, H.L. Fin. Group, San Jose, Calif., 1986—; registered rep. W.S. Griffith Co., securities, 1987-91; pres. Peninsula Fin. Group, Inc., 1991. Bd. dirs. San Francisco 300, 1996—. Recipient various sales and mgmt. awards; mem. Million Dollar Round Table. Mem. Nat. Assn. Life Underwriters, AAUW, U. So. Calif. Alumni Assn., Women Life Underwriters Conf. Republican. Episcopalian. Author: A Study in Changing Youth Values, 1974. Office: Peninsula Fin Group Inc 2995 Woodside Rd Ste 400 Woodside CA 94062-2401

FREMOUW, EDWARD JOSEPH, physicist; b. Northfield, Minn., Feb. 23, 1934; s. Fred J. and Marion Elizabeth (Drozda) F.; m. Rita Lorraine Johnson, June 26, 1960; children: Thane Edrik, Sean Fredrik. BSEE, Stanford U., 1957; MS in Physics, U. Alaska, 1963, PhD in Geophysics, 1966. Asst. prof. geophysics U. Alaska, Fairbanks, 1966-67; physicist Stanford Research Inst., Menlo Park, Calif., 1967-70, sr. physicist, 1970-75; program mgr. SRI Internat., Menlo Park, 1975-77; v.p. Phys. Dynamics, Inc., Bellevue, Wash., 1977-86; pres. Northwest Research Assocs., Inc., Bellevue, Wash., 1986—, also bd. dirs.; cons. Geophys. Inst., College, 1967-68; assoc. La Jolla (Calif.) Inst., 1981-89. Contbr. articles to profl. jours. Trustee East Shore Unitarian Ch., 1984-86; co-chair adv. com. on econ. diversification Wash. State, 1991-96; bd. dirs., pres. Banchero Friends Svc., Inc., 1994-95. Geographic feature Fremouw Peak named in his honor, 1968. Mem. IEEE, Am. Geophys. Union (Excellence in Refereeing award 1984, 89), Union Radio Sci. Internat., Stanford Club of Western Wash. (trustee 1984-86). Democrat. Unitarian Universalist. Home: 2873 W Lk Sammamish Pkwy NE Redmond WA 98052-5913 Office: Northwest Rsch Assocs Inc PO Box 3027 Bellevue WA 98009-3027

FRENCH, JAMES L., performing company executive. Music dir. condr. Maui Symphony Orch., Hawaii. Office: Maui Symphony Orchestra PO Box 788 Wailuku HI 96793*

FRENCH, KIRBY ALLAN, transportation engineer, computer programmer; b. San Angelo, Tex., Oct. 12, 1948; s. Leland Wayne French and Helen Lois (Stennett) French-Vance; m. Verda Jane Amyl Schaffer, Oct. 11, 1970; children: Tammy Lyrae, Adrian Allyn. Diploma in Computer Programming, Mkt. Tng. Inst., 1968. Transp. engr. Calif. Dept. Transp., San Bernardino, 1969—. Author: Speed Math, 1991, Trigonometric Formulas, 1991, Speed Reading, 1994, Microsoft Word 6 Macros for Spec Writers, 1996, Power Macintosh Apple Script Programs, 1996. Mem. Profl. Engrs. in Calif. Govt. Home: 1257 Poplar St San Bernardino CA 92410 Office: Calif Dept Transp 247 W Third St San Bernardino CA 92401

FRENCH, LAURENCE ARMAND, social science educator, psychology educator; b. Manchester, N.H., Mar. 24, 1941; s. Gerald Everett and Juliette Teresa (Boucher) F.; m. Nancy Picthall, Feb. 13, 1971. BA cum laude, U. N.H., 1968, MA, 1970, PhD, 1975; postdoctorate, SUNY, Albany, 1978; PhD, U. Nebr., 1981; MA, Western N.M. U., 1994. Diplomate Am. Bd. Forensic Medicine, Am. Bd. Forensic Examiners; lic. psychologist, Ariz. Instr. U. So. Maine, Portland and Gorham, 1971-72; asst. prof. Western Carolina U., Cullowhee, N.C., 1972-77, U. Nebr., Lincoln, 1977-80; psychologist I N.H. Hosp., Concord, 1980-81; psychologist II Laconia (N.H.) State Sch., 1981-88; sr. psychologist N.H. Divsn. for Children & Youth Svcs., Concord, 1988-89; prof., chair dept. social scis. Western N.Mex. U., Silver City, 1989—; adj. assoc. prof. U. So. Maine, 1980-84; cons. N.C. Dept. Mental Health, 1972-77, Nebr. Indian Commn., Lincoln, 1977-80, Cherokee (N.C.) Indian Mental Health Program, 1974-77; cons. alcohol program Lincoln Indian Ctr., 1977-80; profl. adv. bd. Internat. Coll. Prescribing Psychologists. Author: The Selective Process of Criminal Justice, 1976, Indians and Criminal Justice, 1982, Psychocultural Change and the American Indian, 1987, The Winds of Injustice, 1994, Counseling American Indians, 1997, (with Richard Crowe) Wee Wish Tree: Special qualla Cherokee Issue, 1976, (with Hornbuckle) Cherokee Perspective, 1981, (with Letman et al) Contemporary Issues in Corrections, 1981; spl. issue editor Quar. Jour. Ideology, Vol. II, 1987; contbr. articles to profl. jours. Commr. Pilsbury Lake Village Dist., Webster, N.H., 1985-90. With USMC, 1959-63. U. N.H. fellow, 1971-72, Nebr. U. System fellow, 1978. Fellow APA, Prescribing Psychologists Register; mem. NASP, Am. Soc. Criminology (life), Internat. Coll. Prescribing Psychologists Inc. (profl. adv. bd.), Nat. Assn. Alcohol and Drug Abuse Counselors (nat. chmn., clin. issue com. 1996—), N.Mex. Alcohol and Drug Abuse Counselors Assn., VFW, Phi Delta Kappa (treas. 1990-91, pres. 1991-92). Office: Western NMex U Dept Social Scis Silver City NM 88062

FRENCH, STEPHEN WARREN, art educator, university official; b. Seattle, Sept. 6, 1934; s. George Warren and Madge Evelyn (Marshall) F. m. Hanna Clara Misch, June 10, 1956 (div. May 1971); children: Alexandra, Kenneth, Katharine; m. Toni Virginia Thunen, Aug. 14, 1974 (div. June 1979); 1 child, Elly Kinsell Thunen-French; m. Wanda Waldera, Oct. 19, 1990. BA, U. Wash., 1956, MFA, 1960. Instr. art dept. San Jose (Calif.) State U., 1960-61; from instr. to asst. prof. art dept. U. Wis., Madison, 1961-66; from asst. prof. to prof. art San Jose State U., 1966—, chmn. dept., 1986-90, assoc. dean Coll. Humanities and Arts, 1990—; vis. artist U. Wash., Seattle, 1972, 73, Mont. State U. Boseman, 1970; mem. collections com. San Jose Mus. of Art, 1990—, mem. arts commn. City of San Jose, 1990-93, chair, 1993-94; vice chmn. conv. ctr. art selection com. City of San Jose, 1986-93; chmn. Art in Pub. Places Adv. Panel City of San Jose, 1991-93. One man show San Jose Mus., 1980; exhibited in group shows at Smithsonian Inst., Washington, 1965, Palace of the Legion of Honor, San Francisco, 1967, British Biennial of Graphic Art, 1969, 71, San Francisco Mus. of Modern Art, 1970. Mem. adv. com. San Jose Inst. of Contemporary Art. Sarah Denny fellow U. Wash., 1958. Mem. Coll. Art Assn., Nat. Assn. Schs. of Art & Design, Nat. Conf. of Art Adminstrs., Phi Beta Kappa, Phi Kappa Phi. Unitarian. Home: 1560 Four Oaks Cir San Jose CA 95131-2653 Office: San Jose State U 1 Washington Sq San Jose CA 95112-3613

FRENKLACH, MICHAEL YEHOSHUA, mechanical engineering educator; b. Moscow, Oct. 31, 1947; came to U.S., 1978; m. Kathleen Rose Stevens, Jan. 18, 1981; children: Alan, Anna. MSc in Chem. Tech., Mendeleyev Inst. Chem. Tech., Moscow, 1969; PhD in Phys. Chemistry, Hebrew U., Jerusalem, 1976. Researcher Mendeleyev Inst. Chem. Tech., 1969-71; rsch. assoc. McGill U., Montreal, Que., Can., 1976-78; postdoctoral assoc. MIT, Cambridge, 1978-79; asst. prof. to assoc. prof. chem. engring. La. State U., Baton Rouge, 1979-85; assoc. prof. fuel sci. Pa. State U., University Park, 1985-95; prof. mech. engring. U. Calif., Berkeley, 1995—. Contbr. numerous articles to profl. jours., chpts. to books. Recipient jr. faculty award ARCO Oil & Gas Co., 1981; Alexander van Humboldt Found. fellow, 1985-86. Mem. Am. Chem. Soc., Am. Physics Soc., Combustion Inst., Materials Rsch. Soc., Sigma Xi, Phi Kappa Phi (merit award for rsch. 1983). Office: U Calif Dept Mech Engring Berkeley CA 94720-1740

FREUD, NICHOLAS S., lawyer; b. N.Y.C., Feb. 6, 1942; s. Frederick and Fredericka (von Rothenburg) F.; m. Elsa Doskow, July 23, 1966; 1 child, Christopher. AB, Yale U., 1963, JD, 1966. Bar: N.Y. 1968, Calif. 1970, U.S. Tax Ct. 1973. Assoc. Hughes, Hubbard, Blair & Reed, N.Y.C., 1966-68; assoc. Severson, Werson, Berke et al., San Francisco, 1968-73, ptnr., 1973-78; ptnr. Chickering & Gregory, San Francisco, 1978-85, Russin & Vecchi, San Francisco, 1986-93, Jeffer, Mangels, Butler & Marmaro, LLP, San Francisco, 1993—; Mem. joint adv. bd. Calif. Continuing Edn. of Bar, chair taxation subcom. 1987-87; mem. fgn. income adv. bd. Tax Management Internat. Jour., mem. bd. advs. The Jour. of Internat. Taxation; mem. adv. bd. NYU Inst. on Fed. Taxation. Author: (with Charles G. Stephenson and K. Bruce Friedman) International Estate Planning, rev. edit., 1996; contbr. articles to profl. jours. Fellow Am. Coll. of Tax Counsel (cert. specialist in taxation law) mem. ABA (tax sect. coun. dir. 1995—, chair com. on U.S. activities of foreigners and tax treaties 1989-91, vice chair 1987-89, chair subcom. on tax treaties 1981-87), Calif. State Bar Assn. (taxation sect. exec. com. 1981-85, vice chair 1982-83, chair 1983-84, vice chair income tax com. 1981-82, chair 1982-83, vice chair personal income tax subcom. 1979-80, chair 1980-81, co-chair fgn. tax subcom. 1978-79), N.Y. State Bar Assn. (taxation sect., mem. com. on U.S. activities of fgn. taxpayers and fgn. activities of U.S. taxpayers), Bar Assn. of San Francisco, Bar Assn. of City of N.Y., San Francisco Tax Club (pres. 1988), San Francisco Internat. Tax Group. Office: Jeffer Mangels Butler & Marmaro LLP 1 Sansome St Fl 12 San Francisco CA 94104-4430

FREUDENTHAL, DAVID D., prosecutor. U.S. atty. for Wyo. U.S. Dept. Justice, Cheyenne. Office: US Atty Dist Wyo 2120 Capitol Ave Rm 4002 Cheyenne WY 82001-3633*

FREY, GERRARD RUPERT (GARY FREY), management executive; b. Medicine Hat, Alta., Can., June 7, 1943; s. Walter and Margaret (Materi) F.; m. Karen Martha Johnson, Aug. 27, 1968; children: Samantha Elizabeth, Jonathan Edward. B of Comm. with Distinction, U. Calgary, Alta., 1970; MBA, Harvard U., 1972. Sr. exec. Prin. Group, Edmonton, Alta., 1972-73; dir., v.p. Collective Securities Ltd., Edmonton, 1972-73; program mgr. Banff (Alta.) Ctr. for Mgmt., 1974-75; mgr. fin. svcs. The Banff Ctr., 1976-81, v.p. fin. and adminstrn., 1981-87; v.p. Banff Ctr. for Mgmt., 1981-83; acting pres. The Banff Ctr., 1991-93, exec. v.p., 1987—; chmn., pres., Exdev Cons. Ltd., Banff, 1974—; chmn. Sunshine Village Corp., Banff, 1983-89. Councillor Can. West Found., Calgary, 1983-95; founding dir., chmn. Banff/Lake Louise Tourism Bur., 1990-91; chmn. Assn. for Mountain Parks Protection and Enjoyment, 1994-96; elected trustee Banff Sch. Dist., 1990-92. Capt. Royal Can. Armoured Militia Corps, 1967-70. Recipient Commemorative medal 125th Anniversary of Can. Confedn., 1992. Mem. Can. Com. for Triple E. Senate, Can. assn. Univ. Bus. Officers, Banff Springs Golf Club, Harvard Bus. Sch. Club of Calgary, Riverside Golf and Country Club, Banff Rotary Club, Banff/Lake Louise C. of C. (pres. 1988-90). Home: Box 698, 115 St Julien Rd, Banff, AB Canada TOL OCO Office: The Banff Ctr, Box 1020, Banff, AB Canada TOL OCO

FREY, HARVEY STUART, radiologist, law student; b. N.Y.C., Aug. 9, 1934; s. Louis Elliot and Lillian (Enker) F. BS in Physics, Calif. Inst. Tech., 1955; MD, UCLA, 1960, PhD in Med. Physics, 1968. Diplomate Am. Bd. Radiology (therapy). Asst. prof. radiol. therapy U. So. Calif., L.A., 1968-71; radiol. therapist St. John's Hosp., Santa Monica, Calif., 1971-73, Century City Hosp., Santa Monica, 1973-75, Western Tumor Med. Group, Santa Monica, 1975-85; NIH fellow UCLA, 1964-68; assoc. rsch. biologist UCLA, Santa Monica, 1985-88, clin assoc. prof. radiol. therapy, 1973—. Contbr. numerous articles to profl. jours. Capt. USA Spl. Forces, 1961-63. Mem. AAAS, UCLA Med. Alumni Assn. (sec. 1989), Radiation Rsch. Soc., European Soc. for Therapeutic Radiology & Oncology, Am. Endocurietherapy Soc. (co-founder, 1st pres.). Home: 552 12th St Santa Monica CA 90402-2908

FREYD, WILLIAM PATTINSON, fund raising executive, consultant; b. Chgo., Apr. 1, 1933; s. Paul Robert Freyd and Pauline Margaret (Pattinson) Gardiner; m. Diane Marie Carlson, May 19, 1984. BS in Fgn. Svc., Georgetown U., 1960. Field rep. Georgetown U., Washington, 1965-67; campaign dir. Tamblyn and Brown, N.Y.C., 1967-70; dir. devel. St. George's Ch., N.Y.C., 1971; assoc. Browning Assocs., Newark, 1972-73; regional v.p. C.W. Shaver Co., N.Y.C., 1973-74; founder, chmn. IDC, Henderson, Nev., 1974—. Inventor PHONE/MAIL program. Bd. dirs. Nev. Symphony Orch., 1994, N.J. Symphony Orch., 1991-94; apptd. Nev. Charitable Solicitation Task Force, 1994. Mem. Nat. Soc. Fund Raising Execs. (nat. treas. 1980-81, pres. N.Y. chpt. 1974-76, cert. 1982), Am. Assn. Fund Raising Counsel (sec. 1984-86), World Fund Raising Coun. (bd. dirs. 1995), Georgetown U. Regional Club Coun., N.Y. Yacht Club, Union League Club N.Y., Masons, Nassau Club, Circumnavigators Club. Office: IDC 2920 Green Valley Pky Bldg 5 Henderson NV 89014-0407

FRICK, MR. See GROEBLI, WERNER FRITZ

FRICK, OSCAR LIONEL, physician, educator; b. N.Y.C., Mar. 12, 1923; s. Oscar and Elizabeth (Ringger) F.; m. Mary Hubbard, Sept. 2, 1954. A.B., Cornell U., 1944, M.D., 1946; M.Med. Sci., U. Pa., 1960; Ph.D., Stanford U., 1964. Diplomate: Am. Bd. Allergy and Immunology (chmn. 1967-72). Intern Babies Hosp., Columbia Coll. Physicians and Surgeons, N.Y.C., 1946-47; resident Children's Hosp., Buffalo, 1950-51; pvt. practice medicine specializing in pediatrics Huntington, N.Y., 1951-58; fellow in allergy and immunology Royal Victoria Hosp., Montreal, Que., Can., 1958-59; fellow in allergy U. Calif.-San Francisco, 1959-60, asst. prof. pediatrics, 1964-67, assoc. prof., 1967-72, prof., 1972—, dir. allergy tng. program, 1964—; fellow immunology Inst. d'Immunobiologie, Hosp. Broussais, Paris, France, 1960-62. Contbr. articles papers to profl. publs. Served with M.C., USNR, 1947-49. Mem. Am. Assn. Immunologists, Am. Acad. Pediatrics (chmn. allergy sect. 1971-72, Bret Ratner award 1982), Am. Acad. Allergy (exec. com. 1972—, pres. 1977-78), Internat. Assn. Allergology and Clin. Immunology (exec. com. 1970-73, sec. gen. 1985—), Am. Pediatric Soc. Club: Masons. Home: 370 Parnassus Ave San Francisco CA 94117-3609

FRICKE, MARTIN PAUL, science company executive; b. Franklin, Pa., May 18, 1937; s. Frank Albert and Pauline Jane (Wentz) F.; m. Barbara Ann Blanton, Jan. 3, 1959. BS, Drexel U., Phila., 1961; MS, U. Minn., 1964, PhD, 1967. Program mgr., group leader Gen. Atomics, San Diego, 1968-73; program mgr., divsn. mgr. Sci. Applications Internat. Corp., La Jolla, Calif., 1973-77, v.p., 1977-80, corp. v.p., 1980-84; sr. v.p. Systems Group, The Titan Corp., San Diego, Calif., 1984-87, exec. v.p. Techs Group, 1987-89, sr. v.p. corp. ops., 1989-93; program adminstr. San Diego Supercomputer Ctr., 1995-97; ind. cons., 1997—; mem. cross sect. evaluation working group, Upton, L.I., N.Y., 1970-73, U.S. Nuclear Data Com., Washington, 1970-73. Author publs. in field. Recipient postdoctoral fellowship U. Mich., Ann Arbor, 1967-68, scholarship Pa. Indsl. Chem. Co., 1956-60; grad. fellow Oak Ridge (Tenn.) Assoc. Univs., 1964-67. Fellow Am. Phys. Soc. (panel on pub. affairs 1982-84); mem. Phi Kappa Phi. Roman Catholic. Home and Office: 2211 Caminito Preciosa Sur La Jolla CA 92037-7233

FRIDLEY, SAUNDRA LYNN, internal audit executive; b. Columbus, Ohio, June 14, 1948; d. Jerry Dean and Esther Eliza (Bluhm) F. BS, Franklin U., 1976; MBA, Golden Gate U., 1980. Accounts receivable supr. Internat. Harvester, Columbus, Ohio, San Leandro, Calif., 1972-80; sr. internal auditor Western Union, San Francisco, 1980; internal auditor II, County of Santa Clara, San Jose, Calif., 1980-82; sr. internal auditor Tymshare, Inc., Cupertino, Calif., 1982-84, div. contr., 1984; internal audit mgr. VWR Scientific, Brisbane, Calif., 1984-88, audit dir., 1988-89; internal audit mgr. Pacific IBM Employees Fed. Credit Union, San Jose, 1989-90, Western Staff Svcs., Inc., Walnut Creek, Calif., 1990—; internal audit mgr., 1990-92; dir. quality assurance, 1992—; owner Dress Fore the 9's, Brentwood, Calif., 1994—; pres., founder Bay Area chpt. Cert. Fraud Examiners, 1990. Mem. NAFE, Friends of the Vineyards, Internal Auditors Speakers Bur., Assn. Cert. Fraud Examiners (founder, pres. Bay area chpt., we. regional gov. 1996—), Inst. Internal Auditors (pres., founder Tri-Valley chpt.), Internal Auditor's Internat. Seminar Com., Internal Auditor's Internat. Conf. Com. Avocations: woodworking, gardening, golfing. Home: 19 Windmill Ct Brentwood CA 94513-2502 Office: Western Staff Svcs 301 Lennon Ln Walnut Creek CA 94598-2418 also: Dress Fore The 9's 613 1st St Ste 19 Brentwood CA 94513-1322

FRIED, ELAINE JUNE, business executive; b. L.A., Oct. 19, 1943; grad. Pasadena (Calif.) High Sch., 1963; various coll. courses; m. Howard I. Fried, Aug. 7, 1966; children: Donnoven Michael, Randall Jay. Agt., office mgr. Howard I. Fried Agy., Alhambra, Calif., 1975—; v.p. Sea Hill, Inc., Pasadena, Calif., 1973-95. Publicity chmn., unit telephone chmn. San Gabriel Valley unit; past chmn., vol. lobbyist, recipient certificate appreciation, 1987, Am. Diabetes Assn.; past publicity chmn. San Gabriel Valley region Women's Am. Orgn. for Rehab. Tng. (ORT); chmn. spl. events publicity, Temple Beth Torah Sisterhood, Alhambra, membership chmn., 1991-92, v.p. membership, 1991-93; former mem. bd. dirs., pub. relations com., pers. com. Vis. Nurses Assn., Pasadena and San Gabriel Valley, Recipient Vol. award So. Calif. affiliate Am. Diabetes Assn., 1974-77, 25 Yr. Vol. Svc. award Am. Diabetes Assn., 1996; chmn. outside Sisterhood publicity Congregation Shaarei Torah, 1993—, public rels. chair, 1993—. Co-recipient Ner Tamid award Temple Beth Torah. Contbr. articles to profl. jours. Clubs: ORT, Hadassah, Congregation Shaarei Torah Sisterhood. Speaker on psycho-social aspects of diabetes, insurance and the diabetic, ins. medicine. Home: 404 N Hidalgo Ave Alhambra CA 91801-2640

FRIED, GIL BEN, lawyer, educator, expert witness; b. Van Nuys, Calif., Mar. 27, 1965; s. Louis Lester and Haya Rachel (Greenberg) F.; m. Susan Malka Landes, Aug. 11, 1991; children: Gabriella Aliza, Arieh Leib. BS in Bus., Calif. State U., Sacramento, 1986; M in Sport Adminstrn., JD, Ohio State U., 1990. Bar: Calif. 1992, U.S. Dist. Ct. Calif. 1994. Analyst Paul Kagan Assoc., Carmel, Calif., 1989-92; adj. prof. U. San Francisco, 1993-95; dir. Sports Law Ctr., San Francisco, 1992-95; asst. prof., sports adminstrn. coord. U. Houston, 1995—; of counsel Bisk & Lutz L.L.P., Houston, 1996—; expert witness Expert Resources, San Francisco, 1993—. NASD Arbitrator, 1995, AAA Sports Arbitrator, 1992. Author: Safe at First, 1993; editor Sports Facility Law Reporter, 1992—. Bd. dirs. Palo Alto (Calif.) Cmty. Eruv, 1993-95, Chevre Kadisha, Palo Alto, 1993-95. bd. dirs., Young Israel of Houston, 1995—, Hebrew Acad., 1995—. Recipient Outstanding Contbn. award Sportsplex Owners Assn., 1995. Mem. ABA, Calif. Bar Assn., Sports Lawyers Assn., Stadium mgrs. Assn. Office: Univ Houston 104 Garrison Gym Dept HHP Houston TX 77204-5331

FRIED, LOUIS LESTER, information technology and management consultant; b. N.Y.C., Jan. 18, 1930; s. Albert and Tessie (Klein) F.; m. Haya Greenberg, Aug. 15, 1960; children: Ron Chaim, Eliana Ahuva, Gil Ben. BA in Pub. Adminstrn., Calif. State U., Los Angeles, 1962; MS in Mgmt. Theory, Calif. State U., Northridge, 1965. Mgr. br. plant data processing Litton systems, Inc., Woodland Hills, Calif., 1960-65; dir. mgmt. info. systems Bourns, Inc., Riverside, Calif., 1965-68, Weber Aircraft Co., Burbank, Calif., 1968-69; v.p. mgmt. services T.I. Corp. of Calif., Los Angeles, 1969-75; dir. advanced computer systems dept. Stanford Research Inst., Menlo Park, Calif., 1976-85, dir. ctr. for info. tech., 1985-86, dir. worldwide info. tech. practice, 1987-90; v.p. info. tech. cons. Stanford Rsch. Inst., Menlo Park, Calif., 1990-97; spl. advisor to pres. TELUS Corp., Edmonton, Alta., Can., 1997—; cons. editor Auerbach Pubs., 1978—, Reston Pubs., 1979—; lectr. U. Calif., Riverside, 1965-69, lectr. mgmt. and EDP. Contbr. numerous articles to profl. jours., 2 textbooks. Mem. Assn. Systems Mgmt. Home: 788 Loma Verde Ave Palo Alto CA 94303-4147 Office: Stanford Rsch Inst Menlo Park CA 94025

FRIEDENBERG, WALTER DREW, journalist; b. Meriden, Conn., Dec. 22, 1928; s. Gustav Edward and Adela (Drews) F.; m. Tencha Avila, May 29, 1965; children: Christopher Drew, Eric Avila, Karina Della. BA, Wake Forest U., 1949; AM, Harvard U., 1956; postgrad., U. Chgo., 1959. Reporter Rocky Mount (N.C.) Evening Telegram, 1949-50, Winston-Salem (N.C.) Jour., 1950, Richmond (Va.) Times-Dispatch, 1954, Buffalo Evening News, summer 1956; fellow Inst. Current World Affairs, N.Y., 1956-60; stringer Chgo. Daily News, Fgn. News Svc., 1960; reporter Pitts. Press, 1960-61; fgn. corr. in Europe, Africa and Asia Scripps-Howard Newspaper Alliance, Washington, 1961-66, editl. writer, 1966-69; editor Cin. Post, 1969-77; European corr. Scripps-Howard Newspapers, London, 1977-79; fgn. affairs corr. Scripps Howard News Svc., Washington, 1979-91; exec. editor Santa Fe New Mexican, 1991-92; Scripps Howard vis. prof. sch. journalism Ohio U.; Fulbright lectr. China Sch. Journalism, Beijing, 1996-97. 2d lt. U.S. Army, 1951-53. Mem. Phi Beta Kappa, Omicron Delta Kappa. Office: Route 7 Box 125 B Santa Fe NM 87505

FRIEDERICH, MARY ANNA, gynecology and obstetrics consultant, retired; b. Rochester, N.Y., Nov. 15, 1931; d. Lewis Weniger and Mary Jasper (McGinnis) F.; m. John S. Savage (div. 1987); stepchildren: Steven T. Savage, Scott Allen Savage, Sandra Sue Savage DellaVilla. BA, Cornell U., 1953; MD, U. Rochester, 1957. Diplomate Am. Bd. Ob-Gyn. Intern in ob-gyn. and surgery U. Rochester, N.Y., 1957-58, asst. resident ob-gyn, 1958-59, assoc. resident and fellow ob-gyn and psychiatry, 1959-60, resident and instr. ob-gyn to chief resident, 1960-62, sr. instr. ob-gyn and psychiatry, 1963-66, asst. prof. in ob-gyn and psychiatry, 1966-68, assoc. prof. ob-gyn and psychiatry, 1968-76, clin. assoc. prof. in ob-gyn and psychiatry, 1976-86; med. dir. Planned Parenthood of Cen. and No. Ariz., 1986-89; sr. assoc. cons. in gyn. Mayo Clinc, Scottsdale, Ariz., 1990-91; med. dir. Ariz. Physicians I.P.A., 1989-93; assoc. Maricopa County Medicine Assocs., 1991-94; Maricpar Faculty Assn., 1994-96, retired, 1996; sr. assoc. ob-gyn and psychiatry Strong Meml. Hosp. of U. Rochester, 1976-84, attending ob-gyn, 1985-87; staff in gynecology Good Samaritan Hosp., Phoenix; attending ob-gyn Maricpar Med. Ctr., 1994-96; speaker and presenter in field. Editor: Psychosomatic Medicine, Women's Health, Human Sexuality, Jour. of Psychosomatic Ob-Gyn, Social Sci. Medicine, Jour. of Reproductive Medicine, Ob-Gyn, Jour AMA; contbr. numerous articles to profl. jours. Bd. pensions United Meth. Ch. Western N.Y. Conf., 1975-84; bd. dirs. Rochester United Meth. Homes, Goodman Gardens, 1970-82, pres. 1979-82; chairperson personnel com. Alternatives for Battered Women, 1979-81; adminstrv. bd. Asbury First United Meth. Ch., 1984-86; bd. dirs. United Cancer Coun., 1985-86; chairperson program com. Women's Coalition of Health Ann. Health Confs., 1985-86. Mem. AMA, Am. Coll. Ob-Gyn, Am. Med. Women's Assn., Soc. for Sex Therapy and Rsch. (bd. dirs. 1983-85), Am. Soc. Colposcopy and Cervical Pathology, Am. Soc. for Psychosomatic Ob-Gyn (past pres., sec., treas., historian), Soc. for Menstrual Cycle Rsch. (sec., treas. 1981—), Assn. of Reproductive Health Profls., Phoenix Ob-Gyn Soc., Maricopa County Med. Soc., Ariz. State Med. Soc. Republican. Methodist. Home: 10559 N 104th Pl Scottsdale AZ 85258-4941

FRIEDHEIM, ROBERT LYLE, political scientist, educator; b. N.Y.C., Aug. 1, 1934; s. Joseph and Blanche (Vogel) F.; m. Robin Rudolph; children: Jessica Faulkner, Amy. AB, Columbia Coll., 1955; MA, Columbia U., 1957; PhD, U. Wash., 1962. Teaching asst., predoctoral assoc. U. Wash., 1958-61; from asst. prof. to assoc. prof. polit. sci. Purdue U., 1961-66; dir. law of sea project, profl. staff mem. Ctr. for Naval Analysis, Arlington, Va., 1966-76; prof. internat. rels., assoc. dir. inst. for marine studies U. So. Calif., 1976-89, dir. sea grant program, 1980-89, dir. sch. internat. rels., 1992-96; advisor U.S. Arctic Rsch. Commn., 1986-96; mem. adv. panel Office Tech. Assessment U.S. Congress, 1988-89; mem. internat. ocean sci. policy com. bd. ocean sci. and policy Nat. Rsch. Coun.; lectr., invited visitor Nat. Bur. Oceanography, Beijing, 1984; mem. adv. group Ocean Policy Roundtable, Woods Hole, 1983; del. Commn. of Califs., 1978-80. Editor: Jour. Ocean and Coastal Mgmt., Ocean Devel. and Internat. Law Jour.; contbr. articles to profl. jours. and chpts. to books; author: Negotiating the New Ocean Regime, 1993, The Seattle General Strike, 1964, (with others) Japan and the New Ocean Regime, 1984, Forecasting Outcomes of Multilateral Negotiations: Methodology, Vol. 1, 1977, The Navy and the Common Sea, 1972, others. Grantee NSF, 1978-80, 1977-78, 1974-75, ONR, 1978-80; CNA fellow, 1971-72. Mem. Am. Soc. Internat. Law, Internat. Studies Assn. (chair internat. orgn. sect. 1970-73, mem. adv. bd. environ. studies sect. 1989—). Office: U So Calif Sch Internat Rel Von Kleinsmid Ctr Rm 330 Los Angeles CA 90089

FRIEDLAND, JACK ARTHUR, plastic surgeon; b. East Chicago, Ind., Feb. 10, 1940; s. Peter and Bettye (Manfield) F.; m. Harriet Anita Simensky, July 1, 1962; children: Margo Lynn, Jonathan Elliott, Julie I. Student, U. Wis., 1958-61; BS, Northwestern U., 1962, MD, 1965. Diplomate Am. Bd. of Surgery, Am. Bd. of Plastic Surgery, Nat. Bd. Med. Examiners. Intern in surgery NYU/Bellevue Med. Ctr., N.Y.C., 1965-66, from surg. resident to chief resident, 1966-70; resident in plastic surgery Inst. Reconstructive Plastic Surgery NYU Med. Ctr., N.Y.C., 1972-74; pvt. practice Phoenix, 1974—; chief of staff children's rehab. svc. State of Ariz., 1984-86; asst. chief of staff Phoenix Plastic Surgery Residency Program, 1974-84; attending physician Phoenix Plastic Surgery Fellowship/Mayo Clinic Residency Programs, 1985—; chief of surgery St. Luke's Hosp. Med. Ctr., Phoenix, 1981-83; chief of plastic surgery Children's Hosp., Phoenix, 1984-86; extra-mural asst. prof. plastic surgery, adj. asst. prof. plastic surgery Mayo Med. Sch., 1991—. Contbr. articles to profl. jours.; spkr. in field. Bd. dirs. men's arts coun. Phoenix Art Mus., 1975—, Am. Heart Assn., Phoenix, 1985-89, MADD, Phoenix, 1985-86. Maj. USAF, 1970-72. Fellow ACS; mem. AMA, Am. Soc. for Aesthetic Plastic Surgery, Inc. (pres. 1990-91), Am. Soc. Plastic and Reconstructive Surgeons, Am. Assn. Plastic Surgeons, Am. Cleft-Palate-Craniofacial Assn., Ariz. Med. Assn., Maricopa County Med. Assn., Ariz. Soc. Plastic and Reconstructive Surgeons, U. Club of Phoenix (bd. dirs. 1974-84, past pres.), Alpha Omega Alpha. Office: 101 E Coronado Rd Phoenix AZ 85004-1556

FRIEDLANDER, CHARLES DOUGLAS, investment company executive, space consultant; b. N.Y.C., Oct. 5, 1928; s. Murray L. and Jeane (Sottosanti) F.; m. Diane Mary Hutchins, May 12, 1951; children: Karen Diane, Lauren Patrice, Joan Elyse. BS, U.S. Mil. Acad., 1950; exec. mgmt. program, NASA, 1965; grad., Command and Staff Coll. USAF, 1965, Air War Coll. USAF, 1966. Commd. 2d lt. U.S. Army, 1950, advanced through grades to 1st lt.; officer inf. U.S. Army, Korea, 1950-51; resigned U.S. Army, 1954; mem. staff UN Forces, Trieste, Italy, 1953-54; chief astronaut support office NASA, Cape Canaveral, Fla., 1963-67; space cons. CBS News, N.Y.C., 1967-69; exec. asst. The White House, Washington, 1969-71; pres. Western Ranchlands Inc., Scottsdale, Ariz., 1971-74, Fairland Co. Inc., Scottsdale, 1974—; v.p. bd. dirs. Internat. Aerospace Hall of Fame, San Diego; space program cons., various cos., Boca Raton, Fla., 1967-69; mem. staff First Postwar Fgn. Ministers Conf., Berlin, 1954; radio/TV cons. space program. Author: Buying & Selling Land for Profit, 1961, Last Man at Hungnam Beach, 1952. V.p. West Point Soc., Cape Canaveral, Fla., 1964. Served to lt. col. USAFR, maj. USAR. Decorated Bronze Star V, Combat Inf. badge; co-recipient Emmy award CBS TV Apollo Moon Landing, 1960; recipient medal of honor N.Y.C., 1951. Mem. Nat. Space Club, Explorer's Club, West Point Soc., Chosin Few Survivors Korea, NASA Alumni League, Nat. Space Soc. *Too many young people think that the exciting and adventurous things in life are out of their reach. When there is a career or vocation that represents something you are good at, and that you would enjoy doing - then do it. Get on a plane, train or bus. Line up at the employment office and take any job just to "get your foot in the door". If you apply yourself, in time you will rise in your chosen field. Always remember: "You can do anything you want to do if you make up your mind to do it!".*

FRIEDMAN, ALAN E., lawyer; b. N.Y.C., May 5, 1946. BA, Amherst Coll., 1967; JD, Stanford U., 1970. Bar: Calif. 1971. Atty. Tuttle & Taylor, L.A. Note editor: Stanford Law Rev., 1969-70. Office: Tuttle & Taylor A Law Corporation 355 S Grand Ave 40th Fl Los Angeles CA 90071-3102

FRIEDMAN, DONALD M., English language educator; b. N.Y.C., Apr. 8, 1929; s. Morley Sidney and Lillian (Berlin) F.; m. Stephanie Judith Diamond, June 14, 1959; children: Elliot Michael, Gabriel Diamond. BA, Columbia U., 1949, Trinity Coll., Cambridge, Eng., 1951; MA, Trinity Coll., Cambridge, Eng., 1958; PhD, Harvard U., 1960. Supr. Trinity Coll., Cambridge, 1951-53; instr. Harvard U., Cambridge, Mass., 1960-61; from asst. prof. to prof. English U. Calif., Berkeley, 1961—; cons. Calif. Humanities Project, 1982-87, State Dept. of Edn., 1986-87. Served with U.S. Army, 1954-56, Japan. Author: Marvell's Pastoral Art, 1970. John Simon Guggenheim Found. fellow, 1974-75; U. Calif. Humanities Rsch. fellow, 1969-70, 91. Mem. MLA, Renaissance Soc. Am., Milton Soc. Am. (exec. bd. 1992-94), John Donne Soc., Phi Beta Kappa (exec. bd. 1991—, Excellence in Teaching award 1994). Home: 2933 Magnolia St Berkeley CA 94705-2329

FRIEDMAN, EMANUEL, physician, educator; b. Jersey City, N.J., Nov. 27, 1922. BS in Acctg. cum laude, L.I. U., 1942; BA in Zoology with honors, U. Calif., Berkeley, 1948; MD, U. Calif., San Francisco, 1952. Diplomate Am. Bd. Internal Medicine, Am. Bd. Gastroenterology. Rotating intern Jewish Hosp. of Bklyn., 1952-53; resident in internal medicine VA Hosp., Bronx, N.Y., 1953-55; resident in gastroenterology VA Hosp., West Haven, Conn., 1955-57; mem. hosp. staff Mills-Peninsula Hosp., Burlingame, Calif., Seton Med. Ctr., Daly City, Calif., U. Calif. Hosps., San Francisco; clin. instr. medicine Stanford (Calif.) U., 1959-69; cons. gastroenterology U. Hawaii Postgrad. Med. Edn. Program, Ctrl. Okinawa Hosp., Gushikawa City, 1973, 76, 94; vis. prof. medicine & gastroenterology Hadassah Med. Sch., Jerusalem, Israel, 1980; clin. prof. medicine U. Calif., San Francisco, 1980—; pres. MidPeninsula Physicians Med. Group, Inc., 1985; chief of staff Peninsula Hosp. and Med. Ctr., 1969-71, chmn. divsn. gastroenterology, 1971-96. Pres. bd. dirs. Jewish Home for the Aged, San Francisco, 1989—; past chmn. Jewish Community Rels. Coun., San Mateo County, Jewish Community Fedn. Campaign, San Mateo County; bd. dirs. Jewish Community Fedn. San Francisco, San Mateo & Marin; v.p., bd. dirs. AIPAC No. Calif.; bd. dirs. Holocaust Ctr. No. Calif.; guest lectr. Middle Eastern affairs San Francisco City Coll.; acting med. dir. Am. Joint Distbn. Com. Med. Clinic, Addis Ababa, Ethiopia, 1990. Fellow ACP; mem. AMA, Am. Gastroent. Assn., Am. Soc. for Gastroent. Endoscopy, Am. Soc. for Internal Medicine, No. Calif. Soc. for Clin. Gastroenterology (pres. 1977), Calif. Soc. for Internal Medicine, Calif. Med. Assn., San Mateo County Med. Soc. (bd. dirs., legis. liaison com., fee rev. com., budget & fin. com.).

FRIEDMAN, GARY DAVID, epidemiologist, research facility administrator; b. Cleve., Mar. 8, 1934; s. Howard N. and Cema C. F.; m. Ruth Helen Schleien, June 22, 1958; children: Emily, Justin, Richard. Student, Antioch Coll., 1951-53; BS in Biol. Sci., U. Chgo., 1956, MD with honors, 1959; MS in Biostatics, Harvard Sch. Pub. Health, 1965. Diplomate Am. Bd. Internal Medicine. Intern, resident Harvard Med. Svcs., Boston City Hosp., 1959-61; 2d yr. resident Univ. Hosps. Cleve., 1961-62; med. officer heart disease epidemiology study Nat. Heart Inst., Framingham, Mass., 1962-66; chief epidemiology unit, field and tng. sta., heart disease ctrl. program USPHS, San Francisco, 1966-68; sr. epidemiologist divsn. rsch. Kaiser Permanente Med. Care Program, Oakland, Calif., 1968-76, asst. dir. epidemiology and biostatics, 1976-91, dir., 1991—; rsch. fellow, then rsch. assoc. preventive medicine Harvard Med. Sch., 1962-66; lectr. dept. biomedical and environ. health scis., sch. pub. health U. Calif. Berkeley, 1968—; lectr. epidemiology and biostatics U. Calif. Sch. Medicine, San Francisco, 1980—, asst. clin. prof. 1967-75, assoc. clin. prof., 1975-92 depts. medicine and family and community medicine; mem. U.S.-USSR working group sudden cardiac death Nat. Heart, Lung and Blood Inst., 1975-82, com. on epidemiology and veterans follow-up studies Nat. Rsch. Coun., 1980-85, subcommittee on twins, 1980—, epidemiology and disease ctrl. study sect. NIH, 1982-86, U.S. Preventive Svcs. Task Force, 1984-88, scientific rev. panel on toxic air contaminants State of Calif., 1988—, adv. com. Merck Found./Soc. Epidemiol. Rsch., Clin. Epidemiology Fellowships, 1990-94; sr. advisor expert panel on preventive svcs. USPHS, 1991—. author: Primer of Epidemiology, 1974, 2d edit., 1980, 3d edit., 1987, 4th edit., 1994; assoc. editor, then mem. editl. bd. Am. Jour. Epidemiology, 1988-96; mem. editl. bd. HMO Practice, 1991—, Jour. Med. Screening, 1997—; contbr. over 250 articles to profl. jours., chpts. to books. Oboist San Francisco Recreation Symphony, 1990—; bd. dirs. Chamber Musicians No. Calif., Oakland, 1991—. Sr. surgeon USPHS, 1962-68. Recipient Roche award for Outstanding Performance as Med. Student; Merit grantee Nat. Cancer Inst., 1987, Outstanding Investigator grantee, 1989; named to Disting. Alumni Hall of Fame Cleve. Heights High Sch., 1991. Fellow Am. Heart Assn. (chmn. com. on criteria and methods 1969-71, chmn. program com. 1973-76, coun. epidemiol.), Am. Coll. Physicians; mem. APHA, Am. Epidemiol. Soc. (mem. com. 1982-86), Am. Soc. Preventive Oncology, Internat. Epidemiol. Assn., Internat. Soc. Twin Studies, Soc. Epidemiologic Rsch., Phi Beta Kappa, Alpha Omega Alpha, Delta Omega. Office: Kaiser Permanente Med Care Program Divsn Rsch 3505 Broadway Oakland CA 94611-5714

FRIEDMAN, GEORGE JAY, psychologist; b. N.Y.C., Oct. 15, 1945; s. Martin and Lee (Jones) F.; m. Patricia Ann Cole, June 9, 1969; 3 children. BA in Psychology, Rutgers U., 1969; MA in Psychology, U. Hawaii, 1972, PhD of Psychology, 1978. Lic. psychologist, Hawaii. Instr. dept. psychology U. Hawaii, Honolulu, 1972-78; intern clin. psychology Mercy Cath. Med. Ctr., Phila., 1978-79; psychologist Crozer-Chester (Pa.) Med. Ctr., 1980-86; dir. psychiat. svcs., chief planner cmty. mental health Am. Samoa Govt., Pago Pago, 1986-87; clin. psychologist State of Hawaii, Wailuku, 1987-91; pvt. practice Wailuku, 1991—; instr. dept. psychiatry Thomas Jefferson U., Phila., 1980-86; cons. Kula (Hawaii) Hosp., 1990-92, Maui Assn. Retarded Citizens, Wailuku, 1991-92, Baldwin H.S., Maui, Hawaii, 1987-91. Contbr. articles to profl. jours. Fellow NSF, 1970-74. Mem. APA, Hawaii Psychol. Assn., Maui Assn. Psychologists, Maui Mental Health Assn., Sigma Xi. Office: 2070 W Vineyard St Wailuku HI 96793-1618

FRIEDMAN, JAY SCOTT, internist; b. L.A., Dec. 11, 1956; s. Martin I. and Roberta (Glasser) F.; m. Marypat Gianotti, Feb. 9, 1986; children: Aaron, Adam. BA, UCLA, 1979; MD, U. Tex., 1983. Diplomate Am. Bd. Internal Medicine. Intern Good Samaritan Hosp. & Med. Ctr., Phoenix, 1983-84; resident St. Joseph's Hosp. and Med. Ctr., Phoenix, 1984-86; assoc. med. dir. Mercy Care St. Joseph's Hosp., Phoenix, 1986—; pvt. practice internal medicine, Scottsdale, Ariz., 1986—; med. dir. Hospice of the Valley, Phoenix, 1987—. Fellow Am. Coll. Physicians; mem. Ariz. Med. Assn., Maricopa County Med. Soc., assn. Physicians & Surgeons (bd. dirs. 1994—). Office: Adult Internal Medicine 10290 N 92nd St Ste 300 Scottsdale AZ 85258-4500

FRIEDMAN, JULES DANIEL, geologist; b. Poughkeepsie, N.Y., Oct. 24, 1928; s. Jack and Sophie (Seltzer) F.; m. Linda Diane Wheelock Sluss, May 2, 1988; children from previous marriage: Susanne K., Jack A., Lisa K.; 1 stepchild, Lori Midson. AB, Cornell U., 1950; MS, Yale U., 1952, PhD, 1958. Geologist, br. mil. geology U.S. Geol. Survey, Washington, 1953-64, geologist, br. theoretical and applied geophysics, 1964-72; geologist, br. geophysics U.S. Geol. Survey, Denver, 1973—, chief remote sensing sect., 1982-85; rep. to U.S. Army Corps Engrs. U.S. Geol. Survey, 1959; advisor to Mex. Govt., 1969, NASA, 1969, 70, Brazilian govt., 1970, Nat. Rsch. Coun. Iceland, 1966-71, USN, 1971-72; cons. tech. assistance program UN, 1971; U.S. Geol. Survey rep. Skylab visual observations team Johnson Space Ctr., NASA, 1975. Contbr. numerous articles to profl. jours. Recipient Group Achievement award NASA, 1974, Quality of Scientific Work award, 1979. Fellow Geol. Soc. Am.; mem. Am. Geophys. Union (sec., exec. com., front range br. 1982-83). Home: PO Box 471 Wheat Ridge CO 80034-0471 Office: US Geol Survey MS 964 Denver Fed Ctr Denver CO 80225

FRIEDMAN, LAWRENCE M., law educator; b. Chgo., Apr. 2, 1930; s. I. M. and Ethel (Shapiro) F.; m. Leah Feigenbaum, Mar. 27, 1955; children: Jane, Amy. AB, U. Chgo., 1948, JD, 1951, LLM, 1953; LLD, U. Puget Sound, 1977, CUNY, 1989, U. Lund, Sweden, 1993; LLD (hon.), John Marshall Law Sch., 1995. Mem. faculty St. Louis U., 1957-61, U. Wis., 1961-68; prof. law Stanford U., 1968—, Marion Rice Kirkwood prof., 1976—; David Stouffer Meml. lectr. Rutgers U. Law Sch., 1969; Sibley lectr. U. Ga. Law Sch., 1976; Wayne Morse lectr. U. Oreg., 1985; Childress meml. lectr. St. Louis U., 1987; Jefferson Meml. lectr. U. Calif., 1994. Author: Contract Law in America, 1965, Government and Slum Housing, 1968, A History of American Law, 1973, 2d edit., 1985, The Legal System: A Social Science Perspective, 1975, Law and Society: An Introduction, 1977, (with Robert V. Percival) The Roots of Justice, 1981, American Law, 1984, Total Justice, 1985, Your Time Will Come, 1985, The Republic of Choice, 1990, Crime and Punishment in American History, 1993; co-editor: (with Stewart Macaulay) Law and the Behavioral Sciences, 1969, 2d edit., 1977, (with Harry N. Scheiber) American Law and the Constitutional Order, 1978, Legal Culture and the Legal Profession, 1996, (with Stewart Macaulay and John Stookey) Law and Society: Readings on the Social Study of Law, 1995; contbr. articles to profl. jours. Served with U.S. Army, 1953-54. Recipient Triennial award Order of Coif, 1976, Willard Hurst prize, 1982, Harry Kalven prize, 1992, Silver Gavel award ABA, 1994; Ctr. for Advanced Study in Behavioral Sci. fellow, 1974-75, fellow Inst. Advanced Study, Berlin, 1985. Mem. Law and Soc. Assn. (pres. 1979-81), Am. Acad. Arts and Scis., Am. Soc. for Legal History (v.p. 1987-89, pres. 1990-91). Home: 724 Frenchmans Rd Palo Alto CA 94305-1005 Office: Stanford U Law Sch Nathan Abbott Way Stanford CA 94305-9991

FRIEDMAN, MILTON, economist, educator emeritus, author; b. Brooklyn, N.Y., July 31, 1912; s. Jeno Saul and Sarah Ethel (Landau) F.; m. Rose Director, June 25, 1938; children: Janet, David. AB, Rutgers U., 1932, LLD (hon.), 1968; AM, U. Chgo., 1933; PhD, Columbia U., 1946; LLD (hon.), St. Paul's (Rikkyo) U., 1963, Loyola U., 1971, U. N.H., 1975, Harvard U., 1979, Brigham Young U., 1980, Dartmouth Coll., 1980, Gonzaga U., 1981; DSc (hon.), Rochester U., 1971; LHD (hon.), Rockford Coll., 1969, Roosevelt U., 1975, Hebrew Union Coll., Los Angeles, 1981, Jacksonville U., 1993; LittD (hon.), Bethany Coll., 1971; PhD (hon.), Hebrew U., Jerusalem, 1977; DCS (hon.), Francisco Marroquín U., Guatemala, 1978. Assoc. economist Nat. Resources Com., Washington, 1935-37; mem. research staff Nat. Bur. Econ. Research, N.Y.C., 1937-45, 1948-81; vis. prof. econs. U. Wis., Madison, 1940-41; prin. economist, tax research div. U.S. Treasury Dept., Washington, 1941-43; assoc. dir. research, statis. research group, War Research div. Columbia U., N.Y.C., 1943-45; assoc. prof. econs. and statistics U. Minn., Mpls., 1945-46; assoc. prof. econs. U. Chgo., 1946-48, prof. econs., 1948-62, Paul Snowden Russell disting. service prof. econs., 1962-82, prof. emeritus, 1983—; Fulbright lectr. Cambridge U., 1953-54; vis. Wesley Clair Mitchell research prof. econs. Columbia U., N.Y.C., 1964-65; fellow Ctr. for Advanced Study in Behavioral Sci., 1957-58; sr. research fellow Hoover Inst., Stanford U., 1977—; mem. Pres.'s Commn. All-Vol. Army, 1969-70, Pres.'s Commn. on White House Fellows, 1971-74, Pres.'s Econ. Policy Adv. Bd., 1981-88; vis. scholar Fed. Res. Bank, San Francisco, 1977.

Author: (with Carl Shoup and Ruth P. Mack) Taxing to Prevent Inflation, 1943, (with Simon S. Kuznets) Income from Independent Professional Practice, 1946, (with Harold A. Freeman, Frederic Mosteller, W. Allen Wallis) Sampling Inspection, 1948, Essays in Positive Economics, 1953, A Theory of the Consumption Function, 1957, A Program for Monetary Stability, 1960, Price Theory: A Provisional Text, 1962, (with Rose D. Friedman) Capitalism and Freedom, 1962, (with R.D. Friedman) Free To Choose, 1980, (with Rose D. Friedman) Tyranny of the Status Quo, 1984, (with Anna J. Schwartz) A Monetary History of the United States, 1867-1960, 1963, (with Schwartz) Monetary Statistics of the United States, 1970, (with Schwartz) Monetary Trends in the U.S. and the United Kingdom, 1982, Inflation: Causes and Consequences, 1963, (with Robert Roosa) The Balance of Payments: Free vs. Fixed Exchange Rates, 1967, Dollars and Deficits, 1968, The Optimum Quantity of Money and Other Essays, 1969, (with Walter W. Heller) Monetary vs. Fiscal Policy, 1969, A Theoretical Framework for Monetary Analysis, 1972, (with Wilbur J. Cohen) Social Security, 1972, An Economist's Protest, 1972, There's No Such Thing As A Free Lunch, 1975, Price Theory, 1976, (with Robert J. Gordon et al.) Milton Friedman's Monetary Framework, 1974, Tax Limitation, Inflation and the Role of Government, 1978, Bright Promises, Dismal Performance, 1983, Money Mischief, 1992, (with Thomas S. Szasz) Friedman & Szasz on Drugs: Essays on the Free Market and Prohibition, 1992; editor: Studies in the Quantity Theory of Money, 1956; bd. editors Am. Econ. Rev, 1951-53, Econometrica, 1957-69; adv. bd. Jour. Money, Credit and Banking, 1968-94; columnist Newsweek mag, 1966-84, contbg. editor, 1971-84; contbr. articles to profl. jours. Decorated Grand Cordon of the 1st Class Order of the Sacred Treasure (Japan), 1986; recipient Nobel prize in econs., 1976, Pvt. Enterprise Exemplar medal Freedoms Found., 1978, Presdl. medal of Freedom, 1988, Nat. Medal of Sci., 1988, Prize in Moral-Cultural Affairs, Instn. World Capitalism, 1993; named Chicagoan of Yr., Chgo. Press Club, 1972, Educator of Yr., Chgo. Jewish United Fund, 1973. Fellow Inst. Math. Stats., Am. Statis. Assn., Econometric Soc.; mem. Nat. Acad. Scis., Am. Econ. Assn. (mem. exec. com. 1955-57, pres. 1967; John Bates Clark medal 1951), Am. Enterprise Inst. (adv. bd. 1956-79), Western Econ. Assn. (pres. 1984-85), Royal Economic Soc., Am. Philos. Soc., Mont Pelerin Soc. (bd. dirs. 1958-61, pres. 1970-72). Club: Quadrangle. Office: Stanford U Hoover Instn Stanford CA 94305-6010

FRIEDMAN, MITCH ALAN, conservation biologist; b. Chgo., July 20, 1963; s. Ira Jerome Friedman and Francine (Hirsch) Scully; m. Margo Malone, Sept. 3, 1995; 1 child, Jessie Malone Friedman. Student, Mont. State U., 1981-83; BA in Zoology, U. Wash., 1986. Ranch hand Ferguson Ranch, Cheyenne, Wyo., 1980; wildlife biologist Mont. Dept. Fish, Wildlife and Parks, Savage, Mont., 1981; fork lift operator Lustro Co., Evanston, Ill., 1982-83; framing carpenter Windward Builders, Lake Forest, Ill., 1984-85; fgn. fisheries observer Nat. Marine Fisheries, Seattle, 1985-86; organizer Wash. Earth First, Bellingham and Seattle, 1985-88, Ancient Forest Rescue Expedition, Bellingham, 1989-90; exec. dir., founder Northwest Ecosystem Alliance, Bellingham, 1989—; bd. dirs. The Wildlands Project, Portland, Hells Canyon Preservation Coun., Joseph, Oreg., North Cascades Conservation Coun., Seattle; advisors North Cascades Audubon Soc., Bellingham, 1987—, Atmosphere Alliance, Olympia, Wash., 1992—. Editor: Forever Wild: Conserving the Greater North Cascades Ecosystem, 1988, Cascadia Wild: Protecting an International Ecosystem, 1993 (Regional Bestseller 1993); contbg. editor Wild Earth, 1991; exec. producer video Nature Has No Borders, 1993. Co-chair No on 92-93, Whatcom County, Wash., 1993, Second Dist. Environ. Working Group, Bellingham, 1994. Pole Vault state medalist State of Ill., Champagne, 1981. Mem. Soc. for Conservation Biology, Natural Areas Soc., Nat. Audubon Soc., City Club Bellingham. Office: NW Ecosystem Alliance 1421 Cornwell Ste 201 Bellingham WA 98225

FRIEDMAN, PAUL, food products executive; b. 1951. Ptnr. Cheese & Stuff, Hartford, Conn., 1972-80, P & J's Constrn., 1978-81, Prim Products, 1981-83; pres. Herb Farm, Inc., Encinitas, Calif., 1983—. Office: Herb Farm Inc PO Box 231069 1613 Lake Dr Encinitas CA 92024-5226*

FRIEDMAN, RICHARD ELLIOTT, Hebrew and literature educator; b. Rochester, N.Y.. ThD, Harvard U., 1978. Prof. Hebrew and comparative lit. U. Calif.-San Diego, La Jolla, 1976—. Author: The Exile and Biblical Narrative, 1981, Who Wrote the Bible?, 1987, coll. text edit., 1988, Brit. and internat. edit., 1988, paperback edit., 1988, German, Spanish, Italian, and Japanese edits., 1989, Hebrew edit., 1991, 2d edit., 1997 (N.Y. Times Editors' Recommended Selection 1987, N.Y. Times Notable Books of 1987, The Times London Editors' Recommended Selection 1988, Laymen's Nat. Bible Assn. Citation 1988, N.Y. Times Editors' Recommended Paperback Selection 1989, N.Y. Times Notable Paperback Books of 1989, Book of the Month Club, Quality Paperback Books Club, Readers' Union Book Club Eng., Book Club Assocs. Eng.), The Disappearance of God, 1995, Portuguese, Japanese, Dutch edits. (Pubs. Weekly Best Books of 1995, Book of the Month Club, One Spirit Book Club, Brit. Book Club), The Hidden Face of God, 1997; editor: The Creation of Sacred Literature, 1981, The Poet and the Historian, 1983, (with H.G.M. Williamson) The Future of Biblical Studies: The Hebrew Scriptures, 1987. U. Calif. Presdl. Rsch. fellow in the humanities, 1997; U. Calif. rsch. grantee, 1978, 79, 84, 88. Fellow Am. Coun. Learned Socs.; mem. Bibl. Colloquium, Soc. for Bibl. Lit., Authors Guild. Office: U Calif-San Diego La Jolla CA 92093-0410

FRIEDMAN, ROBERT ERIC, lawyer; b. Berkeley, Calif., June 28, 1949; s. Howard Abraham and Phyllis Ruth (Koshland) F.; m. Kristina Kiehl, Mar. 12, 1977; children: Alison Kiehl Friedman, Anne Kiehl Friedman. AB, Harvard U., 1971; JD, Yale U., 1977. Bar: D.C. 1977. Chief spl. projects Ga. Dept. Natural Resources, Atlanta, 1971-72; fellow Health Policy Program U. Calif., San Francisco, 1972-73; policy analyst Nat. Ctr. for Productivity and Quality of Work Life, Washington, 1977-79; pres., founder Corp. for Enterprise Devel., Washington, 1979-88; chair, dir. Corp. for Enterprise Devel., San Francisco, 1988—; chair, founder Assn. for Enterprise Opportunity, San Francisco, 1990-92; bd. dirs. Levi Strauss Found., San Francisco, Rosenburg Found., San Francisco, EcoTrust, Portland, Oreg. Author: Development Report Card for the States, 1987, Safety Net as Ladder, 1988; editor: Expanding the Opportunity to Produce, 1981. Democrat. Jewish. Office: Corp for Enterprise Devel 353 Folsom St San Francisco CA 94105-2321

FRIEDMAN, RUSSELL PETER, grief recovery educator, restaurant manager; b. Port Chester, N.Y., Jan. 4, 1943; s. Harry and Betty Sybil (Robfogel) F.; m. Jeanne Baier, June 10, 1975 (div. Oct., 1987); 1 child, Kelly Logan. BA, Rollins Coll., 1964. Owner, mgr. Taming of the Stew, L.A., 1970-72, Lost on Larrabee, L.A., 1972-76, Budapest Hungarian, L.A., 1980-86; mgr. Ghengis Cohen, 1986-89; exec. dir. The Grief Recovery Inst., 1989—. Author: (book) Moving Beyond Loss Work Book, 1994; contbr. articles to various publs. Co-founder The Grief Recovery Helpline, L.A., 1989, The Grief Recovery Inst. Ednl. Found., 1992. Office: Grief Recovery Inst Ste 204 7906 Santa Monica Blvd Los Angeles CA 90046

FRIEDMAN, SHELLY ARNOLD, cosmetic surgeon; b. Providence, Jan. 1, 1949; s. Saul and Estelle (Moverman) F.; m. Andrea Leslie Falchook, Aug. 30, 1975; children: Bethany Erin, Kimberly Rebecca, Brent David, Jennifer Ashley. BA, Providence Coll., 1971; DO, Mich. State U., 1982. Diplomate Nat. Bd. Med. Examiners, Am. Bd. Dermatology. Intern Pontiac (Mich.) Hosp., 1982-83, resident in dermatology, 1983-86; assoc. clin. prof. dept. internal med. Mich. State U., 1984-89, adj. clin. prof., 1989—; med. dir. Inst. Cosmetic Dermatology, Scottsdale, Ariz., 1986—. Contbr. articles to profl. jours. Mem. B'nai B'rith Men's Council, 1973, Jewish Welfare Fund, 1973. Am. Physicians fellow for medicine, 1982. Mem. AMA, Am. Osteopathic Assn., Am. Assn. Cosmetic Surgeons, Am. Acad. Cosmetic Surgery, Internat. Soc. Dermatologic Surgery, Internat. Acad. Cosmetic Surgery, Am. Acad. Dermatology, Am. Soc. Dermatol. Surgery, Frat. Order Police, Sigma Sigma Phi. Jewish. Office: Scottsdale Inst Cosmetic Dermatology 5206 N Scottsdale Rd Scottsdale AZ 85253-7006

FRIEDMANN, LYNNE TIMPANI, public relations consultant, writer; b. Lynn, Mass., Oct. 17, 1952; d. Henry and Rita Marie (Despres) Timpani; m. Marc David Friedmann, July 30, 1988. BA, Calif. State U., 1983. With Regis McKenna Pub. Rels., Costa Mesa, Calif., 1983-85; pub. info. rep. U. Calif., Irvine, 1985-88; cons. Friedmann Comms., San Diego, 1988—. Mem. Assn. for Women in Sci. (exec. bd. sec. 1994—, pub. rels. chair 1989-93), Nat. Assn. Sci. Writers, Pub. Rels. Soc. Am. (accredited), Leadership Am. (Class of 1994). Office: Friedmann Comms PO Box 1725 Solana Beach CA 92075-7725

FRIEDMANN, PERETZ PETER, aerospace engineer, educator; b. Timisoara, Romania, Nov. 18, 1938; came to U.S., 1969; s. Mauritius and Elisabeth Friedmann; m. Esther Sarfati, Dec. 8, 1964. DSc, MIT, 1972. Engring. officer Israel Def. Force, 1961-65; sr. engr. Israel Aircraft Industries, Ben Gurion Airport, Israel, 1965-69; research asst. dept. aeronautics and astronautics MIT, Cambridge, 1969-72; asst. prof. mech. and aerospace engring. dept. UCLA, 1972-77, assoc. prof., 1977-80, prof., 1980—; chmn. dept. mech. and aerospace engring. UCLA, Los Angeles, 1988-91. Editor in chief Vertica-Internat. Jour. Rotocraft and Powered Lift Aircraft, 1980-90; contbr. numerous articles to profl. jours. Grantee NASA, Air Force Office Sci. Rsch., U.S. Army Rsch. Office, NSF. Fellow AIAA (recipient Structures, Structural Dynamics and Materials award 1996); mem. ASME (Structures and Materials award 1983), Am. Helicopter Soc., Sigma Xi. Jewish. Office: UCLA MAE Dept Engring IV 48-121 Box 951597 Los Angeles CA 90095-1597

FRIEND, DAVID ROBERT, chemist; b. Vallejo, Calif., Aug. 10, 1956; s. Carl Gilbert and Roberta (Schwarzrock) F.; m. Carol Esther Warren, Dec. 17, 1983; 1 child, Ian, Michael. BS in Food Biochemistry, U. Calif., Davis, 1979; PhD in Agrl. Chemistry, U. Calif., Berkeley, 1983. Polymer chemist SRI Internat., Menlo Park, Calif., 1984-87, sr. polymer chemist controlled release and biomed. polymers dept., 1987-90, assoc. dir. controlled release and biomed. polymers dept., 1990-92, dir. controlled release and biomed. polymers dept., 1992-93; exec. dir. rsch. and product devel. Cibus Pharm., Burlingame, Calif., 1993-94; v.p. rsch. and product devel. Cibus Pharm., Redwood City, Calif., 1994-96, v.p., chief scientific officer, 1996—; leader Biopharms. Rsch. Group, 1990; lectr. U. Calif. Sch. Pharmacy, San Francisco. Assoc. editor Jour. Controlled Release; contbr. articles to scholarly jours.; patentee in field. Mem. Controlled Release Soc., Am. Assn. Pharm. Sci. Democrat. Jewish. Home: 454 9th Ave Menlo Park CA 94025-1802 Office: Cibus Pharm 887 Mitten Rd Burlingame CA 94010-1303

FRIES, ARTHUR LAWRENCE, life health insurance broker, disability claim consultant; b. Bklyn., Aug. 21, 1937; s. Jack Edwin and Sophia (Kabat) F.; m. Cindy Ann Blum, Mar. 27, 1960; children: Stacey Jill, Todd Steven. AB, Nichols Coll., 1956; BS, Syracuse U., 1958. Registered health underwriter. Various positions ins. sales and adminstrn. various firms, N.Y.C., 1962-72; life and health ins. agt. Washington Nat. Ins. Co., Los Angeles, 1973-85; pvt. practice, N.Y.C., Los Angeles and Northridge, Calif., 1962-72, Northridge, 1982—; blood chmn. Washington Nat. Ins. Co., 1976-79; spkr., lectr., cons. on individual disability income ins. claims; cons., expert witness and negotiator for non-can disability ins. claims. Contbr. articles to profl. jours. Chmn. memberships Vista Del Mar Men's Assn. for Orphaned Children, 1975. Recipient Nat. Sales Achievement award L.A. Gen. Agts. and Mgrs. Assn., 1965-94, Health Ins. Quality award, 1965-92, 93, Agt. of Yr. award 1976, 78, Nat. Quality award, 1980-91, Disting. Svc. award D.I.T.C. Rsch. Seminar, 1994. Mem. Am. Bd. Forensic Examiners, Inst. for Forensic Experts, Nat. Forensic Ctr., Nat. Assn. Life Underwriters (blood chmn. 1976-79, spkr. ann. conv. 1988, 90, 93 million dollar roundtable), Nat. Assn. Health Underwriters (life leading prodrs. roundtable), Calif. Assn. Life Underwriters, Calif. Assn. Health Underwriters (charter), Forensic Cons. Assn. of Orange County, L.A. Assn. Health Underwriters (conf. spkr., spkrs. chmn. 1983-84, program chmn. 1984, bd. dirs., membership chmn. 1987-88), Am. Diabetic Assn. Republican. Home and Office: 225 Via San Remo Newport Beach CA 92663-5511

FRIES, DAVID SAMUEL, chemist, educator; b. Manassas, Va., June 22, 1945; s. Basil L. and Ruby (Sperau) F.; m. Mærjie Ann Strayer, May 1, 1964; children: Susan, Jane, Corey. BA in Chemistry, Bridgewater Coll., 1968; PhD in Medicinal Chemistry, Va. Commonwealth U., 1971. Prof. medicinal chemistry U. of Pacific, Stockton, Calif., 1973—, dean grad. sch., 1993-96; vis. rsch. prof. U. Groningen, The Netherlands, 1984-85, German Cancer Rsch. Ctr., Heidelberg, 1989-90; cons. on opioid drug addiction, 1975—. Contbr. articles to profl. jours. and chpts. to books. Rsch. grantee Nat. Inst. on Drug Abuse, NSF; U.S. Fulbright scholar U. Zimbabwe, 1997. Mem. Am. Chem. Soc., Am. Assn. Colls. Pharmacy, Sigma Xi, Phi Kappa Phi, Rho Chi, Phi Delta Chi. Office: U of Pacific Sch of Pharmacy Stockton CA 95211

FRIES, LITA LINDA, school system administrator; b. Merced, Calif., Feb. 16, 1942; d. Alfred Earl and Juanita Lora (Brown) Griffey; m. George Richard Fries, Feb. 3, 1962; 1 child, Damon Brant. BA, U. Calif., Berkeley, 1966; MS, Calif. State U., 1976. Cert. elem. tchr., secondary tchr., ednl. adminstrator, reading specialist. Tchr. Peace Corps, Mwanza, Tanzania, 1963-65; tchr. Oakland (Calif.) Unified Sch. Dist., 1966-74, tchr. spl. assignment, 1974-84, principal, Burckhalter, 1984-85, program mgr., 1985-90, administr., 1990-92, coord. state and fed. programs, 1992—. Mem. East Bay Reading Assn. (editor 1982-83), Pi Lamda Theta (membership chairperson 1986-88), Delta Kappa Gamma, Phi Delta Kappa. Democrat. Office: Oakland Unified Sch Dist 1025 2nd Ave Oakland CA 94606-2212

FRIESECKE, RAYMOND FRANCIS, health company executive; b. N.Y.C., Mar. 12, 1937; s. Bernhard P. K. and Josephine (De Tomi) F.; BS in Chemistry, Boston Coll., 1959; MS in Civil Engring., MIT, 1961. Product specialist Dewey & Almy Chem. div. W. R. Grace & Co., Inc., Cambridge, Mass., 1963-66; market planning specialist USM Corp., Boston, 1966-71; mgmt. cons., Boston, 1971-74; dir. planning and devel. Schweitzer div. Kimberly-Clark Corp., Lee, Mass., 1974-78; v.p. corp. planning Butler Automatic, Inc., Canton, Mass., 1978-80; pres. Butler-Europe Inc., Greenwich, Conn. and Munich, Germany, 1980; v.p. mktg. and planning Butler Greenwich Inc., 1980-81; pres. Strategic Mgmt. Assocs., San Rafael, Calif., 1981-96; chmn. Beyond Health Corp., 1994—; corp. clk., v.p. Bldg. Research & Devel., Inc., Cambridge, 1966-68. Host, prodr. The Ounce of Prevention Show, Sta. KEST, San Francisco, 1994—; author: Management by Relative Product Quality, The New Way to Manage; contbr. articles to profl. jours. State chmn. Citizens for Fair Taxation, 1972-73; state co-chmn. Mass. Young Reps., 1967-69; chmn. Ward 7 Rep. Com., Cambridge, 1968-70; vice chmn. Cambridge Rep. City Com., 1966-68; vice-chmn. Kentfield Rehab. Hosp. Found., 1986-88, chmn., 1988-91; Rep. candidate Mass. Ho. of Reps., 1964, 66; pres. Marin Rep. Coun., 1986-91; chmn. Calif. Acad., 1986-88; sec. Navy League Marin Coun., 1984-91, v.p. 94—; bd. dirs. The Marin Ballet, 1996—. 1st lt. U.S. Army, 1961-63. Mem. NRA, Am. Chem. Soc., Physicians Com. for Responsbile Medicine, Marin Philos. Soc. (v.p. 1991-92), Health Medicine Forum, The World Affairs Coun. Home: 141 Convent Ct San Rafael CA 94901-1335 Office: PO Box 150578 San Rafael CA 94915

FRIESS, DONNA LEWIS, psychology educator, writer; b. L.A., Jan. 14, 1943; d. Raymond W. Lewis, Jr. and Dorothy Gertrude (Borwick) McIntyre; m. Kenneth E. Friess, June 20, 1964; children: Erik, Julina, Daniel. BA in Comm., U. So. Calif., 1964; MA in Comm., Calif. State U., Long Beach, 1966; PhD in Psychology, U.S. Internat. U., San Diego, 1993. Cert. tchr., Calif. Prof. human comm. Cypress (Calif.) Coll., 1966—; lectr. survivors of abuse, 1990—, mental health profls., 1990—; CEO Hurt Into Happiness Publishing, 1990—, Hurt Into Happiness Seminars, 1993—; presenter and keynote presenter in field of child abuse, various confs., convs., cmty. groups, workshops, and lawmakers' groups; guest expert (TV shows) Sally Jessy Raphael, 1993, Leeza Gibbons Talk Show, 1994, Sonja: Live, 1994, Oprah Winfrey Show, 1991, Ron Reagan Show, 1994, CBS This Morning, 1994, Inside Edition, 1991-92, (radio shows) AM-LA, KFI, and 80 radio talk shows and small network TV shows, 1993-94. Author: Relationships, 1995, Just Between Us: A Guidebook for Survivors of Childhood Trauma to Heal Their Important Relationships, 1995, Cry the Darkness, 1993, European edit. 1995, Circle of Love: Secrets to Successful Relationships, 1996; contbr. articles to mags. Recipient Author's award U. Calif. Friends of Libr., 1996, recognition from U.S. Justice Dept. for outstanding efforts to stop child abuse, 1995; nominee for Pres.'s Am. Svc. award, 1996. Mem. Am. Coalition Against Child Abuse (founder), Task Force for ACCA to Educate American Judges on Issues of Sexual Abuse, One Voice, Calif. Psychol. Assn., Western Social Sci. Assn., Child Abuse Listening and Mediating (bd. dirs.), Am. Profl. Soc. on Abuse of Children, Mother Against Sexual Abuse (bd. dirs.), Laura's House for Battered Women (bd. dirs.), Calif. Tchrs. Assn., Faculty Assn. Calif. C.Cs., Speech Communication Assn. of Am., U.S. Internat. U. Alumni Assn. (bd. dirs.). Office: Cypress College Dept Human Communications Cypress CA 90630

FRIGON, JUDITH ANN, electronics executive, office systems consultant; b. Wisconsin Rapids, Wis., Feb. 11, 1945; d. Harold Leslie and Muriel Alice (Berard) Neufeld; m. Gene Roland Frigon, June 17, 1967; children: Shane P., Shannon M., Sean M. Sec., office mgr. George Chapman D.D.S., Fairfax, Va., 1971-75; owner, operator Sunset Motel, Havre, Mont., 1976-78; sec. Wash. State U. Social Research Ctr., Pullman, 1978-80; adminstrv. sec. Wash. State U. Systems and Computing, Pullman, 1980-85, office automation cons., word processing trainer, IBM profl. office system adminstr., 1983-89, microcomputer cons. and trainer, 1989—; systems analyst, programmer Wash. State U. Computing Ctr., Pullman, 1985-97; owner Computer Assistance, Tng. and Svcs., Pullman, 1992—, Valley Bus. Coll., Lewiston, Idaho, 1997—. Pres. Pullman svc. unit Girl Scouts U.S.A., 1983-89, v.p. Inland Empire coun., Spokane, Wash., 1985-89, pres., 1989-95, nat. operational vol., 1995—; mem. Pullman Civic Trust, 1986—; mem.-at-large Pullman United Way, 1988-93, mem. admissions and allocations com., 1990-93, mem. comm. com., 1990-93, fund devel.-major gifts chair, 1995—; host family for State of Wash. Jr. Miss candidates, 1988—, local area judge, 1995—. Recipient Girl Scouts Thanks badge, 1991, Wash. State U. Mom of Yr. award, 1995. Mem. Profl. Secs. Internat., Jaycees (Jayceen of Yr. 1978), Pullman Kiwanis Club. Roman Catholic. Home: 1235 NW Davis Way Pullman WA 99163-2815 Office: Wash State U Computing Ctr 2120 Computer Sci Bldg Pullman WA 99164

FRISBEE, DON CALVIN, retired utilities executive; b. San Francisco, Dec. 13, 1923; s. Ira Nobles and Helen (Sheets) F.; m. Emilie Ford, Feb. 5, 1947; children: Ann, Robert, Peter, Dean. BA, Pomona Coll., 1947; MBA, Harvard U., 1949. Sr. investment analyst, asst. cashier investment analysis dept. 1st Interstate Bank Oreg., N.A., Portland, 1949-52; treas. PacifiCorp, Portland, 1958-60, then v.p., exec. v.p., pres., 1966-73, chief exec. officer, 1973-89, chmn., 1973-94; chmn. emeritus PacifiCorp., Portland, 1994-97; bd. dirs. Wells Fargo Bank. Chmn. bd. trustees Reed Coll.; trustee Safari Game Search Found., High Desert Mus.; mem. cabinet Columbia Pacific coun. Boy Scouts Am.; founder Oreg. chpt. Am. Leadership Forum; mem. exec. com. Oreg. Partnership for Internat. Edn. 1st lt. AUS, 1943-46. Mem. Arlington Club, Univ. Club Multnomah Athletic Club, City Club. Office: 1500 SW 1st Ave Portland OR 97201-5815

FRISCHKNECHT, LEE CONRAD, retired broadcasting executive; b. Brigham City, Utah, Jan. 4, 1928; s. Carl Oliver and Geniel (Lund) F.; m. Sara Jean McCulloch, Sept. 3, 1948; children: Diane Frischknecht Etherington, Jill Frischknecht Taylor, Ellen Frischknecht DePola, Amy Frischknecht Blodgett. BS in Speech, Utah State U., 1951; MA in Radio-TV, Mich. State U., 1957. Announcer sta. KID Radio, Idaho Falls, Idaho, 1951-52; producer-director sta. WKAR-TV, East Lansing, Mich., 1953-57, prodn. mgr., 1958-59, program mgr., 1960-61, gen. mgr., 1962-63; dir. sta. rels. Nat. Ednl. TV, N.Y.C., 1964-67; dir. univ. rels. Utah State U., 1969-70; dir. network affairs Nat. Pub. Radio, Washington, 1971, v.p., 1972, pres., 1973-77; communications cons., 1978—; mgr. ed. telecommunications sta. KAET-TV, Phoenix, Ariz., 1980-86; asst. gen. mgr. sta. KAET-TV, Phoenix, 1987-93; assoc. prof. radio-TV, Mich. State U., 1962-63; assoc. prof. speech Utah State U., 1968-69; lectr. Ariz. State U., 1981-82. Bd. dirs. Nat. Pub. Radio, 1973-78, Ariz. Sch. Svcs. Through Ednl. Tech., 1984-93, PSSC Legacy Fund, 1993—; bd. dirs. Pub. Svc. Satellite Consortium, 1982-90, chmn., 1987-90. Recipient Outstanding Alumnus in Communications award Mich. State U., 1973, Meritorious Svc. award in Communications, Brigham Young U., 1974, Disting. Svc. award Pacific Mountain Network, 1987. Mem. LDS Ch. Home: 8100 E Camelback Rd # 180 Scottsdale AZ 85251-2729

FRISHBERG, NANCY JO, computer company executive, linguist; b. Mpls., Nov. 9, 1948; d. Morton Charles and Alyse Sue (Goldsman) F.; 1 child, Janet Seiden. AB with honors, U. Calif., Berkeley, 1970; MA, U. Calif., San Diego, 1973, PhD, 1976. Rsch. asst. Lab. for Lang. Studies, Salk Inst., LaJolla, Calif., 1970-73; rsch. assoc. Interpreting Svcs. Nat. Tech. Inst. for Deaf-Rochester (N.Y.) Inst. Tech., 1973-75; asst. prof. linguistics Hampshire Coll., Amherst, Mass., 1975-78; dir. sign lang. rsch. NYU Deafness Rsch. and Tng. Ctr., N.Y.C., 1978-80; pvt. practice cons. sign lang. and interpretation N.Y.C., 1980-85; liberal arts specialist IBM-Academic Info. Systems, Milford, Conn., 1985-87; staff asst., dir. sci. ctrs. IBM, Milford, 1987-89; inst. fellow User Interface Inst., IBM Watson Rsch., Yorktown Heights, N.Y., 1989-92; lic. support engr. Apple Computer, 1994-96; exec. dir. New Media Ctrs., San Francisco, 1996—; mem. adv. bd. ENFI Project Gallaudet U., Washington, 1988-90, Project Common Ground, 1991-94. Author: Interpreting: An Introduction, 1986, rev. edit., 1990; mem. editorial bd. Jour. of Interpretation, 1991-95. Mem. Assn. Software Design (bd. dirs.), Registry Interpreters for the Deaf (pres. N.Y.C. metro 1980-82), Assn. for Computers and Humanities (exec. coun. 1989-91), Conf. of Interpreter Trainers (edn. stds. com. 1990—), Sign Instrs. Guidance Network (nat. evaluation team 1977-84), Linguistic Soc. Am., Internat. Interactive Comm. Soc. (Mark of Excellence award 1990).

FRISK, JACK EUGENE, recreational vehicle manufacturing company executive; b. Nampa, Idaho, Jan. 22, 1942; s. Steinert Paul and Evelyn Mildred (Letner) F.; m. Sharon Rose Caviness, Aug. 3, 1959; 1 dau., Toni. With Ideal of Idaho, Inc., Caldwell, purchasing mgr., 1969-75, gen. mgr., sec.-treas., 1975-82; sales mgr. Traveleze Industries div. Thor Industries, Sun Valley, Calif., 1982-88; owner, pres. Crossroads Industry div. Cross Enterprises Inc., Mesa, Ariz., 1988-92; dir. mktg. western divsn. Chariot Eagle, Inc., Ocala, Fla., 1992-95; gen. mgr. Chariot Eagle West, Inc., Phoenix, 1995-96; tool coord. III Mc Donnell Douglas Helicopter Systems, Mesa, 1996—. Episcopalian. Home: 1430 N Parsell Cir Mesa AZ 85203-3713 Office: Mc Donnell Douglas 5000 E McDowell Rd D178 Mesa AZ 85215

FRITCHER, EARL EDWIN, civil engineer, consultant; b. St. Ansgar, Iowa, Nov. 24, 1923; s. Lee and Mamie Marie (Ogden) F.; m. Dorsille Ellen Simpson, Aug. 24, 1946; 1 child, Teresa. BS, Iowa State U., 1950. Registered civil engr., Calif. Project devel. engr. dept. transp. State of Calif., Los Angeles, 1950-74, traffic engr. dept. transp., 1974-87; pvt. practice cons. engr. Sunland, Calif., 1987—; consulting prin. traffic engr. Parsons DeLeuw Inc., 1990—; cons. traffic engr. DeLeuw Cather Internat., Dubai, United Arab Emerates, 1994. Co-author: Overhead Signs and Contract Sign Plans, 1989; patentee in field. Served to 2d lt. USAF, 1942-46, 50-51. Mem. Iowa State U. Alumni Assn. (life). Republican. Methodist. Clubs: Verdugo Hills Numismatic (Sunland), Glendale Numismatic.

FRITTS, MARY MADELYN (MARY BAHR), librarian, writer; b. Bemidji, Minn., May 20, 1946; d. Frederick J. Bahr and Frances Mary Larson; m. Bill James Fritts, Dec. 27, 1969; children: Jason, Joshua, Jordan, Jeremy. BLS, Coll. St. Catherine, St. Paul, 1968. Med. libr. H. A. Bradford Meml. Libr., Denver, 1969-71; registrar Presbyn. Med. Ctr. Nursing Sch., Denver, 1971-74; ch. libr. Father Burger Libr., Overland Park, Kans., 1978-80; asst. libr. Cobb County Pub. Libr., Marietta, Ga., 1981-84; info., reference technician Pikes Peak Libr. Dist., Colorado (Colo.) Springs, 1990—; judge writing contest Colo. Ctr. For The Book, 1990, Soc. Children's Book Writers and Illustrators, 1991. Author: (as Mary Bahr) The Memory Box, 1992, Jordi's Run, 1997; contbng. author: (anthologies) Guiltless Catholic Parenting, 1995, God's Vitamin C for the Christmas Spirit, 1996; columnist New Writers Mag., Sarasota, Fla., 1991-93; book reviewer Five Owls, St. Paul, Minn., 1993-96; contbr. articles to juvenile pubs. Vol. Oak Park Pub. Libr., Queen of Holy Rosary Sch., Overland Park, Kans., 1976-78, St. Ann's Ch., Marietta, 1981-83, Cheyenne Mountain Schs., Colorado Springs, 1988-93; editor St. Paul's Ch. newsletter, Colorado Springs, 1990-91; writing mentor Colorado Springs Sch. Dist. II, 1996. Recipient Chautauqua grant Highlights Found, 1988. Mem. ALA, Soc. Children's Book Writers and Illustrators (Mag. Merit award and grants 1992), Colo. Author's League (bd. mem. 1996-97, Top Hand awards 1993, 94, 95, 96), Rocky Mountain Soc. Children's Book Writers and Illustrators (mem. bd., retreat dir. 1990, 91, workshop spkr., 1994, 95, 96). Home and Office: 807 Hercules Pl Colorado Springs CO 80906

FRITZ, CHARLES JOHN, artist; b. Mason City, Iowa, Feb. 20, 1955; s. John Walter and Doris Beaunette (Lind) F.; m. Joan Mary Markwardt; children: Isaac John, Erik Charles. BS in Edn., Iowa State U., 1978. Tchr.

Boone (Iowa) Cmty. Sch. Dist., 1978-79; artist Billings, Mont., 1980—; guest artist Western Rendezvous of Art, Helena, Mont., 1992, Buffalo Bill Mus. Art Exhibit, Cody, Wyo., 1992—; juror Okla. Art Guild, Oklahoma City, 1996. One-man shows include Turner Art Gallery, Denver, 1988, 90, 92-95, MacNider Art Mus., Mason City, Iowa, 1995; exhibited in group shows at Miniatures exhibit, Mpls., 1988—, Mus. N.Am. Wildlife, Jackson Hole, Wyo., 1988—, Settlers West Gallery, Tucson, 1988—, Nat. Mus. Wildlife Art, Jackson, Wyo., 1988—, C.M. Russell Mus., Great Falls, Mont., 1989—, Western Heritage Ctr. of Yellowstone County, Billings, 1989, 90-96, Albuquerque Mus. Found., 1990—, Gov.'s Invitational Art Show, Cheyenne (Wyo.) Frontier Days, 1992—, Buffalo Bill Hist. Ctr., Cody, Wyo., 1992—, Thomas Gilcrease Mus., Tulsa, 1992-95, Denver Rotary Club, 1994-96, Nat. Cowboy Hall of Fame, Oklahoma City, 1996, 97, Cin. Mus. Ctr., 1996, C.M. Russell Mus., Great Falls, Mont., 1996; represented in permanent collection Denver Art Mus., Charles H. MacNider Art Mus., Mason City, also pvt. and corp. collections. Rep. bd. St. John's Luth. Home, Billings, 1985-86; chairperson Luth. blood drive United Blood Svcs., Billings, 1993-96; numerous com. and bd. positions Luth. Ch. of Good Shepherd, Billings, 1981-96. Recipient award of merit Wildlife and Western Art Exposition, Mpls., 1987, J. K. Ralston award Western Heritage Ctr. Yellowstone County, Billings, 1989, 90, Dale Hawkins Meml. award Western Heritage Ctr. Yellowstone County, Billings, 1990-95, Juror's Choice-Best of Show, C.M. Russell Art Auction, 1992, 96, Peter Hassrict award of merit Buffalo Bill Hist. Ctr., Cody, 1992, Lee M. Loeb Meml. award for landscape Salmagundi Exhibit, N.Y.C., 1993, Spirit of the West award C.M. Russell Mus. and Art Auction, 1997.

FRITZ, ETHEL MAE HENDRICKSON, writer; b. Gibbon, Nebr., Feb. 4, 1925; d. Walter Earl and Alice Hazel (Mickish) Hendrickson; BS, Iowa State U., 1949; m. C. Wayne Fritz, Feb. 25, 1950; children: Linda Sue, Krista Jane. Dist. home economist Internat. Harvester Co., Des Moines, 1949-50; writer Wallace's Farmer mag., Des Moines, 1960-64; free-lance writer, 1960—. Chmn. Ariz. Council Flower Show Judges, 1983-85; media rels. Presdl. Inaugural Com., 1988. Accredited master flower show judge. Mem. Women in Communications (pres. Phoenix profl. chpt.; nat. task force com. 1980—), Am. Soc. Profl. and Exec. Women, Am. Home Econs. Assn., SW Writers' Conf., Ariz. Authors Assn., Phi Upsilon Omicron, Kappa Delta. Republican. Methodist. Club: PEO. Author: The Story of an Amana Winemaker, 1984, Prairie Kitchen Sampler, 1988, The Family of Hy-Vee, 1989.

FRITZSCHE, KATHLEEN (DRAGONFIRE FRITZSCHE), performing arts educator; b. Liverpool, Eng., Apr. 22, 1943; came to U.S., 1964; d. James and Kathleen Honora (Parry) Walker; m. James Dockery, 1966 (div. 1971); 1 child, James Dockery II; m. Francis Frederick Fritzche, Feb. 14, 1978 (div. 1989); 1 child, Rebecca. Student, L.A. Harbor Coll.; studied with, Lawrence J. Wong, Richard Hatch, Dr. Rodney Oakes. Tchg. staff Angels Gate Cultural Ctr., San Pedro, Calif., 1996—. Writer, composer, performer, artist in various media. Home: 335 Viewland Pl San Pedro CA 90731

FRIZELL, SAMUEL, law educator; b. Buena Vista, Colo., Aug. 30, 1933; s. Franklin Guy and Ruth Wilma (Noel) F.; m. Donna Mae Knowlton, Dec. 26, 1955 (div. June 1973); children: Franklin Guy III, LaVerne Anne; m. Linda Moncure, Jul. 3, 1973. AA cum laude, Ft. Lewis Coll., 1957; BA cum laude, Adams State Coll., 1959, EdM, 1960; JD, Hastings U. Calif., 1964. Bar: Calif. 1965. Assoc. atty. McCutcheon, Black, Verleger & Shea, L.A., L.A., 1964-67; atty. Law Offices Samuel Frizell, Santa Ana, Calif., 1967-82; adj. prof. Cerritos Coll., Norwalk, Calif., 1977-81; adj. prof. Western State U., Fullerton, Calif., 1982-84, assoc. prof., 1984-90, prof., 1990-95; cons. Law Offices Samuel Frizell, Mira Loma, Calif., 1982—. Author: Frizell's Torts Tips, 1992; contbr. articles to profl. jours.; editor law jour. Mem. Main St. Adv. Panel, Garden Grove, Calif., 1975-76; judge pro-tem Orange County Superior Ct., Santa Ana, 1979-80; chair, com. atty. advertising Orange County Bar Assn., 1975; bd. dirs. Orange County Trial Lawyers Assn., 1972-75; adv. panel to legal assts. Cerritos Coll., Norwalk, 1982-86. Fellow Soc. Antiquaries; mem. Order of the Coif. Office: Western State U 1111 N State College Blvd Fullerton CA 92631

FROHMADER, FREDERICK OLIVER, lawyer; b. Tacoma, Wash., Mar. 12, 1930; s. Frederick William and Elizabeth May (Farrell) F.; m. Brenda Frohmader (dec.); children: Fred Albert Aubert, Frederick William, Lisa Kim. BCS, Seattle U., 1953; LLB, Gonzaga U., 1960, JD, 1967. Bar: Wash. Lawyer in pvt. practice, Tacoma, 1960—; with Pierce County Prosecutor, Tacoma, 1961-62; represented various Wash. Indians and Indian tribes in their fishing and hunting rights under various treaties signed with U.S., 1962-83. Served to 1st lt. U.S. Army, 1953-56. Mem. Wash. State Bar Assn., Wash. State Trial Lawyers Assn., Elks. Christian. Home: 629 S Winnifred St Tacoma WA 98465-2538 Office: 1130 S 11th St Tacoma WA 98405-4017

FROHNEN, RICHARD GENE, journalism educator; b. Omaha, Mar. 26, 1930; s. William P. and Florence E. (Rogers) F.; student U. Nebr., Omaha, Mo. Valley Coll., 1948-52; BA, Calif. State U., 1954; MS, UCLA 1961; EdD, Brigham Young U., 1976; grad. Army War Coll., 1982 m. Harlene Grace LeTourneau, July 4, 1958; children: Karl Edward, Eric Eugene. Bus. mgr. athletics and sports publicity dir. U. Nebr., Omaha, 1951-52; pub. rels. dir. First Congl. Ch. Los Angeles, 1953-54, 58-59; writer Los Angeles Mirror News, 1959; gen. assignment reporter, religion editor Los Angeles Times, 1959-61; prof. journalism, dean men Eastern Mont. Coll., Billings, 1961-65; N.W. editor, editorial writer Spokesman-Review, Spokane, 1965-67, also editor Sunday mag.; prof. journalism U. Nev., Reno, 1967-79; exec. dir. devel. Coll. of Desert/Copper Mountain, 1982-85, Ariz. Health Scis. Ctr., Tucson, 1986-90; pub. rels. devel. officer Sch. Med. Scis. U. Nev., 1969-75; adj. prof. mgmt., dir. grad. pros. in Mgmt. U. Redlands (Calif.), 1979-85, 91-95; adj. prof. comm. Calif. State U., Dominguez Hills, 1991-95; cons. Instl. Advancement, Long Beach, Calif., Everett, Wash., 1990—. Mem. exec. bd. Nev. area coun. Boy Scouts Am., 1968-76, coun. commr., 1973-74, v.p., 1975-76; mem. exec. bd. Yellowstone Valley coun. Boy Scouts Am., 1961-65, coun. pres. 1963-64; v.p. Catalina coun. Boy Scouts Am., 1987-90; mem. exec. bd. Long Beach Area Coun., 1990-93; founder, mng. dir. Gt. Western Expdns., 1958-90; adminstrv. asst. to Gov. of Nev., 1985; active Nat. Eagle Scout Assn. Served to 1st lt. USMC, 1954-58; now col. Res., ret. Recipient Silver Beaver award Boy Scouts Am., 1974, Pres.' Vol. Action award Coll. Desert/Copper Mountain, 1984, Outstanding Faculty award U. Redlands, 1984; named to Benson High Sch. Hall of Fame, Omaha, 1988. Mem. Assn. Edn. Journalism, Am. Legion, Res. Officers Assn. U.S., Marine Corps Assn., Marine Corps Res. Officers Assn., Am. Humanics Found., Internat. Platform Assn., Nat. Soc. Fund Raising Execs., N.W. Devel. Officers Assn., Planning Execs. Inst., Internat. Communication Assn., Religion Newswriters Assn., Navy League, Semper Fidelis Soc., Am. Mgmt. Assn., Assn. Am. Med. Colls. Group on Pub. Affairs, Counc. for Advancement and Support Edn., The Ret. Officers Assn., U.S., Assn. for Healthcare Philanthropy, Kiwanis, Lions, Rotary, Kappa Tau Alpha, Alpha Phi Omega, Soc. Profl. Journalists, Sigma Delta Chi (sec.-treas. chpt.). Episcopalian. Office: 1614 Meadow Pl Snohomish WA 98290

FROHNMAYER, DAVID BRADEN, university president; b. Medford, Oreg., July 9, 1940; s. Otto J. and MarAbel (Fisher) B. F.; m. Lynn Diane Johnson, Dec. 30, 1970; children: Kirsten, Mark, Kathryn (dec.), Jonathan, Amy. AB magna cum laude, Harvard U., 1962; BA, Oxford (Eng.) U., 1964, MA (Rhodes scholar), 1971; JD, U. Calif., Berkeley, 1967; LLD (hon.), Willamette U., 1988; D Pub. Svc. (hon.), U. Portland, 1989. Bar: Calif. 1967, U.S. Dist. Ct. (no. dist.) Calif. 1967, Oreg. 1971, U.S. Dist. Ct. Oreg. 1971, U.S. Supreme Ct. 1981. Assoc. Pillsbury, Madison & Sutro, San Francisco, 1967-69; asst. to sec. Dept. HEW, 1969-70; prof. law U. Oreg., 1971-81, spl. asst. to univ. pres., 1971-79; atty. gen. State of Oreg., 1981-91; dean Sch. Law U. Oreg., 1992-94, pres., 1994—; chmn. Conf. Western Attys. Gen., 1985-86; mem. Am. Coun. Edn. Govtl. Rels. commn; bd. dirs. South Umpqua Bank. Mem. Oreg. Ho. of Reps, 1975-81; bd. dirs. Fred Hutchinson Cancer Rsch. Ctr., Nat. Marrow Donor Program, Fanconi Anemia Rsch. Fund, Inc., Qualivest Funds; active Oreg. Progress Bd. Recipient awards Weaver Constl. Law Essay competition Am. Bar Found., 1972, 74; Rhodes scholar, 1962. Mem. ABA (Ross essay winner 1980), Oreg. Bar Assn., Calif. Bar Assn., Nat. Assn. Attys. Gen. (pres. 1987, Wyman award 1987), Round Table Eugene, Order of Coif, Phi Beta Kappa, Rotary. Republican. Presbyterian. Home: 2315 McMorran St Eugene OR 97403-1750 Office: U Oreg Johnson Hall Office of Pres Eugene OR 97403

FROMSON, MURRAY, journalism educator; b. N.Y.C., Sept. 1, 1929; s. Alfred and Frances (Segal) F.; m. Dodi H. Grumbach, May 27, 1961; children: Aliza Bental, Derek Ross. AA in Journalism, L.A. City Coll., 1949; cert. Japan studies, Sophia U., Tokyo, 1954. Reporter The Mirror, L.A., 1950; corr. AP, San Francisco, Seoul, Tokyo, Singapore, Bangkok, 1953-60, NBC News, L.A., 1960-62; corr. CBS News, L.A., Bangkok, Saigon, 1962-76, Chgo., Moscow, Hong Kong, 1962-76; moderator, producer Calif. Pub. Broadcasting, Sacramento, 1980-83; producer Eric Sevareid's Chronicle, 1982; prof. U. So. Calif., L.A., 1982—, dir. Ctr. for Internat. Journalism, 1985-94, dir. Sch. Journalism, 1994—; spl. cons. to pres. U. Calif. Systemwide Adminstrn., Berkeley, 1979; dep. campaign mgr. for media Gov. Jerry Brown, Sacramento, 1978; bd. dirs. Calif. First Amendment Coalition, Sacramento; founding mem. Reporters Com. for Freedom of the Press, Washington, D.C., 1970. Staff sgt. U.S. Army, 1951-52, Korea, Japan. Recipient Outstanding Interpretive Reporting from Vietnam, Overseas Press Club, 1975, Outstanding Spot News Reporting from Vietnam, 1975. Mem. Asia Soc., Japan Am. Soc., Nat. Com. U.S.-China Rels., L.A. Com. on Fgn. Rels., Com. to Protect Journalists (N.Y., chmn. western region), Am. Assocs. Ben Gurion Univ. Jewish. Office: Univ So Calif University Park GFS 326A Los Angeles CA 90089-1695

FRONT, THEODORE, music publishing company executive; b. Darmstadt, Germany, Nov. 26, 1909; s. Hersz and Ryfka (Jankowiak) F. Student, Univ. Munich, 1928-29. Asst. stage dir. Hessisches Landestheater, Darmstadt, 1929-31, Staedtische Opera, Berlin, 1931-33; various positions N.Y.C., 1938-50; asst. to the owner Gateway to Music, L.A., 1950-58; founder Theodore Front Musical Literature, Inc., L.A., 1961—. Democrat. Jewish. Home: 360 S Burnside Ave Apt 1B Los Angeles CA 90036-5401 Office: Theodore Front Musical Lit 16122 Cohasset St Van Nuys CA 91406-2909

FRONTIERE, GEORGIA, professional football team executive; m. Carroll Rosenblum, July 7, 1966 (dec.); children: Dale Carroll, Lucia; m. Dominic Frontiere. Pres., owner L.A. Rams, NFL, 1979—; now mng. ptnr. St. Louis Rams. Bd. dirs. L.A. Boys and Girls Club, L.A. Orphanage Guild, L.A. Blind Youth Found. Named Headliner of Yr., L.A. Press Club, 1981. Office: St Louis Rams 1 Rams Way Saint Louis MO 63045*

FROST, CAROL D., geology educator; b. Salem, Oreg., May 23, 1957; d. O.W. and Mary D. (Bills) F.; m. Eric W. Nye, Dec. 21, 1980; children: Charles W., Ellen M. AB, Dartmouth Coll., 1979; PhD, U. Cambridge, 1984. From asst. prof. to prof. U. Wyoming, Laramie, 1983—; NSF panelist, 1992-96. Mem. Mineralogical Soc. Am., Geochem. Soc., Geol. Soc. Am. (edtl. bd. 1990-96). Office: U Wyo Dept Geology/Geophysics Laramie WY 82071-3006

FROST, EVERETT LLOYD, academic administrator; b. Salt Lake City, Oct. 17, 1942; s. Henry Hoag Jr. and Ruth Salome (Smith) F.; m. Janet Owens, Mar. 26, 1967; children: Noreen Karyn, Joyce Lida. BA in Anthropology, U. Oreg., 1965; PhD in Anthropology, U. Utah, 1970. Field researcher in cultural anthropology Taveuni, Fiji, 1968-69; asst. prof. in anthropology Ea. N.Mex. U., Portales, 1970-74, assoc. prof., 1974-76, asst. dean Coll. Liberal Arts and Scis., 1976-78, dean acad. affairs and grad. studies, 1978-80, v.p. for planning and analysis, dean rsch., 1980-91, dean grad. studies, 1983-88, pres., 1991—; cons., evaluator N. Ctrl. Assn. Accreditation Agy. for Higher Edn., 1989—, mem. rev. bd., 1993—; bd. dirs. Quality N.Mex., 1st Savs. Bank of Clovis and Portales, N.Mex., Plains Regional Med. Ctrs., Clovis and Portales; bd. mem. emeritus N.Mex. First; commr. Western Interstate Commn. for Higher Edn., 1993—; pres. Lone Star Athletic Conf. Pres.'s Commn., 1992—; chmn. rsch. com. N.Mex. First, 1989-91. Chmn. N.Mex. Humanities Coun., 1980-88; mem. N.Mex. Gov.'s Commn. on Higher Edn., 1983-86; mem. exec. bd. N.Mex. First, 1987—; bd. dirs. Roosevelt Gen. Hosp., Portales, 1989—; pres. bd. dirs. San Juan County Mus. Assn., Farmington, 1979-82; vice chair Portales Pub. Schs. Facilities Com., 1990—. NDEA fellow, 1969-70; grantee NEW, 1979-80, NSF, 1968-69, Fiji Forbes, Ltd., 1975-76, others. Fellow Am. Anthropol. Assn., Am. Assn. Higher Edn., Soc. Coll. and Univ. Planning, Assn. Social Anthropologists Oceania, Anthropol. Soc. Washington, Sch. Am. Rsch., Western Assn. Grad. Deans, Current Anthropology (assoc.) Polynesian Soc., Phi Kappa Phi. *

FROST, STANLEY, retired judge; b. Clovis, N.Mex., June 1, 1942; m. Bonnie; children: Warren, Wade, Teresa. AB, N.Mex. Highlands U., 1962; JD, George Wahington U., 1967. Bar: N.Mex., 1967. Assoc. Emmett C. Hart, Esq., Tucumcari, N.Mex., 1968-73; chief judge Tenth Judicial Dist., Tucumcari, N.Mex., 1973-91; justice N.Mex. Supreme Ct., Santa Fe, 1991-96; part time instr., N.Mex. Magistrate Coll., 1982, 83; faculty advisor Nat. Judicial Coll. Univ. Nev., 1981, del. Nat. Judicial Conf. on the Rights of Victims of Crime, 1983; lectr. various confs.; mem. Standing Com. on Implementation of the State Bar Task Force Report on Women in the Legal Profession, Region IV Criminal Justice Planning Commn., N.Mex. Judicial Standards Commn. Mem. Am. Judicature Soc., Nat. Coun. of Juvenile and Family Ct. Judges, Nat. Conf. of State Trial Judges (com. on judicial immunity), N.Mex. Outdoor Drama Assn. (mem. bd. dirs.), N.Mex. Dist. Judges Assn. (mem. bd. dirs.), N.Mex. Judicial Standards Commn., Kiwanis Internat. Democrat. Home: 3 Torreon Ct Santa Fe NM 87505*

FROST, STERLING NEWELL, arbitrator, mediator, management consultant; b. Oklahoma City, Dec. 21, 1935; s. Sterling Johnson and Eula Dove (Whitford) F.; m. Patricia Joyce Rose, Aug. 18, 1957; children: Patricia Diane Wiscarson, Richard Sterling, Lindy Layne Harrington. BS Indsl. Engring., U. Okla., Norman, 1957; MS Indsl. Engring., Okla. State U., 1966. Registered profl. engr., Okla. Calif. Asst. mgr. acctg. Western Electric, Balt., 1972-73, mgr. indsl. engring., Chgo., 1973-75, mgr. devel. engring., 1975-76, mgr. acct. mgmt., San Francisco, 1976-78, dir. staff, Morristown, N.J., 1978-79; gen. mgr. distbn. & repair AT&T Techs., Sunnyvale, Calif., 1979-85, area v.p. material mgt. svcs. AT&T Info. Systems, Oakland, Calif., 1985-87, ops. v.p. material mgmt. svcs., San Francisco, 1988-89; dir. configuration ops. Businessland, Inc., San Jose, Calif., 1989-90, dir. svcs. support, 1990-91; exec. v.p. Isotek, Tiburon, Calif., 1991; v.p., gen. mgr. Tree Fresh, San Francisco, 1991-92; CFO Prima Pacific, Inc., Tiburon, 1992-93; mgmt. cons., arbitrator/mediator, Sterling Solutions, Tiburon, 1993—; bd. dirs. Contract Office Group, San Jose, 1983—, chmn., 1984. Bd. dirs. Santa Clara County YMCA, San Jose, Calif., 1981-84, bd. dirs., Northern Calif. Medication Assn., 1994, Recipient Man of Day citation Sta. WAIT Radio, Chgo. Mem. Nat. Soc. Prof. Engrs. (chmn. edn. com. 1969-70), Am. Inst. Indsl. Engrs. (pres. bd. dirs. 1966-68), Okla. Soc. Profl. Engrs. (v.p. 1968-69), No. Calif. Mediation Assn. (bd. dirs. 1996—), Am. Arbitration Assn., Soc. Profls. in Dispute Resolution. Republican. Baptist.

FROST, W. GREGORY, mortgage company executive; b. San Mateo, Calif., Mar. 17, 1949; s. James Homer and Mary Viola (Rael) F.: m. Devon Tyler Young, Aug. 7, 1988; children: W. Gregory Jr., Derek Adam. BS, U. N.Mex., 1971; postgrad., Tex. Tech U., 1979. V.p. Am. Savs. & Loan, Albuquerque, 1972-77; pres., chief exec. officer Devargas Savs. & Loan, Santa Fe, N.Mex., 1977-80; regional v.p. Citi Fed Mortgage, Albuquerque, 1981-84; v.p. Foster Mortgage Corp., Albuquerque, 1985-87; sr. v.p. Banc Plus Mortgage Corp., Albuquerque, 1987-91; pres. Frost Mortgage Banking Group, Albuquerque, 1991—; lectr., mortgage banking sales trainer; profl. motivational sales trainer The Duncan Group, 1990—. Author: Cross Selling the Listing Agent, 1991, Selling to First Time Home Buyers, 1992, The Assistant System, 1994. Chmn. N.Mex. Dem. rules com., 1977-80; mem. pres.'s coun. Dem. Nat. Com., 1977-80; bd. dirs. Albuquerque Civic Light Opera, 1989-92; bd. dirs., pres. U. N.Mex. Alumni Lettermen, Albuquerque, 1990—; N.Mex. state dir. Fellowship Christian Atheletes, 1994—; dir. Nat. Football Found., 1996—; bd. dirs., treas. Albuquerque Sports Coun., 1994—. Named one of Outstanding Young Men Am., 1980, 81. Mem. Albuquerque Petroleum Club, Albuquerque Country Club, UNM Lobo Club (bd. dirs.), Sigma Alpha Epsilon (eminent dep. archon). Roman Catholic. Home: 5425 Eakes Rd NW Albuquerque NM 87107-5531 Office: Frost Mortgage Banking Grp 2051 Wyoming Blvd NE Albuquerque NM 87112-2615

FRUCHTER, JONATHAN SEWELL, research scientist, geochemist; b. San Antonio, June 5, 1945; s. Benjamin and Dorothy Ann (Sewell) F.; m. Cecelia Ann Smith, Mar. 31, 1973; children: Diane, Daniel. BS in Chemistry, U. Tex., 1966; PhD in Geochemistry, U. Calif., San Diego, 1971. Research assoc. U. Oreg., Eugene, 1971-74; research scientist Battelle Northwest, Richland, Wash., 1974-79, mgr. research and devel., 1979-87, staff scientist, 1987-91, 94—, tech. group leader, 1991-94. Contbr. numerous articles to profl. jours. Mem. AAAS, Am. Chem. Soc., Phi Beta Kappa, Phi Kappa Phi. Office: Battelle NW PO Box 999 Richland WA 99352-0999

FRUSETTA, JAMES WALTER, historian, researcher; b. Arlington Heights, Ill., June 7, 1971; s. Walter James Frusetta and Jo Ellen Crow-Epps. B History, U. So. Calif., 1992, B Internat. Rels., 1992; M History, Ariz. State U., 1996; postgrad., U. Md., 1996—. Opinion editor State Press, Tempe, Ariz., 1993-95; grad. asst. Ariz. State U., Tempe, 1994-95; copy editor Mi-An Pub., Skopje, Macedonia, 1995-96; fellow U. Md., College Park, 1996—; rschr. Navigator Pub., Olympia, Wash., 1996—; Ariz. State U. exch. fellow U. Sts. Cyril and Methodius, 1995-96. Lang. grantee Am. Coun. Learned Socs., 1995; fellow Nat. Security Edn. Program, 1995-96. Mem. Am. Assn. for Advancement of Slavic Studies, Internat. Studies Assn., Phi Beta Kappa, Phi Kappa Phi, Phi Alpha Theta.

FRUSH, JAMES CARROLL, JR., real estate development company executive; b. San Francisco, Oct. 18, 1930; s. James Carroll and Edna Mae (Perry) F.; m. Patricia Anne Blake, Oct. 29, 1960 (div. 1977); children: Michael, Gloria; m. Carolyn Fetter Bell, Aug. 23, 1978; 1 child, Stephen. BA, Stanford, 1953; postgrad., U. Calif., San Francisco, 1957-58; MA, Saybrook Inst., 1981, PhD, 1985. Ptnr. James C. Frush Co., San Francisco, 1960-70; v.p., bd. dir. Retirement Residence, Inc., San Francisco, 1964-70, pres., 1970—; pres. Nat. Retirement Residence, San Francisco, 1971-89, Casa Dorinda Corp., 1971-89; chairperson Retirement Residence Inc. Ala., Daphne, 1995—; pres. Marin Shakespeare Festival, 1971-73, James C. Frush Found., 1972-78; adj. prof. gerontology, psychology and theology Spring Hill Coll., Mobile, Ala., 1988—; adj. prof. counseling edn. U. South Ala., Mobile; bd. dirs. Gwynned Inc., Blue Bell, Pa.; dir. Heritage Retirement Housing, Inc., Daphne, Ala., 1996—. Author (with Benson Eschenbach): The Retirement Residence: An Analysis of the Architecture and Management of Life Care Housing, 1968, Self-Esteem in Older Persons Following a Heart Attack: An Exploration of Contributing Factors, 1985; contbr. articles to profl. jours.; producer ednl. films. Bd. dirs. San Francisco Sr. Ctr., 1973-78, Found. to Assist Calif. Tchrs. Devel. Inc., 1987-89; mem. adv. bd. Christus Theol. Inst., Mobile, Ala., 1992-95; mem. ethics com. adv. bd. Westminster Village, Spanish Ft., 1994—; bd. dirs. com. affirmative aging Episc. Diocese Ctrl. Gulf Coast. Mem. Gerontol. Soc., Southeastern Psychol. Assn., Assn. for Anthropology and Gerontology, Stanford Alumni Assn., RSVP (adv. bd. Mobile chpt. 1988-94), C.G. Jung Soc. of Gulf Coast (pres.), Ala. Humanities Found. Speakers Bur. (presenter 1993-94, 94-95). Office: care T Pimsleur 2155 Union St San Francisco CA 94123-4003

FRY, EVA MARGARET, volunteer worker; b. Calgary, Alta., Can.; d. John Robert and Edith Marion (Duckworth) Maeers; m. Albert Norman Fry, Mar. 14, 1959; children: Linda Marie Wright, Laurie Elizabeth Poirier, Kevin Alan. Lic. real estate agt., Calif. Developer, spkr. juvenile motivational program Be A Winner In Life, San Diego. Mem. MADD, WCTU, PHi Rho Pi. Republican. Mem. LDS Ch. Home: 12120 Fry Ln Valley Center CA 92082

FRY, STEPHEN MICHAEL, music librarian; b. Boise, Idaho, Jan. 5, 1941; s. Homer N. and Alice F.; m. Frances Talbott-White, Jan. 26, 1963; children: John, Kenneth. BA in Music, U. Calif., Riverside, 1964; MA in Music, Claremont (Calif.) Grad. Sch., 1965; MSLS, U. So. Calif., L.A., 1969. Music libr. U. Calif., Riverside, 1966-70; prof. of music Ind. U. of Pa., Indian, Pa., 1970-72; music libr. Northwestern U., Evanston, Ill., 1973-75, UCLA, 1975—; presenter confs. in field; cons. Anton Brees Carillon Libr., Mountain Lake Sanctuary, Lake Wales, Fla., 1972-82; reader Project for the Oral History of Music in Am., N.Y., 1976; cons. in field; dir. Westside Jazz Ensemble, 1989—. Author: California's Musical Wealth, 1985, The Story of the All Women's Orchestras in California, 1985; music editor: American National Biography, 1994—; contbr. articles to profl. jours. Mem. Soc. for Preservation of Film Music (trustee 1986—, sec. 1990—), Music Libr. Assn. (bd. dirs. 1979-81, 95—), Soc. for Preservation of Musical Heritage of So. Calif. (bd. advs. 1988—). Republican. Office: UCLA Music Libr 1102 Schoenberg Hall Univ Calif Los Angeles CA 90095-1490

FRYE, HELEN JACKSON, judge; b. Klamath Falls, Oreg., Dec. 10, 1930; d. Earl and Elizabeth (Kirkpatrick) Jackson; m. William Frye, Sept. 7, 1952; children: Eric, Karen, Heidi; 1 adopted child, Hedy; m. Perry Holloman, July 10, 1980 (dec. Sept. 1991). BA in English with honors, U. Oreg., 1953, MA, 1960, JD, 1966. Bar: Oreg. 1966. Public sch. tchr. Oreg., 1956-63; with Riddlesberger, Pederson, Brownhill & Young, 1966-67, Husband & Johnson, Eugene, 1968-71; trial judge State of Oreg., 1971-80; U.S. dist judge Dist. Oreg. Portland, 1980-95; sr. judge U.S. Dist. Ct., Portland, 1995—. Office: US Dist Ct 119 US Courthouse 620 SW Main St Portland OR 97205-3037

FRYE, JUDITH ELEEN MINOR, editor; b. Seattle; d. George Edward and Eleen G. (Hartelius) Minor; student UCLA, 1947-48, U. So. Calif., 1948-53; m. Vernon Lester Frye, Apr. 1, 1954. Acct., office mgr. Colony Wholesale Liquor, Culver City, Calif., 1947-48; credit mgr. Western Distbg. Co., Culver City, 1948-53; ptnr. in restaurants, Palm Springs, L.A., 1948, ptnr. in date ranch, La Quinta, Calif., 1949-53; ptnr., owner Imperial Printing, Huntington Beach, Calif., 1955—; editor, pub. New Era Laundry and Cleaning Lines, Huntington Beach, 1962—; registered lobbyist, Calif., 1975-84. Mem. Textile Care Allied Trade Assn., Laundry & Dry Cleaning Suppliers Assn., Calif. Coin-op Assn. (exec. dir. 1975-84, Cooperation award 1971, Dedicated Svc.award 1976), Nat. Automatic Laundry & Cleaning Coun. (Leadership award 1972), Women Laundry & Drycleaning (past pres., Outstanding Svc. award 1977), Printing Industries Assn., Master Printers Am., Nat. Assn. Printers & Lithographers. Office: 22031 Bushard St Huntington Beach CA 92646-8409

FRYE, SUSAN CAROLINE, English literature educator; b. Palo Alto, Calif., June 14, 1952; d. Bruce Bradford and Caroline (Reid) Frye; m. Thomas Carlisle Hacker, June 19, 1975 (div. Nov. 1988); 1 child, Elizabeth. BA, Smith Coll., 1974; MA, U. N.Mex., 1981; PhD, Stanford U., 1987. Tchr. English and social studies Sutton (Mass.) H.S., 1974-76, Rio Grande H.S., Albuquerque, 1976-82; asst. prof. English U. Wyo., Laramie, 1986-92, assoc. prof., 1992—. Author: Elizabeth I, 1993; co-editor: Women's Alliances in Early Modern England, 1997. NEH fellow, 1995-96; Folger Shakespeare Libr. grantee, 1995; Wyo. Coun. for Humanities grantee, 1987, 89, 92. Mem. MLA, Rocky Mountain Medieval and Renaissance Assn. (exec. bd., pres. 1986—), Spenser Soc. Am. (exec. bd. 1996—), Soc. for Study of Early Modern Women (nominating com. 1997—), Medieval Feminist Newsletter, Renaissance Soc. Am. Democrat. Jewish. Office: U Wyo Dept English PO Box 3353 Laramie WY 82071

FRYE, TODD MICHAEL, counselor; b. Kudjip, Papua New Guinea, Sept. 22, 1969; came to U.S., 1973; s. Harold Frederick and Janice Irene (Toone) F.; m. Melissa Marie Green, June 12, 1993. BA in Psychology, N.W. Nazarene Coll., 1992, MEd in Counseling, 1996. Psychiat. technician N.W. Passages Hosp., Boise, Idaho, Intermountain Hosp., Boise, Idaho; family cons. Idaho Youth Ranch, Boise, Idaho, 1994—. V.p. providence ministries N.W. Nazarene Coll., Nampa, Idaho, 1992. Mem. Am. Counseling Assn., Idaho Counseling Assn., Idaho Mental Health Assn. Republican. Nazarene. Home: 1208 Hawaii Nampa ID 83686 Office: Idaho Youth Ranch 7025 Emerald St Boise ID 83704-8657

FRYE, WILLIAM EMERSON, physicist, engineer; b. Detroit, June 20, 1917; s. Nels and Lillie (Hagman) F.; m. Elizabeth K. Sayler, June 13, 1942 (dec. 1990); children: Ann, James. AA, Danville (Ill.) Jr. Coll., 1935; AB, U. Ill., 1937, MS, 1938; PhD, U. Chgo., 1941. Group leader, then asst. sect. head Naval Rsch. Lab., Washington, 1942-46; group leader N.Am. Aviation, Inc., L.A., 1946-48; staff mem. Rand Corp., Santa Monica, Calif., 1948-56; dept. mgr. Lockheed Missiles and Space Co., Palo Alto, Calif., 1956-59, consulting scientist, 1959-68, staff scientist, 1968—; rsch. adv. com. NASA, Washington, 1960-64; lectr. in engring. UCLA, 1948-56; lectr. in elec. engring. Stanford (Calif.) U., 1960, 62, 64, 68. Editor: Impact of Space Exploration on Society, 1965. Calendar editor Coun. for Arts, Palo Alto, 1964-68. Recipient Meritorious Civilian Svc. award Naval Rsch. Lab., 1947. Assoc. fellow AIAA; mem. Am. Astronautical Soc. (bd. dirs. 1960-64), Am. Phys. Soc., Sigma Xi, Phi Beta Kappa. Democrat. Unitarian. Home: 536 Lincoln Ave Palo Alto CA 94301-3232

FRYER, GLADYS CONSTANCE, retired physician, medical director, educator; b. London, Mar. 28, 1923; came to U.S., 1967; d. William John and Florence Annie (Dockett) Mercer; m. Donald Wilfred Fryer, Jan. 20, 1944; children: Peter Vivian, Gerard John, Gillian Celia. MB, BS, U. Melbourne, Victoria, Australia, 1956. Resident Box Hill Hosp., 1956-57; postdoctoral fellow Inst. of Cardiology, U. London, 1958; med. registrar Queen Victoria Hosp., Melbourne, Australia, 1958; cardiologist Assunta Found., Petaling Jaya, Malaysia, 1961-64; fellow in advanced medicine London Hosp., U. London, 1964; clin. research physician U.S. Army Clin. Research Unit, Malaysia, 1964-66; physician to pesticide program U. Hawaii, 1967-68; internist Hawaii Permanente Kaiser Found., Honolulu, 1968-73; practice medicine specializing in internal medicine Honolulu, 1973-88; med. dir. Hale Nani Health Ctr., Honolulu, 1975-89, Beverly Manor Convalescent Ctr., Honolulu, 1975-89; vis. pediatric cardiac depts. Yale U., Stanford U., U. Calif., 1958; asst. clin. prof. medicine John Burns Sch. Medicine U. Hawaii, 1968-89; vis. geriatrics dept. U. Capetown, 1990; med. cons. Salvation Army Alcohol Treatment Facility, Honolulu, 1975-81; physician to skilled nursing patients VA, Honolulu, 1984-88; preceptor to geriatric nurse practitioner program U. Colo., Honolulu, 1984-85; lectr. on geriatrics, Alzheimer's disease, gen. medicine, profl. women's problems, and neurosci., 1961—; mem. ad hoc due process bd. Med. Care Evaluation Com., 1982-88, Hospice Adv. Com., 1982-88; mem. pharmacy com. St. Francis Hosp. Clin. Staff, 1983-89, chmn. 1983-84. Contbr. articles to med. and sci. jours. Mem. adv. com. Honolulu Home Care St. Francis Hosp., 1974-87; mem. adv. bd. Honolulu Gerontology Program, 1983-89, Straub Home Health Program, Honolulu, 1984-87; mem. sci. adv. bd. Alzheimers Disease and Related Disorders Assn., Honolulu, 1984-89; mem. long term care task force Health and Community Svcs. Coun. Hawaii, 1978-84. Special Ops. Exec., War Office, London, 1943-44. Recipient Edgar Rouse Prize in Indsl. Medicine, U. Melbourne, 1955, Outstanding Supporter award Hawaii Assn. Activity Coordinators, 1987. Fellow ACP; mem. AAAS, AMA, Hawaii Med. Assn. (councillor 1984-89), Honolulu County Med. Soc. (chmn., mem. utilization rev. com. 1973-89), World Med. Assn., Am. Geriatrics Soc., N.Y. Acad. Sci. Episcopalian.

FRYER, ROBERT SHERWOOD, theatrical producer; b. Washington, Nov. 18, 1920; s. Harold and Ruth (Reade) F. B.A., Western Res. U., 1943. Producer: (Broadway plays) (with others) A Tree Grows in Brooklyn, 1951, (with others) By the Beautiful Sea, 1954, Wonderful Town, 1953, The Desk Set, Shangri-La, Auntie Mame, Redhead, There Was a Little Girl, Advise and Consent, A Passage To India, Hot Spot, Roar Like a Dove, Sweet Charity, Chicago, 1975, The Norman Conquests, 1976, California Suite, 1976, On the Twentieth Century, 1977, Sweeney Todd, 1978, Merrily We Roll Along, The West Side Waltz, 1981, Noises Off, 1983, Benefactors, 1985, Wild Honey, 1987, Hapgood, 1989, (films) The Boston Strangler, 1968, Abdication, 1973, Mame, 1973, Great Expectations, 1974, Voyage of the Damned, 1976, The Boys from Brazil, 1978, Prime of Miss Jean Brodie 1969, Travels with My Aunt, 1973, The Shining 1979, Chicago, 1997—, artistic dir., 1972-90; cons., 1990—; Ahmanson Theatre, Ctr. Theatre Group, L.A.; author: Professional Theatrical Management New York City, 1947. Bd. dirs. Kennedy Ctr.; trustee, exec. com. John F. Kennedy Ctr., Washington. Served as capt. AUS, 1941-46; maj. Res. Decorated Legion of Merit.; Rockefeller Found. fellow. Mem. Episcopal Actors Guild (v.p.), League of N.Y. Theatres (bd. govs.). Office: Producer Cir Co 200 W 57th St #1403 New York NY 10019 *I am grateful for all God has given me, and I feel an obligation to Him to return goodness and kindness to my fellowman.*

FRYKMAN, GEORGE AXEL, history educator, researcher; b. South San Francisco, Calif., Apr. 30, 1917; s. Axel George and Esther Sophia (Hultberg) F.; m. Elizabeth Marie Fulton, June 14, 1942; children: Alice, Jean, Mary. BA in History, San Jose State U., 1940; MA in History, Stanford U., 1947, PhD in History, 1955. Cert. gen. secondary edn., Calif. Tchr. English and social studies Kerman (Calif.) H.S., 1941-42; instr. Western civilization Stanford (Calif.) U., 1949-50; instr. history Wash. State U., Pullman, 1950-51, asst. libr., instr. history, 1951-53, from instr. history to prof. history, 1953-87, asst. to dean Grad. Sch., 1961-64, prof. of history emeritus, 1987—. Co-editor: (symposium) Changing Pacific Northwest, 1988; author: (univ. history) Creating the People's University, 1990; adv. editor: Wash. State Ency. Americana, 1959-64; book rev. editor: The Historian, 1964-66; mem. editl. adv. bd. Pacific N.W. Quar., 1980-94. Capt. USAF, 1942-46. Democrat. Lutheran. Home: SE1015 Spring St Pullman WA 99163

FRYMER, MURRY, columnist, theater critic, critic-at-large; b. Toronto, Ont., Can., Apr. 24, 1934; came to U.S., 1945; s. Dave and Sylvia (Spinrod) F.; m. Barbara Lois Grown, Sept. 4, 1966; children: Paul, Benjamin, Carrie. BA, U. Mich., 1956; student Columbia U., 1958; MA, NYU, 1964. Editor Town Crier, Westport, Conn., 1962-63, Tribune, Levittown, N.Y., 1963-64; viewpoints editor, critic Newsday, L.I., N.Y., 1964-72; asst. mng. editor Rochester Democrat & Chronicle, N.Y., 1972-75; Sunday and feature editor Cleve. Plain Dealer, 1975-77; editor Sunday Mag., Boston Herald Am., 1977-79; film and TV critic San Jose Mercury News, Calif., 1979-83, theater critic, 1983—, columnist, 1983—; instr. San Jose State U., Cleve. State U., judge Emmy awards NATAS, 1968. Author, dir. musical revue Four by Night, N.Y.C., 1963; author (play) Danse Marriage, 1955 (Hopwood prize 1955); author, dir. 6th U.S. Army show A Dozen and One, 1958. Served with U.S. Army, 1956-58. Recipient Best Columnist/Critic award Calif. Publishers Assn., 1993; named Best Columnist, Peninsula Calif. Press Club, 1993. Home: 1060 Moongate Pl San Jose CA 95120-2031 Office: San Jose Mercury News 750 Ridder Park Dr San Jose CA 95131-2432

FRYT, MONTE STANISLAUS, petroleum company executive, speaker, advisor; b. Jackson, Mich., Aug. 3, 1949; s. Marion S. and Dorothy A. (Fischman) F.; m. Pollyanna Hayes, May 26, 1990. BS in Aerospace Engring., U. Colo., Boulder, 1971; MBA in Mgmt., U. Colo., Denver, 1988. Field engr. Schlumberger Well Svcs., Bakersfield, Calif., 1971-75; computer R & D engr. Schlumberger Well Svcs., Houston, 1975-77; account devel. engr. Schlumberger Well Svcs., L.A., 1977-78; dist. mgr. Schlumberger Well Svcs., Abilene, Tex., 1978-80, Williston, N.D., 1980-81; v.p. ops. Logmate Svcs. Inc., Calgary, Alta., Can., 1981-84; pres. Fryt Petroleum Inc., Denver, 1984-91; mgr. petrophysics Am. Hunter Exploration, Ltd., Denver, 1991-92; prin. Reservoir Evaluations Group, Denver, 1992—; ptnr., mgr. Monteray Energy LLC, Denver, 1994—; mgr. tech. Anschutz Exploration Corp., 1995—. Mem. Colo. Rep. Com., 1990—, Rep. Nat. Com., Colo. Rep. Leadership Program, 1992-93; mem. exec. com. Colo. Rep. Bus. Coalition, 1993—, vice-chmn., 1996-97, chmn., 1997—. Mem. Am. Assn. Petroleum Geologists, Rocky Mountain Assn. Geologists, Elks, Rockies Venture Club. Roman Catholic. Home: 7400 S Curtice Ct Littleton CO 80120 Office: Ste 2400 555 17th St Denver CO 80202-3941

FU, LEE-LUENG, oceanographer; b. Taipei, Republic of China, Oct. 10, 1950; s. Yi-Chin and Er-Lan (Chen) F.; m. Cecilia C. Liu, Mar. 26, 1977; 1 child, Christine. BS, Nat. Taiwan U., Taipei, 1972; PhD, MIT, 1980. Postdoctoral assoc. MIT, Cambridge, Mass., 1980; mem. tech. staff Jet Propulsion Lab., Pasadena, Calif., 1981-85, tech. group supr., 1986-93, project scientist, 1988—, lead scientist/ocean scis., 1994, sr. rsch. scientist, 1994; chmn. TOPEX/POSEIDON sci. working team NASA, Washington, 1988—, mem. EOS sci. steering com., 1985-87, mem. NSCAT sci. working team, 1986—. Contbr. articles to profl. publs. Recipient Laurels award Aviation Week and Space Tech., 1993, CNES medal French Space Agy., 1994, Exceptional Scientific Achievement medal NASA, 1996. Mem. AAAS, Am. Geophys. Union, Am. Meteorol. Soc., Oceanography Soc. Office: Jet Propulsion Lab MS 300-323 4800 Oak Grove Dr Pasadena CA 91109-8001

FUCHS, ROLAND JOHN, geography educator, university science official; b. Yonkers, N.Y., Jan. 15, 1933; s. Alois L. and Elizabeth (Weigand) F.; m. Gaynell Ruth McAuliffe, June 15, 1957; children: Peter K., Christopher K., Andrew K. BA, Columbia U., 1954, postgrad., 1956-57; postgrad., Moscow State U., 1960-61; MA, Clark U., 1957, PhD, 1959, DSc (hon.), 1995. Asst. prof. to prof. emeritus U. Hawaii, Honolulu, 1958—, chmn. dept. geography, 1964-86, asst. dean to assoc. dean coll. arts and scis., 1965-67, dir. Asian Studies Lang. and Area Ctr., 1965-67, adj. rsch. assoc. East West Ctr., 1980—, spl. asst. to pres., 1986; vice rector UN U., Tokyo, 1987-94; dir. Internat. Start Secretariat, 1994—; vis. prof. Clark U., 1963-64, Nat. Taiwan U., 1974; mem. bd. internat. orgns. and programs Nat. Acad. Scis., 1976-81, chmn., 1980-81, mem. bd. sci. and tech. in devel., 1980-85; mem. U.S. Nat. Commn. for Pacific Basin Econ. Coop., 1985-87; sr. advisor United Nations U., 1986. Author, editor: Geographical Perspectives on the Soviet Union, 1974, Theoretical Problems of Geography, 1977, Population Distribution Policies in Development Planning, 1981, Urbanization and Urban Policies in the Pacific-Asia Region, 1987, Megacities: The Challenge of the Urban Future, 1994; asst. editor Econ. Geography, 1963-64; mem. editl. adv. com. Soviet Geography: Rev. and Translation, 1966-85, Geoforum, 1988—, African Urban Quar., 1987, Global Environ. Change, 1990—, Asian Geographer, 1991—. Ford Found. fellow, 1956-57; Fulbright Rsch. scholar, 1966-67. Mem. Assn. Am. Geographers, Am. Geophys. Union, Internat. Geog. Union (v.p. 1980-84, 1st v.p. 1984-88, pres. 1988-92, past pres. 1992—), Assn. Am. Geographers (Hon. award 1982), Am. Assn. Advancement of Slavic Studies (bd. dirs. 1976-81), Pacific Sci. Assn. (mem. coun. 1978—, mem. exec. com. 1986—, sec. gen-treas. 1991—), Acad. Europaea (fgn.). Home: 1200 N Nash St Arlington VA 22209

FUCHS, THOMAS, writer; b. L.A., Dec. 2, 1942; s. Daniel and Susan (Chessen) F. BA, U. Calif., Santa Barbara, 1965. Freelance writer, 1966—; dir. rsch. Wolper Prodns., L.A., 1966-69; staff writer You Asked for It, L.A., 1982; staff writer Ripley's Believe It or Not ABC-TV, L.A., 1983-85; mem. Theater West, Los Angeles. Writer: (TV series pilot) Escape, (TV spls.) What Would You Pay for Yesterday, Henry Fonda: An American Legacy, Crimes of Passion, Mysteries of the Bible, Ancient Mysteries, Biography, (one-act plays) Two Old Friends, Yea, Beethoven!, (films) Dinosaur, 1987, Two Old Friends, 1987, A Night of Miracles, 1990, (corp. films) Ralson Purina, Occidental Petroleum, Universal Studios Tour, Mobil Oil, Bank of Am., Simon Wiesenthal Ctr.; author: The Hitler Fact Book, 1990; contbr. articles to L.A. Times, New West, WGA Jour., New Obs., Hollywood Reporter, Travel & Leisure; supervising prodr.: Film Roos. Mem. acquisitions com. Hollywood Expn., Los Angeles. Mem. Writers Guild Am.

FUCHS, VICTOR ROBERT, economics educator; b. N.Y.C., Jan. 31, 1924; s. Alfred and Frances Sarah (Scheiber) F.; m. Beverly Beck, Aug. 29, 1948; children: Nancy, Fredric, Paula, Kenneth. BS, NYU, 1947; MA, Columbia U., 1951, PhD, 1955. Internat. fur broker, 1946-50; lectr. Columbia U., N.Y.C., 1953-54, instr., 1954-55, asst. prof. econs., 1955-59; assoc. prof. econs. NYU, 1959-60; program assoc. Ford Found. Program in Econ. Devel. and Adminstrn., 1960-62; prof. econs. Grad. Ctr., CUNY, 1968-74; prof. community medicine Mt. Sinai Sch. Medicine, 1968-74; prof. econs. Stanford U. and Stanford Med. Sch., 1974-95, Henry J. Kaiser Jr. prof., 1988-95, prof. emeritus, 1995—; v.p. research Nat. Bur. Econ. Research, 1968-78, mem. sr. research staff, 1962—. Author: The Economics of the Fur Industry, 1957; (with Aaron Warner) Concepts and Cases in Economic Analysis, 1958, Changes in the Location of Manufacturing in the United States Since 1929, 1962, The Service Economy, 1968, Production and Productivity in the Service Industries, 1969, Policy Issues and Research Opportunities in Industrial Organization, 1972, Essays in the Economics of Health and Medical Care, 1972, Who Shall Live? Health, Economics and Social Choice, 1975; (with Joseph Newhouse) The Economics of Physician and Patient Behavior, 1978, Economic Aspects of Health, 1982, How We Live, 1983, The Health Economy, 1986, Women's Quest for Economic Equality, 1988, The Future of Health Policy, 1993, Individual and Social Responsibility: Child Care Education, Medical Care, and Long-term Care in America, 1996.; contbr. articles to profl. jours. Served with USAAF, 1943-46. Fellow Am. Acad. Arts and Scis., Am. Econ. Assn. (disting.; pres. 1995); mem. Inst. Medicine of NAS, Am. Philos. Soc., Sigma Xi, Beta Gamma Sigma. Home: 796 Cedro Way Stanford CA 94305-1032 Office: NBER 204 Junipero Serra Blvd Stanford CA 94305-6072

FUERST, DAVID JONATHAN, ophthalmologist, educator; b. Bklyn., Apr. 27, 1954; s. Adolph and Shirley Rita (Miller) F.; m. Marie Madeline Perrelli, Jan. 2, 1983; children: Jessica Lauren, Nicole Michelle, Jason Aaron. ScB, Brown U., 1975, MD, 1978. Diplomate Am. Bd. Ophthalmology. Intern in internal medicine L.I. Jewish-Hillside Med. Ctr., New Hyde Park, N.Y., 1978-79; resident in ophthalmology U. Ill. Eye and Ear Infirmary, Chgo., 1979-82, asst. in ophthalmology, 1980-81, instr., 1981-82; fellow in cornea and external disease U. Calif. Proctor Found. for Rsch. in Ophthalmology, San Francisco, 1982-83, clin. instr., 1982-83; pvt. practice, L.A., 1983—; dir. cornea and external disease svc. White Meml. Med. Ctr., L.A., 1983—, dir. residency program, 1990-95; mem. faculty U. So. Calif., L.A., 1983—; mem. attending staff Cedars-Sinai Med. Ctr., L.A.; mem. courtesy staff Midway Hsop. Med. Ctr., L.A., St. Vincent Med. Ctr., L.A.; mem. attending staff Little Company of Mary, Torrance, Calif.; mem. assoc. staff Queen of Valley Hosp., West Covna, Calif.; co-founder Pacific EyeNet; presenter, lectr. in field. Contbr. articles to med. jours., chpts. to books. Fellow Am. Acad. Ophthalmology; mem. Eye Bank Assn. Am., Internat. Soc. Refractive Surgery, Assn. Proctor Fellows, Calif. Med. Assn. (alt. del. 1988-89), Calif. Assn. Ophthalmologists (bd. dirs. dist. 4B 1996—, asst. v.p., v.p. 1988—), L.A. County Med. Assn. (precinct rep. 1986-88), L.A. Soc. Ophthalmology. Democrat. Jewish. Office: Pacific Eyenet Inc 5750 Wilshire Blvd Ste 285 Los Angeles CA 90036-3697

FUGIEL, FRANK PAUL, insurance company executive; b. Chgo., Aug. 23, 1950; s. Richard A. and Sally (McKinney) F.; m. Nancy Campbell, Sept. 15, 1973; children: Michele, Rachelle. Student, SUNY, Albany. CLU. Individual underwriter Prudential Ins. Co., Merrillville, Ind., 1971-80, group claims mgr., 1980-82, underwriting mgr., 1982-84; group claims officer Employers Health Ins. Co., Green Bay, Wis., 1984-86, underwriting officer, 1986-88, managed care officer, 1988; 2d v.p. individual health ins. Washington Nat. Ins. Co., 1988-90, v.p. ops., 1990; exec. v.p. Oak Brook (Ill.) group divsn. Aegon U.S.A., 1990-94; exec. v.p. TPA divsn. Centennial Life Ins. Co., Merriam, Kans., 1994-95; v.p. managed care adminstrn. United Chambers HealthCare Corp., Naperville, Ill., 1995-96; v.p. mktg. and product devel. Insurers Adminstrv. Corp., Phoenix, Ariz., 1996—. Councilman Hobart, Ind. C. of C., 1981. Served as sgt. USMC, 1970-76. Fellow Life Office Mgmt. Inst., Acad. Life Underwriting; mem. Internat. Claims Assn. (assoc. life and health claims), Life Underwriting Edn. Com., Inst. Home Office Underwriters. Home: 17440 W Tatum Blvd Apt 333 Phoenix AZ 85032 Office: Insurers Adminstrv Corp VP Mktg Product Devel 10210 N 25th Ave Ste 300 Phoenix AZ 85024-1605

FUHLRODT, NORMAN THEODORE, former insurance executive; b. Wisner, Nebr., Apr. 24, 1910; s. Albert F. and Lena (Schafersman) F.; student Midland Coll., 1926-28; A.B., U. Nebr., 1930; M.A., U. Mich., 1936; m. Clarice W. Livermore, Aug. 23, 1933; 1 son, Douglas B. Tchr., athletic coach high schs., Sargent, Nebr., 1930-32, West Point, Nebr., 1932-35; with Central Life Assurance Co., Des Moines, 1936-74, pres., chief exec. officer, 1964-72, chmn. bd., chief exec. officer, 1972-74, also dir. Named Monroe St. Jour. Alumnus of Month, U. Mich. Grad Sch. Bus. Adminstrn. Gen. chmn. Greater Des Moines United campaign United Community Service, 1969-70. Former bd. dirs. Des Moines Center Sci. and Industry. Fellow Soc. Actuaries. Home: 230 W Laurel St Apt 606 San Diego CA 92101-1466

FUHRMAN, KENDALL NELSON, software engineer; b. Evansville, Ind., Aug. 1, 1962; s. Ronald Charles and Mildred Elaine (Gulley) F.; m. Susan Ann Bagstad. BS in Computer Sci. and Math., U. Denver, 1984; postgrad., Colo. State U., 1988. Assoc. engr. Am. TV & Communications, Englewood, Colo., 1982-84; mem. tech. staff Hughes Aircraft Corp., Englewood, 1984-85; software engr. Ampex Corp., Golden, Colo., 1985-87, sr. software engr., 1987-88, project leader, 1988-92; project leader Ohmeda, Louisville, Colo., 1992-94; pres. founder Evolving Video Techs., 1994—; cons. in field, Arvada, Colo., 1990—. Contbr. articles to profl. jours.; patentee antialising algorithm, graphics rendering. Mem. Assn. for Computing Machinery, IEEE, Spl. Interest Group Graphics, Spl. Interest Group Computer Human Interaction, Phi Beta Kappa. Home: 8417 Pierson Ct Arvada CO 80005-5238 Office: Evolving Video Tech Corp 7850 Vance Dr Ste 210 Arvada CO 80003-2128

FUHS, TERRY LYNN, emergency room nurse, educator; b. Gallup, N.Mex., Aug. 21, 1957; d. Louie Rube and Wilda (Boardman) Orr; m. Loren Bruce Fuhs, Dec. 11, 1981; children: Melissa Marincell, Misty Fuhs. ADN, U. N.Mex., Gallup, 1979; BSN, U. N.Mex., 1990. Cert. emergency nurse, TNCC-I, ENPC-I, ACLS-I, PALS-I; RN, N.Mex. Med./surg. staff/chg. nurse Rehoboth McKinley Christian Hosp., Gallup, 1979-83, chg. nurse emergency dept., 1983—, critical care educator, 1992—; affiliate faculty PALS/ACLS, N.Mex. chpt. Am. Heart Assn., 1991—, mem. emergency cardiac care com., 1993—, mem. PALS nat. faculty, 1995—. Presenter/coord. Emergency Nurses Cancel Alcohol Related Emergencies, Gallup, 1994—, Safe Sitter Program, Gallup, 1994—. Recipient Meritorious award N.Mex. Hosp. Assn., 1994. Mem. AAUW, ANA, Emergency Nurses Assn. (state coun. mem. 1993—, N.Mex. chpt. trauma com. chmn. 1994—). Democrat. Methodist. Home: 1117 Ridgecrest Ave Gallup NM 87301-4980 Office: Rehoboth McKinley Hosp 1901 Red Rock Dr Gallup NM 87301

FUJITA, BEVERLY YUMI, advertising copywriter; b. Honolulu, Aug. 25, 1963; d. George Shuichi and Kikue (Tomonaga) F. BA in English with highest honors, U. Hawaii Manoa, Honolulu, 1986. Procedure writer Bank of Hawaii, 1986-89; cable guide editor Honolulu Pub., 1989-93, assoc. editor Honolulu Mag., 1991-94; internal comms. writer Bank of Hawaii, Honolulu, 1994-95; asst. dir. mail mgr. Liberty House, Honolulu, 1995—. Bd. dirs. Temari Ctr. for Asian and Pacific Arts, Honolulu, 1994—. Mem. Soc. Profl. Journalists, Asian Am. Journalists Assn., U. Hawaii Alumni Assn., Phi Beta Kappa, Phi Kappa Phi.

FUJITA, JAMES HIROSHI, history educator; b. Honolulu, July 24, 1958; s. George Hideo and Teruko (Miyano) F. BA, U. Hawaii, 1980, MA, 1983. Grad. asst. U. Hawaii at Manoa, Honolulu, 1980-85, lectr. history, 1986—; lectr. history Kapiolani C.C., Honolulu, 1987—; lectr. Elderhostel Program, Honolulu, 1992. Mem. NEA, Hawaii State Tchrs. Assn., World History Assn., U. Hawaii Profl. Assembly, Phi Alpha Theta. Office: Kapiolani C C 4303 Diamond Head Rd Honolulu HI 96816-4421

FUJITANI, MARTIN TOMIO, software quality engineer; b. Sanger, Calif., May 3, 1968; s. Matsuo and Hasuko Fujitani. BS in Indsl. and Systems Engring., U. So. Calif., 1990. Sec. Kelly Svcs., Inc., Sacramento, 1987; receptionist Coudert Bros., L.A., 1988; rsch. asst. U. So. Calif., L.A., 1988-89; math. aide Navy Pers. Rsch. and Devel. Ctr., San Diego, 1989; quality assurance test technician Retix, Santa Monica, Calif., 1989-90; software engr. Quality Med. Adjudication, Inc., Rancho Cordova, Calif., 1990-92; test engr. Worldtalk Corp., Los Gatos, Calif., 1993-94; quality engr. Lotus Devel. Corp., Mountain View, Calif., 1994-95, Gen. Magic, Sunnyvale, Calif., 1995-96; software engr. Sun Microsys. Inc., Mountain View, 1996—. Assemblyman Am. Legion Calif. Boys State, 1985. Recipient Service Above Self award East Sacramento Rotary, 1986. Mem. Am. Soc. Quality Control, Gen. Alumni Assn. U. So. Calif. (life). Home: 205 Milbrae Ln Apt 2 Los Gatos CA 95030-5459 Office: Sun Microsys Inc MS UMPK 17-204 2550 Garcia Ave Mountain View CA 94043-1100

FUKUHARA, HENRY, artist, educator; b. L.A., Apr. 25, 1913; s. Ichisuke and Ume (Sakamoto) F.; m. Fujiko Yasutake, Aug. 18, 1938; children: Joyce, Grace, Rackham, Helen. Student with Edgar A. Whitney, Jackson Heights, N.Y., 1972, Rex Brandt, Corona del Mar, Calif., 1974, Robert E. Wood, 1975, Carl Molno, Woodside, N.Y., 1976. Exhibited in group shows at Friends World Coll., Lloyds Neck, N.Y., 1980, Elaine Benson Gallery, Bridgehampton, N.Y., 1979, 83, Nat. Invitational Watercolor, Zaner Gallery, Rochester, N.Y., 1981, Fire House Gallery, 1982, Parrish Art Mus., 1982, Japan-R.I. Exchange Exhibit, Provincetown, R.I., 1986, Kawakami Gallery, Tokyo, 1986, Setagaya Mus. Art, Tokyo, 1988-91, 5th Ann. Rosoh Kai Watercolor Exhbn. Meguro Mus. Art, Tokyo, 1991, 6th Ann. Rosoh Kai Watercolor Exhbn. Meguro Mus. Art, 1992, Shinju ku Bunka Ctr., Tokyo, 93-96, Stary Sheets Galleries Exhbn., Irvine, Calif., 1992-94, Laguna Beach, 1996—, Living Legends, Mira Mesa Colls., 1994, Miracosta Coll., 1997; represented in permanent collections at Heckscher Mus., Huntington, N.Y., Abilene Mus. Fine art, Nassau Community Coll., SUNY-Stony Brook, Los Angeles County Mus. Art, Blaine County Mus., Chinook, Mont., Ralston Mus., Sydney, Mont., San Bernardino County Mus., Redlands, Calif., 1984, Riverside Mus. Art, Calif., 1985, Gonzaga U., Spokane, Wash., 1986, Nagano Mus. Art, Japan, 1986, Contemporary Mus. of Art, Hiroshima, 1988, Santa Monica (Calif.) Coll., 1988; instr. Watercolor Venice (Calif.) Adult Sch., 1992-93, tchr. watercolor. Recipient Purchase award Nassau Community Coll., 1976; Best in Show, Hidden Pond, Town of Islip, 1978, Strathmore Paper Co., 1979, Creative Connections Gallery award Foothills Art Ctr., Golden, Colo., 1984, Judges Choice, Mont. Minature Art Soc. 7th Ann International Show, Working with Abandoned Control, 1993, Splash 3 and 4 1995/96 in watercolor series, 1996, others. Mem. Nat. Watercolor Soc., Ala. Watercolor Soc., Pitts. Watercolor Soc., Nat. Drawing Assn. Subject of profl. publs. Address: 1214 Marine St Santa Monica CA 90405-5815

FUKUMOTO, LESLIE SATSUKI, lawyer; b. L.A., Mar. 10, 1955; parents: Robert Fukumoto and Florence Teruko Kodama Kuroda. BA, U. Hawaii, 1977; JD, William S. Richard Sch. Law, 1980. Bar: Hawaii 1980, U.S. Dist. Ct. Hawaii 1980, U.S. Ct. Appeals (9th cir.) 1981. Dep. pub. defender State of Hawaii, Honolulu, 1980-81; assoc. Pyun, Kim & Okimoto, Honolulu, 1981-83; ptnr. Pyun, Okimoto & Fukumoto, Honolulu, 1983-84; sole practice Honolulu, 1984-85; ptnr. Fukumoto & Wong, Honolulu, 1985-93, Tanaka & Fukumoto, Honolulu, 1993-94; prin. Fukumoto Law Corp., Honolulu, 1994—; bd. dirs. Ichiryo Enterprises, Inc., Honolulu. Assoc. editor U. Hawaii Law Rev., 1979-80. Mem. ATLA, Honolulu Club. Office: 1001 Bishop St Pacific 2760 Honolulu HI 96813-3429

FULCO, ARMAND JOHN, biochemist; b. L.A., Apr. 3, 1932; s. Herman J. and Clelia Marie (DeFeo) F.; m. Virginia Loy Hungerford, June 18, 1955 (div. July 1985); children: William James, Lisa Marie, Linda Susan, Suzanne Yvonne; m. Doris V.N. Goodman, Nov. 29, 1987. B.S. in Chemistry, UCLA, 1957, Ph.D. in Physiol. Chemistry, 1960. NIH postdoctoral fellow Lipid Labs. UCLA, 1960-61; NIH research fellow dept. chemistry Harvard U., Cambridge, Mass., 1961-63; biochemist, prin. investigator Lab. Nuclear Medicine and Radiation Biology, UCLA, 1963-80; asst. prof. dept. biol. chemistry UCLA (Med. Sch.), 1965-70, assoc. prof., 1970-76, prof., 1976—, prin. investigator lab. biomed. and environ. scis., 1981-93; prin. investigator lab. structural biology/molecular med. UCLA-Dept. of Energy, 1993-95; cons. biochemist VA, Los Angeles, 1968-79; mem. UCLA Molecular Biology Inst., 1991—; co-dir. Lipid-Hormone Core Lab., UCLA, 1989-96; mem. Jonsson Comprehensive Cancer Ctr. UCLA, 1994—. Author: (with J.F. Mead) The Unsaturated and Polyunsaturated Fatty Acids in Health and Disease, 1976; contbr. over 90 articles to sci. jours. Served with U.S. Army, 1952-54. Mem. AAAS, Am. Chem. Soc., Am. Soc. Biochem. and Molecular Biology, Am. Soc. Microbiology, Internat. Soc. for Study of Xenobiotics, Harvard Chemists Assn., Sigma Xi. Office: UCLA Sch Medicine Dept Biol Chemistry 10833 Le Conte Ave Los Angeles CA 90095-1737

FULD, STEVEN ALAN, financial advisor, insurance specialist; b. Balt., Aug. 20, 1963; s. George Joseph Fuld and Nancy (Morstein) Boltz; m. Julie Michelle Glaser, Jan. 21, 1989; children: Zachary Aaron, Jessica Sydney. Student, Calif. State U., Northridge, 1981-85; postgrad., Am. Coll., 1991—. CLU, ChFC. Agt. Lincoln Nat. Life, Tarzana, Calif., 1984-85; mng. ptnr. The Skyline Group, Encino, Calif., 1985—; mem. extended faculty Am. Coll., 1990-92; lectr. Assn. for Advanced Life Underwriting, The Arthritis Found., Georgetown U., Nat. Assn. Health Underwriters, Nat. Assn. Life Underwriters, Calif. Soc. CPAs, Internat. Soc. Appraisers, March of Dimes, City Nat. Bank, L.A. Bus. Jour., Forth Fin. Network, others; bd. advisors Manulife, 1996—, chmn. MFD tech. com., 1996—; co-host TV series: Strategies of the Rich and Smart, 1995—. Contbg. author: Business Insurance Law and Practice, 1989; contbr. articles to profl. jours. Trustee Temple Beth Haverim; bd. trustees, bd. govs. So. Calif. chpt. Arthritis Found., 1995—, mem. planned gift com., mem. exec. com., 1996—, mem. nat. breakthrough century com., chmn. estate planning day, 1996. Named Man of Yr., Pacific S.W. Region, Fedn. Jewish Men's Clubs, 1993; recipient Disting. Svc. award Arthritis Found., 1995. Mem. Am. Soc. CLU and ChFC (lectr., bd. dirs. San Fernando Valley chpt. 1989-92, Disting. Svc. award 1990, 92), Beverly Hills Estate Counselors Forum (bd. dirs. 1992-95), Conejo Valley Estate Counselors Forum (founder), Nat. Assn. Life Underwriters, Assn. for Advanced Life Underwriting, Temple Beth Haverim Men's

Club (pres.), Temple Beth Haverim (trustee, v.p. ways and means 1993-95). Office: The Skyline Group Second Fl 15928 Ventura Blvd Encino CA 91436

FULKERSON, WILLIAM MEASEY, JR., college president; b. Moberly, Mo., Oct. 18, 1940; s. William Measey and Edna Frances (Pendleton) F.; m. Grace Carolyn Wisdom, May 26, 1962; children: Carl Franklin, Carolyn Sue. BA, William Jewell Coll., 1962; MA, Temple U., 1964; PhD, Mich. State U., 1969. Asst. to assoc. prof. Calif. State U., Fresno, 1981—; asst. to pres. Calif. State U.-Fresno, 1971-73; assoc. exec. dir. Am. Assn. State Colls., Washington, 1973-77; acad. v.p. Phillips U., Enid, Okla., 1977-81; pres. Adams State Coll., Alamosa, Colo., 1981-94, State Colls. in Colo., 1994—; interim pres. Met. State Coll., Denver, 1987-88, Western State Coll., 1996—. Author: Planning for Financial Exigency, 1973; contbr. articles to profl. jours. Commr. North Ctrl. Assn., Chgo., 1980—; bd. dirs. Acad. Collective Bargaining Info. Svc., Washington, 1976, Office for Advancement Pub. Negro Colls., Atlanta, 1973-77, Colo. Endowment for Humanities, 1988—. Named Disting. Alumni William Jewell Coll., 1982, Outstanding Alumnus Mich. State U. Coll. Comm., Arts & Scis., 1987. Mem. Am. Assn. State Colls. and Univs. (parliamentarian, bd. dirs. 1992-94), Am. Coun. on Edn. (bd. dirs.), Assn. Pub. Coll.s and Univs. Pres.s (pres. 1994-95), Nat. Assn. Sys. Heads, Alamosa C. of C. (dir., pres. 1984 Citizen Yr. award), Rotary. Office: State Colls in Colo 1580 Lincoln St Ste 750 Denver CO 80203-1509

FULLER, DOLORES AGNES, songwriter, actress; b. South Bend, Ind., Mar. 10, 1923; d. Eugene J. and Leonora (Dahms) Eble; m. Donald Fuller (div. June 1952); children: Donald K., Darrel D.; m. Philip Chamberlin. Student, Hunter Coll., 1956-59. Sec. Nat. Artists Found., Las Vegas, Nev. and L.A., 1987-96; guest of honor Munich Internat. Film Festiva, 1995. Star movies Glen or Glenda? (also known as I Led Two Lives), 1953, The Hidden Face (also known as Jailbait), 1954; appeared in Outlaw Women, 1953, The Glue Gardenia, 1953, The Body Beautiful, 1953, Girls in the Night, 1953, Lost Mesa of Women, 1953, College Capers, 1953, The Moonlighter, 1953, Count the Hours, 1953, Th Playgirl, 1954, The Raid, 1954, This Is My Love, 1954, The Playgirl, 1954, Bride of the Monster, 1955, The Vampire's Tomb, 1955, Look Back in Angora, 1994, The Haunted World of Edward D. Wood, Jr., 1996; regular performer TV show Chevrolet Playhouse, with Dinah Shore, 1951-54, Queen for a Day; guest appearances on TV shows include The Danny Thomas Show, The Bob Hope Show, 1951-56, The Tonight Show, The Red Skelton Show, The Dennis Day Show, The Streets of San Francisco, also others; TV movies include Superman, Hollywood Preview, Lineup, It's a Great Life, The Damon Runyon Series, Gildersleeve, Dragnet; songs include Rock-a-Hula Baby, Big Love, Big Heartache, Spinout, I Got Lucky I'll Take Love, Steppin' Out of Line, Do the Clam, Have a Happy, Cindy, Cincy, Beyond the Bend, You Can's Say No in Acapulco, Barefoot Ballad, Losers Weepers, Someone To Tell It To, Marriage on the Rocks, Crying Guitar. Recipient award for contbn. to motion pictures FANEX, 1996. Mem. ASCAP. Home: 3628 Ottawa Cir Las Vegas NV 89109

FULLER, EDWIN DANIEL, hotel executive; b. Richmond, Va., Mar. 15, 1945; s. Ben Swint and Evelyn (Beal) F.; m. Denise Kay Perigo, July 18, 1970. Student, Wake Forest U., 1965; BSBA, Boston U., 1968; postgrad., Harvard Sch. Bus., 1987. Security officer Pinkerton Inc., Boston, 1965-68; with sales dept. Twin Bridges Marriott Hotel, Arlington, Va., 1972-73; nat. sales mgr. Marriott Hotels & Resorts, N.Y.C., 1973-76; dir. nat. and internat. sales Marriott Hotels & Resorts, Washington, 1976-78; v.p. mktg. Marriott Hotels & Resorts, 1978-82; gen. mgr. Marriott Hotels & Resorts, Hempstead, N.Y., 1982-83, Marriott Copley Place, Boston, 1983-85; v.p. ops. Midwest region Marriott Corp., Rosemont, Ill., 1985-89; v.p. ops. Western and Pacific regions Marriott Corp., Santa Ana, Calif., 1989-90; sr. v.p., mng. dir. Marriott Hotels & Resorts-Internat., Washington, 1990-93; exec. v.p., mng. dir. internat. lodging Marriott Lodging Internat., Washington, 1994-97, pres., mng. dir., 1997—; chmn. bd. dirs. SNR Reservation Sys., Zurich, Switzerland, 1979-81; bd. dirs. Boston U. Hotel Sch., 1984—, Mgmt. Engrs. Inc., Reston, Va., Barnby Books; treas. MEI Pacific Honolulu, 1985—; chmn. Fuller Properties, Laguna Hills, Calif., 1990—. Pres. Boston U. Gen. Alumni Assn., 1993—, v.p., 1990-93; v.p. Boston U. Sch. Mgmt. Alumni Bd., 1985—; mem. adv. bd. Boston U. Hospitality Mgmt. Sch., 1985—; trustee Boston U., mem. exec. com. bd. trustees, 1994—. Capt. U.S. Army, 1968-72, Vietnam. Decorated Bronze Star. Mem. Boston U. Alumni Coun. (v.p.), Harvard Sch. Bus. Advanced Mgmt. Program (fund agt.), Sigma Alpha Epsilon, Delta Sigma Pi. Republican. Home: 25362 Derbyhill Dr Laguna Hills CA 92653-7835 Office: Marriott Hotels & Resorts 1 Marriott Dr Washington DC 20058-0001

FULLER, GLENN STRAITH, minister; b. Tientsin, China, Feb. 17, 1924; came to U.S., 1927; s. Glenn Vincent and Margaret Meldrum (Straith) F.; m. Kathleen Crawford Lester, June 30, 1954; children: Margaret Alicia, Catherine Ann, Mary Wyon. BA, Pomona Coll., 1944; BD, Union Theol. Seminary, 1947, STM, 1961. Sr. pastor Bowen Meml. Meth. Ch., Bombay, 1947-49; various pastor positons worldwide, 1954-69; sr. pastor Seoul (Korea) Union Ch., 1970-73; assoc. pastor Los Altos (Calif.) United Meth. Ch., 1973-76; sr. pastor Almaden Hills United Meth. Ch., San Jose, Calif., 1976-83; assoc. pastor First United Meth. Ch., Palo Alto, Calif., 1983-88; pastor English-Speaking United Meth. Ch., Vienna, 1988-91; chaplain Lytton Gardens, Palo Alto, 1994—; sec. of missions San Jose Dist. Unified Meth. Ch., 1980-88, 92-96; pub. spkr. Gen. Bd. Global Ministries, N.Y.C., 1988—. Mem. World Affairs Coun., San Francisco, 1993—; bd. dirs. United Christian Campus Ministry, Stanford, Calif., 1995—. Mem. Peninsula Dem. Club. Home: 1027 Hollyburne Ave Menlo Park CA 94025-1610

FULLER, JANICE MARIE, secondary school educator; b. Flagler, Colo., Feb. 7, 1948; d. William Harrison and Ruth Elsie (Jensen) Martin; m. William Edward Fuller, Sept. 16, 1966; children: James Edward, David William, John Justin. A.Gen. Studies, Pikes Peak C.C., Colorado Springs, Colo., 1982; BS in Biology, Met. State Coll., Denver, 1986. Gen. office mgr. Schmidt Environ. Enterprises, Commerce City, Colo., 1972-77; v.p., sec. Fuller Constrn., Inc., Larkspur, Colo., 1993—; tchr. math. and sci. Douglas County Schs., Castle Rock, Colo., 1988-92; tchr. sci. Christ the King Sch., Denver, 1992-96; tchr. biology Ellicott Jr.- Sr. High Sch., Calhan, Colo., 1996—; tutor math./sci.; coach track, gymnastics, volleyball Castle Rock Jr. H.S., 1990-92; nominated 1st U.S./Russia Joint Conf. on Edn. in Moscow, U. Iowa Citizen Ambassador Program, 1994; mem. dist. accountability com. Ellicott Sch. Dist., 1996—. Mem. dist. accountability comm. Douglas County Sch. Dist., Castle Rock, 1987-91, dist. comm. com., 1990. Mem. ASCD, NAFE, AAUW, Nat. Assn. Student Activity Advisors, Nat. Sci. Tchrs. Assn., Met. State Coll. Alumni Assn. Office: Ellicott Jr-Sr High Sch 375 S Ellicott Hwy Ellicott CO 80808-8838

FULLER, LAWRENCE ROBERT, newspaper publisher; b. Toledo, Sept. 9, 1941; s. Kenneth M. and Marjory A (Rairdon) F.; m. Suzanne Hovik, May 7, 1967; children: Elizabeth, Michael. BJ, U. Mo., 1963. Reporter Globe Gazette, Mason City, Iowa, 1963-67; reporter, from asst. city editor to city editor Mpls. Star, 1967-75; exec. editor Messenger-Inquirer, Owensboro, Ky., 1975-77; exec. editor Argus Leader, Sioux Falls, S.D., 1977-78, pres., pub., 1978-84, 86—; pres. Gannett News Media, Washington, 1984-85; dir. corp. communications Gannett Co., Inc., Washington, 1985-86; v.p. The Honolulu Advertisers, 1986—, pres. Bd. dirs. Zool. Soc. Sioux Falls, 1986—, YMCA, Sioux Falls, 1986—, United Way, Sioux Falls, 1987—, Forward Sioux Falls, 1988—, U. Hawaii Found., Alohia United Way, Child and Family Svcs., Ronald McDonald Children's Charities, Aloha Festivals; bd. dirs., co-chair econ. task force Hawaii Bus. Roundtable; chair Allen H. Neuharth Fund for Excellence in Journalism. Mem. Am. Newspaper Pubs. Assn., Am. Soc. Newspaper Editors, AP Mng. Editors Assn., S.D. Newspaper Assn. (bd. dirs. 1987-90), Sioux Falls Area C. of C. (bd. dirs. 1986-89), Minnehaha Country Club. Office: Honolulu 605 Kapiolani Blvd Honolulu HI 96813*

FULLER, PAUL NORMAN, retired aerospace executive; b. Highland Park, Ill., Sept. 14, 1927; s. Paul Max and Friedel (Schaer) F.; m. Elizabeth Szajko; children: Janet Fuller Lawrence, Jean Elizabeth. BS in Aero. Engring., U. Ill., 1950. Supr. Thor program Rocketyne, Canoga Park, Calif., 1953-58, project engr. Redstone program, 1958-60, project engr. J-2 engine program, 1960-70, program mgr. J-2 engine program, 1970-73, dir. Nat. Space Tech. Lab. shuttle program, 1974-76, chief program engr. space shuttle engine, 1976-83, program mgr. peacekeeper program, 1983-87, v.p., 1987-94; ret., 1994; cons. Rockwell/Rocketdyne, Colorado Springs, Colo., 1994—; mem. external adv. bd. propulsion space engring. Pa. State U., 1990; sec. adv. com. U.S. Dept. Transp., Washington, 1988—, chmn. to sec. adv. com., 1990-92. With U.S. Army, 1950-52. Recipient Pub. Svc. award NASA, 1973, 81, Pub. Svc. medal NASA, 1981, Engring. Achievement award San Fernando Valley Engring. Coun., L.A., 1982, Disting. Alumni award U. Ill., 1983. Mem. Colorodo Springs C. of C. (mem. task forces 1995—). Home: 2640 Trevor Ln Colorado Springs CO 80919 Office: Boeing NAm Inc Internat-Rockedyne 6633 Canoga Ave Canoga Park CA 91309

FULLER, ROBERT KENNETH, architect, urban designer; b. Denver, Oct. 6, 1942; s. Kenneth Roller and Gertrude Ailene (Heid) F.; m. Virginia Louise Elkin, Aug. 23, 1969; children: Kimberly Kirsten, Kelsey Christa. BArch, U. Colo., 1967; MArch and Urban Design, Washington U., St. Louis, 1974. Archtl. designer Fuller & Fuller, Denver; architect, planner Urban Research and Design Ctr., St. Louis, 1970-72; prin. Fuller & Fuller Assocs., Denver, 1972—. Past pres. Denver East Ctrl. Civic Assn., Country Club Hist. Dist.; bd. dirs. Cherry Creek Steering Com.; pres. Horizon Adventures, Inc. Mem. AIA (past pres. Denver chpt.), Colo. Arlberg Club (past pres.), Phi Gamma Delta, Delta Phi Delta. Home: 2244 E 4th Ave Denver CO 80206-4107 Office: 3320 E 2nd Ave Denver CO 80206-5302

FULLER-MCCHESNEY, MARY ELLEN, sculptor, writer, publisher; b. Wichita, Kans., Oct. 20, 1922; d. Edward Emory and Karen Mabel (Rasmussen) Fuller; m. Robert Pearson, Dec. 17, 1949. AA, U. Calif., Berkeley, 1943. Staff writer Currant; rschr. Archives of Am. Art; publisher Sonoma Mt. Publishing Co. Author: (art book) A Period of Exploration, 1973, Robert McChesney: An American Painter, 1996, also 3 mystery novels, short stories, poems, and articles on art; exhbns. include: (sculpture) Syracuse (N.Y.) Mus., San Francisco Mus., Oakland (Calif.) Mus., Calif. State U. Sonoma, Santa Rosa Civic Ctr., U. Calif. Davis, San Jose (Calif.) State U., U. Calif. Ctr. U. Oaxaca; San Francisco art festivals and many galleries; prin. works include Dos Leones, San Francisco Gen. Hosp., 1974, Children's Scupture Park, Salinas Cmty. Ctr., 1976, Temko Lions, Fresno Ave. Berkeley, Calif., 1976, Falcon, Andrew Hill H.S., San Jose, Calif., 1977, Yuba Totem, Yuba Lion, Dept. Motor Vehicles Bldg., Calif., 1978, Playground, Portsmouth Square, San Francisco, 1982, Olympic Lions, Squaw Valley, Calif., 1983, Stratford Meml. Lion and Bear, Petaluma (Calif.) Libr., 1983, Anshen-Mays Birdbath, Sausalito, Calif., 1984, West Side Pump Sta., San Francisco, 1979; 4 garden sculptures L.A. State Office Bldg., 1987, Walnut Creek Totem, 1992, Seach Park, Santa Cruz, 1993. Ford Found. fellow, 1965-66; Nat. Endowment Arts grantee, 1975. Home and Studio: 2955 Sonoma Mt Rd Petaluma CA 94954

FULLMER, DANIEL WARREN, psychologist, educator, retired; b. Spoon River, Ill., Dec. 12, 1922; s. Daniel Floyd and Sarah Louisa (Essex) F.; m. Janet Satomi Saito, June 1980; children: Daniel William, Mark Warren. B.S., Western Ill. U., 1947, M.S., 1952; Ph.D., U. Denver, 1955. Postdoctoral intern psychiat. div. U. Oreg. Med. Sch., 1958-61; mem. faculty U. Oreg., 1955-66; prof. psychology Oreg. System of Higher Edn., 1958-66; faculty Coll. Edn. U. Hawaii, Honolulu, 1966-95, retired, 1995, prof. emeritus, 1974—; pvt. practice psychol. counseling; cons. psychologist Grambling State U., 1960-81; founder Free-Family Counseling Ctrs., Portland, Oreg., 1959-66, Honolulu, 1966-74; co-founder Child and Family Counseling Ctr., Waianae, Oahu, Hawaii, Kilohana United Meth. Ch., Oahu, 1992, v.p., sec., 1992; pres. Human Resources Devel. Ctr., Inc., 1974—; chmn. Hawaii State Bd. to License Psychologists, 1973-78. Author: Counseling: Group Theory & System, 2d. edit., 1978, The Family Therapy Dictionary Text, 1991, MANABU, Diagnosis and Treatment of a Japanese Boy with a Visual Anomaly, 1991; co-author: Principles of Guidance, 2d. edit., 1977; author (counselor/cons. training manuals) Counseling: Content and Process, 1964, Family Consultation Therapy, 1968, The School Counselor-Consultant, 1972; editor: Bulletin, Oreg. Coop Testing Service, 1955-57, Hawaii P&G Jour., 1970-76; assoc. editor: Educational Perspectives, U. Hawaii Coll. Edn. Served with USNR, 1944-46. Recipient Francis E. Clark award Hawaii Pers. Guidance Assn., 1972, Thomas Jefferson award for Outstanding Pub. Svc., 1993; named Hall of Fame Grambling State U., 1987. Mem. Am. Psychol. Assn., Am. Counseling Assn. (Nancy C. Wimmer award 1963). Methodist. Office: 1750 Kalakaua Ave Apt 809 Honolulu HI 96826-3725 *I grew up along Spoon River. The people of Spoon River had a principle of life: Improve on what you are. The purpose is to be able to help others help themselves. From here, it is like stepping into a river of life; the deeper you got, the stronger the current. Then, suddenly, here you are nearing the delta. Just ahead lies a beautiful ocean.*

FULLMER, DONALD KITCHEN, insurance executive; b. Rockyford, Colo., Apr. 11, 1915; s. George Clinton and Florence E. (Kitchen) F.; m. June 5, 1934 (dec. 1987); children: Robert E., Maxine Fullmer Vogt, Phyllis R. Fullmer Danielson. CLU, Am. Coll. Life Underwriting, 1962. Lic. ins. agt., Wash. Life underwriter N.Y. Life, Aberdeen, Wash., 1954-74; ind. gen. agt. Aberdeen, Wash., 1974-81; life underwriter MONY, Bellingham, Wash., 1983-88; ret. County chmn. Rep. Party, Grays Harbor, Wash., 1964-69, mem. state exec. com., 1971-72. With U.S. Army, 1945. Mem. N.W. Wash. Assn. Life Underwriters, Wash. State Assn. Life Underwriters (pres. 1968-69), Twin Harbor Life Underwriters, Masons. LDS. Home: 5464 Bell West Dr Bellingham WA 98226-9033

FULLMER, STEVEN MARK, systems engineer; b. San Francisco, Mar. 15, 1956; s. Thomas Patrick and Patricia Ann (Carroll-Boyd) F.; m. Rhonda Lynnette Bush, Nov. 8, 1992; children: Wesley Stevenson, Sierra Marin. BA in Chemistry, Willamette U., 1978, BA in Biology, 1978; MBA, Ariz. State U., 1993. Sr. engr., project leader Honeywell Large Computer Products, Phoenix, 1981-86; bank officer, cons., infosecurity cons. First Interstate Bank/Wells Fargo Bank, Phoenix, 1987-96; project mgr. Wells Fargo Bank, 1996; staff engr. AG Comm. Systems, 1996—; cons. J.A. Boyd & Assoc., San Francisco, 1985-96, ImaginInc. Consulting, Phoenix, 1985—. Contbr. articles to profl. jours. Mem. exec. bd. Grand Canyon coun. Boy Scouts Am., scoutmaster, 1983-88, commr., 1988-92, dist. chmn., 1995-96; founder, lt. comdr. Maricopa County Sheriff's Adj. Posse, 1982-93; pres. Heard Mus. Coun., 1995-96; rehabber Liberty Wildlife. Recipient Order of Merit Boy Scouts Am., 1988, Nat. Disting. Commr. award Boy Scouts Am., 1990, Nat. Founder's award Boy Scouts Am., 1991, Silver Beaver award Boy Scouts Am., 1994. Mem. Am. Inst. for Cert. Computer Profls. (cert. data processor 1985), Mensa, KC (membership dir. 1988), Knights Cross (Sovereign Order of St. Stanislas), Phi Lambda Upsilon, Phi Eta Sigma, Kappa Sigma, Alpha Chi Sigma, Sigma Iota Epsilon, Beta Gamma Sigma. Republican. Roman Catholic. Office: AG Comm Systems 2500 W Utopia Rd Phoenix AZ 85027

FULTON, NORMAN ROBERT, consumer credit manager; b. Los Angeles, Dec. 16, 1935; s. Robert John and Fritzi Marie (Wacker) F.; AA, Santa Monica Coll., 1958; BS, U. So. Calif., 1960; m. Nancy Butler, July 6, 1966; children: Robert B., Patricia M. Asst. v.p. Raphael Glass Co., Los Angeles, 1960-65; credit adminstr. Zellerbach Paper Co., Los Angeles, 1966-68; gen. credit mgr. Carrier Transicold Co., Montebello, Calif., 1968-70, Virco Mfg. Co., Los Angeles, 1970-72, Superscope, Inc., Chatsworth, Calif., 1972-79; asst. v.p. credit and adminstrn. Inkel Corp., Carson, Calif., 1980-82; corp. credit mgr. Consumer Electronics, Santa Monica, Calif., 1982-83; br. credit mgr. Sharp Electronics Corp., Carson, Calif., 1983-96. Served with AUS, 1955-57. Fellow Nat. Inst. Credit (cert. credit exec.); mem. Credit Mgrs. So. Calif., Nat. Notary Assn. Home: 9 Vista Loma Dr Rancho Mirage CA 92270

FULTON, RICHARD DELBERT, dean; b. Missoula, Mont., Feb. 5, 1945; s. C. Dulane and E. Benita (Lyon) F.; m. Suzanne Lee Mathews, Nov. 5, 1976; children: David Amil, Effie Lee. BA in English, Ea. Mont. Coll., 1967; MA in English, U. S.D., 1969; PhD in English, Wash. State U., 1975. Instr. U. Md., College Park, 1970-71; asst. dean Wash. State U., Pullman, 1975-82, 83-84; dean in residence Coun. Grad. Schs., Washington, 1982-83; assoc. dean Iona Coll., New Rochelle, N.Y., 1984-86; provost Rocky Mountain Coll., Billings, Mont., 1986-89; dean of faculty Clark Coll., Vancouver, Wash., 1989—; cons. Coun. Grad. Schs., 1983; pres. Wash. Instrnl. Commn., 1995. Co-editor: Henry Fielding: An Annotated Bibliography, 1980, Union List of Victorian Serials, 1985; editor: Victorian Periodicals Rev., 1993-96; contbr. numerous articles and revs. on Victorian periodicals and European lit. Bd. dirs. United Way, Pullman, 1976-78. Mem. Rsch. Soc. for Victorian Periodicals (pres. 1989— bd. dirs. 1984—), North Am. Conf. British Studies, Am. Assn. Higher Edn., Nat. Coun. Instrnl. Adminstrs. Democrat. Episcopalian. Office: Clark Coll 1800 E Mcloughlin Blvd Vancouver WA 98663-3509

FULTZ, BRENT THOMAS, materials scientist, educator, researcher; b. Troy, N.Y., Feb. 24, 1955; s. Stanley Charles and Esther Doris (Richert) F.; m. Colleen Jaye O'Hara, Sept. 30, 1984; children: Emily Elise, Eric Michael, Elissa Katherine. BSc in Physics, MIT, 1975; MSc in Materials Sci., U. Calif., Berkeley, 1978, PhD in Materials Sci., 1982. Staff scientist Lawrence Berkeley (Calif.) Lab., 1982-85; asst. prof. materials sci. Calif. Inst. Tech., Pasadena, 1985-90, assoc. prof., 1991-97, prof., 1997—; prof. U. Udine, Italy, 1992; cons. Everett Charles Technologies, Pomona, Calif., 1986—, Def. Sci. Study Group, Alexandria, Va., 1994-95, Def. Sci. Bd., Washington, 1996. Editor 4 books; contbr. over 150 articles to profl. jours.; patentee in field. Recipient Faculty Devel. award IBM, 1986, 87; NSF Presdl. Young Investigator, 1988-93; Xerox Found. grantee, 1986; Wallenberg Found. scholar, 1988. Mem. Am. Soc. Metals (chmn. atomic transport com. 1994—), Am. Phys. Soc., Minerals Metals Materials Soc. (chmn. chemistry and physics com. 1996—). Home: 269 S Berkeley Ave Pasadena CA 91107 Office: Calif Inst Tech Mail 138-78 Pasadena CA 91125

FULTZ, PHILIP NATHANIEL, management analyst; b. N.Y.C., Jan. 29, 1943; s. Otis and Sara Love (Gibbs) F.; m. Bessie Learleane McCoy, Mar. 11, 1972. AA in Bus., Coll. of the Desert, 1980; BA in Mgmt., U. Redlands, 1980, MA in Mgmt., 1982. Enlisted USMC, 1967, advanced through grades to capt., 1972, served in various locations, 1964-78, resigned commn., 1978; CETA coord. County of San Bernardino, Yucca Valley, Calif., 1978-85; contract analyst Advanced Technology, Inc., Twentynine Palms, Calif., 1985-88; spl. transit analyst Omintrans, San Bernardino, Calif., 1988-89; tech. analyst Atlantic Rsch. Corp. (formerly Calculon Corp.), Twentynine Palms, Calif., 1988—; mgmt. analyst Marine Corps Base, Twentynine Palms, Calif., 1991—; adj. asst. prof. mgmt. Chapman U., Orange, Calif., 1992—. Founding dir. Unity Home Battered Women's Shelter, Joshua Tree, Calif., 1982, Morongo Basin Adult Literacy; bd. dirs. Twentynine Palms Water Dist., 1991-95. Mem. Rotary (sec. Joshua Tree chpt. 1983-85). Republican. Home: 73477 Desert Trail Dr Twentynine Palms CA 92277-2218 Office: Morale Walfare & Recreation Marine Corps Base Twentynine Palms CA 92277-2302

FUNG, SUN-YIU SAMUEL, physics educator; b. Hong Kong, Dec. 27, 1932; came to U.S., 1953; s. Lok-Chi and Lai-Lan Fung; m. Helen Wu, Feb. 9, 1964; children: Eric, Linette. BS, U. San Francisco, 1957; PhD, U. Calif., 1964. Rsch. physicist Rutgers U., New Brunswick, N.J., 1964-66; asst. prof. physics U. Calif., Riverside, 1966-70, assoc. prof., 1970-76, prof., 1976—, chmn. physics dept., 1980-85, 90-91. Chmn. Chinese Meml. Pavilian Com., Riverside, 1985-88. Mem. AAAS, Am. Phys. Soc., Overseas Chinese Physicist Assn., Chinese Am. Faculty Assn. (pres. 1988-89, 90-92). Office: U Calif Riverside CA 92521

FUNK, SUSAN E., management consultant; b. Manhattan, Kans., Oct. 28, 1957; d. John William and Dorothy Elizabeth (Hamilton) F.; m. Gordon Louis Fuglie, June 11, 1994. BA, Yale U., 1979; MBA, Stanford U., 1985. Legis. asst. Congressman Tom Coleman, Washington, 1979-83; assoc. dir. AMI St. Joseph Hosp., Omaha, 1985-89; asst. adminstr. Charter Hosp. Glendale, Ariz., 1989; assoc. Laventhol & Horwath, L.A., 1990; pres. Applied Healthcare Rsch., Inc., Santa Clarita, Calif., 1990-92, The Kailos Group, Inc., L.A., 1993—. Bd. mem. Am. Heart Assn., Greater L.A. affiliate, 1991-97, chair orgnl. planning and devel., 1994-97, chair met. divsn., 1991-93; bd. mem. BeeveFound. for Eye and World Health, Verdugo City, Calif., 1991-94. Recipient Exceptional Svc. award Am. Heart Assn. Greater L.A., 1991. Mem. Am. Coll. Healthcare Execs., Women in Health Adminstrn., Healthcare Fin. Mgmt. Assn., L.A. County Bar Assn. (healthcare law sect.). Office: The Kailos Group Inc 2255 Ronda Vista Dr Los Angeles CA 90027-4641

FUNSTON, GARY STEPHEN, publishing and advertising executive; b. Phila., July 7, 1951; s. Ralph Gaylord and Adele Rose (DeCintio) F.; m. Nancy Eileen Clark (div. 1974); 1 child, Stephen Blake. Student, DeAnza Coll., 1969-73, San Jose State U., 1973-75, London Bus. Sch., 1995; student exec. devel. program, Cornell U., 1996. Store mgr. Smith & Foley Shoes Inc., Sunnyvale, Calif., 1970-75; sales rep. The Hoover Co., San Jose, Calif., 1975-78, GTE Directories Corp., Santa Clara, Calif., 1978-81; ptnr., sec., treas. Mailco Advt. Inc., Milpitas, Calif., 1981-83; owner, cons. ADCOM, San Jose, 1983-85; dir. sales mgr. Lomar Trans Western Publs., Ft. Lauderdale, Fla., 1985-87; mgr. sales, mktg. Ameritel, San Diego, 1987-89; regional sales dir. United Advt. Publs., Union City, Calif., 1989—; sales cons. Republic Telcom, San Jose, 1983-84; mgmt. cons. Norcal Directory Co., San Jose, 1984-85; advt. cons. Yellow Page Programs, San Jose, 1983-85. Contbr. articles to profl. jours. Mem. CAP, Mountain View, Calif., 1983-84; com. mem. Housing Ind. Found., San Jose, 1991-97, dinner sponsor, 1991-97, fundraiser, 1991-97. Mem. Calif. Apt. Assn. (suppliers coun. 1990—, chmn. suppliers com. 1993, 95, 96, industry stds. com. 1994, mem. exec. com. 1995, 96, bd. dirs. 1995, 96), Solano-Napa Rental Housing Assn., Tri-County Apt. Assn. (com. mem. 1989—), Rental Housing Owners Assn. So. Alameda County (bd. dirs. 1994, Mem. of Yr. award 1992), Highland Swingers Golf Club (treas. 1990—). Republican. Roman Catholic. Home: 22135 Sevilla Rd Apt 36 Hayward CA 94541 Office: For Rent Mag 32950 Alvarado Niles Rd # 510 Union City CA 94587-3106

FUNTE-RADFORD, DEIDREA LEA, interior designer, consultant; b. Mason City, Iowa, Oct. 3, 1955; d. William August and Beverly Mae Funte; m. Robert Keith Radford, Oct. 3, 1987; children: Lindsay Rai, Chelsea Kae. BFA in Interior Design, Grandview Jr. Coll., Des Moines, 1977; postgrad., Ariz. State U., 1978. Resident designer, contract mgr. SSC, Phoenix, 1980-88; interior designer, cons. De's Igns, Scottsdale, Ariz., 1988—; archtl. specifications cons., Archs. and Engrs. Svc., Mission Viejo, Calif., 1992-96; new residential bus. mgr. Dunn-Edwards Corp., Tempe, Ariz., 1996—. Mem. Am. Soc. Interior Design (allied, cert.).

FUREN, SHIRLEY ANN, marketing professional; b. Pomona, Calif., Sept. 12, 1936; d. Orville Emmett and Mary Evelyn (Carmack) Strickland; m. Ralph R. Rickel, Sept. 3, 1954 (div.); children: Lynda Diane, Lorrie Anne, Stanley Rupert; m. Walter E. Furen, Sept. 25, 1976. B Univ. Studies with distinction, U. N.Mex., 1975; Massage Therapist, Healing Arts Inst., Roseville, Calif., 1994. Cert. massage therapist, Calif. Adminstrv. asst. Psychiat. Inst. Am., Washington, 1977; exec. sec. Am. Assn. Schs. Podiatric Medicine, Washington, 1978-79; real estate broker Snider Bros/Merrill Lynch Realty, Santa Rosa, Calif., 1980-88; owner Spheres, Roseville, 1991—; model Julie Nation Acad., Santa Rosa, 1996. Vol. Andrea Lambert, M.F.C.C., Gold River, Calif., 1992-95; vol. hostess Ted Gaines for City Coun., Roseville, 1993; vol. fundraiser Matrix Gallery, Sacramento, Crocker Art Mus., Sacramento; staffer Matrix Gallery Aux., 1994—; wedding coord. Culinary Guild, Trinity Cathedral, 1989—. Mem. ASCE (chmn. 1992, 93), Sacramento Capital Club, Mercedes Benz Assn. Episcopalian. Home and Office: Spheres 7 Oak Forest Ln Santa Rosa CA 95409-6313

FURIMSKY, STEPHEN, JR., freelance writer; b. Coalton, Ill., Aug. 4, 1924; s. Stephen Sr. and Anna (Petricko) F.; m. Dorothy Conrad, June 8, 1946 (dec. Nov. 1989); children: Stephen III, Karen Ann Segal, Daniel Michael, Melany; m. Janet Fay Green, Dec. 16, 1991; step-children: Bruce Emerson, Peni Emerson, Kara Welliver, Beth Emerson Levine. AB, U. Chgo., 1951; MS in Internat. Affairs, George Washington U., 1967; grad., Air War Coll., 1967. Instr. in polit. sci. Craven Community Coll., New Bern, N.C., 1975-80; owner San Diego Sod, San Marcos, Calif., 1981-84; spl. advocate juvenile ct. Voices for Children, San Diego, 1985-91; sports editor, health and fitness editor Enterprise Newspaper, Fallbrook, Calif., 1989-91. Candidate state senate, N.C., 1978. Col. USMC, 1942-73. Decorated Legion of Merit, D.F.C., Bronze Star, Air medal, Cross of Gallantry (Vietnam). Mem. VFW (life), Am. Legion, The Order of Daedalians, Mil. Order of World Wars. Republican. Eastern Orthodox. Home: 58 Desert Rain Ln Henderson NV 89014-2915

FURLONG, THOMAS CASTLE, newspaper editor; b. Chgo., Oct. 23, 1945; s. Thomas Raphael and Winifred Harrison (Castle) F.; m. Susan Howlett, Dec. 1, 1985; children: Brendan Howlett, Castle Christina, Cameron Thomas. BA, Denison U., 1967. Reporter City News Bur., Chgo., 1971-72; reporter, editor Pioneer Press, Wilmette, Ill., 1972-75, Chgo. Daily

News, 1976-78; reporter Long Beach Press.-Telegram, Calif., 1978-79; reporter, editor Chgo. Sun Times, 1979-81; reporter L.A. Times, 1981-92, asst. bus. editor, 1993-96, dep. bus. editor, 1996—. Lt. USN, 1967-71. Recipient Best Bus. Articles award L.A. Press Club, 1988. Office: LA Times Times Mirror Sq Los Angeles CA 90053

FURLOTTI, ALEXANDER AMATO, real estate development company executive; b. Milan, Italy, Apr. 21, 1948; came to U.S., 1957; s. Amato and Polonia Concepcion (Lopez) F.; m. Nancy Elizabeth Swift, June 27, 1976; children: Michael Alexander, Patrick Swift, Allison Nicole. BA in Econs., U. Calif. Berkeley, 1970; JD, UCLA, 1973. Bar: Calif. 1973, U.S. Dist. Ct. (9th cir.) 1973. Assoc. Alexander, Inman, Kravetz & Tanzer, Beverly Hills, Calif., 1973-77, ptnr., 1978-80; ptnr. Kravetz & Furlotti, Century City, Calif., 1981-83; pres. Quorum Properties, L.A., 1984—; dir., CEO Transmar N.V., Netherland Antilles, 1984—. Trustee Harvard-Westlake Sch., L.A., 1989-97, Yosemite Nat. Inst., San Francisco, 1990-92. Recipient Grand award Pacific Coast Bldrs. Conf., 1993, Golden Nugget award, 1993, Grand award Nat. Assn. Homebuilders, 1993. Mem. Am. Bar Assn., Urban Land Inst., The Beach Club. Republican. Episcopalian. Office: Quorum Properties 12218 Montana Ave Los Angeles CA 90049

FURLOW, MARY BEVERLEY, English language educator; b. Shreveport, La., Oct. 14, 1933; d. Prentiss Edward and Mary Thelma (Hasty) F.; divorced, 1973; children: Mary Findley, William Prentiss, Samuel Christopher; m. William Peter Cleary, Aug. 1, 1989. BA, U. Tenn., 1955, MEd, 1972; MA, Governors State U., 1975; cert. advanced study, U. Chgo., 1987. Mem. faculty Chattanooga State C.C., 1969-73, Moraine Valley C.C., Palos Hills, Ill., 1974-78; mem. English faculty Pima C.C., Tucson, 1978—; cons. in field. Contbr. author: Thinking on the Edge, 1993. Named one of Outstanding Educators of Am., 1973. Fellow Internat. Soc. Philos. Enquiry; mem. DAR, Internat. Soc. Appraisers, Internat. Soc. Philos. Enquiry, Ariz. Antiquarian Guild, Cincinatus Soc., Jr. League, Mensa, Holmes Socs., Clan Chattan Soc., Daus. of Confederacy, Alpha Phi Omega (Tchr. of Yr. 1973), Pi Beta Phi. Democrat. Episcopalian. Home: 1555 N Arcadia Ave Tucson AZ 85712-4010 Office: Pima CC 8202 E Poinciana Dr Tucson AZ 85730-4645

FURMAN, WILL, film producer, director, cinematographer, writer; b. Washington, D.C., Aug. 29, 1940; s. William Jr. F.; m. Norma Doane, Oct. 1, 1972; children: Laurie, Linda, Rick. BA, San Francisco State U., 1962, MA, 1965. Prodr. Guild, Bascom & Bonfigli, Inc., San Francisco, 1964-66; prodr., dir. Walter Landor & Assoc., San Francisco, 1966-67; prodr., dir., owner Furman Films, San Francisco, 1967-82; prodr., dir., pres. Furman Films, Inc., San Francisco, 1982—. Recipient Cine Golden Eagle award Coun. for Internat. Nontheatrical Events, 1965, 78, 80, 83, 85, 88, 91. Mem. Independent Documentary Assn., Independent Feature Project. Republican. Clubs: Bohemian. Office: Furman Films Inc PO Box 1769 Venice CA 90291

FURNAS, DAVID WILLIAM, plastic surgeon; b. Caldwell, Idaho, Apr. 1, 1931; s. John Doan and Esther Bradbury (Hare) F.; m. Mary Lou Heatherly, Feb. 11, 1956; children: Heather Jean, Brent David, Craig Jonathan. AB, U. Calif.-Berkeley, 1952, MS, 1957, MD, 1955. Diplomate Am. Bd. Surgery, Am. Bd. Plastic Surgery (dir. 1979-85, sr. examiner 1986—), Royal Coll. Surgeons Found. (trustee 1995—). Intern U. Calif. Hosp., San Francisco, 1955-56, asst. resident in surgery, 1956-57; asst. resident in psychiatry, NIMH fellow Langley Porter Neuropsychiat. Inst. U. Calif., San Francisco, 1959-60; resident in gen. surgery Gorgas Hosp., C.Z., 1960-61; asst. resident in plastic surgery N.Y. Hosp., Cornell Med. Center, N.Y.C., 1961-62; chief resident in plastic surgery Cornell U. Svc., VA Hosp., Bronx, N.Y., 1962-63; registrar Royal Infirmary and Affiliated Hosps., Glasgow, Scotland, 1963-64; assoc. in hand surgery U. Iowa, 1965-68, asst. prof. surgery, 1966-68, assoc. prof., 1968-69; assoc. prof. surgery, chief div. plastic surgery U. Calif., Irvine, 1969-74, prof., chief div. plastic surgery, 1974-80, clin. prof., chief div. plastic surgery, 1980—; surgeon East Africa Flying Drs. Svc., African Med. and Rsch. Found., Nairobi, Kenya, 1972-73; plastic surgeon S.S. Hope, Nicaragua, 1966, Sri Lanka, 1968; mem. Balakbayan med. mission Mindanao and Sulu, The Philippines, 1980, 81, 82; overseas vis. prof. plastic surgery Ednl. Found., 1994. Contbr. chpts. to textbooks, articles to med. jours.; author, editor 6 textbooks; assoc. editor Jour. Hand Surgery, Annals of Plastic Surgery, Jour. Craniofacial Surgery. Expedition leader Explorer's Club Flag 171 Skull Surgeons of the Kisii Tribe, Kenya, Flag 44 Skull Surgeons of the Marakwet Tribes, Kenya, 1987. Capt. Med. Corps, USAF, 1957-59; col. Med. Corps., USAR, 1989-92, ret. Recipient Golden Apple award for teaching excellence U. Calif.-Irvine Sch. Medicine, 1980, Kaiser-Permanente award U. Calif.-Irvine Sch. Medicine, 1981, Humanitarian Service award Black Med. Students, U. Calif. Irvine, 1987, Sr. Research award (Basic Sci.) Plastic Surgery Ednl. Found., 1987; named Orange County Press Club Headliner of Yr., 1982. Fellow ACS, Royal Coll. Surgeons Can., Royal Soc. Medicine, Explorers Club, Royal Geog. Soc.; mem. AMA, Calif. Med. Assn., Orange County Med. Assn., Am. Soc. Plastic and Reconstructive Surgeons (bd. dirs. 1970-73), Am. Soc. Reconstructive Microsurgery, Soc. Head and Neck Surgery, Am. Cleft Palate Assn., Am. Soc. Surgery of Hand, Soc. Univ. Surgeons, Am. Assn. Plastic Surgeons (trustee 1983-86, treas. 1988-91, v.p. 1993-94, pres.-elect 1994, pres. 1995), Am. Soc. Aesthetic Plastic Surgery, Am. Soc. Maxillofacial Surgeons, Assn. Acad. Chairmen Plastic Surgery (bd. dirs. 1986-89), Assn. Surgeons East Africa, Assn. Plastic & Reconstructive Surgeons So. Africa (hon.), Pacific Coast Surg. Assn., Internat. Soc. Aesthetic Plastic Surgery, Internat. Soc. Reconstructive Microsurgery, Internat. Soc. Craniomaxillofacial Surgery, Pan African Assn. Neurol. Sci., African Med. and Rsch. Found. (bd. dirs. U.S.A. 1987—), Muthaiga Club, Ctr. Club, Club 33, Univ. Club, Phi Beta Kappa, Alpha Omega Alpha. Office: U Calif Div Plastic Surgery Irvine Med Ctr 101 The City Dr S Orange CA 92668-3201 *A crisis, at the outset, usually augurs nothing but ill. In the long run, however, my crises have more often than not marked a new course for my life, which is more fulfilling, and more exciting than anything in the past. Yes, a bit of good luck is needed, but the special feature of a crisis is that you are suddenly cut off from past patterns, habits, and interdependencies. Along with the distress and pain is freedom! Freedom to build again, with a new foundation and modern structure, using wisdom you didn't have the last time you built.*

FURNISH, DALE BECK, lawyer, educator; b. Iowa City, Iowa, Feb. 11, 1940; s. William Madison and Eula Bernice (Beck) F.; m. Roberta Rae Mahnke, Aug. 23, 1963 (div. Oct. 1975); 1 child, Katherine Elizabeth; m. Hannah Rose Arterian, May 27, 1978 (div. May 1994); children—William, Susannah, Diana, Cordelia; m. Diane Larkey, June 11, 1994. B.A., Grinnell Coll., 1962; J.D., U. Iowa, 1965; LL.M., U. Mich., 1970. Bar: Iowa, 1965, U.S. Ct. Appeals (8th cir.) 1966, Ariz. 1973, U.S. Dist. Ct. Ariz. 1976. Law clk. U.S. Ct. Appeals (8th cir.), Sioux City, Iowa, 1965-66; asst. prof. law U. Iowa, Iowa City, 1966-68; vis. prof. law Ford Found. Internat. Legal Ctr., Santiago, Chile, 1969-70; prof. law Ariz. State U., Tempe, 1970—; ptnr. Molloy, Jones & Donahue, P.C., 1988-92; vis. prof. law U. Nacional Autonoma de Mexico, Mexico City, 1974-75; Fulbright prof. Pontificia U. Católica del Peru, 1984, 88; lectr. USIA, Latin Am., 1972—; chmn. Ariz. Supreme Ct. Project on Judicial Cooperation with Sonora, Mex., 1993—, Nat. Law Ctr. Inter-Am. Free Trade, 1991—. Author: Usury and the Monetary Control Act of 1980, 1981, Legal Aspects of the North American Free Trade Agreement, 1992. Bd. editors Am. Jour. Comparative Law, 1972-89, Revista Peruana del Derecho Internat., 1979—. Mem. Fgn. Relations Com., Phoenix, 1979—, mem. exec. bd. 1986-91; mem. Gov.'s Ariz.-Mex. Commn., 1981—, chmn. legal adv. com., 1988-93. Mem. Am. Assn. Law Schs. (chmn. creditor debtor sect. 1978, chmn. comparative law sect. 1979), ABA, Ariz. Bar Assn., Iowa Bar Assn., Interam. Bar Assn., Am. Bankruptcy Inst. (bd. dirs. 1984-91), Order of Coif. Republican. Presbyterian. Office: Ariz State U Coll Law Tempe AZ 85287-7906

FURNIVAL, GEORGE MITCHELL, petroleum and mining consultant; b. Winnipeg, Man., Can., July 25, 1908; s. William George and Grace Una (Rothwell) F.; m. Marion Marguerite Fraser, Mar. 8, 1937; children: William George, Sharon (Mrs. John M. Roscoe), Patricia M., Bruce A. BSc, U. Man., Can., 1929; MA, Queens U., Can., 1933; PhD, MIT, 1935. Field geologist in Man., Ont., N.W.T., and Que., 1928-36; asst. mine supt. Cline Lake Gold Mines, Ltd., 1936-39; geologist Geol. Survey Can., No. and Southwestern Sask., 1939-42; from 1942-70 employed by the Standard Oil Co. Calif. (Chevron) subs. including following positions: dist. geologist Standard Oil Co. of Calif. (Chevron Standard, Ltd.), Calgary, Alta., 1942-44, asst. to chief geologist, 1944-45, field supt. So. Alta., 1945-46, mgr. land and legal dept., 1949-50, v.p. land and legal, dir., 1950-52, v.p. legal, crude oil sales, govt. rels., dir., 1952-55; pres., dir. Dominion Oil, Ltd., Trinidad and Tobago, 1952-60; v.p. exploration, dir. Calif. Exploration Co., Chevron Overseas Petroleum, Inc., San Francisco, 1955-63; staff asst. land to v.p. exploration and land Standard Oil Co. of Calif., 1961-63; chmn. bd., mng. dir. West Australian Petroleum Pty., Ltd. (Chevron operated), Perth, 1963-70, retired 1970; dir. mines Dept. Mines and Natural Resources, Man., 1946-48; v.p., dir. Newport Ventures, Ltd., Calgary, 1971-72; v.p. ops., dir., mem. exec. com. Brascan Resources subs. Brascan Ltd. (formerly Brazilian Traction Ltd., Calgary, 1973-75, sr. v.p., dir., 1975-77, sr. cons., 1977-78; pres., CEO, dir. Western Mines Ltd. (Brascan), 1978-80, exec. v.p., divsn. gen. mgr. Westmin Resources Ltd. (Brascan), also dir., mem. exec. com., 1981-82; pres., acting gen. mgr. Coalition Mining, Ltd.; pres., COO, dir. Lathwell Resources Ltd., 1983-84; cons. petroleum and mining, 1985—; founder Man. Geol. Survey, 1946; dir. Cretaceous Pipe Line Co., Ltd., Austen & Butta Pty., Ltd., Western Coal Holdings, Inc., Quest Explorations Ltd., San Antonio Resources Inc.; del. Interprovincial Mines Ministers Conf., several years; sec. Winnipeg Conf., 1947. Elected to Order of Can., 1982. Scholarship in mining geology named in his honor, U. B.C., Can. Fellow Royal Soc. Can., Geol. Soc. Am., Geol. Assn. Can., Soc. Econ. Geologists, Am. Assn. Petroleum Geologists (hon. life); mem. Engring. Inst. Can., Canadian Inst. Mining and Metallurgy (hon. life mem., past br. chmn., dist. councillor, v.p., chmn. petroleum div., Distinguished Service award 1974, Selwyn G. Blaylock gold medal 1979), Australian Petroleum Producing Exploration Assn. (hon. life mem., chmn. com. West Australian petroleum legislation, councillor, state chmn. for Western Australia), Australian Am. Assn. in Western Australia (councillor), Assn. Profl. Engrs., Geologists and Geophysicists of Alta. (hon. life mem., Centennial award 1985), Coal Assn. of Can. (bd.dirs.). Clubs: Calgary Golf and Country, Calgary Petroleum, Ranchmen's. Author numerous govt. and co. papers, reports, reference texts, also sci. articles to profl. jours. Home: 1315 Baldwin Cres SW, Calgary, AB Canada T2V 2B7

FURSE, ELIZABETH, congresswoman, small business owner; b. Nairobi, Kenya, 1936; came to U.S., 1958, naturalized, 1972; m. John Platt; 2 children (from previous marriage). BA, Evergreen State Coll., 1974; postgrad., U. Wash., Northwestern U., Lewis & Clark Coll. Dir. Western Wash. Indian program Am. Friends Svc. Com, 1975-77; coord. Restoration program for Native Am. Tribes Oreg. Legal Svc., 1980-86; co-owner Helvetia Vineyards, Hillsboro, Oreg.; mem. 103rd-105th Congresses from 1st Oreg. dist., 1993—, mem. commerce, fin. and hazardous materials, health and environment, energy and power coms., mem. telecomm. and finance com. Co-founder Oreg. Peace Inst., 1985. Office: US House of Reps 316 Cannon HOB Washington DC 20515*

FURST, DAN (DANIEL CHRISTOPHER FURST, III), producer, writer, actor; b. N.Y.C., Sept. 14, 1944; s. Daniel Christopher and Mary Ann Monica (Dolan) F.; m. Kimie Yoshimura, Dec. 17, 1986. BA, Rockhurst Coll., 1966; MA, Columbia U., 1967, PhD, 1974. developer, tchr. intensive courses in English Nippon Steel, Kawasaki Heavy Industries, Kubota Engring., others, 1985-91; guest lectr. Japanese theatre U. Hawaii, New Sch., N.Y.C., 1991; workshop leader Movement, Intuition and Silence, Kyoto, 1992; tchr. multimedia courses Kyoto U., 1993-95; announcer, emcee The Kyoto Global Forum, 1993, The Conf. on Ecol. Responsibility, New Delhi, 1993; artist mgr. Asia Pacific Wave concerts, Osaka, 1993, Count Basie Orch. Japan tour, 1994. Columnist: Mainichi Daily News, Asahi Evening News, Kansai Time Out Mag., Japan Times, Daily Yomiuri, 1985-95; contbr. articles to Edinburgh Internat. Festival Souvenir, Am. Theatre, High Performance, Asia Times, others; actor, fight dir. King Lear, 1987, Macbeth, 1989, Just Between the Three of Us, 1989, f/F Parasite, 1989, Bau Talkie, 1989; appeared in (films) Geisha, 1988, As Is, 1990, Cosmic Itch, 1991, Curious Fish, 1993, City Life White Paper, 1994, Undesirable Elements, 1995; interviewed dir. Peter Brook, actor Sir Ian McKellen, actor Makalo Mofokeng, Kabuki actors Ichikawa Ennosuke, Nakamura Tomijuro, bunraku theater master Takemoto Aioidayu, composer Ikuma Dan; appeared in commls., narrations for Sharp, Daiwa Bank, Hitachi, Osaka Gas, Omron, Mitsubishi Chems., numerous others; founder, artistic dir. Sirius Prodns. theater co., Kyoto, 1988-95, The Play of Freedom, 1995-97. Home: 2151 Mohala Way Honolulu HI 96822

FURST, DANIEL ERIC, medical educator. AB cum laude, Johns Hopkins U., 1964, MD, 1968. Diplomate Nat. Bd. Medicine, Am. Bd. Internal Medicine. Med. intern Johns Hopkins U., Balt., 1968-69, med. resident, 1969-70; fellow rheumatology UCLA Med. Ctr., 1973-75, asst. prof., 1977-82; fellow clin. pharmacology U. Calif. Med. Ctr., San Francisco, 1975-77; assoc. prof. medicine/rheumatolgoy U. Iowa Coll. Medicine, Iowa City, 1982-87; clin. prof. medicine/rheumatology Robert Wood Johnson Med. Sch., U. Medicine/Dentistry of N.J., New Brunswick, N.J., 1987-92; dir. anti-inflammatory/pulmonary clin. rsch. Ciba-Geigy Pharms., Summit, N.J., 1987-92; dir. clin. rsch. programs Va. Mason Med. Ctr., Seattle, 1992-94; clin. prof. medicine U. Washington, Seattle, 1992—; clin. dir. Va. Mason Rsch. Ctr., 1993—, dir. arthritis clin. rsch., 1994—; vis. prof. McMaster U., Hamilton, Ont., Can., 1989, U. Ind., Inpls., 1990, St. Vincent's Hosp., S.I., N.Y., NYU, 1991, Med. Coll. N.Y., Albany, 1993, Hoffman-LaRoche, Switzerland, 1994, Yakima, Wash., 1994; spkr. numerous cons.; cons. Pfizer, Inc., 1993—, Sanofi, 1993—, Hoffman-LaRoche, 1994—; active numerous profl. coms. Editor: (with others) Drugs for Rheumatic Disease, 1987, Immunomodulators in the Rheumatic Diseases, 1990, Second Line Agents (DMARDS) in the Rheumatic Diseases, 1992, Nonsteroidal Anti-Inflammatory Drugs, 2d edit., 1994, Systemic Sclerosis, 1995; editl. reviewer numerous jours.; contbr. articles to profl. jours., chpts. to books. Capt. M.C., USAF, 1970-73. Fellow Am. Coll. Physicians; mem. Am. Rheumatism Assn., Am. Soc. Clin. Pharmacology and Therapeutics, N.Y. Acad. Scis., Washington State Med. Assn., King County Med. Soc. Office: Va Mason Rsch Ctr 1000 Seneca St Seattle WA 98101-2744

FURTAK, THOMAS ELTON, physicist, educator, author, consultant; b. Ord, Nebr., May 23, 1949; s. Sylvester B. and Elsie L. (Pecenka) F.; m. Carolyn Kay Furtak, Jan. 30, 1971; children: Rick Anthony, Erin Marie, Mark Lim. BS, U. Nebr., 1971; PhD, Iowa State U., 1975. Postdoctoral fellow Ames (Iowa) Lab., 1975-77, assoc. physicist, 1977-80; assoc. prof. Rensselaer Poly. Inst., Troy, N.Y., 1980-86; prof. physics Colo. Sch. Mines, Golden, 1986—. Co-author: (textbook) Optics, 1986; co-editor: Surface Enhanced Raman Scattering, 1982; adv. editor Chem. Physics Letters, 1983-93. Mem. Am. Phys. Soc., Optical Soc. Am., Electrochem. Soc., Am. Chem. Soc., Materials Rsch. Soc., Am. Vacuum Soc., Phi Beta Kappa, Sigma Xi, Pi Mu Epsilon. Democrat. Roman Catholic. Office: Colo Sch Mines 16th and Illinois Sts Golden CO 80401

FURUKAWA, DEAN KEILI, psychotherapist; b. Seattle, Mar. 22, 1952. BA in Psychology, Social Psychology and Rsch. cum laude, Calif. State U., Northridge, 1974; M of Social Welfare, UCLA, 1978, D of Social Welfare, 1984. Lic. clin. social worker, Calif., Mont.; cert. facilitator, cons. in eye movement desensitization and reprocessing. Asst. vol. program coord. L.A. County Probation Dept., 1975-76; family counselor Family Svc. L.A., 1976-77; counselor III Harbor Regional Ctr. for Developmentally Disabled Citizens, 1977-80; rsch. interviewer Alcoholism Rsch. Ctr. UCLA Sch. Psychiatry, 1981-82; sr. social worker, clin. coord., acting dir. Gateways Hosp. and Mental Health Ctr., 1983-88; children's social worker III Adoptions Bur. L.A. County Dept. Children's Svcs., 1988-89; primary therapist, social worker Rivendell Psychiat. Ctr., Billings, 1989-91, clin. cons., 1991; psychotherapist, cons. Billings, 1990—; prof. rank lectr. Ea. Mont. Coll., 1990; clin. cons. Yellowstone Treatment Ctrs., 1991-93. Editor: Asian-American Students Assn. Newsletter, 1973-74; contbr. articles to profl. jours. Mem. exec. bd. Asian Pacific Family Outreach, 1978-80; mem. exec. com. Asian-Am. Social Workers, 1978-80; mem. adv. bd. Positive Alternative for Student Success, 1979-80; founder Billings Therapist Support Group, 1990-92, Crow Indian Reservation Vol. Clinic, 1994-95. DHEW Child Welfare Adminstrn. scholar UCLA, 1977-78; pub. health svc. fellow UCLA, 1981-83. Mem. NASW. Office: PO Box 21373 Billings MT 59104-1373

FURUYAMA, RENEE HARUE, association executive; b. Honolulu, Feb. 15, 1957; d. Walter Tadashi and Jane Machie (Kamada) F.; m. Joel Fischer, Oct. 31, 1991; children: Lisa, Nicole. Grad., Tohoku U., Sendai, Japan, 1984; MSW, U. Hawaii, 1988, M.Urban and Regional Planning, 1993. Lic. social worker, Hawaii. Geriatric case mgr. Dept. Human Svcs., Honolulu, 1992-95; pub. policy dir. Mental Health Assn. Hawaii, Honolulu, 1995—; lectr. in field. Bd. dirs. Waianae Clubhouse, Miyagi Kenjinkai, Am. friends Svc. Com.; mem. Unity Organizing Com.; chmn. Hawaii Commn. for Africa. Tohuku U. scholar; recipient numerous scholarships and awards. Mem. NASW, UN Assn. Hawaii (treas. 1988-91). Democrat. Home: 1371-4 Hunakai St Honolulu HI 96816 Office: 200 N Vineyard Blvd Ste 300 Honolulu HI 96817

FUTCH, MARGUERITE ELIZABETH, not-for-profit organization executive; b. Kingston, Pa., Nov. 27, 1951; d. William J. and Shirley Rita (Woods) F.; 1 child, Brandon. BA in English and Psychology, Bloomsburg (Pa.) State U., 1973; MA in Not-for-Profit Mgmt., Regis U., Denver, 1997. Program adminstr. Phila. Urban League, 1975-76; adminstr. Ctr. for the blind, Phila., 1976-78; pres., CEO Colo. Optometric Ctr., Denver, 1979—. Chair Statewide Low Vision Task Force, Colo., 1989, Colo. adv. Coun. Svcs. for the blind, 1989; vice chmn. Guild Urban League Met. Denver, 1993; mem., mktg. chmn. Minoru Yasui Vol. Award Com., 1995—. Nat. Merit scholar, 1968-69. Mem. Assn. United Way Execs. (chmn.), Urban League (life), Denver C. of C., Colo. Assn. Educators and Rehabilitators of Blind and Visually Impaired Persons (chmn.), Zonta (bd. dirs. 1996—). Office: Colo Optometric Ctr 2736 Welton St Ste 200 Denver CO 80205

FYFE, ALISTAIR IAN, cardiologist, scientist, educator; b. Hobart, Tasmania, Australia, Sept. 5, 1960; came to U.S., 1991; s. Ian John and Merrill Millicent (Faragher) F.; 1 child, Alexander Jonathan. B of Med. Sci., U. Tasmania, 1980, B of Med. Sci. with honors, 1981, MBBS, 1984; PhD in Molecular Biology, UCLA, 1995. Diplomate Am. Bd. Internal Medicine and Cardiovasc. Disease. Intern Royal Hobart Hosp., 1985-86; resident in internal medicine U. B.C., Vancouver, Can., 1986-89; cardiology fellow U. Toronto, Ont., Can., 1989-91; cardiac rsch. fellow UCLA, 1991-95, asst. prof. medicine, cardiology, 1995—, dir. Ctr. for Cholesterol and Lipid Mgmt., 1995—, assoc. mem. Molecular Biology Inst., 1996—. Author: (with others) Progress in Pediatric Cardiology, 1993; contbr. articles to profl. jours. Recipient Fellowship Clinician Scientist award Med. Rsch. Coun., Can., 1992. Fellow Royal Coll. Physicians Can., Am. Coll. Cardiology, Coun. Arterial Sclerosis; mem. Internat. Heart Transplant Soc., Am. Heart Assn. (fellow arteriosclerosis coun., reviewer 1993—, Young Investigator award, 1993, 95), Am. Soc. Clin. Investigation, Am. Diabetes Assn. Office: UCLA Cardiology 10833 Le Conte Ave Los Angeles CA 90024-1602

FYLER, PATRICIA ANN, legal nurse consultant, small business owner; b. Pittsfield, Mass., Aug. 20, 1928; d. Clarence Augustus and Elaine Agnes (Carruthers) McConkey; m. Robert Parmelee Fyler, Oct. 4, 1949; children: Deborah, Rebecca, Pamela, Nancy, Cynthia. Student, Bishop Meml. Nursing Sch., 1949, St. Francis, 1954-56; BS, U. Redlands, 1985. CEN. Staff to head nurse Berkshire Med. Ctr., Pittsfield, 1949-54; staff nurse, operating room St. Francis Hosp., Lynwood, Calif., 1954-57; staff nurse, operating room St. Jude Hosp., Fullerton, Calif., 1958-62, relief charge nurse, 1962-67, charge nurse, 1967-78, asst. supr. emergency dept., 1978-80; mgr. emergency dept. St. Jude Hosp., Yorba Linda, Calif., 1980-89; owner, pres. Fyler Assocs./Multi-Specialty Legal Nurse Cons., Brea, Calif., 1990—; staff RN St. Jude Med. Ctr., Fullerton, 1989—. Active cont. learning program, PTA, youth orgns., continuing learning experience; past pres. Orange County, Calif.; pres. L.A. Mem. Am. Assn. Legal Nurse Cons. (past pres. Orange County, past pres. Los Angeles County), Emergency Nurses Assn. (numerous offices). Office: Fyler Assocs 3438 Ashwood Ct Oceanside CA 92054-7001

GAÁL, VIOLETTA, retired social worker, massage therapist; b. Bucharest, Romania, May 1, 1931; came to the U.S., 1957; d. Gábor and Rozália (Turzai) G.; m. Alex Balogh, Sept. 14, 1953 (div. May 1965); 1 chilb, Gábor. BA, Sacramento State U., 1962. Cert. social worker, Calif.; cert. massage therapy, Calif. Adminstr. State Planning Bur., Budapest, Hungary, 1950-54; stock clk. Ladies Dress Shop, Sacramento, Calif., 1957-61; social worker Welfare Dept., Sacramento, 1963-65, Oakland, Calif., 1965-80; pvt. practice massage therapist San Francisco, 1986—; mil. contractor, watch-clock repair, 1978-81. Author: Spiral; Translator: Idegen a Királyok Völgyében, 1993, Jézus Misztikus élete, 1993, The Boys of Pal Street, 1994, Fehr Sierrak, 1994. Republican. Home: 4099 Howe St Apt 101 Oakland CA 94611-5204

GABOW, PATRICIA ANNE, internist; b. Starke, Fla., Jan. 8, 1944; m. Harold N. Gabow, June 21, 1971; children: Tenaya Louise, Aaron Patrick. BA in Biology, Seton Hill Coll., 1965; MD, U. Pa. Sch. Medicine, 1969. Diplomate Am. Bd. Internal Medicine, Am. Bd. Nephrology, Nat. Bd. Med. Examiners; lic. Md., Colo. Internship in medicine Hosp. of U. of Pa., 1969-70; residency in internal medicine Harbor Gen. Hosp., 1970-71; renal fellowship San Francisco Gen. Hosp. and Hosp. of U. Pa., 1971-72, 72-73; instr. medicine divsn. renal diseases, asst. prof. U. Colo. Health Scis. Ctr., 1973-74, 74-79, assoc. prof. medicine divsn. renal diseases, prof., 1979-87; chief renal disease, clin. dir. dept. medicine Denver Gen. Hosp., 1973-81, 76-81, dir. med. svcs., 1981-91; CEO, med. dir. Denver Health and Hosps., 1992—; faculty assoc. U. N.C., Chapel Hill, 1992-93; reviewer Kidney Internat., New Eng. Jour. of Medicine; intensive care com. Denver Gen. Hosp., 1976-81, med. records com., 1979-80, ind. rev. com., 1978-81, continuing med. edn. com., 1981-83, animal care com., 1979-83; student adv. com. U. Colo. Health Scis. Ctr., 1982-87, faculty senate, 1985, 86, internship adv. com., 1977-92; exec. com. Denver Gen. Hosp., 1981—, chmn. health resources com., 1988-90, chmn. pathology search com., 1989, chmn. faculty practice plan steering com., 1990-92. Mem. editorial bd. EMERGINDEX, 1983-93, Am. Jour. of Kidney Disease, 1984—, Western Jour. of Medicine, 1987—, Annals of Internal Medicine, 1988-91, Jour. of the Am. Soc. of Nephrology, 1990-97; contbr. numerous articles, revs. and editorials to profl. publs., chpts. to books. Mem. Mayor's Safe City Task Force, 1993; mem. sci. adv. bd. Polycystic Kidney Rsch. Found., 1984-96, chmn., 1991; mem. sci. adv. bd. Nat. Kidney Found., 1991-94; mem. Nat. Pub. Health and Hosps. Inst. Bd., 1993—. Recipient Sullivan award for Highest Acad. Average in Graduating Class, Seton Hill Coll., 1965, Pa. State Senatorial scholarship, 1961-65, Kaiser Permanente award for Excellence in Teaching, 1976, Ann. award to Outstanding Woman Physician, 1982, Kaiser Permanente Nominee for Excellence in Teaching award, 1983, Seton Hill Coll. Disting. Alumna Leadership award, 1990; named one of The Best Doctors in Am., 1994-95; grantee Bonfils Found., 1985-86, NIH, 1985-90, 91-96. Mem. Denver Med. Soc., Colo. Med. Soc., Am. Soc. Nephrology, Internat. Soc. Nephrology, Am. Coll. Physicians, Am. Fedn. Clin. Rsch., Am. Physiol. Soc., Polycystic Kidney Disease Rsch. Found. (sci. advisor 1984-96), Western Assn. Physicians, Nat. Kidney Found. (sci. adv. bd. 1987-91), Women's Forum of Colo., Inc., Assn. Am. Physicians. Roman Catholic. Office: Denver Health 777 Bannock St Denver CO 80204-4507

GABRIEL, RENNIE, financial planner; b. L.A., July 27, 1948; s. Harry and Milly (Broder) Goldenhar; m. Judi Robbins, Nov. 24, 1968 (div. Feb. 1989); children: Ryan, Davida; m. Lesli Gilmore, May 5, 1990. BA, Calif. State U., Northridge, 1971; CLU, Am. Coll., 1979, Cert. Fin. Planner, 1988. Ins. agt. Prudential and Provident Mutual, Encino, Calif., 1972-78; pension cons. Shadur LaVine & Assocs., Encino, 1978-81; owner Artist Corner Gallery Inc., Encino, 1977-82; pension and fin. planner Gabriel Tolleson & Stroum, Tarzana, Calif., 1983-87; pension cons., fin. planner Shadur LaVine/Integrated Fin., Encino, 1987-90; dir. pensions U.S. Life of Calif., Pasadena, Calif., 1983; fin. planner Pension Alternatives, Encino, 1990-92, The Fin. Coach, Encino, 1993—; instr. UCLA, 1992—. Contbr. articles to fin. publs. Mem. Internat. Assn. Fin. Planning (pres. San Fernando Valley chpt. 1992), Nat. Assn. Life Underwriters (Achievement award 1974, Nat. Quality award 1975, Million Dollar Round Table 1990), Internat. Assn. Fin. Planning, CLUs, Inst. Cert. Fin. Planners, Employee Assistance Profls. Assn. (treas. San Fernando Valley chpt. 1992), Apt. Assn. San Fernando Valley-Ventura County (bd. mem. 1992).

GABRIELIAN, ARMEN, computer scientist, researcher, consultant; b. Tehran, Iran, Aug. 17, 1940; came to U.S. 1959; s. Levon Simon and Eliza Gabrielian; m. Tong Moon, 1974; children: Sonya Emi, Tanya Simone. BS, MIT, Cambridge, Mass., 1963; MS, MIT, 1965, PhD, 1969. Rsch. assoc. U. Waterloo, Ont., Can., 1969-71; postdoctoral fellow U. So. Calif., L.A., 1971-72; ind. cons. L.A., Newport Beach, 1972-77; sr. sys. analyst Fluor Corp., Irvine, Calif., 1977-78; sr. scientist Hughes Aircraft Co., Fullerton, Calif., 1979-87; tech. dir. Thomson-CSF, Inc., Palo Alto (Calif.) Rsch. Ops., Palo

Alto, Calif., 1987-91; pres. UniView Systems, Mountain View, Calif., 1991—. Contbr. articles to profl. jours. Mem. IEEE, Assn. for Computing Machinery, Sigma Xi, Tau Beta Pi, Eta Kappa Nu.

GABRIELSON, SHIRLEY GAIL, nurse; b. San Francisco, Mar. 17, 1934; d. Arthur Obert and Lois Ruth (Lanterman) Ellison; m. I. Grant Gabrielson, Sept. 11, 1955; children: James Grant, Kari Gay. BS in Nursing, Mont. State U., 1955. RN, Mont. Staff and operating room nurse Bozeman (Mont.) Deaconess Hosp., 1954-55, 55-56; staff nurse Warm Springs State Hosp., 1955; office nurse, operating room asst. Dr. Craft, Bozeman, 1956-57; office nurse Dr. Bush, Beach, N.D., 1957-58; pub. health nurse Wibaux County, 1958-59; staff and charge nurse Teton Meml. Hosp., Choteau, Mont., 1964-65; staff pediatric and float nurse St. Patrick Hosp., Missoula, Mont., 1965-70; nurse, insvc. dir. Trinity Hosp., Wolf Point, Mont., 1970-79; ednl. coord. Community Hosp. and Nursing Home, Poplar, Mont., 1979-96; coord. staff devel. Faith Luth. Home, Wolf Point, 1980-81; risk mgr. NEMHS, 1996—; CPR instr. ARC, Am. Heart Assn., Great Falls, Mont., 1979—; condr. workshops and seminars; program coord., test proctor for cert. nursing assts., 1989-96; risk mgr. N.E. Mont. Health Svcs., Poplar, Wolf Point, 1996—; preceptor for student nurses in rural health nursing clin. U. N.D., 1993-96. Author: Independent Study for Nurse Assistants, 1977. Former asst. camp leader Girl Scouts U.S.A.; former mother advisor, bd. dirs. Rainbow Girls; pres. Demolay Mothers Club, 1977; bd. dirs. Mont. div. Am. Cancer Soc., 1984-90, mem. awards com., 1986-89; founder Tri-County Parkinson's Support Group, N.E. Mont. Recipient Lifesaver award Am. Cancer Soc., 1987, Svc. award ARC, 1989, Health and Human Svcs. award Mont. State Dept., 1990, U.S. Dept. Health award, 1990, Outstanding award, U.S. HHS, Mont. Health Promotion award Dept. Health and Environ. Scis. Mem. ANA, Mont. Nurses Assn. (mem. commn. on continuing edn. 1977-91, chmn. 1984-86), Order Eastern Star (Worthy grand matron 1995-96), Alpha Tau Delta (alumni pres. 1956). Presbyterian. Home: 428 Hill St Wolf Point MT 59201-1244 Office: Community Hosp-Nursing Home PO Box 38 Poplar MT 59255-0038

GABRIELSON, WALTER OSCAR, artist; b. Eveleth, Minn., July 25, 9135; s. Walter Oscar and Marie Hope (Harris) G.; m. Nancy Heather Goldberg, Mar. 24, 1983. BS, UCLA, 1958; BFA, MFA, Otis Art Inst., L.A., 1965. Printer Tamarind Lithography Workshop, L.A., 1964-66; prof. art Calif. State U., Northridge, 1966-81. Exhibited at Arco Ctr. for Visual Arts, 1976, others. Author: 41 Airplanes, 1970, Persistence, 1993. Bd. dirs. Santa Barbara (Calif.) Contemporary Arts. Forum, 1991-95. 1st lt. USAF, 1958-61. Ford Found. Tamarind grantee, 1964-66. Studio: 375 Pine Ave Ste 2 Goleta CA 93117-3725

GAGARIN, DENNIS PAUL, advertising agency executive; b. Long Beach, Calif., July 9, 1952. BS in Graphic Design, San Jose State U., 1976. Art dir. Brower, Mitchell, Gum Advt., Los Gatos, Calif., 1976-79, Offield & Brower Advt., Los Gatos, 1979-82; sr. art dir. Tycer, Fultz, Bellack Advt., Palo Alto, Calif., 1982-85; head art dir. TFB/BBDO Advt., Palo Alto, 1985-87; creative dir. Lena Chow Advt., Palo Alto, 1987-90; prin., ptnr. Gagarin/McGeoch Advt. and Design, Redwood City, Calif., 1989—; prof. San Jose (Calif.) State U., 1987-90, now guest lectr.; guest art dir. Western Art Dirs. Club, Palo Alto. Recipient awards for graphic design, art direction. Office: Gagarin/McGeoch Advt-Design 493 Seaport Ct Ste 102 Redwood City CA 94063-2730

GAGGIANO, ANDREA JEAN, secondary education educator; b. Orange, Calif., Jan. 12, 1971; d. Thomas Edward Lareau and Joyce Loreen Molzahn Ours; m. Michael John Gaggiano, June 18, 1994. BA in English, U. Calif., Irvine, 1993, BA in History, 1993. Cert. English and history tchr., Calif. Thcr. English Trabuco Hills H.S., Mission Viejo, Calif., 1994—. Mem. Calif. Tchrs. Assn., Nat. Coun. Tchrs. English. Republican. Quaker.

GAGNEJA, GURCHARAN LOL, health facility administrator; b. Aug. 3, 1939; came to U.S., 1974; s. Balmukand and Ganga Devi (Nagpal) G.; m. Janet Graham Keirs Reid, Oct. 23, 1970 (div. July 1987); children: Sharan Devi, Anita Janet; m. Susan Romatz, May 23, 1992. BSc, Panjab U., 1958; MEng./BSc, Sheffield U., 1967; PhD, Heriot-Watt U., 1970; MSc in Microbiology, Detroit U., 1983; postdoctoral diploma in clin. biochemistry/lab. medicine, Windsor U., Can., 1976. Diplomate Am. Bd. Bioanalysis; cert. lab. dir. Mich. Dept. Pub. Health. Rschr. biotechnology U. Bath, Eng., 1970-73; asst. lab. dir. Bioanalytical Proc. Inc., Allen Park, Mich., 1974-78; lab. dir. Detroit Doctors, Livonia, Mich., 1978-85; pres. Sterling Biochems. Inc., Ferndale, Mich., 1985-91, Esquire Diagnostics, West Bloomfield, Mich., 1991-94, Clin. Lab. Hemet, Calif., 1994, Biotronic Diagnostics Inc., Hemet, 1996—; lab. dir. Diagnostic Rsch. Lab, Bloomfield, 1984-85; pres. Nuclear Diagnostics Inc., Troy, Mich., 1986-91. Fellow Royal Inst. Chemistry U.K., Nat. Acad. Clin. Biochemistry; mem. APHA, Am. Assn. Bioanalysis, Am. Assn. Clin. Chemists, Assn. Clin. Biochemists U.K., N.Y. Acad. Scis. Republican. Home: 850 E Latham Ave Ste A Hemet CA 92543-4391 Office: Biotron Diagnostics Inc 850 E Latham Ave Hemet CA 92543-4391

GAIBER, MAXINE DIANE, museum education director; b. Bklyn., May 6, 1949; d. Sidney and Junia Estelle (Gruberg) Oliansky; m. Stuart Gaiber, May 11, 1971; children: Scott Cory, Samantha Lauren. BA, Bklyn. Coll., 1970; MA, U. Minn., 1972. Tours & curriculum svcs. dir. Mpls. Inst. Arts, 1972-77, assoc. chair edn., 1977-79; cons. mus. edn. Field Mus./Art Inst., Chgo., 1979-82; program coord. Field Mus. of Natural History, Chgo., 1982-83; publs. dir. Art Ctr. Coll. Design, Pasadena, Calif., 1983-85; rsch. dir. Art Ctr. Coll. Design, Pasadena, 1985-86, campaign dir., 1986-88; pub. rels. officer Newport Harbor Art Mus., Newport Beach, Calif., 1988-94, dir. edn. & publs., 1994-96; dir. edn. Orange County Mus. Art, Newport Beach, 1996—; instr. L.A. County Mus. Art, 1985—, Art Ctr. Coll. Design, Pasadena, 1986-89, Coll. DuPage, Glen Ellyn, Ill., 1981-83. Editor: Why Design?, 1987; editor/author: Mus. edn. materials, 1972—. Art vol. Mariners Sch., Newport Beach, 1989-93. Fellow Bush Found. 1976. Mem. Pub. Rels. Soc. Am., Am. Assn. Mus. (Edn. Com. rep. 1979-83). Office: Orange County Mus Art 850 San Clemente Dr Newport Beach CA 92660-6301

GAINES, FRANCIS PENDLETON, III, lawyer; b. Lexington, Va., Sept. 24, 1944; s. Francis Pendleton Jr. and Dorothy Ruth (Bloomhardt) G.; m. Mary Chilton, Dec. 19, 1967 (div. Aug. 1992); children: Elizabeth Chilton, Edmund Pendleton, Andrew Cavett. BA in Hist., U. Ariz., 1967; LLB, U. Va., 1969. Bar: U.S. Dist. Ct. (Ariz.) 1969, Ariz. 1969, U.S. Ct. Appeals (9th cir.) 1972, U.S. Supreme Ct. 1975. Assoc. Evans, Kitchel & Jenckes, Phoenix, 1969-75, ptnr., 1975-89; ptnr. Fennemore Craig, Phoenix, 1989—; mem. panel arbitrators N.Y. Stock Exch., 1984—, NASD, 1984—; judge pro tem Ariz. Ct. Appeals, 1994-95, Maricopa County (Ariz.) Superior Ct., 1994—; mem. State Bar Disciplinary Hearing Com., 1991—, chair, 1995—; mem. nat. litigation panel U. Va. Sch. Law; lectr. and panelist various CLE programs. Author: Punitive Damages-A Railroad Trial Lawyers Guide, 1985. Sr. warden All Saints' Episcopal Ch., 1994-97, parish chancellor, 1997—; chmn. bd. govs. All Saints' Day Sch., Phoenix, 1990-91; chmn. Phoenix planned giving subcom. U. Ariz., 1985. Fellow Am. Bar Found.; mem. ABA, State Bar Ariz., Maricopa County Bar Assn., Nat. Assn. Railroad Trial Coun. (exec. com. Pacific region), Ariz. Assn. Def. Coun., Securities Industry Assn. (law and compliance divsn.), Univ. Club, Internat. Wine & Food Soc. (Phoenix br.). Republican. Episcopalian. Office: Fennemore Craig 3003 N Central Ave Ste 2600 Phoenix AZ 85012-2913

GAINES, HOWARD CLARKE, retired lawyer; b. Washington, Sept. 6, 1909; s. Howard Wright and Ruth Adeline-Clarke Thomas Gaines; m. Audrey Allen, July 18, 1936; children: Clarke Allen, Margaret Anne. J.D., Cath. U. Am., 1936. Bar: D.C. bar 1936, U.S. Supreme Ct. bar 1946, U.S. Ct. Claims bar 1947, Calif. bar 1948. Individual practice law Washington, 1938-43, 46-47, Santa Barbara, Calif., 1948-51; asso. firm Price, Postel & Parma, Santa Barbara, 1951-54; partner Price, Postel & Parma, 1954-88; of counsel, 1989-94, ret., 1994; chmn. Santa Barbara Bench and Bar Com., 1972-74. Chmn. Santa Barbara Police and Fire Comm., 1948-52; mem. adv. bd. Santa Barbara Com. on Alcoholism, 1956-67; bd. dirs. Santa Barbara Humane Soc., 1958-69, 85-92; bd. trustees Santa Barbara Botanic Garden, 1960—, v.p., 1967-69; bd. trustees Cancer Found. Santa Barbara, 1960-77; dir. Santa Barbara Mental Health Assn., 1957-59, v.p., 1959; pres. Santa Barbara Found., 1976-79, trustee, 1979—. Fellow Am. Bar Found.; mem. ABA, Bar Assn. D.C., State Bar Calif. (gov. 1969-72, v.p. 1971-72, tres. 1971-72), Santa Barbara County Bar Assn. (pres. 1957-58), Am. Judicature Soc., Santa Barbara Club. Republican. Episcopalian. Home: 1306 Las Alturas Rd Santa Barbara CA 93103-1600 *Strive for a career in productive work you truly enjoy. Give due respect to others and their opinions. Learn to listen before voicing criticism or giving constructive advice. Season your life with a little humor.*

GAINES, JERRY LEE, secondary education educator; b. Seminole, Okla., Feb. 18, 1940; s. Frank Gaines and Jane M. (Crowe) Gring; m. Lorraine Louise Paulson, Oct. 7, 1961; children: Paul Martin, Mark Edwin. AA, Pasadena City Coll., 1960; BA, Calif. State U., L.A., 1964; MA, Calif. State U., Long Beach, 1969. Tchr. bus. Rolling Hills High Sch., Rolling Hills Estates, Calif., 1965-91, Palos Verdes Peninsula High Sch., Rolling Hills Estates, 1991—; coord. driver edn. Palos Verdes Peninsula Unified Sch. Dist., Palos Verdes Estates, Calif., 1970-91, mentor tchr., 1984-93. Coauthor driver edn. workbook; contbr. articles to traffic safety publs. Chmn. San Pedro (Calif.) Citizens Adv. Com., 1985-88; pres. South Shores Homeowners Assn., San Pedro, 1986-90, 95-96, San Pedro and Peninsula Homeowners Coalition, 1990-93. With USN, 1960-62. Mem. NEA, ASCD, Calif. Tchrs. Assn., Palos Verdes Faculty Assn., Nat. Bus. Edn. Assn., Calif. Bus. Edn. Assn., Am. Driver and Traffic Safety Edn. Assn. (bd. dirs. 1982-88), Calif. Assn. Safety Edn. (pres. 1982-83), Elks, Phi Delta Kappa. Home: 2101 W 37th St San Pedro CA 90732-4707 Office: Palos Verdes Peninsula High Sch 27118 Silver Spur Rd Palos Verdes Peninsula CA 90274-2300

GAIR, KEVIN LINDSEY, learning director; b. Baldwin Park, Calif., Dec. 21, 1958; s. Robert Corrington and Nora Linda (Lindsey) G.; m. Beverly Helen Wood, May 1, 1982; children: Stephanie Renee, Cristine Nicole. BA, Calif. State Poly. U., 1984; MEd in Adminstrn., Point Loma Nazarene Coll., 1990; PhD, LaSalle U., 1996. Clear credential, Calif. Dept. Edn. Police officer Glendora (Calif.) Police Dept., 1981-83; security host Disneyland, Anaheim, Calif., 1983-84; history, computer and sci. tchr. Baldwin Park Unified Sch. Dist., 1984-91; history tchr. Fowler (Calif.) Unified Sch. Dist., 1991-94, mentor tchr., 1994-95; learning dir. Kings Canyon Unified Sch. Dist., Reedley, Calif., 1995—; mem. various sch. coms. including chair history dept., mem. tech. com. Fowler H.S., 1993-95; chair tech. com., mem. Parent Tchr. Club and sch. site coun. Dunlap Sch., 1995-96. Author: Dark Descent, 1993, Dark Descent II, 1995; editor-in-chief Baldwin Park Press, 1988; author of short stories. Mem. Shannon Valley Property Owners, Squaw Valley, Calif., 1991-96, Squaw Valley Coun., 1995-96; vol. firefighter Mountain Valley Fire Dept., Dunlap, Calif., 1995—. Recipient Cert. of Merit, Calif. State Senate, 1990. Mem. Free and Accepted Mason. Home: PO Box 505 Squaw Valley CA 93675-0505 Office: Dunlap Sch Box 100 Dunlap CA 93621

GALANE, MORTON ROBERT, lawyer; b. N.Y.C., Mar. 15, 1926; s. Harry J. and Sylvia (Schenkelbach) G.; children: Suzanne Galane Duvall, Jonathan A. B.E.E., CCNY, 1946; LL.B., George Washington U., 1950. Bar: D.C. 1950, Nev. 1955, Calif. 1975. Patent examiner U.S. Patent Office, Washington, 1948-50; spl. partner firm Roberts & McInnis, Washington, 1950-54; practice as Morton R. Galane, P.C., Las Vegas, Nev., 1955—; spl. counsel to Gov. Nev., 1967-70. Contbr. articles to profl. jours. Chmn. Gov.'s Com. on Future of Nev., 1979-80. Fellow Am. Coll. Trial Lawyers; mem. Am. Law Inst., IEEE, Am. Bar Assn. (council litigation sect. 1977-83), State Bar Nev., State Bar Calif., D.C. Bar. Home: 2019 Bannie Ave Las Vegas NV 89102-2208 Office: 302 Carson Ave Ste 1100 Las Vegas NV 89101-5909

GALARRAGA, ANDRES JOSE, professional baseball player; b. Caracas, Venezuela, June 18, 1961; m. Eneyda G., Feb. 18, 1984; 1 child, Andria. First baseman Montreal Expos, 1979-91, St. Louis Cardinals, 1991-92, Colorado Rockies, 1992—. Named to Nat. League All-Star Team, 1988, 93; recipient Gold Glove award, 1989-90, Silver Slugger award, 1988; Nat. League Batting Champion, 1993; named Comeback Player of Yr., 1993, MVP So. League. 1984. Office: Colorado Rockies 2850 W 20th Ave Denver CO 80211-5103*

GALASSIE, JOHN PERRY, medical supervisor; b. Appleton, Wis., Nov. 3, 1941; s. Philip Anthony and Lylase S. (Voit) G.; m. Dorothy Jean Bristol, Dec. 14, 1963; children: John Perry Jr., Angelina Maria. BS, U. Nebr., 1973. Cert. physician asst. Nat. Commn. on Certification of Physician Assts., 1975; lic. physician asst., Utah, 1990. Med. lab technician USAF, 1960-71, maj., physician asst., 1973-90; physician asst. FHP, Ogden, Utah, 1990-91; med. supr. Pharm. divsn. Bayer Corp., Ogden, 1991—. Fellow Utah Acad. Physician Assts. (Life Svc. award 1991), Soc. Air Force Physician Assts., Am. Acad. Physician Assts.; mem. Am. Legion, Am. Assn. Retired Persons. Home: 935 E 3000 N # 68 Layton UT 84040-6552 Office: Bayer Corp 3073 Harrison Blvd Ogden UT 84403-0828

GALBRAITH, NANETTE ELAINE GERKS, forensic and management sciences company executive; b. Chgo., June 15, 1928; d. Harold William and Maybelle Ellen (Little) Gerks; m. Oliver Galbraith III, Dec. 18, 1948; children: Craig Scott, Diane Frances Galbraith Ketcham. BS with high honors with distinction, San Diego State U., 1978. Diplomate Am. Bd. Forensic Document Examiners. Examiner of questioned documents San Diego County Sheriff's Dept. Crime Lab., San Diego, 1975-80; sole prop. Nanette G. Galbraith, Examiner of Questioned Documents, San Diego, 1980-82; pres., examiner of questioned documents Galbraith Forensic & Mgmt. Scis., Ltd., San Diego, 1982—; one of keynote speakers Internat. Assn Forensic Scis., Adelaide, South Australia, 1990. Contbr. articles to profl. jours. Fellow Am. Acad. Forensic Scis. (questioned documents section, del. to Peoples Rep. of China 1986, USSR, 1988); mem. Am. Soc. Questioned Document Examiners, Southwestern Assn. Forensic Document Examiners (charter), U. Club Atop Symphony Towers, Phi Kappa Phi. Republican. Episcopalian. Office: Galbraith Forensic & Mgmt Scis Ltd 4370 La Jolla Village Dr San Diego CA 92122-1251

GALBREATH, JAMES HOWARD, portfolio manager; b. Pomona, Calif., June 15, 1946; s. Howard Leslie Galbreath and Barbara (Coles) Bradford; m. Kathryn Dougherty, Sept. 1, 1975; children: Shannon Brook, Brittany Nicole. BSBA in Fin., U. Denver, 1969. CFA. Account exec. Dean Witter, Denver, 1969-70; pres. Am. Money Mgmt., Denver, 1971-72; v.p. Chandelle Corp., Denver, 1972-74; ptnr. Stephenson and Co., Denver, 1974-82; pres. Galbreath Fin., Englewood, Colo., 1982-87; mng. dir. NWQ Investment Mgmt. Co., Englewood, 1987—; bd. dirs. Homax Corp., Bellingham, Wash.; pres. The Rockies Fund, Inc., 1983-87. Mem. Leadership Denver Assn. (pres. bd. dirs. 1994-97), Denver Soc. Security Analysis, Metro Denver Exec. Club, Rockies Club (chmn. 1983-90), Colo. Venture Capital Assn. (pres.), Econ. Club Colo. Republican.

GALE, ARNOLD DAVID, pediatric neurologist, consultant; b. Chgo., Nov. 2, 1949; s. Benjamin and Revelle Frances (Steinman) G. AB summa cum laude, Stanford U., 1971; MD, Johns Hopkins U., 1976. Diplomate Am. Bd. Pediatrics, Nat. Bd. Med. Examiners; med. lic., Calif. Resident in pediatrics Mass. Gen. Hosp., Boston, 1976-78; postdoctoral fellow Johns Hopkins Hosp., Balt., 1978-79, resident in neurology, 1979-82; asst. prof. pediatrics and neurology George Washington U. Sch. Medicine, Washington, 1982-89; dir. neurology tng. program Children's Hosp. Nat. Med. Ctr., Washington, 1982-89; med. info. officer Muscular Dystrophy Assn., Tucson, 1992—; consulting neurologist Vaccine Injury Program U.S. Dept. HHS, Rockville, Md., 1989—; adv. panel FDA, Rockville, 1983-89; reviewer Am. Jour. Diseases of Children, 1991, New Eng. Jour. Medicine, 1986. Author: Pediatric Emergency Medicine, 1989; contbr. articles to profl. jours. Support group coord. Muscular Dystrophy Assn., San Jose, Calif., 1989—; mem. Pres.'s Com. Employment of People Disabilities, Washington, 1992—; med. adv. bd. Multiple Sclerosis Soc., Santa Clara, Calif., 1990—; bd. dirs. Muscular Dystrophy Assn., Tucson, 1993—. Recipient Nat. Rehab. award Allied Svcs., Scranton, Pa., 1994. Fellow Am. Acad. Pediatrics; mem. Am. Acad. Neurology, Am. Soc. Neurol. Investigation (founding mem.), Child Neurology Soc., Phi Beta Kappa, Alpha Omega Alpha. Jewish. Office: 2757 Donovan Ave Santa Clara CA 95051-3020

GALE, DANIEL BAILEY, architect; b. St. Louis, Nov. 6, 1933; s. Leone Caryll and Gladys (Wotowa) G.; student Brown U., 1951-53, Ecole Des Beaux Arts, Paris, 1954-55; BArch., Washington U., 1957; m. Nancy Susan Miller, June 15, 1957; children: Caroline Hamilton, Rebecca Fletcher, Daniel Bailey With Gale & Cannon, Architects and Planners, Hellmuth, Obata & Kassabaum, Inc., Architects, St. Louis, and exec. v.p. corp. devel., dir. HOK, Inc., St. Louis, 1961-79; ptnr. Heneghan and Gale, architects and planners, Aspen, Colo., 1967-69; pres., chief exec. officer Gale Kober Assocs., San Francisco, 1979-83; pvt. practice architecture, Belvedere, Calif., 1984—; pres. Program Mgmt. Inc., Belvedere, 1984—. Recipient Henry Adams prize Washington U., 1957. Mem. AIA, Singapore Inst. Architects. Home and Office: 280 Belvedere Ave Belvedere CA 94920-2425

GALE, MARADEL KRUMMEL, public policy and management educator, consultant; b. Bremerton, Wash., June 13, 1939; d. Bernhard Utz and Florence Claire (Choiniere) Krummel; m. Richard Philip Gale, June 10, 1961 (div. 1976). BA, Wash. State U., Pullman, 1961; MA, Mich. State U., East Lansing, 1967; JD, U. Oreg., 1974. Asst. prof. dept. urban and regional planning U. Oreg., Eugene, 1974-83, lectr. Sch. of Law, 1975-77, asst. prof. community svc. and pub. affairs, 1976-77, spl. asst. Office of the Pres., 1979-80, asst. dean Sch. Architecture, 1980-81, assoc. prof. dept. planning, pub. policy and mgmt., 1983—, dir. Micronesia and South Pacific program, 1988—; vis. asst. prof. Sch. Forestry, Oreg. State U., 1979-80; legis. lobbyist City of Eugene, 1975; mem. faculty U.S. Forest Svc. Land Mgmt. Planning Team, 1979-80; cons. Peace Corps./U.S. AID, Senegal, Kenya, Rwanda, 1986. Mem. adv. com. Bur. of Land Mgmt., Eugene, 1980—, The Micronesia Inst., 1992—; project dir. Peace Corps-Yap (Micronesia), 1988. Named Woman of Yr., Lane County Coun. Orgns., 1986; U.S. Info. Agy. grantee Coll. of Micronesia, 1989, U. of South Pacific, 1993, U.S. Dept. Edn. grantee, 1989, U.S. Dept. Interior grantee, 1990—. Mem. Assn. for Women in Devel., Am. Planning Assn. (sec., treas. planning and law divs. 1979-81). Office: U Oreg Dept Planning & Pub Policy Eugene OR 97403

GALES, SAMUEL JOEL, retired civilian military employee, counselor; b. Dublin, Miss., June 14, 1930; s. James McNary McNeil and Alice Francis (Smith) Broadus-Gales; m. Martha Ann Jackson (div. Jan. 1978); children: Samuel II (dec.), Martha Diane Townsend, Katherine Roselein, Karlmann Von, Carolyn B., Elizabeth Angelica McCain. BA, Chapman Univ., 1981, MS, 1987. Ordained Eucharist minister, Episcopal Ch., 1985; cert. tchr., Calif. Enlisted U.S. Army, 1948, advanced through grades to master 1st sgt., 1969, ret., 1976; tchr. Monterey (Calif.) Unified Sch. Dist., 1981-82; civilian U.S. Army Directorate of Logistics, Ft. Ord, Calif., 1982-93; collateral EEOC counselor Dept. Def., U.S. Army, 1987-93; peer counselor, 1982-84. Active Family Svc. Agy., Monterey, 1979-85; rep. Episc. Soc. for Ministry on Aging, Carmel, Calif., 1980-86, Task Force on Aging, Carmel, 1983-87, vestryman, 1982-85, 91-94; ombudsman Monterey County Long-Term Care Program, Calif. Dept. for the Aging, 1993—; vol. guide Monterey Bay Aquarium Found., 1994—, vol. docent Bay Net, Ctr. for Marine Conservation, Monterey Bay Nat. Marine Sanctuary, 1997—. Decorated Air medal. Mem. Am. Legion (post comdr. 1973-74), Forty and Eight (chef-de-gare 1979, 80), Monterey Chess Club, Comdr.'s Club Calif. (pres. Outpost 28 1981-82). Republican. Home: PO Box 919 1617 Lowell St Seaside CA 93955-3811

GALILEY, C. JEROME, secondary education educator; b. Bklyn., Aug. 22, 1948; s. Jerome Clemence and Marion (Szymborski) G.; m. Diane Lynn Nichols, June 10, 1970 (div. June 1975). BA Applied Arts/Scis. with distinction, San Diego State U., 1970, MA in Edn., 1974; student, U. Calif., San Diego, 1992. Cert. vocat. subjects supr. and coord., Calif. Regional occupl. instr. San Diego County Regional Occupl. Program, Poway, Calif., 1970-71; tchr. San Dieguito Union H.S. Dist., Encinitas, Calif., 1971—; cons. Poway Unified Sch. Dist., 1971, 77; mem. vocat. adv. com. Mira Costa C.C., Oceanside, Calif., 1992—. Critical reviewer: Automotive Technology Today, 1989. Mem. Calif. Automotive Tchrs. Assn., Calif. Indsl. and Tech. Edn. Assn., Automotive Svc. Coun. Home: 4707 Norma Dr San Diego CA 92115-3137 Office: San Dieguito Union High Sch Dist 710 Encinitas Blvd Encinitas CA 92024-3357 also: Torrey Pines HS 3710 Del Mar Hts Rd San Diego CA 92130

GALL, DONALD ALAN, data processing executive; b. Reddick, Ill., Sept. 13, 1934; s. Clarence Oliver and Evelyn Louise (McCumber) G.; m. Elizabeth Olmstead, June 25, 1960 (div. 1972); children: Christopher, Keith, Elizabeth; m. Kathleen Marie Insogna, Oct. 13, 1973; 1 child, Kelly Marie. BSME, U. Ill., 1956; SM, MIT, 1958, ME, 1960, ScD, 1964. Rsch. engr. GM, Detroit, 1956-57; staff engr. Dynatech Corp., Cambridge, Mass., 1959-60; mgr. ctr. systems Dynatech Corp., Cambridge, 1962-63; asst., assoc. prof. Carnegie-Mellon U., Pitts., 1964-69; rsch. assoc. prof. surgery and anesthesiology U. Pitts. Sch. Medicine, 1969-73; vis. fellow IBM Research Lab., Rueschlikon, Switzerland, 1970-71; pres. Omega Computer Systems, Inc., Phoenix, 1973—; CEO Omega Legal Systems, Inc., Phoenix, 1995—; bd. dirs. TTI Technologies, Inc., Omaha, 1996—; exec. dir., bd. dirs. M Tech. Assn. Contbr. articles to profl. jours.; inventor fuel injection system. Bd. dirs. Scottsdale Boys and Girls Club, 1982-93; mem. Scottsdale Head Honchos, 1978-87; mem. Verde Vaqueros, 1987—. Recipient Taylor medal Internat. Conf. on Prodn. Rsch., Disting. Alumnus award dept. mech. and indsl. engrng. U. Ill., 1997, bronze tablet. Mem. AAAS, ASME, Sigma Xi, Pi Tau Sigma, Tau Beta Pi, Phi Kappa Phi. Home: 9833 E Cortez St Scottsdale AZ 85260-6012 Office: Omega Computer Sys Inc 3875 N 44th St #200 Phoenix AZ 85018

GALL, SALLY MOORE, librettist, poet, scholar; b. N.Y.C., July 28, 1941; d. John Alexander and Betty (Clark) Moore; m. John Knox Marshall, 1961 (div. 1965); m. W. Einar Gall, Dec. 8, 1967. BA in English cum laude, Harvard U., 1963; postgrad., Columbia U., 1963-65; MA in English, NYU, 1971, PhD, 1976. vis. prof. English Drew U. Grad. Program, Madison, N.J., 1978; adj. asst. prof. English NYU, 1978-81. Opera libretti: Kill Bear Comes Home, 1996, The Singing Violin, 1995, The Little Thieves of Bethlehem, 1997, The Hill, 1997; dramatic cantata: Eleanor Roosevelt, 1996; musical theatre texts: Pinocchio, The Lysistrata Affair; author: (books) Ramon Guthrie's Maximum Security Ward: An American Classic, 1984, (with M.L. Rosenthal) The Modern Poetic Sequence: The Genius of Modern Poetry, 1983 (Explicator Lit. Found. award 1984), 2d edit. 1986; editor: Maximum Security Ward and Other Poems, 1984; versification editor: Poetry in English: An Anthology, 1987; translator Chopin's songs, Schubert's Miriam's Song of Triumph; contbr. articles to profl. jours., poetry to literary jours. Penfield fellow, 1973-74; recipient Key Pin and Scroll award, NYU, 1976. Mem. ASCAP, Dramatists Guild, Nat. Opera Assn., Internat. Alliance for Women in Music, Opera for Youth (bd. dirs.), Poets and Writers, Morning Music Club of Nyack (pres. 1989-91). Democrat. Home and Office: 5820 Folsom Dr La Jolla CA 92037-7323 also: 29 Bayard Ln Suffern NY 10901

GALLAGHER, MICHAEL L., lawyer; b. LeMars, Iowa, Apr. 14, 1944. BA, Ariz. State U., 1966, JD, 1970. Bar: Ariz. 1970. judge pro tem Maricopa County Superior Ct., 1979, Ariz. Ct. Appeals, 1985. Chmn. gov.'s adv. com. profl. football, 1981-87, mayor's adv. com. profl. sports, 1984-91; bd. dirs. Maricopa County Sports Authority, 1989; bd. visitors law sch. Ariz. State U., 1979; dir. Valley of the View YMCA, chmn., 1995, PHoenix Suns Charities; trustee Peter Kiewit Found. Mem. Am. Bd. Trial Advocates (pres. Phoenix chpt. 1988), Fedn. Ins. and Corp. Counsel, Internat. Assn. Defense Counsel, Ariz. Assn. Defense Counsel (pres. 1978), Ariz. C. of C. (dir.). Office: Gallagher & Kennedy PC 2600 N Central Ave Phoenix AZ 85004-3050

GALLAGHER, PATRICK FRANCIS, anthropologist; b. Wilkinsburg, Pa., Apr. 18, 1930; s. Hugh Vincent and Mary Caroline (Denne) G.; m. Mary Ann Bridge, 1954 (div. 1965); children: Patrick Francis III, John Vincent, Lisa Bridge; m. Mary Ann Hammerel, Sept. 16, 1971 (div. 1979); children: Molly Alison, Kingman Cruxent. BA summa cum laude, U. Pitts., 1957; PhD in Anthropology, Yale U., 1964; student, Washington Sch. Psychiatry, 1968. From asst. prof. to prof. George Washington U., Washington, 1961-69; prof., dean Coll. of the Potomac, Washington, 1971-72; assoc. prof. Cerro Coso C.C., Ridgecrest, Calif., 1973-75; prof. anthropology Universidad Nacional Francisco de Miranda, Venezuela, 1979-81; lectr. Chapman Coll. Ctrs., Palmdale, Calif., 1973—; lectr. Smithsonian Instn., Washington, 1966-68, 73, Davis & Elkins Coll., Elkins, W.Va., 1990-91. Author: La Pitia: An Archaeological Sequence in Northwestern Venezuela, 1976; asst. editor: Abstracts of New World Archaeology, 1961-62; illustrator: Sons of the Shaking Earth, 1959, The Entry of Man into the West Indies, 1960, Man Takes Control, 1961, Conservatism among the Iroquois at the Six Nations Reserve,

1961, Mexico, 1962; contbr. articles to profl. jours. NSF grantee, 1965, 67-68. Fellow AAAS, Royal Anthropol. Inst. of Gt. Britain and Ireland, Am. Anthrop. Assn.; mem. Asociacion Venezolana Para el Avance de la Ciencia, Archeol. Assn. Venezuela (corr.), Anthropol. Soc. Washington (coun. 1967-69), Soc. Am. Archaeology (treas.-elect 1968), Phi Beta Kappa, Sigma Xi. Home: PO Box 2693 32538 Bennett Ln Fort Bragg CA 95437-2693

GALLAGHER, TIM, editor, newspaper. Editor Ventura (Calif.) County Star. Office: Ventura County Star 5250 Ralston St Ventura CA 93003

GALLAHER, FREDERICK BLAKE, public health specialist; b. Socorro, N.Mex., Jan. 10, 1947; s. Frederick Eugene Gallaher and Letha Evelyn Morris; m. Josephine Romy Saavedra, Aug. 1, 1981; children: Justin Blake, Patrick James. BA in Theology, San Jose Christian Coll., 1974; MPA, U. N.Mex., 1988; MPH, Harvard U., 1995. LPN, emerg. room mgr. U. N.Mex. Hosp., Albuquerque, 1975-77, 78-79; health facility surveyor State of N.Mex. Health and Environ. Dept., Santa Fe, 1979-82; state tng. coord. emergency med. svcs. State of N.Mex. Health and Environ. Dept., 1988-90; adminstrv. intern City of Albuquerque/Office of the Mayor, 1985-86; dir. admissions, LPN Ladera and Montebello Nursing Homes, Albuquerque, 1987-88; adminstr. Ctr. for Disaster Medicine U. N.Mex. Sch. Medicine, Albuquerque, 1990-93; dir. tng. and quality improvement Brewster Ambulance Co., Boston, 1993-94; spl. forces med. specialist U.S. Army, 1975-94; project mgr. Human Survival Program Harvard U., Cambridge, Mass., 1994-95; pres. High Desert Cons., Santa Fe, 1995—; med. care program mgr. Health Dept., Santa Fe, 1996—; presenter in field. Contbr. articles to profl. publs.; author: A Medical Handbook for Disaster and Refugee Operations, U. N.Mex., 1993. Mem. Nat. Coun. State EMS Tng. Coords. (chmn. practical exam com. 1989-90), Nat. Disaster Med. Sys., Spl. Forces Assn., Harvard-Radcliffe Club, Pi Alpha Alpha. Office: Health Facility Licensing and Certification Ste 2 525 Camino de los Marquez Santa Fe NM 87501

GALLARDO-SALGUERO, HELEN CHRISTINE, social welfare specialist; b. Las Vegas, Nev., Jan. 29, 1966; d. Leonard Hafen and Helen Melvina (Dunton) Skinner Hafen; children: Ambrosia Lee Hafen-Hayes, Jasmine Rona Hafen; m. Luis Enrique Urbina-Cruz, Apr. 9, 1989 (annulment Apr. 1992); m. Pedro Arnoldo Gallardo-Salguero, Feb. 4, 1994. AA in Gen. Studies, C.C. So. Nev., Las Vegas, 1991. Clerical aide Clark County C.C., North Las Vegas, Nev., 1983-89; receptionist Re-Entry Ctr., Las Vegas, 1990; adminstrv. clk., accident claims coord. U.S. Census Bur., Las Vegas, 1990; vol. clerical aide State Nev. Welfare Dept., Las Vegas, 1991; employment security specialist State Nev. Employment Security Dept., Las Vegas, 1991-92; founder, resident agt., dir., pres. Nevadans Acting for Welfare Reform, North Las Vegas, 1990—; bd. dirs. Nev. Acting for Welfare Reform, North Las Vegas, 1990—. Author: Why the Welfare System Fails, 1989. Parent aide Econ. Opportunity Bd., Headstart, Las Vegas, 1989-90; scholarship attendee Govs. Conf. on Women, Ceasar's Palace, Las Vegas, 1990; vol. translator MASH-Homeless Shelter, St. Vincents, Las Vegas, 1994. Democrat. Roman Catholic. Home and Office: PO Box 30070 North Las Vegas NV 89036

GALLAWAY, MARTHINE S., artist; b. Oakland, Calif., June 15, 1913; d. Hector Lorillard and Alma Amelia (Steffensen) Solares; m. Howard Murray Gallaway, June 14, 1936; children: Heather, Bruce, Brian, Kent, Kirk. BA, U. Nev., 1934. Muralist on ceramic tiles. Developer high-fired ceramic glazes allowing refined detail in tile commns.; artist numerous tile commns. churches, restaurants, pvt. homes.; tile commns. published in numerous mags. Past pres. Arundel (Calif.) PTA, Carlmont High Sch. PTA, San Carlos, Calif.; libr. bldg. com. San Carlos, 1965, city hall bldg. com. 1960; vol. Woodside (Calif.) Store County Mus. Mem. Am. Soc. Interior Designers, Hist. Preservation Com. Designers, AAUW (charter mem., pres. 1955), Nat. Mus. of Women in the Arts (charter), Cap & Scroll, Zeta Tau Alpha. Home: 1400 Native Sons Rd Woodside CA 94062-4731

GALLAY, ALAN, history educator; b. N.Y.C., Nov. 26, 1957; s. Harold Herman and Leona (Gittenstein) G.; m. Carol Elizabeth Coleman, Aug. 1985; 1 child, Cyrana Coleman. BA in History, U. Fla., 1978; MA in History, Georgetown U., 1981, PhD in History, 1986. Vis. asst. prof. U. Notre Dame, South Bend, Ind., 1986-87, U. Miss., Oxford, 1987-88; prof. history Western Wash. U., Bellingham, 1988—; vis. prof. Harvard U., Cambridge, Mass., 1990-91; vis. lectr. U. Aukland, New Zealand, 1992. Author: The Formation of a Planter Elite, 1989; editor: Voices of the Old South, 1994, The Colonial Wars of North America, 1512-1763: An Encyclopedia, 1996. Andrew W. Mellon Faculty fellow in the humanities Harvard U., Cambridge, 1990-91, J. William Fulbright fellow U.S. Info. Agy., Washington, 1992, NEH fellow, 1997—. Mem. Am. Hist. Assn., Orgn. Am. Historians, So. Hist. Assn., Ga. Hist. Soc., Inst. Early Am. History and Culture. Office: Dept History Western Wash Univ Bellingham WA 98225

GALLEGLY, ELTON WILLIAM, congressman; b. Huntington Park, Calif., Mar. 7, 1944; married; four children. Attended, Calif. State U., L.A. Businessman, real estate broker Simi Valley, Calif., from 1968; mem. Simi Valley City Coun., 1979; mayor City of Simi Valley, 1980-86; mem. 100th-104th Congresses from the 21st (now 23d) Calif. dist., 1986—; chmn. internat. rels. subcom. on the western hemisphere, mem. judiciary com., mem. resources com.; mem. exec. com. U.S. Ho. Reps. Rep. Study Com.; mem. Congl. Human Rights Caucus, Congl. Fire Svcs. Caucus; formerly vice-chmn., chmn. Ventura County Assn. govts., Calif. Bd. dirs. Moorpark Coll. Found.

GALLEGOS, JOSÉ ESQUIPULA, adult education educator; b. Palma, N.Mex., June 21, 1932; s. Filiberto Bernardino and Felicita Juana (Montaño) G.; m. Rosemary Head, Sept. 2, 1961; children: Alicia, Christopher, Lucia, Monica, David. Student, St. Francis Sem., 1953-55, Duns Scotus Coll., 1956-59, U. Detroit, 1957-58; BA, Ea. N.Mex. U., 1962; postgrad., U. N.Mex., 1974-83. Tchr. Artesia (N.Mex.) Pub. Schs., 1962-91, instr. chpt. 1 math. program, 1991-93; instr., coord. N.Mex. State U., Carlsbad, 1963—. Pres. Am. GI Forum, Artesia, 1962-70; leader Boy Scouts Am., 1963-68, 4H, 1968-79; mem. bd. N.Mex. Adult Edn. Assn., 1965—; mem. Ret. Sr. Vol. Program, Artesia, 1993; eucharistic min. Our Lady of Grace Cath. Ch., Artesia. Recipient Outstanding Tchr. award N.Mex. Adult Edn. Assn., 1974. Democrat. Home: 8 Chalk Bluff Rd Artesia NM 88210

GALLENKAMP, CHARLES, writer; b. Dallas, Apr. 13, 1930; s. Charles O. and Norma (Benton) G.; m. Karen L. Wright, May 19, 1994. Student, U. Tex.; BA in Anthropology and Art History, U. N.Mex., 1954. Asst. dir. Mus. Anthropology, U. N.Mex., 1949-52; asst. curator anthropology Houston Mus. Natural Sci., 1954-57; dir. Maya Rsch. Fund, Interam Found., North Tex. State U., Denton, 1957-62; owner-dir. Janus Gallery, Santa Fe, 1970-78; exhbn. coord. Albuquerque Mus., 1980-87. Author: (juvenile) The Pueblo Indians in Story, Song, and Dance, 1955, 2nd edit., 1980, Finding Out About the Maya, 1963, (with Carolyn Meyer) The Mystery of The Ancient Maya, 1985 (one of Best Books of Yr. Sch. Libr. Jour.); author: Maya: The Riddle and Rediscovery of a Lost Civilization, 1959, 2nd edit., 1976, 3rd edit., 1985; editor: Maya: Treasures of An Ancient Civilization, 1985; contbr. articles to profl. jours. Grantee Interam Found., 1957, Helene Wurlitzer Found., 1962-63, Chapelbrook Found., 1965, Sch. Am. Rsch., 1978-79, Earhart Found., 1992, Ludwig Vogelstein Found., Edward Ewing Barrow Found. Mem. Soc. Am. Archaeology, Archaeol. Inst. Am., Sch. Am. Rsch. (rsch. assoc. 1976-79, 91-93), Explorers Club (emeritus). Home: PO Box 9275 Santa Fe NM 87504

GALLETTA, JOSEPH LEO, physician; b. Bessemer, Pa., Dec. 21, 1935; s. John and Grace (Galletta) G.; m. Teresita Suarez Soler, Feb. 19, 1961; children: John II, Angela, Eric, Christopher, Robert Francis, Michael Angelo. Student, U. Pitts., 1953-56; MD, U. Santo Tomas, Manila, 1962. Intern, St. Elizabeth Hosp., Youngstown, Ohio, 1963-64; family practice medicine, 29 Palms, Calif., 1967-77, Hemet, Calif., 1977—; chief of staff 29 Palms Cmty. Hosp., 1970-71, 73-76; vice chief of staff Hi-Desert Med. Center, Joshua Tree, Calif., 1976-77; chmn. dept. family practice Hemet Valley Hosp., 1981-83, med. dir. chem. dependency dept., 1985-88; med. dir. Loma Linda (Calif.) U. Behavioral Medicine Ctr. Recovery Svc., 1994-96; pres. Flexisplint, Inc.; founding mem. Hemet Hospice; former cons. Morongo Basin Mental Health Assn.; mem. adv. com. on substance abuse Riverside County, 1995—. Hon. mem. 29 Palms Sheriff's Search and Rescue, 1971-77. Bd. dirs. 29 Palms Cmty. Hosp. Dist., Morongo Unified Sch. Dist. Served with M.C. USN, 1964-67. Diplomate Am. Bd. Family Practice. Fellow Am. Geriatric Soc. (founder West Coast chpt.), Am. Acad. Family Practice; mem. Calif. Med. Assn., Riverside County Med. Assn., Am. Holistic Med. Assn. (charter), Am. Soc. Addiction Medicine, Calif. Soc. Addiction Medicine (mem. exec. coun. 1995—), Am. Acad. Family Practice, Calif. Acad. Family Practice. Roman Catholic. Established St. Anthonys Charity Clinic, Philippines, 1965; inventor Flexisplint armboards. Home: 27691 Pochea Trl Hemet CA 92544-8180 Office: Westside Medical Pla 37020 Florida Ave Hemet CA 92545-3520

GALLI, DARRELL JOSEPH, management consultant; b. Ft. Bragg, Calif., Nov. 10, 1948; s. Joseph Germain and Esther Edith (Happajoki) G.; B.A. in Transp./Internat. Bus., San Francisco State U., 1975; BS in Computer Info. Systems, 1985; MBA Golden Gate U., 1980; m. Rondus Miller, Apr. 23, 1977 (div. 1981); 1 dau., Troyan Hulda. With Pacific Gas & Electric Co., Santa Cruz, Calif., 1972-73; with Calif. Western R.R., Ft. Bragg, 1975-77, Sheldon Oil Co., Suisun, Calif, 1978-80; mgr. House of Rondus, Suisun, 1974-79; mgmt. cons., Suisun City, 1979—; instr. Solano Coll., 1979-81, Golden Gate U., 1981; mem. faculty U. Md. European div., Heidelberg, W.Ger., 1982-88; owner, mgr. Old Stewart House Bed and Breakfast, Fort Bragg, Calif., 1990—; lectr. Coll. Redwoods, Ft. Bragg, 1989—; coord. Small Bus. Mgmt. Seminar, 1980. Asst. coordinator Sr. Citizens Survey for Solano Coll. and Sr. Citizens Center, 1980; mem. Ft. Bragg City Coun., 1994—. Served with U.S. Army, 1969-71. Lic. Calif. real estate agt. Mem. Am. Assn. M.B.A. Execs., World Trade Assn., Bay Area Elec. R.R. Assn. Republican. Episcopalian. Club: Odd Fellows. Home: 511 Stewart St Fort Bragg CA 95437-3861 Office: 321 Morrow St Fort Bragg CA 95437-3861

GALLI, JOHN RONALD, academic administrator, physics educator; b. Salt Lake City, Oct. 10, 1936; s. John Lester and Ella Mae (Lewis) G.; m. Marica Lee Jackson Galli, Mar. 21, 1960 (div. July 1, 1977); children: Shawnee Sue Galli Petersen, Sherri Kay Galli; m. Cheryl Maur Corley Galli, June 2, 1978; children: Debora Maur Galli, Diana Lynn Galli, John David Galli. PhD in Physics, U. Utah, 1963. Physicist Naval Weapons Ctr., China Lake, Calif., summer 1958, 59, Aerojet Gen., Downy, Calif., 1963; prof. Physics Weber State U., Ogden, Utah, 1963—; dept. chair Physics, 1964-70, 83-95, dean Coll. of Sci., 1995—. Inventor: Mechanical Twisting Cat, 1993; contbr. various publs. and presentations, 1963-95. Mem. Golden Key, Am. Assn. Physics Tchrs. Mem. LDS Ch.

GALLIAN, RUSSELL JOSEPH, lawyer; b. San Mateo, Calif., Apr. 24, 1948; s. Phillip Hugh and Betty Jane (Boulton) G.; m. Marian Barbara Howard, Sept. 21, 1969; children: Lisa, Cherie, Joseph, Russell, Yvette, Jason, Ryan. BS, U. San Francisco, 1969, JD with highest honors, 1974. Bar: Calif. 1974, Utah 1975, U.S. Ct. Appeals (10th cir.) 1975, U.S. Supreme Ct. 1990; CPA, Calif. Staff acct. Arthur Andersen & Co., CPAs, San Francisco, 1969-71; treas., contr. N.Am. Reassurance Life Svc. Co., Palo Alto, Calif., 1972-74; assoc. VanCott Bagley Cornwell & McCarthy, Salt Lake City, 1975-77; sr. ptnr. Gallian & Westfall, St. George, Utah, 1977—; chmn. bd. dirs. Dixie Title Co., St. George. Chmn. Tooele (Utah) City Planning Commn., 1978; atty. City of Tooele, 1978-80, Town of Ivins, Utah, 1982—, Town of Springdale, Utah, 1987-90, Town of Rockville, Utah, 1987&, Town of Virgin, 1995—; commr. Washington County, 1993-96; chmn. Washington County Econ. Devel. Coun., 1993-96; bd. dirs. Dixie Ctr., 1993-96; mem. Habitat Conservation Plan Steering Com. Mem. ABA, Utah State Bar Assn., Tooele County Bar Assn. (pres. 1978-79), So. Utah Bar Assn. (pres. 1986-87). Republican. Mormon. Office: Gallian & Westfall 59 South 100 East Saint George UT 84770

GALLIHER, NANCY LYNN, elementary education educator; b. Longview, Wash., July 11, 1968; d. Michael Dean and Kathleen Elizabeth Williamson; m. David Allen Galliher, July 24, 1993. BA in Elem. Edn., Wash. State Univ., 1991; student, Heritage Coll., Toppenish, Wash., 1996-97. Cert. sch. counselor. Tchr. Kelso (Wash.) Sch. Dist., 1992, Richland (Wash.) Sch. Dist., 1992—. Grantee, For Those With Dreams, 1993, 94. Mem. ASCD. Methodist. Office: Richland Sch Dist 705 N 62nd Ave West Richland WA 99353-9705

GALLIK, DONNA MARIE, cardiologist; b. Woonsocket, R.I., Feb. 16, 1961; d. Joseph and Barbara Evangeline (Gianco) G. ScB, Brown Univ., 1983, MD, 1987. Diplomate in internal medicine and cardiovascular diseases Am. Bd. Internal Medicine. Cardiologist West L.A. VA Hosp., L.A., 1997—; chief electophysiology UCLA Sch. Medicine, asst. prof. medicine. Contbr. articles to profl. jours. Fellow Am. Coll. Cardiology; mem. AMA, Greater L.A. Electrophysiology Soc. Office: West L A VA Medical Ctr Divsn Cardiology 11301 Wilshire Blvd Los Angeles CA 90073-1003

GALLIMORE, LAURENE ELIZABETH, education educator; b. Indpls., May 16, 1952; d. Frank and Rose Lee (Smith) Simms; married; children: Jed, Rosa, Frank. BS, U. Nebr., 1986; MEd, Western Md. Coll., Westminster, 1987. Home sch./day sch. tchr. Dallas, Oreg., 1979-84; self-contained classrm. tchr. Helen Hyatt Elem. Sch. and Prescott Elem. Sch., Lincoln, Nebr., 1984-86; supervising tchr. elem. dept. Ind. Sch. for the Deaf, Indpls., 1991-95, ast. supt. edn., 1995; asst. prof. spl. edn. in deaf edn. Western Oreg. State Coll., Monmouth, 1995—; part-time instr. Western Oreg. State Coll., 1979, Ball State U., Muncie, Ind., 1990-94, Vincennes U., Indpls., 1990-94. Author: How to Utilize American Sign Language as the Language of Instruction in the Classroom, 1992; (with Gayle Joyce) The Visual Language Cookbook, 1979; contbr. articles to profl. jours.; presenter in field. Mem. TESOL-Teaching English to Deaf and 2d Lang. Students, Conf. Assn. of Instrs. of the Deaf, Assn. Coll. Educators for Deaf and Hard of Hearing, Coun. on Edn. of the Deaf, Nat. Assn. of the Deaf, Oreg. Assn. of the Deaf, others. Office: Western Oreg State Coll 345 Monmouth Ave Monmouth OR 97361

GALLISON, H(AROLD) BAILEY, SR., youth agency administrator, public relations and marketing consultant; b. Orange, N.J., Apr. 6, 1924; s. Harold Hobron and Stella Camilla (Holm) G.; m. Janet Caralee Frazier, Jun. 23, 1951 (div. Jun. 1983); children: Claudia Jean, Harold Bailey II; m. Sharilyn Leone Lemkuil Gallison, Jan. 27, 1984. BA, U. Mo., 1948. Sales mgr., adminstr. Carll Mercury Dealership, La Jolla, Calif., 1951-53; exec. dir. La Jolla Town Council, 1953-63; advt. mgr. Security Pacific Bank, San Diego, 1963-70; dir. pub. rels. Mercy Hosp., San Diego, 1970-83; sr. account exec. Citadel Comm., San Diego, 1983-85; exec. dir. Community Campership Coun., San Diego, 1985—; chmn. adv. bd. La Jolla Capital Fin. Corp., San Diego, 1991—. pres. La Jolla Civic Theatre Assn., 1973-76. With USN, 1943-46, MTO. Named Profl. of Yr., San Diego Pub. Rels. Club, 1973, Outstanding Alumni, U. Mo., 1987, Citizen of Yr., San Diego Boy Scout Coun., 1994. mem. SAR, U.S. Navy League, Ky. Col. So. Calif. (bd. dirs. 1991—), U. Mo. Alumni Assn. (past bd. dirs.), Hon. Dep. Sheriff Assn., Kiwanis Club (named Kiwanian of Yr. La Jolla chpt. 1991), Am. Legion. Republican. Presbyterian. Office: Community Campership Coun Ste 208 7510 Clairemont Mesa Blvd San Diego CA 92111-1539

GALLO, JON JOSEPH, lawyer; b. Santa Monica, Calif., Apr. 19, 1942; s. Philip S. and Josephine (Sarazan) G.; m. Jo Ann Broome, June 13, 1964 (div. 1984); children: Valerie Ann, Donald Philip; m. Eileen Florence, July 4, 1985; 1 child, Kevin Jon. BA, Occidental Coll., 1964; JD, UCLA, 1967. Bar: Calif. 1968, U.S. Ct. Appeals (9th cir.) 1968, U.S. Tax Ct. 1969. Assoc. Greenberg, Glusker, Fields, Claman & Machtinger, L.A., 1967-75, ptnr., 1975—; bd. dirs. USC Probate and Trust Conf., L.A., 1980—, UCLA Estate Planning Inst., chmn. 1992—. Contbr. articles to profl. jours. Fellow Am. Coll. Trust and Estate Counsel; mem. ABA (chair Generation Skipping Taxation com. 1992-95, co-chair life ins. com. 1995—), Internat. Acad. Estate and Trust Law, Assn. for Advanced Life Underwriting (assoc. mem.). Office: Greenberg Glusker Fields Claman & Machtinger LLP Ste 2100 1900 Avenue Of The Stars Los Angeles CA 90067-4501

GALLO, JOSEPH E., vintner; b. 1941. Various positions Gallo Sales Co., South San Francisco, 1962—, now pres. Office: Gallo Sales Co Inc 30825 Wiegman Rd Hayward CA 94544*

GALLUP, MARC RICHMOND, biology educator, paleontologist; b. Glendale, Calif., Sept. 25, 1949; s. Donald Ray and Gloria Muriel (Grimes) G.; m. Susan Holly Smith, Dec. 30, 1971 (div. 1994); m. Vicki Lyn Bradley, July 20, 1996. BA in Zoology, UCLA, 1971, PhD in Biology, 1982; MA in Zoology, U. Tex., 1974. Instr. biology Santa Monica (Calif.) Coll., 1980-84; instr. Calif. State U., Northridge, 1981-83, Los Angeles Mission Coll., San Fernando, Calif., 1981-84, South Pasadena (Calif.) High Sch., 1984-86; instr. dept. biology, target sci. UCLA, 1992—; cons. Jet Propulsion Lab., Pasadena, 1985—. Cons. L.A. librs., 1974-76, Los Angeles County Mus. Natural History, 1975-84; tchr. L.A. H.S., 1994—, Calif. Initiative Network Sci. Grantee Sigma Xi, 1977, Karl Schmidt Field Mus. Natural History, 1977, UCLA Patent, 1975, 77. Mem. NEA, AAAS, NSTA, Am. Soc. Zoologists, Planetary Soc. (sr. v.p.). Democrat. Home: 8816 S 10th Ave Inglewood CA 90305-2327 Office: LA HS Los Angeles CA 90019

GALLUS, CHARLES JOSEPH, journalist; b. Havre, Mont., Jan. 24, 1947; s. Raymond Charles and Anna Jo (Mack) G. BA in Polit. Sci. cum laude, Carroll Coll., 1969; MA in Polit. Sci., U. Mont., 1972. Bookkeeper's asst. Ellen Solem, CPA, Chinook, Mont., 1972; circulation asst. Havre Daily News, 1972-73, wire editor, reporter, photographer, 1973—. Mem. 2 study comms. Havre local govt., 1974-77, 84-86; mem. Hill County Dem. Ctrl. Com., Havre, 1974—. Mem. AP, Glacier Natural History Assn., Sagebrush Athletic Club, Soc. Profl. Journalists, KC, Sigma Delta Chi. Roman Catholic. Home: 112 3rd St # 746 Havre MT 59501-3532 Office: Havre Daily News 119 2nd St # 431 Havre MT 59501-3507

GALTON, ELIZABETH, psychiatrist, psychoanalyst; b. Evesham, Eng., June 16, 1941; came to U.S., 1962; d. Herbert and Herta (Adler) G.; m. John E. Dunkelberger, June 25, 1977; 1 child, Diana. BA, U. Kans., 1963, MD, 1967. Cert. psychiatrist. Asst. clin. prof. psychiatry U. Calif., L.A., 1974—; pvt. practice psychiatry/psychoanalysis Santa Monica, Calif., 1974—. Viola player Santa Monica Symphony Orch. Fellow Am. Psychiat. Assn.; mem. So. Calif. Psychiat. Soc. (pres. 1994-95). Office: 2901 Wilshire Blvd Ste 449 Santa Monica CA 90403-4907

GALTON, STEPHEN HAROLD, lawyer; b. Tulare, Calif., Dec. 23, 1937; s. Harold Parker and Marie Rose (Tuck) G.; m. Grace Marilyn Shaw, Aug. 15, 1964; children—Mark, Bradley, Jeremy, Elisabeth. B.S., U. So. Calif., 1966, J.D., 1969. Bar: Calif. 1970, U.S. Ct. Appeals (9th cir.) 1973, U.S. Dist. Ct. (no. dist.) Calif. 1973, U.S. Dist. Ct. (cen. dist.) Calif. 1970, U.S. Dist. Ct. (ea. and so. dists.) Calif. 1973. Assoc. Martin & Flandrick, San Marino, Calif., 1970-71, ptnr., 1971-72; assoc. Booth, Mitchel, Strange & Smith, Los Angeles, 1973-77, ptnr., 1978-85; ptnr. Galton & Helm, Los Angeles, 1986—. Mem. ABA (litigation, tort, insurance sects.), Calif. State Bar Assn. (del. 1974-81, chair fed. cts. com.), Wilshire Bar Assn. (pres. 1986-87), Los Angeles County Bar Assn. (bd. of trustees 1987—). Republican. Presbyterian. Contbr. articles to profl. jours. Office: Galton & Helm 500 S Grand Ave Ste 1200 Los Angeles CA 90071-2624

GALVAO, LOUIS ALBERTO, import and export corporation executive, consultant; b. Ponta Delgada, Sao Miguel, Portugal, July 5, 1949; came to U.S., 1969; s. Jeremias B. and Margarida M. G.; m. Antonieta A. Galvao, Oct. 26, 1966 (div. 1984); children: Marlene, Vanessa. Degree in Bus. Mgmt., Indsl. & Commerce Sch., Azores, Portugal, 1968; Dr. Universal Life (hon.), Universal Life Ch., 1991. Asst. mgr. sales J.B. Galvao Imports, Azores, 1964-68; asst. supr. Union Carbide Corp., Peabody, Mass., 1969-70, Container Corp. Am., Wakefield, Mass., 1970-73; sales dir. McCulloch Oil Corp., Lake Havash City, Ariz., 1972-74; pres. Sunset Investments Corp., Phoenix, 1974—; v.p. United Universal Enterprises Corp., Phoenix, 1985—; pres. Universal Imports, Inc., Phoenix, 1977—; dir. Global Savings & Loan Ltd., London, 1990—. mem. Nat. Rep. Congl. Com., Washington, 1982— (cert. recognition 1981, 84, 85, Campaign Kickoff award 1984, cert. merit 1992), Rep. Presdl. Task Force, Washington, 1984— (Am. flag dedicated in his honor at Rotunda of U.S. Capital bldg. 1986, life mem., mem. presdl. electiom registry 1992), Rep. Nat. Com. (cert. recognition 1990, 92), European Movement, U.K., 1990—, Social Dem. Party, Portugal, 1990—, Washington Legal Found.; charter mem. U.S. Def. Com.; del. The Presl. Trust, Washington, 1992. Recipient award U.S. Def. Com., 1984; inducted to Rep. Nat. Hall Honor Rep. Nat. Candidate Trust, 1992. Mem. Am. Mgmt. Assn., Nat. Assn. Export Cos., Profl. Fin. Assts., Heritage Bus. Club, Senatorial Club, Universal Life Ch. Roman Catholic.

GALVIN, ELIAS, bishop. Bishop Desert S.W. Diocese, Phoenix, Ariz. Office: Seattle Area/Pac NW Conf 2112 3rd Ave Ste 301 Seattle WA 98121*

GAMACHE, ADRIEN EDMOND, economist, valuation consultant; b. Manchester, N.H., Sept. 21, 1941; s. Wilfred Dolar Gamache and Madeleine Rose Gamache Burrill; children: Christina, Monique, Jennifer. Student, U. N.H., 1959-61; BS, Purdue U., 1963; PhD, U. Wash., 1969. Sr. analyst Arthur Andersen & Co., Seattle, 1969; analyst MacMillan Bloedel Ltd., Vancouver, B.C., Can., 1970-72; economist, analyst Black & Co., Inc., Portland, Oreg., 1973; economist H. C. Mason & Assocs., Inc., Portland, 1974-76; pres. Gamache & Assocs., Inc., Portland and Seattle, 1977-85, Pvt. Valuations, Inc., Seattle, Wash., 1990—; assoc. prof. Coll. Forest Resources U. Wash., Seattle, 1981-86; dir. devel. svcs., appraiser Shorett & Reily, Seattle, 1986; v.p., dir. fin. svcs., dir. real estate valuation Consilium, Inc., Bellevue, 1987-90; instr. Appraisal Inst., U. Wash., Wash. Inst., ITT Rayonier, La.-Pacific Corp.; mem. faculty N.W. Securities Inst., Wash. State Bar Assn., Oreg. State Bar Assn. Editor: Selling the Federal Forests, 1983. NSF fellow, 1963. Mem. Am. Soc. Appraisers (affiliate), Appraisal Inst. (affiliate). Republican. Unitarian. Home: 17301 NE 45th St #92 Redmond WA 98052 Office: Pvt Valuations Inc 1000 2nd Ave Ste 3450 Seattle WA 98104-1046

GAMAL, IRWIN BERT, management consultant; b. Bklyn., Aug. 1, 1943; s. Murray and Rose (Yelinski) G.; m. Karen Ann Sawko, Aug. 24, 1974. AA, Cerritos Coll., Norwalk, Calif., 1965; BA, Calif. State U., Long beach, 1967, MA, 1972. Cert. Calif. cmty. coll. instr. Dir. tng. Vornado, Inc., Whittier, Calif., 1975-77; dir. mgmt. devel. Galardi Group, Newport Beach, Calif., 1977-81; dir. HRD divsn. Arrindell Assocs., Newport Beach, 1981; internal HRD cons. Fluor Corp., Irvine, Calif., 1981-84; dir. tng. Coldwell Banker Residential, Newport Beach, 1984-88; pres. Insight Sys. Group, Laguna Beach, Calif., 1988—; project advisor, class chmn. Pepperdine U., Malibu, Calif., 1990-92; feedback specialist Ctr. for Creative Leadership, La Jolla, Calif., 1993—; seminar leader, keynote spkr. Nat. Seminars Group, Shawnee Mission, Kans., 1993-94. Contbr. articles to profl. jours. Mem. Indsl. League of Orange County. Recipient Cert. of Appreciation ACCET, 1993, Participation award Calif. Assn. Pre-paid Dental Plans, 1991, Outstanding Svc. award Coastline C.C., Fountain Valley, Calif., 1983. Mem. ASTD (dir. profl. devel. 1993—, Service award 1993), World Affairs Coun., Orange County Orgnl. Devel. Network (bd. editors 1993), Calif. State U.-Long Beach Alumni Assn. Republican. Jewish. Office: Insight Systems Group 20875 Klamath Ct Laguna Niguel CA 92677

GAMBARO, ERNEST UMBERTO, lawyer, consultant; b. Niagara Falls, N.Y., July 6, 1938; s. Ralph and Teresa (Nigro) G.; m. Winifred Sonya Gambaro, June 3, 1961 (div.); m. Monica Cuellar, Sept. 30, 1994. B.A. in Aero. Engring. with honors, Purdue U., 1960, M.S. with honors, 1961; Fulbright scholar, Rome U., 1961-62; J.D. with honors, Loyola U., L.A., 1975. Bar: Calif. 1975, U.S. Tax Ct. 1976, U.S. Supreme Ct. 1979, U.S. Ct. Apppeals (9th cir.). With Aerospace Corp., El Segundo, Calif., 1962-80, counsel, 1975-80; asst. gen. counsel, asst. sec. Computer Scis. Corp., El Segundo, 1980-99v.p., gen. counsel, sec. INFONET Svcs. Corp., El Segundo, 1988—; cons. bus. fin.and mgmt., 1968—. Recipient U.S. Air Force Commendation for contbns. to U.S. manned space program, 1969; Purdue U. Pres.'s scholar, 1959-60. Mem. ABA (internat., taxation sects.), Los Angeles Bar Assn. (exec. com. 1976—, founder chmn. sect. law and tech. 1976-78, chmn. bar reorgn. com. 1981-82), Am. Arbitration Assn. Los Angeles Ctr. Internat. Comml. Arbitration (founder, bd. dirs.), Internat. Law Inst. (faculty), St. Thomas More Law Soc., Phi Alpha Delta, Omicron Delta Kappa (past pres.), Tau Beta Pi, Sigma Gamma Tau (past pres.), Phi Eta Sigma. Republican. Newspaper columnist Europe Alfresco; contbr. articles to profl. publs. Home: 6542 Ocean Crest Dr Palos Verdes Peninsula CA 90275-5400 Office: 2100 E Grand Ave El Segundo CA 90245-5024

GAMBINO, JEROME JAMES, nuclear medicine educator; b. N.Y.C., Sept. 13, 1925; m. Jacquelyn Ann Mazzola, Mar. 27, 1948; children: Charles, John, Mary Ellen, Jacquelyn. BA, U. Conn., 1950, MS, 1952; PhD, U.

Calif., 1957. Asst. prof. natural scis. SUNY, New Paltz, 1957-59; research radiobiologist UCLA, 1959-61; mem. research staff Northrop Corp., Hawthorne, Calif., 1961-69; dir. edn. nuclear medicine dept. VA Med. Ctr., Los Angeles, 1969-96; rsch. cons. VA Med. Ctr., L.A., 1996—; lectr. anatomy U. So. Calif., L.A., 1963-89, radiol. scis. UCLA, 1978—. Mem. Radiation Research Soc., Soc. Nuclear Medicine (pres. So. Calif. chpt. 1981-82). Office: West LA VA Med Ctr Nuclear Medicine 115 11301 Wilshire Blvd Los Angeles CA 90073-1003

GAMBLE, BARBARA JEAN, dietitian and consultant; b. Garden City, Kans., June 6, 1950; d. Joe P. and Anna M. (Burgardt) Dreiling; m. Don L. Gamble, Dec. 14, 1973; 1 child, Angelene J. BS in Dietetics and Instnl. Mgmt., Kans. State U., 1972. Dietitian and dir. dietary svcs. Prowers Med. Ctr., Lamar, Colo., 1974—; cons. dietitian S.E. Colo. Hosp. and Long Term Care, Springfield, 1977—, Sand Haven Nursing Home, Lamar, 1972—, Holly Nursing Care Ctr., 1975—. Mem. Am. Dietetic Assn. (registered), Colo. Dietetic Assn., Colo. Cons. Dietitians, Cons. Dietitians with Health Care Facilities. Republican. Home: 402 Willow Valley Dr Lamar CO 81052-3917 Office: Prowers Med Ctr 401 Kendall Dr Lamar CO 81052-3942

GAMBOA, GEORGE CHARLES, oral surgeon, educator; b. King City, Calif., Dec. 17, 1923; s. George Angel and Martha Ann (Baker) G.; m. Winona Mae Collins, July 16, 1946; children: Cheryl Jan Gamboa Granger, Jon Charles, Judith Merlene Gamboa Hiscox. Pre-dental cert., Pacific Union Coll., 1943; DDS, U. Pacific, 1946; MS, U. Minn., 1953; AB, U. So. Calif., 1958, EdD, 1976. Diplomate Am. Bd. Oral and Maxillofacial Surgery. Fellow oral surgery Mayo Found., 1950-53; clin. prof. grad. program oral and maxillofacial surgery U. So. Calif., L.A., 1954—; assoc. prof. Loma Linda (Calif.) U., 1958-94, chmn. dept. oral surgery, 1960-63; pvt. practice oral and maxillofacial surgery, San Gabriel, Calif., 1955-93; dir. So. Calif. Acad. of Oral Pathology, 1995—; clinical supr. dental hygiene program Pasadena City Coll., 1997—. Mem., past chmn. first aid com. West San Gabriel chpt. ARC. Fellow Am. Coll. Dentists, Am. Coll. Oral and Maxillofacial Surgeons (founding fellow), Pierre Fauchard Acad., Am. Inst. Oral Biology, Internat. Coll. Dentists, So. Calif. Acad. Oral Pathology; mem. Am. Assn. Oral and Maxillofacial Surgeons, Internat. Assn. Oral Surgeons, So. Calif. Soc. Oral and Maxillofacial Surgeons, Western Soc. Oral and Maxillofacial Surgeons, Am. Acad. Oral and Maxillofacial Radiology, Marsh Robinson Acad. Oral Surgeons, Profl. Staff Assn. Los Angeles County-U. So. Calif. Med. Ctr. (exec. com. 1976—), Am. Cancer Soc. (Calif. div., profl. edn. subcom. 1977-90, pres. San Gabriel-Pomona Valley unit 1989-90), Am. Dental Assn. (scientific session chmn. section on anesthesiology, 1970), Calif. Dental Soc. Anesthesiology (pres. 1989-94), Calif. Dental Found. (pres. 1991-93), Calif. Dental Assn. (jud. coun. 1990-96), San Gabriel Valley Dental Soc. (past pres.), Xi Psi Phi, Omicron Kappa Upsilon, Delta Epsilon. Seventh-day Adventist. Home: 1102 Loganrita Ave Arcadia CA 91006-4535

GAMBRELL, THOMAS ROSS, investor, retired physician, surgeon; b. Lockhart, Tex., Mar. 17, 1934; s. Sidney Spivey and Nora Katherine (Rheinlander) G.; m. Louise Evans, Feb. 23, 1960. Grad. in pre-medicine summa cum laude, U. Tex., 1953, MD, 1957. Intern Kings County Hosp., Bklyn.; company physician Hughes Aircraft, Fullerton, Calif., 1958-65, Chrysler Corp., Anaheim, Calif., 1962-65, L.A. Angels Baseball Team, Fullerton, 1962-64; pvt. practice medicine Fullerton, 1958-91; with St. Jude Hosp., Anaheim Meml. Hosp., Fullerton Cmty. Hosp., Martin Luther Hosp.; mem. utilization rev. com. St. Mary's Convalescent Hosp., Fullerton Convalescent Hosp., Sunhaven and Fairway Convalescent Hosp.; owner Ranching (Citrus) & Comml. Devel., Ariz., Tex., N.Y., 1962-94. Contbr. articles to profl. jours. Organizer of care for needy elderly, North Orange County, 1962-65; sponsor numerous charity events. Fellow Am. Acad. Family Physicians; mem. AMA, Am. Geriats. Soc., Calif. Med. Assn., Tex. Med. Assn., Tex. Alumni Assn., Orange County Med. Assn., Mayflower Soc., Plantagenet Soc., Sons of Confederacy, SAR, Order Am. Royal Descendants (col.), Order Crown (col.), Baronial Order Magna Carta, Phi Eta Sigma, Delta Kappa Epsilon, Plōu Chi. Office: PO Box 6067 Beverly Hills CA 90212-1067

GAMLIN, JOHN PASCHALL, lawyer; b. Paris, Tenn., Nov. 27, 1964; s. Charles Thomas and Annie Laurie (Paschall) G. BA, Vanderbilt U., 1987; JD, Ohio State U., 1990. Bar: Tenn. 1990, Colo. 1991, U.S. Dist. Ct. Colo., U.S. Ct. Appeals (fed. cir.), U.S. Ct. Appeals (10th cir.). With John P. DiFalco and Assocs., P.C., Ft. Collins, Colo., 1990—. Home: 4500 Seneca St #36 Fort Collins CO 80526 Office: John P DiFalco and Assoc PC 1136 E Stuart St Ste 4102 Fort Collins CO 80525-1173

GAMM, GORDON JULIUS, lawyer; b. Shreveport, La., July 14, 1939; s. Sylvian Willer Gamm and Leona (Gordon) Windes. BA, Drake U., 1963; JD, Tulane U., 1970. Bar: La. 1970, Mo. 1971, Colo. 1993. Atty. pvt. practice, Kansas City, 1977-93, Boulder, Colo., 1993—. Founder Bragg's Symposium, 1980—. Mem. Colo. Bar Assn., Boulder Bar Assn., Boulder Valley Rotary. Office: 4450 Arapahoe Ave Ste 106 Boulder CO 80303-9102

GAMMELL, GLORIA RUFFNER, professional association administrator; b. St. Louis, June 19, 1948; d. Robert Nelson and Antonia Ruffner; m. Doyle M. Gammell, Dec. 11, 1973. AA in Art, Harbor Coll., Harbor City, Calif., 1969; BA in Sociology, Calif. State U., Long Beach, 1971. Cert. fin. planner. Bus. analyst Dun & Bradstreet, Los Angeles, 1971-81; sales rep. Dun & Bradstreet, Orange, Calif., 1971-93; rep. sales Van Nuys, Calif., 1981-90; pres. sec. Gammell Industries, Paramount, Calif., 1993-95, also bd. dirs.; regional dir. Am. Mgmt. Assn., 1995—. Mem. Anne Banning Assistance League, Hollywood, Calif., 1981-82; counselor YWCA, San Pedro, Calif., 1983-84; fundraiser YMCA, San Pedro, 1984-85; mem. womens adv. com. Calif. State Assembly, 1984-89. Recipient Best in the West Presdl. Citation, 1981-86, 89, 90. Home: 991 W Channel St San Pedro CA 90731-1415

GANDHI, OM PARKASH, electrical engineer; b. Multan, Pakistan, Sept. 23, 1934; came to U.S., 1967, naturalized, 1975; s. Gopal Das and Devi Bai (Patney) G.; m. Santosh Nayar, Oct. 28, 1963; children: Rajesh Timmy, Monica, Lena. BS with honors, Delhi U., India, 1952; MSE, U. Mich., 1957, Sc.D., 1961. Rsch. specialist Philco Corp., Blue Bell, Pa., 1960-62; asst. dir. Cen. Electronics Engring. Rsch. Inst., Pilani, Rajasthan, India, 1962-65, dep. dir., 1965-67; prof. elec. engring., rsch. prof. bioengring. U. Utah, Salt Lake City, 1967—; chmn. elec. engring., 1992—; cons. U.S. Army Med. R & D Command, Washington, 1973-77; cons. to microwave and telecom. industry and govtl. health and safety orgns.; mem. Commns. B and K, Internation Union Radio Sci.; mem. study sect. on diagnostic radiology NIH, 1978-81. Author: Microwave Engineering and Applications, 1981; editor: Engineering in Medicine and Biology mag., 1987, Electromagnetic Biointeraction, 1989, Biological Effects and Medical Applications of Electromagnetic Energy, 1990; contbr. over 200 articles to profl. jours. Recipient Disting. Rsch. award U. Utah, 1979-80; grantee NSF, NIH, EPA, USAF, U.S. Army, USN, N.Y. State Dept. Health, others. Fellow IEEE (editor spl. issue Procs. IEEE 1980, co-chmn. com. on RF safety standards 1988—, Tech. Achievement award Utah sect. 1975, Utah Engr. of Yr. 1995), Am. Inst. for Med. and Biol. Engring.; mem. Electromagnetics Acad., Bioelectromagnetics Soc. (bd. dirs. 1979-82, 87-90, v.p., pres. 1991-94, d'Arsonval award 1995). Office: Univ Utah Dept Elec Engring 3280 Merrill Engring Salt Lake City UT 84112

GANDSEY, LOUIS JOHN, petroleum and environmental consultant; b. Greybull, Wyo., May 19, 1921; s. John Wellington and Leonora (McLaughlin) G.; m. Mary Louise Alviso, Nov. 10, 1945; children: Mary M., Catherine K., John P., Michael J., Laurie A. AA, Compton Jr. Coll., 1941; BS, U. Calif. Berkeley, 1943; M in Engring., UCLA, 1958. Registered profl. engr., Calif. With Richfield Oil Corp., L.A., 1943-65, process engr., processing foreman, sr. foreman, mfg. coord., 1943-61, project leader process computer control, 1961-63, light oil oper. supt., 1963-64, asst. refinery supt., 1964-65; mgr. planning Richfield div. Atlantic Richfield Co., L.A., 1966-68, mgr. evaluation products div., L.A., 1968-69, mgr. supply and transp., Chgo., 1969-71, mgr. planning and mgmt. sci., N.Y.C., 1971, mgr. supply and transp., L.A., 1971-72, mgr. coordination and supply, 1972-75, mgr. domestic crude, 1975-77; v.p. refining Lunday-Thagard Oil Co., South Gate, Calif., 1977-82; petroleum cons. World Oil Corp., L.A., 1982-85; gen. petroleum cons., 1986—; instr. chem. and petroleum tech. L.A. Harbor Coll., 1960-65; cons. on oil crops, Austria, 1991; U.S. del. in environ. affairs to Joint Inter-Govtl. Com. for Environ. Protection, USSR, 1991, asphalt tech. to Joint Inter-Govtl. Com. for Highway Design CWS, 1992; U.S. del. Econ. and Environ. Affairs, Portugal, Spain, 1994, Hist. & Econ. Affairs, Mexico, 1995, Basque Country, Spain, 1996. Contbr. articles to profl. jours. Served with C.E., AUS, 1944-45. Mem. AICE, Am. Chem. Soc., Calif. Soc. Profl. Engrs., Environ. Assessment Assn. Home: 2340 Neal Spring Rd Templeton CA 93465-8413

GANDY, H. CONWAY, lawyer, state official; b. Washington, Nov. 3, 1934; s. Hoke and Anne B. (Conway) G.; m. Carol Anderson, Aug. 29, 1965; children: Jennifer, Constance, Margaret. BA, Colo. State U., 1962; JD, U. Denver, 1968. Bar: Colo. 1969, U.S. dist. ct. Colo. 1969. Pvt. practice, Ft. Collins, Colo., 1969-81; adminstrv. law judge div. Adminstrv. Hearings, State of Colo., Denver, 1981—. Dem. candidate for Colo. Senate, 1974, dist. atty., 1976. With USN, 1954-58. Mem. Colo. Bar Assn., Larimer County Bar Assn., Nat. Assn. Adminstrv. Law Judges (pres. Colo. chpt. 1985-86), Sertoma (Centurion award 1973, Tribune award 1975, Senator award 1977, 79, sec. Honor Club 1977-78, pres. Ft. Collins club 1978-79, pres. Front Range club 1988-89). Methodist. Home: 724 Winchester Dr Fort Collins CO 80526-2636 Office: PO Box 8287 Fort Collins CO 80526-8003

GANNETT, DAMON L., lawyer; b. Amarillo, Tex., Apr. 29, 1947; s. Willard L. Gannett and Patricia L. (Restine) Taber; m. Carol A. Leggate, Aug. 30, 1969; children: Amy, Tyler, Jessica, Lindsey, Tobin, Tucker. BBA, U. Mont., 1969, JD, 1972. Bar: Mont. 1972. Assoc. Sandall, Cavan & Edwards, Billings, Mont., 1976, Jones, Olsen & Christensen, Billings, 1976-78; ptnr. Olsen Christensen & Gannett, Billings, 1978-82, Olsen, Christensen, Gannett & Waller, Billings, 1983-84, Olsen, Christensen & Gannett, Billings, 1985-90, Gannett & Ventrell, Billings, 1990-93; pvt. practice Gannett Law Firm, Billings, 1993—; Atty. Child Protection Team, 1978—. Capt. USAF, 1972-76. Recipient Commrs. award Fed. Dept. HHS, 1985. Mem. ABA, State Bar Mont. (chmn. bd. 1987-89, pres. 1990-91), Nat. Assn. Counsel Children (v.p. 1989—). Home: 3222 Durland Dr Billings MT 59102-0443 Office: Gannett Law Firm PO Box 1375st Billings MT 59103

GANS, DENNIS JOSEPH, information technology specialist; b. Yokohama, Japan, Sept. 7, 1949; came to U.S., 1951; s. Harry Leo and Hope Lorene (Everett) G.; m. Carolyn Johnson O'Grady, 1986; 1 child, Erik Christopher. BS in Bldg Constrn. (Engring./Mgmt.), Tex. A&M U., 1971. Project mgr. D.C.B., Inc., 1972-73, 78-79, 86-87; quality control engr. Martin Zachry, Kwajalein, Marshall Islands, 1975-76; co-owner B.G.S.Y. Enterprises, Denver, 1975; project mgr. State of Colo., 1977-78, 79-80; co-owner Denver Skatewear, 1978-80; mgr. scheduling Morrison Knudsen, Zaire, 1980-82; constrn. engr. Bechtel Internat., Jubail, Saudi Arabia, 1982; project mgr. Village at Breckenridge (Colo.) Resort, 1984-86; sr. buyer Hewlett Packard Co, Roseville, Calif., 1988-91, bus. analyst, 1991-95; info. tech. specialist, 1995—. Deacon, Presbyn. Ch. U.S.A. Mem. Tex. A&M U. Assn. Former Students, Sierra Club. Republican. Home: 4611 Nassau Ct Rocklin CA 95765-5210

GANTT, BARRY, secondary school educator; b. Germany, Dec. 18, 1945; s. Chil Meyer and Sarah Gottesman; divorced. BA, Long Island U., 1967; MA, San Francisco State Coll., 1970. Cert. secondary and jr. coll. tchr., Calif. Dir. conf. svcs. Calif. Coll. Arts and Crafts, Oakland, 1984-85; events producer, founding bd. mem. Cartoon Art Mus., San Francisco, 1985-88, adminstr., 1988-89; edn. dir. Artists in Print, San Francisco, 1986-88; English instr. West Valley Coll., Saratoga, Calif., 1990; art cons. Owl Gallery, San Francisco, 1991; English instr. Oakland (Calif.) Pub. Schs., 1992—; instr. ind. studies Hayward Unified Sch. Dist.; judge art contests, San Francisco Bay Guardian, 1980, 81, 82, 84, 85; producer Loonies Humor Salon, 1978—. Editor GRAPHITI (Artists in Print), 1981-83, CENTERLINE (Ctr. for Design), 1981-82; contbr. articles to nat. and local mags. Mem. adv. bd. Ctrl. YMCA, San Francisco, 1978-80; dep. registrar Ctrl Dem. Coun., San Francisco, 1972-80; v.p. Soc. of Separationists, San Francisco, 1980-85. Recipient fellowship PTA, San Francisco State Coll., 1970. Mem. Am. Fedn. Tchrs., Calif. Tchrs. Assn., Golden Gate Tip Toppers. Office: PO Box 20443 Oakland CA 94620-0443

GANTZ, NANCY ROLLINS, nursing administrator, consultant; b. Buffalo Center, Iowa, Mar. 7, 1949; d. Troy Gaylord and Mary (Emerson) Rollins. Diploma in Nursing, Good Samaritan Hosp. and Med. Ctr., Portland, Oreg., 1973; BSBA, City Univ., 1986; MBA, Kennedy-Western U., 1987, PhD, 1991. Nurse ICU, Good Samaritan Hosp., 1973-75; charge nurse Crestview Convalescent Hosp., Portland, 1975; dir. nursing svcs. Roderick Enterprises, Inc., Portland, 1976-78, Holgate Ctr., Portland, 1978-80; nursing cons. in field of adminstrn., 1980-84; coord. CCU; mgr. ICU/CCU Tuality Community Hosp., Hillsboro, Oreg., 1984-86; head nurse intensive care unit, cardiac surgery unit, coronary care unit, Good Samaritan Hosp. & Med. Ctr., Portland, 1986-88, mgr. critical care units, 1988-92, asst. v.p. patient care svcs., 1992-93, dir. heart ctr. Deaconess Med. Ctr., Spokane, Wash., 1992-93; exec. asst. King Faisal Specialist Hosp. and Rsch. Ctr., Riyadh, Saudia Arabia, 1994—; mem. speakers bur. Nurses of Am.; mem. task force Oreg. State Health Div. Rules and Regulations Revision for Long Term Health Facilities and Hosps., 1978-79; numerous internat. and nat. speaking presentations. Contbr. chpts. to books and articles to profl. jours. Mem. Am. Nurses Assn. (cert.), Nat. League Nursing, Am. Assn. Critical Care Nurses (pres. elect greater Portland chpt. 1985-86, pres. 1986-87, bd. dirs. 1985—), Am. Heart Assn., Oreg. Heart Assn., Geriatric Nurses Assn. Oreg. (founder, charter pres.), Clackamus Assn. Retarded Citizens, AACN (chpt. cons. region 18 1987-89, mgmt. SIC region 18, 1990-92), AONE Coun. Nurse Mgrs. (bd. dirs. Region 9 1991-92, Sigma Theta Tau. Seventhday Adventist. Home: 15821 NE 19th St Vancouver WA 98684-4517

GARBARINO, JOSEPH WILLIAM, labor arbitrator, economics and business educator; b. Medina, N.Y., Dec. 7, 1919; s. Joseph Francis and Savina M. (Volpone) G.; m. Mary Jane Godward, Sept. 18, 1948; children: Ann, Joan, Susan, Ellen. B.A., Duquesne U., 1942; M.A., Harvard U., 1947, Ph.D., 1949. Faculty U. Calif., Berkeley, 1949—; prof. U. Calif., 1960-88, dir. Inst. Bus. and Econ. Research, 1962-88, prof. emeritus, 1988—; vis. lectr. Cornell U., 19S9-60, UCLA, 1949, SUNY, Buffalo, 1972; Fulbright lectr. U. Glasgow, Scotland, 1969; vis. scholar U. Warwick; mem. staff Brookings Instn., 1959-60; vis. lectr. U. Minn., 1978; labor arbitrator. Author: Health Plans and Collective Bargaining, 1960, Wage Policy and Long Term Contracts, 1962, Faculty Bargaining: Change and Conflict, 1975, Faculty Bargaining in Unions in Transition. Served with U.S. Army, 1942-45, 51-53. Decorated Bronze Star. Democrat. Roman Catholic. Home: 7708 Ricardo Ct El Cerrito CA 94530-3344

GARCIA, ANDREW B., chemical engineer; b. Las Cruces, N.Mex., Apr. 22, 1949; s. Rudolf A. and Margaret (Rivera) G.; m. Katherine D. Montano, July 5, 1974 (dec. Aug. 1996); children: Lauren, Alexandra. BS in Chem. Engring. with honors, N.Mex. State U., Las Cruces, 1972; MBA, St. Mary's Coll., Moraga, Calif., 1979; postgrad., U. Calif., Berkeley, 1994. Registered environ. assessor; cert. asbestos contractor/supr.; cert. bldg. insp. and mgmt. planner; cert. hazardous materials mgr. Design engr. Gen. Electric Co., San Jose, Calif., 1972-75; chem. engr. Chevron Chem. Co., Richmond, Calif., 1975-78; supr. Chevron Corp., San Francisco, 1978-80; supply product mgr. Chevron USA Inc., Walnut Creek, Calif., 1980-89; project mgr. Chevron Land & Devel. Co., San Francisco, 1989-93; environ. project mgr. Alameda County, Oakland, Calif., 1993-95; environ. support mgr. Computer Scis. Corp., Edwards AFB, Calif., 1995—. Park and recreation commr. City of Martinez, Calif., 1984-89; mem. citizens adv. bd. City of Martinez, 1989-91. Mem. AIChE, Nat. Soc. Profl. Engrs., Project Mgmt. Inst. Roman Catholic. Home: 3331 Saint Marys Rd Lafayette CA 94549-5147 Office: Computer Scis Corp PO Box 446 Edwards CA 93523

GARCIA, ARLEEN ELENA, archaeologist, researcher; b. Miami, Oct. 2, 1972; d. Alfredo and Marlene Lydia (Leyva) G.; m. Guillermo Gonzalez. Student, Fla. Internat. U., 1990-93; BA in Archeaology cum laude, U. Ariz., 1996. Mem. crew Tierra Right-of-Way Svcs., 1994, analyst, 1995; rsch. asst. Desert Archaeology, Ariz., 1996-97; lab., field asst. Ariz. State Mus., 1993-94, student employee Ariz. Site File, 1994-95, curatorial asst. Ctrl. Ariz. Project Repository, 1994, 95—; vol. field asst. Homol'ovi Rsch. Program Ariz. State Mus., Winslow, 1995-96; ground stone analyst Homol'ovi Rsch. Program Lab. Ariz. State Mus., 1996-97. Scholar nat. Hispanic Scholarship Fund, 1994, Byron Cummings Scholarship, 1995, Latino/Latina Leadership Opportunity Program, 1996; recipient Prix de l'Alliance Française, 1996.

GARCIA, CASTELAR MEDARDO, lawyer; b. Conejos, Colo., June 3, 1942; s. Castelar M. Sr. and Anna (Vigil) G.; m. Mary Elizabeth Miller, Apr. 1, 1967; 1 child, Victoria Elisabeth. BA, Adams State Coll., 1965; JD, U. Colo., 1976. Bar: Colo. 1977, U.S. Dist. Ct. Colo. 1977, U.S. Ct. Appeals (10th cir.) 1983, U.S. Ct. Appeals (4th cir.) 1988, U.S. Supreme Ct. 1984. Human resources counselor State of Oreg., Klamath Falls, 1966-68; regional dir. Colo. Civil Rights Com., Alamosa, 1970-73; dep. dist. atty. Denver, 1977-80, chief dep. dist. atty., 1980-84; pvt. practice Manassa, Colo., 1984—; owner Cumbres Ranch; town atty., Romeo, Colo., 1984—; commr. Colo. Dept. Hwys., 1991, Colo. Dept. Transp., 1991—; vice chmn. Colo. Transp. Commn., 1996—. Mem. Colo. delegation to Cam Real Trade Corridor Consortium between U.S., Can. and Mex. With U.S. Army, 1968-70, Vietnam. Decorated Purple Heart. Mem. Colo. Bar Assn., Hispanic Bar Assn., San Luis Valley Bar Assn. Republican. Roman Catholic. Home: PO Box 90 Alamosa CO 81101-2197 Office: 714 S St Manassa CO 81141

GARCIA, DAVID, agricultural products executive; b. 1953. Graduate, U. Wyo., 1975. With We. Nuclear Mining, Lander, Wyo., 1976-78, Diamond Fruit Growers, Inc., Hood River, Oreg., 1978—; now treas. Office: Diamond Fruit Growers Inc PO Box 180 Hood River OR 97031-9436*

GARCIA, DENNIS R., state agency administrator; b. El Rito, N.Mex., Nov. 12, 1954; s. Dennis and Eliza (Lucero) G.; m. Nickie Vigil, Nov. 26, 1986; children: Dennis Joseph, Anna Alyssa, Carlos Lorenzo. BS, N.Mex. State U., 1977. Cert. real estate appraiser, N.Mex. Extention agt. N.Mex. State U., Dulce, 1977-78, Las Vegas, 1978-79; land use specialist N.Mex. State Land Office, Santa Fe, 1979-87, pub. lands resources dir. field divsn., 1987-96, pub. lands resources dir. surface divsn., 1996—. Roman Catholic. Home: 2202 Ardor Santa Fe NM 87504 Office: State Land Office Surface Divsn PO Box 1148 Santa Fe NM 87504-1148

GARCIA, EDWARD J., federal judge; b. 1928. AA, Sacramento City Coll., 1951; LLB, U. Pacific, 1958. Dep. dist. atty. Sacramento County, 1959-64, supervising dep. dist. atty., 1964-69, chief dep. dist. atty., 1969-72; judge Sacramento Mcpl. Ct., 1972-84, U.S. Dist. Ct. (ea. dist.) Calif., Sacramento, 1984—. Served with U.S. Army Air Corps, 1946-49. Office: US Dist Ct US Courthouse 650 Capitol Mall Rm 2546 Sacramento CA 95814-4707*

GARCIA, GORDON STANLEY, physician; b. Washington, July 26, 1959; s. Raymond Garcia and Lois Jane Cobb; m. Renee Jovita Fuentes, June 25, 1983; children: Margaux, Claire. BA, U. Calif., Berkeley, 1981; MD, U. Calif., San Diego, 1987. Diplomate Am. Bd. Pediats., Am. Bd. Internal Medicine, Am. Bd. Allergy and Immunology. Rsch. asst. Cetus Corp., Emeryville, Calif., 1981-83; resident in internal medicine and pediatrics U. Calif., Irvine, 1987-91; fellow in allergy/immunology Kaiser Found. Hosp., L.A., 1991-93; staff physician Permanente Med. Group, Sacramento, 1993—; asst. clin. prof. pediats. U. Calif. Med. Sch., Davis, 1994—. Fellow Am. Acad. Pediats.; mem. Am. Coll. Allergy, Asthma, and Immunology, Am. Thoracic Soc., Am. Acad. Allergy and Immunology, Calif. Med. Assn., Sacramento-El Dorado County Med. Soc. Office: Permanente Med Group 6600 Bruceville Rd Sacramento CA 95823

GARCIA, JERRY, mayor. Mayor South Gate, Calif. Address: 8650 California Ave South Gate CA 90280

GARCIA, JUAN RAMON, historian, educator; b. Sebastian, Tex., July 27, 1947; s. Juan and Maria de la Luz (Perez-Hernandez) G.; m. Rosalind Sigworth, Oct. 18, 1992; children: Mariel Shannon, Michelle Nocole, Alison Marissa. BA, DePaul U., 1971, MA, 1979; MA, U. Notre Dame, 1974, PhD, 1977. From asst. to assoc. prof. U. Mich., Flint, 1975-81; assoc. prof. U. Ariz., Tucson, 1981—, assoc. dean instrn. Coll. Social and Behavioral Scis., 1994—; dir. Mex. Am. studies U. Mich., Flint, 1975-81, chmn. affirmative action com. 1979-81, chmn. student affairs and concerns com. 1978-81; dir. U. Ariz. Teaching Ctr., 1990-94; cons. Nat. Inst. Edn. Women and Minorities divsn., Washington, 1978-81, NEA Program Devel. divsn., Washington, 1979-82; hist. cons., host TV Sta. KUAT, 1989; hist. cons. Los Mineros, 1991; adv. bd. Tucson Pub. Libr. Writers the Purple Sage; liaison Am. with Disabilities Act., 1993—; presenter in field. Author: Operation Wetback, 1980, Mexicans in the Midwest, 1900-32, 1996; editor: Perspectives in Mexican American Studies, 1988-89, 92—; contbr. articles to profl. jours. Chmn. State Bilingual Commn., Mich., 1976-80; Rockefeller Found. rev. panel S.W. Hispanic Rsch. Inst., 1989; libr., archives and pub. records com. mem. State of Ariz., 1988—. Ford Found. fellow, 1972-75; Rsch. grantee U. Ariz., 1986, NSF grantee, 1972; named Disting. prof. U. Mich., 1981. Mem. Nat. Assn. for Chicano Studies (Rocky Mountain rep., exec. coord. com., conf. site com. mem., chmn. editorial com. 1983-88), Western Social Sci. Assn. (coord. Chicano studies sect. 1983). Office: Univ Ariz Dept History 215 Social Science Tucson AZ 85721

GARCIA, STEPHANIE BROWN, aerospace company pricing manager; b. San Jose, Calif., July 18, 1959; d. Thomas Francis III and Martha Caroline (Bramer) B.; m. Markcos Mario Garcia, Apr. 5, 1986; children: Ryan Markcos, Jason Thomas, Corey Lawrence. BBA, James Madison U., 1981; MBA, U. San Diego, 1986. Adminstrv. assoc. Gen. Dynamics Corp., San Diego, 1981-82, estimator, 1982-84, sr. estimator, 1984-85; prin. fin. rep. Sundstrand Corp., San Diego, 1985-87, pricing mgr., 1987-93, 96—, contract compliance and estimating mgr., 1993-96. Fund raiser United Way, San Diego, 1990—; active Tecolote Youth Baseball Assn., San Diego, 1991—. Mem. Nat. Contract Mgmt. Assn. (dir. youth and civic activities 1983-85), U. San Diego Grad. Bus. Alumni Assn., Phi Beta Kappa, Beta Gamma Sigma. Republican. Roman Catholic. Home: 2853 Denver St San Diego CA 92117 Office: Sundstrand Power Sys PO Box 85757 4400 Ruffin Rd San Diego CA 92186-5757

GARCIA-BORRAS, THOMAS, oil company executive; b. Barcelona, Spain, Feb. 2, 1926; came to U.S., 1955, naturalized, 1961; s. Thomas and Teresa (Borras-Jarque) Garcia-Julian; MS, Nat. U. Mex., 1950; postgrad. Rice U., 1955-56; m. Alia Castellanos Lima, Apr. 30, 1952; children: Erik, Angelica, Laureen, Cliff. Chief chemist Petroleos Mexicanos, Veracruz, Mex., 1950-55; rsch. engr. Monsanto, Texas City, Tex., 1956-60; pilot plant mgr. Cabot and Foster Grant Co., 1960-69; engring. mgr. Signal Chem. Co., Houston, 1969-71; mgmt. and engring. cons., Covina, Calif., 1971-73; project mgr. Occidental Petroleum Co., Irvine, Calif., 1973-79; fleet and indsl. mgr. internat. ops. Wynn Oil Co., Fullerton, Calif., 1979-87; dir. export Sta-Lube, Inc., Rancho Dominguez, Calif., 1987-91; prin. U.S. Products Corp., Las Vegas, Nev.; internat. bus. and energy cons. Covina, Calif. Mem. Internat. Mktg. Assn., Am. Inst. Chem. Engrs., Am. Chem. Soc. Author: Manual for Improving Boiler and Furnace Performance, 1983; contbr. articles to profl. jours. Home: 1430 E Adams Park Dr Covina CA 91724-2925 Office: 516 S 4th St Las Vegas NV 89101-6513

GARCIA-RAZANSKAS, ADA ANN, educator; b. L.A., May 27, 1956; d. Adam J. Garcia and Maria Anita (Reyes) Lucero; children: Sara Rae Sheehan, Anne Marie Sheehan. AS, Rio Hondo Coll., 1977; student, UCLA, 1980, Calif. State Poly. U., Pomona, 1988. RN; cert. tchr. nursing edn. and health. Staff nurse Anaheim (Calif.) Meml. Hosp., charge nurse; educator Coastline ROP, Costa Mesa, Calif.; program dir., health careers educator Montebello (Calif.) Unifed Sch. Dist., Health Careers Acad./Pathways; owner A&M Health Careers Edn. Network; cons. Calif. State Poly. U. Pomona; lectr. various high schs.; advisor Health Occupations Students Am.; instr. credentialing programs for tchrs. in health careers. Author: Multi-Cultural Resource Guide, 1989. Mem. Calif. Assn. Health Career Educators, Calif. Assn. Nurses Substance Abuse, Calif. Assn. Regional Occupational Ctrs. Home: 2124 W Mills Dr Orange CA 92868-3430

GARDINER, JOHN JACOB, leadership studies educator; b. Tel Aviv, Feb. 6, 1946; came to U.S., 1952; s. Leon and Zipora (Shalev) Zucker; m. Joanna Meredith Winslow, Dec. 24, 1967; children: James, Katharine. BA, U. Fla., 1967, PhD, 1973; postgrad., U. Oreg., 1978, Stanford U., 1983. Tchr., dept. chair Keystone Heights (Fla.) Sch., 1968-72; instr., asst. to v.p. acad. affairs U. Fla., Gainesville, 1973-75; asst. prof. edn. The Citadel, Charleston, S.C., 1975-77; prof., dept. chair Okla. State U., Stillwater, 1979-91, Seattle U., 1991—; assoc. in edn. Harvard U., 1985; vis. asst. prof. Fla. State U., Tallahassee, 1977-78, U. Oreg., Eugene, 1978-79; chair bd. Pacific N.W. Postdoctoral Inst., Seattle, 1995—. Co-author: UNESCO Guide, 1991, Insights on Leadership, 1996. Permanent fund chair dist. 5030 Rotary, Seattle, 1996-99. Recipient Svc. to State award Gov. and Ho. of Reps., 1991; fellow W. K. Kellogg Found., 1972-73. Mem. Am. Coun. Edn. (bd. dirs. Nat. Leadership Group 1985-96), Assn. Study of Higher Edn. (bd. dirs. 1983-85), Am. Ednl. Rsch. Assn. (bd. dirs. divsn. J 1983-85), Vashon Island Club (bd. dirs. 1995—). Episcopalian. Office: Seattle U 510 Loyola Hall Broadway and Madison Seattle WA 98122

GARDINER, LESTER RAYMOND, JR., lawyer; b. Salt Lake City, Aug. 20, 1931; s. Lester Raymond and Sarah Lucille (Kener) G.; m. Janet Ruth Thatcher, Apr. 11, 1955; children: Allison Gardiner Bigelow, John Alfred, Annette Gardiner Weed, Leslie Gardiner Crandall, Robert Thatcher, Lisa Gardiner West, James Raymond, Elizabeth, David William, Sarah Janet. BS with honors, U. Utah, 1954; JD, U. Mich., 1959. Bar: Utah 1959, U.S. Dist. Ct. Utah 1959, U.S. Ct. Apls. (10th cir.) 1960. Law clk., U.S. Dist. Ct., 1959; assoc. then ptnr. Van Cott, Bagley, Cornwall & McCarthy, Salt Lake City, 1960-67; ptnr. Gardiner & Johnson, Salt Lake City, 1967-72; ptnr. Christensen, Gardiner, Jensen & Evans, 1972-78; ptnr. Fox, Edwards, Gardiner & Brown, Salt Lake City, 1978-87, ptnr. Chapman & Cutler, 1987-89, ptnr. Gardiner & Hintze, 1990-92; CEO and pres. Snowbird Ski and Summer Resort, Snowbird Corp., 1993—; reporter, mem. Utah Sup. Ct. Com. on Adoption of Uniform Rules of Evidence, 1970-73, mem. com. on revision of criminal code, 1975-78; master of the bench Am. Inn of Ct. I, 1980-90; mem. com. bar examiners Utah State Bar, 1973; instr. bus. law U. Utah, 1965-66; adj. prof. law Brigham Young U., 1984-85. Mem. Republican State Central Com. Utah, 1967-72, mem. exec. com. Utah Rep. Party, 1975-78, chmn. state convs., 1980, 81; mem. Salt Lake City Bd. Edn., 1971-72; bd. dirs. Salt Lake City Pub. Library, 1974-75; trustee Utah Sports Found., 1987-91; bd. dirs. Salt Lake City Visitors and Conv. Bur., 1988-91, 93—. Served to 1st lt. USAF, 1954-56. Mem. Utah State Bar Assn., Sons of Utah Pioneers, Utah Ski Assn. (bd. dirs. 1994—), Nat. Ski Areas Assn. (mem. pub. lands com. 1994—, gov. affairs com. 1994—), Rotary. Mormon. Office: Snowbird Corp Snowbird UT 84092

GARDINER, T(HOMAS) MICHAEL, artist; b. Seattle, Feb. 5, 1946; s. Thomas Scott Gardiner and Carolyn Virginia (Harmer) Bolin; m. Kelly Michelle Floyd, Mar. 7, 1981 (div. Dec. 1983); m. Diana Phyllis Shurtlieff Rainwater, Sept. 26, 1986; children: Rita Em, Nigel Gus. BA in Philosophy, Sulpician Sem. N.W., Kenmore, Wash., 1969; student, Cornish Inst. Arts, 1971-73. Seaman Tidewater Barge, Camas, Wash., 1969; pari-mutuel clk. Longacres Racetrack, Renton, Wash., 1969-92; dock worker Sealand, Inc., Seattle, 1970; tchr. Coyote Jr. H.S., Seattle, 1989-95, Sch. Visual Concepts, Seattle, 1990-95; tchr., vis. artist Ctrl. Wash. U., Ellensburg, 1991. Represented in permanent collections Seattle Water Dept., Nordstrom, Seattle City Light, Sultan (Wash.) Sch. Dist., King County Portable Works Collection, SAFECO Ins. Co., Seattle, City of Portland Collection, 1988, Highline Sch. Dist., Seattle; commns. include ARTp Metro Art Project, Seattle, interior painting Villa del Lupo restaurant, Vancouver, B.C., Can.; illustrations included in The New Yorker Mag., Am. Illustration 13, The Seattle Times. Recipient Best Design award Print Mag., 1985; Nat. Endowment for Arts Fellowship grantee, 1989. Democrat. Roman Catholic. Home and Office: 3023 NW 63d St Seattle WA 98107

GARDNER, ARTHUR SPEEDIE, engineering executive; b. Port Chester, N.Y., Dec. 16, 1939; s. Angus John and Mercedes Adele (Speedie) G.; m. Estelle Kulakowski, June 8, 1963 (div. Sept. 1, 1980); children: Keith Speedie, Slade Havelock, Kess Elizabeth; m. Cathy Ann Pfost, Aug. 1, 1981; children: Colby Cameron Hughes, Brennan Allen Hughes. BSChemE, Bucknell U., Lewisburg, Pa., 1963; BAChemE, Bucknell U., 1963; LLB, LaSalle Ext. U., Chgo., 1968. Cert. profl. engr., Colo. Engring. supr., safety dir., environ. staff engr. Mobil Oil Corp., Paulsboro, N.J., 1963-74; dir. govt. and environ. affairs Buckeye Pipeline Co., Allentown, Pa., 1974-77; sr. technologist ChemDesign (subsidiary ChemShare), Houston, 1977-78; chem. engring. supr. Occidental Shale Co., Grand Junction, Colo., 1978-82; v.p. engring., gen. mgr. Wesfrac Inc., Charterhall Refining & Mktg., Wescourt Group, Grand Junction, 1982-91; tech. editor Today's Refinery Percy Pub. Co., Chappaqua, N.Y., 1989—; engring. exec., one of three founders NGL Ptnrs., NGL Inc., Farstad Gas & Oil L.L.C., Minot, N.D., 1991—; chief engr. George Bros. Fabrication, Inc., Midland, Tex., 1995—; mem. tech. sect. (measurement & product handling) Gas Processors Assn., Tulsa, 1986-91, 96—. Contbr. 84 tech. articles to Today's Refinery. Mem., chpt. pres., state v.p., nat. dir. Jaycees, 1964-74 (Outstanding awards 1968, 69, 70); mem. Indian Guides, 1975-77, Indian Princesses, 1977-78, coach and referee Grand Mesa Soccer Assn., 1979-90; mem. Bus-Edn. Partnership, Grand Junction, 1992—; tutor Sch. Dist. 51 high schs., Mesa St. Coll., 1992—. Recipient Individual award Colo. Assn. Ptnrs. in Edn., 1993. Mem. AIChE, NSPE (Ute chpt. treas. 1996). Home: 935 Bader Dr Grand Junction CO 81501-2931 Office: Farstad Gas & Oil LLC PO Box 9093 Grand Junction CO 81501

GARDNER, BARBARA ROGERS, humanities educator; b. St. Louis, June 12, 1935; d. William Houston and Jean (Cadman) Jack; m. David Rogers, Sep. 4, 1952 (div. Apr. 1977); children: Jean, Steven, John; m. Mark Gardner, June 13, 1983. BA, Syracuse U., 1955; MA, U. Iowa, 1986; PhD, Rutgers U., 1971. Prof. Ramapo Coll., Mahwah, N.J., 1972-84; prof. mythol. studies, psychology and lit. Pacifica Grad. Inst., Carpinteria, Calif., 1989-97. Author: The Doomsday Scroll, 1980, Jung and Shakespeare, 1992, (play) Isadora, 1988; exhibited in group show Rannells Art Gallery, 1966. Mem. Sculpture Guild, Santa Barbara Screenwriters Assn. (prize 1996). Democrat. Episcopalian.

GARDNER, BOOTH, governor; b. Tacoma, Aug. 21, 1936; m. Jean Gardner; children—Doug, Gail. B.A. in Bus., U. Wash., 1958; M.B.A., Harvard U., 1963. Asst. to dean Sch. Bus. Adminstrn., Harvard U., Cambridge, Mass., 1966; dir. Sch. Bus. and Econs., U. Puget Sound, Tacoma, 1967-72; pres. Laird Norton County, 1972-80; mem. Wash. Senate, 1970-73; county exec. Pierce County, Tacoma, 1981-84; gov. State of Wash., 1985-89, 89—. Co-founder Central Area Youth Assn. Seattle; trustee U. Puget Sound. recipient Harold W. McGraw, Jr. prize in edn., McGraw-Hill, 1993. Office: 801 2nd Ave Ste 1300 Seattle WA 98104*

GARDNER, CATHY ANNE, defender; b. L.A., Apr. 3, 1951; d. Ulas Howard Gardner and Catherine (Williams) Robinson. AA, L.A. C.C., 1972; BA, Calif. State U., 1973; JD, Peoples Coll. Law, L.A., 1982. Atty. Tulare County Pub. Defender, Visalia, Calif., 1984-86; atty. L.A. County Pub. Defender's Office, L.A., 1986—. Mem. Nat. Lawyers Guild, Calif. Attys. for Criminal Justice, Calif. Pub. Defenders Assn.

GARDNER, CLYDE EDWARD, health care executive, consultant, educator; b. Steubenville, Ohio, Oct. 8, 1931; s. Peter D. and Louella Mary (Gillespie) G.; m. Patricia Jackson, Oct. 4, 1953 (div. Dec. 1977); 1 child, Bruce Stephen. BA, San Francisco State U., 1969, MS, 1971. Adminstr. Gardner Convalescent Hosp., Napa, Calif., 1955-68; exec. dir. Haight Ashbury Free Med. Clinic, San Francisco, 1970-71; lectr. San Francisco State U., 1969-71; dir. planning and rsch. div. N. Country Com. on Area Wide Health Planning, Canton, N.Y., 1971-77; prof. Gov.'s State U., University Park, Ill., 1977-83; sr. ptnr. Health Care Cons., Park Forest, Ill., 1983-86; exec. dir. Mahoning Shenango Area Health Edn. Network, Youngstown, Ohio, 1986-90; pres., chief exec. officer Mahoney Edn. and Tng. Network, Youngstown, Ohio, 1990-92; pres., CEO Health Sci. Assocs., Tucson, 1992—; bd. dirs. rec. sect. Mahoning Shenango Area Health Edn. Network, Youngstown, 1986-90; adj. prof. SUNY, Canton, 1975-76, Youngstown State U., 1987—; bus. rep. Apollo Coll., 1994-95; rschr. FMR Rsch., 1996. Author: Data Book for Health and Institutional Planning, 1981; author of numerous pub. health planning, health edn. studies and funded pvt., state and fed. health care grants, 1971-90. Pres. Found. I Ctr. for Human Devel., Harvey, Ill., 1978-83, U. Profls. of Ill., Chgo., 1982-83; bd. dirs. Blue Cross/Blue Shield Drug and Alcohol Benefit Study, Chgo., 1980-83. Recipient Recognition award Ill. Dangerous Drugs Commn., 1980, 81, Outstanding Svc. award U. Profls. Ill., 1983-84, Outstanding Svc. award Ill. Fedn. Tchrs., 1983. Mem. Disabled Artist Assn. (bd. dirs., chair resource devel. com.). Democrat.

GARDNER, DAVID CHAMBERS, education educator, psychologist, business executive, author; b. Charlotte, N.C., Mar. 22, 1934; s. James Raymond and Jessica Mary (Chambers) Bumgardner m. Grace Joely Beatty, 1984; children: Joshua Avery, Jessica Sarah. BA, Northeastern U., 1960; MEd, Boston U., 1970, EdD, 1974; PhD, Columbia Pacific U., 1984. Diplomate Am. Bd. Med. Psychotherapists. Mgr. market devel. N.J. Zinc Co., N.Y.C., 1961-66, COMINCO, Ltd., Montreal, Que., Can., 1966-68; dir. Alumni Ann. Giving Program, Northeastern U., Boston, 1968-69; dir. career and spl. edn. Stoneham (Mass.) Pub. Schs., Boston, 1970-72; assoc. prof. div. instructional devel. and adminstrn. Boston U., 1974—; sr. ptnr. Gardner Beatty Group, 1990—; chmn. bd. CyberHelp, Inc., 1995—; coord. program career vocat. tng. for handicapped, 1974-82, chmn. dept. career and bus. edn., 1974-79, also dir. fed. grants, 1975-77, 77-79; co-founder Am. Tng. and Rsch. Assocs., Inc., chmn. bd., 1979-83, pres., chief exec. officer, 1984—; dir. La Costa Inst. Lifestyle Mgmt., 1986-87. Author: Careers and Disabilities: A Career Approach, 1978; co-author: (with Grace Joely Beatty) Dissertation Proposal Guidebook: How to Prepare a Research Proposal and Get It Accepted, 1980, Career and Vocational Education for the Mildly Learning Handicapped and Disadvantaged, 1984, Stop Stress and Aging Now, 1985, Never Be Tired Again, 1990; co-author: The Visual Learning Guide Series, 1992, 93, 94, 95, 96, 97, Internet for Windows: America Online Edition, 1995, Cruising America Online for Windows, 1995, Windows 95: The Visual Learning Guide, 1995, Quicken 5 for Windows, 1995, The Visual Learning Guide, 1995, Excel for Windows 95: The Visual Learning Guide, 1995, Word for Windows 95, The Visual Learning Guide, 1995, Windows NT 4.0 Visual Desk Reference, 1997, Discover Netscape Communicator, 1997, Discover Internet Explorer, 1997; editor Career Edn. Quar., 1975-81; contbr. articles to profl. jours. With AUS, 1954-56. U.S. Office Edn. fellow Boston U., 1970, U.S. Office Edn.-Univ. Boston rsch. fellow, 1974. Fellow Am. Assn. Mental Deficiency (Ann. Profl. Tchr. and Rsch. award Region X 1979); mem. Nat. Assn. Career Edn. (bd. dirs., past pres.), Coun. for Exceptional Children, Ea. Ednl. Rsch. Assn. (founding dir.), Am. Vocat. Assn., Phi Delta Kappa, Delta Pi Epsilon. Home and Office: 7618 Nueva Castilla Way Carlsbad CA 92009-8137

GARDNER, HOMER JAY, electrical engineer; b. El Paso, Tex., Apr. 4, 1942; s. George R. and Faye E. (Folkers) G.; m. Roxy Diane Tolley, Jan. 29, 1966; children: Roger, Shannon, Stefanie. BSEE, Brigham Young U., 1968; MS, Colo. State U., 1973. Devel. engr. IBM Corp., Boulder, Colo., 1968-90; sr. engr. Exabyte Corp., Boulder, 1990—. Patentee in field. Mem. Colo. State Electronics Adv. Com., Denver, 1980-83, chmn., 1982. Mem. IEEE. Republican. Mormon. Home: 8138 Captains Ln Longmont CO 80501-7727 Office: Exabyte 1745 38th St Boulder CO 80301-2603

GARDNER, NORD ARLING, management consultant administrator; b. Afton, Wyo., Aug. 10, 1923; s. Arling A. and Ruth (Lee) G.; BA, U. Wyo., 1945; MS, Calif. State U., Hayward, 1972, MPA, 1975; postgrad. U. Chgo., U. Mich., U. Calif.-Berkeley; m. Thora Marie Stephen, Mar. 24, 1945; children: Randall Nord, Scott Stephen, Craig Robert, Laurie Lee. With U.S. Army, 1941 Commd. 2d lt., 1945, advanced through grades to lt. col., 1964; ret., 1966; personnel analyst Univ. Hosp., U. Calif.-San Diego, 1966-68; coordinator manpower devel. U. Calif.-Berkeley, 1968-75; univ. tng. officer San Francisco State U., 1975-80, personnel mgr., 1976-80; exec. dir. CRDC Maintenance Tng. Corp., non-profit community effort, San Francisco, 1980-85; pres., dir. Sandor Assocs. Mgmt. Cons., Pleasant Hill, Calif., 1974-86, 91—; gen. mgr. Vericlean Janitorial Service, Inc.; in-charge bus. devel. East Bay Local Devel. Corp., Oakland, Calif., 1980-85; incorporator and pres. Indochinese Community Enterprises, USA, Ltd., Pleasant Hill, Calif., 1985-87; freelance writer, grantsmanship cons., 1987—; ptnr. Oi Kit Bldg. Maint. Svc., 1988-91; dir. univ. rels. Internat. Pacific U., San Ramon, Calif., 1990—, exec. dir., bd. dirs. Internat. Pacific Inst., 1994— ; cons. Phimmasone Internat. Import-Export, Richmond, Calif., Lao Lanx-Xang Assn., Oakland Refugee Assn., 1988-90; instr. Japanese, psychology, supervisory courses, 1977-78; bd. dirs. New Ideas New Imports, Inc. Author: To Gather Stones, 1978. Adv. council San Francisco Community Coll. Dist. Decorated Army Commendation medal. Mem. Ret. Officers Assn., Am. Soc. Tng. and Devel., No. Calif. Human Resources Council. Am. Assn. Univ. Adminstrs., Internat. Personnel Mgrs. Assn., Coll. and Univ. Personnel Assn., Commonwealth Club of Calif., U. Calif.-Berkeley Faculty Club, San Francisco State U. Faculty Club, Army Counter Intelligence Corp Vets., Inc. Republican. Home: 2995 Bonnie Ln Pleasant Hill CA 94523-4547 Office: Internat Pacific Inst 1 Annabel Ln Ste 214 San Ramon CA 94583-1342

GARDNER, PAUL ALLEN, biology educator; b. Philipsburg, Pa., Nov. 28, 1950; s. Roscoe Bert and Vera Rose (Biddle) G.; m. Ann Hales, Apr. 23, 1975; children: Charity, Katie. BS in Biology, Pa. State U., 1974; MS in Zoology, BYU, 1977; PhD in Zoology, No. Ariz. U., 1987. Rsch. asst. U. Utah, Salt Lake City, 1977-79; surg. technician Flagstaff (Ariz.) Med. Ctr., 1979-89; assoc. prof. biology Snow Coll., Ephraim, Utah, 1989—; mem. steering com., chmn. best mgmt. practices com. Utah Ptnrs. in Flight, Salt Lake City, 1993—. Contbr. articles and photographs to ednl. publs. incl. Ranger Rick and Am. Biology Tchr. Varsity coach, scoutmaster Boy Scouts Am., Flagstaff and Ephraim, 1985-91. With U.S. Army, 1968-71. Mem. Human Anatomy and Physiology Soc., Am. Ornithologists Union. Home: 120 E 100 S # 60 2 Ephraim UT 84627-1449 Office: Snow Coll Dept Biology 150 College Ave Ephraim UT 84627

GARDNER, RAY DEAN, JR., lawyer; b. Huntington Park, Calif., July 9, 1954; s. Ray Dean Gardner Sr. and Wanda Lou (Banks) Goldman; m. Elizabeth Louise Davis, Dec. 28, 1976; 1 child, John Davis. BA, Humboldt State U., 1977; JD, U. Calif., San Francisco, 1981. Bar: Alaska 1981, U.S. Dist. Ct. Alaska 1981, U.S. Ct. Appeals (9th cir.) 1981, U.S. Supreme Ct. 1985, Colo. 1989, Wis. 1991, Utah, 1996. Assoc. Hartig, Rhodes, Norman, Mahoney & Edwards, Anchorage, 1981-85, ptnr., 1985-89; sr. counsel The Pittsburg & Midway Coal Mining Co. (A Chevron Co.), Denver, 1989-95; chief legal officer Kennecott Utah Copper Corp., Magna, Utah, 1995—; bd. dirs. Legal Aid Soc. Salt Lake, 1997. Bd. dirs. Resource Devel. Council for Alaska Inc., 1985-89, Alaska Mineral and Energy Resource Edn. Fund, 1987-89. Alfred C. Piltz scholar Humboldt State U., 1975; Calif. State fellow, 1978-81. Mem. Am. Mining Congress (coal leasing com.), Colo. Bar Assn. (mineral, bus. and environ. sects.), Denver Bar Assn., Alaska Bar Assn. (exec. com. natural resources sect. 1984-87, chmn. bus. law sect. 1985-86, corp. code revision subcom. 1985-87), Wis. Bar Assn., Alaska Assn. Petroleum Landmen, Alaska Miners Assn. (state oversight com. 1985-86), Utah Bar Assn., Anchorage C. of C. (chmn. state legis. com. 1986-88, bd. dirs. 1988-89). Presbyterian. Home: 2715 Comanche Dr Salt Lake City UT 84108-2810 Office: Kennecott Utah Copper Corp PO Box 6001 8315 West 3595 South Magna UT 84044-6001

GARDNER, ROBERT ALEXANDER, career counselor, career management consultant; b. Berkeley, Calif., Sept. 16, 1944; s. Robert Sr. and Eleanor Ambrose (Starrett). BA, U. Calif., Berkeley, 1967; MA, Calif. State U., Chico, 1974; MS, San Francisco State U., 1992. Registered profl. career counselor; nat. cert. career counselor; nat. cert. counselor. Div. personnel officer Wells Fargo Bank, San Francisco, 1977-80; dir. personnel Transamerica Airlines, Oakland, Calif., 1980-84; career counselor, career mgmt. cons. Gardner Assocs., Oakland, 1984—; bd. dirs. Vocats. Svcs.; adj. faculty mem. John F. Kennedy U., Walnut Creek, Calif., 1995-96; career counselor, outplacement cons. Forty Plus of No. Calif., Oakland, 1988-93; instr. Armstrong U., Berkeley, 1980-81, U. Calif. Univ. Ext. Divsn., 1984-96, extended edn., 1981-86, internat. cons., 1984-87. Author: Achieving Effective Supervision, 1984, rev. edit. 1989, Managing Personnel Administration Effectively, 1986, Career Counseling: Matching Yourself to a Career, 1987. Mem. ACA, APA, Soc. Indsl. and Orgnl. Psychology, Nat. Career Devel. Assn., Calif. Career Devel. Assn., Calif. Assn. for Counseling and Devel., Internat. Assn. Career Mgmt. Profls., Rotary (Paul Harris fellow). Home: 1766 Camino Verde Apt C Walnut Creek CA 94596 Office: Gardner Assocs 3873 Piedmont Ave Ste 12 Oakland CA 94611-5370

GAREY, DONALD LEE, pipeline and oil company executive; b. Ft. Worth, Sept. 9, 1931; s. Leo James and Jessie (McNatt) G.; BS in Geol. Engring., Tex. A&M U., 1953; m. Elizabeth Patricia Martin, Aug. 1, 1953; children: Deborah Anne, Elizabeth Laird. Reservoir geologist Gulf Oil Corp., 1953-54, sr. geologist, 1956-65; v.p., mng. dir. Indsl. Devel. Corp. Lea County, Hobbs, N.Mex., 1965-72, dir., 1972-86, pres., 1978-86; v.p., dir. Minerals, Inc., Hobbs, 1966-72, pres., dir., 1972-86, chief exec. officer, 1978-82; mng. dir. Hobbs Indsl. Found. Corp., 1965-72, dir., 1965-76; v.p. Llano, Inc., 1972-74, exec. v.p., chief operating officer, 1974-75, pres., 1975-86, chief exec. officer, 1978-82, also dir.; pres., chief exec. officer, Pollution Control, Inc., 1969-81; pres. NMESCO Fuels, Inc., 1982-86; chmn., pres., chief exec. officer Estacado Inc., 1986—, Natgas Inc., 1987—; pres. Llano Co2, Inc., 1984-86; cons. geologist, geol. engr., Hobbs, 1965-72. Chmn., Hobbs Manpower Devel. Tng. Adv. Com., 1965-72; mem. Hobbs Adv. Com. for Mental Health, 1965-67; chmn. N.Mex. Mapping Adv. Com., 1968-69; mem. Hobbs adv. bd. Salvation Army, 1967-78, chmn., 1970-72; mem. exec. bd. Conquistador coun. Boy Scouts Am., Hobbs, 1965-75; vice chmn. N.Mex. Gov.'s Com. for Econ. Devel., 1968-70; bd. regents Coll. Southwest, 1982-85. Capt. USAF, 1954-56. Registered profl. engr., Tex. Mem. Am. Inst. Profl. Geologists, Am. Assn. Petroleum Geologists, AIME, Rotary. Home: 315 E Alto Dr Hobbs NM 88240-3905 Office: Broadmoor Tower PO Box 5587 Hobbs NM 88241-5587

GARFEIN, ARTHUR DOUGLAS, psychiatrist, psychoanalyst; b. Bklyn., Oct. 29, 1942; s. Abraham and Flora G. (Geshwind) G.; m. Anita B. Burnett, Nov. 18, 1967; children: Jennifer, Joshua. AB, Bucknell U., 1964; MD, U. Louisville, 1968. Diplomate Am. Bd. Psychiatry and Neurology. Intern Jackson Meml. Hosp.-U. Miami (Fla.) Sch. Medicine, 1968-69; resident in psychiatry U. Colo., Denver, 1969-72; pvt. practice Littleton, Colo., 1974—; med. dir. behavioral health svcs. Porter Meml. Hosp., Denver, 1989—; assoc. clin. prof. psychiatry U. Colo. Health Scis., Denver, 1996—; chmn. Colo. PsychCare; mem. faculty Denver Inst. Psychoanalysis, coord. advanced psychotherapy seminar, 1988—; cons. in field. Pres. Goddard Neighborhood Assn., Littleton, Colo., 1988-90, Assn. Mental Affiliation with Israel, Colo. chpt., Highlands Park, Ill., 1986-88. lt comdr. USN, 1972-74. Fellow Am. Psychiat. Assn.; mem. Colo. Psychiat. Assn. (chmn. rev. com. 1984-86), Denver Psychoanalytic Soc. (ethics com. 1988—, treas. 1992—). Home: 3986 W Bowles Ave Littleton CO 80123-6582 Office: 191 E Orchard Rd Ste 202 Littleton CO 80121-8057

GARLAND, G(ARFIELD) GARRETT, sales executive, golf professional; b. Lakewood, Ohio, Dec. 17, 1946; s. Garfield George and Lois Marie (Calavan) G.; m. Debra Ann Threlkel; 1 child, Brandon Palmer. BA, U. Colo., 1974. Broker Marcus & Millichap, Newport Beach, Calif., 1982-84; v.p. Pacific Coast Fed., Encino, Calif., 1984-85; dir. of acquisitions Prudential Investment Fund, L.A., 1985-86; v.p. A.S.A.I., L.A. and Tokyo, 1986-89; dir. sales Lojack Corp., L.A., 1989—; pres. Collegiate Scholarship Svcs. of Am., 1991-92; cons. Centinela Hosp. Fitness Inst. Mem. Pres.'s Coun. on Competitiveness, 1992, Childhelp USA. Capt. U.S. Army, 1967-71. Mem. VFW, PGA of Am., L.I.F.E. Found., Am. Legion, World Affairs Coun., Internat. Platform Assn., U.S. Ski Team, Natural Historic Preservation Trust. Home: 3846 Via Dolce Marina Dl Rey CA 90292-5085 Office: Lojack Corp 9911 W Pico Blvd Los Angeles CA 90035-2703

GARLAND, HARRY THOMAS, research administrator; b. Detroit, Jan. 18, 1947; s. Harry George and Rose (Bonn) G.; m. Roberta Joy Siciliano; children: Eva, Harry, Brad, Ken. BA, Kalamazoo Coll., 1968; PhD, Stanford U., 1972. Lectr. Stanford (Calif.) U., 1972-73, asst. dept. chmn., 1973-76; pres. Cromemco, Inc., Mountain View, Calif., 1976-89; v.p. Canon Rsch. Ctr., Palo Alto, Calif., 1990—; trustee Kalamazoo (Mich.) Coll., 1986—; bd. mem. Industry Initiatives for Sci. and Math Edn., 1994—. Author: Introduction to Microprocessor System Design, 1979; co-author: Understanding IC Operational Amplifiers, 1971, Understanding CMOS Integrated Circuits, 1975; contbr. articles to profl. jours.; patentee in field. Recipient NIH traineeship, Disting. Alumni award Kalamazoo Coll., 1986. Office: Canon Rsch Ctr 4009 Miranda Ave Palo Alto CA 94304-1218

GARLAND, KATHLEEN ANNE, geologist; b. New Kensington, Pa., May 17, 1959; d. Thomas J. and Mildred (Hribar) G. BA/BS, Pa. State U., 1982, PhD, 1989; DEA, U. de Bertagne Occid., France, 1984. Tchg. asst. dept. geosci. Pa. State U., State College, 1984-88; geologist, geophysicist Chevron U.S.A., New Orleans, 1988-92; project mgr., mgr. reimbursement program N.Mex. Environ. Dept., Santa Fe, 1992-95; dir. mining and minerals divsn. Energy, Minerals, and Natural Resources Dept., Santa Fe, 1995—. Mem. Rotary (bd. dirs., sec. 1996, pres.-elect 1997—), Phi Beta Kappa. Roman Catholic. Office: Energy Minerals Natural Res 2040 S Pacheco Santa Fe NM 87505

GARLOUGH, WILLIAM GLENN, marketing executive; b. Syracuse, N.Y., Mar. 27, 1924; s. Henry James and Gladys (Killam) G.; m. Charlotte M. Tanzer, June 15, 1947; children: Jennifer, William, Robert. BEE, Clarkson U., 1949. With Knowlton Bros., Watertown, N.Y., 1949-67, mgr. mfg. svcs., 1966-67; v.p. planning, equipment systems divsn. Vare Corp., Englewood Cliffs, N.J., 1967-69; mgr. mktg. Valley Mould divsn. Microdot Inc., Hubbard, Ohio, 1969-70; dir. corp. devel. Microdot Inc., Greenwich, Conn., 1970-73, v.p. corp. devel., 1973-76, v.p. adminstrn., 1976-77, v.p. corp. devel., 1977-78; v.p. corp. devel. Am. Bldg. Maintenance Industries, San Francisco, 1979-83; pres. The Change Agts., Inc., Walnut Creek, Calif., 1983—; bd. dirs. My Chef Inc.; mem. citizens adv. com. to Watertown Bd. Edn., 1957. Bd. dirs. Watertown Cmty. Chest, 1958-61; ruling elder Presbyn. Ch. With USMCR, 1942-46. Mem. Am. Mgmt. Assn., Inst. Mgmt. Cons. (cert.), Bldg. Svc. Contractors Assn., Internat. Sanitary Supply Assn., Mensa, Am. Mktg. Assn., TAPPI, Assn. Corp. Growth (pres. San Francisco chpt. 1984-85, v.p. chpts. west 1985-88), Lincoln League (pres. 1958), Marine's Meml. Club, Am. Contract Bridge League (life master), Clarkson Alumni Assn. (Watertown sect. pres. 1955), No. N.Y. Contract Club (pres. 1959), No. N.Y. Transp. Club, Tau Beta Pi. Home: 2557 Via Verde Walnut Creek CA 94598-3451 Office: The Change Agts Inc 2557 Via Verde Walnut Creek CA 94598-3451

GARMANY, GEORGE PARKER, neurologist; b. Detroit, Nov. 3, 1947; m. Catharine Doremus, June 12, 1970 (div. 1991); children: Richard, Jeffrey; m. Beverly Reeves, Apr. 8, 1995. BA, U. Va., 1969, MD, 1973. Diplomate Am. Bd. Psychiatry and Neurology. Intern medicine Emory U. Affiliated Hosps., Atlanta, 1973-74; resident neurology U. Colo. Med. Ctr., Denver, 1974-77; pvt. practice Associated Neurologists, Boulder, Colo., 1977—; cons. Jimmie Heuga Ctr., Avon, Colo., 1985—; pres. med. staff United Med. STaff, Boulder, 1986-87. Bd. mem. Nat. Multiple Sclerosis Soc., Colo. chpt., Denver, 1981—, chair profl. adv. com., 1992—, mem. nat. com. profl. adv. com. chairs, 1994—. Named Vol. Faculty of Yr. Denver Gen. Hosp., 1990, Over and Above award Nat. Multiple Sclerosis Soc., Denver, 1994. Fellow Am. Acad. Neurology; mem. Colo. Soc. Clin. Neurologists (pres. 1988-90), Colo. Mayflower Soc. (capt. 1995—), Boulder Rotary. Office: Associated Neurologists 1000 Alpine Ave Ste 291 Boulder CO 80304-3411

GARNER, LYNN EVAN, mathematics educator; b. Ontario, Oreg., July 19, 1941; s. Evan Bowen and Sarah Melba (Despain) G.; m. Marjorie Kaye Waite, Sept. 9, 1960; children: Kaylene, Bradley, Kristen, Alisse, Brian. BS, Brigham Young U., 1962; MA, U. Utah, 1964; PhD, U. Oreg., 1968. Instr. to prof. Brigham Young U., Provo, Utah, 1962—; instr. Waterford Sch., Provo, 1983-89, Meridian Sch., Provo, 1989-96; cons. Hewlett Packard Edn. Adv. Com., Corvallis, Oreg., 1992—. Author: Outline of Projective Geometry, 1981, Calculus and Analytic Geometry, 1988, Calculus with H/P Calculators, 1990, Calculus with the HP48, 1992, 94. Mem. Am. Math. Soc., Math. Assn. of Am., Pi Mu Epsilon, Phi Kappa Phi, Sigma Xi. Mem. Ch. LDS. Office: Brigham Young U 283 Tmcb Provo UT 84602-6549

GARNETT, DANIEL JOSEPH, surgeon; b. Waukegan, Ill., Aug. 21, 1942; s. Robert and Eleanor Elizabeth (Ryan) G.; m. Stephanie Ann McCarty, Nov. 24, 1971; children: David Bryan, Michael Clarke. AB, Dartmouth Coll., 1964, B in Med. Sci., 1965; MD, Columbia U., N.Y.C., 1967. Diplomate Am. Bd. Surgery. Straight surg. intern Harborview Hosp., Seattle, 1969-70; resident in gen. surgery Swedish Hosp. Med. Ctr., Seattle, 1970-73, chief resident, 1973-74; practice surgery Seattle, 1974—. Lt. USNR, 1968-70. Fellow ACS, Seattle Surg. Soc.; mem. AMA, Wash. State Med. Assn., King County Med. Soc., Trout Unltd. Office: 1801 NW Market St Ste 401 Seattle WA 98107-3909

GARR, CHERYL DENISE, research chemist; b. Idaho Falls, Idaho, May 2, 1960; d. Jerry Lee and Jane Ellen (Wise) Gross; m. Westley Dean Garr, June 27, 1987; children: Taylor Kristen, Jamie Lynn. BS in Chemistry, Evergreen State Coll., Olympia, Wash., 1986; PhD in Chemistry, U. Oreg., 1992. Postdoctoral fellow Panlabs Inc., Bothell, Wash., 1992, scientist, 1992-96, group leader, 1995-96, project mgr. synthetic and combinatorial chemistry, 1996—. Contbr. articles to Jour. Am. Chem. Soc., Jour. Inorganic Chemistry, Bio-organic Med. Chemistry, Jour. Biomolecular Screening.

Mem. Am. Chem. Soc., Soc. for Biomolecular Screening, Soc. for Indsl. Microbiologists. Home: 22717 NE 195th St Woodinville WA 98072-7538 Office: Panlabs Inc 11804 N Creek Pky S Bothell WA 98011-8805

GARRETSON, OWEN LOREN, petroleum engineer; b. Salem, Iowa, Feb. 24, 1912; s. Sumner Dilts and Florence (White) G.; m. Erma Mary Smith, Jan. 23, 1932; children: John Albert, Owen Don, Susan Marie, Leon Todd. Student, Iowa Wesleyan Coll., 1930-32; BS, Iowa State U., 1937. Registered profl. engr., Okla., N.Mex., Iowa, Mo. Engr. Bailey Meter Co., Cleve., 1937, St. Louis, 1937-38; engr., dist. mgr. Phillips Petroleum Co., Bartlesville, Okla., 1938-39, Amarillo, Tex., 1939-40; engr., dist. mgr. Phillips Petroleum Co., Detroit, 1940-41, wholesale mgr. liquified petroleum gas sales divsn., 1941-42; mgr. product supply and transp. divsn. Phillips Petroleum Co., Bartlesville, 1942-44, mgr. engring. devel. divsn., 1944-46, mgr. spl. products engring. devel. divsn., 1946-47; pres. Gen. Tank & Steel Corp., Roswell, N.Mex., United Farm Chem. Co.; pres., dir. Garretson Equipment Co., Mt. Pleasant, Iowa; v.p., dir. Valley Industries, Inc., Mt. Pleasant; pres., dir. Garretson Carburetion of Tex., Inc., Lubbock; v.p., dir. Sacra Gas Co. Roswell, 1957-58; exec. v.p., dir. Arrow Gas. Co. & Affiliated Corps., Roswell, N.Mex., Tex., Utah, 1958-60; asst. to pres. Nat. Propane Corp., Hyde Park, N.Y.; pres., chmn. bd. Plateau, Inc. Oil Refining, Farmington, N.Mex., 1960-82, also bd. dirs.; chmn. bd. S.W. Motels, Inc., Farmington; organizing dir. Farmington Nat. Bank, 1964; cons. Suburban Propane Gas Corp. Whippany, N.J. Contbr. articles to profl. jours.; 42 patents issued in several fields; inventor WWII aircraft engine power boost sys., 1942. Mem., past pres. Farmington Indsl. Devel. Svc., N.Mex. Lidquefied Petroleum Gas Commn., 1955-76, chmn., 1956-58; mem. Iowa Gov.'s Trade Commn. to No. Europe, 1970, Iowa Trade Mission to Europe, 1979; mem. com. natural gas/liquefied natural gas Internat. Petroleum Expn. and Congress, 1970-71; mem. Nat. Coun. Crime and Delinquency. Recipient Merit award Iowa Wesleyan Coll. Alumni Assn., 1968, Profl. Achievement Engring. citation Iowa State U., 1986. Mem. ASME, NSPE, Nat. Liquefied Petroleum Gas Assn. (bd. dirs., Disting. Svc. award 1979), Am. Petroleum Inst., Nat. Petroleum Refiner's Assn. (bd. dirs., pres.), Ind. Refiners Assn. Am., Agrl. Ammonia Inst. Memphis (bd. dirs.), N.Mex. Liquefied Petroleum Gas. Assn. (pres., bd. dirs.), Ind. Petroleum Assn. Am., N.Mex. Acad. Sci., Am. Soc. Agrl. Engrs., Am. Soc. Automotive Engrs., N.Mex. Amigos., Am. Inst. Chem. Engrs., Newcomen Soc. N.Am., Soc. Indsl. Archeology, Ancient Gassers (sec., pres.), 25 Yr. Club Petroleum Industry, Masons, Rotary, Phi Delta Theta, Tau Beta Pi. Home: 500 E La Plata St Farmington NM 87401-6940 Office: PO Box 108 Farmington NM 87499-0108

GARRETSON, STEVEN MICHAEL, elementary education educator; b. L.A., Nov. 2, 1950; s. Fredrick Harmon and Mildred (Mason) G.; m. Candice Kay Clouse, Sept. 23, 1972; children: Joshua Steven, Amanda Jeanine. BA, U. Calif., Irvine, 1972, tchr. credential, 1974; postgrad., U. Calif., Santa Barbara, 1973; MA, U. San Francisco, 1980. Cert. tchr., adminstr., Calif. Tchr. Irvine Unified Sch. Dist., 1974—; energy conservation cons. Irvine Unified Sch. Dist., 1981-85, grant writer, 1983—, archtl. design cons., 1975—, mentor tchr., 1984-86; presenter state social studies conf., 1980. Mem. Irvine Tchrs. Assn. (grievance chmn. 1980-82, treas., 1977-78, v.p., 1978-79, contract negotiator, 1976-84, 89-93, benefits mgmt. bd. 1990—, pres. 1993-97), Phi Delta Kappa. Roman Catholic. Office: Irvine Tchrs Assn 4752 Barranca Pkwy Irvine CA 92714

GARRETT, ABIGAIL, health facility administrator, nutritionist; b. Atlanta, Aug. 12, 1957; d. Joseph and Ebony (Thornhill) G.; m. John Garrett, May 5, 1988; children: Chad, Quiana. BS in Nutrition, Cornell U., 1980; postgrad. in Bus. Administrn., Rutgers U., 1980-81. Cert. nutritionist. Mem. cafeteria staff President H.S., N.Y.C., 1980-82; nutritionist Rockwell Rehab. Ctr., Rochester, N.Y., 1982-84, Clearview Hosp., Syracuse, N.Y., 1984-90; prin., nutritionist You Can Werik, Scottsdale, Ariz., 1990—; chef The Office, N.Y.C., 1980-82, Asian Palace, Summit, N.J, 1981-82; dietiton Rahway Health Spa, Syracuse, 1982-89; cons. in field. Author: Just the Weight You Are, 1996, The Way to a Man's Heart is not his Stomach, 1997; mem. editl. bd. Nutrition and Facts, 1995—, Food for Thought, 1996—. active Big Sister Cares Ariz. Youth Found., Scottsdale, 1993—; chmn. bd. dirs. Ariz. Charity Care, Scottsdale, 1994—; nutrition cons. Young Mothers Young Women YWCA, Scottsdale, 1991—; bd. dirs. Universal Arts Ctr. Mem. AAAU, AAAS, NSF, N.Y. Acad. Scis., Ariz. Crops Assn.(mem. field trip com. 1991—). Office: You Can Werik 13610 N Scottsdale Rd Scottsdale AZ 85254-4052

GARRETT, DENNIS ANDREW, police official; b. Phoenix, Feb. 9, 1940; s. Lynn Patrick and Louise A. (Yates) G.; m. Joan Marie Braun, June 12, 1980. AA, Glendale Community Coll., 1975; BS magna cum laude, No. Ariz. U., 1980; MPA, Ariz. State U., 1985. Officer Phoenix Police Dept., 1963-69, sgt., 1969-72, lt., 1972-75, capt., 1975-80, maj., 1980, asst. police chief, 1980-91, police chief, 1991—. Chmn. St. Jerome's Sch. Bd., Phoenix, 1978-79, Boys & Girls Club Met. Phoenix, mem. Valley Leadership, Phoenix, 1985—, NAACP; bd. dirs. Friendly House, YMCA. Mem. ASPA (pres. Ariz. chpt. 1988-89), Internat. Assn. Chiefs Police, Ariz. Assn. Chiefs Police, Nat. Orgn. Black Law Enforcement Execs., Fraternal Order Police, Rotary, Phi Kappa Phi. Republican. Roman Catholic. Office: Phoenix Police Dept 620 W Washington St Phoenix AZ 85003-2186

GARRETT, DON JAMES, philosophy educator; b. Salt Lake City, June 5, 1953; s. James Raymond and Bula (Fisher) G.; m. Frances Clark, Aug. 8, 1975; children: Matthew, Christopher. BA, U. Utah, 1974; PhD, Yale U., 1979. Asst. prof. Harvard U., Cambridge, Mass., 1979-82; asst. prof. U. Utah, Salt Lake City, 1982-85, assoc. prof., 1985-95, prof., 1995—, chair dept. philosophy, 1996—; vis. assoc. prof. Johns Hopkins U., Balt., 1988. Author: Cognition and Commitment in Hume's Philosophy, 1997; editor: The Cambridge Companion to Spinoza, 1996, (jour.) Hume Studies, 1994—. Office: Dept Philosophy 341 OSH Univ Utah Salt Lake City UT 84112

GARRETT, PAUL EDGAR, insurance executive, writer; b. Timpas, Colo., Nov. 18, 1909; s. Charles Calvin and Ida Pauline (Guire) G.; m. Muriel Gladys Goodroad, Mar. 10, 1945 (dec. Aug. 1983); children: Donald (dec.), Gerald (dec.); m. Ornetta Gardner, Oct. 27, 1984. BS, U. Wyo., 1935. CLU. Prin. Pub. Schs., Torrington, Wyo., 1931-32; prin., supt. Territorial Schs., Seward and Kodiak, Alaska, 1932-35; supt. Consol. Schs., Glendo, Wyo., 1935-36; dist. mgr. Ohio Nat. Life, Laramie, Wyo., 1936-37; gen. agt. Ohio Nat. Life, Billings, Mont., 1937-50; mem., chmn. field adv. bd. Ohio Nat. Life, Spokane, 1946-66, gen. agt. for Mont., Idaho and Wash., 1950-66; mem., chmn. Ins. Examining Bd., Olympia, Wash., 1962-70. Author: (poems) Song of the North, 1936, Down By The Sea, 1994; author hunting and fishing stories, short stories, historical stories. Lt. USN, 1943-46, PTO. Mem. Elks, Masons, Brotherhood of Friends, Sigma Chi. Home: 1518 E Cambridge Ln Spokane WA 99203 also: 119 Viscount Ln Lake Havasu City AZ 86403

GARRIDO, AUGIE, university athletic coach. Head coach Calif. State Fullerton Titans, 1973-87, 1991-96, U. Ill., 1987-91, U. Texas, Austin, 1996—. Named 4th Winningnest active divsn. IA coach, 1103 victories. Office: U Tex Austin PO Box 13178 2400 Inner Campus Dr Austin TX 78712*

GARRIGUS, CHARLES BYFORD, retired literature educator; b. Benton, Ill., June 13, 1914; s. Charles Byford and Ailene Marie (Fowler) G.; m. Ferne Marie Fetters, Dec. 28, 1936 (dec.); children: Marmarie (dec.), Charles, Richmond, Karis, Rose Ann. AB, U. Ill., 1936, MA, 1937. Prof. humanities King's River Coll., Reedley, Calif., 1949-73; Calif. poet laureate for life, 1966—. Author: California Poems, 1955, (poems) Echoes of Being, 1975, (novels) Brief Candel, 1987, Chas and The Summer of '26, 1994; editor: Modern Hamlet, 1950. Mem. Calif. Assembly, 1958-66. Democrat. Methodist. Home: 1623 Morgan Dr Kingsburg CA 93631-2619

GARRISON, F. SHERIDAN, transportation executive. CEO Am. Freightways, Harrison, Ark., 1956-79; chmn. bd., pres., CEO Am. Freightways, Inc., Harrison, Ark., 1982—, Am. Freightways Corp., Harrison, 1982—, Garrison Corp., Harrison, 1982—. Office: Am Freightways PO Box 840 2200 Forward Dr Harrison AR 72602-2004*

GARRISON, GENE KIRBY, artist, writer, photographer; b. Clayton, Del., Aug. 11, 1925; d. Leighton Bradley and Adelaide (Stevens) Kirby; m. Elbert Wingate Garrison; children: Robert Kirby, David Andrew. AA, Phoenix Coll., 1964. Author: Widow... or Widow-to-Be?, 1991; co-author: From Thunder to Breakfast, 1978; exhibits include Desert Artists, Inc., Cave Creek, Ariz., 1983—, es Posible Gallery, Scottsdale, Ariz., 1992—, Imagine Gallery, Scottsdale, 1988—. Literary arts com. Foothills Cmty. Found., Carefree, Ariz., 1994—; historian Desert Foothills Cmty. Theater, Carefree, 1975-95. Mem. Desert Foothills Woman's Club, Desert Artists, Inc. (founder).

GARRISON, U. EDWIN, military, space and defense products manufacturing company executive; b. 1928. BSME, Miss. State U., 1951. With Thiokol Corp., Ogden, Utah, 1952—, from v.p. to pres. aerospace group, 1983-89, past pres., CEO, 1989—; chmn. bd. dirs. Thiokol Corp., Ogden, 1991—. With USN, 1946-48. Office: Thiokol Corp 2475 Washington Blvd Ogden UT 84401-2300*

GARRITY, RODMAN FOX, psychologist, educator; b. Los Angeles, June 10, 1922; s. Lawrence Hitchcock and Margery Fox (Pugh) G.; m. Juanita Daphne Mullan, Mar. 5, 1948; children—Diana Daphne, Ronald Fox. Student, Los Angeles City Coll., 1946-47; B.A., Calif. State U., Los Angeles, 1950; M.A., So. Meth. U., Dallas, 1955; Ed.D., U. So. Calif., 1963. Tchr. elem. sch. Palmdale (Calif.) Sch. Dist., 1952-54; psychologist, prin. Redondo Beach (Calif.) City Schs., 1954-60; asst. dir. ednl. placement lectr., ednl. adviser U. So. Calif., 1960-62; asso. prof., coordinator credentials programs Calif. State Poly. U., Pomona, 1962-66; chmn. social sci. dept. Calif. State Poly. U., 1966-68, dir. tchr. preparation center, 1968-71, coordinator grad. program, 1971-73, prof. tchr. preparation center, 1968—, coordinator spl. edn. programs, 1979—; cons. psychologist, lectr. in field. Pres. Redondo Beach Coordinating Council, 1958-60; mem. univ. rep. Calif. Faculty Assns., 1974-76. Served with Engr. Combat Bn. AUS, 1942-45. Mem. Prins. Assn. Redondo Beach (chmn. 1958-60), Nat. Congress Parents and Tchrs. (hon. life), Am. Psychol. Assn., Calif. Tchrs. Assn. Democrat. Office: Calif State U Dept Special Edn Pomona CA 91768 *Empathetic reaching out to others transcends the obvious importance of achievement and intellectual ability. This has been a basic guide for my endeavors in the helping professions.*

GARROP, BARBARA ANN, elementary education educator; b. Chgo., Sept. 2, 1941; d. Marshall and Esther (Barbakoff) Stickles; widowed; children: Alana Beth, Stacy Lynn. AA with honors, Wright Jr. Coll., Chgo., 1961; BA with honors, Roosevelt U., 1963; MS with honors, Calif. State U., Hayward, 1982. Cert. elem. tchr., reading specialist, Calif. Tchr. Von Humboldt Sch., Chgo., 1963-64, Haugan Sch., Chgo., 1964-67; primary grades reading specialist Mt. Diablo Sch. Dist., Concord, Calif., 1979-80, Mills Elem. Sch., Benicia, Calif., 1980-87, Mary Farmar Sch., Benicia, 1987—; mentor tchr. Benicia Unified Sch. Dist., Benicia, 1989, 92, 96—; inst. tchr. leader Calif. Lit. Project, 1991-93; instr. Chapman U. Acad. Ctr., Fairfield, Calif., spring, 1992; mem. reading delegation to China citizen amb. program People to People Internat., 1993. Author phonic manual, 1982; featured in article Woman's Day mag., 1982; contbr. reading program to Excellence In Educational Programs Throughout Solano County, 1994-95, 96-97; contbg. author Celebrating The National Reading Initiative, 1988. Bd. dirs. Sisterhood of Congregation B'nai Shalom, Walnut Creek, Calif., 1987-88. Grantee Reading Is Fundamental, 1979-80. Mem. NEA, Internat. Reading Assn., Calif. Reading Assn. (Achievement award 1984), Constra Costa Reading Assn., Calif. Tchrs. Assn., AAUW, Pi Lambda Theta. Jewish. Lodge: B'nai Brith Women (v.p. Columbus, Ohio 1971-72, pres. Walnut Creek 1973-74). Office: Mary Farmar Sch 901 Military W Benicia CA 94510-2558

GARRUTO, JOHN ANTHONY, cosmetics executive; b. Johnson City, N.Y., June 18, 1952; s. Paul Anthony and Katherine Helen (DiMartino) G.; m. Denise Kitty Conlon, Feb. 19, 1971 (div. May 1978); 1 child, James Joseph; m. Anita Louise, May 12, 1979 (div. Sept. 1984); 1 child, Christopher Russell; m. Debra Lynn Brady (div. Dec. 1986); m. Michelle Bartok, Apr. 2, 1988; 1 child, Catherine Michelle. BS in Chemistry, SUNY, Binghamton, 1974; AAS in Bus. Adminstrn., Broome Coll., 1976. Rsch. chemist Lander Co. Inc., Binghamton, 1974-77; rsch. dir. Lander Co. Inc., St. Louis, 1977-79, Olde Worlde Products, High Point, N.C., 1979-81; v.p. rsch. and devel. LaCosta Products Internat., Carlsbad, Calif., 1981-89; chief ops. officer Randall Products Internat., Carlsbad, 1989-91; pres. Dermasearch Internat., 1991-92; chief tech. officer Innovative Bioscis. Corp., Oceanside, Calif., 1992-95; v.p. rsch. Garden Botanika, Oceanside, Calif., 1995—; cons. Trans-Atlantic Mktg., Binghamton, 1975-78; instr. cosmetic sci UCLA, 1991, UCLA Ext. Mem. AAS, Soc. Cosmetic Chemists (newsletter editor 1980-81, publicity chmn. 1984—, edn. chmn. 1987, employment chmn. 1994—, sec. beauty industry west), Fedn. Am. Scientists, N.Y. Acad. Scis. Office: Garden Botanika # 115 4168 Avenida De La Plata Oceanside CA 92056-6031

GARRUTO, MICHELLE BARTOK, cosmetic company executive; b. Youngstown, Ohio, Feb. 18, 1961; d. Albert James and Judith Ann (Phillips) Bartok; m. John Anthony Garruto, Apr. 2, 1988 (div. 1997); children: Catherine Michelle, Gabrielle Bartok. BS in Physiol. Psychology, U. Calif., Santa Barbara, 1983. EMT, Calif. Asst. to phys. therapist Santa Barbara Phys. Therapy, 1983-84, Escondido (Calif.) Phys. Therapy, 1984-85; regional sales rep. Ft. Dodge Labs., San Francisco, 1985-87; owner North Coast Therapeutics, Oceanside, Calif., 1987-92; CEO, Innovative Bioscis. Corp., Carlsbad, Calif., 1992—. Mem. Nat. Women's Fitness Assn., Women's Enterprise Network, Soc. Cosmetic Chemists, Beauty Industry West (pub. rels. dir. 1991-92, chair symposium 1996), Internat. Spa and Fitness Assn. (sponsor Ironman competition 1989). Home: 178 Grandview Lencadia CA 92023-2839 Office: Innovative Bioscis Corp 2235 Faraday Ave Ste R Carlsbad CA 92008-7215

GARRY, STACEY LYNNE, pathologist; b. Bakersfield, Calif., Sept. 20, 1952; d. Stancil Lee Buchanan and Nona Ethel (Pyle) Finn; m. Edward David Garry, Dec. 18, 1982. Student, Bakersfield Coll., 1970-73; BS in Zoology, Idaho State U., 1982; MD, U. Calif., San Francisco, 1986. Diplomate Am. Bd. Med. Examiners, Am. Bd. Pathology-Anatomic and Clin. Pathology, Am. Bd. Pathology-Hematology. Lab. asst. Kern Med. Ctr., Bakersfield, 1968-72; med. lab. technician Bannock Regional Med. Ctr., Pocatello, Idaho, 1976-77, Pocatello Regional Med. Ctr., 1976-82; resident U. Utah, Salt Lake City, 1986-91; pathologist lab. med. cons. Sunrise Hosp., Las Vegas, Nev., 1991—; dir. LMC Labs., Las Vegas, Nev., 1992—; cons. U. Utah Cardiovascular Inst., Salt Lake City, 1988-91, Associated & Regional Univ. Pathologists, Salt Lake City, 1989-91, Dermatopathology Inc., Murry, Utah, 1987-91, HGM Laser Inc., Salt Lake City, 1987-89, Symbion Inc., Vancouver, B.C., 1987-91; lectr. Utah State Health Dept., Utah, Oreg., Idaho, Ill. and Wis. State Med. Tech. Soc., Bannock Regional Med. Ctr. Fellow Coll. Am. Pathologists (resident forum chmn. 1990-91, vice chmn. 1989-90, resident & young physicians sect. 1991-94, planning com. 1990-93, com. pathology enhancement 1992-95); mem. AMA (del. 1983-85, 86-90, 92-95), Utah State Med. Assn. (del. 1986-90), U. Utah Housestaff Assn. (pres. 1988-90), Soc. for Hematopathology, CAP-HOD (del.), CAP-LAP Nev. State (commn. 1997—), CAP Pathology (mem. com. 1994—), Phi Kappa Phi. Home: 1500 Commanche Dr Las Vegas NV 89109-3113 Office: LMC Labs Sunrise Hosp Maryland Pky Las Vegas NV 89109-1627

GARSH, THOMAS BURTON, publisher; b. New Rochelle, N.Y., Dec. 12, 1931; s. Harry and Matilda (Smith) G.; m. Beatrice J. Schmidt; children: Carol Jean, Thomas Burton, Janice Lynn. B.S., U. Md., 1955. Edn. rep. McGraw Hill Book Co., N.Y.C., 1959-68; mktg. mgr. D.C. Heath & Co., Boston, 1969-71; dir. mktg. Economy Co., Oklahoma City, 1971-72; sr. v.p. Macmillan Pub. Co., N.Y.C., 1972-78; pres. Am. Book Co., N.Y.C., 1978-81; founder, pres., dir. Am. Ednl. Computer, Inc., Palo Alto, Calif., 1981-86; founder, chmn., chief exec. officer OmnyEd Corp., Palo Alto, 1987-91; pres. Silver Burdett & Ginn divsn. of Simon and Schuster, 1991-92; dir. Fifty Plus Fitness Assn., Palo Alto, Calif. Mem. county council Boy Scouts Am., 1963-65; mem. ch. council on Interracial Affairs, 1966-68, pres., 1967; vice-chmn. Madison County Democratic Party, 1967. Mem. Assn. Am. Pubs., Profl. Bookman's Assn., Omicron Delta Kappa, Sigma Alpha Epsilon. Club: Cazenovia Country (founder). Home: 401 Old Spanish Trl Portola Valley CA 94028-8133

GARSIDE, LARRY JOE, research geologist; b. Omaha, May 2, 1943; s. Edwin Joseph and Ruby Anne (Weaver) G.; m. Terri Marie (Nelson), Sept. 11, 1993. BS in Geology, Iowa State U., 1965; MS in Geology, U. Nev., 1968. Lab. asst. Iowa State U., Ames, 1965; rsch. asst. U. Nev., Reno, 1965-68; econ. geologist Nev. Bur. Mines & Geology, Reno, 1968-84, chief geologist, dep. dir., 1985-87, acting dir., 1987-88, rsch. geologist, 1988—; exec. sec. Nev. Oil & GAs Conservation Commn., Reno, 1974-75. Contbr. numerous articles to profl. jours. Fellow Geol. Soc. of Am.; mem. Am. Assn. Petroleum Geologists, Soc. Econ. Geologists, Assn. Exploration Geochemists, Geol. Soc. Nev. (pres. 1973-74, sec., treas. 1969-70), Nev. Petroleum Soc. (sec., treas. 1986, pres. 1996-97), Geothermal Resource Coun. (charter). Home: 2670 Margaret Dr Reno NV 89506-8651 Office: Nev Bur of Mines & Geology U Nev #178 Reno NV 89557-0088

GARSON, ARNOLD HUGH, newspaper publisher; b. Lincoln, Nebr., May 29, 1941; s. Sam B. and Celia (Stine) G.; m. Marilyn Grace Baird, Aug. 15, 1964; children: Scott Arnold, Christopher Baird, Gillian Grace, Megan Jane. BA, U. Nebr., 1964; MS, UCLA, 1965. Reporter Omaha World-Herald, 1965-69; reporter Des Moines Tribune, 1969-72, city editor, 1972-75; reporter Des Moines Register, 1975-83, mng. editor, 1983-88; editor San Bernardino (Calif.) County Sun, 1988-96; pub. Sioux Falls (S.D.) Argus Leader, 1996—. Recipient Pub. Svc. Reporting award Am. Polit. Sci. Assn., 1969, Profl. Journalism award U. Nebr. at Omaha, 1969, John Hancock award for excellence in bus. and fin. journalism, 1979, Mng. Editors Sweepstakes award Iowa AP, 1976, Calif.-Nev. AP award for column writing, 1995. Mem. Am. Soc. Newspaper Editors, Soc. Profl. Journalists. Jewish. Home: 5 Riverview Heights Sioux Falls SD 57105 Office: Sioux Falls Argus Leader PO Box 5034 Sioux Falls SD 57117-5034

GARSTANG, ROY HENRY, astrophysicist, educator; b. Southport, Eng., Sept. 18, 1925; came to U.S., 1964; s. Percy Brocklehurst and Eunice (Gledhill) G.; m. Ann Clemence Hawk, Aug. 11, 1959; children—Jennifer Katherine, Susan Veronica. B.A., U. Cambridge, 1946, M.A., 1950, Ph.D., 1954, Sc.D., 1983. Research assoc. U. Chgo., 1951-52; lectr. astronomy U. Coll., London, 1952-60; reader astronomy U. London, 1960-64, asst. dir. Obs., 1959-64; prof. astrophysics U. Colo., Boulder, 1964-94, chair faculty assembly, 1988-89, prof. emeritus, 1994—; chmn. Joint Inst. for Lab. Astrophysics, 1966-67; cons. Nat. Bur. Standards, 1964-73; v.p. commn. 14 Internat. Astron. Union, 1970-73, pres., 1973-76; Erskine vis. fellow U. Canterbury, N.Z., 1971; vis. prof. U. Calif., Santa Cruz, 1971. Editor: Observatory, 1953-60; Contbr. numerous articles to tech. jours. Recipient Excellence in Svc. award U. Colo., 1990. Fellow Am. Phys. Soc., AAAS, Optical Soc. Am., Brit. Inst. Physics, Royal Astron. Soc.; mem. Am. Astron. Soc., Royal Soc. Scis. Liege (Belgium). Home: 830 8th St Boulder CO 80302-7409 Office: U Colo JILA Boulder CO 80309-0440 *It is a privilege to help others to learn about the wonderful universe in which we live.*

GARTH, JOHN CAMPBELL, physicist, researcher; b. N.Y.C., Sept. 26, 1934; s. Robert Campbell and Sarah Souther (Lingle) G.; m. Nancy Carolyn McCandless, Aug. 20, 1960; children: Lee McCandless, Lynn Virginia. BS in Engring., Princeton U., 1956; MS in Physics, U. Ill., 1958, PhD in Physics, 1965. Teaching asst. U. Ill., Urbana, 1956-59, NSF coop. fellow, 1959-60, rsch. asst., 1960-64; asst. prof. physics Worcester (Mass.) Poly. Inst., 1964-67; rsch. physicist Air Force Cambridge Rsch. Lab., Hanscom AFB, Mass., 1967-76; rsch. physicist (solid state) Rome Air Devel. Ctr. (named changed to Rome Lab. 1990), Hanscom AFB, 1976-91; solid state physicist Phillips Lab., Hanscom AFB, 1991-95, Kirtland AFB, 1995—; presenter in field to profl. socs., symposia, confs., 1970—. Contbr. over 60 articles to sci. jours. Recipient Sci. Achievement award Rome Lab., 1976, Tech. Achievement award, 1981. Mem. IEEE (reviewer Conf. on Nuclear and Space Radiation Effects 1980-90, award com. 1996), ASTM (E10.07 standards com. 1984—), Am. Phys. Soc., Am. Nuclear Soc. (session chmn. methods for neutral- and charged particles transport 1984, alt. session chmn. 1986, session organizer, session chmn. 1994). Evangelical. Home: 7305 New Dawn Ct NE Albuquerque NM 87122 Office: Phillips Lab PL/VTMR 3550 Aberdeen Ave SE Kirtland AFB NM 87117-5776

GARTH-LEWIS, KIMBERLEY ANNE, political science consultant; b. Sacramento, Jan. 21, 1960; d. Nat Garth and Frances (Hopkins) Garth Bradley; children: Shavaugn I., Veronica G. BS, U. San Francisco, 1981; MPA, Golden Gate U., 1985, DPA, 1993. Lic. tchr., Calif. Pvt. cons. Sacramento, 1985—; founder, pres. rsch. firm KAGL & Affiliates, Inc., 1991—; prof. U. San Francisco, Humphrey's Coll.; lectr. in U.S., Can. and Eng., 1985—. Author: Public-Private Partnerships in Corrections, 1996; contbr. articles to reports and transcripts. Ind. rschr. advocate Calif. Correctional Peace Officers Assn.; cons. Legis. Penal Code Com., 1990; aide to State Senator Robert Presley; staff support state task force Blue Ribbon Commn., 1989; advisor Little Hoover Commn., 1993-94, others; mem. Sch. Site Coun., 1991-95. Recipient Golden State Minority award, 1989, NAFE appreciation award, 1991, outstanding Women award, 1992-93, Women's Bus. and Profl. awards, 1997. Mem. IARCA, ASPA, NAFE (chair sect. membership 1991-92), Polit. Sci. Soc., Black Chamber, Beta Sigma Phi. Republican. Office: 1228 N St Sacramento CA 95814-5623

GARTNER, HAROLD HENRY, III, lawyer; b. L.A., June 23, 1948; s. Harold Henry Jr. and Frances Mildred (Evans) G.; m. Denise Helene Young, June 7, 1975; children: Patrick Christopher, Matthew Alexander. Student, Pasadena City Coll., 1966-67, George Williams Coll., 1967-68, Calif. State U., Los Angeles, 1969; JD cum laude, Loyola U., Los Angeles, 1972. Bar: Calif. 1972, U.S. Dist. Ct. (cen. dist.) Calif. 1973, U.S. Ct. Appeals (9th cir.) 1973. Assoc. Hitt, Murray & Caffray, Long Beach, Calif., 1972; dep. city atty. City of L.A., 1972-73; assoc. Patterson, Ritner & Lockwood, L.A., 1973-79; mng. ptnr. all offices Patterson, Ritner, Lockwood, Zanghi & Gartner, L.A., Ventura, Bakersfield, and San Bernardino, Calif., 1991—; instr. law Ventura Coll., 1981. Recipient Am. Jurisprudence award Trusts and Equity, 1971. Mem. ABA, Calif. Bar Assn., Ventura County Bar Assn., Nat. Assn. Def. Counsel, Assn. So. Calif. Def. Counsel, Ventura County Trial Lawyers Assn., Direct Relief Internat. (bd. trustees). Republican. Club: Pacific Corinthian Yacht. Home: 6900 Via Alba Camarillo CA 93012-8279 Office: Patterson Ritner Lockwood Gartner & Jurich Ste 231 260 Maple Ct Ventura CA 93003

GARTZ, PAUL EBNER, systems engineer; b. Chgo., July 17, 1946; s. Friedrich Samuel and Lillian Louise (Koroschetz) G. BSEE, Ill. Inst. Tech., 1969; MSEE, Stanford U., 1970. Engring. co-op Western Electric, Chgo., 1965-69; mem. tech. staff Bell Telephone Labs., Whippany, N.J., 1969-74; sales mgr. Evelyn Wood Reading Dynamics, N.Y.C., 1975-78; owner Gartz Design, Montclair, N.J., 1976-79; mktg. rep. United Computing Systems, Seattle, 1979; sr. prin. engr. Boeing, Seattle, 1980—; bd. dirs. Walla Walla (Wash.) Coll. of Engring.; chmn. bd., pres. SDF, Inc., L.A.; educator Seattle U., 1987—, Walla Walla Coll., 1989, U. Wash., 1992—. Contbr. articles to profl. publs. Recipient Nat. Hist. Preservation award Nat. Hist. Preservation Soc., N.J., 1980. Fellow AIAA (assoc.); mem. IEEE (bd. govs. Aerospace Electronic Sys. Soc., Harry Rowe Mimno award 1987), Sys. Devel. Forum (bd. dirs. 1987—), Internat. Coun. Sys. Engring. (bd. dirs.), assoc. fellow, AIAA. Home: 9912 Arrowsmith Ave S Seattle WA 98118-5907 Office: The Boeing Co MS 05-KA PO Box3707 Seattle WA 98124-2207

GARVENS, ELLEN JO, art educator, artist; b. Omro, Wis., Aug. 15, 1955; d. Leonard Kenneth and Eugenia Mary (Wetter) G.; m. James Patrick Phalen, Oct. 18, 1988; 1 child, Cole Garvens Phalen. BS in Art, U. Wis., 1979; MA, U. N. Mex., 1982, MFA, 1987. Asst. prof. art Oberlin (Ohio) Coll., 1990-94, U. Wash., Seattle, 1994—. Artist: one person shows include: Jayne H. Baum Gallery, N.Y.C., 1986, 89, 93, Wooster (Ohio) Mus. of Art, U. R.I., Kingston. Recipient Wis. Women in Arts award Madison, 1978, Fullbright Hays scholarship Internat. Comm. Agy., Washington, 1979-80; grantee, NEA, Washington, 1986, HC Powers grant, Oberlin Coll., 1991, Royalty Rsch. Fund grant, U. Wash., 1996. Home: 19518 67th Ave Seattle WA 98155 Office: U Wash Sch of Art Box 353440 Seattle WA 98195-3440

GARVEY, DORIS BURMESTER, environmental administrator; b. N.Y.C., Oct. 3, 1936; d. William Henry and Florence Elizabeth (Sauerteig) Burmester; m. Gerald Thomas John Garvey, June 6, 1959; children: Deirdre Anne, Gerald Thomas John Jr., Victoria Elizabeth. BA with honors, Wilson Coll., 1958; MA with honors, Yale U., 1959. Rsch. assoc. Princeton U., N.J., 1967-76; environ. scientist Argonne (Ill.) Nat. Lab., 1976-84; staff mem. Los

Alamos (N.Mex.) Nat. Lab., 1984-86, regulatory compliance officer, 1986-89, sect. leader environ. protection group, 1989-92, dep. group leader, environ. protection group, 1992-94, leader sitewide Environ. Impact Statement project, 1994—. Contbr. articles to profl. jours. Bd. dirs. N.Mex. Repertory Theater, Santa Fe, 1987-88; mem. Environ. Improvement Bd., Glen Ellyn, Ill., 1980-82. Mem. AAUW, N.Mex. Hazardous Waste Soc., Women in Sci., Gov.'s Task Force Emergency Response, Nat. Assn. Environ. Profls., Phi Beta Kappa. Democratic. Roman Catholic. Home: 368 Calle Loma Norte Santa Fe NM 87501-1278 Office: Los Alamos Nat Lab PO Box 1663 MS M889 Los Alamos NM 87545

GARVEY, EVELYN JEWEL, retired mental health nurse; b. Carrizozo, N.Mex., Aug. 23, 1931; d. Everett E. and Jewel A. (Bullard) Bragg; m. Robert J. Garvey, July 10, 1949; children: Nancy, Annie, Catherine, Robert, Michael, Betty. AD, Ea. N.Mex. Coll., 1972. RN, N.Mex.; cert. EMT., N.Mex. Staff nurse N.Mex. Rehab. Ctr., Roswell, 1972; staff nurse Villa Solano State Sch., Roswell, 1972-79, DON, 1979-81; staff nurse Ft. Stanton (N.Mex.) Hosp., 1981-95, Sunset Villa Nursing Home, Roswell, N.Mex., 1995-96; ret., 1996.

GARVEY, JUSTINE SPRING, immunochemistry educator, biology educator; b. Wellsville, Ohio, Mar. 14, 1922; d. John Sherman and Lydia Kathryn (Johnsten) Spring; m. James Emmett Garvey, June 15, 1946; children: Johanna Xandra Kathryn, Michaela Garvey-Hayes. BS, Ohio State U., 1944, MS, 1948, PhD, 1950. Analytical chemist Sun Oil Refinery Lab., Toledo, 1944-46; Office of Naval Rsch. predoctoral fellow in microbiology U. Rochester, N.Y., 1946-47; AEC predoctoral fellow microbiology Ohio State U., Columbus, 1948-50; rsch. fellow chemistry Caltech, Pasadena, Calif., 1951-57, sr. rsch. fellow chemistry, 1957-73, rsch. assoc. chemistry, 1973-74; assoc. prof. biology Syracuse (N.Y.) U., 1974-78, prof. immunochemistry, 1978-89, emeritus, 1990—; vis. assoc. biology Caltech, 1990—; bd. sci. counselors Nat. Inst. Dental Rsch., NIH, Bethesda, Md., 1979-82; ad hoc study sects. NIH, Bethesda, 1979-88. Co-author: (textbook) Methods in Immunology, 1963, 2d edit., 1970, 3d edit., 1977; editl. bd. Immunochemistry Jour., 1964-71, Immunological Methods Jour., 1971-77; contbr. more than 125 articles to profl. jours. Grantee NIAID, 1951-72, NSF, 1977-79, Nat. Inst. on Aging, 1978-87, Nat. Inst. Environ. Health Scis., 1980-88. Mem. AAAS, Am. Assn. Immunologists, N.Y. Acad. Scis., Sigma Xi.

GARVEY, KELLY ANN, secondary education educator; b. Lakewood, Ohio, Jan. 23, 1970; d. Daniel Fueger and Darlene Marie (Slomshek) Gross; m. Travler Franklin Garvey, June 17, 1995. AA in Liberal Arts, West Valley Coll., Saratoga, Calif., 1990; BA in English, San Jose (Calif.) State U., 1992, Calif. state tchg. credential, 1994. Tchr. English Overfelt H.S., San Jose, 1994, Monta Vista H.S., Cupertino, Calif., 1994—. Mem. ASCD, Calif. Tchrs. Assn., Calif. Assn. Tchrs. English. Office: Monta Vista H S 21840 Mcclellan Rd Cupertino CA 95014-4055

GARVIN, PETER GRAHAM, golf industry executive, business educator; b. Buffalo, Mar. 21, 1954; s. Stanley John Garvin and Jane Oliver (Irwin) Wein; m. Linda Susan Ash, Aug. 19, 1978; children: Graham Pierson, Ashton Burns. AA, Paul Smiths Coll., 1974; BSBA, U. Denver, 1976, postgrad., 1978. Asst. treas. Security Pacific Mortgage, Denver, 1977-79; v.p. Mortgage Plus, Inc., Denver, 1979-81; regional v.p. Gill Mortgage Corp., Denver, 1981-84, Criterion Fin., Denver, 1984-85; pres. Fin. Netowrk Corp., Denver, 1985-89, Golf Enterprises, Inc., Denver, 1989-92; pres., Covin Golf LLC, 1995—; adj. prof. bus. U. Denver, Metro State Coll., Denver; adv. bd. com. chmn. Real Estate Sch. U. Denver, 1994-96; chmn. Bus. Econ. Awareness. Contbr. articles to newspapers. Com. chmn. Cub Scouts Am., Denver, 1995-96; mem. mktg. com. Denver Post Champions of Golf, Denver, 1981. Recipient Student award Student Cons. Assn., Washington, 1971. Mem. Mortgage Bankers Am. (mem. edn. com. 1981), Nat. Writers Assn., The CLub at Inverness, Los Verdes Golf Club. Republican. Presbyterian. Home: 8259 Arrowhead Way Littleton CO 80124 Office: Covin Golf LLC 8122 South Park Ln Ste 102 Littleton CO 80120

GARY, WALTER J(OSEPH), entomologist, educator; b. Flower Hill, N.Y., June 8, 1944; s. Walter J. and Mary E. G.; m. Margaret Frances, June 30, 1971; children: Ryan, Sean. BA, BS, Oreg. State U., 1968; MS, U. Nebr., 1973, PhD, 1978. Integrated pest mgmt. specialist U. Nebr., Lincoln, 1973-78; educator agriculture Wash. State U., Pullman, 1978—. Bd. dirs., pres. Walla Walla (Wash.) Valley Pioneer and Hist. Soc.; senator Wash. State U. Faculty Senate, Pullman; com. chair, mem. bd., dirs., Walla Walla Valley C. of C. With U.S. Army, 1968-70. Recipient Disting. Svc. award Nat. Assn. County Agrl. Agts., 1985. Mem. Entomol. Soc. of Am. (bd. cert.). Home: 834 Wauna Vista Dr Walla Walla WA 99362-4260

GARZA, DEBORAH JANE, bilingual education educator; b. L.A., July 25, 1952; d. Nicholas and Mary Jane (Hover) Maloof. AA in Gen. Edn., Rio Hondo Coll., 1973; BA in Sociology, Calif. State U., Fullerton, 1978; MS in Sch. Mgmt., U. La Verne, 1988. Calif. life teaching credential; bilingual cert. competence; cert. sch. adminstr.; profl. adminstr. svcs. credential. Bilingual classroom tchr. Norwalk (Calif.)-La Mirada Unified Sch. Dist., 1981-87, 89—, categorical aid program specialist, 1987-88; instrnl. specialist Whittier (Calif.) City Sch. Dist., 1987-88; master tchr. Norwalk (Calif.)-La Mirada Unified Sch. Dist., 1985-90, dist. mentor tchr., 1989-90, presenter/instr., 1991—; panel mem. ednl. tv. broadcast Schooling and Language Minority Students, 1990. Treas. Edmondson Sch. PTA, Norwalk, 1989-94, sec., 1994—. Recipient Merit Scholarship award U. of La Verne (Calif.) Faculty, 1991, Hon. Svc. award Edmondson Sch. PTA, Norwalk, 1992; named Tchr. of Yr., Edmondson Sch., 1990. Mem. Calif. Assn. for Bilingual Edn., Assn. Calif. Sch. Adminstrs., Norwalk-La Mirada Adminstrs. Assn.

GARZA, OSCAR, newspaper editor. Daily calendar editor-arts L.A. Times, Calif. Office: Los Angeles Times Times Mirror Sq Los Angeles CA 90053*

GASKILL, HERBERT LEO, accountant, engineer; b. Seattle, July 1, 1923; s. Leo Dell and Vesta Rathbone (Dahlen) G.; m. Margaret Helen Jenkins, Mar. 1, 1944 (div.); children—Margaret V., Herbert Leo; m. Opal Jordan, June 13, 1992; 1 child, Ann. B.S. and M.S. in Chem. Engring., U. Wash., 1949, M.B.A., 1976. C.P.A., Wash. Asst. prof. dental materials, exec. officer dept. dental materials Sch. Dentistry, U. Wash., 1950-56; ops. analyst The Boeing Co., Seattle, 1958-71, mktg. cons. govt. programs, 1972-74; pvt. practice acctg., Seattle, 1976-80; hazardous waste mgr. Boeing Co., Seattle, 1980-86, project mgr. Western Processing Remediation, 1986-95, ret. 1995. Active Seattle Art Mus., Pacific Northwest Aviation Hist. Found. Served to lt. (j.g.) USNR, 1941-46. TAPPI fellow, 1956; U. Wash. Engring. Expt. Sta. fellow, 1957. Mem. Wash. Soc. C.P.A.s. Contbr. articles to profl. jours. Home: 1236 NE 92nd St Seattle WA 98115-3135

GASPAR, ANNA LOUISE, retired elementary school teacher, consultant; b. Chgo., May 12, 1935; d. Miklos and Klotild (Weiss) G. BS in Edn., Northwestern U., 1957. Cert. elem. tchr., Calif. Tchr. 6th grade Pacific Palisades Elem. Sch., L.A., 1957-58; tchr. 1st grade Eastman Street Elem. Sch., L.A., 1959, Glassell Park, L.A., 1959-62, Stoner Ave. Elem. Sch., L.A., 1962-67; 2nd-4th grade tchr. Brentwood Elem. Sch., L.A., 1967-78; tchr. 4th and 5th grades Brockton Avenue Elem. Sch., L.A., 1978-90; vol., established Swakopmund Tchrs. Resource Ctr., Peace Corps, Namibia, 1991-93; tchr. English, Atlantic Sr. Primary Sch., Swakopmund, Namibia, 1992; career info. cons. Peace Corps., 1991—; substitute tchr. various schs., Las Vegas, 1994—. Mem. Hadassah, Bet Knesset Bamidbar, and numerous other cmty. clubs. Mem. Internat. Platform Assn., Calif. Ret. Tchrs. Assn., Northwestern U. Alumni Assn., Peace Corps, So. Nev. Peace Corps Assn. Democrat. Jewish. Home: 2700 Hope Forest Dr Las Vegas NV 89134-7322

GASPAR, MAX RAYMOND, surgeon; b. Sioux City, Iowa, May 10, 1915; s. Edgar Mathias and Mabel Agnes (Teefey) G.; m. Virginia Hunter, June 2, 1938 (div. Nov. 1968); children: Karen, Thomas, James, Susan, Mary Ann; m. Lia Sylvia Rista, Jan., 25, 1969. BA, Morningside Coll., 1936; BS, U. S.D., 1938; MD, U. So. Calif., 1941. Diplomate Am. Bd. Surgery, Am. Bd. Surgery with Spl. Competence in Vascular Surgery. Instr. in surgery U. So. Calif., L.A., 1947-48, Coll. Med. Evangelists, L.A., 1948-50, UCLA, 1950-53; asst. clin. prof. surgery Coll. Med. Evangelists, 1953-55, asst. prof. surgery, 1955-59; assoc. clin. prof. surgery Loma Linda U., 1959-63, clin. prof. surgery, 1963-66; clin. prof. surgery U. So. Calif., 1966-90, emeritus prof. surgery, 1990—; chief surgery L.A. County/UCLA Harbor Gen. Hosp., 1958; attending surgeon L.A. County/U. So. Calif. Gen. Hosp., 1955-91, consulting surgeon, 1991—; dir. vascular surgery Loma Linda U., 1956-66. Author: (textbook) Peripheral Arterial Disease, 1981; contbr. numerous articles to profl. jours. and chpts. to books. Dir. Cath. Welfare Bd., Long Beach, Calif., 1960-62, Am. Heart Assn., Long Beach, 1964-65, Am. Cancer Soc., Long Beach, 1967-70; trustee St. Mary's Found., Long Beach, 1985-94. Lt. USN, 1943-46. Recipient Alumnus of Yr. award U. So. Calif., 1979, Disting. Svc. medal L.A. County/U. So. Calif. Med. Ctr., 1983. Fellow Am. Coll. Surgeons; mem. Am. Surg. Assn., Soc. for Clin. Vascular Surgery (pres. 1979-81), Soc. Internat. de Chirurgie, Soc. for Vascular Surgery. Republican. Roman Catholic. Office: 1045 Atlantic Ave Ste 1008 Long Beach CA 90813

GASSER, CHARLES SCOTT, biologist, educator; b. Ft. Benning, Ga., July 26, 1955; s. James Charles and Martha Carson (Clark) G.; m. Judy Callis, Aug. 6, 1989; 1 child, Reta Catherine. BS, U. Calif., Davis, 1973; PhD, Stanford U., 1985. Sr. rsch. biologist Monsanto Co., St. Louis, 1985-89; prof. molecular and cellular biology U. Calif., Davis, 1989—. Recipient Presdl. Young Investigator award NSF, 1990. Office: U Calif Davis Sect Molecular Cell Biology Davis CA 95616

GASSMAN, VICTOR ALAN, cosmetics executive; b. St. Louis, Nov. 7, 1935; s. Samuel and Hilda (Scalla) G.; m. Betty Cohn, Dec. 24, 1961 (div. 1981); children: Susan L., James C.; m. Lynne Hobbs, Jan. 28, 1984; children: Michael S., Christopher S. BS, BA in Retailing, Washington U., 1957. Divisional sales mgr. Famous Barr, St. Louis, 1957-64; mdse. mgr. May Co., L.A., 1965-77; divisional mdse. mgr. J.W. Robinson, L.A., 1977-83; pres. DEPUTE-div. Dep. Corp., L.A., 1983-85, Liz Claiborne Cosmetics, N.Y.C., 1985-88, Victor Gassman & Assocs., N.Y.C., 1988-90; sr. v.p., gen. mgr. Visage Beaute' Cosmetics, Beverly Hills, Calif., 1990-91, sales, mktg. svcs. cons., 1991—. Actor in You Can't Take It With You, Hilton Head Cmty. Playhouse, 1990, The Boys Next Door, 1990, Broadway Bound, 1990; actor in Misbegotten Birthday, Murder Mystery Cruise, 1990, The Madwoman of Chaillot, Readers Theater, 1990, Americas Most Wanted, Fox-TV, 1990, Good Old Days on the Radio, Fine Arts Club, Pasadena, Calif., 1994. Dir. YMCA, Boy Scouts, United Fund, Redlands Art Assn., San Bernardino, 1965-71; v.p. Regional Econ. Devel. Coun., San Bernardino, 1970; pres. Arrowhead Allied Arts Coun., San Bernardino, 1969. Capt. U.S. Army, 1957-65. Recipient Buyer of the Yr. award May Co., 1973, Retailer of Yr. award Fragrance Found., 1982, Career Achievement award So. Calif. Cosmetic Assn., 1984, Best New Packaging / TV award Fragrance Found., 1987. Mem. Foragers Cosmetics Assn., Inland Ctr. Mchts. Assn. (pres. 1971), So. Calif. Cosmetics Assn. (bd. dirs. 1990-93), Beauty Industry West (bd. dirs. 1990—), Rotary Club. Democrat. Jewish.

GAST, NANCY LOU, chemical company executive; b. Appleton, Wis., Aug. 13, 1941; d. Harvey William Gast and June Louella (Mohr) Webster. Med. technologist Palo Alto/Stanford (Calif.) Hosp., 1963-65; med. technologist St. Vincent Hosp., Portland, Oreg., 1965-70, chemistry supr., 1970-81; tech. rep. DuPont-Diagnostic Systems, Claremont, Calif., 1981-83; sales rep. DuPont-Diagnostic Systems, Wilmington, Del., 1983-85; account rep. DuPont-Diagnostic Systems, Claremont, Calif., 1985-87, acct. mgr., 1987-96, exec. coun. med. products sales, 1995-96, territory mgr., 1996; account rep. Dade Internat., Inc., Deerfield, Ill., 1996—. Vol. med. technologist Health Help Ctr., Portland, 1984-88; bd. dirs. Assocs. ofSisters of Holy Names of Jesus and Mary, 1984-93, co-dir, 1994—. Mem. Am. Soc. Med. Technologists, Assn. Oreg. Med. Technologists (treas. 1976-78, chmn. sci. assembly for industry 1992-95), Am. Soc. Clin. Pathologists (cert. med. technologist assoc.). Republican. Roman Catholic. Office: Dade Internat Inc PO Box 778 Deerfield IL 60015-9831

GASTON, MARGARET ANNE, retired business educator; b. Regina, Sask., Can., Aug. 28, 1930; Came to U.S., 1948.; d. William Julius and Mary Josephine (Collins) Grogan; m. Robert F. Gaston, 1955 (dec. Mar. 1970); 1 child, Robert. BA in Bus. Edn., Cen. Wash. U., 1959; MEd, Western Wash. U., 1972; postgrad., Boston U., 1984. Cert. tchr. K-12, cert. vocat. tchr., Wash. Bus. educator Manson (Wash.) Sch. Dist., 1956-59; instr. K-12 Eastmont Sch. Dist., East Wenatchee, Wash., 1959-63; instr. Shoreline Community Coll., Seattle, 1969-70; instr., chmn. dept. bus. Skagit Valley Coll. Whipbey Campus, Oak Harbor, Wash., 1970-90; part-time instr. bus. edn. Wenatchee Valley Coll., 1959-65. Contbr. articles to profl. jours. Fellow Western Wash. U., Bellingham, 1968-69. Mem. AAUW, NEA, Wash. Edn. Assn., Bus. and Profl. Women, Delta Pi Epsilon, Beta Sigma Phi. Home: 118 S 12th St Mount Vernon WA 98274-4036

GASTON, RANDALL WALLACE, police chief; b. Lake Charles, La., Mar. 18, 1944; s. Wallace Howard and Mary Jean (Hubbs) G.; m. Linda Lou Lockwood; children: Debora Gaston Ricks, Aaron, Bryan, Allison. BS, Long Beach State Coll., 1971; MPA with honors, U. So. Calif., 1974; grad., FBI Nat. Acad., 1982. Police officer Anaheim (Calif.) Police Dept., 1965-69, police sgt., 1969-73, police lt., 1973-83, police capt., 1983-94, police chief, 1994—; instr. Orange County (Calif.) C.C.s, 1971-94. Mem. Internat. Police Chiefs Assn., Calif. Police Chiefs Assn., Orange County Police Chiefs Assn., FBI Nat. Acad. Assocs., Kiwanis Club of Greater Anaheim (bd. dirs. 1990-95), Phi Kappa Phi. Office: Anaheim Police Dept 425 S Harbor Blvd Anaheim CA 92805-3704

GATES, BRUCE CLARK, chemical engineer, educator; b. Richmond, Calif., July 5, 1940; s. George Laurence and Frances Genevieve (Wilson) G.; m. Jutta M. Reichert, July 17, 1967; children: Robert Clark, Andrea Margarete. BS, U. Calif., Berkeley, 1961; PhD in Chem. Engring., U. Wash., 1966. Rsch. engr. Chevron Rsch. Co., Richmond, Calif., 1967-69; from asst. prof. to assoc. prof. U. Del., Newark, 1969-77, prof. chem. engring., 1977-85, H. Rodney Sharp prof., 1985-92, assoc. dir. Ctr. Catalytic Sci. & Tech., 1977-81, dir. Catalytic Ctr. Sci. & Tech., 1981-88; prof. chem. engring. U. Calif., Davis, 1992—. Author: Catalytic Chemistry, 1992; co-author: Chemistry of Catalytic Processes, 1979; co-editor: Metal Clusters in Catalysis, 1986, Surface Organometallic Chemistry, 1988, Advances in Catalysis, 1996—. Fulbright Rsch. grantee Inst. Phys. Chemistry U. Munich, 1966-67, 75-76, 83-84, 90-91. Mem. AIChE (Alpha Chi Sigma award 1989, William H. Walker award 1995), Am. Chem. Soc. (Del. sect. award 1985, Petroleum Chemistry award 1993), Catalysis Soc. N.Am. (bd. dirs. 1997—). Office: U Calif Dept Chem Engring & Materials Sci Davis CA 95616

GATES, CHARLES CASSIUS, rubber company executive; b. Morrison, Colo., May 27, 1921; s. Charles Cassius and Hazel LaDora (Rhoads) G.; m. June Scowcroft Swaner, Nov. 26, 1943; children: Diane, John Swaner. Student, MIT, 1939-41; BS, Stanford U., 1943; DEng (hon.), Mich. Tech. U., 1975, Colo. Sch. of Mines, 1985. With Copolymer Corp., Baton Rouge, 1943-46; with Gates Rubber Co., Denver, 1946-96, v.p., 1951-58, exec. v.p., 1958-61, chmn. bd., 1961-96, CEO; chmn. bd. The Gates Corp., Denver, 1982-96, CEO, 1982-96, also bd. dirs.; pres. The Gates Corp., 1994-96; chmn. Cody Co., Denver, 1996—, Gates Capital Mgmt., LLC, Denver, 1996—; bd. dirs. Tejas Gas Corp.; pres. bd. trustees Gates Found.; chmn. Cody Co. Trustee Denver Mus. Natural History, Calif. Inst. Tech., Pasadena, Denver Art Mus. Found., Graland Country Day Sch. Found. Recipient Community Leadership and Service award Nat. Jewish Hosp., 1974; Mgmt. Man of Year award Nat. Mgmt. Assn., 1965; named March of Dimes Citizen of the West, 1987. Mem. Conf. Bd. (dir.), Conquistadores del Cielo, Denver Country Club, Outrigger Canoe Club, Waialae Country Club, Boone and Crockett Club, Club Ltd., Old Baldy Club, Country Club of Colo., Roundup Riders of Rockies, Shikar-Safari Internat., Augusta Nat. Golf Club, Castle Pines Golf Club, The Wigwam Club. Office: Cody Co Ste 680 3773 Cherry Creek North Dr Denver CO 80209

GATES, MELODI MOSLEY, software engineer; b. Dallas, Aug. 29, 1964; d. Dan Roland and Jaynet Marie (Simpson) Mosley; m. Cary L. Gates, Dec. 24, 1985. BS in Math. and Computer Sci., Calif. State U., Long Beach, 1986; MS in Computer Sci. and Engring., U. Colo., 1995. From maintenance programmer to devel. programmer/analyst CaseWare, Inc., Costa Mesa, Calif., 1986-88; staff programmer/analyst US West Knowledge Engring., Inc., Denver, 1988-89; sr. mem. tech. staff, software engr. and software architect US West Info. Techs. Enterprise Architecture Ctr., Denver, 1989—. Home: 750 S Sherman St Denver CO 80209-4037 Office: US West Techs 1475 Lawrence St Denver CO 80202-2219

GATES, MILO SEDGWICK, retired construction company executive; b. Omaha, Apr. 25, 1923; s. Milo Talmage and Virginia (Offutt) G.; m. Anne Phleger, Oct. 14, 1950 (dec. Apr. 1987); children: Elena Motlow, Susan Gates, Virginia Lewis, Anne Symington, Milo T.; m. Robin Templeton Quist, June 18, 1988; stepchildren: Robert L. Quist, Catherine Quist, Sarah Mazzocco. Student, Calif. Inst. Tech., 1943-44; B.S., Stanford U., 1944, MBA, 1948. With Swinerton & Walberg Co., San Francisco, 1955—, pres., 1976—, chmn., 1988-96; ret. Bd. dirs., trustee Children's Hosp. San Francisco; trustee Grace Cathedral, San Francisco; bd. dirs. Calif. Acad. Scis. Lt. (j.g.), USNR, 1944-46. Mem. Pacific-Union Club, Bohemian Club. Republican. Home: 7 Vineyard Hill Rd Woodside CA 94062-2531

GATES, SHELDON WILBUR, publishing executive; b. Benton Harbor, Mich., May 17, 1927; s. Charles Wilbur and Gertrude Caroline (McLane) G.; m. Betty Elaine Sauer, June 17, 1951; 1 child, Lori Kim. BS, U. Mich., 1951; MS, Ariz. State U., 1963. Radio engr. U. Mich., Ann Arbor, 1949-50; intelligence officer U.S. Govt., Washington, 1951-53; electronic engr. Motorola, Inc., Scottsdale, Ariz., 1955-60; pres., founder Jensen Tools & Alloys, Phoenix, 1964-73; cons. Phoenix, 1974-80; pub. McLane Publs., Scottsdale, 1985—. Patentee in field; contbr. articles to profl. jours.; author: (software) PC-Ratios, 1993, (book) 101 Business Ratios, 1993. With U.S. Mcht. Marines, 1945-46, PTO. Mem. Phoenix Direct Mktg. Club, Beta Gamma Sigma. Office: McLane Publs PO Box 9-c Scottsdale AZ 85252

GATES, THEODORE ALLAN, JR., software engineer; b. Washington, May 24, 1933; s. Theodore Allan and Margaret (Camp) G.;m. Anne Bissell, Sept. 8, 1955; children: Virginia Anne, Nancy Bissell, Theodore Allan III (dec.), Margaret Kenyon. Student, U. Md., 1951-53, 56-57, 68-69. Mem. staff Arthur D. Little Sys., Burlington, Mass., 1976-77, Corp. Tech. Planning, Portsmouth, N.H., 1977-78; project mgr. Honeywell Info. Sys., Phoenix, 1978-81; tech. mgr. Honeywell Info. Sys., Seattle, 1981-83; mgr. data and software engring. ISC Sys. Corp., Spokane, Wash., 1983-90; project mgr. Boeing Computer Svcs., Richland, Wash., 1990-96, The Boeing Co., Bellevue, Wash., 1996—. With U.S. Army, 1953-56, Korea. Recipient Superior Performance award Census Bur., 1958. Mem. IEEE, Assn. Computing Machinery, Air Force Assn., Navy League, U.S. Naval Inst., Gorilla Found., Smithsonian Assocs., Nature Conservancy, Commodores Club (Boston), Masons, Shrine. Lutheran. Home: 3203 168th Pl SE Bellevue WA 98008 Office: The Boeing Co m/s 7W-43 PO Box 3707 Seattle WA 98124-2207

GATES, WILLIAM HENRY, III, software company executive; b. Seattle, Wash, Oct. 28, 1955; s. William H. and Mary M. (Maxwell) G.; m. Melinda French, January 1, 1994. Grad. high sch., Seattle, 1973; student, Harvard U., 1975. With MITS, from 1975; founder, chmn. bd. Microsoft Corp., Redmond, Wash., 1976—, now also chief exec. officer. Author: The Future, 1994, The Road Ahead, 1996. Recipient Howard Vollum award, Reed Coll., Portland, Oreg., 1984, Nat. medal Tech. U.S. Dept. Commerce Tech. Adminstrn., 1992; named CEO of Yr., Chief Executive mag., 1994. Office: Microsoft Corp 1 Microsoft Way Redmond WA 98052-8300*

GATLIN, KAREN CHRISTENSEN, English language educator; b. Iowa City, Iowa, Feb. 18, 1943; d. Carl Archibald and Esther Agnes (Bradley) Christensen; m. John Charles Gatlin, Apr. 4, 1964 (div. Sept. 1976); children: Britt Jonene, Shawna Lynne. BS in Secondary Edn., N.E. Mo. State U., 1964; MA in Multicultural Edn., U. N.Mex., 1989. Cert. secondary English tchr., reading K-12, French. Tchr. 8th grade English Ernie Pyle Jr. H.S., Albuquerque, 1964-69; tchr. 7th grade English Truman Mid. Sch., Albuquerque, 1974-81; tchr. 6th/7th grade English and 8th grade French Madison Mid. Sch., Albuquerque, 1981-87; clin. supr. student tchg. U. N.Mex., Albuquerque, 1987-89; French instr. U. N.Mex. Continuing Edn., Albuquerque, 1988-93; tchr. English Sandia H.S., Albuquerque, 1989-96; mem. profl. stds. com. A.F.T.-APS, Albuquerque, 1989-90; mem. restructuring com. APS-Sandia H.S., Albuquerque, 1989-90; participant United World Coll. Restructuring Symposium, Las Vegas, 1990; tour leader, counselor E.F. Inst. for Cultural Exch., France, Gt. Britain and Germany, 1985, 90, 95, 96; guest spkr. multi-cultural tchr. edn. Auburn U., Montgomery, Ala., 1989. Mem. LWV, Albuquerque Tchrs. Fedn., Delta Kappa Gamma, Phi Delta Kappa, Kappa Delta Pi (v.p. 1964). Home: 1038 Claudine NE Albuquerque NM 87112

GAU, WAYNE WATSON, church abbot, educational consultant; b. Honolulu, Dec. 3, 1948; s. Gordon Stanley and Bessie Wo Hop Gau. AS in Police Sci., Honolulu C.C., 1970; BA in History, U. Hawaii, Manoa, 1970; MA, St. Patrick's Sem., Menlo Park, Calif., 1973, MDiv in Theology, 1974; STD, San Francisco Theological Seminary, San Anselmo, Calif., 1992. Ordained to Celtic Evang. ministry, 1979, ordained abbot, 1981. Religion tchr. Damien Meml. H.S., Honolulu, 1974-75; religion lectr. Chaminade U., Honolulu, 1975-78, Leeward C.C., Pearl City, Hawaii, 1977-79, Kapiolani C.C., Honolulu, 1979, Windward C.C., Kaneohe, Hawaii, 1982; rector St. Columba's Ch., Honolulu, 1979-88; presbyter-abbot Cmty. of St. Columba, Honolulu, 1981—; adminstr. gen. Celtic Evang. Ch., Honolulu, 1981—; human resources mgmt. instr. Pepperdine U., Pearl Harbor, Hawaii, 1978; night min. Hawaii Coun. of Chs., Honolulu, 1977-78, 79; sr. night min. Oahu Assn. Evangs., Honolulu, 1981-83; vicar-legate, dir. Cath. Apostolic Ch., Santa Ana, Calif., 1987—; owner-cons. Optimum Edn. and Promotion, Honolulu, 1987-94, 96—; coord. The Iona Inst. for Social Ethics Tng. and Personal Devel., 1994-96, rector, 1996—. Book reviewer Jour. of the Evang. Theol. Soc., 1987, 88, 89. Mem. Neighborhood Bd. for Diamond Head, Kapahulu, St. Louis Heights, Honolulu, 1987-90; dir. St. Louis Heights Cmty. Assn., Honolulu, 1988-90. Named Knight Assn. of St. George the Martyr, 1986, Comdr. Holy Orthodox Order of St. Gregory the Illuminator, 1986, Order of the Holy Cross of Jerusalem, 1987, Ordre Souverain des Chevaliers du Saint-Sepulcre Byzantin, 1987, Knight Most Vnerable and Holy Orthodox Order of St. Basil the Great, 1989. Mem. Honolulu Acad. of Arts, Henry Bradshaw Soc. (Eng.). Republican. Office: Celtic Evang Ch PO Box 90880 Honolulu HI 96835-0880

GAUFIN, SAMUEL OLIVER, lawyer; b. Boise, Idaho, July 14, 1954; s. David Marshall and Monica Jane (Oliver) G. m. Lynn Alison Gaufin, Mar. 22, 1986; children: Samuel O. II, Griffin Bingham. BS, Weber State U., 1975; JD, U. Utah, 1978. Bar: Utah, 1978, U.S. Ct. Appeals (10th cir.), 1979. From assoc. to ptnr. Van Cott Bagley, Cornwall & McCarthy, Salt Lake City, Utah, 1978-87; ptnr. Berman & O'Rorke, Salt Lake City, 1987-93, Berman, Gaufin & Tomsic, Salt Lake City, 1993-95, Berman, Gaufin, Tomsic & Savage, Salt Lake City, 1995—. Assoc. comment editor U. Utah Law Rev., 1972. Mem. Order of the Coif. Democrat. Congregationalist. Office: Berman Gaufin Tomsic & Savage 50 S Main St Ste 1250 Salt Lake City UT 84144-0103

GAULKE, MARY FLORENCE, library administrator; b. Johnson City, Tenn., Sept. 24, 1923; d. Gustus Thomas and Mary Belle (Bennett) Erickson; m. James Wymond Crowley, Dec. 1, 1939; 1 son, Grady Gaulke (name legally changed); m. 2d, Bud Gaulke, Sept. 1, 1945 (dec. Jan. 1978); m. 3d, Richard Lewis McNaughton, Mar. 21, 1983 (div. 1995). BS in Home Econs., Oreg. State U., 1963; MS in L.S., U. Oreg., 1968, PhD in Spl. Edn., 1970. Cert. std. pers. supr., std. handicapped learner, Oreg. Head dept. home econs. Riddle Sch. Dist. (Oreg.), 1963-66; libr. cons. Douglas County Intermediate Edn. Dist., Roseburg, Oreg., 1966-67; head resident, head counselor Prometheus Project, So. Oreg. Coll., Ashland, summers 1966-68; supr. librarians Medford Sch. Dist. (Oreg.), 1970-73; instr. in psychology So. Oreg. Coll., Ashland, 1970-73; libr. supr. Roseburg Sch. Dist., 1974-91; resident psychologist Black Oaks Boys Sch., Medford, 1970-75; mem. Oreg. Gov.'s Coun. Librs., 1979. Author: Vo-Ed Course for Junior High, 1965; Library Handbook, 1967; Instructions for Preparation of Cards For All Materials Cataloged for Libraries, 1971; Handbook for Training Library Aides, 1972. Coord. Laubach Lit. Workshops for H.S. Tutors, Medford, 1972. Fellow Internat. Biog. Assn. (life); mem. ALA, So. Oreg. Libr. Fedn. (sec. 1971-73), Oreg. Library Assn., Pacific N.W. Libr. Assn., Am. Biog. Inst. (lifetime dep. gov. 1987—), Internat. biog. Ctr. (hon., adv. coun. 1990), Delta Kappa Gamma (pres. 1980-82), Phi Delta Kappa (historian, research rep.). Democrat. Methodist. Clubs: Lodge: Order Eastern Star (worthy matron 1956-57). Home: 976 29th St Vero Beach FL 32960 Office: 119 Orchard Ln Ashland OR 97520

GAUSE, CHARLES MARVIN, artist; b. Yakima, Wash., June 20, 1955; s. Paul E. and Margaret J. (Lutz) G.; m. Joyce F. Hayes, Oct. 9, 1976; children: Jonathan, Christel, Charlene. Author: Alaskan Art of Charles Gause, 1991, 2d edit., 1996; one-man shows include Fine Arts Gallery, 1982, 86,; represented in permanent collections Arco and Sea-Land Corp. Ofcl. fund-raising print artist Iditarod Trail Com., Anchorage, 1988-97; ofcl. artist Anchorage Fur Rendezvous, 1991-94. Recipient first lady's vol. award State of Alaska, 1991.

GAWTHROP, DAPHNE WOOD, performing company executive. Exec. dir. Sacramento Ballet. Office: 1631 K St Sacramento CA 95814-4019

GAY, CHARLES W., JR., academic administrator; b. Tulsa, June 30, 1937; s. Charles W. Sr. and Juanita T. (Reeder) G.; m. Sarah E. Frost Smith, Sept. 8, 1953 (div. June 1967); children: Timothy L., Patrick N.; m. Louise M. Kiser, Dec. 22; stepchildren: Beth L., Richard E. Macatee. BS in Forest Mgmt., Okla. State U., 1962, MS in Range and Livestock Mgmt., 1964. Range rsch. asst. Santa Rita Explt. Range/U.S. Forest Svc., Tucson, Ariz., 1962; range mgmt. extension specialist to assoc. prof. N.Mex. State U., 1964-68, chief of party livestock devel. project in Paraguay, 1969-72; gen. mgr. agr. divsn. Collier Cobb and Assocs./Hudson Farms and Farm Svcs., Pike Road, Ala., 1973-79; v.p. Gay Sales and Svcs., Inc., Tulsa, 1979-83; assoc. chief of party, adj. prof. on range mgmt. project Utah State U., Rabat, Morocco, 1983-86; rsch. asst. prof. of range sci. Utah State U., Logan, 1986-87, acting dept. head range scie., 1987-88, asst. to dean for adminstrv. affairs, ext. program leader, 1989—; invited lectr. Bank of Am. Symposium, 1978, Global Natural Resources Monitoring and Assessments Conf., Venice, Italy, 1989, Icelandic Soil Conservation Svc., Iceland, 1989; invited vis. scientist N.W. Plateau Inst. of Biology, Haibei Alpine Rsch. Sta., China, 1992; co-chmn. U.S. Range Mgmt. Task Force/USDA and Mex.'s Dept. Agr. and Water Resources. Editorial bd., assoc. editor: Arid Soil Rsch. and Rehab. jour.; contbr. articles to profl. jours. Pres. bd. dirs. Nora Eccles Harrison Mus. Art, 1994-97; bd. dirs. USU Comty. Credit Union, 1991-97, Utah Festival Opera Co., 1995—; trustee, past dir. Devel. for the Logan Chamber Music Soc., 1988-89; chmn. joint com. for Mendon Ward, Boy Scouts Am., 1989-90; Dem. Party chmn., Mendon, 1990—; mem. Kiwanis Youth Devel. Com., Logan. Recipient Phillips Petroleum Grad. Rsch. scholarship, Ala. Coop. Extension Leadership award 1978, others. Mem. N.Y. Acad. Scis., Soc. Range Mgmt. (sec., chmn. internat. affairs com., others), Soc. Am. Foresters (chair range ecology work group), Am. Mgmt. Assn., Soc. Internat. Devel. (mentor), Utah Soc. Environ. Edn., Intermountain Assn. Environ. Edn. Office: Utah State Univ Coll Natural Resources Logan UT 84322

GAYDOS, GREGORY GEORGE, political scientist, educator; b. Marblehead, Ohio, July 17, 1941; s. George Joseph Gaydos and Dorothy Margaret (Vargosick) Saunders; m. Yoko Okuda, Feb. 14, 1977. BS in Edn., Bowling Green State U., 1963, MA in History, 1965; PhD in Polit. Sci., U. Hawaii, 1977. Rsch. asst. Agy. for Internat. Devel., Honolulu, 1968-69; assoc. prof. polit. sci. Hawaii Pacific U., Honolulu, 1970—; invited participant Hawaii Com. for Humanities, Honolulu, 1979, East-West Ctr. conf. on Asian classics curriculum, Honolulu, 1995, conf. on Confucianism and human rights, Honolulu, 1996. Contbr. articles to profl. jours. Active Mayor's Com. on Pub. TV, Honolulu, 1987—. 1st lt. U.S. Army, 1965-67. Recipient award for Best French Poem of Yr., Vers Jour., 1981, Most Disting. Screenplay, Hawaii Internat. Film Festival, 1983. Mem. Lanikai Lit. League, Hawaii Sociol. Assn. (invited panelist and presenter 1979), Am. Polit. Sci. Assn., Western Polit. Sci. Assn. (invited panelist and presenter 1994). Republican. Roman Catholic. Office: Hawaii Pacific U 1166 Fort Street Mall Honolulu HI 96813-2708

GAYTAN, KARL E., mayor. Mayor City of Colton, Calif. Office: 650 N LaCaldena Dr Colton CA 92324

GAZELL, JAMES ALBERT, public administration educator; b. Chgo., Mar. 17, 1942; s. Albert James and Ann Marion (Bloch) G. BA in Polit. Sci. with honors, Roosevelt U., 1963, MA in Polit. Sci., 1966; PhD in Govt., So. Ill. U., 1968. Instr. Roosevelt U., Chgo., 1965, 67, So. Ill. U., Carbondale, 1966-68; asst. prof. San Diego State U., 1968-72, assoc. prof., 1972-75, prof., 1975—; cons. County San Diego, 1973, Ernst and Ernst, Detroit, 1973. Contbr. articles to profl. jours. Mem. ACLU, Am. Soc. Pub. Adminstrn., Nat. Ctr. for State Cts., Nat. Assn. Ct. Mgmt., Western Govt. Rsch. Assn. Inst. for Ct. Mgmt. Home: 4319 Hilldale Rd San Diego CA 92116-2135 Office: San Diego State U 5402 College Ave San Diego CA 92115-2435

GAZLEY, JEF, psychotherapist; b. Phoenix, Aug. 13, 1951; s. Al and Barbara (Holmes) G.; m. Ilene Walrath, Aug. 7, 1977 (div. Jan. 1980). BA, U. Wash., 1975; MS in Counseling, U. Ore., 1980. Cert. counselor, Ariz. Intake worker Sacred Heart Hosp., Eugene, Ore., 1977-80; social worker Centro de Armistad, Guadalupe, Ariz., 1981-82; head chemical dependence, family svcs. social worker North Behavioral Health Ctr., Phoenix, 1982-86; psychotherapist Affiliated Psychotherapists, Tempe, Ariz., 1986—; mentor, tchr. Prescott (Ariz.) Coll., 1986—. Mem. AACD, NBCC, AAMFT, NACCMHC, AMHCA, Am. Soc. Clin. Hypnosis, Internat. Soc. Clin. Hypnosis, Am. Acad. Pain Mgmt. Office: Affiliated Psychotherapists 1270 E Broadway Rd Ste 208 Tempe AZ 85282-1515

GEARY, DAVID LESLIE, communications executive, educator, consultant; b. Connellsville, Pa., Sept. 30, 1947; s. Harry and Edith Marie (Halterman) G. BA, Otterbein Coll., 1969; MSJ, W.Va. U., 1971; postgrad., U. Denver, 1974-75; diploma, Def. Info. Sch., 1971, exec. communications curriculum, U. Okla., 1978, Def. Dept. Sr. Pub. Affairs Officers Course, 1984, Fgn. Svc. Inst., U.S. Dept. State, 1984, Nat. Def. U., 1986; postgrad., U. Sarasota, 1992—. Admissions counselor Otterbein Coll., 1968-69; instr. English, staff counselor Office of Student Ednl. Svcs. W.Va. U., Morgantown, 1969-71; dir. info. Luke AFB, Ariz., 1971-72; course dir. English and comm. U.S. Air Force Acad., Colo., 1972-76; dir. pub. affairs Loring AFB, Maine, 1976-79; spl. asst. pub. affairs Seymour Johnson AFB, N.C., 1980; dir. pub. affairs USAF Engring. and Svcs., Tyndall AFB, Fla., 1980-84, UN and US Air Forces, Korea, 1984-85; asst. prof., asst. dept. chmn., mem. coun. of assoc. and asst. deans U. Ala., 1985-88; dir., nat. cmty. rels. dir., acting dir. pub. affairs USAFR, 1988-92; prin. Leadership Comm. Counsel, 1992-95; comm. program mgr., dir. pub. affairs U.S. Dept. Energy, Albuquerque, 1995—; adj. prof. pub. rels. Ga. State U., Atlanta, 1993-95; guest lectr. U. Maine, 1976-79, USAF Inst. Tech., 1981-82, Fla. State U., 1982-83, U. Md., 1984-85, U.So. Calif., 1984-85, Seoul (Korea) Nat. U., 1985, U. Ala., 1988, Ga. State U., 1991, U. Ga., 1991. Contbr. articles to profl. jours.; mem. bd. profls. Pub. Rels. Rev.: A Jour. of Rsch. and Comment, 1996—; mem. editl. bd. Jour. of Employee Comm. Mgmt., 1996—. Decorated 4 U.S. Meritorious Svc. medals, 2 Air Force Commendation medals, Air Force Achievement medal, Armed Forces Res. medal, Humanitarian Svc. medal, 2 Nat. Def. Svc. medals, Pres.'s Extraodinary Svc. award Otterbein Coll., 1969, Hon. Citizen of Ariz. award, 1971, Mayor's Community Svc. medallion, Songtan, Korea, 1985, Nat. Disting. Svc. medal Arnold Air Soc., 1986, Nat. citation Angel Flight, 1986, George Washington Honor medal from Freedom's Found., 1988, Outstanding Faculty Advisor award U. Ala. Student Govt. Assn., 1988, Exemplary Svc. award Nat. Com. for Employer Support of Guard and Res., 1991, U.S. Dept. Energy Quality award, 1995, U.S. Dept. Energy Spl. Orgnl. Achievement Recognition, 1995, 96; Readers Digest Found. grantee, 1970. Mem. NATAS, VFW, Assn. for Edn. in Journalism and Mass Commn., Internat. Comm. Assn., Pub. Rels. Soc. Am., Internat. Assn. Bus. Communicators, SAR, Am. Legion, N.Mex. Pub. Affairs Roundtable (founding). Republican. Episcopalian. Office: Office Pub Affairs US Dept Energy PO Box 5400 Albuquerque NM 87185-5400

GEBB, SHELDON ALEXANDER, lawyer; b. Long Beach, Calif., Jan. 12, 1935. AB, U. Calif., Berkeley, 1957; LLB, U. Calif., 1963. Bar: Calif. 1964. Mng. ptnr. Baker & Hostetler, L.A., Long Beach, Silicon Valley, Calif. Chmn. bd. trustees Southwestern U. Sch. Law, 1985-91. Mem. ABA, State Bar Calif., Maritime Law Assn. U.S. Office: Baker & Hostetler 600 Wilshire Blvd Los Angeles CA 90017-3212

GEBBIA PINETTI, KAREN MARIE, lawyer, educator; b. Chgo., July 21, 1958; d. Stephen L. and Doris A. (Melendez) G. BA magna cum laude, Villanova U., 1980; JD cum laude, Georgetown U., 1983. Bar: Ill. 1983, Hawaii, 1995, U.S. Dist. Ct. (no. dist.) Ill. 1983, U.S. Ct. Appeals (7th cir.) 1985. With Nachman, Munitz & Sweig, Chgo., 1983-87, Winston & Strawn, Chgo., 1987-93; asst. prof. law U. Hawaii, Honolulu, 1993—. Contbr. numerous articles to profl. jours. Vol. N.W. Youth Outreach, Chgo., 1990-93, Lakeview Homeless Shelter, 1990-93, La Rabida Children's Hosp., 1991-93; mem. Chgo. Coun. on Fgn. Rels., People to People Internat.; mem. project adv. bd. World Without War Coun.-Midwest; mem. bd. dirs., 2d v.p. Hawaii Ctrs. for Ind. Living, 1995—, Hawaii Cath. Diocesan Women's Concerns Com., 1995—. Mem. ABA (bus. law sect., bus. bankruptcy com., comml. fin. svcs. com.), Ill. Bar Assn., Hawaii State Bar Assn., Seventh Cir. Bar Assn., Chgo. Bar Assn., Assn. Am. Law Schs. (consumer and comml. law sect., debtors' and creditors' rights sect.). Office: U Hawaii W S Richardson Sch Law 2515 Dole St Honolulu HI 96822-2328

GEBBIE, KRISTINE MOORE, health science educator, health official; b. Sioux City, Iowa, June 26, 1943; d. Thomas Carson and Gladys Irene (Stewart) Moore; m. Lester N. Wright; children: Anna, Sharon, Eric. BSN, St. Olaf Coll., 1965; MSN, UCLA, 1968; DPH U. Mich., 1995. Project dir. USPHS tng. grant, St. Louis, 1972-77; coord. nursing St. Louis U., 1974-76, asst. dir. nursing, 1976-78, clin. prof., 1977-78; adminstr. Oreg. Health Div., Portland, 1978-89; sec. Wash. State Dept. Health, Olympia, 1989-93; coord. Nat. AIDS Policy, Washington, 1993-94; asst. prof. Sch. Nursing Columbia U., 1994—; assoc. prof. Oreg. Health Scis. U. Portland, 1980—; chair, U.S. dept. energy secretarial panel on Evaluation of Epidemiologic Rsch. Activities, 1989-90; mem. Presdl. Commn. on Human Imunodeficiency Virus Epidemic, 1987-88. Author: (with Deloughery and Neuman) Consultation and Community Orgn., 1971, (with Deloughery) Political Dynamics: Impact on Nurses, 1975; (with Scheer) Creative Teaching in Clinical Nursing, 1976. Bd. dirs. Luth. Family Svcs. Oreg. and S.W. Wash., 1979-84; bd. dirs. Oreg. Psychoanalytic Found., 1983-87. Recipient Disting. Alumna award St. Olaf Coll., 1979; Disting. scholar Am. Nurses Found., 1989. Fellow Am. Acad. Nursing; mem. Assn. State & Territorial Health Ofcls., 1988 (pres. 1984-85, exec. com. 1980-87, McCormick award 1988), Am. Pub. Health Assn. (exec. bd.), Inst. Medicine, N.Am. Nursing Diagnosis Assn. (treas. 1983-87), Am. Soc. Pub. Adminstrn. (adminstrn. award II 1983). Office: Columbia U Sch Nursing 630 W 168th St New York NY 10032-3702

GEBHARD, BOB, professional baseball team executive. Gen. mgr. Colorado Rockies. Office: Colo Rockies 2001 Blake St Denver CO 80205-2008

GEBHART, JOHN E., III, health products company executive; b. 1954. BS in Acctg., Widener Coll., 1976; MBA, Pepperdine U., 1988. CPA. Svc. audit mgr. Arthur Young& Co., San Jose, Calif., 1976-83; dir. fin. and adminstrn. Catalytica, Inc., Mountain View, Calif., 1984-88; with Access Health Mktg., Inc., Rancho Cordova, Calif., 1989—; now sr. v.p. corp. devel. Office: Access Health Marketing Inc 11020 White Rock Rd Rancho Cordova CA 95670-6010*

GEDDIS, SCOTT WINFIELD, physical education educator; b. Columbus, Ohio, July 17, 1954; s. Malcolm Winfield and Mary Ellen (Causey) G.; m. Carol Willow Vosgler Williams, Aug. 4, 1978 (div. June 1985); 1 child, Dustin Scott. AAS, Phoenix Coll., 1984. Cert. ACLS, PALS instr., paramedic. Paramedic Rural Metro Fire Dept., Scottsdale, Ariz., 1974—; flight medic Survival Flight, Phoenix, 1980-84; mem. faculty Phoenix Coll., 1983—, athletic dir., 1996—; co-founder, dir. Basic Found., Phoenix, 1981—; state coord. Pre-Hosp. Trauma Life Support, Bridgeport, Conn., 1994—. Contbr. columns, mags. to Scholastic Coach, 1990-94. V.p. Cholla Little League, 1990-91, sec.-treas., 1991-92, pres., 1992-93. Recipient Sports Medicine award Ariz. Med. Assn., 1984. Office: Phoenix Coll 1202 W Thomas Phoenix AZ 85013

GEE, DEBBIE, ophthalmologic nurse; b. San Francisco, Apr. 11, 1962; d. Wee Ock and Suey Kim (Chin) G.; m. Welton Wong, June 29, 1986; children: Brian Matthew Wong, Andrew Ryan Wong. BSN, BA Health Edn., San Francisco State U., 1986. RN, Calif. From staff nurse ophthalmology to dir. ambulatory surg. svcs. Marshal Hale Meml. Hosp. then Calif. Pacific Med. Ctr., San Francisco, 1986—; developer ambulatory surgery ctrs. and programs, Calif. Pacific Med. Ctr., 1989—. Mem. Am. Soc. Ophthalmic RNs, Assn. Operating Room Nurses. Office: Calif Pacific Med Ctr 3700 California St San Francisco CA 94118-1618

GEE, GAVIN M., state government official. Dir. dept. finance State of Idaho, Boise. Office: 700 W State St 2d Fl Boise ID 83720-0031

GEE, MARGUERITE, nonprofit organization administrator; b. Houston, June 13, 1944; d. Yum and Mah (Shee) G.; m. James R. Royse, Nov. 4, 1995. BA in Journalism, U. Houston, 1968. Pub. rels./devel. dir. Coun. of Ind. Colls., Washington, 1976-78; editor Corp. for Pub. Broadcasting, Washington, 1979-80; cons. MG Cons., Washington, 1980-85; devel. dir. Comty. Adult Health Svcs., Oakland, Calif., 1986-89; asst. v.p. United Way, San Francisco, 1992-93; exec. dir. Mission Reading Clinic, San Francisco, 1993—; cons. MG Cons., San Francisco, 1990-92; mem. adv. com. Women's Econ. Agenda Project, Oakland, 1985-89; co-founder, bd. dirs. Nat. Inst. for Women of Color, Washington, 1981-91. V.p. Centro del Pueblo, San Francisco, 1993—; treas. Mission Army Found., San Francisco, 1993—; mem. steering com. Comty. Devel. Coalition, San Francisco, 1995—. Mem. Asian Ams./Pacific Islanders in Philanthropy, Devel. Execs. Roundtable. Home: 1946 Marin Ave Berkeley CA 94707-2442

GEE, ROGER ALLAN, accounting educator, writer; b. Ithaca, N.Y., May 9, 1941; s. Charles F. and Helen Elenore (Knuutila) G.; m. Linda Dorman Campbell, June 11, 1966; children: Jennifer Anne, John Allan. BS in Acctg., Ithaca Coll., 1964; MS in Taxation, Nat. U., 1990. CPA, Calif. Staff acct. Touche, Ross & Co., CPAs, San Diego, 1969-71; owner Roger A. Gee, CPA, San Diego, 1971-89; prof. acctg. San Diego Mesa Coll., 1986—; mem. dist. acctg. adv. com. San Diego C.C., 1986—. Author: Computer Accounting Applications Using Microsoft Excel with a Mouse, 1993, Computer Accounting Applications Using Lotus 1-2-3, 1993; Computer Accounting Applications Using BusinessWorks 10.0, 1995. Lt. (j.g.) USN, 1964-67. Mem. AICPA, Am. Acctg. Assn., Calif. Soc. CPAs, Kiwanis (disting. club pres. Scripps-Mira Mesa chpt. 1984). Office: San Diego Mesa Coll 7250 Mesa College Dr San Diego CA 92111-4902

GEFFEN, DAVID, recording company executive, producer; b. Bklyn., Feb. 21, 1943; s. Abraham and Batya (Volovskaya) Geffen. U of Texas, Austin, Brooklyn Coll. of CUNY. Agt. with William Morris, N.Y.C., 1964-68; agt. with Ashley Famous, 1968; exec. V.P. and agent Creative Management Associates, 1969; founder (with Laura Nyro) and pres. Tuna Fish publishing co.; pres. Asylum Records, 1970-73, Geffen-Roberts, Inc., 1970-71, Elektra-Asylum Records, 1973-76; founder and pres. Geffen Records, L.A., 1980—; vice-pres. Warner Bros. Pictures, 1975; now chmn. Geffen Records, L.A.; head Geffen Film Co.; vice-chmn. Warner Brothers Pictures, 1974; exec. asst. to chmn. Warner Communications, 1977; co-founder Dreamworks SKG, Universal City, 1995—; mem. music faculty Yale U., 1978; apptd. Regent U. Calif., Gov. Calif., 1980-87. Producer films including After Hours, Lost in America, Personal Best, 1982, Risky Business, 1983, Lost in America, 1985, Little Shop of Horrors, 1986, Social Security, 1986, Beetlejuice, 1988, Men Don't Leave, 1990; co-producer Master Harold...and the Boys, 1982, Cats, 1982, Good, 1982, Dreamgirls, 1983, Madam Butterfly, 1988 (9 Tony award, Best Play); musical Miss Saigon. Bd. dirs. Los Angeles County Art Mus. Office: Dreamworks SKG Bldg 10 Plz 100 Universal Terrace Pkwy Universal City CA 91608*

GEFFNER, DAVID LEWIS, endocrinologist; b. New York, Mar. 21, 1942; s. Samuel Benjamin and Jeanne (Domb) G.; m. Patricia June Fisher, June 7, 1970; 1 child, Laura Simpson. BA cum laude, NYU, 1962; MD, Georgetown U., 1967. Diplomate Am. Bd. Internal Medicine, Am. Bd. Endocrinology and Metabolism, Am. Bd. Quality Assurance and Utilization Physicians, Nat. Bd. Med. Examiners. Intern in medicine VA Hosp., Bklyn., 1967-68; resident Cornell Cooperating Hosps. Staff Tng. Program, N.Y.C., 1968-71; rsch. fellow in endocrinology N.Y. Hosp., N.Y.C., 1971-72; fellow in endocrinology UCLA Wadsworth VA Hosp., L.A., 1972-73, acting asst. chief endocrinology, 1973-74; dept. head endocrinology and metabolism Friendly Hills Healthcare Network/Cigna Med. Group Calif., L.A., 1974-96; rsch. asst. Sloan-Kettering Inst. Meml. Hosp. for Cancer and Allied Diseases, 1963, chief biology group, epidemiology sect., 1965, clin. attending, admitting and diagnostic svc., 1971-72; clin. fellow in medicine Cornell U. Med. Coll., 1969-72; asst. prof. UCLA Sch. Medicine, 1973-74, asst. clin. prof., 1974-81, assoc. clin. prof., 1981-90, clin. prof., 1990—; Cigna (Ross Loos) INA plans, numerous coms., 1974-96 including chmn. Instn. Rev. Bd., 1990, Health Care Assessment Com., 1981-84; vice chair med. quality rev. com. Med. Bd. Calif., 1986-93. Contbr. articles to profl. jours., chpts. to books, abstracts and exhibits to profl. confs.; invited speaker nat. meetings. Bd. dirs. L.A. chpt. Am. Diabetes Assn., chmn. profl. edn. com. Calif. affiliate, pres.-elect, 1995-96, pres., 1996—; dir. Diabetes Care, Med Ptnrs. West, 1997—. Fellow ACP, Am. Coll. Med. Quality (adv. ethics and policy com. 1991), Am. Assn. Clin. Endocrinology; mem. Am. Coll. Nuclear Medicine, Am. Assn. Clin. Endocrinologists, Endocrine Soc., L.A. County Med. Soc. (com. on patient and physician advocacy, med. staff affairs 1991-93, membership retention 1992-93), Soc. Nuclear Medicine, Calif. Med. Assn. (med. staff survey com. 1991—), Thyroid Found. Am., Human Growth Found., L.A. Clin. Endocrine Rsch. Group (bd. dirs. 1983-86), Crosstown Endocrine Club, Assn. Mil. Surgeons U.S., Phi Delta Epsilon. Office: 1711 W Temple St Los Angeles CA 90026-5446

GEHB, MICHAEL, public relations executive. CFO Copithorne & Bellows, San Francisco. Office: Copithorne & Bellows 100 1st St Ste 2600 San Francisco CA 94105-2637*

GEHRES, JAMES, lawyer; b. Akron, Ohio, July 19, 1932; s. Edwin Jacob and Cleora Mary (Yoakam) G.; m. Eleanor Agnew Mount, July 23, 1960. B.S. in Acctg., U. Utah, 1954; M.B.A., U. Calif.-Berkeley, 1959; J.D., U. Denver, 1970, LL.M. in Taxation, 1977. Bar: Colo. 1970, U.S. Dist. Ct. Colo. 1970, U.S. Tax Ct. 1970, U.S. Supreme Ct. 1973, U.S. Ct. Appeals (10th cir.) 1978, U.S. Ct. Claims 1992. Atty. IRS, Denver, 1965-80, atty. chief counsel's office, 1980—. Served with USAF, 1955-58, capt. Res. ret. Mem. ABA, Colo. Bar Assn., Am. Inst. C.P.A.s, Colo. Soc. C.P.A.s, Am. Assn. Atty.-C.P.A.s, Am. Judicature Soc., Am. Acctg. Assn., Order St. Ives, The Explorers Club, Am. Alpine Club, Colo. Mountain Club (bd. dirs.), Colo. Mountain Club Found. (bd. dirs.), Beta Gamma Sigma, Beta Alpha Psi. Democrat. Contbr. articles to profl. jours. Office: 935 Pennsylvania St Denver CO 80203-3145

GEHRING, GEORGE JOSEPH, JR., dentist; b. Kenosha, Wis., May 24, 1931; s. George J. and Lucille (Martin) G.; m. Ann D. Carrigan, Aug. 2, 1982; children: Michael, Scott. DDS, Marquette U., 1955. Pvt. practice dentistry, Long Beach, Calif., 1958—. Author: The Happy Flosser. Chmn. bd. Long Beach affiliate Calif. Heart Assn.; mem. Long Beach Grand Prix com. of 300; ind. candidate for pres. of the U.S., 1988, 92. Served with USNR, 1955-58. Fellow Internat. Coll. of Denists, Am. Coll. Dentists; mem. Harbor Dental Soc. (dir.), Pierre Fauchard Acad., Delta Sigma Delta. Club: Rotary. Home: 1230 E Ocean Blvd Unit 603 Long Beach CA 90802-6908 Office: 532 E 29th St Long Beach CA 90806-1617

GEHRKE, ROBERT JAMES, physicist; b. Chgo., Nov. 20, 1940; s.Wilhelm August and Gertrude Mary (Kraemer) G.; m. Mary Louise Irwin, Oct. 12, 1963; children: Marie Therese, Julie Christine, Karen Maureen. BS, DePaul U., Chgo., 1962; MS, U. Nev., Reno, 1966. Physicist Phillips Petroleum Co., Idaho Falls, Idaho, 1965-66; sr. physicist Idaho Nuclear Corp., Idaho Falls, 1966-71; assoc. scientist Aerojet Nuclear Corp., Idaho Falls, 1971-76; sci. specialist EG&G Idaho Inc., Idaho Falls, 1976-85, unit mgr., 1985-91, sci. specialist, 1991-94; sci. specialist Lockheed Martin Idaho Techs. Co., Idaho Falls, 1994-95, cons. scientist, 1995—; instr. U. Idaho Ext., Idaho Falls, 1977—; project leader Am. Nat. Stds. Inst.; IAEA expert assignment to Korea Rsch. Inst. of Standards and Science Republic of Korea, 1992. Editorial rev. bd. Radioactivity and Radiochemistry Jour., 1990—; reviewer Analytical Chemistry, 1990, Jour. of Applied Radiation and Isotopes, 1988—; contbr. articles to profl. jours. Pres. Bonneville Assn. for Retarded Citizens, Idaho Falls, 1969-70, Idaho Assn. for Retarded Citizens, Boise, 1970-71. Named Disting. Alumnus, U. Nev.-Reno, 1977; recipient UR & D 100 award "Pins Chem. Assay System", 1992. Mem. Am. Nuclear Soc. (sec. environ. scis. divsn. 1990-95, treas. 1993-94, newsletter editor 1990-93, treas. isotope and radiation divsn. 1993-94, chair 1995-96, vice chair/chair elect 1994-95, nuclear data chmn. 1989-92, chmn. ANS-41 Stds. Subcom. on Environ. Remediation of Radioactively Contaminated Sites 1992-97), Am. Chem. Soc., Health Physics Soc., Am. Nat. Stds. Inst. Roman Catholic. Office: Lockheed Martin Idaho Techs PO Box 1625 Idaho Falls ID 83415-2114

GEHRY, FRANK OWEN, architect; b. Toronto, Ont., Can., Feb. 29, 1929; came to U.S., 1947; s. Irving and Thelma (Caplan) G.; children—Leslie, Brina; m. Berta Aguilera, Sept. 11, 1975; children—Alejandro, Samuel. B. in Architecture, U. So. Calif., 1954; postgrad., Harvard U., 1956-57. Registered profl. architect, Calif. Designer Victor Gruen Assn., Los Angeles, 1953-54, planning, design and project dir., 1958-61; project designer, planner Pereira & Luckman, Los Angeles, 1957-58; prin. Frank O. Gehry & Assocs., Venice, Calif., 1962—. Architect Loyola Law Sch., L.A., 1978-92, Mus. Contemporary Art, L.A., 1983, Calif. Aerospace Mus., L.A., 1984, Frances Goldwyn Regional Br. Libr., Hollywood, Calif., 1986, U.C.I. Info. and Computer Sci./Engring. Rsch. Lab. and Engring. Ctr., Irvine, Calif., 1986-88, Vitra Internat. Mfg. Facility and Design Mus., Weil am Rhein, Germany, 1989, Chiat/Day Hdqs., Venice, Calif., 1991, Am. Ctr., Paris, 1992, Advanced Tech. Labs. Bldg., Iowa City, 1992, U. Toledo Ctr. for Visual Arts, 1992, Wald Disney Concert Hall, L.A., Frederick R. Weisman Art Mus., Mpls., 1993, Vitra Internat. Hdqs., Basel, Switzerland, 1994, Disney Ice, Anaheim, Calif., 1995, EMR Communication and Tech. Ctr., Bad Geynhausen, Germany, 1995, Team Disneyland Adminstrn. Bldg., Anaheim, 1996, ING Office Bldg., Prague, Czech Republic, 1996, Guggenheim Mus., Bilbao, Spain, 1997. Trustee Hereditary Disease Found., Santa Monica, Calif., 1970—. Recipient Arnold W. Brunner Meml. prize in architecture, 1983, Eliot Noyes Design chair Harvard U., 1983, Charlotte Davenport Professorship in architecture Yale U., 1982, 85, 87-89, Pritzker Architecture prize, 1989, Wolf prize in art, 1992, Praemium Imperiale, 1992, Dorothy and Lilian Gish award, 1994. Office: Frank O Gehry & Assocs 1520B Cloverfield Blvd Santa Monica CA 90404-3502*

GEIDUSCHEK, JEREMY MARK, pediatric anesthesiologist; b. Ann Arbor, Mich., Jan. 8, 1958; s. E. Peter and Joyce Barbara (Brous) G.; m. Susan Elaine Thompson, Mar. 26, 1988; children: A. Max, Emma Kate. BS in Biology, Stanford U., 1979; MD, Vanderbilt U., 1983. Diplomate Nat. Bd. Med. Examiners, Am. Bd. Pediatrics, Am. Bd. Anesthesiology. Resident in pediatrics U. Wash., Seattle, 1983-86, resident in anesthesiology, 1986-89, acting asst. prof., dept. of anesthesiology, 1989-92, asst. prof., 1992—; fellow, pediatric anesthesiology Children's Hosp. & Med. Ctr., Seattle, 1988-89, attending physician dept. anesthesia and critical care, 1989—. Contbr. articles to profl. jours.; author: chpt. in books: Risk and Outcome in Anesthesia, Pediatric Anesthesia, 1992, 2d edit. 1994. Mem. Am. Soc. Anesthesiologists, Wash. State Soc. Anesthesiologists, Soc. for Pediatric Anesthesiology, Am. Acad. Pediatrics, Wash. State Med. Soc. Office: Childrens Hosp & Med Ctr 4800 Sand Point Way NE Seattle WA 98105-3901

GEIS, JOHN RICHARD, plastic surgeon; b. Denver, Mar. 18, 1929; s. Eugene Edward and Patricia Lillian (McGowan) G.; m. Joyclyn Jamie Imperatrice, Sept. 30, 1979; 1 child, Paula Marie Long. BA, UCLA, 1951; MS, U. Denver, 1952; MD, Northwestern U., Chgo., 1956. Diplomate Am. Bd. Plastic Surgery. Asst. prof. surgery U. Calif., San Francisco, 1984—; med. cons. Med. Bd. of Calif., Fresno, 1994-95. Capt. USAF, 1958-60. Fellow ACS; mem. Am. Soc. Plastic and Reconstructive Surgery.

GEISEL, HENRY JULES, lawyer; b. Cin., Oct. 3, 1947; s. Albert and Else Geisel; m. Ellyn Anne Levy, Sept. 1, 1975; children: Noah L., Gideon L. BS in Econs., U. Pa., 1969; JD, U. Cin., 1972. Bar: Colo. 1972, U.S. Dist. Ct. Colo. 1972. Dep. dist. atty. 20th Jud. Dist., Boulder, Colo., 1973-74, 10th Jud. Dist., Pueblo, Colo., 1974-76; assoc. John R. Naylor, Pueblo, 1976-82, Naylor & Geisel P.C., Pueblo, 1982—. Pres. Temple Emanuel, Pueblo, 1981-82, 85-88; bd. dirs. Pueblo Youth Svcs. Bur., 1978-93, sec., 1989-93; bd. dirs. Pueblo Intensive Phonics Literacy Ctr., Inc., 1989-96, Parkview Hosp. Found., Pueblo, 1986-93, chmn., 1988. Mem. ABA, Colo. Bar Assn., Pueblo County Bar Assn., Colo. Trial Lawyers Assn. Clubs: Pueblo Country. Office: Naylor & Geisel PC 1123 N Elizabeth St Pueblo CO 81003-2233

GEISER, THOMAS CHRISTOPHER, lawyer; b. Bern, Switzerland, Aug. 13, 1950; came to U.S., 1952; s. Henry Abraham and Pia Margaret (Tschudin) G.; m. Catherine Barlow Yeakle, Oct. 20, 1973 (div. Mar. 1983); m. Donna Lea Schweers, Jan. 3, 1987; 1 child, Kelsey Schweers. BA, U. Redlands, Calif., 1972; JD, U. Calif., San Francisco, 1977. Bar: Calif. 1978. Atty. Internat. Bur. Fiscal Documentation, Amsterdam, The Netherlands, 1977-78; assoc., ptnr. Hanson, Bridgett, Marcus, Vlahos & Stromberg, San Francisco, 1979-85; ptnr. Epstein, Becker, Stromberg & Green, San Francisco, 1985-90, Brobeck, Phleger & Harrison, San Francisco, 1990-93; sr. v.p., gen. counsel, sec. WellPoint Health Networks Inc., Woodland Hills, Calif., 1993-96, exec. v.p., gen. counsel, sec., 1996—. Mem. Nat. Health Lawyers Assn., Calif. Soc. Health Care Attys., Order of Coif. Office: WellPoint Health Networks Inc 21555 Oxnard St Woodland Hills CA 91367

GEISERT, OTTO, food products executive; b. 1928. Various positions Balcom & Moe Inc., Pasco, Wash., 1958—, now pres. *

GEISINGER, PAMELA SUSAN, editor; b. New London, Conn., Feb. 28, 1968; d. James Gary and Nancy Sue (Neece) G. BA, St. Olaf Coll., 1990; M of Journalism, Northwestern U., 1992. Reporter Albert Lea Tribune, Minn., 1990-91; reporter, copy editor The World Newspaper, Coos Bay, Oreg., 1992-94; copy editor, wire editor The Columbian, Vancouver, Wash., 1994—. Methodist. Office: The Columbian 701 W 8th St Vancouver WA 98660-3008

GEISSERT, KATY, mayor; b. Wash., 1926; m. Bill Geissert; children: Bill Jr., Jack, Holly, Doug, Ann. BA in Journalism, Stanford U., 1948. Mem. Torrance (Calif.) City Council, 1974-86; mayor City of Torrance, 1986—; mem. Gov.'s Infrastructure Rev. Task Force, Calif. Past chmn. Torrance Park & Recreation Commn.; past mem. fin. adv. com. Torrance Sch.; past chmn. adv. bd. Calif. State U., Dominguez Hills, Torrance Salvation Army; mem. bond steering com. Torrance Library, 1967; chmn. local park bond issue steering com., 1971, Los Angeles County Sanitation Dist. Bd.; community cons. South Bay Harbor Vol. Bur.; mem. adv. bd. Torrance YWCA; bd. dirs. Switzer Ctr., region III United Way, Torrance LWV; mem. city selection com. Los Angeles County. Recipient PTA Hon. Service award, Woman of Distinction award Soroptimists, Community Service award Riviera Homeowners Assn., spl. citation Nat. Recreation & Park Assn.; named Disting. Citizen of Yr. Torrance Area C. of C., 1973, Woman of Yr. YWCA, Woman of Achievement award Redondo Marina Bus. & Profl. Women's Club. Mem. U.S. Conf. Mayors, League Calif. Cities (del., cities transp. com.), Calif. Elected Women's Assn. (bd. dirs.). Office: City of Torrance Office of Mayor 3031 Torrance Blvd Torrance CA 90503-5015*

GEIST, HOWARD J., orthopedic surgeon; b. Madison, Wis., Aug. 13, 1929; s. Frederick D. and Alice M. (Stewart) G.; m. Sally R. Haase, Dec. 21, 1956; children: Dennis, Alan, Richard, Gary. BA, Dartmouth Coll., 1952; MD, Harvard U., 1955. Intern, asst. resident in surgery Barnes Hosp., St. Louis, 1955-57; resident in orthopedic surgery U. Hosps. Cleve., 1960-63; pvt. practice, Portland, Oreg., 1964—. Capt. M.C., USAF, 1957-60. Fellow Am. Acad. Orthopedic Surgeons. Home and Office: 1425 SW Upland Dr Portland OR 97221-2648

GEIST, KARIN RUTH TAMMEUS MCPHAIL, secondary education educator, realtor, musician; b. Urbana, Ill., Nov. 23, 1938; d. Wilber Harold and Bertha Amanda Sofia (Helander) Tammeus; m. David Pendleton McPhail, Sept. 7, 1958 (div. 1972); children: Julia Elizabeth, Mark Andrew; m. John Charles Geist, June 4, 1989 (div. 1995). BS, Juilliard Sch. Music, 1962; postgrad., Stanford U., 1983-84, L'Academia, Florence and Pistoia, Italy, 1984-85, Calif. State U., 1986-87, U. Calif., Berkeley, 1991, 92. Cert. tchr., Calif.; lic. real estate agt., Calif. Tchr. Woodstock Sch., Musoorie, India, 1957, Canadian, Tex., 1962-66; tchr. Head Royce Sch., Oakland, Calif., 1975-79, 87—, Sleepy Hollow Sch., Orinda, Calif., 1985—; realtor Freeholders, Berkeley, Calif., 1971-85, Northbrae, Berkeley, Calif., 1985-92, Templeton Co., Berkeley, 1992—; organist Kellogg Meml., Musoorie, 1956-57, Mills Coll. Chapel, Oakland, 1972—; cashier Trinity U., San Antonio, 1957-58; cen. records sec. Riverside Ch., N.Y.C., 1958-60; sec. Dr. Rollo May, N.Y.C., 1959-62, United Presbyn. Nat. Missions, N.Y.C., 1960, United Presbyn. Ecumenical Mission, N.Y.C., 1961, Nat. Coun. Chs., N.Y.C., 1962; choral dir. First Presbyn. Ch., Canadian, Tex., 1962-66; assoc. in music Montclair Presbyn. Ch., Oakland, 1972-88; site coord., artist, collaborator Calif. Arts Coun. Artist; cons. music edn. videos and CD Roms Clearvue EAV, Chgo., 1993—. Artist: produced and performed major choral and orchestral works, 1972-88; prodr. Paradiso, Kronos Quartet, 1985, Magdalena, 1991, 92, Children's Quest, 1993—. Grantee Orinda Union Sch. Dist., 1988. Mem. Berkeley Bd. Realtors, East Bay Regional Multiple Listing Svc., Calif. Tchrs. Assn., Commonwealth Club (San Francisco). Democrat. Home: 7360 Claremont Ave Berkeley CA 94705-1429 Office: Templeton Co 3070 Claremont Ave Berkeley CA 94705-2630

GELBER, DON JEFFREY, lawyer; b. L.A., Mar. 10, 1940; s. Oscar and Betty Sheila (Chernitsky) G.; m. Jessica Jeasun Song, May 15, 1967; children: Victoria, Jonathan, Rebecca, Robert. Student UCLA, 1957-58, Reed Coll., 1958-59; AB, Stanford U., 1961, JD, 1963. Bar: Calif. 1964, Hawaii 1964, U.S. Dist. Ct. (cen. and no. dists. Calif.) 1964, U.S. Dist. Ct. Hawaii 1964, U.S. Ct. Appeals (9th cir.) 1964, U.S. Supreme Ct. 1991. Assoc. Greenstein, Yamane & Cowan, Honolulu, 1964-67; reporter Penal Law Revision Project, Hawaii Jud. Council, Honolulu, 1967-69; assoc. H. William Burgess, Honolulu, 1969-72; ptnr. Burgess & Gelber, Honolulu, 1972-73; prin. Law Offices of Don Jeffrey Gelber, Honolulu, 1974-77; pres. Gelber & Wagner, Honolulu, 1978-83, Gelber & Gelber, Honolulu, 1984-89, Gelber, Gelber, Ingersoll, Klevansky & Faris, Honolulu, 1990—; legal counsel Hawaii State Senate Judiciary Com., 1965; adminstrv. asst. to majority floor leader Hawaii State Senate, 1966, legal csl. Edn. Com., 1967, 68; majority counsel Hawaii Ho. of Reps., 1974; spl. counsel Hawaii State Senate, 1983. Contbr. articles to legal publs. Mem. State Bar Calif., ABA (sect. bus. law), Am. Bankruptcy Inst., Hawaii State Bar Assn. (sect. bankruptcy law, bd. dirs. 1991-93, pres. 1993). Clubs: Pacific, Plaza (Honolulu). Office: Gelber Gelber Ingersoll Klevansky & Faris 745 Fort Street Mall Ste 1400 Honolulu HI 96813-3812

GELFAND, ERWIN WILLIAM, immunologist; b. Montreal, Que., Can., Mar. 10, 1941; s. Samuel and Sylvia (Nadler) G.; m. Adele Zilbert, June 22, 1967; children: Lauren, Allison. BS, McGill U., Montreal, 1962, MD, 1966. Diplomate Am. Bd. Pediat. Rotating intern Montreal Gen. Hosp., 1966-67; jr. asst. resident Montreal Children's Hosp., 1967-68; sr. resident Children's Hosp. Med. Ctr., Boston, 1968-69; head divsn. immunology, rheumatology Hosp. for Sick Children, Toronto, Quebec, Can., 1979-87; chmn. Nat. Jewish Med. and Rsch. Ctr., Denver, 1987—. Contbr. over 480 articles to profl. jours.; mem. editl. bd. various sci. jours. Recipient Mead-Johnson award in Pediat., 1981; named McLaughlin Found. prof. Can. Royal Coll., 1986-87, scholar Raymond & Beverly Sackler Found., 1988-92. Fellow Royal Coll. Physicians and Surgeons. Office: Nat Jewish Med and Rsch Ctr Immunology and Respiratory Medicine 1400 Jackson St Denver CO 80206-2761

GELLERT, MICHAEL JOHN, psychotherapist; b. Montreal, Que., Can., Sept. 2, 1953; came to U.S., 1981; s. Leslie and Edith (Reich) G. BA, Concordia U., Montreal, 1976; MA, McMaster U., Hamilton, Ont., Can., 1978; MSW, CUNY, 1984. Sabbatical replacement prof. Vanier Coll., Montreal, 1980-81; asst. coord. personal svc. unit outreach program Dist. Coun. 37, N.Y.C., 1986-88; coord. personal svc. unit outreach program Dist. Coun. 37, 1988-91; clin. mgr. Health Mgmt. Ctr., Cerritos, Calif., 1991-92; pvt. practice Santa Monica, Calif., 1991—; psychotherapist U. So. Calif., L.A., 1992-95. Author: Modern Mysticism, 1991, 94; contbr. articles to profl. jours. Rsch. grantee Ann and Erlo Van Waveren Found., N.Y.C., 1988, 92. Mem. NASW, C.G. Jung Inst. of L.A. (cert. analyst 1996). Office: 1526 14th St Ste 111 Santa Monica CA 90404

GELLERT-ROSS, JULIE CHAREN, psychotherapist; b. Santa Monica, Calif., Dec. 21, 1963; d. Werner and Frances Adeline (Silverman) G. BA cum laude with distinction, San Diego State U., 1991; MA, U. N.Mex., 1993; PhD, Union Inst., 1996. Lic. profl. clin. counselor. Quality controll tech. Transwestern Publ., San Diego, 1986-91; grad. asst. U. N.Mex., Albuquerque, 1991-93; psychotherapist All Walks of Life, Albuquerque, 1993-94; psychotherapist, owner Esperanza Counseling and Psychotherapist Assocs., Albuquerque, 1994—; pres. U. N.Mex. Grad. Students in Counseling, 1992-93. Vol. Youth Diagnostic and Devel. Ctr., Albuquerque, 1992, Davis Spector Shalom House, Albuquerque, 1992-94; vol. coord. Jewish Family Svcs., Albuquerque, 1993-94; guest mem. Sandoval County DWI Task Force, Bernalillo, N.Mex., 1994. Grad. Rehab. scholar U. N.Mex., 1991, Mensa scholar, San Diego, 1991. Mem. Hadassah (life). Democrat. Jewish. Office: Esperanza Counseling Assocs PO Box 820 560 Camino Del Pueblo Bernalillo NM 87004

GELLMAN, GLORIA GAE SEEBURGER SCHICK, marketing professional; b. La Grange, Ill., Oct. 5, 1947; d. Robert Fred and Gloria Virginia (McQuiston) Seeburger; m. Peter Slate Schick, Sept. 25, 1978 (dec. 1980); 2 children; m. Irwin Frederick, Gellman, Sept. 9, 1989; 3 children. BA magna cum laude, Purdue U., 1969; student, Lee Strasberg Actors Studio; postgrad., UCLA, U. Calif.-Irvine. Mem. mktg. staff Seemac, Inc. (formerly R.F. Seeburger Co.); v.p. V.I.P. Properties, Inc., Newport Beach, Calif. Profl. actress, singer, artist, writer; television and radio talk show hostess, Indpls., late 1960s; performer radio and television commls., 1960s—. Mem. Orange County Philharm. Soc., bd. dirs. women's com.; mem. Orange County Master Chorale, Orange County Performing Arts Ctr., v.p., treas. Crescendo chpt. OCPAC Ctr. Stars, 1st v.p. membership; bd. dirs. Newport Harbor (Calif.) Art Mus., v.p. membership, mem. acquisition coun.; bd. dirs., mem. founders soc. Opera Pacific, mem. exec. com. bd. dirs.; patron Big Bros./Big Sisters Starlight Found.; mem. Visionaries Newport Harbor Mus., Designing Women of Art Inst. Soc. Calif.; pres. Opera Pacific Guild Alliance; immediate past pres. Spyglass Hill Philharm. Com.; v.p. Pacific Symphony Orch. League; bd. dirs. Pacific Symphony Orch.; mem. Calif. State Libr. Found. Bd., U. Calif. Irvine Found. Bd., mem. devel. com., honors com., pub. affairs and advocacy com.; chmn. numerous small and large fundraisers; mem. com. Red Cross; bd. dirs. Pacific Symphony Orch.; mem. Fashionables of Chapman U. Recipient Lauds and Laurels award U. Calif., Irvine, 1994, Gellman Courtyard Sculpture honoring contbn. to Sch. of Humanities, U. Calif., Irvine. Mem. AAUW, AFTRA, SAG, Internat. Platform Assn., Actors Equity, U. Calif.-Irvine Chancellor's Club, U. Calif.-Irvine Humanities Assocs. (founder, pres., bd. dirs.), Mensa, Orange County Mental Health Assn., Balboa Bay Club, U. Club, Club 39, Islanders, Covergirls, Alpha Lambda Delta, Delta Rho Kappa. Republican. Home: PO Box 1993 Newport Beach CA 92659-0993

GELL-MANN, MURRAY, theoretical physicist, educator; b. N.Y.C., Sept. 15, 1929; s. Arthur and Pauline (Reichstein) Gell-M.; m. J. Margaret Dow, Apr. 19, 1955 (dec. 1981); children: Elizabeth, Nicholas; m. Marcia Southwick, June 20, 1992; 1 stepson, Nicholas Levis. BS, Yale U., 1948; PhD, Mass. Inst. Tech., 1951; ScD (hon.), Yale U., 1959, U. Chgo., 1967, U. Ill., 1968, Wesleyan U., 1968, U. Turin, Italy, 1969, U. Utah, 1970, Columbia U., 1977, Cambridge U., 1980; D (hon.), Oxford (Eng.) U., 1992. Mem. Inst. for Advanced Study, 1951, 55, 67-68; instr. U. Chgo., 1952-53, asst. prof., 1953-54, assoc. prof., 1954; assoc. prof. Calif. Inst. Tech., Pasadena, 1955-56; prof. Calif. Inst. Tech., 1956-93, now R.A. Millikan prof. physics; vis. prof. MIT, spring 1963, CERN, Geneva, 1971-72, 79-80; dir. physics Santa Fe Inst., 1993—; Mem. Pres.'s Sci. Adv. Com., 1969-72, Pres.'s Adv. Com. on Sci. and Tech., 1994—; mem. sci. and grants com., Leakey Found., 1977—; chmn. bd. trustees Aspen Ctr. for Physics, 1973-79; founding trustee Santa Fe Inst., 1982, chmn. bd. trustees, 1982-85, co-chmn. sci. bd. 1985—. Author: (with Y. Ne'eman) Eightfold Way. Citizen regent Smithsonian Instn., 1974-88; bd. dirs. J.D. and C.T. MacArthur Found., 1979—. NSF post doctoral fellow, vis. prof. Coll. de France and U. Paris, 1959-60; recipient Dannie Heineman prize Am. Phys. Soc., 1959; E.O. Lawrence Meml. award AEC, 1966; Overseas fellow Churchill Coll., Cambridge, Eng., 1966; Franklin medal, 1967; Carty medal Nat. Acad. Scis., 1968; Research Corp. award, 1969; named to UN Environ. Program Roll of Honor for Environ. Achievement, 1988; Nobel prize in physics, 1969. Fellow Am. Phys. Soc.; mem. NAS, Royal Soc. (fgn.), Am. Acad. Arts and Scis. (v.p., chmn. Western ctr. 1970-76), Council on Fgn. Relations, French Phys. Soc. (hon.). Clubs: Cosmos (Washington); Century Assn., Explorers (N.Y.C.); Athenaeum (Pasadena). Address: Santa Fe Institute 1399 Hyde Park Rd Santa Fe NM 87501-8943*

GELPI, MICHAEL ANTHONY, entrepreneur; b. Columbus, Ohio, Dec. 28, 1940; s. Andre and Eleanor (Amorose) G. AB, Georgetown U., 1962. Store mgr. Swan Cleaners, Columbus, 1964-65, dist. supr., 1965-68, v.p., 1968-76, exec. v.p., treas., 1976-81, also dir.; v.p. Rainbow Properties, Columbus, 1971-83, pres., 1983-85, chmn. bd., dir. The Neoprobe Corp., Columbus, 1985-89; pres., dir., CEO M.D. Personal Products, Hayward, Calif., 1992-95; bd. dirs. Health Options; owner The Treasure House, San Francisco. Trustee Am. Cancer Soc., 1978-92 , crusade chmn., 1979-84, 1st v.p., 1981-84, pres., 1984-85, chmn., 1985-87, trustee Ohio div., 1984-86, state spl. gifts chmn., 1984-86. Mem. City of Columbus AIDS Adv. Coalition, 1987-92, chmn., 1988-92; trustee Players Theatre of Columbus, 1981-88, v.p., 1985-86, pres. 1986-87; trustee German Village Hist. Soc., 1980-81; trustee Cen. Ohio Radio Reading Svc., 1982-88, pres., 1983-85, trustee Town-Franklin Hist. Neighborhood Assn., 1979-85, v.p., 1983-85; chmn. advance gifts Bishops Ann. Appeal, 1981-86; bd. dirs. Human Rights Campaign Fund, 1985-88; trustee Geriatric Svc. Orgn., 1988-92, devel. chair, 1988-92; candidate for Ohio 12th dist. U.S. Congress, 1988, 90. 1st lt. U.S. Army, 1962-64. Roman Catholic. Recipient Vol. of Yr. award Am. Cancer Soc., 1981, Community Svc. award Columbus Dispatch, 1984, Mayor's award for Vol. Svc. to City of Columbus, 1982, 84.

GELTZ, ELIZABETH S. See HANDS, ELIZABETH S.

GELVEN, MICHAEL PAUL, marketing executive; b. Boston, June 4, 1946; s. Abraham and Sarah Rebecca (Glick) G.; m. Wendy Ellen Tanzer, Oct. 20, 1968; children: Marc Ian, Shana Lee. Student Boston State Coll., 1964-66, Northeastern U., 1969-71; cert. Southeastern Mass. U., 1978. Cert. wine educator.Mgr. trainee Contan Liquors, Inc., Somerville, Mass., 1967-68, mgr., 1968-73; mgr. Tanza Liquors, Inc., Somerville, 1973-74; pres., chief exec. officer Perry's Liquor Inc., North Dartmouth, Mass., 1974-82 ; pres. GTC Assos. Inc., North Easton, Mass., 1978-85; pres., chief operating officer MPG Mktg. Inc., 1985—; pres. DeRoy's Package Store, Chicopee, Mass., 1979-80; pres. Computer 'N Things, Inc., North Dartmouth, 1982-85; pres. Medi-Save Cos., Hyannis, Mass., 1987-90, Supplies, Inc., Needham, Mass., 1987-91, Phone Mail Co., Inc., North Dartmouth, 1991-95, Calif. Wine Guild, Napa, Calif., 1991—, CWG, Inc., Napa, Calif., 1996—; instr. Bristol C.C., 1979-96. With Army N.G., 1966. Mem. NOPA, NOMDA, Mass. Beverage Assn., Soc. Wine Educators, Les Amis DuVin, La Confrerie Saint-Etienne d'Alsace (Master of Wine candidate 1996-97), Assn. Better Computer Dealers, Mensa. Democrat. Jewish (pres. temple 1978-80, dir. 1980-84, 87-90, 93-95, 97—). Lodges: Lions, Masons, KP, B'nai B'rith (pres. 1973-74). Home: 1008 Stonebridge Dr Napa CA 94558-5345 Office: 520 California Blvd Ste 13 Napa CA 94559-3158

GEMBACZ, GILBERT THADDEUS, judge; b. Lexington, Miss., Aug. 1, 1947; s. Stanley Thaddeus and Mary Dillahunt (Sanders) G.; m. Camille Frances Giraldi, June 27, 1976. BA, Southwestern State Coll., Weatherford, Okla., 1969; JD, Southwestern U., L.A., 1979; MBA in Taxation, Golden Gate U., 1984. Bar: Calif. 1980, U.S. Ct. Appeals (9th cir.) 1980, U.S. Dist. Ct. (cen. dist.) Calif. 1980, U.S. Tax Ct. 1985, U.S. Supreme Ct. 1990. Pvt. practice L.A., 1980-83; staff counsel Calif. State Bd. Equalization, Sacramento, 1983-85; litigation atty. IRS Office of Chief Counsel, L.A., 1985-90; asst. dist. counsel immigration and naturalization svc. U.S. Dept. Justice, L.A., 1990-96; judge U.S. Immigration Ct., L.A., 1996—. Mem. Emergency Preparedness Staff, La Canada, Calif., 1991—. Capt. U.S. Army, 1969-76, col. U.S. Army Res., 1995. Mem. ABA, Calif. Bar Assn., Los Angeles County Bar Assn., Italian Am. Bar Assn. Office: US Immigration Ct 300 N Los Angeles St # 2001 Los Angeles CA 90053

GENDZEL, IVAN BENNETT, psychiatrist, educator; b. N.Y.C., May 14, 1931; s. Irving Meyer and Celia (Handler) G.; m. Rella Eisendorf, June 1953 (dec. Nov. 1954); m. Lolgene Grace Nickel, May 4, 1957; children: Glen Joseph, Amy Grace. BA in Chemistry with distinction, Cornell U., 1952, MD, 1956. Intern in medicine Cornell Med. Ctr.-N.Y. Hosp., N.Y.C., 1956-57, resident in medicine, 1957-58; resident in medicine U. Calif. Med. Ctr., San Francisco, 1958-59; resident in psychiatry Stanford (Calif.) U. Med. Ctr., 1959-60, 62-64, clin. faculty dept. psychiatry and behavioral scis., 1964—, clin. assoc. prof., 1975—; pvt. practice psychiatry Palo Alto, Calif., 1964—; dep. chief psychiatry Stanford Med. Ctr., 1968-70, hosp. med. bd., 1968-70, chmn. credentials com. dept. psychiatry and behavioral scis., 1978-84, concurrent rev. com., 1978-82; staff mem. Stanford U. Hosp., 1964—; profl. adv. bd. Miramonte Mental Health Svcs., 1964-73, chmn., 1970-72. Contbr. articles to profl. jours. Profl. adv. bd. Parents Without Ptnrs., 1964-70; scoutmaster Stanford Area Coun. Boy Scouts Am., 1973-76, staff advanced adult leader tng., 1976-79, course dir., 1979, v.p./Manpower, 1980-82, v.p. ops., 1983-85, coun. pres., nat. coun. rep., 1986-87 (award of merit and Silver Beaver award 1988, v.p. devel. Stanford Area coun. 1987-93, Pacific Skyline coun. 1993-96). With USN, 1960-62. Fellow Am. Group Psychotherapy Assn., Am. Psychiat. Assn.; mem. Mid-Peninsula Psychiat. Soc. (sec. 1969-70, pres. 1978-79), No. Calif. Psychiat. Soc., No. Calif. Group Psychotherapy Soc. (coun. 1978-86, pres. 1980-82), Network Continuing Health Educators (program com. 1985, program com. chmn. 1987). Home: 1019 Harker Ave Palo Alto CA 94301-3419 Office: 900 Welch Rd Palo Alto CA 94304-1805

GENG, HWAI-YU, manufacturing engineer, plant manager; b. Chung-King, People's Republic of China, June 15, 1946; came to U.S., 1971; s. Ruhan Wu and Rubing Geng; m. Li-mei Geng, Mar. 6, 1971; children: Amy, Julie. BS in Indsl. Engring., Chung Yuan U., Chung-li, Taiwan, 1969; MSME, Tenn. Tech. U., 1973; MBA, Ashland U., 1982. Registered engr., Calif. Asst. to plant mgr. Fruehauf Corp., Delphos, Ohio, 1973-84; mgr. indsl. engring. dept. Westinghouse Electric, Sunnyvale, Calif., 1984-93; mgr. new plant constrn. Applied Materials, Santa Clara, Calif., 1993-96, Hewlett Packard, 1996—. Author tech. papers in field; patentee in field. Mem. Inst. Indsl. Engrs. (sr., membership v.p. 1980—), Soc. Mfg. Engrs. (sr.), Inst. Environ. Scis. (sr.). Home: 4182 Coulombe Dr Palo Alto CA 94306-3801

GENGLER, SUE WONG, health educator; b. Hong Kong, Apr. 6, 1959; came to U.S., 1966; d. Tin Ho and Yuet Kum (Chan) Wong; m. Clayton J. Gengler, 1995. BS, UCLA, 1981; MPH, Loma Linda (Calif.) U., 1990; DrPH, Loma Linda U., 1995. Cert. health edn. specialist. Asst. to the dir. Project Asia Campus Crusade for Christ, San Bernardino, Calif., 1982-83, Campus Crusade for Christ-Internat. Pers., San Bernardino, 1983-90; health educator San Bernardino County Pub. Health, 1990-92; community lab. instr., rsch. asst. dept. health promotion and edn. Loma Linda (Calif.) U. Sch. Pub. Health, 1992-95; behaviorist/educator Anaheim Hills Med. Group/St. Jude Heritage Med. Group, Anaheim, Calif., 1995-96; direct svcs. dir. Alternatives to Domestic Violence, Riverside, Calif., 1997—. Mem. Minority Health Coalition, San Bernardino, 1990-92, Com. for the Culturally Diverse, San Bernardino, 1990—; vol. Am. Cancer Soc.; chair Gt. Am. Smokeout, Inland Empire, 1991; bd. dirs. Family Svcs. Agy., San Bernardino, 1994-96. Selma Andrews scholar Loma Linda U., 1994; named Outstanding Young Woman of Yr., 1983, Hulda Crooke Scholar, Loma Linda U., 1989; recipient Am. Cancer Soc. Rose award, 1991 (Calif.), Gaspar award, 1991 (nat.). Mem. APHA, Nat. Coun. for Internat. Health, Soc. Pub. Health Edn.

GENGOR, VIRGINIA ANDERSON, financial planning executive, educator; b. Lyons, N.Y., May 2, 1927; d. Axel Jennings and Marie Margaret (Mack) Anderson; m. Peter Gengor, Mar. 2, 1952 (dec.); children: Peter Randall, Daniel Neal, Susan Leigh. AB, Wheaton Coll., 1949; MA, U. No. Colo., Greeley, 1975, 77. Chief hosp. intake service County of San Diego, 1966-77, chief Kearny Mesa Dist. Office, 1977-79, chief Dependent Children of Ct., 1979-81, chief child protection services, 1981-82; registered rep. Am. Pacific Securities, San Diego, 1982-85; registered tax preparer State of Calif., 1982—, registered rep. (prin.) Sentra Securities, 1985—; assoc. Pollock & Assocs., San Diego, 1985-86; pres. Gengor Fin. Advisors, 1986—; cons. instr. Nat. Ctr. for Fin. Edn., San Diego, 1986-88; instr. San Diego Community Coll., 1985-88. Mem. allocations panel United Way, San Diego, 1976-79, children's circle Child Abuse Prevention Found., 1989—; chmn. com. Child Abuse Coordinating Council, San Diego, 1979-83; pres. Friends of Casa de la Esperanza, San Diego, 1980-85, bd. dirs., 1980—; 1st v.p. The Big Sister League, San Diego, 1985-86, pres., 1987-89. Mem. NAFE, Inst. Cert. Fin. Planners, Internat. Assn. Fin. Planning, Inland Soc. Tax Cons., AAUW (bd. dirs.), Nat. Assn. Securities Dealers (registered prin.), Nat. Ctr. Fin. Edn., Am. Bus. Women's Assn., Navy League, Freedoms Found. Valley Forge, Internat. Platform Assn. Presbyterian. Avocations: community service, travel, reading. Home: 6462 Spear St San Diego CA 92120-2929 Office: Gengor Fin Advisors 4950 Waring Rd Ste 7 San Diego CA 92120-2700

GENINI, RONALD WALTER, history educator, historian; b. Oakland, Calif., Dec. 5, 1946; s. William Angelo and Irma Lea (Gays) G.; m. Roberta Mae Tucker, Dec. 20, 1969; children: Thomas, Justin, Nicholas. BA, U. San Francisco, 1968, MA, 1969. Cert. secondary edn. tchr., Calif.; adminstrv. svcs. credential. Tchr. Ctrl. Unified Sch. Dist., Fresno, Calif., 1970—; judge State History Day, Sacramento, 1986-94; mem. U.S. history exam. devel. team Golden State, San Diego, 1989-93; securer placement of state-registered landmarks. Author: Romualdo Pacheco, 1985, Darn Right It's Butch, 1994, Theda Bara, 1996; contbr. articles to profl. jours. Bd. dirs. Fresno Area 6 Neighborhood Coun., 1973-74, Fresno City and County Hist. Soc., 1975-78, St. Anthony's sch. bd., Fresno, 1980-84. Named one of Outstanding Young Educators Am., Fresno Jaycees, 1978; recipient recognition for Tchr. Cares award Calif. Assembly and Fresno City Coun., 1996. Mem. Calif. Hist. Soc. Libertarian. Roman Catholic. Home: 1486 W Menlo Ave Fresno CA 93711-1305 Office: Ctrl HS 3535 N Cornelia Fresno CA 93722-9643

GENN, NANCY, artist; b. San Francisco; d. Morley P. and Ruth W. Thompson; m. Vernon Chathburton Genn; children: Cynthia, Sarah, Peter. Student, San Francisco Art Inst., U. Calif., Berkeley. lectr. on art and papermaking Am. Ctrs. in Osaka, Japan, Nagoya, Japan, Kyoto, Japan, 1979-80; guest lectr. various univs. and art mus. in U.S., 1975—; vis. artist Am. Acad. in Rome, 1989, 94. One woman shows of sculpture, paintings include, De Young Mus., San Francisco, 1955, 63, Gumps Gallery, San Francisco, 1955, 57, 59, San Francisco Mus. Art, 1961, U. Calif., Santa Cruz, 1966-68, Richmond (Calif.) Art Center, 1970, Oakland (Calif.) Mus., 1971, Linda/Farris Gallery, Seattle, 1974, 76, 78, 81, Los Angeles Inst. Contemporary Art, 1976, Susan Caldwell Gallery, N.Y.C., 1976, 77, 79, 81, Nina Freudenheim Gallery, Buffalo, 1977, 81, Annely Juda Fine Art, London, 1978, Inoue Gallery, Tokyo, 1980, Toni Birckhead Gallery, Cin., 1982, Kala Inst. Gallery, Berkeley, Calif., 1983, Ivory/Kimpton Gallery, San Francisco, 1984, 86, Eve Mannes Gallery, Atlanta, 1985, Richard Iri Gallery, L.A., 1990, Harcourts Modern and Contemporary Art, San Francisco, 1991, 93, 96, Am. Assn. Advancement of Sci., Washington, 1994, Anne Reed Gallery, Ketchum, Id., 1995, Michael PeTronko Gallery, N.Y., 1997; group exhbns. include San Francisco Mus. Art, 1971, Aldrich Mus., Ridgefield, Conn., 1972-73, Santa Barbara (Calif.) Mus., 1974, 75, Oakland (Calif.) Mus. Art, 1975, Susan Caldwell, Inc., N.Y.C., 1974, 75, Mus. Modern Art, N.Y.C., 1976, traveling exhbn. Arts Coun. Gt. Britain, 1983-84, Inst. Contemporary Arts, Boston, 1977; represented in permanent collections Mus. Modern Art, N.Y.C., Albright-Knox Art Gallery, Buffalo, Libr. of Congress, Washington, Nat. Mus. for Am. Art, Washington, L.A. County Mus. Art, Art Mus. U. Calif., Berkeley, McCrory Corp., N.Y.C., Mus. Art, Auckland, N.Z., Aldrich Mus., Ridgefield, Conn., (collection) Bklyn. Mus., (collection) U. Tex., El Paso, Internat. Ctr. Aesthetic Rsch., Torino, Italy, Cin. Art Mus., San Francisco Mus. Modern Art, Oakland Art Mus., L.A. County Mus., City of San Francisco Hall of Justice, Harris Bank, Chgo., Chase Manhattan Bank, N.Y.C., Modern Art Gallery of Ascoli Piceno, Italy, Mills Coll. Art Mus., Oakland, Calif., Mills Coll. of Art, Oakland, Calif., various mfg. cos., also numerous pvt. collections; commd. works include, Bronze lectern and 5 bronze sculptures for chancel table, 1st Unitarian Ch., Berkeley, Calif., 1961, 64, bronze fountain, Cowell Coll., U. Calif., Santa Cruz, bronze menorah, Temple Beth Am, Los Altos Hills, Calif., 1981, 17, murals and 2 bronze fountain sculptures, Sterling Vineyards, Calistoga, Calif., 1972, 73, fountain sculpture, Expo 1974, Spokane, Wash; vis. artist Am. Acad., Rome, 1989. U.S./Japan Creative Arts fellow, 1978-79; recipient Ellen Branston award, 1952; Phelan award De Young Mus., 1963; honor award HUD, 1968. Home: 1515 La Loma Ave Berkeley CA 94708-2033

GENNARO, ANTONIO L., biology educator; b. Raton, N.Mex., Mar. 18, 1934; s. Paul and Mary Lou (Gasperetti) G.; m. Virginia Marie Sullivan, May 15, 1955 (div. 1979); children: Theresa Ann, Carrie Marie, Janelle Elizabeth; m. Marjorie Lou Cox, Sept. 27, 1980. BS, N.Mex. State U., 1957; MS, U. N.Mex., 1961, PhD, 1965. Tchr. biology Las Cruces H.S., N.Mex., 1957-58; asst. prof. biology St. John's U., Collegeville, Minn., 1964-65; prof. biology Eastern N.Mex. U., Portales, 1965—. Contbr. articles to profl. jours. Bd. trustees N.Mex. Mus. of Natural History, 1996—. Served to capt. U.S.

Army, 1958-59; mem. Res., 1959-66. Recipient Presdl. Faculty award Eastern N.Mex. U., 1970, Pres.'s Faculty award for excellence in rsch., 1988, Spirit of Ea. award, 1995; Outstanding Sci. award N.Mex. Acad. Sci., 1975. Mem. Southwestern Naturalists (treas. 1974-78), Am. Soc. Mammalogists, Herpetologists League, Sigma Xi, Phi Kappa Phi (pres. 1970-74). Roman Catholic.

GENRICH, MARK L., newspaper editorial writer, columnist; b. Buffalo, Aug. 28, 1943; m. Allison Forbes, 1967; children: Audrey, Liza, Colby. BA, Bucknell U., 1966. Editl. writer Palladium-Item, Richmond, Ind., 1970; writing exec. Bruce Eberle & Assocs., Inc., Vienna, Va., 1975-77; dep. editor editl. pgs. Phoenix Gazette, 1977—; participant U.S. Army War Coll., Carlisle, Pa., U.S. Naval War Coll., Newport, R.I.; participant arms control, disarmament programs including Space & Arms talks, Geneva; chmn. New Tech. Com., Journalism in Edn. Com.; mem. various coms. Created, hosted cable TV program focus on polit. figures; regional editor The Masthead. Grantee European Cmty. Visitor Programme, 1993; recipient highest honors editl. writing, newspaper design Ariz., Western Region; highest honor Maricopa County Bar Assn.; Stanford U. media fellow, 1985. Mem. Nat. Conf. Editl. Writers (bd. dirs., included vol. Editl. Excellence), First Amendment Cong. (bd. dirs.), Soc. Profl. Journalists/Sigma Delta Chi, ABA (com. prisons, sentencing). Home: 130 W Pine Valley Dr Phoenix AZ 85023-5283 Office: Ariz Republic 120 E Van Buren St Phoenix AZ 85004-2227

GENTRY, JAMES WILLIAM, retired state official; b. Danville, Ill., Aug. 14, 1926; s. Carl Lloyd and Leone (Isham) G.; A.B., Fresno State Coll., 1948; M.J., U. Calif., Berkeley, 1956; m. Dorothie Shirley Hechtlinger, Mar. 18, 1967; 1 stepdau., Susan Mushkin. Field rep. Congressman B.W. Gearhart, Fresno, Calif., 1948, Assemblyman Wm. W. Hansen, Fresno, 1950, sec., 1953-56; exec. asst. Calif. Pharm. Assn., Los Angeles, 1956-69, editor, pub. Calif. Pharmacy Jour., 1956-69; pub. relations dir. PAID Prescriptions, 1963-64; dir. pub. info. comprehensive Health Planning Council, Los Angeles County, 1969; asst. adminstr., dir. pub. info. So. Calif. Comprehensive Health Planning Council, 1969-71, acting adminstr., 1971-72; exec. sec., 1972-73, Calif. Adv. Health Council, 1973-85, fed. cons., 1986-88; Calif. Health Care Commn., 1973-75; acting public info. officer Calif. Office Statewide Health Planning and Devel., 1978-79; interim dir. , 1983; mem. L.A. Civil Svc. Police Interview Bd., 1967-72; asst. sgt.-at-arms Calif. State Assembly, 1950; exec. sec. Calif. Assembly Interim Com. on Livestock and Dairies, 1954-56; mem. adv. bd. Am. Security Council; mem. Calif. Health Planning Law Revision Commn.; former mem. Calif. Bldg. Safety Bd. Mem. Fresno County Republican Central Com., 1950; charter mem. Rep. Presdl. Task Force. Served to col. AUS, 1949-50, 50-53; Korea. Decorated Legion of Merit, Bronze Star medal, Commendation Ribbon with metal pendant ; recipient pub. awards Western Soc. Bus. Publns. Assn., 1964-67. Mem. Am. Assn. Comprehensive Health Planning, Pub. Relations Soc. Am., Ret. Officers Assn. (life), Allied Drug Travelers So. Calif., L.A. Press Club, Mil. Police Assn., Res. Officers Assn. (life), Assn. U.S. Army, U.S. Senatorial Club, The Victory Svcs. Club of London, Pi Gamma Mu, Phi Alpha Delta. Sigma Delta Chi. Editor: Better Health, 1963-67; Orientation Conf. Comprehensive Health Planning, 1969; Commentary, 1969-71. Editorial adv. Pharm. Svcs. for Nursing Homes: A Procedural Manual, 1966. Editor: Program and Funding, 1972; Substance Abuse, 1972. Home: 902 Commons Dr Sacramento CA 95825-6647

GENTRY, JEANNE LOUISE, lecturer, writer; b. Portland, Oreg., Sept. 12, 1946; d. Louis Darell and Mary Louise (Lane) G.; m. Gini Mario Martini, June 13, 1965 (div. 1968); children: Deborah Corinna Martina, Darell James Martini. Student, Northwestern Coll. Bus., Portland, 1968, Mt. Hood Community Coll., Gresham, Oreg., 1986. Receptionist, sec. to pres. Met. Printing Co., Portland, 1969-73; adminstrv. asst. Lifespring, Inc., Portland, 1974-77; cons. Jeanne Mort Co., Boring, Oreg., 1978-80; office mgr. Beef Palace Provisioners, Gresham, 1980-82; bus. cons. Boring, 1983-90; owner Good As New Doll Hosp., Boring, 1990-92; adminstrv. projects mgr. Profl. Svc. Industries, Portland, 1992—. Co-compiler: Lebanon Pioneer Cemetery, 1991, rev. edit. 1995. Apptd. to Oreg. Pioneer Cemetery Commn., 1995 (chair, 1995—). Mem. Geneal. Coun. Orgn. (sec. 1991-94), Nat. Geneal. Soc., Fellowship of Brethren Genealogists, Geneal. Forum of Oreg. (Newsletter staff), Ind. Geneal. Soc. (charter), East Tenn. Hist. Soc., Oreg. Hist. Cemeteries Assn. (pres. 1992-96), Pellissippi Geneal. and Hist. Soc., Lebanon Geneal. Soc. Home: 16385 SE 232nd Dr Boring OR 97009-9124

GEOFFRION, MOIRA MARTI, artist, educator; b. Olney, Md., July 11, 1944; d. Fritz and Gertrude (Austin) Marti; m. Charles Geoffrion, 1965; children: Sabrina, Damien. BFA, Boston U., 1965; MFA, So. Ill. U., 1974. From asst. prof. to full prof. art Notre Dame (Ind.) U., 1974-86; prof. and head dept. art U. Ariz., Tucson, 1986-91, sculpture area dir., 1991—; vis. artist 12 univs. and colls. including U. Colo., Boulder, U. Mont., Missoula, San Jose State U., U. Cin., U. Ind., Bloomington, U. No. Ill., DeKalb. One-woman shows include Art Gallery U. Montemorelais (Mex.), Gallery Route One, Calif., Tucson Mus. Art, Zaks Gallery, Chgo., Plieades Gallery, N.Y., 14 Sculptors Gallery, N.Y.; exhibited in group shows at Process Space Festival Traveling Exhbn., Plovdiv, Sophia, Baltchik, Bulgaria, All Around Ariz., NAU Galleries, Am. Artists Invitational, Gallery 10-10, St. Petersburg, Russia 1990, Chgo. Navy Pier Show, others. Exxon Disting. Scholar grant, ICIP/Fulbright grant for rsch., others. Office: Univ Ariz Dept Art Tucson AZ 85721

GEORGE, ALEXANDER LAWRENCE, political scientist, educator; b. Chgo., May 31, 1920; s. John and Mary (Sargis) G.; m. Juliette Lombard, Apr. 20, 1948; children: Lee Lawrence, Mary Lombard. AM, U. Chgo., 1941, PhD, 1958; DHL (hon.), U. San Diego, 1987; PhD (hon.), U. Lund, Sweden, 1994. Rsch. analyst OSS, 1944-45; dep. chief rsch. br. Info. Control divsn. Office Mil. Govt. for Germany, 1945-48; specialist study of decision-making and internat. rels. RAND Corp., Santa Monica, Calif., 1948-68; head dept. social sci. RAND Corp., Santa Monica, 1961-63; prof. polit. sci. and internat. rels. Stanford (Calif.) U., 1968—; lectr. U. Chgo., 1950, Am. U., 1952-56; chmn. com. on Conflict Resolution NRC/NAS, 1995—. Author: (with Juliette L. George) Woodrow Wilson and Colonel House: A Personality Study, 1956, Propaganda Analysis, 1959, The Chinese Communist Army in Action, 1967, (with others) The Limits of Coercive Diplomacy, 1971, (with Richard Smoke) Deterrence in American Foreign Policy: Theory and Practice, 1974 (Bancroft prize for Deterrence in Am. Fgn. Policy 1975), Towards A More Soundly Based Foreign Policy: Making Better Use of Information, 1976, Presidential Decisionmaking in Foreign Policy, 1980, Managing U.S.-Soviet Rivalry, 1983, (with Gordon Craig) Force and Statecraft, 1983, 3rd edit., 1995; editor: (with others) U.S.-Soviet Security Cooperation: Achievements, Failures, Lessons, 1988, Avoiding War: Problems of Crisis Management, 1991, Forceful Persuasion, 1992, Bridging the Gap: Theory and Practice of Foreign Policy, 1993, (with William E. Simons) The Limits of Coercive Diplomacy, 2d. edit., 1994. Mem. Carnegie Commn. on Preventing Deadly Conflict, 1993—. Fellow Ctr. Advanced Study Behavioral Scis., 1956-57, 76-77, NIMH, 1972-73, MacArthur Prize, 1983-88, Disting. fellow U. S. Inst. Peace, 1990-91, 91-92; Founds. Fund for Rsch. in Psychiatry grantee, 1960, NSF rsch. grantee, 1971-73, 75-77; recipient award for behavioral rsch. relevant to prevention of nuclear war NAS, 1997. Mem. Am. Acad. Arts and Scis., Coun. on Fgn. Rels., Am. Polit. Sci. Assn., Internat. Studies Assn. (pres. 1973-74), Phi Beta Kappa. Home: 944 Lathrop Pl Stanford CA 94305-1060

GEORGE, DEAN CURTIS, state insurance agency administrator; b. Mt. Edgecombe, Alaska, Oct. 11, 1953; s. Jimmie Albert and Lydia Mary (James) G.; m. Dinah Marie Hobson, Sept. 12, 1984; children: Sasha Hobson-George, Annastasia Hobson-George. BS, U. Oreg., 1982. Vol. acct. Tibal House Renovation Project, Angoon, Alaska, 1976-77; accounts payable acct., program auditor, cons. Ctr. Coun. Tlingit Indian Tribes of Alaska, Juneau, 1977-83; internal auditor Office of the Gov. State of Alaska, Juneau, 1984-85; revenue officer IRS, Juneau, 1985-90; revenue auditor Alaska Divsn. Ins., Juneau, 1990-94; fin. examiner Alaska Divsn. Ins., 1994—; bd. dirs. Taquan Air, Inc.; bd. dirs., chmn. Kootznoowoo, Inc. Mem. Alaska Native Brotherhood Camp 2, Soc. Fin. Examiners. Mem. Am. Orthodox Ch. Home: 8162 Threadneedle Juneau AK 99802 Office: Alaska Divsn Ins PO Box 110805 Juneau AK 99811-0805

GEORGE, FRANCIS, bishop; b. Chgo., Jan. 16, 1937. Ordained priest Roman Cath. Ch., 1963. Provincial ctrl. region Oblates of Mary Immaculate, 1973-74, vicar gen., 1974-86; bishop Diocese of Yakima, Wash., 1990-96, Diocese of Portland, Oreg., 1996-97; archbishop Diocese of Chgo., 1997—. Office: Archdiocese of Chicago Pastoral Ctr PO Box 1979 Chicago IL 60690*

GEORGE, LESLIE EARL, protective services official; b. Eldrado, Okla., July 12, 1930; s. Earl Haskel and Cuba Mae (Huddleston) G.; m. Eleanor Mae Hart, Nov. 20, 1955; children: Leslie Earl Jr., Rickie Dwayne, Jeffery Scott, Gregory Allen. AA, East L.A. Coll., 1966; BA in Mgmt., Redlands U., 1983. Reinforcing iron worker Blue Diamond Corp., L.A., 1949-51; reinforcing ironworker foreman Triangle Steel Co., Vernon, Calif., 1953-54; fire fighter City of El Monte (Calif.) Fire Dept., 1955-56, fire engr., 1956-57, fire capt., 1957-61, adminstrv. capt., 1961-66, fire battalion chief, 1966-91, fire chief, 1988—. Bd. dirs., pres. Boys' Club El Monte, 1993. With U.S. Army, 1951-53. Mem. Calif. Conf. Arson Investigators (life, pub., editor), Rotary (pres., sec., program chmn.). Home: 2627 E Maureen St West Covina CA 91792-2215 Office: 3615 Santa Anita Ave El Monte CA 91731-2428

GEORGE, LLOYD D., federal judge; b. Montpelier, Idaho, Feb. 22, 1930; s. William Ross and Myrtle (Nield) G.; m. LaPrele Badouin, Aug. 6, 1956; children: Douglas Ralph, Michele, Cherie Suzanne, Stephen Lloyd. BS, Brigham Young U., 1955; JD, U. Calif., Berkeley, 1961. Ptnr. Albright, George, Johnson & Steffen, 1969-71, George, Steffen & Simmons, 1971-74; judge U.S. Bankruptcy Ct. (Nev. dist.), 1974-84, U.S. Dist. Ct. Nev., 1984—, now chief judge; justice of peace Clark County, Nev., 1962-69. Served with USAF, 1955-58. Office: US Dist Ct RM 316 300 Las Vegas Blvd S Fl 3 Las Vegas NV 89101-5833*

GEORGE, NICHOLAS, criminal defense lawyer, entrepreneur; b. Seattle, July 11, 1952; s. Harry and Mary (Courounes) G.; children: Harry Nicholas, James Michael. BA in Polit. Sci. cum laude, Whitman Coll., 1974; MBA in Mktg. and Corp. Planning, U. Chgo., 1979; JD, U. Puget Sound, 1989. Bar: Wash. 1991, U.S. Dist. Ct. (we. dist.) Wash. 1991, U.S. Ct. Appeals (9th cir.) 1991, U.S. Tax Ct. 1992, U.S. Dist. Ct. (ea. dist.) Wash. 1994, U.S. Supreme Ct. 1994. Fin. cons. Pacific Western Investment Co., Lynnwood, Wash., 1975-77; planning dir. Clinton Capital Ventures, Seattle, 1979-81; corp. planning mgr. Tacoma Boatbldg., 1981-83; pres. MegaProf Investors, Bellevue, Wash., 1983-89; practice trial-settlement law bus., Seattle, 1989—; free-lance coll. counselor, Seattle, 1980—. Author: Legitimacy in Government: Ideal, Goal, or Myth? 1974. Bd. auditor St. Demetrios Greek Orthodox Ch., Seattle, 1982-83; bd. dirs. Hellenic Golfers Assn., Seattle, 1981-83. Mem. ABA, Assn. Trial Lawyers Am., Wash. State Bar Assn., Wash. Assn. Criminal Def. Lawyers, Wash. State Trial Lawyers Assn., Fed. Bar Assn., Nat. Assn. Criminal Def. Lawyers, Tacoma-Pierce County Bar Assn., Seattle-King County Bar Assn., Wash. Defender Assn., Wash. State Hist. Soc., Am. Inst. Archeol., Rotary, Wash. Athletic Club, Phi Alpha Delta. Republican. Greek Orthodox. Home: 8422 NE 27th Pl Bellevue WA 98004-1656 Office: 911 Tacoma Ave S Ste 100 Tacoma WA 98402

GEORGE, PATRICIA BYRNE, artist; b. Cheyenne, Wyo.; d. Vincent Patrick and Margaret Mae (Adams) Byrne; m. Edward Palmer George, Jr.; children: Stacy Elizabeth George O'Reilly, Kristie Anne. BA, UCLA. Artist (mag. covers) Calif. Living, Dec. 1994, Huntington Harbour, July 1994, Family Living, June 1993, Manhattan Arts, Sept. 1993; exhibited in group shows at Hellenic Inst., Athens, 1990, Matrix Gallery, San Francisco, 1991, 92, Neville Gallery, Toronto, Ont., Can., 1991, 92, Chapelle de la Sorbonne, Paris, 1992, Panopoulos Gallery, Athens, 1993, Internat. Artists, Tokyo, 1994, Fine Art Collection, Sausalito, Calif., 1994, Mark Alan Gallery, Laguna Beach, Calif., 1995, Gail Roff Fine Art Gallery, Newport Beach, Calif., 1995, 96, Galerie Klimintiris, Montreal, Que., Can., 1996, Sapporo (Japan) Mus., 1997; represented in numerous pvt., mus. and corp. collections, including Internat. Trade Ctr., Hilton Hotels, Newport Coast Resort, Disney Corp., others. Recipient Laureate award Mayor of Paris, 1990, Spl. award of jury Musee d'art Moderne, France, 1993; Cover Contest winner Manhattan Arts, 1993. Office: European Expressions 4141 Ball Rd # 221 Cypress CA 90630-3400

GEORGE, PETER T., orthodontist; b. Akron, Ohio; s. Tony and Paraskeva (Ogrenova) G.; BS Kent State U., 1952; DDS, Ohio State U., 1956; cert. in orthodontics Columbia U., 1962; children: Barton Herrin, Tryan Franklin. Pvt. practice orthodontics, Honolulu, 1962—; cleft palate cons. Hawaii Bur. Crippled Children, 1963—; asst. prof. Med. Sch., U. Hawaii, Honolulu, 1970—; lectr. in field. Mem. Hawaii Gov.'s Phys. Fitness Com., 1962-68; mem. Honolulu Mayor's Health Coun., 1967-72; mem. med. com. Internat. Weightlifting Fedn., 1980-84; chmn. bd. govs. Hall of Fame of Hawaii, 1984; bd. dirs. Honolulu Opera Theatre, 1986-91, chmn. bd. Hawaii Internat. Sports Found., 1988-91. Served to capt. Dental Corps, U.S. Army, 1956-60. Olympic Gold medallist in weightlifting, Helsinki, 1952, Silver medallist, London, 1948, Melbourne, 1956; six times world champion; recipient Disting. service award Hawaiian AAU, 1968; Gold medal Internat. Weightlifting Fedn., 1976; named to Helms Hall of Fame, 1966; named mem. 100 Golden Olympians, 1996. Diplomate Am. Bd. Orthodontics. Fellow Am. Coll. Dentistry, Internat. Coll. Dentistry; mem. Hawaii Amateur Athletic Union (pres. 1964-65), U.S. Olympians (pres. Hawaii chpt. 1963-67, 80—), Am. Assn. Orthodontists, Honolulu Dental Soc. (pres. 1967-68), Hawaii Dental Assn. (pres. 1978), Hawaii Soc. Orthodontists (pres. 1972). Editor Hawaii State Dental Jour., 1965-67. Inventor appliance to prevent sleep apnea. U.S. weightlifting coach USSR, 1979, asst. coach Olympic weightlifting team, 1980. Home and Office: 1441 Kapiolani Blvd Ste 520 Honolulu HI 96814-4403

GEORGE, RONALD M., judge; b. L.A., Mar. 11, 1940. AB, Princeton U., 1961; JD, Stanford U., 1964. Bar: Calif. 1965. Dep. atty. gen. Calif. Dept. Justice, 1965-72; judge L.A. Mcpl. Ct., L.A. County, 1972-77; judge Superior Ct. Calif., L.A. County, 1977-87, supervising judge criminal divsn., 1983-84; assoc. justice 2d dist., divsn. 4 Calif. Ct. Appeal, L.A., 1987-91; assoc. justice Calif. Supreme Ct., San Francisco, 1991-96, chief justice, 1996—. Mem. Calif. Judges Assn. (pres. 1982-83). Office: Calif Supreme Court 303 2nd St South Tower San Francisco CA 94107

GEORGE, THOM RITTER, conductor, music educator, composer; b. Detroit, June 23, 1942; s. Robert Murray and Virginia Flowers (Ritter) G.; m. Patricia Imogene Dengler , Aug. 14, 1965; children: Samantha, Clara, Alexander. MusB, Eastman Sch. Music, 1964, MusM, 1968; D in Mus. Arts, The Cath. U. Am., 1970. Lectr. music The Cath. U. Am., Washington, 1966-70; music dir., condr. Quincy (Ill.) Symphony Orch., 1970-83; lectr. music John Wood Community Coll., Quincy, 1980-83; assoc. prof. Idaho State U., Pocatello, 1983-88, prof., 1988—; music dir., condr. Idaho State Civic Symphony, Pocatello, 1983—. Composer: Concerto for Bass Trombone, 1964, Proclamations, 1965, Sextet, 1980, numerous others. Bd. dirs. Civic Music Assn., Quincy, 1970-74; bd. sec. Vol. Action Ctr., Quincy, 1976-78. Served with USN, 1966-70. Recipient citation Quincy Coll., 1973, Sigvald Thompson award Fargo (N.D.) Moorhead Symphony, 1975, Composer-in-Residence award Elkhorn Music Festival, Sun Valley, Idaho, 1986. Mem. ASCAP, Am. Music Ctr., Am. String Tchrs. Assn., Nat. Band Assn. Lodges: Rotary (Quincy membership chmn. 1975-83, mem. Pocatello fine arts com. 1985—). Office: Idaho State U Dept Music PO Box 8099 Pocatello ID 83209

GEORGE, VANCE, conductor; b. Bremen, Ind., Sept. 30, 1933. BA in Music Edn., Goshen Coll., Ind., 1955; Grad., Bhatkande Sch. Music and Dance, India, 1959; student, Goethe Inst., Germany, 1961; MusM in Conducting, Ind. Univ., 1963, Mus D in Conducting, 1965; studied with Margaret Hullis, Rene Leibowitz and Otto-Werner Mueller. Chorus master Opera Theater, Ind. Univ., Bloomington, Ind., 1963-65; dir. Women's Chorus, Ind. Univ., Bloomington, Ind., 1963-65; dir. choral activities Univ. Wis., Madison, 1965-71; instr. Choral Inst., Am. Chroral Found., Madison, 1967, 69; dir. choral activities Kent State Univ., Ohio, 1971-82; assoc. chorus conductor Cleveland Orch. Chorus, Cleveland Orch. Chamber Chorus, Ohio, 1977-83; prof. conducting Festival of the Rockies, Whitefish, Mont., 1987; conductor Phoenix Bach Soc., Ariz., 1988-90; dir. San Francisco Symphony Chorus, Calif., 1983—; bd. dirs. Choris Am.; former chmn. Cleve. Orch. Chorus, Sch. of the Cleve. Orch.; guest chorus dir. Kent State Univ. Chorus, Canton Symphony Orch., 1976-77, 80-81; vis. assoc. prof. Univ. Calif., Berkeley, 1983, 85, 87, 88. Condr. San Francisco Symphony, San Francisco Symphony Chorus, oratorio, seasonal concerts, pops, Asian Youth Orch., Asian Youth Chorus; studies in U.S., Europe, Canada, India. Recipient Grammy award for Best Choral Performance, 1992; nominee Grammy award Mahler Symphony #2, 1994. Mem. IFCM, ACDA, Pi Kappa Lambda. Office: San Francisco Symphony Chorus 201 Van Ness Ave San Francisco CA 94102-4507

GEORGESCO, VICTOR, printing company executive; b. Bucharest, Romania, Mar. 17, 1948; came to U.S., 1978; s. Paul D. and Maria C. (Bender) G. B.S., Poly. U., Bucharest, 1968. Overseas br. mgr. Metal Import Export, Bucharest, 1968-77; asst. mgr. Otto Botner GMBH, Duesseldorf, W. Ger., 1977-78; purchasing agt. Trico Industries, Torrance, Calif., 1978-86; exec. v.p. ops. Beverly Ctr. Printing Co., Los Angeles, 1986—. Mem. Purchasing Mgmt. Assn. (Los Angeles chpt.). Office: 8104 W 3rd St Los Angeles CA 90048-4309

GEORGOPOULOS, DEAN ELIAS, film producer, real estate developer; b. Manchester, N.H., Nov. 2, 1963; s. Louis James and Aphrodite (Zoulamis) G. U. N.H. V.p. ops. Famous Ski Togs Factory Outlets, N.H., Vt., Mass., Maine, 1978-82, Jim's Oxford Shop, Manchester, N.H., 1982, 86; gen. mgr. U. N.H. Hockey, Durham, 1982-86, 89; bus. affairs The Bus Boys, L.A., 1986-88; v.p. ops. Am. Computer Products, Salem, N.H., 1990; mgr. The Barn Sporting Goods, Newton, Mass., 1990; sales assoc. Smith Barney Harris Upham Brokerage, White Plains, N.Y., 1991; film prodr. Rocky Point Prodns., L.A., 1990-93; redeveloper The Shannon Co., Woodland Hills, Calif., 1991-94; film prodr. Kosmos Entertainment Group, Malibu, Calif., 1993—; MIS cons. The Mus. of Flying, Santa Monica, Calif., 1990, The Cockpit, N.Y.C., 1991, LMH Prodns., Studio City, Calif., 1993—; prodn. cons. Infinity Vision Entertainment, Delmar, Calif., 1993—. Campaign coord. Georgopoulos for Congress, Manchester, N.H., 1986, Georgopoulos for Gov. Coun., Manchester, N.H., 1984; campaign worker Sununu for Gov., Manchester, N.H., 1982, Nixon re-election, Manchester, N.H., 1972. Mem. U.S. Hockey, 1968—. Republican. Greek Orthodox. Home: 143 Little Bay Rd Newington NH 03801-2700 Office: Kosmos Entertainment Group 20010 Pacific Coast Hwy Malibu CA 90265-5422

GER, SHAW-SHYONG, accountant; b. Kaohsiung, Taiwan, Nov. 19, 1959; s. Jing-Ru and Jui-Mei (Lee) G. BA in econs., Nat. Taiwan U., Taipei, 1981; MBA, Ariz. State U., 1986, M in acctg., 1989. CPA, Ariz. Rsch. asst. Ariz. State U., Tempe, 1988-89; contr. CLH Internat., Inc., Tempe, 1989—. Recipient All Am. Scholar award U.S. Achievement Acad., 1989. Mem. Assn. MBA Exec., Nat. Geog. Soc., Inst. Cert. Mgmt. Accts., Beta Gamma Sigma. Address: PO Box 601 Tempe AZ 85280-0601

GERACIE, MICHAEL LOUIS, JR. (BUD GERACIE), journalist; b. Milw., Oct. 30, 1958; s. Michael Louis and Diane Mary (Doss) G.; m. Janet Kay Smith, Sept. 16, 1989; 1 child, Nicholas Smith. BA in Journalism, U. Wis., 1981. Sports editor UPI, Milw., 1982-83; reporter Milw. Sentinel, 1983-85; reporter San Jose (Calif.) Mercury News, 1985-89, columnist, 1989—. Spokesperson Child Quest Internat., San Jose, 1994; bd. mem. Wender-Weis Found., Palo Alto, Calif., 1995. Office: San Jose Mercury News 750 Ridder Park Dr San Jose CA 95131-2432

GERAGHTY, JOHN VINCENT, mayor; b. Seattle, Feb. 23, 1934; s. John V. and Gladys I (Johnson) G.; m. Marlene Curtis; children: Marcella Maile, Sheila Leek, Brigid Krause, Nora. BA in Comm., U. Wash., 1956; MPA (hon.), Ea. Washington U., 1994. Reporter Spokane (Wash.) Daily Chronicle, 1959-62; sec. to mayor/coun. City of Spokane, 1962-64; county commr. Spokane (Wash.) County, 1964-71; vp. guest rels. EXPO '74 Corp., Spokane, 1971-74; publisher, owner The Falls Newspaper, Spokane, 1974-76; v.p. Haworth & Anderson, Inc., Spokane, 1976-83; owner, pres. Jack Geraghty & Assocs., Spokane, 1983—; pres. Alliance Pacific, Inc., Spokane, 1985-93; mayor City of Spokane, 1994—; bd. dirs., past pres. Future Spokane, 1983-89; cons. Citizens League of Greater Spokane. Bd. dirs. and past pres., Spokane Comty. Mental Health Ctr., 1980-95, mem. and past chmn. Ea. Wash. U. Bd. Dirs., Cheney, Wash., 1985—; mem. and vice chair Spokane Centennial Projects Com., 1988. Mem. Pub. Rels Soc. Am. (pres. Spokane chpt. 1983), Spokane Pub. Rels. Coun. (past pres.), Manito Golf Club, Spokane Club, Beta Theta Pi. Democrat. Roman Catholic. Home: PO Box 251 Spokane WA 99210-0251 Office: City of Spokane 808 W Spokane Falls Blvd Spokane WA 99201-3333

GERARD, NEIL BARRY, educator; b. Bronx, N.Y., Apr. 28, 1947; s. Melvin Bruce and Annette (Neuberger) G.; m. Joan Susan Rosenfeld, June 29, 1969; children: Alison Dawn, Craig Douglas. AA, Nassau Com. Coll., Garden City, 1965; BA, CUNY, Flushing, 1968; MBA, Adelphi U., Garden City, 1972. Dir. student act. Suny Alfred Ag & Tech., Alfred, N.Y., 1968-70; asst. dir. U. Ctr- Adelphi U., Garden City, N.Y., 1970-74; assoc. dir. U. Ctr.- Adelphi U., Garden City, 1974-77; dir./bus. mgr. Calif. Poly. U., Pomona, 1977-93; assoc. dean students, dir. Campus Ctr. Pomona Coll., Claremont, Calif., 1993—. Author: ACUI Bulletin, Coll. Law Enforcement Journal, NACAS Journal. Pres. Temple Beth Israel, Pomona, 1990—. Mem. Prof. Assn. Coll. Unions Internat. (pres. 1987-88, Butts-Whiting award 1996). Democrat Jewish. Home: 2131 Kelly Ave Upland CA 91784-1292 Office: Pomona Coll 575 N College Way Claremont CA 91711-2557

GERBA, CHARLES PETER, microbiologist, educator; b. Blue Island, Ill., Sept. 10, 1945; s. Peter and Virginia (Roulo) G.; m. Peggy Louise Scheitlin, June 6, 1970; children: Peter, Phillip. BS in Microbiology, Ariz. State U., 1969; PhD in Microbiology, U. Miami, 1973. Postdoctoral fellow Baylor Coll. Medicine, Houston, 1973-74, asst. prof. microbiology, 1974-81; assoc. prof. U. Ariz., Tucson, 1981-85, prof., 1985—; cons. EPA, Tucson, 1980—, World Health Orgn., Pan Am. Health Orgn., 1989—; advisor CRC Press, Boca Raton, Fla., 1981—. Editor: Methods in Environmental Virology, 1982, Groundwater Pollution Microbiology, 1984, Phage Ecology, 1987, Pollution Sci., 1996; contbr. numerous articles to profl. and sci. jours. Mem. Pima County Bd. Health, 1986-92; mem. sci. adv. bd. EPA, 1987—. Recipient McKee medal Water Environ. Fedn., 1996; named Outstanding Research Scientist U. Ariz., 1984, 92, Outstanding Rsch. Team, 1994. Fellow AAAS (environ. sci. and engring.), Am. Acad. Microbiology, Am. Soc. Microbiology (divsn. chmn. 1982-83, 87-88, pres. Ariz. chpt. 1984-85, councilor 1985-88); mem. Internat. Assn. Water Pollution Rsch. (sr. del. 1985-91), Am. Water Works Assn. (A.P. Black award 1997). Home: 1980 W Paseo Monserrat Tucson AZ 85704-1329 Office: U Ariz Dept Microbiol & Immunol Water & Soils Tucson AZ 85721

GERBER, LLOYD M., business consultant; b. Mapleton, Utah, Apr. 14, 1927; s. Irvin M. and Emily Aurilla (McKee) G.; m., Dec. 20, 1951; children: Steven, Kathryn, Julie, Lisa, Susan, Lori, Mark, Nathan. BS, Brigham Young U., 1953; LLB, George Washington U., 1957. Bar: N. Mex. 1958, Utah 1960. Lawyer, pvt. practice Farmington, N. Mex., 1958-59; contract adminstr. Thiokol Chems., Salt Lake City, 1960-64, Uta Rsch. and Devel., Salt Lake City, 1960-64; ptnr. Madsen, Tanner, Gerber, Uno, Salt Lake City, 1966-69; v.p., gen. mgr. Robinson Terminal, Alexandria, Va., 1969-80, ceo, pres., 1980-85; cons. real estate, bus. Boise, 1989. Author poems; appeared on Tonight Show NBC, 1989. Mem., chmn. Planning & Zoning, Eagle, Idaho, 1989-93. Republican. Home: 3420 Shadow Hills Dr Eagle ID 83616

GERBER, MICHAEL LEWIS, cardiac surgeon; b. Pitts., Mar. 25, 1938; s. Max H. and Fay F. G.; m. Barbara Schulman, Feb. 23, 1963; children: Michael L., Laurel E., Andrew D. BS, U. Pitts., 1959, MD, 1963, JD, 1990; LLM Georgetown U. Law Ctr., 1992. Intern, Ind. U. Med. Center, 1963-64; resident U. Pitts. Med. Ctr., 1964-68, Allegheny Gen. Hosp., 1968-69; resident plastic surg. EVMC, 1993-94, UMMC, 1994-95; clin. instr. surgery U. Pitts. With USAR, 1963-69. Diplomate Am. Bd. Surgery, Am. Bd. Thoracic Surgery. Mem. ACS, Soc. Thoracic Surgeons, AMA, Am. Coll. Chest Physicians, Pan-Pacific Surg. Assn., Am. Heart Assn., Am. Assn. for Thoracic Surgery, Pitts. Thoracic Surg. Soc. (past pres.). Republican. Home: 1535 El Paseo Real La Jolla CA 92037-6303

GERBER, SANFORD EDWIN, audiologist; b. Chgo., June 16, 1933; s. Leon and Rose (Ely) G.; m. Sharon R. Doyle; children: Howard M., Michael B., Naomi R., Sharon R. BA, Lake Forest Coll., 1954; MS, U. Ill., 1956; PhD, U. So. Calif., 1962. Speech clinician East Whittier City Sch. Dist., Whittier, Calif., 1956-58; Sr. human factors specialist System Devel. Corp., Santa Monica, Calif., 1958-60; head speech and hearing rsch. Hughes Aircraft Co., Fullerton, Calif., 1960-65; asst. prof. audiology U. Calif., Santa Barbara, 1965-69; assoc. prof. U. Calif., 1969-75, prof., 1975-94, coord. speech and hearing scis., 1974-79, chmn. dept. speech and hearing scis., 1979-84; prof. emeritus, 1994—; chair vis. prof. dept. comm. disorders Ea. Wash. U., Cheney, 1994—; adj. prof. Wash. State U., 1994—; mem. sci. bd. Audio-Metric Labs., Inc., Stamford, Conn., 1979-82; cons. CBS Tech. Ctr., Stamford, 1969-80, U.S. Dept. Def., Ft. Meade, Md., 1967-80; bd. dirs. KPBX Spokane Pub. Radio, 1995—. Author: Introductory Hearing Science, 1974, Audiometry in Infancy, 1977, Early Diagnosis of Hearing Loss, 1980, Early Management of Hearing Loss, 1981, The Development of Auditory Behavior, 1983, The Multiply-Handicapped Hearing-Impaired Child, 1983, International Perspectives on Communication Disorders, 1988, Prevention, 1990, Handbook of Pediatric Audiology, 1996, Audiology and Auditory Dysfunction, 1996; contbr. numerous articles to profl. jours. Pres. Congregation B'nai Brith, Santa Barbara, 1972-74, Univ. Religious Conf., 1974-76; trustee Santa Barbara coun. Assn. for Retarded Citizens, 1973-78, 80-88, 89-94, treas., 1977-78, sec., 1990-93; mem. governing bd. Assn. for Retarded Citizens Calif., 1987-94; trustee Santa Barbara Jewish Fedn., 1974-84, Spl. Californian's Found., 1983-89. Fellow So. Ear, Nose, Throat Advances in Children (pres. 1976-77), Am. Acad. Otolaryngology Head and Neck Surgery (assoc.), Am. Speech-Lang.-Hearing Assn.; mem. Pan-Am. Soc. Audiology (pres. 1992—), Internat. Soc. Audiology (exec. com. 1982-92), Am. Auditory Soc., Am. Acad. Audiology, Sigma Xi. Office: 704 East 23d Ave Cheney WA 99004 *While I may be able to comment upon my own standards of conduct, I cannot say if these standards have led to success in another's view. I have endeavored to find and say truth in my scholarly activity and in my daily life; perhaps this is a form of integrity. As a teacher, I hope to help find my students' integrity. I don't believe that I have created my students, but maybe sometimes I have helped them create themselves.*

GERBRACHT, ROBERT THOMAS (BOB GERBRACHT), painter, educator; b. Erie, Pa., June 23, 1924; s. Earl John and Lula Mary (Chapman) G.; m. Delia Marie Paz, Nov. 27, 1952; children: Mark, Elizabeth, Catherine. BFA, Yale U., 1951; MFA, U. So. Calif., 1952. Cert. tchr., Calif. Art tchr. William S. Hart Jr. and Sr. High Sch., Newhall, Calif., 1954-56; stained glass artist Cummings Studios, San Francisco, 1956-58; art tchr. McKinley Jr. High Sch., Redwood City, Calif., 1958-60, Castro Jr. High Sch., San Jose, Calif., 1960-79; portrait artist, tchr. San Jose, San Francisco, 1979—; instr. art Coll. of Notre Dame, Belmont, Calif., 1955-60, San Jose City Coll., 1967-71, Notre Dame Novitiate, Saratoga, 1976-79, U. Calif., Santa Cruz, 1980-81; art cons. Moreland Sch. Dist., Campbell, Calif., 1979-80; instr. nationwide workshops, Calif., Colo., Fla., Mass., N.Mex., N.Y., Oreg., S.C., Vt., Wash., Wis., Mex., 1980—. Represented in permanent collection Triton Mus. Art, Santa Clara, Calif.; portraits include Marie Gallo, Mrs. Bruce Jenner, Austin Warburton, Rev. Cecil Williams; subject of articles in Today's Art and Graphics, Art and Antique Collector, Am. Artist, U.S. ART; work reproduced and included in Best of Pastel and Best of Oil Painting, 1996. Cpl. U.S. Army, 1943-46. Recipient Am. Artist Achievement award Tchr. of Pastels, 1993. Mem. Pastel Soc. Am., Pastel Soc. West Coast (advisor, Best of Show 1988), Soc. Western Artists (trustee 1989-97, Best of Show 1982, 85, 90, Best Portrait award 1984), Oil Painters Am. Home: 1301 Blue Oak Ct Pinole CA 94564-2145

GEREN, LAURIE HEWITT, educator; b. Hanover, N.H., Sept. 20, 1954; d. William Joseph and Florence (Mandigo) Hewitt; m. Deryl S. Geren, Nov. 8, 1975; children: Mark, Jodi Lynn, Megan Lee. AA, Coll. So. Idaho, Twin Falls, 1990; BA, Idaho State U., 1992. Cert. tchr., Idaho. Educator Hansen (Idaho) Elem., 1992-94; educator O'Leary Jr. H.S., Twin Falls, 1994—, impact dir., 1994—. Elder, deacon Presbyn. Ch. Nat. child devel. assoc., 1990. Mem. PEO (guard chpt. D 1994-95), Magic Valley Reading Coun. (pres. 1995-96), Alpha Delta Kappa, Phi Kappa Phi. Home: 810 Chase Dr Twin Falls ID 83301 Office: Twin Falls Sch Dist # 411 201 Main Ave W Twin Falls ID 83301-6103

GERINGER, JAMES E., governor; b. Wheatland, Wyo., Apr. 24, 1944; m. Sherri Geringer; children: Jen, Val, Rob, Meri, Beckie. BS in Mechanical Engring., Kans. State U., 1967. Commd. officer USAF; with contract administration Mo. Basin Power Project's Laramie River Sta., 1977-79; elected mem. Wyo. Legislature, 1982; farm owner, 1987—; Governor State of Wyoming, 1994—; participant in various space devel. programs, Calif., devel. variety Air Force and NASA space boosters including launches of reconnaissance satellites, the NASA Viking Mars lander, an upper stage booster for the space shuttle and the Global Positioning Satellite System; chief of computer programming at a ground receiving station for early warning satellites. Mem. Nat. Fedn. Ind. Bus., Am. Legion, Farm Bur., Farmer's Union, Rotary, Lions, Ducks Unlimited, Pheasants Forever, C. of C. Lutheran. Office: Office of the Gov State Capitol Bldg 124 200 W 24th St Cheyenne WY 82002-0010*

GERKEN, WALTER BLAND, insurance company executive; b. N.Y.C., Aug. 14, 1922; s. Walter Adam and Virginia (Bl) G.; m. Darlene Stolt, Sept. 6, 1952; children: Walter C., Ellen M., Beth L., Daniel J., Andrew P., David A. BA, Wesleyan U., 1948; MPA, Maxwell Sch. Citizenship and Pub. Affairs, Syracuse, 1958. Supr. budget and adminstrv. analysis Wis., Madison, 1950-54; mgr. investments Northwestern Mut. Life Ins. Co., Milw., 1954-67; v.p. finance Pacific Mut. Life Ins. Co., L.A., 1967-69, exec. v.p., 1969-72, pres., 1972-75, chmn. bd., 1975-87; chmn. exec. com. Pacific Mut. Life Ins. Co., Los Angeles, 1987-95, also dir.; sr. advisor Boston Consulting Group; chmn. equity bd. PIMCO Advisors, L.P.; bd. dirs. Mullin Cons., Inc. Bd. dirs. Keck Found.; bd. dirs. Hoag Meml. Presbyn. Hosp.; chmn. bd. Hoag Hosp. Found., 1993-95; trustee emeritus Occidental Coll. L.A., Wesleyan U., Middletown, Conn.; chmn. bd. Nature Conservancy Calif., Exec. Svc. Corp.; mem. Calif. Citizens Budget Com., Calif. Commn. Campaign Fin. Reform, Calif. Commn. on Higher Edn., Nat. Sch. to Work Adv. Coun.; chair Exec. Svc. Corps. So. Calif. Decorated D.F.C., Air medal. Mem. Calif. Club, Dairymen's Country Club (Boulder Junction, Wis.), Balboa Bay Club (Newport Beach, Calif., former bd. dirs.), Automobile Club So. Calif. (bd. dirs.), Calif. Ind. Coll. Network (co-chair), Pauma Valley Country Club. Office: Pacific Mut Life Ins Co 700 Newport Center Dr Newport Beach CA 92660-6307

GERLACH, WILLIAM EDWARD, agricultural marketing executive; b. Eau Claire, Wis., Sept. 28, 1950; s. Edward B. and Marie A. G.; m. Cheryl Ann Hamilton, Aug. 1988; 1 child, Ian Hunter. BA in Econ., U. Wis., 1972; MS Agrl. and Managerial Econ., U. Calif., Davis, 1981. English tchr. Peace Corps., Danané, West Africa, 1972-74; pers. recruiter Peace Corps./Vista, N.Y.C., San Francisco, 1975-79; rsch. asst. U. Calif., Davis, 1980-81; commodity analyst, economist Calif. Farm Bur. Fedn., Sacramento, 1981-88; patent mgmt., mkt. rsch., strategic planning U. Calif. Tech. Transfer Office, Alameda, 1988—. Vol. tchr. Ctr. for New Americans, Concord, 1991-96. With Peace Corps., 1972-74. Home: 775 Miller Ave Martinez CA 94553-1348

GERMAN, DONALD FREDERICK, physician; b. San Francisco, Oct. 2, 1935; m. Marilyn Sue King; children: Susan, Charles, Donald. BS, U. San Francisco, 1956; MD, U. Calif., San Francisco, 1960. Diplomate Am. Bd. Pediats., Am. Bd. Allergy and Immunology. Intern Kaiser Found. Hosp., San Francisco, 1960-61, resident in pediats., 1963-65, resident, fellow in allergy, 1966-68; staff pediatrician Kaiser Med. Ctr., Santa Clara, Calif., 1965-66, staff allergist, 1968-69; chief dept. allergy Kaiser Permanente Med. Ctr., San Francisco, 1969—; clin. prof. pediatrics U. Calif. Med. Sch., San Francisco, 1991—. Capt. USAF, 1961-63. Fellow Am. Acad. Pediats., Am. Coll. Allergy and Immunology, Am. Acad. Allergy and Immunology. Office: Kaiser Permanente Med Ctr Allergy Dept 1635 Divisadero St Ste 101 San Francisco CA 94115-3000

GERMAN, WILLIAM, newspaper editor; b. N.Y.C., Jan. 4, 1919; s. Sam and Celia (Norack) G.; m. Gertrude Pasenkoff, Oct. 12, 1940; children: David, Ellen, Stephen. B.A., Bklyn. Coll., 1939; M.S., Columbia U., 1940; Nieman fellow, Harvard U., 1950. Reporter, asst. fgn., news, mng., exec. editor, editor San Francisco Chronicle, 1940—; editor Chronicle Fgn. Service, 1960-77; mng. editor KQED, Newspaper of the Air, 1968; lectr. U. Calif., Berkeley, 1946-47, 68-70. Editor: San Francisco Chronicle Reader, 1962. Bd. trustees World Affairs Coun. Served with AUS, 1943-45. Mem. AP Mng. Editors Assn., Am. Soc. Newspaper Editors, Commonwealth Club of Calif. (pres. 1995). Home: 150 Lovell Ave Mill Valley CA 94941-1883 Office: San Francisco Chronicle 901 Mission St San Francisco CA 94103-2905

GERNER, ANDRE ANTHONY, air force officer; b. Redwood City, Calif., July 8, 1957; s. Sebastian and Anna (Schmidt) G.; m. Terri Kay Donaldson, Sept. 8, 1984; children: Andre S., Joseph A. Student, U. Santa Clara, 1975-77; BS in Aero. Engring., USAF Acad., 1981; MS in Aero. and Astro. Engring., U. Wash., 1982; postgrad., USAF Test Pilot Sch. Class 91A, 1991. Commd. 2d lt. USAF, 1981, advanced through grades to lt. col., 1997; prin. rschr. NASA Ames Rsch. Ctr., Moffett Field, Calif., 1983; pilot 384th AREFS & 384th BMW, McConnell AFB, Kans., 1984-87, 32d AREFS, Barksdale AFB, La., 1987-90; exptl. test pilot USAF, Edwards AFB, Calif., 1991-94; rsch. fellow RAND, Santa Monica, Calif., 1994-95; instr. aero. engring. USAF Acad., USAFA, Colo., 1995—. Contbr. articles to profl. publs. Mem. AIAA (sr. mem., 1st place award aerospace scis. meeting 1982). Republican.

GEROU, PHILLIP HOWARD, architect; b. Natick, Mass., July 20, 1951; s. James Francis and Enid (Meymaris) G.; m. Cheri Rodgers, Nov. 24, 1979; children: Gregory Bedford, Sara Christine. BArch, U. Nebr., 1974, MArch, 1975. Architect Denver, 1975-77; project mgr. Henningson, Durham, Richardson, Denver, 1978-82; dir. architecture Daniel Mann Johnson Mendenhall, Denver, 1982-85; v.p., dir. comml. design Downing Leach Architects, Boulder, 1985-86; prin., designer Gerou & Assocs. Ltd., Evergreen, Colo., 1986—; design cons. Kilimanjaro Children's Hosp., Tanzania, 1988-91, World Alpine Ski Championships, Vail, Colo., 1988. Pres. Colo. Soc. of Architects Ednl. Fund., Denver, 1986; del. State Rep. Assembly, Denver, 1986; trustee Rockland Community Ch., Denver, 1986-89. Recipient Citation award Nat. Assn. of Remodeling Industry, 1991, 96, Design Excellence Wood, Inc., 1990, Citation award, 1990. Fellow AIA (pres. Colo. chpt. 1986, bd. dirs. 1981-87, nat. dir. 1991-94, v.p. 1995, conf. chair Western Mtn. region 1990, spl. recognition award 1990), Nat. Coun. Archl. Adminstrn. Bds. (examiner 1985). Republican. Mem. United Ch. of Christ. *

GEROW, LYNN BURDETTE, JR., psychiatrist; b. Reno, Nev., Jan. 19, 1942; s. Lynn Burdette and Nell Juanita (Lozano) G.; m. Ann Marie Prida, Dec. 20, 1965; 1 child, James Byron. BS, U. Nev., Reno, 1963; MD, McGill U., Montreal, Quebec, Can., 1967. Diplomate Am. Bd. Psychiatry and Neurology, Nat. Bd. Med. Examiners; lic. Calif., Nev. Intern Walter Reed Gen. Hosp., Washington, 1967-68; resident in psychiatry Letterman Gen. Hosp., San Francisco, 1968-71; fellow in Cmty. Psychiatry, Ctr. for Tng. in Cmty. Psychiatr y, Mental Health Adminstrn., Langley Porter Inst., San Francisco, 1969-71; fellow in child psychiatry Letterman Gen. Hosp. and Langley Porter Neuropsychiat. Inst., San Francisco, 1971-73; asst. chief and dir. tng. Child Psychiatry Svc. Letternam Gen. Hosp., San Francisco, 1973-75; clin. instr. of psychiatry U. Calif. Sch. Medicine, San Francisco, 1974-75; mem. com. for protection of human subjects U. Nev., Reno, 1978-80; pvt. practice psychiatry Reno, Nev., 1975—; from asst. clin. prof. to assoc. clin. prof. dept. psychiatry and behavioral scis. U. Nev. Sch. Medicine, Reno, 1979-86; attending psychiatrist Washoe Med. Ctr., 1975-93, asst. chmn. dept. psychiatry, 1976-77, chmn., mem. exec. com., 1978-80, 82-84; attending psychiatrist St. Mary's Hosp., VA Hosp., Reno, 1975, Truckee Meadows Hosp., Reno, 1981-82, Sparks Family Hosp., Reno, 1983-94; psychiat. cons. Nev. Blue Shield, 1976-84; trustee Washoe Med. Ctr., 1980-86, chmn. budget and fin. com., 1982-86. Lt. col. U.S. Army Med. Corps, 1967-75. Lt. col. U.S. Army Med. Corps, 1967-75. Fellow Am. Acad. Disability Evaluating Physicians; mem. AMA, Am. Psychiat. Assn., Nev. State Med. Assn., Washoe County Med. Soc., Nev. Psychiat. Assn., Am. Acad. Psychiatry and the Law, Am. Acad. Forensic Scis., Nat. Assn. Disability Evaluating Physicians, Am. Occupational Med. Assn. Office: 50 Kirman Ave Ste 301 Reno NV 89502-1178

GERRODETTE, CHARLES EVERETT, real estate company executive, consultant; b. Alderwood Manor, Wash., June 18, 1934; s. Honoré Everett and Marjorie Violet (Stapley) G.; m. Laurine Carol Manley, Mar. 16, 1956 (div. 1977); children: Stephen Everett, Suzanne Gerrodette Prince; m. Diane Marie Drumm, Dec. 6, 1984. BA in Bus. Adminstrn., U. Wash., 1956, postgrad., 1959; postgrad., NYU, 1956-57. Credit analyst and corr. comml. credit dept. Chase Manhattan Bank, N.Y.C., 1956-57; reviewing appraiser Prudential Ins. Co. Am., Seattle, 1959-67; v.p., sr. loan officer real estate group Seattle 1st Nat. Bank, 1967-90; pres., CEO, Portal Pacific Co., Inc., Seattle, 1990—; real estate advisor, fin. cons. Charles E. Gerrodette, MAI, Seattle, 1990—; instr. appraising Shoreline C.C., Seattle, 1974-76. Contbg. author: Prentice Hall Ency. of Real Estate Appraising, 3d edit., 1978. Mem. blue ribbon com. for planning Shoreline Sch. Dist., Seattle, 1974-75. With U.S. Army, 1957-59. Mem. Am. Arbitration Assn. (panel of arbitrators), Appraisal Inst. (MAI designation 1972, officer, bd. dirs. Wash.-B.C. chpt. 1980-89, pres. 1984, nat. fin. and adminstrn. com. 1982-87, nat. governing counselor 1987-89, nat. fin. com. 1990-96), Mortgage Bankers Assn. (income property com.), Columbia Tower Club, Lambda Alpha, N.W. Grad. Assn. Theta Delta Chi (trustee 1960-70, past pres.). Episcopalian. Office: 2125 1st Ave Ste 1204 Seattle WA 98121-2118

GERRY, DEBRA PRUE, psychotherapist; b. Oct. 9, 1951; d. C.O. and Sarah E. Rawl; m. Norman Bernard Gerry, Apr. 10, 1981; 1 child, Gisele Psyche Victoria. BS, Ga. So. U., 1972; MEd, Armstrong State U., 1974; PhD, U. Ga., 1989. Cert. Ariz. Bd. Behavioral Health Examiners. Spl. edn. tchr. Chatham County Bd. Edn., Savannah, Ga., 1972-74; edn. and learning disabilities resource educator Duval County Bd. Edn., Jacksonville, Fla., 1974-77; ednl. resource counselor spl. programs adminstr. Broward County Bd. Edn., Ft. Lauderdale, Fla., 1977-81; pvt. practice Scottsdale, Ariz., 1990—. Contbr. author coll. textbooks; contbr. articles to profl. jours. Vol., fundraiser, psychol. cons., group leader Valley AIDS Orgns., Phoenix, 1990-96; fundraiser Hosp. Health Edn. Programs, Scottsdale, 1992-93; mem. com. for women's issues Plz. Club, Phoenix, 1992-93; pres. Laissez Les Bon Temps Rouler, Wrigley Club, Phoenix, 1993-96; bd. dirs. Sojourner's Ctr., Phoenix; appointee Ariz. Supreme Ct., Foster Care Rev. Bd., Phoenix, 1996-99. Recipient Rudy award Shanti Orgn., 1991. Mem. APA, NOW, ACA, Internat. Soc. Poets (disting., Poet of Merit award 1996), Nat. Assn. Women Bus. Owners, Assn. for Multicultural Coun., Assn. for Specialists in Group Work, Mensa, Phi Delta Kappa, Kappa Delta Epsilon, Sigma Omega Phi, Kappa Delta Pi.

GERSTELL, A. FREDERICK, aggregates and asphalt and concrete manufacturing executive; b. 1938. AB, Princeton U., 1960. Vice pres. mktg., dir. Alpha Portland Cement Co., 1960-75; v.p. Calif. Portland Cement Co., L.A., 1975-81, pres., chief operating officer, 1981-84; pres., chief operating officer CalMat Co., L.A., 1984-88, pres., chief exec. officer, chief operating officer, 1988-90, chmn.bd., pres., chief exec. officer/chief operating officer, 1990-96, chmn. bd., CEO, 1996—. Trustee emeritus The Lawrenceville (N.J.) Sch. With USAR 1960-66. Mem. Merchants and Mfrs. Assn. (dir.), Nat. Stone Assn. (bd. dirs., vice chmn., exec. com.), Calif. C. of C. (bd. dirs.), Ameron, Inc. (dir.). Office: CalMat Co 3200 N San Fernando Rd Los Angeles CA 90065-1415

GERTH, DONALD ROGERS, university president; b. Chgo., Dec. 4, 1928; s. George C. and Madeleine (Canavan) G.; m. Beverly J. Hollman, Oct. 15, 1955; children: Annette, Deborah. BA, U. Chgo., 1947, AM, 1951, PhD, 1963. Field rep. S.E. Asia World Univ. Svc., 1950; asst. to pres. Shimer Coll., 1951; Admissions counselor U. Chgo., 1956-58; assoc. dean students, admissions and records, mem. dept. polit. sci. San Francisco St. U., San Francisco, 1958-63; assoc. dean instnl. relations and student affairs Calif. State Univ., 1963-64; chmn. commn. on extended edn. Calif. State Univs. and Colls., 1977-82; dean of students Calif. State U., Chico, 1964-68, prof. polit. sci., 1964-76, assoc. v.p. for acad. affairs, dir. internat. programs, 1969-70, v.p. acad. affairs, 1970-76; co-dir. Danforth Found. Research Project, 1968-69; coordinator Inst. Local Govt. and Public Service, 1968-70; pres., prof. polit. sci. and public adminstrn. Calif. State U., Dominguez Hills, 1976-84; pres., prof. govt. and adminstrn. Calif. State U., Sacramento, 1984—; past chair Accrediting Commn. for Sr. Colls. and Univs. of Western Coll. Assn.; chmn. admissions coun. Calif. State U.; bd. dirs. Ombudsman Found., L.A., 1968-71; com. continuing edn. Calif. Coordinating Coun. for Higher Edn., 1963-64; lectr. U. Philippines, 1953-54, Claremont Grad. Sch. and Univ. Ctr., 1965-69; chair Sacramento World Trade Ctr.; vice chmn. Calif. State U. Inst. Co-author: The Learning Society, 1969; author, editor: An Invisible Giant, 1971; contbg. editor Education for the Public Service, 1970, Papers on the Ombudsman in Higher Education, 1979. Mem. pers. commn. Chico Unified Sch. Dist., 1969-76, chmn., 1971-74; adv. com. on justice pgorams Butte Coll., 1970-76; mem. Varsity Scouting Coun., 1980-84; chmn. United Way campaign Calif. State Univs., L.A. County, 1981-82; bd. dirs. Sacramento Area United Way, campaign chmn., 1991-92, exec. com., 1991-96, vice chmn., 1992-94, chmn.-elect, 1994-95, chmn., 1995—; mem. bd. dirs. South Bay Hosp. Found., 1979-82; mem. The Cultural Commn., L.A., 1981-84; mem. com. govtl. rels. Am. Coun. Edn. Capt. USAF, 1952-56. Mem. Internat. Assn. Univ. Pres. (pres. 1996—), Am. Polit. Sci. Assn., Am. Soc. Pub. Adminstrn., Soc. Coll. and Univ. Planning, Western Govtl. Rsch. Assn., World Affairs Coun. No. Calif., Assn. Pub. Adminstrn. Edn. (chmn. 1973-74), Western Polit. Sci. Assn., Am. Assn. State Colls. and Univs. (bd. dirs.), Calif. State C. of C. (edn. com.), Assn. Governing Bds. of Univs. and Colls., Sacramento Club (bd. dirs.), Comstock Club. Democrat. Episcopalian. Home: 417 Webster's Ct Roseville CA 95747 Office: Calif State U 6000 J St # 206 Sacramento CA 95819-2605

GERTZ, DAVID LEE, homebuilding company executive; b. Denver, July 30, 1950; s. Ben Harry and Clara (Cohen) G.; m. Bonnie Lee Schulein, June 2, 1973; children: Joshua, Eva. BS, U. Colo., 1972; MBA, U. Colo., Denver, 1993. Real estate broker Crown Realty, Denver, 1972-73; pres. Sunshine Plumbing Co., Lakewood, Colo., 1974-76, Sunshine Diversified, Inc., Lakewood, 1976—, Sunshine Master Builders, Ltd., Lakewood, 1990—; sec.-treas. Wight Lateral Ditch Co., Lakewood, 1987-91. Builder of custom homes and toxin free homes for allergy sensitive people. Cub master pack 135 Cub Scouts Am., Lakewood, 1989-91; asst. scout master troop 135 Boy Scouts Am., Lakewood, 1991-94; co-chair bldg. com. Hebrew Ednl. Alliance; bd. dirs. Hebrew Ednl. Alliance, Denver, 1991-94; mem. Anti-Defamation League, Denver, 1989—. Scholar, Evans Scholars, U. Colo., 1968-72. Mem. Home Builders Assn. of Colo. (energy com. 1986—, Lakewood coord. com. 1986—, Jeffco coord. com. 1986—), Jeffco Bd. Realtors. Office: Sunshine Master Builders 8125 W Belleview Ave Littleton CO 80123-1203

GERWICK-BRODEUR, MADELINE CAROL, marketing and timing professional; b. Kearney, Neb., Aug. 29, 1951; d. Vern Frank and Marian Leila (Bliss) Gerwick; m. David Louis Brodeur; 1 child, Maria Louise. Student, U. Wis., 1970-72, U. Louisville, 1974-75; BA in Econs. magna cum laude, U. N.H., 1979; postgrad., Internat. Trade Inst., Seattle. Cert. profl. cycles cons., 1995; cert. bus. astrologer. Indsl. sales rep. United Radio Supply Inc., Seattle, 1980-81; mfrs. rep. Ray Over Sales Inc., Seattle, 1981-82; sales engr. Tektronix, Inc., Kent, Wash., 1982-83; mktg. mgr. Zepher Industries, Inc., Burien, Wash., 1983-85, Microscan Systems Inc., Tukwila, Wash., 1986.; market devel. URS Electronics, Inc., Portland, 1986-88; sr. product specialist Fluke Corp., 1989-95; owner Astro Cycles Cons. L.L.C., Seattle, 1995—; bd. dirs., sec. Starfish Enterprises Inc., Tacoma, 1984-87; com. chmn. Northcon, Seattle and Portland, 1984-86, 88, 90; speaker to Wash. Women's Employment and Edn., Tacoma, 1983—. Writer daily col. for Zodiac Zone, Online Noetic Network; pub. The Good Timing Bus. Calendar; co-author The Complete Idiot's Guide To Astrology, 1997. Recipient Jack E. Chase award for Outstanding Svc. and Contbr. Northcon Founder's Orgn., 1988. Mem. Electronic Mfrs. Assn. (sec. 1982, sec.-treas. 1988, v.p. 1989), Inst. Noetic Scis., Internat. Soc. for Astrol. Rsch., Wash. State Astrol. Assn. (bd. dirs. 1996—), Phi Kappa Phi. *Since not all days are created equal, Madeline Gerwick-Brodeur offers good timing for new business ventures, product introductions, new team starts or major events, to get them off to a good start and assure the best possible outcomes. Her 15 years of business experience, 20 years of cycle and timing experience, plus astrological certification, uniquely qualifies her for this work. Her Good Timing Calendar provides daily cycles for all types of business activities and includes quarterly newsletters with trends and special opportunity days.*

GERZSO, GUNTHER, painter, graphic artist; b. Mexico City, June 17, 1915. Exhbns. include FIAC Art Contemporain, Grand Palais, Paris, 1978, Inst. Fine Arts, Mex., 1980, El Arbol Fla., 1981-82, Mus du Petit Palais, 1982, Mary-Ann Martin Fine Arts, N.Y.C., 1984, Galeria de Arte Mex., 1990, others. Guggenheim fellow, 1973; recipient Nat Prize Fine Arts, Mex., 1978. Office: care George Belcher Gallery 74 New Montgomery St Ste 750 San Francisco CA 94105-1607*

GESHELL, RICHARD STEVEN, lawyer; b. Colorado Springs, Colo., Aug. 6, 1943; s. Peter Steven and Ann Elizabeth (Irwin) G.; m. Carol Ann Reed, Sept. 6, 1965; 1 child, Carmen Marie. BA in Chemistry, Ariz. State U., 1965; JD, U. Nebr., 1968. Bar: Nebr. 1968, U.S. Dist. Ct. Nebr. 1968, Hawaii 1983, U.S. Dist. Ct. Hawaii 1983, U.S. Ct. Appeals (9th cir.) 1984, U.S. Supreme Ct. 1986. Mem. Robak and Geshell, Columbus, Nebr., 1968-83; ptnr. R. Steven Geshell, Honolulu, 1983—. Served to capt. USAR, 1974-83. Mem. Assn. Trial Lawyers Am., Nebr. Bar Assn., Hawaii Bar Assn., Blue Key (pres. 1964-65), Mid-Pacific C. C., Elks (chief forum 1984, past exalted ruler, trustee), Phi Sigma Kappa (past house mor, past v.p.). Republican. Home: 1155 Kaluanui Rd Honolulu HI 96825-1357 Office: 6600 Kalanianaole Hwy Ste 116 Honolulu HI 96825-1280

GESNER, BRUCE DAVID, consulting company executive; b. Fall River, Mass., May 7, 1938; s. Norval Garfield Jr. and Margaret Lena (Glynn) G.; m. Claudette Jeannine Labreche, June 6, 1959 (div. Apr. 1991); children: Jeannine Catherine, Bruce David Jr., Jacqueline Marie, Michael Steven; m. Barbara Phyllis Whittiker, May 11, 1991. BS in Chemistry, Southeastern U. Mass., 1960; PhD in Physical Organic Chemistry, U. Idaho, 1963. Mem. tech. staff Bell Labs., Murray Hill, N.J., 1963-69; supr. PWB group Bell Labs., Whippany, N.J., 1969-71; supr. materials chemistry Bell Labs., Norcross, Ga., 1971-77; sr. field rep. Bell Labs., Omaha, 1978-82, San Francisco, 1982-84; divsn. mgr., liaison Bellcore, San Francisco, 1985; exec. dir. technology Pacific Bell, San Ramon, Calif., 1986-90; owner, operator Qaulitel Cons. Group, Danville, Calif., 1990—. PAtentee in field. Sec., treas. Puddingstone Heights Country Club, Parsippany, N.J., 1970-71; treas. Smoke Rise (Ga.) Cmty Club, 1976-77. Mass. State scholar, 1959, 60; Nat Defense fellow, 1960-63. Mem. AAAS, Am. Chem. Soc., Calif. Acad. Sci. (pres. cir. 1991-94), Phi Kappa Phi, Sigma Xi. Home: 1300 Fountain Springs Cir Danville CA 94526-5625 Office: Qualitel Cons Group 900 Bush St Apt 903 San Francisco CA 94109-6394

GESSEL, DAVID CLYDE, lawyer; b. Salt Lake City, June 9, 1959; s. Clyde David and Mary Louise (Gardner) G.; m. Diana Marie Allen, Nov. 10, 1987; children: Michael Allen, Megan Elizabeth, James David. BS in Polit. Sci. cum laude, U. Utah, 1983; MA in Polit. Sci. and Pub. Policy, Rutgers U., 1986; grad. cert. in state and local govt., U. Utah, 1986; JD, U. Va., 1991. Bar: Utah 1991. Legis. asst., legis. dir. Congressman Ron Packard, Washington, 1986-88; atty. Jones, Waldo, Holbrook and McDonough, Salt Lake City, 1991-94; v.p. govt. rels. and legal affairs Utah Assn. Healthcare Providers, Salt Lake City, 1994—. Exec. editor Va. Environ. Law Jour., 1990-91. Rep. LDS Ch., Australia, 1978-80. Recipient Elbert D. Thomas award U. Utah, Salt Lake City, 1983; Eagleton fellow Eagleton Inst. Politics of Rutgers U., New Brunswick, N.J., 1985-86. Mem. Am. Soc. Assn. Execs., Am. Acad. of Health Care Attys., Phi Delta Phi, Pi Sigma Alpha. Office: Utah Assn Health Care Providers 2180 S 1300 E Ste 440 Salt Lake City UT 84106

GETIS, ARTHUR, geography educator; b. Phila., July 6, 1934; s. Samuel J. and Sophie Getis; m. Judith M. Marckwardt, July 23, 1961; children: Hilary Hope Tarazi, Victoria Lynn, Anne Patterson Tibbetts. BS, Pa. State U., 1956, MS, 1958; PhD, U. Wash., 1961. Asst. instr. geography U. Wash., 1960-61; asst. prof. Mich. State U., 1961-63; faculty Rutgers U., New Brunswick, N.J., 1963-77; prof. geography Rutgers U., 1969-77, dir. grad. programs in geography, 1970-73, chmn. New Brunswick geography dept., 1971-73; prof. geography U. Ill., Urbana-Champaign, 1977-90; prof. geography San Diego State U., 1990—, doctoral program coord., 1990-92; Stephen/Mary Birch Found. Endowed Chair of Geog. Studies, 1992—, Albert W. Johnson Univ. Rsch. Lectureship, 1995; head dept. U. Ill., 1977-83, dir. Sch. Social Scis., 1983-84; centennial fellow Pa. State U., 1996; vis. lectr. Bristol U., Eng., 1966-67, UCLA, summers 1968, 74, U. B.C., 1969; vis. prof. Princeton U., 1971-74; vis. disting. prof. San Diego State U., 1989; mem. Regional Sci. Research Group, Harvard U., 1970; panelist NSF, 1981-83. Author: (with B. Boots) Models of Spatial Processes, 1978, Point Pattern Analysis, 1988, (with J. Getis and J.D. Fellmann) Geography, 1981, Human Geography, 3d edit., 1992, 4th edit., 1994, 5th edit., 1996, Introduction to

Geography, 4th edit., 1994, (edited with J. Getis) The United States and Canada, 1995; editor Geographical Systems, 1992—; contbg. editor, assoc. editor: Jour. Geography, 1972-74; mem. editl. bd. Nat. Geog. Rsch., 1984-90, Rsch. and Exploration, 1991-95, Geog. Analysis, 1991—. Mem. Urbana Zoning Bd. Appeals, 1980-84; co-pres. Univ. High Sch. Parent-Faculty Orgn., 1982-83. Rutgers U. faculty fellow, 1970; East-West Center sr. fellow, 1974; NSF grantee, 1983-85, 1992-94. Mem. Assn. Am. Geographers (grantee 1964-65, vis. scientist 1970-72, chair math. models and quantitative methods splty. group 1991-92), Western Regional Sci. Assn. (bd. dirs. 1992—), Regional Sci. Assn. (pres. N.E. sect. 1973-74), Inst. Brit. Geographers, Internat. Geog. Union (sec. commn. math. models 1988-96), Sigma Xi. Home: 5135 Jumilla St San Diego CA 92124-1503 Office: San Diego State U Dept Geography San Diego CA 92182

GETREU, IAN E(DWIN), electronics engineer; b. Melbourne, Australia, Sept. 14, 1943; s. Leo and Matylda Getreu; m. Beverly S. Salmenson, June 5, 1983. BE with honors, U. Melbourne, 1965, M Engring. Sci., 1967; postgrad., UCLA, 1966-67; PhD, U. Calif., Berkeley, 1972. Sr. engr. Tektronix Inc., Beaverton, Oreg., 1972-79, mgr. integrated cir. computer aided design devel., 1979-83, mgr. advanced products mktg., 1983-85, scientist advanced products, 1985-86; v.p., modeling Analogy Inc., Beaverton, 1986-92, v.p. engring., 1992-94, v.p. tech. devel., 1994—, also bd. dirs., 1986-90; lectr. U. New South Wales, Sydney, Australia, 1974-75; chmn. Computer Aided Network Design Com., 1980-82. Author: Modeling the Bipolar Transistor, 1976. Bd. dirs. Jewish Fedn. of Portland, 1986-93, v.p., 1989-93; chair Oreg. Am. Israel Pub. Affairs Com., 1994-96. Mem. IEEE (sr.) (cirs. and systems soc. v.p. confs. 1990-91), Internat. Conf. Computer Aided Design (chmn. 1986). Home: PO Box 1356 Beaverton OR 97075-1356

GETREU, SANFORD, city planner; b. Cleve., Mar. 9, 1930; s. Isadore and Tillie (Kuchinsky) G.; B.A. in Architecture, Ohio State U., 1953; M.A. in Regional Planning, Cornell U., 1955; m. Gara Eileen Smith, Dec. 8, 1952 (div. Feb. 1983); children—David Bruce, Gary Benjamin, Allen Dana; m. Kelly Heim, Aug. 8, 1988. Resident planner Mackesey & Reps., consultants, Rome, N.Y., 1955-56; planning dir., Rome, 1956-57; dir. gen. planning, Syracuse, N.Y., 1957-59, dep. commr. planning, 1959-62, commr. planning, 1962-65; planning dir. San Jose, Calif., 1965-74; urban planning cons., 1974—; pres. Sanford Getreu, AICP, Inc., vis. lectr., critic Cornell U., 1960-65, Syracuse U., 1962-65, Stanford, 1965, San Jose State Coll., 1965, Santa Clara U., Calif. State Poly. Coll., DeAnza Coll., San Jose City Coll., U. Calif. at Berkeley; pres. planning dept. League of Calif. Cities, 1973-74; advisor State of Calif. Office of Planning and Research. Past bd. dirs. Theater Guild, San Jose, Triton Mus., San Jose. Mem. Am. Soc. Cons. Planners, Am. Planning Assn., Am. Inst. Cert. Planners, Bay Area Planning Dirs. Assn. (v.p. 1965-74, mem. exec. com. 1973-74), Assn. Bay Area Govts. (regional planning com. 1967-74). Club: Rotary. Home: 105 Coronado Ave Los Altos CA 94022-2222 Office: 4966 El Camino Real Ste 101 Los Altos CA 94022-1406

GETTO, MICHAEL HUTSON, communications consultant; b. Newport News, Va., June 22, 1957; s. Michael Hutson and Clare (Donmoyer) G.; m. Kimberly Lynn Seaber, Oct. 9, 1982. BS, U. Colo., 1979. Newsman KLWN/KLZR, Lawrence, Kans., 1979-81; press sec. U.S. Rep. Larry Winn, Washington, 1981-83; press aide U.S. Senator Pete Wilson, Washington, 1983; asst. to chief (adminstrn. of George Deukmejian) Calif. OSHA, San Francisco, 1985-88; account exec. Ketchum Pub. Rels., San Francisco, 1988-91; ind. cons. Michael Getto Consulting, San Francisco/Moldova, Russia and Romania, 1991—. Mem. Ripon Soc., Washington/San Francisco, 1982—, Calif. Rep. League, San Francisco, 1985-90, Lincoln Club, San Francisco, 1992-93, pres., 1996—. Home: 2 Lower Crescent Ave Apt 1 Sausalito CA 94965 Office: Kamer-Singer and Assocs Inc 74 New Montgomery St # 450 San Francisco CA 94105

GETTY, GORDON PETER, composer, philanthropist; b. Los Angeles, Dec. 20, 1933; s. J. Paul and Ann Rork (Light) G.; m. Ann Getty; 4 children. Studied, voice with Easton Kent, piano with Robert Vetlesen, theory with Sol Joseph, 1961-62; BS, San Francisco Conservatory Music, hon. music degree, 1981; hon. music degree, Pepperdine U., 1985; hon. doctorate, Mannes Coll. Music, N.Y.C., 1986. Former cons. Getty Oil Co., dir.; former chmn. LSB Leakey Found., Pasadena, Calif., now trustee. Works include opera in two acts Plump Jack, commnd. by Globe Shakespeare Ctr., London, performed by San Francisco Symphony, 1985, also Scene One broadcast live from Davies Symphony Hall, San Francisco, Mar. 1985; Emily Dickinson Song Cycle The White Election, 30 performances U.S. and abroad, 1981-85, also broadcast live from Nat. Gallery Art, Washington, 1985; Victorian Scenes, performed San Francisco Girls Chorus U. Calif., Berkeley, WInifred Baker Choral, 1985; Nine Piano Pieces performed by Stewart Gordon, 1985; A Cappella Choruses and Piano Works broadcast live Georgetown U., Washington, Apr., 1985; author monograph on White Election, poems My Uncle's House, 1984, other poetry. Adv. dir. Met. Opera, 1977—; trustee Mannes Coll. Music, 1982—; dir. San Francisco Symphony, 1979—. Recipient Golden Plate award Am. Acad. Achievement, 1985, Achievement Arts award Northwood Inst., 1985. Office: Rork Music Publ One Embarcadero Ctr Ste 1050 San Francisco CA 94111*

GEYER, DAVID WARREN, aerospace scientist, software engineer; b. Pueblo, Colo., Apr. 3, 1936; s. Warren Francis and Donna Maxine (Smith) G.; m. Winifred Jane Geyer, June 1974; children: Michael Harold, Michael David, Thomas, Martha. BSEE, U. Colo.; MSEE, NYU. Mem. tech. staff Bell Telephone Labs., Whippany, N.J., 1957-61; sr. engr., dir. Convair Divsn. Gen. Dynamics, San Diego, 1961-81; v.p. Teledyne Sys. Co., Northridge, Calif., 1981-87; gen. mgr. strategic planning Analex Corp., Albuquerque, 1987-96, Scottsdale, Ariz., 1996—. Author: (with others) Ivertial Guidance by Parson, 1968. Bd. dirs. Highlands Ranch (Colo.) Homeowners Assn., 1990-91. Mem. IEEE (sr.), AIAA, Assn. of Computing Machinery, Profl. Aerospace Contractors Assn. Office: Analex Corp 11462 E Carol Way Scottsdale AZ 85259

GHANDHI, SORAB KHUSHRO, electrical engineering educator; b. Allahabad, India, Jan. 1, 1928; came to U.S., 1947, naturalized, 1960; s. Khushro S. and Dina (Amroliwalla) G.; m. Cecilia M. Ghandhi; children: Khushro, Rustom, Behram. B.Sc. in Elec. and Mech. Engring, Benares (India) Hindu U., 1947; M.S., U. Ill., 1948, Ph.D., 1951. Mem. electronics lab. Gen. Electric Co., 1951-60; mgr. electronic components and functions lab., research div. Philco Corp., 1960-63; prof. elec. engring. Rensselaer Poly. Inst., Troy, N.Y., 1963—, chmn. electrophysics and electronic engring. div., 1968-75, prof. electrophysics, elec., computer and systems engring. dept., 1975-92, active emeritus prof., 1992—; cons. to industry, 1963—. Co-author: (with R.F. Shea editor) Principles of Transistor Circuits, 1953, Transistor Circuit Engineering, 1957, Amplifier Handbook, 1966; author: The Theory and Practice of Microelectronics, 1968, Semiconductor Power Devices, 1977, VLSI Fabrication Principles: Silicon and Gallium Arsenide, 1983, 2d edit., 1994; editor Solid State Electronics, 1993—. J.N. Tata fellow, 1947-50. Fellow IEEE; mem. Electrochem. Soc., Am. Standards Assn., Sigma Xi, Eta Kappa Nu, Pi Mu Epsilon, Phi Kappa Pi. Address: 2716 Cita Ave Escondido CA 92029-5816

GHAREEB, DONALD L., judge; b. East Grand Rapids, Mich., Oct. 28, 1930; s. Phillip Nimey and Hannah (Dabakey) G. AB in Letters and Law, U. Mich., 1952, JD, 1954. Bar: Mich. 1956, Ariz. 1969. Pvt. practice law Grand Rapids, Mich., 1956-68; adminstrv. law judge Ind. Commn. of Ariz., Phoenix, 1970-90, vice chief adminstrv. law judge, 1990—. Speaker and educator Ariz. Workers Compensation Bar, 1987—, chmn., 1993-94. U.S. Jaycees (nat. v.p. senate 1988-89, state pres. Ariz. senate 1987-88). Republican. Eastern Orthodox.

GHAZANFAR, SHAIKH MOHAMMED, economics educator, researcher; b. Jullundar, Brit. India, Apr. 1, 1937; came to U.S., 1958; s. Shaikh Mehboob and Musammat Farhat (Elahi) Bakhsh; m. Rukhsana Sharif, Aug. 16, 1965; children: Farah, Asif, Kashif. BA with honors, Wash. State U., 1962, MA in Econs., 1964, PhD in Econs., 1968. Instr. econs. Wash. State U., Pullman, 1962-64, rsch. economist, 1964, teaching asst., 1965-67, instr., 1967-68; asst. prof. U. Idaho, Moscow, 1968-72, assoc. prof., 1972-77, prof., 1977—, head dept., 1979-81; head, 1993—; coord. internat. studies program U. Idaho, Moscow, 1990-93; vis. prof. U. Punjab, Lahore, Pakistan, fall 1974-75, U. Md., College Park, spring 1974-75, King Abdulaziz U., Jeddah, Saudi Arabia, 1983-866; mem. budget forecast Idaho Legis., 1974-93. Bd. dirs. Daily News community bd., 1992-94. Mem. Martin Luther King Day Com., Moscow, 1986-90, Latah County Task Force on Human Rights, Moscow, 1988-92; chmn. Malcom Kerr scholarship com. for high sch. students Nat. Coun. on U.S.-Arab Rels., Washington, 1988-94. Mem. AAUP, Nat. Tax. Assn., Atlantic Econ. Soc., Amnesty Internat., History of Econs. Soc. Office: U Idaho Dept Econs Moscow ID 83843

GHEEN, BETTY M., food products executive; b. 1924. V.p. Merrill Farms, Salinas, Calif. Office: Merrill Farms 1067 Merrill St Salinas CA 93901-4420*

GHISELIN, BREWSTER, author, English language educator emeritus; b. Webster Groves, Mo., June 13, 1903; s. Horace and Eleanor (Weeks) G.; m. Olive F. Franks, June 7, 1929; children: Jon Brewster, Michael Tenant. A.B., UCLA, 1927; M.A., U. Calif.-Berkeley, 1928, student, 1931-33; student, Oxford U., Eng., 1928-29. Asst. in English U. Calif., Berkeley, 1931-33; instr. English U. Utah, 1929-31, 34-38, lectr., 1938-39, asst. prof., 1939-46, assoc. prof., 1946-50, prof., 1950-71, prof. emeritus, 1971, Distinguished Research prof., 1967-68; dir. Writers' Conf., 1947-66; poetry editor Rocky Mt. Rev., 1937-46; assoc. editor Western Rev., 1946-49; lectr. creativity, cons. Inst. Personality Assessment and Research, U. Calif., Berkeley, 1957-58; editorial adv. bd. Concerning Poetry, 1968—. Author: Against the Circle, 1946, The Creative Process, 1952, new paperback edit., 1985, 95, The Nets, 1955, Writing, 1959, Country of the Minotaur, 1970, (with others) The Form Discovered: Essays on the Achievement of Andrew Lytle, 1973, Light, 1978, Windrose: Poems, 1929-1979, 1980, (with others) Contemporary Authors, 1989; (poems) Flame, 1991. Bd. advisors Silver Mountain Found. Ford Found. fellow, 1952-53; recipient award Nat. Inst. Arts and Letters, 1970; Blumenthal-Leviton-Blonder prize Poetry mag., 1973; Levinson prize, 1978; William Carlos Williams award Poetry Soc. Am., 1981; Gov.'s award for arts Utah Arts Council, 1982; LHD hc, U of Utah, 1994. Mem. MLA, Utah Acad. Scis., Arts and Letters (Charles Redd award), Phi Beta Kappa, Phi Kappa Phi. Home (winter): 1115 Jefferson Way Laguna Beach CA 92651-3022 also (summer): 1747 Princeton Ave Salt Lake City UT 84108-1810 Office: U Utah Dept English 3500 LNCO Salt Lake City UT 84112 *To be human is to be a user of the basic resources of society, those modes and forms of vision and action that by determining the character and quality of men's experience shape everything men do and are.*

GHOSH, ABHIJIT, electrical engineer; b. Calcutta, India, Aug. 22, 1964; came to U.S., 1986; s. Susanta Kumar and Madhuri G.; m. Eliane Setton, Dec. 1, 1993. B in Tech., Indian Inst. Tech., Kharagpur, India, 1986; MS, U. Calif., 1989; PhD, 1991. Rsch. asst. U. Calif., Berkeley, 1987-91, teaching asst., 1986-87; sr. engr. Mitsubishi Electric Rsch. Labs., Sunnyvale, Calif., 1991—; program com. Internat. Test Synthesis Workshop, IEEE, Santa Barbara, Calif., 1993—, Asian Design Automation Conf., IEEE, Japan, 1995. Author: Sequential Logic Testing and Verification, 1991, Logic Synthesis, 1994; patentee ATM Switch Architecture, 1994; contbr. articles to profl. jours. Recipient Best paper award IEEE, ACM, Orlando, Fla., 1990. Mem. IEEE, Assn. for Computing Machinery. Office: Mitsubishi Electric Rsch Labs Inc 1050 E Arques Ave Sunnyvale CA 94086-4601

GHYMN, ESTHER MIKYUNG, English educator, writer; b. Seoul, Korea; came to U.S., 1963; d. Yong Shik and Kyung hee (Park) Kim; m. Kyung-Il Ed Ghymn; children: Jennifer, Eugene. MA, U. Hawaii, 1969; MAT, U. Pitts., 1974; PhD, U. Nev., Reno, 1990. Lectr. U. Nev., Reno, 1993-96, ESL coord., lectr., 1996—. Author: The Shapes and Styles of Asian American Prose Fiction, 1990, Images of Asian American Women Writers, 1995; editor APANN News. Bd. dirs. Asian Americans N. Nev., 1992-95, Multicultural Office, Truckee Meadows C.C., Reno, 1994-96, mem. steering com. Access to Success, 1996. Please spell out NAFSA in MEM section and APANN in CRW section.

GIACOLINI, EARL L., agricultural products company executive. Vice-chmn. Sun Diamond Growers of Calif., Pleasanton; chmn Sun Sweet Growers, Yuba City, CA. Office: Sun Sweet Growers Inc 901 N Walton Ave Yuba City CA 95993-9370*

GIACOMO, GARY CHRISTOPHER, magazine editor, journalist; b. Sacramento, Calif., Dec. 23, 1957; s. James John and Audrey Mary (Huttle) G.; m. Sherry Baker, June 15, 1979; 1 child, Matthew. AA in Cmty. Journalism, Am. River Coll., Sacramento, 1979; BA in Journalism, Calif. State U., Sacramento, 1983; MS in Mass Comms., San Jose State U., 1996. News editor Amador Ledger, Jackson, Calif., 1979-81; computer typesetting trainer Sys. Integrators, Inc., Sacramento, 1981-84, product mgr. newspapers, 1984-87; mag. editor Calif. State Firefighters Assn., Sacramento, 1987—; mem. reader panel Folio mag., Stamford, Conn., 1992-93. Mem. Western Publ. Assn. (Maggie award for Design 1990, Maggie award for Most Improved Mag. 1989), Soc. Profl. Journalists (Enterprise Reporting award 1994). Roman Catholic. Office: Calif State Firefighters 3246 Ramos Cir Sacramento CA 95827-2513

GIANNOTTA, STEVEN LOUIS, neurosurgery educator; b. Detroit, Apr. 4, 1947; s. Louis D. and Betty Jane (Root) G.; m. Sharon Danielak, June 13, 1970; children: Brent, Nicole, Robyn. Student, U. Detroit, 1965-68; MD, U. Mich., 1972. Diplomate Am. Bd. Neurol. Surgeons. Surg. intern U. Mich., Ann Arbor, 1972-73, neurosurg. resident, 1973-78; asst. prof. neurosurgery UCLA, 1978-80; asst. prof. neurosurgery U. So. Calif., Sch. Medicine, L.A., 1980-83, assoc. prof. neurosurgery, 1983-89, prof. neurosurgery, 1989—; sec. Congress Neurol. Surgeons, Washington, 1986-89, v.p., 1993; pres. L.A. (Calif.) Soc. Clin. Neuroscis., 1992-93; bd. dirs. Am. Bd. Neurol. Surgery, 1995—. Fellow ACS, Am. Heart Assn. (stroke coun., rsch. grantee 1980, 84), So. Calif. Neurol. Soc (pres. 1993-94). Democrat. Roman Catholic. Office: Dept Neurosurgery Box 239 1200 N State St Los Angeles CA 90033

GIANNULLI, MOSSIMO, business owner. Owner Mossimo Inc., Irvine, Calif. Office: Mossimo Inc 15320 Barranca Blvd Irvine CA 92618

GIBBONS, JIM, congressman; b. Sparks, Nev., Dec. 16, 1944; m. Dawn Gibbons, 1986; children: Christopher, Jennifer, Jimmy. BS in Geology, U. Nev., 1967, MS in Mining/Geology, 1973; JD, Southwestern Law Sch., 1979; postgrad., U. So. Calif.; grad., USAF Air Command & Staff Coll., 1984, USAF Air War Coll., 1988. Airline pilot Western Airlines, 1979-87, Delta Airlines, 1987—; mem. Nev. State Assembly, 1988-94, 105th Congress from 2d dist. Nev., 1995—; Republican whip Nev. State Assembly, 1993. Col. USAF, 1967-71, Vietnam; vice-comdr. Nev. Air Guard, 1975—, Desert Storm, 1990-91. Office: 1116 Longworth Washington DC 20515

GIBBS, PATRICIA HELLMAN, physician; b. Boston, Oct. 22, 1958; d. Frederick Warren and Patricia Christina (Sander) H.; m. Richard D. Gibbs, Dec. 22, 1984; children: Ruth, Samuel, Matthew, Kate, Frank. BA summa cum laude, Williams Coll., 1982; MD, Yale Univ., 1987. Diplomate Am. Bd. Family Practice. Intern, resident dept. family practice U. Wash., Seattle, 1987-90; ptnr. Tricia Gibbs, MD and Richard Gibbs, MD, San Francisco, 1990-95; co-founder, med. dir. San Francisco Free Clinic, 1993—; supervising physician San Francisco Ballet, 1990-95. Author: (chpt.) Medical and Orthopedic Issues of Active and Athletic Women-Skiing, 1993; co-author: (chpt.) Spine Care-Dance, 1993. Women's scholar Williams Coll., 1982, Class of '25 Athlete scholar, 1982. Mem. AMA, Am. Acad. Family Physicians, Phi Beta Kappa, Sigma Xi. Office: San Francisco Free Clinic 132 Clement St San Francisco CA 94118-2420

GIBBS, WILLIAM HAROLD, university administrator; b. Evanston, Ill., Apr. 10, 1950; s. Harold William and Margaret Rose (Heidbreder) G. BS, Ariz. State U., 1973; MBA, U. Ill., 1975. CPA. Mgr. Price Waterhouse, Phoenix, 1975-82; chief fin. officer Apollo Group Inc., Phoenix, 1983-87; pres. U. Phoenix, 1987—. Office: U Phoenix 4615 E Elwood St Phoenix AZ 85040-1958

GIBBS, WOLCOTT, JR., writer, editor; b. N.Y.C., Apr. 5, 1935; s. Wolcott and Elinor Mead (Sherwin) G.; m. Elizabeth Lucille Villa, 1958 (div. 1979); children: William, Eric; m. Elaine St. James, 1980. BA, Princeton U., 1957. Publicity mgr. Doubleday & Co., N.Y.C., 1958-64; freelance writer Norwalk, Conn., 1964-67, 76-78; editor J.B. Lippincott Co., N.Y.C., 1967-70; book editor Motor Boating & Sailing Mag., N.Y.C., 1970-76, exec. editor, 1978-79; editor Yachting Mag., N.Y.C., 1979-84; exec. editor The New Yorker, N.Y.C., 1984-89; sr. editor Islands Mag., Santa Barbara, Calif., 1989—; cons. Book-of-the-Month Club, N.Y.C., 1973-84. Author: (non-fiction) Practical Sailing, 1971, Power Boating, 1973, Sailing: A First Book, 1974, Backpacking, 1975, Navigation, 1975, Advanced Sailing, 1975, The Coastal Cruiser, 1981, Cruising in a Nutshell, 1983, (fiction) Dead Run, 1988, Running Fix, 1990, Shadow Queen, 1992, Landfall, 1992, Capitol Offense, 1995, Shot in the Dark, 1996. Mem. USCG Aux. Office: Islands Publ Co 3886 State St Santa Barbara CA 93105-3112

GIBBY-SMITH, BARBARA, psychologist, nurse; b. Woodburn, Oreg., Dec. 13, 1938; d. Chester Clifton and Marvel Elizabeth (Hill) Gibby; m. Roy Milton Smith, June 2, 1957 (div. June 1990); children: Thomas Clifton, Jeffery Shawn, Mark Anderson. ADN, Chemeketa C.C., Salem, Oreg., 1972; BS, SUNY, Albany, 1980; MS, Western Oreg. State Coll., 1982; D of Psychology, Pacific U., Forest Grove, Oreg., 1993. Diplomate Am. Bd. Profl. Disability Cons., Am. Bd. Specialist, Am. Bd. Forensics Medicine. Adminstr. Birch St. Manor, Dallas, Oreg., 1973-81; disability determination specialist State of Oreg. Workers' Compensation Dept., Salem, 1983-85; counselor Women's Crisis Ctr., Salem, 1986-88; rehab. counselor Employer Rehab. Svcs., Portland, Oreg., 1985-87; therapist, counselor Pacific U., Hillsboro, Oreg., 1988-89, Forest Grove, 1989-91; intern in psychology Portland State U., 1991-92, Kaiser-Permanente, Salem, 1991-92; resident in psychology Tillamook (Oreg.) Counseling Ctr., 1993-95; hosp. privileges psychology and medicine Tuality Healthcare, 1996—; group therapy counselor Women's Crisis Ctr., Dallas, 1982-83; eating disorders group therapy facilitator, Salem, 1986-88; nat. register Doctoral Addiction Examiner. Active Women's Coalition Orgn., Salem, 1988—. Mem. APA (clin. neuropsychology divsn. 40), Am. Coll. Forensic Examiners (diplomate), Nat. Bd. Addiction Examiners, Oreg. Psychol. Assn., Prescribing Psychologist Assn. (candidate). Democrat. Office: Mountain View Counseling Ctr 1911 Mountain View Ln Ste 500 Forest Grove OR 97116-2221 also: Mountain View Med Ctr Ste 200 1909 Mt View Ln Ste 200 Forest Grove OR 97116

GIBLETT, PHYLIS LEE WALZ, middle school educator; b. Denver, July 17, 1945; d. Henry and Leah (Pabst) Walz; B.S.B.A. (Estelle Hunter scholar 1963, Denver Classroom Tchr.'s scholar 1963, Outstanding Bus. Edn. Student scholar 1967), U. Denver, 1967, MBA, 1969; m. Thomas Giblett, May 31, 1975; children: Leann Ruth, Douglas Henry, John Peter. Tchr. bus. Aurora (Colo.) South Middle Sch., info. specialist, 1996—; tchr. Aurora Pub. Schs., 1967-80, 82-86, 88-96, on leave, 1980-82, 86-88, chmn. bus. dept., 1972-79; evening tchr. S.E. Met. Bd. Coop Services, 1967-68, post secondary/adult classes Aurora Pub. Schs., 1972-75, C.C. Denver, North Campus, 1973, Aurora Pub. Schs. Adult Edn., 1983-84; mem. Aurora Pub. Sch. System, mem. tech. com. 1991—, dist. tech. trainer, 1992—, Program Cadre mem., 1995—, steering com. shared decision making, 1990-94, zero tolerance com., 1992-94, facilitator Mentor com., 1991-92, exploratory tchr. facilitator, 1992—; mem. dist. tech. com. South Middle Sch., Aurora Dist. Tech. Com., 1975-79; adviser chpt. Future Bus. Leaders Am., 1976-78; mem. Colo. Curriculum Specialist Com., 1976-77. Treas. Aurora Coun. PTA, 1987-89, Century Elem. Sch. PTA, 1988-89, reflections chmn., 1987-89, 90-93; mem. PTA. Named Miss Future Bus. Tchr., Phi Beta Lambda of Colo., 1965. Mem. Nat., Mountain-Plains (participant leadership conf. 1977), Colo. Bus. Edn. Assns. (pres. 1976-77), Colo. Educators for/About Bus., Am., Colo. vocat. assns., NEA, Colo., Aurora edn. assns., Delta Pi Epsilon (pres.-elect Eta chpt. 1978, pres. 1980-81). Republican. Lutheran.

GIBNEY, FRANK BRAY, publisher, editor, writer, foundation executive; b. Scranton, Pa., Sept. 21, 1924; s. Joseph James and Edna May (Wetter) G.; m. Harriet Harvey, Dec. 10, 1948 (div. 1957); children: Alex, Margot; m. Harriet C. Suydam, Dec. 14, 1957 (div. 1971); children: Frank, James, Thomas; m. Hiroko Doi, Oct. 5, 1972; children: Elise, Josephine. BA, Yale U., 1945; DLitt (hon.), Kyung Hee U., Seoul, Korea, 1974. Corr., assoc. editor Time mag., N.Y.C., Tokyo and London, 1947-54; sr. editor Newsweek, N.Y.C., 1954-57; staff writer, editorial writer Life mag., N.Y.C., 1957-61; pub., pres. SHOW mag., N.Y.C., 1961-64; pres. Ency. Brit. (Japan), Tokyo, 1965-69; pres. TBS-Brit., Tokyo, 1969-75, vice chmn., 1976—; v.p. Ency. Brit., Inc., Chgo., 1975-79; vice chmn., bd. editors Ency. Brit., Chgo., 1978—; pres. Pacific Basin Inst., Santa Barbara, Calif., 1979—; vis. prof. Pomona Coll., 1995—; bd. dirs. U.S. Com. for Pacific Econ. Cooperation, 1988—, v.p., 1993-95; cons. com. on space and aeros. U.S. Ho. of Reps., Washington, 1957-59; vice chmn. Japan-U.S. Friendship Commn., 1984-90, U.S.-Japan Com. Edn. and Cultural Interchange, 1984-90. Author: Five Gentlemen of Japan, 1953, The Frozen Revolution, 1959, (with Peter Deriabin) The Secret World, 1960, The Operators, 1961, The Khrushchev Pattern, 1961, The Reluctant Space Farers, 1965, Japan: The Fragile Super-Power, 1975, rev. edit., 1996, Miracle by Design, 1983, The Pacific Century, 1992, Korea's Quiet Revolution, 1993; co-author: The Battle for Okinawa, 1995; editor: The Penkovskiy Papers, 1965, Senso, 1995, The Bureaucrats' Kingdom, 1996. Served to lt. USNR, 1942-46. Decorated Order of the Rising Sun 3d Class Japan, Order of Sacred Treasure 2d Class Japan. Mem. Council on Fgn. Relations, Tokyo Fgn. Corr. Club, Am. C.of C. (Tokyo), Japan-Am. Soc., Japan Soc. Roman Catholic. Clubs: Century Assn., Yale (N.Y.C.); Tokyo; Tavern, The Arts (Chgo.). Home: 1901 E Las Tunas Rd Santa Barbara CA 93103-1745

GIBSON, DENICE YVONNE, telecommunications, networking and computer executive; b. Grants Pass, Oreg., Apr. 6, 1955; d. Harry Charles Gibson and Bettye Yvonne Bentley Stein. BS in Psychology, U. San Francisco, 1980; MS in Systems Mgmt., U. So. Calif., 1982; postgrad., Stanford U., 1983; PhD in Instl. Mgmt., Pepperdine U., 1990. Documentation coord./systems analyst Argonaut Ins., Menlo Park, Calif., 1977-78; tech. ops. mgr. Amdahl Corp., Sunnyvale, Calif., 1978-85; sr. dir. worldwide mktg. Candle Corp., L.A., 1985-89; v.p. mktg. Panoramic Inc., San Jose, 1989-90; v.p. devel. Tandem Computers, Plano, Tex., 1990-92; v.p. devel. and support Tandem Corp., Plano, Tex., 1992-93, Cupertino, Calif., 1993—; v.p. quality initiative ctr. Tandem Corp., Cupertino, 1995-96; adj. prof. U. Calif., Santa Cruz, 1993-95; gen. mgr., sr. v.p. Novell Inc., Provo, Utah, 1996—; adj. prof. info. sys. mgmt. U. San Francisco, 1984-86; adj. faculty mem. U. Phoenix, 1995—; guest lectr. Stanford U., U. Calif., Berkeley, U. Calif., Santa Clara; adj. faculty U. Calif., Santa Cruz, 1994, U. San Francisco, 1994; cons. Nat. Sch. Safety Ctr., 1987, Fed. Law Enforcement Tng. Ctr., 1987, Nat. Soc. Secs., 1986, Pacific Bell, 1985, Elxsi Computers, 1983, Trilogy, 1983. Contbr. articles to profl. jours. Mem. IEEE, Engring. Soc., Am. Soc. Tng. and Devel., Am. Mgmt. Assn., Internat. Platform Assn.

GIBSON, ELISABETH JANE, principal; b. Salina, Kans., Apr. 28, 1937; d. Cloyce Wesley and Margaret Mae (Yost) Kasson; m. William Douglas Miles, Jr., Aug. 20, 1959 (div.); m. Harry Benton Gibson Jr., July 1, 1970. AB, Colo. State Coll., 1954-57; MA, San Francisco State Coll., 1967-68; EdD, U. No. Colo., 1978; postgrad. U. Denver, 1982. Cert. tchr., prin., Colo. Tchr. elem. schs., Santa Paula, Calif., 1957-58, Salina, Kans., 1958-63, Goose Bay, Labrador, 1963-64, Jefferson County, Colo., 1965-66, Topeka, 1966-67; diagnostic tchr. Ctrl. Kans. Diagnostic Remedial Edn. Ctr., Salina, 1968-70; instr. Loretto Heights Coll., Denver, 1970-72; co-owner Ednl. Cons. Enterprises, Inc., Greeley, Colo., 1974-77; resource coord. Region VIII Resource Access Project Head Start Mile High Consortium, Denver, 1976-77; exec. dir. Colo. Fedn. Coun. Exceptional Children, Denver, 1976-77; asst. prof. Met. State Coll., Denver, 1979; dir. spl. edn. N.E. Colo. Bd. Coop. Edn. Svcs., Haxtun, Colo., 1979-82; prin. elem. jr. h.s., Elizabeth, Colo., 1982-84; prin., spl. projects coord. Summit County Schs., Frisco, Colo., 1984-92; prin. Frisco Elem. Sch., 1985-91; cons. Montana Dept. Edn., 1978-79, Love Pub. Co., 1976-78, Colo. Dept. Inst., 1974-75; cons. Colo. Dept. Edn., 1984-85, mem. proposal reading com., 1987—; pres. Found. Exceptional Children, 1980-81; pres. bd. dirs. N.E. Colo. Svcs. Handicapped, 1981-82; bd. dirs. Dept. Ednl. Specialists, Colo. Assn. Sch. Execs., 1982-84; mem. Colo. Title IV Adv. Coun., 1980-82; mem. Mellon Found. grant steering com. Colo. Dept. Edn., 1984-85; mem. Colo. Dept. Edn. Data Acquisition Reporting and Utilization Com., 1983, Denver City County Commn. for Disabled, 1978-81; chmn. regional edn. com. 1970 White House Conf. Children and Youth; bd. dirs. Advocates for Victims of Assault, 1986-91; mem. adv. bd. Alpine Counseling Ctr., 1986-92; mem. placement alternatives commn. Dept. Social Svcs., 1986—; mem. adv. com. Colo. North Ctrl. Assn., 1988-91; sec. Child Care Resource and Referral Agy., 1992—; mem. Child Care Task Force Summit County, 1989-92; mem. tchr. cert. task force Colo. State Bd. Edn., 1990-91; chair Summit County Interagy. Coord. Coun., 1989-93. Recipient Vol. award Colo. Child Care Assn., 1992, Ann. Svc.

award Colo. Fedn. Coun. Exceptional Children, 1981; San Francisco State Coll. fellow, 1967-68. Mem. Colo. Assn. Retarded Citizens, Assn. Supervision Curriculum Devel., Nat. Assn. Elem. Sch. Prins., North Cen. Assn. (state adv. com. 1988-91), Order Eastern Star, Kappa Delta Pi, Pi Lambda Theta, Phi Delta Kappa. Republican. Methodist. Author: (with H. Padzensky) Goal Guide: A minicourse in writing goals and behavioral objectives for special education, 1975; (with H. Padzensky and S. Sporn) Assaying Student Behavior: A minicourse in student assessment techniques, 1974; contbr. articles to profl. jours. Home: 14354 E Caley Ave Aurora CO 80016 Office: Sylvan Learning Ctr 8200 S Quebec St Englewood CO 80112-3194

GIBSON, FRANCES, nurse; b. Junction, Tex., Sept. 28, 1936; d. August and Juanita (Corpus-Garcia) Rehwoldt; m. Richard Gibson, July 4, 1954 (dec. July 25, 1962); children; Kenneth, René, Allison. AA, East Los Angeles Coll. Lic. vocat. nurse, 1969; registered nurse 1976, operating room technician, 1971; cert. adult edn. tchr., paralegal. Instr., profl. expert East Los Angeles Coll., Monterey Park, Calif., 1971-74; hostess talk show (in Spanish) Sta. KMEX-TV, Los Angeles, 1970-76; tchr. adult edn. Garvey Sch. Bd., Rosemead, Calif., 1976-77; clin. nurse L.A. County/U. So. Calif. Med. Ctr., 1981-89; case mgr. AIDS Healthcare Found., L.A., 1991-93; AIDS clinician Los Angeles County/U. So. Calif. Med. Ctr., 1993; vol. nurse Lung Assn., L.A., 1970-76, ARC, L.A., 1969—; instr. health classes ARC, also instr. Spanish to ARC pers., mgr. info. booths at health fairs and convs., provider first aid at various gatherings, immunization clinics, chmn. adv. bd., 1971-82, bd. dirs., 1972-75, 79-82; med. editor, legal asst. Ivie & McNeill, L.A., 1986—. Author: Spanish for English-Speaking Personnel, 1972. Recipient Spotlight award ARC, 1972, Clara Barton award, 1976, Associate Womens Students award, 1969; named one of Ten Prettiest Chicanas in East Los Angeles, 1970. Mem. Nat. Assn. Chicano Nurses, Nursing Edn. Associates, AFL CIO, ACLU, Alpha Gamma Sigma. Democrat. Home: 2241 Charlotte Ave Rosemead CA 91770-3624

GIBSON, MELVIN ROY, pharmacognosy educator; b. St. Paul, Nebr., June 11, 1920; s. John and Jennie Irene (Harvey) G. B.S., U. Nebr., 1942, M.S., 1947, D.Sc. (hon.), 1985; Ph.D., U. Ill., 1949. Asst. prof. pharmacognosy Wash. State U., Pullman, 1949-52; assoc. prof. Wash. State U., 1952-55, prof., 1955-85, prof. emeritus, 1985—. Editor: Am. Jour. Pharm. Edn, 1956-61; editorial bd., co-author: Remington's Pharm. Sci, 1970, 75, 80, 85; editor, co-author: Studies of a Pharm. Curriculum, 1967; author over 100 articles. Served as arty. officer AUS, 1942-46. Decorated Bronze star, Purple Heart; sr. vis. fellow Orgn. for Econ. Cooperation and Devel., Royal Pharm. Inst., Stockholm, Sweden and U. Leiden (Holland), 1962; recipient Rufus A. Lyman award, 1972, Wash. State U. Faculty Library award, 1984; named Wash. State U. Faculty Mem. of Yr., 1985. Fellow AAAS; assoc. fellow Am. Coll. Apothecaries; mem. AAUP, N.Y. Acad. Scis., Am. Pharm. Assn., Am. Soc. Pharmacognosy (pres. 1964-65), Am. Assn. Coll. Pharmacy (exec. com. 1961-63, bd. dirs. 1977-79, chmn. coun. faculties 1975-76, pres. 1979-80, Disting. Educator award 1984), U.S. Pharmacopeia (revision com. 1970-75), Am. Found. Pharm. Edn. (hon. life, bd. dirs. 1980-85, exec. com. 1981-85, vice chmn. 1982-85), Acad. Pharm. Sci., Fedn. Internat. Pharm., Am. Inst. History of Pharmacy (sponsor), U. Nebr. Chancellor's Club, U. Nebr. Pres. Club, Sigma Xi, Phi Kappa Phi, Omicron Delta Kappa, Rho Chi, Spokane Club, Kappa Psi (Nat. Svc. citation 1961). Democrat. Presbyterian. Home: 707 W 6th Ave Apt 41 Spokane WA 99204-2813

GIBSON, RICHARD INGRAM, geophysicist; b. Jonesboro, Ark., Aug. 19, 1948; s. Richard D. and Clena Vee (Ingram) G. Student, Flint (Mich.) Jr. Coll., 1966-68; BS in Geology, Ind. U., Bloomington, 1971; postgrad., U. Calif., Davis, 1972-73. Assoc. instr. geology dept. Ind. U., Bloomington, 1970-72; mineralogist Beck Analytical Svcs., Bloomington and Davis, Calif., 1971-75; geophysicist Aero Svc. Corp., Houston, 1975-76, Gulf Oil Exploration and Prodn. Co., Houston, 1976-84; dir., gravity and magnetics Everest Geotech, Denver and Houston, 1984-89; pres. Everest Geotech, Denver, 1989-91; owner Gibson Consulting, Golden, Colo., 1989—; adj. prof. geophysical field exercise, U. Ark., Dillon, Mont., 1986-88; instr. Geologic Field Sta., Ind. U., Cardwell, Mont., 1989—. Author: History of the Earth, 1994; editor, pub. (newsletter) Life After Gulf, 1984-91; contbr. articles to profl. jours. Recipient 1st prize Ednl. Exhibit, Houston Gem and Mineral Soc., 1977, 1st prize Clin. Investigation, Am. Urol. Assn., 1973, Hon. Mention award in Photography, Houston-Galveston Employees Clubs, 1980; named Outstanding Young Man in Am., 1982. Mem. Tobacco Root Geol. Soc. (co-founder, pres. 1974-77, sec., bd. dirs. 1977-81, Svc. award 1979), Am. Assn. Petroleum Geologists, Geol. Soc. Am., Soc. Exploration Geophysicists, Wyo. Geol. Assn., Mont. Geol. Soc., Rocky Mountain Assn. Geologists, Ind. U. Geology Club (pres. Bloomington chpt. 1969-70). Office: Gibson Consulting PO Box 523 Golden CO 80402-0523

GIBSON, TREVA KAY, university official; b. Harrisburg, Ill., Aug. 12, 1938; d. William Clayton and Margaret Pauletta (Heathman) Humphrey; m. Charles Hurbert Gibson, Sept. 6, 1959; children: Charles H. Jr., Eric Clayton. BS, So. Ill. U., 1960; MEd, U. Mo., St. Louis, 1972; DSc (hon.), Kazakh (USSR) State U., 1990; EdD, Ariz. State U., 1991. Tchr. Perry Cen. Jr. High Sch., Southport, Ind., 1961-64, Granite City (Ill.) High Sch., 1964-65; counselor Kelley High Sch., Benton, Mo., 1967-68, Valley Park (Mo.) High Sch., 1968-69, Hazelwood East High Sch., St. Louis, 1969-76, Bradshaw Mountain High Sch., Prescott Valley, Ariz., 1976-80; dir. placement Grand Canyon U., Phoenix, 1980-82, dean of students, 1982-89, spl. asst. to pres. for internat. rels., 1988—. Mem. Nat. Assn. of Fgn. Student Advisors, Internat. Educators, World Coun. for Curriculum and Instrn., World Affairs Coun., Consortium for Global Edn., Christian Higher Edn. Profls. Serving Internat. Students. Baptist. Home: 2406 W Anderson Ave Phoenix AZ 85023-2210 Office: Grand Canyon U 3300 W Camelback Rd Phoenix AZ 85017-3030

GIDDINGS, DEBRA LYNN, marketing executive, computer consultant; b. Steubenville, Ohio, July 27, 1956; m. Dwight Gene Taylor, Jan. 11, 1975 (div. 1987) 1 child, Karisa Lauren; m. Richard Coates Giddings, May 6, 1989. AA in Data Processing with highest honor, Jefferson Tech. Coll., 1981; BA in Mgmt., U. Phoenix, 1997. Computer cons. Toronto, Ohio, 1981-84; programmer analyst John Hancock Ins., Anaheim, Calif., 1984-85; system analyst Chiro-Med, Placentia, Calif., 1985-87; computer instr. CSI, Cerritos, Calif., 1987-88; sr. tech. trainer Symbol MSI, Costa Mesa, Calif., 1988-90; mgr. tech. pubs. Symbol Techs., Costa Mesa, 1990-91; software product mgr. Symbol Techs., Costa Mesa, 1991; market rsch. mgr. Pacific Access Computers, 1992-93; mktg. mgr. Caere Corp., Los Gatos, Calif., 1994-95; client svcs. mgr. Phoenix Pub. Sys., Inc., Monterey, Calif., 1995-96, product mgr., 1996; SMB mktg. mgr. Santa Cruz Ops., 1996—; cons. World Vision, Monrovia, Calif., 1988, AT&T, Morristown, N.J., 1988, Great Western Bank, Chatsworth, Calif., 1988. Author: U Basic Programming, 1988. Mem. SPCA. Republican. Home: 24205 San Pedro Ln Carmel CA 93923-9305 Office: 425 Encinal St Santa Cruz CA 95061

GIEDT, WALVIN ROLAND, epidemiologist, educator; b. Eureka, S.D., Aug. 17, 1905; s. Theodore John Peter and Augusta Elizabeth (Pritzkau) G.; m. Lois Della Hosking, Nov. 4, 1932; children: Carol Augusta, Barbara Ellen. BS in Medicine, U. S.D., 1933; MD, U. Chgo., 1937; MPH, Johns Hopkin's U., 1941. Lab. instr. Sch. of Medicine U. S.D., Vermillion, 1933-36, asst. prof. microbiology Sch. of Medicine, 1938-40; chief epidemiologist div. S.D. Dept. Health, Pierre, 1941-43; chief epidemiologist div. Wash. State Dept. Health, Seattle, 1943-71, ret., 1971. Contbr. articles to profl. jours. With USPHS, 1941-66. Mem. Wash. State Pub. Health Assn. (past pres). Democrat. Address: 409 30th Ave S Seattle WA 98144-2507

GIEM, ROSS NYE, JR., surgeon; b. Corvallis, Oreg., May 23, 1923; s. Ross Nye and Goldie Marie (Falk) G.; student U. Redlands, Walla Walla Coll.; BA, MD, Loma Linda U.; children: John, David, Paul, James, Ross Nye, Matthew, Julie. Intern, Sacramento Gen. Hosp., 1952-53; resident in ob-gyn, Kern County Gen. Hosp., Bakersfield, Calif., 1956-57, in gen. surgery, 1957-61; practice medicine specializing in gen. surgery, Sullivan, Mo., 1961-70; staff emergency dept. Hollywood Presbyn. Med. Center, 1971-73, Meml. Hosp., Belleville, Ill., 1973-87, St. Elizabeth Hosp., Belleville, Ill., 1973-90; St. Luke Hosp., Pasadena, Calif., 1973-89, Doctors Hosp., Montclair, Calif. 1990-93, Harriman Jones Med. Group, Long Beach, Calif., 1993—; instr. nurses, physicians, paramedics, emergency med. technicians, 1973-91. Served with AUS, 1943-46. Diplomate Am. Bd. Surgery. Fellow ACS, Am. Coll. Emergency Physicians; mem. AMA, Ill. Med. Assn., Pan Am. Med. Assn., Pan Pacific Surg. Assn., Royal Coll. Physicians (Eng.)

GIER, KARAN HANCOCK, counseling psychologist; b. Sedalia, Mo., Dec. 7, 1947; d. Ioda Clyde and Lorna (Campbell) Hancock; m. Thomas Robert Gier, Sept. 28, 1968. BA in Edn., U. Mo., Kansas City, 1971; MA Teaching in Math/Sci. Edn., Webster U., 1974; MA in Counseling Psychology, Western Colo. U., 1981; MEd Guidance and Counseling, U. Alaska, 1981; PhD in Edn., Pacific Western U., 1989. Nat. cert. counselor. Instr. grades 5-8 Kansas City-St. Joseph Archdiocese, 1969-73; ednl. cons. Pan-Ednl. Inst., Kansas City, 1973-75; instr., counselor Bethel (Alaska) Regional High Sch., 1975-80; ednl. program coord. Western Regional Resource Ctr., Anchorage, 1980-81; counselor U. Alaska, Anchorage, 1982-83; coll. prep. instr. Alaska Native Found., Anchorage, 1982; counselor USAF, Anchorage, 1985-86; prof. U. Alaska, Anchorage, 1982—; dir. Omni Counseling Svcs., Anchorage, 1984—; prof. Chapman Coll., Anchorage, 1988—; workshop facilitator over 100 workshops on the topics of counseling techs., value clarification, non-traditional teaching approaches, peer-tutor tng. Co-author: Coping with College, 1984, Helping Others Learn, 1985, The Tutor Training Handbook, 1996; editor, co-author: A Student's Guide, 1983; contbg. author developmental Yup'ik lang. program, 1981; contbr. photographs to Wolves and Related Canids, 1990, 91; contbr. articles to profl. jours. Mem. Am. Bus. Women's Assn., Blue Springs, Mo., 1972-75, Ctr. for Environ. Edn., World Wildlife Fund, Beta Sigma Phi, Bethel, Alaska, 1976-81. Recipient 3d place color photo award Yukon-Kuskokwim State Fair, Bethel, 1978, Notable Achievement award USAF, 1986, Meritorious Svc. award Anchorage Community Coll., 1984-88. Mem. Coll. Reading and Learning Assn. (editor, peer tutor sig leader 1988—, Cert. of Appreciation 1986-93, bd. dirs. Alaska state, coord. internat. tutor program, Spl. Recognition award 1994-95), AACD, Alaska Assn. Counseling and Devel. (pres. 1989-90), Alaska Career Devel. Assn. (pres.-elect 1989-90), Nat. Rehab. Assn., Nat. Rehab. Counselors, Greenpeace, Human Soc. of U.S. Wolf Haven Am., Wolf Song of Alaska. Home and Office: Omni Counseling Svcs 8102 Harvest Cir Anchorage AK 99502-4682

GIERLASINSKI, KATHY LYNN, accountant; b. Chewelah, Wash., May 21, 1951; d. John Edward and Margaret Irene (Seefeldt) Rail; m. Norman Joseph Gierlasinski, May 23, 1987. BBA, Gonzaga U., 1984. CPA, Wash. Legal sec. Redbook Pub. Co., N.Y.C., 1974-75, Howard Michaelson, Esquire, Spokane, Wash., 1975-76; sec. Burns Internat. Security Svcs., Spokane, 1977-79; sec. to contr. Gonzaga U., Spokane, 1979-81, acctg. asst., 1981-82; staff acct. Martin, Holland & Petersen, CPA's, Yakima, Wash., 1984-87; acct., supr. Strader Hallet & Co., P.S., Bellevue, Wash., 1988-91; acct. Miller & Co., P.S., Woodinville, Wash., 1991-93; pres. Gierlasinski & Assocs., P.S., Bothell, Wash., 1993—; treas. White Pass Ski Patrol, Nat. Ski Patrol Systems, Wash., 1987-90; editor, chmn. audit com. Mt. Spokane Ski Patrol, 1983-84. Mem. AICPA, Am. Soc. Women Accts. (charter, editor 1987), Wash. Soc. CPA (sec. Sammamish Valley chpt. 1990-92, pres. 1992-93, 93-94), Washington Soc. of Cert. Pub. Accts. (chair adv. coun. 1995-96, tax com., govt. affairs com., dir. 1996—), Bus. and Profl. Women of Woodinville (treas. 1994-95), Northshore C. of C. Republican. Lutheran. Home: 28623 NE 47th Pl Redmond WA 98053

GIESECKE, MARK ERNST, psychiatrist; b. Bloomington, Ill., Apr. 14, 1948; s. Gustav Ernst and Louise Helene (Bittner) G.; m. Susan Lane Bennett, June 20, 1969 (div. Dec. 1976); m. Linda L. Hartz, Apr. 23, 1977; children: Craig, Lauren. AB, Harvard Coll., 1969; MD, U. Pa., 1973. Diplomate Am. Bd. Psychiatry and Neurology; lic. psychiatrist, Ariz. Intern Hosp. U. Pa., 1973-74, resident in psychiatry, 1974-77, med. staff, 1977-90, from asst. dir. to dir. psychiatry svc., 1977-90, from assoc. instr. to clin. assoc. prof. psychiatry, 1976—; med. dir. The Guidance Ctr., Inc., Flagstaff, Ariz., 1990-93, med. dir. outpatient seriously mentally ill svcs., 1993—; staff dept. medicine Flagstaff Med. Ctr., 1990—; staff Aspen Hill Hosp., Flagstaff, Ariz., 1990—; quality assurance com. The Guidance Ctr., Inc., Flagstaff, 1990-93, total quality mgmt. com., medical svcs. com., 1993—; campus emergency procedures com. U. Pa., 1979-81, psychiat. leave policy com., 1982-84, alchol concerns com., 1983-90, coun. com. on sexual harassment, 1986-90, fraternity/sorority adv. bd., 1986-88; com. on lang. retirement U. Pa. Coll. Arts and Scis., 1984-87. Contbr. articles to profl. jours. Recipient Horatio C. Wood prize in pharmacology, 1973, Preceptorship award Am. Soc. Anesthesiologists, 1971. Mem. Am. Psychiat. Assn., Ariz. Psychiat. Soc., No. Ariz. Psychiat. Soc. (charter mem.), Alpha Omega Alpha (pres. U. Pa. chpt., 1972-73). Home: 420 W Havasupai Rd Flagstaff AZ 86001-1510 Office: The Guidance Ctr Inc 2187 N Vickey St Flagstaff AZ 86004-6106

GIESSER, BARBARA SUSAN, neurologist, educator; b. Bronx, N.Y., Jan. 21, 1953; d. David and Evelyn (Cohen) G.; m. Philip D. Kanof, June 17, 1979; children: David, Marisa. BS, U. Miami, 1972; MS, U. Tex., Houston, 1974; MD, U. Tex., San Antonio, 1978. Diplomate Am. Bd. Psychiatry and Neurology. Intern Montefiore Hosp., Bronx, 1978-79; resident Bronx Mcpl. Hosp. Ctr. (Albert Einstein Coll. Medicine), 1979-82; asst. prof. neurology Albert Einstein Coll. Medicine, Bronx, 1983-91; med. dir. Gimbel MS Comprehensive Care Ctr., Teaneck, N.J., 1985-90, Rehab. Inst. of Tucson, 1991-95; assoc. prof. clin. neurology Ariz. Health Scis. Ctr., Tucson, 1993—. Author: Neurology Specialty Board Review, 3d edit., 1986, 4th edit., 1996; contbr. articles to profl. publs. Dean's Tchr. scholar Ariz. Health Scis. Ctr., 1995. Fellow Am. Acad. Neurology; mem. Nat. Multiple Sclerosis Soc. (rsch. grant 1989, mem. profl. adv. com. Desert S.W. chpt. 1994—, bd. dirs. 1994—). Office: Ariz Health Scis Ctr 1501 N Campbell Ave Tucson AZ 85724-0001

GIFFIN, WALTER CHARLES, retired industrial engineer, educator, consultant; b. Walhonding, Ohio, Apr. 22, 1936; s. Charles Maurice and Florence Ruth (Davis) G.; m. Beverly Ann Neff, Sept. 1, 1956; children—Steven, Rebecca. B. Indsl. Engring., Ohio State U., 1960, M.S., 1960, Ph.D., 1964. Registered profl. engr., Ohio. Research engr. Gen. Motors Research Labs., Warren, Mich., 1960-61; research assoc. systems research group Ohio State U., Columbus, 1961-62, instr. indsl. and systems engring., 1962-64, asst. prof., 1964-68, assoc. prof., 1968-71, prof., 1971-87, prof. emeritus, 1987—; prof. engring. U. So. Colo., Pueblo, 1987-92; ret., 1992—; cons. in field. Author: Introduction to Operations Engineering, 1971; Transform Techniques for Probability Modeling, 1975; Queueing: Basic Theory and Applications, 1978. NASA Research grantee, 1978-83. Club: Exptl. Aircraft Assn. (Oshkosh, Wis. and Pueblo, Colo.). Home: 419 Fairway Dr Pueblo West CO 81007-1852

GIFFORD, ARTHUR ROY, publishing executive; b. Buffalo, Jan. 27, 1937; s. William Howard and Dorothy Ellen (Logan) G.; m. Anna Marie Boone, July 9, 1960 (div. Feb. 1974); 1 child, Douglas Alan; m. Carolyn Elaine Crowe, Dec. 20, 1974; children: Christine Michelle, Stephen Michael. BA, Butler U., 1964; postgrad., Pacific Luth. U., Tacoma, 1970; MA, U. Wash., 1975. Cert. provisional and standard secondary tchr., Wash. Passenger svc. agt. United Airlines, Seattle, 1966-67; indsl. engr. The Boeing Co., Seattle, 1967-70, prog. mgr. engring. div. Boeing Community Connection, 1987-91; mgr. assessment reports, corp. safety, health and environ. affairs The Boeing Co., 1991-94; tchr., theatre dir. Fed. Way (Wash.) Sch. Dist., 1971-87; pres. Creative Approaches, Kent, Wash., 1994—. Bd. dirs. Lyric Theatre and Conservatory, Midway, Wash., 1980-82; treas. Wash. Edn. Theatre Assn., 1973-77, 85-89; treas. ArtsTime '89, Wash. State Centennial All-Arts Conf., 1987-89, long-range planning com., Kent (Wash.) View Christian Sch., 1987—; pres. PTA, Kent View Christian High Sch., 1992—; mem. precinct com. Dem. Orgn. King County, Wash., 1973-75, 93—. Democrat. Methodist. Home: 13904 SE 241st St Kent WA 98042-3315 Office: Creative Approaches PO Box 1363 Renton WA 98127-1363

GIFFORD, ERNEST MILTON, biologist, educator; b. Riverside, Calif., Jan. 17, 1920; s. Ernest Milton and Mildred Wade (Campbell) G.; m. Jean Duncan, July 15, 1942; 1 child, Jeanette. A.B., U. Calif., Berkeley, 1942, Ph.D., 1950; grad., U.S. Army Command and Gen. Staff Sch., 1965. Asst. prof. botany, asst. botanist expt. sta. U. Calif.-Davis, 1950-56, assoc. prof. botany, assoc. botanist, 1957-61, prof. botany, botanist, 1962-87, prof. emeritus, 1988—, chmn. dept. botany and agrl. botany, 1963-67, 74-78. Author: (with A. S. Foster) Morphology and Evolution of Vascular Plants, 3d edit., 1989, (with T. L. Rost) Mechanisms and control of Cell Division, 1977; editor in chief Am. Jour. Botany, 1975-79; advisor to editor Ency. Brit.; contbr. articles on anatomy, ultrastructure and morphogenesis of higher plants to profl. jours. Served to maj. U.S. Army, 1942-46; ETO; to col. USAR, 1946-73. Decorated Bronze Star medal; named disting. contbr. Ency. Brit., 1964; NRC fellow Harvard U., 1956; Fulbright research scholar, France, 1966; John Simon Guggenheim Found. fellow, France, 1966; NATO sr. postdoctoral fellow, France, 1974; recipient Acad. Senate Disting. Teaching award U. Calif.-Davis, 1986. Fellow Linnean Soc. (London); mem. Bot. Soc. Am. (v.p. 1981, pres. 1982, merit award 1981), Internat. Soc. Plant Morphologists (v.p. 1980-84), Am. Inst. Biol. Scis., Calif. Bot. Soc., Sigma Xi. Office: U Calif Sect Plant Biology Robbins Hall Davis CA 95616

GIFFORD, LESLIE JANE, artist, writer, educator; b. Chgo., May 20, 1947; d. Wendell W. and Nyma Jane Gifford. BS in Theatre and Dance, Skidmore Coll., 1969; student, Art Students League, N.Y.C., 1989-93, Alliance Francaise, Paris, 1977. Dancer Dance Circle, Boston, 1969-70; publicity dir. Charles Playhouse, Boston, 1969-70, Chelsea Theatre Ctr., Bklyn., 1971-74; artist in residence, choreographer, dir. Am. Ctr., Paris, 1978-81; asst. to exec. prodr. The American Experience, Boston, 1986-91; tchr. N.Y. Open Ctr., N.Y.C., 1991-95; painter, writer N.Y.C. and San Francisco, 1993-95; tchr. Mindful Body, San Francisco, 1995. Dir., choreographer: (theater/dance) Black to Black, Edinburgh Festival, 1978 (Fringe First award); dir., prodr.: (ind. film) September Dogs, 1991; author, illustrator: (screenplay/book) Earth Song, 1993. Mem. San Francisco Art Inst.

GIFFORD, LISA BONNIE, interior designer; b. American Fork, Utah, Mar. 12, 1968; d. Ronald F. and Bonnie L. (Ball) Myers; m. L. Graham Gifford, Feb. 11, 1989; children: Austin, Lincoln, Bronson. Cert. of completion, Mexican-N.Am. Inst. Cultural Rels., Mexico City, 1988; grad., Inst. of Religion, Logan, Utah, 1992; BA magna cum laude, Utah State U., 1993. Sec., receptionist Zion Home Furnishings, Provo, Utah, 1989; dept. mgr. Stokes Bros., Logan, 1989-92; interior designer Design Discovery, Salt Lake City, 1993, Office Essentials, Provo, 1993—; interior designer, prin. Details Drafting & Design, L.L.C., American Fork, 1993—. Acad. scholarships Utah State U., 1987-93. Mem. Am. Soc. Interior Designers (allied), Phi Kappa Phi, Phi Upsilon Omicron. Republican. Mem. LDS Ch. Office: Office Essentials 120 N University Ave Provo UT 84601-2820

GIGLIOTTI, RICHARD JOSEPH, nuclear security executive; b. North Adams, Mass., June 15, 1945; s. Victor and Ida (Antenucci) G.; m. Diane Carol Gigliotti; children: Gina Bianca, Victoria Marie, Richard Joseph Jr. BA, Norwich U., 1968; postgrad., Mass. State Coll., 1968-70. Police officer North Adams Police Dept., 1966-70, Wethersfield (Conn.) Police Dept., 1973-77; security supr. UNC Naval Products, Montville, Conn., 1977-78, corp. security dir., 1984-92; mgr. security UNC Recovery Systems, Charlestown, R.I., 1978-80; dir. loss prevention Colt Firearms, Hartford, Conn., 1980-84; mgr. security RUST Geotech Inc., Grand Junction, Colo., 1992-96; adj. faculty Ea. Conn. State U., Willimantic, Mohegan C.C., Norwich, 1984-92; guest lectr. various colls., univs., and corps., 1978—. Author: Security Design for Maximum Protection, 1984, Emergency Planning for Maximum Protection, 1991; contbr. articles to profl. jours. Active Gov.'s and Gen. Assembly's Task Force on Pvt. Security in Conn., 1983. 1st lt. U.S. Army, 1970-73. Recipient Chief Samuel Luciano award Mcpl. Police Tng. Coun., 1974. Mem. Internat. Assn. Chiefs Police, Am. Soc. for Indsl. Security, Ret. Officers Assn., Blue Knights Law Enforcement Motorcycle Club. Roman Catholic.

GILBERT, BEN W., retired newspaper editor; b. N.Y.C., Feb. 10, 1918; s. Harry and Tessie (Wertheimer) Goldberg; m. Maurine Coffee, Mar. 11, 1941 (dec.); children: Ian R. Gilbert, Amy G. Mann. B of Social Sci., CCNY, 1937; MA in Journalism, U. Mo., 1939. Reporter St. Louis (Mo.) Star Times, 1940-41; reporter Washington Post, Washington, 1941-45, city editor, day mng. editor, assoc. editor, 1945-70; on-air editor newsroom Sta. WETA-TV, Washington, 1970-71; gen. asst. to mayor Washington City Govt., 1972, planning dir., 1972-78; cons. various orgns., Washington, 1979-84; mem. Nat. Capital Planning Commn., Washington, 1973-78. Author, editor: Ten Blocks From White House, 1968. Mem. ethics com. Group Health Wash., Tacoma, 1985—, Landmarks Presdl. Commn., 1985—, chair, 1986-91. Recipient TV Emmy award D.C. TV Assn., 1970, State Historic Preservation award Wash. State Office Hist. Preservation, 1995, Disting. Citizen award Tacoma Mcpl. League, 1995. Mem. City Club Wash. (vol. editor newsletter, rsch. reports, bd. dirs.), City Club Tacoma (bd. dirs. 1986—), Phi Beta Kappa. Democrat. Home and Office: 421 N 6th St Tacoma WA 98403

GILBERT, DONALD R., lawyer; b. Phila., June 6, 1946. BA, Stanford U., 1968; JD, U. Calif., 1971. Bar: Calif. 1972, Ariz. 1972. Ptnr. Fennemore Craig, Phoenix. Mem. ABA, State Bar Ariz., State Bar Calif., Maricopa County Bar Assn. Office: Fennemore Craig 3003 N Central Ste 2600 Phoenix AZ 85012-2913

GILBERT, EDWARD MICHAEL, cardiology educator; b. Portsmouth, Va., Sept. 2, 1952; s. Edward Richard and Elenor (Kroeger) G.; m. Ina Judith Amber, Oct. 18, 1981 (div. June 1991); 1 child, Stephanie Amber; m. Karen Ann Allen, Dec. 7, 1991; 2 children: Robert Michael, Victoria Marie. BA in Chemistry, U. Conn., 1974; MD, Wayne State U., 1978. Diplomate Am. Bd. Internal Medicine, Am. Bd. Cardiovasc. Disease. Resident in medicine Wayne State U., Detroit, 1978-81, fellow in critical care, 1983-84; emergency room physician St. Johns Hosp., Detroit, 1981-83; fellow in cardiology U. Utah, Salt Lake City, 1984-88, asst. prof. medicine, 1988-93, assoc. prof., 1993—, dir. heart failure treatment program, 1992—; clin. assoc. physician NIH, 1988-90; med. dir. CCU, U. Utah Health Sci. Ctr., 1993-94. Contbr. over 75 articles to med. and sci. jours. Fellow Bayer Fund, 1988. Fellow Am. Coll. Cardiology (Merck fellow 1985); mem. Am. Heart Assn. (fellow clin. coun., grantee 1989-91), Am. Fedn. Clin. Rsch., Am. Alpine Club. Office: U Utah Health Sci Ctr 50 N Medical Dr Salt Lake City UT 84132-0001

GILBERT, HEATHER CAMPBELL, manufacturing company executive; b. Mt. Vernon, N.Y., Nov. 20, 1944; d. Ronald Ogston and Mary Lodivia (Campbell) G.; BS in Math. (Nat. Merit scholar), Stanford U., 1967; MS in Computer Sci. (NSF fellow), U. Wis., 1969. With Burroughs Corp., 1969-82, sr. mgmt. systems analyst, Detroit, 1975-77, mgr. mgmt. systems activity, Pasadena, Calif., 1977-82; mgr. software product mgmt. Logical Data Mgmt. Inc., Covina, Calif., 1982-83, dir. mktg., 1983, v.p. bus. devel., 1983-84; v.p. profl. services, 1984-85; mgr. software devel. Unisys Corp., Mission Viejo, Calif., 1985—. Mem. Assn. Computing Machinery, Am. Prodn. and Inventory Control Soc., Stanford U. Alumni Assn. (life), Stanford Profl. Women Los Angeles County (pres. 1982-83), Nat. Assn. Female Execs., Town Hall. Republican. Home: 21113 Calle De Paseo Lake Forest CA 92630-7037 Office: Unisys Corp 25725 Jeronimo Rd Mission Viejo CA 92691-2711

GILBERT, PAUL THOMAS, chemical development engineer; b. Chgo., July 29, 1914; s. Paul T. and Ilse (Forster) G.; m. Phyllis A. Simons, Oct. 17, 1942 (div. July 1955); children: Susan R. Sorensen, John (dec.), Brian (dec.), Wendy E. Levy; m. Hazel L. Dalton, July 9, 1955; children: Michael L. Pinizzotto, Michele L. Urquhart. BS in Chemistry, Northwestern U., 1936; postgrad., U. Wis., 1936-38; MA in Math., U. Minn., 1940; postgrad., Calif. Inst. Tech., 1941, U. Calif., Santa Barbara, 1971-74. Tchg. asst. math. U. Minn., Mpls., 1939-41; instr. math. Utah State Agrl. Coll., Logan, 1941, 43-44, U. Minn., Mpls., 1943; rsch. chemist Metalloy Corp., Mpls., 1944-46; rsch. scientist Beckman Instruments, South Pasadena, Calif., 1946-52, N.Am. Aviation, Downey, Calif., 1952-55, Beckman Instruments, Fullerton, Palo Alto, Calif., 1955-71; devel. engr. Chemistry Dept. U. Calif., Santa Barbara, 1971-93; tchr. math. NW Mil. and Naval Prep. Sch., Mpls., 1939-41, 45; tech. translator, 1946—; cons. Atomics Internat., Canoga Park, Calif., 1956-59, lectr. Fullerton Youth Mus., 1963-65, bd. dirs. Co-author (translator) Chemical Analysis by Flame Photometry, 1963; translator: Fundamentals of Analytical Flame Spectroscopy, 1979; patentee in field; contbr. articles to profl. jours. Racecourse measurer Santa Barbara Athletic Assn., 1978—. Cadet USAF, 1941-43. Mem. AAAS, Am. Chem. Soc., Am. Math. Soc., Phi Beta Kappa, Sigma Xi, Phi Eta Sigma. Home: 715 Via Miguel Santa Barbara CA 93111-2743 Office: Univ Calif Dept Chemistry Santa Barbara CA 93106

GILBERT, RICHARD KEITH, education educator, researcher; b. St. Louis, Apr. 23, 1958; s. William Ray and Janice Sylvia (Rephlo) G. BA, U. Calif., Santa Barbara, 1981, MA, 1990, postgrad., 1993; PhD, U. So. Calif.,

1997. Secondary tchg. credential, Calif. Rschr. Marine Sci. Inst., Santa Barbara, 1979-82; rschr., coord. Catalina Island (Calif.) Marine Inst., 1983-85; tchr. sci. L.A. Unified Sch. Dist., 1985-87; sci. and calculus educator Am. Internat. Sch., Johannesburg, South Africa, 1987-89; rschr. psychotherapy U. Calif., Santa Barbara, 1990-92; cons. advanced tech. divsn. spl. projects Gen. Rsch. Corp., Santa Barbara, 1992-94; instr., rschr. U. So. Calif., L.A., 1993—; rschr., cons. Human Scis. Rsch. Coun., Pretoria, South Africa, 1995; cons. Akela Corp., 1994; team leader, cons. TELP Project USAID, Pretoria, 1996; profl. expert rsch. and evaluation LACOE, DAE. Active re-election campaign Hon. Robert Lagomarsino, Santa Barbara, 1992—. Named Outstanding Tchr. Advanced Biol. Sci., NSF, Calif. State U., Northridge, 1986-87; Grad. fellow Calif. State U., U. So. Calif., 1993. Mem. AAAS, N.Y. Acad. Scis., Comparative Internat. Edn. Soc., Am. Ednl. Rsch. Assn., U.S. Naval Inst., Phoenix Soc. (outstanding mem. 1987). Presbyterian. Home: 6285 Avenida Ganso Goleta CA 93117-2063 Office: U So Calif Dept Edn WPH 904 Los Angeles CA 90089-0031

GILBERT, ROBERT WOLFE, lawyer; b. N.Y.C., Nov. 12, 1920; s. L. Wolfe and Katherine L. (Oestreicher) Wolfe; m. Beatrice R. Frutman, Dec. 25, 1946; children: Frank Richard, Jack Alfred. BA, UCLA 1941; JD, U. Calif., Berkeley, 1943. Bar: Calif. 1944, U.S. Ct. Appeals. (9th cir.) 1944, U.S. Ct. Appeals. (D.C. cir.) 1976, U.S. Supreme Ct. 1959. Pres. Gilbert & Sackman, P.C. and predecessors, L.A., 1944—; judge pro tem Los Angeles Mcpl. and Superior Ct., Commr. City of L.A. Housing Authority 1953-63; bd. dirs. Calif. Housing Coun. 1955-63; U.S. faculty mem. Moscow Conf. on Law and Econ. Cooperation, 1990. Mem. Internat. Bar Assn., Interam. Bar Assn. (co-chmn. labor law and social security com.), ABA (co-chmn. internat. labor law com.), Fed. Bar Assn., L.A. Bar Assn. (past chmn. labor law sect.), Am. Judicature Soc., Order of Coif, Pi Sigma Alpha. Club: Nat. Lawyers. Contbr. articles to profl. jours. Home: 7981 Hollywood Blvd Los Angeles CA 90046-2611 Office: 6100 Wilshire Blvd Ste 700 Los Angeles CA 90048-5114

GILBERT, SANDRA M., English language educator, writer. BA in English with high honors, Cornell U., 1957; MA, NYU, 1961; PhD, Columbia U., 1968; DLitt, Wesleyan U., 1988. Lectr. English CUNY, N.Y.C., 1963-64, 65-66, Calif. State U., Sacramento, 1967-68; asst. prof. English Calif. State U., Hayward, 1968-71; vis. lectr. English St. Mary's Coll., Moraga, Calif., 1972; assoc. prof. English Ind. U., Bloomington, 1973-75; assoc. prof. English U. Calif., Davis, 1975-80, prof. English, 1980-85, 89—; prof. English Princeton (N.J.) U., 1985-89, Charles Barnwell Strout Class of 1923 prof., 1989; chair women's studies subcom. SWADAC U. Calif., Davis, 1976-80; vis. prof. Ind. U., Bloomington, fall 1980, The Johns Hopkins U., Balt., fall 1986; panelist NEH, fall 1982, Rockefeller Found., fall 1982, women's studies Woodrow Wilson Found., fall 1985; dir. Mt. Holyoke Project Gender Context, 1983, summer 1984; mem. exec. com. Humanities Inst., 1983-87; Margaret Bundy Scott vis. prof. Williams Coll., fall 1984; Bonzall vis. prof. Stanford (Calif.) U., winter 1985; Gildersleeve professorship Barnard Coll., fall 1982; Joseph Warren Beach lectr. U. Minn., May, 1984; faculty Sch. Criticism and Theory, Northwestern U., summer 1984; mem. women's studies program com. Princeton U., 1986—, mem. creative writing program com., 1986—, acting dir. creative writing program, spring 1989; Paley lectr. The Hebrew U., Jerusalem, 1990; Danz lectr. U. Wash., Seattle, 1992; bd. advisors Literary Classics in the U.S., 1979-82; lectr. in field. Author: Acts of Attention: The Poems of D. H. Lawrence, 1972, 2d rev. edit., 1990 (alternate selection Readers Subscription 1973), In the Fourth World: Poems, 1979, The Summer Kitchen: Poems, 1983, Emily's Bread: Poems, 1984, Kate Chopin's The Awakening and Selected Stories, 1984, Blood Pressure: Poems, 1988, Wrongful Death: A Medical Tragedy, 1995, Ghost Volcano: Poems, 1995; co-author: (with Susan Gubar) The Madwoman in the Attic: The Woman Writer and the Nineteenth Century Literary Imagination, 1979 (runner-up Pulitzer Prize in non-fiction 1980), A Guide to the Norton Anthology of Literature by Women, 1985, No Man's Land: The Place of the Woman Writer in the Twentieth Century, Vol. 1, The War of the Words, 1987, Vol. 2, Sexchanges, 1989, Vol. 3, Letters From the Front, 1994, Masterpiece Theatre: An Academic Melodrama, 1995; co-editor: (with Susan Gubar) Shakespeare's Sisters: Feminist Essays on Women Poets, 1979, Women of Letters Series, 1984—, The Norton Anthology of Literature by Women: The Tradition in English, 1985, Feminism and Modernism, 1987, (with Susan Gubar and Diana O'lbehin) Mother Songs, 1995, (with Wendy Barker) The House is Made of Poetry: Essays on the Art of Ruth Stone, 1995; editor: So. Ill. U. Press Series in Feminist Criticism, 1984—; poetry editor Calif. Quarterly, 1975-80; mem. editorial bd. Tulsa Studies in Women's Lit., 1980—, Poesis, 1983—, Genre, 1988—; co-editor (with Susan Gubar) Women's Studies, spring 1980, fall 1984; mem. poetry bd. Wesleyan U. Press, 1985-88; contbr. essays, poems and ficiton to profl. jours. and popular mags. Grantee Calif. State Hayward Found., 1969-70, Ind. U., 1974, U. Calif., summer 1976, 78, 79, 81; recipient Columbia U. Pres.'s fellowship, 1964-65, AAUW fellowship, 1966-67, NEH fellowship, 1980-81, Rockefeller Found. Humanities fellowship, 1982, Guggenheim fellowship, 1983, U. Calif.-Davis Humanities Inst. fellowship, 1987-88, U. Calif. Pres.'s fellowship, 1991-92, Eunice Tietjens Meml. prize, 1980, Charity Randall award Internat. Poetry Found., 1990, Woman of the Yr. award Ms. mag., 1986. Mem. MLA (nominating com. 1985-87, William Riley Parker Prize com. 1985-87, exec. com. Lit. Criticism divsn. 1985-87, exec. coun. 1981-84, exec. com. Women's Studies divsn. 1980-84, 2nd v.p., 1st v.p., pres-elect, 1994—), D.H. Lawrence Soc. (mem. exec. com. 1983-85). Office: Univ of Calif Dept of English Davis CA 95616

GILBERT, SCOTT, advertising executive. Co-chmn. bd., CEO Team One Advertising, El Segundo, Calif. Office: 1960 E Grand Ave Ste 700 El Segundo CA 90245*

GILBERT, WILLIAM MARSHALL, retired biologist, educator; b. Huntington, W.Va., July 19, 1935; s. Frank Albert and Eleanor (Marshall) G.; m. Claire Arlene Bohn, Aug. 25, 1985; 1 child, Chantal Louise. BSc, Ohio State U., 1957, MA, 1959; PhD, U. Calif., Davis, 1974. Instr. biology Contra Costa Coll., San Pablo, Calif., 1973-79; environ. rsch. analyst San Francisco Bay Marine rsch. Ctr., Emeryville, Calif., 1979-85; intr. environ. sci. Chabot Coll., Hayward, Calif., 1990-94; pvt. ornithol. rschr. on behavior of orange-corwned and Wilson's warblers, 1981—; lit. reviewer Am. Ornithol. Union, 1996—. Contbr. articles to profl. jours. Mem. Nature Sounds Soc. (bd. dirs. 1983—), Sierra Club (Couples sect. leadership chair 1982—). Home and Office: 4630 Driftwood Ct El Sobrante CA 94803

GILBERT-BUSHNELL, HELEN ODELL, artist, art educator; b. Mare Island, Calif., Apr. 6, 1922; d. Henry Edward Odell and Ruth Stewart Harris; m. Fred Ivan Gilbert Jr., Sept. 18, 1943 (div. 1973); children: Rondi, Kristin, Galen, Gerald, Gil, Lisa, Cara; m. Kenneth W. Bushnell, Apr. 5, 1997. BA, Mills Coll., 1943; postgrad., Cen. Sch. Art, London, 1960-61, U. Calif., Berkeley, 1966; MFA, U. Hawaii, 1968. Employee Dorothy Wright Liebes Studio, San Francisco, 1944-54; ind. artist Honolulu, 1955—; prof. U. Hawaii, Honolulu, 1968—; v.p. Fine Art Projects, Ltd., Honolulu, 1987-91. Artist (books) Contemporary Women Sculptors (by Watson Jones), 1986, Le Strutture Della Visualita (by Heinz Holz), 1985: one-woman shows include Contemporary Art Ctr., Honolulu, 1983, 89, 90, Seasons Galerie, Den Haag, The Netherlands, 1984, Galerie Maghi Bettini, Amsterdam, 1984, Galerie Meissner Edition, Hamburg, Germany, 1984, Sande Webster Gallery, Phila., 1985, 88, 92, Northeastern U., Boston, 1986, Karin Fesel Galerie, Düsseldorf, Germany, 1991, Sidney Mishkin Gallery, N.Y.C., Honolulu Acad. Arts, 1994, (solo) 1995-97; exhibited in group shows 55 Mercer Gallery, N.Y.C., 1989, 97, Portland Art Mus., Internat. Point Exhbn., Baruch Coll., 1996; Salon des Artists Graphiques Actuels, Paris Grande Palaise, 1989, Ulrich Mus., Wichita, Kans., 1992, First Graphic Biennial Invitational Maastricht, The Netherlands, 1993, Noyes Mus., Oceanville, N.J., 1994, N.J. State Mus., Trenton, 1994. Recipient Purchase award State Foun. on Culture and the Arts, Hawaii, 1972, 73, 76, 78, 81, 83, 86; project grantee Ford Found., 1978, rshc. grantee U. Hawaii, 1969, 70, 81, 90. Mem. Am. Abstract Artists Assn., Soc. Am. Graphic Artists, The Nat. Arts Club (N.Y.C.), Honolulu Printmakers (Merit awards 1983, 84, 85), Contemporary Art Mus. (Honolulu, founder), Honolulu Acad. Arts (life, Purchase awards 1962, 71, 77, hon. Acad. Purchase 1995). Home: 2081 Keeaumoku Pl Honolulu HI 96822-2553 Office: U Hawaii Dept of Art 2535 The Mall Honolulu HI 96822-2233

GILBERTSON, OSWALD IRVING, marketing executive; b. Bklyn., Mar. 23, 1927; s. Olaf and Ingeborg (Aase) Gabrielsen; m. Magnhild Hompland, Sept. 11, 1954; 1 child, Jan Ivar. Electrotechnician, Sorlandets Tekniske Skole, Norway, 1947; BSEE, Stockholms Tekniska Institut, Stockholm, Sweden, 1956. Planning engr. test equipment design and devel. Western Electric Co., Inc., Kearny, N.J., 1957-61, planning engr. new prodn., 1963-67, engrng. supr. test equipment, 1963-67, engrng. supr. submarine repeaters and equalizers, 1967-69; engrng. mgr. communication cables ITT Corp., Oslo, Norway, 1969-71, mktg. mgr. for ITT's Norwegian co., Standard Telefon og Kabelfabrik A/S (STK), 1971-87, STK Factory rep., 1987-89, Alcatel Kabel Norge AS Factory rep., 1989-92, Alcatel Can. Wire Inc. Factory rep., 1992-95; div. mgr. Eswa Heating Systems, Inc., 1980-87, pres., 1987-89. Hon. Norwegian consul, 1981—; apptd. Knight First Class Norwegian Order Merit, 1989. Served with AUS, 1948-52. Registered profl. engr., Vt. Mem. IEEE, Norwegian Soc. Profl. Engrs., Soc. Norwegian Am. Engrs., Sons of Norway. Patentee in field. Home and Office: 6240 Brynwood Ct San Diego CA 92120-3805

GILBERTZ, LARRY E., state legislator, entrepreneur; b. Gillette, Wyo., Feb. 3, 1929; s. Jacob A. and Lena E. (Schlautmann) G.; m. Verna Ann Howell, June 18, 1955; children: Katerine, L.D., Susan, Jay. Mgr. Gilbertz Ranch, Gillette, 1953-62, owner, 1963—; sr. ptnr. Gilbertz Co., Gillette, 1971—; pres. Gilbertz Enterprises, Gillette, 1988—; mem. Wyo. Senate, Cheyenne, 1993—; chmn. U. Wyo. Exptl. Farm, Campbell County, 1970-74. Treas. Sch. Bd. Dist. # 9, Campbell County, 1969-71; active Sch. Dist. Reorgn., Campbell County, 1970, Wyo. Ct. Reform, 1971. With U.S. Army, 1951-53, PTO. Recipient Performance Testing award U. Wyo., 1969-74, Chem. Weed Control award, 1969-74. Mem. Am. Farm Bur., Am. Legis. Exch. Coun., Am. Legion. Republican. Roman Catholic. Home: 3934 Hwy 50 HCR 82 Gillette WY 82718

GILBRIDE, KEVIN, professional football coach; b. New Haven, Aug. 27, 1951; m. Deborah DiNuzzo, Jan. 4, 1975; children: Kelly, Kristen, Kevin. Degree in phys. edn., So. Conn. State U.; M in Sports Adminstrn., Idaho State U. Coach Idaho State U., 1974-75; linebacker coach Tufts U., Medford, Mass., 1976-77; defensive coord. Am. Internat., Springfield, Mass., 1978-79; passing game coord. East Carolina, 1987, offensive coord., 1988; head coach So. Conn. State U., 1980-84; quarterbacks/receivers coach Ottawa Rough Ridgers Can. Football League, 1985, offensive coord., 1986; offensive coord. Houston Oilers NFL, 1989-92, asst. head coach Houston Oilers, 1993-94, offensive coord. Jacksonville Jaguars, 1995-96, head coach San Diego Chargers, 1996—. Office: San Diego Chargers PO Box 609609 San Diego CA 92160-9609

GILCHRIST, ANN ROUNDEY, medical/surgical nurse; b. Utica, N.Y., Dec. 21, 1948; d. William Gilchrist and Adele (Cobb) Roundey; divorced; children: Kristie Ann Hughes, Megean Elizabeth Hughes. Student, Cazenovia Coll., 1967-68; LPN, Utica Sch. Practical Nursing, 1972; postgrad., Mohawk Valley C.C., 1972-75; ADN, SUNY, Morrisville, 1976. RN, Nev.; CNOR. Obstetrics and med., surg. staff nurse St. Elizabeth Hosp., Utica, 1972-76; asst. charge nurse CCU and ICU Mohawk Valley Gen. Hosp., Ilion, N.Y., 1976-78; staff nurse operating room Tucson Med. Ctr., 1978-80, El Dorado Hosp., Tucson, 1978-80; staff nurse oper. rm. and post anesthesia care unit Tucson Gen. Hosp., 1980-85; charge nurse oper. rm. Desert Springs Hosp., Las Vegas, 1985-87, staff nurse GI Lab., 1988-90; charge nurse GI Lab, staff nurse operating room Lake Mead Hosp., Las Vegas, 1991-93; supr. operating room Red Rock Surg. Ctr., Las Vegas, 1993-95; agy. nurse Reliable Health Care Svcs., 1995—; charge nurse endoscopy lab. Sunrise Flamingo Surg. Ctr., Las Vegas, 1995—. Mem. NAFE, Am. Orgn. Operating Room Nurses, Soc. Gastroenterology Assts., Nat. Koi Club. Home and Office: 4552 Scott Ave Las Vegas NV 89102-8107

GILDZEN, ALEX, writer; b. Monterey, Calif., Apr. 25, 1943; s. Al and Helen (Kovach) G. BA, Kent (Ohio) State U., 1965, MA, 1966. Intern Gen. Tire & Rubber, Akron, Ohio, 1965; lectr. English Kent State U. Libr., 1967-70, asst. curator, 1970-77, assoc. curator, 1977-84, curator spl. collections, 1984-93; fellow Inst. for Bibliography and Editing, Kent State U., 1986-94; judge poetry contest Kaleidoscope: A Literary/Art Mag. by Persons with Disabilities, Akron, Ohio, 1983-84. Author: The Year Book, 1974, The Avalanche of Time, 1986; co-author: Joseph Chaikin, 1992; co-editor: A Gathering of Poets, 1992. Recipient Ohioana award Ohioana Libr. Assn., Columbus, 1993. Mem. ALA (mem. exhbn. catalog awards com. 1990-92). Home: 2328 Brother Abdon Way Santa Fe NM 87505

GILES, GERALD LYNN, psychology and learning enhancement educator, computer educator; b. Manti, Utah, Jan. 2, 1943; s. Bert Thorne and Sarah Jenett (Carlen) G.; m. Sharon Ruth Bleak, June 12, 1967; children: Kim, David, Kristie, Becky, Michael, Andrew, Brent, Amber. BA, U. Utah, 1968, MA, 1971. Tchr. Granite Sch. Dist., Salt Lake City, 1968-72; prof. Salt Lake Community Coll., Salt Lake City, 1972—; cons. QUE Enterprises, Salt Lake City, 1976—; mem. faculty U. Phoenix, Salt Lake City, 1986—; internat. presenter in field. Author: The Vicious Circle of Life, 1988, The Computer Productivity Planner, 1988. Chmn. Rep. voting dist., Salt Lake City, 1984-86; bishop LDS Ch., 1986-91; adviser Explorer Scouts. Named Outstanding Tchr. of Yr., 1986; recipient Teaching Excellence award, 1986, Excellence award Nisod, 1994. Mem. ASCD, Nat. Assn. Devel. Edn., Southwestern Assn. Devel. Edn., Utah Assn. Adult and Continuing Edn. Home: 4342 Beechwood Rd Salt Lake City UT 84123-2206 Office: Salt Lake C C PO Box 30808 Salt Lake City UT 84130-0808

GILES, JANA MARÍA, writer, editor; b. Aberdeen, Wash., Nov. 2, 1966; d. Garred Allen Giles and Francisca Hernández. BA, St. John's Coll., 1988; MA, U. N.Mex., 1994. Asst. editor CZM Assocs., Annapolis, Md., 1989; publs. asst. Internat. Mgmt. and Devel. Inst., Washington, 1989-90; copy editor Albuquerque Jour., 1990-91; tchg. asst. English dept. U. N.Mex., Albuquerque, 1992-95; assoc. prodr. Writing the Southwest, Albuquerque, 1993-94; assoc. editor Colonial L.Am. Hist. Rev., Albuquerque, 1995—; fiction judge Conceptions Southwest, Albuquerque, 1993; mentor APS Gifted Mentorship, Albuquerque, 1995-96. Contbr. short stories, acad. articles and book revs. to profl. publs.; mem. editl. bd. Hembra, 1992-93; co-editor The Women's Anthology of St. John's College, 1988-90. Vol. Celebrate Youth!, Albuquerque, 1990—, KUNM-FM Pub. Radio, Albuquerque, 1990-91, Unemployment and Poverty Action Fund, Washington, 1989-90; essay judge Acad. Decathlon, Albuquerque, 1993; mem. fiction writer's retreat Vt. Studio Ctr., Johnson, 1997. Named Outstanding Scholar, N.Mex. Tchrs.' Assn., 1984; creative writing fellow dept. English U. N.Mex., 1992-93. Mem. MLA. Office: U NMex Spanish Colonial Rsch Ctr Colonial LAm Hist Rev Zimmerman Libr Albuquerque NM 87131

GILES, WALTER EDMUND, alcohol and drug treatment executive; b. Omaha, Aug. 9, 1934; s. Walter Edmund and Julia Margaret (Shively) G.; m. Ellen M. Garton, June 13, 1953; m. Dona LaVonne Foster, Sept. 29, 1970 (dec. 1990); children: Sue, Stephen, Theresa, Marcy, Kim, Tim, Nadine, Charles; m. Yvonne Marie Fink, Nov. 29, 1991; children: Jessica Nicole Farr, Walter Edmund III, David Michael. BA, U. Nebr., Lincoln, 1972, MA, 1977. Counselor VA Hosp., Lincoln, Nebr., 1969-70; coord. alcohol programs Mcpl. Ct., Lincoln; dir. Orange County Employee Assistance, Santa Ana, Calif., 1977-79; adminstr. Advanced Health Ctr., Newport Beach, Calif., 1979-81; pres. Great West Health Svcs. Inc., Orange, Calif., 1982-86, Pine Ridge Treatment Ctr. Inc., Running Springs, Calif., 1986—. Author (book) The Workbook, 1985, Intervention, 1986; host (radio show) Addictions, 1984. Mem. Nat. Assn. Alcoholism Counselors, Calif. Assn. Alcoholism Counselors.

GILETTI, GREGORY PAUL, military officer; b. Phila., Oct. 17, 1964; s. Ronald Charles and Rosa T. (Tramontana) G.; m. Sharon Anne Hullinger, May 30, 1987; children: Joseph, Andrew, Grace, John. BS, USAF Acad., 1986; MA, Boston Coll., 1993. Commd. 2d lt. USAF, 1986, advanced through grades to capt., 1990; program mgr. USAF, Hanscom AFB, Mass., 1986-89; ops. officer 3245th Air Base Group USAF, Hanscom AFB, 1989, dir. program control, 1990-91; asst. prof. dept. polit. sci. USAF Acad., Colorado Springs, Colo., 1993-96; exec. officer, dean of faculty USAF Acad., 1996—. Capt. USAF. Mem. Assn. Grads. Republican. Roman Catholic. Home: 4206K West Muledeer Dr U S A F Academy CO 80840

GILGER, PAUL DOUGLASS, architect; b. Mansfield, Ohio, Oct. 13, 1954; s. Richard Douglass and Marilyn Joan (Hawkins) G. BArch, U. Cin., 1978. Registered architect, Ohio. Architect Soulen & Assocs., Mansfield, Ohio, 1976-81, PGS Architecture/Planning, Los Gatos, Calif., 1981-82, Bottomline Systems, Inc., San Francisco, 1983-85; pvt. practice San Francisco Bay Area, 1985-90; set designer Nomad Prodns. Scenic Studios, San Francisco, 1985-87; architect James Gillam, Architect, San Francisco, 1987-90, Hedgpeth Architects, Santa Rosa, Calif., 1990—, Home Planners, Inc., Tucson, 1994—; booking mgr. 1177 Club, San Francisco, 1985-86, City Cabaret, San Francisco, 1986-87; bd. dirs San Francisco Coun. Entertainment, 1987-90; project architect Lucasfilm Movie Studio Indsl. Light and Magic, San Rafael, Calif., 1991. Author: "Tune the Grand Up", the Jerry Herman Musical Revue. Recipient Ohio Cmty. Theatre Assn. award, 1980, Theatrewest Acting award, 1983, 3 Bay Area Critics Cir. award, 1984, 85, 4 Cabaret Gold awards San Francisco Coun. Entertainment, 1985, 86, 3 Hollywood Dramalogue awards, 1985, 5 awards. 1996; San Francisco Focus award, 1985. Home: 631 Spencer Ave Apt 6 Santa Rosa CA 95404-3315 Office: Hedgpeth Architects 2321 Bethards Dr Santa Rosa CA 95405-8536

GILHOOLY, DAVID JAMES, III, artist; b. Auburn, Calif., Apr. 15, 1943; s. David James and Gladys Catherine (Schulte) G.; m. Camille Margot Chang, Aug. 23, 1983; children: David James, Andrea Elizabeth, Abigail Margaret, Peter Rodney, Hakan Yuatutsu, Kiril Shintora, Sorgan Subetei. BA, U. Calif., Davis, 1965, MA, 1967. tchr. San Jose (Calif.) State Coll., 1967-69, U. Sask. (Can.), Regina, 1969-71, York U., Toronto, Ont., Can., 1971-75, 76-77, U. Calif.-Davis, summer 1971, 75-76, Calif. State U.-Sacramento, summers 1978-79; lectr. in field. One-man shows include San Francisco Museum Art, 1967, M. H. deYoung Meml. Mus., San Francisco, 1968, Matrix Gallery, Wadsworth Athenaeum, Hartford, Conn., 1976, Mus. Contemporary Art, Chgo., 1976, Vancouver (B.C., Can.), Art Gallery, 1976, ARCO Ctr. for Visual Arts, Los Angeles, 1977, Mus. Contemporary Craft, N.Y.C., 1977, E.B. Crocker Art Mus., Sacramento, 1980, St. Louis Mus. Art, 1981, Smith-Anderson Gallery, Palo Alto, 1985, San Jose Mus. Art, 1992, Solomon Dubnick Gallery, Sacramento, 1997; group shows include U. Calif.-Berkeley Art Mus., 1967, Inst. Contemporary Art, Boston, 1967, Whitney Mus. Am. Art, N.Y.C., 1970, 74, 81, Musee d'art de la Ville Paris, 1973, Chgo. Art Inst., 1975, San Francisco Mus. Art and Nat. Collection Fine Art, Washington, 1976-77, Stedelijk Mus., Amsterdam, The Netherlands, 1979, Everson Mus. Art, Syracuse, N.Y., 1979, Whitney Mus. Am. Art, N.Y.C., 1981, Palm Springs Desert Art Mus., 1984, Oakland Mus., 1985, Stanford Mus. Art, 1987, Inst. Contemporary Art, Boston, 1994; represented in permanent collections S. Bronfman Collection Can. Art, Montreal, Que., San Francisco Mus. Art, Phila. Mus. Art, Vancouver Art Gallery, Art Gallery Greater Victoria (B.C.), Albright-Knox Art Gallery, Buffalo, San Antonio Mus. Art, Oakland (Calif.) Mus. Art, Stedelijk Mus., Stanford U., Palo Alto, Calif., Australian Nat. Gallery, Canberra, Govt. Can., Calgary, Alta., Whitney Mus. Am. Art, Eugene (Oreg.) Ctr. Performing Arts. Can. Council grantee, 1975, 78. Mem. Royal Can. Acad. Republican. Mem. Ch. of Scientology. Address: Solomon Dubnick Gallery 2131 Northrop Ave Sacramento CA 95825 Office: 11140 SE Oak Dr Dayton OR 97114-7447

GILKESON, JERRELL ESTLE, principal; b. Grand Junction, Colo., Apr. 2, 1949; s. Ferrell C. and Jessie Rose (Estle) G.; m. Evelin Harper, June 6, 1971; children: Melody, Julie. BA, So. Coll., 1972; MEd, U. So. Miss., 1992. Tchr. elem. sch. Key West (Fla.) Ch. Sch., 1972-75; chaplain Bass Meml. Acad., Lumberton, Miss., 1976-80, Upper Columbia Acad., Spangle, Wash., 1980-84; pastor Grandview (Wash.) Ch., 1985-89; prin. high sch. Bass Mem. Acad., 1989-93; tchr. mid. sch. Redlands (Calif.) Jr. Acad., 1994-95; prin. high sch. Escondido (Calif.) Adventist Acad., 1995—; prodn. mgr. Harper Foria Optical, Chula Vista, Calif., 1992—. Mem. ASCD, Nat. Assn. Secondary Sch. Prins. Office: Escondido Adventist Acad 1233 W 9th Ave Escondido CA 92029-2202

GILKEY, GORDON WAVERLY, curator, artist; b. Albany, Oreg., Mar. 10, 1912; s. Leonard Ernest and Edna Isabel (Smith) G.; m. Vivian Malone, Oct. 17, 1938 (dec. Sept. 1995); 1 son, Gordon Spencer. BS, Albany Coll., 1933; MFA, U. Oreg., 1936; ArtsD (hon.), Lewis and Clark Coll., 1957. Mem. art staff Stephens Coll., Mo., 1939-42; prof. art, head dept. Oreg. State U., 1947-64; dean Oreg. State U. (Sch. Humanities and Social Scis.), 1963-73, Oreg. State U. (Coll. Liberal Arts), 1973-77; curator prints and drawings Portland (Oreg.) Art Mus., 1978—; prof. and printmaker-in-resident Pacific N.W. Coll. Art, 1978—; spl. asst. to exec. dir. Portland Art Mus., 1988-94; dir. Internat. Exc. Print Exhibits, 1956-78; U.S. adviser IV Bordighera Biennale, Italy, 1957; chmn. Gov.'s Planning Coun. for Arts and Humanities in, Oreg., 1965-67; mem. Gov.'s Commn. on Fgn. Lang. and Internat. Studies. Ofcl. etcher New York World's Fair, 1939, 1937-39; etcher Nat. Broadcasting Co., Radio City, N.Y.C., 1937-39; artist-author: Etchings: New York World's Fair, 1939; contbr. articles on art; major work in permanent collection, Met. Mus. Art, others. Col. U.S. Army Air Corps, 1942-47, ret. Decorated Palmes Academiques (France), officer's cross and comdr.'s cross Order of Merit (Fed. Republic Germany), Order Star of Solidarity (Italy), comdr. Order of Merit (Italy), officer Order Acad. Palms (France), chevalier Legion of Honor (France), Grand Cross Order St. Gregory the Illuminator, comdr. Order Polonia Restituta, chevalier Order of Holy Sepulchre, chevalier mil. and hospitaller Order of St. Lazarus, chevalier mil. and hospitaller Order of Our Lady of Mt. Carmel, chevalier St. Dennis of Zante, knight Grand Cross Order of St. Basil the Great, knight Imperial Order of St. Eugene of Trebizond, Order of the Knights of Sinai, order of Temple of Jerusalem, comdr. Order St. Stephan the Martyr; recipient King Carl XVI Gustaf's Gold Commemorative medal in art Sweden, German Friendship award; Soc. Mayflower Descendants, Aubrey R. Watzek award; named AIA-Carnegie Corp. fellow, summers 1930, 32. Mem. Am. Print Alliance (bd. dirs.), Portland Art Mus. (founder), Soc. Am. Graphic Artists, Calif. Soc. Printmakers, Coll. Art Assn., UN Assn. Oreg. (past pres.), Oreg. Internat. Coun. (bd. dirs.), Print Coun. of Am., N.W. Print Coun. (trustee), Phi Kappa Phi, Kappa Pi. Home: 1500 SW 5th Ave Ste 2401 Portland OR 97201-5458 Office: 1219 SW Park Ave Portland OR 97205-2430

GILL, AJIT SINGH, civil engineer; b. Mullanpur, Ludhiana, India, Sept. 21, 1933; came to U.S., 1955; s. Chanan Singh and Indkaur Gill; m. Sharon Rose, Nov. 24, 1960 (div.); 1 child, Daniel P.; m. Sandra Chloe, Jan. 21, 1972; 1 child, Mira A. BSc in Econs., Brigham Young U., 1961, BSc in Engring. Scis., 1962. Registered profl. engr., Utah. Roadway designer Dept. Transp., Salt Lake City, 1963-66, hydraulic and civil engr., 1966-80; water resources engr. Div. Water Resources State of Utah, Natural Resources & Energy, Salt Lake City, 1980—. Mem. Instrumentation Soc. Am. Home: 4169 Bennion Rd Salt Lake City UT 84119-5467

GILL, BECKY LORETTE, addictionist, psychiatrist; b. Phoenix, Mar. 16, 1947; d. David Franklin and Lorette (Cooper) Brinegar; m. Jim Shack Gill, Jr., Aug. 5, 1978. *Father David F. Brinegar served as a Captain in the Army in World War II and was stationed in the Persian Gulf. After the war, he worked with the Central Arizona Project, and then as an editor of The Arizona Daily Star. Mother Lorette C. Brinegar served in the Red Cross in France in World War II, and then was a high school physical education teacher, counselor, and vice principal at various Arizona high schools. She was a ranked Arizona and Southwest tennis player. Husband Jim S. Gill is a retired Marine Corps Gunnery Sergeant who works as a high school teacher. He graduated magna cum laude from Memphis State University.* BA in Biology, Stanford U., 1968; MD, U. Ariz., 1973. Diplomate Am. Bd. Psychiatry and Neurology; cert. addiction counselor; substance abuse residential facility dir., addictions specialist, clin. supr. Clerk typist Ariz. Med. Ctr. Med. Libr., Tucson, Ariz., 1970; asst. ref. libr. Ariz. Med. Ctr. Med. Libr., Tucson, 1971; surg. extern Tucson Med. Ctr., summer 1970; med. extern Fed. Reformatory for Women, Alderson, W.Va., 1972-73; commd. lt. USN, 1974, advanced through grades to capt., 1992; intern in medicine USPHS Hosp., Balt., 1973-74; resident in psychiatry Nat. Naval Med. Ctr., Bethesda, Md., 1974-77; head alcohol rehab. svc./substance abuse dept., staff psychiatrist Naval Hosp., Camp Lejeune, N.C., 1977-85; head alcohol rehab. svc./substance abuse dept., head psych. Naval Hosp., Millington, Tenn., 1985-88; head alcohol rehab. dept. Naval Hosp., Long Beach, Calif., 1988-94; head Navy Addictions Rehab. and Edn. Dept., Camp Pendleton, Calif., 1994—; mem. tumor bd. Naval Hosp., Camp Lejeune, 1977-85, cons. Tri-Command Consolidated Drug and Alcohol Counseling Ctr. Agy., 1977-85, phys. fitness program com., 1980-85, med. liaison on substance abuse, 1982-85, drug/alcohol program advisor, 1983-85, Tri-Command Consolidated

Drug and Alcohol Adv. Coun., 1983-85, controlled substance abuse review subcom. of pharmacy and therapeutics com., 1984-85; watch officer Acute Care Clinic, Naval Hosp., Millington, 1985-86, cons. Counseling and Assistance Ctr., 1985-88, mem. bioethics com., chmn. med. records, utilization review com., 1985-88, exec. com. med. staff, chmn., 1986-87, psychiatric cons. to NAS Brig, 1986-88, mem. quality assurance com., 1986, mem. credentials com., 1986-87, pharmacy and therapeutics com., 1986, pos. mgmt. com., 1986-87, dir. med. svcs., 1986-88, dir. surgical svcs., 1986, commd. duty watch officer, 1986-87, watch officer acute care clinic, 1987-88, mem. Navy Drug and Alcohol adv. coun., 1987-88, preceptor to social worker, 1987-88, pos. mgmt. com., 1988, mem. commd. retention coun., 1988; also, numerous coms. at Naval Hosp., Long Beach, Calif., Naval Hosp., Camp Pendleton, Calif. Capt. USN. Recipient Commendation medal USN, 1988, meritorious svc. medal, 1994. Mem. Am. Acad. of Psychiatrists in Alcoholism and Addictions (founding mem.), Am. Soc. of Addiction Medicine, Assn. Mil. Surgeons of U.S., Addiction Profls. of N.C. (chmn. pub. info. com. 1979-80, ea. regional v.p. 1981-82, chmn. fall meeting planning com. 1983, sec. 1984-85), Nat. Assn. of Alcoholism and Drug Abuse Counselors, Calif. Assn. Alcohol and Drug Abuse Counselors, Am. Legion, VFW Aux. U.S. Lawn Tennis Assn. (hon. life), Stanford Cap and Gown, Stanford Alumni Assn., U. Ariz. Alumni Assn., Stanford Cardinal Club. Democrat. Home: 32155 Corte Florecita Temecula CA 92592-6319 *While serving as a career officer and physician, Becky Gill became the only board certified addictionist in the Navy. She was instrumental in establishing the Navy's new Continuum of Care model for identifying and treating alcohol abuse and dependence. This model has become the standard for Department of Defense (DoD) treatment programs world-wide and for the civilian health care system (Tri-Care) treating DoD personnel.*

GILL, DAVID, food products executive; b. 1949. Student, Cal Poly San Luis Obispo, 1970-75. With Almaden Vineyards, Napa Valley, Calif., 1975-78; ptnr. Rio Farms, Oxnard, Calif., 1978—. Office: Rio Farms PO Box 3288 Camarillo CA 93011*

GILL, GENE, artist; b. Memphis, June 18, 1933; s. Edward Morris and Annie Zelma (Mondy) G. BFA, Chouinard Art Inst., L.A., 1962. One-man shows include Comara Gallery, L.A., 1970, 71, 74, Orlando Gallery, Sherman Oaks, Calif., 1995; exhibited in group shows Esplanade Gallery, Santa Monica, 1969, L.A. Art Assn. Galleries, 1970, R and W. Gallery, Memphis, 1971, Scripts Coll., 1971, San Diego Fine Arts Mus., 1971, Laguna Beach Mus. Art, 1971, 72, 77, Palm Springs Mus. Art, 1973, L.A. County Mus. Art, 1973, Van Straaten Gallery, Chgo., 1974, Mcpl Art Gallery, L.A., 1976; represented in permanent collections L.A. County Mus. Art, Palm Springs Desert Mus. Art, Atlantic Richfield Corp, Northrop Corp., Container Corp. Am., Home Savings, Pattiz Found., Westside Jewish Cmty. Ctr. With USN, 1954-58. Recipient numerous awards at juried art shows. Home: 2430 Cascadia Dr Glendale CA 91206-1803

GILL, GEORGE WILHELM, anthropologist; b. Sterling, Kans., June 28, 1941; s. George Laurance and Florence Louise (Jones) G.; BA in Zoology with honors (NSF grantee), U. Kans., 1963, M.Phil. Anthropology (NDEA fellow, NSF dissertation research grantee), 1970, PhD in Anthropology, 1971; m. Pamela Jo Mills, July 26, 1975 (div. 1988); children: George Scott, John Ashton, Jennifer Florence, Bryce Thomas. Mem. faculty U. Wyo., Laramie, 1971—, prof. anthropology, 1985—, chair dept. anthropology, 1993-96; forensic anthropologist law enforcement agys., 1972—; sci. leader Easter Island Anthrop. Expdn., 1981; chmn. Rapa Nui Rendezvous: International. Conf. Easter Island Rsch., U. Wyo., 1993. Served to capt. U.S. Army, 1963-67. Recipient J.P. Ellbogen meritorious classroom teaching award, 1983; research grantee U. Wyo., 1972, 78, 82, Nat. Geog. Soc., 1980, Center for Field Research, 1980, Kon-Tiki Mus., Oslo, 1987, 89, 94, 96, World Monuments Fund, 1989. Diplomate Am. Bd. Forensic Anthropology (bd. dirs. 1985-90). Fellow Am. Acad. Forensic Scis. (sec. phys. anthropology sect. 1985-87, chmn. 1987-88); mem. Am. Assn. Phys. Anthropologists, Plains Anthrop. Soc., Wyo. Archael. Soc. Republican. Presbyterian. Author articles, monographs; editor: (with S. Rhine) Skeletal Attribution of Race, 1990. Home: 649 Howe Rd Laramie WY 82070-6885 Office: U Wyo Dept Anthropology Laramie WY 82071

GILL, JO ANNE MARTHA, middle school educator; b. L.A., July 8, 1940; d. James Hurse Wilson and Martha Grace (Hanson) Wilson Horn; m. Richard Martin Gill, Apr. 18, 1959; 1 child, Richard James. BA in Interdisciplinary Studies, Nat. U., San Diego, 1989; MA in Ednl. Adminstrn., Calif. State U., San Bernardino, 1992. Cert. tchr. pre-sch. through adult edn., social sci., adminstrn. Tchr. grades 6 and 7 Palm Springs (Calif.) Unified Sch. Dist., 1989-94, tchr. 8th grade U.S. history, gifted/regular, 1994—; prof. edn. Calif. State U., San Bernardino; cons. Desert Schs. Consortium, Palm Springs, 1993-95, Inland Empire History/Social Studies, Riverside, Calif., 1991-95; adv. bd. Inland Empire Lit. Project, 1994—; mem. leadership team Inland Area History/Social Sci. Summer Inst., U. Calif., Riverside, 1994—. Contbr. articles to profl. jours. Mem. Calif. State History Standards and Course Models Commn.; coach mid. sch. demonstration program. Inland Area History/Social Sci. Adv. Acad. fellow, 1991, NEH fellow, 1993, Calif. History/Social Sci. Project/UCLA fellow, 1994; recipient 1st pl. award/tchr. multimedia group presentation Nat. History Day, 1996. Mem. AAUW (home tour guide 1993), Calif. Coun. for the Social Studies (presenter conf. workshop 1993, 95, 96), Calif. Assn. for Gifted (presenter ann. conf. workshop 1994, 96, Calif. Outstanding Middle Sch. Educator Area 9 1997), Inland Empire Coun. for the Social Studies (pres. 1994-96, Outstanding Middle Sch. Educator area 9 local award 1997), Delta Kappa Gamma (scholarship fundraising com. 1993-94). Democrat. Roman Catholic. Office: Palm Springs Unified Schs 333 S Farrell Dr Palm Springs CA 92262-7905

GILL, REBECCA LALOSH, aerospace engineer; b. Brownsboro, Tex., Sept. 17, 1944; d. Milton and Dona Mildred (Magee) La Losh; m. Peter Mohammed Sharma, Sept. 1, 1965 (div.); m. James Fredrick Gill, Mar. 9, 1985; children: Erin, Melissa, Ben. BS in Physics, U. Mich., 1965; MBA, Calif. State U., Northridge, 1980. Tchr., Derby, Kans., 1966; weight analyst Beech Aircraft, Wichita, Kans., 1966; weight engr. Ewing Tech. Design, assigned Boeing-Vertol, Phila., 1966-67, Bell Aerosystems, Buffalo, 1967; design specialist Lockheed-Calif. Co., Burbank, 1968-79; sr. staff engr. Hughes Aircraft Missile Systems, Canoga Park, Calif., 1979-82, project mgr. AMRAAM spl. test and tng. equipment, 1982-85, project mgr. GBU-15 guidance sect., Navy IR Maverick Missile, Tucson, 1985-89, project mgr. Navy IR Maverick Missile, SLAM Seeker Prodn., 1989-92, TOSH and TOW program mgr., 1992—; sec. Nat. Cinema Corp. Com. chmn. Orgn. for Rehab. through Tng., 1971-75; speaker ednl. and civic groups. Pres. Briarcliffe East Homeowners Assn.; coord. support group Am. Diabetes Assn., chmn. com. fundraising, coun. mem. Tucson chpt.; active NOW; block leader Neighborhood Watch. Recipient Lockheed award of achievement, 1977. Mem. NAFE, Soc. Allied Weight Engrs. (dir., sr. v.p., chmn. pub. rels. com.), Aerospace Elec. Soc. (dir.), Tucson Zool. Soc. (bd. dirs.), Hughes Mgmt. Club (bd. dirs., chmn. spl. events, chmn. programs, parliamentarian, 1st v.p., pres.), Women in Def. (sec., Ariz. chpt.), Las Alturas Homeowners Assn. (v.p., pres.), Tucson Racquet Club. Republican. Office: Hughes Missile Systems Co Bldg 801 MS G25A Tucson AZ 85734

GILL, STEVEN, food products executive; b. 1949. Student, Cal Poly San Luis Obispo, Calif., 1970-75. With Bud Antle Inc., Salinas, Calif., 1975-78; ptnr. Rio Farms, L.A., 1978—. Office: Rio Farms PO Box 3288 Camarillo CA 93011*

GILLAM, DAVID ALLEN, elementary school educator; b. Colorado Springs, Colo., May 25, 1957; s. Ernest Allen and Dorothy Jane (Maphis) G.; m. Lori D. Sheppard, Aug. 16, 1980; children: Colin Nathaniel, Aspen Nichole. BEd, U. Alaska, 1979; MAT, Alaska Pacific U., 1993. Cert. elem. tchr., Alaska. Tchr. Anchorage Sch. Dist., 1979-93, sci. tchr. expert, 1993-94; tchr. Susitna Elem. Sch., Anchorage, 1994—; instr. sci. methods, evaluation of students Alaska Pacific U., Anchorage, 1991-97; instr. U. Alaska, Anchorage, 1994-95. Creek honcho Anchorage Waterway Coun., 1993-96. NSF Presdl. awardee (state finalist), 1995, 96; Milken awardee, 1996. Fellow Alaska Sci. Consortium (exec. bd. 1993-96); mem. Nat. Sci. Tchrs. Assn., Alaska Sci. Tchrs. Assn. (pres. 1995-97), Nat. Coun. Tchrs. Math. Office: Susitna Elementary School 7500 Tyone Ct Anchorage AK 99504-3531

GILLEN, ARTHUR FITZPATRICK, retired lawyer; b. So. St. Paul, Minn., Oct. 10, 1919; s. Leonard Peter and Cecelia (Koppy) G.; m. Louise Rosemary Powers, April 28, 1945; children: Robert, Anne Marie, Theodore, Janice, Peter, Mary. BS, U. Minn., 1941, JD, 1943. Bar: Minn., 1943. Sr. partner LeVander Gillen & Miller, PA Attys., So. St. Paul, Minn., 1943-95, LeVander Gillen & Miller PA Attys., So. St. Paul, 1943-95; bd. dirs., pres. Jr. C. of C., C. of C., and Kiwanis; bd. dirs. Gemstone Products Co. and Twin City Concrete, So. St. Paul, 1982—. State rep Minn. Legislature, 1943-51; state senator, Minn. Legislature, 1951-59. Named Man of Year, So. St. Paul Jr. C. of C., 1951. Named to hall of fame, So. St. Paul (Minn.) C. of C., 1992. Republican. Roman Catholic. Home: 21043-124th Ave Sun City West AZ 85375

GILLEN, KATHERINE ELIZABETH, librarian; b. Washington, May 16, 1951; d. Hugh Chisholm and Norma Marie (Provost) G. BS, U. Md., 1973, MLS, 1976; MA, U. Phoenix, 1989; grad., Citizens Police Acad., Mesa, Ariz., 1993, Air Command and Staff Coll., 1996. Librarian Maricopa County Community Coll., Phoenix, 1982-84; librarian reference and serials Mesa (Ariz.) Pub. Library, 1981-92; libr. mgr. Denver Pub. Libr., 1992; libr. USAF, Luke AFB, Ariz., 1993—. Book reviewer Libr. Jour., 1991—; contbr. short stories to mags.; pub.: Felicia's First Christmas, 1994. Class mem. Mesa Leadership Tng. and Devel., 1991-92. Mem. AAAS (reviewer 1982—), Ariz. State Libr. Assn. (exec. bd. 1991-92, serials roundtable chmn. 1991-92), Serials Specialists of Maricopa County, Mensa. Home: 11301 W Orange Blossom Ln Avondale AZ 85323

GILLER, EDWARD BONFOY, retired government official, retired air force officer; b. Jacksonville, Ill., July 8, 1918; s. Edward Bonfoy and Ruth (Davis) G.; m. Mildred Florana Schmidt, July 2, 1943; children—Susan Ann, Carol Elaine, Bruce Carleton, Penny Marie, Paul Benjamin. B.S. in Chem. Engring, U. Ill., 1940, M.S., 1948, Ph.D., 1950. Chem. engr. Sinclair Oil Refining Co., 1940-41; commd. 2d lt. USAAF, 1942; advanced through grades to maj. gen. USAF, 1968; pilot, 1941-46; chief radiation br. (Armed Forces Spl. Weapons Project), Washington, 1950-54; dir. research directorate Air Force Spl. Weapons Center, Albuquerque, 1954-59; spl. asst. to comdr. (Office Aerospace Rsch.), Washington, 1959-64; dir. sci. and tech. Hdqrs. USAF, 1964-67; asst. gen. mgr. for mil. application U.S. AEC, 1967-72; ret. from USAF, 1972; asst. gen. mgr. for nat. security AEC, 1972-75; dep. asst. adminstr. for nat. security U.S. ERDA, 1975-77; rep. of Joint Chiefs of Staff to Comprehensive Test Ban Negotiations, Geneva, Switzerland, 1977-84; sr. scientist Pacific-Sierra Rsch. Corp., Arlington, Va, 1984-92; v.p. Trans Mar Inc., Spokane, Wash., 1992-96; cons. Sandia Nat. Labs., Albuquerque, 1990—; cons. in the field. Decorated Silver Star, D.S.M., Legion of Merit with oak leaf cluster, D.F.C., Air medal with 17 oak leaf clusters, Purple Heart; Croix de Guerre France). Fellow Am. Inst. Chemists; mem. Am. Inst. Chem. Engrs., Sigma Xi, Alpha Tau Omega. Episcopalian. Home: 216 Wapiti Dr Bayfield CO 81122-9243

GILLESPIE, MARILYN, museum administrator. Dir. Las Vegas Natural History Mus., 1991—; pres. Bd. Mus. and Attractions, Nev., sec. 1997—. Vol. promoting environ. concerns, homelessness issues, spl. edn. Mem. Kiwanis Club (bd. dirs. Las Vegas Territory, program dir. Uptown). Office: Las Vegas Natural History Mus 900 Las Vegas Blvd North Las Vegas NV 89101

GILLESPIE, PENNY HANNIG, business owner; b. Schenectady, N.Y., June 4, 1954; d. William Armand and Freda (Penney) H.; m. Kenneth Scofield Keyes, Jr., Sept. 2, 1984 (div. Aug. 1992). Student, U. Ariz., 1972-74. Cert. EMT, Ariz., N.Y.; completion in skills tng. for profls. in Hakomi psychotherapy, Oreg. Co-founder Ken Keyes Coll., Coos Bay, Ore., 1982-91; pvt. practice counseling Eugene, Ore., 1991-95; founder, pres. The Wellness Network, Eugene, Oreg., 1994—. Co-author: Gathering Power Through Insight and Love, 1986, Handbook to Higher Consciousness: The Workbook, 1989; editor: How to Enjoy Your Life in Spite of It All, 1980, The Hundredth Monkey, 1982, Your Heart's Desire, 1983, Your Life Is a Gift, 1987, Discovering the Secrets of Happiness, 1988, PlanetHood, 1988, The Power of Unconditional Love, 1990. Bd. dirs. Living Love Ch., 1980-91, sec., v.p.; founding bd. dirs., sec., sec.-treas., v.p. The Vision Foundation, Inc., 1982-91; founding bd. dirs., sec., sec.-treas. Cornucopia, The Living Love Ch. of Ky., 1982-91; vol. Victim Advocate Lane County Dist. Attys. Victim/Witness Svcs. Program, Oreg., 1993. Recipient peace award Coalition for Justice and Peace, Ariz. State U. and the Inst. Peace Edn., 1989; award as site mgr. for Anne Frank exhibit Jewish Fedn. Lane County, Ore., 1993. Home: PO Box 21942 Eugene OR 97402-0413

GILLETTE, FRANKIE JACOBS, retired savings and loan executive, social worker, government administrator; b. Norfolk, Va., Apr. 1, 1925; d. Frank Walter and Natalie (Taylor) Jacobs; m. Maxwell Claude Gillette, June 19, 1976. BS, Hampton U., 1946; MSW, Howard U., 1948. Lic. clin. social worker; cert. jr. coll. tchr., life. Youth dir. YWCA, Passaic, N.J., 1948-50; dir. program Ada S. McKinley Community Ctr., Chgo., 1950-53; program dir. Sophie Wright Settlement, Detroit, 1953-64; dir. Concerted Services Project, Pittsburg, Calif., 1964-66, Job Corps Staff Devel., U. Calif., Berkeley, 1966-69; spl. program coordinator U.S. Community Services Adminstrn., San Francisco, 1969-83; pres. G & G Enterprises, San Francisco, 1985—; chmn. bd. dirs. Time Savs. and Loan Assn., San Francisco, 1986-87. Commr. San Francisco Human Rights Commn., 1988-93; bd. dirs. Urban Econ. Devel. Corp., 1980-93, San Francisco Conv. and Visitors Bur.; trustee Fine Arts Mus. of San Francisco, 1993—; chmn. San Francisco-Abidjan Sister City Com., 1990—. Mem. Nat. Assn. Negro Bus. and Profl. Women's Clubs (pres. 1983-87). Office: G & G Enterprises 85 Cleary Ct Apt 4 San Francisco CA 94109-6518

GILLETTE, RICHARD GARETH, neurophysiology educator, researcher; b. Seattle, Feb. 17, 1945; s. Elton George and Hazel I. (Hand) G.; m. Sally A. Reams, Feb. 17, 1978 (div. Nov. 1988); 1 child, Jesse Robert. BS, U. Oreg., 1968; MS, Oreg. Health Sci. U., 1976, PhD, 1993. Rsch. asst. dept. otolaryngology Oreg. Health Sci. U., Portland, 1969-72, grad. rsch. asst., 1973-80; instr. physiology Western State Chiropractic Coll., Portland, 1981-85, asst. prof. physiology, 1985-93, assoc. prof. physiology, 1993—; lectr. neurosci. sch. optometry Pacific U., Forest Grove, Oreg., 1985-86; grad. rsch. asst. R.S. Dow Neurol. Sci. Inst., Portland, 1988-93, vis. scientist, 1993—. Contbr. articles to profl. jours. NIH Predoctoral Tng. fellow Oreg. Health Sci. U., 1973-76; Tarter fellow Med. Rsch. Found. Oreg., 1989; NIH grantee, 1990-93, 94—. Mem. AAAS, Soc. for Neurosci., Am. Pain Soc., Internat. Assn. for Study of Pain, N.Y. Acad. Scis. Office: WSCC 2900 NE 132nd Ave Portland OR 97230-3014

GILLETTE, W. MICHAEL, judge; b. Seattle, Dec. 29, 1941; s. Elton George and Hazel Irene (Hand) G.; m. Susan Dandy Marmaduke, 1989; children: Kevin, Saima, Ali, Quinton. AB cum laude in German, Polit. Sci., Whitman Coll., 1963; LLB, Harvard U., 1966. Bar: Oreg. 1966, U.S. Dist. Ct. Oreg. 1966, U.S. Ct. Appeals (9th cir.) 1966, Samoa 1969, U.S. Supreme Ct. 1970, U.S. Dist. Ct. Vt. 1973. Assoc. Rives & Rogers, Portland, Oreg., 1966-67; dep. dist. atty. Multnomah County, Portland, 1967-69; asst. atty. gen. Govt. of Am. Samoa, 1969-71, State of Oreg., Salem, 1971-77; judge Oreg. Ct. Appeals, Salem, 1977-86; assoc. justice Oreg. Supreme Ct., Salem, 1986—. *

GILLHAM, GRANT DAVID, political consultant; b. Alton, Ill., Jan. 7, 1957; s. Richard Clark and Joan Margaret (Long) G. BA in History, Tulane U., 1979. Sales and mgmt. exec. Kent-Miller, Inc., St. Louis, 1979-81; commd. 2d lt. USAF, 1981, advanced through grades to capt., 1985; pilot 320th bomb wing USAF, Sacramento, Calif., 1982-86; instr. pilot, flight examiner 552d airborne warning control wing USAF, Okla. City, 1986-90; polit. cons. Calif. State Assembly, Sacramento, 1990-95; chief exec. officer Gillham Profl. Group, 1991—; sr. cons. Calif. State Senate, 1995—. Mem. alumni admissions com. Tulane U., Sacramento, Calif., 1988—. Decorated Commendation medal, Air medal and Combat Readiness medal. Republican.

GILLIAM, EARL B., federal judge; b. Clovis, N.Mex., Aug. 17, 1931; s. James Earl and Lula Mae G.; m. Rebecca L. Prater; children: Earl Kenneth, Derrick James. B.A., Calif. State U., San Diego, 1953; J.D., Hastings Coll. Law, 1957. Bar: Calif. 1957. Dep. dist. atty. San Diego, 1957-62; judge San Diego Mcpl. Ct., 1963-74, Superior Ct. Calif., San Diego County, 1975-80, U.S. Dist. Ct. (so. dist.) Calif., San Diego, 1980—; head Trial Practice Dept. Western State U. Law Sch., San Diego, 1969—. Office: US Dist Ct 940 Front St San Diego CA 92101-8994

GILLIAM, ELIZABETH M., illustrator, printmaker, poet; b. Kansas City, Mo., Mar. 1, 1929; d. Urcil Wilford and Ruth Elizabeth (Williams) Smoot; m. Ronald Roy Gilliam, Mar. 28, 1956; children: Ursula Marie, Alessandra Theresa, Pamela Celeste. BS, Kansas City Art Inst., 1953; student, U. Bonn, Germany, 1957-58; pvt. student, Bangkok, 1965-70, Washington, 1960-62. Artist Hallmark Greeting Cards, Kansas City, Mo., 1952-53, Rand Corp., Santa Monica, Calif., 1958. Editor: (poetry anthology) South of San Francisco, 1976; author: (poetry) Traces, 1992. Voting poll judge City of Redondo Beach, Calif., 1988-92. Mem. Yuki Teikei Soc. of Tokyo and Calif., Chapparal Poets of Calif. (chpt. pres.), Commonwealth Club of San Francisco. Home: PO Box 120470 Chula Vista CA 91912

GILLIAM, JACKSON EARLE, bishop; b. Heppner, Oreg., June 20, 1920; s. Edwin Earle and Mary (Perry) G.; m. Margaret Kathleen Hindley, Aug. 11, 1943; children—Anne Meredith, Margaret Carol, John Howard; m. MarKatheryn Allender Brooks, Oct. 17, 1988. A.B., Whitman Coll., 1942; B.D., Va. Theol. Sem., 1948, S.T.M., 1949, D.D., 1969. Ordained to ministry Episcopal Ch., 1948; rector in Hermiston, Ore., 1949-53; canon St. Mark's Cathedral, Mpls., 1953-55; rector Ch. Incarnation, Great Falls, Mont., 1955-68; bishop Episcopal Diocese Mont., 1968-86; vicar St. Jude's Episcopal Ch., Hawaiian Oceanview Estates, 1987—; chmn. com. on pastoral devel., chmn. council on ministry, mem. program, budget and fin. com. Episc. Ch., 1978, pres. Province VI. Served to 1st lt. AUS, World War II. Decorated companion Order of Cross of Nails, companion Coventry Cathedral, Eng., 1974. Home: PO Box 6502 Ocean View HI 96737-6502

GILLIN, JOHN CHRISTIAN, psychiatrist; b. Columbus, Ohio, Apr. 28, 1938; s. John Philip and Helen (Norgord) G.; m. Frances Davis, May 29, 1966. BA, Harvard Coll., 1961; MD, Case Western U., 1966. Intern Cleve. Met. Hosp., 1966-67; resident Stanford U., Palo Alto, Calif., 1987-89; clin. assoc. Nat. Inst. Mental Health, Bethesda, Md., 1969-71, researcher, 1971-82; prof. psychiatry U. Calif., San Diego, 1982—; staff psychiatrist San Diego VA Med. Ctr., 1982—; adj. prof. psychiatry San Diego State U., 1990—. Author: (with W.B. Mendelson and R.J. Wyatt) Human Sleep and Its Disorders, 1977. Capt. USNR, ret. Office: U Calif Dept Psychiatry San Diego CA 92093-0603

GILLIS, JOHN SIMON, psychologist, educator; b. Washington, Mar. 21, 1937; s. Simon John and Rita Veronica (Moran) G.; m. Mary Ann Wesolowski, Aug. 29, 1959; children: Holly Ann, Mark, Scott. B.A., Stanford U., 1959; M.S. (fellow), Cornell U., 1961; Ph.D. (NIMH fellow), U. Colo., 1965. Lectr. dept. psychology Australian Nat. U., Canberra, 1968-70; sr. psychologist Mendocino (Calif.) State Hosp., 1971-72; asso. prof. dept. psychology Tex. Tech U., Lubbock, 1972-76; prof. psychology Oreg. State U., Corvallis, 1976—, chmn. dept. psychology, 1976-84; cons. VA, Ciba-Geigy Pharms., USIA, UN High Commn. for Refugees; commentator Oreg. Ednl. and Pub. Broadcasting System, 1978-79; Fulbright lectr., India, 1982-83, Greece, 1992; vis. prof. U. Karachi, 1984, 86, U. Punjab, Pakistan, 1985, Am. U., Cairo, 1984-86. Contbr. articles to profl. jours. Served with USAF, 1968-72. Ciba-Geigy Pharms. grantee, 1971-82. Mem. Am. Psychol. Assn., Western Psychol. Assn., Oreg. Psychol. Assn. Roman Catholic. Home: 7520 NW Mountain View Dr Corvallis OR 97330-9106 Office: Oreg State U Dept Psychology Corvallis OR 97331 *The real pleasures of life seem to come not from avoiding difficult tasks but rather from involving oneself with them - from working hard on those problems that need attention.*

GILLIS, NELSON SCOTT, financial executive; b. Pitts., May 6, 1953; s. Nelson Williams and Elinor (Miller) G.; m. Vickie Sue Hall, Nov. 22, 1980; children: Michael David, Matthew Daniel, Nathan Alexander, Alexander Joshua, Artyom Jonathan. BS in Acctg., Fla. State U., 1975; postgrad. AEA Exec. Inst., Stanford, 1984. CPA, Ga.; cert. fin. planner. Audit sr., Price Waterhouse & Co., Atlanta, 1975-78; sr. acct. Siemens Energy and Automation, Inc., 1978-80; div. contr., Portland, Oreg., 1980-83; v.p. fin. Integrated Circuits Inc., Redmond, Wash., 1983-85; dir. Controls Evaluation and Audit Kaufman & Broad, Inc., Atlanta, 1985-89; v.p., contr. SunAm. Life Ins. Co., Anchor Nat. Life Ins. Co., First Sun Am. Life Ins. Co., L.A., 1989-94, sr. v.p., controller, 1994—; sr. v.p., cont. Calfarm Life Ins. Co., 1995—, SunAm. Nat. Life Ins. Co., 1996—; John Alden Life Ins. Co. N.Y., 1997—. Master fellow Life . Inst.; mem. AICPA (life ins. and disability plans com., 1991-94, task force on disclosure of risks and uncertainties in the ins. industry, 1992-95, rels. with actuaries com. 1993-96, ins. plans exec. com. 1995—, chmn. personal lines ins. com. 1995—), Inst. CFPs, Ins. Internal Audit Group, Life Office Mgmt. Assn. (fin. controls and reports com. 1987-90), Ga. Soc. CPAs (ins. plans com. 1988-89), Calif. Soc. CPAs (L.A. members in industry, acctg. principles/auditing stds. & ins. industry coms. 1991-94), Ins. Acctg. and Systems Assn., Internat. Assn. for Fin. Planning, Am. Assn. Individual Investors, Fla. State Alumni Assn., Nat. Assn. Securities Dealers (registered prin.), Beta Gamma Sigma, Lambda Chi Alpha. Republican. Office: Sun Life Ins Co Am/Century City 1 Sun Am Ctr MS 36-07 Los Angeles CA 90067-6022

GILLIS, PAUL LEONARD, accountant; b. Montevideo, Minn., Nov. 20, 1953; s. Joseph Hans and Verna Ruth (Sjolie) G.; m. Deborah Ann Roller, Sept. 9, 1978. BA, Western State Coll., 1975; MS, Colo. State U., 1976. CPA, Colo. Tax cons. Price Waterhouse, Denver, 1976-78; tax mgr. Price Waterhouse, Singapore, 1978-82; internat. tax mgr. Price Waterhouse, San Francisco, 1982-84; sr. mgr. Price Waterhouse, Denver, 1984-88, mng. tax ptnr., 1988—, chmn. mining industry practice, 1993—; mem. adv. coun. Colo. State U.; bd. dirs. World Trade Ctr.; mem. Dist. Export Coun.; pres. Forest Hills Metro Dist.; lectr. World Trade Inst., San Francisco, 1982-84. Author: Accounting for Income Tax, 1988. Pres. Forest Hills Metro Dist., 1992—. Recipient 50 for Colo. award, Colo. Assn. Commerce and Industry, Disting. Alumni award Colo. State U., 1996. Fellow Colo. Soc. CPAs; mem. AICPA, Am. Club (Singapore) (treas. 1981-82), Nat. Mining Assn., Glenmoor Country Club, Denver Athletic Club, Harley Owners Group (Denver chpt.), Chatfield Yacht Club. Home: 22616 Forest Hills Dr Golden CO 80401-8022 Office: Price Waterhouse 950 17th St Denver CO 80202-2828

GILLIS, WILLIAM GARETH, fire protection official; b. Agana, Guam, Oct. 10, 1949; s. William Wayne and Florence Theresa Gillis; m. Cheryl Denise Muñoz, Aug. 26, 1972; children: Nathan William, Erin Marie, Leah Nicole. AA, S.J. Delta Coll., Stockton, Calif., 1969; BA, Sacramento State U., 1971. Cert. state fire marshal, paramedic, Calif. With Luckies Stores, Stockton, 1971-72; fire fighter City of Stockton Fire Dept., 1972-79, fire engr., 1979-82, fire capt., 1982-84, paramedic capt., 1984-92, battalion chief, 1992-95, fire marshal, 1995—. Pres. Stockton Firefighters Relief Assn., 1985—, G. Brennan Meml. Scholarship, Stockton, 1994—; v.p. Leadership Stockton Alumni, 1996; bd. dirs. Child Abuse Prevention, San Joaquin County, 1994—. Mem. Internat. Assn. Fire Chiefs, Fire Marshals Assn., Internat. Assn. Firefighters, Nat. Fire Protection Assn., Calif. Fire Prevention Officers Assn. Home: 8655 Treasure Ave Stockton CA 95212-1414 Office: City of Stockton Fire Dept 425 N El Dorado Stockton CA 95202

GILLISPIE, STEVEN BRIAN, systems analyst, researcher; b. Seattle, Oct. 19, 1955; s. Edwin B. and Claudia Mae (Cooper) G. BS in Physics with distinction, U. Wash., 1979, BS in Math., 1979, BS in Psychology, 1983, BA in Gen. Studies, 1983. Software specialist Fla. Computer Graphics, Seattle, 1983-84; data analyst coronary artery surgery study U. Wash., Seattle, 1985-87, sci. programmer dept. radiology, 1987-88, systems analyst dept. radiology, 1988—. Dir. devel. med. imaging software Viewbox, 1992; contbr. articles to profl. jours. Mem. Woodland Park Zool. Soc., Seattle, 1986—; contbg. mem. Nordic Heritage Mus., Seattle, 1991—; patron The High Desert Mus., Bend, Oreg., 1991—. Mem. Soc. for Indsl. and Applied Math., U. Wash. Alumni Assn. (life). Office: U Wash Dept Radiology Box 356004 Seattle WA 98195-6004

GILLMAR, JACK NOTLEY SCUDDER, real estate company executive; b. Honolulu, Oct. 18, 1943; s. Stanley Eric and Ruth Dorothy (Scudder) G.; m. Janet Thebaud, June 12, 1967; children: Emily, Bennett. BA, U. Pa., 1965; MA, Harvard U., 1967, Pacifica Grad. Inst., 1994. Vol. Peace Corps/Micronesia, East Caroline Islands, 1967-70; trustee Scudder Gillmar Estate, Honolulu, 1973—; trustee, sec. Parker Sch. Trust, Kamuela, Hawaii, 1991—.

Author: Impact of an In-country Peace Corps Training Program, 1970, Specimens of Hwaiian Kapa, 1979, Beauty as Experience and Transcendence, 1994. Trustee, pres. Friendship Graden Found., Honolulu, 1971—; owner Nanue (Hawaii) Forest Preserve, 1986—. Fulbright grantee, 1990. Mem. Pacific Club. Office: Scudder Gillmar Estate PO Box 2902 Honolulu HI 96802-2902

GILLMAR, STANLEY FRANK, lawyer; b. Honolulu, Aug. 17, 1935; s. Stanley Eric and Ruth (Scudder) G.; m. Constance Joan Sedgwick; children: Sara Tamsin, Amy Katherine. AB cum laude with high honors, Brown U., 1957; LLB, Harvard U., 1963. Bar: Calif. 1963. Ptnr. Graham & James, San Francisco, 1970-92; of counsel Mackenzie & Albritton, 1993—. Co-author: How To Be An Importer and Pay For Your World Travels, 1979; co-pub.: Travelers Guide to Importing, 1980. Sec. Calif. Council Internat. Trade, 1973-92, hon. counsel, 1980-92, exec. com., 1985-92; mem. Mayor San Francisco Adv. Council Econ. Devel., 1976-82; mem. Title IX Loan Bd., 1982-96, sec. 1986-92; dir. The San Francisco Ministry to Nursing Homes, 1992-94, treas., 1992-94; dir. Inverness Assn., 1995—, pres., 1996—. Served with USNR, 1957-60. Mem. ABA, Calif. State Bar, Bar Assn. San Francisco, Bankers Club (San Francisco); Villa Taverna Club, Inverness Yacht Club. Office: One Post St Ste 500 San Francisco CA 94104

GILLMORE, RICHARD DUANE, nonprofit association director; b. Missoula, Mont., July 9, 1950; s. Duane Cal and Dorothy Mae (Swallow) G.; children: Lissa Kelly, Damiel Richard. BA, Western Wash. U., 1972; MA, U. Mont., 1976. Grant adminstr. King County, Seattle, 1976-81; pvt. practice grant writing cons. Bellevue, Wash., 1981-83; program dir. Boys & Girls Clubs, Seattle, 1983-84, athletic dir., 1984-87; club dir. Boys & Girls Clubs, Federal Way, Wash., 1987-91; assoc. dir. Boys & Girls Clubs, Tacoma, 1991—; bd. mem. King Day Classic, Tacoma, 1994—. Mem. Tacoma Athletic Commn., 1995—. Mem. Assn. Boys and Girls Clubs Profls. (pres. 1993—). Office: Boys & Girls Clubs Pierce County 1501 Pacific Ave Ste 301 Tacoma WA 98402-3301

GILLQUIST, PETER EDWARD, church organization executive; b. Mpls., July 13, 1938; s. William Parker and Louise E. (Blitsch) G.; m. Marilyn Joyce Grinder; children: Wendy, Gregory, Ginger, Terri Beth, Heidi, Peter Jon. BA, U. Minn., 1960; postgrad., Dallas Sem., 1960-61, Wheaton (Ill.) Grad. Sch., 1961-62. Regional dir. Campus Crusade, Chgo., 1960-68; dir. devel., exec. v.p. Found., U. Memphis, 1969-72; sr. editor Thomas Nelson Publs., Nashville, 1975-86; dir. missions Antiochian Orthodox Ch., Santa Barbara, Calif., 1987—; presiding bishop Evang. Orthodox Ch., Santa Barbara, 1979-87; pub. Conciliar Press, Ben Lomond, Calif., 1985—; v.p. Orthodox Christian Mission Ctr., St. Augustine, Fla., 1995—. Author: Becoming Orthodox, 1989, Metropolitan Philip, 1991; editor: Coming Home, 1992, Orthodox Study Bible, 1993. Planning dir. Memphis Mayor's Drug Commn., 1970-72. Mem. Four Freshmen Soc., Order of St. Ignatius, Sigma Alpha Epsilon. Office: Antiochian Orthodox Ch Dept Missions-Evangelism 777 Camino Pescadero Santa Barbara CA 93117-4908

GILMAN, JOHN JOSEPH, research scientist; b. St. Paul, Dec. 22, 1925; s. Alexander Falk and Florence Grace (Colby) G.; m. Pauline Marie Harms, June 17, 1950 (div. Dec. 1968); children: Pamela Ann, Gregory George, Cheryl Elizabeth; m. Gretchen Marie Sutter, June 12, 1976; 1 son, Brian Alexander. BS, Ill. Inst. Tech., 1946, MS, 1948; PhD, Columbia, 1952. Research metallurgist Gen. Electric Co., Schenectady, 1952-60; prof. engrng. Brown U., Providence, 1960-63; prof. physics and metallurgy U. Ill., Urbana, 1963-68; dir. Materials Research Center Allied Chem. Corp., Morristown, N.J., 1968-78; dir. Corp. Devel. Center, 1978-80; mgr. corp. research Amoco Co. (Ind.), Naperville, Ill., 1980-85; assoc. dir. Lawrence Berkeley Lab./U. Calif., Calif., 1985-87; sr. scientist Lawrence Berkeley Lab., Calif., 1987-93; adj. prof. UCLA, 1993—. Author: Micromechanics of Flow in Solids, 1969, Inventivity-The Art and Science of Research Management, 1992; editor: The Art and Science of Growing Crystals, 1963, Fracture of Solids (with D.C. Drucker), 1963, Atomic and Electronic Structures of Metals, 1967, Metallic Glasses, 1973, Energetic Materials, 1993; editl. bd. Jour. Applied Physics, 1969-72; contbg. editor Materials Tech., 1994—; contbr. over 250 papers, articles to tech. jours. Served as ensign USNR, 1943-46. Recipient Mathewson gold medal Am. Inst. Metal Engrs., 1959, Disting. Service award Alumni Assn. Ill. Inst. Tech., 1962, Application to Practice award, 1985. Fellow Am. Phys. Soc., The Materials Soc., Am. Soc. for Metals (Campbell lectr. 1966); mem. Nat. Acad. Engring., Phi Kappa Phi, Tau Beta Pi. Home: 2852 Forrester Dr Los Angeles CA 90064-4662 Office: UCLA 6532 Boelter Hall Los Angeles CA 90095

GILMAN, JUNE ISABELLE BRANDER, rancher; b. Bradley, Mont., June 2, 1917; d. George and Fannie Elizabeth (Markle) Brander; m. Kenneth E. Gilman, May 11, 1947 (dec. Jan. 26, 1973). Grad. H.S., Deer Lodge, Mont., 1937. Office mgr. ins. agy., Deer Lodge, 1941; clk. Selective Svc. Bd., Boulder, Mont., 1942; stenographer Mont. Bd. of Health, Helena, 1942, U.S. Bur. Animal Industry, Helena, 1945-47, Cominco Am. Mining, Garrison, Mont., 1948-88; ranch owner Drummond, Mont., 1952—. Author: (book of poetry) Rhymes of Today and Yesterday, 1987, Sundry Rhymes, 1989, Home Brand Rhymes, 1995. Entertainer Cowboy Poetry Gathering, Elko, Nev., 1986-94, Big Timber and Lewistown, Mont, 1986-94; self-employed Circle Star Rodeo, Avon, Mont., 1932-39. Sgt. WAC, 1943-45, Africa, Italy. Mem. Women in Mil. Svc. Home: PO Box 198 Drummond MT 59832-0198

GILMOR, HELEN W., judge. Judge Honolulu. Office: Prince JK Kuhio Fed Bldg 300 Ala Moana Blvd Rm C-414 Honolulu HI 96850

GILMORE, A. DOUGLAS, retail sales executive; b. Kittery, Maine, July 21, 1947; s. Allen Johnston and Margaret Nell (McIntosh) G.; m. Joy Carolyn Gustafson, Aug. 23, 1969; children: Chelsea Jay, Allison Anne. BA, Willamette U., 1969; M Internat. Mgmt., Am. Grad. Internat. Mgmt., 1971. Acct. exec. Levi Strauss & Co., various locations, 1971-75; dist. sales mgr. Levi Strauss & Co., L.A., 1975-76; regional sales mgr. Levi Strauss & Co., San Francisco, 1977-80; dir. sales and mktg. Levi Strauss & Co., Edmonton, Alta., Can., 1980-82; asst. gen. mgr., mktg. dir. Levi Strauss & Co., Sydney, Australia, 1982-86; v.p. mktg. Winmore Products, Bellevue, Wash., 1986-87; v.p. ops. Trans Am. Glass, Seattle, 1987-93; pres. Mail Movers, Inc., Seattle, 1993—; dir. internat. sales Eddie Bauer, Redmond, Wash., 1993—. Mem. Sydney/San Francisco Sister City Com., Sydney, 1982-85; mem. Boys and Girls Club of Mercer Island. Mem. Internat. Mktg. Soc., Am. Mktg. Assn., Sales and Mktg. Execs., Am. Nat. Club (Sydney). Home: 525 Overlake Dr E Medina WA 98039 Office: Eddie Bauer 15010 NE 36th St Redmond WA 98052-5317

GILMORE, TIMOTHY JONATHAN, executive recruiter, paralegal; b. Orange, Calif., June 24, 1949; s. James and Margaret (Swanson) G.; m. Blanche Jean Panter, Sept. 3, 1984; children: Erin, Sean and Brian (twins). BA, St. Mary's Coll., Moraga, Calif., 1971; grad., Denver Paralegal Inst., 1996. Adminstrv. asst. Gov. Ronald Reagan, Sacramento, Calif., 1971-73; salesman Penn Mutual, Anaheim, Calif., 1973-76; asst. devel. dir. St. Mary's Coll., Moraga, 1976-81; devel. dir. St. Alphonsus Hosp., Boise, Idaho, 1981-83; adminstr. Blaine County Hosp., Hailey, Idaho, 1983-86; exec. dir. Poudre Hosp. Found., Ft. Collins, Colo., 1986-87; nat. recruiting dir. Power Securities Corp., Denver, 1987-89; cons. Horn, Fagan & Lund Exec. Search Cons., Ft. Collins, 1989; v.p. Jackson & Coker Locum Tenens, Inc., Denver, 1990-93; pres. Gilmore and Assocs., Ft. Collins, Colo., 1993—. Mem. Kiwanis (pres. Moraga club 1980-81, sec. Boise club 1982-83). Republican. Mem. LDS Ch. Home and Office: 2914 Bassick St Fort Collins CO 80526-3738

GILPIN, HENRY EDMUND, III, photographer, educator; b. Cleve., Nov. 10, 1922; s. Henry Edmund Jr. and Eloise (Van Der Veer) G.; m. Doris Myers, June 29, 1946; children: Jean Gilpin-Freeman, James Howard. Tchr. Ansel Adams Yosemite Workshop, 1959-82, Monterey (Calif.) Peninsula Coll., 1964—. Photographs included in collections of Amon Carter Mus., Ft. Worth, Walker Mus. Art, Mpls., Nat. Mus. Modern Art, Kyoto, Japan, Art and Sci. Mus., Nashua, N.H., Monterey Peninsula Mus. Art, also univs. Trustee Friends of Photography Ctr., San Francisco, 1969-79, Ctr. for Photographic Art, Carmel, Calif., 1989-93. 1st lt. USAF, 1942-45, ETO. Decorated Air Medal with 5 oak leaf clusters; D.F.C., Croix de Guerre, France, 1946. Home: 1353 Jacks Rd Monterey CA 93940-4910

GILSTRAP, LINDA LEE, fundraising executive; b. San Diego, Apr. 22, 1953; d. Asa Lee and Gloria Helen (Oden) Huffman; m. Philip M. Gilstrap, April 25, 1982. BA, United States Internat. U., 1974. Dir. cmty. health edn. Scripps Meml. Hosp., Chula Vista, Calif., 1982-88; health edn./grants/fund devel. staff Children's Hosp., San Diego, 1988-96; dir. grants and devel. Southwestern Coll., Chula Vista, 1996—; grant devel. cons. Children's Hosp., 1994-96. Chmn., mem. Commn. on Aging, Chula Vista, 1986-92; founding dir. Eastlake Edn. Found., Chula Vista, 1994-96. Innovative Cmty. Health Edn. Project grantee Am. Hosp. Assn., 1987. Mem. Nat. Coun. for Resource Mgmt., Grant Resource Info. Network, Nat. Soc. Fundraising Execs. Democrat. Roman Catholic. Home: 755 Bajo Ct Chula Vista CA 91910-6607 Office: Southwestern College 900 Otay Lakes Rd Chula Vista CA 91910-7223

GIMBOLO, ALEKSEI FRANK CHARLES, artist, philosopher, author; b. Portland, Oreg., Mar. 29, 1956; s. Frank Charles and Elisabeth MacFarlane Gimbolo; m. Lilli M. Colipapa, Dec. 16, 1985; children: Niko Alexander, Romaneé Alexander. Student, U. Hawaii, 1976-78, Coll. Charleston, 1979-80. Winemaker Chateau LaCaia, Hazel Green, Ala., 1980-87; artist, philosopher Portland, 1987—. Author: Illuminati Wisdom of the Enlightened Ones, 1995; painting pub.: Encyclopedia of Living Artist, 7th edit., 1992, 8th edit., 1993; featured in Voice of Am.; exhibits include Seattle Art Resource, Perimeter Gallery, Houston, Signature Galleries, Calif., Hotel Vintage Plz., Portland, Oreg. Vice-chmn. Pre-Law Soc., Charleston, S.C., 1979; exec. com. chmn. Young Reps. of Am., Charleston, 1979; fencing coach Portland (Oreg.) State U., 1993. Office: PO Box 6754 Portland OR 97228-6754

GIN, HAL GABRIEL, university administrator; b. Oakland, Calif., July 2, 1950; m. Rose Y. Lee, Dec. 15, 1979; children: Kevin, Deanna. BA, Calif. State U., Hayward, 1973, MPA, 1983; EdD, U. San Francisco, 1995. Program advisor Calif. State U., Hayward, 1974-84, coord. orientation, dir. ednl. support svcs., 1984-86, dir. student life, 1988-93, exec. dir. student devel. svcs., 1993—. Bd. dirs. San Lorenzo (Calif.) Village Homes Assn., 1984-86; mem. San Lorenzo Village Found., 1995—. Mem. Nat. Assn. Student Pers. Adminstrs. (v.p. Region VI 1989-92, conf. com. 1996-97, exec. com. 1977—), Lions (cabinet sec./treas. Internat. divsn., 1985-86, pres. San Lorenzo chpt. 1979). Office: Calif State U Student Devel Svcs Hayward CA 94542

GINN, SAM L., telephone company executive; b. Saint Clair, Ala., Apr. 3, 1937; s. James Harold and Myra Ruby (Smith) G.; m. Meriann Lanford Vance, Feb. 2, 1963; children: Matthew, Michael, Samantha. B.S., Auburn U., 1959; postgrad., Stanford U. Grad. Sch. Bus., 1968. Various positions AT&T, 1960-78; with Pacific Tel. & Tel. Co., 1978—; exec. v.p. network Pacific Tel. & Tel. Co., San Francisco, 1979-81, exec. v.p. services, 1981-82, exec. v.p. network services, 1982, exec. v.p., strategic planning and adminstrn., 1983, vice chmn. bd., strategic planning and adminstrn., 1983-84; vice chmn. bd., group v.p. PacTel Cos. Pacific Telesis Group, San Francisco, 1984-86; pres. Air Touch Commn., San Francisco, 1984-87; vice chmn. bd., pres., chief exec. officer PacTel Corp. Pacific Telesis Group, San Francisco, 1986; pres., chief operating officer Pacific Telesis Group, San Francisco, 1987-88, former chmn., pres., chief exec. officer; chmn. Air Touch Commn., San Francisco, 1993—; now chmn. bd., CEO Air Touch Commn., San Francisco, Calif.; mem. adv. bd. Sloan program Stanford U. Grad. Sch. Bus., 1978-85, mem. internat. adv. council Inst. Internat. Studies; bd. dir. 1st Interstate Bank, Chevron Corp., Safeway, Inc. Trustee Mills Coll., 1982—. Served to capt. U.S. Army, 1959-60. Sloan fellow, 1968. Republican. Clubs: Blackhawk Country (Danville, Calif.); World Trade, Pacific-Union; Rams Hill Country (Borrego Springs, Calif.), Bankers. Office: Air Touch Commn 1 California St San Francisco CA 94111*

GINSBURG, JERRY HUGH, physician, health facility administrator; b. L.A., Mar. 22, 1943; s. Jack and Pauline (Wald) G.; m. Barbara Rever; children: Dustin, Ian. BA in English Lit., U. Calif., Berkeley, 1966; MD, U. So. Calif., 1970. Dir. Salinas-Monterey (Calif.) Heart Inst., 1985—. Pres. Am. Heart Assn., Salinas, 1988, 92. Fellow Am. Coll. Physicians, Am. Coll. Cardiology, Am. Coll. Rheumatology, Am. Coll. Chest Physicians, Coun. Am. Heart Assn.; mem. Soc. Critical Care Medicine . Office: Salinas-Monterey Heart Inst 230 San Jose St Ste 30 Salinas CA 93901-3932

GINTER, CAROL(YN) AUGUSTA ROMTVEDT, retired bond underwriter; b. Toledo, Oreg., May 24, 1926; d. Fred and Mary Elizabeth (Whitney) Romtvedt; m. Paul Peter Ginter, June 2, 1951 (dec. Dec. 1995); children: Joan Paula, Teresa Ginter Ward, Philip M., Jeffrey G. Student, U. Oreg., 1945-46. Office and dispatch clk. Oregonian Newspaper, Portland, 1943-45; clk. typist USN Supt. of Ships, Portland, 1945; gen. ins. clk. Fidelity & Deposit Co., Portland, 1946-48; bond clk. Aetna Casualty & Surety Fireman's Fund, Transamerica, Portland, 1956-65; surety bond underwriter Cole, Clark & Cunningham/Rollins, Burdick Hunter, Portland, 1965-79; freelance publicity specialist Waldport, Oreg., 1986—. Pub., coord. family history: Fred Romtvedt, His Life and Loves, 1980. Publicity specialist ARC, 1991—; publicity/sec., lay min. Altar Soc., St. Anthony's Cath. Ch., 1990-96. Mem. South County Women's Club (sec. 1984-94, 96), Waldport C. of C. (vol. visitors ctr. 1995—), Lincoln County Hist. Soc., Alsi Hist. Soc. Republican. Home: 1802 NW Canal St Waldport OR 97394

GIORDANO, ANGELA MARIA, military officer; b. Harvey, Ill., Mar. 14, 1965; d. Ronald Raymond Saunders (stepfather) and Claudia Giovanna (Camilli) Pound. BS, U.S. Mil. Acad., 1987; MS in Def. Analysis, Naval Postgrad. Sch., 1997. Commd. 2d lt. U.S. Army, 1987, advanced through grades to capt., 1991; terrain analysis platoon leader 63d engr. airborne co. U.S. Army, Ft. Bragg, N.C., 1988-89, co. exec. officer 175th engr. airborne co., 1989, bn. S-1 adjutant 30th engr. airborne bn., 1989-90, co. exec. officer 1st psychol. ops. airborne bn., 1990, team chief Latin Am. 1st psychol. ops. airborne bn., 1991-92; asst. S-3 constrn. officer 555th Combat Engr. Group, Ft. Lewis, Wash., 1992-93, ops. officer, 1993-94; co. comdr. Hdqs. and Hdqs. Co., 14th Combat Engr. Bn. (Corps), Ft. Lewis, Wash., 1994-96. Author, editor (Spanish handbook): Psychological Operations, 1991. Decorated Joint Svc. Army Achievement medal, Commendation medal, 2 Army Achievement medals, 2 Meritorious Svc. medals. Mem. Am. Mensa, Soc. Am. Mil. Engrs., Assn. Grads. U.S. Mil. Acad., NAFE, Nat. Geographic Soc. Republican. Roman Catholic. Home: 201 Glenwood Circle # 32 C Monterey CA 93940-6772

GIORGI, PETER BONNARD, educator; b. Nice, France, Dec. 25, 1929; came to the U.S., 1935; s. Leonard A. and Donal (Bonnard) G.; m. Detelina Petrova, July 21, 1962; children: Jean-Pierre André, Giséle Elaine. BS in Secondary Edn., Mansfield State U., 1953; MS in Edn., U. Ariz., 1958; postgrad., Johns Hopkins U., U. So. Calif., U. S.C., U. Houston, U. Md., Pa. State U., Temple U., Laverne Coll. Tchr., coach, counselor East Forest H.S., Marienville, Pa., 1953-55; reading specialist, curriculum cons. Spring Jr. High, Tucson, 1955-59; tchr., reading specialist Stephen Decatur H.S., Sigonella, Sicily, Italy, 1959-60, Bitburg (Germany) H.S., 1960-61; tchr., coach, curriculum cons. Dreux (France) H.S., 1961-65; tchr., counselor, work experience coord. Vicenza (Italy) H.S., 1965-95; cons., instr. U. Ariz., Tucson, 1995—; instr., cons. Lincoln U., Jefferson City, Mo., 1956-58, U. Md., 1960-95, Big Bend U., Army Edn. Ctr., Italy, 1985-95; supr. student tchr. program U. Ariz., 1957-59; instr. Air Force Edn. Ctr., Dreux AFB, France, 1960-65; instr., coord. summer sci. program DePauw U., Vicenza, 1980-85. Author: (handbooks) Reading Improvement Methods, 1958, JHS Social Studies Activities, 1987, (curriculum guides) Work Study Programs, 1972, Heritage Museums, 1986. With USN, 1947-49. Recipient Armed Svcs. award Armed Svcs. Recruiting Command, Europe, 1971, 73, 76, Cmty. Svc. award European Task Force-U.S. Army, Vicenza, 1978; GE fellow U. S.C., Columbia, 1973. Mem. NEA, ASCD, Internat. Reading Assn., Internat. Vocat. Guidance Assn., Nat. Geography Assn., Phi Delta Kappa (v.p. 1961-64). Home: 201 N Jessica Box 320 Tucson AZ 85710

GIPSON, GORDON, publishing company executive; b. Caldwell, Idaho, Oct. 26, 1914; s. James Herrick and Esther (Sterling) G.; m. Tryntje Heeling, Dec. 27, 1961; children—Craig, Amy. Student, Coll. Idaho. With The Caxton Printers, Ltd., Caldwell, 1935—; treas. The Caxton Printers, Ltd., 1945—, v.p., 1964—, pub., 1965—, pres., 1991—. Served with USAAF, 1942-45. Club: Elk. Home: 2211 S 10th Ave Caldwell ID 83605-5221 Office: 312 Main St Caldwell ID 83605-3235

GIRAGOSSIANTZ, ROXANA, nursing administrator; b. Kars, Russia, Sept. 18, 1906; came to the U.S., 1909; d. David Michael and Varvar (Der Galoostian) G. RN, St. Francis Coll., San Francisco, 1928; BA and BS, U. San Francisco, 1945; MA, Columbia U., 1950. RN, Calif. Supr. St. Francis Hosp., San Francisco, 1928-42; clin. coord. St. Francis Sch., San Francisco, 1945-47; instr. Lone Mountain, U. San Francisco, 1945-50; chairperson adminstrn. com., vol., adminstr. Calif. Armenian Home; bd. mem., officer NorCal Armenian Home and Sr. Svcs., San Francisco, 1982-96. Author: Armenian Senior Scenes, 1994. Republican. Home: 1069 Via Alta Lafayette CA 94549

GIRARDEAU, MARVIN DENHAM, physics educator; b. Lakewood, Ohio, Oct. 3, 1930; s. Marvin Denham and Maude Irene (Miller) G.; m. Susan Jessica Brown, June 30, 1956; children—Ellen, Catherine, Laura. B.S., Case Inst. Tech., 1952; M.S., U. Ill., 1954; Ph.D., Syracuse U., 1958. NSF postdoctoral fellow Inst. Advanced Study, Princeton, 1958-59; research assoc. Brandeis U., 1959-60; staff mem. Boeing Sci. Research Labs., 1960-61; research assoc. Enrico Fermi Inst. Nuclear Studies, U. Chgo., 1961-63; assoc. prof. physics, research asso. Inst. Theoretical Sci., U. Oreg., Eugene, 1963-67; prof. physics, research assoc. Inst. Theoretical Sci., U. Oreg., 1967—, dir., 1967-69, chmn. dept. physics, 1974-76. Contbr. articles to profl. jours. Recipient Humboldt Sr. U.S. Scientist award, 1984-85. NSF research grantee, 1965-79; ONR research grantee, 1981-87. Fellow Am. Phys. Soc.; mem. AAUP. Home: 2398 Douglas Dr Eugene OR 97405-1711 Office: U Oreg Dept Physics Eugene OR 97403

GIRARDELLI, RONALD K., food products executive; b. 1949. BA, Oreg. State U., 1971. With Blue Cross, Portland, Oreg., 1971-73; pres. Diamond Fruit Growers, Inc., 1973—. Office: Diamond Fruit Growers Inc PO Box 180 Hood River OR 97031-9436*

GIROD, FRANK PAUL, retired surgeon; b. Orenco, Oreg., Aug. 13, 1908; s. Leon and Anna (Gerig)ûG.; m. Nadine Mae Cooper, Aug. 26, 1939; children: Judith Anne, Janet Carol, Franklin Paul, John Cooper. AB, Willamette U., Salem, Oreg., 1929; MD, U. Colo., 1938. Diplomate Am. Bd. Family Practice. Tchr. physics and chemistry, athletic coach Cortez High Sch., Colo., 1929-34; intern U. Colo., Denver, 1938-39; resident surgeon U.S. Marine Hosp., Balt., 1939-41; pvt. practice specializing in family practice and surgery Lebanon, Oreg., 1946-95; ret., 1995; bd. dirs. Lebanon Hosp., 1960—, pres. med. staff. Trustee, sec. Blue Shield Ops., Oreg., 1950-60; grand marshal Lebanon Strawberry Festival, 1988; mem. bd. Coun. of Govts. Sr. Svcs., 1991, 92. Maj. Army Med. Corp, 1942-45. Decorated Bronze Star; recipient Disting. Svc. First Citizen award Lebanon, Oreg., 1989; Frank P. Girod Med. Scholarship named in his honor, 1995. Mem. AMA, Oreg. Med. Assn. (trustee), Am. Acad. Family Practice, Kiwanis (pres. 1947-48). Republican. Methodist. Home: 625 E Rose St Lebanon OR 97355-4544

GIRON, RICK, adminstrative services manager; b. Santa Fe, N.Mex., Feb. 4, 1961; s. Bill and Frances (Chavez) G.; m. Rebecca D. Vigil, Nov. 17, 1986; 1 child, Andy. BBA, Univ. N.Mex., 1984, MPA, 1989. Adminstrn. intern City of Albuquerque Water Resources, 1983-84; systems analyst City of Albuquerque Pub. Works Dept., 1984-89, 89-90; 1st lt. N.Mex. Army Nat. Guard, 1987—, systems analyst, 1990-91, adminstrn. svcs. mgr., 1991—. Del. State Dem. Conv., Albuquerque, 1994; vol. political campaigns, 1980—; mem. adv. bd. U. N.Mex. Sch. Pub. Adminstrn. Named Outstanding Young Man of Am., 1987. Mem. ASPA (bd. dirs., treas. 1989-90, 94-95, pres.-elect 1995-96, pres. 1996—), NG Officers Assn., Assn. U.S. Army, Air Def. Assn., Enlisted Assn., Albuquerque Hispano C. of C. (co-chmn. tourism and conv. com.), N.Mex. Suprs. and Profl. Assn. (bd. dirs., treas. 1991-93, pres. 1993—), KC. Democrat. Roman Catholic. Home: 4628 11th St NW Albuquerque NM 87107-3704 Office: City of Albuquerque PO Box 1293 Albuquerque NM 87103-1293

GIRTON, LANCE, economics educator; b. Brazil, Ind., July 20, 1942; s. John E. and Barbara (Wooland) G.; m. Kathy Marlock, Apr. 30, 1988; children: Derek, Lance Alan. BA in Econs., So. Ill. U., cre, 1964; MA in Econs., U. Chgo., 1967, PhD in Econs., 1976. Instr. econs. Elmhurst (Ill.) Coll., 1968-69; asst. prof. econs. Mich. Technol. U., Houghton, 1969-71; economist internat. fin. div. Bd. Govs. FRS, Washington, 1971-78; prof. Pa. State U., College Park, 1983-84; vis. prof. U. Utah, Salt Lake City, 1977-78, prof., 1978—; assoc. professorial lectr. George Washington U., Washington, 1975-76; v.p., head rsch. Citicorp Homeowners Inc., St. Louis, 1985-86; cons. Investment Cos. Inst., Washington, 1981-83, World Bank, Washington, 1982—, Congl. Budget Office, Washington, 1980; rsch. assoc. Ctr. for the Econ. Analysis of Law, 1996—; Murphy Endowment Fund vis. scholar U. Wis., La Crosse, 1979; presenter papers, participant profl. meetings, 1973—; seminar presenter Brown U., U. Chgo., U. Pa., Pa. State U., UCLA, U. Colo., also others; referee profl. jours. Contbr. articles to profl. jours. Univ. scholar So. Ill. U., 1961-64; fellow NIMH, 1966-68. Mem. Am. Econ. Assn. Office: U Utah Dept Econs Salt Lake City UT 84112

GIRVIGIAN, RAYMOND, architect; b. Detroit, Nov. 27, 1926; s. Manoug and Margaret G.; m. Beverly Rae Bennett, Sept. 23, 1967; 1 son, Michael Raymond. AA, UCLA, 1947; BA with honors, U. Calif., Berkeley, 1950; M.A. in Architecture, U. Calif.-Berkeley, 1951. With Hutchason Architects, L.A., 1952-57; owner, prin. Raymond Girvigian, L.A., 1957-68, South Pasadena, Calif., 1968—; co-founder, advisor L.A. Cultural Heritage Bd., 1961—; vice chmn. Hist. Am. Bldgs. Survey, Nat. Park Svc., Washington, 1966-70; co-founder, mem. Calif. Hist. Resources Commn., 1970-78; co-founder, chmn. governing bd. Calif. Hist. Bldgs. Code, 1976-91, chmn. adminstrv. law, 1992—, chmn. emeritus, 1993—; chmn. Calif. State Capitol Commn., 1985—. Co-editor, producer: film Architecture of Southern California for Los Angeles City Schs, 1965; historical monographs of HABS Landmarks, Los Angeles, 1958-80; historical monographs of Califs. State Capitol, 1974, Pan Pacific Auditorium, 1980, L.A. Meml. Coliseum, 1984, Powell Meml. Libr., UCLA, 1989; designed: city halls for Pico Rivera, 1963, LaPuente, 1966, Rosemead, 1968, Lawndale, 1970 (all Calif.); hist. architect for restoration of Calif. State Capitol, 1975-82, Workman/Temple Hist. Complex, City of Industry, Calif., 1974-81, Robinson Gardens Landmarks, Beverly Hills, Calif., 1983-92, Pasadena (Calif.) Ctrl. Libr., 1982-92, 95-97, Mt. Pleasant House Mus., Heritage Sq., L.A., 1972-95. Mem. St. James Episcopal Ch., South Pasadena, Calif. Served with U.S. Army, 1945-46. Recipient Archtl. Design medal U. Calif., Berkeley, 1947, Outstanding Achievement in Architecture award City of Pico Rivera, Calif., 1968, Neasham award Calif. Hist. Soc., 1982, Preservationist of Yr. award Calif. Preservation Found., 1987, L.A. Mayor's award for archtl. preservation, 1987, Gold Crown award for advancement of arts Pasadena Arts Coun., 1990, Golden Palm award Hollywood Heritage, 1990. Fellow AIA (Calif. state preservation chmn. 1970-75, state preservation coord. 1970-89, co-recipient nat. honor award for restoration Calif. State Capitol 1983, co-recipient honor award for restoration Pasadena Cen. Libr., Pasadena chpt. 1988); mem. Soc. Archtl. Historians, Nat. Trust for Historic Preservation, Calif. Preservation Found., Calif. Hist. Soc. Independent Democrat. Office: PO Box 220 South Pasadena CA 91031-0220 *Raymond Girvigian's pioneering work in the Post War II Historic Preservation Movement includes many firsts. He initiated or assisted in creating over a score of California's (and the nation's) earliest laws, codes, and regulations for historical landmarks. He served as a pro-bono preservation official at local, state, and federal levels (e.g., California Landmark Commission's first historical architect) and led many preservation campaigns in the public interest. His professional resume includes hundreds of landmark examples. He is currently a consulting historical architect. Girvigian's numerous honors and awards recognize his years of innovative contributions to this field. I believe that we must all serve society in whatever way that we are best able; and if a worthy cause I have undertaken appears to have failed, I should ignore that possibility and press on with even greater determination and vigor to succeed. I would hope by that example to encourage others to join the cause and thereby further the likelihood of a successful effort for the good of all.*

GISH, ROBERT FRANKLIN, English language educator, writer; b. Albuquerque, Apr. 1, 1940; s. Jesse Franklin and Lillian J. (Fields) G.; m. Judith Kay Stephenson, June 20, 1961; children: Robin Elaine Butzier, Timothy Stephen, Annabeth. BA, U. N.Mex., Albuquerque, 1962, MA, 1967, PhD, 1972. Tchr. Albuquerque Pub. Schs., 1962-67; prof. U. No. Iowa, Cedar Falls, 1968-91; dir. ethnic studies, prof. English Calif. Poly. State U., San

Luis Obispo, 1991—, prof., 1992—. Author: Hamlin Garland: Far West, 1976, Paul Horgan, 1983, Frontier's End: Life of Harvey Fergusson, 1988, William Carlos Williams: The Short Fiction, 1989, Songs of My Hunter Heart: A Western Kinship, 1992, Frist Horses: Stories of the New West, 1993, North American Native American Myths, 1993, When Coyote Howls: A Lavaland Fable, 1994, Nueva Granada: Paul Horgan and the Southwest, 1995, Bad Boys and Black Sheep: Fateful Tles from the West, 1996, Beyond Bounds: Cross-Cultural Essays, 1996, Beautiful Swift Fox: Erna Fergusson and the Modern Southwest, 1996, Dreams of Quivira: Stories in Search of The Golden West, 1997. Office: Calif Poly State U Ethnic Studies San Luis Obispo CA 93407

GISLASON, IRVING LEE, psychiatry educator; b. Nanaimo, B.C., Can., July 21, 1943; came to U.S., 1977; s. Sverrir and Helga Johina (Gislason) G.; m. Leslie Laura Hope; children: Sarah Jonina, Catherine Adair. MD, U. B.C., Vancouver, 1969. Diplomate Am. Bd. Psychiatry and Neurology; lic. psychiatrist B.C., Calif. Rotating intern Meml. Hosp. Long Beach, Calif., 1969-70; resident in psychiatry dept. psychiatry and human behavior U. Calif.-Irvine, Orange, 1972-74, fellow in child psychiatry dept. psychiatry & human behavior, 1974-76; chief resident dept. psychiatry U. B.C., 1976; staff psychiatrist U. Calif.-Irvine Med. Ctr., Orange, 1977—, dir. Child Study Ctr., 1977-89, acting chief divsn. child and adolescent psychiatry, 1980-81, assoc. dir. Child Inpatient Unit, 1984, acting chief Adolescent Inpatient Unit, 1987, dir. Child Psychiat. and Inpatient Unit, 1989-92, dir. adult psychiat. inpatient unit, 1992—, med. student ednl. coord., 1993—, dir. med. student edn. (psychiatry), 1993—; examiner Am. Bd. Psychiatry and Neurology; clin. instr. psychiatry U. B.C., 1977, U. Calif.-Irvine, 1975; chief child psychiatry consultation liaison program U. Calif.-Irvine Med. Ctr., 1977-89; cons. Greater Vancouver Mental Health Svcs., 1977; staff psychiatrist U. B.C. Sci. Ctr. Hosp., 1977; clin. prof. psychiatry U. Calif.-Irvine, 1987—, cons. staff dept. medicine psychiat. sect. Children's Hosp. of Orange County, 1981—; presenter and lectr. in field. Contbr. articles to profl. jours. Mem. adv. bd. Com. on Children's TV, NBC Studios, 1977-81. Licentiate Med. Coun. Can.; fellow Royal Coll. Physicians Can. (diplomate fellowship exam. in medicine 1976, specialist cert. 1976), Am. Acad. Child Psychiatry; mem. Can. Med. Assn. Home: 688 N Lemon Hill Trl Orange CA 92869-2403 Office: U Calif-Irvine Med Ctr 101 The City Dr S Orange CA 92868-3201

GIST, MARILYN ELAINE, organizational behavior and human resource management educator; b. Tuskegee, Ala., May 9, 1950; d. Lewis A. and Grace (Perry) G. BA in Edn., Howard U., 1972; MBA, U. Md., 1982, PhD in Bus. Aminstrn. Organizational Behavior, 1985. Tchr. Montgomery County Pub. Schs., Rockville, Md., 1972-76; mgmt. intern NASA Goddard Space Flight Ctr., Greenbelt, Md., 1976-79; procurement mgr. NASA Goddard Space Flight Ctr., Greenbelt, 1980-81, staff asst. to dir. mgmt. ops., 1983-85; dir. contracts OAO Corp., Greenbelt, 1981-83; prof. organizational behavior U. N.C., Chapel Hill, N.C., 1985-87; prof. organized behavior and human resources U. Wash., Seattle, 1987—; staff cons. U. Md., Coll. Park, 1979-84, CIA, Langley, Va., 1984-85; adj. prof. human resources Cornell U., 1995-96. Contbr. articles to profl. jours. Recipient Outstanding Student award Alumni Assn. Internat. U. Md., 1985, Alan Nash Outstanding Doctoral Student award U. Md., 1985, Chancellor's Disting. lectr. award U. Calif., Irvine, 1993; U. Md. Academic Research grantee, 1982-85. Mem. Acad Mgmt. (Outstanding Paper award 1987), Am. Psychological Assn., So. Mgmt. Assn. Democrat. Roman Catholic. Office: U Wash Sch Bus Adminstrn MacKenzie Hall DJ 10 Seattle WA 98195

GITT, CYNTHIA E., lawyer; b. York, Pa., Nov. 14, 1946. BA, Wheaton Coll., 1968; JD with high honors, George Washington U., 1971. Bar: D.C. 1971, Calif. 1974, Mich. 1976, U.S. Supreme Ct. 1976, Ariz. 1978. Legis. asst. to Hon. Bella Abzug, 1971; trial atty. Equal Employment Opportunity Commn., Washington, San Francisco, 1971-75; asst. prof. Wayne State Law Sch., Detroit, 1975-77; atty. Morgan, Lewis & Bockus, L.A., 1977-84; mem. Ford & Harrison, L.A., 1984-91, Epstein, Becker & Green, L.A., 1991—. Mem. ABA (labor and employment sect.), Assn. Trial Lawyers Am., State Bar Calif., D.C. Bar, Los Angeles County Bar Assn. (sect. labor law, sect. litigation), Order Coif. Office: Epstein Becker & Green 1875 Century Park E Ste 500 Los Angeles CA 90067-2506

GITTLEMAN, MORRIS, consultant, metallurgist; b. Zhidkovitz, Minsk, Russia, Nov. 2, 1912; came to U.S., 1920, naturalized; s. Louis and Ida (Gorodietsky) G.; B.S. cum laude, Bklyn. Coll., 1934; postgrad. Manhattan Coll., 1941, Pratt Inst., 1943, Bklyn. Poly. Inst., 1946-47; m. Clara Konefsky, Apr. 7, 1937; children—Arthur Paul, Michael Jay. Metall. engr. N.Y. Naval Shipyard, 1942-47; chief metallurgist, chemist Pacific Cast Iron Pipe & Fitting Co., South Gate, Calif., 1948-54, tech. mgr., 1954-57, tech. and prodn. mgr., 1957-58; cons. Valley Brass, Inc., El Monte Calif., 1958-61, Vulcan Foundry, Ltd., Haifa, Israel, 1958-65, Anaheim Foundry Co. (Calif.), 1958-63, Hollywood Alloy Casting Co. (Calif.), 1960-70, Spartan Casting Co., El Monte, 1961-62; Overton Foundry, South Gate, Calif., 1962-70, cons., gen. mgr., 1970-71; cons. Familian Pipe & Supply Co., Van Nuys, Calif., 1962-72, Comml. Enameling Co., Los Angeles, 1963-68, Universal Cast Iron Mfg. Co., South Gate, 1965-71; pres. MG Coupling Co., 1972-79; instr. physics Los Angeles Harbor Coll., 1958-59; instr. chemistry Western States Coll. Engring., Inglewood, Calif., 1961-68. Registered profl. engr., Calif. Mem. Am. Foundrymen's Soc., Am. Foundrymen's Soc. So. Calif. (dir. 1955-57), AAAS, Am. Soc. Metals, N.Y. Acad. Scis., Internat. Solar Energy Soc. (Am. sect.). Contbr. to tech. jours.; inventor MG timesaver coupling, patents worldwide. Home: 17635 San Diego Cir Fountain Valley CA 92708-5243

GIUDICI, FRANCIS, food products executive; b. 1956. Pres. L.A. Heame Co., 1975—. Office: L A Hearne Co 512 Metz Rd King City CA 93930-2503*

GIULIANO, ARMANDO ELARIO, surgical oncologist, educator, author; b. N.Y.C., Oct. 2, 1947; s. Antonio Vincent and Victoria (Squizzaro) G.; m. Cheryl Jane Fallon, June 21, 1970; children: Christopher and Amanda (twins). BA, Fordham U., 1969; MD, U. Chgo., 1973. Diplomate Am. Bd. Surgery. Resident U. Calif., San Francisco, 1973-76, 78-80; fellow in tumor immunology UCLA, 1976-78, asst. prof. surgery, 1980-84, assoc. prof. surgery, 1984-90, dir. Breast Svc., 1980-91, asst. dean Med. Sch., 1988-91, clin. prof. surgery, 1991—, prof. surgery, 1990-91; assoc. dir., chief surg. oncology John Wayne Cancer Inst., Santa Monica, Calif., 1991—; dir. Keefer Breast Ctr. St. John's Hosp., Santa Monica, 1993—; vice chmn. com. on cancer liaison Commn. on Cancer, Chgo., 1993—, mem. com. on edn., 1990—. Mem. editorial bd. Breast Surgery Index and Revs., 1993—; contbr. more than 100 articles to profl. jours. Bd. dirs. Coastal Cities unit Am. Cancer Soc., 1993—; mem. nat. profl. adv. bd. The Wellness Cmty., L.A., 1993—. Mem. ACS (com. on surg. edn. 1989—, commn. on cancer 1990—), Soc. Surg. Oncology (chmn. edn. com. 1993), Soc. Univ. Surgeons, Am. Soc. Clin. Oncology, Pacific Coast Surg. Assn., Western Surg. Assn., Am. Surg. Assocs., Alpha Omega Alpha. Office: John Wayne Cancer Inst 1328 22nd St Santa Monica CA 90404-2032

GIUMARRA, GEORGE, JR., vintner; b. 1942. Prin. ARRA Sales Corp., Edison, Calif., 1975—, Giumarra Farms Inc., Edison, Calif., 1963—; v.p. Giumarra Vineyards Corp., Edison, Calif., 1963—; prin. Giumarra Bros. Fruit Co., Inc., L.A., 1963—. Office: Giumarra Vineyards Corp 11220 Edison Hwy Edison CA 93220*

GIVANT, PHILIP JOACHIM, mathematics educator, real estate investment executive; b. Mannheim, Germany, Dec. 5, 1935; s. Paul and Irmy (Dinse) G.; m. Kathleen Joan Porter, Sept. 3, 1960; children: Philip Paul, Julie Kathleen, Laura Grace. BA in Math., San Francisco State U., 1957, MA in Math., 1960. Prof. math. San Francisco State U., 1958-60, Am. River Coll., Sacramento, 1960—; pres. Grove Enterprises, Sacramento, 1961—; pres. Am. River Coll. Acad. Senate, Sacramento, 1966-69; v.p. Acad. Senate for Calif. Community Colls., 1974-77; mem. State Chancellor's Acad. Calendar Com., Sacramento, 1977-79. Founder, producer Annual Sacramento Blues Music Festival, 1976—; producer Sta. KVMR weekly Blues music program, 1978—, music festivals Folsom Prison, 1979-81, Vacaville Prison, 1985. Pres. Sacramento Blues Festival, Inc., 1985—; mem. Lake Tahoe Keys Homeowners Assn., 1983—, Sea Ranch Homeowners Assn., 1977—. Recipient Spl. Service Commendation, Acad. Senate Calif. Community Colls., 1977, Spl. Human Rights award Human Rights-Fair Housing Commn., Sacramento, 1985, W.C. Handy award for Blues Promoter of Yr. Nat. Blues Found., Memphis, 1987, 1st Critical Achievement award Sacramento Area Mus. Awards Commn., 1992. Mem. Faculty Assn. Calif. Community Colls., Am. Soc. Psychical Research, Nat. Blues Found. (adv. com., W.C. Handy Blues Promoter of Yr. 1987). Home and Office: 3809 Garfield Ave Carmichael CA 95608-6631

GIVENS, STEVEN WENDELL, economic development planner; b. Mayfield, Ky., Sept. 18, 1954; s. Jaynes Wendell and Joanne G.; m. Robyn E. Cockrell, July, 1981 (dec. Oct. 1987); children: Grant Tyler, Paige; m. D'Lyn C. Ford, Apr. 27, 1991. BS, Murray State U., 1976, Western N.M. Univ., 1996. Edn. editor The Hobbs (N.Mex.) Daily News Sun, 1976-80; sports editor, area writer The Duncan (Okla.) Banner, 1980-85; territorial sales rep. Wm. E. Davis & Sons, Oklahoma City, 1985-87; mgr. Connie's Mexico Cafe, Wichita, Kans., 1987-88; sports editor Clovis (N.Mex.) Jour., 1988-90; edn./county govt. editor Carlsbad (N.Mex.) Current Argus, 1990-91; news editor Las Cruces (N.Mex.) Sun News, 1991-93, Rio Grande Gazette, Anthony, Tex., 1993; econ. devel. planner, comm. dir. Doña Ana County Econ. Devel.-MVEDA, Las Cruces, 1994—; bd. dirs. The Messenger Advocate Pub., Mesilla Park, N.Mex.; v.p. AP Mng. Editors, N.Mex., 1992, 93. Contbr. articles to jours. and newspapers. Precinct organizer Clinton-Gore Rapid Response Team, Las Cruces, 1992, 96; mem. Dem. Nat. Com., 1976—; dist. bd. Yucca coun., Boy Scouts Am., 1993—; adv. com. El Paso C.C., 1993—. Named Restaurant Mgr. of the Yr. Wichita River Festival, Old Town Assn., 1988; recipient Resolution of Appreciation, Eddy County, N.Mex., 1991. Mem. Optimist Internat. (club pres. 1980-82, lt. gov. 1982-83, gov. 1985-86, Outstanding Disting. Lt. Gov. award 1982-83, New Club Bldg. award 1982-83). Presbyterian. Office: Dona Ana County MVEDA 2345 Nevada Ave Las Cruces NM 88001-3902

GLAD, DAIN STURGIS, retired aerospace engineer, consultant; b. Santa Monica, Calif., Sept. 17, 1932; s. Alma Emanuel and Maude La Verne (Morby) G.; BS in Engring., UCLA, 1954; MS in Elec. Engring., U. So. Calif., 1963. Registered profl. engr., Calif. m. Betty Alexandra Shainoff, Sept. 12, 1954 (dec. 1974); 1 child, Dana Elizabeth; m. Carolyn Elizabeth Giffen, June 8, 1979. Electronic engr. Clary Corp., San Gabriel, Calif., 1957-58; with Aerojet Electro Systems Co., Azusa, Calif., 1958-72; with missile systems div. Rockwell Internat., Anaheim, Calif., 1973-75; with Aerojet Electrosystems, Azusa, 1975-84; with support systems div. Hughes Aircraft Co., 1984-90; with Electro-Optical Ctr. Rockwell Internat. Corp., 1990-94; cons., 1994—. Contbr. articles to profl. jours. Ensign, U.S. Navy, 1954-56; lt. j.g. Res., 1956-57. Mem. IEEE. Home: 1701 Marengo Ave South Pasadena CA 91030-4818

GLAD, SUZANNE LOCKLEY, retired museum director; b. Rochester, N.Y., Oct. 2, 1929; d. Alfred Allen and Lucille A. (Watson) Lockley; m. Edward Newman Glad, Nov. 7, 1953; children: Amy, Lisanne Glad Lantz, William E. BA, Sweet Briar Coll., 1951; MA, Columbia U., 1952. Exec. dir. New York State Young Reps., N.Y.C., 1951-57; mem. pub. rels. staff Dolphin Group, L.A., 1974-83; scheduling sec. Gov.'s Office, Sacramento, 1983-87; dep. dir. Calif. Mus. Sci. and Industry, L.A., 1987-94; ret. Mem. Calif. Rep. League, Pasadena, 1969—; mem. Assistance League of Flintridge, 1970—, Flintridge Guild Children's Hosp., 1969-89. Mem. Sweet Briar Alumnae of So. Calif. (pres. 1972), Phi Beta Kappa, Tau Phi. Episcopalian.

GLADNER, MARC STEFAN, lawyer; b. Seattle, July 18, 1952; s. Jules A. and Mildred W. (Weller) G.; m. Susanne Tso (div. Feb. 1981); m. Michele Marie Hardin, Sept. 12, 1981; 1 child, Sara Megan. Student, U. Colo., 1970-73; JD, Southwestern U., 1976. Bar: Ariz. 1976, Navajo Tribal Ct. 1978. Law clk. jud. br. Navajo Nation, Window Rock, Ariz., 1976-77, gen. counsel jud. br., 1977-79; pvt. practice law Phoenix, 1979-83; ptnr. Seplow, Rivkind & Gladner, Phoenix, 1983-86, Crosby & Gladner, P.C., Phoenix, 1986—; adj. instr. Coll. Ganado, Ariz., 1978-79. Democrat. Jewish. Office: Crosby & Gladner PC 111 W Monroe St Ste 706 Phoenix AZ 85003-1720

GLADWELL, MARILYN MEILAN, microbiologist; b. Conchas Dam, N.Mex., Nov. 30, 1938; d. Edmund H. and Henrietta M. (Hum) Chun; m. Jack Gladwell, Feb. 7, 1972; children: Linda Sue Poetsch, David S. Bailey. BS in Microbiology, U. Wash., 1960. Microbiologist Cowlitz Gen. Hosp., Longview, Wash., 1960-67; microbiologist, lab. supr., tech. supr. A O N.W., Inc. Med. Lab., The Dalles, Oreg., 1968-94, prin., 1971-94, pres., 1991-94; pres. The Majack Corp., The Dalles, 1994—. Computer specialist The Dalles Pub. Libr., 1994—. Mem. Am. Soc. Med. Technologists, Am. Rose Soc. Republican. Home and Office: The Majack Corp PO Box 1207 The Dalles OR 97058-9207

GLADYSZ, JOHN ANDREW, chemistry educator; b. Kalamazoo, Aug. 13, 1952; s. Edward Matthew and Margean Alice (Worst) G. BS in Chemistry, U. Mich., 1971; PhD in Chemistry, Stanford (Calif.) U., 1974. Asst. prof. U. Calif., L.A., 1974-82; assoc. prof. U. Utah, Salt Lake City, 1982-85, prof., 1985—. Assoc. editor Chem. Revs., 1984—; mem. editorial bd. Organometallics, 1990-92, Bull. de la Société Chemique de France, 1992—. Alfred P. Sloan Found. fellow, 1980-84; Camile and Henry Dreyfus scholar and grantee, 1980-85; Arthur C. Cope scholar, 1988; recipient U. Utah Disting. Rsch. award, 1992, Humboldt award, 1994. Mem. AAAS, Am. Chem. Soc. (award in Organometallic Chemistry 1994), The Chem. Soc., Sigma Xi, Alpha Chi Sigma. Home: 1149 Charlton Ave Salt Lake City UT 84106-2603 Office: U Utah Dept Of Chemistry Salt Lake City UT 84112

GLAHE, FRED RUFUS, economics educator; b. Chgo., June 30, 1934; s. Frederick William and Frances Evelyn (Welch) G.; m. Nancy Suzzanna Behrent, June 24, 1961; 1 child, Charles Dixon. BS in Aero. Engring., Purdue U., 1957, MS in Econs., 1963, PhD in Econs., 1964. Engr. Allison divsn. GM, Indpls., 1957-58, 58-60; ops. analyst Def. Sys. divsn. GM, Detroit, 1960-61; rsch. economist Battelle Meml. Inst., Columbus, Ohio, 1964-65; prof. U. Colo., Boulder, 1965—. Author: Macroeconomics, 1973, 77, 85, Microeconomics, 1981, 88, Concordance to Smith's Wealth of Nations, 1993. Mem. Mt. Pelerin Soc. Roman Catholic. Office: U Colo Campus Box 256 Boulder CO 80309

GLASCO, DONALD GLEE, psychiatrist; b. Wichita, Kans., Oct. 18, 1929; s. James Edward and Nelle Josephine (Lyster) G.; m. JoAnn Lewis, June 12, 1955; children: Cheryl Ann, Suzanne, Mark. AB, U. Kans., 1947-52, MD, 1956; student, U. Zurich, Switzerland, 1953-54; cert. in psychiatry, U. Colo., 1960. Diplomate Am. Bd. Psychiatry. Intern U. Kans. Health Svc. Ctr., Kansas City, 1956-57; resident U. Colo. Health Sci. Ctr., Denver, 1957-60; pvt. practice Littleton, Colo., 1962—; assoc. clin. prof. psychiatry U. Colo., Denver, 1963—; staff psychiatrist Denver VA Med. Ctr., 1963-76, 87—. Lt. comdr. USN, 1960-62. Fellow Am. Psychiatric Assn., Colo. Psychiatric Soc. (pres.), Ctrl. Neuro Psychiatric Assn.; mem. Colo. Med. Soc., Appahoe County Med. Soc. Office: 191 E Orchard Rd Ste 203 Littleton CO 80121-8057

GLASER, DONALD ARTHUR, physicist; b. Cleveland, Ohio, Sept. 21, 1926; s. William Joseph Glaser. B.S., Case Inst. Tech., 1946, Sc.D., 1959; Ph.D., Cal. Inst. Tech., 1949. Prof. physics U. Mich., 1949-59; prof. physics U. Calif., Berkeley, 1959—; prof. physics, molecular and cell biology, divsn. neurobiology U. Calif., 1964—. Recipient Henry Russel award U. Mich., 1955, Charles V. Boys prize Phys. Soc., London, 1958, Nobel prize in physics, 1960, Gold Medal award Case Inst. Tech., 1967, Golden Plate award Am. Acad. of Achievement, 1989; NSF fellow, 1961, Guggenheim fellow, 1961-62, fellow Smith-Kettlewell Inst. for Vision Rsch, 1983-84. Fellow AAAS, Fedn. Am. Scientists, The Exploratorium (bd. dirs.), Royal Soc. Sci., Royal Swedish Acad. Sci., Assn. Rsch. Vision and Ophthalmology, Neurosci. Inst., Am. Physics Soc. (prize 1959); mem. Nat. Acad. Scis., Am. Assn. Artificial Intelligence, N.Y. Acad. Sci., Internat. Acad. Sci., Sigma Xi, Tau Kappa Alpha, Theta Tau. Office: U Calif Dept Molecular & Cell Biology Neurobiology Divsn Stanley Hall Berkeley CA 94720

GLASGOW, JANIS MARILYN, foreign language educator; b. Wooster, Ohio, Aug. 24, 1934; d. Paul Ellsworth and Edna Helen (Smith) G. BA, Case Western Reserve U., 1956; MA, U. Wis., 1958; PhD, UCLA, 1966. Grad. teaching asst. U. Wis., Madison, 1957-58, UCLA, 1958-62; asst. prof. French San Diego State U., 1962-68, assoc. prof., 1968-80, prof. French, 1980-94; maître de confs. U. Paris VIII, 1973-74; exch. prof. French U. Nice (France), 1982; exch. prof. comparative lit. U. Nantes (France), 1985. Author: Une Esthetique de Comparaison: Balzac et George Sand, 1978; editor: George Sand: Collected Essays, 1985, Gabriel, 1988, Questions d'Art et de Littérature, 1991. Fulbright scholar, 1956-57, Robert V. Merrill Grad. scholar, 1961-62. Mem. MLA (regional del. Pacific coast 1974-75, 89-91), Am. Assn. Tchrs. French (pres. 1979-81), Am. Soc. French Acad. Palms, Mensa, Phi Beta Kappa (pres. Epsilon Assn. of Calif. 1972-73, pres. Nu chpt. of Calif. 1976-77, 88-90). Home: 713 N Grant St Wooster OH 44691-2824 also: 1225 Pacific Beach Dr San Diego CA 92109-5279

GLASS, LUIS T.P., retired tennis professional; b. N.Y.C., Mar. 3, 1948; s. Sidney Harris and Virginia Glass. Diploma, Deerfield (Mass.) Acad. Tennis profl. USPTR, 1993; instr. Nat. Jr. Tennis League, San Diego; ret. With U.S. Army, 1969-77. Nat. Pub. Parks Champion, 1993, Masters Champion (3 times) So. Calif. Grand Prix, Masters Champion Caif. Tennis Series, Silver Ballist U.S. Tennis Assn., 1993; recipient Sportsmanship award San Diego dist., 1985, Tennis Family of Yr., San Diego, 1996; tennis scholar UCLA, 1965. Mem. Rancho Valencia Tennis Resort Club, Balboa Tennis Club, North Park Tennis Club. Home: 4061 Texas St San Diego CA 92104

GLASS, RICHARD STEVEN, chemistry educator; b. N.Y.C., Mar. 5, 1943; s. Emanuel David and Sylvia Cynthia (Lucks) G.; m. Susan Stern, Aug. 30, 1970; children: Ethan Charles, Lawrence Craig. BA, NYU, 1963; PhD, Harvard U., 1967. Rsch. assoc. Stanford (Calif.) U., 1966-67; sr. scientist Hoffmann La Roche, Inc., Nutley, N.J., 1967-70; asst. prof. U. Ariz., Tucson, 1970-76, assoc. prof., 1976-82, prof., 1982—; scientific adv. bd. Naxcor, Inc., Menlo Park, Calif., 1987—; cons. several cos. Editor: (book) Conformational Analysis of . . . , 1988; editorial bd. Sulfur Letters, Sulfur Reports, 1993—; patentee in field; contbr. articles to profl. jours. Grantee NSF, NIH, ACS, 1970—; sr. fellow NIH, 1988; guest scientist Hahn-Meitner Inst., Berlin, 1991. Fellow AAAS (pres. S.W. and Rocky Mountain Div. 1988); mem. Am. Chem. Soc. Home: 8200 E Ridgewood Dr Tucson AZ 85750-2489 Office: Univ Ariz Dept Chemistry Tucson AZ 85721

GLASS, TIMOTHY FARON KIT, writer, screenwriter, small business owner; b. Allentown, Pa., May 16, 1951; s. Samuel and Alma M. (Laufer) G.; m. Babette G. Keller, Oct. 11, 1991 (div. Jan. 1996); 1 child, Elise Lyndell. Student, U. N.Mex., 1984. Owner, mgr. Glass Bus. Equipment, Peralta, N.Mex., 1987—; cons. It's A Wrap mag., Albuquerque, Digital Equipment Co., Albuquerque; chief info. and comm. officer BBB, N.Mex. Author: Until the End of Time, 1996 (also screenplay); contbr. over 200 articles to nat. and internat. publs. Sr. mem. task force N.Mex. Atty. Gen.'s Office, 1996. Mem. Authors Guild Am., Authors League Am., S.W. Writers Workshop, Civil War Congress N.Mex. Home and Office: PO Box 287 Peralta NM 87042

GLASSHEIM, JEFFREY WAYNE, allergist, immunologist, pediatrician; b. Far Rockaway, N.Y., Sept. 16, 1958; s. Ronald Alan and Glenda (Deitch) G.; m. Paulette Renée, Apr. 16, 1989; 1 child, Elyssa Gwen. BA, Temple U., 1980; DO, U. New. Eng., 1984. Diplomate Am. Bd. Allergy and Clin. Immunology, Am. Bd. Pediatrics. Commd. 2d lt. U.S. Army, 1980, advanced through grades to maj., 1989; intern Winthrop-Univ. Hosp., Mineola, N.Y., 1984-85; resident Madigan Army Med. Ctr., Tacoma, Wash., 1985-87; fellow Fitzsimons Army Med. Ctr. and Nat. Jewish Ctr. Immunology, Aurora, Colo., 1990-91, chief fellow allergy-clin. immunology, 1990-91; chief allergy-clin. immunology and immunizations svcs. Silas B. Hays Army Community Hosp., Fort Ord, Calif., 1991-93; resigned U.S. Army, 1993; pvt. practice Ziering Allergy and Respiratory Ctr., Calif., 1993-94; dir. allergy-immunology dept. Pediatric Med. Group of Fresno, Calif., 1994-95; dir. allergy-immunology Northwest Med. Group, Fresno, 1995-97; pvt. practice allergy and immunology, 1997—. Contbr. articles to profl. jours. Fellow Am. Acad. Pediatrics (allergy and immunology sect.), Am. Acad. Allergy and Immunology, Am. Coll. Allergy, Asthma and Immunology; mem. AMA, Am. Osteo. Assn., Am. Physicians Fellowship for Medicine in Israel, Calif. Soc. Allergy, Asthma and Clin. Immunology, Ctrl. Calif. Allergy Soc., Fresno-Madera Med. Soc., Calif. Med. Assn., Osteo. Physicians and Surgeons of Calif. Republican. Jewish. Office: Northwest Med Group Inc Ste 102 7710 N Fresno St Fresno CA 93722

GLASSMAN, ARTHUR JOSEPH, software engineer; b. N.Y.C., Apr. 4, 1948; s. Max Samuel and Ruth Rae (Gold) G. SB in Physics, MIT, 1968; MS, Yale U., 1969; PhD, Columbia U., 1977. Sr. programmer Cubic, San Diego, 1978-79; engr. Linkabit, San Diego, 1979-80; sr. scientist Jaycor, San Diego, 1980-91; sr. software engr. SuperSet, San Diego, 1992-93, Document Scis. Corp., San Diego, 1994—. Mem. IEEE, Am. Phys. Soc., Am. Geophys. Union, Am. Stats. Assn., Math. Assn. Am.

GLATZER, ROBERT ANTHONY, marketing and sales executive; b. N.Y.C., May 19, 1932; s. Harold and Glenna (Beaber) G.; m. Paula Rosenfeld, Dec. 20, 1964; m. Mary Ann Murphy, Dec. 31, 1977; children: Gabriela, Jessica, Nicholas. BA, Haverford Coll., 1954. Br. store dept. mgr. Bloomingdale's, N.Y.C., 1954-56; media buyer Ben Sackheim Advt., N.Y.C., 1956-59; producer TV commls. Ogilvy, Benson & Mather Advt., N.Y.C., 1959-62; dir. broadcast prodn. Carl Ally Advt., N.Y.C., 1962-63; owner Chronicle Prodns., N.Y.C., 1963-73; dir. Folklife Festival, Smithsonian Inst., Washington, 1973, Expo 74 Corp., Spokane, Wash., 1973-74; pres. Robert Glatzer Assocs., Spokane, 1974—; ptnr. Delany/Glatzer Advt., Spokane, 1979-84; dir. sales/mktg. Pinnacle Prodns., Spokane; adj. faculty Ea. Wash. U., 1987—. Bd. dirs. Riverfront Arts Festival, 1977-78; bd. dirs. Comprehensive Health Planning Council, 1975-78, Spokane Quality of Life Council, 1976-82, Allied Arts of Spokane, 1976-80, Art Alliance Wash. State, 1977-81, Spokane chpt. ACLU, 1979-83, Wash. State Folklife Council, 1983—; commr. Spokane Arts, 1987—; mem. Spokane Community Devel. Bd., 1988—; mem. Shorelines Update Commn., 1988—; mem. Wash. State Small Bus. Improvement Coun., 1994—. Recipient CINE Golden Eagle award (2). Mem. Dirs. Guild Am. Democrat. Jewish. Author: The New Advertising, 1970; co-searcher Scorpio and other TV prodns. Office: 8607 N Division St Spokane WA 99208-5946

GLAZER, REA HELENE See KIRK, REA HELENE

GLAZIER, RON, zoological park administrator. Dir. Santa Ana Zoo, Santa Ana, Calif. Office: Santa Ana Zoo 1801 E Chestnut Ave Santa Ana CA 92701*

GLEASON, DOUGLAS RENWICK, marketing professional; b. Worcester, Mass., Oct. 27, 1956; s. Sherman M. and Dolores E. (Murad) G. BA, Stanford U., 1978; MBA, UCLA, 1982. Asst. product mgr. Pepsi USA, Purchase, N.Y., 1982-83, assoc. product mgr., 1983-85; product mgr. Carnation Co., Los Angeles, 1985-87; dir. promotion Walt Disney Home Video, Burbank, Calif., 1987-90; dir. film licensing The Walt Disney Co., Burbank, 1990-91; dir. promotion Twentieth Century Fox, Beverly Hills, Calif., 1991-92; v.p. publicity and promotion Twentieth Century Fox Internat., 1993—. Mem. Beta Gamma Sigma. Office: Twentieth Century Fox PO Box 900 Beverly Hills CA 90213-0900

GLEASON, ELISABETH GREGORICH, history educator; b. Belgrade, Yugoslavia, July 8, 1933; d. Danilo and Zora V. Gregorich; m. John Bernard Gleason, Aug. 30, 1954. BA, U. Ill., 1954; MA, Ohio State U., 1956; PhD, U. Calif., Berkeley, 1963. Instr. U. Calif., Berkeley, 1962-63; asst. to assoc. prof. San Francisco State U., 1963-69; assoc. to prof. U. San Francisco, 1969—. Author: Gasparo Contarini: Venice, Rome and Reform, 1993 (H. Marraro prize 1995); assoc. editor: Archive for Reformation History, Valparaiso, Ind., Berlin, 1994—. Bd. dirs. Found. Reformation Rsch., St. Louis, 1985—. Rsch. grantee Gladys K. Delmas Found., N.Y.C., 1980, 92, NEH, Washington, 1980, Am. Philos. Soc., Phila., 1981, others. Mem. Am. Cath. Hist. Assn. (pres. 1994), Am. Hist. Assn., Soc. Reformation Rsch. (pres. 1984-86), Sixteenth Century Studies Conf. (pres. 1990), Renaissance Soc. Am. (coun. mem. 1991-93), Soc. Italian Hist. Soc. (mem. coun. 1996—), Soc. Slovene Studies. Office: U San Francisco Dept History San Francisco CA 94117-1080

GLENN, CONSTANCE WHITE, art museum director, educator, consultant; b. Topeka, Oct. 4, 1933; d. Henry A. and Madeline (Stewart) White;

m. Jack W. Glenn, June 19, 1955; children: Laurie Glenn Buckle, Caroline Glenn Galey, John Christopher. BFA, U. Kans., 1955; postgrad., U. Mo., 1969; MA, Calif. State U., 1974. Dir. Univ. Art Mus. & Mus. Studies program, from lectr. to prof. Calif. State U., Long Beach, 1973—; art cons. Archtl. Digest, L.A., 1980-89. Author: Jim Dine Drawings, 1984, Roy Lichtenstein: Landscape Sketches, 1986, Wayne Thiebaud: Private Drawings, 1988, Robert Motherwell: The Dedalus Sketches, 1988, James Rosenquist: Time Dust: The Complete Graphics 1962-92, 1993, The Great American Pop Art Store: Multiples of the Sixties, 1997; contbg. editor: Antiques and Fine Arts, 1991-92. Vice-chair Adv. Com. for Pub. Art, Long Beach, 1990-95; chair So. Calif. adv. bd. Archives Am. Art, L.A., 1980-90; mem. adv. bd. ART/LA, 1986-94, chair, 1992. Recipient Outstanding Contbn. to Profession award Calif. Mus. Photography, 1986. Mem. Am. Assn. Mus., Assn. Art Mus. Dirs., Coll. Art Assn., Art Table, Long Beach Pub. Corp. for the Arts (arts adminstr. of yr. 1989), Kappa Alpha Theta. Office: Univ Art Mus 1250 N Bellflower Blvd Long Beach CA 90840-0006

GLENN, GUY CHARLES, pathologist; b. Parma, Ohio, May 13, 1930; s. Joseph Frank and Helen (Rupple) G.; m. Lucia Ann Howarth, June 13, 1953; children: Kathryn Holly, Carolyn Helen, Cynthia Marie. BS, Denison U., 1953; MD, U. Cin., 1957. Intern, Walter Reed Army Med. Center, Washington, 1957-58; resident in pathology Fitzsimons Army Med. Center, Denver, 1959-63; commd. 2d lt. U.S. Army, 1956, advanced through grades to col., 1977; demonstrator pathology Royal Army Med. Coll., London, 1970-72; chief dept. pathology Fitzsimons Army Med. Center, Denver, 1972-77; past pres. med. staff St. Vincent Hosp., Billings, Mont.; past mem. governing bd. Mont. Health Systems Agy. Diplomate Am. Bd. Pathology, Am. Bd. Nuclear Medicine. Fellow Coll. Am. Pathologists (chmn. chemistry resources com., chmn. commn. sci. resources, mem. budget program and review com., council on quality assurance, chmn. practice guidelines com., bd. govs., chmn. nominating com.), Am. Soc. Clin. Pathology, Soc. Med. Cons. to Armed Forces (chair emeritus legal and legis. com.), Midland Empire Health Assn. (past pres.), Rotary (bd. dirs. local chpt.). Contbr. to profl. jours. Home: 3225 Jack Burke Ln Billings MT 59106-1113

GLENN, JONATHAN PHILIP, post production producer, editor, consultant; b. Cleve., Nov. 9, 1967; s. Dennis and Eileen H. (Amsterdam) G. BS in Comms., Syracuse U., 1990. Prodn. coord. Dick Clark Prodns., Burbank, Calif., 1990-91; prodn. asst. TV show Anything But Love, Beverly Hills, Calif., 1991-92; asst. to producer Lee Rich Prodns., Burbank, 1992-93; producer, editor Mediaworks, Burbank, 1993—; prodn. cons. in pvt. practice, L.A., 1994—. Office: Mediaworks 4444 Riverside Dr # 300 Burbank CA 91505

GLETNE, JEFFREY SCOTT, forester; b. Mpls., Dec. 10, 1952; s. John Sanford Gletne and Lillian Helen (Berg) Oxford; divorced; 1 child, John Steven Gletne. BS, U. Calif., Berkeley, 1976. Registered profl. forester, Calif. Logger, forester Wickes Forest Industries, Dinuba, Calif., 1975-82; owner Skyline Logging Inc., Dinuba, 1982-89; forester Sierra Forest Products, Terra Bella, Calif., 1989—; mem. Bakersfield (Calif.) Coll. Agrl. Adv. Bd., 1993—; cons. Integrated Forest Mgmt., Springville, Calif., 1994-95. pres. People for the West, Bakersfield, 1994, v.p. People for the West, Porterville, Calif., 1995-96. Mem. Soc. of Am. Foresters (vice-chair, sec.-treas. 1993-94, chmn. 1994-95), Calif. Lic. Foresters Assn., Eagles Lodge. Republican. Home: 10480 Road 261 Terra Bella CA 93270-9727 Office: Sierra Forest Products PO Box 10060 Terra Bella CA 93270

GLEW, ANDREW FORSYTH, computer architect, inventor; b. Monteal, Que., Can., Sept. 10, 1961; came to U.S., 1985; s. Cyril Aubrey and Ruth Jean (Robinson) G. B.Eng., McGill U., 1985; MS, U. Ill., 1991. Programmer Systemes Videotex Formic, St. Laurent, Que., 1985, Gould, Urbana, Ill., 1985-88; performance analyst Motorola, Urbana, 1988-89; computer architect Intel, Hillsboro, Oreg., 1991—; educator U. Wis., Madison, 1996—. Inventor numerous patents in field. Office: Intel Mailstop JF1-19 5200 NE Elam Young Pky Hillsboro OR 97124-6463

GLICK, REUVEN, economist; b. N.Y.C., July 19, 1951; m. Marci Gottlieb, Jan. 6, 1991; 1 child, Marissa Beth. BA, U. Chgo., 1973; MA, Princeton U., 1975, PhD, 1979. Economist Fed. Res. Bank N.Y., N.Y.C., 1977-79; asst. prof. econs. and internat. bus. NYU Grad. Sch. Bus., N.Y.C., 1979-85; economist Fed. Res. Bank San Francisco, 1985-87, sr. economist, 1987-90, rsch. officer, 1990-92, asst. v.p., 1992-95; dir. Ctr. for Pacific Basin Monetary and Econ. Studies, 1992—, v.p., 1995—; vis. assoc. prof. econs. U. Calif., Berkeley, 1989; cons. World Bank, Washington, 1982-85. Contbr. articles to profl. jours. Mem. Am. Econ. Assn., Phi Beta Kappa.

GLICK, SAMUEL DAVID, entertainment and communications executive, shop owner; b. Chgo., Dec. 4, 1951; s. Eugene and Florence G.; m. N. Cheri Pavlov, Sept. 3, 1978; children: Bradley, Jory. BS in Radio and TV Comm., So. Ill. U., 1975. Producer pub. affairs programs WMAQ-TV, Chgo., 1974-76, mgr. on-air promotion, 1976-79; dir. creative svcs. KGW-TV, Portland, Oreg., 1979-82, WNBC-TV, N.Y.C., 1982-84, KTLA-TV, L.A., 1984-85; ptnr. Davis*Glick Prodns., L.A., 1985—; mem. NBC Affiliates Promotion Adv. Com., N.Y.C., 1981-84. Inventor NBC affiliates automated sta. signature sys., 1984. Recipient Silver and Bronze awards N.Y. Internat. Film Festival. Mem. Acad. TV Arts and Scis. (N.Y. local Emmy award), Promotion and Mktg. Execs in the Electronic Media-Promax (Gold Medallion award), Hollywood Radio and TV Soc. (Internat. Broadcasting award). Office: Davis Glick Prodns 3280 Cahuenga Blvd W Los Angeles CA 90068-1378

GLICKMAN, HARRY, professional basketball team executive; b. Portland, Oreg., May 13, 1924; s. Sam and Bessie (Karp) G.; m. Joanne Carol Matin, Sept. 28, 1958; children: Lynn Carol, Marshall Jordan, Jennifer Ann. B.A., U. Oreg., 1948. Press agt., 1948-52; pres. Oreg. Sports Attractions, 1952—; mgr. Multnomah (Oreg.) Civic Stadium, 1958-59; pres. Portland Hockey Club, 1960-73; former exec. v.p. basketball team Portland Trail Blazers, now pres. emeritus. Trustee B'nai B'rith Jr. Camp, 1965; bd. dirs. U. Oreg. Devel. Fund. Served with AUS, 1943-46. Named to Oreg. Sports Hall of Fame, 1986. Mem. Portland C. of C. (bd. dirs. 1968-72), Sigma Delta Chi, Sigma Alpha Mu. Jewish. Office: Portland Trail Blazers 1 Center Ct Ste 200 Portland OR 97227-2103

GLIEGE, JOHN GERHARDT, lawyer; b. Chgo., Aug. 3, 1948; s. Gerhardt John Gliege and Jane Heidke; children: Gerhardt, Stephanie, Kristine. BA, Ariz. State U., 1969, MPA, 1970, JD, 1974. Bar: Ariz. 1974. Pvt. practice Scottsdale, Ariz., 1974-81, Flagstaff, Ariz., 1981-94, Sedona, Ariz., 1994—; prof. paralegal studies No. Ariz. U., Flagstaff, 1981-83, prof. urban planning and cmty. devel., 1984—; prof. paralegal studies Yavapai Cmty. Coll., Prescott, Ariz., 1995—. Mem. Nat. Assn. of Bond Law. Home: PO Box 1388 Flagstaff AZ 86002-1388 Office: 2515 W Hwy Sedona AZ 86336

GLINER, ERAST BORIS, theoretical physicist; b. Kiev, USSR, Feb. 3, 1923; came to U.S., 1980; s. Boris Moses Gliner and Bella Boris (Pauckman) Rubinstein; m. Galina Ilchenko, Dec. 12, 1944; children: Bella, Arkady. MS in Physics, Leningrad U., USSR, 1963; PhD in Physics, Tartu U., Estonia, 1972. Head theoretical dept. Spl. Design Office, Leningrad, 1954-63; sr. scientist A Ioffe Inst. of Soviet Acad. Scis., Leningrad, 1963-80; vis. fellow Inst. Lab. Astrophyiscs U. Colo., Boulder, 1982-83; rsch. assoc. McDonnel Ctr. Space Sci. Washington U., St. Louis, 1983-86; vis. scientist Stanford Linear Acceleration Ctr. Stanford U., Palo Alto, Calif., 1987—. Co-author: Differential Equation of Mathematical Physics (English, Russian, Japanese edits.), 1962; contbr. articles to profl. jours. Polit. prisoner USSR, 1945-54. Sgt. field arty. Soviet Army, 1942-44. Decorated Russian Orders Red Star. Mem. Am. Phys. Soc. Jewish. Office: Stanford U SLAC PO Box 4349 Palo Alto CA 94302-0081

GLINSKY, SIMON, management consultant; b. Atlanta, Sept. 29, 1962; s. Salomon and Rebeca Glinsky. Student, U. Edinburgh, Scotland, 1983; BS in Econs. and Fin. magna cum laude, U. Pa., 1984; MBA, Stanford U., 1989. Bus. planning intern IBM Corp., Atlanta, 1983; rsch. coord. fin. dept. Wharton Sch. U. Pa., Phila., 1983-84; bus. analyst McKinsey & Co., Inc., Atlanta, 1984-87; asst. product mgr. Radius, Inc., San Jose, Calif., 1988; prin. The Glinsky Group, San Francisco, 1990—. Long range planning com. Woodruff Arts Ctr., Atlanta, 1986-87, Alliance Theatre, Atlanta, 1985-86; nursery vol. San Francisco Gen., 1992-94; v.p. STOP AIDS Project, San Francisco, 1993-95. Benjamin Franklin scholar U. Pa.; named one of Outstanding Young Men Am., 1986. Mem. U. Pa. Philomathean Soc. (vice-chmn. 175th anniversary com., moderator 1984, chmn. philomathean endowment trust 1987-94), Commonwealth Club (San Francisco), Sha'ar Zahav Klezmer Band. Jewish. Office: Glinsky Group 4111 18th St Ste 4 San Francisco CA 94114-2407

GLOCK, CHARLES YOUNG, sociologist; b. N.Y.C., Oct. 17, 1919; s. Charles and Philippine (Young) G.; m. Margaret Schleef, Sept. 12, 1950; children: Susan Young, James William. B.S., N.Y. U., 1940; M.B.A., Boston U., 1941; Ph.D., Columbia U., 1952. Research asst. Bur. Applied Social Research, Columbia U., 1946-51, dir., 1951-58, lectr., then prof. sociology, 1956-58; prof. sociology U. Calif. at Berkeley, 1958-79, prof. emeritus, 1979—, chmn., 1967-68, 69-71; dir. Survey Research Center, 1958-67; adj. prof. Grad. Theol. Union, 1971-79; Luther Weigle vis. lectr. Yale U., 1968. Co-author: Wayward Shepherds, The Anatomy of Racial Attitudes, Anti-Semitism in America, American Piety; sr. author: Adolescent Prejudice, To Comfort and To Challenge, Religion and Society in Tension, Christian Beliefs and Anti-Semitism, The Apathetic Majority; contbg. editor Rev. Religious Rsch. Sociological Analysis; editor: The New Religious Consciousness, Survey Research in the Social Sciences, Beyond the Classics, Religion in Sociological Perspective, Prejudice U.S.A., Unison-Newsletter of One Voice, 1990-96; contbr. numerous articles on social scis. Active parish edn. Luth. Ch. Am., 1970-72; mem. mgmt. com. Office Rsch. and Planning, 1973-80; bd. dirs. Pacific Luth. Theol. Sem., 1962-74, 80-86, Inst. Rsch. in Social Behavior, 1962-90, Interplayers, 1990-92, Sandpoint Christian Connection, 1995—; pres. Cornerhouse Fund, 1982-92, One Voice, 1994-95, bd. dirs., 1995—; mem. adv. com. Office Rsch. and Evaluation Evang. Luth. Ch. Am., 1988—; mem. history com. Soc. Study of Religion, 1993-94. Capt. USAAF, 1942-46. Decorated Bronze Star, Legion of Merit; recipient Roots of Freedom award Pacific bd. Anti-Defamation League, 1977; Berkeley citation U. Calif., Berkeley, 1979; Rockefeller fellow, 1941-42; fellow Center Advanced Study Behavioral Scis., 1957-58; fellow Soc. for Religion in Higher Edn., 1968-69. Fellow Soc. Sci. Study Religion (Western rep., pres. 1968-69); mem. Am. Assn. Pub. Opinion Research (v.p., pres. 1962-64, pres. Pacific chpt. 1959-60), Am. Sociol. Assn. (v.p. 1978-79), Religious Research Assn., Sociol. Research Assn. Home: 319 S 4th Ave Sandpoint ID 83864-1219

GLOSS, LAWRENCE ROBERT, fundraising executive; b. Colorado Springs, Colo., Oct. 31, 1948; s. Kenneth Edwin and Clara U. (Haeker) G.; m. Betty Berg, June 4, 1977; children: Alexander Edwin, Carolyn Claire. BA, U. Denver, 1970. Dir. natl. congress on volunteerism and citizenship NCVA, Washington, 1975-76; dir. devel. Vis. Nurses Assn., Washington, 1976-77; devel. cons. Am. Lung Assn., Washington and N.Y.C., 1977-78; exec. dir. Colo. Conservation Fund, Denver, Colo., 1978-79, Rose Med. Ctr., enver, 1985-86; dir. devel. Rose Found., Denver, 1979-86; sr. campaign dir. J. Panas, Young and Ptnrs., San Francisco, 1986-88; pres. Gloss and Assocs., Denver, 1988—; mem. adv. coun. non-profit mgmt. Metro State Coll., Denver, 1994; cons. Native Am. Rights Fund, Boulder, Colo., Arts at the Sta., Denver, 1994, Up With People, 1995, 96, Emily Griffith Ctr. Found., 1995, 96. Guest spkr. Tech. Assistance Ctr., Denver, 1992-94; bd. dirs. Alzeimer's and Related Disorders Assn., Denver, 1985-86; bd. dirs. Woman's Sch. Network, Denver, 1984-85, Colo. PTA, Englewood, 1991-92; active Humane Soc. of Boulder Valley, 1996, Episcopal Ministries of U. Colo., Boulder, 1996, Emergency Family Assistance Assn., Inc., 1996. Mem. NSFRE (Colo. chpt. 1992-94, bd. dirs.), Nat. Assn. of Mus. Exhibitors, Colo. Planning Giving Roundtable, Nat. Com. on Planned Giving, Am. Prospect Rsch. Assn., Assn. of Healthcare Philanthropy (regional XII 1993-94), Rotary Club of Denver. Lutheran. Home: 11126 E Stagecoach Dr Parker CO 80134-8424 Office: Gloss and Company 2755 S Locust St Ste 113 Denver CO 80222-7131

GLOVER, KAREN E., lawyer; b. Nampa, Idaho, Apr. 14, 1950; d. Gordon Ellsworth and Cora (Frazier) G.; m. Thaddas L. Alston, Aug. 17, 1979; children: Samantha Glover Alston, Evan Glover Alston. AB magna cum laude, Whitman Coll., 1972; JD cum laude, Harvard U., 1975. Bar: Wash. 1975, U.S. Dist. Ct. (we. dist.) Wash. 1975. Assoc. Preston, Thorgrimson Ellis & Holman, Seattle, 1975-80; ptnr. Preston Gates & Ellis, Seattle, 1981—. Chmn. bd. dirs. United Way King County, Seattle, 1993-94; chair bd. overseers Whitman Coll., Walla Walla, Wash., 1995—; mem. bd. trustees King County Libr. Sys., Seattle, 1992—. Mem. Wash. State Bar Assn. (corp. and tax sects.), Seattle Pension Roundtable, Columbia Tower Club, Sand Point Country Club, Rainier Club. Episcopalian. Office: Preston Gates & Ellis 701 5th Ave Fl 50 Seattle WA 98104-7016

GLOVER, MARIE ELIZABETH, special education educator, speech pathologist; b. Sacramento, Aug. 19, 1943; d. Melvin Edward and Edith Maria (Brown) Thomas; m. Robert John Glover, May 26, 1967. BA in Speech Pathology, Edn., San Jose State U., 1965; MA in Speech Pathology, Ea. Mich. U., 1980; MS in Spl. Edn., Emporia State U., 1984. Tchr. Calif., N.Y., Wis., Ark., Oreg., Mich., Wash., 1965—; speech pathology cons. Coffey County Hosp., Burlington, Kans., 1983-85. Precinct leader Rep. Party, Ann Arbor, Mich., 1975-80; leader Girl Scouts, London, Ark., 1970-74. Mem. Am. Speech-Lang. Hearing Assn. (cert. speech lang. pathology), Wash. Speech, Hearing and Lang. Assn., Coun. Exceptional Children (state mem.-at-large 1991-94, local pres. 1994-95), Learning Disabilities Assn. (pres. 1989), Internat. Reading Assn., Phi Delta Kappa (v.p. 1990-93). Home: 331 Basalt Springs Way Naches WA 98937-9780

GLOVER, PAULA ELLEN, journalist; b. Greeley, Colo., Apr. 19, 1957; d. Lloyd Ray Stonebraker and Elma Althea (McKenzie) Cropper; m. Jeff Haikara, Mar. 4, 1982 (div.); 1 chld, Karl; m. Frank T. Glover, Aug. 22, 1994; children: Ellen Grisinger, Paul. BS, U. Colo., 1982. Editor Code 109 Denver Police Union, 1982-84; assoc. Stratton, Reiter, Dupree & Durante, Denver, 1984-87; reporter Fairplay, Bailey, Colo., 1990-92, Flume Newspaper, Bailey, Colo., 1990-92; editor Brush (Colo.) News Tribune, 1992-94, Ute Pass Courier, Woodland Park, Colo., 1995-96; owner, editor Mountain Independence, Florissant, Colo., 1996—; mem. faculty Morgan C.C., Ft. Morgan, Colo., 1993-94; mem. adv. bd. UPDATE Drug and Alcohol Task Force, Woodland Park, Colo., 1994. Pub. book: Alternate Guide to Having a Baby, 1986. Bd. dirs. Colo. Holistic Health Network, Denver, 1986-87. Recipient 1st Pl. award for deadline reporting Soc. Profl. Journalists, 1995; Colo. Press Assn. scholar, 1982. Mem. Colo. Press Assn., Soc. Profl. Journalists. Democrat. Roman Catholic. Home: PO Box 499 Divide CO 80814 Office: Mountain Independence Pub Corp PO Box 609 Lake George CO 80827

GLOVSKY, MYRON MICHAEL, medical educator; b. Boston, Aug. 15, 1936; m. Carole Irene Parks; five children. BS magna cum laude, Tufts U., 1957, MD, 1962. Bd. cert. Nat. Bd. Med. Examiners, Am. Bd. Allergy & Immunology, Am. Bd. Diagnostic Lab. Immunology. Intern Balt. (Md.) City Hosp., 1962-63; resident New Eng. Med. Ctr., Boston, 1965-66; spl. NIH fellow allergy and immunology Walter Reed Army Inst. Rsch., Washington, 1966-68; fellow hematology and immunology U. Calif., San Francisco, 1968-69; staff physician dept. internal medicine So. Calif. Permanente Med. Group, L.A., 1969-72, dir. allergy & immunology lab., 1970-84, chief dept. allergy and clin. immunology, co-dir. residency program in allergy & clin. immunology, 1974-84, dir. pheresis unit, 1978-80; dir. L.A. County Gen. Hosp./U. So. Calif. Asthma Clinic; prof. medicine, head allergy and immunology labs. pulmonary divsn., head allergy and clin. immunology divsn. pulmonary medicine. U. So. Calif., Sch. Medicine, 1984-89, prof. pathology, 1986-89; clin. prof. medicine, clin. prof. pathology U. So. Calif., 1989—; dir. asthma and allergy referral ctr. Huntington Meml. Hosp., Pasadena, 1989—; head fellowship and career devel. program Nat. Heart Inst., NIH, Bethesda, Md., 1963-65, fellowship bd. mem., 1964-65; vis. assoc. in chemistry Calif. Inst. Tech., Pasadena, 1977—; acad. assoc. complement and allergy Nichols Inst., San Juan Capistrano, Calif., 1980—, med. dir. immunology, 1980-89; clin. prof. medicine U. Calif., L.A., 1983-84; vis. prof. clin. scholars program Eli Lilly & Co., Indpls., 1988; mem. steering com. Aspen Allergy Conf., 1988—; cons. in field. With USPHS, 1963-65. Fellow Am. Acad. Allergy; mem. AAAS, Am. Assn. Immunologists, Am. Thoracic Soc., Am. Fedn. for Clin. Rsch., Am. Coll. Allergy, Reticuloendothelial Soc., L.A. Soc. Allergy and Clin. Immunology (pres. 1979-80), Collegium Internat. Allergolicum. Home: 1961 Oak St South Pasadena CA 91030-4957 Office: Huntington Meml Hosp Asthma & Allergy Ctr 39 Congress St Pasadena CA 91105-3024

GLOYD, STEPHEN STEWART, physician, educator, health facility administrator; b. Phila., Aug. 29, 1947; s. Park W. Gloyd and Dolores Hope Riddell; m. Tracy Willett, Feb. 1979 (div.); m. Ahoua Roué, June 15, 1990; children: Moussa, Salim. BA, Harvard U., 1969, MPH, 1983; MD, U. Chgo., 1973. Physician Frement Cmty. Clinic, Seattle, 1975-78, Boeing Co., Seattle, 1975-78; dist. med. chief Ministry of Health, Sofala Province, Mozambique, 1979-82; physician Sea-Mar Cmty. Clinic, Seattle, 1983-85, Wash. State Dept. Corrections, Monroe, 1985-86; dir. and assoc. prof. Internat. Health Program U. Wash., Seattle, 1986—; exec. dir. Health Alliance Internat., Seattle, 1987—; mem. governing bd. Nat. Coun. Internat. Health, 1994—. mem. editorial bd. Internat. Jour. Health Svcs., 1989; albums include Kutamba, 1985, Musango, 1992. Leader Seattle Coalition Against Apartheid, 1985-89. Urban Studies fellow Andrew Mellon Found., U. Chgo., 1970-72; Health Policy and Mgmt. fellow W. K. Kellogg Found., Harvard, 1982-83; fellow W. K. Kellogg Found., 1988-91. Office: Univ Wash PO Box 357660 Seattle WA 98195

GLUCKMAN, DALE CAROLYN, art museum curator; b. Detroit, Mar. 25, 1944; d. Sam and Gertrude (Wechsler) Schwartz; m. Jonathan Samuel Gluckman, Dec. 4, 1966. BA cum laude, UCLA, 1967, MA, 1986. Owner Double Happiness, L.A., 1971-76; cons. Fowler Mus. Cultural History, UCLA, 1977-78; lectr. UCLA, 1977, 87-88; advisor Am. Friends Svc. Com. Women-in-Africa Program, Bamako, Mali, 1979-81; rschr., cataloguer L.A. County Mus. Art, 1982-84, asst. curator, 1984-88, assoc. curator, 1988—, acting dept. head, 1993—; mem. adv. bd. dept. home econs., fashion design and merchandising program Calif. State U., Northridge, 1986-88; juror Calif. Fiber Artists, San Diego, 1993-94. Co-author: When Art Became Fashion: Kosode In Edo-Period Japan, 1991 (Millia Davenport award 1993), Inquest of Themes and Skills - Asian Textiles, 1989; co-curator: (exhbn.) When Art Became Fashion: Kosode in Edo-Period Japan, 1992 (Am. Assn. Museums curator's com. award 1993). Founding bd. mem. L.A.-Jakarta Sister City, L.A., 1990—. Implementation grantee Nat. Endowment Arts, Washington, 1989, profl. exch. grantee Asian Cultural Coun., N.Y., 1992, Curatorial Rsch. grantee Andrew W. Mellon Found., 1992. Mem. Costume Soc. Am. (regional bd. 1989-92), Textile Soc. Am. (founding bd. mem., membership sec. 1993-96), Centre Internat D'Etude des Textiles Anciens, Assn. Asian Studies, Coll. Art Assn., Am. Assn. Museums, Internat. Com. on Museums. Office: LA County Mus Art 5905 Wilshire Blvd Los Angeles CA 90036-4523

GLUECK, MARY A., psychiatric and mental health nurse, administrator; b. Bridgetown, Barbados; came to U.S., 1952; d. Hubert and Christina Cumming; m. Stephen G. Glueck (dec.). Grad. sch. nursing, St. Joseph's Mercy Hosp., Georgetown, Guyana. RN, Calif. Clin. svcs. mgr. med.-surg., geropsychiat. rehab. Crystal Springs Rehab. div. San Mateo County Gen. Hosp., San Mateo, Calif. Mem. Mid. Mgrs. Assn., Am. Psychiat. Nurses Assn. Home: 4505 Sandra Ct Union City CA 94587-4853

GLYER, DIANA PAVLAC, English language educator; b. Aberdeen, Md., Jan. 21, 1956; d. James and Christel (Reichelt) Sainsbury. BA, BS, Bowling Green State U., 1978; MS in Edn., No. Ill. U., 1981; PhD in English, U. Ill., Chgo., 1992. Tchr. English and art Valley Luth. High Sch., St. Charles, Ill., 1978-82; dir. skills devel. North Park Coll., Chgo., 1984-88, adj. instr. English, 1988-91; asst. prof. English, Coll. of Ozarks, Point Lookout, Mo., 1991-95; asst. prof. English Azusa (Calif.) Pacific U., 1995—. Mem. MLA, Nat. Coun. Tchrs. English, Internat. Assn. on Fantastic in Arts, Mythopoeic Soc. (bd. dirs. 1985—, pub. rels. com. 1990—). Home: PO Box 1056 Sierra Madre CA 91025-4056 Office: Dept English 901 E Alosta Ave Azusa CA 91702

GLYNN, JAMES A., sociology educator, author; b. Bklyn., Sept. 10, 1941; s. James A. and Muriel M. (Lewis) G.; m. Marie J. Gates, Dec. 17, 1966 (div. Apr. 1995); 1 child, David S. AA, Foothill Coll., 1961; BA in Sociology, San Jose (Calif.) State U., 1964, MA in Sociology, 1966. Instr. in sociology Bakersfield (Calif.) Coll., 1966—, prof. sociology, 1972—; adj. prof. Fresno (Calif.) State U., 1971-72, Chapman Coll., Orange, Calif., 1972, Calif. State U., Bakersfield, 1989—, Chapman U., Visalia, Calif., 1997—; del. acad. senate Calif. C.C., Sacramento, 1980-89; councilmember Faculty Assn. Calif. C.Cs., 1981—. Author: Studying Sociology, 1979, Writing Across the Curriculum Using Sociological Concepts, 1983, Hands On: User's Manual for Data Processing, 1986; (with Elbert W. Stewart) Introduction to Sociology, 1972, 4th edit., 1985; (with Crystal Dea Moore) Guide to Social Psychology, 1992, Understanding Racial and Ethnic Groups, 1992, Guide to Human Services, 1994, Focus on Sociology, 1994; (with Charles F. Hohm and Elbert W. Stewart) Global Social Problems, 1996; contbg. editor Introduction to Sociology, 1996; contbg. author: California's Social Problems, 1997. Recipient Innovator Yr. award League Innovations C.C., 1989, Innovator Yr. award Kern C.C. Dist., 1992. Mem. Am. Sociol. Assn., Calif. Sociol. Assn. (founder, treas. 1990-92, editor newsletter 1991-92, pres. 1992-93, exec. dir. 1993—), Commn. on Tchg., Pacific Sociol. Assn. (mem. editl. bd. Sociol. Perspectives 1996—, Disting. Prof. award for Contbn. to Edn. 1997), Population Reference Bur., World Watch Inst., World Future Soc. Democrat. Home: 4512 Panorama Dr Bakersfield CA 93306-1354 Office: Bakersfield Coll 1801 Panorama Dr Bakersfield CA 93305-1299

GOATES, DELBERT TOLTON, child psychiatrist; b. Logan, Utah, Apr. 14, 1932; s. Wallace Albert and Roma (Tolton) G.; m. Claudia Tidwell, Sept. 15, 1960 (div. Apr. 1994); children: Jeanette, Byron, Rebecca Lynn, Alan, Paul, Jonathan Phillip, Kendra, Michelle, George Milton; m. Julie Anderson Headley, Dec. 29, 1994. BS, U. Utah, 1953, MD, 1962; postgrad., U. Nebr., 1965, 67. Intern Rochester (N.Y.) Gen. Hosp., 1962-63; resident Nebr. Psychiat. Inst., Omaha, 1963-67; pvt. practice medicine specializing in child psychiatry Omaha, 1963-67, Albuquerque, 1967-71, Salt Lake City, 1971—; dir. psychiatry Riverdell Psychiat. Ctr., 1986-92, staff psychiatrist, 1992—; asst. prof. child psychiatry U. N.Mex., 1967-71, dir. children's svcs., 1967-71, asst. prof. pediatrics, 1969-71; clin. dir. Children's Psychiat. Ctr., Primary Children's Med. Ctr., Salt Lake City, 1971-77; med. dir. Life Line, 1990-93, Brightway Adolescent Psychiat. Hosp., 1992—; pres. Magic Mini Maker, Inc., Salt Lake City, 1972-78; chmn. bd. Intermountain Polytex, Inc. Bishop Ch. Jesus Christ Latter-day Sts., 1968-71; bd. dirs. Utah Cancer Soc., Great Salt Lake Mental Health. Served with MC, AUS, 1953-55. Mem. AMA, Orthopsychiat. Assn. Am., Utah Psychiat. Assn., Intermountain Acad. Child Psychiatry (pres. 1974-76), Pi Kappa Alpha, Phi Kappa Phi. Home: 4187 Abinadi Rd Salt Lake City UT 84124-4001 Office: 2738 S 2000 E Salt Lake City UT 84109

GOBALET, JEANNE GALLATIN, demographer; b. San Francisco, June 18, 1944; d. Kenneth Clyde and Eloise Carmelita (Gallatin) G.; m. Garth Lawrence Norton, Jan. 21, 1983; 1 child, Robert Gobalet Norton. AB in Sociology/History with distinction, Stanford U., 1966, MA in Edn., 1967, MA in Sociology, 1976, PhD in Sociology, 1982. Instr. social sci. San Jose (Calif.)/Evergreen C.C. Dist., 1967—; prin. Lapkoff & Gobalet Demographic Rsch. Inc., Saratoga, Calif., 1992—; geographic info. systems cons., 1990—, demography cons., 1989—. Contbr. articles to profl. jours. Mem. accreditation teams Accrediting Commn. for Cmty. and Jr. Colls., 1993—. Mem. Population Assn. Am., Am. Sociol. Assn., Soc. for Applied Sociology, Toastmasters Internat., Phi Beta Kappa.

GOBAR, ALFRED JULIAN, economic consultant, educator; b. Lucerne Valley, Calif., July 12, 1932; s. Julian Smith and Hilda (Millbank) G.; B.A. in Econs., Whittier Coll., 1953, M.A. in History, 1955; postgrad. Claremont Grad. Sch., 1953-54; Ph.D. in Econs., U. So. Calif., 1963; m. Sally Ann Randall, June 17, 1957; children—Wendy Lee, Curtis Julian, Joseph Julian. Asst. pres. Microdot Inc., Pasadena, 1953-57; regional sales mgr. Sutorbilt Corp., L.A., 1957-59; market research assoc. Beckman Instrument Inc., Fullerton, 1959-64; sr. marketing cons. Western Mgmt. Consultants Inc., Phoenix, L.A., 1964-66; ptnr., prin., chmn. bd. Darley/Gobar Assocs., Inc., 1966-73; pres., chmn. bd. Alfred Gobar Assocs., Inc., Placentia, Calif., 1973—; asst. prof. finance U. So. Calif., L.A., 1963-64; assoc. prof. bus. Calif. State U., L.A., 1963-68, 70-79, assoc. prof. Calif. State U.-Fullerton, 1968-69; mktg., fin. adviser 1957—; bd. dirs. Quaker City Bancorp, Inc., So. Calif. Housing Devel.; pub. speaker seminars and convs. Contbr. articles to profl. publs. Trustee Whittier Coll., 1992—. Home: 1100 W Valencia Mesa Dr Fullerton CA 92833-2219 Office: 721 W Kimberly Ave Placentia CA

92870-6343 *I try not to be too quick to cast aside the social protocal that has taken centuries to evolve and test in order to define effective behavior.*

GOCHNOUR, NATALIE, economist. BS in Econs., U. Utah, 1984, MS in Econs., 1988. Rsch. analyst Gov.'s Office Planning and Budget, Salt Lake City, 1985-92, dir. demographic and econ. analysis, 1992—. Bd. dirs. Utahns Against Hunger, Sale Lake City; v.p. Wasatch Front Econ. Forum. Office: Governors Office Planning and Budget 116 State Capitol Salt Lake City UT 84107

GODAGER, JANE ANN, social worker; b. Blue River, Wis., Nov. 29, 1943; d. Roy and Elmyra Marie (Hood) G. BA, U. Wis., 1965; MSW, Fla. State U., 1969. Lic. clin. social worker. Social worker III State of Wis. Dept Corrections, Wales, 1965-71; supervising psychiat. social worker I State of Calif., San Bernardino, 1972-75, La Mesa, 1975-77; psychiat. social worker State of Calif., San Bernardino, 1978-85; supr. mental health services Riverside (Calif.) County Dept. Mental Health, 1985-86; mental health counselor Superior Ct. San Bernardino County, 1986—; mem. adv. bd. Grad. Sch. Social Work Calif. State U., San Bernardino, Mental Health Assn. Mem. Nat. Assn. Social Workers, Acad. Cert. Social Workers (diplomate), Kappa Kappa Gamma Alumnae Assn. Office: Office Mental Health Counselor 700 E Gilbert St Bldg 1 San Bernardino CA 92404-5413

GODDARD, JAMES RUSSELL, producer, writer, actor; b. Anaheim, Calif., May 8, 1955; s. Russell Nathaniel and Marilyn (Carson) G.; m. Laurie Lynn Ragsdale, June 5, 1982; children: Aaron Russell, Joshua James, Nathaniel Carson. AA, Cypress Coll., 1976; student, Calif. State U., Fullerton, 1976-77. Prodr., writer Creation Artists, Anaheim, 1976—, R & R Prodns., Chatsworth, Calif., 1990—; cons. Creation Theatrical Co., Anaheim, 1976-80, Actors Promotional Svcs., Hollywood, Calif., 1989—, R & R Prodns., 1990—; stage mgr. Super Bowl Half-Time Show, Encore! Three Tenors, 1993-94, Three Tenors Concert, L.A., 1994. Author: (screenplays) Son of the Morning, 1988, Wait In Silence, 1990, Jack and Charmian London, 1994; (pub. svc. announcement) Recycling Kids, 1990; appeared in 96 TV and film prodns., 1977—; various positions in over 500 profl. entertainment prodns., 1976—. Leader Boy Scouts Am., Anaheim, 1970-74, asst. scoutmaster, Norco, Calif.; crisis counselor Melodyland Hotline Ctr., Anaheim, 1976-80; mgr. Little League Baseball, various locations. Co-recipient Disneyland Cmty. Svc. award Disneyland, 1976-78; recipient Walter Knott Americanism award Walter Knott Assn. Mem. SAG (mem. ethics com. 1992), Nat. Forensics League, Nat. Thesbians Soc. Republican.

GODFREY, ALDEN NEWELL, communications educator; b. Quincy, Mass., Jan. 8, 1924; s. Edgar and Lela Winifred (Smith) G.; m. Ruth Mildred Mix, July 20, 1949 (div. Sept. 1968); children: Craig Alden, Brian Kent; m. Elvena Marie Ulrich, July 20, 1972. BA, Boston U., 1950; MA, U. Minn., 1951; D Divinity, Missionary of New Truth, Chgo., 1971. Info. officer U.S. Dept. of State, Manila, 1951-55; exec. various newspapers, Boston, Wilmington, N.C. and San Diego, 1955-68; exec. dir. United Way of Desert, Palm Springs, Calif., 1968-73, Combined Arts and Edn. Coun., San Diego, 1973-75, Inland Empire Cultural Found., Colton, Calif., 1975-79; v.p. Campaign Mgmt., Ltd., Palm Springs, Calif., 1979-83, pres., 1983-85; adj. prof. Coll. of Desert, Palm Desert, Calif., 1991—. Pres. Alliance of Calif. Arts Couns., San Francisco, 1975-77, San Diego chpt. Pub. Rels. Soc. Am., 1965-66, San Diego Press Club, 1966-67; v.p. Calif. Confedn. of Arts, L.A., 1978-79; campaign mgr. Maryanov for Mayor, Palm Springs, 1993; chmn. Wilson for Supr., Palm Springs, 1995, Mayor's H.O.S.T. Com., San Diego, 1968; mem. Atty. Gen. Adv. Coun., Sacramento, 1964-68. 1st lt. U.S. Army, 1942-46. Mem. Soc. Profl. Journalists, United Way Exec. Assn., Coll. of Desert Adj. Assn., Kiwanis, Press Club of Desert (treas.). Home: 476 N Calle Rolph Palm Springs CA 92262 Office: Coll of the Desert 43-500 Monterey Ave Palm Desert CA 92260

GODFREY, DOUGLAS, tribologist, consultant; b. Magrath, Alberta, Can., July 12, 1918; came to U.S., 1937; s. Melvin and Eva (Jones) G.; m. Yolanda Babinsky, Jan. 1, 1947; children: Yolanda Plaza, Marsha Dees. BSChemE, U. Utah, 1942. Rsch. scientist NACA (now NASA), Cleve., 1944-55; sr. rsch. engr. Chevron Rsch. Co., Richmond, Calif., 1955-83; cons. Wear Analysis, San Rafael, Calif., 1983—; adj. prof. San Francisco State U., 1983-94; rsch. assoc. Herguth Labs., Vallejo, Calif. Contbr. articles to profl. jours. (3 awards). Pvt. USAF, 1942-43. Fellow Soc. Tribologists and Lubrication Engrs. (life, bd. dirs. 1956-58); mem. ASME. Home and Office: 144 Center St San Rafael CA 94901-1718

GODFREY, PATRICK LEWIS, state government official; b. L.A., Nov. 23, 1942; s. Lew Burl and Lois Jean (Lee) Hodges; m. Margie sue Gray, Oct. 1962 (div. 1963); m. Linda Lee Reed, June 1966 (div. 1978); m. Margery May Southworth, Feb. 18, 1979; children: Tracey, Lee Margaret, John Reed, Patrick Jr. Student, El Camino Coll., Lawndale, Calif., 1960-62, Harbor Coll., San Pedro, Calif., 1963-64, Orange Coast Coll., Costa Mesa, Calif., 1965-66. Cert. med. soc. exec., AMA. Asst. exec. dir. Hawaii Med. Soc., Honolulu, 1966-69; pub. affairs mgr. Nat. Assn. Mfrs., L.A., 1969-75, dir. pub. affairs, 1977-79; regional mgr. Nat. Assn. Mfrs., Tacoma, Wash., 1979-80; assoc. George Young & Assocs., L.A., 1975-76; pres. Target Comm., Federal Way, Wash., 1980-82; sr. staff coord. Wash. State Senate, Olympia, 1982—; cons. in pub. affairs program design and implementation to Fortune 1000 cos., polit. actions coms. include Bus.-Industry Polit. Action Com., AMA Polit. Action Com., Polit. Interest Com., The Dillingham Corp. Polit. Action Com., Calif. Congl. Targeting Com., United for Wash., others. Mgr. former Hawaii Gov. William Quinn senatorial race, 1976, Calif. Congl. Targeting Com., 1974; mem. task force Calif. Roundtable; mem. Rep. Nat. Com., U. So. Calif. Ctr. for Study of Pvt. Enterprise. With USAR, 1963-68. Mem. Am. Assn. Med. Soc. Execs., Nat. Rep. Legislator's assn., L.A. Pub. Affairs Officer's assn., San Francisco Pub. Affairs assn., Future Bus. Leaders of Am. Republican. Office: Wash State Senate 206 Institutional Blvd Olympia WA 98504

GODFREY, RICHARD GEORGE, real estate appraiser; b. Sharon, Pa., Dec. 18, 1927; s. Fay Morris and Elisabeth Marguerite (Stefanak) G.; m. Golda Fay Goss, Oct. 28, 1951; children: Deborah Jayne, Gayle Rogers, Bryan Edward. BA, Ripon Coll., 1949. V.p. 1st Thrift & Loan Assn., Albuquerque, 1959-61; pres. Richard G. Godfrey & Assocs., Inc., Albuquerque, 1961-93, owner, 1993—. Mem. Appraisal Inst. (v.p. 1981-82), Counselors of Real Estate. Baptist. Home: 1700 Columbia Dr SE Albuquerque NM 87106-3311 Office: 523 Louisiana Blvd SE Albuquerque NM 87108-3842

GODWIN, MARY JO, editor, librarian consultant; b. Tarboro, N.C., Jan. 31, 1949; d. Herman Esthol and Mamie Winifred (Felton) Pittman; m. Charles Benjamin Godwin, May 2, 1970. BA, N.C. Wesleyan Coll., 1971; MLS, East Carolina U., 1973. Cert. libr., N.C. From libr. asst. to asst. dir. Edgecombe County Meml. Library, Tarboro, 1970-76, dir., 1977-85; asst. editor Wilson Library Bull., Bronx, N.Y., 1985-89, editor, 1989-92; dir. govt. sales The Oryx Press, Phoenix, 1993-95, dir. mktg. svc., 1995-96, dir. mktg., sales and promotional svcs., 1996—; mem. White House Conf. on Librs. and Info. Svcs. Task Force; bd. dirs. Libr. Pub. Rels. Coun., 1992-95. Bd. dirs. Friends of Calvert County Pub. Libr., 1994, Osborn Sch. Dist. Found.; mem. Ariz. Ctr. for the Book. Recipient Robert Downs award for intellectual freedom U. Ill. Grad. Sch. of Libr. Sci., 1992. Mem. ALA (3M/Jr. Mem. Roundtable Profl. Devel. award 1981), N.C. Libr. Assn. (sec. 1981-83), Info. Futures Inst., Ind. Librs. Exchange Roundtable (v.p., pres. elect 1994, pres. 1995-96). Democrat. Episcopalian. Office: The Oryx Press 4041 N Central Ave Ste 700 Phoenix AZ 85012-3307

GODZIK, CATHLEEN A., orthopaedic surgeon, hand surgeon, educator; b. Mass., Apr. 4, 1954; d. Francis John and Jeannette Barbara Godzik. BA in Biology cum laude, Coll. of Holy Cross, 1976; MD, N.Y. Med. Coll., 1981. Diplomate Am. Bd. Orthopaedic Surgery, Am. Bd. Surgery of Hand; qualified med. evaluator, Calif.; cert. added qualification surgery of hand. Fellow in immunology Rockefeller U., N.Y.C., 1976-77; intern Brown U. Sch. Medicine, Providence, 1981-82, resident in gen. surgery, 1982-83; resident in orthopaedic surgery U. Conn. Sch. Medicine, Hartford, 1983-86; Joseph Boyes fellow in hand surgery U. So. Calif., L.A., 1986-87, clin. assoc. prof.; chief hand svc. Orthopaedic Hosp., L.A., 1988—; dir. Inst. Hand and Upper Extremity Surgery, L.A., 1993—; dir. internat. vol. children's program, Calexico, Calif. and Mexicali, Mex., 1988—. Contbr. articles to med. jours. Chmn. support group for congenital upper extremity anomalies Children's Hosp. LA. Mem. Am. Acad. Orthopaedic Surgeons, Am. Soc. for Surgery of Hand, Western Orthopaedic Assn., Calif. Orthopaedic Assn., AO Alumni Assn., Phi Beta Kappa, Delta Sigma Mu. Republican. Office: Inst Hand and Upper Extremity Surgery 2300 S Hope St Ste 200 Los Angeles CA 90007-2674

GOEHRING, KENNETH, artist; b. Evansville, Wis., Jan. 8, 1919; s. Walter A. and Ruth I. (Rossman) G.; m. Margretta M. MacNicol, Dec. 1, 1945. Student, Cass Tech. Inst., 1933-35, Meinzinger Sch. Applied Art, 1945-46, Colorado Springs Fine Arts Ctr., 1947-50. Works have appeared in over 100 exhibitions in 17 states and 20 museums; 17 one-man shows; exhibitor, Terry Inst., Miami, Symphony Hall, Boston, de Cordova Mus., Fitchburg Mus., Mass., Farnsworth Mus., Maine, Corcoran, Washington, Joslyn Meml. Mus., Nebr., Detroit Inst. Arts, Nebr. Galleries, Stanford U. Galleries, Calif, De Young Mus., San Francisco, Denver Art Mus., Okla. Art Ctr., La Jolla Art Ctr., Calif., others; represented in permanent collections, Sheldon Art Ctr., Lincoln, Nebr., Colorado Springs Fine Arts Ctr., Foothills Gallery, Golden Colo., Canon City Fine Arts Ctr., Colo., Washburn U. Gallery, Wichita, Kans., Swedish Consulate, Washington, El Pomar Found., Colo. Springs, in many pvt. collections throughout U.S. Purchase awards include Colorado Springs Fine Arts Ctr., 1958; Washburn U., 1957; Am. Acad. Design, 1977. Address: 2017 W Platte Ave Colorado Springs CO 80904-3429

GOEI, BERNARD THWAN-POO (BERT GOEI), architectural and engineering firm executive; b. Semarang, Indonesia, Jan. 27, 1938; came to U.S., 1969; naturalized, 1976; s. Ignatius Ing-Khien Goei and Nicolette Giok-Nio Tjioe; m. Sioe-Tien Liem, May 26, 1966; children: Kimberley Hendrika, Gregory Fitzgerald. BA in Fine Arts, Bandung Inst. Tech. State U. Indonesia, 1961, MA in Archtl. Space Planning, 1964; postgrad., U. Heidelberg, Germany, 1967-68. Co-owner, chief designer Pondok Mungil Interiors Inc., Bandung, 1962-64; dept. mgr., fin. advisor Gumarna Architects, Engrs. and Planners, Inc., Bandung, Jakarta, Indonesia, 1964-67; shop supr., model maker Davan Scale Models, Toronto, Ont., Can., 1968-69; chief archtl. designer George T. Nowak Architects and Assocs., Westchester, Calif., 1969-72; sr. archtl. designer Krisel & Shapiro Architects and Assocs., L.A., 1972-74; sr. supervising archtl. designer The Ralph M. Parsons A/E Co. (now Parsons Infrastructure and Tech. Group Inc.), Pasadena, Calif., 1974—; v.p. United Gruno U.S.A. Corp. Import/Export, Monterey Park, Calif., 1980-89. Mem. Rep. Presdl. Task Force, Washington, 1982—, Nat. Rep. Senatorial Com., Washington, 1983—, Nat. Rep. Congrl. Com., Washington, 1981—, Rep. Nat. Com., Washington, 1982—; active Am. Indonesian Cath. Soc. Recipient Excellent Design Achievement commendation Magneto-Hydro-Dynamics Program, 1976, Strategic Def. Initiative "Star Wars" Program, 1988, USAF Space Shuttle Program, West Coast Space-Port, 1984; scholar U. Heidelberg, 1967-68. Mem. NRA, Am. Air Gunner Assn., Tech. Comm. Soc., Indonesian Am. Soc., Dutch Am. Soc., Second Amendment Found., The Right to Keep and Bear Arms Com. Republican. Roman Catholic. Home: 154 Ladera St Monterey Park CA 91754-2125 Office: Parsons Infrastructure & Tech Group Inc 100 W Walnut St Pasadena CA 91124-0001

GOELTZ, THOMAS A., lawyer. BA in Econs. summa cum laude, DePauw U., 1969; JD magna cum laude, Mich. U., 1973. Assoc. Riddell, Williams, Ivie, Bullitt & Walkinshaw, Seattle, 1973-75; dep. prosecuting atty. civil divsn. King County Prosecuting Atty.'s Office, Seattle, 1976-79; prin. Cohen, Keegan & Goeltz, Seattle, 1979-86; ptnr. Davis Wright Tremaine, Seattle, 1986—; cons. state and local govt. agencies on environ. land use issues; adv. shoreline mgmt. City of Seattle; part-time lectr. Law Sch. U. Wash., Seattle, 1976-79. Editor Mich. Law Rev. Active Gov. Task Force on Regulatory Reform, 1993-95. Mem. ABA (urban, state & local govt. law sect.), Wash. State Bar Assn. (real property sect., past chair land use and environ. law sect.), Seattle-King County Bar Assn., Am. Coll. Real Estate Lawyers, Nat. Assn. Indsl. and Office Park, ICSC, Order of Coif. Office: Davis Wright Tremaine 2600 Century Sq 1501 4th Ave Seattle WA 98101-1662

GOERINGER, KABRENA EILEEN, chemist; b. Fairfield, Calif., Jan. 24, 1970; d. Thomas C. and Lynn E. (Fisher) Rodda; m. Scott D. Goeringer, Jan. 29, 1993. BS in Chemistry, USAF Acad., 1992; MS in Project and Sys. Mgmt., Golden Gate U., 1995; MS in Analytical Chemistry, U. Wash., 1996. Commd. capt. USAF, 1996; chief nuclear sys. tech., tech. ops. divsn. USAF, McClellan AFB, Calif., 1992-93, chief chem. analysis br., 1993-95; rsch. asst. Wash. State Toxicology Lab., 1995-96; chemistry instr. USAF Acad., USAF Academy, Colo., 1996—. Choir mem., mus. accompanist Christ Episcopal Ch., Seattle, 1995-96; vol. SAFE Halloween Coords., Rancho Cordova, Calif., 1994. Recipient Leadership award Nat. U., Sacramento, 1993, 94. Mem. Am. Chem. Soc. (accredited chemistry degree), Assn. Women in Sci., Soc. Forensic Toxicologists (assoc.), USAF Acad. Co. Grade Officer's Coun. Republican. Episcopalian.

GOETTSCHE, DENISE STALLINGS, physician; b. Walnut Creek, Calif., Aug. 19, 1961; d. Dale Grow and Reane (Hunter) Stallings; m. Jeffrey Lynn Goettsche, July 26, 1986; children, Shannon Renae, Jessica Noel. BS, Brigham Young U., 1984; DO, Coll. Osteo. Medicine Pacific, Pomona, Calif., 1989. Diplomate Am. Bd. Family Practice. Intern San Bernardino County Med. Ctr., 1989-90, resident, 1990-92; physician Yorba Park Med. Group, Orange, Calif., 1992—. Ch. music singing instr. children LDS Ch., Anaheim, Calif., 1994. Mem. Calif. Med. Assn., Orange County Med. Assn. Republican. Office: Yorba Park Med Group 2501 E Chapman Ave Orange CA 92869-3223

GOETZ, GEORGE DAVID, small business owner; b. Reedley, Calif., Aug. 17, 1936; s. David Henry and Anna Henry (Harder) G.; m. Virginia Kay Croissant, July 23, 1957; children: Perry George, Robyn M. Bettger Goetz. Student, Immanuel Acad., Reedley, Calif. Salesperson Gold Seal Co., Bismarck, N.D., 1965-70; sales mgr. K-H Supply Co., Mountain View, Calif., 1971-73, gen. mgr., 1976-78; dist. mgr. no. Calif. Multi-Clean Products, 1974-76; co-owner Trend Bldg. Svcs., San Jose, Calif., 1979-89; owner/pres. Trend Bldg. Svcs., San Jose, 1989—, maintenance cons., 1995—; owner, pres., CEO Papa's Inc., 1995—. Inventor various recipes. Republican. Home: 877 Hummingbird Dr San Jose CA 95125-2919 Office: Papa's Inc and Trend Bldg Svcs 2100 Curtner Ave San Jose CA 95124-1300

GOETZEL, CLAUS GUENTER, metallurgical engineer; b. Berlin, July 14, 1913; came to U.S., 1936; s. Walter and Else (Baum) G.; m. Lilo Kallmann, Nov. 19, 1938; children: Rodney G., Vivian L. Dipl.-Ing., Technische Hochschule, Berlin, 1935; PhD, Columbia U., 1939. Registered profl. engr., Calif. Research chemist, lab. head Hardy Metall. Co., 1936-39; tech. dir., works mgr. Am. Electro Metal Corp., 1939-47; v.p., dir. research Sintercast Corp. Am., 1947-57; adj. prof. NYU, N.Y.C., 1945-57, sr. research scientist, 1957-60; cons. scientist Lockheed Missiles & Space Co., Sunnyvale, Calif., 1960-78; cons. metall. engring. Portola Valley, Calif., 1978—; lectr., vis. scholar Stanford (Calif.) U., 1961-88; vis. prof. Tech. Univ. Karlsruhe, Germany, 1978-80. Author: Treatise on Powder Metallurgy, 5 vols., 1949-63; co-author: (with Lilo Goetzel) Dictionary of Materials and Process Engineering, vol. 1 English-German, 1995, vol. 2, German-English, 1997; contbr. articles to profl. jours. Recipient Alexander von Humboldt Sr. U.S. Scientist award, Fed. Republic Germany, 1978. Fellow AIAA (assoc.), Am. Soc. Metals Internat.; mem. AIME (life), Am. Powder Metallurgy Inst. (sr.), Materials Sci. Club N.Y. (life, past pres.), Inst. Materials (life, London).

GOETZL, THOMAS MAXWELL, law educator, consultant; b. Chgo., May 31, 1943. AB, U. Calif., Berkeley, 1965, JD, 1969. Bar: Calif. 1970. Prof. law Golden Gate U., Sch. Law, San Francisco, 1972—. Bd. dirs. Calif. Lawyers for Arts, 1979—. Office: Golden Gate U Sch Law 536 Mission St San Francisco CA 94105-2921

GOFFE, RANDAL ANTONIO, administrator; b. Kingston, Jamaica, Sept. 19, 1951; s. Henry Samuel and Joyce Antoinette (Scotland) G.; m. Thelma Marian, July 29, 1979; children: Adeelia Suzette, Andrae Devaughn. BS, U. London, 1974; MS, The City U., London, 1975; PhD, The City U. London, 1978. Postdoctoral fellow dept. chem. engring. Stanford (Calif.) U., 1978-79; assoc. fellow, mgr. Monsanto Co., St. Louis; sr. rsch. specialist Monsanto Co.; mgr., indsl. biol. separations Sepracor Inc., Marlborough, Mass.; co-founder Rainbow Media Ptnrship., CTMS mag., Buyers Guide Publishers; co-founder, dir. product devel. CellPro, Inc.; chief tech. officer Unisys Techs., Inc.; co-founder, pres. Genespan Corp.; affiliate prof. dept. chem. engring. U. Wash. Contbr. articles to profl. jours.; patentee in field. Recipient Kirkpatrick Engring. Achievement award, E. deBarry Barnett Meml. Trust in Chemistry, 1977. Fellow Royal Inst. Pub. Health and Hygiene, Royal Soc. Chemistry, Am. Inst. of Chemistry, AICHE, Electochem. Soc.

GOFMAN, JOHN DAVID, physician, ophthalmologist; b. San Francisco, May 28, 1947; s. John William and Helen (Fahl) G.; m. Betty S. Lawrence, Sept. 5, 1993. BA, U. Calif., Berkeley, 1969; MD, Stanford U., 1974. Intern in internal medicine U. Wash., Seattle, 1974-75, resident in ophthalmology, 1976-79; dept. chief ophthalmology U.S. Pub. Health Hosp., Seattle, 1979-81, Pacific Med. Ctr., Seattle, 1981-89; assoc. clin. prof. ophthalmology U. Wash., Seattle, 1979—; ptnr. Eye Clinic of Bellevue, Wash., 1989—. Recipient Alumni scholarship award Stanford U., 1979. Fellow Am. Acad. Ophthalmology; mem. Phi Beta Kappa. Office: Eye Clinic of Bellevue 1300 116th Ave NE Bellevue WA 98004-3828

GOFORTH, NATHAN DAN, police officer; b. Phoenix, Sept. 12, 1951; s. Nathan and Mabel Lettie (Deal) G.; m. Lori Ann Petersen (div. 1984). AA in Bus. Adminstrn., Glendale Community Coll., Ariz., 1974, AA in Adminstrn. Justice, 1976; BS in Pub. Programs, Ariz. State U., 1985. Second asst. mgr. Smittys Big Town, Phoenix, 1967-73, sales rep., 1975-76; sr. inventory auditor Motorola Semiconductor, Phoenix, 1973-74; police officer City Glendale, Ariz., 1976—; Interpreter for deaf Glendale Police Dept., 1976—, peer counselor, 1989—, field tng. officer, 1980—; vol. tchr. Glendale Community Coll. Police Res. Acad., 1989-94. Res. hwy. patrolman Ariz. Dept. Pub. Safety, Phoenix, 1975-76; advisor Glendale Explorer Post 469, 1978—, instl. head, 1992; bd. dirs. Theater Works, 1994—, v.p., 1995—. Recipient Dedication to DAV award, 1990-91, Cert. of Appreciation award Independence High Sch., 1990, Outstanding Vol. Svc. award MADD, 1991. Mem. NRA, Ariz. State U. Alumni Assn., Internat. Police Assn., Frat. order of Police (treas. 1990-94, v.p. 1994-95, trustee 1995—), Ariz. Cts. Assn., Critical Incident Stress Debriefing (S.W. region), Sons of Am. Legion. Office: Glendale Police Dept 6835 N 57th Dr Glendale AZ 85301-3218

GOGERTY, DAVID CALVIN, economist; b. Phoenix, Ariz., Oct. 24, 1934; s. David Leason and Lora Waunita (Hughes) G.; m. Jean Ann Waggoner, Sept. 20, 1987 (div. Dec. 1991). AB, Stanford U., 1956, AM, 1962. Economist The Rand Corp., Santa Monica, Calif., 1963-74; self employed economist L.A., 1974-75, Newport Beach, Calif., 1976-89, Irvine, Calif., 1990—; cons. Inst. for Defense Analyses, Alexandria, Va., 1988-91. Lt. (j.g.) USN, 1957-60, Japan, the Mediterranean, Antarctica. Mem. Am. Econ. Assn., Inst. Navigation, Ops. Rsch. Soc. Episcopalian.

GOGOLIN, MARILYN TOMPKINS, educational administrator, language pathologist; b. Pomona, Calif., Feb. 25, 1946; d. Roy Merle and Dorothy (Davidson) Tompkins; m. Robert Elton Gogolin, Mar. 29, 1969. BA, U. LaVerne, Calif., 1967; MA, U. Redlands, Calif., 1968; postgrad., U. Washington, 1968-69; MS, Calif. State U., Fullerton, 1976. Cert. clin. speech pathologist; cert. teaching and sch. adminstrn. Speech and lang. pathologist Rehab. Hosp., Pomona, 1969-71; diagnostic tchr. L.A. County Office of Edn., Downey, Calif., 1971-72, program specialist, 1972-74, cons. lang., 1975-76, cons. orgns. and mgmt., 1976-79, dir. adminstrv. affairs, asst. to supt., 1979-95; dep. supt., 1995—; cons. lang. sch. dists., Calif., 1975-79; cons. orgn. and mgmt. and profl. assns., Calif., 1976—; exec. dir. L.A. County Sch. Trustees Assn., 1979—. Founding patron Desert chpt. Kidney Found., Palm Desert, Calif., 1985. Doctoral fellow U. Washington, 1968; named One of Outstanding Young Women Am., 1977. Mem. Am. Mgmt. Assn., Am. Speech/Hearing Assn., Calif. Speech/Hearing Assn., Am. Edn. Research Assn. Baptist. Office: LA County Office Edn 9300 Imperial Hwy Downey CA 90242-2813

GOHLKE, JOSH RANDALL, journalist; b. Tarzana, Calif., Sept. 20, 1974; s. Gordon Andrew and Cyndy (Portnoff) G. BA with distinction in English and Comm., Stanford U., 1996. Police reporter Stanford Daily, 1993-94, staff writer, 1994, columnist, 1995-96; staff writer The Outlook, Santa Monica, Calif., 1994, Kern Valley Sun, Lake Isabella, Calif., 1995, Stanford Chaparral, 1996; mng. editor Kern Valley Sun, Lake Isabella, 1996—. Recipient Rebele Found. award, 1995. Mem. Soc. Profl. Journalists, Phi Beta Kappa, Delta Kappa Epsilon. Democrat. Home: PO Box 1179 Kernville CA 93238-1179 Office: Kern Valley Sun PO Box 3074 Lake Isabella CA 93240

GOINS, RONALD L., art director; b. Austin, Tex., Sept. 10, 1962. Graphic artist San Antonio (Tex.) Light, 1982-85; art dir. San Antonio Light Sunday Mag., San Antonio, 1982-85; graphic artist Houston Chronicle, Houston, 1985-86; graphic artist L.A. Daily News, L.A., 1986, art dir., 1986-90; publ., editor Westside Chronicle, L.A., 1990-91; art dir., creative dir. The Advocate Mag., L.A., 1992-96; creative dir. Liberation Publs., L.A., 1992-96, editl. dir., v.p. editl., 1996—. Mem. Inst. Graphic Arts. Office: Liberation Publs 6922 Hollywood Blvd Fl 10 Los Angeles CA 90028-6117

GOLD, ANNE MARIE, library director; b. N.Y.C., Feb. 24, 1949; d. James Raymond and Marion Rita (Magner) Scully; m. Steven Louis Gold, Aug. 9, 1974; 1 child, Lauren Z. BA in English, St. Lawrence U., 1971; MS in Libr. Svc., Columbia U., 1972. Libr. N.Y. Pub. Libr., N.Y.C., 1972-74, Oakland (Calif.) Pub. Libr., 1975-80; with Solano County Libr., Fairfield, Calif., 1980-90, dir. libr. svcs., 1986-90; county libr. Contra Costa County Libr., Pleasant Hill, Calif., 1990—. Mem. Lafayette Sch. Dist. Sch. Bd., 1993—. Mem. ALA, Pub. Libr. Assn. (bd. dirs. 1992-93, met. librs. sect., pres. 1992-93), Libr. Adminstrn. and Mgmt. Assn. (various coms.), Calif. Libr. Assn. (coun. mem. 1985-87, 90-92, exec. bd. 1991-92, co-chair legis. com. 1992-93, pres.-elect 1997, Mem. of Year award, 1994), Calif. Inst. Librs. (v.p. 1990-91), Restructuring Calif. Pub. Librs. Task Force (1994-95).. Office: Contra Costa County Libr 1750 Oak Park Blvd Pleasant Hill CA 94523-4412

GOLD, HAROLD, retired lawyer, accountant; b. N.Y.C., Jan. 14, 1916; s. Samuel and Freida (Swedlow) G.; m. Ellen Facundus, June 18, 1946; children: Sandra L. Gold Brasier, Fred L. Gold. BS in Acctg., UCLA, 1938; JD, U. Minn., 1948. CPA, Minn., Calif. Lectr. income taxation U. Minn., Mpls., 1946-48; pvt. practice Mpls., L.A., 1946-51; regional counsel Western Regional Renegotiation Bd., L.A., 1951-57; mem. adv. bd. federal contracts reports Bur. Nat. Affairs, Washington, 1969-81. Contbr. articles to profl. jours. Capt. U.S. Army Engrs., 1942-46. Fellow ABA (chmn. Pub. Contract Law sect. 1973-74, mem. coun. sect. on Pub. Contract Law (hon.), Nat. Contracts Mgmt. Assn.

GOLD, JEROME, publisher, novelist; b. Chgo., Sept. 8, 1943; s. Sidney Singman and Edith (Hoffman) G.; m. Clotilde Rita Litchfield, Aug. 20, 1965 (div. Apr. 1978); children: Jack Michael, David Charles, Leah Molina Antonia. AA, Fullerton Coll., 1968; BA, U. Mont., Missoula, 1970, MA, 1976; PhD, U. Wash., 1988. Publ. Black Heron Press, Seattle, 1984—; counselor Dept. Juvenile Rehab., Olympia, Wash., 1991—. Author: The Negligence of Death, 1984, The Inquisitor, 1991, Publishing Lives, The Prisoner's Son, 1995; co-author: Of Great Spaces, 1987; editor: Hurricanes, 1994. Sgt. U.S. Army, 1963-66, Vietnam. Mem. Amnesty Internat. Jewish. Office: Black Heron Press PO Box 95676 Seattle WA 98145-2676

GOLD, LOIS SWIRSKY, research scientist; b. Newark, Nov. 21, 1941; d. Sidney C. and Anna S. (Adler) Swirsky; m. Stuart Milton Gold, Mar. 31, 1968; children: Alissa Sharon, Jenny Anna. Student, U. Geneva, 1961-62; AB, Goucher Coll., Towson, Md., 1963; PhD, Stanford U., 1967. Postdoctoral fellow Sys. Devel. Corp., Santa Monica, Calif., 1967-68; lectr. dept. polit. sci. and Sch. Pub. Policy U. Calif., Berkeley, 1968-73, assoc. specialist dept. biochemistry, 1979-80; sr. fellow Carnegie Commn. on Future of Higher Edn., Berkeley, 1970-73; dir. Carcinogenic Potency Project Lawrence Berkeley Lab. and U. Calif., Berkeley, 1978—; sr. scientist Lawrence Berkeley Nat. Lab., 1986—; mem. ad hoc panel of expert reviewers Nat. Toxicology Program, 1988-91; mem. adv. bd. Harvard Ctr. Risk Analysis, 1993-95, Harvard Group on Risk Mgmt. Reform, 1994-95. Contbr. articles to profl. jours.; book editor: (with Errol Zeiger) Handbook of Carcinogenic Potency and Genotoxicity Databases, 1997. Mem. AAAS, Soc. Regulatory Toxicology and Pharmacology, Soc. Toxicology, Phi Beta Kappa.

Home: 1345 Queens Rd Berkeley CA 94708-2113 Office: U Calif Carcinogenic Potency Database 401 Barker Hall Berkeley CA 94720-3203

GOLD, MICHAEL NATHAN, investment banker, management consultant; b. Chgo., May 3, 1952; s. Julius and Sarah (Blitzblau) G.; m. Cynthia Bilicki, June 19, 1976; children: Aaron Michael, Nathan Matthew. BA, Kalamazoo Coll., 1976; cert. in exec. mgmt., UCLA, 1989. Rsch. fellow Sinai Hosp., Detroit, 1976; rsch. assoc. Molecular Biological Inst., UCLA, L.A., 1976-77; lab mgr., adminstr. Biomed. Engring. Ctr. U. So. Calif., L.A., 1977-80; asst. dir. Crump Inst. for Med. Engring. UCLA, 1980-84, assoc. dir., exec. officer Crump Inst. for Med. Engring., 1984-89; chmn., pres. Therapeutic Environments Inc., Van Nuys, Calif., 1989-91; pres., mng. dir. Michael Gold & Assocs., Van Nuys, 1989—; investment banker Crimson Capital Corp., 1991—; Govt. of Czech Repub., 1992-96. Mem. IEEE, Assn. Advancement Med. Instrumentation, Am. Assn. Med. Systems and Informatics, Sea Edn. Assn., Biomed. Engring. Soc., Internat. Soc. Optical Engring. Office: Michael Gold & Assocs 236 W Mountain St Ste 101 Pasadena CA 91103-2968

GOLD, RICK L., federal government executive; b. Rexburg, Idaho, June 25, 1946; s. Raymond Russell and Thelma (Lee) G.; m. Anamarie Sanone, May 14, 1988; children: Nanette Phillips, Russell. BSCE, Utah State U., 1968, MSCE, 1970. Registered profl. engr., Colo., Mont., Utah. Hydraulic engr. U.S. Bur. Reclamation, Provo, Utah, 1969-73; project hydrologist U.S. Bur. Reclamation, Durango, Colo., 1973-75; regional hydrologist U.S. Bur. Reclamation, Billings, Mont., 1975-81; spl. asst. to regional dir. U.S. Bur. Reclamation, Washington, 1981-82; asst. planning officer U.S. Bur. Reclamation, Billings, 1982-83; projects mgr. U.S. Bur. Reclamation, Durango, Colo., 1983-88; regional planning officer U.S. Bur. Reclamation, Salt Lake City, 1988-90, asst. regional dir., 1990-94, deputy regional dir., 1994—; mem. water quality com. Internat. Joint Commn. Study on Garrison Divsn. Unit, Billings, 1975-77; fed. negotiator Cost Sharing and Indian Water Rights Settlement, Durango, 1986-88; chmn. Cooperating Agy. on Glen Canyon Dam EIS, Salt Lake City, 1990-94. Contbr. articles to profl. jours.; author papers. Mem. Rotary Internat., Durango, 1985-87; bd. dirs. United Way of La Plata County, Durango, 1983-88; chmn. Combined Fed. Campaign, La Plata County, 1985. Mem. ASCE, bd. dirs. U.S. Com. on Irrigation and Drainage. Office: US Bur Reclamation 125 S State St Salt Lake City UT 84138-1102

GOLD, STANLEY P., diversified investments executive; b. 1942. AB, U. Calif., 1964; JD, U. So. Calif., 1967. Ptnr. Gang Tyre and Brown, 1967—, Shamrock Holdings Inc., 1985—; pres., chief exec. officer Shamrock Holdings; chmn., CEO, dir. L.A. Gear Inc., L.A., 1992—; chmn. Koor Industries. Office: Shamrock Holdings Inc 4444 W Lakeside Dr Burbank CA 91505-4054

GOLDANSKY, ALVIN EPHRAIM, physician; b. San Diego, Nov. 28, 1958; s. Armand and Eva Goldansky; m. Robin Jill Goldansky, Sept. 1, 1991; 1 child, Rebecca. MD, U. Nacional Autonoma de Mexico, Mexico City, 1984. Bd. cert. internal medicine. Intern, resident LaGuardia Hosp., Forest Hills, N.Y., 1985-88; with All Care Med. Group, Phoenix, 1988-90; staff physician Thomas Davis Med. Ctrs., Phoenix, 1990-91; ptnr., physician Ariz. Primary Care Physicians, Phoenix, 1991—. Mem. ACP. Office: Ariz Primary Care Physician 1728 W Glendale Ave Ste 301 Phoenix AZ 85021-8864

GOLDAPER, GABRIELE GAY, clothing executive, consultant; b. Amsterdam, The Netherlands, May 4, 1937; came to U.S., 1949; d. Richard and Gertrud (Sinzheimer) Mainzer; married, 1957; children: Carolyn, Julie, Nancy. BA in Econs., Barnard Coll., 1959; BS in Edn., U. Cin., 1960; postgrad., Xavier U., 1962. V.p. planning, systems and material control High Tide Swimwear div. Warnaco, Los Angeles, 1974-79; v.p., customer support cons. Silton AMS, Los Angeles, 1979-80; exec. v.p., ptnr. Prisma Corp., Los Angeles, 1980-84; exec. v.p. Mindstar Prods., Los Angeles, 1984-85; gen. mgr. Cherry Lane, Los Angeles, 1985-86; dir. inventory mgmt. Barco Uniforms, Los Angeles, 1986; mgmt. cons. to clothing industry Santa Monica, Calif., 1986—; dir. corp. operation svcs. Authentic Fitness, L.A., 1993; exec. v.p. corp. LCA Intimates, 1994—; instr. Calif. State U., 1978-79, UCLA Grad. Bus. Mgmt. Sch., 1979-86, Fashion Inst. Design and Merchandising. 1985—; chmn. data processing com. Calif. Fashion Creators, 1980; mediator Los Angeles County Bar Assn.; cons. Exec. Service Corps; lectr. various colls. Author: A Results Oriented Approach to Manufacturing Planning, 1978, Small Company View of the Computer, 1979; also articles. Elected mem. Commn. on Status Women, 1985-89. Mem. Apparel Mfrs. Assn. (mgmt. systems com. 1978-80), Calif. Apparel Industries Assn. (exec. com., bd. dirs. 1980), Am. Arbitration Assn. Home: 37 Village Pky Santa Monica CA 90405-2852

GOLDBERG, EDWARD MORRIS, political science educator; b. N.Y.C., May 18, 1931; s. Harry Abraham and Pauline Goldberg; children: David Powell, Natalie Pauline. BA, Bklyn. Coll., 1953; MA, U. N.Mex., 1956; PhD, U. Pa., 1965. Instr. U. Pa., Phila., 1956-59; asst. dean Calif. State U., L.A., 1968-70, dept. chmn. polit. sci., 1972-77, assoc. dean, 1981-86, asst. prof. polit. sci., 1961-66, assoc. prof. polit. sci., 1966-70, prof. polit. sci., 1970-76, prof. emeritus, 1996—; vis. prof. U. So. Calif., L.A., 1974; vis. asst. prof. San Diego State U., 1960-61, U. N.Mex., Albuquerque, 1959-60; cons. HUD, Washington, 1971-72, Calif. State Assembly, Sacramento, 1965; rsch. polit. scientist U. Calif., Davis, 1966, 67; rsch. cons. Taxpayers Assn. of N.Mex., Santa Fe, 1957, 60. Author more than 30 pubs. in field; assoc. editor Western Polit. Quarterly jour., 1981-84; contbr. articles to profl. jours. With U.S. Army, 1953-55. Recipient Outstanding Prof. award Calif. State U., L.A., 1985, summer fellowships NEH, 1980, 84, 89. Mem. Western Polit. Sci. Assn. (v.p. 1977-78, pres. 1978-79), So. Calif. Polit. Sci. Assn. (v.p. 1972-73, pres. 1973-74), Am. Polit. Sci. Assn., Internat. Polit. Sci. Assn. Democrat. Office: Calif State Univ Dept Polit Sci Los Angeles CA 90032-8226

GOLDBERG, FRED SELLMANN, advertising executive; b. Chgo., Jan. 22, 1941; s. Sydney Norman and Birdie (Cohen) G.; m. Jerrilyn Toby Tager, Apr. 12, 1964; children—Robin Lynn, Susanne Joy. B.S., U. Vt., 1962; M.B.A., NYU, 1964. Mktg. research mgr. P. Ballantine & Sons, Newark, 1964-67; sr. v.p., mgmt. supr. Young & Rubicam, N.Y.C., 1967-78; sr. v.p., gen. mgr. Young & Rubicam, Los Angeles, 1978-82; exec. v.p., gen. mgr. Chiat-Day, Inc., San Francisco, 1982-85; exec. v.p., chief operation officer Chiat-Day, Advt., L.A., 1985-87; pres., chief exec. officer San Francisco office Chiat-Day, San Francisco; vice chmn. Chiat/Day Advt., Inc., L.A., 1987-90; founder, chmn., CEO Goldberg Moser O'Neill Advt., San Francisco, 1990—. Republican. Jewish. Office: Goldberg Moser O'Neill 77 Maiden Ln San Francisco CA 94108-5414

GOLDBERG, FREDRIC I., investment management company executive; b. N.Y.C., July 3, 1941; s. Larry and Frances (Bender) G.; m. Nicole Henri, Jan. 19, 1992. BA, SUNY, Buffalo, 1963; MA, Ohio State U., 1965; PhD, Brandeis U., 1968. Instr. philosophy MIT, Cambridge, 1966-68; prof. San Jose (Calif.) State U., 1968-70, Mont. State U., Bozeman, 1971-73, U. Calif., Santa Cruz, 1976-78; salesman Britannica Corp., N.Y.C., 1980-82; salesman, asst. mgr. Equitable Life Ins. Co., N.Y.C., 1982-84; pres., CEO, Goldberg Capital Mgmt. Inc., Santa Fe, 1984—; writer, prodr. The World of Investments, Sta. KHFM, Albuquerque. Home and Office: RR 2 Box 650 Santa Fe NM 87505-8697

GOLDBERG, HARVEY, financial executive; b. Bklyn., Jan. 30, 1940; s. Joseph and Regina (Goldkrantz) G.; m. Joyce Baron, Nov. 22, 1962; children—Keith, Jodi. BS in Acctg., Bklyn. Coll., 1962; postgrad. CCNY, 1963. CPA, N.Y. Sr. acct. Schwartz, Zelin & Weiss CPA's, N.Y.C., 1962-66; mgr. fin. analysis Columbia Records div. CBS, Inc., N.Y.C., 1966-70; asst. controller Revlon, Inc., N.Y.C., 1970-71; treas. Central Textile, Inc., Jersey City, 1971-74; controller Marcade Group, Inc., Jersey City, 1974-81, v.p., controller, 1981-86; v.p., CFO Paul Marshall Products, Inc., subs. Marcade Group, Long Beach, Calif., 1982-86, v.p., CFO , 1988-93; v.p., CFO, Players Internat., Inc., Calabasas, Calif., 1988-93, sr. v.p., CFO, 1988-93; exec. vp., CFO Adesso, Inc., Culver City, Calif., 1994—. County committeeman Monmouth County Dem. Com., N.J., 1979-80; chmn. adv. bd. High Point Ctr., Marlboro, N.J., 1978-82; mem. Marlboro Twp. Bd. Edn., 1980-82, v.p., 1981-82; bd. dirs. Family Consultation Ctr., Freehold, N.J. , 1982-83. Mem. AICPA, N.Y. State Soc. CPA's, Met. Retail Fin. Execs. Assn. Home: 19798 Greenbriar Dr Tarzana CA 91356-5442 Office: Adesso Inc 5110 W Goldleaf Cir Ste 90 Los Angeles CA 90056-1273

GOLDBERG, HERB, psychologist, educator; b. Berlin, Germany, July 14, 1937; came to U.S., 1941; s. Jacob and Ella (Nagler) G.; 1 child, Amy Elisabeth. BA cum laude, CUNY, 1958; PhD, Adelphi U., 1963. Lic. psychologist, Calif. Pvt. practice, L.A., 1965—; prof. Calif. State U., L.A. Author: Creative Aggression, 1972, The Hazards of Being Male, 1976, Money Madness, 1978, The New Male, 1979, The Inner Male, 1986, The New Male/Female Relationship, 1982, What Men Really Want, 1991. Mem. APA, Phi Beta Kappa. Office: 1100 Glendon Ave Ste 939 Los Angeles CA 90024-3513

GOLDBERG, LEE WINICKI, furniture company executive; b. Laredo, Tex., Nov. 20, 1932; d. Frank and Goldie (Ostrowiak) Winicki; student San Diego State U., 1951-52; m. Frank M. Goldberg, Aug. 17, 1952; children: Susan Arlene, Edward Lewis, Anne Carri. With United Furniture Co., Inc., San Diego, 1953-83, corp. sec., dir., 1963-83, dir. environ. interiors, 1970-83; founder Drexel-Heritage store Edwards Interiors, subs. United Furniture, 1975; founding ptnr., v.p. FLJB Corp., 1976-86, founding ptnr., sec. treas., Sea Fin., Inc., 1980, founding ptnr., First Nat. Bank San Diego, 1982. Den mother Boy Scouts Am., San Diego, 1965; vol. Am. Cancer Soc., San Diego, 1964-69; chmn. jr. matrons United Jewish Fedn., San Diego, 1958; del. So. Pacific Coast region Hadassah Conv., 1960, pres. Galilee group San Diego chpt., 1960-61; supporter Marc Chagall Nat. Mus., Nice, France, U. Calif. at San Diego Cancer Ctr. Found., Smithsonian Instn., L.A. County Mus., San Diego Mus. Contemporary Art, San Diego Mus. Art; pres. San Diego Opera, 1992-94. Recipient Hadassah Service award San Diego chpt., 1958-59; named Woman of Dedication by Salvation Army Women's Aux., 1992, Patron of Arts by Rancho Sante Fe Country Friends, 1993. Democrat. Jewish.

GOLDBERG, LINN, physician; b. Portland, Oreg., June 25, 1947; s. Herman and Anita (Mazurosky) G.; m. Marsha Lynn Serling, Feb. 18, 1979; children: Gabriel, Andrew, Aaron, Michael, Alex. BS, U. Oreg., 1970; MD, George Washington U., 1975. Chmn. ambulatory care com. Oreg. Health Sci. U., Portland, 1985-86, dir. human performance lab, 1983—, dir. gen. med. clinics, 1989-93, sec. faculty, 1988—, chief sect. health promotion and sports medicine, 1994—; spl. cons. Inspector Gen. U.S., Dept. Health and Human Svcs., 1990; tech. panel mem. WHO, 1994; crew chief U.S. Olympic Com., 1995—. Co-author/co-editor: Exercise for Prevention and Treatment of Illness, 1994; contbr. articles to profl. jours.; med. reviewer Jour. AMA, Chest, Adolescent Health Care, Archives of Internal Medicine. Grantee Biomed. Rsch., 1980, 81, Tektronix Found., 1982, Nordictrack and Pro Form, Inc., 1985, Fitness Master Inc., 1985, Amoco Fabrics, Inc., 1985, Bally Fitness Products, 1985, Schering-Plough, 1986, 87, 89, Collin's Found., 1988, Hoechst-Roussel Pharms., Inc., 1991, Alzheimer Disease Ctr. Oreg., 1993, NIH, 1993—, Merck Sharp and Dohme, Inc., 1993, NIH/Nat. Inst. on Drug Abuse, 1993—, Med. Found. Oreg., 1995. Fellow Am. Coll. Sports Medicine, Alpha Omega Alpha. Jewish. Office: Oreg Health Scis Univ 3181 SW Sam Jackson Park Rd Portland OR 97201-3011

GOLDBERG, MARK ARTHUR, neurologist; b. N.Y.C., Sept. 4, 1934; s. Jacob and Bertha (Grushlawska) G.; 1 child, Jonathan. BS, Columbia U., 1955; PhD, U. Chgo., 1959, MD, 1962. Resident neurology N.Y. Neurol. Inst., N.Y.C., 1963-66; asst. prof. neurology Columbia U. Coll. Phys. and Surgs., N.Y.C., 1968-71; assoc. prof. neurology and pharmacology UCLA, 1971-77, prof. neurology and pharmacology, 1977—; chair dept. neurology Harbor UCLA Med. Ctr., Torrance, 1977—. Contbr. articles to profl. jours., chpts. to books. Capt. U.S. Army, 1966-68. Fellow Am. Neurol. Assn., Am. Acad. Neurology; Am. Soc. Neurochemistry, Assn. Univ. Profs. Neurology. Office: Harbor UCLA Med Ctr PO Box 492 Torrance CA 90508-0492

GOLDBERG, MARTIN STANFORD, lawyer; b. Youngstown, Ohio, July 11, 1924; s. George and Bee (Walker) G.; m. Donna Mae Lowry, Nov. 18, 1962; children—Jeffrey A., Jeralyn Goldberg Mercer. B.A., Ohio State U., 1952, J.D., 1952. Bar: Ohio 1952, Calif. 1981. Sole practice law, Youngstown, Ohio, 1952—. Served with USAF, 1941-45, PTO. Decorated D.F.C. Mem. ABA, Calif. Bar Assn., Ohio Bar Assn., Mahoning County Bar Assn., Am. Trial Lawyers Assn. Republican. Jewish. Lodges: Masons, Lions-Friars Club. Avocations: Reading, writing, music. Home: 7413 Old Prospector Trl Palm Desert CA 92260 Office: Martin S Goldberg Co LPA 6600 Summit Dr Canfield OH 44406-9510

GOLDBERG, MELVYN, retired educator; b. Chgo., June 19, 1936; s. Sidney and Rachel (Brower) G.; m. Louise Rusch, June 23, 1957 (div. Dec. 1985); children: Robin Baden, Leslie Moss, Michael. BA, No. Ill. U., 1959; MA, Calif. State U., Long Beach, 1971. Cert. tchr., Calif., Ill., Ariz. Tchr. San Pedro (Calif.) H.S., 1959-71, Wkgn. (Ill.) H.S., 1971-94, Coll. of Lake County, Grayslake, Ill., 1987-94; ret., 1994. Author: (poetry and photography) Cyclic Path, 1989; contbr. to various books and mags. Recipient Fulbright Exch. Tchg. award in Eng., USIA, 1990-91. Mem. Assn. Am. Poets. Home: 40 Pebble Dr Sedona AZ 86351

GOLDBERG, MICHAEL ARTHUR, land policy and planning educator; b. Bklyn., Aug. 30, 1941; s. Harold and Ruth (Abelson) G.; m. Rhoda Lynne Zacker, Dec. 22, 1963 (div. 1987); children: Betsy Anne, Jennifer Heli; m. Deborah Nelson, Sept. 7, 1991. B.A. cum laude, Bklyn. Coll., 1962; M.A., U. Calif., Berkeley, 1965, Ph.D., 1968. Acting instr. Sch. Bus. Adminstrn., U. Calif., Berkeley, 1967-68; asst. prof. Faculty of Commerce and Bus. Adminstrn., U. B.C., Vancouver, 1968-71, assoc. prof., 1971-76, prof., 1976—, assoc. dean, 1980-84, dean, 1991—, Herbert R. Fullerton prof. urban land policy, 1981—; mem. Vancouver Econ. Adv. Commn., 1980-82, Can. dept. Fin. Deposit Ins. adv. group, 1992-94, Can. dept. Internat. Trade, Strategic Adv. Group on Internat. Trade in Fin. Svcs., 1991-96; vice chmn. B.C. Real Estate Found., 1985-87, chmn. 1987-91; mem. IFC Vancouver, 1985—, vice chmn., 1985-88, chmn., 1988-89, exec. dir. 1989-91; commr. B.C. Housing Mgmt. Commn., 1989-92; bd. dirs. Imperial Parking Ltd., 1991-94, VLC Properties Ltd., 1991-93, Redekop Properties, 1993—, Catamaran Ferries Inc., 1996—, Sinorank Petroleum, 1996—; vice chmn. Can. Fedn. Deans of Mgmt. and Adminstrv. Scis., 1991-92, chair, 1992-94, Securities Industry Policy Adv. Com., 1995—; pub.-pvt. partnership task force, 1995-96. Author: (with G. Gau) Zoning: Its Costs and Relevance for 1980's, 1980, The Housing Problem: A Real Crisis?, 1983, (with P. Chinloy) Urban Land Economics, 1984, The Chinese Connection, 1985, (with J. Mercer) The Myth of the North American City, 1985, On Balance, 1989; editor: Recent Perspectives in Urban Land Economics, 1976, (with P. Horwood) North American Housing Markets into the Twenty-first century, 1983, (with E. Feldman) The Rites and Wrongs of Land Use Policy, 1988. Trustee Temple Sholom, 1980-84. Can. Coun. fellow, 1974-75, Social Scis. and Humanities Rsch. Coun. fellow, 1979-80, 84-85, Inst. Land Policy fellow, 1979-80, Urban Land Inst. fellow, 1984—, Homer Hoyt Inst. fellow, 1988—, recipient Can. 125th anniversary medal for service to Can., 1993. Mem. Western Regional Sci. Assn., Regional Sci. Assn., Canadian Regional Sci. Assn., Am. Real Estate and Urban Econs. Assn. (dir. 1978—, pres. 1984), Vancouver Bd. Trade, Lambda Alpha. Home: 4625 Puget Dr, Vancouver, BC Canada V6L 2V9 Office: U BC, Dean Commerce & Bus Adminstrn, Vancouver, BC Canada V6T 1Z2 *On reflection, notions of social justice have been as important as any of the guides that I have looked to in working with others and in doing my own work. Operationally, this has meant that I have attempted to deal with students, colleagues and staff in like ways treating people with a basic respect for the inherent human dignity and abhorring those of my colleagues who have treated people in a less respectful way. It has meant that I answer my mail, respond to phone calls and remain available. The cost in the short run to my work has been high at times, but all in all well worth it.*

GOLDBERG, MORRIS, internist; b. N.Y.C., Jan. 23, 1928; s. Saul and Lena (Schanberg) G.; BS in Chemistry cum laude, Poly. Inst. Bklyn., 1951; MD, SUNY, Bklyn., 1956; m. Elaine Shaw, June 24, 1956; children: Alan Neil, Seth David, Nancy Beth. Intern, Jewish Hosp. Bklyn., 1956-57, resident, 1957-58, 61-62, renal fellow, 1958-59; practice medicine, specializing in internal medicine, N.Y.C., 1962-71, Phoenix, 1971—; instr. to asst. clin. prof. internal medicine State U. N.Y. Coll. Medicine, Bklyn., 1962-71; clin. investigator, metabolic research unit Jewish Hosp. Bklyn., 1962-71; cons. in field; mem. staff Phoenix Bapt., Maryvale Samaritan, Good Samaritan, St. Joseph's Hosp., Vets. Affairs Med. Ctr., Phoenix. Served to capt. M.C., U.S. Army, 1959-61. Diplomate Am. Bd. Internal Medicine. Fellow ACP; mem. AMA, Am. Soc. Internal Medicine, Am. Coll. Nuclear Physicians (charter mem.), Am. Soc. Nephrology, Am. Soc. Hypertension (charter mem.), Ariz. Med. Assn., 38th Parallel Med. Soc. S. Korea, Ariz., Maricopa County Med. Assn., Sigma Xi, Phi Lambda Upsilon, Alpha Omega Alpha. Contb articles to med. jours. Home: 24 E Wagon Wheel Dr Phoenix AZ 85020-4063

GOLDBLATT, HAL MICHAEL, photographer, accountant; b. Long Beach, Calif., Feb. 6, 1952; s. Arnold Phillip and Molly (Stearns) G.; m. Shawn Naomi Doherty, Aug. 27, 1974; children: Eliyahu Yonah, Tova Devorah, Raizel, Shoshana, Reuven Lev, Eliezer Noach, Esther Bayla, Rochel Leah, Zalman Ber, Perle Sara. BA in Math., Calif. State U., Long Beach, 1975. Owner Star Publs., Las Vegas, 1975—; treas. Goldblatt, Inc., Las Vegas, 1980—; pres. SDG Computer Svc., Las Vegas, 1985—; chief fin. officer Martin & Mills Ltd., Las Vegas, 1992-93; controller Amland Devel., Las Vegas, 1993-95; CFO Stewart Constrn., Las Vegas, 1995-96; CEO Goldblatt, Inc., Las Vegas, 1996-97; cost acct. Ameristar Casinos, Inc., Las Vegas, 1997—. Photographer: (photo essays) Mikveh Yisroel, 1978, Chassidic Fabrengen, 1979, A Day at Disneyland, 1985; producer, engr.; (audio cassettes) From the Heart of My Dreams, 1980, Middle Class Dreams, 1981, Uforatzta Trio, 1982. Founder, pres. Jews for Judaism, Long Beach, 1975-82, v.p., 1983—; fundraising chmn. Friends of Lubavitch, Long Beach, 1977; bd. dirs. Congregation Lubavitch, Long Beach, 1987, 91-92; treas. Actor's Repertory Theatre, 1995—. Recipient Gold Press Card award Forty Niner Newspaper, 1973, 74, Floyd Durham Meml. award for Outstanding Community Svc., 1973, Georgie award Actor's Repertory Theatre, 1995, ART Disting. Svc. award, 1996. Office: Ameristar Casinos Inc 777 W Lake Mead Dr Henderson NV 89009

GOLDEN, DONALD MICHAEL, writer, inventor; b. Springfield, Mass., June 5, 1953; s. Donald Leon and Marilyn Ruth (Bush) G.; m. Agnes Bozena Meduna, Nov. 13, 1971; children: Steven Frank, Tina Marie Golden Weaver, Tiffany Lynn. Owner, mgr. painting co., Ashford, Conn., 1971-94; writer, inventor, Colorado Springs, Colo., 1994—. Author: (juvenile) Mulligan Stew Gang, 1996, also various others; inventor magic fingers, painter's mate. Rep. Goodwill industries charity functions, Bridgeport, Conn., 1966-67. Home: 2724 N Nevada Ave Colorado Springs CO 80907

GOLDEN, JULIUS, advertising and public relations executive, lobbyist, investor; b. N.Y.C., Feb. 25, 1929; s. Nathan and Leah (Michlin) G.; m. Constance Lee Carpenter, Dec. 31, 1954 (div. Mar. 1965); children: Andrew Mitchell, Juliet Deborah; m. Diana Zana George, Apr. 30, 1973; 1 child, Jeremy Philip. BA, U. N.Mex., 1952. Asst. dir. info. U. N.Mex., Albuquerque, 1952-53; writer AP, Albuquerque, part-time 1952-53, staff writer, 1953-55, fgn. corr., S.Am., 1956-59; pres. Group West Advt./Pub. Relations Albuquerque, 1959—; dir. Sandia Healthcare Corp., Electrical Products Co., Albuquerque. Author: A Time to Die, 1975. Active Bernalillo County Lung Assn., 1961-64; mem. Met. Crime Commn., Albuquerque, 1967-71; chmn., 1970-71; mem. Albuquerque Police Commn. Task Force, 1988-89. Served with AUS, 1945-48, PTO, Korea. Recipient Nat. Feature Writing award Sigma Delta Chi, 1952, E.H. Shaffer award N.Mex. Press Assn., 1953. Mem. Pub. Rels. Soc. (pres. N.Mex. chpt. 1972), Profl. Journalism Soc. (pres. 1969-70), Pub. Rels. Soc. N.Mex. pres. 1972), Am. Advt. Fedn., Overseas Press of Am. Club, Albuquerque Press Club, Petroleum Club, 4 Hills Country Club, Sigma Delta Chi. Democrat. Jewish. Home: 1408 Stagecoach Ln SE Albuquerque NM 87123-4429 Office: Group West 7005 Prospect Pl NE Albuquerque NM 87110-4311

GOLDEN, MICHAEL, state supreme court justice; b. 1942. BA in History, U. Wyo., 1964, JD, 1967; LLM, U. Va., 1992. Bar: Wyo. 1967, U.S. Dist. Ct. 1967, U.S. Ct. Appeals (10th cir.) 1967, U.S. Supreme Ct. 1970. Mem. firm Brimmer, MacPherson & Golden, Rawlins, Wyo., 1971-83, Williams, Porter, Day & Neville, Casper, Wyo., 1983-88; justice Wyo. Supreme Ct., Cheyenne, 1988—, chief justice, 1994—, assoc. justice; mem. Wyo. State Bd. Law Examiners, 1977-82, 86-88. Capt. U.S. Army 1967-71. Office: Wyo Supreme Ct Bldg PO Box 1737 2301 Capital Ave Cheyenne WY 82002-1737*

GOLDEN, NANCY MCALEER, fundraising consultant; b. Bridgeport, Conn., Mar. 21, 1941; d. Arthur Gordon and Nancy (Stevens) McAleer; m. Frederic Golden, Sept. 27, 1980. BA in English Lit., Russell Sage Coll., 1962; postgrad., NYU, 1978-79. Exec. asst. Pubaid S.A., London, 1965-68; mktg. info. mgr. Time-Life Books Time Inc., N.Y.C., 1968-75, gen. mgr. Selling Areas-Mktg., Inc., 1975-82, mgr. adminstrn. and tng. info. systems svcs., 1982-87; dir. membership Commonwealth Club of Calif., San Francisco, 1988-89; freelance fund-raising cons., San Francisco, 1989—, Santa Barbara, Calif., 1995—. Bd. dirs. Victorian Soc. in Am., 1991—. Mem. Nat. Soc. Fund Raising Execs., Cosmopolitan Club. Office: 2207 Alameda Padre Serra Santa Barbara CA 93103-1707

GOLDEN, RENÉE WAYNE, lawyer; b. N.Y.C., Oct. 20, 1930; d. Benjamn A. Weiner and Ada (Block) Zweig; 1 child, Philip Andrew. JD, San Fernando Valley Coll. Law, L.A., 1977. Bar: Calif. 1977. Pvt. practice Hollywood, Calif., 1977—. Mem. ABA, State Bar Calif., Calif. Lawyers for Arts, L.A. County Bar Assn., L.A. Copyright Soc., Beverly Hills Bar Assn. Home and Office: 8983 Norma Pl West Hollywood CA 90069-4818

GOLDENTHAL, NATHAN DAVID, physician; b. Toronto, Can., Sept. 13, 1951; m. Elaine Zaifman, May 26, 1977. MD, U. Toronto, 1975; MPH, U. N.C., 1990. Diplomate Am. Bd. Forensic Examiners, Am. Bd. Forensic Medicine, Am. Bd. Preventive Medicine. Med. dir. Peoria (Ariz.) Med. Clinic, 1977-85; pvt. cons. Peoria, 1985-89; med. developer U. N.C., Chapel Hill, 1989-90; chief profl. svcs. USAF Logistics Command, Dayton, Ohio, 1990-92; dir. Ariz. Inst. Occupl. Safety and Health, Phoenix, 1992—; site physician TRW-Air Bag Safety, Mesa, Ariz., 1995—. Author: Understanding the American with Disabilities, 1993; manuscript reviewer Am. Indsl. Hygiene Jour., 1994-95; contbr. articles to profl. jours. Med. dir. Lyons Aquatic Rehab. Program, Phoenix, 1994-95; mem. tech. com. State Govern ACERP Project, Phoenix, 1994-95; chmn. occupl. health coun. Dept. Def., Dayton, Ohio, 1991-92, chmn. dept. strategic planning, 1991-92. Recipient Nat. Med. fellowship U. N.C., 1989, Pub. Health traineeship U. N.C., 1989. Fellow Am. Coll. Preventive Medicine; mem. Am. Coll. Occupl. Environ. Medicine, Maricopa County Med. Soc. Office: Ariz Inst Occupl Safety & Health 4105 N 20th St Ste 205 Phoenix AZ 85016-6040

GOLDFARB, ROBERT PAUL, neurological surgeon; b. St. Paul, Minn., July 17, 1936; s. Jack and Frances S. (Singer) G.; m. Lesley G. Zatz, Aug. 11, 1963; children: Jill, Pam. BA with distinction, U. Ariz., 1958; MD, Tulane U., 1962. Diplomate Am. Bd. Neurol. Surgery. Intern Michael Reese Hosp., Chgo., 1962-63; resident gen. surgery Presbyn. St. Luke's Hosp., Chgo., 1963-64; resident neurol. surgery U. Ill. Rsch. Hosp., Chgo., 1963-67; pres. med. staff Crippled Children's Svcs. So. Ariz., Tucson, 1973-75; chief staff Tucson Med. Ctr., 1978-80; neurol. surgeon Western Neurosurgery, Ltd., Tucson, 1980—; bd. dir. Health Ptnrs. Physicians Network, 1997—. Maj. USAFR, 1962-70. Baird scholar U. Ariz., 1958. Fellow ACS; mem. Am. Assn. Neurol. Surgeons, Congress Neurol. Surgeons, Am. Coll. Physician Execs., Rocky Mountain Neurosurg. Soc. (v.p. 1979). Office: Western Neurosurgery Ltd 2100 N Rosemont Blvd # 110 Tucson AZ 85712

GOLDFARB, TIMOTHY MOORE, hospital administrator; b. Jerome, Ariz., Dec. 15, 1949; married. B, Ariz. State U., 1975, MHA, 1978. Adminstrv. resident Univ. Med. Ctr., Tucson, 1977-78, mgr. patient accts., 1978-79; asst. adminstr. Tucson Gen. Hosp., 1979; asst. adminstr. Univ. Med. Ctr., Tucson, 1979-83, assoc. adminstr., 1983-84; assoc. hosp. dir. Oreg. Health Scis. Univ. Hosp., Portland, 1984-89, hosp. dir., 1989—. Office: Univ Hosp 3181 SW Sam Jackson Park Rd Portland OR 97201-3011*

GOLDIE, RAY ROBERT, lawyer; b. Dayton, Ohio, Apr. 1, 1920; s. Albert S. and Lillian (Hayman) G.; student U. So. Calif., 1943-44, JD, 1957; student San Bernardino Valley Coll., 1950-51; JD U. So. Calif., 1957; m. Dorothy Roberta Zafman, Dec. 2, 1941; children: Marilyn, Deanne, Dayle, Ron R.

Elec. appliance dealer, 1944-54; teaching asst. U. So. Calif. Law Sch., 1956-57; admitted to Calif. bar, 1957; dep. atty. gen. State of Calif., 1957-58; pvt. practice, San Bernardino, 1958-87. Pres., Trinity Acceptance Corp., 1948-53. Mem. World Peace Through Law Ctr., 1962—; regional dir. Legion Lex, U. So. Calif. Sch. Law, 1959-75; chmn. San Bernardino United Jewish Appeal, 1963; v.p. United Jewish Welfare Fund San Bernardino, 1964-66, Santa Anita Hosp., Lake Arrowhead, 1966-69. Bd. dirs. San Bernardino Med. Arts Corp.; trustee McCallum Theater, Bob Hope Cultural Ctr., 1996—, Friends of Cultural Ctr. Found. Served with AUS, 1942-43. Fellow Internat. Acad. Law and Sci.; mem. ABA, San Bernardino County Bar Assn., Riverside County Bar Assn., State Bar Calif., Am. Judicature Soc., Am. Soc. Hosp. Attys., Calif. Trial Lawyers Assn. (v.p. chpt. 1965-67, pres. 1967-68), Am. Arbitration Assn. (nat. panel arbitrators), Coachella Valley Desert Bar Assn. (chmn. taxation and estate planning, trusts, wills & probate com. 1992-94), Order of Coif, Lake Arrowhead Country Club (pres. 1972-73, 80-81), Lake Arrowhead Yacht Club, Club at Morningside (CFO 1992-93, sec. 1993-94), Nu Beta Epsilon (pres. 1956-57). Home and Office: 1 Hampton Ct Rancho Mirage CA 92270-2585

GOLDIE, WILLIAM DAVID, neurologist, educator; b. Redlands, Calif., June 7, 1947; s. David and Gwendolyn Ann (Lewis) G.; m. Deborah Michelle Schwartz (div. Feb. 1977); m. Ingrid Reneé Neuberger, Aug. 20, 1977; children: Derrick Roger, Christopher David. BA, Stanford U., 1969; MD, U. Calif.-San Diego, La Jolla, 1973. Cert. Am. Bd. Psych. & Neurology, Spl. competence Child Neurology, 1983, Am. Bd. Pediatrics. Resident in pediat. Johns Hopkins U. Hosp., Balt., 1973-75; resident in neurology Stanford (Calif.) U. Hosp., 1975-78; fellow in neurophysiology Mass. Gen. Hosp., Boston, 1978-79; asst. prof. neurology U. Tex. Health Scis. Ctr., Houston, 1979-86; assoc. prof. U. So. Calif., L.A., 1986—, UCLA, 1992—; neurologist Magan Med. Clinic, Covina, Calif., 1990-91; dir. pediatric neurology, dir. neurophysiology Ventura County Med. Ctr., Ventura, Calif., 1992—; dir. clin. neurophysiology Childrens Hosp. L.A., 1986-90, acting head neurology, 1987-89; asst. dir. pediatric rehab. St. John's Regional Med. Ctr., Oxnard, Calif., 1992—. Fellow Am. Acad. Pediatrics, Am. Acad. Neurology; mem. Child Neurology Soc., Am. Cln. Neurophysiology Soc., Am. Epilepsy Soc. Home: 3152 Calle de Marejada Camarillo CA 93010 Office: Ventura County Med Ctr 3400 Loma Vista Rd Ste 9 Ventura CA 93003

GOLDING, GEORGE EARL, journalist; b. Oakdale, Calif., Aug. 26, 1925; s. Herbert Victor and Elva M. (Leydecker) G.; m. Joyce Mary Buttner, July 15, 1948; children: Earlene Golding Bigot, Brad Leslie, Dennis Lee, Frank Edwin, Charlton Kenneth, Daniel Duane. AA, Modesto Jr. Coll., 1950; BA San Francisco State Coll., 1959. Advt. salesman Riverbank News, 1949; galley bank boy, cub reporter San Bernardino Sun, 1951; editor Gustine Standard, 1952; photographer-reporter Humboldt Times, 1952-56; reporter, asst. city editor San Mateo (Calif.) Times, 1956-90; staff writer, corr. UPI; contbg. writer, photographer Nat. Motorist mag.; aviation writer, columnist Flight Log; co-author: (with Joyce Golding) Empire of Cousins, 1995; co-editor (with Joyce Golding) Empire of Cousins Newsletter, 1996. Pub. relations adviser Powder Puff Derby start. 1972. Served with U.S. Maritime Service, 1943, USAAF, 1944-46, AUS, 1950. Recipient John Swett award Calif. Tchrs. Assn., 1964; nominee McQuaid award Cath. Newsmen, 1965, 68; A.P. and Ency. Brit. photography awards, 1954-55, A.P. newswriting award, 1964. Mem. Am. Newspaper Guild, San Francisco-Oakland News Guild, Aviation/Space Writers Assn. (various awards 1983-84), Peninsula Press Club (founding dir., pres. 1976, co-chmn. awards and installation 1986-87), San Mateo County Arts Council (charter). Home: 1625 Ark St San Mateo CA 94403-1001

GOLDING, SUSAN, mayor; b. Muskogee, Okla., Aug. 18, 1945; d. Brage and Hinda Fay (Wolf) G.; children: Samuel, Vanessa. Cert. Pratique de Langue Francaise, U. Paris, 1965; BA in Govt. and Internat. Rels., Carleton Coll., 1966; MA in Romance Philology, Columbia U., 1974. Asssoc. editor Columbia U. Jour. of Internat. Affairs, N.Y.C., 1968-69; teaching fellow Emory U., Atlanta, 1973-74; instr. San Diego Community Coll. Dist., 1978; assoc. pub., gen. mgr. The News Press Group, San Diego, 1978-80; city council mem. City of San Diego, 1981-83; dep. sec. bus., transp., housing State of Calif., Sacramento, 1983-84; county supr. dist. 3 County of San Diego, 1984—; mayor City of San Diego, 1992—; founder Internat. Trade Commn., San Diego, 1985; chmn. San Diego Drug Strike Force, 1987-88, Calif. Housing Fin. Agy., Calif. Coastal Commn.; mem. San Diego County Commn. on the Status of Women; bd. dirs. San Diego County Water Authority; trustee So. Calif. Water Com., Inc.; founder Mid City Comml. Revitalization Task Force, Strategic Trade Alliance, 1993, Calif. Big 10 City Mayors, 1993; chair Pub. Svcs. and Safety Com. San Diego City Coun., Select Com. on Affordable Rental Housing, Gov. Calif. Mil. Base Reuse Task Force, 1994; co-chair City County Reinvestment Task Force; vice-chair Transp. and Land Use Com. of City Coun.; edtablished San Diego World Trade Ctr., 1993, San Diego City/State/County Regional Permit Assistance Ctr., 1994; mem. adv. bd. U.S. Conf. of Mayors, 1994. Bd. dirs. Child Abuse Prevention Found., San Diego Conv. and Vis. Bur., Crime Victims Fund, United Cerebral Palsy, San Diego Air Quality Bd., San Diego March of Dimes, Rep. Assocs.; adv. bd. Girl Scouts U.S.; trustee So. Calif. Water Comm.; mem. Rep. State Cen. Com.; co-chair com. Presidency George Bush Media Fund, Calif.; chair San Diego County Regional Criminal Justice Coun., race rels. com. Citizens Adv. Com. on Racial Intergration, San Diego Unified Sch. Dist.; hon. chair Am. Cancer Soc's. Residential Crusade, 1988. Recipient Alice Paul award Nat. Women's Polit. Caucus, 1987, Calif. Women in Govt. Achievement award, 1988, Willie Velasquez Polit. award Mex. Am. Bus. and Profl. Assn., 1988, Catalyst of Chance award Greater San Diego C. of C., 1994, Woman Who Means Bus. award San Diego Bus. Jour., 1994, Internat. Citizen award World Affairs Coun., 1994; named One of San Diego's Ten Outstanding Young Citizens, 1981, One of Ten Outstanding Rep. County Ofcls. in U.S.A., Rep. Nat. Com., 1987, San Diego Woman of Achievement Soroptimists Internat., 1988. Mem. Nat. Assn. of Counties (chair Op. Fair Share, mem. taxation and fin. com.), Nat. Women's Forum. Jewish. Office: Office of the Mayor City Administration Bldg 11th Fl 202 C St San Diego CA 92101-4806*

GOLDMAN, ALVIN IRA, philosopher, educator; b. Bklyn., Oct. 1, 1938; s. Nathan and Frances (Krugman) G.; m. Holly Martin Smith, June 15, 1969; children: Raphael, Sidra. BA, Columbia U., 1960; MA, Princeton U., 1962, PhD, 1965. From asst. prof. to prof. U. Mich., Ann Arbor, 1963-80; prof. U. Ill., Chgo., 1980-83; prof. U. Ariz., Tucson, 1983-94, Regents' prof. philosophy, 1994—. Author: A Theory of Human Action, 1970, Epistemology and Cognition, 1986, Liaisons: Philosophy Meets..., 1992, Philosophical Applications of Cognitive Science, 1993. Guggenheim fellow, 1975-76, Ctr. for Advanced Study in Behavioral Scis. fellow, 1975-76, Nat. Humanities Ctr. fellow, 1981-82. Mem. Am. Philos. Assn. (Pacific divsn. pres. 1991-92), Soc. for Philosophy and Psychology (pres. 1987-88). Office: Univ of Ariz Dept Philosophy Tucson AZ 85721

GOLDMAN, LEE, physician, educator, researcher; b. Phila., Jan. 6, 1948; s. Marvin and Kathryn (Schwartz) G.; m. Jill Steinhardt, Mar. 21, 1971; children: Jeff, Daniel, Robyn Sue. BA, Yale U., 1969, MD, 1973, MPH, 1973. Diplomate Am. Bd. Internal Medicine, Am. Bd. Cardiovascular Disease. Intern U. Calif.-San Francisco, 1973-74, resident in med., 1974-75, Mass. Gen. Hosp., Boston, 1975-76; fellow in cardiology Yale-New Haven Hosp., 1976-78; asst. prof. medicine Harvard Med. Sch., 1978-83, assoc. prof., 1983-89, prof., 1989-95; asst. physician-in-chief dept. med. Brigham and Women's Hosp., Boston, 1983-87, vice chmn., 1987-93; dir. div. clin. epidemiology dept. medicine Brigham and Women's and Beth Israel Hosps., 1987-93, chief med. officer, 1993-95; mem. operating com. Ptnrs. Health Care Inc., 1993-95; chair dept. medicine, assoc. dean clin. affairs U. Calif., San Francisco, 1995—, Inst. Medicine, 1995—; bd. dirs. Am. Bd. Internal Medicine, 1996—. Contbr. numerous articles to profl. jours.; assoc. editor New England Jour. Medicine, 1989-95. Bd. dirs. Temple Shir Tikva, Wayland, Mass., 1982-84, v.p. 1985-86, pres. 1986-88. ACP teaching and research scholar, 1980-83; Henry J. Kaiser Family Found. scholar, 1982-87. Fellow ACP and Am. Coll. Cardiology; mem. Am. Soc. Clin. Investigation, Soc. Gen. Medicine (sec.-treas. 1986-88, pres. 1990—), Assn. Am. Physicians (recorder 1993—). Office: U Calif Dept of Medicine 505 Parnassus Ave San Francisco CA 94143

GOLDMAN, LEON, dermatologist, laser surgeon; b. Cin., Dec. 7, 1905; s. Abraham and Fanny (Friedman) G.; m. Belle Hurwitz, Aug. 23, 1936; children: John, Steve, Carol. MD, U. Cin., 1929. Prof. dermatology U. Cin., 1951-76, dir. laser lab., 1961-76, dir. laser treatment ctr., 1961-76; dir. laser lab. Children's Hosp., Cin., 1971-76, Jewish Hosp., Cin., 1979-83; laser cons. U.S. Naval Hosp., San Diego, 1983—. Author 7 books on laser medicine and laser surgery; contbr. numerous articles to profl. jours. Chmn. Cancer Coun., Cin., Ohio, 1978; pres. and co-founder Am. Soc. for Laser Medicine and Surgery, 1980-81; bd. dirs. Am. Soc. for Investigative Dermatology. Named Father of Laser Medicine, Opto-Elektronik Congress, Munich, 1977; recipient W.D. Mark medal, Am. Soc. for Medicine and Surgery, 1981, Fineraud award, Am. Acad. Dermatology, 1984, Polaky medal Polaky U., Czechoslovakia, 1985, Schawlow medal Laser Industry Am., 1985, Pioneer award Internat. Soc. for Optical Engring, 1992, Epstein Photomedicine award, 1992. Mem. Laser Inst. Am. (life), Am. Soc. for Laser Medicine and Surgery (dir. laser art 1993). Jewish. Office: US Naval Hosp Code 43 San Diego CA 92134-5000

GOLDMAN, MITCHEL PAUL, dermatologist; b. Miami Beach, Fla., Apr. 5, 1955; s. Arnold Leonard and Betty (Freedman) G.; children: Risa D., Melissa D. BA in Biology summa cum laude, Boston U., 1977; MD, Stanford U., 1982. Diplomate Am. Bd. Dermatology. Intern U. Calif., San Diego, 1982-83; resident UCLA, 1983-86; with Dermatology Assocs., La Jolla, Calif., 1986—; mem. staff U. Calif. San Diego Med. Ctr., Scripps Meml. Hosps., Encinitas and La Jolla, Children's Hosp., 1987—; assoc. clin. prof. dermatology U. Calif., San Diego. Author 7 med. textbooks; contbr. more than 100 articles to profl. jours. Bd. dirs. San Diego chpt., Am. Cancer Soc. Fellow Am. Soc. for Dermatologic Surgery (bd. dirs. 1995—), Am. Acad. Dermatology, Am. Soc. for Laser Medicine and Surgery; mem. N.Am. Soc. Phlebology (past pres.), Am. Venous Forum (bd. dirs. 1993-95), San Diego County Dermatol. Soc. (past pres.), Sonoran Dermatology Soc. (past pres.), Phi Beta Kappa. Office: Dermatology Assocs 9850 Genesee Ave Ste 480 La Jolla CA 92037-1213

GOLDMAN, SERGEY YURI, programmer, physicist; b. Saratov, Russia, Oct. 19, 1957; came to U.S., 1990; s. Yuri Sergey and Vera Moisey (Minkin) G.; m. Lilia Sheynfeld, Aug. 25, 1991; children: Miriam, Joseph. PhD in Physics and Math., Saratov State U., 1985; MS in Environ. Sci., Oreg. Grad. Inst. Sci. & Tech., 1992. Engr., physicist Rsch. Inst. Agropribor, Saratov, Russia, 1979-90; rsch. scientist Oreg. Grad. Inst. Sci. and Tech., Portland, 1990-94; programmer, analyst Computer Sci. Corp., Portland, 1994-96; sr. programmer Automatic Data Processing, Portland, 1996—. Contbr. articles to profl. jours.; co-inventor 6 inventions including method of determining permeability of porous material; spectroscopic method for determining the diffusion coefficient and solubility of helium and neon in glass. Fellow AAAS. Home: 9349 SW Fast Pl Tigard OR 97223-1206

GOLDRING, STANLEY DONALD, medical instrument designer; b. St. Louis, Apr. 13, 1942; s. Ben and Ruth Goldring. BSEE, Wash. U., 1964; MSEE, U. Calif., Berkeley, 1965. Registered profl. engr., Calif. Sr. mem. of tech. staff ESL Inc., Sunnyvale, Calif., 1965-76; R & D engr., sect. mgr. Abbott Labs., Mountain View, Calif., 1977—. Inventor signal filter method, saturation levels in blood, and electro-optic coupler. Grantee NSF, 1964. Mem. Churchill Club, Eta Kappa Nu, Tau Beta Pi. Jewish. Office: Abbott Labs 1212 Terra Bella Ave Mountain View CA 94043-1824

GOLDSMITH, DONALD WILLIAM, lawyer, astronomer, writer; b. Washington, Feb. 24, 1943; s. Raymond William and Selma Evelyn (Fine) G.; m. Rose Marien, Apr. 10, 1975 (div. 1978); 1 child, Rachel Evelyn. BA, Harvard U., 1963; PhD, U. Calif., Berkeley, 1969, JD, 1983. Asst. prof. earth and space sci. SUNY, Stony Brook, 1972-74; vis. prof. Niels Bohr Inst., Copenhagen, 1977; vis. instr. physics Stanford (Calif.) U., 1983; vis. lectr. astronomy U. Calif., Berkeley, 1980-88, vis. assoc. prof., 1990-93; assoc. Pillsbury, Madison and Sutro, San Francisco, 1985-87; cons. Cosmos TV program, Los Angeles, 1978-80; pres. Interstellar Media Publs., Berkeley, 1978—. Author: Nemesis, 1985, The Evolving Universe, 1985, Supernova!, 1989, Space Telescope, 1989, The Astronomers, 1991; (with others) The Search for Life in the Universe, 1980, 2d edit. 1992, Cosmic Horizons, 1982, Mysteries of the Milky Way, 1991; co-writer (TV programs) Is Anybody Out There, 1986, The Astronomers, 1991. Recipient 1st prize popular essays in astronomy Griffith Obs./Hughes Aircraft Corp., L.A., 1983, Best Popular Writing by a Scientist award Am. Inst. Physics, 1986, Klumpke-Roberts award for lifetime achievement Astronomy Soc. Pacific, 1990, Annenberg Found. award for edn. Am. Astron. Soc., 1995. Home: 2153 Russell St Berkeley CA 94705-1006*

GOLDSMITH, JONATHAN CHARLES, hematologist, internist; b. Dayton, Ohio, Oct. 19, 1945; m. Delores Y. Goldsmith. AB, Dartmouth Coll., 1967; MD, NYU, 1971. Intern then resident Vanderbilt U. Hosps., 1971-74; fellow in hematology U. N.C., 1976-79; dir. Hemophilia Treatment Ctr., Children's Hosp., L.A., 1991-95; prof. pediatrics and medicine U. So. Calif., L.A., 1991-95; v.p. clin. affairs, med. dir. Alpha Therapeutic Corp., L.A., 1995—. Maj. USAF, 1974-76. Office: Alpha Therapeutic Corp 5555 Valley Blvd Los Angeles CA 90032-3520

GOLDSMITH, MARGARET MABEL, critical care nurse; b. St. Louis, Nov. 23, 1949; d. Ralph L. and Ruth E. (Snyder) Underhill; m. Tim Shipman, Aug. 27, 1968 (div. Oct. 1988); children: Timothy, Heather, Joshua; m. Dean Goldsmith, July 4, 1994. AD in Nursing, Boise State U., 1980. CCRN, Colo. Critical care RN Mercy Medical Ctr., Nampa, Idaho, 1980-82, West Nebr. Gen. Hosp., Scottsbluff, Nebr., 1982-84; sch. nurse Morrill County Edn. Svc. Unit., Alliance, Nebr., 1984-88; critical care RN, clin. coord. ICU, cardiac rehab. McKee Medical Ctr., Loveland, Colo., 1989—; mem. new products com. Critical Pathways Practice Coun., Loveland, 1993—. Reg. dir. Am. Cancer Soc., Morrill County, Nebr., 1983-84. Mem. Am. Assn. Critical Care Nurses. Office: McKee Medical Ctr 2000 Boise Ave Loveland CO 80538-5006

GOLDSTEIN, BARBARA JOAN, sculptor; b. Chgo.; d. Charles Martin and Constance Evangeline (Bredeson) Kaplan; m. Michael Louis Goldstein, June 18, 1967; children: Rachel Rebecca, Elizabeth Caroline, Adam Charles. BA, Conn. Coll. for Women, 1967; MA, U. Chgo., 1969; postgrad., U. Utah, 1986-88. Child therapist Pritzker Sch., Chgo., 1969-70, Santa Clara County Health Dept., San Jose, Calif., 1970-71; sculptor Salt Lake City, 1970—. Represented in permanent collections U. Utah Med. Ctr., Nat. Kidney Found. Utah, Jewish Cmty. Ctr. Denver, Utah Mus. of Fine Arts, Salt Lake City Art Ctr., among others. Past pres. Salt Lake City Jewish Cmty. Ctr.; bd. dirs. Salt Lake City Art Ctr., 1992-93; Salt Lake City rep. Interfaith Forum on Religion, Art and Arch., 1992—. Mem. NASW, Phi Beta Kappa. Home and Office: 2720 Shadybrook Ln Salt Lake City UT 84121-1539

GOLDSTEIN, BARRY BRUCE, biologist, food company executive, lawyer; b. N.Y.C., Aug. 2, 1947; s. George and Pauline (Kolodner) G.; m. Jacqueline Barbara Aboulafia, Dec. 21, 1968; children: Joshua, Jessica. BA, Queens Coll., 1968; MA, CCNY, N.Y.C., 1974; PhD, CUNY, N.Y.C., 1980; JD, U. N.Mex., 1994. Microbiologist CPC Internat., Yonkers, N.Y., 1968-71; rsch. scientist U. Tex., Austin, 1977-80; v.p. SystemCulture Inc., Honolulu, 1980-83; bioenergy/aquaculture program mgr. N.Mex. Solar Energy Inst., Las Cruces, 1983-89; pres. Ancient Seas Aquaculture Inc., Roswell, N.Mex., 1989-92, Desert Seas Aquaculture Inc., Roswell, 1990-92, Hawaii Shellfish Co., Las Cruces, 1991—; project leader Sandia Nat. Labs., Carlsbad, N.Mex., 1994—. Editl. bd. Natural Resources Jour.; contbr. articles to profl. jours. Recipient Nat. Energy Innovation award Dept. Energy, Washington, 1985; Grad. fellow CUNY, 1971, Jesse Smith Noyes fellow, 1975, Regents scholar SUNY, 1964. Mem. World Aquaculture Soc., Am. Soc. Microbiology, AAAS. Office: PO Box 1349 Carlsbad NM 88221-1349

GOLDSTEIN, DEBBE, art history educator; b. Akron, Ohio, Sept. 1, 1953; d. Max and Evelyn Eva (Goldner) G. BA, Ohio State U., 1975, postgrad., 1994—. Adminstr. The Kitchen Ctr. for Video Music and Dance, N.Y.C., 1977-78; proprietor Deborah Goldstein Arts, N.Y.C., 1978-81; program asst. L.A. County Mus.; asst. dir. spl. events Mus. Contemporary Art, L.A., 1986-88; asst. dir. admissions Art Ctr. Coll. of Design, Pasadena, Calif., 1988—; adv. bd. graphics Orange (Calif.) Coast Coll., Saddleback Coll., Mission Viejo, Calif.; guest lectr. L.A. County Mus., 1992; presenter, spkr. Bowling Green State U., 1995. Co-curator Terra Moto: The Fallen and the Saved (Robert Morris), 1994, (ltd. edit.) Where's Wallenberg? (James Rosenquist), 1995. Educator MOCA, L.A., 1993, 94; mem. Dem. County Com., County of N.Y., 1984. Mem. (affiliate) Indsl. Design Soc. Am. Democrat. Jewish. Democrat. Jewish. Office: Art Ctr Coll of Design 1700 Lida St Pasadena CA 91103-1924

GOLDSTEIN, HOWARD EDWARD, chemical engineer; b. White Plains, N.Y., June 28, 1937; s. Nathan Goldstein and Matilda (Sussman) Treinis; m. Sheila Carol Singer, June 18, 1961; children: David, Allen, Debra. BS in Chem. Engring., U. Ariz., 1961, MS in Chem. Engring., 1963. Engr. Lockheed Missiles & Space Co., Sunnyvale, Calif., 1963-67; thermodynamic engr. Applied Space Products, Mountain View, Calif., 1967-70; from rsch. sci. to chief thermal protection materials br. NASA Ames Rsch. Ctr., Moffett Field, Calif., 1970-90; chief scientist/sr. staff scientist space tech. div. NASA Ames Rsch. Ctr., 1990—. Served in USAR, 1956-63. Fellow AIAA (thermophysics com. 1978-81, materials com. 1986-89); mem. AAAS, Am. Chem. Soc., Am. Ceramic Soc. Office: NASA Ames Rsch Ctr B229-3 Moffett Field CA 94030

GOLDSTEIN, MARCIA, historian, educator, law office administrator; b. Denver, Jan. 17, 1951; d. Dickerson H. and Phyllis (Selby) Tremmel; m. Jeffrey A. Goldstein, Feb. 28, 1976; 1 child, Deanna. BA in History magna cum laude, Metro. State Coll., 1982; MA in Am. History, U. Colo., 1995, postgrad., 1996—. Mktg. support mgr. NBI, Inc., Boulder, 1983-87; law office adminstr. Goldstein & Dodge, Denver, 1991—; instr. Arapahoe C.C., Littleton, Colo., 1994-95, Met. State Coll. Denver, 1995-96. Mem. Orgn. Am. Historians, Nat. Pub. History Coun., Western History Assn., Colo. Hist. Soc., Colo. Coalition for Women's History (bd. dirs., pres., 1993—), Colo. History Group, Historic Denver, Inc., Denver Woman's Press Club, Denver Westerners, Phi Alpha Theta. Democrat.

GOLDSTEIN, MARK ALAN, information science and research company executive, consultant; b. Suffern, N.Y., Feb. 5, 1951; s. Harry and Betty (Cohen) G.; m. Elizabeth Ann Warren, Jan. 1, 1985. BA, SUNY, Binghamton, 1972. Pres. Advanced Tools for the Arts, Tempe, 1975-94; rsch. and devel. engr. MicroAge, Tempe, 1976-79; mgr. hybrid test engring. Medtronic/Micro-Rel, Tempe, 1980-92; pres. Internat. Rsch. Ctr., Tempe, 1992—; bd. dirs. Gov.'s Strategic Partnership Econ. Devel./Ariz. Tech. and Info. Coun., Phoenix, 1993—. Mem. IEEE, Am. Soc. Info. Sci., Assn. Ind. Info. Profls., Electronic Frontier Found., Soc. competitive Intelligence Profls., World Future Soc., Ariz. Software Assn., Ariz. Libr. Assn., Ariz. Online Users Group, Ariz. Sr. Living Cluster. Office: Internat Rsch Ctr PO Box 825 Tempe AZ 85280-0825

GOLDSTEIN, MICHAEL AARON, finance educator; b. Winchester, Mass., Oct. 9, 1964; s. Norman and Sheila Judith Goldstein. BS, U. Pa., 1986, MBA, 1991, PhD in Fin. Markets, 1993. Investment banker Merrill Lynch Capital, N.Y.C., 1986-88; rsch. assoc. WhartonSch, U. Pa., Phila., 1988-93; adviser Ministry of Privatization, Warsaw, Poland, 1990; asst. prof. U. Colo., Boulder, 1993—. Contbr. articles to profl. jours. Treas., CFO Boulder County Dems., Boulder, Colo., 1996; contr. Boulder County Clinton/Gore, 1995-96; bd. dirs. Hillel of Colo., Denver, 1993-96, chair, Boulder, 1994-96. Recipient Tchg. award U. Colo., 1994; GeeWar Terker fellow, 1988-91. Mem. Am. Fin. Assn., Fin. Mgmt. Assn. (reviewer/referee 1996), Wharton Club of Colo., Phi Beta Kappa, Beta Gamma Sigma, Delta Sigma Pi. Democrat. Jewish. Office: Wallace E Carroll Sch mgmt Boston Coll Asst Prof Finance Fulton Hall Ste 244C Chestnut Hill MA 02167-3808

GOLDSTEIN, MICHAEL SAUL, sociologist; b. N.Y.C., Aug. 1, 1944; s. Abraham J. and Rose G.; m. Laura Geller, Dec. 23, 1979 (div. May 1992); children: Joshua, Adam, Elana. BA, Queens Coll., Flushing, N.Y., 1965; MA, Brown U., Providence, 1967, PhD, 1971. Lectr. Brown U., Providence, 1970-71; asst. prof. Sch. Pub. Health, UCLA, 1971-78, assoc. prof., 1978-88, prof., 1988—, chair dept. community health, 1988-91. Author: The Health Movement, 1992; author, editor: 50 Simple Things You Can Do to Save Your Life, 1992. Mem. APHA, Am. Sociol. Assn. Soc. for Study Social Problems, Hastings Inst. Soc. Ethics and the Life Scis. Office: UCLA Sch Pub Health Los Angeles CA 90024*

GOLDSTEIN, SIR NORMAN, dermatologist; b. Bklyn. July 14, 1934; s. Joseph H. and Bertha (Docteroff) G.; B.A., Columbia Coll., 1955; M.D., SUNY, 1959; m. Ramsay, Feb. 14, 1980; children: Richard, Heidi. Intern, Maimonides Hosp., N.Y.C., 1959-60; resident Skin and Cancer Hosp., 1960-61, Bellevue Hosp., 1961-62, NYU. Postgrad. Center, 1962-63 (all N.Y.C.); ptnr. Honolulu Med. Group, 1967-72; practice medicine specializing in dermatology, Honolulu, 1972—; clin. prof. dermatology U. Hawaii Sch. Medicine, 1973—; bd. dirs. Pacific Laser. Bd. dirs. Skin Cancer Found., 1979—; trustee Dermatol. Found., 1979-82, Hist. Hawaii Found., 1981-87; pres. Hawaii Theater Ctr., 1985-89, Hawaii Med. Libr., 1987; mem. Oahu Heritage Council, 1986-94. Served with U.S. Army, 1960-67. Recipient Henry Silver award Dermatol. Soc. Greater N.Y., 1963; Husik award NYU, 1963; Spl. award Acad. Dermatologia Hawaiiana, 1971, Outstanding Scientific Exhibit award Calif. Med. Assn., 1979, Special award for Exhibit Am. Urologic Assn., 1980, Svc. to Hawaii's Youth award Adult Friends for Youth, 1991, Nat. Cosmetic Tattoo Assn. award, 1993, Cmty. Svc. award Am. Acad. Dermatology, 1993; named Physician of Yr., Hawaii Med. Assn., 1993. Fellow ACP, Am. Acad. Dermatology (Silver award 1972), Am. Soc. Lasers Medicine & Surgery, Royal Soc. Medicine; mem. Internat. Soc. Tropical Dermatologists (Hist. and Culture award), Soc. Investigative Dermatologists, AAAS, Am. Soc. Photobiology, Internat. Soc. Cryosurgery, Am. Soc. Micropigmentation Surgery, Pacific and Asian Affairs Council, Navy League, Assn. Hawaii Artists, Biol. Photog. Assn., Health Sci. Communication Assn., Internat. Pigment Cell Soc., Am. Med. Writers Assn., Physicians Exchange of Hawaii (bd. dirs.), Am. Coll. Cryosurgery, Internat. Soc. Dermatol. Surgery, Am. Soc. Preventive Oncology, Soc. for Computer Medicine, Am. Assn. for Med. Systems and Info., Japan Am. Soc. Hawaii (bd. dirs.), Pacific Telecom Council, Hawaii State Med. Assn. (mem. public affairs com.), Hawaii Dermatol. Soc. (sec.-pres.), Hawaii Public Health Assn., Pacific Dermatol. Assn., Pacific Health Research Inst., Honolulu County Med. Soc. (gov.), Nat. Wildlife Fedn., C. of C., Preservation Action, Am. Coll. Sports Medicine, Rotary, Hemlock Soc. USA (med. bd.), Hawaii Govs. Blue Ribbon Panel on Living and Dying with Dignity, Ancient Gaelic Nobilitary Soc. (named Knight of the Niadh Nask, 1995), Outrigger Canoe Club, Plaza Club (pres. bd. dirs. 1990-92), Chancellor's Club, Oahu Country Club. Editor: Hawaii Med. Jour.; contbr. articles to profl. jours. Office: Tan Sing Bldg 1128 Smith St Honolulu HI 96817-5139

GOLDSTEIN, NORTON MAURICE (GOLDY NORTON), public relations consultant; b. Cleve., Apr. 11, 1930; s. Jacob N. and Phyllis Ruth (Weinstein) G.; m. Judith Marcia Morris, Oct. 29, 1955; 1 child, Ann Dee. Reporter L.A. Daily News, 1952-54; writer, producer Cleve Hermann Radio-TV Sports, L.A., 1952-59; exec. v.p. Kennett Pub. Rels. Assocs., L.A., 1959-71; writer, producer Vin Scully Sports Program, L.A., 1959-64; owner, oper. Goldy Norton Pub. Rels., L.A., 1971—. Author: Official Frisbee Handbook, 1972. Founding dir. U.S. Acad. Decathlon, L.A., 1982. With U.S. Army, 1949-52, Korea. Named to Frisbee Hall of Fame, Internat. Frisbee Assn., Hancock, Mich., 1979. Mem. So. Calif. Sports Broadcasters Assn. (charter). Office: Goldy Norton Pub Rels 6200 Wilshire Blvd Ste 903 Los Angeles CA 90048-5810

GOLDSTEIN, STEVEN EDWARD, psychologist; b. Bronx, N.Y., Nov. 25, 1948; s. Maurice and Matilda (Weiss) G.; BS in Psychology, CCNY, 1970, MS in Sch. Psychology, 1971; EdD in Sch. Psychology, U. No. Colo., 1977. Tchr., N.Y.C. Public Schs., 1970-71, 72-73, tchr., counselor, 1974; extern in sch. psychology N. Shore Child Guidance, 1972; sch. psychologist Denver Pub. Schs., 1975; asst. prof. psychology Northeastern Okla. State U., Tahlequah, 1976-78; coord. inpatient, emergency svcs. Winnemucca (Nev.) Mental Health Center, 1978-80; dir. Desert Devel. Ctr., Las Vegas, Nev., 1980-82; sr. psychologist Las Vegas Mental Health Ctr., 1982-92; pvt. practice psychology, Las Vegas, 1983—; sr. psychologist Desert Regional Ctr., 1992—; participant NSF seminar on biofeedback, 1977. Sec. grad. coun. CUNY, 1971; pres. grad. coun. in edn. CCNY, 1971. Lic. psychologist, Nev.; cert. sch. psychologist, N.Y., Calif. Mem. APA (Nev. coord. office of profl. practice 1987-88), Biofeedback Soc. Nev. (membership dir. 1982-90), Nev. Soc. Tng. and Devel. (dir. 1982-83), So. Nev. Soc. Cert. Psychologists (pres.

1984-86), Jewish Fedn. Las Vegas (bus. & profl. com. 1995—). Presenter papers to profl. confs. Office: 1391 S Jones Blvd Las Vegas NV 89102-1200 also: 3180 W Sahara Ave Ste C-25 Las Vegas NV 89102-6005

GOLDSTEIN, WILLIAM M., composer, producer; b. Newark, Feb. 25, 1942; s. Harry and Sylvia (Hochheiser) G. MusB, Manhattan Sch. Music, 1965, postgrad., 1965-66. Freelance composer, arranger, producer music for TV, film, theater, 1966—; composer-in-residence U.S. Army Band, Ft. Myer, Va., 1966-69. Composer, condr., arranger, producer: (feature films) Hello Again, The Bad Guys, Bingo Long Traveling All Stars, 1976, Eye For an Eye, Force Five, Norman Is That You?, Hello Again, 1987, Shocker, 1989, The Quarrel, 1991, others, (TV films) Connecticut Yankee in King Arthur's Court, 1990, Blood River, 1991, Danielle Steele's Zoya, 1995, (TV spls.) Omnibus, (Emmy award nomination 1980), Happy Endings (Emmy award nomination 1983), Fame (Emmy award nomination 1983), Hero in the Family, Marilyn: The Untold Story, Mobil Showcase Theatre, others, (documentaries) Television's Greatest Commercials, Parts I-V, The Stars Salute the U.S. Olympic Team, The Mysteries of the Mind, Living Sands of Namib, others, (theater prodns.) Marat Sade, Spread Eagle Four, The Peddler, Total Sweet Success, A Bullet for Billy the Kid 1964, others, (commls.) McDonalds, Buick, Noxema, Duncan Hines, Mitsubishi, others, (records) Switched on Classics, There's No Stopping Us (Sister Sledge), My Touch of Madness (Jermaine Jackson), Old Fashioned Man (Smokey Robinson), Guys and Dolls (Grammy award nomination 1977), Oceanscape, others. Bd. dirs. Calif. State Summer Sch. for the Arts. Recipient Golden Horse award Republic of China, 1981. Mem. Acad. Motion Picture Arts and Scis. (vis. artist 1980).

GOLDSTON, BARBARA M. HARRAL, editor; b. Lubbock, Tex., Jan. 26, 1937; d. Leonard Paul and Olivette (Stuart) Harral; m. John Rowell Toman (div. 1963); 1 child, Stuart Rowell; m. Olan Glen Goldston, 1989. BE, Tex. Christian U., 1959; MLS, U. Hawaii, 1968; postgrad., Golden Gate U., 1980-82. Tchr. pub. elem. schs., various cities, Tex. and Hawaii, 1959-66; contracts abstractor, indexer Champlin Oil Co., Ft. Worth, 1963-64; adminstrv. asst. engrng. Litton Industries, Lubbock, Tex., 1964-65; mgr. rsch. library Hawaii Employers' Coun., Honolulu, 1968-72; rsch. cons. Thailand Hotel Study, Touche-Ross Assocs., Honolulu, 1974; dir. med. library U. S.D.-Sacred Heart Hosp., Yankton, 1977-79; editor, adminstrv. coord. book div. ABC-Clio, Inc., Santa Barbara, Calif., 1981-88; free-lance rsch./editorial cons. Albuquerque, 1988-89; instr. Santa Fe Community Coll., 1989—; owner Sandbar Prodns., Albuquerque, 1993—; ptnr. Broome-Harral, Inc., Albuquerque, 1989—. Author, editor with others Hist. Periodical Dir., 5 vols., World Defense Forces compendium. Contbr. Boy's Ranch, Amarillo, Tex., 1987—; mem. Lobero Theater Group, Santa Barbara, 1975-76; mem., treas. Yankton Med. Aux., 1977-79. Mem. ALA, Spl. Libraries Assn., Med. Libraries Assn., Am. Soc. Info. Sci., Albuquerque C. of C., Albuquerque Conv. and Visitors Bur., Better Bus. Bur. Albuquerque, Tex. Christian U. Alumni Assn., Delta Delta Delta. Republican. Episcopalian. Home: 11137 Academy Ridge Rd NE Albuquerque NM 87111 Office: PO Box 3824 Albuquerque NM 87190-3824

GOLDSTONE, JACK ANDREW, sociologist; b. San Francisco, Sept. 30, 1953; s. Jack Robert and Ursula (Weinberg) G.; m. Gina Belinda Saleman, Feb. 9, 1992; children: Alexander, Simone. AB, Harvard U., 1976, AM, 1979, PhD, 1981. Asst. prof. Northwestern U., Evanston, Ill., 1981-84; assoc. prof. Northwestern U., 1984-88; prof. U. Calif., Davis, 1989—; dir. ctr. for comparative rsch., U. Calif., Davis, 1989-91. Author: Revolution and Rebellion, 1991 (disting. pub. award Am. Sociol. Assn. 1993); editor: Revolutions of the Late 20th Century, 1991. ACLS fellow, 1983-84, Ctr. for Advanced Studies fellow Stanford U., 1993-94. Mem. Am. Sociol. Assn., Sociol. Rsch. Assn. Office: U Calif Sociology Dept Davis CA 95616

GOLDSTRAND, DENNIS JOSEPH, business and estate planning executive; b. Oakland, Calif., July 12, 1952; s. Joseph Nelson and Frances Marie (Royce) G.; m. Judy A. Goldstrand. BSBA, Calif. State U., Chico, 1975; CLU, Am. Coll., 1986, CFC, 1988. Asst. mgr. Household Fin. Corp., San Leandro, Calif., 1975-76; registered rep. Equitable Fin. Svcs., San Francisco, 1976-79, dist. mgr., 1979-85; ptnr. Goldstrand & Small Ins. and Fin. Svcs., Stockton, Calif., 1986-89; owner Goldstrand Fin. & Ins. Svcs., Stockton, 1989—; spkr. taxation course Law Sch. Humphreys Coll. Spkr. Calif. Assn. Life Underwriters, 1986, 95; contbr. articles to Life Ins. Selling mag., 1986, 88. Mem. Stockton Estate Planning Coun., bd. dirs. 1995-96, spkr., 1996, 97; past pres. United Way San Joaquin County Endowment Found., Inc., 1994, bd. dirs. Mem. Nat. Assn. Life Underwriters (pres. Stockton chpt. 1990-91, Life Underwriter of Yr. 1994), Am. Soc. CLU (pres. Stockton chpt. 1989-90), Calif. Assn. Life Underwriters (trustee 1995—), Million Dollar Round Table, Greater Stockton C. of C., Rotary, Golden Key Soc. Home: 9215 Stony Creek Ln Stockton CA 95219-4910 Office: Goldstrand Fin & Ins Svcs 5250 Claremont Ave # 230 Stockton CA 95207-5700

GOLDZBAND, MELVIN GEORGE, psychiatrist; b. St. Louis, Nov. 6, 1929; s. Max Morris and Genevieve (Goldenson) G.; m. Marilyn Joan Miller, June 30, 1953; children: Daniel A., Lawrence J., Marjorie J. BS, U. Ill., 1950; MD, Chgo. Med. Sch., 1955. Diplomate Am. Bd. Psychiatry & Neurology. Intern Cook County Hosp., Chgo., 1955-56; resident VA Westside Hosp. Dept. of Psychiatry, Chgo., 1956-59; psychiatrist USNR, San Diego, 1959-61; pvt. practice psychiatry San Diego, 1961—; clin. prof., emeritus dir. forensic psychiat. tng. U. Calif., San Diego, 1967— . Author: Consulting in Child Custody, 1981, Quality Time, 1985, Custody Cases & Expert Witnesses, 2d edit., 1988. V.p. San Diego Symphony Orch., 1963-68. Named disting. alumnus Chgo. Med. Sch., 1992. Fellow Am. Psychiat. Assn. (life), Am. Coll. Psychiatrists, Am. Acad. Forensic Scis.; mem. Am. Acad. Psychiatry and the Law (treas.). Office: 3342 4th Ave San Diego CA 92103-5704

GOLITZ, LOREN EUGENE, dermatologist, pathologist, clinical administrator, educator; b. Pleasant Hill, Mo., Apr. 7, 1941; s. Ross Winston and Helen Francis (Schupp) G.; MD, U. Mo., Columbia, 1966; m. Deborah Burd Frazier, June 18, 1966; children: Carrie Campbell, Matthew Ross. Intern, USPHS Hosp., San Francisco, 1966-67, med. resident, 1967-69; resident in dermatology USPHS Hosp., Staten Island, N.Y., 1969-71; dep. chief dermatology, 1972-73; vis. fellow dermatology Columbia-Presbyn. Med. Ctr., N.Y.C., 1971-72; asst. in dermatology Coll. Physicians Surgeons, Columbia, N.Y.C., 1972-73; vice-chmn. Residency Rev. Com. for Dermatology, 1983-85. Earl D. Osborne fellow dermal. pathology Armed Forces Inst. Pathology, Washington, 1973-74; assoc. prof. dermatology, pathology Med. Sch. U. Colo., Denver, 1974-88; prof., 88-97; chief dermatology Denver Gen. Hosp., 1974-97; med. dir. Ambulatory Care Ctr., Denver Gen. Hosp., 1991-97; clin. prof. Pathol and Derm, 1997—. Diplomate Am. Bd. Dermatology, Nat. Bd. Med. Examiners. Fellow Royal Soc. Medicine; mem. Am. Soc. Dermatopathology (sec., treas. 1985-89, pres.-elect 1989, pres. 1990), Am. Acad. Dermatology (chmn. coun. on clin. and lab. svcs., coun. sci. assembly 1987-91, bd. dirs. 1987-91, chmn. 1991), Soc. Pediatric Dermatology (pres. 1981), Soc. Investigative Dermatology, Pacific Dermatol. Assn. (exec. com. 1979-89, sec.-treas. 1984-87, pres. 1988), Noah Worcester Dermatol. Soc. (publs. com. 1980, membership com. 1989-90), Colo. Dermatol. Soc. (pres. 1978), Am. Bd. Dermatology Inc. (chmn. part II test com. 1989—, exec. com. 1993—, v.p. 1994, pres.-elect 1995, pres. 1996, dir. Emeritus, cons. to bd. 1997—), Colo. Med. Soc., Denver Med. Soc., AMA (residency rev. com. for dermatology 1982-89, dermatopathology test com. 1979-85), Denver Soc. Dermatopathology, Am. Dermatol. Assn. Editorial bd. Jour. Cutaneous Pathology, Jour. Am. Acad. Dermatology, Advances in Dermatology (editorial bd. Current Opinion in Dermatology), Women's Dermatologic Soc., So. Med. Assn., Internat. Soc. Pediatric Dermatology, Am. Contact Dermatitis Soc., Am. Soc. Dermatologic Surgery, Physicians Who Care, Am. Bd. Med. Specialties (del.), N.Y. Acad. Scis., AAAS, Brit. Assn. Dermatologists (hon.), Brazilian Soc. Dermatology (hon.), U. Mo. Med. Alumni Orgn. (bd.govs. 1993—); contbr. articles to med. jours. Home: 130 S Elm St Denver CO 80222 Office: Denver Gen Hosp Dept Dermatology 777 Bannock St # 0146 Denver CO 80204-4507

GOLLEHER, GEORGE, food company executive; b. Bethesda, Md., Mar. 16, 1948; s. George M. and Ruby Louise (Beecher) G.; div.; 1 child, Carly Lynn. BA, Calif. State U., Fullerton, 1970. Supr. acctg. J.C. Penney, Buena Park, Calif., 1970-72; systems auditor Mayfair Markets, Los Angeles, 1973, v.p., CFO, 1982-83; controller Fazio's, Los Angeles, 1974-78; group controller Fisher Foods, Ohio, 1978-79; v.p. fin. Stater Bros. Markets, Colton, Calif., 1979-82; sr. v.p., CFO Boys Markets Inc., Los Angeles, 1983—; CEO Ralph Grocery Co., Compton, Calif. Office: Ralph Grocery Co 1100 W Artesia Blvd Compton CA 90220*

GOLSTON, JOAN CAROL, psychotherapist; b. Vancouver, B.C., Can., Aug. 10, 1947; came to U.S., 1958; d. Stefan and Lydia Barbara (Fruchs) G. Student, Reed Coll.; BA, U. Wash., 1977, MSW, 1979. Cert. social worker; bd. cert. diplomate in clin. social work Am. Bd. Examiners in Clin. Social Work. Clin. supr. Crisis Clinic, Seattle, 1975-77; psychiatric social worker Valley Gen. Hosp., Renton, Wash., 1979-82; psychotherapist pvt. practice, Seattle, 1981—; sch. counselor Northwest Sch., Seattle, Seattle Acad.; clin. cons. outpatient dept. Valley Cities Cmty. Mental Health, Renton, 1991, Seattle Counseling Svcs., 1991-96, emergency svcs., 1975-89; cons., trainer and presenter in field. Contbr. articles to profl. jours. Bd. dirs. Open Door Clinic, Seattle, 1975-76, Northwest Family Tng. Inst., Seattle, v.p., 1990, pres., 1991, mem. exec. com., 1988-91; mem. adv. bd. Ctr. Prevention of Sexual and Domestic Violence, 1993—, AIDS Risk Reduction Project Sch. Social Work U. Wash., 1988-93. Nat. Merit scholar, 1964. Mem. NASW (diplomate), Wash. State chpt. NASW (chmn. com. on inquiry ethics 1996—, mem. com. 1992—), Internat. Soc. Study of Dissociation, Internat. Soc. Trauma Stress Studies, Acad. Cert. Social Workers. Office: 726 Broadway Ste 303 Seattle WA 98122-4337

GOLUBIC, THEODORE ROY, sculptor, designer, inventor; b. Lorain, Ohio, Dec. 9, 1928; s. Ivan and Illonka (Safar) G.; m. Rose Andrina Ieraci-Golubic, Nov. 27, 1958; children: Vincivan, Theodore E., Victor, Georjia. Student Ohio State U., Columbus, 1947-48; BFA in Painting, Miami U., Oxford, Ohio, 1951; student Syracuse U., 1955; MFA in Sculpture, U. Notre Dame, 1957. Asst. to Ivan Mestrovic, 1954-60; guest tchr. U. Notre Dame, 1959; urban planner redevel. dept., South Bend, Ind., 1960-65; sculpture cons., Rock of Ages Corp., 1965-67; instr. Cen. Mo. State U., 1969; instr. San Diego Sculptors' Guild, 1970-71; artist-in-residence Roswell (N.Mex.) Mus. and Art Ctr., 1971-72; sculptor, designer, inventor, 1958—; works include: 4 dimensional sun environ. design, South Bend, Ind., Limestone relief sculpture Cathedral of the Nativity, Dubuque, Iowa, The Crypt Series, ROA Corp., Barre, Vt., bronze St. John Bapt., Lorain, Ohio, 4 pt. surface pick-up, 3 dimensional interconnected integrated cir., multilevel S.I.P. package, isolated heatsink bonding pads, lead form as test, semiconductor chip module (Eureka award Motorola, Inc.), Phoenix, mahogany bas relief U. San Diego. With U.S. Army, 1951-53. Mem. Coll. Art Assn. Am., Internat. Sculpture Ctr. Contbr. articles to profl. jours. Home and Studio: 4015 W Topeka Dr Glendale AZ 85308-7536

GOMAN, JON GIFFORD, university chaplain, educator; b. Corvallis, Oreg., Nov. 7, 1946; s. Edward Gordon and LaVerne Pruden Goman; m. Elizabeth Nisbet Marty; children: Nicholas, Jessica, Timothy. BA with honors, U. Puget Sound, 1968; D of Religion, Claremont Sch. Theology, 1976. Assoc. rector St. Michael & All Angels, Issaquah, Wash., 1976-78; tchr. Episcopal Theol. Sch., Claremont, Calif., 1979-81; priest-in-charge Holy Nativity Episcopal Ch., L.A., 1979-81; Episcopal chaplain Oreg. State U., Corvallis, 1981—; tchr. Linn-Benton C.C., Albany, Oreg., 1984—, Ctr. for the Diaconate, Scio, Oreg., 1984—; chmn. Dept. Ministry in Higher Edn. Diocese of Oreg., 1992—. Author: The Ordination of Women, 1976, A Few Words on the Book of Common Prayer, 1993; author, editor: A Bibliography of Secondary Sources for the Gospel Readings of the Eucharistic Lectionary, 1993. Danforth fellow, 1968. Office: St Anselm of Canterbury 2615 NW Arnold Way Corvallis OR 97330-5308

GOMEZ, DAVID FREDERICK, lawyer; b. Los Angeles, Nov. 19, 1940; s. Fred and Jennie (Fujier) G.; m. Kathleen Holt, Oct. 18, 1977. BA in Philosophy, St. Paul's Coll., Washington, 1965, MA in Theology, 1968; JD, U. So. Calif., 1974. Bar: Calif. 1975, U.S. Dist. Ct. (cen. dist.) Calif. 1975, U.S. Dist. Ct. (ea. dist.) Calif. 1977, Ariz. 1981, US. Dist. Ct. Ariz. 1981, U.S. Ct. Claims 1981, U.S. Ct. Appeals (9th cir.) 1981, U.S. Supreme Ct. 1981; ordained priest Roman Cath. Ch., 1969. Staff atty. Nat. Labor Relations Bd., Los Angeles, 1974-75; ptnr. Gomez, Paz, Rodriguez & Sanora, Los Angeles, 1975-77, Garrett, Bourdette & Williams, San Francisco, 1977-80, Van O'Steen & Ptnrs., Phoenix, 1981-85; pres. David F. Gomez, PC, Phoenix, 1985—; mem. faculty Practicing Law Inst., 1989. Author: Somos Chicanos: Strangers in Our Own Land, 1973; co-author Advanced Strategies in Employment Law, 1988. Mem. ABA, Maricopa County Bar Assn., Los Abogados Hispanic Bar Assn., Nat. Employment Lawyer's Assn., Calif. State Bar Assn., Ariz. State Bar Assn. (com. on rules of profl. conduct 1991—, civil jury instructions com. 1992-94, peer rev. com. 1992—). Democrat.

GOMEZ, FRANK ANTHONY, chemist, researcher; b. San Gabriel, Calif., Apr. 10, 1964; s. Frank Aranda and Irene Marie (Serrato) G.; m. Olivia Corral, Sept. 18, 1993. BS in Chemistry, Calif. State. U., L.A., 1986; PhD, UCLA, 1991. Postdoctoral fellow Harvard U., Cambridge, Mass., 1991-94; asst. prof. Calif. State U., L.A., 1994—. Postdoctoral fellow Damon Runyon-Walter Winchell Cancer Rsch. Fund, 1991-94. Mem. AAAS, Am. Chem. Soc., Soc. Advancement Chicanos and Native Ams. in Sci. (bd. dirs. 1993-96). Democrat. Roman Catholic. Office: Calif State U LA Dept Chemistry & Biochem 5151 State University Dr Los Angeles CA 90032

GOMEZ, LAURA MARIE, mental health therapist; b. Sept. 26, 1958; d. Guadalupe Richard and Benita (Ontiveros) G. BS, Brigham Young U., 1984, M in Health Edn., 1987; MEd, U. Utah, 1995. Cert. biofeedback therapist; cert. gerontologist. Instr. Utah Valley State Coll., Orem, Utah, 1986-87; biofeedback therapist Utah Valley Regional Med. Ctr., Provo, 1986-92; adj. prof. Brigham Young U., Provo, 1988-95; instr. Utah State Correctional Facility, Draper, 1990-95; biofeedback therapist Intermountain Pain Mgmt. Ctr., Orem, 1992-95; mental health therapist Pain & Stress Medicine Inst., Salt Lake City, 1995—; stress mgmt. cons., Utah, 1986—; mental health therapist cons., Provo, Utah, 1992—. Vol. Utah County Hospice, Provo, 1984; crisis counselor Utah County Rape Crisis, Provo, 1985-86; co-therapist Utah County AIDS Support Group, Provo, 1991-94. Mem. Am. Counseling Assn., Assn. for Applied Psychophysiology & Biofeedback, Inst. of Noetic Sciero. Home: 674 W 1870 N Orem UT 84057 Office: Health South Rehab Hosp of Utah 8074 South 1300 East Sandy UT 84094

GOMEZ, LOUIS SALAZAR, college president; b. Santa Ana, Calif., Dec. 7, 1939; s. Louis Reza and Mary (Salazar) G.; m. Patricia Ann Aboytes, June 30, 1962; children: Louis Aboytes, Diana Maria, Ramon Reza. Student, Calif. State Poly. U., 1959-65; BA, Calif. State U., San Bernardino, 1971; MA, Calif. State U., 1975; EdD, U. So. Calif., L.A., 1987. Cert. tchr., counselor, adminstr., Calif. Tchr., counselor San Bernardino City Schs., 1971-76; human rels. coord. San Bernardino Valley Coll., 1976-78, counselor, 1978-82, coord. of counseling, 1982-87; asst. dean student svcs. Crafton Hills Coll., Yucaipa, Calif., 1987-89, dean student svcs., 1989-90, acting pres., 1990-92, pres., 1992—; lectr. Calif. State U., San Bernardino, 1976-81, mem. adv. bd., 1987-95. Bd. dirs. Redlands YMCA. Mem. San Bernardino Valley Coll. Faculty Assn. (treas. 1980-82), Faculty Assn. Calif. Community Colls., San Bernardino Community Coll. Dist. Mgmt. Assn., Kiwanis (pres. San Bernardino chpt. 1982). Democrat. Roman Catholic. Home: 10682 Berrywood Cir Yucaipa CA 92399-5924 Office: Crafton Hills Coll 11711 Sand Canyon Rd Yucaipa CA 92399-1742

GÔMEZ, RICARDO JUAN, philosophy educator; b. Buenos Aires, Jan. 23, 1935; came to U.S., 1976; s. Inocencio A. and Maria T. (Pianzola) G.; m. Maria J. Proaño. MA, Ind. U., 1978, PhD, 1982. Prof. U. LaPlata, Argentina, 1967-76; prof. methodology U. Buenos Aires, 1970-76, prof. logic, 1970-74; prof. philosophy of sci. U. Quito, 1978-82; prof. philosophy and sci. Nat. U., Mex., 1978, 82 summer; asspc. prof. philosophy Calif. State U., L.A., 1983-87, prof., 1987—; dir. Inst. of Logic of Philosophy of Sci., La Plata, 1970-76; dean Sch. of Arts and Letters, La Plata, 1973-74. Author: Scientific Theories, 1977, Neoliberalism and Pseudoscience, 1995; contbr. articles to profl. jours. Recipient Konex's prize, Argentina, 1996. Mem. Philosophy of Sci. Assn., Am. Philos. Assn., N.Am. Kant Soc., Soc. for Philosophy Tech., Honors Soc. for Internat. Scholars, Sogedad Filbosofia Iberoamericana. Office: Philosophy Dept Calif State U 5151 State University Dr Los Angeles CA 90032

GOMEZ, RICHARD JOHN, urban planner; b. Chgo., Dec. 1, 1952; s. John Manuel and Carmen Maria (Alaniz) G.; m. Janet Ruth Hamm, June 11, 1980; children: James Lee, Ricole Marie, Veronica Leigh. BS in Urban Planning, Calif. State Poly. U., 1995. Cmty. devel. dir. City of La Verne, Calif., 1978-82; city planner City of Rancho Cucamonga, Calif., 1982-85; sr. dir. Forma, Newport Beach, Calif., 1985-87; sr. project mgr. Lewis Homes Calif., Upland, 1987-89; dep. city mgr. City of Arcadia, Calif., 1994-95; cmty. devel. dir. City of Rancho Cucamonga, 1989-94, 1995—. Commr. Environment Quality Bd., La Verne, 1983-85, Econ. Devel., San Bernardino County, 1986-87, Am. Youth Soccer Orgn., Upland, 1995—, soccer coach. Named Outstanding Young Man in Am., 1980. Mem. Am. Planning Assn. (Inland Empire sect. pres. 1985-87, Disting. Svc. award 1994). Office: City of Rancho Cucamonga 10500 Civic Center Dr Rancho Cucamonga CA 91730-3801

GONG, HENRY, JR., physician, researcher; b. Tulare, Calif., May 23, 1947; s. Henry and Choy (Low) G.; m. Janice Wong; children: Gregory, Jaimee. BA, U. of the Pacific, 1969; MD, U. Calif., Davis, 1973. Diplomate Am. Bd. Internal Medicine, 1977, Pulmonary Disease subspecialty bd., 1980. Resident in medicine Boston U., 1973-75; fellow in pulmonary medicine UCLA Med. Ctr., 1975-77; asst. prof., then assoc. prof. Sch. Medicine UCLA, 1977-89, prof. medicine, 1989-93; assoc. chief pulmonary div. UCLA Med. Ctr., 1985-92; chief Environ. Health Svc. Rancho Los Amigos Med. Ctr., 1993—; prof. medicine U. So. Calif., 1993—; dir. Environ. Exposure Lab., UCLA, 1988-93; chmn. dept. medicine Rancho Los Amigos Med. Ctr., 1996—; mem. pub. health and socio-econs. task force South Coast Air Quality Mgmt. Dist., El Monte, Calif., 1989-90. Contbr. over 300 articles to rsch. publs., chpts. to books; editorial bd. Jour. Clin. Pharmacology, 1983—, Heart and Lung Jour., 1984-92, Am. Jour. Critical Care, 1992—. Elder on session Pacific Palisades Presbyn. Ch., 1984-86, 89-91. Fellow Am. Coll. Chest Physicians (pres. Calif. chpt. 1991-92), Am. Coll. Clin. Pharmacology; mem. Am. Thoracic Soc., Am. Fedn. Clin. Rsch., Western Soc. Clin. Investigation, Air and Waste Mgmt. Assn., Phi Eta Sigma, Phi Kappa Phi. Office: Environ Health Svc Rancho Los Amigos Med Ctr 7601 Imperial Hwy Downey CA 90242-3456

GONG, MAMIE POGGIO, elementary education educator; b. San Francisco, June 26, 1951; d. Louis and Mary Lee (Lum) G.; m. Andy Anthony Poggio. BA, U. Calif., Berkeley, 1973, postgrad., 1981-83, MEd, 1982. Tchr. Oakland (Calif.) Unified Sch. Dist., 1974-84, Palo Alto (Calif.) Unified Sch. Dist., 1984—; cons., writer Nat. Clearinghouse for Bilingual Edn., Washington, 1984; cons. ARC Assocs., Oakland, 1983; rsch. asst. dept. edn. Stanford U., 1987-89. Co-author: Promising Practices: A Teacher Resource, 1984. Recipient Kearney Found. award, 1969, others. Mem. Tchrs. English to Speakers Other Langs. (presenter 1990 conf.), Calif. Assn. Tchrs. English to Speakers Other Langs. Democrat. Office: Palo Alto Unified Sch Dist 25 Churchill Ave Palo Alto CA 94306-1005

GONYEA, BRUCE EDWARD, mortgage company executive; b. Flint, Mich., Feb. 13, 1944; s. George M. Gonyea and Leona M. (Cooper) Mudd; m. Carol A. Gonyea (div. Nov. 7, 1987); children: Burce E. Jr., Gwen J.; m. Della Telghemti Gonyea, Dec. 7, 1991.. Assoc. in Bus., Baker Coll., 1978. Pres. Pioneer Mortgage, Las Vegas, 1981-88, Westwind Mortgage, Las Vegas, 1988—, Pro-File Mortgage, Henderson, Nev., 1989—. Mem. Rep. Men's Club, Las Vegas, 1981—, past bd. dirs. Home: 376 W Viewmont Dr Henderson NV 89015 Office: Pro-File Mortgage Corp 376 W Viewmont Dr Henderson NV 89015-7044

GONZALES, DANIEL S., lawyer; b. San Antonio, Nov. 10, 1959; s. Sam and Mary Louise (Stewart) G.; m. Mary David McCauley, May 16, 1980 (div. 1983); m. Elaine Devon Cattell, Jan. 1, 1988. BA, U. Notre Dame, 1981; JD, Stanford U., 1984. Bar: Calif. 1986, U.S. Dist. Ct. (no. dist.) Calif. 1986, U.S. Tax Ct. 1987, U.S. Ct. Appeals (9th cir.) 1988, U.S. Dist. Ct. (ea. dist.) Calif. 1990. Trivia game writer Axlon Games, Sunnyvale, Calif., 1984; legal writer Matthew Bender & Co., San Francisco, 1984-86; assoc. Carey & Carey, Palo Alto, Calif., 1986-96, Ferrari, Olsen, Ottoboni & Bebb, San Jose, Calif., 1996—. Mng. editor Stanford Jour. Internat. Law, 1983-84. Candidate Menlo Park (Calif.) City Coun., 1988; bd. dirs. Page Mill YMCA, Palo Alto, 1993—, Project Match, 1997—; pres. Menlo Park Dispute Resolution Svc., 1994, 95. Notre Dame scholar U. Notre Dame, 1977, Nat. Merit scholar, 1977, scholar Nat. Hispanic Scholarship Bd., 1980. Mem. ABA, San Mateo County La Raza Lawyers (pres. 1994), Santa Clara County Bar Assn. (chmn. minority access com. 1994, chmn. judiciary com. 1995). Democrat. Office: Ferrari Olsen Ottoboni & Bebb Ste 700 333 W Santa Clara St San Jose CA 95113-1787

GONZALES, RICHARD L., fire department chief. AA in Fire Sci. Tech., Red Rocks C.C., 1988; BS summa cum laude in Bus. Adminstrn., Regis U., 1991; MA, Harvard U., 1991; student, U. Colo. Firefighter Denver Fire Dept., 1972-75, mem. fire prevention bureau, dist. 5 roving officer, 1976-79, mem. training divsn., 1980-81, dist. roving officer firefighter, 1981-82, capt. firefighter pumper 2 and 27, 1982-85, asst. chief, 1985-87, chief fire dept., 1987—; Mem. Nat. Fire Protective Assn. Urban Fire Forum, Internat. Assn. Fire Chiefs, Metro Fire Chiefs Assn., Denver Metro Fire Chiefs Assn., Colo. State Fire Chiefs Assn., Urban Fire Forum, IAFF Local 858 Negotiating Team; bd. trustees Nat. Fire Protection Assn., 1992-95. Mem. adv. bd. U. Colo. Denver Sch. of Pub. Affairs, Red Rocks C.C., Denver Ptnrs., KAZY Denver Marathon; bd. trustees Nat. Multiple Sclerosis Soc.; bd. dirs. Rocky Mountain Poison Drug Found., Chic Chicana, Golden Gloves Charity. Recipient Outstanding Achievement award Hispanics of Colo., 1987; named Young Firefighter of the Yr., 1981. Office: Denver Fire Dept 745 W Colfax Ave Denver CO 80204-2612*

GONZALES, RICHARD ROBERT, academic administrator; b. Palo Alto, Calif., Jan. 12, 1945; s. Pedro and Virginia (Ramos) G.; m. Jennifer Ayres; children: Lisa Dianne, Jeffrey Ayres. AA, Foothill Coll., 1966; BA, San Jose (Calif.) State U., 1969; MA, Calif. Poly. State U., San Luis Obispo, 1971; grad. Def. Info. Sch., Def. Equal Opportunity Mgmt. Inst. Counselor student activities Calif. Poly. State U., San Luis Obispo, 1969-71, instr. ethnic studies, 1970-71; counselor Ohlone Coll., Fremont, Calif., 1971-72, coord. coll. readiness, 1971; counselor De Anza Coll., Cupertino, Calif., 1972-78, mem. community speakers bur., 1975-78; counselor Foothill Coll., Los Altos Hills, Calif., 1978—, mem. community speakers bur., 1978—; instr. Def. Equal Opportunity Mgmt. Inst., 1984—. Mem. master plan com. Los Altos (Calif.) Sch. Dist., 1975-76; vol. worker, Chicano communities, Calif.; active mem. Woodside (Calif.) Recreation Commn. With Calif. Army N.G., now maj. Adj. Gen. Corps, USAR. Recipient Counselor of Yr. award Ohlone Coll., 1971-72; Masters and Johnson Inst. fellow. lic. marriage family child counselor, Calif. Mem. ACA, Am. Coll. Counseling Assn., Calif. Assn. Marriage and Family Therapists, Calif. Community Coll. Counselor Assn. (former pres.), Calif. Assn. Counseling and Devel. (former pres. Hispanic Caucus), Calif. Assn. for Humanistic Edn. and Devel., Calif. Assn. for Multi-Cultural Counseling, Res. Officers Assn., La Raza Faculty Assn. Calif. Community Colls., Nat. Career Devel. Assn., Phi Delta Kappa, Chi Sigma Iota. Democrat. Office: Foothill Coll Los Altos CA 94022

GONZALES, STEPHANIE, state official; b. Santa Fe, Aug. 12, 1950; 1 child, Adan Gonzales. Degree, Loretto Acad. for Girls. Office mgr. Jerry Wood & Assocs., 1973-86; dep. sec. of state Santa Fe, 1987-90, sec. of state, 1991; bd. dirs. N.Mex. Pub. Employees Retirement, N.Mex. State Convassing Bd., N.Mex. Commn. Pub. Records. Mem. exec. bd. N.Mex. AIDS Svc.; mem. Commn. White House Fellowships. Mem. Nat. Assn. Secs. State, United League United Latin Am. Citizens (women's coun.). Office: Office of the Sec of State State Capitol Rm 420 Santa Fe NM 87503

GONZALEZ, ARTHUR PADILLA, artist, educator; b. Sacramento, July 22, 1954; s. John and Rita (Padilla) G.; m. Christine Carol Ciavarella, Feb. 11, 1988; stepchild, Nick Port. BA, Calif. State U., Sacramento, 1977, MA, 1979; MFA, U. Calif., Davis, 1981. Vis. artist La. State U., Baton Rouge, 1982-83, U. Ga., Athens, summer 1984, R.I. Sch. Design, Providence, 1985; asst. prof. U. Calif., Davis, 1985-86, Berkeley, 1987-88; vis. artist, instr. San Francisco Art Inst., 1990-91; assoc. prof. art Calif. Coll. Arts & Crafts, Oakland, 1991—; mem. adv. bd. Calif. Craft Mus., San Francisco, 1994-95; juror Sacramento Met. Arts Commn., 1994-95. One-person shows include Sharpe Gallery, N.Y.C., 1984, 86, 88, Phyllis King Gallery, N.Y.C., 1995. Recipient awards Nat. Endowment for Arts, 1982, 84, 86, 90. Democrat.

Home: 1713 Versailles Ave Alameda CA 94501-1650 Office: Calif Coll Arts & Crafts 5212 Broadway Oakland CA 94618-1426

GONZALEZ, ELIZABETH FARR, accountant, management consultant; b. San Diego, July 24, 1946; d. Michael Ibs and Elizabeth (Sibley) G. AB in History, Stanford U., 1968; MA in History, U. Calif., Riverside, 1970; post-grad., George Mason U., 1984-87, U. Richmond, 1986, Rice U., 1989. Dir. rsch. and ref. Am. Symphony Orch. League, Washington, 1984-87; dir. fin. Syracuse (N.Y.) Symphony, 1986-87; dir. mktg. and pub. rels. Albany (N.Y.) Symphony, 1986-88, Fla. Philharm., Ft. Lauderdale, 1988; contr. Cellular One-Richmond, Va., 1985-87; Recell produce planner Celltech, Inc., Houston, 1987-90; acct. Camp Fire of the Ctrl. Coast, Arroyo Grande, Calif., 1994-95; contr. Raiice Publishing, Atascadero, Calif., 1995—; cons. Omaha Symphony, 1988, Fla. Philharm. Orch., 1988, Camp Fire of Kern County, Bakersfield, Calif., 1994, various cellular telephone cos., 1990-92. Author: (manual) Financial Planning and Reporting for Symphony Orchestras, 1986. Tutor San Luis Obispo (Calif.) Literacy Coun., 1992-93; mem. City of Morro Bay (Calif.) Cable Bd., 1992-93. Mem. Inst. Mgmt. Accts. (v.p. profl. edn. Ctrl. Coast chpt. 1994—), Ctrl. Coast Women's Soccer Assn. (publicity dir. 1994—), Stanford Club of Ctrl. Coast. Republican. Episcopalian. Home: 1297 15th St Los Osos CA 93402-1415

GONZALEZ, IRMA ELSA, federal judge; b. 1948. BA, Stanford U., 1970; JD, U. Ariz., 1973. Law clk. to Hon. William C. Frey U.S. Dist. Ct. (Ariz. dist.), 1973-75; asst. U.S. atty. U.S. Attys. Office Ariz., 1975-79, U.S. Attys. Office (ctrl. dist.) Calif., 1979-81; trial atty. antitrust divsn. U.S. Dept. Justice, 1979; assoc. Seltzer Caplan Wilkins & McMahon, San Diego, 1981-84; judge U.S. Magistrate Ct. (so. dist.) Calif., 1984-91; ct. judge San Diego County Superior Ct., 1991-92; dist. judge U.S. Dist. Ct. (so. dist.) Calif., San Diego, 1992—; adj. prof. U. San Diego, 1992; trustee Calif. Western Sch. Law. Mem. Girl Scout Women's Adv. Cabinet. Mem. Nat. Assn. Women Judges, Lawyers' Club San Diego, Thomas More Soc., Inns of Ct. Office: Edward J Schwartz US Courthouse 940 Front St Ste 5135 San Diego CA 92101-8913

GONZALEZ, JESUS MANUEL, hospital program administrator; b. Cardenas, Cuba, Feb. 12, 1957. Student, Boston Coll., 1980; BA, Met. State Coll., 1995. Cert. flight attendant. Customer svc. mgr. Air Fla., Miami, 1982-86; airline steward Arrow Air, Miami, 1986-88; cmty. outreach coord. AIDS Edn. Program, Colo. AIDS Project, Denver, 1987-89; epidemiologist II STD/AIDS Edn. and Tng. Program Colo. Dept. Health, Denver, 1989-93; social work assoc. pediatric infectious diseases Children's Hosp., Denver, 1993—. Contbr. articles to profl. jours. Mem. edn. adv. com. Am. Found. AIDS Rsch., Colo. HIV/AIDS Consumer Info. Task Force, material rev. panel ARC, material rev. com. Ctr. for Health Policy Devel., Inc., material rev. panel Colo. Dept. Edn.; bd. dirs. The Masske Project, Denver Health and Hosps., Gay and Lesbian Cmty. Ctr. Colo., 1989-93, Legal Ctr. for People with Disabilities, 1991-92. Home: 1347 Lafayette St Denver CO 80218-2305 Office: Children's Hosp Campus B055 Ped Infectious Diseases 1056 E 19th Ave Denver CO 80218-1007

GONZÁLEZ-TRUJILLO, CÉSAR AUGUSTO, Chicano studies educator, writer; b. L.A., Jan. 17, 1931; s. José Andalón and Camerina (Trujillo) González; m. Bette L. Beattie, Aug. 30, 1969. BA, Gonzaga U., 1953, MA, Licentiate in Philosophy, 1954; MST, Licentiate in Sacred Theology, U. Santa Clara, 1961; postgrad., UCLA, 1962-65. Tchr. Instituto Regional Mex., Chihuahua, Mex., 1954-57; community devel. specialist Centro Laboral Méx., México D.F., Mex., 1965-68; supr. ABC Headstart East L.A., L.A., 1968-69; employment counselor Op. SER, San Diego, 1969-70; prof., founding chair dept. Chicano studies San Diego Mesa Coll., 1970—; founding chairperson Raza Consortium, San Diego, 1971-72; cons. Chicano Fedn. San Diego, Inc., 1987-89. Author poetry, short fiction and criticism; editor, asst. editor lit. jours., 1976—; contbr. numerous articles to profl. jours. Mem. Ednl. Issues Coordinating Com., L.A., 1968-69; founding bd. dirs. Mex.-Am. Adv. Com. to Bd. of Edn., L.A., 1969. Fulbright-Hays fellow, Peru, 1982, NEH fellow, 1984; recipient Cmty. Svc. award Chicano Fedn. San Diego Inc., 1982, Teaching Excellence award Nat. Inst. Staff and Orgnl. Devel., 1983, Outstanding Tchr. San Diego Mesa Coll., 1985, 95, Editor's Choice award Poet Mag., 1993, Cesar Chavez Social Justice award, 1994, Latina Latino Indigenous People Coalition award, 1995; named Outstanding Tchr. and Scholar, Concilio of Chicano Studies for San Diego, Imperial Valley and Baja, Calif., 1990; Spl. Congl. recognition, 1995; AVID Writer of the Yr. award San Diego Imperial Counties, 1997. Mem. Am. Fedn. Tchrs., Nat. Assn. Chicano Studies, La Raza Faculty Assn., Chicano Fedn. San Diego County, Centro Cultural De La Raza (past bd. dirs.), Poets and Writers, Asociación Internacional de Hispanistas. Democrat. Roman Catholic. Office: San Diego Mesa Coll 7250 Mesa College Dr San Diego CA 92111-4902

GOOCH, LAWRENCE BOYD, accounting executive; b. L.A., Oct. 20, 1942; s. John Elmer and Roberta Alice (Grant) G.; m. Barbara Ann Buehrig, June 21, 1970; children: Brenda, Timothy, Ted. BSCE, Stanford U., 1965, MBA, 1970. Cons. Am. Appraisal Co., Milw., 1970-71; v.p. Am. Valuation Cons., Chgo., 1971-78, Stone Webster Appraisal, Woodland Hills, Calif., 1979-80; sr. v.p. Arthur D. Little Valuation, Woodland Hills, 1980-88; prin. Price Waterhouse, L.A., 1988—. Capt. USMC, 1965-67, Vietnam. Mem. Stanford Alumni Assn., Stanford Bus. Sch. Alumni Assn., Am. Soc. Appraisers (sr.). Home: 3939 Freshwind Cir Westlake Vlg CA 91361-3804 Office: Price Waterhouse 400 S Hope St Los Angeles CA 90071-2889

GOOD, EDITH ELISSA, writer; b. Hollywood, Calif., Jan. 10, 1945; d. Jack Brian and Rose Marie (Miller) G.; m. Michael Lawrence Black, Dec. 18, 1986. BA in English, Calif. State U. Northridge, 1974. Author, pub. Gull Press, L.A., 1990-95, Tal-San Publ., Distbg., Glendale, Ariz., 1995—; dancer Hajde Dance Troup, Berkeley, Calif., 1962-66. One-person art shows include librs. and h.s., L.A., 1962-95; pub. author and poet including novel Mad in Craft, 1995. Mem. ASCAP, Mensa. Home and Office: 335 N Stanley Ave #220 Los Angeles CA 90036

GOOD, JANET LOIS, occupational health nurse; b. Coudersport, Pa., Mar. 18, 1938; d. Warren Worth and Jeannette (Britton) Ohlman; m. Robert Jack Good, Feb. 14, 1960; children: Diana Ivy, Robert Warren. Diploma in nursing, Pa. Hosp., 1958; cert. in alcohol studies, U. N.D., 1970; cert. in nurse practition, U. Colo., 1973; BS in Health Care Adminstrn., St. Joseph Coll., 1987. Cert. occupational health nurse, cert. instr. CPR, cert. audiometry, spirometry. Staff and recovery room nurse Children's Hosp., Phila., 1958-60; supr. male div. Pennhurst State Sch. for Mentally Retarded, Spring City, Pa., 1961-65; office nurse Pediatric Clinic, Denver, 1966-69; nurse practitioner mgr. Mountain Bell, Denver, 1969-82; adminstrv. nurse Atlantic Richfield Co., Denver, 1982-94; mgr. faculty/staff health svcs. U. Colo. Wardenberg Student Health Ctr., Boulder, Colo., 1994—; presenter health care topics 1978—; U. Colo. Nightingale Awards com. 1992—; Cardiovascular Disease Bi-annual Conf. Planning com., 1990—. Rep. com. woman Adams County, Northglenn, Colo., 1980; del. Rep. State Conv., Denver, 1980; counselor merit badges Boy Scouts Am., Northglenn, 1984-85. Mem. Am. Nurses Assn. (cert.), Am. Nurses Assn. Primary Coun. Nurse Practitioners, Am. Assn. Occupational Health Nurses (bd. dirs. 1983-87, sec. 1987-91), Colo. Assn. Occupational Health Nurses (corr. sec. 1975-76, pres.-elect 1977-78, pres. 1978-79, named Occupational Health Nurse of Yr. 1979, Schering Occupational Health Nurse 1985), Denver Assn. Occupational Health Nurses. Lodge: Order Eastern Star. Office: Univ Colorado at Boulder Campus Box 119 Boulder CO 80309-0119

GOOD, REBECCA MAE WERTMAN, learning and behavior disorder counselor, grief and loss counselor, hospice nurse; b. Barberton, Ohio, May 13, 1943; d. Frederick Daniel Wertman and Freda Beam Wertman Lombardi; m. William Robert Good Jr., Aug. 15, 1964; children: William Robert III, John Joseph, Matthew Stephan. RN diploma, Akron Gen. Med. Ctr., Ohio, 1964; BS in Psychology, Ramapo Coll., Mahwah, N.J., 1986; MA in Counseling, NYU, 1990. RN, Utah; nat. cert. counselor; cert. psychiat. and mental health nurse. Staff nurse Green Cross Gen. Hosp., Cuyahoga Falls, Ohio, 1965-68; staff nurse, relief supr., psychiat. nurse F.D.R. VA Hosp., Montrose, N.Y., 1971-72; geriatric staff and charge nurse Westledge Extended Care Facility, Peekskill, N.Y., 1972-77; infirmary and ICF nurse St. Dominics Home, Orangeburg, N.Y., 1981-83; allergy and immunology nurse Dr. Andre Codispoti, Suffern, N.Y., 1979-89; rsch. asst. counselor NYU, N.Y.C., 1989-90; Rockland advocate Student Advocacy Inc., White Plains, N.Y., 1989-90; exec. dir. Rockland County Assn. for Learning Disabled, Orangeburg, 1990-91; life skills counselor Bd. Coop. Edn., West Nyack, N.Y., 1991-93; learning and behavior disorders counselor, Suffern, 1991-93, Salt Lake City, 1994—; hospice nurse United Hospice Rockland, 1991-93; assessment and referral counselor/case mgr. CPC Olympus View Hosp., Salt Lake City, 1994—; practitioner, tchr. Therapeutic Touch, 1990—. Co-chmn. Rockland County Coordinating Coun. for Devel. Disabled Offenders, New City, N.Y., 1990-93; bd. visitors Rockland Children's Psychiat. Ctr., Orangeburg, 1991-93, sec., 1992; mem. U.S. Congressman Benjamin Gilman's Handicapped Adv. Com., Rockland County, 1985-94; pres. Ramapo Ctrl. Sch. Dist. Spl. Edn. PTA, 1982-86. Ramapo Coll. of N.J. Pres.'s scholar, 1986. Mem. ACA, Utah Counselors Assn., Children and Adults with Attention Deficit Disorders (coord. Rockland chpt. 1992-93), Hospice Nurses Assn., Nurse Healers Profl. Assn., Utah Networker Nurse Healers Profl. Assn. Episcopalian. Office: 7730 S Quicksilver Dr Salt Lake City UT 84121-5500

GOOD, WILLIAM ZEV, physician; b. Wilno, Poland, Apr. 27, 1924; s. Dov Ber and Chana (Kopelowicz) Gdud; m. Pearl Esterowicz, June 7, 1953; children: Leonard James, Michael Daniel, Anne Margaret. MD, U. Turin, Italy, 1951; postgrad. in comprehensive medicine, NYU Postgrad. Med. Sch., 1953-54. Diplomate Am. Bd. Family Practice. Rotating intern St. Elizabeth Hosp., Elizabeth, N.J., 1952-53; ob-gyn. resident Cumberland Hosp., Bklyn., 1954-55; pvt. practice family medicine La Puente, Calif., 1956—. Mem. Am. Jewish Com., 1980. Mem. AMA, Calif. Med. Assn., Calif. Acad. Family Practice, Am. Acad. Family Practice, Zionist Orgn. of Am. Jewish. Office: 1840 N Hacienda Blvd La Puente CA 91744-1143

GOODALL, JACKSON WALLACE, JR., restaurant company executive; b. San Diego, Oct. 29, 1938; s. Jackson Wallace and Evelyn Violet (Koski) G.; m. Mary Esther Buckley, June 22, 1958; children: Kathleen, Jeffery, Suzanne, Minette. BS, San Diego State U., 1960. With Foodmaker, Inc., San Diego, 1963—, pres., 1970—, chief exec. officer, 1979—, chmn. bd., 1985—; founder, bd. dir. Grossmont Bank, La Mesa, Calif.; bd. dirs. Thrifty Drug Stores Inc., Van Camp Seafood Inc.; owner, dir., bd. dirs. San Diego Padres Baseball Club. Bd. dirs. Greater San Diego Sports Assn.; mem. Pres.'s Coun. San Diego State U.; chmn. Child Abuse Prevention Found.; dir. San Diego Hall Champions. Recipient Golden Chain award, 1982, Silver Plate award Internat. Foodsvc. Mfg. Assn., 1985; named Disting. Alumni of Yr. San Diego State U., 1974, 89, Golden Chain Operator of Yr. Multi Unit Food Svc. Operators, 1988, State of Israel Man of Yr., 1987, Citizen of Yr. City Club of San Diego, 1992, Marketer of Yr. Acad. Mktg. Sci., 1992; inducted into San Diego Bus. Hall of Fame, 1992. Mem. Am. Restaurant Assn., Fairbanks Ranch Country Club (founder), Univ. Club of San Diego, San Diego Intercollegiate Athletic Coun., Kadoo Club of N. Am. Republican. Office: Foodmaker Inc 9330 Balboa Ave San Diego CA 92123-1516

GOOD-BROWN, SUE ANN, nurse, small business owner; b. Webster City, Iowa, Nov. 29, 1960; d. George G. and Faye Joann (Simms) Good; m. Scot Warren Brown, Sept. 24, 1988; 1 child, McKenna; 1 step child, Lindsey. AD in Pol. Sci., Miles Community Coll., Miles City, Mont., 1981, ADN, 1983; cert., Sheffield Sch. of ID, 1990. RN, Mont. Owner, artist Redwater Pearl, Circle, Mont., 1985—; RN McCone County Pub. Health, Circle, 1990—; nurse McCone County Hosp., Circle, 1983-90, McCone County MAF and Nursing Home, Circle, 1992; ind. demonstrator Dozens of Terrific Stamps, Circle, 1996—. Dir. McCone County Ann. Health Fair; active McCone County MSU Ext. Adv. Bd., 1992-94, Mont. State Ext. Adv. Bd., 1992-96; svc. unit mgr. GSUSA. Mem. NRA, NOW, NAFE, Nat. Fedn. Ind. Bus., McCone County Sheepgrowers (bd. dirs.), Make it Yourself with Wool (state dir.), Mont. Woolgrower Women. Methodist. Home: PO Box 138 Circle MT 59215-0138

GOODBY, JEFFREY, advertising agency executive. Grad., Harvard Univ., 1973. Political reporter Boston; began advt. career with J. Walter Thompson; with Hal Riney & Ptnrs. San Francisco; prin., creative dir. Goodby, Silverstein & Ptnrs., San Francisco, 1983—. Office: Goodby Silverstein & Ptnrs 921 Front St San Francisco CA 94111-1426*

GOODCHILD, LESTER FRANCIS, higher education educator; b. Lackawanna, N.Y., Apr. 30, 1948; s. Thomas J. and Mary June (Devoy) Walczak; m. Wynn Evelyn Johnson, Sept. 20, 1980. BA, U. St. Thomas, 1970; MDiv with high honors, St. Meinrad Sch. Theology, 1975; MA, Indiana U., Bloomington, 1979; PhD, U. Chgo., 1986. Dir. project respond St. Meinrad (Ind.) Seminary, 1971-72; assoc. instr. dept religious studies Ind. U., 1973; supr. pastoral edn. St. Meinrad Sch. Theology, 1973-74, teaching asst. dept. ch. hist., 1974; dir. aged ministry program St. Joseph's Hosp., Huntingberg, Ind., 1973-74; deacon St. Andrew's Ch., Joliet, Ill., 1974, St. Paul the Apostle Ch., Joliet, 1975; cons. residential property ops., regional property mgr., property mgr. Lehndorff Mgmt. U.S.A. Ltd., Chgo., 1976-78; property mgr. The Habitat Co., Chgo., 1979-81; rsch. asst. ctr. for continuing edn. U. Chgo., 1979-81; instr., mentor Sch. for New Learning DePaul U., Chgo., 1981-88, dir. suburban campuses, 1987; asst. prof. higher edn. coll. edn. dept. profl. studies Iowa State U., Ames, 1988-89; adjunct rsch. assoc. ctr. for study of higher edn. Pa. State U., University Park, 1989-90; assoc. prof. edn., coord. higher edn. and adult studies program coll. edn. U. Denver, 1990—; vis. lectr. Loyola U. Sch. Edn., Chgo., 1989-90; vis. scholar, prof. Boston Coll. and Pa. State U., 1997; presenter in field. Co-editor Association for the Study of Higher Education Reader on the History of Higher Education, 1989, 2d edit., 1997, Administration as a Profession: Formal Programs in the Study of Higher Education, 1991; asst. editor (refereed jour.) Religion & Edn., 1989—; assoc. editor (annual vol.) Higher Education: Handbook of Theory and Research, 1992-96; mem. editl. bd. Jour. Gen. Edn., 1990-94, Rev. Higher Edn., 1992-95, History of Higher Edn. Ann., 1994—; contbr. articles and book reviews to profl. jours., chpts. to books. Election judge City of Chgo., 1976. Travel grantee U. Notre Dame, 1982, NEH, 1989; mini grantee Iowa State U., 1989; faculty rsch. grantee U. Denver, 1992, faculty internat. rsch. grantee; scholar Meinrad Sch. Theology, 1971-75, Ind. U., 1973. Mem. AAUP, Am. Assn. for Higher Edn., Am. Cath. Hist. Assn., Am. Ednl. Rsch. Assn. (proposal reviewer 1985, 88-92), Am. Hist. Assn., Am. Coll. Pers. Assn., Assn. Study Higher Edn. (registration com. 1984, program com. 1987, futures com. 1987-89, welcoming com. 1988—, chair disseration of yr. award com. 1990, task force on edn. in 21st century, 1990-92, chair cirriculum, learning and instruction com. 1990—, annual conf. evaluation com. 1992, proposal reviewer 1988—), Nat. Orgn. Legal Problems Edn., Hist. Edn. Soc., Midwest Philosophy Edn. Soc., Nat. Coun. on Religion and Pub. Edn. (article reviewer 1990—). Democrat. Roman Catholic. Home: 5667 S Geneva St Englewood CO 80111-3726 Office: U Denver Coll Edn 2450 S Vine St Denver CO 80208

GOODEY, ILA MARIE, psychologist; b. Logan, Utah, Feb. 1, 1948; d. Vernal P. and Leona Marie (Williams) Goodey. BA with honors in English and Sociology, U. Utah, 1976; Grad. Cert. Criminology, U. Utah, 1976, MS in Counseling Psychology, 1984, PhD in Psychology, 1985. Speech writer for dean of students U. Utah, Salt Lake City, 1980-89, psychologist Univ. Counseling Ctr., 1984—; cons. Dept. Social Services, State of Utah, Salt Lake City, 1983—; pvt. practice psychology Consult West, Salt Lake City, 1985-86; pub. relations coordinator Univ. Counseling Ctr., 1985—; cons. Aids Project, U. Utah, 1985—; pvt. practice psychology, Inscapes Inst., Salt Lake City, 1987-88; writer civic news Salt Lake City Corp., 1980—; mem. Senator Orrin Hatch's Adv. Com. on Disability Oriented Legis., 1989—. Author book: Love for All Seasons, 1971, Poemspun, 1994, Echoes, 1995, Rapture, 1996; play: Validation, 1979; musical drama: One Step, 1984. Contbr. articles to profl. jours. Chmn. policy bd. Dept. State Social Service, Salt Lake City, 1986—; campaign writer Utah Dem. Party, 1985; appointed to Utah State Legis. Task Force on svcs. for people with disabilities, 1990; chmn. bd. Utah Assistive Tech. Program, 1990—. Recipient Creative Achievement award Utah Poetry Soc., 1974, English SAC, U. Utah, 1978, Leadership award YWCA, 1989, Nat. Golden Rule award J.C. Penny, Washington, 1989, 90, Volunteerism award State of Utah, 1990; Ila Marie Goodey award named in honor. Mem. AAUW, Am. Psychol. Assn., Utah Psychol. Assn., Internat. Platform Assn., Mortar Board, Am. Soc. Clin. Hypnosis, Utah Soc. Clin. Hypnosis, Soc. Psychol. Study Social Issues, League of Women Voters, Phi Beta Kappa, Phi Kappa Phi, Alpha Lambda Delta. Mormon. Clubs: Mormon Theol. Symposium, Utah Poetry Assn. Avocations: theatrical activities, creative writing, travel, political activities. Office: U Utah Counseling Ctr 2450 SSB Salt Lake City UT 84112

GOODHUE, WILLIAM WALTER, JR., pathologist, army officer medical educator; b. St. Louis, Feb. 5, 1945; s. William W. and Rose Marie (Vahousek) G.; B.S. cum laude with honors, Georgetown U., 1966; M.D., Cornell U., 1970. Diplomate Am. Bd. Pathology. Intern anat. pathology N.Y. Hosp.-Cornell Med. Center, N.Y.C., 1970-71, resident anat. pathology, 1971-74; chief resident pediatric anat. pathology Columbia-Presbyn. Med. Center, N.Y.C., 1974-75; resident clin. pathology Tripler Army Med. Center, Honolulu, 1976-78, chief resident, 1978; practice medicine specializing in pathology, 1975—; instr. pathology U. Hawaii Sch. Medicine, Honolulu, 1975-76; chief dept. pathology U.S. Army Hosp., Ft. Campbell, Ky., 1978-80; chief dept. pathology, med. dir. Sch. Med. Tech., dir. pathology residency tng. Gorgas Army Hosp., C.Z. and assoc. prof. med. tech. Panama Canal Coll., 1980-82; resident officer U.S. Army Command and Gen. Staff Coll., Ft. Leavenworth, Kans., 1982-83, div. surgeon 2d Inf. Div., 1983-84; dep. comdr. clin. services, chief dept. primary care and community medicine, staff pathologist, acting comdr. Bayne-Jones Army Hosp., Ft. Polk, La., 1984-85; chief dept. pathology and area lab. services, dir. pathology residency tng. Dwight David Eisenhower Army Med. Ctr., Ft. Gordon, Ga., 1985-94; clin. assoc. prof. pathology Med. Coll. Ga., Augusta, 1986-94; chief pathology grad. med. edn. Tripler Army Med. Ctr., Honolulu, 1994-97, asst. chief dept. pathology, and area lab. svs., Tripler Army Med. Ctr. Honolulu, Hawaii, 1997—; cons. in pathology Eisenhower health service region to comdg. gen.; cons. ARC, 1978-80; rep. Alt. Army Med. Dept. to Coll. of Am. Pathologists House of Del., Am. Soc. Clin. Pathologist Adv. Coun., 1990—; mem. profl. adv. bd. Med. Lab Observer, 1993-95; Army councillor-at-large Armed Forces Med. Lab. Scientists, 1993—. Served to col., M.C., U.S. Army, 1975—. USPHS research fellow, 1971-74; decorated Order Mil. Med. Merit. Fellow Am. Soc. Clin. Pathologists, Internat. Acad. Pathology, Coll. Am. Pathologists (lab. accreditation insp. inspection and accreditation program 1988—), Am. Soc. Abdominal Surgeons; mem. Soc. for Pediatric Pathology, Med. Assn. Isthmian C.Z. (v.p. 1980-81), Assn. Mil. Surgeons U.S., Am. Assn. Blood Banks, Nashville Pathology Soc., Hawaii Soc. Pathologists, AAAS, N.Y. Acad. Scis., Soc. Armed Forces Med. Lab. Scientists, Assn. Practitioners in Infection Control, Clin. Lab. Mgrs. Assn. (bd. dirs. 1989-92), Central Savannah River Area Assn. Med. Lab. Personnel, Assn. U.S. Army, AMA (Physician's Recognition award 1976, 78, 80, 82, 86, 89, 92, 95), Alliance Francaise, Sigma Xi, Phi Beta Kappa. Republican. Roman Catholic. Clubs: Cornell of N.Y.; Kauai Yacht. Contbr. articles on pathology to profl. jours.; research in clin. pathology. Home: 45-049 Ka-Hanahou Pl Kaneohe HI 96744-3014 Office: TAMC DPALS Honolulu HI 96859-5000

GOODIN, EVELYN MARIE, writer; b. Fullerton, Calif.; d. Theodore Hopper and Nellie Mary (Henger) DeWitt; m. Robert Delmer Goodin, Feb. 23, 1950; 1 child, Michael Warren. AA, Fullerton Jr. Coll., 1942; BA, U. Calif., Santa Barbara, 1946. Tchr. Bakersfield (Calif.) City Schs., 1947-50, Stockton (Calif.) City Schs., 1950-58, San Juan Unified Schs., Carmichael, Calif., 1958-82. Author: (poetry) The Young West Sings, 1940, (children's book) The Greatest Living Scientist, 1993; editor: (poetry anthology) First the Blade, 1942; writer radio show Uncle Punkle Show, 1951. Registrar Selective Svc. Sys., Bakersfield, 1948; vol. tchr. Sacramento Safety Ctr., 1985; sec. Suburban Writers Club, Sacramento, 1986-87; mem. Fremont Presbyn. Fremont Presbyterian Inspiration Recreation Svc., 1992-96; with Friendship Inspiration Recreation Svc. Recipient First Prize in Poetry, Creative Arts Coun. Fullerton Jr. Coll., 1942, Recognition award for extended profl. svc. San Juan Tchrs. Assn., 1982. Mem. Whitney Lunch Bunch, Calif. Ret. Tchrs. Assn. (mailing com. N.E. sect. 1994-96), Sports Leisure Travel Club. Home: 5705 River Oak Way Carmichael CA 95608

GOODING, BARBARA K., marketing executive, consultant, author; b. Scranton, Pa., Oct. 29, 1940; d. Eugene Thomas and Kathryn Dorothy (Loftus) Powderly; m. James Jefferson Gooding, Jan. 13, 1997. Student, Miami (Fla.)-Dade Jr. Coll., 1960. Ordained minister, 1992. Asst. controller Oak Ridge, Inc., Hialeah, Fla., 1959-63; v.p., media dir. Harold Gardner Assocs., Inc., Miami Beach, Fla., 1963-67; media dir., adminstrv. asst. Stern, Hays & Lang Advt., Inc., Miami, 1967-69; exec. asst. Los Angeles Times, 1969-71; media dir., adminstrv. asst. Greenman Advt., Inc., Hollywood, Fla., 1971-73; asst. to gen. mgr. Sta. WGMA-FM, Hollywood, 1974; with acctg. and settlement dept. Fed. Res. Bank, Miami, 1974-75; bus. mgr. Impart Pub. Corp., Reno, 1975-76; adminstrv. asst., office mgr. Edn. Advancement Inst., Reno, 1976-78; ind. contractor Du-Bar Internat., Reno, 1979-80; pres. Capital Advt., Reno, 1980-81; dir. media Mktg. Systems Internat., Reno, 1981-82; owner Dolphin Secretarial Service, Reno, 1982-88, Dolphin Services, Reno, 1983-88, Powderly Assocs., Reno, 1982—; pres. Bus.-Promotional Services, Inc., Reno, 1986-89; ptnr. Investigative Rsch. Report Svcs., Sedona, Ariz., 1993-94, B & B Graphics, Sedona, 1991-94, Beyond Belief Metaphysical & Spiritual Resources, Sedona, 1991-94, Megatrends Mktg. Assocs., Sedona, 1991-93, Atkinson Fine Artist's Reps., Sedona, 1992-94; adminstrv. asst. III lease ops. Transp. Ctr. U. Colo., Boulder, 1994-97, mem. staff coun., 1996-97; ptnr., mktg. cons. cattle and horse breeding ranch, St. Clairsville, Ohio, 1997—; speaker Mktg. Fedn., Inc., N.Y.C., 1986; seminar developer and presenter Advt. and Mktg. for Small Bus., U. Nev. Small Bus. Ctr., 1987-88; editor non-fiction books Atkinson World Pub., Sedona, Longmont, Colo., 1992-94; writer, researcher non-fiction studies. Bd. dirs. March of Dimes, Reno, 1982; mem. Presdl. Task Force, Washington, 1983-85, Reno Women's Network, 1982-84; appointed commr. Reno Commn. on Status of Women, 1987-88. Named one of 2,000 Women of Achievement, London, 1971. Mem. Entrepreneurial Women of Reno (rec. sec., bd. dirs. 1987-88). Metaphysician.

GOODING, GRETCHEN ANN WAGNER, physician, educator; b. Columbus, Ohio, July 2, 1935; d. Edward Frederick and Margaret (List) Wagner; m. Charles A. Gooding, June 19, 1961; children: Gunnar Blaise, Justin Mathias, Britta Meghan. BA magna cum laude, St. Mary of the Springs Coll., Columbus, 1957; MD cum laude, Ohio State U., 1961. Diplomate Am. Bd. Diagnostic Radiology. Intern Univ. Hosps., Columbus, 1961-62; rsch. fellow Boston City Hosp., 1962-63, Boston U., 1963-65; with dept. radiology U. Calif., San Francisco, 1975—, assoc. prof. in radiology, 1981-85, prof., vice chmn., 1986—; asst. chief radiology VA Med. Ctr., San Francisco, 1978-87, chief radiology, 1987—, chief ultrasonography, 1975—; chair com. acad. pers. U. Calif., San Francisco, 1993-94; bd. dirs. commn. accreditation vascular labs. Suter Soc., 1993-96. Co-editor Radiologic Clinics of N.Am., 1993—; mem. editl. bd. San Francisco Medicine, 1986-97, Applied Radiology, 1987-89, Current Opinion in Radiology, 1992-93, The Radiologist, 1993—, Emergency Radiology, 1993—, Jour. Clin. Ultrasound, 1997—; contbr. articles to profl. jours. Fellow Am. Coll. Radiology (mem. commn. on ultrasound 1984-96), Am. Inst. Ultrasound in Medicine (bd. govs. 1981-84, chair convention program 1986-88, Presdl. Recognition award 1984); mem. AMA, San Francisco Med. Soc. (chmn. membership com. 1992-94, bd. dirs. 1996—), RSNA (course com. 1984-88, tech. exhibit com. 1992-96), Bay Area Ultrasound Soc. (pres. 1979-80), Soc. Radiologists Ultrasound (chair membership com. 1991-93), ARRS, AUR, CRS, Calif. Med. Assn., Am. Assn. Women Radiologists (pres. 1984-85, trustee 1991-94), VA Chiefs of Radiology Assn. (pres.-elect, pres. 1994-95), San Francisco Radiological Soc. (pres. 1990-91), Hungarian Radiological Soc. (hon.), Pakistan Radiological Soc. (hon.). Office: VA Med Ctr Radiology Svc 4150 Clement St San Francisco CA 94121-1545

GOODMAN, BEATRICE MAY, real estate professional; b. Rehoboth, Mass., Nov. 12, 1933; s. Manuel Silva and Mercy Elizabeth (Mayers) Bettencourt; m. Sam R. Goodman, Sept. 15, 1957; children: Mark, Stephen, Christopher. BS, Marymount Coll., 1980. Pres. Bettencourt Draperies, Rehoboth, Mass., 1955-56; asst. mgr. Leo H. Spivack Furniture, L.I., N.Y., 1956-57; asst. designer Lillian Decorators, L.I., N.Y., 1957-58; asst. buyer Macy's N.Y., N.Y.C., 1958-59; pres. Beatrice & Beverly, Mt. View, Calif., 1980-82; realtor Coldwell Banker, Menlo Park, Calif., 1984—; pres. The Added Touch, Atherton, Calif., 1984-91; realtor Cornish & Carey Realtors, Menlo Park, Calif., 1991—. Den mother Boy Scouts Am., N.Y.C., 1970-76; active Peninsula Vols., Palo Alto, 1974—, Internat. Friendship Force. Mem. Nat. Bd. Realtors, Orgn. for Rehab. Tng. Home: 60 Shearer Dr Atherton CA 94027-3957 Office: Cornish & Carey 1000 El Camino Real Menlo Park CA 94025-4327

GOODMAN, CHRISTOPHER BETTENCOURT, cytogeneticist; b. N.Y.C., June 8, 1967; s. Sam Richard and Beatrice May (Bettencourt) G. BS in Biol. Scis., Calif. Poly. State U., San Luis Obispo, 1990; MS in Human Cytogenetics, Hofstra U., 1994; postgrad., Foothill Coll., 1995. Tutor for learning disabled students Calif. Poly. State U., 1988-90; student tchr., asst. Hofstra U., Hempstead, N.Y., 1992-94; human cytogeneticist MediGene Inc., Yonkers, N.Y., 1993-94; assoc. lab. dir. Cord Blood Registry, Internat. Cord Blood Found.'s, Stem Cell Cord Blood Bank, U. Ariz., Tucson; technician Outland, Menlo Park, Calif., 1994-96; cons. ShredMax, Atherton, Calif., 1994-96; mem. U.S. Dept. HHS, 1992—. EMT, Emergency Med. Svcs., San Luis Obispo, 1990. Mem. AAAS, Am. Soc. Human Genetics, Genetics Soc. Am., N.Y. Acad. Scis., Churchill Club, Beta Theta Pi. Republican. Jewish. Home and Office: 60 Shearer Dr Atherton CA 94027-3957

GOODMAN, GWENDOLYN ANN, nursing educator; b. Davenport, Iowa, Aug. 7, 1955; d. Merle Erwin and Loraine Etta (Mahannah) Langfeldt; m. Mark Nathan Goodman, Oct. 24, 1982; children: Zachary Aaron, Alexander Daniel. BS in Nursing, Ariz. State U., 1977. RN, Ariz. Staff nurse surg. fl. and intensive care unit St. Luke's Hosp. and Med. Ctr., Phoenix, 1977-81; staff nurse intensive care unit Yavapai Regional Med. Ctr., Prescott, Ariz., 1981-82; instr. nursing Yavapai Coll., Prescott, 1982-88, cons., 1986; part-time staff nurse Ariz. Poison Control Ctr., Phoenix, 1980-81; mem. profl. adv. com. Home Health Agy. Yavapai Regional Med. Ctr., 1988-93. Mem. Sigma Theta Tau. Democrat. Home: PO Box 450 Prescott AZ 86302-0450

GOODMAN, JOEL HARRY, JR., university administrator; b. Seattle, Apr. 18, 1944; s. Joel H. and Edith K.; m. Barbara Guzofsky, May 8, 1976; children: Elliott James, Julia Rose. BA with distinction, Stanford U., 1966; MAT, Harvard U., 1967; MA, Stanford U., 1973 and 76; postgrad., U. Chgo., 1975-76. Asst. dir. admissions Stanford U., Palo Alto, Calif., 1972-74; mktg. services mgr. Bell & Howell Edn. Group, Chgo., 1974-80; dir. planning and devel. Western State U., Fullerton, Calif., 1980-83, dean of admissions, 1983—; v.p., assoc. dean adminstrn., student affairs Western State U., 1984—. Office: Western State Univ 1111 N State College Blvd Fullerton CA 92831-3014

GOODMAN, JOSEPH WILFRED, electrical engineering educator; b. Boston, Feb. 8, 1936; s. Joseph and Doris (Ryan) G.; m. Hon Mai Lam, Dec. 5, 1962; 1 dau., Michele Ann. B.A., Harvard U., 1958; M.S. in E.E., Stanford U., 1960, Ph.D., 1963; DSc (hon.), U. Ala., 1996. Postdoctoral fellow Norwegian Def. Rsch. Establishment, Oslo, 1962-63; rsch. assoc. Stanford U., 1963-67, asst. prof., 1967-69, assoc. prof., 1969-72, prof. elec. engring., 1972—; vis. prof. Univ. Paris XI, Orsay, France, 1973-74; dir. Info. Sys. Lab. Elec. Engring. Stanford U., 1981-83, chmn. dept. of elec. engring., 1988-96, William E. Ayer prof. elec. engring., 1988—, sr. assoc. dean engring., 1996—; cons. to govt. and industry, 1965—; v.p. Internat. Comm. for Optics, 1985-87, pres., 1988-90, past pres., 1991-93. Author: Introduction to Fourier Optics, 1968, 2nd edit. 1996, Statistical Optics, 1985, (with R. Gray) Fourier Transforms: An Introduction for Engineers; editor: International Trends in Optics, 1991; contbr. articles to profl. jours. Recipient F.E. Terman award Am. Soc. Engring. Edn., 1971, Frederic Ives Medal, 1990, Optical Soc. Am., Ester Hoffman Beller award Optical Soc. of Am., 1995. Fellow AAAS, Optical Soc. Am. (dir. 1977-83, editor jour. 1978-83, Max Born award 1983, Frederick Ives award 1990, Esther Hoffman Beller medal 1995, v.p. 1990, pres.-elect 1991, pres. 1992, past pres. 1993), IEEE (edn. medal 1987), Soc. Photo-optical Instrumentation Engrs. (bd. govs. 1979-82, 88-90, Dennis Gabor award 1987), Am. Acad. Arts & Scis.; mem. NAE, Electromagnetics Acad. Home: 570 University Ter Los Altos CA 94022-3523 Office: Stanford U Dept Elec Engring Terman 214 Stanford CA 94305

GOODMAN, LINDSEY ALAN, furniture manufacturing executive, architect; b. L.A., Nov. 17, 1957; s. Ira and Wilma Carolyn (Sanders) G.; m. Joan Frances Radditz, July 7, 1990; children: Alexandra Isabelle, Andrew Nicholas. BA, UCLA, 1980; MArch, Calif. State Poly. U., Pomona, 1983. Registered architect. Project designer Bertram Berenson, Architect, Claremont, Calif., 1983; job capt. Architecture & Planning, San Rafael, Calif., 1985-86, Barry Archtl. Design Group, Santa Barbara, Calif., 1986-87; project architect Architects West, Santa Barbara, 1987-89; prin. L.A. Goodman, Architect, Santa Barbara, 1989-91; v.p. IWI/Internat., Chino, Calif., 1992—; CFO Gourmet Artists Inc., Santa Barbara, 1995—; ptnr. IWI/Capital Devel., Chino, 1991—. Author: (poem) The Camargue, 1987. Mem. adv. coun. Santa Barbara Mus. Natural History, 1988-89, 95-96, trustee, 1989-95, v.p. bd. trustees, 96—; patron Santa Barbara Civic Light Opera, 1992—; mem. Young Pres.'s Orgn., 1995—. Recipient Richard J. Neutra Meml. award, 1983. Mem. AIA, Internat. Platform Assn., Royal Archtl. Inst. Can. (internat.). Office: IWI/Internat 15044 La Palma Dr Chino CA 91710-9669

GOODMAN, MARK PAUL, physician; b. N.Y.C., Mar. 6, 1967; s. Leonard Carl and Alice Belle (Barnum) G. BS in Biology cum laude, UCLA, 1989, MD, 1993. Diplomate Am. Bd. Internal Medicine. Resident physician UCLA Med. Ctr., 1993-96, internist, 1996—; mem. risk mgmt. com., ethics com. UCLA Med. Ctr.; mem. morbidity and mortality com. UCLA Dept. Medicine. Author: The Physician in Sherlock Holmes: The Anatomy of a Legend, 1993 (Donald O'Malley award in med. history). Founder, 1st pres. UCLA Regents Scholar Soc., 1989. U. Calif. Regents scholar, U. Calif. Alumni scholar, L.A. County Med. Assn. scholar. Mem. AMA, ACP, Los Angeles County Med. Assn., UCLA Med. Alumni Assn., Golden Key Honor Soc., Phi Eta Sigma. Home: 870 Hugard Ave Ste 405 Los Angeles CA 90024 Office: 9400 Brighton Way Ste 201 Beverly Hills CA 90210

GOODMAN, MARY A., photographer; b. Hartford, Conn., July 24, 1934; d. Allan S. and Carlyn Rhoda (Leicher) G. BS in Edn., NYU, 1958; MA in Spl. Edn., Columbia U., N.Y.C., 1961; MSW, Simmons Coll. Social Wk., Boston, 1965. Free lance photographer various locations, 1975—. Photography of notable persons include His Royal Highness Prince of Wales, Her Majesty, Queen Elizabeth, The Queen Mother, Sir Michael Tippett, O.M., Sir Yehudi Menuhin, Dame Morgot Fonteyn, Dame Alicia Markova, many others. Mem. Friends of Photography, Ansel Adams Ctr., San Francisco. Mem. Nat. Soc. Arts and Letters (Tucson br.), N.Y. Acad. Sci., Royal Photographic Soc. G.B. (sec./membership sect. Journalism group 1976-79, pictorial portfolio group 1991—), Royal Photographic Soc. Pacific br., Photographic Soc. Am., Internat. Ctr. Photography, The Photographer's Gallery, Ctr. for Creative Photography, Soc. Southwestern Authors, Resources for Women. Home: 6266 N Campbell Ave Tucson AZ 85718-3150

GOODMAN, MAX A., lawyer, educator; b. Chgo., May 24, 1924; s. Sam and Nettie (Abramowitz) G.; m. Marlyene Monkarsh, June 2, 1946; children: Jan M., Lauren A. Packard, Melanie Mirez. A.A., Herzl Jr. Coll., 1943; student, Northwestern U., 1946-47; J.D., Loyola U., 1948. Bar: Calif. 1948; cert. family law specialist, 1980, 85, 90. Sole practice Los Angeles, 1948-53; ptnr. Goodman, Hirschberg & King, Los Angeles, 1953-81; prof. law Southwestern U. Sch. Law, Los Angeles, 1966—; lectr. Calif. Continuing Edn. of the Bar, 1971—; editorial cons. Bancroft Whitney, San Francisco, 1986—. Contbr. articles to profl. jours. Served to cpl. U.S. Army, 1943-45. Mem. ABA (chmn. law sch. curriculum family law sect. 1987-88), State Bar Calif. (del. conf. dels. 1972, 80-87, 91, exec. com. family law sect. 1981-85), Los Angeles County Bar Assn. (chmn. family law sect. 1971-72, editor family law handbook). Office: Southwestern U Sch of Law 675 S Westmoreland Ave Los Angeles CA 90005-3905

GOODMAN, MURRAY, chemistry educator; b. N.Y.C., July 6, 1928; s. Louis and Frieda (Bercun) G.; m. Zelda Silverman; Aug. 26, 1951; children: Andrew, Joshua, David. BS magna cum laude with honors in Chemistry, Bklyn. Coll., 1949; PhD, U. Calif., Berkeley, 1953; DSc honoris causa, CUNY, Staten Island, 1995; PhD (hon.), U. Ioannina, Greece, 1995; D in sci., CUNY, 1995; D (hon.), U. Ioannina, Greece, 1995. Asst. prof. Polytechnic Inst., Bklyn., 1956-60, assoc. prof., 1960-64, prof. chemistry, 1964-71, dir. polymer rsch. inst., 1967-71; prof. chemistry U. Calif.-San Diego, La Jolla, 1971—, chmn. dept. Chemistry, 1976-81; vis. prof. U. Alta., Can., 1981, Lady Davis Vis. Prof., Hebrew U., Jerusalem, 1982; William H. Rauscher lectr. Rensselaer Poly. Inst., 1982. Editor Biopolymers Jour., 1963—; contbr. numerous articles to profl. jours. Recipient Alumnus medal Bklyn. Coll., 1964, Scoffone medal U. Padova, 1980, Humboldt award 1986, Max-Bermann medal 1991, Givaudan-Roure award Assn. Chemo-reception Scis., 1992, Ralph Hirschmann award for peptide chemistry, 1997; NRC fellow Cambridge (Eng.) U., 1955-56. Fellow AAAS; mem. Am. Chem. Soc., Am. Pepetide Soc. (Pierce award 1989), Am. Soc. Biol. Chemists, The Chem. Soc. Engr., Biophys. Soc., Coun. for Chem. Rsch. (sci. adv. bd.), U.S. Nat. Commn., Sigma Xi, Phi Beta Kappa. Home: 9760 Blackgold Rd La Jolla CA 92037-1115 Office: U Calif San Diego Dept Chemistry # 0343 La Jolla CA 92093

GOODMAN, WILLIAM LEE, commercial pilot; b. Butte, Mont., May 15, 1946; s. William Lonzo and Phyllis Hilma (White) G.; m. Susan Margaret Thompson, Nov. 29, 1969; children: Kathryn, Margaret, William. BS in Computer Sci., Oreg. State U., 1968; MBA, City U., Seattle, 1982; postgrad., Seattle U.; postgrad. in def. econs., U.S. Naval War Coll., 1986. Cert. airline transport pilot, flight engr., control tower operator, flight instr., FAA. Systems analyst Mohawk Data Scis. Corp., Portland, Oreg., 1974-76; air traffic controller FAA, Pendleton, Oreg., 1976-78; pilot Trans Internat. Airlines, Oakland, Calif., 1978; aerospace engr. Boeing Comml. Airplane Co., Seattle, 1978-86; pilot USAIR, Washington, 1986—. Editor Boeing Tng. Ctr. newsletter Intercom, 1980-82; contbg. editor Boeing Customer Service mag. Advisor, 1982-86. V.p. Homeowners Assn., Auburn, 1982-85. Served to comdr. USNR, 1968-89, Vietnam. Mem. Airline Pilots Assn. (chmn. local air safety 1994-95). Republican. Home: 2912 202nd Avenue Ct E Sumner WA 98390-9022

GOODSON, JOHN EARL, civil engineering executive; b. Merced, Calif., Oct. 19, 1945; s. Vincent Bernard and Dorothy Mae (Taber) G.; m. Mary Haley Cook, Sept. 5, 1970; children: Montgomery Vincent, Garett Champlin. AA, San Jose City Coll., 1969, BS in Civil Engring., 1971; MS in Civil Engring., Purdue U., 1972. Registered profl. civil engr., Oreg., Calif. Transp. planning specialist Tudor Engring. Co., San Francisco, 1972-73; assoc. transp. planner Sacramento Regional Area Planning Commn., 1973-74; transp. engr. Parsons Brinckerhoff-Quade & Douglas, San Francisco, 1974-75; transp. planning engr. Lane County Pub. Works Dept., Eugene, Oreg., 1975-82, county engr., 1982, pub. works dir., 1982—; student aide-civil engr. Contra Costa County Pub. Works Dept., Martinez, Calif., summers 1968-70; rsch. asst. joint hwy. rsch. project Purdue U., West Lafayette, Ind., 1971-72; mem. trans. tech. adv. com. AOC; supporting mem. Transp. Rsch. Bd. Chmn. prevailing wage adv. com. Oreg. Bur. Labor and Industries, 1995-97. Mem. Nat. Assn. County Engrs. (mem. constitution, bylaws com. 1996-97), Am. Pub. Works Assn., Oreg. Assn. County Engrs. and Surveyors (sec.- treas. 1988, pres.- elect 1989, pres. 1990, Award of Merit 1987, County Engr. of Yr. 1988), Inst. Transp. Engrs. (assoc., mem. com. 5B-8). Home: 792 E 39th Pl Eugene OR 97405-4538 Office: Lane County Pub Works Dept 3040 N Delta Rd Eugene OR 97408-1636

GOODWILL, MARGARET JANE, artist; b. L.A., Sept. 27, 1950; d. David and Erna Pauline (Kremser) G.; m. James Vincent Erickson, Sept. 6, 1980. Student, U. Calif., Santa Barbara, 1968-70; BFA cum laude, Calif. Coll. Arts and Crafts, 1972. Graphic artist Proarts, Oakland, Calif., 1970-71; creative art dir. Am. Analysis Corp., San Francisco, 1974-76; dir. Lone Wolf Gallery, San Francisco, 1982-84; prin., artist Calif. and Hawaii, 1984—. One-woman shows include Lone Wolf Gallery, 1985, Wrubel Gallery, Berkeley, Calif., 1988, 3660 On The Rise, Honolulu, 1995, Livingstons Gallery, Oahu, Hawaii, 1994-95, Gordon Biersch, Honolulu, 1997, Art Plantation, 1997; two-person shows include St. Mary's Coll., Moraga, Calif., 1973, Hewlett-Packard Corp. Hdqrs., 1990, 94, 95, Stanford U., Calif., 1991, 95, 96, C.C.P. Gallery, Honolulu, 1992, PacTel Hdqrs., 1992, SunSoft Hdqrs., Calif., 1992, Tandem Hdqrs., Calif., 1992, Raleigh Studios, Hollywood, Calif., 1993, TRW Hdqrs., Oakland, Calif., 1993, Return to Paradise, Honolulu, 1994; exhibited in group shows San Francisco Art Festival, 1971, 72, A Gallery, Palm Desert, Calif., 1986, Banaker Gallery, Walnut Creek, Calif., 1988, 90, Trans Am., Pyramid, San Francisco, 1990, Recycle Art Hawaii 95, 96, 97, Honolulu, Pacific Bell hdqrs., Concord, Calif., 1992, murals for Prevention to Cruelty to Animals Hdqrs., San Francisco, 1980, Wave Nightclub, Waikiki, Hawaii, 1991, The Pyramids, Honolulu, illustrations for So. poverty Law Ctr., memphis, 1991, Cosmo, CD cover designs: Hawaii Pub. TV, The Breaks: fabric design Sonali Corp.; design and illustration Dolphin Shirt Co., ITP Hawaii. Recipient 1st prize Ossining (N.Y.) Women's Club, 1968, Poughkeepsie (N.Y.) Art Ctr., 1968, merit award Delta Art Show, Antioch, Calif., 1971; N.Y. State Regent's scholar, 1968, Walnut Creek Civic Arts scholar, 1970. Mem. Calif. Coll. Arts and Crafts Alumni Assn., Mus. Contemporary Art of Hawaii, Bishop Mus., Nat. Geog. Soc., Smithsonian Assocs.

GOODWIN, JOHN ROBERT, law educator, author; b. Morgantown, W.Va., Nov. 3, 1929; s. John Emory and Ruby Iona G.; m. Betty Lou Wilson, June 2, 1952; children: John R., Elizabeth Ann Paugh, Mark Edward, Luke Jackson, Matthew Emory. B.S., W.Va. U., 1952, LLB, 1964, J.D., 1970. Bar: W.Va., U.S. Supreme Ct. Formerly city atty., county commr., spl. pros. atty., then mayor City of Morgantown; prof. bus. law W.Va. U.; prof. hotel and casino law U. Nev., Las Vegas; Author: Legal Primer for Artists, Craftspersons, 1987, Hotel Law, Principles and Cases, 1987. Served with U.S. Army, Korea. Recipient Bancroft-Whitney award in Constl. Law'; named Outstanding West Virginian, State of West Virginia. Democrat. Author: Twenty Feet From Glory; Business Law, 3d edit.; High Points of Legal History; Travel and Lodging Law; Desert Adventure; Gaming Control Law; editor Hotel and Casino Letter; past editor Bus. Law Rev., Bus. Law Letter. Home: Casa Linda 48 5250 E Lake Mead Blvd Las Vegas NV 89115-6751

GOODWIN, MARTIN BRUNE, radiologist; b. Vancouver, B.C., Can., Aug. 8, 1921; came to U.S., 1948; m. Cathy Dennison, Mar. 7, 1980; 1 child, Suzanne; stepchildren: Chuck Glikas, Dianna; 1 child from previous marriage, Nancijane Goodwin Hilling. BSA in Agriculture, U. B.C., 1943, postgrad., 1943-44; MD, CM, McGill U. Med. Sch., Montreal, Can., 1948. Diplomate Am. Bd. Med. Examiners, lic. Med. Coun. Can.; cert. diagnostic and therapeutic radiology Am. Bd. Radiology; cert. Am. Bd. Nuclear Medicine. Intern Scott & White Hosp., Temple, Tex., 1948-49; fellow radiology Scott & White Clinic, 1949-52, mem. staff, 1952-53; instr. U. Tex., Galveston, 1952-53; radiologist Plains Regional Med. Ctr., Clovis, N.Mex.; radiologist Plains Regional Med. Ctr., Portales, N.Mex., pres. med. staff; chief radiology De Baca Gen. Hosp., Ft. Sumner, N.Mex.; cons. Cannon AFB Hosp., Clovis; pvt. practice radiology Clovis, Portales, Ft. Sumner and Tucumcari, 1955—; adj. prof. health scis. Ea. N.Mex. U., 1976-77; adj. clin. prof. health scis. We. Mich. U., 1976-78. Apptd. N.Mex. Radiation Tech. Adv. Coun., N.Mex. Bd. Pub. Health; former chmn. N.Mex. Health and Social Svcs. Bd.; mem. Regional Health Planning Coun.; treas. Roosevelt County Rep. Ctrl. Com. Capt. U.S. Army M.C., 1953-55; Col. USAF M.C., 1975-79. Fellow AAAS, Am. Coll. Radiology, Am. Coll. Radiology (past councillor); mem. Am. Soc. Thoracic Radiologists (founder), Radiol. Soc. of N.Am. (past councillor), N.Mex. Med. Soc. (various coms., chmn. joint practice com., councillor bd. dirs.), N.Mex. Radiol. Soc. (past pres.), N.Mex. Thoracic Soc. (past pres.), N.Mex. Med. Review Assn. (bd. dirs. 1970-93), N.Mex. Med. Soc. Found. for Med. Care (bd. dirs. 1975—, former v.p., former treas.), County Med. Soc. (past pres., past v.p., past sec.), Clovis C. of C. (chmn. civic affairs com., bd. dirs.), Clovis Elks Lodge (past exalted ruler), Clovis Noonday Lions Club (past sec.). Republican. Presbyterian. Home: 505 E 18th St Portales NM 88130-9201 Office: Med Radiology Assocs 1001 Pile St Clovis NM 88101-5940

GOODWIN, SAMUEL MCCLURE, officer; b. N.Y.C., Dec. 3, 1916; s. Samuel Rivington and Pearl Estelle (McClure) G.; m. DuVal Rutledge Roberts, July 14, 1949 (div. Aug. 1955); children: Samuel McClure Jr., Charles DuVal; m. Christjane Thom, May 25, 1957; 1 child, Peter Bouton. BS in Mil. Sci., U.S. Military Acad., 1940; MA in Internat. & Pub. Affairs, The George Washington U., 1971. Platoon leader, staff officer, squadron comdr., group comdr. 6th Armored Cavalry, USA, France, Germany, 1940-45; staff officer Dept. Army, 1950-54; div. staff officer 24th Inf. Div., Korea, 1954-55; theater army staff officer Hawaii and Vietnam, 1965-66; sr. advisor 1st Rep. Korea Army, 1966-67; commanding gen. U.S. Army Berlin Brigade, Berlin, Germany, 1967-69; dep. cmdr., chief staff U.S. Army III Corps., Ft. Hood, Tex., 1969-70. Pres. Santa Fe Coun. on Internat. Rels., Santa Fe, N.Mex., 1972-78; bd. dirs. Vol. Involvement Svc., Sante Fe., 1978-84; bd. dirs., treas. Visitor Hospitality Cen., Santa Fe., 1984-90. Decorated Legion of Merit (3), 1945, 67, 69, Silver Star medal, 1945, Bronze Star medal, 1945, Disting. Svc. medal, 1970; named Disting. Alumnus N.Mex. Mil. Inst., 1993. Mem. Kiwanis Internat. (hon.), Assn. U. S. Army, U.S. Armor Assn., U.S. Cavalry Assn., Nat. Assn. Uniformed Svcs., Ret. Officers Assn., Mil. Order WW. Democrat. Home and Office: Crossed Sabers Ranch Cerrillos NM 87010-0779

GOOKIN, THOMAS ALLEN JAUDON, civil engineer; b. Tulsa, Aug. 5, 1951; s. William Scudder and Mildred (Hartman) G.; m. Leigh Anne Johnson, June 13, 1975 (div. Dec. 1977); m. Sandra Jean Andrews, July 23, 1983. BS with distinction, Ariz. State U., 1975. Registered profl. engr., Calif., Ariz., Nev., land surveyor Ariz., hydrologist. Civil engr., treas. Gookin Engrs. Ltd, Scottsdale, Ariz., 1968—. Chmn. adv. com. Ariz. State Bd. Tech. Registration Engring., 1984—. Recipient Spl. Recognition award Ariz. State Bd. Tech. Registration Engring., 1990. Mem. NSPE, Ariz. Soc. Profl. Engrs. (sec. Papago chpt. 1979-81, v.p. 1981-84, pres. 1984-85, named Young Engr. of Yr. 1979, Outstanding Engring. Project award 1988), Order Engr., Ariz. Congress on Surveying and Mapping, Am. Soc. Civil Engrs., Ariz. Water Works Assn., Tau Beta Pi, Delta Chi (Tempe chpt. treas. 1970-71, sec. 1970, v.p. 1971), Phi Kappa Delta (pres. 1971-73). Republican. Episcopalian. Home: 10760 E Becker Ln Scottsdale AZ 85259-3868 Office: Gookin Engrs Ltd 4203 N Brown Ave Scottsdale AZ 85251-3946

GORAB, LAWRENCE NED, urologist; b. Jersey City, Nov. 18, 1938; s. Nadeem and Lillian (McLoof) G.; m. Jane Reilly, May 8, 1965; children: Lawrence N. Jr., Elizabeth J., Edward R., William W. BA, Rutgers U., 1960; MD, Georgetown U., 1964. Diplomate Am. Bd. Urology. Intern Hackensack (N.J.) Hosp., 1964-65; resident in gen. surgery Georgetown U. Hosp., Washington, 1965-66; resident in urology Thomas Jefferson U. Hosp., Phila., 1968-71; urologist Colorado Springs (Colo.) Health Ptnrs., 1971—; staff physician Penrose Hosp., Colorado Springs, 1971—, St. Francis Hosp., Colorado Springs, 1971—, Meml. Hosp., Colorado Springs, 1971—. Capt. U.S. Army, 1966-68. Fellow ACS; mem. AMA, Am. Urol. Assn., Am. Fertility Soc., Am. Assn. Clin. Urologists, Colo. Med. Soc., El Paso County Med. Soc., Rocky Mountain Urol. Soc., South Ctrl. Sect. Am. Urol. Assn. Office: Colorado Springs Med Ctr 209 S Nevada Ave Colorado Springs CO 80903-1994

GORANS, GERALD ELMER, accountant; b. Benson, Minn., Sept. 17, 1922; s. George W. and Gladys (Schneider) G.; m. Mildred Louise Stallard, July 19, 1944; 1 child, Gretchen. BA, U. Wash., Seattle, 1947. CPA, Wash. With Touche, Ross & Co., CPAs and predecessor, Seattle, 1947-88; ptnr. Touche, Ross & Co. (name changed to Deliotte & Touche 1989), 1957-88, in charge Seattle office, 1962-82, mem. policy group, adminstrv. com., 1964-69, dir., 1974-83, sr. ptnr., 1979-88, chmn. mgmt. group, 1982-88, ret., 1988; trustee Washington Inst., 1994-96. V.p. budget and fin. Seattle Worlds Fair, 1962; chmn. budget and fin. com. Century 21 Ctr., Inc., 1963-64; mem. citizens adv. com. Seattle Lic. and Consumer Protection Com., 1965; head profl. div. United Way King County, Seattle, 1963-64, head advanced gifts div., 1965, exec. v.p., 1966, pres., 1967; trustee United Way Endowment Fund, 1984-90; adv. bd. Seattle Salvation Army, 1965-80, treas., 1974-80; fin. com. Bellevue Christian Sch., 1970-77; citizens adv. bd. pub. affairs Sta. KIRO-TV, 1970-71; treas., bd. dirs., exec. com. Scandinavia Today in Seattle, 1981-83; treas., bd. dirs. Seattle Citizens Coun. Against Crime, 1972-80, pres., 1976, 77; bd. dirs. U. Wash Alumni Fund, 1967-71, chmn., 1971; trustee U. Wash. Pres.'s Club, 1980-83; bd. dirs., chmn. devel. com. N.W. Hosp. Found., 1977-83; bd. dirs., treas. N.W. Hosp., 1981-86; chmn. fin. com., vice chmn. bd. Health Resources N.W., 1986-89, bd. dirs., 1986—, chmn. bd., 1989-90; chmn. fin. com. Com. for Balanced Regional Transp., 1981-91; co-chmn. United Cerebal Palsy Seattle Telethon, 1986; chmn. fin. com. fund raising Mus. Flight, 1983-87; mem. assoc. bd. Pacific Scis. Ctr., Seattle, 1986-95; active Japanese/Am. Conf. Mayors and C. of C. Pres. vice chmn. U.S. del., 1989-91; chmn. fin. com. Napa Valley Club Homeowners Assn.; bd. dirs., chmn. fin. com. Napa Valley Club Homeowners Assn., 1992-95; bd. dirs., 1st pres. 600 Pk. Ter. Condominium Assn., 1993—. Lt. (j.g.) USNR, 1943-45. Recipient Honor award Sr. Svcs. of Seattle and King County, 1990. Mem. AICPA (chmn. nat. def. com. 1969-75, spl. investigation com. 1984-87), Wash. Inst. for Policy Study (bd. dirs. 1994-96), Nat. Office Mgmt. Assn. (past pres.), Wash. Soc. CPAs (Outstanding Pub. Svc. award 1988), Seattle C. of C. (chmn. taxation com. 1970-71, bd. dirs. 1971-74, 76-79, 80-81, 85—, exec. com. 1980-83, v.p. 1981-84, 1st vice chmn. 1983-84, chmn. 1984-85, vice chmn. facilities fund dr. 1982-84), Nat. Def. Exec. Res., Nat. Club Assn. (bd. dirs. 1984-93, sec., exec. com. 1991-93), Assn. Wash. Bus. (bd. dirs. 1983-86). Home: 612 Bellevue Way SE Bellevue WA 98004-6633 also: Smith Ranch Homes 400 Deer Valley Rd # 4C San Rafael CA 94903-5515 Office: Deloitte & Touche 700 5th Ave Ste 4500 Seattle WA 98104-5000

GORDER, CHERYL MARIE, book publisher; b. Brookings, S.D., Nov. 7, 1952; d. Shirley William and Arlene Opal (Barenklau) Seas; m. Dale Martin Gorder, Dec. 30, 1972 (June 1, 1992); 1 child, Sarah Lynne. BA, S.D. State U., 1974. Mgr. regional auctions Blue Bird Pub., Tempe, Ariz., 1974-85, pub., 1985—; cons. NIMTEC, Inc., Chandler, Ariz., 1991-92. Author: (book) Home Schools: An Alternative, 1985, Homeless: Without Addresses in America, 1988, Home Business Resource Guide, 1989, Green Earth Resource Guide, 1991, Multicultural Education Resource Guide, 1995, Multicultural Education Resource Guide, 1996, Home Education Resource Guide, 1996, Kindergarten at Home, 1997; editor: Who's Who in Antiques, 1986, Real Dakota, 1988, Home Education Resource Guide, 1989, Spacedog's Best Friend, 1989, Dr. Christman's Learn to Read Book, 1990, They Reached for the Stars, 1990, The Sixth Sense: Practical Tips for Everyday Safety, 1990, Under Two Heavens, 1991, Survival Guide to Step-Parenting, 1992, 1996, Road School, 1995, Preschool Learning Activities, 1995, Heartful Parenting, 1996, Success Starts Early, 1997, Excel at Parenting, 1997, Look, Mr. Kim, I'm Being Haved!, 1997, Write Story for Your Child, 1997, Home Education Resource Guide (4th edit.), Divorced Dad's Handbook. Recipient Benjamin Franklin award Pub.'s Mktg. Assn., 1989. Mem. Pub. Mktg. Assn., Am. Bus. Women's Assn., Ariz. Book Pub. Assn. Office: Blue Bird Pub 2266 S Dobson # 275 Mesa AZ 85202

GORDON, BRADLEY B., pharmaceutical research executive; b. 1954. MBA, U. So. Calif., 1981. Gen. ptnr. EMC Venture Ptnrs., San Diego, 1981-86; pres. Access Ptnrs., San Diego, 1986-87; ptnr. Viagene, Inc., San Diego, 1987-95; v.p. fin., CFO Signal Pharm., Inc., San Diego, 1995—. Office: Signal Pharm Inc 555 Oberlin Dr San Diego CA 92121*

GORDON, DAVID ELIOT, lawyer; b. Santa Monica, Calif., Mar. 8, 1949; s. Sam and Dee G.; m. Mary Debora Lane, Mar. 5, 1978. BA, Harvard U., 1969, JD, 1972. Bar: Calif. 1972. Ptnr. O'Melveny & Myers, Los Angeles, 1980—. Founder, editor ERISA Litigation Reporter; contbr. articles on tax and employee benefits to profl. jours. Fellow Los Angeles County Bar Found. (life, pres. 1984-85, bd. dirs. 1980-86); mem. ABA (employee benefits com. 1986—), Am. Coll. Tax Counsel, Los Angeles County Bar Assn. (tax sect., pres. 1990-91), Nat. Assn. Bond Lawyers (bd. dirs. 1982-84). Republican. Office: O'Melveny & Myers 400 S Hope St Los Angeles CA 90071-2801

GORDON, GLORIA KATHLEEN, business association executive, magazine editor; b. Kerrville, Tex., Feb. 13, 1938; d. Candler Ross and Gertrude (Beitel) Gordon; m. Dale H. Fietz, Feb. 23, 1957 (div. 1983); children: Martha Fietz O'Brien, Diane Fietz, Kathleen Thompson. BA in English, U. Tex., 1958. Prod., quality control assoc. Cahners Pub. Co., Denver, 1961-68; editorial asst. Ski Racing mag., Denver, 1968-69; prod. mgr. Meat Industry mag., Mill Valley, Calif., 1965-71; prod. dir. Guidance Industries, Mill Valley, Calif., 1971-72; cons. pub. rels. Gloria Graphics, Corte Madera, Calif., 1978-80; mng. editor Pacific Food Svc. News, Sausalito, Calif., 1980-83; v.p. communications Internat. Assn. Bus. Communicators, San Francisco, 1983—; bd. dirs. Mill Valley Chamber Music Soc. Editor Communication World mag.; contbr. articles to profl. jours. Recipient Gold Key award Pub. Rels. News, 1991, more than 30 awards of excellence for publ. design and content. Mem. Am. Soc. Assn. Execs., Pub. Rels. Soc. Am. Office: Internat Assn Bus Communicators 1 Hallidie Plz Ste 600 San Francisco CA 94102-2818

GORDON, HELEN WILCOX, church librarian; b. Grand Forks, N.D., Feb. 14, 1919; m. Earl W. Gordon, 1948; children: Paul, Carol. BA, Scripps Coll., Claremont, Calif., 1940; Diploma in Nursing, Johns Hopkins Sch.

Nursing, 1943. RN, Calif. Pub. health nurse Health Dept., Newton County, Mo., 1952-54; sch. nurse Pasadena (Calif.) Sch. Dist., 1966-68; libr. First United Meth. Ch., Pasadena, 1991—. 1st lt. Nurse Corps, U.S. Army, 1945-47. Mem. The Ch. and Synagogue Librs. Assn. (pres. Los Angeles County chpt. 1994). Methodist. Office: First United Methodist Ch 500 E Colorado Blvd Pasadena CA 91101-2027

GORDON, HUGH SANGSTER, JR., fire services administrator; b. Winnipeg, Manitoba, Can., July 6, 1949; s. Hugh Sangster Sr. and Margaret Forbes (Johnston) G. BS, U. N.D., 1973, MS, 1975. Cert. arena and pool mgr., fireman. Gen. mgr. recreation commn. City of Flin Flon, Can., 1978-81; supr. field house City of Saskatoon, Can., 1982-84, arena mgr., 1984-85; mgr. facility ops. dept. park and recreation City of Regina, Can., 1985-87, acting. dir. parks and recreation dept., 1986-87, dir. fire svcs., 1987—. Recipient Cert. of Devoted Civil Svc., City of Saskatoon, 1985. Mem. Can. Assn. Fire Chiefs., Saskatchewan Assn. Fire Chiefs (v.p. 1987—). Mem. United Ch. Can. Office: Regina Fire Dept, Box 1790, Regina, SK Canada S4P 3C8*

GORDON, JERRY ARTHUR, family services organization administrator; b. Rochester, N.Y., Apr. 27, 1939; s. Philip R. and Grace (Itkin) G.; m. Susan G. Gerring, July 11, 1940; children: Julie, Lili. BS, Ithaca Coll., 1962; MS, Syracuse U., 1966; EdD, U. Buffalo, 1979. Film editor WOKR-TV, Rochester, N.Y., 1962-63; tchr. Wayne Ctrl. Sch., Walworth, N.Y., 1963-65; dir. Westhill Ctrl. Sch., Syracuse, N.Y., 1965-66; instr. Fredonia (N.Y.) State Coll., 1966-69; assoc. prof. Alfred (N.Y.) State Coll., 1969-82; dir. U. Calif. Media Resources, Riverside, 1982-95; exec. dir. Jewish Family Svcs., Riverside, 1996—; cons. radio, telecom. and tech. Riverside, 1995—. Mem. Dirs. of Ednl. Tech., Calif. Higher Edn. (pres. 1987-88), Riverside Agy. Exec. Assn. Home: 375 Two Trees Rd Riverside CA 92507-3225 Office: Jewish Family Svcs 6859 Magnolia Ave Ste 3 Riverside CA 92506

GORDON, JUDITH, communications consultant, writer; b. Long Beach, Calif.; d. Irwin Ernest and Susan (Perlman) G.; m. Lawrence Banka, May 1, 1977. BA, Oakland U., 1966; MS in Libr. Sci., Wayne State U., 1973. Researcher Detroit Inst. of Arts, 1968-69; libr. Detroit Pub. Libr., 1971-74; caseworker Wayne County Dept. Social Svcs., Detroit, 1974-77; advt. copywriter Hudson's Dept. Store, Detroit, 1979; mgr. The Poster Gallery, Detroit, 1980-81; mktg., corp. communications specialist Bank of Am., San Francisco, 1983-84; mgr., consumer pubs. Bank of Am., 1984-86; prin. ACTIVE VOICE, San Francisco, 1986—. Contbr. edit. The Artist's Mag., 1988-93; contbr. to book Flowers: Gary Bukovnik, Watercolors and Monotypes, Abrams, 1990. Vol. From the Heart, San Francisco, 1992, Bay Area Book Festival, San Francisco, 1990, 91, Aid & Comfort, San Francisco, 1987, Save Orch. Hall, Detroit, 1977-81, NOW sponsored abortion clinic project. Recipient Nat. award Merit. Soc. Consumer Affairs Profls. in Bus., 1986, Bay Area Best award Internat. Assn. Bus. Communicators, 1986, Internat. Galaxy awards, 1992, 95, Internat. Mercury awards, 1995. Mem. AAUW, Internat. Assn. Bus. Communicators, Nat. Writers Union, Freelance Editl. Assn., Achenbach Graphics Arts Coun., Women's Nat. Book Assn., Assn. for Women in Comms., Friends of City Arts and Lectrs., ZYZZYVA (v.p., bd. dirs.). *Judith Gordon brings a singular combination of capabilities to ACTIVE VOICE, a company she founded in 1986. Since then, she has provided editorial, project management, consulting, and marketing services to diverse clients nationwide. Gordonis the former manager of consumer publications at Bank of America where she directed an award-winning publications program within strict time and cost constraints. Among the publications were the bank's account disclosures, considered models of plain language. The name of Gordon's company reflects its key focus: to communicate clearly and compellingly to specialists and laypersons alike. Her company's primary emphasis is financial services collateral, consumer information/education materials, and customer documents that satisfy legal, compliance, and marketing objectives. For these efforts, Gordon has received frequent recognition.*

GORDON, LEE DIANE, librarian; b. Lafayette, Ind., Oct. 30, 1948; d. Henry Charles and Leonora (Brower) G.; m. James J. Thomas, Aug. 27, 1977 (div. Feb. 1994). BA, Calif. State U., Long Beach, 1970; MEd, U. Nev., Las Vegas, 1980. Cert. tchr., Nev., Calif.; cert. libr., Nev. Tchr. Carmenita Jr. High Sch., Cerritos, Calif., 1971-77; tchr. Jim Bridger Jr. High Sch., North Las Vegas, Nev., 1977-79, libr., 1979-84; libr. Eldorado High Sch., Las Vegas, Nev., 1984—. Co-author: The Overworked Teacher's Bulletin Board Book, 1981; filmstrips, 1983; author: World Historical Fiction Guide for Young Adults, 1996; contbr. articles to profl. jours. Mem. Am. Assn. Sch. Librs. (affiliate del., various coms. 1987—), Nev. Assn. Sch. Librs. (chair 1987), Clark County Sch. Librs. Assn. (pres. 1987-88), Delta Kappa Gamma (Iota chpt. pres. 1990-92). Office: Eldorado High Sch 1139 Linn Ln Las Vegas NV 89110-2628

GORDON, LEONARD, sociology educator; b. Detroit, Dec. 6, 1935; s. Abraham and Sarah (Rosen) G.; m. Rena Joyce Feigelman, Dec. 25, 1955; children: Susan Melinda, Matthew Seth, Melissa Gail. B.A., Wayne State U., 1957; M.A., U. Mich., 1958; Ph.D., Wayne State U., 1966. Instr. Wayne State U., Detroit, 1960-62; research dir. Jewish Community Council, Detroit, 1962-64; dir. Mich. area Am. Jewish Com., N.Y.C., 1964-67; asst. prof. Ariz. State U., Tempe, 1967-70, assoc. prof., 1970-77, prof., 1977—, chmn. dept. sociology, 1981-90, assoc. dean for acad. programs Coll. Liberal Arts and Scis., 1990—; cons. OEO, Maricopa County, Ariz., 1968. Author: A City in Racial Crisis, 1978, (with A. Mayer) Urban Life and the Struggle To Be Human, 1979, (with R. Hardert, M. Laner and M. Reader) Confronting Social Problems, 1984, (with J. Hall and R. Melnick) Harmonizing Arizona's Ethnic and Cultural Diversity, 1992. Sec. Conf. on Religion and Race, Detroit, 1962-67; mem. exec. bd. dirs. Am. Jewish Com., Phoenix chpt., 1969-70. Grantee NSF, 1962, Rockefeller found., 1970, 84. Fellow Am. Sociol. Assn.; mem. AAUP, Pacific Sociol. Assn. (v.p. 1978-79, pres. 1980-81), Soc. Study Social Problems (chair C. Wright Mills award com. 1988, treas. 1989-96), Ariz. State U. Alumni Assn. (faculty dir. 1981-82). Democrat. Jewish. Home: 13660 E Columbine Dr Scottsdale AZ 85259 Office: Ariz State U Coll Liberal Arts and Scis Office for Acad Programs Tempe AZ 85287

GORDON, LONNY JOSEPH, choreographer, dance and fine arts educator; b. Edinburg, Tex., Sept. 21, 1942. BFA, U. Tex., 1965; MFA, U. Wis., 1967; DFA, Nishikawa Sch. of Classical Japanese Dance, Tokyo, 1980. Dir. Kinetic Art Theater, N.Y.C., 1970, Tokyo, 1971-72; dir. modern dance Jacobs Pillow, Lee, Mass., 1970; dir. So. Repertory Dance Theater, So. Ill. U., Carbondale, 1972-76; artist-in-residence Smith Coll., Northampton, Mass., 1975; grad. dir. dance U. Wis., Madison, 1976-86, prof., 1985-91; prof., chmn. dance dept. U. Nev., Las Vegas, 1991-94, dir. devel. Performing Arts Ctr., 1994—; choreographer numerous dance works including Fleetings, artist-in-residence; cons. and lectr. in dance and fine arts to numerous profl. dance cos. and ednl. instns. Contbr. articles to profl. jours. including Japan Modern Dance Quarterly, Okura Lantern, Dance Scope; columnist Capital Times, Asahi Evening News, Korean Times; subject of numerous books and profl. works in dance. One man exhbn. watercolor paintings, collage and mixed media works. Grantee numerous profl. and ednl. instns., fellow Fulbright-Hays, 1967-69, 83, NEA Choreographers, 1982-83, Japan Found. profl., 1979, Mobile Found., 1971-72, Nev. State Arts Coun., 1992, 93, 94, 95, 96. Mem. Asian Dance Assn. (bd. dirs.), Am. Coll. Dance Festival (bd. dirs. 1987—), Fulbright Alumni Assn., Ruth Page Dance Series (bd. dirs.). Office: U Nevada/Las Vegas Performing Arts Ctr 45005 Maryland Pkwy Las Vegas NV 89154

GORDON, MARC STEWART, pharmacist, scientist; b. Cleve., June 13, 1958; s. Eugene and Eileen (Israel) G.; m. Diane Southwell, Aug. 11, 1985; children: Evan, Emma. BS in Pharmacy, U. Mich., 1982. Registered pharmacist, Calif. Staff rschr. II, mgr. Syntex Rsch., Palo Alto, Calif., 1982-95; sr. scientist Inhale Therapeutic Systems, Palo Alto, Calif., 1995—. Contbr. numerous articles to profl. jours. Mem. Am. Assn. Pharm. Scientists, Am. Pharm. Assn., No. Calif. Pharm. Discussion Group, Rho Chi. Home: 1474 Samedra St Sunnyvale CA 94087-4054 Office: Inhale Therapeutic Systems 1060 E Meadow Cir Palo Alto CA 94303-4230

GORDON, MARTIN NEIL, pulmonologist; b. Syracuse, N.Y., July 10, 1947; s. Isadore and Esther M. G.; m. Marie A., June 27, 1975; children: Carrie, Jessica, Justin. BS, Syracuse U., 1969; MD, Mt. Sinai Sch. Medicine, 1973. Intern in internal medicine Mt. Sinai Hosp., N.Y.C., 1973-74; resident in internal medicine Mt. Sinai Hosp., 1974-76; chief med. resident Cedars-Sinai Med. Ctr., L.A., 1976-77; fellow in pulmonary medicine Cedars-Sinai Med. Ctr., 1977-79; asst. clin. prof. UCLA, 1977—; pvt. practice Beverly Hills, Calif., 1979—; dir. bronchoscopy svc. Cedars-Sinai Med. Ctr., 1980-82; dir. med. edn. Midway Med. Ctr., L.A., 1984—, chief of staff, 1989-91. Office: 9001 Wilshire Blvd Ste 307 Beverly Hills CA 90211-1841

GORDON, MILTON ANDREW, academic administrator; b. Chgo., May 25, 1935; s. Herrmann Andrew Gordon and Ossie Bell; m. Margaret Faulwell, July 18, 1987; children: Patrick Francis, Vincent Michael; 1 stepchild, Michael Faulwell. BS, Xavier U. La., New Orleans, 1957; MA, U. Detroit, 1960; PhD, Ill. Inst. Tech., 1968; postgrad., Harvard U., 1984. Teaching asst. U. Detroit, 1958-59; mathematician Lab. Applied Scis. U. Chgo., 1959-62; part-time tchr. Chgo. Pub. Sch. System, 1962-66; assoc. prof. math. Loyola U., Chgo., 1966-67; dir. Afro-Am. Studies Program Loyla U., Chgo., 1971-77; dean Coll. Arts and Scis., prof. math. Chgo. State U., 1978-86; v.p. acad. affairs, prof. math. Sonoma State U., Rohnert Park, Calif., 1986-90; pres., prof. math. Calif. State U., Fullerton, 1990—; bd. dirs. Associated We. Univs., Inc.; hon. admissions counselor United States Naval Acad., 1979; mem. exec. coun. Calif. State U., 1990; rep. for Calif. univs.Am. Assn. State Colls. and Univs., 1992; commn. on leadership devel. Am. Coun. on Edn., 1992; nat. task force on gender equality Nat. Collegiate Athletic Assn., 1992-94, pres.'s commn., 1994—; commr. joint commn. on accoutability reporting project Am. Assn. of State Colls. and Univs./Nat. Assn. of State Univs. and Land Grant Colls., 1994—, Am. Assn. Applied Ethics. Contbr. articles to profl. jours. Chmn. Archdiocese of Chgo. Sch. Bd., 1978-79; bd. govs. Orange County Community Found., Costa Mesa, Calif., 1990—, NCCJ, 1991—; bd. dirs. United Way of Orange County, Irvine, Calif., 1991, Pacific Symphony Orch., Santa Ana, 1993—; bd. adv. St. Jude Med. Ctr., Fullerton, Calif., 1992, Partnership 2010, Orange County, 1994, Black Leadership in Orange County, 1995—; bd. dirs. Orange County Bus. Coun., 1996—. Recipient cert. of appreciation Community Ch. Santa Rosa, Calif., 1988, Tree of Life award Jewish Nat. Fund, 1994, Humanitarian of Yr. award North Orange County YMCA, 1995; named Adminstr. of Yr., Chgo. State U., 1979. Mem. Am.conf. Acad. Deans (chmn. bd. dirs. 1983-85), Am. Assn. Univ. Adminstrs. (bd. dirs. 1983-86), Calif. Coalition of Math., Sigma Xi, Phi Beta Delta. Roman Catholic. Office: Calif State Univ Office of President PO Box 6810 Fullerton CA 92834-6810

GORDON, PETER HOWARD, museum curator; b. 1948. Dir. Plaza Gallery, Albany, N.Y., 1979-81; coord. temporary and travelling exhbns. N.Y. State Mus., Albany, 1982-92; chief curator San Jose (Calif.) Mus. Art, 1992—. Author: The New York Landscape, 1981; editor: Diamonds are Forever: Artists and Writers on Baseball, 1987. Office: San Jose Mus Art 110 S Market St San Jose CA 95113

GORDON, PETER LOWELL, immigration administrator; b. Powell, Wyo., Feb. 16, 1953; s. John Eric Gordon and Carol Mae (Peterson) Olson; m. Mitsuko Natsume, Sept. 18, 1993. BA in Polit. Sci., Criminal Justice, Calif. State U., L.A., 1975. Asst. cook Country Kitchen, LaCrosse, Wis., 1970-71; asst. mgr. Ky. Fried Chicken, Tujunga, Calif., 1975-76, Parasol Restaurant, Alhambra, Calif., 1976-77; border patrol agt. Immigration and Naturalization Svc., Dept. Justice, San Diego, 1977-80; immigration insp. Immigration and Naturalization Svc., Dept. Justice, Anchorage, 1980-83; immigration examiner Immigration and Naturalization Svc., Dept. Justice, L.A., 1983-87; legalization mgr. Immigration and Naturalization Svc., Dept. Justice, Laguna Niguel, Calif., 1987-90, immigration mgr., 1990—. Co-developer (nat. data base) Legalization Adjustment Processing System, 1987 (Commr.'s award 1987); co-designer Calif. Svc. Ctr., 1989; co-author Calif. Svc. Ctr. Guidelines, 1989. Spkr. Am. Immigration Lawyers Assn., So. and Northern Calif. chpts.; contbr. Dedication and Everlasting Love to Animals. Mem. Nat. Space Soc., Fedn. for Am. Immigration Reform. Republican. Lutheran.

GORDON, ROBERT EUGENE, lawyer; b. L.A., Sept. 20, 1932; s. Harry Maurice and Minnie (Shaffer); 1 child, Victor Marten. BA, UCLA, 1954; LLB, U. Calif., Berkeley, 1959, JD, 1960; cert., U. Hamburg, Fed. Republic Germany, 1960. Bar: Calif. 1960. Assoc. Lillick, Geary, McHose, Roethke & Myers, Los Angeles, 1960-64, Schoichet & Rifkind, Beverly Hills, Calif., 1964-67; ptnr. Baerwitz & Gordon, Beverly Hills, 1967-69, Ball, Hunt, Hart, Brown & Baerwitz, Beverly Hills, 1970-71; of counsel Jacobs, Sills & Coblentz, San Francisco, 1972-78; ptnr. Gordon & Hodge, San Francisco, 1978-81; sole practice San Francisco, 1981-84, Sausalito, Calif., 1985-89; pvt. practice Corte Madera, Calif., 1989—; adj. prof. entertainment law Hastings Coll. of Law, San Francisco, 1990-91, U. Calif., Berkeley, 1992. Served to 1st lt. U.S. Army, 1954-56. Mem. ABA (forum com. on entertainment and sports law, exec. com. music sect.), San Francisco Bar Assn., Los Angeles Copyright Soc. (bd. trustees 1970-71), Copyright Soc. of the USA. Home: 35 Elaine Ave Mill Valley CA 94941-1014 Office: 5725 Paradise Dr Ste 840 Corte Madera CA 94925-1222

GORDON, ROBERT WILLIAM, editor; b. N.Y.C., Apr. 29, 1946; s. David William and Elizabeth (Marshal) G. BA in Journalism, CCNY, 1968; MA in English, NYU, 1970. Editor Showcase mag., N.Y.C., 1970-72; freelance reader Players Press Inc., N.Y.C., 1965-72, assoc. editor, 1972-74, editor, 1974-76, sr. editor, 1976-78, v.p. editls., assoc. publ., 1978—; editl./script cons. Empire Entertainment, Hollywood, Calif., 1979-84; editl. cons. New World Studios, Hollywood, 1985-87; bd. dirs. Players U.S.A., Studio City, Calif. Author (play) Once Around the Park, 1985 (Best New Play 1987), (books) Writing for Stage, 1990, Classic Theatre, 1990, Working in the Field, 1990. Bd. dirs. Western Ednl. Theatre, Studio City, 1979—. Office: Players Press Inc PO Box 1132 Studio City CA 91614-0132

GORDON, SALLIE ELIZABETH, psychologist, educator; b. Kansas City, Mo., Mar. 27, 1952; d. Gerald and Sarah (Gardiner) Gordon; children: Erin, Shannon. BA, Calif. State U., Fullerton, 1976, MA, 1978; PhD, U. Ill., Champaign, 1982. Part-time prof. Wright State U., Dayton, Ohio, 1981-82; rsch. scientist Klein & Assocs., Yellow Springs, Ohio, 1983-84; asst. prof. U. Idaho, Moscow, 1984-89; pres. Applied Cognitive Scis., Viola, Idaho, 1984-94; Assoc. prof. U. Idaho, Moscow, 1989-96; prof., 1996—. Co-author: Trends in Ergonomics/Human Factors I, 1984, Artificial Intelligence and Other Innovative Computer Applications in the Nuclear Industry, 1988, Questions and Information Systems, 1992, The Psychology of Expertise, 1992, Human Factors, 1997; Author: Systematic Training Program Design, 1994; contbr. articles to profl. jours. Rsch. grantee USAF, 1984, 88-89, Boeing Mil. Aircraft Co., 1987, Idaho State Bd. Edn., 1989-90, IBM, 1991, Northrop Corp., 1992-94. Mem. AAAS, Am. Assn. Artificial Intelligence, Am. Psychol. Assn., Am. Psychol. Soc., Assn. Computing Machinery, Human Factors Soc. Office: U Idaho Psychology Dept Moscow ID 83844

GORDON, STEVEN ERIC, animator, designer; b. Hollywood, Calif., Mar. 23, 1960; s. Wilfred Isadore and Tamara (Bernstein) G.; m. Judith Katherine Ball, June 27, 1981; children: Scott Conrad, Eric Alexander, Natalie Michelle. Grad. high sch., Granada Hills, Calif. Asst. animator Bakshi Prodns., Hollywood, 1977-79, animator, 1979-80; animation dir. Bakshi Prodns., Sun Valley, Calif., 1981-82; layout artist Filmation Studios, Hollywood, 1980-81; animator Disney Pictures, Burbank, Calif., 1982-87; dir. animation Rich Animation, Burbank, Calif., 1987—; owner The Animator's Gallery, 1994—; story bd. artist Disney TV, Burbank, 1984-91, DIC Enterprises, Burbank, 1986-88, designer, 1994; comml. animator Playhouse Pictures, Hollywood, 1986-88, Baer Animation Co., Inc., Hollywood, 1989-90, Cool Prodn., Burbank, 1990-92, Film Roman, North Hollywood, 1991; designer Saban Ctr., L.A., 1993-96; story board artist Fox Animation, 1995—. Democrat. Home: 32449 Scandia Dr Running Springs CA 92382 Address: PO Box 2829 Running Springs CA 92382-2829

GORDON, WALTER, architect; b. Buffalo, Sept. 8, 1907; s. Walter William and Florence (Green) G.; m. Margaret Murray, July 4, 1936. B.S., Princeton U., 1930, M.F.A. in Architecture, 1932; spl. student, Yale U., 1936-37, U. Paris, France, 1934. Curator San Francisco Mus. Art, 1937-39; asst. dir. Portland (Oreg.) Art Mus., 1939-41; practicing architect Portland, 1946-58; dean Sch. Architecture, U. Oreg., 1958-62; faculty mem. Reed Coll., 1962-65; sr. partner Gordon & Hinchliff, architects, 1962-72; prin. Walter Gordon, architect, 1972—; design cons. Portland Devel. Commn., 1962-76, Eugene Renewal Agy., 1972-80, Salem (Oreg.) Renewal Agy., 1973-82; mem. Gov.'s Adv. Com. for Preservation Yaquina Head, 1977-80, Oreg. Bd. Architect Examiners, 1956-58, Portland Art Commn., 1955-57, Oreg. Capitol Planning Commn., 1959-68. Prin. works include Southwest Hills Libr., Portland, Alpha Phi sorority house, Corvallis, Oreg. libr., dormitories, faculty residence Marylhurst Coll., Portland, Pub. Libr., Toledo, Oreg., visitor's lodge, infirmary Trappist Abbey, Lafayette, Oreg., parish hall, chapel Sacred Heart Ch., Newport, Oreg., numerous residences, Pacific N.W. Trustee Portland Art Mus., 1947-51. Fellow A.I.A. (mem. nat. edn. com. 1960-62); mem. Phi Beta Kappa. Clubs: City of Portland (v.p. 1971-72), University. Home and Office: 105 NW Wade Way Newport OR 97365-1426

GORDY, BERRY, entrepreneur, record company executive, motion picture executive; b. Detroit, Nov. 28, 1929; m. Grace Eaton, July 17, 1990; children: Berry IV, Hazel Joy, Terry James, Kerry A., Kennedy W., Stefan K. Founder Motown Record Corp., from 1961; chmn. The Gordy Co.; exec. producer motion pictures. Dir. motion picture Mahogany, 1975; exec. producer films Lady Sings the Blues, 1972, Bingo Long Traveling All-Stars and Motor Kings, 1975, The Last Dragon, 1984; author: To Be Loved: The Music, the Magic, the Memories of Motown, 1994. Recipient Bus. Achievement award Interracial Coun. for Bus. Opportunity, 1967, 2d Ann. Am. Music award for outstanding contbn. to mus. industry, 1975, Whitney M. Young Jr. award L.A. Urban League, 1980, NARAS Trustees award, 1991; named one of Five Leading Entrepreneurs of Nation Babson Coll., 1978; inducted into Rock and Roll Hall of Fame, 1988; Gordon Grand fellow Yale U., 1985. Mem. Guild Am. (bd. dirs.). Office: Gordy Co 6255 W Sunset Blvd Los Angeles CA 90028-7403

GORE, JAMES FRANKLIN, wildlife biologist; b. Maryville, Mo., Mar. 14, 1941; s. James Franklin Jr. and Faye Allen (Rupe) G.; m. Delores E. Barnhart, Sept. 3, 1961 (div. Aug. 1980); 1 child, Brooklin James. BS, S.D. State U., 1963; MS, U. Maine, 1965. Cert. wildlife biologist. Wildlife law enforcement biologist U.S. Fish and Wildlife Svc., Mpls., 1965-66; waterfowl sr. biologist Tenn. Fish and Game Commn., Nashville, 1965-71; wildlife biologist U.S. Army C.E., Nashville, 1971, St. Louis, 1972-78; endangered species cons. specialist U.S. Fish and Wildlife Svc., Boise, Idaho, 1978-91; endangered species cons. specialist USDA/U.S. Forest Svc., Washington, 1991-94, Ogden, Utah, 1994-96; coord. Grizzly Bear Habitat USDA/U.S. Forest Svc., Missoula, Mont., 1997—; lectr. in field. Contbr. numerous articles to profl. jours.; co-editor workshop proc. Workshop on Raptors and Energy Development, 1980. Recipient Disting. Achievement award Am. Legion, 1959, Centennial Achievement award Idaho Centennial Commn., 1990, Alpha award for profl. excellence and outstanding achievements Idaho Gray Wolf Recovery, Wolf Recovery Found., 1991, Outstanding Leadership and Dedication for Grizzly Bear Recovery award Interagy. Grizzly Bear Com., 1991. Mem. NRA, The Wildlife Soc. (Idaho chpt. pres. 1980-81, pres. Ill. chpt. 1978, named Profl. Wildlifer of Yr. 1989), Zi Sigma Pi.

GOREN, BRUCE NEAL, technical administrator; b. N.Y.C., Jan. 6, 1956; s. Seymour and Elaine (Popkin) G. BA, CUNY, Queens, 1978; MA, Bowling Green State U., 1979. Lic. gen. class FCC radiotelephone operator. Paste-up artist Ad Design, Inc., College Point, N.Y., 1977-78; grad. teaching asst. Bowling Green (Ohio) State U., 1979; prodn. asst. Sta. KGAN-TV (formerly Sta. WMT-TV), Cedar Rapids, Iowa, 1980; broadcast engr. Sta. WQAD-TV, Moline, Ill., 1980-81; master control engr. Cable News Network, Atlanta, 1981-82; engr. Sta. WSB-TV, Atlanta, 1982-84; on-air supr. The Post Group, Hollywood, Calif., 1984; TV engr. Sta. KLCS-TV, Los Angeles, 1984-95; applications engr. CSI Videosystems, L.A., 1995-96; owner, 3D animator Cheap Computer Graphics, Hollywood, 1986-96; contbg. editor, columnist TV Tech. Mag., Falls Church, Va., 1991-96; tech. mgr. Mus. TV and Radio, Beverly Hills, Calif., 1996—. Contbr. numerous articles to profl. jours. and mag. Regents scholar N.Y., 1973, Kodak Visual scholar U. Iowa, 1979. Mem. Spl. Interest Group on Computer Graphics, Assn. for Computing Machinery, Soc. Motion Picture and TV Engrs., Mensa. Home: 28938 Morningside Dr Val Verde CA 91384

GORENBERG, ALAN EUGENE, physician; b. Japan, Apr. 30, 1959; s. Daniel and Louise Gorenberg; m. Beverly J. Juan, June 24, 1984. BS in Biology, U. Calif., Irvine, 1981; MD, Loma Linda U., 1986. Diplomate Am. Bd. Internal Medicine, Am. Bd. Allergy and Immunology. Pvt. practice San Bernardino, Calif., 1991—, Victorville, Calif., 1991—. Office: 2130 N Arrowhead Ave Ste 101 San Bernardino CA 92405-4023 also: 12408 Hesperia Rd Ste 7 Victorville CA 92392

GORENBERG, NORMAN BERNARD, aeronautical engineer, consultant, retired; b. St. Louis, May 18, 1923; s. Isadore and Ethel G.; m. Lucille Richmond, June 10, 1947; children: Judith Allyn Gorenberg Stein, Carol Ann Gorenberg, Gershom Gorenberg. BSME, Washington U., St. Louis, 1949. Registered profl. engr., Mo. Aero. engr. USAF Wright Air Devel. Ctr., Dayton, Ohio, 1949-51; aerodynamicist McDonnell Aircraft Corp., St. Louis, 1951-59; supervisory engr. Boeing Co., Vertol Div., Phila., 1959-62; R & D engr. Lockheed Corp., Burbank, Calif., 1962-89; vertical takeoff and landing aircraft cons. Dana Point, Calif., 1989-94; ret., 1994. Contbr. articles to profl. reports. With USAAF, 1943-46. Mem. AIAA, ASME, Am. Helicopter Soc. (chmn. St. Louis sect. 1955-56, nat. aerodyns. com. 1969-70, tech. dir. western region 1969-70), Nat. Mgmt. Assn. (life). Jewish.

GÖRG, ALAN KENT, media company executive, writer, filmmaker; b. Hollywood, Calif., Oct. 12, 1931; s. Oscar Emmett and Birdie (Galen) G.; m. Gwyndolin Lee Yates, Sept. 27, 1963; children: Galyn, Carter, Gentry, Sunny, Tagi. BS, UCLA, 1952, MFA, 1970; LLB, Stanford U., 1955. Life C.C. tchg. and adult edn. credentials, Calif. Chmn. Project Action, Venice, Calif., 1967-70; tchr. various schs., Calif., 1970—; dir. Media Assocs., Marina Del Rey, Calif., 1986—. Author: The Sixties, 1995, Proof That God Exists, 1996, Encounters with Aboriginal Philosophers, 1996; prodr., dir. feature film Living the Blues, 1986. Com. chmn. CORE, L.A., 1963-67; mem. Com. for Traditional Indian Land and Life, L.A., 1968-73; treas. Venice Ocean Park Coop., 1996. Recipient cert. of merit Am. Film Festival, 1965, 70, Film Trax award Ghent (Belgium) Internat. Festival, 1986. Mem. Assn. Ind. Video and Filmmakers. Office: Media Assocs PO Box 11522 Marina Del Rey CA 90295

GORMAN, BRIAN DEAN, investment professional; b. Rockford, Ill., Feb. 13, 1954; s. Benjamin Lee and Joyce (Bartlett) G.; m. Weezie Dunn, Jan. 4, 1974; children: Kellie, Bill, Charlie, Hunter. Student, Shimer Coll., Mt. Carrol, Ill., 1972; BA in History with honors, Mont. State U., 1987. Staff mgr. Guaranteed Life Ins. Co., Gainesville, Fla., 1974-76; v.p. Furniture City, Consumers Warehouse, Inc., Gainesville, 1976-81; owner So. Furniture Distbrs., Inc. (dba Affordable Furniture and Beds; Affordable Sofas, Alpha Mortgage), Gainesville and Bozeman, Mont., 1981-91; mortgages purchase and sales profl. Alpha Mortgage Investments, Bozeman, 1983—. Home: 8004 Pinion Pl Bozeman MT 59715-8929 Office: E-Z Quick Realestate Loan 517 S 22d Ave Ste 1 Bozeman MT 59715-8929

GORMAN, BRUCE CHARLES, health care executive; b. Washington, Jan. 14, 1949; s. Edward David and Dora (Hallen) G.; m. Judy Ann Jackl, Jan. 1, 1982; children: Marcus, Kate. BA with honors, U. Md., 1972; M in City and Regional Planning, Rutgers U., 1974. Dir. mktg. Select Health, Emeryville, Calif., 1984-87; adminstr. Aetna Life Ins. Co., Walnut Creek, Calif., 1987-89; v.p. Am. Biodyne, South San Francisco, 1989-93, Medco Behavioral Care Corp, South San Francisco, 1993-96; pres. Managed Care Econs. & Planning, Inc., Berkeley, Calif., 1996—; mgmt. cons., Berkeley, Calif., 1976-82. Contbr. articles to profl. jours., chpts. to books. Cons. Community Organizing Project, San Francisco, 1979-82, Galleria de la Raza, San Francisco, 1982-83. Named one of Outstanding Young Men Am., 1982. Mem. No. Calif. Employee Benefits Coun., Behavioral Health Care Inst., Omicron Delta Epsilon. Democrat. Jewish.

GORMAN, MICHAEL STEPHEN, construction executive; b. Tulsa, Aug. 3, 1951; s. Lawrence Matthew and Mary Alice (Veith) G.; m. Sheryl Lane McGee, Feb. 19, 1972; children: Kelley Lane, Michael Ryan. Student, Colo. State U., 1970, 71. With McGee Constrn. Co., Denver, 1972-74, with sales and estimating dept., 1974-78, gen. mgr., 1978-80, pres., owner, 1980-91; pres. Wisor Group, Boulder, 1990—; cons., author, columnist in remodeling and custom home building; mortgage banker, ins. cons., 1995—; presenter seminars in field. Mem. Nat. Assn. Remodeling Industry (chmn. membership svcs. com. 1987-91, bd. dirs. 1982-91, regional v.p. 1987-89, nat. sec. 1990-91, Man of Yr. 1982, Regional Contractor of Yr. 1988).

GORMAN, RUSSELL WILLIAM, marketing executive, consultant; b. Glen Ridge, N.J., Aug. 17, 1927; s. William Francis and Emily (Weldon) G.; m. Mieko Deguchi, June 19, 1956. BS, U.S. Merchant Marine Acad., 1949. Lic. mcht. marine, chief mate. Lic. officer Moore McCormack Lines Inc., N.Y., 1949-53; dir. tng. Chevron Shipping Co., San Francisco, 1957-77; mgr. orgn., adminstrn. Utah Internat. Corp., San Francisco, 1977-84; pres. Lumier Inc., San Francisco, 1984-85; v.p. John F. Perry Assocs., Concord, Calif., 1986; pres. Market Devel. Assocs., Danville, Calif., 1986-94; sr. v.p. Aegis Fin. Svcs., 1993—; pres., dir. Perfect Wash US, 1993-96; ptnr. Two Star Internat., Oakland, Calif., 1993—; bd. dirs., v.p. Norlock Tech. Inc., San Mateo, Calif., 1989—; bd. dirs. Internat. Tech. Assocs. Santa Clara, Calif., 1986—. Chmn. Calif. Vets. Coalition for Bush, 1988; mem. Sec. of Def. Adv. Bd. on Naval History, 1990-97; vice chmn. Sec. of Interior Adv. Commn. on San Francisco Maritime Hist. Park, 1992—; chmn., CEO U.S.S. Missouri and Allied Forces Meml., 1995—; adv. speaker Peter Wilson for Senate Campaign, 1988; bd. dirs. Calif. Mil. Mus., Sacramento, 1996—. Lt. USN, 1954-57, rear adm. USNR, 1980-87. Decorated Legion of Merit with gold star, Navy Commendation medal. Mem. Navy League of U.S. (v.p. Pacific Ctrl. region 1989—), Res. Officer Assn. of U.S. (v.p. Navy sect. 1990-92, chmn. long range planning 1992—), Naval Res. Assn. (nat. v.p. surface/subsurface 1990-95, co-chair long range plan 1995—), Oakland C. of C. (vice chmn. mil. affairs com. 1990-95). Republican. Methodist. Home: 46 Willowview Ct Danville CA 94526-1945

GORMÈZANO, KEITH STEPHEN, arbitrator; b. Madison, Wis., Nov. 22, 1955; s. Isadore and Miriam (Fox) G.; m. Emma Lee Rogers, Aug. 17, 1986 (div. Nov. 1990). BGS, U. Iowa, 1977, postgrad. in pub. affairs, 1979-80; postgrad. in law, U. Puget Sound, 1984-86. Pub. Le Beacon Presse, Seattle, 1980-89; real estate agt. Jim Stacy Realty, Seattle, 1988-89; arbitrator Better Bus. Bur. Greater Seattle, 1987-93; arbitrator Puget Sound Multi-Listing Assn., 1988-89, Nat. Assn. Securities Dealers, 1989-92, Ford Consumer Appeals Bd., 1991-92, Harborview Med. Ctrs., 1990-91, 92-93, Up. Improvement Found., 1980-81; joint labor mgmt. com. Puget Fin. Svcs., U. Wash. Med. Ctr., 1990-91, 92-93; pub. info. officer; vol. VISTA, 1982-83; dir. ACJS, Inc., 1981-82; mem. steering com. Seattle Polyfidelity Group, 1994-96, mem. No Safeword Writers Group, 1996—. Editor M'godolim, 1980-81, Funding Bull. U. Wash. Health Scis. Grantseekers, 1991; pub., editor Beacon Rev., 1980-89. Vice chmn. Resource Conservation Commn., Iowa City, 1979-80; bd. dirs. Seattle Mental Health Inst., 1981-83, Youth Advocates, Seattle, 1984, Atlantic St. Ctr., 1984; mem. City of Seattle Animal Control Commn., 1984-86, vice chmn., 1985-86, chmn., 1986; mem. Selective Svc. System, 1982—, vice chmn. civilian rev. bd. 742, 1985—; mem. Wash. State Local Draft Bd. # 18, mem. controlled choice appeals bd. Seattle Sch. Dist., 1989; patient collection rep. U. Wash., 1990-91, Harborview Med. Ctrs., 1990-91, 92-93; mem. Ford Consumer Appeals Bd., 1991-93, Ford Motor Co. Dispute Settlement Bd., 1991-93, Joint Labor-Mgmt. Com., Patient Fin. Svcs., U. Wash. Med. Ctr., 1990-91, 92-93, Temple B'nai Torah; mem. coordinating com. edn. after dark program Jewish Fedn. Greater Seattle, 1991-92, exec. bd. thirty-something plus Jewish Community Ctr., 1991-92; active Congregation Eitz Or; co-facilitator Polyfidelity Group, 1995. Named Citizen of the Day Sta. KIXI Radio, 1982. Mem. League United Latin Am. Citizens Amigos (chair 1984-86), U. Iowa Alumni Assn., No Safeword Writers' Group. Democrat. Jewish. Office: 501 N 36th St Ste 330 Seattle WA 98103-8653

GORMLEY, FRANCIS XAVIER, JR., social worker; b. Boston, Apr. 27, 1953; s. Francis Xavier and Catherine Caroline (Ireland) G. Student, Massasoit Community Coll., 1973; BA in Psychology, U. Mass., Boston, 1981; MSW, U. Wash., 1984. Lic. social worker, Hawaii. Coordinator Gerontology Career Program Elder Fest, Chico, Calif., 1981; mgr. Arnold's Restaurant, Cardiff, Wales, 1981-82; med. social worker Harborview Med. Ctr., Seattle, 1983-84; psychotherapist Seattle Counseling Svc., 1982-88; clin. social worker Pain Ctr. Swedish Hosp., Seattle, 1984-88, Valley Med. Ctr., Renton, Wash., 1987-88; clin. social worker AIDS program, virology clinic Univ. Hosp., Seattle, 1988-94; mgr. clin. ops. dept. social work The Queen's Med. Ctr., Honolulu, 1994—; speaker U. Wash Sch. Social Work Graduation Class, 1984, Social Sensitivity in Health Care U. Wash., 1985—; coord. Coping with AIDS Swedish Hosp. Tumor Inst., 1985; participant Coun. of Internat. Fellowship Italia, Placement Servizi Socio-Sanitari AIDS-Roma, 1991; guest speaker Sta. KIRO-TV, Seattle, 1985, Sta. KPLZ, Seattle, 1985; presentor psychosocial aspects HIV/AIDS Northwest AIDS Edn. & Tng. Ctr. Program, U. Wash. Med. Ctr., 1992, clin. mgmt. of patient with HIV/AIDS El Rio Health Ctr., Pima Colo. Pub. Health Dept., 1992, Queen's Cancer Inst. Symposium, 1996; cons. Assn. Workers Resources, Seattle, 1985—; practicum instr. U. Wash. Seattle Sch. Social Work, 1989—; preceptor, intern Residency Tng. Project Sch. of Medicine/Health Scis., Univ. Wash; HIV/AIDS planning coun. Seattle/King County Pub. Health Dept., 1993; com. for the 25th health scis. open house U. Wash. Editor abstract form Comprehensive Multi-Disciplinary Documentation, Western U.S.A. Pain Soc., 1986; contbr. articles to profl. jours. Mem. Seattle Aids Network, 1985—. Mem. NASW (mem. bd. Wash. state chpt. 1988-90), Acad. Cert. Social Workers, Occupational Social Work Orgn. of NASW, Coun. Internat. Fellowship, U. Wash. Alumni Assn., U. Mass. Alumni Assn., Green Key Soc. Democrat. Office: Queen's Med Ctr Social Work Dept 1301 Punchbowl St Honolulu HI 96813-2413

GORRIS, WENDY KATHLEEN, English language educator; b. Santa Rosa, Calif., Dec. 9, 1970; d. Norman Merle and Kathleen LaVerne (Westerlund) Jones; m. Brent R. Gorris, June 27, 1992. BA in Psychology, Biola U., 1991. Customer svc. rep. City of Santa Rosa, 1992-94; English tchr. Rincon Valley Christian Sch., Santa Rosa, 1994-96; lang. arts cons. McDougal Littell, Walnut Creek, Calif., 1996—. Republican. Office: Rincon Valley Christian Sch 4585 Badger Rd Santa Rosa CA 95409-2630

GORSUCH, EDWARD LEE, chancellor. Degree in Econ. & Cmty. Devel., U. Mo. Dor/ Inst. Social and Econ. Rsch., 1976-94; dean Sch. Pub. Affairs U. Alaska Anchorage, 1988-94; chancellor, 1994—; bd. Commonwealth North; adv. bd. Alaska Airlines Anchorage Cmty.; civilian adv. bd. ALCOM; adv. bd. dirs. Anstar Natural Gas Co.. Office: Office of Chancellor Univ Alaska Anchorage 3211 Providence Dr Anchorage AK 99508

GORTON, SLADE, senator; b. Chicago, Ill., Jan. 8, 1928; s. Thomas Slade and Ruth (Israel) G.; m. Sally Jean Clark, June 28, 1958; children: Tod, Sarah Jane, Rebecca Lynn. AB, Dartmouth Coll., 1950; LLB with honors, Columbia U., 1953. Bar: Wash. 1953. Assoc. law firm Seattle, 1953-65; ptnr. law firm, 1965-69; atty. gen. State of Wash., Olympia, 1969-81; U.S. Senator from Wash., 1981-87, 89—; ptnr. Davis, Wright & Jones, Seattle, 1987-89; mem. Wash. Ho. of Reps., 1959-69, majority leader, 1967-69, Nat. Republican Senatorial com., Indian Affairs/Labor & Human Resources com., budget com.; chmn. commerce, sci., & transp. subcom. on consumer affairs, fgn. commerce & tourism, appropriations subcom. Interior & Related Agys. Trustee Pacific Sci. Center, Seattle, found. mem., 1977-78; mem. Pres.'s Consumer Adv. Council, 1975-77; mem. Wash. State Law and Justice Commn., 1969-80, chmn., 1969-76; mem. State Criminal Justice Tng. Commn., 1969-80, chmn., 1969-76. Served with AUS, 1946-47; to 1st lt. USAF, 1953-56; col. USAFR (ret.). Mem. ABA, Wash. Bar Assn., Nat. Assn. Attys. Gen. (pres. 1976-77, Wyman award 1980), Phi Delta Phi, Phi Beta Kappa. Clubs: Seattle Tennis, Wash. Athletic (Seattle). Office: US Senate 730 Hart Senate Bldg Washington DC 20510

GOSE, RICHARD VERNIE, lawyer; b. Hot Springs, S.D., Aug. 3, 1927. MS in Engring., Northwestern U., 1955; LLB, George Washington U., 1967; JD, George Washington U., 1968. Bar: N.Mex. 1967, U.S. Supreme Ct. 1976, Wyo. 1979; registered prof. engr., Wyo.; children: Beverly Marie, Donald Paul, Celeste Marlene. Exec. asst. to U.S. Senator Hickey, Washington, 1960-62; mgr. E.G. & G., Inc., Washington, 1964-66; asst. atty. gen. State of N.Mex., Santa Fe, 1967-70; pvt. practice law, Santa Fe, 1967—, Santa Fe/Prescott, 1989—; assoc. prof. engring. U. Wyo., 1957-60; owner, mgr. Gose & Assocs., Santa Fe, 1967-78; pvt. practice law, Casper, Wyo., 1978-83; pres. Argosy Internat., Inc., 1994—; co-chmn. Henry Jackson for Pres., M.Mex., 1976, Wyo. Johnson for Pres., 1960. With U.S. Army, 1950-52. Mem. N.Mex. Bar Assn., Wyo. Bar Assn., Yavapai County Bar Assn., Masons, Phi Delta Theta, Pi Tau Sigma, Sigma Tau. Methodist. Home and Office: PO Box 3998 Prescott AZ 86302-3998

GOSLOW, ROBERT HENRY, consulting mechanical, aeronautical and forensic engineer; b. Detroit, Sept. 16, 1926; s. Harry Jay and Lue Anna (Cunningham) G.; m. Joan Maree Ruihley, Dec. 23, 1950; children: Janet Maree Goslow Bove, Douglas Harlon, Scott William. BS in Aero. Egnring., U. Mich., 1950; cert. in engring. mgmt. practice, U. Calif., Irvine, 1985. Registered profl. engr., Calif.; ordained deacon Presbyterian church. Design engr. Douglas Aircraft Co., Santa Monica, Calif., 1950-61; staff engr. ITEK Corp., Palo Alto, Calif., 1961-63; design specialist Lockheed Missiles & Space Co., Sunnyvale, Calif., 1963-69, 72-76; prin. Advantage Engring. Assocs., Sunnyvale, Calif., 1969-72; prin. engr. LearFan USA, Lear Avia, Reno, Nev., 1976-83; sr. tech. specialist B2 div. Northrop Corp., Pico Rivera, Calif., 1983-89; prin. AdvantagEngring., Anaheim, 1989-91; Douglas Thor rep. NASA Discoverer safe sys. oper. com., Santa Monica, 1961; guest lectr. Truckee Meadows C.C., Reno, 1981-82; instr. LearFan Tng. Acad., Reno, 1982. Composer (instrumental music) Trombone Chorale, 1978, (organ prelude) Reflection, 1971, Lue Anna's Theme, 1985 and various choral anthems. Chmn. Com. for Excellence in Elem. Edn., Cupertino, Calif., 1964. Fellow Inst. for Advancement Engring.; mem. NSPE, AIAA, Brit. Soc. Engrs. (hon. mem. 1995), Nat. Acad. Forensic Engrs. (corr.), Calif. Soc. Profl. Engrs. (pres. Orange County chpt. 1986-88, v.p. 1990-91, pres. Peninsula chpt. 1992-93, 96—, dir. Santa Clara Valley chpt. 1994—, sec., dir. CSPE Edn. Found.), Order of Engrs. (nat. bd. govs. 1990-95, chair No. Calif. Link # 130, dir. Silicon Valley Engring. Coun.), Scabbard and Blade, Am. Legion (comdr. Douglas Aircraft Post 523 Santa Monica 1956-57). Republican. Home: 814 Lusterleaf Dr Sunnyvale CA 94086-8156 Office: Advantage Engring 814 Lusterleaf Dr Sunnyvale CA 94086-8156

GOSS, EILEEN ABEL, editor; b. Cleve., Nov. 12, 1942; d. Henry and Faye (Zelivyansky) Abel; m. Lawrence Allan, Dec. 20, 1964; children: Melissa, Deborah. BS, Ohio U., Athens, 1964. Tchr. Cleve. Bd. of Edn., 1964-68; substitute tchr. Cleve. U. Hts., 1968-72; tchr. Hebrew Acad., Cleve., 1972-77; prodn. editor Am. Metal Mkt. Metalworking News, Des Plaines, Ill.; asst. editor Shelby Report of the SE/SW, Atlanta, 1980-85; editor Leisure Times, 1985-91; recorder Leads Inc., 1988; program chmn. Career Connections, 1988. Editor: Leisure Times, 1985-91; publisher North County Active Lifestyles, 1991-93; copy editor Bamboo Telegraph, Singapore, 1993-94. Tutor Carlsbad Adult Learning Program, 1988-90; mng. editor Jewish Cmty. News, Los Gatos, Calif., 1995—. Mem. Soroptimist Internat., Brandeis Women, B'nai B'rith Women (co-pres. 1992-93), Rotary Internat. (bd. dirs. 1992-93). Home: 13 Trillium Ln San Carlos CA 94070 Office: 14855 Oka Rd Los Gatos CA 95030

GOSS, JEROME ELDON, cardiologist; b. Dodge City, Kans., Nov. 30, 1935; s. Horton Maurice and Mary Alice (Mountain) G.; m. Lorraine Ann Sanchez, Apr. 20, 1986. BA, U. Kans., 1957; MD, Northwestern U., 1961. Diplomate Am. Bd. Internal Medicine, Am. Bd. Cardiology (fellow, bd. govs. 1981-84). Intern Met. Gen. Hosp., Cleve., 1961-62; resident Northwestern U. Med. Ctr., Chgo., 1962-64; fellow in cardiology U. Colo., Denver, 1964-66; asst. prof. medicine U. N.Mex., Albuquerque, 1968-70; practice medicine specializing in cardiology N.Mex. Heart Clinic, 1970—; mem. bd. alumni counsellors Northwestern U. Med. Sch., 1977-89, mem. nat. alumni bd., 1991—; chief dept. medicine Presbyn. Hosp., Albuquerque, 1978-80, mem. exec. com., 1980-82, dir. cardiac diagnostic svcs., 1970-96. Contbr. articles to profl. jours. Bd. dirs. Presbyn. Heart Inst., Ballet West N.Mex., N.Mex. Symphony Orch.; pres. Albuquerque Mus. Found. Lt. comdr. USN, 1966-68. Nat. Heart Inst. research fellow, 1965-66; named one of Outstanding Young Men Am., Jaycees, 1970; recipient Alumni Service award Northwestern U. Med. Sch., 1986. Fellow ACP, ACC, Coun. Clin. Cardiology of Am. Heart Assn., Soc. Cardiac Angiography; mem. Albuquerque-Bernalillo County Med. Soc. (sec. 1972, treas. 1975, v.p. 1980), Alpha Omega Alpha. Republican. Methodist. Office: NMex Heart Clinic 1001 Coal Ave SE Albuquerque NM 87106-5205

GOSSARD, EARL EVERETT, physicist; b. Eureka, Calif., Jan. 8, 1923; s. Ralph Dawson and Winifred (Hill) G.; m. Sophia Poignand, Nov. 21, 1948; children: Linda Margaret, Kenneth Earl, Diane Winifred. BA, UCLA, 1948; MS, U. Calif., San Diego, 1951; PhD in Phys. Oceanography, Scripps Instn. Oceanography, 1956. Meteorologist Navy Electronics Lab., San Diego, 1949-55, head radio meteorol. sect., 1955-61; head radio physics div. Navy Electronics Lab. (name now Naval Ocean Systems Ctr.), San Diego, 1961-71; chief geoacoustics program Wave Propagation Lab., NOAA, Boulder, Colo., 1971-73, chief meteorol. radar program, 1973-82; sr. rsch. assoc. Coop. Inst. for Rsch. in Environ. Scis. U. Colo., Boulder, 1982—. Co-author: (with Hooke) Waves in the Atmosphere (Disting. Authorship award Dept. Commerce 1975), 1973; (with Strauch) Radar Observation of Clear Air and Clouds (Disting. Authorship award Dept. Commerce 1985); editor: Radar Observation of the Clear Air, 1980; contbr. over 74 articles to profl. jours. 1st lt. USAAF, 1943-46, CBI. Recipient Silver medal Dept. Commerce, 1976, Citation Am. Geophys. Union, 1986. Fellow Am. Meteorol. Soc.; mem. Nat. Acad., Internat. Union Radio Sci. (past chmn. U.S. Commn. F.). Republican. Presbyterian. Home: 1088 Kelly Rd W Sugarloaf Star Rt Boulder CO 80302 Office: U Colo Campus Box 449 Boulder CO 80309

GOSSETT, JANINE LEE, middle school educator; b. Carlsbad, N.Mex., Jan. 22, 1950; d. William Adair and Anita Jeanne (Hilty) G. BS, N.Mex. State U., 1974, MA, 1992. Tchr., dir. Sunshine Sch., Parker, Ariz.; tchr. spl. edn. Lubbock (Tex.) State Sch.; tchr. regular and accelerated lang. arts Carlsbad Mcpl. Schs.; tchr. 7th & 8th gr. advanced ednl. placement Carlsbad Mcp. Schs. Mem. Nat. Coun. Tchrs. English, Nat. Mid. Sch. Assn., N.Mex. Coun. Tchrs. English (past treas., directory/membership chair). Office: 408 N Canyon St Carlsbad NM 88220-5812

GOSSETT, JEFFREY ALAN, professional football player; b. Charleston, Ill., Jan. 25, 1957. BS in Phys. Edn., Eastern Ill. U., 1982. With Kansas City Chiefs, 1981-82, Cleve. Browns, 1983-84, 85-87; punter Portland USFL, 1985; with Houston Oilers, 1987; punter L.A. Raiders, 1988—. Named punter The Sporting News NFL All-Pro team, 1991. Office: Oakland Raiders 1220 Harbour Bay Pkwy Alameda CA 94502*

GOSSLEE, MARY JUNE, chiropractor; b. Seattle, Jan. 3, 1957; d. Norman Arthur G. and Carol Mae (Tozier) Eller. BS, Univ. State N.Y., 1988; D of Chiropractic, Logan Coll. Chiropractic, 1991. EMT Shepard Ambulance, Seattle, 1983-85; paramedic Abbott Ambulance, St. Louis, 1985-90; teaching asst. Logan Coll. Chiropractic, St. Louis, 1990-91; assoc. Woodway Chiropractic, Lynnwood, Wash., 1993; chiropractor Family Health Ctr., Bellevue, Wash., 1993—; bd. dirs. Successful Women's Network, Bellevue,; founding dir. Discovery Inst. for Healing Arts, Issaquah, Wash., 1995; speaker in field. Recipient Alumni Rsch. award Logan Coll. Alumni Assn., 1991. Mem. Am. Chiropractic Assn., Women Entrepreneur's Network (v.p. 1993-94), Women Bus. Owners (bd. dirs. 1996-97), Bus. Network Internat. (pres. Bellevue chpt. 1996), Chi Rho Sigma. Office: Evergreen Wellness Ctr 860 106th Ave NE Bellevue WA 98004

GOSZCZYNSKI, STEFAN, chemistry educator; b. Radomsko, Poland, Apr. 14, 1924; came to U.S., 1987; s. Tadeusz and Zofia (Nowak) G.; m. Hanna Jaroslawska, June 28, 1953; children: Peter, Thomas. MSc, Silesian Tech., Gliwice, Poland, 1950; PhD, Silesian Tech., 1960, DSc, 1964. Asst., reader Silesian Tech. U., 1948-60, from asst. to assoc. prof., 1962-68; postdoctoral fellow Birmingham (Eng.) U., 1960-61; from assoc. prof. to prof. Poznan (Poland) Tech. U., 1968-87; vis. prof. U. Idaho, Moscow, 1987—; dir. Inst. Tech. and Engring. Poznan Tech. U., 1968-70, head dept., 1977-80. Patentee in field. Named to Order of Merit Polonia Restituta, 1978, Disting. Prof. Republic of Poland, 1980; recipient medal Nat. Edn. Com., 1984. Home: 115 S Lilley Apt 201 Moscow ID 83843 Office: U Idaho Food Rsch Ctr 103 Moscow ID 83843

GOTHOLD, STUART E., school system administrator, educator; b. L.A., Sept. 20, 1935; s. Hubert Eugene and Adelaide Louise (Erickson) G.; m. Jane Ruth Soderberg, July 15, 1955; children: Jon Ernest, Susan Louise, Eric Arthur, Ruth Ann. BA, Whittier Coll., 1956, MA in Edn., 1961, LLD (hon.), 1988; EdD, U. So. Calif., 1974. Tchr. grades 1-9 El Rancho Sch. Dist., Pico Rivera, Calif., 1956-61, prin. jr. h.s., 1961-66; curriculum cons. L.A. County Office Edn., 1966-70; asst. supt. South Whittier (Calif.) Sch. Dist., 1970-72, supt., 1972-77; asst. supt. L.A. County Office Edn., Downey, 1977-78, chief dep. supt., 1978-79, supt., 1979-94; clin. prof. U. So. Calif., L.A., 1994—; mem. adv. bd. Nat. Ctr. Fgn. Lang., 1984—; charter mem. Edn. Insights, Detroit, 1990—. Author: (book) Inquiry, 1970, Decisions-A Health Edn. Curriculum, 1971. Recipient Alumni Merit award USC, 1993, Alumni Achievement award Whittier Coll., 1986; named Dist. Educator Calif. State U., 1993. Republican. Roman Catholic. Home: 10121 Pounds Ave Whittier CA 90603-1649 Office: U So Calif WPH 902c Los Angeles CA 90090-0031

GOTSHALL, CORDIA ANN, publishing company executive, distributing executive; b. Greenwood, Ark., Jan. 21, 1931; d. Harrison Wages and Mabel Magdalene (Boswell) Wages Moreland; m. Daniel W. Gotshall, Apr. 12, 1952. AA with honors, Foothill Jr. Coll., Los Altos Hills, Calif., 1966; BA magna cum laude, Humboldt State U., Arcata, Calif., 1969; student, Humboldt State U., 1969-71. Clk., typist Indentification Bur. Stanislaus County Sheriff's Office, Modesto, Calif., 1950-55; credit dept. mgr. Brizard's Dept. Store, Arcata, 1955-56; sec.-coord. City of Eureka (Calif.) Recreation Dept., 1956-60; seasonal aide State of Calif. Dept. Fish and Game, Palo Alto, 1961; owner, v.p. Sea Challengers Pub. Co., Monterey, Calif., 1976-83, pres., 1983—; co-editor (with Daniel W. Gotshall) Fishwatcher's Guide, 1977; U.S. rep. Moscow Internat. Book Fair, 1985. Mem. Chi Sigma Epsilon. Office: 4 Sommerset Rise Monterey CA 93940-4112

GOTTFRIED, EUGENE LESLIE, physician, educator; b. Passaic, N.J., Feb. 26, 1929; s. David Robert and Rose (Chill) G.; m. Phyllis Doris Swain, Aug. 16, 1957. AB, Columbia U., 1950, MD, 1954. Cert. Nat. Bd. Med. Examiners, Am. Bd. Internal Medicine. Intern Presbyn. Hosp., N.Y.C., 1954-55, asst. resident in medicine, 1957-58; resident Bronx (N.Y.) Mcpl. Hosp. Ctr., 1958-59, fellow in medicine, 1959-60; asst. instr. medicine Albert Einstein Coll. Medicine Yeshiva U., N.Y.C., 1959-60, instr., 1960-61, assoc., 1961-65, asst. prof., 1965-69; assoc. prof. medicine Cornell U. Med. Coll., N.Y.C., 1969-81, assoc. prof. pathology, 1975-81; clin. prof. dept. lab. medicine U. Calif., San Francisco, 1991-93, prof., 1993—, vice chmn. dept. lab. medicine, 1981—; hosp. appointments include asst. vis. physician Bronx Mcpl. Hosp. Ctr., 1960-66, assoc. attending physician, 1966-69; assoc. attending physician N.Y. Hosp., N.Y.C., 1969-81, assoc. attending pathologist, 1975-81, dir. lab. clin. hematology, 1969-81; chief lab. medicine San Francisco Gen. Hosp. Med. Ctr., 1981—, dir. clin. labs., 1981—. Assoc. editor Jour. Lipid Research, 1971-72, 75-77; mem. editorial bd. Jour. Lipid Research, 1972-77. Lt. comdr. USNR, 1955-57. Recipient Career Scientist award Health Research Council City of N.Y., 1964-72. Fellow ACP, Am. Soc. Hematology, Internat. Soc. Hematology, Acad. Clin. Lab. Physicians and Scientists; mem. AAAS, Nat. Com. for Clin. Lab. Stds., Phi Beta Kappa, Alpha Omega Alpha. Office: San Francisco Gen Hosp Clin Labs 1001 Potrero Ave San Francisco CA 94110-3518

GOTTI, MARGARET LYNN, library administrator; b. Detroit, July 31, 1944; d. Frank Mathias and Betty Louise (Lee) Sieger; m. Cyriac Thannikary, Nov. 13, 1965 (div. Feb. 1973); 1 child, Luke Anthony; m. Marcos T. Perez, Mar. 1973 (dec. Oct. 1973); m. Lui Gotti, Dec. 23, 1984. AB, U. Detroit, 1968; MLS, Pratt Inst., 1969; postgrad., NYU, 1976-77. Cert. librarian, N.Y. Sr. librarian Queens Pub. Library, Jamaica, N.Y., 1969-77; library dir. El Centro Pub. Library, El Centro, Calif., 1977—; county libr./cons. Imperial County Free Libr., 1993—; vice chmn., chmn. Serra Coop. Libr. Sys., San Diego, 1980-82. Pres. Hist. Site Found., El Centro, 1988, 92, sec., 1989, trustee, 1989—, v.p., 1991—; fin. sec. St. Elizabeth Luth. Ch., El Centro, 1988; mem. Downtown El Centro Assn., mem. arches bus. improvement dist.; active numerous civic coms., fundraising events; mem. comm. and arts task force Imperial County Arts Coun.; coord. arts and culture com. City of El Centro Strategic Plan. Title IIB fellow Pratt Inst., 1968-69. Mem. ALA, AAUW (v.p. El Centro 1988), Calif. Libr. Assn., Calif. County Librs. Assn., El Centro C. of C., Toastmasters (v.p. El Centro 1978, corr. sec. 1990-91, 1st v.p. 1991—, pres. 1992-93, 2d v.p. 1995-96, recording sec. 1997-98), Women of Moose (sr. regent El Centro 1988-89). Democrat. Lutheran. Home: 1531 W Heil Ave El Centro CA 92243-3135 Office: El Centro Pub Libr 539 W State St El Centro CA 92243-2928

GOTTLIEB, ALAN MERRIL, advertising, fundraising and broadcasting executive, writer; b. L.A., May 2, 1947; s. Seymour and Sherry (Schutz) G.; m. Julie Hoy Versnel, July 27, 1979; children: Amy Jean, Sarah Merril, Alexis Hope, Andrew Michael. Grad. Georgetown U., 1970; BS, Nuclear Engring., U. Tenn., 1971. Press sec. Congressman John Duncan, Knoxvill, Tenn., 1971, regional rep., Young Ams. for Freedom, Seattle, 1972, nat. dir. Young Ams. for Freedom, Washington, 1971-72; nat. treas. Am. Conservative Union, Washington, 1971—, bd. dirs., 1974—; pres. Merril Assocs., 1974—; chmn. Citizens Com. for Right to Keep and Bear Arms, Bellevue, Wash., 1972—, exec. dir., 1973; pres. Ctr. Def. of Free Enterprise, Bellevue 1976—, Second Amendment Found., Bellevue, 1974—; pub. Gun Week, 1985—, The Gottlieb-Tartaro Report, 1995—; bd. dirs. Nat. Park User Assn., 1988—, Am. Polit. Action Com., 1988—, Coun. Nat. Policy, bd. govs., 1985—, Svc. Bureau Assn., pres., dir., 1974—, Chancellor Broadcasting, Inc, Las Vegas, Nev., 1990-93; pres. Sta. KBNP Radio, Portland, 1990—, Evergreen Radio Network, Bellevue, 1990-93, Westnet Broadcasting Inc., Bellevue, 1990, Sta. KSBN Radio, Spokane, 1995—; chmn. Talk Am. Radio Networks, 1994—. With U.S. Army, 1968-74. Recipient Good Citizenship award Citizens Home Protective Assn., Honolulu, 1978, Cicero award Nat. Assn. Federally Licensed Firearms Dealers, Fla., 1982, Second Amendment award Scope, 1983, 91, Outstanding Am. Handgunner award, Am. Handgunners Award Found., Milwaukee, Wisc., 1984, Roy Rogers award, Nat. Antique Arms Collectors Assn., Reno, Nev., 1987, Golden Eagle award, Am. Fedn. Police, Washington, 1990. Mem. NRA. Republican. Author: The Gun Owners Political Action Manual, 1976, The Rights of Gun Owners, 1981, Rev. edit., 1991, The Gun Grabbers, 1988, Gun Rights Fact Book, 1989, Guns For Women, 1988, The Wise Use Agenda, 1989, Trashing the Economy, 1993, Things You Can Do To Defend Your Gun Rights, 1993, Alan Gottlieb's Celebrity Address Book, 1994, More Things You Can Do To Defend Your Gun Rights, 1995, Politically Correct Guns, 1996.

GOTTLIEB, JANE DREW, artist; b. L.A., July 17, 1946; d. Milton and Pat (Gellman) G.; m. David Obst, Dec. 10, 1992; 1 stepchild, Oliver. BA, UCLA, 1968. Artist, photographer So. Calif.; commr. L.A. County Arts Commn.; bd. dirs. Music Ctr. Arts Edn. Coun., L.A. Artist: (short stories) Garden Tales, 1990, Car Tales, 1991, (mus. catalogue) Jane Gottlieb: Photos, 1987, Jane Gottlieb: Monuments, 1990. Home and Studio: 2411 Foothill Ln Santa Barbara CA 93105

GOTTLIEB, LEONARD, foundation administrator; b. Santa Monica, Calif., Apr. 12, 1923; s. Charles and Sarah Gottlieb; m. M. Elizabeth Gottlieb, 1943; children: Thomas Byron, Robert John, Mary Lou. AA, L.A. Trade Tech. Coll., 1943; student, UCLA, 1958, Calif. State U., L.A., 1960. Chief field dep. L.A. City Coun., 1957-67; campaign mgr. Spencer-Roberts & Assocs., L.A., 1967-69; exec. dir. So. Calif. Kidney Found., L.A., 1969-75; dir. devel. Nat. Kidney Found., N.Y.C., 1975-79; regional dir. Nat. Kidney Found., L.A., 1983-91, dir. planned giving, 1991—; legis. analyst II City of L.A., 1980-83. Author: Fund Raising: The How To's, 1976. Mem. life Calif. PTA, 1954; mem. Friends of Sport. Recipient L.A. City Coun. commendation resolution, 1969. Fellow Nat. Kidney Found. Profl. Staff Assn., Planned Giving Coun. So. Calif., Nat. Com. on Planned Giving, Nat. Health Agys. Planned Giving Roundtable, Ephebian Soc., Venice H.S. Alumni Assn. Office: Nat Kidney Found 3140 Grand View Blvd Los Angeles CA 90066-1027

GOTTSCHALK, ADELE M., surgeon; b. N.Y.C., Dec. 28, 1941; d. Otto George and Ada Mae Gottschalk. BS, CUNY, 1963; MD, SUNY, Buffalo, 1967. Intern and resident surgery U. Chgo. (Ill.) Hosp. and Clinics, 1967-70; resident surgery Michael Reese Hosp., Chgo., 1970-71, U. San Diego (Calif.) Hosp., 1971-73; gen. surgeon Kaiser Hosp. Harbor City, Calif., 1973—.

GOTTSTEIN, BARNARD JACOB, retail and wholesale food company executive, real estate executive; b. Des Moines, Dec. 30, 1925; s. Jacob B. and Anna (Jacobs) G.; children: Sandra, James, Ruth Anne, David, Robert; m. Rachel Landau, July, 1986. BA in Econs. and Bus., U. Wash., 1949; LLD (hon.), U. Alaska, Fairbanks, 1991. Pres. J.B. Gottstein & Co., Anchorage, 1953-90; chmn. bd. Carr-Gottstein Inc., Anchorage, 1974-90; ret., 1990—;

dir. United Bank Alaska, Anchorage, 1975-86. Commr. Alaska State Human Rights Commn., 1963-68; del. Dem. Nat. Conv., 1964, 68, 76, 88, 92; committeeman Dem. Nat. Com., 1976-80; v.p. State Bd. Edn., Alaska, 1983-87, pres., 1987-91. Served with USAF, 1944-45. Jewish. Office: Carr-Gottstein Properties 550 W 7th Ave Ste 1540 Anchorage AK 99501-3567

GOUGH, ROBERT EDWARD, horticulturist, editor, educator, writer; b. Wakefield, R.I., Jan. 31, 1949; s. Robert Edward and Christine Anne (Signorelli) G.; m. Patricia Mae Albro, Aug. 17, 1985; children: Robert, Jonathan, Andrew, Amy. BA, U. R.I., 1970, MS, 1973, PhD, 1977. County agrl. agt. Va. Poly. Tech. Inst., Fairfax, Va., 1973; asst. prof. U. R.I., Kingston, 1977-81, assoc. prof., 1981-88; sr. editor Haworth Press, N.Y.C., 1991-93, asst. pub., 1993-95; assoc. prof. Mont. State U., Bozeman, 1995-97, prof., 1997—. Author: Grow the Best Blueberries, 1982, Glossary of Vital Terms for Home Gardens, 1993, High Bush Blueberry and its Management, 1993, Smart Gardener's Guide to Growing Vegetables, 1996; editor: Blueberries: A Century Research, 1996, Smart Gardener's Guide to Growing Fruit, 1997, Small Fruit in the Home Garden, 1997; editor NACTA Jour., Jour. Small Fruit and Viticulture; contbr. articles to profl. jours. Mem. various sch. coms. Mem. KC (dep. grand knight). Republican. Roman Catholic. Home: 8003 Indian Paint Brush Bozeman MT 59715 Office: Mont State U Dept Plant, Soil and Environ Sci Bozeman MT 59717-0312

GOULART, JANELL ANN, elementary education educator; b. Merced, Calif., July 29, 1936; d. James Riddoch and Rowena Janell (Futrell) Mitchell; m. Frank Goulart, May 19, 1956; children: Robert, Frank, Sharon. BA, Fresno (Calif.) State U., 1972, postgrad.; postgrad., Fresno Pacific Coll., Irvine U. Cert. elem. sci. tchr., Calif. Sci. staff developer Calif. Sci. Implementation Network, Irvine, Calif., 1989-96; tchr. Royal Oaks Sch., Visalia, Calif., 1972-96; tchr. sci. Visalia (Calif.) Unified Sch. Dist., 1995; trainer Calif. Learning Assessment System state testing; sci. and math mentor for Visalia Unified Sch. Dist. Mem. Nat. Sci. Tchrs. Assn., Calif. Sci. Tchrs. Assn., Ctrl. Calif. Sci. Tchrs. Assn., Tulare County Reading Coun., Kappa Delta Pi. Home: 1546 River Way Dr Visalia CA 93291-9212 Office: Royal Oaks Sch 1323 S Clover Dr Visalia CA 93277-4221

GOULD, CATHERINE ANNE, clinical psychologist; b. Seattle, Nov. 14, 1952; d. John Van Wyck and Margaret (Hartman) G.; m. Dennis Stuart Stern, June 27, 1982; 1 child, Jessica Alice Gould. Student, Smith Coll., 1971-73; BS in Psychology, U. Mass., 1977; MA in Clin. Psychology, U. Cin., PhD in Psychology, 1982. Lic. clin. psychologist, Calif. Intern Hirsch Cmty. Mental Health Ctr., Culver City, Calif., 1981-82; pvt. practice psychotherapist Encino, Calif., 1982—; postdoctoral fellow San Fernando Valley Child Guidance Clinic, Northridge, Calif., 1982-83; dir. tng. Intercommunity Child Guidance Ctr., Whittier, Calif., 1984-85; coord. kids in the court sys. Children's Inst. Internat., L.A., 1985-86. Author: (with others) Out of Darkness, 1992; contbr. articles to profl. jours.; presentations at various orgns. Mem. Child Sexual Abuse Network, Believe the Children, Nat. Victim Ctr., Nat. Child Abuse Coalition, Calif. Consortium Prevention Child Abuse; mem. adv. bd. Mothers Against Sexual Abuse. Mem. APA, Internat. Soc. Study Dissociation, Calif. Profl. Soc. Abuse Children, Calif. Psyhol. Assn. Office: 16055 Ventura Blvd # 714 Encino CA 91436

GOULD, JULIAN SAUL, lawyer; b. L.A., Apr. 15, 1924; s. David H. and Jeanette (Palm) G.; m. Norma Patricia Gould; 1 child, Paul Julian. Student, U. So. Calif., 1946-48; JD, Southwestern U., L.A., 1950. Bar: Calif. 1950. Lawyer in pvt. practice L.A., 1950—. Named Alumnus of Yr., Southwestern U., 1972. Mem. Hollywood Bar Assn. (pres. 1978), Am. Legion (comdr. 24th Dist. 1960), Southwestern U. Alumni Assn. (pres. 1972), Masons (32 deg., Shriners. Democrat. Office: 1741 Ivar Ave Ste 213 Los Angeles CA 90028-5115

GOULD, MARTHA BERNICE, retired librarian; b. Claremont, N.H., Oct. 8, 1931; d. Sigmund and Gertrude Heller; m. Arthur Gould, July 29, 1960; children: Leslie, Stephen. BA in Edn., U. Mich., 1953; MS in Library Sci., Simmons Coll., 1956; cert., U. Denver Library Sch. Community Analysis Research Inst., 1978. Childrens librarian N.Y. Pub. Libr., 1956-58; adminstr. library services act demonstration regional library project Pawhuska, Okla., 1958-59; cons. N.Mex. State Libr., 1959-60; childrens librarian then sr. childrens librarian Los Angeles Pub. Libr., 1960-72; acctg. dir. pub. srvices, reference librarian Nev. State Libr., 1972-74; pub. services librarian Washoe County (Nev.) Libr., 1974-79, asst. county librarian, 1979-84, county librarian, 1984-94; ret., 1994. Contbr. articles to jours. Exec. dir. Kids Voting/USA, Nev., 1996; treas. United Jewish Appeals, 1981; bd. dirs. Temple Sinai, Planned Parenthood, 1996-97, Truckee Meadows Habitat for Humanity, 1995—; trustee RSVP, North Nevadans for ERA; No. Nev. chmn. Gov.'s Conf. on Libr., 1990; mem. bd. Campaign for Choice, No. Nev. Food Bank, Nev. Women's Fund (Hall of Fame award 1989); mem. No. Nev. NCCJ, Washoe County Quality Life Task Force, 1992—; chair Sierra (Nev.) Comty. Access TV; presdl. appointee vice-chair Nat. Comn. on Librs. and Info. Sci., 1993—; mem. adv. bd. Partnership Librs. Washoe County; apptd. by Pres. Clinton vice-chair Nat. Comn. on Libr. and Info. Svcs., 1994—. Recipient Nev. State Libr. Letter of Commendation, 1973, Washoe County Bd. Commrs. Resolution of Appreciation, 1978, ACLU of Nev. Civil Libertarian of Yr. 1988, Freedom's Sake award AAUW, 1989, Leadership in Literacy award Sierra chpt. Internat. Reading Assn., 1992, Woman of Distinction award 1992, Nev. Libr. Assn. Libr. of Yr., 1993. Mem. ALA (bd. dirs., intellectual freedom roundtable 1977-79, intellectual freedom com. 1979-83, coun. 1983-86), ACLU (bd. dirs. Civil Libertarian of Yr. Nev. chpt. 1988, chair gov.'s conf. for women 1989), Nev. Libr. Assn. (chmn. pub. info. com. 1972-73, intellectual freedom com. 1975-78, govt. rels. com. 1978-79, v.p., pres.-elect 1980, pres. 1981, Spl. Citation 1978, 87, Libr. of Yr. 1993).

GOULDTHORPE, KENNETH ALFRED PERCIVAL, publisher, state official; b. London, Jan. 7, 1928; came to U.S., 1951, naturalized, 1956; s. Alfred Edward and Frances Elizabeth Finch (Callow) G.; m. Judith Marion Cutts, Aug. 9, 1975; children: Amanda Frances, Timothy Graham Cutts. Student U. Westminster (formerly Regent St. Poly.), 1948-49, Bloomsbury Tech. Inst., 1949-50; diploma City and Guilds of London, 1949; student, Washington U., 1951-52. Staff photographer Kentish Mercury, London, 1949-50, St. Louis Post-Dispatch, 1951-55, picture editor, 1955-57; nat. and fgn. corr. Life mag., Time, Inc., N.Y.C., 1957-61, Paris Bur., 1961-65, regional editor Australia-New Zealand, 1966-68, editorial dir. Latin Am., 1969-70; editor Signature mag., N.Y.C., 1970-73; mng. editor Penthouse mag., N.Y.C., 1973-76, pub. cons., 1976-79; editor, exec. pub. Adventure Travel mag., Seattle, 1979-80; sr. ptnr. Pacific Pub. Assocs., Seattle, 1981-83; editor, pub. Washington mag., 1984-89; vice chmn. Evergreen Pub. Co., 1984-89; dir. tourism, State of Wash., 1989-91; pub./cons., writer, 1991—; dir. Grand Fir Pub. Corp., 1994—; tchr. design, editorial techniques Parsons Sch. Design, N.Y.C.; lectr., contbr. elementary schs. lit. progs. Served with Royal Navy, 1946-48. Decorated Naval Medal and bar; recipient awards of excellence Nat. Press Photographers Assn., AP and UP, 1951-57, Pres.' medal Ea. Wash. U., 1986; certs. excellence, Am. Inst. Graphic Arts, 1971, 72, 73, Communication Arts, 1980, 81, 84; spl. award, N.Y. Soc. Publs. Designers, 1980. Mem. Regional Pubs. Assn. (v.p., pres., Best Typography award 1985, Best Spl. Issue 1989), Western Publs. Assn. (Best Consumer Mag. award, Best Travel Mag. awards, 1980, Best Regional and State Mag. award 1985, 86, 88, Best New Publ. award 1985, Best Column award 1985, Best Signed Essay 1986, 87, Best Four-Color Layout 1985, Best Four Color Feature Design), City and Regional Mag. Assn. (William Allen White Bronze awards), Time/Life Alumni Soc., Assn. Washington Gens. (gen. of state 1995, bd. dirs.), Sigma Delta Chi. Episcopalian. Nominated for Pulitzer Prize for coverage of Andrea Doria disaster, 1956; contbr. articles, photographs to nat. mags., books by Life mag. Home: 3049 NW Esplanade Seattle WA 98117-2624

GOURLEY, STEVEN, mayor. Mayor Culver City, Calif. Address: PO Box 507 4095 Overland Ave Culver City CA 90232-0507

GOUSSÉ, MAGGIE, actress; b. Bklyn., Jan. 5, 1958; d. Ewald and Antoinette G.; m. Serge Lecas, sept. 20, 1975 (div. Sept. 1976); 1 child, Cedrick Lesperance. AA in Theater, L.A. City Coll., 1996; postgrad., Calif. State U., L.A., 1996—. Cert. in psychoedn. Cosmetic assoc. Robinson May Co., L.A.; group therapy counselor Edgemont Hosp., L.A.; lang. interpreter French, Creole Berlitz Translations Svcs., Washington; translator, interpreter French, Creole O'Melveny & Meyers, L.A., Hufstedler & Kaus, L.A.; counselor, fashion coord. Job Corps L.A., 1996; ballet jazz tchr. St. Bruno Ch., Laval, Que., 1972, La Souritheque Nursery, Montreal, 1976; social cultural animator, clown Nature Ctr., Can. Summer Project, Laval, 1983; tchr. LeBlanc Sch., Laval, 1983, John Casablancas Modeling & Career Ctr., N.Y.C., 1986; profl. model Da Silva Photo Studio, L.A., 1986; cons. in fashion coord., modeling tchr. Beauties & Shooting Agy., Montreal, 1988; elem. tchr. Montessori Burbank (Calif.) Pre-Sch., 1992; instructional aide Met. Skill Ctr., L.A., 1992; pvt. French tutor, L.A., 1994. Counselor, tchr. Cité Soleil Little Schs., Haiti, 1990. Home and Office: 1072 West Bl Los Angeles CA 90019

GOVAN, GLADYS VERNITA MOSLEY, retired critical care and medical/surgical nurse; b. Tyler, Tex., July 24, 1918; d. Stacy Thomas and Lucy Victoria (Whitmill) Mosley; m. Osby David Govan, July 20, 1938; children Orbrenett K. (Govan) Carter, Diana Lynn (Govan) Mosley. Student, East Los Angeles Coll., Montebello, Calif., 1951; lic. vocat. nurse, Calif. Hosp. Med. Ctr., L.A., 1953; cert., Western States IV Assn., L.A., 1978. Lic. vocat. nurse, Calif.; cert. in EKG. Intravenous therapist Calif. Hosp. Med. Ctr., cardiac monitor, nurse; ret. Past pres. PTA, also hon. mem., 1963—; charter mem. Nat. Rep. Presdl. Task Force.

GOWEN, BRENT DARRELL, English educator, writer; b. San Diego, July 28, 1956; s. Victor Frederick and Shirley (Mitchell) G.; m. Ellen Susan MacDonald, Dec. 17, 1977; 1 child, Kyle. BA, U. Calif., San Diego, 1979, PhD, 1993; MA, San Diego State U., 1983. Grad. tchg. asst. San Diego State U., 1981-83, lectr., 1983-87; grad. tchg. asst. U. Calif., San Diego, 1987-92; assoc. prof. English Palomar Coll., San Marcos, Calif., 1992—. Author: Textuality and Subjectivity, 1991, The Poetics of Reading, 1993. Named Tchr. of Yr., Alpha Gamma Sigma, San Diego, 1994. Mem. Assn. Literary Scholars and Critics. Office: Palomar Coll 1140 W Mission Rd San Marcos CA 92069

GOYNES, BYRON ANTHONY, state agency administrator; b. L.A., July 12, 1960; s. Theron Hulan and Naomi Delores (Jackson) G.; m. Lydia Melvina Kelly, Nov. 10, 1984; 1 child, Joi Antonitte. BBA, Prairie View (Tex.) A&M Univ., 1983; diploma, Nat. Broadcasting Sch., Las Vegas, 1987. Title-info. tech. customer support rep. Clark County Bus. License, Las Vegas, 1984—. Chmn. Bd. of Zoning Adjustment, Las Vegas, 1985—; bd. dirs. Safe Nest, 1985. Mem. Kappa Alpha Psi. Office: Clark County Bus License 500 S Grand Ctrl Pky Las Vegas NV 89155-1810

GOZANI, TSAHI, nuclear physicist; b. Tel Aviv, Nov. 25, 1934; came to U.S., 1965; s. Arieh and Rivcca (Meiri) G.; m. Adit Soffer, Oct. 14, 1958; children: Mor, Shai Nachum, Or Pinchas, Tal. BSc, Technion-IIT, Haifa, Israel, 1956, MSc, 1958; DSc, Swiss Fed. Inst. Tech. (ETH), Zurich, Switzerland, 1962. Registered profl. nuclear engr., Calif.; accredited nuclear material mgr. Rsch. physicist Israel Atomic Energy Commn., Beer-Sheva, 1962-65; rsch. assoc. nuclear engring. dept. Rensselaer Poly. Inst., Troy, N.Y., 1965-66; sr. staff scientist General-Atomic & IRT, San Diego, 1966-70, 71-75; prof. applied physics Tel Aviv U., 1971; chief scientist, div. mgr. Sci. Applications Internat. Corp., Palo Alto and Sunnyvale, Calif., 1975-84; v.p., chief scientist Sci. Applications Internat. Corp., Sunnyvale, 1984-87; corp. v.p. Sci. Applications Internat. Corp., Santa Clara, Calif., 1987-93, sr. v.p., 1993—; Lady Davis vis. prof. Technion-Israel Inst. Tech., 1983-84; bd. dirs. Radiation Sci. Inst., San Jose State U. Author: Active Non-Destructive Assay of Nuclear Materials, 1981; co-author: Handbook of Nuclear Safeguards Measurement Methods, 1983; contbr. over 150 articles to profl. jours. Recipient 1989 Laurel award Aviation Week Jour., R&D 100 awd, 1988, Most Innovative New Products, nominee for the Safe Skies award Conway Data Inc., 1991, 92, 93. Fellow Am. Nuclear Soc.; mem. Am. Phys. Soc., Inst. Nuclear Materials. Office: Sci Applications Internat Corp 2950 Patrick Henry Dr Santa Clara CA 95054-1813

GRABARZ, DONALD FRANCIS, pharmacist; b. Jersey City, Sept. 18, 1941; s. Joseph and Frances (Zotynia) G.; m. Joan Isoldi, Aug. 13, 1966; children: Christine, Robert, Danielle. BPharm, St. Johns U., N.Y.C., 1964. Lic. pharmacist, N.Y., Vt. Dir. qualtiy control and assurance Johnson and Johnson Co., New Brunswick, N.J., 1965-72; dir. quality assurance and regulatory affairs Bard Parker div. Becton Dickinson, Franklin Lakes, N.J., 1972-76; asst. corp. dir. regulatory affairs Becton Dickinson, 1976-80; corp. dir. regulatory affairs C.R. Bard Inc., Murray Hill, N.J., 1980-85; v.p. regulatory affairs, qualtiy assurance Symbion Inc., Salt Lake City, 1985-86; cons., pres. DFG & Assocs., Inc., Salt Lake City, 1986—; mem., mng. dir. Internat. Regulatory Consultants, L.C., Salt Lake City, Boston, Washington, 1987—; adj. prof. Salt Lake C. C., 1993—; lectr. Inst. for Applied Tech., Inst. Internat. Rsch., Ernst & Young, Salt Lake C.C. Co-author, technical advisor, editor Inspection and Recall Film; co-author: Science, Technology, and Regulation in a Competetive Environment, 1990; contbr. articles to profl. jours. Bd. dirs. v.p., asst. treas. Am. Lung Assn., N.J., 1972-75; chmn. Drug Edn., DuPage County, Ill., 1968. Mem. Health Industry Mfg. Assn. (chmn. Legal and Regulatory commn. 1983), Regulatory Affairs Profl. Soc. (lectr.), Am. Soc. Quality Control, Am. Mfr. Med. Instrumentation Assn., Am. Pharm. Assn., Food and Drug Law Inst., Cottonwood Country Club (bd. dirs., treas. 1995—, v.p. 1996—, pres. 1997). Office: Internat Regulatory Cons, LC PO Box 17801 Salt Lake City UT 84117-0801

GRABER, JONATHAN SCHULTZ, musician, music educator; b. Allentown, Pa., Jan. 26, 1965; s. Ralph Schultz and Theresa Lorraine (Green) G. BA, Muhlenberg Coll., 1986; MusM, New Eng. Conservatory Music, 1989; DMA, U. Wash., 1995. Mem. faculty Northlake Sch. Performing Arts, Bothell, Wash., 1995—; concert master Northwest Symphony Orch., Seattle, 1995-96; mem. faculty Cascade Youth Symphony Orch., Edmonds, Wash., 1996—. contbr. article to Am. String Tchr. jour. Younger scholar grantee N.E.H., 1985. Mem. Nat. Fedn. Musicians, Coll. Music Soc., Phi Beta Kappa. Home: 3030 44th Ave W Seattle WA 98199

GRABER, SUSAN P., judge; b. Oklahoma City, July 5, 1949; d. Julius A. and Bertha (Fenyves) G.; m. William June, May 3, 1981; 1 child, Rachel June-Graber. BA, Wellesley Coll., 1969; JD, Yale U., 1972. Bar: N.Mex. 1972, Ohio 1977, Oreg. 1978. Asst. atty. gen. Bur. of Revenue, Santa Fe, 1972-74; assoc. Jones Gallegos Snead & Wertheim, Santa Fe, 1974-75, Taft Stettinius & Hollister, Cin., 1975-78; assoc., then ptnr. Stoel Rives Boley Jones & Grey, Portland, Oreg., 1978-88; judge, then presiding judge Oreg. Ct. Appeals, Salem, 1988-90; assoc. justice Oreg. Supreme Ct., Salem, 1990—. Mem. Gov.'s Adv. Coun. on Legal Svcs., 1979-88; bd. dirs. U.S. Dist. Ct. of Oreg. Hist. Soc., 1985—, Oreg. Law Found., 1990-91; mem. bd. visitors Sch. Law, U. Oreg., 1986-93. Mem. Oreg. State Bar (jud. adminstrn. com. 1985-87, pro bono com. 1988-90), Ninth Cir. Jud. Conf. (chair exec. com. 1987-88), Oreg. Jud. Conf. (edn. com. 1988-91, program chair 1990), Oreg. Appellate Judges Assn. (sec.-treas. 1990-91, vice chair 1991-92, chair 1992-93), Am. Inns of Ct. (master), Phi Beta Kappa. Office: Oreg Supreme Ct 1163 State St Salem OR 97310-1331

GRABSKI, DANIEL ALEXIS, psychiatrist; b. Cleve., May 22, 1928; s. Alex Jacob and Pauline Josephine (Rutkowski) G.; m. Rosemarie Karl, Dec. 24, 1950; children: Daniel Jacob, Daryl Jeffry. BS, Baldwin-Wallace Coll., 1948; MD, St. Louis U., 1952. Diplomate Am. Bd. Psychiatry and Neurology. Exec. dir. Kern County Mental Health Dept., Bakersfield, Calif., 1962-66, 72-86; chief dept. psychiatry Kern County Med. Ctr., Bakersfield, 1972-81; asst. dep. dir. Calif. Dept. Mental Hygiene, Sacramento, 1966-72; med. dir. Weill Meml. Child Guidance Clinic, Bakersfield, 1986—. Capt. USAR, 1954-56. Fellow Am. Psychiat. Assn. (life, spkr. assembly 1977); mem. AMA, Calif. Med. Assn., Ctrl. Calif. Psychiat. Soc., Kern Med. Soc., Flying Physicians Assn., Am. Med. Fly Fishing Assn. (pres.-elect). Office: Weill Child Guidance Clinic 3628 Stockdale Hwy Bakersfield CA 93309

GRACE, JOHN WILLIAM, electrical company executive; b. Swissville, Pa., May 29, 1921; s. Joseph and Ruth Margaret (Bailey) G.; student Am. TV Inst. Tech., 1950; BEE, Drexel U., 1960; m. Ruth Delores Schroeder, Nov. 25, 1950; children: Martha, Joan, Nancy, John William. Technician missiles and surface radar div. RCA, Moorestown, N.J., 1950-56, design engr., 1956-60, project engr., 1960-66; mgr. engring. and sci. exec. EG & G, Inc., Las Vegas, Nev., 1966-73, mgr. bus. devel. operational test and evaluation, Albuquerque, 1973-77; engring. mgr. Instrumentation div., Idaho Falls, Idaho, 1977-79, mgr. systems project office, 1979, mgr. instrumentation program office, 1979-82, mgr. engring. spl. products div., 1982-84, dir. tech. resources, 1984-91, retired 1991. Active Boy Scouts Am., 1969-71. Served with USNR, 1941-45. Mem. IEEE, Instrument Soc. Am. (dir. sci. instrumentation and research div.), Assn. Old Crows, Am. Legion (post adj. vice comdr. 1950). Episcopalian (pres. couples retreat 1969-70). Patentee contradirectional waveguide coupler. Home: 8311 Loma Del Norte Dr NE Albuquerque NM 87109-4901 Office: EG&G Spl Projects Divsn 821 Grier Dr PO Box 93747 Las Vegas NV 89193-3474

GRACE, KAY SPRINKEL, management consultant; d. Robert Lee and Marian (Boyles) S.; m. Geoffrey C. Beaumont; children: Michael, Andrew, Greg. BA in Comms.-Journalism, Stanford U., MA in Edn. Dir. grad. ann. giving, dir. spl. gifts Santa Clara U.; fund devel. dir. The Children's Health Coun., Palo Alto, Calif.; orgnl. cons. San Francisco, 1987—; cons. clients include Calif. 4-H Found., San Diego State U., Nat. Pub. Radio Found., Am. Red Cross, numerous others; core faculty mem. The Fund Raising Sch., Ind. U.; panelist/speaker numerous orgns. including Nat. Soc. Fund Raising Execs., Assn. Hosp. Philanthropy, Devel. Execs. Roundtable, others; presenter confs. in field. Author Beyond Fundraising, 1997, other publs. in field. Fund-raising vol. Stanford U., nat. chair Ann. Fund. Recipient Gold Spike award, Stanford U., 1979, Outstanding Achievement award, Stanford Assocs., 1989, numerous others.

GRACE, WILLIAM PERSHING, petroleum geologist, real estate developer; b. Mineral Point, Mo., Sept. 19, 1920; s. William Francis and Bertha Luciel (Nephew) G.; m. Jeannette Marie Grace, March 28, 1942 (dec.); children: Joyce Medaris, Pamela Grace, Sonia Scott, Patricia Lawser. Student, Corpus Christi U., 1946-47; B in Geology, Tex. Tech. U., 1947-50; student (GRI), U. Colo. Extension, 1968-69. Capt. USAF, 1940-46; regional geologist Anderson-Prichard Oil Corp., San Antonio, Tex., 1950-62; real estate broker Grace Reality, Aurora, Colo., 1963-66; pres. Kimberley Homes, Construction, Aurora, 1966-72; pres., broker Grace-Scott-Cooper Corp., Aurora, 1972—. pres. Friends of the Aurora Pub. Library, 1967, trustee mem. 1978; chmn. Adams County Rep. Party, 1970-72; mem. vocat. edn. coun. Sch. Dist. 28J, 1989—. Named Colorado of Yr. Colo. State Libr. Assn., 1988. Mem. Am. Assn. Petroleum Geologists (del. House of Dels. 1961-62), Nat. Assn. Realtors, Rocky Mountain Assn. Petroleum Geologists, Colo. Assn. Realtors, Colo. State Friends and Trustee Assn., Denver Petroleum Club, Aurora Bd. Realtors (treas. 1979, Realtor of Yr. 1980), Aurora C. of C. (dir. 1966-68, Man of Yr. 1980), Aurora Kiwanis (internat. del. in Nice, France, 1993, lt. gov. Rocky Mountain divsn. 1992, sec. 1965, pres. 1972), Sixty Five Roses Found., Sigma Gamma Epsilon. Lutheran. Home: 2797 S Xanadu Way Aurora CO 80014

GRADDY, ELIZABETH ANN, economics educator; b. Harrisburg, Ark., Sept. 25, 1950; d. Henry T. and Catherine E. (Burrow) G.; m. Glen A. Reed; children: Acacia, Alexandra. BA with highest honors, Memphis State U., 1974; PhD, Carnegie-Mellon U., Pitts., 1984. Asst. prof. U. So. Calif., L.A., 1984-90, assoc. prof., 1990—; vice dean Sch. Pub. Adminstrn. U. So. Calif., 1994-95; dir. program in public policy, 1995—. Contbr. articles to profl. jours. HEW doctoral fellow, 1980-84. Mem. Am. Econ. Assn., Assn. Pub. Policy Analysis and Mgmt., Western Econ. Assn., Sigma Xi. Office: U So Calif Von Kleinsmid Ctr Los Angeles CA 90089

GRADY, DAVID P., freelance writer, retired air force sergeant; b. Boston, Mar. 17, 1941; s. David G. and Doris L. (St. John) G.; m. Janett L. Hardin, Nov. 10, 1962. Grad. pvt. sch., Lowell, Mass. Enlisted man USAF, 1958, advanced through grades to master sgt., 1972; ret., 1978; contr. Valley Hosp., Palmer, Alaska, 1980-81. Contbr. articles to popular publs., including Am. Cowboy, Early Am. Homes, Dog World, Alaska mag. Home: PO Box 1853 Palmer AK 99645

GRADY, DOLORES ANNE, academic administrator, educator, consultant; b. Wiesbaden, Germany, Apr. 24, 1958. BA, U. No. Colo., Greeley, 1980, MA, 1983. Cert. tchr., 1987, trainer, 1996. Instr. Adelphi Bus. Coll., 1984-87; assoc. prof. Colo. Tech. Coll., 1987-91; project mgr. Advanced Skills Edn. Program/Basic Skills Edn. Program Pikes Peak C.C., Ft. Carson, Colo., 1991-93; tng. mgr. Matrix Mktg., Colo., 1993-96; dir. tng. and devel. Ent Fed. Credit Union, 1996—; adj. prof. Chapman U., Colorado Springs, Colo., 1991-93, Pikes Peak C.C., 1991—. Bd. dirs. Pikes Peak Mental Health Action League, Jr. League Colorado Springs. Mem. Internat. Bd. Cert. Trainers, Internat. Soc. Performance Improvement, Am. Soc. Tng. and Devel. Home: 2111 Lockhaven Dr Colorado Springs CO 80909-2037

GRADY, SEAN MICHAEL, writer; b. Palo Alto, Calif., Oct. 3, 1965; s. Michael Wilmont and Naomi Jane (Gladstone) G. BA, U. So. Calif., 1988. Bus. writer Daily Press, Victorville, Calif., 1988-89; bus. editor The Olympian, Olympia, Wash., 1989-90; freelance writer, 1990—; instrnl. asst. Truckee Meadows C.C., Reno, 1992, part-time instr., 1993. Author: Plate Tectonics: Earth's Shifting Crust, 1991, Ships: Crossing the World's Oceans, 1992, The Importance of Marie Curie, 1992, Submarines: Probing the Ocean Depths, 1994, Illiteracy, 1994, Explosives: Devices of Controlled Destruction, 1995. Mem. Soc. Profl. Journalists, Soc. Children's Book Writers and Illustrators (Sierra Nev. chpt.). Home and Office: 3143 Lida Ln Sparks NV 89434

GRAF, ERVIN DONALD, municipal administrator; b. Crow Rock, Mont., Mar. 9, 1930; s. Emanuel and Lydia (Bitz) G.; m. Carolyn Sue Robinson, Mar. 15, 1956 (div. 1958); m. Eleanor Mahlein, Apr. 13, 1959 (dec. Oct. 1990); children: Debra, Belinda, Corrina, Melanie (dec.), Ervin Jr. Enlisted U.S. Army, 1948; served two tours of duty in Vietnam; ret. U.S. Army, 1972; with office and maintenance staff Greenfields Irrigation Dist., Fairfield, Mont., 1972-77, sec. to Bd. Commrs., 1977-95; ret., 1995. Decorated Bronze star with oak leaf cluster. Mem. Am. Legion (all offices Post #80 and Dist. 8 incl. dist. comdr.). Democrat. Lutheran. Home: 211 6th St N Fairfield MT 59436-9101 Office: Greenfields Irrigation Dist Central Ave W Fairfield MT 59436

GRAF, GARY LYNN, career officer; b. Tucson, Ariz., May 4, 1952; s. Milton Frank and Margret Francis (Prausa) G.; m. Jane Elizabeth Bentley, July 25, 1987. BS, U.S. Naval Acad., 1974. Commd. ensign USN, Annapolis, Md., 1970; advanced through grades to comdr. USN, 1989; div. officer USS Flasher USN, Mare Island, San Diego, Calif., 1975-79; leading engring. officer, Nuclear Prototype Tng. Unit USN, Idaho Falls, Idaho, 1979-81; ops. officer USS Pollack USN, San Diego, 1982-85, ASW officer Carrier Group Seven, 1985-87; exec. officer USS Mariano G. Vallejo USN, Charleston, S.C., 1987-89; chief staff officer Submarine Squadron Seven USN, Pearl Harbor, Hawaii, 1990-91; commdg. officer USS Pintado USN, 1992-95; sup force rep Pearl Harbor Naval Shipyard, 1995—. Decorated Navy Commendation medal (3), Navy Achievement medal, Meritorious Svc. medal. Home: 3159 E Dry Creek Rd Phoenix AZ 85048

GRAF, HANS, conductor; b. Austria, Feb. 15, 1949. Studied with Franco Ferrera and Arvid Jonsons. Music dir. Mozarteum Orch., Salzburg, Austria, 1984-94, Calgary Philharm. Orch., 1995—; guest condr. Vienna Symphony, Vienna Philharm., Orchestre Nat. de France, Leningrad Philharm., Pitts. Symphony, Boston Symphony. Office: Calgary Philharmonic Orchestra, 205 8th Ave SE, Calgary, AB Canada T2G 0K9

GRAFE, WARREN BLAIR, cable television executive; b. N.Y.C., June 22, 1954; s. Warren Edward and Maree Lee (Ahn) G.; m. Pamela Arden Rearick, Mar. 8, 1980 (div. Nov. 1982). Student Kendall Coll., 1974-75, U. Wis., Platteville, 1975-76; BA, Ind. U., 1979. Sales rep., Sta. WGTC-FM, Bloomington, Ind., 1979-84, account exec., coop. coord., 1980-84; nat. sales rep. Stas. WTTS-WGTC, Bloomington, 1984; sales rep. Sta. KLFF-KMZK, Phoenix, 1985; account exec. Rita Sanders Advt. and Pub. Rels. Agy., Tempe, Ariz., 1985, Am. Cable TV, Phoenix, 1985-86, Dimension Media Svcs., Phoenix, 1986-89, Greater Phoenix Interconnect, 1989-95, CableRep/Phoenix, 1995—. Recipient Nat. Sales 1st award, Cable TV Advt. Bur., 1986, 2nd award, 1987, 3rd award, 1991, 4th award, 1994, finalist, 1995, 5th award, 1996; named one of Cable's Best Top Ten Cable Advt. Sales Reps. in Country, Cable Avails, 1995. Mem. Tempe C. of C. (ambassador 1986), Chandler (Ariz.) C. of C., Mesa (Ariz.) C. of C. Home: 5122 E Shea Blvd Apt 1117 Scottsdale AZ 85254-4676 Office: CableRep/Phoenix 2020 N Central Ave # 400 Phoenix AZ 85004

GRAFF, DARRELL JAY, physiology educator; b. Cedar City, Utah, Sept. 8, 1936; s. Glen Reber and Wanda Russell G.; m. Joyce Richens, June 16, 1962; children: Michael, Darla Kaye, Janenne Joyce, Christina Lynn. BS, Utah State U., 1958, MS, 1960; PhD, UCLA, 1963. Post doctoral fellow Rice U., Houston, Tex., 1963-65; prof. Physiology Weber State U., Ogden, Utah, 1965—; cons. Albion Laboratories, Clearfield, Utah, 1969-96; bd. mem. Med. Interpretations, Ogden, Utah, 1970-72. Author: Laboratory Manual Physiology, 1967, Intestinal Absorption, 1985. Office: Weber State U 3750 Harrison Blvd Ogden UT 84408

GRAFFIS, JULIE ANNE, entrepreneur, interior designer; b. Houston, Jan. 4, 1960; d. Robert B. and Dorothy Gean (Weempe) Hyde; m. William B. Graffis, May 29, 1988; 1 child, Aaron James Hehr. Student, U. St. Thomas, Houston, 1977, Portland C.C., The Dalles, Oreg., 1984-85; AA, North Seattle C.C., 1987. Cert. window fashions profl. assoc., specialist, master Window Fashions Cert. Program. Co-owner Mosier (Oreg.) Shell Svc., 1981-85; quality control mgr. Town & Country Jeep-Eagle, Seattle, 1986-87; cons. Giovi Ford-Mercury, Pullman, Wash., 1988-89; prin., CEO, Interiors by JAG, Vancouver, Wash., 1990—; mem. Allied Bd. of Trade; cons. Habitat for Humanity, Vancouver, 1992-93; lectr., presenter interior design workshops. Bus. ptnr. Hough Elem. Found. and Sch.; patron Pilchuck Glass Sch. Mem. NAFE, Window Fashions Edn. and Design Resource Network, Greater Vancouver C. of C. (liaison bus. and edn. partnership 1992—, amb. 1993-95), Inst. Managerial and Profl. Women. Office: Interiors by JAG 1605 F St Vancouver WA 98663-3445

GRAFTON, FREDERICK WELLINGTON, artist; b. Middletown, Conn., May 3, 1952; s. Frederick Meeker and Catherine (Simmons) G. BFA with honors, Calif. Coll. Arts and Crafts, Oakland, 1976. watercolor instr. Assoc. Students U. Calif., Berkeley. Represented in permanent collections at Met. Mus. Art, Chase Manhattan Bank, N.Y., Art Inst. Chgo., Arco Ctr. Visual Art, L.A., Bank Am., San Francisco; one-man shows include Grapestake Gallery, San Francisco, 1980, 83, Galleria Del Cavallino, Venice, Italy, 1981, San Jose (Calif.) Mus. Art, 1982; group shows include Bay Area Works on Paper, Seoul and San Francisco Exch., USIS Gallery, South Korea, 1983, Dealers Choice, San Francisco and L.A., U. Calif., Davis, 1985, Sierra Nevada Mus. Art, 1988, Rockford Art Mus., 1988, Transamerica Pyramid, 1996. Recipient Watercolor award Calif. State Expo, 1978. Mem. Emeryville Artists Coop. Home and Office: 1420 45th St # 30 Emeryville CA 94608-2906

GRAHAM, ALICE VIRGINIA, small business owner, civic worker; b. Garden City, Kans., Oct. 6, 1927; d. Ulysses Virgil and Jessie Marie (Gangwer) Walters; m. Leonard Eugene Graham, Sept. 30, 1945; children: Susan Marie, Max Allen, Ted Nelson. Student, Northland Pioneer Coll., Winslow, Ariz., 1976, 93. Field rep., camp dir. Nat. Farmers Union, Denver, 1963-71; state youth ednl. dir. Rocky Mountain Farmers Union, Denver, 1969-70; instr. swimming City of Winslow, 1971-88; co-owner Graham's Mobile Homes, Winslow, 1971—; sec. North Park Village Homes, Inc., Winslow, 1984—. Contbr. essays and fiction to various mags. Bd. dirs. Northland Pioneer Coll. Found., 1995—; mem. choir Winslow Meth. Ch., 1980—; v.p. Winslow Bicentennial Commn., 1975-79; pres. Winslow Enrichment Commn., 1979-80; pres. Winslow Woman's Club, 1978-80, also former rec. sec. and 1st v.p.; mem. Navajo County local jud. adv. com. Ariz. Dept. Health Svcs., Phoenix, 1990; chmn. internat. policy Ariz. Fedn. Women's Clubs, 1978-79, chmn. leadership divsn., 1979-80, treas., 1980-82, 3d v.p., 1982-84, 2d v.p., 1984-86, 1st v.p., pres.-elect, 1986-88; mem. Ariz. Clean and Beautiful Com., Statewide Chem. Abuse Prevention Interagy. Com.; recruitment chmn. Multiple Sclerosis Super Cities Walk, 1991. Recipient Humanities Heritage award Winslow Enrichment Commn., 1982; named Club Woman of Yr., Gen. Fedn. Women's Clubs, 1988; grantee Ariz. Dept. Energy. Mem. Winslow C. of C. (bd. dirs. 1974-76), Indsl. Devel. Endeavor Assn., PEO (1st v.p. 1994), Gen. Fedn. Woman's Club (pres. 1988-90, leadership internat.-regional chmn. S.W. region 1990-92, Off-A-Lot Energy Conservation grantee 1990). Republican. Home: 2303 N Park Dr Winslow AZ 86047

GRAHAM, ANITA LOUISE, correctional and community health nurse; b. Casa Grande, Ariz., Sept. 17, 1959; d. Therman Louis (dec. 1995) and Annie Clessie (Dornan) Nichols; m. Richard Arthur Christy, Aug. 27, 1990; children: Amanda Sue Foster, Kristi Lynn Foster. AS in Practical Nursing, Ctrl. Ariz. Coll., 1982; AAS, Gateway C.C., Phoenix, 1985, Degree in Health Svc. Mgmt., 1992. RN, Ariz., Okla.; cert. BLS, ACLS, Chemotherapy. Cert. nursing asst. Hoemako Hosp., Casa Grande, 1977-82; lic. practical nurse Mesa (Ariz.) Luth. Hosp., 1982-85; RN Mesa Gen. Hosp., 1985-86, East Mesa Care Ctr., 1986-88; RN, case mgr. Interim Healthcare, Phoenix, 1988-93; RN, nurse clinician PDR Carum Care, Phoenix, 1991-97; correctional RN Ariz. Dept. Corrections, Florence, 1993—; IV nurse clinician Signature Home Care, 1994-97; RN, unit mgr., home health IV specialist Select Care, Globe, Ariz., 1997—; mem. RN adv. bd. Interim Healthcare, 1990-93. Mem. Ariz. Nurses Assn. Republican. Home: 1646 N Pennington Dr Chandler AZ 85224-5115

GRAHAM, ANNA REGINA, pathologist, educator; b. Phila., Nov. 1, 1947; d. Eugene Nelson and Anna Beatrice (McGovern) Chadwick; m. Larry L. Graham, June 29, 1973; 1 child, Jason. BS in Chemistry, Ariz. State U., 1969, BS in Zoology, 1970; MD, U. Ariz., 1974. Diplomate Am. Bd. Pathology. With Coll. Medicine U. Ariz., Tucson, 1974—, asst. prof. pathology, 1978-84, assoc. prof. pathology, 1984-90, prof. Pathology, 1990—. Fellow Am. Soc. Clin. Pathologists (bd. dirs. Chgo. chpt. 1993—, sec. 1995—), Internat. Acad. Pathology, Internat. Acad. Telemedicine, Coll. Am. Pathologists; mem. AMA (alt. del. Chgo. chpt. 1992—), Ariz. Soc. Pathologists (pres. Phoenix chpt. 1989-91), Ariz. Med. Assn. (treas. Phoenix chpt. 1995—). Republican. Baptist. Office: Ariz Health Scis Ctr Dept Pathology Tucson AZ 85724

GRAHAM, DENIS DAVID, retired education curriculum coordinator, marriage and family therapist, education consultant; b. Santa Rosa, Calif., Oct. 21, 1941; s. Elbert Eldon and Mildred Bethana (Dyson) G.; m. Margaret Katherine Coughlan, Aug. 31, 1968; children: Kathleen Ann, Todd Cameron (dec.). BS in Edn., U. Nev., 1964, MEd, 1973, MA, 1982. Cert. for ednl. personnel; lic. marriage and family therapist, Nev.; nat. cert. counselor Nat. Bd. for Cert. Counselors. Tchr. vocat. bus. edn. Earl Wooster High Sch., Reno, 1964-66, chmn. dept. bus. edn., 1966-67; state supr. bus. and office edn. Nev. Dept. Edn., Carson City, 1967-70, adminstr. vocat. edn. field svcs., 1970-74, asst. dir., 1974-78, vocat. edn. cons., 1978-85; edn. curriculum specialist Washoe County Sch. Dist., Reno, 1985-89, curriculum coord., 1989-94; ret., 1994; pres. Midpoint Inc., 1995—. marriage and family counselor Severance & Assocs., Carson City, 1983-85, Mountain Psychiat. Assocs., 1985-87; mem. tng. and youth employment council S.W. Regional Lab. for Ednl. Research and Devel., Los Alamitos, Calif., 1982, mem. career edn. council, 1980-81. Editor Council of Chief State Sch. Officers' Report: Staffing the Nation's Schools: A National Emergency, 1984. Contbr. articles to profl. jours. bd. dirs. U. Nev.-Reno Campus Christian Assn., 1988-90; adv. com. Truckee Meadows Community Coll., Reno, 1988-94; mem. Gov.'s Crime Prevention Com., Carson City, 1979-83, Atty. Gen.'s Anti-Shoplifting Com., Carson City, 1974-78, Gov.'s Devel. Disabilities Planning Council, Carson City, 1977-79; bd. dirs. Jr. Achievement No. Nev., 1989-92, sec., mem. exec. com., 1990-91; bd. dir. Friends of the Coll. of Edn. U. Nev., Reno, 1995—. Recipient award for svc. Bus. Edn. Assn. of No. Nev., 1973, Svc. award YMCA, 1962, 63, Helping Hand award Procter R. Hug High Sch., 1993-94, Bill Trabert Meml. award Nev. Dept. Edn. and Nev. Vocat. Assn., 1994. Mem. Am. Vocat. Assn., Nat. Assn. Vocat. Edn. Spl. Needs Pers. (Outstanding Svc. award region V 1982), Assn. Suprs. & Curriculum Devel., Am. Assn. Marriage and Family Therapy, Am. Counseling Assn., Nev. Vocat. Assn. (Outstanding Svc. award 1991, Bill Trabert Meml. award Excellence in Occupational Edn. 1994), Internat. Assn. Marriage and Family Counselors, U. Nev. Reno Alumni Assn. (exec. com. 1971-75), Phi Delta Kappa, Phi Kappa Phi. Democrat. Methodist. Home: 3056 Bramble Dr Reno NV 89509-6901 Office: PO Box 33034 475 S Arlington Ave Reno NV 89533

GRAHAM, JAMES HERBERT, dermatologist; b. Calexico, Calif., Apr. 25, 1921; s. August K. and Esther (Choudoin) G.; m. Anna Kathryn Luiken, June 30, 1950 (dec. May 1987); children: James Herbert, John A., Angela Joann; m. Gloria Boyd Flippin, July 29, 1989. Student, Brawley Jr. Coll., 1941-42; AB, Emory U., 1945; MD, Med. Coll. Ala., 1949. Diplomate: Am. Bd. Dermatology (dir. 1977-87, v.p. 1985-86, pres. 1986-87, Disting. Service medal 1987); diplomate in dermatopathology Am. Bd. Dermatology and Am. Bd. Pathology. Intern Jefferson-Hillman Hosp., Birmingham, Ala., 1949-50; resident in dermatology VA Center and UCLA Med. Center, 1953-56; clin. asst. instr. in medicine UCLA, 1954-56; Osborne fellow and NRC fellow in dermal pathology Armed Forces Inst. Pathology, Washington, 1956-58; vis. scientist Armed Forces Inst. Pathology, 1958-69, chmn. dept. dermatopathology, 1980-88; registrar Registry of Dermatopathology, Armed Forces Inst. Pathology, 1980-88, also program dir. dermatopathology, 1979-88; program dir. dermatopathology Walter Reed Army Med. Center, Washington, 1979-88; asst. prof. dermatology and pathology Temple U., 1958-61, assoc. prof., 1961-65, prof. dermatology, 1965-69, assoc. prof. pathology, 1965-67, prof. pathology, 1967-69; prof. medicine, chief div. dermatology, prof. pathology, dir. sect. dermal pathology and histochemistry U. Calif., Irvine, 1969-78; chief dermatology U. Calif. Med. Ctr., Irvine, 1977-78; prof. emeritus Coll. Medicine, U. Calif., 1978—; head sect. dermatology Orange County (Calif.) Med. Center, 1969-73; cons. dermatology VA Hosp., Long Beach, Calif., 1969-73; chief dermatology sect. VA Hosp., 1973-78, acting chief med. service, 1976; cons. dermatology, dermal pathology Regional Naval Med. Center, San Diego, 1969-82, Long Beach, 1969-78, Camp Pendleton, Calif., 1972-78; cons. dermatology, dermal pathology Meml. Hosp. Med. Center, Long Beach, 1972-86, Fairview State Hosp., Costa Mesa, Calif., 1969-78; cons. for career devel. for rev. clin. investigator applications VA Central Office, Washington, 1973-78; Disting. Eminent physician VA physician and dentist-in-residence program, 1980-88; mem. organizational com. Am. Registry Pathology, Armed Forces Inst. Pathology, Washington, 1976-77; mem. exec. com. Am. Registry Pathology, Armed Forces Inst. Pathology, 1977-78; prof. dermatology, clin. prof. pathology Uniformed Services U. of Health Scis., Bethesda, Md., 1979-88, prof. emeritus, 1989—; program dir. dermatopathology Naval Hosp. and Scripps Clin. and Rsch. Found., San Diego, 1991-94; head divsn. dermatopathology, dept. pathology Scripps Clinic and Rsch. Found., LaJolla, Calif., 1988-94, ret., 1994. Sr. author: Dermal Pathology, 1972; contbr. articles to profl. publs. Served with M.C. USNR, 1949-53. Named Disting. Alumnus, Med. Coll. Ala., 1994. Mem. AMA and Accreditation Coun. for Grad. Med. Edn. (residency rev. com. for dermatopathology 1984-87, residency rev. subcom. for dermatology 1977-87, chmn. 1984-87, cert. of merit 1960), Soc. Investigative Dermatology, U.S. and Can. Acad. Pathology, Am. Soc. Investigative Pathology (emeritus mem. 1995), Am. Dermatol. Assn. (essay award 1958, v.p. 1986-87), Am. Soc. Dermatopathology (pres. 1975-76, Founder's award 1990, rep. to bd. of mem. Am. Registry Pathology 1988-92), Dermatopathology Club (pres. 1980-81), Assn. Mil. Dermatologists, Am. Acad. Dermatology (life, dir. 1974-77, 82, v.p. 1980-81, rep. to bd. mems. Am. Registry Pathology 1977-78), N.Am. Clin. Dermatologic Soc. (hon.), 1973, Pa. Acad. Dermatology, Pacific Dermatol. Assn. (dir. 1972-75, hon. mem. 1981), Dermatology Found., Leader's Soc. Washington Dermatol. Soc. (spl. hon.), Phila. Dermatol. Soc. (pres. 1967-68, hon mem. 1994), San Diego Dermatol. Soc., Cutaneous Therapy Soc., Alpha Omega Alpha, Cosmos Club (Washington). *I have achieved far more than I dreamed possible but it could only happen in America. Being generally optimistic, enthusiastic and persistent has resulted in my serving society in a positive way.*

GRAHAM, JAN, state attorney general; b. Salt Lake City. BS in Psychology, Clark U., Worcester, Mass., 1973; MS in Psychology, U. Utah, 1977, JD, 1980. Bar: Utah. Ptnr. Jones, Waldo, Holbrook & McDonough, Salt Lake City, 1979-89; soliciter gen. Utah Atty. Gen.'s Office, Salt Lake City, 1989-93; atty. gen. State of Utah, 1993—; adj. prof. law U. Utah Law Sch.; bar commr. Utah State Bar, 1991; master of bench Utah Inns Ct. VII; mem. Utah Commn. on Justice in 21st Century; bd. dirs. Jones, Waldo, Holbrook & McDonough; bd. trustees Coll. Law U. Utah (pres.). Fin. devel. chair YWCA; chair Ctrl. Bus. Improvement Dist.; mem. Salt Lake City Olympic Bid Com. 1988 Games. Named Woman Lawyer Yr. Utah, 1987. Mem. Am. Arbitration Assn. (nat. panel arbitrators), Women Lawyers Utah (co-founder, mem. exec. com.). Office: Office of Attorney General 236 State Capitol Building Salt Lake City UT 84114-1202*

GRAHAM, JOHN MATHEWSON, pediatrician, medical geneticist; b. Wilmington, Del., Mar. 8, 1947; s. John M. Sr. and Dorothy (Channell) G.; m. Elizabeth Spear, July 4, 1977; chldren: Zack, George; 1 child from previous marriage, John M. III. BA in Natural and Behavioral Scis., Johns Hopkins U., 1969, ScD in Pub. Health Adminstrn., 1981; MD, Med. U. S.C., 1975. Diplomate Am. Bd. Med. Genetics, Am. Bd. Pediatrics. Med. dir. genetics svcs. Pub. Health Svcs., Concord, N.H., 1981-88; asst. prof., assoc. prof. maternal and child health Dartmouth Med. Sch., Hanover, N.H., 1981-88, dir. clin. genetics and dysmorphology program, 1981-88; assoc. prof. pediatrics UCLA Sch. Medicine, 1988-90, prof., 1990—; mem. staff Cedars-Sinai Med. Ctr., L.A., 1988—, dir. clin. genetics and dysmorphology, 1988—, dir. craniofacial program, 1990—; dir. fetal dysmorphology and pathology program Cedars-Sinai Med. Ctr., 1991—, co-dir. CSMC med. genetics tng. program, 1991—. Contbr. some 40 chpts. to books, 200 articles to profl. jours. Recipient numerous awards and grants. Fellow Am. Coll. Med. Genetics (founding); mem. AMA, Am. Soc. Human Genetics, European Soc. Human Genetics, Am. Acad. Pediatrics, Soc. Pediatric Rsch., Am. Pediatric Soc., We. Soc. for Pediatric Rsch., European Soc. for Pediatric Rsch., Soc. for Behavioral Pediatrics, Behavioral Genetics Assn., Teratology Soc., West Coast Teratology Soc., Am. Cleft Palate-Craniofacial Assn., Soc. Craniofacial Genetics, Alpha Omega Alpha, Delta Omega. Office: Cedars-Sinai Med Ctr 444 S San Vicente Blvd Ste 1001 Los Angeles CA 90048-4175

GRAHAM, KIRSTEN R., computer science educator; b. Inglewood, Calif., July 20, 1946; d. Ray Selmer and Ella Louise (Carter) Newbury; m. Frank Sellers Graham, July 31, 1981. BS, U. Wis., Oshkosh, 1971; MS, U. Colo., 1980; postgrad., Army War Coll., 1987, Mont. State U., 1997—. Cert. Flight instr. Chief info. svc. Mont. State Dept. Labor and Industry, Helena, Mont.; dir., personal property and bus. lic. div. County of Fairfax, Va.; analyst officer U.S. Army Pentagon, Washington; battalion commdr. U.S. Army, Frankfurt, West Germany; assoc. prof. U.S. Army, West Point, N.Y.; tchr. computer tech. Helena Coll. Tech., U. Mont.; del. People-to-People Women Computer Sci. Profls. program., China. Del. to People's Republic of China Citizen's Amb. Program, 1993. LTC U.S. Army, 1964-88. Mem. Assn. for Computing Machinery, Am. Fedn. Tchrs.

GRAHAM, LOIS CHARLOTTE, retired educator; b. Denver, Mar. 20, 1917; d. James Washington Brewster and Martha Wilhemina (Raukohl) Plunkett; m. Milton Clinton Graham, June 30, 1940 (dec.); children: Charlotte, Milton, Charlene, James. Student, Okla. City U., 1935-36; AB, Ouachita Bapt. U., 1939; postgrad., U. Nev., Reno, 1953, 63, 68, Ark. State U., 1954, 59. Cert. tchr., Colo., Nev., Ark. Tchr. Fairmount Sch., Golden, Colo., 1939-40, Melbourne (Ark.) Sch., 1940-41, Blytheville (Ark.) Jr. H.S., 1944-45, Hawthorne (Nev.) Elem. Sch., 1952-81; substitute tchr. Mineral County Sch. Dist., Hawthorne, 1988-94; sr. resource cons. dept. geriatrics U. Nev.-Reno Med. Sch., 1988-90, del. to Rural Health Conf., Hawthorne, 1990; officer Mineral County Tchrs. Assn., 1955-65; ad hoc com. Nev. State Tchrs., 1965. Mem. Mineral County Emergency Planning Com., 1991—; asst. to pres. High Sch. PTA, Hawthorne, 1958, Elem. PTA, Hawthorne, 1961; pianist, choir dir., tchr. various chs., 1927—; active Older Am. Friends of Libr. Recipient Disting. Svc. award. Mem. AAUW (membership v.p. 1988-91, pres. 1991-92, 94-96), AARP (pres. 1995—), Ret. Pub. Employees of Nev. (membership v.p. 1994-96, v.p. 1994-95, pres. 1995—), Older Ams., Friends Libr., Delta Kappa Gamma (v.p. 1991-92, pres. 1995—). Republican. Baptist. Home: PO Box 1543 Hawthorne NV 89415-1543 *I was raised in a Christian home with Christian morals and ideals. I was very aware of children and their needs, because of this I became a teacher. I have always tried to be a good example both to my children and the ones I taught.*

GRAHAM, MARGARET KATHERINE, secondary school educator; b. Grass Valley, Calif., Dec. 21, 1941; d. Carroll Joseph and Mary Barbara (Clark) Coughlan; m. Denis David Graham, Aug. 31, 1968; 1 child, Kathleen Ann. BA, U. Nev., 1963. Cert. secondary tchr., Nev. Case aide Catholic Social Svcs., San Francisco, 1963-64; tchr. Sparks (Nev.) H.S., 1965-67; history tchr. Carson City (Nev.) H.S., 1968-71; tchr. 7th/8th grades St. Teresa's Catholic Sch., Carson City, 1983-87; sex edn. tchr. Washoe County Sch. Dist., Reno, Nev., 1988—; sex edn. adv. bd. Carson City Sch. Dist., 1984-85. Mem. NEA, Washoe County Tchr.'s Assn., PEO, Serra Club (treas. 1992). Democrat. Roman Catholic. Home: 3056 Bramble Dr Reno NV 89509-6901 Office: Washoe County Sch Dist 425 E 9th St Reno NV 89512-2800

GRAHAM, PAMELA SMITH, distributing company executive, artist; b. Winona, Miss., Jan. 18, 1944; d. Douglas LaRue and Dorothy Jean (Hefty) Smith; m. Robert William Graham, Mar. 6, 1965 (div.); children: Jennifer, Eric; m. Thomas Paul Harley, Dec. 4, 1976; stepchildren: Tom, Janice. Student U. Colo., 1962-65, U. Cin., 1974-76. Cert. notary pub., Colo. Profl. artist, craft tchr., art exhibitor Colo., N.J., Ohio, 1968—; property mgmt. and investor Cin., 1972-77; acct., word processor Borden Chem. Co. div. Borden, Inc., Cin., 1974-78; owner, pres. Hargram Enterprises, Cin., 1977-81; owner, pres. Graham & Harley Enterprises, Morrison, Colo., 1981—; owner Sagebrush Studio, 1985—; tchr.; cons. County committeewoman Bergen County, N.J., 1972, clk. of session, 1975-79, conv. chmn., 1981; campaign chmn. United Appeal, 1977; lifeline telephone counselor Suicide Hotline, 1985—; victim advisor Abusive Men Exploring New Directions, 1986-91. Recipient numerous awards for art exhibits including, bus. achievements, 1962—. Mem. NAFE, United Sales Leaders Assn., Nat. Museum of Women in Arts, Colo. Artists Assn., Evergreen Artists Assn. (bd. dirs., pres. 1990, 91), Colo. Calligraphers Guild, Gilpin County Arts Assn., Foothills Art Ctr., Alpha Gamma Chi, Kappa Kappa Gamma. Republican. Clubs: Mt. Vernon Country Club, Queen City Racquet. Office: Graham & Harley Enterprises and Sagebrush Studio 4303 S Taft St Morrison CO 80465-1425

GRAHAM, ROGER JOHN, photography and journalism educator; b. Phila., Feb. 16; s. William K. and Peggy E. (Owens) G.; divorced; children: John Roger, Robb Curt; m. Debbie Kenyon, Dec. 28, 1991. AA, Los Angeles Valley Coll., 1961; BA, Calif. State U., Fresno, 1962, MA, 1967; postgrad, UCLA, 1976. Cert. in elem., jr. high, high sch., cmty. coll., counseling and adminstrn. Tchr. Riverdale (Calif.) Sch., 1963, Raisin City (Calif.) Sch., 1964; tchr., counselor Calif. State Prison, Jamestown, 1966; tchr. trainer UCLA's Western Ctr., 1967; chmn. media arts dept. Los Angeles Valley Coll., Van Nuys, Calif., 1968—; vis. prof. Pepperdine U., Malibu, Calif., 1976, Calif. Luth. Coll., Thousand Oaks, 1973, Chapman U., Orange, Calif., 1996; del. Calif. Fedn. Tchrs. Conv., 1997. Author: Observations on the Mass Media, 1976, (jour) Jr. Coll. Jour., 1972; photo illustrator: The San Fernando Valley, 1980; contbr. articles to profl. jours.; display advertiser Turlock (Calif.) jour., 1962, Fresno Guide, 1963. Mem. Hayden's Com. for Schs., Santa Monica, Calif., 1984, YMCA, Pacific Palisades, Calif.; pres. Pacific Palisades Dem. Club, 1992; rep. to 41st assembly dist. Calif. Dem. Party State Ctrl. Com., 1993, sec. srs. caucus, 1993—. With USN, 1957. NEH scholar 1981; recipient Mayor's Outstanding Citizen award Los Angeles Mayor's Office, 1974, Extraordinary Service award UCLA, 1971; named one of Outstanding Young Men Am., 1971. Mem. C.C. Journalism Assn. (nat. pres. 1978—, Nat. Dedication Journalism award 1972-76), Journalism Assn. C.C. (pres. Calif. sect. 1972—), Calif. Srs. Caucus (state sec. 1993—), L.A. Prof.'s Club, Dem. Club Pacific Palisades (pres. 1992-93), Am. Legion (sgt. at arms 1986—, Palisades post 238 adminstrv. officer 1996—), Sons of the Desert, Sigma Delta Xi, Phi Delta Kappa, Pi Lambda Theta. Home: The Bluffs View Estates 6516 Riggs Pl Los Angeles CA 90045 Office: Los Angeles Valley Coll 5800 Fulton Ave Van Nuys CA 91401-4062

GRAHAM, STEVEN PIDDINGTON, entertainment production company executive; b. San Juan, P.R., May 26, 1962; s. Charles Paul and Gayle Ann (Piddington) G. BA in Motion Picture and Video, Brooks Inst. Photography, Santa Barbara, Calif., 1988. Freelance photographer, 1980—; prodn. asst. Handmade Films, L.A., 1989; operator, technician Lynn Greenberg Teleprompting, Newhall, Calif., 1989-91; pres. PC Prompting Sys., Sherman Oaks, Calif., 1992—. Author teleprompting software Scrollmaster, 1992; creator, inventor portable jib arm teleprompting equipment, 1992, wireless portable steadicam teleprompting equipment, 1996. Vol. L.A. Works, 1993. Mem. Nat. Assn. Broadcast Employees and Technicians (Local 53), Nat. Parks Assn., Sierra Club. Republican. Lutheran. Home: 4261 Dixie Canyon Ave Apt 4 Sherman Oaks CA 91423-3970

GRAHAM, SUSAN BRANDT, gynecologist, anthropologist; b. Oklahoma City, Oct. 26, 1946; d. Clinton H. and Lois (Casbeer) Brandt; m. G. Gordon Graham, Nov. 28, 1969 (div. Aug. 1994); 1 child, Brandt Gordon. BA, U. Okla., 1967; MA, U. Ariz., 1970, PhD, 1975; MD, U. Kans., Kansas City, 1985. Diplomate Am. Bd. Ob-Gyn.; lic. physician, N.Mex. Lab asst. in anthropology Stovall Mus., U. Okla., Norman, 1965-67; naturalist U.S. Nat. Park Svc., Grand Canyon, Ariz., summers 1968-70; asst. prof. anthropology U. Mo., Kansas City, 1976-81; resident in ob-gyn. U. N.Mex. Hosp., Albuquerque, 1985-89; gynecologist, obstetrician Women's Med. Specialists P.C., Albuquerque, 1989-93; gynecologist, owner Susan Brandt Graham, MD, PhD, PC, Albuquerque, 1994—; mem. gynecology peer rev. com. St. Joseph Healthcare System, Albuquerque, 1993—; mem. U.S. Med. Licensing Examination Test Writing Com., 1995—. Author articles. Woodrow Wilson Nat. fellow, 1967-68, U. Ariz. grad. scholar, 1969-70, U. Kans. med. scholar, 1985-89. Fellow Am. Coll. Ob-Gyn. (mem. com. on Indian affairs 1991-94), Am. Anthrop. Assn.; mem. Soc. for Med. Anthropology, N.Mex. Med. Soc. (mem. med.-legal panel 1990—), Greater Albuquerque Med. Assn., Mensa. Office: Ste 102 4702 Montgomery Blvd NE Albuquerque NM 87109

GRAHAM, TONI, writer; b. San Francisco, June 24, 1945; d. Joseph Foster and Maxine E. (Johnson) Avila; m. J. Richard Graham, Nov. 23, 1972 (div. 1987); 1 child, Salvatore Z. BA, New Coll. Calif., 1989; MA in English, San Francisco State U., 1992, MFA in Creative Writing, 1995. Lectr. dept. creative writing San Francisco State U., 1992; thesis advisor lectr. MA in Writing program U. San Francisco, 1993—; lectr. U. Calif., Santa Cruz, 1995—, Chabot Coll., 1996, Dominican Coll., 1996. Contbr. short fiction to mags., including Playgirl, Am. Fiction 88, Five Fingers Rev., Miss. Rev., Ascent, Clockwatch Rev., Miss. Mud, SFSU Rev., Worcester Rev., ZIPZAP mag., Green Mountain Rev., Chiron Rev. Harrold scholar, 1986; recipient Calif. Short Story Competition award, 1987, Herbert Wilner Meml. Short Story award, 1994; story Shadow Boxing cited in Pushcart Prize XIV-Best of the Small Presses, 1989. Mem. MLA, Nat. Coun. Tchrs. English, Assoc. Writing Programs, Hemingway Soc., Golden Key Honor Soc. Home: 345 Prospect Ave San Francisco CA 94110-5509

GRAJEWSKI, JULIAN, law librarian, educator; b. Porto Potenza Picena, Macerata, Italy, Feb. 10, 1946; came to U.S., 1960; s. Anthony and Santa (Grandinetti) G.; m. Agnes Murray Mutch, Sept. 28, 1970 (div. Dec. 1976); children: Keir Ewan, Naomi Isabel; m. Elisabet Appel, Dec. 31, 1986; 1 child, Janusz Antares. BA, SUNY, Plattsburgh, 1974; MA in English, Concordia U., Montreal, 1977; MLS, U. Ariz., 1991. Instr. Pima County C.C., Tucson, 1983-92; law libr. Dept. of Corrections, Winslow, Ariz., 1992—. Author: Liberation, 1970; contbr. short story to Free Fire Zone: Short Stories by Vietnam Veterans, 1973; contbr. articles to Pig Iron Press, East Campus Caldera, Magill's Critical Survey of Short Fiction. Organizer Dem. Party, various locations, 1975—. With U.S. Army, 1966-68, Vietnam. Mem. MLA. Democrat. Roman Catholic.

GRAMES, GEORGE MILLER, human services administrator, physician; b. Phila., Apr. 28, 1934; s. Constantine and Margaret Louise (Whitcomb) G.; m. Betty Ann Rhodes, June 16, 1957; children: Cheryl Lynn, Rae Ann, Barry Scott. BA, Columbia Union Coll., 1956; MD, Loma Linda U., 1960. Diplomate Am. Bd. Internal Medicine, Am. Bd. Nephrology, Am. Bd. Nuclear Medicine. Intern Walter Reed Gen. Hosp., 1960-61, resident internal medicine, 1961-64; asst. prof. radiology Loma Linda (Calif.) U. Med. Ctr., 1971-76, from assoc. prof. to prof. medicine, 1976-91; adminstr. Redlands (Calif.) Hemodialysis Ctr., 1993—; dir. residency tng. program for internal medicine Loma Linda U. Med. Ctr., 1986-90; cons. in field. Contbr. articles to profl. jours. Pres. Epsilon chpt. Alpha Omega Alpha, 1975. Maj. U.S. Army, 1960-67. Fellow ACP; mem. Am. Soc. Nephrology, Am. Soc. Nuclear Medicine, Inland Soc. Nephrology, Internat. Soc. Internal Medicine, Alpha Omega Alpha. Office: Inland Nephrology 1210 Indiana Ct Redlands CA 92374-2896

GRAMMATER, RUDOLF DIMITRI, retired construction executive; b. Detroit, Nov. 29, 1910; s. D.M. and Amelia (Busse) G.; m. Fredricka W. Cook, Aug. 18, 1943, 1 child, Douglas. Student, Pace Coll., 1928-32; LLB, Lincoln U., 1937. Bar: Calif. 1938; CPA, Calif. With Bechtel Corp., San Francisco, 1941-73, treas., v.p., 1955-62, v.p., 1962-71, dir., 1960-73, cons., 1973, v.p., dir. subsidiaries, 1955-71. Mem. ABA, AICPA, Calif. Soc. CPAs,

Calif. Bar Assn., Menlo Country Club. Home: The Peninsula Regent # 819 One Baldwin Ave San Mateo CA 94401-3852

GRAMMER, MAURINE PARKER, educator, writer, appraiser; b. Kansas City, Mo., Dec. 7, 1903; d. John Henry and Julia (West) Parker; m. David Allen Grammer, Nov. 27, 1925 (dec. Feb. 1959); 1 child, David Allen Jr. BS in Art, U. N.Mex., MA in Anthropology, 1957; student, Wyo U., Stephens Coll. Tchr. Albuquerque Pub. Schs., 1927-68; appraiser estates, art and antiques, especially Indian art, 1943—. Author: The Bear that Turned White, 1991, The Navajo Brothers and the Stolen Herd, 1992; author unit of study on Native Ams. for Columbia Tchrs. Coll.; contbr. articles to profl. jours.; loom patentee. Precinct chair Republican Party, Albuquerque, 1960-79. Inducted into Sr. Found. Hall of Fame, Albuquerque, 1996; named Tchr. of Yr., Kirtland AFB, 1968. Mem. NEA, N.Mex. Educators Fed. Credit Union, Pi Lambda Theta, Delta Kappa Gamma. Home: 1508 Ridgecrest Dr SE Albuquerque NM 87108

GRAMS, THEODORE CARL WILLIAM, librarian, educator; b. Portland, Oreg., Sept. 29, 1918; s. Theodore Albert and Emma Elise (Boehne) G. B.A., U. Wash., 1947; postgrad. Harvard Law Sch., 1947-48; M.S. in L.S., U. So. Calif., 1951. Land title asst. U.S. Bonneville Power Adminstrn., Portland, 1939-45, accountant, 1948-50, librarian, 1951-52; head cataloger, lectr. Portland State U. Library, 1952-59, dir. processing services, 1960-83, prof., 1969-87, prof. emeritus, 1988—. Pres. Portland Area Spl. Librns., 1954-55; panelist on impact new tech. on info. scis. Am. Soc. Info. Sci., 1974, panelist on Libr. Congress svcs., 1976. Author: Allocation of Joint Costs of Multiple-Purpose Projects, 1952, Textbook Classification, 1968; editor: Procs. 4th Am. Soc. Info. Scis. Midyear Meeting, 1975, Special Collections in the Libraries of the Pacific Northwest, 1979, Disaster Preparedness and Recovery, 1983, Technical Services: The Decade Ahead (in Beyond 1984: The Future of Technical Services), 1983. Panelist on community action N.W. Luth. Welfare Assn. Conf., 1969; mem. adv. council Area Agy. on Aging, 1974-75; commr. City-County Commn. Aging, Portland-Multnomah County, 1975-80. Bd. dirs. Hub-Community Action Program, Portland, 1967-70, Project ABLE, 1972-74. HEW Inst. fellow, 1968-69. Mem. ALA, AAUP, Beta Phi Mu. Lutheran. Home: 6653 E Carondelet Dr Tucson AZ 85710-2150

GRAN, ROBERT, engineering company executive; b. 1941. PhD, Calif. Inst. Tech., 1970. Sec. head TRW Sys., Redondo Beach, Calif., 1970-73; sr. rsch. engr., divsn. mgr. Flow Rsch. Inc., L.A., 1973-76; chief sci. Dynamics Tech., Inc., Torrance, Calif., 1976—. Office: Dynamics Tech Inc 21311 Hawthorne Blvd Torrance CA 90503-5602

GRANDY, JAY FRANKLIN, fruit processing executive; b. Murray, Ky., July 21, 1939; s. Rodney Leon and Marion Elizabeth (Birchall) G.; m. Jane Ann Howard, June 26, 1965; children—Joanna, Sharon. B.S. in Physics, Auburn U., 1961; M.B.A., Siena Coll., 1969. With Gen. Electric, 1961-77; mktg. mgr. FMC, Cedar Rapids, Iowa, 1977-81, gen. mgr., Fresno, Calif., 1981-82; pres. Snokist Growers, Yakima, Wash., 1984-95; gen. mgr. Seneca Foods Corp., Prosser, Wash., 1996—. Served to 1st lt. U.S. Army, 1962-64. Home: 4203 Fellows Dr Yakima WA 98908-2266

GRANGER, ARTHUR EARLE, geologist; b. Salt Lake City, Mar. 15, 1911; s. Louis Edwin and Sarah (Dibble) G.; m. Leona Pearce, June 23, 1937; children: Penelope, Arthur, Pamela, Sallee, Christine. BA, U. Utah, 1934; MS, U. Wash., 1937; PhD, Am. Internat. U., Pasadena, Calif., 1960. Registered geologist, Calif. Engr. U.S. Forest Svc., Salt Lake City, 1934-36; teaching asst. U. Wash., Seattle, 1936-38; geologist U.S. Geol. Survey, Washington, 1938-54; chief geol. engr. U.S. Steel Corp., San Francisco, 1954-55; chief geologist U.S. AEC, Grand Junction, Colo., 1955-63; owner Arthur E. Granger Co., Reno, Nev., 1964—. Fellow Soc. Econ. Geologists; mem. Am. Assn. Petroleum Geologists. Home and Office: 3300 Clearacre Ln Reno NV 89512-1408

GRANGER, JEFF ROLAND, military personnel specialist; b. Hornell, N.Y., Mar. 19, 1963; s. Roland Harlen and Marcia Gale (Behrens) G. AAS, SUNY, Alfred, 1983; BS, U. Ga., 1986; cert. of qualification in edn., Daemen Coll., 1988; MPA, Alfred U., 1994. Cert. social studies tchr., N.Y. Asst. mgr. Pizza Pronto, Athens, Ga., 1984-86; mgmt. trainee Domino's Pizza, Rochester, N.Y., 1986-87; asst. mgr. Domino's Pizza, Buffalo, 1989; lifeguard City of Cortland (N.Y.) Youth Bur., 1988; recreation supr. George Jr. Republic, Freeville, N.Y., 1988; agrl. tchr. Wellsville (N.Y.) H.S., 1989; residence hall dir. Alfred State Coll., 1987-94; lifeguard lt. City of Rochester, N.Y., 1994; specialist U.S. Army, Fort Carson, Colo., 1995—; mem. bd. alcohol Alfred State Coll., 1991-93; cons. econ. devel. Wellsville C. of C., 1992-93; cons. on consolidation Angelica (N.Y.) Ctrl. Sch., 1994-95. Developer sch. game Macht Politik, 1992; contbr. articles to profl. publs. Named Hon. Mem. Wellsville Future Farmers Am., 1989. Mem. Audubon Soc., Wilson Ctr. Home: PO Box 13246 Fort Carson CO 80913 Office: HHD 2-10th Spl Forces Group Bldg 7402 Attn:S1 Fort Carson CO 80913

GRANLUND, THOMAS ARTHUR, engineering executive, consultant; b. Spokane, Wash., Mar. 1, 1951; s. William Arthur and Louise (Urie) G.; m. Jean MacRae Melvin, May 25, 1974 (div. Feb. 1991). BS, Wash. State U., 1973, BA, 1973; MBA, Gonzaga U., 1982. Engring. adminstr. Lockheed Aeronautical Systems Co., Burbank, Calif., 1978-91; mgmt. cons., 1991—. Co-author: (screenplay) Identities, 1988, Flash, 1989. 1st lt. USAF, 1973-78. Mem. Wash. State U. Alumni Assn. Home: 20924 Ben Ct Santa Clarita CA 91350-1418

GRANOVETTER, MARK, sociology educator; b. Jersey City, Oct. 20, 1943; s. Sidney and Violet (Greenblatt) G.; m. Ellen Susan Greenebaum, June 14, 1970; 1 child, Sara. AB, Princeton (N.J.) U., 1965; MA, Harvard U., 1967, PhD, 1970. Asst. prof. Johns Hopkins U., Balt., 1970-73; from asst. to assoc. prof. Harvard U., Cambridge, Mass., 1973-77; from assoc. prof. to prof. SUNY, Stony Brook, 1977-92; prof. Northwestern U., Evanston, Ill., 1992-95, Stanford U., 1995—. Author: Getting A Job, 1974; series editor Cambridge U. Press, 1986—; contbr. articles to profl. jours. Ctr. for Advanced Study fellow, 1977, J.S. Guggenheim Found. fellow, 1981. Office: Stanford U Dept Sociology Stanford CA 94305

GRANT, JOHN BARNARD, writer; b. Hartford, Conn., Mar. 23, 1940; s. Ellsworth S. and Marion (Hepburn) G.; m. Ann Halterman, May 28, 1965; children: Jason, Schuyler. BA, U. Calif., Berkeley, 1965. Phys. edn. and outdoor skills tchr. Green Valley Sch., Orange City, Fla., 1966-68; math. and English tchr. Deerborne Sch., Coral Gables, Fla., 1969-70; charter sailboat capt. Bradenton Beach, Fla., 1968-69; dir. devel. Calif. Outward Bound, Palo Alto, 1970-71; writer, editor, and pub. Los Gatos and Sebastopol, Calif., 1971—. Author: The Geocentric Experience, 1972, (with Katharine Houghton) Two Beastly Tales, 1975, Skateboarding, 1976, (with Jim Gault) The World of Women's Gymnastics, 1976, Ins and Outs of Soccer, 1983, (with Laeh Maggie Garfield) Companions in Spirit, 1985, The Unamericans in Paris, 1988, (play) Joan, 1989; contbr. numerous stories and poems to mags. With USMC, 1960-64. Mem. Musicians Union (local 292).

GRANT, JOHN CARRINGTON, advertising executive; b. St. Louis, Feb. 2, 1937; s. George Nelson Whitfield and Mary Frances (Tissier) G.; m. Judith Ann Thompson, Oct. 20, 1962; children: Christopher, Susan. Student Westminister Coll., 1960; BS, Washington U., St. Louis, 1969. Account mgr. Darcy, McManus & Masius, St. Louis, N.Y.C. and San Francisco, 1960-68; with Gardner Advt., St. Louis, 1963-66, McCann-Erickson, Seattle, 1974-75; stockbroker Dean Witter, San Francisco, 1968-74; with Tracy-Locke/BBDO, 1975-80; pres. Grant Pollack Advt., Denver, 1980-85; v.p. Brock & Assocs., Denver, 1985-86; dir. Univ. rels. U. Denver, 1987-89; pres. Grant & Assocs., 1989—; pres. CEO The Advertising Consortium, 1989—; mem. faculty Met. State Coll., Denver, 1981-82. Mem. Denver Advt. Fedn. Clubs: Denver Athletic, Oxford.

GRANT, LEWIS O., agricultural products executive, meteorology educator; b. Washington, Pa., Mar. 29, 1923; s. Lewis F. and Rita J. (Jacqmain) G.; m. Patricia Jean Lovelock, July 23, 1949; children: Ann, Nancy, Brenda, Andrew, Laura. BS, U. Tulsa, Okla., 1947; MS, Calif. Inst. Tech., Pasadena, 1948. Meteorological cons. Water Resources Devel. Corp., Pasadena, Calif., 1948-54, Denver, 1948-54; rschr. and rsch. dir. Am. Inst. Aerological Rsch., Denver, 1954-59; asst. prof., assoc. prof. to prof. atmospheric sci. dept. Colo. State U., Ft. Collins, 1959-93, emeritus prof., 1993—; pres. Piedmont Farms, Inc., Wellington, Colo., 1975—; cons. Colo. Legis., Denver, 1971-73. Contb. to profl. jours. Scout master, com. chmn. Boy Scouts of Am.; pres. Partner Communities, Ft. Collins, Colo., 1988; elder Presbyn. Ch., 1980; 1st lt. U.S. Field Artillery and USAF, 1943-46. Recipient Vincent J. Schaefer award Weather Modification Assn., 1991. Fellow Am. Meterological Assn.; mem. Nat. Sci. Found. (atmospheric sci. sect. adv. com. 1970), Nat. A cad. Sci. (sect. chmn. 1975-76), Organic Farming Rsch. Found. (bd. mem. 1995). Republican. Presbyterian. Office: Piedmont Farms Inc 1020 W County Road 72 Wellington CO 80549-1912 also: Colo State U Dept Atmospheric Sci Fort Collins CO 80523

GRANT, NEWELL M., real estate investment manager; b. Denver, Nov. 2, 1941; s. Edwin Hendrie and Mary Belle (McIntyre) G.; m. Judith G. Wilson, June 19, 1971; children: Margaret, James, Newell, Caroline. BA, Dartmouth Coll., 1964; postgrad, U. Pa., 1967-68. Assoc. Kidder Peabody Realty, N.Y.C., 1969-74; ptnr. Borden, Danielson & Grant, Denver, 1975; cons. N.M. Grant & Co., Denver, 1976-78; ptnr. Grant Mgmt. Co., Denver, 1978—; gen. ptnr. Grant Properties, Denver, 1977-93; chmn. bd. Colo. Nat. Bank Southwest, Littleton, Colo., 1983-89, pres. bd. trustees, 1990-91, pres. Denver Botanical Garden Endowment Inc., 1991—. Trustee vol. for outdoor Colo., 1993—. Pres. bd. trustees Denver Bot. Gardens, 1976—; active Gov.'s Task Force for Efficiency and Economy in Colo. State Govt., Denver, 1976. Served to 1st lt. U.S. Army, 1965-66. Mem. Urban Land Inst. (assoc.). Democrat. Episcopalian. Clubs: Denver; Garden of the Gods (Colo. Springs). Home: 1325 Cherryville Rd Littleton CO 80121-1221

GRANT, RICHARD EARL, medical and legal consultant; b. Spokane, Wash., Aug. 27, 1935; s. Conrad Morrison and Sylva Celeste (Sims) G.; m. Susan Kimberly Hawkins, Mar. 17, 1979; children: Paaqua A., Camber Do'otsie O. BSc cum laude, U. Wash., 1961; MEd, Whitworth Coll., 1974; PhD, Wash. State U., 1980. Cert. ins. rehab. specialist; cert. case mgr. Supr. nursing Providence Hosp., Seattle, 1970-72; asst. prof. nursing Wash. State U., Spokane, 1972-78; dir. nursing Winslow (Ariz.) Meml. Hosp., 1978-79; adminstr. psychiat. nursing Ariz. State Hosp., Phoenix, 1979-80; asst. prof. Ariz. State U., Tempe, 1980-83; assoc. prof. Linfield Coll., Portland, Oreg., 1983-86, Intercollegiate Ctr. for Nursing Edn., Spokane, 1986-88; sr. med. care coord. Fortis Corp., Spokane, 1988-92; med. svcs. cons. CorVel Corp., Spokane, 1992-94; owner Richard Grant & Assoc., Spokane, 1995—; cons. Ariz. State Hosp., 1980-82, Pres.'s Commn., Washington, 1981-83, U. No. Colo., Greely, 1985-86; area med. svcs. cons., 1992—. Author: The God-Man-God Book, 1976, Publications of the Membership (Conaa), 1983, 3d rev. edit., 1985, 4th rev. edit., 1988, Predetermined Careplan Handbook-Nursing, 1988, Duhikya: The Hopi Healer, 1996; contbr. articles to profl. jours. Judge Student Space Shuttle Project, Portland, 1983, N.W. Sci. Expo, Portland, 1983. With U.S. Army, 1953-56. Grantee NIMH, U. Wash., 1961; named one of top Hopi Scholars, Hopi Tribe, Second Mesa, Ariz., 1981. Mem. AAAS, Nat. League for Nursing, Wash. League for Nursing (v.p. 1988-90), Coun. on Nursing and Anthropology (editor 1982-90), N.Y. Acad. Scis., Case Mgmt. Soc. Am., Sigma Theta Tau.

GRANT, THOMAS ARTHUR, television journalist; b. Toasket, Wash., Sept. 19, 1953; s. Joseph Charles and Lorraine (Wiswell) G.; m. Mary Ann Connery, Sept. 1, 1941; children: Sean Connery, Patrick Connery, Thomas Connery. BA in English, Wash. State U., 1975; MS in Journalism, Columbia U., 1986. Vol. VISTA, Mpls., 1978-79; reporter Seaside (Oreg.) Signal, 1979-80; editor News-Guard, Lincoln City, Oreg., 1980-82, Silverton (Oreg.) Appeal-Tribune, 1982-85; reporter KCAU TV, Sioux City, Iowa, 1986-87; reporter/anchor WCAX TV, Burlington, Vt., 1987-91; reporter KREM TV, Spokane, Wash., 1991—. Recipient Feature Reporting prize Nat. Newspaper Assn., 1984, Oscars In Agrl., U. Ill., 1988, Pub. Svc. award Soc. Profl. Journalists, 1992, George Polk award Long Island U., N.Y.C., 1995. Office: KREM-TV 4103 S Regal St Spokane WA 99223-7737

GRANT, WILLIAM WEST, III, banker; b. N.Y.C., May 9, 1932; s. William West and Katherine O'Connor (Neelands) G.; m. Rhondda Lowery, Dec. 3, 1955. BA, Yale U., 1954; postgrad., NYU Grad. Sch. Bus., 1958, Columbia U. Grad. Sch. Bus., 1968, Harvard U. Grad. Sch. Bus., 1971. With Bankers Trust Co., N.Y.C., 1954-58; br. credit adminstr. Bankers Trust Co., 1957-58; with Colo. Nat. Bank, Denver, 1958—; pres. Colo. Nat. Bank, 1975—, chmn. bd., 1986-93; chmn. bd. Colo. Capital Advisors, 1989-94; bd. dirs. Plains PetroleumCo., Channel 6 Pub. TV, Barrett Resources Corp. Trustee Denver Mus. Natural History, Gates Found. Denver, Midwest Rsch. Inst., Kansas City; bd. dirs. Sta. KRMA-TV, Inst. Internat. Edn., Mountain State Employers Coun., World Trade Ctr. Mem. Colo. Bankers Assn., Metro. Denver C. of C. (dir. Internat. Gateway Com.). Episcopalian. Clubs: Denver Country, Denver. Home: 545 Race St Denver CO 80206 Office: KRMA-TV 1089 Bannock St Denver CO 80204-4066

GRAPPE, HAROLD HUGO, civil engineer; b. Portland, Oreg., Feb. 21, 1970; s. Donald Eugene and Anna Elizabeth (Rexroth) G. BSCE, Portland State U., 1994. Registered engr.-in-tng., Oreg. Engring. technician Bonneville Power Adminstrn., Portland, 1990-91, trainee in civil engring., 1991-94, civil engr., 1994—. Team guide Dept. Energy Regional Sci. Bowl, Portland State U., 1995, U. Portland, 1996, 97. Recipient Appreciation cert. for leadership in support of the Rose Festival and a spirit of teamwork Portland Rose Festival Assn., 1996. Mem. ASCE. Home: 8510 SW 42nd Ave Portland OR 97219-3522 Office: Bonneville Power Adminstrn 905 NE 11th Ave Portland OR 97232

GRASS, GEORGE MITCHELL, IV, pharmaceutical executive; b. Bryn Mawr, Pa., Dec. 31, 1957; s. George Mitchell III and Irma Lucy (Schaffer) G. PharmD, U. Nebr., Omaha, 1980; PhD, U. Wis., 1985. Lic. pharmacist. Staff rschr. Syntex Rsch., Palo Alto, Calif., 1985-91; pres. Precision Instrument Design, Tahoe City, Calif., 1987-97; pres., CEO NaviCyte Inc., Reno, 1996—; cons. Costar Corp., Cambridge, Mass., 1990-96, various pharm. cos., 1991—; co-founder Raptor Graphics, Snohomish, Wash. Contbr. numerous articles to profl. jours. Recipient Ebert prize Jour. Pharm. Sci., 1989. Mem. AAAS, Am. Assn. Pharm. Scientists, Sigma Xi.

GRASSA, ROSEMARIE LUCIA, massage therapist; b. Boston, Nov. 9, 1950; d. Peter Cesar and Laura Marie (O'Neill) G.; m. Theodore Thomas, Apr. 30, 1968 (div. June 1970); children: James W., Christina M., Carol L., Richard A., Peter C.; m. William McCormic, June 6, 1971 (div. 1980). Student, Pondville Sch. Nursing, Mass., 1980-81, Sch. Shiatsu and Massage, Calif., 1990-91. Onwer, operator Treetop Nursery, Foxboro, Mass., 1979-80, Rosemarie's Sweet Things, Foxboro, 1980-83, Rosemarie's Nursing Svcs., Forestville, Calif., 1985-89, Guerneville (Calif.) Washboard, 1987-90, Rosemarie's Therapeutic Massage Ctr., Guerneville, 1990—, River Run Weekender, Guerneville, 1996—; tchr. Sch. Shiatsu and Massage, Middletown, Calif., 1990-92. Bd. dirs. Met. Cmty. Ch., Guerneville, 1984; bd. dirs., social dir. Met. Cmty. Ch., Santa Rosa, 1992-94; pres. bd. dirs. Sonoma County Lesbian and Gay Pride, Santa Rosa, 1992-95; elected town rep. N. Attleboro, Mass., 1977-78. Named Vol. of Yr. Met. Cmty. Ch. of Redwoods, Guerneville, 1992, Woman of Yr. Raudy Roland, Santa Rosa, 1995. Office: Rosemarie's Therapeutic Massage 16370 1st St PO Box 1195 Guerneville CA 95446

GRASSO, MARY ANN, theater association executive; b. Rome, N.Y., Nov. 3, 1952; d. Vincent and Rose Mary (Pupa) Grasso. BA in Art History, U. Calif., Riverside, 1973; MLS, U. Oreg., 1974. Dir. Warner Rsch. Collection, Burbank, Calif., 1975-84; mgr. CBS TV/Docudrama, Hollywood, Calif., 1984-88; v.p. Nat. Assn. Theatre Owners, North Hollywood, Calif., 1988—; instr. theatre arts UCLA, 1980-85, Am. Film Inst., L.A., 1985-88. Screen credits: The Scarlet O'Hara Wars, This Year's Blonde, The Silent Lovers, A Bunnies Tale, Embassy. Mem. Nat. Assn. Theatre Owners (exec. dir.), Bus. and Profl. Women's Assn. (Woman of Achievement award 1983), Retinitis Pigmentosa Internat. (The Vision award 1996), Acad. Motion Picture Arts and Scis., Found. of the Motion Picture Pioneers, Earth Comm., Phi Beta Kappa. Democrat. Office: Nat Assn Theatre Owners 4605 Lankershim Blvd # 340 North Hollywood CA 91602-1818

GRASSO, MONICA MARIE, home health nurse; b. Albany, N.Y., July 30, 1964; d. Ralph Joseph and Joanna Anna (Haponski) G. BSN, U. No. Colo., Greeley, 1987. RN, Colo. Staff nurse oncology St. Joseph Hosp., Denver, 1987-90; staff nurse ob-gyn. Univ. Hosp., Denver, 1990-92; home health nurse Presbyn. St. Luke Hosp., Denver, 1992, Denver Vis. Nurses Assn., 1992—. Merit scholar U. No. Colo., 1987.

GRAUBART, JEFFREY LOWELL, entertainment lawyer; b. Chgo., Aug. 18, 1940; s. John H. and Florence R. G.; m. Mary Linda Carey, June 24, 1973; children: Joshua Gordon, Noah Carey. BS in Fin., U. Ill., 1962; JD, Northwestern U., Chgo., 1965. Bar: Ill. 1965, Calif. 1968, N.Y. 1980. Assoc. Curtis Friedman & Marks, Chgo., 1965-67, Capitol Records, Inc., Los Angeles, 1968-70; prin. Hadfield, Jorgensen, Graubart & Becker, San Francisco, 1970-81; counsel Frankfurt, Garbus, Klein & Selz, P.C., N.Y., 1981-85; prin. Strote, Graubart & Ashley, P.C., Beverly Hills, Calif. and N.Y., 1986-87; counsel Cohen & Luckenbacher, L.A., 1988-90, Engel & Engel, L.A., 1991-92; sec. Paramount Growers, Inc., Delano, Calif., 1968-70; v.p., dir. London Internat. Artists, Ltd., Los Angeles, 1969-70, Jazz Images, Inc., N.Y.C., 1983-86; adj. prof. NYU, 1982-85; lectr. Columbia U. Sch. Law, N.Y.C., 1982-85, UCLA, 1988—, U. So. Calif., 1988—. Contbr. articles to profl. jours. and mags. Counsel San Francisco Jazz Found., 1980-81. Recipient Deems Taylor award ASCAP, 1981. Mem. NARAS (San Francisco chtp. legal counsel 1973-93, gov. 1973-85, gov. and legal counsel N.Y. chpt. 1982-85, gov. L.A. chpt. 1988-92), Calif. Copyright Conf. (dir. 1995—), Internat. Fedn. Festival Orgns. (dir. 1994—), Inter-Pacific Bar Assn., Beverly Hills Bar Assn. (chair internat. law sect. 1995—), Internat. Radio and TV Soc., Country Music Assn., Assn. of the Bar of the City of N.Y., Soc. Preservation of Film Music (trustee 1989—), v.p. 1991-94). Lodges: B'nai Brith (N.Y. and Los Angeles); Golden Gate (San Francisco) (v.p. 1974-75), Entertainment Industry Unit L.A. (founder, trustee 1988—). Office: 2029 Century Park E Ste 2700 Los Angeles CA 90067-3013*

GRAVES, DAVID WILLIAM, winery executive; b. Oakland, Calif., Oct. 26, 1952; s. James Washington and Barbara Jean (Wagner) G.; m. Elizabeth Peterson McKinne, July 14, 1990. BS, U. Calif., Santa Cruz, 1975. Cellar worker Chappellet Vineyards, Rutherford, Calif., 1978, Joseph Phelps Vineyards, St. Helena, Calif., 1979, Domaine Chandon, Yountville, Calif., 1980, Mt. Eden Vineyards, Cupertino, Calif., 1981; co-founder Saintsbury, Napa, Calif., 1981—; pres., treas. Carneros Quality Alliance, Napa, 1988—; pres. Pinot Noir: Am., Napa, 1989-90. Mem. Am. Soc. Enology and Viticulture (profl. mem.), U. Calif. Santa Cruz Alumni Assn. (alumni councillor 1987-94), U. Calif. Santa Cruz Found. (bd. dirs. 1994—). Democrat. Office: Saintsbury 1500 Los Carneros Ave Napa CA 94559-9742

GRAVES, EARL WILLIAM, JR., journalist; b. Kodiak, Alaska, June 30, 1950; s. Earl William Graves, Sr. and Lola (Olson) Raab; m. Karin Ann Steichen, July 30, 1972; children: Emma, Mark, Max. BA in English with honors, U. Puget Sound, 1972; MA in English, Western Wash. State U., 1976. Tchr. English Naselle (Wash.) High Sch., 1972-74, Clatskanie (Oreg.) High Sch., 1975-77; police reporter Coeur d'Alene (Idaho) Press, 1978-79, city editor, 1980-82, mng. editor, 1983-84; sr. reporter Bulletin, Bend, Oreg., 1984-86; edn. reporter News and Observer, Raleigh, N.C., 1986-87; state edn. reporter News and Observer/Raleigh Times, 1987-89; edn. reporter The Oregonian, Portland, 1990—. Author: Poisoned Apple, 1995. Recipient Outstanding Svc. award N.C. chpt. Phi Delta Kappa, 1988, Third Prize So. Journalism Feature Reporting award Inst. for So. Studies, 1989, N.C. Sch. Bell award N.C. Assn. Educators, 1989, Benjamin Fine award Nat. Assn. Secondary Sch. Prins., 1989, First Pl. Gen. News Reporting award N.C. Press Assn., 1990, First Pl. Edn. Reporting award Pacific Northwest Excellence in Journalism, Soc. Profl. Journalists, 1991, 92, Media award Assn. Retarded Children Oreg., 1992, Seconad Pl. Spot News Reporting award Best of West, 1992, Second Pl. Best Writing award Oreg. Newspaper Pubs. Assn., 1993, Excellence in Edn. award Oreg. Assn. Supervision and Cirriculum Devel., 1993. Mem. Edn. Writers Assn. (sec., bd. dirs. 1990—, Spl. Citation Nat. Awards for Edn. Reporting 1987, 91, Second Pl. Newspaper Series award 1989, Second Pl. Nat. Awards Edn. Reporting 1989). Democrat. Office: Oregonian 1320 SW Broadway Portland OR 97201-3411

GRAVES, KAREN LEE, high school counselor; b. Twin Falls, Idaho, Dec. 9, 1948; d. Isaac Mason and Agnes Popplewell; m. Frederick Ray Graves, Apr. 2, 1987. BA, Idaho State U., 1971; MEd, Coll. of Idaho, 1978. Cert. tchr. secondary edn., english 7-12, vocat. home econs. 7-12, pupil pers. svcs. K-12, Idaho. Tchr. Filer (Idaho) Sch. Dist., 1971-74, 76-80, Twin Falls (Idaho) Sch. Dist., 1974-76; counselor Mountain Home (Idaho) Sch. Dist., 1980—, dept. chairperson, dir. Mem. probation and parole screening com. Mountain Home; sponsor mem. Rocky Mountain Elk Found.; support person Idaho Donor Network. Mem. NEA, ACA, ASCD, Am. Sch. Counseling Assn., Idaho Counseling Assn., Idaho Sch. Counseling Assn., Idaho Edn. Assn., Idaho Affiliation Supervision and Curriculum Devel. Home: 1105 Maple Dr Mountain Home ID 83647 Office: Mountain Home High School 300 S 11th E Mountain Home ID 83647-3235

GRAVES, RICHARD TRACY, stockbroker, professional golfer; b. Greenwich, Conn., Oct. 14, 1945; s. William Tracy and Ruth Ann (Larson) G. m. Moonie Woo, April 26, 1972; children: Tim, Tracy. BSA, U Fla., Gainesville, 1968. Instr. PGA Nat. Acad. of Golf, 1977-84; stockbroker Painewebber, Vail, Colo., 1991—; CEO, author, Proguide Press, Vail., lect., Women & Investing, Painewebber, Vail, 1991—. Author: (Book) Golf Happens, 1996, (booklet) Yardage Book, 1973, inventor Golf Cart Signage Device, Cartplates, 1987. Capt., U.S. Army, South Korea, 1968-70. Recipient Army Commendation Medal, U.S. Army, Seoul, 1969, PGA Merchandiser of the Year, South Fla. PGA, 1986, Clem Price Trophy, Fla. St. Golf Assn., 1959, 8th U.S. Army Golf Champion, Seoul, Korea, 1969. Republican. Methodist. Home: PO Box 849 Vail CO 81658 Office: Painewebber 108 S Frontage Rd #310 Vail CO 81657

GRAVES, THOMAS DAYLE, psychology educator; b. Concordia, Kans., July 21, 1936; s. Byron W. and Hazel Agnes (McGowan) G.; m. Patricia Louise McGintie, Apr. 22, 1961; children: Kelly, Kerry, Karleen. BA, Adams State Coll., 1965, MA, 1966; EdD, U. No. Colo., 1974. Lic. profl. counselor, Colo. Pers. adminstr. Martin-Marietta Corp., Denver, 1958-64; instr. Mesa State Coll., Grand Junction, Colo., 1966-74, prof. psychology, 1975—; cons. Dixson's Inc., Grand Junction, 1976-77, Occidental Oil Shale, Grand Junction, 1976-77, Job Corps, Colbran, Colo., 1978-79, Union Oil Co.,Grand Junction, 1982-85, U.S. Sack Corp., Grand Junction, 1995. Author: Practicum Manual for Undergraduate Students, 1988, Internship Manual for Undergraduate Students, 1989. With U.S. Army, 1956-58. Mem. APA, Am. Counseling Assn., Am. Mental Health Counseling Assn., Rocky Mountain Psychol. Assn. Democrat. Roman Catholic. Home: 2719 8th Ct Grand Junction CO 81506-8203 Office: Mesa State Coll Box 2647 Grand Junction CO 81502

GRAW, LEROY HARRY, purchasing-contract management company executive; b. Dupree, S.Dak., Jan. 10, 1942; s. Harry Fred and Luella (Eichmann) G.; m. Kyong Hee Yuk, Sept. 25, 1969 (div. Feb. 1979); 1 child, Natasha; m. Anat Harari, July 3, 1981; children: Byron, Karen. BS, U.S. Mil. Acad., 1964; M Commerce, U. Richmond, 1974; EdD, U. So. Calif., 1980. Govt. contracting officer worldwide, 1971-88; mgr. govt. contracts Fluor Corp., Dallas, 1988-89; mgr. contracts Superconducting Super Collider, Dallas, 1989-95; dir. contract adminstr. Los Angeles County MTA, L.A., 1995-96; pres. Nat. Contract Svc. Corp., La Crescenta, Calif., 1996—; ccons., Dallas, 1991-95; adj. prof. U. Dallas, 1990-95, U. Calif., Riverside, 1996—, UCLA, Westwood, 1996—. Author: Service Purchasing, 1994, Cost/Price Analysis, 1994; editor: Global Purchasing, 1990; contbr. articles to profl. jours. Dist. commr. Boy Scouts Am., Portland, Oreg., 1987, mem. troop com. troop 390, La Crescenta, 1996. Capt. U.S. Army, 1964-70, Vietnam. Recipient dist. award of merit Boy Scouts Am., Honolulu, 1985. Fellow Nat. Contract Mgmt. Assn. (cert., chpt. v.p. 1996—); m. Nat. Assn. Purchasing Mgmt. (cert., nat. officer 1992—). Home: 5629 Terrace Dr La Crescenta CA 91214

GRAY, ALFRED ORREN, journalism educator, communications specialist; b. Sun Prairie, Wis., Sept. 8, 1914; s. Charles Orren and Amelia Katherine (Schadel) G.; m. Nicolin Jane Plank, Sept. 5, 1947; children—Robin, Richard. B.A., U. Wis.-Madison, 1939, M.A., 1941. Reporter-correspondent-intern U. Wis.-Madison and Medford newspapers, 1937-39; free-lance writer, 1938-41, 51-57; intelligence investigator U.S. Ordnance Dept., Ravenna, Ohio, 1941-42; hist. editor, chief writer U.S. Office Chief Ordnance Service, ETO, Paris and Frankfurt, Germany, 1944-46; asst. prof. journalism

Whitworth Coll., Spokane, Wash., 1946-48, assoc. prof., 1948-56, head dept. journalism, adviser student publs., 1946-80, prof., 1956-80, prof. emeritus, 1980—, chmn. div. bus. and communications arts, 1958-66, chmn. div. applied arts, 1978-79; rschr. writer Spokane, 1980—; dir. Whitworth News Bur., 1952-58; prin. researcher, writer 12 hist. and ednl. projects. Author: The History of U.S. Ordnance Service in the European Theater of Operations, 1942-46, Not by Might, 1965, Eight Generations From Gondelsheim: A Genealogical Study, 1980; co-author: Many Lamps, One Light: A Centennial History, 1984; editor: The Synod Story, 1953-55; mem. editl. adv. bd. Whitworth Today mag., 1989-90; contbr. articles to newspapers, mags., jours.; reader Am. Presbyns.: The Jour. of Presbyn. History, 1992-94. Scoutmaster Troop 9, Four Lakes Coun., Boy Scouts Am., Madison, Wis., 1937-41; chmn. Pinewood Addition Archtl. Com., Spokane, 1956—; dir. Inland Empire Publs. Clinic, Spokane, 1959-74; mem. ho. of dels. Greater Spokane Council of Chs., 1968-71; judge Goodwill Worker of Yr. awards Goodwill Industries Spokane County, 1972; vice-moderator Synod Wash.-Alaska, Presbyn. Ch. (U.S.A.), 1966-67; bd. dirs. Presbyn. Hist. Soc., 1984-90, 91-94, exec. com., 1986-90, chmn. hist. sites com., 1986-90; mem. Am. Bd. Mission Heritage Commn. for Sesquicentennial of Whitman Mission, 1986; elder Spokane 1st Presbyn. Ch., 1962—, clk. of session, 1984-86, mem. Inland Empire Presbytery Com. for Bicentennial of Gen. Assembly, 1988-89, Presbytery of the Inland Northwest, mem. com. on justice and peacemaking, 1988-95, mem. Care and Equipping of Congregations, 1995—; Dem. precinct official, Spokane, 1988-92. Served with AUS, 1942-46. Decorated Bronze Star and Army Commendation medals; recipient Printers Ink trophy Advt. Assn. West, 1953, citation Nat. Coun. Coll. Publ. Advisers, 1967, Outstanding Teaching of Journalism award Whitworth Coll. Alumni Assn., 1972; named Disting. Newspaper Adviser in U.S. among colleges and univs., Nat. Coun. Coll. Publ. Advisers, 1979. Mem. Assn. for Edn. in Journalism and Mass Comms., Ea. Wash. Hist. Soc., Coll. Media Advisors (hon.), Ea. Wash. Geneal. Soc., N.Am. Mycol. Assn., U. Wis. Alumni Assn. Half Century Club, Phi Beta Kappa (pres. profl. chpt. 1949-50, 67-68, 70-71), Sigma Delta Chi, Phi Eta Sigma. Democrat. Home: 304 W Hoerner Ave Spokane WA 99218-2124

GRAY, DONOVAN MICHAEL, cultural development specialist; b. July 14, 1948; s. Stanley Hermann and Maxine Abbott (Cushing) G. BA in Community Arts Devel., The Evergreen State Coll., 1976, MPA in Cultural Policy, 1982. Grants coord. The Evergreen State Coll., Olympia, Wash., 1980-82; local liaison Oreg. Arts Commn., Salem, 1982-85; fundraiser Meany Hall for Performing Arts, Seattle, 1986-88; dir. Western Arts Mgmt. Inst., Ashland, Oreg., 1987-90; pub. info., grant panel system mgr. Nev. State Coun. on Arts, Reno, 1990-91; ptnr. Withers and Gray Project Mgmt. and Consultancy, Medford, 1991-93; exec. dir. Network of Local Arts Agys. of Wash. State, Olympia, 1993—; part-time devel. assoc. The Evergreen State Coll., Olympia, 1993-95; mem. cultural study tour to No. Ireland, Brit. Coun., 1991. Photographs exhibited in shows at Exclusive Accents Gallery, Jacksonville, Oreg., 1990, Rental/Sales Gallery, Rogue Gallery, Medford, 1990-93, 4th St. Gallery and Garden Cafe, Ashland, Oreg., 1992; author: Cultural Equation: The Sum of the Arts, 1989, The Arts Add Up, 1990, Southern Oregon Media Directory, 1990; contbr. articles to profl. publs.; editor, pub. agy. newsletters, 1972-92. Bd. dirs. western divsn. Assn. Am. Dance Cos., 1973-74; mem. Seattle Ctr. Visual Arts adv. com. Seattle Arts Commn., 1973; mem. dance adv. coun. City of Seattle Parks Dept., 1973-74; mem. adv. bd. Western Humanities Ctr., UCLA, 1974-75; mem. expansion arts panel Nat. Endowment for Arts, 1977-78, mem. arts adminstrn. tng. task force locals program, 1989; treas. bd. dirs. Neighborhood Arts Programs Nat. Orgn. Com., 1978-79; mem. adv. bd. Rural Arts Svcs., Mendocino, Calif., 1988-90; chmn. adv. com. Washington State Bldg. for the Arts, 1994—. Named One of Outstanding Community Arts Developers in U.S., Arts Reporting Svc., 1984. Home: 2327 Log Cabin Rd SE Olympia WA 98501-4223

GRAY, ELIZABETH MARIE, biologist; b. South Bend, Ind., June 29, 1965; d. Henry Froehlich and Joan (Griglun) G. AB, Harvard U., 1987; PhD, U. Wash., Seattle, 1994. Rsch. asst. Monteverde Res., Costa Rica, 1987-88, Punta Tombo Res., Argentina, 1988; asst. molecular biologist U. Ky., Lexington, 1990-93; prof. biology U. Nev., Reno, 1995-96, postdoctoral rsch. assoc., 1996—; sci. cons. Wash. State Dept. Wildlife, Olympia, 1991-93; ind. investigator Indonesia, 1995. Reviewer sci. jours.; contbr. articles to profl. jours. Grantee Ctr. Wildlife Conservation, 1992-93. Mem. AAUW, Am. Ornithologists' Union, Assn. Women in Sci., Animal Behavior Soc., Soc. Conservation Biology. Democrat. Office: Univ Nev Reno 1000 Valley Rd ERS/186 Reno NV 89512

GRAY, GAVIN CAMPBELL, II, computer information engineer, computer consultant; b. Levittown, N.Y., Sept. 16, 1948; s. Gavin Campbell Gray and Pauline Louise (Bauerschmidt) Gowen; m. Catherine Ann West, Aug. 23, 1969; children: Jeffrey William, Tamara Pauline. Student, U. Wis., Milw., 1966-71. Programmer, analyst Equitable Variable Life Ins., Farmingdale, N.Y., 1975-77; analyst, programmer Atty.'s Title Svcs., Orlando, Fla., 1977-78; systems analyst Cert. Grocers, Ocala, Fla., 1978-80; supr. R & D, Clay Electric Coop., Keystone Heights, Fla., 1980-86; mgr. info. svcs. Coldwell Banker Relocation Svcs., Mission Viejo, Calif., 1986-96, Oracle Corp., San Diego, 1996—; mem. Guide Internat. Bus. Rules Stds. Project, 1994—, Am. Nat. Stds. Inst. Accredited Stds. Com. X12, 1994-96, Asymetrix Corp. Adv. Coun. Author: IBM GIS Usage for IMS/DLI, 1979; developer software Map-Paint for CICS, methodology Path Evaluation Method (PEM), TRANS-FLOW Programming, Tier Diagramming Method; contbr. articles to profl. jours. Mem. IEEE, APA, Assn. Computing Machinery, Data Adminstrn. Mgmt. Assn. Internat., Data Warehousing Inst., Math. Assn. Am., Internat. Platform Assn., IEEE Computer Soc., IEEE Engring. Mgmt. Soc., N.Y. Acad. Scis., Am. Mus. Natural History, Zool. Soc. San Diego, Am. Mensa Ltd., Nat. Eagle Scout Assn., Intertel, Data Warehousing Inst. Office: Oracle Corp Ste 300 4350 La Jolla Village Dr San Diego CA 92122

GRAY, HARVEY, museum director. Exec. dir. USS Bowfin Submarine Mus. and Pk., Honolulu. Office: USS Bowfin Submarine Mus & Pk 11 Arizona Meml Dr Honolulu HI 96818

GRAY, JAN CHARLES, lawyer, business owner; b. Des Moines, June 15, 1947; s. Charles Donald and Mary C. Gray; 1 child, Charles Jan. BA in Econs., U. Calif., Berkeley, 1969; MBA, Pepperdine U., 1986; JD, Harvard U., 1972. Bar: Calif. 1972, D.C. 1974, Wyo. 1992. Law clk. Kindel & Anderson, L.A., 1971-72; assoc. Halstead, Baker & Sterling, L.A., 1972-75; sr. v.p., gen. counsel and sec. Ralphs Grocery Co., L.A., 1975—; pres. Am. Presidents Resorts, Custer, S.D., Casper/Glenrock, Wyo., 1983—; owner Big Bear (Calif.) Cabins-Lakeside, 1988—, Sta. KGOS/KERM, Torrington, Wyo., 1993—, Sta. KRAL/KIQZ, Rawlins, Wyo., 1993—, Sta. KZMX, Hot Springs, S.D., 1993—, Sta. KFCR, Custer, S.D., 1992—, Sta. KQLT-FM, Casper, Wyo., 1994—, Sta. KASS-FM, Casper, 1995—, Sta. KVOC-AM, Casper, 1997—, KUOC-AM, Casper, Wyo., 1997—; judge pro tem L.A. Mcpl. Ct., 1977-85; instr. bus. UCLA, 1976-85, Pepperdine MBA Program, 1983-85; arbitrator Am. Arbitration Assn., 1977—; media spokesman So. Calif. Grocers Assn., 1979-90, Calif. Grocers Assn., 1979—, Calif. Retailers Assn., 1979—; real estate broker, L.A., 1973—; pres. Mt. Rushmore Broadcasting, Inc., 1991—. Contbg. author: Life or Death, Who Controls?, 1976; contbr. articles to profl. jours. Trustee South Bay U. Coll. Law, 1978-79; mem. bd. visitors Southwestern U. Sch. Law, 1983—; mem. L.A. County Pvt. Industry Coun., 1982—, exec. com. 1984-88, chmn. econ. devel. task force, 1986-89, chmn. mktg. com. 1991-93; mem. L.A. County Martin Luther King, Jr. Gen. Hosp. Authority, 1984—; mem. L.A. County Aviation Commn, 1986-92, chmn., 1990-91; L.A. Police Crime Prevention Adv. Coun., 1986—; Angelus Plaza Adv. Bd., 1983-85; bd. dirs. RecyCAL of So. Calif., 1983-89; trustee Santa Monica Hosp. Found., 1986-91, adv. bd., 1991—; mem. L.A. County Dem. Cen. Com., 1980-90, L.A. City Employees' Retirement System Commn., 1993—; del. Dem. Nat. Conv., 1980. Recipient So. Calif. Grocers Assn. award for outstanding contbns. to food industry, 1982, appreciation award for No on 11 Campaign, Calif./Nev. Soft Drink Assn., 1983; Tyler Price Meml. award Mex.-Am. Grocers Assn., 1995. Mem. ABA, Calif. Bar Assn., L.A. County Bar Assn. (exec. com. corp. law depts. sect. 1974-76, 79—, chmn. 1989-90, exec. com. barristers sect. 1974-75, 79-81, trustee 1991-93, jud. evaluation com. 1993—, nominating com. 1994), San Fernando Valley Bar Assn. (chmn. real property sect. 1975-77, L.A. Pub. Affairs Officers Assn., L.A. World Affairs Coun., Calif. Retailers Assn. (supermarket com.), Food Mktg. Inst. (govt. rels. com., benefits coun. 1993—, chmn. lawyers and economists 1994—), So. Calif. Bus. Assn. (bd. dirs. 1981—, mem. exec. com. 1982—, sec. 1986—, chair 1991—), Town Hall L.A., U. Calif. Alumni Assn., Ephebian Soc. L.A., Harvard Club of So. Calif., Phi Beta Kappa. Home: 2793 Creston Dr Los Angeles CA 90068-2209 Office: PO Box 54143 Los Angeles CA 90054-0143

GRAY, KARLA MARIE, state supreme court justice. BA, Western Mich. U., MA in African History; JD, U. Calif., San Francisco, 1976. Bar: Mont. 1976, Calif. 1977. Law clk. to Hon. W. D. Murray U.S. Dist. Ct., 1976-77; staff atty. Atlantic Richfield Co., 1977-81; pvt. practice law Butte, Mont., 1981-84; staff atty., legis. lobbyist Mont. Power Co., Butte, 1984-91; justice Supreme Ct. Mont., Helena, 1991—. Mem. Mont. Supreme Ct. Gender Fairness Task Force. Fellow Am. Bar Found., Am. Judicature Soc., Internat. Women's Forum; mem. State Bar Mont., Silver Bow County Bar Assn. (past pres.), Nat. Assn. Women Judges. Office: Supreme Ct Mont Justice Bldg Rm 323 215 N Sanders St Helena MT 59601-4522

GRAY, LAWRENCE CLIFTON, JR., physical education educator; b. San Antonio, Jan. 19, 1948; s. Lawrence Clifton and Janey Lillian G.; m. Marcellea Gailes Fields, Dec. 15, 1973 (div. Jan., 1992); m. Maisha Kito Lateef Hasani. BA in Elem. Edn., U. Evansville, 1978; MA in Secondary Edn., San Francisco State U., 1982. Midnight basketball commr. Ella Hill Hutch Cmty. Ctr., San Francisco, 1981-96; CEO, pres. Capricorn Student-Athlete Referral Svc., San Francisco, 1988—. Democrat. Pentecostal. Home: 119 Margaret St San Francisco CA 94112 Office: Balboa HS 1000 Cayuga Ave San Francisco CA 94112

GRAY, LONNA IRENE, indemnity fund executive; b. Forsyth, Mont., Nov. 10, 1944; d. John Jr. and Inga (Hill) Gray; m. James Dodd, Nov. 26, 1964 (div. Oct. 1988); children: Sheri Dodd, James Dodd, Thaddeus Dodd. BS, Mont. State U., 1967; MPA, Boise State U., 1997. Workers compensation claims monitor Idaho State Ins. Fund, Boise, 1990-92; workers compensation claims examiner Indsl. Spl. Indemnity Fund, Boise, 1992-94, acting mgr., 1994-95, mgr., 1995—; mem. Gov.'s Adv. Com. on Workers Compensation, Boise, 1995—. Mem. Boise City Comprehensive Plan Com., 1993-96; founding mem. Log Cabin Lit. Ctr., Boise, 1996—; mem. Beaux Arts Soc./Boise Art Mus., 1976—; mem. Boise City Planning and Zoning Commn., 1985—. Mem. Workers Compensation Surety Group (sec. 1994-95, pres. 1995-96), Bosie Adjusters Assn. (treas. 1995-96, v.p. 1996—), City Club, Idaho Women's Network. Office: Indsl Spl Indemnity Fund 650 W State St Boise ID 83720-7901

GRAY, PATRICIA JOYCE, court administrator; b. Carlsbad, N.Mex., Feb. 5, 1951; d. Owen Corbett and Bobby Jo (Jones) G.; m. Patrick A. Edwards, Oct. 29, 1981 (div. June 1990). Student, U. Nev., Las Vegas, 1974-77. Receptionist, clk. Nationwide Fin., Las Vegas, 1969-70; dep. clk. U.S. Bankruptcy Ct. for Dist. Nev., Las Vegas, 1970-74, chief dep. clk., 1974-75, chief clk., 1975-79, clk. of ct., 1979—; mem. bankruptcy work measurement subcom. of com. on adminstrn. bankruptcy system Jud. Conf. U.S., 1989-91; mem. tng. and edn. com. U.S. Bankruptcy Cts. Adminstrv. Office U.S. Cts., 1990-91; mem. Bankruptcy Work Measurement subcom. of Clerk's adv. com. Adminstrv. Office U.S. Cts., 1992-93, local rules subcom. Dist. Nev., 1991—. Mem. Space and Facilities Ad Hoc Task Force on Personnel of Adminstrv. Office of U.S. Cts., 1994-95, 9th Cir. Task Force on Race, Religious, and Ethnic Fairness, 1994—; mem. bd. dirs. of Clark County, Nev. chpt. ARC, 1994—. Mem. Nat. Conf. Bankruptcy Clks., Fed. Ct. Clks. Assn., Nat. Assn. Ct. Mgrs. Rebublican. Office: US Bankruptcy Ct Foley Fed Bldg 300 Las Vegas Blvd S Las Vegas NV 89101-5833

GRAY, PAUL WESLEY, university dean; b. Cicero, Ill., Jan. 30, 1947; s. Harry B. and Audrey (Tong) G.; m. Rachel E. Boehr, June 3, 1967; children: John M., Janel E., Robert B. BA, Faith Baptist Bible Coll., Ankeny, Tex., 1970; ThM, Dallas Theol. Sem., 1975; MS in Libr. Sci., East Tex. State U., 1977, EdD, 1980; MA, Tex. Woman's U., 1989. Dorm dir. Buckner Baptist Benevolences, Dallas, 1971-75; dir. community living residence IV Dallas County Mental Health/Mental Retardation, Dallas, 1975-78; cataloger W. Walworth Harrison Pub. Libr., Greenville, Tex., 1978-81; v.p. Golden Triangle Christian Acad., Garland, Tex., 1979-83; dir. libr. LeTourneau U., Longview, Tex., 1983-88; dean computer svc. and univ. libr. Azusa (Calif.) Pacific U., 1989—. Mem. ALA, Calif. Libr. Assn., So. Calif. Area Theol. Libr. Assn., Foothill Libr. Consortium. Republican. Baptist. Office: Azusa Pacific U 901 E Alosta Ave Azusa CA 91702-2701

GRAY, PHILIP HOWARD, retired psychologist, educator; b. Cape Rosier, Maine, July 4, 1926; s. Asa and Bernice (Lawrence) G.; m. Iris McKinney, Dec. 31, 1954; children: Cindelyn Gray Eberts, Howard. M.A., U. Chgo., 1958; Ph.D., U. Wash., 1960. Asst. prof. dept. psychology Mont. State U., Bozeman, 1960-65; assoc. prof. Mont. State U., 1965-75, prof., 1975-92; ret., 1992; vis. prof. U. Man., Winnipeg, Can., 1968-70, U. N.H., 1965, U. Mont., 1967, 74, Tufts U., 1968, U. Conn., 1971; pres. Mont. Psychol. Assn., 1968-70 (helped write Mont. licensing law for psychologists); chmn. Mont. Bd. Psychologist Examiners, 1972-74; spkr. sci. and geneal. meetings on ancestry of U.S. presidents; presenter, instr. grad. course on serial killers and the psychopathology of murder. Organizer folk art exhbns. Mont. and Maine, 1972-79; author: The Comparative Analysis of Behavior, 1966, (with F.L. Ruch and N. Warren) Working with Psychology, 1963, A Directory of Eskimo Artists in Sculpture and Prints, 1974, The Science That Lost Its Mind, 1985, Penobscot Pioneers vol. 1, 1992, vol. 2, 1992, vol. 3, 1993, vol. 4, 1994, vol. 5, 1995, vol. 6, 1996; contbr. numerous articles on behavior to psychol. jours.; contbr. poetry to lit. jours. With U.S. Army, 1944-46. Recipient Am. and Can. research grants. Fellow AAAS, APA, Am. Psychol. Soc., Internat. Soc. Rsch. on Aggression; mem. NRA (life), SAR (v.p. Sourdough chpt. 1990, pres. 1991-96, trustee 1989, v.p. Mont. state soc. 1996-97, pres. 1997—), Nat. Geneal. Soc., New Eng. Hist. Geneal. Soc., Gallatin County Geneal. Soc. (charter, pres. 1991-93), Deer Isle-Stonington Hist. Soc., Internat. Soc. Human Ethology, Descs. Illegitimate Sons and Daus. of Kings of Britain, Piscataque Pioneers, Order Desc. Colonial Physicians and Chirugiens, Flagon and Trencher, Order of the Crown of Charlemagne. Republican. Home: 1207 S Black Ave Bozeman MT 59715-5633 *We are human to the extent that we have bondings and the more bondings we have the more human we are. These attachments include familial bonding (imprinting), friendship bonding, marital bonding, ethnic-religious bonding, possession and goal bondings, and bonding to the land and ocean. My life's work is the study of these bondings and I am thereby more firmly connected to the human race.*

GRAY, RHEA COLLETTE, mental health counselor; b. Salt Lake City, July 9, 1971; d. Edward Clorence and Kathleen Diane (Masini) G. BA, Gonzaga U., 1993, MA, 1995. Cert. profl. counselor trainee, Utah; lic. profl. counselor trainee. Therapist aide Children's Behavior Therapy Unit, Salt Lake City, 1990-91, 91, 92; intervention specialist Nine Mile Falls (Wash.) Sch. Dist., 1994; therapist aide Cmty. Mental Health Ctr., Spokane, Wash., 1994-95; counselor, intern Cath. Family Svcs., Spokane, 1995; program coord. Cmty. Based Transitional Ctr., Salt Lake City, 1995-96; Autism specialist Children's Behavior Therapy Unit, Salt Lake City, 1996—. Mem. ACA.

GRAY, RICHARD ARDEN, transportation executive; b. Ft. Bragg, Calif., Oct. 29, 1935; s. Arden Howard and Marion Florence (Coolidge) G.; m. Roberta Jeanne Montna, Feb. 5, 1955; children: Mark Alan, Laura Ann, Deborah Marie, Lisa Lynn. AA, Yuba Coll., 1955; BA, Calif. State U., 1957. Cert. coll. instr., Calif. Deputy sheriff Yuba County Sheriffs Dept., Marysville, Calif., 1957; traffic officer Calif. Hwy. Patrol, Ventura, 1958-60, Yuba City, 1961-68; sgt. field ops. officer Calif. Hwy. Patrol, Gardena, 1969-71; lt. exec. officer Calif. Hwy. Patrol, Van Nuys, 1972-76; lt. area comdr. Calif. Hwy. Patrol, Chico, 1977-88; wholesale, retail distbr. Dick Gray Enterprises, Chico, 1989-94, 95—; instr. Yuba Coll., Marysville, 1965-67, Calif. fish and game hunter safety program, Chico, 1982-86; profl. driver, transporter motor homes, 1989—. Chmn. citizen rev. com. United Way of Butte County, Chico, 1984 (outstanding achievement 1984-86), fundraising campaign chmn. 1986, pres. bd. dirs. 1985; pres., bd. dirs. No. Calif. Counties Exch. Club Child Abuse Prevention Ctr., Chico, 1987-91. With USNR, 1953-61. Recipient Individual Excellence Outstanding Cmty. Svc. award United Way Butte and Glenn Counties, 1994-95. Mem. Calif. Hwy. Patrolmen Assn., RV Club, Elks (honors 1988, pres. 1988-89), Breakfast Exch. Club (pres., bd. dirs. 1980-81), Exch. Club Greater Chico (sponsor 1983). Republican.

GRAY, RICHARD MOSS, retired college president; b. Washington, Jan. 25, 1924; s. Wilbur Leslie and Betty Marie (Grey) G.; m. Catherine Claire Hammond, Oct. 17, 1943; children: Janice Lynn Gray Armstrong, Nancy Hammond Gray Schultz. BA, Bucknell U., 1942; MDiv summa cum laude, San Francisco Theol. Sem., 1961; PhD, U. Calif., Berkeley, 1972; doctorate degree (hon.), World Coll. West, 1988. Writer, creative dir. N.W. Ayer & Son, Phila., 1942-58; univ. pastor Portland State U., Oreg., 1961-68; founder, pres. World Coll. West, Petaluma, Calif., 1973-88, pres. emeritus, 1988—; bd. dirs. World Centre, San Francisco, Lifelplan Ctr.; co-founder Presidio World Coll., 1992—. Author poetry Advent, 1989. Bd. dirs. Citizens Found. Marin, San Rafael, Calif., 1988—, Marin Ednl. Found., 1989-92; ruling elder Presbyn. Ch. U.S.A. Named Disting. Alumnus of Yr. San Francisco Theol. Sem., 1988, Marin Citizen of Yr. Citizens Found., 1988; recipient Svc. to Humanity award Bucknell U., 1992. Mem. Phi Beta Kappa.

GRAY, SANDRA RAE, retired secondary school educator; b. East Palestine, Ohio, Nov. 8, 1932; d. Kenneth Ray Morris and Nina Olivia (Jamsen) Rex; m. Donald Noel Gray Jr., Nov. 9, 1951; children: Pamela, Donald, Douglas. BA in speech communications, Calif. State U., 1967, MA in speech communications, 1974. Tchr. Tustin (Calif.) Unif. Sch. Dist., 1971-95, ret., 1995; tchr. Riverside (Calif.) Sch. Dist., 1968-71; teaching asst. U. Souther Calif., L.A., 1974-77; tchr. Saddleback Coll., Mission Viejo, Calif., 1982-84, Calif. State U., L.A., 1976. Pres. adv. coun. annual fund Calif. State U., 1992-95; pres. Calif. State Speech Coun., 1976-78; chmn. Nat. Forensic League (Big Orange Chpt.), Ripon, Wis., 1992-93. Recipient Calif. State Speech Coun. Hall of Fame Calif. H.S. Speech Assn., 1982. Mem. AAUW. Republican. Protestant. Home: 13671 Falmouth Dr Tustin CA 92780-5217

GRAY, THOMAS STEPHEN, newspaper editor; b. Burbank, Calif., Aug. 22, 1950; s. Thomas Edgar and Lily Irene (Ax) G.; m. Barbara Ellen Bronson, Aug. 27, 1977; children: Jonathan Thomas, Katherine Marie. BA, Stanford U., 1972; MA in English, UCLA, 1976. Teaching assoc. UCLA, 1976-77; reporter L.A. Daily News, 1977-79, editorial writer, 1979-84, editorial page editor, 1984-95; sr. editor Investor's Bus. Daily, L.A., 1995—. Recipient 1st Place award Editorial Writing Greater L.A. Press Club, 1988, Inland Daily Press Association, 1993. Office: Investors Bus Daily Editl Dept 12655 Beatrice St Los Angeles CA 90066-7300

GRAY, WALTER P., III, museum director, consultant; b. San Francisco, Aug. 8, 1952; s. Walter Patton II and Elsie Josephine (Stroop) G.; m. Mary Amanda Helmich, May 23, 1980. BA in History, Calif. State U., Sacramento, 1976. Rschr. Calif. State R.R. Mus., Sacramento, 1977-80, curator, 1980-81, 85-90, archivist, 1981-85, dir., 1990—; cons. in field, 1976—. Contbr. articles to profl. jours. Democrat. Buddhist. Office: California State Railroad Museum 111 I St Sacramento CA 95814-2204

GRAYBEAL, LYNNE ELIZABETH, lawyer; b. Seattle, May 21, 1956; d. John Olin and Janie Marie (Everly) G.; m. Scott Harron, Oct. 7, 1989. Student, Pomona Coll., 1974-76; BA, Colby Coll., 1979; JD, U. Puget Sound, 1983. Bar: Wash. 1983, U.S. Dist. Ct. (we. dist.) Wash. 1983. Rsch. asst. Charles River Assocs., Boston, 1979-80; assoc. Bogle & Gates, Seattle, summer 1982, 83-85; assoc. Monroe, Stokes, Eitelbach & Lawrence, P.S., Seattle, 1986-89, prin., 1990-92; ptnr. Riddell, Williams, Bullitt & Walkinshaw, 1992-94, Foster Pepper & Shefelman, 1994—. Sec. Bathhouse Theatre, 1984-86, v.p., 1987; bd. dirs. Wash. Vol. Lawyers for ARts, 1985-89; v.p., bd. dirs. Seattle Found. for Motion Picture ARts, 1988-89. Mem. ABA (chmn. unfair competition trade identity subcom. 1987-88), Wash. State Bar Assn. (chmn. intellectual and indsl. property sect. 1988-89), Wash. State Patent Law Assn., Wash. Women Lawyers (treas. 1989-91, pres. 1992), Greater Seattle C. of C. (curriculum com. 1989-91, Leadership Tomorrow class 1988-89). Home: 3037 38th Ave W Seattle WA 98199-2512 Office: Foster Pepper & Shefelman 1111 3rd Ave Ste 3400 Seattle WA 98101-3299

GRAYMAN, GLEN, emergency medicine physician; b. L.A., May 24, 1949; s. Martin Grayman and Elaine Joy (Fagnan) Burakoff; m. Betty Jane Kerling, Aug., 1972 (div. 1978); m. Karla Ellen Rodine, Mar. 19, 1982; children: Dane Martin, Britta Jensen. BA with highest honors, U. Calif., Riverside, 1970; MD, UCLA, 1974. Diplomate Nat. Bd. Med. Examiners, Am. Bd. Emergency Medicine, Am. Bd. Internal Medicine, Am. Bd. Quality Assurance & Utilization Review Physicians, Am. Bd. Med. Mgmt.; BLS, ACLS, ATLS, PALS. Intern L.A. County-Harbor Gen. Hosp., Torrance, Calif., 1974-75, resident, 1975-77; emergency physician Desert Hosp., Palm Springs, Calif., 1977—; med. dir. emergency/trauma ctr. Desert Hosp., 1989—, chmn. dept. emergency medicine, 1990-91; pres. Desert Emergency Physicians Med. Group, Palm Springs, 1989—; med. dir. dept. emergency med. svcs. Crafton Hills Coll., Yucaipa, Calif., 1983-90; med. dir. Heart to Heart Emergency Med. Instrn. Co., 1987-90, Western Nurse Specialists, Inc., 1986-91; physician specialist, cons. 1984 Olympic Games, L.A., 1984; asst. clin. prof. UCLA, 1985—, clin. instr., 1982-85. Contbr. articles to profl. jours. Bd. dirs. Riverside county chpt. Am. Heart Assn., 1981-84. Fellow Am. Coll. Emergency Physicians; mem. Am. Coll. Physician Execs., AMA, Calif. Med. Assn., Riverside County Med. Assn. (bd. councilors 1988-90, mediation and med. care com. 1987-88, disaster and emergency med. care com. 1993—), Palm Springs Acad. Medicine (pres. 1991-92, sec. 1989-90), Phi Beta Kappa, Alpha Omega Alpha. Jewish. Office: Desert Hosp 1150 N Indian Canyon Dr Palm Springs CA 92262-4872

GRAZIANI, ROGER DANIEL, secondary school educator; b. Detroit, Apr. 17, 1949; s. Sante and Margaret Daisy (Palmer) G.; m. Connie Sanchez, Oct. 30, 1952 (div. Apr. 1989); children: Adrianna, Vanessa. BA, Mich. State U., 1972; MFA, U. So. Calif., L.A., 1977. Cert. tchr., Calif. Divsn. mgr. Prudential Ins., L.A., 1972-77; tchr. Pater Noster H.S., Glendale, Calif., 1977, Belvedere Jr. H.S., Los Angeles, Calif., 1977-81; tchr., dept. head Pacoima (Calif.) Jr. H.S., 1981-84; tchr. Taft H.S., Woodland Hills, Calif., 1984-93, Glendora (Calif.) H.S., 1993—; founding theatre team mem. Calif. Arts Project, Northridge, 1991—; Calif. State U., 1991—; faculty Calif. State U., Northridge, 1990; judge Am. Film Inst., L.A., 1996. Mem. Monrovia (Calif.) Bd. Edn., 1983—, pres., 1987, 92, 95; founding mem. Monrovia Cable Commn., 1984-88; adv. mem. Monrovia Redevel., 1987. Calif. Writing Project fellow UCLA, 1982. Mem. Drama Tchrs. Assn. So. Calif. (historian 1987, pres. 1988—), L.A. Film Tchrs. Assn. Democrat. Roman Catholic. Home: 1416 Monterey Ave Apt G Monrovia CA 91016-3905 Office: 1600 Foothill Blvd Glendora CA 91741

GRAZIANO, JOSEPH A., computer company executive; b. 1945. CPA, Merrimack Coll. With Ernst & Whinney, Boston, Rolm Corp., 1976-81; CFO Apple Computer, Inc., Cupertino, Calif., 1981-85, 89-96, also exec. v.p., also dir.; CFO, v.p. finance Sun Microsystems, Inc., 1987-89.

GREAT, DON CHARLES, composer, music company executive; b. Medford, Oreg., Mar. 11, 1951; s. Donald Charles Sr. and Anna Marie (Huff) G.; m. Andrea Louise Gerber, Oct. 31, 1970. Student, UCLA, 1975-76, 83-86, Dick Grove Sch. Music, 1983-87. Freelance songwriter Metro-Goldwyn-Mayer Records, 20th Century Records, Bell Records, Los Angeles, 1968—; pres. Don Great Music, Inc., Los Angeles, 1972—. Composer music for TV shows including Who's the Boss? (ABC), 227 (NBC), The Jeffersons (CBS), Gimme a Break (NBC), A Different World (NBC), Fact of Life (NBC), Unsolved Mysteries (NBC), Amen (NBC), Freddie's Nightmares (Lorimar-Warner Bros. TV), Saved By the Bell (NBC Disney), One Day at a Time (CBS), Married With Children (Fox/Columbia Pictures), Small Wonder (Fox TV), 1978—, Different Strokes (NBC), BJ and the Bear (NBC), Silverspoons (NBC), Sheriff Lobo (NBC), Incredible Hulk (CBS), Sanford (NBC), Real People (NBC), Crimetime After Primetime (CBS), Tje Promised Land (CBS), Candid Camera, Tales From the Crypt, In Living Color (Fox-TV), Laugh-In, Baby Races; composer music score Pres. Reagen Libr. Video, Pres. Carter Presdl. Libr. CD-ROM, 1994. Mem. Broadcast Music, Inc. (Best Music Score of Yr. award 1986, named TV Composer of Yr. 1986).

GREAVER, HARRY, artist; b. L.A., Oct. 30, 1929; s. Harry Jones and Lucy Catherine (Coons) G.; m. Hanne Synnestvedt Nielsen, Nov. 30, 1955; children—Peter, Paul, Lotte. BFA, U. Kans., 1951, MFA, 1952. Assoc. prof. art U. Maine, Orono, 1955-66; exec. dir. Kalamazoo Inst. Arts, 1966-78; dir. Greaver Gallery, Cannon Beach, Oreg., 1978—; mem. visual com. Mich. Coun. Arts, 1976-78. One-man exhbns. include Baker U., Baldwin,

Kans., 1955, U. Maine, Orono, 1958, 59, Pacific U., 1985; group exhbns. include U. Utah Mus. Fine Arts, 1972-73, Purdue U., 1977, Drawings/U.S.A, St. Paul, 1963, San Diego Mus., 1971, Rathbun Gallery, Portland, Oreg., 1988; 10-yr. print retrospective Cannon Beach Arts Assn., 1989. Mem. adv. bd. Haystack Ctr. for the Arts, Cannon Beach, 1988-91. Recipient Purchase award Nat. Endowment Arts, 1971; grantee U. Maine, 1962-64. Mem. Cannon Beach Arts Assn., 1986-88. Address: PO Box 120 Cannon Beach OR 97110-0120

GREAVES, JOHN ALLEN, lawyer; b. Kansas City, Mo., Feb. 18, 1948; s. John Allen Greaves and Nancy Lee (Farmer) Greaves-Meltzer; m. Sharon Louise Peace Ventura, Dec. 23, 1967 (div. Mar. 1971); 1 child, Karen Christine Greaves Calogne; m. Jerri Lynn Crawford, Sept. 5, 1981. BA in Polit. Sci., U. Mo., 1976; MPA, JD with honors, Drake U., 1992. Bar: Iowa 1992, U.S. Dist. Ct. (so. dist.) Iowa 1992, Calif. 1994, U.S. Dist. Ct. (no. and cen. dists.) Calif. 1994, U.S. Dist. Ct. (so. and ea. dists.) Calif . 1995, U.S. Dist. Ct. N.Mex. 1995, U.S. Dist. Ct. S.C. 1995, U.S. Ct. Appeals (9th cir.) 1995, U.S. Dist. Ct. (no. dist.) N.Y. 1996, U.S. Ct. Appeals (4th and 10th cirs.) 1996. Pres., CEO VIPilot Svcs., Inc., Kansas City, 1980-83; pilot Air Illinois, Carbondale, Ill., 1983-84, Wright Airlines, Cleve., 1983-84, ComAir Airlines, Cin., 1984-88; jud. law clk. to Hon. Arthur E. Gamble Iowa Dist. Ct., Des Moines, 1990-91; pvt. practice Des Moines, 1992-94; assoc. Baum, Hedlund, Aristei, Guilford & Downey, L.A., 1994—. Mem. ABA, ATLA, Airline Pilots Assn. (chmn. contract adminstrn. com. 1985-87, Disting. Svc. award 1987), Lawyer/Pilot Bar Assn. Home: 3664 May St Los Angeles CA 90066 Office: Baum Hedlund Aristei et al Ste 950 12100 Wilshire Blvd Los Angeles CA 90025

GREBER, ROBERT MARTIN, financial investments executive; b. Phila., Mar. 15, 1938; s. Joseph and Golda (Rubin) G.; m. Judith Ann Pearlstein, Dec. 23, 1962; children: Matthew, Jonathan. B.S. in Fin., Temple U., 1962; grad., Sch. Mgmt. and Strategic Studies, 1982-84. Account exec. Merrill Lynch, Phila., 1962-68; portfolio mgr. v.p. Afuture Funds Inc., Lima, Pa., 1968-70; instl. account exec. Merrill Lynch, Phila., 1970-75; officer, mgr.-v.p. Merrill Lynch, Los Angeles, 1975-79; chief fin. officer Lucasfilm Ltd., Los Angeles, 1979-80; pres., CEO Lucasfilm Ltd., San Rafael, Calif., 1980-84, Diagnostic Networks, Inc., San Francisco, 1984-87; ptnr. Leon A. Farley Assocs., San Francisco, 1988-90; pres., COO The Pacific Stock Exch., 1990-95, chmn., CEO, 1996—; bd. dirs. Bay View Capital Group. Bd. dirs. KQED Pub. Broadcasting Sys., San Francisco, 1983, chmn. bd., 1988; bd. dirs. Film Inst. No. Calif., Marin Symphony Orch., 1981-83, Sonic Solutions, 1993—; trustee Western Behavior Scis. Inst., La JOlla, 1982-89; vice chmn. Assn. Am. Pub. TV, 1992-94; trustee Beryl Buck Inst. for Edn., 1990-93. With Army NG, 1959-60. Office: Pacific Stock Exchange Inc 115 Sansome St San Francisco CA 94104-3601

GRECO, GINA LYN, French language and literature educator; b. New Orleans, Apr. 23, 1964; d. Claude A. and Beryl E. (Bagert) G.; m. Gaetano DeLeonibus, Dec. 19, 1992. BA, Emory U., 1985; MA, Princeton U., 1989, PhD, 1992. Asst. prof. Portland State U., Portland, Oreg., 1992—. Contbr. articles to profl. jours. Mellon Found. fellow, 1986-92. Mem. MLA (mem. com. emerging techs. pedagogy and rsch. 1994—), Medieval Acad. Am., Medieval Acad. The Pacific, Phi Beta Kappa. Office: Portland State U Dept Fgn Langs & Lit PO Box 751 Portland OR 97207-0751

GREEAR, MICHAEL ALLYN, employment counselor and consultant; b. Chehalis, Wash., Dec. 9, 1962; s. William Allyn and Ina Jeanette (Aust) G. BA in Philosophy and Lit., N.W. Nazarene Coll., Nampa, Idaho, 1987. Job coach, crew leader Reliable Enterprises, Centralia, Wash.; employment counselor/cons. ARC Inc. of Ada County, Boise, Idahl; employment cons. Boise Area businesses, 1991-96; employment dir., net. adminstr. Cmty. Partnerships Idaho. Songwriter, musician (rec.) Boneflower, 1994, Seven Faux Trees, 1989, Figures for Fun, 1991, Bastards Joy, 1991, 96. Supporter Snake River Alliance, Boise, KBSU Pub. Radio, Boise. Office: Cmty Partnerships of Idaho 1076 N Cole Rd Boise ID 83704

GREEN, BETH INGBER, intuitive practitioner, counselor, musician, composer; b. N.Y.C., Feb. 28, 1945; d. Frank and Lillian Ingber; m. John Ingber Green, 1995. BA, Bklyn. Coll., 1970; MA, UCLA, 1978. Cert. in intuitive consulting, counseling, tchg. and learning, body and kinetic intervention. Spiritual dir. and founder The Stream, L.A., 1980-86; ptnr., co-founder The Healing Partnership, L.A. and Ramona, 1986-90; spiritual dir. and founder The Triple Eye Found., Escondido, Calif., 1990-93; intuitive practitioner, counselor, cons. and tchr. Jacksonville, Oreg., 1980—; owner Let's Talk, Jacksonville, Oreg.; spiritual activist, co-founder Rising Mountains Setting Suns, Ramona, 1993-95; co-founder Spiritual Activist Movement, L.A. and Ramona, 1993-95; owner Treehouse Music. Author: The Autobiography of Mary Magdalene, 1988; spoken tapes include: The Healing of God, The Alienation of Love, Spirituality: The Last Block to Freedom; music tapes include Beyond the Mystery, Sara in the Clouds; videotapes include Breaking the "I" Barrier. West Coast coord. Wages for Housework Campaign, L.A., 1974-78; co-founder The Looseleaf Directory: Linking Bodies, Minds and Spirits in the Healing Arts, 1994-95.

GREEN, BRIAN GERALD, marketing executive; b. Missoula, Mont., Sept. 5, 1954; s. Gerald Jay and Ruth Anne (Althaus) G.; m. Robin Lee McIntyre, May 10, 1980; 1 child, Sean Brian. ASEE, Clark Coll., 1976; BS in Electronics Engrng. Tech., Oreg. Inst. Tech., Klamath Falls, 1978; MBA, U. Hartford, 1988. Cert. electronic technician. Field engr. Triad Systems Corp., Hartford, Conn., 1978-79; midwest regional mgr. Triad Systems Corp., Chgo., 1979-81; Northwest regional mgr. Triad Systems Corp., Portland, Oreg., 1981-83; northeast area mgr. Triad Systems Corp., Bristol, Conn., 1983-88, Canadian svc. mgr., 1987-88; western area mgr. Triad Systems Corp., Tracy, Calif., 1988-89; world wide svc. mgr. Sysgen, Inc., Milpitas, Calif., 1989-91; svc. mktg. mgr. Sony Corp. Am., San Jose, 1991-93; self employed cons., 1993; bus. mgr. REPAC, Inc., Forest Park, Ga., 1993-94; dir. authentication AirTouch Cellular, Walnut Creek, Calif., 1994—. Mem. Assn. for Svcs. Mgmt. Internat., Masons (Southington, Conn. and Vancouver, Wash. chpts.), Scottish Rite (Hartford), Sphinx Shrine (Hartford). Republican. Methodist. Home: 12140 Carnegie Dr Tracy CA 95376-9149

GREEN, CYRIL KENNETH, retired retail company executive; b. Portland, Oreg., June 11, 1931; s. Lionel and Nora Evelyn (Walker) G.; m. Beverly Ann Hutchinson, July 24, 1950; children: Kenneth James, Teri Ann, Tamara Jo Green Easton, Kelly Denise Green Van Horn. Student pub. schs., Portland. Salesperson Fred Meyer Inc., Portland, Oreg., 1947-53, mgr. food dept., 1953-57, supr. food div., 1957-60, buyer food div., 1960-64, head buyer food div., 1964-67; gen. mgr. Roundup Co. subs. Fred Meyer Inc., Spokane, Wash., 1967-70; dir. ops. Fred Meyer Inc., Portland, Oreg., 1970-72, pres., 1972-96, chief operating officer, 1972-96; ret. Fred Meyer Inc., Portland, 1996; vice chmn., bd. dirs. Oreg. Trail chpt. ARC, Portland, 1984-89; bd. dirs. Marylhurst Coll., Portland, 1987—.

GREEN, DANIEL FRED, forester; b. Seattle, Feb. 28, 1947; s. Fred Davis and Rowena Anne (Pratt) G.; m. Janice Marie Bachman, Sept. 9, 1967 (div. 1979); children: Kelly Colleen, Wendy Alicia; m. Susan Dell Plaisance, Dec. 28, 1984. BS in Forest Mgmt., Oreg. State U., 1969; MS in Forest Sci., U. Idaho, 1976. Forester Oreg. State Forestry Dept., Forest Grove, 1971-73; Millicoma area forester Oreg. State Forestry Dept., Coos Bay, 1973-76; assoc. prof., extension agt. Oreg. State U., Oregon City, 1976-84; owner Green Tree Farm, Oregon City, 1976—; v.p. Woodland Mgmt. Inc., Lake Oswego, Oreg., 1984—; vis. prof. Tech. Inst. of Costa Rica, Cartago, 1984. Vol., host Experiment in Internat. Living, Oregon City, 1986-93; host World Learning, 1994—; pres. Environ. Learning Ctr., Oregon City, 1978, Environ. Edn. Assn. of Oregn., 1979; chmn. natural resources com. Ptnrs. of the Americas, Oreg. and Costa Rica, 1990-93. Mem. Soc. Am. Foresters (chmn. Portland chpt. 1980, state chmn. 1996), Clackamas County Farm Forestry Assn. (pres. 1986-88), Oreg. State U. Forestry Alumni Bd. (chmn. 1994-97). Republican. Office: Woodland Mgmt Inc Ste 46B 5285 Meadows Rd Lake Oswego OR 97035-3228

GREEN, DAVID LEROY, accountant; b. Pocatello, Idaho, Apr. 27, 1946; s. Urban Lyndon and Rebecca (Jorgensen) G.; m. Tamara Thomson. BS, Brigham Young U., 1970, M in Acctg., 1972. CPA Idaho. Staff acct. M. Green & Co., Tulare, Calif., 1972-75; office mgr. M. Green & Co., Coalinga, Calif., 1974-75; staff acct. Haskins & Sells CPAs, Twin Falls, Idaho, 1975-76; sr. acct. Deloitte Haskins & Sells, Twin Falls, Idaho, 1976-78; mgr. Beckstead Cooper Co., Twin Falls, Idaho, 1978-81; mgr. Beckstead Cooper Jiroves, Las Vegas, Nev., 1981-82, pntr., 1982-83; owner, ptnr. Green, May & Assocs. LLP, Pocatello, 1983—. Mem. AICPA, Idaho Soc. CPAs (chmn. taxation com. 1994-95), Rotary. Home: 444 S 10th Pocatello ID 83201-2613 Office: Green May & Assocs LLP 405 W Whitman PO Box 247 Pocatello ID 83204

GREEN, DAVID OLIVER, JR., sculptor, designer; b. Enid, Okla., June 29, 1908; s. David Oliver Green and Ina (Christmas) McBride; m. Jaxine Rhodes Green, Aug. 20, 1929 (dec. Dec. 1983); m. Lilian Stone DeLey, Mar. 15, 1986 (dec. May 1986). Student, Am. Acad. Art, Chgo., 1926, Nat. Acad. Art, 1927. Letterer Nat. Playhouses, Chgo., 1925-30; with lettering/layout Chgo. Herald-Examiner, Chgo., 1931-32; freelance designer London Guarantee Bldg., Chgo., 1932-33; layout artist Charles Daniel Frey Advt., Chgo., 1933-36; package designer Sears Roebuck, Chgo., 1936-37; art dir. advt. Mills Industries, Chgo., 1947-40; prodn. illustrator McDonald Douglas Aircraft, Long Beach, Calif., 1940-42; draftsman Calif. Inst. Tech., Pasadena, Calif., 1943-45; prof. sculpture Otis Art Inst., L.A., 1946-69; Prin. works include Altadena Libr. Bldg., Calif., Lytton Savs. and Loan, Hollywood, Calif.; author: La Partida/The Contest, 1957. Recipient Golden Crown award Pasadena Arts Coun., 1984. Mem. Pasadena Soc. Artists, Soc. for Calligraphy, Pasadena Photochrome Soc. Home and Studio: 176 Jaxine Dr Altadena CA 91001-3818

GREEN, FRANCIS WILLIAM, investment consultant, former missile scientist; b. Locust Grove, Okla., Mar. 17, 1920; s. Noel Francis and Mary (Lincoln) G.; B.S., Phoenix U., 1955; M.S. in Elec. Engrng., Minerva U., Milan, Italy, 1959; M.S. in Engrng., West Coast U., Los Angeles, 1965; m. Alma J. Ellison, Aug. 26, 1950 (dec. Sept. 1970); children: Sharmon, Rhonda; m. Susan G. Mathis, July 14, 1973 (div. July 1979). With USN Guided Missile Program, 1945-49; design and electronic project engr. Falcon missile program Hughes Aircraft Co., Culver City, Calif., 1949-55; sr. electronic engr. Atlas missile program Convair Astronautics, San Diego, 1955-59; sr. engr. Polaris missile program Nortronics div. Northrop, Anaheim, Calif., 1959-60; chief, supr. electronic engr. data systems br. Tech. Support div. Rocket Propulsion Lab., USAF, Edwards AFB, Calif., 1960-67, dep. chief tech. support div., 1967-69; tech. adviser Air Force Missile Devel. Ctr., Holloman AFB, N.Mex., 1969-70, 6585 Test Group, Air Force Spl. Weapons Ctr., Holloman AFB, from 1970; pvt. investment cons., 1978—. Bd. examiners U.S. CSC; mem. Pres.'s Missile Site Labor Relations Com.; cons. advanced computer and data processing tech. and systems engring.; mem. USAF Civilian Policy Bd. and Range Comdrs. Coun; brig. gen., comdr. 2d brigrade State Milit. Forces; comdr. State Mil. Forces, 1989—; mem. Nat. Guard Assn. U.S. Served as pilot USAAF, 1941-45. Fellow Am. Inst. Aeros. and Astronautics; mem. IEEE, Nat. Assn. Flight Instrs. Contbr. articles to profl. jours. Home and Office: 2345 Apache Ln Alamogordo NM 88310-4851

GREEN, JACK, geology educator; b. Poughkeepsie, N.Y., June 19, 1925; s. Louis and Marie (Harris) G.; m. Renee Jean Utley, Sept. 21, 1952; children: Kathy, Jeffrey, Nathan, Teresa, Terrence, Ronald. BS, Va. Poly. Inst. and State U., Blacksburg, 1950; PhD, Columbia U., 1954. Registered geologist, Calif. Geologist Std. of Calif., La Habra, 1953-59; rsch. geologist Rockwell Internat., Downey, Calif., 1959-65, McDonnell Douglas Corp., Huntington Beach, Calif., 1965-70; prof. geology Calif. State U., Long Beach, 1970—; cons. in field; mem. adv. com. Idaho Nat. Engrng. Lab., 1990—; lectr. in field. Sr. editor: Atlas of Volcanic Landforms, 1971. With U.S. Army, 1943-46. NASA grantee, 1972, fellow, 1981; invitee geothermal rsch. grp. Peoples Rep. of China, Tibet, 1984. Mem. Am. Astron. Soc. Home: 941 Via Nogales Palos Verdes Peninsula CA 90274-1661 Office: Calif State U Long Beach Dept Geolog Scis Long Beach CA 90840

GREEN, JAMES CRAIG, retired data systems company executive; b. Gladstone, Mich., Apr. 19, 1933; s. Albert Keene and Margaret Josephine (Craig) G.; student Coll. of Gt. Falls, 1951-53, UCLA, 1962; m. Catherine Maxwell, Nov. 1, 1957; children: Cindi, Shelley, Nancy, James W., Robert. Clk., carrier U.S. Post Office, Gt. Falls, Mont., 1951-57; clk. office and sales Mont. Liquor Control Bd., Gt. Falls, 1957-59; payroll clk. Herald Examiner, Hearst Publs., L.A., 1959-67, data processing mgr., 1967-75, data processing ops. mgr. corp. hdqrs. Hearst Publs., N.Y.C., 1975-78; gen. mgr., v.p. Computer/Data Inc., Billings, Mont., 1978-83; mgr. customer service Big Sky Data Systems, Billings, Mont., 1983-84; pres. FACTS, Inc., 1985-95; tax cons., L.A., 1962-75. Cub Scout leader, com. chmn., L.A. coun. Boy Scouts Am., 1973-75; pres. Bus. Office Employees Assn. L.A., 1963-66. Area commr. Black Otter coun. Boy Scouts Am., 1982-84, com. chmn., 1982-84; exec. bd. dirs. Family Svcs. Inc.; bd. dirs. Big Sky Air Show 1990—; sec. Yellowstone Valley Model Railway; bd. govs. Spokane unit Shrine Hosp. Crippled Children, 1993—, hosp. chmn. Al Bedoo Shrine, 1992—. With USNR, 1951-59. Recipient degree of Chevalier, De Molay Cross of Honor, Legion of Honor degree.; cert. data processing mgr. Mem. Data Processing Mgrs. Assn., Rainbow Girls Grand Cross of Colors Shrine, L.A. Masonic Press Club. Clubs: Masons, Blue Lodge, York Rite, Scottish Rite, Shrine, Grotto (charter mem. Gt. Falls), DeMolay (chpt. advisor 1983-92, state advisor 1982-92). Writer, negotiator contract Bus. Office Employees Assn., L.A., 1965.

GREEN, JOANTA HERMION, electrical engineer; b. Cleve., Nov. 14, 1960; d. Joseph Ezkiel and Clarece Hermion (Marshall) G. BS in Chemistry and Biology, U. Md., 1983; MS in Econ. Devel., N.H. Coll., 1987; postgrad., U. Malaya, Kuala Lumpur, Malaysia, 1990; PhD in Energy Systems, U. Edinburgh, Scotland, 1992. Lab. tech. USDA, 1980-83; dep. headmistress, tchr. Chepareria (West Pokot, Kenya) Girl's Secondary Sch., 1983-86; project engr. renewable energy R & D div. Bechtel Group Inc., San Francisco, 1992-95; owner J.H. Green Enterprises, Sausalito, Calif., 1995—; ind. expert spl. energy program Deutsche Gesellschaft für Technische Zusammenarbeit GmbH, Eschborn, Germany, 1990-92; vis. fellow energy program Asian and Pacific Devel. Ctr., Kuala Lumpur, 1990-91; rsch. assoc. environmentally compatible energy strategies project Internat. Inst. Applied Systems Analysis Laxenburg, Austria, 1991-92; presenter in field. Contbr. articles to profl. publs. Mem. AAAS, Assn. Energy Engrs., Inst. Energy (U.K.), NAFE. Office: J H Green Enterprises 338 Sausalito Blvd Sausalito CA 94965-2327

GREEN, JOEY, writer; b. Miami, Fla., May 26, 1958; s. Robert Morris and Barbara Sandra Green; m. Deborah Ann White, Sept. 7, 1987; children: Ashley, Julia. BFA, Cornell U., 1980. Contbg. editor Nat. Lampoon, N.Y.C., 1981-83, Spy mag., N.Y.C., 1985-87; copywriter J. Walter Thompson USA, N.Y.C., 1983-85; Hong Kong, 1988; sr. copywriter Walt Disney World, Orlando, Fla., 1990-91. Author: Cornell Widow Hundredth Anniversary Anthology, 1981, Hellbent on Insanity, 1983, The Unofficial Gilligan's Island Handbook, 1987, The Get Smart Handbook, 1993, The Partridge Family Album, 1994, Polish Your Furniture with Panty Hose, 1995, Selling Out, 1996, Hi Bob!, 1996, Paint Your House with Powdered Milk, 1996, Wash Your Hair with Whipped Cream, 1997; TV appearances on The Today Show, 1995, 96, The Tonight Show with Jay Leno, 1996, CBS This Morning, 1996, George & Alana, 1996, Caryl & Marilyn, 1997. Recipient Clio award, 1983. Mem. ACLU, Greenpeace. Democrat.

GREEN, JONATHAN WILLIAM, museum administrator and educator, artist, author; b. Troy, N.Y., Sept. 26, 1939; s. Alan Singer and Frances (Katz) G.; m. Louise Lockshin, Sept. 16, 1962 (div. 1985); children: Raphael, Benjamin; m. Wendy Hughes Brown, Aug. 12, 1988. Student, MIT, 1958-60, Hebrew U., 1960-61; BA, Brandeis U., 1963, postgrad., 1964-67; MA, Harvard U., 1967. Photographer Jonathan Green, Photography, Boston, 1966-76, Ezra Stoller Assocs., Mamaroneck, N.Y., 1967-68; prof. MIT, Cambridge, Mass., 1968-76; dir. Creative Photography Lab MIT, Cambridge, 1974-76; editor Aperture Books and Periodical, N.Y.C., 1972-76; prof. Ohio State U., Columbus, 1976-90; dir. Univ. Gallery Fine Arts, Columbus, 1981-90; founding dir. Wexner Ctr. for the Arts, Columbus, 1981-90; dir. Calif. Mus. Photography, U. Calif., Riverside, 1990—, prof., 1990—; cons. Nat. Endowment for Arts, Washington, 1975-76, 85, 88, 94, Harry N. Abrams, Pubs., N.Y.C., 1982-84, Oxford U. Press, N.Y.C., 1977-82, Polaroid Corp., Cambridge, 1976; co-founder Visible Lang. Workshop, MIT Media Lab., 1973. Author: American Photography, 1984 (Nikon Book of Yr. award 1984, Benjamin Citation 1986), The Snapshot, 1974 (N.Y. Type Dirs. Club award 1974), Camera Work: A Critical Anthology, 1973 (Best Art Book award 1973); editor, essayist Re-framing History in Jean Ruiter Photo Works, 1985-1995, 1996, The Garden of Earthly Delights: Photographs by Edward Weston and Robert Mapplethorpe, 1995, New Photographs by Pedro Meyer: Truths & Fictions, An Interactive CD-ROM, 1993, 5 Celebrations of Leslie J. Payne in Leslie Payne: Visions of Flight, 1991, Algorithms for Discovery, 1989, Pink Noise: Three Conversations concerning a Collaborative acoustic Installation with Philip Glass, Richard Serra, Kurt Munacsi, 1987, Rudolf Baranik Elegies: Sleep Napalm Night Sky, 1987, Straight Shooting in America, 1985, James Friedman: Rephotographing the History of the World in James Friedman, Color Photographs 1979-1982, 1982, Aperture in the 50's: The Word and the Way, in Afterimage, 1979, others; represented in permanent collections Mus. Fine Arts, Boston, Mus. Fine Art, Houston, Cleve. Mus. Art, Va. Mus. Fine Art, Richmond, Princeton U. Art Mus., Bell System Collection, Moderna Museet, Stockholm, Ctr. for Creative Photography, Tucson, De Saisset Art Gallery and Mus., Internat. Ctr. Photography, N.Y.C., MIT, Mpls. Inst. Arts; photographs pub.: American Images: New Work by Twenty Contemporary Photographers, 1979, Aperture, 1972, 73, 74, 25 Years of Record Houses, 1981, Architectural Record, Architecture and Urbanism, Progressive Architecture, A Field Guide to Modern American Architecture. Danforth fellow, 1963-67, NEA Photographer fellow, 1978, AT & T fellow, 1979. Office: California Museum Of Photography Downtown Hist Pedestrian Mall 3824 Main St Riverside CA 92501-3624

GREEN, KATHERINE ELIZABETH, federal agency administrator; b. Seattle, Mar. 30, 1940; d. James Ellis and Sarah Katherine (Morgenroth) Flaherty; m. William Charles Green, Feb. 14, 1971; 1 child, Brian Patrick. AB in Psychology, Whitman Coll., 1962. Claims and field rep. Social Security Adminstrn., San Francisco, 1962-68; ops. supr. Social Security Adminstrn., Walnut Creek, Calif., 1968-69; health ins. specialist Social Security Adminstrn., Balt., 1969-71; ops. supr. Social Security Adminstrn., San Francisco, 1971-72, tng. specialist, 1972-74, quality appraisal/mgmt. info. mgr., 1974-76, fin. mgmt. officer, 1977-91, tng. officer, 1991—. Rschr., compiler book: The Descendants of Patrick and Barbara (Scanlon) Flaherty, 1992. Mem. Sch. Site Coun., Brisbane, Calif., 1984-91, 93-96, chair, 1992-93. Mem. New Eng. Hist. Geneal. Soc., Minn. State Hist. Soc., Ind. State Hist. Soc., Mothers' Club St. Ignatius H.S. Democrat. Roman Catholic. Office: Social Security Adminstrn 75 Hawthorne St San Francisco CA 94105-3919

GREEN, KENNETH NORTON, lawyer, law educator; b. Chgo., Mar. 18, 1938; s. Martin and Sarah (Owens) G.; m. Joan Nemer, Oct. 17, 1968 (div. July 1974); 1 child, Joey. AA, Wright Jr. Coll., 1960; BA, Calif. State U., Los Angeles, 1963; postgrad. Southwestern U., 1965-67; JD, U. San Fernando Valley, 1968; Cert. (hon. teaching) Los Angeles Unified Sch. Dist., 1979. Bar: Calif. 1970, U.S. Dist. Ct. (cen. dist.) Calif. 1970, U.S. Supreme Ct. 1973. Tchr. Los Angeles, Calif., 1964-70; dep. pub. defender Los Angeles County, Calif., 1970-73, 75—; ptnr. Green & Pirosh, Los Angeles, 1973-75; chief pub. defender, 1989; instr. Paralegal dept. U. Calif., Los Angeles, 1975—; judge pro tem Los Angeles Mcpl. Ct., 1978. Contbr. articles to legal publs. Ex officio mem. Prison Preventers, Calif. Dept. of Parole; mayor's com. Project Heavy; bd. dirs. City of Hope; Vista Del Mar; legal adv. panel Jewish Family Service; vol. atty. for indigents UCLA Law Sch.; vol. in Parole Program, com. chmn. Research Prejudice-Pvt. Clubs (Disting. Service award 1971). Served with U.S. Army, 1957-58, Korea. Mem. Pub. Defender Assn. (dir. 1971-74, chief wage negotiator 1973-75) ABA, Los Angeles County Bar Assn. (vice chmn. drug abuse 1975, exec. com. criminal justice 1977). Democrat. Jewish. Lodge: Justice (bd. dirs. 1971-72). Office: Pub Defender Los Angeles County 210 W Temple St Los Angeles CA 90012-3210

GREEN, MARC EDWARD, editor; b. Cleve., Mar. 11, 1943; s. Emery S. and Aileen (Goldman) G.; m. Ellen Wilson, June 29, 1969; children: Alec, Matthew. BA, Amherst Coll., 1965; MA, Harvard U., 1966. Instr. in English George Washington U., Washington, 1971-74; screenwriter Warner Bros., Sydney Pollack Prodn., Martin Ransahoff Prodn., L.A., CBS/Paramount, Tri-Star Pictures, others, L.A., 1970-92; adminstr./editor Nat. Health Law Program, L.A., 1982-87; editor The Grantsmanship Ctr., L.A., 1991—. Co-author: Hollywood Dynasties, 1984, Outrageous Conduct, 1988, Hollywood on the Couch, 1993. Mem. Writers Guild of Am. Office: The Grantsmanship Ctr 1125 W 6th St Los Angeles CA 90017-1811

GREEN, MARJORIE JOAN, elementary education educator; b. Sacramento, Apr. 8, 1938; d. Albert Robertson and Mabel Elizabeth (Wallington) Oughton; m. Norman Everett Green, Mar. 22, 1959; children: Scott Allan, Victoria Elizabeth Green-Spicer. BA, Calif. State U., Sacramento, 1960, MA, 1981. Cert. gen. edn. tchr., lang. devel. specialist, reading specialist, adminstr., Calif. Classroom tchr., reading recovery/title I tchr. San Juan Unified Sch. Dist., Carmichael, Calif., 1967-71, 91-96, reading specialist, 1971-91. Author: (curriculum guide) On the Write Track with Spelling, 1992, Teacher to Teacher: A Professional's Handbook, 1993. Bd. dirs. Fair Oaks (Calif.) Theater Festival, 1984-89, Concert Dance Found., Carmichael, 1976-79, Capital Cadets, Sacramento, 1974-76. Mem. Internat. Reading Assn., Calif. Reading Assn., Sacramento Area Reading Assn. (rec. sec. 1986-87, bd. dirs. 1980-82). Lutheran. Office: Carmichael Sch 6141 Sutter Ave Carmichael CA 95608-2738

GREEN, MARK, mayor. Mayor Union City, Calif. Address: 34009 Alvarado Niles Rd Union City CA 94587

GREEN, MELANIE JANE, speech-language pathologist; b. Fremont, Calif., Nov. 23, 1968; d. Robert Lucian and Frances Eileen (Jones) G. BA in Communicative Disorders, Calif. State U., Fullerton, 1992; MS in Speech Lang. Pathology, U. Redlands, 1994. Child care coord. Calvary Chapel of Fullerton (Calif.), 1986-87; speech pathologist aide Providence Speech and Hearing Ctr., Orange, Calif., 1988-90; activities asst. Western Neuro Care Ctr., Tustin, Calif., 1989-90; speech-lang. pathology paraprofl. Long Beach, Calif., 1990—; speech-lang. pathologist Newport Lang., Speech, and Audiology Ctr., Newport Beach, 1994—. Mem. Autism Soc. Am., Am. Speech and Hearing Assn. Home: PO Box 5679 Newport Beach CA 92662-5679

GREEN, MICHAEL FOSTER, neuropsychologist, educator; b. Sewickley, Pa., July 5, 1956; s. Max J. and Victoria Lia (Grunberg) G. BA, Oberlin Coll., 1979; PhD, Cornell U., 1984. Assoc prof. UCLA, 1992-96, prof., 1996—; health sci. specialist West L.A. VA Hosp., 1992—. Editl. bd. Cognitive Neuropsychiatry; contbr. numerous articles to profl. jours. Grantee NIMH, 1988-94, 96—, Janssen Rsch. Found., 1993—. Mem. Am. Psychol. Soc., Soc. Rsch. Psychopathology (exec. bd. 1995—), Internat. Neuropsychol. Soc. Office: UCLA Neuropsychiat Inst 760 Westwood Plz Los Angeles CA 90024-1759

GREEN, MICHAEL SCOTT, history educator, consultant, columnist; b. Santa Monica, Calif., Mar. 27, 1965; s. Robert W. and Marsha (Greene) G. BA with hons., U. Nev., 1986, MA, 1988; MPhil, Columbia U., 1990. Tchg. asst. U. Nev., Las Vegas, 1986-88, adj. instr., 1988-91; adj. instr. C.C. So. Nev., N. Las Vegas, Nev., 1987-95; tchg. asst. Columbia U., 1989-90; instr. C.C. So. Nev., N. Las Vegas, Nev., 1995—; polit. cons. A "Track"tions Campaign Conductors, Las Vegas, 1994—; columnist Nevada's Washington Watch, Washington, 1996—. Editor: (with Gary E. Elliott) Nevada: Readings and Perspectives, 1997; contbr. articles to profl. jours., chpts. to books. Spkr. Leadership Las Vegas, 1994—; spkr., exhibit author Clark County Heritage Mus., Henderson, Nev., 1990—. Rsch. fellow The Huntington Libr., 1992, 93, Ball Bros. Found., 1992, Pres.'s fellow Columbia U., 1988. Mem. Am. Hist. Assn., Orgn. Am. Historians, We. History Assn., Nev. Hist. Soc., Far West Popular Am. Culture Assn., Phi Kappa Phi, Phi Alpha Theta. Democrat. Office: C C So Nev 3200 E Cheyenne Ave North Las Vegas NV 89030

GREEN, PAUL CECIL, management consultant; b. Oconto, Nebr., Sept. 8, 1919; s. Paul Simpson Green and Ruth Adelaide (Kennedy) Elder; m. Carole Jean Pass, Dec. 21, 1964. BSBA, U. Nebr., 1941; MBA, Harvard U., 1948. CLU. Dir. sales Continental Assurance Co., Chgo., 1948-62, v.p. mktg., 1962-73; v.p. mktg. USLIFE Corp., N.Y.C., 1973-75; sr. v.p. Helmich, Miller and Pasek, Inc., Chgo., 1975-81; pres. Paul C. Green and Assocs., Ltd., Green Valley, Ariz., 1981—; chmn. bd. CLU Jour., Bryn Mar, Pa.

Contbr. articles to profl. jours. Precinct capt. Young Repubs., Chgo.; bd. dirs. Green Valley Recreation, Inc.; exec. bd. Green Valley Coordinating Council; pres. Foothills IV Homeowners Assn., Green Valley. Lt. col. USAF, 1942-46. Recipient Achievement award City of Hope, 1977, 78. Mem. Am. Soc. Chartered Life Underwriters, Internat. Assn. Fin. Planners, Life Ins. Mktg. and Research Assn. (chmn. various coms.), Harvard Bus. Sch. Club (Phoenix chpt.), Country Club of Green Valley. Presbyterian. Home: 551 S Paseo Del Cobre Green Valley AZ 85614-2321 Office: PO Box 1448 Green Valley AZ 85622-1448

GREEN, RONNIE DAVID, education educator; b. Roanoke, Va., June 17, 1961; s. Charles M. and Frances Evelyn (Cahoon) G.; m. Jane O. Pauley, Aug. 2, 1986; children: Justin Lucas, Benjamin Nathaniel, Kelli Noelle, Regan Emily. BS, Va. Polytech. Inst., Blacksburg, Va., 1983; MS, Colo. State U., 1985; PhD, U. Nebr., 1988. Grad. asst. Colo. State U., Ft. Collins, 1983-85, U. Nebr., Lincoln, 1985-88; asst. prof. Tex. Tech. U., Lubbock, 1988-94; assoc. prof. Colo. State U., 1994—. Contbr. articles to profl. jours. Pres. Lubbock Presbyn. Community Ch., 1991-93; ordained elder, vocal soloist Westminster Presbyn. Ch., Lubbock, 1988-94; youth leader Wellington (Colo.) Fed. Ch. Rsch. grantee, 1988-96. Mem. Am. Soc. Animal Sci. (Disting. Tchr. award 1996), Nat. Block and Bridle Club (nat. v.p. 1995—), Nat. Beef Cattlemen's Assn., U.S. Beef Improvement Fedn. (chmn.), Colo. Cattlemen's Assn. Office: Colo State Univ Dept Animal Scis Fort Collins CO 80523

GREEN, VICKIE LEE, gifted and talented educator, music educator; b. Sterling, Colo., Sept. 28, 1954; d. Victor Eugene and Beth Arlene (Hunter) Hanson; m. James Harvey Green, Aug. 6, 1976; 1 child, Erich Alan. B in Music Edn., U. Denver, 1976, MA in Gifted and Talented Edn., 1988. Cert. music edn. tchr., Colo. Elem. vocal tchr. East Otero R-1 Sch. Dist., La Junta, Colo., 1976-83; tchr. music Morgan C.C., Ft. Morgan, Colo., 1983-84; mid. sch. band and vocal tchr. Sch. Dist. RE-3, Ft. Morgan, 1984-89, elem. vocal tchr., 1989-91; elem. music and vocal tchr. Weld 6, Greeley, Colo., 1991—; cons. gifted edn. Colo. Dept. Edn., Denver, 1989-91; mem. artist-in-residence program Colo. Coun. Arts and Humanities, Denver, 1984. Mem. NEA, Nat. Assn. for Gifted Children, Colo. Assn. for Gifted and Talented, Colo. Music Educators Assn., Colo. Edn. Assn., Music Educators Nat. Conf., Greeley Edn. Assn. Home: 2318 Sunset Ln Greeley CO 80631-7608 Office: Meeker Elem Sch 2221 28th Ave Greeley CO 80631-7650

GREEN, WILLIAM PORTER, lawyer; b. Jacksonville, Ill., Mar. 19, 1920; s. Hugh Parker and Clara Belle (Hopper) G.; m. Rose Marie Hall, Oct. 1, 1944; children: Hugh Michael, Robert Alan, Richard William. BA, Ill. Coll., 1941; JD, Northwestern U., Evanston, Ill., 1947. Bar: Ill. 1947, Calif. 1948, U.S. Dist. Ct. (so. dist.) Tex. 1986, U.S. Ct. Customs and Patent Appeals, U.S. Patent and Trademark Office 1948, U.S. Ct. Appeals (fed. cir.) 1982, U.S. Ct. Appeals (5th and 9th cir.), U.S. Supreme Ct. 1948, U.S. Dist. Ct. (cen. dist.) Calif. 1949, (so. dist.) Tex.1986. Pvt. practice L.A., 1947—; mem. Wills, Green & Mueth, L.A., 1974-83; of counsel Nilsson, Robbins, Dalgarn, Berliner, Carson & Wurst, L.A., 1984-91; of counsel Nilsson, Wurst & Green L.A., 1992—; del. Calif. State Bar Conv., 1982—, chmn., 1986. Bd. editors Ill. Law Rev., 1946; patentee in field. Mem. L.A. world Affairs Coun., 1975—; deacon local Presbyn. Ch., 1961-63. Mem. ABA, Calif. State Bar, Am. Intellectual Property Law Assn., L.A. Patent Law Assn. (past. sec.-treas., mem. bd. govs.), Lawyers Club L.A. (past treas., past sec., mem. bd. govs., pres. 1985-86), Los Angeles County Bar Assn. (trustee 1986-87), Am. Legion (past post comdr.), Northwestern U. Alumni Club So. Calif., Big Ten Club So. Calif., Town Hall Calif. Club, PGA West Golf Club (La Quinta, Calif.), Phi Beta Kappa, Phi Delta Phi, Phi Alpha. Republican. Home: 3570 Lombardy Rd Pasadena CA 91107-5627 Office: 707 Wilshire Blvd Ste 3200 Los Angeles CA 90017-3514

GREENAGEL, DEBRA, travel agency executive; b. Beach, N.D., Aug. 13; d. Robert W. and Lucille (Booke) Taylor; m. David K. Greenagel, Sept. 11, 1976; children: Jessica, Jack. BA, Moorhead State U., 1972. Hostess Braniff Airlines, Dallas, 1973-82; acct. mgr. Talent Tree, Englewood, Colo., 1983-88; v.p. sales Corp. Travel Svcs., Englewood, 1988-91, Camelot Travel Svcs., Englewood, 1991—; mem. adv. bd. Nat. Car Rental, Mpls., 1996—, United Airlines Career Sch., Denver, 1996—. Vol. Kerpe Ctr. for Battered and Abused Children, 1993-95. Mem. Nat. Bus. Execs. (pres. 1990-91), Am. Soc. Assn. Execs., Jr. League Denver, South Metro C. of C., Rocky Mountain Bus. Travel (bd. dirs. 1995—), Gamma Phi Beta. Office: Camelot Travel Svcs 8231 E Prentice Ave Englewood CO 80111

GREENAWALD, GLENN DALE, social studies trainer, curriculum developer, researcher; b. Pitts., May 26, 1947; s. Glenn Victor and June (Scheller) G. BA, U. Pitts., 1969; MA, U. Minn., 1973; DA, Carnegie-Mellon U., 1978. Cert. social studies tchr., Pa. Tchr. Anoka (Minn.)-Hennepin Sch. Dist., 1969-70, Hempfield Sch. Dist., Greensburg, Pa., 1970-75; teaching asst., rsch. asst. Carnegie-Mellon U., Pitts., 1975-78; staff assoc. Social Sci. Edn. Consortium, Boulder, Colo., 1978-82, 87-91; dir. social studies W.Va. Dept. Edn., Charleston, 1982-85; dir. Learning Improvement Svcs., Nederland, Colo., 1985—; dir. Ctr. for Teaching Social Sci. U. No. Colo., Greeley, 1991-93; exec. dir. Colo. Close Up, 1985—. Author: (with Betty Dillon Peterson) Staff Development in the Social Studies, 1979, Washington Close Up Current Issues Teachers Guide, 1990, The Railroad Era, 1991. Mem. Amnesty Internat., Sierra Club, Legal Def. Fund, Colo. Mountain Club. Recipient numerous grants. Mem. ASCD, Nat. Coun. for Social Studies (chmn. archives com. 1990—, co-chmn. citizenship com. 1981), Coun. of State Social Studies Specialists; Coll. and Univ. Faculty Assembly, Social Studies Specialist Assn., Wash. Coun. for Social Studies, Minn. Coun. for Social Studies, Colo. Coun. for Social Studies (regional dir. 1992, pres. 1994-96), Phi Delta Kappa. Home and Office: Box 681 Nederland CO 80466

GREENAWALT, SHIRLEY POMERINKE, church youth director; b. Spokane, Wash., July 16, 1955; d. Leonard Gordon and Stella Eileen (Binford) Pomerinke; m. Kirk Douglas Greenawalt, Dec. 27, 1980; 1 child, Jason Michael. Student, Lewis-Clark State Coll., 1973-80; BA, McNeese State U., Lake Charles, La., 1982; postgrad., Okla. State U., 1991-94; tchg. cert., U. Idaho, 1995. Typist clk. III, music libr. McNeese State U., Lake Charles, La., 1983; mgr. video librs., libr. video libr. Jubail (Saudi Arabia) Video Club, 1984-87; Calvert corr. tchr. Jubail, 1988-91, 91-93; tchr. knitting and crochet Saudi Ladies Charitable Soc., Jubail, 1988, tchr. volleyball and mus. games, 1989; substitute tchr. K-8 Weslyan Christian Sch., 1990-91; substitute tchr. K-12 Okla. Sch. Dist., 1990-91; tchr. Jubail Acad., S.A.I.S. Dist., 1993-94; youth dir. 4th-6th grade Grace Luth. Ch., Lewiston, Idaho, 1996—; substitute tchr. Lewiston and Lapwai (Idaho) Sch. Dists.; creator, implementor study skills class 7th grade level, 1993-94; tutor students English grammer, spelling, reading, composition and math. Sunday sch. tchr., Vacation Bible Sch. dir. Grace Luth. Ch., Lewiston, Idaho, 1995-97; sec. McSorley PTA, 1995-96; sec.-treas. Sadaf Ladies Group, Jubail, 1989-90; scorekeeper Tee-Ball, 1991-92, 92-93, 93-94. Recipient Golden Key award, 1993. Mem. Interval Internat. Home: 602 22nd Ave Lewiston ID 83501-3846

GREENBAUM, ALAN HOWARD, rabbi; b. L.A., Nov. 13, 1949; s. Wilbert Jacob and Dorothy Rose (Fabian) G.;

GREENBERG, ARNOLD ELIHU, water quality specialist; b. Bklyn., Apr. 13, 1926; s. Samuel and Minnie (Gurevitz) G.; m. Shirley E. Singer, Aug. 2, 1952; children: Noah J., Seth M. BS, CCNY, 1947; MS, U. Wis., 1948; SM, MIT, 1950; postgrad., U. Calif., Berkeley, 1970-75. Rsch. engr., biologist U. Calif., Berkeley, 1950-54; asst. chief labs. Calif. Dept. Health Svcs., Berkeley, 1954-82; lab. mgr. East Bay Mcpl. Utility Dist., Oakland, Calif., 1982-91; cons., 1991—; instr. in engring. extension U. Calif., 1963—; instr. Contra Costa Coll., San Pablo, Calif., 1968-82; cons. Lawrence Berkeley Lab., 1973-84; vis. fellow Israel Inst. Tech., Haifa, 1981. Editor: Standard Methods for the Examination of Water and Wastewater, 1971, 75, 81, 85, 89, 92, 95, Laboratory Procedures for the Examination of Seawater & Shellfish, 1985. Col. USPHS, 1955—. Recipient APHA award for excellence, 1993. Mem. APHA, Am. Acad. Microbiology, Am. Water Works Assn. (hon.).

GREENBERG, BARRY MICHAEL, talent executive; b. Bklyn., Nov. 9, 1951; s. Aaron Herbert and Alice Rhoda (Strauss) G.; m. Susan Kay Greenberg, Feb. 19, 1990; 1 child, Samuel Jacob; 1 child by previous marriage: Seth Grahame-Smith. BA, Antioch U. Dir. B'nai B'rith, Phila., 1976-80; acting dir. Jewish Nat. Fund, L.A., 1980-81; chmn. Celebrity Connection, Beverly Hills, Calif., 1981—; co-founder Beverly Hills Air Force Co.; ptnr. emeritus U.S. Film Force Co. Mem. Air Force adv. bd. USAF; mem. Wilshire Community police adv. bd. L.A. Police Dept.; mem. 50th Anniversary of WWII com. U.S. Dept. Def.; mem. pub. safety steering com. L.A. 4th Councilmatic Dist.; mem. exec. bd. CDC Bus. Responds to AIDS program; co-founder Windsor Watch; bd. dirs. Windsor Sq. Assn.; charter past pres. entertainment industry unit B'nai B'rith. With USAF, 1969-75. Mem. Def. Orientation Conf. Assn., Air Force Pub. Affairs Alumni Assn. Jewish. Office: Celebrity Connection 8306 Wilshire Blvd # 2659 Beverly Hills CA 90211-2382

GREENBERG, BYRON STANLEY, newspaper and business executive, consultant; b. Bklyn., June 17, 1919; s. Albert and Bertha (Getleson) G.; m. Helena Marks, Feb. 10, 1946; children: David, Eric, Randy. Student, Bklyn. Coll., 1936-41. Circulation mgr. N.Y. Post, 1956-62, circulation dir., 1962-63, bus. mgr., 1963-72, gen. mgr., dir., 1973-79; sec., dir. N.Y. Post Corp., 1966-75, treas., dir., 1975-76, v.p., 1976-81; v.p., dir. Leisure Systems, Inc., 1978-80; pres., chief exec. officer, dir. Games Mgmt. Services, Inc., 1979-80. Bd. dirs. 92d St YMHA, 1970-71, Friars Nat. Found., 1981-82. Served with AUS, 1942-45. Mem. Friars Club. Home and Office: 2560 S Grade Rd Alpine CA 91901-3612

GREENBERG, MORTON PAUL, lawyer, insurance broker, consultant; b. Fall River, Mass., June 2, 1946; s. Harry and Sylvia Shirley (Davis) G.; m. Louise Beryl Schindler, Jan. 24, 1970; 1 child, Alexis Lynn. BSBA, NYU, 1968; JD, Bklyn. Law Sch., 1971. Bar: N.Y. 1972; CLU Am. Coll., 1975. Atty., Hanner, Fitzmaurice & Onorato, N.Y.C., 1971-72; dir., counsel, cons. on advanced underwriting The Mfrs. Life Ins. Co., Toronto, Ont.,Can., 1972—; mem. sales ideas com. Million Dollar Roundtable, Chgo., 1982-83; 4th ann. George M. Graves meml. lectr., 1991; speaker on law, tax, and advanced underwriting to various profl. groups, U.S., Can. Author: (tech. jour.) ManuBriefs. Mem. ABA, N.Y. State Bar Assn., Assn. for Advanced Life Underwriting (mem. bus. ins. and estate planning steering com., 1989-93), Internat. Platform Assn., Nat. Assn. Life Underwriters , Denver Assn. Life Underwriters, Am. Soc. CLU, NYU Alumni Assn., Stern Sch. Bus. Alumni Assn. Office: 7617 E Sunrise Trl Parker CO 80134-6915

GREENBERG, MYRON SILVER, lawyer; b. L.A., Oct. 17, 1945; s. Earl W. and Geri (Silver) G.; m. Shlomit Gross; children: David, Amy, Sophie, Benjamin. BSBA, UCLA, 1967, JD, 1970. Bar: Calif. 1971, U.S. Dist. Ct. (cen. dist.) Calif. 1971, U.S. Tax Ct. 1977; CPA, Calif. Staff acct. Touche Ross & Co., L.A., 1970-71; assoc. Kaplan, Livingston, Goodwin, Berkowitz, & Selvin, Beverly Hills, 1971-74; ptnr. Dinkelspiel, Pelavin, Steefel & Levitt, San Francisco, 1975-80; ptnr. Steefel, Levitt & Weiss, San Francisco, 1981-82; pres. Myron S. Greenberg, a Profl. Corp., Larkspur, Calif., 1982—; professorial lectr. tax. Golden Gate U.; instr. U. Calif., Berkeley, 1989—. Author: California Attorney's Guide to Professional Corporations, 1977, 79; bd. editors UCLA Law Rev., 1969-70. Mem. San Anselmo Planning Commn., 1976-77; bd. dirs. Bay Area Lawyers for Arts, 1979-80, Marin County chpt. Am. Heart Assn. (bd. dirs., pres. 1984-90); mem. adv. bd. cert. program in personal fin. planning U. Calif., Berkeley, 1991—. Mem. ABA, AICPA, Marin County (Calif.) Bar Assn. (bd. dirs. 1994—, treas. 1996—), Real Estate Tax Inst. of Calif. Continuing Edn. Bar (planning com.), Larkspur C. of C. (bd. dirs. 1985-87). Democrat. Jewish. Office: 700 Larkspur Landing Cir Larkspur CA 94939-1715

GREENBERG, PAMELA THAYER, public policy specialist; b. Denver, May 16, 1959; d. Paul Burton and Betty Mae (Clint) Thayer; m. Alan Greenberg, Aug. 7, 1988. BA, U. Colo., 1981, MS, 1994. Rsch. asst. Nat. Assessment of Ednl. Progress, Denver, 1982-83; rsch. coord. Regis Coll., Denver, 1983-86; sr. policy specialist Nat. Conf. State Legislatures, Denver, 1986—. Author: Guide to Legislative Information Technology, 1995; contbr. articles to profl. jours. Named one of Outstanding Young Women of Am., 1984. Mem. LWV (bd. dirs. 1990-91). Office: Nat Conf State Legislatures 1560 Broadway Ste 700 Denver CO 80202

GREENBERG, ROGER L., plastic and reconstructive surgeon; b. Cedar Rapids, Iowa, Feb. 15, 1936; m. Mary F. BS, U. Mich., 1958; MD, Wayne State U., 1962. Diplomate Am. Bd. Plastic Surgeon. Gen. surgery resident Calif. Pacific Med. Ctr., San Francisco, 1962-67, chmn. dept. plastic surgery, 1979-89; plastic surgery fellow Cronin-Brauer Clinic, Houston, 1967-69; pvt. practice San Francisco, 1969—; chmn. dept. plastic surgery Calif. Pacific Med. Ctr. Contbr. articles to profl. jours. Mem. AMA, Am. Soc. Plastic Surgeons, Calif. Med. Soc., Calif. Soc. Plastic Surgeons (pres. 1993; med. dir. Alliance 1992—), San Francisco Med. Soc. Office: 525 Spruce St San Francisco CA 94118-2616

GREENBERG, STUART S., investment banker; b. N.Y.C., Apr. 10, 1932; s. Morris and Mae (Wichner) G.; m. Maryanne Gillespie, May 22, 1977; children: Mary Ann, Jonathan, Adam, Megan. BA, CCNY, 1954; postgrad., Am. Inst. of Banking, 1960. Account exec. Merrill Lynch, N.Y.C.; nat. sales mgr. duPont Glore Forgan, N.Y.C.; pres. Robert A. McNeil Corp., San Mateo, Calif., Univ. Group, Long Beach, Calif., Calif. Capital Markets Group, San Francisco; vice chmn. Midwest Group of Funds, Cin., 1989-90; pres., CEO M.A. Gillespie Investment Corp., Encino, Calif., 1990—; chmn. Royalty Mgmt. Corp., 1992—, Federated Broker Dealer Svc. Corp., 1996—. Contbr. articles to profl. jours. With U.S. Army. Mem. Securities Industry Assn., Nat. Assn. of Securities Dealers, Braemar Country Club, Internat. Assn. of Fin. Planners (charter mem.), N.Y. Stock Exch. (allied mem.), Regional Investment Bankers Assn. Home: 3935 Corbin Ave Tarzana CA 91356-5618 Office: Baraban Capital Corp 14th Fl 2121 Avenue Of The Stars Fl 14 Los Angeles CA 90067-5010

GREENBERGER, MARTIN, computer and information scientist, educator; b. Elizabeth, N.J., Nov. 30, 1931; s. David and Sidelle (Jonas) G.; A.B., Harvard, 1955, A.M., 1956, Ph.D., 1958; m. Ellen Danica Silver, Feb. 2, 1959 (div. June 1974); children: Kari Edwards, David Silver; m. Liz Attardo, Dec. 11, 1982; children: Beth Jonit, Jonah Ben, Jilly Sal. Teaching fellow, resident adviser, staff mem. Computation Lab., Harvard, Cambridge, 1954-58; mgr. applied sci. IBM, Cambridge, 1956-58; asst. prof. mgmt. Mass. Inst. Tech., Cambridge, 1958-61, assoc. prof., 1961-67; prof., chmn. computer sci., dir. info. processing Johns Hopkins U., Balt., 1967-72, prof. math. scis., sr. research asso. Center for Met. Planning and Research, 1972-75, prof. math. scis., 1978-82; IBM chair in tech. and policy UCLA Anderson Grad. Sch. Mgmt., 1982—; dir. UCLA Ctr. Digital Media, 1995—; pres. Council for Tech. and the Individual, 1985—; mgr. systems program Electric Power Research Inst., Palo Alto, Calif., 1976-77; Isaac Taylor vis. prof. Technion-Israel Inst. Tech., Haifa, 1978-79; vis. prof. Internat. Energy Program, Grad. Sch. Bus., Stanford U., 1980; vis. prof. policy and analysis MIT Media Lab., 1988-89. Mem. computer sci. and engring. bd. NAS, 1970-72; chmn. COSATI rev. group NSF, 1971-72; mem. evaluation com. Internat. Inst. for Applied Systems Analysis, Laxenburg, Austria, 1980; mem. adv. panels, Office Tech. Assessment, GAO, U.S. Congress; cons. IBM, A.T.&T., CBS, Rand Corp., Morgan Guaranty, Arthur D. Little, TRW, Bolt, Beranek & Newman, Brookings Inst., Resources for Future, Electric Power Rsch. Inst., Atlantic Richfield, Rockwell Internat., Security Pacific Corp, John F. Kennedy Sch. of Govt. Harvard U. Mem. overseers' vis. com. Harvard U., 1975-81; founder and mem. working groups Energy Modeling Forum, Stanford U., 1978-81; mem. adv. com. Nat. Center Analysis of Energy Systems Brookhaven Nat. Lab., 1976-80, chmn., 1977; mem. rev. com. Energy and Environment div. Lawrence Berkeley Lab., 1983, applied sci. div., 1986-88; chmn. forum on electronic pub., Washington program Annenberg, 1983-84; co-founder ICC Forum, 1985; chmn. Roundtable in Multimedia, 1990—; trustee Educom, Princeton, N.J., 1969-73, chmn. council, 1969-70. With USAF, 1952-54, USAFR, 1954-60. NSF fellow, 1955-56; Guggenheim fellow U. Calif., Berkeley, 1965-66. Fellow AAAS (v.p., chmn. sect. T 1973-75); mem. Phi Beta Kappa, Sigma Xi. Author: (with Orcutt, Korbel and Rivlin) Microanalysis of Socioeconomic Systems: A Simulation Study, 1961; (with Jones, Morris and Ness) On-Line Computation and Simulation: The OPS-3 System, 1965; (with Crenson and Crissey) Models in the Policy Process: Public Decision Making in the Computer Era, 1976; (with Brewer, Hogan and Russell) Caught Unawares: The Energy Decade in Retrospect, 1983. Editor: Management and The Computer of the Future, 1962, republished as Computers and the World of the Future, 1964; Computers, Communications, and the Public Interest, 1971; (with Aronofsky, McKenney and Massy) Networks for Research and Education, 1973; Electronic Publishing Plus: Media for a Technological Future, 1985, Technologies for the 21st Century, Vol. 1, On Multimedia, 1990, Vol. 3, Multimedia in Review, 1992, Vol. 5, Content and Communication, 1994, Vol. 7, Scaling Up., 1996. Office: UCLA Anderson Grad Sch Mgmt Los Angeles CA 90095-1481

GREENE, ALVIN, service company executive, management consultant; b. Pitts., Aug. 26, 1932; s. Samuel David and Yetta (Kroff) G.; BA, Stanford U., 1954, MBA, 1959; m. M. Louise Sokol, Nov. 11, 1977; children: Sharon, Ami, Ann, Daniel. Asst. to pres. Narmco Industries, Inc., San Diego, 1959-62; adminstrv. mgr., mgr. mktg. Whittaker Corp., L.A., 1962-67; sr. v.p. Cordura Corp., L.A., 1967-75; chmn. bd. Sharon-Sage, Inc., L.A., 1975-79; exec. v.p., chief operating officer Republic Distbrs., Inc., Carson, Calif., 1979-81, also dir.; chief operating officer Memel, Jacobs & Ellsworth, 1981-87, 87—; pres. SCI Cons., Inc.; dir. Sharon-Sage, Inc., True Data Corp.; vis. prof. Am. Grad. Sch. Bus., Phoenix, 1977-81. Chmn. bd. commrs. Housing Authority City of L.A., 1983-88 . Served to 1st lt., U.S. Army, 1955-57. Mem. Direct Mail Assn., Safety Helmet Mfrs. Assn., Bradley Group. Office: 11990 San Vicente Blvd Ste 300 Los Angeles CA 90049-6608

GREENE, FRANK SULLIVAN, JR., investment management executive; b. Washington, Oct. 19, 1938; s. Frank S. Sr. and Irma O. Greene; m. Phyllis Davison, Jan. 1958 (dec. 1984); children: Angela, Frank, Ronald; m. Carolyn W. Greene, Sept. 1990. BS, Washington U., St. Louis, 1961; MS, Purdue U., 1962; PhD, U. Santa Clara, Calif., 1970. Part-time lectr. Washington U., Howard U., Am. U., 1959-65; pres., dir. Tech. Devel. Corp., Arlington, Tex., 1985-92; pres. Zero One Systems, Inc. (formerly Tech. Devel. of Calif.) Santa Clara, Calif., 1971-87, Zero One Systems Group subs. Sterling Software Inc., 1987-89; asst. chmn., lectr. Stanford U., 1972-74; bd. dirs. Networked Picture Systems Inc., 1986-94, pres., 1989-91, chmn., 1991-94; mng. mem. New Vista Capital, LLC, Palo Alto, Calif., 1993-97, mng. mem., 1997—; bd. dirs. Beyond Software, Inc., 1996—. Author two indsl. textbooks; also articles; patentee in field. Bd. dirs. NCCJ, Santa Clara, 1980—, NAACP, San Jose chpt., 1986-89; bd. regents Santa Clara U., 1983-90, trustee, 1990—; mem. adv. bd. Urban League, Santa Clara County, 1986-89, East Side Union High Sch., 1985-88; bd. dirs. Am. Musical Theatre of San Jose, 1995—. Capt. USAF, 1961-65. Mem. IEEE, IEEE Computer Soc. (governing bd. 1973-75), Assn. Black Mfrs. (bd. dir., 1974-80), Am. Electric Assn. (indsl. adv. bd., 1975-76), Fairchild Rsch. and Devel. (tech. staff, 1965-71), Bay Area Purchasing Coun. (bd. dir. 1978-84), Security Affairs Support Assn. (bd. dir. 1980-83), Sigma Xi, Eta Kappa Nu, Sigma Pi Phi.

GREENE, JOHN THOMAS, judge; b. Salt Lake City, Nov. 28, 1929; s. John Thomas and Mary Agnes (Hindley) G.; m. Dorothy Kay Buchanan, Mar. 31, 1955; children: Thomas Buchanan Greene, John Buchanan Greene, Mary Kay Greene Platt. BA in polit. sci., U. Utah, 1952, JD, 1955. Bar: Utah 1955, U.S. Dist. Ct. (10th cir.) 1955, U.S. Supreme Ct. 1966. Pvt. practice Salt Lake City, 1955-57, asst. U.S. atty., 1957-59; ptnr. Marr, Wilkins & Cannon (and successor firms), Salt Lake City, 1959-75; ptnr., pres., chmn. bd. dirs. Greene, Callister & Nebeker, Salt Lake City, 1975-85; judge U.S. Dist. Ct., Salt Lake City, 1985—. Author: (manual) American Mining Law, 1960; contbr. articles to profl. jours. Chmn. Salt Lake City Cmty. Coun., 1970-75, Utah State Bldg. Authority, Salt Lake City, 1980-85; regent Utah State Bd. Higher Edn., Salt Lake City, 1982-86. Recipient Order of Coif U. Utah, 1955, Merit of Honor award, 1994. Fellow ABA Found. (life, ABA ho. of dels. 1972-92, bd. govs. 1987-91); mem. Utah State Bar Assn. (pres. 1971-72, Judge of the Yr. 1995), Am. Law Inst. (advisor 1980—), Phi Beta Kappa. Mormon. Office: US Dist Ct 350 S Main St Salt Lake City UT 84101-2106

GREENE, LAURENCE WHITRIDGE, JR., surgical educator; b. Denver, Jan. 18, 1924; s. Laurence Whitridge Sr. and Freda (Schmitt) G.; m. Frances Steger, Sept. 16, 1950 (dec. Dec. 1977); children: Charlotte Greene Kerr, Mary Whitridge Greene, Laurence Whitridge III; m. Nancy Kay Bennett, Dec. 7, 1984. BA, Colo. Coll., 1945; MD, U. Colo., 1947; postgrad., U. Chgo., 1948-50. Diplomate Am. Bd. of Surgery. Intern St. Lukes Hosp., Denver, 1947-48; sr. intern in ob./gyn. U. Chgo. Lying-In Hosp., 1948-49; surg. resident U. Cin. Gen. Hosp., 1952-55, sr. surg. resident, 1955-57, chief surgery resident, 1957-58; clin. surgery asst. Sch. of Medicine U. Colo., Denver, 1958-61, clin. instr. Sch. of Medicine, 1961-67, asst. clin. prof. Sch. of Medicine, 1967-75, assoc. clin. prof. Sch. of Medicine, 1975-87, clin. prof. Sch. of Medicine, 1987—; adj. prof. zoology and physiology U. Wyo., Laramie, 1970-80; mem. staff Ivinson Meml. Hosp., Laramie, 1958—; chmn. Wyo chpt. Com. on Trauma, 1973-89; tchr., mem. adv. staff U. Colo. Med. Sch., Denver, 1958-83; mem. advisor, surgeon U. Wyo. Athletics, Laramie, 1975-80, Wyo. Hwy. Patrol, 1950—. Contbr. numerous articles to profl. jours. Lt. M.C. (s.g.) USN, 1950-52, Korea. Fellow ACS; mem. Am. Assn. for Surgery of Trauma, Southwestern Surgery Congress, Western Surg. Assn., Mont Reed Soc., Masons, Shriners, Sigma Xi. Republican. Episcopalian.

GREENE, MARTIN LEE, internist; b. Omaha, Nov. 5, 1939; s. Irving and Nioma I. Greene; m. Beth Weisberg, June 24, 1962 (div. Dec. 1986); m. Toby Saks, Nov. 1, 1987. BA, Harvard Coll., 1961, MD, 1965. Diplomate Am. Bd. Internal Medicine. Resident in medicine Mass. Gen. Hosp., Boston, 1965-67; clin. assoc. NIH, Bethesda, Md., 1967-69; sr. fellow Sch. Medicine U. Wash., Seattle, 1969-71, clin. prof., 1984—; physician Minor and James Med., Seattle, 1971-95, med. dir., 1995—; chmn. gastroenterology Swedish Med. Ctr., Seattle, 1976—. Contbr. articles to profl. jours. Pres. King County Health Planning Coun., Seattle, 1974-76; bd. dirs. Seattle Youth Symphony, 1987-96. Lt. comdr. USPHS, 1967-69. Named Disting. Physician, Crohns Colitis Assn. Am., 1995. Fellow Am. Coll. Physicians; mem. Am. Gastroent. Assn. (treas. 1991-96), Am. Soc. Internal Medicine (del.), Wash. State Med. Assn. (del.), Physicians Ins. Assn. (bd. dirs. 1995—). Home: 2412 40th Ave E Seattle WA 98112 Office: Minor and James Med 515 Minor # 200 Seattle WA 98104

GREENE, RICHARD BOYD, JR., marketing and sales executive; b. Boston, July 31, 1962; s. Richard B. and Joy C. (Cudd) G.; m. Lynn Susan Lippoldt, Aug. 24, 1991. BBA, U. Wis., Milw., 1985; MBA, U. Phoenix, San Jose, Calif., 1994. Sales rep. Campbell Soup Co., Des Plaines, Ill., 1985, sales specialist, 1985-87; mgr. trade svcs. Selling Areas Mktg., Inc., Chgo., 1987-88; regional dir. Selling Areas Mktg., Inc., San Ramon, Calif., 1988-91; dir. Info. Resources, Inc., San Francisco, 1991-94; v.p. A.C. Nielsen, Fremont, Calif., 1994—. Mem. Am. Mktg. Assn. Republican. Methodist.

GREENE, WENDY SEGAL, special education educator; b. New Rochelle, N.Y., Jan. 9, 1929; d. Louis Peter and Anne Henrietta (Kahan) Segal; m. Charles Edward Smith (div. 1952); m. Richard M. Greene Jr. (div. 1967); children: Christopher S., Kerry William, Karen Beth Greene Olson; m. Richard M. Greene Sr., Aug. 29, 1985 (dec. 1986). Student, Olivet Coll., 1946-48, Santa Monica Coll., 1967-70; BA in Child Devel., Calif. State U., Los Angeles, 1973, MA in Elem. Edn., 1975. Cert. tchr., Calif. Counselor Camp Watitoh, Becket, Mass., 1946-49; asst. tchr. Outdoor Play Group, New Rochelle, 1946-58; edn. sec. pediatrics Syracuse (N.Y.) Meml. Hosp., 1952-53; with St. John's Hosp., Santa Monica, Calif., 1962-63; head tchr. Head Start, L.A., 1966-77; tchr. spl. edn. L.A. Unified Sch. Dist., 1977—, Salvin Spl. Edn. Ctr., L.A., 1977-85, Perez Spl. Edn. Ctr., L.A., 1986-; instr. mktg. rsch. for motivational rsch. Anderson-McConnell Agy., 1966; mentor tchr. L.A. Unified Sch. Dist., 1992—. Contbr. to house organ of St. John's Hosp.; co-editor of newspaper for Salvin Sch., L.A.; contbg. reporter El Aguiler (The Eagle), Perez. Bd. dirs. Richland Ave. Youth House, L.A., 1960-63, Emotional Health Assn., L.A., 1961-66, Richland Ave. Sch. PTA, 1959-63; vol. Hospice of St. Joseph Hosp., Orange, Calif., 1985—; mem. cmty. adv. com. spl. edn. Tustin Unified Sch. Dist., 1994—. Mem. AAUW, So. Calif. Assn. Young Children, Olivet Coll. Alumni Assn., United Tchrs. L.A., Westside Singers (L.A.), Kappa Delta Pi. Jewish. Home: 14291 Prospect Ave Tustin CA 92680-2316

GREENE LLOYD, NANCY ELLEN, infosystems specialist, physicist; b. Worcester, Mass., Nov. 4, 1947; d. William Arthur II and Dorothy Goddard (Fuller) Green; children: Ellen Dorothy, Gwyneth Tegan; m. Stephen C. Lloyd, July 25, 1992. BS in Physics, Ohio State U., 1969, MS in Physics, 1971. Instr. physics U. Colo., Colorado Springs, 1971-73; physics programmer U. N.Mex., Albuquerque, 1973-76; data analyst Los Alamos

(N.Mex.) Nat. Lab., 1975-77, programmer, 1977-78, mem. tech. staff controlled thermonuclear reaction divsn., 1978-81, mem. tech. staff Accelerator Tech. div., 1981-84, mem. tech. staff adminstrv. data processing divsn., 1984-85, mem. tech. staff dynamic experimentation divsn., 1985-94, staff mem. supr., 1989-90, acting sect. leader, 1990-91, acting dep. divsn. leader, 1992, chief ops. explosives tech. and applications divsn., 1992-94, mem. tech. staff environ., safety, and health divsn. Instl. Affairs Office, 1994—; speaker in field. Vol. Los Alamos Schs., 1980-88, Fountain Valley Sch., Colo., 1990-91. Nat. Merit scholar, Mich. State U., 1965, Nat. Defense Edn. Act Title IV fellow, Ohio State U., 1969. Mem. NAFE, IEEE, N.Mex. Digital Equipment Computer Users Soc. (exec. com. 1984-87, 88-90, registration chair computer conf. 1984-87, vice-chair 1988-89, publicity 1989-90), N.Mex. Network for Women in Sci. and Engring., VAX Computer Local Users Group (chmn. 1981-82, sec. 1989-92), N.Mex. Square and Round Dance Assn. (dist. co-chair 1996-97), Toastmasters. Office: Los Alamos Nat Lab PO Box 1663 K491 Los Alamos NM 87545-0600

GREENFIELD, JAMES M., fund raiser; b. Hornell, N.Y., Feb. 12, 1936; s. James M. and Vera E. (Alger) G.; m. Diane Roberts, Aug., 1962 (div. 1973); children: Eryn J., Janine L.; m. Karen G. Gabrielson, Nov. 24, 1984. BA, U. Calif., Riverside, 1958. Exec. dir. U. Calif. Alumni Assn., Riverside, 1962-67; dir. corp. rels. Calif. Inst. Tech., Pasadena, 1967-72; dir. devel. Claremont (Calif.) U. Ctr., 1972-73; dir. spl. projects Childrens Hosp. Med. Ctr., Boston, 1973-76; dir. devel. Univ. Hosp., Boston, 1976-81, New Eng. Bapt. Hosp., Boston, 1981-85; dir. fund devel. Cleve. Clinic Found., 1985-87; sr. v.p., devel. and cmty. rels. Hoag Meml. Hosp. Presbyn., Newport Beach, Calif., 1987—. Author: Fund-Raising: Evaluating and Managing the Fund Development Process, 1991, Fund-Raising Fundamentals: A Guide to Annual Giving for Professionals and Volunteers, 1994, Fund-Raising Cost Effectiveness: A Self-Assessment Workbook, 1996; editor: The Nonprofit Handbook: Fund Raising, 2d edit., 1997. With USNR, 1959-62. Mem. Assn for Healthcare Philanthropy (bd. dirs., Harold J. Seymour award 1993), Nat. Soc. Fund Raising Execs. (bd. dirs. 1979-88, bd. dirs. Found. 1982—, Profl. Fund-Raiser of Yr. award Orange County chpt. 1994). Democrat. Office: Hoag Meml Hosp Presbyn One Hoag Dr Box 6100 Newport Beach CA 92658-6100

GREENHOUSE, LYNN, physician; b. Garden City, Kans., Feb. 11, 1956; d. Arnold Hillel and Louise Lynn Greenhouse; m. Douglas James Bruha, June 10, 1989. BA magna cum laude, Miami U. Ohio, Oxford, 1977; MA, Johns Hopkins U., 1979; MD, U. Nev., 1992. Policy analyst office spl. projects U.S. Dept. Energy, Washington, 1979-81; rep. gas mktg., compliance analyst Petro-Lewis Corp., Denver, 1981-84; asst. v.p. investor rels. Derand Resources Corp., Arlington, Va., 1984-86; med. enrolled health care program U. Nev., Reno, 1987-92; med. resident U. Internal Medicine, Reno, 1992-95; physician pvt. practice, Elko, Nev., 1995—; presenter in field. Contbr. articles and abstracts to profl. jours. Mem. ACP, AMA, Phi Beta Kappa, Phi Kappa Phi, Alpha Omega Alpha.

GREENHUT, SAUL EPHRIAM, biomedical researcher, engineer; b. Detroit, May 27, 1961; s. Frederick Sanford and Lillian (Rosen) G.; m. Nancy Jean Cronk, Sept. 8, 1985; children: Adam, Jonathan, Jordan. BSE summa cum laude, U. Mich., 1983, MS in Bioengring., 1984, PhD in Bioengring., 1991. Rsch. engr. Newark Beth-Israel Med. Ctr., 1984-85; computer coord. William Beaumont Hosp., Royal Oak, Mich., 1985-88; rsch. asst. U. Mich., Ann Arbor, 1986-91; rsch. scientist, mgr. applied rsch. Telectronics Pacing Sys., Englewood, Colo., 1991—. Contbr. articles to profl. jours.; inventor in field. Vol. Families First, Aurora, Colo., 1992-93. Fellow U. Mich., 1983-84. Mem. IEEE, Assn. for Advancement of Med. Instrumentation, Internat. Soc. Computerized Electrocardiology (Young Investigator 1990). Democrat. Jewish. Office: Telectronics Pacing Sys 7400 S Tucson Way Englewood CO 80112-3938

GREENLAW, ROGER LEE, interior designer; b. New London, Conn., Oct. 12, 1936; s. Kenneth Nelson and Lyndell Lee (Stinson) G.; children: Carol Jennifer, Roger Lee. BFA, Syracuse U., 1958. Interior designer Cannell & Chaffin, 1958-59, William C. Wagner, Architect, L.A., 1959-60, Gen. Fireproofing Co., L.A., 1960-62, K-S Wilshire, Inc., L.A., 1963-64; dir. interior design Calif. Desk Co., L.A., 1964-67; sr. interior designer Bechtel Corp., L.A., 1967-70; sr. interior designer, project mgr. Daniel, Mann, Johnson, & Mendehall, L.A., 1970-72, Morganelli-Heumann & Assos., L.A., 1972-73; owner, prin. Greenlaw Design Assos., Glendale, Calif., 1973—, Greenlaw Interior Planning & Design, 1996—; lectr. UCLA; mem. adv. curriculum com. Mt. San Antonio Coll., Walnut, Calif., Fashion Inst. Design, L.A.; bd. dirs. Calif. Legis. Conf. Interior Design. Past scoutmaster Verdugo council Boy Scouts Am.; pres. bd. dirs. Unity Ch., La Crescenta, Calif., 1989-91. Mem. Am. Soc. Interior Designers (treas. Pasadena chpt. 1983-84, 1st v.p. 1985, pres. 1986-87, chmn. So. Calif. regional conf. 1985, nat. dir. 1987—, nat. com. legis., nat. com. jury for catalog award, speaker ho. dels., nat. bd. dirs., medallist award, regional v.p., nat. chair ethics com., nat. exec. com., v.p., treas. 1992 Calif. legislative conf. interior design, chmn. standards task force, pres. 1994—), Glendale C. of C. (bd. dirs.), Adm. Farragut Acad. Alumni Assn., Delta Upsilon. Republican. Lodge: Kiwanis (bd. dirs.). Home: 2100F Valderas Dr Glendale CA 91208-1328 Office: 2155 Verdugo Blvd Montrose CA 91020-1628

GREENLEY, CAROL JEAN, graphics designer, music educator, photographer; b. Cleve., Dec. 2, 1951; d. Gaylord and Joan Greenley; m. Edward J. Hollcraft, Dec. 24, 1980. BA, Principia Coll., 1973; MFA, Mills Coll., 1977. Instr. piano Pleasant Hill, Calif., 1974—; photographer Pleasant Hill, 1981-91, graphics designer, 1994—. Mem. Am. Coll. Musicians, Music Tchrs. Assn. Home: 1961 Rose Ln Pleasant Hill CA 94523

GREENSPAN, ADAM, radiologist, educator; b. Przemysl, Poland, May 28, 1935; s. Bernard and Eugenia (Wert) G.; m. Barbara Lynn Warshofsky, Mar. 31, 1985; children: Ludwig, Samantha, Michael. MD, Med. Acad. Worclaw, Poland, 1958, DMS, 1965. Med. diplomate; cert. in radiology. Asst. prof. radiology Mt. Sinai Sch. Medicine, N.Y.C., 1977-79, assoc. prof. radiology, 1979-85; assoc. prof. radiology N.Y.U. Sch. Medicine, N.Y.C., 1986-87; assoc. prof. radiology and othopaedic surgery Sch. Medicine U. Calif., Davis, 1987-88; prof. radiology and orthopaedic surgery N.Y.U. Sch. Medicine, 1988—. Author: Orthopaedic Radiology, 1988, 2d edit., 1993, Radiology of the Arthritides, 1990, Imaging of the Spine, 1993, Differential Diagnosis of Tumors and Tumor-like Lesions of Bones and Joints, 1997. Recipient Physician's Recognition awards AMA, 1974, 77, 81, 92, 94, 96. Fellow Am. Coll. Radiology, N.Y. Acad. Medicine; mem. Internat. Skeletal Soc., Radiol. Soc. N.Am., Am. Roentgen Ray Soc. Office: Univ Calif Davis Radiology 2516 Stockton Blvd Sacramento CA 95817-2208

GREENSPAN, JOHN S., dentistry educator, educator and administrator; b. London, Jan. 7, 1938; came to U.S., 1976; s. Nathan and Jessie (Dion) G.; m. Deborah, Dec. 1962; children: Nicholas J., Louise C. BSC in Anatomy with 1st class honors, U. London, 1959, B in Dental Surgery, 1962, PhD in Exptl. Pathology, 1967; ScD (hon.), Georgetown U., 1990. Licentiate in dental surgery Royal Coll. of Surgeons of Eng. Asst. house surgeon in conservation and periodontology Royal Dental Hosp. London, 1962; asst. lectr. oral pathology Sch. of Dental Surgery Royal Dental Hosp. of London, U. London, 1963-65, lectr. oral pathology Sch. of Dental Surgery, 1965-68, sr. lectr. oral pathology Sch. of Dental Surgery, 1968-75; prof. oral biology and oral pathology Sch. of Dentisty, U. Calif., San Francisco, 1976—, vice chmn. dept. oral medicine and hosp. dentistry, 1977-82, chmn. div. oral biology, 1981-89, coord. basic scis. Sch. of Dentistry, 1982-96; chmn. dept. stomatology U. Calif., San Francisco, 1989—; cons. oral pathology St. John's Hosp. and Inst. of Dermatology, London, 1973-76; cons. dental surgeon St. George's Hosp., 1972-76; prof. dept. pathology Sch. Medicine U. Calif., San Francisco, 1976—; dir. U. Calif. AIDS Specimen Bank, San Francisco, 1982—, U. Calif. Oral AIDS Ctr., San Francisco, 1987—; asso. dir. dental clin. epidemiology program U. Calif., San Francisco, 1987—; dir. U. Calif. AIDS Clin. Rsch. Ctr., San Francisco, 1992—; presenter, lectr. Author: (with others) Opportunist Infections in Patients with the Acquired Immunodeficiency Syndrome, 1989, Contemporary Periodontics, 1989, Gastroenterology Clinics of North America, 1988, Perspectives on Oral Manifestations of AIDS, 1988, AIDS: Pathogenesis and Treatment, 1988, others; contbr. articles to profl. jours.; editorial cons. Achives of Oral Biology, 1968—, Jour. of Calif. Dental Assn., 1980—; editoral adv. bd. Jour. of Dental Rsch., 1977—; editorial bd. AIDS Alert, 1987-89; sr. editor Oral Diseases, 1994—. Rsch. grantee NIH-Nat. Inst. Dental Rsch., 1978-82, 86-92, U. Calif. Task Force on AIDS, 1983—, rsch. com. Royal Dental Hosp., London, 1964-76, Med. Rsch. Coun. of U.K., 1974-77, chmn. U. Calif. San Francisco Acad. Senate, 1983-85; Nuffield dental scholar, 1958-59; fellow Am. Coll. Dentists, 1982—, AAAS, 1985—; recipient Seymour J. Kreshover Lecture award Nat. Inst. Dental Rsch., NIH, 1989, Rsch. in Oral Biology award Internat. Assn. Dental Rsch., 1992. Mem. ADA, AAAS, Am. Assn. Dental Rsch. (pres. 1988-89), Inst. Medicine of Nat. Acad. Scis., Internat. Assn. Dental Rsch. (pres. 1996-97), Royal Soc. Medicine (U.K.), Pathological Soc. (U.K.), Oral Pathology Soc. (U.K.), Royal Coll. Pathologists (U.K.), Am. Acad. Oral Pathology, Bay Area Tchrs. Oral Pathology, Internat. Assn. Oral Pathologists, San Francisco Dental Soc., Calif. Dental Assn., Calif. Soc. Oral Pathologists Histochem. Soc., Am. Assn. Pathologists. Office: U Calif Dept Stomatology Box 0422 Sch Dentistry San Francisco CA 94143

GREENSTEIN, MERLE EDWARD, import and export company executive; b. Portland, Oreg., June 22, 1937; s. Sol and Tillie Germaine (Schnitzer) G.; children: Randall Dale, Todd Aaron. BA, Reed Coll., 1959. Pres. Acme Trading and Supply Co., Portland, 1963-82; chmn. MMI Group, Portland, 1982-91, Internat. Devel. Assocs., Portland, 1991—; com. mem. ISRI, Washington, 1987-89; mem. dist. export coun. U.S. Dept. Commerce, 1980—, mem. first USA trade Missions to Vietnam, 1996. Chmn. fin. Portland Opera, 1966; bd. dirs. Met. YMCA, 1964-67; del. to China, State of Oreg. Ofcl. Trade Mission, 1979; chmn. Western Internat. Trade Group, 1981-82; mem. State of Oreg. Korea Commn., 1985-90; fin. chmn. Anne Frank exhibit, Portland; joint chmn. bldg. campaign Oreg. Mus. Sci. and Industry; bd. dirs. Waverly Children's Home; bd. cons. Unilearn Corp.; chmn. fin. Oreg. Holocaust Mem. Recipient President's E for Export, U.S. Dept. Commerce, 1969; named Citizen of the Week, City of Portland, 1953. Mem. Rolls Royce Owners Club (London), City Club, Tualatin Country Club, Masons, Shriners. Office: Internat Devel Assocs 6731 NE 47th Ave Portland OR 97218-1205

GREENWADE, LANCE ERIC, scientific visualization specialist, mathematician; b. Napa, Calif., July 4, 1957; s. Gerald Gordon and Karen Rae (Smit) G.; m. Margaret Marie Rosa, July 18, 1981; children: Zachary Ray, Benjamin Gordon. BA, Humboldt State U., 1982; MS, Mont. State U., 1984. Lectr. Mont. State U., Bozeman, 1981-85; staff scientist Los Alamos (N.Mex.) Nat. Lab., 1985-86; sr. scientist Idaho Nat. Engring. Lab., Idaho Falls, 1986-87, cons. scientist, 1987—; Graphics chair Cray User Group, 1992—; INEL rep. Sandia-Los Alamos Tech. Exch. Com., 1987—. Mentor Los Alamos Sci. Program, 1985-86, Science NOW, Idaho Falls, 1990-91. Mem. IEEE, IEEE Computer Soc., Assn. Computing Machinery, SIGGRAPH, AEC Sportsman Club (v.p. 1992-93, pres. 1993-94). Home: 601 E 97th S Idaho Falls ID 83404-7762 Office: Idaho Nat Engring Lab 2525 N Fremont Idaho Falls ID 83402-1835

GREENWELL, RONALD EVERETT, communications executive; b. Louisville, Oct. 28, 1938; s. Woodrow M. and Christine (Comer) Gossett G.; m. Diane J. Greenwell, Mar. 18, 1967; children: Wendy, Robin. With Motorola Inc., Schaumburg, Ill., 1962-94, sr. v.p., gen. mgr. communications internat. group, 1986-94; pres. Motorola Communications Internat. Inc., Schaumburg, Ill., 1986-94, ret., 1994; bd. dirs. Entranosa Water Co., TiJeras, N.Mex. Mem. N.C. Ctr. for World Langs. and Culture (bd. dirs.). Home: 30 Canyon Ridge Dr Sandia Park NM 87047

GREENWOOD, RICHARD M., finance company executive, bank executive; b. Fargo, N.D., 1947. Grad., U. Idaho, 1972, Am. Grad. Sch. Internat. Mgmt., 1974. Formerly exec. v.p., CFO Calfed Inc., L.A.; now pres., CEO, dir. Bank Plus Corp., L.A., 1996—; chmn., CEO Fidelity Federal Bank, FSB, 1992—. Office: Fidelity Federal Bank 4565 Colorado Blvd Los Angeles CA 90039

GREER, HOWARD EARL, former naval officer; b. Tyler, Tex., May 1, 1921; s. Earl Abner and Ollie (Lightfoot) G.; m. Dale Price, Nov. 1, 1986; children—Margaret, Darby, David, Briand, Holly, Howard. Student, Tyler Jr. Coll., 1939-40; B.S., U.S. Naval Acad., 1943; M.B.A., George Washington U., 1965. Commd. ensign U.S. Navy, 1943, advanced through grades to vice adm., 1975; comdr. Aircraft Carrier Hancock, 1967-69, Carrier Force, Vietnam, (4 tours), Naval Air Forces, U.S. Atlantic Fleet, Norfolk, Va., 1975-78; dir. CEDAM Internat. Decorated D.S.M. (2), Legion of Merit (4), Knights of Malta Order St. John of Jerusalem. Mem. Assn. Naval Aviation (trustee), Golden Eagles (early pioneer naval aviators, Tailhook Assn., Naval Res. Assn., Santa Fe Country Club. Republican. Methodist. Home: 8539 Prestwick Dr La Jolla CA 92037

GREER, JERRY DEAN, forester; b. Marshfield, Mo., Sept. 12, 1941; s. Ivan Lee and Mary Ellen (Young) G.; m. Karen Sue Evans, Oct. 7, 1961 (div. Jan. 1979); children: Susan Elaine (dec.), Richard Dean, Mary Kathryn Anne; m. Suzanne Karol French, Jan. 23, 1979 (div. Jan. 1989); 1 child, Cassandra Jeri-Lynn. BS in Forestry, U. Mo., 1964. Work project leader Forest Svc./USDA, Mountainair, N.Mex., 1966-68; recreation/lands staff Forest Svc./USDA, Pecos, N.Mex., 1968-70; recreation/lands/fire staff Forest Svc./USDA, Happy Jack, Ariz., 1970-72; recreation/lands staff Forest Svc./USDA, Flagstaff, Ariz., 1972-75; dist. ranger Forest Svc./USDA, Sedona, Ariz., 1975-78, Albuquerque, 1978-84; project mgr. remote sensing Forest Svc./USDA, Houston/Salt Lake City, 1984-88; resources staff officer Forest Svc./USDA, Bedford, Ind., 1988-91; br. chief planning and ecosys. mgmt. Forest Svc./USDA, McCall, Idaho, 1991-97; reviewer sci. books for children Boston U. Sch. Edn., 1991—. Editor: Remote Sensing in the Forest Service, 1988, 90, 92, 94, 96; contbg. editor Uptime Mag., 1987-88; author: (booklet) Techniques of Supervision of Volunteers, 1987; contbr. numerous articles to profl. jours. Bd. dirs. Keep Sedona Beautiful, 1977-78; trustee, bd. dirs. N.Mex. Crime Prevention Assn., Albuquerque, 1984; sec., bd. dirs. Greater Albuquerque Vols. Assn., 1982, 83; mem. com. Flagstaff Area Transp. Study, 1974-75; mem. N.Mex. Disting. Pub. Svc. Awards Coun., Santa Fe, 1984; trustee McCall-Donnelly Sch. Dist., 1997. Curators Freshman scholar, U. Mo., 1959, Richard M. Higgins Endowment Fund scholar, 1961. Mem. AAAS, Soc. Am. Foresters (chpt. chmn., chpt. sec.-treas.), Am. Soc. Photogrammetry and Remote Sensing, Nat. Mil. Intelligence Assn., Am. Alpine Club, Soc. of Photo-Optical Instrumentation Engrs. Home: PO Box 1971 Mc Call ID 83638

GREEVER, MARGARET QUARLES, retired mathematics educator; b. Wilkensburg, Pa., Feb. 7, 1931; d. Lawrence Reginald and Ella Mae (LeSueur) Quarles; m. John Greever, Aug. 29, 1953; children: Catherine Patricia, Richard George, Cynthia Diane. Cert. costume design, Richmond Profl. Inst., 1952; student, U. Va., 1953-56; BA in Math., Calif. State U., L.A., 1963; MA in Math., Claremont Grad. Sch., 1968. Cert. tchr. specializing in Jr. Coll. math., Calif. Tchr. math. Chaffey Unified H.S. Dist., Alta Loma, Calif., 1963-64, L.A. Unified Sch. Dist., 1964-65, Chino (Calif.) Unified Sch. Dist., 1965-81; from asst. prof. to prof. Chaffey Coll., Rancho Cucamonga, 1981-96; phys. sci. divsn. chmn. Chaffey Coll., Alta Loma, 1985-92, dean, phys., life, health sci., 1992-96. Mem. LWV, Nat. Coun. Tchrs. Math., Am. Math. Assn. Two-Yr. Colls., Calif. Math. Coun., Assn. Calif. C.C. Adminstrs., Assn. Instr. Adminstrs., Women in Higher Edn., Pi Lambda Theta.

GREGG, KENNETH STEPHEN, computer scientist; b. Lakewood, Ohio, July 13, 1960; s. John Frederick and Evelyn Mae (Lutrey) G.; m. Theresa Mae Liska, Sept. 5, 1981. BS, Mich. State U., 1983; MS, U. Tex. at Dallas, Richardson, 1988. Software design engr. Tex. Instruments Inc., Lubbock, 1983; programmer/systems analyst Tex. Instruments Inc., Sherman, 1983-84; software design engr. Tex. Instruments Inc., Dallas, 1984-85; software engr., sr. software engr. InteCom Inc., Allen, Tex., 1985-88, lead sr. software engr., 1989; software design engr. Microsoft Corp., Redmond, Wash., 1989-90, OEM liaison, testing architect, 1990-91, Windows NT base test mgr., 1991-92, Windows NT test and performance mgr., 1992-94; sr. dir. software engring. Artisoft, Inc., Tucson, 1994-95; computer cons., 1996—. Author: Windows NT Server 4.0 Administrator's Bible, 1996. Recipient Sch. award Am. Legion, Lakewood, Ohio, 1978. Mem. Assn. for Computing Machinery. Mormon. Home: 8301 N Westcliff Dr Tucson AZ 85743-1044

GREGGS, ELIZABETH MAY BUSHNELL (MRS. RAYMOND JOHN GREGGS), retired librarian; b. Delta, Colo., Nov. 7, 1925; d. Joseph Perkins and Ruby May (Stanford) Bushnell; m. Raymond John Greggs, Aug. 16, 1952 (dec. 1994); children: David M., Geoffrey B., Timothy C., Daniel R. BA, U. Denver, 1948. Children's librarian Grand Junction (Colo.) Pub. Library, 1944-46, Chelan County Library, 1948, Wenatchee (Wash.) Pub. Library, 1948-52, Seattle Pub. Library, 1952-53; children's librarian Renton (Wash.) Pub. Library, 1957-61, dir., 1962, br. supr. and children's services supr., 1963-67; area children's supr. King County Library, Seattle, 1968-78, asst. coordinator children's services, 1978-86; head librarian Valley View Library of King County Library System, Seattle, 1986-90; cons., organizer Tutor Ctr. Library, Seattle South Community Coll., 1969-72; mem. Puget Sound (Wash.) Council for Reviewing Children's Media, 1974—, chmn., 1974-76; cons. to children's TV programs. Editor: Cayas Newsletter, 1971-74; cons. to Children's Catalog, Children's Index to Poetry. Chmn. dist. advancement com. Kloshee dist. Boy Scouts Am., 1975-78; mem. Bond Issue Citizens Group to build new Renton Libr., 1958, 59; mem. exec. bd. Family Edn. and Counseling Ctr. on Deafness, 1991-94; mem. children's lit. tour People to People, South Africa, 1996. Recipient Hon. Service to Youth award Cedar River dist. Boy Scouts Am., 1971, Award of Merit Kloshee dist., 1977, winner King County Block Grant, 1990. Mem. ALA (Newbery-Caldecott medal com. 1978-79, com. chmn. 1983-84; membership com. 1978-80, Boy Scouts com. children's svcs. div. 1973-78, chmn. 1976-78, exec. bd. dirs. Assn. for Libr. Svc. to Children 1979-81, mem. coun. 1985-92, chmn. nominating com. 1986-87, councillor 1989-92, exec. bd. 1989-92, exec. com. 1989-92, coun. orientation com. 1987-89), Wash. Libr. Assn. (exec. bd. children's and young adult svcs. div. 1970-78, chmn. membership com. 1983-90, publs. com. 1988-92, emeritus 1991, mem. elections com.), King County Right to Read Coun. (co-chmn. 1973-77), Pierce-King County Reading Coun., Wash. State Literacy Coun. (exec. bd. 1971-77), Wash. Libr. Media Assn. (jr. high levels com. 1980-84), Pacific N.W. Libr. Assn. (young readers' choice com. 1981-83, chmn. div. 1983-85, exec. bd. 1983-85). Methodist. Home: 11448 Rainier Ave S Seattle WA 98178

GREGOIRE, CHRISTINE O., state attorney general; b. Auburn, Wash.; m. Michael Gregoire; 2 children. BA, U. Wash.; JD cum laude, Gonzaga U., 1977. Clerk, typist Wash. State Adult Probation/ Parole Office, Seattle, 1969; caseworker Wash. Dept. Social and Health Scis., Everett, 1974; asst. atty. gen. City of Spokane, Wash., 1977-81, sr. asst. atty. gen., 1981-82; dep. atty. gen. City of Olympia, Wash., 1982-88, atty. gen., 1993—; dir. Wash. State Dept. Ecology, 1988-92. chair Puget Sound Water Quality Authority, 1990-92, Nat. Com. State Environ. Dirs., 1991-92, States/B.C. Oil Spill Task Force, 1989-92. Mem. Nat. Assn. Attys. Gen. (consumer protection and environment com., energy com., children and the law subcom.). *

GREGOR, DOROTHY DEBORAH, librarian; b. Dobbs Ferry, N.Y., Aug. 15, 1939; d. Richard Garrett Heckman and Marion Allen (Richmond) Stewart; m. A. James Gregor, June 22, 1963 (div. 1974). BA, Occidental Coll., 1961; MA, U. Hawaii, 1963; MLS, U. Tex., 1968; cert. in Library Mgmt., U. Calif., Berkeley, 1976. Reference libr. U. Calif., San Francisco, 1968-69; dept. libr. Pub. Health Libr. U. Calif., Berkeley, 1969-71, tech. services libr., 1973-76; reference libr. Hamilton Libr., Honolulu, 1971-72; head serials dept. U. Calif., Berkeley, 1976-80, assoc. univ. libr. tech. svcs. dept., 1980-84, univ. libr., 1992-94; ret., 1994; chief Shared Cataloging div. Libr. of Congress, Washington, 1984-85; univ. libr. U. Calif.-San Diego, La Jolla, 1985-92, OCLC asst. to pres. for acad. and rsch. libr. rels., 1995—; instr. sch. libr. and info. studies U. Calif., Berkeley, 1975, 76, 83; cons. Nat. Libr. of Medicine, Bethesda, Md., 1985, Ohio Bd. Regents, Columbus, 1987; trustee Online Computer Libr. Ctr., 1988-96; dir. Nat. Coordinating Com. on Japanese Libr. Resources, 1995—. Mem. ALA, Libr. Info. Tech. Assn., Program Com. Ctr. for Rsch. Librs. (bd. chair 1992-93, Hugh Atkinson award 1994).

GREGOR, EDUARD, laser physicist, consultant; b. Dnepropetrovsk, Ukraine, Jan. 9, 1936; came to U.S., 1955; s. Waldemar and Concordia (Teschke) G.; m. Marie L. Carlin, June 29, 1968; 1 child, Eduard Joseph. BS in Physics, Calif. State U., 1964, MS in Physics, 1966. Instr. Calif. State U., L.A., 1963-66; optical physicist TRW Instruments, El Segundo, Calif., 1966-68; laser physicist Union Carbide (Korad), Santa Monica, Calif., 1968-72; prodn. mgr. holography Quantrad Corp., El Segundo, Calif., 1972-75, ops. mgr., 1975-79; sr. project physicist Hughes Aircraft Co., El Segundo, 1979-82, dept. mgr., 1982-91, project mgr., 1992-93, sci., engr., 1993-95; laser tech. cons. Gregor Consulting, Pacific Palisades, Calif., 1995—. Contbr. over 20 tech. articles on laser tech., coherent optics and holography to profl. jours. Sgt. U.S. Army, 1959-61. Recipient IR 100 award Indsl. Rsch. Mag., 1975. Mem. Optical Soc. Am., Soc. Photo-optical Instrumentation Engrs. Home and Office: 820 Las Lomas Ave Pacific Palisades CA 90272-2428

GREGORY, CALVIN, insurance service executive; b. Bronx, N.Y., Jan. 11, 1942; s. Jacob and Ruth (Cherchian) G.; m. Rachel Anna Carver, Feb. 14, 1970 (div. Apr. 1977); children—Debby Lynn, Trixy Sue; m. 2d, Carla Deane Deaver, June 30, 1979. A.A., Los Angeles City Coll., 1962; B.A., Calif. State U.-Los Angeles, 1964; M.Div., Fuller Theol. Sem., 1968; M.R.E., Southwestern Sem., Ft. Worth, 1969; Ph.D. in Religion, Universal Life Ch., Modesto, Calif., 1982; D.Div. (hon.), Otay Mesa Coll., 1982. Notary pub., real estate lic., casualty lic., Calif.; ordained to ministry Am. Baptist Conv., 1970. Youth minister First Bapt. Ch., Delano, Calif., 1964-65, 69-70; youth dir. St. Luke's United Meth. Ch., Highland Park, Calif., 1969-70; tchr. polit. sci. Maranatha High Sch., Rosemead, Calif., 1969-70; aux. chaplain U.S. Air Force 750th Radar Squadron, Edwards AFB, Calif., 1970-72; pastor First Bapt. Ch., Boron, Calif., 1971-72; ins. agt. Prudential Ins. Co., Ventura, Calif., 1972-73, sales mgr., 1973-74; casualty ins. agt. Allstate Ins. Co., Thousand Oaks, Calif., 1974-75; pres. Ins. Agy. Placement Service, Thousand Oaks, 1975—; head youth minister Emanuel Presbyn. Ch., Los Angeles, 1973-74; owner, investor real estate, U.S., Wales, Eng., Can., Australia. Counselor YMCA, Hollywood, Calif., 1964, Soul Clinic-Universal Life Ch., Inc., Modesto, Calif., 1982. Mem. Apt. Assn. Los Angeles, Life Underwriter Tng. Council. Republican. Clubs: Forensic (Los Angeles); X32 (Ventura). Lodge: Kiwanis (club speaker 1971). Office: Ins Agy Placement Svc PO Box 4407 Thousand Oaks CA 91359-1407

GREGORY, ELEANOR ANNE, artist, educator; b. Seattle, Jan. 20, 1939; d. John Noel and Eleanor Blanche G.; BA, Reed Coll., 1963; MFA, U. Wash., 1966; MEd, Columbia U., 1978, EdD., 1978. Art tchr. Seattle Pub. Schs., 1970-75; instr. N.Y.C. C.C., 1977, Manhattan C.C., N.Y.C., 1978; asst. prof. N.Mex. State U., Las Crucas, 1978-79; asst. prof. art Purdue U., West Lafayette, Ind., 1979-82, West Tex. State U., Canyon, 1982-84; mgr. Watson's Crick Gallery, West Lafayette, 1982-83; lectr. Calif. State U., Long Beach, 1985-87, L.A. Unified Sch. Dist., 1988—. One woman shows: Columbia U. Tchrs. Coll., 1976, Watson's Crick Gallery, West Lafayette, 1980, 81, Gallery I, Purdue U., 1980, W. Tex. State U., 1983, Amarillo Art Ctr., 1984, Sch. Visual Concepts, Seattle, 1985; group shows include: El Paso (Tex.) Art Mus., 1979, Ind. State Mus., Indpls., 1980, Lafayette (Ind.) Art Mus., 1982, T. Billman Gallery, Long Beach, 1987; represented in permanent collection: Portland (Oreg.) Art Mus. Mem. Nat. Art Edn. Assn. (pres. women's caucus chpt. 1988-90, v.p.-elect Pacific region 1994-96, v.p. 1996-98, Pacific region sect. award 1997), N.Y. Soc. Scribes, L.A. Soc. Calligraphy, Internat. Soc. Edn. Through Art, Art Educators of L.A. (pres. 1993-95). Episcopalian.

GREGORY, GEORGE ANN, writer, Native American education consultant; b. Ft. Smith, Ark., Aug. 17, 1945; d. George Eugene Miller and Maxine (Manuel) Eggensperger; m. Gavino Sanchez, June 21, 1995; children: Matthew Gregory, James Smiley. BA, U. Ark., 1969; MA, U. N.Mex., 1987, PhD, 1993. Ordained min., 1977. Grad. asst. U. N.Mex., Albuquerque, 1984-89, 92-93; instr. Oglala Lakota Coll., Kyle, S.D., 1989-90; lectr. No. Ariz. U., Flagstaff, 1990-92; dir. Ho Anumpoli!, Albuquerque, 1995—; adj. prof. U. N.Mex., 1993—; cons., evaluator Indian Edn. Albuquerque, 1988-96; cons. emergency med. svcs. acad. U. N.Mex., 1994-95; cons. Okla. Native Am. Langs. Devel. Inst., 1990. Author: (short story) People Before Columbus, 1993, (poetry) Neon Pow Wow, 1993, (juvenile) Mr. Finnegan and the Bear, 1990 (Honorable Mention), (textbook) Native American Holocaust for Beginners, 1997; editor: Nizhoni mag., 1985; guest poet Writer's Alive, Corrales, N.Mex., 1995, 96. Ednl. task force Commn. on Indian Affairs, 1994—; mem. Multicultural Task Force, Albuquerque, 1995; mem. ops. com. Women Studies U. N.Mex., 1994-95; mem. pres.'s ad hoc com. Native Am. Student Concerns U. N.Mex., 1986-87. Emma Mae

Olson scholar Native Am. Coll. Edn. U. N.Mex., 1986; named Top Ten Native Am. Scholars Cornell U., Ithaca, N.Y., 1993. Mem. Native Am. Tchrs. Assn., Native Writer's Circle of Ams., Soc. Study Indigenous Langs. Scientology. Home: PO Box 40184 Albuquerque NM 87196 Office: Ho Anumpoli! 137 Manzano NE Ste C Albuquerque NM 87108-1309

GREGORY, JAMES, actor; b. N.Y.C., Dec. 23, 1911; s. James Gillen and Axemia Theresa (Ekdahl) G.; m. Ann Catherine Miltner, May 25, 1944. Grad. high sch. Actor, 1936—. Actor: (summer stock prodns.) Deer Lake, Pa., 1936-37, 39, Millbrook, N.Y., 1938, Braddock Heights, Md., 1940, Buck's County Playhouse, New Hope, Pa., 1941, Ivy Tower Playhouse, Spring Lake, N.J., 1951, (Broadway shows) Key Largo, 1939, Journey to Jerusalem, 1940, In Time to Come, 1941, Dream Girl, 1945, All My Sons, 1947, Death of a Salesman, 1948-49 (played Biff on Broadway with 5 Willy Lomans), Dead Pigeon, 1954, Fragile Fox, 1955, Desperate Hours, 1956-57, (films) The Young Strangers, 1955, Al Capone Story, 1955, Gun Glory, 1956, Nightfall, 1956, The Big Caper, 1956, A Distant Trumpet, 1961, Underwater Warrior, 1962, PT-109, 1965, The Sons of Katie Elder, 1967, The Manchurian Candidate, 1967, Captain Newman, M.D, 1967, Million Dollar Duck, 1968, Clam Bake, 1967, Secret War of Harry Frigg, 1968, Beneath the Planet of the Apes, 1970, The Hawaiians, 1970, Shoot Out, 1971, The Late Liz, 1971, $1,000,000. Duck, 1971, The Strongest Man in the World, 1974, The Main Event, 1979, Wait Til Your Mother Gets Home, 1982, X-15, Death of a Salesman, also 5 Matt Helm pictures, (TV shows) Big Valley, Bonanza, Gunsmoke, Rawhide, Playhouse 90, Climax, Alfred Hitchcock Presents, Twilight Zone, Quincy, as Inspector Luger in Barney Miller, Mr. Belvedere, 1986. Served with USNR, USMCR, 1942-45, PTO. Mem. Soc. Preservation and Encouragement Barber Shop Quartet Singing Am. Club: Hollywood Hackers, Golf. Home: 55 Cathedral Rock Dr Unit 33 Sedona AZ 86351-8624

GREGORY, JOEL PATRICK, geologist, consultant; b. Danville, Va., Aug. 19, 1956; s. Andrew Harrison and Christine (Burton) G.; m. Bernardine Gayle Zimmerman, Mar. 27, 1982 (div. May 1986). BS in Geology, Coll. William and Mary, 1978; MS in Geology, U. N.C., 1982. Tchg. tchg. asst. Dept. Geology, U. N.C., Chapel Hill, 1978-79, lab. asst., 1979-80, rsch. asst., 1980-81; rsch. asst. U.S. Geol. Survey, Denver, 1981; prodn. geologist Gulf Oil Exploration and Prodn. Co., Okla. City, 1981-84; exploration geologist Enserch Exploration, Inc., Dallas, 1984-91; consulting geologist Pinedale, Wyo., 1991—; chief geologist Paulson & Cooper, Jackson, Wyo., 1995—. Compiler map; contbr. articles to profl. jours. NSF Rsch. grantee, 1977. Mem. Am. Assn. Petroleum Geologists (cert.), Geol. Soc. Am., Sigma Gamma Epsilon. Home and Office: PO Box 1329 Pinedale WY 82941-1329

GREGORY, LEONARD, publishing executive. Mng. editor Pueble (Colo.) Chieftan. Office: Pueblo Chieftan 825 W 6th St Pueblo CO 81003

GREGORY, LESLIE FINLAYSON, tax accountant, financial consultant, realtor; b. Halifax, N.S., Can., Nov. 18, 1956; d. F. Douglas and Beverley Jeanne (Adams) Finlayson; m. Michael R. Gregory, May 15, 1981 (div. 1982); children from previous marriage: Jarrell (Geno) Hurley II, Jason Douglas Hurley. AA magna cum laude, Diablo Valley Coll., Pleasant Hill, Calif.; BS in Fin., Mktg. and Bus. Adminstrn. Mgmt., Calif. State U., Hayward, 1990. Lic. tax acct.; lic. real estate agt. Investment analyst Camilto Mgmt. Co., Lafayette, Calif., 1980-82; office mgr. Gilbert Constrn., Martinez, Calif., 1982-84; acctg. mgr. Richmond (Calif.) Drydock, 1981-82; A/P mgr. Sassoon-Sherman, Oakland, Calif.; tax acct. Beneficial Tax, Pleasant Hill, 1985-88; realtor Mason-McDuffie Real Estate, Clayton, Calif., 1990—; fin. cons., tax acct. Gregory & Assocs., Sonora, Calif., 1983—; tax/audit. rep., Concord, Calif.; mng. representative Excel Comms., 1994—. Mem. NAFE, Nat. Soc. of Pub. Accts., Nat. Assn. Realtors, Calif. Assn. Realtors, Contra Costa Bd. Realtors (participant canned food dr. Walnut Creek, Calif. 1990—), Moose, BAM, R.E. Fin. Planners. Republican. Office: Mason McDuffie Real Estate 5400 B 1 Ignacio Valley Rd Concord CA 94520

GREGORY, NELSON BRUCE, motel owner, retired naval officer; b. Syracuse, N.Y., Aug. 4, 1933; s. Nelson Bruce and Josephine (Sully) G.; m. Bonnie K. Bannowsky, May 2, 1961 (div. 1970); children: Elizabeth Jo, Jennifer Kay; m. Patricia Ann Greenhalgh, Oct. 15, 1977 (div. 1994); children: Peter Ward, Annette Frances, Michael John, Geoffrey Charles. BS, N.Y. Maritime Coll., 1955; postgrad., USN Pilot Tng., Pensacola, Fla., 1955-57; grad., NATO Weapons Sch., Oberammergau, Fed. Republic of Germany, 1966; diploma, Joint Warfare Sch., Salisbury, Eng., 1967, USN Counter Insurgency, Little Creek, Va., 1968, USAF Space Ops., Montgomery, Ala., 1969. Commd. ens. USN, 1955, advanced through grades to lt. comdr., 1964; operational pilot airborne Early Warning Squadron 2 USN, Patuxent River, Md., 1957-60; flight instr. Airborne Early Warning Tng. Unit USN, Patuxent River, 1960-63; command pilot Air Devel. Squadron 6 USN, McMurdo Sound, Antarctica, 1963-64; airspace control officer NATO, Naples, Italy, 1964-68; chief pilot Naval Support Activity, Danang, Vietnam, 1968-69; space intelligence analyst NORAD, Colorado Springs, Colo., 1969-71; operational pilot Electronic Warfare Squadron 33 USN, Norfolk, Va., 1971-74; ops. officer Nat. Parachute Test Range USN, El Centro, Calif., 1974-75; ret. USN, 1975; owner, gen. mgr. Bonneville Motel, Idaho Falls, Idaho, 1975—; bd. dirs. Am. Travel Inns, 1976-78. Patron Idaho Falls Symphony/Opera Theater, 1980—; mem. Better Bus. Bur., 1989; POW return sponsor, 1973. Decorated Air medals (3) USN; recipient Vietnamese Gallantry Cross Republic of Vietnam, 1969; Gregory Ridge in Antarctica named for him, 1964. Mem. Ret. Officers Assn. (life), Idaho Falls C. of C., Elks. Republican. Presbyterian. Home: 2000 S Yellowstone Hwy Idaho Falls ID 83402-4325

GREGSON, GARRY EVAN, statistical engineer, information consultant; b. Murray, Utah, Dec. 17, 1965; s. Garry Wilbur and Patricia Joan (Rolfson) G.; m. Bonnie Kay Secrist, June 10, 1989; children: Samantha Nishell, Garry William, Maddison Marie. BS in Psychology, BS in Health Adminstrn, Weber State U., Ogden, Utah, 1993. Pesticide applicator Pest Control, Kelonna, B.C., Can., 1987; personal computer functional test operator IOMEGA, Roy, Utah, 1988; statis. engr. Matrixx Mktg., Ogden, 1988—; habilitation technician North Side Ctr., Ogden, 1989; cons., ptnr. Prestige Mktg., Ogden, 1995—; cons. Estate Mgmt., Ogden, 1995. Co-author: Mount Olympus Power System, 1995. Scoutmaster Boy Scouts Am., Ogden, 1995—; missionary LDS Ch., Des Moines, 1985-87. Recipient Chief Scout award Boy Scouts Can., Calgary, 1979, Duty to God award LDS Ch., Calgary, 1980. Mem. Psi Chi. Home and Office: 4239 Monroe Blvd Ogden UT 84403

GREINER, ROBERT PHILIP, lawyer, real estate broker; b. Herkimer, N.Y., July 3, 1930; s. Max Henry and Margaret Mary (O'Hara) G. BA, U. Rochester, 1951; MBA, Syracuse U., 1957; LLB, UCLA, 1964. Bar: Calif. 1965; CPA, Calif.; lic. real estate broker, Calif. Pvt. practice acct., CPA, 1962-64; lawyer L.A. (Calif.) Pub. Defenders Office, 1965-87; pvt. practice lawyer and real estate broker Calif., 1987—. Pres. Guide Dog Boosters, Los Alamitos, Calif., 1984. Staff sgt. USAF, 1951-55. Home and Office: 730 Natalie Dr Windsor CA 95492-8870

GREINER MAKENNA, CARRIE ANN, religious science practitioner; b. Denver, Sept. 25, 1959; d. Rodney Earl and Ruth Ellen (Brunskill) G.; m. Craig Evan Rouse, Oct. 8, 1993. BFA, Colo. State U., 1982. Cert. massage therapist, Jin Shin Jyutsu practitioner; lic. spiritual counselor. Graphic designer office of comm. Colo. State U., Ft. Collins, 1982-83, prodn. artist Collegian newspaper, 1982-83; art dir. Cimarron Prodns., Denver, 1984-85; owner design bus. The Solution Rm., Denver, 1985-86; massage in pvt. practice Denver, 1986-92; religious sci. practitioner Mile Hi Ch., Denver, 1991—; mgr. corp. comm. First Trust Corp., Denver, 1986-95. Democrat.

GRENFELL, GLORIA ROSS, freelance journalist; b. Redwood City, Calif., Nov. 14, 1926; d. Edward William and Blanch (Ross) G.; m. June 19, 1948 (div. Nov. 15, 1983); children: Jane, Barbara, Robert, Mary. BS, U. Oreg., 1948, postgrad., 1983-85. Coll. bd., retail sales Meier & Frank Co., Portland, Oreg., 1945; book sales retailer J.K. Gill & Co., Portland, Oreg., 1948-50; advisor Mt. Hood Meadows Women's Ski Program, Oreg., 1968-78; corp. v.p. OK Delivery System, Inc., Oreg., 1977-82; ski instr. Willamette Pass, Oreg., 1983-85, Mt. Shasta, 1986; Campfire girls leader Portland, 1958-72; freelance journalist Marina, Calif., 1986—. Mem. Assn. Jr. League Internat., 1957-87; mem. Monterey County Mental Health Adv. Commn., 1994—, So. Poverty Law Ctr., 1994—, No. Mariposa County History Ctr., Calif. Recipient Golden Poles award Mt. Hood Meadows, 1975. Mem. Soc. Profl. Journalists, Profl. Ski Instrs. Am., U.S. Ski Assn., Calif. State Sheriffs' Assn. (assoc.), Monterey History and Art Assn., Yosemite Assn., Monterey Sports Ctr., Carmel Women's Club, Mariposa County C. of C., Monterey Bay Area Nat. Alumnae Panhellenic. Order Ea. Star, DAR (Commodore Sloat chpt.), Citizens for Law and Order, Mortar Bd., Kappa Alpha Theta.ADR. Democrat. Episcopalian. Home and Office: 3128 Crescent Ave Lot 9 Marina CA 93933-3131

GRENIER, JUDSON A., JR., history educator; b. Indpls., Mar. 6, 1930; s. Judson A. Sr. and Beatrice Olivia (Bjeldanes) G.; m. Nancy Hicks, Aug. 9, 1954; children: Karen, Eric, Jonathan, Caddie. BA, U. Minn., 1951; MA, U. Calif., Berkeley, 1952; PhD in History, UCLA, 1965. Teaching asst. U. Calif., Berkeley, 1951-52; analyst IPS U.S. Dept. of State, Washington, 1952; reporter L.A. Mirror-News, 1958, 59; instr. El Camino Coll., Torrance, 1956-65; prof. Calif. State U., Dominguez Hills, 1966-94, prof. emeritus, 1994—; vis. lectr. UCLA, 1965-66; mem. acad. senate Calif. State U., 1974-83, sec., 1976-78, vice chmn., 1979-80, dir. oral history project, 1986-89, 94—; cons. El Pueblo St. Historic Park, L.A., 1980-83, City of Gardena, Calif., 1980-87, City of Torrance, Calif., 1980-82, City of Redondo Beach, Calif., 1985-87, L.A. County Dept. of Edn., 1979-81. Author: California Legacy: Watson-Dominguez Family, 1987; edit. cons. Calif. History; contbr. articles to profl. jours. Recipient Community Disting. Svc. award Calif. State U., 1987, Hist. Soc. So. Calif. Pflueger award, 1991, Wheat award, 1993; NEH fellow, 1984, Huntington-Haynes fellow, 1985, Newberry Fellow, 1991. Mem. Am. Hist. Assn., Hist. Soc. of So. Calif. (v.p. 1981-83), L.A. 200 (hist. and edn. coms. 1978-81), L.A. Bicentennial Com. (hist. team 1973-76). Home: 587 33rd St Manhattan Beach CA 90266-3405 Office: Calif State U 1000 E Victoria St Carson CA 90747-0001

GREYTAK, LEE JOSEPH, lender services and real estate development company executive; b. Bridgeport, Conn., Sept. 14, 1949; s. Eugene E. and Dorothy B. Greytak; BA in Acctg., Calif. State U., Fullerton, 1973; m. Judy C. Welch, Aug. 31, 1974; children: Marzette Rachelle, Melissa Renee, Joseph Scott. Sr. acct. Collins Foods Internat., Los Angeles, 1974-75; asst. controller Jack La Lanne European Health Spas, Los Angeles, 1975-77; controller Trammell Crow Co., Los Angeles, 1977-83, corp. sec., 1981-83; exec. v.p., chief fin. officer T.D. Service Fin. 1983—, also bd. dirs., 1983—; pres., Territory Devel., 1983-90. Mem. Nat. Assn. Accts., Am. Mgmt. Assn., Nat. Cash Mgmt. Assn., So. Calif. Cash Mgmt. Assn., Builders, Owners, and Mgrs. Assn., Aircraft Owners and Pilots Assn., C. of C. of U.S., Young Execs. of So. Calif., Christian Businessmens Com. of USA. Home: 2918 Shamrock Ave Brea CA 92821-4748 Office: TD Service Fin 1750 E 4th St Ste 800 Santa Ana CA 92821-3923

GRIBOW, DALE SEWARD, lawyer, business executive; b. Chgo., June 18, 1943; s. Obby and Norma (Howard) G. BA, U. So. Calif., 1965; JD, Loyola U., L.A., 1968; postgrad. legal studies UCLA, U. So. Calif. Bar: Calif. 1969, U.S. Dist. Ct. (cen. dist.) Calif. 1970, U.S. Supreme Ct. 1977, U.S. Tax Ct., 1983. Dep. pub. defender L.A. County, 1970-74; sr. ptnr. Gribow, Benjamin & Sandler, Beverly Hills, Calif., 1974-76; pvt. practice law, Beverly Hills, 1976—; pres., chmn. bd. Nutritional Biol. Corp., L.A., 1981-83; owner Exec. Credit Control, Inc., L.A., 1979-83, DDM Properties, L.A., 1981-86; judge pro tem L.A. Mcpl. Ct., 1977-94, Van Nuys, West L.A., Beverly Hills mcpl. cts., 1983-89; dir. Aspen mktg.; mem. adv. bd. Dist. Atty. L.A., 1976-78; city Atty. L.A., 1980-83; owner Gribow Constrn., Inc., 1992—; guest lectr., faculty Internat. Coll. of Surgeons Conv., 1990-96, interviewee CNN Cable News, Sta. KCOP-TV, KABC, CBS, NBC; weekly columnist Accidentally Yours, Century City News, 1991-94; columnist LA Herald Examiner, Santa Monica Evening Outlook; radio talk show host Accidentally Yours, 1991-94; guest radio host Talk Politics, Sta. KPSI, 1996, 97; legal analyst ABC TV & Radio, 1994—; frequent guest on numerous radio & TV shows; featured in LA Times Soc., 1989-93, Century City News, 1990-93, Club & Sports Society (front cover), 1990, 93, Sand to Sea Mag. (front cover), 1995; contbr. articles to profl. jours. Mem. U.S. Congressional Adv. Bd., 1982-89; selected 1982 fund raising chmn. Loyola Law Sch. Alumni; founder Concerned Adults for Dubnoff Sch., a sch. for handicapped children, 1972, pres., 1974-77, 80-81, bd. dirs., 1974-83; bd. dirs. Thalians, 1975—, exec. bd., 1983—, acting pres., 1992-94, exec. v.p., 1990—, exec. vice chmn., 1988—, program chmn., 1983-84, mem. exec. com. Presidents Club, 1980—, chmn. Thalian Ball, 1987, 88; bd. dirs. Guardians Jewish Home for Aged, 1981—, v.p., 1983-84, chmn. spl. events, 1983; bd. dirs. Westside chpt. Kidney Found., West Side Symphony Assn., 1982-84, Ctr. for Improvement Child Caring, 1983-85, Dubnoff Ctr. for Handicapped Children, 1974-85, Boys and Girls Club L.A., 1982-85, founder, chmn. bd. Beverly Hills Men's Charities, 1981—; chmn. Scopus Soc., 1983-88; mem. nat. com. Presdl. Task Force, 1989; founding mem. Children's Liver Transplant Found., 1983-84; contbg. mem. City of Hope, Nat. Jewish Hosp. and Rsch. Ctr., St. Jude's Hosp., Simon Weisenthal Ctr. for Holocaust Studies, Patrons Art Soc., Greater L.A. Zoo Assn., L.A. County Mus., Natural History Mus., Earl Warren Inst., L.A. World Affairs Council, Mcpl. League Beverly Hills, Am. Film Inst., Commerce Assocs. of U. So. Calif., West L.A. Boosters Assn.; v.p. Am. Friends Hebrew U., 1985-90; trustee U. Judaism Continuing Edn., 1984-86; mem. nat. bd. advisors, founder Gribow Rsch. Found. Sudden Arrythmia Death Syndrome, 1992-95, CARE, 1995—; pres. Inst. Critical Care Medicine 911 PLUS, 1994-95, Childrens Discovery Mus., 1996—; bd. trustees, chair numerous coms. Palm Valley Sch., 1995, chmn. annual fund raiser, 1995, 96, chmn. Larry King Dinner Sheba Med. Ctr., 1995; co-chair Gil Garcetti for DA Dinner, 1994; mem. Palm Desert Civic Arts Com., 1997; bd. dir. Am. Diabetes Assn., 1997, MS Walk, 1997; hon. bd. dirs. Theatre Mirage, 1997; master ceremonies Big Brother Big Sister Man of the Yr. Dinner, 1997. Recipient David Schloss Meml. award, 1974, plaque City of L.A., 1977, 80, 82; named hon. Ky. Col., 1981, Man of Yr., ABI, 1990, 93, City of Hope, 1992, recipient Spirit of Life award 1992; commendation from Gov. Jerry Brown, 1982; resolution Calif. State Assembly and Senate, 1982, 92; award for svc. Ronald McDonald House for Childrens Cancer, 1984; numerous other commendations and proclamations; Dale Seward Gribow Day proclaimed in Beverly Hills, 1982, 88, Dale Seward Gribow Day declared in L.A., 1988; award Scopus Soc., 1988, award Am. Friends Hebrew U., 1988 . Mem. L.A. Jaycees, U. So. Calif. Law Alumni, State Bar Calif., L.A. County Bar Assn. (cert. of appreciation 1984), Beverly Hills Bar Assn. (cert. of appreciation 1984), West Hollywood Bar Assn., San Fernando Valley Bar Assn., Calif. Trial Lawyers Assn. (guest lectr. 1990, pres.' club 1990, Outstanding Achievement award 1991), L.A. Trial Lawyers Assn., L.A. Criminal Cts. Bar Assn., Calif. Attys. for Criminal Justice, San Fernando Valley Criminal Cts. Bar Assn., Scopus Soc. (bd. dir. 1983—, chmn. 1986—), Palm Valley C. of C., Vikings, Blue Key, Phi Alpha Delta. wish. Clubs: Friars (membership com., bd. dirs., chmn. legal com. 1989, 90), Variety (bd. dir. 1982-85), Magic Castle, Marbles (bd. dir.), PIPS (v.p., bd. dir. 1982—), J. Daniels, Lincoln. Lodge: B'nai B'rith, Palm Desert Rotary, Bulls and Bears Pvt. Club (chmn. bd. govs.). Office: 43-585 Monterey Ave # 1 Palm Desert CA 92260

GRIDLEY, GEORGE THOMAS, dean; b. Gridley, Calif., Jan. 5, 1935; s. Samuel Thomas and Bertha Mildred (Matlock) G.; m. Jana Fae Davis, Mar. 31, 1954 (div. 1976); children: Cathy E., Mark D., Michael K., Scott M., Keri D., Marci D.; m. Denise Adele Verbeck, May 18, 1986. BA, Chapman Coll., 1972, MEd, 1974; EdD, U. San Francisco, 1985. Tchr. elecs. Sacramento City Schs., 1974-76, 78-80, tchr. spl. edn., 1976-78; instr. elecs. Am. River Coll., Sacramento, 1980-90, dean engring. tech., 1990—. Lobbyist CITEA, Sacramento, 1990-96. With USAF, 1953-74. Mem. Am. Vocat. Assn., Calif. Indsl. & Tech. Edn. Assn. (pres. 1974-96), Calif. Coun. Elec. Instrs.(sec. 1979-81), Indsl. & Tech. Edn. Assn., Toastmasters, Epsilon Pi Tau. Democrat. Roman Catholic. Home: 9134 River Look Ln Fair Oaks CA 95628-6568 Office: Am River Coll 4700 College Oak Dr Sacramento CA 95841-4217

GRIEGO, ELIZABETH BROWNLEE, college dean; b. Lincoln, Nebr., Nov. 9, 1949; d. John Templeton and Elizabeth (Waugh) B.; m. Robert Frederick Griego, Aug. 19, 1972; children: Ann Elizabeth Brownlee, Paul Christopher. BS Speech, Hearing Pathology/Audiology, U. Nebr., 1971; MS, Ohio State U., 1972; PhD in Higher Edn. Adminstrn., U. Calif., Berkeley, 1983. Residence dir. U. Nebr., Lincoln, 1972-73, summer conf. mgr., 1973, 74, complex program dir. office of univ. housing, 1973-75; dir. student activities for residence halls San Francisco State U., 1975-76; asst. dean students/dir. residential life Mills Coll., 1976-80, assoc. dean students/dir. student activities, 1980-81, dir. planning and rsch., sec. to bd. trustees, 1981-86, dir. planning and rsch./spl. asst. to pres., 1986-89; dean student affairs and rsch. Samuel Merritt Coll., Oakland, Calif., 1989—; condr. numerous workshops in field; evaluator various orgns./instns.; lectr. in field. Contbr. articles to profl. jours.; author: Samuel Merritt College Factbook, 1992, 3d edit. 1994, (monograph) Samuel Merritt College Alumni Profile, 1992. Bd. dirs. Inst. for Hist. Study of Bay Area, 1983-85; organizer Habitat for Humanity, Oakland, 1994—; organizer, mem. cmty. svc. tchr. aide and tutoring program Lakeview Elem. Sch., Oakland, 1995-96; organizer, mem. after-sch. tutoring program santa Fe Elem. Sch., Oakland, 1993—; deacon Piedmont Cmty. Ch., liaison to Oakland Coalition of Cmty. chs. and cmty. organizing chair, 1993-96; bd. dirs. Citizens Highly Interested in Music Edn., Piedmont, 1988-89; prodr. original children's opera The Pillow of Kantan, Piedmont Choirs, 1990; 1st v.p. bd. dirs., chair long range planning com. Camp Fire Internat., Alameda, Contra Costa Coun., 1987-90; bd. dirs. Ctr. for Edn. of the Infant Deaf, 1987-89, Mothers Club of Wildwood Sch., 1987-89; adv. com. Mercy H.S. Project 2000, San Francisco, 1985-86; adv. bd. Displaced Homemakers Assn., 1983-85; pres. Claremont Hills Neighborhood Assn., 1983-85. Recipient Blue Bird award for outstanding leadership Alameda-Contra Costa Coun. of Camp Fire Boys and Girls, 1990, Award of the Wolf for greatest ann. achievement and svc. to multicultural group Samuel Merritt Coll., 1994; Student Body Assn. Yearbook dedication for Educator Who Had Greatest Impact on Students, 1990. Mem. Nat. Assn. Student Pers. Adminstrs. (chair exec. com. for no. Calif. 1994-96), Western Assn. Schs. and Colls. (mem. accreditation team 1991-95), Calif. Assn. Instl. Rsch. (exec. com. 1992-93, pres. 1991-92, mem. reorganizing com. 1986-87, Award recognition for serving on 1st exec. bd. 1989, Pres.'s Award for Leadership 1992, Outstanding Svc. award 1993), Western Assn. Women Historians (bd. dirs., chair com. grad. scholarship award 1986-87). Home: 7 Abbott Way Piedmont CA 94618-2609 Office: Samuel Merritt College 370 Hawthorne Ave Oakland CA 94609-3108

GRIER, JAMES EDWARD, hotel company executive, lawyer; b. Ottumwa, Iowa, Sept. 7, 1935; s. Edward J. and Corinne (Bailey) G.; m. Virginia Clinker, July 4, 1959; children: Michael, Susan, James, John, Thomas. BSc, U. Iowa, 1956, JD, 1959. Bar: Iowa 1959, Mo. 1959. Mng. ptnr. Hillix, Brewer, Hoffhaus & Grier, Kansas City, Mo., 1964-77, Grier & Swartzman, Kansas City, 1977-89; pres. Doubletree Hotels Corp., Phoenix, 1989-94; chmn. Sonoran Hotel Capital, Inc., Phoenix, 1994-96; mng. ptnr. Copa Investments, 1996—; bd. dirs. Iowa Law Sch. Found., Iowa City, Mercy Healthcare Ariz., Phoenix, Homeward Bound, Phoenix. Home: 3500 E Lincoln Dr Phoenix AZ 85018-1010 Office: Copa Investments 4400 N 32d St Ste 105 Phoenix AZ 85018

GRIESCHE, ROBERT PRICE, hospital purchasing executive; b. Berkeley, Calif., July 21, 1953; s. Robert Bowen and Lillian (Price) G.; m. Susan Dawn Albers, June 8, 1985 (div. Apr. 1989); 1 child, Sara Christine. AA, Coll. of the Canyons, Valencia, Calif., 1984. Warehouse supr. John Muir Hosp., Walnut Creek, Calif., 1973-82; purchasing mgr. Henry Mayo Newhall Hosp., Valencia, 1982-85; materials mgr. Foothill Presbyn. Hosp., Glendora, Calif., 1985-87; materials mgmt. dir. Huntington Meml. Hosp., Pasadena, Calif., 1987-96; sys. dir. purchasing So. Calif. Healthcare Sys., Pasadena, 1996—; chmn. Huntington Employee Campaign, 1990-92. V.p. Coll. of Canyons Found., Valencia, 1985-90. Named to Outstanding Young Men of Am., 1988. Mem. Am. Soc. Healthcare Materials Mgmt., Calif. Cen. Svc. Assn. (charter). Republican. Presbyterian. Home: 3651 Cosmos Ct Palmdale CA 93550-5748 Office: Huntington Hosp 1300 E Green St Pasadena CA 91106 also: So Calif Healthcare Sys 1300 E Green St Pasadena CA 91106

GRIESEMER, ALLAN DAVID, retired museum director; b. Mayville, Wis., Aug. 13, 1935; s. Raymond John and Leone Emma (Fisher) G.; m. Nancy Jean Sternberg, June 6, 1959; children: David, Paul, Steven. A.B., Augustana Coll., 1959; M.S., U. Wis., 1963; Ph.D., U. Nebr., 1970. Curator; coordinator ednl. services U. Nebr., Lincoln State Museum, 1965-77, assoc. prof., assoc. dir., 1977-79, acting dir., 1980-81, assoc. dir. and coordinator, 1981-82, interim dir., 1982-84; dir. San Bernardino County Mus., Calif., 1984—; mem. faculty dept. geology U. Nebr., Lincoln, 1968-80; lectr. geology U. Nebr., Lincoln State Mus., 1968-80; CEO, dir., curator Mousley Mus. Natural History, Yucaipa, Calif.; adj. prof. Calif. State U., San Bernardino, 1986. Contbr. articles to sci. jours., mus. publs., 1965—. Bd. dirs. Redlands Music Assn., Prospect Pk., Boys and Girls Club, Juland Harvest, Calif. Desert Studies Consortium; mem. adv. bd. Redlands Cmty. Hosp. Recipient Hon. award Sigma Gamma Epsilon, 1958. Mem. Paleontol. Soc., Nebr. Mus. Conf. (pres. 1976-79), Nebr. Geol. Soc., Nebr. Acad. Scis., Mountain Plains Conf., Mountain Plains Mus. Assn. (pres. 1979), Am. Assn. Museums (v.p. 1983), Am. Assn. State and Local History, Western Museums Conf., Rotary. Lutheran. Home: 306 La Colina Dr Redlands CA 92374-8247 Office: Mousley Mus Natural History 35308 Panorama Dr Yucaipa CA 92399

GRIESON, RONALD EDWARD, economist; b. N.Y.C., Mar. 8, 1943; s. Hans and Stella Grieson; m. Barbara Anne Grieson, Aug. 29, 1970. BA with honors, CUNY, 1964; MA, U. Rochester, 1966, PhD, 1969. Prof. econs. MIT, Cambridge, Mass., 1969-72, CUNY, N.Y.C., 1972-74; assoc. prof. econs. Columbia U., N.Y.C., 1974-79; vis. prof. econs. Princeton U., N.J., 1979-80; prof. econs. U. Calif., Santa Cruz, 1980—; cons. DRI/McGraw-Hill, Lexington, Mass., 1976—. Editor 4 books; editor Jour. Urban Econs., 1974-95, Nat. Tax Jour., 1992-94; contbr. chpts. to books, articles to profl. jours. NSF fellow, 1964; Herbert Lehman fellow, 1966-69; recipient various grants. Mem. Am. Econs. Assn., Econometric Soc., Nat. Tax Assn. Home: 27 Ridgecrest Dr Scotts Valley CA 95066-4174 Office: U Calif Dept Econs/SSI Santa Cruz CA 95064

GRIFFEY, KEN, JR. (GEORGE KENNETH GRIFFEY, JR.), professional baseball player; b. Donora, Pa., Nov. 21, 1969. Grad. high sch., Cin. Outfielder Seattle Mariners, 1987—. Recipient Gold Glove award, 1990-94; named to All-Star team, 1990-95, All-Star game MVP, 1992, , Sporting News Am. League Silver Slugger team, 1991, 93-94, Sporting News All-Star team, 1991, 93-94. Office: Seattle Mariners PO Box 4100 83 King St Seattle WA 98104-2860*

GRIFFIN, DEWITT JAMES, architect, real estate developer; b. L.A., Aug. 26, 1914; s. DeWitt Clinton and Ada Gay (Miller) G.; m. Jeanmarie Donald, Aug. 19, 1940 (dec. Sept. 1985); children: Barbara Jean Griffin Holst, John Donald, Cornelia Caulfield Claudius, James DeWitt (dec.); m. Vivienne Dod Kievenaar, May 6, 1989. BA, UCLA, 1936-38; B.A., U. Calif., 1942. Designer Kaiser Engrs., Richmond, Calif., 1941; architect CF Braun & Co., Alhambra, Calif., 1946-48; pvt. practice architecture Pasadena, Calif., 1948-50; prin. Goudie & Griffin Architects, San Jose, Calif., 1959-64, Griffin & Murray, 1964-66, DeWitt J. Griffin & Assocs., 1966-69; pres. Griffin/Joyce Assocs., Architects, 1969-80; chmn. Griffin Balzhiser Affiliates (Architects), 1974-80; founder, pres. Griffin Cos. Internat., 1980—; founder, dir. San Jose Savs. and Loan Assn., 1965-75, Capitol Services Co., 1964-77, Esandel Corp., 1965-77. Pub. Sea Power mag, 1975-77; archtl. works include U.S. Post Office, San Jose, 1966, VA Hosp, Portland, 1976, Bn. Barracks Complex, Ft. Ord, Calif., 1978. bd. dirs. San Jose Symphony Assn., 1973-84, v.p. 1977-79, pres. 1979-81; active San Jose Symphony Found., 1981-86, v.p. 1988-90; bd. dirs. Coast Guard Acad. Found., 1974-87, Coast Guard Found., 1987-90; founder, bd. dirs. U.S. Navy Meml. Found., 1978-80, trustee, 1980—; trustee Montalvo Ctr. for Arts, 1982-88. Served to comdr. USNR, 1942-46, 50-57. Recipient Navy Meritorious Pub. Svc. medal, 1971, Disting. Service medal Navy League of U.S., 1973; Coast Guard Meritorious Pub. Svc. medal, 1975; Navy Disting. Pub. Svc. medal, 1977; Coast Guard Disting. Pub. Svcs. medal, 1977. Fellow Soc. Am. Mil. Engrs.; mem. AIA (emeritus), U.S. Naval Inst., Navy League U.S. (pres. Santa Clara Valley coun. 1963-66, Calif. state pres. 1966-69, nat. dir. 1967—, exec. com. 1968—, pres. 12th region 1969-71, nat. v.p. 1973-75, nat. pres. 1975-77, chmn. 1977-79), U.S. Naval Sailing Assn., Naval Order of U.S., Confrevre de la Chaine des Rotisseurs, Wash. Athletic Club (Seattle), St. Francis Yacht Club, Commonwealth of San Francisco Club, Phi Gamma Delta. Republican. Congregationalist. Home and Office: 8005 NE Hunt Club Ln Hansville WA 98340-9756

GRIFFIN, DORSEY, author; b. Seattle, Mar. 9, 1920; s. Edwin Ray and Matilda Emma (Coleman) G.; m. Doris Mac Dougall; children: Dennis,

Margaret, Brendan, Bernard, Marcia, Mary, Therresa, Brongaene, Galen. Student, Seattle U., 1946-49. With U.S. Postal Svc., Seattle; tooling inspector Boeing Co., Seattle, 1949-62, bldg. maintenance engr., 1962-82. Author: SILKIE! Seal-Folk Tales, Songs and Ballads, 1985, Who Really Killed Chief Paulina? An Oregon Documentary, 1990, Starting at the Narrows: A History of Southern Harney County, Oregon, 1990, Compendium of Oregon History, 1997. Sgt. U.S. Army, 1942-45. Decorated Bronze Star. Democrat. Roman Catholic. Home: PO Box 1022 Tillamook OR 97141

GRIFFIN, ELAINE BURKS, secondary school educator; b. Westfield, N.Y., Sept. 10, 1947; d. John W. and Aldine K. (Kerr) Burks; m. Edward Hitchcock Griffin, Sept. 21, 1968; children: Vera, Marie, Marjeena. BA, Columbia Univ., 1969; MLS, Univ. Calif., Berkeley, 1971. Cert. secondary sch. tchr. Children's libr. Flagstaff (Ariz.) Pub. Libr., 1971-75; tchr. Akhiok (Alaska) Sch., 1975-81; head tchr. Chiniak (Alaska) Chs., 1981—. Bd. dirs. Chiniak Pub. Libr., 1985-95. Named Nat. Tchr. of Yr., Coun. Chief State Sch. Officers, 1995. Mem. NEA, Kappa Delta Pi. Home: PO Box 5502 Chiniak Kodiak AK 99615 Office: Chiniak Sch Box 5529 Chiniak Kodiak AK 99615

GRIFFIN, GLORIA JEAN, elementary school educator; b. Emmett, Idaho, Sept. 10, 1946; d. Archie and Marguerite (Johnson) G. AA, Boise (Idaho) Jr. Coll., 1966; BA, Boise Coll., 1968; MA in Elem. Curriculum, Boise State U., 1975. Cert. advanced elem. tchr., Idaho. Tchr. music, tutor, Boise; sec. Edward A. Johnson, atty., Boise; tchr. Head Start, Boise; elem. tchr. Meridian (Idaho) Sch. Dist., 1968—; developer multi-modality individualized spelling program; co-developer program for adapting curriculum to student's individual differences. Author: The Culture and Customs of the Argentine People As Applied to a Sixth Grade Social Studies Unit. Sec. PTA. Named Tchr. of Yr., Meridian Sch. Dist., 1981. Mem. NEA, Internat. Reading Assn., Idaho Edn. Assn., Meridian Edn. Assn. (bldg. rep.), Idaho Reading Coun., Horizons Reading Coun., Alpha Delta Kappa (rec. sec.). Office: Silver Sage Elem Sch 7700 Snohomish St Boise ID 83709-5975

GRIFFIN, JAMES EDWARD, real estate consultant; b. Fall River, Mass., Jan. 27, 1941; s. James Edward and Marion Beatrice (Johnsen) G. AA, Napa (Calif.) Coll., 1965; BS, Calif. State U., Sacramento, 1967. CPA, Calif., Nev. Auditor Authur Young & Co., San Francisco, 1967-69, Providence, 1969-71; v.p. fin. R.I. Land Co., Providence, 1971-79; treas. Moss Land Co., Sacramento, 1979-82; chief fin. officer Equi-Real Devel. Co., Sacramento, 1982-84, Am. Nev. Co., Henderson, Nev., 1984-90; exec. v.p., chief oper. officer Am. Nev. Co., 1990-93; prin. cons. Griffin & Co., Las Vegas, 1993—; sec.-treas. acctg. adv. coun. UNLV, 1991, chmn. 1993. Recipient Bus. Adminstrn. award Bank Am., 1965. Fellow Nev. Soc. CPAs; mem. AICPA, Inst. Mgmt. Accts. (treas. Las Vegas chpt. 1991, bd. dirs. 1990). Office: Griffin & Co 7550 Pearwood Ct Las Vegas NV 89123-0546

GRIFFIN, (ALVA) JEAN, entertainer; b. Detroit, June 1, 1931; d. Henry Bethel White and Ruth Madelyn (Gowen) Durham; m. Francis Jay Griffin, July 8, 1958 (dec.); stepchildren: Patra, Rodney; 1 adopted child, Donald; children: Rhonda Jean, Sherree Lee. Student, Anderson Coll., 1952-53; DD (hon.), Ministry of Salvation, Chula Vista, Calif., 1990, Ministry of Salvation, 1990. Ordained minister, 1990. Supr. Woolworth's, Detroit, 1945-46; operator, supr. Atlantic Bell Tel. Co., Detroit, 1947-51, Anderson, Ind., 1952-56; sec. to div. mgr. Food Basket-Lucky Stores, San Diego, 1957-58; owner, mgr. Jay's Country Boy Markets, Riverside, Calif., 1962-87; entertainer, prodr., dir., singer Mae West & Co., 1980—; past owner The Final Touch, Colorado Springs; owner Omega Communique Co., 1997—; tchr. art Grant Sch., Riverside, 1964-65; tchr., adviser Mental Retarded Sch., Riverside, 1976-77; instr. Touch for Health Found., Pasadena, Calif., 1975-79; cons., hypnotist, nutritionist, Riverside, 1976-79; mem., tchr. Psi field parapsychology. Mem. Rep. Presdl. Task Force, 1983. Recipient svc. award Rep. Presdl. Task Force, 1986. Mem. Parapsychology Assn. Riverside (pres. 1981-82). Mem. Ch. of Religious Science New Thought. Home: 201 W Chapel Rd Sedona AZ 86336-7031

GRIFFIN, JEFF, mayor. Mayor City of Reno, Nev. Office: City of Reno 490 S Center St Reno NV 89501

GRIFFIN, LINDA SUE, appraiser; b. Oakdale, Calif., Aug. 23, 1947; d. Raymond Emil and Betty Arlene (Holloway) Anderson; m. Jim A. Griffin, Sept. 2, 1972. AA, Modesto (Calif.) Jr. Coll., 1968; BA, Calif. State U. Stanislaus, Turlock, 1976. Eligibility worker Stanislaus County Dept. Social Svcs., Modesto, Calif., 1969-80; appraiser Stanislaus County Assessor, Modesto, 1980—. Mem. Am. Saluki Assn. (sec. 1991-94, regional v.p. 1996—), Saluki Club Greater San Francisco (sec. 1994-96), LWV (pub. rels. 1995-86, v.p. 1996—). Home: 10607 Workman Rd Oakdale CA 95361-8530 Office: Stanislaus County Assessor PO Box 1068 1100 H St Modesto CA 95353-1068

GRIFFIN, MERV EDWARD, former entertainer, television producer, entrepreneur; b. San Mateo, Calif., July 6, 1925; s. Mervyn Edward and Rita (Robinson) G.; m. Julann Elizabeth Wright, May 18, 1958 (div. June 1976); 1 son, Anthony Patrick. Student, San Mateo Coll., 1942-44; L.H.D., Emerson Coll., 1981. Owner Teleview Racing Patrol Inc., Miami, Fla., Video Racing Patrol Inc., Seattle, Beverly Hilton Hotel, Beverly Hills, Calif., The Scottsdale (Ariz.) Hilton, Wickenburg (Ariz.) Inn; chmn. bd. Griffin Group, Inc., Beverly Hills, Zed Greeting Card Co., Scottsdale, Merv Griffin Prodns., Beverly Hills; owner Merv Griffin Entertainment, Beverly Hills. Performer Merv Griffin Show radio sta. KFRC, San Francisco, 1945-48, vocalist Freddy Martin's Orch., 1948-52; contract player, star So This is Love, Warner Bros., 1953-55; TV master ceremonies, 1958—, Merv Griffin Show, NBC-TV, 1962-63, Westinghouse Broadcasting Co., 1965-69, CBS-TV, 1969-72, syndication, 1972-86; currently exec. producing: Wheel of Fortune, Jeopardy. Club: Bohemian (San Francisco). Office: Merv Griffin Enterprises 9860 Wilshire Blvd Beverly Hills CA 90210-3115 also: The Griffin Group 780 3rd Ave New York NY 10017-2024

GRIFFIN, SYLVIA GAIL, reading specialist; b. Portland, Oreg., Dec. 13, 1935; d. Archie and Marguerite (Johnson) G. AA, Boise Jr. Coll., 1955; BS, Brigham Young U., 1957, MEd, 1967. Cert. advanced teaching, Idaho. Classroom tchr. Boise (Idaho) Pub. Schs., 1957-59, 61-66, 67-69, reading specialist, 1969-90, 91-95, inclusion specialist, 1995—, early childhood specialist, 1990-91, inclusion specialist, 1995—; tchr. evening Spanish classes for adults, 1987-88; lectr. in field; mem. cons. pool U.S. Office Juvenile Justice and Delinquency Prevention, 1991—. Author: Procedures Used by First Grade Teachers for Teaching Experience Readiness for Reading Comprehension, The Short Story of Vowels, A Note Worthy Way to Teach Reading. Advisor in developing a program for dyslexics Scottish Rite Masons of Idaho, Boise. Mem. NEA, AAUW, Internat. Reading Assn., Orton Dyslexia Soc., Horizon Internat. Reading Assn., Idaho Edn. Assn. (pub. rels. dir. 1970-72), Boise Edn. Assn. (pub. rels. dir. 1969-72, bd. dirs. ednl. polit. involvement com. 1983-89), Alpha Delta Kappa. Office: 5007 Franklin Rd Boise ID 83705-1106

GRIFFIN, W. C., bishop. Bishop Ch. of God in Christ, Albuquerque. Office: Ch of God in Christ 3322 Montclaire Dr NE Albuquerque NM 87110-1702*

GRIFFING, BARRY L., school system administrator; b. Sulphur, Okla., Sept. 24, 1933; s. William Ted and Wendell Augusta Griffing; m. Beth Griffing, July 25, 1957; children: Jill, Wendy, Meg. BS, Okla. U., 1956; MA, Gallaudet U., 1957, Calif. State U., Northridge, 1963; EdD, UCLA, 1974. Cert. elem., secondary tchr., adminstr., Ariz. Assoc., asst. state supt. P.I./Chief Bur. Phys. Handicapped, Calif. State Bd. Edn., Sacramento; supt. Ariz. Sch. for Deaf and Blind, Tucson; asst. prof. Idaho State U., Pocatello. Mem. CEC, ASCD, TED/CEC, CEASD, CAID, NSSE, Phi Delta Kappa. Home: 1091 Cherry Ln Pocatello ID 83201

GRIFFIS, STANLEY DOUGLAS, county manager; b. Odum, Ga., Oct. 25, 1942; s. John Randall and Hattie Lou (Dubberly) G.; m. Pamela Stewart, Aug. 8, 1945; children: David, Jeffery, Michelle. BBA, U. Okla., 1963; MBA, Mich. State U., 1969; PhD, St. Louis U., 1981. Commd. 2d lt. USAF, 1968, advanced through grades to maj., 1981; assoc. prof. USAF Acad., 1976-81; ret. USAF, 1982; pres. Griffco, Colorado Springs, 1982-87; dir. fin. and adminstrv. svcs. El Paso County, Colorado Springs, 1987-89; dir. fin. Douglas County, Castle Rock, Colo., 1989; county mgr. Pinal County, Florence, Ariz., 1989—; grad. prof. Regis Coll., Colorado Springs, 1983-87; adj. prof. Ctrl. Ariz. Coll., Florence, 1989—. Decorated with Vietnamese Cross of Gallantry, Bronze star. Democrat. Office: Pinal County PO Box 827 Florence AZ 85232-0827

GRIFFITH JOYNER, FLORENCE DELOREZ, track and field athlete; b. L.A., Dec. 21, 1959; d. Robert and Florence Griffith; m. Al Joyner; 1 child: Mary Ruth Joyner. Student, Calif. State U., Northridge, UCLA; PhD (hon.), Am. U., Washington, 1994. Co-owner NUCO Nails, Camarillo, Calif., 1994—; Designed line of sportswear, and uniforms for NBA Ind. Pacers. Actress (prin. role film) The Chaser, (recurring role TV drama) Santa Barbara, guest 227 TV situation comedies; host, commentator various sports events; guest numerous talk shows. Co-chairperson Pres. Coun. on Phys. Fitness & Sports, 1993—, founder The Florence Griffith Joyner Youth Found. Winner Silver medal Summer Olympics, L.A., 1984, 3 Gold medals, 1 Silver medal Summer Olympics, Seoul, Republic of Korea, 1988; U.S. Olympic Com. Sports Woman of the Year 1988, TAC Jesse Owens outstanding track and field athlete, 1988, Internat. Jesse Owens award Most Outstanding amateur athlete, 1988, Tass News Agy. Sports Personality of Yr., 1988, Internat. Fedn. Bodybuilders Most Outstanding Physique 1980s, 1988, UPI and AP Sportswoman of the year, 1988; named Athlete of Yr. Track and Field, 1988, recipient of the Harvard Found. award for outstanding contribution to the field of athletics, 1989, Essence Mag's. Sports award Extraordinary Accomplishments in Athletics, 1989, Golden Camera award from German Advt. Industry, 1989, James E. Sullivan Meml. award as most outstanding athlete in Am., 1989. Address: NUCO Nails Inc PO Box 67853 Via Alondra Camarillo CA 93012*

GRIFFITHS, ARTHUR R., professional hockey team executive. Chmn., gov. Vancouver (Can.) Canucks. Office: Vancouver Canucks, 800 Griffiths Wy, Vancouver, BC Canada V6B 6G1*

GRIFFITHS, MARIAN E. (MIMI GRIFFITHS), government administrator; b. Chgo., June 9, 1948; d. Robert Henry and Dora Irene (MacAllister) G. BA, Eastern Ill. U., Charleston, 1971, MS in LS, 1973. Audiovisual libr. Vincennes (Ind.)/Knox County Pub. Libr., 1973-74; dir. Olney (Ill.) Carnegie Pub. Libr., 1974-81; coord. adminstrv. code unit Ill. Sec. of State, Springfield, 1981-83, adminstr. adminstrv. code div., 1983-89; rules mgr. Ariz. Sec. of State, Phoenix, 1990-91, dir. pub. svcs. dept., 1991—; cons. Okla. Sec. of State/Div. Librs. Editor: Arizona Blue Book, 1993-1994, 1994, 1995-96, 1996; author, editor: (booklets) Illinois Administrative Code Style Manual, 1985-89, Arizona Notary Public Handbook, 1993; author articles. Mem. Nat. Assn. Secs. of State (exec. sec. adminstrv. codes and registers sect. 1984-87, exec. sec. emeritus 1987—, Plaque of Appreciation 1985, Resolution of Recognition 1987), Nat. Assn. Desktop Pubs. Republican. Methodist. Home: 3620 W Questa Dr Glendale AZ 85310 Office: Ariz Sec of State Office 1700 W Washington St Fl 7 Phoenix AZ 85007-2814

GRIGGS, EMMA, management executive; b. Cleveland, Ark., Feb. 8, 1928; d. James and Frazier (Byers) Wallace; m. Augusta Griggs, Mar. 20, 1954 (dec.); children: Judy A., Terri V. *My two professional daughters, Judy A. Griggs and Terri V. Griggs have been and are still extremely influential in my professional career success. We, my daughters and I, have influenced one another's respective careers and in one another's personal lives* . Grad. h.s., Chgo. Pres., CEO Burlington No. Inc., Inglewood, Calif., 1986—. Republican. *I am privileged to be President and C.E.O of a successful company, "Burlington Northern, Inc.". My career began at BNI in January of 1986. Because of my contribution to the Republican Presidential Task Force in 1996, my name will be permanently enshrined on the National Republican Victory Monument, Ronald Reagan Republican Center, 425 Second Street N.E., Washington, D.C. In 1997, I received from the Speaker of the House, the honorable Newt Gingrich, The Speaker's Citizen Task Force Certificate of Merit.*

GRIGGS, GAIL, marketing executive; b. 1937. Grad., U. Oreg., U. Chgo. Instr. Chgo. Art Inst., Roosevelt U., Chgo., Evergreen State U., Olympia, Wash.; with Griggs-Anderson, Inc., 1979—, now pres. Office: Griggs-Anderson Inc 308 SW 1st Ave Fl 4 Portland OR 97204-3400*

GRIGGS, THERESA, historic site administrator. Site supr. Fort Point Nat. Historic Site, San Francisco. Office: Fort Point Nat Hist Site PO Box 29333 Presidio San Francisco CA 94129

GRILLO, LEO, actor, photographer, animal rescuer; b. Lawrence, Mass., Feb. 6, 1949; s. Leo F. Sr. and Carmela M. (DeLucia) G. BS in speech, Emerson Coll., Boston, 1970. Actor Glendale, Calif., 1965—; pres., founder Dedication and Everlasting Love to Animals Inc., Glendale, 1979—, Living Earth Prodns., 1990—, Horse Rescue Am., 1991—; founder, pres. DELTA Rescue Netherlands, DELTA Rescue Italy; pres. Leo Grillo Prodns. Inc., 1995. Author: (with others) Landscam, 1988, Is This the Place?; producer, host Safe House, (TV show) Delta Rescue Story; actor (feature film) The Crap Game. Mem. Screen Actors' Guild, AFTRA, Actors Equity Assn. Office: DELTA PO Box 9 Glendale CA 91209-0009

GRILLY, EDWARD ROGERS, physicist; b. Cleve., Dec. 30, 1917; s. Charles B. and Julia (Varady) G.; m. Mary Witholter, Dec. 14, 1942 (dec. 1971); children: David, Janice; m. Juliamarie Andreen Langham, Feb. 1, 1973. BA, Ohio State U., 1940, PhD, 1944. Rsch. scientist Carbide & Carbon Chemicals Corp., Oak Ridge, Tenn., 1944-45; asst. prof. Chemistry U. N.H., Durham, 1946-47; mem. staff U. Calif. Nat. Lab., Los Alamos, N.Mex., 1947-80, cons., 1980—. Contbr. articles to books and profl. jours. Mem. N.Mex. House of Reps., Santa Fe, 1967-70, Los Alamos County Coun., Los Alamos, 1976-78. Mem. Am. Physical Soc., Kiwanis Club, Los Alamos Golf Club (pres. 1974-75). Republican. Home: 705 43rd St Los Alamos NM 87544-1807 *The key to my life is discovery. It always amazes me how learning can be so fascinating. Of course, the ultimate is discovery in my own vocation-physics-whether it is of my own doing or learning of a colleague's work. But, I also found that intense involvement in community work can lead to surprising results.*

GRIM, ELLEN TOWNSEND, artist, retired art educator; b. Boone County, Ind., Nov. 1, 1921; d. Horace Wright and Sibyl Conklin (Lindley) Townsend; m. Robert Little Grim, Apr. 5, 1952; children: Nancy Ellen Grim Davis, Howard Robert. BA in Art, U. Wash., 1946; MA in Art, UCLA, 1950; postgrad., Otis Art Inst., L.A., 1970-71. Cert. secondary tchr., Calif. Art tchr., chairperson secondary Calif. and L.A. Unified Sch. Dist., 1947-82; retired, 1982; artist L.A., 1975—; guest speaker on art TV and cable, L.A., 1993. One-woman shows include Ventura County Mus. Art, 1982, Riverside Mcpl. Mus., 1984, Craft and Folk Art Mus., L.A., 1986, S.W. Mus., L.A., 1987, Calif. Heritage Mus., 1991, Brand Libr. Art Galleries, 1996, others; exhibited in more than 100 group shows. 1st lt. USMC, 1943-45. Recipient Purchase prize Gardena Fine Arts Collection, 1982, Watercolor West award San Diego Watercolor Soc. Internat., 1983, N.Mex. Watercolor Soc. award, 1989, 1st pl. award Fine Arts Fedn., 1987, 1st pl. award Art Educators L.A., 1988, 89, others. Mem. Nat. Watercolor Soc. (historian 1989-90, Painting award 1984), Women Painters West (membership chair, mem.-at-large 1983-89, Painting award 1985, 86, 89, 92, 93, 95), L.A. Art Assn. (bd. dirs. 1993-95), Pasadena Soc. Artists (Painting award 1986, 88, 90, 92, 93), Collage Artists Am. (1st pl. award 1995), Women Marines Assn. and Alliance of Women Vets., Alpha Phi, Pi Lambda Theta.

GRIM, J(OHN) NORMAN, biology educator, electron microscopy consultant; b. Santa Barbara, Calif., Sept. 8, 1933; s. John Charles and Meada Fern (VanNorman) G.; m. Carole Ann Werly, June 20, 1954; children: Stephen Jay, Kristine Louise Grim Weisskopf. BA, U. Calif., Santa Barbara, 1956; MA, UCLA, 1960; PhD, U. Calif., Davis, 1967. Rsch. technician Sch. Medicine UCLA, 1959-60; rsch. technician Zoology Dept. U. Calif., Davis, 1960-67; biology professor No. Ariz. U., Flagstaff, 1967-94; prof. emeritus, 1994—; pvt. cons., Flagstaff, 1975—; dir. No. Ariz. U. Electron Microscope Facility, Flagstaff, 1968-90. Reviewer books, rsch. articles; contbr. some 40 articles to profl. jours. Commr. Boy Scouts Am., Flagstaff, 1989-91, 93—. Col. USAR, ret. Grantee NSF, 1980, 89-90, U.S. Dept. of Army, 1971-74. Mem. Am. Microscopical Soc., Soc. Protozoologists, Ariz. Soc. Electron Microscopy (pres. 1970-71, 78-79), Soaring Soc. Am., Am. Aviation Hist. Soc. Home: 3610 N Paradise Rd Flagstaff AZ 86004-1611 Office: No Ariz U Biology Dept Box 5640 Flagstaff AZ 86011

GRIMES, JAMES CAHILL, publishing executive, advertising executive; b. Oklahoma City, July 20, 1918; s. James Arthur G. and Kathryn Shanahan; m. Roma Ellison, Oct. 18, 1958; children: Joseph Edward, Jill. BA in Journalism, U. Okla., 1940. With J.C. Grimes & Assocs., Oklahoma City, 1946-49, 56-97; fundraiser Girl Scouts U.S.A., Kansas City, Mo., 1956-62; ptnr. Grimes-Valentine, Arlington, Tex., 1972-75; co-publ., S.W. Travel & Recreation Quarterly, Casa Grande, Ariz., 1983—; publ. Cochise County Mag., 1988-96, Nogales/Santa Cruz County Mag., 1990-96, Okla. Home Builder Mag., 1946-49; co-publ. Ariz...Discover It! mag., 1992-94. Publ. League of Young Dem. Newspaper, Oklahoma City, 1946-49; pres. O'Odham Tash (Indian Days), 1996-97; chmn. Mining Days, Silver City, N. Mex., 1985; chmn. Winter Art Festival, Sierra Vista, Ariz., 1990; dist. commr. Boy Scouts Am., Phoenix, 1930-96. Maj. U.S. Army, 1942-46. Recipient Silver Beaver award Boy Scouts Am., 1985. Named Tourism Citizen of Yr. C. of C., Silver City, N.M., 1985, Sierra Vista, 94. Mem. Rotary Internat., Masons, Tex. Rabbit Breeders Assn., N. Mex. Rabbit Breeders Assn. (pres.), Ariz. Rabbit Breeders Assn., Sigma Delta Chi, Delta Upsilon Fraternity (gen. sec. 1949-56). Republican. Mem. LDS Ch. Home and Office: 450 W Sunwest Dr #150 Casa Grande AZ 85222

GRIMES, JOSEPH EDWARD, computer science educator; b. Bloomington, Ill., Sept. 28, 1941; s. Edward A. and Mary C. (Kleemann) G.; m. Mary Rae Tures, Aug. 8, 1964; children: Joe, Therese, Christine, Michael, Matthew, Mark. BA, St. Ambrose U., Davenport, Iowa, 1963; MS, Ill. State U., 1968; PhD, Iowa State U., 1973. Tchr., coach Cen. Cath. High Sch., Bloomington, 1963-66; civil engr. McLean County Hwy. Dept., Bloomington, 1966-68; instr. Iowa State U., Ames, 1968-73; prof. computer sci. Calif. Poly. State U., San Luis Obispo, 1973—, mgr. computer svcs., 1986-87; cons. NASA, Moffett Field, Calif., 1974—, Xerox Corp., Santa Clara, Calif., 1989—; mem. Naval Ship Weapons Engring. Sta., Port Huenème, Calif., 1987-90; expert witness NCR Corp., 1984-89, Ford Motor Corp., 1989, State of Calif., 1992; chair CalPoly Instructional Adv. Com. on Computing, 1994—, chair UNIX Team, 1995—. Contbr. articles to profl. jours. Dir. referees San Luis Obispo Youth Soccer, 1982—; chmn. fin. coun., mem. pastoral coun. Old Mission, San Luis Obispo, 1985-89. Mem. Am. Statis. Assn., Assn. for Computing Machinery, Computing Soc. of IEEE, Mu Sigma Rho. Roman Catholic. Home: 650 Evans Rd San Luis Obispo CA 93401-8121 Office: Dept Computer Sci Calif Poly State U San Luis Obispo CA 93407

GRIMES, MARY ANNE, nurse; b. Kansas City, Kans., June 19, 1936; d. John Andy and Bertha Helen (Ball) G. RN, St. Joseph's Hosp. Cert. sch. nurse. Staff nurse St. Joseph's Hosp., Phoenix, 1957-61; office nurse Family Med. Clinic, Phoenix, 1961-62; pvt. duty nurse Central Registery, Phoenix, 1962-65; office nurse, mgr. Phoenix Urologic Clinic, 1965-79; sch. nurse Wilson Sch. Dist. 7, Phoenix, 1980-84, Balsz Sch. Dist. # 31, 1984-94; health svc. coord. Cath. Coalition for Urban Schs., Diocese of Phoenix, 1995-96; nurse, South West Sch. Roosevelt Sch. Dist., 1996—. Primary fund raiser Classical Chorus Bach and Madrigal Soc., also sec., bd. dirs.; campaign worker Republican gubernatorial election, Phoenix, 1968, 70; sec.-treas. Cen. Phoenix Coun. for Child Abuse Prevention, 1991-95; patron Spreckels Organ Soc., San Diego, Cantemus Classical Chorus, Phoenix, 1990. Mem. Am. Bus. Women's Assn. (pres. 1974-75, v.p. Phoenix 1996-97, Woman of Yr. Met. chpt. 1995, chpt. pres. 1995—), Nat. Assn. Sch. Nurses Inc., Ariz. Sch. Nurse Assn. Republican. Roman Catholic. Home: 1805 N 21st Pl Phoenix AZ 85006-2415 Office: SW Sch 1111 W Dobbins Rd Phoenix AZ 85041

GRIMES, ORVILLE FRANK, surgery educator; b. San Bernardino, Calif., Jan. 13, 1916; s. Nathan and Frances Marjorie (Aeillio) G.; m. June Levelle, June 14, 1941; children: Orville Frank Jr., Nancy L., Douglas N., Dianne Wilson. AB, U. Calif., Berkeley, 1937; MS, MD, Northwestern U., Chgo., 1942. Diplomate Am. Bd. Surgery, Am. Bd. Thoracic Surgery. Resident in surgery U. Calif., San Francisco, 1942-44, 46-49, mem. faculty, 1944-46, prof. surgery, 1949—, vice chmn. dept. surgery, 1955-61; cons. in surgery Calif. Med. Rev. Inc., San Jose, 1989-95. Contbr. over 150 articles to med. jours., chpts. to books. Maj. M.C., U.S. Army, 1944-46, ETO. Mem. ACS, Am. Surg. Assn., Pacific Coast Surg. Assn., Soc. Univ. Surgeons, Am. Assn. for Thoracic Surgery, San Francisco Surg. Soc. Republican. Episcopalian. Home: 12 Lagoon Pl San Rafael CA 94901-1521 Office: U Calif 400 Parnassus Ave San Francisco CA 94122-2721

GRIMES, PAMELA RAE, elementary school educator; b. Cumberland, Md., Dec. 30, 1943; d. Robert Elmer and Mary Evelyn (Hill) McFarland; m. George Edward Grimes, Feb. 9, 1962; children: George Edward Jr., Robert Eric, Jonathon William, David James, Richard Allen. AA, Am. River Coll., 1965; BA, Calif. State U., Sacramento, 1975, MA, 1975; cert. in computer literacy, Sacramento Unified Sch. Dist., 1981. Cert. elem. tchr., Calif. Tchr. aide O.W. Erlewine Elem. Sch., Sacramento, 1965-67, elem. gate tchr., 1969-71; tchr. aide Cohen Elem. Sch., Sacramento, 1967-69; libr., tchr. 1st through 6th grades Golden Empire Elem. Sch., Sacramento, 1979-89; tchr. Hubert Bancroft Elem. Sch., Sacramento, 1989-95; staff tng. specialist Literacy Curriculum & Instrn. Dept., 1995—; mentor tchr. Sacramento City Unified Sch. Dist., 1985-95; fellow, mem. Calif. History/Social Sci. course of study, 1991; mem. libr./lit. course of study, 1975, mem. CORE lit. com., 1979, mem. lang. arts assessment com., 1990—, mem. CLAS adv. com., 1993-94, mem. literacy task force, 1995-97, mem. adv. com. on assessment testing, 1995, co-chairperson 20-1 class size reduction program, mem. Young Authors program, mem. curriculum alignment project; literacy leader, facilitator CSIN, 1995—; No. Calif. coord. Ottawa U., 1991—; mem. lang. arts/literacy/ELD Task Force, 1996-97. Ednl. cons. Children's Mus. Com., 1985—, Sacramento History Ctr., 1985. Fellow Calif. Lit. Project, 1989, Area III Writing Project, 1988, Calif. Social Studies Inst., 1990. Fellow Calif. Geog. Inst., East Asian Humanities Inst.; mem. NEA, ASCD, SARA, CRA, IRA, Nat. Coun. Tchrs. English, Geography Inst. (mem. social studies project. stds. com. 1991), Calif. Alliance Elem. Edn., Calif. English Tchrs. Assn., Calif. Tchrs. Assn. Democrat. Methodist. Home: 9005 Harvest Way Sacramento CA 95826-2203

GRIMES, RUTH ELAINE, city planner; b. Palo Alto, Calif., Mar. 4, 1949; d. Herbert George and Irene (Williams) Baker; m. Charles A. Grimes, July 19, 1969 (div. 1981); 1 child, Michael; m. Roger L. Sharpe, Mar. 20, 1984; 1 child, Teresa. AB summa cum laude, U. Calif., Berkeley, 1970, M in City Planning, 1972. Rsch. and evaluation coord. Ctr. Ind. Living, Berkeley, 1972-74; planner City of Berkeley, 1974-76, sr. planner, 1983—, analyst, 1976-83; bd. dirs. Vets. Asssistance Ctr., Berkeley, pres., 1978-93; bd. dirs. Berkeley Design Advisors, treas., 1987-94. Author: Berkeley Downtown Plan, 1988; contbr. numerous articles to profl. jours. and other publs. Bd. dirs. Berkeley-Sakai Sister City Assn., 1994—, pres., 1995—, Ctr. Ind. Living. Honored by Calif. State Assembly Resolution, 1988; Edwin Frank Kraft scholar, 1966. Mem. Am. Inst. Cert. Planners, Am. Planning Assn., Mensa, Lake Merrit Joggers and Striders (sec. 1986-89, pres. 1991-93), Lions Internat. (bd. dirs. Berkeley club 1992-94), U. Calif. Coll. Environ. Design Alumni Assn. (bd. dirs. 1992—, treas. 1994-96). Home: 1330 Bonita Ave Berkeley CA 94709-1925 Office: City of Berkeley 2121 Mckinley Ave Berkeley CA 94703-1519

GRIMLEY, CYNTHIA PATRIZI, rehabilitation consultant, special education educator; b. Sharon, Pa., Mar. 29, 1958; d. James Donald Sr. and Delores Virginia (Maykowski) Patrizi; m. Kevin Neil Grimley, Apr. 11, 1987; children: Ronald James, Jennifer Rose. BS, Youngstown (Ohio) State U., 1981; MS, Calif. State U., 1986. Lic. multiple subject tchr., spl. edn. and elem. tchr., severly handicapped edn. tchr.; specialist credential, Calif.; cert. rehab. counselor, case mgr., human resources generalist. Residential program worker, supr., classroom tchr. Mercer County Assn. for the Retarded, Hermitage, Pa., 1980-82; tchr. spl. edn. Hermitage Sch. Dist., 1982-83; cons. property mgmt. Lorden Mgmt. Co., Covina, Calif., 1983-84; tchr. spl. edn. Fullerton (Calif.) Elem. Sch. Dist., 1984-87; vocat. rehab. cons. Profl. Rehab. Cons., Santa Ana, Calif., 1986-89, Pvt. Sector Rehab., Fullerton, 1989—i. Contbr. curriculum, articles in field. Coach Spl. Olympics, Fullerton, 1982-87; sec. So. Calif. Rehab. Exch., 1989, mem.-at-large, 1990, treas., 1991. Polish Art Club scholar, 1977. Fellow Am. Bd.

Vocat. Experts, Am. Acad. Pain Mgmt., Am. Bd. Disability Analysts; mem. NEA, Nat. Assn. Rehab. Profls. in the Pvt. Sector, Calif. Assn. Rehab. Profls., Assn. Retarded Citizens, Soc. for Human Resource Mgmt. Democrat. Roman Catholic. Office: Pvt Sector Rehab 2555 E Chapman Ave Ste 300 Fullerton CA 92831-3618

GRIMM, BOB, food products executive; b. 1954. With Grimmway Enterprises, Inc., Bakersfield, Calif., 1975—, now v.p. Office: Grimmway Enterprises Inc PO Box 81498 18071 Zerker Rd Bakersfield CA 93312*

GRIMM, LARRY LEON, psychologist; b. Goshen, Ind., Aug. 16, 1950; s. Warren Arden and Elizabeth Ann (Rassi) G.; m. Ann Mae Nelson, July 16, 1977; 1 child, Kirsten Ann. BS in Elem. Edn., No. Ariz. U., 1975, MA in Early Childhood Edn., 1977, EdD in Ednl. Psychology, 1983. Lic. psychologist; cert. sch. psychologist, elem. tchr. Ariz., Nat. Tchr. elem. sch. Page (Ariz.) Unified Dist., 1975-76; grad. asst. Coll. Edn., No. Ariz. U., Flagstaff, 1976; tchr. elem. sch. Litchfield Sch. Dist., Litchfield Park, Ariz., 1976-80; grad. assoc. dept. ednl. psychology No. Ariz. U., Flagstaff, 1980-81; sch. psychologist intern Peoria (Ariz.) Unified Dist., 1981-82; adj. faculty Grand Canyon Coll., Phoenix, 1982; sch. psychologist Child Study Services, Prescott (Ariz.) Unified Sch. Dist., 1982-87; adj. assoc. prof. No. Ariz. U., Flagstaff, 1984—, vis. faculty, 1987-88; postdoctoral fellow in pediatric psychology Child Devel. Ctr. Georgetown U. Med. Ctr., Washington, 1988-89; pvt. practice, 1989—; cons. in field; presenter at convs. Contbr. articles to profl. jours. Chmn. project devel. com. Infant & Toddler Network, 1989-92; mem. family resource ctr. adv. bd. Yavapai Regional Med. Ctr., 1990—. Mem. Am. Psychol. Assn. (publs. com. div. 16), Ariz. Assn. Sch. Psychologists (bd. dirs. No. Ariz., regional dir. 1983-84, pres. 1986-87, newsletter editor, 1986-87, Pres.'s award 1985, 88, 89), Nat. Assn. Sch. Psychologists (Ariz. del. fiscal adv. com. 1987-88, Capitol Network 1988-89), Soc. Pediatric Psychologists, Christian Assn. Psychol. Studies. Republican.

GRIMM, REINHOLD, humanities educator; b. Nuremberg, Germany, May 21, 1931; s. Eugen and Anna (Käser) G.; m. Anneliese E. Schmidt, Sept. 25, 1954; 1 dau., Ruth Sabine. Student, U. Erlangen, Germany, 1951-56, Ph.D., 1956; student, U. Colo., 1952-53; Dr. honoris causa, Georgetown U., 1988. Faculty German lit. U. Erlangen, 1957-61, U. Frankfurt, Germany, 1961-67; vis. prof. Columbia, also N.Y.U., spring 1967, U. Va., fall 1978; Alexander Hohlfeld prof. German U. Wis., 1967-80, Vilas prof. comparative lit. and German, 1980-90; presdl. prof. German and comparative lit. U. Calif., Riverside, 1990-92; mem. Inst. for Research in Humanities, U. Wis., spring 1981. Author: numerous books including Nach dem Naturalismus: Essays zur modernen Dramatik, 1978, Von der Armut und vom Regen: Rilkes Antwort auf die soziale Frage, 1981, Love, Lust and Rebellion: New Approaches to Georg Büchner, 1985, Echo and Disguise: Studies in German and Comparative Literature, 1989, Versuche zur europäischen Literatur, 1994; editor: numerous books, jours. including Monatshefte, 1979-90, German Quar., 1991-94, Deutsche Romantheorien, 2d edit., 1974, Deutsche Dramentheorien, 3d edit., 1981; co-editor: numerous books, yearbooks including Basis, 1970-80, Brecht Yearbook, 1971-81; contbr. articles to profl. jours. Recipient Förderungspreis der Stadt Nürnberg, 1964; Guggenheim fellow, 1969-70; Hilldale award, 1988. Mem. MLA, Am. Assn. Tchrs. German (hon., pres. 1974-75), PEN. Home: 6315 Glen Aire Ave Riverside CA 92506-5304

GRIMM, ROD, food products executive; b. 1946. Pres. Grimmway Enterprises, Inc., Bakersfield, Calif., 1965—. Office: Grimmway Enterprises Inc PO Box 81498 18071 Zerker Rd Bakersfield CA 93312*

GRIMMER, BEVERLEY SUE, consumer products executive; b. Olathe, Kans., June 9, 1950; d. Edward Mathines Rice and Jessie LaVaun (Cade) Waymire; m. Danny Joe San Romani, June 4, 1977 (div. May 1991); 1 child, Justin (dec.); m. Gary G. Grimmer, June 21, 1992. Student, Kans. State Tchrs. Coll., 1968-71, U. Kans., 1975-77. Employee trainer, dept. mgr. T.G.&Y. Stores, Emporia, Kans., 1968-70; office mgr. Office of Staff Judge Adv. 3d Armored Div., Frankfurt, Fed. Republic of Germany, 1971-75, Don W. Lill, Atty. at Law, Emporia, 1976-77; instr., sub. tchr. Kodiak (Ala.) C.C. and Kodiak Pub. Sch. System, 1979-81; legal sec. Kaito & Ishida, Honolulu, 1983-84; adminstr. Alcantara & Frame, Honolulu, 1984-86; ind. contractor Hughes Hubbard & Reed, N.Y., Honolulu, 1986-88; paralegal Carlsmith, Ball, Wichman, Murray, Case, Mukai & Ichiki, Honolulu, 1988-91; spl. agt. Vanuatu (Hawaii) Maritime Agy., 1989—; ch. adminstr. Ctrl. Union Ch., Honolulu, 1991-94; owner Gentle Memories, Kailua, Hawaii, 1995—; Gubernatorial coun. appointee Juvenile Justice State Adv. Coun., 1993-94; mem. women's health week com. State of Hawaii, Commn. on Status of Women, 1994. 1st v.p. Christmas in April Oahu, 1995, bd. dirs., 1995—; auction pub. chair Acad. Arts Guild, 1993; mem. Contemporary Arts Mus.; cmty. rels. and arrangements chairs for Tuxes 'n Tails Black and White Ball, Hawaiian Humane Soc., 1993, 94; mem. Hawaii Lupus Found.; bd. dirs. Armed Forces YMCA, 1995—; mem. vestry St. Christopher's Ch., 1995—. Recipient Order of Golden Swivel Shot award Comdt. USCG, 1981, 89, 1st Runner-up Maritime Week Maritime Employee award Propeller Club U.S., 1986, Letter of Appreciation, Dept. Navy, 1983, Cert. of Commendation, U.S. Army, 1975. Mem. Am. Heart Assn. (chair Celebrity Celebration 1994, silent auction co-chair 1996 Heart Ball, co-chair 1997 Heart Ball), Coast Guard Officers' Spouses Club (nominating chair 1989, pres. 1982, 87, 88), Awa Lau Wahine (Coast Guard rep. 1988, 87, corr. sec. 1983, Boutiki chair 1982), Rotary (vice chair Friends of Foster Kids Picnic 1994, chair 1995), Jr. League (cmty. v.p. 1993, rec. sec. 1990), Navy League, Propeller Club Port of Honolulu (bd. govs. alt. 1990), Hawaii Legal Aux. (v.p. 1994, pub./publs. chair 1994). Republican. Episcopalian. Home and Office: 159 Kakahiaka St Kailua HI 96734-3474

GRIMSBO, RAYMOND ALLEN, forensic scientist; b. Portland, Oreg., Apr. 25, 1948; s. LeRoy Allen and Irene Bernice (Surgen) G.; m. Barbara Suzanne Favreau, Apr. 26, 1969 (div. 1979); children: John Allen, Kimberly Suzanne; m. Charlotte Alice Miller, July 25, 1981 (div. 1994); children: Sarah Marie, Benjamin Allen. BS, Portland State U., 1972; D of Philosophy, Union for Experimenting Colls. & Univs., Cin., 1987. Diplomate Am. Bd. Criminalistics; cert. profl. competency in criminalistics DEA Rschr. Registration. Med. technician United Med. Labs., Inc., Portland, 1969-74; criminalist Oreg. State Police Crime Lab., Portland, 1975-85; pvt. practice forensic science Portland, 1985-87; pres. Intermountain Forensic Labs., Inc., Portland, 1987—; adj. instr. Oreg. Health Scis. U., Portland, 1987-95; adj. prof. Portland State U., 1986-88, adj. asst. prof., 1988—; clin. dir. Intermountain Forensic Labs., Inc., 1988-92, Western Health Lab., Portland; adj. faculty Union Inst.; mem. substance abuse methods panel Oreg. Health Divsn. Contbr. articles to profl. jours. Fellow Am. Acad. Forensic Scientists; mem. ASTM, STM, Soc. Forensic Haemogenetics, N.W. Assn. Forensic Scientists, Internat. Assn. Bloodstain Pattern Analysis, Electrophoresis Soc., Internat. Assn. Identification, internat. Assn. Forensic Toxicologists, Pacific N.W. Forensic Study, New Horizons Investment Club. Home: 16936 NE Davis St Portland OR 97230-6239 Office: Intermountain Forensic Labs Inc 11715 NE Glisan St Portland OR 97220-2141

GRIN, LEONID, conductor; b. Dniepropetrovsk, Ukraine, June 19, 1947; came to U.S., 1981; s. Gavriil and Ita (Sklar) Grinshpun; m. Marina Gusak, Apr. 25, 1970; children: Radmila, Daniel. BMus, Dniepropetrovsk Music Coll., 1966; MusM, Onesin's Music Inst., 1971; MusM in Conducting, Moscow State Conservatory, 1975, DMus, 1977. Assoc. condr. Moscow Philharm. Symphony Orch., 1977-79; prof. conducting U. Houston, 1983-86; prin. guest condr. Tampere (Finland) Philharm Orch., 1988-90, music dir., condr., 1990-94; music dir., condr. San Jose (Calif.) Symphony Orch., 1992—; guest condr. various orchs. in Denmark, Sweden, Norway, Finland, Eng., Scotland, Israel, Germany, The Netherlands, Italy, Belgium, Spain, Portugal, New Zealand, USA, Can., many others. Recs. include music by Tchaikovsky, Procofrev, Shostakovitch, all 6 symphonies by Erkki Mellartin. Office: San Jose Symphony Orchestra 495 Almaden Blvd San Jose CA 95110*

GRINDAL, MARY ANN, sales professional; b. Michigan City, Ind., Sept. 9, 1942; d. James Paxton and Helen Evelyn (Koivisto) Gleason; m. Bruce Theodore Grindal, June 12, 1965 (div. Sept. 1974); 1 child, Matthew Bruce. BSBA, Ind. U., 1965. Sec. African studies program Ind. U., Bloomington, 1965-66; rsch. aide Ghana, West Africa, 1966-68; exec. sec. divsn. biol. scis. Ind. U., Bloomington, 1968-69; office asst. Dean of Students office Middlebury (Vt.) Coll., 1969-70; exec. sec. Remo, Inc., North Hollywood, Calif., 1974-76; sec., asst. to product mgrs. in cosmetic and skin care Redken Labs., Canoga Park, Calif., 1976-79; various sec. and exec. sec. positions L.A., 1979-81, 85-89; exec. sec. Sargent Industries, Burbank, Calif., 1981-85; sales asst. Chyron Graphics, Burbank, Calif., 1989—. Author of poems and essays. Mem. U.S. Navy Meml. Found. Mem. DAR (chpt. registrar 1988-91, chpt. regent 1991-94, chpt. chmn. pub. rels. and pub. 1994—, chpt. chaplain 1994-96, mem. spkrs. staff 1995—, state chmn. Am. Heritage 1994-96, state chmn. Calif. DAR scholarship com. 1996—), Nat. Soc. Colonial Dames (rec. sec. 1989-90), Daus. of Union Vets. of Civil War, 1861-65, Inc., Nat. Soc. Daus. of Am. Colonists, Ladies of Grand Army of the Republic, Inc., Nat. Soc. Dames of the Ct. of Honor. Episcopalian.

GRINELL, SHEILA, museum director; b. N.Y.C., July 15, 1945; d. Richard N. and Martha (Mimiless) G.; m. Thomas E. Johnson, July 15, 1980; 1 child, Michael; stepchildren: Kathleen, Thomas. BA, Radcliffe Coll., 1966; MA, U. Calif., Berkeley, 1968. Co-dir. exhibits and programs The Exploratorium, San Francisco, 1969-74; promotion dir. Kodansha Internat., Tokyo, 1974-77; traveling exhbn. coord. Assn. Sci. Tech. Ctrs., Washington, 1978-80, exec. dir., 1980-82, project dir. traveling exhbn. Chips and Changes, 1982-84; assoc. dir. N.Y. Hall of Sci., 1984-87; exec. dir. Ariz. Sci. Ctr., Phoenix, 1993—; cons. Optical Soc. Am., 1987, Nat. Sci. Ctr. Found., 1988, Interactive Video Sci. Consortium, 1988, Assn. Sci. Tech. Ctrs., 1988-89, Found. for Creative Am., 1989-90, Am. Assn. for World Health, 1990, Children's TV Workshop, 1991, Sciencenter, 1991, SciencePort, 1991, The Invention Factory, 1992, N.Y. Bot. Garden, 1992-93. Author: Light, Sight, Sound, Hearing: Exploratorium '74, 1974; editor A Stage for Science, 1979, A New Place for Learning Science: Starting and Running A Science Center, 1992. Fulbright teaching asst., 1966; hon. Woodrow Wilson fellow, 1967. Fellow AAAS; mem. Am. Assn. Mus., Phi Beta Kappa. Office: Ariz Sci Ctr 600 E Washington St Phoenix AZ 85004

GRISEZ, JAMES LOUIS, physician, plastic surgeon; b. Modesto, Calif., Feb. 25, 1935; s. John Francis and Josephine Marie (Tournahu) G.; m. Diane Madeline Skidmore, Mar. 7, 1989; children: James, Stephen, Suzanne, Kathleen. MD, St. Louis Sch. Medicine, 1960. Diplomate Am. Bd. Plastic and Reconstructive Surgery. Intern D.C. Gen. Hosp., Washington, 1960-61; resident med. ctr. Georgetown U., Washington, 1961-64; resident plastic and reconstructive surgery ctr. St. Francis Meml. Hosp., San Francisco, 1964-66; military surgeon Brook Army Med Ctr., San Antonio, 1966, Second Gen. Hosp., Landstuhl, Germany, 1966-69; pvt. practice Napa, Calif., 1969-82, Salinas, Calif., 1982-90, Kailua-Kona, Hawaii, 1990-93, Gilroy, Calif., 1993—; active staff mem. St. Louise Hosp., South Valley Med. Ctr., Hazel Hawkins; chief staff St. Helena Hosp., 1977-78, exec. com. 1973-80; radio talk show host All About Plastic Surgery, sta. KRNY, 1986-88. Contbr. articles to med. jours. Mem. Am. Cancer Soc. (pres. 1988-90), Am. Soc. Plastic and Reconstructive Surgeons, Calif. Soc. Plastic and Reconstructive Surgeons, Hawaii Plastic Surgery Soc. Home: 8675 Muir Dr Gilroy CA 95020-3725 Office: 8375 Church St Gilroy CA 95020

GRISMORE, ROGER, physics educator, researcher; b. Ann Arbor, Mich., July 12, 1924; s. Grover Cleveland and May Aileen (White) G.; m. Marilynn Ann McNinch, Sept. 15, 1950; 1 child, Carol Ann. BS, U. Mich., 1947, MS, 1948, PhD, 1957; BS in Computer Sci., Coleman Coll., 1979. From asst. to assoc. physicist Argonne (Ill.) Nat. Lab., 1956-62; assoc. prof. physics Lehigh U., Bethlehem, Pa., 1962-67; specialist in physics Scripps Inst. Oceanography, La Jolla, Calif., 1967-71, 75-78; prof. physics Ind. State U., Terre Haute, 1971-74; from mem. staff to sr. scientist JAYCOR, San Diego, 1979-84; lectr. Calif. Poly. State U., San Luis Obispo, 1984-92, rsch. prof., 1992—, lunar sample investigator, 1994—. Contbr. numerous articles to profl. jours. Served as ensign USNR, 1945-46, PTO. Mem. AAAS, Am. Phys. Soc., Am. Geophys. Union, N.Y. Acad. Scis., Sigma Xi. Home: 535 Cameo Way Arroyo Grande CA 93420-5574 Office: Calif Poly State U Dept Physics San Luis Obispo CA 93407 *Experimental research scientist and educator specializing in measurements of natural and manmade gamma radioactivities in environmental and lunar samples. Codiscoverer of the radioisotope Silver-108m in the general marine environment. Developed the technique of radiosilver dating.*

GRISSINO-MAYER, HENRI DEE, research scientist; b. Monterrey, Calif., Dec. 24, 1954; s. Keith Alva and Sigrid Leota (Mayer) Summers. BS, U. Ga., 1985, MS, 1988; PhD, U. Ariz., 1995. Tchg. asst. U. Ga., Athens, 1985-88, rsch. asst., 1986, map rm. asst., 1988; grad. rsch. assoc. U. Ariz., Tucson, 1988-95, rsch. assoc. Lab. Tree-Ring Rsch., 1995—; mem. com. Internat. Tree-Ring Data Bank, Boulder, Colo., 1988—, internet list mgr., 1988—; group leader N.Am. Dendroecological Fieldweek, Ft. Collins, Colo., 1991—; internet list mgr. Biogeography Speciality Group, Tucson, 1992—. Contbr. articles to profl. publs., chpt. to book.; programmer software in field. Sci. grantee USDA Forest Svc., 1990-94, Nat. Park Svc., 1991-95, NOAA, 1992—, SWCA, Inc., 1996—. Mem. Assn. Am. Geographers, Assn. Pacific Coast Geographers, Ariz./Nev. Acad. Sci., Ariz. Archeol. and Hist. Soc., Assn. Southwestern Naturalists, Tree-Ring Soc. Office: U Ariz Lab Tree-Ring Rsch Tucson AZ 85721

GRISSOM, GARTH CLYDE, lawyer; b. Syracuse, Kans., Jan. 24, 1930; s. Clyde and Bernice Minnie (Eddy) G.; m. Elena Joyce Kerst, Aug. 17, 1958; children: Colin, Grady, Cole, Kent. B.S., Kans. State U., 1951; LL.B., Harvard U., 1957. Bar: Colo. 1957, U.S. Dist. Ct. (fed. dist.) Colo., 1957, U.S. Ct. Appeals (10th crct.) 1957, U.S. Supreme Ct. 1989. Ptnr., mem., counsel Sherman & Howard, L.L.C., Denver, 1963—. Sec., counsel, trustee Mile High United Way, Denver, 1985-88; trustee Kans. State U. Found., Manhattan, 1962-89; mem. Colo. Gov.'s Commn. on Life and the Law, 1990—, chmn., 1996—. Mem. ABA, Colo. Bar Assn., Denver Bar Assn. (pres. 1985-86, award of merit 1994), Rotary (sec. Denver 1983-84, bd. dirs. 1983-86, pres. 1989-90), Pi Kappa Alpha (pres. 1968-70). Home: 1777 Larimer St 1610 Denver CO 80202 Office: Sherman & Howard LLC 633 17th St Ste 3000 Denver CO 80202-3660

GRISSOM, LEE ALAN, state official; b. Pensacola, Fla., Sept. 7, 1942; s. Levi Aaron and Virginia Sue (Olinger) G.; m. Sharon Kay Hasty, May 14, 1966; children: David, Jonathan, Matthew, Andrew. BA in Pub. Adminstrn., San Diego State U., 1965, M in City Planning, 1971. Sr. research assoc. Western Behavioral Scis. Inst., La Jolla, Calif., 1965-73; mgr. planning div. Greater San Diego C. of C., 1973-74, gen. mgr., 1974-75, pres., chief operating officer, 1975-92; exec. dir. Coun. on Calif. Competitiveness, Gov's. Coun. Econ. advisors. Host (TV program) The City Game, 1972-75. Trustee Calif. State U., 1984-91, fin. com.; chmn. collective bargaining com., chair legis. com.; bd. dirs. Armed Forces YMCA, Econ. Devel. Corp.; chmn. San Diego Housing Commn., 1983-86, Pres.'s adv. bd., San Diego State U., 1983—; mem. Calif. Econ. Devel. Task Force, 1983—; adv. com. Fed. Home Loan Mortgage Corp.; mem. exec. com. Am.'s Cup Task Force. Named Outstanding Young Citizen San Diego Jaycees, 1976; named Outstanding Young Citizen Calif. Jaycees, 1977, one of 10 Outstanding Young Men in Am. U.S. Jaycees, 1978, Outstanding Alumnus San Diego State U., 1987. Republican. Lodge: Rotary. Office: Office Gov Pete Wilson Sacramento CA 95814

GRISWOLD, MARTHA KERFOOT, social worker; b. Oklahoma City, Mar. 22, 1930; d. John Samuel III and Frances (Mann) Kerfoot; m. George Littlefield Griswold, Jan. 28, 1967. AB, Occidental Coll., 1951; MRE, U. So. Calif., 1956, postgrad., 1962. Cert. social worker. Teen dir. Toberman Settlement, San Pedro, Calif., 1954-56; social worker County of L.A., 1956-62, 1969-72; dir. program to integrate disabled children Internat. Inst., L.A., 1979-80; cons. community orgn. L.A., 1980-84; dir. LIV Disability Resources Ctr., Altadena, Calif., 1984—; instr. Calif. State U., L.A., 1966-68, 1983-84; chair Childrens' Adv. Com. L.A. County Dept. Mental Health, 1985-86; coordinator So. Calif. Conf. on Living Long Term with Disability, 1985-87. Co-host, prodr. radio program on disability Access Unlimited, Sta. KPFK-FM, 1987—, host. prodr. cable TV program on disability issues LIVstyles, 1992—. Mem. Pasadena (Calif.) City Disability Issues Com., 1984-86, Pasadena Strategic Planning Task Force, 1985-86, City of Pasadena commn. disability access; mem. coun. on aging and long-term care Region 2 United Way, L.A., chairperson, 1989-90; mem. Pasadena Awareness: A Cmty. Effort for Disabled (PACED v.p.), 1983—. Recipient award So. Calif. Rehab. Assn., 1986, Disting. Alumna award Claremont Sch. Theology, 1996. Mem. AAUW, NASW, Californians for Disability Rights, Acad. Cert. Social Workers, Health and Social Svc. Workers with Disabilities. Congregationalist. Office: LIV Ctr 943 E Altadena Dr Altadena CA 91001-2033

GRITTER, GORDON WILLIAM, psychiatrist; b. Falmouth, Mich., Apr. 26, 1927; s. John and Jeanette Remerie (Schoolland) G.; m. Willa Kenoyer, Apr. 8, 1961 (div. 1977); children: John W., Judith A., Jeanette D., James L.; m. Dianne N. Long, June 20, 1981; children: Stacy K., Curtis D. AB, Calvin Coll., 1951; MD, Boston U., 1955. Diplomate Am. Bd. Psychiatry and Neurology, Nat. Bd. Med. Examiners, Royal Australian and New Zealand Coll. Psychiatrists. Intern Butterworth Hosp., Grand Rapids, Mich., 1955-56; resident and sr. resident Langley Porter Neuropsychiat. Inst., San Francisco, 1956-61; staff psychiatrist San Francisco (Calif.) Gen. Hosp., 1961-62; pvt. practice San Francisco, 1962-73; chief psychiatrist Shiawassee County Mental Health, Owosso, Mich., 1973-76; cons. psychiatrist Wellington (New Zealand) Hosp. Bd., 1976-79; assoc. prof. Mich. State U., East Lansing, 1979-82; staff psychiatrist Atascadero (Calif.) State Hosp., 1982-84, clin. and med. dir., 1984-96; RET., 1996; clin. asst. and assoc. prof. U. Calif., San Francisco, 1965-73, 1984-96. Lay reader, sr. warden, standing com., dep. Episcopal Ch., Calif. and Mich., 1962—. 1st lt. U.S. Army, 1945-47. Recipient Gov.'s Managerial Performance award State of Calif., 1986, 89. Fellow Am. Psychiat. Assn. (life); mem. AMA, Am. Acad. Psychiatry and Law, Physicians for Social Responsibility, Internat. Physicians for Prevention Nuclear War (Nobel Peace prize 1985), World Psychiat. Assn. Home: PO Box 2352 Avila Beach CA 93424

GRITTS, GERALD LEE, home health nurse, AIDS care nurse, AIDS educator; b. Tulsa, Okla., May 14, 1956; s. Arlie Lee and Kathleen Joyce (Thomas) G. A in Health Sci., Greenville (S.C.) Tech. Coll., 1993. RN, Colo. With Preferred Mobile Nurses, Greeley, Colo., 1993-94; grad. RN Fair Acres Manor, Greeley, Colo., 1993-94; grad. RN Quality Home Healthcare Svcs., Greeley, Colo., 1994—, dir. nursing, 1996—; advisor/cons. HIV svcs. Quality Infusion Svcs., 1994—; adj. instr. nursing U. No. Colo.; adj. instr. death, dying, grief colo. State U. Author: (pamphlets) Losing a Loved One to AIDS, 1994, When Your Partner Has AIDS, 1994; author, co-editor, co-producer: (videos) Tears, Smiles and Remembrances, 1993, Healthcare and AIDS: The PWA, Family, and Medical Professionals, 1996. Co-founder, advisor, media chairperson AIDS Pub. Edn. League, Ft. Collins, Colo., 1994-96; cons. HIV vols.; cons. student HIV svcs. Colo. State U., Ft. Collins, 1993—; vol. HIV patients No. Colo. AIDS Project, Ft. Collins, 1993—, bd. dirs., 1995—, sec., 1997—; vol. Parents, Friends of Lesbians and Gays, Denver, 1986—, Friends of the Names Project Quilt, 1994—. Recipient AIDS Health Educator award Straight, But Not Narrow Group, Ft. Collins, 1994, Profls. for AIDS Edn. award AIDS Pub. Edn. League, Ft. Collins, 1994, award of merit Wednesday Noon Moms Group for AIDS Care of Children, Adolescents and Adults, 1995. Mem. Assn. Nurses in AIDS Care, No. Colo. Aids Project (bd. dirs. 1995—, mem. speakers bur. 1994—), Grief and Loss Task Force of Weld County. also: Bank One Plaza Ste 630 822 7th St Greeley CO 80631

GROAT, JENNY HUNTER (LAVIDA JUNE GROAT), painter, artist, choreographer, writer, curator, reviewer; b. Modesto, Calif., Aug. 30, 1929; d. Leo Hunt and Lola Tuttle (Atwood) Miller; m. Maurice Frederick Groat, Jan. 15, 1955. AA in Music, San Joaquin Delta, 1950. Modern dance tchr. Dominican Schs., San Rafael, Calif., 1952-54; dance dir., tchr. Reed Coll., Portland, Oreg., 1954-56 summers; co-founder, artistic dir., tchr. various dance coops., San Francisco Bay Area, 1951-61; founder, dir., tchr., soloist, choreographer Dance West: The Jenny Hunter Sch. and Dance Co., San Francisco, 1962-68; invited art tchr. Internat. workshops, 1983—; tchr. art calligraphy Coll. of Marin, Kentfield, Calif., 1980-90; tchr.-mentor art classes Lagunitas, Calif., 1987—; tchr., tng. for creative dance Dancers and Artists, Bay area, 1955—; mast classes, dance Bay area groups, colls. and univs., 1958-68; organizer panel discussions on art Jenny Hunter Sch., Dance West, San Francisco, 1963; curator introducing U.S. and European artists to Asahi Art Pictorials, Tokyo, 1995—. One-woman shows include Claudia Chapline Gallery, Stinson Beach, Calif., 1994, 93, Gallery One, Petaluma, 1994, Zen Ctr., San Francisco, 1993, 90, Bechtel Ctr. Stanford U., 1993, Marin County Civic Ctr. Libr., San Rafael, San Geronimo Valley Cultural Ctr., 1990, Detroit Pub. Libr., 1988, Markings Gallery, Berkeley, Calif., 1985, Fairfax (Calif.) Pub. Libr., 1981-82, Lyford Ho., Tiburon, Calif., 1982, Palace Legion of Honor Theatre, 1967, 68, 65; numerous group exhbns. including Klingspor Mus., Germany, 1983, Grand Palais, Paris, 1990, EverArts Gallerie, Paris, 1997; permanent collections include Nat. Mus. Women in Arts, Washington, U. Tex., Austin, Harrison Collection-San Francisco Pub. Libr.; represented in many pvt. collections; contbr. articles to profl. jours. Grantor scholarships for child and adult dancers Jenny Hunter Dance West Sch., 1962-68; founder, mentor, tchr. Grass Root Scribes, Marin County, Calif., 1987-89; curator, art exhbns. Coll. of Marin and Kentfield, and Fairfax (Calif.) Libr., 1980-82. Grantee for art work in modern dance City of San Francisco, 1968; recipient Golden Quill award Calligraphic Soc. of Ariz., 1986. Mem. Colo. Calligrapher's Guild (hon.), Friends of Calligraphy, Marin Soc. of Artists (life, First Prize), Soc. for Calligraphy (L.A.), Marin Arts Coun. Democrat. Buddhist.

GROBER, MICHAEL, computer industry professional; b. St. Petersburg, Russia, Aug. 13, 1955; came to U.S., 1987; s. Miney and Tonya (Nikanorova) G. BA in English, St. Petersburg Coll., 1980; MSME, St. Petersburg Inst. Tech., 1977; M of Engring., Cornell U., 1989. Cert. translator. Design engr. Torgmash Design Co., St. Petersburg, 1977-81; engr., rschr. City Gas Co., St. Petersburg, 1981-87; libr. rschr. Cornell U. Libr., Ithaca, N.Y., 1988-89; engring. counselor JVS, San Francisco, 1989-93; program coord. Sun Mircosystems, Mountain View, Calif., 1993—; cons. Bank of Am., San Francisco, 1991-92; bd. dirs. El Internat., Pacifica, Calif. Contbr. articles to profl. jours. Pres. local chpt. Young Profls. Orgn., St. Petersburg, 1978, 80. Mem. Am. Translators Assn., Assn. for Computing Machinery.

GROBESON, MITCHELL, protective services official; b. L.A., Dec. 12, 1958; s. Morris Samuel and Marilyn Pearl (Golde) G. AA, West L.A. C.C., 1979; BA, Chapman U., 1981; grad., L.A. Police Acad., 1982; postgrad., U. So. Calif., 1986. Explorer Culver City (Calif.) Police Dept., 1974-76; tng. officer L.A. Police Dept., 1985, detective, 1986, sgt., 1986-88, 1993—; capt. State U. Police, San Francisco, 1990-91; officer San Francisco Police Dept., 1991-93; cons. screenplays, various literary works, L.A., 1988—. Author: Outside The Badge, 1996. Founder Calif. Gay Officers Action League, L.A., 1988—, So. Calif. Police AIDS Meml., West Coast Gays and Lesbians in the Mil., UCLA, 1989, Internat. Gay and Lesbian Police Conf., Palm Springs, Fla., 1989-91. Mem. NAACP (Pasadena, Calif. chpt.), No. Calif. Golden State Peace Officers Assn. Jewish. Office: LA Police Dept PO Box 69917 Los Angeles CA 90069

GRODY, MARK STEPHEN, public relations executive; b. Milw., Jan. 1, 1938; s. Ray and Betty (Rothstein) G.; m. Karen Goldstein, Mar. 6, 1965 (div. 1972); 1 child, Laura; m. Susan Tellem, Mar. 25, 1979 (div. 1989); 1 child, Daniel. BS, U. Wis., 1960. Pub. rels. exec. GM, Detroit, 1961-74; v.p. pub. affairs Nat. Alliance of Businessmen, Washington, 1973-74; v.p. Carl Terzian & Assocs., L.A., 1974-75; chmn. Mark Grody Assocs. and Grody Tellem Comm., Inc. (now The Rowland Co.), L.A., 1975-90; pres. Mark Grody Assocs., L.A., 1990-93; exec. v.p., gen. mgr. Ogilvy Adams & Rinehart, L.A., 1993-96; pres. Mark Grody Assocs., L.A., 1996—; ptnr. Mktg. Golf Resources, L.A., 1996—. Co-author: Corporate Golf: How to Play the Game for Business Success, 1996. Capt. U.S. Army, 1960. Mem. Pub. Rels. Soc. Am., Industry Edn. Coun. of Calif. (bd. dirs.), Nat. Alliance of Bus./West (bd. dirs.), Mountain Gate Country Club, L.A. Sports Club .

GRODY, WAYNE WILLIAM, physician; b. Syracuse, N.Y., Feb. 25, 1952; s. Robert Jerome and Florence Beatrice (Kashdan) G.; m. Gaylen Ducker, July 8, 1990. BA, Johns Hopkins U., 1974; MD, Baylor Coll. Medicine, 1977, PhD, 1981. Diplomate Am. Bd. Pathology, Am. Bd. Med. Genetics; lic. physician, Calif. Intern/resident UCLA Sch. Medicine, 1982-85, postdoctoral fellow, 1985-86, asst. prof., 1987-93, assoc. prof., 1993—; panelist Calif. Children's Svcs., 1987—, U.S. FDA, Washington, 1989—; mem. DNA tech. com. Pacific Southwest Regional Genetics Network, Berkeley, Calif., Coll. Am. Pathologists, Am. Coll. Med. Genetics, NIH Task Force on Genetic Testing, others, 1987—; med., tech. cons. and writer Warner Bros., NBC, Tri-Star, CBS, Twentieth Century Fox, others, 1987—; mem. molecular genetics com. Coll. Am. Pathology, Am. Coll. Med. Genetics, Nat. Com. on Clin. Lab. Stds., others. Contbg. editor: MD Mag., 1981-91;

assoc. editor Diagnostic Molecular Pathology, 1993—; contbr. articles to profl. jours. Recipient best paper award L.A. Soc. Pathology, 1984, Joseph Kleiner Meml. award Am. Soc. Med. Technologists, 1990; Basil O'Connor scholar March of Dimes Birth Defects Found., 1989. Mem. AAAS, AMA, Am. Soc. Clin. Pathology (DNA workshop dir. 1988—), Am. Soc. Human Genetics, Coll. Am. Pathologists (scholar award 1987), Soc. Inherited Metabolic Disorders, Soc. Pediat. Rsch., Am. Coll. Med. Genetics (mem. DNA com.). Democrat. Jewish. Office: UCLA Sch Medicine Divsn Med Genetics & Molecular Pathology Los Angeles CA 90095-1732

GROEBLI, WERNER FRITZ (MR. FRICK), professional ice skater, realtor; b. Basel, Switzerland, Apr. 21, 1915; s. Fritz and Gertrud (Landerer) G.; m. Yvonne Baumgartner, Dec. 30, 1954. Student architecture, Swiss Fed. Inst. Tech., 1934-35. Lic. realtor, Calif. Chmn. pub. relations com. Profl. Skaters Guild Am., 1972—. Performed in ice shows, Patria, Brighton, Eng., 1937; command performance in, Marina, London, 1937, Symphony on Ice, Royal Opera House, 1937; mem. Ice Follies, 1939-81, partner (with Hans Mauch) in comedy team Frick & Frack, 1939-53; solo act as Mr. Frick (assisted by comedy team), 1955-81; numerous TV appearances including Snoopy on Ice, 1973, Snoopy's Musical on Ice, 1978, Sportsworld, NBC-TV, 1978, Donnie and Marie Osmond Show, 1978, Mike Douglas Show, 1978, Dinah Shore Show, 1978; films include Silver Skates, 1942, Lady Let's Dance, 1943, Jinxed, 1981; interviewed by Barbara Walters NBC Today, 1974; appeared in Christmas Classics on Ice at Blue Jay Ice Castle, 1991. Served with Swiss Army, 1934-37. Named Swiss jr. skating champion, 1934; named to Madison Sq. Garden Hall of Fame for 10,000 performances in Ice Follies, 1967, U.S. Figure Skating Assn. World Hall of Fame, 1984; recipient Hall of Fame Ann. award Ice Skating Inst. Am. Mem. SAG, Profl. Skaters Guild Am., Swiss Club of San Francisco (hon.). Office: care US Figure Skating Assn 20 1st St Colorado Springs CO 80906-3624

GROENIER, JAMES SCOTT, civil engineer; b. Madison, Wis., Jan. 17, 1963; s. James Edward and Darlene Gelaine (Frye) G.; m. Mary Elizabeth Ruhland Groenier, May 17, 1986 (div. Jan. 26, 1988). BS in Civil Engring., U. Wis., Madison, 1986; MS in Civil Engring., Mont. State U., Bozeman, 1995. Registered profl. engr. Wis. Civil engr. Ill. Dept. Transp., Dixon, 1987-88; staff engr. Ayres & Assocs., Eau Claire, Wis., 1988-90; rsch., teaching asst. Mont. State U., Bozeman, 1990-92; civil engr. USDA Forest Svc., Petersburg, Alaska, 1992-95, Vernal, Utah, 1995—. Contbr. technical papers in field. Baseball Coach, 1993—, soccer coach Petersburg Youth Soccer, 1992, 95, Eau Claire Youth Soccer, 1989, 90. Mem. ASCE.

GROESBECK, ROBERT A., mayor. BA, U. Nev.; MBA, Nat. U.; JD, Thomas M. Cooley Law Sch. Bar: Nev. 1990, Mich. 1990, U.S. Dist. Ct. (so. dist.) Nev. 1990. Atty. Harding & Groesbeck, Las Vegas, 1990-91, Thorndal, Backus, Armstrong & Balkenbush, Las Vegas, 1992-94; mayor City of Henderson, Nev., 1993—; gen. counsel Silver Strate Disposal Svc., Las Vegas, 1994—; bd. dirs. So. Nev. Water Authority, Colo. River Commn., Civilian Mil. Coun., Nev. League Cities, Arts Coun. Henderson & Green Valley, Nev. Devel. Authority, exec. com., Las Vegas Convention & Vis. Authority, vice-chmn.; tchg. asst. Thomas M. Cooley Law Sch. Contbr. articles to profl. jours. Bd. dirs. Boys and Girls Club Henderson; commr. Mayors Blue Ribbon Commn. on Ednl. Excellence, Govs. Commn. on Aging; little league baseball coach Henderson Parks and Recreation, 1979-80, 87, 91. Mem. ABA, Clark County Bar Assn., Nev. Trial Lawyers Assn. Address: 240 Water St Henderson NV 89015

GROEZINGER, LELAND BECKER, JR., investment professional; b. San Francisco, Dec. 6, 1941; s. Leland Becker Sr. and Clara Catherine (Hudson) G. BS and BA, U. Ariz., 1964, MS in Fin., 1967. Asst. legis. adv. Leland B. Groezinger Sr., Sacramento, 1970-78; personal investor Sacramento, 1978—. Mem. Episcopal Cmty. Svcs. for the Diocese of No. Calif., Sacramento, 1983-91, bd. dirs., 1984-91, treas., 1985-91; mem. Sacramento Traditional Jazz Soc., Sacramento, 1985—, bd. dirs., 1992—, treas., 1994-95, v.p., 1996-97, pres. 1998—. Republican.

GROGAN, STANLEY JOSEPH, educational consultant; b. N.Y.C., Jan. 14, 1925; s. Stanley Joseph and Marie (Di Giorgio) G.; AA, Am. U., 1949, BS, 1950, MA, 1955; degree, Industrial Coll. of Armed Forces Air War Coll., 1972; MS, Calif. State Coll., Hayward, 1973; EdD, Nat. Christian U., 1974; m. Mary Margaret Skroch, Sept. 20, 1954; 1 child, Mary Maureen. Pers. asst., recruitment asst. CIA, Washington, 1954-56; disting. grad. acad. instr., allied officer course, Maxwell AFB, Ala., 1962; asst. prof. air sci. U. Calif., Berkeley, 1963-64, Chabot Coll., 1964-70, Oakland Unified Sch. Dist., 1962-83, Hayward Unified Sch. Dist., 1965-68; instr. ednl. methods, edn. rsch. methods of instrn. Nat. Christian U., 1975—, Nat. U. Grad. Studies, Belize, 1975—; pres. SJG Enterprises, Inc., cons., 1963—. Asst. dir. Nat. Ednl. Film Festival, 1971. Pub. rels. cons., 1963—. Bd. dirs. We T.I.P., Inc., 1974. With AUS, 1945; lt. col. USAFR, 1948-76; col. Calif. State Mil. Res. Decorated Air medal with oak leaf cluster; recipient citation Korea, 1963; RCVP Korean Vets. Assn. medal, 1994; named to Hon. Order Ky. Cols. Commonwealth of Ky., 1970, Outstanding Secondary Educators of Am. 1972. Fellow Indian Inst. of Security and Safety Mgmt.; mem. NRA (life), VFW (life), DAV (life), Am. Def. Preparedness Assn. (life), Night Fighter Assn. (nat. publicity chmn. 1967), Air Force Assn., Res. Officers Assn., Phi Delta Kappa, Am. Soc. Indsl. Security (cert. protection profl.), Nat. Def. Exec. Res./FEMA, Marines Meml., Contbr. articles to profl. jours. and newspapers. Home: 2585 Moraga Dr Pinole CA 94564-1236

GROGAN, SUZANN JEANETTE-WYMAN, artist; b. L.A., July 6, 1962; d. Frank Adelbert Jr. and Beverly Ann (Burge) Wyman; m. Marvin John Grogan, June 1, 1985. AA, Fullerton Coll., 1984. Drafter Cetec Corp., Southgate, Calif., 1983-85; drafter, illustrator MegaTape Corp., Duarte, Calif., 1985-94; design drafter Magellan Systems Corp., San Dimas, Calif., 1994—; writer Victorville, Calif., 1988—, artist, 1990—; dir. pub. Mojave Inst. Arts, Apple Valley, Calif., 1994. Artist (painting) Art of the West mag., 1993; contbr. articles to U.S. Art, Art Trends., Western Horseman. Charter mem. Nat. Mus. Am. Indian, Washington, 1993—; mem. Nat. Mus. Women in Arts, Washington, 1993—; signature mem. Western Acad. Women Artist; mem. High Desert Cultural Arts Found., Apple Valley, 1994—. Adopted Hon. mem. Wappo Tribe, Sonoma County, Calif., 1994. Mem. Oil Painters Am. (assoc.), Laguna Art-A-Fair Coop. Address: PO Box 3265 Victorville CA 92393-3265

GRONLI, JOHN VICTOR, college administrator, minister; b. Eshowe, South Africa, Sept. 11, 1932; s. John Einar and Marjorie Gellet (Hawker) G.; came to U.S., 1934, naturalized, 1937; BA, U. Minn., 1953; MDiv, Luther Theol. Sem., 1958, DMin, 1978; MA, Pacific Luth. U., 1975; m. Jeanne Louise Ellertson, Sept. 15, 1952; children: Cheryl Marie Mundt, Deborah Raechel Hokanson, John Timothy, Peter Jonas, Daniel Reuben. Ordained to ministry, 1958; pastor Brocket-Lawton Luth. Parish, Brocket, N.D., 1958-61; Harlowton (Mont.) Luth. Parish, 1961-66; sr. pastor St. Luke's Luth. Ch., Shelby, Mont., 1966-75; missionary Paulinum Sem., Otjimbingwe, Namibia, 1975-76; dean, chmn. dept. philosophy and humanities Golden Valley Luth. Coll., Mpls., 1976-85; dir. Summer Inst. Pastoral Ministry, Mpls., 1980-85, sr. pastor Pella Luth. Ch., Sidney, Mont., 1985-95; pres., CEO Ctrl. Mont. Concrete, Harlowton, GEHM Inc., Martinsdale, Mont., 1991—, cons. for orgnl. comms., 1995—. Bd. dirs. Mont. Assn. Chs., 1973-75, Richland Homes, Sidney, Mont., 1990-94, Ea. Mont. Mental Health Assn., 1993-94; sec. bd. for comm. and mission support Am. Luth. Ch., 1973-75; mem. dist. coun. Rocky Mountain Dist., 1963-75, sec., 1963-70; mem. S.African affairs task force SEM Dist., 1978-79; dean S.W. Mont. Conf. Evang. Luth. Ch. in Am.; faculty No. Rockies Inst. Theology, 1986—; trustee Luth. Bible Inst., Seattle, 1986-92. Mem. personnel and guidance assns., Am., Minn. coll. personnel assns. Editor: Rocky Mountain Dist. Yearbook, 1963-70; Rocky Mountain Views, 1973-75; contbr. to Lutheran Standard, 1973-77; contbr. articles to religious jours.

GROOMS, HENRY RANDALL, civil engineer; b. Cleve., Feb. 10, 1944; s. Leonard Day and Lois (Pickell) G.; m. Tonie Marie Joseph; children: Catherine, Zayne, Nina, Ivan, Ian, Athesis, Shaneya, Yaphet, Rahsan, Dax, Jevay, Xava. BSCE, Howard U., 1965; MSCE, Carnegie-Mellon U., 1967, PhD, 1969. Hwy. engr. D.C. Hwy. Dept., Washington, 1965; structural engr. Peter F. Loftus Corp., Pitts., 1966; structural engr., engring. mgr. Rockwell Internat., Downey, Calif., 1969—. Contbr. articles to profl. jours. Scoutmaster Boy Scouts Am., Granada Hills, Calif., 1982-87; basketball coach Valley Conf., Granada Hills, 1984—; coach Am. Youth Soccer Orgn., Granada Hills, 1985-90, 94—; tutor Watts Friendship Sports League, 1989—; co-founder Project Reach, 1993. Recipient Alumni Merit award Carnegie-Mellon U., 1985; named Honoree Black History Project Western Res. Hist. Soc., 1989. Mem. ASCE, Tau Beta Pi, Sigma Xi. Office: Rockwell Internat Mail Code AD 69 12214 Lakewood Blvd Downey CA 90242-2655

GROSE, ANDREW PETER, foundation executive; b. Washington, July 16, 1940; s. Peter Andrew and Mildred (Holston) G.; m. Jacqueline Stamm, Aug. 17, 1963; children: Peter Andrew II, Tracey Christine. BS with high honors, U. Md., 1962, MA, 1964. Mem. legis. staff Fla. Ho. of Reps., Tallahassee, 1972-74; rsch. dir. Nev. Legislature, Carson City, 1974-83; chief of staff Office of Gov. Nev., Carson City, 1983-84, dir. econ. devel., 1984-90; dir. Western region Coun. of State Govt., San Francisco, 1990-95; CFO Pub. Policy Inst. Calif., 1995—; mem. exec. com. Nat. Conf. State Legislatures, Denver, 1982-83. Author: Florida Model City Charter, 1974; mem. editl. bd. Nev. Rev. of Bus. and Econs., Reno, 1976-90. Trustee Temple United Meth. Ch., San Francisco, 1996—; active Habitat for Humanity. Capt. USAF, 1964-70, to brig. gen., Res. Recipient Spl. citation Nev. Libr. Assn., Carson City, 1981. Mem. Air Force Assn., Res. Officers Assn., Nat. Assn. State Devel. Agys. (1st v.p.), Western Govt. Rsch. Assn. (pres. 1993-95), Kiwanis (pres. 1981-82, bd. dirs. 1994—). Democrat. Home: 405 Hazelwood Ave San Francisco CA 94127-2129 Office: Public Policy Inst of California Suite 800 500 Washington Street San Francisco CA 94111

GROSE, ELINOR RUTH, retired elementary education educator; b. Honolulu, Apr. 23, 1928; d. Dwight Hatsuichi and Edith (Yamamoto) Uyeno; m. George Benedict Grose, Oct. 19, 1951; children: Heidi Diane Hill, Mary Porter, John Tracy, Nina Evangeline. AA, Briarcliff Jr. Coll., 1948; postgrad., Long Beach State U., 1954-55; BS in Edn., Wheelock Coll., Boston, 1956; MA in Edn., Whittier Coll., 1976. Cert. tchr., Mass., N.Y., Calif. Reading tchr. Cumberland Head Sch., Plattsburgh, N.Y., 1968-70; master tchr. Broadoaks Sch., Whittier (Calif.) Coll., 1971; reading tchr. Phelan/Washington Schs., Whittier, 1971-73; elem. tchr. Christian Sorensen Sch., Whittier, 1977-94, ret., 1994; cons. Nat. Writing Projet, 1987—, South Basin Writing Project, Long Beach, 1987—; team tchr. first Young Writers' Camp, Long Beach State U., 1988. Author: Primarily Yours, 1987, Angel Orchid Watercolor, 1994. First v.p. Women's League of Physicians Hosp., Plattsburgh, 1970; asst. to Christian, Jewish and Muslim pres., v.p.s of Acad. Judaic, Christian and Islamic Studies 6th Assembly World Coun. Chs., Vancouver, 1983. Mem. AAUW, NEA, Calif. Tchrs. Assn., Whittier Elem. Tchrs. Assn., English Coun. of Long Beach, Acad. Judaic, Christian and Islamic Studies (named companion Order of Abraham 1987, assoc. in dialogue 1996—), Orange County Soc. Calligraphy. Presbyterian. Home: 6085 E Brighton Ln Anaheim CA 92807-4702

GROSS, BRUCE LEON, financial services representative; b. Butte, Mont., Aug. 13, 1944; s. Raymond Leon and Eudessa May (Evans) G.; m. Dorna Parkinson, July 15, 1967 (dec. 1980); m. Carolyn O. Hart, Sept. 5, 1980; children: Shellie, Jason, Robert, Michael, Alex, Jill. BS in Bus. Mgmt., Ariz. State U., 1967, MS in Criminal Justice, 1978. Gen. mgr. Rays Markets, Inc., Kingman, Ariz., 1972-75; dir. vending ops. Ariz. State U., Tempe, 1975-78; dir. R&D Collegiate Products, Inc., Tulsa, 1978-79; owner, CEO Lafayette Electronics, Prescott, Ariz., 1979-80; pres., CEO Groco, Inc., Provo, Utah, 1980-84, Intermountain Planning, Inc., Provo, 1984-89, Ind. Systems, Inc., Salt Lake City, 1989-96; sr. plan rep. FHP of Utah, Inc., Salt Lake City, 1996—; bd. dirs., mem. ethics com. Nat. Indian Gaming Assn., Mpls.; mem. Pollard Bd. Govs., Houston, 1986-88. Capt. U.S. Army, 1968-72, Viet Nam. Mem. Internat. Legion Intelligence, Mensa. Republican. Mem. LDS Ch. Home: 1645 E 480 S Pleasant Grove UT 84062-3303

GROSS, CATHERINE MARY (KATE GROSS), writer, educator; b. Seattle, Jan. 21, 1931; d. Daniel Bergin Hutchings and Eleanor Paris (Miller) Bold. Student, Northwestern U., Evanston, Ill., 1958; BA, U. Wash., 1962, postgrad, 1984, cert. fiction grad., 1996. Cert. vocat. tchr. Copywriter Pacific Nat. Advt., Seattle, 1963; prodn. coordinator Sta KRON-TV, San Francisco, 1963-65, acting program mgr., 1965; chief copywriter, TV and radio producer Teawell-Shoemaker Advt., San Diego, 1966-68; asst. pub. relations dir. San Diego Zoo, 1968-70; pub. relations dir. Univ. Village, Seattle, 1975-77, Seattle/King County Bd. Realtors, 1978; cons. advt. various orgns. including Internat. Assn. Osteopaths, Seattle, 1980-85; adj. instr. bus. Seattle Pacific U., 1980-89; instr. ASUW Exptl. Coll., 1980—; instr. humanities Heritage Inst. Antioch U., 1991—; instr. humanities Bellevue C.C., 1992-96; instr. U. Wash. Exptl. Coll., 1985—. Author: Advertising for a Small Business, 1984, Fund Raising Magic, 1984, Conversations With Writers, 1993, Sunshine the Magician's Rabbit, 1996 (Juvenile Fiction award Wash. Press Assn. 1996); editor: Hiking and Bushwalking in Papua, New Guinea, 1987; tech. editor oceanography and medicine U. Wash., 1974-75; contbr. short stories to Compass and Sea Classics, 1982. Vol. sponsor Big Sisters of Puget Sound, Seattle, 1978-87, Seattle Parks; vol. coordinator World Affairs Council, Seattle, 1986; bd. dirs. Seattle Aquarium, 1985-87. Recipient Non-Fiction Book award Pacific Northwest Writers' Conf., 1979, Juvenile Story award Pacific Northwest Writers' Conf., 1984, Short Story award Fictioneers, 1993, Juv. Fiction award Washington Press Assn., 1997. Mem. AAUW (internat. rep. 1988), Seattle Freelance Writers Assn., Wash. Press Assn., Rocky Mountain Outdoor Writers, Mountaineers, Issaquah Alps Trails Club, Audubon Soc. Republican.

GROSS, GEORGE CLAYBURN, English language educator; b. Wilmington, Calif., May 14, 1922; s. Henry and Rebecca Ada (Bachman) G.; m. Marlo Vane Mumma, Apr. 30, 1941; children: George Timothy, John Henry. BA in English, San Diego State Coll., 1948, MA in English, 1950; PhD in English, U. So. Calif., L.A., 1963. Cert. gen. secondary tchr., Calif. Tchr. English Grossmont H.S., El Cajon, Calif., 1948-49; instr. English San Diego State Coll., 1949-51; head English dept. Grossmont H.S., El Cajon, 1951-61; grad. teaching asst. U. So. Calif., L.A., 1959-60; from asst. to assoc. to full prof. San Diego State U., 1961-85, assoc. dean faculty pers., 1970-72, dean of faculty affairs, 1972-81, prof. English, 1981-85, prof. English emeritus, 1985—; cons. Sweetwater Sch. Dist., Chula Vista, Calif., 1967-68, Calif. State Com. on Pub. Edn., Berkeley, 1967; lectr. in field. Contbr. articles to scholarly jours. 2d lt. U.S. Army, 1943-45, ETO. Scholar U. So. Calif., 1960. Mem. AAUP (officer 1969-70, chpt. v.p.), MLA, Keats-Shelley Assn., Mortar Board (svc. award 1995), Phi Beta Kappa (chpt. sec. 1977-80, spl. award 1985), Phi Delta Kappa, Phi Kappa Phi (chpt. pres. 1969-70, svc. award 1985). Home: 4025 Citradora Dr Spring Valley CA 91977-1127 Office: San Diego State U Dept English San Diego CA 92182

GROSS, JEFFREY, software engineer; b. Chgo., Feb. 23, 1963; s. Mickey and Evelyn (Udwin) G. BSEE, Ill. Inst. Tech., Chgo., 1985. Software engr. Gen. Dynamics, San Diego, 1986-91; sci. programmer Biosym Technologies, San Diego, 1991-94; sr. software engr. Qualcomm, San Diego, 1994—. Ill. State scholar; recipient Gen. Dynamics Excel award. Mem. Assn. Computing Machinery, San Diego Macintosh Users Group, Mensa. Home: 4092 Riviera Dr # 3 San Diego CA 92109-5370

GROSS, JOEL EDWARD, consultant, safety and security executive; b. Paterson, N.J., Mar. 15, 1939; s. Herman and Virginia (Bivens) G.; m. Maria Helena Perides, Sept. 3, 1995. B.A. cum laude, Seton Hall U., 1977. Cert. protection profl., fraud examiner; assoc. in risk mgmt. Lab. technician Nabisco, Inc., Fairlawn, N.J., 1957-60; detective Lincoln Park (N.J.) Police Dept., 1966-79; tng. specialist Agway, Inc., Syracuse, N.Y., 1980-81; mgr. safety Drake Bakeries-Borden, Inc., Wayne, N.J., 1981-85; dir. risk mgmt. Pinkerton's Inc., N.Y.C., 1986; mgr. safety N.J. Transit, 1986-87; sr. ptnr. Hunter-Rumsen Group, 1987-91; mgmt. cons. Joel E Gross & Assocs., Pompton Plains, N.J., 1991-95, Risk Strategies Internat., Albuquerque, 1995—; dir. corp. risk strategies Investigative Group Internat., N.Y.C., 1990-95; lectr. safety, security, risk mgmt., fraud investigations, emergency disaster planning. State del. N.J. State Policemen's Benevolent Assn., Silver Life mem. Recipient commendation Sec. of Navy and Mayor of Lincoln Park, Morris County Prosecutors Office; cert. breathalyzer operator, N.J., instr. and instr. trainer defensive driving Nat. Safety Council. Served as petty officer, USN, 1960-65. Decorated Navy Commendation medal. Mem. Am. Soc. Indsl. Security, Am. Soc. Safety Engrs., Nat. Coun. Investigative and Security Svcs., U.S. Naval Cryptographic Vets. Assn., Navy Intelligence Profls., Nat. Assn. Certified Fraud Examiners, Fire Protection Assn., Am. Legion, Nat. Rifle Assn., Computer Security Inst. Contbr. articles on fleet safety programs to periodicals. Research on juvenile delinquents. Home: 2101 Buckingham Ct NW Albuquerque NM 87120 Office: 3101-R Coors Rd NW # 186 Albuquerque NM 87120

GROSS, RICHARD PHILIP, retired business executive; b. San Francisco, Aug. 13, 1903; s. Louis and Ida (Solomon) G.; m. Marion Brownstone, Dec. 7, 1924 (dec. 1981); 1 child, Richard P. Jr. (dec.); m. Lila North, Jan. 8, 1982 (dec. 1982); m. Ruth Heller, Mar. 21, 1987. Student, Stanford U., 1924. Sec. Nat. Smelting Co., San Francisco, 1923-26; salesman Louis Forester, San Francisco, 1926-28; gen. ptnr. Richard P. Gross and Co., San Francisco, 1928-41, Kanter and Gross, San Francisco, 1941-46; gen. ptnr. Stone and Youngberg, San Francisco, 1946-75, ltd. ptnr., 1975—; bd. dirs. David Rabb Real Estate Investment Trust, Dark-to-Light, Inc.; gov. San Francisco Curb Exch., 1932-38, pres. 1935-38; gov. San Francisco Stock Exch., 1949-50, Pacific Coast Stock Exch., San Francisco, 1957, 58, 68. Mem. Concordia-Argonaut Club (bd. dirs. 1935), City Club. Republican. Jewish. Home: 999 Green St San Francisco CA 94133-3662

GROSS, SHARON RUTH, forensic psychologist, researcher; b. L.A., Mar. 21, 1940; d. Louis and Sylvia Marion (Freedman) Lackman; m. Zoltan Gross, Mar. 1969 (div.); 1 child, Andrew Ryan; m. Ira Chroman, June 1994. BA, UCLA, 1983; MA, U. So. Calif., L.A., 1985, PhD, 1991. Tech. Rytron, Van Nuys, Calif., 1958-60; computress on tetrahedral satellite Space Tech. Labs., Redondo Beach, Calif., 1960-62; owner Wayfarer Yacht Corp., Costa Mesa, Calif., 1962-64; electronics draftsperson, designer stroke-writer characters Tasker Industries, Van Nuys, 1964-65; pvt. practice cons. Sherman Oaks, Calif., 1965-75, 77-80; printed circuit bd. designer Systron-Donner, Van Nuys, Calif., 1975-76; design checker, tech. writer Vector Gen., Woodland Hills, Calif., 1976-77; undergrad. adv. U. So. Calif., L.A., 1987-89, rsch. asst. prof., rsch. assoc. social psychology, 1991—; owner Attitude Rsch. Litigation and Orgn. Cons. Contbr. articles to profl. jours., chpts. to books. Recipient Haynes Found. Dissertation fellowship U. So. Calif., 1990. Mem. APA, AAAS, Computer Graphics Pioneers, Am. Psychol. Soc., Western Psychol. Assn. Democrat. Jewish. Office: U So Calif Dept Psychology Los Angeles CA 90089-1061

GROSSETETE, GINGER LEE, retired gerontology administrator, consultant; b. Riverside, Calif., Feb. 9, 1936; d. Lee Roy Taylor and Bonita (Beryl) Williams; m. Alec Paul Grossetete, June 8, 1954; children: Elizabeth Gay Blech, Teri Lee Zeni. BA in Recreation cum laude, U. N.Mex., 1974, M in Pub. Adminstrn., 1978. Sr. ctr. supr., Office of Sr. Affairs, City of Albuquerque, 1974-77, asst. dir. Office of Sr. Affairs, 1977-96; conf. coord. Nat. Consumers Assn., Albuqeruque, 1978-79; region 6 del. Nat. Coun. on Aging, Washington, 1977-84; conf. chmn. Western Gerontol. Soc., Albuqerque, 1983; N.Mex. del. White House Conf. on Aging, 1995; mem. adv. coun. N.Mex. Agy. on Aging, 1996-99. Contbr. articles to mags. Campaign dir. March of Dimes N.Mex., 1966-67; pres. Albuquerque Symphony Women's Assn., 1972; mem. exec. com. Jr. League Albuquerque, 1976; mem. Gov.'s Coun. on Phys. Fitness, 1987-91, chmn. 1990-91; mem. bd. dirs. N.Mex. Sr. Olympics, 1995—. Recipient N.Mex. Disting. Pub. Service award N.Mex. Gov.'s Office, 1983, Disting. Woman on the Move award YWCA, 1986, Outstanding Profl. award N.Mex. State Conf. on Aging, 1995, Presdl. citation S.W. Soc. on Aging, 1995. Fellow Nat. Recreation and Pk. Assn. (bd. dirs. S.W. regional coun. rep., bd. dirs. leisure and aging sect., pres. N.Mex. chpt. 1983-84, bd. dirs. N.Mex. Sr. Olympics, 1994—, Outstanding profl. award 1982); mem. ASPA (pres. N.Mex. coun. 1987-88), S.W. Soc. on Aging (pres. 1984-85, bd. dirs., Outstanding Profl. award 1991, Presdl. citation 1996), U. N.Mex. Alumni Assn. (bd. dirs. 1978-80, Disting. Alumni award 1985), Las Amapolas Garden Club (pres. 1964), Phi Alpha Alpha, Chi Omega (pres. alumni 1959-60), Pi Lambda Theta. Home: 517 La Veta Dr NE Albuquerque NM 87108-1403

GROSSKOPF, BARRY, psychiatrist, consultant; b. Breslau, Germany, Nov. 1, 1945; came to U.S., 1949; s. Israel and Evelyn (Mendelowicz) G.; m. Myrna Ethel Slotsky, Aug. 14, 1966 (div. July 1983); children: David Dylan, Lauren Rebecca; m. Wendy Lustbader, Mar. 1, 1987. BS with high honors, U. Fla., 1966; MD, U. Miami, 1970. Diplomate Am. Bd. Psychiatry and Neurology. Intern Va. Mason Hosp., Seattle, 1970-71; resident in psychiatry U. Wash., Seattle, 1974-77; med. dir. involuntary treatment program Queenslake Hosp, 1977-84; pvt. practice, 1977-91; med. dir. Highland West SEattle Mental Health, 1987-90; cons. psychiatrist Cedar Hills, Maple Valley, Wash., 1990-96, Spl. Offenders Ctr., 1995—; Helped establish migrant worker clinic, Perrine, Fla., 1968, outreach program Dade County Jail, Miami, 1968; with Appalachia Project AMSA, Lebanon, Va., 1969; gen. practice Group Health Coop. Puget Sound, Burien, Wash., 1971; founder Comprehensive Cmty. Family Practice Clinic, Glenville, W.Va., 1972; county pub. health officer Gilmer County, W.Va., 1972-74; physician cons. outreach for older adults King County Dept. Pub. Health, Seattle, 1977-78; spkr., lectr. in field. With USPHS, 1972-74. Recipient Pioneer award Nat. Health Svc. Corps, 1992. Mem. Am. Psychiat. Assn., Wash. State Psychiat. Assn., Wash. Assn. Community Psychiatrists, King County Med. Soc. Jewish. Office: Cedar Hills 15900 227th Ave SE Maple Valley WA 98038-6207

GROSSMAN, ARNOLD JOSEPH, writer, producer; b. Jersey City, May 10, 1934; s. Alex and Pearl (Dynkine) G.; m. Katherine Chorley, Dec. 28, 1958 (div. Aug. 1980); children: Alex, Rachel, Daniel. BA, U. Denver, 1959. Asst. editor Redbook Mag., N.Y.C., 1960-62, Good Housekeeping, N.Y.C., 1962-63; pres. Grossman & Bartholomew, Denver, 1969-76; owner Grossman Prodns., Denver, L.A., 1976—; cons. Patricia Schroeder for Congress, Colo., 1972-74, Richard Lamm for Gov., Colo., 1976-84, Gary Hart for U.S. Senate, 1974-80, Timothy Wirth for U.S. Senate, 1986. Author: 1988, 1985, California Conspiracy, 1988; prodr.: (movie) Cries Unheard, 1993; contbr. articles to profl. jours. Chmn. bd. dirs. Denver Internat. Film Festival, 1980-82; bd. dirs. Hist. Denver, Inc., 1979-81; commr. Colo. Film Commn., Denver, 1984-85. With USN, 1952-56. Democrat. Jewish. Home and Office: 2143 Old Topanga Cyn Rd Topanga CA 90290

GROSSMAN, DOROTHEA G., consulting services administrator, poet; b. Phila., Aug. 27, 1937; d. Nathan Theodore and Shirley (Gerson) Dwartzin; m. Richard Grossman, June 29, 1958 (dec. Oct. 1992). BA in English Lit., Temple U., 1959. Registrar So. Calif. Inst. Architecture, Santa Monica, 1987-91; office mgr. Gerontological Svcs., Inc., Santa Monica, 1993—. Author: (books of poetry) Cuttings, 1988, Poems from Cave 17, 1996. Performance grantee Meet the Composer, Calif., 1996. Home: Apt 302 2414 S Barrington Ave Los Angeles CA 90064

GROSSMAN, MARC RICHARD, media consultant; b. L.A., Sept. 11, 1949; s. Morris Grossman and Esther Beatrice (Wishnow) Goldstein; m. Maria Luisa Lopez, Sept. 23, 1987; children: Joshua, Aaron, Matthew. BA, U. Calif., Irvine, 1972; M of Journalism, UCLA, 1973. Press sec., personal aide to Pres. Cesar Chavez, United Farm Workers, 1975-81; legis. cons. to Spkr. Willie Brown, Calif. Assembly, Sacramento, 1981-87; media cons. Words in Public, Sacramento, 1987—. Ghostwriter speeches, columns and pieces for dozens of pub. figures; contbr. articles to daily newspapers and mags. Democrat. Jewish. Office: Words in Public 1700 L St Sacramento CA 95814

GROSSMAN, RICHARD, obstetrician/gynecologist; b. Phila., July 13, 1943; s. Louis I. and Emma May (MacIntyre) G.; m. Gail Sise, June 18, 1966; children: David, Bryan. BA, Swarthmore Coll., 1965; MD, U. Pa., 1969; MPH, Loma Linda U., 1993. Diplomate Am. Bd. Ob-Gyn. Med. intern Hartford (Conn.) Hosp., 1969-70; gen. practitioner Presbyn. Med. Svcs., Questa, N.Mex., 1970-73; resident in ob-gyn. U. N.Mex., Albuquerque, 1973-76; obstetrician-gynecologist, shareholder Durango (Colo.) OB-GYN Assocs. PC, 1976-95; ind. physician Durango, 1995—; contract gynecologist Planned Parenthood of the Rocky Mountains, Durango, 1976—; obstetrician-gynecologist Hosp. General Castañer, P.R., 1983-84; clin. asst. prof. U. N.Mex., Albuquerque, 1976—, U. Colo., Denver, 1990—; preceptor U. N.Mex. Dept. Family Practice, Albuquerque, 1976—. Patentee for Improved Condom, Needle Safety Guard; contbg. author gynecologist's column Woman's World, 1984-88; contbr. articles to profl. jours. Recipient Cert. of Appreciation Colo. Assist Alliance, Denver, 1993, Plaques of Appreciation Hosp. General Castañer, P.R., 1984, Planned Parenthood of Rocky Mountains, Denver, 1991, LaPlata County Prevention Ptnrs., Durango, 1994. Fellow Am. Coll. Ob-Gyn.; mem. APHA (sect. population family planning and reproductive health), Assn. Reproductive Health Profls., Nat. Coun. for Internat. Health, Soc. for Advancement of Contraception. Quaker. Office: Durango Ob-Gyn Assocs #3C 375 E Park Ave Ste 3C Durango CO 81301-5012

GROSSMAN, SEYMOUR, retired gastroenterologist; b. Newark, July 5, 1933; s. Abraham and Sally Gertrude (Pilchman) G.; m. Bonnie Jane Simon Grossman, June 26, 1955; children: Michael Joseph, Deborah Joan. Student, MIT, 1950-53; MD, NYU Coll. Medicine, 1957; postgrad., Calif. State U., Hayward, 1995—. Diplomate Am. Bd. Internal Medicine, 1964; cert. Gastroenterology, 1969. Rotating intern Cleve. Metro. Gen. Hosp., 1957-58; internal medicine resident, 1958-61; rsch. fellow, clin. trainee N.Y. Hosp.-Cornell Med. Ctr., 1961-63; clin. instr. Cornell U. Med. Ctr., 1963-65, U. Calif. Sch. Medicine, San Francisco, 1965-67; clin. asst. prof. U. Tex. Sch. Medicine, San Antonio, 1967-69; asst. clin. prof. U. Calif. San Francisco, 1967-75, assoc. clin. prof., 1975-84, clin. prof., 1984—; sr. physician Kaiser Permanente, Oakland, Calif., 1965-67, chief gastroenterology, 1969-95, clin. dir. colon cancer prevention program, 1993—. Contbr. articles to profl. jours. Mem. Am. Gastroent. Assn., Am. Soc. for Gastrointestinal Endoscopy, No. Calif. Soc. for Clin. Gastroenterology (pres. 1984), Phi Lambda Upsilon. Home and Office: 2661 Cedar St Berkeley CA 94708-1933

GROSSMANN, RONALD STANYER, lawyer; b. Chgo., Nov. 9, 1944; s. Andrew Eugene and Gladys M. Grossman; m. Jo Ellen Hanson, May 11, 1968; children: Kenneth Frederick, Emilie Beth. BA, Northwestern U., 1966; JD, U. Mich., 1969. Bar: Oreg., 1969. Law clk. Oreg. Supreme Ct., Salem, 1969-70; assoc. Stoel Rives Boley Jones & Grey, Portland, Oreg., 1970-76, ptnr., 1976—. Mem. ABA, Oreg. Bar Assn. Office: Stoel Rives LLP 900 SW 5th Ave Ste 2300 Portland OR 97204-1232

GROSZ, PHILIP J., lawyer; b. Oshkosh, Wis., Feb. 1, 1952; s. Joseph Otto and Marjorie (Berkhoel) G.; m. Linda Marie Ondrejka, Dec. 29, 1973. BA with honors, U. Wis., 1973; JD, Yale Law Sch., 1977. Bar: Calif. Ptnr. Loeb & Loeb, L.A., 1983-92, mng. ptnr., 1992-96. founder, bd. dirs. Love is Feeding Everyone, L.A., 1983-94. Mem. Calif. Bar Assn. Democrat. Office: Loeb & Loeb 10100 Santa Monica Blvd Los Angeles CA 90067-4003

GROTH, MICHAEL JOSEPH, oculoplastic surgeon; b. Phila., June 17, 1959; s. William Henry Jr. and Dorothy Ann (Tewksbury) G.; m. Ileana E. Zapatero, May 26, 1984; children: Michael, Gabriela, Caroline. BS in Chemistry, U. Fla., 1980; MD, U. Miami, 1984. Intern Mt. Sinai Med. Ctr., Miami, Fla., 1984-85; resident UCLA Jules Stein Eye Inst., L.A., 1985-88; plastic and reconstructive surgeon pvt. practice, Beverly Hills, Calif., 1989—; asst. clin. prof. UCLA Jules Stein Eye Inst., 1989—; clin. instr. Wodsworth VA Hosp., L.A., 1990—. Contbr. articles to profl. jours. Ophthalmic plastic surgery fellow UCLA Jules Stein Eye Inst., 1988-89. Mem. Am. Acad. Ophthalmology, Calif. Med. Assn., Calif. Assn. Ophthalmology, L.A. County Med. Assn., L.A. Soc. Ophthalmology. Office: 9675 Brighton Way Ste 410 Beverly Hills CA 90210-5135

GROUT, MARILYN ANN, geologist, researcher, consultant; b. Albion, N.Y., July 10, 1943; d. Harold Miller and Arline Caroline (Klafehn) Higley; m. Richard Vernon Grout, Nov. 26, 1965. BS in Edn., SUNY, Brockport, 1964; MS in Geology, U. Colo., 1981, PhD in Geology, 1990. Tchr. Centereach (N.Y.) Schs., 1964-65, Dept. Def., Yokota AFB, Japan, 1966-69, Paxton (Mass.) Schs., 1969-70; tchg. asst. dept. geology U. Colo., Boulder, 1978-79; geol. field asst., geologist U.S. Geol. Survey, Denver, 1981-88, rsch. geologist, 1988-95, consulting geologist, 1995—. Developed and implemented methods of studying natural fracture systems. Fellow Geol. Soc. Am.; mem. Am. Assn. Petroleum Geologists (Best Paper award 1992), Internat. Assn. Structural/Tectonic Geologists, Rocky Mountain Assn. Geologists, Fluorescent Mineral Soc., Franklin/Ogdensburg Mineral Soc. Office: 5407 SW View Point Ter Portland OR 97201-3961

GROVE, ANDREW S., electronics company executive; b. Budapest, Hungary, 1936; married; 2 children. B.S., CCNY, 1960, DSc (hon.), 1985; Ph.D., U. Calif.-Berkeley, 1963; DEng (hon.), Worcester Poly. Inst., 1989. With Fairchild Camera and Instrument Co., 1963-67; pres., COO, Intel Corp., Santa Clara, Calif., 1967-87, pres., CEO, 1987—, also bd. dirs. Recipient medal Am. Inst. Chemists, 1960, Merit cert. Franklin Inst., 1975, Townsend Harris medal CCNY, 1980, Enterprise award Profl. Advt. Assn., 1987, George Washington award Am. Hungarian Found., 1990, Citizen of Yr. award World Forum Silicon Valley, 1993, Exec. of Yr. award U. Ariz., 1993, Achievement medal Am. Electronics Assn., 1993, Heinz Family Found. award for tech. and economy, 1995, John von Neumann medal Am. Hungarian Assn., 1995, Steinman medal City Coll. N.Y., 1995, Statesman of the Yr. award Harvard Bus. Sch., 1996, Internat. Achievement award World Trade Club, 1996, Cinema Digital Technols. award Internat. Faton Festival, 1997. Fellow IEEE (Achievement award 1969, J.J. Ebers award 1974, Engring. Leadership Recognition award 1987, Computer Entrepreneur award 1997), Acad. Arts and Scis.; mem. Nat. Acad. Engring. Office: Intel Corp PO Box 58119 2200 Mission College Blvd Santa Clara CA 95052-8119

GROVE, DOUGLAS DAVID, insurance company executive; b. Corona, Calif., Aug. 6, 1957; s. David Malley and Kathleen Lillian (Hogan) G.; m. Gail DeBenedictis, Sept. 12, 1992. BS in Bus. Adminstrn., U. Pacific, Stockton, Calif., 1980. CPCU, ARM. Package underwriter Kemper Group, San Francisco, 1980-85; comml. account underwriter Northbrook Property & Casualty Co., San Francisco, 1985-86, Chubb Ins. Cos., San Francisco, 1986-87; sr. underwriter nat. accounts Fireman's Fund Ins. Cos., San Rafael, Calif., 1987-88, exec. underwriter nat. accounts, 1989-93; exec. underwriter nat. brokerage unit Fireman's Fund, Novato, Calif., 1993-96; comml. lines product mgr. product mgmt. dept. Home Office Product Devel. Dept., 1996—. Mem. Underwriters Forum of San Francisco (sec. 1987, v.p. 1988, pres. 1989), Nat. Assn. Clock and Watch Collectors, Commonwealth Club of San Francisco, Alpha Kappa Lambda (chpt. sec., v.p., pres.). Office: Fireman's Fund Ins Co Target Industries 777 San Marin Dr Novato CA 94998-0001

GROVER, JAMES ROBB, chemist, editor; b. Klamath Falls, Oreg., Sept. 16, 1928; s. James Richard and Marjorie Alida (van Groos) G.; m. Barbara Jean Ton, Apr. 14, 1957; children: Jonathan Robb, Patricia Jean. BS summa cum laude, valedictorian, U. Wash., Seattle, 1952; PhD, U. Calif., Berkeley, 1958. Rsch. assoc. Brookhaven Nat. Lab., Upton, N.Y., 1957-59, assoc. chemist, 1959-63, chemist, 1963-67, chemist with tenure, 1967-77, sr. chemist, 1978-93, rsch. collaborator, 1993—; cons. Lawrence Livermore (Calif.) Nat. Lab., 1962; assoc. editor Ann. Rev. of Nuclear Sci., Ann. Revs., Inc., Palo Alto, Calif., 1967-77; vis. prof. Inst. for Molecular Sci., Okazaki, Japan, 1986-87; vis. scientist Max-Planck Inst. für Strömungsforschung, Göttingen, Fed. Republic Germany, 1975-76. Contbr. numerous articles to profl. jours. With USN, 1946-48. Mem. Am. Chem. Soc. (chmn. nuclear chemistry and tech. 1989), Am. Phys. Soc., Triple Nine Soc., Sigma Xi, Phi Beta Kappa, Phi Lambda Upsilon, Zeta Mu Tau, Pi Mu Epsilon. Libertarian. Presbyterian. Home and Office: 1536 Pinecrest Ter Ashland OR 97520-3427

GROVER, STUART RALPH, management consultant; b. Newark; s. Sidney and Edith Norma (Glazer) G. BA, U. Wis., 1965, MA, 1966, PhD, 1971. Asst. prof. history Vanderbilt U., Nashville, 1971-75, Witteberg U., Springfield, Ohio, 1975-77; asst. prof. history Ohio State U., Columbus, 1977-78, assoc. dir. continuing edn., 1979-81; pub., editor Northside Herald, Columbus, Ohio, 1981-82; dir. pub. rels. Mus. History & Industry, Seattle, 1982-84; pres. Stuart Grover & Assocs., Seattle, 1984-90, The Collins Group, Inc., Seattle and Portland, Oreg., 1990—; nat. panelist NEH Challenge Grant Program, 1989, 90; presenter in field. Contbr. articles to profl. jours. Bd. dirs. Allied Arts, 1987-88, Artist Trust, 1987-88, Seattle/King County Conv. and Visitors Bur., 1984-89, Friends of Chamber Music, Portland, Oreg., 1992-97; mem. oversight com. African-Am. Heritage Ctr. Project City of Seattle Dept. Community Devel., 1987; mem. tech. adv. group for hist. bldg. code State Bldg. Code Coun., 1990; founder Oreg. Artist Trust, 1993-94, Group Health Found., 1994-96, Providence Child Ctr. Found., 1995—, Robison Jewish Home Found., 1996—; active Seattle Leadership Tomorrow, 1987. Recipient Young Scholar award NEH, 1975-75, Mayor's Small Bus. award, Seattle, 1995. Home: 2204 NE Klickitat St Portland OR 97212-2461 Office: The Collins Group Inc 101 Stewart St Ste 840 Seattle WA 98101-1048

GROVES, MARTHA, newspaper writer. Computer writer L.A. Times. Office: LA Times Times Mirror Sq Los Angeles CA 90053*

GRUBB, DAVID H., construction company president; b. 1936; married. BSCE, Princeton U.; MSCE, Stanford U. With Swinerton and Walberg Co., San Francisco, 1964—, then exec. v.p. Structural divsn., exec. v.p. ops., pres., also bd. dirs.; pres. Swinerton Incorp., 1993—, now chmn. bd.; chmn. bd. Swinerton & Walberg Co., SW Indsl., Inc., Conelly Swinerton Constrn., Inc., Westwood Swinerton Constrn., Swinerton & Walberg Property Svcs., Inc. Office: Swinerton Incorp 580 California St San Francisco CA 94104

GRUBER, ANDRAS, physician, researcher; b. Budapest, Hungary, Jan. 10, 1954; came to U.S., 1986; s. Gyula Foky Gruber and Edit Kardos; m. Anna Szemere, Nov. 1, 1975; 1 child, Nora. BS, Radnòti Sch. of Eötvös L. U., Budapest, 1972; MD, Semmelweis Med. U., Budapest, 1979. Cert. in internal medicine. Resident Postgrad. Med. Sch., Budapest, 1979-84, mem. med. staff, 1984-85; mem. med. staff Szönyi Tibor Hosp., Vác, Hungary, 1985-86; postdoctoral fellow Scripps Clinic and Rsch. Found., La Jolla, Calif., 1986-89, rsch. assoc., 1989-91; sr. rsch. assoc. The Scripps Rsch. Inst., La Jolla, 1991—, asst. mem., 1992—, adj. asst. mem., 1994—; assoc. med. dir. DepoTech Corp., San Diego, 1994-96, dir. med. affairs, 1996—; lectr. in field, 1986—. Contbr. 33 articles to profl. jours., also book chpts., abstracts; patentee in field. Rsch. fellow Immuno Ag. Austria/Scripps Clinic, 1986, Am. Heart Assn./Calif. Affiliate, 1989; rsch. grantee U. Calif. Tobacco-Related Disease Rsch. Program, 1991. Mem. Soc. of Fellows of Scripps Clinic & Rsch. Found., Internat. Soc. Thrombosis & Hemostasis, Am. Heart Assn. Coun. on Thrombosis, N.Y. Acad. Scis., Am. Pain Soc., Am. Soc. of Regional Anesthesia, Am. Assn. Pharm. Physician. Office: DepoTech Corp 10450 Science Ctr Dr San Diego CA 92121

GRUBER, GEORGE MICHAEL, accountant, business management and financial systems consultant; b. Euclid, Ohio, Sept. 9, 1951; s. George and Cecilia Marie (Cantwell) G.; m. Alice Armas Peralta, June 22, 1985; 1 child, Christian Alexander. BS in Acctg. and Fin., San Francisco State U., 1983, MBA in Fin., 1991. Letterpress printer Custom Printing Assocs., San Francisco, 1973-78; voucher examiner U.S. Dept. Labor, San Francisco, 1980-81; teamster United Courier, Inc., San Francisco, 1979-81; bookkeeper, tile setter Curry Tile, Albany, Calif., 1982; sr. staff acct. divsn. Marriott Corp. Farrells Restaurants Inc., San Francisco, 1983-85; asst. contr. Bay Area Seating Svc., Oakland, Calif., 1985-87; mgr. acctg. and fin. divsn. Grand Met. Plc (Pillsbury) The Häagen Dazs Co. Inc., Hayward, Calif., 1987-90; corp. contr. Andronico's Park & Shop Inc., Albany, Calif., 1991; div. contr. Core-Mark Internat., Hayward, 1991-93; founder, owner Gruber Fin. Svcs. (GFS), 1993—; mid-Pacific regional fin. acctg. contr. DFS, L.P., Tamuning, Guam, 1993-95; guest lectr. fin. San Francisco State U., 1990-91. With USMC, 1969-72, Vietnam. Mem. Inst. Mgmt. Accts. (v.p. edn. 1991-92, pres. 1992-93, cert. of appreciation 1992-93), Nat. Soc. Pub. Accts. Home and Office: Gruber Fin Svcs Co 432 Congo St San Francisco CA 94131-3111

GRUCHALLA, MICHAEL EMERIC, electronics engineer; b. Houston, Feb. 2, 1946; s. Emeric Edwin and Myrtle (Priebe) G.; m. Elizabeth Tyson, June 14, 1969; children: Kenny, Katie. BSEE, U. Houston, 1968; MSEE, U. N.Mex., 1980. Registered profl. engr., Tex. Project engr. Tex. Instruments Corp., Houston, 1967-68; group leader EG&G Washington Analytical Services Ctr., Albuquerque, 1974-88; engring. specialist EG&G Energy Measurements Inc., Albuquerque, 1988-94, Allied Signal FM&T, Albuquerque, 1994—; cons. engring., Albuquerque; lectr. in field, 1978—; expert witness in field; presenter sci. testimony before Ho. of Reps. Sci. Com., 1996. Contbr. articles to tech. jours.; patentee in field. Judge local sci. fairs, Albuquerque, 1983—. Served to capt. USAF, 1968-74. Recipient R&D 100 award, 1991, Gen. Mgr.'s Vision award Dept. Energy, 1994. Mem. IEEE, Instrumentation Soc. Am., Planetary Soc., N.Mex. Tex. Instruments Computer Group (pres. 1984-85), Electric Auto Assn. (v.p. Albuquerque chpt. 1994—), Sigma Xi, Tau Beta Pi, Eta Kappa Nu. Office: Allied Signal KCD Kirtland Ops PO Box 4339 Albuquerque NM 87196-4339

GRUEN, CLAUDE, economist, consultant; b. Bonn, Aug. 17, 1931; came to U.S., 1938; s. Walter and Elsbet (Bronne) G.; m. Nina Jaffe Gruen, Sept. 11, 1960; children: Les, Dale, Adam, Joshua, Aaron. BBA, U. Cin., 1954, MA, 1962, PhD, 1964. Instr. Xavier U., Cin., 1963-64; lectr. U. Calif., Berkeley, 1964-70; economist Arthur D. Little Inc., San Francisco, 1964-70; pres., prin. economist Gruen Gruen & Assocs., San Francisco, 1970—; dir. Rreef Am. Reit, Inc., 1994—. Co-author: Low and Moderate Income Housing, 1972; contbg. editor Instl. Real Estate Letter, 1991—; contbr. articles to profl. jours. Capt. USAF, 1954-57. Mem. Urban Land Inst. (indsl. and office coun.), Western Regional Sci. Assn., Am. Assn.Econs., Lambda Alpha Real Estate. Jewish. Office: Gruen Gruen & Assocs 564 Howard St San Francisco CA 94105-3002

GRUENWALD, GEORGE HENRY, new products development management consultant; b. Chgo., Apr. 23, 1922; s. Arthur Frank and Helen (Duke) G.; m. Corrine Rae Linn, Aug. 16, 1947; children: Helen Marie Gruenwald Orlando, Paul Arthur. BS in Journalism, Northwestern U., 1947; student, Evanston Acad. Fine Arts, 1937-38, Chgo. Acad. Fine Arts, 1938-39, Grinnell Coll., 1940-41. Asst. to pres. UARCO, Inc., Chgo., 1947-49; creative dir., mgr. mdse. Willy-Overland Motors Inc., Toledo, 1949-51; new products, brand and advt. mgr. Toni Co./Gillette, Chgo., 1951-53; v.p., creative dir., account supr. E.H. Weiss Agy., Chgo., 1953-55; exec. v.p., mgmt. supr. North Advt., Chgo., 1955-71; pres., treas., dir. Pilot Products, Chgo., 1963-71; pres., dir. Advance Brands, Inc., Chgo., 1963-71; owner Venture Group, 1971—; exec. v.p., dir. Campbell Mithun Inc., Mpls. and Chgo., 1971-72; pres., dir. Campbell Mithun Inc., 1972-79, chmn., dir., 1979-81, CEO, dir., 1981-83, chief creative officer, dir., 1983-84; vice-chmn., dir. Ted Bates Worldwide, N.Y.C., 1979-80; mgmt. cons. new products, 1984—. Author: New Product Development-What Really Works, 1985, 2d edit., New Product Development-Responding to Market Demand, 1992, How to Create Profitable New Products, 1997, (workbook) New Product Development Checklists: From Mission to Market, 1991, (videos) New Products Seven Steps to Success, 1988, New Product Development, 1989; editor-in-chief Oldsmobile Rocket Ctr. mag., 1955-65, Hudson Family mag., 1953-56; expert columnist Mktg. News, 1988-95; contbr. articles to profl. jours. Trustee Chgo. Pub. TV Assn., 1969-73, Mpls. Soc. Fine Arts, 1975-83, Linus Pauling Inst. Sci. and Medicine, Palo Alto, 1984-92, 95-96; advisor Linus Pauling Inst., Oreg. State U., Corvallis, 1996—; chmn., v.p., chmn. class reps. Northwestern U. Alumni Fund Coun., Chgo., 1965-68; trustee, chmn., chmn. exec. com. Twin Cities Pub. TV Corp., 1971-84; trustee Minn. Pub. Radio Inc., 1973-77, vice chmn., 1974-75; bd. dirs., mem. exec. com. PBS, Alexandria, Va., 1978-86, 88-94, mem. comm. adv. com., 1993-95, vice chmn. task force on funding, 1991-92; chmn. task force on tech. applications, lay rep., 1971—; del. Am.'s Pub. TV Stas., Washington, 1971—; bd. dirs. St. Paul Chamber Orch., 1982-84, San Diego Chamber Orch., 1986-88; mem. adv. bd. San Diego State U. Pub. Broadcasting Comty., 1986—, pub. rels. specialist, editor. With USAAF, 1943-45, MTO. Recipient Hermes award Chgo. Federated Advt. Clubs, 1963, Ednl. TV awards, 1969, 71, 86; inductee Medill Sch. Journalism Hall of Achievement, 1997. Mem. Am. Mktg. Assn., Am. Assn. Advt. Agys. (mgmt. com. 1976-84), Nat. Soc. Profl. Journalists, Am. Inst. Wine and Food (bd. dirs. 1985-92), So. Calif. Advt. Media Soc. Office: PO Box 1696 Rancho Santa Fe CA 92067-1696 *To learn. To teach. To make a difference.*

GRUNDBERG, ANDY, cultural organization administrator. Dir. Ansel Adams Ctr. Photography, San Francisco. Office: Ansel Adams Ctr Photography 250 Fourth St San Francisco CA 94103

GRUNDTISCH, JEFFERY LYNN, lawyer, medical and environmental consultant; b. Lancaster, Ohio, Nov. 6, 1948; s. Howard Hamilton and Joan Mary (Burnworth) G.; m. Dawn Girvan, July 17, 1984. BA cum laude, Miami U., 1971; JD cum laude, Capital U., 1974. Bar: Ohio 1974, U.S. Dist. Ct. (so. dist.) Ohio 1975, U.S. Ct. Mil. Appeals 1975, U.S. Tax Ct. 1978, U.S. Ct. Claims 1978, U.S. Ct. Internat. Trade 1981, U.S. Supreme Ct. 1985. Commd. capt. USAF, 1975, advanced through grades to lt. col., 1988; chief of civil law 46th Air Base Group, Del Rio, Tex., 1975-77; forensic medicine cons. Keesler Med. Ctr., Biloxi, Miss., 1977-80; med. law cons. U.S. Med. Ctr., Wiesbaden, Germany, 1980-84; chief gen. law 8th Air Force, Shreveport, La., 1984-87; staff judge advocate 40th Air Divsn., Great Falls, Mont., 1987-90; dep. staff judge advocate U.S. Forces Japan and 5th Air Force, Tokyo, 1990-93; chief environ. law Def. Contract Mgmt. Dist. West, El Segundo, Calif., 1993—; mem. environ. cost task force Def. Logistics Agy., Cameron Station, Va., 1993-94; legal cons. to air force surgeon gen., 1980-84; mem. U.S. negotiation team U.S./Japan Status of Forces Agreement, U.S. Force Japan, Tokyo, 1990-91. Author: Current Status of Death with Dignity, 1979, Medical Malpractice Liability in Genetic Counseling and Testing, 1979, Involuntary Hospital and Involuntary Medication of Mental Health Patients, 1980, Quick Reference Guide to Medical Law Topics, 1983, 84, 85, Legal Issues Related to AIDS, 1987, Historical Overview of CA Water Law, 1994, Environmental Insurance Litigation, 1995. Mem. adv. bd. Mont. chpt. Salvation Army, Great Falls, 1989-90; mem. Mil. AIDS Task Force, Walter Reed Med. Ctr., 1981; med. law sect. Ohio Bar Assn., Columbus, 1980. Decorated Air Force Meritorious Svc. medal (4). Mem. Environ. Law Assn. (pres. 1994-96), Toxic Concern Alert Assn. (v.p. 1990-96), European Hosp. Atty. Assn. (pres. 1980-84), Med. Law Cons. Assn. (v.p. 1980-90), Varsity M Club, Order of Curia, Phi Beta Kappa, Alpha Theta Phi, Phi Alpha Theta, Delta Theta Phi. Office: Def Contract Mgmt Dist 222 N Sepulveda Blvd El Segundo CA 90245

GRUTTER, JUDITH APPLEY, career counselor; b. Montclair, N.J., Nov. 24, 1942; d. Lawrence Asa and Ruth (Wilson) Appley; m. Karl Grutter, Aug. 26, 1966 (div. Jan. 1971); m. William Karl Schatz, Nov. 26, 1976. BA in English, Syracuse U., 1969; MS in Counseling, Calif. State U., 1976. Cert. career counselor; registered profl. career counselor Calif. Career counselor Calif. State U., L.A., 1971-76, L.A. County Schs., 1976-81; coord. grad. programs in career counseling Calif. State U., Northridge, 1981-90; ptnr. Webb, Grutter, Helander & Assocs., Pasadena, Calif., 1990-94; prin. G/S Cons., So. Lake Tahoe, Calif., 1978—; trainer, conf. presenter in field, 1976—. Mem. Nat. Career Devel. Assn. (recipient merit award 1993, named career counselor of yr. 1994), Calif. Career Devel. Assn. (exec. bd. 1983—, pres. 1989-90), Assn. for Psychol. Type (tng. faculty 1993—). Democrat. Office: G/S Consultants PO Box 7855 South Lake Tahoe CA 76158

GRUVER, WILLIAM RAND, II, journalist, educator; b. N.Y.C., June 18, 1936; s. Henry and Anne Catherine (Lauer) G.; m. Lila Hean Gruver, Sept. 15, 1961 (dec.); children: Catherine, Robin; m. Barbara Anne Boone, Mar. 4, 1984; 1 child, Renée. BA in Polit. Sci., Columbia U., 1960, MA in Journalism, 1961. Pub. affairs exec. Carl Byoir & Assocs., N.Y.C., 1964-69; dep. press sec. to Senator Robert Kennedy, U.S. Senate, Washington, 1967-68; polit. editor CBS News, N.Y.C. and L.A., 1969-76; polit. corr. Jack Anderson Column, Washington, 1976-82; news dir., anchor U.A. Columbia Cable, Nutler, N.J., 1983-85; commentator, corrs. Stas. KFYI, KFLR, KHEG and KHEP, Phoenix, 1992—; mng. editor Fourth Estate News Svc., Phoenix; mem. faculty Ariz. State U. Walter Cronkite Sch. Journalism and Telecom., Tempe, 1986—. Author: Since 1789, 1971, Last Act, Ed Meese, Man in the Middle, 1994; contbr. numerous articles to mags. and newspapers. Former exec. sec. Calif. Dem. Com., L.A.; former chmn. Ft. Lee (N.J.) Consumer Commn.; media cons. 3 to U.S. senators, Washington. Ensign USN, 1953-57. Mem. AFTRA (sec., bd. dirs.), Soc. Profl. Journalists, Assn. Univ. Tchrs., Am. Legion, Beta Sigma Tau. Home: 3341 W Pershing Ave Phoenix AZ 85029-1236 Office: Fourth Estate News Svc PO Box 39094 Phoenix AZ 85069-9094

GRYC, GEORGE, geologist; b. St. Paul, Minn., July 27, 1919; s. Anthony Stanley and Lillian (Teply) G.; m. Jean L. Funk, Feb. 4, 1942; children: James, Stephen, Christina, Paula, Georgina. BA, U. Minn., 1940, MS, 1942; postgrad., Johns Hopkins U., 1946-49. Geologist Alaskan Br. U.S. Geol. Survey, Washington, 1943-63; chief Alaskan br. U.S. Geol. Survey, Menlo Park, Calif., 1963-76, regional geologist, 1976; chief Office of Nat. Petroleum Resource in Alaska U.S. Geol. Survey, Anchorage, 1976-82; dirs. rep. Western region U.S. Geol. Survey, Menlo Park, 1982-95, gen. chmn. Circum-Pacific Map Project, 1982—. Recipient Meritorious Svc. award Dept. of Interior, Washington, 1974, Disting. Svc. award, 1978; named Hon. Mem., Alaska Geol. Soc., 1987. Fellow Geol. Assn. Am., Sigma Xi; mem. Am. Assn. Petroleum Geologists (editor), Paleontological Soc., Cosmos Club Washington. Office: US Geol Survey MS 901 345 Middlefield Rd Menlo Park CA 94025-3561

GRZANKA, LEONARD GERALD, writer, consultant; b. Ludlow, Mass., Dec. 11, 1947; s. Stanley Simon and Claire Genevive Grzanka. BA, U. Mass., 1972; MA, Harvard U., 1974. Asst. prof. Gakushiun U., Tokyo, 1975-78; pub. rels. specialist Pacific Gas and Electric Co., San Francisco, 1978-80; sales promotion writer Tymshare Transaction Svcs., Fremont, Calif., 1980-81; account exec. The Strayton Co., Santa Clara, Calif., 1981-82; mng. editor Portable Computer Mag., San Francisco, 1982-84; prin. Grzanka Assocs., San Francisco, 1984-86; San Francisco bur. chief Digital News, 1986-91; battery program cons. Bevilacqua Knight Inc., Oakland, Calif., 1991—; staff asst. Electric Power Rsch. Inst./U.S. Advanced Battery Consortium, Palo Alto, Calif., 1991-96; lectr. Golden Gate U., San Francisco, 1985-87. Author: Neither Heaven Nor Hell, 1978; translator, editor: (art catalog) Masterworks of Japanese Crafts, 1977; translator: (book chpt.) Manajo: The Chinese Preface to the Kokinwakashu, 1984 (Literary Transl. award 1984), Spanish translation, 1994. Sgt. USAF, 1965-69. Fellow Danforth Found., 1974. Mem. United Anglers Calif., Harvard Club of San Francisco (bd. dirs. 1984-88, Cert. Appreciation 1986, 88), Phi Beta Kappa, Phi Kappa Phi. Home: 2909 Madison St Alameda CA 94501-5426 Office: BKI 501 14th St # 210 Oakland CA 94612-1405

GUAJARDO, ELISA, educator; b. Roswell, N. Mex., Nov. 13, 1932; d. Alejo Najar and Hortensia (Jiminez) Garcia; m. David Roberto Guajardo, Oct. 15, 1950; 1 child, Elsie Edith. BS, Our Lady of the Lake U., 1962, MEd, 1971; MA, Chapman U., 1977. Cert. tchr., adminstr., counselor, Calif. 5th grade tchr. San Antonio (Tex.) Sch. Dist., 1962-63; soc. sci. tchr. Newport Mesa Sch. Dist., Costa Mesa, Calif., 1963-67; soc. sci. tchr. Orange (Calif.) Unified Sch. Dist., 1967-70, project dir., 1970-71, English tchr., 1972-73, counselor, 1973—; pres. Bilingual, Bicultural Parent Adv. Bd., Orange, Calif., 1971-72; reader bilingual projects Calif. State Dept. Edn., Orange, 1971-72; vis. lectr. We. Wash. Univ., Bellingham, 1972-73; mem. curriuculum and placement couns., Orange Unified Sch. Dist., 1973-78, 95-96. Author: (Able)Adaptations of Bilingual/Bicultural Edn, Fed. Project Proposal. Mem. NEA, AAUW, Calif. Tchrs. Assn., Orange Unified Edn. Assn, Hon., Alpha Chi, Our Lady of Lake U., Tex. chpt. Democrat. Mem. Assemblies of God Church. Office: Canyon HS 220 S Imperial Hwy Anaheim CA 92807

GUAMBAÑA, TEODORO I., government executive; b. Cuenca, Ecuador, Jan. 28, 1943; s. Alberto E. and Maria S. (Morales) G.; m. Abeyta Valdez, Aug. 5, 1972 (div. Dec. 1993); children: Anacarmen, Consuelo-Marie, Simone-Felice. BA in Econs., U. N.Mex., 1969, MPA, 1971. Dir. N.Mex. Budget, Santa Fe, 1980-84; dep. cabinet sec. Dept. Health and Environ., Santa Fe, 1984-86; v.p. fin. Coll. of Santa Fe, 1986-90; dir. adminstrn. Gen. Svcs. Dept., 1995—; adj. prof. U. N.Mex., Albuquerque, 1981—. Author Motorcycle Driver Safety 5 Yr. Plan for New Mexico, 1995. Legis. lobbyist, 1986, 93-94. Named Outstanding Alumni Assn., U. N.Mex., 1993. Mem. Am. Mgmt. Assn., Cmty. Devel. Assn. Home: 2379 Camino Pintores Santa Fe NM 87505 Office: Gen Svcs Dept Atla Vista 716 Santa Fe NM 87503

GUARDINO, SAL, food executive; b. 1922. Farmer Stockton, Calif., 1942—; v.p. Sunniland Fruit Inc., Stockton. Office: Sunniland Fruit Inc 1350 Report Ave Stockton CA 95205-3054*

GUAY, GORDON HAY, postal service executive, marketing educator, consultant; b. Hong Kong, Aug. 1, 1948; came to U.S., 1956; s. Daniel Bock and Ping Gin (Ong) G. AA, Sacramento City Coll., 1974; BS, Calif. State U., Sacramento, 1976, MBA, 1977; PhD, U. So. Calif., 1981. Mgmt. assoc. U.S. Postal Svc., Sacramento, 1980-82, br. mgr., 1982-83, fin. mgr., 1983-84, mgr. quality control, 1984-86, mgr. tech. sales and svcs. divsn., 1986-91, dir. mktg. and comm., 1991-95, postmaster, 1996—; assoc. prof. bus. adminstrn., mktg. and mgmt. Calif. State U., Sacramento, 1981-85; prof. mktg. Nat. U., San Diego, 1984—; pres. Gordon Guay and Assocs., Sacramento, 1979—; cons. Mgmt. Cons. Assocs., Sacramento, 1977-79. Author: Marketing: Issues and Perspectives, 1983; also articles to profl. jours. With U.S. Army, 1968-70. Recipient Patriotic Svc. award U.S. Treasury Dept., San Francisco, 1985. Fellow Acad. Mktg. Sci.; mem. NEA, AAUP, Am. Mgmt. Assn.,

Am. Mktg. Assn. (Outstanding Mktg. Educator award 1989), Am. Soc. Pub. Adminstrn., Soc. Advancement Mgmt. (Outstanding Mem. 1976), Assn. MBA Execs. Democrat. Office: US Postal Svc 4131 S Shingle Rd Shingle Springs CA 95682-9341

GUELKER-CONE, MICHAEL ALFRED, elementary education educator; b. Bakersfield, Calif., Oct. 31, 1953; s. Alfred Russell and Debbie Marie (Welch) C.; m. Leslie Kay Guelker-Cone, July 1, 1977; 1 child, Katie Rebecca. AA, Merced Coll., 1974; BA, Calif. State Coll., 1979; cert. tchr., St. Mary's Coll., Moraga, Calif., 1986. Cert. tchr., Calif., Wash. Dir., head tchr. Benicia (Calif.) Montessori Sch., 1981-85; tchr. Jackson Elem., Fresno, Calif., 1986-94; tchr. spl. edn. Waiakeawaena Elem., Hilo, Hawaii, 1994-95; tchr. Lincoln Elem. Sch., Mt. Vernon, Wash., 1995—; adv. bd. Project Astro, San Francisco, 1992-96. Author: (with others) Project SPICA: A Teacher Resource to Enhance Astronomy Education, 1994, Primarily Earth, 1996. Project SPICA grantee NSF, 1991, Project ARIES grantee, 1993. Mem. Nat. Sci. Tchrs. Assn., Phi Delta Kappa. Congregationalist. Home: 2213 W Birch St Bellingham WA 98226

GUENTER, SCOT MICHAEL, social sciences educator; b. Port Allegany, Pa., July 30, 1956; s. Fritz Edward and Mary (Connors) G. BA, Pa. State U., 1978; MA, U. Md., 1981, PhD, 1986. Tchg. asst., lectr. U. Md., College Park, 1978-86; lectr. Johannes Gutenberg U., Mainz, Germany, 1981-82; asst. prof. Wichita (Kans.) State U., 1986-87, Dickinson Coll., Carlisle, Pa., 1987-89; asst. to assoc. prof. San Jose (Calif.) State U., 1989—; v.p. AIDS Resources, Info. and Svcs. (ARIS), 1995-96, bd. dirs. Author: The American Flag 1777-1924, 1990; editor Raven: A Journal of Vexillology, 1994—; mem. editorial bd. Proteus: A Jour. of Ideas, 1990—; contbr. articles to profl. jours. Nat. merit scholar, 1974. Mem. Am. Studies Assn., Calif. Am. Studies Assn. (v.p. 1992-94, pres. 1994-95), Am. Culture Assn., N.Am. Vexillological Assn. (v.p. 1989-91, pres. 1991-94, Driver award 1985), Golden Gate Area Vexillological Assn., Phi Beta Kappa. Democrat. Roman Catholic. Home: 201 S 4th St Apt 617 San Jose CA 95112-3661 Office: San Jose State U Dept Am Studies San Jose CA 95192-0092

GUENTHER, ROBERT STANLEY, II, investment and property executive; b. Orange, Calif., Sept. 29, 1950; s. Robert Stanley and Fanny Newman (Shaw) G. BA in Psychology, U. Calif., Santa Barbara, 1975; BA in Sociology, U. Calif., 1975. Cert. radio telephone 3rd class operator. Pvt. practice Templeton, Calif., 1975—. Mem. Templeton Hist. Soc. (life), Space Explorers Network, Internat. Platform Soc. Assn., The Planetary Soc., Nat. Geog. Soc., Canine Companions for Independence, U. Calif. Santa Barbara Alumni Assn. Home and Office: 150 White Hawk Ln Templeton CA 93465-8641

GUERARD, ALBERT JOSEPH, retired modern literature educator, author; b. Houston, Nov. 2, 1914; s. Albert Leon and Wilhelmina (McCartney) G.; m. Mary Maclin Bocock, July 11, 1941; children: Catherine Collot, Mary Maclin, Lucy Lundie. AB, Stanford U., 1934, PhD, 1938; AM, Harvard U., 1936. Instr. Amherst (Mass.) Coll., 1935-36; mem. faculty Harvard U., Cambridge, Mass., 1938-61, successively instr. English, asst. prof., assoc. prof., 1948-54, prof., 1954-61; prof. Stanford (Calif.) U., 1961-85, Albert L. Guerard prof. lit., 1965-85. Author: The Past Must Alter, 1937, Robert Bridges, 1942, The Hunted, 1944, Maquisard, 1945, Joseph Conrad, 1947, Thomas Hardy, 1949, Night Journey, 1950, Andre Gide, 1951, Conrad the Novelist, 1958, The Bystander, 1958, The Exiles, 1963, The Triumph of the Novel: Dickens, Dostoevsky, Faulkner, 1976, The Touch of Time: Myth, Memory and the Self, 1980, Christine/Annette, 1985, Gabrielle, 1992, The Hotel in the Jungle, 1996; co-editor: The Personal Voice, 1964. Served as tech. sgt. psychol. warfare br. AUS, World War II. Rockefeller fellow, 1946-47; Fulbright fellow, 1950-51; Guggenheim fellow, 1956-57; Ford fellow, 1959-60; Nat. Found. Arts fellow, 1967-68; Nat. Found. Humanities fellow, 1974-75; recipient Paris Review Fiction prize, 1963. Mem. Am. Acad. Arts and Scis., Phi Beta Kappa, Pen Cen. West. Home: 635 Gerona Rd Stanford CA 94305-8452

GUERBER, STEPHEN CRAIG, historical society director; b. Corvallis, Oreg., Oct. 2, 1947; s. Allen Lewis and Thelma Mae (Gilson) G.; m. Donna Kay Panko, Feb. 4, 1968; children: Dani Mofit, Patrick Jason, Suzanne Crupper. BA, Idaho State U., 1969. Bus. editor The Idaho Statesman, Boise, 1970-73; info. svcs. dir. Jim Hawkes Advt., Boise, 1973-74; asst. alumni dir. Idaho State U., Pocatello, 1974-76; pub. rels. mgr. U.S. West Communications, Boise, 1978-88; dir. info. U.S. West Found., Boise, 1988-91; mgr. community affairs U.S. West Communications, Boise, 1991-93; exec. dir. Idaho Cmty. Found., 1993-96; dir. Idaho State Hist. Soc., 1996—. Councilman City of Eagle, 1984-88, mayor, 1988-96; bd. dirs. Assn. Idaho Cities, 1988-94, Silver Sage coun. Girls Scouts USA, 1990-93, Am. Festival Ballet, 1984-88; mem. Ada Planning Assn., 1985-96, Fourth Idaho Dist. Jud. Coun., 1988-96, Ada County Centennial Commn., 1989-90. Recipient Outstanding Pub. Svc. award Social Svc. Adminstrn., 1983, Profl. Achievement award Idaho State U. Coll. Arts and Scis., 1991, Simplot Vol. award, 1988; named Idaho Disting. Citizen The Idaho Statesman, 1988. Democrat. Baptist. Home: 699 Ranch Dr Eagle ID 83616-5115 Office: Idado State Hist Soc 1109 Main St Ste 250 Boise ID 83702

GUEST, LINDA SAND, education educator; b. Ft. Morgan, Colo., Sept. 9, 1945; d. Robert E. and Leona Mae (Prettyman) Sand; m. Richard E. Guest, June 5, 1966; children: Elise M., Gregory D. BA, Colo. State U., 1967, MEd, 1983; EdD, Harvard U., 1990. Cert. elem. and secondary tchr., prin., supt. Ednl. cons. Nat. Office for Rural Edn., Ft. Collins, Colo.; tchr. Denver Pub. Schs., East Maine Sch. Dist. 63, Niles, Ill., Poudre R-1 Sch. Dist., Ft. Collins, 1979-91; asst. prof. curriculum and instrn. U. Denver Sch. Edn., 1991-94; project coord. Rocky Mountain Tchr. Edn. Collaborative, Greeley, Colo., 1994—. Mem. ASCD, Am. Ednl. Rsch. Assn., Phi Delta Kappa. Home: 2943 Silverwood Dr Fort Collins CO 80525-2347 Office: U No Colo 518 McKee Hall Greeley CO 80639

GUEST, RATIMA L., educator, counselor; b. Bakersfield, Calif., Aug. 6, 1971; d. Choice and Bessie Marie (Jones) G. BA in Social Work, San Diego State U., 1993, MA in Edn., 1994. Social worker Neighborhood House, San Diego, 1992-94; sch. counselor Jackson Elem. Sch., San Diego, 1993-94; transer prep advisor Mesa C.C., San Diego, 1993-94; sch. rels. officer San Diego State U., San Diego, 1994—; rsch. asst. Ford Found. Grant, San Diego, 1993-94; proposal co-author Charter S ch., San Diego, 1993, Mental Health Counseling Program, 1994. Pres. African Am. Panhellenic Coun., San Diego, 1992-94. Mem. ACA, Sigma Gamma Rho (pres, treas, 1991-93). Home: 7272 Saranac St Apt 44 La Mesa CA 91941-3337

GUETTICH, BRUCE MICHAEL, sporting goods company executive; b. Lansing, Mich., Aug. 4, 1957; s. Randolph Otto and Ingiborg (Lintner) G.; m. Shelby Angela Kindig, June 21, 1956. Grad. h.s., Portland, Oreg. Ski and binding technician Glacier's Edge, Portland, 1972-76; ski shop mgr. Glacier's Edge West, West Slope, Oreg., 1976-79, Beyond Repair, Steamboat Springs, Colo., 1979-81; sales and promotions dir. Kenncorp Internat., Vancouver, Wash., 1981-83; founder, pres., dir. World Footbag Assn., Golden, Colo., 1983—; founder, dir. Internat. Footbag Adv. Bd., Golden, 1983—. Author, editor: (mag.) Footbag World, 1983—; author: (manual) Footbag Instructional Manual, 1986; actor, author: (instrnl. video) Footbag Basics, 1987; author, editor: (instrnl. video) Tricks of the Trade, 1990. Office: World Footbag Assn PO Box 775208 Steamboat Springs CO 80477

GUGELCHUK, GARY MICHAEL, academic administrator; b. Williamson, W.Va., May 25, 1953; s. Tony and Sally E. (Bevins) G. BA, Ohio State U., 1975, MA, 1976, PhD, 1985. Curriculum developer Ohio U., Athens, 1985-86; asst. prof. Health Profl. Edn. Coll. Osteo. Medicine Pacific, Pomona, Calif., 1986-92; assoc. prof. Health Profl. Edn. Coll. Osteo. Medicine Pacific, Pomona, 1992—, dir. office of grants, 1989-96, asst. to v.p. acad. affairs, 1993-96; dean Coll. Allied Health Professions Western U. of Health Scis., Pomona, 1996—; mem. adv. com. IGC project Soc. Tchrs. of Family Medicine, Kansas City, Mo., 1993—; cons. Am. Assn. Colls. of Osteopathic Medicine, Rockville, Md., 1994. Contbr. articles to profl. jours. Adv. com. Cmty. Wellness Partnership, Violence Prevention project, Pomona, 1994—; adv. com. LULAC Nat. Edn. Ctr., Pomona, 1988-92. Fellow Am. Anthropol. Assn., Soc. for Applied Anthropology; mem. Am. Ednl. Rsch. Assn., Am. Folklore Soc., Phi Beta Kappa, Phi Kappa Phi. Office: Western U Health Scis 309 E 2nd St Pomona CA 91766-1854

GUGGENHEIM, SUZANNE, company executive; b. Budapest, Hungary, June 6, 1944; came to U.S., 1981; d. Elisabeth Marton; m. Alan A. Guggenheim, Mar. 20, 1974; 1 child, Valerie. BA in Polit. Sci., Inst. of Polit. Sci., Paris, 1968; M in Law, U. Paris, 1968, MA in English, 1970. COO UNI, Paris, 1968-77; chancellor U. of French Antilles and Guyana, Guadeloupe, 1977-80; pres. Apasica, 1980-81; COO DBCS, Stockton, Calif., 1982-88; realtor Wine County Realtors, Lodi, Calif., 1988-89; real estate broker Camino Realty, Oxnard, Calif., 1989-92; exec. v.p., broker CIS Real Estate, Newbury Park, Calif., 1992—; exec. v.p. CYCOM Technology Corp. Mem. Calif. Rep. Party, 1991—; alt. Ventura County Ctrl. Com., 1991-95; mem. Thousand Oaks City Social Svcs. Funding Com.; pres. Conejo Valley Rep. Women, 1993-95, Conejo Valley Women's Club, 1992-94; chmn. Sch. Site Coun. Maple Elem., 1993-94; mem. Parent Assn., 1st v.p. 1993-95; mem. Conejo Valley Sch. Dist. Adv. Coun., 1992-95; pres. Thousand Oaks CRA. Mem. Rotary Club of Newbury Park (bd. dirs. 1992-94). Home: 3265 Peppermint St Thousand Oaks CA 91320-5039 Office: CYCOM 1560 Newbury Rd # 204 Thousand Oaks CA 91320-3452

GUGGENHEIM-BOUCARD, ALAN ANDRE ALBERT PAUL EDOUARD, business executive, international consultant; b. Paris, May 12, 1950; came to U.S., 1981, naturalized, 1991; s. Jacques and Micheline (Rafalovich) Guggenheim; m. Suzanne Marton, Mar. 20, 1974; 1 child, Valerie. BS, U. Paris, 1971; MSCE, Ecole Speciale des Travaux Publics, Paris, 1974; MBA in Finance, U. Paris, 1975; grad., French Command-Gen. Staff Res. Coll., 1981. Asst. prof. math. Nat. Sch. Arts and Architecture, Paris, 1972-75; civil engr. Societe Routiere Colas, Paris, 1976-77, French Antilles, 1977-78; chief exec. officer, exec. dir. C.R.P.G., Pointe A Pitre, Guadeloupe, 1978-81; chief exec. officer, chmn. San Joaquin Software Systems, Inc., Stockton, Calif., 1982-86, CalCar Investment Svcs., Inc., Newbury Park, Calif., 1983—; chmn., CEO CYCOM Tech. Corp., 1996—; bd. mem. Sucmanu, Paris, 1976-82; bd. of organizers Pacific State Bank, Stockton, Calif., 1985-87. Exec. Editor newsletter L'Action Universitaire, 1970-76. Mem. French Res. Policy Rev. Bd., Paris, 1971-77; mem. Ventura County Rep. Cen. Com., Rep. Presdl. Task Force, Rep. Campaign Coun.; mem. bd. Calif. Rep. Assembly; candidate Rep. 37th Assembly Dist., Calif.; mem. cen. com. Calif. Rep. Party, 1992—. Maj. French Res., 1981. Recipient Gold Medal Omnium Technique Holding, 1975. Fellow Engr. and Scientist France; mem. AAAS, ADPA, Assn. U.S. Army, Rotary. Roman Catholic. Home: 3265 Peppermint St Newbury Park CA 91320-5039 Office: 1560 Newbury Rd # 204 Newbury Park CA 91320-3452

GUGGENHIME, RICHARD JOHNSON, lawyer; b. San Francisco, Mar. 6, 1940; s Richard E. and Charlotte G.; m. Emlen Hall, June 5, 1965 (div.); children: Andrew, Lisa, Molly; m. Judith Perry Swift, Oct. 3, 1992. AB in Polit. Sci. with distinction, Stanford U., 1961; JD, Harvard U., 1964. Bar: Calif. 1965, U.S. Dist. Ct. (no. dist.) Calif. 1965, U.S. Ct. Appeals (9th cir.) 1965. Assoc. Heller, Ehrman, White & McAuliffe, 1965-71, ptnr., 1972—; spl. asst. to U.S. Senator Hugh Scott, 1964; bd. dirs. Comml. Bank of San Francisco, 1980-81, Global Savs. Bank, San Francisco, 1984-86, North Am. Trust Co., 1996—. Mem. San Francisco Bd. Permit Appeals, 1978-86; bd. dirs. Marine World Africa USA, 1980-86; mem. San Francisco Fire Commn., 1986-88, Recreation and Parks Commn., 1988-92; chmn. bd. trustees San Francisco Univ. High Sch., 1987-90; trustee St. Ignatius Prep. Sch., San Francisco, 1987-96. Mem. Am. Coll. Probate Counsel, San Francisco Opera Assn. (bd. dir.), Bohemian Club, Wine and Food Soc. Club, Olympic Club, Chevaliers du Tastevin Club (San Francisco), Thunderbird Country Club (Ranch Mirage, Calif.). Home: 2621 Larkin St San Francisco CA 94109-1512 Office: Heller Ehrman White & McAuliffe 333 Bush St San Francisco CA 94104-2806

GUGLIELMO, EUGENE JOSEPH, software engineer; b. Bklyn., Nov. 23, 1958; s. Anthony and Carlotta Sylvia (Grossi) G.; m. Nancy Eleanor Booth, Aug. 13, 1983; children: Tiffany, Trevyn, Kyle, Quentyn. BS in Computer Sci., St. John's U., 1979; MS in Computer Sci., Calif. State U., Chico, 1987; PhD in Computer Sci., Naval Postgrad. Sch., 1992. Computer asst. St. John's U., Jamaica, N.Y., 1977-79; mem. tech. staff Bell Telephone Labs., Whippany, N.J., 1979-80; sys. designer AT&T Comm., Piscataway, N.J., 1980-85; computer scientist Naval Air Warfare Ctr., China Lake, Calif., 1985-94; cons. IBM Cons. Group, Boulder, Colo., 1994; software engr. Monterey Bay Aquarium Rsch. Inst., Moss Landing, Calif., 1994-96; sr. software engr. BEA Systems, Sunnyvale, Calif., 1996—. Contbr. articles to profl. jours. Mem. IEEE, IEEE Computer Soc., Assn. for Computational Linguistics, Assn. Computing Machinery (Info. Retrieval, Artificial Intelligence), N.Y. Acad. Scis. Roman Catholic. Home: 35 Bayview Rd Castroville CA 95012-9725

GUICE, JOHN THOMPSON, retired air force officer; b. Kosciusko, Miss., Nov. 5, 1923; s. Gustave Nathaniel and Anne Mae (McCool) G.; m. Charlotte Webb, Mar. 8, 1949; children—John Thompson, James G., Steven L., Thomas A., Joseph D. B.S. in Engring, U.S. Mil. Acad., 1947; M.S. in Internat. Relations, George Washington U., 1966; disting. grad., Air Command and Staff Coll., 1962, Air War Coll., 1966. Commd. 2d lt. U.S. Army, 1947; advanced through grades to maj. gen. USAF, 1974; tactical and interceptor pilot, 1947-55; officer Air N.G. and N.G., 1956—; dep. dir. Air N.G., 1974-77, dir., 1977-81, ret., 1981. Decorated Legion of Merit, Air Force D.S.M. Mem. Air Force Assn., N.G. Assn., Sigma Chi. Home: 4901 N Calle Luisa Tucson AZ 85718-4925

GUICHETEAU, JOHN EDWARD, internist, respiratory therapy physician; b. Vineland, N.J., Apr. 26, 1947; m. Patricia White; children: Michael, Lauren, Robert. BS in Biology, St. Joseph U., Phila., 1969; MD, Creighton U., 1973. Diplomate Nat. Bd. Med. Examiners, Am. Bd. Internal Medicine, Am. Bd. Geriatric Medicine. Resident Wake Forest U., Winston-Salem, N.C., 1973-76; lt. USN/U.S. Health Corp., 1976-77; med. dir. Miners' Respiratory Clinic, Rock Springs, Wyo., 1978—; med. dir. respiratory therapy program Western Wyoming Coll., Rock Springs, 1978—; pvt. practice Rock Springs, 1984—; cons. Meml. Hosp. Sweetwater County, Rock Springs, 1977-84, chief of medicine, 1977-86, 91, dir. intensive care, 1980—, pres.-elect med. staff, 1984, pres. med. staff, 1985. Mem. affiliate faculty, course dir. CPR, ACLS Am. Heart Assn; med. dir. Am. Cancer, Soc. Sweetwater County, 1983; med. co-dir. Wyo. State Respiratory Therapy Soc., 1981-90, 93—; mem. State Bd. Med. Examiners, 1989—, sec., 1993, v.p., 1994, pres., 1995; med. dir. Hospice of Sweetwater County, 1989—. Fellow ACP, Fedn. State Med. Bds.; mem. AMA, Wyo. State Med. Soc. (counselor 1977-86, regional chmn. Physician Rev. Orgn. 1977-78), Sweetwater County Med. Soc. (pres. 1987-89). Home: 2023 Carson Rock Springs WY 82901 Office: 430 Broadway St Rock Springs WY 82901-6245

GUIDI, LARRY MICHAEL, mayor; b. L.A.; m. Marilyn Ruisbroek; children: Nicole, Michelle, Gabriella, Adriana. Student, Harbor Coll., 1989. Exec. v.p. Keihin Am. Corp.; mayor City of Hawthorne, Calif., 1993—. Advisor Dana Sch. Bldrs. Club; adv. com. Centinela Valley Union H.S. Dist.; chmn. Citizens and Bus. for Drug & Gang Free Zones; founder Ann. Mayors Motorcycle Ride to Benefit Pediat. AIDS and Richstone Family Ctr. for the Prevention Child Abuse, St. Margarets Ctr. Food Dr.; active Challengers Sports Program. Recipient Commendation award Calif. Assembly Resolution, Calif. State Senate Rules Com. Resolution, Cert. Recognition award Calif. State Senate, Outstanding Leadership award Gardena Valley Dem. Club, Svc. to Edn. award Assn. Calif. Sch. Adminstrs., Cert. Appreciation Centinela Valley Union H.S. Dist. Bd. Trustees, AYSO, Hawthorne Pres. Coun. and City Coun., Richstone Ctr., U.S. Conf. Mayors, Spl. Olympics, Svc. award Hawthorne Sch. Dist. Bd. Edn., Outstanding Cmty. Svc. award Del Aire Assembly God Ch. Hawthorne, Honors award Kenny Nickelson Meml. Found. for Homeless Vets., Nat. Red Ribbon Week award. Mem. Long Beach Police Motor Patrol Assn. (hon.). Office: 4455 W 126th St Hawthorne CA 90250

GUILFOYLE, BILL, securities executive; b. 1957. With Benham Group, San Francisco; sr. v.p. mktg. G T Global Fin. Svcs., San Francisco, 1987—. Office: G T Global Financial Svc 50 California St Fl 27 San Francisco CA 94111-4624*

GUILLEMIN, ROGER C. L., physiologist; b. Dijon, France, Jan. 11, 1924; came to U.S., 1953, naturalized, 1963; s. Raymond and Blanche (Rigollot) G.; m. Lucienne Jeanne Billard, Mar. 22, 1951; children: Chantal, Francois, Claire, Helene, Elizabeth, Cecile. B.A., U. Dijon, 1941, B.Sc., 1942; M.D., Faculty of Medicine, Lyons, France, 1949; Ph.D., U. Montreal, 1953; Ph.D. (hon.), U. Rochester, 1976, U. Chgo., 1977, Baylor Coll. Medicine, 1978, U. Ulm, Germany, 1978, U. Dijon, France, 1978, Free U. Brussels, 1979, U. Montreal, 1979, U. Man., Can, 1984, U. Turin, Italy, 1985, Kyung Hee U., Korea, 1986, U. Paris, Paris, 1986, U. Barcelona, Spain, 1988, U. Madrid, 1988, McGill U., Montreal, Can., 1988, U. Claude Bernard, Lyon, France, 1989. Intern, resident univs. hosps. Dijon, 1949-51; asso. dir., asst. prof. Inst. Exptl. Medicine and Surgery, U. Montreal, 1951-53; asso. dir. dept. exptl. endocrinology Coll. de France, Paris, 1960-63; asst. prof. physiology Baylor Coll. Medicine, 1953-57, assoc. prof., 1957-63, prof., dir. labs. neuroendocrinology, 1963-70, adj. prof., 1970—; resident fellow, chmn. labs. neuroendocrinology Salk Inst., La Jolla, Calif., 1970-89, adj. rsch. prof., 1989-94; Disting. Sci. prof. Whittier Inst., 1989—; med. and sci. dir., 1993-94; dir. Whittier Inst.; adj. prof. medicine U. Calif., San Diego, 1995—. Decorated chevalier Legion d'Honneur (France), 1974, officer, 1984; recipient Gairdner Internat. award, 1974; U.S. Nat. Medal of Sci., 1977; co-recipient Nobel prize for medicine, 1977; recipient Lasker Found. award, 1975; Dickson prize in medicine, 1976; Passano award sci., 1976; Schmitt medal neurosci., 1977; Barren Gold medal, 1979; Dale medal Soc. for Endocrinology U.K., 1980, Ellen Browning Scripps Soc. medal Scripps Meml. Hosps. Found., 1988. Fellow AAAS; mem. NAS, Am. Physiol. Soc., Am. Peptide Soc. (hon.), Assn. Am.Physicians, Endocrine Soc. (pres. 1986), Soc. Exptl. Biology and Medicine, Internat. Brain Rsch. Orgn., Internat. Soc. Rsch. Biology Reprodn., Soc. Neuro-scis., Am. Acad. Arts and Scis., French Acad. Scis. (fgn. assoc.), Academie Internationale de Medecine (fgn. assoc.), Swedish Soc. Med. Scis. (hon.), Academie des Scis. (fgn. assoc.), Academie Royale de Medecine de Belgique (corr. fgn.), Internat. Soc. Neurosci. (charter), Western Soc. Clin. Rsch., Can. Soc. Endocrinal Metabolism, (hon.), Club of Rome. Office: Whittier Inst 9894 Genesee Ave La Jolla CA 92037-1221

GUILMET, GLENDA JEAN, artist; b. Tacoma, Wash., Mar. 28, 1957; d. Cody Calvin Black and Maria Isabel Rivera; m. George Michael Guilmet, May 24, 1980; children: Michelle Rene, Douglas James. Student, Clover Park Vocat. Tech. Inst., 1982-83; BA in Bus. Adminstrn., U. Puget Sound, 1981, BA in Art, 1989. Freelance photographer Tacoma, 1976—; women's sports photographer U. Puget Sound, Tacoma, 1977-78, asst. photographer, 1978-79; visual artist Tacoma, 1982—; photographic cons. Puyallup Tribe of Indians, Tacoma, 1984; on-call photographer Puyallup Tribal Health Authority, Tacoma, 1984-86; represented by Sacred Circle Gallery Am. Indian Art, Seattle, Mahler Fine Arts, Seattle, Arts Comm. Internat., Phila.; instr. sculpture Tacoma Arts Commn., 1989; guest lectr. U. Puget Sound, 1990, 94; grants juror Artist Trust, Seattle, 1990; video festival juror Tacoma Mcpl. TV, 1990; photography competition juror Washington State PTA Reflections Com., 1995. Contbr. photographs to various publs.; one-woman shows include Stage Door Gallery, Tacoma Little Theatre, 1993, Seattle U. Women's Ctr., 1994, Instituto de Cultura Puertorriquena, Jayuya, Carolina and Caguana, P.R., 1994, 95, Galleria on Broadway, Tacoma, 1996, Sacred Cir. Gallery of Am. Indian Art, Seattle, 1996; exhibited in group shows at Nat. Mus. of Women in the Arts, Washington, 1989-90, U. Puget Sound, Tacoma, 1989, Windhorse Gallery, Seattle, 1990, Chase Gallery, Spokane City Hall, 1990, Hanforth Gallery, Tacoma, 1990, 91, Wash. State Capital Mus., Olympia, 1990, Foyer of the Okean Theater, Vladivostok, Russia, 1992, First Night Gallery, Tacoma, 1992, 96, Sacred Cir. Gallery of Am. Indian Art, 1993, 96, Cunningham Gallery U. Wash., 1993, Western Gallery, Western Wash. U., Bellingham, 1993, Seattle Art Mus., 1993, Bibliotheque Nat. de France, 1994, Street Level Photography Gallery, Glasgow, Scotland, 1995, Tacoma Art Mus., 1995, Park Ave. Armory, N.Y.C., 1995, Westfalische Mus. fur Naturkunde, Munster, Germany, 1995, 96, others; represented in permanent collections at Steilacoom (Wash.) Tribal Mus., Bibliotheque Nat. de France, U. Puget Sound, Puyallup Tribe of Indians, also corp. collections. Recipient 1st Place Photography award, Crosscurrents Art Contest, 1988. Mem. Artist Trust, En Foco, Atlatl. Home and Studio: 1211 S Tyler St Tacoma WA 98405-1135

GUINN, KENNY C., utility company executive; b. 1936; married. BA, Calif. State U., Fresno, MA; EdD, Utah State U. Supt. Clark County Sch. Dist.; v.p. adminstrn. Nev. Savs. and Loan Assn. (PriMerit Bank), 1978-80, pres., chief operating officer, 1980-85, chief exec. officer, 1985-92, now chmn. bd.; pres. Southwest Gas Corp., 1987-88, chmn., chief exec. officer, 1988-93; now chmn. bd. S.W. Gas Corp. also: SW Gas Corp 5241 Spring Mountain Rd Las Vegas NV 89150-0001 address: Ste 600 3800 Howard Hugh Pkwy Las Vegas NV 89109*

GUINN, LINDA ANN, lawyer; b. Idaho Falls, Idaho, Feb. 5, 1956; d. Denzel K. and Wanda Alice (Woodruff) Jenson; m. Gary Douglas Guinn, Oct. 9, 1976; children: Mindy, Aaron. AAS in Radiation Safety, Ea. Idaho Tech. Coll., Idaho Falls, 1981; BS in Systematics and Ecology, U. Kans., 1988, JD, 1990. Bar: Idaho 1991, Colo. 1995; cert. environ. mgr. Health physics technician Westinghouse Idaho Nuclear, Idaho Falls, 1981-84; pres. Radon & Environ. Profls., Lawrence, Kans., 1986-88; atty. EG&G Idaho, Idaho Falls, 1990-93, sr. atty., 1993-94; sr. cons. EG&G Environ., Denver, 1994-95; gen. counsel Rocky Mountain Remediation Svcs., LLC, Golden, Colo., 1995—; instr. undergrad. and grad. U. Idaho, Idaho Falls, 1991-94; bd. dirs., mem. environ. law sect. Idaho Bar, 1993-94; mem. adv. com. environ. law sect. Colo. Bar. Author articles. Atty. coach Idaho Students Mock Trials, Eagle Rock Jr. H.S., 1992-93; precinct committeeman Idaho Republican Party, Idaho Falls, 1973-74; active Girl Scouts of Am., Kans., 1984-89. Named Best Oralist Nat. Environ. Law Moot Ct., 1989. Mem. ABA, Idaho Health Physics Soc. (chair pub. rels. com. 1983-84), Idaho Assn. Commerce and Industry (environ. com. 1992-94), Kans. U. Environ. Law Soc. (pres. 1988-89), Mensa (pres.). Home: 7148 Estes Dr Arvada CO 80004

GUINN, STANLEY WILLIS, lawyer; b. Detroit, June 9, 1953; s. Willis Hampton and Virginia Mae (Pierson) G.; m. Patricia Shirley Newgord, June 13, 1981; children: Terri Lanae, Scott Stanley. BBA with high distinction, U. Mich., 1979, MBA with distinction, 1981; MS in Taxation with distinction, Walsh Coll., 1987; JD cum laude, U. Mich., 1992. CPA, Mich.; cert. mgmt. acct., Mich. Tax mgr. Coopers & Lybrand, Detroit, 1981-87; tax cons. Upjohn Co., Kalamazoo, 1987-89; litigation atty. Brobeck, Phleger & Harrison, 1992-94, Coughlan, Semmer & Lipman, San Diego, 1994-95; consumer fin. atty. Bank Am. NT & SA, San Diego, 1995—. Served with USN, 1974-77. Mem. AICPA, ABA, Calif. State Bar Assn., San Diego County Bar Assn., Inst. Cert. Mgmt. Acctg., Phi Kappa Phi, Beta Gamma Sigma, Beta Alpha Psi, Delta Mu Delta. Republican. Presbyterian. Home: 3119 Quiet Hills Pl Escondido CA 92029-7307 Office: Bank of Am NT & SA 10124 Old Grove Rd San Diego CA 92131

GUINN, SUSAN LEE, lawyer; b. Langhorne, Pa., July 22, 1965; d. Walter William and Setsuko (Yamada) G. BSN, U. N.Mex., 1988; JD, U. Denver, 1991. Bar: Calif. 1991, U.S. Dist. Ct. Calif. (so. and cen. dists.) 1991. Ptnr. Robinson, Phillips & Calcagnie, San Diego, 1992—. Mem. ATLA (poliction action mgmt. com. 1995, publ. com. 1993—), Calif. Trial Lawyers Assn. (bd. govs. 1994—, chair women's caucus 1995, edn. com. 1994-95), Attys. Info. Exch. Group, Western Trial Lawyers Assn. (bd. govs., edn. chmn. 1993—), San Diego Trial Lawyers Assn. Office: Robinson Phillips & Calcagnie 110 Laurel St San Diego CA 92101-1419

GUINOUARD, DONALD EDGAR, psychologist; b. Bozeman, Mont., Mar. 31, 1929; s. Edgar Arthur and Venabell (Ford) G.; m. Irene M. Egeler, Mar. 30, 1951; children: Grant M., Philip A., Donna I. BS, Mont. State U., Bozeman, 1954; MS, Mont. State U., 1955; EdD, Wash. State U., Pullman, 1960; postdoctoral, Stanford U., 1965; grad., Indsl. Coll. of the Armed Forces, 1964, Air War Coll., 1976. Lic. psychologist, Ariz., counselor, Wash., Mont.; cert. secondary tchr. and sch. adminstr., Wash., Mont. Advanced through grades to col. USAFR, 1946-84, ret., 1984; dir. counseling Consol. Sch. Dist., Pullman, Wash., 1955-60; assoc. prof. Mont. State U., Bozeman, 1960-66; field selection officer Peace Corps, U.S., S.Am., 1962-68; prof. counseling, counseling psychologist Ariz. State U., Tempe, 1966-90; prof. emeritus, 1990; co-owner Forensic Cons. Assocs., Tempe, 1970—; pvt. practice, 1990—; admissions liaison officer USAF Acad., Colo. Springs, 1967-84; assessment officer Fundamental Edn. Ctr. for the Devel. of the Latin American Community, Patzcuaro, Mex., 1963-64; expert witness on vocat. and psychol. disability for fed. and state cts. Contbr. articles to profl. jours. Mem. Ariz. Psychol. Assn., Am. Assn. Counseling & Devel., Reserve

Officers Assn. Democrat. Methodist. Home and Office: 112 E Cairo Dr Tempe AZ 85282-3606

GUINOUARD, PHILIP ANDRE, restaurant executive; b. Pullman, Wash., Apr. 9, 1960; s. Donald Edgar and Irene (Egeler) G.; m. Miquela Teresa Padilla, Feb. 16, 1988; childern: Mia, Angela. Student, Mesa (Ariz.) Community Coll. Dir. quality Garcia's, Phoenix, 1978-84; area spr. El Pollo Asado Inc., Phoenix, 1985-89; gen. mgr. Quinto Patio, Evergreen, Colo., 1989-90, Garcia's, Littleton, Colo., 1990—, Quila's Fresh Mexican Cantina, 1993-94; field tng. mgr. Internat. House of Pancakes, 1994-95; pres., CEO Sub & Munch, 1995—. Mem. Colo. Restaurant Assn. Home: 1714 W Manor St Chandler AZ 85224-5105 Office: 230 W Baseline Rd Ste 103B Tempe AZ 85283-1261

GULA, WILLIAM PETER, physicist; b. Cleve., Dec. 5, 1939; s. Steve William and Anna Regina (Dudek) G.; m. Anne Amy Albrink, May 27, 1972 (div. July 1980); m. Dolores Jeanne Tory, June 11, 1983. BS, Spring Hill Coll., 1964; MS, Columbia U., 1968, PhD, 1972. Tech. staff mem. Los Alamos (N.Mex.) Nat. Lab., 1972—; sci. advisor Dept. Energy, Germantown, Md., 1990-92; advisor Nat. Rsch. Coun., Washington, 1989-93. Mem. IEEE, AAAS, Assn. for Computing Machinery, Am. Phys. Soc. Home: 116 La Vista Dr Los Alamos NM 87544-3437 Office: Group XTM MS B226 Los Alamos Nat Lab Los Alamos NM 87545

GULASEKARAM, BALASUBRAMANIAM, psychiatrist, educator; b. Sri Lanka, Mar. 10, 1946. MBBS, U. Ceylon, Colombo, Sri Lanka, 1970. Diplomate Am. Bd. Psychiatry and Neurology. Resident Westchester County Med. Ctr. N.Y. Med. Coll., 1976-79; sr. psychiatrist Met. State Hosp., Norwalk, Calif., 1984—; asst. clin. prof. dept. psychiatry U. Calif., Irvine, 1991—. Mem. AMA, Am. Psychiat. Assn. Office: 16510 Bloomfield Ave Cerritos CA 90703-2115

GULDAHL, MARTIN GRANVILLE, software engineer; b. Seattle, Oct. 1, 1961; s. Alf and Harriet Florence (Houghton) G. BSEE, U. Utah, 1991. Design engr. Evans & Sutherland Computer Corp., Salt Lake City, 1992—. Mem. IEEE, Phi Kappa Phi, Tau Beta Pi. Home: 1418 S 1100 E Apt 18 Salt Lake City UT 84105-2428 Office: Evans & Sutherland Computer Corp 600 Komas Dr Salt Lake City UT 84108-1229

GULL, PAULA MAE, renal transplant coordinator, nephrology nurse, medical-sugical nurse; b. L.A., Mar. 7, 1955; d. Gerald Henry and Artemis (Cubillas) Balzer; m. Randell Jay Gull, July 10, 1976. AA, Cypress (Calif.) Coll., 1976; AS with high honors, Rancho Santiago Coll., Santa Ana, Calif., 1985; BSN with high honors, Calif. State U., 1993; MSN, Long Beach U., 1996. Cert. med. surg. nurse, nephrology nurse, nurse practitioner, clin. transplant coord. Staff RN U. Calif. Irvine Med. Ctr., Orange, Calif., 1986-87, asst. nurse mgr., 1987-88, nurse mgr., 1988; med.-surg. nurse N000, 1990—; coord. renal transplant U. Calif.-Irvine Med. Ctr., Orange, 1992—. Mem. Am. Nephrology Nurses Assn., N.Am. Transplant Coord. Orgn., Calif. Coalition Nurse Practitioners. Mormon. Home: 24974 Enchanted Way Moreno Valley CA 92557-6410

GULLER, TODD JAIME, marketing and communications executive; b. St. Louis, Mar. 19, 1960; s. Harold and Mildred G.; m. Mara E. Applebaum. BSBA in Advt. Copywriting, Syracuse U., 1986. Asst. producer Sta. KPLR-TV Channel 11, St. Louis, 1981-83; producer/dir. McCaw Cablevision, Syracuse, N.Y., 1983-84; copywriter Beber, Silverstein & Ptnrs., Miami, Fla., 1984-85; copywriter, producer The Savan Co. Advt., St. Louis, 1986-87; mgr. corp. promotions cor. comms. dir., St. Louis, 1987-93; dir. mktg. SuperFlow Corp., 1993-95; dir. mktg. programs Optika, Colorado Springs, 1995-96; pres., CEO Hometenders Colo., Inc., 1996—; producer, dir. Little Apple Prodn. Group, St. Louis, 1984—. Publicist St. Louis Variety Club Children's Charity, 1990—. Recipient Marconi award for: 60 Sec. Radio, 1985, 86. Mem. Advt. Fedn., Am. Film Inst., Jr. Achievement (instr.). Office: Hometenders of Colo Inc PO Box 691 Palmer Lake CO 80133

GULLICKSON, NORMAN ANTHONY, graphic designer, educator; b. Stoughton, Wis., Jan. 26, 1943; s. Norman Martin and Marian (Elizabeth) G.; m. Diana Lee Kadinger, Aug. 28, 1965; children: Heidi Clarene, Michele Marie, Craig Anthony. BS, U. Wis., Stout, 1965, MS, 1966; EdD, U. No. Colo., 1974. Cert. sr. indsl. technologist. Indsl. tchr. asst. U. Wis., Stout, 1965-66; instr. indsl. edn. Winona (Minn.) State U., 1966-70; prof. indsl. tech. Calif. State U. Fresno, 1971—; owner Multi-Media Promotional Advt., 1981—. Fellow Graphic Arts Tech. Foundation, Screen Printing and Graphic Imaging Assn. Internat.; mem. Nat. Assn. Indsl. Tech. (sr. technologist), Flexographic Tech. Found., Internat. Graphic Arts Edn. Assn., Phi Delta Kappa. Home: 1146 E San Bruno Ave Fresno CA 93710 Office: Calif State Univ Fresno 2255 E Barstow Ave Fresno CA 93740-0009

GULLIVER, EDWARD QUENTIN, marine consultant, writer; b. Needham, Mass., July 30, 1919; s. Everett Lee and Fanny Maude (Pullen) G.; m. Kathryn Ellen, Jan. 4, 1957 (div. Jan. 1974); children: Willard, Priscilla, Timothy Lee, Jonathan Edward, Christopher Alan, Susan Kay. Grad., Bishop-Lee Coll., 1937-40. Announcer WNAC, Boston, 1941-43, Answer Man feature program, WOR, N.Y.C., 1943-53; dist. supr. Crown Life Ins. Co., L.A., 1954-64; yacht dealer Gulliver's Sea Travels, St. Thomas, V.I., 1965-79; bus. broker Calif. Bus. Brokers, San Diego, 1980-86; cons. San Diego, 1987—. Author: Puretic Power Block; contbr. articles to profl. jours. Mem. Larchmont Yacht Club, Royal Hong Kong Yacht Club, St. Thomas Yacht Club, Virgin Islands Charter Boat League. Presbyterian. Office: Business Ventures 3707 5th Ave Ste 415 San Diego CA 92103-4221

GULLIXSON, JOHN, mayor. Mayor Yorba Linda, Calif. Address: PO Box 87014 Yorba Linda CA 92686

GULMAN, PAUL JAMES, engineer; b. Staten Island, N.Y., Nov. 24, 1951; s. Marcel John and Margaret Mary (Ferrick) G. B of Engring., The Cooper Union, N.Y.C., 1973. Registered profl. engr., Colo. Mech. design engr. Bindery Systems div. Harris Corp., Easton, Pa., 1973-77; mech. project engr. Colo. Conveyor Corp., Lakewood, 1977-78; prodn. engr. Ball Corp., Westminster, Colo., 1978-85; staff engr. Martin Marietta Corp., Denver, 1985-90; engring. cons. in pvt. practice Wheat Ridge, Colo., 1990-93, 96—; prin. EVA West, Inc., Denver, 1993-96; mem. NASA Space Assembly and Servicing Working Group, Houston, 1991-92. Mem. Mass Transit Com., City of Wheat Ridge, 1979-83, chair, 1980-83. Mem. AIAA, NSPE, Profl. Engrs. Colo. (dir. 1983-85, chair Mathcounts com. 1987-92, pres. Met. chpt. 1986-87, Outstanding Svc. award 1984, 89, 91, Appreciation award 1992), Aircraft Owners and Pilots Assn., Denver Electric Vehicle Coun. Republican. Roman Catholic. Home: 4315 Ammons St Wheat Ridge CO 80033-4445

GUND, GEORGE, III, financier, professional sports team executive; b. Cleve., May 7, 1937; s. George and Jessica (Roesler) G.; m. Mary Theo Feld, Aug. 13, 1966; children: George, Gregory. Student, Western Res. U., Menlo (Calif.) Sch. Bus. Engaged in personal investments San Francisco, 1967—; cattle ranching Lee, Nev., 1967—; partner Calif. Seals, San Francisco, 1976-77; pres. Ohio Barons, Inc., Richfield, 1977-78; chmn. bd. Northstar Fin. Corp., Bloomington, Minn., from 1978; formerly chmn. bd. Minn. North Stars, Bloomington; chmn., co-owner San Jose Sharks, NHL, San Jose, CA, 1991—; dir. Ameritrust Cleve.; vice-chmn. Gund Investment Corp., Princeton, N.J.; chmn. North Stars Met Center Mgmt. Corp., Bloomington; v.p. hockey Sun Valley Ice Skating, Inc., Idaho. Chmn. San Francisco Internat. Film Festival, 1973—; mem. sponsors council Project for Population Action; adv. council Sierra Club Found.; mem. internat. council Mus. Modern Art, N.Y.C.; collectors com. Nat. Gallery Art; bd. dirs. Calif. Theatre Found., Bay Area Ednl. TV Assn., San Francisco Mus. Art, Cleve. Health Museum, George Gund Found., Cleve. Internat. Film Festival, Sun Valley Center Arts and Humanities, U. Nev. Reno Found., Sundance Inst. Served with USMCR, 1955-58. Clubs: Calif. Tennis (San Francisco), University (San Francisco), Olympic (San Francisco); Union (Cleve.), Cleve. Athletic (Cleve.), Kirkland Country (Cleve.), Rowfant (Cleve.); Ranier (Seattle). Office: 1821 Union St San Francisco CA 94123-4307 also: Nationwide Advt Svc 1228 Euclid Ave Ste 600 Cleveland OH 44115-1831*

GUNDERSEN, JOAN REZNER, historian, educator; b. Chgo., Nov. 9, 1946; d. Charles Louis and Lois Gladys (Baskin) Rezner; m. Robert Peter Gundersen, Sept. 13, 1969; 1 child, Kristina. BA, Monmouth Coll., 1968; MA, Coll. William and Mary, 1969; PhD, U. Notre Dame, 1972. Adj. faculty Ind. U., South Bend, 1971-74; vis. asst. prof. Vanderbilt U., Nashville, 1974-75; asst. to full prof. St. Olaf Coll., Northfield, Minn., 1975-90; founding prof. Calif. State U., San Marcos, 1989—. Author: Before the World Confessed, 1987, The Anglican Ministry in Virginia, 1989, To Be Useful to the World, 1996; co-author: American History at a Glance, 1974, 78, 94, America: Changing Times, 1980, 83; bd. editors: Mid-America, 1988—, Virginia Magazine of History, 1992—; contbr. articles to profl. jours. Bd. dirs., pres. Northfield Hist. Soc., 1980-89; mem. exec. bd. Episcopal Women's History Project, 1988-96; bd. dirs. San Marcos Boys and Girls Club, 1991—. Named Outstanding Young Alumnus, Monmouth Coll., 1978, Outstanding Faculty Advisor, Phi Alpha Theta, 1989, Outstanding Course grant Am. Soc. for 18th Century Studies, 1992. Mem. AAUW, Am. Hist. Assn. (Pacific Coast br. coun. mem.), So. Hist. Assn. (membership com. 1986, 88, 89, 93), Women Historians of the Midwest (pres. 1988-90), Alpha Xi Delta (chpt. treas. 1966-68, chpt. advisor 1996—). Episcopalian. Home: 1218 Huntington Rd San Marcos CA 92069-5436 Office: Calif State Univ San Marcos CA 92096

GUNDERSON, BERNICE BLOWER, retired nurse, genealogy researcher; b. Kelseyville, Calif., Jan. 8, 1925; d. Richard Marion and Ruth Emily (Flint) Blower; m. Bill Dean Neff, Apr. 10, 1949 (div. Nov. 1960); children: Brenda Elaine, Beverly Ellen, Bruce Elbert; m. Gilbert M. Gunderson, Aug. 8, 1965 (dec.). BS, Loma Linda U., 1960. RN, Calif. Nurse White Meml. Hosp., L.A., 1948-49, Vancouver (B.C.) Gen. Hosp., Can., 1950, Avenal (Calif.) Dist. Hosp., 1952-53, Long Beach (Calif.) Cmty. Hosp., 1953-55, 86-96; nursing supr. Rancho Los Amigos County Hosp., Downey, Calif., 1955-80, St. Frances Hosp., Lynwood, Calif., 1982-86; spkr. in field. Contbg. author The Searcher, 1980-96; editor Durkee Family History newsletter, 1982-96; co-author article to profl. nursing jour. Singer Sweet Adelines, Downey, 1960-65. Mem. So. Calif. Geneal. Soc. (bd. mem.), Native Daughters of Golden West (2d v.p. 1960-65, officer), Solbakken Lodge Sons of Norway, (libr. 1987-90, sec. 1990-93, treas. 1993-95, found. chmn. 1995-96, circulation mgr. 1997—), Freya Club (pres. 1997—). Republican. Home: 3753 E 15th St Long Beach CA 90804

GUNDERSON, CLEON HENRY, management consultant corporation executive; b. Great Falls, Mont., June 5, 1932; s. Leon H. and Mona (Emmett) G.; m. Virginia Ellen Hudson, Aug. 26, 1972; children: Craig H., Robert S., Laura E. BS, Inst. Tech., Dayton, Ohio, 1971, Mont. State U., 1957; MAPA, U. Okla., 1975. Communications engr. Mountain States Tel & Tel, Helena, Mont., 1953-54; aerospace engr. Boeing Co., Seattle, 1957-58; commd. 2nd lt. USAF, 1958, advanced to col., 1974, ret., 1976; pres. Precision Prodn. & Engring., Walla Walla, Wash., 1976-79, Western Skies Energy Systems, Spokane, Wash., 1979-88, Computer Central, Olympia, Wash., 1988-90, C.H. Gunderson & Assocs., Littlerock, Wash., 1990—; Mem. Am. Inst. Elec. Engrs., Seattle, 1957-60, Am. Inst. Indsl. Engrs., Spokane, 1982-85. Inventor heatexchange solar panels, comml. solar panels. Decorated Silver Stars, Disting. Flying Crosses, Purple Heart, Air medals. Mem. Soc. Mfg. Engrs. (sr. mem.), Soc. Mil. Engrs., Nat. Assn. Small Businesses, Toastmasters Internat., Walla Walla C. of C., Canto Blanco Gun Club (Madrid, v.p. 1973-75, Scott Air Force Base Gun Club (v.p. 1975-76), Spokane Gun Club. Republican. Home: 13001 Littlerock Rd PO Box 246 Littlerock WA 98556-0246 Office: C H Gunderson & Assocs PO Box 246 Littlerock WA 98556-0246

GUNDERSON, MARY ALICE, writer, educator; b. Sheridan, Wyo., Jan. 18, 1936; d. Bernard Graham and Leah Mary (Gilkeson) Wright; m. Edwin Donald Gundersen, July 16, 1964; 1 child, James Nelson. BA in Elem. Edn., U. Wyo., 1957, postgrad., 1971-86. Elem. tchr. Sweetwater County, Green River, Wyo., 1957-58, Natrona County Sch. Dist., Casper, Wyo., 1958-68; homebound instr. Natrona County Sch. Dist., Casper, 1969-73; pub. info. officer Natrona County Libr., Casper, 1976-79; artist in residence Wyo. Arts Coun., Cheyenne, 1973-88; instr. creative writing Casper Coll., 1993-96, devel. studies in English, 1986-94; freelance writer, 1968—; poetry editor/cons. High Plain Press, Glendo, Wyo., 1994—; mem. lit. adv. com. Casper Coll., 1988-92; grants panelist Wyo. Coun. on Arts, Cheyenne, 1988—. Author: Devils Tower: Stories in Stone, 1988 (Nat. Fedn. Presswomen award 1989), Land Marked: Collected Curry Stories, 1992 (Wyo. State Hist. Soc. award 1992); contbr. essays, fiction, poetry to numerous lit. mags. Dir. PressWomen H.S. Journalism Contest, 1987-88; contest dir., booklet editor Wyo. Writers, Inc., 1983; bd. dirs. Cmty. Concert Assn., Casper, 1988. Writing and Rsch. grantee Wyo. Coun. for Humanities, 1980, Individual Artist grantee Wyo. Coun. on Arts, 1995-96, Fiction fellow Wyo. Coun. on Arts, 1987, Ucross Found. resident, 1986, others. Mem. Wyo. Alumni Assn., Am. Assn. Ret. Persons. Democrat. Presbyterian. Home: 318 W 14th St Casper WY 82601

GUNDZIK, MICHAEL JOHN, health insurance executive; b. Berkeley, Calif., July 27, 1961; s. Michael George Gundzik and Arline Martineau Rustin. BS cum laude, U. Colo., 1983; MBA, U. Chgo., 1986. Computer programmer/analyst Am. Mgmt. Systems, Lakewood, Colo., 1983-84; freelance computer programmer/analyst Denver, 1984; summer intern Citicorp, Port-Au-Prince, Haiti, 1985; assoc. The First Boston Corp., N.Y.C., 1986-88; health ins. broker Gundzik & Assocs., Inc., Denver, 1988—. Mem. Nat. Assn. Life Agts., Centennial Assn. Life Agts., Assn. of Health Ins. Agts. Office: Gundzik & Assocs Inc 1801 Broadway Ste 250 Denver CO 80202-3800

GUNN, MICHELA FAITH, psychiatrist; b. Chgo., Feb. 27, 1940; d. Samuel Albert and Elsie (Chestler) G.; m. Martin B. Gelber, Jan. 22, 1970. BS in Chemistry, U. Miami, 1961, MD, 1965. Intern L.A. County-U. So. Calif. Med. Ctr., 1965-66, resident, 1966-68, 68-70, ward chief, 1971-87, clin. instr. psychiatry, 1971-73, clin. asst. prof., 1973-79, clin. assoc. prof., 1979-95; clin. prof., 1995—; psychiatrist pvt. practice, Beverly Hills, Calif., 1970—. Mem. Women's Archtl. League, L.A., 1971—, Gamble House, PAsadena, Calif., 1974—. L.A. County-U. So. Calif. fellow, 1970-71. Mem. So. Calif. Psychiat. Soc. (mem. ethics com. 1987—). Demcorat. Jewish. Home and Office: 12268 Canna Rd Los Angeles CA 90049-1437

GUNNELL, DALE RAY, hospital administrator; b. Logan, Utah, May 21, 1936; married. BA, U. Utah, 1963, MA, 1977. Dir. med. records U. Utah Hosp., Salt Lake City, 1969-70, dir. budget, 1970-74, asst. adminstr., 1974-81, assoc. adminstr., 1981-92, COO, 1992—, now assoc. v.p. Contbr. articles to profl. jours. Home: 269 Shari Cir Bountiful UT 84010-3017 Office: Univ of Utah Hospital & Clinics 50 N Medical Dr Salt Lake City UT 84132-0001*

GUNTER, EMILY DIANE, communications executive, marketing professional; b. Atlantic City, N.J., Apr. 5, 1948; d. Fay Gaffney and Verlee (Wright) G.; children: Saliha, Kadir, Amin, Shedia. BA in Math. Stats., Am. U., 1970, postgrad. computer sci., 1971; postgrad. mktg., San Diego C.C., 1986. Traffic engr. C&P Bell, Washington, 1970-71; market analyst Market Towers Inc., Atlantic City, N.J., 1978-79; outside plant engr. N.J. Bell, Atlantic City, 1979-81; market analyst Empcor Group, Atlantic City, 1981-83; outside plant engr. Pacific Bell, San Diego, 1983-91, account exec., 1991-93; v.p. Black Am. of Achievement, Inc., San Diego, 1994-95; founder Women's Wholistic Enpowerment Ctr., 1996—; pres. Gunter Devel. Enterprises, 1987—; lectr. women and minorities in engring. and math. Princeton (N.J.) U., 1979-81, Atlantic C.C., Atlantic City, 1979-81; customer coord. Pacific Bell-Telsam, San Diego, 1983-85; prof. math. Grossmont Coll., 1992-94, instr. super learning skills seminar, 1992—; motivational spkr. Author: Superlearning 2000: The New Technologies of Self-Empowerment, 1993, Supermath 2000: How to Learn Math Without Fear, 1993, Achieve Goals 2000: A Personal Handbook for the Lifelong Learner, 1995, Living, Learning & Healing Through The Right Use of Your Mind, 1996. Bd. dirs. Lead, San Diego, Atlantic City Transp. Authority, 1981-82, San Diego Urban Math. Collaborative; trustee Reuben H. Fleet Sci. Found., 1989, San Diego Sci. Found., 1989—, 1990 class Lead-Leadership Edn. Awareness Devel., San Diego; mem. steering com. United Negro Coll. Fund, San Diego; mem. Atlantic City Urban Area Transp. Commn., 1982-83; mem. Am. Humanics Bd. U. San Deigo, 1991-94; pres. bd. World Beat Cultural Ctr., Balboa Park, Calif., 1992-93. Mem. African Am. Womens Conf., Women on Tour (exec. bd. 1992—), Coalition Women's Groups (bd. dirs. 1996—). Democrat. Islamic. Home: PO Box 152121 San Diego CA 92195-2121 also: Gunter Devel Enterprises PO Box 152121 San Diego CA 92195-2121

GUNTER, ROBERT L., lawyer; b. Tacoma, Wash., Aug. 25, 1945. BA cum laude, Seattle Pacific U., 1967; JD, U. Wash., 1970. Bar: Wash. 1970. Law clk. to Hon. Walter T. McGovern Wash. State Supreme Ct., 1970-71, U.S. Dist. Ct. Wash., 1970-71; with Preston Gates & Ellis, Seattle. Mem. Wash. Law Rev., 1969-70. Mem. ABA (forum com. constrn. industry, pub. contracts sect.), Wash. State Bar Assn. (pub. procurement and pvt. constrn. sect.), Christian Legal Soc. Office: Preston Gates & Ellis 5000 Columbia Seafirst Ctr 701 5th Ave Seattle WA 98104-7016

GUNTER, WILLIAM DAYLE, JR., physicist; b. Mitchell, S.D., Jan. 10, 1932; s. William Dayle and Lamerta Berniece (Hockensmith) G.; m. Shirley Marie Teshera, Oct. 24, 1955; children—Maria Jo, Robert Paul. B.S. in Physics with distinction, Stanford U., 1957, M.S., 1959. Physicist Ames Research Ctr. NASA, Moffett Field, Calif., 1960-81, asst. br. chief electronic optical engring., 1981-85; pvt. practice cons. Photon Applications, San Jose, Calif., 1985—. Patentee in field. Contbr. articles to profl. jours. Served with U.S. Army, 1953-55. Recipient Westinghouse Sci. Talent Search award, 1950; various awards NASA; Stanford U. scholar, 1950. Mem. Am. Assn. Profl. Cons., Optical Soc. Am., IEEE (sr.), Am. Phys. Soc., Soc. Photo-Optical Instrumentation Engrs., Planetary Soc., Nat. Space Soc., NASA Alumni League. Office: Photon Applications 5290 Dellwood Way San Jose CA 95118-2904

GUPTA, BARBARA MACKAY, mathematics educator; b. Berkeley, Calif., Nov. 6, 1948; d. William Robert and Joanne Coby (Williams) Mackay; m. Yogendra Mohan Gupta, June 21, 1975; 2 children. BA in Elem. Edn., Wash. State U., 1970, PhD, 1996. Cert. tchr., Wash. Tchr. Edison Elem Sch., Walla Walla, Wash., 1970-75; tchr., math. dept. chair, prin. middle campus Pinewood Pvt. Sch., Los Altos, Calif., 1976-81; curriculum cons. Pullman, Wash., 1981—. Eisenhower Spl. Project grant Office the Supt. Pub. Instrn., Pullman, Wash., 1993-94. Mem. ASCD, AAUW, Nat. Coun. Tchrs. Math., Am. Ednl. Rsch. Assn., Assn. for Women in Sci. Home and Office: 845 SW Mies Pullman WA 99163

GUPTA, BIMLESHWAR PRASAD, mechanical engineer, manager; b. Jaipur, Raj, India, May 17, 1946; s. Hari Prasad and Sarla D. (Agarwal) G.; m. Rajni Garg, Dec. 10, 1974; children: Anjli, Neeraj. BSME, U. Jodhpur, India, 1968; MSME, U. Minn., 1971, MBA, 1974. Registered profl. engr., Colo. Engr. Honeywell Inc., Mpls., 1971-76, sect. mgr., 1976-78; program and div. ops. mgr. Nat. Renewable Energy Lab., Golden, Colo., 1978—; lectr. in field; chairperson nat. and internat. confs. on solar thermal rsch. Guest editor spl. edit. The Energy Jour., 1987; contbr. articles to profl. jours. Mem. ASME (assoc. editor jour. 1983-85, guest editor spl. issue 1984), Internat. Solar Energy Soc., India Assn. Colo. (exec. com. 1983-84, pres. 1991), U. Minn. Alumni Assn., Toastmasters (pres. Lakewood 1985, bd. govs. F-2 area 1988-89). Home: 14373 W Bayaud Pl Golden CO 80401-5339 Office: Nat Renewable Energy Lab 1617 Cole Blvd Golden CO 80401-3305

GUPTA, PRAVEEN, engineering executive, software engineer; b. Sambhal, India, May 24, 1959; came to U.S., 1983; s. Jai P. and Kanti (Baranwal) Vaish; m. Reeta Gupta, Dec. 4, 1985; 1 child, Ankur. BS in Physics, M.S. U., Baroda, India, 1978; MSc, U. Roorkee, India, 1980; MTech, Indian Inst. Sci., Bangalore, 1982; MS in Computer Sci., U. Tex., Arlington, 1988; MBA, Golden Gate U., 1995. Systems analyst Tata Consultancy Svcs., Delhi, 1982-84; sr. software engr. Gearhart Industries, Inc., Ft. Worth, 1984-88; sr. electronic systems engr. Electrocom Automation, Inc., Arlington, 1988-90; engring. mgr. Internat. Computers Ltd., Santa Clara, Calif., 1990-94, Raynet Corp., Menlo Park, Calif., 1994-95, Octel Comm. Corp., Milpitas, Calif., 1995-96; prin., founder Anchor Mgmt. Solutions, Fremont, Calif., 1996—. Mem. IEEE. Home: 34712 Teal Common Fremont CA 94555-2857

GUPTA, SUNEEL KUMAR, pharmacologist; b. Yamuna Nagar, India, Sept. 6, 1957; came to U.S., 1987; s. Inder Sain and Kaushalaya (Devi) G.; m. Shahida Naseem, May 24, 1991. MPharm with 1st class honors, Indu U., Varanasi, India, 1981; student, Inst. of Cost and Works Acctg., Calcutta, 1983-84; PhD, U. Manchester, Eng., 1987. Mfg. pharmacist Hindustan Ciba-Geigy Ltd., Kandla, India, 1981-85; postdoctoral fellow U. Calif., San Francisco, 1987-89; staff scientist ALZA Corp., Palo Alto, Calif., 1989-91, rsch. scientist, 1991-92, mgr. clin. pharmacology, 1992-93, assoc. dir. clin. pharmacology, 1994-96; sr. assoc. dir. clin. pharmacology ALZA Corp., Palo Alto, 1996—. Contbr. articles to profl. jours. Recipinet Frederick Craven Moore award U. Manchester, 1985-87. Mem. Am. Soc. Clin. Pharmacology and Therapeutics, Am. Assn. Pharm. Scientists, Am. Coll. Clin. Pharmacology. Office: ALZA Corp 2400 Hanover St Palo Alto CA 94304-1113

GURDJIAN, ANNETTE OVSANNA, artist; b. Providence, Aug. 11, 1950; d. Antranik and Alice Gurdjian; m. Dennis Clay. BFA in Visual Design, U. Oreg., 1984. Exhibited in solo shows at Benton County Hist. Mus., Philomath, Oreg., Spokane Falls C.C., Blackfish Gallery, Portland, Mt. Angel (Oreg.) Abbey Libr., Corvallis (Oreg.) Arts Ctr.; group shows include Mus. Art/U. Oreg., Maude Kerns Art Ctr.,Eugene, Bockrath Gallery, Cleve., Blue Sky Gallery, Portland, Pub. Image Gallery, N.Y.C., Waukesha Fine Arts Gallery/U. Wis., Holter Art Mus., Helena, Mont., U. Puget Sound., Bellevue (Wash.) Art Mus., Wiseman Gallery, Grants Pass, Oreg. Oreg. Arts Commn. Visual Arts fellow, 1992. Home: PO Box 50083 Eugene OR 97405 Office: 303 S 5th St # 300 Springfield OR 97477

GURLEY, CURTIS R., lawyer; b. Joplin, Mo., Apr. 5, 1959; s. Carl R. and Glenda (Cummins) G.; m. Rebecca Lynn Miller; 1 child, Jackson M. BA, U. Mo., 1986, JD, 1989. Bar: N.Mex., Mo. Ptnr. Hynes, Hale & Gurley, Farmington, N.Mex. Mem. San Juan County Bar (pres. 1993), N.Mex. Trial Lawyers Assn. (bd. dirs.), N.Mex. Criminal Def. Attys. Assn., Nat. Criminal Def. Attys. Assn., Elks. Republican. Presbyterian. Office: Hynes Hale & Gurley 1000 W Apache Farmington NM 87401

GURWITZ-HALL, BARBARA ANN, artist; b. Ayer, Mass., July 7, 1942; d. Jack and Rose (Baritz) Gurwitz; m. James M. Marshall III, Mar. 12, 1966 (div. 1973); m. William D. Hall, May 3, 1991; 1 ward: Samantha Hollinger, 1994-96. Student, Boston U., 1960-61, Katherine Gibbs Sch., Boston, 1961-62. Represented by Karin Newby Gallery, Tubac, Ariz.; represented by Wilde-Meyer Gallery, Scottsdale, Ariz.; Artist-in-residence Desert House of Prayer, Tucson, 1989-91; oblate mem. Benedictine Sisters Perpetual Adoration, 1986—. One-woman show Henry Hicks Gallery, Bklyn., 1978, Misty-Mountain Gallery, Tubac,Ariz., 1987, Karin Newby Gallery, Tubac, 1989; exhibited in group shows YWCA, Bklyn, 1977, Heary Hecks Gallery, Becket (Mass.) Art Ctr., 1977-79, Winter Gallery, Tucson, 1980, Johnson Gallery, Bisbee, Ariz., Hilltop Gallery, Nogales, Ariz., 1981, Scharf Gallery, Santa Fe, 1982, Data Mus., Ein Hod, Israel, 1985, C.G. Rein Gallery, Santa Fe, 1986, Tubac Ctr. for Arts, 1985, Mesquite Gallery, Patagonia, Ariz., 1986, Beth O'Donnel Gallery, Tucson, 1989, Karin Newby Gallery, 1989—, Wilde-Meyer Gallery, Scottsdale, Ariz., 1991—, Art Collector's Gallery, Tulsa, 1992, Contemporary Landscape Show Wilde-Meyer, 1996, Mountain Oyster Club, Tucson, 1994, Phoenix Mus. League, 1994, Santa Cruz Valley Art Assn., 1994, 96, Brewster Ctr., 1994, 95, 96, Tubac Biennial Gala, 1994, 96, Tubac Ctr. for Arts Annual Members Show, 1980-94, 96; represented in permanent collections Diocese of Tucson, Data Mus., Desert House of Prayer, Tucson, Ethical Culture Soc., Bklyn., St. Andrews Episcopal Ch., Nogales, Tubac Elem. Sch., Sheraton Corp., also numerous corp. and pvt. collections in U.S. and Europe. Mem. Tubac Village Coun., 1979-86; bd. dirs. Pimeria Alta Hist. Soc., Nogales, Ariz., 1982-84; creator Children's Art Walk, Tubac Sch. Sys. and Village Coun., 1980; set designer, choreographer DeAnza Ann. Pageant, Tubac Ctr. Arts, 1982—; pastoral asst. St. Ann's Parish, Tubac, 1986-89, religious com. mem., 1996-98; team mem. R.C.I.A. Our Lady of the Valley Parish, Green Valley, Ariz., 1994—. Mem. Nat. League Am. PEN Women, Inc. (Sonoran Desert br.), Rose and Jack Baritz Gurwitz Found. (bd. dirs.), Santa Cruz Valley Art Assn. (hon. mention ann. juried show 1989-95, Best of Show award 1989, award for excellence 1992), Assn. Contemplative Sisters.

GUSSIN, CLARK LOUIS, multimedia graphic designer, fine artist; b. Washington, Aug. 14, 1948; s. Theodore Boris and Alice Lucille (Mercer-

Smith) G.; m. Janice Eilleen Kile, July 5, 1969 (div. May 1981); children: Sarah, Natalie; m. Lyn Alleen McCuistion, Dec. 3, 1983; children: Allison Justin. BFA, Calif. Coll. Arts and Crafts, Oakland, 1975. Staff graphic designer IBM, San Jose, Calif., 1978—. One-man shows include Saratoge Gallery, Calif., 1978; exhibited in group shows at Portrait Gallery, 1986, Wild Wings Gallery, San Francisco, 1986, Western Art Show Sunbird Gallery, 1986, Buffalo Gallery, Old Alexandria, Va., 1987-88, The Phoenix Gallery, San Jose, 1987, John Clymer Mus., Ellensburg, Wash., 1992-97, others; videographer, photographer, illustrator, oil painter, watercolorist. Recipient Best of Show award Nat. Western Art Show, Ellensburg, Wash., 1996. Mem. Western Art Assn. Home: 2521 Nightingale Dr San Jose CA 95125

GUSTAFSON, KIRK, performing company executive. Student, U. Colo.; D in Mus. Arts, U. Wash. Music dir. Grand Junction (Colo.) Symphony Orch.; guest condr. Rogue Valley (S.D.) Symphony, Salt Lake Symphony, Boulder Philharmonic, Arapahoe Philharmonic, Arvada Chamber Orch., Colo. Festival Orch.; soloist various orchs.; lectr. Mesa State Coll. Boeing fellow U. Wash. Office: Grand Junction Symphony Orch PO Box 3039 Grand Junction CO 81502

GUSTAFSON, RANDALL LEE, city manager; b. Sidney, Nebr., Nov. 11, 1947; s. Robert John and Hilda Lydia (Sims) G.; m. Cynthia Ann Taylor, Oct. 18, 1974. Student, U. Kans., 1965-68, Rockhurst Coll., 1968-70; BS in Pub. Adminstrn., Upper Iowa U., 1992. City mgr. City of Bonner Springs, Kans., 1970-77; bus. owner Lambquarters, Dix, Nebr., 1977-83; city mgr. City of Aurora, Mo., 1983-85, City of Sterling, Colo., 1985—; bd. dirs. Logan Area Devel. Co., Sterling. Bd. dirs. Fire and Police Pension Assn. Colo., Denver, 1987-95, 13th Jud. Dist. Cmty. Corrections, Brush, Colo., 1988-90; mem. Colo. Mcpl. League Policy Com., Denver, 1987-89. Recipient Disting. Svc. award Jaycees, 1976. Mem. Internat. Assn. City Mgmt. (full mem.), Colo. Assn. City Mgmt., Am. Soc. for Pub. Adminstrn., Govs. Fin. Assn., Rotary, Elks. Republican. Lutheran. Office: Centennial Sq Sterling CO 80751

GUSTAVSON, CARRIE, museum director. Dir. Bisbee (Ariz.) Mining and Hist. Mus. Office: Bisbee Mining and Hist Mus PO Box 14 # 5 Copper Queen Plz Bisbee AZ 85603

GUSTAVSON, JOAN ELLEN CARLSON, psychologist; b. Bingham Canyon, Utah, Feb. 26, 1947; d. Leonard Alfred and Melba Ellen (Brown) Carlson; m. Carl Roger Gustavson, June 6, 1964 (dec. July 1996); children: Andrew Roger, Eric Cris. BS, N.D. State U., Fargo, 1982. Interviewer coord. Galveston (Tex.) Family Health Mental Health Survey Project, 1986-87; asst. rsch. dir. Psychiat. Ethology Lab., U. Tex. Med. Br., Galveston, 1985-89; owner Body Image Distortion and Dissatisfaction Evaluation; owner, pres. Bio-Behavioral Tech.; evaluator ComCare/Comty. Partnership for Behavioral Health Care, Phoenix, Ariz., 1996—; faculty assoc., recruiter, interviewer family bereavment project Prevention Rsch. Ctr., Ariz. State U., Tempe, 1995-96. Editor: Roses and Catails: A Collection of Readings in Human Sexuality, 1981; contbr. articles to profl. jours. Named One of the Outstanding Young Women of Am., 1982. Mem. Am. Inst. Biol. Sci., Am. Psychol. Soc., Western Psychol. Assn., N.Y. Acad. Sci., Sigma Xi, Phi Kappa Phi. Home: 243 W Calle Monte Vista Dr Tempe AZ 85284-2261

GUSTAVSON, MARK STEVEN, lawyer; b. Berkeley, Calif., Jan. 3, 1951; s. Dean Leonard and Barbara (Knight) G.; m. Janet Daly, Jan. 24, 1974; children: Eric Karl, Stephen Earl, Jennifer Ann. BA in Philosophy magna cum laude, U. Utah, 1973, JD, 1976. Bar: Utah 1976. Gen. counsel The Gustavson Group, Inc., Salt Lake City, 1976-91; pvt. practice Salt Lake City, 1976-82; sr. ptnr. Gustavson & Williams Attys., 1983-85, Gustavson, Hall & Williams, Salt Lake City, 1985-86, Gustavson, Schultz, Hall & Williams, Salt Lake City, 1986-93; corp. counsel, sec. Christensen Boyles Corp., Salt Lake City, 1993-96; pvt. practice Law Offices of Mark S. Gustavson, 1996—; pres. Concours Automotive Restoration, Inc., 1981—; adj. prof. philosophy Utah C.C., 1991; mem. devel. com. Tanner Humanities Ctr., U. Utah. Columnist Scale Auto Enthusiast, Car Modeler, Model Car Jour., IPMS Jour.; contbr. articles to profl. jours. Founder Nat. Model Car Builders' Mus, GSL Internat. Model Car Championship. Faculty scholar, U. Utah, 1972-73. Mem. Utah Bar Assn., Salt Lake County Bar Assn., Sunstone Found., Owl and Key. Libertarian. Mormon.

GUSTIN, DAVID JOSEPH, food products executive; b. Boston, Oct. 31, 1950; s. Otto Thomas and Ruth Clark (Cox) G.; m. Fran Davis Solomor, Jan. 17, 1978; children: Robert, Daniel, Sarah. AB, Dartmouth Coll., 1972, MBA, 1973. Mktg. profl. Gen. Foods, White Plains, N.Y., 1973-87; gen. mgr. frozen desserts Gen. Foods, White Plains, 1987-89; sr. v.p. mktg. Frito Lay, Plano, Tex., 1989-92; pres. La Choy, Rosario, other divsns. Hunt Wesson, Fullerton, Calif., 1992-95; pres. Hunt Wesson, Fullerton, 1995-96; pres., COO Con Agra Grocery Products, Fullerton, 1996—. Office: Con Agra Grocery Products 1645 W Valencia Dr Fullerton CA 92833

GUSTUS, STACEY A., legal secretary; b. Lakewood, Colo., Sept. 10, 1961; d. Norman Gaylord and Sandra S. (Melton) Holder; m. Wayne A. Gustus, Jr., June 14, 1980; children: Gregory K., Cynthia Jo. Student, U. North Colo., 1979-80. Cert. paralegal. County court tech Adams County DA, Brighton, Colo., 1980-83; legal sec. Peter L. Mattisson, Esq., Westminster, Colo., 1983-85, Hall & Evans, Denver, 1985-90; paralegal Machol & Machol, Denver, 1990-91; legal sec. McKenna & Cuneo, Denver, 1991—. Mem. Nat. Contract Mgmt. Assn. (treas., newsletter editor, seminar registrar 1994—). Office: McKenna & Cuneo LLP 370 17th St Ste 4800 Denver CO 80202

GUTHRIE, DAVID NEAL, marketing executive; b. Paris, Tex., Feb. 12, 1941; s. Wesley Neal and Marie (Oliver) G.; m. Ramona Jeanne Busch, Feb. 6, 1959; children: David Jr., Scott, Laure. Student, San Antonio Coll., 1959-62, U. Tex., 1962-63, U. Tex., Arlington, 1965-66, U. Mo., 1970-72. From systems analyst to sales mgr. Sperry Univac, St. Louis, 1967-80; sales rep. Computer Sharing Svcs. Inc., St. Louis, 1980-83, Tandem Computers, Inc., St. Louis, 1983-84, Sykes Datatronics, Inc., St. Louis, 1984-85; sales rep. Cray Rsch., Inc., Colorado Springs, 1985-88, mktg. mgr., 1988-93; sales mgr. Thinking Machines Corp., 1993—. With USMCR, 1957-59. Fellow Mensa. Republican. Home: 42 Jessana Hts Colorado Springs CO 80906-7902 Office: Thinking Machines Corp 102 S Tejon Ste 1100 Colorado Springs CO 80903-2013

GUTHRIE, EDGAR KING, artist; b. Chenoa, Ill., May 12, 1917; s. David McMurtrie and Emily Henrietta (Streid) G.; m. Eva Ross Harvey, Dec. 8, 1945 (dec. Jan. 1978); children: Melody Bliss Johnson, Mark King Guthrie. BEd, Ill. State U., 1939; MA, Am. U., 1958; graduate, Command and General Staff Coll., Ft. Leavenworth, Kan., 1967. Artist W.L. Stensgaard Co., Chgo., 1939-40, The Diamond Store, Phoenix, 1941-42; presentation artist CIA, Washington, 1955-72; instr. Columbia Tech. Inst., Arlington, Va., 1966-72; owner, later ptnr. Guthrie Art & Sign Co., Winchester, Va., 1976—; instr. U. Hawaii, Lihue, 1980-81; cartoonist The Kauai Times, Lihue, 1981-90; owner Alo-o-oha-ha-ha Caricatures, Lihue, Honolulu, 1980—; cons., artist Shenandoah Apple Blossom Festival, Winchester, 1975-78; cartoonist Internat. Salon of Caricature, Montreal, Can., 1976-77; co-chmn. Kauai Soc. of Artists Art Show, Lihue, 1981. One man shows include 50 Yrs. of Painting-A Retrospective, Lihue, 1984; inventor Artists' Kit; Filmic Artist: (documentary film) The River Nile, 1960 (NBC Emmy Award). Bd. dirs. Civil Def., Virginia Hills, 1954; publicity com. Frederick County Taxpayers Assn., Winchester, 1973, Exch. Club, Winchester, 1977. Lt. col. U.S. Army, 1942-54. Decorated Purple Heart, Bronze Star with oak leaf cluster; recipient Spl. Merit award Boy Scouts Am. Aloha Coun., Lihue, 1982. Mem. Mus. of Cartoon Art, U.S. Naval Combat Artist, Daniel Morgan Mus. (contbr. 1976), Nat. Soc. Mural Painters (contbr. 1976), Allied Artists of Am. (contbr. 1977), Pastel Soc. Am. (contbr. 1977-78), Am. Watercolor Soc. (contbr. 1982—), Greek Expeditionary Forces (hon.). Mem. Ch. LDS. Home and Office: 2444 Hihiwai St Apt 703 Honolulu HI 96826-5104 *Have short term and long term righteous goals. Be able to take risks in those things that most interest you, and gain wisdom from those risks that are least effectual. Instead of merely abandoning a project, try to give it more quality.*

GUTHRIE, PATRICIA SUE, newspaper reporter, free-lance writer; b. Buffalo, Sept. 27, 1958; d. Robert and Margaret Ann (Flagsted) G. Student, Buffalo State Coll., 1976-78, U. Buffalo, 1978-79; BS in Journalism, No. Ariz. U., 1983; MA in Journalism, Ohio State U. Freelance reporter DesertWest News Svc., Flagstaff, Ariz., 1983-85; reporter The Gallup (N.Mex.) Independent, 1985-88; freelance writer The Ariz. Republic and other news orgns., 1985-88; reporter, outdoors editor The Albuquerque Tribune, 1988—. Recipient Don Bolles award Ariz. Press Club, 1986, George Polk award L.I. U., 1988, Best Investigative Series award N.M. AP Mng. Editors, 1988, Team Reporting award Scripps Howard Newspapers, 1988-89, Nat. Headliner award Atlantic City Press Club, 1989, Unity Awards in Media Lincoln U. of Mo., 1989, Pub. Svc. award N.Mex. Press Assn., 1989, Pub. Svc. award Mng. Editors AP, 1989, Amicus Honor for Pub. Svc. N.M. Trial Lawyers Amicus Found., 1989, Julilee Yr. Disting. Alumnus award No. Ariz. U., 1990; named Outstanding Alumna of the Yr. No. Ariz. U. Sch. Journalism, AP, 1994; Kiplinger fellow Ohio State U. Journalism Grad. Sch., 1990—; Nieman fellow Harvard U., 1995-96. Mem. N.M. Press Women (awards for writing, 1987), Edn. Writers Assn., Women in Communications (Clarion award, 1989), Investigative Reporters and Editors, Sigma Delta Chi (v.p. Flagstaff student chpt. 1982-83). Office: Albuquerque Tribune PO Drawer T Albuquerque NM 87103*

GUTHRIE, TIMOTHY SEAN, art educator, artist; b. Omaha, Nebr., May 11, 1965; s. Robert U. and Dorothy (Booth) G.; m. Elizabeth Ann Broderick, Apr. 11, 1966. BFA, Creighton U., 1989; MFA, U. Idaho, 1996. Supr. artist Larson Co., Tucson, 1990-91, Rock & Waterscape, Irvine, Calif., 1992-93; instr. asst. U. Idaho, Moscow, 1993-96, art instr., 1995-96; vis. artist, instr. U. Mont., Missoula, 1997—. Exhbns. include Boise Art Mus., 1995, Paris-Gibson Mus. Art, Great Falls, Mont., 1995 (Juror's Choice award, Mus. Purchase award), Applalachian State U., Boone, N.C., 1996 (Summa Composite Purchase award), Internat. Sculpture Ctr., Washington, 1996; permanent collections Boise Art Mus., Paris-Gibson Square Mus. Art, Appalachian State U.

GUTSCHE, STEVEN LYLE, physicist; b. St. Paul, Nov. 10, 1946; s. Lyle David and Phyllis Jane (Stubstad) G.; divorced; children: Kristina, Angela; m. Marilyn D. Maloney, Oct. 4, 1980; children: Taylor Steven, Daniel Mark. BS, U. Colo., 1968; MS, U. Calif., Santa Barbara, 1970. Physicist USN Pacific Missile Range, Point Mugu, Calif., 1968-71; staff scientist Mission Rsch. Corp., Santa Barbara, 1971-76, group leader, 1977-79, div. leader, 1979—, v.p., 1987—; pres., 1989—; also bd. dirs. Mission Rsch. Corp., Santa Barbara. Contbr. articles to tech. publs. Presbyterian. Office: Mission Rsch Corp 735 State St Santa Barbara CA 93101-3351*

GUTTENTAG, WILLIAM SIDNEY, television producer, writer, director; b. Bklyn., Jan. 27, 1958; s. Jack and Doris W. G.; m. Marina Brodskaya. BA, U. Pa., 1979; postgrad., Am. Film Inst., 1979-80. Writer, producer CBS News, N.Y.C., 1989; writer, producer, dir. ABC News, N.Y.C., 1990-93, Nat. Geographic TV, Washington, 1993, Home Box Office, N.Y.C., 1986—. Writer, prodr. (documentary film) You Don't Have to Die, 1988 (Acad. award 1989); writer, prodr., dir. Crack USA: County Under Siege, 1989 (Acad. award nomination 1990), Death on the Job, 1991 (Ace award, Acad. award nomination 1992), (ABC news spl.) The Cocaine War: Lost in Bolivia, 1992, Blues Highway, 1994 (Acad. award nomination 1995), (Nat. Geog. TV) 5 American Handguns-5 American Kids, 1995 (nomination Primetime Emmy award 1995), (HBO documentary spl.) Memphis PD: War on the Streets, 1996, (CBS spl.) Images of Life: Photographs that Changed the World, 1996. Recipient Ace awards Nat. Acad. Cable TV, 1990, 93, Scott Newman award Scott Newman Found., 1990. Mem. Acad. Motion Picture Arts and Scis.

GUTTERSEN, MICHAEL, rancher, investor; b. San Francisco, Mar. 26, 1939; s. William L. and Grace Tooee (Smith) Vogler; m. Penny Leonora Quinn, Aug. 29, 1959; children: Michael William, Arthur Roy, Shawn Patrick. Student, U. Col., 1957-58. Foreman Crow Creek Ranch, Ault, Colo., 1960-61; owner/mgr. Flying G Ranch, Briggsdale, Colo., 1961-86; pres. Two E Ranches Inc., Greeley, Colo., 1969-86, PX Ranch, Elko, Nev., 1969-71, Indian Creek Ranch, Encampment, Wyo., 1970-83, Lake Farms Co., Eaton, Colo., 1969-86; gen. ptnr. Guttersen & Co./Guttersen Ranch, Kersey, Colo., 1986—; mgr. ins. agy. Am. Nat. Ins. Co., Greeley, 1962-70; owner FGF Ins. Brokers, Inc., Greeley, 1962-70. Bd. dirs. United Way, Weld County, Colo., 1979-81, Greeley Philharmonic Orch., 1991-94, Nat. Cowboy Hall of Fame, Oklahoma City, 1994—. With U.S. Army, 1958-60. Mem. Nat. Cattlemens Assn., Colo. Cattlemens Assn., Colo. Cattle Feeders Assn., Tex. and S.W. Cattle Raisers Assn., Weld County Livestock Assn., Greeley Country Club. Republican. Roman Catholic. Home: Woods Lake Farm 13696 RD 74 Eaton CO 80615 Office: Guttersen Ranch PO Box 528 Kersey CO 80644-0528

GUTTMAN, IRVING ALLEN, opera stage director; b. Chatham, Ont., Can., Oct. 27, 1928; s. Shea and Bernetta (Schaffer) G. Opera student, Royal Conservatory Music, Toronto, 1947-52; LittD (hon.), U. Winnipeg, 1996. Asst. to Herman Geiger Torel of Can. Opera Co., Toronto, 1948-52; dir., under Pauline Donalda Montreal (Que., Can.) Opera Guild, 1959-68; mem. adv. com. Can. Coun. Founding artistic dir., Vancouver (B.C., Can.) Opera Assn., 1960-74, artistic dir., Edmonton (Alta., Can.) Opera Assn., from 1966, Man. (Can.) Opera Assn., Winnipeg, from 1972; dir. numerous TV productions of opera, including first full-length TV opera for, CBC French Network, 1953, operatic productions for numerous U.S. opera cos., also Can. and European cos.; founding artistic dir., Opera Group, Courtenay Youth Music Camp; author: The Unlikely Pioneer-David Watmough, 1987. Decorated Centennial medal, Queen Elizabeth Jubilee medal, Order of Can., Alberta Govt. award of Excellence, 1989, Gov. Gen.'s Can.'s 125th medal for contbn. to arts in Can., Opera Am. Achievement award for 25 yrs. of disting. svc., 1996; named to Edmonton Hall of Fame, 1989, Vancouver Hall of Fame, 1994, Montreal Hall of Fame, 1996. Mem. Canadian Equity, Am. Guild Musical Artists.

GUTZMAN, PHILIP CHARLES, aerospace executive, logistician; b. Salmon, Idaho, June 23, 1938; s. Lester Theodore and Mildred Cordelia (Hinchey) G.; m. Karen Diane Withington, June 17, 1957 (div. Sept. 30, 1957); m. Linda Ann Young, Aug. 28, 1960; children: Kevin Raeder, Lance. BS, U. Ariz., 1962, BA, 1962; MPA, U. Okla., 1977. Cert. Profl. Logistician. Hardrock miner Calera Mining Co., Cobalt, Idaho, 1955; enlisted U.S. Army, 1955-62, commd. 2d lt., 1962, advanced through grades to maj., 1970; supr. logistics engring. Gen. Dynamics Land Systems, Detroit, 1983-84, chief advance systems, 1984-85; ops. mgr. Gen. Dynamics Svcs., St. Louis, 1985-87, dir. ground elec., 1987-88; dep. program mgr. Gen. Dynamics Svcs., Taif, Saudi Arabia, 1988-89; dir. logistics Gen. Dynamics Svcs., Detroit, 1989-91, program mgr. Saudi Arabian Tank program, 1992-93; sr. cons. Shipley Assocs., Boise, 1994—; adj. prof. mgmt. Boise State U., 1995. Author: Dictionary of Military Acronyms, 1990; contbr. numerous mil. articles to profl. jours., 1972—. Decorated Bronze Star (3), Purple Heart (5), Air medal, Meritorious Svc. medal (2), Cross of Gallantry with Palm. Mem. Soc. Logistics Engrs. (chpt. chmn. 1990-93, bd. dirs. 1992). Republican. Office: Franklin Quest Cons Group 2150 W Pkwy Blvd Salt Lake City UT 84119

GUY, ANDREW A., lawyer; b. Kansas City, Mo., May 11, 1952. AB summa cum laude, Princeton U., 1974; JD, U. Va., 1979. Bar: Wash. 1979. Mem. Bogle & Gates, P.L.L.C., Seattle. Mem. ABA (trial practice, creditor/debtor law sects.), Wash. State Bar Assn. (litigation sect.), King County Bar Assn. Office: Bogle & Gates PLLC Two Union Sq 601 Union St Seattle WA 98101-2327

GUY, MILDRED DOROTHY, retired secondary school educator; b. Brunswick, Ga.; d. John and Mamie Paul (Smith) Floyd; BA in Social Sci., Savannah State Coll., 1949; MA in Am. History, Atlanta U., 1952; postgrad. U. So. Calif., U. Colo.; m. Charles H. Guy, Aug. 18, 1956 (div. 1979); 1 child, Rhonda Lynn. Tchr. social studies L.S. Ingraham H.S., Sparta, Ga.; tchr. English and social studies North Jr. H.S., Colorado Springs, 1958-84; ret., 1984; cooperating tchr. Tchr. Edn. Program, Col. Coll., 1968-72. Fund raiser for Citizens for Theatre Auditorium, Colorado Springs, 1979; bd. dirs. Urban League, 1971-75; del. to County and State Dem. Conv., 1972, 76, 80, 84, 92; mem. Pike's Peak C.C. Coun., 1976-83; mem. Colo. Springs Opera Coun. of 500, 1984-88; mem. nominating com. Wagon Wheel coun. Girl Scouts U.S.A., 1985-87; active Fine Arts Ctr., Pikes Peak Hospice. Recipient Viking award North Jr. H.S., 1973, Woman of Distinction award Girls Scouts Wagon Wheel Coun., 1989, 94; Outstanding Black Woman of Colorado Springs award, 1975; named Pacesetter, Atlanta U., 1980-81, Outstanding Black Educator of Yr., Black Educators of Dist. II, Colorado Springs, 1984; Outstanding Ednl. Service award Colo. Dept. and State Bd. Edn., 1983, Dedicated Svc. award Pikes Peak C.C., 1983; Outstanding Community Leadership award Alpha Phi Alpha, 1985; award Colo. Black Woman for Polit. Action, 1985, Sphinx award, 1986; named in recognition sect. Salute to Women, Colorado Springs Gazette Telegraph, 1986. Mem. LWV (Colo. chpt.), Negro Hist. Assn., Women's Found. Colo.; life mem. NAACP (Golden Heritage), NEA, AAUW, Colo. Coun. Social Studies, Assn. Study Afro-Am. Life and History, Women's Ednl. Soc. Colo. Coll. (bd. mgrs. 1992—), Alpha Delta Kappa, Alpha Kappa Alpha (pres. 1985). Baptist. Home: 3132 Constitution Ave Colorado Springs CO 80909-2177

GUY, RICHARD P., state supreme court justice; b. Coeur d'Alene, Idaho, Oct. 24, 1932; s. Richard H. and Charlotte M. Guy; m. Marilyn K. Guy, Nov. 16, 1963; children: Victoria, Heidi, Emily. JD, Gonzaga U., 1959. Bar: Wash. 1959, Hawaii 1988. Former judge Wash. Superior Ct., Spokane, from 1977; now justice Wash. Supreme Ct., Olympia. Capt. USAS. Mem. Wash. State Bar, Spokane County Bar Assn. Roman Catholic. Office: Wash Supreme Ct PO Box 40929 Temple of Justice Olympia WA 98504-0929

GUYAN, CHERYL ANN, nurse; b. Worcester, Mass., June 4, 1964; d. Ronald John and Linda Ellen (Stone) Denault; m. William James Guyan, July 19, 1986; children: Jeffrey, Kelsey. BS in Nursing, Salve Regina Coll., Newport, R.I., 1986. RN, Calif.; cert. CCRN; cert. instr. ACLS, BLS, PALS. Nurse St. Joseph's Hosp., Tucson, 1986-87; charge nurse Univ. Med. Ctr., Tucson, 1987-90; nurse clinician St. Joseph's Hosp., Savannah, 1990-92, ICU nurse mgr., 1992-94; CCRN Meth. Hosp., Arcadia, Calif., 1994—, critical care educator, 1995—; mem. numerous coms. St. Joseph's Hosp., Savannah, Ga., 1990-94, Meth. Hosp., Arcadia. Mem. AACN, Ga. Assn. Nursing Execs., Sigma Phi Sigma. Republican. Home: 6881 Rovato Pl Alta Loma CA 91701-8586

GUYER, J. PAUL, civil engineer, architect, consultant; b. Sacramento, Feb. 12, 1941; s. Paul Marline and Vivian Ruth (Mosher) G.; m. Judith Mae Overholser, June 28, 1968; children: J. Paul Jr., Christopher Meador. BS, Stanford U., 1962; postgrad., McGeorge Law Sch., 1962-65. Registered profl. engr., architect, Calif. Engr. State of Calif., Sacramento, 1962-67; ptnr. Guyer and Santin, Sacramento, 1967-75; pres. Guyer Santin, Inc., Sacramento, 1975—. Author: Planning and Development Manual, Calif. Dept. Parks and Recreation, 1984; editor: Recreation Planning and Devel., 1983, Infrastructure for Urban Growth, 1987; author tech. reports. Bd. dirs. Davis (Calif.) Sci. Ctr., 1991-92. Fellow ASCE (Harland Bartholemew award for contbns. to field of urban planning 1991); mem. ASME, Sacramento Symphony Assn., Sacramento Opera Assn., Sacramento Met. C. of C., El Macero Country Club, Capital Club, Comstock Club. Home: 44240 Clubhouse Dr El Macero CA 95618

GUYTON, SAMUEL PERCY, retired lawyer; b. Jackson, Miss., Mar. 20, 1937; s. Earl Ellington and Eulalia (Reynolds) G.; m. Jean Preston, Oct. 11, 1959; children: Tamara Reynolds, William Preston, David Sage. BA, Miss. State U., 1959; LLB, U. Va., 1965. Bar: Colo. 1965, U.S. Dist. Ct. Colo. 1965, U.S. Tax Ct. 1977, U.S. Ct. Appeals (10th cir.) 1965, U.S. Ct. Appeals (5th cir.) 1981. Ptnr., Holland & Hart, Denver, 1965-92; ret., 1992; faculty Am. Law Inst. ABA, 1976-88. Sec., trustee Colo. Hist. Found., 1971-92, pres., 1983-87; trustee Music Assn. Aspen and Aspen Music Festival, 1980-88; precinct com. chmn. Dem. Party, 1968-70; mem. Gov.'s mansion preservation com., 1989-92, mem. adv. com., 1989-92; bd. advisors Coll. Arts and Scis., Miss. State U. Capt. USAF, 1959-62. Fellow Am. Coll. Tax Counsel (bd. regents 1985-92, chmn., pres. 1989-91), Am. Tax Policy Inst. (trustee 1989-92, v.p. 1989-92); mem. ABA (sect. taxation 1967-92, chmn. sect.'s com. on agr. 1980-82), Colo. Bar Assn. (tax coun. 1983-86, sec. 1983, chmn. 1985-86), Colo. Bar Found., Greater Denver Tax Csls. Assn. (chmn. 1978), Law Club Denver, Little River Lectures Assn. (bd. dirs., v.p. 1985-96, pres. 1996—), Am. Alpine Club (life), Colo. Mountain Club (life, planned giving com.), Eleanore Mullen Weckbaugh Found. (trustee 1983-95), Humphreys Found. (sec., treas., trustee), Colo. Trail Found. (trustee), Colo. Mountain Club Found. (dir.), Colo. Hist. Soc. (mem. bd. dirs., chmn. nominating com.), Hampshire Coll. (Govt. and Legal Affairs Com.). Mem. Unity Ch. Co-author: Cattle Owners Tax Manual, 1984, Supplement to Federal Taxation of Agriculture, 1983, Colorado Estate Planning Desk Book, 1984, 90; contbr. articles to jours., mags.; bd. advs. Agrl. Law Jour., 1978-82; mem. editorial bd. Jour. Agrl. Tax and Law, 1983-92. Home and Office: 12345 W 19th Pl Lakewood CO 80215-2516 *To live fully and consciously in the present is both challenge and reward.*

GUZAK, KAREN JEAN WAHLSTROM, artist; b. Cambridge, Mass., May 21, 1939; d. Ernest E. and Kathryn E. (Kemp) Wahlstrom; m. Steven V. Guzak, Aug. 29, 1959 (div. 1983); children: Gretchen, Christopher, Lauren. BS, Univ. Colo., 1961; BFA, Cornish Sch. Allied Arts, Seattle, 1976. Pres. Karen Guzak Inc., Seattle, 1982—. One-woman shows in various exhibits including Davidson Galleries, Seattle, 1981, 84, 87, Tom Luttrell Gallery, San Francisco, 1981, Harris Gallery, Houston, 1982, Laura Russo Gallery, Portland, Oreg., 1987, 89, 91, 96, Musee Hyacinth Rigaud, Perpignan, France, 1988; group exhibitions in various exhibits including Bklyn. Mus., 1981, Brentwood Gallery, St. Louis, 1982, Seattle Art Mus., 1983, San Francisco Mus., 1983, Portland Art Mus., 1985, Davidson Gallery, 1992, Stifel Fine Arts Ctr., Wheeling, W.Va., 1993, Bellevue (Wash.) Art Mus., 1988, 90, 95, 96; represented in permanent collections So. Oreg. State Coll., King County Coun. Chambers. Mem. bd. commrs. King County Arts Commn., Seattle, 1981-86, commr., 1984-85; mem. arts adv. com. METRO Arts Program, Seattle, 1985-91; bd. dirs. Ctr. Contemporary Art, 1987-88; mem. contemporary coun. Seattle Art Mus., 1990-96; pres., developer Sunny Arms Coop., Seattle, 1988-90; co-developer, pres. Union Arts Coop., Seattle, 1992-93; pres. bd. dirs. Artist Trust, Seattle, 1996—. Boettcher scholar Univ. Colo., 1957-61; recipient Housing Designs that Work award, Seattle Design Commn., 1991, Home of Yr. award, Seattle Times and AIA, 1994. Democrat. Home & Office: Karen Guzak Inc 707 S Snoqualmie St Ste 5A Seattle WA 98108-1700

GÜZELDERE, GÜVEN, philosophy and cognitive educator, computer science consultant; b. Ankara, Turkey, Jan. 23, 1963; came to U.S., 1986; s. Selçuk and Aylâ (Ülkmen) G. BS in Computer Engring., Boğaziçi U., Istanbul, Turkey, 1986; MA in Philosophy, MS in Computer Sci., Indiana U., 1989; PhD in Philosophy and Symbolic Sys., Stanford U., 1997. Fellow Humanities Ctr. Stanford (Calif.) U., 1992-93, coord. symbolic sys. program, 1993-94, Whiting fellow, 1994-95; asst. prof. philosophy and cognitive sci. Duke U., Durham; cons. Stanford Data Ctr., 1991-92, Xerox PARC, Palo Alto, Calif., 1991-97. Editor: (jour.) Stanford Humanities Rev., 1994-95, (book) The Nature of Consciousness, 1997. Mem. Assn. for Sci. Study of Consciousness (bd. dirs. 1994—), Soc. for Philosophy and Psychology, Soc. for Machines and Mentality, Behavioral and Brain Scis. (assoc.), Am. Philos. Assn., Cognitive Neurosci. Soc. Office: Duke U 201 W Duke Bldg Durham NC 27708

GUZY, MARGUERITA LINNES, secondary education educator; b. Santa Monica, Calif., Nov. 19, 1938; d. Paul William Robert and Margarete (Rodowski) Linnes; m. Stephen Paul Guzy, Aug. 25, 1962 (div. 1968); 1 child, David Paul. AA, Santa Monica Coll., 1959; student, U. Mex., 1959-60; BA, UCLA, 1966, MA, 1973; postgrad. in psychology, Pepperdine U., 1988-92; cert. bilingual competence, Calif., 1994. Cert. secondary tchr., quality review team ednl. programs, bilingual, Calif. Tchr. Inglewood (Calif.) Unified Sch. Dist., 1967—, chmn. dept., 1972-82, mentor, tchr., 1985-88; clin. instr. series Clin. Supervision Levels I, II, Ingelwood, 1986-87; clin. intern Chem. Dependency Ctr., St. John's Hosp., Santa Monica, 1988-92; lectr. chem. and codependency St. John's Hosp., Santa Monica, 1992—; tchr. Santa Monica Coll., 1975-76; cons. bilingual edn. Inglewood Unified Sch. Dist., 1975—, lead tchr. new hope program at-risk students, 1992; cons. tchr. credentialing fgn. lang. State of Calif., 1994; sch. rep. restructuring edn. for state proposal, 1991—; mem. Program Quality Rev. Team Pub. Edn., Calif., 1993; mem. Supt.'s Com. for Discrimination Resolution, 1994-95. Author: Elementary Education: "Pygmalian in the Classroom", 1975, English Mechanics Workbook, 1986. Recipient Teaching Excellence cert. State of Calif., 1986; named Tchr. of Yr., 1973, 88. Mem. NEA, Calif. Tchrs.

Assn., Inglewood Tchrs. Assn. (local rep. 1971-72, tchr. edn. and profl. svcs. com. 1972-78), UCLA Alumnae Assn. (life), Prytanean Alumnae Assn. (bd. dirs. 1995-96, 1960's rep., 2d v.p. membership 1996-98). Republican. Office: Monroe Jr High Sch 10711 S 10th Ave Inglewood CA 90303-2015

GWARTNEY, PATRICIA ANNE, sociology educator; b. Glendale, Calif., Mar. 30, 1951; d. Robert Alan and Marilyn Arline (Sanborn) G.; m. Stanley Morshead Gibbs, July 31, 1971 (div. Feb. 1994); children: Loren, Spencer; m. George Gordon Goldthwaite Jr., Apr. 29, 1995; children: Emily Eleanor, Lisa Margaret, Adam Michael. AB, U. Calif., Berkeley, 1973; MA, U. Mich., 1979, PhD, 1981. Asst. prof. U. Oreg., Eugene, 1981-88, assoc. prof., 1988-96, prof. sociology, 1996—, affiliate Ctr. for Study of Women in Soc., 1984—, founding dir. Oreg. Survey Rsch. Lab., 1992—. Contbr. articles to profl. publs.; editl. bd. Jour. Marriage and the Family, 1995-97. Rsch. advisor Lane County Domestic Violence Coun., Eugene, 1996—; cons. Task Force on Gender Fairness Oreg. Supreme Ct., 1996—. Fulbright fellow U. Auckland, New Zealand, 1986. Mem. AAAS (sect. K nominating com.), AAUP, Am. Sociol. Assn., Pacific Sociol. Assn. (com. on coms.), Population Assn. Am. Democrat. Congregationalist. Home: 2875 Spring Blvd Eugene OR 97403-2510 Office: U Oreg Dept Sociology Eugene OR 97403-1291

GWINN, MARY ANN, newspaper reporter; b. Forrest City, Ark., Dec. 29, 1951; d. Lawrence Baird and Frances Evelyn (Jones) G.; m. Richard A. King, June 3, 1973 (div. 1981); m. Stephen E. Dunnington, June 10, 1990. BA in Psychology, Hendrix Coll., 1973; MEd in Spl. Edn., Ga. State U., 1975; MA in Journalism, U. Mo., 1979. Tchrs. aide DeKalb County Schs., Decatur, Ga., 1973-74, tchr., 1975-78; reporter Columbia (Mo.) Daily Tribune, 1979-83; reporter Seattle Times, 1983—, internat. trade and workplace reporter, 1992-96, asst. city editor, 1996—; instr. ext. divsn. U. Wash., Seattle, 1990; journalism instr., Seattle U., 1994. Recipient Charles Stewart Mott Found. award for edn. reporting, 1980, C.B. Blethen award for enterprise reporting Blethen Family, Seattle, 1989, Pulitzer Prize for nat. reporting, 1990. Mem. Newspaper Guild. Office: Seattle Times PO Box 70 1120 John St Seattle WA 98111

GWINN, MARY DOLORES, philosopher, author, speaker; b. Oakland, Calif., Sept. 16, 1946; d. Epifanio and Carolina (Lopez) Cruz; m. James Monroe Gwinn, Oct. 23, 1965; 1 child, Larry Allen. Student, Monterey Peninsula Jr. Coll., 1965. Retail store mgr. Consumer's Distbg. divsn. May Co., Hayward, Calif., 1973-78; mktg. rep. Dale Carnegie Courses, San Jose, Calif., 1978-79; founder, pres. Strategic Integrations, Ariz.'s Innovative Bus. Devel. Ctr., Scottsdale, 1985—; speaker St. John's Coll. U. Cambridge, England, 1992, INC. Mag., U.S.A., 1996, Clemson Univ., 1996; founder, pres. Internat. Inst. for Conceptual Edn., Scottsdale, 1993—, Gwinn Genius Inst., 1995—. Founder new fields of study Genetics and NeuroBus.; profiled the Thought Process of Genius; conceived Whole Brain Business Theory, 1985; author: Genius Leadership Secrets From The Past For the 21st Century, 1995; writer bus. column: SmartBiz, IMAGE Networker, Colo., 1996; contbr. articles to profl. jours. Republican. Home and Office: 5836 E Angela Dr Scottsdale AZ 85254-6410

GWON, ARLENE, ophthalmologist; b. N.Y.C., Sept. 21, 1943; d. William and Mamie Gwon; m. Patrick Francis Sheehy, 1970; children: Brian, Laura. BA, City U. N.Y., 1964; MD, SUNY, 1968. Diplomate Am. Bd. Ophthalmology. Ophthalmologist pvt. practice, Newport Beach, Calif., 1973—; assoc. clin. prof. U. Calif., Irvine, 1991—; med. rsch. investigator Allergan Inc., Irvine, 1993—; chmn. Hoag Meml. Hosp. IRB, Newport Beach, 1991—. Patentee in field. Office: Allergan Inc 2525 Dupont Dr Irvine CA 92612-1531 also: 1401 Avocado Ave Ste 903 Newport Beach CA 92660-7719

GWYNN, ANTHONY KEITH (TONY GWYNN), professional baseball player; b. L.A., May 9, 1960; m. Alicia; children: Anthony, Anisha Nicole. Student, San Diego State U. Player minor league teams Walla Walla and Amarillo, Hawaii, 1981-82; with San Diego Padres, 1981—. Winner Nat. League batting title, 1984, 87, 88, 89, 95; recipient Gold Glove award, 1986-87, 89-91; mem. All-Star team, 1984-87, 89-94; named MVP N.W. League, 1981, Sporting News Nat. League Silver Slugger team, 1984, 86-87, 89, 94, Sporting News Nat. League All-Star Team, 1984, 86-87, 89, 94. Office: San Diego Padres PO Box 2000 San Diego CA 92112-2000*

GYLSETH, DORIS (LILLIAN) HANSON, retired librarian; b. Helena, Mont., May 26, 1934; d. Richard E. and Lillie (Paula) Hanson; m. Arlie Albeck, Dec. 26, 1955 (div. Apr. 1964); m. Hermann M. Gylseth, Apr. 29, 1983 (dec. Aug. 1985). BS in Edn., Western Mont. Coll. Edn., 1958; MLS, U. Wash., 1961. Tchr. Helena Sch. Dist., 1955-56, Dillon (Mont.) Elem. Sch., 1957-59, Eltopia (Wash.) Unified Sch. Dist., 1959-60; sch. libr. Shoreline Sch. Dist., Seattle, 1960-64, Dept. of Def., Chateauroux, France, Hanau, Fed. Republic Germany, Tachikawa, Japan, 1964-68, Long Beach (Calif.) Unified Sch. Dist., 1968-70; br. libr. Long Beach Pub. Libr., 1970-74, coord. children's svcs., 1974-85; libr. Long Beach (Calif.) Unified Sch. Dist., 1986-94; realtor Century 21, All Pacific, 1994-96. Bd. dirs. Children's Svcs. divsn. Calif. Libr. Assn., 1985, Literary Guild of Orange County, 1993—; co-chmn. Long Beach Authors Festival, 1978-86; mem. planning coun. Third Pacific Rim Conf. on Children's Lit., UCLA, 1986. Mem. So. Calif. Coun. on Lit. for Children and Young Poeple (bd. dirs. 1974-88, pres. 1982-84), Helen Fuller Cultural Carrousel (bd. dirs. 1985—), Friends of Long Beach Pub. Libr. (bd. dirs. 1988—), Zonta (pres. 1978-80). Home: 5131 Kingscross Rd Westminster CA 92683-4832

HA, CHONG WAN, state government executive; b. Chin-ju, Kyung-Nam, South Korea, Oct. 25, 1938; came to U.S., 1963; s. Kyung-sik and Kyung-Nam (Park) H.; m. Karen Hye-Ja Han, Aug. 19, 1968; children: Jean Frances, Julie Ann. BA in Econs., UCLA, 1970; cert. in exec. mgmt., The Peter F. Drucker Mgmt. Ctr., 1984; MA in Mgmt., Claremont (Calif.) Grad. Sch., 1985; PhD in Bus. Mgmt., La Salle U., La., 1995. Sr. systems analyst Atlantic Richfield Co., Los Angeles, 1972-78; asst. v.p. 1st Interstate Services Co., Los Angeles, 1978-85; v.p. Ticor Title Ins. Co., Los Angeles, 1985-91; assoc. dir. MCA/Universal Studios, 1991; dir. State of Calif. Stephen P. Teale Data Ctr., Sacramento, 1991—; mem. exec. com. Calif. Forum on Info. Tech.; mem. adv. bd. Govt. Tech. Conf., 1994. Res. police officer Monterey Park (Calif.) Police Dept., 1981-82; bd. dirs. Asian Pacific Alumni Assn., UCLA, 1988, Asian Pacific Am. Legal Found., L.A., 1988, Korean Youth Ctr., Korean Am. Music Acad.; mem. alumni coun. Claremont Grad. Sch., 1993. Recipient Peter Drucker Ctr. Alumni award, 1994, Calif. State Atty. Gen. award, 1994. Mem. Soc. of Info. Mgmt., Leadership Edn. for Asian Pacifics, UCLA Chancellers Circle. Home: 5625 Adobe Rd Rocklin CA 95765-4529

HAAG, CARRIE H., former sports association executive. BA, Purdue U., 1972; MA, Ea. Ky. U., 1977, EdS, 1978; postdoctoral work, U. N.C., 1978-79. Phys. edn. tchr. Sch. Dist. # 65, Evanston, Ill., 1973-76; grad. asst. Ea. Ky. U., Richmond, 1977-78, U. N.C., Greensboro, 1978-79; asst. to exec. dir. Assn. for Intercollegiate Athletics for Women, Washington, D.C., 1979-80; dir. nat. championships Assn. for Intercollegiate Athletics for Women, Washington, 1980-82; asst. dir. athletics Dartmouth Coll., Hanover, N.H., 1982-84; cons. Washington, D.C., 1989-90; asst. dir. athletics Cen. Conn. State U., New Britain, 1990-92; exec. dir. U.S. Field Hockey Assn., Colorado Springs, Colo., 1984-88, 92-96; del., moderator New Agenda I: Nat. Women in Sports Conf., Washington, 1983; panelist U.S. Olympic Acad. X, Colorado Springs, 1986; U.S. del. Internat. Hockey Fedn. Congress, Brussels, Belgium, 1986, Internat. Olympic Acad., Olympia, Greece, 1987; del. House of Dels. U.S. Olympic Com., 1985-88; grant author and project dir. U.S. Olympic Found., 1986-88; mem. safety com. U.S. Olympic Tng. Ctr. Complex, 1988; mem. applied strategic planning team Nat. Assn. for Girls and Women in Sport, 1988, v.p. bd. dirs., 1990-92. *

HAAG, KEN LEE, civil engineer, management consultant; b. Columbus, Mont., Dec. 20, 1939; s. Edward Peter and Ruth Virginia (Bell) H.; m. Marie Eileen Carlson, Oct. 24, 1959; children: Pamela Marie Clower, Vincent E., Richard Lee. BSCE, Mont. State U., 1962. Civil engr. U.S. Dept. of Interior, Billings and Miles City, Mont., 1962-65; sales engr. Armco Steel Corp., Billings, 1965-69; field and office engr. N.L. Garrick Constr. Co., Missoula, Mont., 1969-71; asst. city engr. City of Billings, 1971-72, city engr., 1972-77, pub. works dir., 1977-97; cons. in field, 1997—. Mem. Mont. League of Cities and Town Program Com., Helena, 1991-94, State of Mont. Solid Waste Mgmt. Plan com., Helena, 1992-93, Regional Tech. Assistance Program, Bozeman, Mont., 1990-92; bd. dirs. Billings Bright n' Beautiful Bd., 1990-94, Keep Am. Beautiful, 1997—. Mem. ASCE (Ea. br. Mont. sect. pres. 1973-74, Outstanding Young Engr. award 1973, Disting. Svc. award 1994), Am. Pub. Works Assn. (pres.-elect 1994-95, pres. 1995-96, region IX dir. 1991-94, Rocky Mountain chpt. pres. 1984-85), Billings C. of C. (managed growth com.).

HAAGE, ROBERT MITCHELL, retired history educator, organization leader; b. Garden City, Kans., Mar. 10, 1924; s. William Russell and Mayme Levice (Mitchell) H.; m. Lila Marie Baker, Sept. 7, 1947; children: Lori Deane, Lisa Anne, Melanie Sue. BA, Southwestern Coll., 1947; MDiv, Garrett Bibl. Inst., 1952. Cert. tchr., Kans., Calif. Min. Meth. Ch., Copeland, Kans., 1947-48, Meth. Chs., Ingleside, Spring Grove, Ill., 1948-50; asst. min. First Meth. Ch., Emporia, Kans., 1952-53; tchr. core curriculum Marshall Intermediate Sch., Wichita, Kans., 1953-56; tchr. U.S. history Bellflower (Calif.) High Sch., 1956-57; tchr. math. Chaffey Joint Union High Sch. Dist., Ontario, Calif., 1957-59; tchr. U.S. history and econs. Chaffey Joint Union High Sch. Dist., 1959-85; 1st faculty pres. Montclair High Sch., 1959-60; founding pres. Inland Empire Counties Coun. for Social Studies, San Bernardino, Calif., 1961-62; dean student activities Western CUNA Mgmt. Sch., Pomona Coll., Claremont, Calif., 1980-84; treas. Tchrs. Adv. Group/Tchrs. Farm and Ranch Co-op, 1984-93. Conservation editor Desomount Dustings Newsletter, 1990-92, gen. editor, 1993—. Founding officer Chaffey Dist. Employees Fed. Credit Union, Ontario, 1964-69; pres., bd. dirs. Chaffey Fed. Credit Union, Ontario, 1979-87, dir., 1969—; officer, bd. govs. Mt. Baldy chpt. Calif. Credit Union League, Pomona, 1977-86; bd. dirs., treas. Upper Westwood Homeowners Assn., Pomona, 1982-84, 91-92; conservation chair Desomount Environ. Orgn.; mem. Nat. Wildlife Fedn. Recipient We Honor Ours award Calif. Tchrs. Assn., 1985, Outstanding Svc. award Associated Chaffey Tchrs., 1985. Mem. Univ. Club Claremont (sec.-v.p.-pres. 1986-92, editor newsletters 1986-90, bd. dirs. 1993-96, chair fin. com. 1993—, Leadership award 1992), Toastmasters Club 12 (pres. 1964-65, Best Evaluator award 1982, 83, 85), Sierra Club, Fedn. of Western Outdoor Clubs (v.p. So. Calif. chpt. 1990—, gen. v.p. 1994-95, treas. 1995—), Phi Delta Kappa (pres. 1977-78, Disting. Svc. award 1978), Kappa Delta Pi (hon. soc. in edn. 1953—). Democrat. Home: 9541 Tudor Ave Montclair CA 91763-2219

HAARSAGER, SANDRA LYNN, author, communications educator; b. West Plains, Mo., Sept. 17, 1946; Victor Everett and Melba Louise (Rowlett) Smith; m. James Barry Watkinson, June 15, 1969 (div. Oct. 1975); m. Dennis Lee Haarsager, Jan. 1, 1977; children: Anna Lynn, Andrew Lee, Jennie Ella. BA in English Lit. and Psychology, Coll. of Idaho, Caldwell, 1968; MPA, Boise State U., 1982; PhD in Am. Studies, Wash. State U., 1990. Reporter and spl. edits. editor Times-News, Twin Falls, Idaho, 1965-69; health & edn. reporter, reviewer and consumer affairs editor Idaho Statesman, Boise, 1972-75; asst. to supt. pub. instrn. Idaho Dept. Edn., Boise, 1975-78; asst. dir. devel. Wash. State U., Pullman, 1978-79; dir. univ. info. svcs. U. of Idaho, Moscow, 1979-83, from instr. to assoc. prof., 1988—, coord. Am. Studies Program, 1994-96; reporter and editor Idahonian/Daily News, Moscow, 1983-85; gen. mgr. News-Rev. Pub. Co., Moscow, 1985-88; columnist Daily News, Moscow, 1986-94; bd. dirs. N.W. Region, Coun. for Advancement and Support of Edn., 1981-82, pub. reviewer; condr. seminars in field; lectr. in field. Author: Bertha Knight Landes of Seattle - Big City Mayor, 1994, Organized Womanhood: Cultural Politics in the Pacific Northwest, 1840-1920, 1997; author monograph: Student Rights and Responsibilities, 1978; contbr. articles, book revs. to profl. jours.; referee Journalism Monographs, 1991—, Journalism Quar., 1991—, Canon-Jour. of Rocky Mountains Am. Studies Assn., 1992—, Am. Journalism, 1993—, Journalism History, 1996—; editl. adv. bd. Idaho--The University Mag., 1983-84. Mem. cmty. adv. coun. Lewiston (Idaho) Tribune, 1981-82; task force leader Idaho Conf. on Women, Boise, 1977; mem. juvenile justice coun. Idaho Law Enforcement Planning Commn., Boise, 1976-78; mem. Wash. Idaho Symphony Chorus, 1981-84, 90-93; bd. dirs. Boise Hotline, 1974-75. Recipient Edn. Media award for columns and editls. on edn. Idaho Assn. Sch. Adminstrs., 1984, Excellence in Pub. Info., Coun. for Advancement and Support of Edn., 1981, Excellence in Broadcast Media, 1979, 80; grantee John Calhoun Smith Fund, 1991-92, 92-93, 93-94, U. Idaho Rsch. Found., 1990, 94, Office of Acad. Affairs of U. Idaho, 1990. Mem. Pacific N.W. Am. Studies Assn. (sec.-treas. 1990-94), Soc. History of Tech., Am. Journalism Historians Assn., Assn. for Edn. in Journalism and Mass Comm. (rsch. chair, sec., qualitative studies 1993-95), U. Idaho Alumni Assn. (bd. dirs. 1992-95), N.W. Comm. Assn., Ida State Parent Tchr. Assn. (life, Svc. to Edn. award 1977), Idaho Press Club (Best Columnist award 1988, Best Feature Writer 1975, others), Moscow C. of C. (bd. dirs. 1982-83), Phi Kappa Phi. Unitarian. Office: Univ of Idaho Sch of Communication Moscow ID 83844-1072

HAAS, BRADLEY DEAN, pharmacy director, clinical pharmacist, consultant; b. Albion, Nebr., Nov. 24, 1957; s. Ernest Duane Jr. and Joy Lou (Fusselman) H. Student, Kearney State Coll., 1976-78; PharmD with distinction, U. Nebr., Omaha, 1981. Registered pharmacist, Nebr., Colo.; cert. hosp. pharmacy residency, basic life support instr. and provider, advanced cardiac life support instr. and provider. Resident hosp. pharmacy U. Nebr. Med. Ctr., Omaha, 1981-82; intensive care clin. pharmacist Mercy Med. Ctr., Denver, 1982-85; home care pharmacist Am. Abbey Homecare, Englewood, Colo., 1985; pharmacy dir. Charter Hosp. of Aurora, Colo., 1989-90; clin pharmacy coord. Porter Meml. Hosp., Denver, 1987-92; asst. dir. clin. pharmacy svcs. Luth. Med. Ctr., Wheat Ridge, Colo., 1992-94; dir. pharmacy Integrated Pharmacy Solutions, Inc./Pru Care Pharmacies, Denver, 1994-96; med. info. scientist Astra-Merck, 1996—; cons. Porter Meml. Hosp. Chronic Pain Treatment Ctr., 1987-89, Charter Hosp., 1989-90; adj. asst. prof. pharmacy U. Colo., 1983—; mem. leadership adv. coun. sch. pharmacy U. Colo., 1987-89; mem. adv. bd. Instl. and Managed Healthcare, Ortho Biotech, Inc., 1992—; mem. State Colo./ Medicare D.U.R. Com., 1992—. Author, co-author in field. Vol. Colo. Hosp. Pharmacists Week, Poison Prevention Week, KUSA-TV Health Fair; lectr. Pathfinder's Youth Group- Careers Day; active Colo. Trust. Named Disting. Young Pharmacist of the Year Marion Labs., Colo., 1987, one of Outstanding Young Men of Am., 1987; recipient Acad. Scholarship U. Nebr. Med. Ctr, 1978-81, Excellence in Pharmacy Practice award U. Colo. Sch. Pharmacy, 1988; Marjorie Merwin Simmons Meml. scholar U. Nebr. Found. Fund., 1980; scholar VFW, 1978-81. Mem. Am. Soc. Hosp. Pharmacists (state chpt. grants program selection com. 1989, nominations com. 1990-91, ho. of dels. 1987, 90-92), Acad. Managed Care Pharmacy, Colo. Managed Care Pharmacy Dirs., Colo. Soc. Hosp. Pharmacists (presdl. officer 1987-89, chmn. numerous couns. and coms., Hosp. Pharmacy Practitioner Excellence award 1988, 89). Home: 10115 Granite Hill Dr Parker CO 80134 Office: Astra Merck Inc 10115 Granite Hill Dr Parker CO 80134

HAAS, PETER E., SR., company executive; b. San Francisco, Dec. 20, 1918; s. Walter A. and Elise (Stern) H.; m. Josephine Baum, Feb. 1, 1945; m. Mimi Lurie, Aug., 1981; children: Peter E., Michael Stern, Margaret Elizabeth. Student, Deerfield Acad., 1935-36; A.B., U. Calif., 1940; MBA cum laude, Harvard, 1943. With Levi Strauss & Co., San Francisco, 1945—, exec. v.p., 1958-70, pres., 1970-81, CEO, 1976-81, chmn. bd., 1981-89, chmn. exec. com., 1989—, also bd. dirs.; chmn. exec. com., bd. dirs. Levi Strauss Assocs. Inc. Holding Corp.; dir. emeritus AT&T. Trustee San Francisco Found., 1984—; assoc. Smithsonian Nat. Bd., 1988—; bd. dirs. No. Calif. Grantmakers, 1989—; former mem. exec. com. Strive for Five; former mem. Golden Gate Nat. Recreation Area Adv. Com.; Former pres. Jewish Welfare Fedn.; former trustee Stanford U.; former dir., vice chmn. San Francisco Bay Area Council; former trustee United Way of San Francisco Bay Area; former pres. Aid to Retarded Children; former bd. govs. United Way of Am. Recipient Alexis De Tocqueville Soc. award, United Way Am., 1985; named CEO of Yr., Fin. World mag., 1981, Bus. Statesman of Yr., Harvard Bus. Sch., 1982; Baker scholar, 1940. Office: Levi Strauss & Co PO Box 7215 San Francisco CA 94120-7215*

HAAS, RAYMOND P., lawyer; b. Corpus Christi, Tex., Dec. 9, 1942. BA cum laude, Yale U., 1964, LLB, 1967. Bar: Calif. 1967. Law clk. to Hon. Roger J. Traynor Supreme Ct. of Calif., 1967-68; atty. Howard, Rice, Nemerovski, Canady, Falk & Rabkin, San Francisco. Trustee San Francisco U. High Sch., 1973-78, 85-88, chmn., 1973-76, treas., 1986-88; trustee Pacific Presbyn. Med. Ctr., 1979-91, vice chmn. 1986-91. Mem. ABA (forum com. on franchising, antitrust law sect., bus. law sect., internat. law sect., patent, copyright and trademarks sect., sci. and tech. sect.), State Bar Calif., Bar Assn. San Francisco (computer law sect.), Licensing Execs. Soc., Computer Law Assn., Order of Coif. Office: Howard Rice Nemerovski Canady Falk & Rabkin 3 Embarcadero Ctr Ste 7 San Francisco CA 94111-4003

HAAS, ROBERT DOUGLAS, apparel manufacturing company executive; b. San Francisco, Apr. 3, 1942; s. Walter A. Jr. and Evelyn (Danzig) H.; m. Colleen Gershon, Jan. 27, 1974; 1 child, Elise Kimberly. BA, U. Calif., Berkeley, 1964; MBA, Harvard U., 1968. With Peace Corps, Ivory Coast, 1964-66; fellow White House, Washington, 1968-69; assoc. McKinsey & Co., 1969-72; with Levi Strauss & Co., San Francisco, 1973—, sr. v.p. corp. planning and policy, 1978-80, pres. new bus. group, 1980, pres. operating groups, 1980-81, exec. v.p., COO, 1981-84, pres., CEO, 1984-89, CEO, chmn. bd., 1989—, also bd. dirs.; pres. Levi Strauss Found., mem. global leadership team. Hon. dir. San Francisco AIDS Found.; trustee Ford Found.; bd. dirs. Bay Area Coun.; past bd. dirs. Am. Apparel Assn. White House fellow, 1968-69. Mem. Brookings Inst. (trustee), Bay Area Com., Conf. Bd., Coun. Fgn. Rels., Trilateral Commn., Calif. Bus. Roundtable, Meyer Freidman Inst. (bd. dirs.), Phi Beta Kappa. Office: Levi Strauss & Co 1155 Battery St San Francisco CA 94111-1230*

HAAS, THOMAS L., artist, art gallery owner; b. Saginaw, Mich., Sept. 27, 1952; s. William Jr. and Alma Elizabeth (Stahl) H.; m. Vicki Van Gaal, Jan. 14, 1972. Student, Scottsdale Artists Sch., 1986-87. Artist, designer Giltspur Exhibits, Phoenix, 1988-90; artist, design dir. Habitat, Inc., Tempe, Ariz., 1990-93; artist, owner Tom Haas Studio, Phoenix, 1993-96, Tom Haas Gallery, Phoenix, 1996—; featured artist Carefree (Ariz.) Wine and Art Festival, 1996. One-man show Sun Cities (Ariz.) Art Mus., 1996; represented in permanent collections Hensley & Co., Phoenix, Hanes by Dave Brown, Tempe, Ariz., Echo Canyon Guest Ranch, Le Veta, Colo. Recipient award for mus. quality and 2d place for drawing George Phippen Meml. Found., 1995, award 3d place for oil painting Phippen Western Art Mus., 1996; 2d place award for oil painting Lake Powell Scenic S.W. competition, Page, Ariz., 1996. Office: 1219 E Glendale Ste 3 Phoenix AZ 95020

HABBESTAD, KATHRYN LOUISE, writer; b. Spokane, Wash., Sept. 29, 1949; d. Bernard Malvin and Gertrude Lucille (Westberg) H. BA, U. Wash., 1971; postgrad., Seattle U., 1981-82. Mgr. bus. Seattle Sun, 1974-75; analyst, dep. dir. Research and Planning Office, Seattle, 1975-83; account exec. Southmark Fin. Services, Seattle, 1983-84; stockbroker Interstate Securities, New Bern, N.C., 1985-86; co-founder, assoc. pub. Havelock (N.C.) News, 1986-87; owner ISIS Enterprises, Spokane, 1988—; writer Spokane; sec.-treas. Seattle Sun Pub. Co., 1974-75, Veritas Services, Seattle, 1978-83; chmn. Energy Com. Nat. Congress for Community Econ. Devel., Washington, 1979-82; pub. The Gnus, 1988. Treas. Havelock Chili Festival, 1985-87. Mem. Internat. Platform Assn., Mensa. Home and Office: 3822 131st Ln SE # L-6 Bellevue WA 98006-1362 *You cannot win if you do not play.*

HABERLIN, WILLIAM EARL, economist, consultant; b. Honolulu, Mar. 26, 1925; s. Earl William Haberlin and Mary Constance (Ferreira) Burroughs; m. Mildred Frances Copley, July 1, 1945; children: James William, Laura Joyce, Judith Ann, Brian Jon. AA, U. Calif., Berkeley, 1944; MBA, Harvard U., 1956. Asst. v.p. United Calif. Bank, L.A., 1963-65; sr. economist Stanford Rsch. Inst., South Pasadena, Calif., 1965-67; sr. v.p. Union Bank, L.A., 1967-81; v.p., corp. sec. Watson Land Co., L.A., 1981-95; pres. Haberlin & Assocs., La Canada, Calif., 1995—. Contbr. articles to profl. jours. Mem. Pvt. Industry Coun., L.A., 1990-95. Comdr. USN, 1943-63. Mem. Rotary Club of L.A., Harvard-Radcliff Club of So. Calif., Harvard Bus. Sch. Alumni Assn., Assn. for Corp. Growth, Assn. for Bus. Economists, Jonathan Club.

HACHMEISTER, JOHN H., lawyer, educator, mediator; b. Chgo., Nov. 24, 1944; s. Howard E. and Leah (Mace) H.; m. Lydia E. McCarver, Jan. 8, 1982; children: Steven, David, Mellissa, Rachel. BA in Polit. Sci., Cen. State U., Edmond, Okla., 1978; postgrad., Oklahoma City U., 1980-82; JD, Southwestern U., L.A., 1984. Bar: Calif. Technician Am. Chain & Cable, Franklin Park, Ill., 1972-76; assoc. Somers, Hall, et al., Gardena, Calif., 1985-90, Spray, Gould & Bowers, L.A., 1990-92, Fiore, Nordberg, et al, Irvine, Calif., 1992-94; pvt. practice Redondo Beach, Calif., 1994—; owner Jack's Imagination Enterprises, Redondo Beach, 1988—; asst. prof. Calif. State U., Northridge; cons., facilitator Oklahoma City Coalition of Neighborhood Assns., 1972-82; speaker in field. Author: (poetry) Colorado Cowboy Poetry Gathering, 1993; co-inventor solder jig for multi-wire cables, 1992. Candidate for state sen. Dem. party, Torrance, Calif., 1990, Ho. of Reps., Oklahoma City, 1978; del. Dem. party convs. Okla. and Calif., 1974-92; mem. Mayor's Transp. Task Force, Oklahoma City, 1976-80; lt. gov. Okla. Intercollegiate Legis., 1977-78; judge Southwestern U. Moot Ct. Competition, Santa Ana, Calif., 1993. Named to Outstanding Young Men of Am. Mem. Calif. Bar Assn., Greenpeace. Home and Office: 2112 Warfield Ave unit 4 Redondo Beach CA 90278-1447

HACK, ELIZABETH, artist; b. Frankfurt, Germany, Feb. 27, 1954; d. Sidney and Eleanor Barbara (Bermak) H. BFA, U. Miami, Coral Gables, Fla., 1976; M Media Arts, U. S.C., 1979. Art instr. Berkeley, Calif., 1991—; art instr. W. Contra Costa (Calif.) Adult Sch., 1994—; lectr., workshops Nat. League Am. Pen Women, El Cerrito Cmty. Ctr., Albany Sr. Ctr., 1992—. Featured artist Commonwealth Club gallery, San Francisco, 1994; solo exhbns. Henry Hardy Gallery, Univ. Club, San Francisco, 1992, Gallery 57, Fullerton, Calif., 1992, AMEX, San Rafael, Informative Edge, San Francisco, 1991, Conv. Plz. Bldg., San Francisco, 1990, Heller Gallery, U. Calif. Berkeley, Sumitomo Bank, San Francisco, ASUC Studio, U. Calif. Berkeley, 1988, Musical Offering, Berkeley, Coldwell Banker, Kensington home, French Hotel Berkeley, 1987, Coffee Cantata, San Francisco, 1985; group exhbns. include Gloria Delson Fine Art, L.A., 1995, 96, Cameo Art Gallery, Columbia, S.C., 1992, 94, Ashkenazy Galleries, L.A., 1991. Curator multiple abstractions W. Contra Costa Adult Sch., 1995, 4th ann. Gift of Life Ctr. for Visual Arts, Oakland, 1996—, AIDS auction, 1994. Recipient Critic's Choice award San Francisco Bay Guardian, 1990, award of distinction Berkeley Art Ctr., 1989. Mem. Nat. League Am. Pen Women (sec. 1994-96, v.p. 1996—). Home and Office: PO Box 8057 Berkeley CA 94707-8057

HACKENMILLER, THOMAS RAYMOND, writer, publisher; b. Riceville, Iowa, May 15, 1951; s. Clarance Joseph and Angela Rose (Miller) H.; m. Joyce Marie Wingenbach, Dec. 18, 1971 (div. June 1980); children: Andrew, Timothy, Anna; m. Kathie D. Teeley, Mar. 21, 1985. AAS, Yakima (Wash.) Valley Coll., 1973; BA in Edn., Ctrl. Wash. U., 1985, MA in History, 1986. Tchr. Lake Chelan Sch. Dist., Chelan, Wash., 1986-94; author, pub. Point Pub., Manson, Wash., 1994—; adj. prof. City U., Bellevue, Wash., 1991-92. Author: Wapato Heritage: The History of the Chelan and Entiat Indians, 1995. Chmn. Tech. 2000 Com. Lake Chelan Sch. Dist., Chelan, 1993-94; mem. State WEDNET Com., Office Supt. of Pub. Instns., Olympia, Wash., 1993-94; mem. exec. com. State History Day, Ellensburg, Wash., 1987-89; bd. dirs. Lake Chelan Cmty. Hosp. Found., Chelan, 1991-93. Mem. Am. Registry Radiologic Technologists. Home: PO Box 355 Manson WA 98831-0355 Office: Point Pub PO Box 355 Manson WA 98831

HACKER, THOMAS OWEN, architect; b. Dayton, Ohio, Nov. 4, 1941; s. Homer Owen and Lydia (McLean) H.; m. Margaret (Brooks) Stewart, Mar. 21, 1965; children: Jacob, Sarah, Alice. BA, U. Pa., 1964, MArch, 1967. Registered arch., Oreg.; registered Nat. Coun. Archtl. Registration Bds. Intern architect Office of Louis I. Kahn, Phila., 1964-70; mem. faculty architecture U. Pa., Phila., 1967-69, U. Oreg., Eugene, 1970-84; design prin. Thomas Hacker and Assocs. Architects P.C., Portland, Oreg., 1983—; vis. profl. architecture, U. Oreg., 1985—. Prin. works include Biomed. Info. Comm. Ctr., Oreg. Health Scis. U. (Design Excellence award AIA), Sch. Nursing, Oreg. Health Scis. U. (Design Excellence award 1992, Regional Honor award AIA 1993), Portland Art Mus., High Desert Mus., Bend, Oreg.; designer crystal vase for Steuben Inc., Spokane Pub. Libr., Yellowstone Art Ctr., Billings, Mont., Lewis & Clark Coll. Signature Project, Multnomah County Midland Libr., Columbia Gorge Interpretive Ctr. Mem. Portland Design Commn., 1989—. Mem. AIA. Office: 34 NW 1st Ave Ste 406 Portland OR 97209-4017 Home: 2762 SW Montgomery Drive Portland OR 97201-1693

HACKETT, CAROL ANN HEDDEN, physician; b. Valdese, N.C., Dec. 18, 1939; d. Thomas Barnett and Zada Loray (Pope) Hedden; BA, Duke, 1961; MD, U. N.C., 1966; m. John Peter Hackett, July 27, 1968; children: John Hedden, Elizabeth Bentley, Susanne Rochet. Intern. Georgetown U. Hosp., Washington, 1966-67, resident, 1967-69; clinic physician DePaul Hosp., Norfolk, Va., 1969-71; chief spl. health services Arlington County Dept. Human Resources, Arlington, Va., 1971-72; gen. med. officer USPHS Hosp., Balt., 1974-75; pvt. practice family medicine, Seattle, 1975—; mem. staff, chmn. dept. family practice Overlake Hosp. Med. Ctr., 1985-86; clin. asst. prof. Sch. Medicine U. Wash. Bd. dirs. Mercer Island (Wash.) Preschool Assn., 1977-78; coordinator 13th and 20th Ann. Inter-profl. Women's Dinner, 1978, 86; trustee Northwest Chamber Orch., 1984-85. Mem. AAUW, Am. Acad. Family Practice, King County Acad. Family Practice (trustee 1993-96), King County Med. Soc. (chmn. com. TV violence), Wash. Acad. Family Practice, Wash. State Med. Soc., DAR, Bellevue C. of C., NW Women Physicians (v.p. 1978), Seattle Symphony League, Eastside Women Physicians (founder, pres.), Sigma Kappa, Wash. Athletic Club, Columbia Tower, Seattle Yacht Club. Episcopalian. Home: 4304 E Mercer Way Mercer Island WA 98040-3826 Office: 1414 116th Ave NE Bellevue WA 98004-3801

HACKETT, RALPH, agricultural products supplier; b. 1954. With Suma Fruit Internat., Phila., 1975-89; with Suma Fruit Internat. USA, 1989—, now CEO. Office: Suma Fruit International USA 1810 Academy Ave Sanger CA 93657-3739*

HACKLEY, CAROL ANN, public relations educator, consultant; b. Sacramento, Mar. 20, 1940; d. Charles Peter and Alice Marian (Schmidt) Cusick; m. William E. Hall, Sept. 1, 1966 (dec. Aug. 1991); children: Kevin Dennis, Kimberlee Marian Hall Floyd; m. T. Cole Hackley, Apr. 10, 1993. BA, Calif. State U., Sacramento, 1961; MA, Ohio State U., 1984, PhD, 1985. Pub. rels. dir., tchr. Lincoln Unified Schs., Stockton, Calif., 1961-63; advt. promotion copy writer, columnist Honolulu (Hawaii) Star-Bulletin, Hawaii Newspaper Agy., 1964; instr. U. Nebr., Lincoln, 1964-66, Ohio State U., Columbus, 1972-80, 82-85; exec. dir. Jour. Assn. Ohio Schs., Columbus, 1974-80, 82-85; asst. prof. U. Hawaii, Honolulu, 1980-82; assoc. prof. pub. rels. comm. dept. U. Pacific, Stockton, 1985—, chair comm. dept., 1992-94; pub. rels. cons. Hackley Ent. Inc., 1995—; sr. cons., ptnr. Kim Floyd Pub. Rels., 1996—; pub. rels. cons. Hall and Hall Prescriptive Pub. Rels., Stockton, 1987-91; prof.-in-residence Edelman Pub. Rels. Worldwide, Sydney, London and San Francisco, 1990—. Chmn. bd. Mountain Valley Multiple Sclerosis, Stockton, 1989-91. Mem. Pub. Rels. Soc. Am. (accredited, internat. sect., internat. pub. rels. exec. com. 1995, v.p. Oakland/East Bay chpt. 1994, del. nat. assembly 1995-97, pres.-elect 1997), Internat. Comm. Assn. Home: 2618 Sheridan Way Stockton CA 95207-3246 Office: Univ of the Pacific 3601 Pacific Cir Stockton CA 95211-0110

HACKMAN, VIDA BERNICE, artist; b. Bakersfield, Calif., Jan. 16, 1935; d. David Henry and Irma Louise (Pankratz) Ratzlaff; m. Kenneth Landis Hackman, Apr. 26, 1966; 1 child, Jonathan David. BA, U. Calif., Santa Barbara, 1956, MFA, 1967; MA, Calif. State U., Northridge, 1965. Instr. art West L.A. Coll., Culver City, Caif., 1969-77; part-time lectr. art Calif. State U., Northridge, 1978-83; vis. lectr. art U. Calif., Santa Cruz, 1983-85; adj. prof. Franklin and Marshall Coll., Lancaster, Pa., 1989; instr. art Bakersfield Coll., 1990-93; trustee Adobe Krow Archives, Bakersfield, 1993—; ptnr. Triad Graphic Workshop, North Hollywood, Calif., 1968-78; juror Calif. State Poly. U., Pomona, 1977, Carnegie Art Mus., Oxnard, Calif., 1987, L.A. Printmaking Soc., 1992, Faulkner Gallery, Santa Barbara, 1994; bd. dirs. Arts Coun. of Kern, 1996; guest lectr. U. Calif., Long Beach, 1980, Santa Barbara City Coll., 1979-80; lectr. Fresno (Calif.) Mus. Art Graphic Arts Coun., 1995; guest artist Douglass Coll., Rutgers U., 1988, Franklin and Marshall Coll., 1987, Black Dolphin Workshop, Calif. State U., Long Beach, 1977; artist-in-resident San Fernando Valley Arts Coun., Northridge, 1983. One woman shows include ADI Gallery, San Francisco, 1975, Coll. of St. Catherine, St. Paul, 1976, L.A. Louver Gallery, Venice, Calif., 1976, M. Shore & Son Gallery, Santa Barbara, 1979, Orlando Gallery, Sherman Oaks, Calif., 1984, 85, 87, 90, 92, 94, L.A. Valley Coll. Fine Arts Gallery, 1986, Soho 20, N.Y.C., 1986, Franklin and Marshall Coll. Fine Arts Gallery, 1988, Douglas Coll., Rutgers U., New Brunswick, N.J., 1988; exhibited in numerous group exhbns., including Achenbach Found., San Francisco, 1972, Santa Barbara Mus. Art, 1974, U. Calif., Riversde, 1975, Johnson Mus. Art, Cornell U., Ithaca, N.Y., 1976, Print Club, Phila., 1977, 82, Calif. State U., L.A., 1978, Long Beach, 1978, Occidental Coll., L.A., 1979, Artworks, Venice, 1980, U. Calif., Santa Cruz, 1983, Kauffmann Galleries, Houston, 1983, Long Beach Mus. Art, 1983, Otis Art Inst. of Parson Sch. Design, L.A., 1984, El Camino Coll. Gallery, Torrance, Calif., 1984, Brand Art Gallery, Glendale, Calif., 1985, Calif. State Poly. U., Pomona, 1985, Tex. Women's U., 1987, U. Wis. Milw. Art Mus. Fine Arts Gallery, 1987, Fla. State U. Fine Arts Gallery, Tallahassee, 1988, San Francisco Internat. Airport, 1988, San Antonio Art Inst., 1991, U. Tex., San Antonio, 1991, Armory Ctr. for Arts, Pasadena, Calif., 1992, Santa Monica Coll. Art Gallery, 1994, Rachele Lozzi Gallery, L.A., 1995, others; represented in permanent collections, including AT&T, N.Y.C. and Chgo., Calif. Exposition, Sacramento, Calif. State U., Long Beach and Northridge, Chase Manhattan Bank, N.Y.C., Coos Art Mus., Coos Bay, Oreg., numerous others. Recipient numerous awards for art, including Purchase award Libr. of Congress and Nat. Collection of Fine Arts, 1973, Cert. of Appreciation Woman's Bldg. Ann. Vesta Awards, 1984, award 2d N.H. Internat. Graphics Internat., 1974, James D. Phelan award in Printmaking, 1969; grantee Nat. Endowment for Arts, 1984. Mem. L.A. Printmaking Soc., Women's Caucus for Art, Coll. Art Assn. Democrat. Methodist. Office: Adobe Krow Archives 430 18th St Bakersfield CA 93308

HACKNEY, ROBERT WARD, plant pathologist, nematologist, parasitologist, molecular geneticist, commercial arbitrator; b. Louisville, Dec. 11, 1942; s. Paul Arnold and Ovine (Whallen) H.; m. Cheryl Lynn Hill, June 28, 1969 (div. Dec. 1995); 1 child, Candice Colleen; m. Jacqueline Monica Eisenreich, Dec. 27, 1995. BA, Northwestern U., 1965; MS, Murray State U., 1969; PhD, Kans. State U., 1973. Postgrad. rsch. nematologist U. Calif., Riverside, 1973-75; plant nematologist Calif. Dept. Food and Agr., Sacramento, 1975-85, sr. plant nematologist, supr. 1985-89, sr. plant nematologist, specialist, 1989—; comml. arbitrator Am. Arbitration Assn., 1980—; chmn. Calif. Nematode Diagnosis Adv. Commn., Sacramento, 1981—. Contbr. articles to profl. jours. Hon. dep. Sheriff, Sacramento, 1982-83. Served with USMC, 1966. NSF grantee, 1974. Mem. Soc. Nematologists, Internat. Council Study of Viruses and Virus Diseases of the Grape, Delta Tau Delta, Sigma Xi. Democrat. Baptist. Office: Calif Dept Food & Agriculture Plant Pest Diagnostic Ctr 3294 Meadowview Rd Sacramento CA 95832-1448

HACKWORTH, MARK STEVEN, chemical company executive; b. San Gabriel, Calif., Jan. 3, 1968; s. Gerald Wayne and Argentina (Sequira) H. AA in Liberal Arts, Mt. San Antonio Coll., Walnut, Calif., 1990; BS in Bus. and Mgmt., U. Redlands, 1996. Technician Nogales Pharmacy, Rowland Heights, Calif., 1986-87; owner, mgr. Champion Chem Dry, Walnut, 1988; small bus. cons. Dry-Fast, Phillips Ranch, Calif., 1991-94. Mem. Lé Tip.

HACKWORTH, THEODORE JAMES, JR., city official; b. Denver, Nov. 7, 1926; s. Theodore James and Thelma B. (Hill) H.; m. Doris Evelyn Larson, Dec. 31, 1947; children—James Robert, Joan Evelyn Grady, Linda Jean Hoffman. B.A., U. Denver, 1955. Sales mgr. Continental Baking Co., Denver, 1950-64; mktg. exec. Sigman Meat Co., Denver, 1964-76; v.p. sales Pierce Packing Co., Billings, Mont., 1976-79; city councilman City of Denver, 1979—, pres., 1983-84; cons. EPA. Mem. Denver pub. schs. bd. edn., 1971-77; dir. Urban Drainage and Flood Control Dist., 1981-84; dir. Met. Wastewater Reclamation Dist., 1982—, sec., 1984-85, chmn. elect 1988-89, chmn., 1989—; mem. Denver Regional Council Govts., 1979-94, vice chmn., 1981-83, chmn., 1984-86; neighborhood commr. Boy Scouts Am., 1968-69, Western Dist. commr., 1970-71; pres. Harvey Park Improvement Assn., 1969; chmn. Denver Met. Library Task Force, 1982. Served with USAF, 1945-47. Mem. Nat. Assn. Regional Council (bd. dirs. m., chmn. surface trans. task force, pres. 1987-89). Republican. Club: Mt. Vernon Country. Contbr. articles to EPA jours. Home: 3955 W Linvale Pl Denver CO 80236-2212 Office: 3110 S Wadsworth Blvd Ste 304 Denver CO 80227-4810

HADA, JOHN JUJI, East Asian international affairs educator; b. San Francisco, Apr. 16, 1927; s. Jutaro James and Katsuyo (Noma) H.; m. Mitzi Mutsumi Egusa, May 27, 1951; children: Elayne Naomi, Matthew Stuart Jun, Sterling Theodore, Leslie Anne. BA in Philosophy and History, U. San Francisco, 1972, MA in History, 1973, EdD in Edn., 1981; PhD in Anthrop. Linguistics, U. Tokyo, Japan, 1986. Col. U.S. Army, 1944-71; fgn. svc. officer Embassy of U.S.A., Tokyo, 1982-86; sr. Fulbright fellow Nat. Lang. Rsch. Inst., Tokyo, 1986-88; prof. Tohoku Nat. U., Sendai, Japan, 1988-93, U. San Francisco, 1993—, Coll. of Notre Dame, Belmont, Calif., 1994—; rschr. Ctr. for the Pacific Rim, U. San Francisco, 1993—. Author: The Anatomy of the All Japan Federation of Self-Governing Students: Its Evolution and Dimensions of Japanese Student Activism in the Postwar Period, Indictment and Trial of Iva Ikuko Toguri D'Aquino, 1973, The Romanization Movement of the Japanese Language During the Allied Occupation of Japan, 1981. Decorated D.S.C., Legion of Merit; recipient Dr. Edward J. Griffin award U. San Francisco Alumni Assn., 1996, Disting. Faculty award U. San Francisco, 1995. Mem. Nat. Japanese Am. Hist. Soc. (dir. 1994—). Democrat. Roman Catholic. Home: 1429 23rd Ave San Francisco CA 94122-3305 Office: U San Francisco 2130 Fulton St San Francisco CA 94117-1080

HADAS, ELIZABETH CHAMBERLAYNE, publisher; b. Washington, May 12, 1946; d. Moses and Elizabeth (Chamberlayne) H.; m. Jeremy W. Heist, Jan. 25, 1970 (div. 1976); m. Peter Eller, Mar. 21, 1984. A.B., Radcliffe Coll., 1967; postgrad. Rutgers U., 1967-68; M.A., Washington U., St. Louis, 1971. Editor U. N.Mex. Press, Albuquerque, 1971-85; dir., 1985—. Mem. Assn. Am. Univ. Presses (pres. 1992-93). Democrat. Home: 2900 10th St NW Albuquerque NM 87107-1111 Office: U New Mexico Press 1720 Lomas Blvd NE Albuquerque NM 87106-3807

HADDAD, EDMONDE ALEX, public affairs executive; b. Los Angeles, July 25, 1931; s. Alexander Saleeba and Madeline Angela (Zail) H.; m. Harriet Ann Lenhart; children: Mark Edmonde, Brent Michael, John Alex. AA, Los Angeles City Coll., 1956; BA, U. Southern Calif., 1958; MA, Columbia U., 1961. Staff writer WCBS Radio News, New York, 1959-61; news commentator, editor KPOL AM/FM Radio, Los Angeles, 1961-67, dir., pub. affairs, 1967-73; exec. dir. Los Angeles World Affairs Council, 1973-84; pres. L.A. World Affairs Coun., 1984-88; deputy asst. sec. of State for Pub. Diplomacy Dept. State, U.S. Govt., Wash., 1987-88; mem. steering com., moderator Conf. environ., L.A., 1989-90; pres. Nat. Coun. World Affairs Orgns., 1981-83; pres. Radio and TV News Assn. So. Calif., 1965-66; sr. fellow Ctr. Internat. Rels., U. Calif., L.A., 1991-94; bd. dirs. Pen Ctr. USA West. Contbg. author: How Peace Came to the World,, 1985; founder, pub. World Affairs Jour. Quar., 1981. Bd. dirs. PEN Ctr. USA West, 1994—, World Affairs Coun., Ventura County, 1995—. Recipient Am. Polit. Sci. Assn. award for Disting. Reporting of Pub. Affairs, 1967. Mem. Am. Assn. Ret. Persons (team mem. congl. dist. 23 AARP/Vote 1995—), Friends of Wilton Park (exec. com. So. Calif.), Brit. Fgn. Office Conf. Ctr. Democrat. Home: 582 Pacific Cove Dr Port Hueneme CA 93041-2175

HADDAD, EDWARD RAOUF, civil engineer, consultant; b. Mosul, Iraq, July 1, 1926; came to U.S., 1990.; s. Raouf Sulaiman Haddad and Fadhila (Sulaiman) Shaya; m. Balquis Yousef Rassam, July 19, 1961; children: Reem, Raid. BSc, U. Baghdad, Iraq, 1949; postgrad., Colo. State U., 1966-67; PhD (hon.), 1995. Project engr., cons. Min. Pub. Works, Baghdad, 1949-63; arbitrator Engring. Soc. & Ct., Kuwait City, Kuwait, 1963-90; tech. advisor Royal Family, Kuwait, 1987-90; cons. pvt. practice Haddad Engring., Albuquerque, 1990-95; owner, pres. Overseas Contacts-Internat. Bus. and Consulting, Albuquerque, 1995—; organizer reps abroad, Kuwait, 1990. Pres. Parents Assn., U. N.Mex., 1995. Recipient Hon. medal Pope Paul VI of Rome, 1973, Men of Achievement award Internat. Biog. Ctr., 1994. Mem. ASCE, NSPE, ABA (assoc.), Am. Arbitration Assn. (mem. adv. bd.), Sierra Cath. Internat. (trustee), Lions (bd. dirs. 1992), Inventors Club (bd. dirs. 1992), KC (chancellor 1992). Address: 143 General Arnold St NE Apt A Albuquerque NM 87123-2535

HADDAD, FARID SAMI, educator; b. N.Y.C., May 4, 1922; s. Sam Abraham and Lamia Nicholas (Morcos) H.; m. Huda F. Fawaz, Sept. 18, 1949; children: Sami, Ranwa, Ziad. BA, Am. U., 1941, MD, 1948. Intern Am. U. Hosp., Beirut, Lebanon, 1948-49; resident Orient Hosp., Beirut, Lebanon, 1949-50, Presbyn. Hosp., Chgo., 1951-53; asst. in urology U. Ill., Chgo., 1951-53; spl. fellow Meml. Hosp., N.Y.C., 1953-54; attending urologist, attending surgeon, chief of staff Orient Hosp., Beirut, 1957-74; attending urologist, attending surgeon Marj'uyun (Lebanon) Govt. Hosp., 1972-77; chief urologist, chief surgeon Obeid Hsop., Riyadh, Saudi Arabia, 1977-81, chief of staff, 1979-81; chief urology VA Med. Ctr., Phoenix, 1981-93; clin. assoc. prof. surgery U. Ariz., Tucson, 1987—. Author: Directory of Medical Alumni, 1957-67, The Prostate - Your Gland, 1963, Directory of AUB, 1967, Hadith from Omar, 2d edit., 1969, Medical Ethics Law, 1969, Bareme des honoraires chirurgicaux, 1970, Catalogue of Medical Manuscripts, 1984, Guide to Diagnostic Imaging Vol. 4, 1984, Vol. 5, 1984; editor: History of Arab Medicine, 1975; contbr. over 1100 articles to profl. jours. Mem. AMA, Atheneum of History of Medicine Buenos Aires (corr. mem.), Syrian Soc. History of Scis., Am. Assn. History of Sci., Maricopa County Med. Assn., Phoenix Urological Assn., Ariz. Med. Assn., Assn. VA Surgeons, Ariz. Urological Soc., Assn. Mil. Surgeons N.Am., History Sci. Soc., Arab Am. Med. Assn., Alpha Omega Alpha. Evangelical. Home and Office: 4332 E Piccadilly Rd Phoenix AZ 85018-5447

HADDAD, WISAM BOULOS, surgeon; b. Amman, Jordan, Mar. 4, 1954; came to U.S., 1973; s. Boulos Somail and Tammam Mufaddi (Hawatmeh) H.; m. Rozanne Charlie Carrubba, June 12, 1977; children: Angie, Laila, Laura. BS, Andrews U., 1976; MD, Loma Linda U., 1979. Diplomate Am. Bd. Surgery. Intern, resident in surgery Loma Linda (Calif.) U. Sch. Medicine, 1980-85, instr. Sch. Medicine, 1984-85, asst. prof. surgery, 1988—; assoc. in surgery Riverside (Calif.) Gen. Hosp., 1985-95, chmn. tumor bd., 1988-94; dir. trauma svcs. Riverside (Calif.) Gen. Hosp, 1994-95; spkr., lectr. to med. socs., med. convs., among others. Chmn. tobacco task force Am. Cancer Soc., Inland Empire, Calif., 1993-95. Fellow ACS; mem. Soc. Loma Linda U. Surgeons (pres. 1993-95). Home: 969 Talcey Ter Riverside CA 92506-7517 Office: Beaver Med Clinic 2 W Fern Ave Redlands CA 92373-5916

HADDIX, CHARLES E., legislative and regulatory consultant; b. Astoria, Oreg., Nov. 23, 1915; s. Charles H. and Mattie Lee (Wilson) H.; grad. U.S. Maritime Officers Sch., 1943; grad. in traffic mgmt. Golden Gate U., 1951; m. Betty Lee Wylie, Aug. 22, 1948; children: Bruce W., Anne C., C. Brian. Nat. sales mgr. Radio Sta. KLX, Oakland, Calif., 1953-55; West Coast mgr. Forjoe & Co., 1955-60; v.p. Calif. Spot Sales, 1958-60, Radio Calif., KLIP, Fowler, Calif., 1961-63; med. sales rep. Ives Labs., Inc., Sanger, Calif., 1964-73; state govt. rels. cons. Marion Merrill Dow Labs., Inc., 1973-87; Calif. legis. advocate, 1968-85; Ariz., Nev., N.Mex., Oreg., Wash., Idaho, Utah and Mont. legis. advocate, 1975-85. Mem. Central Calif. Forum on Refugee Affairs, 1983—, chmn. 1987-88, state forum chmn., 1988; mem. Calif. State Adv. Coun. on Refugee Assistance and Svcs., 1988-90; field cons. U.S. Sen. Alan Cranston, 1987-90, Calif. State Sen. Rose Ann Vuich, 1991-92; Refugee coord. Dooley for Congres Campaign, 1990, Bustamente for Assembly Campaign, 1993-94, Carter Ctr., Atlanta, 1994—;comm. Fresno County Econ. Opportunities Commn., 1992-93; mem. Clinton Presdl. Transition Planning Found., 1993; mem. U.S. Senate Staff Club, 1987-90; field cons. Assemblyman Cruz Bustamente; dist. rep. State Sen. Jim Costa, 1995—; dist. delegate Calif. Dem. 29th Assembly, 1997—; hon. mem. Dem. Nat. Com., 1997—. Author: Reminiscenses of an Old Astoria House, 1992, River Travel Memories on the Columbia, 1992, An Adventure in Dredging, 1993, The Astor Street Mystery, 1994. Served with Marina Mercante Nat., Republic of Panama, 1945, U.S. Mcht. Marine, 1939-41, USCG, 1942-45. Mem. U.S. Naval Inst., Ctrl. Tex. Geneaol. Soc., Historic Waco Found., Oreg. Hist. Soc., Manuscript Soc., Clatsop County Hist. Soc., Columbia River Maritime Mus., Am. Merchant Marine Vets. (ctrl. calif. chpt. 1994—, CEO 1994-96), Commonwealth Club of Calif. (San Francisco). Address: 3218 N Mccall Ave Sanger CA 93657-9385

HADGES, THOMAS RICHARD, media consultant; b. Brockton, Mass., Mar. 13, 1948; s. Samuel Charles and Ethel Toli (Prifti) H.; m. Beth Evelyn Rastad, Oct. 22, 1988. BA in Biology magna cum laude, Tufts U., 1969; student, Harvard Sch. Dental Med., 1969-71. Announcer Sta. WOKW, Brockton, 1965-67, Sta. WTBS-FM, MIT, Cambridge, 1966-68; announcer, program dir. Sta. WTUR, Medford, Mass., 1967-69; announcer Concert Network, Sta. WBCN-FM, Boston, 1968-78, program dir., 1977-78; program dir. Sta. WCOZ-FM, Blair Broadcasting, Boston, 1978-80, Sta. KLOS-FM, ABC, L.A., 1980-85; sr. programming advisor Pollack Media Group, Pacific Palisades, Calif., 1985-89, pres., 1989—; pres. Pollack/Hadges Enterprises, Pacific Palisades, 1985-89. Named Program Dir. of Yr., L.A. Times, 1981. Mem. Phi Beta Kappa. Office: Pollack Media Group 860 Via De La Paz Ste D2 Pacific Palisades CA 90272-3608

HADLEY, ELEANOR MARTHA, economist; b. Seattle, July 17, 1916; d. Homer More and Margaret Sarah (Floyd) H. BA, Mills Coll., 1938; MA, Radcliffe/Harvard U., 1943; PhD, Harvard U., 1949. Rsch. analyst Office Strategic Svcs., Washington, 1943-44; economist Dept. State, Washington, 1944-46, GHQ-SCAP, Tokyo, 1946-47; staff mem. Pres. Trumans Commn. Migratory Labor, Washington, 1950-51; assoc. prof. Smith Coll., Northampton, Mass., 1956-65; economist U.S. Tariff Commn., Washington, 1967-74; professorial lectr. George Washington U., Washington, 1972-84; group dir. internat. div. Gen. Acctg. Office, Washington, 1974-81; vis. scholar U. Washington, Seattle, 1984-94; class dean Smith Coll., Northampton, 1958-62; participant Occupation of Japan series Brit. Broadcasting Co., London, 1989; participant Power in the Pacific KCET, L.A. and Australian Broadcasting Co., 1989. Author: Antitrust in Japan, 1970; contbg. author: Political Power of Economic Ideas, 1989; contbr. to Kodansha Ency. of Japan; author articles. Vol., bd. dirs. Seattle Pub. Libr. Found., 1987—, Blakemore Found., 1995—. Recipient Sacred Treasure award Emperor of Japan, 1986; Fulbright rsch. scholar, Japan, 1962-64. Mem. Assn. for Asian Studies (regional coun. mem., dir. nat. orgn., bd. dirs., 1987-89, named Disting. Lectr. 1985), U. Wash. Mortar Bd. (hon. mem.). Home: 807 SW 207th Pl Seattle WA 98166-4163

HADLEY, JANE FRANCIS, family nurse practitioner; b. Fort Knox, Ky., Oct. 15, 1953; d. Richard Aloyisius and Mary Elizabeth (Davis) Walsh; m. P.C. McNamara, Dec. 20, 1975 (div. Jan. 1986); 1 child, Joel; m. William Melvin Hadley, Oct. 13, 1990. BSN, U. N.Mex., 1977; MSN, U. Tex., El Paso, 1986; cert. family nurse practitioner, Tex. Tech U. Health Scis. Ctr., 1995. RN, N.Mex. Staff nurse U. N.Mex. Hosp., Albuquerque, 1978-81; faculty Maternal Child U. Albuquerque, 1980; staff nurse Step-down Unit Presbyn. Hosp., Albuquerque, 1981; clin. faculty pediatrics Luna Vocat.-Tech. Inst., Las Vegas, N.Mex., 1982; from diabetes educator to rsch. coord. Lovelace Med. Ctr., Albuquerque, 1982-88; pharmacology faculty Diabetes Ctr. U. Va., Charlottesville, 1989; clin. educator St. Jospeh's Med. Ctr., Albuquerque, 1989-90; clin. nurse specialist Post Traumatic Stress Disorder Vet. Affairs Med. Ctr., Albuquerque, 1990-93, nurse mgr. Acute Psychiatric, 1993-95; family nurse practitioner Primary Care Clinic, 1995—. Grantee U.S. Govt., 1979-81, ANA, 1994-95. Mem. ANA (cert. family nurse practitioner, clin. nurse specialist, psychiat. adult mental health nurse), Am. Assn. Diabetes Educators (chpt. coun. chair 1986-87, bd. dirs. 1987-90, fin. com. chair 1987-90), Zia Assn. Diabetes Educators (pres. 1985-86), N.Mex. Nurses Assn. (com. 1992—, bd. dirs. 1995—). Home: 12712 Piru Blvd SE Albuquerque NM 87123-3825

HADLEY, PAUL BURREST, JR. (TABBIT HADLEY), chef services manager, photographer; b. Louisville, Apr. 26, 1955; s. Paul Burrest and Rose Mary (Ruckert) H. Grad. in Computer Ops. and Programming, No. Ky. Vocat. Sch., 1975. Floor mgr. reconciling dept. Cen. Trust Co., Cin., 1974-76; freelance photographer Ky., Ohio, Colo., 1975—; chef mgr. The Floradora, Telluride, Colo., 1978-96; pres. Tabbit Enterprises; freelance recipe writer, Telluride, 1978—. Author poetry (Golden Poet award 1989, Silver Poet award 1990); actor: (plays) Of Mice and Men, The Exercise, Crawling Arnold, A Thousand Clowns, The Authentic Life of Billy The Kid, others. Actor The Plunge Players, Telluride; v.p. Telluride Coun. for Arts and Humanities, 1989. Mem. Plan Internat. USA, Christian Children's Fund. Home: PO Box 923 Telluride CO 81435-0923

HADREAS, PETER JAMES, philosophy educator; b. San Diego, Apr. 22, 1945; s. James D. and Catherine (Mountanos) Hadreas. BA, U. Calif., Berkeley, 1966, MA, 1969, PhD, 1975. Lectr. U. Calif., Berkeley, 1978-86; assoc. prof. philosophy San Jose (Calif.) State U., 1986—; actor (stage play) One Flew Over the Cuckoo's Nest, San Francisco, 1970-75; composer, 20th Century Fox, L.A., 1979; assoc. dir. Inst. for Social Responsibility, San Jose, 1993. Author: In Place of Flawed Diamond, 1986; contbr. articles to profl. jours. Home: 155 Gardenside Dr Apt 31 San Francisco CA 94131-1389

HADSALL, DEBRA JUNE, business service and consulting executive; b. Wichita, Kans., Aug. 28, 1951; d. Doyle I. and June I. (Lonnon) Loveridge; m. Terry B. Hadsall; 1 child, Isaac J. Student, Kans. State U., Manhattan, 1969-72; BS in Bus. Adminstrn., Regis U., Denver, 1991. Program analyst in logistics and facilities planning Air Force Acctg. and Fin. Ctr., Denver, 1986-91; program analyst in planning Def. Fin. and Acctg. Svc., Denver, 1991-94; pres. Shared Visions, Inc., Aurora, Colo., 1993—; prin. Hadsall & Assocs, Aurora, 1996—. Vol. in strategic planning Cherry Creek (Colo.) Sch. Dist. Mem. Tech. Transfer Soc., Tech. Assocs. Colo. (bd. dirs.). Methodist. Office: 12273 E Bates Cir Aurora CO 80014-3309

HAERTEL, GENEVA DILUZIO, educational researcher; b. Hazleton, Pa., July 18, 1947; d. Daniel Anthony and Eva (Socker) DiLuzio; m. Edward Henry Haertel, July 12, 1975 (div. June 1991). BS in Edn., Kent State U., 1968, PhD in Edn., 1975. Cert. tchr. K-8, Ohio. Evaluator dept. rsch. and evaluation Chgo. Pub. Schs., 1975-77; rsch. assoc. Office Ednl. Rsch., U. Ill., Chgo., 1978-80; rsch. assoc. Ctr. Rsch. in Human Devel. & Edn., Temple U., Phila., 1985-88, sr. rsch. assoc. (part time) 1990—; rsch. assoc. (part time) RMC Rsch. Corp., Mountain View, Calif., 1990-91, Evaluation Ctr., Western Mich. U., Kalamazoo, 1991-94; cons. NSF, Washington, 1977-78, Office Ednl. Rsch. and Improvement, Dept. Edn., Washington, 1991, EREAPA Assocs., Livermore, Calif., 1993—, The Rebus Inst., Burlingame, Calif., 1994—. Author: (with Patricia Wheeler) Resource Handbook on Performance Assessment and Measurement, 1993, (with H.J. Walberg) Assessment Reform, Phi Delta Kappan Fastback, 1994. Mem. APA, ASCD, Am. Ednl. Rsch. Assn., Am. Evaluation Assn., Phi Delta Kappa. Home: 501 Forest Ave Apt 310 Palo Alto CA 94301-2613

HAFER, JOHN RICHARD, musician; b. Wyomissing, Pa., May 29, 1927; s. John Jacob and Kathryn Marie (Reifsynder) H.; m. Betty D. DiMascio, July 22, 1953; children: Timothy John, Lisa Marie. Grad., Wyomissing (Pa.) H.S., 1945. Musician Charles Barnet Orchestra, 1949-51, Woody Herman Orch., 1951-55, Claude Thornhill, 1952, Benny Goodman, N.Y.C., 1960-63; musician Merv Griffin Show, New York, 1965-71, L.A., 1971-82; Musician leader (CD rec.) Prez Impressions, In a Sentimental Mood. Recordings include Prez Impressions, In A Sentimental Mood, Charles Mingus Village Vanguard (2 CDs, Mingus The Saint and the Sinner Lady and Mingus, Mingus, Mingus), 1963. Mem. N.Y.C. Local 802, L.A. Local 47. Home: 10500 Reseda Blvd Northridge CA 91326-3129

HAFEY, EDWARD EARL JOSEPH, precision tool company executive; b. Hartford, Conn., June 7, 1917; s. Joseph Michael and Josephine (Pyne) H.; B.S. in Mech. Engring., Worcester Poly. Inst., 1940; postgrad. Johns Hopkins U., 1943, 44; m. Loyette Lindsey, Oct. 21, 1971; children—Joseph M., Barbara Hafey Beard, Edward F. Instr. dept. mech. enging. Worcester Tech. Inst., 1940-41; mgr. Comfort Air Inc., San Francisco, 1946-47; owner, mgr. Hafey Air Conditioning Co., San Pablo, Calif., 1947—, pres. Hafey Precision Tool, Inc., Laguna Beach, Calif., 1982—; cons. air conditioning U.S. Navy, C.E., Japan, Korea, Okinawa. Served to comdr. USNR, 1941-46. Registered profl. engr., Calif.; named Man of Year, San Pablo, 1962. Mem. Assn. Energy Engrs., Calif. Air Conditioning Service Engring. Soc., Am. Legion, Ret. Officers Assn., Sigma Alpha Epsilon. Republican. Roman Catholic. Clubs: Exchange of Laguna Beach, Marine's Meml. Office: PO Box 417 Laguna Beach CA 92652-0417

HAFNER-EATON, CHRIS, health services researcher, educator; b. N.Y.C., Dec. 9, 1962; d. Peter Robert and Isabelle (Freda) Hafner; m. James Michael Eaton, Aug. 9, 1986; children: Kelsey James, Tristen Lee. BA, U. Calif., San Diego, 1986; MPH, UCLA, 1988, PhD in Health Svcs., 1992. Cert. health edn. specialist; internat. bd. cert. lactation cons. Cons. dental health policy UCLA Schl. Dentistry, 1989; grad. teachng asst. UCLA Sch. Pub. Health, 1987-92; health svcs. researcher UCLA, 1987-92; cons. health policy U.S.

Dept. Health & Human Svcs., Washington, 1988—; analyst health policy The RAND/UCLA Ctr. Health Policy Study, Santa Monica & L.A., 1988-94; asst. prof. health care adminstrn. Oreg. State U. Dept. Pub. Health, Corvallis, 1992-95; pres. Health Improvement Svcs. Corp., 1994—; dir. rsch. rev. La Leche League Internat., 1996—; adj. faculty pub. health Linn-Benton Coll., 1995—; bd. dirs. Benton County Pub. Health Bd., Healthy Start Bd.; mem. Linn-Benton Breastfeeding Task Force, Samaritan Mother-Baby Dyad Team, Am. Public Hlth. Assn. (sect. Council Med. Care). Contbr. articles to profl. jours. Rsch. grantee numerous granting bodies, 1988-94. Mem. AAUW, NOW, La Leche League Internat. (area profl. liaison for Oreg.), AM. Pub. Health Assn. (med. care sect., women's caucus), Am. Assn. World Health, Oreg. Pub. Health Assn., Oreg. Health Care Assn., Assn. Health Svcs. Rsch., Soc. Pub. Health Edn., Physicians for Social Responsibility, UCLA Pub. Health Alumni Assn., Delta Omega. Home: 1807 NW Beca Ave Corvallis OR 97330-2636

HAGA, ENOCH JOHN, computer educator, author; b. L.A., Apr. 25, 1931; s. Enoch and Esther Bouncer (Higginson) H.; student Sacramento Jr. Coll., 1948-49; AA, Grant Tech. Coll., 1950; student U. Colo., Denver, 1950, U. Calif., Berkeley, 1954, Midwestern U., 1950-54; AB, Sacramento State Coll., 1955, MA, 1958; PhD, Calif. Inst. Integral Studies, 1972, diploma tchr. Asian Culture, 1972; m. Elna Jo Wright, Aug. 22, 1957. Tchr. bus. Calif. Med. Facility, Vacaville, 1956-60; asst. prof. bus. Stanislaus State Coll., Turlock, Calif., 1960-61; engring. writer, publs. engr. Hughes Aircraft Co., Fullerton, Calif., 1961-62, Lockheed Missiles & Space Co., Sunnyvale, Calif., 1962, Gen. Precision, Inc., Glendale, Calif., 1962-63; sr. adminstrv. analyst Holmes & Narver, Inc., L.A., 1963-64; tchr., chmn. dept. bus. and math. Pleasanton Unified Dist., Pleasanton, Calif., 1964-92, coordinator computer svcs., adminstrn. and instrn., 1984-85; vis. asst. prof. bus. Sacramento State Coll., 1967-69; instr. bus. and computer sci. Chabot Coll., Hayward, Calif., 1970-89; instr. bus. and philosophy Ohlone Coll., Fremont, Calif., 1972; prof., v.p., mem. bd. govs. Calif. Inst. Asian Studies, 1972-75; pres., prof. Pacific Inst. East-West Studies, San Francisco, 1975-76, also mem. bd. govs.; dir. Certification Councils, Livermore, Calif., 1975-80; mem., chmn. negotiating team Amador Valley Secondary Educators Assn., Pleasanton, Calif., 1976-77, pres., 1984-85. With USAF, 1949-52, with USNR, 1947-49, 53-57. Mem. Internat. Assn. for Computer Information Systems (exec. dir. 1970-74). Coordinating editor Total Systems, 1962; editor Automation Educator, 1965-67, Automated Educational Systems, 1967, Data Processing for Education, 1970-71, Computer Techniques in Biomedicine and Medicine, 1973; contbg. editor Jour. Bus. Edn., 1961-69, Data Processing mag., 1967-70; author and compiler: Understanding Automation, 1965; author: Simplified Computer Arithmetic, Simplified Computer Logic, Simplified Computer Input, Simplified Computer Flowcharting, 1971-72, Before the Apple Drops, 15 Essays on Dinosaur Education, 1994, Exploring Prime Numbers on Your PC, 1994, TAROsolution, A Complete Guide to Interpreting the Tarot, 1994, The 2000-Year History of the Haga-Helgøy and Krick-Keller Families, Ancestors and Descendants, 1994; editor Data Processor, 1960-62, Automedica, 1970-76, FBE Bull., 1967-68. Home: 983 Venus Way Livermore CA 94550-6345

HAGAN, ALFRED CHRIS, federal judge; b. Moscow, Idaho, Jan. 27, 1932; s. Alfred Elias and Irene Lydia (Wells) H.; m. Doreen M. Auve, July 10, 1953; children: Chris E., Martha Ann, Peter M. BA, U. Idaho, 1953, JD, 1958. Bar: Idaho 1958, U.S. Dist. Ct. Idaho 1958. Asst. atty. gen. State of Idaho, Boise, 1958, dist. judge, 1967-77; dep. pros. atty. Ada County, Boise, 1959; pvt. practice Boise, 1960-67, 77-84; U.S. bankruptcy judge Dist. of Idaho, Boise, 1985—. 1st lt. USAF, 1953-55. Mem. Nat. Conf. Bankruptcy Judges. Office: MSC 040 550 W Fort St Boise ID 83724-0101

HAGAN, RICHARD FRANCIES, computer system educator; b. Austin, Minn., June 11, 1949; s. Milo F. and Ardella D. (Anderson) H.; m. Betty J. Manthey, Aug. 16, 1980 (div. Mar. 1992); children: Linda, Carl, Ken, Ty, Terry, Gary, Francies. BS, Mankato State U., 1986, MBA, 1991. Driver Wild Bus Svc., Austin, 1968-69, Austin Cab Co., 1969-73; truck driver Armstrong Reality, So. St. Paul, 1973-75, mechanic, 1975-77, shop foreman, 1977-80; driver Midtown Auto Clinic, 1981-94; instr. computer systems Rasmussen Bus. Coll., Mankato, Minn., 1986-93, Mankato (Minn.) State U., 1994; instr. computer info. syss. San Juan Coll., Farmington, N. Mex., 1994—. Home: 3802 English Rd Apt F7 Farmington NM 87402 Office: San Juan Coll 4601 College Blvd Farmington NM 87402-4609

HAGE, STEPHEN JOHN, radiology administrator, consultant; b. Chgo., July 22, 1943; s. Steve and Irene (Lewandowski) H.; m. Constance Louise Simonis, June 10, 1967. AAS, YMCA C.C., Chgo., 1970. Registered radiol. tech. Staff tech. Highland Park (Ill.) Hosp., 1966-68; chief radiotherapy tech. VA Hines (Ill.) Hosp., 1968-70; chief radiology tech. Gottlieb Meml. Hosp., Melrose Park, Ill., 1970-71; radiology adminstr. S. Chgo. Cmty. Hosp., 1971-79; adminstrv. dir. radiology Cedars-Sinai Med. Ctr., L.A., 1979-93; CEO HumiPerfect Co., Chatsworth, Calif., 1994—; cons. Computer Sci. Corp., El Segundo, Calif., 1983—. Contbr. articles to profl. jours. Served with USMC, 1961-64. Recipient 1st pl. Essay award Ill. State Soc. Radiol. Technicians, 1966. Mem. Am. Hosp. Radiology Adminstrs. (charter), Am. Soc. Radiol. Technologists, AAAS, Phi Theta Kappa. Home and Office: HumiPerfect 22115 Halsted St Chatsworth CA 91311-4027

HAGEMAN, JAMES C., rancher; b. Douglas, Wyo., Mar. 2, 1930; s. Fred August and Ruth (Shaw) H.; m. Marion Malvin, May 19, 1956; children: Julia Newman, James P., Rachel Rubino, Hugh, Harriet Dewey, Ted Yellowwolf. Owner, operator ranch Ft. Laramie, Wyo., 1961—. Chair edn. com. Wyo. Ho. of Reps., Cheyenne, 1990—; chmn. sch. bd. exec. com. Wyo. tockgrows, Torrington. Republican. Home: HC 72 Box 340 Fort Laramie WY 82212-9601

HAGEN, DAVID W., judge; b. 1931. BBA, U. Wis., 1956; LLB, U. San Francisco, 1959. Bar: Washoe County 1981, Nev. 1992. With Berkley, Randall & Harvey, Berkeley, Calif., 1960-62; pvt. practice Loyalton, Calif., 1962-63; with Guild, Busey & Guild (later Guild, Hagen and Clark Ltd. and Guild & Hagen Ltd.), Reno, 1963-93; judge U.S. Dist. Ct. Nev., Reno, 1993—; lectr U. Nev., 1968-72; acting dean Nev. Sch. of Law, 1981-83, adj. prof., 1981-87; mem. Nev. Bd. Bar Examiners, 1972-91, chmn., 1989-91; chmn. Nev. Continuing Legal Edn. Com., 1967-75; mem. Nev. Uniform Comml. Code Com. S/sgt. USAF, 1949-52. Mem. ABA, Nev. Bar Assn., Calif. Bar Assn., Washoe County Bar Assn., Am. Coll. Trial Lawyers (state chmn. 1983-85), U.S. Supreme Ct. Hist. Soc., Nat. Maritime Hist. Soc., U.S. Rowing Assn., U.S. Sailing Assn., Vets. Fgn. Wars. Office: US Dist Ct Fed Bldg & US Courthouse 400 S Virginia St Reno NV 89501

HAGEN, JEFFREY AUGUST, thoracic surgeon; b. Milw., Oct. 1, 1959; s. Francis Dale and Darleen Marie (Day) H.; m. Mary Kathleen Slevin, June 16, 1984; children: Kaitlin Marie, Daniel August, Madison Margaret, Alexander Spalding. BS in Math., Creighton U., 1982, MD, 1986. Diplomate Am. Bd. Surgery, Am. Bd. Thoracic Surgery. Intern surgery Creighton U., Omaha, Nebr., 1986-87; resident surgery Creighton U., Omaha, 1987-91; esophageal surgery fellow U. So. Calif. Med. Ctr., L.A., 1991-92; thoracic surgery fellow Barnes Hosp. Washington U., St. Louis, 1992-94; asst. prof. surgery U. So. Calif., L.A., 1994—. Fellow Am. Coll. Surgeons, Soc. Thoracic Surgeons. Office: U So Calif Dept Surgery 1510 San Pablo St Ste 415 Los Angeles CA 90033-4586

HAGEN, KIRK DEE, mechanical engineer, educator; b. Ogden, Utah, July 12, 1953; s. Darius and Ellen Virginia (Hicks) H.; m. Jan Rowley, June 9, 1978; children: Kathryn, Jennifer, Alec, Daniel. BS in Physics, Weber State Coll., Ogden, 1977; MSME, Utah State U., 1981; PhD in Mech. Engring., U. Utah, 1989. Sr. engr. Hercules Aerospace, Magna, Utah, 1980-86; prin. engr. Unisys Corp., Salt Lake City, 1986-92; assoc. prof. mech. engring. tech. Weber State U., Ogden, 1993—; adj. prof. engring. Salt Lake C.C., Salt Lake City, 1991-93. Contbr. articles to profl. jours. Blazer scoutleader Boy Scouts Am., Centerville, Utah, 1990-91. Mem. ASME, ASHRAE, Am. Soc. Engring. Edn., Boy Scouts Am. (varsity scoutleader), N.Y. Acad. Scis., Sigma Xi. Mem. LDS Ch. Home: 582 N 220 E Centerville UT 84014-1836 Office: Weber State U Ogden UT 84408

HAGENBUCH, JOHN JACOB, investment banker; b. Park Forest, Ill., May 31, 1951; s. David Brown and Jean Iline (Reeves) H.; m. Christy Ann Nichols; children: Henry, Hunter, Hilary, Hunter Scott, Will. AB magna cum laude, Princeton U., 1974; MBA, Stanford U., 1978. Assoc., Salomon Bros., N.Y.C., 1978-80, v.p., San Francisco, 1980-85; gen. ptnr. Hellman & Friedman, 1985-93; owner, John J. Hagenbuch & Co., San Francisco, 1993—; gen. ptnr. M&H Realty Ptnrs., L.P., 1993—; bd. dirs. AOF II, Inc. Bd. govs. San Francisco Symphony, Town Sch. for Boys. Mem. Burlingame Country Club, Pacific-Union Club, Calif. Tennis Club, Villa Taverna Club, Menlo Circus Club. Office: M&H Realty Ptnrs Ste 2160 353 Sacramento St San Francisco CA 94111

HAGENS, WILLIAM JOSEPH, state official, public health educator; b. Bay City, Mich., June 3, 1942; s. Francis Bernard and Lillian May (O'Neill) H.; m. Noel Scantlebury, Apr. 15, 1967; children: Clara O'Neill, Nicholas Barlow. BA, Saginaw Valley Coll., 1969; MA, Wayne State U., 1971. Mem. adj. faculty Wayne State U., Detroit, 1971; VISTA vol. Pierce County Legal Assistance, Tacoma, 1971-73; sr. policy analyst Wash. Ho. of Reps., Olympia, 1974—; instr. Pacific Luth. U., Tacoma, 1979-81; clin. prof. Sch. Pub. Health U. Wash., Seattle, 1984—, mem. vis. com. Sch. Nursing, 1993; mem. health policy project George Washington U., Washington, 1985—; bd. dirs. Area Health Edn. Ctr., Seattle, 1988-90; mem. Nat. Acad. State Health Policy, 1990—; mem. adv. com. Wast. State Ctr. Health Stats.; mem. Nat. Conf. State Legislatures' Forum for Health Policy Leadership. Contbg. author: Analyzing Poverty Policy, 1975. Participant AIDS symposium Pasteur Inst., Paris, 1987. Recipient Pres. award Wash. State Pub. Health Assn., 1986, Animal award Wash. State Pub. Health Assn., 1994; NIMH fellow, 1979, WHO internat. travel fellow, 1992. Mem. Am. Pub. Health Assn., Am. Polit. Sci. Assn., Policy Studies Orgn., English Speaking Union, World Affairs Coun., Pi Sigma Alpha. Home: 3214 N 27th St Tacoma WA 98407-6208 Office: Wash State Ho of Reps PO Box 40600 Olympia WA 98504-0600

HAGENSTEIN, WILLIAM DAVID, forester, consultant; b. Seattle, Mar. 8, 1915; s. Charles William and Janet (Finigan) H.; m. Ruth Helen Johnson, Sept. 2, 1940 (dec. 1979); m. Jean Kraemer Edson, June 16, 1980. BS in Forestry, U. Wash., 1938; MForestry, Duke, 1941. Registered profl. engr., Wash., Oreg. Field aid in entomology U.S. Dept. Agr., Hat Creek, Calif., 1938; logging supt. and engr. Eagle Logging Co., Sedro-Woolley, Wash., 1939; tech. foreman U.S. Forest Svc., North Bend, Wash., 1940; forester West Coast Lumbermen's Assn., Seattle and Portland, Oreg., 1941-43, 45-49; sr. forester FEA, South and Central Pacific Theaters of War and Costa Rica, 1943-45; mgr. Indsl. Forestry Assn., Portland, 1949-80; exec. v.p. Indsl. Forestry Assn., 1956-80, hon. dir., 1980-87; pres. W.D. Hagenstein and Assocs., Inc., Portland, 1980—; H.R. MacMillan lectr. forestry U. B.C., 1952, 77; Benson Meml. lectr. U. Mo., 1966; S.J. Hall lectr. indsl. forestry U. Calif. at Berkeley, 1973; cons. forest engr. USN, Philippines, 1952, Coop. Housing Found., Belize, 1986; mem. U.S. Forest Products Trade Mission, Japan, 1968; del. VII World Forestry Congress, Argentina, 1972, VIII Congress, Indonesia, 1978; mem. U.S. Forestry Study Team, West Germany, 1974; mem. sec. Interior's Oreg. and Calif. Multiple Use Adv. Bd., 1975-76; trustee Wash. State Forestry Conf., 1948-92, Keep Oreg. Green Assn., 1957—, v.p., 1970-71, pres., 1972-73; adv. trustee Keep Wash. Green Assn., 1957-95; co-founder, dir. World Forestry Ctr., 1965-89, v.p., 1965-79; hon. Dir. for Life, 1990. Author: (with Wackerman and Michell) Harvesting Timber Crops, 1966; Assoc. editor: Jour. Forestry, 1946-53; columnist Wood Rev., 1978-82; contbr. numerous articles to profl. jours. Trustee Oreg. Mus. Sci. and Industry, 1968-73. Served with USNR, 1933-37. Recipient Hon. Alumnus award U. Wash. Foresters Aumni Assn., 1965, Forest Mgmt. award Nat. Forest Products Assn., 1968, Western Forestry award Western Forestry and Conservation Assn., 1972, 79, Gifford Pinchot medal for 50 yrs. Outstanding Svc., Soc. Am. Foresters, 1987, Charles W. Ralston award Duke Sch. Forestry, 1988, Lifetime Achievement award Oreg. Soc. Am. Foresters, 1995. Fellow Soc. Am. Foresters (mem. coun. 1958-63, pres. 1966-69, Golden Membership award 1989); mem. Am. Forestry Assn. (life, hon. v.p. 1966-69, 74-92, William B. Greeley Forestry award 1990), Commonwealth Forestry Assn. (life), Internat. Soc. Tropical Foresters, Portland C. of C. (forestry com. 1949-79, chmn. 1960-62), Nat. Forest Products Assn. (forestry adv. com. 1949-80, chmn. 1972-74, 78-80), West Coast Lumbermen's Assn. (v.p. 1969-79), David Douglas Soc. Western N. Am., Lang Syne Soc., Hoo Hoo Club, Xi Sigma Pi (outstanding alumnus Alpha chpt. 1973). Republican. Home: 3062 SW Fairmount Blvd Portland OR 97201-1439 Office: 921 SW Washington St Ste 803 Portland OR 97205-2826

HAGERDON, KATHY ANN (KAY HAGERDON), electric power industry executive; b. Fremont, Ohio, Mar. 20, 1956; d. Willis Harold and Lillian Mae (Bahnsen) Lehmann; m. Michael Lee Hagerdon, Apr. 21, 1979; children: Patrick Michael, Robert Joseph, Andrew Richard. BSBA, Ohio State U., 1978; MBA, Ashland U., 1991. Budget analyst Small Motors divsn. Westing House, Bellefontaine, Ohio, 1978-80; fin. analyst Aerospace Elec. divsn. Westing House, Lima, Ohio, 1980-82, fin. cost analyst, 1982-85; sr. fin. analyst Elec. Sys. divsn. Westing House, Lima, 1985-91, lead profl., 1991-92; sr. fin. analyst Sund Strand Electric Power Sys., Lima, 1992-96; plant controller Sund Strand Electric Power Sys., Phoenix, 1996—; chmn. supervisory com. Westing House Credit Union, 1991-94; part-time prof. Tiffin U., Lima, 1994-96, Northwestern Bus. Coll., Lima, 1994-95. Mem. Inst. Mgmt. Accts. (v.p. membership 1994-96), Toastmasters Internat. (pres. 1993-95, Com. award 1991). Roman Catholic. Home: 12232 N 40th Dr Phoenix AZ 85029

HAGGARD, JOEL EDWARD, lawyer; b. Portland, Oreg., Oct. 10, 1939; s. Henry Edward and Kathryn Shirley (O'Leary) H.; m. Mary Katherine Daley, June 8, 1968; children: Kevin E., Maureen E., Cristin E. BSME, U. Notre Dame, 1961; M in Nuclear Engring., U. Okla., 1963; JD, U. Wash., 1971. Bar: Wash. 1971, U.S. Dist. Ct. (we. dist.) Wash. 1971, U.S. Ct. Appeals (9th cir.) 1971, U.S. Supreme Ct. 1971. Nuclear engr. Westinghouse Corp. Bettis Atomic Power Lab., Pitts., 1963-67; research engr. aerospace div. The Boeing Co., Seattle, 1968; engr., mgmt. cons. King County Dept. Pub. Works, Seattle, 1969-71; assoc. Houghton, Cluck, Coughlin & Riley, Seattle, 1971-74, ptnr., 1975-76; pvt. practice law Seattle, 1977, 85—; ptnr. Haggard, Tousley & Brain, Seattle, 1978-84; judge marriage tribunal, Archdiocese of Seattle, 1975-90; chmn. Columbia River Interstate Compact Commn., 1975—; arbitrator King County Superior Ct., 1986—. Contbr. articles to profl. jours. Past trustee, mem. exec. com., past sec. Seattle Symphony. Mem. ABA, Wash. Bar Assn. (past chmn. environ. law sect., fee arbitration com., past mem. rules of profl. conduct com.), Seattle-King County Bar Assn., Rainier Club, Wash. Athletic Club, Astoria Golf and Country Club, Magnolia Cmty. Club (past pres., bd. dirs.). Office: 1200 5th Ave #1200 Seattle WA 98101-1127

HAGGERSON, NELSON LIONEL, JR., education educator; b. Silver City, N.Mex., June 11, 1927; s. Nelson L. and Gladys Lenore (Jackson) H.; m. B. Kate Baldwin, June 1, 1949; children: Patrick, Frederick, Teresa, Rebecca, Lionel, Mary. BA, Vanderbilt U., 1949; MS, Western N.Mex. U., 1952; PhD, Claremont Grad. U., 1960. Cert. secondary tchr.; cert. adminstr. Dir. Exptl. Sch. Webster Coll., Webster Groves, Mo.; asst. prof. edn. Western N.Mex. U., Silver City; prin. Cobre High Sch., Bayard, N.Mex.; prof. emeritus edn. Ariz. State U., Tempe; vis. prof. U. West Indies, St. Augustine, Trinidad and Tobago, 1993-97, U. Pitts., 1982, 91, 92, R.I. Coll., 1991, Western N.Mex. U., 1988, 97. Author: Secondary Education Today, 1967, To Dance With Joy, 1971, Naturalistic Research Paradigms: Theory and Practice, 1983, Informing Educational Policy and Practice Through Interpretive Inquiry, 1992, From Geronimo's Lookout, Growing Up and Living in the Southwest: An Autobiography, 1993, Oh Yes I Can!, A Biography of Arlena Seneca, 1994, also 11 book chpts.; guest editor: Education in Asia, Silver Ann Edit., World Coun. Curriculum and Instrn., Winter, 1995; contbr. over 50 articles to profl. jours. With USN, 1945-46. Fulbright fellow, 1986; recipient Award in Curriculum, MacDonald, 1986; named Outstanding Researcher, Coll. Edn., 1987, Outstanding Tchr., 1988; Rsch. grantee Deakin U., Victoria, Australia, 1988. Mem. AERA, ASCD, Profs. Curriculum, Soc. for Study of Curriculum History, World Coun. for Curriculum and Instrn. (program chmn. 1989), Phi Delta Kappa, Phi Kappa Phi, Kappa Delta Pi. Home: PO Box 24177 Tempe AZ 85285-4177

HAGGERTY, CHARLES A., electronics executive. Student, U. St. Thomas. Pres., chief exec. officer, chmn. bd. dirs. IBM, 1964-92; pres., COO Western Digital Corp., Irvine, Calif., 1992-96. Office: Western Digital Corp PO Box 19665 8105 Irvine Ctr Dr Irvine CA 92718*

HAGLUND, THOMAS ROY, research biologist, consultant, educator; b. Beloit, Wis., Jan. 19, 1950; s. Roy Wilhelm and Marguerite Jean (Anderson) H.; m. Doris Anne Mendenhall, Oct. 22, 1988. BS in Earth Sci., U. Wash., 1972; postgrad., U. Ill., Chgo., 1972-74; PhD in Biology, UCLA, 1981. Lectr., biology Calif. State Univ., L.A., 1981-83; sci. chair Windward Sch., L.A., 1983—; rsch. biologist UCLA, L.A., 1985—; adj. prof. biology Calif. State Poly. U., Pomona, 1991—; cons. U.S. Army C.E., L.A., 1979-80, Calif. Dept. Fish and Game, 1986—, Met. Water Dist., L.A., 1991, 93, 94, Dept. Pub. Works, Los Angeles County, 1991, 94—, U.S. Fish Wildlife Svc., 1992—; sec. So. Calif. Native Fishes Working Group, 1996—. Contbr. chpt. to Historical Biogeography of North American Fish, 1991; contbr. articles to Jour. paleontology, Evolution Paleobiology, Biochem. Systematics Ecology, Copeia. Grantee NSF, 1978, Calif. Dept. Fish and Game, 1986, 87, 90, 91, 92, 93, 94. Mem. AAAS, Am. Soc. Ichthyology and Herpetology, Am. Fisheries Soc., Desert Fishes Coun. Office: UCLA Dept Biology Los Angeles CA 90024-1606 also: Windward Sch 11350 Palms Blvd Los Angeles CA 90066-2104

HAGMAN, JEAN CASSELS, museum publisher, writer; b. Des Moines, Sept. 17, 1947; d. Harlan Lawrence and Mary Anna (Cassels) H. BA in Art History, Mich. State U., 1969; MA in Art History, Wayne State U., 1971; grad., Mus. Mgmt. Inst., 1990. Dir. edn. Grand Rapids (Mich.) Art Mus., 1970-78; dir. pub. rels. programs, edn. Flint (Mich.) Inst. Arts, 1978-81; v.p. edn. Philbrook Art Mus., Tulsa, Okla., 1981-84; prin. Hagman & Assocs., Tulsa, 1984-87; exec. dir. Mus. of S.W., Midland, Tex., 1987-92, Okla. City Art Mus., 1992-94; exec. dir., editor Mus. Info. Svcs., Denver, 1995—. Author: Museum Volunteers: The 4th Dimension, 1985; (booklet) Museum Trustees: An Orientation, 1985; editor (mus. info. svcs.) Quarterly; contbr. articles to profl. jours. V.p. adv. bd. Tulsa County Childrens Svcs., 1983-86; active tourism com. Midland C. of C., 1990-92. Mem. South Metro Denver C. of C., Ind. Pubs. Group. Episcopalian. Office: Mus Info Svcs PO Box 6540 Denver CO 80206

HAGMAN, RICHARD HARLAN, minerals company executive; b. Hinsdale, Ill., May 24, 1946; s. Harlan Lawrence and Mary (Cassels) H.; m. Sandra Lynn Joyner, Sept. 7, 1968; children—Jeffrey Carl, Elizabeth Mary. BA (with honors), Wayne State U., 1969; A.M., U. Chgo., 1973, Ph.D., 1977. Asst. to chmn. grad. dept. edn. U. Chgo., 1976-78; asst. dean Coll. Arts and Scis. Northwestern U., Evanston, Ill., 1978; adminstrv. dir. Grad.Sch. of Pub. Policy, U. Chgo., 1979-81; sr. political econ. research analyst Amoco Corp., Chgo., 1982, sr. pub. and govt. affairs advisor, Denver, 1983-85; v.p. pub., govt. and investor rels. Cyprus Minerals Co., Englewood, Colo., 1985-93, corp. officer, Cyprus Minerals Co, 1994, prin. Mountain Minerals Internat., 1994—, pres. CEO, R H Hagman & Co. Corp. Fin. & Operational Strategies, prin. The Furlong Group, CEO Strategic Coaching, 1996—. Served with U.S. Army, 1969-71. Office: 5445 DTC Pkwy #1000 Englewood CO 80111

HAHN, BETTY, artist, photographer, educator; b. Chgo., Oct. 11, 1940; d. Eugene Joseph and Esther Josephine (Krueger) H.; widowed. A.B., Ind. U., 1963, M.F.A., 1966. Asst. prof. photography Rochester (N.Y.) Inst. Tech., 1969-75; prof. art U. N.Mex., Albuquerque, 1976—. One-woman shows include Smithsonian Instn., Washington, 1969, Ctr. Photographic Studies, Louisville, 1971, Focus Gallery, San Francisco, 1974, Sandstone Gallery, Rochester, N.Y., 1978, Blue Sky Gallery, Portland, Oreg., 1978, Susan Spiritus Gallery, Newport Beach, Calif., 1977, 82, Witkin Gallery, N.Y.C., 1973, 79, Washington Project for the Arts, 1980, Ctr. Creative Photography, Tucson, 1981, Columbia Coll. Gallery, Chgo., 1982, Port Washington Pub. Library, N.Y., 1984, Mus. Fine Arts, Mus. N.Mex, Santa Fe, 1986, Lehigh U., 1988, U. Mass., Amherst, 1989, Andrew Smith Gallery, Santa Fe, 1991, U. N.Mex. Art Mus., Albuquerque, 1994. Named Honored Educator, Soc. for Photog. Edn., 1984; Nat. Endowment Arts grantee, 1977-78, 82-83; N.Y. State Council Arts grantee, 1976. Mem. Soc. Photog. Edn., Coll. Art Assn., Evidence Photographers Internat. Council. Office: Univ N Mex Art Dept Albuquerque NM 87131

HAHN, ELLIOTT JULIUS, lawyer; b. San Francisco, Dec. 9, 1949; s. Leo Wolf and Sherry Marion (Portnoy) H; m. Toby Rose Mallen; children: Kara Rebecca, Brittany Atira Mallen, Michael Mallen, Adam Mallen. BA cum laude, U. Pa., 1971, JD, 1974; LLM, Columbia U., 1980. Bar: N.J. 1974, Calif. 1976, D.C. 1978, U.S. Dist. Ct. N.J. 1974, U.S. Dist. Ct. (cen. dist.) Calif. 1976, U.S. Supreme Ct. 1980. Assoc. von Maltitz, Derenberg, Kunin & Janssen, N.Y.C., 1974-75; law clk. L.A. County Superior Ct., 1975-76; atty. Atlantic Richfield Co., L.A., 1976-79; prof. Summer in Tokyo program Santa Clara Law Sch., 1981-83; assoc. prof. law Calif. Western Sch. Law, San Diego, 1980-85; atty. Morgan, Lewis & Bockius, L.A., 1985-87; assoc. Whitman & Ransom, L.A., 1987-88, ptnr., 1989-93; ptnr. Sonnenschein Nath & Rosenthal, L.A., 1993—; vis. scholar Nihon U., Tokyo, 1982; vis. lectr. Internat. Christian U., Tokyo, 1982; adj. prof. law Southwestern U. Sch. Law, 1986—, Pepperdine U. Law Sch., 1986—; lectr. U. Calif., Davis, Law Sch. Orientation in U.S.A. Law Program, 1994—. Author: Japanese Business Law and the Legal System, 1984; contbr. chpt. on Japan to The World Legal Ency.; internat. law editor Calif. Bus. Law Reporter. Vice-chmn. San Diego Internat. Affairs Bd., 1981-85; bd. dirs. San Diego-Yokohama Sister City Soc., 1982-85, L.A.-Nagoya Sister City Soc., 1986—; mem. master planning com. City of Rancho Palos Verdes, Calif., 1989-91; advisor, exec. com. Calif. Internat. Law Sect., 1990-91, 95, appointee exec. com., 1991-94, vice-chmn., 1992-93, chair, 1993-94; appointee, trustee Palos Verdes Libr. Dist., 1993. Mem. ABA, State Bar of Calif., L.A. County Bar Assn. (bd. dirs. internat. sect., exec. com. Internat. Legal Sec. 1987—, sec. 1995-96, 2d v.p. 1996—, appointee pacific rim com. 1990—, chmn. 1991-92, 95—), Assn. Asian Studies, U. Pa. Alumni Club (pres. San Diego chpt. 1982, pres. coun. Phila., 1983), Anti-Defamation League, Japanese-Am. Soc. Legal Studies (book rev. editor Seattle 1983-85). Jewish. Office: Sonnenschein Nath & Rosenthal 601 S Figueroa St Ste 1500 Los Angeles CA 90017-5720

HAHN, HAROLD THOMAS, physical chemist, chemical engineer; b. N.Y.C., May 31, 1924; s. Gustave Hahn and Lillie Martha (Thomas) H.; m. Bennie Joyce Turney, Sept. 5, 1948; children: Anita Karen, Beverly Sharon, Carol Linda, Harold Thomas Jr. Student, Hofstra U., 1941-43; BSChemE, Columbia U., 1943-44; PhD in Chemistry, U. Tex., 1950-53. Chem. engr. Manhattan Dist. U.S. Army, Los Alamos, N.Mex., 1945-47; chem. engr. U. Calif., Los Alamos, 1947-50; sr. scientist Gen. Electric Co., Hanford, Wash., 1953-58; sect. chief, chem. research dept. Phillips Petroleum Co., Idaho Falls, Idaho, 1958-64; sr. staff scientist Lockheed Missiles & Space Co., Palo Alto, Calif., 1964-92; private cons., 1992—. Contbr. articles to profl. jours.; patentee in field. Pres. Edgemont Gardens PTA, Idaho Falls, 1963-64; commr. cub scout div. Stanford area council Boy Scouts Am., Palo Alto, 1973-76, also cubmaster pack 36, 1973-80, chmn. troops 36 and 37, 1975-77; mem. adminstrv. bd. Los Altos Meth. Ch. Served to col. U.S. Army, 1944-46, with res., 1946-84, col. res. ret. Humble Oil Co. fellow, 1952, Naval Bur. Ordnance fellow, 1953. Fellow Am. Inst. Chemists; mem. AIAA, Magnetics Soc. IEEE (elected sr. mem.), Calif. Acad. Scis., Internat. Platform Assn., Am. Chem. Soc., Sigma Xi, Phi Lambda Upsilon, Kappa Rho. Home and Office: 661 Teresi Ln Los Altos CA 94024-4162

HAHN, HONG THOMAS, mechanical engineering educator; b. Dolma-Myun, Kyungki-Do, Republic of Korea, Feb. 5, 1942; came to U.S., 1966; s. Baek Hyo and Sang Soon (Lee) H.; m. Hoon Pat Paek, Sept. 16, 1967; children: Heryun, Hejin, Jeanie. BS, Seoul Nat. U., Republic of Korea, 1964; MS, Pa. State U., 1968, PhD, 1971. Rsch. engr. U. Dayton (Ohio) Rsch. Inst., 1974-77, Air Force Materials Lab., Wright-Patterson AFB, Ohio, 1972-74, 77-78; mech. engr. Lawrence Livermore (Calif.) Nat. Lab., 1978-79; prof. Washington U., St. Louis, 1979-86, Pa. State U., University Park, 1986-91, UCLA, 1992—; cons. Lawrence Livermore Nat. Lab., Livermore, 1979-90, UN Devel. Programme, 1987-88, Dow Chem., 1990-92; disting. lectr. NASA-Va. Poly. Inst. Composites Program, Blacksburg, 1988; lectr. SW mechanics Series, 1989; Hughes Aircraft Co. chair in mfg. engring., UCLA, 1992. Co-author: Introduction to Composite Materials, 1980; editor: Composite Materials-Fatigue & Fracture, 1986, Jour. Composite Material, 1981—; contbr. over 100 articles to profl. jours. Mem. sci. adv. bd. Swedish Inst. Composites, Pitea, Sweden, 1989-91. Lt. Korean Army, 1964-66. Recipient Outstanding Rsch. award Pa. State Engring. Soc., 1991, Medal of Excellence U. Del. Ctr. Composite Materials, 1996; Harry and Arlene Schell professorship in engring. Pa. State U., 1991. Fellow ASME, Am. Soc. Composites (pres. 1996—); mem. AIAA, Materials Rsch. Soc., Soc. for the

Advancement of Material and Process Engring., Soc. Mfg. Engrs., Am. Ceramic Soc., Am. Soc. for Engring. Edn. Office: MAE Dept Engring IV UCLA Los Angeles CA 90024

HAHN, JOAN CHRISTENSEN, retired drama educator, travel agent; b. Kemmerer, Wyo., May 9, 1933; d. Roy and Bernice (Pringle) Wainwright; m. Milton Angus Christensen, Dec. 29, 1952 (div. Oct. 1, 1971); children: Randall M., Carla J. Christensen Teasdale; m. Charles Henry Hahn, Nov. 15, 1972. BS, Brigham Young U., 1965. Profl. ballroom dancer, 1951-59; travel dir. E.T. World Travel, Salt Lake City, 1969—; tchr. drama Payson High Sch., Utah, 1965-71, Cottonwood High Sch., Salt Lake City, 1971-95; retired, 1995; dir. Performing European Tours, Salt Lake City, 1969-76; dir. Broadway theater tours, 1976—. Bd. dirs. Salem City Salem Days, Utah, 1965-75; regional dir. dance Latter-day Saints Ch., 1954-72. Named Best Dir. High Sch. Musicals, Green Sheet Newspapers, 1977, 82, 84, 90, Utah's Speech Educator of Yr., 1990, 91, named to Nat. Hall of Fame Ednl. Theatre Assn., 1991; recipient 1st place award Utah State Drama Tournament, 1974, 77, 78, 89, 90, 91, 94, 95, Tchr. of Yr. award Cottonwood High Sch., 1989-90, Limelight award, 1982, Exemplary Performance in teaching theater arts Granite Sch. Dist., Salt Lake City, 1982; named to Nat. Hall of Fame, Ednl. Theatre Assn., 1991, Cottonwood H.S. Hall of Fame, 1995; Joan C. Hahn Theatre named in her honor Cottonwood H.S., 1997; named Outstanding Educator, Utah Ho. Reps., 1995. Mem. Internat. Thespian Soc. (sponsor 1968—, internat. dir. 1982-84, trustee 1978-84), Utah Speech Arts Assn. (pres. 1976-78, 88-90), NEA, Utah Edn. Assn., Granite Edn. Assn., Profl. Travel Agts. Assn., Utah High Sch. Activities Assn. (drama rep. 1972-76), AAUW (pres. 1972-74). Republican. Mormon. Avocations: reading; travel; dancing. Home: 685 S 1st E PO Box 36 Salem UT 84653-0036

HAHN, WOODY, sports association executive. Grad., Wash. State U. Athletic dir. Ea. Mont. Coll., until 1987; commr. Great Northwest Conf., 1988—, Continental Divide Conf., 1989—, Pacific West Conf., Billings, Mont.; active NCAA West Region Men's Basketball Adv. Com. Mem. Nat. Assn. Collegiate Dirs. Athletics, Volleyball Coaches' Assn., Basketball Coaches' Assn., NCAA Divsn. II Commrs. Assn. Office: Pacific West Conf PO Box 2002 Billings MT 59103-2002*

HAHN, YUBONG, electro-optics company executive; b. Seoul, Oct. 26, 1942; came to U.S., 1961; s. Chi-Gin Hahn and Bok-Hee Chung; m. Myung-Ok Hahn, June 6, 1970; children: Steven, Denise. PhD in Physics, U. Mo., Rolla, 1971. V.p. CVI Laser Corp., Albuquerque, 1972-79; with Optics Co., Seoul, Korea, 1979-83; pres. Rocky Mountain Instrument Co., Longmont, Colo., 1983—. Mem. Soc. Photog. Instrument Engrs., Soc. Photo-Optical Instrumentation Engring. Office: Rocky Mountain Instruments 1501 S Sunset St Longmont CO 80501-6750

HAILE, BENJAMIN CARROLL, JR., retired chemical and mechanical engineer; b. Shanghai, China, Apr. 6, 1918; came to U.S., 1925; s. Benjamin Carroll and Ruth Temple (Shreve) H.; m. Lola Pauline Lease, Dec. 28, 1957; children: Thomas Benjamin, Ronald Frederick. BS, U. Calif., Berkeley, 1941; cert., Harvard-MIT, 1945; postgrad., U. So. Calif., 1950-51. Registered profl. chem. and mech. engr., Calif. Chem. engr. Std. Oil of Calif. (Chevron), San Francisco, El Segundo, Calif., 1941-43, 46-48; sr. project chem. engr. C.F. Braun & Co., Alhambra, Calif., 1948-50, 54-56, 67-71, 72; contract chem. and mech. engr. Dow Chem., Stearns-Roger, Fluor et al, Tex., Colo., Ill., 1951-54, 56-57; sr. process engr. Aerojet-Gen. Corp., Sacramento and Covina, Calif., 1957-67; mech. engr. So. Calif. Edison Co., Rosemead, Calif., 1972-84; pvt. practice chem. engr. Fontana and Montclair, Calif., 1986, 88, 92; sr. mem. tech. staff Ralph M. Parsons Co., Pasadena, Calif., 1971, 88-91. 2d lt. USAAF, 1943-46. Mem. NSPE (life, Sacramento chpt. pres. 1960-62), Am. Inst. Chem. Engrs. (mem. emeritus), Toastmasters Internat. (chpt. v.p. 1979, Outstanding Toastmaster 1984), Psi Upsilon. Republican. Home: 159 N Country Club Rd Glendora CA 91741-3919

HAILE, LAWRENCE BARCLAY, lawyer; b. Atlanta, Feb. 19, 1938; m. Ann Springer McCauley, March 28, 1984 (dec. Apr. 1994); children: Gretchen Vanderhoof, Eric McKenzie (dec.), Scott McAllister. BA in Econs, U. Tex., 1958, LLB, 1961. Bar: Tex. 1961, Calif. 1962. Law clk. to U.S. Judge Joseph M. Ingraham, Houston, 1961-62; pvt. practice law San Francisco, 1962-67, L.A., 1967—; instr. UCLA Civil Trial Clinics, 1974, 76; lectr. law Calif. Continuing Edn. of Bar, 1973-74, 80-89; mem. nat. panel arbitrators Am. Arbitration Assn., 1965—. Assoc. editor: Tex. Law Rev, 1960-61; Contbr. articles profl. publs. Mem. State Bar Calif., Tex., U.S. Supreme Ct. Bar Assn., Internat. Assn. Property Ins. Counsel (founding mem., pres. 1980), Vintage Auto Racing Assn. (bd. dirs.), Vintage Motorsports Coun. (pres.), Phi Delta Phi, Delta Sigma Rho. Office: 9925 Lancer Ct Beverly Hills CA 90210 *Gold is like brass/Except less crass.*

HAILE, MARCUS ALFRED, retired chemistry educator; b. Haviland, Kans., Oct. 14, 1930; s. William Oral and Myrna May (Stotts) H.; m. Lynne Helene Hunsucker, Mar. 20, 1964; children: Marta Helene, Cavan William. BS, Pepperdine U., 1955; Master, U. No. Iowa, 1968. Cert. secondary tchr., Calif. Tchr. chemistry Hamilton High Sch., L.A., 1957-67; prof. chemistry L.A. City Coll., 1969-94, also pres. acad. senate, 1972-73. Author: Experimental General Chemistry, 1973, 76, Gen. Analytical Chemistry, 1987; contbr. articles to profl. jours. Chmn. Amateur Athletic Union So. Calif. Swimming U.S. Swim, Los Angeles, Ventura and Santa Barbara Counties, Calif., 1980-81. Served with U.S. Army, 1950-52. NSF grantee, 1967-68. Mem. Am. Chem. Soc., Am. Fedn. Tchrs., Thoroughbred Owners Calif. Democrat. Home: 22404 Kearny St Calabasas CA 91302-5861

HAINES, IRENE LOIS, librarian; b. Nespelem, Wash., Aug. 1, 1951; d. William H. Haines and Eula Jean (Roberts) Rogers. BA with hons., Fort Wright Coll., 1976; MLS, U. Wash., 1987. Cert. libr., Wash. Br. team leader Seattle (Wash.) Pub. Libr., 1988—; human diversity trainer. Contbr. articles to jours. Bd. dirs. AFSCME Local 2083C, Seattle, 1984-88; bd. dirs. Colville Indian Libr. Assn., 1981-82. Mem. Colville Confederated Tribes. Democrat. Office: Magnolia Br Libr 2801 34th Ave W Seattle WA 98199-2602

HAINING, JEANE, psychologist; b. Camden, N.J., May 2, 1952; d. Lester Edward and Adina (Rahn) H. BA in Psychology, Calif. State U., 1975; MA in Sch. Psychology, Pepperdine U., 1979; MS in Recreation Therapy, Calif. State U., 1982; PhD in Psychology, Calif. Sch. Profl. Psychology, 1985. Lic. clin. psychologist 1987, lic. ednl. psychologist 1982. Crisis counselor Calif. State U., Northridge, 1973-74; recreation therapist fieldwork Camarillo (Calif.) State Hosp.-Adolescent/Children's Units, 1974; Intern recreation therapist UCLA Neuropsychiatric Inst., L.A., 1975-76; substitute tchr./recreation therapist New Horizons Sch. for Mentally Retarded, Sepulveda, Calif., 1976-79; intern sch. psychologist Los Nietos (Calif.) Sch. Dist., 1977-79; sch. psychologist Rialto (Calif.) Unified Sch. Dist., 1979-82; clin. psychologist field work San Joaquin County Dept. Mental Health, Stockton, Calif., 1982-83; intern clinical psychologist Fuller Theol. Sem. Psychology Ctr., Pasadena, Calif., 1984-85; clin. psychologist U.S. Dept. Justice, Terminal Island, Calif., 1985-86; cmty. mental health psychologist L.A. County Dept. Mental Health, 1987-89; clin. psychologist Calif. Dept. Corrections, Parole Outpatient Clinic, L.A., 1990—, Mary Magdeline Project, Commerce, Calif., 1992—; mem. psychiat.-psychol. panel adult and juvenile Superior Ct., L.A., 1992—; mem. psychiat. panel U.S. Dist. Ct. (cen. dist.) Calif., L.A., 1989—; clin. psychologist O. Carl Simonton Cancer Ctr., Pacific Palisades, Calif., 1993—. Adv. bd. Camarillo (Calif.) State Hosp., 1994—, vice-chmn. adv. bd., 1996—; examiner Lic. Ednl. Psychologist Oral Examinations, Calif. Bd. Behavioral Sci. Examinations, Sacramento, 1985. Recipient award Outstanding Achievement Western Psychology Conf., Calif., 1974. Mem. APA, Calif. Psychol. Assn., Forensic Mental Health Assn. (con. planning com. 1993). Democrat. Lutheran.

HAIR, KITTIE ELLEN, secondary educator; b. Denver, June 12, 1948; d. William Edward and Jacqueline Jean (Holt) H. BA, Brigham Young U., 1971; MA in Social History, U. Nev., Las Vegas, 1987, cert. paralegal, 1995. cert. tchr., Nev. Health educator Peace Corps, Totota, Liberia, 1971-72; tchr. Clark County Sch. Dist., Las Vegas, Nev., 1972-77, 1979—; chair dept. social studies Clark County Sch. Dist., Las Vegas, 1993-95; missionary Ch. Jesus Christ Latter-Day Saints, Alta., Can., 1977-79. Recipient Outstanding Faculty award U. Nev./Southland Corp., Las Vegas, 1991. Mem. So. Nev. Peace Corps Assn., Phi Kappa Phi, Phi Alpha Theta, Delta Kappa Gamma (pres. Iota chpt. 1996—). Democrat. Office: Advanced Technologies Acad 2501 Vegas Dr Las Vegas NV 89106-1643

HAKIM, BESIM SELIM, architecture and urban design educator, researcher; b. Paris, July 31, 1938; came to U.S., 1978; s. Selim D. and Meliha M. (Yamulki) H.; m. Fatina S. Hijab, Oct. 31, 1963 (div. July 1983); children: Omar, Lena, Sara; m. Mariam B. Bashayan, Dec. 31, 1984; 1 child, Malak. BArch, Liverpool (Eng.) U., 1962; MArch in Urban Design, Harvard U., 1971. Registered architect, Ariz. Asst. prof. Tech. U. of Nova Scotia, Halifax, Can., 1967-74, assoc. prof., 1974-80, adj. rsch. prof., 1980-83; adj. assoc. prof. U. N.Mex., Albuquerque, 1982-83; assoc. prof. King Fahd U. of Petroleum and Minerals, Dhahran, Saudi Arabia, 1984-85; assoc. prof. Coll. of Architecture and Planning King Faisal U., Dammam, Saudi Arabia, 1985-93; ind. scholar and cons., 1994—; vis. prof. McGill U., Montreal, 1974, Tech. Inst. Architecture and Urbanism, Tunis, Tunisia, 1975, King Saud U., Riyadh, Saudi Arabia, 1982, 87, 89, 92, MIT, 1977; vis. scholar MIT, 1981, Cornell U., 1995; cons. to Skidmore, Owings and Merrill, Architects/Engrs., Chgo., Keith Graham & Assocs., Architects, Halifax, Nova Scotia and others; architect, engr. King Khaled Internat. Airport, Riyadh, Saudi Arabia, 1983-84; lectr. numerous univs. and profl. confs. in U.S., Can., Eng., Japan, Greece, Turkey, Tunisia, Jordan, United Arab Emirates, Saudi Arabia, Morocco. Prin. works include urban design downtown Halifax, N.S., 1971-74, Coors Corridor Study, Albuquerque, Hist. Old Town, Albuquerque, 1981-83, 11 custom-built houses, an eight-story office bldg., hosp. renovations/additions, apt. bldgs. and a religious facility, U.S., Can., Mid-East; author: Arabic-Islamic Cities: Building and Planning Principles, 1986, 2d edit., 1988, Japanese edit., 1990, (monograph) Sidi Bou Sa'id, Tunisia: A Study in Structure and Form, 1978; contbr. numerous articles, revs. and tech. reports to profl. publs. Recipient citation for rsch. Progressive Architecture, 1987, Edn. Honors award AIA, 1990. Mem. AIA, Am. Inst. Cert. Planners, Am. Planning Assn., Assn. Collegiate Schs. of Architecture, Middle East Studies Assn. N.Am., Halifax Bd. Trade (civic affairs com.), Am. Inst. Maghrib Studies. Home: 1832 Field Dr NE Albuquerque NM 87112-2834

HAKKILA, EERO ARNOLD, retired nuclear safeguards technology chemist; b. Canterbury, Conn., Aug. 4, 1931; s. Jack and Ida Maria (Lillquist) H.; m. Margaret W. Hakkila; children: Jon Eric, Mark Douglas, Gregg Arnold. BS in Chemistry, Cen. Conn. State U., 1953; PhD in Analytical Chemistry, Ohio State U., 1957. Staff mem. Los Alamos (N.Mex.) Nat. Lab., 1957-78, assoc. group leader safeguard systems, 1978-80, dep. group leader, 1980-82, group leader, 1982-83, project mgr. internat. safeguards, 1983-87, program coord., 1987-95; ret., 1995. Editor: Nuclear Safeguards Analysis, 1978; contbr. numerous articles to profl. jours. Fellow Am. Inst. Chemists; mem. N.Mex. Inst. Chemists (pres. 1971-73), Am. Chem. Soc., Am. Nuclear Soc. (exec. com. fuel cycle and waste mgmt. div. 1984-86), Inst. Nuclear Materials Mgmt. Office: Los Alamos Nat Lab PO Box 1663 Los Alamos NM 87544-0600

HALBERT, RONALD JOEL, preventive medicine physician, educator; b. Jacksboro, Tex., June 11, 1958; s. Arthur Joel and Ollie Matilda (Havens) H. BS in Biology magna cum laude, Abilene Christian U., 1979; MD, Baylor U., 1982; MPH in Epidemiology, U.C.L.A., 1990. Diplomate Am. Bd. Preventive Medicine. Pvt. practice Tex., 1985-95, Calif., 1985-95; assoc. dir. preventive medicine residency U.C.L.A., 1992—, lectr. Sch. Pub. Health, 1994—; med. dir. Internat. Med. Corps., L.A., 1988, cons., 1992; epidemiologist Immunization Demonstration Project, L.A., 1991-93, Roybal Immunization Coalition, L.A., 1995; preventive medicine practitioner, Mission City Comty. Network, Sepulveda, Calif., 1993; cons. U.S. Dept. Labor, Washington, 1993, Ctr. for the Study of Latino Health, L.A., 1995-96. Contbr. articles to profl. jours. Pres. Pan-Am. Inst. of Maritime Archaeology, San Francisco, 1993-95; dir. Internat. Med. and Ednl. Found., L.A., 1991-93, Westside Cmty. Outreach for Prevention & Edn., L.A., 1995—. Rsch. fellow Internat. Med. Corps., 1987, divsnl. fellow U.C.L.A. Sch. Pub. Health, 1988-89; recipient Humanitarian Med. award Com. for a Free Afghanistan, Washington, 1985. Fellow Am. Coll. Preventive Medicine, Adventurers' Club of L.A., Explorers Club; mem. APHA, Nat. Coun. for Internat. Health, Am. Coll. Emergency Physicians. Office: UCLA Prev Med Residency Box 951772 Los Angeles CA 90095-1772

HALE, BRUCE DONALD, retired marketing professional; b. Oak Park, Ill., Dec. 21, 1933; s. Edward Garden and Mildred Lillian (Pelc) H.; m. Nancy Ann Novotny, July 2, 1955 (div. 1976); children: Jeffrey Bruce, Karen Jill Hale; m. Connie Luella Green Gunderson, Apr. 21, 1979. BA in Econs., Wesleyan U., Middletown, Conn., 1955. Trainee Caterpillar Tractor Co., Peoria, Ill., 1955-56, dealer tng. rep., 1956-59; dist. rep. Caterpillar Tractor Co., Albuquerque, 1959-62; asst. sales mgr. Rust Tractor Co., Albuquerque, 1962-65; gen. sales mgr. Rust Tractor Co., Albuqerque, 1965-71, v.p. sales, 1971-81, v.p. mktg., 1981-96; ret., 1996. Mem. Am. Mining Congress, Soc. Mining Engrs., Associated Contractors N.Mex., Associated Equipment Distbrs., Rocky Mountain Coal Mining Inst., N.Mex. Mining Assn., Albuquerque Country Club. Home: 9508 Layton Pl NE Albuquerque NM 87111-1368

HALE, DAVID FREDRICK, health care company executive; b. Gadsden, Ala., Jan. 8, 1949; s. Millard and Mildred Earline (McElroy) H.; BA, Jacksonville State U.; m. Linda Carol Sadorski, Mar. 14, 1975; children: Shane Michael, Tara Renee, Erin Nicole, David Garrett. Dir. product mgmt. Ortho Pharm. Corp. Divsn. Johnson & Johnson, Raritan, N.J., 1978-80; v.p. mktg. BBL Microbiology Systems divsn. Becton Dickenson & Co., Cockeysville, Md., 1980-81, v.p., gen. mgr., 1981-82; sr. v.p. mktg. and bus. devel. Hybritech, Inc., San Diego, 1982, pres. 1983-86, CEO, 1986-87; pres., CEO Gensia Sicor, Inc., San Diego, 1987—, also bd. dirs.; bd. dirs. Dura Pharmaceuticals, Scandipharm Inc., Collateral Therapeutics, Children's Hosp., Francis Parker Sch., U. Calif. San Diego Found., San Diego Econ. Devel. Corp., Biotechnology Ind. Orgn., Calif. Healthcare Inst., Biocom San Diego; founder CONNECT; mem. bd. advisors U. Calif. San Diego Found.; mem. Mayor's Bus. and Econ. Devel. Coun. Mem. Young Pres.'s Orgn. Republican. Episcopalian Home: PO Box 8925 16596 Via Lago Azul Rancho Santa Fe CA 92067 Office: Gensia Sicor Inc 9360 Towne Centre Dr San Diego CA 92121-3030

HALE, DEAN EDWARD, social services administrator; b. Balt., Aug. 4, 1950; s. James Russell and Marjorie Elinor (Hoerman) H.; m. Lucinda Hoyt Muniz, 1979; children: Christopher Deane, Lydia Alice JeeSoo. BASW, U. Pa., 1975; postgrad. U. Oreg., 1976, U. London, 1974, U. Mont., 1968-71, Portland State U., 1993, 95—. Dir. recreation Hoffman Homes for Children, Gettysburg, Pa., 1970; social worker Holt Adoption Program, Inc., Eugene, Oreg., 1975-78; supr. social svcs. Holt Internat. Children's Svcs., Eugene, 1978-84, Asia rep., 1984-90, program mgr., 1990-94, interim dir. internat. programs, 1994-95, dir., China, 1995—; guest lectr. U. Oreg.; cons. internat. child welfare, 1982—; co-founder Family Opportunities Unltd. Inc., 1981—. Author: Adoption, A Family Affair, 1981, When Your Child Comes Home, 1986. Pres. Woodtique Heights Homeowners Assn., 1980-91, bd. dirs.; pres. Our Saviour's Luth. Ch., 1981-85; bd. dirs. Greenpeace of Oreg., 1979-84; cons., campaign worker Defazio for Congress 1988, 1987-90; mem. Westside Neighborhood Quality Project, 1988—. Named Outstanding New Jaycee, Gettysburg Jaycees, 1971. Mem. Nat. Assn. Social Workers (bd. dirs. 1978-80, sec. 1979-80), Nat. Assn. Christian Social Workers, Acad. Cert. Baccalaureate Social Workers. Home: 931 Taylor St Eugene OR 97402-4451 Office: PO Box 2880 1195 City View St Eugene OR 97402-3325

HALE, JAMES LEROY (JOHN HALE), forensic document analyst, consultant; b. Prescott, Ariz., Oct. 30, 1941; s. James LeRoy Sr. and Grace Viola (Nichols) H.; m. Cathy Jo Johnsmiller, Feb. 21, 1951; children: Kathryn, Lora Ann, Debra Lynn; m. Susan Gail Jeffries, July 4, 1964 (div. Sept. 1974). AA in Police Sci., Glendale C.C., 1974; student, Ariz. State U., 1974-78. Diplomate Am. Bd. Forensic Document Examiners. Surveyor's aide U.S. Bur. Reclamation, Phoenix and Yuma, Ariz., 1964-65; with Ariz. Hwy. Patrol, Yuma and Wickenburg, Ariz., 1965-70; undercover narcotics enforcement agt. Ariz. Dept. Pub. Safety, 1970-72; forensic document analyst Ariz. Dept. Pub. Safety Questioned Document Lab., Phoenix, 1972-85, No. Ariz. Forensic Lab., Chino Valley, 1985—; cons. and expert witness; lectr.-instr. Am. Inst. Banking, Phoenix, 1982-90; instr. Ariz. law enforcement officer adv. coun. acads., 1978-85. Editor forensic newsletter Southwestern Examiner, 1981-83; author rsch. articles; presenter in field. Mem. Chino Valley Town Coun., 1988-93; pres., bd. dirs. Hi-Desert Artists, Chino Valley, 1988-90, 92-93. Served with U.S. Army, 1959-62, Korea. Recipient numerous appreciation awards. Mem. Southwestern Assn. of Forensic Document Examiners (founder, past pres., bd. dirs.). Republican. Baptist. Home: 3200 N Pine View Dr Prescott Valley AZ 86314 Office: No Ariz Forensic Lab PO Box 411 Chino Valley AZ 86323

HALE, VIOLET ELAINE, inventor, retired food service executive; b. Atwood, Kans.; d. Frank and Lola Mae (Threlkel) Wederski; m. Everett David Hale, June 25, 1948; children: Diana Elaine, Chester Duane, Ray Don. Student, IGAS, 1980. Asst. food svc. dir. Manitou Springs (Colo.) Sch., 1967-84, ret., 1984. Author poems, songwriter; inventor cap shaper dryer, sliced bread stacker. Mem. Manitou Springs Hist. Soc. (v.p. 1989-92). Methodist.

HALER, LAWRENCE EUGENE, technology educator, councilman; b. Iowa City, Iowa, Jan. 24, 1951; s. Eugene Hilbert and Mary Elizabeth (Hans) H.; m. Jenifer Lea Leitz, June 1, 1974. BA, Pacific Luth. U., 1974. Reactor operator UNC Nuclear Industires, Richland, Wash., 1974-80, lead cert. instr., 1980-81, mgr. tng. adminstrn., 1981-82, sr. ops. analyst, 1982-85; sr. specialist Gen. Physics Corp., Columbia, Md., 1985-86; sr. instr. Rockwell Hanford Ops., Richland, 1986-88; tech. instr. Westinghouse Hanford Co., Richland, 1988-89, sr. specialist instr., 1989-96, Fluor Daniel Hanford team leader, 1996—; chmn. bd. dirs. Benton-Franklin County Bd. Health, Richland, 1994-95, Sci. and Tech. Park, Richland; vice chmn. Benton-Franklin Regional Coun. Govts., 1994. Chmn. Benton County Reps., Richland, 1976-78, state committeeman, 1988-90; councilman, mayor pro-tem City of Richland, 1990-96, mayor, 1996—; active cmty. econ. devel. steering com. Nat. League of Cities. Mem. Richland C. of C. (chmn. legis. affairs com. 1988-93), Richland Kiwanis (pres. 1994-95). Lutheran. Home: PO Box 1319 Richland WA 99352-1319 Office: Richland City Coun 505 Swift Blvd Richland WA 99352-3510

HALEY, ANNE ELIZABETH, library director; b. Oct. 4, 1946; m. James F. Shepherd. BA in History, French, U. Puget Sound, 1968; MLS, U. Wash., 1970. Libr. trainee San Diego (Calif.) Pub. Libr., 1968-69; libr. Pierce County Libr., Tacoma, 1970-73; ext. coord. Fort Vancouver (Wash.) Regional Libr., 1973-77; dir. Walla Walla Pub. Libr., Wash., 1977—; commr. Wash. State Libr. Commn., 1995—; lectr. U. Wash. Grad. Sch. Libr. and Info. Sci., 1986, 89, 91, 92; speaker/panelist various libr. assns.; del. head US Observer Del., UNESCO, Paris, 1990; chair statements writing process Wash. Gov.'s Conf. on Librs., 1991; chmn. Wash. Adv. Coun. on Librs., 1979-81; chmn. S.E. Libr. Svc. Area, 1979; chmn. Interstate Libr. Planning Coun., 1975-76. Book reviewer; contbr. articles to profl. jours. Planning facilitator Moscow/Latah County Libr., 1991; chmn. Libr. Legis. Day, Olympia, 1985, 86; mem. Walla Walla Art Club, Walla Walla Woman's Reading Club, PEO, Walla Walla Country Club, Walla Walla Symphony Guild; chmn. Symposium on Creativity, Walla Walla Symphony Soc. 75th Celebration, 1981; parliamentarian Jr. Club Walla Walla, 1982-83; 2d v.p. Camp Fire Coun., 1986-88, treas., 1988-80, sec., 1985-86, chmn. ct. svc. com., 1980-83; pub. svc. divsn. chair United Way Campaign, 1985-87; bd. dirs. Exchange Club, 1988-89; pres. Allied Arts Coun., 1981-82, treas., 1980-81, 82-90; founding pres. Project Read, Walla Walla, 1986-89; chmn. budget and allocations com. United Way, 1991-93, mem., 1989-93; day leader Leadership Walla Walla C. of C., 1992, 93; mem. steering com. City Mgr. Recruitment, 1992; chmn. adv. com. Helpline, 1992-94; pres. United Way Walla Walla County, 1993-94. Recipient Disting. Alumnus award U. Wash. Grad. Sch. Libr. & Info. Sci., 1994. Mem. ALA (chmn. internat. rels. com. 1990-91), Pacific N.W. Libr. Assn. (1st v.p./pres. 1993-95, rep. 1977-79, chmn. pub. libr. divsn. 1977-79, chmn. local arrangements 1972), Wash. Libr. Assn. (ALA councilor 1987-92, ALA coun. 1995—, pres. 1983-85, 1st v.p., chmn. legis. planning com., chmn. budget com. 1981-83, Pres.'s award 1992), Exch. Club (Builders of Pride recognition award 1988). Home: 644 Boyer Ave Walla Walla WA 99362-2308 Office: Walla Walla Pub Libr 238 E Alder St Walla Walla WA 99362-1943

HALEY, JOHN DAVID, petroleum consulting company executive; b. Denver, Mar. 16, 1924; s. Peter Daniel and Margaret Dorothy (O'Haire) H.; m. Annie Loretta Breeden, June 20, 1951; children: Laura, Patricia, Brian, Sharon, Norine, Kathleen. Profl. engr. Colo. Sch. Mines, 1948. Registered profl. engr., Colo., Okla. Petroleum engr. Creole Petroleum, Venezuela, 1948-50, field engr. Texaco Inc., La., 1950-52; staff engr. Carter Oil (Exxon), Tulsa, 1954-56; petroleum cons. Earlougher Engring., Tulsa, 1956-61, resident mgr., Denver, 1961-62; v.p. prodn. Anschutz Corp., Denver, 1962-86; v.p. Circle A Drilling, Denver, 1967-78; dir. Circle A Mud, Denver, 1983-86; pres. Greylock Pipeline, Denver, 1983-86, Anschutz Pipeline, Denver, 1984-86; pres. Haley Engring. Inc., 1987—; mem. pres.'s council Colo. Sch. Mines, 1985—; bd. dirs. Alumni Assn., 1992-97, pres., 1995. Bd. dirs. CSM Found., 1996—; Rep. committeeman, Littleton. Lt. comdr. USNR, 1943-46, 52-54. Recipient Outstanding Alumnus award Alumni Assn., 1997. Mem. Soc. Petroleum Engrs. (bd. dirs. Denver chpt. 1965), Soc. Petroleum Evaluation Engrs. (bd. dirs. 1992-95), Ind. Petroleum Assn. Mountain States, Am. Petroleum Inst. (citation for service), Internat. Assn. Drilling Contractors, Rocky Mountain Oil & Gas Assn. (bd. dirs. 1988—), Soc. Profl. Well Log Analysts, Petroleum Club (Denver chpt.). Roman Catholic. Home: 561 E Caley Dr Littleton CO 80121-2212

HALEY, RICHARD EDWARD, JR., computer scientist; b. Boston, Nov. 21, 1958; s. Richard Edward, Sr. and Margaret Anne (McLellan) H.; m. Lisa Ann Gillespie, Aug. 13, 1988. Grad. high sch., Plano, Tex. With U. Dallas, Irving, Tex., 1976-84, Dallas Co. Deaf Edn., Tex., 1982-87; dir. transp. Tex. Sch. Deaf, 1987-91; owner Writeswright Word Processing, Dallas, Tex., 1986-91; independent game devel., 1987-91; graphics programer Origin Sys., Austin, Tex., 1991-92; network programmer Data Interface, Austin, 1993-94; lan adminstrn. Infinity Group, Albuquerque, N.M., 1994-95; computer tech. Presbyn. Hosp., Albuquerque, 1995—; owner WWWritch, 1996—, ran for N. Mex. Congress Dist. #3, 1997. Author (web page) Abraham Gutmann for Senate, 1996, Slugbaby, 1996; prodr., dir. Roundtable, 1995-96 (Cmty. Impact award 1995); prodr. ABQ Pub. Access TV, 1994—; crew mem. (TV show) Good Health, Good Life, 1995, Freedom Hour, 1996. Rep. Green Coun., N.M., 1994; vice chairperson Albuquerque Regional Greens, 1994. Mem. Delta-9.

HALEY, SALLY FULTON, artist; b. Bridgeport, Conn., June 29, 1908; d. John Poole and Elizabeth (Akers) H.; m. Michele Russo, June 29, 1935; children: Michael Haley, Gian Donato. BFA, Yale U., 1931. One-woman shows include Marylhurst Coll., 1965, Maryhill Mus. Fine Arts, Washington, 1975, Portland Art Mus., 1960, 75, Woodside Gallery, Seattle, 1971, 76, 79, Gov's. Office, Oreg. State Capitol, 1976, Wentz Gallery, Pacific N.W. Coll. Art, 1984, Fountain Gallery Art, Portland, 1962, 72, 77, 80, 81, 84, 86; exhibited in group shows Stewart Gallery, Boston, 1947, San Francisco Mus. Art, 1949, Walker Art Ctr., Mpls., 1954, Denver Art Mus., 1956, 57, 3d Pacific Coast Biennial Exhbn., 1960, Francis J. Newton's Collection, Bush House, 1964, Seattle Ctr. Art Pavilion, 1976, Womans Bldg., L.A., 1977, Laura Russo Gallery, 1993, Oreg. Group Show, Expn. '86 World's Fair, Vancouver, B.C.; represented in permanent collections Fred Myer Trust, Wash. State U., State Capitol Bldg., Salem, Portland Art Mus., The Laura Russo Gallery, Portland, Lynn McAllister Gallery, Seattle, Barby Investment Co., AT&T, Kaiser Found., numerous others; retrospective, Marylhurst Coll., 1993. Named Artist of Yr. Neighbor Newspaper Community, Portland, 1984; recipient Woman of Achievement award YWCA, 1988, Govs. award for the Arts, 1989, Poster award, 1982, Hubbard award Hubbard Mus., Ruidoso Downs, N.Mex., 1990-91.

HALFERTY, FRANK JOSEPH, middle school music educator; b. Seattle, May 7, 1954; s. Edward A. and Eva Mae (Ellis) H.; m. Margaret A. Taylor, Mar. 17, 1979 (div. June 1991); children: Bryan W., Patrick Joseph; m. Melissa A. Rowland, July 31, 1992. BA in Music Edn., Seattle Pacific U., 1976, BA in Music Theory and Lit., 1976; MA in Music Competition, N.Mex. State U., 1982. Cert. tchr., Wash. Band and choral tchr. Raymond (Wash.) Sch. Dist., 1976-77; band and orch. tchr. Bellevue (Wash.) Sch. Dist., 1977-80; MA in Music Composition N.Mex. State U., Las Cruces, 1980-82; band tchr. Lake Washington Sch. Dist., Kirkland, Wash., 1982-93; band tchr. Shoreline Sch. Dist., Seattle, 1993—, head music dept., 1994—; mem. site-based mgmt. coun. Einstein Mid. Sch., Seattle, 1994—; dir. Lake Washington All-Dist. Band, Kirkland, 1984-92. Composer, arranger numerous musical works for band, instrumental ensembles, string orch. and choral groups. Crimson scholar, 1982; named Tchr. of Yr. by students, tchrs. and parents of Kirkland Jr. H.S., 1990; recipient Golden Acorn award Einstein Mid. Sch. PTSA, 1997. Mem. ASCAP, NEA, Music Educators Nat. Conf., Sno-King Music Edn. Assn. (sec. 1994-96), Phi Kappa Phi, Alpha Kappa Sigma. Home: 6155 NE 187th St Seattle WA 98155-3221 Office: Einstein Mid Sch 19343 3rd Ave NW Seattle WA 98177-3012

HALL, ALAN HERMAN, toxicologist, educator; b. South Bend, Ind., Jan. 8, 1949; s. Herman and Thelma D. (Dennie) H.; m. Priscilla K. Hall, July 8, 1967; 1 child, Stephanie A. BA with honors, Ind. U., South Bend, 1973; MD, Ind. U., Indpls., 1977. Diplomate Am. Bd. Emergency Medicine and subspecialty board in med. toxicology, Am. Bd. Med. Toxicology; lic. physician, Tex., Colo. Intern Thomason Gen. Hosp., El Paso, 1977; resident U. Tex. Health Scis. Ctr., San Antonio, 1978-79; fellow U. Colo. Health Scis. Ctr., Denver, 1984-86, sr. cons. Rocky Mountain Poison and Drug Ctr., 1986—, asst. prof. pediatrics, 1987-92, clin. asst. prof. preventive medicine and biometrics, 1992—; mem. faculty U. Colo.; editor-in-chief Tomes and Tomes Plus Info. Sys., Micromedex, Inc., Denver. Guest editor study cases; reviewer jours.; contbr. numerous articles to profl. jours. Mem. peer rev. com. Agy. for Toxic Substances and Disease Registry, 1988-90; mem. State of Colo. Air Quality Sci. Adv. Bd., 1992—. Maj., MC, USAFR, hon. ret. Fellow Am. Coll. Emergency Physicians; mem. AMA, Soc. Toxicology, Am. Coll. Emergency Physicians, Am. Acad. Clin. Toxicology, Am. Coll. Occupl. and Environ. Medicine, Am. Coll. Med. Toxicology, Colo. Med. Soc., Colo. Coll. Emergency Physicians, Rocky Mountain Acad. Occupl. and Environ. Medicine, Denver Med. Soc., Nat. Environ. Health Assn., Aerospace Medicine Assn., Soc. USAF Flight Surgeons, others. Republican. Home: Mile 5.0 Passcreek Rd Carbon County Rd 404 Elk Mountain WY 82324

HALL, ANTHONY R., photographer; b. London, Mar. 18, 1950; s. Reynolds A. and Lilly Elizabeth Hall; m. Marie Hall, Feb. 14, 1991; children: Coloma, Everest. AA English, Pierce Coll., 1969; BA in English, Calif. State U., 1971. Profl. photographer specialisting in people, in comml. and fashion advt.; clients include: Warner Bros., A&M Records, L.A., UCLA, W.W. Norton Books, CableVision Industries, SpeakEasy Mag., Paris, Playboy Agy., Max Agy., Smash Agy., L.A., Brooks Coll. Fashion Design, Damen Industries, Dorothy Shreve Talent Agy., Palm Springs, many others; photography in pubs. including: L.A. Times, Image Mag., Valley Family, L.A. Family Mag., Dama Dinamica, Churokoron, Profl. Photographer, Black Pasion Vol. 2, ArtWeek, others; exhbns. include: Living Arts Gallery, 1983, Photography World Concerts for Humanity, 1984, L.A.V.A., 1985, Calif. State Regional Photographic, 1986, Calif. State U., Choco, 1989, Profl. Photographers Am. Western States, 1990, Internat., 1990, Chgo. Art Inst., 1990, Showcase 91, Beaverton Arts, Oreg., 1991, Soc. for Contemporary Photography, 1991, Orlando Gallery, sherman Oaks, 1991, Fla. Nationals, 1992, Mo. State U., Kirksville, 1992, FotoFest Internat., Houston, 1992, Orlando Gallery, 1993. Recipient 1st place award Calif. State U. Regional, 1986, Fla. Nationals, 1992, Cert. of Merit, Profl. Photographers of Am., 1990. Mem. Kodak Profl. Network of Photographers. Office: 12782 Sky Line Dr Desert Hot Springs CA 92240-4338

HALL, BLAINE HILL, retired librarian; b. Wellsville, Utah, Dec. 12, 1932; s. James Owen and Agnes Effie (Hill) H.; m. Carol Stokes, 1959; children: Suzanne, Cheryl, Derek. BS, Brigham Young U., 1960, MA, 1965, MLS, 1971. Instr. English, Brigham Young U., Provo, Utah, 1963-72, humanities librarian, 1972-96; book reviewer Am. Reference Book Ann., 1984—. Author: Collection Assessment Manual, 1985, Saul Bellow Bibliography, 1987, Jerzy Kosinski Bibliography, 1991, Jewish American Fiction Writers Bibliography, 1991, Conversations with Grace Paley, 1997; editor: Utah Libraries, 1972-77 (periodical award ALA 1977); contbr. articles to profl. jours. Bd. dirs. Orem (Utah) Pub. Libr., 1977-84; mem. Orem Media Rev. Commn., 1984-86; chmn. Utah Adv. Commn. on Librs. With U.S. Army, 1953-54, Korea. Mem. ALA (coun. 1988-92), Utah Libr. Assn. (pres. 1980-81, Disting. Svc. award 1989), Mountain Plains Libr. Assn. (bd. dirs. 1978-83, editor newsletter 1978-83, pres. 1994-96, grantee 1979, 80, Disting. Svc. award 1991), Phi Kappa Phi. Mormon. Home: 230 East 1910 South Orem UT 84058

HALL, BOOKER TELEFERIO, broadcaster; b. Chgo., June 29, 1952; s. Booker and Pearl Hall. BJ, N.E. La. U., 1973. Pub. Singles N.W. Mag., Richland, Wash., 1978-80; cmty. rels. dir. Wash. Pub. Power Supply, Richland, 1980-89; broadcaster Sta. KTOO-TV-FM, Juneau, Alaska, 1989—. Author: Juneau City Museum, 1993, Capital Crimes, 1993, Crime and Punishment: A History of Criminal Justice in Alaska's Capital City, 1993. With USN, 1974-78. Home: PO Box 34182 Juneau AK 99803 Office: KTOO TV FM 360 Egan Dr Juneau AK 99801

HALL, BRONWYN HUGHES, economics educator; b. West Point, N.Y., Mar. 1, 1945; d. Richard Roberts and Elizabeth (Flandreau) Hughes; m. Robert Ernest Hall, June 25, 1966 (div. Apr. 1983); children: Christopher Ernest, Anne Elizabeth. BA, Wellesley Coll., 1966; PhD, Stanford U., 1988. Programming analyst Lawrence Berkeley (Calif.) Lab., 1963-70; sr. programmer econometric programming Harvard U., Cambridge, Mass., 1971-77; owner, opr. TSP Internat., Palo Alto, Calif., 1976—; from rsch. economist to rsch. assoc. Nat. Bur. Econ. Rsch., Stanford, Calif., 1977—; from asst. prof. to assoc. prof. U. Calif., Berkeley, 1987—; internat. rsch. assoc. Inst. for Fiscal Studies, London, 1995—; data base rev. com. U.S. SBA, Washington, 1983-84; ind. econometric programming cons. ednl. instns., Cambridge, 1970-77; Terry prof. econs. Oxford Univ., 1996—. From mem. editorial bd. to assoc. editor Econ. of Innovation and New Tech., Uxbridge, Eng., 1989—; contbr. articles on econs. to profl. publs. Sloan Found. dissertation fellow, 1986-87, Nat. fellow Hoover Inst. on War, Revolution, and Peace, Stanford U., 1992-93, Nutfield Coll. fellow, 1996—; NSF rsch. grantee, 1989—. Mem. Am. Econ. Assn. (census adv. com. 1990-95), Am. Fin. Assn., Am. Statis. Assn., Econometric Soc., Assn. for Computing Machinery. Home: 123 Tamalpais Rd Berkeley CA 94708-1948 Office: U Calif Dept Econs 611 Evans Hall Berkeley CA 94720

HALL, CHARLES FREDERICK, space scientist, government administrator; b. San Francisco, Apr. 7, 1920; s. Charles Rogers and Edna Mary (Gibson) H.; m. Constance Vivienne Andrews, Sept. 18, 1942; children—Steven R., Charles Frederick, Frank A. B.S., U. Calif., Berkeley, 1942. Aero. research scientist NACA (later NASA), Moffett Field, Calif., 1942-60; mem. staff space projects NACA (later NASA), 1960-63; mgr. Pioneer Project, NASA, 1963-80. Recipient Disting. Service medal NASA, 1974, Achievement award Am. Astronautical Soc., 1974, Spl. Achievement award Nat. Civil Service League, 1976, Astronautics Engr. award Nat. Space Club, 1979. Home: 817 Berry Ave Los Altos CA 94024-5416

HALL, CHARLES MCALLISTER, writer; b. Mt. View, Wyo., Nov. 27, 1930; s. Henry Vernon and Eleanor (McAllister) H.; m. Frankie Jane Taylor, Oct. 11, 1957; children: Kathy Jenine, Jonathan, Jared, James, Jeanette, Juli. BA, Brigham Young U., 1958, MA, 1960. Tchg. asst. French Brigham Young U., Provo, Utah, 1958-60; tchr. German Pasco (Wash.) H.S., 1960-63; instr. French Columbia Basin Coll., Pasco, 1963-72; tchg. asst. Russian U. Utah, Salt Lake City, 1968-69; profl. genealogist Global Rsch. Sys., Salt Lake City, 1978-82; freelance writer Salt Lake City, 1972—. Author: Atlantic Bridge to Germany, vols. 1-10, 1974-96. With U.S. Army, 1953-55. Mem. Fedn. East European Family History Societies (pres. 1992-95), Palatines to Am. (pres. 1975-77). Mem. LDS Ch. Home and Office: 4874 S 1710 E Salt Lake City UT 84117-5928

HALL, CYNTHIA HOLCOMB, federal judge; b. Los Angeles, Feb. 19, 1929; d. Harold Romeyn and Mildred Gould (Kuck) Holcomb; m. John Harris Hall, June 6, 1970 (dec. Oct. 1980);. A.B., Stanford U., 1951, J.D., 1954; LL.M., NYU, 1960. Bar: Ariz. 1954, Calif. 1956. Law clk. to judge U.S. Ct. Appeals 9th Circuit, 1954-55; trial atty. tax div. Dept. Justice, 1960-64; atty.-adviser Office Tax Legis. Counsel, Treasury Dept., 1964-66; mem. firm Brawerman & Holcomb, Beverly Hills, Calif., 1966-72; judge U.S. Tax Ct., Washington, 1972-81, U.S. Dist. Ct. for central dist. Calif., Los Angeles, 1981-84; cir. judge U.S. Ct. Appeals (9th cir.), Pasadena, Calif., 1984—. Served to lt. (j.g.) USNR, 1951-53. Office: US Ct Appeals 9th Cir 125 S Grand Ave Pasadena CA 91105-1621

HALL, DAVID BICKNELL, marketing company executive; b. Chico, Calif., Dec. 27, 1945; s. Sankey M. Hall Jr. and Jane (Hall) Meierdiercks; (div.); children: Aimee N., Russell L. Postgrad., John F. Kennedy U. Owner Hall & Assoc., Chico, 1966-77, Hall Petroleum Co., Chico, 1978-85, Sierra Planning Group LLC, Chico, 1986—, Cascade Mgmt. Co., Portland, Oreg., 1984—; pres. Sierra Family Life, Portland, 1992—, Charter Adminstrn. Calif., Portland, 1994—; ptnr. Family Heritage LLC, 1995—. Capt. USAFR. Office: Cascade Mgmt Co 5335 SW Meadows Rd Ste 350 Lake Oswego OR 97035

HALL, DAVID RAMSAY, architect; b. Lansing, Mich., Oct. 24, 1945; s. Harold Wendell and Sarah Katherine (Schlademan) H.; m. Catherine Anne Weeks, Dec. 23, 1967; children: Sarah Catherine, Rebecca Jane. BArch, Wash. State U., 1968. Registered architect, Wash. Designer, draftsman Earl Flansburgh & Assocs., Cambridge, Mass., 1968-70, NBBJ, Seattle, 1970, Mel Streeter & Assoc., Seattle, 1971-72; designer, ptnr. Henry Klein Partnership, Architects, Mt. Vernon, Wash., 1972—. Author, designer, contbr. articles to profl. publs. Commr. Dike Dist. # 19, Skagit County, Wash., 1984-95; mem. adv. bd. Wash. State U., Pullman, 1990-96; bd. dirs. Self Help Housing, Mt. Vernon, 1980-84. Recipient Progressive Architecture Design award, 1972, Honor award Cedar Shake & Shingle, 1991, Am. Wood Coun., 1993, Sunset Mag. Western Home award. 1995. Mem. AIA (bd. dirs. N.W. chpt. 1985-88, Honor award Seattle chpt. 1991, N.W. chpt. 1991, 94, 96, Commendation award Seattle chpt. 1987). Home: 585 Farm To Market Rd Bow WA 98232-9213 Office: Henry Klein Partnership 314 Pine St Ste 205 Mount Vernon WA 98273-3899

HALL, ELTON A., philosophy educator; b. San Fernando, Calif., Sept. 18, 1940; s. Harwood Harry and Verna Florentina (Engelhardt) H.; m. Katherine May Lennard, Aug. 27, 1961; children: Helena Louise, Anita Virya. BA, Occidental Coll., 1963; MA, U. Calif., Santa Barbara, 1965, U. Calif., Santa Barbara, 1967. Asst. prof. philosophy Moorhead (Minn.) State U., 1967-69, Calif. State U., Fresno, 1969-75; head dep. social sci. Oxnard (Calif.) Coll., 1987-90, prof. philosophy, 1975-92, acting div. dir. arts, letters and sci., 1990-91, acting dean gen. edn., 1991-92; prof. philosophy Moorpark (Calif.) Coll., 1992—; pres. acad. senate, 1996—; adj. prof. sociology Calif. Luth. U., 1994; tchr. trainer Calif. Assn. Schs. Cosmetoloty, Sacramento, 1988-91, Calif. Assn. Pvt. Postsecondary Schs., 1991-93. Contbr. articles to profl. jours. Chief negotiator local 1828 AFT, 1996—. Mem. Internat. Soc. Neoplatonic Studies, Muyiddin Ibn 'Arabi Soc. (fellow rep.). Office: Moorpark Coll 7075 Campus Rd Moorpark CA 93021-1605

HALL, GEORGIANNA LEE, special education educator; b. Greeley, Colo., Apr. 2, 1947; d. John Russell and Lois Louise (Urich) Martin; m. William James Bailey, 1970 (div. June 1972); m. Rex Henry Hall, Dec. 22, 1984; 1 stepchild, Jorri Colleen. AA, Fullerton (Calif.) Jr. Coll., 1967; BA, Calif. State U., Fullerton, 1969, elem. edn. credential, 1971, learning handicapped credential, 1976. Cert. resource specialist, lang. devel. specialist. Tutor Edn. Project for Disadvantaged Youth Savanna Sch. Dist., Stanton, Calif., 1965-69; math. tchr. Norwalk (Calif.)-LaMirada Sch. Dist., 1971-72; tchr. Cypress (Calif.) Sch. Dist., 1972-74, tchr. learning disability, 1974-80, tchr. learning handicapped, 1976, tchr. communicatively handicapped, 1981—, resource specialist, 1981—, dist. mentor tchr. for spl. edn., 1993—; dist. spl. edn. rep. for writing of Original Greater Anaheim Consortium Plan for Spl. Edn., 1980; dist. interview team for tchrs., prins., and aides, Cypress, 1985—, dist. staff devel. com., tchg. and assessment com., 1994-95; compliance program quality reviewer dist. leadership team rep. State Calif., Orange County, 1991—; Cypress dist. rep. for drug free schs. Cypress Sch. Dist.-U. Calif., Irvine, 1992—; King sch. rep. dist. drug alcohol tobacco edn.; mem. leadership team King Elem. Sch., Cypress, 1989—; lead tchr. for conflict mgr. tng., 1993—; coord. sch. intervention team, 1989—; coord. activities Svcs. for At-Risk Students, King Elem. Sch., 1990—, crisis intervention team, 1994—; dist. coord. CCR, 1994—; mem. Dist. Coord. Curriculum Com., 1994—; mem. dist. adv. com. Medi-Cal, 1994—; mem Dist. Testing and Assessment Com., 1994—; ACT tchr. rep. interview team for dir. instrn. and spl. edn., 1996, dist. interview team for instrnl. aides. Neighborhood rep. Muscular Dystrophy Assn., Huntington Beach, Calif., 1988—, Coun. for Paralyzed vets., Huntington Beach, 1989—; vol. reading tutor PLUS, Huntington Beach, 1992; publicity chmn. King Sch. PTA, 1992-93, 93-94; coord. resources needy families, King elem. sch. Recipient Hon. Svc. award PTA King Sch., Cypress, 1982; named Spl. Edn. Tchr. of Yr. Resource Specialists Calif., 1989. Mem. NEA, Calif. Tchrs. Assn., Assn. Cypress Tchrs. (sch. rep. 1974-76, 79-82, sec. 1976-77, 2d v.p. 1978-79, 1st v.p. 1979-80), Calif. Assn. Resource Specialists, Children with Attention Deficit Disorder, Learning Disability Assn., Calif. Assn. for Supervision and Curriculum Devel., Orange County Math. Assn., Coun. Exceptional Children, Coun. Learning Disabilities. Office: King Elem Sch 8710 Moody St Cypress CA 90630-2220

HALL, GORDON R., retired state supreme court chief justice; b. Vernal, Utah, Dec. 14, 1926; s. Roscoe Jefferson and Clara Maud (Freestone) H.; m. Doris Gillespie, Sept. 6, 1947; children: Rick Jefferson, Craig Edwin. B.S., U. Utah, 1949, LL.B., 1951. Bar: Utah 1952. Solo practice Tooele, Utah, 1952-69; county atty. Tooele County, 1958-69; judge 3d Jud. Dist. Utah, 1969-77; assoc. justice Supreme Ct. Utah, 1977-81, chief justice, 1981-94; of counsel Snow, Christensen & Martineau, Salt Lake City, 1994—; chmn. Utah Jud. Coun., 1983-94; pres. Conf. Chief Justices, 1988-89; chmn. Nat. Ctr. State Cts., 1988-89; pres. Utah Assn. Counties, 1965; mem. Pres.'s Adv. Com. OEO, 1965-66. Served with U.S. Maritime Svc., 1944-46. Mem. ABA, Utah Bar Assn. Office: Snow Christensen Martineau 11th Fl PO Box 45000 10 Exchange Pl Salt Lake City UT 84145

HALL, HAROLD ROBERT, retired computer engineer; b. Bakersfield, Calif., Feb. 7, 1935; s. Edward Earl and Ethel Mae (Butner) H.; m. Tenniebee May Hall, Feb. 20, 1965. BS, U. Calif., Berkeley, 1956, MS, 1957, PhD, 1966. Chief engr. wave-filter div. Transonic, Inc., Bakersfield, 1957-60; chief design engr. Circuit Dyne Corp., Pasadena and Laguna Beach, Calif., 1960-61; sr. devel. engr. Robertshaw Controls Co., Anaheim, Calif., 1961-63; research engr. Naval Command, Control and Ocean Surveillance Ctr., rsch. and devel. divsn. Navy Research Lab., San Diego, 1966-95; bd. dirs. Circuit Dyne Corp., Pacific Coil Co. Treas. Pacific Beach Town Coun., San Diego, 1996—, Friends of Ostomates Worldwide-U.S.A., Akron, Ohio, 1992—. Recipient Thomas Clair McFarland award U. Calif., Berkeley, 1956, NSF fellow, 1957. Mem. IEEE, Acoustical Soc. Am., Phi Beta Kappa. Home: 5284 Dawes St San Diego CA 92109-1231

HALL, HOWARD PICKERING, engineering and mathematics educator; b. Boston, July 8, 1915; s. George Henry and Elizabeth Isabel (McCallum) H.; m. Ellen Marguerite Ide, June 25, 1945 (dec. 1984); children: Charlotte McCallum, Stephanie Wilson, Lindsey Louise, Gretchen Elizabeth. AB, Harvard U., 1936, MS, 1937, DSc, 1951. Registered structural engr., Ill., 1953. Instr., civil engring. Brown U., Providence, 1937-38; structural analyst Mark Linenthal, Engr., Boston, 1938-39; instr., asst. prof., assoc. prof. civil engring. Northwestern U., Evanston, Ill., 1939-56; design engr, field engr. Porter, Urquart, Skidmore, Owings, Merrill, Casablanca, Fr. Morocco, 1951-53; dean, sch. engring., acad. v.p. Robert Coll., Istanbul, Turkey, 1956-68; dir. of studies, acting headmaster St. Stephen's Sch., Rome, 1968-72; prof. math. Iranzamin Internat., Tehran, Iran, 1973-80; math. tchr. Vienna Internat. Sch., 1980-83, Copenhagen Internat. Sch., 1983-86; cons. S.J. Buchanan, Bryan, Tex., Eng., 1955. Contbr. articles to profl. jours. Served to Capt. U.S. Army, 1942-46, ETO. Recipient Clemens Herschel award Boston Soc. Civil Engrs., 1954. Mem. Sigma Xi. Home: 301 SW Lincoln St Apt 1101 Portland OR 97201-5031

HALL, J. TILLMAN, physical education educator, administrator, writer; b. Big Sandy, Tenn., Jan. 16, 1916; s. Travis M. and Sophia (Kirk) H.; m. Louise Babb, June 16, 1940; children: Nancy Sweeny, Jody Esser. BA, Pepperdine U., L.A., 1940; MA, U. So. Calif., 1947, EdD, 1951. Head dept. phys. edn. Pepperdine U., L.A., 1946-50; head dept. phys. edn. U. So.Calif., L.A., 1950-87, dir. Emeriti Ctr., Emeriti Coll., 1988-96. Author 10 books on phys. edn., recreation and dance; editor books on golf and tennis. Mem. Area Agy. on Aging. With USN, 1941-45. Recipient R. Tait McKenzie Disting. Prof. award AAHPERD, 1978, Disting. Retiree award, 1997. Mem. Internat. Sr. Citizen Assn.

HALL, JAMES BYRON, college provost, author; b. Midland, Ohio, July 21, 1918; s. Harry and Florence (Moon) H.; m. Elizabeth Cushman, Feb. 14, 1946 (dec.); children—Elinor, Prudence, Kathryn, Millicent, James M.M. Student, Miami U., Oxford, Ohio, 1938-39, U. Hawaii, 1938-40; B.A., State U. Iowa, 1947, M.A., 1948, Ph.D., 1953; postgrad., Kenyon Coll., 1949. Writer-in-residence Miami U., 1948-49, U. N.C., Greensville, 1954, U. B.C., 1955, U. Colo., 1963; instr. Cornell U., 1952-53; asst. prof. English U. Oreg., 1954-57, asso. prof., 1958-60, prof., 1960-65; prof. English, dir. The Writing Center, U. Calif.-Irvine, 1965-68; provost U. Calif.-Santa Cruz, 1968-75, emeritus, 1983—; cons. editor Doubleday & Co., 1960-65. Author: Not by the Door, 1954, The Short Story, 1955, 15X3, 1957, Racers to the Sun, 1960, Us He Devours, 1964, Realm of Fiction, 1965-77, Modern Culture and Arts, 1967-75, Mayo Sergeant, 1967, The Hunt Within, 1973, (stories) The Short Hall, 1981, Bereavements: Selected and Collected Poems, 1991, I Like It Better Now, 1992, Art and Craft of The Short Story, 1995; contbr. stories, poetry to anthologies; lit. archive Miami U., Oxford, Ohio. Founder Summer Acad. Contemporary Arts, 1959; cultural specialist U.S. Dept. State, 1964. Served with AUS, 1941-46. Recipient Octave Thanet prize, 1950, Oreg. Poetry prize, 1958, Emily Clark Balch Fiction prize, 1967, Chapelbrook award, 1967, Inst. Creative Arts award.; Rockefeller grantee, 1955; James B. Hall Gallery named in his honor U. Calif. Regents, 1985; James B. Hall traveling fellowships founded by U. Calif.-Santa Cruz, 1985. Mem. AAUP, Nat. Writers Union (pres. local 7, 1983, nat. grievance officer 1985-87), Pasatiempo Men's Golf Club (pres. 1987-88). Democrat. Methodist. Home: 4926 SW Corbett #404 Portland OR 97201

HALL, JEAN ANN, veterinarian, educator; b. Roseburg, Oreg., July 26, 1957; d. Robert A. and Eleanor Carol (Barter) H.; m. Stephen F. Callahan, Aug. 13, 1988; children: Ty, Clay, Travis. BS, Oreg. State U., 1981; DVM summa cum laude, Wash. State U., 1982; MS, Colo. State U., 1987, PhD, 1989. Diplomate Am. Coll. Vet. Internal Medicine; lic. vet. Oreg., Wash., Mass. Intern Angell Meml. Animal Hosp., Boston, 1982-83; clinician in medicine and surgery Brookline Animal Hosp., Boston, 1983-84; resident in small animal internal medicine Colo. State U., Ft. Collins, 1984-87; postdoctoral fellow Oreg. Health Scis. U., Portland, 1989-90; asst. prof. vet. medicine Oreg. State U., Corvallis, 1990—; lectr., cons., and presenter in field. Contbr. chpts. to books and articles and abstracts to profl. jours. Recipient Travel award Fedn. Am. Socs. Exptl. Biology, 1987; grantee Ralston-Purina Co., 1991, faculty Oreg. State U., 1993, IAMS Co., 1994, Mark Morris Inst., 1994, 96. Mem. AVMA, Am. Motility Soc. (Travel award 1986, 88), Am. Animal Hosp. Assn., Oreg. Vet. Med. Assn., Comparative Gastroenterology Soc., Phi Kappa Phi, Alpha Psi, Phi Zeta. Home: 560 SW Lookout Dr Corvallis OR 97333-4032 Office: Oreg State U Coll Vet Medicine Magruder Hall 105 Corvallis OR 97331-4802

HALL, JOSEPHINE WEISSMAN, obstetrician/gynecologist; b. N.Y.C., Dec. 29, 1937; d. Jacob Eliah and Sonia Hall; m. Jearld Wayne Hall, June 20, 1971; children: Michael, Gillian, James, Jesse, Cameron. BA, Swarthmore Coll., 1959; MD, Chgo. Med. Sch., 1963. Diplomate Am. Bd. Ob-gyn. Resident Albert Einstein Coll. Medicine, N.Y.C., 1964-68; pvt. practice Washington, 1968-69; with Mound Bayou (Miss.) Cmty. Hosp., 1969-70; ob-gyn. Ross Coos Med. Group, L.A., 1970-71; instr. dept. Ob-gyn. U. So. Calif. Coll. Medicine, L.A., 1972-73; clin. prof. ob.-gyn. U. So. Calif., L.A., 1989—; pvt. practice L.A., 1973—; bd. dirs. alumni bd. govs. Chgo. Med. Sch. mem. Glendale (Calif.) Nat. Charity League. Recipient Disting. Alumnus award The Chgo. Med. Sch., 1988. Fellow Am. Bd. Ob-gyn. Office: 1910 W Glenoaks Blvd Glendale CA 91201-1616

HALL, KATHRYN O'NEIL, photographic company official; b. St. Joseph, Mo., Apr. 16, 1952; d. Monte Virgil O'Neil and Ardyce Marie (Hartman) Couch; m. Bruce Edwin Hall, June 8, 1974; children: Nathan Estes, Patrick O'Neil. BSBA, U. Denver, 1974. Master scheduler Colo. div. Kodak, Windsor, 1974-79, adminstrv. mgr., 1979-81, prodn. mgr., 1982-84, materials mgr., 1985-95. Pres. sch. bd. St. Vrain Valley Sch. Dist., Longmont, Colo. Mem. AAUW (bull. chmn. 1996-97), Am. Prodn. and Inventory Control Soc. (cert. in prodn. and inventory mgmt., program chmn. 1988-89). Home: 502 Collyer St Longmont CO 80501-5543

HALL, LARRY D., energy company executive, lawyer; b. Hastings, Nebr., Nov. 8, 1942; s. Willis E. and Stella W. (Eckoff) H.; m. Jeffe D. Bryant, July 5, 1985; children: Scott, Jeff, Mike, Bryan. BA in Bus., U. Nebr., Kearney; JD, U. Nebr. Bar: Nebr., Colo. Ptnr. Wright, Simmons, Hancock & Hall, Scottsbluff, Nebr., 1967-71; atty., asst. treas. KN Energy Inc., Hastings, 1971-73, dir. regulatory affairs, 1973-76; v.p. law divsn. KN Energy Inc., Lakewood, Colo., 1976-82, sr. v.p., 1982-85, exec. v.p., 1985-88, pres., COO, 1988-94, pres., CEO, 1994—, also bd. dirs., 1988-94, chmn., CEO, pres., 1996—; bd. dirs. Colo. Assn. Commerce and Industry, Gas Rsch. Inst., Colo. Alliance for Bus., MLA, Rocky Mountain Oil and Gas Assn. Mem. ABA, INGAA (chmn. 1997), MGA, CAB (bd. dirs.), Fed. Energy Bar Assn., Nebr. Bar Assn., Colo. Bar Assn., Pres. Assn., Midwest Gas Assn. (chmn.), Hiwan Country Club, Elks, Club 30. Presbyterian. Home: 1892 Sugarbush Dr Evergreen CO 80439 Office: KN Energy Inc PO Box 15265 Lakewood CO 80215

HALL, LIZA FORSTER, writer, artist; b. Newark, July 29, 1961; d. Jon Clive and Jeanne Claire (Tambornino) Forster; m. Edd Hall, June 7, 1985; children: Gilda Claire, Samuel Henry. Student, Pratt Inst., 1978-81. Talent booker, segment prodr. The Paula Poundstone Show HBO, L.A., 1991-92; segment prodr. The Paula Paoundstone Show HBO, L.A., 1992-93; talent exec. The Carol Burnett Show CBS, L.A., 1992-93; talent, tv writers' mgr. Burns & Burns Mgmt., L.A., 1992-93; talent exec. The Nora Dunn Show HBO, L.A., 1993. Author: Perk, 1997. Vol., spkr. Teens with Eating Disorders, L.A., 1994—. Mem. Soc. Children's Book Writers and Illustrators (assoc., Fiction award Young Adult 1995). Democrat.

HALL, LOIS RIGGS, former state senator, former symphony orchestra administrator; b. Beeville, Tex., May 22, 1930; d. Ira Franklin and Pearl Ophelia (McCoy) Riggs; m. Walter William Hall, Dec. 28, 1950 (dec.); children: Robert Macfarlane, Elaine Denise, Judith Lea. Student, Tex. Women's U., 1947-49, U. Tex., Austin, 1949-50. Exec. sec. N.Mex. Symphony Orch., Albuquerque, 1975-93; mem. N.Mex. Senate, 1980-85, ret. . Active Boy Scouts Am., Girl Scouts U.S.A., Officers Wives Clubs; 2d v.p. Albuquerque Symphony Women's Assn.; bd. dirs. Friends of Music, 1986-88; treas., publicity dir. N.Mex. Aviation Assn. Republican. Home: 620 Ortiz Dr NE Albuquerque NM 87108-1447

HALL, MADELYN GAEL PRIEBE, medical librarian; b. Seattle, May 4, 1951; d. Thomas Taylor and Donna Marie (Moore) Priebe; m. Dennis Earl Hall, Sept. 30, 1972; children: Christopher, Kilmeny. BA in Elem. Edn., Western Wash. U., 1973; MEd in Early Childhood Edn., Columbus (Ga.) Coll., 1984; cert. program in libr. mgmt., U. Wash., 1991. Libr. asst. Whatcom County Libr. System, Bellingham, Wash., 1973-75; substitute tchr., Raymond, Wash., 1976-77; gen. clk. libr. br. U.S. Army Recreation Svcs., Ft. Polk, La., 1977-78; libr. technician U.S. Army Recreation Svcs., Aschaffenburg, Germany, 1979-81; acad. coord., head tchr. basic skills edn. program U.S. Army, Ft. Benning, Ga., 1982-85; libr. Merrill Reeh Ophthalmology Libr., Good Samaritan Hosp. and Med. Ctr., Portland, Oreg., 1985-92, dir. librs., 1992-94; med. libr. S.W. Wash. Med. Ctr. Libr., Vancouver, 1994—; presenter in field; rep. regional adv. com. from Oreg. to Regional Med. Libr., Nat. Library Medicine, 1994-96. Author: Pediatric Ophthalmology Consumer Resource File, 1988, 3d edit., 1993. Mem. Med. Libr. Assn. (chmn. registration and hospitality Pacific N.W. chpt. 1993), Oreg. Health Scis. Libr. Assn. (sec. 1993), Assn. Visual Sci. Librs. (sec. 1990-91, chmn. 1992-93), Wash. Med. Libr. Assn., Portland Area Health Scis. Librs., Kappa Delta Pi. Democrat. Episcopalian. Office: SW Wash Med Ctr Libr Svcs 400 NE Mother Joseph Pl PO Box 1600 Vancouver WA 98668

HALL, MARIAN ELLA See ROBERTSON, MARIAN ELLA

HALL, MYRNA ANNE, marketing professional, development professional; b. Eugene, Oreg., Sept. 6, 1952; d. Laverne Marvel Hansey and Evelyn Lillian (Nielsen) Mishler; m. David Lee Harding, Aug. 15, 1970 (div. 1979); m. Keith Lester Hall, May 15, 1981. BS in Sociology, U. Oreg., 1977; MA in Am. Studies, Wash. State U., 1992. Adminstrv. asst. U. Oreg., Eugene, 1975-77; escrow officer trainee Lane County Escrow, Eugene, 1977-78; asst. escrow officer Safeco Title Ins., Seattle, 1978-80; mktg. dir. Antek Dental

Lab., Bremerton, Wash., 1980-85; owner HMS Mktg. Services, Mt. Vernon, Wash., 1983-86; dir. devel. and spl. gifts San Diego State U., 1994-96, interim v.p. u. rels. and devel., 1996—; devel. coordinator Coll. Arts and Scis. Wash. State U., Pullman, 1986-88; counselor, instr. Skagit Valley Coll., Mt. Vernon, 1986; dir. annual giving, pres.'s assocs. and donor rels. Wash. State U., 1991-93. Author, editor: (monthly newspaper sect.) Skagit Valley Working Women, 1985-86. Vol. Mt. Baker Planned Parenthood, Bellingham, Wash., 1980-86, Skagit Valley Family YMCA, Mt. Vernon, 1984-86, campaign dir., 1985-86; founder, chairperson Skagit Women's Alliance and Network, Mt. Vernon, 1984-87; bd. dirs., v.p. Mt. Vernon Women in Bus., 1984-87; v.p. Wash. State U. Found., 1989-903. Recipient numerous civic vol. awards. Mem. Council for Advancement and Support of Edn. (awards). Office: San Diego State Univ 5500 Campanile Dr San Diego CA 92182-0001

HALL, PAUL J., lawyer; b. San Diego, Jan. 13, 1951. AB with highest honors, U. Calif., Santa Cruz, 1972; postgrad, Yale U.; JD, U. Calif., Berkeley, 1975. Bar: Calif. 1975. Mem. Manatt, Phelps & Phillips, L.A., 1975-94, Stein & Lubin LLP, San Francisco, 1995—; bd. regents U. Calif., 1992-93, regent designate, 1991-92. Trustee U. Calif. Santa Cruz Found., 1986—. Mem. Calif. State Bar, Boalt Hall Alumni Assn., U. Calif. Santa Cruz Alumni Assn.(bd. dirs. 1982-91, treas. 1985-86, sec. 1986-87, v.p. 1987-89, pres.-elect 1989-90, pres. 1990-91). Address: 600 Montgomery St Ste 14 San Francisco CA 94111-2703

HALL, PHYLLIS CHARLENE, therapist, counselor; b. L.A., Mar. 18, 1957; d. Clellan James Jr. and Yvonne Rayedith (Ralls) H. BA, Whittier Coll., 1979; MS in Phys. Edn., Calif. State U., Fullerton, 1985, MS in Counseling, 1988; PhD in Psychology, U.S. Internat. U., 1996. Coach varsity girls basketball, softball Calif. High Sch., Whittier, 1979-80; counselor Rio Hondo Coll., Whittier, 1980-88; coach asst. girls varsity basketball Long Beach (Calif.) Wilson High Sch., 1985-88; therapist intern Turning Point Counseling, Garden Grove, Calif., 1988-89; counselor Long Beach City Coll., 1988—, girls acad. advisor, 1989-94, asst. coach girls basketball, 1993-94; psychologist asst./intern Family Svcs. Long Beach, 1994—; bd. dirs. Long Beach City Coll.; mem. adv. bd. U. Calif. C.C., 1997—. Author: Liberators from Planet Liberx, 1985. Mem. comty. adv. coun. U. Calif., 1996-97; co-sponsor African Am. in Unity Long Beach City Coll., 1990-92; com. mem. 1st Annual African Am. Achievement Conf., San Diego, 1994. Recipient PhD Student Achievement award USIU Dept. MFT, 1996. Mem. Calif. Tchrs. Assn., Long Beach City Coll. Counselors Assn., Women in Arts (founding mem.). Office: Long Beach City Coll 1305 E Pch Long Beach CA 90806

HALL, RICHARD DENNIS, agribusiness and international trade writer; b. Troy, N.Y., Apr. 12, 1935; s. Dennis John and Clara Eleanor (Hanson) H.; m. Joyce Ann Huntington, June 7, 1957; children: Brian Huntington, Roger Hanson. BS, Boston U., 1957. Gen. assignment reporter Worcester (Mass.) Telegram and the Evening Gazette, 1957-60; city hall reporter, columnist Springfield (Mass.) Union, 1960-65; reporter Fresno (Calif.) Bee, 1965-77, agr. water reporter, 1977-79; Washington corr. McClatchy Newspapers, 1979-83; agribus. writer Fresno (Calif.) Bee, 1983-91, ret., 1991; mem. 9th Ann. Conf. European and Am. Journalists, Maastricht, The Netherlands, 1985. Author: Fresno County in the 20th Century, 1987, Hanford Hometown America, 1990. Docent local history tours, Hanford, Calif., 1987; participant Vols. for Overseas Cooperative Assistance, Armenia, 1993. Recipient Agribus. Invitation award, Taiwan, 1983. Home and Office: 1978 Mulberry Dr Hanford CA 93230-2046

HALL, RICHARD LEE, engineering manager; b. Little Rock, May 1, 1947; s. James Montague and Virginia Norma (Hughes) H.; m. Sharon Lee Farrell, June 13, 1970; children: David Scott, Melissa Anne Page. BSME, U. Ark., 1970. Registered profl. engr.; cert. Ark. State Bd. Registration for Profl. Engrs. and Land Surveyors. Plant engr. Alum. Co. of Am., Bauxite, Ark., 1970-72; assoc./mech. engr. BCCLW Arch./Engrs., Little Rock, 1973-82; assoc./dept. head Garver & Garver Engrs., Little Rock, 1982-90; assoc./sr. mech. engr. ADP Fluor Daniel, Tucson, 1991—, dir. health facilities engring., 1992-94, mech. discipline mgr., 1994—. State zone leader Gideons Internat., Ariz., 1994-96. Mem. NSPE, ASHRAE, Nat. Fire Protection Assn., Inst. for Environ. Scis., Ark. Acad. Mech. Engrs., Profl. Engrs. in Pvt. Practice (state chmn. 1980-81). Southern Baptist. Home: 5755 E 9th St Tucson AZ 85711 Office: ADP Marshall 2480 N Arcadia Ave Tucson AZ 85712-5735

HALL, RICHARD MURRAY, JR., finance executive, consultant; b. St. Joseph, Mo., Jan. 1, 1947; s. Richard Murray and Alice Elaine (Huff) H.; m. Joyce Ann Stearns, Mar. 28, 1971 (div. Nov. 1983). BBA in Econs., Wichita State U., 1969, MS in Fin., 1972; Grad. Degree in Banking, So. Meth. U., 1975. Asst. v.p. Fourth Nat. Bank & Trust, Wichita, Kans., 1969-75; v.p. Citizens Frost Bank, San Antonio, 1975-77, United Bank Denver, 1977-84; pres. Am. Nat. Bank/United Bank-City Ctr., Aurora, Colo., 1984-86; sr. v.p. Corp. Fin. Asocs., Denver, 1987-89; dir. Colo. Nat. Leasing, Inc., Denver, 1989-95, pres., 1989-95, chmn. bd. dirs., 1993-95; v.p. and gen. mgr. comml. banking divsn. Colo. Nat. Bank, Denver, 1992-94; pres., chmn. bd. dirs. Colo. Bus. Leasing, Inc., Denver, 1995—. Dir. Am. Heart Assn. Colo., 1980—, pres., 1987-88; mem. Leadership Denver Assn., 1981, dir., 1990-95, pres. 1994-95; chmn. ArtReach, Inc., Denver, 1988, 89; bd. dirs. Colo. Spl. Olympics, 1994—, vice chmn., 1997. Mem. Denver Athletic Club, Meridian Golf Club. Republican. Office: Colo Bus Leasing Inc 999 18th St Ste 2400 Denver CO 80202

HALL, ROBERT EMMETT, JR., investment banker, realtor; b. Sioux City, Iowa, Apr. 28, 1936; s. Robert Emmett and Alvina (Faden) H.; m. Marna Thiel, 1969. BA, U. S.D., 1958, MA, 1959; MBA, U. Santa Clara, 1976; grad. Am. Inst. Banking, Realtors Inst. Grad. asst. U. S.D., Vermillion, 1958-59; mgr. ins. dept., asst. mgr. installment loan dept. Northwestern Nat. Bank of Sioux Falls, S.D., 1959-61, asst. cashier, 1961-65; asst. mgr. Crocker Nat. Bank, San Francisco, 1965-67, loan officer, 1967-69, asst. v.p., asst. mgr. San Mateo br., 1969-72; v.p., Western regional mgr. Internat. Investments & Realty, Inc., Washington, 1972—; owner Hall Investment Co., 1976—; pres. Almaden Oaks Realtors, Inc., 1976—; instr. West Valley Coll., Saratoga, Calif., 1972-82, Grad. Sch. Bus., U. Santa Clara (Calif.), 1981—. Treas., Minnehaha Leukemia Soc., 1963, Lake County Heart Fund Assn., 1962, Minnehaha Young Republican Club, 1963. Mem. Am. Inst. Banking, San Mateo C. of C., Calif. Assn. Realtors (vice chmn.), Beta Theta Pi. Republican. Roman Catholic. Clubs: Elks, Rotary (past pres.), K.C., Almaden Country, Mercedes Benz Calif. Home: 6951 Castlerock Dr San Jose CA 95120-4705 also: PO Box 458 Tahoma CA 96142 also: 8864 Rubicon Dr Rubicon Bay CA 96142 Office: Hall Enterprises 6501 Crown Blvd Ste 106 San Jose CA 95120-2903

HALL, TENNIEBEE M., editor; b. Bakersfield, Calif., May 21, 1940; d. William Elmer and Lillian May (Otis) Hall; m. Harold Robert Hall, Feb. 20, 1965. BA in Edn., Fresno State Coll., 1962; AA, Bakersfield Coll., 1960. Cert. tchr., Calif. Tchr. Edison (Calif.) Sch. Dist., 1962-65; substitute tchr. Marin and Oakland Counties (Calif.), Berkeley, 1965-66; engring. asst. Pacific Coil Co., Inc., Bakersfield, 1974-81; editor United Ostomy Assn., Inc., Irvine, Calif., 1986-91. Co-author: Treating IBD, 1989, Current Therapy in Gastroenterology, 1989; author, designer: Volunteer Leadership Training Manuals, 1982-84; contbr. articles to Ostomy Quar., 1973—. Mem. Pacific Beach Town Coun., San Diego, 1977—; campaign worker Maureen O'Connor (1st woman mayor of city), San Diego, 1986; mem. Nat. Digestive Diseases Adv. Bd., NIH, Washington, 1986-91; mem. planning and devel. bd. Scripps Clinic and Rsch. Found. Inflammatory Bowel Disease Ctr., San Diego, 1993—; various vol. activities, 1966-74, 81-86. Recipient Outstanding Svc. award VA Vol. Svc., Bur. of Vets. Affairs, Washington, 1990. Mem. Nat. Assn. Parliamentarians, United Ostomy Assn. Inc. (regional program dir. 1980-84, pres. 1984-86, Sam Dubin award 1983, Industry Adv. award 1987), Crohn's and Colitis Found. Am. (nat. trustee 1986-95, nat. v.p. 1987-92). Home and Office: 5284 Dawes St San Diego CA 92109-1231

HALL, THOMAS LINWOOD, real estate broker, investment portfolio manager; b. Richmond, Va., Aug. 27, 1935; s. Thomas S. and Marion Hall. Pres. Ananda Constrn., 1978—, Realty Investment Concepts, Inc., Las Vegas, Nev., 1986—, Resource Investment Capital, LLC; chmn. Comml. Investment Divsn., Greater Las Vegas Assn. Realtors, 1989-90; pres. Cert. Exchangors, 1992, Soc. of Las Vegas Equity Mktg. Specialists, 1983-93, pres. Millionaire Motors Inc., 1996. Musician R. Palombi Orch., Riviera Hotel, Las Vegas, 1969-94; v.p. Nev. Soc. for Prevention of Cruelty to Animals, Las Vegas. Mem. Internat. Factoring Inst., Nat. Mortgage Investors Inst., Comml. Investment Real Estate Inst., Nat. Coun. Exchangors (equity mktg. specialist, Hall of Fame 1992), Foresters. Home: PO Box 14951 2213 Paradise Rd Las Vegas NV 89104

HALL, WILLIAM E., engineering and construction company executive; b. Washington, Sept. 5, 1942; s. George W. and Jane F. (Brogger) H.; m. Lavinia Swift, Sept. 21, 1974; children: Deborah A., Douglas E., L. Jane, Elizabeth D. BSChemE, Va. Poly. Inst. and State U., 1963, MSChemE, 1964; postgrad., Stanford U., 1991. Process engr. Stone & Webster Engring. Co., Boston, 1967-70; project mgr. Stone & Webster Engring. Co., London, 1970-76, N.Y.C., 1976-78; regional bus. devel. mgr. Stone & Webster Engring. Co., Houston, 1978-79; prin. project mgr. RM Parsons Co., Pasadena, Calif., 1979-81, sr. v.p., 1989-92; pres. Ralph M. Parsons Co., Pasadena, Calif., 1992—; prin. project mgr. Saudi Arabia Parsons Ltd., Yanbu, 1981-84, mng. dir., 1984-89; bd. dirs. Proye Parsons, Caracas, Venezuela, Latisa; alt. dir. Constrn. Industry Inst., Austin, Tex., 1990-92, dir. 1992—. CHmn. Tournament of Life, Pasadena, 1990-92. Mem. Am. Inst. Chem. Engrs. Republican. Lutheran. Office: Ralph M Parsons Co 100 W Walnut St Pasadena CA 91124-0001 also: Parsons Process Group 5 Greenway Plz Houston TX 77046*

HALLENBECK, HARRY C., architect. Dir. State of Calif., Sacramento. Recipient Edward C. Kemper award Archtl. Inst. Am., 1994. Office: Seismic Safety Implementati State & Consumer Svc Agy 1300 I St Ste 750 Sacramento CA 95814-2913 also: 7485 Rush River Dr # 333 Sacramento CA 95831-5259

HALLENBECK, POMONA JUANITA, artist; b. Roswell, N.Mex., Nov. 12, 1938; d. Cleve and Juanita Henriette (Williams) H.; children: Cheryl Ellis, Cynthia Ellis-Ralph, Catherine Ellis-Timmons. AA, Ea. N.Mex. U., 1965; BFA, Art Student's League, 1976; postgrad., Pan Am. Art Sch., 1976-77. Mgr. Paul Anderson Photography, San Antonio, Tex., 1951-54; tchr. Roswell (N.Mex.) Ind. Sch. Dist., 1960-64; dir., instr. Sketchbox Sch. Art, Galveston, Tex., 1965-71; monitor etching class Art Student's League, N.Y.C., 1975-77; dir., instr. Alleyworks Atlier, Austin, Tex., 1978-81; dir., proprietor, artist Sketchbox Studio, Roswell, 1982-94; instr. Elderhostel program Ghost Ranch, Abiquiu, N.Mex., 1984-94; coord. Calender project Ghost Ranch, Abiquiu, N.Mex., 1992—; owner, proprietor Pomona's Accent Line, Roswell, 1986-94, cons., 1988-94; artist, demonstrator Roswell (N.Mex.) Mus. and Art Ctr., 1981-90, Roswell (N.Mex.) Ind. Sch., 1982-90. Illustrator: (book covers) Julian of Norwich, Nachman, Pseudo Dionysius, Classics of Western Spirituality, Naming the Powers, Unmasking the Powers, Engaging the Powers, Ghost Ranch Cookbook; exhibited in Southwest Expressions Gallery, Chgo., 1990, 91, Claire's Mountain Village, Ruidoso, N.Mex., 1990-94, Roswell Fine Art Mus., 1994, Artisan Gallery, Austin, 1995, Blaire Carnehan Fine Art, San Antonio, 1995, Cimmaron (N.Mex.) Art Gallery, 1995, Trading Post, 1995, Bitzer & Johnson, Roswell, 1996, 97, Potter's Guild Sho, 1997. Mem. World Wildlife, 1996, Roswell Assurance Home for Children, 1990, Ghost Ranch Compadres, Santa Fe, 1990-96, People for the Ethical Treatment of Animals, 1996; arts convener silent auction, Ghost Ranch, 1995. Recipient scholarship Altrusa Club, 1973, Purchase award Am. Artist, 1975; named Best of Show, Ghost Ranch Compadre Show, 1990, Altusa Fashion Show, 1990; grantee Whitney Enterprises, 1990, Artist-in-Residence grantee Ghost Ranch, 1992, McKee grantee, 1995-96. Mem. AAUW, Internat. Platform Assn., Nat. Platform Assn., Soc. Illustrators, Taos Fine Arts Assn., N.Mex. Watercolor Soc., Western Colo. Watercolor Soc., Supts. Salon of Paris (Bronze medal 1988), Ghost Ranch Found. Ctr., Roswell Mus. and Art Ctr., U.S. Humane Soc., Roswell Humane Soc., Mus. Women Artists, Knickerbocher (N.Y.C.). Democrat. Office: Sketchbox Studio of Art 3737 E Grand Plains Rd Roswell NM 88201-9005

HALLER, ANN CORDWELL, secondary school educator; b. Denver, July 2, 1944; d. Robert William and Dorothy Warne (Dahlberg) Cordwell; m. Frederick Ray Haller, Sept. 18, 1965; children: Michael Frederick, Lori Ann. BA in Pre-Med. Scis., Univ. Montana, 1966; MA in Anatomy, Univ. N.D., 1969; PhD in Anatomy, La. State Univ., 1975. Instr. dept. anatomy, sch. medicine Univ. N.D., Grand Forks, 1969-71; instr. dept. biol. scis. Univ. New Orleans, 1975-76; tchr. Kellogg (Idaho) Joint Sch. Dist. #391, 1978—; head class adv. Kellogg H.S., 1980—; mem. faculty adv. com. Nat. Honor Soc., Kellogg. Bd. dirs. Nat. Sci. Scholars Program, Idaho, other scholarship bds., West Shoshone Hosp., Kellogg, 1977-79; mem. Idaho health Sys. Agy., Boise, 1976-79. Recipient Centennial Tchr. Idaho award NIH, 1986. Mem. DAR, Am. Soc. Psychoprophylaxis in Obstetrics (Lamaze instr. 1978—), Nat. Sci. Tchrs. Assn., Philanthropic Ednl. Orgn., Sigma Xi, Delta Kappa Gamma. Lutheran. Home: PO Box 923 804 Country Club Ln Pinehurst ID 83850 Office: Kellogg Joint Sch Dist 391 Jacobs Gulch Rd Kellogg ID 83837

HALLER, EUGENE ERNEST, materials scientist, educator; b. Basel, Switzerland, Jan. 5, 1943; s. Eugen and Maria Anne Haller; m. Marianne Elisabeth Schlittler, May 27, 1973; children: Nicole Marianne, Isabelle Cathrine. Diploma in Physics, U. Basel, 1967, PhD in Physics, 1970. Postdoctoral asst. Lawrence Berkeley (Calif.) Lab., 1971-73, staff scientist, then sr. staff scientist, 1973-80, faculty sr. scientist, 1980—; assoc. prof. U. Calif., Berkeley, 1980-82, prof. materials sci., 1982—; co-chmn. Materials Rsch. Soc. Symposia, Boston, 1982, 89, Internat. Conf. on Shallow Levels in Semiconductors, Berkeley, 1984, 94; mem. rev. com. instrument div. Brookhaven Nat. Lab., Upton, N.Y., 1987-93; mem. Japanese tech. panel on sensors NSF-Nat. Acad. Sci., Washington, 1988; vis. prof. Imperial Coll. Sci., Tech. and Medicine, London, 1991. Editorial adv. bd. Jour. Phys. and Chem. Solids, 1993—; contbr. to numerous profl. publs. U.S. Sr. scientist award Alexander von Humboldt Soc., Germany, 1986, Max-Planck Rsch. award, 1994; rsch. fellow Miller Inst. Basic Rsch., Berkeley, 1990. Fellow Am. Phys. Soc.; mem. AAAS, Materials Rsch. Soc., Swiss Phys. Soc., Sigma Xi. Office: U Calif Berkeley 553 Evans Hall Berkeley CA 94720

HALLETT, JANE MARTIN, writer, educator; b. Belleville, Ill., May 9, 1933; d. Cecil Lawrence and Clara Harriet (Haskins) M.; m. Christian E. Heiligenstein, Aug. 29, 1953 (div.); children: Eric Lee Heiligenstein, Lynn Heiligenstein Caffrey. BA, U. Ill., 1955; MA, Ill. State U., 1984. Mgr. Spanish Internat. Tourist Office, St. Louis, 1968-70; promotional dir. Northwoods Mall, Peoria, Ill., 1971-73; tour leader Fine Arts Soc. and Peoria Art Guild, 1982-85; arts coord. Meth. Med. Ctr., Peoria, 1984-85; mus. educator U. Okla. Mus. Art, Norman, 1985-87; freelance writer, reporter Peoria Observer, WCBU, WHOI-TV, Peoria, The Pantagraph, Bloomington, Ill., New Art Examiner, Chgo., 1974-79; guest curator Laumeier Sculpture Park, St. Louis, 1983; mus. rep. Okla. Art Edn. Assn., Oklahoma City, 1985-87; mem. Okla. Alliance for Art Edn., Oklahoma City, 1985-87; grants com. Tucson/Pima Arts Coun., Tucson, 1991-93. Co-author children's activity book series, 1988—. Co-chair Pub. Arts Com. of Peoria City Beautiful, 1975-78; mem. Pub. Art and Cmty. Design Com., Tucson, 1991—, chair, 1995—. Multi-cultural heritage grantee Tucson/Pima Arts Coun., 1992, 93. Mem. Internat. Sculpture Ctr., Am. Assn. Museums, Pub. Rels. Soc. Am., Spanish Colonial Arts Soc., Assocs. Art History U. Ariz. (cmty. bd.). Office: PO Box 64216 Tucson AZ 85728-4216

HALLICK, RICHARD BRUCE, biochemistry educator; b. Glendale, Calif., Jan. 15, 1946; s. John and Rosa Elizabeth (Coates) H.; m. Margaret Ann Thomas West, Feb. 14, 1989; 1 child, Deborah Hallick Mundorf. BA, Pomona Coll., 1967; PhD, U. Wis., 1971. Postdoctoral rsch. assoc. U. Calif., San Francisco, 1971-73; asst. prof. U. Colo., Boulder, 1973-79, assoc. prof., 1980-83, prof., 1983-84; prof. biochemistry U. Ariz., Tucson, 1984—; vis. scientist Weizmann Inst. Sci., Rehovot, Israel, 1982; cons. Agrigenetics, Boulder, 1981-87; expert witness on DNA evidence, U.S. Dist. Ct., Pima, Cochise, Maricopa Counties, 1992—, in dist. and superior cts., Phoenix, Albbuquerque, 1992—; faculty senator U. Ariz., 1994-96. Exec. editor: Nucleic Acids Rsch. jour., 1989—. Rsch. grantee NIH, 1993-97. Mem. AAAS, Am. Soc. Biol. Chemists, Internat. Soc. Plant Molecular Biologists, Am. Soc. Biochemists and Molecular Biologists, Am. Soc. Plant Physiologists. Episcopalian. Office: Univ Ariz Biosciences West 524 Tucson AZ 85721

HALLIDAY, JOHN MEECH, investment company executive; b. St. Louis, Oct. 16, 1936; s. William Norman and Vivian Viola (Meech) H.; m. Martha Layne Griggs, June 30, 1962; children: Richard M., Elizabeth Halliday Traut. BS, U.S. Naval Acad., 1958; MBA, Harvard U., 1964. Dir. budgeting and planning Automatic Tape Control, Bloomington, Ill., 1964-66; dir. planning Ralston-Purina, St. Louis, 1966-67, v.p. subsidiary, 1967-68, dir. internat. banking, 1967-68; v.p. Servicetime Corp., St. Louis, 1968-70; assoc. R.W. Halliday Assocs., Boise, Idaho, 1970-87; v.p. Sawtooth Comm. Corp., Boise, 1970-73, Comdr. Corp., 1979-81; pres., CEO, bd. dirs. ML, Ltd., San Francisco, 1979—, H.W.L. Inc., San Francisco, 1985-93; pres. Halliday Labs., Inc., 1980-91; exec. v.p., bd. dirs. Franchise Fin. Corp. Am., Phoenix, 1980-85; bd. dirs., v.p. Harvard Bus. Sch. Assn. No. Calif., 1980-87; pres., CEO, bd. dirs. Cycletorl Diversified Industries, Inc., 1992—; guest lectr. U. Calif. Berkeley, 1991—, Calif. Bus.-Higher Edn. Forum, 1995—; mem. Senator Bill Lockyer's Ad-Hoc Bus. Adv. Group on Corrections, 1995-96. Pres. Big Bros. San Francisco, 1978-81; trustee, pres. U. Calif.-Santa Cruz Found., 1988—; mem. ad hoc com. on corrections Calif. State Senate, 1995-96. Mem. Restaurant Assn. (v.p. 1969-70), Olympic Club (San Francisco), Scott Valley Tennis Club (Mill Valley, Calif.). Republican. Episcopalian. Home: 351 Corte Madera Ave Mill Valley CA 94941-1013 Office: 625 Market St Ste 602 San Francisco CA 94105-3308

HALLIDAY, WILLIAM ROSS, retired physician, speleologist, writer; b. Atlanta, May 9, 1926; s. William Ross and Jane (Wakefield) H.; m. Eleanore Hartvedt, July 2, 1951 (dec. 1983); children: Marcia Lynn, Patricia Anne, William Ross III; m. Louise Baird Kinnard, May 7, 1988. BA, Swarthmore Coll., 1946; MD, George Washington U., 1948. Diplomate Am. Bd. Vocat. Experts. Intern Huntington Meml. Hosp., Pasadena, Calif., 1948-49; resident King County Hosp., Seattle, Denver Children's Hosp., L.D.S. Hosp., Salt Lake City, 1950-57; pvt. practice Seattle, 1957-65; with Wash. State Dept. Labor and Industries, Olympia, 1965-76; med. dir. Wash. State Div. Vocat. Rehab., 1976-82; staff physican N.W. Occupational Health Ctr., Seattle, 1983-84; med. dir. N.W. Vocat. Rehab. Group, Seattle, 1984, Comprehensive Med. Rehab. Ctr., Brentwood, Tenn., 1984-87; dep. coroner, King County, Wash., 1964-66. Author: Adventure Is Underground, 1959, Depths of the Earth, 1966, 76, American Caves and Caving, 1974, 82; co-author: (with Robert Nymeyer) Carlsbad Cavern: The Early Years, 1991; editor Jour. Spelean History, 1968-73; contbr. articles to profl. jours. Mem. Gov.'s North Cascades Study Com., 1967-76; mem. North Cascades Conservation Coun., v.p., 1962-63; pres. Internat. Speleological Found., 1981-87; asst. dir. Internat. Glaciospeleological Survey, 1972-76. Served to lt. comdr. USNR, 1949-50, 55-57. Recipient medal Geol. Soc. China; named Alumnus of Yr., George Sch., 1992. Fellow Am. Coll. Chest Physicians, Nat. Speleological Soc. (hon. mem. 1965, bd. govs. 1950-94), Explorers Club; mem. AMA, Nat. Trust (Scotland), Mountaineers Club (past trustee), Seattle Tennis Club.

HALLIN, KARL-ELIV JOHANN, industrial process control company executive; b. Stockholm, Sweden, Apr. 14, 1951; s. Emil Lennart Teodor and Liv Anna (Skogvang) H. BS, U. Alberta, Edmonton, Alberta, Can., 1973; PhD in Chemistry/Spectroscopy, U. B.C., Vancouver, B.C., Can., 1977. Rsch. assoc. Nat. Rsch. Coun./Herzberg Inst. of Astrophysics, Ottawa, Ont., Can., 1978-79; engr. Sentrol Systems Ltd., Downsview, Ont., Can., 1979-82; prin. scientist Valmet Sentrol, Downsview, 1982-89; sr. scientist Devron Hercules, Inc., North Vancouver, B.C., Can., 1989-92; sr. staff scientist Measurex Corp., Cupertino, Calif., 1992-95; sr. sys. arch. Electroglas Inc., Santa Clara, Calif., 1995—. Recipient Sci. scholarship Nat. Rsch. Coun. Can., U. B.C., 1973-77. Mem. Instrument Soc. of Am., IEEE. Office: Electroglas Inc MS/3001 2901 Coronado Dr Santa Clara CA 95054-3991

HALLIWELL, BETTY MARY, writer; b. Houston, Sept. 6, 1942; d. Clarence Tolbert and Mary Evangeline (Shively) Ladd; m. Michael John Halliwell, Sept. 17, 1966. MA, U. Chgo., 1964, UCLA, 1967; PhD, UCLA, 1972. Asst. prof. Calif. State U., Dominguez Hills, 1971, Loyola U., L.A., 1971-73; assoc. prof. Pepperdine U., Malibu, Calif., 1973-78; freelance writer Washington, 1978—, Santa Monica, Calif., 1978—. Author: (series) The Bjorklund Legacy: Philanth at 25, 1995, Bjorklund's Daughter, 1995, The Farber-Bjorklund Presidency Ended Strangely, 1995 (distributed in 80 countries). Recipient poetry prize U. Chgo., 1965; Woodrow Wilson fellow, 1963-64. Mem. Nat. Space Soc., Am. Astronautical Soc., Nat. Peace Corps Assn., Ams. for Death with Dignity, Ams. for Separation of Ch. and State, Character Edn. Partnership, Vegetarian Soc., Phi Beta Kappa. Home: 2930 Colorado Ave Apt D-18 Santa Monica CA 90404-3647

HALLOCK, C. WILES, JR., athletic official; b. Denver, Feb. 17, 1918; s. Claude Wiles and Mary (Bassler) H.; m. Marjorie Louise Eldred, Mar. 23, 1944; children: Lucinda Eldred Hallock Rinne, Michael Eldred. A.B., U. Denver, 1939. Sports info. dir. U. Wyo., 1949-60, track coach, 1952-56; sports info. dir. U. Calif., Berkeley, 1960-63; dir. pub. relations Nat. Collegiate Athletic Assn., 1963-68; dir. Nat. Collegiate Sports Services, 1967-68; commr. Western Athletic Conf., 1968-71; exec. dir. Pacific-8 Conf. (now Pacific-10 conf.), San Francisco and Walnut Creek, Calif., 1971-83; historian Pacific 10 Conf., 1983. Mem. Laramie (Wyo.) City Council, 1958-60. Served to lt. comdr. USNR, World War II. Decorated Air medal; mem. Nat. Football Found. and Hall of Fame Honors Ct. Mem. Nat. Collegiate Athletic Assn., Nat. Assn. Collegiate Dirs. Athletics (Corbett award 1983), Collegiate Commrs. Assn., Coll. Sports Info. Dirs. Am. (Arch Ward award 1963), Football Writers Assn. Am. (past dir.), U.S. Basketball Writers Assn., Lambda Chi Alpha. Presbyn. Home: 235 Western Hills Dr Pleasant Hill CA 94523-3167 Office: 800 S Broadway Walnut Creek CA 94596-5218

HALLORAN, JAMES VINCENT, III, technical writer; b. Greenwich, Conn., May 12, 1942; s. James Vincent and Rita Lucy (Keator) H.; m. Barbara Sharon Case, Sept. 7, 1974. BME, Cath. U. Am., 1964; MBA, U. Chgo., 1973. Mktg. rep. Rockwell Internat., El Segundo, Calif., 1973-76, bus. area mgr., 1976-80, bus. analysis mgr., 1980-84; asst. dir. market analysis H. Silver & Assocs. Inc., Torrance, Calif., 1984-87, dir. mktg., 1987-90; program mgr. Tech. Tng. Corp., Torrance, 1990-91; prin. Bus. Info. & Analysis, Redondo Beach, Calif., 1991-94; mgr. spl. projects Wyle Labs., El Segundo, Calif., 1994—. Commr. Redondo Beach Housing Adv. and Appeals Bd., 1985-89; mem. citizens adv. bd. South Bay Union High Sch. Dist., Redondo Beach, 1983; dir., newsletter editor Project Tomahawk, Curtiss-Wright Hist. Assn., 1995—. Capt. USAF, 1964-68. Libertarian. Home: 612 S Gertruda Ave Redondo Beach CA 90277-4245 Office: Wyle Labs 128 Maryland St El Segundo CA 90245-4115

HALLSTROM, ROBERT CHRIS, government actuary; b. Sacramento, June 8, 1953; s. Clifford Clarence and Billee June (Plunkett) H.; m. Pamela Jane Pracht, Apr. 25, 1987; 1 child, Kelsey Kathlene. BA in Math. with honors, Calif. State U., Sacramento, 1974, MS in Math., 1976. Cert. math. tchr. c.c., Calif. Asst. actuary Transam. Ins. Co., L.A., 1976-80; actuary Cal-Farm Ins. Co., Sacramento, 1980-84; instr. math. Sacramento City Coll., 1985, Sierra Coll., Rocklin, Calif., 1985; sr. casualty actuary Calif. Dept. Ins., San Francisco, 1985—. Fellow Casualty Actuarial Soc.; mem. Internat. Actuarial Assn. Office: Calif Dept Ins 45 Fremont St 21st Fl San Francisco CA 94105

HALOPOFF, WILLIAM EVON, industrial designer, consultant; b. Los Angeles, May 31, 1934; s. William John Halopoff and Dorothy E. (Foote) Lawrence; m. Nancy J. Ragsdale, July 12, 1960; children: Guy William and Carolee Nichole. BS, Art Ctr. Coll. Design, 1968. Internat. indsl. design cons. FMC Corp. Cen. Engring. Lab., Santa Clara, Calif., 1969-81; mgr. indsl. design Tandem Computers, Cupertino, Calif., 1981-93; design cons. Halopoff Assocs., San Jose, Calif., 1984—. Patentee in field. Served with U.S. Army, 1957-59. Mem. Indsl. Designers Soc. Am., Soc. Automotive Engrs. (chmn. subcom. 29 1979-85). Home: 17544 Holiday Dr Morgan Hill CA 95037-6303

HALPENNY, DIANA DORIS, lawyer; b. San Francisco, Jan. 18, 1951; d. William Frederick and Doris E. Halpenny. BA, Calif. State Coll., 1973; JD, Univ. Pacific, 1980. Bar: Calif. 1980. Bookkeeper, sales clk. Farmers Empire Drugs, Santa Rosa, Calif., 1971-73; activity dir. Beverly Manor Convalescent Hosp., Anaheim, Calif., 1973-74; instructional aide LA County Supt. Schs., Downey, Calif., 1974-76, sub. tchr., 1976-77; assoc. Littler, Mendelson, Fastiff & Tichy, San Jose, Calif., 1980-82, Walters & Shelburne, Sacramento,

1982-84, Kronick Moskovitz Tiedemann & Girard, Sacramento, 1984-85; legal advisor Pub. Employment Rels. Bd., 1985-87; gen. counsel San Juan Unified Sch. Dist., 1987—. Founding mem. In-house Sch. Attys No. Calif.; past pres. no. sect. Sch. Law Study Sect. County Counsels Assn., 1991-92; past pres. Calif. Coun. of Sch. Attys., 1995; legal adv. com. Calif. Sch. Bd. Assn. Edn. Legal Alliance; exec. bd. Calif. Edn. Mandated Cost Network, 1987—. Mem. Calif. Coun. Sch. Attys. (v.p. programs 1993, pres. elect 1994, pres. 1995. Office: San Juan Unified Sch Dist 3738 Walnut Ave Carmichael CA 95608-3054

HALPERIN, KRISTINE BRIGGS, insurance sales and marketing professional; b. Pocatello, Idaho, July 25, 1947; d. Fergus and Shirley (Tanner) Briggs; m. Michael Lauren Halperin, Aug. 5, 1995; children: Anthony Ted Rojas, Nancy Kristine Rojas. Student, Idaho State U., 1965-66. Tech. coord. Farmers Ins. Group, Pocatello, 1971-81; svc. rep. All Seasons Ins. Agy., Ventura, Calif., 1982; sr. comml. underwriting asst. Royal Ins. Co., Ventura, 1982-85; sr. comml. lines underwriter Andreini & Co., Ventura, 1985-88; large comml. account unit coord. Frank B. Hall, Inc., Oxnard, Calif., 1988-93; supr. comml. lines dept. Fox Ins. Agy. Inc., Camarillo, Calif., 1993—. Editor (bulletin) News Waves, 1985-87; artist various works specializing in charcoal portraits. Mem. NAFE, Ins. Women Ventura County (treas. 1987-88, v.p. 1988-90, 96—, pres. 1990-91, corr. sec. 1991-92, bd. dirs. 1986, Woman of Yr. 1989-90), Nat. Assn. Ins. Women. Republican. Baptist. Home: 2197 Brookhill Dr Camarillo CA 93010-2107 Office: Fox Ins Agy Inc 2301 Daily Dr Ste 200 Camarillo CA 93010-6613

HALPERN, LEON (HAL PERRIN), composer; b. Bklyn., May 15, 1908; s. Jacab and Vera (Greenberg) H.; m. Fleurette Segalle, Dec. 6, 1936; 1 child, Tamara Ann. Student, Inst. of Musical Art, N.Y.C., 1924-32. Accompanist Isadora Duncans Group, N.Y.C., 1936-37, various dance groups, N.Y.C., 1935-37. Composer numerous ballets, piano music. Scholar Inst. Musical Art, 1925. Mem. ASCAP. Home: 5356 Village Green Los Angeles CA 90016

HALPERT, LESLIE DEAN, engineering executive; b. N.Y.C., Oct. 25, 1953; s. Albert Lee and Charlotte (Batcher) H.; m. Mary Elise Copley, Oct. 23, 1988. Student, Calif. Poly. U., 1971-76; BS in Aerospace Engring., Northrop U., 1987. Design engr. NAA, Rockwell Internat., El Segundo, Calif., 1976-80, sr. master dimensions engr., 1981-93; sr. design engr. Lockheed Corp., Burbank, Calif., 1980-81; pres., chief exec. officer Allen Indsl. Supply, Inc., Burbank, 1993—. Mem. AIAA. Office: Allen Indsl Supply Inc 1711 W Burbank Blvd Burbank CA 91506-1312

HALSELL, GEORGE KAY, music educator; b. Bryan, Tex., Oct. 23, 1956; s. Kay and Jo Inez (Wootten) H.; m. Melanie Lynn Marsh, Aug. 4, 1984; 1 child, Simon Godric. MusB, Johns Hopkins Univ., 1979; MusM, U. Tex., 1980, DMA, 1989. Instr. music West Va. Univ., Morgantown, 1983-84; adj. instr. music Frederick (Md.) C.C., 1985-90; asst. prof. music Adams State Coll., Alamosa, Colo., 1990-91; instr. music Pikes Peak C.C., Colorado Springs, 1992-94; asst. prof. Music Coll. So. Idaho, Twin Falls, 1994—; adj. instr. music Essex C.C., Balt., 1985-90; instr. music Univ. So. Colo., Pueblo, 1992-94; freelance musician; lectr. Pueblo Symphony Orch., 1992-94. Office: Coll So Idaho 315 Falls Ave Twin Falls ID 83301-3367

HALSEY, MINOR, computer company executive. Degree, U. Va. Founder Global Pub. Corp.; founder, chmn., CEO Russell Reynolds, Jr.; chmn., CEO CNET: The Computer Network, 1992—. Office: C-Net The Computer Network 150 Chestnut St San Francisco CA 94111

HALSEY-BRANDT, GREG, mayor. BA in Geography, U. B.C., MA in Geography. Town planner, alderman, 1981-90; mayor City of Richmond, B.C., 1990—; mem. Vancouver Regional Transit Commn.; chmn., dir. Greater Vancouver Regional Dist., 1993-96. Mem. Planning Inst. B.C., Richmond C. of C. Office: Office of the Mayor, 6911 No 3 Rd, Richmond, BC Canada V6Y 2C1

HALVORSEN, JAN LA RAYNE, library services manager; b. Chgo., Aug. 30, 1941; d. La Vern Grant and Dorothy Ethelyn (Johnston) Kelley; m. Wayne Lee Halvorsen, Nov. 5, 1958 (div. Feb. 1975); children: Jon Alan, Kathryn Lynn. BA in Polit. Sci. with honors, Calif. State Poly. U., 1975; M in Pub. Adminstrn., U. Calif., Riverside, 1977; MLS, UCLA, 1990. Ops. supr. City of Huntington Beach (Calif.) Libr., 1984-90, libr. svcs. mgr. circulation, tech. svcs., branches, 1991—; guest lectr. mcpl. fin. Calif. State Poly. U., Pomona, 1986, 87; guest lectr. libr. mgmt. UCLA, 1989; intenr devel. office UCLA, 1988, Mayor Tom Bradley's city econ. devel. office City of L.A., 1989; spkr. Women's Fedn. for World Peace, Anjo, Japan, 1996. Founder family literacy program U.S. Dept. Health Edn. and Welfare, Huntington Beach, 1993, svc. club for teenage girls Valley (Vista H.S.) Club, Fountain Valley, Calif., 1996; dir. ARIDAY, Costa Mesa, Calif., 1994; v.p. Mgmt. Employees Orgn., Huntington Beach, 1986, pres., 1987; sister city rep. from Huntington Beach to Anjo, Japan, 1996. Community Devel. grantee Huntington Beach Dept. Housing Urban Devel., 1994, 97, Calif. League of Cities Helen Putnam award for Excellence, Top award for Cultural Diversity for New Oak View Branch, 1995, Internat. award for svc. for founding Teen Svc. Club, Soroptimist Internat. of Americas, 1997. Mem. ALA, Am. Soc. Pub. Adminstrn., Calif. Libr. Assn. (chair women's devel. conf. 1991-92), Acad. Polit. Sci., Soroptimist Internat. (newsletter, del. 1991-92, 92-93, v.p. 1993-94, pres. 1994-95, Desert Coast region dist. II sec. 1996—, rep. UN 4th World Women's Conf. Beijing 1995), UN Assn. Home: 15682 Mayflower Ln Huntington Beach CA 92647-2807 Office: Huntington Beach Libr 7111 Talbert Ave Huntington Beach CA 92648-1232

HALVORSEN, ROBERT ALFRED, JR., radiologist, educator; b. N.Y.C., Oct. 12, 1948; s. Robert Alfred and Dorothy Deeble (Stalcup) H. BS in Chemistry, U. Miami, 1970, MD, 1974. Rotating intern St. Mary's Med. Ctr., Long Beach, Calif., 1974-75; resident in radiology U. Tex., San Antonio, 1977-80, instr., 1980; fellow ABD imaging Duke U., Durham, N.C., 1980-81, from asst. prof. to assoc. prof., 1981-87; assoc. prof. U. Minn., Mpls., 1987-90; prof., vice-chmn. radiology and medicine U. Calif., San Francisco, 1990—; chief radiology San Francisco Gen. Hosp.; vice chmn. IPA, 1994-97; mem. steering com. County Info. Sys. Network. Contbr. numerous papers to sci. jours., 15 book chpts. Alternate del. Rep. Party, Mpls., 1989. Cadet USCG, 1966-67. Fellow Am. Coll. Radiology, Soc. Emergency Radiologists (chmn. program com. 1995-96, exec. com. 1995-97); mem. Soc. Computed Body Tomography and Magnetic Resonance (chmn. standards com. 1993-95), Soc. Gastrointestinal Radiology (Roscoe Miller award for best paper 1989), Assn. Univ. Radiologists (exec. com. 1990-95, chmn. Stauffer award com. 1993-95). Home: 56 Issaquah Dock Sausalito CA 94965 Office: San Francisco Gen Hosp Dept Radiology 1001 Potrero Ave San Francisco CA 94110-3518

HALVORSON, ALFRED RUBIN, retired mayor, consultant, education educator; b. Milan, Minn., Jan. 22, 1921; s. Chris and Alice (Kleven) H.; m. Dorothy F. Boxrud, Apr. 23, 1944; children: Gary A., Joan D. Halvorson Felice. BS, U. Minn., 1944, PhD, 1949. County extension agt. Agr. Extension Svc. of Minn., St. Paul, 1945; soil fertility researcher Oreg. State U., Klamath Falls, 1949-54; extension agronomist Purdue U., Lafayette, Ind., 1954-57; extension soil scientist Wash. State U., Pullman, 1957-86, prof. emeritus, 1986—; cons. ACF & Shirley Fetilizer Ltd., Brisbane, Australia, 1964, Saudi Arabia Farming Ops., Riyadh, 1984, U.S. AID, Sanaa, North Yemen, 1987. City councilman, City of Pullman, 1987-91, mayor, 1991-95. With M.C. U.S. Army, 1945. Mem. Kiwanis (chair com. Pullman chpt.). Republican. Lutheran. Home and Office: 325 SE Nebraska St Pullman WA 99163-2239

HALVORSON, MARY ELLEN, education educator, writer; b. Salem, Ohio, Apr. 23, 1950; d. Robert J. and Betty June (Bear) Batzli; m. Thomas Henry Halvorson, June 10, 1972; children: Christine Lynn, Matthew Thomas, Rebecca Lynn. BS in Edn. with distinction, No. Ariz. U., 1972, postgrad., 1973-92; postgrad., U. Ariz., 1974-76, Ariz. State U., 1975-76, U. Phoenix, 1989-90; Calif. Coast U., 1994—. Cert. elem. tchr., libr., Ariz. Tchr. Prescott (Ariz.) Unified Schs., 1972-77, dir. community nature ctr., 1978, reading tutor, 1985-88, family math. tchr., 1989-90, part-time libr., 1991-92; dir. Prescott Study Ctr., 1987-90; writer ednl. materials Herald House, Independence, Mo., 1994—; instr. Yavapai C.C., 1994—; edn. coord. Yavapai Prescott Indian Tribe, 1996—; guest speaker Abia Judd Young Authors, Prescott, 1992; math. enthusiast instr. Ariz. Dept. Edn., Prescott, 1989-92; asst. instr. outdoor edn. Ariz. State U., Prescott, 1977-78; tutor English grammar No. Ariz. U., Flagstaff, 1971-72. Co-author: Arizona Bicentenial Resource Manual, 1975; contbr. book rev. column to Prescott Courier, 1993, also articles to profl. publs. Cert. adult instr. Temple Sch., Independence, Mo., 1985—; sec., bd. dirs. Whispering Pines, Prescott, 1989-93; music docent Prescott Symphony Guild, 1982-85; state Christian edn. dir. Cmty. of Christ. Ch., Ariz., 1977-82, elder, counselor to pastor, 1993—; spokesperson Franklin Heights Homeowners, Prescott, 1985; leader Prescott Pioneers 4-H Club, 1989—, Christian Youth Group, 1985—; fundraiser Graceland Coll., 1993; craft demonstrator Sharlott Hall Mus.; master of ceremonies Prescott Summer Pops Symphony, 1995. Recipient 4-H Silver Clover Svc. award, 1995; named Outstanding Young Educator, Prescott Jaycees, 1976, Outstanding Young Women of Am., 1985. Mem. Phi Kappa Phi, Kappa Delta Pi, Sigma Epsilon Sigma. Home: 2965 Pleasant Valley Dr Prescott AZ 86301-7116

HAM, GARY MARTIN, psychologist; b. Lincoln, Nebr., Feb. 6, 1940; s. Wendell E. and Sally Bertha (Lind) H.; children: Jeffery M. BS in Psychology, Wash. State U., 1963, MS in Psychology, 1965; PsyD, Newport U., 1988. Lic. psychologist, Calif.; cert. tchr., Calif, counselor. Clin. psychologist Riverside (Calif.) County Dept. Mental Health, 1967—; tchr., cons., pub. speaker, researcher Riverside County Dept. Mental Health, 1967—; instr. U. Calif. Riverside, Chapman U. Clin. psychologist Riverside County, Critical Incidents Disaster Response Team, 1985—, ARC Disaster Team. 1st lt. USAF, 1964-67. Mem. APA, ASCD, Am. Mental Health Counselors Assn., Am. Critical Incident Stress Found., Calif. Psychol. Assn., Air Force Soc. Psychologists, Psi Chi, Sigma Phi Epsilon. Office: Riverside County Dept Mental Health PO Box 52567 Riverside CA 92517-3567

HAM, STEPHANIE ANN, interior architect; b. Elgin, Ill., Oct. 29, 1950; d. Erwin Joseph and Adele Lou (Wagner) Seyk; m. Arthur Daniel Vermeire, Aug. 14, 1970 (div. 1978); 1 child, Holly Ann Vermiere; m. Jay Todd Ham, Jan. 1, 1987. BS in Interior Architecture, Ariz. State U., 1987. Interior designer United Bank, Phoenix, 1987-88, Architecture One, Phoenix, 1988-89, CBS Property Svcs. Inc., Phoenix, 1989-93; interior designer, sr. planner McCarthy Nordburg, Ltd., Phoenix, 1993-94; facilities project planner City of Phoenix, 1994—. Mentor Ariz. Womens' Found., Phoenix, 1990. Recipient First Place Elderly Care Housing award Del Webb Corp., 1986. Mem. NAFE, Assn. of U. Women. Republican. Roman Catholic. Office: City of Phoenix 200 W Washington St Fl 14 Phoenix AZ 85003-1611

HAMADA, DUANE TAKUMI, architect; b. Honolulu, Aug. 12, 1954; s. Robert Kensaku and Jean Hakue (Masutani) H.; m. Martha S.P. Lee, Dec. 22, 1991; children; Erin, Robyn. BFA in Environ. Design, U. Hawaii, 1977, BArch, 1979. Registered architect, Hawaii, Guam, Florida, Puerto Rico, Saipan. Intern Edward Sullam, FAIA & Assocs., Honolulu, 1979-80; assoc. Design Ptnrs., Inc., Honolulu, 1980-86; prin. AM Ptnrs., Inc., Honolulu, 1986—. Chmn. 31st Ann. Cherry Blossom Festival Fashion Show, Honolulu, 1982, 32d Ann. Cherry Blossom Festival Cooking Show, 1983, mem. steering com., 1982, 83. Recipient Gold Key award for Excellence in Interior Design Am. Hotel and Motel Assn., 1990, Renaissance '90 Merit award Nat. Assn. Home Builder's Remodeler Coun., Merit award Honolulu mag., 1990, Cert. of Appreciation PACDIV USN, 1992. Mem. AIA (Sch. medal 1979), Constrn. Specifications Inst., Nat. Coun. Archtl. Registration Bds., Colegio de Arcquitectos de P.R., Japanese C. of C. Hawaii, Japan-Am. Soc., Hawaiian Astron. Soc. Office: AM Ptnrs Inc 1164 Bishop St Ste 1000 Honolulu HI 96813-2824

HAMANN, JANET M., educational psychology educator; b. San Francisco, Feb. 29, 1936; d. Lawrence Henry and Esther Abigail (Long) H.; m. Wayne R. Sutton, July 30, 1957 (div. July 1969); children: Karin, Jessica, Paul, Roger. BA, UCLA, 1958, MA, 1976, PhD, 1989. Cert. secondary sch. tchr., Calif. Tchr., counselor L.A. City Schs., 1959-74; sr. rsch. asst. UCLA Sch. Edn., 1978-86; lectr., evaluator Mt. St. Mary's Coll., L.A., 1982-92; lectr. Loyola Marymount U., L.A., 1989-90, Calif. Poly. U., Pomona, 1991-92; rschr. UCLA Sociobehavioral Group, 1989-93; instrnl. specialist Moorpark (Calif.) Coll., 1993-96; asst. prof. tchr. edn. Calif. State U., Bakersfield, 1996—. Contbr. articles to profl. jours. Recipient UCLA Dissertation award, 1988; Pi Lambda theta scholar, 1987; UCLA Sociobehavioral Group Postdoctoral fellow, 1989. Mem. World Federalist Assn., Internat. Found. for Integral Psychology, AERA, Sierra Club. Democrat. Home: 6001 Auburn St Apt 222 Bakersfield CA 93306 Office: California State Univ-Bakersfield Dept Tchr Edn 9001 Stockdale Hwy Bakersfield CA 93306

HAMBRECHT, WILLIAM R., venture capitalist; b. 1935; married; 5 children. Student, Princeton U. Broker Francis I. DuPont & Co., San Francisco; mng. ptnr. Hambrecht & Quist, San Francisco, pres., chief exec. officer, dir., now chmn.; bd. dirs. People Express, Inc. Office: Hambrecht & Quist One Bush St San Francisco CA 94104*

HAMBURGER, ROBERT N., pediatrics educator, consultant; b. N.Y.C., Jan. 26, 1923; s. Samuel B. and Harriet (Newfield) H.; m. Sonia Gross, Nov. 9, 1943; children: Hilary, Debre (dec.), Lisa. BA, U. N.C., 1947; MD, Yale U., 1951. Diplomate Am. Bd. Pediatrics, Am. Bd. Allergy and Immunology. Instr., asst. clin. prof. sch. medicine Yale U., New Haven, 1951-60; assoc. prof. biology U. Calif. San Diego, La Jolla, 1960-64, assoc. prof. pediatrics, 1964-67, prof., 1970-90, prof. emeritus, 1990—, asst. dean sch. medicine, 1964-70, lab. dir., 1970—, head fellows tng. program allergy and immunology divsn., 1970-90; pres. RNA and Co., Inc., 1997—; cons. various cos., Calif., Sweden, Switzerland, 1986—; bd. dirs. La Jolla Diagnostics, Inc. Author 1 book; contbr. articles to profl. jours.; patentee allergy peptides, allergen detector. Vol. physician, educator Children of the Californias, Calif. and Baja California, Mex., 1993—. 1st lt. Air Corps, U.S. Army, 1943-45. Grantee NIH and USPHS, 1960-64, 64-84; Fulbright fellow, 1980, Disting. fellow Am. Coll. Allergy, Asthma, Immunology, 1986. Mem. U. Calif. San Diego Emeriti Assn. (pres. 1992-94). Office: U Calif San Diego Allergy Immunology Lab La Jolla CA 92093-0950

HAMBURGER, RONALD OWEN, structural engineering executive; b. N.Y.C., May 22, 1952; s. Stanley Cellar and Claire (Oppenheimer) H.; m. Deborah Ann Osborne, Aug. 26, 1979; children: Kathryn Marie, Robert Steven. BS in Civil Engring., Poly. Inst. N.Y., 1974, MS in Civil Engring., 1974; MBA in Project Mgmt., Golden Gate U., 1986. Registered profl. civil engr. Calif., L.A., Utah, Guam; registered profl. structural engr. Calif., Guam. Engr. Bechtel Assocs. Profl. Corp., N.Y.C., 1974-76; supervising engr. Bechtel Corp., San Francisco, 1976-86; sr. v.p. EQE Internat., Inc., San Francisco, 1986—; project dir. SAC Joint Venture, Sacramento, 1994—; chair tech. subcom. 2 Bldg. Seismic Safety Coun., 1995—. Contbr. articles to profl. publs. Commr. Pacifica (Calif.) Transp. and Safety Commn., 1982-85; commr. bikeway com. San Mateo (Calif.) Regional Planning Commn., 1985. Mem. Structural Engrs. Assn. Calif. (dir. 1995—), Structural Engrs. Assn. No. Calif. (chair seismology com. 1993-94, pres. 1995-96), Earth Engring. Rsch. Inst. (dir. 1997—, chair existing bldgs. forum 1995—). Republican. Jewish. Office: EQE Internat Inc 44 Montgomery St Fl 32 San Francisco CA 94104-4602

HAMBY, DRANNAN CARSON, chemist, educator; b. Duncan, Okla., Nov. 16, 1933; s. Wellington Vernon and Dessie A. (Miller) H.; m. Beverly R. Reinhart, Apr. 3, 1951; children: Mark, Marcy. BA, Linfield Coll., McMinnville, Oreg., 1955; MA, Oreg. State U., Corvallis, 1962, PhD, 1968. Chemist Linfield Rsch. Inst., McMinnville, 1956—, dir., 1962-78; from asst. prof. to prof. chemistry Linfield Coll., 1962—; vis. rsch. engr. UCLA, 1975-76, Brigham Young U., Provo, Utah, 1991-92; instr. Nat. Ourdoor Leaders Sch., Lander, Wyo., 1983—. Mem. McMinnville City Coun., 1976-80. Fulbright scholar, Germany, 1955-56. Mem. Electrochem. Soc., Mt. Hood Ski Patrol, Sierra Club, Sigma Xi. Democrat. Home: 232 NE Oregon St Mcminnville OR 97128-4328 Office: Chemistry Dept Linfield College Mcminnville OR 97128

HAMI, LISA SUZANNE, laboratory supervisor, medical technologist; b. Balt., July 24, 1964; d. Paul Frederick Jr. and Marjorie Anne (Cook) Fox; m. Aliakbar Hami, Mar. 16, 1991; children: Nima John, Maryam Melissa. BS, U. Md., 1986. Med. tech. U. Md. Med. Sys., Balt., 1985-90; supr. stem cell engring. lab. and cord blood bank U. Colo. Hosp., Denver, 1990—; lectr. CACMLE, Denver, 1994. Contbr. articles to profl. jours. Mem. Internat. Soc. Hematother and Graft Engring. (bd. dirs. 1993—). Office: U Colo U Hosp 4200 E 9th Ave Box B-190 Denver CO 80262

HAMILTON, ALLEN PHILIP, financial advisor; b. Albany, Calif., Oct. 17, 1937; s. Allen Philip Sr. and Barbara Louise (Martin) H.; m. Mary Williams, July 18, 1981 (div. Mar. 1987). BA in Bus. Mgmt., St. Mary's U., San Jose, Calif., 1961; AA, Contra Costa State Coll., 1957; Bus. Assoc. degree, NW Mo. State U., 1969; postgrad., San Jose State U., 1959-61. Cert. fin. planner. Fin. advisor Consolidated Investment Svcs., Kansas City, Mo., 1968-70; pres., chief exec. officer Balanced Mgmt. Assn., Mission, Kans., 1969-72, Advanced Svc. Assn., Overland Park, Kans., 1971-78; divisional mgr. Waddell & Reed, Inc., Kansas City, 1978-81; sr. v.p., regional dir. WZW Fin. Svcs., Kansas City, 1981-86; exec.v.p. Skaife & Co., Orinda, Calif., 1986-88; v.p., mktg. dir. Consolidated Securities Corp., Walnut Creek, Calif., 1988; sr. dir. and cert. trainer Club Am., Inc., L.A., 1990—; CFP, prin. Hamilton Fin. Adv., Am. Investment Svcs., Pleasant Hill., Calif., 1989—; silver mktg. distbr., corp. trainer, Can. mktg. distbr. and trainer Nikken, Inc. Internat., numerous fgn. countries, 1991—; sales mgr., ind. distributor, sales trainer Alpine Industries, 1992—; prin. advisor Environ. Solutions Internat.; exec. dir., C.E.O. Environ. Air Quality and Health Found. (Environ. Solutions Internat.); sr. dir. Club Am. OTC Pink Shts., L.A., 1990-92; presdl. dir. FundAmerica, Irvine, Calif., 1988—; guest speaker in field. Author: (with others) The Financial Planner A New Profession, 1986. Asst. dist. commr. Boy Scouts Am., Kansas City, Kans., 1970-79; corp. dir. United Campaign, Overland Park, Kans., 1965-73; active TV show Kidney Found., Kansas City, Mo., 1969-70; sr. arbitrator San Francisco Bay Area Better Bus. Bur., 1986—. Lt. U.S. Army, 1963-65. Recipient Citation Nat. Campaign Re-election 1992, 1992m Senatorial Commn. Rep. Senatorial Inner Circle, 1991. Mem. Inst. Cert. Fin. Planners, Internat. Assn. for Fin. Planning (v.p., bd. dirs. 1982-87, practitioner div.), Registry of Fin. Planning Practitioners, Mt. Diablo Distbrs. Assn. Republican. Home: 2265 Gladwin Dr Walnut Creek CA 94596-6332

HAMILTON, ARTHUR MARKELL, state legislator; 3 children. Mem. Ariz. Ho. of Reps., 1973—; pub. affairs rep. Salt River Project, Phoenix, 1969—; leader Dem. Caucus, 1983—; mem. various coms. including Ways and Means, Rules, Legis. Coun.; mem. labor-mgmt. task force Sec. of Labor, 1994-96; mem. State Legis. Leaders Found. Mem. Nat. Conf. State Legislatures (past pres.), Dem. Legis. Leaders Assn. (vice-chair), Ariz. Dem. Leadership Coun. (founding mem.). Office: Ariz Ho of Reps Dem Caucus 1700 W Washington Phoenix AZ 85007

HAMILTON, CHARLES HOWARD, metallurgy educator; b. Pueblo, Colo., Mar. 17, 1935; s. George Edwin and Eva Eleanor (Watson) H.; m. Joy Edith Richmond, Sept. 7, 1968; children: Krista Kathleen, Brady Glenn. BS, Colo. Sch. Mines, 1959; MS, U. So. Calif., 1965; PhD, Case Western Res. U., 1968. Research engr. Space div. Rockwell Internat., Downey, Calif., 1959-65; mem. tech. staff Los Angeles div. Rockwell Internat., 1968-75; tech. staff, phys. metallurgy Sci. Ctr., Thousand Oaks, Calif., 1975-77, group mgr. metals processing, 1977-79, prin. scientist, 1979-81, dir. materials synthesis and processing dept., 1982-84; assoc. prof. metallurgy Wash. State U., Pullman, 1984-87, prof., 1987—; chmn. Rockwell Corp. tech. panel, materials research and engring; co-organizer 1st Internat. Symposium Superplastic Forming, 1982, Internat. Conf. on Superplasticity and Superplastic Forming, 1988. Sr. editor Jour. Materials Shaping Tech.; dep. editor Scripta Metallurgica et Materialia, 1989—; contbr. tech. articles to profl. publs.; patentee advanced metalworking and tech. Named Rockwell Engr. of Yr., 1979; recipient IR 100 award Indsl. Research mag., 1976, 80. Fellow Am. Soc. Metals; mem. AIME (shaping and forming com.), Sigma Xi. Home: 410 SE Crestview St Pullman WA 99163-2213

HAMILTON, DARDEN COLE, flight test engineer; b. Pitts., Nov. 28, 1956; s. Isaac Herman Hamilton and Grace osborne (Fish) thorp; m. Linda Susanne Moser, Aug. 7, 1976; children: Christopher Moser Hamilton, Elijah Cole Hamilton. BS in Aeronautics, St. Louis U., Cahokia, Ill., 1977; postgrad. in aeronautical tech., Ariz. State U. Lic. pilot, airframe and power mechanic; cert. instr. NRA. Engr. McDonnell Douglas Aircraft Co., St. Louis, Mo., 1977-80; group leader, engring. Cessna Aircraft Co., Wichita, Kans., 1980-83, sr. flight test engr., 1983-85; sr. flight test engr. Allied-Signal Aerospace Co., Phoenix, 1986-92; flight test engr. specialist Allied-Signal Aerospace Co., 1992—. Editor Family Proponent Newsletter, 1994—. Apptd. mem. Ariz. Gov.'s Constnl. Commemoration Com., 1997-2001; bd. dirs. Ariz. House and Senate Chaplaincy; Desert Sky precinct committeeman Rep. Party; vol. coord. legis. dist. 16 campaign John Shadegg for Congress; mem. adult edn. dept. Rivers Comty. Ch.; del. Ariz. dist. 16 Ariz. Rep. Conv., 1995—; mem. resolutions com. Ariz. Rep. Party. Mem. Soc. Flight Test Engrs., Am. Helicopter Soc., Ariz. State Rifle and Pistol Assn. (life). Republican. Home: 5533 W Christy Ln Glendale AZ 85304 Office: Allied-Signal Aerospace Co Allied Signal Engines Inc 111 S 34th St Phoenix AZ 85034-2802

HAMILTON, DAVID BOYCE, economist, economics educator; b. Pitts., Aug. 31, 1918; s. David Boyce andNell Gaston (Blackburn) H.; m. Elizabeth Teal, Dec. 21, 1946 (div. 1982); children: Betsy, David; m. Pauline Turner, May 11, 1985; stepchildren: David, Scott. BA, U. Pitts., 1940, MA, 1941; PhD, U. Tex., 1951. Instr. econs. U. Pitts., 1946-47, U. Tex., Austin, 1947-49; from asst. prof. econs. to prof. econs. U. N. Mex., Albuquerque, 1949-88, prof. emeritus; vis. assoc. prof. econs. Columbia U., N.Y.C., 1956-57; mem. N. Mex. Labor and Indsl. Commn., Santa Fe, 1975-86. Author: The Consumer In Our Economy, 1962, A Primer on the Economics of Poverty, 1968, Evolutionary Economics, 1991; contbr. over 115 articles, reviews to profl. jours., quarterlies. Mem. City of Albuquerque Campaign Ethics, 1977-84, labor bd. City of Albuquerque, 1982-89; campaign mgr. Sen. Joseph M. Montoya, N. Mex., 1970, 76; treas. Robert Kennedy for Pres. campaign, N.Mex.,1968. Maj. USAF, 1941-46, 51-52. Mem. Assn. Evolutionary Econs. (pres. 1972, Veblen/Cummins award 1982), Assn. Instl. Thought, Western Social Sci. Assn., Southwestern Social Sci. Assn. Democrat. Home: 1715 Morningside Pl SE Albuquerque NM 87108 Office: U N Mex Dept Econs Albuquerque NM 87131

HAMILTON, DAVID MIKE, publishing company executive; b. Little Rock, Feb. 25, 1951; s. Ralph Franklin and Mickey Garnette (Chappell) H.; m. Carol Nancy McKenna, Oct. 25, 1975; children: Elisabeth Michelle, Caroline Ellen. BA, Pitzer Coll., 1973; MLS, UCLA, 1976. Cert. tchr. library sci., Calif. Editor Sullivan Assocs., Palo Alto, Calif., 1973-75; curator Henry E. Huntington Library, San Marino, Calif., 1976-80; mgr. prodn., mktg. William Kaufmann Pubs., Los Altos, Calif., 1980-84; pres. The Live Oak Press, Palo Alto, 1984—; cons. editor, gen. ptnr. Sensitive Expressions Pub. Co., Palo Alto, 1985—; consulting dir. AAAI Press, 1994—. Author: To the Yukon with Jack London, 1980, The Tools of My Trade, 1986; contbg. editor and webmaster AAAI world-wide web site, 1995—; contbg. author Small Press jour., 1986, Making a Digital Book, 1995, (books) Book Club of California Quarterly, 1985, Research Guide to Biography and Criticism, 1986. Sec. vestry Trinity Parish, Menlo Park, 1986, bd. dirs., 1985-87; trustee Jack London Ednl. Found., San Francisco; bd. dirs. ISYS Forum, Palo Alto, 1987-96; pres. site coun., mem. supt.'s adv. com. Palo Alto Unified Sch. Dist. Mem. ALA, Coun. on Scholarly, Med. and Ednl. Publs., Am. Assn. Artificial Intelligence (bd. dirs. 1984—, dir. publs.), Bookbuilders West (book show com. 1983), Author's Guild, Soc. Tech. Communication (judge 1984), Assn. Computing Machinery (chmn. pub. com. 1984), Soc. Scholarly Pubs., Sierra Club, Book Club Calif. Democrat. Episcopalian. Home: 2620 Emerson St Palo Alto CA 94306-2310 Office: The Live Oak Press PO Box 60036 Palo Alto CA 94306-0036

HAMILTON, JAMES DOUGLAS, economics educator; b. Denver, Colo., Nov. 29, 1954; s. Warren Bell and Alcita Victoria Hamilton; m. Marjorie Ann Flavin, Aug. 6, 1983; children: Laura Diane, Richard Gregory. BA, Colo. Coll., 1977; MA, U. Calif., Berkeley, 1981, PhD, 1983. From asst. prof. to assoc. prof. to prof. econs. U. Va., Charlottesville, 1981-92; prof. econs. U. Calif., San Diego, 1992—; vis. prof. U. Calif., San Diego, 1984-85; rsch. advisor Fed. Res. Bank, Richmond, Va., 1989-92. Assoc. editor Jour. Econ. Dynamics and Control, 1988—, Jour. Bus. and Econ. Statistics, 1991—, Econometrica, 1992-95, Rev. Econs. and Statistics, 1993—, Jour. Money, Credit and Banking, 1993—. Grad. fellow NSF U. Calif., 1978-81; rsch. grantee NSF, 1988—. Fellow Econometric Soc.; mem. Am. Econ.

Assn., Soc. Econ. Dynamics and Control. Office: U Calif San Diego Dept Econs San Diego CA 92093-0508

HAMILTON, JAY MARTIN, genealogist, author; b. Salt Lake City, Oct. 29, 1921; s. Ernest Jacob and Pearl Edna Bernstrom (Norvald) H.; m. Ingeborg Marianne Haase, Aug. 9, 1947 (dec. Mar. 1976); children: Stephen Ernest Robert, Catherine Ann, Margaret Mary Elizabeth, Mark Antony Thomas; stepchildren: Barbara Josephine Prack Benson, Anton Otto Prack; m. Edith Barbara Vogt, Feb. 18, 1977. Student, Utah State Agrl. Coll., 1940-43; BA Sociology, So. Oreg. State Coll., 1968. Commd. 2nd lt. U.S. Army, 1944, advanced through grades to lt. col., 1963, ret., 1963; exec. dir. Winema Girl Scout Coun., Medford, Oreg., 1964-67; owner/operator Tree of Love Christian Bookstore, Medford, Grants Pass, Oreg., 1977-89. Author: Korean-English Language Collection of Grammatical Patterns, 1959, Hamilton Family History, 1983, Etymology of the Hamilton Name, 1984, Jay M. Hamilton Autobiography, 1985, The Hambleton-Reed Hamilton History, 1988, The Bernstrom-Helgeson Family History, 1996, Chronology of the 76th Infantry Division U.S. Army, 1988. Chmn. emergency med. com. Dist. 8 Comprehensive Health Coun. Jackson-Josephine County, Medford, 1973-76. Recipient Cert. of Svcs. Dist. 8 Comprehensive Health Coun., 1976. Mem. DAV (comdr., numerous awards), Ret. Officers assn. (life), Nat. Assn. for Uniformed Svc., 76th Inf. Divsn. Assn. Republican. Roman Catholic. Home: 308 Medford Heights Ln Medford OR 95704-7550

HAMILTON, JIMMY RAY, secondary education educator; b. McDowell, Ky., Mar. 4, 1949; s. Victor and Lola (Tackett) H.; children: Victor William, Madelin Mae Reinersmann; m. Christa Karin Weinkotz, Apr. 7, 1974; children: Margaret Ann Long, Nathaniel Ray. Student, Def. Info. Sch., 1969, 70, 72; BA in English and Secondary Edn., Ariz. State U., 1987; postgrad., U. Phoenix, 1994-95, Grand Canyon Coll., 1994-95. Cert. English and secondary edn. tchr., ESL and bilingual edn. Tchr. adult based edn. Marcos DeNiza H.S., Tempe, Ariz., 1987-89; tchr. English IV Red Mesa (Ariz.) H.S., 1989-90; tchr. English and drama, drama coach Many Farms (Ariz.) H.S., 1991-96; head coach boys' varsity basketball, 1996—; head coach girls' volleyball Ariz. Interscholastic Assn., Phoenix, 1993—. Mem. Pres. Nixon Inaugural Com., Washington, 1973. Recipient Dir.'s award for best play Native Am. Drama Festival, Tuba City, 1991-92, 92-93, Dir.'s award Four Corners Classic Drama and Fine Arts Festival, 1994, 95. Home: Box 65 Many Farms AZ 86538

HAMILTON, JODY ANN, personal manager, film producer; b. Santa Monica, Calif., Jan. 18, 1967; d. Joseph Henry and Carol Creighton (Burnett) H. BA, U. Pacific, Stockton, Calif., 1988; assoc. degree, Colo. Inst. Art, Denver, 1990. Exec. asst. Cinema Music Group, Hollywood, Calif., 1990-91; CEO JH Entertainment, Valley Village, Calif., 1991—. Author, producer (film) Relativity 3 The Movie, 1995; prodr. Conway/Steckler Show for Real Radio, L.A., 1997. Mem. AFI.

HAMILTON, PATRICIA ROSE, artist's agent; b. Phila., Oct. 21, 1948; d. William Alexis and Lillian Marie (Sloan) Hamilton. B.A., Temple U., 1970; M.A., Rutgers U., 1971. Sec. to curator Whitney Mus., N.Y.C., 1971-73; sr. editor Art in Am., 1973; curator exhbns. Crispo Gallery, 1974-75; dir. Hamilton Gallery, 1976-84; artist's agt., 1984—. Democrat. Avocations: tennis; swimming; cooking. Home and Office: 2040 N Catalina St Los Angeles CA 90027-1826

HAMILTON, PENNY RAFFERTY, research executive, writer, educator; b. Altoona, Pa., Feb. 18, 1948; d. William E. and Lois B. (Noel) Rafferty; m. William A. Hamilton, Dec. 21, 1971. AA, Temple U., 1968; BA, Columbia (Mo.) Coll., 1976; MA, U. Nebr., 1978, PhD, 1981; postdoctoral studies, Menninger Found., Topeka, 1984. Community educator U.S. Forces in Europe, Fulda, Fed. Republic of Germany, 1972-74; health educator Nebr. State Govt., Lincoln, 1974-84; v.p. Advanced Rsch. Inst., Winter Park, Colo., 1984—; spl. features editor, newspaper columnist Sun Newspapers/Capital Times, Lincoln, 1982-91; dir. pub. affairs Sta. KHAT-KMXA, Lincoln, 1986-92. Bd. dirs. Grand County Pet Pals, 1992—, Grand County Aviation Assn., 1992—, Friends of Granby Airport, 1992—. Set world and nat. aviation speed record, 1991. Home: PO Box 2001 Granby CO 80446-2001 Office: Advanced Rsch Inst PO Box 3499 Winter Park CO 80482-3499

HAMILTON, RANDY HASKELL, city manager; b. N.Y.C., Dec. 27, 1921; s. Harry and Adelaide Beatrice (Haskell) H.; m. Ruth Manning (div. May 1961); children: Sarah Beth, Leander Munhall III; m. Louanne McKernan, Apr. 29, 1962; children: Jill Katherine, Jennifer Sabrina. BA, U. N.C., 1943, MA in Pub. Adminstrn., 1947, MA in City and Regional Planning, 1949; PhD, U. Zurich, Switzerland, 1963. City mgr. City of Carolina Beach, N.C., 1949-52; dir., assoc. dir. Nat. League Cities, Washington, 1952-56; city mgr., mcpl. adv. Royal Govt. Thailand, Bangkok, 1956-64; dir. comparative urban studies project UN/IPA, N.Y.C., 1964-65; spl. project dir. League Calif. Cities, Berkeley, Calif., 1965-73; dean Grad. Sch. Pub. Adminstrn., Golden Gate U., San Francisco, 1973-90; vis. scholar Inst. Govtl. Studies, U. Calif., Berkeley, 1990—. Mem. editl. bd. Pub. Adminstrn. Rev., 1970-75, Internat. Jour. Pub. Adminstrn., 1977—, State and Local Govt. Rev., 1980-86; editor Western Govtl. Rsch. Jour., 1990-92. Chmn. Gov.'s Adv. Coord. Coun. Pub. Personnel, Sacramento, 1973; chmn. adv. com. Calif. State Welfare Grant, Sacramento, 1972, State Calif., Sacramento, 1975; chmn. grant adv. com. Highland Hosp. Found., Oakland, Calif., 1991-93. Capt. USAF, 1943-46. Decorated comdr. Royal Order of Crown (Thailand); named Man of Yr., N.C. Lion's Club, 1950; recipient spl. citation U.S. CSC, 1975. Fellow Nat. Acad. Pub. Adminstrn.; mem. Internat. City Mgmt. Assn. (Stephen B. Sweeney award 1980). Republican. Presbyterian. Office: U Calif Inst Govtl Studies 109 Moses Hall Berkeley CA 94720

HAMILTON, SCOTT SCOVELL, professional figure skater, former Olympic athlete; b. Toledo, Aug. 28, 1958; adopted s. Ernest Scovell and Dorothy (McIntosh) H. Grad. high sch., Bowling Green, Ohio, 1976; student, Metro State Coll., 1979. nat. spokesman Discover Card youth programs, 1995—. Amateur competitive career includes Nat. Figure Skating Championships: jr. men's 1st pl., 1976, sr. men's 9th pl., 1977, 3d pl., 1978, 4th pl., 1979, 3d pl., 1980, 1st pl., 1981, 82, 83, 84, Mid-Western Figure Skating Championships: sr. men's 3d pl., 1977, 78, 79, Norton Skate Championships (now Skate Am.): men's divsn. 1st pl., 1979, 80, 81, 82, South Atlantic Figure Skating Championships: sr. men's divsn. 1st pl., 1980, Eastern Figure Skating Championships: sr. men's 1st pl., 1980, 81, 82, 83, 84, World Figure Skating Championships: men's divsn. 5th pl., 1980, 1st pl. 81, 82, 83, 84, Nat. Sports Festival Championships: 1st pl. men's divsn., 1981; Winter Olympics: men's divsn. 5th pl., Lake Placid, N.Y., 1980, 1st pl., Sarajevo, Yugoslavia, 1984, Nippon Hoso Kykai Figure Skating Championships, men's divsn. 1st pl., 1982, Golden Spin of Zagreb Championships, men's divsn. 1st pl., 1983; Profl. competitive career includes Nutrasweet/NBC-TV World Profl. Figure Skating Championships mens. divsn., 1st pl., 1984, 86, 2d pl., 85, 87, 88, 89, 91; World Challenge Champions/ABC-TV men's divsn., 2d pl., 1985, 1st pl., 1986; U.S. Open men's divsn. 1st pl., 1990, 2d pl., 1991, Diet Coke Profl. Skaters Championship men's divsn. 1st pl., 1992, Hershey's Kisses Pro-Am. Figure Skating Championships 2d Place Men's divsn. 1993, Sun Valley Men's Outdoor Championship 2d pl., 1994, The Gold Championship men's divsn. 1st pl., 1994, Can. Profl. Skating Championship men's divsn. 1st pl., 1994, Fox's Rock and Roll Skating Championship men's divsn. 1st pl., 1994; profl. performances include Nat. Arena Tour Ice Capades, 1984-85, 85-86, star Scott Hamilton's Am. Tour, 1986-87, 1990-91, co-star Concert On Ice, Harrah's Hotel, Lake Tahoe, Nev., 1987, spl. guest star Festival On Ice, Nat. Theatre Tour, 1987, star Discover Card Stars On Ice Nat. Arena Tour, 1987-88, 88-89, star Festival On Ice, Harrah's Hotel, 1988, guest star ABC-TV spl. Ice Capades With Kirk Cameron, 1988, A Very Special Christmas, ABC-TV, 1988, An Olympic, Calgary Christmas, ABC-TV, 1988, star and mus. comedy and acting debut Broadway On Ice, Harrah's Hotel and Nat. Theatre Tour, 1989; CBS-TV Sports Figure Skating Commentator 1984-91 various skating competitions and CBS-TV coverage Winter Olympics, Albertville, France, 1992, Lillehammer, Norway, 1994; star, dir., producer Scott Hamilton's Celebration On Ice, Sea World of Calif., 1988, Scott Hamilton's Time Traveler: An Odyssey On Ice, Sea World of Calif., 1989; host, guest star TV spl. A Salute To Dorothy Hamill, 1988; star, co-producer Discover Card Stars On Ice, Nat. Arena Tour, 1989-91; guest star CBS-TV spl. Disney's Christmas on Ice, 1990; co-producer, star Discover Card Stars on Ice Nat. Arena Tour, 1991-92; co-host, star HBO TV spl. Vail Skating Festival, 1992; co-prodr., star Discover Card Stars on Ice Nat. Arena Tour, 1992-93, 93-94, 94-95, Canadian Nat. Tour, 1995; guest TV spl. A Disney Christmas on Ice, 1992, CBS-TV spl. Disney on Ice, 1992, HBO-TV spl. Vail Skating Festival, 1993, Skates of Gold I, Boston, 1993, Skates of Gold II, Cin., 1994, CBS-TV Disney Fantasy on Ice, 1993, CBS-TV spl. Nancy Kerrigan & Friends, 1994, CBS-TV spl. Disney's Greatest Hits, 1994, CBS-TV spl. Dreams on Ice, 1995; creator original concepts in arena figure skating. Cons. Friends of Scott Hamilton Found. named in his honor to fundraise and benefit youth oriented causes throughout U.S., 1988, Scott Hamilton's Friends and Legends 1st Annual Celebrity Charity Golf Tournament, Ford's Colony, Williamsburg, Va., 1991; participant fund-raising Athletes for Reagan, March of Dimes, Am. Cancer Soc., Spl. Olympics, Starlight Found., United Way Adoption Home Socs., Make A Wish Found, Big Bros., 1984—, Athletes For Bush, Adult and Ped. AIDS Rsch., Edn. and Funding, 1988—, Homeless, 1989—, Great Am. Workout for Pres.'s Coun. Phys. Fitness & Sports, 1990, 92; nat. spokesman Discover Card youth programs, 1995—. Winner Olympic Gold medal, Sarajevo, 1984; U.S. Olympic Com. awards and honors include carrier Am. Flag in opening ceremonies Lake Placid, 1980, Figure Skating Athlete of Yr., 1981, 82, 83, 84, Athlete of Yr., 1981, Olympic Spirit award, 1987; recipient Olympia award Southland Corp., 1984, Achievement award March of Dimes, 1984, Colo. Athlete of Yr. award Denver Athletic Club, 1984, Most Courageous Athlete award Phila. Sportswriters Assn., 1985, Profl. Skater of Yr. award Am. Skating World mag., 1986, Jacques Favart award Internat. Skating Union, 1988, The Crown Royal Achievement award from House of Seagrams and Jimmy Heuga Ctr., 1991, Clairol's Personal Best award, 1991, Spirit of Giving award U.S. Figure Skating Assn., 1993, 9th Ann. Great Sports Legends award Nick Buonoconti Fund The Miami Project, 1994, Ritter F. Shumway award U.S. Figure Skating Assn., 1994; inducted U.S. Olympic Hall of Fame, 1990, World Figure Skating Hall of Fame, 1990; honoree nat. com. for adoption, 1992. Hon. mem. Phila. Skating Club, Humane Soc. Republican. Office: 4242 Van Nuys Blvd Sherman Oaks CA 91403-3710*

HAMILTON, SOLOMON MAXIMY, physiologist, educator; b. Marigot, Dominica; came to U.S., 1992; s. Samuel and Euthelie (Joseph) H. AA, Caribbean Union Coll., Trinidad and Tobago, 1983, BA, 1987; PhD, Loma Linda (Calif.) U., 1986. Asst. mgr. Ebenezer Mktg. Corp., Caribbean, Dominica, 1977-78, mgr., 1978-81; tchr. chemistry/physics Dominica SDA H.S., 1988-91; rsch. asst. Loma Linda U., 1992-93, rsch. assoc., 1993-96; asst. prof. physiology La Sierra U., Riverside, Calif., 1996—. Contbr. articles to profl. jours. Pres. No. Dist. Youth Assn., Caribbean, 1980; elder SDA Ch., 1979-90. Mem. AAAS, N.Y. Acad. Scis. Office: La Sierra U Dept Biology 4700 Pierce St Riverside CA 92515

HAMILTON, THOMAS PERCY, preventive medicine physician, military officer; b. Buffalo, July 11, 1932; s. James Alexander and Charlot Clara (Krathwohl) H.; m. Elsie Marie Myers, Apr. 2, 1971; children: Stephen, Patricia, Beverly, Susan. BS, Case-Western Res. U., 1954; MD, SUNY, Buffalo, 1957; MPH, U. Mich., 1969. Diplomate Am. Bd. Preventive Medicine, Pub. Health Adminstrn.; lic. MD, Calif., Ga., Mich., Nev., N.J., Pa. Internship U.S. Naval Hosp., Charleston, S.C., 1958; sr. med. officer, squadron flight surgeon U.S. Navy, various locations, S.C., N.J., 1958-61; regional flight surgeon FAA, Atlanta, 1961-62; family practitioner Levittown (Pa.) Med. Ctr., 1962-63; staff physician, asst. med. dir. Rutgers U., New Brunswick, N.J., 1963-64, 64-66; dir. health dept., cons. in local health adminstrn. various health depts., Adrian, Detroit, Lansing, Mich., 1966-71; dir. health and human svcs., health officer various counties, Santa Ana, Pasadena, L.A., Calif., 1971-84; dep. comdr. U.S. Army Aeromed., med. staff officer Health Svcs. Command, Ft. Rucker/Sam Houston, Ala., Tex., 1984-86, 88-89; chief preventive medicine svc., dep. comdr., comdr. Brooke Army Med. Ctr., Fort Sam Houston, 1989-90, 90-92; prof. and chief preventive medicine, ret. Army Med. Dept. Ctr. and Sch., Fort Sam Houston, 1992-93, 93—; assoc. clin. prof. community and environ.medicine U. Calif., Irvine, 1972—; asst. clin. prof. dept. preventive medicine U. So. Calif., 1977—; asst. clin. prof. dept. family medicine Loma Linda U., 1983—; residency dir. preventive medicine L.A. and Riverside County Health Depts., 1979-84; acad. chair continuing med. edn. Health Officers Assn. of Calif., 1977-84. Contbr. numerous articles to profl. jours. Fellow Am. Coll. Preventive Medicine, Am. Pub. Health Assn.; mem. Am. Coll. Physician Execs., Assn. U.S. Army, Assn. Army Flight Surgeons, Calif. Med. Assn., Res. Officers Assn., Riverside County Med. Assn., The Ret. Officers Assn.

HAMILTON, WALTER NICHOLAS, newspaper reporter, editor; b. Queens, N.Y., Oct. 25, 1964; s. Walter Nicholas and Diane Antonia (Howath) H. BA, Vassar Coll., 1986. Reporter The Patent Trader, Mount Kisco, N.Y., 1987-88, Glendale (Calif.) News Press, 1988-89; fin. writer L.A. Daily News, 1989-95, Investor's Bus. Daily, L.A., 1995—. Mem. Soc. Bus. Editors Writers. Home: 10475 National Blvd # 8 Los Angeles CA 90034

HAMIT, FRANCIS GRANGER, freelance writer; b. N.Y.C., Oct. 6, 1944; s. Harold Francis and Ethel Cordelia (Granger) H.; m. Doris Elaine Pratt Kaesser, May 31, 1974 (div. Mar. 1978). B of Gen. Studies, U. Iowa, 1972, MFA in English, 1976. Freelance writer Iowa City, Chgo., L.A., 1975—; area capt. RRS Security, Ill., 1977; sales rep. Wells Fargo Co. Inc., Chgo., 1979-80; assoc. editor Video Action Mag., Chgo., 1982; factory rep. Hoover Co., L.A., 1987-88; v.p. sales and mktg. EPIC Pvt. Security, West Covina, Calif., 1989-90. Author: Virtual Reality and the Exploration of Cyberspace, 1993; author, dir.: (play) Marlowe: An Elizabethan Tragedy, 1988; contbg. editor: Security Technology and Design Mag., 1993—, Advanced Imaging Mag., 1994—; contbr. 15th edit. Ency. Britannica, 1981-82. With U.S. Army, 1967-71, Vietnam. Mem. Am. Soc. Indsl. Security, Nat. Mil. Intelligence Assn., Shakespeare Soc. Am. (bd. dirs. 1989-91), L.A. Sci. Fantasy Soc., Assn. Former Intelligence Officers. Democrat. Buddhist.

HAMLIN, BEVERLY, gifted education educator; b. Portland, Oreg.; Children: Michael, Shawn, Jamic. BA, Long Beach State U., 1979; MA, Nat. U., San Diego, 1985. Educator Lynwood (Calif.) Unified Sch. Dist., pentathalon coach, marathon coach, oratorical coach, 1980-94, student coun. facilitator, 1984—. Fund raiser PTA, Lynwood. Mem. Mid-cities Nat. Alliance of Black Sch. Educators (parliamentarian).

HAMLIN, DON AUER, financial executive; b. Klamath Falls, Oreg., Oct. 6, 1934; s. Don Fessler and Margaret May (Auer) H.; m. Karen Ruth Wagner; children by previous marriage: Michael, Kathryn, Stephen, Mary, Mark, John, Matthew. BBA, Loyola U. of South, New Orleans, 1955; grad. USAF Command and Staff Coll., 1967; MS in Bus. Adminstrn., George Washington U., 1968. Commnd. 2d lt. U.S. Army, 1955, advanced through grades to lt. col., 1975; served with inf., ordnance, M.P., various locations, 1955-64; inf. comdr. and staff officer, Alaska, Hawaii, Vietnam, 1964-68; cost analyst and dep. agy. comdr. Pentagon Gen. Staff, Washington, 1968-72; inf. adviser, Vietnam, 1972; comptroller Ft. Sam Houston, Tex., 1972-75; ret., 1975; comptroller Severance & Assos., San Antonio, 1975-81; sec.-treas., dir. Severance Reference Lab., Inc., San Antonio, Tex., 1981-82; co-founder, pres. Engring. Cybernetics, Inc., San Antonio, 1982-85; dir. fin. Whittaker Health Services, Austin, Tex., 1985-86; v.p. fin. Metlife Healthcare Network, 1986-88; Harris Meth. Health Plan, Ft. Worth, 1989-91; sr. v.p./CEO, Harris Meth. Health Plan, pres. Harris Meth. Health Ins. Co., 1991-94; CEO Heritage Southwest Med. Group, Irving, Tex., 1994-96; healthcare mgmt. cons., 1996—; pvt. investor, 1983—; dir. Data Terminal Corp., San Antonio, 1981; pres. Balance Point Youth Ranch, San Antonio, 1980-81. Pres., St. Pius X Bd. Edn., San Antonio, 1979. Decorated Legion of Merit with oak leaf cluster, Bronze Star with oak leaf cluster, Air medal with oak leaf cluster, Purple Heart with oak leaf cluster, Mem. San Antonio Med. Mgrs. Assn. (pres. 1982-84), Med. Group Mgrs. Assn., San Antonio Mus. Assn., Mexican-Am. Cultural Center, San Antonio C. of C. Home and Office: PO Box 5162 Silver City NM 88062-5162

HAMLIN, EDMUND MARTIN, JR., engineering manager; b. Utica, N.Y., June 9, 1949; s. Edmund Martin and Catherine Mary (Humphreys) H.; m. Nancy Ann Christensen, June 26, 1971; children: Benjamin John (dec.), Eleanor Mary, Edmund Alexander. BSEE, Clarkson U., 1971; MBA, UCLA, 1993. Lic. airframe and powerplant mechanic, 1994. Engr. NASA Flight Rsch. Ctr., Edwards, Calif., 1971-75; sr. engr. NASA Flight Rsch. Ctr., Edwards, 1976-79; project engr. Sundstrand Energy Systems Div., Belvidere, Ill., 1975-76; sr. engr. Teleco Oilfield Svcs., Meriden, Conn., 1979-80, mgr. electronic systems, 1980-83, the sr. staff engr., 1984; sr. engr. NASA Ames-Dryden, Edwards, Calif., 1984-85; asst. chief flight sys. NASA Ames-Dryden, Edwards, 1985-90, chief flight instrumentation, 1990-94, asst. dir. rsch., 1994—. Inventor: position measurement system, 1976, method for determining and correcting magnetic interference in boreholes, 1988, method for computing borehold azimuth while rotating, 1989. Pres. bd. trustees Tehachapi (Calif.) Unified Sch. Dist., 1989-94. Mem. AIAA, Instrument Soc. Am., Aircraft Owners and Pilots Assn., Exptl. Aircraft Assn. Home: 22220 Valley Vista Dr Tehachapi CA 93561-9549 Office: NASA Ames-Dryden Flight Rsch Facility PO Box 273 Edwards CA 93523-0273

HAMLIN, SUSAN ELIZABETH, lawyer, educator; b. Boise, Idaho, Nov. 15, 1966. BA, U. Idaho, 1989, JD, 1992. Bar: Idaho 1992. Lectr. U. Idaho, Moscow, 1990-92; legal extern U.S. Atty.'s Office, Boise, 1991; law clk. Atty. Gen., Boise, 1992, Idaho Dist. Judge and Snake River Adjudication, 1992-93; dep. atty. gen. Idaho Dept. Water Resources, Boise, 1993-95, Idaho Pub. Utilities Commn., Boise, 1995—. Assoc. mem. Idaho Law Rev., 1990-91. Named Outstanding Young Women of Am., 1988. Mem. ABA, Idaho Trial Lawyers Assn., Idaho Vol. Lawyers for the Arts, Idaho Water User Assn., Phi Alpha Theta (pres. 1987-88), Alpha Gamma Delta (pres. 1987-88). Office: Idaho Pub Utilities Commn 472 W Washington St Boise ID 83702-5983

HAMMAN, STEVEN ROGER, vocational rehabilitation specialist; b. Santa Monica, Calif., Nov. 2, 1946; s. Roy Ernest H. and Joan Barbara (Werner) Scott; m. Christine Frances Solomon, May 29, 1976; children: Zachary Charles, Tamara Edith, Bryan Joseph. AA, Northeastern Colo. U., 1967; BA, Colo. State Coll., 1970; MA, U. No. Colo., 1972; MS, Drake U., 1981. Cert. vocat. expert, rehab. counselor, ins. rehab. specialist. Social worker Poudre-Thompson Transp. Corps, Ft. Collins, Colo., 1974-78; placement specialist Missoula (Mont.) Rehab. Ctr., 1978-80; rehab. counselor Adolph Coors Co., Golden, Colo., 1981; rehab. counselor, br. mgr. Nat. Rehab. Cons., Duluth, Minn., 1981-82; Mont. case svcs. dir. Nat. Rehab. Cons., Missoula, 1982-83; case svcs. dir. Northwest U.S. Nat. Rehab. Cons., Spokane, Wash., 1983-86; rehab. cons., pres., chief exec. officer Vocability, Inc., Post Falls, Idaho, 1986—; pvt. practice as Social Security claimant's rep.; counselor, trainer Community Corrections Program, Ft. Collins, 1976. Cmty. organizer VISTA, Clay, W.Va., 1973-74; pres., bd. dirs. Mountain Van Spl. Transp., Missoula, 1980; bd. dirs. Heritage Place I and II, Coeur d'Alene Homes Inc., 1991-94; advanced master gardner Univ. Idaho Coop. Extention Ctr. Mem. Nat. Assn. Rehab. Practitioners in the Private Sector., Vocat. Evaluation and Work Adjustment Assn. (registered cons. Americans with Disabilities Act), Am. Bd. Disability Analysts (diplomate, sr. disability analyst), Nat. Orgn. Social Security Claimants Reps. Office: Vocability Inc PO Box 772 Post Falls ID 83854-0772

HAMMARGREN, LONNIE, lieutenant governor; b. Dec. 25, 1937; married. BA, U. Minn., 1958, MA in Psychol., 1960, BS, 1964, MD, 1964, MS in Neurosurgery, 1974. Diplomate Am. Bd. Neurological Surgery; med. license Nev., Minn. Flight surgeon for the astronauts NASA Manned Space Craft Ctr.; lt. gov., pres. of the senate State of Nev., 1995—; assoc. clin. prof. neurosurgery U. Nev. Sch. Medicine, Reno; clin. assoc. prof. surgery U. Calif., San Diego, 1982; chair Commn. Econ. Devel., Commn. Tourism; bd. dirs. Nev. Dept. Transp. Bd. regents U. and C.C. Sys. Nev., 1988-94; adv. bd. mem. Gov.'s com. for Employment of Handicapped; mem. State Bd. Edn., 1984-88; bd. mem. March of Dimes, Aid to Adoption of Spl. Kids. Mem. Spinal Cord Injury Program of Nev. (pres.), Cancer Soc., Aerospace Med. Assn., U Med. Ctr. Rehabilitation Unit (dir.), U. Med. Ctr. (chmn. neurosurgery dept.), Help Them Walk Again Found. (Nat. Dir.), Spina Bifida and Hydrocephalus Soc. (med. dir.), Internat. Ctr. for Rehabilitation Engring. (med. dir.), Pacific World Med. Found. (treas.), Paramed. and Emergency Care Bd. (adv.). Office: Office of Lt Gov Sawyer Bldg 555 E Washington Ave Ste 5500 Las Vegas NV 89101-1050

HAMMER, SHARON ARLENE, library director; b. Seattle, July 26, 1938; d. Chauncey Rockhold Marshall and Dorothy Elizabeth (Antic) Ulbrickson; m. M. Wayne Mullins, Sept. 2, 1957 (div. June 1967); 1 child, Michael Wayne (dec.); m. Donald Jay Hammer, Aug. 23, 1969; children: Marjory Backstrum, Bonnie Moore, Polly Collier, Robert, Andy. BA in History, U. Wash., 1969, MLS, 1971, mgmt. program cert., 1982. Supr. serials and circulation Boeing Aerospace Libr./Seattle U. Libr., 1961-69; establisher basic libr. for learning disabled Bellevue (Wash.) Adaptive Learning Ctr., 1971; handicapped/elderly libr. program dir. Seattle Pub. Libr., 1972-74, dir. Wash. libr. for blind and physically handicapped, 1974-78; asst. dir. undergrad. libr. svcs. U. Wash. Librs., Seattle, 1978-83, acting libr. pers. officer, 1980-81; county libr. Marin County Free Libr., San Rafael, Calif., 1983-88; dir. Ft. Vancouver Regional Libr., Vancouver, Wash., 1988—; conf. speaker, workshop presenter, libr. edn. instr. Contbr.: Against All Odds: Case Studies on Library Financial Management, 1994. Mem. Am. Libr. Assn. (Wash. chpt. councilor 1975-79, coun.-at-large 1983-87, chair coun. resolutions com.), Pub. Libr. Assn. (mem. polit. effectiveness com., pub. policy for pub. librs. sect. transition, nominating and fee-based svcs. coms.), Assn. Specialized and Coop. Libr. Agys., Assn. Coll. and Rsch. Librs., Assn. Com. on Orgn., Libr. Info. and Tech. Assn., Libr. Instrn. Roundtable, Washington Libr. Assn. (pres. 1994-96, Pres. award 1993, mem. exec. bd., numerous coms.). Office: Ft Vancouver Regional Libr 1007 E Mill Plain Blvd Vancouver WA 98663-3504

HAMMER, SUSAN M., lawyer; b. Salem, Oreg., Dec. 14, 1948. BA, U. Puget Sound, 1971; JD, Willamette U., 1976. Bar: Oreg. 1976, Wash. 1977. Law clk. to Hon. James Dolliver Wash. State Supreme Ct., 1976-77; mem. Stoel Rives Boley Jones & Grey, Portland, Oreg.; investigator Wash. State Human Rights Commn., 1971; mem. Oreg. State Bd. Bar Examiners, 1981-84. Mem. ABA (labor and employment law sect.), Tri-County Affirmative Action Assn. (bd. dirs.). Office: Stoel Rives Boley Jones & Grey 900 SW 5th Ave Ste 2300 Portland OR 97204-1232

HAMMER, SUSAN W., mayor; b. Altadena, Calif., Dec. 21, 1938; d. James Nathan and Katrine (Krutzsch) Walker; m. Philip Hammer, Sept. 4, 1960; children: Philip, Hali, Matthew. BA in History, U. Calif., Berkeley, 1960. Svc. rep. Pacific Telephone Co., Berkeley, 1960-61; staff asst. Peace Corps, Washington, 1962-63; councilwoman City of San Jose, Calif., 1980-81, 83-90, spl. asst. to mayor, 1981-82, vice mayor, 1985-87, mayor, 1991—; chair, pres. Adv. Com. on Trade Policy and Negotiations, 1994—. Bd. dirs. San Jose Mus. Art, 1971-90, pres., 1978-80; mem. governing bd. NCCJ, 1978—; mem. adv. bd. Cmty. Found. Santa Clara County, 1978—; mem. Santa Clara County Transp. Com., 1976-77, Santa Clara County Juvenile Justice Commn., 1980, Victim-Witness Adv. Bd., 1977-90, Children's Health Coun., San Jose, 1981-89, Santa Clara Valley Leadership Program, 1986-90, Childrens Shelter Project, 1991—, Am. Leadership Forum, 1992—; past chmn. parents adv. com. Trace Sch.; chair Pres.' Adv. Com. on Trade Policy and Negotiation; mem. San Jose Fine Arts Commn., 1980. Recipient Rosalie M. Stern Community Svc. award U. Calif., 1975, Disting. Citizen of San Jose award Exch. Club, 1979, Investment in Leadership award Coro Found., 1985, Tzedek award for honor, compassion and community svc. Temple Emanu-El, 1987, Recognition award YWCA, Santa Clara County, 1989, resolution of commendation Assn. for Responsible Alcohol Control, 1990, Woman of Achievement award The Women's Fund, 1990, Dox Quixote award Nat. Hispanic U., 1991, Friends of Bay Area Mcpl. Elections Com. award, 1991. Democrat. Office: Office of Mayor 801 N 1st St Rm 600 San Jose CA 95110-1704

HAMMERBACK, JOHN CLARK, communications educator; b. San Francisco, Oct. 6, 1938; s. William Joseph and Susan (Ridzik) H.; m. Jean Melton, Aug. 29, 1965; children: Kristen, Karen. BA, San Francisco State Coll., 1962; MA, U. Okla., 1965; PhD, Ind. U., 1970. Teaching asst. dept. speech communication U. Okla., Norman, 1963-65, Ind. U., Bloomington, 1965-68; prof. speech communication Calif. State U., Hayward, 1968—, chmn. dept. speech and drama, 1972-79, affirmative action liason officer, 1986-88, asst. v.p. rsch. faculty affairs, 1988-91, assoc. dean, 1993-95; lectr. U. N.Mex., Albuquerque, 1977, Oreg. State Coll., 1989, San Jose State U., 1993, U. Nev., Las Vegas, 1996, No. Ariz. U., 1996, N.C. State U., 1997, Rotary, Kiwanis, Lions; speechwriter for local polit. candidates, Fremont, Calif., 1978—; dir. Conf. in Rhetorical Criticism, 1987-93. Author: A War of Words: Chicano Rhetoric of the 1960s and 1970s, 1985, In Search of Justice: Studies in Speech Communication in the Indiana Tradition, 1987; editl. bd. Howard Jour. of Comm., 1997—; contbr. 30 articles and chpts. to profl. publs. Bd. dirs. Community Counseling and Edn. Ctr., Fremont; v.p.

Greater Kimber Area Homeowners Assn., 1984. Faculty Research grantee Calif. State U., Hayward, 1975; Meritorious Service award, 1985. Mem. Western Speech Comm. Assn. (2d v.p. 1979-80, mem. legis. assembly 1974-77, chmn. 1980, 1st v.p. 1981-82, chief conv. planner 1982-83, pres. 1983-84, assoc. editor jour. 1979-81, 84-87, 90—, disting. svc. award com. 1985, nominating com. 1984, chmn. mem. com. 1980, mem. search com. 1989, internat. group com. 1996), Rhetoric Soc., Speech Comm. Assn. (com. on coms. 1985, program planner and vice chmn., chmn. pub. address divsn. 1994, nominating com. and legis. assembly 1995, intercultural com. 1995, Disting. Scholarship award, Pub. Addy, 1993), Execs. Club (pres. 1991). Home: 203 Fisalia Ct Fremont CA 94539-3028 Office: Calif State U Hayward CA 94539

HAMMERBECK, WANDA LEE, artist; b. Lincoln, Nebr., Mar. 24, 1945; d. Thomas Earl and Juanita (Arthur/Lee) Matthews; m. Edward Cox Hammerbeck, June 8, 1968 (dec. Aug. 1969); m. Drake Paul Silliman, Feb. 5, 1986; children: Samantha, Alexandra. BA in Psychology, U. N.C., 1967, MA in Higher Edn., 1971; postgrad., Yale U., 1968; MFA in Photography, San Francisco Art Inst., 1977. lectr., panel discussion Art Ctr. Coll. of Design, 1996; vis. artist lectr. Mills. Coll., Oakland, Calif., 1982, leader photography workshops Mus. Photographic Arts, San Diego, 1988, 89, 90, 91, others. Author: (photography books) Depositions, 1978, California Views, 1979, Object, Illusion, Reality, 1979, The Center of the Eye, 1983, Photography 150 Years, 1989, A River Too Far: The Past and Future of Water in the West, 1991, Arid Waters: Photographs from the Water in the West, 1992, Nature Through Her Eyes, 1994; one-woman shows include Camerawork Gallery, San Francisco, 1974, San Francisco Mus. Modern Art, 1978, O.K. Harris, N.Y.C., 1979, Delahunty, Dallas, 1982, Mus. Photographic Art, San Diego, 1983, Carpenter-Hochman, Dallas, 1984, Etherton Gallery, Tucson, Ariz., 1986, Scheinbaum and Russek Gallery, Santa Fe, 1986, Mus. of Art of Am. West, Houston, 1988; exhibited in group shows at San Francisco Art Inst., 1977, DeCordova Mus., Lincoln, Mass., 1981, MIT, Cambridge, 1981, Tyler Sch. Art, Phila, 1981, Mus. Modern Art, Belgrade, Yugoslavia, 1981, Palais des Beaux Arts, Brussels, 1982, Photokina, Cologne, Germany, 1982, Oakland (Calif.) Mus., 1983, San Francisco Mus. Modern Art, 1983, Houston Mus. Fine Arts, 1984, 87, Burden Gallery, N.Y.C., 1987, San Jose Inst. Contemporary Art, 1988, Visual Studies Workshop, Rochester, N.Y., 1989, Tokyo Inst. Polytechnics and Coll. Art, Nihon U., 1990, Mass. Coll. Art, Huntington Gallery, Boston, 1992, Art Mus. Princeton U., 1993, Spencer Art Mus., U. Kans., 1996, Nev. Art Mus., 1996, others; represented in permanent collections at Australian Nat. Gallery, Denver Art Mus., Oakland Mus., Mus. of Modern Art, Princeton Art Mus., Ctr. for Creative Photography, Wellesley Coll., Canberra, Calif. Mus. Photography, Riverside, Fogg Art Mus., Harvard U., Houston Mus. Fine Arts, Lehigh U. Art Galleries, Pa., others; also pvt. and corp. collections. Active various vol. and charity benefits. Recipient 1st pl. all media San Francisco Art Inst., 1977, award Nat. Endowment for the Arts, 1979, 80, 81. Home: 1852 Foothill Blvd Flintridge CA 91011-2927

HAMMERLY, MILT, physician; b. Takoma Park, Md., Apr. 6, 1958; s. Hector and Ethel (Pidoux) H.; m. Joan Anne Vasta, Oct. 4, 1991; children: Aaron, Brett, Matthew. BSc in Kinesiology, Simon Fraser U., 1981; MD, Med. Coll. Wis., 1986. Diplomate Am. Bd. Family Practice. Physician ROmed, Denver, 1989-90, Accord Med. Ctrs., Littleton, Colo., 1990-92, Family Health Assocs., Lewisville, Tex., 1992-94, Plum Creek Med., Castle Rock, Colo., 1994-96; med. dir. Am. Holistic Ctr., Littleton, 1996—. Inventor Electrostatic Massage, 1995. Seventh Day Adventist. Office: Am Holistic Ctr 5161 E Arapahoe Rd #290 Littleton CO 80122

HAMMERSLEY, FREDERICK HAROLD, artist; b. Salt Lake City, Jan. 5, 1919; s. Harold Frederick and Anna Maria (Westberg) H. Student, U. Idaho, 1936-38, Chouinard Art Sch., 1940-42, 46-47, Ecole des Beaux Arts, Paris, France, 1945, Jepson Art Sch., 1947-50. Tchr. Jepson Art Sch., L.A., 1948-51, Pomona Coll., Claremont, Calif., 1953-62, Pasadena (Calif.) Art Mus., 1956-61, Chouinard Art Sch., L.A., 1964-68, U. N.Mex., Albuquerque, 1968-71; guest artist Tamarind Inst., Albuquerque, 1973, 88, 91. On-man shows include Owings-Dewey Fine Arts, Santa Fe, 1992, Richard Levy Gallery, Albuquerque, 1993, Mulvane Art Mus., Washburn U., Topeka, 1993, Corcoran Gallery, 1994, Modernism, San Francisco, 1995, others; works shown in gruop exhibits at M. Knoedler Gallery, Smithsonian Inst., Corcoran Gallery of Art, Albright-Knox Mus. Art, Butler Inst. Am. Art, others; represented in permanent collections Corcoran Gallery Art, San Francisco Mus. Modern Art, LA County Mus. Art, others. Sgt. U.S. Signal Corps and Infantry, 1942-46. John Simon Guggenheim fellow in painting, 1973; grantee Nat. Endowment for the Arts, 1975-77; recipient numerous purchase awards. Home and Office: 608 Carlisle Blvd SE Albuquerque NM 87106-1510

HAMMETT, BENJAMIN COWLES, psychologist; b. L.A., Nov. 18, 1931; s. Buell Hammett and Harriet (Cowles) Graham; m. Ruth Finstrom, June 18, 1957; children: Susan Hood, Sarah, Carol Bress, John. BS, Stanford U., 1957; PhD, U. N.C., 1969. Lic. psychologist, Calif. Staff psychologist Children's Psychiat. Ctr., Butner, N.C., 1965-67; sr. psychologist VA Treatment Ctr. for Children, Richmond, Va., 1968-71; asst. prof. child psychiatry Va. Commonwealth U., Richmond, 1968-71; instr. psychology Western Grad. Sch. Psychology, 1980—; pvt. practice clin. psychology Palo Alto, Calif., 1972-92; rsch. psychologist, 1992—; affiliate staff mem. O'Connor Hosp., San Jose, Calif., 1980-84; v.p. bd. dirs. Mental Rsch. Inst., Palo Alto, 1982-83, pres. bd. dirs., 1983-85, treas., 1990-92, mem. staff, 1992—, bd. dirs. emeritus, 1992—, rsch. affiliate, 1992-95, rsch. assoc., 1995—; bd. dirs. Weestern Grad. Sch. Psychology, 1993—. Co-author chpts. two books. Scoutmaster Boy Scouts Am., 1952-54; 1st lt. Civil Air Patrol, 1969; vol. Peninsula Conservation Ctr., Palo Alto, 1983—, Calif. Acad. Scis., San Francisco, 1987—; treas. John B. Cary Sch. PTA, Richmond, Va., 1969-70; trustee Nat. Parks and Conservation Assn., 1995—; bd. dirs. Western Grad. Sch. Psychology, 1993—. Named Eagle Scout, 1947; grantee NIMH, 1970. Mem. APA, Am. Psychol. Soc., Am. Group Psychotherapy Assn., Internat. Transactional Analysis Assn. (cert. clin. mem.), Assn. Applied Psychophysiology and Biofeedbck, Biofeedback Soc. Calif., Calif. Psychol. Assn., Assn. for the Advancement of Gestalt Therapy, El Tigre Club Stanford U. (sec. 1954). Democrat. Unitarian. Home: 301 Lowell Ave Palo Alto CA 94301-3812

HAMMOND, ALAN DAVID, public speaker; b. Bristol, Eng., Dec. 21, 1936; s. Alan Trevor and Edith Cavell (Tucker) H.; m. Jean Louise Hobson, Sept. 15, 1967. BEd, U. B.C., Vancouver, 1967. Pub. speaking counselor The Emissaries, Loveland, Colo., 1966-90, exec. dir., 1982-92; founder, pres. The Auralia Found., Loveland, 1993—; founder, pres. Emissary Found. Internat., Loveland, 1982-90, Renaissance Bus. Assocs., Loveland, 1983-90, Renaissance Ednl. Assocs., Loveland, 1985-91; adv. to bd. dirs. Whole Health Inst., 1984-89, Assn. for Responsible Comm., Corona, Calif., 1984-89. Co-author anthology-talks, 1979; author numerous booklets; contbr. articles to profl. jours. With RAF, 1955-57. Home and Office: The Auralia Found PO Box 214 Masonville CO 80541

HAMMOND, CHUCK, mayor; m. Barbara Hammond; children: Jeff, Rod. AA Bus., City Coll., San Francisco, 1970; BA in Edn., San Francisco State U., 1972. Coach football & track Fairfield H.S., 1979-84; mem. city coun. Fairfield, Calif., 1984-93, mayor, 1993—; ins. agent, 1987—. Youth coach basketball, track, baseball, football, 1977—. Office: 1000 Webster St Fairfield CA 94533

HAMMOND, HOWARD DAVID, retired botanist and editor; b. Phila., Feb. 10, 1924; s. Clarence Elwood Jr. and Myrtle Iva (Sprowles) H.; m. Sarah Lichtenberg, Apr. 30, 1955; 1 child, Julia Ethel. BS, Rutgers U., 1945, MS, 1947; PhD, U. Pa., 1952. Asst. prof. U. Del., Newark, 1957-58, Howard U., Washington, 1958-68; from asst. prof. to assoc. prof. SUNY, Brockport, 1968-83; assoc. editor N.Y. Bot. Garden, Bronx, 1984-92. Co-editor: Floristic Inventory Tropical Countries, 1989, Southwestern Rare and Endangered Plants: Proceedings of the Second Conference/USDA Forest Service, 1996. Vol. Deaver Herbarium, No. Ariz. U., 1993—. Mem. Am. Inst. Biol. Scis., Bot. Soc. Am., Torrey Bot. Soc.(editor 1976-82, 87-92, pres. 1992), Sigma Xi. Home: 4025 Lake Mary Rd Apt 33 Flagstaff AZ 86001-8608

HAMMOND, JOSEPH CARROLL, III, flight service specialist, genealogist; b. Terrell, Tex., Apr. 22, 1916; s. Joseph Carroll II and Kate Mae (Gullette) H.; m. Ethel Sue Whipple (dec. Apr. 1969); m. Helen M. Parkinson, July 31, 1976. Student, Tyler C.C., 1939; Assoc. degree, Ea. N.Mex. U., 1976; postgrad., U. Okla., 1966-68, 75, Ea. N.Mex. U. With U.S. Airway Svc., 1941-74; family rschr., 1986-95. Compiler: Tucker Snow Genealogies, 1950-68. Active Ret. Sr. Vol. Program, Roswell, N.Mex., 1976-97. Mem. Masons (Master Roswell Lodge # 18 1996, York Cross 1997, Illustrious Master Roswell coun. 1991, Silver Trowel, High Priest Roswell chpt. 7 1991, Comdr. Roswell chpt. 6 1992, pres. Roswell chpt. 731 1980). Democrat. Baptist. Home: 707 Mission Arch Dr Roswell NM 88201-7864 Office: Hammond Locksmith Svc 1702 N Delaware Roswell NM 88201

HAMMOND, JUDY MCLAIN, business services executive; b. Downey, Calif., June 24, 1956; d. Ernest Richard and Bernice Elaine (Thompson) McLain; m. Dennis Francis Hammond, Aug. 15, 1981. BS in Mgmt., Pepperdine U., 1982; MBA, U. So. Calif., 1986. Br. mgr. Kelly Svcs., Encino, Calif., 1978-81; mktg. mgr. Payco Am. Corp., Encino, 1981-83, GC Svcs. Corp., Santa Ana, Calif., 1983-86; pres. Resource Mgmt. Svcs. Inc., Norwalk, Calif., 1986—; founder, pres. The Debt Marketplace, Inc., Norwalk, 1994—; founder, pres. The Debt Marketplace, Inc., 1994—; cons., expert in collection and recovery. Author: Collect More From Collection Agencies. Mem. Toastmasters. Office: 10440 Pioneer Blvd Ste 2 Santa Fe Springs CA 90670-3742

HAMMOND, LARRY AUSTIN, lawyer; b. Wichita, Kans., Sept. 17, 1945. BA, U. Tex., 1967, JD, 1970. Bar: Calif. 1971, Ariz. 1975. Law clk. to Hon. Carl McGowan U.S. Ct. Appeals (D.C. cir.), 1970-71; law clk. to Hon. Hugo L. Black U.S. Supreme Ct., 1971, law clk. to Hon. Lewis F. Powell Jr., 1971-73; asst. spl. prosecutor Watergate spl. prosecution force U.S. Justice Dept., 1973-74, dep. asst. atty. gen. office legal counsel, 1977-80; mem. Osborn Maledon P.A., Phoenix; adj. prof. law Ariz. State U., 1977, 85—, U. Ariz., 1983, U. Mex., 1983; judge pro tempore Ariz. Ct. Appeals, 1992. Editor-in-chief Tex. Law Rev., 1969-70. Mem. ABA, Order of Coif. Office: Osborn Maledon PO Box 36379 2929 N Central Ave Ste 2100 Phoenix AZ 85012-2765

HAMMOND, LAUREN ROCHELLE, senate consultant; b. L.A., Nov. 27, 1955; d. David Frederick and Percy Winona (McIntyre) H. BA in Govt., Calif. State U., Sacramento, 1977; AA in Gen. Edn., Sacramento City Coll., 1977; postgrad., U. of Pacific, 1978-81. Fellow State Atty. Gen., Sacramento, 1980-81; asst. spl. svcs. Calif. Senate, Sacramento, 1981-85, prodn. asst. newsletter program, 1985-88, adminstrv. asst. rules com., 1988-93, cons. rules com., 1993—; cons. Sacramento County Bd. Edn., 1992; advisor various Dem. candidates L.A., Sacramento, 1991-96; mem. Assembly Dist. 9 Com. Mem. County Health Coun., Sacramento, 1994; treas. African Am. caucus Calif. Dem. Party, 1994-96; vice chair, commr. County Project Planning Com., Sacramento, 1995-97; del. Dem. Nat. Conv., Chgo., 1996; elected mem. Sacramento City Coun., Dist. 5, 1997. Recipient Cmty. Svc. award Women's Civic Improvement Club, Sacramento, 1992. Mem. NAACP, Africa's Daughters Rising PAC (founding officer, sec. 1993-95), Calif. State U. Sacramento Alumni Assn. (Svc. award 1993). Roman Catholic. Office: Senate Rules Com Calif Legislature 1020 N St Ste 255 Sacramento CA 95814-5624 also: City Hall Rm 205 Sacramento CA 95814-2672

HAMMOND, TEENA GAY, editor; b. Louisville, Dec. 3, 1967; d. Jimmie Howard and Roseta (Gay) H. Student, U. Louisville, 1985-87, Ariz. State U., 1989-93. Bus. reporter Bus. Jour., Phoenix, 1993-95; dir. mktg. and pub. rels. Murro Cons., Phoenix, 1995-96; bus. reporter Bus. Press, Ontario, Calif., 1996-97; West Coast retail editor Women's Wear Daily, Fairchild Publs., L.A., 1997—; West Coast fashion and features editor W mag., Fairchild Publs., L.A., 1997—. Recipient 2nd place Journalistic Achievement Ariz. Newspaper Assn., 1994, 1st place Gen. Reporting, Ariz. Press Club, 1994, 1st place Sustained Coverage Series, 1994, 3rd place Gen. Reporting, 1994. Office: Womens Wear Daily and W Mag Fairchild Publs 1900 S Bundy Dr Ste 850 Los Angeles CA 90025

HAMMOND-BLESSING, DIANN A., elementary education educator; b. Cedar Rapids, Iowa, May 24, 1943; d. Russell Irving and Ola Arline (Leonard) Hammond; m. Dale Fredrick Blessing, June 10, 1979. BA in Edn., U. Wyo., 1966, MEd, 1973. Cert. elem. tchr., Colo. Tchr. German and social studies Deaver-Frannie Schs., Deaver, Wyo., 1966-68, Alliance (Nebr.) City Schs., 1968-70; tchr. elem. Jefferson County Schs., Arvada, Colo., 1971—; del. Colo. Del. Assembly, 1974-79; sec. Argonauts Investment Group, 1986-87, v.p., 1989, pres., 1990, treas.-elect, 1993, treas., 1994. Co-author curriculum units Our Changing Langauge, 1978. mem. Record Keeping Task Force, Jefferson County, Colo., 1974-75, 84; del. Dem. County and State Convention, Colo., 1976, 80; mem. polit. action com. Jefferson County Schs., 1979-80; precint chair Dem. Com., Colo., 1984. Mem. NEA, AAUW (editor newspaper 1985-87), PTA, Colo. Edn. Assn., Colo. Reading Assn., Jefferson County Edn. Assn. (mem. com., rep. 1973-82, 94-95, 96-97, bd. dirs. 1974-79), Jefferson County Reading Assn., Instrnl. Profl. Devel. Home: 6626 S Yukon Way Littleton CO 80123-3070 Office: Warder Elem Sch 7840 Carr Dr Arvada CO 80005-4420

HAMP-LYONS, LIZ, language educator, consultant; b. Northampton, Eng., May 25, 1946; came to U.S., 1986; m. Brian Wood; 1 child, Nicholas; m. Michael Lyons; 1 child, Christopher. DipEd, U. Exeter, Eng., 1975, MEd, 1977; PhD, U. Edinburgh, 1986. Asst. lectr. Tech. Coll., Northampton, 1971-72; lectr. Coll. of Further Edn., Northampton, 1972-75; dir. studies Am. Ednl. Coll., Patras, Greece, 1977-78; lectr. U. Azebaijan, Tabriz, Iran, 1978; sr. lectr. Universiti Sains Malaysia, Pinang, 1978-80; ESL curriculum coord. We. Ill. U., Macomb, 1980-82; fellow U. Edinburgh, 1982-86; asst. prof. U. Mich., Ann Arbor, 1986-90; assoc. prof. U. Colo., Denver, 1990-96; prof. English, chair dept. English Hong Kong Polytechnic U., Kowloon, Hong Kong, 1996—; cons. in writing assessment Brit. Coun., London, 1983-89, Australian Ministry of Immigration and Employment, Sydney, 1993, 94, Ednl. Testing Svc., Princeton, N.J., 1992—. Author: Research Matters, 1984, Study Writing, 1987; author, editor: Assessing Second Language Writing in Academic Contexts, 1991. Recipient Duke of Edinburgh's prize English Speaking Union, 1984; U. Colo. Denver fellow, 1994-95. Mem. Internat. Lang. Testing Assn. (founding mem.), TESOL, Coll. Composition and Comm. Assn.

HAMPTON, CAROLYN SEEBA, small business owner, minister; b. Palo Alto, Calif., Nov. 11, 1949; d. Robert F. and Beverly M. (Engley) Seeba; m. David Charles Hampton, Apr. 22, 1972; children: Nathan Christopher, Rebekah Ruth. BA, Lewis and Clark Coll., 1971; MDiv, San Francisco Theol. Sem., 1978; cert. in small bus. mgmt., Tillamook Bay C.C., 1994. Ordained to ministry Presbyn. Ch. (USA), 1978; cert. Christian educator. Various clerical positions librs. and shops, Calif., Oreg., 1968-71; mem. clerical staff Lewis and Clark Libr., Portland, Oreg., 1971-75; libr. aide San Francisco Theol. Sem., San Anselmo, Calif., 1975-76; intern St. John's Presbyn. Ch., Camas, Wash., summer 1976; curriculum libr. San Francisco Theol. Sem., San Anselmo, 1976-78; co-assoc. pastor Bethany Presbyn. Ch., Grants Pass, Oreg., 1978-84; co-pastor 1st Presbyn. Ch., Phoenix, Oreg., 1984-85; contract curriculum writer Presbyn. Ch. (U.S.A.), Louisville, 1986-87; temp. supply pastor Mount Laki Presbyn. Ch., Klamath Falls, Oreg., 1987; chaplain Phoenix (Oreg.) Vol. Fire Dept., 1986-88; co-pastor Yoked Parish Presbyn. Ch., Pacific City & Cloverdale, Oreg., 1988-92; chaplain Nestucca Rural Fire Protection Dist., Cloverdale, 1988—; owner Circuit Rider Books of Oreg., Pacific City, 1993—; cons. Christian edn. to various chs., workshops and tchrs., 1987-88; mem. Chrsistian nurture div. Cascades Presbytery, 1979-81, 84-92, chmn. ch. officer devel. team, 1986-88; commr. to 199th Gen. Assembly, Presbyn. Ch. (USA), 1987. Author: (instrnl. text) Teaching Media: A Guide to Making and Using Your Own Audio-Visual Materials, 1973, (Sunday sch. curriculum) The Big Little School Curriculum, 1981-84, (ch. sch. course) Bible Discovery, 1987. Active Tillamook Emergency Svcs. Chaplaincy, 1994—, United Presbyn. Women, 1977—; troop leader Girl Scouts U.S.A., 1988-93; den leader, chmn. pack com. Cub Scouts, 1986-88; program parent Block Home, 1984-88; convenor Rogue C.C. United Campus Ministry Bd., 1981-84; vol. mgr. Cascades Remote Bookshore, 1988-91. Mem. AAUW (life). Home and Office: Circuit Rider Books Oreg PO Box 788 35625 Lower Loop Rd Pacific City OR 97135-0788

HAMPTON, RICHARD OWEN, research plant pathologist and virologist, educator; b. Dalhart, Tex., Feb. 17, 1930; s. Christopher C. and Marian Martha (Wise) H.; m. Willa Mae Johnson, June 12, 1954; children: Kevin Ray, Audrey C. BS in Agr., U. Ark., 1951; MS in Plant Pathology, Iowa State U., 1954, PhD in Plant Pathology, 1957. Asst. plant pathologist Wash. State U., Prosser, 1957-61; rsch. plant pathologist USDA Agr. Rsch. Svc., Prosser, 1961-65, Corvallis, Oreg., 1965-95; project and lab. dir. USDA Agr. Rsch. Svc., Oreg. State U., Corvallis, 1965-95; crop adv. com. USDA Agr. Rsch. Svc. Crop Germplasm Coordination, 1980-95. Author: Serological Detection and Identification of Viral and Bacterial Pathogens, 1990; contbr. over 160 articles to profl. jours. Recipient grants for rsch., several seed cos., Idaho, Wash., Oreg., 1965-95. Mem. Am. Phytopathological Soc. (chair virology 1985-86, chair germplasm 1993-95), Nat. Pea Improvement Assn. (pres. 1988-90, exec. com. 1986-95, Meritorious Svc. award 1991), Nat. Assn. Scholars. Republican. Baptist.

HAMPTON, SHELLEY LYNN, hearing impaired educator; b. Muskegon, Mich., Nov. 27, 1951; d. Donald Henry and Ruth Marie (Heinanen) Tamblyn; m. John Pershing Hampton Jr., Aug. 10, 1985; 1 child, Sarah Elizabeth. BA, Mich. State U., 1973, MA, 1978. Cert. tchr., Wash., Mich., N.Y. Tchr. presch. thru 3d grade N.Y. State Sch. for Deaf, Rome, 1973-78; cons. Ingham Intermediate Sch. Dist., Lansing, Mich., 1978-81; hearing impaired coord. Shoreline Sch. Dist., Seattle, 1981—; N.W. rep. Bur. of Edn. Handicapped, N.Y.C., 1978; N.Y. del. Humanities in Edn., 1977; adv. bd. State Libr. for the Blind, Lansing, 1980-81; adj. prof. Mich. State U., 1979-81, Seattle Pacific U., 1984-86; participant World Cong. Edn. and Tech., Vancouver, B.C., 1986; computer resource technician Spl. Programs, 1988-92, collegial team leader, 1992—; rep. Site-Based Mgmt. Coun., Seattle, 1992—. Writer: Social/Emotional Aspects of Deafness, 1983-84. Del. N.Y. State Assn. for Edn. of Deaf, N.Y.C., 1974-78; N.Y. del. Humanities in Edn., 1977; mem. bd. Plymouth Congl. Ch., Seattle, 1983-87. Recipient Gov.'s Plaque of Commendable Svc., State of Mich., 1981; grantee State of Wash., 1979, 82, Very Spl. Arts Festival, 1979-81; recipient Outstanding Svc. award Mich. Sch. for the Blind, 1980. Mem. NEA, Wash. State Edn. Assn., Shoreline Edn. Assn., Alexander Graham Bell Assn., Regional Hearing Impaired Coop. for Edn., Internat. Orgn. Educators of the Hearing Impaired, Auditory-Verbal Internat., U.S. Pub. Sch. Caucus, Conf. Ednl. Adminstrs. Serving the Deaf. Home: 14723 62nd Dr SE Everett WA 98208-9383 Office: Shoreline Hearing Program 16516 10th Ave NE Seattle WA 98155-5904

HAMREN, NANCY VAN BRASCH, bookkeeper; b. L.A., Feb. 2, 1947; d. Milton Carl and Winifred (Taylor) Van Brasch; m. Jerome Arthur Hamren, Feb. 14, 1981; children: Emily Allison, Meredith Ann. Student, Pasadena City Coll., 1964-65, San Francisco State Coll., 1966-67, U. Oreg., 1975-79. Bookkeeper/office mgr. Springfield Creamery, Eugene, Oreg., 1969—, also bd. dirs.; originator Nancy's Yogurt, Nancy's Cultured Dairy Products. Active mem. Oreg. Shakespearean Festival, Ashland, 1986, Oreg. Nat. Abortion Rights Action League, Sta. KLCC-PBS Radio; bd. dirs. BRING Recycling. Mem. Oreg. Dairy Assn., Audubon Soc., N.Am. Truffling Soc., The Wilderness Soc., Oreg. Pub. Broadcasting, Buhl (Idaho) Arts Coun., Conservation Internat. Democrat. Unitarian. Home: 1315 Ravenswood Dr Eugene OR 97401-1912 Office: Springfield Creamery 29440 Airport Rd Eugene OR 97402-9524

HAMRICK, JOSEPH EUGENE, JR., information services specialist; b. Chapel Hill, N.C., Feb. 4, 1954; s. Joseph Eugene Sr. and Emily Southerland (Cole) H.; m. Elaine Kay Metcalf, Oct. 2, 1982; children: Aubrie Nicole, Allison Laurel, Wendy-Anne Alisa, Claire Elise. BS in Computer and Mmt. Sci., Met. State Coll., Denver, 1989. Cert. system profl. Inst. for Cert. Computer Profls. Programmer, analyst Aviation Mgmt. Systems, Denver, 1980-83; mgr., AVsoft devel. PHH Aviation Systems, Golden, Colo., 1983-86; programmer, analyst Columbine Systems, Inc., Golden, 1986-88; dir., info. svcs. Property Asset Mgmt., Denver, 1988—; cons., pres. Bridgeware, Denver, 1985—. Cons. Terry Considine U.S. Senate Campaign, Denver, 1985-86. Sgt. USAF, 1975-79. Presbyterian. Home: 2272 S Grape St Denver CO 80222-6263 Office: Property Asset Mgmt 1873 S Bellaire St Denver CO 80222-4358

HAN, ITTAH, lawyer, political economist, high technology, computer engineering and financial strategist; b. Java, Indonesia, Jan. 29, 1939; came to U.S., 1956, naturalized, 1972; s. Hongtjioe and Tsuiying (Chow) H. BS in Mech. Engring. and Elec. Engring., Walla Walla Coll., 1960; MA in Math., U. Calif., Berkeley, 1962; BA in French, U. Colo., 1965, MS in Elec. Engring., 1961; MSE in Computer Info. and Control Engring., U. Mich., 1970; MS in Computer Sci., U. Wis., 1971; MBA in Mgmt., U. Miami, Fla., 1973; BA in Econs., U. Nev., 1977; MBA in Tax, Golden Gate U., 1978, MBA in Real Estate, 1979, MBA in Fin., 1979, MBA in Banking, 1980, MPA in Adminstrv. Orgn. and Mgmt., 1984, ME in Computer Engring. U. Idaho, 1991, JD, Whittier Coll., 1991, PhD. in Ethics & Tech. The Union Inst., 1994; MS in Computer-Based Learning Nova Southeastern U., 1994, MA in Edn. & Human Devel. George Washington U., 1995, MS in Instructional & Performance Tech. Boise State U., 1995, MA in Humanities Calif. State U., Dominguez Hills, 1995. Bar: Calif. 1992; cert. fin. planner. Salesman, Watkins Products, Walla Walla, Wash., 1956-60; instr. Sch. Engring. U. Colo., Denver, 1964-66; systems engr. IBM Corp., Oakland, Calif., 1967-69, Scidata Inc., Miami, Fla., 1971-72; chief of data processing Golden Gate Bridge, Hwy. and Transp. Dist., San Francisco, 1973-74; mgr. info. systems tech. and advanced systems devel. Summa Corp., Las Vegas, Nev., 1975-78; mgr. systems devel. Fred Harvey Inc., Brisbane, Calif., 1978-80; chmn. corp. systems steering com., mgr. systems planning Amfac Hotel & Resorts, Inc., 1978-80; tax strategy planner, innovative turnaround fin. strategy planner, chief exec. Ittahhan Corp., 1980-95; exec. v.p. Developers Unltd. Group, Las Vegas, 1982-84; v.p. Fidelity Fin. Co., Las Vegas, 1984-85; exec. v.p. John H. Midby and Assocs., Las Vegas, 1982-84, 1986-95; sec., treas., dir. River Resorts Inc., Las Vegas, 1983-84; sec., treas. Goldriver Ltd., Las Vegas, 1983-84; pres. Weststar Gen. Ptnr. Co., 1984-85, Developers Group Service Co., 1984-86; chief exec. officer, pres. Very High Tech. Polit. Economy Turnaround Management Strategist, Inc., 1986-95; chief exec. officer, pres. Artificial Intelligence Computer Engring. and Expert Systems Engring., Inc. (name changed to Turnaround Strategist & Artificial Intelligence Engring., Inc.), 1986—; pres. Orion Land Devel. Co., Las Vegas, 1987-89, Very High Tech. Computer Engring., Inc., Las Vegas, 1988-95; instr. U. Nev. Sch. Elec. Engring., Reno, 1981; systems designer, cons. in field. Mem. IEEE, Internat. Bd. of Stds. and Practices for CFP, Inc., Calif. Bar Assn., Assn. Computing Machinery, Am. Assn. Artificial Intelligence, Am. Math. Assn., Inst. Cert. Fin. Planners, Am. Contract Bridge League. Republican. Home and Office: 2501 Fulano Way Las Vegas NV 89102-2034

HAN, JIAWEI, computer scientist, educator; b. Shanghai, China, Aug. 10, 1949; came to U.S., 1979; arrived in Can., 1987; s. Yu-chang Han and Jia-zhi Wang; m. Yandong Cai, July 3, 1979; 1 child, Lawrence. BSc, USTC, Beijing, China, 1979; MSc, U. Wis., 1981, PhD, 1985. Asst. prof. Northwestern U., Evanston, Ill., 1986-87, Simon Fraser U., Burnaby, B.C., Can., 1987-91; assoc. prof. Simon Fraser U., Burnaby, 1991-95, prof., 1995—. Editor Jour. Intelligent Info. Sys., Jour. of Knowledge Discovery and Data Mining, IEEE Trans. Knowledge and Data Engring.; contbr. articles to profl. jours. Mem. IEEE, ACM, Assn. Logic Programming. Office: Simon Fraser Univ, Sch Computing Sci, Burnaby, BC Canada V5A 1S6

HAN, MAO-TANG, surgeon, researcher; b. Jinan, Shandong, China, Aug. 28, 1934; came to U.S., 1989; s. Houngwen Han and Shie Sun; m. Hui-Fong Wang, Aug. 28, 1960; children: Han Qiang, Han Shan. Student, Chee-Loo U., 1951-52; MD, Tongj Medical Sch., Wuhan, China, 1952-57. Resident gen. surgery Simo (Province of Yunan) Dist. Hosp., 1957-60, Tonjee Teaching Hosp. Medical U. Tonjee, Wuhan, Province of Hubei, 1960-61; resident in pediatric surgery Tianjin Children's Hosp., Tianjin, 1963-64, chief resident in pediatric surgery, 1964-65, attending surgeon, 1965-79; postgrad. fellow Shanghai Chest Hosp., 1975-76; vis. physician, fellow dept. surgery The Mayo Clinic, Rochester, Minn., 1979-82; chief surgeon dept. surgery Tianjin Children's Hosp., Tianjin, 1984-89; assoc. editor Chinese Jour. Pediat. Surgery; organizer 1st and 2d Internat. Symposia on Pediat. Surgery of China, 1984, 88. Contbr. chpts. to books; contbr. articles to profl. jours. Mem. Assn. of Chinese Pediatric Surgery, Chinese Medical Assn., Am. Coll. Chest Physicians, Asian Assn. Pediatric Surgeons, Pacific Assn. Pediatric Surgeons. Home: 4009 NE 70th St Seattle WA 98115-6021

HAN, ZHONG-SHENG, neurobiologist, researcher; b. Cheng Cheng, Shaanxi, China, Apr. 15, 1953; came to U.S., 1992; s. Hong-Bin and Pei-Qin (Wang) H.; m. Xiu-Ying Qiao, Oct. 1, 1982; children: Lee Han, Fee Han. BS, Shanxi Med. Coll., 1976, MS, 1982; PhD, Fourth Med. U., 1988; postgrad., Oxford U., 1990-91, Barrow Neurol. Inst., 1992—. Resident doctor for occupational diseases Weinan (Shaanxi) Inst. Sanitation and Antiepidemic, 1977-78; rsch. fellow dept. physiology Shaanxi Acad. Chinese Medicine and Pharmacology, Xian, 1983-84; lectr. dept. neurobiology Inst. Neurosci., Fourth Med. U., Xian, 1988-89; postdoctoral fellow MRC unit dept. pharmacology Oxford (Eng.) U., 1990-91; postdoctoral fellow dept. neurobiology Barrow Neurol. Inst., Phoenix, 1992-94; rsch. assoc. Dow Neurol. Scis. Inst., Portland, Oreg., 1995—; lectr. dept. physiology Fourth Mil. Med. U., Xi'an, China, 1983; lectr. dept. brain rsch. Xi'an Med. U., 1984; lectr. dept. physiology Shanxi Med. Coll., Taiyuan, China, 1987, lectr. dept. neurobiology, 1988; lectr. Shanghai (China) Inst. Physiology, 1989; lectr. summer sch. on neurosci. program U. Oxford, 1991. Author revs. and abstracts; contbr. articles to profl. jours. Mem. Pain Mgmt. Delegation to S.E. Asia, U.S. Citizen Ambassador Programs, 1993. Grantee Nat. Natural Sci. Found. China, 1985-88, 1988-89. Mem. U.S. Soc. Neurosci., Chinese Anatomy Soc., Chinese Physiology Soc. Office: Dow Neurol Inst 1120 NW 20th Ave Portland OR 97209

HANAN, LAURA MOLEN, artist; b. Fort Monmouth, N.J., Jan. 30, 1954; d. Richard Eugene Molen and Agnes Arlene (Stahlhacke) Rose; m. John Morris Hanan, Apr. 26, 1985; 1 child, Whitney Anne. BS, U. Calif. Berkeley, 1978; BA in Journalism, Humboldt State U., 1980; AOS in Visual Comm., Northwest Coll. Art, 1992. Reporter, city editor Contra Costa Sun, Moraga, Calif.; sports reporter, photographer The Canby (Oreg.) Herald; sr. technical writer MDS Qantel Bus. Computers, Hayward, Calif.; bus. mgr., owner, designer Hanan Constrn. and Design Co., Inc., Alameda, Calif., 1986-90; dir. admissions Northwest Coll. Art, Poulsbo, Wash., 1992-93; fine artist, graphic artist Laura Hanan Art, Gig Harbor, Seattle, Wash., 1993—; creative dir. Pacific Pipeline, Kent, Wash., 1992-93; co-owner The Watermark Gallery, Village Art Gallery, Freighthouse Gallery, Gig Harbor, Tacoma, 1993-96; art dir., cons. Exec. Office Svcs., Gig Harbor, Beaverton, Oreg., 1996—. Represented in permanent collections Pierce County Libr., John Madden; exhibited at Emerald City Fine Art Gallery, Seattle, 1996—, Peninsula Br. Libr., Gig Harbor, 1994, 95, 96. Recipient First Place prize Peninsula Art League, 1995, 2d place, 1996. Office: Emerald City Fine Art 317 1st Ave S Seattle WA 98104

HANCE, ANTHONY JAMES, retired pharmacologist, educator; b. Bournemouth, Eng., Aug. 19, 1932; came to U.S., 1958; s. Walter Edwin and Jessie Irene (Finch) H.; m. Ruth Anne Martin, July 17, 1954; children: David, Peter, John. BSc, Birmingham U., 1953, PhD, 1956. Rsch.fellow in electrophysiology Birmingham U., Eng., 1957-58; rsch. pharmacologist UCLA, 1959-62; rsch. assoc. pharmacology Stanford U., Palo Alto, Calif., 1962-65, asst. prof., 1965-68; assoc. prof. U. Calif., Davis, 1968-94, ret. prof. emeritus, 1994. Contbr. articles to profl. jours. Mem. Am. Soc. for Pharmacology and Exptl. Therapeutics, Biomed. Engring. Soc., Assn. for Computing Machinery. Home: 1103 Radcliffe Dr Davis CA 95616-0944 Office: U Calif Med Sch Dept Med Pharmacology & Toxicology Davis CA 95616-8654

HANCHETT, WILLIAM A. BARTON, mechanical engineer, designer; b. San Francisco, June 11, 1928; s. William A. Barton Sr. and Tempest Caroline (Wilder) W.; m. Jane Elizabeth Connell, Apr. 6, 1948; children: William A. Barton III, Barbara Lee, Marc Connell. BSBA, SUNY, 1976; BSME, Cath. U. Am., 1980, MSME, 1981. Cert. sr. safety engr. Commd. 2d lt. U.S. Army, 1952, advanced through grades to col., 1971, retired, 1975; dir. Hanchett Engring., Springfield, Va., 1975-81, Ojai, Calif., 1981—; program dir. Advanced Tech., Camarillo, Calif., 1982-88; dist. mgr. Am. Mgmt. Systems Inc., Port Hueneme, Calif., 1988-93. Named hon. mayor Bretten-Badden, Fed. Republic of Germany, 1964-66; decorated Legion of Merit (twice), Joint Svcs. Commendation medal, Army Commendation medal (three times), Vietnam medal of Valor (twice); recipient Engring. Recognition award Cath. U. Amer., 1980. Mem. ASME, Soc. Am. Mil. Engrs. (bd. govs. 1986-89), Am. Soc. Safety Engrs., Systems Safety Soc., Am. Soc. Indsl. Security (vice-chmn. 1989-90, 95, chmn. 1996-97), Am. Soc. Naval Engrs. Republican. Home and Office: 2585 Valley Meadow Ct Oak View CA 93022-9513

HANCOCK, EUGENE MERRILL, dietitian; b. Blackfoot, Idaho, Feb. 14, 1939; s. Clawson Brott and Margaret Amanda (Poulsen) H.; m. Barbara Jean Anderson, May 29, 1965; children: Susan, Douglas, Jean, Rebecca, Amanda, Rachel. Diploma, Ricks Coll., Rexburg, Idaho, 1959; BS, Brigham Young U., 1966. Registered dietitian. Dietetic intern Olka, State U., Stillwater, 1966-67; prodn. mgr. U. N.Mex. Food Svc., Albuquerque, 1967-69; asst. mgr. Brigham Young U. Dining Svc., Provo, Utah, 1969—. Voting dist. chmn. Rep. Party, Orem, Utah, 1986-87. With USAR, 1962-65. Mem. Am. Dietetic Assn., N.Mex. Dietetic Assn., Utah Dietetic Assn., Nat. Assn. Coll. and Univ. Food Svc. LDS. Home: 1541 N 200 W Orem UT 84057-2650 Office: Brigham Young Univ 180 SASC PO Box 21840 Provo UT 84602-1840

HANCOCK, N(EWELL) LES(LIE), accountant; b. Pitts., Apr. 13, 1943; s. Newell Francis and Mildred Helen (Bouverot) H.; m. Margaret Ann Kendrick, Nov. 30, 1968; children: Michelle Lynn, Jennifer Ann, Marie Noelle. BSBA, U. Denver, 1966; postgrad., various schs., 1969—. CPA, Colo. Supr. Pannell, Kerr, Forster, Denver and Atlanta, 1969-78; mgr. Wolf & Co. of Colo., Inc., Denver, 1978-79, 83-84; supr. Kafoury, Armstrong & Co., Reno, 1979-82; pvt. practice acctg. Arvada, Colo. and Reno, 1982—; mgr. Ashby, Armstrong & Co., Denver, 1984-87; asst. contr. 1st Resorts Inc. and Great Am. Mgmt. Group Inc., Lakewood, Colo., 1987-89; team leader subcontract audit Nat. Renewable Energy Lab., Golden, Colo., 1989—. Served to 1st lt. U.S. Army, 1966-69. Mem. AICPA, Colo. Soc. CPAs (report rev. com. 1984-90, pvt. co. practice com. 1990-93, accountancy regulation com. 1993-94, mem. rels. com. 1994-96, mem. svcs. 1996—), Nev. Soc. CPAs (bd. dirs. Reno chpt. 1982-83, auditing stds. com. 1981-82, vice chmn. acctg. principles com. 1981-83), Hospitality Accts. Assn. (sec. 1976-77). Republican. Baptist. Office: PO Box 740535 Arvada CO 80006-0535

HANCOCKS, DAVID MORGAN, museum director, architect; b. Kinver, Worcestershire, Eng., May 5, 1941; came to U.S., 1972; s. Cecil and Eva Alice (Morgan) H.; m. Anthea Page Cook, Feb. 16, 1982; children: Samuel Morgan, Thomas David, Morgan Page. BSc with honors, U. Bath, Eng., 1966, BArch with honors, 1968. Registered architect, U.K. Architect Zool. Soc. London, 1968-69, West of Eng. Zool. Soc., Bristol, 1970-72; design coord. Woodland Pk. Zool. Gardens, Seattle, 1973-74, dir., 1975-84; pvt. practice design Melbourne, Australia, 1985-89; exec. dir. Ariz.-Sonora Desert Mus., Tucson, 1989-97; cons. Singapore Zool. Gardens, 1979-89, Zool. Soc. Victoria, Australia, 1986-89, Mus. of Victoria, 1994. Author: Animals and Architecture, 1971, Master Builders of the Animal World, 1973 (writing award State of Wash. Govs. 1974), 75 Years: A History of Woodland Park Zoological Gardens, 1979. Bd. dirs. Allied Arts, Seattle, 1976-85, Chamber Music Soc., Seattle, 1984-85; adv. coun. Sch. of Renewable Natural Resources, U. Ariz.; adv. bd. U. Ariz. Press. Fellow Discovery Inst., Seattle; recipient Disting. Svc. award Am. Soc. Landscape Architects, 1975, Outstanding Pub. Employee of Yr. award Seattle Mcpl. League, 1983, WPZS medal Woodland Pk. Zool. Soc., 1991. Mem. Am. Assn. Mus., Am. Assn. Zool. Pks. and Aquariums, Am. Assn. Bot. Gardens and Arboreta, Internat. Coun. Mus., Royal Inst. Brit. Architects (assoc.). Home: 3761 N Avenida Flamante Tucson AZ 85716 Office: Ariz-Sonora Desert Mus 2021 N Kinney Rd Tucson AZ 85743-9719

HAND, DALE L., pharmacist; b. Boise, Idaho, Oct. 21, 1947; s. Robert Ray and Evelyn Mabel (McKenzie) H.; m. Gloria J. Lassen, Dec. 19, 1970; children: Travis D., Jason D. Student, Walla Walla Coll., 1965-66; B Pharmacy, Idaho State U., 1970; MS in Health Svcs. Adminstrn., Coll. St. Francis, Joliet, Ill., 1985. Intern Clinic Pharmacy, Pocatello, Idaho, 1968-70; pharmacognosy lab. tchng. asst. Idaho State U., 1969-70; hosp. pharmacy internship St. Luke's Hosp., Boise, 1970-71, clin. staff pharmacist, 1971-77; various to dir. pharmacy svcs. Porter Meml. Hosp., Denver, 1981-92, adminstrv. dir. dept. pharm. care, 1992—; pharmacy extern preceptor U. Colo., 1981—; cons. pharmacist McNamara Hosp. and Nursing Home, Fairplay, Colo., 1981-83; cons. Edn. Design, Inc., 1993—; lectr. in field.; chmn. various hosp. coms. Contbr. articles to profl. jours. Bd. dirs. Arapahoe Sertoma, 1991—. Mem. Am. Soc. Health Sys. Pharmacists, Colo. Soc. Health Sys. Pharmacists. Seventh-Day Adventist. Home: 7269 W Chestnut Dr Littleton CO 80123-5699 Office: PorterCare Hosp 2525 S Downing St Denver CO 80210-5817

HAND, HARLAND JULIUS, garden designer, consultant, retired educator; b. Fairmont, Minn., July 17, 1922; s. Ernest Richard and Emma Lena Louise (Saggau) H. Student, U. Minn., 1940,-42, 45; BA, MA, U. Calif., Berkeley, 1952. Florist Sheridan & Bell, San Francisco, 1948-58; tchr. biology, physiology, art Oakland (Calif.) Pub. Schs., 1952-82; science dept. head McClymond's High Sch., Oakland, 1965-74; garden designer pvt. practice, San Francisco Bay area, 1970—; garden writer various publs., 1977—; lectr. various Calif. Garden Clubs, 1976-80. Contbr. articles on gardening to various mags. and newspapers, chpt. to book, The American Man's Garden. Vol. designer of plantings for City of El Cerrito, Calif., 1975-85. Sgt. U.S. Infantry, 1942-45, ETO. Recipient Commendation City of El Cerrito, 1986; named Man of Yr. Calif. Garden Clubs, Inc., 1978. Mem. Calif. Horticultural Soc. (pres. 1975-76, coun. 1972-76, lectr., Garden award 1990), Friends of U. Calif. Botanical Gardens, Berkeley (lectr., bd. dirs.), Am. Rock Garden Soc. (lectr.), Strybing Arboretum Soc. (lectr.). Home and Office: Harland Hand Garden Design and Consultation 825 Shevlin Dr El Cerrito CA 94530-3050

HAND, HEATHER DENISE, human resources executive, educator; b. L.A., Apr. 28, 1964; d. David Lee and Patricia Lu (Pickette) H.; m. Gerald F. Ruger, Jr., Dec. 21, 1986 (div. June 1996). BA in Psychology, Claremont Mens Coll., 1981; MBA in Bus., Pepperdine U., 1985. Dir. adminstrn. Environ. Diagnostics, Burlington, N.C., 1984-90; dir. human resources Cooperative of Am. Physicians Mutual Protection Trust Fund, L.A., 1990-92; assoc. dir. human resources City of Hop, Duarte, Calif., 1992-94, adminstrv. dir. human resources, 1994-95, v.p. human resources, 1995—. Mem. Am. Soc. Tng. and devel. Am. Soc. Healthcare Human Resources (pres. 1994-95), Soc. Human Resources Mgmt. (cert.), Personnel Indsl. Rels. Assn., L.A. Human Resources Assn., Healthcare Human Resources Mgmt. Assn. Calif. Home: 3759 Canehill Ave Long Beach CA 90808 Office: City of Hope 208 W Spring Std Duarte CA 91010

HANDEL, NEAL, plastic surgeon, researcher; b. L.A., Sept. 2, 1947; s. Max and Ruth H. BA, Columbia U., 1969; MD, Yale U., 1973. Diplomate Am. Bd. Plastic Surgery. Resident UCLA, 1975-76, Tulane U., New Orleans, 1976-78, U. Colo., Denver, 1978—; plastic and reconstructive surgeon The Breast Ctr., Van Nuys, Calif., 1982—, assoc. med. dir., 1982—; mem. adv. bd. Ctr. for Devel. Biology Calif. State U., Northridge, 1985—. Contbr. articles to profl. jours. Rsch. grantee Am. Soc. Aesthetic Plastic Surgery, 1991. Fellow ACS; mem. Am. Soc. Plastic and Reconstructive Surgery, Calif. Soc. Plastic and Reconstructive Surgeons. Office: The Breast Ctr 14624 Sherman Way Ste 506 Van Nuys CA 91405-2241*

HANDEL, WILLIAM KEATING, advertising and sales executive; b. N.Y.C., Mar. 23, 1935; s. Irving Nathaniel and Marguerite Mary (Keating) H.; m. Margaret Inez Sitton; children: William Keating II, David Roger. BA in Journalism, U. S.C., 1959, MA in English Lit. 1960. Account supr. Ketchum, MacLeod & Grove, Pitts., 1960-67; mgr. advt. and pub. rels. ITT Gen. Controls, Glendale, Calif., 1967-80; mgr. corp. comm. Fairchild Camera and Instrument Corp., 1980-84; dist. mgr. Cahners Pub. Co., 1984-90; founder, CEO Tri-Dimensional Mktg. Comm. Agy., 1990-91, Penton Pub. Co., 1991-96, account supr. ADVO, 1996—; ind. sales/mktg. cons. Tri-D Cons., 1996—; pub. rels. counsel Calif. Pvt. Edn. Schs., 1978-87; chmn. exhibits Mini/Micro Computer Conf., 1977-78. Bd. dirs. West Valley Athletic League; bd. dir. L.A. chpt. USMC Scholarship Found.; pub. rels. cons. Ensenada, Mexico Tourist Commn., 1978; chmn., master of ceremonies USMC Birthday Ball, L.A., 1979-82. With USMC, 1950-53. Decorated Silver Star, Bronze Star, Purple Heart (4), Navy Commendation medal with combat V; recipient Pub. Svc. award L.A. Heart Assn., 1971-73. Mem. Bus. and Profl. Advt. Assn. (cert. bus. communicator, past pres.), 1st Marine Divsn. Assn., Navy League (bd. dir.), AdLinx Golf Club of So. Calif., Torrey Pines Golf Club, Griffith Pk. Golf Club, Nueva España Boat Club, Bajamar Country Club, Ensenada Country Club, Baja Country Club, Ensenada Fish and Game Club (Baja, Mex.), U. S.C. Alumni Club (founder/pres. L.A. chpt.), Sigma Chi (chpt. adv.). Republican. Roman Catholic. Home: 2428 Badajoz Pl Rancho La Costa CA 92009-8006

HANDFORD, JACK, fashion education consultant; b. Piedmont, Mo., Aug. 4, 1917; s. Jack and Ethel Collins (Bunyard) H.; m. Virginia Lee Snigg, Sept. 19, 1942 (dec. 1983). BFA, Chouinard Art Inst., L.A., 1946; MFA, Kensington U., Glendale, Calif., 1977; EdD, Kensington U., 1978. Apparel designer Chic Lingerie, L.A., 1946-50; instr. Chouinard Art Inst., L.A., 1946-61; apparel designer Calif. Girl, L.A., 1952-56; designer/owner Handford Ent., Inc., L.A., 1956-72; dir./owner Calif. Fashion Inst., L.A., 1961-72; instr. UCLA Ext., 1972-83; assoc. chmn. fashion dept. Otis/Parsons, L.A., 1981-89; guest lectr. Calif. Dept. Edn., Sacramento, 1964-69, Calif. State U., L.A., 1969-79; part-time instr. Fullerton Coll., 1975-83; conductor/planner in field; mem. various fashion adv. bds. Author: Professional Patternmaking, 1974, 2nd edit. 1984, Professional Pattern Grading, 1980; contbr. articles to profl. jours. With USNR, 1942-45. Fellow Costume Soc. Am. (nat. bd. dirs. 1977-86, reg. pres. 1977-79); mem. Calif. Fashion Designers (pres. 1950-52), Costume Coun. (bd. dirs. 1978-80). Episcopalian. Home: 2500 Honolulu Ave Apt 105 Montrose CA 91020-1876

HANDLEMAN, MARTIN IAN, music teacher; b. Bronx, N.Y., Sept. 3, 1938; s. Harry Aaron and Laura S. (Payman) H.; m. Judith Lee Osler, Aug. 18, 1963; 1 child, Michael. AA, L.A. City Coll.; BA in Music Edn., Calif. State U., Northridge. Cert. elem. educator, secondary music educator. Elem. music tchr. Lancaster (Calif.) Sch. Dist., 1962-64; jr. high music tchr. William S. Hart Union High Sch. Dist., Newhall, Calif., 1964-65; elem. music tchr. San Bernardino (Calif.) Schs., 1965—. Named Outstanding Tchr., 1989; recipient Svc. award So. Calif. Sch. Band & Orch. Assn., 1988. Mem. San Bernardino Tchrs. Assn. (v.p. 1979), So. Calif. Sch. Band & Orch. Assn. (festival adjudicator 1969—, v.p. adjudication 1986-88). Democrat. Office: San Bernardino City Sch 777 N F St San Bernardino CA 92410-3017

HANDLER, EVELYN, science administrator; b. Budapest, Hungary, May 5, 1933; U.S. citizen; m. 1965; two children. BA, Hunter Coll., 1954; MSc, NYU, 1962, PhD in Biology, 1963; LHD (hon.), Rivier Coll., 1982, U. Pitts., 1987, Hunter Coll., 1988. Rsch. assoc. Sloan-Kettering Inst., 1958-60, Merck Inst. Therapeutic Rsch., 1958-60; lectr. Hunter Coll., 1962-64, from asst. to prof. biol. sci., 1965-80, dean sci. and math., 1977-80; pres. U. N.H., 1980-83, Brandeis U., 1983-91; exec. dir. Calif. Acad. Scis., San Francisco; vis. scientist Karolinska Inst., 1971-72; evaluator Com. Higher Edn., Middle States Assn., 1972—; vice chmn. univ. faculty senate CUNY, 1974-76; generalist, mem. Am. Coun. Pharm. Edn., 1978-83; bd. dirs. New Eng. Life Ins. Co., Student Loan Corp. Trustee Bay Area Biosci. Ctr., 1995—, Mills Coll., 1995—. Sr. fellow Carnegie Found. Advanced Tchg., 1990-92; scholar in residence Harvard U., 1991-92, assoc. in edn. 1992-93; rsch. grantee NIH, 1964-69, 73-76, NSF, 1965-67, 70-72, CUNY, 1972-74. Fellow AAAS, N.Y. Acad. Sci.; mem. Internat. Soc. Hematology, Harvey Soc. Office: Calif Acad Scis Golden Gate Park San Francisco CA 94118*

HANDS, D(OUGLAS) WADE, economics educator; b. Lafayette, Ind., Apr. 22, 1951. BS in Econs., U. Houston, 1973; MA in Econs., Ind. U., 1977, PhD in Econs., 1981. Assoc. instr. dept. econs. Ind. U., Bloomington, 1976-79; asst. prof. econs. U. Puget Sound, Tacoma, 1980-86, assoc. prof., 1986-92, prof., 1992—; vis. assoc. prof. U. Notre Dame, Ind., fall 1991. Author: Introductory Mathematical Economics, 1991, Testing, Rationality and Progress: Essays on the Popperian Tradition in Economic Methodology, 1993; contbr. articles and books revs. to profl. jours. Recipient Lieber Assoc. Instr. award Ind. U., 1980; John Lantz jr. faculty fellow U. Puget Sound., 1984, Burlington No. Found. grantee, 1986, 92, Martin Nelson grantee, 1987, 89, 91, John Lantz sr. sabbatical fellow, 1994. Mem. Am. Econ. Assn., History of Econs. Soc., Internat. Network for Econ. Method, Philosophy of Sci. Assn. Home: 4826 Marine View Dr Tacoma WA 98422-2713 Office: U Puget Sound Dept Econs Tacoma WA 98416

HANDS, ELIZABETH S. (ELIZABETH S. GELTZ), nutrition analysis software company executive; b. Richmond, Va.; d. Benjamin Franklin and Tempe (Stewart) Hunt; m. Robert B. Geltz, Nov. 9, 1974; children: Terese Hands, James Hands, David Hands. Student, MIT, 1957-58; BA, Willamette U., 1969. Planner, statistician Gov.'s Planning Dept., Salem, Oreg., 1969-70; self employed in mktg. and fin. cons. Salem, 1970-74; sr. mgmt. analyst Gov.'s Exec. Dept., State of Oreg., Salem, 1974-75, sr. budget analyst, 1975-79; mgr. budget and fin. Port of Portland, Oreg., 1979-81; founder, CEO, pres. ESHA Rsch., Salem, 1981—; co-founder, bd. dirs. Capitol Health Care/HMO Ins., 1972-88. Author: The Food Finder, several edits., 1987-94; editor, author: (software) The Food Processor, 1985-94, Genesis, 1981-94. Mem. urban renewal planning coms., Salem, 1966-70. Mem. Focus Group. Home: 606 Juntura Way SE Salem OR 97302-3964 Office: ESHA Rsch 4263 Commercial St SE Salem OR 97302-3938

HANDSCHUMACHER, ALBERT GUSTAVE, retired corporate executive; b. Phila., Oct. 20, 1918; s. Gustave H. and Emma (Streck) H.; children: Albert, David W., Megan, Karin, Melissa. B.S., Drexel Inst. Tech., 1940; diploma, U. Pitts., 1941, Alexander Hamilton Inst., 1948. Prodn. mgr. Jr. Motors Corp., Phila., 1938-40; sales engr. Westinghouse Electric Co., Pitts., 1941; with Lear, Inc., Grand Rapids, Mich., 1945-57; beginning as sales mgr. central dist., successively asst. to pres., asst. gen. mgr., v.p. and gen. mgr., sr. v.p., dir. sales, pres., dir. Lear, Inc., 1959-62; v.p., gen. mgr. Rheem Mfg. Co., 1957-59; pres., dir. Lear Siegler, Inc., 1962-65; underwriting mem. Lloyd's of London. Trustee Drexel U., Am. Heart Assn. Maj. USAAF, 1942-45. Recipient 60th Anniversary Alumni award for outstanding achievements and services field of indsl. mgmt. Drexel U., 1951, Outstanding Alumni award, 1971; Man of Year award City of Hope, 1970; Man of Year award Nat. Asthma Assn., 1978; named to Abington High Sch. Hall of Fame, 1989. Mem. Astro Club (Phila.). Home: 1100 Stone Canyon Rd Los Angeles CA 90077-2918

HANDWERKER, LISA, medical anthropologist, public health consultant; b. Bklyn., May 2, 1958; d. Sol and Minnie (Geller) H. Student, Emory U., 1976-78; BA, Oberlin Coll., 1980; MPH, U. Calif., Berkeley, 1985; PhD, U. Calif., San Francisco, Berkeley, 1993. Cert. labor coach, ARC standard first aid, CPR for Profl. Rescuer, sr. life saving, swim instr. Pvt. tchr. ESL Tapei, Taiwan, 1981, Jackson Mann Cmty. Sch., Boston, 1982-83, Beijing (China) Med. U., 1985; tchg. asst. U. Calif. Berkeley, U. Calif. Berkeley Ext. Program, 1987-89; post-doctorate rsch. scholar U. Calif., Berkeley, 1994—, rsch. scholar Beatrice M. Bain Rsch. Ctr., 1994—; policy and legis. analyst, cons. World Inst. on Disability, Berkeley, 1995—; assoc. prof. integral health, adj. prof. anthropology Calif. Inst. Integral Studies, San Francisco, 1995—; rsch. affiliate Stanford (Calif.) U., Rsch. Inst. Study of Women and Gender, 1996—; field rschr., exchange student Sch. Pub. Health, Policy and Planning Program, U. Guadalajara, Mexico, 1984; cons. Internat. Child Resource Inst., Berkeley, 1985-86; rschr. Western Consortium for the Health Professions, San Francisco, 1986-87; field rschr. Highland Hosp. Ob-Gyn. Clinic, Oakland, Calif., 1988, others; presenter in field. Editor: Coun. on Anthropology and Reproduction Newsletter, 1993—; contbr. articles to profl. jours. Labor coach, translator Highland Hosp. and Asian Health Svcs., Oakland, 1987-88, 91—; cmty. health worker Berkeley (Calif.) Free Clinic, 1984-85. Recipient Oberlin Coll. Grad. Student Alumni award, 1988-89, Predoctoral award Assn. for Women in Sci., 1990, NSF Doctoral Dissertation Improvement award, 1990-91, Fulbright-Hays Doctoral Dissertation award, 1990-91, Sorpotomist Internat. award, 1991-92, Wenner-Gren Anthropol. Assn. doctoral dissertation award, 1995. Office: 9 Peter Yorke Way San Francisco CA 94109

HANDZLIK, JAN LAWRENCE, lawyer; b. N.Y.C., Sept. 21, 1945; s. Felix Munso and Anna Jean Handzlik; children: Grant, Craig, Anna. BA, U. So. Calif., 1967; JD, UCLA, 1970. Bar: Calif. 1971, U.S. Dist. Ct. (cen. dist.) Calif. 1971, U.S. Ct. Appeals (9th cir.) 1971, U.S. Supreme Ct. 1975, U.S. Tax Ct. 1979, U.S. Dist. Ct. (no. dist.) Calif. 1979, U.S. Dist. Ct. (ea. dist.) Calif. 1981, U.S. Dist. Ct. (so. dist.) Calif. 1982, U.S. Ct. Appeals (2d cir.) 1984, U.S. Ct. Internat. Trade 1984. Law clk. to Hon. Francis C. Whelan, U.S. Dist. Ct. (cen. dist.) Calif., L.A., 1970-71; asst. U.S. atty. fraud and spl. prosecutions unit criminal div. U.S. Dept. Justice, L.A., 1971-76; assoc. Greenberg & Glusker, L.A., 1976-78; ptnr., prin. Stilz, Boyd, Levine & Handzlik, P.C., L.A., 1978-84; prin. Jan Lawrence Handzlik, P.C., L.A., 1984-91; ptnr. Kirkland & Ellis, L.A., 1991—; del. U.S. Ct. Appeals for 9th cir. Jud. Conf., L.A., 1983-85; counsel to ind. Christopher Commn. Study of the L.A. Police Dept., 1991; dep. gen. counsel to Hon. William H. Webster, spl. advisor to L.A. Police Commn. for Investigation of Response to Urban Disorders, 1992; mem. adv. com. for Office of L.A. County Dist. Atty., 1994—. Mem. editl. adv. bd. DOJ Alert, 1994-95. Bd. dirs. Friends of Child Advs., L.A., 1987-91, Inner City Law Ctr., L.A., 1993—; mem. bd. judges Nat. and Calif. Moot Ct. Competition Teams, UCLA Moot Ct. honors program. Mem. ABA (sect. criminal justice nat. com. on white collar crime 1991—, co-chair securities fraud subcom. 1994—, west coast white collar crime com., exec. com. 1993—, vice-chair 1994-96, chair 1996—, mem. sect. litigation, criminal litigation com. 1989—), Fed. Bar Assn., State Bar Calif. (sects. on criminal law and litigation), L.A. County Bar Assn. (coms. on fed. cts. 1988—, chair criminal practice subcom. 1989-90, fed. appts. evaluation 1989-93, white collar crime com. 1991—, exec. com. 1991—), Nat. Assn. Criminal Def. Lawyers. Office: Kirkland & Ellis 300 S Grand Ave Ste 3000 Los Angeles CA 90071-3140

HANES, JOHN GRIER, lawyer, state legislator; b. Cheyenne, Wyo., 1936; s. Harold H. and Mary Elizabeth (Grier) H.; m. Liv Paul; children: Greg, Clint. BS in Bus. Adminstrn., U. Wyo., 1958, JD, 1960. Bar: Wyo. 1960, U.S. Ct. Appeals (10th cir.) 1960, U.S. Ct. Mil. Appeals, 1960, U.S. Supreme Ct. 1964. Dep. sec. of state State of Wyo., 1963-65; prijn. Burke, Woodard & Bishop, Cheyenne, 1965-90, of counsel, 1990—; atty. Wyo. Senate, 1967-71; mcpl. judge City of Cheyenne, 1970-73; mem. Burke, Woodard & O'Donnell, Cheyenne, Wyo., until 1990; of counsel Burke & Woodard, P.C. and predecessor firms, Cheyenne, Wyo., 1990—; mem. Wyo. Ho. of Reps., 1993—. Vol. Cheyenne Frontier Days; mem. Heels; Rep. precinct committeeman, 1976-94. With U.S. Army JAGC. Mem. C. of C., Rotary (pres. 1982-83, dist. gov. 1990-91), Sigma Nu. Home: 848 Creighton St Cheyenne WY 82009-3231 Office: 600 Boyd Bldg 1720 Carey Ave Cheyenne WY 82001-4429

HANEY, ROBERT LOCKE, retired insurance company executive; b. Morgantown, W.Va., June 14, 1928; s. John Ward and Katherine Eugenia (Locke) H. BA, U. Calif., Berkeley, 1949. Sr. engr. Pacific Telephone Co., San Francisco, 1952-58; mgmt. analyst Lockheed Missiles & Space Co., Sunnyvale, Calif., 1958-64; sr. cons. John Diebold, N.Y.C., 1964-65; sr. indsl. economist Mgmt. & Econs. Research, Inc., Palo Alto, Calif., 1965-67; prin. economist Midwest Research Inst., Kansas City, Mo., 1967-69; dir. mktg. coordination Transam. Corp., San Francisco, 1969-73; staff exec. Transam. Ins. Corp., L.A., 1974-82; 2d v.p. Transam. Life Cos., L.A., 1982-93; ret., 1993; cons. in field. Co-author: Creating the Human Environment, 1970. Lt. (j.g.) USN, 1949-52. Mem. Scabbard & Blade. Republican. Episcopalian. Home: 2743 Tiburon Ave Carlsbad CA 92008-7908

HANF, JAMES ALPHONSO, poet, government official; b. Chehalis, Wash., Feb. 3, 1923; s. William G. and Willa DeForest (Davis) H.; m. Ruth G. Eyler, Aug. 16, 1947; 1 child, Maureen Ruth. Grad. Centralia Jr. Coll., 1943, DLitt (hon.) World U. Ariz., 1980 Naval architect technician P.F. Spaulding, naval architects, Seattle, 1955-56, Puget Sound Bridge & Dredge Co. (Wash.), 1953-55, Puget Sound Naval Shipyard, 1951-53, 56-93; cons. Anderson & Assocs., ship bldg.; cons. The Rsch. Bd. Advs., Am. Biographical Inst., Inc.; guest lectr. on poetry and geneal. rsch. methods to various lit. socs., 1969—; contbr. hundreds of poems to lit. jours., anthologies and popular mags.; poetry editor Coffee Break, 1977-82. Recipient Poet Laureate Recognition award Internat. Biog. Centre of Cambridge, Eng., grand prize World Poetry Soc. Conv., 1985, 86, , 90, Golden Poet award World of Poetry in Calif., 1985-90, Silver Poet award Calif. sponsored nat. contest, 1989, numerous other awards. Judge poetry contest, Australia and India, 1985; named Man of Yr. Abaas, 1989—; named Internat. Eminent Poet Internat. Poet Acad. of Madras, India, 1987. Mem Internat. Poetry Soc. (Poet Laureate Wash. State award 1981), World of Poetry Soc. (Golden Poet award 1985-88, Poet Laureate award 1979), Kitsap County Writers Club (pres. 1977-78), Internat. Fedn. Tech. Engrs., Nat. Hist. Locomotive Soc., Kitsap County Hist. Soc., Puget Sound Geneal. Soc., Western World Haiku Soc., Olympic Geneal. Soc. (pres. 1974-75), N.Y. Poetry Forum, World Poets Resource Ctr., Literarische Union, Académie Européenne des Scis., Des Arts

Et Des Letters (corr.), Internat. Soc. Poets Md. (hon. charter), Internat. Platform Assn., Calif. Fedn. Chaparral Poets, World Sadhak Soc. (hon.), Nat. Libr. Poetry (hon. mem.). Baptist. Home: PO Box 374 Bremerton WA 98337-0075

HANFF, PETER EDWARD, librarian, bibliographer; b. Jacksonville, Fla., Jan. 23, 1944; s. George E. and Mildred Todd (Stringer) H.; m. Judith A. Baker, Jan. 22, 1974 (div. 1979). BA, U. Calif., Santa Barbara, 1966; MLS, UCLA, 1967. Libr. Library of Congress, Washington, 1967-69; libr., fellow Lilly Libr. Ind. U., Bloomington, 1969-70; libr. Bancroft Libr. U. Calif., Berkeley, 1970—, acting dir. Bancroft Libr., 1990-95, coord. spl. projects Bancroft Libr., 1995-96, dep. dir. Bancroft Libr., 1996—; lectr. on book collecting U. Calif. Extension, 5 campuses, 1978, 79. Author: Bibliographia Oziana, 1976, 2d edit., 1988; mem. editl. bd. Rare Books and Manuscripts Librarianship, 1986-93; contbr. articles to various publs. Mem. ALA, Assn. Coll. and Rsch. Librs. (appointments and nominating com. 1989-90), Am. Pty. Hist. Assn. (trustee 1993-96, v.p. programs 1996—), Internat. Wizard of Oz Club (bibliography editor 1976—, pres. 1978-86, 95—, recipient L. Frank Baum Meml. award 1978), Grolier Club (N.Y.C.), Colophon Club (San Francisco), Roxburghe Club (San Francisco). Home: 1083 Euclid Ave Berkeley CA 94708-1639 Office: U Calif Bancroft Library Berkeley CA 94720

HANFT, MARGIE EVELYN, librarian; b. Hobart, Ind., Jan. 14, 1933; d. Herman C. and Pauline B. (Harmon) Johnson; m. John Hanft, Dec. 22, 1959 (div.1976); children: Scott, Steven. BA, Northwestern U., 1955; MLS, Immaculate Heart Coll., 1969. Libr. Calif. Inst. of Arts, Valencia, 1969—; mem. adv. bd. Total Interlibrary Exchg. Network, Ventura, Santa Barbara, San Luis Obispo Counties, Calif., 1991-92. Office: Calif Inst of Arts 24700 Mcbean Pkwy Valencia CA 91355-2340

HANIFEN, RICHARD CHARLES, bishop; b. Denver, June 15, 1931; s. Edward Anselm and Dorothy Elizabeth (Ranous) H. B.S., Regis Coll., 1953; S.T.B., Cath. U., 1959, M.A., 1966; J.C.L., Pontifical Lateran U., Italy, 1968. Ordained priest Roman Catholic Ch., 1959; asst. pastor Cathedral Parish, Denver, 1959-66; sec. to archbishop Archdiocese Denver, 1968-69, chancellor, 1969-76; aux. bishop of Denver, 1974-83; 1st bishop of Colorado Springs, Colo., 1984—. Office: Bishop of Colo Springs 29 W Kiowa St Colorado Springs CO 80903-1403

HANKET, ARTHUR ANTHONY, actor, marketing and sales analyst, consultant; b. Ft. Belvoir, Va., June 23, 1954; s. Arthur P. and Jimsy A. (Murphree) H.; m. Stephanie A. Erb, 1 child, Peter Colot. BA in Theater Arts, U. Va., 1976; MFA in Acting, Fla. State U., 1978. Mktg. profl. Metler Assocs., N.Y.C., 1979-82; mktg./sales prof. The N.Y. Times, N.Y.C., 1982-84; mktg./rsch./mgmt. profl. Atwood Richards Inc., N.Y.C. and Irvine, Calif., 1985—; sole propr., pres. TeleMarketing Cons., L.A. Author: National Poetry Review, 1994; appearences include (TV shows) The Lazarus Man, Knots Landing, Married with Children, Andre's Mother, Beauty, One Life to Live, Another World; (theatre) Playwright's Horizons, N.Y.C., Pub. Theater, N.Y.C., Lamb's Theater, N.Y.C., N.Y. Theater Workshop, Hudson Guild Theater, N.Y.C., WPA Theater, N.Y.C., CSC Repertory, N.Y.C., Guthrie Theater, Mpls., The Actor's Gang, La Jolla (Calif.) Playhouse, Long Beach (Calif.) Opera Co., Hartford (Conn.) Stage So., Alley Theater, Phila. Drama Guild, Calif. Shakespeare Festival, Ala. Shakespeare Festival.

HANKINS, HESTERLY G., III, computer systems analyst, inventor, educator; b. Sallisaw, Okla., Sept. 5, 1950; s. Hesterly G. and Ruth Faye (Jackson) H. BA in Sociology, U. Calif., Santa Barbara, 1972; MBA in Info. Systems, UCLA, 1974; postgrad., Golden Gate U., 1985-86, Ventura Coll., 1970, Antelope Valley Coll., 1977, La Verne U., 1987; student, NRI McGraw-Hill Sch. Writing, Washington, 1993—. Cert. community coll. tchr., Calif. Applications programmer Xerox Corp., Marina Del Rey, Calif., 1979-80; computer programmer Naval Ship Weapon Systems Engring. Sta. of Port Hueneme, Oxnard, Calif., 1980-84; spl. asst. to chief exec. officer Naval Air Sta. of Moffett Field, Mountain View, Calif., 1984-85; mgr. computer systems project Pacific Missile Test Ctr., Oxnard, 1985-88; mgr. computer systems project MIS Def. Contract Adminstrn. Svcs. Region, L.A., 1988-94, ret., 1994; instr. writing Nat. U., Inglewood, Calif., 1994—; instr. bus. West Coast U., Camarillo, Calif., 1985; core adj. faculty Nat. U., L.A., 1988—; lectr. bus. Golden Gate U., Los Altos, Calif., 1984; instr. computer sci. Chapman Coll., Sunnyvale, 1984, Ventura (Calif.) Coll., 1983-84; cons. L.A. Police Dept., Allison Mortgage Trust Investment Co.; minority small bus. assn. cons. UCLA. Author: Campus Computing's Accounting I.S. As A Measurement of Computer Performance, 1973, Campus Computer, 1986, Network Planning, 1986, Satellites and Teleconferencing, 1986, Quotations, 1992, Quotable Expressions and Memorable Quotations of Notables, 1993, Idea Bank, 1993, Product Rating System, 1993, Training Base Model, 1993, Sound Seal/Shield, 1994, My Biographical Profile. Mem. St. Paul United Meth. Ch., Oxnard, Calif., 1986-87; fundraiser YMCA Jr. Rodeo, Lake Casitos, Calif.; key person to combine fed. campaign United Way. Named One of Outstanding Young Men in Am. U.S. Jaycees, 1980, Internat. Leader of Achievement and Man of Achievement, Internat. Biog. Centre, Cambridge, Eng., 1988, 20th Century award for achievement Internat. Biog. Centre, Cambridge, Eng., 1994. Mem. Nat. Assn. Accts., Calif. Assn. Accts., Intergovtl. Council on Tech. Info. Processing, Assn. Computing Machinery (recipient Smart Beneficial Suggestion award 1984), IEEE Computer Soc., Fed. Mgrs. Assn., Alpha Kappa Psi (sec. 1972-73). Home and Office: PO Box 7165 Culver City CA 90212

HANKS, EUGENE RALPH, land developer, cattle rancher, retired naval officer; b. Corning, Calif., Dec. 11, 1918; s. Eugene and Lorena B. Hanks; m. Frances Elliot Herrick, Mar. 4, 1945; children: Herrick, Russell, Stephen, Nina. Student, Calif. Poly. Coll., 1939-41, U. So. Calif., 1949-50, Am. U., 1958-59; grad., Command and Staff Coll., Norfolk, Va., 1960. With Naval Aviation Flight Tng.,V-5 Program USN, 1941-42, commd. ensign, 1942, advanced through grades to capt., 1963; carrier fighter pilot, Am. Ace, six victories, 1942-45; test pilot Naval Air Test Ctr., 1946-48; mem. Navy Flight Exhbn. Team Blue Angels, 1950; commdg. officer fighter squadrons including Navy's 1st squadron of F4 Phantoms, Mach II Missile Fighters, Miramar, Calif., 1952-61; 1st ops. officer U.S.S. Constellation, 1961-62; dir. ops. Naval Missile Test Ctr., 1963-66; test dir. Joint Task Force Two, Albuquerque, 1966-69; ret., 1969; owner, developer Christmas Tree Canyon, Cebolla Springs and Mountain River subdivs., Mora, N.Mex., 1969-91. Decorated Navy Cross, DFC with star (2), Air medal (7), Legion of merit; named Citizen of Yr., Citizen's Com. for Right to Bear Arms, 1987, 93, to Dun and Bradstreet's Million Dollar Club. Mem. Ret. Officers Assn., Am. Fighter Aces Assn., Combat Pilots Assn., Assn. Naval Aviation, Am. Forestry Assn., NRA, Blue Angels Assn., Naval Aviation Museum Found., Legion of Valor. Republican. Home and Office: Christmas Tree Canyon PO Box 239 Mora NM 87732-0239

HANKS, MERTON EDWARD, professional football player; b. Dallas, Tex., Mar. 12, 1968. BA, liberal arts, U. Iowa, 1990. With San Francisco 49ers, 1991—. Named to Sporting News NFL All-Pro Team, 1994-95, Pro Bowl, 1994-96. Office: San Francisco 49ers 4949 Centennial Blvd Santa Clara CA 95054-1229

HANKS, SUSAN BUDLONG, physical therapist; b. Evanston, Ill., May 13, 1942; d. Joseph Lyman and Geraldine (Handley) Budlong; divorced; children: Paul Joseph, Nicole Susanne. BS in Phys. Medicine, U. Wis., 1964. Staff phys. therapist Rehab. Inst. Oreg., 1964-66; staff phys. therspist Oreg. Health Scis. U., Child Devel. and Rehab. Ctr., 1967—; pvt. practice phys. therapy Portland, Oreg., 1978-89; cons. Albany (Oreg.) Pub. Schs., 1977, Salem (Oreg.) Pub. Schs., 1978-79, Idaho State Hosp. and Tng. Ctr., Nampa, 1978-79, Ea. Oreg. State Hosp. and Tng. Ctr., Pendleton, 1980, Clark Inst. for Restorative Tech., Battleground, Wash., 1980, Newberg Sch. Dist., 1980-82, McMinnville Sch. Dist., 1981-82, Woodburn Sch. Dist., 1982, Fairview State Hosp., 1981-89; presenter workshops in field. Author: Education and Therapeutic Interventions in Rett Syndrome, 1989; contbr. articles to profl. jours. Mem. Am. Phys. Therapy Assn., Oreg. Phys. Therapy Assn., Neurodevel. Treatment Assn., Phi Kappa Phi. Anglican. Office: Child Devel & Rehab Ctr PO Box 574 Portland OR 97207

HANLEY, JOAN CORETTE, vineyard owner; b. Missoula, Mont., Jan. 25, 1933; d. John Earl and Elsie (Pauly) Corette; m. Donald Lee Hanley, Mar. 26, 1953; children: Lee, Dean, Scott, Mark, Elise. Student, Stanford U., 1951-52, Mont. State Coll., 1953, Northwestern U., 1953; BA in Speech, U. Wash., 1955. Cert. clin. competence speech pathology and audiology. Speech pathology and audiologist, 1955-74; owner, gen. ptnr. Miramonte Vineyards, Temecula, Calif., 1973—; dir. Ctrl. City Speech and Hearing Clinic, Calif. State U., Long Beach, 1978-80; dir. pub. affairs Monaghan Co., Rancho Palos Verdes, Calif., 1990-91; corp. dir. So. Calif. Edison Co., Edison Internat., 1980—; bd. dirs. Harbor-UCLA Rsch. and Edn. Inst., 1995—. Trustee Pomona Coll., Claremont, Calif., 1982—; bd. dirs. Calif. Agrl. Edn. Found., 1989—, Greater L.A. United Way, Inc., 1971-94; co-chair So. Calif., Campaign for U. Wash., 1989-92; chmn. Harbor S.E. region bd. dirs. Greater L.A. United Way, 1992-93; chmn. fundraising com. Holy Trinity Cath. Ch., San Pedro, Calif., 1991-95; bd. dirs., exec. com. Greater L.A. United Way; mem. Commn. on Agr. and Higher Edn. State Calif., 1994-95. Republican. Roman Catholic.

HANLEY, KEVIN LANCE, maintenance manager; b. Oil City, Pa., Nov. 25, 1961; s. Harold Edward and Helen Louise (Banta) H.; m. Patricia Yolanda DeLeon, Sept. 29, 1984; children: Jennifer Jessica, Kevin Lance Jr. Grad. high sch., Titusville, Pa.; diploma, McDonald's Regional Hdqs., L.A., 1986. Maintenance supr. Paschen Mgmt. Corp. McDonald's, Camarillo, Calif., 1980-86, asst. mgr., 1986-88, 95, maintenance cons., 1988-89; mgr. phys. plant Westmont Coll., Santa Barbara, Calif., 1988—; apartment mgr. Bartlein & Co., Ventura, Calif., 1990—; storekeeper USNR, Port Hueneme, Calif., 1994—; gen. cons. "R" Cleaning Maintenance, Santa Paula, Calif., 1989-91; owner Custodial-Plus Svcs., Ventura, Calif., 1996—. Sec.-treas. Ch. of God of Prophecy, Ventura, Calif., 1987-95, co-pastor, 1988-95. With USNR, 1994—. Republican. Office: Westmont Coll 955 La Paz Rd Santa Barbara CA 93108-1023

HANLY, JERI RYAN, computer science educator; b. Evansville, Ind., Oct. 31, 1949; d. Charles Keith and Elizabeth (McIntyre) Ryan; m. Brian Vaughan, Aug. 25, 1968; children: Eric Josef, Kevin Frederick. BS in Edn., U. So. Ala., 1970; MA in Romance Langs., U. Mich., 1975; MS in Computer Sci., U. Wyo., 1984. Instr. of French and Russian Interlochen (Mich.) Arts Acad., 1970-73; lectr. in computer sci. U. Wyo., Laramie, 1980—; rsch. collaborator Naval Weapons Ctr., China Lake, Calif., 1984-92; software engring. seminar instr. IBM-US Edn., 1988-91. Author: Problem Solving and Program Design in C, 1993, 2d edit., 1996, C Program Design for Engineers, 1994, Essential C for Engineers and Scientists, 1997. Mem. Assn. for Computing Machinery. Baptist. Office: U Wyo Computer Sci Dept PO Box 3682 Laramie WY 82071-3682

HANNA, NABIL, biomedical engineer; b. 1944. PhD in Immunology, Hebrew U., Israel. Lectr. Hebrew U., Israel, 1973-78; rsch. sci. NCI-Frederick Cancer Rsch. Ctr., 1978-81; dir. SmithKline Beecham, 1981-90; now with IDEC Pharm. Corp., San Diego, 1991—. Office: IDEC Pharm Corp 11011 Torreyana Rd San Diego CA 92121-1104*

HANNAN, BARBARA ELLON, philosophy educator, lawyer; b. Pulaski, Va., May 21, 1958; d. William Seaton Jr. and Nancy Ellon (Baker) H. BA, Randolph-Macon Woman's Coll., 1979; JD, U. Ariz., 1982, PhD, 1989. Bar: Ariz. 1982. Clk. Slutes, Browning, Sakrison & Grant, Tucson, 1982-83; assoc. Tohono O'Odham Legal Svcs., Sells, Ariz., 1983-84; tchg. asst. U. Ariz., Tucson, 1984-89; asst. prof. U. Idaho, Moscow, 1989-92; vis. asst. prof. U. Ark., Fayetteville, 1993; asst. prof. philosophy U. N.Mex., Albuquerque, 1993-96, assoc. prof., 1996—. Author: Subjectivity and Reduction, 1994; contbg. author (anthology) Love Analyzed, 1996; contbr. articles to profl. jours. Mem. cathedral choir St. John's Episcopal Cathedral. Fellow NEH, 1992. Mem. Am. Philos. Assn., State Bar Ariz., Phi Beta Kappa. Democrat. Episcopalian. Office: U NMex Dept Philosophy Humanities Bldg Albuquerque NM 87131

HANNI, GERALDINE MARIE, therapist; b. Salt Lake City, Nov. 14, 1930; d. John Henry and Theresa Justine (Keirce) Gold; m. Kenneth J. Hanni, Mar. 14, 1951; children: Debra, Valerie, Kathleen, Cynthia, Kristine. BS, U. Utah, 1951, MSW, 1983. Lic. clin. social worker. Tchr. Hillside Jr. High Sch., Salt Lake City, 1970-73; intern Davis County Schs., Farmington, Utah, 1981-82, Westside Mental Health, Salt Lake City, 1982-83; group leader LDS Social Services, Salt Lake City, 1985; therapist ISAT, Salt Lake City, 1983-90, clin. dir., 1987-90; clin. instr. U. Utah, Salt Lake City, 1986-90; pvt. practice, 1990—; mem. bd. Salt Lake County Sexual Abuse Task Force, Salt Lake City; cons. LDS Social Services, Salt Lake City, 1984-86. Contbg. author: Abuse and Religion, Confronting Abuse—an LDS Perspective. Sect. dir. Mortar Bd. Honor Soc., western U.S., 1970; pres. Highland High PTA, Salt Lake City, 1980; chairperson Highland High Community Sch. Orgn., Salt Lake City, 1981. Mem. Nat. Assn. Social Workers (Utah chpt.). Democrat. Mormon.

HANNUM, GERALD LUTHER (LOU HANNUM), retired tire manufacturing company official; b. Syracuse, N.Y., May 31, 1915; s. Ralph Charles and Coral (Snyder) H.; m. Carolyn Russell Osgood, Nov. 29, 1941; children: Nancy, Susan, Jean. AB, Syracuse U., 1937; MA, Kent State U., 1971. Supr. forecasting and inventory control B.F. Goodrich, Arkon, Ohio, 1961-67; econ. planning specialist, staff for v.p. planning B.F. Goodrich Co., 1967-75, econ. planner, 1946-75; ret., 1975. Councilman City of Medford, Oreg., 1977-82, 89-92, mayor, 1983-86; bd. dirs. United Way, Medford, 1986—; pres. Crater Lake coun. Boy Scouts Am., 1987-90. Lt. USNR, 1943-52, PTO. Recipient Silver Beaver award Boy Scouts Am., 1987. Mem. League Oreg. Cities (pres. 1983, Richards award 1989), Rotary. Home: 2900 Seckel St Medford OR 97504-8150

HANOWELL, ERNEST GODDIN, physician; b. Newport News, Va., Jan. 31, 1920; a. George Frederick and Ruby Augustine (Goddin) H.; m. Para Jean Hall, June 10, 1945; children: Ernest D., Deborah J. Hanowell Orick, Leland H., Dee P. Hanowell Martinmaas, Robert G. Diplomate Am. Bd. Internal Medicine. Intern USPHS Hosp., Norfolk, Va., 1948-49; resident in internal medicine USPHS Hosp., Seattle, 1952-55; fellow cardiology New Eng. Ctr. Hosp., Boston, 1961-62; chief medicine USPHS Hosp., Ft. Worth, 1955-57; dept. chief medicine USPHS Hosp., Boston, 1957-59; chief medicine USPHS Hosp., Memphis, 1964-65, Monterey County Gen. Hosp., 1969-70; ret. med. dir., col. USPHS; mem. IM and Cardiology staff Kaiser Permanente Med. Group, Sacramento, 1971-87; writer Auburn, Calif., 1987-; clin. asst. Tufts Med. Sch., 1960-61; cons. chest disease Phila. Gen. Hosp., 1960-61; asst. prof. U. Md. Med. Sch., 1961-64; instr. U. Tenn. Med. Sch., 1964-65; asst. clin. prof. Sch. Medicine, U. Calif., Davis, 1973-81; mem. attending staff Cardiac Clinic Stanford U. Med. Sch. 1967-69. Mem. sch. bd. Salinas, Calif., 1968-69; bd. dirs. Am. Heart Assn., Tb and Health Assn. Served with AUS, 1943-46. Fellow ACP, Am. Coll. Chest Diseases; mem. AWA, Crocker Art Mus. Assn., Comstock Club (Sacramento), Phi Chi. Home and Office: 1158 Racquet Club Dr Auburn CA 95603-3042

HANSEN, ANNE KATHERINE, poet, retired elementary education educator; b. Coulter, Iowa, Oct. 29, 1928; d. Carl Christian and Else Katherine (Paulsen) H. BA, Chapman U., 1958; MA, U. Redlands, 1971. Life credential, Calif. Elem. tchr. Bloomington (Calif.) Schs., 1958-60, San Bernarndino (Calif.) Unified Sch. Dist., 1960-87; ret., 1987. Contbr. poetry to anthologies. Recipient Golden Poet award World of Poetry, 1988, 89, 90, 91, 92, Poet of Merit award Internat. Soc. Poets, plaque, 1993, 94, 96, medallion, 1996. Home: 1632 N Sepulveda Ave San Bernardino CA 92404

HANSEN, BERNT ALLAN, lawyer; b. Longview, Wash., Mar. 29, 1941; s. Bernt Andrew and Wilma Leah Hansen; m. Carole Tuttle, June 8, 1968; children: Matthew, Nicolai, Rachel. BS, Portland State U., 1965; JD, U. Oreg., 1971. Bar: Oreg. 1972, U.S. Dist. Ct. Oreg. 1981. Dep. dist. atty. Lane County, Oreg., 1972-73; sr. dep. dist. atty. Yamhill County, Oreg., 1973-80; pvt. practice McMinnville, Oreg., 1980—. Planning commr. City of McMinnville, 1977-84, councilman, 1985-93. With U.S. Army, 1965-68. Mem. Yamhill County Bar Assn. (pres. 1981-82), ATLA, Oreg. Trial Lawyers Assn., Oreg. Criminal Def. Lawyers Assn., 12th Jud. Dist. Bar Assn. (pres. 1975-76), Rotary (pres. 1995-96). Home: 922 N Galloway St Mcminnville OR 97128-3831 Office: 638 E 5th St PO Box 597 Mcminnville OR 97128

HANSEN, BRETT JAMES, music educator; b. Gary, Ind., June 2, 1958; s. James R. and Mary Lee Hansen; m. Patricia Hansen; children: Melissa, Shala, John, Shayna, Burke, DeeAnna, Hobbs. BME, U. Colo., 1980; postgrad., Utah State U., 1996. Music dir. Jefferson County Schs., Lakewood, Colo., 1980-84; music dir., coach Western H.S., Las Vegas, Nev., 1984-86; music dir. Griffin H.S., Springfield, Ill., 1986-87; pvt. instr., 1987-90; band dir. Carbon H.S., Price, Utah, 1989-90; music dir. Round Mountain (N.Y.) Schs., 1990-92; band dir. Orem (Utah) Jr. H.S., 1992—; state solo/ensemble chair Nev. Music Educators, 1985-86. head precinct judge Jefferson County Rep. party, Arvada, Colo., 1988; Earth Day music coord. City of Round Mountain, 1991; scouting chair Hunter 27th Ward, West Valley, Utah, 1994; bd. dirs. Arvada Ctr. for Arts, 1987-88. Mem. ASCD, Am. Fedn. Tchrs., Utah Fedn. Tchrs., Utah Music Educators, Music Educators Nat. Conf. Republican. Mem. LDS Ch. Office: Orem Jr HS 765 N 600 W Orem UT 84057-3757

HANSEN, CARL FREDERICK, chemistry educator; b. Owatonna, Minn., June 11, 1921; s. Clifford Franklin and Lumetta Gladys (Swanson) H.; m. Alice Adelaide Underleak, July 11, 1946 (div. 1968); children: David R., Richard F., George H. BA, Carleton Coll., 1943; MS, Stanford U., 1948; D of Engring., Nagoya U., 1982. Aeronautical rsch. scientist Ames Aerospace Lab. NACA, Mountain View, Calif., 1950-59; chief physics br. Ames Rsch. Ctr. NASA, Mountain View, Calif., 1959-61, 67-82; head earth & astro scis. GM Defense Rsch. Lab., Santa Barbara, Calif., 1961-67; pres. JAI Assoc., Inc., Mountain View, 1985-89; rsch. prof. chem. physics inst. U. Oreg., Eugene, 1989—; vis. prof. aerospace engring. Nagoya (Japan) U., 1982, Indian Inst. Sci., Bangalore, 1983, Nat. Cheng Kung U., Taiwan, 1984-85, vis. prof. mech. engring. MIT, Cambridge, 1965-66; pres. Hansen Rsch. Assocs., Eugene, 1989—. Author: Molecular Physics of Equilbrium Gases, 1976, Rate Process in Gas Phase, 1983; contbr. articles to profl. jours. Treas. Com. Sch. Improvement, Palo Alto, Calif., 1958-59; bd. dirs. Orchard Farms Assn., San Jose, Calif., 1969-81. Sgt. USAF, 1943-46. Fellow AIAA (assoc., v.p. No. Calif. chpt. 1960); mem. Aircraft Owners and Pilots Assn., Elks. Independent. Office: U Oreg Physics Dept Eugene OR 97403

HANSEN, CAROL LOUISE, English language educator; b. San Jose, Calif., July 17, 1938; d. Hans Eskelsen and Thelma Josephine (Brooks) Hansen; m. Merrill Chris Davis, July 17, 1975 (div. 1978). BA in English, San Jose State U., 1960; MA in English Lit., U. Calif., Berkeley, 1968; PhD in English Lit., Ariz. State U., 1975. Asst. prof. English City Coll. San Francisco, Calif., 1985—, Coll. San Mateo, Calif., 1987—; coord. writing Calif. State U., Monterey Bay, 1996; presenter in field. Author: Woman as Individual in English Renaissance Drama, 1993, 2nd edit., 1995. Active Grace Cathedral, San Francisco. NDEA fellow, English-Speaking Union fellow for rsch. in Eng. Ariz. State U., 1972. Mem. MLA (exec. com. discussion group on two-yr. colls.), Virginia Woolf Soc. Episcopalian.

HANSEN, CHRISTINE MERRI, music educator; b. Inglewood, Calif., Dec. 26, 1954; d. Oluf Steffen and Betty Jane (Henderson) H. PharmD, U. So. Calif., L.A., 1979; AA in Music, piano tchg. cert., Golden West Coll., 1993. Cert. pharmacist; cert. piano tchr. Clin. pharmacist, lectr. pharmacology Cottage Hosp., Santa Barbara, Calif., 1979-87; pvt. math and sci. tutor Calif., 1987—; math. and sci. tutor Golden West Coll. Tutoring Ctr., Huntington Beach, Calif., 1991-93; model La Belle Agy., 1990-91, John Robert Powers Agy., 1991-93; pvt. piano tchr. Writer, pub.: (newsletter) Our Generation. City of Huntington Beach and Mercury Savs. scholar Golden West Coll., 1975, Gift of Music scholar Golden West Coll., Huntington Beach, 1993.

HANSEN, CLIFFORD PETER, rancher, former governor and senator; b. Zenith, Wyo., Oct. 16, 1912; s. Peter Christofferson and Sylvia Irene (Wood) H.; m. Martha Elizabeth Close; children: Mary Elizabeth, Peter Arthur. BS, U. Wyo., 1934, LLD (hon.), 1965. County commr. Teton County, Jackson, Wyo., 1943-51; v.p. Jackson State Bank, 1952-68; gov. State of Wyo., Cheyenne, 1963-66; mem. U.S. Senate, Washington, 1967-78. Trustee U. Wyo., Laramie, 1946-62, Goetische Found., Thermopolis, Wyo., 1979—, Buffalo Bill Mus., Cody, Wyo., 1979—, Jackson Lake Lodge Co., Moran, Wyo., 1960-85; chmn. livestock adv. com. USDA, Washington, 1956-62; pres. Wyo. Stock Growers Assn., Cheyenne, 1956-58; mem. compact com. Who.-Idaho Snake River, 1946-49; mem. Columbia Basin Devel., Portland, Oreg., 1946-52. Named Outstanding Alumnus U. Wyo., 1964, Citizen of the West Nat. Western Stock Show, 1996; named to Hall of Great Westerners, Nat. Cowboy Hall of Fame, 1995. Mem. Masons (past master), Rotary (past pres.), Elks, Teton Pines Country Club, Sun City Country Club. Republican. Episcopalian.

HANSEN, CURTIS LEROY, federal judge; b. 1933. BS, U. Iowa, 1956; JD, U. N.Mex., 1961. Bar: N.Mex. 1961. Law clk. to Hon. Irwin S. Moise N.Mex. Supreme Ct., 1961-62; ptnr. Snead & Hansen, Albuquerque, 1962-64, Richard C. Civerolo, Albuquerque, 1964-71, Civerolo, Hansen & Wolf, P.A., 1971-92; dist. judge U.S. Dist. Ct., N.Mex., 1992—. Mem. State Bar N.Mex., Albuquerque Bar Assn., Am. Coll. Trial Lawyers, Am. Bd. Trial Advocates, Albuquerque Country Club. Office: Fed Bldg & US Courthouse 500 Gold Ave Sw 13th Fl PO Box 1309 Albuquerque NM 87103

HANSEN, DONALD CURTIS, retired manufacturing executive; b. Marinette, Wis., Mar. 13, 1929; s. Curtis Albert and Dagmar Anne (Johnson) H.; m. Joan Mary Crant, Nov. 9, 1973. BBA, Carroll Coll., 1952. Purchasing agt. Prescott/Sterling Co., Menominee, Mich., 1954-62; mfrs. rep. Don C. Hansen Assocs., Phoenix, 1962-63; sales mgr. Karolton Envelope Co., San Francisco, 1964-72; owner, pres. San Francisco Envelope Co., 1972-79; owner Curtis Swann Cards, San Francisco, 1977-79; pres., owner Don C. Hansen, Inc. (doing bus. as The Envelope Co.), Oakland, Calif., 1979-95; ret., 1995. Mgr., organizer Twin City Civic Chorus, Menominee, 1959; bd. dirs. Menominee C. of C., 1958. Served with U.S. Army, 1952-54. Mem. Envelope Printing Specialists Assn. (bd. dirs. 1983—, pres. 1983-84), Envelope Mfrs. Assn. Am., San Francisco Lithograph and Craftsmans Club, Printing Industries of No. Calif. (bd. dirs. 1980-94), San Francisco Tennis Club (bd. govs. 1989-92), Terravita Country Club (Scottsdale, Ariz.), Masons, Shriners. Republican.

HANSEN, ELIZABETH JEAN, appraiser, author; b. Redwood City, Calif., Sept. 14, 1930; d. Conrad and Macil (Gibbsen) H. Postgrad., U. So. Calif., L.A. Antique entrepreneur, appraiser, estate liquidator; founder, owner Hansen's Assn. Appraisers and Liquidators, Watsonville, Calif. Contbg. writer antique pubs. including The West Coast Peddler, Antique Today, Tri-State Weekly, Arts and Antiques mag., Antiques and Collecting Hobbies mag., Antique Dealer, Art and Antique Adventure, Antique Gazette's eastern pub., others; author: Furniture Manuals Vol. I-V, Appraisal Manuals Vol. I and II, Oriental Art Manual Vol. I-IV, Book of Marks, Porcelain/Pottery, 15 State of the Art manuals of bus. and antiques, Porcelain Manual Vol. I, Silver Manual Vol. I and II, Art and Pattern Glass Manual Vol. I, Jewelry Manuals Vol. I-IV, Textile Manual Vol. I and II, Cut Glass Working Manual, Business Manuals Vol. I-V, Code of Ethics and Standards for Appraisers. Recipient Cert. of Merit for Disting. Svc., Cambridge, Eng., 1988. Home and Office: 49 Blanca Ln Spc 305 Watsonville CA 95076-2155

HANSEN, FLORENCE MARIE CONGIOLOSI (MRS. JAMES S. HANSEN), social worker; b. Middletown, N.Y., Jan. 7, 1934; d. Joseph James and Florence (Harrigan) Congiolosi; m. James S. Hansen, June 16, 1959 (dec. Nov. 1989); 1 child, Florence M. BA, Coll. New Rochelle, 1955; MSW, Fla. State U., 1960; PhD, Union Inst., 1992. Caseworker, Orange County Dept. Pub. Welfare, N.Y., 1955-57, Cath. Welfare Bur., Miami, Fla., 1957-58; supr. Cath. Family Service, Spokane, Wash., 1960, Cuban Children's Program, Spokane, 1962-66; founder, dir. social service dept. Sacred Heart Med. Ctr., 1968-85, dir. Kidney Ctr., 1967-91. Asst. in program devel. St. Margaret's Hall, Spokane, 1961-62; trustee Family Counseling Svc. Spokane County, 1981—, also bd. dirs.; mem. budget allocation panel United Way, 1964-76, mem. planning com., 1968-77, mem. admissions com., 1969-70, chmn. projects com. 1972-73; mem. kidney disease adv. com. Wash.-Alaska Regional Med. Program, 1970-73. Mem. Spokane Quality of Life Commn., 1974-75; vol. Primary Health Care Nangoma Health Ctr., 1992—; cons. CARE Internat., Zambia, 1993-95. Recipient Ursula Laurus citation Coll. New Rochelle, 1990, Angela Merici medal, 1995. Mem. Nat. Assn. Social Workers (Wash. chpt. pres. 1972-74, Wash. State Social Worker of Yr. 1991, Nat. Social Worker of Yr. 1991), Acad. Cert. Social Workers (charter). Roman Catholic. Home: 5609 W Northwest Blvd Spokane WA 99205-2039 Office: Nangoma Health Ctr. Box 830022, Mumbwa Zambia

HANSEN, HAROLD B., JR., elementary school educator; b. Sewickley, Pa., July 3, 1955; s. Harold B. and Mary Clara (VanderVort) H.; m. Patty Jo Gabhart, Sept. 19, 1976; children: Jeremiah James, Joshua Andrew, Esther Beth, Christopher Seth. BA in Elem. Edn., Purdue U., 1980; MA in Sch. Adminstrn., Western N.Mex. U., 1987. Cert. secondary lang. arts and spl. edn. tchr., instrnl. leader, sch. adminstr., elem. tchr., coach, N.Mex. Resource rm. tchr. Flossmoor/Homewood (Ill.) Pub. Schs., 1981, Newcomb (N.Mex.) H.S., 1981-82; tchr. self-contained spl. edn. Chester (Mont.) Pub. Schs., 1982-84; adminstr., prin., tchr. Bennett (Colo.) Bapt. Ch. Sch., 1984; propr., tutor Hemispheric Learning Tutorial Svcs., 1982—; tchr. resource room, coach cross county, wrestling, track and field Gallup-McKinley County Pub. Schs., Tohatchi/Navajo Reserv., N.Mex., 1985-90; elem. tchr. phys. edn. and health, at-risk tchr. Tohatchi Elem. Sch. Gallup-McKinley County Pub. Schs., Tohatchi, 1990—, 5th grade track & field head coach, 1991—, 5th grade boys' and girls' basketball asst. coach, 1995—; mem. various sch. coms. Gallup-McKinley County Pub. Schs., 1990—; seminar leader on hemispherecity; dep. registration officer McKinley County, N.Mex., 1986—. Past pres. Village of Hope, substance abuse tng. ctr.; co-founder, past bd. dirs. Christian Home Educators Assn.; past bd. dirs. Approved Workmen Are Not Ashamed; coord. Jump Rope for Heart, Am. Heart Assn. Named to Outstanding Young Men of Am., 1987. Mem. ASCD, N.Mex. Assn. Health, Phys. Edn., Recreation and Dance, Christian HomeEducators Assn., Aesthetic Realism Found. Home: PO Box 1485 Tohatchi NM 87325-1485

HANSEN, J. WOODFORD, agricultural products supplier; b. 1948. Owner of affiliate Hansen Ranch, Camarillo, Calif., 1968—; with Seaboard Produce, Oxnard, Calif., 1979—, now pres. Office: Seaboard Produce 601 Mountain View Ave Oxnard CA 93030-7203*

HANSEN, JAMES LEE, sculptor; b. Tacoma, Wash., June 13, 1925; s. Hildreth Justine and Mary Elizabeth Hansen; m. Annabelle Hair, Aug. 31, 1946 (dec. Sept. 1993); children: Valinda Jean, Yauna Marie; m. Jane Lucas, May 13, 1994. Grad., Portland Art Mus. Sch. Mem. faculty Oreg. State U., Corvallis, 1957-58, U. Calif., Berkeley, 1958, Portland State U., 1964-90. One-man shows include Fountain Gallery, Portland, Oreg., 1966, 69, 77-81, U. Oreg. Art Mus., Eugene, 1970, Seligman (Seders Gallery), Seattle, 1970, Portland Art Mus., 1971, Cheney Cowles Meml. Mus., Spokane, Wash., 1972, Polly Freidlander Gallery, Seattle, 1973, 75, 76, Smithsonian Instn., Washington, 1974, Hodges/Banks Gallery (now Linda Hodges Gallery), Seattle, 1983, Abanté Gallery, Portland, 1986, 88, 92; group exhbns. include N.W. Ann. Painters and Sculptors, Seattle, 1952-73, Oreg. Ann. Painters and Sculptors, Portland Art Mus., 1952-75, Whitney Mus. Am. Art, N.Y.C., 1953, Santa Barbara (Calif.) Mus. Art, 1959-60, Denver Art Mus., 1960, San Francisco Art Mus., 1960, Smithsonian Instn., Washington, 1974, Wash. State U., Pullman, 1975; represented in permanent collections Graphic Arts Center, Portland State Capitol, Olympia, Wash., U. Oreg., Eugene, Salem (Oreg.) Civic Center, Clark Coll., Vancouver, Wash., Portland Art Mus., Transit Mall, Portland, Fresno (Calif.) Mall, Seattle Art Mus., Gresham Town Fair (Oreg.), Oreg. Health Scis. U., Portland, various banks and schs., numerous commns.; represented by Abanté Gallery, Portland, Hansen Studio, Vancouver. Address: 28219 NE 63rd Ave Battle Ground WA 98604-7107

HANSEN, JAMES V., senator. Senator 1st dist. Utah Washington. Office: 2466 Rayburn Washington DC 20515-4401

HANSEN, JAMES VEAR, congressman; b. Salt Lake City, Aug. 14, 1932; s. J. Vear and Sena C. H.; m. Ann Burgoyne H., 1958; children—Susan, Joseph James, David Burgoyne, Paul William, Jennifer. BS, U. Utah, 1960. Mem. Utah Ho. of Reps., 1973-80, speaker of house, 1979-80; mem. 97th-105th Congresses from 1st Utah dist., Washington, 1981—; pres. James V. Hansen Ins. Agy., Woodland Springs Devel. Co.

HANSEN, JAMES VERNON, computer science, information systems educator; b. Idaho Falls, May 31, 1936; s. Heber Lorenzo and Myrtle Jane (Simmons) H.; m. Diane Lynne Bradbury, Sept. 18, 1963; children: Tamsin, Jeffrey, Dale, Peter. BS, Brigham Young U., 1963; PhD, U. Wash., 1973. Systems analyst TRW, Redondo Beach, Calif., 1966-69; sr. rsch. scientist Battelle Meml. Inst., Richland, Wash., 1972-74, also cons.; asst. prof. Ind. U., Bloomington, 1974-77, assoc. prof., 1977-81; William F. Edwards prof. Brigham Young U., Provo, Utah, 1982—; instr. EDI Group, Chgo., 1987-91. Author: Controls in Microcomputer Systems, 1984, Data Communications: Concepts and Controls, 1987, Database Management and Design, 1992, 2d edit., 1995, Artificial Intelligence and Decision Making, Machine Learning, Distributed Artificial Intelligence. Served with U.S. Army, 1959-62. Grantee Peat, Marwick, Mitchell Found., 1982, 83, 84. Mem. Assn. Computing Machinery, Inst. for Ops. Rsch. and Mgmt. Sci., IEEE Computer Soc., Am. Assn. Artificial Intelligence, Sierra Club. Mormon. Office: Brigham Young U Provo UT 84602

HANSEN, JULIA, music educator; b. Peoria, Ill., Feb. 5, 1934; d. Sherman and Mabel (Nubson) Almanrode; m. Joseph Shakes, June 1, 1957 (div.); children: David Shakes, Diane Shakes, Jonathan Shakes. BMusic with honors, Oberlin Conservatory Music, 1955; MMusic with highest honors, Mich. State U., 1956; MS in Counseling, U. LaVerne, Calif., 1986. Cert. tchr. music and counseling Calif. Community Colls. Tchr. Skyline Coll., San Bruno, Calif., 1977—, counselor, 1988-89; pvt. tchr. piano, music theory and composition, 1958—; tchr. piano, theory and ensembles San Francisco City Coll., 1972-76; guest lectr. in field. Author: Music Reading for Beginners, 1986, Handbook for Counselors and Music Students, 1988, The Art of Performing Bamboo Instruments of Bali, 1992 Book 1, 1992, Book 2, 1994, Joged Bumbung, 1996; contbr. articles to Piano Guild Notes. Mem. Coun. for the Arts, Palo Alto, Calif. Oberlin Conservatory scholar, 1951-55; Mich. State U. fellow, 1955-56. Mem. Coll. Music Soc., Nat. Guild Piano Tchrs., Music Assn. Calif. Cmty. Colls., Soc. for Ethnomusicology. Office: Skyline Coll Creative Arts Dept San Bruno CA 94066

HANSEN, KENT, public relations professional, consultant; b. Alliance, Ohio, Dec. 1, 1947; s. Robert Kent and Sue (Shiflet) H.; m. Grace Goffredo, Oct. 30, 1971; children: Emily, Melissa, Gabriel, Megan, P.J., Katie. BA in History/Theater Arts, U. of State of N.Y., 1988; MS in Human Resource Mgmt., Chapman U., 1991. Commd. ensign USN, 1967, advanced through grades to chief petty officer; pub. affairs officer Naval Air Res. Unit, Whidbey Island, Wash., 1977-81; pub. affairs office mgr. USS Coral Sea, Alameda, Calif., 1981-83; chief of bur. Pacific Stars and Stripes, Tokyo, 1983-86; dep. pub. affairs officer Comdr. U.S. Naval Forces Japan, Yokosuka, Japan, 1986-89; exec. prodr. (Japan) Navy Broadcasting Svc., Yokosuka, 1989-92; exec. prodr. (west coast) Navy Broadcasting Svc., San Diego, 1992-93; comty. rels. dir. Utah Dept. Transp., Salt Lake City, 1994—; ret., 1993; cons. joint task force aesthetic design Am. Assn. State Hwy and Transp. Ofcls., Washington, 1996, mem. subcom. pub. affairs, 1994—. Author: (play) Something's Rotten at the Sawmill, 1995; illustrator: (periodical) U.S. C. of C. in Tokyo Jour., 1986, (fgn. lang. texts) Conversational Spanish for Professionals, 1977. Artistic dir. Terrace Plaza Playhouse, Ogden, Utah, 1995. Mem. Pub. Rels. Soc. Am. (Golden Spike award of excellence 1995). Mormon. Office: Utah Dept Transp 4501 S 2700 West Salt Lake City UT 84119

HANSEN, LEONARD JOSEPH, author, journalist; b. San Francisco, Aug. 4, 1932; s. Einar L. and Margie A. (Wilder) H.; m. Marcia Ann Rasmussen, Mar. 18, 1966 (div.); children: Barron Richard, Trevor Wilder. AB in Radio-TV Prodn. and Mgmt., San Francisco State U., 1956, postgrad. 1956-57; cert. IBM Mgmt. Sch., 1967. Jr. writer Sta. KCBS, San Francisco, 1952-54; assoc. producer and dir. Ford Found. TV Sch. Project, San Francisco State U., 1955-57; crew chief on live and remote broadcasts Sta. KPIX-TV, San Francisco, 1957-59, air promotion dir. and writer Sta. KPIX-TV, San Francisco, 1959-60; pub. rels. mgr. Sta. KNTV-TV, San Jose, Calif., 1961; radio and TV promotion mgr. Seattle World's Fair, 1962; pub. relations and promotion mgr. Century 21 Ctr., Inc., Seattle, 1963-64; pub. rels. dir. Dan Evans for Gov. Com., Seattle, 1964; propr., mgr. Leonard J. Hansen Pub. Rels., Seattle, 1965-67; campaign mgr. Walter J. Hickel for Gov. Com., Anchorage, 1966; exec. cons. to Gov. of Alaska, Juneau, 1967; gen. mgr. No. TV, Inc., Anchorage, 1967-69; v.p. mktg. Sea World, Inc., San Diego, 1969-71; editor, pub. Sr. World Publs., Inc., San Diego, 1973-84; chmn. Sr. Pubs. Group, 1977-89; speaker and mktg. cons. to sr. citizens, 1984-92; panelist, pub. affairs radio programs, 1971-92; lectr. journalism San Diego State U., 1975-76. Writer weekly syndicated column Mainly for Seniors, 1984—, syndicated column Travel for Mature Adults, 1984—; writer, journalist The Mature Market; contbg. editor Mature Life Features, news/feature syndicate, 1987-90; chmn. Mature Mkt. Seminars, 1987-90; author Life Begins at 50-The Handbook for Creative Retirement Planning, 1989; pres., pub. Mature Market Editorial Svcs., 1991—. Founding mem. Housing for Elderly and Low Income Persons, San Diego, 1977-78; mem. Mayor's Ad Hoc Adv. Com. on Aging, San Diego, 1976-79; vice chmn. Housing Task Force, San Diego, 1977-78; bd. dirs. Crime Control Commn., San Diego, 1980; del. White House Conf. on Aging, 1981. Served with U.S. Army, 1953-55. Nat. Press Found. fellow, 1994; recipient numerous service and citizenship awards from clubs and community orgns. Fellow Nat. Press Found.; mem. Pub. Rels.Soc. Am. (accredited), Soc. Profl. Journalists (Best Investigative Reporting award 1979), Internat. Platform Assn., San Diego Press Club (Best Newswriting award 1976-77, Headliner of Yr. award 1980), Am. Assn. Travel Editors (profl. mem.), Nat. Press Club (profl. mem.) Home and Office: 10 Town Plz Ste 313 Durango CO 81301-5104

HANSEN, LOWELL HOWARD, physician; b. Clay Center, Kans., Dec. 26, 1929; s. Howard E. and Emma E. (Nochtigal) H.; m. Jesse J. Johnson, Sept. 1, 1951; children: Susan, Rebecca, Sheree, Kathryn, Peter. BS, Wheaton (Ill.) Coll., 1951; MD, U. Colo., 1955. Diplomate Am. Bd. Radiology. Pvt. practice Denver, 1958-64; resident in radiology Denver Gen. Hosp., 1964-66; radiologist Met. Radiologists, P.C., Denver, 1966-95, locum tenens, 1995—. With USPHS, 1955-58. Fellow Am. Coll. Radiology; mem. Radiol. Assn. N.Am., Rocky Mountain Radiol. Soc. (pres. 1978).

HANSEN, MARGARET, food executive; b. 1952. With affiliate Hansen Ranch, Camarillo, Calif., 1973—; sec. Seaboard Produce, Oxnard, Calif., 1979—. Office: Seaboard Produce 601 Mountain View Ave Oxnard CA 93030-7203*

HANSEN, MARK H., retired speech pathologist, consultant; b. Milford, Nebr., Sept. 5, 1936; s. Burdette and Belva (Harrold) H.; m. Sally Jo High, June 14, 1958; children: Laurie Jo, Mark. AB, U. Redlands, 1958, MA, 1959. Cert. spl. edn., elem. and secondary tchr., Calif.; lic. speech pathologist, family and marriage counselor, Calif.; gen. adminstrv. credential. Pvt. practice marriage and family counseling Newport Beach, Calif.; pvt. practice speech pathology Newport Beach; speech cons. San Gabriel (Calif.) Sch. Dist., 1960-61; speech cons. Newport-Mesa Unified Sch. Dist., Newport Beach, 1961-68, dir. spl. edn. local plan areas, 1968-96; vis. prof. Calif. State U., Fullerton, 1970-72; cons. in field. Mem. Am. Speech and Hearing Assn. (clin. cert.), Calif. Coun. Adminstrn. Spl. Edn. (pres. 1985-87, 89-91), Coun. for Exceptional Children (Exemplary Svc. award), U. Redlands Alumni Bd., Phi Delta Kappa (v.p. 1984-86), Omicron Delta Kappa. Home: 2024 Aliso Ave Costa Mesa CA 92627-2109 Office: Newport-Mesa Unified Sch Dist 1601 E 16th St Newport Beach CA 92663-5976

HANSEN, MICHAEL JOSEPH, association executive, writing educator; b. Chgo., Nov. 18, 1930; s. Max J. and Helen J. Hansen; m. Alice Pauline Hamilton, Jan. 19, 1957; 1 child, Michael Hamilton. AA in Acctg., City Colls. Chgo., 1950; student, Syracuse U., 1953; BA in English, U. Chgo., 1958, MA in English, 1960. C.C. tchg. cert. in English and Russian. Russian lang. specialist USAF, Europe, 1951-55; instr. Valparaiso (Ind.) U., 1960-61; adminstr., asst. prof. City Colls. Chgo., Ill., 1962-72; asst. dir. Pima Assn. Govts., Tucson, 1973—; adj. writing instr. Pima C.C., Tucson, 1983—. Author: (novelet) Ransom, 1977. Chmn., mem. Pima Coll. Bd. Govs., Tucson, 1978-82; mem. Ariz. Juvenile Justice Adv. Coun., Phoenix, 1981-87; vice chmn. Crime Resisters Exec. Bd., Tucson, 1983; arbitrator Better Bus. Bur., Tucson, 1987—.

HANSEN, NANCY C. URDAHL, special education educator; b. Tacoma, May 17, 1940; d. Arthur Selmer and Doris Lavina (Perry) Urdahl; m. John Raymond Hansen, Apr. 2, 1966 (div.); children: John Raymond, Julia Amy. BA, U. Puget Sound, 1969; postgrad., Gov.'s State U., 1972-73; AA, Seattle C.C., 1978; MEd, U. Wash., 1979. Cert. spl. edn. tchr., Wash. Tchr. Grace Migrant Sch., Park Forest, Ill., 1970-71, Rainbow Valley Child Care Ctr., Seattle, 1977-78; tchr. aide Highline Pub. Schs., Seattle, 1978, Experimental Edn. Unit U. Wash., Seattle, 1978; vol. coord. Camp Fire Inc., Seattle, 1979-80; researcher Mott Rehab. Svcs., Mountlake Terrace, Wash., 1980-82; tchr. South Kitsap Sch. Dist., Port Orchard, Wash., 1980-82, resource rm. tchr., 1982—; advisor, tchr. Micro-Society (econ. model for sch.), 1994-96; interviewer King County Interagy. Project U. Wash., Seattle, 1978-80; sec. Queen Anne Juvenile Ct. Conf. Com., Seattle, 1976-78. Contbr. articles to profl. jours. Mem. citizen adv. group Piecre County Comprehensive Plan, Tacoma, 1992; co-coord. Keep Wash. Liveable, Tacoma, 1990; sec., co-founder Peninsula Neighborhood Assn., Gig Harbor, Wash., 1988-91, bd. dirs., 1992; coord. & co-founder Peninsula Stream Monitors, Gig Harbor, 1992-95. Mem. Wash. Edn. Assn., South Kitsap Edn. Assn., Learning Disabilities Assn. Wash., Alpha Phi Sorority.

HANSEN, ROBERT DENNIS, educational administrator; b. San Francisco, July 17, 1945; s. Eiler Cunnard and Muriel Lenore (Morrison) H.; BA, U. San Francisco, 1967, MA in Counseling and Guidance, 1971, MA in Supervision and Adminstrn., 1973; EdD, U. La Verne, 1988; children from a previous marriage: April Michelle, Alison Nicole, Andrew Warren. Tchr., dept. chmn., counselor, dir. student affairs, attendance officer South San Francisco Unified Sch. Dist., 1968-74, coord., asst. prin. Jurupa Unified Sch. Dist., Riverside, Calif., 1974-78; prin., asst. supt. San Gabriel (Calif.) Sch. Dist., 1978-91; supt. Rosemead (Calif.) Sch. Dist., 1991—; adj. prof. U. La Verne, Calif., 1988—. Mem. exec. bd. South San Francisco PTA, 1968-74; bd. dirs. West San Gabriel YMCA; mem. parade formation com. Pasadena (Calif.) Tournament of Roses. Recipient Hon. Svc. award Calif. State PTA. Mem. U. San Francisco Edn. Alumni Soc. (pres. 1972-73), Nat. Assn. Year-Round Edn., U. San Francisco Alumni Assn., ASCD, Am. Assn. Sch. Adminstrs., Assn. Calif. Sch. Adminstrs., Phi Delta Kappa. Republican. Presbyterian. Masons (32 degree). Home: 2650 Country Club Dr Glendora CA 91741 Office: Rosemead Sch Dist 3640 Rio Hondo Ave Rosemead CA 91770-2041

HANSEN, ROBERT GUNNARD, philatelist, entrepreneur; b. Chgo., Aug. 16, 1939; s. Earl F. and Mildred E. (Hargrave) H.; A.A., Lincoln Coll., 1960; B.A., Culver Stockton Coll., 1962; M.B.A., U. So. Calif., 1966; postgrad. UCLA Extension, 1962-67; m. Bertha Golds, Aug. 10, 1960; children—Karin Lee, Lisa Marie. With Litton Industries, 1962-63, Sterer Engring., 1963-69; mktg. and contracts ofcl. Santa Barbara Research Ctr., 1969-73; pres., chief exec. officer, R.G. Hansen & Assocs., Santa Barbara, 1974— ; pres., owner The Silver Penny and Santa Barbara Stamp & Coin, 1969—; owner, CEO, pres. Univ. Travel Bureau, 1990-95; guest lectr. Santa Barbara City Coll. Mem. Am. Vacuum Soc., Am. Philatelic Soc. (life), Am. Numismatic Assn., Hawaii Numismatic Assn., Sci. and Engring. Coun. Santa Barbara (pres. 1989), Token and Medal Soc., Masons, York Rite. Scottish Rite, Shriners, Royal Order of Scotland, Channel City, Royal Arch Masons, trustee Santa Barbara Historical Soc., Rotary Internat. (Paul Harris fellow 1990). Research and publs. on cryogenics, electro-optics, infrared radiation; patentee in field. Republican. Presbyterian. Office: 631 Chapala St Santa Barbara CA 93101-3311

HANSEN, RONALD GREGORY, civil engineer; b. Waipahu, Hawaii, Aug. 22, 1929; s. Erling M. and Geraldine J. (Nettleton) H.; m. Theresa J. Cunningham, Feb. 5, 1955; children: Eric L., Karen A., Maureen A., Timothy E. BCE, U. Santa Clara, 1952; MSCE, U. So. Calif., 1958, postgrad., 1958-66; M in Pub. Adminstrn., U. Alaska, 1981. Lic. civil engr., Alaska, Wash., Oreg., Calif. Engr. Calif. Dept. Water Resources, Los Angeles, 1957-67; sr. engr. Water Quality Control Bd., Los Angeles, 1967-71; chief water pollution control State of Alaska, Juneau, 1971-79; sr. engr. KCM Inc. and EMPS Engring, Juneau, 1980-85; pres. Hansen Engring., Juneau, 1985—. Former scoutmaster, mem. bldg. com. S.E. Alaska, Boy Scouts Am.; mem., chmn. Juneau Parks and Recreation Adv. Com., 1983-91. Served to lt. col., C.E., USAR. Mem. ASCE, NSPE (nat. dir. 1993—), Am. Water Works Assn., Water Environ. Fedn., Am. Acad. Environ. Engrs., Rotary (Juneau-Gastineau club pres. 1995-96). Republican. Roman Catholic. Home and Office: Hansen Engring 4117 Birch Ln Juneau AK 99801-8909

HANSEN, SALLY JO, school system coordinator; b. San Fernando, Calif., Sept. 8, 1937; d. Kenneth Morris Sr. and Carmen (Woods) High; m. Mark Herman Hansen, June 14, 1958; children: Laurie Jo, Mark. BA, U. Redlands, 1959. Cert. lang. devel. specialist, Calif., cert. crosscultural lang. and acad. devel. specialist, Calif. Tchr. elem. Covina (Calif.) Unified Sch. Dist., 1959-60; tchr. remedial reading Newport-Mesa Unified Sch. Dist., Newport Beach, Calif., 1965-80, tchr. ESL, 1980-88; title VII coord. Newport-Mesa Unified Sch. Dist., Newport Beach, 1988—, ESL bilingual project coord., 1990—, coord. Healthy Start, 1992—; presenter and staff trainer in field. Author and editor: ESL Guide for Classroom Teachers, 1992. Pres. PTA, Newport Beach/Costa Mesa, 1965-70 (bd. dirs. 1965-80); legis. rep. Orange County Tchr. of Speakers of Other Langs., 1985-87. Mem. Nat. Assn. Bilingual Edn., Calif. Assn. Bilingual Edn., Nat. Charity League (past officer), Rep. Women, U. Redlands Alumni Assn. Presbyterian. Office: Newport Mesa Unified Sch Dist 1050 Arlington Dr Costa Mesa CA 92626-5626

HANSEN, SHARON M., state agency administrator, policy analyst; b. Port Angeles, Wash., Sept. 28, 1935; d. Herbert Milton and Caryl (Heslin) McGee; m. Janis T. Hansen, Sept. 2, 1956; children: Andrew John, Matthew Thomas. BA, U. Wash., 1957, cert. in Mgmt., 1988. Planner Office of Cmty. Devel., State Wash., Olympia, Wash., 1974-75; exec. dir. Pierce County Assn. for Retarded Citizens, Tacoma, 1975-80; resource mgr. Dept. Social and Health Svcs., State Wash., Tacoma, 1980-82; planner Dept. Social and Health Svcs., State Wash., Olympia, Wash., 1982-84; exec. dir. Developmental Disabilities Planning Coun., State Wash., Olympia, Wash., 1984-91; analyst Family Policy Coun., State Wash., Olympia, Wash., 1992-94; dir. Tacoma-Pierce County Commn. on Children, Youth and Families, 1994—; bd. dirs. Nat. Assn. Developmental Disabilities Coun., Washington, 1985-90, v.p. 1990-91; bd. dirs. Prevention Partnership for Children, 1995—, Washington Family Resource Coalition; cons. Westside Regional Ctr., Calif., 1987, N.J. Developmental Disabilities Coun., 1991, Govt. India Ministry of Welfare, 1991. Contbd. articles to profl. jours. Fulbright Hayes lectureship, 1991. Home: 714 N Stadium Way Tacoma WA 98403-2826 Office: Tacoma-Pierce County Com on Children 3629 S D St Tacoma WA 98408-6813

HANSEN, STEVEN ALAN, custom builder; b. Key West, Fla., July 5, 1949; s. Baron Hansen and June (Feree) Correll; m. Sally Jo Cooper, Nov. 13, 1976; children: Blake, Carter, Reid. BS in Religion and Polit. Sci., Ind. U., 1972. Custom builder Hansen Constrn. Inc., Aspen, Colo., 1982—. Bd. dirs. Aspen Art Mus., 1993-95, Com. for Housing Size, Aspen, 1995; mem. steering com. Recreation Dist. and Facility, Aspen, 1996. Office: Hansen Construction Inc 310 AABC Aspen CO 81611

HANSEN, THOMAS CARTER, college athletics conference commissioner; b. Seattle, Nov. 30, 1937; s. Herbert and Marjorie Jean (Jordan) H.; m. Melva Marie Fuhr, Oct. 11, 1962; children: Sarah Marie Hansen Reeves, Bryan Thomas. BA, U. Wash., 1959. Reporter The Columbian, Vancouver, Wash., 1959-60; dir. pub. rels. Pacific-10 Conf., San Francisco, 1960-67; dir. pub. rels. NCAA, Kansas City, Mo., 1967-71, asst. exec. dir., 1971-83; commr. Pacific-10 Conf., Walnut Creek, Calif., 1983—. Author: (chpt.) Administration for Athletic Programs, 1987. Mem. Kiwanis Club, Vancouver, 1959-60, San Francisco, 1960-67, Kansas City, 1967-83. Mem. Nat. Assn. Collegiate Dirs. of Athletics (exec. com. 1988-92, Adminstrv. Excellence award 1994), Collegiate Commrs. Assn. (pres. 1992, 93), Football Found. Hall of Fame (honors ct. 1994—). Republican. Lutheran. Office: Pacific 10 Conf 800 S Broadway Ste 400 Walnut Creek CA 94596-5218

HANSEN, WAYNE W., lawyer; b. Clintonville, Wis., June 7, 1942; s. William W. and Berniece M. (Kuehn) H.; m. Carolyn M. Lemke, Dec. 21, 1969; children: Drew D., Janna J. BBA, U. Wis., 1964, JD, 1967. Bar: Wis. 1967, U.S. Dist. Ct. (we. dist.) Wis. 1971, U.S. Ct. Appeals (7th cir.) 1972, U.S. Dist. Ct. (ea. dist.) Wis. 1975, Wash. 1979, U.S. Dist. Ct. (we. dist.) Wash. 1979, U.S. Ct. Appeals (9th cir.) 1982, U.S. Dist. Ct. (ea. dist.) Wash. 1986. Atty. NLRB, Mpls., 1967-70, Schmitt Nolan Hansen & Hartley, Merrill, Wis., 1970-79; ptnr. Lane Powell Spears Lubersky, Seattle, 1979—. Contbg. author: Developing Labor Law, 1971, Doing Business in Washington State—Guide for Foreign Business, 1989. Office: Lane Powell Spears Lubersky 1420 5th Ave Ste 4100 Seattle WA 98101-2333

HANSON, BONNIE BLANCHE, author, artist; b. Morrow, Ohio, Dec. 11, 1931; d. Harold and Nellie Virginia (Caudill) Compton; m. Don John Hanson, Feb. 15, 1958; children: Robin Dale, Caht Patrick, Jay Bryan. AB in Art, U. Ky., 1953; postgrad., Wheaton (Ill.) Coll., 1957-59, U. San Diego, 1967, San Diego State U., 1968, Pepperdine U., 1985-87. Editor lit. mags. U. Ky., Lexington, 1951-53; interior decorator Shillito's, Cin., 1953-56; asst. editor Scripture Press, Wheaton, Ill., 1957-62; conf. staff Australian Inst. Evangelism, Wollagong, N.S.W., 1959-60; curriculum writer David C. Cook Pub. Co., Elgin, Ill., 1962-74; elem. tchr. Elgin Pub. Schs., 1966, San Diego Pub. Schs., 1971-74; curriculum writer Am. Learning Corp., Huntington Beach, Calif., 1976-78, Union Gospel Press, Cleve., 1978, Std. Pubs., Cin., 1980-84; comm. supr. Pacific Investment Mgmt. Co., Newport Beach, Calif., 1979-92, comm. specialist, 1992-94; faculty Biola U. Writers Inst. Co-author: Church History Correspondence Course, 1959, Making the Most of Your Golden Years, 1984, Hattie's Surprising Discovery, 1992 (CBA Gold Medallion finalist 1992), Poems for a Sunday Afternoon, Winkie Bear Preschool Program Guidebook; lyricist/composer: God's Four Seasons, 1959-60, God's Loving Care; contbr. poetry, articles, stories, puzzles, quizzes, cartoons to profl. jours.; illustrator: Kidnapped!. Active Child Evangelism, Pioneer Girls, Boy Scouts Am., Open Air Campaigners, Bapt. Student Union. Hon. Ky. Col., 1996. Mem. Nat. Writers Assn., Christian Writers Guild, Soc. Children's Book Writers and Illustrators, R.I. Hist. Soc., Christian Writers Fellowship (founding mem.). Home: 3330 S Lowell St Santa Ana CA 92707

HANSON, CAPPY LOVE, writer, musician, singer, composer; b. Berkeley, Calif., May 12, 1946; d. David Nathaniel and Jeanne Ardath (Warner) Taylor. Contbr. poems to Writer's Digest, Transworld Snowboarding, ByLine, The Los Alamos Monitor, The Santa Fe New Mexican, New Frontiers, Blue Mesa Rev., Poetpourri, three anthologies. Placed 1st Writer's Digest Annual Poetry Competition, 1993, 2nd New Mexican, 1993, 3rd Poetry Soc. Tenn., 1995; recipient Hougthon award New England Poetry Club, 1994. Home: 131 Peak Pl #121 Santa Fe NM 87501

HANSON, EDWARD ALVIN, chemist; b. Pomona, Calif., Sept. 28, 1950; s. Donald Raymond Hanson and Joan Lillian (Beisner) Stout; m. Maureen McDonald, Apr. 28, 1980 (div. Jan. 1995); 1 child, Terra Lowansa. AS in Geology, Chaffey C.C., 1970; AS in Computer Sci., Victor Valley Coll., 1987. Chemist Occidental Rsch. Corp., LaVerne, Calif., 1975-78, Scott Specialty Gases, San Bernardino, Calif., 1985-91, Geneva Pharms., Broomfield, Colo., 1993—. Contbr. poems to profl. publs. (Pres. award 1995, Diamond award 1996). Mem. Internat. Soc. Poets. Home: 7630 Leyden Ln Commerce City CO 80022

HANSON, GEORGE, music director, conductor; m. Dawn Hanson. Degree, Ind. U. Resident conductor Atlanta Symphony; asst. to Leonard Bernstein Vienna Stae Opera; asst. Giuseppe Patane La Scala, Covent Garden, Munich Opera Houses; mus. dir. Anchorage Symphony; asst. conductor N.Y. Philharmonic; conductor Tucson Symphony Orchestra; appeared with sixty orchestras and operas in sixteen countries. Named Winner of the Leopold Stokowski Competition at Carnegie Hall, N.Y.C., Hungarian Internat. Coducting Competition, Budapest, Young Musician of 1990 Musical Am. Office: Tucson Convention Ctr Music Hall 443 S Stone Ave Tucson AZ 85701-2399

HANSON, GEORGE PETER, retired research botanist, real estate investor; b. Conde, S.D., July 20, 1933; s. George Henry and Rosa Wilhelmina (Peterson) H.; m. Barbara Jean Graves, Aug. 20, 1958; children: David, Carole, Heather, Peter; m. Gloria Ann Gauntt, June 1, 1969. BS in Agronomy, S.D. State U., 1956, MS in Plant Breeding, 1958; PhD in Genetics, Ind. U., 1965. Asst. prof. biology Thiel Coll. Greenville, Pa., 1962-65; asst. prof. botany Butler U., Indpls., 1965-67; sr. biologist L.A. State and County

Arboretum, Arcadia, Calif., 1968-82; real estate investor, 1971—. Mem. Apt. Assn. of Greater L.A. Methodist. Contbr. numerous articles in field to profl. jours. Home: 1345 W Haven Rd San Marino CA 91108-2018

HANSON, GERALD WARNER, retired county official; b. Alexandria, Minn., Dec. 25, 1938; s. Lewis Lincoln and Dorothy Hazel (Warner) H.; m. Sandra June Wheeler, July 9, 1960; 1 child, Cynthia R. AA, San Bernardino Valley (Calif.) Coll., 1959; BA, U. Redlands (Calif.), 1979; MA, U. Redlands, 1981; EdD, Pepperdine U., 1995. Cert. advanced metrication specialist. Dep. sealer San Bernardino (Calif.) County, 1964-80, div. chief, 1980-85, dir. weights and measures, 1985-94; CATV cons. City of Redlands, 1996—; substitute tchr. Redlands Unified Sch. Dist., 1996—. Chmn. Redlands Rent Rev. Bd., 1985—; bd. dirs. House Neighborly Svc., Redlands, 1972-73, Boys Club, Redlands, 1985-86; mem. Redlands Planning commn., 1990—. With USN. Fellow U.S. Metric Assn. (treas. 1986-88, 92—); mem. NRA (life), Nat. Conf. on Weights and Measures (asst. treas. 1986-94), Western Weights and Measures Assn. (pres. 1987-88), Calif. Assn. Weights and Measures Ofcls. (1st v.p. 1987), Calif. Rifle and Pistol Assn. (life), Masons, Shriners, Kiwanis (treas. Redlands club 1983-95), Over the Hill Gang (San Bernardino). Home: 225 E Palm Ave Redlands CA 92373-6131

HANSON, KENNETH MERRILL, physicist; b. Mt. Vernon, N.Y., Apr. 17, 1940; s. Orville Glen and Marion (Chamberlain) H.; m. Earle Marie Low, June 1964 (div. July 1989); m. Jeannene Masterson, Dec. 1996; children: Jennifer Anne, Keith Merrill. BE in Physics, Cornell U., 1963; MS in Physics, Harvard U., 1967, PhD in Physics, 1970. Rsch. assoc. Lab. of Nuclear Studies, Ithaca, N.Y., 1970-75; mem. staff Los Alamos (N.Mex.) Nat. Lab., 1975—. Author: (with others) Radiology of Skull and Brain, 1979, Image Recovery, 1987; contbr. articles to profl. jours. Recipient Award Excellence, Dept. Energy, 1986, 92. Fellow Soc. Photo Optical Instrumentation Engrs. (program com. imaging conf. 1984-95, chair 1996—); mem. IEEE (sr.), Am. Phys. Soc., Opt. Soc. Am. Office: Los Alamos Nat Lab MS-P940 Los Alamos NM 87545

HANSON, MARY LOUISE, retired social services administrator; b. Walsenburg, Colo., Nov. 8, 1928; d. Norman Francis and Ellen Matilda (Peterson) Kastner; m. Peter R. Hanson, Sept. 1, 1951 (dec. Dec. 1991); children: Sherod Day, Janell Marie, Kari Annette. BA, U. Wyo., 1951, MA, 1958. Bookkeeper Rawlins Nat. (Wyo.) Bank, 1948-49; scholarship sec. U. Wyo., Laramie, 1962-64; dist. counselor Vocational Rehab., Laramie, 1964-71; exec. dir. Laramie Sr. Ctr., 1973-92; ptnr. First St. Gallery, Laramie, 1996—; pres. Laramie Sr. Housing, Inc., 1982-92, Laramie Housing, Inc., 1988—. Developer 1st counseling and tng. programs for vocat. rehab. Albany and Platte Counties, Wyo., 1964-71; dir. renovation hist. bldgs., Laramie, 1973-92. Fed. and Wyo. State grantee, 1964-71, Divsn. Aging., 1973-92. Mem. Albany County Hist. Soc., Laramie Plains Mus., Colo. Reservation Assn., U. Wyo. Alumni Assn. Home: 703 Ivinson Ave Laramie WY 82070 Office: First St Gallery 121 S 1st St Laramie WY 82070

HANSON, WENDY KAREN, chemical engineer; b. Mpls., May 29, 1954; d. Curtis Harley Hanson and Patricia Lou (Vogler) Schweiger. BS, U. Minn., 1976; BA, U. Colo., Denver, 1984; postgrad., U. Calif., La Jolla, 1984-87. Chem. technician Shasta Beverages, Mpls., 1977-78, Conwed, Roseville, Minn., 1978-80; geologist Century Geophys. Corp., Grand Junction, Colo., 1980, Tooke Engring., Grand Junction, 1980-82; sr. scientist Sci. Ventures, San Diego, 1987-96; engr. Parker-Hannifin Corp., San Diego, 1996—. Patentee magnesium separation from Dolomitic phosphate by sulfuric acid leaching. Judge San Diego (Calif.) Sci. and Engring. Fair, 1987—; leader, publs. editor San Diego (Calif.) Wilderness Assn., 1989—. Mem. Am. Chem. Soc. Office: Parker-Hannifin Corp 7664 Panasonic Way San Diego CA 92173-4206

HANSON, WILLIAM LEWIS, lawyer; b. Shanghai, China, Oct. 1, 1924; came to U.S., 1927; s. Victor and Lucia Mae (Parks) H.; m. Elen Stella Hanson, June 26, 1949; children: Raiha Ballard, Victoria Berman, Emily Hanson-McMullen. AB, U. Redlands, Calif., 1946; JD, Harvard U., 1950. Bar: Wash., Fed. Tax Ct., 1976, U.S. Supreme Ct., 1983, U.S. Ct. Appeals (9th cir.), 1969. Coll. and peace edn. sec. Am. Friends Svc., Seattle, 1954-59; pvt. practice law Seattle, 1959-70, 73—; tchr. law/history Lakeside Sch., Seattle, 1970-73; arbitrator Arbitration Panel of Superior Ct. of King County. Co-author: A New China Policy, 1965, Uncommon Controversy: Indian Fishing Rights in the Northwest, 1970; author: (booklet) Peace in China, 1958. Bd. dirs., vol. atty. Am. Friends Svc., 1959-69, ACLU, 1965-78; bd. dirs., commentator Jack Straw Found., Seattle, 1972—; bd. dirs. Inst. for Global Security Studies, Seattle, 1991—; vol., past pres. World Peace Through Law Sect. of Wash. Bar Assn., 1970—; planner, chmn. Bar Assn. Conf. on World Law, 1985—. Recipient Cmty. Svc. for Peace Ann. award Unitarian Ch., Seattle, 1968. Democrat. Soc. of Friends. Home and Office: 4819 NE 103d St Seattle WA 98125-8141

HANSON-SMITH, ELIZABETH, English language educator, computer consultant; b. Bridgeport, Conn., Oct. 28, 1942; d. Arthur Christian and A. Elizabeth H.; m. Jack H.L. THompson, Nov. 25, 1979; children: Aaron Virgil, Paul, Cairbre A.H. Smith. AB in English, Smith Coll., 1964; postgrad., Hochschule St. Gallen, 1964-65; MA in English, Stanford U., 1967; postgrad., U. Paris, 1967-68; PhD in English and Comparative Lit., Stanford U., 1972. Dir. writing adj. program Calif. State U., Sacramento, 1976-80; tchr.-trainer Ministry of Edn., China, 1980-81, Maurice Thorez Inst. Fgn. Langs. and Am. Coun. for Collaboration in Lang. Study, Moscow, 1989-90; prof. English Calif. State U., Sacramento, 1971-95, coord. TESOL grad. program, 1984-95; chair Ryan Act com. arts. and scis. Calif. State U., Sacramento, 1974-75; bd. govs. Calif. Maritime Acad., Vallejo, 1978-80; English lang. cons. Univ. Grants Commn. and Asia Found., Sri Lanka, 1984; curriculum cons. Ministry of Edn. and USAID, Belize, 1986; coord. conv. computer room Calif. Assn. TESOL, 1991-93. Contbg. editor CAELL Jour., 1992—; contbr. articles to profl. jours. Stanford Dissertation fellow, 1967-70; Smith Coll. Alumnae scholar, 1960-64. Mem. TESOL (chair CALL IS 1994-95), Calif. Assn. TESOL, Phi Beta Delta.

HANUSEY, RICHARD DMYTRO, library director; b. Phila., Nov. 30, 1945; s. Richard and Adela Francias (Mackunas) H.; m. Kathleen Mary Morrow, Oct. 2, 1971; children: Keala, Amanda. Student, E. Stroudsburg State U., 1971; Diploma in Libr. Sci., U. Hawaii, 1973. Cert. libr. Libr. asst. dept. planning State of Hawaii, Honolulu, 1973-75; libr. Picatinny Arsenal, Dover, N.J., 1975-77; adminstrv. libr. U.S. Army Area Spt. Group, Livorno, Italy, 1977-80; libr. dir. U.S. Army, Norddeutschland, Bremerhaven, Germany, 1980-86; adminstrv. libr. Fort Drum/10th Mt. Divsn., Watertown, N.Y., 1986-88; libr. dir. U.S. Army, Pacific, Schofield Bar, Hawaii, 1988—; chmn. mng. info systems U.S. Army/Dept. Community Action, Fort Shafter, Hawaii, 1992—; mem. army libr. com. dept. info. resources, U.S. Army, Washington, 1991—, libr. career planning bd., 1991—; mem. joint army-state ednl. schs. adv. coun., Honolulu, 1992—. Mem. Parent's Sch. Assn., Honolulu, 1994. Fellow Hawaii Libr. Assn., ALA. Office: U S Army/Pacific Appe-CFA Libr ACTV Fort Shafter HI 96858-5100

HANZLIK, RAYBURN DEMARA, lawyer; b. L.A., June 7, 1938; s. Rayburn Otto and Ethel Winifred (Membery) H.; children: Kristina, Rayburn N., Alexander, Geoffrey. B.S., Principia Coll., 1960; M.A., Woodrow Wilson Sch. Fgn. Affairs, U. Va., 1968; J.D., U. Va., 1974. Bar: Va. 1975, D.C. 1977. Staff asst. to Pres. U.S., Washington, 1971-73; asso. dir. White House Domestic Council, 1975-77; of counsel firm Danzansky Dickey Tydings Quint & Gordon, Washington, 1977-78, Akin Gump Hauer & Feld, Washington, 1978-79; individual practice law Los Angeles, 1979-81; adminstr. Econ. Regulatory Adminstrn., Dept. Energy, Washington, 1981-85; ptnr. Heidrick and Struggles, Inc., 1985-91, McKenna & Hanzlik, Irvine, Calif., 1991-92; chmn. Lanxide Sports Internat., Inc., San Diego, 1992-95, Stealth Propulsion Internat., Ltd., San Diego, Calif. and, Melbourne, Australia, 1994-97; exec. v.p. Commodore Corp., N.Y.C. and Vienna, Va., 1997—. Contbg. author: Global Politics and Nuclear Energy, 1971, Soviet Foreign Relations and World Communism, 1965. Alt. del. Republican Nat. Conv., 1980; dir. Calif. Rep. Victory Fund, 1980. Served to lt. USN, 1963-68, Vietnam. Mem. ABA, Va. Bar Assn., D.C. Bar Assn. Republican. Christian Scientist.

HAO, LAWRENCE KAHOLO, state official, clinical hypnotherapist; b. Paahau, Hawaii, Aug. 24, 1937; s. Louis Kanoa and Mona Doris (Kaholo) H.; m. Ramona Kay Newton, Apr. 15, 1960; children: Debra Lynn Kelani, Melanie Pualani, Lance Kanoa, Sean Lani Newton. BS, Ind. U., 1962, MS, 1970. Recreational therapist Beatty Meml. Hosp., Westville, Ind., 1962-63; tchr. Russiaville (Ind.) Elem. Sch., 1963-65; tchr. phys. edn. Western Elem. Sch., Russiaville, 1965-67; aquatic dir. Ea. H.S., Greentown, Ind., 1967-69; grad. asst. Ind. U., Bloomington, 1969-70; asst. prof. Western Ill. U., Macomb, 1970-72, U. Hawaii, Honolulu, 1973-76; asst. coord. hwy. safety Hawaii Dept. Transp., Honolulu, 1972-76, adminstr. motor vehicle safety, 1976—. Mem., chmn. Med. Adv. Bd. Hawaii, 1972—, Hawaii Hwy. Safety Coun., 1972—. With USAR, 1956-62. Mem. MADD (profl.), Am. Assn. Motor Vehicle Adminstrs. (profl., regional rep. 1978—), Nat. Hwy. Traffic Safety Adminstrn. (profl., regional rep. 1972—). Office: Motor Vehicle Safety Office Ste 214 1505 Dillingham Blvd Honolulu HI 96817

HAPPEL, STEPHEN KENT, business educator, dean; b. Northfield, Minn., Sept. 18, 1947; s. Gus Joseph and Vera Ruth (Hermsmeier) H.; m. Deborah Anne Sullivan, July 23, 1972 (div. May 1992); children: Margaret Elizabeth, Sarah Elizabeth; m. Elizabeth Setzer, July 24, 1992; 1 child, Graydon Joseph. BA, U. Mo., 1969; MA, Duke U., 1972, PhD, 1976. Instr. econs. N.C. State U., Raleigh, 1973-75; asst. prof. bus. Ariz. State U., Tempe, 1975-81, dir. honors program, 1989—, dir. MBA for execs. program, 1989-92, assoc. prof., 1981-92, prof. econs., assoc. dean undergrad. programs, 1992—; instr. Pacific Coast Banking Sch., Seattle, 1985—, BAI Grad. Sch. Banking, Madison, Wis.; bd. dirs. Dean's Bd. of Excellence, Tempe, 1994—. Author: Modern Managerial Economics, 1987; contbr. articles to profl. jours. Recipient Alumni Assn. Disting. Tchg. award Ariz. State U., 1983-84, Ariz. Prof. of Yr. award Coun. for Advancement and Support of Edn., 1991; NIH Population fellow, 1969-72. Mem. Am. Econ. Assn., Populatoin Assn. Am., Western Econ. Assn., Nat. Collegiate Honors Coun., Phi Beta Kappa. Lutheran. Home: 641 N Cordoba Ave Chandler AZ 85226 Office: Ariz State Univ College of Bus BAC 219 Tempe AZ 85287-3506

HARA, TADAO, educational administrator; b. Shimoneseki, Japan, Oct. 21, 1926; s. Ikuhisa and Chitose Hara; m. Suzuko Hara, May 12; children: Nobumichi, Izumi. BA, Tamagawa U., Machida, Japan, 1952; MA in Bibl. Theology, N.W. Coll., 1958; MA in Ednl. Psychology, Calif. State U., Long Beach, 1965; LittD (hon.), N.W. Coll., 1990. Ordained to ministry Assembly of God Ch. Fgn. student counselor Calif. State U., Long Beach, 1965-68; prof. edn. Tamagawa U., 1969-79, dean students, 1973-77, dir. internat. edn., 1976-79; founder, prin. Internat. Bilingual Sch., Palos Verdes Estates, Calif. Mem. adv. bd. Calif. State U. Long Beach Coll. Edn., 1985-88. Recipient Disting. Alumnus award Coll. Edn., Calif. State U., Long Beach, 1994. Mem. ASCD, Nat. Assn. Fgn. Student Affairs, Delta Upsilon Chi. Home: 3992 Toland Cir Los Alamitos CA 90720-2261 Office: 300 Paseo Del Mar # B Palos Verdes Estates CA 90274-1272

HARAD, GEORGE JAY, manufacturing company executive; b. Newark, Apr. 24, 1944; m. Beverly Marcia Harad, June 12, 1966; children: Alyssa Dawn, Matthew Corde. BA, Franklin and Marshall Coll., 1965; MBA with high distinction, Harvard Bus. Sch., 1971. Staff cons. Boston Cons. Group, 1970-71; asst. to sr. v.p. housing Boise (Idaho) Cascade Corp., 1971; asst. to v.p. Boise Cascade Corp., Palo Alto, Calif., 1971; fin. mgr. Boise Cascade Realty Group, Palo Alto, Calif., 1972-76; mgr. corp. devel. Boise (Idaho) Cascade Corp, Palo Alto, Calif., 1976-80; dir. retirement funds, risk mgmt. Boise (Idaho) Cascade Corp., 1980-82, v.p., contr., 1982-84, sr. v.p., chief fin. officer, 1984-89, exec. v.p., chief fin. officer, 1989-90, exec. v.p. paper, 1990-91; pres., COO Boise (Idaho) Cascade Corp., Palo Alto, Calif., 1991-94; pres., CEO Boise (Idaho) Cascade Corp, Palo Alto, Calif., 1994-95; chmn., CEO Boise (Idaho) Cascade Corp, 1995; chmn., bd. dirs. Boise (Idaho) Cascade Corp., 1995—; chmn., dir. Boise Cascade Office Products Corp.; chmn., pres., CEO Boise Cascade Corp., Palo Alto, Calif.; bd. dirs. Allendale Ins. Co., Inst. Paper Sci. and Tech.; bd. govs. Nat. Coun. of Paper Industry for Air and Stream Improvement Inc. Founder, pres. Boise Coun. for Gifted and Talented Students, 1977-79; bd. dirs. Boise Philharm. Assn., 1983-84; dir. bd. trustees Coll. Idaho, 1986-91. Grad. Prize fellow Harvard Grad. Sch. Arts and Scis., 1965-69, Frederick Roe fellow Harvard U. Sch. Bus., 1971; George F. Baker scholar, 1970-71. Mem. NAM (bd. dirs.), Am. Forest and Paper Assn. (bd. dirs., mem. exec. com. 1984-94), Century Club (Boston), Arid Club, Crane Creek Country Club, Phi Beta Kappa. Home: 224 E Braemere Rd Boise ID 83702-1710 Office: Boise Cascade Corp PO Box 50 Boise ID 83728-0050

HARA-ISA, NANCY JEANNE, graphic designer; b. San Francisco, May 14, 1961; d. Toshiro and Masaye Hara; m. Stanley Takeo Isa, June 15, 1985. Student, UCLA, 1979-82; BA in Art and Design, Calif. State U., L.A., 1985. Salesperson May Co., L.A., 1981; svc. rep. Hallmark Cards Co., L.A., 1981-83; prodn. artist Calif. State U., L.A., 1983, Audio-Stats Internat. Inc., L.A., 1983; prodn. asst. Auto-Graphics Inc., Pomona, Calif., 1984-85, lead supr., 1985-86; art dir., contbg. staff writer CFW Enterprises, Burbank, Calif., 1987-88; graphic designer, prodn. mgr. Bonny Jularbal Graphics, Las Vegas, Nev., 1988-90; graphic designer Weddle Caldwell Advt., Las Vegas, 1990-92; owner Nancy Hara-Isa Designs, 1992—; graphic artist Regional Transp. Commn. of Clark County, Las Vegas, 1993—; freelance designer Caesars Palace. Writer Action Pursuit Games mag. Parade asst., mem. carnival staff Nisei Week, L.A., 1980-84; asst., mem. Summit Orgn., L.A., 1987—; grad. Clark County Leadership Forum, 1996. Mem. NAFE, Women in Profl. Graphic Svcs. (acting 1st v.p. 1990, 2d v.p. 1991), Women in Comms. Republican. Presbyterian. Home: 367 Cavos Way Henderson NV 89014-3555

HARALICK, ROBERT MARTIN, electrical engineering educator; b. N.Y.C., Sept. 30, 1943; s. David and Yetta (Stier) H.; m. Joy Gold, Aug. 20, 1967 (div. July 1977); 1 child, Tammy-Beth; m. Linda G. Shapiro, Feb. 12, 1978 (div. Aug. 1992); 1 child, Michael Aaron; m. Ihsin T. Phillips, Dec. 1993. BA, U. Kans., 1964, BS, 1966, MS, 1967, PhD, 1969. Asst. prof. elec. engring. U. Kans., Lawrence, 1969-71, assoc. prof., 1971-75, prof., 1975-78; prof. Va. Poly. Inst. and State U., 1979-84; v.p. rsch. Machine Vision Internat., Ann Arbor, Mich., 1984-86; Boeing Clairmont Egtvedt prof. elec. engring., adj. prof. computer sci. U. Wash., Seattle, 1986—; pres. Mnemonics Inc., 1979—; co-dir. NATO Advanced Study Inst. Image Processing, 1978; co-chmn. NATO Advanced Study Inst. on Image Processing, 1980, Robust Computer Vision Workshop, 1990, 92, 94; vice chmn. 5th Internat. Conf. on Pattern Recognition, Miami, 1980; dir. NATO Advanced Study Inst. on Pictorial Data Analysis, 1982; adj. prof. Ctr. Bioengring. U. Wash., Seattle, 1988—; program chmn. 10th annual ICPR Conf. on Pattern Recognition Systems and Applications, 1990; program co-chmn. Internat. Conf. on Document Analysis and Recognition, 1991. Author: (with T. Creese) Differential Equations for Engineers, 1977; Pictorial Data Analysis, 1983, (with L. Shapiro) Computer and Robost Vision, Vol I and II, 1992, The Inner Meaning of Hebrew Letters, 1995, (with M. Glazerson) The Torah Codes and Israel Today, 1996; editor: (with J. C. Simon) Issues in Digital Image Processing, 1980, Digital Image Processing, 1981; assoc. editor Computer Vision, Graphics and Image Processing, 1975-93, Pattern Recognition, 1977-93, Communication of the ACM, Image Processing, 1982-92, IEEE Transactions on Systems, Man and Cybernetics, 1979-88, IEEE Transactions on Image Processing, 1992—, Jour. of Electronic Imaging, 1994—; mem. editorial bd. IEEE Transactions on Pattern Analysis and Machine Intelligence, 1981-84, IEEE Expert, 1986-90, Machine Vision and Applications, 1987—, Real Time Imaging, 1994—, mem. editl. com. IEEE Transactions on Pattern Analysis and Machine Intelligence, 1979-84, mem. adv. bd. IEEE Transactions on Pattern Analysis and Machine Intelligence, 1984-93, Image and Vision Computing, 1984-93; mem. adv. program com. Structural & Syntactic Pattern Recognition, 1990; contbr. over 425 articles to profl. jours.; digital computer art exhibitions include William Rockhill Nelson Gallery, Kansas City, Mo., 1971, Nat. History Mus., U. Kans., 1971, Dulin Gallery Art, 1971 (2 purchase awards), Nat. Invitational Print Show, U. R.I., 1972, Fla. State U., 1972, San Diego State Coll., 1972. Recipient Dow Chem. Young Outstanding Faculty award Am. Soc. Engring. Educators, 1975, Outstanding Young Elec. Engrs. Honorable Mention award Eta Kappa Nu, 1975, Best Paper award 5th Ann. Symposium on Automatic Imagery Pattern Recognition, 1975, Best Paper award Pattern Recognition Soc., 1989; NSF faculty fellow, 1977-79. Fellow IEEE, IAPR; mem. IEEE Computer Soc. (chmn. pattern analysis and machine intelligence tech. com. 1975-82, acoustics, signal and speech processing, sys., man and cybernetics, pattern recognition tech. subcom. 1975-81, data structures and pattern recognition subcom. 1975-81, biomed. pattern recognition subcom. 1975-81, internat. assn. for pattern recognition gov. bd. 1986—, program com. pattern and image processing conf. 1978, 4th internat. joint conf. on pattern recognition 1978, conf. B-pattern recognition methods and sys. program com. 11th internat. conf. on pattern recognition 1992, structural and syntactic pattern recognition 1992, 2d internat. conf. on document analysis and recognition 1993, chairperson various workshops and confs., Cert. Appreciation award 1978, 84), Pattern Recognition Soc., Internat. Assn. for Pattern Recognition (pres. 1996—), Am. Assn. Artificial Intelligence, Assn. Computing Machinery. Home: 8651 Inverness Dr NE Seattle WA 98115-3987 Office: U of Wash Dept of Elec Engring Seattle WA 98195

HARALSON, LINDA JANE, communications executive; b. St. Louis, Mar. 24, 1959; d. James Benjamin and Betty Jane (Myers) N.; married. BA summa cum laude William Woods Coll., 1981; MA, Webster U., 1982. Radio intern Stas.-KFAL/KKCA, Fulton, Mo., 1981; paralegal Herzog, Kral, Burroughs & Specter, St. Louis, 1981-82; staffing coordinator, then mktg. coordinator Spectrum Emergency Care, St. Louis, 1982-85, mktg. mgr., 1985-87; dir. mktg. and recruitment Carondelet Rehab. Ctrs. Am., Culver City, Calif., 1987—; mktg. dir. outpatient and corp. services Calif. Med. Ctr., Los Angeles, 1987-88; mktg. dir. Valley Meml. Hosp., Livermore, Calif., 1988-89; account exec. Laurel Communications, Medford, Oreg., 1989-91; community rels. dir. Rogue Valley Med. Ctr., Medford, 1991-95; pub. rels. dir. Rogue Valley Manor, Medford, 1995—; Party chmn. Heart Assn., St. Louis, 1982—; bd. dirs. Am. Lung Assn. Oreg. Recipient Flair award Advt. Fedn. St. Louis, 1984, Hosps. award Hagen Mktg. Research and Hospitals mag., 1984; presdl. acad. scholar William Woods Coll., Fulton, 1977-81. Mem. IABC, NAFE, Am. Mktg. Assn., So. Oreg. Advt. Profls., Britt Music Festivals, Alpha Phi Alumnae Assn. (pres. chpt. 1985-87). Republican. Presbyterian. Avocations: running, travel, sports, French, needlepoint. Home and Office: 4546 NE East Devils Lake Otis OR 97368

HARARY, KEITH, psychologist; b. N.Y.C., Feb. 9, 1953; s. Victor and Lillian (Mazur) H.; m. Darlene Moore, Oct. 22, 1985. BA in Psychology, Duke U., 1975; PhD, Union Inst., 1986. Crisis counselor Durham (N.C.) Mental Health Ctr., 1972-76; rsch. assoc. Psychical Rsch. Found., Durham, 1972-76; rsch. assoc. dept. psychiatry Maimonides Med. Ctr., Bklyn., 1976-79; dir. counseling Human Freedom Ctr., Berkeley, Calif., 1979; rsch. cons. SRI Internat., Menlo Park, Calif., 1980-82; design cons. Atari Corp., Sunnyvale, Calif., 1983-85; pres., rsch. dir. Inst. for Advanced Psychology, San Francisco, 1986—; freelance sci. journalist, 1988—; editor-at-large Omni Mag., 1996—; invited lectr. Duke U., 1995; lectr. in field; adj. prof. Antioch U., San Francisco, 1985, 86; guest lectr. Lyceum Sch. for Gifted Children, 1985-89; vis. rschr. USSR Acad. Scis., 1983; rsch. cons. Am. Soc. for Psychical Rsch., 1971-72, Found. for Rsch. on Nature of Man, 1972, sci. applications Internat. Corp., 1991-93. Co-author: The Mind Race, 1984, 85, 30-Day Advanced Psychology Series, 1989-91, Who Do You Think You Are? Explore Your Many-Sided Self With the Berkeley Personality Profile, 1994, CD-ROM edit., 1996; featured monthly columnist in The Omni Mind Brain Lab in Omni Mag., 1995—; contbr. over 100 articles to profl. jours., other publs. Mem. APA, Am. Psychol. Soc., Assn. for Media Psychology, Am. Soc. for Psychical Rsch. (bd. dirs. 1994—). Home and Office: 98 Main St # 637 Tiburon CA 94920-2566

HARBART, GERTRUDE CAROL, artist, educator; b. Michigan City, Ind., Dec. 25, 1908; d. Charles H. and Maude A. (Hackett) Felton; m. Frank F. (dec. 1977); children: James, Joy. Student, U. Ind., 1930, U. Ohio, 1940, Art Inst. Chgo., 1950; studies with Hans Hoffman, Provence Town, Mass.; studies with Aron Borad, U. Ohio. Tchr. Pub. Schs., Ind., 1957-61, South Bend (Ind.) Art Ctr., 1960-70, Michigan City Art Ctr., 1976—; officer South Bend No. Ind. Art Assn., 1960—, So. Ariz. Watercolor Guild, Tucson, 1978, Michigan City Art Ctr. Guild, 1979—; instr. Pima Coll., Tucson, 1990-97. One-man shows include Chgo. Pub. Library, St. Mary's Notre Dame, Hoosier Salon Indpls., So. Bend Art Ctr., Murphy Gallery, Tucson; group exhibitions include Chgo. and Vicinity Show, Art Inst. Chgo., Old NW Territory, Springfield, Ill, Sarasota Art Assn., Kalamazoo Art Ctr.; nat. competitions include Art U.S.A., Corcoran Gallery, Washington, Acad. of Design N.Y.C., Butler Inst. Am. Art, Youngstown, Ohio, Nat. Painters in Casein, N.Y.; one-mans show Tucson Murphy Gallery, Hooser Salon, Gallery North, New Buffalo, Mich., 1990; permanent collections include Ind. U., Purdue U., Indiana State U., Community Ctr. for the Arts, Michigan City; group shows include Tubal (Ariz.) Art Ctr., Artbarn Valparaiso, Ind., Sarasota (Fla.) Art Assn. Mem. So. Ariz. Water Color Guild, Skyline Women's Club, Tucson Women's Club. Home: 5578 N La Casita Dr Tucson AZ 85718-5310

HARBAUGH, DANIEL PAUL, lawyer; b. Wendell, Idaho, May 18, 1948; s. Myron and Manuelita (Garcia) H. BA, Gonzaga U., 1970, JD, 1974. Bar: Washington 1974, U.S. Dist. Ct. (ea. dist.) Wash. 1977, U.S. Ct. Appeals (9th cir.) 1978. Asst. atty. gen. State of Wash., Spokane, 1974-77; ptnr. Richter, Wimberley & Ericson, Spokane, 1977-83, Harbaugh & Bloom, P.S., Spokane, 1983—; bd. dirs. Spokane Legal Svcs., 1982-86; bd. govs. LAWPAC, Seattle, 1980-92. Bd. dirs. Spokane Ballet, 1983-88; chpt. dir. Les Amis du Vin, Spokane, 1985-88; mem. Spokane County Civil Svc. Commn., 1991—, Gonzaga U. Pres'. Coun., 1991—. Mem. ABA, ATLA, Wash. State Bar Assn. (spl. dist. counsel 1982-95, mem. com. rules for profl. conduct 1989-92, mem. legis. com. 1995-97), Spokane County Bar Assn. (chair med.-legal com. 1991), Wash. State Trial Lawyers Assn. (v.p. 1988-89, co-chair worker's compensation sect. 1992, 93, spl. select. com. on workers' corp. 1990—, forum 1994—, vice chmn. 1994—, mem. legis. com. 1995—), Nat. Orgn. Social Security Claimants Reps., Internat. Wine and Food Soc. (pres. local chpt. 1989-91, cellar master 1994-96), Spokane Club, Spokane Country Club (adminstrv. com. 1991—, chmn. 1995—, bd. trustees 1996—), Alpha Sigma Nu, Phi Alpha Delta. Roman Catholic. Office: Harbaugh & Bloom PS PO Box 1461 N 9 Post Ste 210 Spokane WA 99210

HARBORD, ANNE MARIE, consulting dietetics company executive; b. Detroit, Nov. 9, 1954; d. Lionel Joseph and Mary Ellen (Beaushaw) H.; m. Scott H. Reed, May 27, 1978 (div. Apr. 1980); m. Charles Bloom, June 18, 1988; children: Erica, Mark Alexander. BS in Dietetics, Mich. State U., 1976; MS Nutrition, Food Mgmt., Calif. Poly. U., 1985. Registered dietitian, Calif. Clin. dietitian Saga Foods Co., Kalamazoo, 1976-78; cardiac dietition Anaheim (Calif.) Meml. Hosp., 1978; dir. dietary svcs. Care Enterprises, Orange, Calif., 1978-88; owner, mgr. Geriatric Nutrition Mgmt., Oceanside, Calif., 1988—; dir. nutrition svcs. Kennon Shea & Assoc., El Cajon, Calif., 1988—; speaker in field; quality assurance cons. Health Care div. ARA Living Ctrs. and Retirement Homes, Verduga Hills, Calif., 1979; spl. project coord. Calif. Dieticians in Health Care, 1995—. Pub. (continuing edn. prog.) Nutritional Problems in the Elderly; editor: Dietary Policy and Procedure Manual for Long-Term Care, 1984, Recipes Standardized for Long-Term Care, 1986. Calif. Dietetic Assn. grad. scholar, 1984. Mem. Am. Dietetic Assn., Calif. Assn. Health Facilities (chmn. cons. dietitian practice group 1981-85, treas. 1990-91), Am. Soc. Enteral and Parenteral Nutrition, San Diego Dietetic Assn. (edn. chmn. 1988-89, dist. rep. 1989-91). Roman Catholic. Home and Office: Geriatric Nutrition Mgmt 5027 Nighthawk Way Oceanside CA 92056-5447

HARCOURT, MICHAEL FRANKLIN, retired premier of Province of British Columbia, lawyer, educator; b. Edmonton, Alta., Can., Jan. 6, 1943; s. Frank Norman and Stella Louise (Good) H.; m. Mai-Gret Wibecke Salo, June 26, 1971; 1 son, Justen Michael. B.A., U. B.C., 1965, LL.B., 1968. Bar: B.C. 1969. Founder dir. Vancouver Community Legal Assistance Soc., 1969-71; partner firm Lew, Fraser & Harcourt, 1971-79; pres. Housing & Econ. Devel. Consulting Firm, Vancouver, from 1977; alderman City of Vancouver, 1972-80; mayor, 1980-86, mem. Legis. Assembly, 1986-96, leader, New Dem. Party of British Columbia, 1987-96; premier Province of B.C., 1991-96, ret., 1996; former leader of opposition, leader of govt.; sr. assoc. Sustainable Devel. Inst., 1996—; asst. dir. Justice Devel. Commn., Vancouver; dir. Housing Corp. B.C.; adj. prof. faculty grad. studies U. B.C., 1996—. Bd. dirs. Asia-Pacific Found. Mem. Law Soc. B.C., Nat. Rountable Environ. and Economy (chmn. fgn. rels. com.), Jericho Tennis Club. New Democrat. Mem. United Ch. Can.

HARCOURT, ROBERT NEFF, educational administrator, journalist; b. East Orange, N.J., Oct. 19, 1932; s. Stanton Hinde and Mary Elizabeth (Neff) H. BA, Gettysburg Coll., 1958; MA, Columbia U., 1961. Cert.

guidance, secondary edn., career and vocat. guidance, N.Mex. Social case worker N.J. State Bd. Child Welfare, Newark and Morristown, 1958-61; asst. registrar Hofstra U. and asst. to evening dean of students CCNY, 1961-62; housing staff U. Denver, 1962-64; fin. aid and placement dir. Inst. Am. Indian Arts, Santa Fe, 1965-95; appointed by corp. pres. to adv. bd. Genre Ltd. Art Pubs., L.A., 1986—; nat. color ad participant The Bradford Exchange, Chgo., 1986—. Donor Am. Indian Libr. collection Gettysburg (Pa.) Coll.; active Santa Fe Civic Chorus, 1977-78; art judge 3d, 4th ann. Aspen Fundraiser Nat. Mus. Am. Indian, 1993, 94; vol. Inst. Am. Indian Arts Mus. With U.S. Army, 1954-56; Ger. Named Hon. Okie, Gov. Okla., 1970; decorated Nat. Def. medal; postmasters fellow U. Denver, 1962-64; col. a.d.c. to N.Mex. Gov. David F. Cargo, 1970; Disting. Alumni award Gettsburg Coll. Alumni Assn., 1995. Mem. Am. Contract Bridge League (exec. bd. Santa Fe unit; life master), SAR, Santa Fe Coun. Internat. Rels., Am. Assn. Counseling and Devel., Internat. Platform Assn., New England Historic Genealogical Soc., Assn. Specialists in Group Work (charter), Adult Student Personnel Assn. (charter), Southwestern Assn. Indian Affairs, Neff Family Hist. Soc., St. Andrew Scottish Soc. of N. Mex., Gen. Soc. Mayflower Descendents, Order of the Founders and Patriots of Am., Mil. Order of the Loyal Legion of the U.S., Phi Delta Kappa (past mem. exec. bd. local chpt.), Alpha Tau Omega, Alpha Phi Omega, Safari Club Internat. Home: 2980 Viaje Pavo Real Santa Fe NM 87505-5344

HARDEN, CLINTON DEWEY, JR., restaurant owner, state official; b. Belen, N.Mex., Apr. 12, 1947; s. Clinton Dewey and Doretha E. (Miller) H.; m. Kathrine H. Harden, Aug. 5, 1968; children: Danielle, Dionne, Dustin. BS in Bus. Mgmt., U. Utah, 1970; MBA, Ea. N.Mex. U., 1994. Account exec. Continental Ins., Salt Lake City, 1970-78; owner restaurant Twin Cronnie Enterprises, Clovis, N.Mex., 1978—; cabinet sec. Dept. Labor, Albuquerque, 1995—; chmn. Cabinet Coun. on State Pers., Santa Fe, 1995—. Mem. Sch.-to-Work Adv. Bd., Santa Fe, 1995—, Pardons and Parole Com., Santa Fe, 1995—, Human Resource Investment Coun., Santa Fe, 1995—; pres. Clovis chpt. Amateur Athletic Union; mem., coach Clovis Girls Athletic Assn.; mem. Mayor's Coun. on Juvenile Crime, Clovis; mem. Children Youth and Families Interagy. Coord. Group, 1995—; bd. dirs. Interstate Conf. of Employment Security Agencies, 1995—; rep. Nat. Gov.'s Assn. Human Resources Coun., 1995—; lead sec. Workforce Devel. Reform, 1996—. Mem. Clovis C. of C. (v.p.). Republican. Methodist. Office: Labor Dept PO Box 1928 Albuquerque NM 87103-1928

HARDEN, MARVIN, artist, educator; b. Austin, Tex.; s. Theodore R. and Ethel (Sneed) H. BA in Fine Arts, UCLA, 1959, MA in Creative Painting, 1963. Tchr. art Calif. State U., Northridge, 1968-97, prof. emeritus, 1997—; Tchr. art Santa Monica (Calif.) City Coll., 1968; mem. art faculty UCLA Extension, 1964-68; prof. emeritus Calif. State U., 1997; mem. visual arts fellowship, painting panel NEA, 1985. One-man shows include Ceeje Galleries, L.A., 1964, 66, 67, L.A. City Coll., 1968, Occidental Coll., L.A., 1969, Whitney Mus. Am. Art, N.Y.C., 1971, Eugenia Butler Gallery, L.A., 1971, Rath Mus., Geneva, Switzerland, 1971, Irving Blum Gallery, L.A., 1972, Los Angeles Harbor Coll., 1972, David Stuart Galleries, L.A., 1975, Coll. Creative Studies, U. Calif., Santa Barbara, 1976, James Corcoran Gallery, L.A., 1978, Newport Harbor Art Mus., 1979, L.A. Mcpl. Art Gallery, 1982, Conejo Valley Art Mus., 1983, Simard Gallery, L.A., 1985, The Armory Ctr. for the Arts, Pasadena, Calif., 1994; group shows include U.S. State Dept. Touring Exhbn., USSR, 1966, Oakland (Calif.) Mus. Art, 1966, UCLA, 1966, Mpls. Inst. Art, 1968, San Francisco Mus. Art, 1969, Phila. Civic Ctr. Mus., 1969, Mus. Art, R.I. Sch. Design, 1969, N.S. State Mus., 1969, Everson Mus. Art, Syracuse, 1969, La Jolla (Calif.) Mus., 1969, 70, High Mus. Art, Atlanta, 1969, Flint (Mich.) Inst. Arts, 1969, Ft. Worth Art Center Mus., 1969, Contemporary Arts Assn., Houston, 1970, U. N.Mex., 1974, U. So. Calif., 1975, Bklyn. Mus., 1976, Los Angeles County Mus. Art, 1977, 96, Newport Harbor Art Mus., 1977, Frederick S. Wight Gallery, UCLA, 1978, Cirrus Editions, Ltd., L.A., 1979, Franklin Furnace, N.Y.C., 1980, Art Ctr. Coll. Design, L.A., 1981, Alternative Mus., N.Y.C., 1981, Laguna Beach Mus. (Calif.), 1982, L.A. Inst. Contemporary Art, 1982, Mus. Contemporary Art, Chgo., 1983, Mint Mus., Charlotte, N.C., 1983, DeCordova and Dana Mus. and Park, Lincoln, Mass., 1983, Equitable Gallery, N.Y.C., 1984, L.A. Municipal Art Gallery, 1984, 1985, Cirrus, L.A., 1986, 1990, Heal the Bay, Surfboard Art Invitational, 1990, Pasadena Armory Ctr. for the Arts, 1992, Claremont Coll. West Gallery, L.A., 1992, Grolier Club, N.Y.C., 1993, Calif. State U., San Luis Obispo, 1994, Cheney Cowles Mus., Spokane, Wash., 1995, Louis Stern Fine Art, L.A., 1995, Porter Troup Gallery, San Diego, 1995, Armory Ctr. for the Arts, Pasadena, 1996; represented in permanent collections include Whitney Mus. Am. Art, N.Y.C., Mus. Modern Art, N.Y.C., N.Y. Pub. Libr. Spence Collection, Getty Ctr. for Arts and Humanities, L.A. County Mus. Art, Atlantic Richfield Co. Corp. Art Coll., Grunwald Ctr. Graphic Arts UCLA, City of Los Angeles, Metromedia, Inc., L.A., San Diego Jewish Community Center, Berkeley (Calif.) U. Mus., Home Savs. & Loan Assn., L.A., also pvt. collections. Bd. dirs. Images & Issues, 1980-86; mem. artists adv. bd. L.A. Mcpl. Art Gallery Assn., 1983-86. Recipient UCLA Art Council award, 1963, Disting. Prof. award Calif. State U. Northridge, 1984, Exceptional Merit Service award Calif. State U. Northridge, 1984; Nat. Endowment Arts fellow, 1972; awards in Visual Arts, 1983; Guggenheim fellow, 1983. Mem. L.A. Inst. Contemporary Art (co-founder 1972). Home: PO Box 1793 Cambria CA 93428-1793

HARDER, KELSIE T., artist, educator; b. Trenton, Tenn., Mar. 8, 1942; s. Kelsie Brown Harder and Geneva Lee (Tomlin) Carlson; m. Kumiko Tanaka, Oct. 2, 1991; children: Michon Skyler, Samuel Armstrong, Tsunami Tomlin and Tanaka Solomon (twins). Student, Claremont (Calif.) Men's Coll., 1960-61, Escuela de Bellas Artes, Morelia, Mex., 1961, Ventura (Calif.) Coll., 1961-62; BA, U. Nev., 1973-75. Artist self-employed, 1957—; prof. Truckee Meadows C.C., Reno, 1978—; chmn. art dept. Truckee Meadows C.C., 1982-91; art exhibit judge over 30 regional competitions. Contbr. articles to profl. jours., mags., textbooks; 28 one-man shows; represented in over 100 collections. Recipient numerous regional and nat. awards including YWCA Silver cert. for Outstanding Cmty. Svc., No. Nev., 1972, 88. Office: Truckee Meadows CC 7000 Dandini Blvd Reno NV 89512-3901

HARDER, WENDY WETZEL, communications executive; b. Oceanside, Calif., Feb. 14, 1951; d. Burt Louis and Marjorie Jean (Evans) W.; m. Peter N. Harder, Dec. 1, 1984; 1 child, Jonathan Russell. AA, Palomar Coll., 1971; BA in Communications, U. So. Calif., 1973; MBA, Pepperdine U., 1988. Pub. rels. dir. Orange County Community Devel. Coun., Santa Ana, Calif., 1975-76; assoc. producer Sta. KOCE-TV, Huntington Beach, Calif., 1976-77, reporter, 1977-79, anchor, assoc. producer, 1979-82; sr. adminstr. communications Mission Viejo (Calif.) Co., 1983-84, mgr. corp. affairs, 1984-85, dir. corp. affairs, 1985-91, v.p. corp. affairs, 1991-93, v.p. mktg. and corp. comm., 1993—. 1st v.p. Aliso Viejo (Calif.) Cmty. Found., 1988-93, pres., 1993—, Saddleback Coll. Found., Mission Viejo, 1989-94; co-chmn. The Ctr. on Tour-Schs. Com., Orange County, Calif., 1989-92; v.p. Found. for Vocat. Visions, 1996—, Found. for Vocat. Visions, 1996—; bd. dirs. Dunaj Internat. Dance Ensemble, Orange County, 1985—. Recipient Golden Mike award Radio & TV News Assn., 1981; co-recipient Best Spl. Event award, Pub. Rels. Soc. Am., 1986, Golden Mike award Radio & TV News Assn., 1979. Mem. Orange County Press Club (Best Feature Release award 1983), Royal Scottish Country Dance Assn., Orange County Folk Dancers. Republican. Lutheran. Office: Mission Viejo Co 26137 La Paz Rd Mission Viejo CA 92691-5309

HARDING, ANNA KRISTINE, education educator; b. Mercersburg, Pa., June 2, 1950; d. Obed Jalmer and Anna Ruth (Guss) Williamson; children: Anika Sarah, Benjamin Joel, Paul Steven. BS in Cmty. Health and Health Edn., U. Oreg., 1972; PhD in Health, Oreg. State U., 1990. Registered environ. sanitarian, Oreg.; cert. tchr., Oreg. Environ. sanitation trainee and lab. technologist Lane County Health Dept., Eugene, Oreg., 1972-73; subs. tchr. Corvallis (Oreg.) Sch. Dist., 1973; environ. sanitarian Linn County Health Dept., Albany, Oreg., 1974-75; water quality specialist Timberhill Homeowners Assn., Corvallis, 1984-87; grad. teaching asst., instr. Oreg. State U., Corvallis, 1987-90, asst. prof., dir. environ. health program, 1990—; instr. Linn Benton C.C., Corvallis, 1974-75; rschr. Coimbatore, Tamil Nadu, India, 1988-89; environ. justice task group, 1993—; mercury working group Oreg. Dept. Environ. Quality, 1994; nat. environ. goals roundtable group U.S. EPA, 1994—; presenter in field. Contbg. author: Access to Health, 2nd Edit., 1990; contbr. articles to profl. jours. Composting edn. com. Benton County, 1991-93, AIDS edn. com., 1989-92; unit coord. Health and Human Performance Combined Funds, 1991; vol. Boy Scouts Am., Corvallis, 1990—; mission and outreach bd. First Congl. Ch., 1992-93. Grantee Internat. Pub. Health Conf., 1991, 94, Oreg. Dept. Eniron. Quality, 1992-93, Internat. Environ. Health Conf., 1992-93, Coll. Health and Human Performance, 1992-94, Oreg. State U. Rsch. Office, 1993-94, EPA, 1994-95, 95-96, Nat. Inst. Environ. Health Scis., 1996—, Am. Water Works Assn., 1996-97. Mem. APHA (environ. sect. rep. 1995—), Am. Assn. for World Health, Assn. Oreg. Faculties, Nat. Coun. for Internat. Health, Nat. Environ. Health Assn., Oreg. Environ. Health Assn. Democrat. Congregationalist. Office: Oreg State Univ Waldo Hall Dept Public Health Corvallis OR 97331-6406

HARDING, CAROL ELAINE, English language educator; b. Bellingham, Wash., Oct. 22, 1953; d. Bruce C. and Lenna J. (Deutsch) H.; m. Kyle R. Jansson, June 26, 1982; children: Bryn, Tyra. BA, U. Oreg., 1974, MA, 1976; PhD, Ind. U., 1985. Instr. Wash. State U., Pullman, 1982-84; vis. prof. Linfield Coll., McMinnville, Oreg., 1985-86; instr. Chandler-Gilbert C.C., Chandler, Ariz., 1992-94; lectr. Western Oreg. U., Monmouth, 1994-95, asst. prof., 1995—, writing coord., 1995—. Author: Merlin and Legendary Romance, 1988. Mem. Medieval Acad. Am., Internat. Arthurian Soc., Mid-Valley Writing Consortium. Office: Western Oregon Univ Dept of English Monmouth OR 97361

HARDING, F(RED) VICTOR, fitness consultant; b. San Juan, P.R., May 7, 1954; s. Warren G. and Martha Lee (Pinkston) H.; m. Linda Ruth Yocum, June 11, 1977; children: James Matthew, Bryan David, Rachael Christine. BA, Azusa Pacific U., 1980; Ma, U. So. Calif., 1985. Cert. fire fitness coord., ARA human factors. Asst. football coach Azusa (Calif.) Pacific U., 1982, 1984-85; grad. teaching asst. U. So. Calif., L.A., 1981-84; instr. Calif. State U., Fullerton, 1984-86, 88; instr., asst. football coach Citrus Coll., Glendora, Calif., 1986-89, asst. football coach, 1990; instr. PACE program, asst. football coach L.A. Harbor Coll., Wilmington, Calif., 1989; dir. fitness programs and rsch. Fortanasce & Assoc. Physical Therapy/Sports Medicine, 1992—; presenter in field; rschr. in field; cons. corp. fitness Bally's Nautilus/Aerobics Plus; instr. fitness preparation Valley Fire Edn. Assn., Ventura, Calif. Mem. AAHPERD, Am. Coll. Sports Medicine, Nat. Strength and Conditioning Assn. Republican. Baptist.

HARDING, JIM, state agency executive, energy policy specialist; b. Oakland, Calif., Aug. 17, 1952; s. Robert Eugene and Ebba (Bisgaard) H. Student, Bowdoin Coll., 1969-72; BA, U. San Francisco; postgrad., U. Calif., Berkeley, 1989-90. Energy program dir. Friends of the Earth, Inc., San Francisco, 1972-76; advisor to commr./chmn. Calif. Energy Commn., Sacramento, 1976-79; exec. dir. Internat. Project for Safe Energy Paths, San Francisco, 1979-85; sr. assoc. MHB Tech. Assocs., Inc., San Jose, Calif., 1985-90; asst. dir. Wash. State Energy Office, Olympia, 1990-92, acting dir., 1993, asst. dir., 1994—; policy dir. Northwest Power Planning Coun., 1995—; dir. power planning and forecasting Seattle City Light, 1996—; cons. Can. Internat. Devel. Agy., Ottawa, Ont., 1980-85, Calif. Pub. Utilities Commn., San Francisco, 1985-90, Paul, Weiss, Rifkind, Wharton & Garrison, N.Y.C., 1987-90, Md. Pub. Counsel, Balt., 1988-90. Author: Nuclear Power in the U.S., Europe and U.S.S.R., 1985, Plutonium 1986, 1986, Washington State Energy Strategy, 1992; co-author: Social and Economic Criteria for High Level Waste Management, 1984. Mem. steering com. Keystone (Colo.) Ctr. for Conflict Resolution, 1977-82; mem. Calif. Regulatory Reform Commn., Sacramento, 1979-80; com. mem. NAS, Washington, 1980-84; gov.'s rep. Nat. Marine Fisheries Svc., Portland, Oreg., 1991—. Recipient Adminstr.'s award for exceptional pub. svc. Bonneville Power Adminstrn., 1991, award of merit Soc. for Tech. Communication, 1991. Mem. AAAS. Home: 1725 Arbutus St NE Olympia WA 98506-3201 Office: 700 Fifth Ave Ste 2834 Seattle WA 98104

HARDING, KAREN ELAINE, chemistry educator and department chair; b. Atlanta, Sept. 5, 1949; d. Howard Everett and Ruth Evangeline (Lund) H.; m. Bruce Roy McDowell, Aug. 30, 1975. BS in Chemistry, U. Puget Sound, Tacoma, 1971; MS in Environ. Chemistry, U. Mich., 1972; postgrad., Evergreen State Coll., 1972, 84, Yale U., 1986, Columbia U., 1991. Chemist Environ. Health Lab., Inc., Farmington, Mich., 1972-73, U. Mich. Med. Sch., Ann Arbor, 1973-75; instr. chemistry Schoolcraft Coll., Livonia, Mich., 1975-77; chair chemistry dept. Pierce Coll., Tacoma, 1977—; adj. prof. U. Mich., Dearborn, 1974-77; instr. S.H. Alternative Learning Ctr., Tacoma, 1980-83, Elderhostel, Tacoma, 1985-89; mem. exec. com. Chemlinks project NSF. Mem. County Solid Waste Adv. Com., Tacoma, 1989—, Superfund Adv. Com., Tacoma, 1985-89, Sierra Club, Wash., 1989—; mem., past pres. Adv. Com. Nature Ctr., Tacoma, 1981-87. Faculty Enhancement grantee Pierce Coll., 1990; recipient Nat. Teaching Excellence award, 1991. Mem. NW Assn. for Environ. Studies (treas. 1985—), Am. Chem. Soc., Ft. Steilacoom Running Club (race dir. 1986—). Office: Pierce Coll 9401 Farwest Dr SW Tacoma WA 98498-1919

HARDING, RAY MURRAY, JR., judge; b. Logan, Utah, Nov. 23, 1953; s. Ray M. Sr. and Martha (Rasmussen) H.; children: Michelle, Nicole, Justin. BS, Brigham Young U., 1975; JD, J. Reuben Clark Law Sch., 1978. Bar: Utah 1978, U.S. Dist. Ct. 1995. Ptnr. Harding & Harding, American Fork and Pleasant Grove, Utah, 1978-85; owner Harding & Assoc., American Fork and Pleasant Grove, 1986-95; judge 4th Jud. Dist. Ct. Utah County, State of Utah, 1995—; atty. Lindon City and Pleassant Grove City, Utah, 1983-95, Alpine City, 1985-94, American Fork, Utah, 1985-95. Bd. trustees Utah Valley State Coll., 1986-95, chmn., 1991-93. Named Businessman of Yr., Future Bus. Leaders of Am., 1983. Mem. ABA, ATLA, Utah State Bar Assn., Utah Trial Lawyers Assn., Utah County Bar Assn., Pleasant Grove C. of C. (pres. 1983), Kiwanis (local bd. dirs. 1982-83). Home: 11165 N Yarrow Cir Highland UT 84003 Office: 4th Judicial Dist Ct 125 N 100 W Provo UT 84601-2849 also: 306 W Main St American Fork UT 84003-2230

HARDING, RICHARD EVANS, pastor; b. Moberly, Mo., Dec. 17, 1937; s. Charles L. and Lois E. (Evans) H.; m. Susan Patterson; children: Nancy Harding Harris, John Charles. BA, U. Calif., Riverside, 1961; MDiv, Am. Bapt. Sem. of the West, Covina, Calif., 1969. Ordained to ministry Bapt. Ch., 1969. Tchr. Pasadena City Schs., Calif., 1961-62, Jurupa Unified Sch. Dist., Riverside, Calif., 1962-65; pastor First Bapt. Ch.-Rubidoux, Riverside, Calif., 1966-75; pastor, missionary Cordova Cmty. Bapt. Ch., Alaska, 1975—; cons. Am. Bapt. Ch. and Inst., Alaska, 1990-96. Columnist Cordova Times, 1995—. Mem. Chem. People, Cordova. Recipient Vol. award Gov. of Alaska, 1990. Mem. Alaska Assn. Bapt. Chs. and Instns. (past pres. 1992-94). Home: 2nd and Adams Sts PO Box 728 Cordova AK 99574 Office: Cordova Cmty Bapt Ch 702 2nd Ave Cordova AK 99574

HARDING, TERESA J., interior designer; b. L.A.; d. Edward Joseph Harding and Jane Elizabeth (Gunter) Kruse; divorced. BA, U. Okla. Cert. interior designer, Calif. Buyer lamps and accesories W & J Sloane, San Francisco; interior designer W & J Sloane, Beverly Hills, Calif.; interior designer, owner Harding Interior, L.A. Mem. Brentwood Homeowners Assn., L.A., 1994; treas. Nat. Charity League, 1994—. Mem. Nat. Charity League (treas. 1994-96), Achievement Rewards for Coll. Scientists, Colleagues Helpers in Philanthropic Svcs. (hon.), Am. Soc. Interior Design.

HARDING, WAYNE EDWARD, III, software company executive, accountant; b. Topeka, Sept. 29, 1954; s. Wayne Edward and Nancy M. (Gean) H.; BS with honors in Bus. Administrn., U. Denver, 1976, MBA, 1983; m. Janet Mary O'Shaughnessy, Sept. 5, 1979 (div. Mar. 1985); m. Karen Ruttan, Oct. 10, 1987. Partner, HKG Assocs., Denver, 1976-77; staff auditor Peat, Marwick, Mitchell & Co., Denver, 1976-78; auditor Marshall Hornstein, P.C., Wheat Ridge, Colo., 1978-79; sr. auditor Touche Ross & Co., Denver, 1979-80; controller Mortgage Plus Inc., 1980-81; sec.-treas. Sunlight Systems Energy Corp., 1980-81; ptnr. Harding, Newman, Sobule & Thrush, Ltd., Denver, 1981-82; pvt. practice specializing in microcomputer applications and litigation support, 1982-89; acct., v.p. Great Plains Software, Fargo, N.D., also dir. CPA ptnr. rels.; founder Discount Computer Rentals, Inc., 1985; dir. Harding Transp., Harding Tech. Leasing, Crown Parking Products; lectr. to various profl. groups on computer tech. Class agt., mem. alumni council Phillips Exeter Acad., Exeter, N.H., 1973-83, class agt., 1993—; bd. dirs., treas. Legal Center for Handicapped Citizens, Denver, 1979-80; vol. Denver Bridge, 1984-85. Mem. AICPA (instr., mem. tech. rsch. com. 1994—), Colo. Soc. CPAs (chmn. CPE com. 1987-89, instr., mem. bd. dirs. 1994-97, v.p. 1996-97), Beta Alpha Psi, Pi Gamma Mu, Beta Gamma Sigma. Libertarian. Mem. editorial bd. Practical Acct. Mag.; contbr. articles in field of microcomputers to profl. jours. including Jour. Acctg. on Micro Computers. Home and Office: 6029 S Kenton Way Englewood CO 80111-5727

HARDISON, DEE, mayor. Tchr. spl. edn. Torrance Unified Sch. Dist., 1980-89, program specialist, 1989-94; mem. Torrance City Coun., 1986-94; mayor City of Torrance, 1994—. Office: 3031 Torrance Blvd Torrance CA 90503

HARDISON, ROY LEWIS, marketing professional; b. Brea, Calif., Sept. 5, 1929; s. Arthur Abbott and Norma Doris (Lovering) H.; m. Frances Lucille Jacobsen, Aug. 21, 1949; children: Martin Arthur, Bradley Lewis, Steven Dean. BS in Econ. Entom., U. Calif., Berkeley, 1951. With sales Calif. Spray Chem., Modesto, 1951-59; asst. br. mgr. Chevron Chem. Co. (formerly Calif. Spray Chem.), Lindsay, Calif., 1960-61; br. mgr. Chevron Chem. Co., Yuba City, Calif., 1962-67; asst. dist. mgr. Chevron Chem. Co., Woodland, Calif., 1968-70; dist. mktg. specialist Chevron Chem. Co., Modesto, Calif., 1970-73; cen. coast dist. rep. Chevron Chem. Co., Salinas, Calif., 1973-75; mgr. East Asia Chevron Chem. Internat., Inc., Tokyo, 1976-84; prod. prom. specialist Chev. Chem. Co., Fresno, Calif., 1984-86; with regulatory affairs Moyer Products, Inc., Fresno, 1987-92; tech./market devel. profl. Best Sulfur Products, Fresno, Calif., 1992—. Mem. Hazardous Materials Control Resources Inst., Lions (sec., pres. 1954—). Republican. Presbyterian. Home: 7332 N Pacific Ave Fresno CA 93711-0571 Office: Best Sulfur Products 5427 E Central Ave Fresno CA 93725-9336

HARDWAY, JAMES EDWARD, vocational and rehabilitative specialist; b. Pueblo, Colo., Nov. 26, 1944; s. William Jeremiah and Margaret Ann (Rinker) H.; m. Mary Frances Walker, Sept. 9, 1967; children: Tina Marie, Catherine Ann, William James. BA, U. So. Colo., 1969; MS, U. Wis.-Stout, Menomonie, 1971; postgrad., U. Toledo, 1972—. Cert. vocat. evaluator, work adjustment specialist. Counselor Pueblo (Colo.) Diversified Industries, 1969-70; vocat. evaluator Penta County Vocat. Schs., Perrysburg, Ohio, 1971-82; dept. mgr. Magic City Enterprises, Cheyenne, Wyo., 1982-88; case mgr. Profl. Rehab. Mgmt., Cheyenne, 1989-91, regional mgr., 1992-94; pvt. practice vocational expert Cheyenne, 1994—; speaker State of Ohio Spl. Needs Conf., Ohio, 1972-80; cons. Wyo. State Tng. Sch., Lander, 1977. Pres. bd. dirs. Laramie County Community Action, Cheyenne; bd. dirs. Handicapped Employment Agy., Cheyenne, Wyo. Alzheimer's Assn. With U.S. Army, 1962-65. Fellow Am. Bd. Vocat. Experts; mem. Kiwanis (bd. dirs.). Home: 12309 White Eagle Rd Cheyenne WY 82009-9634

HARDY, BEN(SON B.), orchid nursery executive; b. Oakland, Calif., Nov. 22, 1920; s. Lester William and Irene Isabell (Bliss) H.; student pub. schs., Oakland, Calif., Concord, Calif.; grad. photo Intelligence Sch., Denver, 1949. Served as enlisted man U.S. Navy, 1942-48; joined USAF, 1948, advanced through grades to capt., 1957; with 67th Reconnaissance Squadron, Korea, 1951-52, Hdqrs. Squadron, Thule AFB, 1956, resigned, 1957; material requirements analyst-coord. Teledyne Ryan Aero. Co., San Diego, 1958-73, 83—; dispatcher-coord. Cubic Western Data Co., San Diego, 1977-80; owner-ptnr. orchid nursery. Pres. Exotic Plant Soc., 1976-78, 81-84, San Diego Gesneriad Soc., 1978; dir. 23d Western Orchid Congress, 1979. Author: (with John Klemme) The Orchid Badge Collector's Guide, 1993. Decorated Bronze Star; recipient Letter of Commendation NASA, also others. Mem. Am. Orchid Soc. (life), N.Z. Orchid Soc., San Diego County Orchid Soc. (life, pres. 1972-73, 75-76), Pacific Orchid Soc. Hawaii, Hoya Soc. Internat. (pres. 1981-83, 95—), Cymbidium Soc. Am., Orchid Digest Corp., Auckland Orchid Club, Orchid Badge Club Internat. (found. 1988, pres. 1991—). Home: 9443 E Heaney Cir Santee CA 92071-2919

HARDY, BETH BENITA, nurse; b. Vallejo, Calif., Sept. 11, 1964; d. Agre Abaloc Sanchez and Benita (Licopit) Ionin; m. Troy Allen Hardy, Dec. 16, 1983; children: Tylina Marie, Darryl Allen. AA in Vocat. Nursing, Merced Coll., 1991, ASN, 1993; BSN, Ea. N.Mex. U., 1995. LVN, Calif.; RN, N.Mex., Tex. Float pool LVN Mercy Hosp., Merced, Calif., 1991; staff Anberry Health Care, Atwater, Calif., 1991, Chowchilla (Calif.) Dist. Meml. Hosp., 1991-92; staff RN Plains Regional Med. Ctr., Clovis, 1993-95; staff Clovis Vets. Primary Care Clinic, 1994—. Asst. troop leader Girl Scouts U.S.A., Atwater, 1990-92, troop leader, Clovis, 1994-95. Mem. ANA, Nat. League Nursing, N.Mex. Nurses Assn., Sigma Veta Ni (pres. 1989-90).

HARDY, BLAINE CARMON, history educator; b. Vernal, Utah, Dec. 24, 1934; s. Blaine C. and LaRue Mignon (Hunting) H.; m. Kamillia Marlene Compton, July 31, 1954; children: Melody, Cristine, David, Amelia, Robin. BA, Wash. State U., 1957; MA, Brigham Young U., 1959; PhD, Wayne State U., 1963. Asst. prof. Brigham Young U., Provo, Utah, 1961-66; prof. history Calif. State U., Fullerton, 1966—. Author: Solemn Covenant, 1992 (Best Book award Mormon Hist. Assn. 1993); contbr. articles to profl. publs. Home: 465 Noble St Orange CA 92869-3008 Office: Calif State U Fullerton Dept History 800 N St College Blvd Fullerton CA 92834

HARDY, BRIDGET MCCOLL, screenwriter; b. Laramie, Wyo., Oct. 2, 1959; d. Eugene Nicholas and Deborah Wells Hardy. BA cum laude with honors, Smith Coll., 1984; MA, Jackson Sch. Internat. Studies, 1993; cert. in lit. fiction, U. Wash. Ext., 1995. Founder, pres. Am. Beyond Lang. Edn., Tokyo, Seattle, 1986-91; freelance screenwriter Seattle, 1995—; Japan-Am. cross-cultural cons. Am. Beyond Lang. Edn., Tokyo, Seattle, 1984-92, design asst. lang. immersion camp, Seattle, 1990; various positions Microsoft, Redmond, Wash., 1995-96.; Vol. and hospitality chair Japan-Am. Soc., 1990—; orientation tchr. Youth for Understanding, Seattle, 1991; vol. and interpreter Internat. Children's Festival, Seattle, 1991, 92, 95; vol. Greenworks, Seattle, 1994—; youth team leader Youth Vol. Corps, Redmond, 1994. Recipient Metro Bus Poetry award Seattle Metro, 1996; Earthwatch scholar, 1982.

HARDY, DAVID WHITTAKER, III, artist, educator; b. Dallas, Oct. 5, 1929; s. David Whittaker and Elnora Virginia (Randlett) H.; m. Sally Hofman; 1 child, Anne Louise. Student, Austin Coll., 1947-48, So. Meth. U., 1949-50, U. Colo., 1949, Am. Acad., 1953-56, Art Students League, 1956-59, Sch. Visual Art, 1957-58, Laney Coll., 1972-75, Calif. Coll. Arts & Crafts, 1979-85; studied with, Marion Virginia Randall Randlett, 1941-49, Ramon Froman, 1950-53, William Moseby, 1954-56, Joseph Van Der Brock, 1953-56, Antonin Sterba, 1953, Frank Mason, 1957-58, Robert Beverly Hale, 1958-59, Jack Potter, 1958. Instr. pvt. art classes, 1960—; owner, operator 13th Street Crafts Garden, Oakland, Calif., 1973-76; instr. art Mendocino (Calif.) Art Ctr., 1973-74, Calif. Coll. Arts and Crafts, Oakland, 1979-86; collection buyer Hall of Justice, Hayward, Calif.; guest Wurlizer Found., Taos, N.Mex., 1965; docent tng. program Fine Arts Mus., San Francisco, 1982, 86; guest lectr. U. Calif., Berkeley, 1981, 82. one-man shows include North Park, Dallas, 1964, Pantechnicon Gallery, San Francisco, 1970, Arden Van Wijk Gallery, Saratoga, Calif., 1984, Hemisfair Art, Witte Meml. Mus., San Antonio, 1968, Soc. Western Artists, M.H. De Young Mus., San Francisco, 1970, San Francisco Ann., 1971, Audubon Artists, Nat. Acad., N.Y., 1973, Alma Gilbert Galleries, Inc., Burlingame, Calif., 1992, J.J. Brookings Gallery, San Francisco, 1996, others; numerous pvt. collections in U.S. and abroad. Recipient 1st pl. painting Alameda County Fair, 1973. Mem. Berkeley Art Festival Guild (pres. 1972-77), Soc. Western Artists, Lillian Paley Ctr. Visual Arts (bd. trustees 1974-78). Home: 4220 Balfour Ave Oakland CA 94610-1750 Office: The Atelier 4920 Telegraph Ave Oakland CA 94609-2014

HARDY, GARY WAYNE, financial planner; b. Dayton, Ohio, Aug. 6, 1955; s. Allen J. and Betty J. Hardy; m. Heather E. Robertson, Aug. 9, 1980 (div. July 1990); 1 child, Brian; m. Sherry G. Wegman, Dec. 28, 1991. Degree in music edn., Grand Canyon U., 1981; degree in fin., Ariz. State U., 1984. CFP. Fin. planner Allmerica Fin., Phoenix, Ariz., 1981—; sales mgr., retirement plan specialist Allmerica Fin., Phoenix, 1984—, seminar leader, 1988—. Youth pastor Ch. on Mill, Tempe, Ariz., 1981-86; actor Bethany Cmty. Theatre, Tempe, 1991—; percussionist Bethany Comty. Orch., Tempe, 1986—. Mem. Internat. Assn. Fin. Planners, Nat. Assn. Life Underwriters. Office: Allmerica Fin 2929 E Camelback Rd Ste 124 Phoenix AZ 85016-4425

HARDY, LOIS LYNN, educational training company executive; b. Seattle, Aug. 20, 1928; d. Stanley Milton and Helen Berniece (Conner) Croonquist; m. John Weston Hardy, July 29, 1951 (div. 1974); children: Sarah Lynn, Laura Lynn; m. Joseph Freeman Smith, Jr., Apr. 18, 1981; stepchildren: Nancy Smith Willis, Martha Smith Dahlquist. BA, Stanford U., 1950, MA, 1952; postgrad., U. Calif., Berkeley, 1957-78, U. San Francisco, 1978-81. Cert. life secondary tchr., life counselor, adminstr., Calif.; lic. career and ednl. counselor, Calif. Tchr., counselor Eastside Union High Sch. Dist., San Jose, Calif., 1951-55; dir. Lois Lynn Hardy Music Studio, Danville, Calif., 1955-69; high sch. tchr. San Ramon Unified Sch. Dist., Danville, 1969-71, counselor, 1971-83; dir. Growth Dynamics Inst., Alamo, Calif., 1976—; instr. Fresno (Calif.) Pacific Coll., 1976-79, Dominican Coll., San Rafael, Calif., 1979—; cons., trainer Personal Dynamics Inst., Mpls., 1976—, Performax Internat., Mpls., 1979—, San Jose Unified Sch. Dist., 1986-86, Novato (Calif.) Unified Sch. Dist., 1985-86, IBM, San Francisco, 1984, corp. and ednl. cons., 1951—. Author: How To Study in High School, 1952, 3d edit., 1973; (with B. Santa) How To Use the Library, 1954; How To Learn Faster and Succeed: A How to Study Workbook For Grades 1-14, 1982, rev., 1985; author various seminars; contbr. numerous articles to profl. jours. Choir dir., organist Community Presbyn. Ch., Danville, 1966-68, elder, 1974-75; speaker to numerous orgns., 1955—. Named Musician of Yr., Contra Costa County, 1978, Counselor of Yr., No. Calif. Personnel and Guidance Assn., 1980; Olive S. Lathrop scholar, 1948, AAUW scholar, 1950; recipient Colonial Dames prize in Am. History, 1950. Mem. Am. Assn. Counseling and Devel., Calif. Assn. Counseling and Devel., Calif. Tchrs. Assn., Calif. Career Guidance Assn., Nat. Speakers Assn., Am. Guild Organists, Stanford U. Alumni Assn., Calif. Assn. for the Gifted, Delta Zeta. Democrat. Presbyterian. Office: Growth Dynamics Inst PO Box 1053 Alamo CA 94507-7053

HARDY, WAYNE RUSSELL, insurance broker; b. Denver, Sept. 5, 1931; s. Russell Hinton and Victoria Katherine (Anderson) H.; m. Carolyn Lucille Carvell, Aug. 1, 1958 (July 1977); children: James Russell Hardy, Jann Miller Hardy. BSCE, U. Colo., 1954; MS in Fin. Svcs., Am. Coll., 1989. CLU; ChFC. Western dist. mgr. Fenestra, Inc., San Francisco, 1956-63; ins. and investment broker John Hancock Fin. Svs., Denver, 1963—, Wayne R. Hardy Assocs., Denver, 1963—; speaker convs. and sales seminar, 1977, 81, 84, 85, 89; chmn. John Hancock Agt.'s Adv. Com., 1983-84; active State of Colo. Ins. Adv. Bd., 1991-93. Chmn. Colo. Coun. Camera Clubs, Denver, 1962; bd. dirs. Porter Charitable Found., Denver, 1983-85; deacon, class pres. South Broadway Christian Ch., 1961-65; mem. Denver Art Mus., Denver Botanic Gardens, Rocky Mountain Estate Planning Coun., Alliance Francaise. Capt. U.S. Army, 1954-56. Mem. Am. Soc. CLU and ChFC (pres. Rocky Mountain chpt. 1990-91), Nat. Assn. Life Underwriters (pres. Denver chpt. 1983-84, Nat. Quality award 1968—, expert witness ins. litigation), Nat. Football Found. (bd. dirs. Denver chpt. 1992—), Million Dollar Round Table (life), U. Colo. Alumni (bd. dirs. 1990-92), U. Colo. Alumni C Club (bd. dirs. 1972-74), Univ. Club, Greenwood Athletic Club, Village Tennis Club, Rocky Mountain Optimist Club (pres. 1984-85). Republican. Home and Office: 6178 E Hinsdale Ct Englewood CO 80112-1534

HARDY, WILLIAM TAYLOR, psychologist, educator; b. Port Huron, Mich., Dec. 6, 1946; s. David Mark and Virginia Beard (Taylor) H.; m. Cindy Lyn Hopkins, 1977. BA, Pomona Coll., 1969; MA, U. Calif. San Diego, La Jolla, 1971, PhD, 1976. Lectr., asst. prof. U. NSW, Randwick, Australia, 1977-87; instr. Sierra Coll., Rocklin, Calif., 1989—. Contbr. articles to profl. jours. Mem. APA (charter), We. Psychol. Assn. Home: 9449 Golden Dr Orangevale CA 95662 Office: Sierra Coll Psychology Dept 5000 Rocklin Rd Rocklin CA 95677

HARDY-VALDEZ-WOODWARD, NANCY GREAVES, educational administrator; b. Preston, Idaho, Sept. 29, 1939; d. Donald Kidd and Idana (Swainston) Greaves; 1 child, Susan Rainey. BS, Utah State U., 1961; MS, U. Utah, 1970. Cert. in adminstrn., supervision, Utah; cert. Nat. Bd. Cert. Counselors. Tchr. Granite Sch. Dist., Salt Lake City, 1966-70; sch. counselor Olympus Jr. High Sch., Salt Lake City, 1970-87; pres. Am. Sch. Counselors Assn., Alexandria, Va., 1987-88; supr. pupil svcs. Salt Lake City Sch. Dist., 1988—. Columnist Adolescence Mag., 1988-93. Recipient Lifetime Achievement award, Utah Sch. Counseling Assn.; named Utah Sch. Counselor of Yr., Utah Sch. Counseling Assn. Mem. ACA (governing coun. 1987-92, chmn. western region 1990-91, svc. awards 1988-92), Nat. Assn. Pupil Svcs. Adminstrs. (treas. 1993-94, pres. 1996). Office: Salt Lake City Sch Dist 440 E 1st S Salt Lake City UT 84111-1802

HARE, PAUL DEHAVEN, public safety director; b. Salamanca, N.Y., Feb. 3, 1936; s. Edwin Lawrence and Mary Elizabeth (DeHaven) H.; m. Gene Marie Hurlbut, May 5, 1959; children: Scott, Shawn, Shelly. BS in Sociology, U. Rochester, 1973. Cert. polygraphist Nat. Acad. Lie Detection. Investigator L.A. Sheriff's Dept., 1962-70, Palm Springs (Calif.) Police Dept., 1976-83; security cons. Paul Hare & Assocs., Palm Springs, 1984-90; dir. pub. safety Cabazon Band Mission Indians, Indio, Calif., 1991—; bd. advisor Calif. Polygraph Examination Assn., 1984-88; security advisor, cons. Cabazon Band Mission Indians, 1984-90. City commr., mem. personnel bd. City of Palm Springs, 1983-86. Sgt. USAF, 1954-62. Mem. Internat. Assn. Chiefs of Police, Masons (sr. deacon 1973—), Royal Arch (high priest 1975-76), Scottish Rite, Am. Legion (comdr. 1973—), Rotary (Palm Springs pres. 1988-89, Indio bd. dirs. 1993-94). Office: Cabazon Pub Safety Dept 84-245 Indio Springs Dr Indio CA 92203-3405

HARGISS, JAMES LEONARD, ophthalmologist; b. Manhattan, Kans., June 15, 1921; s. Meade Thomas and Julia Baldwin (Wayland) H.; m. Helen Natalie Berglund, July 19, 1947; children: Phillip M., Craig T., D. Reid. BS, U. Wash., 1942; MD, St. Louis U., 1945, MSc in Medicine, U. Pa., 1952. Diplomate Nat. Bd. Med. Examiners, Am. Bd. Ophthalmology. Intern U.S. Naval Hosp., PSNS Bremerton, Washington, 1945-46; resident physician G.F. Geisinger Meml. Hosp. and Foss Clinic, Danville, Pa., 1949-51; practice medicine specializing in ophthalmic surgery Seattle, 1951-58; ophthalmic surgeon Eye Clinic of Seattle, 1958-94, pres., 1962-91, CEO, 1985-91; ophthalmic cons. Eye Assocs. N.W., Seattle, 1994—; asst. clin. prof. Sch. Medicine, U. Wash., 1995—. Contbr. chapter to book, 1987, articles to Ophthalmology, 1964-80. Dist. chmn. King County Rep. Cen. Com., 1962-70. Served as physician/surgeon with USNR, 1945-48. Recipient Citation of Merit Washington State Med. Assn., 1959; Wendell F. Hughes fellow, 1960. Fellow AMA (Cert. of award 1960), Am. Coll. Surgeons, Am. Acad. Ophthalmology (Honor award 1975), Am. Soc. Ophthalmic Plastic and Reconstructive Surgery (charter) (Lester T. Jones award 1979), De Bourg Soc. of St. Louis U., Pacific Coast Oto-Ophthalmology Soc. (v.p.), Lions (Lake City pres. 1960-61), Gullwing Group Internat., Alpha Omega Alpha. Office: Eye Assocs NW 1101 Madison St Ste 600 Seattle WA 98104-1320

HARGREAVES, MATHEW D., printer, publishing executive; b. Renton, Wash., Apr. 8, 1955; s. Thomas William and Shirley Grace (Woodcox) H. BA in Law Enforcement, Highline C.C., Midway, Wash., 1975. Pressman Safeco Ins. Co., Seattle, 1978—. Author: Enya: A Beginning Discography, 1991, (bibliography) Anne Inez McCaffrey 40 Years of Publishing, 1992; co-author: (discography) Voices in the Dunes: The Tangerine Dream, 1991. Office: PO Box 66099 Seattle WA 98166-0099

HARGROVE, DON, state senator; b. Bozeman, Mont., Mar. 16, 1933; s. Ora Augustus and Helen Victoria (Drizle) H.; m. Eloise Marilyn Fellbaum, Aug. 20, 1955; children: Mark, Dan, David. BS, Mont. State U., 1956; MS, U. So. Calif., L.A., 1966. Commd. 2d lt. USAF, 1956, advanced through grades to col., 1976, comdr. 41st Mil. Airlift Squadron, comdr. 3d Mil. Airlift Group, def. attache to Bolivia; senator Mont. State Senate, Helena, 1995—; aviation advisor Colombian Nat. Narcotics Police, 1986-91. Republican. Home: 37 Big Chief Trail Bozeman MT 59715 Office: Montana State Senate State Capitol Dist 16 Helena MT 59620

HARKEN, ALDEN HOOD, surgeon, thoracic surgeon; b. Boston, 1941. MD, Case Western Reserve U., 1967. Diplomate Am. Bd. Surgeons, Am. Bd. Thoracic Surgeons. Intern Peter Bent Brigham Hosp., Boston, 1967-68, resident surgery, 1968-70, resident thoracic surgery, 1971-73; fellow cardio-vascular surgery Boston Children's Hosp., 1970-71; surgeon U. Colo. Hosp., Denver; prof., chmn. surgery dept. U. Colo. Sch. Medicine, Denver; part time pvt. practice surgery Denver. Mem. Am. Assn. Thoracic Surgeons, Soc. Univ. Surgeons, AATS. Office: U Colo Med Sch Dept Surg 4200 E 9th Ave Box C-305 Denver CO 80262-0001

HARKER, ROBERT TWAITES, retired insurance executive, archaeology educator; b. Billings, Mont., Oct. 14, 1929; s. Oliver Ellsworth and Florence Emily (Batteen) H.; m. Frances Caroline Ketcham, Mar. 16, 1951 (dec. Mar. 1983); children: Scott Coleman, Sharon Lynn, Steven Charles. BA in Bus. Adminstrn., U. Mont., 1951. Asst. br. mgr., underwriting mgr. Indsl. Indemnity Co., L.A., 1953-60; mgr. workers compensation and liability Parks & Co., L.A., 1960-63; owner Robert T. Harker, Broker, L.A., 1963-66; gen. mgr. Calif. Compensation and Fire Co., L.A., 1966-70; asst. divsn. mgr. Argonaut Ins., San Francisco, 1971-77; regional mgr. workers compensation and liability Aetna Ins., San Francisco, 1977-82; dir. workers compensation Mission Ins. Co., San Francisco, 1982-83; archaeology instr. So. Calif., 1989—; instr. Ins. Edn. Assn., Ins. Sch. Pacific, U. Calif.-Berkeley ext., San Francisco, 1971-77; archaeologist Earthwatch expdns., 1989—. Author: Development of Transportation in State of Montana, 1951. Pres., chmn. bd. Cimarron Homeowner's Assn., Escondido, Calif., 1987-91. With USN, 1946-48, WWII. Recipient Wall St. Jour. Student Achievement award, 1951. Mem. Archaeol. Inst. Am. (mem. nat. and Calif. chpts.), USN League (life, Commodore 1983), Smithsonian Assocs. (assoc.), Mus. Natural History (assoc.). Home: 2038 Skyview Glen Escondido CA 92027 *Robert Twaites Harker's archaeological discoveries in Santorini, Greece, have been shown on The Learning Channel (TLC), broadcast nationwide and in Canada. His comments on archaeological discoveries in Central America were shown on CNN International News. His great discoveries in Bermuda and on dolphins in Hawaii have been detailed in the Bermuda Royal Gazette, Mid-Ocean News, London Times, Hispanos Unidos, and the Times Advocate News. He has visited 65 countries and participated in more than 55 expeditions worldwide.*

HARKIN, MICHAEL EUGENE, anthropologist, educator, writer; b. Muncie, Ind., Aug. 16, 1958; s. Roy Eugene and Sandra Arlene (Satterthwaite) H.; m. Alison Margaret Quaggin; children: Caroline Margaret, James Michael. BA with honors, U. N.C., 1980; AM, U. Chgo., 1984, PhD, 1988. Vis. asst. prof. U. Wyo., Laramie, 1989-90, asst. prof., 1993-96, assoc. prof. anthropology, 1996—; vis. asst. prof. Mont. State U., Bozeman, 1990-91; asst. prof. Emory U., Atlanta, 1991-93. Author: The Heiltsuks, 1997; assoc. editor Ethnohistory, 1997—; contbr. articles to profl. jours. Fellow Am. Anthrop. Assn.; mem. Am. Soc. for Ethnohistory, Am. Ethnol. Soc., Am. Soc. for Psychol. Anthropology. Democrat. Episcopalian. Office: University of Wyoming Dept Anthropology PO Box 3431 Laramie WY 82071-3431

HARKINS, CRAIG, management consultant; b. Boston, May 1, 1936; s. Edwin Craig and Shirley Nadine (Pike) H.; m. Betty Letitia Hester, June 17, 1961 (div. 1985); children: Daniel, Sean, Lance; m. Donna Marie Hamlin, Sept. 1, 1990; 1 child Angelika. BA, Colby Coll., Waterville, Maine, 1958; MA, NYU, 1959; Profl. Dipl., Columbia U., N.Y.C., 1963; PhD, Rensselaer Poly. Inst., Troy, N.Y., 1978. Computer operator Pacific Mutual, L.A., 1957; reporter Evening Independent, St. Petersburg, Fla., 1960-61; pub. rels. mgr. IBM, N.Y./Calif, 1961-82; mgmt. cons. Hamlin Harkins Ltd., San Jose, 1982—. Co-editor: Guide to Writing Better Technical Papers, 1982; contbr. numerous articles to profl. jours. Sec. Hudson River Sloop Restoration, Poughkeepsie, N.Y., 1972-76; communications/mktg. com. United Way, Santa Clara, Calif., 1981—; mem. mktg. com. San Jose Cleve. Ballet, 1991—. With USMCR, 1961-66. Mem. Internat. Communication Assn., Peninsula Mktg. Assn., Soc. for Tech. Communication (bd. dirs. 1980-81), IEEE Profl. Communications Soc. (sec. 1977-80). Democrat. Roman Catholic. Home: 1301 Mariposa Ave San Jose CA 95126-2624 Office: Hamlin Harkins Ltd 1611 The Alameda San Jose CA 95126-2202

HARKONEN, WESLEY SCOTT, physician; b. Mpls., Dec. 17, 1951; s. Wesley Sulo and Frances (Fedor) H.; m. Barbara Jean Harkonen, Feb. 14, 1986; children: Kirsten, Alan. BA summa cum laude, U. Minn., 1973, MD, 1977. Resident internal medicine U. Minn., Mpls., 1977-81; fellow allergy and immunology U. Calif., San Francisco, 1983-85, fellow clin. pharmacology, 1984-85; project dir. Xoma Corp., Berkeley, Calif., 1983-87; rsch. assoc. Stanford U., 1987-88; assoc. med. dir. Becton Dickinson, Mountain View, Calif., 1988-89; v.p. med. affairs Calif. Biotechnology, Mountain View, Calif., 1989-91; v.p. med. and regulatory affairs Univax Biologics, Rockville, Md., 1991-95; sr. v.p. devel. and ops. Connective Therapeutics, Palo Alto, Calif., 1995—. Author: Traveling Well, 1984; contbr. articles to profl. jours. J. Thomas Livermore Rsch. award, U. Minn., 1977. Mem. Am. Fedn. for Clin. Rsch. Office: Connective Therapeutics 3400 W Bayshore Palo Alto CA 94303

HARLAN, KATHLEEN T. (KAY HARLAN), business consultant, professional speaker and seminar leader; b. Bremerton, Wash., June 9, 1934; d. Floyd K. and Rosemary (Parkhurst) Troy; m. John L. Harlan, Feb. 16, 1952 (div. 1975); children: Pamela Kay, Kenneth Lynwood, Lianna Sue; m. Stuart Friedman, Nov. 10, 1991. Chair Kitsap-North Mason United Way, 1968-70; owner, operator Safeguard N.W. Systems, Tacoma, 1969-79; devel., mgr. Poulsbo (Wash.) Profl. Bldg., 1969-75; pres. Greenapple Graphics, Inc., Tacoma, 1976-79; owner, mgr. Iskrem Hus Restaurant, Poulsbo, 1972-75; pres. Bus. Seminars, Tacoma, 1977-82; owner, mgr. Safeguard Computer Ctr., Tacoma, 1982-91; owner Total Systems Ctr., Tacoma, 1983-88; Mem. Orgnl. Renewal, Inc., Tacoma, 1983-88; assoc. mem. Effectiveness Resource Group, Inc., Tacoma, 1979-80; pres. New Image Confs., Tacoma, 1979-82; spkr. on mgmt. and survival in small bus.; CEO Manage Ability, Inc., profl. mgmt. firm, 1991—; exec. dir. Another Door to Learning, 1996—. Contbg. author: Here is Genius!, 1980; author small bus. manuals. Mem. Wash. State br. Boundary Rev. for Kitsap County, 1970-76, Selective Svc. Bd. 19, 1969-76; co-chair Wash. State Small Bus. Improvement Coun., 1986; del. White House Conf. on Small Bus., 1986; chair Wash. State Conf. on Small Bus., 1987; founder, mem. exec. bd. Am. Leadership Forum, 1988-94; dir. Bus. Leadership Week, Wash. State, 1990-96; chair Pro-Tech Pierce County, 1992-94; chair Allenmore Hosp., 1993-96; founding mem. Multicare Health Found., 1995—. Recipient Nellie Cashman award; named Woman Entrepreneur of Yr. for Wash. State, 1986, 87. Mem. Tacoma-Pierce County C. of C. (lifetime exec. bd. 1985—, chair spl. task force on small bus. for Pierce County 1986-89, treas. 1987-88, chair-elect 1988-90, chair 1990-91).

HARLAN, RAYMOND CARTER, communication executive; b. Shreveport, La., Nov. 13, 1943; s. Ross E. and Margaret (Burns) H.; m. Nancy K. Munson, Sept. 3, 1966 (div. 1978); children: Kathleen Marie, Patrick Raymond; m. Sarah J. Kinzel, Sept. 1, 1979 (div. 1982); m. Linda Frances Gerdes, Mar. 30, 1985; stepchildren: Kimberly Jo Gillis, Kellie Leigh Raffa, Ryan William Gerdes. BA in Speech and Drama cum laude, Southwestern U., 1966; MA in English, U. Tex., 1968; MA in Speech & Theatre Arts, Bradley U., 1976. Commd. 2d lt. USAF, 1968, advanced through grades to maj., 1980, ret., 1988; pres. ComSkills Tng., Aurora, Colo., 1988—; asst. prof. Bradley U., Peoria, Ill., 1972-76; instr., asst. prof., course dir. Air Force Acad., Colorado Springs, 1976-81; asst. prof. Air Force Inst. Tech., Dayton, Ohio, 1987-88; internat. trainer Inst. for Internat. Rsch., London, 1990-92; presenter in field. Author: The Confident Speaker, 1993; co-author: Telemarketing That Works, 1991, Interactive Telemarketing, 1995; contbr. articles and revs. to profl. jours. Decorated Air Force Commendation medal with three oak leaf clusters, Air Force Meritorious Svc. medal with one oak leaf cluster; recipient George Washington Honor Medal Freedom Found., 1983, Leo A. Codd award Am. Def. Preparedness Assn., 1st Prize ann. poetry contest Ariz. State Poetry Soc., 1979. Mem. ASTD, Nat. Writers Assn., Air Force Assn., Ret. Officers Assn., Soc. for Tech. Comm. Lutheran. Office: ComSkills Tng 17544 E Wesley Pl Aurora CO 80013-4174

HARLEY, ROBISON DOOLING, JR., lawyer, educator; b. Ancon, Panama, July 6, 1946; s. Robison Dooling and Loyde Hazel (Goehenauer) H.; m. Suzanne Purviance Bendel, Aug. 9, 1975; children: Arianne Erin, Lauren Loyde. BA, Brown U., 1968; JD, Temple U., 1971; LLM, U. San Diego, 1985. Bar: Pa. 1971, U.S. Ct. Mil. Appeals 1972, Calif. 1976, U.S. Dist. Ct. (cen. and so. dists) Calif. 1976, N.J. 1977, U.S. Dist. Ct. N.J. 1977, U.S. Supreme Ct. 1980, D.C. 1981, U.S. Ct. Appeals (9th cir.) 1982, U.S. Dist. Ct. (ea. dist.) Pa. 1987, U.S. Ct. Appeals (3rd cir.) 1986. Cert. criminal law specialist Calif. Bd. Legal Specialization, 1981, recertified 1986, 91, 96; cert. criminal trial adv. Nat. Bd. Trial Advocacy, 1982, recertified, 1987, 92-97. Asst. agy. dir. Safeco Title Ins. Co., L.A., 1975-77; ptnr. Cohen, Stokke & Davis, Santa Ana, Calif., 1977-85; prin. Harley Law Offices, Santa Ana, Calif., 1985—; adj. prof. Orange County Coll. Trial Advocacy, adj. prof., paralegal program U. Calif., trial adv. programs U.S. Army, USN, USAF, USMC; judge pro-tem Orange County Cts. Author: Orange County Trial Lawyers Drunk Driving Syllabus; contbr. articles to profl. jours. and reports. Bd. dirs. Orange County Legal Aid Soc. Served to lt. col. JAGC, USMCR, 1975-94; trial counsel, def. counsel, mil. judge, asst. staff judge adv. USMC, 1971-75, regional def. counsel Western Region, 1986-90, instr., program coord. Army, Navy, Air Force, Marines, Coast Guard Trial Adv. Programs worldwide. Recipient Commendation medal U.S. Navy, Nat. Defense Svc. medal, Reserve medal, 23 Certs. of Commendation and/or Congratulations. Mem. ABA, ATLA, Orange County Bar Assn. (judiciary com., criminal law sect., adminstrn. of justice com.), Orange County Trial Lawyers Assn., Calif. Trial Lawyers Assn., Calif. Attys. for Criminal Justice, Calif. Pub. Defenders Assn., Nat. Assn. for Criminal Def. Attys., Assn. Specialized Criminal Def. Advs., Orange County Criminal Lawyers Assn. (found. com.), Res. Officers Assn., Marine Corps Reserve Officers Assn., Marine Corps Assn. Republican. Avocations: sports, physical fitness, reading. Home: 12 Bayberry Way Irvine CA 92612-2727 Office: Harley Law Offices 825 N Ross St Santa Ana CA 92701-3419

HARLOW, CHARLES VENDALE, JR., finance educator, consultant; b. Long Beach, Calif., May 18, 1931; s. Charles Vendale and Lucille (Morris) H.; m. Luann Jones, July 6, 1956; children: Jeffrey, Pamela, John. BA, Stanford U., 1953; MBA, U. So. Calif., 1960, DBA, 1968. Ptnr. Harlow & Harlow Investments, Long Beach, 1955-68; pres. Cambistics, Inc., Long Beach, 1968-88; asst. prof. Calif. State U., Long Beach, 1968-71, assoc. prof., 1971-75, prof. fin., 1975-94; prof. fin. Pepperdine U., 1995—; mng. dir. Cambistics Securities Corp., Long Beach, 1990—. Co-author: The Commodity Futures Trading Guide, 1969 (100 Best Books in Bus. award), The Futures Game, 1974, How to Shoot From the Hip Without Getting Shot in the Foot: Making Smart Strategic Choices Every Day, 1990. 1st lt. USMC, 1953-55. NSF grantee, 1968. Republican. Office: Cambistics PO Box 15596 Long Beach CA 90815-0596

HARLOW, STEVEN MICHAEL, banker; b. Houston, Sept. 15, 1963; s. Harvey Lee Harlow and Dorothy Jean Boulton; m. Angelia D. Wesch, Oct. 9, 1993. BBA, U. Tex., 1986. CPA, Tex. Credit analyst Bank One Tex. N.A., Houston, 1986-87, credit analyst supr., 1987, comml. loan rep., 1987-88, comml. loan officer, 1988-89, asst. v.p., 1989-91, v.p., 1991-92; v.p. Seafirst Bank, Tacoma, Wash., 1992—; youth job program advisor Seafirst Bank, 1994-96. Vol. income tax asst. IRS, various locations, 1988-89; recruiting chmn. Multiple Sclerosis Club, 1989-90; pres. jr. bd. Am. Cancer Soc., 1989-90, bd. dirs., treas. Houston unit, 1989-92; bd. dirs. S.W. Alternate Media Project, 1990-91; mem. Tacoma-Pierce County C. of C. (leadership program 1995); mem. Met. Park Dist. of Tacoma Bus. Adv. Coun., 1996—. Mem. AICPA, Tex. Soc. CPAs (bd. dirs. Houston chpt. 1992, chmn. young CPA com. Houston chpt. 1991-92), Wash. Soc. CPAs (pres. Tacoma chpt. 1996—), U. Tex. Ex-Students Assn., Forum Club (Houston), Houston Sierra Club (bd. dirs., vice chmn., 1990-91, outings leaders 1989-93), Rotary Internat. (G.S.E. team to the Netherlands 1992), Tacoma Country and Golf Club. Home: 4102 N 38th St Tacoma WA 98407-5619 Office: Seafirst Bank PO Box 1493 820 A St Ste 350 Tacoma WA 98401

HARMAN, JANE FRANK, congresswoman, lawyer; b. N.Y.C., June 28, 1945; d. A. N. and Lucille (Geier) Lakes; m. Sidney Harman, Aug. 30, 1980; children: Brian Lakes, Hilary Lakes, Daniel Geier, Justine Leigh. BA, Smith Coll., 1966; JD, Harvard U., 1969. Bar: D.C. 1969, U.S. Ct. Appeals (D.C. cir.) 1972, U.S. Supreme Ct. 1975. Spl. asst. Commn. of Chs. on Internat. Affairs, Geneva, Switzerland, 1969-70; assoc. Surrey & Morse, Washington, 1970-72; chief legis. asst. Senator John V. Tunney, Washington, 1972-73; chief counsel, staff dir. Subcom. on Rep. Citizen Interests, Com. on Judiciary, Washington, 1973-75; adj. prof. Georgetown Law Ctr., Washington, 1974-75; chief counsel, staff dir. Subcom. on Constl. Rights, Com. on Judiciary, Washington, 1975-77; dep. sec. to cabinet The White House, Washington, 1977-78; spl. counsel Dept. Def., Washington, 1979; ptnr. Manatt, Phelps, Rothenberg & Tunney, Washington, 1979-82, Surrey & Morse, Washington, 1982-86; of counsel Jones, Day, Reavis & Pogue, Washington, 1987-92; mem. 103rd Congress from 36th Calif. dist., 1992—; mem. vis. coms. Harvard Law Sch., 1976-82, Kennedy Sch. Govt., 1990—. Counsel Dem. Platform Com., Washington, 1984; vice-chmn. Ctr. for Nat. Policy, Washington, 1981-90; chmn. Dem. Nat. Com. Nat. Lawyers' Coun., Washington, 1986-90. Mem. Phi Beta Kappa. Democrat. Office: US House Reps 325 Cannon House Office Bldg Washington DC 20515-0536 Office: 5200 W Century Blvd Ste 960 Los Angeles CA 90045-5900 also: 3031 Torrance Blvd Torrance CA 90503-5015*

HARMAN, WALLACE PATRICK, lawyer; b. El Paso, Tex., Jan. 22, 1949; s. Wallace Irvin and Dorothy Louise (Pearson) H.; m. Gina Marie Ries, Dec. 31, 1988; children: Loren Patrick, Claire Marie. BA, Stanford U., 1972; JD, U. Calif., 1977. Bar: Calif. 1977, U.S. Ct. Appeals (9th cir.) 1977, N.Mex. 1978, U.S. Dist. Ct. N.Mex. 1978, U.S. Ct. Appeals (10th cir.) 1978. Zone adminstrn. mgr. Am. Motors Corp., Burlingame, Calif., 1972-74; atty., shareholder Sutin, Thayer & Browne, APC, Albuquerque, N.Mex., 1977-87, group leader comml. group, 1985-87; atty., shareholder, mng. atty. bus. group The Payne Law Firm, P.C., Albuquerque, 1987-91; atty., ptnr. Hisey & Wainwright, P.A., Albuquerque, 1991-92; atty., pres., chief exec. officer The Harman Law Firm, P.C., Albuquerque, 1992—; mem. N.Mex. Supreme Ct. Med.-Legal Panel, Albuquerque, 1978-80, 91—; mem. N.Mex. Supreme Ct. Lawyers Assistance Com., Albuquerque, 1991—; area rep. The Taft Sch., Watertown, Conn., 1992—; mem. mentorship program Hatings Coll. Law. Co-author: Recent Developments in Commerical Law, University of New Mexico Law Review, 1989. Bd. advisors Lovelace Med. Ctr., Albuquerque, 1980-89; mem. state bd. trustees The Nature Conservancy, N.Mex., 1984-88; adv. bd. Assistance League Albuquerque, 1982-89, Jr. League Albuquerque, 1984-87, Make-a-Wish Found. of N.Mex., Inc., 1996-97. Recipient AV Rating award Martindale-Hubbell, 1990. Mem. ABA, Albuquerque Bar Assn. Democrat. Office: The Harman Law Firm PC Ste 100 4501 Indian School Rd NE Albuquerque NM 87110-3929

HARMEL, HILDA HERTA See PIERCE, HILDA

HARMON, CLIFF F., artist; b. L.A., June 26, 1923; s. Artemas Henry and Helen Leone (Lindsey) H.; m. Barbara Sayre; 1 child, Jonathan Henry. Student, Bisstram Sch. Fine Arts, Taos Valley Art Sch., Black Mountain Coll. Wood tool pattern maker Douglas Aircraft Co., Santa Monica, Calif., 1954-59; wood model builder Electronic Splty. Co., L.A., 1959-61; owner art gallery Taos, N.Mex., 1962—. One-man shows include N.Mex. Mus. Fine Art, Santa Fe, 1952, Stables Art Gallery, Taos, 1965-69, 71, 73, 75, 77, 79, 96, Total Arts Gallery, Taos, 1978, 96, Suzanne Brown Gallery, Ariz., 1985, New Directions Gallery, Taos, 1989; exhibited in group shows at Dallas Mus. Fine Arts, 1949, Mus. N.Mex. Art Gallery, Santa Fe, 1952, Arts & Humanities Coun. Invitational Travelling Exhibit, 1971, Cunningham Meml. Art Gallery, Bakersfield, Calif., 1971, Phoenix Art Mus., N.Mex. Mus. Fine Arts, Rotunda Gallery, London, 1973, Okla. Art Ctr., Oklahoma City, 1974, Colo. Women's Coll., Denver, 1975, 17th Ann. Eight State Exhbn., Okla., 1975, Munson Gallery, Santa Fe, 1978, Fall Festival of Arts, Taos, 1984-96, Taos Invites Taos, El Cielo Grande de Taos, 1986-89, Harwood Mus., Taos, 1987, 91, Taos Art Assn., 1991, 93, 94, 95, 96 (1st pl., Blue Ribbon 1994); represented in various permanent pub. collections. With USCG, 1942-46, PTO. Recipient 1st, 2d and 3d prizes Glendale Art Assn., 1960, 1st premium N.Mex. State Fair Art Exhbn., 1968, 3d prize 1st Biennial Five State Art Exhibit, 1971. Mem. Taos Art Assn. (artist mem., pres.). Home and Office: Torreon Gallery PO Box 6584 234 Las Cruces Rd Taos NM 87571

HARMON, WARREN WAYNE, geography educator; b. Colton, Calif., Feb. 13, 1936; s. Renick Elkin and Henrietta Frances (Stüwich) H.; m Margaret Ann Schonberger, Nov. 21, 1959; children: Andrea Jane, Fritz Warren. AA, San Bernardino Valley Coll., 1958; BA, San Diego State Coll., 1961, MA, 1964. Geography instr. Mesa Coll., San Diego, 1966; geography instr. Grossmont Coll., El Cajon, Calif., 1967-84, div. coord., 1984, prof. geography, dept. chmn. of earth scis., 1984-89, dean humanities & social scis., 1989-90, dean math., phys. and behavioral scis. div., 1990-92, prof. geography, 1992—; geog. cons. UCLA, 1986-88. Author: Geography of

California, 1976; co-author Geographic Perspectives on American Westward Expansion, 1986; contbr. articles to profl. jours. Co-founder So. Calif. Tourette Syndrome Assn., Mission Viejo, Calif, 1974; chief Indian Guides, La Jolla, Calif., 1978. Named Outstanding Educator of Am., Fuller and Dees, 1974, Disting. Chair of Sci. Grossmont Coll., 1988-89. Mem. Nat. Coun. for Geog. Edn., Calif Geography Soc. (exec. bd. mem. 1978), Calif. Geog. Alliance (charter mem.), Fulbright Alumni Assn. (Fulbright scholar 1970-71), Nature Conservancy, Audubon Soc., La Jolla Play Readers Club, Gamma Theta Upsilon. Democrat. Methodist. Office: Grossmont Coll 8800 Grossmont College Dr El Cajon CA 92020-1765

HARNEY, FRANCIS PAUL, mechanical engineer, consultant; b. Rochester, N.Y., July 18, 1960; s. James Joseph and Regina Dolores H. BSME, U. Rochester, 1983; M Engring. in Engring. Mgmt., U. Colo., Boulder, 1995. Registered profl. engr., Colo. Media devel. engr. Storage Tech., Inc., Louisville, Colo., 1986-90, staff engr. libr. devel., 1990-93, staff engr. libr. enhancements, 1993-94, staff engr. mechanical integrity, 1994-96; sr. devel. engr. OEM Disk Dr. Sourcing, Louisville, Colo., 1996—; cons. in field Boulder, Colo., 1991—. Mem. ASME, Nat. Eagle Scout Assn. Home: 535 W Hackberry St Louisville CO 80027 Office: Storage Tech Inc 2270 S 88th St # 2140 Louisville CO 80028-2140

HARNSBERGER, THERESE COSCARELLI, librarian; b. Muskegon, Mich.; d. Charles and Julia (Borrell) Coscarelli; B.A. cum laude, Marymount Coll., 1952; M.L.S., U. So. Calif., 1953; postgrad. Rosary Coll., River Forest, Ill., 1955-56, U. Calif., Los Angeles Extension, 1960-61; m. Frederick Owen Harnsberger, Dec. 24, 1962; 1 son, Lindsey Carleton. Free-lance writer, 1950—; librarian San Marino (Calif.) High Sch., 1953-56; cataloger, cons. San Marino Hall, South Pasadena, Calif., 1956-61; librarian Los Angeles State Coll., 1956-59; librarian dist. library Covina-Valley Unified Sch. Dist., Covina, Calif., 1959-67; librarian Los Angeles Trade Tech. Coll., 1972—, mem. acad. senate, 1996—; med. librarian, tumor registrar Alhambra (Calif.) Community Hosp., 1975-79; tumor registrar Huntington Meml. Hosp., 1979—; pres., dir. Research Unltd., 1980—; free lance reporter Los Angeles' Best Bargains, 1981—; med. library cons., 1979—; reviewer various cookbooks, 1991—. Author numerous poems. Chmn. spiritual values com. Covina Coordinating Council, 1964-66; chmn. Neighborhood Watch, 1976—. Winner poetry contest Pasadena Star News, 1993. Mem. ALA, Internat. Women's Writing Guild, Calif. Assn. Sch. Librarians (chmn. legis. com.), Acad.Com. Partimers Rep., 1996 Covina Tchrs. Assn., AAUW (historian 1972-73), U. So. Calif. Grad. Sch. Libr. Sci. (life), Am. Nutrition Soc. (chpt. Newsletter chmn.), Nat. Tumor Registrars Assn., So. Calif. Tumor Registrars Assn., Med. Libr. Assn., So. Calif. Libr. Assn., So. Calif. Assn. Law Libr., Book Publicists So. Calif., Am. Fedn. Tchrs. (exec. bd. part-timers 1994, alt. exec. bd. local # 1521 coll. guild 1994—, acad. senate part-timers rep. 1996—), Coll. Guild, Calif. Libr. Assn., Assn. Poetry Bibliographers, Faculty Assn. Calif. Community Colls., Immaculate Heart Coll. Alumnae Assn., Assistance League Pasadena, Loyola Marymount Alumnae Assn. (coord. 1986), Pi Lambda Theta. Author: (poetry) The Journal, 1982, To Julia: in Memoriam; author: (words to choral music by Lindsay C. Harnsberger) Haiku Poem for Vanigals, 1996; contbr. articles to profl. jours., poems to newspapers. Office: 2809 W Hellman Ave Alhambra CA 91803-2737

HARO, ROBERTO PEDRO, university official, education educator; b. Sacramento, Sept. 9, 1936; s. Tereso Nunez and Catalina (Herreros) H.; m. Pauline J. Kessemeier, June 10, 1961 (div. Aug. 1972); children: Richard, Robert. BA, U. Calif., Berkeley, 1958, MA, 1959, MLIS, 1962; EdD, U. San Francisco, 1979. Librarian Calif. State U., Hayward, 1962-63; adminstrv. intern Columbia U., N.Y.C., 1963-65; head librarian InterGovtl. Affairs Library, U. Calif., Davis, 1965-69; dir. rsch. President's Cabinet Com. on Spanish-Speaking, Washington, 1969-71; assoc. dir. libraries U. So. Calif., L.A., 1972-75; assoc. dir. profl. devel. program U. Calif., Berkeley, 1976-79, mgmt. fellow Chancellor's Office, 1980-81, asst. vice chancellor, 1982-87, asst. chancellor, 1988-90, also sr. lectr., 1982; prof., dir. Monterey County campus San Jose State U., 1990-95; vis. prof. San Francisco State U., 1995—; rsch. cons. Border States Consortium, San Diego, 1978-79, Calif. Spanish Lang. Data, Hayward, 1981-84; prin. investigator Hispanic Info. Exchange, Oakland, Calif., 1984-86; vice chmn. adv. com. Coll. Bd., N.Y.C., 1986-89. Author: Latin Americana Resources, 1971, Developing Library and Information Services, 1981; contbr. articles to profl. jours. Chmn. New Oakland Commumity Ednl. Task Force, 1984-89. Sgt. U.S. Army, 1959-61. Am. Coun. on Edn. fellow, 1987, Inst. for Ednl. Mgmt. fellow, 1988. Mem. Am. Assn. Higher Edn., Nat. Assn. Student Personnel Adminstrs., Leadership San Francisco. Roman Catholic. Home: 3398 Balboa St Apt 6 San Francisco CA 94121-2770 Office: San Francisco State U Cesar E Chavez Inst 608 Font Blvd San Francisco CA 94132

HAROLD, FRANKLIN MARCEL, research scientist; b. Frankfurt Germany, Mar. 16, 1929; came to U.S., 1947; s. Walter Morton and Hermine (Reiss) H.; m. Ruth Laura Catsiff, Feb. 7, 1954; 1 dau., Lynn Stephanie. BS, CCNY, 1952; PhD, U. Calif.-Berkeley, 1955; D in Natural Scis. (hon.), U. Osnabrück, 1984. Various positions Nat. Jewish Ctr. for Immunology and Respiratory Medicine, Denver, 1959—, U. Colo. Med. Sch., Denver, 1963—; rsch. prof. Colo. State U., Ft. Collins, 1989-96, prof. emeritus, 1996—; vis. fellow Australian Nat. U., Canberra, 1975. Author: The Vital Force-A Study of Bioenergetics, 1986. Served with U.S. Army, 1955-57. Fulbright fellow, Teheran, 1969-70. Mem. Am. Soc. Biol. Chemists, Am. Soc. Microbiology. Home: 908 Edwards St Fort Collins CO 80524-3824 Office: Colorado State U Dept Biochemistry Fort Collins CO 80523-0001

HAROLD, RUTH LAURA, research biologist; b. N.Y.C., July 16, 1931; d. Oscar and Mae (Remstein) Catsiff; m. Franklin M. Harold, Feb. 7, 1954; 1 child, Stephanie L. BA, U. Ariz., 1952; MA, U. Calif., Berkeley, 1954. Various tech. rsch. positions U. Calif., Berkeley, 1954-56, Calif. Inst. Tech., Pasadena, 1957-59, U. Colo., Denver, 1959-61; rsch. biologist Nat. Jewish Hosp. and Rsch. Ctr., Denver, 1961-72, rsch. assoc., 1978-89; rsch. assoc. Colo. State U., Ft. Collins, 1989-95, ret., faculty affiliate; hon. mem. staff dept. molecular and cell biology U. Aberdeen, U.K., 1995. Editor Newsletter of the Zoosporic Fungi, Ft. Collins, 1992-96; artist watercolor paintings, India ink wash drawings, bot. illustrations, 1988—; scientist-author 20 scholarly rsch. articles in peer-reviewed jours., 1956-96. Precinct com. chair Dem. Party, Denver, 1972-74; del. Dem. State Conv., Denver, 1972, 74; mem., com. chair LWV, Denver, 1966-68. Mem. Am. Soc. Microbiology, Am. Mycological Soc., Am. Soc. Bot. Artists. Office: Colo State U Dept Biochem & Molec Biol Fort Collins CO 80523

HAROUN, ANSAR M., forensic psychiatrist; b. Pakistan, Nov. 29, 1947; m. Nasra Haroun, 1977. Student, U. London; MD, King Edward Med. Coll., 1975; M in Med. Sci. in Cmty. Medicine, U. Nottingham, Eng., 1979. Diplomate Am. Bd. Psychiatry and Neurology. Fellow in cmty. medicine U. Nottingham Med. Sch., 1976-79; med. intern, resident physician in psychiatry Yale U. Sch. Medicine, 1980-84; fellow in psychiat. pub. health Yale U. Sch. Pub. Health, 1984-85; fellow in pediatric psychiatry Columbia U. Coll. Physicians and Surgeons, N.Y.C., 1985-87; forensic psychiatrist Superior Ct. Calif., San Diego, 1987—; assoc. clin. prof. psychiatry and pediats. U. Calif. Sch. Medicine, San Diego; adj. prof. Sch. Law U. San Diego. Author: Insomnia and Depression in General Practice, 1979, Clinical Guidelines for Involuntary Outpatient Treatment, 1990. Lt. col. M.C., USAR, 1984—. Recipient Ciba award Royal Soc. Medicine; Royal, Religious and Ancient Found. of Christ's Hosp. scholar, Roosevelt scholar. Fellow Royal Soc. Health, Am. Coll. Forensic Psychiatry; mem. Am. Acad. Psychiatry and Law, Am. Psychiat. Assn., Am. Soc. Law and Medicine. Office: Superior Ct of Calif Forensic Psychiatry Clinic County Courthouse Rm 1003 San Diego CA 92101-3814

HARPER, ANTHONY, counselor, singer; b. Clarksville, Tenn., Jan. 6, 1952; s. Hal L. and Kathryn A. (Reding) H.; m. Mary K. McGrane, July 1972 (div. Nov. 1974); 1 child, Amy; m. Mary J. Breshears, Aug., 1980. BA, USNY, 1984; MEd, Coll. Idaho, 1986; postgrad., Liberty U., Calif. Coast U., 1989—; PhD, Calif. Coast U., 1996. Tv switcher engr. KISU TV, Pocatello, Idaho, 1977-78, KIFI TV, Idaho Falls, Idaho, 1979; singer various locations, 1978—; founder, exec. dir., counselor Shiloh Counseling Ctr., Boise, Idaho, 1987—; guest spkr. in field. Author: (test and manual) Spiritual Relationship Scale, 1990. Republican. Office: PO Box 1829 Boise ID 83701-1829

HARPER, DONALD CALVIN, dean; b. Claresholm, Alta., Can., Oct. 31, 1942; s. William James and Effie Mabel (Slonaker) H.; m. Kathleen Ann Paton, May 18, 1968; children: Christopher Bradley, Angela Dawn. BA, U. Alta., Edmonton, 1963, MA, 1970. Rsch. asst. coun. Province of Alta., 1966-67, rsch. asst. dept. of youth, 1967-69; instr. sociology Grande Prairie Regional Coll., Alta., 1969-71, registrar, 1971-74, registrar, dir. student svcs., 1974-79, dir. student and community svcs., 1979-80, instr. humanities and social scis., 1980-81, chairperson acad. devel., 1981-84, dean acad. and applied studies, 1984-93; project coord. Aboriginal Head Start, Grande Prairie Friendship Ctr., 1996—; instl. mediator/family and divorce, 1995—; mem. task force Worth Royal Com. Ednl. Planning, 1970-71; mem. Alta Coun. Admissions & Transfer, 1974-77, 79-82, 89-92; chairperson com. Sr. Acad. Officers, Alta, 1990-92. Pres. Grande Prairie Little Theatre, 1978-80, 94-95, Crohn's and Colitis Found. of Can., G.P. chpt.; bd. dirs. Prairie Gallery, 1980-81, 84-86, other community bds.; regional dir. Alta. Fedn. Home and Sch. Assns., 1990-92; mem. Can. Program adv. com. Assn. Can. C.C., 1991-93. Home: 8517 100A St, Grande Prairie, AB Canada T8V 3C4

HARPER, GLORIA JANET, artist, educator; children: Dan Conyers, Jan Girvan. Student, Famous Artists Sch., 1967-69, 69-71; BA in Comml. Art, Portland C.c., 1981; postgrad., Valley View Art Sch., 1982-89, Carrizzo Art Sch., 1983-89, Holdens Portrait Sch., 1989; studied with Daniel Greene, 1989, postgrad. in paralegal studies. Cert. art educator. Artist, art instr. Art By Gloria, 1980—; owner Art By Gloria Art Sch. and Gallery, Pendleton, Oreg., 1991—; lectr., workshop presenter in field, 1980—. Paintings and prints included in various mags. Mem. NAFE, Nat. Assn. Fine Artists, Water Color Soc. Am., Nat. Mus. Women in Arts, So. Career Inst. Profl. Legal Assts. (area rep.), Profl. Legal Assts., Pendleton C. of C. Home: PO Box 1734 Pendleton OR 97801-0570 Office: Art By Gloria 404 SE Dorion Ave Ste 204 Pendleton OR 97801-2531

HARPER, RICHARD HENRY, film producer, director; b. San Jose, Calif., Sept. 15, 1950; s. Walter Henry and Priscilla Alden (Browne) H.; m. Ann Marie Morgan, June 19, 1976; children: Christine Ann, Paul Richard, James Richard. Show designer Walt Disney Imagineering, Glendale, Calif., 1971-76; motion picture producer, dir. Harper Films, Inc., La Canada, Calif., 1976—. Producer, dir. (films) Impressions de France, Disney World, Fla., 1982, Magic Carpet Round the World, Disneyland, Tokyo, 1983, American Journeys, Disneyland, Calif., 1985, Collecting America, Nat. Gallery Art, Washington, 1988, Hillwood Mus., Washington, 1989, Journey Into the 4th Dimension for Sanrio World, Journey Into Nature for Sanrio World, Japan, 1990, Masters of Illusion, Nat. Gallery of Art, Washington, 1992. Recipient more than 150 awards world-wide for outstanding motion picture prodn. including Silver trophy Cannes Internat. Film Festival, 2 Gold awards Internat. Festival of the Ams., 1981, 82, 14 Golden Eagle C.I.N.E. awards, 1977-92, Emmy award Nat. Acad. TV Arts and Scis., 1993. Mem. Acad. of Motion Picture Arts and Scis.

HARPER, ROB MARCH, artist, educator; b. Chico, Calif., Oct. 5, 1942; s. Robert Wreathal and Lorene Marie (March) H.; m. Georgia Lee Schiller, May 31, 1971. BFA, San Francisco Art Inst., 1971; MFA, Washington U., St. Louis, 1974. Artist/illustrator Oakland, Calif., 1974-88; tchr. adult edn. Alameda County Pub. Schs., Oakland, Hayward, 1988—; tchr./artist Oakland Parks and Recreation dept., 1988—. One person show at Lucien Labaudt Art Gallery, San Francisco, 1974; exhibited in shows including Nelson Gallery Art, Kansas City, Mo., 1974, St. Louis Art Mus., 1974, Butler Inst. Am. Art, Youngstown, Ohio, 1975, Cooperstown (N.Y.) Art Assn., 1975, 77, E.B. Crocker Art Gallery, Sacramento, Calif., 1976, Civic Arts Gallery, Walnut Creek, Calif., 1976, Marrietta (Ohio) Coll., 1976, Chautauqua (N.Y.) Art Assn., 1977, Miniature Painters, Sculptors and Gravers Soc. Washington, Arts Club of Washington, 1977, 79, Nat. Soc. Painters in Casein and Acrylic, Inc., The Am. Acad. and Inst. Arts and Letters, N.Y.C., 1979, Lynn House Gallery, Antioch, Calif., 1994, Chico (Calif.) Art Ctr., 1994, Sarratt Gallery, Vanderbilt U., Nashville, 1996, Maude Kerns Art Ctr., Eugene, Oreg., 1996, Spartanburg (S.C.) County Mus. Art, 1996; represented in permanent collection. O.K. Harris Gallery, N.Y.C. Recipient Hallmark award-purchase, 1973-74, Butler Inst. Am. Art purchase prize, 1975. Home: 3099 California St Oakland CA 94602

HARPER, ROBERT, actor; b. N.Y.C., May 19, 1951. BA in English with high distinction, Rutgers Coll., 1974. Mem. repertory co. Arena Stage, Washington, 1974-76; actor, 1974—; guest artist Rutgers U., New Brunswick, N.J., 1977, 84. Actor Long Wharf Theater, New Haven, Conn., 1978, 84, Theater for New City, N.Y.C., 1981, (Broadway) Once in a Lifetime, 1978, The Inspector General, 1978, (featured actor Broadway) The American Clock, 1980, (TV films) J. Edgar Hoover, The Wrong Man, Not Quite Human, Payoff, Running Mates, The Story of Bill W, Paper Angels, Ruby Ridge, (guest actor TV series) Newhart, Roseanne, Murphy Brown, Wiseguy, L.A. Law, (featured actor TV series) Frank's Place, 1987-88, (films) Creepshow, 1982, Once Upon a Time in America, 1984, Twins, 1991, Final Analysis, 1992. Advisor charity events The Laugh Factory, Hollywood, 1981—. Recipient Regents fellowship U. Calif., 1974, Kennedy Ctr. award Am. Coll. Theater Festival, 1974. Mem. MLA, ACLU (sponsor Garden Event 1994), Acad. Motion Picture Arts and Scis., Acad. TV Arts and Scis., Am. Soc. Aesthetics, Screen Actor's Guild, Actor's Equity Assn. Office: Ste 151 8721 Santa Monica Blvd West Hollywood CA 90069

HARPER, ROBERT LEVELL, pharmaceutical company executive; b. Wichita, Kans., Nov. 11, 1942; s. Cleo Levell and Mary Florence (Weaver) H.; m. Margaret Lucille Madden, Jan. 20, 1961 (div. 1980); children: Douglas Warren, Susan Denise; m. Maria Elain Davis, June 20, 1981; stepchildren: Laura Elaine Emery, Melissa MacAlpin Emery. Cert. med. rep., Sterling Mgmt. Inst. Sales rep. Dorsey Labs. div. Sandoz Pharms., Tulsa, 1967-70; mgr. key accounts Sandoz Pharms., Houston, 1970-72; div. mgr. Dorsey Pharms. div. Sandoz Pharms., Kansas City, Mo., 1972-85; mgr. govt. affairs Sandoz Pharms., Sacramento, 1985—; rotating mgr. Sandoz Pharms., East Hanover, N.J., 1985. Donor Kansas City Coll. Osteo. Medicine, 1973; co-founder first aid program state CAP, Oklahoma City, 1973; leader youth program YMCA, Johnson County, Mo., 1977-79; leader youth baseball Johnson County, 1976-79; del. Nat. Baseball Congress, Houston, 1971, 72, 73; mem. med. edn. for srs. SRx Regional Program, 1985—. With USAFR, 1960-64. Recipient appreciation award Calif. State Firemen's Assn., Sacramento, 1987. Mem. Nat. Assn. Legis. Svcs., Calif. Medication Edn. Coalition, Calif. Mfrs. Assn., Pharm. Mfrs. Assn., Calif. Derby. Home: 11370 Tunnel Hill Way Gold River CA 95670-7240

HARRELL, GARY PAUL, lawyer; b. Texas City, Tex., July 8, 1952; s. James Eugene Jr. and Mary Alice (Worley) H.; m. Leigh Evans, May 27, 1978. BS, U. Tex., 1977, MA, 1979; cert. mgmt. healthcare facilities, UCLA, 1984; JD cum laude, Lewis & Clark Coll., 1991. Bar: Oreg. 1991, U.S. Dist. Ct. (fed. dist.) Oreg. 1991; diplomate Am. Coll. Healthcare Execs. Staff/charge nurse Healthcare Facilties, Austin, Tex., 1972-78; gen. mgr. Nursing Support Svcs., Austin, 1978-80; dir. edn. Downey (Calif.) Cmty. Hosp., 1980-84; v.p. patient care Grande Ronde Hosp., La Grande, Oreg., 1984-88; assoc. Lane Powell Spears Lubersky, Portland, Oreg., 1990-94; ptnr. Harrell & Nester, LLP, Portland, 1994—; adj. prof., asst. prof. Calif. State U., Long Beach, 1980-84; pres. Oreg. State Bd. Nursing, Portland, 1987-90. With USNR, 1970-74. Recipient Am. Jurisprudence award, 1989. Fellow Healthcare Fin. Mgmt. Assn. (treas. Oreg. chpt.); mem. Oreg. Assn. Nurse Attys. (treas., past. pres.), Am. Coll. Health Care Adminstrs. (pres. Oreg. chpt.). Office: Harrell & Nester LLP 1515 SW 5th Ave Ste 510 Portland OR 97201-5450

HARRICK, JIM, university athletic coach. Head coach NCAA Divsn. 1A basketball, ranked #4 UCLA Bruins, 1992, head coach NCAA Divsn. 1A basketball champions, 1995-96; head coach basketball U. R.I., Kingston, 1996. Office: U RI 3 Keaney Rd Ste 1 Kingston RI 02881-0810*

HARRIE, DANIEL ANDREW, newspaper reporter; b. Salt Lake City, May 1, 1955; s. Delmar P. and Lenore (Gregerson) H.; m. Billie D. Hunsaker, June 28, 1980; children: Sam, Andrew, Ryan. BA in Comm., U. Utah, 1985. Staff writer UPI, Salt Lake City, 1985-90; staff writer/polit. The Salt Lake Tribune, 1990—. Recipient William H. Cowles III Meml. award AP, 1996. Mem. Soc. Profl. Journalists (state chpt. pres. 1995, state bd. dirs. 1986—, 1st place winner in investigative reporting 1996, 1st place in deadline reporting 1996). Office: The Salt Lake Tribune 143 S Main St Salt Lake City UT 84111

HARRIGAN, NICHOLAS PAUL, military officer; b. Santa Monica, Calif., Aug. 27, 1969; s. Michael John and Kathleen Karyl (Krock) H. BSME, Carnegie Mellon U., 1991. Commd. USN, advanced through grades to lt., 1991-97; instr. Carnegie Mellon U. Naval ROTC, Pitts., 1991; student NFO CTW-6, Pensacola, Fla., 1991-93; radar intercept officer VF-2 USN, San Diego, Calif., 1993-96, Va. Beach, 1996—.

HARRIMAN, JOHN HOWLAND, lawyer; b. Buffalo, Apr. 14, 1920; s. Lewis Gildersleeve and Grace (Bastine) H.; m. Barbara Ann Brunmark, June 12, 1943; children—Walter Brunmark, Constance Bastine, John Howland. A.B. summa cum laude, Dartmouth, 1942; J.D., Stanford U., 1949. Bar: Calif. 1949. Assoc. firm Lawler, Felix & Hall, Los Angeles, 1949-55; asst. v.p., then v.p. Security Pacific Nat. Bank, Los Angeles, 1955-72; sr. v.p. Security Pacific Nat. Bank, 1972-85; of counsel Argue Freston Pearson Harbison & Myers, 1985-86; sec. Security Pacific Corp., 1971-85; dir. Master Metal Works. Mem. L.A. adv. coun. Episcopal Ch. Found., 1977-79; mem. Republican Assocs., 1951—, trustee, 1962-72; mem. Calif. Rep. Central Com., 1956-69, 81—, exec. com., 1960-62, 81-84; mem. L.A. County Rep. Central Com., 1958-70, exec. com., 1960-62, vice chmn., 1962; chmn. Calif. 15th Congl. Dist. Rep. Central Com., 1960-62, Calif. 30th Congl. Dist. Rep. Central Com., 1962; treas. United Rep. Fin. Com. L.A. County, 1969-70; chmn. L.A. County Reagan-Bush campaign, 1980, co-chmn., 1984; exec. dir. Calif. Rep. Party, 1985-86. With USAAF, 1943-46. Mem. Am. Bar Assn., Am. Soc. Corp. Secs. (pres. Los Angeles region 1970-71), State Bar Calif., Los Angeles Bar Assn., Town Hall Los Angeles, Phi Beta Kappa, Theta Delta Chi, Phi Alpha Delta. Clubs: Beach (Santa Monica, Calif.); California (Los Angeles); Lincoln, Breakfast Panel (pres. 1970-71).

HARRINGTON, CHARLES LEE, retired judge; b. Berkeley, Calif., Feb. 5, 1932; s. Harris Clifford and Thelma Aileen (Lee) H.; m. Febe Forster, Dec. 29, 1956; children: Kathleen Harrington Guerra, Aileen Harrington Parsons, Jane Harrington Erdiakoff, Charles Lee II. BSBA, U. Calif., Berkeley, 1953; JD, U. Calif., San Francisco, 1963. Bar: N.Mex., Calif. Pvt. practice Albuquerque and Roswell, N.Mex., 1964-68; dep. county counsel Alameda County Counsel's Office, Oakland, Calif., 1969-86; ct. commr./judge pro tem Alameda County Superior Ct., Oakland, 1986-94; mem. bioethics com. Alameda-Contra Costa Med. Assn., Oakland; panelist on continuing edn. of the Bar, Berkeley, calif., 1972-80; panelist The Rutter Group, Encino, Calif., 1989. Bd. dirs., pres. Moraga (Calif.) Hist. Soc., 1975-78; bd. dirs. Big C Soc., Berkeley, 1979-83; bd. dirs., v.p., sec. Friends of Cal Crew, Berkeley, Calif., 1987—; bd. dirs. Oakland (Calif.) Strokes, 1975-83. 1st lt. USAF, 1954-58; lt. col. USAF Res., retired 1984. Decorated 2 Air Force Commendation medals. Mem. Friends of Cal Crew (bd. dirs., sec. 1987—), Moraga Hist. Soc. (pres. 1975—), Alameda County Bar Assn., State Bar of N.Mex., Calif. State Bar. Republican. Home: 105 La Quinta Moraga CA 94556-1024 Office: PO Box 185 Moraga CA 94556-0185

HARRINGTON, MARY EVELINA PAULSON (POLLY HARRINGTON), religious journalist, writer, educator; b. Chgo.; d. Henry Thomas and Evelina (Belden) Paulson; m. Gordon Keith Harrington, Sept. 7, 1957; children: Jonathan Henry, Charles Scranton. BA, Oberlin Coll., 1946; postgrad., Northwestern U., Evanston, Ill., Chgo., 1946-49, Weber State U., Ogden, Utah, 1970s, 80s; MA, U. Chgo.-Chgo. Theol. Sem., 1956. Publicist Nat. Coun. Chs., N.Y.C., 1950-51; mem. press staff 2d assembly World Coun. Chs., Evanston, Chgo., 1954; mgr. Midwest Office Communication, United Ch. of Christ, Chgo., 1955-59; staff writer United Ch. Herald, N.Y.C., St. Louis, 1959-61; affiliate missionary to Asia, United Ch. Bd. for World Ministries, N.Y.C., 1978-79; freelance writer and lectr., 1961—; corr. Religious News Svc., 1962—; prin. lectr. Women & Family Life in Asia series to numerous librs., Utah, 1981, 81-82; pub. rels. coord. Utah Energy Conservation/Energy Mgmt. Program, 1984-85; tchr. writing Ogden Community Schs., 1985-89; adj. instr. writing for publs. Weber State U., 1986—; instr. Acad. Lifelong Learning, Ogden, 1992—, Eccles Community Art Ctr., Ogden, 1993—; dir. communication Shared Ministry, Salt Lake City, 1983—; chmn. communication Intermountain Conf., Rocky Mountain Conf., Utah Assn. United Ch. of Christ, 1970-78, 82—, Ind. Coun. Chs., 1960-63; chmn. communication Ch. Women United Utah, 1974-78, Ogden rep., 1980—. Editor: Sunshine and Moonscapes: An Anthology of Essays, Poems, Short Stories, 1994, (booklet) Family Counseling Service: Thirty Years of Service to Northern Utah, 1996; contbr. numerous articles and essays to religious and other publs. Pres. T.O. Smith Sch. PTA, 1976-78, Ogden City Coun. PTA, 1983-85; assoc. dir. Region II, Utah PTA, Salt Lake City, 1981-83, mem. State Edn. Commn., 1982-87; chmn. state internat. hospitality and aid Utah Fedn. Women's Clubs, 1982-86; v.p. Ogden dist., 1990-92, pres. Ogden dist., 1992-96, state resolutions com., 1996—; trustee Family Counseling Svc. No. Utah, Ogden, 1983-95, emeritus trustee, 1995—; Utah rep. to nat. bd. Challenger Films, Inc., 1986—; state pres. Rocky Mountain Conf. Women in Mission, United Ch. of Christ, 1974-77, sec., 1981-84, vice moderator Utah Assn., 1992-94. Recipient Ecumenical Svc. citation Ind. Coun. Chs., 1962, Outstanding Local Pres. award Utah PTA, 1978, Outstanding Latchkey Child Project award, 1985, Cmty. Svc. award City of Ogden, 1980, 81, 82, Celebration of Gifts of Lay Woman Nat. award United Ch. of Christ, 1987, Excellence in the Arts in Art Edn. award Ogden City Arts Commn., 1993, Spirit of Am. Woman in Arts and Humanities award Your Cmty. Connection, Ogden, 1994; Utah Endowment for Humanities grantee, 1981, 81-82. Mem. Nat. League Am. Penwomen (chmn. Utah conv. 1973, 11 awards for articles and essays 1987-95, 1st pl. news award 1992), AAUW (state edn. rep. 1982-86). Democrat. Home and Office: 722 Boughton St Ogden UT 84403-1152

HARRINGTON, WALTER HOWARD, JR., judge; b. San Francisco, Aug. 14, 1926; s. Walter Howard and Doris Ellen (Daniels) H.; B.S., Stanford, 1947; J.D., Hastings Coll., U. Calif., 1952; m. Barbara Bryant, June 1952 (div. 1973); children: Stacey Doreen, Sara Duval; m. 2d, Hertha Bahrs, Sept. 1974. Admitted to Calif. bar, 1953; dep. legislative counsel State of Calif., Sacramento, 1953-54, 55; mem. firm Walner & Harrington, Sacramento, 1954; dep. dist. atty. San Mateo County, Redwood City, Calif., 1955-62; pvt. practice in Redwood City, 1962-84; judge San Mateo County Mcpl. Ct., 1984-90, Superior Ct., 1990-96. Chmn., San Mateo County Criminal Justice Council, 1971-76, San Mateo County Adult Correctional Facilities Com., 1969-71; pro tem referee San Mateo County Juvenile Ct., 1967-72. Served as ensign USNR, 1944-46. Mem. San Mateo County Bar Assn. (pres. 1969, editor publs. 1964-74), State Bar Calif. (editorial bd. 1968-81, vice chmn. 1969, 74-75, chmn., editor 1975-76), San Mateo County Legal Aid Soc. (pres. 1971-72), Order of Coif, Delta Theta Phi. Republican. Episcopalian. Office: Hall of Justice 401 Marshall St Redwood City CA 94063-1636

HARRIS, ANTHONY JOSEPH, physical therapist; b. Kansas City, Mo., Feb. 29, 1956; s. John Joseph and Evelyn Jane (Climer) H.; m. Diane Marie Beilmann, June 10, 1978; children: John, Clinton, Mitchell, Emily. BS in Edn. and Phys. Edn., Baker U., Baldwin City, Kans., 1978; MS in Phys. Therapy, U. Indpls., 1986. Cert. athletic trainer. Head athletic trainer Shadow Mountain H.S., Paradise Valley, Ariz., 1980-81, Scottsdale (Ariz.) Pub. Schs., 1981-82, Phoenix Coll., 1982-83; asst. athletic trainer Indpls. Colts, 1984-87; head athletic trainer Ind. Ctrl. U., Indpls., 193-86; dir. sports medicine Caylor-Nickel Med. Ctr., Bluffton, Ind., 1986-88; pvt. practice phys. therapy Ind. Phys. Therapy and Sports Medicine, Ft. Wayne, 1988-89; phys. therapist, athletic trainer, travel sec. Phila. 76ers/NBA, 1989-92, Detroit Pistons/NBA, Auburn Hills, Mich., 1992-95; facility mgr. Novacare Outpatient Rehab., Phoenix, 1995-96; phys. therapist Strength Tng., Inc., 1996—; athletic trainer U.S. Olympic Festival, L.A., 1990, R. Jones Cup, Taiwan, 1991, World Univ. Games, Buffalo, 1993, U.S. Boxing Team, Olympic Games, Atlanta, 1996. Mem. Nat. Athletic Trainers Assn., Am. Phys. Therapy Assn., Nat. Basketball Trainers Assn., Nat. Strength Coaches Assn.

HARRIS, BARBARA HULL (MRS. F. CHANDLER HARRIS), social agency administrator; b. L.A., Nov. 1, 1921; d. Hamilton and Marion (Eimers) Baird; m. F. Chandler Harris, Aug. 10, 1946; children: Victoria, Randolph Boyd. Pres., Victoria Originals, 1955-62. Student, UCLA, 1939-41, 45-47. Ptnr.J.B. Assocs., cons., 1971-73; statewide dir. vols. Children's Home Soc. Calif., 1971-75. L.A. County Heart Sunday chmn. L.A. County Heart Assn., 1965, bd. dirs., 1966-69; mem. exec. com. Hollywood Bowl

Vols., 1966-84, chmn. vols., 1971, 75; chmn. Coll. Alumni of Assistance League, 1962; mem. exec. com. Assistance League So. Calif., 1964-71, 72-80, 83-89, pres., 1976-80; bd. dirs. Nat. Charity League, L.A., 1965-69, 75, sec., 1967, 3d v.p., 1968; ways and means chmn., dir. L.A. Am. Horse Show, 1969; dir. Coronet Debutante Ball, 1968, ball bd. chmn., 1969-70, 75, 84, 96—, mem. ball bd., 1969—; pres. Hollywood Bowl Patroness com., 1976; v.p. Irving Walker aux. Travelers Aid, 1976, 79, pres., 1988-89; pres. So. Calif. alumni council Alpha Phi, 1961, fin. adviser to chpts. U. So. Calif., 1961-72, UCLA, 1965-72; benefit chmn. Gold Shield, 1969, 1st v.p., 1970-72; chmn. Golden Thimble III Needlework Exhbn., Hosp. of Good Samaritan, 1975; bd. dirs. UCLA Affiliates, 1976-78, KCET Women's Council, 1979-83, Region V United Way, 1980-83; pres. Jr. Philharmonic Com., 1981-82; bd. dirs. L.A. Founder chpt. Achievement Rewards for Coll. Scientists, 1980-91, pres., 1984-85; pres. L.A. County chpt. Freedom Found. of Valley Forge; mem. com. for the Hollywood Bowl 75 yr. history, 1994-96. Recipient Outstanding Svc. award L.A. County Heart Assn., 1965, Outstanding Alumna Ivy award Alpha Phi, 1969, Outstanding Alumni award for community service UCLA, 1978, Mannequin's Eve award, 1980, Outstanding Bd. Mem. of Yr. award Assistance League of So. Calif., 1989-90. Mem. Hollywood C. of C. (dir. 1980-81). Home: 7774 Skyhill Dr Los Angeles CA 90068-1232

HARRIS, BENJAMIN KEITH, rheumatologist; b. Stambaugh, Mich., Dec. 24, 1937; s. Edward and Dorothy M. Harris; m. Janis Lee Finkleman, May 24, 1985; children: Eric, Jason, Jay, Jamie, Jill. BA with highest distinction, Northwestern U., 1959; MD cum laude, Yale U., 1963. Diplomate Am. Bd. Internal Medicine (internal medicine and rheumatology). Intern Univ. Hosps. Cleve., 1963-64, resident in internal medicine, 1966-68, fellow in rheumatology, 1968-70; pvt. practice Phoenix, 1970—; rheumatology sect. chief Good Samaritan Med. Ctr., Phoenix, 1973-80, St. Joseph's Hosp. and Med. Ctr., Phoenix, 1974—; clin. lectr. internal medicine U. Ariz. Coll. Medicine, Tucson, 1986—. Bd. dirs. Phoenix Chamber Music Soc., 1976-86, Greater Phoenix chpt., Austism Soc. Am., 1973-76, Ctrl. Ariz. chpt., Arthritis Found., 1973—. Capt. M.C., 1964-66. Recipient Nat. Vol. Svc. citation Arthritis Found., 1978. Fellow ACP, Am. Coll. Rheumatology (network physician, com. rheumatologic care); mem. Phi Beta Kappa. Republican. Jewish. Office: Phoenix Rheumatology Specialists 926 E McDowell Ste 206 Phoenix AZ 85006

HARRIS, BERNICE LEE, educator; b. Emmett, Idaho, Apr. 3, 1946; d. Orville Lee and Aloisia W. (Odermott) H.; 1 child, Peregrin Harris-Marshall. BA in English Edn., U. Wyo., 1974, MA in English, 1981; PhD in English, U. Tulsa, 1993. Freelance film producer San Francisco, 1969-71; media cons. Anchorage Sch. Dist., 1973-77; lectr. media and edn. U. Alaska, Anchorage, 1973-78; tchr. English, women's history and film history Anchorage Sch. Dist., 1977-78; dir. humanities, cons. women's studies Wyo. Coun. for Humanities, Laramie, 1981-84; lectr. women's studies and English U. Wyo., Laramie, 1984-85; mem. humanities faculty Alaska Pacific U., Anchorage, 1985-86; instr. humanities Tulsa Jr. Coll., 1988; grad. asst. U. Tulsa, 1987-93; asst. prof. English, 1993-95; asst. prof. Lewis Clark State Coll., Lewiston, Idaho, 1995—; co-dir. Wyo. Women's Oral History Project, Laramie, 1979-81; co-founder, pres. Wyo. Oral History Assn., Laramie, 1980-84; coord. lecture series Alaska Pacific U., 1985-86; cons. in field. Author of short stories and poems. Bd. dirs. Alaska Women's Resource Ctr., Anchorage, 1976-78, Women's Ctr., Laramie, 1978-79, 82-85; bd. dirs. Call Rape Inc., Tulsa, 1988, crisis line vol., 1987-91. U. Wyo. scholar, 1973, 79; Coe fellow, U. Wyo., 1973. Mem. MLA, Shakespeare Assn., Am. Renaissance Soc. Office: Lewis Clark State Coll 500 8th Ave Lewiston ID 83501-2691

HARRIS, BOB, investment company executive; b. 1948. MBA, U. Calif., Berkeley, 1970. With Alex Brown & Sons, San Francisco, 1970-89; gen. ptnr. Harris Unterberg, San Francisco, 1989—. Office: Harris Unterberg 275 Battery St Ste 2980 San Francisco CA 94111-3339*

HARRIS, CAROL SUE, small business owner; b. Biloxie, Miss., Sept. 23, 1954; d. Carl Allen Huffman and Ada Lee (Rutherford) Smith; m. Timothy Arthur Harris, June 21, 1979; 1 child, Chris. AA magna cum laude, Antelope Valley Coll., 1996. Asst. mgr. Straw Hat Pizza Inc., Lancaster, 1975-80; owner, v.p. Pet Oasis, Inc., Lancaster, 1980—; mem., advisor Bus. Retention Com., 1993. Author: Home Cookin', 1992; contbr. to Stock-Dog mag. Mem. Com. to Elect Phil Wyman, Lancaster, 1996. Mem. Rotary (sgt. at arms 1996—), Trade Club of Antelope Valley (sec. 1988-96). Republican. Home: 7523 West Ave A Lancaster CA 93536 Office: Pet Oasis Inc 43749 15th W Lancaster CA 93534

HARRIS, CLAUDE, fire department chief. Fire chief Seattle Fire Dept., ret., 1996. Office: Seattle Fire Dept Office of the Chief 301 2nd Ave S Seattle WA 98104-2618

HARRIS, DALE RAY, lawyer; b. Crab Orchard, Ill., May 11, 1937; s. Ray B. and Aurelia M. (Davis) H.; m. Toni K. Shapkoff, June 26, 1960; children: Kristen Dee, Julie Diane. BA in Math., U. Colo., 1959; LLB, Harvard U., 1962. Bar: Colo. 1962, U.S. Dist. Ct. Colo. 1962, U.S. Ct. Appeals (10th cir.) 1962, U.S. Supreme Ct. 1981. Assoc. Davis, Graham & Stubbs, Denver, 1962-67, ptnr., 1967—, chmn. mgmt. com., 1982-85; spkr., instr. various antitrust seminars; bd. dirs. Lend-A-Lawyer, Inc., 1989-94. Mem. campaign cabinet Mile High United Way, 1986-87, chmn., atty. adv. com., 1988, sec., legal counsel, trustee, mem. exec. com. 1989-94, chmn. bd. trustees, 1996, 97; trustee The Spaceship Earth Fund, 1986-89; trustee, Legal Aid Found. Colo., 1989-95; mem. devel. coun. U. Colo. Arts & Scis. dept., 1985-93; area chmn. law sch. fund Harvard U., 1978-81; bd. dirs. Colo. Jud. Inst., 1994—, Colo. Lawyers Trust Account Found., 1996—; steering com. Youth-At-Work, 1994, School-To-Work, 1995. With USAR, 1962-68. Fellow Am. Bar Found.; mem. ABA (antitrust and litigation sects.), Colo. Bar Found., Colo. Bar Assn. (chmn. antitrust com. 1980-84; coun. corp. banking and bus. law sect. 1978-83, bd. govs. 1991-95, exec. com. 1993-94, chmn. family violence task force 1996-97), Denver Bar Assn. (chmn. Centennial Com. 1990-91, pres.-elect 1992-93, pres. 1993-94, bd. trustees 1992-95, Merit award, 1997), Colo. Assn. Corp. Counsel (pres. 1973-74), Denver Law Club (pres. 1976-77, Lifetime Achievement award, 1997), The Two Percent Club (exec. com., 1994—), Citizens Against Amendment 12 Com. (exec. com. 1994). Phi Beta Kappa, Univ. Club, Union League Club (Chgo.), Rotary (Denver). Home: 2032 Bellaire St Denver CO 80207-3722 Office: Davis Graham & Stubbs 370 17th St PO Box 185 Denver CO 80201

HARRIS, DAVID JACK, artist, painter, educator; b. San Mateo, Calif., Jan. 6, 1948; s. Jack McAllister and Audrey Ellen (Vogt) H. BA, San Francisco State U., 1971, MA, 1975. Dir. Galerie de Tours, San Francisco, 1971-72; lectr. Chabot Coll., Hayward, Calif., 1975-80; interior designer David Harris Assocs., San Mateo, 1975-85; freelance artist, painter San Mateo, 1975—; ptnr. Harris & Kasten, Archs. & Designers, 1990—; art cons. David Harris Assocs., Belmont, Calif., 1980—; v.p. Coastal Arts League Mus., Half Moon Bay, Calif., 1988—; ptnr., art dir. Fine Art Pub., Palo Alto, Calif., 1989—; bd. dirs. 1870 Gallery and Studios, Belmont, 1978—, gallery dir., 1989—, owner, partner HSW Gallery, San Francisco. Painter murals Chartered Bank of London, 1979, Caesar's Hotel, Las Vegas, 1984, Pacific Telephone, San Francisco; author mus. catalog California Concepts, 1988; represented in permanent collections at Ask Computer, Palo Alto, shared Fin., Harris Corp., Bain and Co., San Francisco, Verilink, Litton Industries, Foothill Bank, Los Altos, Chartered Bank of London, San Francisco, Stanford U., Palo Alto, Golden Nugget Hotel, Atlantic City, Nat. Bank of Detroit, Crisafi, Sciabica, Woodward, D.J. Crisafi and Co., Sheraton Grande, L.A., 1st am. Title Guaranty Co., Walt Disney, Voysys Corp., Spieker Pntrs., Storm & Co., Menlo Park, Calif., others. Recipient Purchase award North Cen. Washington Mus., 1988. Mem. Internat. Soc. Interior Designers, Coastal Arts League Mus. (v.p. 1988—, Zoe Tierny award 1988). Home and Office: 1870 Ralston Ave Belmont CA 94002-1859

HARRIS, DAVID JOEL, foundation executive; b. Miller, S.D., Sept. 22, 1950; s. Joel Chips and Amy Ruth (Rietz) H.; m. Susan Claire Hagius, June 30, 1979 (div. 1997); children: John, Jennifer. BA, Earlham Coll., Richmond, Ind., 1972; MS, Purdue U., 1975; PhD, U. Hawaii, 1983. Vis. rsch. asst. Internat. Ctr. Tropical Agr., Cali, Colombia, 1975-76; rsch. assoc. U. Hawaii, Honolulu, 1976-83; sr. rsch. fellow Internat. Ctr. Tropical Agr., 1984-87; mgr. Calif.-Nev. United Meth. Found., San Francisco, 1988-92; exec. v.p. Calif.-Nev. United Meth. Found., Sacramento, 1992—; treas. Nat. Assn. United Meth. Found., 1992-94. Contbr. articles to profl. jours. Pres. Mothers Against Drunk Driving, Sonoma County, Calif., 1989-91. Grad. fellow Purdue U., 1972, fellow NSF, 1973, 75-77. Mem. Nat. Com. on Planned Giving, Commonwealth Club Calif., Phi Beta Kappa. Methodist. Home: 355 Gemma Cir Santa Rosa CA 95404-2733 Office: Calif Nev United Meth Found 1579 Farmers Ln Ste 283 Santa Rosa CA 95405-7535

HARRIS, DAVID THOMAS, immunology educator; b. Jonesboro, Ark., May 9, 1956; s. Marm Melton and Lucille Luretha (Buck) H.; m. Francoise Jacqueline Besencon, June 24, 1989; children: Alexandre M., Stefanie L. BS in Biology, Math. and Psychology, Wake Forest U., 1978, MS, 1980, PhD in Microbiology and Immunology, 1982. Fellow Ludwig Inst. Cancer Rsch., Lausanne, Switzerland, 1982-85; rsch. asst. prof. U. N.C., Chapel Hill, 1985-89; assoc. prof. U. Ariz., Tucson, 1989-96, prof., 1996—; cons. Teltech, Inc. Mpls., 1990—, Advanced Biosci. Resources, 1994—; bd. sci. advisors Cryo-Cell Internat., 1992—; bd. dirs. Ageria, Inc., Tuscon; dir. Cord Blood Stem Cell Bank, 1993—; sci. dir. Gene Therapy, 1994—; mem. Ariz. Cancer Ctr., Steele Meml. Children's Rsch. Ctr., Ariz. Arthritis Ctr. Program, sci. adv. bd. Cord Blood Registry, Inc., chief sci. div. Cord Blood Registry, Inc. Co-author chpts. to sci. books, articles to profls. jours.; reviewer sci. jours.; co-holder 3 scientific patents. Grantee local and fed. rsch. grants, 1988—. Mem. AAAS, Am. Assn. Immunologists, Reticuloendothelial Soc., Internat. Soc. Hematotherapy and Graft Engring., Internat. Soc. Devel. and Comparative Immunology, Scandanavian Soc. Immunology, Sigma Xi. Democrat. Mem. Ch. of Christ. Office: U Ariz Dept Microbiology Bldg 90 Tucson AZ 85721

HARRIS, DEL WILLIAM, professional basketball coach. BA, Milligan Coll., Tenn., 1959; MA, Ind. U., 1965. Ordained minister, Christian Ch., 1958. High sch. coach, 1959-64; head basketball coach Earlham Coll., Richmond, Ind., 1965-74; asst. coach Utah Stars, Am. Basketball Assn., 1974-75, U. Utah, 1975-76; asst. coach Houston Rockets, NBA, 1976-79, basketball coach, 1979-83; scout Milw. Bucks, Nat. Basketball Assn., 1983-86, asst. coach, 1986-87, head coach, 1987-91; v.p. ops. Milw. Bucks, from 1987; head coach Los Angeles Lakers, 1994—; speaker on motivation Intercontinental Tng. Systems Inc., 1982-84. Author: Multiple Defenses, 1971, Zone Offense, 1975, Winning Defense, 1995; juvenile novel Playing the Game, 1982; appeared in (movie) Space Jam, 1996, (TV) Diagnosis Murder, 1996. Bd. dirs. Wis. Leukemia Soc., 1989, Milw. Athletes Against Childhood Cancer Fund; hon. chairperson Easter Seals Milw. High Sch. Classic, Vince Lombardi Golf Classic, Leukemia 6 Hours for Life Telethon; spokesperson St. Francis Children's Ctr., Milw., Spl. Olympics. Recipient Disting. Houstonian award, 1981, Coach of Yr. award NBA, 1995; Eli Lilly fellow, 1965. Office: Los Angeles Lakers 3900 W Manchester Blvd Inglewood CA 90305-2200

HARRIS, ELIHU MASON, mayor; b. L.A., Aug. 15, 1947; m. Kathy Neal, Aug. 14, 1982. BS in Polit. Sci. with honors, Calif. State U., 1968; M in Pub. Adminstrn., U. Calif., Berkeley, 1969; JD, U. Calif., Davis, 1972. Bar: Calif., D.C. Pvt. practice Calif., 1977-78; formerly mem. Calif. Legis. Assembly, from 1978; now mayor City of Oakland, Calif.; prof. pol. sci. and adminstrn. of justice Calif. State U., Hayward and Sacramento campuses. Former chmn. Joint Legis. Audit Com., Assembly Com. on Fair Employment Practices and the Select Com. on Judicial Efficiency and Improvement, also former mem. Ways and Means, Judiciary, and Health and Transp. coms.; mem. Niagara Movement Dem. Club. Dr. Martin Luther King Rsch. fellow U. Calif. Davis Sch. Law; finalist White House Fellowships competition, 1977-78. Mem. ABA (exec. dir. 1975-77), NAACP, Charles Houston Bar Assn., Calif. Assn. Black Lawyers, Black Am. Polit. Assn. Calif. (former chmn.), Kappa Alpha Psi. Office: Office of Mayor 1 City Hall Plz Oakland CA 94612-1901

HARRIS, EMMA EARL, nursing home executive; b. Viper, Ky., Nov. 6, 1936; d. Andrew Jackson and Zola (Hall) S.; m. Ret Haney Marten Henis Harris, June 5, 1981; children: Debra, Joseph, Wynona, Robert Walsh. Grad. St. Joseph Sch. Practical Nursing. Staff nurse St. Joseph Hosp., Bangor, Maine, 1973-75; office nurse Dr. Eugene Brown, Bangor, 1975-77; dir. nurses Fairborn Nursing Home, Ohio, 1977-78; staff nurse Hillhaven Hospice, Tucson, 1979-80; asst. head nurse, 1980. Author: Thoughts on Life, 1988. Vol. Heart Assn., Bangor, 1965-70, Cancer Assn., Bangor, 1965-70. Mem. NAFE. Democrat. Avocations: theatre, opera. Home: 530 E Flores St Tucson AZ 85705-5723

HARRIS, F. CHANDLER, retired university administrator; b. Neligh, Nebr., Nov. 5, 1914; s. James Carlton and Helen Ayres (Boyd) H.; m. Barbara Ann Hull, Aug. 10, 1946; children: Victoria, Randolph Boyd. AB, UCLA, 1936. Assoc. editor Telegraph Delivery Spirit, Los Angeles, 1937-39; writer, pub. service network radio programs University Explorer, Sci. Editor, U. Calif., 1939-61; pub. information mgr. UCLA, 1961-75, dir., 1975-82, dir. emeritus, 1982—. Mem. pub. relations com., western region United Way, 1972-75; bd. dirs. Am. Youth Symphony, Los Angeles, 1978—, v.p., 1983—; bd. dirs. Hathaway Home for Children, 1982-88. Recipient 1st prize NBC Radio Inst., 1944; Harvey Hebert medal Delta Sigma Phi, 1947, Mr. Delta Sig award, 1972; Adam award Assistance League Mannequins, 1980, Univ. Service award UCLA Alumni Assn., 1986. Mem. Western Los Angeles Regional C. of C. (dir. 1976-80), U. Calif. Retirees Assn. Los Angeles (pres. 1985-87), Sigma Delta Chi, Delta Sigma Phi (nat. pres. 1959-63). Club: UCLA Faculty (sec. bd. govs. 1968-72). Editor Interfraternity Research Adv. Council Bull., 1949-50, Carnation, 1969-80, Royce Hall, 1985. Home: 7774 Skyhill Dr Los Angeles CA 90068-1232

HARRIS, FREDERICK PHILIP, retired philosophy educator; b. Portland, Oreg., Aug. 28, 1911; s. Philip Henry and Nellie Louise (Humpage) H.; m. Hester Almira Larson, July 15, 1943; children: Judith, Jacquelyn, Jennifer, Elizabeth, Marcia, Frederick (dec.). AB, Willamette U., 1935; MA, Columbia U., 1937, PhD, 1944; cert. in Japanese, U. Mich., 1944. Tutor Horace Mann Sch. for Boys, N.Y.C., 1935-41; instr. English Rutgers U., New Brunswick, N.J., 1941-42; psychologist Bur. Psychol. Svcs., U. Mich., Ann Arbor, 1946; assoc. prof. philosophy Case Western Res. U., Cleve., 1946-55, chmn. dept., 1948-57; headmaster Am. Sch. in Japan, Tokyo, 1957-66; prof. Oreg. State U., Corvallis, 1967-80, chmn. dept. philosophy, 1967-76; Fulbright vis. prof. faculty edn. Kyoto (Japan) U., 1955-57; prof. Rockefeller Found. Am. Studies Seminar, Doshisha U. Japan, 1956; vis. prof. U. Oreg., Eugene, summer 1950, U. Hawaii, Honolulu, summer 1966, Lewis & Clark Coll., Portland, 1966-67; dir. Oreg. Study Ctr. Waseda U., Tokyo, 1977-80; vis. prof. Grad. Sch. Commerce Waseda U., 1980, Open Coll., 1982-92; pres. Tokyo Internat. Co., 1986-92; advisor Japan Intercultural Comm. Soc., Tokyo, 1980-82. Author: The Neo-Idealist Political Theory, 1944; editor: The Teaching of Philosophy, 1950; editor Perspectives, Japan Intercultural Comm. Soc., 1981-82. Trustee Internat. Sch., Nagoya, Japan, 1963-66, Sendai Am. Sch., Japan, 1963-65. Staff sgt. U.S. Army, 1942-45. Fulbright grantee Kyoto U., 1955, 56; Frederick Philip Harris Libr. named in his honor Am. Sch. in Japan, Tokyo, 1966. Mem. Am. Philos. Assn., Asiatic Soc. Japan (counselor 1986-89), Japan English Forensics Assn., Dem. Nat. Com., Common Cause, Nature Conservancy, Wilderness Soc., Nat. Wildlife Fedn. Methodist. Home: 3050 SW Ridgewood Ave Portland OR 97225-3363

HARRIS, GODFREY, public policy consultant; b. London, June 11, 1937; s. Alfred and Victoria H.; came to U.S., 1939, naturalized, 1945; BA with gt. distinction, Stanford U., 1958; MA (disting. mil. grad.), UCLA, 1960; m. Linda Berkowitz, Dec. 21, 1958 (div. 1982); m. Barbara DeKovner-Mayer, Nov. 5, 1984; children—Gregrey, Kennith, Mark. Fgn. svc. officer U.S. State Dept., Washington, Bonn, Germany and London, 1962-65; mgmt. analyst Office Mgmt. and Budget, Washington, 1965-67; spl. asst. to pres. IOS Devel. Co., Geneva, 1967-68; pres. Harris/Ragan Mgmt. Group, L.A., 1968—; lectr. Rutgers U., 1960-61. Mem. adv. com. on gifted Santa Monica Unified Sch. Dist. (chmn. 1978-79); mem. L.A. World Affairs Coun., Town Hall L.A.; mem. Am. Friends of Ctr. for Ednl. Tech. Israel; former West Coast rep. Panamanian Export Promotion and Investment Devel. Ctr. 1st lt. U.S. Army, 1958-60. Decorated Commendation medal. Fellow Am. Acad. Cons.'s; mem. Assn. Mgmt. Cons.'s, Stanford U. Alumni Assn. (membership sec. N.Am. chpt.), London C. of C. and Industry. Democrat. Jewish. Author: History of Sandy Hook, N.J., 1961; (with F. Fielder) The Quest for Foreign Affairs Officers, 1966; Panama's Position, 1973; (with C. Sonabend) Commercial Translations, 1985; (with B. DeKovner-Mayer) From Trash to Treasure, 1985; (with K. Katz) Promoting International Tourism, 1986, 2nd edit., 1996, The Panamanian Perspective, 1987, The Ultimate Black Book, 1988, (with Kennith Harris), 2nd edit., 1996, (with D. Behar) Invasion, 1990, The Fascination of Ivory, 1991, (with Gregrey Harris) Talk is Cheap, 1991, (with Guillermo de St. Malo Arias) The Panamanian Problem, 1993, How to Generate Word of Mouth Advertising, 1995, (with Adelheid Hasenknopf and Hans Jorgen Groll) European Union Almanac, 1995, 96; founder, editor Almanac of World Leaders, 1957-62, Consultants Directory, 1975-76. Office: Harris Ragan Mgmt Group Ste 404 9200 W Sunset Blvd Los Angeles CA 90069-3506

HARRIS, HARRY H., television director; b. Kansas City, Mo., Sept. 8, 1922; s. Harry Howard Sr. and Jennie Harris; m. Patricia A. Pulici, Aug. 18, 1939; children: Susanne and Joanne. Student, UCLA, 1940-41. film editor Desilu Prodns., 1949-57. Prodr., dir. (TV movie): Eight is Enough Reunion, 1987; dir (TV movies): Alice in Wonderland, 1984, The Waltons Thanksgiving Special, 1993, The Runaways, 1974, Swiss Family Robinson,1976, Rivkin Bounty Hunter, 1980, The Young Pioneers, 1978; dir. (TV pilots): House Detective, 1985, Private Life of T.K. Dearing, 1975, Carousel Horse, 1986 (Emmy nomination), Kowalski Loves Ya, 1986, Tom Swift, 1982, Apple's Way, 1975, The Home Front, 1980, Scamps, 1969; dir (TV episodes): In the Heat of the Night, 1988-93, Remington Steele, 1984-88, Magnum P.I., 1985-88, Cagney & Lacey, 1983, Bodies of Evidence, 1992, Spenser for Hire, Jake and the Fatman, 1991, MacGyver, 1989-90, Father Dowling Mysteries, 1990, Scarecrow and Mrs. King, 1984, Hawaii 5-0, 1976, Blue Knight, 1985, Hunter, 1976, Oldest Rookie, 1987, Naked City, 1972, Mission Impossible, 1972, Perry Mason, 1972, Shell Game, 1976, Shaft, 1975, The D.A., Adam-12, 1974, T.H.E. Cat, 1965, Fame, 1982 (Emmy award 1982), The Waltons, 1972-82 (Emmy award nominee 1973, Humanitas award 1976), Eight is Enough, 1977-80, Our House, 1986, Boone, Apple's Way, 1975, Sisters, 1992-96 (Genesis award 1992, Golden Reel award 1995), Tom Swift, 1982, Falcon Crest, 1982-87, Dallas, 1981, 85, Hotel, 1983, Kung-Fu, 1975, A Fine Romance, 1989, Nurse, 1981, Mississippi, 1983, Supercarrier, 1988, Love American Style, 1968, Doc Elliot, 1975, Gibbsville, 1976, Spencer's Pilots, 1976, The Islanders, 1959, McCall of the Wild, 1989, Hearts are Wild, 1982, Dante's Inferno, 1968, Stick With Me Kid, 1994, The Cape, 1996, 7th Heaven, 1996—, Eight Is Enough Reunion, 1987, University Hospital, 1994-95, Savannah, 1995, Dr. Quinn Medicine Woman, 1994, Gunsmoke, 1961-66, Guns of Paradise, 1991, Wanted Dead or Alive, 1958-60, Rawhide, 1963-64, Jesse James, 1963, Wells Fargo, High Chapparral, 1967-70, Bonanza, 1968, Daniel Boone, 1964-68, Pistols N' Petticoats, 1967, Hondo, 1968, Stagecoach West, 1959, MacKenzies of Paradise Cove, 1978, Swiss Family Robinson, 1976, Man from Atlantis, 1977, Voyage to the Bottom of the Sea, 1968-72, Land of the Giants, 1968-70, Lost in Space, 1965-68, Time Tunnel, 1966, Road West, 1969, The Texan, 1958-59, Death Valley Days, 1968, Man Called Shenandoah, 1965, The Virginian, 1970, Men of Shiloh, 1970, Branded, 1964-66, Young Pioneers, 1978. 2nd Lt. USAF, 1944. Mem. Dirs. Guild Am., Motion Picture Film Editors (life).

HARRIS, HOWARD JEFFREY, marketing and printing company executive; b. Denver, June 9, 1949; s. Gerald Victor and Leona Lee (Tepper) H.; m. Michele Whealen, Feb. 6, 1975; children: Kimberly, Valerie. BFA with honors, Kansas City Art Inst., 1973; M. of Indsl. Design with honors, Pratt Inst., 1975; postgrad. Graphic Arts Research Center, Rochester Inst. Tech., 1977; cert. mktg. exec., U. Utah, 1987. Indsl. designer Kivett & Myers, Architects, 1970-71; indsl. designer United Research Corp., Denver, 1971-72; indsl. designer, asst. to v.p., pres. JFN Assos., N.Y.C., 1972-73; dir. facility planning Abt & Assos., Cambridge, Mass., 1973-74; v.p. design, prodn., and research Eagle Direct, Denver, 1974—; pres. Eagle Direct, Denver. Vol. Stepping Stones. Recipient SBA Small Bus. Person of the Year award for State of Colo., 1997. Mem. Indsl. Designers Soc. Am., Graphic Arts Tech. Found., Design Methods Group, The Color Group, Nat. Assn. Counsel for Children, Am. Advt. Fedn., Nat. Assn. Printers and Lithographers (bd. dirs., chmn. mktg. com.). Democrat. Jewish. Office: 5105 E 41st Ave Denver CO 80216-4420

HARRIS, JAMES MARTIN, architect; b. Lead, S.D., Apr. 30, 1928; s. James Reynolds and Amy B. (Martin) H.; m. Enid Lou Vondy, June 26, 1955; children—Jini Lynn Harris Selig, Kristen Marie Harris Landau. B.Arch., U. Oreg., 1954. Registered architect, Wash., Oreg. Founder James M. Harris Architect, Tacoma, Wash., 1960; with Harris, Reed, Litzenberger & Tsang; of counsel to Harris Tsang Architects, 1988—. Co-author: Norway, 1969; contbr. articles to profl. jours. Pres. Downtown Tacoma Assn., 1984; founding co-chmn. Downtown Area Revitalization Task Force, Tacoma, 1980; bd. dirs. Better Bus. Bur., 1981-84; chmn. bd. visitors U. Oreg. Sch. Architecture and Allied Arts; chmn. Tacoma-Vladivostok (Russia) Sister City Com., 1990-91, founding chair, 1991; mem. exec. bd. Rainier coun. Boy Scouts Am., 1992—. Lt. (j.g.) USNR, 1946-48. Mem. AIA (coll. fellows, nat. bd. dirs. 1976-78, nat. v.p. 1979, nat. long-range planning com., del. people to people exch. to China, 1981, to Australia and New Zealand, 1988, various commns. and design juries), Tacoma Lawn and Tennis Club, Tacoma Rotary (dist. 5020, bd. dirs. 1981-84, pres. 1993-94, gov. 1997—), Elks. Republican. Episcopalian. Office: 3624 N Union Ave Tacoma WA 98407-6139

HARRIS, JAMES MICHAEL, sales executive; b. San Francisco, Mar. 24, 1947; s. Alfred James and Pearl Olga (Slavich) H.; m. Vivian Toni Ferrara, Mar. 20, 1987 (div. Mar. 1992); 1 child, Michael James. BA, San Diego State U., 1971. Rsch. assoc. San Diego State U., 1971-73; assoc. dir. San Diego Taxpayers Assn., 1973-75, exec. dir., 1976-79; govt. rels. dir. Rohr Industries, San Diego, 1975-76; chief of staff City of San Diego, 1979-83; CEO Harris & Lee, San Diego, 1983-90; exec. dir. San Diego Auto Mus., 1990-96; dir. corp. sales Rely, Inc., San Diego, 1996—; cons. Souplantation Restaurants, San Diego, 1977-83, Fuego Zero, San Diego, 1989-90, Couveé Comm., San Diego, 1989-90, Deanna Kay Products, Carlsbad, Calif., 1989-90; bd. dirs. Ctrl. Balboa Park Assn., Inter-Mus. Promotional Coun. Rschr. (book) Public Finance in the San Diego S.M.S.A., 1972, Shifting Public Functions and the Distribution of Tax Burden by Economic Class, 1972. Bd. dirs. Alumni Assn. San Diego State U., 1977-79; San Diego county coord. Yes on Lottery Campaign, Woodward/McDowell, San Diego, 1984; expert witness San Diego County Grand Jury, 1977, 78; charter rev. com. mem. San Diego County, 1984. Recipient 20 Outstanding Young Citizens of San Diego award San Diego Jr. C. of C., 1977, Man of Distinction award San Diegans Inc., 1979. Office: Rely Inc 9750 Miramar Rd San Diego CA 92126

HARRIS, JAN C., health care administrator; b. Ithaca, N.Y., Jan. 15, 1944; d. Frank and Shirley Ellen (Rickard) Caplan; m. Sonny G. Harris, Mar. 23, 1990; children: Josh, Greg, Irene, Mike, Ginger, Morgan, J.B. BSN, Cornell U., 1966; MA in Liberal Studies, Dartmouth Coll., 1974; MS in Healthcare Adminstrn., U. Colo., 1989. Coord. fed. programs, dir. instrn., tech. ctr. Northwest Arctic Sch. Dist., Kotzebue, Alaska, 1976-82; dir. planning and devel., interim pres., ops. exec. Maniilaq Assn., Kotzebue, 1985-93; adminstr., v.p. health svcs. Maniilaq Health Ctr., Kotzebue, 1993—; cons. Walrus Works, Anchorage, 1982-85. Recipient Svc. award PHS/Indian Health Svc. Mem. Am. Coll. Healthcare Execs., Am. Soc. Quality Control, Healthcare Forum. Home: PO Box 62 Kotzebue AK 99752-0062 Office: Maniilaq Health Ctr Box 43 Kotzebue AK 99752

HARRIS, JEFFREY SAUL, physician executive; b. Pitts., Mar. 13, 1949; s. Aaron Wexler and Janet Mary (Szerlip) Harris; m. Mary V. Anderson, Jan. 2, 1981; children: Sarah Ariel, Noah Aaron, Susannah Leia. BS in Molecular Biophysics/Biochemistry, Yale U., 1971; MD, U. N.Mex., 1975; MPH, U. Mich., 1982; MBA, Vanderbilt U., 1988. Diplomate Am. Bd. Preventive Medicine in Occupl. Medicine & Gen. Preventive Medicine & Pub. Health, Emergency Medicine, Medicine Quality, Ind. Med. Examination; lic. Md., Calif., Tenn., Alaska. Gen. med. officer USPHS, Juneau, Alaska, 1976-78; clin. dir. S.E. Alaska Native Health Corp, Juneau, 1978-79; asst. to commr. Tenn. Dept. Health and Environment, Nashville, 1980-83; dir. health care mgmt. Northern Telecom Inc., Nashville, 1983-88; pres. HDM, Inc., Nashville, 1988-90; med. dir. Aetna Health Plans of Tenn., Nashville, 1990-91; leader nat. practice, health strategy Alexander & Alexander Cons. Group, San Francisco, 1991-94; chief prevention, health and disability officer Indsl. Indemnity, San Francisco, 1994—; pres. Harris Associates, Anchorage, Nashville, Mill Valley, Calif., 1979—. Author: Strategic

Health Management, 1994; author, editor: Managing Employee Health Care Costs, 1992, Manual of Occupational Health and Safety, 1992, 96, Occupational Medicine Practice Guidelines: Evaluation and Management of Common Health Problems and Functional Recovery in Workers, 1997; author, co-editor: Health Promotion in the Work Place, 1994; mem. editl. bd. Am. Jour. Health Promotion, 1985—, Occupl. Environment Med. Report, 1988—; contbg. editor JAMA, Am. Jour. Pub. Health, 1988—; contbr. articles to profl. jours. Fellow Am. Acad. Family Practice, Am. Coll. Occupl. Environ. Medicine (dir., practice guidelines com., Presdl. award 1996), Am. Coll. Preventive Medicine, Am. Coll. Med. Quality, Am. Bd. Ind. Med. Examiners. Home: 386 Richardson Way Mill Valley CA 94941 Office: Indsl Indemnity 255 California St San Francisco CA 94111

HARRIS, JEREMY, mayor; s. Ann Harris; m. Ramona Sachiko Akui Harris. BA, BS in Marine Biology, U. Hawaii, 1972; M in Population and Environmental Biology and Urban Ecosystems, U. Calif., Irvine. Lectr. oceanography, biology Kauai C.C.; instr. on reef walks on Kauai U. Hawaii Sea Grant Program; del. Hawaii Constl. Conv., 1978; chmn. Kauai County Council; exec. asst. to Mayor Frank F. Fasi City and County of Honolulu, 1985-86, mng. dir. of Honolulu, 1986-94, mayor, 1994—. Named Pub. Adminstr. of Yr. Am. Soc. Pub. Adminstrn., 1993, 94; recipient Merit award Internat. Downtown Assn., others. Office: Office of the Mayor 530 S King St Ste 300 Honolulu HI 96813-3014*

HARRIS, JOHN CARSON, editor; b. Washington, July 7, 1950; life ptnr., Jim Davis. BA, Middlebury Coll., 1972; MA, U. Va., 1974, U. Calif., Berkeley, 1986. Editor Smithsonian Instn., Washington, 1978-81; sr. editor Getty Museum, Malibu, Calif., 1988—. Contr. articles to profl. jours. Home: 831-1/2 N Sweetzer Ave Los Angeles CA 90069

HARRIS, JOSEPH, retired biochemistry educator; b. Balt., Dec. 2, 1919; s. Philip and Bess (Green) H.; m. Irene Dorothy Brown, Mar. 5, 1944; children: Donald Jeffrey, Mark Lindsay. BS, U. Md., 1947; MA, Johns Hopkins U., 1949, PhD, 1952. Responsible investigator Baxter Labs., Inc., Morton Grove, Ill., 1952-54; instr. U. Colo., Denver, 1954-55; asst. prof. biochemistry Albany (N.Y.) Med. Coll., 1955-62; head neurochemistry lab. Barrow Neurol. Inst., Phoenix, 1962-75; rsch. prof. Ariz. State U., Tempe, 1965-75, prof., 1975-89; prof., assoc. chmn. dept. chemistry, 1975-86; prof. emeritus Ariz. State U., Tempe, 1990—; vis. rsch. prof. Royal N. Shore Hosp., Sydney, N.S.W., 1969; exchange scientist U.S. Nat. Acad. Scis., Hungary, 1971; vis. prof. Oxford U., Oxford, U.K., 1981. Cons. editor monograph, Pi-Interactions in Biological Systems, 1969; co-editor: Metal Ions in Neurology and Psychiatry, 1985; contbr. articles to profl. jours. Bd. dirs. Am. Heart Assn., Ariz., 1971-90; project advisor Ariz. Commn. Post Secondary Edn., Phoenix, 1985-87; adv. bd. Cen. Ariz. Consortium Internat. Edn., 1987-89. Capt. U.S. Army, 1944-46; ETO. Travel grantee Burroughs Wellcome Found., 1981. Fellow AAAS, N.Y. Acad. Scis.; mem. Am. Chem. Soc., Am. Soc. for Neurochemistry, Biochem. Soc., Biophys. Soc., Sigma Xi. Home: 2131 E Geneva Dr Tempe AZ 85282-4039 Office: Ariz State Univ Dept Chemistry & Biochemistry Tempe AZ 85287-1604

HARRIS, KEVIN MICHAEL, library manager, investigative specialist; b. Falls City, Kans., Nov. 14, 1950. AA, Skagit Valley Jr. Coll., 1971; BA in English, Western Wash. U., 1973; cert. legal asst., Bellingham Tech. Sch., 1986; cert. investigative specialist, Exec. Security Internat., 1992. Asst. mgr. Whatcom County Libr. System, Bellingham, 1982—; investigative legal asst. Vol. Lawyer Program, Bellingham, 1986-93; investigative specialist Harris and Assocs., Ferndale, Wash., 1992—; res. police officer Ferndale Police Dept., 1993—. Mem. Custer Sportsmen's Club (life, legis. chmn. 1991—, chief instr. 1993—), Double Action Tng. Acad. (staff mem. 1995). Office: Ferndale Community Libr PO Box 1209 Ferndale WA 98248-1209

HARRIS, LINDA GRADYNE, publishing executive; b. Shawnee, Okla., Jan. 3, 1944; d. Robert Alexander and Mary Edythe (Murphy) Thompson; m. James Edward Harris, Dec. 22, 1962; children: James E. Jr., Christine Ann Harris Strickland. BA in Journalism, N.Mex. State U., 1980. Publicity dir. Belleville (Ill.) YMCA, 1975-76; asst. dir. pub. rels. St. Mary's Hosp., East St. Louis, Ill., 1976-78; newswriter N.Mex. State U., Las Cruces, 1980-81; info. coord. N.Mex. Water Resources Rsch. Inst., Las Cruces, 1981-88; pub. Arroyo Press, Las Cruces, 1989—; history rschr. 1st Nat. Bank, Las Cruces, 1979; pub. participation coord. City of Las Cruces, 1980; instr. Dona Ana Branch C.C., Las Cruces, 1992—. Author: New Mexico Water Rights, 1984, Las Cruces Illustrated History, 1993 (S.W. Book award 1994); author, editor: Water: Lifeblood of New Mexico, 1988; author, prodr. (video) N.Mex. Water Rights: A Legal Perspective, 1986. Mem. Rio Grande Hist. Collections, Las Cruces, 1990—; bd. mem., past pres. Dona Ana County Hist. Soc., Las Cruces, 1990—; cultural com. mem. Downtown Revitalization Com., Las Cruces, 1994; bd. mem. Branigan Cultural Ctr., Las Cruces, 1995—. Recipient Book award Dona Ana County Hist. Soc., Las Cruces, 1994; named N.Mex. del. White House Conf. on Librs., State of N.Mex., 1990; Linda G. Harris Day named in honor Gov. N.Mex., Santa Fe, 1988; scholar N.Mex. Endowment for Humanities, Santa Fe, 1994-95. Mem. N.Mex. Press Women (sec. 1992-94, bd. mem.), N.Mex. Book Assn., Rocky Mountain Book Pub. Assn., Border Book Festival, Writers Without Borders, Libr. Assocs.-N.Mex. State U. Democrat. Methodist. Home: 4932 Tobosa Rd Las Cruces NM 88011 Office: Arroyo Press PO Box 4333 Las Cruces NM 88003

HARRIS, MARTIN STEPHEN, aerospace engineering executive; b. Greenville, S.C., Nov. 23, 1939; s. Vitruvius Aiken and Clara Margaret (Thackston) H.; m. Helen C. Dean, Sept. 7, 1963 (div. May 1980); children: Dean, Susan, James; m. Prudence Cooper Bolstad, Jan. 20, 1990 (dec. Mar. 10, 1993). BS in Physics, Furman U., 1962; MS in Physics, Fla. State U., 1967; ret., USAF, 1982. Commd. 2d lt. USAF, 1962, advanced through grades to maj., 1973, ret., 1982; sr. project engr. Hughes Aircraft Co., El Segundo, Calif., 1982-84, section head, 1984-86, space vehicle mgr., 1986-89, asst. program mgr., 1989—. Mem. Sigma Alpha Epsilon.

HARRIS, MICHAEL GENE, optometrist, educator, lawyer; b. San Francisco, Sept. 20, 1942; s. Morry and Gertrude Alice (Epstein) H.; m. Dawn Block; children: Matthew Benjamin, Daniel Evan, Ashley Beth, Lindsay Meredith. BS, U. Calif., 1964, M. Optometry, 1965, D. Optometry, 1966, MS, 1968; JD, John F. Kennedy U., 1985. Bar: Calif., U.S. Dist. Ct. (no. dist.) Calif. Assoc. practice optometry, Oakland, Calif., 1965-66, San Francisco, 1966-68; instr., coord. contact lens clinic Ohio State U., 1968-69; asst. clin. prof. optometry U. Calif., Berkeley, 1969-73, dir. contact lens extended care clinic, 1969-83, chief contact lens clinic, 1983—, assoc. clin. prof., 1973-76, asst. chief contact lens svc., 1970-76, assoc. chief contact lens svc., 1976—, lectr., 1978-80, sr. lectr., 1980—, vice chmn. faculty Sch. Optometry, 1983-85, 95—, prof. clin. optometry, 1984-86; clin. prof. optometry, 1986—, dir. residency program, 1993—, asst. dean, 1994-95, assoc. dean, 1995—; John de Carle vis. prof. City U., London, 1984; vis. rsch. fellow U. New South Wales, Sydney, Australia, 1989; sr. vis. rsch. scholar U. Melbourne, Australia, 1989, 92; pvt. practice optometry, Oakland, Calif., 1973-76; mem. ophthalmic devices panel, med. device adv. com. FDA, 1990—, interim chair, 1994; lectr., cons. in field; mem. regulation rev. com. Calif. State Bd. Optometry; cons. hypnosis Calif. Optometric Assn., Am. Optometric Assn.; cons. Nat. Bd. Examiners in Optometry, Soflens div. Bausch & Lomb, 1973—, Barnes-Hind Hydrocurve Soft Lenses, Inc., 1974-87, Pilkinton-Barnes Hind, 1987—, Contact Lens Rsch. Lab., 1976—, Wesley-Jessen Contact Lens Co., 1977—, Palo Alto VA, 1980—, Primarius Corp., Cooper Vision Optics Alcon, 1980—; co-founder Morton D. Sarver Rsch. Lab., 1986; Planning commr. Town of Moraga, Calif., 1986, vice-chmn., 1987-88, chmn. 1988-90; mem. Town Coun., Moraga, Calif., 1992—, vice mayor, 1994-95, Medi-Cal. Adv. Planning Commn., 1993-95, chair, 1994—; with Managed Care Commn., 1995—, chair, 1996—; with City County Rels. Com., Contra Costa County; founding mem. Young Adults div. Jewish Welfare Fedn., 1965—, chmn. 1967-68; commr. Sunday Football League, Contra Costa County, Calif., 1974-78. Charter Mem. Jewish Community Ctr. Contra Costa County; founding mem. Jewish Community Mus. San Francisco, 1984; Para-Rabbinic, Temple Isaiah, Lafayette, Calif., 1987, bd. dirs., 1990; life mem. Bay Area Coun. for Soviet Jews, 1976; bd. dirs. Jewish Community Rels. Coun. of Greater East Bay, 1979—, Campolindo Homeowners Assn., 1981-85; pres. student coun. John F. Kennedy U. Sch. Law, 1984-85. Fellow U. Calif., 1971; Calif. Optometric Assn. Scholar 1965, George Schneider Meml. scholar, 1964, Max Shapero Meml. Lectr., 1995. Fellow Am. Acad. Optometry (diplomate cornea and contact lens sect.; chmn. contact lens papers; mem. contact lens com. 1974—, vice chmn. contact lens sect. 1980-82, chmn. 1982-84, immediate past chmn. 84-86, chmn. jud. com. 1989—, chmn. by-laws com. 1989—), Assn. Schs. and Colls. Optometry (coun. on acad. affairs), AAAS, Prentice Soc. (pres.- elect 1994-96, pres. 1996—); mem. Assn. for Rsch. in Vision and Ophthalmology, Am. Optometric Assn. (proctor 1969—, cons. on hypnosis, mem. contact lens sect., mem. position papers com., com. on ophthalmic standards, sub-com. on testing and certification, cons. editor Jour.), Calif. Optometric Assn., Assn. Optometric Contact Lens Educators, Am. Optometric Found., Mexican Soc. Contactology (hon.), Nat. Coun. on Contact Lens Compliance, Internat. Soc. Contact Lens Rsch., Calif. State Bd. Optometry (regulation rev. com.), Calif. Acad. Scis., U. Calif. Optometry Alumni Assn. (life), ABA, Calif. Young Lawyers Assn., Contra Costa Bar Assn., Mus. Soc., JFK U. Sch. Law Alumni Assn., Benjamin Ide Wheeler Soc. U. Calif., Mensa. Democrat. Lodge: B'nai B'rith. Editor current comments sect. Am. Jour. Optometry, 1974-77; editor Eye Contact, 1984-86, assoc. editor The Video Jour. Clin. Optometry, 1988—, consulting editor Contact Lens Spectrum, 18—; author: Contact Lenses: Treatment Options for Ocular Disease, Contact Lenses for Pre & Post-Surgery; editor: Problems in Optometry, Special Contact Lens Procedures; Contact Lenses and Ocular Disease, 1990; contbr. chpts. to books; author various syllabuses; contbr. articles to profl. pubs. Office: U Calif Sch Optometry Berkeley CA 94720-2020 Office: U of Calif Sch of Optometry Berkeley CA 94720

HARRIS, PATRICIA CAROL, business executive, consultant; b. Spokane, Wash., Aug. 30, 1943; d. Arthur Laverne and Hazel Kathryn (Wingegar) Fisk; m. Bernard J. Harris Jr., Sept. 14, 1962; children: Heather Kathryn, Holly Marie. BS in Bacteriology and Pub. Health, Wash. State U., 1965; MS in Clin. Microbiology and Immunology, U. Wash., 1977. Microbiologist San Francisco Health Dept., 1965-67, Seattle-King County Health Dept., 1967-68; chief microbiologist Gen. Hosp. of Everett, Wash., 1968-86; tech. specialist Bartels, Inc. Divsn. of Baxter, Issaquah, Wash., 1986-92, tech. mgr., 1992-95; dir. sales and mktg. Bartels, Inc. Divsn. of Dade, Issaquah, Wash., 1995-96; v.p. bus. devel. Bartels, Inc., Issaquah, Wash., 1996—; cons. clin. microbiologist, Everett, 1970-86; software devel. cons. CLINREL Micro Sys., Everett, 1983-86. Contbr. articles to profl. jours. Mem. Am. Soc. for Microbiology, Am. Soc. Clin. Pathologists, Clin. Lab. Mgrs. Assn. Home: 3617 255th Ln SE Apt 27 Issaquah WA 98029-5754 Office: Bartels Inc 2005 NW Sammamish Rd Issaquah WA 98027-5364

HARRIS, RICHARD JEROME, psychology educator; b. Vicksburg, Miss., May 17, 1940; s. Frederick Arthur and Mary Elizabeth (Gieselbreath) H.; m. Mary Margaret Bierman, June 14, 1965; children: Jennifer Mary, Christopher Richard, Alexander Norman. Student, Calif. Inst. Tech., 1958-61; BS, U. Wis., 1963; MA, Stanford U., 1966, PhD, 1968. Instr., acting co-chmn. psychology & sociology dept. Talladega (Ala.) Coll., 1965-66; psychology rsch. assoc. Palo Alto VA Hosp., Mountain View, Calif., 1967-68; lectr. Stanford (Calif.) U., 1968; asst. prof. U. N.Mex., Albuquerque, 1968-72; assoc. prof. psychology U. N.Mex., 1972-83, prof. psychology, 1983—; vis. assoc. prof. Ohio State U., Columbus, 1974-75, vis. prof. U. Ga., Athens, 1988-89; action editor Jour. Personality Social Psychology, 1979; mem. edit. bd. Jour. Experimental Social Psychology, 1977-90. Author: A Primer of Multivariate Statistics, 1975, 2d rev. edit., 1985, An Analysis of Variance Primer, 1994; contbr. articles to profl. jours. Vis. fellow, U. New South Wales, Kensington, Australia, 1981-82. Fellow Am. Psychol. Soc., Soc. Personality and Social Psychology; mem. Soc. Multivariate Experimental Psychology, Soc. Experimental Social Psychology, Psychonomic Soc., Soc. Applied Multivariate Rsch. (pres. 1977-79), Soc. Advancement Social Psychology. Democrat. Home: 1719 Rita Dr NE Albuquerque NM 87106-1129 Office: U N Mex Dept Psychology Albuquerque NM 87131

HARRIS, ROBERT DALTON, history educator, researcher, writer; b. Jamieson, Oreg., Dec. 24, 1921; s. Charles Sinclair and Dorothy (Cleveland) H.; m. Ethel Imus, June 26, 1971. BA, Whitman Coll., Walla Walla, Wash., 1951; MA, U. Calif., Berkeley, 1953, PhD, 1959. Tchg. asst. U. Calif., Berkeley, 1956-59; instr. history U. Idaho, Moscow, 1959-61, asst. prof., 1961-68, assoc. prof., 1968-74, prof. history, 1974-86, prof. emeritus, 1986—. Author: (Book) Necker, Reform Statesman of Ancient Regime, 1979, Necker & Revolution of 1789, 1986. 1st lt., U.S. Army, 1942-46; Ballet Folk of Moscow, Idaho, (bd. dirs., 1971-73), Historian, First United Methodist Church, Moscow, Idaho, 1989—. Mem. Am. Hist. Assn., Am. Assn. of U. Prof. Democrat. Methodist. Home: 928 E 8th St Moscow ID 83843

HARRIS, ROBERT FRANCIS, psychoanalyst, psychiatrist; b. Wellington, Kans., May 4, 1944; s. Francis Benjamin and Cleta Catherine (Wempe) H.; m. Stephanie Diane Brown, Sept. 9, 1978; 1 child, Makenzie Brown-Harris. BS summa cum laude, St. Louis U., 1966; MD, Stanford U., 1971; grad., San Francisco Psychoanalytic Inst., 1991. Diplomate Am. Bd. Psychiatry and Neurology. Intern St. Mary's Hosp., San Francisco, 1971-72; resident Stanford (Calif.) U., 1972-75; pvt. practice Palo Alto, 1975—; psychiatrist Stanford U. Hosp., 1975—; vol. clin. faculty Stanford U., 1975—, clin. assoc. prof., 1986—, mem. clin. faculty com., 1978-82, chmn. clin. faculty com., 1980-81, mem. task force on psychiat. edn., 1987-89, mem. curriculum com., 1988—; personal and supervising analyst Psychoanalytic Inst. No. Calif., San Francisco, 1991; mem. ext. divsn. San Francisco Psychoanalytic Inst., 1981—; asst. prof. Pacific Grad. Sch. Psychology, Menlo Park, Calif., 1980-84, 86-90; mem. clin. faculty psychiat. residency program Dept. Mental Health Svcs., County of San Mateo, Calif., 1984-89; vol. faculty Family Svcs. Assn. of the Mid-Peninsula, Palo Alto, 1978-80. Author: (with others) Violence and the Struggle for Existence, 1970; contbr. articles to profl. jours. Mem. Am. Psychoanalytic Assn., San Francisco Psychoanalytic Soc., Am. Psychiat. Assn., Am. Group Psychotherapy Assn., No. Calif. Group Psychotherapy Soc. Office: 780 Welch Rd Ste 207 Palo Alto CA 94304-1518

HARRIS, ROBERT W., lawyer; b. Hindsdale, Ill., Feb. 5, 1948. BA, U. Kans., 1970; JD, U. Denver, 1973. Bar: Colo. 1973. Formerly ptnr. Hall & Evans, Denver; pres. Harris, Karstaedt, Jamison & Powers, P.C., Englewood, Colo., 1995—. Mem. ABA. Office: Harris Karstaedt et al 5299 Dtc Blvd Ste 1130 Englewood CO 80111-3305

HARRIS, ROGER J., mortgage company executive, entrepreneur; b. Chgo., Nov. 20, 1930; s. Stanley and Mary (Koba) Pokwinski; married, 1948 (div. Jan. 1970); 1 child, Linda; m. Betty J. Henry, Nov. 21, 1971. BS in Commerce, Roosevelt U., Chgo., 1956; postgrad., Loyola U. Law Sch., Chgo., 1959-62. Systems sales rep. Univac, Chgo., 1953-55; merchandising systems analyst Montgomery Ward, Chgo., 1956-62; cons. Haskins & Sells, Chgo., 1962-65; prin. A.T. Kearney, L.A., 1965-70; bus. cons. Roger J. Harris and Assocs., Inc., Calif. and Alaska, 1970—; chmn. bd. dirs., CEO Mortgage Co. Alaska; chmn. bd. dirs. MBI Corp.; conf. reader Am. Mgmt. Assn., L.A., 1970-82. Mem. Am. Soc. of Accts., Small Bus. Adminstrn. (chmn. score/ACE program 1990-91). Office: PO Box 210707 Anchorage AK 99521-0707

HARRIS, SIGMUND PAUL, physicist; b. Buffalo, Oct. 12, 1921; s. Nathan N. and Ida (Lebovitz) H.; m. Florence Katcoff, Sept. 19, 1948; 1 child, Roslyn. BA cum laude, SUNY, Buffalo, 1941, MA, 1943; postgrad., Yale U., 1943; PhD, Ill. Inst. Tech., 1954. Physicist Metall. Lab. U. Chgo., 1943-44; jr. scientist Los Alamos (N.Mex.) Nat. Lab., 1944-46; assoc. physicist Argonne Nat. Lab., Chgo., 1946-53; sr. physicist Tracer Lab., Inc., Boston, 1954-56; sr. research engr. Atomics Internat., Canoga Park, Calif., 1956-64; head physics sect. research div. Maremont Corp., Pasadena, Calif., 1964-66; from asst. prof. to full prof. L.A. Pierce Coll., Woodland Hills, Calif., 1966-86, prof. physics emeritus, 1986—; cons. Space Scis. Inc., Monrovia, Calif., 1968—. Author: Introduction to Air Pollution, 1973. Patentee method for measuring power level of nuclear reactor, apparatus for producing neutrons. Mem. Am. Nuclear Soc., Am. Assn. Physics Tchrs., Am. Phys. Soc., Phi Beta Kappa, Sigma Xi. Home: 5831 Saloma Ave Van Nuys CA 91411-3018 Office: 6201 Winnetka Ave Woodland Hills CA 91371-0001

HARRIS, WARREN LYNN, development engineer; b. Albuquerque, May 8, 1966; s. Jerry Dale and Viola Guadalupe (Gutierrez) H. BS, Ariz. State U., 1988. Programming mgr. I.P.C. Computer Svcs., Inc., Tempe, Ariz., 1985-89; software sys. engr. Intel Corp., Chandler, Ariz., 1990; dir. software R & D Pics, Inc., Tempe, 1990-91; dir. software R & D parics divsn. Ansoft Corp., Tempe, 1991-94; devel. engr. Ansoft Corp., Phoenix, 1994—. Mem. IEEE, Assn. for Computing Machinery, Mortar Bd., Golden Key, Upsilon Pi Epsilon. Office: Ansoft Corp Parics Divsn 4949 W Phelps Rd Glendale AZ 85306-9999

HARRIS, WILSON, psychiatrist, research scientist; b. Arroyo, P.R., Mar. 30, 1952. Grad., S.W. Sch. Hypnotherapy, La.; MD, Columbia U., 1972; ThD, Am. Bapt. Sem., W.Va., 1974. Co-dir., rsch. scientist, psychiatrist, tchr. U.S. Indsl. Rsch. Labs., Washington, 1972-78, 85—, legal cons., 1972-78, 85—; dir. World Industries Internat. Rsch. Facilities, Washington, 1982-90; pres. Nat. Cons. Network, Sacramento, Calif., 1993—; host Do It With Dr. Harris, TV and radio program, 1985—, DownTowners (variety show); staff Carolina Christian U., Linwood, N.C. Prodr. Open Forum, 1980-82. Dir., founder Haven Home for Children, dir. childrens devel. programs; overseer United Full Gospel Ministries and Chs., Calif. Recipient Charles Neville Humanitarian award, 1979, 84, 89, Piedmont Humanitarian award, 1985, 90, Nat. Journalist award Owens Sci. Acad. Collegiate Assn., 1995. Mem. Am. Guild Hypnotherapists, Am. Assn. Nutritional Counselors Therapists, Internat. Assn. Christian Pastoral Counselors, Am. Guild Variety Artists, Investigators, Reporters, Editors Assn., Am. Fedn. Fed. Investigators Reporters, Am. Soc. Rsch. Scientists, N.C. Assn. Christian Counselors Therapists (diplomate), Nat. Chaplains Assn. (juvenile officer). Democrat. Office: Nat Cons Network PO Box 340792 Sacramento CA 95834-0792

HARRISON, AIDAN TIMOTHY, chemist; b. York, England, July 26, 1960; came to U.S., 1988; s. Bernard and Mary Winifred (Brown) H. BSc, Liverpool Polytech., England, 1982; PhD, Warwick U., Coventry, England, 1986; MBA, Cornell U., 1995. Rsch. intern Imperial Chem. Industries, Runcorn, Eng., 1979-80, Shell Rsch. Ltd., Sittingbourne, Eng., 1981; post-grad. rsch. assoc. Warwick U., Coventry, 1982-85, postdoctoral rsch. fellow, 1986-88; dir. NMR facility Cornell U., Ithaca, N.Y., 1988-95; ctrl. region sales exec. Nalorac Corp., Martinez, Calif., 1995-97; tech. sales N&K Tech., Santa Clara, Calif., 1997—. Contbr. articles to profl. jours. Bd. dirs. Commonland Community Residents Assn., Ithaca. Grantee NATO Advanced Sci. Inst. 1988. Mem. AAAS, Am. Chem. Soc., Royal Soc. Chemistry. Office: N&K Tech 3150 Deha Cruz Blvd Ste 105 Santa Clara CA 95054

HARRISON, ANTHONY ROBERT, public relations executive; b. Boise, Idaho, Mar. 6, 1964; s. Robert Marvin and Geraldine Louise (Givens) H.; m. Taynia Lynn Kerner, July 21, 1990. BS in Comm., U. Idaho, 1990. Account rep. Burson-Marsteller, N.Y.C., 1987; asst. account exec. Nelson Comm. Group, Phoenix, 1987-89; pub. rels. dir. Steele, Stoltz & Assocs., Boise, 1989-92; v.p., client svc. mgr. Oliver, Russell & Assocs., Boise, 1992—; profl. advisor U. N.D. Pub. Rels. Student Soc. of Am. Prodr. CD-ROM: Trus Joist MacMillan Multimedia Press Kit, 1996; editor The Haunted Homepage. Named Outstanding Profl. Advisor, Pub. Rels. Student Soc. Am., Midwest Dist., 1995; recipient Gold Rockie for pub. rels. Idaho Advt. Fedn., 1993, 95, Silver Rockie for sales promotion, 1994. Mem. Pub. Rels. Soc. Am. (Bronze Anvil 1994, 96). Office: Oliver Russell & Assocs Inc PO Box 1930 Boise ID 83701

HARRISON, CAROLE ALBERTA, museum curator, restaurateur, civic worker; b. Dayton, Ohio, Jan. 16, 1942; d. Chester Arthur and Mildred Irene (Focke) Shaw; student U. Dayton, 1959-60, U. Colo., 1960-61; children: Amelia Holmes, Ann Elizabeth, Abigail Shaw. With Council for Pub. TV, Channel 6, Inc., Denver, 1972-78, Hist. Denver, Inc., 1973-93; owner Harrison Enterprises, Inc., 1982—; general mgr. The Denver Petroleum Club, The Denver Club; dir. devel. Sewall Rehab. Center, Denver, 1979-80; exec. v.p. Marilyn Van Derbur Motivational Inst., Inc., 1980-82. Bd. dirs. Center for Public Issues, Denver, 1979-82, Passages, 1982-88, Hall of Life, 1981-83, Historic Denver, 1982-84, Denver Firefighters Mus., 1979—; bd. dirs. KRMA-TV Vols., 1970—, pres., 1973-74; founder Com. for Support of Arts, Denver, 1978-79; chmn. Graland Country Day Sch. Auction, 1979, 80, Channel 6 Auction, 1971, 72, Colo. Acad. Auction, 1980, The Hundred Most Interesting Women in Denver, 1988; mem. Denver Mayor's Task Force on Infrastructure Fin., 1988-90; bd. dirs. Met. Denver and Colo. Conv. and Visitors Bur. Named Outstanding Bus. Woman of the Yr. Colo. Woman's C. of C., 1991. Mem. Leadership Denver Alumni Assn. (dir. 1980-82), Colo. Restaurant Assn., Denver C. of C. (govt. relations com. 1983-87, state local affairs council 1987-88, urban affairs), Women's Forum. Home: 490 Jackson St Denver CO 80206 Office: 555 17th St Ste 3700 Denver CO 80202-5555

HARRISON, CHARLES WAGNER, JR., applied physicist; b. Farmville, Va., Sept. 15, 1913; s. Charles Wagner and Etta Earl (Smith) H.; m. Fern F. Perry, Dec. 28, 1940; children—Martha R., Charlotte J. Student, U.S. Naval Acad. Prep. Sch., 1933-34, U.S. Coast Guard Acad., 1934-36; BS in Engring., U. Va., 1939, EE, 1940; SM, Harvard U., 1942, M of Engring., 1952, PhD in Applied Physics, 1954; postgrad., MIT, 1942, 52. Registered profl. engr., Va., Mass. Engr. Sta. WCHV, Charlottesville, Va., 1937-40; commd. ensign U.S. Navy, 1939, advanced through grades to comdr., 1948; research staff Bur. Ships, 1939-41, asst. dir. electronics design and devel. div., 1948-50; research staff U.S. Naval Research Lab., 1944-45, dir.'s staff, 1950-51; liaison officer Evans Signal Lab., 1945-46; electronics officer Phila. Naval Shipyard, 1946-48; mem. USN Operational Devel. Force Staff, 1953-55; staff Comdg. Gen. Armed Forces Spl. Weapons project, 1955-57; ret. U.S. Navy, 1957; cons. electromagnetics Sandia Nat. Labs., Albuquerque, 1957-73; instr. U. Va., 1939-40; lectr. Harvard U., 1942-43, Princeton U., 1943-44; vis. prof. Christian Heritage Coll., El Cajon, Calif., 1976. Author: (with R.W.P. King) Antennas and Waves: A Modern Approach, 1969; contbr. numerous articles to profl. jours. Fellow IEEE (Electronics Achievement award 1966, best paper award electromagnetic compatibility group 1972); mem. Internat. Union Radio Sci. (commn. B), Electromagnetics Acad., Famous Families Va., Sigma Xi. Home: 2808 Alcazar St NE Albuquerque NM 87110-3516 *Research is like saving - if postponed until needed, it is too late to start. One should keep expanding his mind.*

HARRISON, ETHEL MAE, financial executive; b. Ft. Dodge, Iowa, June 11, 1931; d. Arthur Melvin and Grace Gwendolyn (Hall) Cochran; m. Cleo Arden Goss, June 17, 1951 (div. 1962); m. Clarence Hobert Harrison, Dec. 23, 1965 (dec. Feb. 1993). Dipl., Internat. Corres. Schs., Riverside, Calif., 1986. Tax preparer Goss Tax Svc., Riverside, 1953-61; tax preparer H & R Block, Inc., Riverside, 1972-84, supr./bookkeeper, 1974-79; owner, pres. Ethel Harrison's Tax Svc., Riverside, 1984—. Mem. NAFE, Riverside Tax Cons. Assn. (sec. 1988—), Am. Soc. Profl. and Exec. Women, Am. Inst. Profl. Bookkeepers, Soc. of Calif. Tax Profls., Nat. Assn. Tax Cons., Nat. Soc. Tax Profls., Nat. Assn. Tax Preparers, Inland Soc. Tax Cons., Nat. Taxpayers Union. Home and Office: 10460 Gramercy Pl Riverside CA 92505-1300

HARRISON, GARTH TREVIER, artist, retired social worker; b. Hiawatha, Utah, Jan. 24, 1928; s. George Trevier and Alda L. (Jackson) H.; m. Norma Muir, Oct. 2, 1956 (div. June 1977); m. Carmen Ramirez-Perez; children: Rosemary Carter, Celeste Moss, Annette Ross, Theresa Cook, Victor T. BS in Sociology, U. Utah, 1952, MSW in Psychiat., 1954. Child welfare worker Utah State Dept. Pub. Welfare, Provo, 1953-56; clin. social worker Idaho Dept. Mental Health, Blackfoot, Pocatello, 1957-60; psychiat. social worker, dir. pub. edn. South Ctrl. Mental Health Ctr., Owatonna, Minn., 1961-65; dir. Josephine County Child Guidance Clinic, Grants Pass, Oreg., 1965-68; mgr. pub. info. svcs. Utah State Dept. Pub. Welfare, Salt Lake City, 1968-70; dist. mental health specialist Utah State Dept. Social Svcs., Vernal, 1970-78, adult svcs. worker, 1978-90. Chmn. rsch. com. Utah Coun. Family Rels., Provo, 1964-65; mem. Wintah County Sheriff's Adv. Com., 1996—. With USN, 1946-48; Capt. USAR. Mem. Am. Soc. Classical Realism, Knickerbocker Artists, Utah Sheriffs' Assn. (hon.). Home: PO Box 745 Vernal UT 84078 Office: Alpine Studio 659 N 500 E Vernal UT 84078

HARRISON, GEORGE HARRY, III (HANK HARRISON), publishing executive, author; b. Monterey, Calif., June 17, 1940; s. Edith Cooke; 1 child, Courtney Love. BA in Psychology, San Francisco State Univ., 1965; post-grad., Univ. London, 1978-81. Mgr. Grateful Dead (formerly Warlocks), Palo Alto, Calif., 1965-66; founder, counselor LSD rescue Inst. Contemporary Studies, San Francisco, 1967; pvt. practice counselor San Francisco, 1967-78; pub., founder Archives Press, San Francisco, 1979—; writer-in-residence Montalvo Ctr. Arts, Saratoga, Calif., 1974; founder Media Assocs., Los Altos, Calif., 1991—; presenter, expert witness in field;

lectr. in the field. Author: The Dead Trilogy, 1972-97, Quest for Flight, 1975, 2nd edit., 1995, The Cauldron and the Grail, 1992, The Secret Book: Revelations of the Grail, 1994, Kurt Cobain: Beyond Nirvana, 1995, Ace of Cups The Grail in Tarot, 1995, Confessions of a Naked Beekeeper, 1996, The Stones of Ancient Ireland, 1996, Hamburger Zen, 1997; contbr. San Francisco Oracle, The Berkeley Barb, The Ga. Straight and L.A. Free Press; editor emeritus Doctor Dobb's Jour.; tech., staff writer Info World, A Plus; radio, TV guest including Geraldo, Am. Jour., Inside Edition, Hard Copy. With USN Med. Corps., 1958-61. Rocky Mountain Writer's Conf. scholar, 1968, Warburg Inst. scholar Univ. London, 1981, Applied Materials Corp. scholar, 1984. Mem. Press Club, Ind. Pub. Assn. Democrat. Home & Office: PO Box 46 Wilton CA 95693

HARRISON, HELEN HERRE, writer, volunteer, advocate; b. Harrisburg, Pa., Aug. 23, 1946; d. Edward Albert Herre Jr. and Rebecca Irene (Allen) Webster; (stepfather) Donald Steele Webster; m. Alfred Craven Harrison Jr., Apr. 4, 1970; children: Edward Alfred, Amy Ruth. AB, U. Calif., Berkeley, 1968. Writer St. Martin's Press, 1976—. Author: The Premature Baby Book: A Parent's Guide for Coping and Caring in the First Years, 1983; edited: Parent to Parent Newsletter, 1978-80, Support Lines, 1984; contbg. column for Twins Mag., 1984-88; editorial adv. bd. Twins Mag., 1988—. Mem. Phi Beta Kappa. Home: 1144 Sterling Ave Berkeley CA 94708-1757

HARRISON, ISOM, librarian. BS in Chemistry, Rust Coll., 1970; MS in Organic Chemistry, U. of the Pacific, 1978. Tech. info. specialist Lawrence Livermore (Calif.) Nat. Lab., 1973-82, supr. br. librs., 1980-82, asst. mgr. rsch. info. group, 1983-86, libr. divsn. mgr., 1991—; tech. info. specialist Chem. Info. System, 1982-83; libr. svcs. mgr. Clorox Co., Pleasanton, Calif., 1986-91; presenter, tchr., coord. workshops in field. Contbr. articles to profl. publs. Home: 1648 Bonaire Cir Stockton CA 95210-5677

HARRISON, JOHN CONWAY, state supreme court justice; b. Grand Rapids, Minn., Apr. 28, 1913; s. Francis Randall and Ethlyn (Conway) H.; m. Ethel M. Strict; children—Nina Lyn, Robert Charles, Molly M., Frank R., Virginia Lee. LLD, George Washington U., 1940. Bar: Mont. 1947, U.S. Dist. Ct. 1947. County atty. Lewis and Clark County, Helena, Mont., 1934-60; justice Mont. Supreme Ct., Helena, 1961—. Pres. Mont. TB Assn., Helena, 1951-54, Am. Lung Assn., N.Y.C., 1972-73, Mont. coun. Boy Scouts Am., Great Falls, Mont., 1976-78. Col. U.S. Army. Mem. ABA, Mont. Bar Assn., Kiwanis (pres. 1953), Sigma Chi. Home: 215 S Cooke St Helena MT 59601-5143 Office: Mont Supreme Ct 215 N Sanders St Helena MT 59601-4522

HARRISON, RUTH FEUERBORN, retired literature and writing educator; b. Garnett, Kans., Aug. 23, 1930; d. Vincent Herman and Mary Jane (Weaver) Feuerborn; m. Bryce Robert Howard, Sept. 14, 1949 (div. Aug. 1973); children: Sam Bryce Howard, Bryan Jeffrey Howard, Gregory Robert Howard; m. Frederick Charles Harrison, Sept. 13, 1973. BA in English, Portland State U., 1966, MA in English, 1968; PhD in Medieval Comparative Lit., U. Oreg., 1974. Asst. prof. English dept. Portland (Oreg.) State U., 1969-74; freelance editor, cons. Editing, Inc., 1974-77; textbook reviewer Prentice-Hall, 1974-77; adj. prof. English dept. Linfield Coll., McMinnville, Oreg., 1977-82; tech. writer, tech. editor Bendix (aka UNC Geotech), Grand Junction, Colo., 1983-87; adj. prof. English dept. Oreg. Coast C.C., Newport, Oreg., 1987-93; textbook reviewer Prentice-Hall, 1974-77; poetry workshop leader Moon Fish, Yachats (Oreg.) Lit. Festival, others. Author: (textbooks) Punctuation: A Programmed Text, 1969, English 101: Survey of English Literature, 1972, (collected poems) Bone Flute, 1996; author hist. booklet for Little Log Ch. Hist. Mus., Yachats, 1994. Joint honor scholar, 1947; NEH grantee, 1981; grad. assistantships Portland State U., 1966-68, U. Oreg., 1968-69. Mem. NOW, South County Tuesday Writing Group, Acad. Am. Poets. Democrat. Home: 2710 NW Bayshore Loop Waldport OR 97394

HARRISON, THOMAS JOSEPH, Italian and comparative literature educator; b. Izmir, Turkey, Oct. 9, 1955; came to U.S., 1973; s. Robert Pogue and Vera Maria (Aliotti) H.; m. Nanette Barrutia, 1991. BA, Sarah Lawrence Coll., 1977; MPhil in Comparative Lit., CUNY, 1982, PhD in Comparative Lit., 1984. Asst. prof. Italian and comparative lit. U. Utah, 1984-88, dir. comparative lit. program, 1986-88; asst. prof. Italian and comparative lit. La. State U., 1988-89; asst. prof. Italian and comparative lit. U. Pa., Phila., 1989-94, Italian lang. coord., 1989-94, undergrad. dir. Italian program, 1990-94, dir. summer instr. Florence, 1991; vis. assoc. prof. Italian NYU, 1992, UCLA, 1994-97. Author: Essayism: Conrad, Musil, and Pirandello, 1992, 1910: The Emancipation of Dissonance, 1996; editor: Nietzsche in Italy, 1988; translator, editor: The Favorite Malice: Ontology and Reference in Contemporary Italian Poetry, 1983; co-translator: The Adventure of Difference (Gianni Vattimo), 1993; contbr. articles to profl. jours. Fellow Gardner Rsch., 1986-87, NEH Petrarch Inst., Yale, 1989, Lilly, 1989-90. Home: 1650 Veteran Ave Los Angeles CA 90024-5533 Office: UCLA Dept Italian Los Angeles CA 90024

HARRISON, WENDY JANE MERRILL, university official; b. Waterbury, Conn., Dec. 4, 1961; d. David Kenneth and Jane Joy (Nevius) Merrill; m. Aidan T. Harrison; children: Christopher, Charlotte. BA in Journalism, George Washington U., Washington, 1981; MBA in mgmt., Cornell U., 1992. Intern in edn. HEW, Washington, summer 1978, writer, summer 1979; rsch. asst. dep. health svcs. adminstrn. George Washington U., Washington, 1979-81; sec. Nat. Assn. Beverage Importers, Washington, 1981; account exec. Staff Design, Washington, 1982; adminstrv. aide Internat. Food Policy Rsch. Inst., Washington, 1983-86; program assoc. Acad. for Ednl. Devel., Washington, 1986-87; pvt. practice cons. Washington, 1987-88; adminstrv. mgr. food and nutrition policy program Cornell U., Ithaca, 1988-92; cons. in mgmt. of med. practices Med. Bus. Mgmt., Ithaca, 1994-95; realtor Century 21 Alpha, 1995-97; compensation mgr. Santa Clara (Calif.) U., 1996—; cons., editor George Washington U., 1986; cons., rapporteur Internat. Food Policy Restaurant Inst., Washington and Copenhagen, Denmark, 1987; cons., adminstr. Hansell & Post, Washington, 1987-88, Cornell U., Washington and Ithaca, 1988. Sponsor Worldvision, Tanzania, 1988-91. George Washington U. scholar, 1979-81. Mem. Milpitis Host Lions Club (1st v.p.), Sigma Delta Xi (scholar 1980). Democrat. Episcopalian. Home: 1891 Anne Marie Ct San Jose CA 95132 Office: Santa Clara U 500 El Camino Real Santa Clara CA 95053

HARRISON, WILLIAM ALAN, judge, arbitrator; b. Detroit, Mar. 13, 1947; s. Roger Holmes and Grace Jane (Campbell) H.; m. Janet Ellan Harrison, May 16, 1970; 1 child, Mark Campbell. BBA, U. Mich., 1969; JD, Wayne State U., 1974. Bar: Wash. 1974. Adminstrv. appeals judge Environ. Hearings Office State of Wash., Olympia, 1975—; arbitrator, 1984—. Vol. Safari Club, 1995—, Rocky Mountain Elk Found., 1970—. With USAR, 1970-76. Mem. ABA (exec. com. Nat. Conf. of Adminstrv. Law Judges 1993—), Columbia Tower Club (charter), Wash. Athletic Club. Office: Environmental Hearings Office PO Box 40903 Olympia WA 98504-0903

HARRISON, WILLIAM CRAIG, computer company executive; b. Chickasha, Okla., June 5, 1940; s. Odie Webb and Sarah (Boone) H.; m. Susan Marie Jenne, Sept. 10, 1970; children: Richard Scot, Robin Alaine. BS in Physics, Tex. Tech. U., 1962; PhD in Physics, Fla. State U., 1970; MBA in Fin., Temple U., 1983. Rsch. fellow Harvard U., Cambridge, Mass., 1970-71, Rutgers, The State U. N.J., New Brunswick, 1972-74; sr. sci. programmer Boeing Computer Svcs., Phila., 1974-76, supr. sci. computing, 1976-78, mgr. sci. computing, 1978-90; mgr. sci. computing Boeing Computer Svcs., Seattle, 1990-92, mgr. delivery sys., 1992-95; dir. Delivery Sys., 1995—. Mem. Am. Phys. Soc., Assn. Computing Machinery. Home: 1528 E Interlaken Blvd Seattle WA 98112-2125 Office: Boeing Info & Support Svcs Boeing Internat & Support Svcs Seattle WA 98112

HARRISON, WILLIAM ORVILLE, physician; b. Longview, Wash., July 9, 1938; s. Orville William and Ruth Ellen (McMilan) H.; m. Susan Marie Connelly, Dec. 29, 1965 (div. Jan. 1994); children: Scott William, John Andrew. Student, U. Vienna, Austria, 1960; AB in Biology, Stanford U., 1961; postgrad., U. Oreg., Eugene, 1961-62; MD, U. Md., 1962-66. Diplomate Am. Bd. Preventive Medicine, Am. Bd. Internal Medicine; cert. med. rev. officer. Commd. ensign USN, 1962, advanced through grades to capt., 1979; intern Oak Knoll Naval Hosp., Oakland, Calif., 1966-67; med. submarine officer U.S.S. Kamehameha USN, Pearl Harbor, Hawaii, 1967-69; resident in internal medicine Naval Regional Med. Ctr., Oakland, 1969-72; sr. rsch. fellow U. Wash., Seattle, 1972-74; head infectious diseases br. U.S. Naval Hosp., San Diego, 1974-81, chmn. clin. investigation dept., 1981-84, dir. HIV/AIDS br., 1985-88, commdg. officer med. clinics NTC, 1984-85, ret., 1988; AIDS specialist San Diego, 1988-94; clin. svcs. dir. Reynolds Electrical Engring. Co., Las Vegas, Nev., 1994-95, Bechtel Nev. Corp., Las Vegas, 1996—; cons. epidemiologist Calif. Dept. Health Svcs., Sacramento, 1985-95; cons. physician Calif. Dept. Corrections, Frontera, Calif., 1991-94. Contbr. articles to profl. jours. Recipient Sir Henry Wellcome medal Assn. Mil. Surgeons of U.S., 1980. Fellow ACP, Am. Coll. Preventive Medicine, Infectious Diseases Soc. Am.; mem. Christian Med. and Dental Soc. (trustee 1988-92), Am. Venereal Disease Assn. (sec.-treas. 1980-88), Alpha Omega Alpha. Republican. Office: 2621 Losee Rd Bldg C-1 PO Box 98521 Las Vegas NV 89193-8521

HARRISVILLE, ROY ALVIN, III, pastor, educator; b. Mason City, Iowa, Nov. 26, 1954; s. Roy Alvin and Norma Alice (Haggerty) H.; m. Mary Lee, June 3, 1978; children: Kendra Megan, David Alexander. BA, Concordia Coll., Moorhead, Minn., 1977; MDiv, Luther Northwestern Sem., 1981; PhD, Union Theol. Sem., Va., 1990. Ordained min. Luth. Ch., 1981. Vis. instr. Luther Northwestern Sem., St. Paul, 1981, Wartburg Coll., Waverly, Iowa, 1984, Union Sem., Richmond, Va., 1986, 87; assoc. pastor 1st Luth. Ch., Litchfield, Minn., 1989; prof. biblical studies and dir. continuing studies Lutheran Bible Inst. Seattle, Issaquah, Wash., 1994—; adj. faculty mem. St. Cloud (Minn.) State U., 1993. Author: The Figure of Abraham in the Epistles of Saint Paul, 1992; co-author: Augsburg Sermons 3: Gospels, Series A, 1992. Mem. Soc. Biblical Literature.

HARROP, DIANE GLASER, shop owner, mayor; b. Lafayette, Ind., June 2, 1953; d. Donald Anthony and Mary Ophelia (Rohner) G.; m. Randolph Allen Harrop, Aug. 7, 1976; children: William Donald, Steven Randolph. BE, U. Kans., 1975. Researcher U. Kans. Speech Dept., Lawrence, 1973-75; clk., book designer Pruett Pub. Co., Boulder, Colo., 1975; debate coach, English tchr. Olathe (Kans.) High Sch., 1975-76; cash items teller Converse County Bank, Douglas, Wyo., 1976-79; owner, mgr. R-D Pharmacy & Books, Douglas, 1979—; mayor City of Douglas, 1989-91, councilmember, 1991-93; columnist Casper Star Tribune, 1993—; weekly columnist Douglas Budget Newspaper, 1994; appt. Wyo. Econ. Devel. and Stabilization Bd., 1991-97, vice chmn. 1994-96; grants chmn. Wyo. Cmty. Found. Bd. Creator original jewelry (silverwork 1st prize winner Wyo. State Fair 1978). First woman councilmember City of Douglas, 1987-89; gov's. appointee, 1st chmn. State Adv. Coun. on Innovative Edn., Wyo., 1991; charter pres. Converse County Hosp. Aux., 1985; sec.-treas. Converse County Joint Powers Bd., 1987; bd. dirs. Nicolaysen Art Mus., 1987; mem. Wyo. Mcpl. League Legis. Com. (chmn. 1988—); mem., exhibitor Firearms Engravers Guild of Am., 1988, 89; moderator Congl. Ch.; Douglas chpt. pres. Wyo. Jaycee Women, 1984-85; mem. P.E.O. Sisterhood Chpt. N, 1983-84, Zonta Internat. (treas. 1982-83); pres. Friends of Wyoming State Fair, 1990—; bd. dirs. Ea. Wyoming Mental Health, 1991, Converse County United Way, 1993—; Wyo. adv. com. Dwight D. Eisenhower Math. and Sci. Grant, 1992; mem. parents adv. coun. Douglas H.S., 1994—. Recipient Celebrate Literacy award Internat. Reading Assn. Wyo., 1988, Outstanding Community Svc. award Douglas C. of C., 1991, Apple for Edn. award Gov. Mike Sullivan, 1992, Kellogg Found. scholarship to Heartland Ctr. for Leadership Devel. Seminars, 1993; named one of Outstanding Young Women in Am., 1983-86. Mem. Mountains and Plains Booksellers (bd. dirs. 1992-94), Douglas C. of C., Am. Booksellers Assn., Nat. Fedn. Ind. Businesses, Kiwanis (Douglas chpt. sec. 1994-95, pres. 1996-97). Republican. Office: R-D Pharmacy & Books 206 Center St Douglas WY 82633-2543

HARROWER, THOMAS MURRAY, electro-mechanical design engineer; b. Alloa, Scotland, Jan. 4, 1918; arrived in U.S., 1952; s. William and Sarah Osbourne Boyes (Murray) H.; m. Dora Adkin; children: Sheila Murray, Sandra Murray. BSEE, BSME, Royal Tech. Coll., Glasgow, Scotland, 1942. Sr. rsch. engr. Lockheed Missile & Space, Van Nuys, Calif., 1960-63; engr., scientist McDonnell Douglas Missile, Santa Monica, Calif., 1965-69; sales-mktg. engr. Whittaker Controls, Culver City, Calif., 1973-75; engring. adminstr. HTL Kinetics, Santa Barbara, Calif., 1981-82; sr. proposal specialist Whittaker, EGG-Spectrolab., Litton, So. Calif., 1982-85; staff engr. VSE Corp., 1991-94; ret., 1994. Author: The Sea Pirates of Singapore, Sudan, The Tenement, The Tenement Goes to War, The Deadly Metamorphis, John Harrower: Colonial, Glenmannan, King's Warlock, The Condottiere, Son of Vittorio, The Modernized Elizabethan Guide to a Winning Proposal, The Rules Will Kill You, Clydeside Lass, It Started in Belfast, Cambus, An Illustrated Anthology of African Art, (children's fiction) Zig and Zag, Wiggly-Woo, The Magic Carpet. With Brit. Territorial Forces, 1940-46. Mem. Masons. Republican. Home: 729 Ivywood Dr Oxnard CA 93030

HARRUS, ALAIN SIMON, marketing professional; b. Casablanca, Morocco, Aug. 25, 1955; came to U.S., 1979; s. David and Helen (Ifergan) H.; m. Carol Beth Ronis, July 26, 1981; children: Isaac Alexander, Rachel Beth Julie. BS in Math. and Physics, U. Paris, 1978, MS in Physics, 1979; PhD, Temple U., 1984. Tech. staff AT&T Bell Labs., Allentown, Pa., 1985-89; sr. tech. Novellus Systems, San Jose, Calif., 1989-90, dir. chem. vapor deposition, 1990-93, dir. strategic mktg., 1994-96; v.p., chief tech. officer, 1996—; dir. chem. vapor desosition LAM Rsch., Fremont, Calif., 1993-94. Patentee in field; contbr. articles to profl. jours. Mem. IEEE, Am. Phys. Soc., Electrochem. Soc. Home: 517 Patricia Ln Palo Alto CA 94303-2856 Office: Novellus Systems 81 Vista Montana San Jose CA 95134-1510

HARSHA, PHILIP THOMAS, aerospace engineer; b. N.Y.C., Feb. 22, 1942; s. Palmer and Catherine (Redinger) H.; m. Jean Ann Quinn, Oct. 23, 1965; children: Peter Charles, Evan Michael. BS in Engring. Sci., SUNY, Stony Brook, 1962, MS in Engring. Sci., 1964; PhD in Aerospace Engring., U. Tenn., 1970. Combustion rsch. engr. Gen. Electric Co., Cin., 1964-67; lead rsch. engr. Aro, Inc., Arnold Engring. Devel. Ctr., Tenn., 1969-74; rsch. specialist R&D Assoc., Marina Del Rey, Calif., 1974-76; div. mgr. Sci. Applications Internat. Corp., Chatsworth, Calif., 1976-85; chief aero. scientist Lockheed Aero. Systems Group, Burbank, Calif., 1985-88; chief project engr. Rocketdyne div. Rockwell Internat., Canoga Park, Calif., 1988-90; dep. program dir. Nat. Aero-Space Plane Program, 1990-95; program mgr. Boeing North American, Inc., Seal Beach, Calif., 1994—. Contbr. articles to profl. jours. Recipient Disting. Alumnus award U. Tenn. Space Inst., 1984. Mem. AIAA, ASME, N.Y. Acad. Sci., Sigma Xi. Republican. Methodist. Home: 1607 Ocean Ave Seal Beach CA 90740-6548 Office: Boeing North American Inc PO Box 3644 Seal Beach CA 90740

HARSHMAN, VIRGINIA ROBINSON, writer, historical researcher; b. L.A., June 29, 1920; d. Paul Edward and Hazel (Reed) Robinson; m. Walter Neill Harshman, Jr., Apr. 24, 1942; children: Loren James, Walter Neill III, David Alan, Anne Elizabeth. Grad. h.s., Inglewood, Calif., 1937. Draftsman So. Calif. Edison, San Bernardino, Calif., 1961-76; freelance writer Lytle Creek, Calif., 1950-94, Rialto, Calif., 1994—. Author: The Story of Lytle Creek Canyon, 1992. Mem. com. Lytle Creek Cmty. Plan, 1980-82; docent, spl. collections Feldhym Libr., San Bernardino, Calif., 1985-95; historian, dir. Citizens for a Safe Environment, Rialto, 1996—. Mem. San Bernardino Valley Geneal. Soc. (editor, bd. dirs.), Lytle Creek Cmty. Ctr. (editor The Canyon, 1956-59, 79-81).

HART, ANNE, author; b. N.Y.C., Nov. 18, 1941; BS in Creative Writing, English, NYU, 1964; MA in Creative Writing, English, San Diego State U., 1979; diploma Hollywood Scriptwriting Inst., 1984; diploma Alexandra Inst. Painting, San Diego, 1988. Pres. Anne Hart Prodns., Writing Cons. Author more than 40 books including In The Chips: 101 Ways to Make Money with your Personal Computer, 1985, High Paying Jobs in Six Months or Less, 1984, Understanding Robotics, 1985, Careers in Robotics, 1985, Careers in Aerospace, 1985, Homehealth Careers, 1993, Winning Resumes for Computer Personnel, 1994; (novels) Psyche Squad, The One Who Invented Writing, 1991, Psychege, 1996; (CD-ROM) How To Write Video & Multimedia Scripts, The Idealist Adventures, 1994, How to Write for Multimedia Markets, 1996; and various short stories; co-author: Winning Tactics for Women Over 40, 1988, (screenplay and novel) Midnight Shift, 1989, Playpen Hostages, 1989, (screenplay) Black Snow Melting, 1990, Why so Many Thousands of American Children Are MIssing Overseas, 1991, Midnight Shift, Writing For the New Media, 1994; columnist Careers and the Internet; contbr. articles to various publs., film scripts, 2 novelettes and collections of short stories. Office: PO Box 4333 San Diego CA 92164-4333*

HART, BONITA ELLEN, registered dietitian analyst; b. Rolla, N.D., Aug. 3, 1940; d. Delmar Lee and Ellen Vivien (Nicholas) Lovitt; m. Patrick Dennis Hart; children: Patrick Michael Hart, Lorene Ellen Hart. BS, Colo. State U., 1963; post grad., U. Calif. Berkeley, 1963-65, Seattle City U., 1978-84. Cert. dietitian. Clin. instr., dietetic intern Letterman Gen. Hosp., San Francisco, 1964-66; chief prodn. and svc. Letterman Gen. Hosp., 1964-66; food svc. dir. North Hollywood (Calif.) Cmty. Hosp., 1966-71; v.p. Hyatt Med. Enterprises, Encino, Calif., 1971-87, Am. Med. Internat., Beverly Hills, Calif., 1971-87; pres. Food and Nutrition Mgmt. Svcs., Inc., North Hollywood, 1987—. Author, editor: Clinical Diet Manual, 1971—, tng. manuals, pamphlets; lectr. in field. Mem. adv. coun. Calif. Polytech. San Luis Obispo and Calif. State U., L.A. 1st lt. U.S. Army, 1962-66. Mem. AFTRA, Am. Dietetic Assn., Am. Soc. for Hosp. Food Svc. Adminstrs., Calif. Dietetic Assn., L.A. Dist. Dietetic Assn., Washington Dietetic Assn. Roman Catholic. Home: 22200 Chatsworth St Chatsworth CA 91311

HART, DARREL GENE, government agency administrator, consultant; b. Rolla, Mo., Sept. 21, 1958; s. Valgene Ezra and Wilma Lou (Baker) H.; m. Kimberly White, July 4, 1983 (div. Jan. 1996); children: Dawn Marie, Casey Joseph Gene; m. Susan Marie Moine, Nov. 9, 1996. BS in Police Sci., BA in Econs., N.Mex. State U., 1982; MA in Pub. Adminstrn., U. N.Mex., 1996. Cert. law enforcement officer, N.Mex. Dispatcher N.Mex. State U. Police Dept., Las Cruces, 1978-79; officer N.Mex. State U. Police Dept., 1979-80, sgt., 1980-85; instr. N.Mex. Law Enforcement Acad., Santa Fe, 1985-86; bur. chief N.Mex. Law Enforcement Acad./N.Mex. Dept. Pub. Safety, Santa Fe, 1986-88; dep. dir. N.Mex. Law Enforcement Acad./N.Mex. Dept. Pub. Safety, 1988-90; dir. divsn. tng. and recruiting N.Mex. Dept. Pub. Safety, 1990—; cons., expert witness D. Hart & Assocs., Santa Fe, 1985—. Mem. adv. com. Fed. Law Enforcement Tng. Ctr., Glynco, Ga., 1992—. Mem. Nat. Sheriffs Assn., Internat. Assn. Chiefs of Police, Internat. Assn. Dirs. Law Enforcement Stds. and Tng. (pres. 1993-94). Office: NMex Dept Pub Safety 4491 Cerillos Rd Santa Fe NM 87505

HART, DAVID KIRKWOOD, management educator, consultant; b. Samta Maria, Calif., Sept. 30, 1933; s. David F. and Dale (Davis) H.; m. Mary Emily Winther, June 21, 1957; children: Karen Dale, Susan Lee, David Winther, Andrea Lynne. BS in Polit. Sci. with honors, Brigham Young U., 1957; MA in Polit Sci., U. Calif., Berkeley, 1960; PhD in Govt. with distinction, Claremont Grad. Sch., 1965. Teaching asst. dept. Polit. Sci. U. Calif., Berkeley, 1959-60; asst. prof. dept. Polit. Sci. San Francisco U., 1966-68; from asst. prof. dept. bus., govt. and soc. to prof. Sch. Bus. Adminstrn. U. Wash., Seattle, 1968-83; from instr. to asst. prof. Brigham Young U., Provo, Utah, 1960-66; prof. Inst. Pub. Mgmt., Marriott Sch. of Mgmt. Brigham Young U., Provo, 1983—, J. Fish Smith prof. of free enterprise studies, 1987-96, Alumni prof., 1996—; mem. editorial adv. bd. Sage Profl. Papers in Adminstn. and Policy Studies, 1975-76; reviewwr Acad. of Mgmt. Review, Western Political Quarterly, and others; bd. editors Adminstrn. and Soc., 1980—, Pub. Adminstrn. Rev., 1986-89, Bus. Ethics Quarterly, 1990—, Jour. Socio-Econs., 1990—, Internat. Jour. Pub. Adminstrn., 1992—, Socio Economic Series JAI Press, 1990—; occasional commentator on polit. or econ. conditions for various TV and radio stas., occasional editorial writer for newspapers, polit. cons. Co-author: (with William G. Scott) Organizational America, 1979, Organizational Values in America, 1989; co-editor: (with James V. Downton, Jr.) Pespectives on Political Philosophy: Thucydides through Machiavelli, 1971, Perspectives on Political Philosophy: Machiavelli through Marx, 1971, Perspectives on Political Philosophy: Marx through Marcuse, 1973; contbr. numerous articles, including award wnners, to profl. jours., chpts. to books, also reviews and papers presented at confs. in field. Missionary for Church of LDS, in England, 1954-56; editor The Millennial Star, Ch. mag., 1955-56; chmn. Rep. County Ctrl. Com. Utah County, 1962-63, mem. State Ctrl. Com., 1962-63; spl. asst. to chmn. Rep. State Ctrl. Com. Calif., 1965, field rep. 1960. 2d lt. USAF, 1957-58, 1st lt. Res. and N.G., 1961-68. Selected one of 32 Super-Professors in nat. survey of univs. by Esquire Mag., 1966; recipient Peck Inspirational Teaching award, Sch. Exec. Devel., Inst. Fin. Edn., 1974, 75, U. Wash. Alumnbi Disting. Tchr. award, 1974, Danforth Found. fellowship, 1963-65, Disting. Alumnus award Claremont Grad. Sch., 1993; nmaed Falk Found. fellow 1960, MBA Assn. U. Wash., Prof. of Yr., 1981-82, 87-88, MPA Assn. Brigham Young U. Tchr. of Yr., 1985, Beta Gamma Sigma Disting. Tchr., U. Wash., 1974, and others. Mem. Soc. for Advancement Socio-Econs., Acad. Mgmt., Am. Soc. Pub. Adminstrn., Am. Polit. Sci. Assn., Nat. Assn. Scholars, Reserve Officers Assn., Am. Alpine Club. Golden Key, Blue Key, Beta Gamma Sigma , Phi Eta Sigma, Pi Sigma Alpha. Home: 3537 N Little Rock Dr Provo UT 84604-5286 Office: Brigham Young Univ Marriott Sch Mgmt 766 Tanner Bldg Provo UT 84602

HART, DONALD PURPLE, bishop; b. N.Y.C., Apr. 22, 1937; s. Donald Buell Hart and Ann Wentworth (Ayres) Herrick; m. Elizabeth Ann Howard, Sept. 8, 1962; children: Sarah, Thomas. BA, Williams Coll., 1959; B of Divinity, Episc. Div. Sch., Cambridge, Mass., 1962. Curate Ch. of the Redeemer, Chestnut Hill, Mass., 1962-64; priest-in-charge Good Shepherd Mission, Huslia, Alaska, 1964-69; diocesan staff Native Ministry, Anchorage, Alaska, 1969-73; rector St. Matthew's Ch., Fairbanks, Alaska, 1973-83, St. James Ch., Keene, N.H., 1983-86; bishop Diocese of Hawaii, Honolulu, 1986-94; asst. bishop Diocese of Conn., Hartford, 1995—. Chmn. St. Andrew's Priory Sch., Honolulu, 1986—, Seabury Hall Sch., Makawao, Hawaii, 1986—, St. John's Sch., Tumon Bay, Guam, 1986—; bd. govs. Iolani Sch., Honolulu, 1986—. Office: 1335 Asylum Ave Hartford CT 06105-2295

HART, EDWARD LEROY, poet, educator; b. Bloomington, Idaho, Dec. 28, 1916; s. Alfred Augustus and Sarah Cecilia (Patterson) H.; m. Eleanor May Coleman, Dec. 15, 1944 (dec. Dec. 1990); children: Edward Richard, Paul LeRoy, Barbara, Patricia; m. Leah Yates Bryson, Apr. 30, 1993. BS, U. Utah, 1939; MA, U. Mich., 1941; DPhil (Rhodes scholar), Oxford (Eng.) U., 1950. Instr. U. Utah, Salt Lake City, 1946; asst. prof. U. Wash., Seattle, 1949-52; asst. prof. Brigham Young U., Provo, Utah, 1952-55, assoc. prof., 1955-59, prof., 1959-82, prof. emeritus, 1982—; vis. prof. U. Calif., Berkeley, 1959-60, Ariz. State U., summer 1968. Author: Minor Lives, 1971, Instruction and Delight, 1976, Mormom in Motion, 1978; (poems) To Utah, 1979, Poems of Praise, 1980; More Than Nature Needs, 1982, God's Spies, 1983; contbr. articles to profl. jours. Lt. USNR, 1942-46. Am. Philos. Soc. grantee, 1964; First prize in poetry and biography Utah State Arts Coun., 1973, 75; Fulbright-Hays sr. lectr. Pakistan, 1973-74; recipient Charles Redd award Utah Acad., 1976, Coll. Humanities Disting. Faculty award Brigham Young U., 1977. Fellow Am. Coun. Learned Socs., Found. Econ. Edn.; mem. Phi Beta Kappa, Phi Kappa Phi. Democrat. Mormon. Home: 1401 Cherry Ln Provo UT 84604-2848 Office: Brigham Young U Dept English Provo UT 84602 *As a young writer in graduate school, I made the shocking discovery one day that I had written some things I did not really believe. I wanted to be a writer, but I made a vow in my journal that I would not do so at the expense of my integrity: that I would never write anything again that I did not believe and accept with all my being. I have kept that promise, and at the same time have tried to be creative and resourceful. I do not believe that my writing has suffered from the attempt to be honest, but if it has, that is a small price to pay for self-respect.*

HART, HOWARD FRANKLIN, lawyer; b. Syracuse, N.Y., Sept. 5, 1947; s. Earl E. and Leona (Altman) H.; m. Helene Hayat, May 23, 1985 (separated 1994); 1 child, Sarah. AB, Cornell U., 1969; JD, Harvard U., 1972. Bar: N.Y. 1973, Calif. 1982. Assoc. Hughes Hubbard & Reed, N.Y.C., 1972-80; ptnr. Hughes Hubbard & Reed, N.Y.C., L.A., 1980-86, Rodi, Pollock, Pettker, Galbraith, & Phillips, L.A., 1986-89; v.p., gen. counsel Carlsberg Mgmt. Co., Santa Monica, Calif., 1989-97; of counsel Hughes Hubbard & Reed LLP, L.A., 1997—.

HART, JOHN, artistic director; b. London, 1924. Student, Sch. Sadler's Wells Ballet. Dancer Sadler's Well (became Royal Ballet), London, 1938-55, ballet master, 1955-62, asst. dir. to Dame Ninette de Valois, 1962-63, asst. dir. to Sor Frederick Ashton, 1963-70; artistic dir. Ballet West, Salt Lake City, 1985—; formerly artistic dir. PACT Ballet Co., S. Africa; formerly chmn. dance div. U.S. Internat. U., San Diego; formerly dance dir. San Diego Opera. Author: Ballet and Camera, The Royal Ballet. Recipient 1st Adeline Genee Gold Medal Royal Acad. Dancing, Queen Elizabeth award outstanding achievement in ballet, 1970, Salt Lake City's C. of C. Honors in the Arts award, 1995; decorated comdr. Order Brit. Empire, 1971. Office: Ballet West 50 W 200 S Salt Lake City UT 84101-1642*

HART, JOHN LEWIS (JOHNNY HART), cartoonist; b. Endicott, N.Y., Feb. 18, 1931; s. Irwin James and Grace Ann (Brown) H.; m. Bobby Jane Hatcher, Apr. 26, 1952; children: Patti Sue, Perri Ann. Ed. pub. schs. Freelance cartoonist, 1954-58; commerical artist GE, Johnson City, NY, 1957-58; syndicated cartoonist, 1958—. Comic strip, B.C., nationally syndicated, 1958—, (with Brant Parker) The Wizard of Id, 1964—; collections include: Hey B.C., 1958, Hurray for B.C., 1958, Back to B.C., 1959, B.C. Strikes Back, 1961, What's New B.C., 1962, B.C.- Big Wheel, 1963, B.C. is Alive and Well, 1964, The King is a Fink, 1964, Take a Bow, B.C., 1965, The Wonderous Wizard of Id, 1965, B.C. on the Rocks, 1966, The Peasants are Revolting, 1966, B.C. Right On, 1967, B.C. Cave In, 1967, Remember the Golden Rule, 1967, There's A Fly in My Swill, 1967, The Wizard's Back, 1968, B.C., 1972, B.C. Cartoon Book, 1973. Served with USAF, 1950-53, Korea. Recipient Best Humor Strip awards, Nat. Cartoonists Soc., 1967-71; Reuben Award, Nat. Cartoonist Soc., 1969, named Outstanding Cartoonist of Year, 1968; Yellow Kid award, 1970; Internat. Congress Comics for best cartoonist, Lucca, Italy; Best Humor Strip award, French Comics Council, 1971; Public Service Award, NASA, 1972. Mem. Nat. Comics Council, Nat. Cartoonists Soc. Office: care Creators Syndicate 5777 W Century Blvd Ste 700 Los Angeles CA 90045-5677*

HART, JOSEPH H., bishop; b. Kansas City, Mo., Sept. 26, 1931. Ed., St. John Sem., Kansas City, St. Meinrad Sem., Indpls. Ordained priest Roman Catholic Ch., 1956; consecrated titular bishop of Thimida Regia and aux. bishop Cheyenne Wyo., 1976; apptd. bishop of Cheyenne, 1978. Office: Bishop's Residence Chancery Office 2121 Capitol Ave PO Box 426 Cheyenne WY 82003-0426

HART, MARIAN GRIFFITH, retired reading educator; b. Bates City, Mo., Feb. 5, 1929; d. George Thomas Leon and Beulah Winiferd (Hackley) Griffith; m. Ashley Bruce Hart, Dec. 23, 1951; children: Ashley Bruce Hart II, Pamela Cherie Hart Gates. BS, Cen. Mo. State Coll., 1951; MA, No. Ariz. U., 1976. Title I-Chpt. I reading dir. Page (Ariz.) Sch. Dist.; Title I dir. Johnson O'Malley Preschool, Page Sch. Dist.; dist. reading dir. Page Sch. Dist.; bd. dirs. Lake Powell Inst. Behavioral Health Svcs., sec., 1993-95, mem. fin. com., 1995—, chmn. fin. com., 1995. Author; contbr. articles to profl. jours., childrens mags. Vol., organizer, mgr., instr. Page Cmty. Adult Literacy Program, 1986-91, Marian's Literacy Program, 1991-95; lifetime mem. Friends of Page Pub. Libr., sec. bd., 1990-91. Mem. Delta Kappa Gamma (pres. chpt. 1986-90, historian 1990-92, Omicron state coms., scholarship 1988-89, nominations 1991, Omicron State Coms. comms. 1995-97), Beta Sigma Phi (pres. chpt., v.p. chpt.). Home and Office: 66 S Navajo Dr PO Box 763 Page AZ 86040

HART, MICHAEL JOHN, environmental management; b. Manchester, N.H., July 7, 1946; s. Wilfred Norman and Agnes Hedvega (Filipowitz) H.; m. G. Mary Falvey, Aug. 15, 1976; children: Jocelyn Elizabeth, Catherine Mary. BA, Colo. U., 1968; MBA, Denver U., 1989. Radio announcer Sta. KRNW, Boulder, Colo., 1971-73; resource mgr. Flatiron Cos., Boulder, Colo., 1973-79; v.p. Flatiron Sand & Gravel, Boulder, Colo., 1979-89; pres. Hart & Assocs., Boulder, Colo., 1989—; chmn. of bd. Thorne Ecol. Inst., Boulder, 1991-93; pres. Colo. Rock Products Assoc., Denver, 1989; bd. dirs. Nat. Aggregates Assoc., Silver Springs, Md., 1992, Nat. Sand and Gravel Assoc., Silver Spring, 1983-86, bd. dirs. M&S div. Nat. Stone Assn. Contbr. articles to profl. jours. Mem. LWV, BOulder, 1992, Pvt. Industry Coun., Boulder, 1989, Sch. Dist./Capital Needs Com., Boulder, 1990-92. Named Man of Yr., Colo. Sand & Gravel Assoc., 1979. Mem. Soc. for Ecol. Restoration, Assn. State Wetland Mgrs., Environ. Law Inst., Colo. Water Congress, Nat. Stone Assn. (bd. dirs. 1995), Nat. Aggregates Assn., Beta Gamma Sigma. Office: Hart Environ 2255 Meadow Ave Boulder CO 80304-1626

HART, MILFORD E., psychotherapist, counselor; b. Cambridge, Mass., Apr. 10, 1945; s. I. Lester and Florence D. (Robinson) H.; m. Magdalena Herrera, Jan. 14, 1977; children: Joaquin, Norma, Jeremy, Thomas, Katherine. BA, U. No. Colo., 1968, MA, 1992. Lic. profl. counselor, hypnotherapist; nat. cert. counselor. Real estate broker ERA Ken Rice, Aurora, Colo., 1980-83; pvt. practice psychotherapy and hypnosis Greeley & Ft. Morgan, Colo., 1992—; real estate broker ERA Questor Real Estate Corp., Aurora, 1984-85, pvt. real estate broker, Denver, 1985-89; instr. psychology Morgan C.C., Ft. Morgan, 1993—; fin. counselor CCCS, Greeley, Colo., 1989—; mem. adv. bd. Family Self-Suffeciency, Greeley, 1993-94. Author poems; contbr. articles to profl. jours. Mem. Weld County Dem. Com., Greeley, 1967-68; vol. United Farm Workers, Weld County, 1966-69, Cath. Cmty. Svcs., Greeley, 1989—, Pro Bono Project of Weld County; area dir. women's program U.S. Slowpitch Softball Assn., Weld County, 1990-93; chair grievance com. Aurora Bd. Realtors; chair polit. affairs Greeley Bd. Realtors. Recipient John A. Love Book award U. No. Colo., 1968; grantee Cmty. Correction, 1993-94, Morgan C.C., 1994. Mem. ACA, Am. Mental Health Counseling Assn., Colo. Housing Counseling Coalition (v.p. 1994), Internat. Critical Incident Stress Found. Democrat. Office: 800 8th Ave Ste 317 Greeley CO 80631-1100

HART, PAMELA JUNE, educator; b. Ft. Worth, Tex., Apr. 6, 1955; d. Thomas Jefferson Jr. and Betty Marie (Briggs) Coats; m. Joe Ballard Lucke Jr., Mar. 19, 1974 (div. Apr. 1991); children: Thomas Joe, Geoffrey Brent; m. George Randall Hart, Jan. 18, 1992. AA with distinction, N.Mex. Jr. Coll., 1991; BS in Edn. cum laude, Coll. of the Southwest, 1992. Cert. tchr. Tchr. Hobbs, N.Mex., 1991—. Recipient Trustee scholarship Coll. of the Southwest, 1989-90. Mem. N.Mex. Assn. Classroom Tchrs. (local v.p. 1994-95, local pres. 1995-96, internal v.p. 1996-97), Delta Kappa Gamma. Republican. Methodist. Home: 1510 Cordoba Hobbs NM 88240

HART, RUSS ALLEN, telecommunications educator; b. Seguin, Tex., June 30, 1946; s. Bevelly D. and Hattie V. (Reeh) H.; m. Judith Harwood, 1984 (div. 1986); m. Patricia Barrios, Mar. 22, 1987. BA, Tex. Tech. U., 1968; MA, U. Ariz., 1976; PhD, U. Wyo., 1984. Chief cinematographer, producer-dir. dept. med-TV-film, health sci. ctr. U. Ariz., Tuscon, 1973-77; instr., coord. ednl. TV and cinematography U. Wyo., Laramie, 1977-81; assoc. prof., dir. biomed. communication Mercer U., Macon, Ga., 1981-84; prof., dir. instructional telecommunications Calif. State U., Fresno, 1984-92, prof., assoc. dir. computing, comm. and media svcs., 1992-95, prof., assoc. dir. Acad. Innovation Ctr., 1995—; condr. ednl. confs.; tech. cons. for distance edn. Contbr. articles to profl. jours. Served to capt. USAF, 1968-73. Recipient Cert. Merit, Chgo. Internat. Film Festival, 1975, 1st pl. INDY Indsl. Photography award, 1976, 2d pl. INDY Indsl. Photography award, 1975, Silver plaque Chgo. Internat. Film Festival, 1978, Winner of case study competition Internat. Radio and TV Soc., 1989, Bronze Telly award, 1992-93, 95, Crystal Shooting Star award, 1993, 94, Cine Golden Eagle award, 1994. Mem. Assn. for Ednl. Comms. and Tech. (rsch. session chmn. 1983), Am. Assn. Adult and Continuing Educators (mem. eval. task force 1986), Broadcast Edn. Assn., Health Sci. Comms. Assn. (mem. continuing edn. subcom. 1983), Biol. Photog. Assn. (film judge 1975), Alliance for Distance Edn. in Calif. (founding mem. 1991), Ednl. Telecom. Consortium of Ctrl. Calif. (founding mem. 1993), Phi Delta Kappa, Phi Kappa Phi. Office: Calif State U Acad Innovation Ctr Fresno CA 93740

HART, TIMOTHY RAY, lawyer, dean; b. Portland, Jan. 5, 1942; s. Eldon V. and Wanda J. (Hillyer) H.; m. Mary F. Barlow, Aug. 31, 1964 (div. Dec. 1975); children: Mark, Matthew, Marisa, Martin; m. Annette Bryant, Aug. 8, 1981. AA, San Jose City Coll., 1968; BA, San Jose State U., 1970; MA, Wash. State U., 1973; JD, San Joaquin Coll. Law, Fresno, Calif., 1983. Bar: Calif. 1983, U.S. Dist. Ct. (ea. dist.) Calif. 1983. Police officer City of Santa Clara, Calif., 1965-71; chief of police U. Idaho, Moscow, 1971-73; crime prevention officer City of Albany, Oreg., 1973-75; instr. criminal justice Coll. of Sequoias, Visalia, Calif., 1975-81, dir. paralegal dept., 1981-83, chmn., dir. adminstrn. justice div., 1983-88; assoc. dean instruction, 1988—; sole practice, Visalia, 1983—; apptd. dep. chief police City of Sanger (Calif.), 1996—. Bd. dirs. Sprout Ranch for Deaf Children, Tulare County Humane Soc. With USAF, 1960-63. Mem. ABA, Calif. Bar Assn., Assn. Trial Lawyers Am., Assn. Criminal Justice Educators, Am. Criminal Justice Assn., Delta Phi. Mennonite. Home: 1012 W Hemlock Ave Visalia CA 93277 Office: Coll of Sequoias 915 S Mooney Blvd Visalia CA 93277-2214

HARTENBACH, DAVID LAWRENCE, school system administrator; b. St. Louis, Dec. 6, 1934; s. Henry Charles and Loretta S. (Schwarz) H. BA, St. Louis U., 1958, MEd, 1960; EdD in Sacred Theology, U. No. Colo., 1981. Cert. adminstr., Colo. Adminstrv. intern St. Louis U. H.S., 1966-67, asst. prin., 1967-68; prin. Regis H.S. Archdiocese of Denver, 1968-70; prin. Benton Harbor (Mich.) H.S., 1970-72; prin. W.C. Hinkley H.S. Aurora (Colo.) Pub. Schs., 1972-77, exec. dir. H.S.'s, 1977-86, assoc. supt. instrn., 1986-89, assoc. supt. aux., 1989-93, supt. schs., 1993—; mem. state com. Colo. North Ctrl. Assn., Greeley, 1976-83. Membership chmn. Centennial Dist. Unit PTA, Aurora, 1993—; mem. human rels. com. City of Aurora, 1978-84. Named Colo. Supt. of Yr., Nat. Sch. Bds. Assn., 1995; grantee Ford Found., 1965-66, Nat. Acad. Rsch. in Vocat. Edn., 1979. Mem. ASCD, Nat. Assn. Secondary Sch. Prins. (nat. com. large secondary schs. 1980-83, adminstrv. intern J. Lloyd Trump grantee 1966-67), Am. Assn. Sch. Adminstrs., Colo. Assn. Sch. Bds., Colo. Assn. Sch. Execs., Kiwanis (past pres. Centennial chpt.). Office: Aurora Pub Schs 1085 Peoria St Aurora CO 80011-6203*

HARTER, CAROL CLANCEY, university president, English language educator; m. Michael T. Harter, June 24, 1961; children: Michael R., Sean P. AB, SUNY, Binghamton, 1964, MA, 1967, PhD, 1970; LHD, Ohio U., 1989. Instr. SUNY, Binghamton, 1969-70; asst. prof. Ohio U., Athens, 1970-74, ombudsman, 1974-76, v.p., dean students, 1976-82, v.p. for adminstrn., assoc. prof., 1982-89; pres., prof. English SUNY, Geneseo, 1989-95; pres. U. Nev., Las Vegas, 1995—. Co-author: (with James R. Thompson) John Irving, 1986, E.L. Doctorow, 1990; author dozens of presentations and news columns; contbr. articles to profl. jours. Office: U Nev Las Vegas Office of Pres 4505 S Maryland Pkwy # 1001 Las Vegas NV 89154-9900

HARTER, LAFAYETTE GEORGE, JR., economics educator emeritus; b. Des Moines, May 28, 1918; s. Lafayette George and Helen Elizabeth (Ives) H.; m. Charlotte Mary Toshach, Aug. 23, 1950; children—Lafayette George III, James Toshach, Charlotte Helen. B.A. in Bus. Adminstrn, Antioch Coll., 1941; M.A. in Econs, Stanford, 1948, Ph.D., 1960. Instr. Menlo Coll., Menlo Park, Cal., 1948-50; instr. Coll. of Marin, Kentfield, Calif., 1950-60; prof. econs. dept. Oreg. State U., 1960-85, prof. emeritus, 1985—, chmn. dept., 1967-71; mem. panel arbitrators Fed. Mediation and Conciliation Service, 1965—, Oreg. Conciliation Service, 1967—; mem. Univ. Centers for Rational Alternatives. Author: John R. Commons: His Assault on Laissez-faire, 1962, Labor in America, 1957, Economic Responses to a Changing World, 1972; editorial bd. Jour. Econ. Issues, 1981-84. Assoc. campaign chmn. Benton United Good Neighbor Fund, 1970-72, campaign chmn., v.p., 1972-73, pres., 1973-74, vice chmn.; pub. mem. Adv. Commn. on Unemployment Compensation, 1972, 73, chmn., 1974-78; Bd. dirs. Oreg. Coun. Econ. Edn., 1971-89; pub. mem. local profl. responsibilities Oreg. State Bar Assn., 1980-83; pub. mem. Oreg. Coun. on Ct. Procedures, 1985-93, bd. mem. Community Econs. of Corp., Community Econ. Stabilization Corp. Lt. comdr. USNR, 1941-46. Mem. AAUP, Am. Arbitration Assn. (pub. employment disputes panel 1970-92), Am. Western Econ. Assns., Indsl. Rels. Rsch. Assn., Am. Assn. for Evolutionary Econs., Oreg. State Employees Assn. (v.p. faculty chpt. 1972, pres. 1973), Am. Assn. Ret. Persons (pres. local chpt. 1992-93), Corvallis Retirement Village (fin. com., bd. dirs.). Democrat. Mem. United Ch. of Christ (moderator 1972, 73; mem. fin. com. Oreg. conf. 1974-82, dir. 1978-81, mem. personnel com. 1983-85). Home: 3755 NW Van Buren Ave Corvallis OR 97330-4952

HARTER, PENNY, poet, English educator; b. N.Y.C., Apr. 9, 1940; d. George and Barbara (Kingsley) H.; m. Charles H. Bihler, 1960 (div. 1980); children: Charles, Nancy Etline; m. William J. Higginson, May 31, 1980. BA in English Edn., Douglass Coll., New Brunswick, N.J. Tchr. Woodbridge Twp. Bd. Edn., Woodbridge, N.J., 1978-83; tchr. English Madison (N.J.) High Sch. and Jr. Sch., 1983-91; instr. English Santa Fe (N.Mex.) Prep. Sch., 1991—; adj. instr. English, Union County Coll., Cranford, N.J., 1987-89; editor From Here Press, Santa Fe, 1979—; cons. in writing and teaching of writing, 1972—. Author: (poems) House by the Sea, 1975, Lovepoems, 1981, White Flowers in the Snow, 1981, Hiking the Crevasse: Poems on the Way to Divorce, 1983, In the Broken Curve, 1984, The Price of Admission, 1986, The Monkey's Face, 1987, At the Zendo, 1993, Stages and Views, 1994, Shadow Play: Night Haiku, 1994, Grandmother's Milk, 1995, Turtle Blessing, 1996, others; contbr. to numerous anthologies and periodicals. Recipient Arnold Gingrich Meml. award N.J. State Coun. on Arts, 1978, Honorable Mention awrd Chester H. Jones Found. Nat. Poetry Competition, 1988, Mary Carolyn Davies Meml. award Poetry Soc. Am., 1987; N.J. State Coun. on Arts fellow in writing, 1985, 88, Geraldine R. Dodge Found. fellow in teaching of writing, 1985. Mem. PEN N.Mex., PEN Internat., Poetry Soc. Am., Haiku Soc. Am. (pres. 1986). Office: care From Here Press PO Box 2740 Santa Fe NM 87504-2740

HARTFORD, CHARLES EDWARD, surgeon; b. Palmerton, Pa., June 8, 1932; s. Arthur William and Ruth Sarah (Sheaffer) H.; m. Kathryn Mary Delich, Sept. 5, 1953; children: Lois Ann Burkett, Jean Louise Boatman, John William Hartford. BS in Chemistry, Franklin & Marshall Coll., 1955; MD, Temple U., 1959. Diplomate Am. Bd. Surgery, Am. Bd. Surg. Critical Care. Dir. of burn unit U. Iowa Hosp., Iowa City, 1969-76; prof. surgery U. Iowa, 1976; dir. burn treatment ctr. Crozer Chester Med. Ctr., Chester, Pa., 1977-87; clin. prof. surgery U. Pa., Phila., 1986-88; dir. burn unit U. Colo. Health Sci., Denver, 1988—, prof. surgery, 1988—. Lt. USN, 1959-64. Fellow ACS, Am. Assn. for the Surgery of Trauma; mem. Am. Burn Assn. (sec. 1976-78, pres. 1991), Western Surg. Assn., Assn. of Program Dirs. in Surgery, Alpha Omega Alpha. Office: U Colo Health Sci Ctr Campus Box C298 4200 E 9th Ave Denver CO 80220-3706

HARTFORD, JANE DAVIS, textile artist; b. Erick, Okla., Aug. 21, 1927; d. Bunyon Hoyt and Lonie Lee (Jeter) Davis; m. Thomas James Hartford, Jr., June 15, 1951; children: Jane Anne, Thomas James III. BFA, U. Okla., 1949; postgrad., Parson's Sch. Design, 1949; MA, U. Louisville, 1960. Interior designer Marshall Field and Co., Chgo., 1950-51; art therapist Norton Meml. Infirmary, Louisville, 1958-59; artist, tchr. Utah Arts Coun., Salt Lake City, 1980; bd. dirs., founding mem., chmn. ways and means com. Intermountain Weavers Conf., Phoenix, 1980-83. Exhibited in group shows at Small Expressions '85, Mass., 1985, Small Expressions '87, Calif., 1987, Convergence '86, Toronto, Can., 1991, Conf. So. Calif. Handweavers, 1991, Nat. Cathedral, Washington, 1992, Fiber & Textile Exhibit, U. Wis., 1995, Fiber Arts Fiesta, Albuquerque, 1997. Vol. demonstrator Pioneer Trails State Park, Salt Lake City, 1976-88. Mem. Handweavers Guild Am. (bd. dirs. 1980-88, pres. 1983-85, chmn. bd. dirs. 1985-88), MM Atwater Weavers Guild Utah (life, pres. 1974-75), Las Tejedoras de Santa Fe y los Alamos (v.p. 1991-93,chair 1993-95), P.E.O. (recording corr. sec., guard 1991-92), Pi Beta Phi (historian 1946-47). Episcopalian. Home: 500 Washington Ave Santa Fe NM 87501-1123

HARTFORD, MARGARET ELIZABETH (BETTY HARTFORD), social work educator, gerontologist, writer; b. Cleve., Dec. 12, 1917; d. William A. and Inez (Logan) H. BA, Ohio U., 1940; MS, U. Pitts., 1944; PhD, U. Chgo., 1962. Dir. youth svc. YWCA, Canton, Ohio, 1940-42; program cons. Intercultural Rels. Am. Svc. Inst., Pitts., 1943-48, exec. dir., 1948-50; prof. social work Case Western Res. U., Cleve., 1950-75; founding dir. Sch. Gerontology U. So. Calif., L.A., 1975-77, prof. gerontology, social work, 1977-83, prof. emeritus, 1983—; instr. Claremont (Calif.) Adult Sch. Dist., 1983—, mentor/tchr. adult edn., 1990-95; instr. retirement Pasadena (Calif.) City Coll., 1983-84, Mt. San Antonio Coll., 1988-90; cons. pre-retirement, retirement planning to corps. and ednl. systems, various cities, 1980—; cons., lectr. 1970—; instr. gerontology/mental health Kaiser Permanente, 1997—. Author: Groups in Social Work, 1973, (workbook) Making the Best of the Rest of Your Life, 1982, rev. edit., 1996, Leaders Guide to Making the Best of the Rest of Your Life, 1986; contbr. monthly column on successful aging Pomona Valley Cmty. Svcs. on Aging Newsletter; contbr. numerous articles to profl. publs. Commr. human svcs. City of Clairmont, 1986-89, city coun. observer LWV, 1994-95; trustee Mt. San Antonio Gardens Retirement Com., 1985-92, sec., 1988-91; v.p. Mt. San Antonio Gardens Club Coun., bd. dirs. admissions com. 1996—, nominating com. 1992-97, health svcs. com. 1996—, chmn. task force on wellness/fitness; trustee Corp. Pilgrim Pl. Ret. Cmty., chmn. health and svcs. com., 1987-94, 96—; bd. dirs., trustee Vol. Assn. Rancho Santa Ana Bot. Gardens, 1991—; chmn. vol. pers. com., goals and evaluation com. St. Ambrose Episcopal Ch., Claremont, 1988—. Named Outstanding Contbn. to Social Work, Alumni Assn. Schs. Social Work U. So. Calif., 1984, Outstanding Contbr. Social Group Work, Com. Advancement of Group Work, Toronto, Ont., Can., 1985, Woman of Yr., Trojan Women U. So. Calif., 1976, Woman of Yr., YWCA of Pomona Valley, 1989, Vol. of Yr., L.A. County Coun. on Aging, 1990; recipient Dart award for Innovative Tchg., U. So. Calif., 1974, 1st pl. award at juried show Am. Assn. Chinese Brush Painting, 1987, 2nd pl. short story Sedona Writers Contest, Hon. Mention non-fiction, 1989, County Commr. Citation State of Calif. Ho. of Reps., Outstanding Contbn. award Mt. San Antonio Gardens Retirement Cmty., 1994, Contbn. to Srs. award Pomona Valley Cmty. Svcs., 1994, Spl. Recognition award, Social Work, U. So. Calif., 1996. Fellow Gerontol. Soc. Am.; mem. AAUW, Nat. Assn. Social Workers (cert., nat. chmn. 1962-64, group work sect., chmn. Cleve. chpt. 1969-72), Am. Soc. Aging (chmn. program com. 1983-85, City of Claremont com. on aging 1983—, chmn. 1991, program chair 1985-94), Audubon Soc., Delta Kappa Gamma, Alpha Xi Delta. Episcopalian. Home: 918 Harrison Ave Claremont CA 91711-4129

HARTGRAVES, JEFFREY BURTON, editor; b. Phoenix, Ariz., Sept. 9, 1961; s. J. E. and Florence Marie (Ramarini) H. BA, Ariz. State U., 1986. Freelance writer Phoenix and N.Y.C., 1989-92; assoc. artistic dir. Planet Earth Multicultural Theater, Phoenix, 1993-95; ptnr. Chavez/Hartgraves Advt., San Francisco, 1995—; editor Myriad An Arts Jour., San Francisco, 1995—; founding mem. The Writer's Cir., Phoenix, 1994-96; assoc. mem. The Ensemble, Tempe, Ariz., 1990-95. Author: (stage plays) Every Other Saturday, 1994, Moments, 1994, Bloodwater Mirage, 1996. Barclay Arts grantee Barclay Found., 1994. Democrat. Home and Office: Myriad-An Arts Jour 207 Gough St # 30 San Francisco CA 94102

HARTH, ROBERT JAMES, music festival executive; b. Louisville, June 13, 1956; s. Sidney and Teresa O. H.; m. Melanie Lynn Pope; 1 child, Jeffrey David Harth Curtis. B.A. in English, Northwestern U., 1977. Assoc. mgr. Ravinia (Ill.) Festival Assn., 1977-79; v.p., gen. mgr. Los Angeles Philharm. Assn., 1979-89, Hollywood Bowl, 1979-89; pres., chief exec. officer Aspen (Colo.) Music Festival and Sch., Music Assocs. of Aspen, Inc., 1989—. Office: Aspen Music Festival Sch 2 Music School Rd Aspen CO 81611-8500

HARTH-BEDOYA, MIGUEL, conductor; b. Lima, Peru, 1968. Degree, Curtis Inst. Music, Juilliard Sch. Music dir. Eugene (Oreg.) Symphony Orch.; music dir., condr. N.Y. Youth Symphony Carnegie Hall; guest condr. N.Y. Philharm., Quebec Symphony, Auckland Philharmonia, New Zealand, Puerto Rico Symphony, Buenos Aires Philharmonia, Evansville Philharm. Orch., Ind., others; condr. Juilliard Orch. tour, France, 1993, Japan, 1995, St. Luke's Orch., 1995; founder, artistic dir. New Opera Co. Peru, Orquestra Filarmonica de Lima; mem. conducting faculty Juilliard Sch. Condr. (opera) Il Tutore Burlato, 1994, Italy, recording, 1995. Office: Eugene Symphony Orch 45 W Broadway Ste 201 Eugene OR 97401*

HARTING, TRIP, equine trainer; b. Takoma, Md., Jan. 8, 1946; s. Frederick George Jr. and Claire Charlotte (McMullen) H. BA, Roanoke Coll., 1968; MA, Georgetown U., 1971. Dressage judge Am. Horse Shows Assn., N.Y.C., 1972; chmn. dressage com. U.S. Pony Clubs, Lexington, Ky., 1994; chmn. jr. young rider com. U.S. Dressage Fedn., Lincoln, Nebr., 1991. Sgt. U.S. Army, 1968-70. Mem. Calif. Dressage Soc. (chmn. L.A. chpt. 1994). Office: PO Box 691842 West Hollywood CA 90069-8842

HARTLE-SCHUTTE, DAVID, elementary school educator; b. Chgo., June 27, 1950; s. Lawrence E. and Dorothea R. (Elliott) Schutte; m. Maureen Hartle, Sept. 5, 1977; children: Erika, Brett. BS, Miami U., 1972; MEd, Antioch U., 1975; EdD, U. Ariz., 1988. Cert. elem. tchr., Hawaii, Ariz. Elem. tchr. Window Rock Sch. Dist., Ft. Defiance, Ariz., 1975-80; title I tchr. Window Rock Sch. Dist., Ft. Defiance, 1980-89; asst. prof. U. Hawaii, Hilo, 1989-95; tech. coord. Keaukaha Elem. Sch., Hilo, 1995—; cons. literacy devel. Hawaii Dept. Edn., 1989-95; bd. dirs. Literature and Hawaiian Children, Honolulu, 1993-95. Contbr. articles to profl. jours. Mem. ASCD, NEA, Internat. Reading Assn., Nat. Coun. Tchrs. English, Hawaii Tchrs. Assn. Office: Keaukaha Elem Sch 240 Desha Ave Hilo HI 96720

HARTLING, EARLE CHARLES, environmental engineer; b. L.A., May 5, 1956; s. Earle Vaughn and Edna Catherine (Wireman) H.; m. Shirley Lorraine Gjurgevich, Nov. 24, 1990; 1 child, Vaughn Thomas. BS in Biology, Loyola Marymount U., L.A., 1978, MS in Environ. Sci. and Engring., 1981. Cert. qualified environ. profl. (Inst. of Profl. Environ. Practice). Project engr. Sanitation Dists. of L.A. County, Whittier, 1981-94, water recycling coord., 1994—; guest lectr. Environ. Sys. Engring. Program, Calif. State U., Long Beach, 1993-94. Prodr. video: Water for a Dry Land, 1989 (Best Video award Calif. Water Pollution Control Assn. 1989); contbr. articles to profl. jours. Founding mem. Recycling and Conservation Task Force, Culver City, Calif., 1989—, L.A. County Reclaimed Water Adv. Com., 1990—. Mem. Water Reuse Assn. of Calif. (Outstanding Svc. award 1995), Water Environ. Fedn., Calif. Water Environment Assn. (chmn. groundwater mgmt. subcom. 1984—), Mensa, Tau Beta Pi, Alpha Sigma Nu. Roman Catholic. Home: 4314 Jasmine Ave Culver City CA 90232-3427 Office: Sanitation Dist LA County PO Box 4998 Whittier CA 90607

HARTMAN, DIANE LAWRENCE, communication professional; b. Mobile, Ala., May 10, 1943; d. Archiebald Nightingale and Leah Nora (Davis) Lawrence; m. Jeff Hartman, Aug. 1965 (div. 1972); 1 child, Sasha Lyn. BA, U. Ala., 1972, MA, 1973. Staff news dept. South Ctrl. Bell, Birmingham, Ala., 1973; reporter, editor The Anniston (Ala.) Star, 1973-76, The Denver Post, 1976-83; dir. comm. Colo. and Denver Bar Assn., 1983—; asst. prof. Auburn (Ala.) U., 1988-89. Recipient First Place Features, Ala. Press Assn., 1975, 2nd Place Newsletter, Am. Soc. Assn. Execs., 1994. Mem. ACLU (bd. dirs. Denver) 1995-96), Denver Women's Press Club (spl. events com.). Mem. Unity Church. Office: Colo Bar Assn Ninth Fl 1900 Grant St Denver CO 80203-4301

HARTMAN, GLORIA JEAN, janitorial executive; b. Sebastopol, Calif., Jan. 28, 1944; d. Clarence Ernest Kearbey and Christena Noramona (Lancaster) Hugill; m. Seth Wayne Hartman Sr., July 22, 1961; children: Seth Wayne Jr., Tony David, Rebecca Lynn, Peter Andrew, Virgle Eugene. Counselor, bookkeeper Teen Challenge, San Francisco, 1965-68; bookkeeper S&M Janitorial Supply, Santa Rosa, Calif., 1969-75; office mgr. Paul Bunyan Supply, Alturas, Calif., 1976-92; plant mgr. Backpacker's Pantry, Boulder, Colo., 1991-92; owner Hart Clean, Klamath Falls, Oreg., 1992—. Author: Race for Doroon, 1990. Mem. VFW. Republican. Home and Office: 3630 Crest St Klamath Falls OR 97603

HARTMAN, HYMAN, biochemist; b. Montreal, June 5, 1936; s. Cecil Nathan and Hadassah (Weissenberg) H.; m. Berl Mendelson Hartman, Sept. 15, 1960; children: Rebecca, Deborah. BSc in Biochemistry, McGill U., Montreal, 1957; PhD in Biochemistry, Columbia U., 1963. Postdoctoral fellow dept. molecular biology MIT, Cambridge, Mass., 1964-68; rsch. assoc. dept. molecular biology U. Calif., Berkeley, 1968-74; asst. prof. dept. human genetics Sackler Med. Sch., U. Tel-Aviv, Israel, 1974-76; rsch. scientist Children's Hosp., Harvard Med. Sch., Boston, 1977-80; rsch. scientist dept. earth scis. MIT, 1980-87; rsch. assoc. dept. computer sci. U. Calif., Berkeley, 1988-90, rsch. assoc. dept. soil sci., 1991—; dir. Inst. for Advanced Studies in Biology, Berkeley, 1991—; mem. NASA Exobiology Peer Rev. Panel, 1980-85; mem. com. on planetary biology and chem. evolution Space Sci. Bd., Nat. Acad. Sci., 1984-87. Co-editor: Search for the Universal Ancestor, 1987, Clay Minerals and the Origin of Life, 1986, The Origin and Evolution of the Cell, 1992; contbr. articles to profl. jours. Office: Inst Advanced Studies Biol 880 Spruce St Berkeley CA 94707-2043

HARTMAN, PHIL EDWARD, actor; b. Brantford, Ont., Can., Sept. 24, 1948; came to U.S., 1957; Appeared in films Cheech and Cong's Next Movie, 1980, Weekend Pass, 1984, Pee-Wee's Big Adventure (also co-writer), The Last Resort, 1985, Blind Date, Three Amigos, 1986, The Brave Little Toaster (voices), Amazon Women on the Moon, 1987, Fletch Lives, Quick Change, 1989, CB4, 1993, So I Married An Axe Murderer, 1993, Coneheads, 1993, Greedy, 1994, The Pagemaster, 1994 (voice), Houseguest, 1995; mem. cast TV program Saturday Night Live, 1986-94, News Radio, 1995—. Sgt.

Bilko, 1996, Jingle All the Way, 1996, The Second Civil War, 1997. Recipient Emmy award for best writing in a musical or variety program, 1990.

HARTMAN, ROBERT LEROY, artist, educator; b. Sharon, Pa., Dec. 17, 1926; s. George Otto and Grace Arvada (Radabaugh) H.; m. Charlotte Ann Johnson, Dec. 30, 1951; children: Mark Allen, James Robert. B.F.A., U. Ariz., 1951, M.A., 1952; postgrad., Colo. Springs Fine Arts Center, 1947, 51, Bklyn. Mus. Art Sch., 1953-54. Instr. architecture, allied arts Tex. Tech. Coll., 1955-58; asst. prof. art U. Nev., Reno, 1958-61; mem. faculty dept. art U. Calif., Berkeley, 1961—, prof., 1972-91, prof. emeritus, 1991—, chmn. dept., 1974-76; mem. Inst. for Creative Arts, U. Calif., 1967-68. One man exhbns. include, Bertha Schafer Gallery, N.Y.C., 1966, 69, 74, Santa Barbara Mus. Art, 1973, Cin. Art Acad., 1975, Hank Baum Gallery, San Francisco, 1973, 75, 78, San Jose Mus. Art, 1983, Bluxome Gallery, San Francisco, 1984, 86, U. Art Mus., Berkeley, 1986, Instituto D'Arte Dosso Dossi, Ferrara, Italy, 1989, Victor Fischer Galleries, San Francisco, 1991, Triangle Gallery, San Francisco, 1992, 93, 95; group exhbns. include Richmond Mus., 1966, Whitney Mus. Biennial, 1973, Oakland Mus., 1976, San Francisco Arts Commn. Gallery, 1985 (award), Earthscape Expo '90 Photo Mus., Osaka, Japan, 1990, In Close Quarters, American Landscape Photography Since 1968, Princeton Art Mus., 1993, Facing Eden: 100 Years of Landscape Art in The Bay Area, San Francisco, 1995; represented in permanent collections, Nat. Collections Fine Arts, Colorado Springs Fine Arts Center, Corcoran Gallery, San Francisco Art Inst., Roswell Mus., Princeton Art Mus. U. Calif. humanities research fellow, 1980. Office: U Calif Dept Art Berkeley CA 94720

HARTMAN, ROSEMARY JANE, special education educator; b. Gainesville, Fla., Aug. 24, 1944; d. John Leslie and Irene (Bowen) Goddard; m. Alan Lynn Gerber, Feb. 1, 1964 (div. 1982); children: Sean Alan, Dawn Julianne Silva, Lance Goddard; m. Perry Hartman, June 27, 1992. BA, Immaculate Heart Coll., 1967; MA, Loyola U., 1974. Cert. resource specialist. Tchr. L.A. Unified Schs., 1968-78; resource specialist Desert Sands Unified Sch. Dist., Palm Desert, 1978-83, Palm Springs Unified Schs., 1983—. Co-author: The Twelve Steps of Phobics Anonymous, 1989, One Day At A Time in Phobics Victorious, 1992; founder Phobics Victorious, 1992. Mem. Am. Assn. Christian Counselors (charter), Internat. Platform Assn. Office: Phobics Victorious PO Box 695 Palm Springs CA 92263-0695

HARTMAN, RUTH GAYLE, rancher; b. San Francisco, Apr. 17, 1948; d. William James and Doris June (Reinhold) Nixon; m. Marcus Max Hartman, Dec. 14, 1968; children: William Marcus Hartman, Alicia Marlene Hartman. Grad. high sch., Sunnyvale, Calif. Cert. cosmetologist. Cosmetologist Palo Alto, Calif., 1966-68; engring. clk. Pacific Telephone, San Francisco, 1968-69, traffic data clk., 1969-76; owner, mgr. Coffee Creek (Calif.) Ranch Inc., 1976—. Appointed parent mem. Act Testing Secondary Adv. Bd., Sacramento, 1988-90; mem. Trinity High Sch. Curriculum Com., Weaverville, Calif., 1984, 85. Mem. Dude Ranch Assn., Trinity County C. of C., U.S. C. of C., Calif. Hotel and Motel Assn. (bd. dirs. 1992—, mem. ednl. com., mem. govtl. affairs com.), Internat. Platform Assn. Episcopalian. Home and Office: HC 2 Box 4940 Trinity Center CA 96091-9505

HARTMAN, SUSAN P(ATRICE), adult education administrator. Dir. adult edn. Front Range C.C., Westminster, Colo. Recipient Regional Person of Yr. award, 1992. Office: Front Range Community Coll Westminster CO 80030

HARTMAN, TERRY A., filmmaker; b. Waukegan, Ill.. BFA, Art Ctr. Sch., L.A., 1971. Fellow in clin. hypnotherapy. Dir. Terry Hartman Studio, Portland, Oreg., 1974-82; creative dir. Needham Worldwide, Auckland, New Zealand, 1983-85; dir. Hong Kong Films, 1986; writer, dir. Hartman Films, Portland, 1988—; dir. PSI Creative Internat., Portland; v.p. Making the Difference, Inc.; owner Tuka Art Originals. Producer: (TV commls.) Am. Cancer Soc., 1990 (Nat. Citation/Telly 1992), (video) New Voice Club, 1993 (Telly), (documentary) Perrier Investments, 1994 (Telly), N.Y. Film Fstivals, Internat. Med. Film Festival, San Francisco. Mem. Am. Indian Alaskan Native Coun. Mem. Assn. Ind. Film/Video Makers.

HARTMAN-IRWIN, MARY FRANCES, retired language professional; b. Portland, Oreg., Oct. 18, 1925; d. Curtiss Henry Sabisch and Gladys Frances (Giles) Strand; m. Harry Elmer Hartman, Sept. 6, 1946 (div. June 1970); children: Evelyn Frances, Laura Elyce, Andrea Candace; m. Thomas Floyd Irwin, Apr. 11, 1971. BA, U. Wash., 1964-68; postgrad., Seattle Pacific, 1977-79, Antioch U., Seattle, Wash., 1987, Heritage Inst., Seattle, Wash., 1987. Lang. educator Kennewick (Wash.) Dist. # 17, 1970-88; guide Summer Study Tours of Europe, 1971-88. Sec. Bahai Faith, 1971-94, libr., Pasco, Washington, 1985-88; trustee Mid. Columbia Coun. Girl Scouts U.S.; mem. Literacy Coun. Fulbright summer scholar, 1968. Mem. NEA, Wash. Edn. Assn., Kennewick Edn. Assn., Nat. Fgn. Lang. Assn., Wash. Fgn. Lang. Assn., Literacy Coun. Home: PO Box 247 Netarts OR 97143-0247

HARTMANN, STEVEN MARTIN, freight company executive; b. Aurora, Ill., June 30, 1958; s. Terry Martin and Barbara Lynn (Foster) H.; m. Rochelle Thatcher, June 23, 1982; children: Jordan, Tyler, Haylee, Cameron, Braden, Jessica. BA in Econs., Brigham Young U., 1982; postgrad., John Marshall Law Sch., Chgo., 1985. Adminstrv. mgr. Aurora (Ill.) Fast Freight, 1982-83, account exec., 1983-85, dir. maint., 1985-86, v.p., 1987-91; dir. pricing and quality Oak Harbor Freight Lines, Auburn, Wash., 1991-94, v.p., 1995—; mem. Nat. Classification Com., Alexandria, Va., 1984—, chmn., 1996—; bd. dirs., chmn. Pacific Inland Tariff Bur., Portland, 1992-95; Ill. Transp. adv. bd. Ill. Trucking Assn., Springfield, 1990-91. Author, editor Directions mag., 1992—. Leader Boy Scouts Am., Sumner, Wash., 1991—. Mem. Chgo. Traffic Club. Republican. LDS. Home: 3508 197th Avenue Ct E Sumner WA 98390-9041 Office: Oak Harbor Freight Lines Inc 1225 37th St NW Auburn WA 98001-2417

HARTNELL, AGNES E., dietitian, educator; b. Covington, Ohio; d. Richard Fowler and Margaret Louella (Crook) Albery; m. William F. Hartnell; divorced; children: Jan Hancock, Hanna. BS in Home Econs., Ohio State U., 1937; BS in Edn., U. Akron, 1955; MS in Edn., U. Ariz., 1962; EdD in Adminstrn. and Supervision, Ariz. State U., 1968. Cert. tchr., Ariz. Home economist Columbus (Ohio) Electric Co.; educator in univ. and H.S. Ohio, Calif., Ariz., 1953-57; home econs. dept. chair Phoenix Coll., 1977-88; cons., instr. Ctrl. Ariz. Coll., Coolidge, 1988—; TV/radio instr. PBS, Ariz. State U., Tempe, 1970-88; registered dietician, cons., Phoenix, 1988—; cons. prisons, Native Ams., colls., Ariz., 1970-77; mem. nat. adv. bd. Future Homemakers Am., 1958, 70, State of Ariz., Ariz. Dietetic Assn., Home Econs. Assn., Hero, Phoenix Coll., Ctrl. Ariz. Coll., 1970—. Author: (study guide) Nutrition Concepts and Controversies, 3d edit., 1988, (textbooks) Child Nutrition Practicum, 1994, Dietary Triggers for Migraine, 1996; contbr. articles to profl. jours. Resource nutrition spkr. 1st United Meth. Ch., Phoenix, 1990—; resident mem. The Mountain Club, Prescott, Ariz., 1982-95; del. China Asns. for Sci.-Tech., Peking, 1988. Recipient Star award Chandler, Ariz., 1967-68, Hosp. Aux. Mem. Am. Dietetic Assn., Am. Home Econs. Assn. (cert.), Am. Soc. of Interior Designers, Ret. Edn. Assn., Home Econs. in Bus., Ohio State U. Alumni Assn., Ariz. State U. Alumni Assn., Delta Gamma, Omicron Nu. Republican. Home and Office: 520 W Clarendon Ave Unit E5 Phoenix AZ 85013-3428

HARTNETT, JIM, mayor. Mayor City of Redwood City, Calif. Office: City of Redwood City 1017 Middlefield Rd Redwood City CA 94063

HARTNETT, KATHLEEN CAMBLIN, counselor; b. N.Y.C., July 17, 1942; d. John Hutchinson and Margaret (Donovan) Camblin. BA, St. Mary's Coll., 1964; MEd, Lewis &Clark Coll., 1977; postgrad., Portland State U., 1996—. Lic. profl. counselor, Oreg. Missionary Extension Lay Vols., Anadarko, Okla., 1964-65; social worker Cook County Pub. Aid, Chgo., 1965-67, Cath. Svcs. for Children, Portland, 1967-68; dir. social work Patterson (N.J.) Orphanage, 1968-69; cancer counselor St. Vincent Med. Ctr., Portland, 1974-79; asst. dir. cancer counseling Kaiser Permanente, Portland, 1979-84; dir. cancer counseling Providence Health System, Portland, 1984—; cons. in field. cons. pub. edn. Portland Pub. Schs., Am. Cancer Soc., Portland, Lewis and Clark Coll., Portland, Portland Ctr. Hearing and Speech, Oreg. Comprehensive Cancer Program, Nat. Psoriasis Assn., all 1976—. Mem. Am. Counseling Assn. (mental health spl. interest 1990—), Oreg. Counseling Assn. Office: Providence Health System care Cancer Counseling Svcs 5050 NE Hoyt Level B Portland OR 97213

HART-SCHULZ, TABITHA BERNIER, alternative education educator; b. Seattle, June 10, 1954; d. William Kenneth and Lucille (Sampson/Whitefoot) Bernier; m. Eric Elmore Schulz, Sept. 12, 1977; children: Amber Hart Schulz, Serena Marie Schulz. BA in Fine Art, Lewis and Clark Coll., M of Tchg. Cert. in basic tchg., std. tchg. Mem. Oreg. tchr. intern program Oreg. State U., Corvallis, 1976-77; title IV tutor Salem (Oreg.) Pub. Schs., 1978-79; ABE instr. DES program Cen. Oreg. C.C., Bend, 1989-94; flex instr. Sisters (Oreg.) Sch. Dist., 1993-94; alt. tchr. Warm Springs Reservation Jefferson County Schs. 509-J, Madras, Oreg., 1994—; honorarium lectr. Lewis and Clark Coll., 1993. Mem. ednl. adv. com. Native Peoples wing Oreg. High Desert Mus., Bend, 1993; alt. rep. Title IX Parent Com., Warm Springs, 1995-97; stage mgr. Cascade Festival of Music, Bend Sr. H.S., 1986—; mem. Oreg. Hist. Soc., Oreg. High Desert Mus. Mem. Oreg. Assn. for Alts. in Edn., Oreg. Devel. Studies Orgn., Oreg. Indian Edn. Assn. Home: 1591 NW Saginaw Ave Bend OR 97701

HARTSOUGH, GAYLA ANNE KRAETSCH, management consultant; b. Lakewood, Ohio, Sept. 16, 1949; d. Vernon W. and Mildred E. (Austin) Kraetsch; m. James N. Heller, Aug. 20, 1972 (div. 1977); m. Jeffrey W. Hartsough, Mar. 12, 1983; 1 child, Jeffrey Hunter Kraetsch Hartsough. BS, Northwestern U., 1970; EdM, Tufts U., 1973; MEd, U. Va., 1978, PhD, 1978. Vol. VISTA, Tenn., 1970-71; asst. tchr. Perkins Sch. for the Blind, Watertown, Mass., 1971-72; resource tchr. Fairfax (Va.) County Pub. Schs., 1972-76; asst. dir. ctr. U. Va., Charlottesville, 1976-78; sr. program officer Acad. for Edn. Devel., Washington, 1978-80; mng. cons. Cresap/Towers Perrin, Washington and L.A., 1980-86; pres. KH Consulting Group, L.A., 1986—; mem. adv. coun. Northwestern U. Sch. Speech, Evanston, Ill., 1992—. Contbr. more than 20 articles to profl. jours. Co-founder L.A. Higher Edn. Roundtable, L.A., 1987—. Recipient Outstanding Woman of Achievement award Century City C. of C., 1991. Mem. Orgn. Women Execs. (bd. dirs. L.A. 1986-95). Home: 15624 Royal Ridge Rd Sherman Oaks CA 91403-4207 Office: KH Consulting Group 1901 Ave Of Stars Fl 18 Los Angeles CA 90067-6001

HARTWICK, THOMAS STANLEY, technical management consultant; b. Vandalia, Ill., Mar. 19, 1934; s. William Arthur and Bernice Elizabeth (Daniels) H.; m. Alberta Elaine Lind, June 10, 1961; children: Glynis Anne, Jeffrey Andrew, Thomas Arthur. BS, U. Ill., 1956; MS, UCLA, 1958; PhD, U. So. Calif., 1969. Mgr. quantum electronics dept. Aerospace Corp., El Segundo, Calif., 1973-75, asst. dir. electonics research lab., 1975-79; mgr. electro-optical devel. lab. Hughes Aircraft Co. subs. Gen. Motors Corp., El Segundo, 1979-82, chief sci. advanced tactical programs, 1982-83; mgr. electro-optics research ctr. TRW Corp., Redondo Beach, Calif., 1983-86, mgr. microelectrics ctr., 1986-90, program mgr., 1990-96; chmn., bd. dirs. Laser Tech., Inc., Hollywood, Calif., 1990-94; cons. mem. U.S. Dept. Def. Adv. Group on Electronic Devices, Washington, 1977—, group C chmn., 1988-94; mem. Japan/U.S. Tech. Assessment Team, Washington, 1984; mem. Army Rsch. Labs. Adv. Bd., 1993-95; mem. com. optical sci. and engring. Nat. Rsch. Coun., 1995—. Contbr. articles to profl. jours.; inventor FAR Infrared Laser, 1975. Mem. Am. Phys. Soc., Optical Soc. Am., (com. mem. 1976-79), Am. Def. Preparedness Assn. (dep. chmn. West Coast seminar 1987-88), mem. Nat. Res. Coun. Comm. Optical Sci and Engring., 1995—.

HARTZELL, IRENE JANOFSKY, psychologist; b. L.A. Vor-Diplom, U. Munich, 1961; BA, U. Calif., Berkeley, 1963, MA, 1965; PhD, U. Oreg., 1970. Lic. psychologist, Wash., Ariz. Psychologist Lake Washington Sch. Dist., Kirkland, Wash., 1971-72; staff psychologist VA Med. Ctr., Seattle, 1970-71, Long Beach, Calif., 1973-74; dir. parent edn. Children's Hosp., Orange, Calif., 1975-78; clin. psychologist Kaiser Permanente, Woodland Hills, Calif., 1979—; clin. instr. dept. pediatrics U. Calif. Irvine Coll. Medicine, 1975-78. Author: The Study Skills Advantage, 1986; contbr. articles to profl. jours. Intern Oreg. Legislature, 1974-75. U.S. Vocat. Rehab. Adminstrn. fellow U. Oreg., 1966-67, 69. Mem. APA, Pi Lambda Theta.

HARVEY, ARTHUR WALLACE, music educator; b. Boston, May 20, 1939; s. Ernest L. and Euphemia C. (Forsyth) H.; m. Patricia Wilgus, Aug. 22, 1959; children: Debbie, Laurie, Charles, Lois, Cathy. BS, Gordon Coll., Wenham, Mass., 1959; MM, Boston U., 1965; DMA, Temple U., 1974. Ordained to ministry, Baptist Ch. Dir. bands Vineland (N.J.) Sr. H.S., 1966-71; asst. prof. Barrington (R.I.) Coll., 1971-73; prof. music Ea. Ky. U., Richmond, 1973-90; exec. dir. Music for Health Svcs., Honolulu, 1986—; minister of music Waialae Bapt. Ch., Honolulu, 1991-94; adj. prof. U. Hawaii, Honolulu, 1991—; dir. music and worship Calvary by the Sea Luth. Ch., Honolulu, 1996—; vis. prof. Potsdam Coll./SUNY, 1980-89; mem. Very Spl. Arts Internat., Washington, 1977—. Contbr. numerous articles to profl. jours.; co-prodr.: (video series) Music and the Brain. Bd. dirs. IC Fine Arts Inst. Mem. Internat. Soc. for Music in Medicine, Internat. Arts Medicine Assn., Very Spl. Arts Hawaii (bd. dirs.), Hawaii Music Educators Assn. (pres.-elect). Home and Office: Music for Health Svcs 521 Hahaione St 10H Honolulu HI 96825

HARVEY, DONALD, artist, educator; b. Walthamston, Eng., June 14, 1930; s. Henry and Annie Dorothy (Sawell) H.; m. Elizabeth Clark, Aug. 9, 1952; children—Shan Mary, David Jonathan. Art tchrs. diploma, Brighton Coll. Art, 1951. Art master Ardwyn Grammar Sch., Wales, 1952-56; mem. faculty dept. art U. Victoria, B.C., Can., 1961-95; now prof. emeritus painting U. Victoria. One man exhbns. include, Albert White Gallery, Toronto, 1968, retrospective, Art Gallery of Victoria, 1968; represented in permanent collections, Nat. Gallery Can., Montreal Mus., Albright-Knox Mus., Seattle Art Mus. Mem. accessions com. Art Gallery of Victoria, 1969-72. Can. Council fellow, 1966. Mem. Royal Can. Acad. of Arts (full academician), Can. Group Painters, Can. Painters and Etchers. Home: 1025 Joan Crescent, Victoria, BC Canada V8S 3L3

HARVEY, ELLEN MAE, county official; b. Chewy, Okla., Mar. 4, 1926; d. William P. and Rose M. (Phelps) Patterson; m. Leonard V. Owens, Mar. 11, 1942 (div. Aug. 1953); children: Mary E., Nellie R., Leonard J., Patrick E.; m. James V. Jones, 1953 (div. 1962); 1 child, Russell V. Jones. Provider adult foster home Jackson County Mental Health, Medford, Oreg., 1965—. Mem. Eagles, Moose. Hoe: 2914 Far West Rd Medford OR 97501

HARVEY, GREGORY ALAN, microcomputer technology educator, consultant; b. Harvey, Ill., Feb. 15, 1949; s. Kenneth Herman and Mildred Faye (Pounds) H. BA, U. Ill., 1970; teaching credential, San Francisco State U., 1982. Mem. drafting and design staff Bechtel Engring., San Francisco, 1973-81; computer cons., prin. Harvey & Assocs., San Francisco, 1981-96; prin. Media of the Minds, 1993-96; pres. Mind Over Media, Inc., 1995—; computer cons. PCTeach, Inverness, Calif., 1984-91; profl. lectr. Golden Gate U., 1992. Author: Communication in Writing, 1984, Mastering SuperCalc 3, 1985, Mastering Q&A, 1986, Lotus 1-2-3 Desktop Companion, 1987, WordPerfect Desktop Companion, 1987, Mastering WordStar, 1987, Lotus 1-2-3 Instant Reference, 1988, DOS Instant Reference, 1988, Understanding HyperCard, 1988, HyperTalk Instant Reference, 1988, The Complete Lotus 1-2-3 Handbook, 1989, Mastering PageMaker on the MacIntosh, 1990, Encyclopedia WordPerfect, 1990, Que's WordPerfect Windows QuickStart, 1991, Que's Lotus 1-2-3 Window QuickStart, 1991, PC World's WordPerfect Windows, 1991, Greg Harvey's Excel 4 Handbook Windows, 1992, Greg Harvey's Excel 4 Handbook MacIntosh, 1992, IDG's 1-2-3 for Dummies, 1992, IDG's DOS for Dummies Command Reference, 1993, Windows for Dummies Command Reference, 1993, WordPerfect for Dummies Command Reference, 1993, WordPerfect 6 DOS Handbook, 1993, More Excel for Dummies, 1994, Excel 5 for Mac for Dummies, 1994, Windows 95 for Dummies Quick Reference, 1995, Dummies 101: Excel 5 for Windows 95, 1995, Shockwave for Director for Dummies, 1996, Que's Net Savvy Office, 1997, IDG's Director Studio Secrets, 1997. Mem. Internat. Interactive Comm. Soc., Berkeley Macintosh Users Group. Democrat. Zen Buddhist. Home: 60 Kyleswood Pl Inverness CA 94937-9717 Office: Mind Over Media Inc PO Box 1175 Point Reyes Station CA 94956-1175

HARVEY, JAMES GERALD, educational counselor, consultant, finanicial director, researcher; b. California, Mo., July 15, 1934; s. William Walter and Exie Marie (Lindley) H. BA Amherst Coll., 1956; MAT (fellow), Harvard U., 1958, MEd, 1962. Asst. to dean grad. sch. edn. Harvard U., Cambridge, Mass., 1962-66, dir. admissions, fin. aid, 1966-69; dir. counseling service U. Calif., Irvine, 1970-72; ednl. cons., Los Angeles, 1972—. Author: (ednl. materials) HARVOCAB Vocabulary Program, 1985—. 1st lt. USAF, 1958-61. Amherst Mayo-Smith grantee, 1956-57; UCLA Adminstrv. fellow, 1969-70. Mem. Am. Ednl. Research Assn., Nat. Council Measurement in Edn. Address: 1845 Glendon Ave Los Angeles CA 90025-4653

HARVEY, JOSEPH EMMETT, construction executive; b. L.A., Dec. 4, 1951; s. Emmett Allan and Mary Summerall (Anderson) H. BA in Psychology with distinction, U. Hawaii, 1974; postgrad., U.S. Internat. U., 1975-76, San Diego State U., 1976-77. Ops. mgr. C.S. Goodale Co., San Diego, 1977-84; sales mgr. Dunn & Co., San Diego, 1985-89; constrn. mgr. Comml. Shelving, Inc., Honolulu, 1989-92; constrn. exec. Skylights of Hawaii, Honolulu, 1992—. Program coord. Crisis House, El Cajon, Calif., 1975-79. Mem. Bldg Industry Assn., Constrn. Specifications Inst. (dir. 1994-96, asst. chair western region tech. com. 1994-95, awards chair 1995—, Constrn. Document Technician cert. 1995, merit award 1993, Pacesetter award 1994), Rotary (Svc. award 1993), Phi Beta Kappa.

HARVEY, O.J., retired psychology educator; b. Corinne, Okla., Aug. 27, 1927; s. Joseph Marion and Nina Inez (Little) H.; m. Mary Christine Minton, Nov. 17, 1950. BA, U. Okla., 1950, MA, 1951, PhD, 1954. Fellow Yale U., New Haven, Conn., 1954-55; asst. prof. psychology Vanderbilt U., Nashville, 1955-58; asst. prof. U. Colo., Boulder, 1958-60; assoc. prof. U. Colo., 1960-62, prof., 1964-91, prof. emeritus, 1991—. Author Conceptual Systems and Personality Organization, 1961; editor 2 books; contbr. over 100 articles to profl. jours. With USN, 1946-47. Fellow Ctr. for Advanced Study, Palo Alto, Calif., 1964-65; recipient Career Devel. award NIMH, Washington, 1965-70. Home: 435 S 68th St Boulder CO 80303-4308

HARVEY, RAYMOND CURTIS, conductor; b. N.Y.C., Dec. 9, 1950; s. Shirley Nathaniel and Doris Louise (Walwin) H. BMus, MMus, Oberlin Coll., 1973; M. in Musical Arts, Yale U., 1978, D in Musical Arts, 1984. Choral dir. Northfield (Mass.) Mt. Hermon Sch., 1973-76; asst. conductor Des Moines Metro Opera, Indianola, Iowa, 1977-80; music dir. Tex. Opera Theater, Houston, 1978-80; Exxon/arts endowment conductor Indpls. Symphony, 1980-83; assoc. conductor Buffalo Philharmonic, 1983-86; music dir. Marion (Ind.) Philharmonic, 1982-86, Springfield (Mass.) Symphony, 1986-94; Fresno Philharm. Orch., 1993—; guest conductor Minn. Orch., 1991, 92, Detroit Symphony, 1990, 92, N.Y. Philharmonic, 1987, Atlanta Symphony, 1992, Louisville Orch., 1990, 93, Utah Symphony, 1993. Democrat. Methodist. Office: Fresno Philharm Orch 2610 W Shaw Ave Ste 103 Fresno CA 93711

HARVEY, SIMON, actor, writer; b. Tel Aviv, July 17, 1958; came to U.S., 1959; s. Eric and Esther (Tabori) S. BA, Columbia U., 1980; MFA, U. So. Calif., 1988. Actor television and theatre; freelance speechwriter, 1996—. Appeared in TV on Munsters Today, 1989-90, Lifestories, 1990, Knots Landing, 1990, Parker Lewis Can't Lose, 1991, Reasonable Doubts, 1992, Beverly Hills 90210, 1992, Days of Our Lives, 1992, The Young and the Restless, 1992, Friends, 1996; mem. Free Shakespeare Co., Chgo., 1980-82, Players Workshop of Second City, Chgo., 1981-82, Kern Shakespeare Festival, Bakersfield, Calif., 1987, Utah Shakespeare Festival, 1988, Theater of N.O.T.E., L.A., 1990-92; appeared in L.A. Theater prodns.; writer Frontiers Newsmag., 1994. Mem. SAG (awards nominating com. 1995), AFTRA, AEA. Office: The Levin Agy 8484 Wilshire Blvd Ste 745 Beverly Hills CA 90211

HARVEY, STEWART CLYDE, retired pharmacologist, educator; b. Denver, Feb. 16, 1921; s. John Alden and Marie Bronson (Barfoot) H.; m. Joyce Contance Payne, Dec. 27, 1947 (dec. June 1964); children: Janet Ann Harding, Stephen John; m. Eunice Marie Munk, July 2, 1965. BA, U. Colo., 1943, postgrad., 1946; PhD, U. Chgo., 1948. Instr. U. Colo., Boulder, 1943-46; instr., chmn. pharmacology Dental Coll. U. Tex., Houston, 1948-49; instr. pharmacology U. Utah, Salt Lake City, 1949-51, asst. prof. pharmacology, 1951-53, assoc. prof. pharmacology, 1953-74, prof. pharmacology, 1974-88, prof. emeritus, 1988—; vis. prof. U. Southampton, Eng., 1972-73; mem. rev. panel on pharmacology and toxicology NIH, Bethesda, Med., 1965-66; mem. Utah Heart Rsch. Com., Salt Lake City, 1955-66; cons. com. on drugs AMA, Chgo.; mem. panel on rev. antacids FDA, Bethesda, 1972-74; ad hoc cons. Med. Letter, NSF; cons., expert witness on alcohol and drugs to various cts., 1952-90. Author chpts. in books; assoc. editor Remington's Pharm. Scis., 1963-90, Circulation Rsch., 1958-63. Chmn. 1st senatorial dist. Utah Dem. Party, Salt Lake City, 1953-62; scoutmaster Boy Scouts of Am., Salt Lake City, 1957-65; charter mem. Utah Environ. Ctr., Salt Lake City, 1970-72; mem. Citizens Adv. Panel to U.S. Army Engrs., Ogden, Utah, 1970-72; conservation chmn. Great Salt Lake Audubon, 1995-96. Rsch. grantee NIH, Am. Heart Assn., Utah Heart Assn., Gividan-Delawana. Democrat. Home: 1652 Yale Ave Salt Lake City UT 84105-1720

HARVEY, VIRGINIA ISHAM, curator, fiber artist; b. Hot Springs, S.D., July 5, 1917; d. Russell Raymond and Goldie Marguerite (Coles) Isham; m. William A Harvey, Aug. 27, 1937 (dec. Apr. 1994); children: William A Jr., Russell Wilson. Student, Mills Coll., Oakland, Calif., 1935-36, U. Wash., 1936-37, Cornish Sch. Arts, Seattle, 1955-59. Curator Collections Textile Study Ctr., U. Seattle, 1958-78; cons. Tethers Unltd., Freeland, Wash., 1995—; workshop tchr., lectr. in field. Contbr. articles to profl. jours.; author books and monographs, including Macrame, The Art of Creative Knotting, 1967, Color and Design in Macrame, 1970, Techniques of Basketry, 1976, Threads in Action; exhbns. include N.W. Craftsman Exhbn., 1955-68, Calif. Palace of the Legion of Honor, San Francisco, 1957, Frye Mus., 1959, 60, 61, Contemporary Crafts Gallery, Portland, Oreg., 1961, Mus. History and Industry, Seattle, 1962, Mills Coll., 1963, 64, Kentucky Train, 1966, Mus. Contemporary Crafts, N.Y.C., 1966, Bainbridge Arts and Crafts Festival, 1965, Wash. State Mus., Olympia, 1967, Edmonds Arts and Crafts Festival, 1969, Grand Rapids (Mich.) Art Mus., 1970, Ea. Mich. U., 1973, Boise Mus. Art, 1974, Allied Arts of Tacoma, 1972, Peninsula Textile Exhibit, Port Townsend, 1979, Fiberworks, 1988, others. Panel mem. basketry symposium Wing Luke Mus., Seattle, 1988; judge weaving Skagit County Fair, 1989, 90. Recipient N.W. Craftsmen Exhbn. award, 1957, Rsch. award Pacific N.W. Arts and Crafts Fair, Bellevue, Wash., 1957, 64, Fiberworks award, 1988; Am. Crafts Coun. Hon. fellow, 1996. Mem. Seattle Weavers Guild (pres. 1956), Whidbey Weavers Guild, Pacific N.W. Needlarts Guild (hon.), N.W. Designer Craftsmen (hon.), PEO Sisterhood (rec. sec. 1951-54).

HARVIE, J. JASON, administrative aide, private secretary; b. Seattle, Wash., Dec. 12, 1937; s. James Joseph Harvie and Betty Clair (Walton) Krussow; m. Maureen W.Y. Johnson, June 12, 1970 (div. Sept. 1980). Cert. Law Enforcement, U. Guam, Agana, 1973, Grad. Basic Police Acad., 1973, Advanced Police Technology, 1974; Diploma, San Francisco Police Acad., 1980. Police officer II Gov. of Guam/Dept. Pub. Safety, Agana, 1972-77; chief dept. safety and secutiy U. Calif. Hastings/Coll. of Law, San Francisco, 1978-82; chief patrol officer San Francisco Parking Authority, 1982-84; aide H.E. Sheik Abdullah O. Mahdi, Pebble Beach, Calif., 1984-96. Decorated Navy Achievement medal USN; named Knight Chevalier, Grand Knight/Police Hall of Fame, Miami, 1989; recipient Legion of Honor award Am. Police Hall of Fame, Miami, 1990. Mem. Am. Fedn. Police, Calif. Peace Officers Assn., Marine's Meml. Club, Am. Police Hall of Fame. Republican. Episcopalian. Home and Office: PO Box 1018 Pebble Beach CA 93953

HARVIE, KEITH WILLIAM, orthopaedic surgeon; b. Cornith, N.Y., July 20, 1940; s. Donald Edwin and Gussie (Sclar) H.; m. Betty Kramer, June 10, 1964; children: Lois Rebecca, Joel Seaton. BA, Yeshiva U., 1961; DO, Kirksville Coll., 1965. Pvt. practice Orthopedic Cons. Ltd., Albuquerque, 1974—; chmn. dept. surgery St. Joseph Heights Hosp., Albuquerque, 1981-92. Pres. Jewish Fedn. Greater Albuquerque, 1992-94. Fellow Am. Osteo. Bd. Surgery, Internat. Coll. Surgeons, Am. Acad. Orthopedic Surgeons, AOAO, NASS, ITS. Office: 4325 Carlisle Blvd NE Albuquerque NM 87107-4810

HARWICK, BETTY CORINNE BURNS, sociology educator; b. L.A., Jan. 22, 1926; d. Henry Wayne Burns and Dorothy Elizabeth (Menzies) Routhier;

m. Burton Thomas Harwick, June 20, 1947; children: Wayne Thomas, Burton Terence, Bonnie Christine Foster, Beverly Anne Carroll. *Betty is a third generation Californian. Her husband, Burton Thomas Harwick from Deer Lodge, Montana, is a founder and president of Dynatrol National Corporation which principally produces electronic motor controllers and water purity monitors. He received an AB in physics from the University of California at Berkeley in 1951 and did postgraduate work at the University of California at Los Angeles. He was a project engineer for Atomics International, a division of North American Aviation. He was a chief electronic technician in the U.S. Navy during WWII. Betty and Burton met at Intervarsity Christian Fellowship at University of California at Berkeley.* Student, Biola, 1942-45, Summer Inst. Linguistics, 1945, U. Calif., Berkeley, 1945-52; BA, Calif. State U., Northridge, 1961, MA, 1965; postgrad., MIT, 1991. Prof. sociology Pierce Coll., Woodland Hills, Calif., 1966-95, pres. acad. senate, 1976-77, pres. faculty assn., 1990-91, chair dept. for philosophy and sociology, 1990-95, co-founder/faculty advisor interdisciplinary religious studies program, 1988-95; chmn. for sociology L.A. C.C. Dist., 1993-95. Author: (with others) Introducing Sociology, 1977; author: Workbook for Introducing Sociology, 1978. faculty rep. Calif. C.C. Assn., 1977-80. Alt. fellow NEH, 1978. Mem. Am. Acad. Religion, Soc. Bibl. Lit., Am. Sociol. Assn. Presbyterian. Home: 19044 Superior St Northridge CA 91324-1845

HARWICK, MAURICE, lawyer; b. L.A., Feb. 6, 1933. AA, L.A. City Coll., 1954; JD, Southwestern U., 1957. Bar: Calif., 1958; U.S. Supreme Ct., 1962. Dep. dist. atty. County of Los Angeles, 1958-60; pvt. practice law, Santa Monica, Calif., 1960—; judge pro tem Municipal Ct., 1966-67, 80-81, 85—; past advisor to dist. atty. Los Angeles County. Chmn. bd. rev. Los Angeles Community Colls. and City Schs.; mem. Project Safer Calif. gov.'s com., 1974-75. Mem. Calif. Bar Assn., Los Angeles County Bar Assn., Dist. Attys. Assn. L.A., Criminal Cts. Bar Assn. (pres. 1972, bd. govs.), Assn. Trial Lawyers Am., Los Angeles County Dist. Attys. Assn., Vikings. Office: Ste 22 7401 Laurel Canyon Blvd North Hollywood CA 91615

HARWICK, WAYNE THOMAS, economist; b. Oakland, Calif., Feb. 29, 1948; s. Burton Thomas and Betty Corinne (Burns) H. BA in Econs., Calif. State Univ., Northridge, 1970, MA in Econs., 1975; BA in Math., Calif. State Univ., L.A., 1983. Planner Ventura (Calif.) County Schs., 1975-76; labor market economist Calif. Employment Data Rsch., L.A., 1976-83; cost analyst TRW, Redondo Beach, Calif., 1983-88; engring. specialist Northrop-Grumman, Pico Rivera, Calif., 1988-92, 96—; cost economist Aerojet, Azusa, Calif., 1992-94; sr. assoc. Mgmt. Consulting Rsch., Oxnard, Calif., 1994-95; instr. Oxnard Coll., 1975-78; owner Industry Metrics, Torrance, Calif., 1995—; spkr. in field. Bd. dirs. Homeowners Assn., Torrance, 1993-95. Mem. Soc. Cost Estimating Analysis (cert. cost analyst), Internat. Soc. Parametric Analysts (So. Calif. bd. dirs. 1997), Assn. Proposal Mgmt. Profls., World Affairs Coun., West End Tennis Club. Presbyterian. Home: 4404 Spencer St Torrance CA 90503 Office: Northrop Grumman Corp 8900 Washington Blvd Pico Rivera CA 90660-3765

HASAN, MAHMOOD UL, secondary school educator; b. Dibai, India, Aug. 12, 1945; came to U.S. 1981; s. Qazi Saeed and Khursheed (Zehra) Ahmad; m. Olga Marie Feixova, Dec. 4, 1976 (div. July 1993); children: Shaun, Talib; m. Ghazala Qamar Omar, Sept. 10, 1993; 1 child, Afreen. BSc with honors, U. Karachi, Pakistan, 1964; MSc, U. Karachi, 1965; BEd, U. New Brunswick, Fredericton, Can., 1973. Lectr. Habib Tech. Inst., Nawabshah, 1965-66, S.M. Sc. Coll., Karachi, 1966-67; tchr. Lake Manitoba Sch., Vogar, 1975-81; instructional asst. San Jose (Calif.) City Coll., 1985-88; tchr. San Francisco Unified Sch. Dist., 1988—. Author (computer software) Pascal Tutor, 1993. Mem. Calif. Tchrs. Assn., San Francisco Math. Tchrs. Assn., Pakistan Engrs. and Scientists Assn. Islam. Home: 4176 Sophia Way San Jose CA 95134-1522 Office: Phillip and Sala Burton Acad High Sch 400 Mansell St San Francisco CA 94134-1829

HASELBUSH, RUTH BEELER, retired newspaper editor; b. Kansas City, Mo., July 19, 1922; d. Maxwell Newton and Mary Springer Beeler; m. Weber F. Trout, Aug. 15, 1942 (dec. May 1985); m. Willard C. Haselbush, May 22, 1988; children: Gregory, Jeffrey Trout. BA, U. Denver, 1946; postgrad., U. Kans., 1939, 40, 41, U. Wis., 1940. Editor Park Ridge Adv. Pioneer Press, Chgo., 1967-88; ret., 1988. Charter mem. Park Ridge (Ill.) Hist. Soc., 1971. Named Mem. of Yr., Park Ridge C. of C., 1980. Mem. DAR (sec. Colo. chpt. 1990-94, chaplain 1994-96), Denver Post Retirees, Denver Press Club, Soc. Profl. Journalists (sec., mem. chmn. Headline club 1974-76), Alpha Chi Omega (pres. 1956-57), U. Denver Alumni. Republican. Baptist. Home: 370 Forest St Denver CO 80220-5753

HASENKAMP, BRUCE HENRY, foundation executive; b. Bklyn., May 12, 1938; s. Henry Ernst Hasenkamp and Ruth Frances (Hoyer) Savage; m. Inta Sarma Macs, May 13, 1973; 1 child, Peter Andris Henry. AB cum laude, Dartmouth Coll., 1960; JD, Stanford U., 1963. Bar: Calif. 1964, N.Y. 1964, U.S. Dist. Ct. (no. dist.) Calif. 1964, U.S. Ct. Appeals (9th cir.) 1964, U.S. Dist. Ct. (so. dist.) N.Y. 1968, U.S. Supreme Ct. 1968. Assoc. Simpson Thacher and Bartlett, N.Y.C., 1963-68; asst. dean law sch. Stanford (Calif.) U., 1968-73; dir. Pres.'s Commn. on White House Fellowships, Washington, 1974-77; dir. pub. affairs Shaklee Corp., San Francisco, 1978-82; exec. v.p. The Hannaford Co., San Francisco, 1983-85; v.p. The Asia Found., San Francisco, 1985-86; v.p. pub. affairs Hosp. Council No. Calif., San Mateo, 1986-89; exec. dir. St. Francis Found., San Francisco, 1989—; mem. Pres.'s Commn. on White House Fellowships, 1981-92, Calif. Med. Bd., 1987—, pres., 1993-94; dir. Direct Selling Assn. Trustee World Affairs Coun. No. Calif., San Francisco, 1981-88, Hillsborough City Sch. Dist., 1985-93, pres., 1986-87, 92-93; vice chmn. Hillsborough Recreation Commn., 1989-91; steering com. Bay Area Coun., San Francisco, 1980-82, dep. Calif. Roundtable, San Francisco, 1980-82; pres. Calif. Rep. League, 1971-73; asst. sec. Calif. Reps., 1973-74; dir. Coun. of Better Bus. Bur., 1980-84, Nat. Commn. for Certification of Physician Assts., 1992—. Mem. Nat. Assn. Corp. Dirs., Calif. State Bar Assn. (ho. dels. 1971), Fedn. of State Med. Bds. of U.S. (editl. bd. 1989-95, bd. dirs. 1993—, treas. 1995—), Commonwealth Club of Calif. (gov. 1981-85), Univ. Club, Capitol Hill Club (Washington), Sigma Phi Epsilon (nat. dir. 1973-87, grand pres. 1991-93). Mem. Anglican Ch. Home: 2435 Skyfarm Dr Hillsborough CA 94010-6343 Office: St Francis Found Ste 1208 900 Hyde St San Francisco CA 94109

HASHIMOTO, LLOYD KEN, communications executive; b. Cheyenne, Wyo., Sept. 21, 1944; s. Harry H. and Bettie M. (Kadota) H. Student in chemistry, 1963-65, student in elec. engring., 1969-72, student in edn., 1979; BSin Vocat. Edn., U. Wyo., 1992. Prin. Teltron Electronics, Laramie, Wyo., 1972—; audio visual technician U. Wyo., Laramie, 1972—; mem. internat. panel Electronics Mag., 1974, 76; instr. workshops and seminars High Tech to a Lay Person, 1978; instr. workshop radio direction finding, 1988—; mem. edn. steering com. U. Wyo. Grad. Mountain Folk Sch., 1993-94. Contbr. articles to profl. jours. Program chmn., unit and dist. commr. Snowy Range dist. Boy Scouts Am., Laramie, 1985—, instr. Longs Peak Coun. With U.S. Army, 1965-69. Recipient award of merit Boy Scouts Am., 1991, Silver Beaver award Boy Scouts Am., 1993, Disting. Commr. award Boy Scouts Am., 1994. Mem. IEEE, Assn. Ednl. Comms. Tech. (assoc. audio visual technician S.E. Wyo. chpt.), Soc. Internat. Devel., Assn. for Field Svc. Mgrs. Internat., Am. Legion, Masons (cryptic Masons youth leadership award for Wyo. 1994), Shriners. Home: 504 S 26th St Laramie WY 82070-4932 Office: Teltron Electronics PO Box 1049 Laramie WY 82070-1049

HASKELL, DONALD, agricultural products executive; b. 1928. Chmn. bd. M.H. Sherman Co., Newport Beach, Calif., 1960—, Tejon Ranch Co., Lebec, Calif. Office: Tejon Ranch Co 4436 Lebec Rd Lebec CA 93243*

HASLAM, GERALD WILLIAM, writer, educator; b. Bakersfield, Calif., Mar. 18, 1937; s. Fredrick Martin and Lorraine Hope (Johnson) H.; m. Janice Eileen Pettichord, July 1, 1961; children: Frederick W., Alexandra R., Garth C., Simone B., Carlos V. BA, San Francisco State U., 1963, MA, 1965; PhD, Union Grad. Sch., 1980. Instr. English San Francisco State U., San Francisco, 1966-67; asst. prof. English Sonoma State U., Rohnert Park, Calif., 1967-70, assoc. prof. English, 1970-74, prof. English, 1971—; adj. prof. Union Grad. Sch., Cin., 1984—, The Nat. Faculty, Atlanta, 1984—. Editor various anthologies; author various booklets, monographs, film scripts, (fiction) Okies: Selected Stories, 1973, Masks: A Novel, 1976, The Wages of Sin: Collected Stories, 1980, Hawk Flights: Visions of the West, 1983, Snapshots: Glimpses of the Other California, 1985, The Man Who Cultivated Fire and Other Stories, 1987, That Constant Coyote: California Stories, 1990, Condor Dreams and Other Fictions, 1994, The Great Tejon Club Jubilee, 1995, (non-fiction) Voices of a Place, 1987, Coming of Age in California, 1990, The Other California, 1990, The Great Central Valley: California's Heartland, 1993. With U.S. Army, 1958-60. Creative Writing fellow Calif. Arts Coun., 1989; recipient Benjamin Franklin award, 1993, Bay Area Book Reviewers' Non-fiction award, 1994, Commonwealth Club medal for Calif., 1994, award of merit Assn. State & Local History, 1994. Mem. PEN U.S.A. West (Josephine Miles award 1990), Western Lit. Assn. (bd. dirs., past pres.), Calif. Studies Assn. (steering com., founding mem.), Calif. Hist. Assn., Calif. Tchrs. Assn., San Francisco State U. Alumni Assn. (life), Union Inst. Alumni Assn., Multi-Ethnic Lit. of U.S. (founding mem.), Robinson Jeffers Assn. (founding mem.), Sierra Club, The Nature Conservancy, Calif. Trout (founding mem.), The Commonwealth Club, Tulare Basin Archeology Group, Save the American River Assn. Roman Catholic. Office: Sonoma State U 1801 E Cotati Ave Rohnert Park CA 94928-3613

HASNEY, CHRISTOPHER WILLIAM, retired investment company executive, educator; b. Pasadena, Calif., Aug. 4, 1951; s. James Francis and Sherry (Locke) H. BS, Santa Clara Coll., 1976; MS, Coll. for Fin. Planning, 1994. Fin. planner Sierra Vista, Ariz., 1983-86; assoc. v.p. investments Dean Witter Reynolds, Inc., Sierra Vista, Ariz., 1986-96; ret., 1996; assoc. faculty Cochise Coll., Sierra Vista, 1988-94. Contbr. articles to profl. jours. Asst. tech. dir. Sierra Repertory Co., 1984—. Capt. U.S. Army, 1976-84. Mem. Am. Contract Bridge Assn., Rotary (pres. Sierra Vista South 1993-94, Paul Harris fellow 1992), PDs Men's Golf Club. Republican. Home: PO Box 2792 Sierra Vista AZ 85636-2792

HASPIEL, GEORGE SIDNEY, writer, illustrator; b. St. Louis, Jan. 1, 1929; s. Harry Hyman and Ceilia (Edelstein) H.; m. Margaret Fleming, Dec. 22, 1973; children: Erica, Adam, Lisa. AB, Washington U., St. Louis, 1951; MS, 1953; PhD, Pa. State U., 1961. Dir. Audiology Clinic Tulane U., New Orleans, 1953-54; clin. audiologist Northwestern U., Evanston, Ill., 1954-56; co-dir. Outpatient Audiology Pa. State U., State College, 1956-60; dir. Hunter Coll., N.Y.C., 1960-64; co-dir. Pa. State U., State College, 1964-69; pvt. practice St. Lukes Hearing and Speech Ctr., San Francisco, 1969-91; exec. dir. St. Lukes Corr. Dental-Facial Deformities, San Francisco, 1988-91, St. Lukes Cognition and Learning Ctr., San Francisco, 1988-91; dir. Dragon Press Pub. Co., San Francisco, 1988—; dir. Lang. Rsch. Jewish Guild for the Blind, N.Y.C., 1962-66; dir. Title III Project Cupertino (Calif.) Pub. Schs., 1973-76; adv. bd. Sr. Adv. Group, San Francisco, 1987-90. Author: (test) Discrimination By Identification of Pictures, 1961, Children's Articulation Test, 1990, (books) Lipreading for Children, 1988, Language Activities for Children, 1989. Fellow Am. Speech and Hearing Assn. (life). Democrat. Jewish. Home: 127 Sycamore Ave Mill Valley CA 94941-2821

HASSER, CHRISTOPHER JOHN, electrical engineer; b. N.Y.C., Sept. 5, 1968; s. Charles John and Clayton (Raker) H. BSEE, Cornell U., 1991; MSEE, U. Dayton, 1995. Bio-environ. engr. Sch. Aerospace Medicine USAF, San Antonio, 1991; biorobotics engring. project leader USAF, Dayton, Ohio, 1991-96; chief rsch. engr. Immersion Human Interface Corp., San Jose, Calif., 1996—. EMT Lansing (N.Y.) Fire Dept. Ambulance Co., 1987-91, Beavercreek (Ohio) Fire Dept., 1991-96. Capt. USAF, 1991-96. Named Mil. Person of Yr., Beavercreek C. of C., 1991; scholar USAFR Officer Tng. Cors, Cornell U., 1986-90. Mem. Robotics and Automation Soc. of IEEE, Nat. Assn. EMT's, Sigma Alpha Epsilon. Office: Immersion 2158 Paragon Dr San Jose CA 95131-1305 Home: 1436 Gordy Dr San Jose CA 95131

HASSON, STEVEN J., chairman board of county commissioners; b. Spokane, Wash., July 29, 1950; s. John W. Higgins and Arden L. (Whitehead) H.; m. Janet S., June 12, 1982; children: Jenny Lynn, Nicholas Ryan, Paul Andrew. BA in Urban & Regional Planning, Eastern Wash. U., 1982, BA in Earth Sci. cum laude, 1982. Cert. journeyman carpenter. Self-employed bldg. contractor Wash., 1973-82; urban planner Spokane (Wash.) County Planning Dept., 1983; pk. and recreation planner Spokane (Wash.) Pks. Dept., 1984; utility planner Spokane (Wash.) County Utilities Dept., 1985, mgr. aquifer protection area, 1986, mgr. sewer and water protection svcs., 1987; county commr. Spokane County, 1988-92, 1992—, hearing examiner officer, 1993—. Past chmn., mem. Spokane County Health Dist., 1989—; vice chmn. Eastern Wash. Area Agy. on Aging, 1989—; past pres. Magnuson Club, Spokane, 1986—; exec. bd. Spokane Transit Authority, 1989—; exec. bd. mem. Solid Waste Authority, 1995—; chmn. Spokane County Air Pollution Control Authority, 1995—; exec. bd. Spokane Regional Transp. Coun., Spokane Valley Festival Orgn., 1996, Spokane Regional Conv. & Visitors Bur., 1996, Spokane County Growth Mgmt. Bd., 1996; mem. New Century Plan, 1996, Wash. Dept. Ecology Air Quality adv. bd., 1996; mem. Spokane County Law & Justice adv. bd.; adv. bd. Habitat for Humanity. With U.S. Army, 1975-76. Recipient Cert. of Merit, Nat. Dean's List, 1981, 82, Achievement award Planning Assn. of Wash., 1984. Mem. Spokane Valley Bus. Assn., Am. Planning Assn., Wash. State Assn. Counties, Citizens League (founding mem. 1986—), Spokane Club, Spokane Valley C. of C., Spokane City C. of C. Republican. Home: 2020 S Pierce Rd Spokane WA 99206-5687 Office: Spokane County Commr Office 1116 W Broadway Ave Spokane WA 99260-2052

HASTINGS, ELISA KIPP, English language educator; b. L.A., May 14, 1956; d. Charles F. and Margaret Heaney) Kipp; m. Robert Allan Hastings Jr., July 18, 1987; 1 child, Trevor Carlyle. BA in Theatre Arts, Calif. State U., Northridge, 1978; postgrad., Calif. State U., Dominguez Hills, 1996—. Cert. single subject credential English, English lang. devel. Tchr. Horance Mann Jr. H.S., L.A., 1983-88, Bell Gardens (Calif.) H.S., 1988-92; tchr. Bellflower (Calif.) H.S., 1993—, sch. site coun., 1994-96; festival judge Drama and Shakespeare Festivals, L.A., 1990-92; judge regional speech competition, Cyrpess, Calif., 1995; mem. curriculum devel. com. Bellflower Sch. Dist., 1996—; advisor Calif. Scholarship Fedn., 1994-96. Prodr., dir.: (video prodn.) Tartuffe, 1991; dir. sch. plays and festivals, 198-96. Sponsor Christian Children's Fund, 1984-96; mem. Klanwatch-So. Poverty Law Ctr., 1990-96; guild mem. Shakespeare Festival, L.A., 1995-96. Recipient Cert. of Appreciation Sch. Site Coun., Bellflower H.S., 1996. Mem. Drama Tchrs. Assn. So. Calif., RESOLVE Nat. Home: 6115 John Ave Long Beach CA 90805-3633 Office: Bellflower HS 15301 Mcnab Ave Bellflower CA 90706-4101

HASTINGS, L(OIS) JANE, architect, educator; b. Seattle, Mar. 3, 1928; d. Harry and Camille (Pugh) H.; m. Norman John Johnston, Nov. 22, 1969. B.Arch., U. Wash., Seattle, 1952, postgrad. in Urban Planning, 1958. Architect Boeing Airplane Co., Seattle, 1951-54; recreational dir. Germany, 1954-56; architect (various firms), Seattle, 1956-59, pvt. practice architecture, 1959-74; instr. archtl. drafting Seattle Community Coll., part-time 1969-80; owner/founder The Hastings Group Architects, Seattle, 1974—; lectr. design Coll. Architecture, U. Wash., 1975; incorporating mem. Architecta (P.S.), Seattle, 1980; pres. Architecta (P.S.), from 1980; mem. adv. bd. U. Wash. YWCA, 1967-69; mem. Mayor's Com. on Archtl. Barriers for Handicapped, 1974-75; chmn. regional public adv. panel on archtl. and engring. services GSA, 1976; mem. citizens adv. com. Seattle Land Use Adminstrn. Task Force, from 1979; AWIU guest of Soviet Women's Con., 1983; speaker Pacific Rim Forum, Hong Kong, 1987; guest China Internat. Conf. Ctr. for Sci. and Tech. of the China Assn. for Sci. and Tech., 1989; mem. adv. com. Coll. architecture and urban planning U. Wash., 1993; mem. accreditation team U. Oreg. Coll. Architecture, 1991, N.J. Inst. Tech. Sch. Architecture, 1992. Design juror for nat. and local competitions, including Red Cedar Shingle/AIA awards, 1977, Current Use Honor awards, AIA, 1980, Exhibit of Sch. Architecture award, 1981; Contbr. to: also spl. features newspapers, articles in profl. jours. Sunset mag. Mem. bd. Am. Women for Internat. Understanding, del. to, Egypt, Israel, USSR, 1971, Japan and Korea, 1979, USSR, 1983; mem. Landmarks Preservation Bd. City of Seattle, 1981-83; mem. Design Constrn. Rev. Bd. Seattle Sch. Dist., 1985-87; mem. mus. con. Mus. History and Industry, 1987—; leader People to People del. women architects to China, 1990. Recipient AIA/The Seattle Times Home of Month Ann. award, 1968; Exhbn. award Seattle chpt. AIA, 1970; Environ. award Seattle-King County Bd. Realtors, 1970, 77,; AIA/House and Home/The American Home Merit award, 1971, Sp. Honor award Wash. Aggregates and Concrete Assn., 1993, Prize bridge Am. Inst. Steel Contrn., 1993; Honor award Seattle chpt. AIA, 1977, 83; Women Achievement award Past Pres. Assembly, 1983, Washington Women and Trading Cards, 1983; Nat. Endowment for Arts grantee, 1977; others; named to West Seattle High Sch. Hall of Fame, 1989, Woman of Achievement Matrix Table, 1994; named Woman of Distinction, Columbia River Girl Scout Coun., 1994. Fellow AIA (pres. Seattle chpt. 1975, pres. sr. coun. 1980, state exec. bd. 1975, N.W. regional dir. 1982-87, Seattle chpt. found. bd. 1985-87, Bursar Coll. Fellows 1989-90, Coll. of Fellows historian 1994—, internat. rels. com. 1988-92, vice chancellor 1991, chancellor 1992, Seattle chpt. medal 1995), Internat. Union Women Architects (v.p. 1969-79, sec. gen. 1985-89, del. UIA Congress, Montreal 1990), Am. Arbitration Assn. (arbitrator 1981—), Coun. of Design Professions, Assn. Women Contrs., Suppliers and Design Cons., Allied Arts Seattle, Fashion Group, Tau Sigma Delta, Alpha Rho Chi (medal). Office: The Hastings Group-Architects 603 Stewart St Ste 915 Seattle WA 98101-1229 *It is not the quantity but the quality of space that is important.*

HASTINGS, MERRILL GEORGE, JR., publisher, marketing consultant; b. Dedham, Mass., May 12, 1922; s. Merrill G. and Emita E. (Zeil) H.; m. Priscilla G. Brayton, July 31, 1948; children: William, Deborah. Educ., Bowdoin Coll., 1946. Chmn. bd., pres. Skiing Pub. Co., Denver, 1950-64, Colorado Mag., Inc., Denver, 1964-77, Mountain Bus. Pubs., Denver, 1972-77, Hastings, Johnsus & White, Vail, Colo., 1977-79, Energy Pub. Co., Denver, 1980-82, Pulse Pubs., Denver, 1985-87, Living Will Ctr., Denver, 1990—, Colo. Mag. LLC, Denver, 1994-96; chmn. bd. Continental Divide Trail Alliance, 1996; founder of The Colo. Trail, 1974. Founder Colo. Trail, 1974,. Recipient Austrian IXth Winter Olympic medal, Innsbruck, 1964. Home: Sunnyvail Rnch Mc Coy CO 80463 Office: 1250 Poppy Creek Rd Mc Coy CO 80463-9705

HASTINGS, NANCY PETERS, editor, publisher; b. Lincoln, Nebr., Jan. 3, 1952; d. Jim N. and Doris (Dunn) Peters; m. Robert Martin Hastings, Sept. 5, 1987; 1 child, Keighley Tenaya. BS summa cum laude, U. Nebr., 1973, MA in English, 1977, MA in Classical Greek, 1985; MA in Creative Writing, N.Mex. State U., 1987. Artist in the schs. Nebr. Arts Coun., Omaha, 1975—; instr. Latin dept. fgn. langs. N.Mex. State U., Las Cruces, 1988-89; elderhostel instr. Elderhostel, Las Cruces, 1986—; instr. English dept. N.Mex. State U., Las Cruces, 1985-87; coll. instr. dept. classics U. Nebr., Lincoln, 1980-82, 84-85; instr. Greek and world history Doane Coll., Crete, Nebr., 1984-85; state poetry coord. Nebr. Arts Coun., Omaha, 1978-80; editor, pub. Whole Notes Press, Las Cruces, 1984—, 1988—; judge S.W. Creative Writing Awards for High Sch., N.Mex. State U., 1986—; speaker poetry symposium S.E. C.C., Lincoln, 1990; approved artist NEA, Nebr., N.Mex., Utah, Wyo., 1975—. Author: (poetry) A Quiet I Carry With Me, 1994; guest editor Cafe Solo, 1996—. Vice chair Gov.'s Career Devel. Conf. for Women, Las Cruces, 1987, chair, 1988; exec. dir. A Children's Theatre Co., 1997; exec. dir. ACT, 1996—. Mem. Coordinating Coun. of Literary Mags., Las Cruces Press Women (treas.). Democrat. Methodist. Office: Whole Notes Press PO Box 1374 Las Cruces NM 88004-1374

HASTINGS, RICHARD (DOC HASTINGS), congressman; b. Spokane, Wash., Feb. 7, 1941; m. Claire; 3 children. Student, Columbia Basin Coll., 1959-81, Ctrl. Wash. U., 1953-64. Pres. Columbia Basin Paper & Supply, 1967—; mem. Wash. State Ho. of Reps., 1979-87, 104th Congress from 4th Wash. dist., 1994—; bd. dirs. Yakima Fed. Savings & Loan; chmn. Franklin County Republican Com., 1974-78; served on Ways & Means, Energy and Utilities, Agriculture, Judiciary, Constitution & Elections, Rules Coms. Office: US House Reps 1323 Longworth House Office Bldg Washington DC 20515-4704*

HATAI, THOMAS HENRY, international marketing professional; b. Tokyo, Dec. 27, 1937; came to U.S., 1951; s. Isamu Herbert and Kiyoko (Kume) H.; m. Geraldine Hatai, Jan. 19, 1970 (div. 1978); children: Dickson Y.V.P., Keio Gijuku Yochisha. BS, Woodbury Univ., 1965. Supr. internat. dept. Union Bank, L.A., 1964-66; with mgmt. United Airlines, L.A., 1966-69; v.p. far east Travel Systems Internat., Oakbrook, Ill., 1969-75; pres. Hatai Internat., L.A., 1975-78; pres., chief exec. officer Pace Mktg., Inc., La Habra, Calif., 1978—; founder, pres. Pace Products, Inc., 1983-91, DBH Global Ltd., 1983—; founder, vice chmn. bd. dirs., CEO Yamamo Cosmetics Inc., 1991—; pres., CEO Yamamo Products Inc. (dba AVEC), 1992—; bd. dirs. Gradn Five Corp., Bangkok, Thailand. Illustrators: The Marty Story, 1954, The St. Meinrad Story, 1954. Mem. United Internat. Club (bd. dirs. 1969 Japan), U.S. C. of C. Republican. Home: 8544 Buena Tierra Pl Buena Park CA 90621-1002 Office: D B H Global Ltd 1251C S Beach Blvd La Habra CA 90631-6301

HATCH, ELVIN JAMES, anthropology educator; b. Tulare, Calif., Sept. 20, 1937; s. Raymond K. and Elvera (Anderson) H.; m. Deanna Elizabeth Fries; children: Kristen Lee, Catherine Anderson. BA, Fresno State Coll., 1959; PhD, UCLA, 1968. Lectr. anthropology U. Calif., Santa Barbara, 1967-68, asst. prof. anthropology, 1968-74, assoc. prof. anthropology, 1974-79, prof. anthropology, 1979—, chair dept. anthropology, 1978-84; mem. editorial com. U. Calif. Press, Berkeley, 1986-91, co-chair editorial com., 1988-91. Author: Theories of Man and Culture, 1973, Biography of a Small Town, 1979, Culture and Morality, 1983, Respectable Lives, 1991. Mem. Am. Anthropol. Assn. Office: Dept Anthropology Univ Calif Santa Barbara CA 93106

HATCH, GARY LAYNE, English educator, writer; b. South Jordan, Utah, Sept. 15, 1964; s. LaRelle J. and Jacqueline Deanna (Roberts) H.; m. AnneMarie Henrichsen, May, 31, 1986; children: Aubrey, Carson, Maren. BA in English, Brigham Young U., 1988; PhD in English, Ariz. State U., 1992. Field rep. LDS Ch., Copenhagen, Denmark, 1983-85; instr. LDS Missionary Tng. Ctr., Provo, Utah, 1986-88; teaching assoc. Ariz. State U., Tempe, 1988-92; asst. prof. Brigham Young U., Provo, 1992—; composition coord. English dept. Brigham Young U., 1993—; moderator H-Rhetor Electronic Conf., Mich. State. U., 1993—. Author: Arguing in Communities, 1996; contbr. articles to profl. jours. Kennedy Ctr. rsch. grantee Brigham Young U., Provo, 1994, 97; Regent scholar 1991, 92. Mem. Nat. Coun. Tchrs. of English, Internat. Soc. Social Argumentation, Internat. Soc. for History of Rhetoric, 18th Century Scottish Studies Soc., Brigham Young Scholar Assn. (pres.). Democrat. Office: English Dept Brigham Young U 3146 JKHB Provo UT 84604-2724

HATCH, GEORGE CLINTON, television executive; b. Erie, Pa., Dec. 16, 1919; s. Charles Milton and Blanche (Beecher) H.; m. Wilda Gene Glasmann, Dec. 24, 1940; children: Michael Gene Zbar, Diane Glasmann Orr, Jeffrey Beecher, Randall Clinton, Deepika Hatch Avanti. AB, Occidental Coll., 1940; MA in Econs., Claremont Coll., 1941; HHD (hon.), So. Utah U., 1988. Pres. Comms. Investment Corp., Salt Lake City, 1945-95; chmn. Double G Comm. Corp., Salt Lake City, 1956—; dir. Republic Pictures Corp., Los Angeles, 1971-94; pres. Sta. KVEL, Inc., 1978-94; pres. Standard Corp., Ogden, 1993—; past mem. Salt Lake adv. bd. First Security Bank Utah; past chmn. Rocky Mountain Pub. Broadcasting Corp.; past chmn. bd. govs. Am. Info. Radio Network; past bd. govs. NBC-TV Affiliates. Past pres. Salt Lake Com. on Fgn. Relations; past mem. Utah Symphony Bd., Salt Lake City; past chmn., past mem. Utah State Bd. Regents, 1964-85. Recipient Svc. to Journalism award U. Utah, 1966, silver medal Salt Lake Advt. Club, 1969, Disting. Svc. award Utah Tech. U., 1984, Disting. Utahan Centennial Yr. award Margaret Thatcher U.K., Utah Festival, 1996. Mem. Nat. Assn. Broadcasters (past pres., radio bd. dirs., ambassador to Inter-Am. mtgs. in Latin Am. 1962), Utah Broadcasters Assn. (past pres., Mgmt. award 1964, Hall of Fame award 1981), Salt Lake City Advt. Club (silver medal 1969), Phi Beta Kappa, Phi Rho Pi (life). Democrat. Office: The Std Corp 1537 Chandler Dr Salt Lake City UT 84103-4220 *George Hatch commenced his broadcast career as manager of KLO-AM in Ogden, Utah in 1941. He served as chairman of Intermountain Radio Network, 1941-87, and constructed KALL-AM in Salt Lake City, Utah, in 1945, and KALL-FM, in 1968. He operated radio stations: KGHL-AM and KIDX-FM, Billings, KYSS-AM-FM, Missoula, KMON-AM, Great Falls, KOPR-AM, Butte, Montana; KGEM-AM and KJOT-FM, Boise, KUPI-AM and KQPI-FM, Idaho Falls, KLIX-AM, Twin Falls, Idaho; KULA-AM, Honolulu, Hawaii; WISH-AM-FM, Indianapolis, and WTHI-AM, Terre Haute, Indiana. He also operated television stations KUTV-TV, Salt Lake City, Utah; KARD-TV, Wichita, KSNT-TV, Topeka, Kansas; KTVJ-TV, Joplin, Missouri; and KGMB-TV, Honolulu, Hawaii. He co-founded Telecommunications, Inc., in 1968, and served as Vice-Chairman until 1980.*

HATCH, KELLEY MARIE, journalist, television news anchor, writer; b. Balt., June 16, 1958; d. Roland W. and Ava Marie (Jackson) Marsh; m. James R. Johnson II (div.); children: Jeremiah Shawn, Joshua Adam; m. Brett Wilder Hatch, Feb. 22, 1992. Student, Lincoln Meml. U., 1976-77, U. Mich., Flint, 1987-88, N.Mex. State U., 1989. Mktg.cons. Sta. KPSA, Alamogordo, N.Mex., 1989-90; dir. mktg. Temporarily Yours, Inc., Farmington, N.Mex., 1991; account exec. Sta. KOBF-TV, Farmington, 1991-92, news anchor, 1992-96; exec. dir. Fairbanks Drama Assn. and Fairbanks Children's Theatre, Inc., 1996—. Pres. Am. Heart Assn., 1994, bd. dirs., sec., 1991-92; bd. dirs. Childhaven, 1992—, San Juan Stage Co., 1991—; bd. dirs., fin. devel. com. ARC, 1992—. Recipient Best Investigative News award, AP, 1993, 95, Honorable Mention Gen. News award, AP, 1994, Top Story of Yr. award N.Mex. Broadcasters, 1995. Mem. Am. Bus. Women's Assn. (pres. 1991). Republican. Office: Fairbanks Drama Assn Children's Theatre Inc PO Box 73610 Fairbanks AK 99707

HATCH, LYNDA SYLVIA, education educator; b. Portland, Oreg., Feb. 19, 1950; d. Marley Elmo and Undine Sylvia (Crockard) Sims. BA, Wash. State U., 1972; MS, Portland State U., 1975; EdD, Oreg. State U., 1984. Cert. tchr., Oreg. Tchr. 5th grade, outdoor sch. specialist Clover Park Sch. Dist. 400, Tacoma, 1971-72; tchr. 6th grade, outdoor sch. specialist Hillsboro (Oreg.) elem. Dist. 7, 1972-78; tchr. 6th grade, outdoor sch. specialist Bend (Oreg.)-La Pine Sch. Dist., 1978-82, elem. curriculum specialist, 1983-85, tchr. 4th grade gifted and talented, 1985-90; grad. teaching asst. Oreg. State U., Corvallis, 1982-84; asst. prof. various methods, chair instrnl. leadership area No. Ariz. U., 1991—; ednl. cons., tchr. workshops, 1973—; presenter workshop Soviet-Am. Joint Conf., Moscow State U., 1991, Meeting of Children's Culture Promoters, Guadalajara, Mex., 1994; faculty Ariz. Journey Schs. for Math. and Sci. Tchg. Improvement; coord. Odyssey of the Mind, Bend, 1985-89, tchr.-mentor program for 1st-yr. tchrs., Beaverton, Oreg., 1982-83. Author: Pathways of America: Lewis and Clark, 1993, Pathways of America: The Oregon Trail, 1993, Pathways of America: The California Gold Rush Trail, 1994, Pathways of America: The Santa Fe Trail, 1995, Fifty States, 1997, U.S. Presidents, 1997, U.S. Map Skills, 1997; contbr. articles to profl. jours. Vol., leader, bd. dirs. Girl Scouts U.S., 1957—; elder First Presbyn. Ch., Bend, 1980—; vol. hist. interpretation High Desert Mus., Bend, 1987-91; docent Mus. No. Ariz.; bd. dirs. The Arboretum at Flagstaff. Recipient Excellence in Teaching award Bend Found., 1985-86, 86-87; named Tchr. of Yr. Oreg. Dept. Edn., 1982; Celebration Teaching grantee Geraldine Rockefeller Dodge Found., 1989, 90, 91, 92, 93, 94, 95. Mem. NEA, Nat. Coun. Tchrs. Math., Nat. Sci. Tchrs. Assn., Nat. State Tchrs. of Yr. (nat. pres. 1988-90), Oreg. Coun. Tchrs. Math. (b. dirs. 1981-82), Oreg. Coun. Tchrs. English (bd. dirs. 1981-82), Ariz. Reading Assn., Ariz. Sci. Tchrs. Assn., No. Ariz. Reading Coun. (exec. bd. 1991-92, 92-93), Ariz. State Adv. Couns. Nat. Coun. for Social Studies, Assn. Tchr. Educators, Coun. for Elem. Sci. Internat. (bd. dirs. 1995—), Internat. Reading Assn., Oreg.-Calif. Trails Assn., S.W. Oreg.-Calif. Trails Assn., Phi Delta Kappa (found. rep. 1991-92, v.p. programs 1992-93, historian 1993-94, v.p. membership 1994-95), Kappa Delta Pi (past chpt. counselor), others. Home: 1480 W University Heights Dr N Flagstaff AZ 86001-8970

HATCH, ORRIN GRANT, senator; b. Homestead Park, Pa., Mar. 22, 1934; s. Jesse and Helen (Kamm) H.; m. Elaine Hansen, Aug. 28, 1957; children: Brent, Marcia, Scott, Kimberly, Alysa, Jess. B.S., Brigham Young U., 1959; J.D., U. Pitts., 1962; LLD (hon.), U. Md., 1981; MS (hon.), Def. Intelligence Coll., 1982; LLD (hon.), Pepperdine U., 1990, So. Utah State U., 1990. Bar: Pa. 1962, Utah 1962. Ptnr. firm Thomson, Rhodes & Grigsby, Pitts., 1962-69, Hatch & Plumb, Salt Lake City, 1976; mem. U.S. Senate from Utah, 1977—, past chmn. labor and human resources com., chmn. Senate judiciary com., joint com. on taxation, com. on Indian affairs. Author ERA Myths and Realities, 1983; contbr. articles to newspapers and profl. jours. Recipient Outstanding Legislator award Nat. Assn. Rehab. Facilities, Legislator of Yr. award Am. Assn. Univ. Affiliated Programs, Legis. Leadership award Health Profl. Assn., many others. Mem. Am., Nat., Utah, Pa. bar assns., Am. Judicature Soc. Republican. Mormon.

HATCH, STEVEN GRAHAM, publishing company executive; b. Idaho Falls, Idaho, Mar. 27, 1951; s. Charles Steven and Margery Jane (Doxey) H.; BA, Brigham Young U., 1976; postgrad. mgmt. devel. program U. Utah, 1981; m. Rhonda Kay Frasier, Feb. 13, 1982; children: Steven Graham, Kristen Leone, Cameron Michael, Landon Frasier, McKell Margery. Founder, pres. Graham Maughan Enterprises, Provo, Utah, 1975—, Internat. Mktg. Co., 1980—, Mcht. Acct. Svcs., 1996—; chmn. AuthorizeNet, Inc., 1996—; pres. Cardservice Interant. Provo; dir. Goldbrickers Internat., Inc. Sec., treas. Zions Estates, Inc., Salt Lake City, Kansas City, Mo. Eagle Scout Boy Scouts Am., 1970; trustee Villages of Quail Valley, 1984-88. Recipient Duty to God award, 1970; missionary France Mission, Paris 1970-72, pub. rels. dir. 1972. Mem. Provo Jaycees, Internat. Entrepreneurs Assn., Mormon Booksellers Assn., Samuel Hall Soc. (exec. v.p. 1979), U.S. C. of C., Provo C. of C. (chmn. legis. action com. 1981-82, mem. job svc. employer com.), Rotary Club (Provo pres. 1995-96, area rep. 1996—). Republican. Mormon. Office: Graham Maughan Pub Co 50 E 500 S Provo UT 84606-4809

HATCHER, HERBERT JOHN, biochemist, microbiologist; b. Mpls., Dec. 18, 1926; s. Herbert Edmond and Florence Elizabeth (Larson) H.; m. Beverly J. Johnson, Mar. 28, 1953 (dec. July 1985); children: Dennis Michael, Steven Craig, Roger Dean, Mark Alan, Susan Diane, Laura Jean; m. Louise Fritsche Nelson, May 24, 1986; children: Carlos Howard Nelson, Kent Robert Nelson, Carolyn Louise Tyler. BA, U. Minn., 1953, MS, 1964, PhD, 1965. Bacteriologist VA Hosp., Wilmington, Del., 1956-57; microbiologist Smith, Kline, French, Phila., 1957-60, Clinton (Iowa) Corn Processing, 1966-67; microbiologist, biochemist Econs. Lab. Inc., St. Paul, 1967-84; biochemist EG&G Idaho Inc., Idaho Falls, 1984-90; co-owner B/CG Cons. Svcs., Idaho Falls, 1990—; affiliate prof. U. Idaho; adj. prof. Mont. State U., Bozeman; cons. EG&G Idaho, Inc., Idaho Falls, Henkel Corp. N.J., 1986. Chmn. bd. edn. Cross of Christ Luth. Ch., Coon Rapids, Minn., 1974-76; pres. chpt. Aid Assn. Luths., Idaho Falls, 1986; pres.-elect St. Johns Luth. Ch., 1988, pres., 1989. With USNR, 1945-46.

HATFIELD, BRIAN ALLEN, state legislator; b. Aberdeen, Wash., July 8, 1966; s. Stanley Allen and Gail Louise (Briney) H.; m. Freddie Lynn Goodin, July 31, 1993; 1 child, Tarrah Lynn Lavinder. AA, Grays Harbor Coll., Aberdeen, Wash., 1987; BA in Polit. Sci. cum laude, Wash. State U., Pullman, 1989. Adminstrv. asst. Wash. State Senate, Olympia, 1989-94; mem. Wash. Ho. of Reps., Olympia, 1994—. Bd. dirs. Wash. Wildlife and Recreation Coalition, 1996—, Lower Columbia Cmty. Action Coun., Longview, Wash., 1995—; chiar 19th Dist. Dems., S.W. Wash., 1990-94. Named Dem. of Yr., Pacific County Dems., 1995-96. Mem. Raymond Elks, Raymond Kiwanis. Home: 226 Fir St Raymond WA 98577 Office: Wash State Ho of Reps PO Box 40600 Olympia WA 98504

HATFIELD, CHARLES DONALD, newspaper executive; b. Huntington, W.Va., June 15, 1935; s. Howard Donald and LaUna (Wilson) H.; m. Sandra Gail Soto, June 11, 1955; children: John Christopher, Lisa, Joel Thomas. BA, Marshall Coll., 1977. Mem. sports staff Huntington Advertiser, 1953-60, asst. news editor, 1960-67, mng. editor, 1972-79; news editor Herald-Advertiser, Huntington, 1967-69, mng. editor, 1969-72; exec. editor Herald-Dispatch, Huntington, 1979-82, pub., editor, 1982-85; regional v.p. Gannett Co., Inc. E., Huntington, 1985-86; pub., editor and regional v.p. Tucson Citizen and Gannett West, 1986—. Author: Don Hatfield Cleans Out His Attic, 1986. Bd. dirs. United Way, Tucson, 1987-95, Greater Tucson Econs. Coun., 1988—, Tucson Mus. Art, 1989—. Mem. AP Mng. Editors Assn. (treas. 1986-88), Am. Soc. Newspaper Editors, Am. Newspapers Pubs. (pres.), Ariz. Newspaper Assn., La Paloma Club, Tucson Country Club. Office: Tucson Citizen PO Box 26767 Tucson AZ 85726-6767*

HATFIELD, MARK O., former senator; b. Dallas, Oreg., July 12, 1922; s. Charles Dolen and Dovie (Odom) H.; m. Antoinette Kuzmanich, July 8, 1958; children: Mark, Elizabeth, Theresa, Charles. A.B., Willamette U., 1943; A.M., Stanford U., 1948. Instr. Willamette U., 1949, dean students, asso. prof. polit. sci., 1950-56; mem. Oreg. Ho. of Reps., 1951-55, Oreg. Senate, 1955-57; sec. State of Oreg., 1957-59, gov., 1959-67; U.S. senator from Oreg., 1967-97, chmn. appropriations com.; mem. energy and natural resources com., rules and adminstrn. com., joint printing com., joint libr. com.; mem. select com. Indian Affairs, Republican Policy Com.; chmn. Appropriations subcom. on transp. & related agencies. Author: Not Quite So Simple, 1967, Conflict and Conscience, 1971, Between A Rock and A Hard Place, 1976; co-author: Amnesty: The Unsettled Question of Vietnam, 1976, Freeze! How You Can Help Prevent Nuclear War, 1982, The Causes of World Hunger, 1982; co-author: What About the Russians, 1984. Served to lt. j.g. USN, 1943-45, PTO. Recipient numerous hon. degrees. Republican. Baptist. Home: 6036 SW Riverpoint Ln Portland OR 97201 Office: 4380 SW Macadam Ste 460 PO Box 8639 Portland OR 97201*

HATFIELD, PAUL GERHART, federal judge, lawyer; b. Great Falls, Mont., Apr. 29, 1928; s. Trueman LeRoy and Grace Lenore (Gerhart) H.; m. Dorothy Ann Allen, Feb. 1, 1958 (dec. Aug. 1992); children: Kathleen Helen, Susan Ann, Paul Allen. Student, Coll. of Great Falls, 1947-50; LL.B., U. Mont., 1955. Bar: Mont. bar 1955. Asso. firm Hoffman & Cure, Gt. Falls, Mont., 1955-56, Jardine, Stephenson, Blewett & Weaver, Gt. Falls, 1956-58, Hatfield & Hatfield, Gt. Falls, 1959-60; chief dep. county atty. Cascade County, Mont., 1959-60; dist. ct. judge 8th Jud. Dist., Mont., 1961-76; chief justice Supreme Ct. Mont., Helena, 1977-78; U.S. Senator from Mont., 1978-79; U.S. dist. judge for Dist. of Mont., Gt. Falls, 1979—; chief judge, 1990-96; Vice chmn. Pres.'s Council Coll. of Great Falls. Author standards for criminal justice, Mont. cts. Served with U.S. Army, 1951-53, Korea. Mem. Am., Mont. bar assns., Am. Judicature Soc. Roman Catholic. Office: US Dist Ct PO Box 1529 Great Falls MT 59403-1529

HATFIELD, SAMUEL FAY, JR., educator, small business owner; b. Sumter, S.C., May 6, 1945; s. Samuel Fay and Mary Louise (Geddings) H.; m. Valerie Jean Widding, Dec. 31, 1964; children: John Michael, David Andrew. BSBA, U. Nebr., 1967; MS in Indsl. Mgmt., U. N.D., 1970. Securities and life ins. lic. Commd. 2d. lt. USAF, 1967, advanced through grades to col., 1990; registered rep. Fortis Investments, Inc., Torrance, Calif., 1990-91; project mgr. B-2 Div. Northrop Grumman Corp., Pico Rivera, Calif., 1991-94; sales mgr. Primerica Fin. Svcs., Longmont, Colo., 1994—; owner Java House, Louisville, Colo., 1995—; substitute tchr. Dist. 50 Adams County, Westminister, Colo., 1996—, St. Vrain Valley Sch. Dist., Longmont, Colo., 1996—. Chmn., deacon Parkwood Bapt. Ch., Fairfax, Va., 1979; deacon 1st Bapt. Ch. Palos Verdes, Calif. 1987; v.p. Baywatch Home Owners Assn., San Pedro, Calif., 1992; assoc. pastor Front Range Cmty. Ch., Superior, Colo., 1995—, clk., 1996—. Mem. Nat. Contract Mgmt. Assn., Village Square Mchts. Assn. (treas. 1996—). Republican. Home: 1995 Keota Ln Superior CO 80027

HATFIELD, WENDELL BENTON, physician; b. Wichita, Kans., Sept. 21, 1931; s. Harold Benton and Ruth Wilhelmina (Schmidt) H.; m. Charlotte Behre, Sept. 1, 1954; children: Christopher, Catherine, Dana Wendell, Susan. BA, Columbia Coll., 1953; MD, Columbia U., 1956. Diplomate Am. Bd. Internal Medicine. Intern Presbyn. Hosp., N.Y.C., 1956-57, asst. resident in medicine, 1957-59, fellow in rheumatology, 1959-60, chief resident in medicine, 1960-61; instr. in medicine Columbia U., N.Y.C., 1963-65, assoc. in medicine, 1966-69; assoc. clin. prof. of medicine U. Colo., Denver, 1978-89, clin. prof. of medicine, 1990—; asst. prof. clin. medicine Columbia U., Englewood, Colo., 1970-74; practice of rheumatology Colorado Arthritis Ctr., Englewood, Colo., 1977—; acting dir. Divsn. of Rheumatology, Columbia U./Presbyn. Hosp., N.Y.C., 1975-77; chmn. dept. medicine, Swedish Med. Ctr./Porter Hosp., Denver, 1982-86. Contbr. articles to profl. jours. Bd. dirs. Swedish Med. Ctr. Found., Englewood, Colo., 1987-93, v.p., 1993-94. Capt. U.S. Army, 1961-63, PTO. Recipient Harvard Book award Harvard Club of Colo., 1948, Woodbury medal Woodbury B., 1949, Van Amringe medal Columbia Coll., 1952. Fellow Am. Coll. Rheumatology; mem. Rocky Mountain Rheumatism Soc. (pres. 1987-88), Rocky Mountain Metabolic Bone Soc., Am. Soc. for Clin. Densitometry, Colo. Med. Soc., Arapahoe County Med. Soc. Home: 7585 S Prince St Littleton CO 80120 Office: Colorado Arthritis Ctr 701 E Hampden Ave Englewood CO 80110-2736

HATHAWAY, LOLINE, zoo and botanic park curator; b. Whittier, Calif., June 27, 1937; d. Richard Franklin and F. Nadine (Applegate) H.; 1 child, Patrick Paul Kundtz. BA, Reed Coll., Portland, Oreg., 1959; PhD, Washington U., St. Louis, 1969. Instr. St. Louis U., 1966-68; curator of edn. Chgo. Zool. Soc., Brookfield, Ill., 1968-71; cons. on terrestrial biology Ryckman, Edgerly, Tomlinson & Assocs., St. Louis, 1972-75; marina mgr. Lake Piru (Calif.) Recreation Area, 1976-77; curator, dir. Navajo Nation Zool. and Botanical Park, Window Rock, Ariz., 1983—. Vice chmn., chmn. City of Santa Fe Springs (Calif.) Traffic Commn., 1979-83; mem. Navajo Estates Vol. Fire Dept., Yah-ta-hey, N.Mex., 1984-85; bd. dirs. Hathaway Ranch Mus., Santa Fe Springs, 1986-93, Gallup Cmty. Concerts Assn., 1994—; leader 4-H Club, 1989—. Mem. AAAS (vice chmn. S.W.-Rocky Mountain div. sci. edn. sect. 1983-84, chmn. 1984-85), AAUW (scholarship com. Gallup 1992—), Am. Assn. Zool. Parks and Aquariums, Am. Assn. Bot. Gardens and Arboretums, Assn. Living. Hist. Farms and Agr. Mus., Am. Inst. Biol. Scis., Sierra Club (Ozarks chpt. founder, bd. dirs., sec. Gt. Lakes chpt. 1963-72). Democrat. Home: 27 S LaChee PO Box 4172 Yah-ta-hey NM 87375 Office: Navajo Nat Zool and Bot Pk PO Box 9000 Window Rock AZ 86515-9000

HATHAWAY, STANLEY KNAPP, lawyer; b. Osceola, Nebr., July 19, 1924; s. Franklin E. and Velma Clara (Holbrook) H.; m. Roberta Louise Harley, Nov. 26, 1948; children—Susan Garrett, Sandra D'Amico. A.B., U. Nebr., 1948, LL.B., 1950; LL.D., U. Wyo., 1975. Bar: Nebr. 1950, Wyo., 1950, U.S. Dist. Ct. Wyo., Nebr., Mont. 1950, U.S. Supreme Ct. 1964. Sole practice, Torrington, Wyo., 1950-66; gov. Wyo., 1967-75; assoc. Hathaway, Speight & Kunz, Cheyenne, Wyo., 1975—; dir. Apache Corp., Houston; county atty. Goshen County (Wyo.), 1955-62; gov. State of Wyo., 1967-75; sec. U.S. Dept. Interior, 1975. Served with USAAF, 1943-45. Decorated Air medals with 5 clusters. Mem. ABA, Wyo. State Bar Assn. Republican. United Episcopalian. Clubs: Masons (Cheyenne); Shriners (Rawlins, Wyo.). Office: Hathaway Speight & Kunz 2515 Warren Ave Cheyenne WY 82001-3162

HATHAWAY, WILLIAM ELLISON, pediatrics educator; b. Ardmore, Okla., Jan. 13, 1929; s. Elmer Gray and Bertha Mae (Underwood) H.; m. Helen Sue White, Aug. 23, 1956; children: Elizabeth, Jennifer, William, Thomas, Margaret, Joseph, Katherine. BA, U. Okla., 1950, MD, 1954. Intern USN Hsop., Bremerton, 1954-55; resident in pediatrics N.Y. Hosp., N.Y.C., 1957-59; fellow in hematology U Colo. Sch. Med., Denver, 1959-60, asst. prof. pediatrics, 1964-67, assoc. prof., 1967-73, prof. pediatrics, 1973-88, prof. emeritus, 1989—; pvt. practice pediatrics Colorado Springs, Colo., 1960-61; instr. pediatrics U. Ky. Med. Ctr., Lexington, 1961-63, asst. prof. pediatrics, 1963-64; dir. hemophilia programs U. Colo. Med. Ctr., Denver, 1967-89; vis. prof. U. Ariz. Med. Ctr., Tucson, 1992-95. Author: (with others) Immunologic Deficiency Diseases in Man, 1968, (with others) Hemophilia and New Hemorrahagic States, 1970, , Advances in Pediatrics, 1972, Care of the Critically Ill Cild, 1972, (with others) Immunologic Disorders in Infants and Children, 1973, Clinics in Perinatology, 1975, Current Problems in Pediatric Hematology, 1975, Current Pediatric Therapy, 1976, The Critically Ill Child, 1977, (with R.R. Montgomery) Kidney Disease: Hematologic and Vascular problems. 1977, (with J. Bonnar) Perinatal Coagulation, 1978, (with R.R. Montgomery) Pediatric Clinics of North America, 1980, Haemostasis and Thrombosis, 1981, Pediatrics, 1982, Current Pediatric Therapy, 1982, Standardization of Coagulation Assays: An Overview, 1982, Current Pediatric Therapy, 1984, Current Therapy in Neonatal-Perinatal Medicine, 1985, Practical Pediatric Therapy, 1985, Management of Musculoskeletal Problems in Hemophilia, 1986, Blood Component Therapy of Neonatla Disease, 1986, Primary Pediatric Care, 1987, Current Pediatric Diagnosis and Treatment, 1987, 1987 Yearbook of Pediatrics, 1987, Haemostasis and Thrombosis, 1987, Pediatrics, 1987, Current Therapy in Pediatrics-2, 1989, Immunologic Disorders in Infants and Children, 1989, Hematologic Disorders in Maternal-Fetal Medicine, 1990, Current Pediatric Diagnosis and Treatment, 10th edit., 1991, Perinatal Thrombosis and Haemostasis, 1991, Hematology: Basic Principles and Practice, 1991, (with others) Vitamin K and Vitamin-K Dependent Proteins: Analytical, Physiological and Clinical Aspects, 1993, Pediatric Therapy, 1993, Haemostasis and Thrombosis in Obstetrics and Gynaecology, 1992, Fetal and Neonatal Physiology, 1992; (with W.W. Hay, J.R. Groothuis, J.E. Paisley) Current Pediatric Diagnosis and Treatment, 1993; (with S.H. Goodnight Jr.) Disorders of Hemostasis and Thrombosis: A Clinical Guide, 1993; contbr. numerous articles to profl. jours. Comdr. USNR, 1955-57. Recipient Career Tchg. scholar award, 1996. Mem. Internat. Soc. Thrombosis Haemostasis, Am. Soc. Hematology, Am. Pediatric Soc., Soc. Pediatric Rsch. Home: 450 N Mountain Side Pl Tucson AZ 85745-9126 Office: U Colo Health Sci Ctr Campus Box C-220 4200 E 9th Ave Denver CO 80220-3706

HATHERILL, JOHN ROBERT, toxicologist, educator; b. Waterford, Mich., Aug. 20, 1953; s. John William and Anna Marie (Morin) H. MS, Ea. Mich. U., 1978; PhD, U. Mich., 1985. Med. technologist U. Mich., Ann Arbor, 1976-78, sr. clin. chemist, 1979-86, rsch. assoc., 1980-85; sr. scientist Ciba-Geigy Pharms., Summit, N.J., 1986-87; rsch. dir. Stanford (Calif.) U., 1987-89; prof. U. Calif., Santa Barbara, 1990—; adj. prof. UCLA, 1990—. Contbr. articles to profl. jours., chpts. to books. Judge, mem. adv. bd. Calif. State Sci. Fair, L.A., 1992. Fellow World Ctr. for Exploration (bd. dirs. 1985); mem. Soc. Toxicology, Am. Soc. Clin. Pathologists, N.Y. Acad. Sci., Sigma Xi, Gamma Alpha. Home: 535 E Arrellaga St Apt 14 Santa Barbara CA 93103-2246

HATTAR, MICHAEL MIZYED, mathematics educator; b. El-Salt, Jordan, Mar. 17, 1934; came to U.S., 1954; s. Mizyed Zedan and Rif'a (Naber) H.; m. Helen Jean Sharbrough, June 30, 1962; children: Mai Michelle, Amiel Michael, Khalid Mikhail, Muna Michelle. BA, Greenville (Ill.) Coll., 1958; MS, Western Wash. State U., 1968; postgrad., Oxford U., 1989. Tchr. Don Bosco Tech. Inst., Rosemead, Calif., 1962-76, 95—, chmn., 1968-76; part-time tchr. Rio Hondo Coll., 1983—; tchr. Mt. Sac Coll., 1969—, Ontario (Calif.) High Sch., 1976-92, Rancho Cucamonga (Calif.) High Sch., 1992-95; with Don Bosco Tech. Inst., Rosemead, Calif., 1995—; speaker math. confs. Participant U.S./Russian Joint Conf. on Math. Edn., Moscow, 1993. Recipient Tchr. of Yr. award Industry Edn. Coun. San Gabriel Valley, 1970, Award of Excellence, U.S. Orgn. Med. and Edn. Needs South Bay chpt., 1975, Citation, Assn. Arab-Am. Univ. Grads., 1977, Man of Yr. award Am. Arab Soc., 1978, Commendation, Olympic Neighbor Program, 1984, Tchr. of Yr. award Ontario H.S., 1987-88, Award of Excellence, U.S. Orgn. Med. and Edn.; named Tchr. of Yr. Inland Valley, Calif. Mem. ASCD, Nat. Coun. Tchrs. of Math., Calif. Math. Coun., San Bernardino County Math. Coun. (Tchr. of Yr. award 1991, pres. 1992-93). Home: 1247 E Dore St West Covina CA 91792-1313 Office: Don Bosco Tech Inst 1151 San Gabriel Blvd Rosemead CA 91770

HATTER, TERRY JULIUS, JR., federal judge; b. Chgo., Mar. 11, 1933. A.B., Wesleyan U., 1954; J.D., U. Chgo., 1960. Bar: Ill. 1960, Calif. 1965, U.S. Dist. Ct. 1960, U.S. Ct. Appeals 1960. Adjudicator Chgo., 1960-61; assoc. Harold M. Calhoun, Chgo., 1961-62; asst. pub. defender Cook County Chgo., 1961-62; asst. U.S. atty. No. Dist. Calif., San Francisco, 1962-66; chief counsel San Francisco Neighborhood Legal Assistance Found., 1966-67; regional legal svcs. dir. Exec. Office Pres. OEO, San Francisco, 1967-70; exec. dir. Western Ctr. Law and Poverty, L.A., 1970-73; exec. asst. to mayor, dir. criminal justice planning L.A., 1974-75; spl. asst. to mayor, dir. urban devel., 1975-77; judge Superior Ct. Calif., L.A., 1977-80, U.S. Dist. Ct. (cen. dist.) Calif., L.A., 1979—; lectr. Police Acad., San Francisco Police Dept., 1963-66, U. Calif., San Diego, 1970-71, Colo. Jud. Conf., 1973; assoc. clin. prof. law U. So. Calif. Law Ctr., L.A., 1970-74, mem. bd. councilors; prof. law Loyola U. Sch. Law, L.A., 1973-75; mem. faculty Nat. Coll. State Judiciary, Reno, 1974. V.p. Northbay Halfway House, 1964-65; vice chmn. Los Angeles Regional Criminal Justice Planning Bd., 1975-76; mem. Los Angeles Mayor's Cabinet Com. Econ. Devel., 1976-77, Mayor's Policy Com., 1973-77, chmn. housing econ. and community devel. com., City Los Angeles, 1975-77, chmn. housing and community devel. tech. com., 1975-77; vice chmn. Young Dems. Cook County, 1961-62; chmn. bd. Real Estate Coop; bd. dirs. Bay Area Social Planning Coun., Contra Costa, Black Law Center L.A., Nat. Fedn. Settlements & Neighborhood Ctrs., Edn. Fin. & Governance Reform Project, Mexican Am. Legal Def. & Ednl. Fund, Nat. Health Law Program, Nat. Sr. Citizens Law Ctr., Calif. Law Ctr., L.A. Regional Criminal Justice Planning Bd.; mem. exec. com. bd. dirs. Constl. Rights Found; trustee Wesleyan Univ. Meth. Ch.; mem. bd. visitors U. Chgo. Law Sch. Mem. NAACP (exec. com., bd. dirs. Richmond chpt.), Nat. Legal Aid & Defender Assn. (dir., vice chmn.), L.A. County Bar Assn. (exec. com.), Am. Judicature Soc., Charles Houston Law Club, Phi Delta Phi, Order Coif. Office: US Dist Ct 312 N Spring St Rm 175 Los Angeles CA 90012-4701*

HATTON, GLENN IRWIN, neuroscientist, educator; b. Chgo., Dec. 12, 1934; s. Irwin Alfred and Anita Hatton; m. Patricia Joann Hatton, Sept. 4, 1931; children: James Daniel, William Graham, Christopher Jay, Jennifer Kay, Tracey Elisabeth. BA, North Ctrl. Coll., 1960; MA, U. Ill., 1962, PhD, 1964. Asst. prof., assoc. prof., prof. Mich. State U., East Lansing, 1965-91; prof., chair U. Calif., Riverside, 1992—. Contbr. numerous articles to profl. jours. Fellow NIH, 1982, Guggenheim Fellow, 1989; recipient Javits Neurosci. Investigator award NINDS, 1985, 93. Fellow AAAS; mem. Assn. Neurosci. Depts. and Programs (pres. 1994-95), Am. Physiol. Soc., Am. Assn. Anatomists, Soc. Neurosci. Office: U Calif Dept Neurosci Riverside CA 92521

HAUBER, JANET ELAINE, mechanical engineer; b. Milw., July 21, 1937; d. Ralph Joseph and Ethel Esther (Forsyth) H. BME, Marquette U., 1965; MS, Stanford U., 1967, PhD, 1970. Rsch. metallurgist dept. chemistry Lawrence Livermore (Calif.) Nat. Lab., 1970-73, project leader, 1973-74, sect. leader, facility mgr., 1974-76, dep. div. leader, 1976-78, dep. div. leader mech. engring. dept., 1978-86, dep. assoc. dept. head, 1986-87, sect. leader, 1987-93; engr.-at-large, 1993—. Contbr. articles to profl. jours. Ford Foudn. fellow Stanford U., 1965, ASTM fellow, 1967. Mem. AAUW (v.p. 1992-93), Soc. Women Engrs., Interplast, Inc. (adv. coun. 1996—), Sigma Xi, Math./Sci. Network (bd. dirs. 1994—, treas. 1995-96, pres. 1996—). Office: Lawrence Livermore Nat Lab PO Box 808 Livermore CA 94551-0808

HAUCK, DENNIS WILLIAM, writer; b. Hammond, Ind., Apr. 8, 1945; s. Floyd William and Wilma (Frey) H. AA in Math., Ind. U., 1964-67; MS in Math., U. Vienna, Austria, 1972. Editor IUFOR Svcs. Inc., Munster, Ind., 1973-76; mng. editor Countrywide Publs., N.Y.C., 1976-80; tech. writer EPCO Inc., Reno, 1980-83, Odenberg Inc., Sacramento, Calif., 1984-91; freelance writer Sacramento, 1991—; cons. in field. Editor Jour. of Ufology, 1973-76; author: William Shatner: A Biography, 1992, The Alchemical Works of Gottlieb Latz, 1992, Haunted Places Guidebook, 1993, First Matter, 1993, Captain Quirk, 1995, Haunted Places, 1996. Active mem. Greenpeace, San Francisco. Mem. Authors Guild, Nat. Spkrs. Assn., Calif. Writers Club, Nat. Writers Union. Office: Hauck Editorial Svcs PO Box 22201 Sacramento CA 95822-0201

HAUCK, JOANN RAE, secondary education educator; b. San Bernardino, Calif., Sept. 27, 1946; d. Victor Ray and Irene Theresa (Schumacher) Starkweather; m. Robert James Hauck, Nov. 18, 1992. BS in Secondary Edn., Idaho State U., 1987; MEd in Sch. Counseling, Albertson Coll. of Idaho, 1994. Cert. vocat. guidance counselor, secondary vocat. bus. edn. tchr., Idaho. Bus. tchr. Mackay (Idaho) Jr./Sr. H.S., 1987-96; guidance counselor K-12 Carey (Idaho) Carey Sch., 1996—. Mem. ACA, NEA, Idaho Counselors Assn., Idaho Edn. Assn. Home: PO Box 599 Mackay ID 83251-0599 Office: Carey Sch PO Box 266 Carey ID 83320

HAUENSTEIN, DONALD HERBERT, JR., computer company executive; b. Canton, Ohio, Dec. 29, 1942; s. Donald Herbert and Mary Alice (Andrichs) H.; m. Maria Del Socorro Moreno, June 5, 1965 (div. Apr. 1979); children: Carlos Ian, Marissa Renee; m. Carol King, May 28, 1988. B in Indsl. Engring., Ohio State U., 1970, MS in Indsl. Engring., 1970; MBA, U. Houston, 1977; exec. mgmt. program, UCLA, L.A., 1986. Indsl. engr. Schlumberger Well Svcs., Houston, 1970-72, supr. of methods, 1972-75; mgr. engring. svcs. Dresser Atlas, Houston, 1975-80; mgr. mfg. engring. VETCO Offshore, Ventura, Calif., 1980-83; dir. mfg. engring. HR Textron, Valencia, Calif., 1983-88; dir. spl. projects HR Textron, Valencia, 1988-90; owner, retail Abacus Computer Svcs., Saugus, 1990—. Pres. St. Christopher's Sch. Bd., Houston, 1976-79, bd. dirs. Orchard Ln. Condominium Assn., Oxnard, Calif., 1986, Arbor Park Condominium Assn., 1987. With USAF, 1961-65. Mem. Tau Beta Pi, Alpha Pi Mu. Republican. Roman Catholic. Home: 28025 Tupelo Ridge Dr Santa Clarita CA 91354-1326 Office: Abacus Computer Svcs 23001 Soledad Canyon Rd Saugus CA 91350-2635

HAUER, JAMES ALBERT, lawyer; b. Fond du Lac, Wis., Apr. 3, 1924; s. Albert A. and Hazel M. (Corcoran) H.; children: Stephen, John, Paul, Christopher, Patrick. BCE, Marquette U., 1948, LLB, 1949; bank mgmt. cert., Columbia U., 1957, U. Wis., 1959. Bar: Wis., U.S. Dist. Ct., U.S. Ct. Appeals. Patent counsel Ira Milton Jones, Milw., 1949; chief counsel Wauwatosa Realty, Milw., 1950-57; v.p. Wauwatosa (Wis.) State Bank, 1957-67; pres. Milw. We. Bank, 1967-69, Prem Constrn. Co., Milw., 1969-73; pvt. practice Elm Grove, Wis., 1973-86, Sun City, Ariz., 1986—. Pres., bd. dirs. Sunshine Svc., Sun City, Meals on Wheels, Sun City. With USMCR, 1942-45. Mem. Wis. Bar Assn., Ariz. Patent Law Assn. (charter). Roman Catholic. Office: 10221 W Edgewood Dr Sun City AZ 85351-1605

HAULENBEEK, ROBERT BOGLE, JR., government official; b. Cleve., Feb. 24, 1941; s. Robert Bogle and Priscilla Valerie (Burch) H.; BS, Okla. State U., 1970; m. Rebecca Marie Talley, Mar. 1, 1965; children—Kimberly Kaye, Robert Bogle, III. Micro paleon. photographer Pan Am. Rsch. Co., Tulsa, 1966-67; flight instr. Okla. State U., 1970; air traffic control specialist FAA, Albuquerque, 1970-73, Farmington, N.Mex., 1973-78, flight svc. specialist, Dalhart, Tex., 1978-80, Albuquerque, 1980—; staff officer CAP, Albuquerque, 1970-73, Farmington, 1974-78, advanced through grades to col., 1988, dir. ops. for hdqrs., 1981-86, N.Mex. Wing dep. commdr., 1986-88, N.Mex. Wing comdr., 1988-91, N.Mex. Wing dir. sr. programs, 1993-95; mem. faculty Nat. Staff Coll., Gunter Air Force Sta., Montgomery, Ala., 1981-82; dir. South West Region Staff Coll., Albuquerque, 1986; mem. 1995 Nat. Air Traffic Control Facility of Yr. With U.S. Army, 1964-65. Recipient Meritorious Svc. award CAP, 1978, 81, 82, Lifesaving award, 1982, 95, Exceptional Svc. award, 1981, Distng. Svc. award, 1991. Mem. Exptl. Aircraft Assn., Nat. Assn. Air Traffic Specialists (facility rep. 1978-86), Nat. Assn. Flight Instrs., Aircraft Owners and Pilots Assn. Republican. Presbyterian. Home: 5229 Carlsbad Ct NW Albuquerque NM 87120-2322

HAUN, DAVID HARDING, government official; b. Ogden, Utah, Oct. 11, 1953; s. Wallace Edmund and Nadine (Harding) H. BA, Weber State U., 1975; MPA, Am. U., 1979. Staff asst. com. on aeronautical and space scis. U.S. Senate, 1975-77, staff mem., 1977; rsch. analyst gov.'s com. on exec. reorgn. State of Utah, 1977-78; dist. office mgr. no. Utah office U.S. Bur. of the Census, 1980; rsch. analyst Gov.'s Agenda for the 80's Commn., 1981; dep. assessor Weber County Assessor's Office, 1985-88, dept. assessor, reappraisal supr., 1988-91, sys. adminstr., reappraisal supr., 1991-92; city councilman 3d mcpl. ward Ogden City Coun., 1989-92; assessor Weber County, 1992—; adj. prof. Weber State U., 1991; mem. human devel. policy com. Nat. League of Cities, 1990-91, energy, environ. and natural resources policy com., 1982-83; ; mem. Ogden City budget adv. com. on fin. affairs, 1985-86; mem. Utah League of Cities and Town Resolutions Com., 1983; mem. Utah Energy Devel. and Conservation Coun., 1983, Weber Area Coun. of Govts., 1981-83; mgr. TCS Printing Svcs., 1982-84; mem. Ogden Energy Commn., 1983. Mem. Am. Soc. of Pub. Adminstrn., Internat. Assn. of Assessing Officers, Utah Assn. of Counties (mem. legis. com. 1992—, bylaws revision com. 1992-93). Office: Weber County Assessor 2380 Washington Blvd Ogden UT 84401

HAUN, JOHN DANIEL, petroleum geologist, educator; b. Old Hickory, Tenn., Mar. 7, 1921; s. Charles C. and Lydia (Rhodes) H.; m. Lois Culbertson, June 30, 1942. AB, Berea Coll., 1948; MA, U. Wyo., 1949, Ph.D., 1953. Registered profl. engr., Colo. Geologist Stanolind, Amoco, Vernal, Utah, 1951-52; v.p. Petroleum Research Corp., Denver, 1952-57; mem. faculty dept. geology Colo. Sch. Mines, Golden, 1955-80; prof. Colo. Sch. Mines, 1963-80, part time, 1980-85, emeritus prof., 1983—; cons. Barlow & Haun, Inc., Evergreen, Colo., 1957-90; cons. Potential Gas Agy., 1966-78, mem. com., 1978—; mem. adv. com. Colo. Water Pollution Control Commn., 1969-70; mem. adv. council Kans. Geol. Survey, 1971-76; del. Internat. Geol. Congress, Sydney, Australia, 1976; U.S. rep. Internat. Com. on Petroleum Res. Classification UN, N.Y.C., 1976-77; mem. oil shale adv. com. Office of Tech. Assessment, Washington, 1976-79, mem. U.S. natural gas availability adv. panel, 1983; mem. Colo. Oil and Gas Conservation Commn., 1977-87, vice-chmn., 1983-85, chmn. 1985-87; mem. energy resources com. Interstate Oil and Gas Compact Commn., 1978—; mem. exec. adv. com. Nat. Petroleum Coun., 1968-70, 79-89, mem. com. on unconventional gas sources, 1978-80; com. on Arctic oil and gas resources, 1980-81; mem. U.S. Nat. Com. on Geology Dept. Interior and NAS, 1982-89, chmn., 1985-87; mem. com undiscovered oil and gas resources, 19881-91, com. status and rsch. objectives in solid-earth scis.: critical assessment, 1988-92, Nat. Rsch. Coun.; del. Internat. Geol. Congress, Paris, 1980, Moscow, 1984; mem. Colo. Oil and Gas legis. com., 1993-94. Editor: The Mountain Geologist, 1963-65, Future Energy Outlook, 1969, Methods of Estimating the Volume of Undiscovered Oil and Gas Resources, 1975; asst. editor: Geologic Atlas of the Rocky Mountain Region, 1972; co-editor: Subsurface Geology in Petroleum Exploration, 1958, Symposium on Cretaceous Rocks of Colorado and Adjacent Areas, 1959, Guide to the Geology of Colorado, 1960; contbr. articles to profl. jours. Served with USCG, 1942-46. Recipient Disting. Svc. award Am. Assn. Petroleum Geologists, 1973. Fellow Geol. Soc. Am., AAAS; mem. Am. Assn. Petroleum Geologists (editor 1967-71, pres. 1979-80, hon. mem. 1984, Sidney Powers Meml. award 1995), Am. Inst. Profl. Geologists (v.p. 1974, pres. 1976, exec. com. 1981-82, Ben H. Parker Meml. award 1983), Am. Geol. Inst. (governing bd. 1976, 79-82, sec.-treas. 1977-78, v.p. 1980-81, pres. 1981-82, Ian Campbell medal 1988, William B. Heroy Jr. award 1996), Rocky Mountain Assn. Geologists (sec. 1961, 1st v.p. 1964, pres. 1968, hon. mem. 1974), Soc. Econ. Paleontologists and Mineralogists, Am. Petroleum Inst. (com. exploration 1971-73, 78-88), Nat. Assn. Geology Tchrs., Wyo. Geol. Assn. (hon. life), Colo. Sci. Soc. (hon. life), Sigma Xi, Sigma Gamma Epsilon, Phi Kappa Phi. Home: 1238 County Road 23 Evergreen CO 80439

HAUPTMANN, RANDAL MARK, biotechnologist; b. Hot Springs, S.D., July 6, 1956; s. Ivan Joy and Phyllis Maxine (Pierce) H.; m. Beverly Kay Suko, May 22, 1975; 1 child, Erich William. BS, S.D. State U., 1979; MS, U. Ill., 1982, PhD, 1984. Postdoctoral rschr. Monsanto Corp. Rsch., St. Louis, 1984-86; vis. rsch. scientist U. Fla., Gainesville, 1986-88; asst. prof. No. Ill. U., DeKalb, 1988-90, dir. plant molecular biology ctr., 1989-90; sr. rsch. scientist Amoco Life Sci. Techs., Naperville, Ill., 1990-94; comml. mgr. advanced tech. Seminis Vegetable Seeds, Woodland, Calif., 1994—. Author: (with others) Methods in Molecular Biology, 1990; contbr. articles to profl. jours. Mem. Internat. Assn. Plant Tissue Culture, Internat. Soc. Plant Molecular Biology, Am. Soc. Plant Physiologists, Tissue Culture Assn. (Virginia Evans award 1982), Sigma Xi, Gamma Sigma Delta. Republican. Office: 37437 State Hwy 16 Woodland CA 95695

HAUSDORFER, GARY LEE, mortgage banker; b. Indpls., Mar. 26, 1946; s. Walter Edward and Virginia Lee (Bender) H.; AA, Glendale Coll., 1966; BS, Calif. State U.-L.A., 1968; children: Lisa Ann, Janet Lee. Rsch. officer Security Pacific Bank, L.A., 1968-73; v.p., mgr. W. Ross Campbell Co., Irvine, Calif., 1973-81; sr. v.p. Weyerhaeuser Mortgage Co., Irvine, 1982-87; exec. v.p., ptnr. L.J. Melody & Co. of Calif., 1987-89; pres. Hausdorfer Co., 1989—. pres. The Diamond Group, 1994—; Councilman, City of San Juan Capistrano, 1978-94, mayor, 1980-81, 84-85, 88-90; chmn. Capistrano Valley Water Dist., 1980-81, San Juan Capistrano Redevel. Agy., 1983-84, 85-86, South Orange County Leadership Conf.; bd. dirs. Orange County Trans. Corridor Agy., Orange County Transit Dist.; chmn. Orange County Transp. Authority. Recipient cert. of commendation Orange County Bd. Suprs., 1981, congl. commendation, 1985, Theodore Roosevelt Conservation award Pres. Bush, 1990. Republican.

HAUSEL, WILLIAM DAN, economic geologist, martial artist; b. Salt Lake City, July 24, 1949; s. Maynard Romain and Dorthy (Clark) H.; m. Patricia Kemp, Aug. 14, 1970; children: Jessica Siddhartha, Eric Jason. BS in Geology, U. Utah, 1972, MS in Geology, 1974. Astronomy lectr., Hansen Planetarium, Salt Lake City, 1968-72; rsch. asst. U. Utah, 1972-74; teaching asst. U. N.Mex., Albuquerque, 1974-75; project geologist Warnock Cons., Albuquerque, 1975; geologist U.S. Geol. Survey, Casper, Wyo., 1976-77; staff geologist Geol. Survey of Wyo., Laramie, 1977-81, dep. dir., 1981-91, sr. econ. geologist, 1991—; cons. Western Gold Exploration and Mining, Anchorage, 1988, 89, Chevron Resources, Georgetown, Mont., 1990, Fowler Resources, Phillipsburg, Mont., 1992, Bald Mountain Mining, U.S., 1993, A and E Diamond Exploration, Calif., 1993, Echo Bay Exploration, U.S., 1994; assoc. curator mineralogy Wyo. State Mus., Cheyenne, 1983-90; state rep. and divsn. head Shorin-Ryu Karate, JUKO-KAI Internat., Wyoming, 1994—; U.S. dir. open divsn. Shorin-Ryu Karate, 1996, divsn head, Shorin-Ryu Karate and Kobudo (Juko-Kai: Internat), 1997. Author: Partial Pressures of Some Lunar Lavas, 1972, Petrogenesis of Some Representative Lavas, Southwestern Utah, 1975, Exploration for Diamondiferous Kimberlite, 1979, Gold Districts of Wyoming, 1980, Ore Deposits of Wyoming, 1982, Geology of Southeastern Wyoming, 1984, Minerals and Rocks of Wyoming, 1986, The Geology of Wyoming's Precious Metal Lode and Placer Deposits, 1989, Economic Geology of the South Pass Greenstone Belt, 1991, Economic Geology of the Cooper Hill Mining District, 1992, Mining History and Geology of Wyoming's Metal and Gemstone Districts, 1993, Geology, Mining Districts, and Ghost Towns of the Medicine Bow Mountains, 1993, Diamonds, Kimberlite and Lamproite in the United States, 1994, Pacific Coast Diamonds-An Unconventional Source Terrane, 1995, Economic Geology of the Seminoe Mountains Greenstone Belt, 1994, The Great Diamond Hoax of 1872, 1995, Geology and Gold Mineralization of the Rattlesnake Hills, Granite Mountains, Wyoming, 1996; contbr. over 300 articles to profl. jours. and 3 books. Grantee NASA, 1981, Office of Surface Mining, 1979, U. Wyo., 1981-92, U.S. Geol. Survey Coop. Geologic Mapping Initiative, 1985-88, Union Pacific Resources, 1991, 92, 93, 94; recipient Pres.'s cert. excellence in presentation Am. Assn. Petroleum Geologists, 1992. Mem. Wyo. Geol. Assn. (cert. of appreciation 1992), Wyo. Profl. Geologists, Soc. Econ. Geologists, U. Utah Geology Club (pres. 1969-71), Laramie Bushido Dojo Karate (pres. 1985-88), U. Wyo. Campus Shotokan Karate Club (instr. 1988-93), Shorin-Ryu Karate Club (U. Wyo. Campus headmaster 1993—), Juko-Kai Internat., Internat. Okinawan Martial Arts Union. Avocations: karate (7th degree black belt/Dai-shihan), jujutsu, sketching. Home: 4238 Grays Gable Rd Laramie WY 82070-6911 Office: Geol Survey of Wyo PO Box 3008 Laramie WY 82071-3008

HAUSER, GERARD ALAN, communication educator; b. Buffalo, N.Y., May 20, 1943; s. Albert Clement Hauser and Ann John Michalakes; m. Jean Marie Brown, Aug. 14, 1965; children: Gerard, Jr., Kirsten. BA, Canisius Coll., 1965; MA, U. Wis., 1966, PhD, 1970. Asst. prof. Pa. State U., University Park, 1969-73, assoc. prof., 1973-87, prof., 1987-93; prof. U. Colo., Boulder, 1993—; dir. univ. scholars program, Pa. State U., 1987-93; chmn. comm. dept. U. Colo., Boulder, 1993—, chmn. coun. of chairs, 1996—. Author: Introduction to Rhetorical Theory, 1986; co-editor: Philosophy and Rhetoric jour., 1990-93. Mem. Internat. Soc. for History of Rhetoric, Rhetoric Soc. of Am. (bd. dirs. 1997—), Speech Comm. Assn., We. States Commn. Assn. Office: Univ Colo 94 Hellems Hall Boulder CO 80309-0270

HAVENS, CANDACE JEAN, planning consultant; b. Rochester, Minn., Sept. 13, 1952; d. Fred Z. and Barbara Jean (Stephenson) H.; m. Bruce Curtis Mercier, Feb. 22, 1975 (div. Apr. 1982); 1 child, Rachel; m. James Arthur Renning, Oct. 26, 1986; children: Kelsey, Sarah. Student, U. Calif., San Diego, Darmouth Coll., 1970-72, Am. U., Beirut, 1973-74; BA in Sociology, U. Calif., Riverside, 1977; MPA, Harvard U., 1994. Project coord. social svc. orgn. Grass Roots II, San Luis Obispo, Calif., 1976-77; planner City San Luis Obispo, 1977-86, city parking, spl. projects mgr., 1986-88; spl. asst. to city adminstr. City of San Luis Obispo, 1989, planning cons., 1991—; mgmt. rsch. specialist Bank of Boston, 1995-96. Past pres. Nat. Charity League, Riverside; mem. San Luis Obispo Med. Aux., 1986-93, San Luis Obispo Arts Coun., 1986—; pres. bd. dirs. San Luis Obispo Children's Mus., 1990-91, CFO, 1993; mediator in Newton (Mass.) Cts., 1996, San Luis Obispo, 1996—,. Mem. AAUW, SPIDR, Am. Inst. Cert. Planners, Toastmasters (sec. 1986-87, v.p. 1987-88, pres. 1989-90, treas. 1991-92), Am. Planning Assn., Mass. Assn. Mediation Profls. and Practitioners. Office: 1555 Higuera St Ste 120 San Luis Obispo CA 93401

HAVILAND, MARLITA CHRISTINE, elementary school educator; b. Moses Lake, Wash., Sept. 4, 1952; d. Marvin Curtis and Delita F. (Grout) McCully; m. James A Haviland, June 18, 1971. BS in Edn., So. Nazarene U., Bethany, Okla., 1973; MA in Edn., No. Ariz. U., 1987. Cert. elem. tchr., Ariz., Colo., ESL, basic edn., spl. edn. tchr., c.c., Ariz., early childhood edn., Colo,. Elem. tchr. St. Paul (Ark.) Pu. Sch., Twin Wells Indian Sch., Sun Valley, Ariz., Navajo Gospel Mission, Kykotsmovi, Ariz., Shonto (Ariz.) Boarding Sch. (now Shonto Prep Sch.); instr. Northland Pioneer Coll.; coord. Sch. Wide Book Fair. Coord. Children Inc., Shonto. Mem. Nat. Fedn. Fed. Employees (past pres., sec.-treas., steward), Nat. Sci. Tchrs. Assn., Ariz. CADRE, Alpha Nu, Phi Kappa Phi. Home: PO Box 7427 Shonto AZ 86054

HAVIS, ALLAN STUART, playwright, theatre educator; b. N.Y.C., Sept. 26, 1951; s. Mickey and Esther H. BA, CCNY, 1973; MA, Hunter Coll., 1976; MFA, Yale U., 1980. Film animation tchr. Guggenheim Mus., N.Y.C., 1974-76; playwriting tchr. Dramatist Guild, N.Y.C., 1985-87, Ulster County C.C., Stoneridge, N.Y., 1985-88; prof. theatre, head playwriting program U. Calif.-San Diego, La Jolla, 1988—. Author: (novel) Albert the Astronomer, 1979, (plays) Morocco, 1986 (HBO award), Lilith, 1991, (anthology) Plays by Allan Havis, 1989, A Daring Bridge, 1997, Ladies of Fisher Cove, 1997, Sainte Simone, 1997, (play) A Vow of Silence, 1996. Dramaturg Young Playwrights Festival, N.Y.C., 1984, juror, 1993; juror N.J. Arts Coun., Trenton, 1987; panelist Theatre Communications Group, N.Y.C., 1987; juror McKnight Playwriting Fellowship, 1995; v.p. Literary Mgrs. and Dramaturgs of Am., So. Calif. region, 1995—. Playwriting fellow Nat. Endowment for the Arts, 1986, Rockefeller Found., 1987, Guggenheim Found., 1987-88; recipient New American Plays award Kennedy Ctr./Am. Express, Washington, 1988, Dramatists Guild/CBS award, 1995, HBO award, 1996. Democrat. Jewish. Office: Dept of Theatre Univ Calif-San Diego La Jolla CA 92093

HAVIVI, ABRAHAM, psychiatrist; b. N.Y.C., Feb. 24, 1958; s. Moshe and Sylvia (Bartzoff) H. BA, Brown U., 1980; MD, U. Pa., 1990. Diplomate Am. Bd. Psychiatry and Neurology. Intern Coopa Hosp., Camden, N.J., 1990-91; resident psychiatry UCLA Neuro-Psychiatric Inst., L.A., Calif., 1991-94; fellow in child adolescent psychiatry UCLA Neuro-Psychiatric Inst., L.A., 1994-96; pvt. practice L.A., Calif., 1996—. Mem. Am. Psychiatric Assn., Am. Acad. Child and Adolescent Psychiatry, So. Calif. Psychiatric Soc. Office: 8306 Wilshire Blvd #830 Beverly Hills CA 90211

HAVLEN, ROBERT JAMES, astronomer, non-profit society administrator; b. Utica, N.Y., Sept. 16, 1943; s. Frank James and Marian Whitmore (Briggs) H.; m. Carolyn Anne Wolf, Sept. 2, 1967; children: Pamela Ruth, Naomi Lynn. BS, U. Rochester, 1965; PhD, U. Ariz., 1970. Staff astronomer European So. Obs., Santiago, Chile, 1970-77; vis. lectr. U. Va., Charlottesville, 1977-79; asst. to dir. Nat. Radio Astronomy Obs., Charlottesville, 1979-88; head obs.svcs. Nat. Radio Astronomy Obs., Socorro, N.Mex., 1988-93; exec. dir. Astron. Soc. Pacific, San Francisco, 1993—. Contbr. rsch. papers to profl. jours. Mem. Am. Astron. Soc., Internat. Astron. Union. Office: Astron Soc Pacific 390 Ashton Ave San Francisco CA 94112-1722

HAWES, SUE, lawyer; b. Washington, Mar. 30, 1937; d. Alexander Boyd and Elizabeth (Armstrong) H.; m. James E. Brodhead, June 21, 1963; children: William James Pusey Brodhead, Daniel Alexander Hawes Brodhead. BA, Sarah Lawrence Coll., 1959, MA, 1963; JD, Whittier (Calif.) Sch. of Law, 1983. Bar: Calif. 1988, U.S. Dist. Ct. (cen. dist.) Calif. 1990. Dancer and choreographer N.Y.C., Washington, Latin Am., Europe, 1959-62; instr., dir. dance program dept. theatre and phys. edn. Smith Coll., Northampton, Mass., 1963-65; instr. dept. dance UCLA, 1973-75; freelance script supr. L.A., 1976-80; prin. Law Office of Sue Hawes, L.A., 1988-96. Articles editor Whittier Law Rev., 1982-83. Active Santa Barbara Symphony League. Mem. AAUW, State Bar Calif., Santa Barbara County Bar Assn., Actors' Equity Assn. Democrat.

HAWK, DAWN DAVAH, secondary education educator; b. Dodge, Nebr., Apr. 14, 1945; d. Fred John and Marcella Martha (Kunes) Lerch; m. Floyd Russell Hawk, June 14, 1969. BAE, Wayne State Coll., 1967. Cert. tchr., Nebr., Iowa, Ariz. English tchr. Tekamah (Nebr.) Pub. Sch., 1967-69, West Lyon Community Schs., Inwood, Iowa, 1970-74, Norfolk (Nebr.) Cath. Schs., 1974-85; English tchr., libr. Beemer (Nebr.) Pub. Schs., 1969-70; English and reading tchr. San Manuel (Ariz.) Sch. Dist., 1986—; chair adaptive edn. dept. San Manuel (Ariz.) High Sch., 1992-93; tutor in field. Active Catalina Luth. Ch., Tucson. Recipient Cooper Found. award for excellence in teaching U. Nebr., 1983; NEH edn. grantee, 1987, 89, 91, 95; Ariz. Reading Assn. grad. scholar, 1995. Mem. NEA, Nat. Coun. Tchrs. English, Internat. Reading Assn., Ea. Pinal Lit. Coun., Ariz. English Tchrs. Assn., Tucson Area Reading Coun. (bd. advisors), San Manuel Tchrs. Assn. Republican. Home: 3950 E Hawser St 5 Tucson AZ 85739-9534 Office: San Manuel HS PO Box 406 San Manuel AZ 85631-0406

HAWK, FLOYD RUSSELL, secondary school educator; b. Fresno, Calif., Oct. 7, 1945; s. Floyd Edward and Velma Irene (Lyon) H.; m. Dawn Davah Lerch, June 14, 1969. BA in Bus., Wayne State Coll., 1971. Cert. tchr. Ariz. Tchr. W. Lyon Pub. Schs., Inwood, Iowa, 1970-74, Norfolk (Nebr.) Cath. Schs., 1974-76, Madison (Nebr.) Pub. Schs., 1977-85, Young (Ariz.) Pub. Schs., 1985-86, San Manuel (Ariz.) High Sch., 1986--; state rep. Nat. Coaches Assn., Madison, Nebr., 1980-82; bd. dirs. Pinal County Adult Literacy, San Manuel. Mem. adv. bd. Multiple Sclerosis Soc. NEH grantee, 1995. Mem. NEA, Ariz. Edn. Assn., Nat. Coun. Social Studies, Ariz. Bus. Edn. Assn., Ariz. Hist. Soc., Optimist Club (pres. 1972, lt. gov. 1973). Republican. Lutheran. Office: San Manuel HS PO Box 406 Tucson AZ 85739

HAWK, STEVE J., magazine editor; b. Pensacola, Fla., Aug. 14, 1955; s. Frank Hagen and Nancy Jo (Skaggs) H.; m. Pamela Mary Higgins; 1 child, Wilson Henry. BA in Eng., U. Calif., Santa Barbara, 1977. Staff writer The Citizen, Solana Beach, Calif., 1979-80, Blade-Tribune, Oceanside, Calif., 1980-81, Times-Advocate, Escondido, Calif., 1981-84, Orange County Register, Santa Ana, Calif., 1984-90; editor Surfer Magazine, San Juan Capistrano, Calif., 1990—; freelance writer Us, Harper's, Alaska Airlines Mag., L.A. Times, 1980-94. Editor: Notes from the Jungle's Edge: The Journalism of Barry Farrell, 1988. Office: Surfer Magazine PO Box 1028 Dana Point CA 92629-5028

HAWKE, BERNARD RAY, planetary scientist; b. Louisville, Oct. 22, 1946; s. Arvil Abner and Elizabeth Ellen (Brown) H. B.S. in Geology, U. Ky., 1970, M.S., 1974; M.S., Brown U., 1977, Ph.D. in Planetary Geology, 1978. Geologist U.S. Geol. Survey, 1967-68; researcher U. Ky., 1972-74, Brown U., 1974-78; planetary scientist Hawaii Inst. Geophysics, U. Hawaii, Honolulu, 1978—; dir. NASA Pacific Regional Planetary Data Ctr., 1981—; prin. investigator NASA grants; assoc. dir. Hawaii Space Grant Coll. Author papers in field. Served with USAR, 1970-72. Decorated Bronze Star. Mem. Geochem. Soc., Meteoritcal Soc., Am. Geophys. Union, Am. Chem. Soc., Geol. Soc. Am., Sigma Xi, Sigma Gamma Epsilon, Alpha Tau Omega. Republican. Office: U Hawaii SOEST Hawaiian Inst Geophysics Honolulu HI 96822

HAWKE, DEBORAH SUE, academic counselor; b. Woodland, Calif., Dec. 11, 1953; d. Fred Henry III and Harriett Grace (Kies) Abbott; children: Jamie Abbott, Robert Stewart. Student, Napa Jr. Coll., 1972-74, U. Calif., Davis, 1976—. Lic. real estate broker, Calif. Sec. Lucas, Landucci & Bick, Davis, 1974-75; sec. dept. sociology U. Calif., Davis, 1975-76, sec., advising asst. dept. psychology, 1976-84, acad. counselor sect. neurobiology, physiology and behavior, 1984—; mem. steering com. Systemwide Acad. Advisor/Counselors Conf., Davis, 1987, 95; chair Execution for Agrl. and Environ. Scis. Coll. Celebration, 1993, 94; pres. Acad. Adv. Workshop, Davis, 1991, 92. Recipient Debbie Hawke Day award Undergrad. Physiology Club, Davis, 1989, Mem. of Month award Cross Court Athletic Club, 1990. Republican. Home: 809 W Gibson Woodland CA 95695 Office: U Calif Sect Neurobiology Physiology & Behavior Davis CA 95616

HAWKE, SIMON NICHOLAS, writer, educator; b. N.Y.C., Sept. 30, 1951; s. Valentin Michael and Helga Ellen (Hartewelt) Yermakov. Student, Am. U., 1969-70; BA in Comms., Hofstra U., 1974; postgrad., U. Ariz., 1993-94; MA in English and History, Western N.Mex. U., 1994. instr. Colo. Mountain Coll. Summer Writers Conf., instr. in composition and fiction writing, Pima C.C., Tucson, 1992—; instr. Pima Writers workshop, 1992; instr. Gila Writers Conf., Western N.Mex. U., Silver City, 1994; dir. Sonora Writers Workshop, 1995—. Author: (pub. as Nicholas Yermakov) Journey from Flesh, 1981, Last Communion, 1981, Fall into Darkness, 1982, Epiphany, 1982, Clique, 1982, Jehad, 1984; (pub. as Simon Hawke) The Ivanhoe Gambit, 1984, The Timekeeper Conspiracy, 1984, The Pimpernel Plot, 1984, The Zenda Vendetta, 1985, The Nautilus Sanction, 1985, The Khyber Connection, 1986, The Argonaut Affair, 1987, Psychodrome, 1987, The Wizard of Fourth Street, 1987, The Shapechanger Scenario, 1988, The Dracula Caper, 1988, The Wizard of Whitechapel, 1988, Steele, 1989, The Lilliput Legion, 1989, Cold Steele, 1989, The Wizard of Sunset Strip, 1989, Killer Steele, 1990, Jagged Steele, 1990, The Hellfire Rebellion, 1990, Renegade Steele, 1990, The Wizard of Rue Morgue, 1990, Target Steele, 1990, The Cleopatra Crisis, 1990, To Stalk a Spectre, 1991, Samurai Wizard, 1991, The Wizard of Santa Fe, 1991, The Sixgun Solution, 1991, The Reluctant Sorcerer, 1992, The Nine Lives of Catseye Gomez, 1992, Sons of Glory, 1992, The Romulan Prize, 1993 (N.Y. Times Bestseller), The Outcast, Call to Battle, 1993, The Inadequate Adept, 1993, The Wizard of Camelot, 1993, The Wizard of Lovecraft's Cafe, 1993, The Patrian Transgression, 1994, The Seeker, 1994, The Nomad, 1994, Whims of Creation, 1995, The Broken Blade, 1995, The Iron Throne, The Ambivalent Magician, 1996, WAR, 1996, A Thief in the Tombs of Horror, 1997, Wizard of Dragon Storm, 1997, The Knight's Apprentice, 1997; author numerous sci. fiction. short stories to anthologies. Home: HCR-1 Box 466 Tucson AZ 85736

HAWKES, GLENN ROGERS, psychology educator; b. Preston, Idaho, Apr. 29, 1919; s. William and Rae (Rogers) H.; m. Yvonne Merrill, Dec. 18, 1941; children—Kristen, William Ray, Gregory Merrill, Laura. B.S. in Psychology, Utah State U., 1946, M.S. in Psychology, 1947; Ph.D. in Psychology, Cornell U., 1950. From asst. prof. to prof. child devel. and psychology Iowa State U., Ames, 1950-66, chmn. dept. child devel., 1954-66; prof. human devel., rsch. psychologist U. Calif., Davis, 1966-89, prof. emeritus, 1990—, acad. coord. Hubert Humphrey fellowship program, 1990—, assoc. dean applied econs. and behavioral scis., 1966-83, chmn. dept. applied behavioral scis., 1982-86, chmn. teaching div., 1970-72, prof. behavioral scis. dept. family practice, Sch. Medicine; acting dir. Internat. Programs, U. Calif., Davis, 1994—; vis. scholar U. Hawaii, 1972-73, U. London, 1970, 80, 86; bd. dirs. Creative Playthings Inc., 1962-66. Author: (with Pease) Behavior and Development from 5 to 12, 1962; (with Frost) The Disadvantaged Child: Issues and Innovations, 1966, 2d edit., 1970; (with Schultz and Baird) Lifestyles and Consumer Behavior of Older Americans, 1979; (with Nicola and Fish) Young Marrieds: The Dual Career Approach, 1984. Contbr. numerous articles to profl. and sci. jours. Served with AUS, 1941-45. Recipient numerous research grants from pvt. founds. and govtl. bodies; recipient Iowa State U. faculty citation, 1965, Outstanding Service citation Iowa Soc. Crippled Children and adults, 1965, citation Dept. Child Devel., 1980, Coll. Agrl. and Environ. Scis., 1983; named hon. lt. gov. Okla., 1966. Home: 1114 Purdue Dr Davis CA 95616-1736 Office: U Calif Internat House 10 College Park Davis CA 95616-3607

HAWKEY, PHILIP A., city manager; b. Lima, Ohio, Sept. 26, 1946; s. George D. and Beatrice A. (Coon) H.; m. Dena Spanos, Oct. 18, 1969; children: George, Aaron, Ann. BA, Baldwin-Wallace Coll., 1968; MA, Ohio State U., 1972; JD, Cleve. State U., 1975. Bar: Ohio, 1976. Adminstrv. asst. City of Cleve., 1972-76; city adminstr. City of Wooster, Ohio, 1976-79; city mgr. City of Kettering, Ohio, 1979-82; dep. city mgr. City of Cin., 1982-86; city mgr. City of Toledo, 1986-90, City of Pasadena, Calif., 1990—. Mem. Internat. City Mgmt. Assn. (v.p.). Home: 1136 Wotkyns Dr Pasadena CA 91103-2838 Office: City Hall 100 N Garfield Ave Rm 237 Pasadena CA 91109-7215

HAWKINS, DAVID RAMON, psychiatrist, writer, researcher; b. Milw., June 3, 1927; s. Ramon Nelson and Alice-Mary (McCutcheon) H.; children: Lynn Ashley, Barbara Catherine. BS, Marquette U., 1950; MD, Med. Coll. Wis., Milw., 1953; PhD, Columbia Pacific U., 1995. Med. dir. North Nassau Mental Health Ctr., Manhasset, N.Y., 1956-80; dir. rsch. Brunswick Hosp., L.I., N.Y., 1968-79; pres. Acad. Orthomolecular Psychiatry, N.Y.C., 1970-80; dir. Inst. Spiritual Rsch., Sedona, Ariz., 1979-88, The Rsch. Inst., Sedona, 1988—; pres. Attractor Rsch., Sedona, 1989—, Veritas Pub., Sedona, 1995—; chmn. Inst. Advaned Theoretical Rsch., 1993—; guest lectr. U. Notre Dame, Harvard U., U. W.Va., U. Mich., 1970-88, U. Calif., San Francisco, 1997; guest on TV news and interview shows including McNeal-Lehrer, Barbara Walters, Today, 1972-76; chief of staff Mingus Mountain RTC, 1995; cons. psychiatrist MJL Hosp., Cottonwood, Ariz., 1995; cons.

USN, Dept. Health Edn. Welfare, Congress. Author: (with Linus Pauling) Orthomolecular Psychiatry, 1973, Force vs. Power, 1995; contbr. articles to profl. jours. With U.S. Navy, 1945-46, PTO. Decorated knight Sovereign Order St. John of Jerusalem; Rsch. grantee N.Y. State Dept. Mental Hygiene, annually, N.Y. State Legis., 1967-87; recipient Mosby Book award, 1953. Mem. AMA, APA, Ariz. Med. Soc., Ariz. Psychiat. Soc., Alpha Omega Alpha. Office: Rsch Inst 151 Keller Ln Sedona AZ 86336-9711 *Our lives are created more by our vision of the future then they are by the details of our past.*

HAWKINS, ROBERT LEE, health facility administrator; b. Denver, Feb. 18, 1938; s. Isom and Bessie M. (Hugley) H.; m. Ann Sharon Hoy, Apr. 28, 1973; children: Robert, Jeanne, Julia, Rose. AA, Pueblo Jr. Coll., 1958; BS, So. Colo. State Coll., 1965; MSW, U. Denver, 1967. Psychiat. technician Colo. State Hosp., Pueblo, 1956-58, 1962-63, occupl. therapist asst., 1964-65, clin. adminstr. psychiat. team, 1969-75, dir. cmty. svcs., 1975-92, supr. vol. services, 1975—, mem. budget com., 1975—; asst. supt. clin. svcs., 1992—; supt. Colo. Mental Health Inst., Pueblo, 1996—; counselor (part-time) Family Svc. Agy., Pueblo, 1968-69, exec. dir., 1969-70; mem. faculty U. So. Colo., 1968-75; ptnr. Human Resource Devel., Inc., 1970-75; mem. Nat. Adv. Com. on Instnl. Quality and Integrity, U.S. Dept. Edn., Washington, 1993—. Mem. Pueblo Positive Action Com., 1970; chmn. adv. bd. Pueblo Sangre de Cristo Day Care Center, 1969-72; chmn. Gov.'s So. Area Adv. Council of Employment Service, 1975-76, chmn. Pueblo's City CSC, 1976-77, Pueblo Cmty. Corrections, 1985-87, Pueblo Civil Svc. Commn., 1988—; commr. Pueblo Housing Authority, 1986—, Colo. Commn. Higher Edn., 1987—, USED Commn. for Ednl. Quality & Integrity, 1993—; mem. gov's. adv. com. Mental Health Stds., 1981—; mem. Colo. Juvenile Parole Bd., 1977; bd. dirs. Pueblo United Fund, 1969-74, pres., 1973; bd. dirs. Pueblo Community Orgn., 1974-76, Spanish Peaks Mental Health Center, 1976—, Neighborhood Health Center, 1977-79, Pueblo Community Corrections, 1983—, Pueblo Legal Svcs., 1983—, Girl Scouts USA, 1996—; mem. Pueblo Colo. 2010 Commn., 1994—, adv. com. YWCA, 1994—, Healthy Pueblo 2000 Task Force, 1993—. Bd. dirs. Posada Shelter for Homeless, 1990—, Boys Girls club, 1991—, ARC, 1994—, pres., 1994—. With U.S. Army 1958-62. Mem. Nat. Assn. Social Workers (nominating com. 1973-76), ACLU (dir. Pueblo chpt. 1980—), NAACP, Broadway Theatre Guild. Democrat. Methodist. Mem. Kiwanis. Home: 220 Melrose Ave Pueblo CO 81004 Office: Colo State Hosp 1600 W 24th St Pueblo CO 81003-1411

HAWKINS, ROBERTA ROSENTHAL, theater educator; b. L.A., Dec. 16, 1951; d. Robert and Mary Lu (Clayton) R.; m. Joseph Angelo Carter, Feb. 21, 1986; 1 child, Jessica Clayton. BA in English, U. Mass., 1973; MFA in Theatre Arts, Brandeis U., 1981. Cert. secondary tchr. Mass., N.Y., Calif. Tchr. English and drama Maynard (Mass.) H.S., 1973-76, J.F.K. Mid. Sch., Hudson, Mass., 1978-79; English dept. coord. dist. 6 mid. sch. N.Y.C., 1981-86; English, speech advisor Park West H.S., N.Y.C., 1986-90; chmn. dept. fine arts Rancho Verde H.S., Moreno Valley, Calif., 1991-96; adminstrv. dir. The Players' Conservatory, Riverside, Calif., 1996—; stage dir. 13th St. Theatre, N.Y.C., 1983-86, various summer stock, off-off Broadway, 1974-86; singer/actor various roles; adj. prof. DeVry Inst. of Tech., 1997—. Prodr./dir. over 30 plays; actress/singer over 30 performances. Mem. Calif. Tchrs. Assn.

HAWLEY, NANCI ELIZABETH, public relations and communications professional; b. Detroit, Mar. 18, 1942; d. Arthur Theodore and Elizabeth Agnes (Fylling) Smisek; m. Joseph Michael Hawley, Aug. 28, 1958; children: Michael, Ronald, Patrick (dec.), Julie Anne. Pres. Tempo 21 Nursing Svcs., Inc., Covina, Calif., 1973-75; v.p. Profl. Nurses Bur., Inc., L.A., 1975-83; cons. Hawley & Assocs., Covina, 1983-87; exec. v.p. Glendora (Calif.) C. of C., 1984-85; dir. membership West Covina (Calif.) C. of C., 1985-87; exec. dir. San Dimas (Calif.) C. of C., 1987-88; mgr. pub. rels. Soc. for Advancement of Material and Process Engrs., Covina, 1988-92; small bus. rep. South Coast Air Quality Mgmt. Dist., 1992-94; bus. counselor Commerce and Trade Agy., Small Bus. Devel. Ctr., 1994; exec. v.p. Ont. (Calif.) C. of C., 1994—. V.p. Sangabriel valley chpt. Women in Mgmt. Recipient Youth Motivation award Foothill Edn. Com., Glendora, 1987. Mem. NAFE, Pub. Rels. Soc. Am., Soc. Nat. Assn. Publs., Am. Soc. Assn. Execs., Nat. Assn. Membership Dirs., Profl. Communicators Assn. So. Calif., Western Assn. Chamber Execs. (Spl. merit award for mag. pub. 1995), Kiwanis Internat. (sec. 1989-90, pres. West Covina 1990-91, Kiwanian of Yr. 1989), Rotary Internat. Office: Ontario C of C Ste 203A Convention Center Way Ontario CA 91764

HAWLEY, PHILIP METSCHAN, retired retail executive, consultant; b. Portland, Oreg., July 29, 1925; s. Willard P. and Dorothy (Metschan) H.; m. Mary Catherine Follen, May 31, 1947; children: Diane (Mrs. Robert Bruce Johnson), Willard, Philip Metschan Jr., John, Victor, Edward, Erin (Mrs. Kevin Przybocki), George. BS, U. Calif., Berkeley, 1946; grad. advanced mgmt. program, Harvard U., 1967. With Carter Hawley Hale Stores, Inc., L.A., 1958-93, pres., 1972-83, chief exec. officer, 1977-93, chmn., 1983-93; bd. dirs. Atlantic Richfield Co., Johnson & Johnson, Weyerhaeuser Co. Trustee Calif. Inst. Tech., U. Notre Dame; chmn. L.A. Energy Conservation Com., 1973-74. Decorated hon. comdr. Order Brit. Empire, knight comdr. Star Solidarity Republic Italy; recipient Award of Merit L.A. Jr. C. of C., 1974, Coro Pub. Affairs award, 1978, Medallion award Coll. William and Mary, 1983, Award of Excellence Sch. Bus. Adminstrn. U. So. Calif., 1987, Bus. Statesman of Yr. award Harvard Bus. Sch., 1989, 15th ann. Whitney M. Young Jr. award L.S. Urban League, 1988; named Calif. Industrialist of Yr. Calif. Mus. Sci. and Industry, 1975. Mem. Calif. Retailers Assn. (chmn. 1993—, dir.), Beach Club, Calif. Club, L.A. Country Club, Bohemian Club, Pacific-Union Club, Newport Harbor Yacht Club, Multnomah Club, Links Club, Phi Beta Kappa, Beta Alpha Psi, Beta Gamma Sigma. Office: 400 S Hope St Ste 1900 Los Angeles CA 90071

HAWTHORNE, NAN LOUISE, publisher, internet resources consultant, trainer; b. Hawthorne, Nev., Jan. 3, 1952; d. Louis Frederick Haas and Merle Forrest (Ohlhausen) Ritter; m. James Denver Tedford, Dec. 20, 1981. BS, No. Mich. U., 1981. Mng. dir. Sound Vol. Mgmt., 1993—; mgr. vols. Seattle Commns., 1993-94; columnist Seattle Vol., 1994—; co-host TV program on TCI Pub. Access: Volunteer!. Author: Loving the Goddess Within, 1991, Building Better Relatinships with Volunteers, 1997. Mem. Wash. State Coun. on Volunteerism and Citizen Svcs., 1992-94; trainer United Way of King County Vol. Ctr., 1993—; bd. dirs., dir. vols. Dovia of King County, 1992, 96—; mem. adv. bd. Retired Sr. Vol. Program, 1995—; bd. dirs. Cmty. Vol. Svcs.; pres., bd. dirs. Cmty. Vol. Svcs., 1996—. Office: Sound Vol Mgmt 9594 1st Ave NE Ste 413 Seattle WA 98115-2028

HAY, ANDREW MACKENZIE, merchant banking and commodities company executive; b. London, Apr. 9, 1928; came to U.S., 1954, naturalized, 1959; s. Ewen Mackenzie and Bertine (Buxton) H.; MA in Econs., St. John's Coll., Cambridge U., 1950; m. Catherine Newman, July 30, 1977. Commodities trader, London and Ceylon, 1950-53; v.p. Calvert Vavasseur & Co. Inc., N.Y.C., 1954-61, pres., 1962-78, pres. Calvert-Peat Inc., N.Y.C., 1978—, Andrew M. Hay, Inc.; chmn. Barretto Peat Inc., N.Y.C., 1974-88; Pacific NW cons. Am. Assn. Exporters and Importers, 1982—; radio and TV appearances. Mem. adv. com. on tech. innovation Nat. Acad. Scis., 1978; bd. dirs. Winston Churchill Found.; treas., trustee World Affairs Coun. Oreg., 1986—; apptd. Her Majesty's hon. Brit. consul, 1987; dean Oreg. Counsular Corps, 1991. Capt. Brit. Army. Decorated comdr. Order Brit. Empire. Mem. Am. Importer Assn. (pres. 1977-79), Pacific N.W. Internat. Trade Assn. (exec. dir. 1986—), Brit. Am. C. of C. (pres. 1966-68), Philippine Am. C. of C. (pres. 1977-79), St. George's Soc. (bd. dir.), St. Andrew's Soc. (bd. dir.), Recess Club, Downtown Assn. (N.Y.C.), U. Club, Arlington Club. Episcopalian. Author: A Century of Coconuts, 1972. Home and Office: 3515 SW Council Crest Dr Portland OR 97201-1403

HAY, JOHN LEONARD, lawyer; b. Lawrence, Mass., Oct. 6, 1940; s. Charles Cable and Henrietta Dudley (Wise) H.; m. Ruth Murphy, Mar. 16, 1997; 1 child, Ian. AB with distinction, Stanford U., 1961; JD, U. Colo., 1964. Bar: Colo. 1964, Ariz. 1965, D.C. 1971. Assoc. Lewis and Roca, Phoenix, 1964-69, ptnr., 1969-82; ptnr. Fannin, Terry & Hay, Phoenix, 1982-87, Allen, Kimerer & LaVelle, Phoenix, 1987-94, Gust Rosenfeld, Phoenix, 1994—; bd. dirs. Ariz. Life and Disability Ins. Guaranty Fund, 1984-95, chmn., 1993-95. Co-author: Arizona Corporate Practice, 1996, Representing Franchises, 1996. Mem. Dem. Precinct Com., 1966-78, Ariz. State Dem. Com., 1968-78; chmn. Dem. Legis. Dist., 1971-74; mem. Maricopa County Dem. Cen. Com., 1971-74; bd. dirs. ACLU, 1973-78; bd. dirs. Community Legal Svcs., 1983-89, pres., 1987-88; bd. dirs. Ariz. Club, 1994-96. Mem. ABA, Ariz. Bar Assn., Maricopa County Bar Assn. (bd. dirs. 1972-85), Assn. Life Ins. Counsel, Ariz. Licensors and Franchisors Assn. (bd. dirs. 1985—, pres. 1988-89), Ariz. Civil Liberties Union (bd. dirs. 1967-84, 95—, pres. 1973-77, Disting. Citizen award 1979), Phoenix C. of C. (chmn. arts and culture task force 1997—). Home: 201 E Hayward Ave Phoenix AZ 85020-4037 Office: Gust Rosenfeld 201 N Central Ave Ste 3300 Phoenix AZ 85073-0033

HAY, JOHN WOODS, JR., retired banker; b. Rock Springs, Wyo., Apr. 23, 1905; s. John Woods and Mary Ann (Blair) H.; A.B., U. Mich., 1927; m. Frances B. Smith, Dec. 28, 1948; children—Helen Mary, John Woods III, Keith Norbert, Joseph Garrett. Pres., dir. Rock Springs Nat. Bank, 1947-95, Rock Springs Grazing Assn., 1939-95, Blair & Hay Land & Livestock Co., Rock Springs, 1949—. Former trustee, v.p. William H. and Carrie Gottsche Found. Mem. Masons, Shriners, Jesters, Rotary, Sigma Alpha Epsilon. Republican. Episcopalian. Home: 502 B St Rock Springs WY 82901-6213 Office: 333 Broadway St Rock Springs WY 82901-6242

HAY, RICHARD LAURENCE, theater scenic designer; b. Wichita, Kans., May 28, 1929; s. Laurence Charles and Ruth Mary (Rhoades) H. BA, Stanford U., 1952, MA, 1955. Tech. dir., designer Oreg. Shakespeare Festival, Ashland, 1953-55, prin. scenic designer, 1970—; instr. drama Stanford U., Palo Alto, Calif., 1957-62, assoc. prof., 1965-69; assoc. artistic dir. for design Denver Ctr. Theater Co., 1984-91; freelance scenic designer Guthrie Theater, Mpls., Am. Conservatory Theater, San Francisco, Mo. Repertory Theater, Kansas City, Mark Taper Forum, Los Angeles, Old Globe Theater, San Diego, Berkekey (Calif.) Repertory Theater, others; theater designer: Source and Space Theatres, Denver Ctr. Theatre Co., New Old Globe Theatre and Festival Stage, Old Globe Theatre, San Diego, Intiman Theatre, Seattle, Black Swan, Angus Bowmer Theatre, Elizabethan Stage, Oreg. Shakespeare Festival. Author: (with others) A Space for Magic: Stage Settings by Richard L. Hay, 1979; exhibitor Prague Quadriennial, 1987, U.S. Inst. Theatre Tech. Biennial Scenography Expn., 1984, 88, 90. Bd. dirs. U.S. Inst. Theatre Tech., 1994-97. Recipient Critics award Hollywood (Calif.) Drama-Logue, 1982, 85, 86, 89, Gov's. award for the Arts State of Oreg., 1989; Fulbright grantee, 1955. Mem. United Scenic Artists, U.S. Inst. Theatre Tech. (bd. dirs.), League Hist. Am. Theaters. Democrat. Congregationalist. Home: 707 Liberty St Ashland OR 97520-3140 Office: Oreg Shakespeare Festival PO Box 158 Ashland OR 97520-0158

HAY, WILLIAM CHARLES, professional hockey team executive; b. Saskatoon, Sask., Can., Dec. 9, 1935; s. Charles and Florence (Miller) H.; m. Nancy Ann Woodman, Aug. 24, 1957; children: Pam, Penny, Donald. B.S. in Geology, Colo. Coll., 1958. Profl. hockey player Chgo. Black Hawks, 1958-67; mgr. Sedco Drilling Co., Calgary, Alta., 1967-70, gen. mgr., from 1970; gen. mgr. Hi-Tower Drilling Co., Calgary, Alta., from 1970; formerly pres., chief operating officer Hockey Can.; pres. Calgary Flames Hockey Club, NHL, 1991—; also alternate governor Calgary Flames; now planning advisor Canadian Hockey Association. Office: Canadian Hockey Asso, 2424 Univ Dr, Calgary, AB Canada T2N 3Y9*

HAYASHI, ALAN T., mathematics educator; b. Honolulu, Mar. 10, 1954; s. Harold T. and Sally S. (Nakamoto) H.; married. BSc, AB, U. Calif., Riverside, 1975; postgrad., Ohio State U., 1983-84. Cert. secondary tchr., single subject teaching and community coll. instr.'s credentials, Calif. Tchr., coach boys track and girls basketball Jurupa Jr. High Sch., Jurupa Unified Sch. Dist., Riverside, Calif., 1976-79; tchr. math., coach acad. decathlon and knowledge bowl Channel Islands High Sch., Oxnard (Calif.) Union High Sch. Dist., 1979-91; instr. Oxnard Coll., Ventura County C.C. Dist., 1989—, dept. chmn., 1995; casino dealer Harrah's Hotel & Casino, Stateline, Nev., 1980-81; teaching asst., instr. Ohio State U., Columbus, 1983-84; mathematician Pacific Missile Test Ctr., U.S. Dept. Def., Point Mugu, Calif., 1990; textbook reviewer Calif. Dept. Edn., 1981, 89; statistician Channel Islands High Sch. football team, 1980-92; asst. dir. summer inst. Calif. State Math. Project/Tri-County Math Project, 1996, co-dir., 1997. Newsletter editor Internat. Rels. Coun. Riverside, 1975-77. Recipient Chpt. Outstanding Tchr. award Calif. Mini-Corp., 1991-92, Tandy Tech. scholar nat. semi-finalist, 1990-91; named Tchr. of Yr., Calif. Scholastic Fedn. chpt., 1989, Channel Islands H.S. Tchr. of Yr., 1983, Oxnard Coll. Acad. Senate Treas., 1994, 97; NSF fellow, 1981, 82, Calif. Math Project/Tri-County Math Project fellow, 1994, sr. fellow, 1995, TCMP Leadership Network fellow, 1995—. Mem. NEA, Math. Assn. Am., Nat. Coun. Tchrs. Math., U. Calif.-Riverside Alumni Assn., Calif. Fedn. Tchrs., Ventura County Math. Coun. Office: Oxnard Coll 4000 S Rose Ave Oxnard CA 93033-6699

HAYDEN, CEDRIC L., state legislator, dentist; b. Eugene, Oreg., Aug. 4, 1934; s. Jesse and Gwendolen (Lampshire) H.; m. Marilyn Adele Jaekel, Dec. 27, 1961; children: Jonathan, Christopher, Matthew, Cedric Ross, Kaminda. BS, U. Oreg., 1957; DMD, Washington U., St. Louis, 1960; MPH, Loma Linda U., 1979. Dentist Antioch (Calif.) Dental Group, 1963-65; missionary Seventh Day Adventist Ch., Port of Spain, Trinidad, 1965-69; dentist Hayden Family Dentistry Group, Eugene, Oreg., 1970—; legislator Oreg. Ho. of Reps., Salem, 1985-97, chmn. house com. on transp., house com. on gen. govt., 1991-95, asst. majority leader, asst. caucus leader, 1991-95. Lt. (s.g.) USN, 1960-63. Fellow Am. Dental Soc. Anesthesiology. Home: 43676 E Bilyeu Creek Dr Scio OR 97374-9378

HAYDEN, JAMES WALWORTH, emergency physician, medical director; b. Gardner, Ma., Apr. 25, 1942; s. Robert Hawley and Dorothea Wallace (Ward) H.; m. Lauren Shanks, Dec. 10, 1982; children: David Ward, Mark Stevenson. BS in Chemistry, U. N.C., 1963; PhD in Organic Chemistry, U. Kans., 1968; MD, U. Tex., Houston, 1977. Bd. cert. Am. Bd. Forensic Examiners, Am. Bd. Med. Examiners; cert. Am. Assn. Med. Rev. Officers, Am. Soc. Addiction Medicine; cert. ACLS provider and instr., advanced trauma life support provider, BLS instr., pediat. advanced life support provider. Rsch. chemist Shell Devel. Co., Emeryville Rsch. Ctr., Houston, 1968-72; asst. to the dir. Inst. Clin. Toxicology, Houston, 1973-75; sr. rsch. assoc. U. Tex. Med. Sch., Houston, 1975-76; intern and resident Baylor Coll. Medicine, Houston, 1977-78; program physician Inst. Clin. Toxicology Ctrl. Methadone Clinic, Houston, 1978-79, med. dir., 1979-80; emergency dept. physician Gulf Coast Emergency Physicians, St. Luke's Episcopal Hosp., Houston, 1978-79, Houston Emergency Physicians Assocs., Meml. Hosp. Sys., Houston, 1979-80; med. dir. Chem. Dependence Assocs. and Huntsville (Tex.) Clinic, Houston, 1980-87; emergency dept. physician S.E. Tex. Emergency Physicians, West Houston Med. Ctr., 1986-87, Newport (Wash.) Cmty. Hosp., 1989-90; exec. dir. Chem. Dependence Assocs., Priest River, Idaho, 1987—; emergency dept. physician Emergency Physician Svcs., Holy Family Hosp., Spokane, Wash., 1989—; assoc. med. dir., med. rev. officer Cascade Transp. Svcs., Spokane, 1994—; adj. instr. dept. pharmacology U. Tex. Med. Sch., Houston, 1973-77, adj. asst. prof. dept. pharmacology, 1981-88, clin. instr. family practice and cmty. medicine, 1981-88; presenter in field. Contbr. articles to profl. jours. Fellow Am. Acad. Family Physicians; mem. Am. Coll. Emergency Physicians, Assn. Emergency Physicians, Am. Soc. Addiction Medicine, Am. Assn. Med. Rev. Officers, Tex. Med. Assn., Idaho Med. Assn., Bonner County Med. Soc., Wilderness Med. Soc. Home: PO Box 40 Rt 1 Box 111 Priest River ID 83856 Office: Chem Dependence Assocs PO Box 40 Priest River ID 83856

HAYDEN, RON L., library director; b. San Pedro, Calif., Dec. 24, 1948; s. Larnie Alphonsis and Myrtie Louise (Pilcher) H.; m. Marilee Ann Brubaker, May 30, 1971 (dec. June 1978); m. Susan Ann Huffman, Jan. 1, 1982. AA, Golden West Coll., 1969; BA, Long Beach State U., 1972; MLS, Fullerton U., 1974. Reference sr. libr. Huntington Beach (Calif.) Libr., 1975-79, pub. svc. libr., 1979-86, libr. dir., 1986—; liason Libr. Patrons Assn., Huntington Beach, 1986—. Author: Collection Development Library Journal, 1979. Recipient Award of Excellence Calif. S.W. Recreation Park Conf., 1990. Mem. ALA (Libr. in Media award, Best of Show award 1990), Calif. Libr. Assn., Friends Libr., So. Calif. Tennis Assn., Rotary (bd. dirs., vocat. chmn. 1988—). Office: Huntington Beach Libr 7111 Talbert Ave Huntington Beach CA 92648-1232*

HAYEK, CAROLYN JEAN, retired judge; b. Portland, Oreg., Aug. 17, 1948; d. Robert A. and Marion L. (DeKoning) H.; m. Steven M. Rosen, July 21, 1974; children: Jonathan David, Laura Elizabeth. BA in Psychology, Carleton Coll., 1970; JD, U. Chgo., 1973. Bar: Wash. 1973. Assoc. firm Jones, Grey & Bayley, Seattle, 1973-77; sole practice law, Federal Way, Wash., 1977-82; judge Federal Way Dist. Ct., 1982-95; ret., 1995. Task force mem. Alternatives for Wash., 1973-75; mem. Wash. State Ecol. Commn., 1975-77; columnist Tacoma News Tribune Hometown Sect., 1995-96; bd. dirs. 1st Unitarian Ch. Seattle, 1986-89, vice chair 1987-88, pres., 1988-89; den leader Cub Scouts Mt. Rainier coun. Boy Scouts Am., 1987-88, scouting coord., 1988-89; bd. dirs. Twin Lakes Elem. Sch. PTA. Recipient Women Helping Women award Federal Way Soroptimist, 1991, Martin Luther King Day Humanitarian award King County, 1993, Recognition cert. City of Federal Way Diversity Commn., 1995. Mem. AAUW (br. pres. 1978-80, 90-92, chmn. state level corr. com. 1986-87, mem. diversity com. 1991—, state bd. mem. 1995-97, dir. ESL project), ABA, Wash. Women Lawyers, Wash. State Bar Assn., King County Dist. Ct. Judges Assn. (treas., exec. com. 1990-91, 92-93, com. chmn., chair and rules com. 1990-91, 92-94), Elected Wash. Women (dir. 1983-87), Nat. Assn. Women Judges (nat. bd. dirs., dist. bd. dirs. 1984-86, chmn. rules com. 1988-89, chmn. bylaws com. 1990-91), Fed. Way Women's Network (bd. dirs. 1984-87, 88-91, 95-97, pres. 1985, program co-chair 1989-91, co-editor newsletter), Greater Fed. Way C. of C. (dir. 1978-82, sec. 1980-81, v.p. 1981-82), Sunrise Rotary (com. svc. chair, bd. dirs., membership com., Federal Way chpt. 1991-96, youth exchange officer 1994-95), Washington Women United (bd. dirs. 1995-97), Unitarian Universalist Women's Assn. (chair bylaws com. 1996), Eliot Inst. (bd. dirs. 1996). *The challenge of our decade is to prevent our country from polarizing between the "haves" and the "have-nots" and to modify our institutions to reflect the diversity of our population, to allow all persons access to the basic necessities of life and to recognize that the family life of our workers must be accommodated by employers.*

HAYES, BYRON JACKSON, JR., lawyer; b. L.A., July 9, 1934; s. Byron Jackson and Caroline Violet (Scott) H.; m. DeAnne Saliba, June 30, 1962; children: Kenneth Byron, Patricia DeAnne. Student, Pomona Coll., 1952-56; BA magna cum laude, Harvard U., LLB cum laude, 1959. Bar: Calif. 1960, U.S. Supreme Ct. 1963. Assoc., McCutchen, Black, Verleger & Shea, L.A., 1960-68, ptnr., 1968-89; ptnr. Baker & Hostetler, 1990—. Trustee L.A. Ch. Extension Soc. United Meth. Ch., 1967-77, pres., 1974-77, chancellor ann. conf. Pacific and S.W., 1979-86; Dir., pres. Pacific and S.W. United Meth. Found., 1978-84. Named Layperson of yr. Pacific and S.W. Ann. Conf., United Meth. Ch., 1981; recipient Bishop's award United Meth. Ch., 1992. Mem. ABA, Am. Coll. Mortgage Attys. (regent 1984-93, pres. 1993-94), Calif. Bar Assn., L.A. County Bar Assn. (chmn. real property sect. 1982-83), Toluca Lake Property Owners Assn. (sec. 1990-94), Pomona Coll. Alumni Assn. (pres. 1984-85), Lakeside Golf Club (Toluca Lake, Calif.). Office: Baker & Hostetler 600 Wilshire Blvd Fl 10 Los Angeles CA 90017-3212

HAYES, CECIL EDWARD, physicist; b. Memphis, May 11, 1941; s. Thomas Jackson and Laura Katherine (West) H.; m. Joyce Elaine Wittebort, June 21, 1969; children: Elaine Marie, John Alexander. BS in Engring. Physics, Cornell U., 1964; AM in Physics, Harvard U., 1966, PhD in Physics, 1973. Rsch. asst. dept. physics Harvard U., Cambridge, Mass., 1968-73; rsch. assoc. dept. physics Rutgers U., New Brunswick, N.J., 1973-76; postdoctoral rsch. assoc./teaching fellow physics U. Utah, Salt Lake City, 1976-79, rsch. asst./rsch. assoc. prof., 1979-82; sr. physicist Applied Sci. Lab., GE Med. Sys., Milw., 1982-91; adj. asst. prof. dept. med. physics U. Wis., Madison, 1988-93; assoc. prof. dept. radiology U. Wash., Seattle, 1991—; cons. GE Med. Sys., Milw., 1991—, Superconductor Technologies, Santa Barbara, Calif., 1993-94. Patentee in field (12); contbr. numerous articles and abstracts to jours., chpts. to books. NSF fellow, 1964-66; John McMullen Regional scholar, 1959-62, Owens-Ill. scholar, 1962-64. Mem. Am. Phys. Soc., Soc. for Magnetic Resonance in Medicine, Phi Eta Sigma, Tau Beta Pi (Meml. prize for best 5th yr. rsch. project in engring. physics). Office: Univ of Washington Dept Radiology Box 356004 1959 NE Pacific St Seattle WA 98195-0004

HAYES, CLAUDE QUINTEN CHRISTOPHER, research scientist; b. N.Y.C., Nov. 15, 1945; s. Claude and Celestine (Stanley) H. BA in Chemistry and Geol. Sci., Columbia U., 1971, postgrad., 1972-73; postgrad., N.Y. Law Sch., 1973-75; JD, Western State Law Sch., 1978. Cert. community coll. tchr. earth scis., phys. sci., law, Calif. Tech. writer Burroughs Corp., San Diego, 1978-79; instr. phys. scis. Nat. U., San Diego, 1980-81; instr. bus. law, earth scis. Miramar Coll., 1978-82; sr. systems analyst Gen. Dynamics Convair, 1979-80, advanced mfg. technologist, sr. engr., 1980-81; pvt. practice sci. and tech. cons. Calif., 1979—; instr. phys. sci., phys. geography, bus. law San Diego Community Coll. Dist., 1976-82, 85-90; U.S. Dept. Def. contractor Def. Nuclear Agy., Strategic Def. Initiative Agy., USAF, Def. Advance Rsch. Projects Agy., 1986—, U.S. Army, 1991—; adj. prof. phys. chemistry San Diego State U., 1986-87; bus. and computer sci. def. rsch. contractor to Maxwell Labs., Naval Ocean Sys. Ctr.; tech. cons. Pizza Hut, Inc., Carts of Colo., Smiths Industries. Contbr. articles to profl. jours.; patentee in field. Mem. Am. Chem. Soc., N.Y. Acad. Sci., Am. Inst. Aero. and Astronautics. Home and office: 3737 3rd Ave Apt 308 San Diego CA 92103-4133

HAYES, DEBORAH, musicology educator, college administrator; b. Miami, Fla., Dec. 13, 1939; d. Lauffer Truby Hayes and Margaret Hayes Parsons. AB, Oberlin Coll., 1960; AM, Stanford U., 1961, PhD, 1968. Instr. U. Colo., Boulder, 1968-70, asst. prof., 1970-78, assoc. prof. musicology, 1978-95, assoc. dean Coll. of Music, 1994—, prof. musicology, 1995—. Author: Peggy Glanville-Hicks: A Bio-Bibliography, 1990, Peter Sculthorpe: A Bio-Bibliography, 1993; contbr. articles to profl. publs.; feature editor Internat. Alliance for Women in Music, 1993-94; contbr. articles to profl. jours. Mem. Am. Musicological Soc. (com. on status of women 1991 94), Sonneck Soc. Home: 3290 Darley Ave Boulder CO 80303-6412 Office: U Colo Campus Box 301 Boulder CO 80309

HAYES, DELBERT J., athletic company executive; b. 1935. BA, Wash. State U., 1957. CPA, Wash. Acct. Price, Waterhouse & Co., 1961-69, Linn-Pacific, 1969-70; ptnr. Hayes, Nyman & Co., 1972-75; treas. Nike, Inc., Beaverton, Oreg., 1975-80, exec. v.p., 1980—, also bd. dirs. Office: Nike Inc One Bowerman Dr Beaverton OR 97005-2319*

HAYES, E. HOPE, museum director. Exec. dir. African-Am. Mus. and Libr. at Oakland, Calif. Office: African-Am Mus and Libr at Oakland 5606 San Pablo Ave Oakland CA 94608

HAYES, G. JERRY, automobile dealer executive; b. Ogden, Utah, May 10, 1928; s. Grant E. and Lena (Black) H.; m. Joyce Rasmussen, Sept. 8, 1950; children—Brent, Timothy. Banking and fin. degree U. Utah-Salt Lake City. Vice pres. Hayes Bros. Buick-Jeep, Salt Lake City, 1953—. Sec. Better Bus. Bur., Salt Lake City, 1971-73; pres. Salt Lake Safety Council, 1972-82. Served as sgt. USAF, 1950-52. Mem. Nat. Automobile Dealers Assn. (dir. 1975-87), Utah Automobile Dealers Assn. (pres. 1973, CEO, exec. pres. 1990-96). Republican. Home: 2168 Parkway Ave Salt Lake City UT 84109-1505

HAYES, GEORGE NICHOLAS, lawyer; b. Alliance, Ohio, Sept. 30, 1928; s. Nicholas John and Mary Irene (Fanady) H. B.A., U. Akron, 1950; M.A., Western Res. U., 1953, LL.B., 1955. Bar: Ohio 1955, U.S. Dist. Ct. Alaska 1957, Alaska 1959, U.S. Ct. Appeals (9th cir.) 1958, U.S. Supreme Ct. 1964, Wash. 1972. Mcpl. ct. prosecutor, asst. county prosecutor Portage County, Ravenna, Ohio, 1955-57; asst. U.S. atty. Fairbanks and Anchorage (Alaska), 1957-59; dep. atty. gen. State of Alaksa, 1959-62; dist. atty. 3d Jud. Dist., Anchorage, 1960-62; atty. gen., Juneau, Alaska, 1962-64; spl. counsel to Gov., State of Alaska on earthquake recovery program at Washington, 1964; stockholder Delaney, Wiles, Hays, Reitman & Brubaker, Inc. (name now Delaney, Wiles, Hayes, Gerety & Ellis, Inc.), Anchorage, 1964-92, of counsel, 1992, ret. 1992. Mem. ABA, Washington State Bar Assn., Alaska Bar Assn., Ohio Bar Assn., Anchorage Bar Assn., Am. Coll. Trial Lawyers. Democrat. Office: Delaney Wiles Hayes 1007 W 3rd Ave Anchorage AK 99501-1917

HAYES, GLADYS LUCILLE ALLEN, state community care official, poet, writer; b. Havelock, Nebr., Nov. 29, 1913; d. Harry Arthur and Louise (Vogel) Allen; m. James Franklin Hayes, Oct. 5, 1943; children: J. Allen, Warren Andrew. Secretarial diploma, Lincoln (Nebr.) Sch. Commerce,

1932; student, Santa Clara U., 1950-60; BS in Media Studies, Sacred Heart U., Fairfield, Conn., 1989, exec. MBA, 1991. Cert. profl. religion tchr. Archdiocese of San Francisco. Exec. tech. sec. McCormick-Selph divsn. Teledyne Corp., Hollister, Calif., 1960-65; adminstrv. asst. to v.p. Greater Bridgeport Regional Narcotics Program, Inc., Bridgeport, Conn., 1979-81; adminstrv. asst. to scientists and engrs. CBS Lab. div. CBS Inc., Stamford, Conn., 1968-76; sec. to Nobel laureate and physicist Dennis Gabor, Dsc, FRS U. London, U.S., 1971-79; corp. sec. Automated Power Systems, Inc., Bridgeport, 1976-90; owner, mgr. GA Secretarial Svc., Stratford, Conn., 1980-91; med. sec. Conn. Community Care, Inc., Stratford, Conn., 1986-91; sec., environ. resources U.S. Army Corps Engrs., Elmendorf AFB, Anchorage, Alaska, 1992-93; substitute tchr. Anchorage Sch. Dist., 1992-93, Juneau (Alaska) Sch. Dist., 1994-95; cmty. svc. rep. Alaska Dept. Corrections, Juneau, 1994-95; radio broadcaster Fairfield U., 1985-91; owner, mgr. G A Secretarial Svc., 1985-96. Former residential fund raising chmn. ARC, Gilroy, Calif.; former motion picture chmn. St. Mary's Sch., Gilroy, also past pres. Mothers' Guild, former mem. Edn. Commn.; former fundraiser March of Dimes; mem. various choirs and choral groups, Calif., Conn., Alaska, Utah; mem. Nat. Coun. on Aging; tchr. religion Archdiocese of San Francisco, Diocese of Lincoln, 1933-67, Archdiocese of Bridgeport, 1968-72. Recipient Excellence in Aging award Conn. Community Care, Inc., 1989, prize for photograph City of Bridgeport, 1987, Pope Pius X Medal of Honor, 1959. Mem. Nat. Honor Soc. Republican. Roman Catholic.

HAYES, JAMES C., mayor; b. Sacramento, Calif.; m. Murilda Hayes; 2 children. BA in Edn., U. Alaska, 1970, postgrad. in counseling psychology. Elected mem. Fairbanks (Alaska) North Star Borough Sch. Bd., 1973; elected mem. Fairbanks City Coun., 1987-90, re-elected, 1990-92; elected mayor City of Fairbanks, 1992-95, re-elected, 1995—; former mem. City of Fairbanks transp. and human rights commns., State of Alaska gov.'s task force; former mem. pub. utilities bd., Nat. League of Cities steering com. Recipient Polit. Awareness award, Anchorage (Alaska) Black Caucus; selected Outstanding Young Man of Am., Nat. Jaycees; featured subject numerous mags., including Jet, Ebony, and Essence. Office: Office of Mayor 410 Cushman St Fairbanks AK 99701-4683

HAYES, MARY ESHBAUGH, newspaper editor; b. Rochester, N.Y., Sept. 27, 1928; d. William Paul and Eleanor Maude (Seivert) Eshbaugh; B.A. in English and Journalism, Syracuse (N.Y.) U., 1950; m. James Leon Hayes, Apr. 18, 1953; children—Pauli, Eli, Lauri Le June, Clayton, Merri Jess Bates. With Livingston County Republican, Geneseo, N.Y., summers, 1947-50, mng. editor, 1949-50; reporter Aurora (Colo.) Advocate, 1950-52; reporter-photographer Aspen (Colo.) Times, 1952-53, columnist, 1956—, reporter, 1972-77, assoc. editor, 1977-89, editor in chief, 1989-92, contbg. editor, 1992—; Author, editor The Story of Aspen, 1996; contbg. editor Destinations Mag., 1994-97, Aspen Mag., 1996—. tchr. Colo. Mountain Coll., 1979. Mem. Nat. Fedn. Press Women (1st prizes in writing and editing 1976-80), Colo. Press Women's Assn. (writing award 1974, 75, 78-85, sweepstakes award for writing 1977, 78, 84, 85, 91, 92, 93, also 2d place award 1976, 79, 82, 83, 94, 95, Woman of Achievement 1986). Mem. Aspen Community Ch. Photographer, editor: Aspen Potpourri, 1968, rev. edit., 1990. Home: PO Box 497 Aspen CO 81612-0497 Office: Box E Aspen CO 81612 *At age 8, Mary Eshbaugh and her brother, John Paul, were photographed for a third-grade textbook, Adventures in Science, published by Allyn and Bacon. Fascinated with the book project, Mary decided to follow that formula and become a writer, using real people in photographs. She followed her dream of becoming a writer;today her award-winning feature stories and profiles appear in newspapers and magazines. She has written a cookbook, Aspen Potpourri, featuring Aspen residents and their recipes. Her history book, The Story of Aspen, features photographs of Aspen residents with their stories.*

HAYES, MAXINE DELORES, physician; b. Nov. 29, 1946; children: Leon Williams, Kevin Williams. AB in Biology, Spelman Coll., 1969; MD, SUNY Buffalo, 1973; MPH, Harvard U., 1977. Intern pediat. Vanderbilt Hosp., Nashville; resident Children's Hosp., Boston; dir. Divsn. Parent-Child Health Svcs., Olympia, Wash., 1988-90; asst. sec. Divsn. Parent-Child Health Svcs., Olympia, 1990-93, Cmty. and Family Health, Olympia, 1993—; pres. Assn. Maternal and Child Health Programs, Washington, 1995-97; nat. program dir. Robert Wood Johnson Child Health Initiative, 1994-97. Recipient Outstanding Contbns. in Field of Pub. Health award Wash. State Pub. Health Assn., 1994, Guardian of Women's Health award Aradia Women's Health Ctr., 1996. Fellow Am. Acad. Pediatrics; mem. APHA. Office: Cmty and Family Health PO Box 47830 Olympia WA 98504-7830

HAYES, ROBERT B., communications executive; b. Seattle, Mar. 9, 1942; m. Donna-Marie Hayes; children: Robert Jr., Kendall, Justin. BA in Pub. Rels., San Jose State U., 1965. Pub. rels. rep. Sylvania Electronic Systems, 1965-66; account exec. Ruder & Finn, Inc., 1967-68; pub. rels. mgr. paper group Boise Cascade Corp., Boise, Idaho, 1968-71, press rels. mgr. corp. comms., 1971-72, dir. corp. comms., 1972-80, 81—; v.p. pub. affairs Gould, Inc., 1980; mem. Pub. Rels. Seminar. Past trustee Boise Art Mus.; past chmn. pub. rels. com. United Way Ada County; past pres. FUNDSY, Inc., bd. dirs.; bd. dirs. Boise River Festival. Mem. Pub. Rels. Soc. Am., Am. Forest & Paper Assn. (comms. steering com.), Nat. Assn. Mfrs. (past mem. pub. rels. coun.), Greater Boise C. of C. (past chmn. pub. rels. com.). Office: Boise Cascade Corp PO Box 50 Boise ID 83728-0050

HAYES, ROGER MATTHEW, deputy sheriff; b. Youngstown, Ohio, May 27, 1943; s. Roger and Edith (Wellendorff) H.; m. Carolyn Starr; children: Troy, Matthew, Todd, Adam, Trent, Sarah. BA, Columbia Coll., 1992; postgrad., U. Colo.; MA, Regis U., 1996. Dep. sheriff Arapahoe County (Colo.) Sheriff Dept., 1986—. Past pres. Arapahoe County Rep. Men's Club; pres. Fraternal Order of Police, Greenwood Village, Colo., West Metro Found.; mem. mil. acad. selection com. U.S. Senator William Armstrong, Denver, 1982, White House Adv. Team, Reagan/Bush, Denver, 1982, West Metro Fire Found. Sgt. USMC, 1963-66, Vietnam. Recipient medal of Merit Air Force Assn., Washington, 1984. Mem. Am. Soc. Pub. Adminstrs., Am. Sociol. Assn. Home: 9883 W Progress Pl Littleton CO 80123-2177

HAYES, STEVEN LEE, lawyer; b. Ft. Smith, Ark., Oct. 12, 1947; s. Fred B. and Frances S. (Stanley) H.; m. Paula M. Webster, Apr. 30, 1990; 1 child, Nicole S. BA in History, U. Ark., 1969; LLB, U. San Francisco, 1979. Bar: Calif. 1979. Ptnr. Pritzker & Hayes, L.A., 1979-83, pres., 1983-92; pvt. practice L.A., 1992—; ptnr. Bowles & Hayes, L.A.; pres. Citizens for an Alt. Tax System, L.A., 1990—. Contbr. articles to profl. jours. Mem. Phi Beta Kappa. Home and Office: Citizens for an Alt Tax System 1015 Oneonta Dr Los Angeles CA 90065-4255

HAYES, SUSAN WYLIE, non-profit medical organization executive; b. Greenwood, S.C., Feb. 10, 1952; d. Gene Wylie and Mary Louisa (Barnes) H.; m. John Barron Boyd Jr., July 28, 1973. BA, U. S.C., 1972, MA, 1975; MA, Syracuse U., 1977. Rsch. assoc. S.C. State Legislature, Columbia, 1973-74; instr. U. S.C., Columbia, 1974-75, rsch. assoc., 1980-81; instr. Syracuse (N.Y.) U., 1976-77; rsch. assoc. Syracuse Rsch. Corp., 1978-81; devel. assoc. Sta. WCNY-TV-FM, Syracuse, 1981-83, dir. devel., 1983-86; dir. devel. Stas. WNED-TV-AM-FM and WNEQ-TV, Buffalo, 1986-88, v.p. devel. and publicity, 1988-96; pres. and CEO Interplast, Inc., Mountain View, Calif., 1996—, also bd. dirs. Contbr. articles to profl. jours. Bd. dirs. Ctrl. N.Y. Health Sys. Agy., Syracuse, 1980, YWCA Santa Clara County, San Jose, Calif., 1996—. Recipient various awards PBS, 1983, 87, 88, 90, 91, 94. Democrat. Office: Interplast Inc 300 B Pioneer Way Mountain View CA 94041

HAYMAN, RICHARD WARREN JOSEPH, conductor; b. Cambridge, Mass., Mar. 27, 1920; s. Fred Albert and Gladys Marie (Learned) H.; m. Maryellen Daly, June 25, 1960; children: Suzanne Marie, Olivia Kathryn. D Hum. (hon.), Detroit Coll. Bus., 1980. Free-lance composer, arranger 20th Century Fox, Warner Bros., MGM, Universal Film Studios; music arranger, dir. Vaughn Monroe Orch. records and TV show, N.Y.C., 1945-50; chief arranger Arthur Fiedler and Boston Pops Orchestra, 1950-95; mus. dir. Mercury Record Corp., N.Y.C., 1950-65, Time-Mainstream Records, N.Y.C., 1960-70; prin. pops condr. Detroit Symphony Orchs., St. Louis, Birmingham (Ala.), Hartford (Conn.), Calgary (Can.), Grand Rapids (Mich.) Symphony Orch., London (Ont., Can.) Orch. Composer: No Strings Attached, Dansero, Skipping Along, Carriage Trade, Serenade to a Lost Love, Olivia, Suzanne, Freddie the Football; recorded and released 50 C.D. recordings on Naxos Internat. Records with Richard Hayman and His Symphony Orch., 1991—. Recipient Best Instrumental Record award Sta. WERE, Cleve., 1963, Best TV Comml. Jingle award Nat. Acad. Rec. Arts and Scis., (N.Y.C.), 1960; star dedicated to him on Hollywood Blvd Walk of Fame. Mem. Nat. Acad. Rec. Arts and Scis., ASCAP, Am. Fedn. Musicians. Roman Catholic. Office: Richard Hayman Prodns 784 US Highway 1 Ste 22-b North Palm Beach FL 33408-4413 also: St Louis Symphony Orch 718 N Grand Blvd Saint Louis MO 63103-1011

HAYNES, MICHAEL SCOTT, SR., resource specialist; b. Hancock, Mich., Feb. 16, 1948; s. Russell L. and Hildegard Eleanor (Habel) H.; m. Joan Loree Donaldson, July 25, 1968; children: Michael Jr., Andrew Lloyd, Gregory Alan. BA in History, Calif. Luth. U., 1970; MS in Spl. Edn., Learning Disabled, Calif. State U., Long Beach, 1993. Cert. tchr. elem. edn., Calif., cert. resource specialist tchr., handicapped specialist, Calif. Tchr. elem. edn. Rio Lindo Sch., El Rio, Calif., 1970-71, Trinity Luth. Day Sch., Hawthorne, Calif., 1973-82; tchr. elem. edn. L.A. Unified Sch. Dist., 1982—, learning handicapped specialist, 1988-90, resource specialist tchr., 1990—; tchr. chair Am. Luth. Edn. Assn., 1979-82; trustee L.A. Edn. Alliance Restructuring, 1992—; sec. sch. site United Tchrs. L.A., 1991-94. Scoutmaster Boy Scouts Am., 1983-90. With USCG, 1975-85. Recipient Wood badge Boy Scouts Am., 1983. Mem. Calif. Assn. Resource Specialists (univ. liaison 1991-92), So. Calif. Chihuahua Club, Inc. (sec. 1992-94, v.p., 1995), Orange Empire Dog Club, Kappa Delta Pi, Phi Delta Kappa.

HAY-ROE, VICTOR, plastic surgeon; b. Edmonton, Alta., Can., Dec. 23, 1930; s. Edmund Archer and Ruth Mildred (Maddison) Hay-Roe; m. Elizabeth Mae Davison, May 8, 1953 (div. 1978); children: Glenn Cameron, Elizabeth Diane, Scott Richard; m. Lynn Siu, Apr. 19, 1980. BSc, U. Alta., 1953, MD, 1955. Resident in surgery Queen's Hosp., Honolulu, 1956-59; resident in plastic surgery U. Pitts. Sch. Medicine, 1963-66; chief of plastic surgery Honolulu Med. Group, Inc., 1967—; clin. assoc. prof. plastic surgery, U. Hawaii, Honolulu, 1973—; trip leader, Interplast plastic surgery team to Samoa, 1978, Jamaica, 1988, 90. Mem. Hawaii Plastic Surgery Soc. (pres. 1986-88), Northwest Soc. Plastic Surgeons, Am. Soc. Plastic and reconstructive Surgeons. Republican. Home: 2277 Halekoa Dr Honolulu HI 96821-1056 Office: Honolulu Med Group Inc 550 S Beretania St Honolulu HI 96813-2405

HAYS, DIANA JOYCE WATKINS, consumer products company executive; b. Riverside, Calif., Aug. 29, 1945; d. Donald Richard and Evelyn Christine (Kolvoord) Watkins; m. Gerald N. Hays, Jan 30, 1964 (div. Jan. 1970), 1 child, Tad Damon. BA, U. Minn., 1975, MBA, 1982. Dir. environ./phys. sci. Sci. Mus. Minn., St. Paul, 1972-76; dir. mktg. rsch. No. Natural Gas Co., Omaha, 1977-78; mktg. asst., asst. product mgr. Gen. Mills, Inc., Mpls., 1978-81; product mgr. ortho pharms. Consumer Products div. Johnson & Johnson, Raritan, N.J., 1981-82, product dir. home diagnostics, 1982-86; mktg. dir. new market devel. Consumer Products div. Becton Dickinson & Co., Franklin Lakes, N.J., 1986-90; dir. home diagnostics worldwide program Becton Dickinson Advanced Diagnostics Div. Becton Dickinson & Co., Balt., 1990-93; founder, pres. Exec. Computing Solutions, Inc., Vista, Calif., 1991—; product mktg. mgr. Jostens Learning Corp., San Diego, 1994-95; mgr. MIS Circus Distbn., Inc., Vista, Calif., 1995-96; product mktg. mgr. St. Bernard Software, San Diego, Calif., 1997—; chmn. energy exhibit com. Assn. Sci.-Tech. Ctrs., Washington, 1974-75. Producer Ecologenie, 1975. Recipient Tribute to Women and Industry award YWCA, 1989. Mem. Am. Mktg. Assn., NAFE, Twin Mgmt. Forum, Am. Assn. of Health Svcs. Mktg., Capital PC User Group, Beta Gamma Sigma (life). Republican. Roman Catholic. Office: St Bernard Software 16882 W Bernardo Dr San Diego CA 92128

HAYS, E. EARL, youth organization administrator; b. Uniontown, Kans.; s. Earl Loren and Avis Marie (Mccollum) H.; m. Betty Ann Frigo, Nov. 21, 1966. BA, Whittier Coll., 1962; MA, Ottawa U., 1993; PhD, Pacific Western U., 1993. Dir. pub. rels., fin., dist. exec. Boy Scouts Am. L.A. Area Coun., 1962-71; asst. dir. exploring Boy Scouts Am. Nat. Coun., North Brunswick, N.J., 1971-73; dir. fin. svcs. Boy Scouts Am. Golden Empire Coun., Sacramento, 1973-75; dir. field svc. Boy Scouts Am. Santa Clara County, San Jose, Calif., 1975-77; scout exec., CEO Boy Scouts Am. Clinton Valley Coun., Pontiac, Mich., 1977-82, Boy Scouts Am. Grand Canyon Coun., Phoenix, 1982—. Bd. dirs. Pontiac Oakland Symphony, 1980-82; pres. United Way Exec. Dirs. Assn., Phoenix, 1984-85. Fellowship honor Boy Scouts Am., 1991, James E. West fellow, 1994. Mem. Ottawa U. Alumni Assn. (bd. dirs. 1995—), Nat. Eagle Scout Assn. (life), Rotary (pres. Pontiac 1982, bd. dirs., sec.) Phoenix 100 Club (Paul H. Harris fellow). Democrat. Lutheran. Office: Grand Canyon Coun 2969 N Greenfield Rd Phoenix AZ 85016-7715 *E. Earl Hays has more than 35 years progressively responsible experience as a professional Scouting Executive. While Chief Executive Officer in Phoenix, Arizona, youth membership has grown by 75%, ranking among the top 12 out of 335 local councils nationwide. Honored as a member of the Chief Scout Executive's Winners' Circle for Balanced Youth Membership Growth (51,468 youth members), Sound Fiscal Operations, Quality Program, and as a National Quality Council. In 1996, he received the Ansel Adams Mountain Portrait Award for Endowment Development, and the Excellence in Marketing the Scouting Program award from the Western Region Boy Scouts of America.*

HAYS, MYRNA GRACE, educational association administrator, fashion consultant; b. Bowling Green, Ohio, Mar. 8, 1939; d. Ora Vernon and Vita (Eishen) Mantel; m. Peter L. Hays, Sept. 14, 1963; children: Melissa, Eric, Jeffrey. BS, Bowling Green State U., 1961; MA, Ohio State U., 1963. Editor, writer U. Calif., Davis, 1966-67, exec. dir. faculty assn., 1979—; tchr., dir. Discovery Pre-Sch., Davis, 1975-77; image cons. Beauty for All Seasons, Davis, 1985-92; fashion cons. CMCE Custom Fashions, Davis, 1987—, area dir., 1988-94; legis. coord. Coun. Univ. Calif. Faculty Assn., Davis, 1992—. Bd. dirs. PTA, Davis, 1967-87, pres., 1981-83; co-chair county sch. bd. campaign State Supr. Pub. Instrn., Davis, 1985. Home and Office: 1129 Fordham Dr Davis CA 95616

HAYS, RONALD JACKSON, naval officer; b. Urania, La., Aug. 19, 1928; s. George Henry and Fannie Elizabeth (McCartney) H.; m. Jane M. Hughes, Jan. 29, 1951; children: Dennis, Michael, Jacquelyn. Student, Northwestern U., 1945-46; B.S., U.S. Naval Acad., 1950. Commd. ensign U.S. Navy, 1950, advanced through grades to adm., 1983; destroyer officer Atlantic Fleet, 1950-51; attack pilot Pacific Fleet, 1953-56; exptl. test pilot Patuxent River, Md., 1956-59; exec. officer Attack Squadron 106, 1961-63; tng. officer Carrier Air Wing 4, 1963-65; comdr. All Weather Attack Squadron, Atlantic Fleet, 1965-67; air warfare officer 7th Fleet Staff, 1967-68; tactical aircraft plans officer Office Chief Naval Ops., 1969-71; comdg. officer Naval Sta., Roosevelt Roads, P.R., 1971-72; dir. Navy Planning and Programming, 1973-74; comdr. Carrier Group 4, Norfolk, Va., 1974-75; dir. Office of Program Appraisal, Sec. of Navy, Washington, 1975-78; dep. and chief staff, comdr. in chief U.S. Atlantic Fleet, Norfolk, Va., 1978-80; comdr. in chief U.S. Naval Force Europe, London, 1980-83; vice chief naval ops. Dept. Navy, Washington, 1983-85; comdr. in chief U.S. Pacific Command, Camp H.M. Smith, Hawaii, 1985-88; pres., chief exec. officer Pacific Internat. Ctr. for High Tech. Rsch., Honolulu, Hawaii, 1988-92; tech. cons., 1992—. Decorated D.S.M. with 3 gold stars, Silver Star with 2 gold stars, D.F.C. with silver star and gold star, Legion of Merit, Bronze Star with combat V, Air Medal with numeral 14 and gold numeral 3, Navy Commendation medal with gold star and combat V. Baptist. Home and Office: 869 Kamoi Pl Honolulu HI 96825-1318

HAYWARD, FREDRIC MARK, social reformer; b. N.Y.C., July 10, 1946; s. Irving Michael and Mildred (Feingold) H.; m. Ingeborg Beck, Aug. 18, 1971 (div. 1974); 1 child, KJ. BA, Brandeis U., Waltham, Mass., 1967; MA, Fletcher Sch. Law & Diplomacy, Medford, Mass., 1968, MALD, 1969. Exec. dir. Men's Rights, Inc., Boston, 1977—; vis. lectr. Tufts U., Medford, Mass., 1979; lectr. in field; conductor workshops in field; mem. adv. bd. Ctr. for Men's Studies, 1988-93; host, prodr. The SacraMENshow. Author 3 published anthologies; contbg. editor: The Liberator, Forest Lake, Minn., 1988-89; contbg. writer Spectator, Berkeley, Calif., 1988—; contbr. articles to profl. jours. Farrell fellowship on Men, 1989; Fletcher Sch. Law and Diplomacy fellow, 1967-69; recipient award of Excellence Nat. Coalition of Free Men, 1993. Mem. Nat. Congress for-Men (bd. dirs. 1981-90), Am. Fedn. TV and Radio Artists, Men. Internat. (bd. dirs. 1982-86), Sacramento Valley Men's Coun., Children's Rights Coun. Office: Mr Inc PO Box 163180 Sacramento CA 95816-9180

HAYWORTH, JOHN DAVID, JR., congressman, sportscaster, commentator, broadcaster; b. High Point, N.C., July 12, 1958; s. John David and Gladys Ethel (Hall) H.; m. Mary Denise Yancey, Feb. 25, 1989; children: Nicole Irene, Hannah Lynne, John Micah. BA in Speech and Polit. Sci., N.C. State U., 1980. Sports anchor, reporter Sta. WPTF-TV, Raleigh, N.C., 1980-81, Sta. WLWT-TV, Cin., 1986-87; sports anchor Sta. WYFF-TV (formerly Sta. WFBC-TV), Greenville, S.C., 1981-86, Sta. KTSP-TV, Phoenix, 1987-94; congressman, Ariz. U.S. House Reps., Washington, D.C., 1995—; radio commentator; play-by-play broadcaster. Dist. committeeman Ariz. Rep. Com., Scottsdale, 1988-89; bd. dirs. Am. Humanics Found., Ariz. State U., Tempe, 1991-92; chmn. Scout-A-Rama, Theodore Roosevelt coun. Boy Scouts Am., 1991-92. Recipient honor roll award Atlantic Coast Conf., 1977, Young Am. award Unharrie coun. Boy Scouts Am., 1979, Friend of Edn. award Sch. Dist. Greenville County, 1985, Sch. Bell/Friend of Edn. award S.C. Dept. Edn., 1985. Mem. Rotary (bd. dirs. Phoenix 1989-90). Baptist. Office: US House Reps 1023 Longworth House Office Bldg Washington DC 20515-0306

HAZEKAMP, PHYLLIS WANDA ALBERTS, library director; b. Chgo.; d. John Edward and Mary Ann (Demski) Wojciechowski. BA, De Paul U., 1947; MSLS, La. State U., 1959; postgrad., Santa Clara U., U. Chgo. Cert. tchr., Calif., Ariz. Libr. Agrl. Experiment Sta., U. Calif., Riverside, 1959-61; tech. libr. Lockheed Tech. Libr., Palo Alto, Calif., 1962-63; asst. law libr. Santa Clara (Calif.) U. Law Sch., 1963-72; libr. dir. Carmelite Seminary, San Jose, Calif., 1973-78; reference libr. San Jose State U., 1978-79; libr. dir. SAI Engrs., Santa Clara, 1980-81, Palmer Coll. Chiropractic, San Jose, 1981-90, Camp Verde (Ariz.) Community Libr., 1990—; mem. Cultural Commn., Santa Clara, 1968-72; pres. Santa Clara Art Assn., 1973-74. Bd. dirs. House of Ruth, 1995—. Mem. Kiwanis Internat., House of Ruth (bd. dirs. 1995—). Office: Camp Verde Community Libr 130 Black Bridge Loop Rd Camp Verde AZ 86322

HAZEN, DEAN SCOTT, meteorologist; b. Columbus, Ohio, June 30, 1961; s. Claude B. Jr. and Joan Marilyn Hazen; m. Tammy A. Evans, Aug. 1, 1981. BS, Fla. State U., 1983; MS, U. Okla., 1988. Commd. 2d lt. USAF, 1983, advanced through grades to capt., 1987; weather officer 363d Tactical Fighter Wing, Shaw AFB, S.C., 1983-85, 8th Tactical Fighter Wing, Kunsan Air Base, Republic of Korea, 1985-86; staff meteorologist Air Force Astronautics Lab., Air Force Flight Test Ctr., Edwards AFB, Calif., 1988-92; staff meteorologist 45th Space Wing, Kennedy Space Ctr., Cape Canaveral, Fla., 1992-94; resigned, 1994; sci. and ops. officer Nat. Weather Svc., Pocatello, Idaho, 1994—; instr. Cerro-Coso C.C., Edwards AFB, 1990-92. Contbr. articles to profl. jours. Mem. Portneuf Valley Cmty. Adv. Panel, Pocatello, 1995—. Mem. Am. Meteorology Soc. (sec. Ea. Idaho chpt. 1996—), Nat. Eagle Scout Assn. Office: Nat Weather Svc 1320 Beechcraft Ave Pocatello ID 83204

HAZEN, PAUL MANDEVILLE, banker; b. Lansing, Mich., 1941; married. BA, U. Ariz., 1963; MBA, U. Calif., Berkeley, 1964. Asst. mgr Security Pacific Bank, 1964-66; v.p. Union Bank, 1966-70; chmn. Wells Fargo Realty Advisors, 1970-76; with Wells Fargo Realty Advisors, San Francisco, 1979—, exec. v.p., mgr. Real Estate Industries Group, 1979-80, mem. exec. office Real Estate Industry Group, 1980, vice-chmn. Real Estate Industries Group, 1980-84, pres., chief oper. officer Real Estate Industries Group, 1984—, also dir. Real Estate Industries Group, 1984—; pres., treas. Wells Fargo Mortgage & Equity Trust, San Francisco, 1977-84; with Wells Fargo & Co., San Francisco, 1978—, from exec. v.p. to vice-chmn., pres., chief operating officer, 1978-95, chmn, CEO, 1995—, also dir.; trustee Wells Fargo Mortgage & Equity Trust; bd. dirs. Pacific Telesis Group. Office: Wells Fargo Bank NA PO Box 63710 San Francisco CA 94163-1205*

HAZEWINKEL, VAN, manufacturing executive; b. L.A., Oct. 2, 1943; s. Ben J. and Betty J. (Bishop) H.; m. Linda Bennett, Sept. 11, 1965; children: Van, Karey. BS, Calif. State U., Long Beach, 1967. With Daily Indsl. Tools Inc., Costa Mesa, Calif., 1959—, v.p., 1966-78, pres., 1978—. Founding mem. bd. dirs. Greater Irvine (Calif.) Indsl. League, 1970-73. Mem. Soc. Mfg. Engrs. Office: 3197D Airport Loop Dr Costa Mesa CA 92626-3420

HAZLETT, MARK A., lawyer; b. N.Y.C., Aug. 18, 1948. BA, Stanford U., 1970, JD, 1973. Bar: Hawaii 1973. Ptnr. Cades, Schutte, Fleming & Wright, Honolulu; mem. adv. com. to Commr. of Fin. Insts., 1984-86; adj. prof. of law U. Hawaii Law Sch., 1995—. Co-editor: Hawaii Commercial Real Estate Manual, 1988; co-editor, co-author: Hawaii Real Estate Financing Manual, 1990. Mem. ABA, Hawaii State Bar Assn. (dir. fin. svcs. divsn. 1982-83, chmn. real property and fin. svcs. sect. 1984, bd. dirs. 1982-95). Office: Cades Schutte Fleming & Wright PO Box 939 1000 Bishop St Honolulu HI 96808

HE, XIANGUO, chemist, consultant; b. Shanghai, People's Republic of China, Nov. 6, 1941; came to U.S., 1989; s. Shihuai and Cuiju (Fang) H.; m. Lizhi Lian, Oct. 1, 1972; 1 child, Li Wei. BS, Fudan U., Shanghai, 1963. Rsch. asst. Shanghai Inst. Materia Medica Chinese Acad. Scis., Shanghai, 1963-78; rsch. assoc. Chinese Acad. Scis., Shanghai, 1978-81; postdoctoral rschr. Purdue U., West Lafayette, Ind., 1981-82, Ohio State U., Columbus, 1983-84; assoc. prof. Chinese Acad. Scis., Shanghai, 1985-89; vis. prof. U. Wash., Seattle, 1989-92; rsch. dir. East Earth Herb, Inc., Eugene, Oreg., 1992—. Co-author: The Handbook of Identification of Flavonoids Compounds, 1980, High Performance Liquid Chromatography and its Applications on Medical Research, 1981, Extraction and Separation of Active Compounds from Chinese Medicine, 1983, Natural Products Chemistry, 1991. Mem. Am. Chem. Soc., Internat. Assn. Ofcl. Analytical Chemistry, Am. Soc. Pharmaconosy. Home: 3847 Ashford Dr Eugene OR 97405 Office: East Earth Herb Inc 4091 W 11th Ave Eugene OR 97402

HEAD, SAMUEL, management consultant; b. Tampa, Nov. 20, 1948; m. Karen Theresa Grant, Oct. 24, 1988; children: Samuel Sherman, Shaunda Denise, Jonathan Spencer. BS, Fla. A&M U., 1970; MA in Mgmt., Nat. U., San Diego, 1989; MPA, Golden Gate U., 1993. Dir. comml. revitalization Nev. Econ. Devel. Co., Las Vegas, 1984-85; sr. mgmt. analyst Clark County, Las Vegas, 1985-92; interim city mgr. City of Seaside, Calif., 1993-94, asst. city mgr., cmty. devel. dir., 1992-95; pres. The HEAD Group, Henderson, Nev., 1995—. Commr. Monterey County Film Commn., Monterey, Calif., 1992-94. Mem. Nat. Assn. Black County Ofcls., Nat. Forum for Black Pub. Adminstrs., Am. Soc. Pub. Adminstrn., Uptown Kiwanis (Las Vegas) (pres., sec., 1986-92, Meritorious award 1988), Alpha Phi Alpha (pres., sec. 1967—, 25 yr award 1992). Republican. Baptist. Office: The HEAD Group PO Box 50252 Henderson NV 89016

HEADDING, LILLIAN SUSAN (SALLY HEADDING), writer, forensic clairvoyant; b. Milw., Jan. 1, 1944; d. David Morton and Mary Davis (Berry) Coleman; m. James K. Hill (div. 1976); children: Amy Denise; m. John Murray Headding (div. 1987). BA, U. Nev., 1975; MA, U. Pacific, 1976. With Gimbels, Milw., 1963-65; spl. assignment G2 USAPIC U.S. Womens Army Corp., 1963; retail mgr. Frandisco Corp., N.Y.C., 1965-66; dist. mgr. Anita Shops, Los Angeles, 1966-68; store mgr. Clothes Closet, Sunnyvale, Calif., 1969-70; owner Lillian Headding Interiors & Comml. Design, Pittsburg, Calif., 1976-88; mfrs. rep. and assoc. J.G. West, San Francisco, 1989-91; Karate instr. Sch. of the Tiger, Pleasant Hill, Calif., 1988-94, 1st degree black belt, 1973; clairvoyant, psychic cons. on numerous crime and missing persons cases, U.S., Can., Eng. and France, 1972—. Author short stories, poetry. Bd. dirs. and co-founder Cmty. Action Against Rape, Las Vegas, 1972-75; self-def. expert Las Vegas Met. Police Dept., 1972-75, North Las Vegas (Nev.) Police Dept.; co-supr. Family & Children's Svcs., Contra Costa County, Calif., 1985-86. Mem. AAUW, People for Ethical Treatment of Animals, Sister's in Crime Nat. Writers Assn., Philippine Hawaiian Black Belters Assn., Humane Farming Assn., Am. Assn. Profl. Psychics. Democrat. Jewish. Office: care Helen Rees Lit Agy 308 Commonwealth Ave Boston MA 94521-3718 Also: Apt 33 5333 Park Highlands Blvd Concord CA 94521-3718 *Through many confrontations with the monster of ignorance, I have found that patience, a sincere smile, and a good sense of humor will tear down closed doors with more ease than a battering ram, and that these doors when opened this way, will remain open.*

HEADLEE, ROLLAND DOCKERAY, professional society administrator; b. Los Angeles, Aug. 27, 1916; s. Jesse W. and Cleora (Dockeray) H.; m. Alzora D. Burgett, May 13, 1939; 1 dau., Linda Ann (Mrs. Walter Pohl). Student, UCLA, 1939. Asst. mgr. Par Assocs., Los Angeles, 1935-43, Finance Assocs., 1946-58; financial cons., lectr., 1958-63; account exec. Walter E. Heller & Co., Los Angeles, 1963-66; exec. dir. emeritus Town Hall Calif., Los Angeles, 1966—; dir. Am. Internat. Bank, Mfrs. Assocs., R.H. Investment Corp. Mem. adv. bd., bd. dirs., Los Angeles council Boy Scouts Am. Served to 1st lt. AUS, 1943-46. Mem. Mensa, Los Angeles World Affairs Council, Newcomen Soc. Methodist. Clubs: Commonwealth of Calif, Economic of Detroit, Los Angeles Stock Exchange. Home: 8064 El Manor Ave Los Angeles CA 90045-1434 *The single most important word in managing is why. Why do we do it this way? Why is "John" the best choice to do it? Why can't we simplify it? Why doesn't it sell? Then comes how.*

HEADY, FERREL, retired political science educator; b. Ferrelview, Mo., Feb. 14, 1916; s. Chester Ferrel and Loren (Wightman) H.; m. Charlotte Audrey McDougall, Feb. 12, 1942; children—Judith Lillian, Richard Ferrel, Margaret Loren, Thomas McDougall. A.B., Washington U., St. Louis, 1937, A.M., 1938, Ph.D., 1940; hon. degrees, Park Coll., 1973, John F. Kennedy U., 1974, U. N.Mex., 1993. Jr. adminstrv. technician, also adminstrv. asst. Office Dir. Personnel, Dept. Agr., 1941-42; vis. lectr. polit. sci. U. Kansas City, 1946; faculty U. Mich., 1946-67, prof. polit. sci., 1957-67; dir. Inst. Pub. Adminstrn., 1960-67; acad. v.p. U. N.Mex., Albuquerque, 1967-68; pres. U. N.Mex., 1968-75, prof. pub. adminstrn. and polit. sci., 1975-81, prof. emeritus, 1981—; Asst. to commr. Com. Orgn. Exec. Br. of Govt., 1947-49; dir., chief adviser Inst. Pub. Adminstrn., U. Philippines, 1953-54; mem. U.S. del. Internat. Congress Adminstrn. Scis., Spain, 1956, 80, Germany, 1959, Austria, 1962, Poland, 1964, Mexico, 1974; exec. bd. Inter-Univ. Case Program, 1956-67; sr. specialist in residence East-West Center, U. Hawaii, 1965; mem. Conf. on Pub. Service, 1965-70; chmn. bd. Assoc. Western Univs., 1970-71; commr. Western Interstate Commn. Higher Edn., 1972-77; mem. commns. on bus. professions and water resources, mem. exec. com. Nat. Assn. State Univs. and Land Grant Colls., 1968-75. Author: Administrative Procedure Legislation in the States, 1952, (with Robert H. Pealy) The Michigan Department of Administration, 1956, (with Sybil L. Stokes) Comparative Public Administration: A Selective Annotated Bibliography, 1960, Papers in Comparative Public Administration, 1962, State Constitutions: The Structure of Administration, 1961, Public Administration: A Comparative Perspective, 1966, rev. edit., 1979, 5th edit., 1995; contbr. profl. jours. Chmn. state affairs com. Ann Arbor Citizens Coun., Mich., 1949-52; mem. exec. com. Mich. Meml.-Phoenix Project and Inst. Social Rsch., 1960-66; mem. Gov. Mich. Constl. Revision Study Commn., 1960-62; schs. and univs. adv. bd. Citizens Com. for Hoover Report, 1949-52, 54-58; cons. to Ford Found., 1962; chmn. Coun. on Grad. Edn. in Pub. Adminstrn., 1966; mem., vice chmn. N.Mex. Gov.'s Com. on Reorgn. of State Govt., 1967-70; mem. N.Mex. Am. Revolution Bicentennial Commn., 1970-73, N.Mex. Gov.'s Com. on Tech. Excellence, 1969-75, Nat. Acad. Pub. Adminstrn.; mem., vice chmn. N.Mex. Constl. Revision Commn., 1994-95. Served to lt. USNR, 1942-46. Recipient Faculty Disting. Achievement award U. Mich., 1964, N.Mex. Disting. Pub. service award, 1973, award of distinction U. N.Mex. Alumni Assn., 1975, Outstanding Grad. Tchr. award U. N.Mex., 1981-82, Fulbright sr. lectureship, Colombia, 1992, Waldo award for career contbns. to lit. and leadership of pub. adminstrn., 1994. Mem. Am. Polit. Sci. Assn., Am. Soc. Pub. Adminstrn. (pres. 1969-70), AAUP (chmn. com. T 1957-61), Am. Council Edn. (mem. commn. on fed. relations 1969-72), Phi Beta Kappa, Phi Kappa Phi. Presbyterian. Home: 2901 Cutler Ave NE Albuquerque NM 87106-1714

HEALEY, DEBORAH LYNN, education administrator; b. Columbus, Ohio, Sept. 15, 1952; d. James Henry and Marjorie Jean Healey; 1 child, Jesse Healey Winterowd. BA in German/Religion, Queen's U., 1974; MA in Linguistics, U. Oreg., 1976, PhD in Edn., 1993. Instr. Lane C.C., Eugene, Oreg., 1976-77; instr., materials developer Rogue C.C., Ashland, Oreg., 1977-79; instr. Chemeketa C.C., Salem, Oreg., 1979-80; instr., computer ops. English Lang. Inst. Oreg. State U., Corvallis, 1979-85, 88-93; instr., computer ops. Yemen-Am. Lang. Inst., Sana'a, Yemen, 1985-88; programmer, cons. Internat. Soc. for Tech. in Edn., Eugene, 1989-91; coord. instr. English Lang. Inst. Oreg. State U., Corvallis, 1993-95, tech. coord., 1995—; Macintosh support Computer-Enhanced Lang. Instrn. Archive, 1993—; computer cons. in field. Author: (book) Something To Do On Tuesday, 1995; co-author: (chpt.) A Handbook for Language Program Administrators, 1997; editor, author Computer-Assisted English Lang. Learning Jour., 1990—; co-editor (ann. publ.) CALL Interest Sect. Software List, 1990—; co-author (software) The House, At The Zoo, 1993. Mem. TESOL (interest sect. chair 1992-92), Oreg. TESOL (newsletter editor 1981-84), Nat. Assn. Fgn. Student Advisors-Assn. Internat. Educators, Am. Ednl. Rsch. Assn., Computer Assn. Lang. Instrn. Consortium. Office: ELI Oreg State Univ 301 Snell Hall Corvallis OR 97331-8515

HEALEY, MARK CALVIN, biologist, educator; b. Salt Lake City, Mar. 7, 1947; children: Rachelle, Jeffrey, Christopher. BS, U. Utah, 1971, MS, 1973; PhD, Purdue U., 1976; DVM, Miss. State U., 1981. Lic. veterinarian, Utah; lic. accredited veterinarian in Utah by USDA. Teaching asst., teaching fellow U. Utah, 1970-73; grad. instr. Sch. of Vet. Medicine Purdue U., Lafayette, Ind., 1973-76; instr. Tex. A&M U., College Station, 1976-77; resident Coll. of Vet. Medicine Miss. State U., 1978-81; rsch. asst. prof. Dept. Animal, Dairy and Vet. Scis. Utah State U., Logan, 1981-83, asst. prof. Dept. Animal, Dairy and Vet. Scis., 1983-86, asst. prof. joint appointment with Dept. of Biology, 1984—, assoc. prof. Depts. Biology and Animal, Dairy and Vet. Scis., 1986-91, asst. head Dept. Animal, Dairy and Vet. Scis., 1990—, prof., 1991—; outside peer reviewer USDA/Competitive Rsch. Grants Program, 1985—. Patentee bacterial extract vaccines for veterinary application; contbr. numerous articles to profl. jours. Recipient Phi Sigma Soc. award U. Utah, 1970, Outstanding Young Men of Am. Ann. award, 1982, Prof. of Yr. award Utah State U., 1986. Mem. Am. Soc. Parasitologists, Am. Assn. Vet. Parasitologists, Rocky Mountain Conf. Parasitologists, Am. Vet. Med. Assn., Intermountain Vet. Med. Assn., Utah Vet. Med. Assn., Vet. Med. Assn. of No. Utah, Am. Soc. Microbiology, Intermountain Br. of Am. Soc. for Microbiology, Conf. Rsch. Workers in Animal Disease, Western Food Animal Disease Rsch. Conf. Office: Utah State U Coll of Agriculture Dept Animal Dairy Vet Scis Logan UT 84322-5600

HEALY, ANNE, sculptor; b. N.Y.C., Oct. 1, 1939; d. Robert Timothy and Mary Rita (Essig) H.; m. Richard Alois Synek, Feb. 28, 1960 (div. 1962); 1 child, Deirdre Leigh. BA, Queens Coll., 1961. One-woman exhbns. include U.S. Theatre Technicians Symposium, 1971, Solow Bldg., N.Y.C., 1971, A.I.R. Gallery, N.Y.C., 1972, 74, 78, 81, 83, CUNY Grad. Ctr., 1974, Hammarskjold Pla. Sculpture Garden, N.Y.C., 1974, 88 Pine St., N.Y.C., 1974-75, Zabriskie Gallery, N.Y.C., 1975, 78, Contemporary Art Ctr., Cin., 1976, Am.'s Cup Ave., Newport Art Assn., Susie Schochet Gallery, R.I., 1976, U. Mass., Amherst, 1976, A.I.R., N.Y.C., 1978, U. of South, Tex., 1979, San Francisco M.O.M.A. Rental Gallery, 1989; group exhbns. include Outdoor Installations, Basel, Switzerland, 1976, Paris, 1976; represented in permanent collections Mus. Contemporary Crafts, N.Y.C., Mich. State U., Allen Art Mus., Oberlin, Ohio, CUNY Grad. Ctr.; commns. include Wayne State U. Health Care Inst., Detroit, 1979, Springfield Mus. Fine Art, Mass., 1979, City of Pitts., 1981, Prudential Life Ins., Newark, N.J., 1984, State of Wash., 1985, City of Oakland, Calif., 1986, Litton Industries, Los Colinas, Tex., 1986, Stanford U., 1990, Wash. State Art Coun., 1996; instr. sculpture St. Ann's Sch., Bklyn., 1973-79; adj. asst. prof. Baruch Coll., CUNY, 1976-81; guest lectr. Mich. State U., 1973; vis. artist Mich. State U., 1973; guest lectr. U. Cin., 1974, 76, Smith Coll., Northampton, Mass., 1975, U. R.I., Kingston, 1975; vis. prof. U. Iowa, Iowa City, 1979; asst. prof. U. Calif. Berkeley, 1981-85, assoc. prof., 1985-94, prof. 1994—. Arts commr. for sculpture City of San Francisco, 1989-96, pres. arts commn., 1992-95. Featured in numerous popular mags. and profl. jours.; contbr. articles to profl. jours. Office: U Calif Dept Art Kroeber Hall Berkeley CA 94720

HEALY, BARBARA ANNE, insurance company executive, financial planner; b. Chgo., May 21, 1951; d. William James Healy and Eileen Mary (Dooley) Dashiell; m. Joel Feldman, June 25, 1991. BA, No. Ill. U., 1973; MBA, DePaul U., 1976. Cert. fin. planner. Dept. head, instr. St. Benedict High Sch., Chgo., 1973-76; account rep. Xerox Corp., Chgo., 1976-78, mktg. specialist, 1978-79, high volume sr. sales exec., 1979-81; western dist. mgr. McGraw Hill, N.Y.C., 1981-82; fin. planner United Resources Ins. Service, Torrance, Calif., 1982-83, sales mgr., 1983-85, exec. v.p., 1985-86; regional v.p. United Resources Ins. Service, Foster City, Calif., 1986-89; v.p., nat. mktg. dir. Met. Life Resources (formerly United Resources Ins. Svcs.), Phoenix, 1990—; Tempe, Ariz.; instr. Trenton Coll., Riverside, Ill., City Coll. Chgo., Northeastern Ill. U., Chgo., Prairie State Coll., Chicago Heights, 1976-81. Author: Financial Planning for Educators, 1987; contbr. articles to prof. jours.; speaker in field. Mem. Internat. Assn. Fin. Planners, Inst. Cert. Fin. Planners, Registry Fin. Planning Practitioners, Nat. Council Fin. Edn. Republican. Roman Catholic. Home: 20791 Chartwell Dr Kildeer IL 60047 Office: Met Life Resources 426 N 44th St Phoenix AZ 85008

HEALY, DANIEL THOMAS, secondary education educator; b. Wenona, Ill., May 25, 1930; s. Timothy John and Helen Ann (Duller) H.; m. Beverly Ann Imm, Oct. 1, 1966; 1 child, Owen Jay. AA, Fresno (Calif.) City Coll., 1972; BS, Calif. State U., Fresno, 1974; MA, Azusa (Calif.) Pacific U., 1980. Farmer Wenona, 1948-58; mgr. Garfield Grain Elevator, Wenona, 1958-66; supt. Cargill Inc., San Joaquin, Calif., 1966-69; educator Redlands (Calif.) Unified Sch. Dist., 1974—; advisor Future Farmers of Am., Redlands High Sch., 1974-88; leader Osage Livewires 4-H Club, Wenona, 1950-55. Performer on nat. TV, movies including Hero and Hot Shots II, appearances as Pres. Bush celebrity look-alike, 1990—. Sgt. U.S. Army, 1953-54. Fellow Am. Legion (life mem.), Elks (life). Mem. Christian Ch. Office: Orangewood High Sch 515 Texas St Redlands CA 92374-3071

HEALY, JAMES BRUCE, cooking school administrator, writer; b. Paterson, N.J., Apr. 15, 1947; s. James Burn and Margaret Mercy (Patterson) H.; m. Alice Fenvessy, May 9, 1970; 1 child, Charlotte Alexandra. BA, Williams Coll., 1968; PhD, The Rockefeller U., 1973. Mem. faculty Inst. Advanced Study, Princeton, N.J., 1973-75; J.W. Gibbs instr. physics Yale U., New Haven, Conn., 1975-77, research affiliate, 1977-80; dir. Healy-Lucullus Sch. French Cooking, New Haven, 1978-80, Boulder, Colo., 1980—; cons. Claudine's, Denver, 1985-86; vis. instr. Salem (Mass.) State Coll., 1984, and various culinary schs. Author: Mastering the Art of French Pastry, 1984, The French Cookie Book, 1994; contbr. articles and revs. on restaurants and cooking to mags. and profl. jours. Mem. Internat. Assn. Cooking Profls. (cert.), Confederation Nationale des Patissiers, Glaciers, et Confiseurs de France. Methodist. Home and Office: Healy-Lucullus Sch French Cooking 840 Cypress Dr Boulder CO 80303-2820

HEALY, KIERAN JOHN PATRICK, lighting designer, consultant; b. London, June 6, 1957; came to U.S., 1980; citizen of Ireland.; s. Denis Finbarr and Dawn Josephine (O'Hannigan) H.; m. Debra Leslie Liebling, Jan. 6, 1990; 1 child, Conor Thomas. Student, Isleworth Polytechnic, Middlesex, Eng., 1975-76. Lighting designer The Who, 1976-80, The Rolling Stones, 1980; v.p. Showlites, L.A., 1980-81; freelance lighting designer various TV prodns., 1982-89; dir. photography Design Ptnrs., Inc., Hollywood, Calif., 1989—. Lighting designer for TV programs, including Live Aid, ESPY Awards, Arsenio Hall, Gracelands in Africa, The Tonight Show with Jay Leno, other spls. Mem. Nat. Acad. Cable Programming (ACE nomination 1988), Acad. TV Arts and Scis. (Emmy nominations 1984, 87, 89, 92, 94), Assn. Cinemotograph Techs. and Allied Trades, Internat. Photographers Guild. Roman Catholic. Office: Design Partners Inc 1438 N Gower St Los Angeles CA 90028-8383

HEALY, SONYA AINSLIE, health facility administrator; b. Sudbury, Ont., Can., Apr. 7, 1937; came to U.S., 1949; d. Walter B. and Wilma A. Scott; m. Richard C. Healy, Jr., Dec. 16, 1961. Diploma, Good Samaritan Hosp., West Palm Beach, Fla., 1958; student, U. Mass., 1963-64, NYU, 1964-66; BS, Boston U., 1969, MS in Med.-Surg. Nursing, 1974. Various staff nursing, charge nurse positions, suprs., med.-surg. and obstet. nursing, 1958-69; chmn. jr.-sr. teaching team Sch. of Nursing Melrose (Mass.) Wakefield Hosp., 1969-73; asst. dir. nurses Boston State Hosp., 1973-74; asst. dir., DON Mt. Zion Hosp. and Med. Ctr., 1974-75; asst. dir. patient care svcs., DON St. Elizabeth's Hosp., Boston, 1975-80, St. Joseph's Hosp., Nashua, N.H., 1980-82; adminstr. U. Calif. Med. Ctr., San Diego, 1982-91, corp. chief nursing officer, 1991, assoc. dir. hosp. and clinics, dir. patient care svcs., 1982-93; cons. health care Noyes & Assocs. Ltd., Chgo., 1993—; mem. acad. affairs com., bd. trustees U. San Diego; clin. assoc. Ul. San Diego, 1984—; mem. adj. faculty San Diego State U.; mem. clin. faculty UCLA Sch. of Nursing; presenter in field. Author: The 12-hour Shift: Is It Viable?-Nursing Outlook, 1984, (handbook) Human Resource Management Handbook, 1987, Human Resources Management Handbook, 1987, Nursing Economics, 1989; mem. editl. adv. bd. dirs. OR Nurse Today, 1989-96; editl. rev. Nursing Economics; contbr. articles to profl. jours. Mem. ASNSA (nominations com. 1978, cert.), Am. Orgn. of Nurse Execs. (bd. dirs. 1990-92, by laws com. 1990-92), Mass. Soc. of Nursing Svcs. Adminstrs. (pres. pres. 1977), Calif. Soc. of Nursing Svc. Adminstrs. (task force on orgns. program com. 1984-85, bd. dirs. 1985-87, mem. com. 1987-88, long range planning com.), San Diego Dirs. of Nurses (sec. 1982-83, pres. 1988-89), Sigma Theta Tau (Zeta Mu chpt.).

HEANEY, DOROTHY PHELPS, nurse, nursing administrator; b. Elmer, N.J., Apr. 8, 1963; d. Joseph Francis and Dorothy Ruth (Andrews) Phelps; m. Bradley George Heaney, June 8, 1985. AS in Nursing, Gloucester County Coll., Sewell, N.J., 1984. Nursing asst. Pine Crest Nursing Home, Sewell, 1982-84, staff nurse, 1984, charge nurse, 1984-85; charge nurse Le Havre Convalescent Hosp., Menlo Park, Calif., 1985-86, dir. staff devel., 1986-87, asst. dir. nursing, 1986, dir. nursing, 1986-87; dir. nursing Hillhaven Convalescent Hosp., Menlo Park, 1987-90, Brookside Convalescent Hosp., San Mateo, Calif., 1990-92; owner, mgr. Friendly Vending, 1992-93; cons. in pvt. practice skilled nursing and geriatric care, legal nurse cons. Mountain View, Calif., 1993—; med., legal cons., 1997—. Home: 148 Promethean Way Mountain View CA 94043-4863

HEAP, SUZANNE RUNDIO, elementary school educator; b. Long Beach, Calif., June 10, 1935; d. George Lionel and Jennie Bolton (Rundio) Heap; children: Katharine Trent, Cecily Gullett. BA, Mary Washington Coll., Fredericsburg, Va., 1957; MA in Edn., Azua-Pacific U., 1978; student, Calif. Western-USIU, San Diego, 1970. Cert. elem. tchr. K-8, Calif., Level I Orff-Schulwerk nat. cert; cert. in master gardening, Calif. Tchr. 5th and 6th grades Chula Vista (Calif.) Elem. Sch. Dist., kindergarten tchr., ret., 1991; cons. bargaining team Chula Vista Edn. Assn. Vol. with U. Calif. Cooperative Extension/U.S. Dept. Agr. Vol. numerous civic orgns.; past exec. com. bd., recording sec. U. Calif. Coop. Ext. Master Gardener, San Diego County. Recipient Instruction grant, ORFF Instrumentarium, We Honor Ours award San Diego county svc. ctr. coun. Calif. Tchrs. Assn., 1991. Mem. Calif. Ret. Tchrs. Assn., NSF Math. Inst. Univ. Calif. San Diego, Am. ORFF-Schulwerk Assn. (bd. sec. San Diego chpt. 1991-93), Crown Garden Club Coronado (pres.), San Diego Floral Assn. Home: 620 1st St Coronado CA 92118-1202

HEARLE, KEVIN JAMES, poet, educator; b. Santa Ana, Calif., Mar. 17, 1958; s. H. David and L. Patricia (Flaherty) H.; m. Elizabeth Ellen Henderson, Nov. 26, 1983. AB in English with distinction, Stanford U., 1980; MFA in English, U. Iowa, 1983; MA in Lit., U. Calif., Santa Cruz, 1990, PhD in Lit., 1991. Poet, 1979—; teaching asst. U. Calif., Santa Cruz, 1987-91, lectr., 1993; lectr. San Jose (Calif.) State U., 1992-94, Calif. State U., L.A., 95-96; poet-in-the-schs. Iowa Ctr. for the Arts, Iowa City, 1982; teaching asst. U. Iowa, Iowa City, 1982-83; instr. Coe Coll., Cedar Rapids, Iowa, 1983-84; participant Nat. Endowment for Humanities Summer Seminar on Am. Indian Lit., U. Ill., Chgo., 1994. Author: Each Thing We Know Is Changed Because We Know It and Other Poems, 1994; poetry co-editor Quarry West, 1988-92; reviewer Am. Lit., 1992—, We. Am. Lit., 1992—, Steinbeck Newsletter, 1992—; editl. bd. Steinbeck Newsletter, 1995—; asst. editor Viking Critical Library Edition of The Grapes of Wrath, 2d edit., 1995; contbr. poetry and articles to jours. Mem. MLA, Robinson Jeffers Assn., Internat. John Steinbeck Soc., We. Lit. Assn., PEN Ctr. USA West. Home: 102 Hobart Ave San Mateo CA 94402-2808

HEARN, CHARLES VIRGIL, minister; b. Westport, Ind., Sept. 4, 1930; s. Forrest V. and Emma Florence (Marsh) H.; PhD., Thomas A. Edison U., 1972; D.D., Trinity Hall Coll. and Sem., 1977; diploma Palm Beach Psychotherapy Tng. Center, 1976; m. Linda Elmendorf; children by previous marriage—Debra Lynn, Charles Gregory, Martin Curtis. Ordained to ministry Methodist Ch., 1958; pastor various Meth. chs., Ind., Tex., Wyo., Calif., 1958-70; interpersonal minister St. Alban's Ch. of the Way, San Francisco, 1974—; clergyman and counselor Green Oak Ranch Boys Camp, Calif., 1969-70; dir. rehab. Mary-Lind Found., Los Angeles, 1970-71; med. asst. Fireside Hosp., Santa Monica, Calif., 1971-72; dir. alcoholism program Patrician Hosp., Santa Monica, 1972-74; propr., exec. dir. Consultation & Referral, Santa Monica, 1974—. Vice chmn. Western Los Angeles Alcoholism Coalition, 1974-78; pres. bd. dirs. Trinity Hall Coll. and Sem. Served with U.S. Army, 1951-53; Korea. Decorated Bronze Star; diplomate Am. Bd. Examiners in Psychotherapy, Bd. Examiners in Pastoral Counseling. Fellow Am. Acad. Behavioral Sci., Internat. Council Sex Edn. and Parenthood of Am. U.; mem. Am. Ministerial Assn. (pres. 1981—), Nat. Assn. Alcoholism Counselors, Calif. Assn. Alcoholism Counselors, Cons. on Alcoholism for Communities, Nat. Council Family Relations, Am. Coll. Clinic Adminstrs., Assn. Labor-Mgmt. Adminstrs. Democrat. Contbr. numerous articles on psychotherapy to profl. publs. Office: 1244 11th St Apt D Santa Monica CA 90401-2018

HEARNE, JOHN Q., telecommunications executive; b. San Francisco, June 10, 1948; s. John P. and Genevieve (Carolan) H.; m. Elizabeth Michaels, 1977; children: Jennifer, Brendan, Megan. BA in Math. summa cum laude, UCLA, 1970; JD, Stanford U., 1973. Bar: Calif. 1974, D.C. 1977. Assoc. Fisher, Wayland, Cooper & Leader, Washington, 1977-82, ptnr., 1983-89, of counsel, 1990—; owner, chmn., pres. Point Telesys., Inc. (formerly Pont Comms. Co.), 1988—, Point Broadcasting Co. and Point Enterprises, Inc., $D, 1994—; chmn. Gold Coast Broadcasting Co., 1994—, High Desert Broadcasting Co., 1996—. Contbr. articles to profl. jours. Woodrow Wilson Nat. fellow, 1970. Mem. Fed. Comm. Bar Assn. (chmn. common carrier practice com. 1984-87, chmn. access com. 1987-88), Cellular Telecomm. Industries Assn. (bd. dirs. 1990-94), Surfrider Found., U.S. Surfing Fedn., Nat. Scholastic Surfing Assn., Malibu Surfing Assn., Rotary (chmn. environ. com. 1994-95), Phi Beta Kappa. Office: 100 Wilshire Blvd Ste 1000 Santa Monica CA 90401-1113

HEARST, JOHN EUGENE, chemistry educator, researcher, consultant; b. Vienna, Austria, July 2, 1935; came to U.S., 1938; s. Alphonse Bernard and Lily (Roger) H.; m. Jean Carolyn Bankson, Aug. 30, 1958; children: David Paul, Leslie Jean. B.E., Yale U., 1957; Ph.D., Calif. Inst. Tech., 1961; D.Sc. (hon.) Lehigh U., 1992. Postdoctoral rschr. Dartmouth Coll., Hanover, N.H., 1961-62; prof. chemistry U. Calif., Berkeley, 1962-95, prof. emeritus, 1996—, Miller rsch. prof., 1970-71, sr. rsch. scientist Lawrence Berkeley Lab., 1980—, dir. divsn. chem. biodynamics, 1986-89; Disting. lectr. Purdue U., 1986; Merck Centennial lectr. Lehigh U., 1992, Robert A. Welch Found. lectr., 1992-93; founder, sr. cons. Advanced Genetics Rsch., Inc., Oakland, Calif., 1981-84; founder, dir. HRI Rsch. Inc., 1978—, Steritech Inc., Concord, Calif., 1992-96, Cerus Corp., 1996—, v.p. new sci. opportunities, 1996—; cons. Codon, Inc., 1993—. Author: Contemporary Chemistry, 1976. editor: General Chemistry, 1974; exec. editor Nucleic Acids Rsch., 1990-93; inventor, patentee in field. Bd. dirs. U. No. Calif., 1993-95. Recipient NSF sci. profl. devel. award, 1977-78; John Simon Guggenheim fellow, 1968-69, European Molecular Biology Orgn. sr. fellow, 1973-74. Mem. AAAS, Am. Chem. Soc., Biophys. Soc., Am. Soc. Biol. Chemists, Am. Soc. for Photobiology (coun., pres. elect 1990-91, pres. 1991-92, Rsch. award 1994), Am. Phys. Soc. Home: 101 Southampton Ave Berkeley CA 94707-2036 Office: U Calif Dept Chemistry #1460 Berkeley CA 94720-1460

HEARST, ROSALIE, philanthropist, foundation executive; b. Oklahoma City, Mar. 7; d. Mathis O. and Audell Bertha (Clary) Wynn; m. George Randolph Hearst, Sr., July 16, 1958. Student, Oklahoma City Coll., UCLA. Hearst rep. U.S. Senate Youth Program; pres. George Randolph Hearst Meml. Found. for Diabetic Edn.; pres. Rosalie Hearst Ednl. Found.; bd. dirs. Elvirita Lewis Found; life mem. Eisenhower Med. Ctr., Pathfinders, Tiempo de Los Ninos, Desert Hosp. Aux., Desert Press Club, Coll. of the Desert Aux., Internat. Orphans; bd. dirs. Pathfinder's Ranch Boys' Club; past bd. dirs. numerous charitable orgns.; trustee emeritus The Bob Hope Cultural Ctr.; coord. Officers' Wives Vol. Svcs. Dibble Gen. Hosp., Palo Alto; coord. Am. Women's Vol. Svcs. Sawtelle Hosp. L.A.; created Rosalie and George Hearst Fellowship in Ophthalmology U. Calif Berkeley. Named Woman of Yr. City of Hope, 1971, Disting. Woman Northwood Inst. Midland, Mich., 1988; recipient award for Lifetime Achievement in Community Service Palm Springs Women's Press Club. Home: 550 Camino Del Norte Palm Springs CA 92262-4216

HEARST, WILLIAM RANDOLPH, III, newspaper publisher; b. Washington, June 18, 1949; s. William Randolph and Austine (McDonnell) H.; m. Margaret Kerr Crawford, Sept. 23, 1990; children: William, Adelaide, Caroline. A.B., Harvard U., 1972. Reporter, asst. city editor San Francisco Examiner, 1972-76, publisher, 1984—; editor Outside Mag., 1976-78; asst. mng. editor Los Angeles Herald Examiner, 1978-80; mgr. devel. Hearst Corp., 1980-82; v.p. Hearst Cable Communications Div., 1982-84. Bd. dirs. Sun Microsystems; trustee Carnegie Inst. Washington. Office: San Francisco Examiner 110 5th St San Francisco CA 94103-2918

HEART, TRACY, psychotherapist, counselor, facilitator; b. La Jolla, Calif., Mar. 25, 1961; d. Palmer and Sandra Lee (Sweeney) Osborn. BA in Psychology, Lewis & Clark Coll., 1983, MA in Counseling Psychology, 1992. Practicum and contract therapist Luth. Family Svcs., Portland, Oreg., 1991-92; on-call therapist Ryles Ctr. for Evaluation & treatment, Portland, 1992-93; triage, intake therapist Network Behavioral Health, Portland, 1993—, Ceres Behavioral Health, Portland, 1995—; psychotherapist, counselor Tigard, Oreg., 1995—; instr., spkr. Portland C.C., 1996—. Mem. Am. Counseling Asn., Oreg. Mental Health Counselors Alliance. Office: 6970 SW Sandburg Ste 340 Portland OR 97223

HEATH, BERTHANN JONES, education administrator; b. Dallas, May 4, 1938; d. James Lafayette and Allie Mae (Hudson) Jones; m. John William Heath, Jr., July 14, 1963 (div. 1975); 1 child, John William, III. BS cum laude, Pepperdine U., 1959; MS, UCLA, 1960. Cert. nat. family and consumer scientist. Tchr., dept. chair L.A. Unified Sch. Dist., 1960-69, dist. resource tchr., 1972-75; counselor L.A. H.S., 1968-72; regional supr., home econs. edn. L.A. Regional Office Calif. State Dept. Edn., 1975-85; program mgr., sch.-to-career transition San Diego City Schs., 1985—; trustee Consumer Credit Counselors of San Diego and Imperial Counties, Calif., 1986—; mem. adv. com. Calif. State Dept. Edn. Home Econs. and Health Careers, Sacramento, 1985—; mem. articulation team SDUSD and San Diego C.C.s, 1987—. Contbr. to pamphlets and leaflets. V.p. San Diego chpt. The Links, Inc., 1995—. Recipient Appreciation/Commendation award Calif. Dept. Edn., 1987, Nat. Gourmet Cook award Nat. Assembly, Links, Inc., 1996. Mem. Am. Vocat. Assn. (bylaws chair F&CS divsn. 1993—), Nat. Assn. Local Suprs. of family and Consumer Scientists (pres. 1992-93), Am. Vocat. Assn. (mem. policy and planning com. 1991-97), Am. Assn. Family and Consumer Scientists, Calif. Assn. F&CS (mem. San Diego chpt., chair secondary edn. 1985-95), Southern Calif. Biotech. Consortium (founder, co-chair articulation 1994—), San Diego Nutrition Coun., Delta Sigma Theta. Office: San Diego Unified Sch Dist Dana Ctr # 193 1775 Chatsworth Blvd San Diego CA 92107

HEATH, EDWARD V., rubber company executive; b. Denver, Mar. 11, 1938; s. Raymond J. and Lois Heath; m. M. Jane Jobe, Aug. 15, 1961; children: Kent, Gregory. BA, Colo. Coll., 1960; B of Fgn. Trade, Thunderbird Sch., 1962; MBA, U. Denver, 1963. Sales corr. Gates Export Co., Denver, 1962-63; spl. rep. Mid. East Gates Export Corp., Beirut, 1963-67; mgr. mktg. devel. Gates Europe, Brussels, 1967-68; export mgr. Millers Falls Co., Greenfield, Mass., 1968-71; mgr. mktg. Latin Am. Stanley Works, New Britain, Conn., 1971-76; gen. mgr. Stanley Colombia, Cali, 1976-79; pres. Huge & Sons Inc., Houston, 1979-84; dir. internat. mktg. Gates Rubber Co., Denver, 1984-85, dir. export ops., 1985-94, mng. dir. Latin Am. ops., 1994—. Mem. Soc. Mfg. Engrs., Overseas Automotive Coun. Republican. Presbyterian. Home: 4272 E Orchard Pl Littleton CO 80121-3172

HEATH, GARY BRIAN, manufacturing firm executive, engineer; b. Pueblo, Colo., Nov. 5, 1954; s. William Sidney Heath and Eleanor Aileen (Mortimer) Svedman, (stepfather) Donald Svedman; m. Francine Marie Tamburelli, Apr. 28, 1990. BSME, U. So. Colo., 1979; MBA, U. Phoenix, 1984. Engr. ADR Ultrasound Corp., Tempe, Ariz., 1979-81; sr. engr. Technicare Ultrasound, Englewood, Colo., 1981-83; engring. mgr. COBE Labs., Inc., Lakewood, Colo., 1983-89; dir. mfg. COBE BCT, Inc., Lakewood, 1989-96, v.p. mfg., 1996—; Patentee fluid flow transfer device, pressure diaphragm for fluid flow device. Mem. Soc. Mfg. Engrs., Soc. Plastics Engrs. Home: 2436 S Dover Ct Lakewood CO 80227-3109 Office: COBE BCT INC 1201 Oak St Lakewood CO 80215-4409

HEATON, DEBBIE ANN, mental health services worker; b. El Paso, Tex., Jan. 28, 1959; d. Joe Harrison and Patricia Ann (Major) Williams; m. Donald Esplin Heaton, Aug. 10, 1978 (div. Aug. 1981); 1 child, Marsha Camille. BSBA, Chadwick U., 1993; BS, La Salle U., 1995, postgrad., 1995—. Cert. substance abuse counselor, Ariz. Receptionist Gallup (N.Mex.) Animal Hosp., 1980-82; clk. Allsup's, Gallup, 1983-85; security guard Giant Refinery, Gallup, 1985-86; asst. mgr. Circle K, Thatcher, Ariz., 1986-87; asst. house mgr. Graham/Greenlee Counseling, Safford, Ariz., 1987-89; adult case mgr. Southeastern Behavioral Health Svcs., Willcox, Ariz., 1989-96; adult mental health case mgr. Ariz. Physicians IPA, Safford, 1996—. Recipient Case Mgmt. Svc. award U. Ariz. Divsn. Rehab. Svcs., 1995. Mem. Assn. Social Work Mgrs., Nat. Assn. Case Mgmt. (conf. workshop presenter 1996). Home: 3405 S Sage Trail Thatcher AZ 85552

HECHT, HAROLD MICHAEL, retail executive; b. Buffalo, Oct. 17, 1939; s. Harold Michael and Elizabeth (Liveright) Hl; m. Brenda Clucas, June 16, 1962; children: Elizabeth, Thomas, John, Christopher. BSBA, Dartmouth Coll., 1961, MBA, 1962. Merchandise mgr. br. store Stewart & Co., Balt., 1965-68; v.p. br. stores Hecht Co., Washington, 1968-69; v.p., mgr. gen. merchandise Meier & Frank, Portland, Oreg., 1969-72; exec. v.p. G. Fox & Co., Hartford, Conn., 1972-75; exec. v.p. sales promotions and merchandising The Broadway Dept. Stores, Los Angeles, 1975-90, chmn. bd. dirs., chief exec. officer; exec. v.p. Carter Hawley Hale Stores Inc., Los Angeles, 1990, pres., 1991-92; pres. Builders Emporium, 1992-94; cons., 1995; pres. Dickson Trading (North Am. Inc.), 1996—. Mem. adv. bd. Fashion Inst., Los Angeles; bd. dirs. NCCJ, San Marino Schs. Found., 1984—. Mem. Merchants and Manufactors Assn. (bd. dirs.). Clubs: Jonathan (Los Angeles); Princeton (N.Y.C.); Annandale Golf (Pasadena, Calif.). Office: 70 South Lake Ave Ste 630 Pasadena CA 91101

HECHT, IRENE MARGRET, lawyer; b. Edmonton, Alta., Can., Dec. 2, 1956; came to U.S., 1964; d. Erich Ernst and Auguste (Schindler) H. BA in Speech Comm. magna cum laude, U. Wash., 1977, JD with honors, 1980. Bar: Wash., 1980. Assoc. Keller Rohrback, Seattle, 1980-85; ptnr. Keller Rohrback LLP, Seattle, 1986—. Mem. Internat. Assn. Def. Counsel, Rainier Club. Office: Keller Rohrback LLP 1201 3d Ave Ste 3200 Seattle WA 98101

HECHT, SCOTT JAMES, mechanical engineering executive; b. Powell, Wyo., Oct. 6, 1959; s. Robert N. and Jackie Louise (Corbett) H.; m. Janice Neilson, Aug. 21, 1981; children: Kristin, Jessica, Nathan, Jason. BSME, Brigham Young U., 1984, MSME, 1985. Registered professional engineer, Wyo., Mont., Idaho. Staff engr. SSR Engrs., Billings, Mont., 1985-90; pres. Western Engring. Inc., Powell, 1990—. Mem. IEEE, ASME, Nat. Assn. Corrosion Engrs. Republican. Mem. LDS Ch. Office: Western Engring Inc 871 Road 19 Powell WY 82435-9510

HECHTER, MARC STEVEN, management consultant; b. N.Y.C., May 25, 1952; s. Leon Hechter and Rebecca Naomi Hall Hoge; div. 1985; children: Brandon Christopher, Whitney Marie; m. Mamie May Chinn, Dec. 20, 1987. BA, U. Nev., Las Vegas, 1975, MPA, 1979. Mgmt. analyst Regional Transp. Commn., Las Vegas, 1978-79; prin. planner Clark County Dept. Comprehensive Planning, Las Vegas, 1979-83; adminstr. Nev. Housing Div., Carson City, 1983-86; v.p. Donaldson, Lufkin and Jenrette Securities Corp., N.Y.C. and L.A., 1986-87; sr. mgmt. analyst Clark County Dept. Fin., Las Vegas, 1987-88; exec. asst. to gov. State of Nev., Carson City, 1988-89; contract lobbyist, polit. cons. Wadhams and Assocs., Inc., Las Vegas and Carson City, 1989, 90-91; v.p. Zions First Nat. Bank, Las Vegas, 1989-90; asst. gen. mgr. State Indsl. Ins. System, Carson City, 1991-93; prin., CEO Jayne, Hechter and Co., Inc., Las Vegas, 1993-95; sr. v.p. fin. Saxton Inc., Las Vegas, Nev., 1995—; adj. instr. polit. sci. and history We. Nev. C.C. Past bd. dirs. Nev. Opera Assn.; head coach Silver State Girls Soccer League U-19. Mem. Pi Kappa Phi, Pi Sigma Alpha. Republican. Episcopalian. Home: 3456 Distinction Ct Las Vegas NV 89129-6728

HECK, GARY L., security management company executive; b. Great Lakes, Ill., Oct. 31, 1952; s. Walter John and Alice Edna (Vogan) H.; children: Tera Lee, Breyana Marie. AAS, Delta Coll., 1972; BS, Mich. State U., 1974. Cert. protection profl. Police officer Ludington (Mich.) Police Dept., 1974-75; undercover narcotics investigator Thumb Intelligence Group, Cass City, Mich., 1975-77, Jefferson County Sheriffs Dept., Madras, Oreg., 1977-78; police patrolman Lansing Police Dept., 1978-86; chief of security Trammell Crow Co., Dallas, 1986-88; security mgr. Am. Patrol and Guard, Denver, 1988-90; dir. life safety and security Trammell Crow Co., Denver, 1990-95, Vector Property Svcs., Denver, 1995—; cons. emergency response task force Bldg. Owners and Mgrs. Assn., Denver, 1992—. Contbr. North Shore Animal League, Chgo., 1992—; walker March of Dimes, Denver, 1993. Mem. Am. Soc. for Indsl. Security, Downtown Denver Security Assn. (bd. dirs.), Nat. Fire Protection Assn., Nat. Parks and Conservation Assn., Sierra Club, World Wildlife Fund, Planetary Soc. Home: PO Box 18429 Denver CO 80218-0429 Office: Vector Property Svcs 1200 17th St Ste 1130 Denver CO 80202-5835

HECK, THOMAS S., civil engineer, management consultant; b. Chgo., Feb. 8, 1954; s. Robert Elgin and Eva (Prystasz) H.; m. Robin L. Landry, Jan. 31, 1992. BS, U.S. Air Force Acad., 1977; MPA, Troy State U., 1986; EdS, George Washington U., 1991. Commd. 2LT USAF, 1972—; advanced through grades to lt. col. USN; AFIT student Brown & Root Inc., Houston, 1984-85; chief ops. CES, Lajes, Azores, Portugal, 1986-87; chief ops. and tng. Tactical Air Command AC Hdqs., Langley AFB, Va., 1986-90; chief saber 1 Civil Engring. Squadron, Langley AFB, Va., 1990-91; chief ops. 60 Civil Engring. Squadron, Travis AFB, Calif., 1991-94; dep. command engr. Southcom Engring., Corozal, Panama, 1994-96; base civil engr. 61/ABG/CE, L.A. AFB, 1996—. Mem. Assn. Grad. Home: 31 Titan Dr San Pedro CA 90732

HECKENLIVELY, JOHN ROBERT, ophthalmology educator; b. Denver, Jan. 24, 1946; s. H.M. and Dora H. AB, Oberlin Coll., 1968; MD, U. Colo., 1972. Intern U. Utah Med. Ctr., Salt Lake City, 1972-73; resident in ophthalmology U. Ky. Med. Ctr., Lexington, 1973-76; fellow in retina UCLA/Jules Stein Eye Inst., L.A., 1976-77; asst. prof. ophthalmology UCLA/Jules Stein Eye Inst., 1978, assoc. prof. ophthalmology, 1983, prof. ophthalmology, 1988—; fellow in genetics Johns Hopkins Hops., Balt., 1977-78; dir. UCLA Visual Physiology Lab., 1979—, Hereditary Retinal Disease Ctr., Jules Stein Eye Inst., 1992—. Author: (textbook) Retinitis Pigmentosa, 1988; author/editor: Principles and Practice of Clinical Electrophysiology of Vision, 1992; editor: Pattern Electroretinogram, 1984, Retinal Diseases, 1992; editorial bd. Metabolic and Pediatric Ophthalmology, Documenta Ophthalmologica; ad hoc reviewer NIH; editor Internat. Soc. for Clin. Electrophysiology of Vision, 1982-90. Adv. bd. Blue Cross of Calif., 1987—. Recipient Jules Stein Tribute award RP Internat. Found., Woodland Hills, Calif., 1986, award NIH, Bethesda, Md., 1987-96. Fellow Am. Acad. Ophthalmology (chair retina sec. 1988-92), Royal Coll. Ophthalmologists; mem. Macula Soc., Ophthalmic Genetic Study Club, Am. Soc. Human Genetics, Oxford Ophthal. Congress, Am. Ophthal. Soc., L.A. Acad. Medicine. Office: UCLA Jules Stein Eye Inst 100 Stein Plaza Los Angeles CA 90024

HECKER, MICHAEL HANNS LOUIS, electrical engineer, speech scientist; b. Hamburg, Germany, Mar. 30, 1936; came to U.S., 1948; s. Hanns Ewald Hecker and Wilhelmine (Corinth) Klopfer; m. Elizabeth Ann Bowen, Sept. 3, 1960 (div.); 1 child, Serena Suzanne; m. Dorothy Louise Dunlap, Mar. 12, 1971. BSEE with honors, Northeastern U., 1959; MSEE, MIT, 1961; PhD in Speech & Hearing Scis., Stanford U., 1974. Sr. rsch. engr. Bolt Beranek and Newman Inc., Cambridge, Mass., 1964-67, SRI Internat., Menlo Park, Calif., 1967-95; cons. forensic acoustics, Los Altos, Calif., 1967—; retained by White House during Watergate investigation to examine presdl. tapes; sci. cons. Nat. Commn. Rev. Fed. & State Laws Relating to Wiretapping & Electronic Surveillance, 1974-76. Author: Speaker Recognition, 1971; co-editor: Speech Evaluation in Psychiatry/Medicine, 1981; contbr. articles to profl. jours., chpts. to med. books. 1st lt. U.S. Army, 1962-64. NIH grantee, 1982-88. Fellow Am. Acad. Forensic Scis., Acoustical Soc. Am. (chmn. tech. com. on speech), Eta Kappa Nu, Tau Beta Pi, Sigma Xi. Office: 585 Giralda Dr Los Altos CA 94024-3826

HECKMAN, RICHARD AINSWORTH, chemical engineer; b. Phoenix, July 15, 1929; s. Hiram and Anne (Sells) H.; m. Olive Ann Biddle, Dec. 17, 1950; children: Mark, Bruce. BS, U. Calif., Berkeley, 1950, cert. hazardous mgmt. U. Calif., Davis, 1985, int. solid waste mgmt., U. Calif., Berkeley. Registered profl. engr., Calif. With radiation lab. U. Calif., Berkeley, 1950-51; chem. engr. Calif. Rsch. & Devel. Co., Livermore, 1951-53; assoc. div. leader Lawrence Livermore Nat. Lab., 1953-77, project leader, 1977-78, program leader, 1978-79, energy policy analyst, 1979-83, toxic waste group staff engr., 1984-86, waste minimization project leader, 1986-90; div. dir. hazardous waste mgmt. Nationwide Technologies, Inc., Oakland, 1990-91; mng. dir. Heckman & Assocs., 1991-92; v.p. environ. scis. Pan Am. Resources Inc., Pleasanton, Calif., 1992—, also bd. dirs.. Mem. Calif. Radioactive Materials Forum. Co-author: Nuclear Waste Management Abstracts, 1983; patentee in field. Bd. dirs. Calif. Industries for Blind, 1977-80, Here and Now Disabled Svcs. for Tri-Valley, Inc., 1980. Calif. Fellow Am. Inst. Chemists, Acad. Hazardous Materials Mgmt.; mem. AAAS, Am. Acad. Environ. Engrs. (diplomate), Am. Chemistry Soc., Am. Inst. Chem. Engrs., Am. Nuclear Soc., Soc. Environ. Mgmt. & Tech., Solid Waste Assn. N.Am., Soc. Profl. Engrs., Water Environ. Fedn., Air and Waste Mgmt. Assn., Internat. Union Pure and Applied Chemistry (assoc.), Nat. Hist. Soc., N.Y. Acad. Scis., Internat. Oceanographic Soc., Environ. Assessment Assn., World Trade Club, San Francisco, Commonwealth Club San Francisco, Richmond Yacht Club, Island Yacht Club (commodore 1971), Midget Ocean Racing Club (sta. 3 commodore 1982-83), U.S. Sailing Assn., Midget Ocean Racing Assn. No. Calif. (commodore 1972). Home and Office: Pan Am Resources Environ Scis Dept 5683 Greenridge Rd Castro Valley CA 94552-2625

HECKMANN, RICHARD ANDERSON, zoology educator; b. Salt Lake City, Dec. 7, 1931; married; 5 children. BS in Zoology, Utah State U., 1954, MS in Zoology, 1958; postgrad., U. Calif., Davis, 1958-60, U. Pacific, 1959, U. Hawaii, 1960-61, U. Wash., 1963, U. Calif., Berkeley, 1963, 66; PhD in Zoology, Mont. State U., 1970; postgrad., Imperial Coll., Eng., 1976, U. Utah, 1985-86. Teaching asst. Utah State U., 1957; rsch. asst. U. Calif., 1958-59, teaching asst., 1959-61; instr. Contra Costa Coll., 1962-67; teaching asst. Mont. State U., 1968-70; asst. prof. Calif. State U., Fresno, 1970-72; prof. Brigham Young U., Provo, Utah; lectr. Calif. State U., Fresno, 1970; cons. U.S. Forest Svc., 1962, Niagara Chem. Co., 1964, 65, 67, Westinghouse Electric Corp., 1974, 75, 76, Central Utah Project, 1974, Diking Utah Lake Proposal Team, 1976, BLM Deep Creek Mts. and Big Creek Impact Studies, Vaughn Hansen Assocs., 1978, NARL Nielsen, Maxwell & Wangsgaard Engrs., Noorlander Corp., 1979, 80; dir. Rsch. Team to Guatemala; vis. prof. USSR, Poland, NAS, 1989; vis. prof. U. Ain Shams, U. Cairo, Egypt, 1996; alumni prof. Brigham Young U., 1995-97. Author: Laboratory Manual for Biology Part I and II, 1966, Healing and Bacteriocidal Properties of Selected Herbal Extracts, 1988; co- author: (Clark, Glen) Atlas of Animal Parasites, 1974; editorial bd. Calif. Fish and Game Mag., 1974, Jour. Wildlife Diseases, 1974; patentee in field; Contbr to numerous profl. jours. Recipient Faculty Rsch. awards, 1972, 73, 74, 75, Silver Beaver award Boy Scouts of Am., 1989; grantee NSF, 1971, 72, 75, Utah Divsn. Wildlife Resources, 1975, 78, 79, Westinghouse Corp., 1976, Ariz. Fuels Corp., 1977, 78, 79, Naval Artic Rsch. Lab. U. Alaska, 1979, Utah Power and Light, 1979, Schering Corp., 1984, Brigham Young U., 1987-89, Binational Agrl. Rsch. Devel. Fund, 1986, 87, 88, 89, Nev. Divsn. Wildlife Resources, 1986, 87, 88-89; Pauley Rsch. fellow, 1960, 61, NSF, 1963, 66; Carl Raymond Grey scholar, 1950; honored by Farmer to Farmer Program USAID, 1988, 89. Mem. Am. Inst. Fishery Rsch. Biologist, Soc. of Protozoologist, Soc. of Parasitologists, Am. Fisheries Soc. (fish health sect., fish culture sect., pub. com., chmn. profl. standards com., mem. endangered species com.), World Malocologist's Soc., Utah Pub. Health Assn. Office: Brigham Young U Dept Zoology Provo UT 84602

HEDDEN, THOMAS DEXTER, translator; b. Chgo., Dec. 2, 1953; s. Gregory Dexter and Genevieve (Groves) H.; m. Heather Behn, Nov. 28, 1992; 1 child, Henry Dexter. BA, U. Wis., 1976; MA, UCLA, 1979; PhD, U. Calif., Berkeley, 1988. Accredited translator Russian-English, German-English, Polish-English, French-English. Project mgr. Am. Translators, Palo Alto, Calif., 1990-92; sr. project mgr. SimulTrans, Mountain View, Calif., 1992-94; German quality assurance engr. Consilium, Mountain View, 1995-96; grader Am. Translators Assn., Alexandria, Va., 1994—. Editor: Sovereign Rescheduling: Risk and Portfolio Management, 1988; translator manuals; author jour. articles. Mem. Am. Translators Assn., No. Calif. Translators Assn., Soc. for Tech. Comms., Am. Assn. for Advancement of Slavic Studies. Democrat. Home: 10 Mulberry Ct Apt 2 Belmont CA 94002

HEDLER, KENNETH BRUCE, journalist; b. San Bernardino, Calif., June 29, 1955; s. Herbert Roland and Julia (Barahl) H. AA, Coll. of the Desert, 1975; student, Calif. State U., Fresno, 1975-76; BA, Calif. State U., Fullerton, 1978. Reporter Palo Verde Valley Times, Blythe, Calif., 1984-86; reporter, bus. editor The Union, Grass Valley, Calif., 1986-89; copy editor Appeal-Democrat, Marysville, Calif., 1989-92; bus., agr. reporter Imperial Valley Press, El Centro, Calif., 1992-93; reporter Mobile Homes Courier, Hemet, Calif., 1993-94; copy editor Adams/Green Industry Pub., Cathedral City, Calif., 1994-95; staff writer Elsinore Valley Sun-Tribune, Lake Elsinore, Calif., 1996—; stringer AP, L.A., Phoenix and Sacramento, 1985-89. Treas. Comms. Workers Am., Grass Valley, Calif., 1988-89. Mem. Soc. Profl. Journalists, Desert Press Club (bd. dirs. 1995-96, editor newsletter).

HEDLUND, PAUL JAMES, lawyer; b. Abington, Pa., June 26, 1946; s. Frank Xavier and Eva Ruth (Hoffman) H.; m. Marta Louise Brewer, Dec. 7, 1985; children: Annemarie Kirsten, Brooke Ashley, Tess Kara. BSME, U. Mich., 1968; JD, UCLA, 1973. Bar: Calif. 1973, D.C. 1994, U.S. Dist. Ct. (ctrl. dist.) Calif. 1977, U.S. Dist. Ct. (ea. dist.) Calif. 1991, U.S. Dist. Ct. (no. dist.) N.Y. 1994, U.S. Patent and Trademark Office 1978, U.S. Ct. Appeals (9th cir.) 1994. Staff engr. So. Calif. Edison, L.A., 1968-70; ptnr. Hedlund & Samuels, L.A., 1974-88, Kananack, Murgatroyd Baum & Hedlund (and predecessor firms), L.A., 1988-92; shareholder Baum, Hedlund, Aristei, Guilford & Downey (and predecessor firms), L.A., 1993—; mem. discovery team, mem. trial team MDL 817 United Airlines Aircrash at Sioux City, Iowa, Chgo., 1989. Office: Baum Hedlund Aristei Guilford & Downey 12100 Wilshire Blvd Ste 950 Los Angeles CA 90025-7114

HEDRICK, BASIL CALVIN, state agency administrator, ethnohistorian, educator, museum and multicultural institutions consultant; b. Lewistown, Mo., Mar. 17, 1932; s. Truman Bloice and M. LaVeta (Stice) H.; m. Anne Kehoe, Jan. 19, 1957 (div. 1979); 1 dau., Anne Lanier Hedrick Caraker; m. Susan Elizabeth Pickel, Oct. 2, 1980. A.B., Augustana Coll., Rock Island, Ill., 1956; MA, U. Fla., 1957; PhD, Inter-Am. U., Mex., 1965; cert., U. Vienna, Strobl, Austria, 1956. Asst. prof., assoc. prof., prof. So. Ill. U., Carbondale, 1967-74, asst. dir. univ. Mus., 1967-70, dir. Univ. Mus. and Art Galleries, 1970-77, dean internat. edn., 1972-74; asst. dir. Ill. Div. Mus., Springfield, 1977-80; prof. history U. Alaska, Fairbanks, 1980-88, dir. U. Alaska Mus., 1980-88, dir. inter. affairs, 1985-87; founder, dir. Div. Mus., Archaeology and Publs. State of Mich., Lansing, 1988-91; multicultural cons., 1991—; dir. mktg. Rosalie Whyel Mus. Doll Art, Bellevue, Wash., 1991—; Fulbright sr. lectr., Brazil, 1972; mem. nat. register adv. panel, Ill., 1977-80; mem. Alaska Coun. on Arts, Anchorage, 1983-85; chmn. Fairbanks Hist. Preservation Commn., 1982-88; mem. Alaska Land Use Coun.; bd. dirs. Alaska Hist. Preservation Found., 1986-88; mem. Gov.'s Revitalization Task Force, Lansing, Mich., mem. ethnic coun., Mich., 1988-89; bd. dirs. East King County Visitors Bur., 1993—; officer, bd. dirs. Wash. Mus. Assn., 1993—. Author: (with others) A Bibliography of Nepal, 1973, (with Carroll L. Riley) The Journey of the Vaca Party, 1974, Documents Ancillary to the Vaca Journey, 1976, (with C.A. Letson) Once Was A Time, a Wery Good Time: An Inquiry into the Folklore of the Bahamas, 1975, (with J.E. Stephens) In the Days of Yesterday and in the Days of Today: An Overview of Bahamian Folkmusic, 1976, It's A Natural Fact: Obeah in the Bahamas, 1977, Contemporary Practices in Obeah in the Bahamas, 1981; compilations and collections, 1959-69; editor: (with J. Charles Kelley and Riley) The Classic Southwest: Readings in Archaeology, Ethnohistory and Ethnography, 1973, (with J. Charles Kelley and Riley) The Mesoamerican Southwest: Readings in Archaeology, Ethnohistory and Ethnology, 1974, (with Riley) Across the Chichimec Sea, 1978; (with others) New Frontiers in the Archaeology and Ethnohistory of the Greater Southwest, 1980; Trans. of Ill. Acad. Sci., 1979-81, (with Susan Pickel-Hedrick) Ethel Washington: The Life and Times of an Eskimo Dollmaker, The Role of the Steamboat in the Founding and Development of Fairbanks, Alaska, 1986, (with Susan Savage) Steamboats on the Chena, 1988; co-editor: Led Zeppelin live, 1993, 94, 97, Beautiful Children, 1996; author and editor of various other publications; contbr. articles to profl. jours. Chmn. Goals for Carbondale, 1972; active various local state, nat. polit. campaigns. Mem. NMA (bd. dirs. 1989-91), Am. Assn. Mus. (leader accreditation teams 1977—, sr. examiner), Ill. Archaeol. Soc. (pres. 1973-74), Mus. Alaska, Assn. Sci. Mus. Dirs., Midwest Mus. Conf. (treas. 1977-80), Western Mus. Assn., Wash. Mus. Assn. (bd. dirs. 1994—, v.p. 1995—), BD Arts (bd. dirs. 1995-96), Phi Kappa Phi. *Pragmatism has been the ruling factor in both my personal and professional life. I have never assumed that anything is immutable and, therefore, I have rarely been overly surprised or disappointed in changes which have occurred. In our rush to succeed and excel, we often forego the realities of daily life in order to attempt the literally impossible. The better rule is, to adapt to reality without losing ethical and moral principle. Relax and learn.*

HEDRICK, WALLACE EDWARD, business executive; b. Malad, Idaho, Nov. 11, 1947; s. Clarence Franklin and Beth S. Hedrick; BS, U. Nev., Reno, 1970; MA, U. No. Colo., Greeley, 1974; m. Jerrie S. Deffenbaugh, Nov. 20, 1980; children: Ann Elizabeth, Ryan Wallace, Hallie Sue. Regional dir. No. Idaho, Idaho Planning and Cmty. Affairs Agy., Moscow, 1970-73, assoc. chief, Boise, 1973-75; project dir. Pacific N.W. Regional Commn., Boise, 1975-76; pres. Resources N.W., Inc., Boise, 1976-88; dir. Idaho State Lottery, 1988-95; pres. Tri West Lotto Bd., 1993-95; pres. Resources Northwest, Boise, 1995—. Sec.-treas. Idaho Citizens for Responsible Govt., 1978-80; trustee, chmn. Joint Sch. Dist. 2, 1985—; trustee Meridian Sch. Bd.; bd. dirs. Boise Family YMCA, 1994—; exec. com. North Am. Assn. State and Provincial Lotteries. Served with USAR, 1971. Mem. Multi State Lottery Assn. (pres. 1994-95), N.Am. Assn. of State and Provincial Lotteries (regional dir.). Democrat. Home: 9413 Knottingham Dr Boise ID 83704-2234 Office: Resources Northwest PO Box 578 Boise ID 83704

HEDRICK, WALLY BILL, artist; b. Pasadena, Calif., 1928; s. Walter Thomas and Velma Laurel (Thurman) H. Student, Otis Art Inst., Los Angeles, 1947, Calif. Coll. Arts and Crafts, 1954; B.F.A., Calif. Sch. Fine Arts, 1955; MA, San Francisco State U., 1958. Instr. San Francisco State U., 1958-59, Calif. Sch. Fine Arts, 1960-64, Art Inst. San Francisco, 1964-70, San Francisco Acad. Art, 1971, San Jose State U., 1972-73, Indian Valley Coll., 1974—; instr. summer session Art. Inst. San Francisco, 1978; instr. U. Calif., Davis, 1984, 86. One-man shows include Pasadena (Calif.) Arts Ctr., 1950, M.H. de Young Meml. Mus., San Francisco, 1955, Calif. Sch. Fine Arts, San Francisco, 1956, Oakland (Calif.) Mus., 1958, Isaacs Gallery, Toronto, Can., 1961, New Mission Gallery, San Francisco, 1963, San Francisco Art Inst., 1967, Sonoma Satte Coll., Calif., 1968, 63 Bluxome St., San Francisco, 1975, Gallery Paule Anglim, San Francisco, 1982, 84, 89, 90, Emanuel Walter Gallery, 1985, Atholl McBean Gallery, 1985, Natsoulas-Novelozo Gallery, Davis, Calif., 1989, Mills Coll. Art Gallery, 1994, Gallery Paule Anglim, 1994; group exhbns. include Pasadena Art Mus., L.A. County Mus. Art, 1953, San Francisco Mus. Modern Art, 1954, 57, 60, 66, Santa Barbara Mus. Modern Art, 1956, Mus. Modern Art, N.Y.C., 1959, 76, Calif. Palace Legion Honor., 1961, San Francisco Art Inst., 1962, San Francisco Mus. Art, 1962, 66, Norton Simon Mus. Art, Pasadena, 1962, Richmond (Calif.) Art Ctr., 1964, Calif. State U. Sonoma, Rhonert Park, 1968, Dallas Mus. Fine Arts, 1974, Wadsworth Antheneum, Hartford, Conn., 1975, San Francisco Mus. Modern Art, 1977, Gallery Paule Anglim, San Francisco, 1981, 83, 86, 92, South Market Cultural Ctr., 1982, Columbus (Ga.) Mus. Arts and Scis., 1984, Sheldon Meml. Art Gallery, U. Nebr., Licoln, 1984, Chgo. Internat. Arts Expo., 1984, Old Waterhouse Cabaret, Oakland, 1985, Arts Coun. San Mateo County, Belmont, Calif., 1985., Emanuel Walter Gallery, 1985, Atholl McBean Gallery, 1985, Newport Harbor Art Mus., Newport Beach., Calif., 1986, L.A. County Mus. Art, 1986-87, Mus. Contemporary Art, Chgo., 1986-87, Natsoulas Novelozo Gallery, 1990; group exhibitions include Gallery Paule Anglim, San Francisco, 1992, ACGI Gallery, Berkeley, Calif., 1993, The Crocker Mus., Sacramento, 1994, The Oakland Mus., Calif., 1994, San Francisco Art Inst., 1994, Richmond Art Ctr., Calif., 1995, San Francisco Women Artists Gallery, 1995, Whitney Mus. Am. Art, N.Y.C., 1995, Walker Art Ctr., Mpls., 1996, M.H. de Young Meml. Mus., 1996; represented in permanent collections, Aldrich Mus. Contemporary Art, Ridgefield, Conn., Mus. Modern Art, N.Y.C., Smithsonian Instn., San Francisco Mus. Modern Art, City and County San Francisco, L.A. County Mus. Art, Laguna (Calif.) Mus., Mus. Contemporary Art, Ridgefield, Conn., Oakland Mus., Calif. State U. Sonoma, U. Calif. San Francisco. San Francisco Art Commn., San Francisco Art Inst., San Francisco Internat. Airport, Univ. Art Mus., Berkeley, Calif., Mills Coll., Oakland; represented by Gallery Paule Anglim. Served with AUS, 1950-52. Recipient Adeline Kent award, 1985, Golden Bear award Calif. State Fair, 1990, merit award, 1991, award of excellence, 1996; grantee Nat. Endowment Arts, 1962, 82, 93, Marin Arts Coun.-Bucks Found., individual artist grantee San Francisco Found., 1985-86, Adolph and Esther Gottlieb Found. grantee, 1997. Office: PO Box 94 Bodega CA 94922-0094

HEDVIG, MICHAEL ELLIOTT, management consultant; b. Urbana, Ill., Oct. 12, 1960; s. Thomas Ivan and Eleanor Barbara (Herson) H. BA, Calif. State U. Northridge, 1984; BBA, Nat. U., 1992; MSBA, Tex. A&M, 1994. Mgmt. intern Army Material Command, Texarkana, Tex., 1993-94; logistician Army Corps of Engrs., Seattle, 1994-95; contract adminstr. Weapons Divsn. Naval Air Warfare Ctr., Point Mugu, Calif., 1995-96; contract adminstr. Naval Facilities Engring. Command, Port Hueneme, Calif., 1996—. Mem. Nat. Contract Mgmt. Assn. (publicity chair 1996-97). Office: Naval Facilities Engring NCBC Code 27 Bldg 41 Port Hueneme CA 93043

HEEGER, DAVID J., psychology educator; b. Berkeley, Calif., Oct. 3, 1961; s. Alan J. and Ruth (Chadacoff) H.; m. Anne Gelman, Oct. 21, 1990; 1 child. BA, U. Pa., 1983, MS in Engring., 1985, PhD, 1987. Rsch. assoc. Stanford (Calif.) U., 1990-91; rsch. scientist NASA-Ames Rsch. Ctr., Moffett Field, Calif., 1991; asst. prof. Stanford U., 1991—. Contbr. articles to profl. jours.; patentee in field. Rsch. fellow U. Pa., Phila., 1983-87, Vis. fellow SRI Internat., Menlo Park, Calif., 1984-85, Postdoctoral Rsch. fellow MIT Media Lab., Cambridge, Mass., 1987-90, Fairchild Found. Postdoctoral fellow, 1987, Sloan Rsch. Found. fellow, 1994; NIH Rsch. grantee, 1993; recipient David Marr prize Internat. Conf. Computer Vision, London, 1987. Office: Stanford U Dept Psychology Stanford CA 94305

HEEGER, JACK JAY, public relations consultant; b. Sioux City, Iowa, Oct. 18, 1930; s. Lester and Etta (Grossman) H.; m. Fern E. Rubenstein, Feb. 14, 1954 (dec. May 1987); children: Lloyd, Marshall, Laurie; m. Heddy L. Swierstra, Sept. 2, 1989. MBA, Calif. State U., 1985. Accredited in pub. rels. Reporter Sioux City (Iowa) Jour., 1954-55, UPI, L.A., 1955-57; asst. dir. pub. rels. Revell, Inc., Venice, Calif., 1957-59; mgr. west coast Carl Byoir & Assoc., L.A., 1959-69; owner, cons. Jack J. Heeger Pub. Rels., L.A., 1969-70, 84—; exec. staff mem. Braun & Co., L.A., 1970-74; v.p. pub. affairs Sunkist Growers, Inc., Sherman Oaks, Calif., 1974-84; lectr. Calif. State U., L.A., 1986-87; assoc. prof. Calif. State U., Long Beach, 1987-92; assoc. prof. emeritus Calif. State U., 1992—. Contbr. articles to profl. jours. Sgt. USMC, 1951-53. Fellow Pub. Rels. Soc. Am. (pres. L.A. chpt. 1973, named disting. profl. 1976, Cmty. Svc. award 1991).

HEEKIN, VALERIE ANNE, telecommunications technician; b. Santa Monica, Calif., Nov. 7, 1953; d. Edward Raphael and Jane Eileen (Potter) H. AA, L.A. Valley Coll., 1980; BS magna cum laude, Calif. Baptist Coll., 1987. Telecommunications technician Pacific Bell Co., N. Hollywood, Calif., 1971—; pres. Odyssey Adventures, Inc., Sylmar, Calif., 1987—. Pres. Parkwood Sylmar Homeowners Assn., 1981-89; activist civil rights. Republican. Roman Catholic. Office: Odyssey Adventures PO Box 221477 Newhall CA 91322-1477

HEERMANS, JOHN MICHAEL, electrical, chemical engineer; b. The Dalles, Oreg., Nov. 24, 1958; s. Donald Jerome and Motrona A. H.; m. Karen Marie Hudson, Nov. 8, 1987. BS in Chem. Engring., U. Calif., Santa Barbara, 1983; MSEE, U. So. Calif., L.A., 1989. Engr. Grumman Aerospace Corp., Nas Pt. Mugu, Calif., 1983-86; project engr. Hughes Aircraft Co., El Segundo, Calif., 1986-94; engr. specialist Lockheed Martin Tactical Def. Sys., Litchfield Park, Ariz., 1994—. Republican. Seventh-day Adventist. Office:

Lockheed Martin Tactical Def Sys MS 5122 PO Box 85 Litchfield Park AZ 85340

HEFFELFINGER, DAVID MARK, optical engineer; b. Ft. Worth, Jan. 10, 1951; s. Hugo Wagner and Betty Lu (Graf) H.; m. Gail Patricia Lindsay, Dec. 10, 1995; children: Jakob, Leon, Stacy. MS in Physics, Wayne State U., 1984. Project scientist GM Rsch. Lab., Warren, Mich., 1978-90; grad. rsch. asst. Wayne State U., Detroit, 1982-84; engring. dept. mgr. Bio-Rad Labs., Hercules, Calif., 1990—. Contbr. articles to Jour. Applied Physics, Bull. Am. Phys. Soc., Biotechniques; patentee in field. Recipient Vaden Miles award Wayne State U., 1982. Mem. AAAS, Internat. Soc. Optical Engring., Optical Soc. Am. Office: Bio Rad Labs 2000 Alfred Nobel Dr Hercules CA 94547-1801

HEFFLINGER, LEROY ARTHUR, agricultural manager; b. Omaha, Feb. 14, 1935; s. Leroy William and Myrtle Irene (Lampe) H.; m. Carole June Wickman, Dec. 23, 1956; children: Dean Alan, Andrew Karl, Roger Glenn, Dale Gorden. BS in Fin., U. Colo., 1957. Mgr. Hefflinger Ranches, Inc., Toppenish, Wash., 1963-97; pres. Hefflinger Ranches, Inc., 1973—; bd. dirs. Hop Adminstrv. Com., Portland, Oreg., 1980-86; trustee Agr. and Forestry Edn. Found., Spokane, Wash., 1988-94, vice chmn., 1993-94; mem. adv. bd. Ctrl. Bank, Toppenish, Wash., 1995—. Vestryman, bd. dirs. St. Michael's Ch., Yakima, Wash., 1969-74; mem. capital campaign com. Heritage Coll., Toppenish, 1990-91; bd. dirs. Am. Hop Mus., 1997—. Capt. USAF, 1958-63. Mem. Hop Growers Am. (past pres. 1982-95, bd. dirs.), Hop Growers Wash. (past treas. 1978-83, bd. dirs.), Beta Theta Pi. Republican. Episcopalian. Office: Hefflinger Ranches Inc PO Box 47 Toppenish WA 98948-0047

HEFFRON, MICHAEL EDWARD, software engineer, computer scientist; b. Battle Creek, Mich., Dec. 18, 1949; s. Michael Richard and Maxine Beverly (Piper) H.; m. Louella Mae Thompson, Apr. 12, 1969; children: Karen, Jennifer. BS in Computer Sci., Ariz. State U., 1986. Engring. asst. Motorola, Inc., Scottsdale, Ariz., 1977-81; calibration lab. supr. ADR Ultrasound, Tempe, Ariz., 1982-83; engring. aide Motorola, Inc., Scottsdale, 1983-86; v.p. CyberSoft, Inc., Tempe, Ariz., 1986-90; engr. Injection Rsch. Specialists, Inc., Colorado Springs, Colo., 1990-91; software devel. mgr. Injection Rsch. Specialists Co. div. Pacer Industries, Colorado Springs, 1991-92; sr. systems engr. Computer Data Systems Inc., Rockville, Md., 1992-93; software engr. Coergon, Inc., Boulder, Colo., 1993-95, Loral Comm. Systems (purchased by Lockheed Martin 1996), Colorado Springs, Colo., 1995-96, Lockheed Martin, Colorado Springs, 1996-97, L-3 Comms. Corp. (formerly Lockheed Martin Wideband Sys.), Colo. Springs, 1997—. Patentee in field. Served with USAF, 1970-77. Fellow IEEE; mem. Assn. Computing Machinery, Soc. Reliability Engrs. Republican. Pentecostal Ch. Office: L-3 Comms Corp 1150 Academy Park Loop Ste 240 Colorado Springs CO 80910-3716

HEFLEY, JOEL M., congressman; b. Ardmore, Okla., Apr. 18, 1935; s. J. Maurice and Etta A. (Anderson) H.; m. Lynn Christian, Aug. 25, 1961; children: jana, Lori, Juli. BA, Okla. Baptist U., 1957; MS, Okla. State U., 1963. Exec. dir. Community Planning and Research, Colorado Springs, Colo., 1966-86; mem. Colo. Ho. of Reps., 1977-78, Colo. Senate, 1979-86, 100th-104th Congresses from 5th Colo. dist., 1987—; mem. armed svcs. com., mem. natural resources com., mem. small bus.-SBA com. Republican. Baptist. Clubs: Rotary, Colorado Springs Country. Office: House of Representatives 2351 Rayburn Bldg Washington DC 20515-0005

HEGEDUS, JOHN S., medical products executive; b. 1929. With Am. Home Products, N.Y., 1968-77, Revlon Health Care, N.Y., 1977-86, Sterling Drug, N.Y., 1986-92, Genelabs Tech. Inc., Redwood City, Calif., 1992—. Office: Genelabs Tech Inc 505 Penobscot Dr Redwood City CA 94063-4737

HEICKSEN, MARTIN HENRY, retired archaeology and biblical literature educator; b. Columbus, Mont., Apr. 17, 1911; s. Henry Martin and Bertha Ann (Crawford) H.; m. Amanda Eldora Bolstad, July 18, 1938; children: Byron Homer, Gerald Eugene, Darlene Joyce. AB, San Francisco State U., 1955, MA, 1957. Life C.C. anthropology credential, Calif. Min., pastor 4 Assemblies of God chs., Mont., 1936-42; exec. sec.-treas. Mont. dist. coun. Assembly of God, 1942-47; instr. Ctrl. Bible Coll., Springfield, Mo., 1947-48; prof. bibl. lit. Bethany Coll., Santa Cruz, Calif., 1948-67; assoc. prof. archaeology Wheaton (Ill.) Coll., 1967-71; vis. prof. archaeology Cabrillo Coll., Aptos, Calif., 1974-76; prof. archaeology and O.T., Omega Tng. Ctr., San Jose, Calif., 1976-79, St. James Coll., Pacifica, Calif., 1980-90; ret., 1990; field archaeologist San Francisco State U. and U. Calif., Berkeley, 1950-63; archaeologist, photographer Dothan (Jordan) Archaeol. Expdn., 1964; dir. Tekoa (Israel) Archaeol. Expdn., 1968-71; cons. archaeologist, Santa Cruz, 1971-76. Author: Settlement Patterns in Jordan, 1966, Tekoa: Excavations in 1968, 1969, Tekoa, Historical and Cultural Profile, 1970; author, photographer: Zondervan, Pictorial Ency.-Bible, 5 vols., 1975. Rsch. grantee Am. Philos. Soc., 1964. Mem. Near East Archaeol. Soc. (sec. 1969-94). Republican. Baptist. home: 412 Gay Pl Billings MT 59102-4730

HEIDBREDER, GAIL, architect, educator; b. Balt., Jan. 20, 1941; d. Gerald August and Ora Henderson (Longley) H.; children: Laura Temple Lundin, John Temple. BA, Stanford U., 1966, postgrad., 1975-78, 93—. Registered architect, Calif. With various firms, 1969-85; owner Gail Heidbreder, AIA-Architect, Porterville, Calif., 1985—; instr. architecture, constrn. and CADD, Coll. of Sequoias, Visalia, Calif., 1990—. Mem. AIA. Office: Coll of Sequoias 915 S Mooney Blvd Visalia CA 93277-2214

HEIDINGSFIELD, MICHAEL J., protective services official; b. Phila.. BS in Criminology, Fla. State U., 1973; M in Liberal Arts, Tex. Christian U., 1990; postgrad., Andrew Jackson U., 1997—. Police officer/sgt.-in-charge criminal investigation divsn. U. Tex. Sys. Police, Arlington, Ariz., 1975-78; police officer, field tng. officer, officer patrol divsn. Arlington Tex. Police Dept., 1978-81, sgt. patrol divsn., 1981-82, sgt. crimes specific task force criminal investigations, 1982-84, comdr., lt. internal affairs divsn., 1984-86, comdr., lt. spl. investigations divsn., 1986-87, shift comdr., lt. patrol divsn., 1987-88, comdr., capt. south patrol divsn., 1988-89, dep. chief of police Uniformed Svcs. Bur., 1989-91; chief of police, dir. pub. safety Scottsdale (Ariz.) Police Dept., 1991—; assoc. faculty Ottawa U. Phoenix, 1996—, Scottsdale C.C., 1993—; security cons. to the Commr. of Major League Baseball, N.Y.C., 1987-96; assessor Commn. on Accreditation for Law Enforcement Agys., Inc., Fairfax, Va., 1990—. Contbr. articles to profl. jours. Gov.'s appointee State of Ariz., Ariz. Criminal Justice Commn., 1993-97, Auto Theft Prevention Authority, 1992-93. With USAF, 1974-75, USAFR, 1980—. Recipient Exec. of Yr. award Scottsdale (Ariz.) chpt. Profl. Secs. Internat., 1991. Mem. Internat. Assn. Chiefs of Police, Police Exec. Rsch. Forum, Ariz. Assn. Chiefs of Police. Office: Scottsdale Justice Ctr 3700 N 75th St Scottsdale AZ 85251

HEIDT, RAYMOND JOSEPH, insurance company executive; b. Bismarck, N.D., Feb. 28, 1933; s. Stephen Ralph and Elizabeth Ann (Hirschkorn) H.; BA, Calif. State U., San Jose, 1963, MA, 1968; PhD, U. Utah, 1977; m. Joyce Ann Aston, Jan. 14, 1956; children: Ruth Marie, Elizabeth Ann, Stephen Christian, Joseph Aston. Claims supr. Allstate Ins. Co., San Jose, Calif., 1963-65; claims mgr. Gen. Accident Group, San Francisco, 1965-69; owner, mgr. Ray Heidt & Assocs., Logan, Utah, 1969-76; v.p. claims Utah Home Fire Ins. Co., Salt Lake City, 1976—; with Utah State U., 1970-76; dir. Inst. for Study of Pacifism and Militarism; vice-chmn. Benton County Parks and Recreation Bd., 1987-90. Active Kennewick Hist. Preservation Commn., 1989-90, 1st chmn., 1989-90, Magna Area Coun., 1992, pres. 1993-94; bd. trustees, sec. treas. Utah Ethnic and Mining Mus., 1994—. With U.S. Army, 1952-57. Decorated Bronze Star. Mem. Southeastern Wash. Adjusters' Assn. (pres. 1988-90), Utah Claims Assn. (pres. 1977-78), Lions, Am. Legion. Mormon. Republican. Home: 437 Pleasants Dr Nampa ID 83651

HEIFETS, LEONID, microbiologist, researcher; b. Russia, Jan. 5, 1926; came to U.S., 1979; s. Boris and Luba Heifets; m. Seraphima Apsit, Jan. 1955 (div. July 1978); children: Michael, Herman. MD, Med. Inst., Moscow, 1947, PhD, 1953; DSc, Acad. Med. Scis., Moscow. Asst. prof. Med. Inst., Arkhangelsk, Russia, 1950-54, assoc. prof., 1954-57; lab. dir. Mechnikov Rsch. Inst., Moscow, 1957-69; sr. rschr. Inst. for Tb, Moscow, 1969-78; rsch. fellow Nat. Jewish Hosp., Denver, 1979-80; lab. dir. Nat. Jewish Ctr., Denver, 1980—; asst. prof. Colo. U., Denver, 1980-86, assoc. prof., 1986-92, prof. microbiology, 1992—; mem. com. on bacteriology Internat. Union Against Tb, Paris, 1986—. Author: Effectiveness of Vaccination, 1968, Clinical Mycobaceriology (Clinics in Laboratory Medicine), 1996; author, editor: Drug Susceptibility, 1991; assoc. editor Tubercle; contbr. articles to profl. jours. Mem. Am. Soc. Microbiology. Office: Nat Jewish Ctr Immunology Respiratory Med 1400 Jackson St Denver CO 80206-2761

HEIL, NANCY, mayor; b. Buffalo; m. Jacob Heil; 4 children. City councillor City of Westminster, Colo., 1983-91, mayor, 1991—. Co-founder Drug and Alcohol Resource Effort; founder Cmty. Edn. Found., 1988. Recipient Disting. Citizen award Affiliated Nat. Bank, Westminster, 1983, Spirit award Rotary, 1987; named Westminster Woman of Yr. Westminster Sentinel, 1987. Office: 4800 W 92nd Ave Westminster CO 80030

HEILMAN, JUNE E., general surgeon; b. Rapid City, S.D., Jan. 29, 1947; d. Henry C. and Edna L. (Baum) H. BA, U. S.D., 1969; MD, NYU, 1973. Diplomate Am. Bd. Surgery. Fellow in trauma U. Wash., Seattle, 1974-75, fellow in cardiothoracic surgery, 1979-80, resident in gen. surgery, 1975-80; intern in surgery Parkland Meml. Hosp., Dallas, 1973-74; attending surgeon Pocatello (Idaho) Regional Med. Ctr., 1980—. Fellow ACS, S.W. Surg. Congress. Office: 333 N 18th Ave Pocatello ID 83201-3358

HEILMAN, MARLIN GRANT, photographer; b. Tarentum, Pa., Sept. 29, 1919; s. Marlin Webster and Martha (Grant) H.; widowed; 1 child, Hans. BA in Econs., Swarthmore Coll., 1941. Prin. Grant Heilman Photography, Inc., Lititz, Pa., 1948—. Author and photographer: Farm Town, 1974, Wheat Country, 1977, FARM, 1988; photographer: Psalms Around us, 1970. Capt. U.S. Army, 1941-45. Decorated Bronze Star, Croix de Guerre, French Army, 1945, Hon Legionaire Firs Clas, French Fgn. Legion, 1943.

HEIM, VICTORIA LYNNE, writer; b. Denver; d. Kenneth Carlton and Fleta Jean (Gwyn) Fagan. BA in History, U. Ariz., 1981. Poetry writer, lectr. internat. topics; lectr. U. Ariz., Ariz. Dept. Corrections, pub. schs., Ariz.; freelance writer; creator Elko (Nev.) Internat. Forum. Mem. Toastmasters (area gov. 1990-91, DTM 1992).

HEIMANN, JANET BARBARA, volunteer trail consultant; b. Santa Cruz, Calif., Dec. 18, 1931; d. John Louis and Charlotte Lucina (Burns) Grinnell; m. Richard Frank Gustav, July 10, 1953; children: David Robert, Gary Alan, Kathleen Janet. BS, U. Calif., Berkeley, 1954. Vol. trail rschr. Monterey County Pks. Dept.; appointee Carmel Valley Trail Adv. Com., 1993—. Pres. Folsom Freedom Trails, Placer County, Calif., 1980-83; chmn. Adopt-a-Trail, Folsom Lake Trail Patrol, Placer County, 1986-88; bd. dirs. Loomis Basin Horseman Assn., Placer County, 1986-87. Mem. AAUW. Republican. Home: 11565 Mccarthy Rd Carmel Valley CA 93924-9239

HEIN, KENNETH CHARLES LAWRENCE, priest, educator; b. Longmont, Colo., June 2, 1938; s. Peter Joseph and Lena Josephine (Keller) H. BA in Latin, St. Benedict's Coll., Atchison, Kans., 1964; STB, Coll. di Sant'Anselmo, Rome, Italy, 1967; ThD, U. Tübingen, Fed. Republic Germany, 1973. Benedictine monk Holy Cross Abbey, Canon City, Colo., 1960—, bus. mgr., 1985-88, treas., 1988-92; priest Roman Cath. Ch., 1969—; sem. tchr. St. Thomas Theol. Sem., Denver, 1972-74; tchr. high sch.modern langs. The Abbey Sch. Theology, Canon City, 1974-83, acad. dean, 1981-83; tchr. St. Anselm's Coll., Manchester, N.H., 1983-85; chaplain Fitzsimon's Army Med. Ctr., Aurora, Colo., 1989-92; adminstr. Holy Cross Abbey, Canon City, Colo., 1992—; bd. dirs. Theol. Inst. Holy Cross Abbey, 1974-78; mem. Med.-Moral Bd. St. Thomas More Hosp., 1980—; presenter in Anglican Roman Cath. dialog, 1975-76, med.-moral issues, 1979—; presenter in Benedictine/Meth. Conf., Rome, 1994. Contbr. numerous articles to profl. jours.; translater Psalms of Bible, 1989. Founder Abbey Students Aid to Poor, 1974-83. Office: Holy Cross Abbey 2951 E Us Highway 50 Canon City CO 81212-2781

HEINDL, CLIFFORD JOSEPH, physicist; b. Chgo., Feb. 4, 1926; s. Anton Thomas and Louise (Fiala) H. B.S., Northwestern U., 1947, M.S., 1948; A.M., Columbia U., 1950, Ph.D., 1959. Sr. physicist Bendix Aviation Corp., Detroit, 1953-54; orsort student Oak Ridge Nat. Lab., 1954-55; asst. sect. chief Babcock & Wilcox Co., Lynchburg, Va., 1956-58; research group supr. Jet Propulsion Lab., Pasadena, Calif., 1959-65, mgr. research and space sci., 1965—. Served with AUS, 1944-46. Mem. AIAA, Am. Nuclear Soc., Health Physics Soc., Planetary Soc., Am. Phys. Soc. Home: 179 Mockingbird Ln South Pasadena CA 91030-2047 Office: 4800 Oak Grove Dr Pasadena CA 91109-8001

HEINE, JOHN PARKER, urologist, medical administrator; b. San Francisco, Sept. 18, 1944; s. Parker F. and Anne (Bruper) H.; m. Janet K. Nederhus, May 25, 1966; children: David J., Erika L. BS, Loyola U., 1966; MD, U. Calif., San Francisco, 1970. Diplomate Am. Bd. Urology. Intern San Francisco Gen. Hosp., 1971; resident in urology U. Calif. Med. Ctr., San Francisco, 1976; pvt. practice Fremont, Calif.; chief of staff Washington Hosp., Fremont, Calif., 1985; pres. Found. Alameda Contra Costa County Med. Assn., 1995-96, pres., 1996—. Maj. USAF NG, 1970-78. Roman Catholic. Office: John P Heine MD 1999 Mowry Ave Ste 2M Fremont CA 94538-1723

HEINER, DOUGLAS CRAGUN, pediatrician, educator; b. Salt Lake City, July 27, 1925; s. Spencer and Eva Lillian (Cragun) H.; m. Joy Luana Wiest, Jan. 8, 1946; children: Susan, Craig, Joseph, Marianne, James, David, Andrew, Carolee, Pauli. *Great grandparents Martin and Adelgunda Heiner left Waldorf, Germany in 1847 for the United States. Grandfather Daniel Heiner migrated west with his family in 1859, helping to settle Morgan, Utah in 1863. He later became mayor of Morgan and a member of the first Utah Legislature. Great grandfather Roswell Stevens headed west in 1847 and joined the "Mormon Battalion" on its historic march from Council Bluffs to San Diego. His daughter Martha married Daniel Heiner. Great great great grandfather Patrick Cragun was a member of the 1775 Boston Tea Party, which lead to the Revolutionary War.* BS, Idaho State Coll., 1946; MD, U. Pa., 1950; PhD, McGill U., 1969. Intern Hosp. U. Pa., Phila., 1950-51; resident, fellow Children's Med. Ctr., Boston, 1953-56; asst. prof. pediatrics U. Ark. Med. Ctr., Little Rock, 1956-60; assoc. prof. pediatrics U. Utah Med. Ctr., Salt Lake City, 1960-66; fellow in immunology McGill U., Montreal, 1966-69; prof. of pediatrics Harbor-UCLA Med. Ctr., Torrance, 1969-84; disting. prof. of pediatrics UCLA Sch. Medicine, 1985-94, prof. emeritus, 1994—. Author: Allergies to Milk, 1980; mem. editl. bd. Jour. Allergy and Clin. Immunology, 1975-79, Allergy, 1981-88, Jour. Clin. Immunology, 1981-87, Pediat. Asthma, Allergy and Immunology, 1986-94; contbr. over 150 original articles to profl. jours. and chpts. to books. Scoutmaster Boy Scouts Am., Salt Lake City, 1963; com. chmn. Rancho Palos Verdes, 1979-81; high coun. mem. Mormon Ch., Rancho Paos Verdes, 1983-86. 1st lt. med. corps U.S. Army, 1952-53, Korea. Recipient Disting. Alumni award Idaho State U., 1987. Fellow Am. Pediatric Soc., Am. Acad. Allergy and Clin. Immunology (food allergy com. 1981—), Am. Coll. Allergy and Immunology; mem. Soc. for Pediatric Rsch., Western Soc. for Pediatric Rsch. (Ross award 1961), Am. Assn. Immunologists, Clin. Immunology Soc., Am. Acad. Pediatrics. Republican.

HEINLEIN, OSCAR ALLEN, former air force officer; b. Butler, Mo., Nov. 17, 1911; s. Oscar A. and Katherine (Canterbury) H.; B.S., U.S. Naval Acad., 1932; M.S., Calif. Inst. Tech., 1942; M.S. in Mech. Engring., Stanford, 1949; certificate in mining U. Alaska, 1953; grad. Air War Coll., 1953; student spl. studies U. Ariz., 1956-57, Eastern Wash. U., Clark County Community Coll., Las Vegas, Nev., 1988, U. Nice, France; D.D., Universal Sem., 1970; AA Clark County Community Cm. Catharine Anna Bangert, May 1, 1933 (div. Apr. 1937); 1 dau., Catharine Anna; m. 2d, Mary Josephine Fisher, Aug. 25, 1939 (dec. Dec. 1977); 1 son, Oscar Allen III; m. 3d, Suzanne Birke, Feb. 23, 1980; 1 son, Michael Andre Bertin. Marine engr. Atlantic Refining Co., Phila., 1934; civil engr. Annapolis Mineral Devel. Co., Calif., 1935-37; enlisted as pvt. U.S. Army, 1937, advanced through grades to col., 1944; comdr. Ladd AFB, Alaska, 1953-54, 11th Air Div., Fairbanks, Alaska, 1954, Air Force Logistics Command Support Group, Vandenberg AFB, Calif., 1960-65, prof. air sci. U. Ariz., Tucson, 1955-58; insp. Gen. Mobile Air Material Area, Ala., 1958-60; ret. 1965; now cons.; pres. O.A. Heinlein Merc. Co., Butler, Mo., 1934—; vis. prof. U. Nev., Reno; dep. dir. civil def. Boulder City, Nev., 1967; dir., sec. Boulder Dam Fed. Credit Union, 1973-79; mem. Boulder City Police Adv. Com., 1976; ordained minister Bapt. Ch., 1976. Active Boy Scouts Am. Mem. Clark County (Nev.) Republican Central Com., 1966, Exec. com., 1970; mem. Rep. Central Com., 1966; Rep. candidate Nev. Assembly, 1972; mem. Boulder City Charter Commn. Mem. community coll. adv. bd. U. Nev., 1970. Served with USN, 1928-32; to 2d lt. USMC, 1932-34. Decorated Legion of Merit, Air medal, Army, Navy and Air Force commendation medals. Mem. Inst. Aero. Scis., Am. Meteorol. Soc., Nat. Research Assn., Am. Radio Relay League, SAR, Am. Polar Soc., VFW, Daedalians, Mensa, So. Nev. Amateur Radio Club, Inst. Amateur Radio, Quarter Century Wireless Assn., Ret. Officers Assn., Air Force Assn., Nat. Rifle Assn. (life), Armed Forces Communications and Electronics Assn., USS Nevada Assn., CAP, Am. Legion, Am. Assn. Ret. Persons, West Coast Amateur Radio Service, Soc. Wireless Pioneers. Mason, Nev. Rifle and Pistol Assn. (bd. dirs.), Vet. Wireless Operator's Assn. Clubs: MM (San Diego); Intertel (Ft. Wayne, Indiana); Missile Amateur Radio (pres. 1961-65 Vandenberg AFB); Explorers (N.Y.C.); Arctic Circle Prospectors', High Jumpers (Fairbanks, Alaska); Boulder City Gem and Mineral; Stearman Alumnus; Marines Memorial (San Francisco). Author: Big Bend County, 1953. Inventor. Home: 107 Wyoming St Boulder City NV 89005-2818

HEINS, MARILYN, college dean, pediatrics educator, author; b. Boston, Sept. 7, 1930; d. Harold and Esther (Berow) H.; m. Milton P. Lipson, 1958; children: Rachel, Jonathan. A.B., Radcliffe Coll., 1951; M.D., Columbia U., 1955. Diplomate Am. Bd. Pediatrics. Intern, N.Y. Hosp., N.Y.C., 1955-56; resident in pediatrics Babies Hosp., N.Y.C., 1956-58; asst. pediatrician Children's Hosp. Mich., Detroit, 1959-78; dir. pediatrics Detroit Receiving Hosp., 1965-71; asst., assoc. dean student affairs Wayne State U. Med. Sch., Detroit, 1971-79; assoc. dean acad. affairs U. Ariz. Med. Coll., Tucson, 1979-83, vice dean, 1983-88, prof. pediatrics, 1985-88. Author: (with Anne M. Seiden) Child Care/Parent Care, 1987; mem. editorial bd. Jour. AMA, 1981-91; contbr. articles to profl. jours. Bd. dirs. Planned Parenthood So. Ariz., 1983, pres., 1988-89, Ariz. Ctr. for Clin. Mgmt.,1991—, Nat. Bd. Med. Examiners, 1983-88; mem. adv. bd. So. Ariz. Women's Fund, 1992—, Ariz. State Hosp., 1985-88. Recipient Alumni Faculty Service award Wayne State U., 1972, Recognition award, 1977, Women on the Move Achievement award YWCA Tucson, 1983, Tuscon women of Vision award Weizmann Inst., 1997, pres.'s disting. svc. award Ariz. Med. Assn., 1997; mem. Ariz. Ctr. Clin. Mgmt. 1990—. Home: 6530 N Longfellow Dr Tucson AZ 85718-2416

HEINZ, RONEY ALLEN, civil engineering consultant; b. Shawano, Wis., Dec. 29, 1946; s. Orville Willard and Elva Ida (Allen) H.; m. Judy Evonne Olney, Oct. 30, 1965. *Beyond the business world, life in engineering and construction management, Roney Heinz is involved in the spiritual world as the international director of the Canaan Christians Fund. The primary project of this nonprofit, volunteer organization has been the survival of several thousand people through the horrid conditions of a five-year war in Sierra Leone, West Africa. A call for help came to Roney Heinz when several designated Christian safehaven villages were totally destroyed by the warfare. The fund helped the survivors with food, clothing, medications, and shelter. Now the task is rebuilding and getting the people back to self sufficiency.* BSCE, Mont. State U., 1973. Surveyor U.S. Army Corps Engrs., Seattle, 1966-73; civil engr. Hoffman, Fiske, & Wyatt, Lewiston, Idaho, 1973-74, Tippetts-Abbott-McCarthy-Stratton, Seattle, 1977-79; asst. editor Civil Engring. Mag. ASCE, N.Y.C., 1974-77; constrn. mgr. Boeing Co., Seattle, 1979-83; owner, gen. mgr. Armwavers Ltd., South Bend, Wash., 1983—; pres. Great Walls Internat. Inc., Elma, Wash., 1993-95, Heinz Internat., Inc., 1995—; mem. dams and tunnels del. to China, People to People Internat., Spokane, 1987; mem. U.S. com. on Large Dams. Asst. editor Commemorative Book Internat. Congress on Large Dams, 1987; contbr. articles to profl. publs., including Civil Engring. Mag., Excavator Mag., Internat. Assn. for Bridge and Structural Engring., Japan Concrete Inst., others. Dir. Canaan Christians Fund, Aberdeen, 1993—; bd. dirs. Seaman's Ctr., Aberdeen, Wash., 1990—. Recipient First Quality award Asphalt Paving Assn. Wash., 1991. Mem. ASCE (sec. met. sect. 1975-76, assoc. mem. forum), ASTM (Student award 1973)., USCOLD. Republican. Lutheran. Office: Armwavers Ltd PO Box 782 South Bend WA 98586-0782 *Construction project management is the specialty of the firms owned and operated by Roney Heinz. Heinz International, Inc. is developing a network of mostly retired engineers nationwide and internationally. The concept of working with retired engineers is beneficial to all parties. Retired engineers can work without long term commitments but with a network of other engineers backing them. The client gets the benefit of engineers with an entire career of experience and a firm specializing in construction management rather than engineering design. The clients are normally the design firm, the owner, or the financier. The projects can be anywhere.*

HEINZE, DAVID C., business administration educator; b. Paterson, N.J., June 3, 1941; s. E. Charles and Susan (Jen) H. BS in Math., Ariz. State U., 1963, PhD in Quantitative Bus. Analysis, 1969; MS in Actuarial Sci., U. Wis., 1964. Prof. bus. Rochester (N.Y.) Inst. Tech., 1969-74, Va. Commonwealth U., Richmond, 1974-79, No. Ariz. U., Flagstaff, 1979-81, Calif. State U., Chico, 1981—; cons. Eastman Kodak, Rochester, 1971-74, Omark, Oroville, Calif., 1984. Author: Statistical Decision Analysis for Management, 1973, Management Science, 1978, 82, Fundamentals of Managerial Statistics, 1980; contbr. articles to profl. jours. Knapp fellow, NDEA fellow. Mem. Phi Kappa Phi, Beta Gamma Sigma. Office: Calif State U. Dept Bus Chico CA 95929

HEINZE, RUTH-INGE, Asian studies educator, researcher, writer; b. Berlin, Nov. 4, 1919; came to U.S., 1955; d. Otto and Louise (Preschel) H. Gr. Latinum, Interpreter Coll., Berlin, 1967; BA, U. Calif., Berkeley, 1969, MA, 1971, PhD, 1974. Producer, writer Ednl. Broadcast, Berlin, 1963-73; lectr. U. of Chiang Mai, Thailand, 1971-72; staff rsch. asst. human devel. dept. U. Calif., San Francisco, 1974, rsch. assoc. Ctr. for S.E. Asian Studies, 1974—; lectr. Mills Coll., Oakland, Calif., 1974; adj. faculty Saybrook Inst., San Francisco, 1984—, Calif. Inst. for Integral Studies, 1984-93,. Author: The Role of the Sangha in Modern Thailand, 1977, Tham Khwan - How to Contain the Essence of Life, 1982, Trance and Healing in Southeast Asia Today, 1988, Shamans of the 20th Century, 1991, The Search for Visions, 1994. Prodr. Universal Dialogue Series, Berkeley, 1979—; nat. dir. Ind. Scholars of Asia, 1981—; bd. dirs. Oakland Asian Cultural Ctr., 1987-93. Recipient grant Am. Inst. for Indian Studies, 1975,78, Fulbright-Hays Rsch. grant, 1978-79. Mem. Internat. Assn. for Study of Traditional Asian Medicine, Internat. Soc. for Shamanic Rsch., Parapsychology Rsch. Group, Spiritual Emergency Network, Nat. Pictographic Soc., Ind. Scholars of Asia, Assn. for Asian Studies, Oakland Asian Cultural Ctr. Home and Office: 2321 Russell St Apt 3C Berkeley CA 94705-1959

HEISLER, BRADLEY PAUL, lawyer. BS in Engring., Walla Walla Coll., 1988; JD, U. Calif., Davis, 1991. Bar: Calif. 1991, U.S. Dist. Ct. (ea. dist.) Calif. 1991, U.S. Patent and Trademark Office, 1992. Pvt. practice Roseville, Calif., 1994—. Office: 3017 Douglas Blvd Ste 300 Roseville CA 95661-3850

HEISSER-METOYER, PATRICIA, psychologist, organizational consultant; b. L.A., May 15, 1946. BA in Psychology, Calif. State U., L.A., 1966; PhD, U. Calif., Irvine, 1976. Clin. psychology fellow UCLA Neuro-Psychiat. Inst., Westwood, Calif., 1971-72; sr. staff psychologist Cedar-Sinai Med. Ctr., L.A., 1973-84; dir. clin. tng., asst. prof. Antioch U., Marina Del Rey, Calif., 1993—; cons. Fed. Emergency Mgmt. Agy., L.A., 1992-94, Musicians Assistance Program, L.A., 1995-96, Internat. Ho. of Blues, 1994-96, County Dept. Mental Health, L.A.; bd. dirs. , dir. contbns. and devel. L.A. Jazz Soc. Mem. AFTRA, APA, NAACP, Am. Mgmt. Assn., Alpha Kappa Alpha. Office: Antioch U 13274 Fiji Way Marina Del Rey CA 90292

HEISTER, CARLA GAYLE, library director; b. Rock Falls, Ill., May 16, 1950; d. Andrew George and Elizabeth Mary (Brooks) Fisher; m. Robert Allen Heister, Aug. 2, 1980; children: Leah Elizabeth, Ellen Clare. BS in Biology, No. Ill. U., 1979, MA in Libr. Sci., 1982; MS in Biol. Scis., U. Ill., 1989. Libr. Ill. Natural History Survey, Champaign, 1982-92; dir. Quinney Libr. Utah State U. Coll. Natural Resources, Logan, 1992—. Co-compiler: The Natural Resources of Illinois, 1987. Mem. Am. Soc. Info. Sci., Utah

Soc. for Environ. Edn., Spl. Librs. Assn. (chair environ. and resource mgmt. div. 1993-94). Presbyterian. Office: SJ and Jessie E Quinney Nat Resources Rsch Libr UMC 5260 Logan UT 84322

HEITLER, BRUCE F., entrepreneur; b. Denver, June 12, 1945; s. Emmett H. and Dorothy (Shwayder) H.; m. Susan Kaye McCrensky, June 6, 1971; children: Abigail, Sara, Jesse, Jacob. BA, Yale U., 1967, JD, 1972; MCP, U. Calif., Berkeley, 1969. Bar: Colo. 1973. Assoc. Holme Roberts & Owen, Denver, 1972-74; project mgr. Cen. Devel. Group, Denver, 1974-76; pres. Heitler Devel., Inc., Denver, 1976-96; vice chmn., bd. dirs. Nexus Greenhouse Corp., Northglenn, Colo., 1982—; pres., bd. dirs. Colo. Biogenix, Inc., Denver; owner, operator Discovery Door Children's Ctr., Denver, 1990—; chmn. Lowry AFB Redevel. Authority, 1994—. Trustee E. Roosevelt Inst. for Cancer Rsch., Denver, 1975-94, Social Sci. Found. U. Denver, 1989—; active Yale Devel. Bd., New Haven, 1986-90. Mem. Colo. Yale Assn. (pres. 1991-93), Assn. Yale Alumni (bd. govs. 1994—), Cactus Club (pres. 1986-88). Jewish. Office: Heitler Devel Inc Ste D315 1410 Grant St Denver CO 80203-1846

HEITMAN, GREGORY ERWIN, state official; b. Lewiston, Idaho, June 7, 1947; s. Elmer William and Carmelita Rose Ann (Kinzer) H.; m. Phyllis Ann Pryor, Sept. 25, 1982. BS in Math., U. Idaho, 1969, MBA, 1971; student, Wash. State U., 1965-67. Student communications dir. Assoc. Students U. Idaho, Moscow, 1970-72, advisor, apt. mgr. dept. housing, 1971-72; traffic fatality analyst Idaho Dept. Transp., Boise, 1973-74; ops. mgr. Region IV Health & Welfare State of Idaho, Boise, 1974-78, supr. computer svcs., div. environ. in health and welfare, 1978-85; coord. field svcs., program dir. Idaho Ctr. for Vital Stats. and Health Policy, Boise, 1985—; acting dir. Idaho Ctr. for Health Statistics, Boise, 1988-89, spl. asst. program and policy devel., 1989—; mem. med. records adv. com. Boise State U., 1987—, cons., lectr. 1987—. Active various charitable orgns.; precinct committeeman Dem. of Latah County, 1972; election day coord. Ada County, 1986; vol. Am. Cancer Soc., 1990, Easter Seals, 1992, Arthritis Found., 1996. Mem. Idaho Pub. Health Assn., Assn. Vital Records and Health Statistics, Idaho Pub. Employees Assn., Assn. Govt. Employees. Roman Catholic. Home: 5103 Shalecrest Ct Boise ID 83703-3442 Office: Idaho Vital Stats PO Box 83720 Boise ID 83720-0036

HEJHALL, ROY CHARLES, electrical engineer; b. Duluth, Minn., Aug. 11, 1932; s. Charles Joseph Hejhall and Florence Mary (Patwell) Wales; m. Virginia Lee Hoke, June 9, 1956 (div. 1968); children: Jeffrey, Jody, Julie; m. Audrey Ruth Bailey, June 28, 1970. BS in Engring., U.S. Naval Acad., 1956.; Commd. ensign USN, 1956, advanced through grades to lt., 1961; tech. staff Motorola, Phoenix, 1961-96; ret.; tech. advisor Am. Radio Relay League, Newington, Conn., 1977—. Contbr. articles to profl. jours. Mem. Elks. Republican.

HELANDER, TERRILL WEBB, educational psychologist; b. Pasadena, Calif., Apr. 11, 1958; d. Allen Paul and Dorothy Winder (Cannon) Webb; m. Wayne Richard Helander, June 27, 1982; children: Margaret, Thomas, David, Andrew. BA, Pitzer Coll., Claremont, Calif., 1980; MA, Calif. State U., Northridge, 1982; PhD, U. So. Calif., L.A., 1990. Lic. ednl. psychologist, Calif. advanced pupil pers. credential. Sch. psychologist Hacienda-La Puente (Calif.) Unified Sch. Dist., 1982-89, Placentia (Calif.) Unified Sch. Dist., 1989-91; pvt. practice Pasadena, Calif., 1990—; cons. Young & Healthy, Pasadena, 1991—; advisor dist. adv. com. Claremont (Calif.) Unified Sch. Dist., 1994-95; supr. interns Pasadena Mental Health Ctr., 1990-91; presenter workshop on stress Orange County Dept. Edn., 1991. Mem. Pasadena Symphony Jrs., 1985-87; bd. mem. B'nai Simcha Presch., Arcadia, Calif., 1991; sch. vol. Parent Faculty Assn., Condit Elem. Sch., Claremont, 1994—. Recipient award Harry Steele Found., 1978. Republican. Office: Youth & Healthy 325 S Oak Knoll Pasadena CA 91101

HELBOCK, RICHARD WILLIAM, editor, publisher; b. Portland, Oreg., Mar. 24, 1938; s. Earnest Richard and Lola Anita (Mobley) H.; m. Lucille C. Cook, Aug. 24, 1963 (div. June 1979); children: Richard Cook, Shannon Noel; m. Cathy R. Clark, May 5, 1991. BS in Engring., U.S. Mil. Acad., 1960; MA in Geography, U. Pitts., 1965, PhD in Geography, 1973. Rsch. assoc. Regional Econ. Devel. Inst., Pitts., 1965-68; from asst. to assoc. prof. N.Mex. State U., Las Cruces, 1968-81; editor, pub. La Posta Publs., Las Cruces and Portland, 1969—; rsch. assoc. Pakistan Inst. Devel. Econs., Islamabad, 1974-75. Author: Postmarks on Postcards, 1985, Combat Infanty Mail, 1991, Western Post Offices, 1993; editor in charge La Posta: Jour. of the Am. Postel history, 1969—. Named Disting. Philatelist, U.S. Classics Soc., 1991. Mem. Am. Philatelic Soc. Office: La Posta Publs PO Box 135 Lake Oswego OR 97034

HELD, NANCY B., perinatal nurse, lactation consultant; b. Winchester, Mass., Sept. 4, 1957; d. Ann and Laurence Babine; m. Lew Held, May 22, 1976; children: David, Jessica. BSN, NYU, 1979; MS, U. Calif., San Francisco, 1992. Cert. lactation and childbirth educator, Am. Soc. Psychoprophylaxis Obstetrics; internat. bd. cert. lactation cons. Labor/delivery nurse Pascack Valley Hosp., Westwood, N.J., 1979-83; obstetrics educator Drs. Pinski, Wiener & Grasso, Westwood, N.J., 1982-85; ob/gyn office nurse Drs. Power Hagbom Holter & Clark, San Francisco, 1986-87; asst. to dir. maternity svcs. Women's Health Assn., Greenbrae, Calif., 1987-89; perinatal edn. and lactation ctr. clin. coord. Calif. Pacific Med. Ctr., San Francisco, 1989—; owner North Bay Lamaze, 1988—; speaker and cons. in field. Recipient Founders Day award, NYU. Fellow Am. Coll. Childbirth Educators; mem. Assn. Women's Health Obstetric and Neonatal Nursing (spkr. nat. con. 1993, nat. rsch. utilization team 1993), Am. Soc. Psychoprophylaxis (chpt. co-pres.), Nurses Assn. of Am. Coll. Ob/Gyn, Internat. Childbirth Educators Assn., Internat. Lactation Cons. Assn., Sigma Theta Tau.

HELDER, DAVID ERNEST, artist, educator; b. Seattle, Feb. 4, 1947; s. Reinard Wright and Maxine Edda (Spiva) H.; m. Sallye Ann Giles, Aug. 7, 1976; 1 child, Julian Oliver. AA, Yuba Coll., Marysville, Calif., 1966; BA in Sculpture, Calif. Coll. Arts and Crafts, Oakland, 1969, MFA, 1971; MA in Aesthetic Edn., Stanford U., 1975. Aesthetic edn. and art direction cons. U. Mpls. Super Computer Inst., 1988—. San Francisco Arts Festival, 1980, Stamford (Conn.) Art Assn., 1988, Exhibited in solo shows at Wake Gallery, Cape Town, South Africa, 1972, Margaret Jensen Gallery, San Francisco, 1976, Park Gallery, San Francisco, 1977, Lyle Tuttle Gallery, San Francisco, 1979, Jaymark Gallery, San Francisco, 1981; group shows include San Diego Art Inst., 1988, Alligator Gallery, San Francisco, 1988, Helio Gallery, N.Y.C., 1991, Rayco Gallery, San Francisco, 1991, North East Juried Exposition, Mass., 1993. Home: 644 Stanyan St San Francisco CA 94117-1807 Studio: 636 Stanyan St San Francisco CA 94117-1807

HELDT, JEAN-PAUL, management consultant; b. Bischviller, Alsace, France, May 1, 1951; came to U.S., 1979; s. Paul C. and Marthe L. (Heinrich) H.; children: Jeremy, Juliane, Jonathan. MD, Louis-Pasteur U., Strasbourg, 1975; MA in Cross-Cultural Studies, Loma Linda (Calif.) U., 1982, MPH, 1987; Diploma in Cmty. Health, U. London, 1986. Diplomate Am. Bd. Ophthalmology. Dir. nat. blindness prevention program Ministry Pub. Health, Internat. Eye Found., Conakry, Guinea, 1982-83; med. dir. Afghan Refugee Eye Care Program League of Red Cross Socs., Mardan, Pakistan, 1984-85; prof. ophthalmology, pub. health U. Montemorelos, Mex., 1987-89; health programs coord. World vision Internat., Hanoi, Vienam, 1992-93; health programs cons. World vision Internat., Bangkok, 1993; area dir. Asia-Pacific Habitat for Humanity Internat., 1994-95; cons., founder Genesys Mgmt. Sys. 2000, Newbury Park, Calif., 1982—; lectr. in field; condr. workshops in field; bd. dirs. Internat. Cons. Network, 1991, health devel. internat. coord., 1990-92. Corrs. Internat. Rev. of Trachoma, Paris, 1982-84; contbr. articles to profl. jours. McGill U. Postdoctoral fellow, 1979-80; Fuller Theol. Sem. Sch. World Mission vis. scholar, 1993-94. Mem. Am. Pub. Health Assn. (Outstanding Student award 1987), Nat. Coun. for Internat. Health, Am. Acad. Ophthalmology (mem. book/jour. link subcom., disaster relief subcom.). Home and Office: 4210 Greenwood St Newbury Park CA 91320-5229

HELFERT, ERICH ANTON, management consultant, author, educator; b. Aussig/Elbe, Sudetenland, May 29, 1931; came to U.S., 1950; s. Julius and Anna Maria (Wilde) H.; m. Anne Langley, Jan. 1, 1983; children: Claire L., Amanda L. BS, U. Nev., 1954; MBA with high distinction, Harvard U., 1956, DBA, 1958. Newspaper reporter, corr., Neuburg, Fed. Republic of Germany, 1948-52; rsch. asst. Harvard U., 1956-57; asst. prof. bus. policy San Francisco State U., 1958-59; asst. prof. fin. and control Grad. Sch. Bus. Adminstrn., Harvard U., 1959-65; internal cons., then asst. to pres., dir. corp. planning Crown Zellerbach Corp., San Francisco, 1965-78, asst. to chmn., dir. corp. planning, 1978-82, v.p. corp. planning, 1982-85; mgmt. cons., San Francisco, 1985—; co-founding dir. Modernsoft, Inc.; mem. Dean's adv. coun. San Francisco State Bus. Sch., sch. fin. Golden Gate U.; bd. dirs., past chmn. and pres. Harvard U. Bus. Sch. No. Calif.; trustee Saybrook Inst. Author: Techniques of Financial Analysis, 1963, 9th ed. 1997, Valley of the Shadow, 1997, Valuation, 1966, (with others) Case Book on Finance, 1963, Controllership, 1965; contbr. articles to profl. jours. Exch. student fellow U.S. Inst. Internat. Edn., 1950; Ford Found. doctoral fellow, 1956. Mem. Assn. Corp. Growth (past pres., bd. dirs. San Francisco chpt.), Inst. Mgmt. Cons., Commonwealth Club, Phi Kappa Phi. Roman Catholic. Home: 111 W 3rd Ave # 401 San Mateo CA 94402-1521 Office: 1777 Borel Pl Ste 508 San Mateo CA 94402-3514

HELFFERICH, MERRITT RANDOLPH, technology transfer administrator; b. Hartford, Conn., Aug. 10, 1935; s. Reginald Humphrey and Virginia (Merritt) H.; m. Carla Anne Ostergren, July 11, 1959 (div. 1977); children: Deirdre Alida, Tryntje Bronwyn; m. April Evalyn Crosby, Aug. 24, 1985. BA, U. Alaska, 1966; MPA, Harvard U., 1990. Surveyor Golden Valley Electric Assn., Fairbanks, Alaska, 1965-66; engring. technician Geophys. Inst., U. Alaska, Fairbanks, 1966-69, field technician, rocket flight meteorologist Poker Flat Rsch. Range, 1969-76, head tech. svcs., 1976-83, asst. dir., 1986-88, assoc. dir., 1988-93; ice technician Humble Oil Co./U. Alaska, S.S. Manhattan, Northwest Passage Voyage, 1969; assoc. v.p. human resource devel. U. Alaska, Fairbanks, 1983, asst. to chancellor, 1983-86, dir. Elvey addition/Internat. Arctic Rsch. Ctr. project, 1994-95; exec. v.p. U. Alaska Tech. Devel. Corp., Fairbanks, 1994—; legis. liaison U. Alaska, Fairbanks, 1983-86; adv. bd. NSF Polar Ice Coring Office, Fairbanks, 1989-94; bd. dirs. Internat. Small Satellite Orgn., Washington, Snedden Parks Found., Northern Alaska Environ. Ctr., 1994-95. Mem. editl. bd. U. Alaska Press, Fairbanks, 1986-94. Commr. Alaska Women's Commn., Juneau, 1988-89; mem., co-chair Main St. Fairbanks, 1990-94; mem. Fairbanks Native Cultural Ctr. Com., 1991-93; chair Fairbanks North Star Borough Riverfront Commn., 1992-95, mem., 1995—; bd. dirs. Suedden Parks Found., 1993—, No. Alaska Environ. Ctr., 1994-95; pres. Interior Alaska Land Trust; bd. dirs. Alaska High-Tech Bus. Coun. Helfferich Glacier named in his honor U.S. Bd. Geographic Names, 1971; recipient Antarctic Svc. medal NSF, 1971, Nick Begich Scholarship Fund award, 1989, Alumni Achievement award U. Alaska Alumni Assn., 1993; elected Coll. of Fellows, U. Alaska, Fairbanks, 1997. Fellow Explorers Club (chair exploration com. Alaska Yukon chpt. 1991-92, chair 1995); mem. AAAS, Soc. Rsch. Adminstrs., Am. Geophys. Union, Assn. Univ. Tech. Mgrs., Rotary Club of Fairbanks. Democrat. Home: PO Box 80769 Fairbanks AK 99708-0769 Office: U Alaska Tech Devel Corp 250 Chushman St Ste 3D Fairbanks AK 99701

HELFORD, PAUL QUINN, communications educator, academic administrator; b. Chgo., June 27, 1947; s. Norman and Eleanor (Kwin) H.; m. Leslie Gale Weinstein, July 11, 1971; children: Ross Michael, Benjamin Keith. BA, U. Ill., 1969; MA, Northeastern Ill. U., 1977. Cert. tchr., Ill., Oreg., Ariz. Tchr. John Hersey H.S., Arlington Heights, Ill., 1969-73; freelance writer Mill Valley, Calif., 1973-75; mgr., program dir. Sta. KOZY-TV, Eugene, Oreg., 1976-88, mktg., sales, and program dir. Group W Cable, 1984-88; prodr., with mktg. Northland Broadcasting, Flagstaff, Ariz., 1989-91; lectr. cinema and broadcasting No. Ariz. U., Flagstaff, 1989—, acad. coord. for instrnl. TV, 1995—; dir. Native Am. Video Workshops, 1991—, Flagstaff Festival of the Arts Film Festival, 1992, No. Ariz. U. Instrnl. TV Programming, 1994—; writer New Times, Phoenix, 1992, Flagstaff Live!, 1996—. Writer, prodr. Paul Helford's Hollywood Oldies, 1976-81, In Review, 1981, Live from the Fair, 1981-85, Group W Cable Minutes, 1984-85, Bad Horror and Sci. Fiction, 1985 (Award for Cable Excellence 1986), KOZY movie promotional spots 1976-88 (Award for Cable Excellence 1984, 88, CLIO award nomination 1988, 1989); contbr. articles to profl. jours. Recipient CLIO award 1984, 86, Cable Mktg. Grand award, 1981, 85. Mem. Nat. Assn. Cable Programmers.

HELGESON, DUANE MARCELLUS, retired librarian; b. Rothsay, Minn., July 2, 1930; s. Oscar Herbert and Selma Olivia (Sateren) H.; B.S., U. Minn., 1952. Librarian, Chance-Vought Co., Dallas, 1956-59, System Devel. Corp., Santa Monica, Calif., 1959-62, Lockheed Aircraft, Burbank, Calif., 1962-63, C.F. Braun Co., Alhambra, Calif., 1963-74; chief librarian Ralph M. Parsons Co., Pasadena, Calif., 1974-79; pres. Mark-Allen/Brokers-in-Info., Los Angeles, 1976-80; phys. scis. librarian Calif. Inst. Tech., Pasadena, 1980-84; corp. librarian Montgomery Watson, Pasadena, 1985-94, ret. 1994. mem. adv. bd. Los Angeles Trade Tech. Coll., 1974-79, U. So. Calif. Library Sch., 1974-79. Served with USAF, 1952-54. Mem. Spl. Libraries Assn. (chmn. nominating com. 1974). Co-editor: (with Joe Ann Clifton) Computers in Library and Information Centers, 1973. Home: 2706 Ivan Hill Ter Los Angeles CA 90039-2717

HELLER, DEAN, state official. Sec. of state State of Nev., Carson City. Home: 1520 Andorra Dr Carson City NV 89703-2308 Office: Sec of State Capitol Complex 101 S Carson St Carson City NV 89710*

HELLER, JOSEPH, health professional; b. Tarnopol, Poland, June 15, 1940; came to U.S., 1956; s. Simon and Hinda (Kaufman) H. Group supr. JCT Propulsion Lab., Pasadena, Calif., 1962-71; pres. Rolf Inst., Boulder, Colo., 1972-78; founder, pres. Hellerwork, Mt. Shasta, Calif., 1979—. Author: Bodywise. Office: Hellerwork 406 Berry St Mount Shasta CA 96067

HELLER, JULES, artist, writer, educator; b. N.Y.C., Nov. 16, 1919; s. Jacob Kenneth and Goldie (Lassar) H.; m. Gloria Spiegel, June 11, 1947; children: Nancy Gale, Jill Kay. AB, Ariz. State Coll., 1939; AM, Columbia U., 1940; PhD, U. So. Calif., 1948; DLitt, York U., 1985. Spl. art instr. 8th St. Sch., Tempe, Ariz., 1938-39; dir. art and music Union Neighborhood House, Auburn, N.Y., 1940-41; prof. fine arts, head dept. U. So. Calif., 1946-61; vis. asso. prof. fine arts Pa. State U., summers 1955, 57; dir. Pa. State U. (Sch. Arts), 1961-63; founding dean Pa. State U. (Coll. Arts and Architecture), 1963-68; founding dean Faculty Fine Arts York U., Toronto, 1968-73; prof. fine arts Faculty of Fine Arts, York U., 1973-76; dean Coll. Fine Arts, Ariz. State U., Tempe, 1976-85; prof. art Coll. Fine Arts, Ariz. State U., 1985-89; prof. emeritus, dean emeritus, 1990—; vis. prof. Silpakorn U., Bangkok, Thailand, 1974, Coll. Fine Arts, Colombo, Sri Lanka, 1974, U. Nacional de Tucumán, Argentina, 1990, U. Nacional de Cuyo, Mendoza, Argentina, 1990; lectr., art juror; Cons. Open Studio, 1975-76; mem. vis. com. on fine arts Fisk U., Nashville, 1974. Printmaker; exhibited one man shows, Gallery Pascal, Toronto, U. Alaska, Fairbanks, Alaskaland Bear Gallery, Visual Arts Center, Anchorage, Ariz. State U., Lisa Sette Gallery, 1990, Centro Cultural de Tucumán, San Miguel de Tucumán, 1990; exhibited numerous group shows including Canadian Printmaker's Showcase, Pollack Gallery, Toronto, Mazelow Gallery, Toronto, Santa Monica Art Gallery, L.A. County Mus., Phila. Print Club, Seattle Art Mus., Landau Gallery, Kennedy & Co. Gallery, Bklyn. Mus., Cin. Art Mus., Dallas Mus. Fine Arts, Butler Art Inst., Oakland Art Mus., Pa. Acad. Fine Arts, Santa Barbara Mus. Art, San Diego Gallery Fine Arts, Martha Jackson Gallery, N.Y.C., Yuma Fine Arts Assn., Ariz., Toronto Dominion Centre, Amerika Haus, Hannover, Fed. Rep. Germany, U. Md., Smith-Andersen Galleries, Palo Alto, Calif., Grunewald Ctr. Graphic Arts, L.A., Univ. So. Fla., Tampa, Sheldon Meml. Gallery, Lincoln, Nebr., Santa Cruz (Calif.) Mus., Drake U., Iowa, Bradley U., Ill., Del Bello Gallery, Toronto, Honolulu Acad. Fine Arts; represented in permanent collections, Nat. Mus. Am. Art Smithsonian Instn., Washington, Long Beach Mus. Art, Library of Congress, York U., Allan R. Hite Inst. of U. Louisville, Ariz. State U., Tamarind Inst., U. N.Mex., Zimmerli Mus. Rutgers U., N.J., Can. Council Visual Arts Bank, also pvt. collections; author: Problems in Art Judgment, 1946, Printmaking Today, 1958, revised, 1972, Papermaking, 1978, 79; co-editor: North American Women Artists of the Twentieth Century, 1995; contbg. artist: Prints by California Artists, 1954, Estampas de la Revolucion Mexicana, 1948; illustrator: Canciones de Mexico, 1948; author numerous articles. Adv. bd. Continental affairs com. Americas Soc., 1983-86. With USAAF, 1941-45. Can. Coun. grantee; Landsdowne scholar U. Victoria; Fulbright scholar, Argentina, 1990. Mem. Coll. Art Assn. (Disting. Teaching of Art award 1995), Authors Guild, Internat. Assn. Hand Papermakers (steering com. 1986—), Nat. Found. Advancement in the Arts (visual arts panelist 1986-90, panel chmn. 1989, 90), Internat. Assn. Paper Historians, Internat. Coun. Fine Arts Deans (pres. 1968-69). Home: 6838 E Cheney Dr Paradise Valley AZ 85253-3525

HELLER, PHILIP, lawyer; b. N.Y.C., Aug. 12, 1952; s. Irving and Dolores (Soloff) H.; divorced; 1 child, Howard Philip. BA summa cum laude, Boston U., 1976, JD, 1979. Bar: Mass. 1979, N.Y. 1980, U.S. Ct. Appeals (1st and 9th cirs.) 1980, U.S. Supreme Ct. 1983, Calif. 1984, U.S. Dist. Ct. (all dists.) Calif., U.S. Dist. Ct. (ea. and so. dists.) N.Y., U.S. Dist. Ct. Mass. Law clk. to judge Cooper U.S. Dist. Ct. (so. dist.) N.Y., N.Y.C., 1979; ptnr. Fagelbaum & Heller LLP, L.A. Mem. ABA (litigation sect.), Calif. Bar Assn., L.A. County Bar Assn. Democrat. Office: Fagelbaum & Heller LLP Ste 3270 2029 Century Park E Los Angeles CA 90067

HELLMAN, F(REDERICK) WARREN, investment advisor; b. N.Y.C., July 25, 1934; s. Marco F. and Ruth (Koshl) H.; m. Patricia Christina Sander, Oct. 5, 1955; children: Frances, Patricia H., Marco Warren, Judith. BA, U. Calif., Berkeley, 1955; MBA, Harvard U., 1959. With Lehman Bros., N.Y.C., 1959-84, ptnr., 1963-84; exec. mng. dir. Lehman Bros., Inc., N.Y.C., 1970-73; pres. Lehman Bros., Inc., 1973-75; ptnr. Hellman Ferri Investment Assocs., 1981-89, Matrix Ptnrs., 1981—; gen. ptnr. Hellman & Friedman, San Francisco; bd. dirs. DN & E Walter, APL Ltd., Levi Strauss & Co., Williams-Sonoma, Inc., Il Fornaio (Am.) Corp., Franklin Resources, Inc., Mobile Media Comms., Powerfood, Inc.; trustee The Brookings Inst., chmn. com. on jobs. Bd. dirs. Children Now; trustee The San Francisco Found. Mem. Bond Club, Piping Rock Club, Century Country Club, Pacific Union Club. Office: Hellman & Friedman 1 Maritime Plz Fl 12 San Francisco CA 94111-3404

HELLYER, CONSTANCE ANNE, communications executive, writer; b. Puyallup, Wash., Apr. 22, 1937; d. David Tirrell and Constance (Hopkins) H.; m. Peter A. Corning, Dec. 30, 1963 (div. 1977); children: Anne Arundel, Stephanie Deak; m. Don W. Conway, Oct. 12, 1980. BA with honors, Mills Coll., 1959. Grader, researcher Harvard U., Cambridge, Mass., 1959-60; researcher Newsweek mag., N.Y.C., 1960-63; author's asst. Theodore H. White and others, N.Y.C., 1964-69; freelance writer, editor Colo., Calif., 1969-75; writer, editor Stanford (Calif.) U. Med. Ctr., 1975-79; communications dir. No. Calif. Cancer Program, Palo Alto, 1979-82; comm. dir. Stanford Law Sch., Palo Alto, 1982—. Founding editor (newsletters) Insight, 1978-80, Synergy, 1980-82, Stanford Law Alum, 1992-95; editor (mag.) Stanford Lawyer, 1982—; contbr. articles to profl. jours. and mags. Recipient silver medal Coun. for Advancement and Support Edn., 1985, 89, award of distinction dist. VII, 1994. Mem. No. Calif. Sci. Writers Assn. (co-founder, bd. dirs. 1979-93), Phi Beta Kappa. Democrat. Home: 2080 Louis Rd Palo Alto CA 94303-3451 Office: Stanford Law Sch Stanford CA 94305-8610

HELMER, DAVID ALAN, lawyer; b. Colorado Springs, May 19, 1946; s. Horton James and Alice Ruth (Cooley) H.; m. Jean Marie Lamping, May 23, 1987. BA, U. Colo., 1968, JD, 1973. Bar: Colo. 1973, U.S. Dist. Ct. Colo. 1973, U.S. Ct. Claims, 1990, U.S. Ct. Appeals (10th cir.) 1993, U.S. Supreme Ct. 1991. Assoc., Neil C. King, Boulder, Colo., 1973-76; mgr. labor rels., mine regulations Climax Molybdenum Co., Inc. div. AMAX, Inc., Climax, Colo., 1976-83; prin. Law Offices David A. Helmer, Frisco, Colo., 1983—; sec., bd. dirs. Z Comm. Corp., Frisco, 1983-90; cmty. bd. dirs. Norwest Bank Colo., N.A., Frisco. Editor U. Colo. Law Rev., 1972-73; contbr. articles to legal jours. Bd. dirs. Summit County Council Arts and Humanities, Dillon, Colo., 1980-85, Advisor Advocates for Victims of Assault, Frisco, 1984—; legal counsel Summit County United Way, 1983-95, v.p., bd. dirs., 1983-88; bd. dirs., legal counsel Summit County Alcohol and Drug Task Force, Inc., Summit Prevention Alliance, 1984—, Pumpkin Bowl Inc./Children's Hosp. Burn Ctr., 1989—. Chmn. Summit County Reps., 1982-89; chmn. 5th Jud. Dist. (Colo.) Rep. Com., 1982-89; chmn. resolutions com. Colo. Rep. Conv., 1984, del. Rep. Nat. Com., 1984; chmn. reaccreditation com. Colo. Mountain Coll., Breckenridge, 1983; founder, bd. dirs. Dillon Bus. Assn., 1983-87, Frisco Arts Coun., 1989—; atty. N.W. Colo. Legal Svcs. Project, Summit County, 1983—; mcpl. judge Town of Dillon, Colo., 1982—, Town of Silverthorne, Colo., 1982—. Master sgt. USAR, 1968-74. Mem. ABA, Colo. Bar Assn. (bd. govs. 1991—, mem. exec. com. 1995—), Continental Divide Bar Assn. (pres. 1991-95, v.p. 1995-97), Summit County Bar Assn. (pres. 1990—), Dillon Corinthian Yacht Club (commodore local club 1987-88, 95—, vice commodore, 1994, club champion 1989-91, 94, 95, Winner of Colo. Cup, Colo. State Sailing Championships 1991), Phi Gamma Delta. Lutheran. Home: PO Box 300 352 Snake River Dr Dillon CO 80435-0300 Office: PO Box 868 611 Main St Frisco CO 80443-0868

HELMER, M. CHRISTIE, lawyer; b. Portland, Oreg., Oct. 8, 1949; d. Marvin Curtis and Inez Bahl (Corwin) H.; m. Joe D. Bailey, June 23, 1979; children: Tim Bailey, Bill Bailey, Kim Easton. BA in English magna cum laude, Wash. State U., 1970; JD cum laude, Lewis & Clark Coll., 1974. Bar: Oreg. 1974, U.S. Supreme Ct. 1975, U.S. Ct. Appeals (9th cir.) 1975. Assoc. Miller Nash, Portland, 1974-81, ptnr., 1981—; mem. Oreg. Bd. Bar Examiners, Portland, 1978-81; del. 9th Cir. Jud. Conf., 1984-87, mem. exec. com., 1987-90. Author: Arrest of Ships, 1985. Mem. ABA, Oreg. Bar (bd. govs. 1981-84, treas. 1983-84), Maritime Law Assn., Internat. Bar Assn., Classical Chinese Garden Soc. (bd. dirs.), Multnomah Athletic Club, Phi Beta Kappa. Office: Miller Nash 111 SW 5th Ave Ste 205-24 Portland OR 97204-3639

HELMINIAK, CLARE, public health service officer; b. Woodruff, Wis., Mar. 12, 1956; d. Harry H. and Catherine (Specht) H.; m. Gene Carnicom; children: Whitney Alexis, Heath Britten, J. Kirk. BS in Zoology summa cum laude, U. Wis., 1978; MD, Med. Coll. Wis., 1982, MPH. Intern Edward W. Sparrow Hosp., Lansing, Mich., 1982-83; gen. med. officer Mescalero (N.Mex.) IHS Hosp., 1983-84; gen. med. officer dept. pediatrics Alaska Native Med. Ctr., Anchorage, 1984-85; adminstr. hepatitis B program Alaska Native Health Bd., Anchorage, 1985-88; asst. dir. hepatitis B program Alaska Area Native Health Svc., Anchorage, 1985-88; med. officer Parker (Ariz.) Indian Health Svc. Hosp., 1989—; diabetes com. officer Parker Indian Health Svc. Hosp., intermittent acting clin. dir., Phoenix area pharmacy and therapeutics com., Phoenix area Patient Care Component physician trainer, 1989—; preceptorship in radiology St. Bincent's Hosp., Dublin, Ireland, 1981; preceptorship in internal medicine and rural medicine Nat. Health Svc. Corps., Appalachian Regional Hosp., Hazard, Ky., 1981; externship in family medicine Wis. Acad. Family Physicians, Kaukauna (Wis.) Clinic and Cmty. Hosp., 1979. Treas. Parker Piranha Swim Team, 1994—; active La Paz County 4H, 1994—. Decorated Bronze Star; recipient Phoenix Area Exceptional Performance award, 1992, Outstanding Svc. award Intertribal Coun. Ariz., 1992, USPHS Unit Commendation medal, 1996. Mem. AAUW, Am. Soc. for Circumpolar Health, MUMPS Users Group, Assn. Mil. Surgeons the U.S. (Ribbon award), Commd. Officers Assn. USPHS (Ribbon award), Res. Officers Assn. (Ribbon award), Mo. Foxtrotting Horse Assn. Democrat. Roman Catholic. Office: USPHS/IHS RR 1 Box 12 Parker AZ 85344-9703

HELMKE, BEATE HELEN, administrator; b. Dortmund, Federal Republic of Germany, Feb. 14, 1941; came to U.S., 1971; d. Hugo and Maria (L.) H. BA, Paedagogische Hochschule, 1967; MA in Linguistics, U. Mich., 1972; PhD, Mich. State U., 1978. Cert. data user (U.S. Dept. Commerce); gerontologic counseling. Program dir. SCS Engrs., Redmond, Wash., 1979, Wash. State Dept. of Social and Health Svcs., Olympia, 1980, Bolte Homes Corp., Seattle, 1981—. Contbr. articles to profl. jours. Disting. scholar, Heinrich Hertz Fund, 1971; Teaching fellow, U. Mich., 1972; recipient Dissertation award, 1977. Mem. Wash. State Alt. Care Orgn. (past pres.), Phi Delta Kappa.

HELMUTH, PHILIP ALAN, tax consultant; b. Alhambra, Calif., Dec. 29, 1965; s. Melvin I. and Elsie (Borkholder) H. Student, MiraCosta Coll., 1985-89, Palomar Coll., 1989-90. Data entry operator Melco Bus. Svc., Vista, Calif., 1980-83, bookkeeper, 1983-91, ptnr., tax cons., 1992-95, owner, 1995—; bookkeeper Underwater Schs. of Am., Oceanside, 1985-86; owner, notary pub. Vista, 1987—; owner Melco Bus. Svcs., Vista, 1995—. Mem. Nat. Notary Assn. (com. mem. editl. adv. com. 1990-93, pub. image com. 1990-93), Nat. Assn. Enrolled Agts., Calif. Soc. Enrolled Agts. (Palomar chpt. dir. 1995-96, 2d v.p. 1996—), Escondido Grad. Spokesman Club (sec. 1991-92, pres. 1992-93, treas. 1993-95). Office: Melco Bus Svc Ste 102 410 S Santa Fe Ave Vista CA 92084-6163

HELSPER, JAMES T., surgical oncologist, researcher, educator; b. Mpls., Mar. 29, 1924; s. Salvius John and Gretchen Louise (Gleissner) H.; m. Mildred Ann Belinsky, June 11, 1951 (div. Aug. 1972); children: James Thomas Jr., Richard Scott, Paige Carla; m. Carolyn Marie Harrison, Dec. 26, 1975; 1 child, Brian Harrison Helsper. BS, St. Vincent Coll., 1945; MD, Jefferson Med. Coll., 1947; postgrad., U. Pa., 1949-50. Diplomate Am. Coll. Surgeons, Am. Bd. Surgery, 1956; lic. Calif., N.Y., N.J., Fla., Mass. Intern Med. Ctr., Jersey City, N.J., 1947-48, residency, 1948-49; resident surgery U.S. Naval Hosp., Portsmouth, Va., 1951-52; chief resident surgery Queens Gen. Hosp., N.Y., 1952-53; asst. resident surgery Med. Ctr. for Cancer and Allied Diseases, N.Y., 1953-54, spl. fellow head and neck svc., 1954, sr. resident surgery, 1955-57; mem. surg. staff Huntington Meml. Hosp., Pasadena, Calif., Kenneth Norris Jr. Cancer Hosp.; attending surgeon L.A. County U. So. Calif. Med. Ctr.; assoc. clin. prof. surgery U. So. Calif. Sch. Medicine, L.A., prof. clin. surgery, 1996—; head melanoma site team U. So. Calif. Comprehensive Cancer Ctr., L.A.; mem. head and neck site team U. So. Calif. Comprehensive Cancer Ctr.; asst. clin. prof. surgery Loma Linda (Calif.) U. Sch. Medicine; chmn. tumor bd. L.A. County Gen. Hosp., 1963, 70, 81-82; cancer liaison fellow Am. Coll. Surgeons L.A. County/USC Med. Ctr., Norris Cancer Hosp.; from student and corpsman to capt. USNR, 1943-84. Mem. AMA, ACS (bd. govs. 1994), Am. Cancer Soc. (Calif. divsn., L.A. county unit chmn. profl. edn. com., 1965-67, v.p. for program 1967-69, 84—, pres. elect 1969-70, 85-86, pres. 1970-71, 86-87, chmn. nom. com. 1971-72, Calif. divsn. chmn. profl. edn com. 1974-75, mem. profl. edn. com. 1971-76, mem. bd. dirs. 1967—, mem. pub. info. com. 1969-71, mem. Macomber Legacy Com. 1975-82, mem. rsch. com. 1987-88, named Man of The Year 1991), Am. Fedn. Clin. Oncologic Socs., Am. Radium Soc., Am. Soc. Clin. Oncology, Calif. Med. Assn. (mem. com. on cancer), Calif. Med. Assn. (mem. com. on cancer), N.Y. Acad. Medicine, L.A. County Med. Assn. (mem. com. on cancer, jr. sect. pres. 1966), L.A. Surg. Soc., L.A. Acad. Medicine, Pasadena Med. Soc., Internat. Union Against Cancer (mem. sci. com.), Pan-Pacific Surg. Assn., Soc. Surg. Oncology (James Ewing Soc.), Soc. Head and Neck Surgeons (pres. 1988-89), Flying Physicians Assn., The Adventurer's Club, Quiet Birdmen. Home: 580 Arbor St Pasadena CA 91105-1536 Office: 50 Bellefontaine St Ste 301 Pasadena CA 91105-3132

HEMANN, RAYMOND GLENN, research company executive; b. Cleve., Jan 24, 1933; s. Walter Harold Marsha Mae (Colbert) H.; BS, Fla. State U., 1957; postgrad. U.S. Naval Postgrad. Sch., 1963-64, U. Calif. at Los Angeles, 1960-62; MS in Systems Engring., Calif. State U., Fullerton, 1970, MA in Econs., 1972, cert. in tech. mgmt. Calif. Inst. Tech., 1990; m. Lucile Tinnin Turnage, Feb. 1, 1958; children: James Edward, Carolyn Frances; m. Pamela Lehr, Dec. 18, 1987. Aero. engring. aide U.S. Navy, David Taylor Model Basin, Carderock, Md., 1956; analyst Fairchild Aerial Surveys, Tallahassee, 1957; research analyst Fla. Rd. Dept., Tallahassee, 1957-59; chief Autonetics div. N.Am. Rockwell Corp., Anaheim, Calif., 1959-69; v.p., dir. R. E. Manns Co., Wilmington, Calif., 1969-70; mgr. Avionics Design and Analysis Dept. Lockheed-Calif. Co., Burbank, 1970-72, mgr. Advanced Concepts div., 1976-82; gen. mgr. Western div. Arinc Research Corp., Santa Ana, 1972-76; dir. Future Requirements Rockwell Internat., 1982-85; dir. Threat Analysis, Corp. Offices, Rockwell Internat., 1985-89; pres., chief exec. officer Advanced Systems Rsch., Inc., 1989—; adj. sr. fellow Ctr. Strategic and Internat. Studies, Washington, 1987—; bd. dirs. Fla. State U. Rsch. Found., 1995—, bd. dirs. Mgmt Svc. Inc.; bd. dirs., pres. Associated Aviation, Inc., 1980—; chmn. adv. com. Coll Engring. Fla State U./Fla. A&M U., 1995—; cons. various corps. U.S. govt. agys.; sec., bd. dirs. Calif. State U., Fullerton, Econs. Found.; mem. naval studies bd. panels NAS, 1985—, Arms Control Working Group; asst. prof. ops. analysis dept. U.S. Naval Postgrad. Sch., Monterey, Calif., 1963-64, Monterey Peninsula Coll., 1963; instr. ops. analysis Calif. State U., Fullerton, 1963, instr. quantitative methods, 1969-72; program developer, instr. systems engring. indsl. rels. ctr. Calif. Inst. Tech., 1992-96; lectr. Brazilian Navy, 1980, U. Calif., Santa Barbara, 1980, Yale U., 1985, Princeton U., 1986, U.S. Naval Postgrad. Sch., 1986, Ministry of Def., Taiwan, Republic of China, 1990; Calif. Inst. Tech. Assocs., 1992—; mem. exec. forum Calif. Inst. Tech., 1991—; Chmn. comdr.'s adv. bd. CAP, Calif. Wing; reader Recording for the Blind, 1989—. With AUS, 1950-53. Syde P. Deeb scholar, 1956; recipient honor awards Nat. Assn. Remotely Piloted Vehicles, 1975, 76; named to Hon. Order Ky. Cols., 1985. Comml., glider and pvt. pilot. Fellow AAAS, AIAA (assoc.); mem. IEEE, Ops. Rsch. Soc. Am., Air Force Assn., Nat. Coalition for Advanced Mfg. (adv. bd. 1990—), N.Y. Acad. Scis., Assn. Old Crows, L.A. World Affairs Coun., Phi Kappa Tau (past pres.). Episcopalian. Contbr. articles to profl. jours. and news media. Office: Advanced Sys Rsch Inc 33 S Catalina Ave Ste 202 Pasadena CA 91106-2426

HEMION, DWIGHT ARLINGTON, television producer, director; b. New Haven, Mar. 14, 1926; s. Dwight Arlington and Bernice Ruby (Berquist) H.; m. Katherine Bridget Morrissy, Sept. 1, 1973; children—Katherine, Dwight Gustav. Student pub. schs., Verona, N.J. Asso. dir. ABC-TV, N.Y.C., 1946-49; TV dir. Tonight Show, NBC-TV, N.Y.C., 1950-60; dir. Perry Como TV show, N.Y.C., 1960-67; producer/dir. Yorkshire Prodns., N.Y.C., 1967-70; producer/dir. TV spls. in assn. with ATV, London; producer/dir. Smith-Hemion Prodns., Los Angeles, 1975-90. Dir.: Frank Sinatra: A Man and His Music, 1965 (Emmy award TV Acad. Arts and Scis.); The Sound of Burt Bacharach, 1969, Singer Presents Burt Bacharacn, 1970, Barbra Streisand and Other Musical Instruments, 1973, Steve and Eydie-Our Love is Here to Stay, 1975, America Salutes Richard Rodgers: The Sound of His Music, 1976, Bette Midler-Ol' Red Hair is Back, 1977, Ben Vereen ... His Roots, 1977, Steve and Eydie Celebrate Irving Berlind, 1978, IBM Presents Baryshinikov on Broadway, 1979 (Emmy award), Goldie and Kids ... Listen to Us!, 1982 (Emmy award), Sheena Easton...Act I, 1983 (Emmy award), Anne Murray's Winter Carnival...From Quebec, 1984, 4 Emmy Award Shows, 5 Christmas in Wasington shows, 6 TV Acad. Hall of Fame shows, 50th Predl. Inaugural Gala, Neil Diamond Hello Again, opening cermemonies Liberty Weekend, Barbra Streisand One Voice, We The People Contitutional Gala, Julie Andrews the Sound of Christmas, All Star Salute to Our Troops, Barbra Streisand...The Concert, Disney's Young Musicians Symphony Orchestra, Disney's American Teachers Awards, and many others. Served in AC U.S. Army, 1944-46. Named Dir. of Year in TV Dirs. Guild Am., 1965. Mem. Purcival Country Club. Office: Smith-Hemion Prodns Inc PO Box 15 1438 N Gower Los Angeles CA 90028-0015*

HEMMERS, OLIVER ANDREAS, physicist; b. Berlin, Aug. 23, 1963; s. Hans-Joachim and Margot Erna (Laskowski) H.; m. Anne Pantelas, Nov. 22, 1992. Diploma, Tech. U. Berlin, 1988, postgrad., 1988-92, Dr.rer.nat. in Physics, 1993. Rsch. assoc. Fritz-Haber-Inst. Max Planck Gesellschaft, Berlin, 1993-94; rsch. assoc. U. Las Vegas, 1994—. Author: Korrelationseffekte in kleinen Molekulen, 1993; contbr. articles to profl. jours. Mem. Am. Phys. Soc., German Phys. Soc., Chess Club. Office: U Las Vegas Dept Chemistry Box 454003 4505 S Maryland Pkwy Las Vegas NV 89154-9900

HEMMES, PAUL RICHARD, JR., health products executive; b. Staten Island, N.Y., June 14, 1944; s. Paul Richard and Wanda (Wisniewski) H.; m. Sonja D. Hansen, June 19, 1965; children: Paul C., Jeffrey M. BS in Chemistry, Clarkson Coll., 1966; PhD in Physical Chemistry, Polytechnic Inst. Bklyn., 1970; postdoctoral, U. Utah, 1969-70. Prof. physical chemistry Rutgers U., Newark, 1970-81; supr. Miles Labs. Research and Devel., Elkhart, Ind., 1981-85; dir. Miles Labs. Mfg., Elkhart, 1985-88; v.p. mfg. Angenics Inc., Cambridge, Mass., 1988-89; v.p. rsch. & devel. Environ. Test Syss., Elkhart, 1989-96; v.p. ops. Abaxis Inc., Sunnyvale, Calif., 1996—. Mem. edit. bd. Microchem. Jour., 1974-81, assoc. editor; mem. edit. bd. Jour. of Molecular Liquids, 1978-81; also articles; patentee in field. Office: Abaxis Inc 1320 Chesapeake Terr Sunnyvale CA 94009

HEMMINGS, PETER WILLIAM, orchestra and opera administrator; b. London, Apr. 10, 1934; s. William and Rosalind (Jones) H.; m. Jane Frances Kearnes, May 19, 1962; children—William, Lucy, Emma, Rupert, Sophie. Grad. Gonville and Caius Coll., Cambridge, 1957; LL.D. (hon.), Strathclyde U., Glasgow, 1978. Clk., Harold Holt Ltd., London, 1958-59; planning mgr. Sadlers Wells Opera, London, 1959-65; gen. adminstr. Scottish Opera, Glasgow, 1962-77; gen. mgr. Australian Opera, Sydney, 1977-79; mng. dir. London Symphony Orch., 1980-84; gen. dir. Los Angeles Music Ctr. Opera Assn., 1984—; gen. mgr. New Opera Co., London, 1956-65, dir. Royal Acad. Music; gen cons. Compton Verney Opera Project. Served to lt. Brit. Signal Corps, 1952-54; Fed. Republic Germany. Fellow Royal Scottish Acad. Music, Royal Acad. Music (hon.); mem. Am. Friends of Sadeer Wells (pres. 1994—), Internat. Assn. Opera Dirs., 1977-79, Opera Am. (v.p.). Anglican. Club: Garrick (London). Home: 775 S Madison Ave Pasadena CA 91106-3831 Office: LA Music Ctr Opera 135 N Grand Ave Los Angeles CA 90012-3013

HEMP, CHRISTINE ELIZABETH, poet, educator; b. Seattle, July 22, 1956; d. Peter La Tourette and Mary (McClinton) H. Student, Bowdoin Coll., 1976-77; BA in Humanities, Willamette U., 1978; postgrad., Oxford (Eng.) U., 1984-85; MA in English, Middlebury Coll., 1986. Poet-in-the-schs. Mass. Edn. Cultural Collaborative, 1987-92; instr. expository writing Harvard U. Ext. Sch., 1987-92; instr. writing seminars various cos., 1990—; art critic SAnta Fe Mag. of Arts, 1992—; instr. poetry U. N.Mex., 1993—; writer Recursos of Santa Fe, 1995; instr. Haystack Mountain Sch. Crafts, Deer Isle, Maine, 1995, writing retreat at Ghost Ranch, Abiquiu, N.Mex., 1996; poet-in-residence Voyageurs Nat. Pk., Minn, 1996. Contbr. poems Simon Schuster Anthology, 1996. Named Poet of Yr., New Eng. Assn. Tchrs. of English, 1982; fellow Bread Loaf Writers Conf., 1986; grantee Mass. Arts Lottery, Somerville, 1986, 87, Money for Women grantee Barbara Deming Found., N.Y.C., 1994. Home and Office: PO Box 541 Taos NM 87571

HEMPENIUS, GERALD EDWARD, real estate broker; b. Chgo., Sept. 6, 1934; s. John Garrett and Jessie Fern Hempenius; m. Patricia A. Woodcock, Jan. 28, 1955; children: Sharyl Lynn Hempenius Britt, Jeffrey Alan. BS, Whittier Coll., 1956; MS, NYU, 1957. Cert. Comml. Investment Mem. Nat. Assn. Realtors, Grad. Realtors Inst., Exchange Mktg. Specialist, Cert. Hotel Adminstr. Store mgr. J.C. Penney, various cities, Calif., 1957-75; real estate agt. Gold Coast Realty, Morro Bay, Calif., 1976-77; real estate broker, owner Com-Spec Properties, Inc., San Luis Obispo, Calif., 1977—, cons., 1986—; pres., bd. dirs. Calif. Lodging Industry Assn., Sacramento, 1984-88; mem. conf. com. Calif. Hotel and Motel Assn. and Forte Hotels Calif., 1991-96. Bd. dirs. Visitors and Conf. Bur., San Luis Obispo, 1991-96. Mem. Citizen Amb. Program, Seattle, 1996. Mem. Nat. Assn. Realtors, Nat. Coun. Exchangors, Nat. Assn. Counselors, Calif. Assn. Realtors, Morro Bay C. of C. (pres., bd. dirs. 1980-86), Rotary (pres. 1990, Paul Harris fellow 1984, Rotarian of Yr. award 1984). Republican. Office: Com-Spec Properties Inc 1422 Monterey St Ste A-201 San Luis Obispo CA 93401

HEMPHILL, WILLIAM ALFRED, III, marketing executive; b. Pitts., Mar. 3, 1949; s. William Alfred II and Virgie Mae (Fisher) H.; m. Sandra Lynn von Lohen, Feb. 17, 1973; 1 child, Michelle Ellise. BS, USAF Acad., 1972; postgrad., Air Force Squadron Officer's Sch., 1977, Ariz. State U., 1981-85, Air Force Command and Staff Coll., 1995-96. Commd. 2d lt. USAF, 1972, advanced through grades to capt., 1976; radar navigator SAC USAF, Blytheville AFB, Ark., 1974-77; B-52 radar navigator SAC USAF, Rapid City, S.D., 1977-79; resigned USAF, 1979; maj. USAFR, 1988, area res. liaison officer, 1988-96; wings res. coord., 1996—; mktg. rep. Sperry Def. Systems, Phoenix, 1979-82, Sperry Space Div., Phoenix, 1982-83; product devel. mgr. Motorola Govt. Electronics Group, Tempe, Ariz., 1983-84; mktg. dir. Conrac SCD Div., Duarte, Calif., 1984-88; cons. Upland, Calif., 1988; nat. sales mgr. TEAC Am., Inc., Montebello, Calif., 1989-92; mktg. mgr. Mekel Engring, Walnut, Calif., 1992-94; venture devel. mgr. Thermo Tech. Ventures, Idaho Falls, 1994-96; deputy program mgr. TTV, Idaho Falls, 1996—. Author: (with other) A Programmable Display Generator System, 1982. Position paper writer Rep. Nat. Com., 1980; pres. bd., performer Concert Dance Theater, 1988-92; mem. West End Rep. Club, Ontario, Calif.; vestry mem. St. Mark's Episc. Ch., Upland, Calif., 1988-91, dir. Homeless Shelter, 1991—. Mem. Am. Mgmt. Assn., Tech. Mktg. Soc. Am., Air Force Assn., USAF Acad. Grad. Assn. Episcopalian. Lodge: Elks.

HEMRY, LARRY HAROLD, former federal agency official, writer; b. Seattle, Jan. 4, 1941; s. Harold Bernard and Florence Usborne (Achilles) H.; m. Nancy Kay Ballantyne, July 10, 1964 (div. Apr. 1976); children: Rachel Dalayne, Aaron Harold, Andrew LeRoy. BA, Seattle Pacific Coll., 1963; postgrad., Western Evang. Sem., Portland, Oreg., 1969, 70. Ordained to ministry Free Meth. Ch., 1968. Clergyman Free Meth. Ch., Vancouver, B.C., Can., 1963-64, Mt. Vernon, Wash., 1968-69; clergyman Colton (Oreg.) Community Ch., 1969-71; edit clk. Moody Bible Inst., Chgo., 1964-66; pres., founder Bethel Enterprises, Colton, 1969-71; immigration insp. U.S. Immigration and Naturalization Svc., Sumas, Wash., 1972-96. Author, historian: Some Northwest Pioneer Families, 1969, The Hemry Family History Book, 1985; author: An Earnest Plea to Earnest Christians, 1969. chmn. com. to establish and endow the James A. Hemry meml. scholarship fund Seattle Pacific U., 1975. żellow Seattle Pacific U. (Centurians Club); mem. The Nature Conservancy, The Sierra Club, The Audubon Soc. Home: PO Box 532 Sumas WA 98295-0532

HEMSLEY, DAVID LEE, computer company executive; b. Salzburg, Austria, Oct. 19, 1950; came to U.S., 1953; s. Glen Merrill and Arlene Lofthouse (Pulsipher) H.; m. Donna Elizabeth Hoover, Aug. 10, 1973; children: Richard, Melody, Jill, Teresa, Ryan, Amy, Justin, Darren. BA in Math., San Jose State U., 1976, MS in Math., 1983. Software engr. CSC, Mountain View, Calif., 1976-77, Link Flight Simulation, Sunnyvale, Calif., 1977-82, Ford Aerospace, Palo Alto, Calif., 1982-84, Kaiser Electronics, San Jose, Calif., 1984-89, Prodata, Inc., Citrus Heights, Calif., 1991-92, Jones Futurex, Rocklin, Calif., 1993-94; pres. System Design Automation, Placerville, Calif., 1989—. Inventor software, 1989. Republican. Mem. LDS Ch. Office: System Design Automation PO Box 2171 Placerville CA 95667-2171

HENAGER, CHARLES HENRY, civil engineer; b. Spokane, Wash., July 11, 1927; s. William Franklin and Mary Agnes (Henry) H.; m. Dorothy Ruth Parker, May 6, 1950; children: Charles Henry, Jr., Donald E., Roberta R. BS in Civil Engring., Wash. State U., 1950. Registered profl. engr., Wash. Instrumentman Wash. State Dept. Hwys., Yakima, 1950-52; engr. Gen. Electric Co., Richland, Wash., 1952-62; shift supr., reactor GE, Richland, Wash., 1962-63, sr. engr., 1963-65; sr. devel. engr. Battelle Pacific N.W. Labs., Richland, 1965-68, sr. rsch. engr., 1968—. Contbr. articles to profl. jours.; patentee in field. With USN, 1945-46. Fellow Am. Concrete Inst. (tech. activities com. 1987-89, Del Bloem award 1986), ASTM (subcom. 1980-92), ASCE (pres. Columbia sect. 1961-62); mem. Kennewick Swim Club (pres. 1962-63), Sigma Tau, Tau Beta Pi, Phi Kappa Phi. Republican. Methodist. Home: 3413 S Huntington Loop Kennewick WA 99337-2572

HENCH, PHILIP KAHLER, physician; b. Rochester, Minn., Sept. 19, 1930; s. Philip Showalter and Mary Genevieve (Kahler) H.; m. Barbara Joan Kent, July 10, 1954; children: Philip Gordon, John Kahler, Amanda Kent. BA, Lafayette Coll., 1952; MD, U. Pitts., 1958; MSc in Medicine, U. Minn., 1965. Dir. emeritus staff & alumni affairs Scirpps Clinic Med. Group; intern U. Colo. Med. Ctr., 1958-59; fellow in medicine and rheumatology Mayo Graduate Sch., Rochester, Minn., 1959-63; with Inst. for Arthritis and Metabolic Diseases, NIH, Bethesda, Md., 1963-64; asst. div. rheumatology Scripps Clinic and Rsch. Found., La Jolla, Calif., 1965-66, assoc., 1966-70, assoc. mem., 1970-74, mem., head, 1974-82, sr. cons., 1982—, adj. asst. mem. dept. neuropharmacology, mem. dept. acad. affairs; asst. clin. prof. U. Calif. Sch. Medicine, San Diego; cons. to pharm. cos.; mem. People to People Mission to China on study of Aging. Contbr. articles on rheumatic diseases, pain and sleep disorders to profl. jours.; mem. editorial com. Rheumatism Revs., 1974-84; editorial reviewer Arthritis and Rheumatism, Jour. Rheumatology, 1985—; bd. spl. cons. Patient Care mag., 1987—. Mem. bd. advisors San Diego Opera; mem. U. Calif. San Diego Police Dept. Sr. Vol. Program. Recipient Arthritis Found. award (6), San Diego chpt., 1971-80; Philip S. Hench scholar Mayo Grad. Sch. Medicine, 1965. Fellow ACP, Am. Coll. Rheumatology (chmn. nonarticular rheumatism study group 1975-82, com. on preventive and rehab. medicine 1984-85, com. on rheumatologic practice 1975-77); mem. AMA, Nat. Soc. Clin. Rheumatologists (sec., treas.) Am. Pain Soc., Calif. Med. Assn., Internat. Assn. for Study Pain, La Jolla Acad. Medicine (pres. 1994-96), Arthritis Found (bd. govs. San Diego chpt., Best Doctors in Am. award 1992-93, 94-95, 96-97), San Diego Hist. Soc., San Diego Mus. Fine Arts, San Diego Opera (bd. advisors). Republican. Home: 7856 La Jolla Vista Dr La Jolla CA 92037-3530 Office: Scripps Clinic & Rsch Found 10666 N Torrey Pines Rd La Jolla CA 92037-1027

HENDERSON, D. AUSTIN, computer scientist; b. London, Ont., Can., Jan. 25, 1943; came to U.S., 1966; s. Dugald Austin and Nancy (Gilbert) H.; m. Lynne Ellen McHugh, Aug. 29, 1981; children: Kimberly, Mark, Brooke. Honors BSc in Math. and Sci., Queen's U., Kingston, Ont., 1965; MS in Computer Sci., U. Ill., 1967; PhD in Elec. Engring., MIT, 1975. Rsch. asst. computation structures and programming MIT, Cambridge, 1967-75; cons. on computer graphics and networks MIT Lincoln Lab., Lexington, Mass., 1968-75; cons. computer graphics and applications programmin Bolt Beranek and Newman Inc., Cambridge, 1970-75, computer scientist, 1975-78; mem. rsch. staff Xerox Palo Alto (Calif.) Rsch. Ctr., 1978-86; PARC-EuroPARC liaison Rank Xerox Cambridge (Eng.) EuroPARC, 1987-89; v.p. Fitch Richardson Smith, Worthington, Ohio, 1989; area mgr. design, use and shared spaces Sys. Scis. Lab., Xerox Palo Alto Rsch. Ctr., 1989-90; mgr. user interface architecture Xerox Corp., Palo Alto, 1990-94; user experience architect advanced tech. group Apple Computer, Inc., Cupertino, Calif, 1994-95, mgr. user experience lab., 1995-96, mgr. discourse architecture lab. Apple Rsch. Labs., 1996-97; prin. Rivendale Consulting, La Honda, Calif., 1997—. Contbr. articles to profl. jours.; patentee in field. Mem. Assn. Computer Machinery Spl. Interest Group on Computer Human Interaction (vice chair 1988-89, co-chair 1989-91, 91-93, past chair 1994-95, conf. chair 1985, disting. svc. award 1995). Home and Office: 8115 La Honda Rd PO Box 334 La Honda CA 94020

HENDERSON, FREDA LAVERNE, elementary education educator; b. Parker County, Tex., June 18, 1939; d. Johnnie C. and Golda Arlene (Porter) Holbrooks; m. Ronald S. Henderson, Apr. 12, 1958; children: Ronald Kevin, Kelly Doyle, Chetley Brian, Terry Dean. AA, Am. Inst. Art, 1960; BEd, U. Colo., 1991; MEd, Lesley Coll., 1997. Pvt. tchr. art, Calhan, Colo., 1981-86; elem. tchr. art Ellicott Schs., Colo., 1987-90, tchr. chpt. I, 1991-96; classroom tchr. Ellicott Schs., 1996—. Sec. Ellicott Sch. PTA; chmn. High Sch. Booster Club, 1979-80; active vol. activities, 1964-79. Home: 1975 Buck Rd Calhan CO 80808-8515 Office: Ellicott Schs # 22 350 S Ellicott Hwy Calhan CO 80808-8838

HENDERSON, JAI, museum director. CEO Calif. Afro-Am. Mus., L.A. Office: Calif Afro-Am Mus 600 State Dr Exposition Pk Los Angeles CA 90037

HENDERSON, JAMES, JR., senator; b. Ganado, Ariz., May 16, 1942; m. Deborah Henderson; children: Valencia, Clarissa, Jaime Jamesina, Marcus. Cert. in career counseling, Utah State U., 1962. Employment svcs. mgr. Ariz. Dept. Econ. Security-Employment Svcs., Phoenix, 1968-74; vocat. devel. specialist Bur. Indian Affairs, Ft. Defiance, Ariz., 1974-77; dir. divsn. resources The Navajo Tribe, 1977-84, dir. office legis. affairs, 1986-90; senator State of Ariz., 1990—. With U.S. Army, 1966-68. Decorated Purple Heart; recipient Feed My People Internat. award, 1990, Outstanding Svc. award Navajo Nat. Coun. Resolution, 1990, Chief Manuelito Appreciation award Navajo Tribal Coun. Democrat. Presbyterian. Office: PO Box 3348 Window Rock AZ 86515

HENDERSON, JAMES HAROLD, entrepreneur, business executive, financial planner; b. Knoxville, Tenn., June 18, 1948; s. Harold Alpheus and Joanna Elizabeth (McCammon) H.; m. Jane Frances Dewey, Jan. 22, 1977; children: Jeanette Marie, Joanne Reneé, Joshua McCammon. BS in Mgmt. and Econs., U. North Ala., 1971; MS in Systems Mgmt., U. So. Calif., Los Angeles, 1981. Cert. fin. planner; registered investment advisor. Commd. U.S. Army, 1971, advanced through grades to capt., 1975, resigned, 1979; owner Worldwide Merchantile and Co., Clarksville, Tenn., Oscoda, Mich. and Cowley, Wyo., 1979—, Worlwide Merchantile and Co., Cowley, Wyo., 1979—; freelance fin. planner Clarksville, Tenn. and Oscoda, Mich., 1979-92; investment advisor James H. Henderson and Co., Oscoda, Mich., 1987-92; counselor Christian Fin. Concepts, Inc., 1985-89. Lt. col. USAR, 1971—; asst. army attache to India, USAR, 1991—, def. and army attache to Nepal, 1994. Mem. Inst. Cert. Fin. Planners (cert.), Officer's Christian Fellowship (area coord. 1984-90), Nat. Eagle Scout Assn. Home and Office: PO Box 742 Cowley WY 82420-0742

HENDERSON, LAVELL MERL, retired biochemistry educator; b. Swan Lake, Idaho, Sept. 9, 1917; s. George Merl and Nellie Marie (Gambles) H.; m. Maurine Criddle, Aug. 16, 1939; children: Janet Louise, Jeanne, Linda Marie. BS, Utah State U., 1939; MS, U. Wis., 1941, PhD, 1947. Instr. U. Wis., Madison, 1947-48; asst. prof. U. Ill., Urbana, 1948-57; prof., head Okla. State U., Stillwater, 1957-63; prof., head U. Minn., St. Paul, 1963-74, prof, assoc. dean, 1974-84, prof. emeritus, 1984—; mem. food and nutrition bd. NAS, Washington, 1965-71; mem. nutrition study sect. NIH, Washington, 1973-77, nutrition sci. tng. com. Nat. Inst. Gen. Med. Sci., Washington, 1965-69. Editor: Advances in Nutrition Research, 1976-84; editorial bd. Jour. Nutrition, 1965-68, 83-86; contbr. articles to profl. jours. Bd. dirs. Hormel Inst., Austin, Minn., North Star Rsch. & Devel., Mpls.; site visitor U.S. Office Edn., Title II, Washington, 1964-65. Grantee NIH, 1951-84; recipient Borden award Am. Inst. Nutrition, 1970. Mem. Am. Chem. Soc., Am. Soc. Biochemistry & Molecular Biology, Am Inst. Nutritin (pres. 1977, fellow 1986). Home: 8612 Mt Majestic Rd Sandy UT 84093-1833

HENDERSON, NANCY GRACE, marketing and technical documentation executive; b. Berkeley, Calif., Oct. 23, 1947; d. John Harry and Lorraine Ruth (Johnson) H. BA, U. Calif., Santa Barbara, 1969; MBA, U. Houston, 1985; teaching credential, U. Calif., L.A., 1971. Chartered Fin. Analyst. Tchr. Keppel Union Sch. Dist., Littlerock, Calif., 1969-72, Internat. Sch. Prague, Czechoslovakia, 1972-74, Sunland Luth. Sch., Freeport, Bahamas, 1974-75; tchr., dept. head Internat. Sch. Assn., Bangkok, Thailand, 1975-79; exec. search Diversified Human Resources Group, Houston, Tex., 1979-82; data processing analyst Am. Gen. Corp., Houston, 1982-83, personnel and benefits dept., 1983-85, investment analyst, 1985-86, equity security analyst/quantitative portfolio analyst, 1986-87; dir. mktg. and communications Vestek Systems Inc., San Francisco, 1987-90, dir. technical publs., 1990—; tchr. English as Second Language program Houston Metro. Ministries, 1980-81. Pres., bd. dirs. Home Owners Assn., Walnut Creek, Calif., 1988-90; tchr. English to refugees Houston Metro Ministries, 1982; exec. dir. Internat. Child Abuse Prevention Found., 1989; ch. choir, session, fundraising and com. chmn. Presbyn. Ch.; active Crisis Hotline, 1978-79, 92-93; dir. project Working in Networks for Good Shelter, 1993-95. Named a Notable Woman of Tex., 1984-85. Mem. Assn. for Investment Mgmt. and Rsch., Toastmasters (pres. Houston chpt. 1983, v.p. 1982-83). Office: Vestek Systems 388 Market St Ste 700 San Francisco CA 94111-5314

HENDERSON, SCOTT, jazz guitarist; b. West Palm Beach, Fla., Aug. 26, 1954; s. Charles and Geneva (Mavity) H. Guitarist Jean Luc Ponty, L.A., Chick Corea, L.A., Joe Zawinul, L.A.; co-band leader Tribal Tech, L.A.; guitar instr. Musicians Inst., L.A.; columnist Guitar World mag., N.Y.C. Author; (videos) Jazz Fuzion Improvisation, Melodic Phrasing; bandleader albums: Spears, Dr. Hee, Nomad, Tribal Tech., Illicit, Face First, Reality Check, Dog Party, Tore Down House. Named Best Jazz Guitarist, Guitar Player mag., 1991, Best Blues Album award, 1995, Best Jazz Guitarist, Guitar World mag., 1992.

HENDERSON, THELTON EUGENE, federal judge; b. Shreveport, La., Nov. 28, 1933; s. Eugene M. and Wanzie (Roberts) H.; 1 son, Geoffrey A. B.A., U. Calif.–Berkeley, 1956, J.D., 1962. Bar: Calif. 1962. Atty. U.S. Dept. Justice, 1962-63; assoc. firm FitzSimmons & Petris, 1964, assoc., 1964-66; directing atty. San Mateo County (Calif.) Legal Aid Soc., 1966-69; asst. dean Stanford (Calif.) U. Law Sch., 1968-76; ptnr. firm Rosen, Remcho & Henderson, San Francisco, 1977-80; judge U.S. Dist. Ct. (no. dist.) Calif., San Francisco, 1980—, chief judge; asso. prof. Sch. Law, Golden Gate U., San Francisco, 1978-80. Served with U.S. Army, 1956-58. Mem. ABA, Nat. Bar Assn., Charles Houston Law Assn. Office: US Dist Ct US Courthouse PO Box 36060 Rm 18-6652 San Francisco CA 94102*

HENDERSON-DIXON, KAREN SUE, psychologist; b. Bloomington, Ill., Mar. 25, 1946; d. Charles Lewis and Faye Lanore (Wantland) Henderson; m. David Thomas Biggs, Dec. 2, 1967 (div. 1972); m. Dean Eugene Dixon Jr., Jan. 13, 1973 (div. 1995); children: Christopher, Matthew. BA, U. Calif., Berkeley, 1966; MS, San Jose (Calif.) State Coll., 1971; PhD, Union Inst., 1991. Lic. clin. psychol., Alaska; cert. community coll. tchr. Pvt. practice clin. psychology, pvt. practice, Anchorage, 1980—; adj. prof. U. Alaska, Anchorage, 1994-95; cons. Alaska Youth and Parent Found., Anchorage,

1989—, Kenai Peninsula Counseling Svcs., 1995—, Parents United, Anchorage, 1989; mental health cons. Rural Alaska Community Action Program, Anchorage, 1988; cons., mem. adolescent treatment team Charter North Hosp., Anchorage, 1985-88; cons. Infant Impaired Hearing Program, Anchorage, 1984-85, Parent Tng. Ctr., Anchorage, 1980-82; psychiat. social worker Langdon Psychiat. Clinic, Anchorage, 1976-80; instr. in psychology U. Alaska Community Coll., Anchorage, 1974-81; parole agt. narcotic outpatient program State Dept. Corrections, Oakland, Calif., 1972-74; group counselor II, caseworker Alameda County Probation Dept., Oakland, Calif., 1971-72; cons. psychologist Alviso (Calif.) Econ. Devel. Program, 1971-72; instr. psychology Coll. of Alameda, 1973; faculty adv. for coop. edn. U. Alaska C.C., 1975-76. Sec., liaison to bd. Susitna Sch. PTA, Anchorage, 1983-84; co-chmn. optional bd. Susitna Sch., 1984-85, chmn., 1985-86, vol. coord., 1988-89; mem. adv. bd. Steller Alt. Sch., 1992-95. Mem. APA, Alaska Psychol. Assn. Democrat. Office: 912 W 6th Ave Anchorage AK 99501-2024

HENDIN, BARRY ALLEN, physician; b. St. Louis, Apr. 23, 1942; s. Gus and Lillian (Shanker) H.; m. rita Ellen Scissors, Aug. 2, 1964; children: Julie ann Hendin Thikoll, Lori Beth Hendin Travis, Holly Hendin. AB, Washington U., St. Louis, 1964, MD, 1968. Intern Jewish Hosp., St. Louis, 1968-69; resident in neurology Washington U., 1969-72, instr., 1972; clin. lectr. U. Ariz., 1988-95, clin. prof. of neurology, 1995—; chief neurology svc. Good Samaritan Med. Ctr., Phoenix, 1979—, chmn. Divsn. Neuroscis., 1991-92, vice chief of staff, 1993-95; bd. dirs. Samaritan Health System, 1995—. Contbr. articles to profl. jours. Mem. Gov.'s Coun. on Head and Spinal Cord Injuries, Ariz. State Govt., Phoenix, 1994, 95; mem. Parke-Davis Epilepsy Speakers' Bur., 1992—. Maj. USAF, 1972-74. Fellow Am. Acad. Neurology; mem. Maricopa County Med. Soc., Royal Soc. of Medicine. Office: Phoenix Neurol Assocs 2720 N 20th St Ste 125 Phoenix AZ 85006-1340

HENDLER, ROSEMARY NIELSEN, business owner, computer artist; b. Sydney, Australia, Oct. 18, 1946; came to U.S., 1954, naturalized, 1970; d. Robert Stanley McFarlane and Joyce Elizabeth (Annetts) Nielsen; m. Joel Arnold Hendler, June 1, 1977; 1 child, Stewart Maxwell. BA, U. Calif., Berkeley, 1968; postgrad., Acad. Art San Francisco, 1974-76, UCLA, 1985-87. Buyer linens Breuners Home Furnishings, Oakland, Calif., 1969-71; buyer textiles Liberty House, San Francisco, 1971-73, Bullock's, Palo Alto, 1973-75; graphic artist Montclarion Pubs., Oakland, 1975-77; pres., owner Cordeaux River Trading Co., L.A., 1986-93; owner, ptnr. Hendler Graphics, Orinda, Calif., 1995—. Advisor (CD-ROM) Visionary Stampede, Multimedia Project, San Francisco; exhibited computer art in numerous one-woman shows, 1994, 95, 96. Bd. dirs. docent coun. L.A. County Mus. Art, 1981—; VIP hostess Olympic Games, L.A., 1984; bd. dirs. Young Audiences, L.A., 1985-87; exec. bd. Orinda Arts Coun., 1991—, pres., 1993-94; mem. art guild Oakland Mus., 1991—; mem. task force Arts and Cultural Coun. of Contra Costa County, 1994—. Recipient Design award Levi Strauss, 1975, Honorable Mention awrd Manhattan Arts Internat., 1996, others. Mem. NAFE, Nat. Assn. Local Arts Agys., Nat. Assn. Desktop Pubs., Calif. Assn. Local Arts Agys., Jr. League L.A., Costume Coun., L.A. County Mus. Art, Lamorinda Arts Alliance, Artists in Tech., Orinda C. of C. Republican. Office: 16 El Verano Orinda CA 94563-1912

HENDREN, DEBRA MAE, critical care nurse; b. Belle Fourche, S.D., Apr. 27, 1959; d. Clyde Leslie and Kathryn Ann (Daughters) F.; m. Anthony Ray Martinez, May 21, 1983 (div.); m. Cecil B. Hendren, Nov. 21, 1992. AD, Casper Coll., 1987, cert. EMT, 1990. RN, Colo., Wyo.; CCRN. Nurse Wyo. Med. Ctr., Casper, North Suburban Med. Ctr. (formerly Humana Hosp. Mountain View), Thornton, Colo.; nurse Swedish Med. Ctr., Englewood, Colo., charge nurse ICU, 1993—; asst. nurse mgr. North Suburban Med. Ctr., Thornton, Colo., 1996—. Mem. Wyo. Nurses Assn., Colo. Nurses Assn., AACN. Home: 5168 E 126th Ct Thornton CO 80241-3001

HENDREN, ROBERT LEE, JR., academic administrator; b. Reno, Oct. 10, 1925; s. Robert Lee and Aleen (Hill) H.; m. Merlyn Churchill, June 14, 1947; children: Robert Lee IV, Anne Aleen. BA magna cum laude, Coll. Idaho, LLD (hon.); postgrad., Army Univ. Ctr., Oahu, Hawaii. Owner, pres. Hendren's Inc., 1947—; pres. Albertson Coll. Idaho, Caldwell, 1987—; bd. dirs. 1st Interstate Bank Idaho. Trustee Boise (Idaho) Ind. Sch. Dist., chmn. bd. trustees, 1966; chmn. bd. trustees Coll. Idaho, 1980-84; bd. dirs. Mountain View coun. Boy Scouts Am., Boise Retail Merchants, Boise Valley Indsl. Found., Boise Redevel. Agy., Ada County Marriage Counseling, Ada County Planning & Zoning Com., Blue Cross Idaho. Recipient Silver and Gold award U. Idaho, Nat. award Sigma Chi. Mem. Boise C. of C. (pres., bd. dirs.), Idaho Sch. Trustees Assn., Masons, KT, Shriners, Rotary (Paul Harris fellow). Home: 3504 Hillcrest Dr Boise ID 83705-4503 Office: Albertson Coll Idaho 2112 Cleveland Blvd Caldwell ID 83605-4432

HENDRICK, HAL WILMANS, human factors educator; b. Dallas, Mar. 11, 1933; s. Harold Eugene and Audrey Sarah (Wilmans) H.; m. Mary Francis Boyle; children: Hal L., David A., John A. (dec.), Jennifer G. BA, Ohio Wesleyan U., 1955; MS, Purdue U., 1961, PhD, 1966. Cert. profl. ergonomist; bd. cert. forensic examiner. Asst. prof. U. So. Calif., L.A., assoc. prof., 1979-86; exec. dir. Inst. of Safety and Systems Mgmt., U. So. Calif., L.A., 1986-87; prof., dean Coll. of System Sci., U. Denver, 1987-90; prof. U. So. Calif., 1986-95; prof. emeritus U. So. Calif., L.A., 1995—; dir. Rocky Mountain region Error Analysis, Inc., 1996—; pres. Bd. Cert. in Profl. Ergonomics, 1992-94. Author: Behavioral Research and Analysis, 1980, 2d edit., 1989, 3rd edit., 1990; editor 10 books; contbr. articles to profl. jours. Lt. col. USAF, 1956-76. Fellow APA, Am. Psychol. Soc., Human Factors Ergonomics Soc. (pres. L.A. chpt. 1986-87, pres. Rocky Mountain chpt. 1989-90, 95-96); mem. Internat. Ergonomics Assn. (pres. Geneva 1990-94, immediate past pres. 1994-97, sec. gen. 1987-89, exec. com. 1984—, U.S. rep. 1981-87), Ergonomics Soc. (U.K.), Soc. for Indsl. and Orgnl. Psychology. Democrat. Home and Office: 7100 E Crestline Ave Englewood CO 80111-1600

HENDRICK, JAMES T., lawyer; b. Fostoria, Ohio, Mar. 21, 1942. BA with honors and distinction in econs., U. Ill., 1963; JD, Harvard U., 1967. Bar: Ill. 1967, Calif. 1970. Ptnr. Thelen, Marrin, Johnson & Bridges, San Francisco. Mem. Ill. Bar Assn. Office: Thelen Marrin Johnson & Bridges Two Embarcadero Ctr San Francisco CA 94111

HENDRICKS, DELOY G., nutrition educator; b. Pocatello, Idaho, Dec. 18, 1938; s. Gerald Kenneth and Jennie Rachael (Bloxham) H.; m. Cora Jean Wood, June 13, 1962; children: Judy Lee, JaLee, Jolene, Janet Sue, Jerrae, Joy Marie, Clint Elwin. BS, U. Idaho, 1961; PhD, Mich. State U., 1967. Asst. prof. Utah State U., Logan, 1967-72, assoc. prof., 1972-77, prof., 1977—. Co-inventor for method for improving meat quality, 1988; author: (book chpt.) Introduction to Chemical Analysis of Food, 1994. Councilman City Coun., Providence, Utah, 1982-86. Lt. U.S. Army, 1961-63. Mem. Am. Inst. Nutrition (grad. edn. com. 1980-84), Sigma Xi. Office: Utah State U Dept Nutrition UMC 8700 Logan UT 84322-8700

HENDRICKS, MARK KENNETH, animator, artist; b. Detroit, Feb. 20, 1952; s. Burton Neal and Shirley Elizabeth (Cochrane) H.; m. Debra Sue Harbourne, June 17, 1972 (div. Sept. 1984); children: Deirdra Isis, Dustin Quake; m. Brenda Kae Cooper, Sept. 22, 1986. BFA, Ea. Mich. U., 1975; BA in Psychology, Sonoma State U., 1978; postgrad., Laney Coll., 1978-80, U. Calif., Berkeley, 1980-82. Illustrator Brown and Caldwell, Walnut Creek, Calif., 1981-84; animator Fed. Res. Bank, San Francisco, 1984—; mem. Sta. KQED-TV, San Francisco, 1986, KETH-TV, San Jose, Calif., 1990, KCET, San Mateo, Calif., 1992; cons. Lockheed Aerospace, Sunnyvale, Calif., 1986—, Journalism dept. U. Calif., Berkeley, 1987—, Wells Fargo Bank, San Franciso, 1987—, Opta Imaging, Sunnyvale, 1991—; mem. Modern Mus., San Franciso, 1988, Folk Art Mus., San Francisco, 1990, Smithsonian Instn., 1990. Animator: (ednl. videos) Signs of the Times, 1986, How Banks Create Money, 1987, Velocity, 1988, Striking a Balance, 1989, Grass Roots, 1990, The FED Our Central Bank, 1991, Capacity, 1992, Money, 1993, Trade in Action, 1994, www.frbsf.org, 1995, Money Matters, 1996. Mem. ASIFA, Spl. Interest Group on Computer Graphics. Home: 2448 Monticello Ave Oakland CA 94601-5543 Office: Fed Res Bank 101 Market St San Francisco CA 94105-1530

HENDRICKSON, DAVID CALVIN, political science educator; b. Oklahoma City, Okla., Mar. 22, 1953; s. Calvin Wesley and Frances (Hewitt) H.; m. Clelia de Moraes; children: Whitney, Wesley, Marina. BA in History, Colo. Coll., 1976; MA in Polit. Sci., Johns Hopkins U., 1981, PhD in Polit. Sci., 1982. Coord. undergrad. internat. rel. program Johns Hopkins U., Balt., 1979-81; legis. asst. Daniel P. Moynihan, Washington, 1981; asst. prof. polit. sci. Colo. Coll., Colorado Springs, 1983-89, assoc. prof. polit. sci., 1989-96, prof. polit. sci., 1996—; book reviewer (U.S.) Fgn. Affairs, N.Y.C., 1994—; editl. bd.: Ethics and Internat. Affairs, 1995—. Author: The Future of American Strategy, 1987, Reforming Defense: The State of American Civil-Military Relations, 1988; author: (with Robert W. Tucker): The Fall of the First British Empire: Origins of the War of American Independence, 1982, Empire of Liberty: The Statecraft of Thomas Jefferson, 1990, The Imperial Temptation: The New World Order and America's Purpose, 1992; contbr. articles to profl. jours. Grantee NEH, 1990, 95; Rsch. fellow The Lehrmann Inst., 1984-85, John M. Olin Found. fellow, 1986-87; recipient Burlington No. Faculty Achievement award Colo. Coll., 1989. Mem. Am. Polit. Sci. Assn., Coun. on Fgn. Rels. (Whitney Shepardson fellow 1991-92)., Pacific Coun. Internat. Policy, Am. Soc. Internat. Law. Democrat. Unitarian. Office: Colo Coll Dept Polit Sci 14 E Cache La Poudre St Colorado Springs CO 80903-3243

HENDRICKSON, L. BRUCE, state banking commissioner; b. Omaha, Oct. 14, 1945. Student, U. Nebr., 1964-68. Auditor to 2d v.p. investments Omaha Nat. Bank (now First Bank); v.p. investments First Nat. Bank (now Sunflower Banks), Salina, Kans.; sr. v.p. investments First Wyoming Bancorp (now Key Bank), Cheyenne, Key Bank of Wyo., Cheyenne; nationwide investment portfolio mgr. KeyCorp, Albany, N.Y.; CFO Key Bank of Wyo.; sr. v.p., regional mgr. Rocky Mountain states KeycCorp; banking commr. State of Wyo., Cheyenne; mem. Western Govs. Assn. Health Passport task force, 1994-95; mem. legis. com. to re-codify Wyo. State Investment Statutes, 1995-96. Bd. dirs. Wyo. State 4-H Found., 1986-93, chmn., 1992-93; Jr. Achievement advisor, 1973-84; elder, mariners 1st Presbyn. Ch. Recipient Ptnr. in 4-H award, 1993. Mem. Wyo. Bankers Assn. (chmn. coordinating com. with State Treas., designated expert banker to Wyo. Legislature 1984-96). Office: Wyo Dept Audit Divsn Banking Herschler Bldg 3 E Cheyenne Way Cheyenne WY 82002

HENDRICKSON, ROBERT J., educational administrator; b. West Chester, Pa., Dec. 3, 1935; s. Carl W. Sr. and Ethel A. (Butler) H.; m. Barbara M. Nale, June 18, 1960; children: Robert J., Jr., Susan E. Hendrickson. BS, West Chester State U., 1957; MEd, Seton Hall U., 1963. Tchr., adminstr. Newark Acad., Livingston, N.J., 1957-79; v.p. Internat. Trading and Commodities, N.Y.C., 1979-80; athletic dir. The Hun Sch., Princeton, N.J., 1980-84; regional dir. of sales and mktg. Aramis, St. Louis and N.Y.C., 1984-87; dean of students Phoenix Country Day Sch., Paradise Valley, Ariz., 1987—. Chmn. edn. com. Youth Vol. Assn., Maricopa County, Ariz., 1993-95. Named to Hall of Fame, Newark Acad., 1984; honored by Newark Police Dept. for svc. to youth, 1975. Mem. Ariz. Coaches Assn., Ariz. Assn. Sch. Coun. Advs., others. Home: 4256 E Rosemonte Dr Phoenix AZ 85024-3344 Office: Phoenix Country Day Sch 3901 E Stanford Dr Paradise Valley AZ 85253-7536

HENDRICKSON, WILLIAM LEE, French language educator; b. Denver, Feb. 13, 1936; s. William Francis and Virginia Maria (Maloney) H.; m. Ruth Suzanne Bader, Dec. 29, 1976; 1 child, Matthew Lee. BA, Ariz. State U., 1959; postgrad., U. Strasbourg, France, 1959-60; MA, U. Kans., 1962; PhD, Princeton U., 1969. Asst. instr. U. Kans., Lawrence, 1960-62, Princeton (N.J.) U., 1963-64; instr., then asst. prof. Brown U., Providence, 1965-72; asst. prof. Washington U., St. Louis, 1972-76; asst. prof. Ariz.. State U., Tempe, 1976-78, assoc. prof., 1978—. Co-author: Quinze Lecons de francais, 1972; co-editor: Jean Misrahi Memorial Volume, 1977, Studies on Seven Sages of Rome, 1978; editor: Contrastes: Contrastive Studies, 1989. Mem. Balsz Sch. Dist. Planning Assessment Com., Phoenix, 1992-94. Fulbright grantee, 1959-60, NEH grantee, 1973-74; fellow Camargo Found., Cassis, France, 1983. Mem. MLA, Soc. Rencesvals, Internat. Arthurian Soc., Am. Assn. Tchrs. of French (v.p. 1979-81, co-pres., 1989-93, exec. com. 1986-89), Cen. Ariz. Consortium on Internat. Edn., Phi Kappa Phi. Democrat. Roman Catholic. Home: 2422 N 56th St Phoenix AZ 85008-2626 Office: Ariz State U Dept Langs and Lit Tempe AZ 85287-0202

HENDRIX, JILL E., artist; b. Jackson, Mich., July 12, 1956; d. Daryl D. and Katherine L. (Ott) Raymond; m. Dennis G. Hendrix, Jan. 11, 1975; 1 child, Ragina M. Student, Ea. Wyo. Coll., Torrington, 1986-94. One-woman shows include Anderson Americana Galleries, Denver, 1995—, Las Vegas, Nev., 1996—; featured artist Atty. Gen.'s Conv., 1993.

HENDRIX, LOUISE BUTTS, retired educator, author; b. Portland, Tenn., June 16, 1911; d. Luther Edward and Johnny Henrietta (McNeill) B.; m. Edwin Alonzo Hendrix, Aug. 1, 1934 (dec. May 1991); children: Lynette Louise, Edwin Alonzo Jr. AB, Chico (Calif.) State Coll., 1932; postgrad., Sacramento State U., 1934-62, Coll. Pacific, 1934-62; Diploma of merit, U Delle Arti, Parma, Italy, 1982. Tchr. jr. high sch. Rio Vista, Calif., 1932-34; newspaper worker Chico Enterprise, 1930-32; tchr. jr. high sch. Al,-augh, Calif., 1944-45; newspaper corr. Sacramento Bee, Marysville Appeal Dem., Live Oak, Calif., 1945-52, Oroville Mercury Register Marysville Appeal Dem., Biggs, Calif., 1935-40; tchr. jr. high sch. Live Oak, 1952-69; ret., 1969. Author: Better Reading and Writing with Journalism, 1974, Sutter Buttes-Land of Histum Yani, 1980, 6th edit., 1992, Petals and Blossoms, 1983, Squaw Man, 1987; contbr. poetry to profl. jours. Mem. Sutter County Parks and Recreation Commn., Yuba City, 1977-80; founder Save Sutter Buttes Assn., Inc., Yuba City, 1978, sec., treas., 1978-90. Recipient Poet of Yr. award World Congress Poets, Orlando, Fla., 1986, Gold Poet award World of Poetry Conv., Anaheim, Calif., 1988. Fellow Internat. Poetry Soc.; mem. AAUW, Calif. Retired Tchrs. Assn., Sierra Club (Conservationist of Yr. 1974), Woman's Club (pres. Yuba City chpt. 1978-79). Democrat. Roman Catholic. Home: Covell Gardens 1111 Alvarado Ave #249 Davis CA 95616

HENDRIX, TIMOTHY DALE, highway construction company manager; b. Poplar Bluff, Mo., Dec. 7, 1954; s. Ralph Alexander Jr. and Bernice Ann (Nadeau) H.; m. Linda Lee Savage, Mar. 6, 1982; children: Christopher Michael, Jeremy Raymond, Brian James. BSCE, Worcester Poly. Inst., 1975; MSCE, Stanford U., 1976. Registered profl. engr., Calif., Oreg. Estimator, constrn. engr. Wildish Corvallis (Oreg.) Constrn. Co., 1976-77; estimator, project engr. Wildish Constrn. Co., Eugene, Oreg., 1977-78; project mgr. Wildish Constrn. Co., Bend, Oreg., 1979; mgr. Wildish Corvallis Cos., 1979-81; chief estimator Wildish Cos., Eugene, 1981-84, project mgr., 1983-86; project mgr. Wildish Standard Paving Co., Eugene, 1986-88, mgr., 1989—. Mem. AGC (bd. dirs. Columbia chpt. 1992—), Downtown Athletic Club (Eugene). Office: Wildish Standard Paving Co PO Box 7428 3600 County Farm Rd Eugene OR 97408-4616

HENDRY, JOHN EASTON, III, physician, surgeon; b. San Jose, Calif., Oct. 21, 1943; s. John Easton Jr. and Katherine E. Hendry. BA cum laude, Stanford U., 1966; MD, McGill U., Montreal, Can., 1970. Diplomate Am. Bd. Ob-Gyn., Nat. Bd. Med. Examiners. Inter Santa Clara Valley Med. Ctr., San Jose, Calif., 1969-70; resident in ob-gyn. Wash. U.-Barnes Hosp., St. Louis, 1972-75, chief resident, 1974-75; mem. sr. active staff Mercy San Juan Hosp., Carmichael, Calif., 1975—, Mercy Am. River Hosp., Carmichael, Calif., 1975—; mem. courtesy staff Sutter Roseville (Calif.) Hosp., 1975—; mem. Sacramento Ind. Physicians, Inc., 1989—; peer reviewer Med. Bd. Calif., Blue Shield HMO Physician Adv. Com.; mem. panel of arbitrators Am. Arbitration Assn.; mem. panel Physicians for Quality. Fellow ACOG; mem. AMA, Calif. Med. Assn., No. Calif. Obstet. and Gynecol. Soc., Am. Assn. Gynecologic Laparoscopists, Sacramento-El Dorado Med. Soc. Office: 5525 Dewey Dr Ste 104 Fair Oaks CA 95628-3130

HENG, STANLEY MARK, military officer; b. Nebraska City, Nebr., Nov. 4, 1937; s. Robert Joseph Sr. and Margaret Ann (Volkmer) H.; m. Sharon E. Barrett, Oct. 10, 1959; children: Mark, Nick, Lisa. Student, Command and Gen. Staff Coll., 1969, Nat. Def. U., 1979; BA, Doane Coll., 1987. Commd. adj. Nebr. N.G., 1966, advanced through grade to major gen., 1966-87; adj. Nebr. Mil. Dept., Lincoln, 1966-77, adminstrv. asst., 1978-86; adj. gen. emergency mgmt. State of Nebr., Lincoln, 1987—. Mem. N.G. Assn. U.S., N.G. Assn. Nebr. (exec. sec. 1967-71, Svc. award 1970), Adj. Gens. Assn., Am. Legion. Democrat. Mem. United Ch. of Christ. Office: Mil Dept 1300 Military Rd Lincoln NE 68508-1090

HENGSTLER, DENNIS DEAN, university program director; b. Wapakoneta, Ohio, Aug. 21, 1952; s. Luther C. and N. Delphine Hengstler. BS, Ball State U., 1974; MA, U. Ill., 1978, PHD, 1980. Evaluation specialist, lectr. U. N.C., Greensboro, 1979-82; lectr. dept. psychology U. N.C., Asheville, 1982-85, dir. office instl. rsch., 1982-85; dir. office instl. rsch., 1985-91; dir. office planning and policy analysis U. Houston, 1985-91; lectr. grad. sch. edn. U. Calif., Santa Barbara, 1991—, dir. office instl. rsch and planning, 1991—; instr. Command Coll. Calif. Law Enforcement, 1996—. Contbr. articles to profl. jours. Mem. Assn. Instl. Rsch., Calif. Assn. Instl. Rsch. (pres. 1997—), N.C. Assn. Instl. Rsch. Office: Office of Budget and Planning U Calif Santa Barbara Santa Barbara CA 93106

HENIG, SUZANNE, medical biological research company executive; b. N.Y.C., Jan. 12, 1936; d. Samuel G. and Gicia (Gottesdiener) Henig. BA, NYU, 1957, MA, 1961, PhD, 1968. V.p. Am. Heritage Soc., Washington, 1975-80; editor Va. Woolf Quar., San Diego, 1976-79; pres. India Expo, San Diego, 1976-81, Aeolian Press, San Diego, 1976—; v.p. Centro Internationale Biologica, S.A., Tiajuana, Mex., 1996; pres. Jenesse Found. for Med. Rsch., San Diego, 1995—, Double Helix, San Diego, 1995—, Genesis Prodns. of Hollywood, San Diego, 1990—. Editor Internat. Jour. Medicine, 1996; contbr. articles to profl. jours. V.p. N.Y. Young Reps., N.Y.C., 1953-54. Recipient Thomas Wolfe award for poetry NYU, 1957; grantee ACLS, Leopold Schepp Found., Am. Philos. Soc. Home: 4082 Carmel Springs Way San Diego CA 92130-2275

HENKEL, CATHY, newspaper sports editor. Office: The Seattle Times 1120 John St Seattle WA 98109-5321

HENKIN, WILLIAM ASHER, psychotherapist; b. Bklyn., July 17, 1944; s. William Ascher and Ethel Henkin. BS, Northwestern U., 1965, MA, 1967; MA, Calif. Inst. Integral Studies, 1985; PhD, Inst. Advanced Study Sexuality, 1993. Instr. Northwestern U., Evanston, Ill., 1967-69; editor various publs., Chgo., 1970-73, N.Y.C., 1970-73, San Francisco, 1970-73; freelance writer San Francisco, 1973—; psychotherapist pvt. practice, San Francisco, 1987—; adj. prof. Profl. Sch. Psychology, San Francisco, 1992-94; faculty Advanced Mgmt. Inst., San Francisco, 1994—; adj. prof. Calif. Sch. Profl. Psychology, 1994—. Author: The Spiral Tapestry, 1981, co-author: The Physic Healing Book, 1978, Bodywise, 1985. Fellow Am. Acad. Clin. Sexuality; mem. Calif. Assn. Marraige & Family Therapists, Soc. Scientific Study of Sex (past pres., San Francisco chpt.ú, Harry Benjamin Internat. Gender Dysphoria Assn. Office: 1801 Bush St Ste 111 San Francisco CA 94109-5239

HENLEY, ERNEST MARK, physics educator, university dean emeritus; b. Frankfurt, Germany, June 10, 1924; came to U.S., 1939, naturalized, 1944; s. Fred S. and Josy (Dreyfuss) H.; m. Elaine Dimitman, Aug. 21, 1948; children: M. Bradford, Karen M. B.E.E., CCNY, 1944; Ph.D., U. Calif. at Berkeley, 1952. Physicist Lawrence Radiation Lab., 1950-51; research assoc. physics dept. Stanford U., 1951-52; lectr. physics Columbia U., 1952-54; mem. faculty U. Wash., Seattle, 1954—; prof. physics U. Wash., 1961-95; prof. emeritus, 1995—; chmn. dept. U. Wash., 1973-76, dean Coll. Arts and Scis., 1979-87, dir. Inst. for Nuclear Theory, 1990-91; assoc. dir. Inst. for Nuclear Theory U. Wash., 1991—; rschr., author numerous publs. on symmetries, nuclear reactions, weak interactions and high energy particle interactions; chmn. Nuclear Sci. Adv. Com., 1986-89. Author: (with W. Thirring) Elementary Quantum Field Theory, 1962, (with H. Frauenfelder) Subatomic Physics, 1974, 2nd edit. 1991, Nuclear and Particle Physics, 1975. Bd. dirs. Pacific Sci. Ctr., 1984-87, Wash. Tech. Ctr., 1983-87; trustee Associated Univs., Inc., 1989—, chmn. bd., 1993-96. Recipient sr. Alexander von Humboldt award, 1984, T.W. Bonner prize Am. Physics Soc., 1989, Townsend Harris medal CCNY, 1989; F.B. Jewett fellow, 1952-53, NSF sr. fellow, 1958-59, Guggenheim fellow, 1967-68, NATO sr. fellow, 1976-77. Fellow AAAS (chmn. physics sect. 1989-90), Am. Phys. Soc. (chmn. div. nuclear physics 1979-80, pres. 1992), Am. Acad. Arts and Scis.; mem. NAS, Sigma Xi. Office: Univ Wash Physics Dept Box 351560 Seattle WA 98195-1560

HENLEY, JEFFREY O., restaurant executive; b. Phoenix, Nov. 6, 1948; s. Justin Oniel and Jane Ellen (Rice) H.; children—Amy, Julie, Todd. B.A., U. Calif.-Santa Barbara, 1966; M.B.A., UCLA, 1967. Cost acctg. supr. Hughes Aircraft Co., Culver City, CA, 1967-70; div. controller Tridair Industries, Redondo Beach, Calif., 1970-72, Fairchild Camera & Instrument, Mountain View, Calif., 1972-75; dir. fin. Memorex Corp., Santa Clara, Calif., 1975-79; v.p., controller Saga Corp, Menlo Park, Calif., 1979-82, exec. v.p., 1982—; pres. Fast Service Restaurant Group, Menlo Park, Calif., 1985—; Exec. v.p., CFO Oracle Corp., Redwood City, Calif. Bd. dirs. Herbert Hoover Boys' & Girls' Club, Menlo Park, Calif., 1983, pres., 1984—. Mem. Fin. Exec. Inst., Sigma Phi Epsilon. Republican. Presbyterian. Office: Oracle Corp 500 Oracle Pkwy MS 50P6 Redwood City CA 94065-1600*

HENLEY, PRESTON VANFLEET, former banker, financial consultant; b. Fort Madison, Iowa, July 7, 1913; s. Jesse vanFleet and Ruth (Roberts) H.; m. Elizabeth Artis Watts, Mar. 31, 1940 (div. June 1956); children: Preston Edward VanFleet, Stephen Watts, John vanFleet; m. 2d, Helena Margaret Greenslade, Nov. 29, 1964; 1 adopted son, Lawrence D. Student Tulane U., 1931-34, Loyola U., New Orleans, 1935-36; A.B., Calif. State Coll. at Santa Barbara, 1939; postgrad. U. Wash., 1939-40, N.Y. U., 1943, 46. Teaching fellow U. Wash., 1939-40; sr. credit analyst, head credit dept. Chase Nat. Bank, 45th St. br. N.Y.C., 1942-49; Western sales rep. Devoe & Raynolds, Inc., N.Y.C., 1949-51; v.p., comml. loan officer, mgr. credit dept. U.S. Nat. Bank, Portland, Oreg., 1951-72; loan adminstr. Voyageur Bank Group, Eau Claire, Wis.; v.p. Kanabec State Bank, Mora, Minn., Montgomery State Bank (Minn.), Park Falls State Bank (Wis.), Montello State Bank (Wis.), 1972; v.p., mgr. main office, sr. credit officer So. Nev. region Nev. Nat. Bank, Las Vegas, 1973-75; bus. and fin. cons., 1975—; loan cons. Continental Nat. Bank, Las Vegas, 1983-89; instr. Am. Inst. Banking, Portland, 1952-65, Multomah Coll., Portland, 1956-62, Portland State U., 1961-72, Mt. Hood Community Coll., 1971-72, Clark County Community Coll., 1979-83; adv. dir. Vita Plus, Inc., 1979-83; exec. dir. Nev. Minority Purchasing Council, 1979-80; dir., treas. Consumer Credit Counselling Service of Oreg. 1965-72. Treas., Ore. chpt. Leukemia Soc., 1965-66; mem. Menninger Found. 1965-67; trustee, exec. com. St. Rose delima Hosp. Found., 1982-87;dir. So. Nev. chtp. Assn. Part-Time Profls., 1985-87. Served with USNR, 1943-45. Mem. Oreg. Bankers Assn., Robert Morris Assos. (pres. Oreg. chpt. 1959-60, nat. dir. 1961-64), Nat., Oreg. assns. credit mgmt., Credit Research Found., Inst. Internal Auditors, S.A.R., Beta Mu, Leaf and Scarab, Alpha Phi Omega, Portland C. of C., Oreg. Retail Council. Republican. Episcopalian. Mason (32 deg., Shriner). Contbr. articles to profl. jours. Home and Office: 7778 Locke Haven Dr Las Vegas NV 89123-0734

HENNE, ANDREA RUDNITSKY, business educator; b. Phila., Sept. 11, 1952; d. Isadore and Florence (Sanders) Rudnitsky; m. Lawrence Michael Henne, May 27, 1984; children: Laura Joy, Michael Andrew. BS, Temple U., 1974; MA in Edn., UCLA, 1975, EdD, 1983. Prof. L.A. City Coll., 1975-90; dir. curriculum devel. Bridges Learning Ctr., Solana Beach, Calif., 1992-94; instr. San Diego Mesa Coll., 1995—; bus. cons., San Diego, 1994—. Author: Intensive Records Management, 4th edit., 1997. Vol. Solana Beach Elem. Sch., San Diego, 1990—, Girl Scouts U.S.A., San Diego, 1995—. Edn. Professions Devel. Act fellow UCLA, 1975; named Outstanding Young Careerist, Bus. and Profl. Women, L.A., 1979. Mem. ASCD, Assn. Records Mgmt. and Adminstrn., Inc., Nat. Bus. Edn. Assn., Calif. Bus. Edn. Assn. (sec., v.p. and pres. 1976-79), Delta Pi Epsilon.

HENNEMAN, STEPHEN CHARLES, counselor; b. Chgo., June 17, 1949; s. Charles Philip Jr. and Marion Louise (Eichberger) H.; m. Patrica Ann York, Feb. 14, 1975 (div. Sept. 1980); 1 child Charles Philip III; m. Marion Jean McDermand, Oct. 4, 1980; stepchildren: Ervin F. Schrock Jr., Lisa Ann Schrock, Thomas M. Schrock. BA in Journalism, Colo. State U., 1971; MA in Counseling, U. N.D., 1987. Commd. 2d lt. USAF, 1971, advanced through grades to maj., 1984; missile launch officer 570th Strategic Missile Squadron, Davis Monthan AFB, Ariz., 1972-76; info. officer 321st Strategic Missile Wing, Grand Forks AFB, N.D., 1976-79; missile combat crew flight comdr. 446th Strategic Missile Squadron, Grand Forks AFB, 1980-82; missile combat crew comdr. evaluator 321st Strategic Missile Wing, Grand Forks AFB, 1982, wing nuclear surety officer, 1982-83, chief weapon safety branch, 1983-85; asst. ops. officer 320th Strategic Missile Squadron, F E Warren AFB, Wyo., 1985-86; dep. wing inspector 90th Strategic Missile Wing, F E Warren AFB, 1986-88; ops. officer 319th Strategic Missile Squadron, F E Warren AFB, 1988-89; dep. chief war res. materiel div. Hdqrs. U.S. Air Forces in Europe, Ramstein Air Base, Fed. Republic Germany, 1989-92; vol. and outreach coord. Safe House/Sexual Assault Svcs., Inc., Cheyenne, Wyo., 1992-93; quality control investigator Dept. Employment State of Wyoming, Cheyenne, 1993-95; counselor Wyo. State Penitentiary, Rawlins, 1995-96, counseling team leader, 1996—. Advocate, counselor Safehouse/Sexual Assault Svcs., Inc., Cheyenne, 1985-89; bd. dirs. Carbon County Citizens Organized to See Violence Ended. Mem. Am. Counseling Assn., Am. Correction Assn., Internat. Assn. Marriage and Family Counselors, Internat. Assn. Addictions and Offender Counselors, Wyo. Counseling Assn., Wyo. Corrections Assn., Air Force Assn., Ret. Officers Assn., Nat. Coalition Against Domestic Violence, Nat. Coalition Against Sexual Assault, Am. Legion.

HENNER, MARTIN E., arbitrator, mediator; b. N.Y.C., Aug. 6, 1940; s. Isidore and Rose (Zabar) Henner; m. Karen Elaine Hemmingsen, Mar. 24, 1978 (div. Sept. 1984). BA, U. Chgo., 1960; JD, U. Wis., 1969; ADB, Columbia U., 1978. Bar: Wis. 1969, Calif. 1970, Oreg. 1974. Adminstrv. asst. to commr. U.S. Equal Employment Opportunity Commn., Washington, 1965; exec. dir. U.S. Equal Employment Opportunity Commn., 1969; compliance officer, affirmative action specialist, dir. Mich. Civil Rights Divsn., Detroit, 1965-67; atty. Henner, Wolpman, Constantinides & Cohen, 1970-71; pvt. practice, 1971-75, 95—; rschr. U.S. Vets. Adminstrn. Hosp., Palo Alto, Calif., 1976; adminstr., trainer U. Conn., 1977-79; dep. pub. defender Orange County (Calif.), 1980; atty./staff rep. Am. Fedn. State County and Mcpl. Employees, 1981-86; legis. aide to Senator William Dwyer Oreg. State Senate, 1995; vis. asst. prof. San Jose (Calif.) State U., 1976, 77; asst. prof. U. Conn., 1977-79, Calif. State U., Long Beach, 1979-82; Fulbright lectr. U. Paris, 1980-81; instr. Oreg. State U., Corvallis, 1986-88. Contbr. articles to profl. jours. Mem. Am. Arbitration Assn., Oreg. Mediation Assn., Oreg. Assn. Adminstrv. Law Judges, Oreg. State Bar Assn. (state bar counsel region 2), Indsl. Rels. Rsch. Assn. (trustee Oreg. chpt. 1995—), Soc. Profls. in Dispute Resolution (treas. Pacific NW chpt. 1988-89). Home: 2675 Baker Blvd Eugene OR 97403 Office: PO Box 1558 Eugene OR 97440

HENNESSEY, ALICE ELIZABETH, forest products company executive; b. Haverhill, Mass., May 24, 1936; d. H. Nelson and Elizabeth E. (Johnson) Pingree; A.B. with honors, U. Colo., 1957; cert. with distinction Harvard-Radcliffe Program in Bus. Adminstrn., 1958; m. Thomas M. Hennessey, June 13, 1959; children—Shannon, Sheila, Thomas N. With Boise Cascade Corp. (Idaho), 1958—, sec. to pres., 1958-60, adminstrv. asst. to pres., 1960-61, 65-71, corp. sec., 1971—, v.p., 1974-82, sr. v.p., 1982-96; pres., CEO Idaho Cmty. Found., 1996—. Bd. dirs. Boise Pub. Libr. Found., U. Idaho Found.; sustaining mem. Boise Jr. League; mem. Phi Beta Kappa, Alpha Chi Omega. Office: Boise Cascade Corp PO Box 50 Boise ID 83728-0001

HENNING, MARTHA LOUISE, English language educator; b. Monterey, Calif., Nov. 14, 1948; d. Robert J. and Ruth J. (Udden) H.; m. Peter M. Stock; children: Nathan C. Hamilton, Sarah L. Hamilton. AB in English, Stanford U., 1970; MA in Humanities, SUNY, Buffalo, 1972; PhD in Rhetoric and Composition, U. Louisville, 1993. Lectr. U. Ind. S.E., New Albany, 1985, U. Louisville, 1987, Jefferson C.C., Louisville, 1989-90, Bellarmine Coll., Louisville, 1990-91; prof. English Portland (Oreg.) C.C., 1991—; bd. dirs., co-chair Young Rhetoricians' Conf., Monterey, Calif., 1991—. Author: Beyond Understanding: Appeals to the Imagination, Passions, and Will in Mid-Nineteenth Century American Women's Fiction; contbr. articles to profl. publs. Mem. MLA, Assn. Profl. Comms. Cons., Internat. Soc. for History of Rhetoric, Nat. Coun. Tchrs. English, Rhetoric Soc. Am., Stanford Alumnae Assn. (life). Home: 7430 SW 76th Ave Portland OR 97223-7489 Office: Portland CC PO Box 19000 Portland OR 97280-0990

HENNING, WILLIAM THOMAS, museum director; b. Denver, Mar. 5, 1937; s. William Thomas Sr. and Rosalee (Bennett) H.; m. Eleanor Ann Whiteley, May 29, 1958; children: Cynthia Diane, Thomas Reed, David Randal. BFA, Phillips U., Enid, Okla., 1959; MA, U. Denver, 1963; postgrad., U. Iowa, 1966-69. Instr. Ariz. Western Coll., Yuma, 1963-66; asst. prof. Phillips U., 1969-75; curator Colorado Springs Fine Art Ctr., 1976-79, Hunter Mus. Art, Chattanooga, 1980-87, Ark. Arts Ctr., Little Rock, 1987-91, U. Ky. Art Mus., Lexington, 1991-96; dir. Rosemount Mus., Pueblo, Colo., 1996—; adj. faculty U. Ark., Little Rock, 1990-91, U. Ky., Lexington, 1995, U. So. Colo., Pueblo, 1997. Author: A Catalogue of the American Collection. Hunter Museum of Art, 1985; co-author: A Spectacular Vision: The George and Susan Proskauer Collection, 1994. Mem. Am. Assn. Museums, Mountain-Plains Mus. Assn., Nat. Trust for Historic Preservation, Rotary Coub, Blue Key. Episcopalian. Home: 6B Windbridge Ln Pueblo CO 81001 Office: Rosemount Mus 419 W 14th St Pueblo CO 81003

HENNION, CAROLYN LAIRD (LYN HENNION), investment executive; b. Orange, Calif., July 27, 1943; d. George James and Jane (Porter) Laird; m. Reeve L. Hennion, Sept. 12, 1964; children: Jeffrey Reeve, Douglas Laird. BA, Stanford U., 1965; grad. Securities Industry Inst., U. Pa., 1992. CFP, fund specialist; lic. ins. agt.; registered gen. securities prin. Portfolio analyst Schwabacher & Co., San Francisco, 1965-66; adminstrv. coord. Bicentennial Commn., San Mateo County Calif., 1972-73; dir. devel. Crystal Springs Uplands Sch., Hillsborough, Calif., 1973-84; tax preparer Household Fin. Corp., Foster City, Calif., 1982, freelance, 1983-87; sales promotion mgr. Franklin Distbrs., Inc., San Mateo, 1984-86, v.p. and regional sales mgr. of N.W., 1986-91, Mid-Atlantic, 1991-94; v.p. Viatech, Inc., 1986-92; v.p. Keypoint Svcs. Internat., 1992—; pres. Brock Rd. Corp., 1993—; v.p. Strand, Atkinson, Williams & York, Medford, Oreg., 1994—. Editor: Lest We Forget, 1975. Pres. South Hillsborough Sch. Parents' Group, Calif., 1974-75; sec. Vol. Bur. of San Mateo County, Burlingame, Calif., 1975; chmn. Community Info. Com., Town of Hillsborough, 1984-86, mem., sub-com. chmn. fin. adv. com., 1984-86, Jackson Co. Airport adv. com., 1996—; mem. coun. Town of Buncom, Oreg., 1990—; bd. dirs. Pacific N.W. Mus. Natural History, 1995-96; chmn. Jackson County Applegate Trail Sesquicentennial Celebration, 1995-97; treas. Sesquicentennial Wagon Train, 1995-97; v.p. and sec. So. Oreg. Hist. Soc. Found., 1995—; trustee Oreg. Shakespeare Festival Endowment Fund, 1996—, sec., treas., 1997—; mem. planned giving com. Providence Cmty. Health Found., 1996—; dir. Rogue Valley Manor Cmty. Svcs., 1996—; adv. com. Jackson Co. Airport, 1996—. Recipient awards Coun. for Advancement and Support of Edn., 1981, Exemplary Direct Mail Appeals Fund Raising Inst., 1982, Wholesaler of Yr. Shearson Lehman Hutton N.W Region, 1989, Golden Mic award Frederic Gilbert Assocs., 1993. Mem. Securities Industry Assn. (chmn. state membership 1989-91), Internat. Assn. Fin. Planners (sec. Oreg. chpt. 1988-89, bd. dirs.), So. Oreg. Estate Planning Coun. (bd. dirs. 1997—), Buncom Hist. Soc., Oreg. Shakespeare Festival, Britt Festivals, So. Oreg. Hist. Soc., Arts Coun. So. Oreg., Jr. League. Republican. Home: 3232 Little Applegate Rd Jacksonville OR 97530-9303 Office: Strand Atkinson Williams & York 1 North Holly Medford OR 97501

HENRICKSON, EILER LEONARD, retired geologist, educator; b. Crosby, Minn., Apr. 23, 1920; s. Eiler Clarence and Mabel (Bacon) H.; m. Kristine L. Kuntzman; children: Eiler Warren, Kristin, Kurt Eric, Ann Elizabeth. BA, Carleton Coll., 1943; PhD, U. Minn., 1956. Geologist U.S. Geol. Survey, Calif., 1943-44; instr. Carleton Coll., 1946-47, 48-51, asst. prof., 1951-53, 54-56, assoc. prof., 1956-62, prof., 1962-70, Charles L. Denison prof. geology, 1970-87, chmn. dept., 1970-78, wrestling coach, 1946-58, 83-87; prof. geology, chmn. dept. Colo. Coll., 1987-96; pres. Concentrating Systems of Am., 1996—; instr. U. Minn., 1947-48, 53-54; vis. lectr. numerous univs., Europe, 1962; cons. Jones & Laughlin Steel Corp., 1946-58, Fremont Mining Co., Alaska, 1958-61, G.T. Schieldahl Co., Minn., 1961-62, Bear Creek Mining Co., Mich., 1965-66, U. Minn. Messenia Expdn., 1966-75, Exxon Co., 1977-78, Cargill Corp., Mpls., 1983-84, Leslie Salt Co., San Francisco, 1985-86, various other cos.; research scientist, cons. Oak Ridge (Tenn.) Nat. Lab., 1985-86; cons. Argonne Nat. Lab., 1966-78, research scientist, summers, 1966-67; field studies metamorphic areas, Norway and Scotland; dir. young scholars program NSF, 1988-90. Author: Zones of Regional Metamorphism, 1957. Dir. Northfield Bd. Edn., 1960-63; steering com. Northfield Community Devel. Program, 1966-67. Served as 1st lt. USMCR, 1943, AUS, 1944-46. Fulbright research scholar archeol. geology, Greece, 1966-87. Mem. AAAS, Mineral Soc. Am., Nat. Assn. Geology Tchrs., Minn. Acad. Sci (vis. lectr.), Am. Geol. Inst., Geol. Soc. Am., Soc. Econ. Geologists, Rocky Mountain Assn. Geologists, Nat. Wrestling Coaches and Ofcls. Assn., Archaeol. Inst. Am. (vis. lectr.), Sigma Xi. Home: 19560 Four Winds Way Monument CO 80132-9309

HENRICKSON, MARK, social worker, priest; b. Wilmington, Del., Nov. 28, 1955; s. Bruce and Elaine Mary (Fowler) H.; m. T. A. Bennett, Jan. 15, 1982. BA, Trinity Coll., 1977; MDiv, Episcopal Div. Sch., 1980; MSW, U. Conn., 1990; PhD, UCLA, 1996. Ordained priest, Episc. Ch., 1981. Curate Trinity Episcopal Ch., Torrington, Conn., 1980-82; chaplain resident Hartford (Conn.) Hosp., 1982-83; priest-in-charge St. Monica's Episcopal Ch., Hartford, 1983-85; pvt. practice Hartford, 1985-91; dir. AIDS/HIV program Hartford Health Dept., 1988-91; NIMH, AIDS rsch. tng. fellow UCLA, 1992-94; field unit supervisor immunization program L.A. County Dept. Health Svcs., 1995-96; HIV divsn. dir. Northeast Valley Health Corp., 1996—; mem. Permanent Task Force on AIDS, Conn., 1989-91; cons. AIDS Ministries Regional Care Team, Hartford, 1990-91; mem. adj. faculty St. Joseph's Coll., Hartford, 1991. Contbr. articles to profl. jours. Active Conn. Coalition for Lesbian/Gay Civil Rights, Hartford, 1986-91; mem. Commn. on Ministry Episcopal Diocese L.A. Recipient various civic and profl. awards. Mem. NASW, Social Work AIDS Network. Office: 8215 Van Nuys Blvd Ste 306 Panorama City CA 91402

HENRICKSON, PAUL ROBERT, artist; b. Boston, Dec. 25, 1928; s. Jacob and Gunhild Marie (Nielsen) H. BFA, R.I. Sch. Design, 1951; MEd, U. Mass., 1954; PhD, U. Minn., 1962. Head art dept. Tantasqua High Sch., Sturbridge, Mass., 1954-56, Valley City (N.D.) State Coll., 1956-59, Radford (Va.) U., 1961-64, U. Guam, Agana, 1964-68; chmn. div. fine arts, exec. dir. insular art couns. U. No. Iowa, Cedar Falls, 1968-71, prof. art, dir. creativity rsch., 1968-71; prof. art. Coll. of Sante Fe, N.Mex., 1971-72; advisor Torrance Creativity Ctr., U. Ga., Athens, 1988—. Candidate Sec. of State, N.Mex., 1990; bd. dirs. Scandinavian Film Festival, N.Mex., 1984, Hammer of Thor Found., N.Mex., 1985—, Baltic Film Festival, N.Mex., 1990—. With USNR, 1954-59. Home and Office: PO Box 3731 Santa Fe NM 87501 also: RR 11 Box 73B Santa Fe NM 87501-8798

HENRIKSEN, MELVIN, mathematician, educator; b. N.Y.C., N.Y., Feb. 23, 1927; s. Kaj and Helen (Kahn) H.; m. Lillian Viola Hill, July 23, 1946 (div. 1964); children—Susan, Richard, Thomas; m. Louise Levitas, June 12, 1964. B.S., Coll. City N.Y., 1948; M.S., U. Wis., 1949, Ph.D. in Math, 1951. Asst. math., then instr. extension div. U. Wis., 1948-51; asst. prof. U. Ala., 1951-52; from instr. to prof. math. Purdue U., 1952-65; prof. math., head dept. Case Inst. Tech., 1965-68; research assoc. U. Calif. at Berkeley, 1968-69; prof., chmn. math. dept. Harvey Mudd Coll., 1969-72, prof., 1972-97, prof. emeritus, 1997—; mem. Inst. Advanced Study, Princeton, 1956-57, 63-64; vis. prof. Wayne State U., 1960-61; rsch. assoc. U. Man., Winnipeg, Can., 1975-76; vis. prof. Wesleyan U., Middletown, Conn., 1978-79, 82-83, 86-87, 93-94. Author: (with Milton Lees) Single Variable Calculus, 1970; assoc. editor: Algebra Universalis, 1993—, Topology Atlas, 1996—, Topological Commentary, 1996—; author articles on algebra, rings of functions, gen. topology. Sloan fellow, 1956-58. Mem. Am. Math. Soc., Math. Assn. Am. (assoc. editor Am. Math. monthly 1988-91, assoc. editor Algebra Universalis 1993—). Home: 504 W Bowling Green Dr Claremont CA 91711-2716

HENRY, DAVID ALLEN, advertising executive; b. Cedar Rapids, Iowa, Apr. 16, 1950; s. Don Albert and Anna Mae (Manwiller) H.; m. Elise Marie Cohen, June 7, 1981 (div. Apr. 1988); children: Lauren, Erica, Sylvia. BBA, U. Iowa, 1972. V.p. mktg. Movie Systems, Inc., Denver, 1975-77; chmn., chief exec. officer Henry Gill Advt., Denver, 1977—; mem. bd. advisors Entrepreneurial Inst. Denver, 1989. Bd. dirs. Direction 2,000 Found., Littleton, Colo., 1990-93, Littleton Pub. Schs. Found., 1993—; nat. advisor White House Conf. for Drug-Free Am., Washington, 1988. Recipient Award of Merit, United Way Mile High Child Care, Denver, 1988, Cert. of Appreciation, Communities for Drug-Free Colo., 1989, Sch. Restructuring Program, Gov. of Colo., 1990, Cert. of Merit, Keep Denver Beautiful, 1990. Mem. Am. Mktg. Assn., Am. Assn. Advt. Agys. (mem. western bd. govs. 1988-92, chmn. bd. dirs. Rocky Mountain Coun. 1988), Denver Advt. Fedn. (bd. dirs. 1987-91), Denver Press Club, Greater Denver C. of C. (mem. bd. advisors 1990, Cert. of Appreciation 1989). Office: Henry Gill Advt 1225 17th St Ste 2500 Denver CO 80202-5525

HENRY, KAREN HAWLEY, lawyer; b. Whittier, Calif., Nov. 5, 1943; d. Ralph Hawley and Dorothy Ellen (Carr) Hawley; m. John Dunlap, 1968; m. Charles Gibbons Henry, Mar. 15, 1975; children: Scott, Alexander, Joshua; m. Don H. Phemister, June 21, 1991; children: Justin Phemister, Jonathan Phemister, Keith Phemister. BS in Social Scis., So. Oreg. Coll., 1965; MS in Labor Econs., Iowa State U., 1967; JD, U. Calif., 1976. Instr., Medford (Oreg.) Sch. Dist., 1965-66; rsch. asst. dept. econs. Iowa State U., Ames, 1966-67; dir. rsch. program Calif. Nurses Assn., San Francisco, 1967-72; labor rels. coord. Affiliated Hosps. of San Francisco, 1972-79; ptnr. Littler, Mendelson, Fastiff & Tichy, San Francisco, 1979-89; mng. ptnr. labor and employment law Weissburg and Aronson, Inc., San Francisco, 1989-90; prin. Karen H. Henry, Inc., Auburn, Calif., 1991—. Author: Health Care Supervisor's Legal Guide, 1984, Nursing Administration Law Manual, 1986, ADA: Ten Steps to Compliance, 1992, 5th edit., 1997; editl. bd. Health Care Supervisor; contbr. articles on employment law issues to profl. jours. Mem. Calif. Soc. Healthcare Attys. (bd. dirs. 1986-87, pres. 1987-88), Am. Hosp. Assn. (ad hoc labor atty. com.), State Bar of Calif., Sacramento Bar Assn., Thurston Soc., Order of Coif. (law jour.). Office: Karen H Henry Inc 1141 High St Auburn CA

HENRY, KEITH DOUGLAS, architect; b. Winnipeg, Man., Can., Oct. 25, 1957; s. Charles Eric and Ruth Elva (McDonald) H.; m. Elizabeth Anne McNulty, June 19, 1993. B of Environ. Studies, U. Man., Winnipeg, 1978, MArch, 1982. Design architect Ferguson Folstad Friggstad Architects, Saskatoon, Regina, Sask., Can., 1982-86; assoc. ptnr. Folstad & Friggstad Architects, Saskatoon, 1986-92; ptnr. Friggstad Downing Henry Architects-Wilson Bailey Tech., Saskatoon, 1992—. Prin. works include John Paul II Collegiate (Award of Merit Sask. Assn. Architects 1991), Bedford Rd. Collegiate (City of Sask. Heritage award 1996), Can. Nat. Inst. Blind Svc. Ctr. (Award of Excellence Sask. Masonry Inst. 1993). Recipient Marion M. Graham Collegiate award Am. Assn. Sch. Adminstrs./AIA, 1985, Heritage award City of Saskatoon, 1996. Mem. Royal Archtl. Inst. Can., Sask. Assn. Architects (registered, mem. coun. 1993—, pres. 1995-96), North Saskatoon Bus. Assn., Aurum Club. Office: Friggstad Architects, 2233 Avenue C North, Saskatoon, SK Canada S7L 5Z2

HENRY, MARIE ELAINE, poet; b. San Francisco, Oct. 4, 1948; d. Norbert Francis and Katharyne Elizabeth (Hedman) H. BA in English with honors, San Jose State U., 1970; MA in Creative Writing, San Francisco State U., 1972. Contbg. poet/short fiction writer various lit. jours. and anthologies including: The Reed, Panjandrum, Gallimaufry, Beautitude, Alcatraz, Center, Boulevards, Rapscallions Dream, Yellow Silk, Another Small Magazine, California Oranges, Peace or Perish: A Crisis Anthology, Co-Evolution Quar., Apalachee Quar., Squaw Valley Community of Writers Poetry Anthology, Canvass, Noe Valley Voice, Only Morning in Her Shoes, Pudding Mag., Sacred River, Out of Season, Disability Rag, Range of Motion, Watch Out! We're Talking, Through the Mill, Bite to Eat Place, Poetry at the 33 Review, Dream Machinery, Buffalo Bones, Convolvulus, Exquisite Corpse, Full Court: A Literary Anthology of Basketball, Barnabe Mountain Rev. Recipient James D. Phelan writing awards San Jose State U., 1970. Mem. Marin Poetry Ctr., Bay Area Folk Harp Soc. Home: 855 C St #408 San Rafael CA 94901

HENRY, MICHAEL FITZROY, psychotherapist; b. Port of Spain, Trinidad, Sept. 14, 1949; came to U.S., 1970; s. Francis and Vilma R. (Haynes) H.; m. Margaret J. Baker, May 30, 1976; 1 child, Anthony. AA, Walla Walla (Wash.) C.C., 1972; BA, Whitman Coll., 1975, Whitworth Coll., 1983; PhD, Pacific Western U., 1994. Diplomate Am. Acad. Forensic Counseling; nat. cert. group psychotherapist. Counselor Carondelet Psychiat. Ctr., Richland, Wash., 1976-78, Luth. Family Svcs., Kennewick, Wash., 1989—; pvt. practice Richland, 1989—; cons. Juvenile Justice Ctr., Kennewick, 1983—; cons., tchr. Leadership Inst. Seattle, 1991-92. Mem. NAACP, Tri Cities, Wash., 1984—. Mem. Am. Assn. Marriage and Family Therapy, Am. Counseling Assn., Nat. Assn. of Drug and Alcohol Counseling, Assn. for the Treatment of Sex Abusers, Exch. Club Am. (Mem. of Yr. award 1993). Office: 750 Swift Blvd Ste 3 Richland WA 99352-3521

HENRY, PHILIP LAWRENCE, marketing professional; b. Los Angeles, Dec. 1, 1940; s. Lawrence Langworthy and Ella Hanna (Martens) H.; m. Claudia Antonia Huff, Aug. 9, 1965 (div. 1980); children: Carolyn Marie, Susan Michelle; m. Carrie Katherine Hoover, Aug. 23, 1985. BS in Marine Engring., Calif. Maritime Acad., 1961. Design engr. Pacific Telephone Co., San Diego, 1963-73; service engr. Worthington Service Corp., San Diego, 1973-78; pres. Realmart Corp., San Diego, 1978-81; dir. mktg. Orbit Inn Hotel and Casino, Las Vegas, 1981-84; pres. Comml. Consultants, Las Vegas, 1984—, Gray Electronics Co., Las Vegas, 1986—. Inventor electronic detection device, 1986. Served to lt. (j.g.) USNR, 1961-67. Republican. Home: 1843 Somersby Way Henderson NV 89014-3876

HENRY, SAMUEL DUDLEY, educator; b. Washington, Oct. 9, 1947; s. Dudley and Shendrine Eugene (Boyce) H.; m. Ana Maria Meneses, Dec. 23, 1988; children: Antonia, Adsilla. BS, D.C. Tchrs. Coll., 1969; MA in Edn., Columbia U., 1974, EdD, 1978. Tchr. engring. D.C. Pub. Schs., 1969-71, Binghamton Pub. Schs., Bing, N.Y., 1971-73; asst. prof. U. Mass., Amherst, 1977-79; dir. Tchrs. Coll., N.Y.C., 1979-81, San Jose (Calif.) State U., 1981-88, 89-92; assoc.dean Calif. State U., Northridge, 1988-89; exec. dir. , assoc. prof. Portland State U., 1992—. Mem. Multi-County Com. Child & Family Svcs., Portland, 1993—, Evelyn Robinson Scholar Com., San Jose, 1985-92; mem., pres. exec. bd. United Campus Christian Ctr., San Jose, 1984-87; assoc. campaign mgr. Learned for City Coun., San Jose, 1986. With U.S. Army. Recipient Shiny Apple award L.A. Tchrs. Ctr., 1989, Disting. Svc. award Evelyn Robinson Sch. Com., San Jose, 1992. Mem. ASCD, Smithsonian Inst. Home: 1186 SW 12th Ct Troutdale OR 97060-1495 Office: Portland State U Box 751 Portland OR 97207

HENRY, WILLIAM RADER, mechanical engineering consultant; b. Conover, N.C., Feb. 27, 1943; s. William Huit and Madolyn Floy (Rader) H.; m. Violeta Belen Mercado, Sept. 30, 1969; children: Michelle Lynn, Thomas Vincent. AA, Allan Hancock Jr. Coll., 1966; BS in Mech. Engring., U. Mo., 1969. Registered profl. engr., N.Y., Calif. Engr. B.F. Goodrich, Akron, Ohio, 1969-70; sr. engr. B.F.G. Internat., Akron, 1971-73; area maintenance engr. B.F.G. Tire Co., Oaks, Pa., 1974-75; maintenance mgr. Tropical do Brazil, Fieria de Santana, Okla., 1976-77; area maintenance mgr. B.F.G. Tire Co., Miami, Okla., 1978-79; project engr. GE, Schenectady, N.Y., 1980-81; project mgr. Kinetic Systems, Inc., Santa Clara, N.Y., 1982-84; v.p. Facilitech, Inc., Santa Clara, 1985-91; prin. Facilities Tech. Inc., Santa Clara, 1992-95; owner Energy Tech. Sales & Engring., San Jose, Calif., 1996—. With USAF, 1962-66. Mem. ASME, ASHRAE. Republican. Roman Catholic. Home: 5918 Silver Leaf Rd San Jose CA 95138-1811 Office: Energy Tech Sales and Engring 5918 Silver Leaf Rd San Jose CA 95138

HENSEL, JEFFREY, geologist, consultant; b. Detroit, Nov. 15, 1962; s. Manfred Karl and Liane Bertha (Freuck) H.; m. Kimberly Ann Habel, Sept. 6, 1986; children: Rachael Anna, Kayla Marie. BS in Geology, Wayne State U., 1984; MS in Environ. Studies, Calif. State U., Fullerton, 1992. Registered geologist, Wyo., Calif., Ky.; registered environ. assessor, Calif. Geologist GMC Assocs. Inc., Northville, Mich., 1985-86, BCL Assocs. Inc., Long Beach, Calif., 1986-89; sr. geologist Radian Internat. LLC, Irvine, Calif., 1989—; advisor environ. affairs dept. and environ. studies bd. Calif. State U., Fullerton, 1990-92. Mich. Indsl. Soc. grantee, 1984. Mem. Nat. Water Well Assn., Ducks Unltd. Republican. Roman Catholic. Office: Radian Internat LLC 16845 Von Karman Ave # 100 Irvine CA 92614

HENSLEY, DAVID LAWRENCE, music educator; b. Santa Monica, Calif., June 2, 1957; s. Benjamin R. and Peggy (Zapton) H.; m. Tamara Louise Walters, June 29, 1985; children: Benjamin, Catherine. BA in Music, Calif. State U., Fullerton, 1980; MusM, No. Ariz. U., 1991. Calif. tchg. credential. Music tchr., choral dir. Lompoc (Calif.) H.S., 1980-94; prof. music, choral dir. Porterville (Calif.) Coll., 1994—; founding condr. Lompoc (Calif.) Valley Master Chorale, 1991-94. Arts adv. Santa Barbara Arts Coun., 1987. Mem. Am. Choral Dirs. Assn. (editor western divsn. newsletter 1993-95), Music Educators Nat. Conf., So. Calif. Vocal Assn., Calif. Music Educators Assn., Music Assn. Calif. C.C. Home: 1511 W Brian Ln Porterville CA 93257-1090 Office: Porterville Coll 100 E College Ave Porterville CA 93257-6058

HENSLEY, DOROTHY SUE, elementary educator; b. Louisville, Ky., Apr. 30, 1946; d. Vincent and Dorothy Mae (Staab) H. BA, U. Louisville, 1968; MA, U. Denver, 1972. Tchr. Louisville Pub. Schs., 1968-71, Jefferson County Pub. Schs., Golden, Colo., 1972—. Pres. of bd. Denver Mus. of Miniatures Dolls and Toys, Denver, 1992-94, bd. dirs., 1988-92. Mem. NEA, Jefferson County Edn. Assn., Colo. Edn. Assn., Colo. Coun. of Internat. Reading Assn., Nat. Assn. of Miniature Enthusiasts, Wee Wonders of Arvada.

HENSLEY, JACKSON MOREY, artist; b. Portales, N.Mex., Sept. 6, 1940; s. E.T. Jr. and E.M. Hensley; m. Carolyn Brown Hensley, Aug. 5, 1961 (dec. 1989); children: Michael M., Janet M.; m. Tresa Vorenberg Hensley; Aug. 14, 1989; 1 child, Morika Rose Hensley. Student, Nat. Acad. Design, N.Y.C. Prin. works exhibited in numerous group shows including Knickerbocker Artist Exhibit, N.Y.C., Hudson River Artist Exhibit, White Plains, N.Y., IBM Gallery, Washington, Salmagundi Club, N.Y.C., Stamford (Conn.) Mus., Nat. Arts Club, N.Y.C., La. State Mus., many others; paintings represented in numerous collections including Madewood Plantation House Mus., New Orleans, Desert Caballeros Mus., Wickensburg, Ariz., Diamond T. Found. Mus., Tex., Arabian Horse Trust Mus., Denver, L.A. Mus. West Collection, others. Mem. Salmagundi Club, Cliff Dwellers Club, Arts and Letters Club, Arts Club (Montreal, Washington), Nat. Arts Club, Royal British Club, Savage Club, Chelsea Art Club, Art et Amicite, Providence Art Club. Home: 10 Highview Ln Santa Fe NM 87505

HENSLEY, WILLIAM LYNN (WILLIE HENSLEY), state senator, corporate executive; b. Kotzebue, Alaska, June 17, 1941; s. John and Priscilla Hensley; m. Abigale Ryan; children: Priscilla, Mary Lynn, James, Elizabeth. Student, U. Alaska, 1960-62; BA in Polit. Sci., George Washington U., 1966; postgrad., U. Alaska, spring 1966, LLD (hon.), 1980; postgrad., UCLA, fall 1968. Mem. Alaska Ho. of Reps., 1966-70; senator State of Alaska, 1970-74, 86-88; chmn. United Bank Alaska, Anchorage, 1976-86; pres. N.W. Alaska Native Assn. Devel. Corp., Kotzebue, 1976-94; pres., sr. v.p., dir., founder N.W. Alaska Native Assn. Regional Corp., Kotzebue, 1986-94; commr. Dept. Commerce and Econ. Devel. State of Alaska, 1994—; pres. Alaska Village Electric Coop., 1967-71; chmn., chmn., bd. dirs. Tundra Times, 1979—. Chmn. Alaska Dem. Party, 1968, 84-86, Rural Affairs Commn., 1968-74, Capital Site Selection Com., 1975-76, Reapportionment Commn., 1985, nat. committeeman; bd. regents U. Alaska, 1985-87, bd. dirs. Northwest Regional Ednl. Lab., 1969-71; bd. dirs. Nat. Coun. on Indian Opportunity, 1968-70, Alascom, 1977—, Alaska Fedn. Natives, 1966-80, exec. dir., pres., co-chair; mem. Providence Hosp. Adv. Bd., 1979-87; mem. Clinton Transition Staff, Little Rock, 1992; dir. South-Ctrl. Red Cross, apptd. mem. Pacific regional com. Recipient Nat. Pub. Svc. award Rockefeller Found., 1980; named Citizen of Yr. Alaska Fedn. Natives, 1981. Home: 7045 Tree Top Cir Anchorage AK 99516-6828 Office: Commerce and Econ Devel PO Box 110800 Juneau AK 99811

HENTHORNE, JASON FITZGERALD, explosives consultant; b. Wooster, Ohio, Apr. 17, 1970; s. Jay Geiger Jr. and Mary Beth (Sammons) H. BA in Environ. Studies, Geology, U. Pa., 1993. Field cons. Rucker & Assocs., Charleston, W.Va., 1993-94; cons., pres. J&B Ent., Chapel Hill, N.C., 1994-96; explosives cons./3D CAD modeling Yenter Blasting Cos., Golden, Colo., 1996—. Mem. Rocky Mountain Explosives, Hells Fire Club (co-founder, v.p. 1992—). Republican. Home: 28661 Moss Rock Rd Golden CO 80401 Office: Yenter Companies PO Box 1188 Golden CO 80402

HENTZ, VINCENT R., surgeon; b. Jacksonville, Fla., Aug. 29, 1942. MD, U. Fla., 1968. Intern Stanford (Calif.) Hosp., 1968-69, resident in plastic surgery, 1969-74, now hand surgeon; fellow in hand surgery Roosevelt

Hosp., N.Y.C., 1974-75. Office: Stanford Univ Dept Hand Surgery PO Box 61000 Dept 1415 San Francisco CA 94161*

HENZINGER, THOMAS ANTON, computer science educator; b. Linz, Austria, Dec. 8, 1962; came to U.S., 1985; s. Sigmund A. and Elisabeth H. Diplomas in computer sci. with distinction, Kepler U., Linz, 1984, 87; MS in Computer and Info. Sci., U. Del., 1986; PhD in Computer Sci. with distinction, Stanford U., 1991. Asst. prof. computer sci. Cornell U., Ithaca, N.Y., 1992-95; asst. prof. elec. engring., computer scis. U. Calif., Berkeley, 1996—; visitor AT&T Bell Labs., Murray Hill, N.J., 1991, 92, 93, 94, 95; vis. scientist dept. applied math. Weizmann Inst. Sci., Rehovot, Israel, 1989, 90; postdoctoral visitor Inst. Computer Sci. and Applied Math. Fourier U., Grenoble, France, 1991; jour. referee Distributed Computing, Formal Aspects of Computing, Formal Methods in System Design, Info. and Computation, Jour. Automated Resaoning, Jour. Symbolic Computation; lectr. in field. Contbr. articles to profl. jours. Recipient George E. Forsythe Meml. award Stanford U., 1989, Career Devel. award NSF, 1995, Young Investigator award Office Naval Rsch., 1995; Fulbright fellow, 1985-86, Grad. fellow IBM, 1988-91. Mem. AAAS, Math. Assn. Am., Assn. Computing Machinery (jour. referee conf. referee), IEEE (jour. referee, conf. referee), Assn. Symbolic Logic (jour. referee), Soc. Indsl. and Applied Math. (jour. referee, conf. referee), European Assn. Theoretical Computer Sci. (jour. referee), N.Y. Acad. Scis., Sigma Xi. Office: U Calif EECS Dept 519 Cory Hall Berkeley CA 94720-1770

HEPLER, KENNETH RUSSEL, manufacturing executive; b. Canton, Ohio, Mar. 31, 1926; s. Clifton R. and Mary A. (Sample) H.; m. Beverly Best, June 9, 1945; 1 child, Bradford R. Student, Cleve. Art Inst., 1946-47, Case Western Res. U., 1948-50. V.p., adminstr. A. Carlisle and Co., San Francisco, 1954-67; pres. K.R. Hepler and Co., Menlo Park, Calif., 1968-73, Paramount Press., Jacksonville, Fla., 1974-75; pvt. practice printing broker, 1976-80; chmn. Hickey and Hepler Graphics Inc., San Francisco, 1981—; instr. printing prodn., San Francisco City Coll. With USAAC, 1943-45. Mem. San Francisco Litho Club (pres. 1972), Phila. Litho Club (sec. 1975-76), Newtown Exchange Club (pres. 1976), Elks. Republican. Presbyterian. Office: Hickey & Hepler Graphics Inc 1633 Bayshore Hwy Ste 222 Burlingame CA 94010

HEPLER, MERLIN JUDSON, JR., real estate broker; b. Hot Springs, Va., May 13, 1929; s. Merlin Judson and Margaret Belle (Vines) H.; m. Lanova Helen Roberts, July 25, 1952; children: Nancy Andora, Douglas Stanley. BS in Bus., U. Idaho, 1977; grad., Realtors Inst., 1979. Cert. residential specialist. Enlisted USAF, 1947, advanced through grades to sgt., 1960, ret., 1967; service mgr. Lanier Bus. Products, Gulfport, Miss., 1967-74; sales assoc. Century 21 Singler and Assn., Troy, Idaho, 1977-79; broker B&M Realty, Troy, 1979—. Mem. Nat. Assn. Realtors, Am. Legion, U. Idaho Alumni Assn., Air Force Sgts. Assn. Republican. Lodge: Lions. Home: 1081 Driscoll Ridge Troy ID 83871-9605 Office: B&M Realty W 102 A St PO Box 187 Troy ID 83871-0187

HEPLER, OVID MANSFIELD, minister; b. Englewood, Colo., Jan. 25, 1922; s. Edgar W. and Evalyn (Parks) H.; m. Marian A. Milburn, Jan. 6, 1941; 1 child, Judith Anne. BA, U. Colo., 1966; DD, Faith Sem., Elkins Park, Pa., 1988. Various clerical positions Denver & Rio Grande RR, Denver, 1939-44; editor 1st Bapt. Ch. and Western Voice Pubs., Englewood, Colo., 1945-55; pvt. contractor Littleton, Colo., 1956-66; pastor Haven Bapt. Ch., Denver, 1967—; bd. dirs. Rocky Mt. Evangel. Assn., 1948-68; exec. com. Internat. Coun. Christian Chs., 1983—; pres. Coun. Bible Believing Chs., USA, 1987—. Editor: Western Voice, 1950-55, 85—. Home and Office: Haven Bapt Ch 6600 S Windermere St Littleton CO 80120-3204

HEPPE, KAROL VIRGINIA, lawyer, educator; b. Vinton, Iowa, Mar. 14, 1958; d. Robert Henry and Audry Virginia (Harper) H. BA in Law and Society, U. Calif., Santa Barbara, 1982; JD, People's Coll. of Law, 1989. Cmty. organizer Oreg. Fair Share, Eugene, 1983; law clk. Legal Aid Found. L.A., summer 1986; devel. dir. Ctrl. Am. Refugee Ctr., L.A., 1987-89; exec. dir. Police Watch-The Police Misconduct Lawyer Referral Svc., L.A., 1989-94; instr. People's Coll. of Law, L.A., 1992-94; dir. alternative sentencing project Ctr. Juvenile and Criminal Justice, 1994-95; cons. Bay Area Police Watch, 1996; vol. law clk. Legal Aid Found. L.A., 1984-86, Lane County Legal Aid Svc., Eugene, 1983. Editor (newsletters) Law Studies in Action, 1986, Ctrl. Am. Refugee Ctr., 1986-89, Prison Break, 1994. Bd. dirs. People's Coll. of Law, 1985-90, Law Student Civil Rights Rsch. Coun., N.Y.C., 1986; bd. dirs., law student organizer Nat. Lawyers' Guild, L.A., 1984-87; mem. Coalition for Human Immigrants Rights, 1991-92, So. Calif. Civil Rights Coalition, 1991-92. Scholar, Kramer Found., 1984-88, Law Students' Civil Rights Rsch. Coun., 1986, Davis-Putter Found., 1988, Assn. for Cmty.-Based Edn. Prudential, 1988.

HERB, EDMUND MICHAEL, optometrist, educator; b. Zanesville, Ohio, Oct. 9, 1942; s. Edmund G. and Barbara R. (Michael) H.; divorced; children—Sara, Andrew; m. Jeri Herb. O.D., Ohio State U., 1966. Pvt. practice optometry, Buena Vista, Colo., 1966—; past prof. Timberline campus Colo. Mountain Coll.; past clin. instr. Ohio State U. Sch. Optometry. Mem. Am. Optometric Assn., Colo. Optometric Assn. Home: 16395 Mt Princeton Rd Buena Vista CO 81211-9505 Office: 115 N Tabor St Buena Vista CO 81211 also: Leadville Colorado Med Ctr Leadville CO 80461

HERBAUGH, ROGER DUANE, computer and software company executive; b. Mt. Vernon, Wash., May 20, 1957; s. Donald Lloyd and Kathleen Joyce (Anderson) H.; m. Anne Louise Finlayson, May 8, 1993; children: Andrew David Miller, Celeste Jane Miller, Trevor Allan Miller, Vanessa Anne Herbaugh, Deirdre Rose Herbaugh. AA, Skagit Valley Coll., 1984; BA, Western Wash. U., 1986. Cert. Microsoft profl. Computer programmer Stockmar Northwestern, Mt. Vernon, 1986-87; CEO, computer cons. Herbaugh & Assocs., Inc. Computer Support Group, Mt. Vernon, 1987—; also pres. bd. dirs. Herbaugh & Assocs., Inc., Mt. Vernon; cons. Shell Oil Co., Anacortes, Wash., 1986—, BP Oil Co., Ferndale, Wash., 1986-93, ARCO, Blaine, Wash., 1989—, Tosco, Ferndale, Wash., 1993-97, Tosco, Seattle, 1993-97; Microsoft Solutions provider; bd. dirs., pres. Software Plus, Inc., Mt. Vernon, 1991—. Sgt. U.S. Army, 1975-81. Mem. Burlington C. of C., Mt. Vernon C. of C., Kiwanis (pres., bd. dirs. Mt. Vernon chpt.). Republican. Mem. LDS Ch. Office: Herbaugh & Assocs Inc Computer Support Group 1754 S Burlington Blvd Burlington WA 98233-3224

HERBERT, CAROL SELLERS, farming executive, lawyer; b. Durham, N.C., Mar. 2, 1943; d. George Grover and Mae (Savage) Sellers; m. James Keller Herbert, Nov. 13, 1980; children: John, Katherine, Paul, Barry. BA, Duke U., 1964; JD cum laude, Whittier Coll., 1976. Bar: Calif. 1976, U.S. Dist. Ct. (cen. dist.) Calif. 1976. Tchr. h.s. Wasatch Sch. Dist., Heber, Utah, 1964-67; dir., tchr. Pinedale (Mont.) Sch. Dist., 1967-71; adminstr. Whittier Law Sch., L.A., 1971-76; lawyer Katz Granof Palarz, Beverly Hills, Calif., 1976-79; exec. dir. MBJ Legal and Profl. Pub., Inc., L.A., 1979-83; dean San Joaquin Coll. Law, Fresno, Calif., 1981-85; pres., co-founder Barrister Project, L.A., 1985-90, Herbert Found., Fresno and Lindsay, Calif., 1990—; dir., CFO HerCal Corp., Lindsay, Calif.; trustee Domus Mitus Found., Fresno, 1994-96; founder Beverly Hills Bar Assn. Com. on Women and Law, 1977; dir. CLI DreamWeavers Divsn., Lindsay, Calif., 1995; reiki master Usui Shiki Ryoho, 1996. Prodr. Lang. of Dreams (video series), 1994-97. Mem. ABA, Calif. State Bar Assn.

HERBERT, CHESLEY C., psychiatrist, educator; b. Charlotte, N.C., June 7, 1943; m. Marie Genevieve Groszko, Aug. 10, 1975; Rachel G., Andrew G. AB in History, Duke U., 1961-65; MD, Columbia U., 1965-69. Diplomate Am. Bd. Psychiatry and Neurology; lic. physician and surgeon, Calif., Nat. Bd. Med. Examiners, DEA. Intern Harlem Hosp. Ctr., N.Y.C., 1969-70; resident in psychiatry U. Calif., San Francisco, 1970-73, fellow in social psychiatry, 1973-75; pvt. practice San Francisco, 1973—; asst. clin. prof. psychiatry U. Calif., San Francisco, 1975-83, assoc. clin. prof., 1983—; staff psychiatrist On Lok Sr. Health Svcs., San Francisco, 1980—; cons. Psychopathic divsn. Superior Ct., San Francisco, 1974-78, North of Market Sr. Alcohol Program, San Francisco, 1979-80; psychiatrist srs. unit N.E. Mental Health Ctr., San Francisco, 1975-79; chief divsn. psychiatry and psychology dept. medicine Davies Med. Ctr., San Francisco, 1996—; mem. courtesy staff mem. St. Francis Meml. Hosp., Calif. Pacific Med. Ctr., Chinese Hosp. Contbr. articles to profl. jours. Mem. Am. Psychiat. Assn., No. Calif. Psychiat. Soc., Calif. Med. Assn., San Francisco Med. Soc. Office: 45 Castro St Ste 302 San Francisco CA 94114-1010

HERBERT, CHRISTOPHER JAY, marketing professional, management consultant; b. Flint, Mich., May 8, 1953; s. Clarence LaVern and Doris Julia (Potter) H.; m. Nancy Ellen Welch, Dec. 19, 1987. BA, Lewis and Clark Coll., 1975; MBA, Ariz. State U., 1984. Cert. neuro-linguistic programming practitioner. Planner Maricopa Employment and Tng. Adminstrn., Phoenix, 1977-78; asst. dir. for planning and program devel. Maricopa County Human Resources Dept., Phoenix, 1978-81, CETA adminstr., 1981; v.p. Cons. Assocs., Inc., Phoenix, 1981-82; pres. C.J. Herbert & Co. Inc., Scottsdale, Ariz., 1982-85; v.p. Behavior Rsch. Ctr., Inc., Phoenix, 1985-89; pres. The Insight Group Inc., Tempe, Ariz., 1989—; mem. mktg. com. Phoenix Symphony, 1988-90. Bd. dirs. Grand Canyon Assn., 1992—, pres. 1994-96, chair governance com., 1996—, bd. dirs. Grand Canyon Fund, 1995—, v.p. 1995—; bd. dirs. The Phoenicians, 1994. Mem. Qualitative Rsch. Cons. Assn. (chair professionalism com. 1992-95, conv. speaker 1993, 94, 95, treas. bd. dirs. 1995), Am. Assn. Polit. Cons., Am. Assn. Pub. Opinion Rsch., Am. Inst. Wine and Food (chmn. Ariz. chpt. 1993, mem. nat. membership com. 1994), Brotherhood of Knights of the Vine (Master Knight, bd. dirs. Phoenix chpt. 1991-95), Phoenix C. of C. (bd. dirs. 1987-89, chmn. small bus. coun. 1986-87, mem. health coun. 1993—). Office: The Insight Group Inc 2105 E Vaughn St Tempe AZ 85283-3343

HERBERT, GAVIN SHEARER, health care products company executive; b. Los Angeles, Mar. 26, 1932; s. Gavin and Josephine (D'Vitha) H.; children by previous marriage Cynthia, Lauri, Gavin, Pam; 2d. m. Ninetta Flanagan, Sept. 6, 1986. B.S., U. So. Calif., 1954. With Allergan, Inc., Irvine, Calif., 1950—, v.p., 1956-61, exec. v.p., pres., 1961-77, chmn. bd., CEO, 1977-91, chmn. bd., 1992-95, chmn. emeritus; pres. Eye and Skin Care Products Group Smith Kline Beckman Corp., 1981-89; exec. v.p. Smith Kline Beckman Corp., 1986-89; bd. dirs. Beckman Instruments, Inc., Calif. Healthcare Inst. Mem. Rsch. to Prevent Blindness (bd. dirs.), Big Canyon Country Club, Newport Harbor Yacht Club, Pacific Club, Beta Theta Pi. Republican. Office: Allergan Inc PO Box 19534 2525 Dupont Dr Irvine CA 92715-1531

HERBERT, KENNETH GEORGE, management consultant; b. Fairfax, Va., Mar. 30, 1968; s. Gary Arthur Herbert and Helen Marjorie (Schade) Craft; m. Isabelle Bouilly, Aug. 9, 1991. BA in Politics, U. Calif., Santa Cruz, 1991. Industry analyst Def. Forecasts, Washington, 1991-92; sr. analyst Frost & Sullivan, Mountain View, Calif., 1992-94, rsch. dir., 1994-97; corp. dir. Frost & Sullivan, Mountain View, 1997—. Mem. Santa Clara Valley Armed Forces Comm. and Electronics Assn. (bd. dirs. 1994—). Home: 721 Independence Ave Mountain View CA 94043-2655 Office: Frost and Sullivan 2525 Charleston Rd Mountain View CA 94043-1626

HERBERT, MARY KATHERINE ATWELL, freelance writer; b. Grove City, Pa., Dec. 9, 1945; d. Stewart and Luella Irene (Brown) Atwell; m. Roland Marcus Herbert; children: Stephen Todd, Amy Elizabeth, Jill Anne. BA, Ariz. State U., 1968, MA, 1973; film cert., U. So. Calif., 1978. Film writer Scottsdale Daily Progress, 1976-79; dir. pub. relations Phoenix Theatre, 1980-85; script analyst, 1985-86; exec. asst. to v.p. prodn. DeLaurentiis Entertainment Group, 1986; producer's assoc. film TRAXX, 1986-87; devel. dir. Devin/DeVore Prodns., 1988-89; free-lance script analyst and writer Glendale, Calif., 1989—. Script writer: (TV shows) Trial By Jury, Dick Clark Prodn., Dry Heat, Blind Desire, others; author: Writing Scripts Hollywood Will Love, 1994. bd. mgrs. Hollywood-Wilshire YMCA, 1992-96. Mem. Ariz. Forum, Kappa Delta Pi, Pi Lambda Theta.

HERBERT, ROBERT NORMAN, engineering company executive; b. Cotati, Calif., Jan. 13, 1924; s. William Fulton and Abbie May (Churchill) H.; m. Helen Jane Osgood, Feb. 25, 1945 (div. 1948); 1 child, Susan Jane; m. Helen Elizabeth Hardy, Feb. 17, 1951; children: Elizabeth Lee, Justine Ann. AA, Santa Rosa (Calif.) Jr. Coll., 1942; BS, MIT, 1947. Registered profl. engr., Wash. Ship supt. Todd Shipyards, Alameda, Calif., 1948-51; naval architect P.F. Spaulding & Assocs., Seattle, 1953-63; cons. naval architect Robert N. Herbert, NA, San Francisco, 1963-75; pres. Herbert Engring. Corp., San Francisco, 1975-83, chmn. bd., 1983—. Contbr. articles to profl. jours. Mem. Soc. Naval Architects and Marine Engrs. (chmn. North Calif. sect. 1974-75, v.p. 1983-84, David W. Taylor medal 1986), Internat. Forest Products Transport Assn. (sec.-treas. 1982—). Republican.

HERBST, DAVID W., lawyer; b. Pomona, Calif., June 17, 1952. BA magna cum laude, Pomona Coll., 1974; JD, Stanford U., 1977. Bar: Calif. 1977, U.S. Tax Ct. 1979. Mem. Wise & Shepard, Palo Alto, Calif. Mem. ABA, State Bar Calif., Santa Clara County Bar Assn., Palo Alto Bar Assn. Office: Holtzmann Wise & Shepard 3030 Hansen Way Palo Alto CA 94304-1006

HERDECK, DONALD ELMER, publishing executive, retired humanities educator; b. Chgo., Nov. 19, 1924; s. Elmer and Violet (Cotter) H.; m. Margaret L. Laniak. BA, MA, U. Chgo., 1948; PhD, U. Pa., 1968. Tchr. French and English Girard Coll., Phila., 1952-54; fgn. svc. officer U.S. Dept. State, Washington, 1955-64; assoc. prof. humanities Georgetown U., Washington, 1965-87; pub., chmn., pres. Three Continents Press, Colorado Springs, 1973-96; pres., editor, publ. Passeggiata Press, Pueblo, Colo., 1996—. Author: African Authors: A Bio-Critical Bibliographical Ency., 1971, Caribbean Writers: A Bio-Critical Bibliographical Ency., 1974; editor, contbr. Three Dynamite Authors: Derek Walcott, Naguib Mahfouz, Wole Soyinka, 1994, Appreciating the Difference: The Biography of Three Continents Press, 1996. Pres. Cabin John Citizens Assn., Bethesda, Md., 1969-70. With U.S. Army, 1943-46, ETO. Mem. African Lit. Assn., 103d Infantry Assoc.

HERDEG, HOWARD BRIAN, physician; b. Buffalo, Oct. 14, 1929; s. Howard Bryan and Martha Jean (Williams) H.; m. Beryl Ann Fredricks, July 21, 1955; children: Howard Brian III, Erin Ann Kociela. Student Paul Smith's Coll., 1947-48, U. Buffalo, 1948-50, Canisius Coll., 1949; DO, Phila. Coll. Osteopathic Medicine, 1954; MD, U. Calif.-Irvine Coll. Medicine, 1962. Diplomate Am. Acad. Pain Mgmt. Intern, Burbank (Calif.) Hosp., 1954-55; practice medicine specializing in gen. medicine, surgery and pain mgmt., Woodland Hills, Calif., 1956—; chief med. staff West Park Hosp., Canoga Park, Calif., 1971-72, trustee, 1971-73; chief family practice dept. West Hills Regional Med. Center (formerly Humaua Hosp. West Hills, 1982-83, 84-85, 88-89), mem. exec. com., 1984-85, 88-89, Mem. Hidden Hills (Calif.) Pub. Safety Commn., 1978-82; bd. dirs. Hidden Hills Community Assn., 1971-73, pres., 1972; bd. dirs. Hidden Hills Homeowners Assn., 1973-75, pres., 1976-77; bd. dirs. Woodland Hills Freedom Season, 1961-67, pres., 1962; mem. Hidden Hills City Council, 1984—, mayor pro tem, 1987-90, mayor, 1990-92. Recipient disting. service award Woodland Hills Jr C. of C., 1966. Mem. Woodland Hills C. of C. (dir. 1959-68, pres. 1967), Theta Chi, Gamma Pi. Republican. Home: 24530 Deep Well Rd Hidden Hills CA 91302-1210 Office: 22600 Ventura Blvd Woodland Hills CA 91364-1414

HERENDEEN, DAVID LOUIS, software company executive; b. Niagara Falls, N.Y., July 12, 1946; s. Donald George and Lois Irene (Stewardson) H.; m. Carol Ann Coulter, Dec. 3, 1966 (div. Dec. 1980); 1 child, Melissa Ann; m. Lenora May Linabury, Dec. 21, 1980. AS in Math., Niagara County C.C., 1966; BS in Computer Sci., UCLA, 1975. Assoc. engr. Bell Aerospace Corp., Buffalo, N.Y., 1966-72; mng. Hughes Aircraft Co., El Segundo, Calif., 1972-73, 78-79, MacNeal-Schwedler Corp., Pasadena, Calif., 1979-82; v.p. Universal Analytics, Inc., Torrance, Calif., 1973-77, 82—; bd. dirs. Universal Analytics, Inc. Contbr. articles to profl. jours. Recipient Douglas Michel Nastran Achievement award NASA, 1993. Mem. AIAA, IEEE Computer Sci., Assn. for Computing Machinery. Office: Universal Analytics Inc 3625 Del Amo Blvd Ste 370 Torrance CA 90503-1689

HERETH, LYLE GEORGE, electrical engineering technologist; b. Everett, Wash., Oct. 14, 1947; s. L. Walter and Alvina Katharina (Weber) H.; m. Margaret Sue Brewer, Dec. 19, 1978; children: Christopher, Walter, Emilie, Jennifer, Jacob. BS in Elec. Engring. Tech., Weber State Coll., 1975; M of Engring. Adminstrn., U. Utah, 1981. Quality engr. Nat. Semiconductor, Salt Lake City, 1975-78, Beehive Internat., Salt Lake City, 1978-80; quality mgr. Sperry Univac, Salt Lake City, 1980-82; sys. devel. mgr. LDS Ch., Salt Lake City, 1982-85, dir. tech., arch., 1985-90, asst. coord., 1990-93, cons. emerging tech., 1993—; chmn. info. sys. VIM, CDC Corp., Minn., 1984-89; project mgr. geneal. sys. FamilySearch, 1987 (Smith award 1992, 95). Chmn. planning and zoning South Salt Lake City Govt., 1986-94. Recipient Pub. Svc. awards South Salt Lake Govt., 1983, 94. Mem. Am. Soc. Quality Control, Assn. for Info. and Image Mgmt. Mem. LDS Ch. Office: LDS Ch FHD 50E N Temple Salt Lake City UT 84150

HERGER, WALLY W., congressman; b. Yuba City, Calif., May 20, 1945. Formerly mem. Calif. State Assembly; mem. 100th-102d Congresses from 2d Calif. dist., 1987—; mem. agr., mcht. marine and fisheries coms. 100th-103rd Congresses from 2d Calif. dist.; mem. budget com., mem. ways and means com.; owner Herger Gas, Inc. Office: US House of Representatives 2433 Rayburn Bldg Washington DC 20515-0005

HERING, WILLIAM MARSHALL, medical organization executive; b. Indpls., Dec. 26, 1940; s. William Marshall and Mary Agnes (Clark) H.; m. Suzanne Wolfe, Aug. 10, 1963. BS, Ind. U., 1961, MS, 1962; PhD, U. Ill., Urbana, 1973. Tchr. Indpls. pub. schs., 1962-66; asst. dir. sociol. resources project Am. Sociol. Assn., 1966-70; dir. social sci. curriculum Biomed. Interdisciplinary Project, Berkeley, Calif., 1973-76; staff assoc. Tchrs. Ctrs. Exchange, San Francisco, 1976-82; dir. research Far West Lab. Ednl. Research and Devel., San Francisco, 1979-82, sr. research assoc., 1982-85; mgr. human resource devel. Bank Am., San Francisco, 1985-94; dir. programs Am. Acad. Ophthalmology, San Francisco, 1994—; mem. Nat. Adv. Bd. Educ. Resource Info. Ctr.; cons. U.S. Dept. Edn.; pres. Social Sci. Educ. Consortium, 1981-82, bd. dirs., 1979-81; bd. dirs. San Francisco Chamber Orch., 1986—. Nat. Inst. Educ. grantee, 1979-82. Mem. Am. Soc. Tng. and Devel. (v.p. 1986), Golden Gate Soc., Nat. Audubon Soc., Phi Delta Kappa. Republican. Episcopalian. Contbr. over 100 articles on social studies edn., staff devel., ednl. research and evaluation to profl. jours. Home: 731 Duboce Ave San Francisco CA 94117-3214 Office: 655 Beach St San Francisco CA 94109-1336

HERMAN, ANDREA MAXINE, newspaper editor; b. Chgo., Oct. 22, 1938; d. Maurice H. and Mae (Baron) H.; m. Joseph Schmidt, Oct. 28, 1962. BJ, U. Mo., 1960. Feature writer Chgo.'s Am., 1960-63; daily columnist News Am., Balt., 1963-67; feature writer Mainichi Daily News, Tokyo, 1967-69; columnist Iowa City Press-Citizen, 1969-76; music and dance critic San Diego Tribune, 1976-84; asst. mng. editor features UPI, Washington, 1984-86, asst. mng. editor news devel., 1986-87; mng. editor features L.A. Herald Examiner, 1987-91; editor/culture We/Mbl Newspaper, Washington, 1991—. Recipient 1st and 2d prizes for features in arts James S. Copley Ring of Truth Awards, 1982, 1st prize for journalism Press Club San Diego, 1983. Mem. Soc. Profl. Journalists, Am. Soc. Newspaper Editors, AP Mng. Editors, Women in Communications. Office: We/Mbl Newspaper 1350 Connecticut Ave NW Washington DC 20036-1701

HERMAN, GEORGE ADAM, writer; b. Norfolk, Va., Apr. 12, 1928; s. George Adam and Minerva Nevada (Thompson) H.; m. Patricia Lee Glazer, May 26, 1955 (div. 1989); children: Kurt, Erik, Karl, Lisa, Katherine, Christopher, Jena, Amanda; m. Patricia Jane Piper Dubay, Aug. 25, 1989; children: Lizette, Paul, Kirk, Victoria. PhB, Loyola Coll., 1950; MFA, Cath. U., 1954; cert. fine arts, Boston Coll., 1951,52,53. Asst. prof. Clarke Coll., Dubuque, Iowa, 1955-60, Villanova (Pa.) U., 1960-63; asst. prof., playwright in residence Coll. St. Benedict, St. Joseph, Minn., 1963-65; chmn. theatre dept. Coll. Great Falls, Mont., 1965-67; media specialist Hawaii State Dept. Edn., Honolulu, 1967-75, staff specialist, 1975-83; sr. drama critic Honolulu Advertiser, 1975-80; artistic dir. Commedia Repertory Theatre, Honolulu, 1978-80; freelance writer, lectr. Portland, Oreg., 1983—; lectr. Portland State U., 1985—; film actor SAG, L.A., 1975—. Author: (plays) Company of Wayward Saints, 1963 (McKnight Humanities award 1964), Mr. Highpockets, 1968, A Stone for Either Hand, 1969, Tenebrae, 1984, (novels) Carnival of Saints, 1994 (finalist Oreg. Book Awards 1994), A Comedy of Murders, 1994, Tears of the Madonna, 1995. Pres. local chpt. Nat. Sch. Pub. Rels. Assn., Honolulu, 1981-83; bd. dirs. Honolulu Community Theatre, 1981-82, Hawaii State Theatre Coun., Honolulu, 1981. With U.S. Army, 1950-52. Named Genesian Jewel Nat. Cath. Theatre Conf., 1949; recipient Hartke Playwrighting award Cath. U., 1954, Excellence award Am. Security Coun., 1967. Mem. Am. Legion, Amnesty Internat., Ednl. Theatre Assn. (bd. dirs. 1990—). Office: PO Box 3238 Newberg OR 97132-5238

HERMAN, JAMES JEROME, electronics engineer, lawyer; b. Sheboygan, Wis., July 23, 1929; s. Jacob and Amalia (Biel) H.; m. Lynn R. Willis, Sept. 8, 1951; children: Mark, Julie, Matthew. BA, Ripon (Wis.) Coll., 1952; BS in Elec. Engring., MIT, 1952; MSEE, U. Wis., 1956; JD, U. Santa Clara, 1979. Electronics engr. Raytheon, Waltham, Mass., 1952; grad. sch. rsch. asst. U. Wis., Madison, 1955-56; sr. electronics engr. Convair divsn. Gen. Dynamics, San Diego, 1956-59; prin. engr. Link Divsn. Gen. Precision Corp., Palo Alto, Calif., 1959-60; rsch. specialist, staff engr., sr. staff engr., tech. cons. Lockheed Missiles & Space Co., Sunnyvale, Calif., 1960-90; vol. atty. Sr. Citizens Legal Svcs., Santa Cruz, Calif., 1994. Vol. Habitat for Humanity, Santa Cruz, 1995-97. 1st lt. USAF, 1953-55. Recipient Pub. Svc. Group Achievement award NASA, 1981. Mem. AIAA, IEEE, Calif. State Bar. Republican. Lutheran. Home: 3040 Wisteria Way Aptos CA 95003-3318

HERMSEN, JAMES R., lawyer; b. Orange, Calif., Oct. 2, 1945. BA, U. Wash., 1967, JD, 1970. Bar: Wash. 1971. Ptnr. Miller, Nash, Wiener, Hager & Carlsen, Seattle; mem. Bur. of Competition Fed. Trade Commn., 1971-73. Mem. ABA, Seattle-King County Bar Assn., Wash. State Bar Assn., Am. Bar Assn., Phi Beta Kappa, Omicron Delta Epsilon, Phi Delta Phi. Office: Miller Nash Wiener Hager & Carlsen 4400 Two Union Sq 601 Union St Seattle WA 98101-2327

HERNANDEZ, CARROL, social services administrator. Dir. mental health divsn. Dept. Social Svcs., Olympia, Wash. Office: Dept Social Svcs PO Box 45320 Olympia WA 98504

HERNANDEZ, FRANK, university educator, federal agency administrator, educator; b. Saginaw, Mich., Oct. 4, 1931; s. Jesus A. and Paula (Soliz) H.; m. Lupe Marie Silva, Apr. 11, 1959; children: Nora Clark, Judy Krohn, Daniel Hernandez. BS in Psychology, Ctrl. Mich. U., 1958; MA in Edn., San Francisco State U., 1973; MPA, U. So. Calif., 1975. Juvenile probation officer Saginaw County Juvenile Ct., Saginaw, 1959-61, asst. county juvenile agt., 1961-62; welfare coord., adult probation officer City of Saginaw, 1962-65; mediator family ct., adult probation officer San Mateo County, Belmont, Calif., 1965-86; lectr. dept. pub. adminstrn. San Francisco State U., 1989-92; acad. ctr. advisor Embry-Riddle Aero. U., Moffett Field, Calif., 1988—; rschr. Family Court Svcs., San Mateo (Calif.) County, 1977; lectr. dept. polit. sci. San Jose (Calif.) State U., 1977-94; expert witness Family Law Specialist Calif. State Bar, San Francisco, 1980; honorarium panel spkr. continuing edn. of the bar U. Calif. Law Sch., Berkeley, 1979; tng. admihnstr. human resources NASA/Ames, 1996—; spkr., presenter, Internat. Conf. Mexico City, 1990. Mem. Free and Accepted Masons of Calif., Tau Kappa Epsilon. Home: 4910 Birmingham Dr San Jose CA 95136-2908

HERNANDEZ, JO FARB, museum curator, consultant; b. Chgo., Nov. 20, 1952. BA in Polit. Sci. & French with honors, U. Wis., 1974; MA in Folklore and mythology, UCLA, 1975; postgrad., U. Calif., Davis, 1978, U. Calif., Berkeley, 1978-79, 81. Registration Mus. Cultural History UCLA, 1974-75; Rockefeller fellow Dallas Mus. Fine Arts, 1976-77; asst. to dir. Triton Mus. Art, Santa Clara, Calif., 1977-78, dir., 1978-85; adj. prof. mus. studies John F. Kennedy U., San Francisco, 1978; grad. advisor arts adminstrn. San Jose (Calif.) State U., 1979-80; dir. Monterey (Calif.) Peninsula Mus. Art, 1985-93, cons. curator, 1994—; prin. Curatorial and Mus. Mgmt. Svcs., Watsonville, Calif., 1993—; lectr., panelist, juror, panelist in field USIA, Calif. Arts Coun., Calif. Confedn. for Arts, Am. Folklore Soc., Calif. Folklore Soc., others; vis. lectr. U. Wis., 1980, Northwestern U., 1981, San Jose State U., 1985, UCLA, 1986, Am. Cultural Ctr., Jerusalem, 1989, Tel Aviv, 1989, Binat. Ctr., Lima, Peru, 1988, Daytona Beach Mus. Art, 1983, UCLA, 1986, Israel Mus., 1989, U. Chgo., 1981, Northwestern U., 1981, Mont. State U., 1991, Oakland Mus., 1996, others; guest curator San Diego Mus. Art, 1995—; guest on various TV and radio programs. Contbr. articles to profl. publs.; author: (mus. catalogs) The Day of the Dead: Tradition and Change in Contemporary Mexico, 1979, Three from the Northern Island:

Contemporary Sculpture from Hokkaido, 1984, Crime and Punishment: Reflections of Violence in Contemporary Art, 1984, The Quiet Eye: Pottery of Shoji Hamada and Bernard Leach, 1990, Alan Shepp: The Language of Stone, 1991, Wonderful Colors: The Paintings of August Francois Gay, 1993, Jeannette Maxfield Lewis: A Centennial Celebration, 1994, Armin Hansen, 1994, Jeremy Anderson: The Critical Link/A Quiet Revolution, 1995, A.G. Rizzoli: Architect of Magnificent Visions, 1997, among others. Bd. dirs. Bobbie Wynn and Co. of San Jose, 1981-85, Santa Clara Arts and Hist. Consortium, 1985; bd. dirs. Non-Profit Gallery Assn., 1979-83, v.p., 1979-80; mem. nat. adv. bd. The Fund for Folk Culture, Santa Fe, 1995-98. Recipient Golden Eagle award Coun. Internat. Non-theatrical Events, 1992, Leader of Decade award Arts Leadership Monterey Peninsula, 1992. Mem. Am. Assn. Mus. (mus. assessment program surveyor 1990, 94, lectr. 1986, nat. program com. 1992-93), Calif. Assn. Mus. (chair ann. meeting 1990, chair nominating com. 1988, 90, 93, bd. dirs. 1985-94, v.p. 1987-91, pres. 1991-92), Artable, Am. Folklore Soc., Western Mus. Conf. (bd. dirs., exec. com. 1989-91, program chair 1990), Nat. Coun. for Edn. in Ceramic Arts, Phi Beta Kappa. Office: Curatorial and Mus Mgmt Svcs 345 White Rd Watsonville CA 95076-0429

HERNANDEZ, LILLIAN A., health facility administrator; b. Inglewood, Calif., May 12, 1959; d. John Erling and Lillian Alice (Hastings) Johnson; m. David Robert Hernandez, Aug. 11, 1979; children: Linda Marie, Amber Michelle, Christine Lee. AA, Cerritos Jr. Coll., 1981; BS in Bus., Calif. State U., Long Beach, 1986. Cert. quality circle facilitator. Note teller Bank of Am., Bellflower, Calif., 1978-79; computer operator Piping Products West, Vernon, Calif., 1981; counselor/asst. mgr. Zoe Employment Agy., Los Alamitos, Calif., 1981-82; pers. asst./quality circle facilitator Hazel of Calif. Inc., Santa Fe Springs, 1982-86; employment coord. PARTNERS Nat. Health Plans, San Bernardino, Calif., 1987-89; owner Cream Whippeeze, Riverside, Calif., 1989-91; Riverside County media coord. William Dannemeyer for U.S. Senate, 1991-92; human resources dir. Manor Care Health Svcs., Hemet, Calif., 1993—; Interview panalist City of Riverside, Calif., 1990. Chmn. Citizens' Adv. Affirmative Action Com., Riverside, Calif., 1990; founding mem. Riverside Citizens for Responsible Behavior, 1990—; bd. dirs. Greater Riverside Hispanic Chamber, 1989-91; mem. Community Rels. Commn., 87-94; chmn. recreation and culture, 1989-90, parliamentarian, 1988-90; assoc. mem. Calif. Rep. State Cen. Com., 1989-92; mem. Calif. Rep. State Com., Riverside County Ctrl. Com.; vice-chair 2d supervisoral dist.; adv. com. law enforcement policy, Calif. Rep. State Party, 1989-92, del., 1992—; founding mem. v.p. Riverside Citizens for Responsible Behavior, 1990—, assoc. mem., 1989-92, del., 1992—, sec. health and human svcs. commn., 1995—; mem. Cmty Rels. Commn., 1987-89. Mem. Personnel and Indsl. Rels. Assn., Profls. in Human Resources Assn., Soc. Human Resource Mgmt. Republican. Office: Manor Care Health Svcs 1717 W Stetson Ave Hemet CA 92545-6882

HERNANDEZ, SAM, sculptor, educator; b. Hayward, Calif., Jan. 23, 1948; s. Ferdinand Rudolph and Martha (Pelaez) H.; m. Jo Farb, Sept. 5, 1976; 1 child, Larissa Anne. BA in Art, Calif. State U., Hayward, 1970; diploma (hon.), U. Sonora, Mexico, 1972; MFA in Art, U. Wis., 1974. Dir. sculpture program East Tex. State U., Commerce, 1974-77; asst. prof. Santa Clara (Calif.) U., 1977-83, assoc. prof., 1983-96, chair art dept., 1980-86, prof., 1996—; vis. lectr. U. Wis., Madison, 1980; artist in residence Skopje (Macedonia) U., 1986; vis. artist Honolulu (Hawaii) Acad. Arts, 1992; vis. instr. Anderson Ranch, Snowmass Village, Colo., 1994, 95, Haystack Sch., Deer Isle, Maine, 1994. One man shows include Palm Springs Desert Mus., Oakland Mus., San Jose Mus. Art, Fresno Art Mus., Honolulu Acad. Arts, U. Oreg. Mus. Art.; group shows include San Francisco Mus. Modern Art, Crocker Art Mus., Sacramento, Am. Craft Mus., N.Y.C., Philbrook Mus. Art, Tulsa, Mexican Mus., San Francisco, Contemporary Mus., Honolulu, Contemporary Art Ctr., Cin., Mus. of Macedonia, Skopje, New Orleans Mus. Art, Milw. Art Mus., Lowe Art Mus., Coral Gables, Fla., Des Moines Art Ctr., Denver Art Mus., Chgo. Cultural Ctr., Laguna Art Mus., Va. Mus. Fine Art; co-author: The Day of the Dead: Tradition and Change in Contemporary Mexico, 1979. Individual Artist fellow Cultural Coun. Santa Clara (Calif.) County, 1983, Visual Artist fellow Nat. Endowment for the Arts, Washington, 1984, Sr. Fulbright fellow Fulbright Program, 1986; Individual Artist grantee No. Calif. Grantmakers/NEA, Santa Cruz, 1989. Office: Santa Clara U Art Dept Bellomy at the Alameda Santa Clara CA 95053

HEROLD, RALPH ELLIOTT, motion picture arts educator; b. L.A., Dec. 5, 1919; s. Henry Danelle and Isabelle (Baker) H. BS, St. Andrews Coll., 1951; PhD in Mgmt. Sci., Clayton U., 1978. Instr. media sci. L.A. City Schs., 1949-56; staff asst. flight ops. Hughes Aircraft Co., Culver City, Calif., 1955-57; mgr. logistics & program control N.Am. Aviation, L.A., Canoga Park, Downey, Calif., 1957-67; mgr. quality assurance McDonnell Douglas Astronautics, Huntington Beach, Calif., 1967-70; dir. motivational sci. Systematics, Fullerton, Calif., 1970-74; pers. dir. Chapman U., Orange, Calif., 1974-75; instr. Am. film heritage Rancho Santiago Coll., Santa Ana, Calif., 1976—. Contbr. numerous articles to profl. jours.; prodr. film-to-video Objective Kobe, own color footage of Kobe, Japan in WWII. Lt. col. U.S. Army Signal Corps, 1940-63. Mem. Theater Hist. Soc. Am., Ret. Officers Assn., Cinecon, Hollywood Stuntman's Assn. Home: 5892 Amberdale Dr Yorba Linda CA 92886

HERPIN, WILLIAM BERNARD, JR., program manager; b. St. Petersburg, Fla., Aug. 16, 1943; s. William Bernard Herpin Sr. and Mary Louise (Johnston) Murrah; m. Linda Elaine Bjornerud, June 6, 1965; children: Tiffany, Nikki, Kari. BS in Aerospace Engring., U. Kans., 1973; MA in Computer Resource Mgmt., Webster U., 1985. Comm. officer USS John Marshall, Vallejo, Calif., 1974-75; asst. weapons officer USS John Marshall, Pearl Harbor, Hawaii, 1975-77; tng. support officer Naval Submarine Tng. Ctr. Pacific, Pearl Harbor, Hawaii, 1977-79; ops. officer USS Robert E Lee, Pearl Harbor, Hawaii, 1979-80; br. chief Air Force Space Command, Colorado Springs, 1980-85; task leader Nat. Systems & Rsch. Co., Colorado Springs, 1985-94, program mgr., 1994—; mem. accountability com. Sch. Dist. 11, Colorado Springs, 1984-85. V.p. Pikes Peak Chpt. MADD, Colorado Springs, 1983-86; sr. victim asst. team caseworker Colorado Springs Police Dept., 1987—, handicap parking enforcement officer, 1993—; pres. Our Savior Luth. Ch., Colorado Springs, 1989-94. Lt./Capt. USN/USAF, 1965-85. Named Colo. lifesaver Colo. Dept. Hwy. Safety, 1986, Outstanding vol. Colorado Springs Police Dept. Traffic, 1988. Mem. The Ret. Officers Assn., Law Enforcement Alliance of Am., Pikes Peak Computer Application Soc. (treas. Sysop 1980—), NRA, Pikes Peak Chpt. MADD (v.p. treas. 1984—). Republican. Lutheran. Home: 532 Potter Ct Colorado Springs CO 80909-5427 Office: Nat Systems & Rsch Co 5475 Mark Dabling Blvd Ste 200 Colorado Springs CO 80918-3848

HERRERA, JOHN, professional football team executive; married; 8 children. BA in History, U. Calif., Davis. Tng. camp asst. Oakland Raiders, 1963-68, pub. rels. asst., 1968, dir. pub. rels., 1978-80, sr. exec., 1985—; dir. player pers. B.C. Lions, 1981-82; gen. mgr. Sask. Roughriders, 1983-84; with scouting depts. Tampa Bay Buccaneers, 1975-76, Washington Redskins, 1977. Office: Oakland Raiders 1220 Harbor Day Pkwy Alameda CA 94502

HERRERA, ROBERT BENNETT, retired mathematics educator; b. L.A., July 24, 1913; s. Royal Robert and Rachel (Mix) H.; AA, L.A. City Coll., 1934; AB, UCLA, 1937, MA, 1939; m. Agnes Mary MacDougall, May 18, 1941; children: Leonard B., Mary Margaret, William R. Tchr. high sch., Long Beach, Calif., 1939-41; statistician U.S. Forest Survey, Berkeley, Calif., 1941-45; faculty L.A. City Coll., 1946-79, prof. math., 1966-79, chmn. math. dept., 1975-79, ret., 1979; lectr. math. UCLA, 1952-75; cons. Ednl. Testing Svc., Princeton, 1965-68, Addison Wesley Pub. Co., 1966-68, Goodyear Pub. Co., 1970-76. Mem. AAAS, Math. Assn. Am. (past sec. So. Calif. sect., past gov.), Am. Math. Soc., Internat. Oceanic Soc., Phi Beta Kappa, Pi Mu Epsilon. Democrat. Author: (with C. Bell, C. Hammond) Fundamentals of Arithmetic for Teachers, 1962. Home: 2737 S Kihei Rd # 159 Kihei HI 96753-9609 Office: PO Box 134 Kihei HI 96753-0134

HERRERA, SHIRLEY MAE, personnel and security executive; b. Lynn, Mass., Apr. 5, 1942; d. John Baptiste and Edith Mae Lagasse; m. Christian Yanez Herrera, Apr. 30, 1975; children: Karen, Gary, Ivan, Iwonne. AS in Bus., Burdette Bus. Coll., Lynn, 1960; student, Wright State U., 1975-78. Cert. facility security officer, med. asst. in pediatrics. Med. asst. Christian Y. Herrera, M.D., Stoneham, Mass., 1972-74; human resource adminstr. MTL Systems, Inc., Dayton, Ohio, 1976-79; dir. pers. and security Tracor GIE, Inc., Provo, Utah, 1979-95; cons. on family dynamics family enrichment program Hill AFB, Utah, 1980-82; cons. on health care memt. Guam 7th Day Adventist Clinic, 1983; cons. on basic life support and CPR, Projecto Corazon, Monterrey, Mex., 1987—; faculty mem. Inst. for Reality Therapy, 1991—. Contbg. editor Inside Tractor, 1991—. Chmn. women's aux. YMCA Counselling Svcs., Woburn, Mass., 1970; chmn. youth vols. ARC, Wright-Patterson AFB, Dayton, 1974-76; trustee Quail Valley Homeowner's Assn., Provo, 1988-89; rep. A Spl. Wish Found., Provo, 1989. Recipient James S. Cogswell award Def. Investigative Svc., Dept. Def., 1987. Mem. Inst. for Realty Therapy (cert.), Pers. Assn. Ctrl. Utah, Women in Mgmt. (coun. mem. 1991-95), Nat. Classification Mgmt. Soc. (chairperson Intermountain chpt. 1992-94). Republican. Home: 3824 Little Rock Dr Provo UT 84604-5234

HERRICK, TRACY GRANT, fiduciary; b. Cleve., Dec. 30, 1933; s. Stanford Avery and Elizabeth Grant (Smith) H.; B.A., Columbia U., 1956, M.A., 1958; postgrad. Yale U., 1956-57; M.A., Oxford U. (Eng.), 1960; m. Maie Kaarsoo, Oct. 12, 1963; children: Sylvi Anne, Alan Kalev. economist, Fed. Res. Bank, Cleve., 1960-70; sr. economist Stanford Research Inst., Menlo Park, Calif., 1970-73; v.p., sr. analyst Shuman, Agnew & Co., Inc., San Francisco, 1973-75; v.p. Bank of Am., San Francisco, 1975-81; pres. Tracy G. Herrick, Inc., 1981—; lectr. Stonier Grad. Sch. Banking, Am. Bankers Assn., 1967-76; commencement speaker Memphis Banking Sch., 1974; bd. dirs. Jefferies Group, Inc. (chmn. bd. audit com. 1989-96, chmn. bd. compensation com. 1991-96, dir. 1996—), Jefferies & Co., Inc., Anderson Capital Mgmt., Inc. Fellow Fin. Analysts Fedn.; mem. Assn. Investment Mgmt. Rsch., San Francisco Soc. Security Analysts, dir. Com. for Monetary Rsch. and Edn., Inc. Republican. Congregationalist. Author: Bank Analyst's Handbook, 1978; Timing, 1981; Power and Wealth, 1988; contbr. articles to profl. jours. Home: 1150 University Ave Palo Alto CA 94301-2238

HERRINGER, FRANK CASPER, diversified financial services company executive; b. N.Y.C., Nov. 12, 1942; s. Casper Frank and Alice Virginia (McMullen) H.; m. Maryellen B. Cattani; children: William, Sarah, Julia. AB magna cum laude, Dartmouth, 1964, MBA with highest distinction, 1965. Prin. Cresap, McCormick & Paget, Inc. (mgmt. cons.), N.Y.C., 1965-71; staff asst. to Pres., Washington, 1971-73; adminstr. U.S. Urban Mass Transp. Adminstrn., Washington, 1973-75; gen. mgr., chief exec. officer San Francisco Bay Area Rapid Transit Dist., 1975-78; exec. v.p., dir. Transam. Corp., San Francisco, 1979-86, pres., 1986—, CEO, 1991—, chmn., 1996—; bd. dirs. Unocal Corp., Occidental Life Ins. Co., Transam. Fin. Group, Transam. Leasing, Charles Schwab & Co. Trustee Calif. Pacific Med. Ctr. Mem. Cypress Point Club, San Francisco Golf Club, Olympic Club, Pacific Union Club, Phi Beta Kappa. Office: Transam Corp 600 Montgomery St San Francisco CA 94111-2702*

HERRIOTT, DAVID NEIL, aerospace engineer; b. Pasadena, Calif., Dec. 26, 1967; s. Gerald Don and Mildred Violet (Herforth) H.; m. Pamela Jo Burke, July 2, 1994. B in Aerospace Engring., U. So. Calif., 1989; M in Orgnl. Mgmt., U. Phoenix, Diamond Bar, Calif., 1994. Cert. unigraphics instr. Rsch. asst. U. So. Calif., L.A., 1985-89; structural designer McDonnell Douglas, Long Beach, Calif., 1990-94, CAD tools process leader, 1994-95, instr. unigraphics, 1994-95; pres., CEO Jovian Technologies, Inc., 1996—. Vol. Am. Cancer Soc., Long Beach, 1991—, Big Sisters, L.A., 1991—, Long Beach Meml. Hosp., 1990-91. Mem. AIAA, Sigma Xi. Republican. Methodist.

HERRMAN, MARCIA KUTZ, child development specialist; b. Boston, June 16, 1927; d. Cecil and Sonia (Schneider) Kutz; m. Bayard F. Berman, July 23, 1949 (div. 1960); m. William H. Herrman, June 23, 1961; 1 child, Fred. BA, Smith Coll., 1949; MA, Pacific Oaks Coll., 1974. Cert. tchr., Calif. NIMH intern Cedars-Sinai Med. Ctr., L.A., 1966-67; ednl. therpist L.A. Child Guidance Clinic, 1967-69, Child and Family Study Ctr., Cedars-Sinai Med. Ctr., 1969-71; dir. tng., asst. project dir. handicapped early edn. program Dubnoff Ctr., North Hollywood, Calif., 1972-76; child devel. cons. schs., agys. and families Studio City, Calif., 1969—; cons. L.A. Child Guidance Clinic, Head Start, Child Care and Devel. Svcs., 1969-73; profl. expert L.A. Unified Sch. Dist., 1976-80; vis. faculty Pacific Oaks Coll., Pasadena, Calif., 1970-76. Vol. Alliance for Children's Rights, 1992-94, Child Advocate's Office, Superior Ct., L.A., 1983—; mem. Dependency Ct. Com., 1988-92, Task Force on Rep. of Children in Dependency Ct., L.A. County, 1994; mem. placement com., joint com. of PPAC and Cmty. Adv. Coun., 1995—; mem. steering com. Cmty. Based Placement Project, Joint Effort of Youth Law Ctr., L.A. Dept. Children. & Family Svcs. and Calif. Dept. Social Svcs., 1995; mem. L.A. Foster Care Network, 1987-94, L.A. County MacLaren Children's Ctr. Task Force, 1990-95; mem. cmty. adv. com. St. Joseph's Ctr., 1992—. Recipient Vol. of Yr. award L.A. County Bd. Suprs., 1986, Commendation for Dedicated Svc. to Community, 1991, Recognition award for Outstanding Svc. to Children L.A. County Inter-Agy. Coun. on Child Abuse, 1991; Sophia Smith scholar, 1949. Fellow Am. Orthopsychiat. Assn. (life); mem. N.Y. Acad. Scis., Assn. Child Devel. Specialists, Nat. Ct. Appointed Spl. Advocate Assn. Democrat. Jewish. Home and Office: 3919 Ethel Ave Studio City CA 91604-2204

HERRMANN, MARK LEONARD, economics educator, consultant; b. Berkeley, Calif., Oct. 1, 1959; s. Leonard Ralph and Jean Francis (Padovan) H.; m. Diane Marie Long, Aug. 28, 1982; 1 child, Jake. B, U. Calif., Davis, 1982; M, U. Calif., 1985; D, Wash. State U., 1990. Instr. MTI Western Bus. Coll., Sacramento, 1982-83; cons. Mudge, Rose, Guthrie, Alexander & Ferdon, Pullman, Wash., 1990, R.J. Solie and Assocs., Fairbanks, Alaska, 1990-93; asst. prof. U. Alaska, Fairbanks, 1991-94, assoc. prof., 1994—. Contbr. articles to profl. jours. Mktg. fellow USDA, Pullman, 1985-88; Halibut grantee Alaska Sea Grant, Fairbanks, 1996, Crab grantee Alaska Dept. Fish and Game, Fairbanks, 1996. Mem. Am. Agrl. Econs. Assn., Am. Econ. Assn., Am. Fisheries Soc., Internat. Inst. Bayesian Economists, Internat. Inst. Fisheries Econs. and Trade, World Aquaculture Soc. Methodist. Office: Dept Econs U Alaska Fairbanks AK 99775

HERRON, ELLEN PATRICIA, retired judge; b. Auburn, N.Y., July 30, 1927; d. David Martin and Grace Josephine (Berner) Herron; A.B. Trinity Coll., 1949; M.A., Cath. U. Am., 1954; J.D., U. Calif.-Berkeley, 1964. Asst. dean Cath. U. Am., 1952-54; instr. East High Sch., Auburn, 1955-57; asst. dean Wells Coll., Aurora, N.Y., 1957-58; instr. psychology and history Contra Costa Coll., 1958-60; dir. row Stanford, 1960-61; assoc. Knox & Kretzmer, Richmond, Calif., 1964-65. Bar: Calif., 1965. Ptnr. Knox & Herron, 1965-74, Knox, Herron and Masterson, 1974-77 (both Richmond, Calif.); judge Superior Ct. State of Calif., 1977-87; pvt. judge, 1987-90; pvt. judge Jud. Arbitration and Mediation Svc., Inc. (JAMS- Endispute), 1990—; ptnr. Real Estate Syndicates, Calif., 1967-77; owner, mgr. The Barricia Vineyards, 1978—. Active numerous civic orgns. Democrat. Home: 51 Western Dr Richmond CA 94801-4011

HERRON, GAYLE ANN, mental health consultant, psychotherapist, health facility administrator; b. L.A., Sept. 21, 1953; d. Robert Owen Sr. and Rachel Rebecca (Lemley) Colvin; m. Curtic William Herron, Feb. 14, 1997. AA in Psychology, Okla. City Community Coll., Oklahoma City, 1986; BS in Sociology, Okla. State U., 1990, BS in Psychology, 1991, MS in Counseling, 1992; MSW, U. Nev., Las Vegas, 1996. Adminstr., fin. cons. Security Fin. Cons., Oklahoma City, 1980-88; case worker Big Bros./Big Sisters, Stillwater, Okla., 1988-89; counselor Payne County Family Practices, Stillwater, 1989; social worker Dept. Human Svcs. Child Welfare, Stillwater, 1990; instr. Langston (Okla.) U., 1992; counselor Payne County Dept. Guidance Clinics and Health, Stillwater and Cushing, Okla., 1992-93, Christian Counseling Assocs., Stillwater, 1993-95; clin. dir., CEO New Beginnings Clin. Svcs. Corp., Las Vegas, 1996—. Disaster vol. ARC, Oklahoma City, 1987-88, disaster injury team vol., 1995; vita site coord. IRS, Oklahoma City, 1982-84; emergency room EMT Hillcrest Hosp., Oklahoma City, 1994; EMT/intermediate paramedic Amcare Ambulance Svcs., 1994. mem. ACA, APA, NASW, Am. Assn. for Christian Counselors, Nat. Assn. Social Workers, Okla. Psychol. Assn., Okla. Assn. Counseling and Devel., Assn. for Humanist Psychology, Phi Theta Kappa, Psi Chi. Democrat. Mem. LDS Ch. also: Fairway Villas 35 Gatel Calabash NC 28467 Address: PO Box 71146 Las Vegas NV 89170-1146

HERSCHENSOHN, MICHAEL J., museum administrator. Exec. dir. Mus. of History and Industry, Seattle. Office: Mus History & Industry 2700 24th Ave E Seattle WA 98112*

HERSHEY, JOHN C., retired rancher; b. Bakersfield, Calif., Apr. 18, 1918; s. John and Arnola (Beck) H.; m. Juanita M. hershey, June 20, 1940 (dec. Feb. 1984); children: John C. III, Janice Cauline Marcello; m. Faye M. Hershey, Nov. 2, 1985. AA, Bakersfield Coll., 1938. Owner, operator Rivermere A.A. Ranches, Bakersfield, 1938-95; ret. Pres. Kern County Farm Bur. Mem. Nat. Farm Bur., Calif. Farm Bur., Nat. Cattlemen's Assn., Calif. Cattlemen's Assn., Kern County Cattlemen's Assn. (pres.). Republican. Baptist. Home: 4407 Glencannon Bakersfield CA 93388 Office: Rivermere AA Ranches PO Box 5095 Bakersfield CA 93388

HERSHMAN, LYNN LESTER, artist; b. Cleve.; 1 dau., Dawn. B.S., Case-Western Res. U., 1963; M.A., San Francisco State U., 1972. Prof. U. Calif., Davis, 1984—; Vis. prof. art U. Calif., Berkeley, Calif. Coll. Arts and Crafts, San Jose State U., 1974-78; assoc. project dir. Christo's Running Fence, 1973-76; founder, dir. Floating Mus., 1975-79; ind. film/video producer and cons., 1979—. Author works in field; one-man shows include Santa Barbara Mus. Art, 1970, Univ. Art Mus., Berkeley, Calif., 1972, Mills Coll., Oakland, Calif., 1973, William Sawyer Gallery, 1974, Nat. Galleries, Melbourne, Australia, 1976, Mandeville Art Gallery, U. Calif., San Diego, 1976, M.H. de Young Art Mus., 1978, Pallazo dei Diamonte, Ferrara, Italy, 1978, San Francisco Art Acad., 1980, Portland Center Visual Arts, 1980, New Mus., New Sch., N.Y.C., 1981, Inst. Contemporary Art, Phila., 1981, Anina Nosai Gallery, N.Y.C., 1981, Contemporary Art Center, Cin., 1982, Toronto, Los Angeles Contemporary Exhibits, 1986, Univ. Art Mus. Berkeley, 1987, Madison (Wis.) Art Ctr., 1987, Intersesction for the Arts, San Francisco, Pacific Film Archive, A. Space, "Guerilla Tactics" Toronto, Can., Venice Bienalle Global Village; group exhbns. include Cleve. Art Mus., 1968, St. Paul Art Ctr., 1969, Richmond (Calif.) Art Ctr., 1970, 73, Galeria del Sol, Santa Barbara, Calif., 1971, San Francisco Art Inst., 1972, Richard Demarco Art Gallery, Edinburgh, Scotland, 1973, Laguna Beach (Calif.) Art Mus., 1973, Univ. Art Mus., Univ. Calif., Berkeley, 1974, Bronx (N.Y.) Mus., 1975, Linda Ferris Gallery, Seattle, 1975, Madenville Art Gallery, San Diego, Contemporary Arts Mus., Houston, 1977, New Orleans, 1977, Ga. Mus. Art, Athens, 1977, New Mus., N.Y., 1981, Calif. Coll. Arts and Crafts, 1981, San Francisco Mus. Modern Art, 1979, 80, 90, Art-Beaubourg, Paris, 1980, Ars Electronica, 1989, Am. Film Inst., 1989, Mus. Moving Image Internat. Ctr. for Photography, 1989, Kitchen Ctr. for Video-Music, N.Y., 1990, Robert Koch Gallery, San Francsico, 1990, Inst. Contemporary Art, London, 1990, Frankfurt (Germany) Art Fair, 1990, Inst. Conteporary Art, Boston, 1991, Oakland (Calif.) Mus., 1991, La Cite des Arts et des Nouvelles Technologies, Montreal, 1991, Richard F. Brush Art Gallery, Canton, N.Y., 1992, Jack Tilton Gallery, N.Y., 1992, Southeastern Ctr. for Contemporary Art, Winston-Salem, N.C., 1992, Bonner Kunstverein, Bonn, Germany, 1992, Chgo. Ave. Armory, 1992, Retrospective, Tribute, 1994, Nelson Gallery, Paris, 1994, Hess Collection, 1994. Bd. dirs. San Francisco Art Acad., Spectrum Found., Motion a Performance Collective. Western States Regional fellow (film/video), 1990; grantee Nat. Endowment for the Arts, (2) Art Matters Inc., San Francisco Found., N.Y. State Coun. for the Arts, Zellerbach Family Fund, Inter Arts of Marin, Gerbode Found., The Women's Project; recipient Dirs. Choice award San Francisco Internat. Film Festival, 1987, tribute 1987 Mill Valley Video Festial, Exptl. Video award 1988, 1st prize Montbelliard, France, 1990, 2d prize, Vigo, Spain, 1992, 1993 Ars Electronica, Austria, WRO Poland, Nat. Film Theatre, London, Gerber award Seattle Art Mus., 1994, ZKM/Siemans award, 1995. Mem. Assn. Art Pubs. (dir., Annie Gerber award 1995). Office: 1935 Filbert St San Francisco CA 94123-3503*

HERSLEY, DENNIS CHARLES, environmentalist, software systems consultant; b. Idaho Falls, Idaho, July 11, 1947; s. Cyril R. and Bardella (Webb) H.; m. Jane Anne Lilly, Jan. 16, 1993; children: Cary Connolly, Laura Lilly, Claire Lilly. Student, U. So. Calif., 1964-65; electronics tech. cert., Idaho State U., 1970; postgrad., U. Santa Clara, 1979. Cert. FCC 1st class radio engr. with TV and radar endorsements.;. Ptnr. Intensive Care Tech. Svcs., Pocatello, Idaho, 1972-74; test engring. mgr. Nat. Semiconductor, Sunnyvale, Calif., 1975-76; test ops. mgr. Amdahl Ireland, Ltd., Dublin, 1978; engr., planner, analyst Amdahl Corp., Sunnyvale, 1979-85; CFO, chmn. Provista Software Internat., San Jose, Calif., 1985-86; pres. Almaden Consulting, Santa Cruz, Calif., 1985—; co-founder, pres., dir. non profit sci. rsch. Citizens United for Responsible Environmentalism, Inc., Santa Cruz, Calif., 1994—; planner, sponsor Fusewest Regional Tech. Conf., Scottsdale, Ariz., 1988-89; tech. curriculum advisor Idaho State U., 1970-75. Inventor calculator design, 1975. Recipient Outstanding Alumnus award Idaho State U., 1975, Honored Donor award Monterey Bay Aquarium, 1996. Mem. Calif. Assn. Non-Profits, No. Calif. Focus Users Group (asst. editor 1988-90), Santa Cruz Tech. Alliance. Office: CURE 2375 Benson Ave Santa Cruz CA 95065-1674

HERSMAN, MARION FRANK, professional administrator, lawyer; b. Huntington, W.Va., Nov. 12, 1932; s. Marion Rockefeller and Frances Mae (Peabody) H.; m. Carole Anne Birthright, Oct. 1960 (div.); 1 child, Frank Eric Birthright; m. Nina Claire Mohay, Dec. 24, 1976 (div.); 1 child, Alicia Claire; m. Eleonora Georgi Hivrina, April 11, 1995; 1 child, Elizabeth Anne. B.S. in Chemistry, Physics and Math, Ohio State U., 1953; Ph.D. in Chemistry (Victor Chem. fellow, Colgate Palmolive-Peet fellow, Univ. fellow), U. Ill., 1956; J.D., George Washington U., 1958, LL.M., 1960; M.A., New Sch. for Social Research, 1964. Bar: Va. 1958, N.Y. 1959, D.C. 1960, U.S. Supreme Ct. 1960, U.S. Ct. Appeals (D.C. cir.) 1960. Teaching fellow U. Ill.; patent examiner U.S. Patent Office, Washington, 1956-57; assoc. firm Burns Doane, Benedict & Irons, Washington, 1957-59, Arthur, Dry & Dole, N.Y.C., 1959-60, Fish, Richardson & Neave, N.Y.C., 1960-64; staff assoc. office sci. resources planning NSF, Washington, 1964-67; office of planning and policy studies NSF, 1967-69, head office intergovtl. sci. programs, 1969-72, dir. office intergovtl. sci. and research utilization, 1972-75; exec. dir. Colo. Planning Coordinating Council, 1976; spl. asst., sci. and tech. advisor to Gov. Colo., 1976; sci. and tech. advisor Fedn. Rocky Mountain States, Denver, 1977; dir. Rocky Mountain Tech. Sharing Task Force, 1977; dir. Div. Water Resources Hillsborough County, Tampa, Fla., 1977, dir. Div. Pub. Utilities, 1977-78; dir. Office of Planning and Intergovtl. Relations Hillsborough County, Tampa, 1978-79; asst. county adminstr. Hillsborough County (Fla.) Div. Pub. Utilities, 1978-79; vice chmn. Hillsborough Intergovtl. Resource Recovery Mgmt. Com.; mem. Fla. Community Conservation Com., 1978-80, Urban Consortium, 1978-80; spl. asst. to pres. U. South Fla., 1979-80; atty. NSF, 1980-82; dir. com. on hazardous materials Fed. Emergency Mgmt. Agy., 1981-83; vis. disting. prof. Nova U., 1982, spl. asst. to pres. for program devel., 1982; asst. city mgr. for health and human services City of Austin, (Tex.), 1982-84; exec. v.p. Lawyers Title of Ky., 1983-85; ptnr. LTK Enterprises, 1983-85; exec. v.p., chief operating officer Automation Telecommunications and Management Inc., Austin, Tex., 1984-85; dir. research and state services The Council of State Govts., Lexington, Ky., 1985-87; town mgr. Town of Snow Hill, Md., 1988; county mgr. Nye County, Nev., 1988-90; pres. RH Mgmt. Assocs., 1990—; dir. social svcs. Louis Berger Internat. Cons., Sasatov Oblast, Russia, 1996—; spkr. in field; tchg. assoc. George Washington U., 1957-59; chmn., exec. dir. com. on intergovtl. sci. rels. Fed. Coun. Sci. and Tech., Exec. Office of Pres., 1979-83; mem. Agrl. Yearbook adv. bd. USDA, 1979, mem. tech. adv. bd. nat. rural cmtys. facilities assessment, 1978; chmn. com. on policy mgmt. and assistance U.S. Office Mgmt. and Budget, Washington, 1974-75; mem. com. on tech. sharing President's Office Sci. and Tech., 1972-74; chmn. So. Nev. Rural Health Fair, 1991; prof. urban engring. Nat. U. Mex., Mexico City, 1975; vis. faculty CSC, Kings Point, N.Y., 1975, Fed. Exec. Inst., Charlottesville, Va., 1977, Golden Gate U., 1979-80; vis. prof. U. Colo. Grad. Sch. Pub. Affairs, 1976-77, U. South Fla., 1978, Martin Sch., U. Ky., 1986-88; spl. asst. to dir. NSF, 1976-80; cons. Office Sci. and Tech., Exec. Office of Pres., 1976-80, Western Govs.' Task Force on Regional Policy Mgmt., 1976-77; cons. USDA, 1978; mem. Subcom. on Rsch. Itilization Transp. Rsch. Bd./NRC/NAS, 1981-82; adminstr. Pahrump Valley Med. Ctr., 1991-92; pres. Nev. Health and Med. Found., 1991-92; U.S. exec. advisor mayor and city coun. City of Narva, Estonia, 1994-96; U.S. exec. advisor City of Tartu, Estonia, 1994, Internat. Exec. Svcs. Corps, 1994; U.S. trade rep. City of Narva, Estonia, 1994—; exec. advisor Internat. Exec. Svc. Corps. City of Vladimir, Russia, 1995-96. Contbg. author: Science and Technology Policies, 1973; bd. editors and consultants: Scholar and Educator, 1977; mem. editorial bd.: Jour. Edn. and Scholar, 1977-87; contbr. articles to profl. jours.

Bd. dirs. Warwick Assn., 1980-81; chmn. consumers and bus. affairs com. D.C. Area Neighborhood Council; mem. Washington Mayor's Planning and Budget Adv. Com., 1980-82; vol. exec. Internat. Exec. Svcs. Corps., 1994—; Pahrump Arts Coun., 1994—. Recipient Pub. Service award states of Ga., La., Ala., Pa., Okla., N.C., Pub. Service award So. Interstate Nuclear Bd., Pub. Service award Nat. Conf. State Legislatures; Picatinny Arsenal fellow, Victor Chem. fellow, Colgate Palmolive-Peet fellow, Ohio State Univ. fellow; U.S. Govt. grantee. Mem. Va., D.C., Fed. bar assns., Am. Chem. Soc., Am. Soc. Pub. Adminstrn. (chmn. sect. on intergovtl. adminstrn. and mgmt. 1977-79, Public Service award), AAAS, Sigma Xi, Phi Lambda Upsilon, Delta Theta Phi (chmn. scholarships), Alpha Chi Sigma, Kappa Sigma. Home and Office: PO Box 3434 2070 S Page St Pahrump NV 89041

HERTEL, HOWARD JAY, photographer; b. Oakland, Calif., Apr. 25, 1924; s. Elmer Joseph and Lillian Ruth (Hultberg) H.; m. Laverne Wilson, June 1949 (div. June 1965); children: Douglas Jay (dec.), Kenneth Bruce. Grad. H.S., Lafayette, Calif. Comml. photographer Waters and Hainlin Studio, Oakland, 1942-43; photographer, photo lab. tech. Army Air Forces, 1943-45; photographer Stanford Rsch. Inst., Menlo Park, Calif., 1950-53; freelance photographer San Francisco; faculty mem. Stanford (Calif.) U., 1950-53; market rsch. interviewer Field Rsch. Corp., San Francisco, 1994. Pres. Young Reps., Sacramento. Staff sgt. USAFR, 1964; active Sr. Ctr.-Aquatic Park San Francisco, 1994. Named assoc. Royal Photographic Soc., Bath, Eng., 1955. Mem. Air Force Assn. (life).

HERTLEIN, FRED, III, industrial hygiene laboratory executive; b. San Francisco, Oct. 17, 1933; s. Fred and Herta (Komning) H.; m. Clara Kam Fung Tse, Apr. 1958 (div. Apr. 1982); children: Fritz, Hans Wernher, Lisa Marie, Gretel Marga. BS in Chemistry, U. Nev., 1956; postgrad., U. Hawaii, Manoa, 1956-58. Cert. profl. chemist, indsl. hygienist, safety profl., hazard control mgr., bldg. insp. and mgmt. planner, biol. safety profl. Grad. teaching ast. in chemistry U. Hawaii, Honolulu, 1956-58; air pollution sampling sta. operator Truesdail Labs., Honolulu, 1957; chemist oceanographical research vessels Dept. Interior, 1957-59; with Bechtel-Hawaiian Dredging, 1959; co-owner marine survey co. Honolulu, 1959-60; radiochemist Pearl Harbor (Hawaii) Naval Shipyard, 1959-62, indsl. hygienist med. dept., 1962-69, head indsl.hygiene br., 1969-72; indsl. hygiene program mgr. Naval Regional Med. Clinic, Pearl Harbor Naval Sta., 1972-78; pres., dir. lab. and indsl. hygiene, co-owner Indsl. Analytical Lab., Inc., Honolulu, 1978-; pres. F. Hertlein & Assocs., 1970-78; asst. clin. prof. U. Hawaii Sch. Pub. Health, 1973—. Contbr. articles to profl. jours. Named Outstanding Male Fed. Employee, Honolulu Fed. Exec. Council, 1967, Citizen of Day citation Sta. KGU76, Honolulu, 1972, cert. of achievement Toastmasters Internat., 1974, expression of appreciation U. Hawaii Sch. Pub. Health, 1985. Fellow Am. Inst. Chemists (life); mem. Am. Acad. Indsl. Hygiene, Am. Chem. Soc., Am. Indsl. Hygiene Assn., Gesellschaft fü Aerosolforschung, Profl. Assn. Diving Instrs. (instr. emeritus), Tubists Universal Brotherhood Assn. (life). Home: 1493 Kaweloka St Pearl City HI 96782-1513 Office: Indsl Analytical Lab Inc 3615 Harding Ave Ste 305 Honolulu HI 96816-3759

HERTLING, GUNTER HELMUT, Germanics educator; b. Pasadena, Calif., June 14, 1930; m. Darlene M. Little; children: Sonja, Dieter. BA, U. Calif., Berkeley, MA, PhD, 1963. From instr. to asst. prof. to assoc. prof. U. Wash., Seattle, 1961-74, prof., 1974—; mem. senate U. Wash., Seattle. Author books and articles on 18th, 19th and 20th century German lit. Mem. MLA, Am. Assn. Tchrs. German, Pacific Ancient and Modern Lang. Assn. (v.p. 1994, pres. 1995). Office: Dept Germanics U Wash Box 353130 Seattle WA 98195-3130

HERTNEKY, RANDY LEE, optometrist; b. Burlington, Colo., Jan. 9, 1955; s. Harry Francis and Darleen Mae (Walters) H.; m. Laura Ann Ciaccio, Nov. 28, 1981; children: Lisa Kay, Erin Elizabeth. BA, U. Colo., 1977; OD, So. Calif. Coll. Optometry, Fullerton, 1981. Pvt. practice optometry Yuma and Wray, Colo., 1982—. Precinct committeeman Yuma County Rep. Com., 1986—; mem. bd. rev. Boy Scouts Am., Yuma, 1982—; chmn. bldg. com. Yuma H.S., 1987-89; bd. dirs. Yuma Hosp. Found., 1990—, vice chmn., 1994—; chmn. Yuma Sch. Curricculum Com., 1993. Mem. APHA, KC (sec. 1990-95, dep. grand knight 1995-96, grand knight 1996—), Am. Optometric Assn. (coord. Colo. Polit. Action Com. 1995—), Colo. Optometric Assn. (trustee 1989-90, vice chmn. legis. com. 1994—, nominee Optometrist of Yr. 1996), Coll. Optometrists in Vision Devel. (assoc.), Yuma C. of C. (Bus. of Yr. 1996), Wray C. of C., Lions (treas. 1987-88, pres. 1991-92, Lion of Yr. award 1992). Roman Catholic. Office: 107 S Main St Yuma CO 80759-1913

HERTWECK, ALMA LOUISE, sociology and child development educator; b. Moline, Ill., Feb. 6, 1937; d. Jacob Ray and Sylvia Ethel (Whitt) Street; m. E. Romayne Hertweck, Dec. 16, 1955; 1 child, William Scott. A.A., Mira Costa Coll., 1969; B.A. in Sociology summa cum laude, U. Calif.-San Diego, 1975, M.A., 1977, Ph.D., 1982. Cert. sociology instr., multiple subjects teaching credential grades kindergarten-12, Calif. Staff research assoc. U. Calif.-San Diego, 1978-81; instr. sociology Chapman Coll., Orange, Calif., 1982-87; instr. child devel. MiraCosta Coll., Oceanside, Calif., 1983-87, 88-89; instr. sociology U.S. Internat. U., San Diego, 1985-88 ; exec. dir., v.p. El Camino Preschools, Inc., Oceanside, 1985—. Author: Constructing the Truth and Consequences: Educators' Attributions of Perceived Failure in School, 1982; co-author: Handicapping the Handicapped, 1985. Mem. Am. Sociol. Assn., Am. Ednl. Research Assn., Nat. Council Family Relations, Nat. Assn. Edn. Young Children, Alpha Gamma Sigma (life). Avocations: foreign travel; sailing; bicycling. Home: 2024 Oceanview Rd Oceanside CA 92056-3104 Office: El Camino Preschs Inc 2002 California St Oceanside CA 92054-5673

HERTWECK, E. ROMAYNE, psychology educator; b. Springfield, Mo., July 24, 1928; s. Garnett Perry and Nova Gladys (Chowning) H.; m. Alma Louise Street, Dec. 16, 1955; 1 child, William Scott. BA, Augustana Coll., 1962; MA, Pepperdine U., 1963; EdD, Ariz. State U., 1966; PhD, U.S. Internat. U., 1978. Cert. sch. psychologist, Calif. Night editor Rock Island (Ill.) Argus Newspaper, 1961; grad. asst. psychology dept. Pepperdine Coll., L.A., 1962; counselor VA, Ariz. State U., Tempe, 1963; assoc. dir. Conciliation Ct., Phoenix, 1964; instr. Phoenix Coll., Phoenix, 1965; prof. Mira Costa Coll., Oceanside, Calif., 1966—, mem. senate coun., 1968-70, 85-87, 89-91, chmn. psychology-counseling dept., 1973-75, chmn. dept. behavioral sci., 1976-82, 87-88, 90-91; part-time lectr. dept. bus. adminstrn. San Diego State U., 1980-84, Sch. Human Behavior U.S. Internat. U., 1984-89; prof. psychology Chapman Coll. Mem. World Campus Afloat, 1970; pres. El Camino Preschs., Inc., Oceanside, Calif., 1985—; CEO Nutri-Cal, Inc., Cardiff, Calif., 1996—. Bd. dirs. Lifeline, 1969, Christian Counseling Center, Oceanside, 1970-82; mem. City of Oceanside Childcare Task Force, 1991—; mem. City of Oceanside Community Rels. Commn., 1991-96, vice chair, 1994; mem. steering com. Healthy Cities Project City of Oceanside, Calif., 1993-95. Mem. Am., Western, North San Diego County (v.p. 1974-75) psychol. assns., Am. Assn. for Counseling and Devel., Nat. Educators Fellowship (v.p. El Camino chpt. 1976-77), Am. Coll. Personnel Assn., Phi Delta Kappa, Kappa Delta Pi, Psi Chi, Kiwanis (charter mem. Carlsbad club, dir. 1975-77). Home: 2024 Oceanview Rd Oceanside CA 92056-3104 Office: Mira Costa Coll PO Box 586312 Oceanside CA 92058-6312 also: El Camino Preschs Inc 2002 California St Oceanside CA 92054-5673

HERWIG, KARL ROBERT, physician; b. Phila., Nov. 12, 1935; s. Louis and Elizabeth Frances (Myers) H.; m. Barbara K. Bosscher, Oct. 26, 1963; children: Susan Elizabeth, K. Robert. BS, Ursinus Coll., 1957; MD, Jefferson Med. Coll., 1961. Diplomate Am. Bd. Urology. Intern U. Mich., Ann Arbor, 1961-62, resident gen. surgery, 1962-64; fellow Peter Sent Brigham Hosp., Boston, 1964; urology resident U. Mich., Ann Arbor, 1964-67; staff urologist U.S. Naval Medical Ctr., Bethesda, Md., 1967-69; urology faculty U. Mich., 1969-77; staff urologist Scripps Clinic, La Jolla, Calif., 1977—; instr., assoc. prof. U. Mich., 1969-77; urology div. head Scripps Clinic, 1977-95, sr. cons., 1994; clinical assoc. prof. U. Calif., San Diego, 1977—. Contbr. articles to profl. jours. With U.S. Navy, 1967-69. Recipient Faculty Achievement award U. Mich., 1972. Fellow Am. Coll. Surgeons; mem. Am. Urological Assn., Cen. Surgical Soc., Am. Assn. Endocrine Surgeons, Collier Surgical Soc., Am. Med. Soc., Rotary. Republican. Presbyterian. Office: Scripps Clinic 10666 N Torrey Pines Rd La Jolla CA 92037-1027

HERZ, MICHAEL JOSEPH, marine environmental scientist; b. St. Paul, Aug. 12, 1936; s. Malvin E. and Josephine (Daneman) H.; m. Joan Klein Levy, Feb. 3, 1962 (div. 1982); children: David M., Daniel J., Ann K.; m. Naomi Brodie Schalit, Aug. 21, 1984 (div. 1996); children: Nathaniel B., Hallie R. BA, Reed Coll., 1958; MA, San Francisco State U., 1962; PhD, U. So. Calif., 1966. Program coord. postdoctoral tng. program U. Calif., San Francisco, 1969-73, asst. prof., 1969-73, assoc. prof. in residence, 1973-74; exec. dir., dir. water quality tng. program San Francisco Bay. chpt. Oceanic Soc., 1974-77; exec. v.p., co-dir. rsch. and policy Oceanic Soc., San Francisco, 1977-84; sr. rsch. scientist San Francisco State U., 1984-88; exec. dir. and baykeeper San Francisco BayKeeper, 1989-95; pvt. cons. Alna, Maine, 1995—; chmn. bd. govs. Tiburon Ctr. Environ. Studies, San Francisco State U., 1985-86; NRC com. mem. Effectiveness of Oil Spill Disperants, Washington, 1985-87; mem. com. on ocean disposal of radwaste Calif. Dept. Health, Sacramento, 1985-92; mem. tech. adv. com. Calif. Office of Oil Spill Prevention and Response, 1992-95; bd. dirs. Friends of the Earth, Washington, 1989—, Aquatic Habitat Inst., 1986-89; mem. Alaska Oil Spill Commn., 1989-90; mem. NRC com. Risk Assessment and Mgmt. of Marine Systems, Washington, 1996—. Author, co-editor: (books) Memory Consolidation, 1972, Habituation I & II, 1973; contbr. reports to profl. publs. Chmn. community adv. bd. Sta. KQED (Pub. Broadcast System affiliate), 1979-85, San Francisco, citizens adv. com. San Francisco Bay Conservation and Devel. Commn., 1979—, chmn. 1984; mem. tech. adv. com. San Francisco Bay Regional Water Quality Control Bd., Oakland, Calif., 1979-82, Assn. Bay Area Govts., Oakland, 1983-84; mem. bay area adv. com. Sea Grant Marine Adv. Program, San Francisco, 1983-89; mem. com. Bur. Land Mgmt., Pacific States Regional Tech. Working Group, 1979-83; bd. dirs. Maine Initiatives, 1996—. Served with U.S. Army, 1958-59. Predoctoral fellow NIMH, U. So. Calif., 1963-64; postdoctoral fellow NIMH, UCLA Brain Research Inst., 1966-68. Mem. AAAS, Calif. Acad. Scis., San Francisco Bay and Estuarine Assn., Oceanic Soc. (bd. dirs. 1984-89), Sheepscot Valley Conservation Assn. (bd. dirs. 1995—.

HERZBERG, DOROTHY CREWS, middle school educator; b. N.Y.C., July 8, 1935; d. Floyd Houston and Julia (Lesser) Crews; m. Hershel Zelig Herzberg, May 22, 1962 (div. Apr. 1988); children: Samuel Floyd, Laura Jill, Daniel Crews. AB, Brown U., 1957; MA, Stanford U., 1964; JD, San Francisco Law Sch., 1976. Legal sec. various law firms, San Francisco, 1976-78; tchr. Mission Adult Sch., San Francisco, 1965-66; tchr. secondary and univ. levels Peace Corps, Nigeria, 1961-63; investigator Office of Dist. Atty., San Francisco, 1978-80; sr. adminstr. Dean Witter Reynolds Co., San Francisco, 1980-83; registered rep. Waddell and Reed, 1983-84; fin. services rep. United Resources, Hayward, Calif., 1984-86; tax preparer H&R Block, 1987; revenue officer IRS, 1987-89; now tchr. ESL, West Contra Costa Sch. Dist., El Cerrito, Calif., 1989—. Editor: (newsletters) Coop. Nursery Sch. Council, 1969-71, Miraloma Life, 1976-82, Dem. Women's Forum, 1980-81, Stanford Luncheon Club, 1984-85. Bd. dirs. LWV, San Francisco, 1967-69, mem. speakers bur., 1967-80; pres. Council Coop. Nursery Schs., San Francisco, 1969-71; bd. dirs. Miraloma (Calif.) Improvement Club, 1977-88, pres., 1980-81; alt. for supr. San Francisco Mayor's Commn. on Criminal Justice, 1978. Democrat. Unitarian. Home: 1006 Richmond St El Cerrito CA 94530-2616

HERZING, ALFRED ROY, computer executive; b. Kitchener, Ont., Can., June 23, 1958; naturalized, 1982; s. Alfred Georg and Kaethe (Binder) H.; m. Marjorie, Aug. 20, 1983; 1 child, Adam. BSEE, Calif. Poly. Inst., 1981. Telecom. engr. Union Oil Co., L.A., 1982-84; computer planning analyst Union Oil-UNOCAL, 1984-86; supr. facilities mgmt. UNOCAL Corp. Info. Svcs., Anaheim, Calif., 1986-89, bus analyst, 1989, mgr. planning and analysis, 1989-91, mgr. tech. & bus. assessment, 1991—; speaker ENTELEC, Dallas, San Antonio, 1983, 85. Host athletic tournament Alfred Roy Herzing Invitational Frisbee Golf Tournament, 1980—. Mem. IEEE, Toastmasters (L.A. chpt. pres. 1986-87, gov. area 12 1987-88, arminstrv. lt. gov. dist. 52 1988-89, edn1. lt. gov. dist. 52 1989-90, dist. gov. 1990-91, Toastmaster of Yr. 1990, region II conf. edn. presenter 1992, 93, chmn. dist. 52 1992-93, 93-94, pres. speakers forum club 1993-94, CTM/ATY.DTM chmn. founder's dist. 1993-94, 94-95, internat. dir. 1995-97), Yorba Linda Achievers Club (charter mem., pres. 1993-94). Republican. Home: 20365 Via La Vieja Yorba Linda CA 92887-3211 Office: UNOCAL 2929 E Imperial Hwy Brea CA 92821

HERZOG, COLLEEN DIANE, special education educator; b. Seattle, Oct. 17, 1967; d. Robert Paul and Diane Grace (George) H.; m. Paul Robert Piguet, Aug. 20, 1994. BA in Edn., Western Wash. U., 1992; postgrad., Cen. Wash. U., 1994—. Cert. K-8 gen. edn., K-12 spl. edn. Substitute spl. edn. tchr. Kent (Wash.) Sch. Dist., 1992; spl. edn. tchr. Edns. Svcs. Dist. 112, Vancouver, Wash., 1992-93, Battle Ground (Wash.) Sch. Dist., 1993—. Mem. CEC. Roman Catholic. Office: Amboy Mid Sch 22115 NE Chelatchie Rd Amboy WA 98601-3813

HERZOG, WHITEY (DORREL NORMAN ELVERT HERZOG), former professional baseball team executive; b. New Athens, Ill., Nov. 9, 1931. Infielder, outfielder Washington Senators, 1956-58, Kansas City Athletics, 1958-60, Balt. Orioles, 1961-62, Detroit Tigers, 1963; scout Kansas City Athletics, 1964, coach, 1965; coach N.Y. Mets, 1966, dir. player devel., 1967-72; mgr. Tex. Rangers, 1973; coach Calif. Angels, 1974-75, interim mgr., 1974; mgr. Kansas City Royals, 1975-79; mgr. St. Louis Cardinals, 1980-90, v.p., 1990; sr. v.p., dir. player pers. Calif. Angels, 1991-94; retired, 1994. Named Sporting News Man of Yr., 1982, Nat. League Mgr. of Yr., 1982, 85, 87, A.L. Mgr. of Yr., 1976, UPI Exec. of Yr., 1981-82.

HESKETH, THOMAS A.E., lawyer, arbitrator; b. Toronto, July 22, 1951; s. Thomas William Hesketh and Mary Patricia Bell Kindermann. BA, Claremont Men's Coll., 1975; JD, U. Calif., San Franciso, 1979. Bar: Calif. 1980, U.S. Supreme Ct. 1989. Tchr. Peace Corps, Morocco, 1973-76; atty. Law Offices of Daryl R. Hawkins, San Francisco, 1980-87, Dinkelspiel & Dinkelspiel, San Francisco, 1987-90; instr. legal rsch. and writing Hastings Coll. of the Law, U. Calif., San Francisco, 1985-88; atty., arbitrator Chickering & Gregory, San Francisco, 1990-94, Law Offices of Thomas A.E. Hesketh, San Francisco, 1995—; judge pro tem, arbitrator San Francisco Mcpl. Ct., 1988—; settlement judge pro tem, arbitrator San Francisco Superior Ct., 1992—; arbitrator Am. Arbitration Assn., 1992—, Nat. Assn. Securities Dealers, 1988—, N.Y. Stock Exch., 1994—, Pacific Coast Stock Exch., 1992—. Sr. articles editor Hastings Constnl. Law Quar., 1978-79. Mem. Civil Grand Jury, San Francisco, 1991-92. Calif. State scholar, 1969-73. Mem. Bar Assn. San Francisco (vol. legal svcs. program). Democrat. Office: Law Offices of Thomas AE Hesketh 303 31st Ave San Francisco CA 94121-1706

HESS, CATHERINE MARY, museum curator; b. L.A., Mar. 27, 1957; d. Harry Joseph and Myrtle (Klein) H.; m. Laurence Bradley Frank, Dec. 31, 1988; 1 child, Julian Guthrie. BA, UCLA, 1979, MA cum laude, 1983. Curatorial asst. J. Paul Getty Mus., Malibu, Calif., 1984-86, asst. curator, 1987-90, assoc. curator, 1991—; guest lectr. L.A. County Mus. Art, 1987, 90, 94, Calif. State U., Long Beach, 1990, George R. Gardiner Mus., Toronto, Ont., Can., 1988, 89, Pescara, Italy, 1989, San Diego Mus. Art, 1994, St. Louis Art Mus., 1994. Author: Italian Maiolica: Catalogue of the Collections J. Paul Getty Museum, Malibu, 1988; co-author: Looking at European Ceramics 1400-1900, 1993, Decorative Arts: An Illustrated Summary Catalogue J. Paul Getty Museum, Malibu, 1993, Checklist of Sculpture, 1997, Masterpieces of Decorative Arts, 1997, European Glass: A Catalogue of the Collections, 1997. Office: J Paul Getty Museum 1200 Getty Center Dr Los Angeles CA 90049

HESS, FREDERICK DANA, science administrator, educator; b. Tacoma, Mar. 22, 1946; s. Willard Frederick and Sylvia R. (Rogers) H. BS, Mich. State U., 1969; MS, U. Calif., Davis, 1973, PhD, 1975. Grad. asst. U. Calif., Davis, 1970-75; prof. Colo. State U., Ft. Collins, 1975-76, Purdue U., West Lafayette, Ind., 1976-85; dir. rsch. Sandoz Agro Inc., Palo Alto, Calif., 1985-94; v.p. rsch. Sandoz Agro Inc., Palo Alto, 1995-96, Novartis Crop Protection, Inc., Palo Alto, 1997—; lectr. Purdue U., West Lafayette, 1986—, U. Calif., Davis, 1996—; cons. in field, 1976-85. Editor: Biochemical Responses Induced by Herbicides, 1982; contbr. chpts., articles to profl. jours. Grantee NSF, 1984. Fellow Weed Sci. Soc. Am. (Outstanding Grad. Student 1975, Outstanding Young Scientist 1985, Outstanding jour. article 1986, abstract editor 1989-91, bd. dirs. 1993-95, v.p. 1996, pres. elect 1997); mem. Am. Soc. Plant Physiology, Electron Microscope Soc. Am., Internat. Weed Sci. Soc. Office: Novartis Crop Protection 975 California Ave Palo Alto CA 94304-1104

HESS, HELEN ELIZABETH, retired secondary school educator, musician; b. Elkader, Iowa, Feb. 22, 1930; d. James Dale and Helen Louise (Wahl) Welsch; m. Roger Merle Hess, Dec. 18, 1966. BA, U. So. Miss., 1952, MA, 1955. Tchr. Natchez (Miss.) Pub. Schs., 1952-54; tchr. Bakersfield (Calif.) City Schs., 1955-89, ret., 1989; staff mem. Bakersfield Symphony Orch., 1989—. Life mem. Washington Jr. H.S. PTA; mem. Assistance League Bakersfield, 1990—; bd. dirs. Bakersfield Masterworks Chorale. Named Outstanding Classroom Tchr., Bakersfield Rotary Club, 1970. Mem. Local and State Ret. Tchrs. Assn. Republican. Presbyterian. Office: Bakersfield Symphony Orch 1401 19th St Ste 130 Bakersfield CA 93301-4400

HESS, IVAN EDWARD, set designer, educator; b. Pasadena, Calif., Aug. 3, 1945; s. Robert Edward and Virginia (Yerxa) H.; div.; 1 child, Jedediah Nathaniel. BA, Calif. State U., Hayward, 1967; MFA in Theatrical Design, Stanford U., 1971; postgrad. spl. masters class J. Svoboda, San Francisco, 1973; postgrad., Lindisfarne Inst., N.Y.C., 1977-82. Designer, tech. dir. Hayward (Calif.) Cmty. Theatre, 1965; staff tech. dir. Mills Coll., 1967-68; designer, tech. dir. Calif. Theatre Arts, 1969; designer, instr. Calif. State U., Hayward, 1970; assoc. prof., designer Humboldt State U., Arcata, Calif., 1971-78, 80-81; prof., designer Humboldt State U., Arcata, 1983—; substitute instr. San Joes State U., 1968, part time designer Calif. State U., Hayward, 1964-67; designer Oakland Repertory Theatre, 1968. San Mateo (Calif.) Light Opera, 1968, Santa Rosa Repertory Theatre, 1978; vis. artist, Tufts U., Boston, 1978-80, faculty, site architect, Lindiafarne Inst., 1981-82; prof., designer London U. Goldsmiths, 1982-83; instr., designer Hartnell Coll., 1990, Cypress Coll., 1990-91; cons. Minor Theatre, 1988-93, Pier Two, San Francisco, 1987, other Ednl. theatres. Set designs include Son of the Wilderness, Caucasion Chalk Circle, Penny for a Song, The Physicist, Caligula, The Magic Hand, Marat/Sade, Ballad of an Outcast, The Time of Your Life, What the Butler Saw, Il Travotore, Blythe Spirit, Beaux Strategem, Cyrano de Bergerac, Flea in her Ear, Rimers of Eldritch, The Tooth of Crime, The Ghost Sonata, Vanities, Good Woman of Szechuan, Too True To Be Good, Vinegar Tom, The Bacchae, The Road Not Taken, Annie Get Your Gun, Hair, Two Sisters on the Old Road, One Man's Hero, Mr & Mrs Coffee, Echo Location, Song of Hydrogen, Schwyek in the Second World War, I, Lionel, Sheetrock and the Piano Tuner, Architect and the Emperor of Assyria, Taking Leave, Heidi Chronicles; tech. dir. The Hostage, Arms and the Man, The Visit, A Little Night Music, Cabaret; lighting design Chopin in Space. Mem. AAUP, U.S. Inst. Theatre Tech., Calif. State Employees Assn., Lindisfarne Assn., Western Mining Coun., Calif. Faculty Assn., Am. Coll. Theatre Festival (chmn. region XIII, past regional chair Kennedy Ctr.), New Dramatists (N.Y.C.), Calif. Ednl. Theatre Assn., Assn. for Theatre in Higher Edn., Calif. Ednl. Theatre Assn., Am. Theatre in Higher Edn. Home: 1190 Tilley Ct Arcata CA 95521-6720 Office: Humboldt State U Theatre Arts Dept Arcata CA 95521

HESS, RICHARD NEAL, plastic surgeon; b. Phila., June 16, 1957. MD, U. Ariz., 1983. Chmn. plastic surgery Northwest Hosp., Tucson. Office: Aesthetic Surg of Tucson 5585 N Oracle Rd Tucson AZ 85704-3821

HESS, ROBERT, JR., ambulance service executive; b. East Cleveland, Ohio, Oct. 22, 1957; s. Robert and Patricia Lou Hess; m. Susan Hole, Jan. 28, 1983; children: Christine Renee, Robert III, Jessica Marie. Student Cuyahoga C.C., 1977-78; MBA Case Western Reserve U., 1992. With Physician's Ambulance Svc., South Euclid, 1972-94, v.p. in charge fin., data processing, med. assurance, 1978-86, sr. v.p., COO, 1986-94; pres., CEO PhysMed, Inc., South Euclid, Ohio, 1986-94; sr. v.p., COO Physician's/Medic Transport, Inc., Columbus, Ohio, 1990-94; EMS project mgr. Rural/Metro Corp., Scottsdale, Ariz., 1994—, dir. bus. devel., 1996—; bd. dirs. Hess Enterprises, Inc.; adj. faculty Cuyahoga C.C., vice chmn. Emergency Med. Technician Tng. Dept., 1986-90, mem. paramedic admissions com. Dir. rsch. U.S. Emergency Med. Technician Assn., 1981. Instr. advanced cardiac life support Am. Heart Assn., 1981-88; mem. Ohio Bd. Regents Paramedic Adv. Com., 1980-86; alternate mem. emergency med. svc. adv. com. Ohio Bd. Edn., 1986-92; mem. United Way Cleve., eagle com., 1987; paramedic adv. coun. Hillcrest Hosp.; mem. Ohio EMS Bd Ohio Dept. Edn., 1986-88; bd. dir. Commn. on Accreditation of Ambulance Svcs., 1990-96, vice chair, 1990-94, treas. 1995-96; mem. golf tournament com. March of Dimes, 1990-94; bd. dirs. March of Dimes Birth Defects Found., No. Ohio Chpt., 1993-94, chmn. campaign com. March of Dimes Metro Divsn., 1993-94; mem. exec. com. March of Dimes, 1993-94; bd. dirs. Ariz. Children's Found., 1996, chmn. major gifts com.; mem. City of Scottsdale Gang Task Force, 1996; Mem. Ohio Ambulance Assn. (pres. 1981-82, trustee 1980-81, chmn. govtl. affairs com. 1985-87), Am. Ambulance Assn. (dir. 1980-83, 90-94, fin. com. 1987, govtl. affairs com., accreditation com., bd. dirs. 1990-96, vice chmn. industry image com. 1993-95), Am. Ambulance Assn. Found. (exec. dir. 1993-95), Nat. Assn. Emergency Med. Technicians, Ohio Assn. Emergency Med. Services. Republican. Roman Catholic. Office: 8401 E Indian School Rd Scottsdale AZ 85251-2855

HESSE, CHRISTIAN AUGUST, mining and underground construction consultant; b. Chemnitz, Germany, June 20, 1925; s. William Albert and Anna Gunhilda (Baumann) H.; B. Applied Sci. with honors, U. Toronto (Ont., Can.), 1948; m. Brenda Nora Rigby, Nov. 4, 1964; children: Rob Christian, Bruce William. Registered profl. engr., Can.; chartered engr., U.K. In various mining and constrn. positions, Can., 1944-61; jr. shift boss N.J. Zinc Co., Gilman, Colo., 1949; asst. layout engr. Internat. Nickel Co., Sudbury, Ont., 1949-52; shaft and tunnel engr. Perini-Walsh Joint Venture, Niagara Falls, Ont., 1952-54; constrn. project engr. B. Perini & Sons (Can.) Ltd., Toronto, Ottawa, and New Brunswick, 1954-55; field engr. Aries Copper Mines Ltd., No. Ont., 1955-56; instr. in mining engring. U. Toronto, 1956-57; planning engr. Stanleigh Uranium Mining Corp. Ltd., Elliot Lake, Ont., 1957-58, chief engr., 1959-60; subway field engr. Johnson-Perini-Kiewit Joint Venture, Toronto, 1960-61; del. Commonwealth Mining Congress, Africa, 1961; with U.S. Borax & Chem. Corp., 1961-90; mng. dir. Yorkshire Potash, Ltd., London, 1970-71, gen. mgr., pres. Allan Potash Mines Ltd., Allan, Sask., Can., 1974, chief engr. U.S. Borax & Chem. Corp., L.A., 1974-77, v.p. engring., 1978-81, 87-90, v.p. and project mgr. Quartz Hill molybdenum project, 1981-90; v.p. Pacific Coast Molybdenum Co., 1981-90, v.p. mining devel., 1984-90. Co-author publs. on submarine tailings disposal. Sault Daily Star scholar, Sault Sainte Marie, Ont., Can., 1944. Fellow Inst. Mining and Metallurgy; mem. SME/AIME (chmn. So. Calif. mining sect. 1994-95), Can. Inst. Mining and Metallurgy (life), Assn. Profl. Engrs. Ont., Prospectors and Developers Assn., N.W. Mining Assn., Alaska Miners Assn., L.A. Tennis Club. Lutheran.

HESSLER, DOUGLAS SCOTT, screenwriter; b. Hagerstown, Md., July 22, 1948; s. Chester Scott and Betty Jane (Martin) H.; m. Fumiko Hamada, June 11, 1993. BFA, Va. Commonwealth U., 1971; MFA, Md. Inst. Coll. of Art, 1974; Postgrad. Degree, Am. Film Inst., L.A., 1985. Painter, filmmaker, N.Y.C., 1974-82; creative dir. J. Walter Thompson Advt., N.Y.C., 1977-83; prodn. exec. Cannon Films, L.A., 1985-88, Walt Disney Co., L.A., 1988-90; artistic dir. Landmark Entertainment, L.A., 1990-92; condr. screenwriting workshops, L.A., Germany, 1995-96. Screenwriter: Over the Line, 1993, Eye of the Storm, 1993, Judgement Day, 1994, Adrenaline, 1995, Code Red, 1996, Side Swipe, 1996; prodr. Intruder, Paramount Picturs, 1990. Staff sgt. USAFR, 1967-72. Recipient Adolf-Grime award, Germany, 1995, award Houston Film Internat. Festival, 1996, N.Y. Film Festival, 1996; N.Y. State Arts grantee N.Y. State Coun. on Arts, 1979, 80, 81; Am. Film Inst. Writer/Dir. fellow, 1984-85.

HETFELD, ELIZABETH ANN, industrial engineer; b. Oshkosh, Wis., Feb. 28, 1954; d. Frederick Damler and Connie Steiger Dempsey; children: Hunter H. Student, U. Autonima, Guadalajara, Mex., 1974; BA in Architecture, U. N.Mex., 1979. Project mgr. drafting Hutchinson, Brown & Ptnrs., Architects, Albuquerque, 1978-80; engr. facilities constrn. mgmt. divsn. Albuquerque Ops. Office, 1982-90, engr. quality engring. divsn., 1982-90, engr. budget and resources mgmt., 1982-90, site mgr. uranium mill tailings remedial action project, 1982-90; sect. chief indsl. tech. Bonneville Power Adminstrn., Portland, Oreg., 1990—; mem. employee support sounding bd. Bonneville Power Adminstrn., Portland, 1990-91, mem. women's resource group, 1990-93. Mem. City Club Portland, 1990-91.

HETLAND, JOHN ROBERT, lawyer, educator; b. Mpls., Mar. 12, 1930; s. James L. and Evelyn (Lundgren) H.; m. Mildred Woodruff, Dec. 1951 (div.); children: Lynda Lee Catlin, Robert John, Debra Ann Allen; m. Anne Kneeland, Dec. 1972; children: Robin T. Willcox, Elizabeth J. Pickett. B.S.L., U. Minn., 1952, J.D., 1956. Bar: Minn. 1956, Calif. 1962, U.S. Supreme Ct. 1981. Practice law Mpls., 1956-59; assoc. prof. law U. Calif., Berkeley, 1959-60, prof., 1960-91; prof. emeritus, 1991—; prin. Hetland & Kneeland, PC, Berkeley, 1959—; vis. prof. law Stanford U., 1971, 80, U. Singapore, 1972, U. Cologne, Fed. Republic Germany, 1988. Author: California Real Property Secured Transactions, 1970, Commercial Real Estate Transactions, 1972, Secured Real Estate Transactions, 1974, 1977; co-author: California Cases on Security Transactions in Land, 2d edit., 1975, 3d edit., 1984, 4th edit., 1992; contbr. articles to legal, real estate and fin. jours. Served to lt. comdr. USNR, 1953-55. Fellow Am. Coll. Real Estate Lawyers, Am. Coll. Mortgage Attys., Am. Bar Found.; mem. ABA, State Bar Calif., State Bar Minn., Order of Coif, Phi Delta Phi. Home: 20 Red Coach Ln Orinda CA 94563-1112 Office: 2600 Warring St Berkeley CA 94704-3415

HETT, JOAN MARGARET, civic administrator; b. Trail, B.C., Can., Sept. 8, 1936; s. Gordon Stanley and Violet Thora (Thors) Hett; B.Sc., U. Victoria (B.C., Can.), 1964; M.S., U. Wis., Madison, 1967, Ph.D., 1969. Ecologist, Eastern Deciduous Forest Biome, Oak Ridge Nat. Lab., 1969-72; coor. sites dir. Coniferous Forest Biome, Oreg. State U., Corvallis and U. Wash., Seattle, 1972-77; ecol. cons., Seattle, 1978-84; plant ecologist Seattle City Light, 1984-86; supr. Rights-of-Way, Seattle City Light, 1986-91, vegetation mgmt. mgr., Seattle City Light, 1991—. Mem. Ecol. Soc. Am., Brit. Ecol. Soc., Am. Inst. Biol. Scis., Am. Forestry Assn., Sigma Xi. Contbr. articles to profl. jours.; research in plant population dynamics, land use planning, forest sucession.

HEUMAN, DONNA RENA, lawyer; b. Seattle, May 27, 1949; d. Russell George and Edna Inez (Armstrong) H. BA in Psychology, UCLA, 1972; JD, U. Calif., San Francisco, 1985. Cert. shorthand reporter, 1978—; owner, Heuman & Assocs., San Francisco, 1978-86; real estate broker, Calif., 1990—; co-founder, chair, CFO Atherton Park Foods, Inc., 1996—. Mem. Hastings Internat. and Comparative Law Rev., 1984-85; bd. dirs. Saddleback, 1987-89. Jessup Internat. Moot Ct. Competition, 1985, N. Fair Oaks Mcpl. Adv. Coun., vice chair, sec., 1993-95. Mem. ABA, NAFE, ATLA, AOPA, Nat. Shorthand Reporters Assn., Women Entrepreneurs, Mensa, Calif. State Bar Assn., Nat. Mus. of Women in the Arts, Calif. Lawyers for the Arts, San Francisco Bar Assn., Commonwealth Club, World Affairs Coun., Zonta (bd. dirs.). Home: 750 18th Ave Menlo Park CA 94025-2018 Office: Superior Ct Calif Hall Of Justice Redwood City CA 94063

HEURING, WAYNE ROBERT, newspaper journalist; b. East St. Louis, Ill., Sept. 8, 1947; s. Allen B. and Esther E. (Baldus) H.; m. Ellen Zucker, June 29, 1970 (div. Jan. 1974); m. Laura Appelbaum, Apr. 21, 1974 (div. Jan. 1975). BA in Psychology, U. Ill., 1969, MS in Journalism, 1971. Sports dir. WPGU Radio, Urbana, Ill., 1966-68; sportswriter Champaign-Urbana (Ill.) News-Gazette, 1969-71; reporter, copy editor Champaign-Urbana Courier, 1971-75; copy editor Milw. Sentinel, 1975-79; night bus. desk chief Chgo. Tribune, 1979-86; night copy desk chief San Francisco Examiner, 1986—; writing coach San Francisco State U., 1989—; journalism instr. Marquette U., Milw., 1976-78. Co-chmn. judging com. Nat. Ednl. Media Network, Oakland, Calif., 1994-96, mem. judging com. 1993—, trustee 1995-96. Home: 60 Parkridge Dr Apt 6 San Francisco CA 94131-1428 Office: San Francisco Examiner 110 5th St San Francisco CA 94103-2918

HEUSCHELE, WERNER PAUL, veterinary researcher; b. Ludwigsburg, Federal Republic of Germany, Aug. 28, 1929; came to U.S., 1932, naturalized, 1951; s. Karl August and Margarete Anna (Wagner) H.; m. Carolyn Rene Bredeson, Jan. 1, 1983; children: Eric W.K., Mark R. (dec.), Jennifer M. Student, San Diego State Coll., 1947-50; BA in Zoology, U. Calif., Davis, 1952, DVM, 1956; student, NIH, Bethesda, Md., 1966; PhD in Med. Microbiology, Virology, Immunology, U. Wis., 1969. Diplomate Am. Coll. Vet. Microbiologists, Am. Coll. Zoological Medicine. Mgr. veterinary hosp. Zool. Soc. San Diego, 1956-61, head, microbiology/virology, 1981-86, dir. research, 1986—; research veterinarian Plum Island Animal Disease Lab., Orient Point, N.Y., 1961-70; tng. resident in vet. pathology Armed Forces Inst. Pathology, Washington, 1965-66; assoc. prof. infectious disease Kansas State U., Manhattan, 1970-71; head, virology, research and devel. Jensen-Salsbery Labs., Kansas City, Kans., 1971-76; prof. vet. preventive medicine Ohio State U., Columbus, 1976-81; cons. Syntro Corp., San Diego, 1985-88, SIBIA, San Diego, 1983-90, UN-FAO-UNDP, Maracay, Venezuela, 1979, 80; grant rev. panelist USDA, Washington; mem. com. on bovine tuberculosis eradication, com. on animal health and vet. medicine, bd. on agrl. NRC, 1992-96. Contbr. articles to profl. jours. Recipient U. Calif.-Davis Sch. of Vet. Medicine Alumni Achievement award, 1991. Mem. USDA (VS adv. blue-ribbon panel 1987-91), Am. Assn. Zool. Pks. and Aquariums (profl. fellow), Am. Assn. Zoo Veterinarians (pres. 1958-59, sec., treas. 1959-62, Life Mem. award 1993), Am. Vet. Med. Assn., Wildlife Disease Assn. (v.p. 1985-87, Disting. Svc. award 1995), Internat. Union for Conservation of Nature and Natural Resources Vet. Specialist Group, Captive Breeding Specialist Group (species survival com.), Columbus Zoo Assn. (bd. dirs. 1977-81), Am. Coll. Vet. Microbiologists (bd. govs. 1984-87), U.S. Animal Health Assn., Sigma Xi, Phi Zeta. Home: 4690 59th St San Diego CA 92115-3830 Office: Zool Soc San Diego PO Box 551 San Diego CA 92112-0551

HEWITT, CONRAD W., state superintendant of banks. Supt. of banks State of Calif. Office: 111 Pine St Ste 1100 San Francisco CA 94111-5613

HEWITT, JERENE CLINE, English language educator; b. Chinook, Mont., Dec. 25, 1917; d. Charles G. and Dorothy Elizabeth (Strother) Grobee; m. Ronald A. Cline, 1938 (dec.); children: Alan, Scott, Mike; m. William F. Hewitt, June 25, 1977 (dec.). BA, U. Calif., Irvine, 1966, MFA, 1968, PhD, 1981. Mgr. dept. correspondence Dun & Bradstreet, L.A., 1939-41; statistician Lockheed, 1941-44; freelance writer, editor, 1948—; teaching asst. U. Calif., Irvine, 1966-67, teaching assoc., 1967-68; asst. prof. English Calif. State U., L.A., 1968-71; assoc. prof. Pasadena (Calif.) City Coll., 1971-80, prof., 1980-83, dir. creative writing program dept. English, 1973-83, prof. emerita, 1983—; owner Words, Inc., Big Bear City, Calif. Author: Selected Poems, 1968, Essentials, 1972, The Epigram in English, 1981; contbr. poetry, articles and short stories to publs. Mem. AAUP, MLA, Acad. Am. Poets, Writers' Club Whittier (pres. 1962-64, bd. dirs.). Home: 1071 G St Erwin Lake CA 90601-4423 Office: Box 2498 Big Bear City CA 92314

HEWITT, WILLIAM JAMES, municipal official; b. Apr. 29, 1944; m. Sharon Hewitt; 3 children. BS, Brandon (Can.) U.; cert. in adult edn., Red River C.C., Winnipeg, Can.; cert. in pub. adminstrn., Assiniboine Coll., Brandon; cert. in fire svc. mgmt., Internat. City Mgmt. Assn. cert. fire fighter, fire prevention officer, fire svc. instr., Can. Vol. fire fighter Virden Vol. Fire Dept., 1964-68; fire fighter City of Brandon Fire Dept., 1968-73; asst. fire commr. Office Manitoba Fire Commr., 1973-78, mgr. field svcs. sect., 1978-86; fire chief City of Saskatoon, Can., 1986—; developer Manitoba Fire Coll., apptd. prin., 1978; past chair Manitoba Fire Svcs. Mobile Radio Comm. Com., Manitoba Fire Coll. Protection Tech. Adv. Com., Manitoba Pub. Fire Safety Edn. Com. Contbr. articles to profl. jours.; presenter confs. in Boston, Memphis, Cin., Toronto, Regina, Yellowknife, Winnipeg, Ottawa, others; speaker in field. Mem. Internat. Soc. Fire Svc. Instrs. (bd. dirs. 1976-92), Internat. City Mgmt. Assn. (instr. firesvc. adminstrn. program), Internat. Fire Svcs. Tng. Assn. (fire svc. instr. textbook and fire dept. ops. textbook coms. 1976-81), Internat. Assn. Fire Chiefs (1st v.p. Can. divsn.), Nat. Fire Protection Assn., Can. Fire Chief's Assn. (pres.), Sask. Fire Chief's Assn. (past pres.), Sask. Profl. Qualifications and Standards Bd. (chmn.), Sask. C. of C., N.D. State Fireman's Assn. (hon. life). Office: Fire Dept, 125 Idylwyld Dr S, Saskatoon, SK Canada S7M 1L4

HEWLETT, WILLIAM (REDINGTON), manufacturing company executive, electrical engineer; b. Ann Arbor, Mich., May 20, 1913; s. Albion Walter and Louise (Redington) H.; m. Flora Lamson, Aug. 10, 1939 (dec. 1977); children: Eleanor Hewlett Gimon, Walter B., James S., William A., Mary Hewlett Jaffe; m. Rosemary Bradford, May 24, 1978. BA, Stanford U., 1934, EE, 1939; MS, MIT, 1936; LLD (hon.), U. Calif., Berkeley, 1966, Yale U., 1976, Mills Coll., 1983, Marquette U., 1994; DSc (hon.), Kenyon Coll., 1978, Poly. Inst. N.Y., 1978; LHD (hon.), Johns Hopkins U., 1985; EngD (hon.), U. Notre Dame, 1980, Utah State U., 1980, Dartmouth Coll., 1983; PhD, Rand Grad. Inst.; D Electronic Sci. (hon.), U. Bologna, Italy, 1989; HHD (hon.), Santa Clara U., 1991. Electromedical researcher, 1936-39; co-founder Hewlett-Packard Co., Palo Alto, Calif., 1939, ptnr., 1939-46, exec. v.p., dir., 1947-64, pres., 1964-77, chief exec. officer, 1969-78, chmn. exec. com., 1977-83, vice chmn. bd. dirs., 1983-87, emeritus dir., 1987—; mem. internat. adv. council Wells Fargo Bank, 1986-92; trustee Rand Corp., 1962-72; trustee Carnegie Inst., Washington, 1971-90, trustee emeritus, 1990—, chmn. bd. 1980-86; dir. Overseas Devel. Council, 1969-77; bd. dirs. Inst. Radio Engrs. (now IEEE), 1950-57, pres. 1954; coord. chpt. on rsch. in industry for 5-Yr. Outlook Report, NAS, 1980-81; mem. adv. coun. on edn. and new techs. The Tech. Ctr. of Silicon Valley, 1987-88; past bd. dirs. Chrysler Corp., FMC Corp., Chase Manhattan Bank, Utah Internat. Inc. Contbr. articles to profl. jours.; patentee in field. Trustee Stanford U., 1963-74, Mills Coll., Oakland, Calif., 1958-68; mem. Pres.'s Gen. Adv. Com. on Fgn. Assistance Programs, Washington, 1965-68, Pres.'s Sci. Adv. Com., 1966-69; mem. San Francisco regional panel Commn. on White House Fellows, 1969-70, chmn., 1970; pres. bd. dirs. Palo Alto Stanford Hosp. Ctr., 1956-58, bd. dirs., 1958-62; dir. Drug Abuse Council, Washington, 1972-74, Kaiser Found. Hosp. & Health Plan Bd., 1972-78; chmn. The William and Flora Hewlett Found., 1966-94, chmn. emeritus, 1994—; bd. dirs. San Francisco Bay Area Council, 1969-81, Inst. Medicine, Washington, 1971-72, The Nat. Acads. Corp., 1986—, Monterey Bay Aquarium Rsch. Inst., 1987—, Univ. Corp. for Atmospheric Rsch. Found., 1986-88. Lt. col. AUS, 1942-45. Recipient Calif. Mfr. of Yr. Calif. Mfrs. Assn., 1969, Bus. Statesman of Yr. Harvard Bus. Sch. No. Calif., 1970, Medal of Achievement Western Electronic Mfrs. Assn., 1971, Industrialist of Yr. (with David Packard) Calif. Mus. Sci. and Industry and Calif. Mus. Found., 1973, Award with David Packard presented by Scientific Apparatus Makers Assn., 1975, Corp. Leadership award MIT, 1976, Medal of Honor City of Boeblingen, Germany, 1977, Herbert Hoover medal for disting. service Stanford U. Alumni Assn., 1977, Henry Heald award Ill. Inst. Tech., 1984, Nat. Medal of Sci. U.S. Nat. Sci. Com., 1985, Laureate award Santa Clara County BUs. Hall of Fame Jr. Achievement, 1987, World Affairs Coun. No. Calif. award, 1987, Degree of Uncommon Man award Stanford U., 1987, Laureate award Nat. Bus. Hall of Fame Jr. Acievement, 1988; Decorated Comdr.'s Cross Order of Merit Fed. Republic Germany, 1987, John M. Fluke Sen. Meml. Pioneer award, Electronics Test Mag., 1990, Silicon Valley Engring. Hall of Fame award Silicon Valley Engring. Coun., 1991, Exemplary Leader award Am. Leadership Forum, 1992, Alexis de Tocqueville Soc. award United Way, Santa Clara County, 1991, Nat. Inventors Hall of Fame award Nat. Inventors Hall of Fame Found. Akron, 1992, Howard Vollum Leadership award Oreg. Grad. Inst. Sci. and Tech., 1993, Internat. Citizens award World Forum of Silicon Valley, 1994, Lifetime Achievement award Lemelson-MIT prize, 1995; named to Lowell H.S. Alumni Assn. Wall of Fame, 1995; named hon. fellow Harris-Manchester Coll. Oxford U., 1996. Fellow NAE (Founders award 1993), IEEE (life fellow, Founders medal with David Packard 1973), Franklin Inst. (life, Vermilye medal with David Packard 1976), Am. Acad. Arts and Scis.; mem. NAS (panel on advanced tech. competition 1982-83, president's circle 1989—), Instrument Soc. Am. (hon. life), Am. Philos. Soc., Calif. Acad. Sci. (trustee 1963-68), Assn. Quadrato della Radio, Century Assn. N.Y.C. Office: Hewlett-Packard Co 3000 Hanover St Palo Alto CA 94304-1112

HEYCK, THEODORE DALY, lawyer; b. Houston, Apr. 17, 1941; s. Theodore Richard and Gertrude Paine (Daly) H. BA, Brown U., 1963; postgrad. Georgetown. U., 1963-65, 71-72; JD, N.Y. Law Sch., 1979. Bar: N.Y. 1980, Calif. 1984, U.S. Ct. Appeals (2nd cir.) 1984, U.S. Supreme Ct. 1984, U.S. Dist. Ct. (so. and ea. dists.) N.Y. 1980, U.S. Dist. Ct. (we. and no. dists.) N.Y. 1984, U.S. Dist. Ct. (cen. and so. dists.) Calif. 1984, U.S. Ct. Appeals (9th cir.) 1986. Paralegal dist. atty. Bklyn., 1975-79; asst. dist. atty. Bklyn. dist., Kings County, N.Y., 1979-85; dep. city atty., L.A., 1985—; bd. dirs. Screen Actors Guild, N.Y.C., 1977-78. Mem. ABA, AFTRA, NATAS, SAG, Bklyn. Bar Assn., Assn. Trial Lawyers Am., N.Y. Trial Lawyers Assn., N.Y. State Bar Assn., Calif. Bar Assn., Fed. Bar Council, L.A. County Bar Assn., Actors Equity Assn. Home: 2106 E Live Oak Dr Los Angeles CA 90068-3639 Office: Office City Atty City Hall E 200 N Main St Los Angeles CA 90012-4110

HEYER, CAROL ANN, illustrator; b. Cuero, Tex., Feb. 2, 1950; d. William Jerome and Merlyn Mary (Hutson) H. BA, Calif. Lutheran U., 1974. Freelance artist various cos., Thousand Oaks, Calif., 1974-79; computer artist Image Resource, Westlake Village, Calif., 1979-81; staff writer, artist Lynn-Davis Prodns., Westlake Village, Calif., 1981-87; art dir. Northwind Studios Internat., Camarillo, Calif., 1988-89; illustrator Touchmark, Thousand Oaks, 1989—; cons. art dir., writer Lynn-Wenger Prodns., 1987-89; guest spkr. Thousand Oaks Libr., Author's Faire, Calif. Luth. U., Soc. Children's Book Writers and Illustrators, Illustrators Day, Ventura County Reading Assn.'s Author's Faire; guest artist/spkr. Oxnard Libr.; booksignings/appearances Anaheim Conv. Ctr., L.A. Conv. Ctr., Am. Booksellers Assn.; guest 1996 Readout, grand opening Barnes and Noble, Thousand Oaks; represented by Art Works, N.Y.C. Illustrator (children's books) A Star in the Pasture, 1988, The Dream Stealer, 1989, The Golden Easter Egg, 1989, All Things Bright and Beautiful, 1992, Rapunzel, 1992, The Christmas Carol, 1995, Prancer, Gift of the Magi, Dinosaurs, Here Come the Brides, (adult book) The Artist's Market, also L.A. Times, Daily News, The Artist's Mag., News Chronicle; also cover art for Dragon mag., Dungeon mag., Aboriginal Sci. Fiction mag., F.X. Schmid - Puzzle Wizards of the Coast (fantasy collector cards) and various novels, books and games; illustrator Bugs Bunny Coloring Book, Candyland Work Book, The Dragon Sleeps Step Ahead Workbook, City of Sorcers, CD-ROM cover for Memorex/Roaring Mouse Prodns.; interior art for various publs. including (mags.) Amazing Stories two covers, Interzone, Aboriginal Sci. Fiction Mag., Alfred Hitchcocks Myster Mag., Ideals mag., Realms of Fantasy mag., Sci. Fiction Age mag., Tomorrow mag., (book) Tome of Magic (also art for game cards); writer (screenplay) Thunder Run, 1986; illustrator, writer (children's books) Beauty and the Beast, 1989, The Easter Story, 1989, Excalibur, Robin Hood, 1993, Sleeping Beauty in the Wood, 1996, The Christmas Story, 1996; paintings for line of Fantasy Art Prints, Scafa/Tornabene, religious art prints; rep. by Every Picture Tells a Story Gallery, Worlds of Wonder; 2 covers for young adults Hyperion/Disney Press; one-woman show Adventures for Kids Gallery; illustrator poster for motion picture and TV fund; writer Disney ednl. prodns., others; freelance artist Disney Interactive. Recipient Lit. award City of Oxnard Cultural Arts Commn. and Carnegie Art Inst., 1992, Best Cover Art Boomerang award, 1989, Cert. of Merit, Career Achievement award Calif. Luth. U., 1993, Cert. of Excellence Alumni Career Achievement award, 1993, Print's Regional Design Ann. award, 1992, Best Paper Backs award Internat. Reading Assn./Children s Book Coun. Joint Com., 1994, Spectrum Internat. Competition for Best in Contemporary Fantastic Art. Mem. Soc. Children's Book Writers (judge 1990, Mag. Merit award 1988, Keynote spkr.), Assn. Sci. Fiction and Fantasy Artists, Soc. Illustrators (Cert. of Merit 1990-92). Home and Office: Touchmark 925 Ave Arboles Thousand Oaks CA 91360

HEYL, ALLEN VAN, JR., geologist; b. Allentown, Pa., Apr. 10, 1918; s. Allen Van and Emma (Kleppinger) H.; student Muhlenberg Coll., 1936-37; BS in Geology, Pa. State U., 1941; PhD in Geology, Princeton U., 1950; m. Maxine LaVon Hawke, July 12, 1945; children: Nancy Caroline, Allen David Van. Field asst., govt. geologist Nfld. Geol. Survey, summers 1937-40, 42; jr. geologist U.S. Geol. Survey, Wis., 1943-45, asst. geologist, 1945-47, assoc. geologist, 1947-50, geologist, Washington and Beltsville, Md., 1950-67; staff geologist, Denver, 1968-90; cons. geologist 1990—; disting. lectr. grad. coll. Beijing, China and Nat. Acad. Sci., 1988; disting. invited lectr. Internat. Assn. Genesis Ore Deposits 9th Symposium, Beijing, 1994; chmn. Internat. Commn. Tectonics of Ore Deposits. Fellow Instn. Mining and Metallurgy (Gt. Brit.), Geol. Soc. Am., Am. Mineral. Soc., Soc. Econ. Geologists; mem. Inst. Genesis of Ore Deposits, Geol. Soc. Wash., Colo. Sci. Soc., Rocky Mountain Geol. Soc., Friends of Mineralogy (hon. life), Evergreen Naturalist Audubon Soc., Sigma Xi, Alpha Chi Sigma. Lutheran. Contbr. numerous articles to profl. jours., chpts. to books. Home: PO Box 1052 Evergreen CO 80439-1052

HEYMAN, IRA MICHAEL, federal agency administrator, museum executive, law educator; b. N.Y.C., May 30, 1930; s. Harold Albert and Judith (Sobel) H.; m. Therese Helene Thau, Dec. 17, 1950; children: Stephen Thomas (dec.), James Nathaniel. AB in Govt., Dartmouth Coll., 1951; JD, Yale U., 1956; LLD (hon.), U. Pacific, 1981, Hebrew Union Coll., 1984, U. Md., 1986, SUNY, Buffalo, 1990. Bar: N.Y. 1956, Calif. 1961. Legis. asst. to U.S. Senator Ives, 1950-51; assoc. Carter, Ledyard & Milburn, N.Y.C., 1956-57; law clk. to presiding justice U.S. Ct. Appeals (2d cir.), New Haven, 1957-58; chief law clk. to Supreme Ct. Justice Earl Warren, 1958-59; acting assoc. prof. law U. Calif., Berkeley, 1959-61, prof. law, 1961-66, prof. city and regional planning, 1966-93, prof. emeritus, 1993—, vice chancellor, 1974-80, chancellor, 1980-90; counselor to Sec. of Interior Dept. Interior, Washington, 1993-94; sec. Smithsonian Inst., Washington, 1994—; vis. prof. Yale Law Sch., 1963-64, Stanford Law Sch., 1971-72. Editor Yale Law Jour.; contbr. articles to profl. jours. Sec. Calif. adv. com. U.S. Commn. Civil Rights, 1962-67; trustee Dartmouth Coll., 1982-93, chmn., 1991-93; mem. Lawyers' Com. for Civil Rights under Law, 1977-95; chmn. exec. com. Nat. Assn. State Univs. and Land Grant Colls., 1986; bd. regents Smithsonian Instn., 1990-94. 1st lt. USMC, 1951-53, capt. Res. ret. Decorated chevalier Legion of Honor (France).

HEYNEMAN, NICHOLAS ERNEST, psychologist; b. Glendale, Calif., May 22, 1954; s. Ernest A. and Emma (Melideo) H.; children: Alexandra, Jonah. BA, U. Calif., San Diego, 1979; MA, W.Va. U., 1982, PhD, 1985. Lic. psychologist, Pa., Idaho. Psychologist Meml. Med. Ctr., Long Beach, Calif., 1985-87; asst. prof. Pa. State Coll. Medicine, Hershey, 1987-89, Idaho State U., Pocatello, 1989—; pvt. practice Pocatello, 1989—. Author: (book/software) Dreamscape, 1996. Mem. APA. Office: Ste 172 775 Yellowstone Ave Pocatello ID 83201

HIATT, HOLLY MARLANE, history educator; b. Mesa, Ariz., Sept. 28, 1972; d. Phillip Rudger and Roma Lee (Willis) H. BA in Edn., Ariz. State U., 1994. Cert. secondary edn., Ariz. Tchr. history Snowflake (Ariz.) Unified Sch. Dist., 1994—. Bd. dirs. local chpt. Gov.'s Alliance Against Drugs, Snowflake, 1988-90. Mem. Ariz. Coun. Social Studies, Nat. Coun. Social Studies, Lambda Delta Sigma (pres. 1993-94), Phi Alpha Theta. Republican. Mem. Latter-Day Saints Ch. Home: 325 S 1st St E Snowflake AZ 85937

HIATT, PETER, librarian studies educator; b. N.Y.C., Oct. 19, 1930; s. Amos and Elizabeth Hope (Derry) H.; m. Linda Rae Smith, Aug. 16, 1968; 1 child, Holly Virginia. B.A., Colgate U., 1952; M.L.S., Rutgers U., 1957, Ph.D., 1963. Head Elmora Br. Library, Elizabeth, N.J., 1957-59; instr. Grad. Sch. Library Service Sci. Rutgers U., 1960-62; library cons. Ind. State Library, Indpls., 1963-70; asst. prof. Grad. Library Sch., Ind. U., 1963-66, assoc. prof., 1966-70; dir. Ind. Library Studies, Bloomington, 1967-70; dir. continuing edn. program for library personnel Western Interstate Commn. for Higher Edn., Boulder, Colo., 1970-74; dir. Grad. Sch. Library and Info. Sci., U. Wash., Seattle, 1974-81, prof., 1974—; prin. investigator Career Devel. and Assessment Center for Librarians, 1979-83, 90-93; dir. library insts. at various colls. and univs.; adv. project U.S. Office Edn.-ALA, 1977-80; bd. dirs. King County Libr. Sys., pres., 1991, 95, sec., 1993, 94; prin. investigator Career Devel. and Assessment Ctrs. for Lib109rs.: Phase II, 1990-93. Author: (with Donald Thompson) Monroe County Public Library: Planning for the Future, 1966, The Public Library Needs of Delaware County, 1967, (with Henry Drennan) Public Library Services for the functionally Illiterate, 1967 (with Robert E. Lee and Lawrence A. Allen) A Plan for Developing a Regional Program of Continuing Education for Library Personnel, 1969, Public Library Branch Services for Adults of Low Education, 1964; dir., gen. editor: The Indiana Library Studies, 1970; author: Assessment Centers for Professional Library Leadership, 1993; mem. editorial bd. Coll. and Rsch. Librs., 1969-73; co-editor Leads: A Continuing Education Newsletter for Library Trustees, 1973-75, Octavio Noda; author chpts., articles on library continuing edn., staff devel. and libr. adult svcs. Mem. ALA (officer), Pacific N.W. Libr. Assn., Assn. Libr. and Info. Sci. Educators (officer, Outstanding Svc. award 1979), ACLU. Home: 19324 8th Ave NW Seattle WA 98177-3023 Office: U Wash Grad Sch Libr and Info Sci Seattle WA 98195 *I know of no other profession which helps so many people and organizations change and grow--from pre-school years through retirement, as does librarianship. It is a joy to be part of that.*

HIBBARD, CHARLES GUSTIN, historian; b. Climax, Mich., May 14, 1925; s. Byron C. Hibbard and B. Todd; m. Shirley Van Drunen, Nov. 29, 1952 (div. Mar. 1976); children: Elizabeth, Catherine, Rebecca, Robert; m. Mavis Hardy, Dec. 22, 1979. BS, U. Utah, 1960, PhD, 1980; MA, U. So. Calif., 1969. Cert. secondary tchr., Utah. Enlisted USAF, 1949, advanced to chief master sgt., air traffic contr., air traffic contr., 1949-70; historian USAF, various locations, 1982-89; postal clk. U.S. Postal Svc., Salt Lake City, 1972-77; pres. Ft. Douglas (Utah) Mil. Mus. Assn., 1993—; bd. dirs. Hill AFB (Utah) Mus., 1986-89. Author: 509th Composite Group Trains at Wendover, 1995 Fall Air Power History; editor, contbr. to book History of Hill AFB, Utah, 1988; contbr. to Ency. of Am. West, 1994, Hist. Dictionary of USAF, 1992. Decorated Bronze Star. Mem. Utah Hist. Soc., Wasatch Westerners (pres. 1991-92), Oreg.-Calif. Trails Assn., Western History Assn. Home: 5100 S 1050 W Trlr 220A Ogden UT 84405-3771 Office: Ft Douglas Mus Assn 32 Potter St Salt Lake City UT 84113-5046

HIBBARD, RICHARD PAUL, industrial ventilation consultant, lecturer; b. Defiance, Ohio, Nov. 1, 1923; s. Richard T. and Doris E. (Walkup) H.; BS in Mech. Indsl. Engring., U. Toledo, 1949; m. Phyllis Ann Kirchoffer, Sept. 7, 1948; children: Barbara Rae, Marcia Kae, Rebecca Ann, Patricia Jan, John Ross. Mech. engr. Oldsmobile div. Gen. Motors Corp., Lansing, Mich., 1950-56; design and sales engr. McConnell Sheet Metal, Inc., Lansing, 1956-60; chief heat and ventilation engr. Fansteel Metall. Corp., North Chicago, Ill., 1960-62; sr. facilities and ventilation engr. The Boeing Co., Seattle, 1962-63; ventilation engr. environ. health div. dept. preventive medicine U. Wash., 1964-70, lectr. dept. environ. health, 1970-82, lectr. emeritus, 1983—; prin. Indsl. Ventilation Cons. Svcs., 1983—; chmn. Western Indsl. Ventilation Conf., 1962; mem. com. indsl. ventilation Am. Conf. Govtl. Indsl. Hygienists, 1966—; mem. staff Indsl. Ventilation Conf., Mich. State U., 1955—. With USAAF, 1943-45, USAR, 1946-72. Recipient Disting. Svc. award Indsl. Ventilation Conf., Mich. State U., 1975, 93. Mem. Am. Soc. Safety Engrs. (R.M. Gillmore Meml. award Puget Sound chpt.), ASHRAE, Am. Inst. Plant Engrs., Am. Indsl. Hygiene Assn. (J.M. Dallevalle award 1977), Am. Foundryman's Soc. Lodges: Elks, Masons. Contbr. articles on indsl. hygiene and ventilation to profl. jours. Home: 41 165th Ave SE Bellevue WA 98008-4721

HIBBS, JOHN DAVID, software executive, engineer, business owner; b. Del Norte, Colo., Jan. 26, 1948; s. Alva Bernard and Frances Ava (Cathcart) H.; m. Ruthanne Johnson, Feb. 28, 1976. BSEE, Denver U., 1970. Elec. engr. Merrick and Co., Denver, 1972-73; lighting engr. Holophane div. Johns Manville, Denver, 1973-79; lighting products mgr. Computer Sharing Svcs., Inc., Denver, 1979-83; pres., owner Computer Aided Lighting Analysis, Boulder, Colo., 1983-86, Hibbs Sci. Software, Boulder, Colo., 1986—; chmn. bd. Sport Sail Inc., 1996—; co-founder Sport Sail, Inc. Author CALA, CALA/Pro and PreCALA lighting programs; patentee in field. With USNR, 1970-72. Recipient 1st prize San Luise Valley Sci. Fair, 1963. Mem. IEEE, Illuminating Engring. Soc. North Am. (chmn. computer com. 1988-91), Computer Soc. IEEE (chmn. computer problem set com. 1991-95). Home and Office: PO Box 400 Fraser CO 80442-0400

HIBLER, JUDE ANN, photojournalist; b. Portland, Oreg., Apr. 6, 1943; d. William Eliot and Myrtle Winifred (Johnson) Henderson; m. Jeffrey Charles Hibler, Jan. 27, 1962; 1 child, Beth Karen. Student, Portland State Coll., 1960-61, Pima C.C., 1980, U. Colo., Boulder, 1982, Antioch U. West, 1981-82. Alcohol counselor Whole Person Health Ctr., Boulder, 1984; adminstrv. mgr. Nordstrom, San Diego, 1985-88; publ., editor, owner Jazz Link Mag., San Diego, 1988-91; co-owner, photojournalist Jazz Link Enterprises, Longmont, Colo., 1991—; cons. El Cajon (Calif.) Jr. High Sch., 1989, Long Beach (Calif.) High Sch., 1990. Co-author: Joe Pass: Improvising Ideas, 1994; contbg. writer: Encyclopedia of Jazz, 1995, The Dale Bruning Jazz Guitar Series Vol. 1: Phrasing & Articulation, 1997; co-prodr. CD: Dale Bruning Quartet's Tomorrow's Reflections, 1995; co-prodr., leader, author: Jazz Music & Media Clinic Book, 1996; publ./editor: Jazz Link Mag., 1988 (best jazz pub. 1988); editor The Gift of Jazz mag., 1995-96; photographer: (book covers) Joe Pass Note by Note, 1994, Improvising Ideas, 1994; photojournalist Jazzscene of Oreg., JazzNow Mag., 1992-94, Concord Jazz. Named Outstanding Svc. Nat. Assn. Jazz Educators, 1989, First Friend of

Jazz Dr. Billy Taylor's Soundpost, 1991. Mem. San Diego Musicians Union (hon. mem.). Democrat. Home and Office: 3721 Columbia Dr Longmont CO 80503-2117

HICE, MICHAEL, editor, marketing professional; b. Carlsbad, N.Mex., June 8, 1946; s. William Elmer and Jewell Irene (Holcomb) H. BA, Tulane U., 1968. Asst. dir. ESL Lang. Ctrs., Houston, 1970-77; program dir. St. Marys Coll., Moraga, Calif., 1977-78; with Savin Corp., San Francisco, 1978-82; gen. sales mgr. Radio Sta. KLSK, Santa Fe, N.Mex., 1983-90; ptnr., v.p. Mountain Time Tours, Santa Fe, N.Mex., 1987-88; ptnr., v.p. sales mktg. cons. Nightingale Hice Inc., Santa Fe, N.Mex., 1990-96; ptnr., editor Indian Artist, Inc., Santa Fe, N.Mex., 1994—; co-founder, arts dir., promoter Homogenesis, San Francisco, 1981-82. Editor Indian Artist, 1994; co-author: (play) Song of Myself, 1984. Co-founder AID and Comfort, Santa Fe, 1989, Bus. for Social Responsibility, 1993. Recipient Best of Show award N.Mex. Advt. Fedn., 1990, Best Multi-Media Pub. Svc. Campaign award, 1993. Mem. Nat. Mktg. Assn. Home: 361 Ojo de la Vaca Santa Fe NM 87505 Office: Indian Artist Inc 1807 2nd St # 61 Santa Fe NM 87505-3499

HICK, KENNETH WILLIAM, business executive; b. New Westminster, B.C., Can., Oct. 17, 1946; s. Les Walter and Mary Isabelle (Warner) H. BA in Bus., Eastern Wash. State Coll., 1971; MBA (fellow), U. Wash., 1973, PhD, 1975. Regional sales mgr. Hilti, Inc., San Leandro, Calif., 1976-79; gen. sales mgr. Moore Internat., Inc., Portland, 1979-80; v.p. sales and mktg. Phillips Corp., Anaheim, Calif., 1980-81; owner, pres., chief exec. officer K.C. Metals, San Jose, Calif., 1981-87; owner, pres., chief exec. officer Losli Internat. Inc., Portland, Oreg., 1987-89; pres. Resources N.W. Inc., 1989—; communications cons. Asso. Pub. Safety Communication Officers, Inc., State of Oreg., 1975-93; numerous cons. assignments, also seminars, 1976—. Contbr. to numerous publs., 1976—. Mem. Oreg. Gov.'s Tax Bd., 1975-76; pres. Portland chpt. Oreg. Jaycees, 1976; bd. fellows U. Santa Clara, 1983—. Served with USAF, 1966-69. Decorated Commendation medal. Mem. Am. Mgmt. Assn., Am. Mktg. Assn., Assn. M.B.A. Execs., Assn. Gen. Contractors, Soc. Advancement Mgmt., Home Builders Assn. Roman Catholic. Home: 17627 Kelok Rd Lake Oswego OR 97034-6655 Office: Resources N/W Inc PO Box 1909 Lake Oswego OR 97035-0209

HICKCOX, LESLIE KAY, health educator, consultant, counselor; b. Berkeley, Calif., May 12, 1951; d. Ralph Thomas and Marilyn Irene (Stump) H. BA, U. Redlands, 1973; MA, U. of the Pacific, 1975; MEd, Columbia U., 1979; MEd in Health Edn., Oreg. State U., 1987, MEd in Guidance & Counseling, 1988, EdD in Edn., 1991. Cert. state C.C. instr. (life), Calif. Instr. health curriculum and supervision Concordia Coll., Portland, Oreg., 1992; health and phys. edn. instr. Portland C.C., 1994-95; instr. human studies and comm. Marylhurst (Oreg.) Coll., 1987—; edn. supr., instr. Oreg. State U., Corvallis, 1988-90; phys. edn. instr., dir. intramurals SUNY, Stony Brook, 1981-83; phys. edn. instr., dir intramurals Health Edn. Inst. U. (New Zealand) Auckland, 1991; coord., instr. dept. health, phys. edn. and recreation Rogue C.C., Grants Pass, Oreg., 1995-97; founder Experiential Learning Inst., 1992—; Lilly N.W. High Edn. Tchg. Conf., 1996. Contbr. articles to profl. jours. Mem. ASCD, Nat. Ctr. for Health Edn., Assn. for Advancement of Health Edn., Higher Edn. R & D Soc. Australasia, Coun. for Adult and Exptl. Learning, Kappa Delta Phi, Phi Delta Kappa.

HICKEL, WALTER JOSEPH, investment firm executive, forum administrator; b. nr. Claflin, Kans., Aug. 18, 1919; s. Robert A. and Emma (Zecha) H.; m. Janice Cannon, Sept. 22, 1941 (dec. Aug. 1943); 1 child, Theodore; m. Ermalee Strutz, Nov. 22, 1945; children: Robert, Walter Jr., Jack, Joseph, Karl. Student pub. schs., Claflin; D.Eng. (hon.), Stevens Inst. Tech., 1970, Mich. Tech. U., 1973; LL.D. (hon.), St. Mary of Plains Coll., St. Martin's Coll., U. Md., Adelphi U., U. San Diego, Rensselaer Poly. Inst., 1973, U. Alaska, 1976, Alaska Pacific U., 1991; D.Pub. Adminstrn. (hon.), Willamette U. Founder Hickel Investment Co., Anchorage, 1947—; gov. State of Alaska, 1966-69, 90-94; sec. U.S. Dept. Interior, 1969-70; sec. gen. The Northern Forum, 1994—; former mem. world adv. council Internat. Design Sci. Inst.; former mem. com. on sci. freedom and responsibility AAAS; nominated for pres. at 1968 Republican Nat. Convention; co-founder Yukon Pacific Corp.; founder Inst. of the North, 1996—. Author: Who Owns America?, 1971; contbr. articles to newspapers. Mem. Republican Nat. Com., 1954-64; bd. regents Gonzaga U.; bd. dirs. Salk Inst., 1972-79, NASA Adv. Coun. Exploration Task Force, 1989-91; mem. Governor's Econ. Com. on North Slope Natural Gas, Alaska, 1982. Named Alaskan of Year, 1969, Man of Yr. Ripon Soc., 1970; recipient DeSmet medal Gonzaga U., 1969, Horatio Alger award, 1972, Grand Cordon of the Order of Sacred Treasure award His Imperial Majesty the Emperor of Japan, 1988. Mem. Pioneers of Alaska, Alaska C. of C. (former chmn. econ. devel. com.), Equestrian Order Holy Sepulchre, Knights Malta, KC. Home: 1905 Loussac Dr Anchorage AK 99517-1225 Office: PO Box 101700 Anchorage AK 99510-1700 *We shall never understand peace, justice and the living of life until we recognize that all people are human and that humans are the most precious things on earth.*

HICKERSON, GLENN LINDSEY, leasing company executive; b. Burbank, Calif., Aug. 22, 1937; s. Ralph M. and Sarah Lawson (Lindsey) H.; m. Jane Fortune Arthur, Feb. 24, 1973. BA in Bus. Adminstrn., Claremont Men's Coll., 1959; MBA, NYU, 1960. Exec. asst. Douglas Aircraft Co., Santa Monica, Calif., 1963; sec., treas. Douglas Fin. Corp., Long Beach, Calif., 1964-67, regional mgr. customer financing, 1967; exec. asst. to pres. Universal Airlines, Inc., Detroit, 1967-68, v.p., treas., asst. sec., 1968-69, pres., 1969-72; v.p., treas., asst. sec. Universal Aircraft Service, Inc., Detroit, 1968-69, chmn. bd., 1969-72; v.p., treas. Universal Airlines Co., Detroit, 1968-69, pres., 1969-72; group v.p. Marriott Hotels, Inc., Washington, 1972-76; dir. sales Far East and Australia Lockheed Calif. Co., 1976-78, dir. mktg. Americas, 1978-79, dir. mktg. Internat., 1979-81, v.p., internat. sales, 1981-83; v.p. comml. mktg. internat. Douglas Aircraft Co., McDonnell Douglas Corp., 1983-89; mng. dir. GPA Asia Pacific, El Segundo, Calif., 1989-90; exec. v.p. GATX Air Group, San Francisco, 1990-95, pres., 1995—. Bd. govs. Keck Ctr. for Internat. Strategic Studies; mem. Calif. Export Adv. Council. Served to lt. (j.g.) USCGR, 1960-62. H.B. Earhart Found. fellow, 1962. Mem. Internat. Assn. Charter Airlines (exec. com. 1971), Pacific Union Club. Home: 3233 Pacific Ave San Francisco CA 94118-2026 Office: GATX Air 4 Embarcadero Ctr San Francisco CA 94111-4106

HICKEY, LYNN ZWERG, visual and performing arts school coordinator; b. L.A., Apr. 16, 1941; d. Henry Otto and Evelyn Lucille (Pritchard) Zwerg; m. Guy Charles Hickey, Feb. 14, 1965; 1 child, Megan Zwerg Hickey. BA, Calif. State U., Northridge, 1964; MA, Calif. State U., 1978, Calif. State U., L.A., 1985; EdD, U. La Verne, 1995. Mentor tchr. L.A. Unified Sch. Dist., 1965-85, middle schs. humanities, interdisciplinary programs coord., 1987-91, visual and performing arts magnet sch. K-8, 1992—; coord. visual and performing arts technology in curriculum State of Calif. Dept. of Edn., Downey, 1986-87; cons. Nat. Arts Edn. Rsch. Ctr., N.Y.C., 1988-93; coord. Inst. The Calif. Arts Project, 1990, 94, 95; curriculum cons. SDE ednl. tech. unit, Sacramento, 1988-89, SDE/WASC, 1987—, mid. schs. unit, Sacramento, 1991—. Coord. Resource Guide, Arts and Tech. Edn., 1986; author, editor Humanities Resource Guide and Planning Charts, 1990. Adv. Performing Tree, L.A., 1986—, Folk and Traditional Arts, Cultural Affairs Dept., L.A., 1990-93; mem. Multicultural Com., L.A. County Office of Edn., Downey, 1985. Winner Community Svc. award, Performing Tree, 1988, Bravo award, L.A. Music Ctr., 1985, Douc Langer award, Calif. Art Educators Assn., 1985. Mem. Nat. Art Edn. Assn. (prof. rels. chair), Calif. Art Edn. Assn., Nat. Mid. Sch. Assn., Calif. League Mid. Schs., The Calif. Arts Project. Democrat. Office: 32nd St/USC Visual and Performing Arts Magnet Sch 822 W 32nd St Los Angeles CA 90007-3601

HICKEY, SHIRLEY LOUISE COWIN, elementary education educator; b. Moscow, Idaho, Nov. 20, 1950; d. George Theodore and Shirley Phyllis (Stokes) Cowin; m. Leonard Arnold Hickey, Aug. 19, 1973 (div. Sept. 1994); 1 child, Alisa Hadley. BA, Mt. Holyoke Coll., 1973; MA, Gonzaga U., Spokane, Wash., 1977. Cert. tchr., Wash. Substitute tchr. Cen. Valley Sch. Dist. and West Valley Sch. Dist., Spokane, Wash., 1973-77; svc. rep. Pacific NW Bell Telephone, Seattle, 1978-83; substitute tchr. Tahoma Sch. Dist., Maple Valley, Wash., 1983-87, St. Anthony Sch., Renton, Wash., 1983-87, St. James Sch., Kent, Wash., 1983-87; elem. tchr. Cedar Valley Sch., Kent, 1987-93, tchr., 1996—; pvt. tchr. piano, 1983-93. Cellist Women in Music Internat., 1990-91; class agt. Mt. Holyoke Coll., South Hadley, Mass., 1972-89, class libr. chmn., 1989-92; bd. dirs. Cedar Valley PTA, Kent, 1989-90. Mem. Kent Edn. Assn. (bldg. rep. 1988-92, polit. action com. 1990-93, crisis team 1990-91, sec. 1992-93, pres. 1993-96), Music Tchrs. Nat. Assn., Wash. State Music Tchrs. Assn., Mt. Holyoke Alumnae Assn. (bd. dirs. 1990-93), Mt. Holyoke Coll. Club (western rep. 1987-90, com. chmn. 1990-93). Episcopalian. Home: 19609 SE 259th St Kent WA 98042-5045

HICKEY, WINIFRED E(SPY), former state senator, social worker; b. Rawlins, Wyo.; d. David P. and Eugenia (Blake) Espy; children: John David, Paul Joseph. BA, Loretto Heights Coll., 1933; postgrad. U. Utah, 1934, Sch. Social Service, U. Chgo., 1936; LLD (hon.) U. Wyo., 1991. Dir. Carbon County Welfare Dept., 1935-36; field rep. Wyo. Dept. Welfare, 1937-38; dir. Red Cross Club, Europe, 1942-45; commr. Laramie County, Wyo., 1973-80; mem. Wyo. Senate, 1980-90; dir. United Savs. & Loan, Cheyenne; active Joint Powers Bd. Laramie County and City of Cheyenne. Pub. Where the Deer and the Antelope Play, 1967. Pres., bd. dirs. U. Wyo. Found., 1986-87; pres. Meml. Hosp. of Laramie County, 1986-88, Wyo. Transp. Mus., 1990-92; chmn. adv. council div. community programs Wyo. Dept. Health and Social Services; pres. county and state mental health assn., 1959-63; trustee, U. Wyo., 1967-71, St. Mary's Cathedral, 1986—; active Nat. Council Cath. Women, Gov. Residence Found., 1991-93, Wyo. Transp. Mus., 1993—; chair Am. Heritage Assocs. of U. Wyo., 1992—; com. chair Citizen of the Century State of Wyo.. Named Outstanding Alumna, Loretto Heights Coll., 1959, Woman of Yr. Commn. for Women, 1988, Legislator of Yr. Wyo. Psychologists Assn., 1988, Family of the Yr. U. Wyo., 1995. Mem. Altrusa Club (Cheyenne).

HICKLIN, RONALD LEE, music production company executive; b. Burlington, Wash., Dec. 4, 1937; s. Wendell C. and Theodora (Van Voorhis) H.; children: Jennifer Lynn, Mark Allan; m. Trudi Takamatsu, Oct. 23, 1994. Student, U. Wash., 1956-57. Pres. S.A.T.B. Inc., L.A., 1979—, Killer Music, Inc., Hollywood, Calif., 1982—, T.T. B.B. Inc., Hollywood, 1989—; ptnr. Killer Tracks, Primat Am., Hollywood, 1990-96. Lead tenor The Eligibles, 1958-62; vocal dir., singer Piece of Cake Inc., 1968-81; arranger, producer Calif. Raisin Adv. Bd., 1982 (recipient 2 Clios 1983); producer/co-writer Wheaties, 1983 (Clio award); producer/composer Gatorade, 1983; producer/performer Levi's 501 Blues, 1984. With USAF, 1959-65. Mem. NARAS (MVP award 1973, 75), AFTRA (nat. bd. dirs. 1970-85, local bd. dirs. 1968-85), Screen Actors Guild (nat. bd. dirs. 1975), Am. Fedn. Musicians, Hollywood C. of C. Home: 30 Kewen Pl San Marino CA 91108-1104 Office: Killer Music Inc Ste 108 3518 Cahuenga Blvd W Los Angeles CA 90068-1335

HICKMAN, CRAIG RONALD, author; b. Borger, Tex., Dec. 5, 1949; s. Winston Whitehead and Verla (Bingham) H.; m. Pamela Lewis, Nov. 17, 1972; children: Jared Winston, Kimberly Michelle, Leigh Megan. BA in Econs. cum laude, Brigham Young U., 1974; MBA with honors, Harvard U., 1976. Cons. Ernst & Ernst (now Ernst & Young), L.A., 1976-77; sr. planning analyst Dart Industries, L.A., 1977-79; campaign mgr. Wright for Gov., Salt Lake City, 1980; mgr. cons. svcs. Arthur Young & Co. (now Ernst & Young), 1980-83; pres. Bennett Info. Group, Salt Lake City, 1983-85; chmn., pres. Mgmt. Perspectives Group, Provo, Utah, 1985-91; author, cons. Provo, 1985—; cons. Frito-Lay, Dallas, 1985, Procter & Gamble, Cin., 1986, AT&T, ea. U.S., 1986, Fla. Power & Light, 1987, Systematic Mgmt. Svcs., Phila., 1988, Geneva Steel, Vineyard, Utah, 1989, Found. Health Corp., Sacramento, 1990, Centex, Dallas, Am. Express, N.Y.C., 1994; keynote speaker numerous corp. confs., U. Md., Notre Dame, Head Start Program, Dalhousie U., numerous assns. and USIA, India, Israel, Egypt, Saudi Arabia, 1985-94; bd. dirs. Am. Parts sys. Co-author: Creating Excellence, 1984 (nat. bestseller paperback 1986), The Future 500, 1987; author: Mind of a Manager, Soul of a Leader, 1990 (internat. bestseller paperback 1992), Practical Business Genius, 1991, The Strategy Game, 1993, The Oz Principle, The Organization Game, 1994, The Productivity Game, 1995; contbr. articles and commentaries to profl. jours. Mem. ASTD. Republican. Mem. LDS Ch. Home: 1007 East 150 South Springville UT 84663-4100

HICKMAN, DONN MICHAEL, plastic surgeon; b. Tampa, Fla., 1951. MD, U. Miami, 1976. Plastic surgeon Meml. Med. Ctr., Long Beach, Calif. Office: 4401 Atlantic Ave Ste 101 Long Beach CA 90807-2239*

HICKMAN, GRACE MARGUERITE, artist; b. Reno, Nev., Nov. 7, 1921; d. Charles Franklin and Jeannie (McPhee) Wolcott; m. Robert Frederick Hickman, Apr. 10, 1943; children—John Charles, Carol Ann Hickman Harp, David Paul. Student Emily Griffiths Opportunity Sch., Denver, 1968-71, Red Rocks Community Coll., Golden, Colo., 1974-75, Loretto Heights Coll., Denver, 1983-85. Tchr. art Aurora Parks & Recreation, Colo., 1979-81; instr. paint workshop Marine Resource Ctr., Atlantic Beach, N.C., 1981, 82; lectr. color theory Aurora Artists Club, 1985; instr. creative color Acapulco Art Workshops, 1987, 88; tchr. color theory and art fundamentals Colo. Free U., 1991-92. One woman shows include Internat. House, Denver, 1974, Foothills Art Ctr., Golden, Colo., 1975, Greek Market Place, Denver, 1976, Marine Resource Ctr., Atlantic Beach, N.C., 1983, Depot Art Ctr., Littleton, Colo., 1984, Sheraton DTC, Women's Bank Denver, 1986, NYU Sch. Environmental Medicine, Tuxedo, 1987, Studio Paul Kontny, Denver, 1988. group shows include: Wellshire Presbyn. Ch., Denver, 1975, Brass Cheque Gallery, Denver, 1978, Colo. Women in Arts, Denver, 1979, Garelick's Gallery, Scottsdale, Ariz., 1982; Bold Expressions, Littleton, Colo., 1983. represented in permanent collections: Augustana Luth. Ch., Denver, South Shores Ins. Agy., Huntington Beach, Calif., Texon Gen. Partnership, Englewood, Colo., others. Coordinator figure study Bicentennial Art Ctr., Aurora, 1986; pres. Depot Art Ctr., Littleton, Colo., 1980-82. Mem. Nat. Mus. for Women in the Arts, Artists Equity Assn., Colo. Artists Equity Assn. (chmn. publicity Colo. 1% for Art 1976-77), Pastel Soc. Am., Littleton Fine Arts Guild (pres. 1976-77), Art Students League, Colo. Speakers Bur. (coordinator), Nat. Mus. Women in Arts. Democrat. Lutheran. Club: Aurora Athletic. Avocations: swimming; reading; art history. Home: 12361 E Bates Cir Aurora CO 80014-3311

HICKMAN, MAXINE VIOLA, social services administrator; b. Louisville, Miss., Dec. 24, 1943; d. Everett and Ozella (Eichelberger) H.; m. William L. Malone, Sept. 5, 1965 (div. 1969); 1 child, Gwendolyn. BA, San Francisco State U., 1966; MS, Nova U., 1991; postgrad., Calif. Coast U., 1991—. Lic. State of Calif. Dept. Social Svcs. IBM profl. mechanic operator Wells Fargo Bank, San Francisco, 1961-65; dept. mgr. Sears Roebuck & Co., San Bruno, Calif., 1966-77; adminstr. Pine St. Guest House, San Francisco, 1969-88; fin. planner John Hancock Fin. Svcs., San Mateo, Calif., 1977-81; chief exec. officer Hickman Homes, Inc., San Francisco, 1981—; cons. BeeBe Meml. Endowment Found., Oakland, Calif., 1990—, Calif. Assn. Children's Home-Mems., Sacramento, 1989—. Mem. NAACP, San Francisco. Named Foster Mother of Yr., Children's Home Soc. Calif., 1985, Woman of Yr., Gamma Nu chpt. Iota Phi Lambda, 1991. Mem. Foster Parents United, Calif. Assn. Children's Homes, Nat. Bus. League, Order of Ea. Star, Masons (worthy matron), Alpha Kappa Alpha. Democrat. Baptist. Office: Hickman Homes Inc 67 Harold Ave San Francisco CA 94112-2331

HICKS, BETHANY GRIBBEN, lawyer, commissioner; b. N.Y., Sept. 8, 1951; d. Robert and DeSales Gribben; m. William A. Hicks III, May 21, 1982; children: Alexandra Elizabeth, Samantha Katherine. AB, Vassar Coll., 1973; MEd, Boston U., 1975; JD, Ariz. State U., 1984. Bar: Ariz. 1984. Pvt. practice Scottsdale and Paradise Valley, Ariz., 1984-91; law clk. to Hon. Kenneth L. Fields Maricopa County Superior Ct. (S.E. dist.), Mesa, 1991-93, judge pro tem, 1993—; commr. Maricopa County Superior Ct., Mesa, 1994-95, Phoenix, 1995—; magistrate Town of Paradise Valley, Ariz., 1993-94. Mem. Jr. League of Phoenix, 1984-91; bd. dirs. Phoenix Children's Theatre, 1988-90; parliamentarian Girls Club of Scottsdale, Ariz., 1985-87, 89-90, bd. dirs., 1988-91; mem. exec. bd., sec. All Saints' Episcopal Day Sch. Parents Assn., 1991-92, pres., 1993-94; mem. Nat. Charity League, 1995—. Mem. ABA, State Bar Ariz., Maricopa County Bar Assn. Republican. Episcopalian. Club: Paradise Valley Country. Office: 9th Flr 101 West Jefferson Phoenix AZ 85003-2205

HICKS, DAVID EARL, author, inventor; b. Indpls., Jan. 1, 1931; s. John Arthur and Marguerite (Barnes) H.; m. Shirlene Lavan Barlow, Jan. 22, 1958 (div. June 1973); children: Sharon Lynn, Brenda Kay; m. Margaret Leigh Payne, Feb. 17, 1977; children: David Bradley, Leslie Ann, Brian Patrick. Grad., Nat. Radio Inst., 1953; student, Purdue U., 1959-60, Miami-Dade Community Coll., 1971-72. Cert. advanced paramedic. Tech. writer, editor Howard W. Sams, Inc., Indpls., 1958-64; tech. writer Systems Engring. Labs, Inc., Ft. Lauderdale, Fla., 1964-67; publs. mgr. Novatronics, Inc., Pompano Beach, Fla., 1967-69; pres. Datatek, Inc., Ft. Lauderdale, 1969-71; tech. writer Systems Devel. Corp., Colorado Springs, Colo., 1973-74, Ford Aerospace Corp., Colorado Springs, 1974-76; pres. Nutronics Corp., Colorado Springs, 1982-87; tech. writer Digital Equipment Corp., Colorado Springs, 1978-88; pres. Innovation USA Mag., Colorado Springs, 1989; tech. cons., inventor pvt. practice, Colo. Springs, 1964-65, 75-92; novelist Colo. Springs, 1992—; tech. cons. Japan Electronics, Tokyo, 1962-63, Nutronics Corp., Longmont, Colo., 1987. Author of eight tech. books (two made best seller list) including: Citizens Band Radio Handbook, 1961, Amateur Radio-VHF and Above, 1965, CB Radio Operating Procedures, 1976; contbr. articles to electronics jours.; inventor of new electric charging system, 1978, awarded U.S. patent, 1981; lectr. numerous sci. and invention seminars, 1978—. Communications officer CD, Indpls., 1962-63; judge sci. fair Pub. Sch. System, Colorado Springs, 1986-87. Served with USN, 1948. Recipient Red Cross Hall of Fame, Indpls., 1963; grantee U.S. Dept. of Energy, 1984; recipient Nat. Energy Resources Tech. Innovation award, 1989, Disting. Leadership award Am. Biog. Inst. 1990, cert. of merit Internat. Biog. Ctr., 1990. Mem. Soc. of Am. Inventors (bd. dirs., Pres. award 1989), Am. Radio Relay League, Author's Guild, Author's League of Am. Republican. Office: PO Box 25053 Colorado Springs CO 80936-5053

HICKS, NORM, airport operations executive; b. 1941. BBA, Golden Gate U., 1964; postgrad., U.S. Naval Postgrad. Sch., 1971. Exec. dir., COO Mohave County Airport Authority, Bullhead City, Ariz. Office: Mohave County Airport Auth 600 Highway 95 Bullhead City AZ 86429*

HICKS, PHILIP STANLEY, psychiatrist; b. St. Louis, May 25, 1928; s. Thomas Ross and Mabel Louise (Kinnecome) H.; m. Marilyn Fenton, Apr. 15, 1951 (div. Sept. 1973); children: Catherine, Elizabeth, John, Sara; m. Penny Linda Harris, Nov. 17, 1979; 1 child, Michael Harris. BA in Chemistry, U. N.D., 1948; MD, Boston U., 1948-52. Diplomate Am. Bds. Medical Examiners, Psychiatry and Neurology; lic. physician and surgeon, Calif. Intern Boston City Hosp., 1952-53; resident neuropsychiatry Michael Reese Hosp., Chgo., 1953-55; resident psychiatry The Langley Porter Clinic, San Francisco, 1955-56; candidate, clin. assoc. The San Francisco Psychoanalytic Inst., 1956-65; med. dir. The Family Rehab. Ctr., San Rafael, Calif., 1965-68; asst. clin. prof. dept. psychiatry Univ. Calif., San Francisco, 1968—; med. dir. Cowell Treatment Ctr. of Sacramento Childrens Home, 1968-69, Lane Childrens Ctr., Sebastopol, 1969-75; chief dept. psychiatry and neurology 5th Gen. Hosp., Bad Cannstatt, West Germany, 1975-77; asst. chief dept. psychiatry Letterman Army Med. Ctr., San Francisco, 1977-79; chief dept. psychiatry Silas B. Hays Army Community Hosp., Fort Ord, Calif., 1979-81; chief med. officer Correctional Tng. Facility, Soledad, Calif., 1981-83; chief psychiatrist Natividad Med. Ctr., Salinas, Calif., 1983-84, Calif. State Prison, San Quentin, Calif., 1986-91; pvt. practice, 1991—; pvt. practice San Rafael, 1956-75; clin. instr. U. Calif., San Francisco, 1956-68; psychiatrist Calif. State Prison, San Quentin, 1956-57, San Francisco Gen. Hosp., 1957-58, Clearwater Ranch Childrens Home, Philo, Calif., 1957-64, Correctional Tng. Facility, Soledad, 1984-86, Forensic Program Napa (Calif.) State Hosp., 1991-94, Contra Costa County Mental Health Svcs., 1994—; faculty Letterman Army Med. Ctr., San Francisco, 1977-79, dir. forensic module, 1987-91; vis. faculty residency tng. program Tripler Army Med. Ctr., Honolulu, 1982-92; faculty residency tng. program. Calif. Pacific Med. Ctr., San Francisco, 1992-94; cons. Contra Costa County Cmty. Mental Health Activity, 1956-60, Marin County Health Dept., San Rafael, 1957-58, Family Svc. Agy. of Marin, San Rafael, 1957-58, Atascadero (Calif.) State Hosp., 1978-81, Aetna Fed. Health Programs, 1994—, Med. Bd. Calif. Author, presenter and lectr. in field. With USNR, 1945-52; col. M.C. USAR, 1975-81, res. duty, 1981-96. Mem. Am. Acad. Psychiatry and the Law, Am. Psychiatric Soc. (life), No. Calif. Psychiatric Soc. (life), Forensic Mental Health Assn. Calif., Marin Psychiatric Soc. (pres. 1960-75), Begg Soc. Boston U. Honor Med. Soc., Alpha Omega Alpha Honor Med. Soc. Home and Office: 26 Mount Rainier Dr San Rafael CA 94903-1078

HICKSON, ERNEST CHARLES, financial executive; b. L.A., July 14, 1931; s. Russell Arthur and Marilyn Louise (Mambert) H.; m. Janice Beleal, Sept. 5, 1959; children: Arthur, Jennifer, Barton. BS, U. So. Calif., 1961; postgrad., UCLA Grad. Sch. of Bus. Admin., 1961-63. Lic. real estate broker, Calif., 1986. Credit supr. ARCO (Richfield Oil), L.A., 1955-60; asst. v.p. Union Bank L.A., 1960-64; v.p. County Nat. Bank (now Wells Fargo), Orange, Calif., 1964-67; v.p., sr. loan ofcr. City Bank, Honolulu, 1967-70; pres., CEO Shelter Corp., 1968-72; exec. v.p., dir. U.S. Fin., Inc., San Diego, 1970-73; pres., CEO USF Investors, 1971-73; exec. v.p. Sonnenblick Goldman, L.A., 1973-76; pres., CEO First Hawaiian Devel., Honolulu, 1976-82; CEO TMH Resources, Laguna Niguel, Calif., 1982—; cons. and expert witness in fin. Author: (novel) The Developers, 1978; editor: (monthly newsletter) Financial Marketing, 1978-83. Staff sgt. USAF, 1950-53. Recipient Exec. award Grad. Sch. of Credit and Fin. Mgmt., Stanford U., 1964, Assocs. award The Nat. Inst. of Credit, UCLA, 1959. Mem. U. So. Calif. Assocs., U. So. Calif. Pres.'s Circle, Urban Land Inst., Town Hall, Center Club (Costa Mesa), Pacific Club (Honolulu), Outrigger Canoe Club (Honolulu), Phi Gamma Delta.

HIDDLESTON, RONAL EUGENE, drilling and pump company executive; b. Bristow, Okla., Mar. 21, 1939; s. C.L. and Iona D. (Martin) H.; m. Marvelene L. Hammond, Apr. 26, 1959; children: Michael Scott, Mark Shawn, Matthew Shane. Student, Idaho State U., 1957-58. With Roper's Clothing and Bishop Redi-Mix, Rupert, Idaho, 1960-61; pres., chmn. bd., gen. mgr. Hiddleston Drilling, Rupert, 1961-66, Mountain Home, Idaho, 1966—; bd. dirs. Ground Water Pub., Baker Mfg. Mem. Mountain Home Airport Adv. Bd., 1968—; hon. mem. Idaho Search and Rescue. Mem. Nat. Ground Water Assn. (dir., past pres., chmn. fund raising new hdqrs.), Idaho Ground Water Assn. (dir. past pres.), Pacific N.W. Water Well Assn., N.W. Mining Assn., Nat. Fedn. Ind. Businessmen, Ground Water Inst. (bd. dirs.), Aircraft Owners and Pilots Assn., Ducks Unltd., Nat. 210 Owners Club, Nat. Sporting Clays Assn., Masons, Royal Arch, Scottish Rites, El Korzh Shrine. Home: 645 E 17 N Mountain Home ID 83647-1629 Office: RR 3 Box 610D Mountain Home ID 83647-9806

HIENTON, JAMES ROBERT, lawyer; b. Phoenix, July 25, 1951; s. Clarence J. Jr. and Lola Jean (Paxton) H.; m. Diane Marie DeBrosse, July 22, 1977. BA, U. Ariz., 1972; MBA, Ariz. State U., 1975, JD, 1975; LLM, Washington U., St. Louis, 1977. Bar: Ariz. 1975, U.S. Dist. Ct. (Ariz.) 1975. Corp. atty. Ariz. Pub. Service, Phoenix, 1975-76; asst. prof. Ariz. State U., Tempe, 1977; assoc. then ptnr. Gust, Rosenfeld, Divelbess et al, Phoenix, 1978-85; sr. tax ptnr. Evans, Kitchel and Jenckes, Phoenix, 1985-89; ptnr. Jennings, Strouss and Salmon, Phoenix, 1989-93; sr. shareholder Bonnett, Fairbourne, Friedman, Hienton, Miner & Fry, P.C., Phoenix, 1993-95, Ridenour, Swenson, Cleere & Evans, P.C., Phoenix, 1995—. Officer, bd. dirs. Charter Govt., Phoenix, 1978-82; mem. Phoenix Citizens Charter Rev. Com., 1982; participant Phoenix Together; participant 1st Phoenix Town Hall, 1981, 2d, 1982, 3d, 1983, recorder, 1983, 85; mem. Balanced Govt. Com., 1983; mem Phoenix Police and Fire Pension Bds., 1982-89; bd. dirs. Ariz. Theater Co., 1979-89; mem. class V, Valley Leadership, 1983-84; founding life mem. Ariz. Mus. Sci. and Industry. Mem. ABA, Ariz. Bar Assn., Maricopa County Bar Assn., Phi Kappa Phi. Republican. Club: Phoenix City. Home: 441 W Mclellan Blvd Phoenix AZ 85013-1141 Office: Bonnett Fairbourne et al 40 N Central Ave Ste 1400 Phoenix AZ 85004-4457

HIGASHIDA, RANDALL TAKEO, radiologist, neurosurgeon, medical educator; b. L.A., Oct. 26, 1955; s. Henry and Alice Higashida; m. Jean Kim, May 17, 1986. BS, U. So. Calif., 1976; MD, Tulane U. Diplomate Am. Bd. Radiology. Intern Harbor UCLA Med. Ctr., 1980-81, resident in radiology, 1981-84, fellow in diagnostic/interventional neuroradiology, 1984-85; asst. prof. radiology UCLA Med. Ctr., 1985-86; assoc. prof. radiology U. Calif. San Francisco Med. Ctr., 1986-94, prof. radiology and neurosurgery, 1994—; cons. Target Therapeutics Corp., Fremont, Calif., 1989-93, Interventional Therapeutics Corp., Fremont, 1986-93, Cordis Corp., Miami Lakes, Fla., 1993-96; mem. exec. com. stroke rsch. grants Abbott Labs., Chgo., 1994-96. Mem. editl. bd. Jour. Endovasc. Surgery, 1994-96, Jour. Minimally Invasive Neurosurgery, 1994-96; manuscript reviewer Am. Jour. Neuroradiology, 1992—. Recipient rsch. award Am. Heart Assn., Dallas, 1978-79. Mem. AMA; sr. mem. Am. Soc. Neuroradiology, Soc. Cardiovasc.

and Interventional Radiology, Am. Soc. Interventional and Therapeutic Neuroradiology (exec. com. 1994-96), Joint Sect. of Cerebrovasc. Surgery (exec. com. 1994-96), Internat. Soc. Endovasc. Surgery. Republican. Protestant. Office: UCSF Medical Ctr 505 Parnassus Ave # L352 San Francisco CA 94143-0628

HIGDON, BERNICE COWAN, retired elementary education educator; b. Sylva, N.C., Feb. 26, 1918; d. Royston Duffield and Margaret Cordelia (Hall) Cowan; m. Roscoe John Higdon, Aug. 12, 1945; children: Ronald Keith, Rodrick Knox, Krista Dean. BS, Western Carolina U., 1941; cert. tchr., So. Oreg. Coll., 1967; student, Chapman Coll., 1971. Cert. tchr., Calif. Prin., tchr. Dorsey Sch., Bryson City, N.C., 1941-42; expeditor Glenn L. Martin Aircraft Co., Balt., 1942-45; tchr. elem. sch. Seneca, S.C., 1945-46, Piedmont, S.C., 1946-47; tchr. elem. sch. Columbia, S.C., 1950-51, Manteca, Calif., 1967-68; kindergarten tchr. 1st Bapt. Ch., Medford, Oreg., 1965-67; tchr. elem. sch. Marysville (Calif.) Unified Sch. Dist., 1968-83; tchr. Headstart, Manteca, 1968. Past counselor Youth Svc. Bur., Yuba City, Calif.; troop leader Girl Scouts U.S.A., Medford, 1962-63; past Sunday sch. tchr. 1st Bapt. Ch., Medford; bd. dirs. Christian Assistance Network, Yuba City, 1984-85; aux. vol. Fremont Med. Ctr., Yuba City, 1984-94; deaconess Evang. Free Ch., Yuba City, 1991-93. Recipient cert. of appreciation Marysville Unified Sch. Dist., 1983, Christian Assistance Network, 1985; cert. of recognition Ella Elem. Sch., Marysville, 1983. Mem. Calif. Ret. Tchrs. Assn., Nat. Ret. Tchrs. Assn., Sutter Hist. Soc., AAUW, Am. Assn. Ret. Persons. Home: 1264 Charlotte Ave Yuba City CA 95991-2804

HIGGINBOTHAM, LLOYD WILLIAM, mechanical engineer; b. Haydentown, Pa., Nov. 24, 1934; s. Clarence John and Nannie Mae (Piper) H.; m. Genevieve Law, Oct. 17, 1953 (div.); 1 child, Mark William; m. Mary Bannaian, July 23, 1966; 1 child, Samuel Lloyd. With rsch. and devel. TRW Inc., Cleve., 1953-57; pres. Higginbotham Rsch., Cleve., 1957-64, Higginbotham Assocs., Woodland Hills, Calif., 1964—; founder, CEO Engrs. of World, Woodland Hills, Calif., 1993—; founder, pres., CEO Enhance Engring. Edn. Found., Inc., Woodland Hills, 1993—; pres., CEO Engrs. Coun., 1993—; cons. grad. engring. programs UCLA, Calif. State U., L.A., U. So. Calif.; pres. adv. com. Pierce Coll., L.A.; adv. com. So. Calif. Productivity Ctr.; cons. various Calif. legislators. Mem. Town Hall Calif. Recipient Community Svc. award City of Downey, Calif, 1974, Archimedes award NSPE, Outstanding Contbr. Recognition, 1986, Outstanding Leadership Recognition, 1987, William B. Johnson Meml. Internat. Interprofl. award, 1992. Fellow Inst. Advancement Engring. (class of 1982, exec. dir., exec. mgr. 1984-93); mem. Soc. Carbide and Tool Engrs. (chmn., 1974-76), Soc. Mfg. Engrs. (chmn. San Fernando Valley chpt. 1977-79, numerous awards), San Fernando Valley Joint Coun. Engrs. (now Engrs. Coun., Inc., advisor, pres. 1981-82, 92-94), San Fernando Valley engrs. Coun. (pres., CEO 1992—), Profl. Salesmen's Assn., Am. Soc. Assn. Execs., L.A. Coun. Engrs. and Scientists (exec. mgr. 1984-93), N.Y. Acad. Scis., L.A. Area C. of C., Toastmasters, Masons. Republican. Office: Higginbotham Assocs 24310 Calvert St Woodland Hills CA 91367-1113

HIGGINS, ELLEN M., physician assistant; b. Balt., Sept. 18, 1949; d. Kenneth J. and Helen A. (Hagerty) Coughlin; m. William J. Higgins, Oct. 16, 1971; children: Daniel, Bridget, Aileen. BA, Emmanuel Coll., 1971; MS, U. Colo., 1987. Cert. physician assistant. Physician asst. Ptnrs. in Pediatrics, Englewood, Colo., 1988—; clin. instr. U. Colo. Health Scis. Ctr., Denver, 1985-95, asst. clin. prof., 1995—; mem. med. adv. bd. Mother's Milk Bank, Denver, 1986-91; mem. adv. bd. Adam's Camp, 1996—. Mem. Colo. Assn. Physician Assts. Office: Ptnrs in Pediat 8100 S Quebec St Unit B-10 Englewood CO 80112-3100

HIGGINS, JAMES BRADLEY, dentist; b. Richmond, Ind., July 3, 1941; s. James Randall and Mildred Ethel (White) H.; m. Dorothy Campbell, Dec. 29, 1964; children: Kimberly, Amy, Michaelle Ann, James. DDS, Ind. U., Bloomington, 1966. Resident dentist Ind. State Mental Hosp., Richmond, 1966; pvt. practice dentistry San Jose, Calif., 1968—; lectr. hypnosis Calif. Dental Assts. Assn., 1974-88; cons. Calif. State Bd. Dental Examiners, 1978-80; co-chmn. Santa Clara County Dentist Peer Rev. Com., 1982-84; dental lectr. San Jose Unified Sch. Dist. Bd. dirs. Santa Clara County Health Dept., San Jose, 1986-90, Noble Sch. Parent Tchr. Adv. Bd., San Jose. Capt. Dental Corp, USAF, 1966-68. Mem. ADA, NAACP (life), Nat. Dental Assn., Calif. Dental Assn., Santa Clara County Dental Soc., 100 Black Men of San Jose Assn. (charter). Democrat. Office: 4600 Alum Rock Ave San Jose CA 95127-2463

HIGGINS, RUTH ANN, social worker, family therapist; b. Rock Valley, Iowa, Sept. 23, 1944; d. Neal and Tillie (Feekes) Vonk; m. 1972 (div. Sept. 1986); children: Ashlie Kay, Steven Grant. BA, Northwestern Coll., 1966; MA, U. Colo., 1978; LCSW, U. Denver, 1983. Cert. profl. tchr., Colo., social worker, Colo. Tchr. Adams County Dist. 12, Northglenn, Colo., 1967-69, Dept. Def., Clark AFB, The Philippines, 1969-70, Jefferson County Schs., Lakewood, Colo., 1970-75; social worker Boulder (Colo.) County Mental Health Ctr., 1977, Boulder Community Counseling Ctr., 1979-81, Columbine Counseling Ctr., Broomfield, Colo., 1981—; sch. social worker Adams County Sch. Dist. 12, Northglenn, Colo., 1985—; part time social worker Hospice of Metro Denver, 1984-85, Boulder Valley Pub. Schs., 1985, Lutheran Hospice Care, Wheatridge, Colo., 1985. Author, editor: Nothing Could Stop the Rain, 1976. Recipient Hon. Mention Counselor of Yr. award Colo. Sch. Counselors Assn., 1994. Mem. Nat. Assn. Social Workers. Democrat.

HIGGINS, SHAUN O'LEARY, media executive; b. Princeton, Ind., Mar. 22, 1948; s. John Frank and Laura Dorothea (Thompson) H.; m. Ann Glendening, Nov. 23, 1975; children: Flannery Maeve, Ian Dashiell. BA in Comm., DePauw U., 1971. Reporter, city editor Lu-Mar Newspapers, Inc., Bloomington, Ind., 1967-69; mng. editor The Times, Brazil, Ind., 1969-72; congl. cand. 7th Dist. Ind. Dem., Brazil, 1972; cons. Keep's Creek Assocs., Indpls., 1972-73; wire editor Times & Times World, Roanoke, Va., 1973-74; freelance writer, editor self-employed, N.Y.C., 1974-75; news editor, state bur. chief Lee Newspapers, Inc., Billings, Helena, Mont., 1975-79; asst. mng. editor Cowles Pub. Co., Spokane, Wash., 1973-83; mktg. dir. Cowles Pub. Co., Spokane, 1983-88, dir. mktg. and sales, 1988—; pres., COO New Media Ventures, Inc., Cowles Pub. Co., Spokane, 1993—; chmn., CEO Print Mktg. Concepts, Inc., 1996—; cons. in field; instr. in field; owner The Oxalis Group, Spokane, 1979—. Co-prodr. "Good Paper" TV comml., 1986 (Telly award 1988; 2 Emmy awards 1987); dir. "The Arts Can Change Your Life," 1988 (MAX award 1988); author: Review Tower, 1985 (MAX award 1985), Toward Greater Understanding, 1989, Database Marketing Applications for Newspapers, 1995, Effective Direct Mail Letters for Newspapers, 1995, Ice Storm '96, The Newspaper in Art, 1997; editor: Ice Storm '96, 1996; contbr. more than 50 articles to profl. publs. Bd. dirs., trustee Wash. Commn. for Humanities, Seattle, 1988-93, United Way of Spokane County, 1988-91; mem. pub. rels. adv. bd. DePauw U., 1996—; bd. dirs. Spokane Regional Conv. and Visitors Bur., 1991-94, Spokane Symphony Orch., 1991-96, Cmty. Devel. Bd., Spokane, 1986-88; trustee, chmn. Spokane Area Econ. Devel. Coun., 1983-91, chair, 1990; chmn. Festival of Four Cultures, 1989. Recipient Emmy(s) N.A.T.A.S., 1987, Telly award Cin. Broadcasters, 1988, MAX Best of Show award Spokane Advt. Fedn., 1988, Best of Show award Internat. Newspaper Mktg. Assn., 1987, Silver Strand award INMA-West, 1993; named Spokane Advt. Profl. of Yr., 1988, Media, Inc. Northwest Print Media Person of the Year, 1992. Mem. Spokane Advt. Fedn. (pres. 1988-89), Direct Mktg. Assn., Pub. Rels. Soc. Am., Soc. Profl. Journalists, Am. Statis. Assn., Internat. Newspaper Mktg. Assn. (trustee, internat. pres. 1993—, Silver Shovel award 1996), Newspaper Assn. Am. (retail coun., bus. devel. com., chair nat. polit. task force), Fedn. Internationale des editeurs des Journaux (exec., dir.), Chautauqua Soc. of Eastern Wash. U., Voltaire Soc. Am. (founding mem.). Home: 428 W 27th Ave Spokane WA 99203-1854 Office: Cowles Pub Co 999 W Riverside Ave Spokane WA 99201-1006

HIGHLANDER, RICHARD WILLIAM, communications executive; b. Beckley, W.Va., Feb. 17, 1940; s. Ronald William and Lucille Bernice (Bland) H.; m. Ida Mae Canterbury, June 26, 1965; one child, Alison Renee. BA, Rutgers U., 1963; MA, U. Ga., 1972. Commd. 2d lt. U.S. Army, 1963, advanced through grades to lt. col., 1979, ret., 1984; dir. communications, def. systems group FMC Corp., Santa Clara, Calif., 1984-94; v.p. comm. United Def. LP, Santa Clara, 1994—. Contbr. articles to profl. jours., Freedom Found. award 1966, 81. Trustee San Jose Repertory Co., 1985. Decorated Legion of Merit with bronze oak leaf cluster, Bronze Star with two bronze oak leaf clusters, Purple Heart. Mem. PRSA (accredited), Assn. U.S. Army, Internat. Assn. Bus. Communicators, Calif. Mfrs. Assn. (bd. dirs. 1985, chmn. bd. 1993), Aerospace Industries Assn. (comm. coun.), Rotary, San Jose Met. C. of C. (bd. dirs.), Chi Psi. Republican. Methodist. Home: 1486 Oak Canyon Dr San Jose CA 95120-5711

HIGHT, HAROLD PHILIP, retired security company executive; b. Crescent City, Calif., Apr. 17, 1924; s. Vernon Austin and Mary Jane (Gontau) H.; m. Margaret Rose Edelman, Nov. 19, 1945 (div. 1949); children: Linda Marie, Beverly Sue; m. Doris Louise Dunn, June 20, 1982. Student police sci., Coll. of Redwoods, 1969. With Pan Am. World Airways, South San Francisco, Calif., 1945-51, 52; officer Richmond (Calif.) Police Dept., 1952-54; aircraft electrician Internat. Atlas Svc., Oakland, Calif., 1954-56; security officer radiation lab. AEC, Livermore, Calif., 1956-58; chief police Port Orford (Oreg.) Police Dept., 1958-61; dep. sheriff, sgt., evidence technician Del Notre County Sheriff's Dept., Crescent City, 1961-85; security officer, sgt. Del Notre Security Svc., Crescent City, 1985. With USN, 1941-45, 51-52. Mem. Internat. Footprint Assn. (sec., treas. bd. dirs. Crescent City 1985—), Navy League U.S. (2d v.p. Crescent City 1984—), Tin Can Sailors, Masons, Scottish Rite (32d degree), Elks, Grange. Republican. Roman Catholic. Home: 110 Lafayette Way Crescent City CA 95531-8351

HIGLEY, DEBRA KAY, geologist; b. Scotia, Calif., Apr. 16, 1954; d. Floyd and Charlotte E. (Abbott) H. BS in Geology, Mesa State Coll., 1977; MS in Geochemistry, Colo. Sch. Mines, 1983, PhD in Geology, 1994. Geologist Nuclear Assurance Corp., Grand Junction, Colo., 1976-81, N.Am. Exploration, Kaysville, Utah, 1981, U.S. Geol. Survey, Lakewood, Colo., 1982—. Cartoonist: Geology and Wildflowers of Western Colorado, 1977; contbr. articles to profl. jours. Mem. Am. Assn. Petroleum Geologists, Soc. Luminescent Microscopy and Spectroscopy, Rocky Mountain Assn. Geologists, Soc. for Sedimentary Geology (pres. Rocky Mountain sect. 1994). Republican. Office: US Geol Survey MS 940 Bldg 25 DFC Lakewood CO 80225

HILBERS, BETTY GAYLOR, poet; b. Muncie, Ind., Nov. 21, 1930; d. Ernest Clinton and Constance Irene (Hutson) Gaylor; m. Vernon Wesley Hilbers, June 10, 1951; children: David vernon, Kathleen Lynn. spkr./presenter Western Cowboy Poetry gatherings, Ariz., N.Mex., 1989-95. Author: (book) Moods and Inspirations, 1990; poetry published various books and jours.; songwriter: Under the Master's Care Gospel Album Hallelujah, 1993. Recipient Poet of Merit Trophy Am. Poet Assn., 1989, Medallion of Merit, Ariz. Pioneers Soc., 1993. Mem. Ariz. Pioneers Soc. Home: 706 Salt Mine Rd Camp Verde AZ 86322

HILBERT, STEPHANIE MAYER, actress, director, producer; b. Detroit, Mar. 28, 1943; d. Zygmunt S. and Florence (Bart) Mayer; m. Morton Shelly Hilbert, July 3, 1972; 1 child, Stephen Bart. BFA, U. Conn., 1965, MA, 1967. Assoc. Conn. Commn. on the Arts, Hartford, 1967-69; Caribbean cons. Nat. Endowment for Arts, Washington, 1969-70; project dir. Environ. Awareness Film Project U.S. Virgin Islands Govt., St. Thomas, 1969-70; rsch. assoc. lectr. U. Mich., Ann Arbor, 1970-73; comm. cons. Commn. on Profl. and Hosp. Activities, Ann Arbor, 1973-74; pres. video prodn. and program devel. Comm. Cons. Co., Ann Arbor, 1974-76, Hilbert Prodns. Co., Ann Arbor, 1974-86, Environ. Cons. Co., Bellevue, Wash., 1992—; prodr. East Shore Readers Theatre, 1992—; comm. cons. Nile River Project, Cairo and Aswan, Egypt, 1974, 75, 76, Pan Am. Health Orgn., San Jose, Costa Rica, 1977; performing arts cons. U.S. Mil., Bangkok, Thailand, 1972; bd. mem. Theatre Puget Sound, Encore Playhouse. Pres. Internat. Study Group, Brussels, 1989-91; bd. mem. Am. Theatre Co., Brussels, 1987-92; performing arts cons. Internat. Festival, Brussels, 1987-92; entertainment producer Am. Club, Brussels, 1989-91; v.p. Seattle Repertory Orgn. of Seattle Repertory Theatre, 1996—. Recipient Alexander Barnes Meml. Scholarship Adelphi (N.Y.)U., 1961-63, Victor Borge Scholarship U. Conn., 1963-65, Appreciation awards Charlotte Amalie Inter-Island Film Co., 1970, Am. Podiatry Assn. Aux., 1976; U. Conn. acting fellow, 1965-67. Mem. Actors' Equity. Unitarian. Home: 14635 NE 13th Pl Bellevue WA 98007-4008

HILBRECHT, NORMAN TY, lawyer; b. San Diego, Feb. 11, 1933; s. Norman Titus and Elizabeth (Lair) H.; m. Mercedes L. Sharratt, Oct. 24, 1980. B.A., Northwestern U., 1956; J.D., Yale U., 1959. Bar: Nev. 1959, U.S. Supreme Ct. 1963. Assoc. counsel Union Pacific R.R., Las Vegas, 1962; ptnr. Hilbrecht & Jones, Las Vegas, 1962-69; pres. Hilbrecht, Jones, Schreck & Bernhard, 1969-83, Hilbrecht & Assocs, 1983—, Mobil Transport Corp., 1970-72; gen. counsel Bell United Ins. Co., 1986-94; mem. Nev. Assembly, 1966-72, minority leader, 1971-72; mem. Nev. Senate, 1974-78; legis. commn., 1977-78; asst. lectr. bus. law U. Nev., Las Vegas. Author: Nevada Motor Carrier Compendium, 1990. Mem. labor mgmt. com. NCCJ, 1963; mem. Clark County (Nev.) Dem. Ctrl. Com., 1959-80, 1st vice chmn., 1965-66; del. Western Regional Assembly on Ombudsman; chmn. Clark County Dem. Conv., 1966, Nev. Dem. Conv., 1966; pres. Clark County Legal Aid Soc., 1964, Nev. Legal Aid and Defender Assn., 1965-83; assoc. for justice Nat. Jud. Coll., 1993, 94, 95, 96. Capt. AUS, 1952-67. Named Outstanding State Legislator Eagleton Inst. Politics, Rutgers U., 1969, Best Lawyers in Am., Bar of Nev., 1993. Mem. ABA, ATLA, Am. Judicature Soc., Am. Acad. Polit. and Social Sci., State Bar Nev. (chmn. adminstrv. law 1991-94, chmn. sect. on adminstrv. law 1995), Nev. Trial Lawyers (state v.p. 1966), Am. Assn. Ret. Persons (state legis. com. 1991-94), Elks, Phi Beta Kappa, Delta Phi Epsilon, Theta Chi, Phi Delta Phi. Lutheran. Office: 723 S Casino Center Blvd Las Vegas NV 89101-6716

HILDE, REUBEN LYNN, plastic surgeon; b. L.A., 1943. Plastic surgeon, Loma Linda U., 1971. Plastic surgeon Presbyn. Inter. Comm Hosp., Whittier, Calif. Office: 7957 S Painter Ave Ste 203 Whittier CA 90602-2414*

HILDEBRAND, CAROL ILENE, librarian; b. Presho, S.D., Feb. 15, 1943; d. Arnum Vance and Ethel Grace (Cole) Stoops; m. Duane D. Hildebrand, Mar. 21, 1970. BA, Dakota Wesleyan U., Mitchell, S.D., 1965; M in Librarianship, U. Wash., 1968. Tchr. Watertown (S.D.) H.S., 1965-67; libr. dir. Chippewa County Libr., Montevideo, Minn., 1968-70, The Dalles (Oreg.)-Wasco County Libr., 1970-72; libr. Salem (Oreg.) Pub. Libr., 1972-73; libr. dir. Lake Oswego (Oreg.) Pub. Libr., 1973-82; asst. city libr. Eugene (Oreg.) Pub. Libr., 1982-91, acting city libr., 1991-92, libr. dir., 1993—; cons., condr. workshops in field. Vice chmn. LWV, Lane County, 1987; bd. dirs. People for Oreg. Librs. Polit. Action Com., 1986—; sec. Citizens for Lane County Libr., 1985-88. Named Woman of Yr., Lane County Coun. of Orgns., 1995, Oreg. Libr. of Yr., 1993. Mem. ALA (chpt. councilor 1990-94), AAUW (bd. dirs. 1986, sec. 1995-96), Pacific N.W. Libr. Assn. (pres. 1989-90), Oreg. Libr. Assn. (pres. 1976-77), Rotary, Phi Kappa Phi. Methodist. Office: Eugene Public Library 100 W 13th Ave Eugene OR 97401-3433

HILDEBRAND, MILTON, zoology educator, retired; b. Phila., June 15, 1918; s. Joel Henry and Emily J. (Alexander) H.; m. Viola Memmler, Aug. 11, 1943; children: Ross, Kern, Joan. AB, U. Calif., Berkeley, 1940, MA, 1948, PhD, 1951. Lectr. U. Calif., Davis, 1948-52, asst. prof., 1952-56, assoc. prof., 1956-62, prof., 1962-86, prof. emeritus, 1986—; mammalogist expdn. to Ctrl. Am., U. Calif., Berkeley, 1941-42. Author: Anatomical Preparations, 1968, Analysis of Vertebrate Structure, 1974, 4th edit., 1995, Laugh and Love, 1979; contbr.: Functional Vertebrate Morphology, 1985. Recipient Disting. Teaching award Acad. Senate of U. Calif., Davis, 1973. Mem. Am. Soc. Zoologists (sec. div. vertebrate morphology 1963-68, chair 1968-70).

HILDEBRANDT, DARLENE MYERS, information scientist; b. Somerset, Pa., Dec. 18, 1944; d. Kenneth Geary and Julia (Klim) Myers; m. Peter Anton Hildebrandt, May 26, 1983; 1 child, Robin Adaire. BA, U. Calif., Riverside, 1969; MA, U. Wash., 1970. Info. specialist U. Wash. Acad. Computer Ctr., Seattle, 1970-73, library assoc., 1974-75, mgr. computing info. services adminstr., 1976-85, adminstr. computing info. services, 1986-91; head sci. librs. Wash. State U., Pullman, 1991—; spl. librs. rep. Wash. State Adv. Coun. Librs., 1992-98. Editor: (newsletter) Points Northwest (Elaine D. Kaskela award 1973, 75, Best ASIS 1974); compiler and editor Computing Info. Directory, 1985-96. Recipient Civitan award, 1963. Mem. Am. Soc. for Info. Sci. (founding mem. Pacific Northwest chpt. 1971, chairperson 1975, 76, bd. dirs. 1980-83, chpt. award 1978). Office: Wash State U Owen Sci & Engring Libr Pullman WA 99164-3200

HILDEBRANT, ANDY MCCLELLAN, retired electrical engineer; b. Nescopeck, Pa., May 12, 1929; s. Andrew Harmon and Margaret C. (Knorr) H.; m. Rita Mae Yarnold, June 20, 1959; children: James Matthew, David Michael, Andrea Marie. Student, State Tchrs. Coll., Bloomsburg, Pa., 1947-48, Bucknell U., 1952-54, UCLA, 1955-57, Utica Coll., 1965-70. Rsch. analyst Douglas Aircraft Co., Santa Monica, Calif., 1954-57; specialist engring. GE, Johnson City, N.Y., 1957-58, Ithaca, N.Y., 1958-64; elec. engr. GE, Utica, N.Y., 1964-70, Sylvania Electro Systems, Mountain View, Calif., 1970-71, Dalmo-Victor Co., Belmont, Calif., 1971-72, Odetics/Infodetics, Anaheim, Calif., 1972-75, Lear Siegler, Inc., Anaheim, 1975-78, Ford Aerospace, Newport Beach, Calif., 1978-79, THUMS Long Beach Co., Long Beach, Calif., 1979-94; ret., 1994; elec. engring. cons. Perkin-Elmer, Auto Info. Retrieval, Pi-Gem Assn., Pasadena, Calif., Palo Alto, Calif., 1971-73. Patentee AC power modulator for a non-linear load. Juror West Orange County Mpcl. Ct., Westminster, Calif., 1979, U.S. Dist. Ct., L.A., 1991-92. With USN, 1948-52. Recipient Cert. Award in Indsl. Controls Tech., Calif. State U., Fullerton, 1991-92. Mem. Orange County Chpt. Charities (sec. 1988), KC (past grand knight 1987-88). Republican. Roman Catholic. Home: 20392 Bluffwater Cir Huntington Beach CA 92646-4723

HILDENBRAND, DONALD GERALD, editor; b. Klamath Falls, Oreg., Dec. 18, 1941; s. Gerald Edward and Mary Elizabeth (Lasater) H. BS in Gen. Studies, Southwestern Oreg. Coll., 1972; MFA in Creative Writing, U. Oreg., 1975. Cert. black belt Chinese Gung Fu; cert. instr. Hsing-i Kung Fu, Taiwan Martial Arts Inst., 1978. Instr. phys. activities Lane C.C., Eugene, Oreg., 1978—; editor Poetic Space Mag., Eugene, 1989—. Home: PO Box 11157 Eugene OR 97440

HILDERBRAND, JOHN ORMAND, real estate agent, retired rancher; b. Portland, Oreg., Apr. 10, 1927; s. Ormand George and Lois Marion (Barnett) H.; m. Wanda Fay Tucker, June 11, 1950; children: Ormand, Jill, Jeff. BS, Oreg. State U., 1950. Ranch owner, operator Sherman County, Oreg., 1950—; real estate agt. J. Freedman Realtor, Bend, Oreg., 1987—; mem. Sherman County Co-op bd. dirs., bd. dirs. soil conservation, Sherman County. Bd. edn. Wasco Grade Sch., Sherman Union High Sch.; charter mem. Sherman Rd. Adv. Bd. With U.S. Navy, 1945-46. Mem. Sherman County Wheat Growers (pres.), Masons (master, pres. Mid-Columbia Shrine Club 1994), Elks. Home: 96247 Hilderbrand Ln Wasco OR 97065-3043 Office: J Freedman & Co Realtor 15 SW Colorado Ave Bend OR 97702-1150

HILER, EMERSON GARD, psychiatrist; b. Passaic, N.J., July 9, 1919; s. Edward Everett and Pauline Chatfield (Gard) H.; m. Carolyn Alice Montgomery, 1944 (div. 1971); children: Beth Swanson, Craig Hiler, Wendy Hewitt, Ellen Ruona; m. Sara Louise Spriggs, Jan. 14, 1973; stepchildren: Laura Schroeder, Alice Regan. BS, Stanford U., 1942, MD, 1945. Diplomate Am. Bd. Psychiatry and Neurology in Psychiatry. Rotating intern Orange County (Calif.) Hosp., 1945-46; psychiat. resident Brentwood Neuropsychiat. Hosp./VA Ctr., L.A., 1948-51; pvt. practice psychiatry Ontario, Calif., 1951-52; various to unit chief Brentwood Neuropsychiat. Hosp./VA Ctr., L.A., 1964-66; asst. chief psychiatry svc., chief consultation sect. VA Hosp., Long Beach, Calif., 1966-70, chief psychiatry svc., 1970-71, chief consultation sect., 1972-77; psychiatrist Orange County Mental Health Svcs., Santa Ana, Calif., 1977-84; forensic psychiatrist Riverside County Dept. Mental Health/Pub. Guardian's Office, Riverside, Calif., 1984—; clin. instr. dept. psychiatry, Stanford U., Sch. of Medicine, Palo Alto, Calif., 1954-56; asst. clin. prof. psychiatry, Loma Linda Sch. of Medicine, L.A., 1960-64; asst. clin. prof. psychiatry, UCLA Sch. of Medicine, L.A., 1964-66; asst. clin. prof. of psychiatry and human behavior, U. Calif., Irvine, 1966—. Contbr. articles to profl. jours. Capt. U.S. Army, 1946-48. Recipient Disabled Am. Vets. Nat. award 1974. Fellow APA (life); mem. So. Calif. Psychiat. Soc. Office: Pub Guardians Office Riverside Cty Mental Health PO Box 1405 Riverside CA 92502

HILGERT, ARNIE D., management educator; b. Detroit, Feb. 24, 1944; d. Norris Bersford and Romayne Catherine (Kent) Clarke; m. Jeffrey L. Hilgert, Dec. 21, 1964 (div. Dec. 1981); children: Michele LEanne, Tracy Lee. BA, U. Redlands, 1982; MBA, Claremont Grad. Sch., 1984, MA, 1991, PhD, 1992. Ptnr. Durawood Shasta Pacific Industries, Chico, Calif., 1971-78; mgr., owner Homefront Home Improvement Stores, Chico, Calif., 1975-78; rsch. assoc. exec. mgmt. program The Claremont (Calif.) Grad. Sch., 1984-85, adminstr. exec. mgmt. program, 1985-89; sponsored rsch. analyst Calif. State U., L.A., 1989-90; asst. prof. bus. adminstrn. and higher edn. No. Ariz. U., Yuma, 1992—. Contbr. articles to profl. jours. Participant Rio Colorado Commn., Yuma, 1993—. State of Calif. Grad. fellow, Claremont, 1982-84; Econs. scholar John Randolph Haynes and Dora Haynes Found., 1981, Elizabeth Malpass scholar Zonta Club Redlands, 1980. Mem. Acad. Bus. Adminstrn., Acad. Mgmt., Acad. Internat. Bus., Ctr. for Study of Intellectual Devel., Claremont Grad. Sch. Womens Scholars. Home: 11843 Calle del Cid Yuma AZ 85367 Office: No Ariz U PO Box 6236 Yuma AZ 85366

HILKER, WALTER ROBERT, JR., lawyer; b. L.A., Apr. 18, 1921; s. Walter Robert and Alice (Cox) H.; children: Anne Katherine, Walter Robert III. BS, U. So. Calif., 1942, LLB, 1948. Bar: Calif. 1949. Sole practice Los Angeles, 1949-55; ptnr. Parker, Milliken, Kohlmeier, Clark & O'Hara, 1955-75; of counsel Pacht, Ross, Warne, Bernhard & Sears, Newport Beach, Calif., 1980-84. Trustee Bella Mabury Trust; bd. dirs. Houchin Found. Served to lt. USNR, 1942-45. Decorated Bronze Star. Mem. ABA, Calif. Bar Assn., Orange County Bar Assn. Republican. Clubs: Spring Valley Lake Country (Apple Valley, Calif.); Balboa Bay (Newport Beach, Calif.). Home and Office: 17 Navarre Irvine CA 92612

HILL, ALICE LORRAINE, history, genealogy and social researcher, educator; b. Moore, Okla., Jan. 15, 1935; d. Robert Edward and Alma Alice (Fraysher) H.; children: Debra Hrboka, Pamela Spangler, Eric Shiver, Lorraine Smith. Grad., Patricia Stevens Modeling Sch., Orlando, Fla., 1963; student, Draughton Sch. Bus., Oklahoma City, 1968-69, Troy State U., 1970-71, Ventura Coll., 1974; AA in Gen. Edn., Rose Coll., Midwest City, Okla.; BS in Bus. and Acctg., Ctrl. State U., 1977; student, U. Okla., 1977-78; postgrad., Calif. Luth. U., 1988; ed. Sch. Edn., UCLA, 1990. Cert. cmty. coll. life instr. acctg., bus. and indsl. mgmt., computer and related techs., and real estate, Calif.; ordained min., Gospel Ministry, 1982; lic. in real estate sales. Former model, 1990-95; with L.A. Unified Sch. Dist., 1990-95; founder A. Hill & Assocs. (formerly America, We Love You), Oxnard, Calif., 1993—; co-founder Law of Moses Common Law Legal Assn., Kingfisher, Okla., with Internat. Hdqs. at Brussett, Mont., 1994; founder The Los Artistas for creative activities for young people, 1996; rschr. Americana 2000. Author: America, We Love You (Congl. Record Poem, made into World's 1st Internat. Patriotic song), 1975, Land of Lands (now world's first internat. patriotic song); ghost writer book for Shafenberg Rsch. Found., 1981; author: (lyrics) Come Listen to the Music, 1996, Someday John, 1996; contbr. various articles and poems to profl. publs. Named hon. grad. Patricia Stevens Modeling Sch. (Fla.); recipient scholarship Leadership Enrichment Program, Okla., 1977, Hon. recognition Okla. State Bd. of Regents for Higher Edn., 1977, Presdl. citations for Pres. Ford, 1975, 76, Admired Woman of the Decade award, 1994, Life Time Achievement award, 1995, Most Gold Record award, 1995, Key award for Rsch., Internat. Cultural Diploma of Honor, 1995, Woman of Yr. award, 1995, Internat. Woman of Yr. award Order Internat. Fellowship, 1994/95, Disting. Mem. Internat. Poetry Soc.; named to Internat. Hall of Fame Internat. Poetry Soc., 1996. Mem. NAFE, NEA, AAUW, Internat. Platform Assn., Ventura County Profl. Women's Networking. Home: 1646 Lime Ave Oxnard CA 93033-6897

HILL, ANNA MARIE, manufacturing executive; b. Great Falls, Mont., Nov. 6, 1938; d. Paul Joseph and Alexina Rose (Doyon) Ghekiere. AA, Oakland Jr. Coll., 1959; student, U. Calif., Berkeley, 1960-62. Mgr. ops. OSM, Soquel, Calif., 1963-81; purchasing agt. Arrow Hiuss, Scotts Valley, Calif., 1981-82; sr. buyer Fairchild Test Systems, San Jose, Calif., 1982-83; materials mgr. Basic Test Systems, San Jose, 1983-86; purchasing mgr. Beta Tech., Santa Cruz, Calif., 1986-87; mgr. purchasing ICON Rev., Carmel, Calif., 1987-88; materials mgr. Integrated Components Test System, Sunnyvale, Calif., 1988-89; mfg. mgr. Forte Comm., Sunnyvale, 1989-94; new products mgr. Cisco Sys., San Jose, 1994—; cons., No. Calif., 1976—. Counselor Teens Against Drugs, San Jose, 1970, 1/2 Orgn., Santa Cruz, 1975-76. Mem. Am. Prodn. Invention Control, Nat. Assn. Female Execs., Nat. Assn. Purchasing Mgmt., Am. Radio Relay League. Democrat. Home: 733 Rosedale Ave # 4 Capitola CA 95010-2248 Office: Cisco Systems 110 W Tasman Dr San Jose CA 95134-1700

HILL, CAROL ANN, geologist, writer, researcher; b. Detroit, Aug. 8, 1940; d. Glenn George and Evelyn Alberta (Read) Havens; m. Alan Eugene Hill, Mar. 26, 1960; children: Larry Glenn, Roy Leon. BS, U. N.Mex., 1973, MS, 1978. V.p. Plasmatronics, Albuquerque, 1978-83; mem. staff U. N.Mex., 1990—. Author: Cave Minerals, 1976, Cave Minerals of the World, 1986, 2nd edit., 1997, Geology of Carlsbad Cavern, 1987, Geology of Delaware Basin, 1996; author, editor Saltpeter Symposium, 1981. Mem. Geol. Soc. Am., N.Mex. Geol. Soc., Union Internat. Speleologie, Nat. Speleol. Soc. (fellow 1976, Cert. of Merit 1983), Soc. Econ. Paleontologists and Mineralogists, West Tex. Geol. Soc., Caver Rsch. Found.

HILL, DALE RICHARD, military officer; b. Charleston, W.Va., Dec. 20, 1939; s. Cecil Thomas Jr. and Frances Eileen (Gillespie) H.; m. Linda Lee Ergeson, Apr. 20, 1962 (dec. 1971); m. Debbie Kay Hildebrant, Feb. 19, 1972; children: Mark, Bret, Lara, Dale, Adam. BS, W.Va. State Coll., 1967; MA, Cen. Mich. U., 1977; grad., USA Command and Gen. Staff Coll., 1982. Commd. 2d lt. U.S. Army, Ft. Benning, Ga., 1968; advanced through grades to lt. col. U.S. Army, 1984; aide-de-camp USA Operational Test and Evaluation Agy., Falls Church, Va., 1976-80; ops. officer Hdqrs. 3 Bde, 2 Infantry divsn., Camp Howze, Republic of Korea, 1980-81; emergency action officer Hdqr. Readiness Command, MacDill AFB, Fla., 1981-82; plans tng. officer Hdqrs. Multinat. Force & Observers Sinai, El Gorah, 1982-83; chief current ops. Hdqr. I Corps., Ft. Lewis, Wash., 1983-86; commdr. Yakima (Wash.) Firing Ctr., 1986-89. Democrat. Home: 161602 W North River Rd Prosser WA 99350-8789

HILL, DANIEL WEBB, retired reference librarian; b. Chgo., Sept. 10, 1930; s. Arthur Remsen and Mary Margaret Hill; m. Marie Eva Schichtel, Oct. 24, 1959 (dec. Oct. 1985); children: Robert Francis, Karl Edward, Mary Rose, Janet Ruth Schichtel. BS in English, U. San Francisco, 1952; BLS, U. Calif., Berkeley, 1953. Std. tchg. credential with specialization in jr. coll. tchg., Calif. Asst. libr. So. Calif. Edison Co., L.A., 1954-59; rsch. info. analyst N.Am. Aviation, Downey, Calif., 1959-64; rsch. info. specialist Lockheed Missile and Space, Sunnyvale, Calif., 1965-70; libr. IV Oreg. State Libr., Salem, 1970-88. Mem. N.W. Assn. Book Pubs. Home: 3023 Honeysuckle Way NE Salem OR 97303

HILL, DAVID MICHAEL, cardiologist; b. Frankfurt, Germany, Dec. 29, 1950; came to U.S., 1953; s. Harold Weymouth and Jacqueline Francis (Wilson) H.; m. Chantal Leslie Underwood, Sept. 11, 1982; children: Nicole Jennifer, Kristiane Michele. BS in Chemistry, Presbyn. Coll., Clinton, S.C., 1972; MD, Med. Coll. Ga., Augusta, 1976. Diplomate Am. Bd. Internal Medicine in cardiovascular diseases. Categorical medicine intern Naval Hosp. San Diego, 1976-77, resident internal medicine, 1977-79, fellow cardiovascular disease, 1979-81; staff cardiologist Naval Hosp. Long Beach, Calif., 1982-85; chief internal medicine Naval Hosp. Long Beach, 1985-87; chief cardiology Naval Hosp. Oakland, Calif., 1987-92; chief of cardiology Scripps Meml. Hosp., Encinitas, Calif., 1997—; bd. dirs. Critical Air Medicine, Inc., San Diego, 1979—; CEO Spectrum Environ., Inc., Reno, Nev., 1995—; bd. dirs. San Diego Cardiovascular Network, 1995—, San Diego Cardiovascular Assocs., 1995—. Contbr. articles to profl. jours. Comdr. USN, 1972-92. Recipient Meritorious Svc. medal Pres. U.S., Oakland, 1992. Fellow Am. Coll. Cardiology; mem. Calif. Med. Assn., San Diego County Med. Soc. Republican. Presbyterian. Office: San Diego Cardiovascular Assocs 351 Santa Fe Dr Ste 100 Encinitas CA 92024-5137

HILL, DAVID PAUL, geophysicist; b. Livingston, Mont., June 18, 1935; s. Sanford and Gerda (Sevareid) H.; m. Ann Rivers, June 17, 1961; 1 child, Peter M. BS in Geology, San Jose State U., 1958; MS in Geophysics, Colo. Sch. Mines, 1961; PhD in Geophysics, Calif. Inst. Tech., 1971. Geophysicist U.S. Geol. Survey, Denver, 1961-64, Hawaiian Volcano Obs., 1964-66, Pasadena, Calif., 1966-71, Menlo Park, Calif., 1971-77; chief seismology br. U.S. Geol. Survey, Menlo Park, 1977-82, chief scientist Long Valley Caldera, 1983—; U.S. chmn. U.S.-Japan Panel on Earthquake Prediction, 1978-83. Assoc. editor Jour. Geophys. Rsch., 1985-88, Bull. Seismol. Soc. Am., 1996—; contbr. articles to profl. jours. Mem. Mono County (Calif.) Unified Command, 1985—. Fellow Am. Geophys. union; mem. AAAS, Seismological Soc. Am. (assoc. editor bull. 1996—). Office: US Geol Survey 345 Middlefield Rd Menlo Park CA 94025-3561

HILL, DEBRA LEE, school counselor, educator; b. Flint, Mich., Feb. 22, 1955; d. Charles Lynn and Barbara Hattie (Kerr) Bugbee; m. Randy Steve Hill, Sept. 2, 1978; children: Heather Leigh, Christopher Thomas. BA, Olivet Nazarene U., 1977; postgrad., Memphis State, 1987-88; MA, Gov.'s State, 1987; MS, Nat. U., 1992. Emergency rm. crisis specialist Riverside Hosp., Kankakee, Ill., 1976-77; coord. adult program Riverside Mental Health Unit, Kankakee, 1977-85; psychotherapist Eastwood Mental Health Unit, Memphis, 1986-88; with Beginning Alcohol and Addictions Basic Edn. Studies alcohol/drug edn. Ctr. Creative Alternatives, Huntington Beach, 1988-90; dir./counselor intervention program Westminster (Calif.) Sch. Dist., 1990—; with counseling ministries Cmty. Ch., Westminster, 1988—; mem. sch. attendance rev. bd. Westminster Sch. Dist., 1992—; peer leadership advisor City of Westminster/Westminster Sch. Dist., 1993—. Vol. phone counselor Suicide Crisis Ctr., Memphis, 1987-88; coord. religious cmty. Red Ribbon Steering Com., Huntington Beach, 1992-93. Recipient Golden Bell award Calif. Sch. Bd. Assn., 1994; Leadership scholar Nat. U., 1991. Mem. Am. Counseling Assn., Am. Sch. Counselor Assn., Am. Assn. Christian Counselors, Assn. Specialists Group Work, Assn. Counseling, Edn. and Supervision, Assn. Spiritual, Ethical Values Counseling, Counseling Guidance & Devel. Assn. (H.B. McDaniel award 1996). Home: 8812 Tamarisk Cir Westminster CA 92683-6840 Office: Westminster Sch Dist Intervention Program 14171 Cedarwood St Westminster CA 92683-4503

HILL, DONALD WAIN, education accreditation commission executive; b. Montfort, Wis., June 14, 1924; s. Victor Charles and Emma Grace (Carr) H.; m. Phyllis Kay Hogan, July 2, 1949; children: Leslie Scott Hill Barnett, Lance Howlett Hill, Lawson Wain Hill. BBA, U. Wis., 1949, MBA, 1953. Budget analyst City of Milw., 1950-53; adminstrv. analyst State of Wis., Madison, 1953-54; bus. mgr. U. Wis., Milw., 1954-56; mem. joint staff Coord. Comm. for Higher Edn., Madison, 1956-59; asst. supt. schs. Chgo. Pub. Schs., 1959-66; exec. vice chancellor City Colls. of Chgo., 1966-84; ednl. cons. Hill Assocs., Carlsbad, Calif., 1984-86; asst. dir., sr. accreditation specialist for western U.S. Accreditation Commn. of Career Sch. and Colls. of Tech., Arlington, Va., 1986—; chmn. fin. com. Ill. Task Force on Edn., Springfield, 1965-66; mem. Ill. Higher Edn. Master Plan Com., Urbana, 1963-64; chmn. facilities com. Task Force to Form U. of Wis.-Milw., 1956; mem. fin. study com. U.S. Office Edn., Washington, 1963. Contbr. articles to profl. jours. Mem. ednl. credentials and credit rev. team Am. Coun. on Edn., Abu Dhabi, 1987; mem. task force on collective bargaining Carnegie Found., N.Y.C., 1975-76. With U.S. Infantry, 1942-46, ETO. Mem. Wis. Acad. Scis., Arts and Letters (higher edn. rep. for Wis. Acad. Rev. 1957-59), Econ. Club Chgo. Presbyterian. Home: 3459 Pontiac Dr Carlsbad CA 92008-2135 Office: Accreditation Commn Career Schs and Colls Tech 2101 Wilson Blvd Ste 302 Arlington VA 22201

HILL, EARL MCCOLL, lawyer; b. Bisbee, Ariz., June 12, 1926; s. Earl George and Jeanette (McColl) H.; m. Bea Dolan, Nov. 22, 1968; children: Arthur Charles, John Earl, Darlene Stern, Tamara Fegert. BA, U. Wash., 1960, JD, 1961. Bar: Nev. 1962, U.S. Ct. Clms. 1978, U.S. Ct. Apls. (9th cir.) 1971, U.S. Sup. Ct. 1978. Law clk. Nev. sup. ct., Carson City, 1962; assoc. Gray, Horton & Hill, Reno, 1962-65, ptnr. 1965-73; ptnr. Marshall Hill Cassas & de Lipkau (and predecessors), Reno, 1974—, Sherman & Howard, Denver, 1982-91; judge pro tem Reno mcpl. ct., 1964-70; lectr. continuing legal edn.; mem. Nev. Commn. on Jud. Selection 1977-84; trustee Rocky Mountain Mineral Law Found. 1976-95, sec. 1987-88. Contbr. articles to profl. jours. Mem. ABA, ATLA, State Bar Nev. (chmn. com. on jud. adminstrn. 1971-77), Washoe County Bar Assn., Am. Judicature Soc., Lawyer Pilots Bar Assn., Soc. Mining Antiquarians (sec.-treas. 1975—), Prospectors Club. Office: Holcomb Profl Ctr 333 Holcomb Ave Ste 300 Reno NV 89502-1664

HILL, ERIK BRYAN, newspaper photographer; b. Eugene, Oreg., Feb. 17, 1957; s. Robert Donald and Dagmara (Grislis) H.; m. Robin Mackey, Aug. 30, 1986; children: Mara, Emma. BA in Internat. Rels., Stanford U., 1979; MS in Journalism, Ohio U., 1987. Photographer, photo editor The Kansas City (Mo.) Star, 1981-84; photographer The Anchorage Daily News, 1984—; adj. instr. U. Alaska, Anchorage, 1990—. Recipient Pulitzer prize gold medal for pub. svc. Columbia U., 1989, finalist Pulitzer prize for feature photography, 1990. Mem. Nat. Press Photographers Assn. Office: Anchorage Daily News 1001 Northway Dr Anchorage AK 99508-2030

HILL, GEOFFREY WILLIAM, publisher; b. Cirencester, Eng., Oct. 7, 1941; came to the U.S., 1947; s. Ceril Hill and Olive Dora (Belcher) Colburn; m. Vicki Lynn Hill; children: Kari, Kelli, Kimi. Grad. H.S., Portland, Oreg. Journeyman's cert. in typography. Delivery boy Paul O. Giesey, Adcrafters, Portland, 1958-61, typography apprentice, 1962-66, typography journeyman, 1967-69, typography dept. head, 1970-71; ptnr. advt. prodn. Feiring & Hill Ad Agy., Bend, Oreg., 1972-73; owner advt. prodn. Geoff Hill Advt., Bend, 1974-90; owner Sun Pub., Bend, 1976—; entertainer and singer, Oreg., 1960-74. Editor: (quar. mag.) Cascades East Mag., 1976, (book) Fishing Central Oregon, 1996. Mem. Bend C. of C., Sisters C. of C., Redmond C. of C. Home: PO Box 5784 Bend OR 97708-5784

HILL, GREG, newspaper bureau chief. San Francisco bur. chief Wall St. Jour. Office: Wall St Jour 201 California St Ste 1350 San Francisco CA 94111-5015*

HILL, HARRY DAVID, city official, human resources professional; b. Whittier, Calif., Oct. 29, 1944; s. Harry Boreman and Winifred Nell (Purvis) Hill; m. Linda Mae Price, Nov. 8, 1969; 1 child, Jon Ryan. AA, Los Angeles Harbor Coll., Wilmington, Calif., 1964; BA in Polit. Sci., UCLA, 1966; M of Pub. Adminstrn. in Human Resources, U. So. Calif., 1972. Personnel aide City of Anaheim, Calif., 1966-67, personnel analyst, 1967-71, sr. personnel analyst, 1971-75, personnel services mgr., 1975-83, asst. human resources dir., 1983-88, asst. labor rels. dir., 1988-94, dir. human resources, 1994—; chmn. supervisory com. Anaheim Area Credit Union, 1981-89, bd. dirs., 1989-95. Mem. So. Calif. Pub. Labor Coun. (treas. 1986-87, pres. 1988), Internat. Pers. Mgmt. Assn. (pres. western region 1983-84), So. Calif. Pers. Mgmt. Assn. (pres. 1978-79), Coop. Pers. Svcs. (bd. dirs. 1987—). Democrat. Office: City of Anaheim 200 S Anaheim Blvd Fl 3 Anaheim CA 92805-3820

HILL, JIM, state official; 1 child, Jennifer. BA in Econs., Mich. State U., 1969; MBA, Indiana U., 1971, JD, 1974. Asst. atty. gen. Oreg. Dept. of Justice, 1974-77; hearing referee Oreg. Dept. of Revenue, 1977-81; personnel specialist and cons. State Farm Ins., 1984-86; elected mem. Oreg. House of Reps., 1983-87, Oreg. State Sen., 1987-93; dir. mktg. PEN-NOR, Inc., Portland Gen. Contractors, 1986-88; corp. accts. mgr. for Latin Am. Mentor Graphics, 1988-93. Office: Oreg State Treasury 159 State Capitol Salem OR 97310-0840

HILL, JOHN EARL, mechanical engineer; b. Ely, Nev., July 18, 1953; s. Earl M. and Florence (Lagos) H.; m. Terry Lynn Biederman, Oct. 3, 1981; 1 child, Felicia Biederman. BA in Social Psychology, U. Nev., 1974, BSME, 1981. Cert. engr. in tng. Machinist B&J Machine and Tool, Sparks, Nev., 1977-78; designer, machinist Screen Printing Systems, Sparks, Nev., 1978, Machine Svcs., Sparks, 1978-81; computer programmer U. Nev., Reno, 1980-81; design engr. Ford Aerospace and Communications Corp., Palo Alto, Calif., 1981-82, 86-88; contract design engr. Westinghouse Electric Corp., Sunnyvale, Calif., 1982-83; contract project engr. Adcotech Corp., Milpitas, Calif., 1983-84; sr. engr. Domain Tech., Milpitas, 1984-85; project engr. Exclusive Design Co., San Mateo, Calif., 1985-86; automation mgr. Akashic Memories Corp., San Jose, Calif., 1988-94; ptnr. Automated Bus. Svcs., San Jose; dir. automation engring. Seagate Rec. Media, Fremont, Calif., 1994—. Mem. Robotics Internat. of Soc. Mfg. Engrs., Tau Beta Pi, Pi Mu Epsilon, Phi Kappa Phi. Home: 147 Wildwood Ave San Carlos CA 94070-4516 Office: Seagate Rec Media 47010 Kato Rd Fremont CA 94538-7332

HILL, JUDITH DEEGAN, lawyer; b. Chgo., Dec. 13, 1940; d. William James and Ida May (Scott) Deegan; children: Colette M., Cristina M. BA, Western Mich. U., 1960; JD, Marquette U., 1971; cert. U. Paris, Sorbonne, 1962; postgrad. Harvard U., 1984. Bar: Wis. 1971, Ill. 1973, Nev. 1976, D.C. 1979. Tchr., Kalamazoo (Mich.) Bd. Edn., 1960-62, Maple Heights (Ohio), 1963-64, Shorewood (Wis.) Bd. Edn., 1964-68; corp. atty. Fort Howard Paper Co., Green Bay, Wis., 1971-72; sr. trust adminstr. Continental Ill. Nat. Bank & Trust, Chgo., 1972-76; atty. Morse, Foley & Wadsworth Law Firm, Las Vegas, 1976-77; dep. dist. atty., criminal prosecutor Clark County Atty., Las Vegas, 1977-83; atty. civil and criminal law Edward S. Coleman Profl. Law Corp., Las Vegas, 1983-84; pvt. practice law, 1984-85; atty. criminal div. Office of City Atty., City of Las Vegas, 1985-89, pvt. practice law, 1989—. Bd. dirs. Nev. Legal Svcs., Carson City, 1980-87, state chmn., 1984-87; bd. dirs. Clark County Legal Svcs., Las Vegas, 1980-87; mem. Star Aux. for Handicapped Children, Las Vegas, 1986-96; Greater Las Vegas Women's League, 1987-88; jud. candidate Las Vegas Mcpl. Ct, 1987, Nev. Symphony Guild, Variety Club Internat., 1992-93, Las Vegas Preservation Group. Recipient Scholarship, Auto Specialties, St. Joseph, Mich., 1957-60, St. Thomas More Scholarship, Marquette U. Law Sch., Milw., 1968-69; juvenile law internship grantee Marquette U. Law Sch., 1970. Mem. Nev. Bar Assn., So. Nev. Assn. Women Attys., Ill. Bar Assn., Children's Village Club (pres. 1980) (Las Vegas, Nev.). Home: 521 Sweeney Ave Las Vegas NV 89104-1436 Office: Ste 211 726 S Casino Center Blvd Las Vegas NV 89101-6700

HILL, KATHLEEN LOIS, performing art school executive; b. Denver, Sept. 11, 1955; d. James Jenkins and Elaine (Marcella) Hill; 1 child Terrence Drake. BA, Colo. Women's Coll., 1977. Choreographer Fashion Bar TV Comml., Denver, 1981, Pure Gold Cheerleaders USFL, Denver, 1985, Kenny Rodgers Western Wear, Denver, 1990; exec., art dir. Hill Acad. of Dance and Dramatics, Denver, 1976—; bd. dirs. Colo. Dance Alliance, Denver, 1986-89; guest judge I Love Dance, Portland, Oreg., 1991-93. Performer Met. Troupers Charity Entertainers, Colo., 1970-76. Named Young Careerist, Bus. and Profl. Women of Am., 1978; recipient Scholastic scholarships Colo. Women's Coll., 1973-77. Mem. Colo. Dance Alliance (bd. dirs. 1986-89), Colo. Dance Festival, Internat. Tap Assn. Democrat. Roman Catholic. Office: Hill Acad Dance/Dramatics 1338 S Valentia St Ste 110 Denver CO 80231-2167

HILL, LELAND R., real estate appraiser, consultant; b. Santa Monica, Calif., May 16, 1956; s. Leland R. and Phyllis M. (Audt) H.; m. Diane C. Jones, Aug. 25, 1984; children: Jessica LeAnne, Amanda Mary. BS in Acctg. & Real Estate, Calif. State U., 1980. Lis. real estate broker, Calif.; cert. gen. appraiser, Calif. Staff appraiser Paul Jackle & Assocs., Huntington Beach, Calif., 1979-82; v.p. Real Estate Appraisal Co., Newport Beach, Calif., 1982-83, Real Estate Svcs. Co., Tustin, Calif., 1983-84; owner, pres. Assoc. Appraisers of Am., Westminster, Calif., 1984—, Hill Cons. Svcs., Westminster, 1995—; instr. Jim Morgan & Assoc., Roseville, Calif., 1996—; dir. Assoc. of Cons., Appraisers and Inspectors, Hurcules, Calif., 1995—. Author: Residential Real Estate Appraiser's Protable Handbook, 1990. Mem. Calif. Assn. Mortgage Brokers (L.A. chpt. bd. dirs. 1995—), Huntington Beach Elks Lodge (assoc.), Westminster Elks Lodge (loyal knight 1996—, esquire 1994-95), Good Sam Club (life), Kids at Heart. Republican. Lutheran. Office: Assoc Appraiser of Am 14340 Bolsa Chica Rd Ste J Westminster CA 92683-4868

HILL, LORIE ELIZABETH, psychotherapist; b. Buffalo, Oct. 21, 1946; d. Graham and Elizabeth Helen (Salm) H. Student, U. Manchester, Eng., 1966-67; BA, Grinnell Coll., 1968; MA, U. Wis., 1970, Calif. State U., Sonoma, 1974; PhD, Wright Inst., 1980. Instr. English U. Mo., 1970-71; adminstr., supr. Antioch-West and Ctr. for Ind. Living, San Francisco, Berkeley, 1975-77; dir. tng. Ctr. for Edn. and Mental Health, San Francisco, 1977-80, exec. dir., 1980-81; pvt. practice Berkeley and Oakland, Calif., 1976—; instr. master's program in psychology John F. Kennedy U., Orinda, Calif., 1985, 94—; founder group of psychotherapists against racism; spkr. on cross-cultural psychology; creater Jump Start, a violence prevention and unlearning racism program for youth; trainer for trainers 3rd Internat. Conf. Conflict Resolution, St. Petersburg, Russia; sr. facilitator Color of Fear. Organizer against nuclear war; founding mem. Psychotherapists for Social Responsibility; psychologist Big Bros. and Big Sisters of the East Bay, 1986-88; vol. instr. City of Oakland Youth Skills Devel. Program; active Rainbow Coalition for Jesse Jackson's Presdl. Campaign, Ron Dellums Re-election Com.; campaigner for Clinton-Gore; founder, chair Psychotherapists against Violence; creator JumpStart program. Recipient Helen Margulies Mehr Pub. Svc. award, 1996. Mem. Calif. Psychol. Assn. (chairperson pub. interest divsn. 1997). Democrat-Socialist. Office: 2955 Shattuck Ave Berkeley CA 94705-1808

HILL, MELODIE ANNE, special education educator; b. Cortez, Colo., May 24, 1959; d. DaleWentworth and Lette Belle (Green) Higman; m. Jeffrey A. Hill, Feb. 16, 1985; children: Kevin Patrick, Virginia Laurel. BA in Edn. & Psychology, U. Denver, 1983; MA in Curriculum, Adams State Coll., 1987; postgrad., N.Mex. State U., 1995—. Reading specialist Kemper Elem. Sch., Cortez, Colo., 1983-85, sci. specialist, 1985-89; mem. sci. curriculum team Lewis-Arriola Elem. Sch., Cortez, Colo., 1989-93; sci. tchr. trainer Ctrl. Consolidated Elem. Sch. Dist., Shiprock, N.Mex., 1989—; tchr. spl. edn. Nataani Nez Elem. Sch., Shiprock, N.Mex., 1993—; presenter in field. Sec. Cortez Vol. Fire Dept., 1995-96; mem. GoodSamaritan Ctr., Cortez, 1990—, Colo. Rep. Women, Cortez, 1996—. NSF grantee, 1990; Honrbeck scholar, 1983. Mem. ASCD, AAUW, Nat. Assn. Sci. Tchrs., Colo. Assn. Sci. Tchrs., N.Mex. Coun. Exceptional Children. Episcopalian. Office: Ctrl Consolidated Sch Dist PO Box 280 Shiprock NM 80402

HILL, NATHAN SCOTT, educator, writer, cultural consultant; b. Fremont, Calif., Jan. 6, 1962; s. N. Eugene and Patricia (Yeager) H.; m. Laura S. Weir, Aug. 19, 1984. BA in Polit. Sci., George Washington U., 1985; MA in Govt., U. Va., 1988; postgrad., U. Calif.-Davis. Co-dir. Calif. Art Rsch., Dixon, 1991—; sr. rsch. and policy analyst Calif. Sch. Bds. Assn., West Sacramento, 1993-96; dir. comm. George Lucas Ednl. Found., Nicasio, CA, 1996—. Author, editor, presenter articles, chpts., papers on art history, cultural policy and planning, polit. sci., and edn. Commr. City of Davis Peace & Justice Commn. 1990-92, chmn., 1991-92; commr. City of Davis Civic Arts Commn., 1992-93; bd. dirs. Napa County Legal Assistance Agy., Napa, Calif., 1995-96; mem. policy adv. bd. U. Calif. Calif. Alliance for Math. and Sci., Oakland, 1995-97. World Affairs Coun. scholar U. Calif.-Davis, 1983; du Pont fellow U. Va., 1985-86; adminstrn. fellow Nat. Endowment for Arts, Washington, 1991; rsch. fellow U. Calif. Washington Ctr., 1992-93. Mem. Am. Edn. Rsch. Assn. Home: 1545 Ingrid Dr Dixon CA 95620 Office: The George Lucas EdnFound PO Box 34961 San Rafael CA 94912

HILL, PHILIP RICHARDSON, management consultant; b. Boston, Aug. 5, 1930; s. Philip Cushing and Marie Teresa (Whiting) H.; m. Lenita Lillian Patronelle Louise Quiroz del Campos, Nov. 1954 (div. Nov. 1965); children: Gregory Richardson, David Cushing, Christopher Whiting; m. Gudrun Randolph, June 1966 (div. Feb. 1974); children: Derek Peter, Marc Alan; m. Hatsue Akimoto, Mar. 27, 1977. BS, Calif. State U., L.A., 1957; MS, Calif. State U., Northridge, 1962. Dir. corp. planning Litton Industries GmbH, Bonn, Germany, 1963-65, Levitt & Sons, Lake Success, N.Y., 1966-68; v.p. BRC, L.A., 1968-71; pres. IIT-Bldg. System Far East, Tokyo, 1971, ESI Japan, Tokyo, 1971-73, Am. Wirewrap, San Jose, Calif., 1979-90, Micon Industries, Oakland, Calif., 1980-81, Philip R. Hill & Co., Inc., Corvallis, Oreg., 1970—. Author: The Apartment Management Guide, 1977, Planning for Company Growth, 1979, Smart Management, 1980, The Peter Hill Family in the Americas from 1663, 1992; contbr. articles to profl. jours. Served with U.S. Army, 1953-55. Republican. Office: Philip R Hill & Co Inc 3558 NW Fillmore Ave Corvallis OR 97330-4941

HILL, RICK ALLAN, congressman; b. Grand Rapids, Minn., Dec. 30, 1946; m. Betti Christie, June 10, 1983; children: Todd, Corey, Mike. BA in Econs. and Polit. Sci., St. Cloud State U., 1968. Surety bonding businessman, owner InsureWest, 1968-90; real estate and investment ptnr., 1983—; committeeman State Rep. Party, 1990-94; legis. liaison to Gov. Marc Racicot, Mont., 1993; mem. at large 105th Congress from Mont., 1997—; fin. chair State Rep. Party, 1989-91, state chair, 1991-92. Bd. dirs. Mont. Sci. and Tech. Alliance, 1992. Office: 1037 Longworth Washington DC 20515

HILL, ROBERT MARTIN, police detective, consultant, lecturer; b. Hammond, Ind., Dec. 10, 1949; s. Donald Edwin and Norma Jeanne (Beal) H.; m. Connie Carolina Nordquist, Dec. 19, 1970. BA, U. Minn., 1974; postgrad., U. Phoenix; cert. in fin. fraud, IRS, Glynco, Ga., 1984; cert. in questioned documents, U.S. Secret Service, Glynco, Ga., 1986. Cert. police officer, Ill., Minn., Ariz.; cert. fraud examiner. Police officer Rolling Meadows (Ill.) Police Dept., 1970-72, St. Paul Police Dept., 1972-79; police officer Scottsdale (Ariz.) Police Dept., 1980-81, police fraud detective, 1981—; com. mem. Fraud Ariz. Banker's Assn., 1985-86; lectr. various colls. and orgns. Recipient Dirs. Commendation U.S. Secret Svc., Washington, 1986, Commendation, Dept. Defense, 1993; named Investigator of Yr. Econ. Crime Investigators, 1991. Mem. Internat. Assn. Credit Card Investigators (v.p. 1985-86, pres., bd. dirs. 1986-88, Nat. Law Enforcement Officer of the Yr. award 1986, Ariz. chpt. Police Officer of the Yr. 1984, 86, 93), Internat. Assn. Auto Theft Investigators, Internat. Police Assn., Assn. Cert. Fraud Examiners. Republican. Baptist. Office: 9065 E Via Linda Scottsdale AZ 85258-5400

HILL, ROGER EUGENE, physicist; b. San Bernardino, Calif., Feb. 12, 1936; s. George Eugene and Alice Marie (Greek) H.; m. Bette Cerf Ross, Aug. 14, 1955 (div. Dec. 1974); children: Catherine Marie, Teresa Jean, Diana Louise; m. Louise Mary Jackson, May 8, 1993. BS, St. Mary's Coll., Moraga, Calif., 1957; PhD, U. Calif., Berkeley, 1964. Rsch. assoc. U. Chgo., 1963-66; prin. sci. officer Rutherford High Energy Lab., Chilton, Didcot, Berks, U.K., 1966-68; vis. scientist CERN, Geneva, 1968; tech. mgr. Geonuclear Nobel Paso, S.A., Paris, 1969-78; sr. rsch. scientist U. N.Mex., Albuquerque, 1982-86; sect. leader Los Alamos (N.Mex.) Nat. Lab., 1986—; sci. liaison officer Joint Verification Experiment, USSR, 1988; tech. advisor U.S. Delegation Nuclear Testing Talks, Geneva, 1988-89. Contbr. articles and papers to profl. jours. Recipient Excellence award Dept. Energy, 1990. Mem. Am. Phys. Soc., Am. Assn. Physics Tchrs. Office: Los Alamos Nat Lab Ms H803 Los Alamos NM 87545

HILL, STEVEN JOHN, journalist, educator; b. New London, Conn., June 6, 1958; s. William John and Patricia (Rogers) H. BA in Geology and Geophysics, Yale U., 1982. Child devel. counselor Martin Psychiat. Ctr., Cath. Cmty. Svcs. N.W., 1985-90; freelance journalist San Francisco, 1991—; program dir. Labor Net @ IGC, San Francisco, 1995-96; west coast dir. Ctr. for Voting and Democracy, San Francisco, 1993—. Contbr. articles to newspapers, profl. publs., and mags., including Ms., Seattle Times, Cleve. Plain Dealer, Christian Sci. Monitor, L.A. Times, On the Issues, Capital Times, San Francisco Chronicle, The Nation, The Humanist, others, also poetry and short fiction to small publs. Mem. adv. com. Citizens for Proportioned Representation, San Francisco, 1993-96; mem. steering com. LaborNet @ IGC, 1996; campaign mgr., chmn. San Franciscans for Preference Voting, 1996. Mem. Green Party.

HILL, WILLIAM U., lawyer, prosecutor. Atty. gen. Cheyenne, Wyo., 1995—. Office: 123 State Capitol Cheyenne WY 82002*

HILLER, ARTHUR, motion picture director; b. Edmonton, Alta., Can., Nov. 22, 1923. Ed., U. Toronto and U. B.C., Alta., Toronto and B.C.; F.V.Ch.C., Victoria Coll., Glasgow, 1967; MA in Psychology; LHD, London Inst. Applied Research, 1973; DFA (hon.), U. Victoria, 1995; LLD, U. Toronto, 1995. Dir. TV prodns. Matinee Theatre, Playhouse 90, Alfred Hitchcock Presents, Route 66, Naked City; dir. films Americanization of Emily, 1965, Out of Towners, 1970, Love Story, 1970, Plaza Suite, 1971, Hospital, 1971, Man of La Mancha, 1972, The Man in the Glass Booth, 1975, Silver Streak, 1976, The In-Laws, 1979, Making Love, 1982, Teachers, 1984, Outrageous Fortune, 1987, The Babe, 1992. Decorated comdr. Internat. Order Sursam Corda; doctor laureate Imperial Order Constantine Brussels, 1972; recipient Can. radio awards, 1951, 52; awards for edn. by radio Ohio U., 1952, 53; best dir. nomination Nat. Acad. TV Arts and Scis., 1962; best dir. nomination Acad. Motion Picture Arts and Scis., 1970;

Golden Globe award for best dir., 1970; Dir.'s award nomination Dirs. Guild Am., 1970; Best Dir. award N.Y. Fgn. Press, 1970. Mem. Directors' Guild of Am. (pres. 1988-92), Acad. Motion Picture Arts and Scis. (pres. 1993-97). Office: Golden Quill 8899 Beverly Blvd Ste 702 Los Angeles CA 90048-2429

HILLERSTROM, PER ROGER, psychotherapist; b. N.Y.C., Jan. 28, 1954; s. Per and Gully (Johanson) H.; m. Beth Marlene Neese, July 15, 1979; children: Karlyn Beth, Per Lukas, Rebekah Marlene. AA, Skyline Coll., 1974; BS cum laude, Bethel Coll., 1979; MS, Biola U., 1982. Cert. mental health counselor, Wash. Mktg. mgr. Professor's Restaurants, St. Paul, 1978-80; chem. dependency counselor Bremer House, St. Paul, 1978-79; mortuary aide Hilgenfeld Mortuary, Anaheim, Calif., 1980-82; sutdent svcs. counselor Biola U., La Mirada, Calif., 1980-82; seminar instr. Christian Marriage Enrichment, Santa Ana, Calif., 1982-85; clin. family therapist Crista Counseling, Seattle, 1982-95; clin. family therapist, ptnr. Heritage Assocs., Edmonds, Wash., 1996—; field advisor master's program Antioch U., Seattle, 1990-92; radio host counsline program KCIS Radio, Seattle, 1983-95, KGNW Radio, Seattle, 1996—. Author: Intimate Deception, 1989 (Book of Yr. award Cornerstone 1990), Your Faily Voyage, 1993, Rewriting Your Family Script, 1995. Mem. Am. Assn. Christian Counselors (charter), Am. Assn. Marriage and Family Therapists, Christian Assn. Psychol. Studies. Office: Heritage Assocs 555 Dayton Ste C Edmonds WA 98020

HILLESTAD, CHARLES ANDREW, lawyer; b. McCurtain, Okla., Aug. 30, 1945; s. Carl Oliver and Aileen Hanna (Sweeney) H.; m. Ann Ramsey Robertson, Oct. 13, 1973. BS, U. Oreg., 1967; JD, U. Mich., 1972. Bar: Colo. 1972, U.S. Dist. Ct. Colo. 1972, U.S. Ct. Appeals (10th cir.) 1972, Oreg. 1993; lic. real estate broker, Colo. Law clk. to presiding justice Colo. Supreme Ct., Denver, 1972-73; ptnr. DeMuth & Kemp, Denver, 1973-83, Cornwell & Blakey, Denver, 1983-90, Scheid & Horlbeck, Denver, 1990-93, Gablehouse & Epel, Denver, 1993-94; pvt. practice Cannon Beach, Oreg., 1994—; co-developer award winning Queen Anne Inn, Capitol Hill Mansion and Cheyenne Canyon Inn hotels; mem. ad hoc com. Denver Real Estate Atty. Specialists. Co-author: Annual Surveys of Real Estate Law for Colorado Bar Association; contbr. articles to profl. jours.; assoc. editor Inn Times. Former coun. mem. Denver Art Mus.; former chmn. Rocky Mountain chpt. Sierra Club; former bd. dirs. Hist. Denver, Inc. Staff sgt. U.S. Army, 1968-70. Recipient Colo. Co. of Yr. award Colo. Bus. Mag., Award of Honor Denver Ptnrship., Newsmaker of Yr. and Outstanding Achievement awards Am. Assn. Hist. Inns, Tourism Person of Yr. award Denver Conv. and Visitor's Bur., Rocky Mountain Spectacular Inn award B&B Rocky Mountains Assn., Best Inns of Yr. awards County Inns Mag. and Adventure Rd. Mag., Best of Denver award Westward newspaper. Mem. ABA, Colo. Bar Assn., Oreg. Bar Assn., Denver Bar Assn., Colo. Lawyers for the Arts, POETS, Seaside C. of C. (v.p. bd. dirs.). Office: PO Box 1065 1347 S Hemlock Cannon Beach OR 97110

HILLINGER, CHARLES, journalist, writer; b. Evanston, Ill., Apr. 1, 1926; s. William Agidious H. and Caroline Bruning; m. Arliene Otis, June 22, 1948; children: Brad, Tori. BS in Polit. Sci., UCLA, 1951. Circulation mgr., columnist Park Ridge (Ill.) Advocate, 1938-41; copy boy, libr., feature writer Chgo. Tribune, 1941-43; reporter, feature writer, syndicated columnist L.A. Times, 1946-92, ret., 1992. Author: California Islands, 1957, Bel-Air Country Club, A Living Legend, 1993, Charles Hillinger's America, 1996, Charles Hillinger's California Islands, 1997, Charles Hillinger's California, 1997. Mem. adv. bd. Sant Cruz Is. Found., Santa Barbara, Calif., 1992—; treas. 8-Ball Welfare Found. Greater L.A. Press Club, 1992—. With USN, 1943-46. Mem. Greater L.A. Press Club (sec. 1978-88, v.p. 1988-90, pres. 1990-92), Dutch Treat Club W. Home: 3131 Dianora Dr Rancho Palos Verdes CA 90275-6200

HILLIS, RICK, writer, educator; b. Nipawin, Sask., Can., Feb. 3, 1956; came to U.S., 1988; s. Lyle Arthur and Joyce (Morgan) H.; m. Patricia Mary Appelgren, Aug. 26, 1988; children: Cullen, Cassidy. BED, U. Sask., Saskatoon, 1979; MFA, U. Iowa, 1984; postgrad., Stanford U., 1988-90. Tchr. h.s. various cities, Sask., 1979-81; Jones fiction lectr. Stanford (Calif.) U., 1990-94; writer-in-residence Reed Coll., Portland, Oreg., 1994-96; vis. asst. prof. English Lewis and Clark Coll., Portland, 1996-97. Author: (book) Limbo River, 1990 (Drue Heinz and Calif. Commonwealth medal 1990), (book of poems) The Blue Machines of Night, 1988, (screenplay) Rumors of Foot, 1993. Stegner fellow Stanford U., 1988-90. Home: 4634 SE 34th Ave Portland OR 97202

HILLIS, STEPHEN KENDALL, secondary education educator; b. Hillsboro, Oreg., Jan. 5, 1942; s. Earnest Howard Hillis and Phyllis Noreen (Bagley) Gortner; m. Sharon Ione Arbogast, Aug. 5, 1967; children: Jeff Wise, Teryl Dorothy, Tonya Noreen. BA, Pacific U., 1965. Cert. Std. Oreg. Dept. Edn. H.s. tchr. Eagle Grove, Iowa, 1967-73, Madras, Oreg., 1973—. Precinct com. Jefferson County Dems., Madras, 1978-89, chair precinct com. 1988-91. With USAR, 1959-65. Mem. ASCD, NEA (human civil rights com. 1990-96, bd. dirs. 1993—), Oreg. Edn. Assn. (bd. dirs. 1983—, v.p. 1988-93). Democrat. Home: 375 NE Chestnut Madras OR 97741-1910 Office: 509J Sch Dist 390 S Tenth St Madras OR 97741

HILLMAN, LEILANI GENÉ, artist, gallery owner; b. Ottumwa, Iowa, Aug. 6, 1939; d. Glen Randal and LuCeil Irene (Clossen) shepp; m. Donald Earl Hillman, Sept. 12, 1959; children: Darci Ann, Lance Randal. Student, Ea. N.Mex. U., 1957-59, Diablo Valley Coll., 1975. Owner Marhaba by Lani, Mesa, Ariz., 1993—; co-owner White Mountain Creekside Gallery, Pinetop, Ariz., 1996—; tchr. art, Mesa, Overgaard and Apache Junction, Ariz., 1995-96. Mem. N.E. Ariz. Fine Arts Assn. (pres. 1995—), Mesa Art League, Nat. Acrylic Painters Assn. (signature mem.).

HILLMANN, LEO CHARLES, real estate company executive; b. White Plains, N.Y., Nov. 11, 1946; s. David Augustine and Mary Isabel (Healy) H.; m. Irene Marie May, Feb. 14, 1986; children: Evan Carter, Raegan Lynn, Christine Marie. BCE, Villanova U., 1969; MS in Ops. Rsch., George Washington U., 1978; grad., Naval War Coll., 1989; AS in Real Estate, Cuyamaca Coll, 1990; MA in History, San Diego State U., 1993. Commd. ensign USN, 1969, advanced through grades to comdr., 1983, active submarine svc., 1969-89; pres., CEO Shilo Enterprises, Spring Valley, Calif., 1989—; mem. fac. history dept Mesa Coll., San Diego, Calif., 1995—. Author: Naval Engineering, 1976, The Public at the Creation, 1993. Staff Rep. Conv. Orgn., San Diego, 1996. Mem. Navy League U.S., U.S. Naval Inst., Ret. Officer's Assn., Am. Legion, Calif. Assn. Realtors, San Diego County Assn. Realtors, San Diego State U. Alumnae Assn., U.S. Navy Meml. Assn., USS Constitution Mus., San Diego Zool. Soc., Phi Alpha Theta. Roman Catholic. Home: 9787 Avenida Colino Spring Valley CA 91977 Office: 10174 Austin Dr Ste 2693 Spring Valley CA 91978

HILLS, LINDA LAUNEY, advisory systems engineer; b. New Orleans, June 21, 1947; d. Edgar Sebastien and Isabel (James) Launey; m. Marvin Allen Hills Sr. Jan. 29, 1977 (div. July 1982); 8 stepchildren. Student, Navy Avionics Schs., Memphis and San Diego, 1979-89; certs. in tech. tng., IBM, Chgo. and Kingston, N.Y., Sys. Mgmt. Schs., Chgo. and Dallas. Cert. disaster recovery planner. Sec. Calhoun and Barnes Inc. Co., New Orleans, 1965; clk.-typist, stenographer, med. transcriptionist, teletypist Social Security Adminstrn., New Orleans, 1965-67; dep. U.S. marshal U.S. Marshal's Office, New Orleans, 1967-69; supr. U.S. Atty.'s Office, New Orleans, 1969; with clk.'s office, dep. U.S. clk., courtrom dep. U.S. clk. U.S. Dist. Ct. (ea. dist.) La., New Orleans, 1969-73; steno, sr. sec. Kelly Girl and Norrell Temp Services, New Orleans, 1974; customer engr. trainee IBM, Dallas, 1979; customer engr., sys. mgmt. specialist IBM, San Diego, 1979-84; sys. ctr. rep. NSD Washington System Ctr. IBM, Gaithersburg, Md., 1984-87; ops. specialist mktg. dept. IBM, San Diego, 1987—, adv. sys. engr., 1988-91; lectr., cons. in field. Author 3 workbooks on recovery mgmt., also presentation guide for execs. with cost evaluation, presentation guide for company coms. Vol. Touro Infirmary, Dialysis Unit, New Orleans, 1965-67, New Orleans Recreation Dept. 1964-68, PALS-Montgomery County Mental Health Orgn., Bethesda, Md., 1984-87, various polit. candidates, 1963—; mem. Calif. Gov.'s Subcom. on Disaster Preparedness. Petty officer USN, 1974-78. Mem. NAFE, ACP, DAV, Info. System Security Assn., Women Computer Profls. San Diego, Data Processing Mgmt. Assn., San Diego Zoolog. Soc., Assn. System Mgmt., Smithsonian Instn. (resident assoc.), Nat. Trust Hist. Preservation. Office: PO Box 261806 San Diego CA 92196-1806

HILLS, REGINA J., journalist; b. Sault Sainte Marie, Mich., Dec. 24, 1953; d. Marvin Dan and Ardithanne (Tilly) H.; m. Vincent C. Stricherz, Feb. 25, 1984. B.A., U. Nebr., 1976. Reporter UPI, Lincoln, Nebr., 1976-80, state editor, bur. mgr., 1981-82; state editor, bur. mgr. UPI, New Orleans, 1982-84, Indpls., 1985-87; asst. city editor Seattle Post-Intelligencer, 1987—; panelist TV interview show Face Nebr., 1978-81; vis. lectr. U. Nebr., Lincoln, 1978, 79, 80; columnist weekly feature Capitol News, Nebr. Press Assn., 1981-82. Recipient Outstanding Coverage awards UPI, 1980, 82. Mem. U. Nebr. Alumni Assn., Zeta Tau Alpha. Office: Seattle Post-Intelligencer 101 Elliott Ave W Seattle WA 98119-4220

HILLYARD, LYLE WILLIAM, lawyer; b. Logan, Utah, Sept. 25, 1940; s. Alma Lowell and Lucille (Rosenbaum) H.; m. Alice Thorpe, June 24, 1964; children: Carrie, Lisa, Holly, Todd, Matthew. BS, Utah State U., 1965; JD, U. Utah, 1967. Bar: Utah 1967, U.S. Supreme Ct. 1977. Pres. Hillyard, Anderson & Olsen, Logan, 1967—; senator State of Utah, Salt Lake City, 1985—. Rep. chmn. Cache County, Logan, 1970-76; Utah State Rep., 1981-84; pres. Cache County C. of C., 1977. Named one of Outstanding Young Men of Am., Utah Jaycees, 1972; recipient Disting. Svc. award, Logan Jaycees, 1972, Merit award Cache Valley coun. Boy Scouts Am., 1981. Mem. ABA, Utah State Bar Assn., Cache County Bar Assn., Assn. Trial Lawyers Am., Am. Bd. Trial Advocates. Mormon. Club: Big Blue (Logan). Lodge: Kiwanis. Office: Hillyard Anderson & Olsen 175 E 1st N Logan UT 84321-4601

HILTON, BARRON, hotel executive; b. Dallas, 1927; s. Conrad Hilton. Founder, pres. San Diego Chargers, Am. Football League, until 1966; v.p. Hilton Hotels Corp., Beverly Hills, Calif., 1954; pres., chief exec. officer Hilton Hotels Corp., Beverly Hills, 1966—, chmn., 1979—, also dir.; chmn., pres., dir. Hilton Equipment Corp, Beverly Hills, Calif; mem. gen. adminstrv. bd. Mfrs. Hanover Trust Co., N.Y.C. Office: Hilton Hotels Corp 9336 Civic Center Dr Beverly Hills CA 90210-3604*

HILTON, STANLEY GOUMAS, lawyer, educator, writer; b. San Francisco, June 16, 1949; s. Loucas Stylianos and Effie (Glafkides) Goumas; m. Raquel Estrella Villalba, Feb. 25, 1996. BA with honors, U. Chgo., 1971; JD, Duke U., 1975; MBA, Harvard U., 1979. Bar: Calif. 1975. Libr. asst. Duke U. Libr., Durham, N.C., 1972-75, Harvard U. Libr., Cambridge, Mass., 1977-79; minority counsel U.S. Senator Bob Dole, Washington, 1979-80; adminstrv. asst. Calif. State Senate, Sacramento, 1980-81; pvt. practice San Francisco, 1981—; adj. assoc. prof. Golden Gate U., San Francisco, 1991—. Author: Bob Dole: American Political Phoenix, 1988, Senator for Sale, 1995. Pres. Com. to Stick With Candlestick Park, San Francisco, 1992-96, Value Added Tax Now, San Francisco, 1994—, Save the 4th Amendment, San Francisco, 1995—. Mem. Hellenic Law Soc., Bechtel Toastmasters Club. Democrat. Office: PO Box 27575 San Francisco CA 94127

HILYARD, DAVID FRANKLIN, optician; b. Hartland, Maine, Mar. 16, 1949; s. Clarence Emery and Glenda Irene (Doughty) H.; m. Darrie Jean Young, Sept. 28, 1984; children: Lisa, Chad, Wyatt, Spenser. Student, Norwalk Tech. Inst., 1968-69. Optical technician Laser Optics, Inc., Danbury, Conn., 1966-69, 71-76; radio team chief, sgt. U.S. Army, 1969-71; master optician, supr. Zygo Corp., Middlefield, Conn., 1976-85; specialist, chief optician UCO/Lick Observatory, U. Calif., Santa Cruz, 1985—. Author: (manual) Conventional Optical Polishing Procedures, 1982, Keck Telescope High Resolution Spectograph Optical Components, 1993; co-author: (technical report) University of California Tech. Report #49 Mosaic Project, 1988, Keck Telescope High Resolution Spectograph Design Review, 1990, UCO/Lick Tech. Report #75, 1994. Mem. Am. Inst. of Physics, Optical Soc. of Am., Soc. of Photo-Optical Instrumentation Engrs. Home: 255 Cottini Way Santa Cruz CA 95060-9467 Office: Univ of California Lick Observatory 1156 High St Santa Cruz CA 95064-1077

HIMMERICH Y VALENCIA, ROBERT THERON, historian, farmer; b. Ipswich, S.D., Dec. 13, 1932; s. Fred and Florence Lucille (Angel-Barnard) Himmerich; m. Eva Margaret Valencia, Sept. 24, 1953; 1 child, Marc Valencia Himmerich. BA, Calif. State U., Fullerton, 1970, MA, 1975; PhD, UCLA, 1984. Enlisted U.S. Marine Corps, 1950, commd. 2d lt., 1953, advanced through grades to maj., 1967, served in Korea, Vietnam, Hawaii among others, 1950-73, ret., 1973; owner Himmerich Trucks, Tustin, Calif., 1973-75; v.p. Jaskulski, Himmerich & Horan Brokerage Inc., Costa Mesa, Calif., 1975-91; vis. asst. prof. dept. history U. N.Mex., Albuquerque, 1985-90, assoc. dir. acad. programs Latin Am. Inst., 1990-92, assoc. prof. dept. history, 1994—; lectr. dept. history UCLA, 1985; editor N.Mex. Hist. Rev., Albuquerque, 1992—; farmer, Pena Blanca, N.Mex., 1985—. Author: Encomenderos of New Spain, 1991. Bd. dirs. Santa Fe Fiesta Found., 1989—, N.Mex. Endowment for the Humanities, Albuquerque, 1993—; mem. Santa Fe Rodeo Assn., 1991—. Mem. We. History Assn., Rocky Mountain Coun. on Latin Am. History, Marine Corps Assn. Libertarian. Roman Catholic. Office: U NMex Dept History Albuquerque NM 87131

HINCHEY, BRUCE ALAN, environmental engineering company executive; b. Kansas City, Mo., Jan. 24, 1949; s. Charles Emmet and Eddie Lee (Scott) H.; m. Karen Adele McLaughlin, Nov. 27, 1969 (div. Nov. 1983); children: Scott Alan, Traci Denise, Amanda Lee, Richard Austin; m. Karen Robitaille, Apr. 10, 1993. Student, U. Mo., Rolla, 1967-71. Source testing crew chief Ecology Audits, Inc., Dallas, 1971-76; lab. mgr. Ecology Audits, Inc., Casper, Wyo., 1976-78; mgr. ops. Ecology Audits, Inc., Dallas, 1978-79; v.p. Kumpe & Assoc. Engrs., Casper, 1979-81; pres. Western Environ. Svcs. and Testing, Inc., Casper, 1981—; v.p. Hawk Industries, Inc., 1993—; pres. Mining Assocs. Wyo., Cheyenne, 1986-87. Mem. Wyo. State Ho. of Reps., Cheyenne, 1989—, spkr. of house, mgmt. coun., rules com., energy coun., select water com., active Natrona County Rep. precinct, Casper, 1986—, Am. Legis. Exch. Coun., 1989; chair Natrona County Rep. Party, 1988-89. Mem. Am. Inst. Mining Engrs., Nat. Fedn. Ind. Bus. (Guardian award), Air Pollution Control Assn., Casper C. of C., Rotary, Shriners, Masons. Baptist. Office: Western Environ Svcs and Testing Inc 913 N Foster Rd Casper WY 82601-1640

HINCKLEY, GORDON B., church official; s. Bryant S. and Ada (Bitner) H.; m. Marjorie Pay, Apr. 29, 1937; children: Kathleen Hinckley Barnes, Richard G., Virginia Hinckley Pearce, Clark B., Jane Hinckley Dudley. Asst. to Council of Twelve Apostles, Church of Jesus Christ Latter Day Saints, 1958-61, mem. council, 1961-81, Counselor of the First Presidency, 1981-82, Second Counselor of the First Presidency, 1982-85, First Counselor to the First Presidency, 1985-95; pres. of ch., 1995—. Office: First Presidency LDS Ch 47 E South Temple Salt Lake City UT 84150-1005

HINCKLEY, TED C., historian, educator, writer; b. N.Y.C., Oct. 4, 1925; s. Theodore Charles and Eunice Marguerite (Platt) H.; m. Caryl Fay Chesmore, June 17, 1948; children: Susan Platt Hinckley Koester, Deborah Christine Hinckley Riche. BS in Bus. Adminstrn., Claremont McKenna Coll., Claremont, Calif., 1950; BS in History, N.W. Mo. State U., Maryville, 1951; MA in Edn., U. Mo., Kansas City, 1953; PhD in History, Ind. U., 1961. Jr. exec. Chesmore Seed Co., St. Joseph, Mo., 1965; tchr. history Barstow Sch., Kansas City, Mo., 1951-53; asst. to pres. Claremont McKenna Coll., 1953-55; headmaster St. Katharine's Sch., Davenport, Iowa, 1955-57; tchg. asst. Ind. U., Bloomington, 1957-59; prof. history San Jose (Calif.) State U., 1959-90; adj. prof. Western Wash. U., Bellingham, 1991—; lectr. Fulbright Assocs., Yogyakarta, Indonesia, 1994-95. Author: John G. Brady, 1982, The Canoe Rocks, 1995, War, Wings. . .1945, 1996, The Americanization of Alaska, 1972; mem. editl. bd. Pacific N.W. Quar., 1974-93, Alaska History, 1984—, Jour. of the West, 1977—. Mem. Calif. Hist. Preservation Commn., Sacramento, 1980-85; elder Saratoga (Calif.) Presbyn. Ch., 1968-70; assoc. Danforth Found., St. Louis, 1962—. With USN, 1943-46, 2d lt. U.S. Army Res., 1950-53, ensign USN, 1953-56. Huntington Libr. summer fellow, 1971; grantee Am. Philos. Soc., 1962, 66, Alaska Hist. Commn., 1983-94. Mem. Am. Hist. Assn., Western Hist. Assn. (coun. 1987-90), Alaska Hist. Soc., Wash. State Hist. Assn., Fulbright Assn., Phi Beta Kappa. Christian. Home: 950 Chesley Park Dr Sedro Woolley WA 98284

HINDE, ELIZABETH ROSE, elementary education educator; b. Atlantic City, N.J., Sept. 30, 1961; d. William Munroe and Frances (Galati) Wyand; m. Brent William Hinde, March 26, 1988; children: Spencer, Andrew. BA, U. Ariz., Tucson, 1983; MEd, Ariz. State U., Tempe, 1991. Cert. tchr., Ariz.; middle sch. endorsement. 5th grade tchr. Stevenson Elem. Sch., Mesa Pub. Schs., Mesa, Ariz., 1983-85, 6th grade tchr., 1985-96; 6th grade tchr. Porter Elem. Sch., Mesa Pub. Schs., Mesa, Ariz., 1996—. Mem. Assn. Supervision and Curriculum Devel., Nat. Coun. Social Studies, Ariz. Coun. Social Studies, Ariz. Geographical Alliance, Nat. Edn. Assn. Office: Porter Elem Sch 1350 S Lindsay Rd Mesa AZ 85207

HINDS, EDWARD DEE, insurance and investment professional, financial planner; b. Madera, Calif., May 13, 1949; s. Edward Dee Jr. and Donna (Parker) H.; m. Olga P. Hinds; children: Sarah, Stephen, Rebekah. Grad., Life Underwriting Tng. Coun. CLU; registered investment adviser. Sr. acct. agt. Allstate, Lemoore, Calif., 1983-90; gen. agt. Ohio Nat. Life Ins. Co.'s and Midland Nat. Life Ins., Paso Robles, Calif, 1990—; gen. ptnr. Edward D. Hinds, Ins. and Fortress Fin. Strategies, Paso Robles, 1990—, Edward D. Hinds, Ins., 1995—; founder, gen. ptnr. Fortress Fin. Strategies, A Registered Investment Adviser, 1995—; benefits cons. U-Haul Dealers, Cen. Calif., 1992—. Mem. Am. Soc. CLU and ChFC, Internat. Assn. Fin. Planners, Nat. Assn. of Life Underwriters, Nat. Assn. of Health Underwriters.

HINES, GAROLD PAUL, utilities executive. BS, U. Nev., 1973, MS, 1980. cert. secondary tchg. credential, Nev. Asst. U. Nev., Reno, 1974-75; tchr. San Francisco Christian Sch., 1975-76, Winnemucca Jr. H.S., 1981-83; utility operator Valmy Power Plant, 1984-86; asst. control operator Tracy (Nev.) Plant, 1987-89, control rm. operator, 1990—. Trademark (Christian bd. game) ProSeed, 1993; contbr. stories to profl. jours. U. Nev. fellow, 1979-80; named Olympic Torch runner, 1996. Home: 793 C St Fernley NV 98408 Office: Tracy Power Sta 191 Wunotoo Rd Sparks NV 89434-6609

HINES, MELISSA, neuroscientist, psychologist; b. Moline, Ill., Nov. 27, 1951; d. William Joseph and Janice Ethel (Sersig) H.; m. Richard Green; 1 child, Adam Hines-Green. BA, Princeton (N.J.) U., 1973; PhD, UCLA, 1981. Lic. clin. psychologist, Calif. Postdoctoral scholar U. Calif., Anatomy and Brain Rsch. Inst., L.A., 1981-84; vis. scientist St. Bartholomews Hosp., U. of London Endocrinology, 1992, Wis. Primate Ctr., U. Wis., Madison, 1981-82; rsch. scientist dept. psychiatry and anatomy UCLA, 1984-89, asst. prof. dept. psychiatry, 1989-93, assoc. prof., 1993—; pvt. practice psychology L.A., 1989—; reviewer, site visitor Pub. Health Svc., Washington, 1989—. Contbr. articles to profl. jours. Rsch. grantee NIH, 1981—; fellowship grant Giannini Found., 1983-84. Mem. Brain Rsch. Inst., Internat. Acad. of Sex Rsch., Am. Psychol. Soc., Sigma Xi. Office: UCLA Dept Psychiatry 760 Westwood Plz Los Angeles CA 90024-8300

HINES, WILLIAM EVERETT, publisher, producer, cinematographer, writer; b. San Bernardino, Calif., Apr. 2, 1923; s. Everett Ellsworth and Etta Elvira (Gillard) H. Student, UCLA, 1941-43, 46; BA, U. So. Calif., L.A., 1950, MA, 1951. Cameraman, film editor N.Am. Aviation, Inc., L.A. and Downey, Calif., 1951-53; founder, pres. Ed-Venture Films, L.A., 1954—; sec., treas. Sampson Prodns., S.A., Panama, 1956-60; v.p. Intro-Media Prodns., Inc., L.A., 1971-75; pres., pub. Ed-Venture Films/Books, L.A., 1985—; cons., expert witness, L.A., 1965—; lectr., instr., L.A., 1958—. Author: Job Descriptions...For Film & Video, 4 edits., 1961-84, Operating Tips for Film and Video, 1993; writer Operating Tips column for Internat. Photographer mag., 1987—; contbr. numerous features to profl. jours.; producer: (ednl. film) Running For Sheriff, 1954 (Merit award 1955, 56); producer films., commls. Mem. profl. adv. bd. Calif. State U., Long Beach, 1973—, Northridge, 1974—; chmn. bd. trustees Producers and Film Craftsmen Pension and Health Plans, L.A., 1965-79. Sgt. USAAF, 1943-46. Recipient Spl. citation City of L.A., 1966. Mem. Nat. Assn. Broadcast Employees and Technicians, Internat. Photographers Guild, Internat. Alliance Theatrical Stage Employees (exec. bd. dirs. 1989—, dir. tng. 1992—), Soc. Oper. Cameramen (charter, sec. 1984—, corp. liaison 1991—), Am. Film Inst., Publishers Mktg. Assn., Nat. Geog. Soc., Assn. Film Craftsmen (pres., mem. exec. bd. 1957-79), Masons, Shriners, Ephebian Soc., Sigma Nu (Epsilon Pi chpt.). Office: Ed-Venture Films/Books 1122 Calada St Los Angeles CA 90023-3115

HING, LAWRENCE STEWART, lawyer, management consultant; b. Englewood, N.J., Mar. 4, 1963; s. Jin Hing and Lily Cheng Goon; m. Denise Marie Kieszkowski, Sept. 5, 1992. BA, Yale U., 1985; JD, NYU, 1988; MBA, U. Calif., Berkeley, 1996. Bar: Calif. 1988, D.C. 1990. Assoc. Orrick, Herrington & Sutcliffe, San Francisco, 1988-90; atty. Securities and Exchange Commn., San Francisco, 1990-94; sr. counsel Securities and Exch. Commn., San Francisco, 1994-96; cons. Andersen Consulting, San Francisco, 1996—. Recipient Scottish Univ. Internat. Summer Schs. grant U. Edinburgh, Scotland, 1984; U.K.-Berkeley MBA scholarBritish Consulate-Gen., 1995. Mem. Phillips Exeter Alumni Assn. Northern Calif., Yale Alumni Assn. Home: 1200 Francisco St Apt 7 San Francisco CA 94123-2318 Office: Andersen Consulting Strategic Svcs Group 1 Market Plz San Francisco CA 94105

HINMAN, FRANK, JR., urologist, educator; b. San Francisco, Oct. 2, 1915; s. Frank and Mittie (Fitzpatrick) H.; m. Marion Modesta Eaves, Dec. 3, 1948. AB with great distinction, Stanford U., 1937; MD, Johns Hopkins U., 1941. Diplomate Am. Bd. Urology (trustee 1979-85). Intern Johns Hopkins Hosp., 1941-42; resident Cin. Gen. Hosp., 1942-44, U. Calif. Hosp., 1945-47; pvt. practice medicine specializing in urology San Francisco, 1947-85; assoc. clin. prof. urology U. Calif., San Francisco, 1954-62, clin. prof., 1962—; urologist-in-chief Children's Hosp., 1957-85; mem. adv. council Nat. Inst. Arthritis, Diabetes, Digestive and Kidney Diseases, 1983-86. Served to lt. USNR, 1944-46. Named Disting. Alumnus, Johns Hopkins U., 1995. Fellow ACS (regent 1972-80, vice-chmn. 1978-79, v.p. 1982-83), Royal Coll. Surgeons (hon., Eng.); mem. Am. Urol. Assn. (hon.), Am. Assn. Genito-Urinary Surgeons (hon., pres. 1981), Clin. Soc. Genito-Urinary Surgeons (pres. 1979), Internat. Urol. Soc. (pres. Am. sect. 1980-84), Am. Assn. Clin. Urologists, Am. Fedn. Clin. Research, Soc. Pediatric Urology (founder, pres. 1971), Soc. Univ. Urologists (founding mem., pres. 1973), Am. Acad. Pediatrics (pres. urology sect. 1986), Urodynamics Soc. (founding mem., pres. 1980-82), Genito Urinary Reconstructive Soc. (founding mem.), Pan Pacific Surg. Assn. (v.p. 1980-83), Internat. Continence Soc., Brit. Assn. Urologic Surgeons (hon.) (St. Paul Medalist 1991), Société Française d'Urologie, Australasian Soc. Urologic Surgeons (hon.), Phi Beta Kappa, Alpha Omega Alpha. Clubs: Bohemian, St. Francis Yacht, San Francisco Yacht. Home: 1000 San Francisco St San Francisco CA 94109 Office: U Calif Med Ctr San Francisco CA 94143-0738 *Devoting two afternooons each week to research, teaching and other academic pursuits, uninterrupted by surgery and clinical practice, can result in satisfying advances.*

HINMAN, GEORGE WHEELER, physics educator; b. Evanston, Ill., Nov. 7, 1927; s. Norman Seymour and Bess (Bryan) H.; m. Mary Louise Cauffield, June 19, 1952; children: Norman Field, Lydia Hinman Tukey, Nancy Wheeler. BS in Physics and Math., Carnegie Mellon U., 1947, MS in Physics, 1950, DSc in Physics, 1952. Asst. prof., then assoc. prof. physics Carnegie Mellon U., Pitts., 1952-63; chmn. physics Gen. Atomic Co. subs. Gulf Oil Corp., San Diego, 1963-69; prof. physics, dir. Applied Energy Studies Wash. State U., Pullman, 1969-82, 83—; dir. N.Mex. Energy Research & Devel. Inst., Santa Fe, 1982-83; chair environ. sci. & regional planning, 1989—; cons. Los Alamos (N.Mex.) Nat. Lab., 1976-90, GAO, 1977—, Nat. Nuclear Accreditation Bd., 1992—. Author: Dictionary of Energy, 1983; contbr. articles to profl. jours. Grantee NSF, others. Fellow Am. Phys. Soc.; mem. Am. Nuclear Soc., AAAS, Am. Soc. Engring. Edn. Democrat. Home: 925 SW Fountain St Pullman WA 99163 Office: Wash State U Room 305 Troy Hall Pullman WA 99164

HINSON, ROGER MACK, physician; b. Waynesboro, Tenn., June 6, 1963; s. Gayther McKinley and Betty Frances (Wisdom) H.; m. Denice Elizabeth Moewes, Apr. 28, 1990. BA, David Lipscomb Coll., 1985; MD, George Washington U., 1989. Diplomate Nat. Bd. Med. Examiners, Am. Bd. Pediatrics. Intern, pediatrics Madigan Army Med. Ctr., Tacoma, Wash., 1989-90, resident, pediatrics, 1990-92; fellow neonatal-perinatal medicine Walter Reed Army Med. Ctr., Washington, 1992—. Contbr. articles to profl. jours. Maj. USAR, 1985—. Fellow Am. Acad. Pediatrics (tng.). Mem. Ch. of Christ. Office: Madigan Army Med Ctr Dept Pediatrics Tacoma WA 98431

HINSVARK, DON GEORGE, social services agency professional; b. Helena, Mont., Mar. 27, 1934; s. Almer Burton and Carmen Christine Hinsvark; m. Jacqueline Rica Sarfati, July 10, 1958; children: Jon Felix, Timothy Joel, Michael David, Symone Hinsvark Sass. BA, U. So. Calif., 1956; MA in

Tchg. and Counseling, San Diego State U., 1967; postgrad., sch. adminstrn. cert., U. La Verne, 1984-86; Cert. Career Counseling/Legal Asst., U. Calif.-San Diego, 1994. Cert. tchr. gen. elem. and jr. high edn., sch. adminstrn., sch. counselor, Calif. Tchr. San Diego (Calif.) City Schs., 1962-65, dist. counselor, 1965-85, dist. counselor team leader, 1985-91, chmn. sch. attendance rev. bd., 1992; career counselor Dyasayd Consultation, San Diego, 1993; program supr. Voices for Children, San Diego, 1994—; mem. San Diego Commn. on Children, Youth and Families, 1994—, adv. bd. San Diego State U. Sch. Social Work, 1993-95; adv. bd., instr. U. La Verne (Calif.), Edn. Dept., 1984-88; presenter in field. Joint author: Crisis Team Handbook, 1988; contbr. articles to profl. jours. Coach Age Group Swim Team, Coronado, Calif., 1962, Pop Warner Football, Coronado, 1970-71; coach and mgr. Little League Baseball, Coronado, 1970-75, Sr. Little League Baseball, Coronado, 1976-77. Lt. USN, 1956-61, Atlantic and Pacific; capt. USNR; commdg. officer Res. Naval Spl. Warfare Staff unit, 1980-82, 84-86. Recipient NROTC scholarship USN, 1952-56; scholar Nat. Def. Edn. Inst., U.S. Govt. 1966, 68. Mem. Calif. Sch. Social Workers Assn. (pres. San Diego chpt. 1972, state area rep. 1979), San Diego City Student Svcs. Assn. (pres. 1983-84, 86-87), Calif. Sch. Counselors Assn. (area rep. 1982-83, 92-93, Area Counselor of Yr. 1992), Calif. Assn. for Counseling and Devel. (pres. San Diego chpt. 1992-93), Kiwanis (v.p., sec. San Diego chpt. 1987, Educator of Yr. 1991), Am. Counseling Assn. Home: 720 Country Club Ln Coronado CA 92118-2038 Office: Voices for Children 2851 Meadow Lark Dr San Diego CA 92123-2709

HINTHORN, MICKY TERZAGIAN, volunteer, retired; b. Jersey City, N.J., July 5, 1924; d. Bedros H. and Aznive (Hynelian) Terzagian; m. Wayne L. Hinthorn, Aug. 11, 1957. BS in Occupational Therapy, U. So. Calif., 1953; MBA, Coll. Notre Dame, Belmont, Calif., 1984. Registered occupational therapist. Gen. office worker Drake Secretarial Coll., Jersey City, 1941-42; sec., expediter Western Electric Co., Kearny, N.J., 1943-45; sec. div. edn. CBS, NYC, 1945-46; sec. to v.p. sales Simon and Schuster, Inc., NYC, 1947-51; gen. office worker in Sch. of Edn. U. So. Calif., L.A., 1951-52; occupational therapist Palo Alto (Calif.) Clinic, 1954-55; chief occupational therapist Children's Health Coun., Palo Alto, 1954-56; sec. to chief mil. engr. Lenkurt Electric Co., San Carlos, Calif., 1956-58; sr. sec. re-entry program Bank of Am., Redwood City, Calif., 1979-80; ret., 1980; organizer occupational therapy dept. Children's Health Coun., Palo Alto, Calif., 1954, chief 1954-56. Author, editor numerous newsletters and orgns.' papers. Charter mem., membership chair U. So. Calif. Pres. Cir., San Francisco, 1978-80; treas. North Peninsula chpt. San Francisco Opera Guild, San Mateo, Calif., 1979; vol. pub. info. chair re-election San Mateo County Supr., Redwood City, Calif., 1978; founder, charter pres. Friends of Belmont (Calif.) Libr., 1974-75; mem. Coastside Fireworks Com., 1989-94, chair corp. sponsorship, 1992-93. Recipient Hon. Mem., Friends of San Francisco Pub. Libr., 1974. Mem. AAUW (pres. San Mateo br. 1976-77; Half Moon Bay br. chair local scholarships 1992, historian 1992-94, corr. sec. 1995-96, name grant honoree Edn. Found. Jodi Gordon Endowment 1991-92), Half Moon Bay Coastside C. of C. (chair bus. edn. scholarships 1992, 93, Recognition award 1993), Seton Med. Ctr. Coastside Aux. (assoc., scholarship com. 1996-97), U. So. Calif. Alumni Assn. (life), Coll. of Notre Dame Alumni Assn., Friends of Filoli, Friends of Half Moon Bay Libr. Home: PO Box 176 Half Moon Bay CA 94019-0176

HINTON, LESLIE FRANK, media executive; b. Bootle, Lancashire, Eng., Feb. 19, 1944; came to U.S., 1976, naturalized, 1985; s. Frank Arthur and Lilian Amy (Bruce) H.; m. Mary Christine Weadick, Mar. 30, 1968; children: Martin Frank, Thomas Adam, William Daniel, James Arthur, Jane Amy. Reporter Adelaide News, South Australia, 1960-65; desk editor Brit. United Press, London, 1965-66; reporter The Sun, London, 1966-69, 71-76; writer, editor Adelaide News, South Australia, 1969-70; U.S. corr. News Internat., N.Y.C., 1976-78; news editor The Star, N.Y.C., 1978-80, mng. editor, 1980-82; assoc. editor Boston Herald, 1982-85; editor-in-chief Star Mag., 1985-87; exec. v.p. Murdoch Mags., N.Y.C., 1987-90, pres., 1990-91; pres., chief exec. officer News Am. Pub., Inc., N.Y.C., 1991-93; chmn., CEO Fox TV Stations Inc, Fox News Inc., L.A., 1993-94; exec. v.p. strategic planning Fox TV Group, Nowin, London, 1994—. Office: Fox TV Group, 31-32 Soho Sq, London 6AP, England*

HINZ, SHIRLEY SORENSEN, administrative secretary; b. Denver, Sept. 28, 1942; m. Dale Edward Hinz, Sept. 3, 1966; children: Andrew Christian, Tammy Lynn Dahl. Student, Ft. Lewis Coll., 1961, Barnes Bus. Coll., 1982; diploma in spl. pub., Inst. Children's Lit., 1994. Adminstrv. asst. USDA, Ft. Collins, Colo., 1989; divsn. sec. U.S. Dept. Energy, Golden, Colo., 1991; sect. sec. U.S. Dept. Interior, Ft. Collins, 1992—; mem. labor mgmt. partnership coun. U.S. Dept. Interior, 1994-95. Contbr. poems to Inten Publs., 75th anniversary edit. CPPA Law Enforcement Jour. Active Ault (Colo.) Sr. Ctr., 1989—. Recipient Editor's Choice award Nat. Libr. Congress, Nat. Libr. Poetry, 1995, 96, Accomplishment of Merit award Creative Arts & Sci. Enterprises, 1996, Nat. Merit Award cert. Larimer County Fed. Exec. Assn., 1996. Mem. Internat. Soc. Poets (disting.), Famous Poets Soc. (Diamond Homer award 1996). Lutheran. Home: PO Box 1063 304 Cherry Ln Ault CO 80610 Office: US Dept of Interior 4512 McMurry Ave Fort Collins CO 80525

HIRANO, IRENE ANN YASUTAKE, museum director; b. L.A., Oct. 7, 1948; d. Michael S. and Jean F. (Ogino) Yasutake; 1 child, Jennifer. BS in Pub. Adminstrn., U. So. Calif., 1970, MPA in Pub. Adminstrn., 1972. Project adminstr. U. So. Calif., 1970-72; assoc. dir. Asian Women's Ctr., 1972-73; nat. project coord., Japanese site supr. Nat. Asian Am. Field Study, L.A., 1973-75; cons. U.S. Dept. Health, Edn. and Welfare, Adminstn. on Aging, San Francisco, 1975; exec. dir. T.H.E. Clinic for Women, Inc., L.A., 1975-88; exec. dir., pres. Japanese Am. Nat. Mus., L.A., 1988—; lectr., spkr. in field. Mem. L.A. Ednl. Alliance for Restructuring Now, 1993—, Pres's. Com. on Arts & Humanities, 1994—, Commn. on Future of Smithsonian Inst., 1993—, L.A. Coalition, 1993—; trustee Malborough Sch., 1993—; co-founder Leadership Edn. for Asian Pacifics, 1983, pres. 1983-86, v.p. 1986-90; pres., bd. dirs. Asian Pacific Am. Support Group, U. So. Calif., 1984-88; bd. dirs. Liberty Hill Found., 1984-88, community funding bd., 1981-84, chairperson Calif. Commn. on the Status of Women, 1981-82, commn. mem., 1976-83, many others. Recipient Nat. Outstanding Asian/Pacific Islander award NEA, 1983, Outstanding Women of the '90's, Robinson's Corp., 1992, Outstanding Svc. award Nat. Women's Polit. Caucus, 1986, Nat. Inst. Women of Color, 1984, Outstanding Alumni award U. So. Calif., 1994, So. Calif. Hist. Soc. Cmty. award, 1995. Office: Japanese Am Nat Mus 369 E 1st St Los Angeles CA 90012-3901*

HIROHATA, DEREK KAZUYOSHI, air force reserve officer; b. Dos Palos, Calif., June 26, 1963; s. Vincent Yoshinobu and Gertrude Sumiko (Kimura) H. BA in Polit. Sci., Calif. State U., Fresno, 1987; grad., Italian Mil. Jump Sch., 1989, USAFE Command & Control Sch., 1990, Brit. Army Jump Sch., 1990; MA in Aerospace Sci., Embry riddle U., Carbondale, 1992; JD, So. Ill. U., Carbondale, 1996. Bar: Calif. Commd. 2d lt. U.S. Air Force, advanced through grades to capt., 1991; ground launched cruise missile launch control officer Italy and U.K., 1988-90; emergency actions officer 501 Tactical Missile Wing, RAF Greenham Common, U.K., 1989-90; chief force mgmt. 513 Svcs. Squadron, RAF Mildenhall, U.K., 1990-92; billeting & food svc. coord., laison officer Air Fete, Eng.; treaty inspector escort Conventional Forces Europe; USAFR, 1993—, 932 SVS ops. officer. Contbr. to poetry anthologies Am. Poetry Soc., 1993, Poets Pen Quarterly, 1993, Memories Anthology, 1994, Delta. Coord. peer support network Sch. Law So. Ill. U., Carbondale, founder, capt. trial advocacy competition team, 1994-95; mem. Jessup Internat. Moot Ct. team. Mem. ABA, ATLA (founder So. Ill. U.-Carbondale chpt.), Calif. State Bar Assn. Am. Psychology and Law Soc., Christian Legal Soc., Internat. Law Soc., So. Ill. U.-Carbondale Student Bar Assn., So. Ill. U.-Carbondale Law & Medicine Soc., Air and Space Smithsonian, Officers' Christian Fellowship, Airforce Assn., Air Force Edn. Soc., U.S. Capitol Hist. Soc., Calif. State U.-Fresno Alumni Orgn., West Coast Karate Assn., Assn. Air Force Missileers (assoc.), Sigma Nu (alumni advisor So. Ill. U.-Carbondale chpt., dist. commdr.), Ill. State Bar Assn., State Bar Calif., Lawyer-Pilots Bar Assn. Republican. Methodist. Home: PO Box 243 South Dos Palos CA 93665-0243

HIRONDELLE, ANNE ELIZABETH, ceramic artist; b. Vancouver, Wash., July 8, 1944; d. John Wayne and Alice G. (Tokola) Harvey; m. Robert Lee Schwiesow, Aug. 26, 1967. BA in English, U. Puget Sound, 1966; MA in Counseling Psychology, Stanford U., 1967; postgrad. Sch. Law, U. Wash., 1972-73; student ceramics program, Factory of Visual Art, Seattle, 1973-74; postgrad., U. Wash., 1974-76. Assoc. dir. U. Wash. YMCA, Seattle, 1967-69, dir., 1969-72; lectr., artist-in-residence, workshop leader Pacific Luth. U., Tacoma, 1980, Multnomah Art Ctr., Portland, 1982, Brookhaven Coll., Farmers Branch, Tex., 1988, Internat. Clay Seminar, Calgary, Alta., Can., 1989, Sonoma State Coll., Santa Rosa, Calif., 1990, Emily Carr Sch. Art and Design, Vancouver, B.C., Can., 1990, Tulane U., New Orleans, 1991, Santa Rosa Jr. Coll., 1991, Newport H. S., Bellevue, 1992, Arrowmont Sch. Arts and Crafts, Gatlinburg, Tenn., 1993, Boise State U., 1993, Craft Students League, N.Y.C., 1994. One person shows include Pacific Luth. U., Tacoma, Wash., 1980, Seattle Ctr., 1985, Lawrence Gallery, Portland, Oreg., 1986, 88, Foster/White Gallery at Frederick & Nelson, Seattle, 1986, Martha Schneider Gallery, Highland Park, Ill., 1987, Franklin House Gallery, Port Townsend, Wash., 1985, 87, 90, Garth Clark Gallery, Kansas City, Mo., 1990, Maveety Gallery, Salishan, Oreg., 1991, Schneider-Bluhm-Loeb Gallery, Chgo., 1992, Joanne Rapp Gallery, Scottsdale, Ariz., 1991, 93, The Works Gallery, Phila., 1991, 94, Garth Clark Gallery, N.Y.C., 1992, 94, Garth Clark Gallery, L.A., 1987, 89, 90, 93, 95; exhibited in group shows Oreg. Sch. Arts and Crafts, Portland, 1979, Sussler Gallery, U. Mich., Ann Arbor, 1980, Henry Gallery, U. Wash., Seattle, 1981, Lawrence Salishan Gallery, Gleneden Beach, Oreg., 1982, Hockaday Ctr. for Arts, Kalispel, Mo., 1983, Bellevue (Wash.) Art Mus., 1984, Tacoma Art Mus., 1984, Foster/White Gallery, Seattle, 1985, 87, 93, Gallery Eight, La Jolla, Calif., 1986, 87, 93, Martha Schneider Gallery, Chgo., 1986, 90, Safeco Plaza, Seattle, 1986, Garth Clark Gallery, N.Y.C., 1986, 87, 88, 89, 91, 92, Susan Cummings Gallery, Walnut Creek, Calif., 1987, Pewabic Pottery, Detroit, 1987, Athenaem Mus., Alexandria, Va., 1988, Lawrence Gallery, Portland, 1988, Faith Nightingale Gallery, San Diego, 1988, 91, Nora Eccles Harrison Mus. Art, Utah State U., Logan, 1989, Cedar Creek Gallery, Creedmore, N.C., 1989, Sonoma State U. Art Gallery, Rohnert, Calif., 1990, Moira-James Gallery, Green Valley, Nev., 1990, 91, Swidler Gallery, Royal Oak, Mich., 1989, 90, 91, The Works Gallery, Phila., Pa., 1990, Am. Craft Mus., N.Y.C., 1991, Conterprary Crafts gallery, Portland, 1991, Pro Art Gallery, St. Louis, 1992, 93, Kirkland (Wash.) Arts Ctr., 1992, MacKenzie Fine Arts Ctr, Dearborn, Mich., 1993, The 1004 Gallery, Port Townsend, Wash., 1993, Craft Alliance, St. Louis, 1993, 94, Ferrin Gallery, Northampton, Mass., 1993, Art Ctr. Gallery Seattle Pacific U., 1993, Schmidt-Bingham Gallery, N.Y.C., 1994, Galleries of Dept. Art Tex. Tech. U., 1994, Artworks Gallery, Seattle, 1994; represented in numerous pub. and pvt. permanent collections including Am. Craft Mus., Ariz. State U. Art Mus., Boise State U., Gateway Tower, Newark Mus., Nora Eccles Harrison Mus. Art, Pacific Lut. U., Oreg. Arts Commn., U. Iowa Mus. Art, The White House, Charles A. Wustum Mus. Fine Arts, others; featured in numerous profl. jours., art. mags., mags. and newspapers. Recipient 1st pl. awards, 1989; Nat. Endowment for Arts visual artist fellow, 1988. *

HIRONO, MAZIE KEIKO, state official; b. Fukushima, Japan, Nov. 3, 1947; came to U.S., 1955, naturalized, 1957; d. Laura Chie (Sato) H. B.A., U. Hawaii, 1970; J.D., Georgetown U., 1978. Dep. atty. gen., Honolulu, 1978-80; house counsel INDEVCO, Honolulu, 1982-83; sole practice, Honolulu, 1983-84, Shim, Tam, Kirimitsu & Naito, 1984-88; mem. Hawaii Ho. of Reps., Honolulu, 1980-94; elected lt. gov., 1994. Del., State Democratic Party Conv., Honolulu, 1972-82; bd. dirs. Nuuanu YMCA, Honolulu, 1982-84, Moiliili Community Ctr., Honolulu, 1984, Mem. U.S. Supreme Ct. Bar, Hawaii Bar Assn., Phi Beta Kappa. Democrat. Office: State Capitol Lt Governor's Office PO Box 3226 Honolulu HI 96801*

HIRSCH, ANTHONY T., physician; b. N.Y.C., Jan. 29, 1940; s. Robert S. and Minna Hirsch; m. Barbara Hershan, July 8, 1961; children: Deborah, Kenneth, Steven. BS cum laude, Tufts U., 1961, MD, 1965. Diplomate Am. Bd. Pediatrics, Am. Bd. Allergy-Immunology. Pvt. practice pediatrics Children's Med. Group, L.A., 1973-84; chair dept. pediatrics, dir. residency tng. program in pediatrics White Meml. Med. Ctr., L.A., 1984—. Capt. USAF, 1969-71. Fellow Am. Acad. Pediatrics (chair access task force Calif. br., mem. nat. access task force, chair coun. on pediatric practice), Am. Acad. Allergy-Immunology. Office: White Meml Med Ctr Dept Pediatrics 414 N Boyle Ave Los Angeles CA 90033-2410

HIRSCH, BETTE G(ROSS), college administrator, foreign language educator; b. N.Y.C., May 5, 1942; d. Alfred E. and Gladys (Netburn) Gross; m. Edward Raden Silverblatt, Aug. 16, 1964 (div. Feb. 1975); children: Julia Nadine, Adam Edward; m. Joseph Ira Hirsch, Jan. 21, 1978; stepchildren: Hillary, Michelle, Michael. BA with honors, U. Rochester, 1964; MA, Case Western Res. U., 1967, PhD, 1971. Instr. and head French dept. Cabrillo Coll., Aptos, Calif., 1973-90, divsn. chair fgn. langs. and comms. divsn., 1990-95, interim dir. student devel., 1995-96, dean, transfer edn., 1996—; mem. steering com. Santa Cruz County Fgn. Lang. Educators Assn., 1981-86; mem. liaison com. fgn. langs. Articulation Coun. Calif., 1982-84, sec., 1983-84, chmn., 1984-85; workshop presenter, 1982—; vis. prof. French Mills Coll., Oakland, Calif., 1983; mem. fgn. lang. model curriculum stds. adv. com. State Calif., 1984; instr. San Jose (Calif.) State U., summers 1984, 85; reader Ednl. Testing Svc. Advanced Placement French Examination, 1988, 89; peer reviewer for div. edn. programs, NEH, Washington, 1990, 91, 93; grant evaluator, NEH, 1995; mem. fgn. lang. adv. bd. The Coll. Bd., N.Y.C., 1986-91. Author: The Maxims in the Novels of Duclos, 1973; co-author (with Chantal Thompson) Ensuite, 1989, 93, Moments Litteraires, 1992 (with Chantal Thompson and Eline Phillips) Mais Oui! workbook, lab. manual, video manual, 1996; contbr. revs. and articles to profl. jours. Pres. Loma Vista Elem. Sch. PTA, Palo Alto, Calif., 1978-79; bd. dirs. United Way Stanford, Palo Alto, 1985-90, mem. allocations com., 1988, bd. dirs. Cabrillo Music Festival, 1996—, Cmty. TV of Santa Cruz County, 1996—. Grantee NEH, 1980-81, USIA, 1992; Govt. of France scholar, 1982. Mem. Am. Coun. on Teaching of Fgn. Langs., Am. Assn. Tchrs. French (exec. coun. No. Calif. chpt. 1980-85), Assn. Calif. C.C. Adminstrs., Assn. Depts. Fgn. Langs. (exec. com. 1985-88, pres. 1988), Modern Lang. Assn. (mem. adv. com. on fgn. langs. and lits. 1995—). Democrat. Jewish. Home: 4149 Georgia Ave Palo Alto CA 94306-3813 Office: Cabrillo College 6500 Soquel Dr Aptos CA 95003-3119 *Treat life like a work of art in progress. Strive for the creative, the exceptional. Do it all with style.*

HIRSCH, DANIEL OREN, public policy organization executive; b. Oakland, Calif., Feb. 12, 1950; s. Werner Zvi and Hilde Esther (Swirn) H. AB magna cum laude, Harvard U., 1972. Pres. Com. to Bridge the Gap, L.A., 1972—; coord. S. Calif. Amnesty Internat., Calif., 1975-77; lectr. UCLA, 1975-83; dir. Adlai E. Stevenson Program on Nuclear Policy U. Calif., Santa Cruz, 1983-89; energy and environment fellow Fedn. Am. Scientists, Washington, 1989; pres. Com. to Bridge the Gap, L.A., 1990—; co-chmn. adv. panel Santa Susana Nuclear Epidemiology Study, 1992—; panel mem. EPA/Inter-Agy. Work Group for Dept. of Energy/Energy Tech. Engrng. Ctr., 1992—. Contbr. articles to profl. jours. Recipient Environment award UN Environment Programme, 1996, Jennings award So. Calif. Fedn. Scientists, 1997; Stevenson Coll. fellow, 1984-89. Mem. Fedn. Am. Scientists (nat. coun. 1988). Office: Committee to Bridge the Gap 1637 Butler Ave #203 Los Angeles CA 90025

HIRSCH, RICHARD G., lawyer; b. L.A., June 15, 1940; s. Charles and Sylvia (Leopold) H.; m. Claire Renee Recsei, Mar. 25, 1967; 1 child, Nicole Denise. BA, UCLA, 1961; JD, U. Calif., Berkeley, 1965. Bar: Calif. 1967, U.S. Dist. Ct. (ctrl. dist.) Calif. 1967, U.S. Supreme Ct. 1972, U.S. Ct. Appeals (9th cir.) 1989, U.S. Dist. Ct. (ea. dist.) Calif. 1991. Dep. dist. atty. L.A. Dist. Atty.'s Office, 1967-71; ptnr. Nasatir, Hirsch & Podberesky, Santa Monica, Calif., 1971—; commr. Calif. Coun. Criminal Justice, 1977-81; mem. Spl. Com. on Cts. in the Media/Judicial Coun. Calif., 1979. Co-author: California Criminal Law Proceedings/Practice, 1986, 2d edit. 1994. Pres. bd. trustees Santa Monica Mus. Art, 1984-91; chmn. Greek Theatre Adv. Com., L.A., 1976-79; mem. L.A. Olympic Organizing Com., 1981-84; bd. dirs. Ocean Park Cmty. Ctr., 1995—. Recipient Spl. Merit Resolution, L.A. City Coun., 1984, Criminal Def. of Yr. award Century City Bar Assn., 1996. Fellow Am. Bd. Criminal Lawyers; mem. Calif. Attys. Criminal Justice (pres. 1987, bd. trustees), Criminal Cts. Bar Assn. (pres. 1981, Spl. Merit award 1988), Santa Monica C. of C. (bd. dirs. 1995—). Office: Nasatir Hirsch Podberesky 2115 Main St Santa Monica CA 90405-2215

HIRSCH, STEVEN A., lawyer; b. Ariz., 1955. BA with distinction, U. Ariz., 1977, JD with high distinction, 1980. Bar: Ariz. 1980; cert. real estate specialist State Bar Ariz. Law clerk to Hon. James D. Hathaway Ariz. Ct. Appeals Divsn. 2, 1980-81; ptnr. Bryan Cave, Phoenix, Ariz. Editorial bd. Ariz. Bar Jour., 1986-89. Fellow Ariz. Bar Found. (bd. dirs. 1989-97, pres. 1995); mem. ABA (del. and dist. rep. young lawyers divsn. assembly 1990-92), Maricopa County Bar Assn. (bd. dirs. 1987-88), Order of Coif. Office: Bryan Cave 2800 N Central Ave Fl 21 Phoenix AZ 85004-1007

HIRSCH, WALTER, economist, researcher; b. Phila., Apr. 21, 1917; s. Arnold Harry and Ann Belle (Feldstein) H.: m. Leanore Brod, Feb. 12, 1939 (dec. 1985); stepchild, Stephen M. Gold; children: Jeffrey A., Robert A.; m. June Freedman Gold Clark, Dec. 16, 1986. BS in Econs., U. Pa., 1938; LLD (hons.), Chapman Coll., 1968. Economist U.S. Bur. Stats., Washington and N.Y.C, 1946-50, Dept. USAF, Washington, 1950-51, Nat. Prodn. Auth., Washington, 1952-53; dir. indsl. mobilization Bur. Ordnance Dept. USN, Mechanicsburg, Pa., 1954-56; ops. rsch. analyst Bur. Supplies and Accts. Dept. USN, Arlington, Va., 1956-58; economist, ops. rsch. analyst Internat. Security Affairs Office Sec. of Def., Arlington, 1958-61; chief ops., rsch. analyst Gen. Svcs. Adminstrn., Washington, 1961-63; ops. rsch. analyst Spl. Projects Office Sec. of Def., Arlington, 1963-67; dir. ednl. rsch. U.S. Office Edn., San Francisco, 1967-72; cons. on loan to Office of Dean Acad. Planning San Jose (Calif.) State U., 1972-74. Author: Unit Man-Hour Dynamics for Peace or War, 1957, Internal Study for Office Secretary of Defense: Sharing the Cost of International Security, 1961. Vol. De Young Mus., San Francisco, 1981-84, Calif. Palce of Legion of Honor, Phila. Mus. Art, 1984-86; pres. Met. Area Reform Temples, Washington, Nat. Fedn. Temple Brotherhoods; supporter Phila. Orch., San Francisco Symphony, San Francisco Conservatory Music, Curtis Inst. With USAAF, 1942-46. Recipient Meritorious Civilian Svc. award Navy Dept., 1956. Mem. Pa. Athletic Club, Commonwealth Club of Calif., World Affairs Council, Press Club of San Francisco, Phi Delta Kappa.

HIRSCH, WERNER ZVI, economist, educator; b. Linz, Germany, June 10, 1920; came to U.S., 1946, naturalized, 1955; s. Waldemar and Toni (Morgenstern) H.; m. Hilde E. Zwirn, Oct. 30, 1945; children: Daniel, Joel, Ilona. BS with highest honors, U. Calif., Berkeley, 1947, PhD, 1949. Instr. econs. U. Calif., 1949-51; econ. affairs officer UN, 1951-52; economist Brookings Instn., Washington, 1952-53; asst. rsch. dir. St. Louis Met. Survey, 1956-57; prof. econs. Washington U., St. Louis, 1953-63, dir. Inst. of Urban and Regional Studies; economist Resources for Future, Inc., Washington, 1958-59; dir. Inst. Govt. and Pub. Affairs UCLA, 1963-73, prof. econs., 1963—; mem. senate acad. coun. U. Calif., 1985-87, 89-91; mem. acad. senate faculty welfare com. U. Calif., 1984-96, exec. bd. acad. senate UCLA, 1996—, chairperson univ. faculty welfare com., 1985-87, 89-91, mem. restructure task force, 1993-95, long-range planning com., 1995—, scholar in residence Rockefeller Study Ctr., 1978; cons. Rand Corp., 1958—, U.S. Senate Com. on Pub. Works, 1972, Calif. Senate Select Com. on Structure and Adminstrn. Pub. Edn., 1973, Joint Econ. Com. of Congress, 1975-76, OECD, 1977-80; mem. com. to improve productivity of Govt. Com. Econ. Devel., 1975-76; chmn. L.A. City Productivity Adv. Com., 1982-85; active Transit Rsch. Panel of NRC, 1993-96. Author: Introduction to Modern Statistics, 1957, Analysis of the Rising Costs of Education, 1959, Urban Life and Form, 1963, Elements of Regional Accounts, 1964, Regional Accounts for Public Decisions, 1966, Inventing Education for the Future, 1967, The Economics of State and Local Government, 1970, Regional Information for Government Planning, 1971, Fiscal Crisis of America's Central Cities, 1971, Program Budgeting for Primary and Secondary Public Education, 1972, Governing Urban America in the 1970s, 1973, Urban Economic Analysis, 1973, Local Government Program Budgeting: Theory and Practice, 1974, Recent Experiences with National Planning in the United Kingdom, 1977, Law and Economics: An Introductory Analysis, 1979, 2d rev. edit., 1988, Higher Education of Women: Essays in Honor of Rosemary Park, 1978, Social Experimentation and Economic Policy, 1981, The Economics of Municipal Labor Markets, 1983, Urban Economics, 1984, Economist's Role in Government at Risk, 1989, Public Finance and Expenditures Under Federalism, 1990, Privatizing Government Services, 1991; mem. editl. bd. Pakistani Jour. Applied Econs., 1980—, Internat. Rev. Law and Econs., 1985-88, Urban Affairs Quar., 1991-94. Bd. dirs. Calif. Coun. Environ./Econ. Balance, 1974—, Calif. Found. on Economy, 1979-89, U. Calif. Retirement Sys., 1986-94, Wilstein Inst.; mem. bd. govs. Edmund G. Brown Inst., 1981-86; mem. UCLA Bldg. Authority, 1984-87, UCLA Coun. on Planning and Budget, 1995—; pres. Am. Friends of Wilton Pk., 1983-85, Friends of Graphic Arts, 1974-79; mem. exec. com. regional bd. Anti-Defamation League, 1986—; trustee U. Art Mus., Berkeley, 1991—; gov. U. Calif. Faculty Ctr., 1992-94. Mem. Am. Econ. Assn., Am. Farm Econs. Assn., Western Regional Sci. Assn. (bd. dirs., pres. 1978-80), Law and Econs. Assn., Soc. for Advancement of Socio-Econs., Town Hall West (pres. 1978-79), L.A. World Affairs Coun., Phi Beta Kappa, Sigma Xi. Home: 11601 Bellagio Rd Los Angeles CA 90049-2112 Office: U Calif Dept Econs Los Angeles CA 90024-1477

HIRSCHFELD, A. BARRY, printing executive; b. Denver, Aug. 18, 1942; m. Arlene Friedman; 2 children. BS, Calif. State Poly. U., 1964; MBA, U. Denver, 1966. Pres. A.B. Hirschfeld Press, Denver, 1966—. Mem. Colo. Concern; past bd. chmn. Denver Art Mus.; past chmn., exec. com. Denver Met. Conv. and Visitors Bur., life trustee; bd. dirs. Pub. Svc. Co. of Colo.; bd. govs. 9Who Care; mem. endowment com., past bd. Allied Jewish Fedn.; bd. dirs. Boettcher Found., Boy Scouts Am., Mountain States Employers Coun., pres. 1997—, Nat. Conf. Christians and Jews, Rocky Mountain Multiple Sclerosis Ctr.; mem. Mayor's Adv. com., Denver, many others. Recipient U. Denver Founders Day Award for cmty. svc., 1991, Humanitarian of Yr. award Nat. Jewish Ctr., 1988, Martin Luther King Jr. Social Responsibility award, 1987, Best of Bus. award Colo. Bus. Mag., 1996. Mem. Met. Denver Exec. Club (past pres., past bd. dirs.), Mile Hi Stadium Club (v.p.), One Hundred Club of Denver. Office: 5200 Smith Rd Denver CO 80216

HIRSCHFELD, GERALD JOSEPH, cinematographer; b. N.Y.C., Apr. 25, 1921; s. Ralph and Kate (Zirker) H.; m. Sarnell Ogus, June 5, 1945 (div. June 1972); children—Alec, Marc, Eric, Burt; m. Julia Warren Tucker, July 28, 1981. Student, Columbia U., 1938-40. Cinematic instr. New Inst. for Film, Bklyn., 1947-49; freelance dir. photography for TV and Film N.Y.C., 1949-54; dir. photography, v.p. MPO Videotronics, Inc., N.Y.C., 1954-72; free-lance dir. and cameraman, cinematographer, N.Y.C. and Hollywood, Calif., 1972—; cinema instr. Am. Film Inst., L.A., 1980, Tahoe Film and Video Workshop, Lake Tahoe, Nev., 1984, Washington Film and Video Assn., 1987; staff mem. Internat. Film and Video Workshops, Rockport, Maine, 1996-97. Cinematographer for films including: Young Frankenstein, My Favorite Year, Diary of a Mad Housewife, The Neon Empire (ACE award nomination 1990); author: Image Control, 1992 (Kraszna-Krausz Internat. Book Award 1994). With Signal Corps, U.S. Army, 1941-45. Recipient Billy Bitzer award Internat. Photographers of the Motion Picture Industry, 1994. Mem. Internat. Photographer's Union, Internat. Alliance Theatrical Stage Employees, Am. Soc. Cinematographers. Home and Office: 361 Scenic Dr Ashland OR 97520-2623

HIRSCHFIELD, ALAN J., entrepreneur. B.S., U. Okla.; M.B.A., Harvard U. V.p. Allen & Co., Inc., 1959-67; v.p. fin., dir. Warner Bros. Seven Arts, Inc., 1967-68; with Am. Diversified Enterprises, Inc., 1968-73; pres., chief exec. officer Columbia Pictures Industries, N.Y.C., 1973-78; vice chmn., chief operating officer 20th Century-Fox Film Corp., L.A., 1979-81; chmn. bd., chief exec. officer 20th Century-Fox Film Corp., 1981-85; cons., investor entertainment industries, L.A., 1985-89; mng. dir. Wertheim Schroder & Co., L.A., 1990-92; co-CEO Data Broadcasting Corp., 1990—; bd. dirs. Cantel Internat., Inc., Chyron Inc., George Gustav Heye Ctr. Nat. Mus. Am. Indian, 1997. Bd. dirs. George Gustav Heye Ctr. Nat. Mus. Am. Indian, 1997—. Office: PO Box 7443 Jackson WY 83002-7443

HIRSCHLER, MARCELO MIGUEL, fire science consultant; b. Buenos Aires, Argentina, May 8, 1947; came to U.S., 1984; s. Esteban Jorge and Ana Margarita Sussman (Fraenkel) H.; m. Nora Victoria Idelsohn, Aug. 15, 1973; children: Georgina Evelyn, David Derek. Licentiate in Chemistry, U. Buenos Aires, 1970, D of Chemistry, 1975. Undergrad. tchg. asst. Sch. Exact & Natural Scis. U. Buenos Aires, 1970-71, postgrad. rsch. asst. Sch. Pharmacy & Biochemistry, 1971-75; rschr. R&D Dept. ALUAR Aluminio Argentino, Buenos Aires, 1975; temporary lectr. physical chemistry The City U., London, 1977-84; R&D assoc. chem. group BF Goodrich Co., Avon

Lake, Ohio, 1984-86, sr. R&D assoc. geon vinyl divsn., 1986-91; fire sci. cons. GBH Internat., Rocky River, Ohio, 1995, Mill Valley, Calif., 1995—. Author: The Combustion of Organic Polymers, 1981; assoc. editor Fire and Materials Jour., 1991—, Fire Hazard and Fire Risk Assesment, 1992, Carbonmonoxide and Human Lit., 1993, Fire Colorinary, 1995; mem. editl. bd. Fire Safety Jour., Jour. Fire Scis., Fire and Flammability Bulletin; contbr. 300 articles to profl. jours. Sec. bd. dirs. Beth Israel The West Temple, Cleve., 1987-91; bd. trustees Oakwood Beach Assn., Rocky River, 1989-95. Mem. ASTM (E-5 Cert. Appreciation 1989, Frank W. Reinhardt award 1990, E-5 Award Recognition 1995, chmn. subcom. fire and furnishings, sec. subcoms. planning fire standards, U.K. Royal Soc. Chemistry (chartered chemist), Soc. Fire Protection Engrs., Nat. Fire Protection Assn. (mem. tech. com. on fire tests, nat. electric code panel 15, nat. life safety code com. on furnishings & contents, com. on hazard and risk of contents & furnishings), Combustion Inst. , Fire Retardant Chems. Assn., Internat. Assn. Fire Safety Sci., Soc. Plastics Engrs., Soc. Plastics Industry.

HIRSH, DWIGHT CHARLES, III, microbiologist; b. L.A., Oct. 5, 1938; s. Dwight Charles and Elizabeth Curtice H.; m. Lucy M. Tuschak; children: Dwight C. IV, Elizabeth M. BS, Loyola U., L.A., 1960; DVM, U. Calif., Davis, 1966; PhD, Stanford U., 1972. Asst. prof. microbiology U. Mo., Columbia, 1972-74; from asst. to assoc. prof. microbiology U. Calif., Davis, 1974-83, prof. microbiology, 1983—. Recipient Norden Disting. Tchr. award U. Calif. Sch. Vet. Med., 1980, 90, Disting. Tchr. award U. Calif. Acad. Senate, 1994. Mem. K.C. (fin. sec. 1990—). Republican. Roman Catholic. Office: Univ Calif Sch Vet Med Davis CA 95616

HIRST, WILMA ELIZABETH, psychologist; b. Shenandoah, Iowa; d. James H. and Lena (Donahue) Ellis; m. Clyde Henry Hirst (dec. Nov. 1969); 1 child, Donna Jean (Mrs. Alan Robert Goss). AB in Elementary Edn., Colo. State Coll., 1948, EdD in Ednl. Psychology, 1954; MA in Psychology, U. Wyo., 1951. Lic. psychologist, Wyo. Elem. tchr., Cheyenne, Wyo., 1945-49, remedial reading instr., 1949-54; assoc. prof. edn., dir. campus sch. Nebr. State Tchrs. Coll., Kearney, 1954-56; sch. psychologist, head dept. spl. edn. Cheyenne (Wyo.) pub. schs., 1956-57, sch. psychologist, guidance coordinator, 1957-66, dir. rsch. and spl. projects, 1966-76, also pupil personnel, 1973-84; pvt. cons., 1984—; vis. asst. prof. U. So. Calif., summer 1957, Omaha U., summer 1958, U. Okla., summers 1959, 60; vis. assoc. prof. U. Nebr., 1961, U. Wyo., summer 1962, 64, extension divsn., Kabul, Afghanistan, 1970, Cath. U., Goias, Brazil, 1974; investigator HEW, 1965-69; prin. investigator effectiveness of spl. edn., 1983-84; participant seminar Russian Press Women and Am. Fedn. Press Women, Moscow and Leningrad, 1973. Sec.-treas. Laramie County Coun. Community Svcs., 1962; mem. speakers bur., mental health orgn.; active Little Theatre, 1936-60, Girl Scout Leaders Assn., 1943-50; mem. Adv. Coun. on Retardation to Gov.'s Commn.; mem., sec. Wyo. Bd. Psychologist Examiners, 1965-71 vice chmn., 1971-74; chmn. Mayor's Model Cities Program, 1969; mem. Gov.'s Com. Jud. Reform, 1972; adv. council Div. Exceptional Children, Wyo. Dept. Edn., 1974; mem. transit adv. group City of Cheyenne, 1974; bd. dirs. Wyo. Children's Home Soc., 1968, treas., 1978-84; rsch. on women's prisons State of Wyo., 1989; bd. dirs. Goodwill Industries Wyo., chmn., 1981-83; mem. Wyo. exec. com. Partners of Americas, 1970-86; del. Internat. Conv. Ptnrs. of Ams., Jamaica, 1987; del., moderator pers. com. Presbytery of Wyo., 1987-90, mem. mission program com., 1991-95, spl. gifts com. 1994—; bd. dirs. workforce opportunities adv. com. AARP, 1992-94; Friendship Force ambassador to Honduras, 1979; chmn. bd. SE Wyo. Mental Health Center, 1969; elder 1st Presbyn. Ch., Cheyenne, 1978—, also bd. deacons; chmn. adv. assessment com. Wyo. State Office Handicapped Children, 1980, 81; mem. allocations com. United Way of Laramie County, active People to People Internat., Child Welfare Project, 1992; participant People to People Internat. Citizen Amb. Program, child welfare project assist Lithuania, Latvia, Estonia, 1992. Named Woman of Year, Cheyenne Bus. and Profl. Women, 1974. Diplomate Am. Bd. Profl. Psychology. Fellow Am. Acad. Sch. Psychology; mem. APA, ASCD, Internat. Council Psychologists (chmn. Wyo. div. 1980-85), AAUP, Am. Assn. State Psychology Bds. (sec.-treas. 1970-73), Wyo. Psychol. Assn. (pres. 1962-63), Laramie County Mental Health Assn. (bd. mem., corr. sec. 1963-69, pres.), Wyo. Mental Health Assn. (bd. mem.), Internat. Platform Assn., Am. Ednl. Research Assn., Assn. for Gifted (Wyo. pres. 1964-65), Am. Personnel and Guidance Assn., Am. Assn. Sch. Adminstrs., NEA (life, participant seminar to China 1978), AAUW, Cheyenne Assn. Spl. Personnel and Prins. (pres. 1964-65, mem. exec. bd. 1972-76), Nat. Fedn. Press Women (dir. 1979-85), DAR (vice regent Cheyenne chpt. 1975-77), AARP (state coordinator 1988—, preretirement planning specialist 1986-88, state coord. work force program, 1992—, leadership coun., state del. nat. conv. 1990, pilot project Wyo. state delivery for retirement planning 1990—, AARP Works, op. project state govt. edn. assn. and AARP work force vols. video for retirement planning statewide 1993, master trainer retirement planning 1993—, employment planning master trainer, 1994—, planning com. Area 8 Conf., leadership meeting 1994, mem. adv. coun. Laramie County Widowed Persons Svcs. 1995—, bd. dirs. 1996—), Psi Chi, Kappa Delta Pi, Pi Lambda Theta, Alpha Delta Kappa (pres. Wyo. Alpha 1965-66). Presbyn. Lodge Soc. Colonial Dames XVII Century, Order Eastern Star, Daus. of Nile. Clubs: Wyo. Press Women, Zonta (pres. Cheyenne 1965-66, treas. dist. 12 1974). Author: Know Your School Psychologist, 1963; Effective School Psychology for School Administrators, 1980. Home and Office: 3458 Green Valley Rd Cheyenne WY 82001-6124 *I've found that life's greatest satisfaction comes from making a positive difference.*

HIRSTEL, ROBERT, labor relations consultant; b. Portland, Oreg., Oct. 10, 1917; s. Edward and Pearl (Jacob) H.; m. Aida Dibar, June 14, 1944; children: Coco, Denise Hirstel Shaughnessy. BS, Oreg. State U., 1941; MS, NYU, 1942. Supt., pers. dir. Dept. Store Lipman North, Portland, Oreg., 1947-55; labor rels. cons. Seattle and Portland, 1955—. Capt. U.S. Army, 1942-47, ETO. Mem. Met. Opera Nat. Coun., Wash. Athletic Club, Rainzer Club, Seattle Opera Assn. (bd. dirs. 1975-90). Home: 9228 SE 59th St Mercer Island WA 98040-5021 Office: 1218 3rd Ave Ste 2101 Seattle WA 98101-3072

HIRT, CYRIL WILLIAM, physicist; b. Flushing, N.Y., Dec. 20, 1936; s. Cyril W. and Margret E. (Plumb) H.; m. Virginia L. Warren, June 22, 1968; children: Heather, Amber. BS, U. Mich., 1958, MS, 1959, PhD, 1963. Staff scientist Los Alamos (N.Mex.) Nat. lab., 1963-72, group leader, 1973-80; chief scientist Sci. Applications Inc., La Jolla, Calif., 1972-73; founder, pres. Flow Sci. Inc., Los Alamos, 1980—. Contbr. numerous articles to profl. jours. Office: Flow Sci Inc 1257 40th St Los Alamos NM 87544-3217

HISAKA, ERIC TORU, plastic surgeon; b. Stockton, Calif., 1951. MD, U. Calif., Davis, 1977. Plastic surgoen Valley Care Hosp., Pleasanton, Calif.; also with Tri Valley Surgical Ctr., Pleasanton, Calif. Office: 5720 Stoneridge Mall Rd # 13 Pleasanton CA 94588-2828*

HISE, MARK ALLEN, dentist; b. Chgo., Jan. 17, 1950; s. Clyde and Rose T. (Partipilo) H. AA, Mt. San Antonio Coll., Walnut, Calif., 1972; BA with highest honors, U. Calif., Riverside, 1974; MS, U. Utah, 1978; DDS, UCLA, 1983. Instr. sci. NW Acad., Houston, 1978-79; chmn. curriculum med. coll. prep program UCLA, 1980-85; instr. dentistry Coll. of Redwoods, Eureka, Calif., 1983; practice dentistry Arcata, Calif., 1983—; participant numerous radio and TV appearances. Editor: Preparing for the MCAT, 1983-85; contbr. articles to profl. jours.; speaker in field. Henry Carter scholar U. Calif., 1973, Calif. State scholar 1973, 74, Rgents scholar U. Calif., 1973; Calif. State fellow, 1975, NIH fellow, 1975-79. Mem. AAAS, ADA, Calif. Dental Assn., Acad. Gen. Dentistry, Nat. Soc. for Med. Rsch., North Coast Scuba Club. Roman Catholic. Home and Office: 1225 B St Arcata CA 95521-5936

HISERT, GEORGE A., lawyer; b. Schenectady, N.Y., Sept. 18, 1944. BS summa cum laude, Brown U., 1966, MS, 1966; JD cum laude, U. Chgo., 1970. Bar: Calif. 1971. Law clk. to Hon. Sterry R. Waterman U.S. Ct. Appeals (2nd cir.), 1970-71; ptnr. McCutchen, Doyle, Brown & Enersen, San Francisco, 1977-93; now ptnr. Brobeck, Phleger & Harrison. Mem. editl. bd. Chgo. Law Rev., 1969-70; ABA sect. on bus. law liaison to UCC Permanent Editl. Bd. Mem. ABA (subcom. letter of credit, subcom. secured trans. of uniform comml. code com. bus. law sect., subcom. on syndications and loan participations of comml fin. svc. com., bus. law sect.), Internat. Bar Assn. (banking law com., bus. law sect.), State Bar Calif. (uniform comml. code com. bus. law sect., vice-chair 1992-93, chair 1993-94), Am. Coll.Comml. Fin. Lawyers, Order of Coif, Sigma Xi. Office: Brobeck Phleger & Harrison Spear St Tower One Market Plz San Francisco CA 94105

HISKES, DOLORES G., educator; b. Chgo.; d. Leslie R. and Dagmar (Brown) Grant; m. John R. Hiskes; children: Robin Caproni, Grant. Student, U. Ill., Chgo. Presenter workshops in devel. and implementation of tutoring programs and ednl. materials. Author/illustrator: Phonics Pathways, Pyramid, The Dorbooks, The Short-Vowel Dictionary; developer ednl. games: The Train Game, Blendit!, Wordwatch. Mem. Orton Dyslexia Soc., Learning Disabilities Assn., Nat. Right to Read Found., The Calif. Reading Assn., Pubs. Mktg. Assn., Marin Small Pubs. Assn., Pacific Ednl. Mktg. Assn., Calif. Watercolor Soc., Commonwealth Club of Calif. Office: Dorbooks PO Box 2588 Livermore CA 94551

HISLOP, KARE ELIZABETH, music director, educator; b. Calif., Aug. 20, 1948; m. Donald Lindsay Hislop, Sept. 9, 1967; children: Victoria, Laurel. BA, Chico State Coll., 1969; MA, Calif. State U., Chico, 1976. Cert. elem. and secondary tchr., Calif. Tchr. Red Bluff (Calif.) H.S., 1971-89, Evergreen Sch. Dist., Cottonwood, Calif., 1980, Elkins Sch., Paskenta, Calif., 1989-93; music dir. First United Meth. Ch., Red Bluff, 1980—. Author: Recipies From the Adobe, 1993; co-author: Murder at the Grand Hotel, 1991, Murder in Paradise, 1992, Murder at Mugsy's, 1993, Death in the West, 1994, Death in the Caribbean, 1995, The Speakeasy Caper, 1996. Facilitator Tehama County Child Assault Prevention, Red Bluff, 1990-92; leader, trainer, cons. Sierra Cascade Girl Scout Coun., Red Bluff, 1971—; dir. Christie Hill Ch. Camp, Red Bluff, 1979—. Mem. IDE Adobe Interpretive Assn. (pres. 1991—), Am. Lung Assn. (murder mystery chair 1990-94), Mystery Weavers (pres. 1994—), Kappa Delta Pi. United Methodist.

HISLOP, MERVYN WARREN, health advocate administrator, psychologist; b. Vancouver, B.C., Apr. 26, 1937; s. George and Freda (Wickenden) H.; m. Marilyn Gail Johnson, July 24, 1965; children: Lawren Nyall, Mylene Lorelle. B.A. with honors, U. B.C., 1965; M.A., McMaster U., 1967, Ph.D., 1970. Cert. health adminstr. Dir. behaviour mgmt. services Surrey Place Centre, Ministry of Health, Toronto, Ont., 1970-73; dir. psychol. services Woodlands Ministry of Human Resources, New Westminster, B.C., 1973-78; coordinator life edn. program New Westminster, 1975-77; exec. dir. Riverview Hosp., Port Coquitlam, B.C., 1978-85, Valleyview Hosp., Port Coquitlam, B.C., 1985-86; dir. legis. and regulatory affairs Mental Health Services Div., B.C. Ministry of Health, 1986-89; psychiat. adv. Govt. Alberta, Can., 1989—; research proposal submission cons. Can. Council, 1973; mem. edn. adv. com. Douglas Coll., 1983-86. Demonstration model grantee Province Ont., 1971; province Ont. grad. fellow McMaster U., 1969; recipient David and Jean Bolocan Meml. prize U. B.C., 1965; Nat. Rsch. Coun. Can. scholar, 1965, 66, 67, 68. Mem. Can. Coll. Health Service Execs. (cert.), Can. Inst. Law and Medicine. Home: 17203-57 Ave, Edmonton, AB Canada T6M 1B8

HITCHCOCK, VERNON THOMAS, farmer, lawyer; b. Selma, Ind., Feb. 21, 1919; s. Lucian Elmer and Loda Alice (King) H.; m. Betty Kathryn Orr, May 24, 1949; children: Brenda, Linda, Nancy, Debra, Randolph. BS in Agr., Purdue U., 1940; JD, Stanford U., 1953. Bar: Calif. 1954, U.S. Supreme Ct. 1961. Pilot Southwest Airways, San Francisco, 1946, TWA, Kansas City, Mo., 1947-51; pvt. practice Healdsburg, Calif., 1954-55; dep. atty. gen. State of Calif., Sacramento, 1956; dep. county counsel Sonoma County, Santa Rosa, Calif., 1957-65; exec. dir. Libyan Aviation Co., Tripoli, 1966-67; legal counsel Sonoma County Schs., 1967-82; farm mgr. Selma, Ind., 1975—; originator Freedom Under Law program. Author: The Airline to Infinity. Active Am. Security Council, 1965—. Served to comdr. USNR, 1941-79. Mem. Res. Officers Assn., Naval Order U.S., Commonwealth Club San Francisco, Quiet Birdmen, Odd Fellows. Republican. Episcopalian.

HITCHENS, DAVID WILLIAM, purchasing and health materials management consultant; b. Evanston, Ill., Oct. 16, 1955; s. Matthew Eugene and Annamae (De Caluwe) H.; m. Barbara Steiner, Apr. 26, 1980; children: Sharon, Collette. BA, Marquette U., 1977. Dir. materials mgmt. The Children's Hosp., Denver, 1983-88; materials mgr. Nat. Jewish Ctr. Immunology and Respiratory Medicine, Denver, 1988-95. Roman Catholic. Home: 6800 S Sherman St Littleton CO 80122-1000

HITE, JANET SUE, elementary education educator; b. Logansport, Ind., Feb. 22, 1948; d. Joseph William and Ruth Elizabeth (McVay) H. AA, Palomar Coll, San Marcos, Calif., 1968; BA in English, Pepperdine U., L.A., 1970; MA in Edn., Pepperdine U., Malibu, Calif., 1980. Tchg. and preliminary adminstrv. svcs. credentials, profl. adminstrv. svcs. credential, Calif. Tchr. Graham Elem. Sch., L.A., 1971-75, 76-82, Uniontown (Ky.) Pub. Sch., 1975-76; tchr. Paseo del Rey Fundamental Magnet Sch., Playa del Rey, Calif., 1982-90, magnet coord., 1990-94; magnet coord. Paseo del Rey Natural Sci. Magnet Sch., Playa del Rey, 1994—; master tchr. Pepperdine U., L.A., 1979-90; adj. prof. Loyola Marymount U., Westchester, Calif., 1993—; cons. program quality rev. team L.A. Unified Sch. Dist., 1993-95. Editor: (booklet) Creative Writings, 1980. Co-founder, co-dir. Cultural and Urban Environ. Studies Inc., L.A., 1979-84; active San Dieguito United Meth. Ch. Grantee L.A. Edn. Partnerships, 1983, 90, L.A. Unified Sch. Dist., 1984; recipient Red Apple award Tchr. Remembrance Day Found., 1972, Outstanding Tchr. of Yr. award Westchester C. of C., 1990. Mem. ASCD, Phi Delta Kappa (charter, Pepperdine chpt., newsletter editor 1979-80, treas. 1980-81, 3d v.p. 1981-82, 1st v.p. 1982-83, pres. 1983-84, advisor 1985-95), Loyola Marymount U. chpt. Kappa Delta Pi (charter). Republican. Methodist. Home: 7740 Redlands St Apt M3073 Playa Del Rey CA 90293-8452 Office: Paseo del Rey Natural Sci Magnet Sch 7751 Paseo Del Rey Playa Del Rey CA 90293-8372

HITTLE, GEORGE F., state agency administrator; b. Rawlins, Wyo., Feb. 20, 1935. BS in Agr., U. Wyo., 1962, postgrad., 1974, 82; postgrad., Laramie County (Wyo.) C.C., Cheyenne, 1984, 87, 93, 94. Cert. weed and pest supr.; cert. pesticide applicator. Range conservationist U.S. Dept. of Interior/Bur. Land Mgmt., Rock Springs and Worland, Wyo., 1962-68; weed and pest supr. Hot Spring County Weed and Pest Control Dist., Thermopolis, Wyo., 1971-73; weed and pest coord. Wyo. Dept. Agr., Cheyenne, 1974—. Organizer, project coord.: (videos) Enhancing Resources through Integrated Management Systems, 1992, Explosion in Slow Motion-Weeds on Western Lands, 1994, A Kid's Journey to Understanding Weeds, 1996. Co-author amendment to Fed. Noxious Weed Act, 1990, Guidelines for Coordinated Mgmt. of Undesirable Plants in Wyo., 1990, Wyo. Environ. Pesticide Control Act, 1973, Leafy Spurge Control Act, 1978, 83, rewrite of Wyo. Weed and Pest Control Act, 1979, rewrite of Wyo. Seed Law, 1983, Wyo. Weed and Pest Spl. Mgmt. Program, 1989, rewrite of Fed. Noxious Weed Act; co-founder Intermountain Agr. Found., 1987—; developer, co-organizer Regional Forage Certification Program for Noxious Weed-Free Forage, 1986, 87; co-developer, co-implementer Colo./Wyo. Operation and Inspection Stds. for recycling plastic agr. pesticide containers, 1993; organizer 1st trip to Wash. with Wyo. del. on weed-related issues, 1975. With U.S. Army, 1954-56. Recipient Alvah Elledge award Wyo. Weed and Pest Coun., 1977, Outstanding Svc. award, 1976. Mem. Western Soc. Weed Sci., Weed Sci. Soc. Am., Soc. Range Mgmt., Wyo. Weed and Pest Control Dists., Wyo. Weed and Pest Coun., Intermountain Agr. Found., Intermountain Noxious Weed Adv. Coun. (organizer 1987), Western Weed Coordinating Com. (organizer 1988), Elks. Republican. Office: Wyo Dept Agr PO Box 1901 Cheyenne WY 82003

HIX, PHYLLIS MARIE, lawyer; b. Bloomfield, Iowa, Mar. 28, 1936. Student, U. Iowa, 1954-56; BS in Occupational Therapy cum laude, U. So. Calif., 1959, JD, 1962. Bar: Calif. 1963. Assoc. Lawler, Felix & Hall, 1963, Overton, Lyman & Prince, 1963-66, Dryden, Harrington & Swartz, 1967-74; pvt. practice Kernville, Calif., 1974-76, 88—; ptnr. Kurlander & Hix, San Marino, Calif., 1976-88; mem. commn. on jud. nominees evaluation State of Calif., 1979-81, arbitration panel Los Angeles County Superior Ct.; Mcpl. Judge Pro Tem; Superior Ct. Settlement Officer, arbitrator. Co-author (column) Strange As It Seems. Bd. dirs. Pasadena Tournament of Roses Found., 1994—, treas., 1997. Mem. Calif. Bar Assn. (chmn. resolutions com. 1977, state bar ct., asst. presiding referee, exec. com. 1976-80, bd. govs. 1981-84), L.A. County Bar Assn. (exec. com. 1969-72, chmn. legal med. com. 1974-75, adv. com.), Assn. So. Calif. Def. Counsel (bd. dirs. 1973-75, 77-79), Am. Bd. Trial Advs. (mem. exec. com. 1975-76), Def. Rsch. Inst., Calif. Women Lawyers (founding mem.), Am. Arbitration Assn. (nat. bd. dirs. 1976-80), Am. Indian Bar Assn., Internat. Assn. Def. Counsel, Back Country Horsemen of Calif. (v.p. 1988—), U.S. Marshals Posse, Kern County Sheriff's Mounted Posse. Office: 112 Buena Vista PO Bin DD Kernville CA 93238

HIXON, ROBIN RAY, food service executive, writer; b. Vancouver, Wash., May 4, 1954; s. Charles Donovan and Leona Margaret (Teske) Hixson. Exec. chef, Am. Culinary Fedn., 1972-77; BA in Bus., Purdue U., 1992. Cert. Am. Restaurant Assn., 1992. Apprentice Redlion Inns, Vancouver, 1972-77, exec. chef, 1977-80; exec. chef Hilton Hotel, Baton Rouge, 1981; chief steward Delta Queen Steamboat Co., New Orleans, 1981-86, gen. mgr., 1986-88; exec. chef Icicle Seafoods Inc., Seattle, 1989-92, Sea Spirit Cruise Lines, Inc., 1992-93, Petersburg Fisheries, Inc., Alaska, 1993-96; dir. ops. The Calzone-Co. Inc., Duncan & Ptnrs., Pete's Pizza Inc., Spokane, Wash., 1996—; cons. RSVP Travel Prodns., Inc., Mlps., 1992—. Author: American Regional Cuisines, 1987; contbr. articles to profl. jours. Mem. Nat. Trust for Hist. Preservation, 1982-92, Wash. Hist. Preservation, 1990-92, Oreg. Pub. Broadcasting, 1990-92, N.Y. Met. Opera, 1973-80; performer Peruvian Singers, 1972-74, A Chorus-Line, 1975-76, Spokane's Mens Chorus, 1996—. Mem. Am. Culinary Fedn. (writer 1985-91), Chefs De Cuisine Soc. Oreg. (sgt. at arms 1974-80), N.Y.C. Acad. Theatre and Dance, Am. Film Inst. Democrat. Home: 1701 Broadway St # 262 Vancouver WA 98663-3436 Office: 821 E Sharp Ave Spokane WA 99202-1934

HJELMSTAD, WILLIAM DAVID, lawyer; b. Casper, Wyo., Apr. 4, 1954; s. Alvin Gordon and A. Thecla (Walz) H.; m. Jenny M. Dube, Nov. 27, 1993; children: Jennifer Ashley, Allison Caitlin. AA in Social Sci., Casper Coll., 1974; BS in Psychology, U. Wyo., 1976, JD, 1979. Bar: Wyo. 1979, U.S. Dist. Ct. Wyo. 1979. Dept. county pros. atty. Hot Springs County, Thermopolis, Wyo., 1979-80; asst. pub. defender Natrona County, Casper, Wyo., 1980-82; sole practice, Casper, 1981—. Mem. ATLA, ABA (mem. family law com. 1983-84, adoption com. 1983-84), Wyo. State Bar Assn. (mem. alcohol and substance abuse com., lawyers assistance com. 1988-95), Natrona County Bar Assn., Wyo. Trial Lawyers Assn., Am. Judicature Soc., Acad. Family Mediators, U. Wyo. Alumni Assn., Casper Coll. Alumni Assn., Wyo. Cowboy Shootout Com., Elks, Kiwanis. Home: PO Box 90001 Casper WY 82609-1001

HJORTSBERG, WILLIAM REINHOLD, author; b. N.Y.C., Feb. 23, 1941; s. Helge Reinhold and Anna Ida (Welti) H.; m. Marian Souidee Renken, June 2, 1962 (div. 1982); children—Lorca Isabel, Max William.; m. Sharon Leroy, July 21, 1982 (div. 1985). BA, Dartmouth Coll., 1962; postgrad., Yale U., 1962-63, Stanford U., 1967-68. Ind. author, screenwriter, 1969—; adj. prof. media and theatre arts Mont. State U., 1991—. Author: Alp, 1969, Gray Matters, 1971, Symbiography, 1973, Toro! Toro! Toro!, 1974, Falling Angel, 1978, Tales & Fables, 1985, Nevermore, 1994, films: Thunder and Lightning, 1977, Legend, 1986; co-author TV film: Georgia Peaches, 1980; contbg. editor Rocky Mountain Mag., 1979; contbr. fiction to Realist, Playboy, Cornell Rev., Penthouse, Oui, Sports Illustrated; contbr. criticism to N.Y. Times Book Rev. Recipient Playboy Editorial award, 1971, 78; Wallace Stegner fellow, 1967-68; Nat. Endowment Arts grantee, 1976. Mem. Authors Guild, Writers Guild Am. Home and Office: Main Boulder RT Mc Leod MT 59052

HO, IWAN, research plant pathologist; b. Souzhou, Jiangsu, China, Apr. 15, 1925; came to U.S., 1956; m. Mei-Chun Chang, Nov. 29, 1975; 1 child, Tomur M. BS, Nat. Shanghai U., 1946; MS, La. State U., 1958; PhD, Oreg. State U., 1984. Microbiologist Seattle Pub. Health Dept., 1962-66; research plant physiologist Forestry Scis. Lab., Corvallis, Oreg., 1970—; courtesy asst. prof. Coll. Forestry, Oreg. State U. Mem. Mycol. Soc. Am., Am. Soc. Plant Physiologists, Internat. Soc. Plant Molecular Biology, Sigma Xi. Democrat. Episcopalian. Home: 1686 SW Bullevard St Philomath OR 97370-9538 Office: Forestry Sci Lab Pacific NW Rsch Sta 3200 SW Jefferson Way Corvallis OR 97331-8550

HO, WAN CHUEN, plastic surgeon; b. Hong Kong, China, 1933. MD, U. Hong Kong, 1958. Plastic surgeon Kaiser Permanente Hosp., Bellflower, Calif.; also vol. hand surgeon U. So. Calif. County Hosp. Office: Kaiser Permanente Hosp 9400 Rosecrans Ave Bellflower CA 90706-2217*

HOADLEY, JOSEPH E., retired physician; b. Cainsville, Mo., Jan. 12, 1913; s. Archie Guy Hoadley and Ada Pontius; m. Frances Louise Ross, Aug. 30, 1943; children: Frank R., Jeannette, David Allen, Clyde J. BS in Chemistry, Park Coll., Parkville, Mo., 1938; MD, St. Louis Sch. Medicine, 1943. Tchr. Campbell County Sch. Sys., Gillette, Wyo., 1933-35; med. officer U.S. Army/Tripler Gen. Hosp., Honolulu, 1945-46; chief med. staff Gillette Hosp., 1947-53, 53-79; mem. med. staff VA Hosp., Sheridan, Wyo., 1980-92. Author, pub.: The Homestead Doctor, 1995. Pres. Wyo. divsn. Am. Cancer Soc., Gillette, 1956-59; mem. Campbell County Hosp. Bd., Gillette, 1975-79, Northeastern Wyo. Mental Health Bd., Campbell County, 1976-79. Recipient Svc. award N.E. Mental Health Assn., 1979, Campbell County Meml. Hosp., 1979. Mem. Internat. Coll. Surgeons, Masons, Shriners, Lions. Baptist. Home: 26 N Piney Rd Story WY 82842

HOAG, JOHN ARTHUR, retired bank executive; b. Freeport, N.Y., Sept. 29, 1932; s. John Hoag and Viola (Babcock) Hobson; m. Jeanette Makaio, Dec. 5, 1959; children: Steve, Vanessa, Kanani. BS, U. Mo., 1955; grad., Pacific Coast Banking Sch., Wash., 1970; MBA, U. Hawaii, 1977. Account exec. Walston & Co., N.Y.C., 1960; mgmt. trainee 1st Hawaiian Bank, Honolulu, 1960, br. mgr., Hilo, 1968, Island v.p., 1970-76, sr. v.p., mgr., 1976, exec. v.p. loan group, 1979, pres., 1989-94, also bd. dirs.; vice chmn. bd. dirs., 1994; retired 1st Hawaiian Bank, 1995; pres. 1st Hawaiian Inc., Honolulu, 1991-95, also bd. dirs.; vice chm. 1st Interstate Bank Hawaii, Honolulu, 1991—; vice chmn. of bd., 1994—, ret., 1995; pres., chmn. bd. Hawaii Reserves, Inc.; vice chmn. Pioneer Fed. Savs. Bank. Bd. regents Tokai Internat. Coll., 1992-95, U. Hawaii, 1995—; bd. dirs. Hawaii Med. Svc. Assn., 1981-93, Honolulu Polynesian Cultural Ctr, 1990-93, Kapiolani Med. Ctr. for Women and Children, Honolulu, 1989-95. Capt. USMC, 1955-60. Mem. Pres.' Club U. Hawaii, C. of C. of Hawaii (chmn. bd. 1992-93). Mem. LDS Ch. Office: 1st Hawaiian Bank 1132 Bishop St Ph Honolulu HI 96813-2830 also: 1st Hawaiian Bank PO Box 3200 Honolulu HI 96847-0001

HOANG, DUC VAN, theoretical pathologist, educator; b. Hanoi, Vietnam, Feb. 17, 1926; came to U.S. 1975, naturalized 1981; s. Duoc Van and Nguyen Thi (Tham) H.; m. Mau-Ngo Thi Vu, 7 children. M.D., Hanoi U. Sch. Medicine, Vietnam, 1952; DSc, Open Internat. U., Sri Lanka, 1989. Dean Sch. Medicine Army of the Republic of Vietnam, Saigon, 1959-63; dean Minh-Duc U. Sch. Medicine, Saigon, 1970-71; clin. prof. theoretical pathology U. So. Calif. Sch. Medicine, L.A., 1978—; adj. prof. Emperor's Coll. Traditional Oriental Medicine, Santa Monica, Calif., 1988-91; initiator of attitudinal immunology. Author: Towards an Integrated Humanization of Medicine, 1957; The Man Who Weights the Soul, 1959; Eastern Medicine, A New Direction?, 1970; also short stories; author introdn. to work of Maria Noël, Vietnamese transl. of The Red Rose; translator: Pestis, introduction to the work of Albert Camus, Vietnamese translation of La Peste; editor: The East (co-founder); jour. Les Cahiers de l'Asie du Sud-Est. Founder, past pres. Movement for Fedn. Countries S.E. Asia; co-founder, past v.p. Movement for Restoration Cultures and Religions of Orient; active Vo-Vi Meditation Assn. Am.; mem. The Noetic Inst., 1988—, Internat. Found. for Homeopathy, 1987; founder, pres. Intercontinental Found. for Electro-Magnetic Resonance Rsch., 1989—; coord. Unity and Diversity World Health Coun., 1992—. Named hon. dean The Open Internat. U. of Complementary Medicines, Sri Lanka, 1989; Unity-and-Diversity World Coun. fellow, 1990—. Mem. AAUP, Assn. Clin. Scientists, Am. Com. for Integration Eastern and Western Medicine (founder), Assn. Unitive Medicine (founder, pres.), U. So. Calif. Faculty Member Club (L.A.). Republican. Roman Catholic. Home: 3630 Barry Ave Los Angeles CA 90066-3202

HOARE, TYLER JAMES, sculptor; b. Joplin, Mo., June 5, 1940; s. Melvin James and Dorotha Maude (Beadle) H.; m. Kathy Joyce Quinn, Mar. 9, 1963; 1 dau., Janet Elaine. Student, U. Colo., 1959-60, Sculpture Center, N.Y.C., 1960-61; BFA, U. Kan., 1963; postgrad., Calif. Coll. Arts and Crafts, 1965-67. instr. extension U. Calif. at Berkeley, 1973—; guest lectr. San Francisco Art Inst., San Francisco State Coll. One-man shows include

New Center U.S. Art Gallery, Kansas City, Mo., 1964, Jewish Community Center Gallery, Kansas City, Studio C, Berkeley, Calif., 1965, Derby Gallery, Berkeley, Lucien Labaudt Gallery, San Francisco, 1966, U. Calif.-Berkeley, 1966, Free U. Berkeley Gallery, Fredric Hobb's San Francisco Art Center, 1967, Green Gallery, San Francisco, 1968, St. Mary's Coll., 1969, John Bolles Gallery, San Francisco, 1969, 71, San Francisco State Coll., 1970, Camberwell Sch. Art, London, Eng., 1971, SUNY, Albany, Atherton Gallery, Menlo Park, Calif., 1972, Stanford, 1973, Richmond (Calif.) Art Ctrs., 1983, Calif. State U. Hayward, Keokuk (Iowa) Art Ctr., Olive Hyde Art Ctr., Fremont, Calif., John Bolles Gallery, San Francisco, Cen. Sch. Art & Design, London, 1974, Daly City (Calif.) Civic Ctr., San Mateo (Calif.) Arts Coun./Sunshine Gallery, County of San Mateo Hall of Justice, 1975, Purdue U. Gallery 1, 1976, Spiva Art Ctr., Mo. So. State Coll., 1977, Manner of Speaking, San Franciso, Stuart Gallery, Berkeley, 1978, Studio 718, San Francisco, 1980, Geotrope Gallery, Berkeley, 1981, Studio Nine, Benicia, Calif., Marin County Civic Ctr., San Rafael, 1982, Solano Community Coll., Suison City, Calif., 1983, Oakland Art Assn. Gallery, 1986, Coastal Art League Mus., Half Moon Bay, Calif., 1989, Barrett Art Gallery, Utica Coll. Syracuse U., 1993, Bedford Gallery, Ctr. for Arts, Walnut Creek, Calif., 1994, Copy Art, Barcelona, 1994, Mus. Artpool, Budapest, 1994, CopyArt, Berlin, 1994, Gallery Without Walls, Australia, 1994, LeSabord Exchange, Quebec, 1994, Internat. MailArt Exposition, Paris, 1994, Xantus Janos Mus., 1994, Group A-Z Vasarely Mus. Budapest, 1994, Santa Barbara Mus. Art, 1994, Artists Stamps, Dallas, 1994, A.I.M. Internat., Seattle, Wash., 1994, Bunnell St. Gallery, Homer, Alaska, 1994, Madrid, Spain, 1994, Osaka, Japan, 1994, Internat. Archive, Piza, Italy, 1994, U. Calif., San Francisco, 1994, Oakland City Hall, 1994, Tarragona Spain, 1994, Galerie Arts Technologiques, Montreal, 1994; exhibited in group shows The Trading Co. II, U. Calif., Berkeley, 1989, Western Wash. U. Bellingham, 1989, Calif. Mus. of Photography, 1989, U. Calif., Riverside, 1989, Eye Tahoe, Venice, Calif., 1989, Holsum Roc Gallery, Chgo., 1989, Cleve. Inst. of Art, 1989, Sonoma State U. Art Gallery, 1989, Rohnert Park, Calif., 1989, Gallery 25, Fresno, Calif., 1989, The Art Store Gallery, L.A., 1989, Art-Pool, Buda-Ray U. Budapest, Hungary, 1989, Jr. Coll. Albany, N.Y., 1989, Ohlone Coll. Art Gallery, Fremont, Calif., 1990, Alcorcon Culture Office, Madrid, N.Y., 1990, Corr. Sch., N.Y.C., Balley Art Gallery, Walnut Creek, Calif., 1990, Mercer Gallery, 1990, Monroe Community Coll. Rochester, N.Y., 1990, Acad. of Art Coll. Gallery, San Francisco, 1990, Sonama State U., 1990, Can. Union, Scarborough, Ont., Can., 1990, Sangamon State U., Springfield, Ill., 1990, Jr. Coll. of Albany, 1990, Adirondack Community Coll., Glen Falls, N.Y., 1990, Contemporary Tech. Art, Museo Internat. De Electrografia, 1990, Monroe Community Coll., Mercer Gallery, Rochester, N.Y., 1991, Wilder Gallery, Los Gatos, Calif., 1991, Buda-Ray U., 1991, Guy Bleus Archives, Belgium, 1991, Art Electro-Images, Paris, 1991, Action Art Internat., Chgo., 1991, Goodwill, Kent, Wash., 1991, Electrografia Museo Internat., Spain, 1991, Contemporary Art Gallery, Aono, Japan, 1991, Shadow Archive, Kenosha, Wis., 1991, U. Art Gallery, Calif. State U., Hayward, 1993, A.C.C.I. Gallery, Berkeley, 1993, Ctr. Visual Arts, Oakland, Calif., 1993, 94, Art Rsch. Ctr., Budapest, 1993, Steering Wheel W. Art Gallery, San Francisco, 1993, Photocopier Art, Ace Art, Winnipeg, Can., 1993, Irvine Arts Ctr., 1993, U. Tex., Dallas, 1993, 10,000 Humans Edicions, Barcelona, 1993, Culver City, Calif., 1993, Monroe C.C., Rochester, N.Y., 1993, Hockey 100 Calgary, Alta., 1993, Fresno Art Mus., 1993, Luther Coll., Decorah, Iowa, 1993, 94, Corridor Gallery Tex. Tech U., Lubbock, 1993, Ctr. d'Art de Baie, St. Paul, Quebec, 1993, AUA Gallery, Lebabnon, N.H., 1993, Artists Book Works, Chgo., 1993, Les Vraies Folies Bergeres, Paris, 1993, Arlington (Va.) Art Ctr., 1993; represented in permanent collections Oakland Mus., Calif., Pasadena Mus., Calif., Calif. Palace of Legion of Honor, San Francisco, San Francisco Mus., Library of Congress, Pratt Graphics Center, Los Angeles County Mus., Cin. Mus., USIA, Washington, SUNY-Albany, Oakland Mus., Calif. Coll. Arts and Crafts, others. Studio: 30 Menlo Pl Berkeley CA 94707-1533

HOBART, BILLIE, education educator, consultant; b. Pitts., Apr. 19, 1935; d. Harold James Billingsley and Rose Stephanie (Sladack) Green; m. W.C.H. Hobart, July 20, 1957 (div. 1967); 1 child, Rawson W. BA in English, U. Calif., Berkeley, 1967, EdD, 1992; MA in Psychology, Sonoma State U., 1972. Cert. tchr., Calif. Asst. prof. Coll. Marin, Kentfield, Calif., 1969-78; freelance cons., writer, 1969—; asst. prof. Contra Costa Coll., San Pablo, Calif., 1986—. Author: (cookbook) Natural Sweet Tooth, 1974, (non-fiction) Expansion, 1972, Purposeful Self: Coherent Self, 1979, (non-fiction) Talking to Dead People, 1996; contbr. articles to profl. jours. Served with WAC, 1953-55. Mem. No. Calif. Coll. Reading Tchrs. Assn. (pres. 1996-98), Mensa, Commonwealth Club San Francisco, Phi Delta Kappa. Home and Office: PO Box 1542 Sonoma CA 95476-1542

HOBART, JEAN ADRIAN, lawyer; b. Lynn, Mass., Aug. 14, 1943; d. Jean Renan and Alison (Norie) Adrian; m. Terry W. von Talge, Feb. 14, 1988; children: Robert, Stephen, Paul, Gary; m. Gerard W. Von Talge, Feb. 14, 1988; stepchildren: Kirsten, Von Talge, Gregory W. Von Talge. AA, Fullerton Coll., 1973; BSL, Western State U., 1976, JD, 1977. Bar: Calif. 1978, U.S. Claims Ct. 1990, U.S. Dist. Ct. (cen. dist.) Calif. 1979, U.S. Dist. Ct. (no. dist.) Calif. 1992. Assoc. Carter & Hobart, Santa Ana, Calif., 1978-80; ptnr. Bostrom & Hobart, Newport Beach, Calif., 1980-82; prin. Law Office Jean Hobart, Irvine, Calif., 1982—. Named to Hall of Fame, Western State U., 1991. Mem. Orange County Women Lawyers (bd. dirs.), Orange County Trial Lawyers Assn. (past bd. dirs., past pres.), Pub. Law Ctr. Orange County (past bd. dirs., v.p. 1988), Orange County Bar Assn. (past bd. dirs.), Consumer Attys. Calif. (past bd. dirs.). Office: 38 Corporate Park Ste 200 Irvine CA 92606-5130

HOBART, WILLIS LEE, editor; b. Corvallis, Oreg., Sept. 15, 1942; s. Irvin Edwin and Lillian Lucille (Wilson) H.; children: Todd, Ryan, Bradley. BS in Fish and Wildlife Mgmt., Oreg. State U., 1965. Reporter Lincoln County Leader, Toledo, Oreg., 1966; editor Sandy (Oreg.) Post, 1967; editor edn. and agr. Daily Courier, Grants Pass, Oreg., 1967-68; asst. dir. conservation dept. NRA, Washington, 1968-73; mng. editor Marine Fisheries Rev. U.S. Nat. Marine Fisheries Svc., Seattle, 1973-76, editor Marine Fisheries Rev., 1977—, office dir. sci. publs., 1991—; freelance outdoor writer and photographer, 1965—. Author, editor: Conservation Action Handbook, 1968, Baird's Legacy: History of U.S.F.C.-NMFS, 1995; co-editor: Our Living Oceans, 1991, Molluscan Shellfisheries of Europe and North America, 3 vols., 1997; editor: (jour.) Marine Fisheries History, 1988. Mem. Am. Fisheries Soc., Outdoor Writers Assn. Am., Wildlife Soc., Northwest Outdoor Writers Assn. Office: Nat Marine Fisheries Svc Sci Publ Office 7600 Sand Point Way NE Seattle WA 98115-6349

HOBBS, GREGORY J., JR., judge; b. Gainesville, Fla., Dec. 15, 1944; s. Gregory J. Hobbs and Maryann (Rhodes) Frakes; m. Barbara Louise Hay, June 17, 1967; children: Daniel Gregory, Emily Mary Hobbs Wright. BA, U. Notre Dame, 1966; JD, U. Calif., Berkeley, 1971. Bar: Colo. 1971, Calif. 1972. Law clk judge William E. Doyle 10th U.S. Cir. Ct. Appeals, Denver, 1971-72; assoc. Cooper, White & Cooper, San Francisco, 1972-73; enforcement atty. U.S. EPA, Denver, 1973-75; asst. atty. gen. State of Colo. Atty. Gen.'s Office, Denver, 1975-79; ptnr. Davis, Graham & Stubbs, Denver, 1979-92; shareholder Hobbs, Trout & Racey, P.C., Denver, 1992-96; justice Colo. Supreme Ct., Denver, 1996—; counsel No. Colo. Water Conservancy, Loveland, Colo., 1979-96. Contbr. articles to profl. jours. vol. Peace Corps-S.Am., Colombia, 1967-68; vice chair Colo. Airquality Control Com., Denver, 1982-87; mem. ranch com. Philmount Scout Ranch, Boy Scouts Am., Cimarron, N.Mex., 1988—; co-chair Eating Disorder Family Support Group, Denver, 1992—. Recipient award of merit Denver Area Coun. Boy Scouts, 1993, Pres. award Nat. Water Resources Assn., Washington, 1995. Mem. Colo. Bar Assn., Denver Bar Assn. Office: Colo Supreme Ct 2 E 14th Ave Denver CO 80203

HOBBS, GUY STEPHEN, financial executive; b. Lynwood, Calif., Feb. 23, 1955; s. Franklin Dean and Bette Jane (Little) H.; m. Laura Elena Lopez, Jan. 6, 1984; 1 child, Mariah Amanda. BA, U. Calif., Santa Barbara, 1976; MBA, U. Nev., 1978. Sr. rsch. assoc. Ctr. for Bus. and Econ. Rsch., Las Vegas, Nev., 1978-80; pvt. practice mgmt. cons. Las Vegas, 1979-82; mgmt. analyst Clark County, Las Vegas, 1980-81, sr. mgmt. analyst, 1981-82, dir. budget and fin. planning, 1982-84, comptroller, dir. fin., chief fin. officer, 1984-96; pres. Hobbs, Ong & Assocs., Inc., 1996—; lectr. in mgmt. Coll. Bus. and Econs., U. Nev., Las Vegas, 1977-88; pres. Pacific Blue Ent., 1991—; mem. Interim Legis. Com. Infrastructure Fin., 1993-94; mem. Interim Legis. Com. Studying Laws Relating to the Distbn. of Taxes in Nev., 1995-96. Author publs. in field. Mem. exec. bd. Miss Nevada USA and Miss NEVADA Teen USA, 1996—. Mem. Am. Soc. Pub. Adminstrn. (Pub. Adminstr. of Yr. 1987), Govt. Fin. Officers Assn. (Fin. Reporting Achievement award 1984-95, Disting. Budget Presentation, award 1993-96), Nev. Taxpayers Assn., Las Vegas C. of C., Govt. Rsch. Assn. Republican. Office: Hobbs Ong & Assocs Inc 3900 Paradise Rd Ste 152 Las Vegas NV 89109-0928

HOBBS, STEPHEN CRAIG, management consultant; b. Monroe, Wis., Jan. 8, 1950; s. Howard W. and Mayme (Terry) H.; m. Leila B. Paulson, Oct. 22, 1989. BS in Labor and Indsl. Rels., Mich. State U., 1972, BA in Econs., 1972; postgrad., U. Colo., 1976-78. Cert. mgmt. acct. Mgr. Saunders Leasing Systems, Inc., Denver, 1972-74; ops. mgr. Best Brands, Inc., Denver, 1974-76; contr., purchasing mgr. R & L Distbg. Co., Denver, 1976-80; contr. Ctr. Equipment Co., Denver, 1980-87; cons. C & S Assocs., Denver, 1987-90; CFO Bell Plumbing & Heating Co., Denver, 1990-94; ptnr. Telesis Cons. Co., Englewood, Colo., 1994-97; info. mgmt. cons. Berger and Co., Denver, 1997—; small bus. cons. South Met. Denver C. of C., Littleton, 1992—, bus. issues com., 1992—. Mem. Inst. Mgmt. Accts. (nat. com. mem. 1993—, past pres. coun. Centennial chpt. 1992—, chpt. pres. 1991-92, v.p. 1988-91), Constrn. Fin. Mgmt. Assn., Am. Fin. Assn. Office: Berger and Co 1350 17th St Ste 300 Denver CO 80202

HOBERG, MICHAEL DEAN, management analyst, educator; b. Pipestone, Minn., Feb. 27, 1955; s. Dennis Edwin and Beverly Ann (Voss) H.; 1 child, Heather; m. Janet Lee Freeman. BS in Park Adminstrn., Calif. State U., Sacramento, 1977; MPA, Calif. State U., Turlock, 1982; PhD in Pub. Adminstrn., Greenwich U., 1993; postgrad., U. Calif., Berkeley, 1996—. Cert. govt. fin. mgr. Park ranger Nat. Park Svc., State of Calif., and San Joaquin County, Calif., 1977-82; park svcs. specialist San Joaquin County, Stockton, Calif., 1983-86, mgmt. analyst, 1986—; adj. instr. Delta Coll., Stockton, 1987-90; dir. Hoberg Mgmt. and Consulting, Stockton, 1987—. Fencing Champion foil No. Calif. Intercollegiate Athletic Conf., 1977, 9th Place award USFA Nat. Championships, 1988; High Jump champion City of Stockton, 1971-73; inducted into Sacramento C. of C. Athletic Hall of Fame, 1977. Mem. Mensa. Democrat. Home: 2209 Meadow Ave Stockton CA 95207-1428 Office: San Joaquin County 7000 S Canlis Blvd French Camp CA 95231

HOBGOOD, E(ARL) WADE, college dean; b. Wilson, N.C., June 28, 1953; s. Max Earl and Mary (Carpenter) H.; m. Dianne Bland, Apr. 24, 1977; children: Courtney, Heather. BFA, E. Carolina U., 1975, MFA, 1977. Asst. prof. art Ark. State U., Jonesboro, 1977-78; design dir. and asst./assoc. prof. art Western Carolina U., Cullowhee, N.C., 1978-84; chmn., assoc. to full prof. art and design Winthrop U., Rock Hill, S.C., 1984-88, acting chmn. dept. music, 1991-92, assoc. dean and prof. Sch. Visual and Performing Arts, 1988-92; dean Coll. of Fine Arts Stephen F. Austin State U., Nacogdoches, Tex., 1992-93; dean Coll. of Arts, exec. dir. Carpenter Performing Arts Ctr Calif. State U., Long Beach, 1993—; panelist ann. conf. Coun. Coll. Arts & Scis., 1995; panelist Internat. Coun. Fine Arts Dean's Ann. Conf., 1995; faculty cons. Ednl. Testing Svcs., 1993—; field reader/evaluator, field-initiated studies grants U.S. Dept. Edn., 1992—; sr. evaluator Nat. Assn. Schs. of Art and Design, 1987; chair grants rev. panel Pub. Corp. for Arts, 1994, mem. allocations com., 1996—; mem. cultural planning com. City of Long Beach; evaluator/cons. Arts Edn. Partnership Grants, Ky. Arts Coun., 1992; evaluator/panelist Challenge grants, NEA, 1991, correspondent/cons. Arts Edn. Rsch. Briefing, 1991; cons. in field. One-person exhibit Limestone Coll., 1985; group shows include SFA Art Faculty Exhbn., 1992, Black Mountain Invitational, 1981, High Point Invitational, 1980, State of S.C. Traveling Exhbn., 1984-85, others. Mem. selection com. Pub. Corp. for the Arts, Long Beach, 1993; bd. dirs. Rock Hill Arts Coun., 1985-89; mem. planning com. Cultural/City of Rock Hill, 1988-92, County of York, S.C., 1989-92; mem. Long Beach Mus. of Art, 1993—, Univ. Art Mus., 1993—, KLON Jazz Radio, 1993—; mem. Mayor's Task Force on Smithsonian, City of Long Beach, 1996—. Recipient medallion in arts edn. Kennedy Ctr. for Performing Arts, Washington, 1988, 1st place award U.S. Bicentennial Com., Keep America Beautiful mural design, 1976, A&M Records Advt. award, 1975, R.J. Reynolds Permanent Collection purchase, 1975, 1st place Southern Visions Photography, 1984, others. Mem. Internat. Coun. Fine Arts (editor publs., mem. futures com., chair editl. bd. 1996—), Long Beach C. of C., Japan Am. Soc., Greater L.A. World Trade Assn., Long Beach Mus. Art, Phi Kappa Phi. Office: Calif State Univ Coll of the Arts 1250 N Bellflower Blvd Long Beach CA 90840-0006

HOBSON, WAYNE K., humanities educator; b. Moscow, Idaho, July 1, 1941; s. Karl and Dorothy Hobson; m. Nancy Robinson, Aug. 20, 1966; children: Jeffrey, Emily. BA, U. Oreg., 1965; MAT, Reed Coll., 1966; MA, Stanford U., 1969, PhD, 1977. From asst. to assoc. prof. Calif. State U., Fullerton, 1973-86; prof. Calif. State U. Fullerton, Fullerton, 1986—. Author: American Legal Profession and the Organizational Society, 1890-1930, 1986. Mem. Am. Studies Assn., Orgn. Am. Historians, Am. Soc. for Legal History. Democrat. Home: 915 Miramar St Laguna Beach CA 92651-3707 Office: Dept Am Studies Calif State Univ Fullerton CA 92634

HOCH, ORION LINDEL, corporate executive; b. Canonsburg, Pa., Dec. 21, 1928; s. Orion L.F. and Ann Marie (McNulty) H.; m. Jane Lee Ogan, June 12, 1952 (dec. 1978); children: Andrea, Brenda, John; m. Catherine Nan Richardson, Sept. 12, 1980. BS, Carnegie Mellon U., 1952; MS, UCLA, 1954; PhD, Stanford U., 1957. With Hughes Aircraft Co., Culver City, Calif., 1952-54; with Stanford Electronics Labs., 1954-57; sr. engr., dept. mgr., divsn. v.p., divsn. pres. Litton Electron Devices div., San Carlos, Calif., 1957-68; group exec. Litton Components divsn., 1968-70; v.p. Litton Industries, Inc., Beverly Hills, Calif., 1970, sr. v.p., 1971-74, pres., 1982-88, chief exec. officer, 1986-93, chmn., 1988-94, also dir.; pres. Intersil, Inc., Cupertino, Calif., 1974-82; chmn. exec. com., dir. Western Atlas, Inc., Beverly Hills, 1994—; bd. dirs. Litton Industries, Inc., Bessemer Trust Cos. Trustee Carnegie-Mellon U. Served with AUS, 1946-48. Mem. IEEE, Sigma Xi, Tau Beta Pi, Phi Kappa Phi. Office: Western Atlas Inc 360 N Crescent Dr Beverly Hills CA 90210-4802

HOCHMAN, JOHN IRA, psychiatrist; b. Birmingham, Ala., Nov. 3, 1945; s. Harold and Laura Hochman; m. Janice Lutwick, Feb. 1972; children: Noah, Rachel, Jared. BS magna cum laude in Physics/Chemistry, CUNY, 1966; MD, NYU, 1969. Diplomate Am. Bd. Psychiatry and Neurology. Extern Guys Hosp., London U., 1969, N.Y. State Psychiat. Inst., 1969; intern Huntington Meml. Hosp., Pasadena, Calif., 1969-70; resident dept. psychiatry U. So. Calif., L.A., 1970-73; pvt. practice Encino, Calif., 1974—; asst. clin. prof. psychiatry & biobehavioral scis. UCLA Sch. Medicine, 1987—; clin. assoc. So. Calif. Psychoanalytic Inst., Beverly Hills, Calif., 1972-80, instr., 1981-82; mem. staff various hosps., L.A. County, 1973—; staff psychiatrist Dept. Mental Health, L.A., 1973-74; cons. L.A. County Probation Dept., L.A., 1976; forensic psychiat. cons., Encino, 1978—; mem. task force on cults Cmty. Rels. Coun. L.A., 1982-90; mem. faculty panel L.A. County Superior Ct., L.A., 1984-85; mem. bd. advisors Am. Family Found., 1991; mem. sci. adv. bd. False Memory Syndrome Found., Phila., 1993—; mem. conf. faculty Johns Hopkins Med. Inst. & False Memory Syndrome Found., 1994, 96; presenter and lectr. in field. Mem. editl. bd. Jour. Cultic Studies, 1988—; editl. cons./reviewer Psychiat. Annals, Am. Jour. Psychiatry; contbr. articles to profl. jours. and newspapers. Mem. southwestern regional bd. Anti-Defamation League, 1982-85; bd. dirs. West Coast Orthodox Unit, 1992-95. Capt. USAFR, 1970-75. Recipient John G. Clark award Am. Family Found., 1990. Mem. AMA, Am. Psychiat. Soc., Am. Psychiat. Assn., Am. Assn. Psychiatry & Law, Calif. Med. Assn., So. Calif. Psychiat. Soc. (mem. com. psychiatry and religion, 1988-89), L.A. County Med. Assn. (mem. sect. indsl. medicine and surgery 1980-86, pres. 1983). Jewish. Office: Bldg 3 #255 6345 Balboa Blvd Encino CA 91316

HOCHSCHILD, CARROLL SHEPHERD, medical equipment and computer company executive, educator; b. Whittier, Calif., Mar. 31, 1935; d. Vernon Vero and Effie Corinne (Hollingsworth) Shepherd; m. Richard Hochschild, July 25, 1959; children: Christopher Paul, Stephen Shepherd. BA in Internat. Rels., Pomona Coll., 1956; Teaching credential U. Calif., Berkeley, 1957; MBA, Pepperdine U., 1985; cert. in fitness instrn., U. Calif., Irvine, 1988. Cert. elem. tchr., Calif. elem. tchr. Oakland (Calif.) Pub. Schs., 1957-58, San Lorenzo (Calif.) Pub. Schs., 1958-59, Pasadena (Calif.) Pub. Schs., 1959-60, Huntington Beach (Calif.) Pub. Schs., 1961-63, 67-68; adminstrv. asst. Microwave Instruments, Corona del Mar, Calif., 1968-74; co-owner Hoch Co., Corona del Mar, 1978—. Rep. Calif. Tchrs. Assn., Huntington Beach, 1962-63. Mem. AAUW, P.E.O. (projects chmn. 1990-92, corr. sec. 1992-94, chpt. pres. 1994-95), Internat. Dance-Exercise Assn., NAFE, ASTD (Orange County chpt.), Assistance League Newport-Mesa. Republican. Presbyterian. Clubs: Toastmistress (corr. sec. 1983), Jr. Ebell (fine arts chmn. Newport Beach 1966-67).

HOCHSCHILD, RICHARD, medical instruments executive, researcher; b. Berlin, Germany, Aug. 28, 1928; came to U.S., 1939; s. Paul and Ann Ida (Schosstag) H.; m. Carroll Corinne Shepherd, July 25, 1959; children: Christopher Paul, Stephen Shepherd. BA in Physics, Johns Hopkins U., 1950; MA in Physics, U. Calif., Berkeley, 1957. Tech. adv. U.S. Atomic Energy Commn., N.Y.C., 1951-53; chief 300 area U.S. Atomic Energy Commn., Hanford, Wash., 1953-54; pres. Metrol, Inc., Pasadena, Calif., 1957-60, Microwave Instruments Co., Corona del Mar, Calif., 1962-74; chief exec. officer Hoch Co., Corona del Mar, 1975—; developer computerized med., physiol. and psychol. testing and measuring instruments; specialist in biomarkers of aging; pioneer devel. eddy current and microwave methods of nondestructive testing, automated instrumentation for biol. age testing; cons. in field. Patentee and author in field. Office: Hoch Co 2915 Pebble Dr Corona Del Mar CA 92625-1518

HOCKMUTH, JOSEPH FRANK, physicist, psychotherapist; b. Buffalo, N.Y., Mar. 6, 1942; s. Joseph Frank and Gertrude Marie (Merkley) H.; m. Sharon Louise Van Deusen Tiernan, June 30, 1965 (div.); children: Joseph Fess, Catherine Marie; m. Katherine Nancy Genco, June 1, 1991 (div.). BS in Physics, Calif. State U., 1965; MA in Psychology, Norwich U., 1992. Cert. substance abuse counselor, Ariz. Bd. Behavioral Health Examiners; cert. coll. instr., Ariz. State Bd.; cert. profl. counselor. Rsch. engr. Westinghouse Astroelectronics, Newbury Park, Calif., 1965-66; rsch. engr. Lockheed Missile & Space Co., Sunnyvale, Calif., 1966-69, sr. rsch. engr., 1972-78; radiation effects engr. IRT Corp., San Diego, 1969-72, staff scientist, 1984-87; addictions counselor Charter Hosp., Glendale, Ariz., 1992-93; prin. staff engr. Motorola Govt. Sys. & Tech. Group, Scottsdale, Ariz., 1978-84; tech. staff engr. Motorola GSTG, Scottsdale, Ariz., 1987—, divsn. cons. for radiation effects, 1987—; psychotherapist Fountain Hills, Ariz., 1992—. Contbr. Awakenings mag., 1992—. Funds coord. United Way, Scottsdale, 1988-90; class sponsor Wounded Knee (Wyo.) Tribal Elem. Sch., 1992—. Sgt. Calif. NG, 1960-68. Fellow Am. Counseling Assn., Ariz. Counselors Assn., Noetic Scis. Inst.; mem. ASTM (com. 1985—), IEEE (ofcl. tech. paper reviewer 1993). Roman Catholic. Home: 15024 E Windyhill Rd Fountain Hls AZ 85268-1323 Office: Motorola GSTG 8201 E Mcdowell Rd # H2550 Scottsdale AZ 85257-3812

HODARA, EDEN, artist; b. Cleve., Oct. 31, 1924; d. Samuel Alexander and Cecelia (Klein) Baruch; m. Henri Hodara, Aug. 1, 1951; 1 child, Paul. Student, Huntington Hartford Art Sch., Cleve.; student of Walter Kuhn, Art Students League, N.Y.C., 1943, 44; student, Acad. Beaux Arts, Paris, Acad. de la Grand Chaumiere, 1952. One-woman show Miami Mus. Modern Art, 1961, Yamada Art Gallery, Kyoto, Japan, 1962, Kovler-Heman Gallery, Chgo., 1962, Comsky Gallery, L.A., 1970, NAS, Washington, 1987, Mat. Acad. Scis. & Engring., Irvine, Calif., 1991; exhibited in group shows Galerie Craven, Paris, 1953, Art Inst. Chgo., 1959, 62, Pan Am. Festival, Chgo., 1959, Long Beach (Calif.) Art Mus., 1966, San Francisco Art Mus., 1966, San Diego Art Mus., 1970, L.A. Inst. Contemporary Art, 1975, others; represented in permanent collections Gutai Mus., Osaka, Japan, Insho Damoto Mus. Modern Art, Kyoto, numerous pvt. collections. Home and Studio: 33761 Cabrillo Isle Dana Point CA 92629-4215

HODASH, BOB (ROBERT A. HODASH), educational program specialist; b. Bronx, N.Y., Aug. 25, 1957; s. Robert and Anne Marie (Buckley) H.; m. Wendy Kapstrom, Apr. 7, 1990; 1 child, Liam Kapstrom Hodash. BA, Lehman Coll., 1980, MS, 1981. Profl. clear tchg. credential sci. and phys. edn.; preliminary adminstrv. svcs. credential. Health and phys. edn. chair athletic dir. Beth Am/Herzl Sch., Beverly Hills, Calif., 1982-84; assoc. athletic dir. Windward Sch., Mar Vista, Calif., 1984-86; tchr. phys. edn. and sci. L.A. Unified Sch. Dist., 1986-91, chair sci. dept., 1987-91; sci. tchr. Curran Jr. H.S. Bakersfield (Calif.) City S.D., 1991-95, sci. mentor tchr., 1994-95, program specialist, 1995—; press rels. asst. dir. L.A. Olympics, 1984; pres. Ocean Valley Athletic League, L.A. County, 1984-86; advisor MESA (Math, Engring., Sci. Achievement), L.A. and Bakersfield, 1986-95. Author: Historical Trail of the Bronx, 1976; prodr. (animated films) Anti Smoking Shorts, 1990. Water safety instr. trainer ARC, N.Y., 1976-81; com. mem. Anti Grafitti Program, Bakersfield, 1995—. Named Presdl. Vol. of the Yr., Pres. of the U.S., 1984; IBM Assist grantee IBM, L.A., 1990, Middle Sch. Restructing grantee State of Calif., 1990, 91. Mem. ASCD, Nat. Sci. Tchrs. Assn., Calif. Sci. Tchrs. Assn., Calif. State Tchrs. Assn., Phi Delta Kappa. Home: 9501 Benet Way Bakersfield CA 93311-1423 Office: Frank West Sch 2400 Benton St Bakersfield CA 93304-5052

HODGDEN, HUGH JERRY, geological consulting executive; b. Manhattan, Kans., July 12, 1931; s. Frank Burton and Emily Elizabeth (Bennett) H.; 1 adopted child, Dewey L. Pleake. BS in Geol. Engring., U. Kans., 1953, MS in Geology, 1960. Archtl. draftsman Hercules Powder Co., Sunflower Ord Works, Kans., 1951-53; asst. instr. geology U. Kans., Lawrence, 1953-54; geologist Continental Oil Co., Colo., Wyo. and La., 1957-63; western regional mgr. Info. Handling Svcs., Chgo. and L.A., 1963-67; nat. sales mgr. Share Rsch. Corp., Santa Barbara, Calif., 1967-68; asst. to pres., geologist Internat. Nuclear Corp., Denver and Calgary, Can., 1968-70; pres., CEO Rangeland Resources, Inc., Denver, 1970-72; owner Hodgden & Assocs., Denver, 1972—; owner, pres., CEO Hodgden Oil Co., Denver and Golden, Colo., 1980—; founder, pres., CEO Alaska Platinum Ltd., Golden, Colo. & Platinum, Alaska, 1992-96; v.p. Corral Creek Corp., Denver, 1996—; mem. Kans. U. Geol. Assocs. Bd., 1993—. Contbr. articles to profl. jours. Active various civic orgns., Golden, 1978—; mem. All Breed Rescue, Denver, 1992—; vice-chmn. Golden Parks and Recreation Bd., 1995—; mem. Leadership Golden, 1996—. Capt. USAF, 1954-56. Mem. Am. Assn. Petroleum Geologists (cert. petroleum geologist), Soc. Ind. Profl. Exploration Scientists (cert. profl. geologist), Rocky Mountain Assn. Geologists, Kans. Geol. Soc., Denver Internat. Petroleum Soc. Office: Hodgden Oil Co 408 18th St Golden CO 80401-2433

HODGDON, LINWOOD L., sociology educator; b. Plainfield, Vt., Mar. 19, 1917; married; 3 children. BA, Am. Internat. Coll., 1941; MA, Mich. State U., 1947, PhD, 1952; DPA (hon.), Am. Internat. Coll., 1996. From asst. prof. to prof. dept. econ. and sociology Kans. State U., Manhattan, 1949-58; Fulbright prof. sociology/anthropology Inst. Social Scis., Agra (India) U., 1958-59; acting dir. Cmty. Devel. Br. U.S. Ops. Mission, Seoul, Korea, 1061-62, cons. cmty. devel., 1960-62; cons. cmty. devel. Ford Found., New Delhi, 1962-64; dir. Office Internat. Programs Colo. State U., Ft. Collins, 1964-68, prof. sociology, 1968-82, prof. sociology emeritus, 1982—; cons. Australian govt., 1964, State Dept./AID, India, 1978, Malaysian govt./Asian Devel. Bank, 1979-80; mem. planning team Consortium for Study of Nigerian Rural Devel., AID/Govt. Nigeria, 1965, 66, 67, vice chmn. consortium coun., 1966-67; seminar participant Am. Assn. Colls. for Tchr. Edn., Egypt, 1973; Fulbright prof. sociology of devel. Nat. U., Bangi, Malaysia, 1985-86; sociology prof. Semester at Sea, U. Pitts., fall 1990; papers presented at numerous internat. profl. confs. Contbr. chpts. to books, papers to conf. procs. and profl. jours. Pres. Lesher Jr. High Sch. PTA, 1968-69; pres. Ft. Collins Poudre Golden K Kiwanis Club, 1988-89; bd. dirs. Ft. Collins Kiwanis Club, 1966-69, 76-78, South Coll. Cmty. Assn., 1965-68. Lt. USNR, 1942-46, PTO. Grantee Mich. Med. Soc. and pvt. founds., 1947-48, Kans. Acad. Sci., 1953, AID, 1960-61, 62, Ford Found., 1963-64, Colo. State U. Faculty Coun. Rsch. Com., 1973. Mem. Alpha Kappa Delta, Gamma Sigma Delta, Sigma Xi, Phi Kappa Delta, Phi Kappa Phi. Home: 1121 Robertson St Fort Collins CO 80524-3924

HODGES, JOSEPH GILLULY, JR., lawyer; b. Denver, Dec. 7, 1942; s. Joseph Gilluly Sr. and Elaine (Chanute) H.; m. Jean Todd Creamer, Aug. 7, 1971; children: Ashley E., Wendy C., Elaine V. BA, Lake Forest Coll., 1965; JD, U. Colo., 1968. Bar: Colo. 1968, U.S. Dist. Ct. Colo. 1969, U.S. Ct. Mil. Appeals 1969. Assoc. Hodges, Kerwin, Otten & Weeks, Denver, 1969-73; assoc. Davis, Graham & Stubbs, Denver, 1973-76, ptnr., 1976-86; pvt. practice, Denver, 1986—. Bd. dirs. Arapahoe Colo. Nat. Bank, Littleton, Colo., 1971-90, Cherry Creek Improvement Assn., Denver, 1979-91; bd. trustees Lake Forest (Ill.) Coll., 1977-87; pres. Colo. Arlberg Club, Winter Park, Colo., 1984-85; treas. St. Johns Episcopal Cathedral, Denver, 1981-96; chmn. bd. Spalding Cmty. Found., 1995—. Capt. USAR, 1969-74. Named Best Lawyers in Am., Woodward/White, N.Y.C., 1994-95. Fellow Am. Coll. Trust and Estate Counsel (state chmn. 1991-96); mem. ABA (chmn. probate divsn. G-2 Tech. 1990-95, coun. mem. real property, probate and trust law sect. 1996—), Am. Judicature Soc., Colo. Bar Assn. (chair probate coun. 1981-82), Denver Bar Assn., Denver Estate Planning Coun., Colo. Planned Giving Roundtable (bd. 1991-94), Rotary Club Denver, Kappa Sigma, Phi Alpha Delta. Republican. Office: 3300 E 1st Ave Ste 600 Denver CO 80206-5809

HODGES, JUDITH ANNE, artist, art educator; b. San Antonio, Sept. 22, 1951; d. Robert Marc and Betty A. H.; 1 child, Elan Young. BA in Liberal Arts, Prescott Coll., 1973; student, San Antonio Art Inst., 1985; Profl. Clear Multiple Subject Tchg. Credential, Nat. U., 1989; student, Monart Sch. of Arts, 1989, Otis Art Inst., 1990, Idylwild Sch. Music and the Arts, 1990, Art Ctr., Pasadena, 1997. Message therapist pvt. practice, San Antonio, 1981-86, Murrieta Hot Springs, Calif., 1986-90; art tchr. Creative Arts Group, Temecula, Calif., 1988-90; tchr., artist Butterfield Visual and Performing Arts Magnet Sch., Moreno Valley, Calif., 1991—; tchr. Art Club Butterfield Elem. Sch. of Arts, Moreno Valley, 1973, 94-97; juror Temecula Student Art Fair, 1990; art cons. Fallbrook (Calif.) Union Elem. Sch. Dist., 1990; site organizer Festival of Arts Moreno Valley Unified Sch. Dist., 1992-96; active gifted and talented and visual and performing arts student assessment Moreno Valley Unified Sch. Dist., 1995-96. Exhibited in group shows at Upstairs Gallery, Claremont, Calif., 1994, 95, Newport Beach Jazz Festival, Calif., 1996, Tubac Ctr. for Arts, Ariz., 1997, Art 2000 Group Exhbn., 1997 (hon. mention), Ariz. Aqueous XI Nat. Juried Exhibit, 1997, Riverside (Calif.) Art Mus., 1997, Fallbrook Wildlife Art Show, Calif., 1997; artist: (published prints) The Bug Collection, 1997. Recipient San Antonio Art Inst. grant., 1985. Mem. Art 2000.

HODGKIN, JOHN E., pulmonologist; b. Portland, Oreg., Aug. 22, 1939; s. Williard E. and Dorothy (Rigsby) H.; m. Jeanie Walker, Sept. 6, 1980; children: Steve, Kathryn, Carolyn, Jonathan, Jamie. BS, Walla Walla Coll., 1960; MD, Loma Linda U., 1964. Fellow in pulmonology Mayo Clinic, Rochester, Minn., 1970-72; chief pulmonary sect. Loma Linda (Calif.) U., 1974-80; clin. prof. medicine U. Calif., Davis, 1983—; med. dir. respiratory care St. Helena Hosp., Deer Park, Calif., 1983—, med. dir. pulmonary rehab., 1983—, med. dir. ctr. for health promotion, 1983-96; med. dir. Adventist Health No. Calif., Roseville, Calif., 1995—, Calif. Med. Found., 1995—. Editor: Chronic Obstructive Pulmonary Disease: Current Concepts, 1987, Respiratory Care: A Guide to Clinical Practice, 1997, Pulmonary Rehabilitation: Guidelines to Success, 1993, Lung Sounds: A Practical Guide, 1996. Decorated bronze star U.S. Army, 1968. Fellow Am. Assn. Cardiovas. & Pulmonary Rehab. (pres. 1995-96), Am. Coll. Chest Physicians, Am. Coll. Physicians, Am. Thoracic Soc., Nat. Assn. Med. Direction of Respiratory Care, Am. Assn. Respiratory Care (bd. med. advisors). Home: 1330 Crestmont Dr Angwin CA 94508-9634 Office: Saint Helena Hosp Lloyd Bldg Ste 502 Deer Park CA 94576

HODGSON, GREGORY BERNARD, software systems architect; b. Chgo., July 17, 1946; s. John George and Lucille (Nass) H.; m. Kathleen Patricia, Aug. 11, 1972 (div. July 1974); m. Kathryn Marie Maytum, Feb. 14, 1976. BS in Computer Engring., U. Ill., 1972. Computer programmer specialist Lockheed Missiles and Space Co., Sunnyvale, Calif., 1972-81, software systems engr., 1981-89; software sys. cons. Lockheed Missiles and Space Co., Sunnyvale, 1989-95; engr./scientist Hewlett-Packard Co., Sunnyvale, Calif., 1995; software system architect Lockheed Martin Missile and Space Ctr., Sunnyvale, Calif., 1995—; cons. in field. Served with U.S. Army, 1966-69. State of Ill. VA scholar, 1970-72. Mem. Ill. VA Assn. (coord. fed. and state affairs 1970-72). Roman Catholic. Home: 469 1/2 Curie Dr San Jose CA 95123-4925

HODSON, CHRISTINE ANN, psychologist; b. Chgo., Oct. 19, 1951; d. Roger Mithoff and Patricia Ann (Hill) H.; m. Gerard Fischer Jr., May 10, 1986; 1 child, Nathan David. BA, U. Calif., Santa Cruz, 1974; MS, Calif. State U., 1976; PhD, U. Md., 1982. Lic. psychologist, Calif. Therapist U. Md. Parent/Child Svc., College Park, 1978-80; psychometrist Prince George's Sch. Dist., Prince George's County, Md., 1979-80; trainee Alameda County Mental Health, Oakland and Fremont, Calif., 1980-82; pvt. practice Oakland, 1983—; family ct. counselor Alameda County Family Ct. Svcs., 1982—, supr. to interns, tchr. to profls., 1983—; cons. to schs. and shelters, 1980-93; presenter at profl. confs. and to profl. orgns. Contbr. to profl. publs. NIMH fellow, 1976. Mem. APA, Assn. Family and Conciliation Cts., No. Calif. Mediation Assn. Office: Alameda County Family Ct Svcs 1221 Oak St Oakland CA 94612

HODSON, SARA SUZANNE, manuscripts curator; b. Whittier, Calif., June 3, 1949; d. C. Hartley and Elizabeth M. (Holland) H.; m. Peter J. Blodgett, Mar. 26, 1988. BA with honors, Whittier Coll., 1971, MA in English, 1977; MLS, UCLA, 1979. Libr. asst. The Huntington Libr., San Marino, Calif., 1973-77, curator of lit. manuscripts, 1979—; adv. bd. DuPlessis Archives, Fuller Sem., Pasadena, Calif., 1994-95; adj. instr. Claremont (Calif.) Grad. Sch., 1994; mem. faculty Western Archives Inst., Pomona, Calif., 1994, Pasadena, 1995, 96. Contbr. essays to Conrad Aiken: A Priest of Consciousness, 1989, Dictionary of Literary Biography Yearbook, 1992, Pre-Raphaelites in Context, 1992; editor: Guide to Literary Manuscripts, 1979; contbr. articles to profl. jours. Recipient scholarship Calif. Scholarship Fedn., 1967. Mem. Am. Libr. Assn., Soc. Am. Archivists (chair manuscripts repositories sect. 1994-95, vice chair/chair elect privacy and confidentiality roundtable, 1994-95, chair 1996-97), Soc. Calif. Archivists (treas. 1986-88, v.p. 1990-91, pres. 1991-92, Lifetime Achievement award 1996), Jack London Soc. (adv. bd. 1996—), Renaissance Conf. of So. Calif.

HOEFER, GREGORY ALLEN, banker; b. Seattle, Wash., Aug. 15, 1952; s. Roland Glen and Joyce Marwite (Pearson) H.; m. Gail Jean Anderson, Aug. 25, 1973 (div. Dec. 1986); m. Maryn Lyn Jacobson, Nov. 12, 1992; children: Jedidiah, Anna. BS, Seattle Pacific U., 1974; MTh, Freelandia Inst., Fredonia, Mo., 1978; PhD, Clayton Sch. Theology, California, 1979. Fellow Seattle Pacific U., 1976; mgr. Western Appraisal Co., Seattle, 1975-82; chief appraiser State of Wash., Olympia, 1982-84; chief appraiser, west region U.S. Treasury/Banks & Thrifts, Seattle, 1984-92; regional mgr., comml. appraisal Bank of Am., Las Vegas, 1992-96; regional appraisal mgr. Am. Savs., Las Vegas, 1996—; cons. Hoefer Corp., Seattle, 1980-90; tchr. Appraisal Inst., USA, 1982—; preacher Evangel. Ch. Alliance, Olympia, 1982-84. Co-author publs. in field. Recipient award of Excellence Fed. Fin. Instns. Examination Coun., 1990. Mem. Nat. Soc. Appraisers. Office: Am Savs 2625 S Rainbow # A-100 Las Vegas NV 89102

HOEFFLIN, STEVEN M., plastic surgeon; b. Seattle, Wash., 1946. MD, UCLA, 1972. Plastic surgeon Santa Monica (Calif.) Hosp.; also clin. prof. UCLA. Office: 1530 Arizona Ave Santa Monica CA 90404-1208

HOEFLE, KAREN MARIE, hospice executive; b. Ann Arbor, Mich., Mar. 9, 1949; d. Fred W. and Helen Marie (Woodworth) Morgan; m. Brian Lee Hoefle, May 1, 1970 (div. July 1984); children: Jennifer Marie, Scott Everett. BAS magna cum laude, U. Mich., 1971. Staff nurse children's psychiat. ward U. Mich. Med. Ctr., Ann Arbor, 1971-72; staff nurse pediat. unit U. Ariz. Med. Ctr., Tucson, 1972-75; staff nurse pulmonary unit Tucson Med. Ctr., 1975-83; account exec. home respiratory unit Baxter, Tucson, 1983-88; regional sales trainer infusion divsn. Caremark, Tucson and Phoenix, 1988-92, regional contract mgr. women's health divsn., 1992-93; regional dir. admissions Hospice Family Care, Tucson and Phoenix, 1993-95; v.p. bus. devel. for Ariz. and Calif. Hospice Family Care, Mesa, Ariz., 1995—; cons. Ariz. Lung Assn., Tucson, 1983-88; mem. Phoenix Managed Care, 1994—; sustaining mem. Ariz. Continuity of Care, Tucson, 1994—. Mem. ways and means com. Enrichment for Parents, Tucson, 1977. Mem. Nat. Hospice Orgn., U. Mich. Alumni Assn., Sigma Theta Tau. Democrat. Methodist. Office: Hospice Family Care 1125 E Southern Ave Ste 201 Mesa AZ 85204-5011

HOEFT, CARL EDWARD, chemist; b. Mankato, Minn., Mar. 6, 1966; s. Jeffrey Lynn and Marlys Jean (Hoffman) H.; m. Judith Irene Vacek, Aug. 23, 1986; children: Jared Corwin, Summer Rose. BA in Chemistry, Hamline U., 1988; MSChemE, Wash. State U., 1992, PhD in Chem. Engring., 1994. Quality assurance technician Hutchinson (Minn.) Tech., Inc., 1984, chem. technician, 1985-86; tech. aide 3M Care Specialties Lab., St. Paul, 1987-89; tchg./rsch. asst. Wash. State U., Pullman, 1990-94; sr. rsch. chemist Dionex Corp., Sunnyvale, Calif., 1994—. Mem. coun. on ministries Simpson United Meth. Ch., Pullman, 1993. Melvin M. Smith scholar, 1992, 93, 94, 3M scholar, 1985, 86, 87, Hutchinson Tech., Inc. scholar, 1984-88. Mem. Am. Chem. Soc. (sec. student chpt. Hamline U. 1987-88). Methodist. Office: Dionex Corp 1228 Titan Way PO Box 3603 Sunnyvale CA 94086

HOEHN, ROBERT J., plastic surgeon, educator; b. East St. Louis, Ill., 1929; m. Margaret M. Guest Maier (div. Oct. 1987); children: Robert Anthony Till, Margaret Eve; m. Nancy Ruth Vincent Baum. MD, Washington U., St. Louis, 1956. Diplomate Am. Bd. Plastic Surgery. Intern Vancouver (B.C., Can.) Gen. Hosp., 1956-57; resident in internal medicine, 1957-58; resident McGill U., Montreal, Que., Can., 1960-61; resident in gen. surgery Boston City Hosp., 1961-62; fellow in orthopaedic surgery, 1962; fellow in transplantation immunology Westminster Hosp., London, 1962-63; resident in plastic surgery N.Y. Hosp.-Cornell, 1963-65; clin. prof. plastic surgery U. Colo., 1978—; with Aurora Presbyn. Hosp., 1978—, Aurora Regional Med. Ctr., 1978—, Denver Children's Hosp., 1978—, Porter Meml. Hosp., 1982—, Swedish Hosp., 1982—; pvt. practice. Fellow ACS; mem. AAPS, Am. Soc. Plastic and Reconstructive Surgeons, Plastic Surgery Rsch. Coun. Home: 2601 S Quebec St # 3 Denver CO 80231 Office: # 205 3535 Cherry Cr N Dr Denver CO 80209

HOELL, NOEL LARAMIE, psychiatrist; b. Helena, Mont., July 31, 1939; s. Edward J. and Bessie P. (Laramie) H.; children: Geoffrey K., Andrea B. MD, U. Chgo., 1964. Cert. psychiatrist. Intern U. Oreg., 1964-65; resident in pscyhiatry U. Colo., 1965-69; asst. prof. U. Calif. Davis Med. Sch., Sacramento, 1972-77; staff psychiatrist Western Mont. Regional Community Mental Health Ctr., Missoula, 1977-78; pvt. practice Missoula, 1978—. Maj. U.S. Army Med. Corps, 1969-72. Mem. Am. Psychiat. Assn., Mont. Psychiat. Assn. (legis. rep., sec., pres., dep. rep., rep. 1979—), Western Mont. Med. Soc. Office: 554 W Broadway St Missoula MT 59802-4051

HOEPER, GEORGE WILLIAM, JR., editor; b. Auburn, Calif., Mar. 8, 1918; s. George William and Blanche (Shock) H.; m. Alice Mary Silvester, Oct. 23, 1948; 1 child, Dale William. AA, Placer Jr. Coll., Auburn, 1939; student, U. Calif., San Diego, 1946. Pub. information officer Contractors Pacific Naval Air Bases, Honolulu, 1941-43; news reporter San Diego Tribune, 1946; reporter, state editor Sacramento Union, 1947-62; cons. State of Calif., Sacramento, 1963-65; bur. chief Stockton (Calif.) Record, 1965-86; editor Calaveras County Hist. Soc., San Andreas, Calif., 1986—. Author: Bacon and Beans from a Gold Pan, 1971, rev. edit., 1983, Black Bart, Boulevardier Bandit, 1995, Water for the Thirsty Hills, 1996; contbr. over 40 articles to profl. publs. With U.S. Air Corps., 1943-46. Mem. Mother Lode History Network, Calaveras Hist. Soc. Office: Calaveras County Hist Soc 30 Main St San Andreas CA 95249-9547

HOERNER, MICHAEL DUANE, beauty salon executive; b. Spokane, May 31, 1957; s. John Valentine and Maxine W. (Moffit) H.; m. Monya J. Patterson, Sept. 8, 1990. Lic. in Cosmetology, M'Lady Sch. of Beauty, Spokane, 1978; Lic. in Ins. Sales, Combined Ins. Sch., Portland, Oreg., 1981. Lic. in securities sales. Stylist Laurel & Hardys, Spokane, 1978-79, Trimmers-The Crescent, Spokane, 1979-80; bookkeeper Stratton Electronics, Spokane, 1980-81; sales mgr., acct. exec. Combined Ins., Spokane, 1981-84; shift mgr., stylist Supercuts, Spokane, 1984-86; sales dir., broker Allied Capital Group, Spokane, 1986-88; asst. mgr., stylist Cutter's Edge Hair Design, Spokane, 1988-90; mgr., founder Shear Satisfaction Salon, Seattle, 1990-93; pres., CEO Shear Satisfaction Salons, Inc., Seattle, 1993—. Mem. Civitan, Palm Beach, Fla., 1988. Ship serviceman USN, 1975-76. Office: Shear Satisfaction Salons 19505 44th Ave W Ste H Lynnwood WA 98036-5658

HOFERT, JACK, consulting company executive, lawyer; b. Phila., Apr. 6, 1930; s. David and Beatrice (Schatz) H.; m. Marilyn Tukeman, Sept. 4, 1960; children: Dina, Bruce. BS, UCLA, 1952, MBA, 1954, JD, 1957. Bar: Calif. 1957; CPA, Calif. Tax supr. Peat, Marwick Mitchell & Co., L.A., 1959-62, tax mgr., 1974-77; v.p. fin. Pacific Theaters Corp., L.A., 1962-68; freelance cons. L.A., 1969-74; tax mgr. Lewis Homes, Upland, Calif., 1977-80; pres. Di-Bru, Inc., L.A., 1981-87, Scolyn, Inc., L.A., 1988-95; bus. cons., 1995—; dir. Valley Fed. Savs. and Loan Assn., 1989-92. Mem. UCLA Law Rev., 1956-57; contbr. articles to tax, fin. mags. Served with USN, 1948-49. Home and Office: 2479 Roscomare Rd Los Angeles CA 90077-1812

HOFF, BERNADINE RYAN, management consultant; b. Creighton, Nebr., Aug. 29, 1926; d. Ralph Russell and Ella Helma (Boysen) Ryan; m. Edwin J. Hoff, Jan. 15, 1962 (div. June 1973); 1 child, Denise Kelly. BA in Secondary Edn., Northeastern Ill. U., 1970; MA in Diversified Edn., U.S. Internat. U., 1974, PhD in Mgmt., 1979. Ops. asst. Spiegel, Inc., Chgo., 1957-64; dir. off-campus grad. program U.S. Internat. U., San Diego, 1973 76; cons. pvt practice, San Diego, 1973—; dir. program devel. Pepperdine U., Santa Ana, Calif., 1976-77; program dir., continuing mgmt. edn. U. Minn., Mpls., 1977-80; dir. continuing edn. San Diego State U., 1980-81; pres., CEO Nat. Cons. Referrals, Del Mar, Calif., 1980-85; v.p. acad. affairs LaJolla U., San Diego, 1992-93; adj. faculty Nat. U., San Diego, 1981—; mktg. advisor, cons. Link Data Corp., San Diego, 1992—, Saddleback Coll., Mission Viejo, Calif., 1982-83, others. Trainee Peace Corps, Rabat, Morocco, 1997. Mem. NAt. Mgmt. Assn. (pres., v.p.). Home: 8931 Jana Ct Spring Valley CA 91977

HOFFENBLUM, ALLAN ERNEST, political consultant; b. Vallejo, Calif., Aug. 10, 1940; s. Albert A. and Pearl Estelle (Clarke) H. BA, U. So. Calif., 1962. Mem. staff L.A. County Rep. Com., 1967-71; staff dir. Rep. Assembly Caucus Calif. legislature, Sacramento, 1973-75; polit. dir. Rep. Party of Calif., L.A., 1977-78; owner Allan Hoffenblum & Assocs., L.A., 1979—. Capt. USAF, 1962-67, Vietnam. Decorated Bronze Star medal. Mem. Internat. Assn. Polit. Cons., Am. Assn. Polit. Cons. Jewish. Office: 9000 W Sunset Blvd Ste 707 West Hollywood CA 90069-5804

HOFFLUND, PAUL, lawyer; b. San Diego, Mar. 27, 1928; s. John Leslie and Ethel Frances (Cline) H.; m. Anne Marie Thalman, Feb. 15, 1958; children: Mark, Sylvia. BA, Princeton (N.J.) U., 1950; JD, George Washington U., 1956. Bar: D.C. 1956, U.S. Dist. Ct. D.C. 1956, U.S. Ct. Appeals (D.C. cir.) 1956, Calif. 1957, U.S. Dist. Ct. (so. dist.) Calif. 1957, U.S. Ct. Mil. Appeals 1957, U.S. Ct. Claims 1958, U.S. Ct. Appeals (9th cir.) 1960, U.S. Supreme Ct. 1964, U.S. Tax Ct. 1989. Assoc. Wencke, Carlson & Kuykendall, San Diego, 1961-62; ptnr. Carlson, Kuykendall & Hofflund, San Diego, 1963-65, Carlson & Hofflund, San Diego, 1965-72; Christian Sci. practitioner San Diego, 1972-84; arbitrator Mcpl. Cts. and Superior Ct. of Calif., San Diego, 1984—; pvt. practice San Diego, 1985—; adj. prof. law Nat. U. Sch. Law, San Diego, 1985-94; judge pro tem Mcpl. Ct. South Bay Jud. Dist., 1990—; disciplinary counsel to U.S. Tax Ct., 1989—; asst. U.S. atty. U.S. Dept. of Justice, L.A., 1959-60, asst. U.S. atty. in charge, San Diego, 1960-61, spl. hearing officer, San Diego, 1962-68; asst. corp. counsel Govt. of D.C., 1957-59. Author: (chpt. in book) Handbook on Criminal Procedure in the U.S. District Court, 1967; contbr. articles to profl. jours. Treas. Princeton Club of San Diego; v.p. Community Concert Assn., San Diego; pres. Sunland Home Found., San Diego, Trust for Christian Sci. Orgn., San Diego; chmn. bd. 8th Ch. of Christ, Scientist, San Diego. With USN, 1950-53, comdr. JAGC, USNR, 1953-72, ret. Mem. ABA, San Diego County Bar Assn., Inst. Global Ethics, World Affairs Coun., Phi Delta Phi. Democrat. Home and Office: 6146 Syracuse Ln San Diego CA 92122-3301 *Decisions should be based on divine direction rather than human determination. Pray first; then act. A life devoid of sprirituality lacks dimention. The steps of a good man are ordered by the lord: And he delighteth in his way.*

HOFFMAN, CHARLES FENNO, III, architect; b. Greenwich, Conn., May 28, 1958; s. Harrison Baldwin Wright and Louise Elkins (Sinkler) H.; m. Pia Christina Ossorio, Dec. 27, 1980; children: Wilhelmina C. L., Frederic W. S., Henry F., C. Fenno IV. BA in Environ. Design, U. Pa., 1983; MArch, U. Colo., 1986. Designer Fenno Hoffman & Assocs., Boulder, Colo., 1983—; pvt. practice designer Boulder, 1985; assoc. William Zmistowski Assoc. Architects, 1987—, Pellecchia-Olson Architects, Boulder, 1989—; prin. Fenno Hoffman Architects PC, Boulder, Colo., 1991—; cons. Summit Habitats, Inc., 1984—; design cons. The Denver Partnership, 1985, Downtown Denver, Inc., 1985; guest critic U. Colo., 1990—, guest lectr., 1991-92, 94, 95, 96, 97, design instr., 1995—. Prin. works include Ca'Venier Mus. for Venice Bienalle, 1985, Cleveland Pl. Connection, Denver, 1985 (1st prize 1985), hist. renovated house Boulder, 1986, 3 Gates 3 Squares, Denver, 1986, Geneva Ave. House, 1992, Jarrow Sch. master plan, 1994; numerous residential and multi-family projects, 1991—, Northeast Classroom, 1995; author: Urban Transit Facility, A Monorail for Downtown Denver, 1985, US Navy Marine Corps., Facilities Assessments, 1996. Bd. dirs. Jarrow Sch. Mem. Architects & Planners ofBoulder. Democrat. Episcopalian. Clubs: Rallysport Racquet (Boulder). Office: 505 Geneva Ave Boulder CO 80302-7139

HOFFMAN, DAVID WAYNE, III, real esate appraiser; b. Sarra Polichie, Luciana, Italy, Sept. 22, 1955; came to U.S., 1959; s. Desurondro Augustine Cozza and Hazel Annabelle (Rosenthal) Ankley; m. Janie Louise Charbonal, May 6, 1974 (div. Sept. 1974). MA in Econs., Gonzaga U., 1979; BA, Wash. State U., 1983; cert. in property mgmt., Spokane C.C., 1986. Lic. real estate appraiser, Wash. Rep. Gus J. Cozza Constrn. Co., Spokane, Wash., 1973-75; regional rep. Brouner, Gottlieb, Inc., Seattle, 1975-80; v.p., sec.-treas. Washco Corp., Spokane, 1980—; property mgr., ptnr. real estate sales Diversified Apt. Realty Co., Inc., Seattle, 1989—; ptnr. Girtz Bakery, Spokane, 1985-87, Foxes Bar, Albuquerque; owner Page One Books & Records, Albuquerque, 1997—. Mem. Spokane Club, Wash. Athletic Club, Athletic Round Table, Seattle Tennis Club, Manito Country Club, Moose, Brotherhood of Friends Lodge, Albuquerque Social Club. Republican. Roman Catholic. Home: 9900 Spain NE Ste H-1041 Albuquerque NM 87111 Office: D A R C O Inc 420 E Howell St Seattle WA 98122-2126

HOFFMAN, DONALD DAVID, cognitive and computer science educator; b. San Antonio, Dec. 29, 1955; s. David Pollock and Loretta Virginia (Shoemaker) H.; m. Geralyn Mary Souza, Dec. 13, 1986; 1 child from previous marriage, Melissa Louise. BA, UCLA, 1978; PhD, MIT, 1983. MTS and project engr. Hughes Aircraft Co., El Segundo, Calif., 1978-83; rsch. scientist MIT Artificial Intelligence Lab, Cambridge, Mass., 1983; asst. prof. U. Calif., Irvine, 1983-86, assoc. prof., 1986-90, full prof., 1990-97; cons. Fairchild Lab. for Artificial Intelligence, Palo Alto, Calif., 1984; panelist MIT Corp. vis. com., Cambridge, 1985, NSF, Washington, 1988; conf. host IEEE Conf. on Visual Motion, Irvine, 1989; conf. host Office of Naval Rsch. Conf. on Vision, Laguna Beach, Calif., 1992; vis. prof. Zentrum für Interdisziplinäre Forschung, Bielefeld, Germany, 1995-96. Co-author: Observer Mechanics, 1989; mem. editl. bd. Cognition, 1991—, Psychol. Rev., 1995—; contbr. articles to profl. jours. Vol. tchr. Turtle Rock Elem. Sch., Irvine, 1988-90. Recipient Distinguished Scientific award, Am. Psychol. Assn., 1989, Troland Rsch. award U.S. Nat. Acad. Scis., 1994; grantee NSF, 1984, 87. Mem. AAAS. Office: U Calif Dept Cognitive Sci Irvine CA 92697

HOFFMAN, DONALD JAMES, management consultant; b. Urbana, Ill., Nov. 20, 1948; s. Harold L. and Dorothy P. (McCarty) H.; m. Susan L. Hoffman, Mar. 20, 1971. BSBA, Biola U., 1970; MBA, Calif. State Poly. U., Pomona, 1974. Cert. in mgmt. acctg. Contr. Biola U., La Mirada, 1970-75; area contr. Calif. ops. Internat. Paper Co., 1975-77, project mgr. Calif. ops., 1977-78, mng. planning western ops., 1978-80, product mgr. wood products, 1980-81, timber and wood products, 1981-83, mng. lumber and plywood, 1983-85; pres., CEO Hudson Group, Inc., 1985-88; prin. The Crest Co., 1989—; bd. dirs. Kewennaw Land Assn., Ltd., Ironwood, Mich. Commr. Wasco County Planning Commn., 1994; chmn. ARC, Hood River, Oreg. Named Outstanding Young Men of Am. U.S. Jaycees, 1980. Baptist. Office: The CREST Co 2080 State Rd Mosier OR 97040-9781

HOFFMAN, GARY ALLAN, retail executive, human resource consultant; b. Jacksonville, Fla., Aug. 31, 1949; s. Louis A. and Myrna H.; m. Silvia Patricia Biscar, Oct. 14, 1979; children: Andrea, Brooks. BA in Polit. Sci. magna cum laude, Calif. State U., San Francisco, 1971. No. Calif. regional dir. St. Jude Children's Rsch. Hosp. Found., Memphis, Tenn., 1972-74; program devel. specialist Calif. Credit Union League, Pomona, 1975-77; sr. tng. specialist Crocker Nat. Bank, San Francisco, 1977-78; program coord. Inst. for Profl. Devel., San Jose, Calif., 1978-79; mgr., sr. acct. exec. Sales Cons., San Mateo, Calif., 1979-86; pres., CEO Serramonte Candle Co., Inc., Daly City, Calif., 1986-93, Lumiere, San Bruno, Calif., 1993-94; human resources cons. HR Easy Key Account Mgr., Charlotte, N.C., 1997—; western regional dir. Internat. Edn. Forum, Bayshore, N.Y., 1994-97; chpt. v.p. ASTD, L.A., 1974. Campus coord. Dem. Nat. Com., San Mateo, 1968, precinct chairperson, 1972. Mem. Green Hills Country Club, Anti-Defamation League. Democrat. Home: 231 Bridgeport Dr Half Moon Bay CA 94019-4238

HOFFMAN, GEORGE ALAN, consulting company executive; b. Albany, N.Y., May 16, 1937; s. Irving Marshall and Margaret (Coyne) H.; m. Kim Thi Nguyen, Oct. 10, 1971; children: Caroline, Christine. AB, U. Calif., Berkeley, 1980, MBA, 1982. Mgmt. analyst Am. Can Co., N.Y.C., 1966-69; cons. Vietnamese Air Force, Bien Hoa, Vietnam, 1970-74, Puslitbang, Jakarta, Indonesia, 1974-75; v.p. Union Bank, Oakland, Calif., 1987—. Author: Indonesian Production-sharing Oil Contracts, 1982, The Guns of T.E. Lawrence, 1996. Mem. Mensa. Club: Commonwealth (San Francisco). Office: 460 Hegenberger Rd Oakland CA 94621-1404

HOFFMAN, GEORGE BERNARD, estate planner; b. St. Louis, Dec. 11, 1942; s. George Bernard and Ethel Eva (Drobina) H.; m. Suzanne Carol Johnson, May 9, 1970 (div. Feb. 1992). AA, Mt. San Antonio Coll., Walnut, Calif., 1966; BA, Calif. State Coll., L.A., 1971; MBA, Calif. State U., L.A., 1974. Cert. estate planner; cert. paralegal. Pers. specialist Alpha Beta Mkts., La Habra, Calif., 1965 69, mgr., 1969-79; dir. mktg. Auburn Cord Dusenberg of Calif., L.A., 1979-81; sr. planner Bertcourt Securities Corp., Upland, Calif., 1981-88; gen. mgr. Penita Investment Ltd., Hong Kong, 1988-92; owner George B. Hoffman Estate Planning, Whittier, Calif., 1992—. With U.S. Army, 1966-68; Vietnam. Decorated Army Commendation medal, Air medal. Mem. VFW, Am. Legion. Democrat. Roman Catholic.

HOFFMAN, NEIL EUGENE, cell biologist; b. N.Y.C., Jan. 9, 1956; s. Edward Martin and Aza H.; m. Setsuko Tsukamoto, Dec. 11, 1981; children: Aaron, Masa. BS, Cornell U., 1978; PhD, U. Calif., Davis, 1982. Postdoctoral fellow Mich. State U., East Lansing, Mich., 1983-86, Rockefeller U., N.Y.C., 1986-87, U. Pa., Phila., 1987-88; staff scientist Carnegie Inst., Stanford, Calif., 1988—. Contbr. articles to profl. jours. Recipient First award NIH, 1989-95; postdoctoral fellow NSF, 1986-88. Mem. Am. Soc. Plant Physiology, Am. Chem. Soc., Internat. Soc. Plant Molecular Biology, Am. Soc. Cell Biology. Office: Carnegie Inst Washington 290 Panama St Stanford CA 94305-4101

HOFFMAN, ROBERT JAMES, retired electronics engineer; b. Portland, Oreg., Dec. 23, 1924; s. William Charles and Myra (Mayo) H. BS in Gen. Sci., MIT, 1951; MBA, Stanford U., 1956; postgrad., U. So. Calif., 1966. Lic. gen. radiotelephone FCC. Field engr. Western Elec. Co., Winston-Salem, N.C., 1951-53; engr. Lenkurt Elec. Co., San Carlos, Calif., 1956-58; group leader The Martin Co., Littleton, Colo., 1959-60; sr. reliability engr. Librascope, Glendale, Calif., 1962-68; proprietor Pinewood Electronics, LaPine, Oreg., 1977-81, Rideway, San Diego, 1990—; rschr. earthquake precursors, 1970—; developer sewing machine empty bobbin alarm, 1984, telephone remote control, 1992. Pub.: (book) Semiconductor Data, 1962. Mem. Project Area Com., San Diego City Heights, 1993. With USN, 1943-46. Home: # 11 5330 Orange Ave Apt 15C San Diego CA 92115

HOFFMAN, WILLIAM YANES, plastic surgeon; b. Rochester, N.Y., 1952. MD, U. Rochester, 1977. Plastic surgeon U. Calif. San Francisco Med. Ctr.; also prof. plastic surgery U. Calif., San Francisco. Office: UC San Fran Plastic Surgery 350 Parnassus Ave Ste 509 San Francisco CA 94117-3608*

HOFFMANN, JON ARNOLD, aeronautical engineer, educator; b. Wausau, Wis., Jan. 13, 1942; s. Arnold D. and Rita J. (Haas) H.; m. Carol R. Frye. BSME, U. Wis., 1964, MSME, 1966. Register profl. engr., Calif. Research engr. Trane Co., 1966-68; prof. aeronautical engring. Calif. Poly. State U., San Luis Obispo, 1968—; research engr. Stanford U. NSF Program,

1970; research fellow Ames Research Ctr. Ctr. NASA/ASEE, 1974-75; tech. cons. NASA/AMES Research Ctr., 1977; design engr. Cal/ Poly ERDA contract, 1976-77; prin. investigator NASA-ARC Cooperative Agreement, 1983. Contbr. articles to profl. jours. Grantee NASA, NSF. Mem. ASME. Home: 1044 Via Chula Robles Arroyo Grande CA 93420-4915 Office: Calif Poly State U Dept Aero Engring San Luis Obispo CA 93407

HOFFMANN, KATHRYN ANN, humanities educator; b. Rockville Centre, N.Y., Oct. 26, 1954; d. Manfred and Catherine (Nanko) H.; m. Brook Ellis, Nov. 25, 1987. BA summa cum laude, SUNY Buffalo, 1975; MA, The Johns Hopkins U., 1979, PhD, 1981. Asst. prof. French lit. and lang. U. Wis., Madison, 1981-88, U. Hawaii-Manoa, Honolulu, 1992—; mng. ptnr. Yuval Design Partnership, Chgo., 1988-92. Author: Society of Pleasures: Interdisciplinary Readings in Pleasure in Power during the Reign of Louis XIV, 1997; assoc. editor Substance, 1982-87; contbr. articles to profl. jours.; designer clothing accessories. Grantee NEH, 1993, 95; fellow Inst. Rsch. in Humanities, 1984-85, Am. Coun. Learned Socs., 1984-85. Mem. MLA, Hawaii Assn. Lang. Tchrs., N.Am. Soc. for 17th Century French Literature, Soc. for Interdisciplinary French 17th Century Studies (exec. com. 1994-96), Soc. for Interdisciplinary Study of Social Imagery, Phi Beta Kappa. Home: 3029 Lowrey Ave Apt Q2224 Honolulu HI 96822-1800 Office: U Hawaii Manoa Dept European Languages & Lit 1890 E West Rd # 483 Honolulu HI 96822-2318

HOFFMANN, TIMOTHY JAY, computer networking executive; b. Milw., Aug. 2, 1958; s. Thomas R. and Lorna G. Hoffmann. B in Computer Sci., U. Minn., 1980. Analyst United Computing Svcs., Kansas City, Mo., 1980-84; sr. analyst Control Data Corp., Kansas City, 1984-89; sr. network analyst Power Computing, Dallas, 1989-93; mgr. info. svcs. Infonet Svcs. Co., El Segundo, Calif., 1993—. Co-author: (textbook) Fortran: A Structured, Disciplined Style, 1st, 2d, 3d edits., 1980—. Office: Infonet Svcs Co 2100 E Grand Ave El Segundo CA 90245-5024

HOFFMANN, WAYNE THOMAS, financial services executive; b. Milw., Sept. 25, 1955. BA in Fin., U. Wis., Milw., 1977; MBA, U. Wis., 1978. Credit mgr. 1st Wis. Nat. Bank, Madison, 1978-80; reg. v.p., other positions Prudential Capital Corp., Milw. and Mpls., 1980-91; v.p. Great West Life Assurance Co., Denver, 1991—. Office: Great West Life Assurance Co 8515 E Orchard Rd Englewood CO 80111-5002

HOFFMEISTER, GERHART, German language educator; b. Giessen, Germany, Dec. 17, 1936; came to U.S., 1966, naturalized citizen, 1993; s. Johannes and Inge Caecilie (Johannsen) H.; m. Margaret von Poletika, May 28, 1966 (div. Dec. 1988); 1 child, George A. Degree, U. Bonn, Fed. Republic Germany, 1963, U. Cologne, Fed. Republic Germany, 1966; PhD, U. Md., 1970. Student tchr. U. Cologne, 1964-66; instr. U. Md., 1966-70; asst. prof. U. Wis., Milw., 1970-74; assoc. prof. Wayne State U., Detroit, 1974-75; assoc. prof. U. Calif., Santa Barbara, 1975-79, prof., 1979—, bd. dirs. Comparative Lit. program, 1991-97. Author: (with others) Germany 2, 000 Years III, 1986; editor: Goethe in Italy, 1988, French Revolution, 1989, European Romanticism, 1989. Recipient award Am. Philos. Assn., 1974, Max Kade Found., 1986, 88. Mem. MLA, Pacific Ancient and Modern Lang. Assn., Am. Assn. Tchrs. German, Goethe Soc. N.Am. Home: 117 Calle Alamo Santa Barbara CA 93105-2818 Office: U Calif Dept German Santa Barbara CA 93106

HOFMANN, ALAN FREDERICK, biomedical educator, researcher; b. Balt., May 17, 1931; s. Joseph Enoch and Nelda Rosina (Durr) H.; m. Marta Gertrud Pettersson, Aug. 15, 1969 (div. 1976); children: Anthea Karin, Cecilia Rae; m. Helga Katharina Aicher, Nov. 3, 1978. BA with honors, Johns Hopkins U., 1951, MD with honors, 1955; PhD, U. Lund, Sweden, 1965; MD honoris causis, U. Bologna, Italy, 1988; hon. fellow, Royal Coll. Physicians, 1996. Intern, then resident dept. medicine Columbia Presbyn. Med. Ctr., N.Y.C., 1955-57; clin. assoc. clin. ctr. Nat. Heart Inst., NIH, Bethesda, Md., 1957-59; postdoctoral fellow, dept. physiol. chemistry U. Lund, Sweden, 1959-62; asst. physician Hosp. of the Rockefeller U., N.Y.C., 1962-64; outpatient physician N.Y. Hosp., N.Y.C., 1963-64; assoc. physician Hosp. of the Rockefeller U., N.Y.C., 1964-66; cons. in medicine, assoc. dir. gastroenterology unit Mayo Clinic, Rochester, Minn., 1966-77; attending physician Med. Ctr. U. Calif.-San Diego, 1977—; asst. prof. dept. medicine Rockefeller U., N.Y.C., 1964-66; assoc. prof. medicine and biochemistry U. Minn. Mayo Grad. Sch., 1966-69, assoc. prof. medicine and physiology, 1969-70, prof. medicine and physiology, 1970-73; prof. medicine and physiology Mayo Med. Sch., 1973-77; cons. physiology Mayo Clinic, Rochester, 1975-77; prof. medicine U. Calif., San Diego, 1977—, adj. prof. pharmacy, U. Calif., San Francisco, 1986—; vis. prof. pharmacy U. Mich., Ann Arbor, 1980-85. Patentee solvent for direct dissolution of cholesterol gallstones, breath test for pancreatic exocrine function, bile acid replacement therapy; contbr. numerous articles to profl. jours., books, films. Recipient Travel award Wellcome Trust, 1961-63, Travel award NSF, 1964, Sr. Scientist award Humboldt Found., Fed. Republic of Germany, 1976, 91 (shared prize) Eppinger Prize, Falk Found., 1976, Disting. Achievement award Modern Medicine mag., 1978 Chancellor's Rsch. Excellence award U. Calif., 1986; Nat. Fedn. fellow, 1959-61, USPHS fellow, 1962-63, Fogarty Internat. Sr. fellow NIH, 1986; Rockefeller Found. scholar, Bellagio, Italy, 1980. Fellow AAAS, Royal Soc. Medicine; mem. Am. Assn. Study of Liver Disease (numerous coms., pres. 1984), Swedish Soc. for Gastroenterology (hon.), Soc. for Gastrointestinal Radiology (hon.), Gastroent. Soc. Australia (hon.), Chilean Soc. Gastroenterology (hon.), Brit. Soc. Gastroenterology (hon.), Royal Flemish Acad. for Medicine (hon., fgn. corr. mem.), German Soc. for Digestive and Metabolic Disease (hon. mem., Siegfried Thannhauser medal 1996), Am. Soc. Clin. Investigation, Assn. Am. Physicians, Am. Liver Found. (chmn. sci. adv. bd. 1986-91), Am. Physiol. Soc. (Horace Davenport medal 1996), Am. Gastroent. Assn. (chmn. biliary diseases coun. 1991-92, Disting. Achievement award 1970, co-winner Beaumont prize 1979, Friedenwald medal 1994), Phi Beta Kappa, Sigma Xi, Alpha Omega Alpha, Omicron Delta Kappa. Home: 5870 Cactus Way La Jolla CA 92037-7069

HOFMANN, PAUL BERNARD, health care consultant; b. Portland, Oreg., July 6, 1941; s. Max and Consuelo Theresa (Bley) H.; m. Lois Bernstein, June 28, 1969; children: Julie, Jason. BS, U. Calif., Berkeley, 1963, MPH, 1965, DPH, 1994. Research assoc. in hosp. adminstrn. Lab. of Computer Sci., Mass. Gen. Hosp., Boston, 1966-68; asst. dir. Lab. of Computer Sci., Mass. Gen. Hosp., 1968-69; asst. adminstr. San Antonio Community Hosp., Upland, Calif., 1969-70; assoc. adminstr. San Antonio Community Hosp., 1970-72; dep. dir. Stanford (Calif.) U. Hosp., 1972-74, dir., 1974-77; exec. dir. Emory U. Hosp., Atlanta, 1978-87; exec. v.p., chief ops. officer Alta Bates Corp., Emeryville, Calif., 1987-91; cons. Alta Bates Corp., Emeryville, 1991-92, Alexander & Alexander, San Francisco, 1992-94; disting. vis. scholar Stanford (Calif.) U. Ctr. for Biomed. Ethics, 1993—; sr. fellow Stanford (Calif.) U. Hosp., 1993-94; sr. cons. stragetic healthcare practice Alexander & Alexander Cons. Group, San Francisco, Calif., 1994—; instr. computer applications Harvard U., 1968-69; lectr. hosp. adminstrn. UCLA, 1970-72, Stanford U. Med. Sch., 1972-77; assoc. prof. Emory U. Sch. Medicine, Atlanta, 1978-87. Author: The Development and Application of Ethical Criteria for Use in Making Programmatic Resource Allocation Decisions in Hospitals, 1994; contbr. articles to profl. jours. Served with U.S. Army, 1959. Fellow Am. Coll. Hosp. Adminstrs. (recipient Robert S. Hudgens meml. award 1976); mem. Am. Hosp. Assn., Assn. Univ. Programs in Health Adminstrn., U. Calif. Alumni Assn.

HOFSTETTER, JANE ROBINSON, artist, educator; b. Oakland, Calif., Feb. 23, 1936; d. Thomas O. and Fern (Worstell) Robinson; m. William R. Hofstetter, Aug. 3, 1958; children: David, Glen. Student, U. Calif., Berkeley, San Francisco Sch. of Design, Chouinard Art Inst., L.A. lectr. in field. Represented in permanent collections Triton Mus. Art, Santa Clara, Calif., State of Calif. Collection, Asilomar, San Ramon and Santa Clara City Halls, Kayser Hosp., Calif., IBM Hdqs. and Gen. Facilities, Gould Inc., No. Calif. Savings and Loan, Systems Control Inc., Zerox Corp., Finance Am. Recipient Trinton Art Mus. award and numerous others. Mem. Nat. Watercolor Soc., Watercolor West Soc., Midwest Watercolor Soc., Soc. Western Artists. Studio: 308 Dawson Dr Santa Clara CA 95051-5806

HOGAN, CLARENCE LESTER, retired electronics executive; b. Great Falls, Mont., Feb. 8, 1920; s. Clarence Lester and Bessie (Young) H.; m. Audrey Biery Peters, Oct. 13, 1946; 1 child, Cheryl Lea. BSChemE, Mont. State U., 1942, Dr. Engring. (hon.), 1967; MS in Physics, Lehigh U., 1947, PhD in Physics, 1950, D in Engring. (hon.), 1971; AM (hon.), Harvard U., 1954; D in Sci. (hon.), Worcester Poly. U., 1969. Rsch. chem. engr. Anaconda Copper Mining Co., 1942-43; instr. physics Lehigh U., 1946-50; mem. tech. staff Bell Labs., Murray Hill, N.J., 1950-51, sub-dept. head, 1951-53; assoc. prof. Harvard U., Cambridge, Mass., 1953-57, Gordon McKay prof., 1957-58; gen. mgr. semi-conductor products divsn. Motorola, Inc., Phoenix, 1958-60, v.p., 1960-66, exec. v.p., dir., 1966-68; pres., chief exec. officer Fairchild Inst., Mt. View, Calif., 1968-74, vice chmn. bd. dirs., 1974-85; gen. chmn. Internat. Conf. on Magnetism and Magnetic Materials, 1959, 60; mem. materials adv. bd. Dept. Def., 1957-59; mem. adv. coun. dept. electrical engring. Princeton U.; mem. adv. bd. sch. engring. U. Calif., Berkeley, 1974—, adv. bd. dept. chem. engring. Mont. State U., 1988—; mem. nat. adv. bd. Desert Rsch. Inst., 1976-80; mem. vis. com. dept. electric engring. and computer sci. MIT, 1975-85; mem. adv. coun. div. electrical engring. Stanford U., 1976-86; mem. sci. and ednl. adv. com. Lawrence Berkeley Lab., 1978-84; mem. Pres.'s Export Coun., 1976-80; mem. adv. panel to tech. adv. bd. U.S. Congress, 1976-80. Patentee in field; inventor microwave gyrator, circulator, isolator. Chmn. Commn. Found. Santa Clara County, Calif., 1983-85; mem. vis. com. Lehigh U., 1966-71, trustee, 1971-80, also life trustee; trustee Western Electronic Edn. Fund; mem. governing bd. Maricopa County Jr. Coll.; bd. regents U. Santa Clara. Lt. (j.g.) USNR, 1942-46. Recipient Community Svc. award NCCJ, 1978, Medal of Merit Am. Electronics Assn., 1978, Berkeley Citation U. Calif., 1980; named Bay Area Bus. Man of Yr. San Jose State U., 1978, One of 10 Greatest Innovators in Past 50 Yrs. Electronics Mag., 1980. Fellow AAAS, IEEE (Frederick Philips gold medal 1976, Edison silver medal Cleve. Soc. 1978, Pioneering medal for microwave theory and tech. 1993), Inst. Elec. Engrs. (hon.); mem. NAE, Am. Phys. Soc., Menlo Country Club, Masons, Sigma Xi, Tau Beta Pi, Phi Kappa Phi, Kappa Sigma. Democrat. Baptist. Home: 36 Barry Ln Atherton CA 94027-4023

HOGAN, EDDY, library director; b. San Antonio, May 26, 1952; s. Robert and Susie (Morales) H. BA in English, U. Houston, 1976; MLS, U. Tex., 1978, postgrad., 1979. Reference libr. Main Libr. U. Colo. Univ. Libr., Boulder, 1979-84, U. Calif. Gen. Libr., Berkeley, 1984-87; data & info. svcs. libr. Cecil H. Green Libr. Stanford (Calif.) U. Univ. Librs., 1987-90; electronic info. svcs. libr. Calif. State U. Univ. Libr., Sacramento, 1990-95; dir. libr. svc. Calif. State U., 1996—; presenter, keynote spkr. in field. Mem. bd. editors Jour. Acad. Librarianship, 1993—; contbr. articles to profl. jours. H.E.A. Title II-B minority fellow U. Tex., 1977-78; grantee Calif. State U., Sacramento Hornet Found., 1992; Microsoft CD-ROM Libr. scholar, 1989. Mem. ALA (vice-chair, chair elect, 1996—, systems and svcs. sect. 1990-93, libr. adminstrn. and mgmt. assn. 1994-97, current topics planning com., chmn. Assn. Coll. and Rsch. Librs. univ. librs. sect. 1990-92, chmn. publs. com., libr. instrn. roundtable 1983-84, chmn. com. libr. svcs. to Spanish-speaking), Calif. State U. Librs.-North (pres. 1992—). Home: 1318 Patch Ct Marina CA 93933-5036 Office: Calif State U Monetary Bay Libr 100 Campus Ctr Seaside CA 93955

HOGAN, MERVIN BOOTH, mechanical engineer, educator; b. Bountiful, Utah, July 21, 1906; s. Charles Ira and Sarah Ann (Booth) H.; m. Helen Emily Reese, Dec. 27, 1928; 1 son, Edward Reese. BS, U. Utah, 1927, ME, 1930; MS, U. Pitts., 1929; PhD, U. Mich., 1936, postgrad.; Sterling fellow, Yale U., 1937-38. Registered profl. engr., Conn., Mich., N.Y., Utah, Va. chartered engr., U.K. Design engr. Westinghouse Electric Corp., East Pittsburgh, Pa., 1927-31; asst. prof. mech. engring. U. Utah, Salt Lake City, 1931-36, asso. prof., 1936-39, prof., 1939-56, chmn. dept. mech. engring., 1951-56, prof., 1971-76, prof. emeritus, 1976—; mgr. product design engring. GE, Syracuse, N.Y., 1956-65; mgr. design assurance engring. GE, Phoenix, 1965-70; cons. engr. GE, Waynesboro, Va., 1970-71; cons. Chgo. Bridge & Iron, 1950-56. Author: Mormonism and Freemasonry: The Illinois Episode, 1977, The Origin and Growth of Utah Masonry and Its Conflict with Mormonism, 1978, Mormonism and Freemasonry under Covert Masonic Influences, 1979, Freemasonry and the Lynching at Carthage Jail, 1981, Freemasonry and Civil Confrontation on the Illinois Frontier, 1981, The Involvement of Freemasonry with Mormonism on the American Midwestern Frontier, 1982; contbr. articles to engr. jours., numerous articles to Masonic publs. Recipient Merit of Honor award U. Utah, 1981. Fellow ASME, Inst. Mech. Engrs. (London), Yale Sci., Engring. Assn.; mem. IEEE (sr.), Nat. Eagle Scout Assn., DeMolay Legion of Honor, S.R. in State N.Y., Utah Soc. SAR (pres. 1983-84), Aztec Club, Timpanogos Club, Elfun Soc., Rotary, Masons (33 deg.), Shriners, Prophets, KT, DeMolay, Quatuor Coronati Lodge 2076, Sigma Xi, Phi Kappa Phi, Tau Beta Pi, Pi Tau Sigma, Sigma Nu, Theta Tau, Alpha Phi Omega, Phi Lambda Epsilon. Home: Douglas Park 921 Greenwood Terr Salt Lake City UT 84105 Office: U Utah 3008 Merrill Engring Bldg Salt Lake City UT 84112

HOGAN, MICHAEL R(OBERT), judge; b. Oregon City, Oreg., Sept. 24, 1946; married; 3 children. A.B., U. Oreg. Honors Coll., 1968; J.D., Georgetown U., 1971. Bar: Oreg. 1971, U.S. Ct. Appeals (9th cir.) 1971. Law clk. to chief judge U.S. Dist. Ct. Oreg., Portland, 1971-72; assoc. Miller, Anderson, Nash, Yerke and Wiener, Portland, 1972-73; magistrate judge U.S. Dist. Ct. Oreg., Eugene, 1973-91, dist. judge, 1991—, chief judge, 1995—; bankruptcy judge U.S. Dist. Oreg., Eugene, 1973-80. Mem. ABA, Oreg. State Bar Assn. Office: US Courthouse 211 E 7th Ave Eugene OR 97401-2722

HOGE, ROBERT WILSON, museum curator; b. Wilmington, Del., Jan. 5, 1947; s. George Lee and Rosalie Jessie (Colton) H.; m. Laura Lee Brown, June 20, 1980 (div. Mar. 1991). BA, U. Colo., 1969. Cert. tchr., Colo., Iowa. Dir. Sanford Mus., Cherokee, Iowa, 1976-81; curator Am. Numismatic Assn., Colorado Springs, Colo., 1981—. Contbg. editor The Numismatist, 1989—; columnist The Numismatist, 1981—. Mem. Am. Assn. Museums (Internat. Mus. Ptnr. award 1989), Am. Numismatic Soc., Royal Numismatic Soc., Mountain-Plains Mus. Assn., Colo.-Wyo. Assn. Museums, Numismatics Internat., Phi Beta Kappa. Office: Am Numismatic Assn 818 N Cascade Ave Colorado Springs CO 80903-3208

HOGLE, JERROLD EDWIN, English language educator; b. L.A., May 15, 1948; s. Howard Clinton and Jane (Reynard) H.; m. Pamela Jean Wesp, Aug. 22, 1970; children: Karen, Joanne. BA summa cum laude, U. Calif., Irvine, 1970; MA, Harvard U., 1971, PhD, 1974. Tchg. fellow in humanities Harvard U., Cambridge, Mass., 1971-74; asst. prof. English U. Ariz., Tucson, 1974-80, assoc. prof. English, 1980-89, prof. English, 1989—, assoc. dean humanities, 1990-93, acting dean humanities, 1991, univ. disting. prof., 1996—, chair faculty, 1997—. Author: (book) Shelley's Process, 1988; editor: (book) Evaluating Shelley, 1996, mem. editl. bd. Keats Shelby jours.; mem. adv. bd. (website) Romantic Crossings, 1995—; mem. editl. adv. bd. Gothic Studies jour., 1995—; contbr. articles to lit. and essays collection, jours. Pres. Butterfield Elem. PTO, Tucson, 1983-84; pres. Mountain View H.S. PTO, Tucson, 1989-90; local pres., state bd. dirs. Ariz. Assn. Gifted/Talented, Tucson, 1982-91; founder, Marana Found. for Edn., Tucson, 1991-92. Sgt. USAR, 1971-77. Guggenheim fellow, 1989-90, Mellon Huntington Libr. fellow, 1990. Mem. MLA, N.Am. Soc. for Study of Romanticism (conf. chair 1991—), Internat. Gothic Assn. (pres., 1995—), Keats-Shelley Assn. (mem. editl. adv. bd. 1989—). Democrat. Office: U Ariz Dept English Tucson AZ 85921

HOGOBOOM, WILLIAM PERRY, judge, arbitrator, mediator; b. Pasadena, Calif., Oct. 31, 1918; s. William Coryell and Grace Wise (Hogsett) H.; m. Betty Cornwell, June 30, 1944 (dec. Jan. 1991); children: William, Christian, Katherine, Lissa. BA, Occidental Coll., 1939; MPA, U. So. Calif., L.A., 1941, JD, 1949, LLD (hon.), 1978; LLD (hon.), W. L.A. Sch. Law, 1977. Bar: Calif. 1949, U.S. Ct. Appeals (9th cir.) 1950, U.S. Dist. Ct. (so. dist.) Calif. 1949, U.S. Supreme Ct. 1967. Ptnr. Iverson & Hogoboom, L.A., 1950-68; judge Superior Ct. of Calif., L.A., 1968-83; v.p., gen. counsel U. So. Calif., L.A., 1983-91; arbitrator, mediator L.A., 1993—. Author: California Family Law Practice, 1979. Lt. USN, 1944-46. Fellow Internat. Acad. Trial Judges; mem. L.A. County Bar Assn. (trustee 1975-77), Calif. Judges Assn., Order of Coif, Phi Beta Kappa. Home and Office: 192 Annandale Rd Pasadena CA 91105

HOHENSTEIN, HENRY JOHN, land use planner, educator; b. Cohoes, N.Y., Sept. 28, 1931; s. Charles Henry and Ann Mildred (Eldon) H.; m. Mary Arline Kennedy, Aug. 29, 1953 (div. May 1974); children: Anne, Henry, Ellen, Elizabeth, Frederick; m. Susan Natalie Carroll, Oct. 2, 1988. BS, Rutgers U., 1953; M in City and Regional Planning, Calif. Poly. State U., 1985. Owner 7-H Co., 1974-84; redevel. dir. City of Desert Hot Springs, Calif., 1984-86; assoc. planner City of Indio, Calif., 1986-88; cmty. devel. dir. City of Indio, 1992-96; dir. planning Interactive Design, Palm Springs, Calif., 1988-92; adj. faculty Coll. of the Desert, Palm Desert, 1986-96. Author: Peanut Butter and Jelly, IRS Conspiracy, 1974. Planning commr. Planning Commn., City of Desert Hot Springs, 1987-91. Maj. USMC, 1953-56. Recipient Disting. Leadership award Calif. chpt. Am. Planning Assn., 1994. Mem. Am. Inst. Cert. Planners. Home: 9090 Calle Escorial Desert Hot Springs CA 92240-1647

HOHNER, KENNETH DWAYNE, retired fodder company executive; b. St. John, Kans., June 24, 1934; s. Courtney Clinton and Mildred Lucile (Forrester) H.; m. Sherry Eloi Anice Edens, Feb. 14, 1961; children: Katrina, Melissa, Steven, Michael. BS in Geol. Engring., U. Kans., 1957. Geophysicist Mobil Oil Corp., New Orleans, Anchorage, Denver, 1957-72; sr. geophysicist Amerada Hess Corp., Houston, 1972-75, ARAMCO, London, 1975-79; far east area geophysicist Hamilton Bros., Denver, 1979-83; owner Hohner Poultry Farm, Erie, Colo., 1979-94; pres. Hohner Custom Feed, Inc., Erie, Colo., 1982-94. Mem. Soc. Exploration Geophysicists. Home: 1201 W Thornton Pkwy Denver CO 80221

HOHNHORST, JOHN CHARLES, lawyer; b. Jerome, Idaho, Dec. 25, 1952; m. Raelene Casper; children: Jennifer, Rachel, John. BS in Polit. Sci./Pub. Adminstrn., U. Idaho, 1975, JD cum laude, 1978. Bar: Idaho 1978, U.S. Dist. Ct. Idaho 1978, U.S. Ct. Appeals (9th cir.) 1980, U.S. Ct. Claims 1983, U.S. Supreme Ct. 1987. Adminstrv. asst. to Sen. John M. Barker Idaho State Senate, 1975; ptnr. Hepworth, Lezamiz & Hohnhorst, Twin Falls, Idaho, 1978—. Contbr. articles to profl. jours. Mem. planning & zoning commn. City of Twin Falls, 1987-90. Mem. ABA, Assn. Trial Lawyers Am., Idaho State Bar (commr. 1990-93, pres. 1993), Idaho Trial Lawyers Assn. (regional dir. 1985-86), 5th Dist. Bar Assn. (treas. 1987-88, v.p. 1988-89, pres. 1989-90), Greater Twin Falls C. of C. (chmn. magic valley leadership program 1988-89, bd. dirs. 1989-92), Phi Kappa Tau (Beta Gamma chpt., Phi award 1988). Office: Hepworth Nungester & Lezamiz PO Box 389 133 Shoshone St N Twin Falls ID 83303

HOILAND, ANDREW CALVIN, architect; b. Great Falls, Mont., Aug. 3, 1926; s. Andrew C. and Ida (Mohondro) H.; m. Patricia Ruth Willits, Aug. 13, 1950; children: William H., Richard C., Diana Ruth. B.S. in Architecture, Mont. State Coll., 1949. Draftsman A.V. McIver (architect), Great Falls, 1949-52; prin. A. Calvin Hoiland (architect), Great Falls, 1952-54; partner Hoiland & Lund (architects), Great Falls, 1953-63, Hoiland-Zucconi (architects), Great Falls, 1964-74, A. Calvin Hoiland (Architect), 1974—; Pres. Mont. Bd. Archtl. Examiners, 1968. Assoc. editor Am. Architects Directory, 1969-70; mem. editorial adv. bd. Symposia mag., 1968-78, Northwest Archtl. mag., 1983-85; important works include: Great Falls swimming pools, 1963, Mountain View Sch., Great Falls, 1968-69, Great Falls fire stas., 1969-71, Gregson Hot Springs swimming pools, 1972, Great Falls PCA-FLBA Office, 1978, I.F.G. Leasing Bldg, Great Falls, 1980, Heritage Inn, French Quarter, Great Falls, 1979-80, Giant Springs Trout Hatchery, Great Falls, 1984, Midgetman Launcher Facility, Malmstron AFB, 1988. Chmn. charity ball for Great Falls Rehab. Center, 1961-62; chmn. master plan com. Great Falls Swimming Pool, 1962-65; chmn. adv. council Great Falls chpt. DeMolay; bd. dirs. Great Falls Camp Fire Girls. Served with USAAC, World War II. Named to Legion of Honor Order DeMolay, 1956, Cross of Honor, 1976. Mem. AIA (pres. Mont. 1961-62, editor Mont. publ. 1965-71), Great Falls Soc. Architects (charter pres. 1953), Mont. Tech. Council (charter pres. 1960-61), Sigma Chi. Methodist (chmn. bd. trustees, mem. bldg. com. Wesley Center, mem. Mont. bd. missions). Lodges: Masons (master 1979), Scottish Rite (33 degree, master 1980), Royal Order of Scotland, York Rite, Shriners, Kiwanis (pres. Great Falls 1964). Home and Office: 2826 3rd Ave S Great Falls MT 59405-3110 *I believe we should learn from the past, enjoy the present, and prepare for the future.*

HOIVIK, THOMAS HARRY, military educator, international consultant; b. Mpls., June 6, 1941; s. Tony Horace and Helen Lenea (Carlsen) H.; m. Judith Lisa Kohn; children: Todd, Gregory. BA, U. Minn., 1963; grad. with distinction, Naval Test Pilot Sch., 1969; MS with distinction, Naval Postgrad. Sch., 1973; grad. with distinction, Naval War Coll., 1976; MA, Salve Regina U., 1988. Cert. exptl. test pilot, air transport pilot, jet aircraft, helicopter, glider single and multi-engine. Commd. ensign USN, 1963, advanced through grades to capt., 1963-91; test pilot Naval Air Test Ctr., Patuxent River, Md., 1968-71; program mgr. H-53 aircraft Naval Air Systems Command, Washington, 1976-78; comdg. officer Helicopter Mine Countermeasure Squadron 14, Norfolk, Va., 1978-80; dir. U.S. Naval Test Pilot Sch., Patuxent River, 1980-82; fed. exec. fellow Ctr. for Strategic and Internat. Studies, Washington, 1982-83; chair tactical analysis Naval Postgrad. Sch., Monterey, Calif., 1983-85; comdg. officer Naval Air Sta., Willow Grove, Pa., 1985-87; ret. USN, 1991; chair applied systems analysis Naval Postgrad. Sch., Monterey, 1987-91, prof. acquisition mgmt. and ops. rsch., 1991—; ret. capt. USN, 1991; dir. test and evaluation sr. level curriculum Defense Acquisition U., 1993—; mem. U.S. Congrl. Study Group on Nat. Strategy, Washington, 1982-83, World Economy, 1982-83; cons. U.S., Internat. Govt. Orgns., 1990—; founder, pres. Lysonics Rsch. Internat., 1993; flight demonstration pilot Paris Internat. Air Show, 1967. Contbr. articles to profl. jours. Bd. dirs. Vocat. Edn. Bd., Montgomery County, Pa., 1985-87, Congrl. Svc. Acad. Appointment Bd., Phila., 1985-87; youth leader, counselor YMCA, St. Paul, 1955-61. Recipient Legion of Merit Pres. of U.S., 1987, Outstanding Youth Leadership award YMCA, 1960; established U.S. Helicopter Speed Record, 1966. Mem. AIAA, Soc. of Exptl. Test Pilots, Internat. Test and Evaluation Assn., Nat. Contract Mgmt. Assn., Ops. Rsch. Soc. Am., Mil. Ops. Rsch. Soc., U. Minn. "M" Club, Disable Am. Vets, Sigma Alpha Epsilon. Office: Naval Postgrad Sch Monterey CA 93943

HOKANA, GREGORY HOWARD, engineering executive; b. Burbank, Calif., Nov. 24, 1944; s. Howard Leslie and Helen Lorraine (Walker) H.; m. Eileen Marie Youell, Apr. 29, 1967; children: Kristen Marie, Kenneth Gregory. BS in Physics, UCLA, 1966. Design engr. Raytheon Co., Oxnard, Calif., 1967-74; staff engr. Bunker Ramo Corp., Westlake Village, Calif., 1974-84; mgr. analog engring. AIL Systems, Inc., Westlake Village, 1984-91; mgr. product devel. Am. Nucleonics Corp., Westlake Village, 1991-93; tech. mgr. Litton Data Sys., Agoura Hills, Calif., 1994—. Mem. IEEE, Assn. Old Crows. Democrat. Methodist. Home: 3485 Farrell Cir Newbury Park CA 91320-4333 Office: Litton Data Systems PO Box 6008 Agoura Hills CA 91376-6008

HOLBROOK, JAMES RUSSELL, lawyer; b. Kansas City, Mo., Sept. 24, 1944; s. Newell James and Martha Inez (Russell) H.; m. Meghan Zanolli, Feb. 12, 1983. Student, MIT, 1962-63; BA, Grinnell (Iowa) Coll., 1966; MA, Ind. U., 1968; JD, U. Utah, 1974. Bar: Utah 1974, U.S. Dist. Ct. Utah 1974, U.S. Ct. Appeals (10th cir.) 1977, U.S. Supreme Ct. 1980. Law clk. to chief judge U.S. Dist. Ct. Utah, Salt Lake City, 1973-75; pvt. practice Salt Lake City, 1975-78, asst. U.S. Atty. of Utah, 1978-80; ptnr. Giauque & Williams, Salt Lake City, 1980-82; gen. counsel Intermountain Power Agy., Murray, Utah, 1982-83; ptnr. Callister Nebeker & McCullough, Salt Lake City, 1983—; mem. adv. com. on revisions to local rules of practice U.S. Dist. Ct. Utah, 1989—, mem. alt. dispute resolution subcom., 1991—; mem. alt. dispute resolution com. Utah Jud. Coun., 1993—; adj. assoc. prof. U. Utah Coll. Law, Salt Lake City, 1984-88, 90—. Articles editor Jour. Contemporary Law, 1973-74; contbr. articles to profl. jours. Mem. bd. Internat. Visitors Utah Coun., Salt Lake City, 1984-96; mem. exhbns. coun. Utah Mus. Fine Arts, Salt Lake City, 1986-92, 94-97; bd. govs. Salt Lake Found., Salt Lake City, 1987-92; mem. Ctr. for Humanitarian Outreach and Inter-Cultural Exch., Salt Lake City, 1996—; trustee Utah Mus. Natural History, Salt Lake City, 1996—. With U.S. Army, 1968-70, Vietnam. Decorated Bronze Star, Army Commendation medal; NSF fellow, 1966-68, Woodrow Wilson Found. fellow, 1966. Mem. ABA, Utah Bar Assn. (commr. 1988-90), Fed. Bar Assn. (pres. Utah chpt. 1984-85), Am. Arbitration Assn. (bd. dirs. N.Y.C. 1996—), Sutherland Inn of Ct. (master of the bench 1984—), Alta Club, Phi Beta Kappa, Sigma Phi Epsilon. Democrat. Home: 775 Hilltop Rd Salt Lake City UT 84103-3311 Office: Callister Nebeker & McCullough Gateway Tower East Ste 900 10 East South Temple Salt Lake City UT 84133

HOLBROOK, PETER GREENE, artist; b. N.Y.C., Apr. 13, 1940; s. Richard Greene and Margaret Primrose (Henderson) H.; children: Acacia, Sean. BA, Dartmouth Coll., 1961; Cert., Bklyn. Mus. Art Sch., 1963. Tchr. Oxbow Summer Sch. Painting, Saugatuck, Mich., 1968, U. Ill., Chgo., 1968-70, North Shore Art League, Winnetka, Ill., 1968, Calif. State U., Hayward, 1970-71, Ctr. for Arts and Humanities, Sun Valley, Idaho, 1988. One-man shows include Carpenter Galleries, Hanover, N.H., 1960, Richard Gray Gallery, Chgo., 1964, 66, 67, 69, 70, 73, 76, Unitarian Ch., Chgo., 1968, Indpls. Mus. Art, 1970, William Sawyer Gallery, San Francisco, 1975, Nautilus Gallery, Arcata, Calif., 1976, ADI Gallery, San Francisco, 1977, 78, Frumkin Struve Gallery, Chgo., 1980, 82, Mattingly-Baker Gallery, Dallas, 1982, Kauffman Gallery, Houston, 1983, Struve Gallery, Chgo., 1985, Larry Munson Gallery, Santa Fe, 1986, Capricorn Galleries, Bethesda Md., 1987, 89, 90, 92, Louis Newman Galleries, Beverly Hills, Calif., 1988, 89, 90, Bell Gallery, Woodstock, N.Y., 1988, Shaklee Terrace Gallery, San Francisco, 1991, Jan Cicero Gallery, Chgo., 1991, John Pence Gallery, San Francisco, 1991, Equitable Life Gallery, San Francisco, 1992, Mesa (Ariz.) SW Mus., 1996; exhibited in group shows at Frumkin Struve Gallery, Chgo., 1980, Kauffman Galleries, Houston, 1981, Cultural Ctr., Eureka, Calif., 1981, Frumkin Struve Gallery, Chgo., 1982, Hamline U., St. Paul, 1983, Scottsdale (Ariz.) Ctr. for Arts, 1984, Coll. Redwoods, Eureka, 1985, Bell Gallery, Rhinebeck, N.Y., 1986, John Pence Gallery, San Francisco, 1987, 88, 89, 90, Sun Valley Art Ctr., Idaho, 1987, Payne Gallery Moravian Coll., Bethlehem, Pa., 1988, Atlee and Atlee Fine Arts, Eureka, 1989, Jan Cicero Gallery, Chgo., 1989-90, 90, Internat. Art Expo Navy Pier, Chgo., 1990, and more; mus. exhbns. include Civic Arts Gallery, Walnut Creek, Calif., 1980, Pa. Acad. Fine Art, Phila., 1982, U. Wis. and Ill. State U., 1982, Springfield (Mo.) Art Mus., 1982, 86, Ft. Wayne (Ind.) Mus. Art, 1983, Rahr-West Mus., Manitowoc, Wis., 1984, San Francisco Mus. Modern Art, 1985, Nat. Mus. Art, Washington, 1987, Butler Inst., Youngstown, Ohio, 1987, Mesa (Ariz.) Southwest Mus., 1987, 94, Hunter Art Mus., Chattanooga, 1994; represented in permanent mus. collections Ind. State U., Indpls., Nat. Collection Fine Arts Smithsonian, Washington, No. Ill. U., De Kalb, Bklyn. Mus., N.Y.C., Art Inst. Chgo., Cornell Coll., Mt. Vernon, Iowa, Mus. S.W., Midland, Tex., U. Nebr., Lincoln, Boise Art Mus., Springfield Art Mus., 1997, Achenbach Collection Palace of Legion of Honor, San Francisco, Oakland (Calif.) Mus., Tucson Mus. Art; represented in permanent corp. collections Am. Fedn. Arts, N.Y.C., Bank of Am., San Francisco, Dolby Labs., San Francisco, Gulf Pipeline, Houston, Ill. Bell Telephone, Chgo., Koffler Found., Chgo., Minn. Mining & Mfg., St. Paul, Western Electric, N.Y.C., H.J. Heinz Co., Pitts., Continental Bank, Singapore, FMC Corp., Chgo., Kemper Ins. Co., Chgo., Shaklee Corp., San Francisco, Plz. of Ams., Dallas, Clorox Co., Oakland, Stroud & Waller, Chgo., R.J. Reynolds Co., Winston-Salem, N.C., Frito-Lay Corp, Dryers Corp., Oakland. Recipient Walter H. Stevens award Watercolor USA, 1981, Raffael prize for watercolor Cultural Ctr., 1981, Max Beckman Meml. fellowship Bklyn. Mus. Sch., 1962-63, James B. Reynold Fgn. Study fellowship, Paris, 1961-62, Marcus Heiman award for creative arts Dartmouth Coll., 1960; recipient Emily L. Wild prize Art Inst. Chgo., 1968, Bartels prize, 1967, James Clark prize, 1965.

HOLBROOK, RICHARD L., investment manager; b. Tachikawa, Japan, Dec. 29, 1952; s. Eldon G. and Marian L. Holbrook; m. Cynthia Ann Williams; children: Natalie, Melanie Lindsay. BA in Econs., Brigham Young U., 1977; MBA, STanford U., 1979. Investment counselor Bailand Biehl & Kaiser, San Mateo, Calif., 1979-95; portfolio mgr. Bailand Biehl & Kaiser, $, Calif., 1987-95; investment counselor in pvt. practice, Foster City, Calif., 1995—. Author investment column for San Mateo newspaper, 1992—. Bishop local congregation Ch. of Jesus Christ of Latter Day Saints, Foster City, 1992—. Home: 505 St Thomas Ln Foster City CA 94404-3977

HOLBROOK, SALLY DAVIS, author; b. L.A., July 2, 1932; d. Elias Kaylor and Elisabeth (Jackson) Davis; m. William Sumner Holbrook III, Sept. 22, 1956; children: William Sumner IV (dec.), Robert Davis. AB, Pomona Coll., Claremont, Calif., 1954. Author: Sun, Sand and Sausage Pie, 1992, Party Perfect and Pampered, 1995. Mem. Jr. League of Pasadena; assoc. Children's Hosp.-Pasadena Guild. Mem. The Town Club of Pasadena, The Valley Hunt Club. Republican. Episcopalian. Home: 1440 Vista Ln Pasadena CA 91103-1938 Address (summer): 1230 E Ocean Blvd Apt 303 Long Beach CA 90802

HOLDCROFT, LESLIE THOMAS, clergyman, educator; b. Man., Can., Sept. 28, 1922; s. Oswald Thomas and Florence (Waterfield) H.; student Western Bible Coll., 1941-44; BA, San Francisco State Coll., 1950; MA, San Jose State Coll., 1955; postgrad. Stanford, 1960, 63, U. Cal., 1965-67; DDiv., Bethany Bible Coll., 1968; m. Ruth Sorensen, July 2, 1948; children: Cynthia Ruth, Althea Lois, Sylvia Bernice. Instr. Western Bible Coll., 1944-47; instr. Bethany Bible Coll., 1947-55, dean edn., 1955-68, v.p., 1967-68; pres. Western Pentecostal Bible Coll., 1968-87; acad. cons., researcher, Abbotsford, B.C., 1991—; pastor Craig Chapel, 1959-68; dir. Can. Pentecostal Corr. Coll., Abbotsford, 1985-90, 95—. Pres., Assn. Canadian Bible Colls., 1972-76. Author: The Historical Books, 1960, The Synoptic Gospels, 1962, The Holy Spirit, 1962, The Pentateuch, 1951, 96, Divine Healing, 1967, The Doctrine of God, 1978, The Four Gospels, 1988, 94, Anthropology: A Biblical View, 1990, Soteriology: Good News in Review, 1990, Ecclesiology: Christ's Treasure on Earth, 1992. Home: 34623 Ascott Ave, Abbotsford, BC Canada V2S 5A3 Office: Box 700, Abbotsford, BC Canada V2S 6R7

HOLDEN, FRED STEPHEN, industrial tree farmer; b. Seattle, Aug. 5, 1927; s. Charles Ray and Mary Frances (Hull) H.; m. Carole Kathryn Kronsteiner, Sept. 3, 1950; children: Lisl Kathryn, Miles Frederick. Student, Wash. State U., 1947-50, U. Oreg., 1950-51. Lumber buyer Bacon Lumber Co., Portland, Oreg., 1952-54; mill supt. Holden Lumber Co., Prescott, Oreg., 1955-58; timber broker Longview, Wash., 1958-67; real estate broker Ridgefield (Wash.) Agy., 1968-71; br. mgr. Tranasam. Title Ins. Co., Portland, 1972-76; lead examiner Tranasam. Title Ins. Co., Bellevue, Wash., 1977-89; owner, mgr. Pvt. Indsl. Tree Farm, Kirkland, Wash., 1983—. Author: Land and Trees, 1991. Ombudsman Wash. State Long-Term Care Ombudsman's Office, Bellevue, 1992-96. With U.S. Army, 1946-47. Home and Office: 9821 Forbes Creek Dr Kirkland WA 98033

HOLDEN, GEORGE FREDRIC, brewing company executive, public policy specialist, author; b. Lander, Wyo., Aug. 29, 1937; s. George Thiel Holden and Rita (Meyer) Zulpo; m. Dorothy Carol Capper, July 5, 1959; children: Lorilyn, Sherilyn, Tamilyn. BSChemE, U. Colo., 1959, MBA in Mktg., 1974. Adminstr. plastics lab. EDP, indsl chems. plant, prodn. process engring., tool control supervision, aerospace (Minuteman, Polaris, Sparrow), Parlin, N.J., Salt Lake City, Cumberland, Md., 1959-70; by-product sales, new market and new product devel., resource planning and devel. and pub. rels. Adolph Coors Co., Golden, Colo., 1971-76; dir. econ. affairs corp. pub. affairs dept., 1979-84, dir. pub. affairs rsch., 1984-86; owner Phoenix Enterprises, Arvada, 1986—; mgr. facilities engring. Coors Container Co., 1976-79; instr. brewing, by-products utilization and waste mgmt. U. Wis.; cons., speaker in field. Mem. bd. economists Rocky Mountain News, 1990—; mem. Heritage Found. Ann. Guide to Pub. Policy Expert, 1987—, Speakers Bur., Commn. on the Bicentennial U.S. Constitution, 1991-93; del. Colo. Rep. Conv., 1976—; adv. Cost of Govt. Day; bd. dirs. Colo. Pub. Expenditures Coun., 1983-86, Nat. Speakers Assn., Colo. Speakers Assn. (bd. dirs. 1987-90, 91-93), Nat. Assn. Bus. Economists, Colo. Assn. Commerce and Industry Excs. Ednl. Found. Sr. fellow budget policy Independence Inst. Colo. "ThinkTank". Mem. U.S. Brewers Assn. (chmn. by-products com. 1983-86, ednl. found. 1984-85, Hon. Gavel, 1975), Am. Inst. Indsl. Engrs. (dir. 1974-78), Washingtons Am. for Tax Reform Found. Co-author: Secrets of Job Hunting, 1972; The Phoenix Phenomenon, 1984; author: Total Power of One in America, 1991; contbr. articles to Chem. Enging. mag., 1968-76, over 400 published articles, white papers in field; over 900 speeches, 560 appearances on radio talk shows nationwide. Home: 6463 Owens St Arvada CO 80004-2732 Office: Phoenix Enterprises PO Box 1900 Arvada CO 80001-1900

HOLDEN, MICHAEL JOHN, lawyer; b. Sheboygan, Wis., Sept. 29, 1955; s. John Robert and Hilda H.; m. Mary Louise Turkovich, Apr. 9, 1983; children: John, Anne. AB, U. Mich., 1977; JD, Duke U., 1980. Bar: Ariz. 1980, U.S. Dist. Ct. Ariz. 1980, U.S. Ct. Appeals (9th cir.) 1980. Assoc. Lewis and Roca, Phoenix, Ariz., 1980-85; ptnr. Lewis and Roca, Phoenix, 1985—. Mem. ABA, Am. Subcontractors Assn. Ariz. (bd. dirs. 1993), Associated Gen. Contractors Ariz. (assoc.), Ariz. State Bar (chmn. constrn. law sect. 1987-89). Office: Lewis and Roca Ste 1900 40 N Central Ave Phoenix AZ 85004-4424

HOLDEN, WILLIAM WILLARD, insurance executive; b. Akron, Ohio, Oct. 5, 1958; s. Joseph McCullem and Lettitia (Roderick) H.; m. Kim Homan, Aug. 31, 1985; 1 child, Jennifer Catharine. BA, Colgate U., 1981. Crime ins. trainee Chubb & Son, Inc., N.Y.C., 1981-82; exec. protection dept. mgr. Chubb & Son, Inc., San Jose, Calif., 1982-85, Woodland Hills, Calif., 1986-91; sr. v.p., mgr. Fin. Svcs. Group, Inc., Rollins, Hudig, Hall, Aon Fin. Svcs. Group, L.A., 1991—; tng. analyst Chubb & Son, Inc., Warren, N.J., 1985-86. Co-author manual: Chubb Claims Made Training, 1985; contbr. articles to Colgate alumni mag. Mgr., coach Campbell (Calif.) Little League, 1983-85; pres. Le Parc Homeowners Assn., Simi Valley, Calif., 1987-89; mem. Community Assn. Inst., L.A., 1986—. Mem. Profl. Liability Underwriting Soc. (L.A. steering com.), Forum for Corp. Dirs. Republican. Office: Aon Fin Svcs Group Inc 707 Wilshire Blvd Los Angeles CA 90017

HOLDER, J. HAL, food products executive; b. 1954. With Griffin-Holder Co., Rocky Ford, Colo., 1972—, now pres. Office: Griffin-Holder Co PO Box 511 Rocky Ford CO 81067-9407*

HOLDER, THOMAS JAY, art educator; b. Kansas City, Mo., Jan. 21, 1940; s. Ward Leonard and Olive (Henrie) H.; m. Martha H. Hofmann, 1961 (div. 1971); children: Barbara L., Sheridan W.; m. Jacqueline E. Jacobs, Dec. 27, 1991; children: Rachel C., Kiersten N. BA in Painting, San Diego State U., 1965; MFA, U. Wash., 1969. Part-time instr. San Diego City Coll., Mesa Coll., 1965-67; teaching asst. San Diego State U., 1967; part-time instr. Highline Coll., 1968-69; instr. U. Wash., 1969-70; prof. art U. Nev., Las Vegas, 1971—, chair dept. art, 1972-74, 82-86; dir. Donna Beam Fine Art Gallery, 1984-91; founding dir. Nev. Inst. for Contemporary Art, 1985-91. Paintings represented in numerous collections including Brenau Coll., 1991, Bank of Am., Nev., 1977-89, First Interstate Bank, Las Vegas, 1987, Internat. Athletic Club, Kansas City, 1984, Nev. Mus. Art, Reno, 1983, others; exhibited in numerous one-person and group shows incuding William Traver Gallery, Seattle, 1990, Nev. Inst. Contemporary Art, 1993, Brendan Walter Gallery, Santa Monica, Calif., 1992, No. Ariz. U. Art Mus., Flagstaff, 1992. Visual arts fellow Nev. State Coun. on Arts, 1992, grantee, 1991; recipient Best in Show award Brenau Coll. Nat. Invitational, 1989, 1st place award 23d S.W. Ann., 1989. Mem. Coll. Art Assn. Home: 740 N Magic Way Henderson NV 89015 Office: U Nev 4505 S Maryland Pky Las Vegas NV 89154-9900

HOLDING, CAROL PIERSON, brand positioning consultant; b. St. Louis, Feb. 4, 1956; d. Emery Lancaster and Joan Marcia (Godwin) Pierson; m. Reynolds Walker Holding, June 7, 1986; 1 child, Carolyn Walker. AB in Econs., Smith Coll., 1976; MBA, Harvard U., 1980. V.p. Ally & Gargard, N.Y.C., 1980-86, Citibank, N.Y.C., 1986-88; sr. v.p. Siegel-Gale, N.Y.C., 1988-91, McCann-Erickson, San Francisco, 1991; pres. Holding Assocs., San Francisco, 1992—. Bd. dirs. Planned Parenthood, San Francisco, 1993-96, Bill T. Jones/Arnie Zane and Co., N.Y.C., 1986-91; bd. dirs., v.p. Youth Advocates, 1996—, Metro. Club, 1996; head planning com. Swedenborgian Ch., San Francisco, 1993-95. Mem. San Francisco Ad Club, Commonwealth Club, Met. Club, Mechanics Inst., Bus. Mktg. Assn. Office: Holding Assocs 65 Carmelita St San Francisco CA 94117-3312

HOLDSWORTH, JANET NOTT, women's health nurse; b. Evanston, Ill., Dec. 25, 1941; d. William Alfred and Elizabeth Inez (Kelly) Nott; children: James William, Kelly Elizabeth, John David. BSN with high distinction, U. Iowa, 1963; M of Nursing, U. Wash., 1966. RN, Colo. Staff nurse U. Colo. Hosp., Denver, 1963-64, Presbyn. Hosp., Denver, 1964-65, Grand Canyon Hosp., Ariz., 1965; asst. prof. U. Colo. Sch. Nursing, Denver, 1966-71; counseling nurse Boulder PolyDrug Treatment Ctr., Boulder, 1971-77; pvt. duty nurse Nurses' Official Registry, Denver, 1973-82; cons. nurse, tchr. parenting and child devel. Teenage Parent Program, Boulder Valley Schs., Boulder, 1980-88; bd. dirs., treas. Nott's Travel, Aurora, Colo., 1980—; nurse Rocky Mountain Surgery Ctr., 1996—; instr., nursing coord. ARC, Boulder, 1979-90, instr., nursing tng. specialist, 1980-82. Mem. adv. bd. Boulder County Lamaze Inc., 1980-88 ; mem. adv. com. Child Find and Parent-Family, Boulder, 1981-89; del. Rep. County State Congl. Convs., 1972-96, sec. 17th Dist. Senatorial Com., Boulder, 1982-92; vol. Mile High ARC, 1980; vol. chmn. Mesa Sch. PTO, Boulder, 1982-92, bd. dirs., 1982-95, v.p., 1983-95; elder Presbyn. ch. Mem. ANA, Colo. Nurses Assn. (bd. dirs. 1975-76, human rights com. 1981-83, dist. pres. 1974-76), Coun. Intracultural Nurses, Sigma Theta Tau, Alpha Lambda Delta. Republican. Home: 1550 Findlay Way Boulder CO 80303-6922 Office: Rocky Mountain Surgery Ctr 2405 Broadway St Boulder CO 80304-4108

HOLIDAY, LINDA FREYA, educator, school administrator; b. Oakland, Calif., Aug. 18, 1952; d. Wayne Richard and Ruth D. Hultgren; m. Alan Wells Holiday, July 29, 1984; 1 child, Nathan Wells. BA in Japanese and Chinese Studies, U. Calif., Santa Cruz, 1979; MA in East Asian Studies, Stanford U., 1983. English instr. YMCA, Mitsubishi, others, Japan, 1973-80; lectr. in phys. edn. (Aikido) U. Calif., Santa Cruz, 1976-82; exec. dir., chief instr. North Bay Aikido, Inc., Santa Cruz, 1982—; seminar instr. various Aikido schs., U.S. and Can., 1977—; mem. examining bd. Aikido Assn. No. Calif., San Francisco Bay area, 1980-87. Cons. Sister City Commn., Santa Cruz, intermittently 1973—. Nat. Resource fellow U.S. Govt., 1982-83; Alice Liu Meml. scholar, U. Calif., Santa Cruz, 1979. Office: North Bay Aikido Inc 306 Mission St Santa Cruz CA 95060

HOLL, WALTER JOHN, architect, interior designer; b. Richardton, N.D., May 14, 1922; s. John and Rose Mary (Raskop) H.; m. Eleanor Mary Triervieler, Jan. 23, 1943; children: Mark Walter, Michael John, Randolph Gregory, Linda Michelle, Timothy James, John Walter. Student in architecture Internat. Corr. Schs., 1946-47, structural engring., 1959; student in interior design U. Nebr., 1976; student in photography Clarke Coll., 1981. Licensed architect, Calif, interior designer, Ill.; cert. Nat. Coun. for Interior Design Qualifications. Steel detailer, estimator E.J. Voggenthaler Co., Dubuque, Iowa, 1941-42; engr., also methods developer Marinship Corp. Sausalito, Calif., 1942-44; ptnr. Holl & Everly, Dubuque, 1946-47; prin. Holl Designing Co., also W. Holl & Assocs., Dubuque and San Francisco, 1947-87; prin. Walter J. Holl, Burlingame, Calif, 1987, 89, San Diego, 1989—; mem. convoy USCG Ofcl. Presdl. Security Patrol, 1979; cons. Clarke Coll. Art Students, Dubuque, 1953-61; commd. architect, interior designer and constructor renovations and hist. preservation Dubuque County Couthouse, 1978-85; oral exam commr. Calif. Bd. Archtl. Examiners, 1994—; cert. mem. Calif. State Office Emergency Svc.; participant The Brit. Coun.-Archs. Study Tour, Belfast, No. Ireland, 1995; juror Nat. Coun. for Interior Design Qualification, 1996. Patentee castered pallet. Chmn. Dubuque Housing Rehab. Commn., 1976-77. Served with AUS, 1944-46, ETO. Decorated 2 bronze stars; recipient Nat. Bldg. Design awards, 1968, 69, 73, 94. Mem. AIA (bd. dirs. 1993—, pres.-elect north county sect. San Diego chpt. 1995, pres. 1996), USCG Aux. (comdr. 1975-78), Am. Soc. Interior Designers (profl.), Am. Arbitration Assn. (panel arbitrators), Inst. Bus. Designers (profl. Chgo. chpt.). Roman Catholic. Clubs: Dubuque Golf and Country (bldg. commn. 1953-54), Julien Dubuque Yacht (commodore 1974-75), Mchts. and Mfrs. (Chgo.). Home and Office: Walter J Holl AIA ASID Architect 11255 Tierrasanta Blvd San Diego CA 92124-2890 *As client's architect, my customary advice was: Why widen Main Street for a parade once a year."*

HOLLAND, GARY NORMAN, ophthalmologist, educator; b. Long Beach, Calif., July 30, 1953; s. Richard L. and Edith (Hewson) H. MD, UCLA, 1979. Diplomate Am. Bd. Ophthalmology, Nat. Bd. Med. Examiners; lic. MD, Calif., Ga. Intern in internal medicine UCLA, 1979-80; resident in ophthalmology Jules Stein Eye Inst., L.A., 1980-83; fellowship in uveitis rsch. Proctor Found. U. Calif. San Francisco, 1983-84; cornea fellowship Emory U. Med. Sch., Atlanta, 1984-85; prof. ophthalmology Jules Stein Eye Inst. UCLA, 1985—. Assoc. editor Am. Jour. Ophthalmology, 1993—. Mem. Am. Uveitis Soc. (chmn. edn. and rsch. com. 1994—). Office: UCLA Jules Stein Eye Inst 100 Stein Plz Los Angeles CA 90095-7003

HOLLAND, H. RUSSEL, federal judge; b. 1936; m. Diane Holland; 3 children. BBA, U. Mich., 1958, LLB, 1961. With Alaska Ct. System, Anchorage, 1961, U.S. Atty.'s Office, Dept. Justice, Anchorage, 1963-65; assoc. Stevens & Savage, Anchorage, 1965-66; ptnr. Stevens, Savage, Holland, Erwin & Edwards, Anchorage, 1967-68; sole practice Anchorage, 1968-70; ptnr. Holland & Thornton, Anchorage, 1970-78, Holland, Thornton & Trefry, Anchorage, 1978, Holland & Trefry, Anchorage, 1978-84, Trefry & Brecht, Anchorage, 1984; judge U.S. Dist. Ct. Alaska, Anchorage, 1984—. Mem. ABA, Alaska Bar Assn., Anchorage Bar Assn. Office: US Dist Ct 222 W 7th Ave Rm 281 Anchorage AK 99513-7504*

HOLLAND, HENRY NORMAN, marketing consultant; b. Norfolk, Va., Oct. 13, 1947; s. Henry Norman and Edith Leigh (O'Bryan) H.; m. Linda Diane Eggerking, June 1, 1968 (div. 1983); 1 child, Steven Frederick; m. Jane Elizabeth Bond, Dec. 27, 1983. BA, Chaminade Coll., 1972; MBA, U. Hawaii, 1977. Lic. ins. broker, Calif. Mgr. Chevron USA, Honolulu, 1965-75; dealer Dillingham Chevron, Honolulu, 1975-82; gen. mgr. Barcat Enterprises, San Francisco, 1982-85; counselor E.K. Williams of San Francisco, 1985; gen. mgr. Woodside (Calif.) Oil Co., 1985-88; cons. Holland Bus. Mgmt., San Francisco, 1989—; dir. Chevron Fed. Credit Union, Honolulu, 1971-75. Author: Make Yours Service, tng. seminars, newsletter, safety programs; contbr. articles to profl. jours. Loaned mgr. United Way, Honolulu, 1972; nation chief YMCA Indian Guides, Kailua, Hawaii, 1976-79. With U.S. Army, 1967-69, Vietnam. Mem. English Speaking Union, Met. League San Francisco Symphony, Golden Gate Nat. Parks Assn., Nat. Trust for Historic Preservation, San Francisco Mus. Soc., Chevron Adv. Coun., Nat. Assn. Enrolled Agts., Calif. Assn. Enrolled Agts., Sovereign Order of Saint John of Jerusalem Knights Hospitaller, VFW. Republican. Presbyterian.

HOLLAND, MICHAEL JAMES, computer services administrator; b. N.Y.C., Nov. 20, 1950; s. Robert Frederick and Virginia June (Wilcox) H.; Anita Garay, Jan. 5, 1981 (Aug. 1989); 1 child, Melanie. BA in Comparative Lit., Bklyn. Coll., 1972. Enlisted USN, 1975, advanced to CPO, 1989; field med. technician 3rd Marine Divsn., Okinawa, Japan, 1976-77, 1st Marine Divsn., Camp Pendleton, Calif., 1978-79; clin. supr. Naval Hosp. Subic Bay, Philippines, 1979-81; dept. head Tng. Ctr. USMCR, Johnson City, Tenn., 1981-84; clin. supr. No. Tng. Area, Okinawa, 1984-85, 3rd Marine Air Wing, Camp Pendleton, 1985-88; cons. Naval Regional Med. Command, San Diego, 1988-90; system analyst Naval Med. Info. Mgmt. Ctr. Detachment, San Diego, 1990-92; computer svcs. adminstr. U.S. Naval Hosp., Guam, 1993-95; ret., 1995. Mem. Fleet Res. Assn., Nat. City C. of C. (com. 1989-91), Assn. for Computing Machinery.

HOLLAND, ROBERT DEBNAM, SR., investment company executive; b. Norfolk, Va., Mar. 5, 1922; s. Ralph Frederick and Erma Gwendoly (Debnam) H.; m. Frances Lee Hodges, Dec. 1,26, 1934 (div. June 1987); children: Robert Debnam Jr., Elizabet Lee, William Peyton; m. Anne Marie Lamb, Aug. 10, 1988. BA, U.S. Merchant Marine Acad., 1943, Centre Coll., Danville, Ky., 1949; postgrad., U. Va., 1950. Salesman IBM Corp., 1952-56; salesman Burroughs Corp., 1956-61, mgr. indsl. mktg., 1956-65; v.p. fin. CIER, Inc., Washington; pres. Photomatrics Corp., L.A., 1985-88; mng. ptnr. Transnat. Corp., Las Vegas, Nev., 1988—; treas., bd. dirsn. Internat. Lable Co., Las Vegas, 1992—; chmn. exec. com. Network Recovery Sys., San Ramon, Calif., 1994—. Lt. comdr. USNR, 1942-55. Mem. AIM, Inst. Automation Rsch., Am. Mgmt. Assn., Sigma Chi, Omicron Delta Kappa, Phi Kappa Delta. Democrat. Episcopalian. Home: 3115 Pradera Cir Las Vegas NV 89121 Office: U Nev 5975 Spencer St Ste 166 Las Vegas NV 89119

HOLLAND, ROBIN JEAN, personnel company executive; b. Chgo., June 22, 1952; d. Robert Benjamin and Dolores (Levy) Shaeffer; 1 child, Robert Gene. BA in Pub. Rels. magna cum laude, U. So. Calif., 1977. Account exec., pub. rels. firm, 1977-79, Mgmt. Recruiters, 1979; owner, operator Holland Exec. Search, Marina Del Rey, Calif., 1979—; pres. Bus. Communications, 1983—; cons. on outplacement to bus.; condr. seminars on exec. search; guest lectr. Active Ahead with Horses, Audubon Soc., conservation orgns. Recipient numerous local honors. Mem. Am. Coaster Enthusiasts, LK.A. Can., Mensa, Peruvian Paso Horse Owners and Breeders N.Am. Office: Holland Exec Search 4766 Admiralty Way Ste 9774 Marina Del Rey CA 90295-2174

HOLLENBECK, DOROTHY ROSE, special education educator; b. Yakima, Wash., May 8, 1941; d. George Milford and Blance Mary (McCarthy) Hollenbeck; BS in Speech and Lang. Therapy, Marquette U., 1964; MA in Spl. Edn., San Francisco State U., 1969; m. Thomas M. Chambers, Aug. 14, 1971; adopted children—David, Monique, Christopher, George, Elizabeth. Speech pathologist Mpls. Pub. Schs., 1964-65, Milbrae (Calif.) Sch. Dist., 1965-68; reading specialist Dept. Def., Landstuhl, Germany, 1970-71; tchr. children with extreme learning problems Portland (Oreg.) Public Schs., 1971-80, dept. chmn. spl. edn., 1980-84, program specialist program devel., 1984-86, diagnostic specialist assessment program spl. edn., 1986-94, speech and lang. pathologist, 1994-95; spch. and lang. pathologist, spl. edn. tchr., Chinacum, Washington Sch. Dist. 1995 —; cert. instr. develop. therapy U. Ga., 1982; instr. Portland State U., D.C.E., 1982, 83. HEW Dept. Rehab. fellow, 1969. Mem. Am. Speech and Hearing Assn. (cert. in clin. competence), Common Cause, Cousteau Soc., NEA, Oreg. Edn. Assn., Nat. Council Exceptional Children (presenter nat. conv. 1984). Democrat. Roman Catholic. Author: PEACHES (Pre-Sch. Ednl. Adaptation for Children Who Are Handicapped), 1978. Home: 1212 Garfield St Port Townsend WA 98368-3515 Office: Chinacum Pub Schs PO Box 278 Chimacum WA 98325

HOLLEY, ELIZABETH SHELBY, educational therapist; b. Lennox, Calif., Dec. 4, 1926; d. Guy Sheldon and Bessie Edna (Humphreys) Bedwell; m. Erwin Dale Thomson, Apr. 26, 1943 (dec. Feb. 1963); m. Kenneth Gunnar Holley, Apr. 10, 1963; children: Edward, Evonne, Fiona, Luana, Raymond, Jean, Kevin. AA, L.A. City Coll., 1959; BA, L.A. State Coll., 1961, MA, 1963. Lic. marriage, family and child counselor. Ednl. therapist Marianne Frostig Ctr., L.A., 1959-64, West Valley Ctr. for Ednl. Therapy, Canoga Park, Calif., 1964-80; dir. Studio for Acad. Achievement, Sherman Oaks, Calif., 1980-87; vol. Peace Corps, Jamaica, 1987-89; ednl. therapist in pvt. practice Woodland Hills, Calif., 1990—; cons. Kaiser/Permanente, Woodland Hills, Calif., 1992—. Author: A Practical Parents Handbook on Teaching Children with Learning Disabilities, 1994. Bd. dirs. Orton Dyslexia Soc., L.A., 1980-87; vol. Juvenile Justice Connection, Van Nuys, Calif. Mem. Assn. of ednl. Therapists (founding mem., bd. dirs. 1979-87). Democrat. Home: 5656 Manton Ave Woodland Hills CA 91367-3028

HOLLEY, JACK K., journalist; b. Denver, Jan. 2, 1937; s. W. Jack and Grace H. (Hood) H.; m. Mary B. Holley; children: Richard T., Laura A., Michael D. BA in Journalism, U. Colo., 1960. Reporter The Chieftain, Pueblo, Colo., 1959; copy editor The World-Herald, Omaha, 1961-63, reporter, columnist, 1963-67, urban affairs reporter, 1967-70, asst. city editor, 1970-72, city editor, 1972-74, asst. to exec. editor, 1974-76, news editor, 1976-79, day mng. editor, 1979-81, mng. editor for adminstrn., 1981-82; asst. prof.Medill Sch. Journalism Northwestern U., 1982-90; news editor The Press-Enterprise, Riverside, Calif., 1990-91, asst. mng. editor news, 1991—; dir. undergraduate studies Northwestern U., 1983-85, dir. Evanston Programs, 1985-86; mem. mgmt. com. conf. on newsroom tech. AP Mng. Editors, 1986; moderator regional job seminar Am. Soc. Newspaper Editors, 1985; mem. 1st amendment watchdog group instrumental in Stuart vs. Nebr. Press Assn., Media of Nebr.; participant in continuing edn. seminars Inland Press Assn. Small Newspaper Conf., Itasca, Ill., Poyntner Inst. for Media Studies Program in Media Mgmt., St. Petersburg, Fla., Am. Press Inst., Reston, Va., ABA Fair Trial-Free Press Seminar, Reno, Nev., among others. Ford Found. fellow, 1967, Fellow Inst. for Modern Comm., Northwestern U., 1986-87. Mem. Soc. Profl. Journalists, Calif. Soc. Newspaper Editors (instr. 1993, 94), Am. Assn. Pub. Opinion Rsch. (panelist 1988-90), Midwest Assn. Pub. Opinion Rsch., Soc. Profl. Journalists. Home: 5401 Telefair Way Riverside CA 92506-3574 Office: The Press-Enterprise 3512 14th St Riverside CA 92501-3814

HOLLIE, GLADYS MIRIAM, nurse; b. Coupland, Tex., Nov. 2, 1932; d. John Charles and Cora Rebecca (Atkinson) H.; m. Simon Jackson Davis, Oct. 25, 1956 (div. 1961); 1 child, Harold Gene Holli Johnson. AD, McClennen Community Coll., Waco, Tex., 1980. Vocat. nurse St. Paul Hosp., Dallas, 1955-58, Tex. Children's Hosp., Dallas, 1958-60, Long Beach (Calif.) VA Med. Ctr., 1960-77, VA Med. Ctr., Waco, 1977-82; RN VA Med. Ctr., Fresno, Calif., 1982-95, ret., 1995. Vol. Am. Cancer Soc., Fresno,

1991, YWCA, Fresno, 1991, Ch. Women United. Mem. Order Ea. Star (asst. matron 1983—). Democrat. Mem. African Methodist Episcopal Ch.

HOLLINGER, DAVID ALBERT, historian, educator; b. Chgo., Apr. 25, 1941; s. Albert Jr. and Evelyn Dorothy (Steinmeier) H.; m. Joan Heifetz, Sept. 17, 1967; children: Jacob, Julia. BA, U. La Verne, 1963; MA, U. Calif., Berkeley, 1965, PhD, 1970. From asst. to assoc. prof. SUNY, Buffalo, 1969-77; prof. U. Mich., Ann Arbor, 1977-92, U. Calif., Berkeley, 1992—. Author: Morris R. Cohen and the Scientific Ideal, 1975, In the American Province, 1985, Postethnic America, 1995, Science, Jews, and Secular Culture, 1996. Guggenheim Found. fellow, 1983. Mem. Am. Hist. Assn., Am. Studies Assn., Soc. Am. Historians, Orgn. Am. Historians, History Sci. Soc. Office: Dept History U Calif Berkeley CA 94720

HOLLINGSWORTH, MARGARET CAMILLE, financial services administrator, consultant; b. Washington, Feb. 20, 1929; d. Harvey Alvin and Margaret Estelle (Head) Jacob; m. Robert Edgar Hollingsworth, July 14, 1960 (div. July 1980); children: William Lee, Robert Edgar Hollingsworth Jr., Barbara Camille, Bradford Damion. AA, Va. Intermont Coll., 1949. Bookkeeper Fred A. Smith Real Estate, Washington, 1949-53; adminstrv. mgr. Airtronic, Inc., Bethesda, Md., 1953-61; pers. adminstr. Sears Roebuck, Washington, 1973-74; adminstrv. mgr., communication mgr. Garvin GuyButler Corp., San Francisco, 1980-88, exec. sec., pers. mgr., 1989-95, adminstrv. cons., ret., 1996; adminstrv. cons., Concord, Calif.; assoc. Robert Hollingsworth Nuclear Cons., Walnut Creek, Calif., 1975-79. Bd. dirs. Civic Arts, Walnut Creek, 1975-97; bd. dirs., mem. pub. rels. com. Valley Art Ctr., Walnut Creek, 1997—. Recipient Spl. Recognition award AEC, 1974. Mem. Internat. Platform Assn., Commonwealth Club, Beta Sigma Phi (pres. 1954). Democrat. Presbyterian. Home: 1108 Limeridge Dr Concord CA 94518-1923

HOLLINGSWORTH, MEREDITH BEATON, enterostomal therapy clinical nurse specialist; b. Danvers, Mass., Oct. 5, 1941; d. Allan Cameron and Arlene Margaret (Jerue) Beaton; m. William Paul Hollingsworth, Nov. 19, 1983; stepchild, Brendon R. Diploma, R.I. Hosp. Sch. Nursing, Providence, 1968; BS in Nursing, U. Ariz., 1976; MS in Human Resource Mgmt., Golden Gate U., 1984; postgrad., U. Tex., 1988; EdD, U. N.Mex., 1995, postgrad., 1996—. Cert. enterostomal therapy nurse, health edn. specialist. Commd. ensign USN, 1968, advanced through grades to lt. comdr., 1979; charge nurse USN, USA, PTO, 1968-88; command ostomy nurse, head ostomy clinic Naval Hosp. Portsmouth, Va., 1985-88; pres., chief exec. officer Enterostomal Therapy Nursing Edn. and Tng. Cons. (ETNetc), Rio Rancho, N.Mex., 1989—; mgr. clin. svcs. we. area Support Systems Internat., Inc., Charleston, S.C., 1990-92; pres., CEO Paumer Assocs. Internat., Inc., Rio Rancho, N.Mex., 1992—; sr. cons. enterostomal therapy nursing, edn., & tng. cons.; provost N.Mex. Sch. Enterostomal Nursing, Rio Rancho, 1996—; enterostomal therapy nurse, clin. nurse specialist, educator Presbyn. Health Care Svcs., Albuquerque, 1992-95; sr. cons. Enterstomal Therapy Nursing Edn. & Tng. Cons. A Divsn. of Paumer Assocs., Rio Rancho, N. Mex., 1995—; provost N.Mex. Sch. ET Nursing, Rio Rancho, 1995—; lectr. in field. Mem. adminstrv. bd. Baylake United Meth. Ch., Virginia Beach, 1980-83; chmn. bd. deacons St. Paul's United Ch., Rio Rancho; active Am. Cancer Soc. Mem. Wound, Ostomy and Continence Nurses Soc. (nat. govt. affairs com., govt. affairs com. Rocky Mountain region, newsletter editor, pub. rels. com., regional pres. 1989-93, nat. sec. 1994-95), United Ostomy Assn., World Coun. Enterstomal Therapists, N. Mex. Health Care Assn., N. Mex. Assn. for Home Care, N. Mex. Assn. for Continuity of Care. Republican. Office: PO Box 44395 Rio Rancho NM 87174-4395

HOLLINS, SID, mayor; m. Marion Hollins. BA in Bus. Mgmt., MS in Pub. Sch. Adminstrn. Tchr., prin., personnel dir., dep. supt., supt. various schs., Escondido, Calif.; sch. bd. mem., pres. Escondido, Calif., 1985-90; mem. Escondido City Coun., 1990-94; mayor City of Escondido, 1994—. Present and past cmty. svc. includes: mem. Escondido Parks and Recreation commn., mem. Escondido Humane Soc., pres. 5 yrs., mem. Escondido Child Care Advocacy and Coordinating Coun., founding mem. Escondido Edn. Compact, mem. Mayor's Resource Panel, chmn. Escondido Gen. Plan Revision Com., founding mem. Escondido Cmty. Dialogue; founding mem. Escondido Arts in Edn. Found.; bd. mem. Calif. Ctr. for Arts, Escondido; chmn., mem. United Crusade. Inducted into Grad. Hall of Fame, 1994-95, Escondido Union High Sch. Dist.; recipient Veteran of Yr. Leadership award, 1995, San Diego Veterans Svcs., Heart of the City award, 1995, Palomar Family Counseling Svc., Significant Contbn. to Pub. Edn. and its Students award, 1995, San Diego County Sch. Bds. Assn. Mem. Escondido C. of C. (edn. com.), Escondido Noon Optimist Club (past pres., lt. gov., youth work chmn.). Office: Mayors Office City Hall 201 N Broadway Escondido CA 92025

HOLLIS, MARY FRANCES, aerospace educator; b. Indpls., Sept. 18, 1931; d. Lucian Albert and Clara Frances Coleman; divorced; 1 child, Booker Albert Hollis. BS, Butler U., 1952, MS, 1962; postgrad., Stanford U., 1975, San Francisco State U., 1980-81. Cert. elem. tchr., Ind., Calif. Kindergarten tchr. Lockerbie Nursery Sch., Indpls., 1952, Indpls. Pub. Schs., 1952-69; tchr. K-6 San Mateo (Calif.) City Sch. Dist., 1969-91; summer sch. prin. San Mateo City Sch. dist., Foster City, Calif., 1983-91; aerospace educator, 1982—; bd. dirs. Coun. of Math./Sci. Educators of San Mateo County, Belmont, Calif. Editor: San Mateo County Math./Sci. Coun. quarterly newsletter, 1988-90. Bd. dirs. Arts Coun. of San Mateo County, 1986-91, Mid-Peninsula chpt. ACLU, San Mateo, 1990—, Unitarian-Universalist Ch. San Mateo, 1996—, Peninsula Funeral and Meml. Planning Soc., 1996—; office mgr. Roger Winston Campaign for San Mateo Union H.S. Dist. Bd. Trustees, 1993; mem. adv. com. USAF-Pacific Liaison Region-CAP, 1988-94. Recipient Life Down to Earth award NASA, Moffet Field, Mt. View, Calif., 1985-86, Earl Sams Tchr. of Yr. award Calif. Assn. Aerospace Educators, 1989, award of merit Am. Legion, San Bruno, Calif., 1989, citation Air Force Assn., Mountain View, Calif., 1991, Aviation Summer Sch. cert. of appreciation Am. Legion Dept. Calif. Aerospace Commn., 1994. Mem. NEA (life), AAUW (bd. dirs. San Carlos chpt. 1993-95), NAACP, Am. Bus. Women's Assn. (rec. sec. Foster City chpt. 1985), World Aerospace Edn. Orgn. Democrat. Unitarian-Universalist. Office: PO Box 625 Belmont CA 94002-0625

HOLLMANN, MARTIN, aircraft design engineer; b. Berlin, Germany, Dec. 6, 1940; s. Hans Erich and Gisella (Schimmelbusch) H.; married; children: Eric Matthew, Christian. BS in Aeronautical Ops., Calif State U., San Jose, 1969; MS in Mech. Engring., U. Cen. Fla., 1974. Design engr. Convair Aerospace/Divsn. of Gen. Dynamics, Inc., San Diego, Calif., 1969-72; sr. engr. Martin Marietta Corp., Orlando, Fla., 1972-74; sr. design engr. Lockheed Missiles and Space Co., Inc., Palo Alto, 1974-78; program engr. Ford Aerospace and Comms. Corp., Palo Alto, Calif., 1978-80; sr. engr. Westinghouse Electric Corp., Sunnyvale, Calif., 1980-82; sr. project engr. FMC Corp., San Jose, 1982-84; prin. engr. Kaiser Electronics Corp., San Jose, Calif., 1984-86; pres. Aircraft Designs, Inc., Monterey, Calif., 1986—; projects include all graphite MX-missile canister, world's first composite armored personnel carrier, Stallion (high performance, cross country airplane), Star Kraft six-passenger aircraft, Lancair series of aircraft, structural design and anlysis of the hydrofoil for Catalina Flyer, 1991, others; clientele include Lockheed, DuPont, NASA, Beechcraft, TASK Rsch., Inc., Westfoil Internat., Westinghouse, Universal Studios, NEICO Aviation, Hughes Aircraft, California Microwave, others. Author: (books) Modern Aircraft Design, Vol. 1, Vol. 2, Composite Aircraft Design, Modern Gyroplane Design, Flying the Gyroplane, Succeed in Aviation, Modern Aerodynamic Flutter Analysis, Modern Aircraft Drafting, ABCs of Desktop Finite Element Analysis, others. Mem. AIAA. Republican. Lutheran.

HOLLOWAY, CINDY, mortgage company executive; b. Queens, N.Y., Aug. 8, 1960; d. Richard Stephen and Beverly Bunny (Harris) Tannenbaum; m. David Milton Holloway (div. Mar. 1986); 1 child, Benjamin Jerome. BA, Calif. State U., Fullerton, 1981. Lic. real estate broker. Waitress Bob's Big Boy, San Bernardino, Calif., 1984-85; receptionist RNG Mortgage Co., San Bernardino, 1985; loan processor Quality Mortgage Co., Colton, Calif., 1985-88, loan officer, 1988-91; loan officer RNG Mortgage, 1991-92; v.p., br. mgr. Mountain West Fin., 1992—. Mem. San Bernardino Bd. Realtors (spl. events com. 1988—, comm. com. 1990—), Nat. Trust for Hist. Preservation, San Bernardino Execs. Assn., Assn. Profl. Mortgage Women (bd. dirs. 1989-90, v.p. 1992-93, Affiliate of Yr. award 1990), San Bernardino Execs. Group (bd. dirs. 1994—). Home: PO Box 3187 Crestline CA 92325-3187

HOLLOWAY, DEBRA LINN, humanities educator; b. Norwood, Mass., Jan. 2, 1966; d. Paul Jackson and Anna Grace (Baer) H. BA in English, U. N.H., 1988, MA in Lit., 1993. Asst. dean admissions U. N.H., Durham, 1989-91, instr. writing, 1991-94; instr. tchg. writing U. Colo., Boulder, 1995-96, rsch. assoc. Colo. Humanities Ctr., 1995-96; rsch. assoc. Boulder Sch. Arts, 1996-97; Mem. adv. bd. The Art Gallery, Durham, 1994-97; mem. greater Piscataqua diversity com., Portsmouth, N.H., 1993-94. Mem. AAUW, Am. Ednl. Rsch. Assn. Office: Sch Edn Campus Box 249 Boulder CO 80309-0249

HOLLOWAY, ROBERT WESTER, radiochemist; b. Morrilton, Ark., Jan. 3, 1945; s. Otho and Bessie Vance (Woolverton) H.; m. Mary Ella Hamel, Dec. 31, 1970; children: David, Jason. BS, Harding Coll., 1967; postgrad., U. Okla., 1968; PhD, U. Ark., 1977. Asst. prof. U. Ark., Pine Bluff, 1976-79; research chemist DuPont Corp., Aiken, S.C., 1979-81; supervisory chemist EPA, Las Vegas, 1981-94; pres. Nev. Tech. Assocs., Inc., 1994—. Contbr. articles to profl. jours. Served to capt. USAF, 1967-72. Mem. Am. Chem. Soc., Health Physics Soc., Toastmasters, Optimists. Republican. Home: 311 E Desert Rose Dr Henderson NV 89015-8107 Office: Nev Tech Assocs Inc PO Box 90748 Henderson NV 89009-0748

HOLM, DARRELL VAUGHN, oil company consultant; b. Ft. Benton, Mont., June 21, 1951; s. Einer A. and Kathleen E. (Vaughn) H.; m. Anna Marie Moscolic, June 10, 1972; children: Sarah, Andrea, Matthew, Ryan. BS in Geophys. Engring., Mont. Tech., 1973, MS in Environ. Engring., 1990. Registered profl. civil engr., Mont. Geophysicist Union Tex. Petroleum, Midland, 1976-78; staff geophysicist Marathon Oil Co., Casper, Wyo., 1978-80; petroleum geophysicist Milestone Petroleum, Inc., Billings, Mont., 1980-81; sr. geophysicist Hunt Oil Co., Denver, 1981-89; sr. staff geophysicist Burlington Resources, Inc., Billings, 1985-89; project engr. Maxim Technologies, Inc., Billings, 1990-96; oil company cons. Billings, 1996; environ., oil exploration cons., 1996; fin. mgmt. cons., Billings, 1988-96. Fundraiser YMCA, Midland, Tex., 1977, Billings, 1984; co-leader Boy Scouts Am., Billings, 1994. Mont. Mining Coun. Rsch. grantee, 1989. Mem. NSPE, Soc. of Exploration Geophysicists, Mont. Soc. Engrs. Home: 2220 Boulder Ave Billings MT 59102

HOLMAN, KAREN MARIE, purchasing agent; b. Anchorage, Sept. 6, 1962; d. Joseph Willie and Rose Millicent (Watson) Anderson; m. Robert L. Holman Jr., Nov. 27, 1982. AA in Bus. Adminstrn., Anchorage Community Coll., 1984; BA in Orgnl. Adminstrn., Alaska Pacific U., 1991. Cert. purchasing mgr.; accredited purchasing practitioner. Sr. office clk. Bur. of the Census, Anchorage, 1980; premium audit clk. Providence Wash. Ins., Anchorage, 1981-82; info. systems clk. G.A Ltd., Anchorage, 1982-83; purchasing agt. State of Alaska, Anchorage, 1984-89, U. Alaska, Anchorage, 1989-92, ATU Telecommunications, 1992—. Del. Dem. Group State Caucuses, Anchorage, 1989; mem. Greater Friendly Temple Ch. of God in Christ, state dir. pub. rels. Alaska Ecclesiastical Jurisdiction; bd. dirs. Alaska Women's resource Ctr., 1989-91. Mem. Nat. Assn. Purchasing Mgmt. Home: 3722 Randolph St Anchorage AK 99508-4529

HOLMAN, PAUL DAVID, plastic surgeon; b. Waynesboro, Va., Mar. 13, 1943; s. Wallace D. and Rosalie S. Holman. BA, U. Va., 1965; MD, Jefferson Med. Coll., 1968. Intern, George Washington U. Hosp., Washington, 1968-69, resident in gen. surgery, 1969-70, 72-74; resident in plastic surgery Phoenix Plastic Surgery Residency, 1974-76; practice medicine specializing in plastic surgery, Phoenix, 1977—; mem. staff Good Samaritan Hosp., Phoenix, St. Joseph's Hosp., Phoenix, Phoenix Children's Hosp. Served to lt. comdr. USNR, 1970-72. Diplomate Am. Bd. Surgery, Am. Bd. Plastic Surgery. Mem. AMA, ACS, Am. Soc. Plastic and Reconstructive Surgeons, Phi Beta Kappa. Office: 2111 E Highland Ave Ste 105 Phoenix AZ 85016-4732

HOLMBERG, BRANTON KIETH, management consultant; b. Tacoma, Mar. 6, 1936; s. Victor August and Ann Irene (Warren) H.; BA, Central Wash. U., 1962, MEd, 1964; EdD, U. Idaho, 1970; m. Margaret Ann Nelson, Sept. 17, 1960; children: James Michael, Ann Marie, Nelson John. Asst. prof. Pacific Lutheran U., 1964-70; assoc. prof. Cen. Wash. U., Ellensburg, 1970-76, asso. dir. Orgn. Devel. Ctr., 1972-73; PhD program dir. U.S. Internat. U., McChord AFB, 1977-78; pres. Holmberg Assoc., mgmt. and orgn. devel. cons., Bellingham, 1975—, Northpoint Corp., geriatric care ctrs., Bellingham, 1978-84, Northwest Horticulture, Inc., 1979-90, Internat. Highpoint Corp., 1983-91, Advanced Laundry Svc., 1984-88, assoc. dean Northwest Indian Coll., 1993-94; dean Northwest Indian Coll, 1994-95. Mem. Ellensburg Criminal Law and Justice Planning Com., 1972-73. Served with USAF, 1954-58. U. Idaho fellow, 1968. Mem. Am. Psychol. Assn., Am. Mgmt. Assn., Am. Personnel and Guidance Assn., Internat. Assn. Quality Circles, Internat. Registry Orgn. Devel. Cons., Acad. Mgmt., AAUP, Orgn. Devel. Network, Phi Delta Kappa. Home: 14115 Goodrich Dr NW Gig Harbor WA 98329-8645

HOLMES, BARBARAANN KRAJKOSKI, secondary education educator; b. Evansville, Ind., Mar. 21, 1946; d. Frank Joseph and Estella Marie (DeWeese) Krajkoski; m. David Leo Holmes, Aug. 21, 1971; 1 child, Susan Ann Sky. BS, Ind. State U., 1968, MS, 1969, specialist cert., 1976; postgrad. U. Nev., 1976-78. Acad. counselor Ind. State U., 1968-69, halls dir., 1969-73; dir. residence halls U. Utah, 1973-76; sales assoc. Fidelity Realty, Las Vegas, Nev., 1977-82. cert. analyst Nev. Dept. Edn., 1981-82; tchr. Clark County Sch. Dist., 1982-87, computer cons., adminstrv. specialist instructional mgmt. systems, 1987-91, chair computer conf., 1990-92, adminstrv. specialist K-6, 1990-93, dean of students summer sch. site adminstr. Eldorado H.S., 1991-96; asst. prin. Garrett Middle Sch., Boulder City, Nev., 1997—. Named Outstanding Sr. Class Woman, Ind. State U., 1969; recipient Dir's. award U. Utah Residence Halls, 1973, Outstanding Sales Assoc., 1977; Tchr. of Month award, 1983, Dist. Outstanding Tchr. award, 1984, Dist. Excellence in Edn. award, 1984, 86, 87, 88. Mem. Nev. Assn. Realtors, AAUW, Am. Assn. Women Deans, Adminstrs. and Counselors, Am. Personnel and Guidance Assn., Am. Coll. Personnel Assn., Nevadans for Equal Rights Amendment, Alumnae Assn. Chi Omega (treas. Terre Haute chpt. 1971-73, pres., bd. officer Las Vegas 1977-81), Clark County Panhellenic Alumnae Assn. (pres. 1978-79), Computer Using Educators So. Nev. (sec. 1983-86, pres.-elect 1986-87, pres. 1987-88, state chmn. 1988-89, conf. chmn. 1989-92, sec. 94—, Hall of Fame 1995), Job's Daus. Club (guardian sec. 1995—), Order Ea. Star, Phi Delta Kappa (Action award 1990-96, newspaper editor 1992-93). Developed personal awareness program U. Utah, 1973-76. Home: 1227 Kover Ct Henderson NV 89015-9017 Office: Garrett Middle Sch 1200 Avenue G Boulder City NV 89005

HOLMES, CHRISTOPHER, public relations executive; b. Sydney, Australia, Feb. 4, 1946; came to U.S., 1984; s. Ronald David and Charlotte (Fisher) H.; m. Stephanie Anne, July 7, 1980; children: Georgina Lawyer, Anna Lawyer. Student, St. Johns Coll., Sussex, Eng., 1960-64, Balliol, Oxford, Eng., 1965-69, L'Inst. Touraine, France, 1970. Publicity mgr. Fred Muller, Inc., London, 1972-75; publicity dir. Cassell, Inc., London, 1975-79; pub. rels. mgr. Hong Kong Tourist Assoc., Hong Kong, 1980-82; publicity dir. Holmes Publicity, Hong Kong, 1982-83; publicity mgr. Book Mktg. Coun., London, 1983-87; publicity dir. Secker Warburg, London, 1987-94; sr. acct. exec. Waggener Edstrom, Bellevue, Wash., 1995-96; editor Svc. Intelligence Inc., Seattle, 1996—. Author: Royal Hong Kong Jockey Club, 1988 (Silver Pen award 1989). Mem. Publ. Publicity Cir. (sec. 1973-75), Fgn. Corres. Club, Spl. Forces Club. Office: Svc Intelligence Inc 1417 4th Ave Seattle WA 98101

HOLMES, DAVID LEO, recreation and leisure educator; b. Hammond, Ind., Jan. 4, 1943; s. Leo Victor and Hannah Marget (Robertson) H.; m. Barbara Ann Krajkoski, Mar. 21, 1971; 1 child, Susan Ann Sky. AA, Vincennes U., 1967; BS, Ind. State U., 1969, MS, 1970; PhD, U. Utah, 1976. Tchr., dir. sch. recreation and outdoor edn. Rockville (Ind.) Jr. Ctr., Ind. State Dept. Corrections, 1970-72; instr. Nat. Outdoor Leadership Sch., Washington, Conn., 1972; teaching fellow U. Utah, Salt Lake City, 1973-76; from asst. to prof. program coord. sport and leisure dept. U. Nev., Las Vegas, 1976-91, prof. dept. leisure studies, 1991—; adj. asst. prof. dept. recreation Ind. State U., Terre Haute, 1972-73; lectr. in field. Contbr. more than 50 articles to profl. jours.; author 5 monographs; editor 5 jours. Active State Comprehensive Outdoor Recreation Planning Com., Nev., 1988; planning team Clark Country Nev. Sch. Dist., 1987-88; adv. bd. Clark Country Nev. Parks and Recreation, 1979-88, vice-chmn., 1984. With USMCR, Desert Storm, 1990-91. Recipient Pacemaker award, Faculty Citation Vincennes U., 1990, Spl. Pres. award Nat. Assn. Country Parks & Recreation Officials, 1986; named Outstanding Alumni U. Utah, 1987; recipient Spl. Recognition award Ind. State U., 1987, Hon. Mem. Wings, Blue Parachute Team, # 1 USAF Acad., 1982; grantee various institutions. Mem. AAHPERD (life, Cmty. Svc. award 1987), Nat. Recreation and Park Soc. (Excellence award 1995), Am. Assn. for Leisure and Recreation (bd. dirs. 1981-82, v.p. recreation S.W. dist. 1981), Nev. Parks and Recreation Soc., Nev. State Parks Coop. Assn. (bd. dirs. 1991-92, 93-94), Nev. Assn. for Health, Phys. Edn. and Recreation (pres. 1979-80, Profl. of Yr. 1983-84), U. Nev. Alumni Assn. (Prof. Worthy of Recognition 1995). Methodist. Home: 1227 Kover Ct Henderson NV 89015-9017 Office: Univ Las Vegas Dept Leisure Studies 4505 S Maryland Pky Las Vegas NV 89154-9900

HOLMES, DOROTHY SPARHAWK, writer, retired nurse; b. Rowley, Alta., Can., Nov. 30, 1914; d. Lafayette Freemont and Bertha Emily (Whipp) Sparhawk; m. George F. Holmes, Apr. 13, 1936; children: Delores Jean, Ramone Joan, Debra Lee. GED, Ctrl. Oreg. C.C., 1964, LPN, 1967. Nurse St. Charles Hosp., Bend, Oreg., 1967-69, with admitting office, 1969; mem. staff Elzora Convalescent Home, Milton-Freewater, Oreg., 1969-70, Blue Mountain Convalescent Ctr., 1970073; ret., 1973. Author: Sir Chester Cricket, 1990, Songs of a Singing Heart, 1996. Home: 519 E Court St Goldendale WA 98620-9235

HOLMES, MICHAEL, oil and gas consultant; b. London, Oct. 6, 1936; came to U.S., 1963, naturalized, 1975; s. Norman Edward and Iris I. (Fisher) H.; m. Francoise J. Charlet, July 14, 1962 (div.); children: Antony I., Dominic M.; m. Sally Haven, July 13, 1973. (div.). B.S.C., U. London, 1957, Ph.D., 1961; M.S., Colo. Sch. Mines, 1973. Geologist, Brit. Petroleum, London, 1960-66, Shell Can., Edmonton, Alta., 1966-68; research scientist Marathon Oil, Denver, 1968-73; exploration mgr. Berry Wiggins, London, 1973-74; v.p. H.K. Van Poollen, Denver, 1974-78; prin. Michael Holmes, Denver, 1978—; dir. Cibola Energy Corp., Albuquerque. Author: (with others) Reservoir Economics and Engineering Manual, 1973. Bd. dirs. English Speaking Union, Denver, 1970-73. Mem. Arapahoe C. of C. (bd. dirs. 1970-73), Am. Assn. Petroleum Geologists, Soc. Petroleum Engrs., Soc. Profl. Well Log Analysts, Rocky Mountain Assn. Geologists, Am. Inst. Profl. Geologists.

HOLMES, PAUL LUTHER, political scientist, educational consultant; b. Rock Island, Ill., Mar. 7, 1919; s. Bernt Gunnar and Amanda Sophia (Swenson) H.; m. Ardis Ann Grunditz, Nov. 1, 1946; children: Mary Ann, David Stephen. BA, U. Minn., 1940; MA, Stanford U., 1949, EdD, 1968; MA, George Washington U., 1964. Career officer U.S. Navy, 1941-64, ret. as capt.; adminstr. Laney Coll., Oakland, Calif., 1965-70; dean Contra Costa Coll., San Pablo, Calif., 1970-71; pres. Coll. of Alameda (Calif.), 1971-75, prof. polit. sci., 1975-80; dir. doctoral studies program No. Calif., Nova U., 1975-80; cons. in higher edn., Gig Harbor, Wash., 1981—; regent Calif. Luth. U., 1973-76. Mem. Stanford Univ. Alumni Assn., Rotary, Phi Delta Kappa. Lutheran.

HOLMES, RALPH EDWARD, plastic surgeon; b. San Diego, Calif., Dec. 8, 1943. MD, Boston U., 1967. Prof., head divsn. plastic surgery U. Calif. San Diego Med. Coll. Office: U Calif San Diego Med Ctr 200 W Arbor Dr San Diego CA 92103-8890

HOLMES, RICHARD ALBERT, software engineer, consultant; b. Santa Barbara, Calif., May 7, 1958; m. Janet M. Dunbar; children: Brian D., Kevin M. AA in Music summa cum laude, City Coll. San Francisco, 1987; BS in Computer Sci. summa cum laude, Nat. U., 1991; postgrad., Stanford U., 1993—. Ind. software cons. San Francisco, 1986-88; software quality assurance contractor Oxford & Assocs., Mountain View, Calif., 1988-89; microkernel diagnostics engr. Apple Computer, Cupertino, Calif., 1990-93, file system engr., 1994-96; operating sys. engr. Hewlett Packard, Cupertino, Calif., 1996—. CCSF tchr. & faculty scholar, 1986, 87, Alpha Gamma Sigma scholar, 1987. Mem. IEEE, Assn. for Computing Machinery, Alpha Gamma Sigma (treas. 1986-87). Office: Hewlett-Packard Co MS 47LA1 19447 Pruneridge Ave Cupertino CA 95014

HOLMES, RICHARD BROOKS, mathematical physicist; b. Milw., Jan. 7, 1959; s. Emerson Brooks Holmes and Nancy Anne Schaffter. BS, Calif. Inst. Tech., 1981; MS, Stanford (Calif.) U., 1983. Sr. sys. analyst Comptek Rsch., Vallejo, Calif., 1982-83; staff scientist Western Rsch., Arlington, Va., 1983-85; sr. scientist AVCO Everett (Mass.) Rsch. Lab., 1985-88; prin. rsch. scientist North East Rsch. Assocs., Woburn, Mass., 1988-90; sr. mem. tech. staff Rocketdyne divsn. Rockwell Internat., Canoga Park, Calif., 1990-95; sr. staff scientist Lockheed Martin Rsch. Labs., Palo Alto, Calif., 1995—; cons. North East Rsch. Assocs., 1990. Contbr. Matched Asymptotic Expansions, 1988; contbr. articles to Phys. Rev. Letters, Phys. Rev., Jour. of the Optical Soc. Am. and IEEE Jour. of Quantum Electronics. Mem. No. Calif. Scholarship Founds., Oakland, 1977; mem. Wilderness Soc., Washington, 1989. Stanford fellow Stanford U., 1982; fellow MIT, 1990; recipient Presdl. Medal of Merit, 1992. Mem. AAAS, Am. Phys. Soc., Optical Soc. Am. Office: Lockheed Martin Rsch Labs Bldg 202 Org 97-01 3251 Hanover St Palo Alto CA 94304

HOLMES, ROBERT EDWARD, photographer; b. Ilkeston, Derbyshire, Eng., Mar. 21, 1943; came to the U.S., 1979; s. Maurice E. and Marjorie E. (Jones) H.; m. Barbara Jane Perez, Aug. 16, 1979; children: Emma S., Hannah S. BS, U. London, 1964; diploma in town planning, Nottingham (Eng.) Coll. Art, 1967. Dep. planning officer Broxtowe Dist. Coun., Nottinghamshire, Eng., 1971-79; freelance photographer and writer Calif., 1979—; bd. mem. Survival Internat., London, 1973-79; pres. Am. Soc. Media Photographers, N.Y., 1984-85. Author, photographer: Thomas Cook Guide to California, 1993, Thomas Cook Guide to New England, 1994, Thomas Cook Guide to Hawaii, 1995; photographer: (series) Day in the Life, 1990-96, Spirits in Stone, 1993. Named Travel Photographer of Yr., Soc. Am. Travel Writers, 1990, 92. Fellow Royal Geog. Soc.; mem. Reform Club (London). Home: PO Box 556 Mill Valley CA 94942-0556 Office: Robert Holmes Photography 3000 Bridgeway Sausalito CA 94965-1492

HOLMES, ROBERT EUGENE, state legislative consultant, journalist; b. Shelbyville, Ind., June 5, 1928; s. Eugene Lowell and Sarah Lucinda (Hughes) H.; m. Retha Carolyn Richey, June 27, 1955 (div. Sept. 1966); children: Enid Adair Offley, William Houstoun (dec.), Holly Ann Holmes. BA in Polit. Sci., DePauw U., 1950; MA in Journalism, Ind. U., 1953; MA in Communs. and Urban Affairs, Stanford U., 1976. Staff reporter Elkhart, Ind. Truth, 1954-57; city editor, investigative editor Press-Enterprise, Riverside, Calif., 1957-70; sr. cons. Calif. State Senate Dem. Caucus, Sacramento, 1971-74, dep. dir., 1978-79; press sec. Lt. Gov. of Calif., Sacramento, 1975-77; project dir. Border Area Devel. Study, U.S. Econ. Devel. Adminstrn., Sacramento, 1978; staff dep. dir. Calif. Senator Robert Presley, Sacramento, 1979-83; chief cons. Joint Legis. Ethics Com., Calif. Legislature, Sacramento, 1981-82; staff dir. Joint Com. on Prison Constrn. and Ops., Calif. Legislature, Sacramento, 1983-94; rsch. cons. Calif. Rsch. Bur., Calif. State Libr., Sacramento, 1991-92; cons. Calif. Hist. State Capitol Commn., 1995-96. Author, editor rschr. legis. reports; contbg. editor creative writing quar. Noah's Hotel, Inverness, Calif., 1991—; contbr. articles to mags., short stories, 1961—. Pres., Golden Bear Dem. Club, Sacramento, 1972-74; media dir. Lt. Gov. Campaign, Sacramento and L.A., 1974. Sgt. USMC, 1951-53. Recipient Silver Gavel award ABA, 1969, 1st Place media award Calif. State Bar Assn., 1968, 1st Place award Calif. Newspaper Pubs. Best Series, 1969, 70, 71, Jack Anderson award for excellence in journalism Calif. Correctional Peace Officers Assn., 1993; Am. Polit. Sci. Assn. Ford Found. fellow Stanford U., 1970. Mem. NAACP, ACLU, Calif. Writers Club, Common Cause. Democrat. Home: 416 Florin Rd Sacramento CA 95831-2007

HOLMES, SANDRA FAYE, elementary school educator; b. Memphis, May 1, 1951; d. Elmore Howard and Lillian (Blackburn) Denton; children: Rudy Gerald, Jason ryan. BS in Elem. Edn., Memphis U., 1977, MA in Adminstrn./Supervision, 1988. Cert. prin., Wash. Tchr. Memphis City Schs.,

1973-90; tchr. Oakwood Elem. Sch./Clover Park Sch. Dist., Lakewood, Wash., 1990—, adminstrv. intern, acting prin., 1994-95; tchr., acting prin. Lochburn Mid. Sch., Lakewood, 1996—, assemblies coord., 1996-97. Mem. NAACP, 1994-95, Women of the Well, St. John Bosco Cath. Ch., Lakewood, 1993-96, chairperson cmty. bldg., 1993-96, pastoral advisor parish coun., 1993-96, rep. strategic planning com., 1993-96, rep. rev. for Cath. schs. ednl. study, 1993-94. Mem. NEA, Wash. Edn. Assn. (chairperson pub. rels. Soundview Uniserve 1993-94, pub. rels. commn. 1993-94), Assn. of Wash. Sch. Prins. Democrat. Roman Catholic. Home: Oak Terrace 42 Thunderbird Pky # 108 Lakewood WA 98498 Office: Clover Park Sch Dist 10220 Gravelly Lake Dr SW Lakewood WA 98499

HOLMES-SMITH, DAVID MICHAEL, computer engineer, consultant, priest, dean; b. Whittier, Calif., Nov. 25, 1955; s. Norman Kenneth Smith and Joanne Sherwood (Jackman) Chace; m. Kathleen Martha Holmes, Apr. 15, 1989; children: Kelly Leilani, Jennifer Puanani. BA in Performing Arts, U. Hawaii, 1990, MEd, 1992; MS in Info. Sys., Hawaii Pacific U., 1993; postgrad., Internat. Grad. Sch. Theology, Honolulu, 1994—. Ordained Anglican priest Episcopal Ch., 1993. Instr. Hawaii Pacific U., Honolulu, 1990-94; owner, designer Holmes-Smith Engring., Honolulu, 1992—; instr. Mid-Pacific Inst., Honolulu, 1994—; priest St. Michaels Mission, Honolulu, 1994-95, Missionary Episcopal Ch., 1995—; dean Abbot Holy Order of the Culdee, Honolulu, 1995—; archdean Culdee Coll., Honolulu, 1995—; cons. edn., computer tech., 1992—. Author/producer: (musical) Forgotten Legend, 1988, Tabernacle Liturgy, 1990. Chair edn. and comm. com. Anglican Episcopal Diocese of Okla., 1993-95; mem. Ruthe rford Inst., Honolulu, 1992. Cmdr. Mid Pacific Squadron Civil Air Patrol, 1996. Iona Inst. rsch. fellow. Mem. Internat. Soc. for Teaching in Edn., Epsilon Delta Phi, Phi Eta Sigma, Delta Mu Delta. Home: 1914 University Ave Apt 209 Honolulu HI 96822-2473 Office: Holy Order of the Culdee 1914 University Ave Ste 106 Honolulu HI 96822

HOLMGREN, JANET L, college president; b. Chgo., Dec. 1, 1948; d. Kenneth William and Virginia Ann (Rensink) H.; m. Gordon A. McKay, Sept. 7, 1968 (div. 1990); children: Elizabeth Jane, Ellen Katherine. BA in English summa cum laude, Oakland U., Rochester, Mich., 1968; MA in Linguistics, Princeton U., 1971, PhD in Linguistics, 1974. Asst. prof. English studies Federal City Coll. (now U. D.C.), Washington, 1972-76; asst. prof. English U. Md., College Park, 1976-82, asst. to chancellor, 1982-88; assoc. provost Princeton (N.J.) U., 1988-90, vice-provost, 1990-91; pres. Mills Coll., Oakland, Calif., 1991—; mem. external adv. bd. English dept. Princeton U. Bay Area Biosci. Ctr. Author: (with Spencer Cosmos) The Story of English: Study Guide and Reader, 1986, Narration and Discourse in American Realistic Fiction, 1982; contbr. articles to profl. jours. Faculty rsch. grantee U. Md., 1978; fellow NEH, 1978, Princeton U., 1968-69, 70-72, NSF, 1969-70; recipient summer study aid Linguistic Soc. Am., Ohio State U., 1970. Mem. Assn. Ind. Caif. Colls. and Univs. (exec. com.), Nat. Assn. Ind. Colls. and Univs., Am. Coun. on Education (chair office of women in higher edn.), Calif. Acad. Sci. (coun.). Democrat. Episcopal. Office: Mills Coll Office Pres 5000 Macarthur Blvd Oakland CA 94613-1301

HOLMGREN, RICHARD S., JR., environmental engineering executive; b. 1928. BS in Civil Engring., MIT, 1950; MS in Sanitary Engring., U. Calif., Berkeley, 1957. With Montgomery Watson, 1958—, now chmn. Office: Montgomery Watson Ams 300 N Lake Ave # 1200 Pasadena CA 91101-1829*

HOLNESS, ALLAN DELANO, JR., real estate developer; b. Louis Store, St. Mary, Jamaica, Mar. 7, 1955; came to U.S., 1975; s. Allan and Daphne (Mullings) H.; div.; children: Traona Mona, Ali Gail, Marcus Aureilius. BS, Warner Pacific Coll., Portland, Oreg., 1979; student, Univ. Alaska, Anchorage, 1981-83. Asst. acct. Can. Imperial Bank Commerce, Kingston, Jamaica, 1973-75; internat. banker First Nat. Bank Oreg., Portland, 1978; intern, legis. aid U.S. Senator Mark O. Hatfield, Washington, 1977; CEO A.D. Holness Co., Anchorage, 1979—. Treas. Nat. Youth Coun., Kingston, 1974-75; organizer campaign Jim Campbell for Gov., Anchorage, 1994; mem. Alaska Sch. to Work Coun. Mem. Lions Club, Alpha Chi. Republican. Presbyterian.

HOLO, SELMA REUBEN, museum director, educator; b. Chgo., May 21, 1943; d. Samuel and Ghita (Hurwitz) Reuben; children from previous marriage: Robert, Joshua; m. Fred Croton, June 18, 1989. BA, Northwestern U., 1965; MA, Hunter Coll., 1972; PhD, U. Calif., Santa Barbara, 1980; postgrad., Mus. Mgmt. Inst., 1985. Lectr. Art Ctr. Coll. of Design, Pasadena, Calif., 1973-77; curator of acquisitions Norton Simon Mus., Pasadena, 1977-81; dir. Fisher Gallery and mus. MA art history/mus. studies program U. So. Calif., L.A., 1981—; guest curator, cons. Getty Mus., Malibu, Calif., 1975-76, 81; guest curator Isetan Mus., Tokyo, 1982, cons. Nat. Mus. for Women in Arts, Washington, 1984; reviewer grants Inst. Mus. Svcs., Washington, 1986-87, Getty Grant Program, 1988-90; panel chmn. Internat. Com. on Exhbn. Exch., Washington, 1984; panelist NEA, Washington, 1985, 91-93, Idaho Commn. on the Arts; admission panel mem. Mus. Mgmt. Inst., 1990; hon. curator Tokyo Fuji Mus.; lectr. museology IVAM, Valencia, Spain, 1994, Complutense U. Masters in Museology, 1994, U. Castilla La Mancha in Museology, 1995; presenter Museo/Mus. Conf., Barcelona, Spain, 1996, Bilbao (Spain) Mus. Fine Arts Conf. on Mus. Edn., 1996; co-author survey com. mus. studies programs, 1986. Author: (catalogues) Goya: Los Disparates, 1976; co-author: La Tauromaquia: Goya, Picasso and the Bullfight, 1986; editor: Keepers of the Flame, The Unofficial Artists of Leningrad, 1990; guest editor New Observations, 1990; contbr. articles to profl. jours. and mag. Fellow La Napoule Art Found., 1988, Fulbright Found , 1994; Kress Found. grantee, N.Y., 1979, Internationes Fed. Republic of Germany grantee, 1985, 92; recipient Fuj Fine Art award, 1990, Sr. Rsch. Fulbright fellowship to Spain, 1994, award from program for cooperation between the program for the Ministry of Culture of Spain and N.Am. Univ. Mem. Am. Assn. Mus., Art Table. Office: U So Calif Fisher Gallery 823 Exposition Blvd Los Angeles CA 90007-4005

HOLOWAY, SUSAN E., writer; b. Ilwaco, Wash., Dec. 26, 1944; d. Theodore Woodruff and Ruth Virginia (Tartar) H.; m. Richard John Pakenen, Aug. 6, 1966 (div. Nov. 1984). BA, Wash. State U., 1967, MA, 1988. Cert. English tchr., Wash., Oreg. English, French, speech and drama tchr. Ilwaco H.S., 1969-74, 78-80, substitute tchr., 1988-89; editor Finnish-Am. Lit. Heritage Found., Portland, Oreg., 1983-84; grad. asst., tchr., publicist theater dept. Portland State U., 1987-88; English instr. Clatsop C.C., Astonia, Oreg., 1989-95; freelance writer Oysterville, Wash., 1995—. Author: (poetry and play) Remember Where You Started From, 1992, Woodruff Family Genealogy, 1995, numerous plays and oral histories. Mem. Ocean Beach Sch. Bd., Ilwaco, 1991—, legis. rep., 1995—; mem. choir, coms. Ocean Park United Meth. Ch., Ocean Park, 1985—; bd. dirs., co-chair Water Music Festival, Seaview, Wash., 1991-95; bd. dirs. Grays Harbor C.C. Satellite, Ilwaco, 1970-80; founder, chair Finnish-Am. Folk Fest, Noselle, Wash., 1982—; mem. leadership conf. WSS Dirs. Assn., Olympia, Wash., 1996-97, Willapa Alliance, Ilwaco, 1996. Recipient Cultural Spl. award Snomk-Seura, 1995-96. Mem. CCCC, Ilwaco Heritage Mus., Maritime Mus., South Bend Pacific County Hist. Soc., Oysterville Cmty. Club (v.p. 1996—). Home: Box 25 Oysterville WA 98641

HOLST, WENDELL, marketing professional, consultant, writer; b. Edgar, Nebr., Sept. 15, 1920; s. Gustav Adolph and Johanna Rebecca Maria (Rahmann) H.; m. Imogene Perkins, Oct. 18, 1947; children: Mark W. Holst, Marilyn J. Holst Thore. Student, Northwestern Coll. Law, 1946-47; grad., Ins. Inst., 1951. Payroll auditor U.S. Dept. Interior, Portland, Oreg., 1941-43, social security adminstr., 1946-47; acct. sys. specialist to intermountain mgr. Oreg. Mutual Ins. Co., McMinnville, 1947-53; asst. sec., exec. v.p. Western Pacific Ins. Co., Seattle, 1953-70; exec. v.p. Groninger & Co., Seattle, 1970-72; pres. Consumers United Ins. Co., Seattle, 1972-75, Forest Industries Ins., Albany, Oreg., 1975-77, Timber-Line Gen. Agy., McMinnville, 1975-77, Inter-West Ins. Co., McMinnville, 1979-85; mktg. cons. various cos., Oreg., 1985—. Author: Getting Most Out of Small Business, 1993, Getting Most Out of Your Insurance, 1993, Getting Most Out Of Your Travels, 1993, Getting Most Out of Just Thinking, 1993, Getting Most Out of Your Retirement, 1995, Getting Ahead? Oh Yes You Can, 1995, Little Thinkers, 1996, Spoof's Letters of Laughter, 1996; inventor short-cut endorser. Del. Indsl. Conf. Bd., Seattle, 1955-70; campaign mgr. Ins. Commr. Cand., Seattle, 1970-74; sec. Little League Baseball, Seattle, 1959-64; chmn. bd. YMCA, Seattle; com. chmn. Boy Scouts Am., Seattle, 1957. With USN, 1942-46. Mem. Ins. Acctg. and Sys. Assn. (nat. pres. 1972-73), Masons, Shriners, Elks. Presbyterian. Home and Office: 2205 Saint Andrews Dr Mcminnville OR 97128-2455

HOLT, DENNIS F., media buying company executive. Student, U. So. Calif. Salesman RKO, L.A.; founder, pres. chief exec. officer, chmn. Western Internat. Media Corp., L.A. Office: Western Internat Media Corp 8544 W Sunset Blvd West Hollywood CA 90069-2310*

HOLT, RONALD LAWRENCE, anthropologist, educator; b. Sweetwater, Tex., Dec. 3, 1949; s. William Hazelwood and Minnie Louise (Crider) H.; m. Elisa Karen Holt, July 3, 1987; children: Ian Ari, Robin Nikko. BA, Tex. Tech U., 1974, MA, 1976; PhD, U. Utah, 1987. Tchr. So. Utah U., 1981-82; T U. Utah, 1983-86; dir. of honours, assoc. prof. anthropology Weber State U., Ogden, Utah, 1986—. Author: Beneath These Red Cliffs: An Ethnohistory of the Utah Pointes, 1992. Founding trustee Utah Dem. Leadership Coun., 1995; Dem. candidate U.S. Congress, 1992. Mem. Am. Anthrop. Assn., Nat. Collegiate Honors Assn., Exchange Club. Buddhist. Office: Weber State University 2904 University Cir Ogden UT 84408-2904

HOLT, STEVEN HAMILTON SKOV, industrial designer, educator; b. Hartford, Conn., Sept. 24, 1957; s. John Nicholas Holt and Alice Claire (Humphrey) Lund; m. Mara Elizabeth Skov, Aug. 27, 1994. AB in Cognitive Sci., Brown U., 1982; MFA in Design Studies, Stanford U., 1992. Celia Siegel fellow Cooper-Hewitt Mus., N.Y.C., 1982; editor I.D. Mag., N.Y.C., 1983-85; designer Smart Design, N.Y.C., 1986; dir. product design studies Parsons Sch. Design, N.Y.C., 1986-90; ptnr. Zebra Design, Cologne, Germany, 1987-90; visionary frogdesign, inc., Sunnyvale, Calif., 1992—; chmn. indsl. design dept. Calif. Coll. Arts & Crafts, San Francisco, 1995—. Contbg. editor: Axis Mag., Tokyo, 1986-93, Indsl. Ontwerpen Mag., Rotterdam, The Netherlands, 1989-93; contbg. editor, columnist Met. Home Mag., N.Y.C., 1988-91, Graphis Mag., N.Y.C., 1993—; contbr. articles to profl. jours. Mem. Indsl. Design Soc. Am., Soc. Archtl. Historians. Office: frogdesign inc 1327 Chesapeake Ter Sunnyvale CA 94089

HOLT, SUSAN LYNNE, mental health counselor; b. Columbus, Ohio, Sept. 28, 1954; d. Robert Charles and Faith Margaret H. Cert. in non-violent crisis intervention. Counselor, coord. domestic violence program L.A. Gay and Lesbian Ctr., 1987-89; acting asst. dir. counseling svcs. dept. L.A. Gay and Lesbian Cmty. Svc. Ctr., 1990-91, mental health clinician, 1990—, clin. tng. coord., 1991-96, program coord., domestic violence prevention, outreach, and treatment, 1996—; group counselor U. Judaism, L.A., 1986-90, mgr. support group facilitator program, 1988-90; counselor rep., mem. counseling adv. bd. L.A. Gay and Lesbian Ctr., 1988-93, chmn. clin. svcs. and tng., 1990-93, mem. planning and adminstrn. com., 1991-92; mem. Domestic Violence Task Force, Hollywood, 1996—. Mem. Coun. on Jewish Life, Commn. on Cmty. Outreach, Jewish Fedn. Coun. of L.A., 1985-88, chmn. spkr. bur., 1985-88; presenter Domestic Violence Hearings, Office of Criminal Justice Planning, State of Calif., L.A., 1992; mem. Domestic Violence Task Force Gay and Lesbian Cmty. Svcs. Ctr., L.A., 1993—, City of West Hollywood, Calif. Domestic Violence Task Force, 1996—. Mem. Am. Counseling Assn., Am. Mental Health Counselors Assn. Office: 1625 Schrader Blvd Los Angeles CA 90028-6213

HOLT, VONNIE, counselor, educator; b. Chewelah, Wash., Feb. 25, 1950; d. Kiel Adonis Ganoung and Gladys Mary (McClurg) Walker; children: Mark B. Wasson, Jeremy C. Wasson., Michael L. Holt; stepchildren: Joshua, Courtney. BSc in Psychology, Wash. State U., 1990, EdM, 1992. Registered mental health counselor, Wash. Counselor YWCA, Lewiston, Idaho, 1990-96; counselor group co-facilitator Valley Treatment Spltys., Clarkston, Wash., 1991—, V.T.S. & Assocs./Adult Counseling & Ednl. Svc., Clarkston, 1994—; tchr./counselor Walla Walla C.C., Clarkston, 1995—; cons. Valley Treatment Specialties, 1991—, YWCA of Lewiston/Clarkston, 1990-96; adj. faculty Walla Walla C.C. Mem. ACA. Office: Adult Counseling & Ednl Svcs 717 Elm St Clarkston WA 99403-2049

HOLT, WILLIAM E., lawyer; b. Phila., Aug. 31, 1945. BBA, U. Iowa, 1967, JD with distinction, 1970. Bar: Iowa 1970, Wash. 1971. Law clk. to Hon. William T. Beeks U.S. Dist. Ct. (we. dist.) Wash., 1970-71; ptnr. Gordon, Thomas, Honeywell, Malanca, Peterson & Daheim, Tacoma; adj. prof. U. Puget Sound Law Sch., 1974-75. Note editor Iowa Law Rev., 1969-70. Mem. ABA, Wash. State Bar Assn. (exec. com. real property, probate and trust sect. 1987-89), Phi Delta Phi. Office: Gordon Thomas Honeywell Malanca Peterson & Daheim PO Box 1157 Ste 2200 Tacoma WA 98401-1157

HOLTAN, RAMER B., JR., lawyer; b. Wilmington, Del., Oct. 20, 1944. AB, Harvard U., 1966; JD cum laude, U. Ill., 1972; postgrad., U. Freiburg, West Germany. Bar: Wash. 1973. Mem. Perkins Coie, Seattle. Articles editor U. Ill. Law Rev., 1971-72. Mem. Order of the Coif. Office: Perkins Coie 40th Fl 1201 3rd Ave Fl 40 Seattle WA 98101-3099

HOLTKAMP, SUSAN CHARLOTTE, elementary education educator; b. Houston, Feb. 23, 1957; d. Clarence Jules and Karyl Irene (Roberts) H. BS in Early Childhood Edn., Brigham Young U., Provo, Utah, 1979, MEd, 1982. Cert. tchr., Utah. 2d grade tchr. Nebo Sch. Dist., Spanish Fork, Utah, 1979-84, kindergarten tchr., 1984-85; tchr. 2d grade DODDS, Mannheim, Fed. Republic Germany, 1985-86; tchr. 3d grade Jordan Sch. Dist., Salt Lake City, 1987-92, tchr. 5th grade, 1992—. Mem. NEA, JEA, Utah Edn. Assn., ASCD.

HOLTON, WILLIAM CHESTER, engineer, consultant; b. Caldwell, Idaho, May 2, 1939; s. Chester Clayton and Margaret Ann (MacLaren) H.; m. Rhoberta Phaigh Romo, June 1, 1958 (div. Sept. 1976); children: William Lee, Robert Charles, Ronald Clayton. AS, Regents Coll., 1986. lic. FCC. Electronic technician Litton Industries, L.A., 1963-66; applications engr. 3M Co., Camarillo, Calif., 1966-74; program analyst USN, Port Magu, Calif., 1974-75; video supr. U. Calif., Santa Barbara, 1975-77; cons. Great Am. Tech. Services, L.A., 1977—. Creator digitally controlled screenings theater for Steven Spielberg at Universal Studios, first high speed sound-on-film editing suite in People's Republic of China, variable speed projection control system for Eddie Murphy. Mem. IEEE Computer Soc.

HOLTZ, JOSEPH NORMAN, marketing executive; b. Matawan, N.J., Oct. 11, 1930; s. Joseph Antone and Catherine Martina (Crosby) H.; m. Irene Strano, July 15, 1951; children: Joseph Jr., Karl, Gary, Robert, Eric. AA, De Vry Tech. Inst., 1954; student, Monmouth Coll., 1955-56; BBA, Nat. U., 1988, MBA, 1989; grad., Realtor Inst. Lic. real estate agent Nat. Assn. Realtors, Cert. Factoring Specialist designation Internat. Factoring Inst., Cert. Mortgage Investor designation Nat. Mortgage Investors Inst. Engr. Bendix Aviation, Red Bank, N.J., 1952-56, Hughes Aircraft Co., L.A., 1956-73; pres. Jo-Rene Assocs., Orange, Calif., 1973-86; asst. v.p. Builders Sales Corp., Santa Ana, Calif., 1986-87; exec. v.p. The Lehnert Group, Irvine, Calif., 1987-88; pres. J.N. Holtz Assocs., Orange, 1988—; CEO Holtz Funding Group, Orange, 1994—; v.p., corp. broker Mortgage Outlet Corp., 1992-94; corp. broker Shancie Real Estate Corp., 1992-94. Com. mem. United Way, Santa Ana, 1987—. Mem. IEEE, Inst. Residential Mktg., Sales and Mktg. Coun., Nat. Assn. Factoring Profls., Nat. Real Estate and Mortgage Investors Assn., Phoenix Club, Am. Soc. for Quality Control. Republican. Home: 5045-2 E Almond Ave Orange CA 92869-4245 Office: J N Holtz Assocs PO Box 11917 Santa Ana CA 92711-0014

HOLUB, ROBERT FRANTISEK, nuclear chemist, physicist; b. Prague, Czechoslovakia, Sept. 19, 1937; came to U.S., 1966; s. Stanislav and Marie (Prochazkova) H.; m. Johnna S. Thames, Dec. 27, 1977; children: Robert M., John F., Elisabeth J. BS, Charles U., Prague, 1958, MS, 1960; PhD, McGill U., 1970. Research assoc. Fla. State U., Tallahassee, 1970-73; teaching intern U. Ky., Lexington, 1973-74; rsch. physicist Bur. Mines, U.S. Dept. Interior, Denver, 1974-95; prof. dept. physics Colo. Sch. of Mines, Golden, 1995—; cons. IAEA, Vienna, Austria, 1984-89, key participant radon metrology program, 1990—; faculty affiliate Colo. State U., Ft. Collins, 1982—. Patentee continuous working level exposure apparatus. Contbr. articles to sci. jours. NRC Can. scholar, 1967-70. Mem. Am. Phys. Soc., Health Physics Soc., Am. Assn. for Aerosol Rsch.

HOLWAY, JAMES MICHAEL, regional planner, state agency administrator; b. Balt., Aug. 22, 1958; m. Rita Jo Anthony; 1 child, Joseph. BA in Polit. Sci., Cornell U., 1981; M in Regional Planning, U. N.C., 1987, PhD in Environ. Planning, 1990. Cert. planner. Asst. dir. Ariz. Dept. Water Resources, 1996—; faculty assoc. Ariz. State U., Tempe, 1993—, mem. external adv. bd. Herberger Ctr. for Design Excellence, 1996—. Mem. adv. com. City of Phoenix Sonoran Preserve, 1994—. Mem. Am. Planning Assn., Ariz. Planning Assn., Ariz. Hydrolic Soc., Am. Water Works Assn., Lambda Alpha Internat.

HOLZBERLEIN, KURT W., news director; b. Meeker, Colo., July 14, 1962; s. John Monte and Sally Anne (Mohar) H. BA in Am. Studies, U. Notre Dame, 1985. Announcer Sta. KMKR, Meeker, 1980-86; vol. prodr. Sta. KBDI-TV, Denver, 1986-88; bur. reporter, anchor Sta. KREX-TV Network, Grand Junction, Colo., 1988-89; reporter, anchor Columbine Cablevision, Ft. Collins, Colo., 1989-91, news dir., 1991-96. Recipient Cableace award for newscast Nat. Acad. Cable Programmers, 1993, 94, gen. reporting award for newscast AP, Denver, 1993. Mem. Soc. Profl. Journalists (award for gen. reporting and series Denver 1992, 1st pl. spot news reporting 1996, Tatshoff fellow 1996), Radio and TV News Dirs. Assn.

HOLZBOG, THOMAS JERALD, architect, planner; b. Milw., Oct. 25, 1933; s. Walter Charles and Dorothy (Van Holten) H.; divorced; children: Jessica Jane, Arabella Laura. BArch, Yale U., 1960; M Urban Design, Harvard U., 1968. Registered architect, N.Y., Mass., Calif., Wis. Nev. Field supr. Walter C. Holzbog, Wis.; draftsman Paul Rudolph, New Haven, 1958-59; rschr., draftsman Candilis, Josic & Woods, Paris, 1960; deisgner draftsman Sir Leslie Martin, Cambridge, Eng., 1960-61; project designer Sir Denys Lasdun & Ptnrs., London, 1961-64; job capt. I. M. Pei & Ptnrs., N.Y.C., 1965-67; pres. T. J. Holzbog Architect, L.A. and Boston, 1967—; speaker, educator in field; adj. prof., lectr. Harvard U., Columbia U., Pratt Inst., R.I. Sch. Design, Tufts U., Calif. Poly. State U., UCLA; vis. critic various univs. Work exhibited and pub. in profl. publs. Co-founder, mem. Westwood Design Rev. Bd., 1989-91; mem. bd. advisors UCLA Extension, 1987-88; past chmn. Design Adv. Com., Lexington, Mass.; past mem. Hist. Dist. Commn., Lexington; past bd. dirs. Interfaith Housing Corp., Lexington; past mem. edn. and urban design com. Boston Soc. Architects; past mem. Mayor's Task Force on Urban Design, N.Y.C. Capt. U.S. Army, 1954-56. Recipient numerous design awards; Fulbright scholar, 1960. Mem. AIA (past chmn., co-founder L.A. Found., past chmn., co-founder student affiliate com.), Am. Inst. Cert. Planners, Am. Soc. Landscape Architects, Nat. Coun. Archtl. Registration Bds., Archtl. Assns. London, Nat. Inst. Archtl. Edn., Scarab, Sigma Chi. Home and Office: 1301 Warnall Ave Los Angeles CA 90024-5355

HOLZER, THOMAS LEQUEAR, geologist; b. Lafayette, Ind., June 26, 1944; s. Oswald Alois and Ruth Alice (Lequear) H.; children: Holly Christine, Elizabeth Alice. BSE, Princeton U., 1965; MS, Stanford U., 1966, PhD, 1970. Asst. prof. geology U. Conn., Storrs, 1970-75; adj. environmentalist Griswold & Fuss, Manchester, Conn., 1973-75; research geol. U.S. Geol. Survey, Menlo Park, Calif., 1975-82, rsch. geologist, 1984-88, 93—; dep. asst. dir. rsch. U.S. Geol. Survey, Reston, Va., 1982-84, chief br. engring. seismology and geology, 1989-93; cons. assoc. prof. geology and environ. sci. Stanford U., 1994—. Contbr. numerous articles to profl. jours. Coach Am. Youth Soccer Orgn., Palo Alto, Calif., 1979-82. Recipient Superior Svc. award U.S Geol. Survey, 1981, Outstanding Pub. Svc. award U.S. Geol. Survey, 1991. Fellow Geol. Soc. Am. (chmn. engring. geology divsn. 1988-89, councilor 1995—, Disting. Svc. award hydrogeology divsn. 1995); mem. AAAS, Am. Geophys. Union, Assn. Groundwater Scientists and Engrs., Sigma Xi. Republican. Presbyterian. Home: PO Box 851 Palo Alto CA 94302-0851 Office: US Geol Survey 345 Middlefield Rd Menlo Park CA 94025-3561

HOM, GLORIA SUN, social science educator; b. San Francisco, Mar. 19, 1940; d. Patrick Pichi and May Lan (Chew) Sun; m. Peter D. Hom, Feb. 9, 1963; children: Patricia Sun Hom Hoo, Jennifer Lin, Leslie Frances. BA in Econs. and Polit. Sci., Dominican Coll., San Rafael, Calif., 1962; MA in Scons./Polit. Sci., San Jose State U., 1967; EdD in Orgn./Mgmt., U. San Francisco, 1990. Cert. cmty. coll. adminstr., counselor, tchr. econs., polit. sci., history, psychology. Instr. polit. sci. West Valley Coll., Saratoga, Calif., 1970-80; chmn., faculty dept. econs. Mission Coll., Santa Clara, Calif., 1981—, chmn. social sci. divsn., 1996—; faculty fgn. trade dept. Wuxi, China, 1987, Fu Dan U., Shanghai, 1987; faculty Asian studies U. Calif.-Santa Cruz, 1973-87; faculty econs. San Jose State U., 1980-90; cons. OSRR, U.S. Dept. Edn., 1991; gen. ptnr. Ideograph Assocs., Palo Alto; realtor, assoc. Hokono Bus. Investments, Inc.; rsch. asst. Stanford U., 1962; price economist Bur. Labor Stats., Dept. Labor, Washington, N.Y.C., 1963; tax auditor IRS, Dept. Treasury, San Francisco, 1964. Author/editor: History Chinese Argonauts, 1991. Bd. trustees Dominican Coll., San Rafael, 1987—, Castilleta Sch., Palo Alto, Calif., 1995—, Calif. State U., 1993-95, Calif. Maritime Acad.; mem. Calif. Bd. Edn., Sacramento, 1989-93; bd. dirs. Sallie Mae, Washington, 1991-94, YWCA; chmn. Rep. Party, Santa Clara County, 1992 94, chmn. edn. com., 1989-90; mem. Calif. Rep. Ctrl. Com.; pres. South Bay chpt. Calif. Chinese Am. Rep. Assn.; chmn. candidate devel. com. Santa Clara County Rep. Party, 1985-87; alt. Nat. Rep. Conv., New Orleans, 1988, Dallas, 1984, Detroit, 1980; attendee inauguration of George Bush, 1989, Ronald Reagan, 1980, 84; active numerous polit. campaigns; mem. White House Conf. on Librs., 1988-90; bd. dirs. Sr. Coord. Coun., 1990-95, Haigh Scaten Found., 1991—; adv. bd. San Jose Hist. Mus., 1990-94, Chinese Hist. and Cultural Project, 1990-94; mem. econ. devel. com. Calif. Commn. of the Califs., 1980-84; vol. Am. Cancer Soc.; bd. dirs. Campfire; mem. Com. on Status of Women in the Econs. Profession; active Girl Scouts U.S., Heart Fund, LWV, Peninsula Children's Ctr., San Jose Hist. Mus., United Way, World Affairs Coun., YMCA, others. Named to Outstanding Educators of Am., 1973; recipient Cert. of Appreciation, U.S. Dept. Edn., 1985, Cert. of Extraordinary Svc., Chinese Am. Citizens League, 1972, Seal of Appreciation, Bd. Edn., Sacramento, 1992. Mem. AAUP, AAUW, Western Assn. Schs. and Colls. (accrediting commn. for cmty. and jr. colls.), Palo Alto Rep. Women Federated (pres. 1981-82), Am. Acad. Polit. and Social Scis., Asian Am. Mfr. Assn., Asian Bus. League, Assn. of Cert. Employees West Valley Coll., Calif. Tchrs. Assn., Chinese Am. C. of C. (pres. 1997—), Chinese Hist. Soc., Faculty assn. of C.C., South Bay Polit. Sci. Assn., Stanford Alumni Assn., Western Social Sci. Assn., Women in Higher Edn., Art History Club of San Jose, Chinese Am. Women's Club, Kenna Club of U. Santa Clara, Lawyers Wives of Santa Clara County, Rotary of Palo Alto, Stanford Area Chinese Club, Stanford Club of Palo Alto, Palo Alto Women's Club. Republican. Roman Catholic. Home: 660 Towle Pl Palo Alto CA 94306-2535 Office: Mission College 3000 Mission College Blvd Santa Clara CA 95054-1804

HOM, RICHARD YEE, research engineer; b. Phoenix, July 26, 1950; s. Tommy Look and Betty (Mah) H.; m. Kathleen Chien; 1 child, Matthew Richard Chien; BS in Engring. Sci. and Aero. and Aerospace Tech., Ariz. State U., 1973. Asst. engr. Sperry Flight System, Phoenix, 1973; sr. engr., composite tool engring. Boeing Comml. Airplane Co., Seattle, 1973-84; specialist engr. 1984-88, sr. specialist engr. R & D, metall. processing and advanced projects Boeing Aerospace Co., 1984-90, also automation tech.; with customer svcs. and airline support Boeing Comml. Airplane Group, 1990-91; prin. rsch. engr. metallics rsch. and devel. Boeing Def. and Space Group, 1991—. Mem. AIAA, SMA, Air Force Assn., Soc. Mfg. Engrs., Aircraft Owners and Pilots Assn., ASM Internat. Home: 28704 15th Ave S Federal Way WA 98003-3161 Office: Boeing Def and Space Group M/S 8J-74 PO Box 3999 # 74 Seattle WA 98124-2499

HOMAN, RALPH WILLIAM, finance company executive; b. Wilkes-Barre, Pa., June 7, 1951; s. Norman Ryan and Adelaide Bernice (Sandy) H.; m. Donna Marie Webb, Jan. 25, 1975. BS in Acctg., Wheeling Coll., 1977; MBA in Mktg., Nat. U., 1986. Paymaster Dravo Corp., Pitts., 1974-75; tax preparer H&R Block, Wheeling, W.Va., 1977; fin. services exec. NCR Credit Corp., Sacramento, 1977-84; leasing exec. CSB Leasing, Sacramento, 1984-85; pres. Convergent Fin. Svcs., Colorado Springs, Colo., 1985—; bd. dirs. Concord Coalition, Colorado Springs. cons. Jr. Achievement, 1990—. Co-winner Name the Plane Contest Pacific Southwest Airlines, 1984. Mem. The 30/40 Something Social Club (founder, pres. Sedona chpt.), Am. Assn. Boomers (pres. Pikes Peak chpt. 1992-93), Toastmasters (treas. Oak Creek chpt. 1988-89), Kiwanis (sec. 1988-89, founder, chmn. adult soccer league),

Concord Coalition (bd. dirs., pres. Colorado Springs chpt.). Home and Office: Convergent Fin Svcs 5720 Escapardo Way Colorado Springs CO 80917-3340

HOMEK, PETER EDWARD, gas company executive; b. N.Y.C., Aug. 9, 1961; s. Peter and Helen Marie (Casey) H. BS, Poly. U., N.Y.C., 1983; MBA, U. So. Calif., 1995. Commd. 2d lt. USMC, 1983, advanced through grades to capt., 1988, resigned, 1990; fin. cons. Merrill Lynch, Pasadena, Calif., 1990-91; econ. analyst Dept. of State, Washington, 1991-93; mergers and acquisitions specialist Pacific Enterprises, L.A., 1994-96; mgr. S.Am. divsn., dir. ops. Pacific Enterprises, Buenos Aires, 1996—; bus. planner HPRL, L.A., 1993-94. Bd. dirs. Internat. Visitors Coun., 1996—. Office: Pacific Enterprises Internat 555 W 5th St Los Angeles CA 90013-1010

HONAKER, CHARLES RAY, health facility administrator; b. Charleston, W.Va., Jan. 13, 1947; s. Charles Frederick and Avis Linda (McCarthy) H.; m. Sarah Powers, Aug. 30, 1969; children: Charles Erik, Cara Powers, Katherine Powers, Erin Powers. BA, U. Del., 1977; M in Health Sci., Johns Hopkins U., 1981. Cert. nursing home adminstr., cert. healthcare exec.; diplomate Am. Coll. Healthcare Execs. Dir. residential treatment Gov. Bacon Health Ctr.-State of Del., Delaware City, 1975-80; sr. health planner State of W.Va., Charleston, 1980-83; assoc. hosp. adminstr. Pinecrest State Hosp., Beckley, W.Va., 1983-84; nursing home adminstr. Arthur B. Hodges Ctr., Charleston, W.Va., 1984-86, Carondelet Holy Family Ctr., Tucson, 1986-89; hosp. adminstr. Carondelet Holy Cross Hosp., Nogales, Ariz., 1989—; bd. mem., v.p. So. Ariz., Am. Cancer Soc., 1989-94; chair, bd. mem. Office of Rural Health, U. Ariz., Tucson, 1990—; chmn. bd. Ariz. Rural Health Assn., Phoenix. Bd. mem. Sahuarita (Ariz.) Unified Sch. Dist., 1987-91, C. of C., Nogales, 1995. Fellow Am. Acad. Med. Adminstrs., Am. Coll. Health Care Adminstrs.; mem. U.S.-Mex. Border Health Assn., Ariz.-Mex. Commn. (pub. health coms.). Republican. Roman Catholic. Home: 17211 S La Canada Dr Sahuarita AZ 85629 Office: Cardondelet Holy Cross Hosp 1171 W Target Range Rd Nogales AZ 85621-2415

HONAKER, JIMMIE JOE, lawyer, ecologist; b. Oklahoma City, Jan. 21, 1939; s. Joe Jack and Ruby Lee (Bowen) H.; children: Jay Jimmie, Kerri Ruth. BA, Colo. Coll., 1963; MA, U. No. Colo., 1991; JD, U. Wyo., 1966, MS, 1995; postgrad., Utah State U., 1995—. Bar: Colo. 1966, U.S. Dist. Ct. Colo. 1966, U.S. Ct. Appeals (10th cir.) 1982. Pvt. practice Longmont, Colo., 1966-91. Incorporator Longmont Boys Baseball, 1969; chmn. Longmont City Charter Commn., 1973; chmn. ch. bd. 1st Christian Ch., Longmont, 1975, 76; chmn. North Boulder County unit Am. Cancer Soc., 1978, 79. Recipient Disting. Svc. award Longmont Centennial Yr., 1971; named Outstanding Young Man, Longmont Jaycees, 1973. Mem. Colo. Bar Assn. (interprofl. com. 1972-91), Christian Legal Soc., Internat. Assn. Approved Basketball Ofcls. (cert.), Nat. Eagle Scout Assn., Ecol. Soc. Am., Colo. Mountain Club, Uintah Mtn. Club, Phi Alpha Delta. Address: USU Box 1320 Logan UT 84322-0199

HONDL, EDELTRAUD A., retired psychiatrist; b. Česky Trêbova, Czech Republic, Jan. 8, 1939; came to the U.S., 1961; d. Josef and Emma (Blaschke) H.; m. Arthur A. Murray, Nov. 19, 1972; six stepchildren. AA, Holy Ghost Coll., 1962; BS, DePaul U., 1965; MD magna cum laude, Marquette U., 1968. Diplomate Am. Bd. Psychiatry. Resident in gen. psychiatry and child psychiatry U. Wash. Hosps., Seattle, 1969-73; med. dir. Mental Health North, Seattle, 1973-83; pvt. practice adult and child psychiatry Harvard Psychiat. Group, Seattle, 1983-95; cons. Child Devel. Ctr. Program, Seattle, 1974-80; med. dir. Luther Child Ctr., Everett, Wash., 1990-93. Regional dir. AMA, Pacific N.W., 1979-90. Fellow Am. Psychiat. Assn. (treas. 1978-93), Wash. State Psychiat. Assn., Seattle Chpt. Psychiat. Assn., Am. Med. Women's Assn. (life), Wash. State Med. Assn. Democrat. Roman Catholic. Home: 19219 Richmond Beach Dr NW Shoreline WA 98177-2943

HONE, MICHAEL CURRAN, law educator, venture capitalist; b. San Francisco, June 21, 1937; s. Leo B. and Hazel J. (Curran) H.; children: Michael E., Lisa A. BS, U. Calif., Berkeley, 1960, JD, 1963. Dir. Dynamic Materials, Lafayette, Colo., 1984—; pres. HMS Capital, San Francisco, 1980-86; ptnr. HMS Capital, Menlo Park, Calif., 1987—; prof. U. San Francisco Law Sch., 1996—; dir. Stanford U. Book Store, 1995—, Multipoint Networks, Belmont, Calif., 1995—; vis. prof. Stanford Law Sch., 1996. With U.S. Army, 1956. Mem. Order of the Coif. Office: U San Francisco Kendrick Hall 2199 Fulton St San Francisco CA 94117-1004

HONEYCHURCH, DENIS ARTHUR, lawyer; b. Berkeley, Calif., Sept. 17, 1946; s. Winston and Mary Martha (Chandler) H.; m. Judith Ann Poliquin, Oct. 5, 1969; children: Sean, James, Thomas. BA, UCLA, 1968; JD, U. Calif., San Francisco, 1972. Bar: Calif. 1972, U.S. Dist. Ct. (no. dist.) Calif. 1972, U.S. Ct. Appeals (9th cir.) 1972. Dep. pub. defender Sacramento County Calif., Sacramento, 1973-75; supervising asst. pub. defender Solano County, Fairfield, Calif., 1975-78; ptnr. Honeychurch & Finkas and predecessor firm, Fairfield, 1978—. Bd. dirs. Fairfield-Suisun Unified Sch. Dist., Fairfield, 1979-83, Solano Coll., Fairfield, 1985—; chmn. bd. dirs. Downtown Improvement Dist., Fairfield, 1980-82; mem. Dem. Ctr. Com. Solano County, 1994—. Mem. ABA, Nat. Assn. Criminal Def. Lawyers, Calif. Trial Lawyers Assn., Calif. Attys. Criminal Justice, Calif. Pub. Defenders Assn., Solano County Bar Assn. (pres. 1991), Calif. Bd. Legal Specialization (cert.), Nat. Bd. Trial Advocacy (cert.). Democrat. Office: Honeychurch & Finkas 823 Jefferson St Fairfield CA 94533-5513

HONGO, FLORENCE MAKITA, educational association administrator; b. Cressey, Calif., Nov. 21, 1928; d. Haruzo and Shizu M.; m. Andrew Yoshiwara, Oct. 28, 1950 (div. May 1974); children: Janice Lee, Kim Ann, Jon Noel, Sue Ellen, J. Paul; m. Masanori Hongo, Dec. 25, 1981. BA in History, San Francisco State U., 1972. Gen. mgr. Asian Am. Curriculum Project, Inc., San Mateo, Calif., 1970—; instr. humanities & ethnic studies dept. Coll. San Mateo, 1978-92; adv. specialist title IV San Mateo City Elem. Sch. Dist., 1969-72; cons., lectr. and presenter in field. Contbr. chpts. to books and articles to profl. jours. Office: AACP Inc 234 Main St PO Box 1587 San Mateo CA 94401

HONNING, BENGT EUGENE, chiropractic physician, consultant, biochemist; b. Sundsvall, Sweden, Sept. 8, 1927; came to U.S., 1931; s. Walfrid Eugen and Julia Margareta (Vestine) H.; m. Mary Lou Neely, Feb. 7, 1948; children: Sharon Ann, Dale Eldred. BS, Calif. State U., 1964; MS, Wm. Darren U., 1965, PhD in Biochemistry, 1967; LLB, Blackstone Sch. Law, 1978; DC, L.A. Coll. Chiropractic, 1969. Diplomate Nat. Bd. Chiropractic Examiners; lic. clin. lab. scientist, Calif. Biochemist Am. Med. Labs., L.A., 1956-69; chiropractor, neurologist Long Beach, Calif., 1969—; biochemist Biochem. Consultants, Long Beach, 1967-88; prof. biochemistry L.A. Coll. Chiropractic, 1967-69. Author: Self Winding Clock Company, 1980; contbr. articles to profl. jours. Chief libr. Self Winding Clock Assn., Long Beach, 1979—. Served with USN, 1945-47. Mem. Am. Chem. Soc., CAMLT, Am. Astron. Soc., Nat. Assn. of Watch and Clock Collectors (cert. of merit 1993, chpt. 4 pres. 1980-84). Lutheran. Home: 1161 E Marcellus St Long Beach CA 90807-1609 Office: 1165 E San Antonio Dr Ste A Long Beach CA 90807-2374

HONOUR, LYNDA CHARMAINE, research scientist, educator, psychotherapist; b. Orange, N.J., Aug. 9, 1949; d. John Henry, Jr. and Evelyn Helena Roberta (Pietrowski) H. BA, Boston U., 1976; MA, Calif. State U., Fullerton, 1985, UCLA, 1989; PhD, U. So. Calif., 1997. Lic. marriage, family and children psychotherapist, Calif. Prof. psychology Pepperdine U., Malibu, Calif., 1989-95; pvt. practice psychotherapy, West Los Angeles, Calif., 1991—; clin. and vis. prof. throughout so. Calif., including Calif. Sch. Profl. Psychology, Calif. State U., L.A., 1989—; rsch. scientist in neuroendocrinology and neurochemistry in numerous labs.; condr. rsch. Neuropsychiat. Inst., Brain Rsch. Inst., Mental Retardation Rsch. Ctr., UCLA, Tulane U. Med. Sch., V.A. Med. Ctr., New Orleans, Salk Inst. Biol. Studies; rsch. cons. U. Calif. Med. Ctr., Irvine; cons. in rsch. or psychotherapy, 1976—. Contbr. articles to Hosp. Practice, Peptides, Physiology and Behavior, Pharmacology, Biochemistry and Behavior, also others. Rsch. grantee Organon Internat. Rsch. Group, The Netherlands, 1984-88. Mem. AAAS, AAUP, Am. Psychological Assn. (assoc.), Am. Psychological Soc., Calif. Assn. Marriage, Family and Child Psychotherapists, N.Y. Acad. Scis., Sons and Daus. of Pearl Harbor Survivors, Psi Chi, Sigma Delta Epsilon. Roman Catholic.

HOOD, EDWARD, data processing executive; b. L.A., Nov. 5, 1954; s. Thomas Leslie and Mary (Jewell) H.; m. Carmenita Feu. AA in Adminstrn. of Justice, L.A. City Coll., 1977; BA in Phys. Edn., Calif. State U., L.A., 1980. Ordained to ministry, Bapt. Ch., 1983. Dir. pub. rels. and fin. Greater Revelation Bapt. Ch., L.A., 1979-83, assoc. minister, 1981-92; assoc. minister Gospel Truth Ch., L.A., 1981-84; owner Compusys, L.A., 1989—; chmn. and pres. Video Documentary, L.A., 1988—; asst. prin. and tchr. Grace Luth. Christian Elem. Sch., L.A., 1990-91; pastor Bright and Morning Star Cmty. Christian Ch., San Bernardino, 1992—; athletic and audio-visual equip. person Nat. Youth Sports Program, summers 1983-90; athletic equip. attendant II, Calif. State U., L.A., 1981-90, part-time lectr., 1989-90; substitute instructional aide San Bernardino County, Calif., 1992—. Author: The Philosophy "Paradoxism:; creator "Black Jesus or Compassion collection"; inventor Airskate. Pres. Menlo Ave. Block Club Neighborhood Watch, L.A., 1984-87; asst. coach "B" football, instr. K-coll., Manual Arts High Sch., 1979. With USMC, 1972-74. Mem. NAACP. Democrat. Home: 16324 Merrill Ave D103 Fontana CA 92335-2935

HOOD, PAUL, reservoir engineer; b. Barton-on-Sea, Hants., Eng., Mar. 18, 1948; came to U.S., 1987; s. Robert James and Olga Margaret (Lark) H.; m. Gillian Patricia Eisele, Nov. 30, 1974 (div. May 1979); 1 child, Miriam Eleanor Eisele; m. Linda Dee Stafford, Oct. 27, 1989 (div. Oct. 1991); children: Sonya Ray, Tasha Marie; m. Mary Jane Saxton, June 28, 1992. BSc in Math. Physics, Birmingham (Eng.) U., 1969; MSc in Civil Engring., Swansea (Wales) U., 1972, PhD in Civil Engring., 1974. Rsch. asst. U. Wales, Swansea, 1972-74; rsch. fellow U. Reading, U.K., 1974-75; rsch. programmer Seismograph Svc. Ltd., Keston, Kent, U.K., 1975-77; rsch. geophysicist British Petroleum, London, 1978-80; staff reservoir engr. British Petroleum, various locations, 1980-89; prin. cons. British Petroleum, Houston, 1990-92; mgr. reservoir engring. Sci. Software Intercomp, Denver, 1992-95; ind. reservoir engring. cons., 1995—; CEO, pres. IPCA, SSI. Contbr. articles to profl. jours., chpts. to books. G.B. rep. NATO CIOR Competition, Oslo, 1973, Athens, Greece, 1974. Capt. Brit. Army Res., 1968-83. Mem. Soc. Petroleum Engrs., Soc. Exploration Geophysicists, European Assn. Exploration Geophysicists (Van Weelden award 1978).

HOOFARD, JANE MAHAN DECKER, elementary education educator; b. Grand Junction, Colo., Apr. 29, 1946; d. Nat Don and Bernita Margaret (Williams) Mahan; m. William Edward Hoofard, Mar. 6, 1982; children: Lynna Kay Decker, Keith Dale. BA, Ft. Lewis Coll., 1968. Cert. tchr., Calif. Tchr. 3rd, 6th grades Shasta Lake Union Sch. Dist., Summit City, Calif., 1968-73; tchr., MGM cons., coord., brain drain writer Shasta County Schs., Redding, Calif., 1975-81; tchr. 2nd, 3rd grades Manton (Calif.) Joint Union Sch. Dist., 1987-89; elem. and mid. sch. tchr. Mineral (Calif.) Elem. Sch. Dist., 1989—. Writer, editor, pub. AAUW. Mem. Calif. Tchrs. Assn., Shasta Lake Tchrs. Assn. (past pres.). Home: PO Box 104 Mineral CA 96063-0104 Office: Mineral School PO Box 130 Mineral CA 96063-0130

HOOK, RALPH CLIFFORD, JR., business educator; b. Kansas City, Mo., May 2, 1923; s. Ralph Clifford and Ruby (Swanson) H.; m. Joyce Fink, Jan. 20, 1946; children—Ralph Clifford III, John Gregory. BA, U. Mo., 1947, MA, 1948; PhD, U. Tex., 1954. Instr. U. Mo., 1947-48; asst. prof. Tex. A&M U., 1948-51; lectr. U. Tex., 1951-52; co-owner, mgr. Hook Buick Co., also Hook Truck & Tractor Co., Lee's Summit, Mo., 1952-58; assoc. prof. U. Kansas City, 1953-58; dir. Bur. Bus. Research and Services, Ariz. State U., 1958-66, prof. mktg., 1960-68; dean Coll. Bus. Adminstrn., U. Hawaii, 1968-74; prof. mktg. U. Hawaii, 1974-96, prof. mktg. emeritus, 1996—; vis. Disting. prof. N.E. La. U., 1979; dir. Hook Bros. Corp., Family Bus. Ctr. Hawaii, Pan Pacific Inst. Ocean Scis., Mauna Loa Macademia Ptnrs., ltd. partnerships; mem. Nat. Def. Exec. Res., Dept. Commerce. Author: (with others) The Management Primer, 1972, Life Style Marketing, 1979, Marketing Service, 1983; contbr. (with others) monograph series Western Bus. Roundup; founder, moderator monograph series Western Bus. Roundup radio series, 1958-68. Bd. dirs. Jr. Achievement Hawaii; trustee Tokai U. Honolulu Ctr., 1987—. Served to 1st lt. F.A. AUS, 1943-46; col. Res. Recipient alumni citation of merit U. Mo. Coll. Bus. and Pub. Adminstrn., 1969; Distinguished Service award Nat. Def. Transp. Assn., 1977, God and Service award United Meth. Ch./Boy Scouts Am., 1986; named to Faculty Hall Fame Ariz. State U. Coll. Bus. Assn., 1977, Hawaii Transp. Hall of Fame, 1986. Fellow Internat. Coun. for Sml. Bus. (pres. 1963); mem. Hawaii World Trade Assn. (pres. 1973-74), Am. Mktg. Assn. (v.p. 1965-67, pres. Cen. Ariz. chpt. 1960-61, pres. Honolulu chpt. 1991-92, Wayne A. Lemberg award for disting. svc. 1995), Western Assn. Collegiate Schs. Bus. (pres. 1972-73), Sales and Mktg. Execs. Internat. (life), Nat. Def. Transp. Assn. (Hawaii v.p. 1978-82), Newcomen Soc. N.Am. (Hawaii chmn.), Pi Sigma Epsilon (v.p. for edn. programs 1990-94), Mu Kappa Tau (sec. - treas. 1991-94, v.p. 1994-96, pres. 1996—), Beta Gamma Sigma, Omicron Delta Kappa, Beta Theta Pi, Delta Sigma Pi (gold coun.). United Methodist. Home: 311 Ohua Ave Apt 1104D Honolulu HI 96815-3658 Office: U Hawaii Coll Bus Adminstrn 2404 Maile Way Bldg C Honolulu HI 96822-2223

HOOK, VIVIAN YUAN-WEN HO, biochemist, neuroscientist; b. Oakland, Calif., Mar. 21, 1953; d. Timothy T. and Cheng-Ping (Wang) Ho; m. Gregory R. Hook, July 9, 1976; children: Lisa, Michelle. AB, U. Calif., Berkeley, 1974; PhD, U. Calif., San Francisco, 1980. From postdoctoral fellow to sr. scientist NIMH, NIH, Bethesda, Md., 1980-85; asst. prof. Uniformed Svcs. U., Bethesda, 1986-90, assoc. prof., 1991-94; assoc. prof. U. Calif., San Diego, 1994-95, prof., 1996—; biochemistry and neuroscience study sect. Nat. Inst. Drug Abuse, Bethesda, 1989-92. Contbr. articles to profl. jours. NIH grantee, 1987—; Wellcome Sr. Scientist fellow NIH, 1983-86, Pharmacology Rsch. Assoc. fellow, 1980-82; recipient Ind. Scientist award NIH, 1994—. Mem. Soc. for Neurosci., Am. Soc. Biochemistry and Molecular Biology, Endocrinology Soc.

HOOKE, MICHAEL PETER, secondary education educator; b. San Francisco, Nov. 6, 1965; s. Dennis Michael and Jacklyn Ellen Hooke. BA, Gonzaga U., 1987; Master Catechist, Diocese of Oakland, 1990; MA in Systematic Theology, Dominican Sch. Philosophy and Theology, Berkeley, Calif., 1991. Educator St. Joseph Notre Dame H.S., Alameda, Calif., 1988—, religion dept. chair, 1996—; guest lectr. Roman Cath. Diocese of Oakland, 1988—. Mem. DAV, KC, ASCD, Nat. Cath. Ednl. Assn., Nat. Assn. of Social Studies Tchrs., Nat. Thespian Soc. Democrat. Roman Catholic. Office: St Joseph Notre Dame HS 1011 Chestnut St Alameda CA 94501-4315

HOOKER, JO, interior designer; b. Evanston, Ill., Dec. 13, 1932; d. Armand Francis and Josephine Margaret (Daus) Conto; m. Donald E. Hooker, Feb. 11, 1956 (div. 1975); children: Elizabeth Ann Hooker Gilbertson, Kathryn Maura Hooker. BFA, U. Ill., 1955; postgrad., Ariz. State U., 1972-76. Cert. Nat. Coun. for Interior Design Qualification, 1980; ASID. Interior designer Barrows Design Studio, Phoenix, 1976-94; interior designer, owner Jo Hooker Interior Design, Scottsdale, Ariz., 1994—. Designer showcases for Phoenix Home and Garden, 1986, 87, 91. Mem. Am. Soc. Interior Designers (cert. profl., bd. dirs. Ariz. North chpt. 1996—, ethics chair 1994-97, hist. com. 1996, Design Excellence award Ariz. North chpt. 1985), Soc. Illustrators. Office: Jo Hooker Interior Design 6615 N Scottsdale Rd Scottsdale AZ 85250-4421

HOOLEY, DARLENE, congresswoman, county commissioner; b. Williston, N.D., Apr. 4, 1939; d. Clarence Alvin and Alyce (Rogers) Olsen; m. John Hooley; children: Chad, Erin. BS in Edn., Oreg. State U., 1961, postgrad., 1963-65; postgrad., Portland State U., 1966-67. Tchr. Woodburn (Oreg.) & Gervais Sch., 1962-65, David Douglas Sch. Dist., Portland, Oreg., 1965-67, St. Mary's Acad., Portland, 1967-69; mem. West Linn (Oreg.) City Coun., 1976-80; state rep. Oreg. State Ho. of Reps., 1980-87; county commr. Clakamas County (Oreg.) Bd., 1987-96; mem. 105th U.S. Congress from 5th dist. Oreg., 1996—. Vice-chair Oreg. Tourism Alliance, Portland, 1991—. bd. dirs. Pub. Employees Ret. Bd., Portland, 1989—, Cmty. Corrections Bd., Oregon City, 1990—, Providence Med. Ctr., Portland, 1989—; acting chair Oreg. Trail Found. Bd., Oregon City, 1991—; mem. Urban Growth Policy Adv. Com., Portland, 1991—. Named Legislator of the Year Oreg. Libr. Assn., 1985-86, Oreg. Solar Energy Assn., 1985; recipient Spl. Svc. award Clackamas City Coun. for Child Abuse Prevention, 1989. Mem. LWV, Oreg. Women's Polit. Caucus (Women of the Yr. 1988). Democrat. Office: 1517 Longworth Washington DC 20515-3705

HOOPER, CATHERINE EVELYN, senior development engineer; b. Bklyn., Nov. 10, 1939; d. Frederick Charles Jr. and Catherine Veronica (Heaney) Podeyn; m. Melvyn Robert Lowney, Nov. 30, 1957 (div. 1970); children: Denise Lowney Andrade, Michele Lowney Budris; m. William White Hooper, Sept. 21, 1974. Student, San Jose (Calif.) City Coll., 1969, De Anza Coll., 1980. Insp. Amelco Semiconductor, Mountain View, Calif., 1966-68; lab. technician Fairchild R & D, Palo Alto, Calif., 1968-73; sr. lab. technician Varian Cen. Rsch., Palo Alto, 1973-84; sr. devel. engr. Hughes Rsch. Labs., Malibu, 1984—. Contbr. articles to profl. jours. Pres. Conejo Valley chpt. Nat. Women's Polit. Caucus., 1994—. Mem. Am. Vacuum Soc., Materials Rsch. Soc., Grad. Women in Sci. (L.A. pres. 1990-92), Internat. Soc. Optical Engrs., Sigma Xi (sec. 1987-90, 94). Office: Hughes Rsch Labs 3011 Malibu Canyon Rd Malibu CA 90265-4737

HOOPER, EDWIN BICKFORD, physicist; b. Bremerton, Wash., June 18, 1937; s. E.B. and Elizabeth (Patrick) H.; m. Virginia Hooper, Dec. 28, 1963; children: Edwin, Sarah, William. SB, MIT, 1959, PhD, 1965. Asst. prof. applied sci. Yale U., New Haven, 1966-70; physicist, asst. dep. assoc. dir. Lawrence Livermore (Calif.) Nat. Lab., 1970—. Contbr. articles to profl. jours. Pres. Danville (Calif.) Assn., 1982-84; pres. Friends Iron Horse Trail, 1984-86; v.p. San Ramon Valley Edn. Found., 1989-90; dir. Leadership, San Ramon Valley, 1990-92. Fellow Am. Phys. Soc. (bd. dirs. div. Plasma Physics 1990-91); mem. AIAA, Am. Assn. for Advancement Sci. Office: Lawrence Livermore Nat Lab L 637 Livermore CA 94550

HOOPER, ROGER FELLOWES, architect, retired; b. Southampton, N.Y., Aug. 18, 1917; s. Roger Fellowes and Justine Van Rensselaer (Barber) H.; m. Patricia Bentley, Aug. 10, 1946; children: Judith Bayard Teresi, Rachel Bentley Zingg, Roger Fellowes III. AB, Harvard U., 1939, MArch, 1948. Ptnr. Malone & Hooper, San Francisco, 1949-60; ptnr., pres. Hooper Olmsted & Emmons, San Francisco, 1964-79; chmn. Hooper Olmsted & Hrovat, San Francisco, 1980-94, retired, 1994. Bd. mgr. Marin YMCA, San Rafael, Calif.; bd. dirs., pres. Marin Conservation League, San Rafael. Lt. comdr. USNR, 1941-45, WWII. Mem. AIA.

HOOPES, SIDNEY LOU, marketing consultant, educational association administrator; b. Monterey, Calif., Oct. 24, 1944; d. Jack Sidney Wayne Combs and Alta Virginia (Lane) Combs-Snow; m. Dan Fredrick Hoopes, Oct. 11, 1969; children: Rachel Virginia, Sarah Elizabeth. BSBA in Mktg., U. Ark., 1964. Market rschr. Procter & Gamble, Cin., 1964-65; asst. press sec. U.S. Senator J. W. Fulbright, Washington, 1966-68; adminstr. regional office Tex. Chapparal Basketball Team, Lubbock, 1970-71; office adminstr., sec. Tex. Tech. U., Lubbock, 1971-72; office adminstr. Hoopes Law Office, Idaho Falls, Idaho, 1973-82; cons. mktg. and advt. Idaho Falls, 1983—; field rep. to Richard H. Stallings U.S. Congressman; exec. dir. Edn. Found., Idaho Falls, 1994-95; dir. mktg., co-exec. dir. Idaho Falls Opera Thatre, 1995—. Environ. educator Sch. Dist. #91, Idaho Falls, 1982-86; treas. Bonneville County Dem. Party, 1975-76, sec., 1988—; chief fund raiser Yellowstone Nat. Park Inst., 1983-84; bd. dirs. Idaho Falls Opera Theatre, 1984—; dist. field. mgr. U.S. Ho. of Reps. in 2d Congl. Dist. of Idaho. Named One of Outstanding Young Women Dems. in Idaho, 1975; proclaimed Sidney Hoopes Appreciation Day, Idaho Falls Opera Theatre, 1989. Mem. Greater Yellowstone Coalition (charter). Episcopalian. Home: 1950 Alan St Idaho Falls ID 83404-5722

HOOPS, WILLIAM JAMES, clergyman; b. Welch, Okla., June 10, 1957; s. Paul Raymond and Bertha Lue (Stillwell) H.; m. Susan Denise Towers, May 12, 1983; 1 child, Robert Paul. BA, Okla. Bapt. U., 1983; MDiv, Golden Gate Sem., 1987. Ordained to ministry So. Bapt. Ch., 1987. Ministerial intern 1st Bapt. Ch., Concord, Calif., 1984-87; pastor 1st Bapt. Ch., Marina, Calif., 1987-91; chaplain USAFR, Travis AFB, Calif., 1975—; instl. min. Fed. Bur. Prisons, Fed. Correctional Instn., Lompoc, Calif., 1991—, Intensive Confinement Ctr., Lompoc, 1996—. Producer TV documentary Insights, 1986-87. Bible tchr. 1st So. Bapt. Ch., Lompoc, 1991—. Capt. USAFR, 1975—. Mem. Air Force Assn., Res. Officers Assn., Calif. So. Bapt. Conv. (revival steering com. 1988-90), Ctrl. Coast Bapt. Assn. (vice moderator 1987-88, dir. evangelism 1988-91), Pacific Coast Bapt. Assn., Lompoc Fed. Correctional Instn. Employees Club (sec. 1991-92), Ctrl. Coast Ministrial Alliance (pres. 1988-89), Calif. Campers on Mission (pres. 1995—).

HOOVER, KENNETH R., political science educator, writer; s. Lee Armstrong and Margaret Anne Hoover; m. Judith Ann Maybee; children: Andrew, Erin. BS, Beloit (Wis.) Coll., 1962; MS, U. Wis., 1965, PhD, 1970. Asst. prof. U. Wis., Whitewater, 1964-70; assoc. prof. Coll. of Wooster, Ohio, 1970-78, U. Wis.-Parkside, Kenosha, 1978-88; prof. Western Wash. U., Bellingham, 1988—; chair dept. polit. sci. Western Wash. U., 1988-95, pres. faculty senate, 1995-96. Co-author: Cons. Capitalism, 1989, Ideology and Political Life, 2d edit., 1994, Elements of Social Science, 6th edit., 1995. Recipient Best Article award Utopian Studies Jour., 1994; hon. fellow U. Southampton Internat. Ctr., 1987-88. Office: Dept Polit Sci Western Wash U Arntzen Hall 415 MS 9082 Bellingham WA 98225

HOOVER, ROBERT ALLAN, university president; b. Des Moines, May 9, 1941; s. Claude Edward and Anna Doris H.; m. Jeanne Mary Hoover, Feb. 22, 1968; children: Jennifer Jill Jacobs, Suzanne Elizabeth. BS, Ariz. State U., 1967, MA, 1969; PhD, U. Calif., Santa Barbara, 1973. Instr. polit. sci. Utah State U., Logan, 1971-73, asst. prof. polit. sci., 1973-79, assoc. prof. polit. sci., chair polit. sci. dept., 1979-84, prof. polit. sci., 1984-91, dean Coll. Humanities, Arts and Social Scis., 1984-91; v.p. for acad. affairs U. Nev., Reno, 1991-96; pres. U. Idaho, Moscow, 1996—. Author: The Politics of MX: A New Direction in Weapons Procurement?, 1982, The MX Controversy: A Guide to Issues and References, 1982, Arms Control: The Interwar Naval Limitation Agreements, 1980. Bd. dirs. United Way, Reno, 1994-96, Channel 5, Reno, 1991-95, St. Scholastica Acad., Canon City, Colo., 1991-96. Office: Univ Idaho President's Office Adminstrn Bldg Rm 105 Moscow ID 83844-3151

HOOVER, ROBERT CLEARY, retired bank executive; b. Highland Park, Ill., July 26, 1928; s. Howard Earl and Dorothy (Higgs) H.; m. Beatrice Leona Burroughs, June 21, 1949 (div.); children: Catherine, Robert C. II, Holly; m. Nancy Ellen Pitman, July 25, 1959 (div.); children: John, Elizabeth, Courtney; m. Cecilia Susan Flournoy, July 3, 1981; 1 child, Whitney Suzanne. BA, U. Calif., Berkeley, 1950. Asst. advt. mgr. Hoover Co., North Canton, Ohio, 1951-54; v.p., asst. gen. mgr. Golden State Linen Svc., Oakland, Calif., 1954-61; asst. mgr. Wells Fargo Bank, San Francisco, 1961-66; v.p. Bank Calif. Assn., San Francisco, 1966-84, v.p., spl. asst. to chmn. bd. and chief exec. officer, 1984-94; ret. Bd. mem. Providence Hosp., Oakland, 1985-91, Bay Area Tumor Inst., 1975—. Mem. Am. Inst. Banking, Naval War Coll. Found. (life), Navy League United States (life), Naval Order U.S. (life), Bohemian Club, Claremont Country Club, Pacific Union Club. Republican. Episcopalian. Home: 46 Sotelo Ave Piedmont CA 94611-3535

HOOVER, WILLIAM R(AY), computer service company executive; b. Bingham, Utah, Jan. 2, 1930; s. Edwin Daniel and Myrtle Tennessee (McConnell) H.; m. Sara Elaine Anderson, Oct. 4; children—Scott, Robert, Michael, James, Charles. B.S., M.S., U. Utah. Sect. chief Jet Propulsion Lab., Pasadena, Calif., 1954-64; v.p. Computer Scis. Corp., El Segundo, Calif., 1964-69, pres., 1969-94, chmn. bd., 1972—, also CEO. *

HOPE, GERRI DANETTE, telecommunications management executive; b. Sacramento, Feb. 28, 1956; d. Albert Gerald and Beulah Rae (Bane) Hope. AS, Sierra Coll., Calif., 1977; postgrad. Okla. State U., 1977-79. Instructional asst. San Juan Sch. Dist., Carmichael, Calif., 1979-82; telecomm. supr. Delta Dental Svc. of Calif., San Francisco, 1982-85; telecomm. coordinator Farmers Savs. Bank, Davis, Calif., 1985-87; telecomm. officer Sacramento Savs. Bank, 1987-95; owner GDH Enterprises, 1993—; telecomm. analyst II dept. ins. State Calif., 1995—; sr. telecomm. engr. Access Health Inc., Rancho Cordova, Calif., 1996—; sr. telecomms. engr. Access Health, Inc., 1996—; founder Custom Label Designer, Sacramento; mem. telecomm. adv. panel Golden Gate U., Sacramento; lectr. in field. Mem. NAFE, Telecomm.

Assn. (v.p. membership com. Sacramento Valley chpt., 1993, v.p. dir. programs 1997), Am. Philatelic Soc., Sacramento Philatelic Assn., Errors, Freaks and Oddities Club, Philatelic Collectors. Republican. Avocations: writing, computers, philately, animal behavior, participating in Christian ministry. Home: 3025 U St Antelope CA 95843-2513 Office: Access Health Inc 11020 White Rock Rd Rancho Cordova CA 95670

HOPKIN, JOHN BARTON, publisher, editor; b. Evanston, Ill., Mar. 23, 1952; s. Arthur McMurrin and Jean (Delaney) H.; m. Janet Dawn Gillies, Apr. 30, 1987; 1 child, Shane. BA magna cum laude, Harvard U., 1974; BA in Music Edn., San Francisco State U., 1981. Tchr. Holy Trinity Secondary Sch., Kingston, Jamaica, 1974-76; tchr., performing musician pvt. practice, Point Reyes Station, Calif., 1976-78; instr. Jamaica Sch. Music, Kingston, 1978-79; tchr. Millbrook (N.Y.) Sch., 1981-83; publisher, editor Experimental Music Instruments, Nicasio, Calif., 1984—. Author: Making Simple Musical Instruments, 1995, Musical Instrument Design, 1996, Gravikords, Pyrophones and Whirlies, 1996. Home and Office: Experimental Musical Instruments PO Box 784 Nicasio CA 94946

HOPKINS, CECILIA ANN, business educator; b. Havre, Mont., Feb. 17, 1922; d. Kost L. and Mary (Manaras) Sofos; B.S., Mont. State Coll., 1944; M.A., San Francisco State Coll., 1958, M.A., 1967; postgrad. Stanford U.; Ph.D., Calif. Western U., 1977; m. Henry E. Hopkins, Sept. 7, 1944. Bus. tchr. Havre (Mont.) High Sch., Mateo, Calif., 1942-44; sec. George P. Gorham, Realtor, San Mateo, 1944-45; escrow sec. Fox & Cars 1945-50; escrow officer Calif. Pacific Title Ins. Co., 1950-57; bus. tchr. Westmoor High Sch., Daly City, Calif., 1958-59; bus. tchr. Coll. of San Mateo, 1959-63, chmn. real estate-ins. dept., 1963-76, dir. div. bus., 1976-86, coord. real estate dept., 1986-91; cons. to commr. Calif. Div. Real Estate, 1963-91, mem. periodic rev. exam. com.; chmn. C.C. Adv. Com., 1971-72, mem. com., 1975-91; projector direction Calif. State Chancellor's Career Awareness Consortium, mem. endowment fund adv. com., c.c. real estate edn. com., state c.c. adv. com.; mem. No. Calif. adv. bd. to Glendale Fed. Savs. and Loan Assn.; mem. bd. advisors San Mateo County Bd. Suprs., 1981-82; mem. real estate edn. and rsch. com. to Calif. Commr. Real Estate, 1983-90; mem. edn., membership, and profl. exchange coms. Am. chpt. Internat. Real Estate Fedn., 1985-92. Recipient Citizen of Day award KABL, Outstanding Contbns. award Redwood City-San Carlos-Belmont Bd. Realtors, Nat. Real Estate Educators Assn. award emeritus, 1993; named Woman of Achievement, San Mateo-Burlingame br. Soroptimist Internat., 1979. Mem. AAUW, Calif. Assn. Real Estate Tchrs. (state pres. 1964-65, life hon. dir. 1962—, Outstanding Real Estate Educator of Yr. 1978-79), Real Estate Cert. Inst. (Disting. Merit award 1982), Calif. Bus. Edn. Assn. (certificate of commendation 1979), San Francisco State Coll., Guidance and Counseling Alumni, Calif. Real Estate Educators' Assn. (dir. emeritus, hon. dir. 1990), Real Estate Nat. Educators Assn. (award emeritus for outstanding contributions, 1993), San Mateo-Burlingame Bd. Realtors (award emeritus Outstanding Contbrs. to Membership), Alpha Delta, Pi Lambda Theta, Delta Pi Epsilon (nat. dir. interchpt. rels. 1962-65, nat. historian 1966-67, nat. sec. 1968-69), Alpha Gamma Delta. Co-author: California Real Estate Principles; contbr. articles to profl. jours. Home: 504 Colgate Way San Mateo CA 94402-3206

HOPKINS, DAVID MOODY, geologist; b. Nashua, N.H., Dec. 26, 1921; s. Donald Wheeler and Henrietta (Moody) H.; m. Joan Prewitt, Dec. 27, 1949 (dec. Sept. 1955); children: Dana, Chindi Ann; m. Martha Bryant, Sept. 25, 1957 (div. June 1970); 1 child, Alexander Carrier Hopkins; m. Rachel Chouinard Stanley, Aug. 23, 1970. BS, U. N.H., 1942; MS, Harvard U., 1948, PhD, 1955. From geologist to sr. rsch. geologist U.S. Geol. Survey, Washington, 1942-55, Menlo Park, Calif., 1955-84; disting. prof. U. Alaska, Fairbanks, 1985-94; ret., 1994; cons. U.S. Nat. Park Svc., Anchorage, 1986—, Alaska Divsn. Geol. and Geophys. Surveys, 1995. Editor, contbr. The Bering Land Bridge, 1967; co-editor, contbr. Paleoecology of Beringia, 1982; contbr. articles to profl. jours. With USAF, 1945-47. Recipient Franklin Burr award Nat. Geographic Soc., 1993. Felow Geol. Soc. Am. (chmn. Geomorphology and Quaternary Geology divsn. 1969-70, Archaeol. Geology divsn. 1984-85, Kirk Bryan award 1968, Career award in Geoarcheology 1990, Career award in Quaternary Geology and Geomorphology 1995), Arctic Inst. N.Am. (editl. bd. 1979—), Calif. Acad. Sci.; mem. Am. Quaternary Assn. (pres. 1974), Soc. Am. Archaeology (Fryxell award 1988). Democrat. Home: 40 Steelhead Rd Fairbanks AK 99709-3201 Office: U Alaska Dept Geology and Geography Fairbanks AK 99709-5780

HOPKINS, GLENN ERNEST, artist, educator; b. Washington, May 19, 1949; s. Wilford Clyde and Dorothy Mary (Ruffner) H.; m. Phyllis Goodwin, Oct. 7, 1972 (div. 1980); 1 child, Gary Buckminster; m. Christina Jeon, 1995; 1 child, Choice Jhun. BS, Western Md. Coll., 1971; MFA, UCLA, 1979. Cert. tchr., Calif. Dir. acting program Buck's Rock Camp, New Milford, Conn., 1969-73; prodr., dir. Mootney Theatre Co., Venice, Calif., 1975—; advisor Calif. State Adult Curriculum, 1977—; instr. divsn. career and continuing edn. L.A. Unified Sch. Dist., 1977—; guest lectr. numerous orgns. Bd. dirs. Nomenus, Inc.; active Santa Monica Meth. Ch., Com. to Monitor Poppers; convener Westside Greens, Indian Springs Com. Mem. Dramatists Guild Am., Va. Ctr. Creative Arts, UTLA (chpt. chairperson 1991—), Ragdale Inst. Home and Office: Venice Mootney Theatre 1532 Berkeley Ave #3 Santa Monica CA 90404

HOPKINS, HENRY TYLER, museum director, art educator; b. Idaho Falls, Idaho, Aug. 14, 1928; s. Talcott Thompson and Zoe (Erbe) H.; children—Victoria Anne, John Thomas, Christopher Tyler. BA, Sch. of Art Inst., Chgo., 1952, MA, 1955; postgrad., UCLA, 1957-60; PhD (hon.), Calif. Coll. Arts and Crafts, 1984, San Francisco Art Inst., 1986. Curator exhbns., publs. Los Angeles County Mus. of Art, 1960-68; dir. Fort Worth Art Mus., 1968-74, San Francisco Mus. of Modern Art, 1974-86; chmn. art dept. UCLA, 1991-94, dir. F.S. Wight Gallery, 1991-95, dir. Armand Hammer Mus. Art and Cultural Ctr., 1994—; lectr. art history UCLA Ext.; instr. Tex. Christian U., Ft. Worth, 1968-74; dir. U.S. representation Venice (Italy) Biennial, 1970; dir. art presentation Festival of Two Worlds, Spoleto, Italy, 1970; co-commr. U.S. representation XVI Sao Paulo (Brazil) Biennale, 1981; cons. NEA, mem. mus. panel, 1979-84, chmn., 1981; cons., mem. mus. panel NEH, 1976. Contbr. numerous articles to profl. jours., also numerous mus. publs. Served with AUS, 1952-54. Decorated knight Order Leopold II, Belgium); recipient special internat. award, Art L.A., 1992. Mem. Assn. Art Mus. Dirs. (pres. 1985-86), Coll. Art Assn., Am. Assn. Museums, Western Assn. Art Museums (pres. 1977-78). Home: 939 1/2 Hilgard Ave Los Angeles CA 90024-3032 Office: UCLA/Armand Hammer Mus Art 10899 Wilshire Blvd Los Angeles CA 90024-4314

HOPKINS, JAMES CLARENCE, insurance company executive; b. Dallas, Sept. 26, 1930; s. Clarence C. and Vinnie Lee (Feemster) H.; m. Mary C. Pittman, Dec. 27, 1952; children: Nola C., Lauren L., Linda M., J. David. BS, North Tex. U., 1953; cert. CLU, U. Pa., 1966; cert. in chartered fin. cons., Am. Coll., 1983. CLU. Agy. mgr. Travelers Ins. Co., Houston, 1956-64; agy. dir. Ranger Nat. (Anderson Clayton Co.), Houston, 1964-66; regional dir. Phila. Life Ins. Co. (Tenneco), Denver, 1966-86; pres. Ins. Designers, Inc., Denver, 1987—; pres., exec. dir. Ins. Designers Am., Inc. Editor: U.S. Army Training Battalions, 1954; contbr. articles to profl. jours. Ann. conf. del. Meth. Ch., Odessa, Tex., 1973-74, Parker, Colo., 1978-79, 80, bd. chmn., 1980. 1st lt. M.S.C., U.S. Army, 1953-56. Mem. Colo. Assn. Life Underwriters, Colo. Assn. Chartered Life Underwriters, Denver Assn. Life Underwriters, Masons. Home: 6895 S Norfolk St Foxfield CO 80016-1451 Office: Ins Designers of Am Inc 4155 E Jewell Ave Ste 1007 Denver CO 80222-4514

HOPKINS, LEE WALLACE, writer; b. L.A., June 30, 1934; s. Leon Wallace and Eva (Bong) H.; m. Barbara Franklin, Aug. 15, 1958 (div. 1963); m. Carol Porter, Sept. 15, 1970 (div. 1984); children: Alison Christina, Carolyn Alexandra. BA with honors, UCLA, 1957. Dir. pub. rels. and advt. Calif. Blue Shield, San Francisco, 1959-67; account exec. Doremus & Co., San Francisco, 1967-70; pres. Lee Hopkins Pub. Rels., San Francisco, 1970-90, Task Force 2000 Communications, San Francisco, 1990—; press sec. to King Kigeli V of Rwanda. Contbr. book revs. to profl. jours. and newspapers; author: After They Learn to Dance, 1974, The Origin of Design, 1986, The Dream of Regulus, 1988, The Feast of Tantalus, 1991. Sgt. U.S. Army, 1957-59. Mem. Marines' Meml. Club, Soc. King Charles the Martyr. Democrat. Episcopalian. Office: Task Force 2000 Comms 69 Whitney St Ste C San Francisco CA 94131-2769

HOPKINS, MARTHA JANE, education educator; b. Astoria, Oreg., Mar. 21, 1938; d. Willie Lester and Della May (Solmon) H. BA, N.W. Nazarene Coll., 1959; MS, Ind. U., 1961; EdD, U. Idaho, 1971. Tchr. Lynch Elem. Sch., Portland, Oreg., 1959-60, Corvallis (Oreg.) High Sch., 1961-64, Bethany (Okla.) Nazarene Coll., 1964-66; athletic dir. N.W. Nazarene Coll., Nampa, Idaho, 1984-87, acad. dean, 1987-89, prof. health and phys. edn., 1966—, chair dept. bus., 1992-95; chmn. Div. Profl. Studies, Nampa, 1985—. Bd. dirs. Coll. Ch. of Nazarene, Nampa, 1989. Named to Idaho New Agenda Hall of Fame, 1988, NAIA Coaches Hall of Fame, 1982, N.W. Nazarene Coll. Athletic Hall of Fame, 1990. Mem. AAHPERD, Am. Assn. for Higher Edn., Idaho Assn. Health Phys. Edn. and Dance (pres. 1971-72), DAR (chair nat. def. com. EEDAHHOW chpt. 1989—), Nat. Wellness Inst., IAHPER (disting. svc. award 1996). Home: 204 Mirage Ave Nampa ID 83651-2282 Office: NW Nazarene Coll Holly St Nampa ID 83686

HOPKINS, PHILIP JOSEPH, journalist, editor; b. Orange, Calif., Dec. 10, 1954; s. Philip Joseph and Marie Elizabeth H.; m. Susan Lisa Ingman Hopkins, Oct. 5, 1991; 1 child, Robin Genevieve Hopkins. BA in Journalism, San Diego State U., 1977. Cert. tissue therapist Center for Decubitis Ulcer Research, 1981. Reporter, La Jolla Light & Journal (Calif.), 1973; editorial cons. San Diego Union, 1974; asst. producer Southwestern Cable TV, San Diego, 1974; corr. Mission Cable TV, San Diego, 1975; photojournalist United Press Internat., San Diego, 1976; editor Rx Home Care mag., L.A., 1981, Hosp. Info. Mgmt. mag., 1981; editor, assoc. pub. Arcade mag., 1982; mng. editor Personal Computer Age, L.A., 1983-84; bur. chief Newsbytes syndicated column, 1985-86; v.p. Humbird Hopkins Inc., L.A., 1978-88; personal fin. writer Hume Pub. Co., 1987-89; writer, editor and researcher Ind. Rsch. and Info. Svc., 1988-90; writer, analyst Geneva Bus. Rsch., 1990; sci. writer, The Cousteau Soc., 1990; pub. cons. U. So. Calif., 1989; group lead Kaiser Permanente, 1991—. Recipient 1st and 4th place awards Nikon, Inc., Photo Contest, 1974; 3rd prize Minolta Camera Co. Creative Photography awards, 1975; Best Feature Photo award Sigma Delta Chi Mark of Excellence contest, 1977. Pres. Ind. Writers of So. Calif., 1988. Mem. Computer Press Assn. (life, hon.). Co-author: The Students' Survival Guide, 1977, 78; photographs have appeared in Time and Omni mags., The Mythology of Middle Earth, Parenting Your Aging Parents, Beginners Guide to the SLR, NBC-TV's Saturday Night Live. Home: 2373 Brigden Rd Pasadena CA 91104 Office: Kaiser Permanente 393 E Walnut ITSD/992 Pasadena CA 91188

HOPKINS, ROBERT ARTHUR, retired industrial engineer; b. Youngstown, Ohio, Dec. 14, 1920; s. Arthur George and Margaret Viola (Brush) H.; m. Mary Madelaine Bailey, Apr. 6, 1946; 1 child, Marlaine Hopkins Kaiser. BBA, Case Western Reserve U., 1949; cert. loss control engr., U. Calif., Berkeley, 1969. Ins. agt. Nat. Life and Accident Ins. Co., Lorain, Akron, Ohio, 1951-56, San Mateo, Calif., 1951-56; ins. agt., engr. Am. Hardware Mt. Ins. Co., San Jose, Fresno, Calif., 1956-60; loss control engr. Manhattan Guarantee-Continental Ins. Co., Calif., 1967-77. Organizer Operation Alert DC, Lorain, 1951-52; prin. spkr. DC, Fresno, 1957; active Pleasant Hill (Calif.) Civil Action Com., 1981-83; civilian coord. Office Emergency Svcs., Pleasant Hill, 1983-85; advisor, coord. airshows and warbird aircraft, 1980—; chmn. bd. Western Aerospace Mus., Oakland, Calif., 1988; ops. asst. for tower and ops. 50th Anniversary Golden Gate Bridge, San Francisco, 1987; advisor, coord. Travis AFB Air Expo '90, 1990; advisor Air Expo '96, NAS Alameda (Calif.) 50th Anniversary, 1990; advisor NAS Moffett Field Air Show, 1990, 92, Calif. Coast Air Show, Half Moon Bay, 1993-94, Dixon May Fair honoring WWII 50th anniversary, 1995; warbird coord. Port of Oakland Airshow, 1987; warbird advisor/coord. Beale AFB, 1993—; mem. Smithsonian Mus, Smithsonian Air & Space Mus; charter mem. Nat. Mus. of Am. Indian. Served with USAAC, 1942. Recipient Letter of Appreciation Fresno DC, 1957, cert. of appreciation City of Pleasant Hill, 1986, cert. of recognition and spl. citizenship award Calif. State Senate, 1995. Mem. No. Calif. Safety Engrs. Assn. (v.p., pres., chmn. 1974-77), Confederate Air Force (mem. staff, leader Pacific wing 1980—), Nat. Aero. Assn., Aero. Club No. Calif., Hamilton Field Assn. (dir. ops. Wings of Victory Air Show 1987, coord. 1988, 89—, asst. to pres. 1989—, advisor contr. 1990—), VFW (life, state civil disaster chmn. Area 5 Calif. 1991), Air Force Assn., Kiwanis (chpt. sec.-treas.). Republican. Roman Catholic. Home: 48 Mazie Dr Pleasant Hill CA 94523-3310

HOPKINS, STEPHEN DAVIS, mining company executive; b. N.Y.C., Oct. 31, 1907; s. Louis Davis and Margaret Hall (Daly) H.; m. Hildegarde Lupprian, 1942 (dec. 1983). BA, Yale U., 1935. Page N.Y. Stock Exch., N.Y.C., 1928, specialist clk., 1929-31; teller 1st Nat. Bank, Greenwich, Conn., 1935-37; editor Commerce & Fin. mag., 1938-41; chief adminstrv. officer Jensvold Mfg. Co., Olympia, Wash., 1945-46; account exec. Conrad, Bruce & Co., Seattle, 1947-48; investment counsel Pacific Rsch. & Mgmt. Co., Seattle, 1949-63; gen. mgr. plywood coop., Tacoma, 1951-52; writer nat. media on domestic currency consumer point view Deer Lodge, Mont., 1962—; advisor, cons. trading gold placer futures N.Y. Merc. Exch., 1971; advisor, cons. to U.S. currency mgrs., 1962—; advisor to currency mgrs. Republic of Russia, 1992, 93, CFO, gold placer mining co. Dawson/Klondike area, Yukon Territory, Can., 1994—. Editor: U.S. Coin and Currency Laws from 1775—, Inflation-Watch (registered trademark), 1978-83. Head usher St. George's Episcopal Ch., N.Y.C., 1975-76; mem. western Wash. enrollment and scholarship com. Yale U., 1948-52. 1st lt. C.E., U.S. Army, 1943-45. Mem. Mil. Order World Wars (officer Seattle chpt. 1950). Home and Office: 525 W 3rd Ave Anchorage AK 99501-2240

HOPKINSON, SHIRLEY LOIS, library science educator; b. Boone, Iowa, Aug 25, 1924; d. Arthur Perry and Zora (Smith) Hopkinson; student Coe Coll., 1942-43; AB cum laude (Phi Beta Kappa scholar 1944), U. Colo., 1945; BLS, U. Calif., 1949; MA (Honnold Honor scholar 1945-46), Claremont Grad. Sch., 1951; EdM, U. Okla., 1952, EdD, 1957 Tchr. pub. sch. Stigler, Okla., 1946-47, Palo Verde High Sch., Jr. Coll., Blythe, Calif., 1947-48; asst. librarian Modesto (Calif.) Jr. Coll., 1949-51; tchr., librarian Fresno, Calif., 1951-52, La Mesa, Cal., 1953-55; asst. prof. librarianship, instructional materials dir. Chaffey Coll., Ontario, Calif., 1955-59; asst. prof. librarian ship, San Jose (Calif.) State Coll., 1959-64; assoc. prof., 1964-69, prof., 1969—; bd. dirs. NDEA Inst. Sch. Librs., summer 1966; mem. Santa Clara County Civil Service Bd. Examiners. Recipient Master Gardner cert. Oreg. State U. Extension Svc. Book reviewer for jours. Mem. ALA, Calif. Library Assn., Audio-Visual Assn. Calif., NEA, AAUP, AAUW (dir. 1957-58), Bus. Profl. Women's Club, Sch. Librs. Assn. Calif. (com. mem., treas. No. sect. 1951-52), San Diego County Sch. Librs. Assn. (sec. 1945-55), Calif. Tchrs. Assn., LWV (bd. dirs. 1950-51, publs. chmn.), Phi Beta Kappa, Alpha Lambda Delta, Alpha Beta Alpha, Kappa Delta Pi, Phi Kappa Phi (disting. acad. achievement award 1981), Delta Kappa Gamma (sec. 1994—). Author: Descriptive Cataloging of Library Materials; Instructional Materials for Teaching the Use of the Library. Contbr. to profl. publs. Editor: Calif. Sch. Libraries, 1963-64; asst. editor: Sch. Library Assn. of Calif. Bull., 1961-63; book reviewer profl. jours. Office: 1340 Pomeroy Ave Apt 408 Santa Clara CA 95051-3658

HOPP, RICHARD A., lawyer; b. Seattle, Dec. 11, 1946. BA, San Luis Rey Coll., 1969; JD, U. Wash., 1976. Bar: Wash. 1976. Mem. Stoel, Rives, Boley, Jones & Grey, Seattle; chmn. Seattle Pension Roundtable, 1987—. Articles editor Washington Law Review, 1975-76. Mem. ABA, Wash. State Bar Assn. (bd. dirs. Seattle chpt., western pension conf. 1985-87, tax coun., taxation sect.), Seattle-King County. Office: Stoel Rives Boley Jones & Grey 1 Union St Seattle WA 98101-2070

HOPPING, WILLIAM RUSSELL, hospitality industry consultant and appraiser; b. Balt., May 3, 1947; s. Russell Leroy and Janet Louise (Cloud) H.; m. Catherine Wilson; 1 child, William Alexander. BS in Hotel Adminstrn., Cornell U., 1969; MBA, U. Denver, 1978. Mgr. Sylvania (Ohio) Country Club, 1972-77; sr. cons. Pannell Kerr Forster, Denver, 1978-82; cons. Ginther Wycoff Grp., Denver, 1982-85; pres. W.R. Hopping & Co., Inc., Denver, 1985—. Vol., Big Bros., Inc., Denver, 1990—; chmn. adv. bd. U. Denver Profl. Career Devel. Prog., 1987-88, chmn. task force, Career and Placement Ctr., 1989. 1st lt. U.S. Army, 1970-72. Mem. Appraisal Inst., Internat. Soc. Hospitality Cons. (pres. 1990-91, chmn. 1991-93, chmn. emeritus, 1993—), Cornell Soc. Hotelmen (pres. Rocky Mountain chpt. 1984-85). Office: W R Hopping & Co Inc 6334 S Yates Ct Littleton CO 80123-6738

HOPPLE, JANET LYNETTE, medical technologist; b. Clyde, Ohio, Nov. 10, 1942; d. Clarence A. and Gretta I. (Baker) Ferree; m. C. Earl Hopple, Apr. 4, 1964; children: Kent E., Cory E. Med. Lab. Technician, Carnegie Coll., 1961, Med. Technologist, 1964. Mem. Am. Med. Technologists. Med. lab. technician St. Joseph's Hosp., Warren, Ohio, 1961-62, Mercy Hosp., Tiffin, Ohio, 1962-64, Samuel H. Williams, MD, Alexandria, Va., 1964-65; med. technologist Mercy Hosp., Tiffin, 1965-73; med. technologist/lab. mgr. Doctor's Park Clin. Lab., Lake Jackson, Tex., 1975-79; med. technologist Chandler (Ariz.) Med. Surg. Group, 1983-85; med. technologist/lab. mgr. Casa Grande (Ariz.) Clinic, 1984-89; med. technologist/sr. technician, lab. newsletter editor Casa Grande Regional Med. Ctr., 1989—. Mem. Am. Med. Technologists (del. Reno, Nev. 1994), Ariz. State Soc. of Am. Med. Technologists (state conv. com. 1994-95, 97, nat. level Disting. Achievement award 1995, McCoy Boyd award 1995, state level Med. Technologist of Yr. 1995), Ariz. State Am. Motors Club (treas. 1994-96), Casa Grande 4 Wheelers Club. Republican. Home: 19325 W Hopi Dr Casa Grande AZ 85222 Office: Casa Grande Regional Med Ctr 1800 E Florence Blvd Casa Grande AZ 85222

HORAN, ADEL EDWARD, sociology and psychology educator; b. Salt, Jordan, Sept. 17, 1943; came to U.S., 1976; s. Awad and Martha (Neshweiwat) H.; m. Samira A., May 11, 1966; 1 child, Marsha. BFA, Da Vinci Art Acad., 1964; MFA, Sussex Coll., 1981; MA in Psychology, Liberty U., 1981; PhD in Human Svcs., Walden/Ind. U., 1994. Art dir. Nesco Advt., Jordan, 1960-65, Kuwait Oil Co., 1965-71, Samira Advt., Toronto, Can., 1971-76, Readers Digest, Pleasantville, N.Y., 1976-79, Yonkers (N.Y.) Gazette, 1979-82; fine artist Horan Art Studio, Phoenix, 1982-85; instr. Rio Salado Coll., Phoenix, 1985-88, Horan Art Sch., Phoenix, 1988-94; counselor St. John of the Desert, Phoenix, 1990-93; prof. sociology and psychology Ariz. Inst. Bus. and Tech., 1995—. Author: Origins and Early Egyptian Art, 1982, Art in the Middle East, 1982, Arab-Americans Acculturation into the American Society, 1995, Israeli-Arab Conflict 1917-2000, 1996; publisher (mag.) The Immigrant, 1978, The Arab World, 1978. Mem. Am. Assn. Counseling Devel., Am. Assn. Christian Counseling, Am. Assn. Family Therapists, Am. Assn. of the Aged, Am. Multicultural Assn., Am. Portrait Soc., Phoenix Guild, Calif. Reference, Scottsdale Artists League, Paradise Valley (Ariz.) C. of C., Gibran Khalil Scholar Found. N. Am. Republican. Roman Catholic.

HORAN, MARY ANN THERESA, nurse; b. Denver, July 4, 1936; d. John Paul and Lucille (Somma) Perito; m. Stephen F. Horan, Sr., Dec. 28, 1957; children: Seanna, Dana, Michelle, Annette, Stephen Jr., Christine, David. BSN, Loretto Heights Coll., Denver, 1958; postgrad. Pima Community Coll., 1982. RN, Ala. Staff nurse Med. Ctr. Hosp., Huntsville, Ala., 1978-79, Crestwood Hosp., Huntsville, 1980-81, St. Joseph Hosp. Eye Surgery, Tucson, 1981—; v.p. Success Achievement Ctr., Tucson, 1987—; Shaklee distbr., 1996—. Contbr. articles to nursing jours., poetry to lit. jours. Republican. Roman Catholic. Home: 8311 E 3rd St Tucson AZ 85710-2550

HORII, NAOMI, editor; b. West Lafayette, Ind., Jan. 12, 1968; d. Yoshiyuki and Nobuko Ruth (Abe) H. BS, U. Colo., 1989; MA, U. Mo., 1993. Editor MYU Pub., Tokyo, 1989-91; tchr., talented and gifted program Boulder, Louisville, Colo., 1994—; editor Many Mountains Moving, Boulder, 1994—; also bd. dirs. Many Mountains Moving. Vol. Takarazuka Exch. Program, Boulder, 1993—, Nightwalk Women's Safety Program, Boulder, 1987-89. Recipient Rocky Mountain Women's Inst. fellowship for fiction, 1996-97, Gary Higa Found. Meml. scholarship for essay, 1988. Mem. NAFE, Nat. Assn. Asian Am. Profls., Rocky Mountain Book Pub. Assn., Visiones. Home and Office: Many Mountains Moving 420 22d St Boulder CO 80302

HORN, CHRISTIAN FRIEDRICH, venture capital company executive; b. Dresden, Germany, Dec. 23, 1927; came to U.S., 1954, naturalized, 1959; s. Otto Hugo and Elsa H.; m. Christa Winkler, Feb. 13, 1954; 1 child, Sabrina. MS, Technische Hochschule, Dresden, 1951; PhD, Technische Hochschule, Aachen, Germany, 1958. Rsch. scientist German Acad. Sci., Berlin, 1951-53, Farbwerke Hoechst, Germany, 1953-54; rsch. mgr. Union Carbide, N.Y.C., 1954-65; pres. Polymer Tech. Inc., N.Y.C., 1965-74; v.p. W.R. Grace & Co., N.Y.C., 1974-81, sr. v.p., 1981-95, also bd. dirs.; pres. Horn Venture Ptnrs. (formerly Grace Horn Ventures), Cupertino, Calif., 1983—, mng. ptnr., 1987—; pres. Horn Investment Corp., Cupertino, 1996—; bd. dirs. Buffets, Inc., Cariopulmonary, Timothy's Coffees of the World, Roadhouse Grill, Inc., Rosti, Inc., Sonoma Valley Bagel Co. Patentee in field. With German Army, 1944-45. Decorated Iron Cross. Lutheran. Home: 27827 Via Feliz Los Altos CA 94022-2421 Office: Horn Venture Ptnrs 20300 Stevens Creek Blvd Cupertino CA 95014-2240

HORN, KENNETH PORTER, aeronautical/astronautical engineering administrator; b. Ft. Worth, Dec. 10, 1937; s. John Melton and Hilda Marjorie (Teitelbaum) H.; m. Ann Harper, July 28, 1979. BA in Mech. Engring., Rice U., 1960, MS in Mech. Engring., 1962; PhD in Aeronautics/Astronautics, Stanford U., 1966. Engr. NASA Manned Spacecraft Ctr., Houston, 1961; rsch. engr. Aerospace Corp., El Segundo, Calif., 1966-72, sect. head, 1972-75; assoc. program dir. Rand Corp., Santa Monica, Calif., 1978-85, project leader, 1975—, dept. head, 1988-90, program dir., 1985—. Contbr. articles to profl. jours. Recipient fellowship Ford Found., 1964-66, scholarship Mission Mfg., 1961. Fellow AIAA (assoc.); mem. Am. Phys. Soc., Sigma Tau, Sigma Xi. Office: Rand Corp 1700 Main St Santa Monica CA 90401-3208

HORN, (JOHN) STEPHEN, congressman, political science educator; b. San Juan Bautista, Calif., May 31, 1931; s. John Stephen and Isabelle (McCaffrey) H.; m. Nini Moore, Sept. 4, 1954; children: Marcia Karen, John Stephen. AB with great distinction, Stanford, 1953, postgrad., 1953-54, 55-56, PhD in Polit. Sci, 1958; M in Pub Adminstrn., Harvard, 1955. Congl. fellow, 1958-59; adminstrv. asst. to sec. labor Washington, 1959-60; legislative asst. to U.S. Senator Thomas H. Kuchel, 1960-66; sr. fellow The Brookings Instn., 1966-69; dean grad. studies and research Am. U., 1969-70; pres. Calif. State U., Long Beach, 1970-88, Trustee prof. polit. sci., 1988-93; mem. 103rd Congress from 38th Calif. dist., 1993—; sr. cons., host The Govt. Story on TV, The Election Game (radio series), 1967-69, vice chmn. U.S. Commn. on Civil Rights, 1969-80 (commr. 1980-82); chmn. Urban Studies Fellow Adv. Com., U.S. Dept. HUD, 1969-70; mem. Law Enforcement Ednl. Prog. Adv. Com., U.S. Dept Justice, 1969-70; adv. bd. Nat. Inst. Corrections, 1972-88 (chmn. 1984-87),. Author: The Cabinet and Congress, 1960, Unused Power: The Work of the Senate Committee on Appropriations, 1970, (with Edmund Beard) Congressional Ethics: The View from the House, 1975. Active Pres.-elect Nixon's Task Force on Orgn. Exec. Br., 1968, Kutak Found.; vice chmn. Long Beach Area C. of C., 1984-88; co-founder Western U.S. Com. Arts and Scis. for Eisenhower, 1956; chmn. Am. Assn. State Colls. and Univs., 1985-86; mem. Calif. Ednl. Facilities Authority, 1984-93. USAR, 1954-62. Fellow John F. Kennedy Inst. Politics Harvard U., 1966-67. Fellow Nat. Acad. Pub. Adminstrn.; mem. Stanford Assocs., Stanford Alumni Assn. (pres. 1976-77), Phi Beta Kappa, Pi Sigma Alpha. Republican. Office: 129 Cannon House Office Bldg Washington DC 20515

HORNADAY, ALINE GRANDIER, publisher, independent scholar; b. San Diego, Sept. 14, 1923; d. Frank and Lydia Landon (Weir) Grandier; m. Quinn Hornaday, Oct. 9, 1965. BA, Union of Experimenting Colls., San Diego, 1977; PhD, U. Calif., San Diego, 1984. Pub. San Diego Daily Transcript, 1952-72, columnist, 1972-74; dir. San Diego Ind. Scholars, 1985-87, 94-95; co-pub. Jour. Unconventional History, Cardiff, Calif., 1989—; vis. scholar U. Calif., San Diego, 1984—; speaker at profl. confs. Co-author: The Hornadays, Root and Branch; contbr. articles to profl. jours. and books. Commr. San Diego City Libr. Commn., 1964-70. Mem. San Diego Ind. Scholars, Nat. Coalition Ind. Scholars, Med. Assn. of Pacific, Am. Hist. Assn., Medieval Acad. Am., Nat. Soc. Colonial Dames of Am., Wed. Club (pres. 1964-65). Home and Office: 6435 Avenida Cresta La Jolla CA 92037-6514

HORNER, ALTHEA JANE, psychologist; b. Hartford, Conn., Jan. 13, 1926; d. Louis and Celia (Newmark) Greenwald; children: Martha Horner

Hartley, Anne Horner Benck, David, Kenneth. BS in Psychology, U. Chgo., 1952; PhD in Clin. Psychology, U. So. Calif., 1965. Lic. psychologist, N.Y., Calif. Tchr. Pasadena (Calif.) City Coll., 1965-67; from asst. to assoc. prof. Los Angeles Coll. Optometry, 1967-70; supr. Psychology interns Pasadena Child Guidance Clinic, 1969-70; pvt. practice specializing in psychoanalysis and psychoanalytic psychotherapy, N.Y.C., 1970-83; supervising psychologist dept. psychiatry Beth Israel Med. Ctr., N.Y.C., 1972-83, coordinator group therapy tng., 1976-82, clinician in charge Brief Adaptation-Oriented Psychotherapy Research Group, 1982-83; assoc. clin. prof. Mt. Sinai Sch. Medicine, N.Y.C., 1977-91, adj. assoc. prof., 1991—; mem. faculty Nat. Psychol. Assn. for Psychoanalysis, N.Y.C., 1982-83; sr. mem. faculty Wright Inst. Los Angeles Postgrad. Inst., 1983-85; pvt. practice specializing in psychoanalysis and psychoanalytic psychotherapy L.A., 1983—; clin. prof. dept. Psychology UCLA, 1985-95. Author: (with others) Treating the Neurotic Patient in Brief Psychotherapy, 1985, Object Relations and the Developing Ego in Therapy, 1979, rev. edit., 1984, Little Big Girl, 1982, Being and Loving, 1978, 3d edit. 1990, Psychology for Living (with G. Forehand), 4th edit., 1977, The Wish for Power and the Fear of Having It, 1989, The Primacy of Structure, 1990, Psychoanalytic Object Relations Therapy, 1991; mem. editorial bd. Jour. of Humanistic Psychology, 1986—, Jour. of the Am. Acad. of Psychoanalysis; contbr. articles to profl. jours. Mem. AAAS, APA, Calif. State Psychol. Assn., Am. Acad. Psychoanalysis (sci. assoc.), So. Calif. Psychoanalytic Soc. and Inst. (hon.). Office: 3579 E Foothill Blvd # 256 Pasadena CA 91107-3119

HORNER, ANTHONY ADAM, pediatrician, educator; b. N.Y.C., May 24, 1960; s. Harry and Joan Ruth (Frankel) H. BA in Biochemistry, U. Calif. San Diego, 1983; MD, St. Louis U., 1987. Diplomate Am. Bd. Pediatrics, Am. Bd. Allergy and Immunology. Resident in pediatrics UCLA Med. Ctr., 1990; fellow in pediatric immunology Boston Children's Hosp., 1994; asst. prof. pediatrics med. sch. U. Calif. San Diego, San Diego, 1994—; dir. pediatric allergy and immunology med. ctr. U. Calif. San Diego, 1994—; co-principle investigator Children's Asthma Mgmt. Program, San Diego, 1994—. Fellow Am. Acad. Pediatrics, Am. Acad. Allergy and Immunology. Office: U Calif San Diego Med Ctr 200 West Arbor Dr San Diego CA 92103-8448

HORNER, ELAINE EVELYN, secondary education educator; b. Portales, N.Mex., Feb. 26, 1941; d. Carlton James and Clara C. (Roberson) Carmichael; m. Bill G. Horner, Feb. 2, 1959; children: Billy G. Sr., Frances E. Moreau, Aaron J. BA, Ea. N.Mex. U., 1973, MEd, 1978. Tchr. Artesia (N.Mex.) Jr. High Sch., 1973—. Recipient Honor of Excellence award Navajo Refining, 1993. Mem. NEA, Nat. Coun. Tchrs. Math., N.Mex. Coun. Tchrs. Math., Artesia Edn. Assn. (v.p. 1987-88), Delta Kappa Gamma (treas. 1988—). Democrat. Baptist. Home: 2406 N Haldeman Rd Artesia NM 88210-9435 Office: Artesia Jr High Sch 15th And Cannon Artesia NM 88210

HORNER, HARRY CHARLES, JR., sales executive, theatrical and film consultant; b. Pitts., Oct. 30, 1937; s. Harry Charles and Sara Marie (Hysong) H.; m. Patricia Ann Hagarty, June 15, 1965 (div. 1981); m. Sharon Kae Wyatt, Dec. 30, 1983; children: Jeffrey Brian, Jennifer Leigh, Mark Gregory. BFA, U. Cin., 1963; postgrad., Xavier U., Cin., 1963-64. Mgr. Retail Credit Co., Atlanta, 1964-68; ops. mgr. Firestone Tire and Rubber Co., L.A., 1968-80; exec. v.p. Romney/Ford Enterprises Inc., Scottsdale, Ariz., 1980-85; sales mgr. Environ. Care Inc., Calabassas, Calif., 1985-93; ops. v.p. Albuquerque (N.Mex.) Grounds Maintenance, Inc., 1993—; pres., chief exec. officer The Cons. Group Cos. Ltd., Palm Desert, Calif., 1984—; pres. E. Valley Theatre Co., Chandler, Ariz., 1984-86. Cons. Ariz. Commn. on Arts, Phoenix, 1983-84. Republican. Mem. LDS Ch. Office: Albuquerque GroundsMaintenance Inc 8442 Washington Pl NE Albuquerque NM 87113-1671

HORNER, JENNIE LINN, retired educational administrator, nurse; b. Memphis, Tex., Feb. 27, 1932; d. Lester C. and Cecil T. (Knight) Linn; m. Billy A. Gooch, June 4, 1951 (dec.); children: Brenda Michael, Patricia Lynn Magneson, Robert Allen; m. 2d Donald M. Horner, July 26, 1975. RN, U. Tex., 1955; BS, No. Ariz. U., 1977, MA, 1978, EdD, 1984. Cert. tchr., registered nurse, Ariz., Tex. Indsl. nurse Lipton Tea Co., Galveston, Tex., 1955-56; head nurse U. Tex. Med. Br., Galveston, 1956-58; sch. nurse Wash. Sch. Dist., Phoenix, 1970-77; tchr. middle sch., 1977-80; asst. prin. Murphy Sch. Dist., Phoenix, 1980-82; assoc. prin. middle sch. Madison Sch., Phoenix, 1982-84; lang. arts coordinator Madison Sch. Dist., Phoenix; prin. Dysart Unified Sch. Dist., El Mirage, Ariz., 1984-87; adminstr. for ednl. svcs., 1987-91, ret., 1991; med. cons. Medahab, Phoenix. Mem. Assn. Supervision and Curriculum Devel., Sch. Nurses Orgn. Ariz. (past pres.), Am. Vocat. Assn., Am. Sch. Health Assn., Nat. Assn. Sch. Nurses, Nat. Assn. Elem. Sch. Prins., Nat. Sch. Health Assn., Ariz. Sch. Health Assn. (bd. dirs.), Ariz. Adminstrs. Assn., Aware West, Phi Delta Kappa. Democrat. Home: 14239 N 50th Ln Glendale AZ 85306-4447

HORNER, LEE, foundation executive, speaker, consultant, computer specialist; b. Sault Ste. Marie, Ont., Can., Mar. 18, 1944; came to U.S., 1976; d. William E. and Gladys (Boomhower) H.; m. Claude Lavallee, Jan. 21, 1960 (div. Sept. 1969); children—Kevin Lauren Lavallee/Petalos, Cynthia Lee Lavallee; m. James G. Petalos, Jan. 9, 1970 (dec. Jan. 1977). Student Concordia U., Montreal, Que., Can., 1975-76, U. Nev.-Las Vegas, 1977, 90. Pres., LHP Investments, Inc., Las Vegas, 1978—; v.p. Casa Mobile Corp., real estate, San Francisco, 1979—; founder, chmn. bd. PMS Research Found., Las Vegas, 1982—; pub. speaker Premenstrual Syndrome, health, wellness, cycles. Author: How to Chart Your Course to Freedom, 1983; Mini-Nutrition and Exercise Manual, 1983; PMS Minder, 1983; PMS Wellness Workbook, 1985, PMS Support Group Manual, 1985. Mem. Am. Soc. Fund Raising Execs., Am. Bus. Women's Assn., Nat. Speakers Assn. (founding pres. Las Vegas chpt. 1984-85, 88—). Club: Windjammer, Toastmasters (ednl. v.p. 1980, adminstrv. v.p. 1983, 88, pres. 1989—). Home: 2754 El Toreador St Las Vegas NV 89109-1710 Office: LHP Investments Inc PMS Rsch Found PO Box 14574 Las Vegas NV 89114-4574

HOROWITZ, BEN, medical center executive; b. Bklyn., Mar. 19, 1914; s. Saul and Sonia (Meringoff) H.; m. Beverly Lichtman, Feb. 14, 1952; children: Zachary, Jody. BA, Bklyn. Coll., 1940; LLB, St. Lawrence U., 1940; postgrad. New Sch. Social Rsch., 1942. Bar: N.Y. 1941. Dir. N.Y. Fedn. Jewish Philanthropies, 1940-45; assoc., ea. regional dir. City of Hope, 1945-50, nat. exec. sec., 1950-53, exec. dir., 1953-85, gen. v.p., bd. dirs., 1985—, bd. dirs. nat. med. ctr., 1980—; bd. dirs. Beckman Rsch. Inst., 1980—. Mem. Gov.'s Task Force on Flood Relief, 1969-74. Bd. dirs., v.p. Hope for Hearing Found., UCLA, 1972-96; bd. dirs. Forte Found., 1987-92, Ch. Temple Housing Corp., 1988-93, Leo Baeck Temple, 1964-67, 86-89, Westwood Property Owners Assn., 1991—. Recipient Spirit of Life award, 1970, Gallery of Achievement award, 1974, Profl. of Yr. award So. Calif. chpt. Nat. Soc. Fundraisers, 1977; Ben Horowitz chair in rsch. established at City of Hope, 1981. City street named in his honor, 1986. Jewish. Formulated the role of City of Hope as pilot ctr. in medicine, sci., and humanitarianism, 1959. Home: 221 Conway Ave Los Angeles CA 90024-2601 Office: City of Hope 208 W 8th St Los Angeles CA 90014-3208

HOROWITZ, JED H., plastic surgeon, reconstructive surgeon; b. N.Y.C., Dec. 29, 1952; s. Bernard Joseph Horowitz and Ruth Zimmerman; m. Joanne Harrington Mayers, Dec. 19, 1980; children: Jamie, Jessica, Jodie. BS summa cum laude, SUNY, Stony Brook, 1973; MD, SUNY, Buffalo, 1977. Diplomate Am. Bd. Plastic Surgery. Categorical surgical internship Boston U. Affiliated Hosps., 1977-78; gen. surgical resident Grady Meml. Hosp. & Emory U. Sch. of Medicine, Atlanta, 1978-79, 1980-82; gen. surgical rsch. fellow clinical rsch. facility Emory U. Hosp. and Sch. of Medicine, 1979-80; fellowships in craniofacial, microsurgery and hand surgery dept. Plastic and Maxillofacial Surgery U. Va. Med. Ctr., Charlottesville, 1982-83; resident plastic and maxillofacial surgery U. Va. Med. Ctr., 1983-84; chief resident dept. Plastic and Maxillofacial Surgery U. Va. Med. Ctr., 1984-85; clin. asst. prof. divsn. plastic surgery Plasticos Inst. for Plastic Surgery, Long Beach, Calif.; clin. instr. dept. plastic and maxillofacial surgery U. Va. Med. Ctr., 1984-85; emergency room cons. Boston U. Hosp., 1977-78, Grady Meml. Hosp. Surgical Emergency Clinic, Atlanta, 1978-79. Contbr. articles to profl. jours.; speaker in field. Mem. ACS, Am. Soc. Plastic and Reconstructive Surgeons, Am. Cleft Palate Assn., L.A. County Med. Assn., Calif. Med. Assn., Calif. Soc. Plastic Surgery, Long Beach Surgical Soc., Orange County Med. Assn. Office: 2880 Atlantic Ave Ste 290 Long Beach CA 90806-1716 also: 1441 Avocado Ste 808 Newport Beach CA 92660

HOROWITZ, MYER, retired university president, education educator; b. Montreal, Que., Can., Dec. 27, 1932; s. Philip and Fanny Cotler H.; m. Barbara Rosen, 1956; children: Carol Anne, Deborah Ellen. BA, Sir George Williams U., 1956; MEd, U. Alta., 1959; EdD, Stanford U., 1965; LLD (hon.), McGill U., 1979, Concordia U., 1982, Athabasca U., 1989, U. B.C., 1990, U. Alta., 1990. Tchr. elem. and high schs., Montreal, Que. area, 1952-60; lectr. in edn. McGill U., 1960-62, asst. prof., 1963-65, assoc. prof., 1965-67, prof., 1967-69, asst. dean, 1965-69; prof., chmn. dept. elem. edn. U. Alta., 1969-72, dean of edn., 1972-75, v.p. (acad.), 1975-79, pres., 1979-89, prof. emeritus, 1990—. Contbr. articles to profl. jours. Decorated officer Order of Can. Fellow Can. Coll. Teachers. Jewish. Office: U of Alta, 845B Edn Centre, Edmonton, AB Canada T6G 2G5

HOROWITZ, ZACHARY I., entertainment company executive; b. N.Y.C., Apr. 27, 1953; s. Ben and Beverly (Lichtman) H.; m. Barbara J. Natterson; 1 child, Jennifer Lily. BA summa cum laude, Claremont Mens Coll., 1975; JD, Stanford U., 1978. Bar: Calif. 1978. Assoc. Kaplan, Livingston, Goodwin, Berkowitz & Selvin, Beverly Hills, Calif., 1978; from sr. atty. to dir. bus. affairs West Coast CBS Records, L.A., 1978-83; v.p. bus. and legal affairs MCA Records, Universal City, Calif., 1983-84, sr. v.p. bus. and legal affairs, 1984-88; from sr. v.p. bus. and legal affairs to COO Universal Music Group, Universal City, 1986-95, pres., 1995—; bd. dirs. MCA Victor Japan; mem. op. com. Motown Recording Co., L.A., 1988-93. Mem. bd. editors Stanford Law Rev., 1977-78. Nat. bd. dirs. City of Hope, 1989—, vice chmn. Music Industry chpt., 1985-86, chmn. maj. gifts com., 1986-90, nat. campaign co-chmn., 1990-91, pres., 1991-92, chmn., 1993-94, endowment chair, 1995—, adv. bd. Nashville Celebrity Baseball Game, 1995—. Mem. NARAS (presdl. adv. com. 1996—), Record Industry Assn. Am. (bd. dirs. 1990—, fin. com. 1993—). Office: Universal Music Group 70 Universal City Plz Universal City CA 91608-1011

HORRIGAN, THERESA MARIE, publishing executive; b. San Francisco, Jan. 30, 1947; d. Raymond Joseph and Dorothy Louise (Purnell) Polasky; m. Richard William Horrigan, June 3, 1967; 1 child, Jennifer Dorothy. BA, U. San Francisco, 1967. Elem. sch. tchr. St James Sch. for Girls, San Francisco, 1967-69; owner Protean Press, San Francisco, 1983—; mem. Pacific Ctr. for Book Arts, San Francisco, 1983—, sec., 1993; mem. Friends of Calligraphy, San Francisco, 1992—. Editor, pub.: (poetry) Oh Mother and Other Poems, 1991, A Small Box of Poets, 9 books, 1994, Hobo Traveling Notes, 1990; author, pub.: Kokopelli, 1993, Ellis Island, 1995, Bekop, 1997, The Ogham, 1997; author, artist, pub.: The People in the Rock, 1993; artist, pub.: Stonemasons' Marks, 1990; pub.: Jeramy's Book, 1985. Vol. dispatcher Food Runners, San Francisco, 1989—. Democrat. Office: Protean Press 287 28th Ave San Francisco CA 94121-1001

HORST, RANDY, museum director. Dir. Western Mont. Coll. Gallery Mus., Dillion. Office: Western Mont Coll Mus 710 S Atlantic Dillon MT 59725

HORTON, GWENDOLYN, nursing educator emeritus; b. Moose Jaw, Sask., Can., June 7, 1914; came to U.S., 1919; d. Orville A. and Myrtle (King) H. AA, L.A. City Coll.; BS, Calif. State U., L.A., 1968, MS, 1974. RN; cert. pub. health. Policewoman L.A. Police Dept., 1940-45; prof. nursing L.A. City Coll., Trade Teck Coll., East L.A. Coll., Harbor Coll.; prof. nursing L.A. Pierce Coll., 1972-83, prof. emeritus, 1983—. Mem. Descanso Gardens Guild, LaCanada, Calif., 1953-56, San. Fernando Valley Bd. Realtors, Van Nuys, Calif., 1980-91; bd. dirs. Owners of Subsidized Housing; pres. L.A. Garden Club, 1988-90. Mem. Water and Power Assocs. L.A. (bd. dirs. 1989-94), Apt. Assn. Greater L.A. (v.p. 1990-91, bd. dirs.), Calif. Nurses Assn., L.A. Cinema Club, L.A. Breakfast Club (emergency aid com.), Los Feliz Rep. Women Federated, So. Calif. Rep. Women, Calif. Rep. Women. Home: 2041 N Vermont Ave Los Angeles CA 90027-1952

HORTON, JOHN MICHAEL, psychoanalyst; b. Boston, Feb. 13, 1946; s. William Donald and Cecilia Frances Horton; m. Jane Ellen Howell, Sept. 2, 1973; 1 child, Jesse Ellen. BA, U. Wash., 1968, MD, 1972. Diplomate Am. Bd. Psychiatry and Neurology. Intern Mt. Zion Hosp., San Francisco, 1972-73, resident, 1973-75; asst. clin. prof. psychiatry U. Calif. Sch. Medicine, San Francisco, 1975-86, U. Wash. Sch. Medicine, Seattle, 1987—; pvt. practice psychiatry and psychoanalysis San Francisco, 1978-86, Seattle, 1986—. Mem. Am. Psychiat. Assn., Am. Psychoanalytic Assn. Roman Catholic. Office: John M Horton MD Ste 105 4033 E Madison St Seattle WA 98112-3117

HORTON, JONATHAN CHARLES, neuroscientist, neuro-ophthalmologist; b. Edmonton, Alta., Can., Nov. 16, 1954; came to U.S., 1960; s. George Klaus and Pamela (Fairbrother) H.; m. Lidia Mucia, Dec. 22, 1984; children: Nathanael Carroll, Matthew David, Christina Ixmukane. AB in History, Stanford U., 1976; MD, Harvard U., 1984, PhD, 1984. Diplomate Am. Bd. Ophthalmology. Med. intern Mass. Gen. Hosp., Boston, 1984-85, neurology resident, 1985-86; ophthalmology resident Georgetown U. Hosp., Washington, 1986-89; neuro-ophthalmology/pediatric ophthalmology fellow U. Calif., San Francisco, 1989-90, asst. prof. ophthalmology and neurology, 1990-96, assoc. prof. ophthalmology, neurology and physiology, 1996—. Contbr. articles to profl. jours. Grantee: N. Calif. Soc. to Prevent Blindness, San Francisco, 1990, Nat. Eye Inst., Washington, 1993. Fellow N. Am. Neuro-Ophthalmology Soc., Am. Acad. Ophthalmology; mem. AAAS, Soc. for Neurosci., Assn. for Rsch. in Vision and Ophthalmology, Cordes Eye Soc., Phi Beta Kappa. Home: 2230 Sheraton Pl San Mateo CA 94402 Office: U C San Francisco Dept Ophthalmology 10 Kirkham St # K301 San Francisco CA 94143-0730

HORTON, KATHRYN LYNNE, marketing executive; b. Troy, Ohio, Sept. 12, 1950; d. Fred and Bonnie June (Perry) Nolls; m. Brad VanDyck, Dec. 25, 1978 (div. June 1985); children: Scott Allen, Geoffrey Randall. BA in Bus., ITO, L.A., 1985, mktg. specialist, 1986. Customer svc. rep. Nationwide Ins., Akron, Ohio, 1974-76, Polymetrics, Santa Clara, Calif., 1976-79; fin. dir. SCS, Santa Clara, 1979-85; mktg. mgr. Ch. of Scientology Internat., L.A., 1985-90; customer svc. rep. Steven Tomczak & Assocs., Burbank, Calif., 1990-92; sr. mktg. v.p. Exec. Software, Glendale, Calif., 1992-94; owner The Mktg. Biz, La Crescenta, Calif., 1994—. Mem. NAFE. Office: The Mktg Biz # 208 143 S Glendale Ave Glendale CA 91205

HORTON, KENNETH, investor; b. Newport, Nebr., May 11, 1921; s. Fred and Clara E. (Cottrel) H.; m. Evelyn H. Shafer, Dec. 29, 1939 (div. 1961); children: Kenneth Eugene, Helen Clara Catherine; m. Arlene J. Mitchell, July 23, 1962. AA, Valley Coll., San Bernardino, Calif., 1951. Crew leader 1st suppression fire crew Civilian Conservation Corp, Glendora, Calif., 1937-39; journeyman R.R. Car Shop/Santa Fe R.R., San Bernardino, 1940-44; boy's counselor San Bernardino County Juvenile Hall, 1948-53; supr. state champion drill team Calif. Youth Authority, Whittier, 1954; layout carpenter Bectal Constrn. Co., Oro grande, Calif., 1954-55; patrolman, vice officer Police Dept., San Bernardino, 1956-66; ind. investor Thousand Oaks, Calif., 1950—. Sustaining mem. Rep. Nat. Com., Washington, 1978—. With U.S. Army, 1944-45. Decorated Bronze Star medal; recipient Letter of Appreciation for apprehending holdup man Security Pacific Bank, 1974. Lutheran. Home: PO Box 1432 Thousand Oaks CA 91358

HORTON, LAWRENCE STANLEY, electrical engineer, apartment developer; b. Hanston, Kans., July 25, 1926; s. Gene Leigh and Retta Florene (Abbott) H.; m. Margaret Ann Cowles, Nov. 26, 1946 (dec. 1964); children: Craig, Lawrence Stanley, Steven J.; m. Julia Ann Butler Wirkkula, Aug. 15, 1965; stepchildren: Charles Wirkkula Horton, Jerry Higginbotham Horton. BSEE, Oreg. State U., 1949. Elec. engr. Mountain States Power Co., Calif. Oreg. Power Co., Pacific Power and Light Co., 1948-66; mgr. Ramic Corp., 1966-69; cons. elec. engr. Marquess and Assocs., Medford, Oreg., 1969-85, sec., bd. dirs.; pres., owner Medford Better Housing Assn., 1985—; ptnr. Terpening Terrace, Jackson St. Properties, T'Morrow Apts., Johnson Manor, Fountain Pla., Champion Pk.; bd. dirs. Valley of Rogue, developer various apt. complexes, 1969—, Northwood Apts., Horton Plz.; bd. dirs. Medford Hist. Commn. Active Medford Planning Commn., Archtl. Review Commn., Housing Authority; bd. govs. State of Oreg. Citizens Utility; pres. United Fund, 1963-64. With USN, 1945-46. Named Rogue Valley Profl. Engr. of Yr., 1969. Mem. IEEE, Nat. Soc. Profl. Engrs., Profl. Engrs. of Oreg., So. Oreg. Rental Owners Assn. (pres.), Rogue Valley Geneol. Soc. (pres.), Medford C. of C. (dir.), Rogue Valley Yacht Club (commodore 1974-75, dir., local fleet capt., champion), Rogue Valley Knife and Fork (past pres.), San Juan 21 Fleet Assn. (western vice commodore, Top Ten San Juan Sailor West Coast, 1980), Jackson Toastmasters (founder 1957), Medford Rotary, Kiwanis (life, pres. Crater Golden 1990-91). Republican. Methodist. Grad. instr. Dale Carnegie course, 1955, 56; contbr. elec. articles to profl. assns., 1956-61. Office: Medford Better Housing Assn 1118 Spring St Medford OR 97504-6272

HORTON, MICHAEL L., mortgage company executive, publishing executive; b. Pasadena, Calif., Oct. 19, 1961; s. Jerry S. and Mary L. Horton. BA in Bus. Econs., Claremont McKenna Coll., 1983. Lic. real estate broker. Gen. mgr. I.W.S., Pasadena, 1976-80; proprietor NBB Svcs. Orgn., Upland, Calif., 1980-85; regional mgr. Sycamore Fin. Group Inc., Rancho Cucamonga, Calif., 1984-87; CEO, pres. Boulder Fin. Corp., Rancho Cucamonga, 1987—, M.C.M. Pub. Corp., Rancho Cucamonga, 1992—; pres., CEO Sandstone Realty Group, Inc., 1995—; chm. C.H.A.M.P. Inc., 1996—; chmn. Champeon Inc., 1996—. Author: A Real Estate Professional's Guide to Mortgage Finance, 1985; author Mortgage Fin. Newsletter, 1984—; author fin. workshop. Mem. Rep. State Ctrl. Com., Calif., 1980—, Bldg. and Industry Assn., Rancho Cucamonga, 1988—, Res Publica Soc., Claremont, Calif., 1986—; donor mem. L.A. World Affairs Coun., 1988—. Claremont McKenna Coll. scholar, 1981-83; recipient Dons D. Lepper Meml. award Exec. Women Internat., 1981, So. Calif. Edison Bus. Competition award, 1979, 81. Mem. Nat. Assn. Realtors, Inland Empire West Bd. Realtors. Office: Boulder Fin Corp 9121 Haven Ave Ste 180 Rancho Cucamonga CA 91730-5453

HORTON, SHIRLEY, mayor. BS in Acctg., San Diego State U. Pres. Grasser/Tate Real Estate Co., Calif.; planning commr. City of Chula Vista, Calif., 1985-91, elected councilwoman, 1991-94, elected mayor, 1994—; past govt. svc. positions include: bd. del. San Diego Assn. Govts.; Met. Transit Devel. Bd. alternate, mem. Otay Valley (Calif.) Regional Park Policy com., mem. San Diego Interagy. Water Quality panel, mem. South County Econ. Devel. Coun., mem. Interagy. Water Task Force, mgm. Gang Issues com., mem. Bayfront subcom., mem. Appropriate Techs. subcom. Mem. San Diego County Assessment Appeals bd., 1982-86, pres. South San Diego Bay Cities Bd. Realtors, 1987, mem. Scripps Meml. Hosp. Cmty. Adv. Bd., 1990-91, mem. South Bay YMCA Support Campaign com., 1990. Mem. Calif. Assn. Realtors (regional v.p. 1989, dir. 1980-90), Chula Vista C. of C. (econ. devel. com. 1984-85). Office: Mayor and Council Office City of Chula Vista 216 4th Ave Chula Vista CA 91910

HORWIN, LEONARD, lawyer; b. Chgo., Jan. 2, 1913; s. Joseph and Jennie (Fuhrmann) H.; m. Ursula Helene Donig, Oct. 15, 1939; children—Noel Samuel, Leonora Marie. LLD cum laude, Yale U., 1936. Bar: Calif. 1936, U.S. Dist. Ct. (cen. dist.) Calif. 1937, U.S. Ct. Appeals (9th cir.) 1939, U.S. Supreme Ct. 1940. Assoc., Lawler, Felix & Hall, 1936-39; ptnr. Hardy & Horwin, Los Angeles, 1939-42; counsel Bd. Econ. Warfare, Washington, 1942-43; mem. program adjustment com. U.S. War Prodn. Bd., 1942-43; attache, legal advisor U.S. Embassy, Madrid, Spain, 1943-47; sole practice, Beverly Hills, Calif., 1948—; dir., lectr. Witkin-Horwin Rev. Course on Calif. Law, 1939-42; judge pro tempore Los Angeles Superior Ct., 1940-42; instr. labor law U. So. Calif., 1939-42. U.S. rep. Allied Control Council for Ger., 1945-47; councilman City of Beverly Hills, 1962-66, mayor, 1964-65; chmn. transp. Los Angeles Goals Council, 1968; bd. dirs. So. Calif. Rapid Transit Dist., 1964-66; chmn. Rent Stabilization Com., Beverly Hills, 1980. Fellow Am. Acad. Matrimonial Lawyers; mem. ABA, State Bar Calif., Order Coif, Balboa Bay Club, Aspen Inst., La Costa Country Club. Author: Insight and Foresight, 1990, Plain Talk, 1931; contbr. articles to profl. jours. Office: 121 S Beverly Dr Beverly Hills CA 90212-3002

HORWITZ, DAVID LARRY, pharmaceuticals company executive, researcher, educator; b. Chgo., July 13, 1942; s. Milton Woodrow and Dorothy (Glass) H.; m. Gloria Jean Madian, June 20, 1965; children: Karen, Laura. AB, Harvard U., 1963; MD, U. Chgo., 1967, PhD, 1968; MBA, Lake Forest Grad. Sch. Mgmt., 1991. Diplomate Am. Bd. Internal Medicine. Resident in internal medicine U. Chgo. Hosp., 1971-72; fellow in endocrinology U. Chgo., 1972-74, asst. prof., 1974-79; assoc. prof. U. Ill., Chgo., 1979-90, clin. prof. medicine medicine, 1990-92; med. dir. Baxter Healthcare Corp., Deerfield, Ill., 1982-91, v.p. med. and profl. affairs, 1991-92; v.p. med. and regulatory affairs SciClone Pharms., San Mateo, Calif., 1992-95, exec. v.p., 1995—. Contbr. articles to profl. jours. Bd. dirs. No. Ill. affiliate Am. Diabetes Assn., 1976-92, pres. 1987-89. Comdr. USNR, 1969-71. Recipient Research and Devel. award Am. Diabetes Assn., 1974-76; Outstanding Young Citizen of Chgo. award Chgo. Jr. C. of C., 1976; Outstanding Young Citizen Ill. award Ill. Jaycees, 1977. Fellow ACP; mem. Endocrine Soc., Am. Diabetes Assn. (chmn. com. on planning and orgn. 1986-88), Am. Assn. Clin. Nutrition. Research in clinical diabetes and insulin physiology. Office: SciClone Pharms 901 Mariners Island Blvd San Mateo CA 94404-1593

HOSACK, KATHLEEN ELIZABETH, counselor, arts consultant, artist; b. Portland, Oreg.; d. Harold Ferdinand and Elizabeth Magdalene (Ramser) Jacobsen; m. Charles Weeks Hosack, June 20, 1973; children: Geoffrey, Cameron. BA, Boise State U., 1974; MA, U. Idaho, 1987, MS, 1996. Lic. profl. counselor, clin. hypnotherapist. Tchr. Lake Hazel Elem., Boise, 1974-77; comm. cons. Shasta Pacific, Portland, 1979-80; pub., editor arts and entertainment guide, Coeur d'Alene, Idaho, 1981-83; dir. Downtown Bus. and Profl. Assn., Coeur d'Alene, 1982-83; coord. Community Concepts, Coeur d'Alene, 1984-85; arts writer, corr. The Spokesman-Review, Spokane, 1989-90; drawing instr. North Idaho Coll. Community Educ., Coeur d'Alene, 1989-92; cons. Idaho Arts Adv. Network, Coeur d'Alene, 1991—; artist in residence Citizens Coun. for the Arts, Coeur d'Alene Pub. Schs., 1988-90. Exhibited in group shows including Western Women's Art Showcase, 1985, 1986, Cheney Cowles Art Mus., 1988, Art on the Green Juried Exhbn. (Holmberg award 1987, Jurors award 1986, 88, 89, Pres. award 1991), Blake Gallery, Seattle, 1990, Inland Artists Invitational Exhbn., Coeur d'Alene, 1990. Pres. Coeur d'Alene Cultural Ctr., 1988-90, mem. adv. bd., 1992—; arts commr. City of Coeur d'Alene, 1989-91; Cultural Ctr. chairperson, Kootenai County Centennial, Coeur d'Alene, 1989-90; bd. dirs. Performing Arts Alliance Com., Citizens Coun. for the Arts. Recipient Upbeat Citizen award Coeur d'Alene C. of C., 1983, Golden "K" award Kiwanis, Coeur d'Alene, 1985, Career Excellence award in Arts and Culture Women's Forum, 1990. Mem. Am. Counseling Assn., Nat. Career Devel. Assn., U. Idaho Grad. Rehab. Assn., Tau Kappa Sigma. Home: 1020 E Mountain Coeur D Alene ID 83814

HOSEK, JAMES ROBERT, economist; b. Evanston, Ill., Aug. 31, 1944; s. Walter Frank and Frances Miriam (Hoffman) H.; m. Susan DeWire, Sept. 10, 1966; children: Katherine, Adrienne, Peter. BA, Cornell U., 1966; MA, U. Chgo., 1970, PhD, 1975. Rsch. analyst Nat. Bur. Econ. Rsch., New Haven, 1970-73; assoc. economist RAND, Santa Monica, Calif., 1973-79, economist, 1979-83, sr. economist, 1983—, dir. def. manpower rsch. ctr., 1981-85, head dept. econs. and stats., 1985-90, corp. rsch. mgr., human capital, 1990-94, human capital and material resource policy, 1994-96; mem. panel NAS, Washington, 1988; mem., chair econ. adv. coun. Calif. Inst. Fed. Policy Rsch., 1994—. Editor RAND Jour. of Econs., 1988—; assoc. editor Abstracts of Working Papers in Econs., 1986—; contbr. articles to profl. jours. Recipient numerous rsch. grants. Fellow Interuniversity Sem. on Armed Forces and Soc.; mem. Am. Econ. Assn., Western Econ. Assn., Phi Eta Sigma.

HOSHMAND, AHMAD REZA, agricultural and resources economist; b. Kabul, Afghanistan, Feb. 2, 1947; came to U.S., 1968; s. Ghulam Reza and Saleha (Azim) H.; m. Lisa Lai Sang Tsoi, July 18, 1973; children: Anthony, Andrea. BS, U. Hawaii, 1971; MS, U. Wis., Platteville, 1972; PhD, U. Md., 1978. Lectr. Calif. State U., Fresno, 1979-80; assoc. prof. Calif. State Poly. U., Pomona, 1980-84, prof., 1985-94, assoc. dean Coll. of Agr., 1985-90; prof. U. Hawaii-West Oahu, Pearl City, 1994—; cons. U.S. Agy. for Internat. Devel., San Jose, Costa Rica, 1981, Yavundee, Cameroon, 1988; cons. Govt. Hong Kong, Kowloon, 1990; dir. Small Bus. Inst., U. Hawaii-West Oahu, 1996—. Author: Statistical Methods for Agricultural Sciences, 1988, Experimental Research Designs, 1994, Statistical Methods for Environmental and Agricultural Sciences, 1997; contbr. articles to profl. jours. Recipient scholarship Am. Field Svc., 1964-65, scholarship East-West Ctr., Honolulu, 1968-71, Meritorious Profl. Promise award for excellence in tchg. Calif. State U., 1989. Mem. Am. Econ. Assn., Am. Agrl. Econ. Assn., Hawaiin Econ. Assn., Western Agrl. Econ. Assn., Phi Beta Delta. Home: 1294-D Moanalualani Ct Honolulu HI 96819 Office: Univ Hawaii West Oahu 96-043 Ala Ike St Pearl City HI 96782-3366

HOSKER, DONALD, materials research technician; b. Boston, June 21, 1961; s. Donald and Carlene Mary (Womack) H. BS in Math., Northeastern U., Boston, 1991, cert. mgmt. and bus. adminstrn., 1993. Lic. real estate sales assoc., Mass. Supr. New Eng. Duct Cleaning Co., Braintree, Mass., 1977-88; sales assoc. Ginino Realtors, Brockton, Mass., 1987-88; sr. materials rsch. technician rsch. and engring. group Morton Internat., Woburn, Mass., 1988-95; materials rsch. technician CVD rsch. dept. Thermo Trex Corp., Waltham, Mass., 1995-96, San Diego, Calif., 1996—. Mem. AAAS, MENSA, N.Y. Acad. Scis. Home: 4060 Huerfano Ave # 347 San Diego CA 92117

HOSKINS, THOMAS RICHARD, JR., corporate securities agent; b. Wichita, Kans., Mar. 21, 1959; s. Thomas Richard and Doris Jewell (Riddle) H. AA of Applied Bus. in Acctg., U. Cin., 1980; BS in Bus. Adminstrn., U. Nev., Reno, 1984. Tax examiner IRS, Covington, Ky., 1979-82; asst. mgr. MGM Grand Hotel and Casino, Reno, 1985-86; sales analyst Internat. Game Technol., Reno, 1987-90; investigative agt. Nev. Gaming Control Bd., Carson City, Nev., 1990-95, corp. securities agent, 1995—. Mem. Nat. Rep. Com. Named Dean's List U. Nev., Reno, 1984. Mem. U. Cin. Alumni Assn. Republican. Office: State of Nevada Gaming Control Board 1150 E William St Carson City NV 89710

HOSLER, LADDIE, editor; b. Allentown, Pa., June 13, 1926; d. Edwin William Cheesbrough and Evelyn (Lilly) Foster; children: Sharon, Lynn, David, Peter. BA, Pa. State U., 1948, BS, 1967, MEd, 1968; MS in Counseling, San Diego State U., 1988. Tchr. fine arts/crafts Bellefonte (Pa.) Jr. High Sch., 1969-71; editor pub. a contact svc. for women "The Wishing Well" (Laddie's Ventures II), San Diego, 1974—. Office: The Wishing Well PO Box 178440 San Diego CA 92177-8440

HOSLEY, EDWARD HOWARD, career development organization executive; b. Oakland, Calif., Nov. 12, 1930; s. Howard Herman and Grace Marguerite (Swim) H.; m. Harriet Esther Howells, Apr. 27, 1958. BA in Geology, U. Calif., Berkeley, 1956; MA in Anthropology, UCLA, 1962, PhD in Anthropology, 1966. Instr. El Camino Coll., Torrance, Calif., 1964-65; asst. prof. Calif. State U., Fullerton, 1965-66, U. Alaska, Fairbanks, 1966-68; assoc. prof. Eastern Oreg. State Coll., LaGrande, 1968-71; prof., assoc. dean Eisenhower Coll., Seneca Falls, N.Y., 1971-78; prof., assoc. v.p. acad. affairs SUNY, Potsdam, 1978-90; pres. Career Devel., Beaverton, Oreg., 1990—. Author: Alaska Natives, 1968, The Kolchan, 1968, Eskimo Prehistory, 1969; contbr. articles to profl. jours. and chpts. in books. With U.S. Army, 1952-54. Research fellow NSF, 1962, NEH, 1968; grantee Nat. Mus. Can., 1966; recipient McConnell Found., 1975. Fellow Am. Anthrop. Assn., Soc. for Applied Anthropology; mem. ACA, Assn. for Psychol. Type, Nat. Assn. Practicing Anthropologists. Episcopalian. Home: 4401 Wagon Wheel Cir Forest Grove OR 97116-3328 Office: Career Devel PO Box 850 Forest Grove OR 97116-0850

HOSSEINIYAR, MANSOUR M., software engineer, financial consultant; b. Tehran, Iran, Jan. 18, 1957; came to U.S., 1976; s. Ali and Maryam Hosseiniyar. AS, Delta Coll., Univ. Ctr., Mich., 1978; BS, Calif. State U., Fresno, 1980; MS, U. So. Calif., L.A., 1984, Engr. in Elec. Enging. Degree, 1988. Cert. Nat. Assn. Realtors, Calif. Assn. Realtors. Asst. prof. Delta Coll., 1976-78, Calif. State U., Fresno, 1979-80; tech. staff, software engr. Versys Corp., Torrance, Calif., 1981-83; rsch. assist. U. So. Calif., 1983-89; tech. staff, software engr. Teledyne Corp., L.A., 1985-88; tech. staff, engr. Rockwell Corp., Canoga Park, Calif., 1989-95; mem. tech. staff, engr. Jet Propulsion Lab., Calif. Inst. Tech., Pasadena, 1995-96, MICROPOLIS Corp., Chatsworth, Calif., 1996—; corp. officer, broker, Equal Financial, Encino, Calif., 1992-97, Capital Financial, Tarzana, Calif., 1990-97. Precinct officer nat. election, Calabasas, Calif., 1996. Mem. IEEE, Nat. Assn. Securities Dealers (cert.), Southland Regional Assn. Realtors. Democrat. Moslem. Home: 24763 Via Del Llano Calabasas CA 91302-3020 Office: MICROPOLIS Corp 21211 Nordhoff St Chatsworth CA 91311

HOSSLER, DAVID JOSEPH, lawyer, law educator; b. Mesa, Ariz., Oct. 18, 1940; s. Carl Joseph and Elizabeth Ruth (Bills) H.; m. Gretchen Anne, Mar. 2, 1945; 1 child, Devon Annagret. BA, U. Ariz., 1969; JD, 1972. Bar: Ariz. 1972, U.S. dist. ct. Ariz. 1972, U.S. Supreme Ct. 1977. Legal intern to chmn. FCC, summer 1971; law clk. to chief justice Ariz. Supreme Ct., 1972-73; chief dep. county atty. Yuma County (Ariz.), 1973-74; ptnr. Hunt, Tallen and Hossler, Yuma, Ariz., 1974—; instr. in law and banking, law and real estate Ariz. Western Coll.; instr. in bus. law, mktg., ethics Webster U; co-chmn. fee arbitration com. Ariz. State Bar, 1990—; instr. agrl. law U. Ariz. Mem. precinct com., Yuma County Rep. Cen. Com., 1974—, vice chmn., 1982; chmn. region II Acad. Decathalon competition, 1989; bd. dirs. Yuma County Ednl. Found., Yuma County Assn. Behavior Health Svcs., also pres., 1981; coach Yuma High Sch. mock ct. team, 1987—; bd. dirs. Friends of U. Med. Ctr. With USN. Recipient Man and Boy award Boys Clubs Am., 1979, Freedoms Found. award Yuma Chpt., 1988, Demolay Legion of Honor, 1991; named Vol. of Yr., Yuma County, 1981-82. Mem. Assn. Trial Lawyers Am., Am. Judicature Soc., Yuma County Bar Assn. (pres. 1975-76), Navy League, VFW, Am. Legion, U. Ariz. Alumni Assn. (nat. bd. dirs., past pres.), Rotary (pres. Yuma club 1987-88, dist. gov. rep. 1989, dist. gov. 1992-93, findings com. 1996, dist. found. chair 1996—, Van Houton award 1996). Editor-in-chief Ariz. Adv., 1971-72. Episcopalian (vestry 1978-82). Home: 2802 S Fern Dr Yuma AZ 85364-7909 Office: Hunt Tallen & Hossler 330 W 24th St Yuma AZ 85364-6455 also: PO Box 2919 Yuma AZ 85366

HOST, LAWRENCE A., conservation biologist; b. Chgo., 1953. BS, U. Mass., 1982; MS, Wash. State U., 1988. Wildlife biologist Bur. Land Mgmt., Winnemucca, Nev., 1989-93, Fish and Wildlife Svc., Sacramento, 1993—. With USN, 1975-79. Office: US Fish and wildlife Svc 3310 El Camino Ave #130 Sacramento CA 95821-6340

HOSTETLER, KARL YODER, internist, endocrinologist, educator; b. Goshen, Ind., Nov. 17, 1939; s. Carl Milton and Etta LaVerne (Yoder) H.; m. Margaretha Steur, Dec. 17, 1971; children: Saskia Emma, Kirsten Cornelia, Carl Martijn. BS in Chemistry, DePauw U., 1961; MD, Western Res. U., 1965. Diplomate Am. Bd. Internal Medicine, Am. Bd. Endocrinology and Metabolism. Intern, resident in medicine Univ. Hosp. Cleve., 1965-69; fellow endocrinology Cleve. Clinic Found., 1969-70; postdoctoral fellow, lipid chemistry U. Utrecht, The Netherlands, 1970-73; asst. prof. medicine U. Calif., San Diego, 1973-79, assoc. prof. medicine, 1979-82, prof. medicine, 1982—; dir., sr. v.p. Vical Inc., San Diego, 1987-92; bd. dirs. Triangle Pharms., Durham, N.C. Assoc. editor: Jour. of Clin. Investigation, 1993-97; contbr. numerous articles to scholarly and profl. jours. Pres. San Diego County chpt. Am. Diabetes Assn., 1982-83. Recipient fellowship John Simon Guggenheim Found., 1980-81, Japan Soc. for Promotion of Sci., Tokyo, 1986. Mem. Am. Soc. Clin. Investigation, Am. Soc. Biochemistry and Molecular Biology, Western Soc. Clin. Investigation, Western Assn. Physicians, Am. Soc. Microbiology, Internat. Soc. Antiviral Rsch. Office: U Calif San Diego Dept Medicine 0676 La Jolla CA 92093

HOSTLER, CHARLES WARREN, international affairs consultant; b. Chgo., Dec. 12, 1919; s. Sidney Marvin and Catherine (Marshall) H.; 1 son, Charles Warren, Jr. B.A., U. Calif. at Los Angeles, 1942; M.A., Am. U., Beirut, Lebanon, 1955, Georgetown U., 1950; Ph.D., Georgetown U., 1956. Commd. 2d lt. U.S. Air Force, 1942, advanced through grades to col., 1963; ret., 1963; dir. internat. ops. McDonnell Douglas Corp., Middle East, N.Africa, Beirut, 1965-67; mgr. internat. ops. McDonnell Douglas Corp., Paris, 1963-65; mgr. internat. mktg., missiles and space McDonnell Douglas Corp., 1967-69; pres. Hostler Investment Co., Newport Beach, Calif., 1969-74; chmn. bd. Irvine (Calif.) Nat. Bank, 1972-74; dir. Wynn's Internat., Inc., Fullerton, Calif., 1971-74; dep. asst. sec. for internat. commerce, dir. Bur. Internat. Commerce, U.S. Dept. Commerce, Washington, 1974-76; regional v.p. Mid-East and Africa, E-Systems Inc., Cairo, Egypt, 1976-77; pres. Pacific SW Capital Corp., San Diego, 1977-89; ambassador U.S. Govt., Bahrain, 1989-93; hon. consul gen. State of Bahrain, 1993—; adj. prof. Sch. Internat. Svc., Am. U., Washington, 1955-63; pres. San Diego Consular Corps. Author: Turkism and the Soviets, 1957, The Turks of Central Asia, 1993; contbr. articles to econ., comml. and mil. jours. Chmn. Calif. Contractors State Lic. Bd., 1973-79, San Diego County Local Agy. Formation Commn., 1979-89; chmn. Calif. State Park and Recreation Commn., 1983-89; pres. San Diego Consular Corps, 1996—. Decorated Legion of Merit; recipient Fgn. Affairs award for pub. svc. U.S. State Dept. Mem. Am. Polit. Sci. Assn., Am. Ordnance Assn., Middle East Inst. (bd. govs. 1962-80, 93—). Office: # 302 1101 First St Coronado CA 92118-1474

HOTCHKISS, VIVIAN EVELYN, employment agency executive; b. Fulda, Germany, May 5, 1956; came to U.S., 1957; d. Fred Roy and Rosemary Krug. Student, Pierce Coll., 1974-75, Calif. State U., Northridge, 1976, UCLA, 1991—. Adminstrv. sec. Taurus Fin. Corp., Hollywood, Calif., 1976-79; adminstrv. asst. Peoples Fin. Corp., Encino, Calif., 1979-81, Thor Employment Agy., L.A., 1981-83, Creative Capital Corp., L.A., 1983—; owner, pres. Bus. Systems Staffing & Assocs., L.A., 1985—; exec. dir. Edn., Counseling & Placement Program, L.A., 1990—. Author: (newsletter) The Leader; contbr. articles to newspaper, 1996-97. Mem. Execs. Assn. L.A. (membership dir. 1989-96, Member of Yr. 1990). Office: Bus Sys Staffing & Assocs Inc 10680 W Pico Blvd Ste 210 Los Angeles CA 90064-2223

HOTZ, HENRY PALMER, physicist; b. Fayetteville, Ark., Oct. 17, 1925; s. Henry Gustav and Stella (Palmer) H.; m. Marie Brase, Aug. 22, 1952; children: Henry Brase, Mary Palmer, Martha Marie. B.S., U. Ark., 1948; Ph.D., Washington U., St. Louis, 1953. Asst. prof. physics Auburn U., Ala., 1953-58, Okla. State U., Stillwater, 1958-64; assoc. prof. Marietta Coll., Ohio, 1964-66; physicist, scientist-in-residence U.S. Naval Radiol. Def. Lab., San Francisco, 1966-67; assoc. prof. U. Mo., Rolla, 1967-71; physicist Qanta Metrix div. Finnigan Corp., Sunnyvale, Calif., 1971-74; sr. scientist Nuclear Equipment Corp., San Carlos, Calif., 1974-79, Envirotech Measurement Systems, Palo Alto, Calif., 1979-82, Dohrmann div. Xertex Corp., Santa Clara, Calif., 1982-86; sr. scientist Rosemount Analytical Div. Dohrmann, 1983-91; cons. Burlingame, Calif., 1991—; cons. USAF, 1958-62; mem. lectr. selection com. for Hartman Hotz Lectrs. in law, liberal arts U. Ark. Served with USNR, 1944-46. Mem. Am. Phys. Soc., Am. Assn. Physics Tchrs., AAAS, Phi Beta Kappa, Sigma Xi, Sigma Pi Sigma, Pi Mu Epsilon, Sigma Nu. Methodist. Lodge: Masons. Home: 290 Stilt Ct Foster City CA 94404-1323 Office: Hotz Assocs 525 Almer Rd Apt 201 Burlingame CA 94010-3955

HOTZ, ROBERT LEE, science writer, editor; b. Hartford, Conn., Mar. 7, 1950; s. Robert B. and Joan (Willison) H.; m. Jennifer Hall Arlen, May 21, 1988; children: Michael Arlen, Robert Arlen. BA magna cum laude, Tufts U., 1973, MA, 1973. Tech. editor Intermetrics, Inc., Cambridge, Mass., 1973-76; reporter The News-Virginian, Waynesboro, 1976-79, The Pitts. Press, 1979-84; sci. writer The Atlanta Jour.-Constn., 1984-90, projects editor, 1991-93; sci. editor, 1993; sci. writer The L.A. (Calif.) Times, 1993—; participant NSF Antarctica Expeditions, 1987, 95. Author: Designs on Life: Exploring the New Frontiers of Human Fertility, 1991; contbr. articles to profl. publs. Recipient AAAS-Westinghouse award, 1977, 88, Ga. Best Reporting award AP, 1986, Metro Staff Pulitzer Prize spot news, 1995, Walter Sullivan award Am. Geophys. Soc., 1995, Journalism award ASCE, 1995. Mem. Nat. Assn. Sci. Writers, Soc. Profl. Journalists (Ray Sprigle Meml. award 1982, 84), Nat. Press Club. Episcopalian. Home: 236 21st St Santa Monica CA 90402-2416 Office: The LA Times Times Mirror Sq Los Angeles CA 90012

HOUCHIN, KENNETH WAYNE, ophthalmologist, neuro-opthalmologist, educator; b. Phoenix, Apr. 19, 1958; s. Merle Cleo and Mildred Elizabeth (Knittle) H. BA with highest honors, Union Coll., 1981; MD, Loma Linda U., 1985. Intern in internal medicine Loma Linda (Calif.) U. Med. Ctr., 1985-86, resident in neurology, 1986-89, resident in ophthalmology, 1990-93; fellow in neuro-ophthalmology U. Minn., Mpls., 1989-90; instr., neuro-ophthalmologist Loma Linda U. Sch. Medicine, 1993—; gen. ophthalmologist Inland Eye Inst., Colton, Calif., 1993—; lectr., presenter in field; clk. in third-world ophthalmology Maluti Adventist Hosp., Lesotho, Africa. Contbr. articles to profl. publs., photographs to NBC Today Show, 1979-80, book Kansas in Color, 1982, also greeting cards and calendar. Mem. AMA, Am. Acad. Neurology, Am. Acad. Ophthalmology (subcom. internat. ophthalmology com. 1991-93), Assn. for Rsch. in Vision and Ophthalmology, Calif. Med. Assn., N.Am. Neuro-Ophthalmology Soc., San Bernardino County Med. Soc., (bd. dir., 1996—), Tri-County Eye Soc. (pres. Riverside, San Bernardino, Ea. L.A. Counties 1995, v.p. 1996). Office: Loma Linda U Inland Eye Inst FMO # 1800 11370 Anderson St Loma Linda CA 92354

HOUGH, J. MARIE, real estate company official; b. Trenton, N.J., Oct. 15, 1940; d. Michael J. and Evelyn M. (Klink) Mazur; m. Gary T.M. Hough, Apr. 7, 1990. Degree in bus. adminstrn., Rider Bus. Coll., 1964; AA, L.A. City Coll., 1967; B of Edn., Cin. Coll., 1970; MEd, Azusa Pacific U., 1982. Cert. tchr., Calif. Vocat. tchr. Papua New Guinea Inst., 1972-80, adminstrv. asst. Princeton (N.J.) U., 1980-82; bus. instr. Criss Coll., Anaheim, Calif., 1983-87; instr. office occupations Regional Occupational Program, Santa Ana, Calif., 1987-90; bus. instr. Somos Hermandas Unidas, Anaheim, 1991-92; office tech. instr. United Cambodian Community Vocat. Ctr., Long Beach, Calif., 1992-93; bus. mgr. Hough Enterprises, San Clemente, Calif., 1993-95; realtor First Team Real Estate, Mission Viejo, Calif., 1995, The Prudential Calif. Realty, Mission Viejo, 1995-96; Prudential-Jon Douglas Realty Co., Laguna Niguel, Calif., 1996—. Ind. rep. Nat. Telephone and Comms., Inc., Irvine, 1996—. Mem. Am. Vocat. Assn. Home: 26002 View Point Dr E Capo Beach CA 92624-1224 Office: Prudential-Jon Douglas Realty Co 25461 Rancho Niguel Rd Laguna Niguel CA 92677

HOUGH, MICHAEL JAMES, sculptor, educator; b. Anaheim, Calif., Jan. 20, 1960; s. Richard Guy Hough and Barbara Jean (Dierberger) Moody; m. Ronelle Bingham, July 28, 1984; m. Tracy Lee Watts, Mar. 23, 1991; children: Timothy Michael Enke, Alden Richard Thomas. BA in Art, Calif. State U., Sacramento, 1983, MA in Art, 1989; MFA in Ceramic Sculpture, RISD, 1993. Graphic designer J.K. Bonum, Sacramento, Calif., 1980-86; mem. TV prodn. staff Sta. KVIE Channel 6, Sacramento, Calif., 1983-89; art tchr. El Sereno H.S., Fair Oaks, Calif., 1987-90; ceramics instr. RISD, Providence, 1991-93; art tchr. Snake River Correctional Facilities, Ontario, Oreg., 1993-96, Boise (Idaho) State U., 1994—, Treasure Valley C.C., Ontario, 1994—; ceramic artist Weiser (Idaho) Sculpture Works, 1983—; vis. artist Foresthill and Auburn Union Sch. Dists., Calif., 1984-91; mural painter Taylor Studios, Sacramento, South Lake Tahoe, and Carson City, Nev., 1988—; presenter Raku demonstrations Sacramento Open Studio Tours, 1989, 90; fin. dir., mem. 750 Gallery, Sacramento, 1987-89; dir. Witt Gallery, Calif. State U., Sacramento, 1985-86; kiln rm. mgr. RISD, 1991-93. One-man shows include 750 Gallery, Sacramento, 1987, ArtWorks Gallery, Fair Oaks, Calif., 1987, 89, Michael Himovitz Gallery, Sacramento, 1990, 93, 95, 96, Himovitz Pavillions, Sacramento, 1991, Habatat/Shaw Gallery, Farmington Hills, Mich., 1994, Gallery at Glendeven, Mendocino, Calif., 1994; group shows include Thesis Exhbn. RISD Roitman Gallery, Providence, Rhode Island, Grad. Exbhn., 1993, Habatat/Shaw Gallery, Mich., 1993, Farrell Collection, Washington, 1993, Holmes Fine Art Gallery, San Jose, Calif., 1993, Cafe au Clay Cup Invitational Lincoln Arts, Calif., 1994, Contemporary Crafts Gallery, Portland, 1994, The Potters Ctr., Boise, 1994, Michael Himovitz Gallery, 1994, Galos Fine Art, Idaho, 1995, San Bernardino Mus. Art, 1997, Coos Art Mus., Oreg., 1997; represented in permanent collections at Faviana Olivier, Boston, Pac-Tel Corp., Calif., Embassy Suites Hotel, South Lake Tahoe, Calif., Sacramento First Nat. Bank, Tower Corp., Sacramento, Hewlett Packard Co., Roseville, Calif.; author: (books) Raku Pottery, 1991, Raku: A Practical Approach, 1991; contbr articles to profl. jours. Invitational-promotion fundraiser Sta. KXJZ, Sacramento, 1991. Home and Studio: 527 E Court St Weiser ID 83672-2214

HOUGHTON, ROBERT CHARLES, secondary education educator; b. Dover, N.H., Apr. 12, 1958; s. Raymond David and Barbara Jean (Lyle) H. Student, USCG Acad., New London, Conn., 1976-77; BA with honors, U. Calif., Riverside, 1987, postgrad., 1987-89. Teaching credential, Calif. Various teaching positions, 1977-80; pharmacy technician Anaheim (Calif.) Meml./Brea (Calif.) Cmty., 1980-85; teaching asst. U. Calif., Riverside, 1988-90; instr. Mt. San Jacinto (Calif.) Coll., 1989-90; tchr. Desert Sands Unified, Indio, Calif., 1990—; counselor Chem. Awareness Network, Indio, Calif., 1990—; computer cons. Desert Sands Unified Sch. Dist., Indio, 1994—; resident tchr. Calif. State U., San Bernardino, 1994-95; asst. tour dir. Lakeland Tours, Washington, 1991-95. Mem. NEA, Nat. Coun. Social Studies, Nat. Geographic Soc., Calif. Tchrs. Assn., Nat. Trust Historic Preservation, Civil War Trust. Republican. Home: 72600 Fred Waring Dr Apt 407 Palm Desert CA 92260-5223 Office: 81195 Miles Ave Indio CA 92201-2807

HOUPIS, HARRY LOUIS FRANCIS, research physicist; b. Johnson City, N.Y., Jan. 18, 1954; s. Louis Harry and Annamarie Houpis.; m. Carole Lynn Turner, Jan. 28, 1984; children: Demetrius Vesalius, Carissa Selena. BS in Math., MIT, 1976, BS in Physics, 1976; MS in Physics, U. Calif. San Diego, La Jolla, 1978, PhD in Physics, 1981. Asst. rsch. physicist U. Calif. San Diego, La Jolla, 1981-87; vis. rsch. physicist Max Planck Inst. for Aeronomie, Katlenburg-Lindau, Fed. Republic Germany, 1985, Cen. Rsch. Inst. for Physics, Budapest, Hungary, 1986, Supercomputer Computations Rsch. Inst. Fla. State U., Tallahassee, 1986-87; vis. and assoc. rsch. physicist Space Physics Rsch. Lab. U Mich., Ann Arbor, 1987-88; tech. staff Mission Rsch. Corp., Monterey, Calif., 1988-90; dir. we. region Ctr. for Remote Sensing, Missoula, Mont., 1990-94; pres. EnviroSens, Inc., Missoula, Mont., 1995—; lectr. in physics Hartnell C.C., Salinas, Calif., 1989-90; proposal refree NASA, NSF, Washington, 1985—; manuscript referee Jour. Geophys. Rsch. and Icarus, 1981-92. Author: The Physics of Comets; contbr. numerous articles to profl. jours. Pub. lectr. San Diego Speakers Bur., 1979-86. Fulbright sr. scholarship Coun. for Internat. Exch. of Scholars, 1985-86; Max Planck Soc. fellowship, Max Planck Inst., 1983, 85. Mem. Am. Geophys. Union, Am. Phys. Soc. Home: 3509 Norman Dr Missoula MT 59804-3001 Office: EnviroSens Inc 415 N Higgins Ave Ste 124 Missoula MT 59802-4522

HOURIZADEH, ARASH, espresso manufacturing company executive, physician; b. Hackensack, N.J., May 29, 1972; s. Richard and Vida (Monify) H. BS, UCLA, 1994, BA, 1994; postgrad., U. Calif., San Diego, 1994—. Archtl. fabricator Perspective Models, Van Nuys, Calif., 1991-92; realtor Jon Douglas Co., Encino, Calif., 1990-94; v.p. Astra Mfg. Co., Canoga Park, Calif., 1993—; rschr. depts. immunology and econs. UCLA, 1992-94; mem. bioethics com. U. Calif. San Diego Med. Ctr., 1994—. Mng. editor Jour. Molecular Investigations, 1992-94, Cancer Update, 1992-94. Outreach dir. Career Network, L.A., 1992; mem. mktg. and promotions com. UCLA Mardi Gras, 1991-93. UCLA Alumni scholar, 1990, Alumni Achievement award, 1994. Mem. UCLA Alumni Assn., UCLA Alumni Scholars, Phi Beta Kappa, Phi Eta Sigma. Home: 15221 Antelo Pl Los Angeles CA 90077-1602

HOUSE, DAVID L., electronics components company executive; b. 1943. With Raytheon, 1965-69, Honeywell, 1969-72, Microdata, 1972-74; v.p., gen. mgr. Intel Corp., 1974-96; chmn., pres., CEO Bay Network Computers, Santa Clara, 1996; now sr. v.p. Intel Corp. address: PO Box 58185 Santa Clara CA 95052*

HOUSE, EDWARD BRILEY, JR., librarian; b. Newport News, Va., June 21, 1948; s. Edward Briley and Susie Marie (Davenport) H.; children: Sarah Elizabeth, Caitlin Marie. AA in Social Scis., Canal Zone Coll., 1968; BS in Secondary Edn., U. Nebr., 1970; MLS, U. Wash., 1983. Owner Ed House Housepainting, Central Point, Oreg., 1975-81; dir. G.H. and L.E. Brown Pub. Libr., Washington, N.C., 1983-85; supervising libr. Albany (Oreg.) Pub. Libr., 1985-90, dir., 1990—. Mem. budget com. Linn-Benton Cmty. Coll., Albany, 1992-94, chair, 1995-97; mem. bd. edn. Linn Benton C.C., 1995—. Mem. ALA, Oreg. Libr. Assn. (v.p./pres. elect 1995-96, pres. 1996-97, chair pub. libr. divsn. 1993-94), Greater Albany Rotary Club (sec. 1990-94). Home: 2887 44th Ave SE Albany OR 97321 Office: Albany Pub Libr 1390 Waverly Dr SE Albany OR 97321-6945

HOUSE, MARY DONNA, dean; b. Decatur, Ill., Jan. 2, 1942; d. Donald Edward and Mary Catherine (Doolin) Brown; m. Ernest R. House, Feb. 1, 1964; children: Kristin Diane, Colby Patton. RN, Decatur Mason County Sch. Nsg., 1962; BS in Occupl./Practical Arts, U. Ill., 1979, MS in Occupl./Practical Arts, 1982; PhD in Vocat. Adminstrn., Colo. State U., 1990. RN, Colo., Ill.; vocat. tchg. cert. Colo. C.C. and Occupl. Edn. Bd. RN Alton (Ill.) State Mental Hosp., 1962-64; head nurse Carle Clinic, Urbana, Ill., 1964-66; instr. health occupations Urbana (Ill.) Adult Edn., 1978-85; staff devel. dir. Urbana (Ill.) Americana, 1983-85; instr. health occupations Emily Griffith Opportunity Sch., Denver, 1985-95, instrnl. dean health occupations, 1995—; mem. Work Force Initiative, Piton Found., Denver, 1995—. Contbr. articles to profl. jours. Mem. Am. Vocat. Assn. (program chair 1994-95), Colo. Vocat. Assn. (pres.-elect 1991-92, pres. 1992-93, past-pres. 1993-94, Outstanding Svc. award 1994, pres. health occupations divsn. 1988-90), Kappa Delta Pi, Phi Delta Kappa. Home: 856 F Walnut St Boulder CO 80302

HOUSE-HENDRICK, KAREN SUE, nursing consultant; b. San Francisco, July 16, 1958; d. Mathas Dean and Marilyn Frances (Weigand) House. Casa Loma Coll., 1985; AS in Nursing, SUNY at Albany, 1987. Psychiat. charge nurse Woodview Calabasas (Calif.) Hosp., 1985-87, Treatment Ctrs. Am., Van Nuys, Calif., 1987-88; cons., RN Valley Village Devel. Ctr., Reseda, Calif., 1988; plastic surg. nurse George Sanders, M.D., Encino, Calif., 1986—; nurse New Image Found., 1989—, Mid Valley Youth Ctr., 1991—; dir. nursing Encino Surgicenter (Sanders), 1992—; dir. nursing Devel. Tng. Svcs. for Devel. Disabled, 1988—; nurse cons. New Horizons for Developmentally Disabled, 1993. Instr., vol. ARC. Recipient Simi Valley Free Clinic Scholarship. Mem. Encino C. of C. Home: 29748 Saguaro St Santa Clarita CA 91384-3567 Office: 16633 Ventura Blvd Ste 110 Encino CA 91436-1834

HOUSEWORTH, DEREK EUGENE, software test engineer; b. Nacodoches, Tex., Jan. 25, 1969; s. Donald Eugene and Vera Jean (Draper) H. BS in Bus. with high honors, Mont. State U., 1992. Systems software analyst Applied Systems Tech., Kalispell, Mont., 1988-89; computer operator II Mont. State U., Bozeman, 1990; software tng. cons. Bozeman, 1990-92; lead software test engr. Microsoft Corp., Redmond, Wash., 1992—. Named SBI Case of Yr., Undergrad., U.S. SBA, Washington, 1993. Mem. Phi Kappa Phi, Beta Gamma Sigma. Office: Microsoft Corp One Microsoft Way Redmond WA 98052

HOUSEWORTH, LAURA JENNINGS, lawyer; b. Kansas City, Kans., Mar. 22, 1927; d. Frank Harvey and Lucile (Pollock) Jennings; m. Richard Court Houseworth, Nov. 1, 1952; children: Louise, Lucile, Court II. BA magna cum laude, Lake Forest Coll., 1949; MEd, U. Mo., 1951; JD, Ariz. State U., 1974. Bar: Ariz. 1975, D.C. 1989. Nat. rep. Chi Omega, Cin., 1949-50; asst. dean women U. Kans., Lawrence, 1951-52; dep. county atty. Maricopa County, Phoenix, 1975-88, juvenile div., 1979—, sr. trial atty., asst. supr. juvenile div., 1985—, extradition atty., 1987—, grand jury, 1987—; lectr. Nat. Family Support Assn., San Diego, 1977; arbitrator Superior Ct., 1986; judge pro tem Ariz. Ct. Appeals, 1986. Founding bd., pres. Vol. Bur., Tucson, 1969; founding bd. Girl's Club Tucson, 1970; founding bd., 1st v.p. Crisis Nursery, Phoenix, 1978; exec. bd. United Way, Legal Aid, Family Svc.; nat. trustee Lake Forest Coll., 1992—. Mem. ABA, ATLA, Maricopa County Bar Assn., Ariz. Women's Lawyers Assn., Ariz. Acad. Republican. Episcopalian. Club: Jr. League Phoenix. Home: Colonia Miramonte # 83 Paradise Valley AZ 85253

HOUSEWORTH, RICHARD COURT, banker; b. Harveyville, Kans., Jan. 18, 1928; s. Court Henry and Mabel (Lynch) H.; m. Laura Louise Jennings, Nov. 1, 1952; children: Louise, Lucile, Court. B.S., U. Kans., 1950. Mgmt. trainee Lawrence Nat. Bank, Kans., 1951-52; pres. 1st Nat. Bank, Harveyville, 1952-55; exec. v.p. Ariz. Bank, Phoenix, 1955-87, cons., 1987-88; dir. Export-Import Bank of the US, Washington, 1988-91; alt. U.S. exec. dir. The Inter-American Devel. Bank, Washington, 1991-93; supt. of banks, Banking Dept. State of Ariz., 1993—. Past pres. Better Bus. Bur., Tucson; past chmn. bd. Pacific Coast Banking Sch. U. Wash.; past pres. Barrow Neurol. Inst. of St. Joseph's Hosp.; past chmn. Valley of the Sun Visitors and Conv. Bur. Served with U.S. Army, 1946-48. Recipient 1st Disting. Service award Scottsdale Jaycees, 1962. Mem. Ariz. C. of C. (1st pres., dir.), Tucson C. of C. (past pres.), Am. Inst. Banking (past pres. Maricopa chpt.), Ariz. Bankers Assn. (past pres.), Urban League of Phoenix (past chmn.), Paradise Valley Club, Met. Club, Phi Delta Theta. Republican. Episcopalian. Home: 83 Colonia Miramonte Paradise Vly AZ 85253 Office: Supt of Banks 2910 N 44th St Ste 310 Phoenix AZ 85018-7256

HOUSEWORTH, STEVEN MICHAEL, court counselor; b. St. Cloud, Minn., Mar. 19, 1951; s. John Leman Houseworth and Lovina Francis (Sand) Bystrom; children: Sherry Lynn, Lisa Lynn, Bradley Steven. BS, Portland State U., 1974; postgrad., Lewis and Clark Coll., 1997—. Ct. counselor Clackamas County Juvenile Ctr., Oregon City, Oreg., 1975—; exec. dir. Theft Talk Counseling Svc., Portland, Oreg., 1983—; instr. Clackamas C.C., Oregon City, 1983-95; spl. commn. instr. Portland C.C., 1990—; dep. sheriff Clackamas County Sheriff, Oregon City, 1983—. Author: (manual) Teacher's Manual-Stealing, 1989. Mem. Toastmasters, Canby, Oreg., 1984-92; sustaining mem. Rep. Nat. Com., Washington, 1994. Mem. APA (affiliate). Republican. Office: Theft Talk Counseling Svcs 3530 SE 52nd Ave Portland OR 97206-2912

HOUSTON, ELIZABETH REECE MANASCO, correctional education consultant; b. Birmingham, Ala., June 19, 1935; d. Reuben Cleveland and Beulah Elizabeth (Reece) Manasco; m. Joseph Brantley Houston; 1 child, Joseph Brantley Houston III. BS, U. Tex., 1956; MEd, Boston Coll., 1969. Cert. elem. tchr., Calif., cert. spl. edn. tchr., Calif., cert. community coll. instr., Calif. Tchr., elem. Ridgefield (Conn.) Schs., 1962-63; staff, spl. edn. Sudbury (Mass.) Schs., 1965-68; staff intern Wayland (Mass.) High Sch., 1972; tchr., home bound Northampton (Mass.) Schs., 1972-73; program dir. Jack Douglas Ctr., San Jose, Calif., 1974-76; tchr. specialist spl. edn., coord. classroom svcs., dir. alternative schs. Santa Clara County Office Edn., San Jose, Calif., 1976-94; instr. San Jose State U., 1980-87, U. Calif., Santa Cruz, 1982-85, Santa Clara U., 1991—; cons. Houston Rsch. Assocs., Saratoga, Calif., 1981—. Author: (manual) Behavior Management for School Bus Drivers, 1980, Classroom Management, 1984, Synergistic Learning, 1988, Learning Disabilities in Psychology for Correctional Education, 1992. Recipient President's award Soc. Photo-Optical Instrumentation Engrs., 1979, Classroom Mgmt. Program award Sch. Bds. Assn., 1984, Svc. to Youth award, Juvenile Ct. Sch. Adminstrs. of Calif., 1989, 90, 91, 92; grantee Santa Clara County Office Edn. Tchr. Advisor Program U.S. Sec. Edn., 1983-84. Home: 12150 Country Squire Ln Saratoga CA 95070-3444

HOUSTON, JAMES RUSSELL, retired minister; b. Gloversville, N.Y., Oct. 15, 1922; s. Cyril Wyshart and Anna Belle (Wilson) H.; m. Shirley Joan Walters, July 29, 1952; children: Jeffrey, Shawn, Kurt, Kim, Traci. BA, Ky. Christian Coll., 1945, Butler U., 1947; MDiv, Christian Theol. Sem., 1957. Ordained minister Christian Ch. (Disciples of Christ), Aug. 12, 1945. Pastor First Christian Ch., Cayuga, Ind., 1948-54, Park Christian Ch., Dennison, Ohio, 1954-60, Bethany Christian Ch., Evansville, Ind., 1960-64; pastor Ctrl. Christian Ch., Pocatello, Idaho, 1964-86, ret. min. emeritus, 1987—; morning devotions pastor KSEI Radio, Pocatello, 1966-81; asst. chaplain VA, Pocatello, 1994—; bd. dirs. N.W. Region Christian Ch., Beaverton, Oreg., 1970-75. Chaplain Greater Cleve. BSA Res., Clendening, Ohio, 1957-59; rep. ecumenical ministery Idaho State U., Pocatello, 1964-68; pres. Pocatello Ministerial Assn., 1966-67, 69-70; bd. dirs. Idaho-Oreg. Sight Conservation Found., Boise, 1965, ARC, Pocatello, 1970-77; chaplain CAP, Pocatello, 1968-78; instnl. rev. rep. Bannock Regional Med. Ctr., Pocatello, 1990-95, Pocatello Regional Med. Ctr, 1990-95. Named Lion of Yr., Lions Club Internat., 1963, Lifetime Hon. Tail Twister, Pocatello Lions Club, 1987; recipient Svc. award Bannock Regional Med. Ctr., 1986. Home: 1771 N Honeysuckle Ln Inkom ID 83245

HOUSTON, JANE HUNT, retired educator; b. Upper Montclair, N.J., Dec. 22, 1919; d. MacLean and Mary Hunt (Young) H. BA, Duke U., 1941; MEd, U. Wyo., 1960. Cert. tchr., Wyo. Field worker Glendale (Calif.) coun. Girl Scouts U.S., 1941-45; exec. dir. Sacramento coun. Girl Scouts U.S., 1945-46, Cheyenne (Wyo.) coun. Girl Scouts U.S., 1946-56; tchr. Laramie County Sch. Dist. # 1, Cheyenne, 1956-79; ret., 1979. Co-author: Centennial, Wyoming 1876-1976-the Real Centennial. Bd. dirs. Carbon Power and Light Inc., Saratoga, Wyo., 1983—, Centennial Water and Sewer Dist., 1988—. Mem. LWV, Centennial Valley Hist. Assn. (sec. 1975—), Wyo. State Hist. Soc. (charter), Laramie County Ret. Tchrs. (com. chmn. 1980-95). Republican. Episcopalian. Office: Centennial Valley Hist Soc PO Box 200 Centennial WY 82055

HOUSTON, JOHN ALBERT, political science educator; b. Spokane, Dec. 24, 1914; s. John Alexander and Ethel (Robinson) H.; m. Marjorie Anne Robinson, Aug. 14, 1939 (dec. Sept. 1968); children: Alexandra Louise (Mrs. Lee Benham), John Alexander II (dec. Aug. 1979), Ann Celeste; m. Pollyanna Turner, Nov. 1, 1969. A.B. in Econs, Stanford, 1936, M.A. in Internat. Relations, 1947; Ph.D. in polit. sci, U. Mich., 1951. Ins. broker Johnson & Higgins, San Francisco, 1936-37; case aide Calif. Relief Adminstrn., 1938-40; asst., then asso. prof. polit. sci. U. Miss., 1949-54; faculty Knox Coll., Galesburg, Ill., 1954—; prof. polit. sci. Knox Coll., 1957-80, prof. emeritus, 1980—, Philip Sydney Post disting. prof., 1961-80; sec.-treas. Midwest Collegiate Athletic Conf., 1961-67. Author: Latin America in the United Nations, 1956, Book; rev. editor: Midwest Jour. Polit. Sci, 1962-65. Mem. Galesburg Planning Commn., 1956-57. Served to lt. comdr. USNR, 1941-45. Social Sci. Research Council fellow, 1956. Mem. Am. Polit. Sci. Assn., Midwest Conf. Polit. Scientists, Omicron Delta Kappa, Pi Sigma Alpha, Scabbard and Blade, Sigma Alpha Epsilon. Home: 565 Henley Way Ashland OR 97520-3119

HOUTSMA, PETER C., lawyer; b. Denver, 1951. BA in Polit. Sci. and Econs. magna cum laude, U. Colo., 1973; JD magna cum laude, Cornell U., 1976. Bar: Colo. 1976. Mem. Holland & Hart, Denver. Mem. Am. Arbitration Assn. (panel arbitrators), Order of Coif, Phi Beta Kappa. Office: Holland & Hart PO Box 8749 555 17th St Ste 3200 Denver CO 80201

HOUX, MARY ANNE, investments executive; b. Kansas City, Mo., Aug. 16, 1933; d. Rial Richardson Oglevie and Geraldine Marie (McHale) Oglevie; m. Phillip Clark Houx, May 12, 1962 (dec. Dec. 1974); 1 child, Clark Oglevie. BS in Edn., U. Kans., 1954. Tchr. Kirkwood (Mo.) Pub. Schs., 1954-55, Kansas City (Kans.) Pub. Schs., 1955-57; asst. to v.p. Woolf Bros., Kansas City, Mo., 1957-59; Midwest dir. C.A.R.E., Inc., Kansas City, 1959-62; legal sec. Phillip C. Houx, Chico, Calif., 1962-74; owner Mary Anne Houx Investments, Chico, 1974—. Trustee Chico Unified Sch. Dist. Bd., 1977-90; coun. person City of Chico, 1990-91; 3rd dist. supr. County of Butte, Calif., 1991—. Mem. Calif. Sch. Bds. Assn. (pres. 1987-88), Greater Chico C. of C. (Athena award 1993). Republican. Roman Catholic. Office: PO Box 1087 Chico CA 95927-1087

HOVEY, LESLIE MORRIS, plastic surgeon, educator; b. Anaheim, Calif., Aug. 6, 1936; s. Morris and Georgia M. (Guss) H.; m. Loretta (Szluk) Hovey, June 8, 1963; children: Kevin A., Christopher A., Jason D., Justin D. BA in Physiology, U. Calif., Berkeley, 1959; MD, George Washington U., 1963. Diplomate Am. Bd. Surgery, Am. Bd. Plastic Surgery. Intern Tripler Army Med. Ctr., Hawaii, 1963-64, surgery resident, 1964-68; commdg. officer 43rd Surgical Hosp., Korea, 1968-69; fellow head & neck surgery Walte Reed Army Med. Ctr., Washington, 1969-70; resident plastic surgery U. Miami Sch. of Medicine, Fla., 1971-72; plastic surgeon U.S. Army, 1972-76; pvt. practice San Francisco, 1977-87; clinical assoc. prof. plastic surgery Stanford U., Palo Alto, Calif., 1987—; chief of staff St. Francis Med. Hosp., San Francisco, 1985-87; bd. dirs. Plastic Surgery Ednl. Found., Chgo., 1986-92. Mem. of surgical teams to fgn. countries Reconstructive Surgery Found., 1977—. U.S. Army Res. Fellow ACS; mem. Am. Soc. Plastic & Reconstructive Surgery, Am. Burn Assn., Calif. Soc. Plastic Surgery, Soc. Head & Neck Surgeons, Santa Clara County Med. Assn. Office: Santa Clara Vly Med Ctr Divsn Plastic Surgery 751 S Bascom Ave San Jose CA 95128-2604

HOVIND, DAVID J., manufacturing company executive; b. 1940. BA, U. Wash., 1964; postgrad., Stanford U., 1984. With PACCAR Inc., Bellevue, Wash., 1964—, sr. v.p., 1986-87, exec. v.p., 1987-93; now pres. PACCAR Inc., 1993—. Office: PACCAR Inc PO Box 1518 777 106th Ave NE Bellevue WA 98004-5001*

HOVIOUS, GREGORY PAUL, municipal contract officer, contract consultant; b. Tripoli, Libya, June 26, 1956; came to U.S., 1959; s. Charles Raymond and Thelma Kathryn (Arnett) H.; m. Kimberly Ann Steed, Dec. 21, 1985; children: Christopher Gregory, Kathryn Ann. BA in Psychology, Calif. State U., Sacramento, 1981; JD, U. of the Pacific, 1984. Staff atty. Allen, Farley and Welch, Sacramento, 1981-84; v.p. Constrn. Contract Mgmt. Svcs., Sacramento, 1984-87; owner Hovious Consulting, Sacramento, 1987-88; gen. mgr. Yancey Co., Sacramento, 1988-90; contract officer City of Sacramento, 1990—; staff cons. Mayor's Minority Bus. Enterprise/Women Bus. Enterprise Adv. Com., Sacramento, 1994—; chmn. City Contracting Policy Com., Sacramento, 1994—. Author: Standard Specifications City of Sacramento, 1991. Bd. dirs. St. Johns the Evangelist Sch., Sacramento, 1996. With U.S. Army, 1975-76. Named Trainee of the Cycle, Assn. of U.S. Army, 1975; named to Outstanding Minority Program, Minority Enterprise Devel. Conf., 1993; recipient Best Program/Outstanding and Dedicated Svc. award Bay Area Contract Compliance Assn., 1996. Mem. Nat. Contract Mgmt. Assn., Project Mgmt. Inst., Constrn. Specification Inst., Constrn. Mgmt. Assn. Am., Am. Pub. Works Assn. Republican. Roman Catholic. Office: City of Sacramento 927 10th St Rm 100 Sacramento CA 95814

HOVSEPIAN, ABRAHAM, metal products executive; b. Windsor, Ont., Canada, Feb. 4, 1926; came to the U.S., 1926, naturalized, 1945; s. Minas and Sophia (Apelian) H.; children: Paul George, Carol Grace. BS, Wayne State U., 1949; postgrad., U. So. Calif., 1960-61, Calif. State U., 1962-63. cert. mfg. engr. Engr. Ford Motor Engring. Rsch., Dearborn, Mich., 1949-51, carboloy divsn. Gen. Electric, Detroit, 1951-54; pres. Sci. Platters Inc., Alhambra, Calif., 1954—; dir. Progressive Savings & Loan Assn., 1967-74; founder, dir., treas. Diversified Industries, L.A., 1968—; dir., treas. Diversified Ins. Svcs., L.A., 1970—; dir. Continental Bank, Alhambra, 1973-81, Comco Inc., Sun Valley, Calif., Tokai Bank of Calif., 1981—; chmn. bd. dirs. Ingleside Psychiatric Mental Health Ctr., Rosemead, Calif.; chmn. bd. trustees Alhambra Cmty. Hosp.; pres. Alhambra CSC; mem. Pasadena Tournament of Roses Assn. Gov.'s appointee Calif. Coun. on Mental Health, 1984-92. With USN, 1944-46. Recipient Outstanding Citizenship award Civitan Club, 1968, cert. of honor Alhambra City Coun., 1968, Alhambra Redevelopment Agy., 1969, Ingleside Psychiat. Mental Health Ctr., 1970, Alhambra Cmty. Hosp., 1972. Mem. Nat. Assn. Metal Finishers, Soc. Mfg. Engrs., Metal Finishing Assn. So. Calif., Alhambra C. of C. (pres. 1969). Clubs: Rotary Internat. (pres.), Mason (Alhambra). Republican. Congregationalist. Home: 317 La France Ave Apt 3 Alhambra CA 91801-1757 Office: 318A S Palm Ave Alhambra CA 91803-1524

HOVY, EDUARD HENDRIK, computer science researcher, educator; b. Johannesburg, South Africa, Feb. 20, 1956; came to U.S., 1981; s. Willem H. and Rosemarie Hovy. BSc, Rand Afrikaans U., Johannesburg, 1979; MS, Yale U., 1983, PhD, 1987. Project leader Info. Scis. Inst. U. So. Calif., L.A., 1987—. Author: Natural Language Generation, 1988; co-editor: Automated NL Generation, 1992, Burning Issues in Discourse, 1996. Mem. Assn. Computational Linguistics (exec. bd. 1994-96), Assn. Machine Translation in Ams. (pres. 1996—), Am. Assn. Artificial Intelligence. Office: USc Info Scis Inst 4676 Admiralty Way Marina Dl Rey CA 90292-6601

HOWARD, BRADFORD REUEL, travel company executive; b. Honolulu, Aug. 6, 1957; s. Joseph DeSylva and Marguerite Evangeline (Barker) H.; m. Marcia Andresen, June 23, 1985; children: Evan DeSilva Andresen, Blair Marguerite. BS in Bus., U. Calif., Berkeley, 1979. Owner, operator Howard Janitorial Svcs., Oakland, Calif., 1970-80; prodn. mgr. Oakland Symphony Orch., 1976-80; brand mgr. The Clorox Co., Oakland, 1980-85; gen. mgr., corp. sec. Howard Tours, Inc./Howard Enterprises, Oakland, 1985—; co-owner Howard Mktg. Cons., Oakland, 1985—; cons. Marcus Foster Found., Oakland, 1984-85; pres., gen. mgr. Piedmont (Calif.) Community Theater, 1976-92. Mem. Calif. Alumni Assn. (bd. dirs. 1991-95), U. Calif. Bus. Alumni Assn. (v.p. 1986-88, pres. 1988-89, Bay Area chpt. 1983-84), U. Calif. Devel. Coun., Oakland-Sunrise Rotary (sec. 1985-87, pres. 1987-88), Lake Merrit Breakfast Club. Office: Howard Tours Inc 526 Grand Ave Oakland CA 94610-3515

HOWARD, CHRISTOPHER PHILIP, business consultant; b. N.Y.C., Aug. 6, 1947; s. Murray and Hope (McGurn) H.; m. Danina Mary Hill, June 29, 1987; children: Sean, Stephen, Coby, Katherine, Sara. BA in Econs., Stanford U., 1968; MBA, Santa Clara U., 1970. Cert. mgmt. cons.; cert. profl. mgmt. cons.; cert. profl. cons. to mgmt. Cons. Ernst & Ernst, CPAs, Phoenix, 1972-74; ops. mgr. Jensen Tools & Alloys Inc., Phoenix, 1974-77; CFO Pioneer Industries, Inc., Phoenix, 1977-80; sr. v.p. Health-Tech Mgmt., Inc., Phoenix, 1980-84; mng. prin. Howard and Assocs., Inc., Phoenix, 1984-87; consulting mgr. Grant Thornton, CPAs, Reno, 1987-89; mng. dir. Howard Consulting Group, Inc., Reno, 1989—; faculty mem. U. Nev., Reno, 1991-95. 1st lt. USAF, 1970-72. Mem. Inst. Cert. Mgmt. Accts., Cons. Bur., Nat. Bur. Profl. Mgmt. Cons., Inst. Cert. Mgmt. Cons., Inst. Bus. Appraisers, Stanford U. Alumni Assn. Episcopalian. Office: Howard Consulting Group 6880 S Mccarran Blvd # A-10 Reno NV 89509-6122

HOWARD, DAVID HAL, journalist; b. Albany, Oreg., July 21, 1944; s. Hal and Vera Louise (Bond) H.; m. Veronica Sue Kind, Sept. 4, 1966 (div. 1971); 1 child, Daniel Wayne; m. Georgetta Lavelle Cooper, Aug. 3, 1973. BA in Journalism, Whitworth Coll., 1966. Owner, operator printing shop, Spokane, Wash., 1968-69; social worker State of Wash., Spokane, 1969-70, 72-76; labor union rep. Wash. Fedn. of State Employees, Spokane, 1970-72; freelancer real estate sales Albany, 1976-82; editor, dir. info. The Grange News, Seattle, 1982-88, 93—. Author: News Handbook for Granges, 1984, People, Pride and Progress: 125 Years of the Grange in America, 1992; editor The Universal Message, 1973-77, The Grange News, 1982-88, 93—. Assoc. dir. United Way of Linn County, Oreg., 1989-93. Mem. Nat. Grange (master Fairmount chpt. 1977-79, Editor of Yr. 1983), Freedom from Religion Found., Lebanon (Oreg.) C. of C. Lodges: Masons, Eastern Star (assoc. patron 1981). Home: 38281 Mountain Home Dr Lebanon OR 97355-9367 Office: Grange News/Wash State Grange PO Box 1186 Olympia WA 98507-1186

HOWARD, EDWARD PAXSON, IV, law center executive; b. Santa Monica, Calif., Sept. 21, 1963; s. Edward Paxson and Marilyn (Webb) H.; m. Dina Elaine Bernstein, Aug. 12, 1995. BA in Polit. Sci., George Washington U., 1986; JD, Loyola Marymount U., L.A., 1990. Bar: Calif. 1991. Assoc. Paul, Hastings, Janofsky & Walker, L.A., 1990-91, Hall & Phillips, L.A., 1991-94, Hall & Assocs., L.A., 1994-96; exec. dir. Ctr. for Law in the Pub. Interest, L.A., 1996—; adj. prof. law Loyola Law Sch., L.A., 1995—. Elected mem. Los Angeles County Dem. Ctrl. Com., 1993; co-author Proposition 186, Calif., 1994, Propositions 214 and 216, Calif., 1996; apptd. State Bar Com. on Consumer Advocacy; mem. Assembly and Senate Task Force on Personal Privacy. Recipient Am. Jurisprudence award Loyola Law Sch., 1990. Office: Ctr for Law in Pub Interest 10951 W Pico Blvd Los Angeles CA 90064-2126

HOWARD, GEORGE HARMON, management consultant; b. St. John, Wash., Nov. 14, 1934; s. George Philip and Corrinne Cadwallader (Rippeteau) H.; m. Elizabeth Ann Ogden, Dec. 22, 1956 (dec. July 1991); children: Debra Ann Leming, Keith Philip, Corrie Lou Govostis, Stacia Elizabeth. BA, Wash. State U., 1957; MBA, Harvard U., 1967. Sales rep. Burroughs Corp., Spokane, Wash., 1957; various positions USAF, Kirtland AFB, 1958-77; vice commdr. AF Contract Mgmt. Div., Kirkland AFB, N.Mex., 1978; mgr. corp. devel. Leisure Dynamics, Evergreen, Colo., 1978-80; pres. HBK Assocs., Inc., Evergreen, 1981-87; dir. ops. ILX Lightwave Corp., Bozeman, Mont., 1988-89; sr. cons. Matrix Mgmt. Group, Seattle, 1990-94; owner HBK Assocs., Auburn, Wash., 1994—; pres. Howard Farms, Inc., St. John, Wash., 1986—. Co-author: TFX Acquisition, 1966. Instr. Red Rocks Community Coll., Denver, 1986-87; del. Colo. Rep. Conv., Denver, 1984. Recipient Outstanding Sr. award Wash. State U., 1957, Legion of Merit award USAF, 1978, Bronze star USAF, 1968. Mem. Shrine, York Rite Bodies, Masonic Lodge, Order of Eastern Star, Wheatland Grange, Air Force Assn., The Ret. Officers Assn. Republican. Episcopalian. Home: 6358 S 298th Pl Auburn WA 98001-3040 Office: HBK Assocs 6358 S 298th Pl Auburn WA 98001-3040

HOWARD, JAMES WEBB, investment banker, lawyer, engineer; b. Evansville, Ind., Sept. 17, 1925; s. Joseph R. and Velma (Cobb) H.; m. Phyllis Jean Brandt, Dec. 27, 1948; children: Sheila Rae, Sharon Kae. BS in Mech. Engring, Purdue U., 1949; postgrad., Akron (Ohio) Law Sch., 1950-51, Cleve. Marshall Law Sch., 1951-52; MBA, Case Western Res. U., 1962; J.D., Western State Coll. Law, 1976. Registered profl. engr., Ind., Ohio. Jr. project engr. Firestone Tire & Rubber Co., Akron, 1949-50; gen. foreman Cadillac Motor Car div. GM, 1950-53; mgmt. cons. M.K. Sheppard & Co., Cleve., 1953-56; plant mgr. Lewis Welding & Engring. Corp., Ohio, 1956-58; underwriter The Ohio Co., Columbus, 1959; chmn. Growth Capital, Inc., Chgo., 1960—; pvt. practice law San Diego, 1979-85; pres. Meister Brau, Inc., Chgo., 1965-73, The Home Mart, San Diego, 1974-82; mng. agt., fin. instn. specialist FDIC/RTC, 1985-90; specialist in charge Office of FDIC-DOL, Portland, Oreg., 1986-87; pres. Creative Mgmt. Group, Scottsdale, Ariz., 1991—. Developer of "Lite" beer. Co-chmn. Chgo. com. Ill. Sesquicentennial Com., 1968. Served with AUS, 1943-46. Decorated Bronze Star, Parachutist badge, Combat Inf. badge. Mem. ASME, Nat. Assn. Small Bus. Investment Cos. (past pres.), State Bar Calif., Grad. Bus. Alumni Assn. Western Res. U. (past gov.), Masons, Tau Kappa Epsilon, Pi Tau Sigma, Beta Gamma Sigma. Methodist.

HOWARD, JANE OSBURN, educator; b. Morris, Ill., Aug. 12, 1926; d. Everett Hooker and Bernice Otilda (Olson) Osburn; B.A., U. Ariz., 1948; M.A., U. N.Mex., 1966, Ph.D., 1969; m. Rollins Stanley Howard, June 5, 1948; children—Ellen Elizabeth, Susan (Mrs. John Karl Nuttall). Instr. U. N.Mex. Sch. Medicine, Albuquerque, 1968-70, mem. staff pediatrics, deaf blind children's program, Albuquerque, 1971-72, asst. dir. N.Mex. programs for deaf blind children, 1972—, instr. psychiatry, instr. pediatrics, coordinator deaf-blind children's program, 1972-76, edn. cons., 1976—, publicity and pub. relations cons., 1983—; Cons. Mountain-Plains Regional Ctr. for Services to Deaf-Blind Children, Denver, 1971-74, Bur. Indian Affairs, 1974. Active Cystic Fibrosis, Mother's March, Heart Fund, Easter Seal-Crippled Children. Recipient fellowships U. N.M., 1965, 66, 66-67, 67-68, U. So. Calif. John Tracy Clinic, 1973. Fellow Royal Soc. Health; mem. Council Exceptional Children, Am. Assn. Mental Deficiency, Nat. Assn. Retarded Children, AAUW, Pi Lambda Theta, Zeta Phi Eta, Alpha Epsilon Rho. Republican. Methodist. Home: 615 Valencia Dr SE Albuquerque NM 87108-3742

HOWARD, JO ANN, business owner; b. L.A., Nov. 22, 1937; d. John George and Lucile Anne (Farish) Heinzman; m. William Harold Howard, Dec. 2, 1958; children: Teri Lynn Wilson, Tracey Ann Currie, Randall William, Richard John. Student, Mt. San Antonio Coll., 1957. Escrow officer, mgr. So. Cities Escrow, Hemet, Calif., 1970-75; escrow officer Hemet Escrow, 1975-76; ptnr. Ramona Escrow, Hemet, 1976-79; pres., supr. Howard Escrow, Hemet, 1979—; pres. Recon Enterprises, Inc., Hemet, 1976—, Chaparral Accomodators, Inc., Hemet, 1990-96; retired, 1996. Pres. Sorpotimists Internat., San Jacinto-Hemet Valley, Calif., 1979. Named one of Disting. Pres.'s, Soroptimists, 1978-80; recipient Woman of Distinction award Soroptimist Internat. (San Jacinto-Hemet Valley 1990). Mem. Women's Coun. Bd. Realtors (affiliate, treas.), Hemet-San Jacinto Bd. Realtors (affiliate), San Jacinto C. of C., Hemet C. of C., Calif. Escrow Assn. (pres. Calif. chpt. 1991), Riverside County Escrow Assn. (bd. dirs. 1985—), Escrow Inst. of Calif. (bd. dirs. 1992—). Republican. Presbyterian. Office: Howard Escrow 166 E Main St Ste 8 San Jacinto CA 92583

HOWARD, JOHN WAYNE, lawyer; b. Newport, R.I., Dec. 17, 1948; s. Joseph Leon and Irene Elizabeth (Silver) H.; m. Kathleen Amanda Busby, Oct. 7. 1978. B.A., U. Calif.-San Diego, 1971; J.D. Calif. Western Sch. Law, 1976; postgrad. San Diego Inn of Ct., 1979, Hastings Coll. Advocacy, 1981. Harvard Law Sch., Program of Instructions for Lawyers, 1992, Bar: Calif. 1978, U.S. Dist. Ct. (so. dist.) Calif. 1978, U.S. Supreme Ct. 1989, Colo. 1989, U.S. Dist. Ct. (cen. dist.) Calif. 1991, U.S. Dist Ct. (no. dist.) Calif., U.S. Dist. Ct. (ea. dist.) Calif., U.S. Ct. of Appeals (9th cir.) 1995, U.S Ct. Appeals (D.C. cir.) 1996, U.S. Ct. of Claims, 1996. Assoc. Robert T. Dierdorff, San Diego, 1978-79; sole practice, San Diego, 1979-82; ptnr. Howard & Neeb, San Diego, 1982-84; prin. John W. Howard and Assocs., San Diego, 1984-86; gen. counsel Ace Parking, Inc., 1986-89, CCCA Inc., 1989-93; pres. Individual Rights Found. Inc., 1993-95, pres. Inst. for Constitutional Rights, Inc., 1995—, John W. Howard and Assoc., 1995—; jud. arbitrator Superior Ct. Calif., 1983—. Chmn., San Diego County Indigent Def. Adv. Bd., 1981-84, mem. subcom. on def. monitoring and budget for Office Defender Services of San Diego County; mem. select com. on small bus. Calif. State Assembly, 1983-90; chmn. San Diego Pub. Arts Adv. Bd.; mem. San Diego County Council of Com. Chairs; chmn. precinct orgn. Roger Hedgecock for Supt. Campaign Com., 1976, mem. steering com., 1976; chmn. Muscular Dystrophy Telethon, San Diego, 1983; vice chmn. San Diego Festival of Arts, 1983-84; pres. Bowery Theatre, San Diego, 1984-89; pres., bd. dirs. La Jolla Stage Co.; founder, bd. dirs. San Diego Theatre League; 1st v.p., bd. dirs. Muscular Dystrophy Assn.; bd. dirs. Patrick Henry Meml. Found., Brookneal, Va., The Poe Mus., Richmond, Va., San Diego Med. Oncology Research Found., Ilan-Lael Found., Multiple Sclerosis Soc., Am. Ballet Found., Wellness Community, Teatro Mascara Magica; bd. dirs., chmn. legal affairs subcom. Calif. Motion Picture Council; mem. adv. bd. dirs. San Diego Motion Picture Bur.; mem. pub. edn. com. Am. Cancer Soc.; founder, bd. dirs. San Diego Theatre Found., 1984—; mem. 44th Congl. Dist. Adv. Com.; mem. Com. to Re-Elect Congressman Bill Lowery; mem. San Diego County 4th Dist. Adv. Com. Mem. ABA, Calif. State Bar, Assn. Trial Lawyers Am., Am. Corp. Counsel Assn., U. Calif.-San Diego Alumni Assn. (past v.p., bd. dirs.), Calif. Western Sch. Law Alumni Assn., Friendly Sons of St. Patrick, Delta Kappa Epsilon, Phi Alpha Delta. Republican. Lodge: Rotary.

HOWARD, JOSEPH B. (JOE HOWARD), actor; b. Yonkers, N.Y., Nov. 24, 1948; s. Joseph Bernard and Mary Irene (Crimmins) H.; m. Sharon Atkinson Hess, Nov. 29, 1975; children: Jeremy Patrick, Julia Rosamond. BA, Hamilton Coll., 1970. Pvt. investigator Pinkerton's Nat. Detective Agy., Albany, N.Y., 1970-71; profl. actor, 1971—; tchr. music Antilles Sch., St. Thomas, V.I., 1972-73; bd. dirs and gen. dir. Theatre of Light, Inc., L.A., 1977-82; bd. dirs. Robinson's Books & Creative Arts, Ventura, Calif., 1982-92; founder and bd. dirs. All Am. Entertainment Cluster, L.A., 1996—. Appeared in Broadway plays So Long, 174th St., 1976, Shenandoah, 1976-77; (TV show) MATHNET; (film) Grumpy Old Men, 1994. Founder and dir. Citizens Alliance for Responsible Edn., Eden Prairie, Minn., 1993-94; campain mgr. sch. bd. election, Eden Praire, 1994. Mem. SAG (vol. income tax asst., L.A. 1997), AFTRA, Actors Equity Assn. Home and Office: 13610 Valley Vista Blvd Sherman Oaks CA 91423

HOWARD, LUCIA FAKONAS, lawyer; b. East St. Louis, Mo., July 21, 1951. BA summa cum laude, Ariz. State U., 1972; JD cuml laude, Harvard U., 1975. Bar: Ariz. 1975. Law clerk to Hon. Christopher Armstrong Mass. Ct. Appeals, 1975-76; spl. asst. on econ. devel. office of mayor City of Phoenix, Ariz., 1985, 89—; mem. Ariz. Ctr. for Women and the Law, 1979-82, Ariz. Commn. on Salaries for Elected Ofcls., 1982-84. Commr. Phoenix Commn. on Excellence in Edn., 1989—. Mem. State Bar Ariz. (chair inst. on estate planning 1978-80, com. on pub. edn. 1979-80), Ariz. Women Lawyers Assn. (pres. 1978-81), Maricopa County Bar Found. (bd. dirs. 1984-85), Kappa Delta Pi, Alpha Lambda Delta. Office: Fakonas Howard Ltd 4436 E Camelback Rd Unit 34 Phoenix AZ 85018-2833

HOWARD, MARK W., surgeon; b. San Jose, Calif., Mar. 7, 1959; s. Berwyn Jones and Anne Linnea (Madsen) Howard-Kwder; m. Kristina M. Athanas, Aug. 25, 1986; children: Mark Christopher, Tyler Joseph Berwyn. AB in Physiology, U. Calif., Berkeley, 1981; MD, Harvard Med. Sch., 1985. Diplomate Am. Bd. Orthopedic Surgery. Intern, resident UCLA Med. Ctr., Torrance, Calif., 1985-90; fellowship in spinal surgery UCLA Med. Ctr., Westwood, Calif., 1990-91; active staff Community Hosp. of Monterey Peninsula, Monterey, Calif., Salinas Valley Meml. Hosp., Calif. Contbr. articles to profl. jours. and publs. Mem. AMA, Am. Acad. Orthopaedic Surgeons, N.Am. Spine Soc., Calif. Med. Assn., Calif. Orthopaedic Assn., Monterey County Med. Assn., Phi Beta Kappa.

HOWARD, NANCY E., lawyer; b. Ft. Wayne, Ind., Aug. 13, 1951. BA, Stanford U., 1973, JD, 1977. Bar: Calif. 1977. Mem. Tuttle & Taylor, L.A. Contbr. articles to profl. jours. Mem. Order of Coif., Phi Beta Kappa. Office: Tuttle & Taylor 355 S Grand Ave Los Angeles CA 90071-1560

HOWARD, SEYMOUR, art history educator; b. Chgo., Jan. 20, 1928; s. Max and Sarah Leah (Linn) H.; m. Ilia Goebel, July 27, 1958; children—Catherine Anne, Sarah. A.M., U. Chgo., 1952, Ph.D., 1958. Prof. U. Calif.-Davis, 1958—. Author: A Classical Frieze by Jacques Louis David, 1975 (NEA award); Lansdowne Herakles, 1978 (Getty award); Jacob Merz,

1981 (Swiss govt. award); Bartolomeo Cavaceppi, 1982; Antiquity Restored, 1990. Editor 18th Century Studies, Calif. Art Commn. Contbr. articles to profl. jours. Mem. Archeol. Inst. Am., Coll. Art Assn. Am., Art Historians Pacific Northwest (pres. 1965-72). Office: Art Dept U Calif Davis CA 95616

HOWARD, VICTOR, management consultant; b. Montreal, Que., Can., Aug. 12, 1923; s. Thomas and Jean (Malkinson) H.; BA, Sir George Williams U., 1947; BSc, 1948; PhD, Mich. State U., 1954; m. Dorothy Bode, Dec. 25, 1953. Mech. design engr. Canadian Vickers Ltd., Montreal, 1942-46; with Aluminum Co. Can., 1946-48, E.B. Badger Co., Boston, 1948-50; asst. prof. Mich. State U., 1952-56; social scientist Rand Corp., 1956-58; staff exec., personnel dir. System Devel. Corp., Santa Monica, Calif., 1958-66; staff cons. Rohrer, Hibler & Replogle, San Francisco, 1966-69; mng. dir. Rohrer, Hibler & Replogle Internat., London and Brussels, 1969-74, ptnr. 1974, mgr. San Francisco, 1974-88, dir., 1979-88; pres. V. Howard and Assocs., 1988—, The Inst. on Stress and Health in the Work Place, 1988—; vice chair State Bd. Psychology, 1989-93. Fellow Brit. Inst. Dirs.; mem. Am. Psychol. Assn., Western Psychol.Assn., U.S. Power Squadrons (comdr. Sequoia Squadron 1981, dist. comdr. 1987), Calif. State Mil. Res. (col. 1984), Reform Club, Hurlingham (London) Club, Thames Motor Yacht Club (Molesey, Eng.), Order of St. John of Jerusalem (chevalier)Sovereign Mil. Order of the Temple (prior Priory of St Francis, Grand Cross), Masons (33 degree), Shriners, Sigma Xi. Home and Office: 530 Los Altos Ct Santa Rosa CA 95403-1329

HOWATT, SISTER HELEN CLARE, human services director, former college library director; b. San Francisco, Apr. 5, 1927; d. Edward Bell and Helen Margaret (Kenney) H. BA, Holy Names Coll., 1949; MS in Libr. Sci., U. So. Calif., 1972; cert. advanced studies Our Lady of Lake U., 1966. Joined Order Sisters of the Holy Names, Roman Cath. Ch., 1945. Life teaching credential, life spl. svcs. credential, prin. St. Monica Sch., Santa Monica, Calif., 1957-60, St. Mary Sch., L.A., 1960-63; tchr. jr. high sch. St. Augustine Sch., Oakland, Calif., 1964-69; tchr. jr. high math St. Monica Sch., San Francisco, 1969-71, St. Cecilia Sch., San Francisco, 1971-77; libr. dir. Holy Names Coll., Oakland, Calif., 1977-94; activities dir. Collins Ctr. Sr. Svcs., 1994—. Contbr. math. curriculum San Francisco Unified Sch. Dist., Cum Notis Variorum, publ. Music Libr., U. Calif., Berkeley. Contbr. articles to profl. jours. NSF grantee, 1966, NDEA grantee, 1966. Mem. Cath. Libr. Assn. (chmn. No. Calif. elem. schs. 1971-72). Home and Office: 2550 18th Ave San Francisco CA 94116-3005

HOWE, BRYANT RICHARD, legislative staff member; b. Salt Lake City, Mar. 28, 1956; s. Richard Cuddy and Juanita (Lyon) H.; m. Sandra Kay Swander, Aug. 7, 1981; children: Alicia, Taylor, Megan, Miquelle, Alexander. BA with honors, U. Utah, 1980; MPA, Brigham Young U., 1982. Rsch. and pub. policy analyst Utah Legis., Salt Lake City, 1982—. Recipient Outstanding History Student award Utah State Hist. Soc., 1980. Mem. Nat. Conf. State Legis. Health Policy Staff Network (staff chair children and family svcs. com. 1994-95). Mem. LDS Ch. Office: Office Legis Rsch 436 State Capitol Building Salt Lake City UT 84114-1202

HOWE, DEBRA ANN, therapist; b. Galveston, Tex., Aug. 7, 1959; d. Jesse and Gloria (Garza) Cortez; m. Michael Brian Howe, Apr. 23, 1983; children: Annika Michelle, Ryan Michael. BS in Home Econs., Tex. Tech. U., 1981; MEd in Counseling, Boston U., 1986. Cert. adoption profl. Group facilitator Bright Horizons, Albuquerque, 1986-91; ct. clinician I 2d Judicial Dist. Ct., Albuquerque, 1989-95; divorce mediator in pvt. practice Albuquerque, 1995—; adoption profl. Triad Counseling Inc., Albuquerque, 1995-97; parent edn. trainer All Indian Pueblo Coun., Albuquerque, 1996-97; therapist Minirth Meier Clinic, Albuquerque, 1996—; intern supr. U. N.Mex., Albuquerque, 1993—, Webster U., Albuquerque, 1993—, Highlands U., Albuquerque, 1995-96; workshop presenter Assn. of Family Conciliation Cts., 1991; adoption profl. Child Rite Adoption Svcs., Albuquerque, 1997—. Vol. coord. Escuela del Sol Montessori, Albuquerque, 1994—, v.p. parent action com., 1994-96. Named Supr. of the Yr., U. N.Mex., 1995, Outstanding Contbr., ARC, Woodbridge, Eng., 1984. Mem. ACA. Home: 4315 Rancho Largo Albuquerque NM 87120-5363 Office: Minirth Meier Clinic 5345 Wyoming Blvd NE # 105 Albuquerque NM 87109-3199

HOWE, DRAYTON FORD, JR., lawyer; b. Seattle, Nov. 17, 1931; s. Drayton Ford and Virginia (Wester) H.; m. Joyce Arnold, June 21, 1952; 1 son, James Drayton. A.B., U. Calif.-Berkeley, 1953; LL.B., Hastings Coll. Law, 1957. Bar: Calif. 1958, C.P.A. Calif. Atty. IRS, 1958-61; tax dept. supr. Ernst & Ernst, San Francisco, 1962-67; ptnr. Bishop, Barry, Howe, Haney & Ryder, San Francisco, 1968—; lectr. on tax matters U. Calif. extension, 1966-76. Mem. Calif. Bar Assn., San Francisco Bar Assn. (chmn. client relations com. 1977), Calif. Soc. C.P.A.s. Office: Bishop Barry Howe Haney & Ryder 275 Battery St 12th Fl San Francisco CA 94111-3305

HOWE, JOHN THOMAS, film director, educator; b. Toronto, Ont., Can., Aug. 30, 1926; s. Thomas and Margret Ogilvy (Manzie) H.; m. Beverley Jean Luchuck, Oct. 23, 1974; children: Natalie Elaine, Nicholas Thomas. BA, U. Toronto, 1950. Freelance radio, TV staff producer Can. Broadcasting Corp., 1945-55; staff mem. Can. Repertory theatre, 1950-51; dir., producer Nat. Film Bd. Can., 1955-83; prof. dept. cinema-TV U. So. Calif., L.A., 1983—. Dir., composer feature film Why Rock the Boat?, 1974; producer, dir., editor, composer feature film A Choice of Two, 1981; dir., producer numerous feature documentaries, theatrical shorts, TV dramas, others. Capt. Royal Can. Arty., 1944-46, ETO. Mem. Assn. Can. TV and Radio Artists, Dir.'s Guild Am., Soc. Filmmakers (past pres.), Soc. Composers, Authors, and Music Pubs. Can., Can. Coun. Film Orgns. (past pres.), Syndicat Gen. Cinema (past pres.). Office: Sch Cinema Univ So Calif University Park Los Angeles CA 90007

HOWE, LEE MARTIN, electronics marketing executive, army officer; b. Oakland, Calif., Nov. 7, 1952; s. Nate Houghton and Helen J. (Martin) H.; m. Donna G. Keuper, June 6, 1976; children: Christine Ann, Kenneth Martin. BA in Bus. and Pub. Adminstrn., U. San Francisco, 1974, MA in Mktg. and Internat. Rels., 1976; MA in Mil. Sci. and Strategy, Command and Gen. Staff Coll., 1988. Lic. comml. pilot. Storekeeper, buyer Officers Open Mess, Nas Alameda, Calif., 1968-70; computer systems operator Bank of Am., San Francisco, Calif., 1970-74; dist. salesman Clairol Corp., San Mateo, Calif., 1974-76; reconnaissance officer 2d Mil. Intelligence Bn., Europe, 1979-82; dist. sales mgr. Rockbestos Wire & Cable Co., New Haven, 1984-85; sr. govt. account mgr., regional specialist Gould Computer Systems, Santa Clara, Calif., 1985-86; mgr. internat. sales and mktg. Walkins-Johnson Co., Palo Alto, Calif., 1986-92; pres. ID. Internat. Mtkg., Redwood City, Calif., 1992—. Author: Aerial Reconnaissance Handbook, 1981; editor (area studies) Tech. Transfer into the Pacific Rim, 1988. Mem. spl. com. on youth employment City and County of San Francisco, 1974-75; mem. spl. com. Assn. Bay Area Govts., Berkeley, Calif., 1974-76; active U.S. Little League, Fremont, Calif., 1988—; spokesperson Nat. Crime Prevention Coun., San Francisco Bay Area, Calif., 1994; vol. World Cup Soccer USA, 1994. Lt. col. USAR, 1984—. Decorated 3 Army Commendation medals, 2 Meritorious Svc. medals, Presdl. Award Excellence. Mem. Assn. Old Crows (chpt. rep. 1986-88), Alumni Assn. U. San Francisco (chmn.), Animal Rescue Found., Nat. Crime Prevention Coun. (spokesperson 1994—). Office: ID Internat Mktg 1647 Kentfield Ave Redwood City CA 94061-2746

HOWE, RICHARD CUDDY, state supreme court justice; b. South Cottonwood, Utah, Jan. 20, 1924; s. Edward E. and Mildred (Cuddy) H.; m. Juanita Lyon, Aug. 30, 1949; children: Christine Howe Schultz, Andrea Howe Reynolds, Bryant, Valerie Howe Winegar, Jeffrey, Craig. B.S., U. Utah, 1945, J.D., 1948. Bar: Utah. Law clk. to Justice James H. Wolfe, Utah Supreme Ct., 1949-50; judge city ct. Murray, Utah, 1951; individual practice law Murray, 1952-80; assoc. justice Utah Supreme Ct., 1980—, justice; mem. Utah Constnl. Revision Commn., 1976-85. Chmn., original mem. Salt Lake County Merit Coun.; mem. Utah Ho. of Reps., 1951-58, 69-72, Utah Senate, 1973-78. Named Outstanding Legislator Citizens' Conf. State Legislatures, 1972. Mem. ABA, Utah Bar Assn., Sons of Utah Pioneers. Mem. LDS Ch. Office: Utah Supreme Ct 332 State Capitol Building Salt Lake City UT 84114-1202

HOWE, SUSAN LEONE, artist, printmaker, design consultant; b. Sarasota, Fla., June 16, 1947; d. James Leo and Mary Jeanne (Johnson) Lefholz; m. Kenneth J. Campagna, Dec. 12, 1970 (div. 1985); m. William Clarence Howe, Apr. 23, 1987. BA, San Jose State U., 1973. Art dir. Scale Models Unltd., Menlo Park, Calif., 1969-78; pres., owner Campagna & Assocs., Palo Alto, Calif., 1978-87; artist, printmaker, Two Hat Studios, Aptos, Calif., 1987—. One-woman shows include Maturango Mus., Ridge Crest, Calif., 1994, Santa Cruz (Calif.) County Bldg., 1994, U. Calif. YWCA, Berkeley, 1995; works exhibited in group shows Internat. Print Exhbn., U. Hawaii, 1993, San Bernardino (Calif.) County Mus., 1993, ARC Nat. Print Exhbn., Chgo., 1994, St. Francis Found., San Francisco, 1996, Atelier Gallery, Santa Cruz, 1996, Desert Art, Palm Desert, Calif., 1996-97, Takara Gallery, Houston, 1997. Mem. Arts Guild Santa Cruz County, Arts Guild Sonoma. Office: Two Hat Studios 1570 Cox Rd Aptos CA 95003

HOWE, VERNON WESLEY, mathematics educator; b. Burundi, Aug. 4, 1942; came to U.S., 1945; s. Parshall L. and Adelia F. (Swingle) H.; m. Winona R. Scott, July 25, 1965; children: Andrew, Stephanie. MA in Math., U. Calif., Berkeley, 1966; PhD in Math., Dartmouth Coll., 1971; MS in Computer Sci., Calif. State U., Fullerton, 1986. Instr. math. Atlantic Union Coll., South Lancaster, Mass., 1966-67; asst. prof. math. U. Ark., Fayetteville, 1971-74; prof. math. and computing La Sierra U., Riverside, Calif., 1974—; vis. prof. math. Colgate U., Hamilton, N.Y., 1982-83; cons. computing Comarco Corp., Anaheim, Calif., 1985-90. Recipient G.T. Anderson award for teaching La Sierra U., 1994, Zapara award for coll. teaching, 1986, Tchr. of Yr. award Loma Linda U., 1976. Mem. Am. Math. Soc., Math. Assn. Am., Soc. Indsl. and Applied Math., Assn. for Computing Machinery, Am. Birding Assn. Seventh-day Adventist. Home: 11238 Rogers St Riverside CA 92505 Office: La Sierra U 4700 Pierce St Riverside CA 92515

HOWE, WARREN BILLINGS, physician; b. Jackson Heights, N.Y., Oct. 25, 1940; s. John Hanna and Francelia (Rose) H.; m. Hedwig Neslanik, Aug. 7, 1971; children: Elizabeth Rose, Sarah Billings. BA, U. Rochester, 1962; MD, Washington U., St. Louis, 1965. Diplomate Am. Bd. Family Practice with CAQ in Sports Medicine, Nat. Bd. Med. Examiners. Intern Phila. Gen. Hosp., 1965-66; resident physician Highland Hosp./U. Rochester, 1969-71; family physician Family Medicine Clinic of Oak Harbor (Wash.), Inc., PS, 1971-92; student health physician, univ. team physician We. Wash. U., Bellingham, 1992—; team physician Oak Harbor High Sch., 1972-92; head tournament physician Wash. State High Sch. Wrestling Championships, Tacoma, 1989—; attending physician Seattle Goodwill Games, 1990; clin. asst. prof. U. Wash. Sch. Medicine, 1975-82. Contbr. articles to profl. jours. and chpts. to books. Bd. dirs. Oak Harbor Sch. Dist. #201, 1975-87; chmn. Oak Harbor Citizen's Com. for Sch. Support, 1988-90. Lt. comdr. USN, 1966-69, Vietnam. Recipient Disting. Svc. award City of Oak Harbor, 1984; Paul Harris fellowship Oak Harbor Rotary Club. Fellow Am. Coll. Sports Medicine (chair membership com.), Am. Acad. Family Physicians; mem. AMA, Wash. State Med. Assn., Am. Med. Soc. for Sports Medicine, Am. Coll. Health Assn. Presbyterian. Home: 4222 Northridge Way Bellingham WA 98226-7804 Office: WWU Student Health Ctr 25 High St Bellingham WA 98225-9112

HOWELL, SCOTT NEWELL, computer company executive, state legislator; b. Provo, Utah, Sept. 28, 1953; s. Varon L. and Kathryn (Tuttle) H.; m. Linda Skanchy, Sept. 8, 1978; children: Bryan, Bradley, Jason, Jeffrey. BA, U. Utah, 1978. With sales IBM Corp., mgr.; mem. Utah State Senate, 1992—; chmn. Nat. Acad. Fin., Salt Lake City, 1991-93. Bd. dirs. Utah Chpt. Nat. Children's Protection of Child Abuse, Salt Lake City, 1992-93, visually handicapped divsn. United Way, Salt Lake City, 1992-93. Democrat. Mormon. Home: 9711 S 3725 E Sandy UT 84092-6047 Office: IBM Corp 420 E S Salt Lake City UT 84111-2316*

HOWELLS, R. TIM, professional sports team executive; m. Patty Howells; four children. Grad., U. Utah, 1968. With Howells, Inc., Salt Lake City, 1968-82; v.p., co-owner, pvt. investor Howells, Inc., from 1982; gen. mgr. Utah Jazz NBA, 1989—. Office: Utah Jazz 301 W South Temple Salt Lake City UT 84101-1216*

HOWER, DONNA WILSON, elementary education educator; b. Petaluma, Calif., Sept. 9, 1948; d. Loran Richard and Marie Libby (Turner) Wilson; m. John C. Hower, July 14, 1973; 1 child, Alaina Marie. BA, U.S. Internat. U., 1970. Calif. gen. elem. tchg. credential. Tchr. Juarez-Lincoln Elem., Chula Vista, Calif., 1970-73, Hillsborough (Calif.) City Schs., 1974—; computer mentor, tchr. Hillsborough (Calif.) Schs., 1985-87, grant writer, 1990-91; regional fellow Calif. Ctr. for Sch. Restructuring, 1992—. Pres. Hillsborough Tchrs. Assn., 1979. Recipient Kent awards San Mateo County Bd. Edn., 1990, Golden Bell award Calif. State Sch. Bds. Assn., 1991. Mem. ASCD, Nat. Coun. Tchrs. Math., Calif. Math. Coun., Calif. League Middle Schs., Calif. Tchrs. Assn. (local pres. 1978-79). Office: Crocker Middle Sch 2600 Ralston Ave Hillsborough CA 94010-6544

HOWES, WILLIAM CRAIG, English educator; b. Huntsville, Ont., Can., Feb. 23, 1955; came to U.S., 1977; s. William Hay and Merle Eleanor (Luck) H.; m. Sara Lois Collins, July 1, 1979; 1 child, William Seth. BA with honours, U. Toronto, 1977; MA, Princeton U., 1978, PhD, 1980. Asst. prof. English U. Hawaii, Honolulu, 1980-87, assoc. prof., 1987-94, prof., 1994—. Author: Voices of the Vietnam POWs, 1993; contbr. articles to profl. jours. Bd. dirs. Poets in the Schs., Honolulu, 1985—. Recipient Pres. citation for teaching, 1986. Mem. Coun. Editors Learned Jours. (v.p. 1996—), Hawaii Lit. Arts Coun. (pres. 1982—, Elliott P. Cades award Lit. 1994), Modern Lang. Assn. Office: U Hawaii Dept English 1733 Donaghho Rd Honolulu HI 96822-2315

HOWLAND, PETER MCKINNON, academic administrator; b. Corvallis, Oreg., Apr. 2, 1956; s. James Chase and Ruth Louise (Meisenhelder) H. BA, Linfield Coll., 1978; postgrad., Boise State U., 1981-82; MA in Interdisciplinary Studies, Oreg. State U., 1985. Travel agt. Sather Tours and Travel, Salem, Oreg., 1979-81; office asst. then devel. asst. Linfield Coll., McMinnville, Oreg., 1985-90, devel. asst. for rsch., 1990-94, dir. of rsch. and records, 1994—. Mem. Pi Sigma Alpha. Republican. Mormon. Office: Linfield Coll Office Coll Rels 900 SE Baker St Mcminnville OR 97128-6894

HOWLETT, JOHN DAVID, government relations; b. Akron, Colo., July 16, 1952; s. John Butler and Reavis Lavina (Smith) H. BA, U. Nebr., 1975, M in Urban and Regional Planning, 1977. Urban and regional planner Oblinger-McCaleb, Denver, 1979-80; staff project mgr. Greater Denver C. of C., 1980-83; dir. econ. devel. City of Littleton, Colo., 1983-87; dir. civic and econ. devel., interim pres. The Denver Partnership, Denver, 1987-91; mng. assoc. Linton, Mields, Reisler & Cottone, Inc., Denver, 1991-95; prin., owner Price Howlett, Inc., Denver, 1995—; mem. Arapahoe/Douglas Pvt. Industry Coun., Englewood, Colo., 1984-87; mem. steering com. New Bus. and Industry Coun., Denver, 1985-87; mem. exec. com. Met. Denver Network, 1987-91. Mem. profl. adv. coun. Coll. Arch. U. Nebr., Lincoln, 1980—; vice chmn. C-470 Inter-Camber Task Force, Denver, 1984-87; trustee AMC Cancer Rsch. Ctr., Lakewood, Colo., 1985-87; mem. exec. bd. Friends Auraria Libr., Denver, 1989-90; mem. vocat. adv. com. Mental Health Corp., 1990-94. Mem. Am. Planning Assn. (pres. Colo. chpt. 1985-87, Karen Smith Chpt. award 1987), City Club Denver (pres. 1984-85). Democrat. Presbyterian. Home: 3026-L Prentice Ave Littleton CO 80123-7785 Office: Price Howlett Inc 2547 W 32nd Ave Denver CO 80211

HOWRY, JOE, newspaper editor. Mng. editor Ventura (Calif.) County Star. Address: 5250 Ralston St Ventura CA 93003

HOWSLEY, RICHARD THORNTON, lawyer, regional government administrator; b. Medford, Oreg., Jan. 31, 1948; s. Calvin Nevil and Arvilla Constance (Romine) H.; m. Susan Erma Johnson, Oct. 23, 1971; children: James Denver, Kelly Ann. BA, Willamette U., 1970; MS, Va. Poly. Inst. and State U., 1974; JD, Lewis and Clark Law Sch., 1984. Bar: Oreg. 1984, Wash. 1985, U.S. Dist. Ct. (we. dist.) Wash., 1985. Tech. editor U.S. Bur. Mines, Arlington, Va., 1971-72; program mgr., sr. planner KRS Assos., Inc., Reston, Va., 1972-74; exec. dir. Rogue Valley Council Govts., Medford, 1974-78; exec. dir. Regional Planning Council of Clark County, Vancouver, Wash., 1978-84; pres. Landerholm, Memovich, Lansverk & Whitesides, Vancouver, 1985-92; pvt. practice, Vancouver, 1992—; vice chmn. Oreg. Council of Govts. Dirs. Assn., 1976-77, chmn., 1977-78; mem. regional adv. com. So. Oreg. State Coll., 1975-78. Mem. Medford-Ashland Air Quality Adv. Com., 1977-78. Carpenter Found. scholar, 1966-70, Leonard B. Mayfield Meml. scholar, 1966-67, Albina Page Found. scholar, 1966-70. Mem. ABA, Oreg. State Bar Assn., Wash. State Bar Assn., Am. Planning Assn., Am. Inst. Cert. Planners, Internat. City Mgmt. Assn. (10-yr. service award), Nat. Assn. Regional Councils (10-yr. service award). Democrat. Methodist. Home: PO Box 61448 Vancouver WA 98666-1448 Office: Richard T Howsley PS 1400 Washington St Ste 200 Vancouver WA 98660-2968

HOWSMON, ALAN JOHNSTON, consulting engineer; b. Columbus, Ohio, Mar. 27, 1934; s. Wayne Johnston and Julia Ann (Haas) H.; m. Martha Marie Zeeveld, Dec. 17, 1977; children: Gregg, Christina, Andrea, Brent, Rebecca. BSME, Purdue U., 1956, MS in Engrng. Sci., 1960, PhD, 1966. Asst. prof. div. interdisciplinary studies SUNY, Buffalo, 1964-67; assoc. prof. Inst. Aerospace Studies, U. Toronto, Ont., Can., 1967-70; rsch. assoc. prof. dept. physics U. Ill., Champaign, 1969-70; dir. rsch. Legis. Coun. State of Vt., Montpelier, 1970-72; pres., owner Woods & Meadows, Inc., Waterbury Center, Vt., 1972-78; v.p., gen. mgr. Ashtabula (Ohio) Erectors, Inc., 1978-85; postdoctoral rsch. assoc. Purdue U., West Lafayette, Ind., 1989-91; prin. H & H Cons., Seattle, 1990—. Named Tchr. of Yr., SUNY Sch. ENGRING., 1967; Standard Oil Ind. fellow Purdue U., 1958, GM fellow, 1959. Mem. Assn. Profl. Engrs. Ont. (cert.), Am. Phys. Soc. Home: 2410 Boyer Ave E Apt 6 Seattle WA 98112-2141 also: RR 1 Box 9425 Waterbury Center VT 05677-9748

HOY, HAROLD HENRY, artist; b. Spokane, Wash., May 16, 1941; s. James K. and Rose Hoy; m. Pei-In Kathy Chen, Arp. 5, 1942. BA, Ctrl. Wash. State U., Ellensburg, 1965; MFA in Painting, U. Oreg., 1967, MFA in Sculpture, 1969. Art instr. Lane Cmty. Coll., Eugene, Oreg., 1970—; lectr. U. Oreg., Eugene, 1974, Lower Columbia Coll., Longview, Wash., 1979, Eastern Wash. U., Cheney, 1979, U. Kans., Lawrence, 1982. One-man shows include William Sawyer Gallery, San Francisco, 1979, U. Oreg. Art Mus., Eugene, 1979, Eastern Wash. U., Cheney, 1979, Blackfish Gallery, Portland, Oreg., 1981, Jackson St. Gallery, Seattle, 1982, Northwest Artists Workshop, Portland, 1982, Project Space Gallery, Eugene, 1982, 84, New Zone Gallery, Eugene, 1985, Internat. Firehouse Cmty. Ctr., Portland, 1987, U. No. Iowa, Cedar Falls, 1989, Portland State U., 1991, Hunt Ctr. Performing Arts, Eugene, 1991, Quartersaw Gallery, Portland, 1991, 93, 95, others; exhibited in group shows at Jackson St. Gallery, Seattle, 1983, Northwest Artists Workshop, Portland, 1983, Project Space Gallery, Eugene, 1983, Artquake, Portland, 1983, 84, Oreg. State U., Corvallis, 1983, Marylhurst (Oreg.) Coll., 1983, Weber State Coll., Ogden, Utah, 1983, Wing Lake Meml. Mus., Seattle, 1984, Pub. Image Gallery, N.Y.C., 1984, Portland Art Mus., 1985, U. Hawaii, Honolulu, 1985, Clark Coll., Vancouver, Wash., 1986, New Zone Gallery, Eugene, 1984, 85, 86, 88, 90, 91, 92, Lane Cmty. Coll., Eugene, 1983, 86, 88, 91, Blackfish Gallery, Portland, 1984, 86, Thinking Eye Gallery, L.A., 1987, Newport (Oreg.) Art Mus., 1984, Kerns Art Ctr., Eugene, 1989, Erb Meml. Union Gallery, U. Oreg., Eugene, 1988, 89, Clackamas Cmty. Coll., Oregon City, Oreg., 1987, 90, Corvallis (Oreg.) Art Ctr., 1989, 90, Art Gallery U. Hawaii, Honolulu, 1991, 94, William Sawyer Gallery, San Francisco, 1993, Hult Ctr. for Performing Arts, Eugene, 1986, 88, 89, 93, 94, Maude Kerns Art Ctr., Eugene, 1985, 87, 88, 90, 92, 94, 95, others. Co-founder, bd. dirs. New Zone Gallery, Eugene, 1984-87; founder, bd. mem. Project Space Gallery, Eugene, 1980-83. Recipient Individual Artist fellowships Oreg. Arts Commn., 1971, 77. Democrat. Office: Lane Cmty Coll 4000 E 30th Ave Eugene OR 97405-0640

HOYE, WALTER BRISCO, retired college administrator; b. Lena, Miss., May 19, 1930; s. William H. and LouBertha (Stewart) H.; m. Vida M. Pickens, Aug. 28, 1954; children—Walter B. II, JoAnn M. B.A., Wayne State U., 1953. Sports/auto editor Detroit Tribune, 1958-65; sports editor Mich. Chronicle, 1965-68; assoc. dir. pub. relations San Diego Chargers Football Co., 1968-76; media liason NFL, 1972-75; community services officer San Diego Coll. Dist., 1976-78; placement officer Ednl. Cultural Complex, San Diego, 1978-80, info. officer, 1980-82, placement officer, adminstrv. asst., 1982-83, placement/program support supr., 1983-91, supr. program support svcs., 1989—; cons. in field. Bd. dirs. San Diego County ARC; active San Diego Conv. and Tourist Bur., Joint Ctr. Polit. Studies, Am. Cancer Soc., San Diego Urban League, Neighborhood Housing Assn., Public Access TV. Named San Diego County Citizen of Month, May, 1979; recipient United Way Award of Merit, 1974. Mem. Internat. Assn. Auditorium Mgrs., Am. Personnel and Guidance Assn., San Diego Career Guidance Assn., Nat. Mgmt. Assn., Assn. Calif. Community Coll. Adminstrs., Calif. Community Coll. Placement Assn., Rocky Mountain Assn. Student Fin. Aid Adminstrs. Home: 6959 Ridge Manor Ave San Diego CA 92120-3146

HOYT, DIANA VAUGHN, fundraising executive; b. Denver, Jan. 26, 1945; d. Michael and Virginia Rose (Barnes) Grega; m. Michael Lee, Dec. 1967 (div. Dec. 1973); m. Roy Alan Flegenheimer, July 28, 1974 (div. Jan. 1992); m. Robert L. Hoyt, Jan. 9, 1994; children: Elon Michael, Rachel Anne. AA, Hutchinson (Kans.) Jr. Coll., 1965; BS, Kans. U., 1967; MA, Ariz. State U., 1972. Cert. high sch. tchr., Ariz., cert. fundraising, Nat. Soc. of Fund Raising Exec. Math tchr. various high schs., Ariz. and Mo., 1967-75; devel. officer Ariz. Mus. Sci. and Tech., Phoenix, 1986-88, Desert Bot. Garden, Phoenix, 1988-89, Actors Theatre, Phoenix, 1989-91, TERROS Behavioral Health Svcs., Phoenix, 1991-95, Ariz. Cactus Pine Girl Scout Coun., Phoenix, 1995—. Mem. Samaritans, 1987-96; women's campaign chmn. United Jewish Appeal, 1984-86; mem. Valley Leadership, 1986-87. Recipient Lee Amada Young Leadership award Jewish Fedn. Greater Phoenix, 1981, Golda Meir award, 1990. Mem. Nat. Soc. Fund Raising Execs. (bd. dirs. Greater Ariz. chpt., pres. 1995), Jewish Bus. and Profl. Women's Nat. Coun., Coun. for Jews with Special Needs (pres.), Rotary Internat., Beta Gamma Sigma, Phi Lambda Theta, Phi Theta Kappa. Democrat. Jewish. Home: 4929 E Laurel Ln Scottsdale AZ 85254-4640 Office: Ariz Cactus Pine Girl Scout Coun PO Box 21776 Phoenix AZ 85036

HOYT, EARL WESLEY, materials scientist, accelerator technologist; b. Chgo., July 28, 1927; s. Wesley Henry Hoyt and Elsa Bernice Plank; m. Virginia L. Rocco, Nov. 12, 1949 (div. July 1974); children: Noelle R., Randall C., Wayne W., Mark W.; m. Dorothy J. Franklin, July 1, 1984. Student, Wilson Coll., Chgo., 1947-50, Ill. Inst. Tech., Chgo., 1950-52, U. Chgo., 1952-54. Assoc. staff. Argonne Nat. Lab., Lemont, Ill., 1947-57; metallurgist, ceramist Gen. Electric Lab., Pleasanton, Calif., 1957-63; materials scientist Stanford (Calif.) Linear Accelerator Ctr., 1963—; cons. Stanford U., 1970—. Author more than 100 tech. publs., reports and jour. articles in fields of nuclear and accelerator tech. Served with USMCR, 1945-47. Home: 3655 Kentucky Ave Riverbank CA 95367-2911 Office: Stanford U PO Box 4349 Palo Alto CA 94309-4349

HOYT, JACK WALLACE, engineering educator; b. Chgo., Oct. 19, 1922; s. Claire A. and Fleta M. (Wheeler) H.; B.S., Ill. Inst. Tech., 1944; M.S., UCLA, 1952, Ph.D., 1962; m. Helen Rita Erickson, Dec. 27, 1945; children: John A., Katheryn M. (Mrs. Richard Everett), Annette M. (Mrs. Walter Butler), Denise M. (Mrs. Paul Kruesi). Research engr. gas turbines Cleve. Lab., NACA, 1944-47; mem. staff Naval Ocean Systems Center, Navy Dept., DOD, San Diego, 1948-79, asso. for sci. fleet engring. dept., 1967-79, now cons.; vis. prof. mech. engring. Rutgers U., New Brunswick, N.J., 1979-81; Benjamin Meaker vis. prof. U. Bristol (Eng.), 1987; prof. mech. engring. San Diego State U., 1981-94; active in research, 1994—. Fellow ASME (Freeman scholar 1971); mem. N.Y. Acad. Scis., Soc. Naval Architects and Marine Engrs. Author, patentee in field. Spl. rsch. propulsion and hydrodynamics. Home: 4694 Lisann St San Diego CA 92117-2441

HOYT, LEEZA LEE, public relations and advertising firm executive; b. Cairo, Egypt, Nov. 27, 1955; (parents Am. citizens); d. Harry Grant and Lucille H. Hoyt. BA cum laude in Pub. Relations, U. So. Calif., 1977; MBA, Loyola U., L.A., 1983. Lic. in real estate sales, Calif. Real estate salesperson Ladera Realty, L.A., 1976-78; account coordinator/jr. account exec. Lewis & Assocs., L.A., 1978-79; jr. account exec. Ayer Jorgensen Macdonald (now N.W. Ayer, ABH Internat.), advt. firm, Los Angeles, 1979; recruitment adminstr. Lawler, Felix & Hall, L.A., 1980-81; account exec. Clive Hoffman Assocs., L.A., 1981-83; sr. account exec. Rifkind, Pondel & Parsons, L.A., 1983-84; founder, pres. Hoyt Orgn., Torrance, Calif., 1984—. Fund-raising chmn. for 1980 Spl. Olympics, L.A. Jr. C. of C.; mem. L.A. Hdgrs. City Assn., Archtl. Guild U. S.C. Recipient 2d pl. Award of Excellence, Pro Awards, Pub. Communicators of L.A., 1994, 96, 1st pl. award, 1995; named to Outstanding Young Women Am., U.S. Jaycees, 1980. Mem. Pub. Rels. Soc. Am., Soc. Mktg. Profl. Svcs., L.A. C. of C., Torrance C. of C., U. So. Calif. South Bay Young Alumni (2d v.p. bd. dirs. 1982), Trojan Jr. Aux. (dir. 1978-80), Trojan Fourth Estate (bd. dirs.), Town and Gown Jrs., Alpha Gamma Delta Alumni (exec. coun. 1983-84), Internat. Coun. of Shopping Ctrs. Office: 22750 Hawthorne Blvd Ste 230 Torrance CA 90505-3614

HRUT, CHRISTOPHER BOLESLAW, sales and marketing executive; b. Szczecin, Poland, Apr. 18, 1958; came to U.S. 1986; s. Zdzislaw and Halina (Maj) H. MSc, Gdansk U., Poland, 1982; Dipl.Eng., Tech. U. Gdansk, 1983; MSc, MIT, 1987; MBA, Harvard U., 1989. Sr. supr. Gdansk Shipyard, 1983-86; exec. asst. Fuji-Xerox, Tokyo, 1988; mng. exec. Network Equip. Technologies, 1989-90; dir. Trimble Navigation & Navigation Techs., Sunnyvale, Calif., 1991—; gen. ptnr. Renaissance Capital, Boston, 1993—; gen. ptnr. European Renaissance Ptnrs.; cons. in field. Contbr. articles to profl. jours. MIT grantee, Harvard Bus. Sch. fellow, Kosciuszko Found. grantee. Mem. Harvard Bus. Sch. Club No. Calif., MIT Club No. Calif., Commonwealth Club of Calif., Harvard U. Club No. Calif., Churchill Club, Kosciuszko Found., Harvard U. Club of Poland (founding chmn. 1991—), Harvard U. Club of Hungary (founding chmn. 1990—), Harvard U. Club of Czechoslovakia (founding chmn. 1990—). Home: 445 Encinal Ave Apt H Menlo Park CA 94025 Office: Oracle Corp 500 Oracle Pkwy Box 659106 Redwood Shores CA 94065 also: Zaruskiego 26, PL-80-299 Gdansk-Osowa Poland

HSIAO, CHIE-FANG, neuroscientist; b. Chi-Yei, Taiwan, Jan. 15, 1945; came to U.S., 1983; s. Zu-Chin and Chiao (Ching) H.; m. Shu-Lan Lin, Jan. 29, 1976; children: Kathryne, Amy. BS in Pharmacology, Taipei (Taiwan) Med. Coll., 1976; PhD in Med. Sci., Osaka (Japan) U., 1983. Rsch. assoc. SUNY, Stony Brook, 1983-85, U. Colo., Boulder, 1985-89; rsch. instr. U. Mo., Kansas City, 1989-92; neuroscientist U. Calif., L.A., 1992—; lectr. U. Mo., Kansas City, 1988-89; rsch. instr. Osaka U. Med. Sch., 1981-83, U. Calif., L.A., 1992—. Advisor Taipei Med. Sch. Alumni, Calif., 1993, Taiwanese Assn., Colo., 1985. Recipient Nat. Rsch. Svc. award NIH, 1992, fellowship Fight for Sight Inc., 1984, scholarship Japan Rotary, 1982. Mem. AAAS, Soc. for Neurosci., Naturalistic Soc. USA. Home: 1437 S Westgate Ave Apt 12 Los Angeles CA 90025-2241 Office: Univ Calif 405 Hilgard Ave Los Angeles CA 90024-1301

HSIEH, STEWART, lawyer; b. L.A., Apr. 5, 1953; s. Donald and Eva (Moe) H.; m. Victoria Parrott, Mar. 29, 1979 (div. 1996); children: Joshua, Christine. BS, Calif. State U., L.A., 1975; JD, Southwestern U., 1978. Atty., ptnr. Frye & Hsieh, L.A., 1988—; bd. dirs. Med. Bd. Calif., v.p., 1992-94, 95-96, pres., 1997; mem. low income housing adv. com. Calif. State Treas., 1995—, chmn., 1996. Mem. com. Boy Scouts Am., 1994, vice chmn; statewide co-fin. chair Matt Fong for State Treas., 1993—, Matt Fong for State Contr., 1989-90; mem. ctrl. com. Calif. Rep. Party, 1991—, regional co-chair Asian Outreach Project, 1989-90; bd. dirs. RIMPAC, 1990—; mem. Asian adv. com. Natural Mus. History, County of L.A., 1990-94. Mem. Nat. Assn. Bond Lawyers, Calif. Soc. Healthcare Attys., State Bar of Calif., L.A. County Bar Assn. (co-chmn. sr. citizen outreach com. 1992-93), L.A. Athletic Club (chmn. bd. 1996). Republican. Office: Frye and Hsieh LLP 626 Wilshire Blvd # 800 Los Angeles CA 90017-3209

HSIEH, YOU-LO, fiber and polymer scientist, educator; b. Taipei, Taiwan, Republic of China, Feb. 16, 1953; came to U.S., 1975; d. Men-Chu and Tze-hue (Hsiao) Hsieh; m. A. Bruce Playle, May 11, 1980; children: Arlo, Alma. BS, Fu-Jen U., Taipei, 1975; MS, Auburn (Ala.) U., 1977; PhD, U. Md., 1981. Asst. prof. U. Calif., Davis, 1981-88, assoc. prof., 1988-94, prof. div. textiles and clothing, 1994—. Author rsch. papers. Recipient German Acad. Exch. Svcs. award, N.Y.C.; NSF grantee; Cotton Inc. grantee. Mem. Am. Chem. Soc., Am. Phys. Soc., Am. Textile Chemists and Colorists Soc., The Fiber Soc. Office: U Calif Davis Div Textiles and Clothing Davis CA 95615-8722

HSU, CHARLES, venture capitalist; b. N.Y.C., Oct. 31, 1957; s. Chichang and Ujjala (Deb) H. AB in Biochemistry magna cum laude, Harvard U., 1979; PhD in Genetics, Stanford U., 1984, MBA, 1990. Tchg. fellow Harvard U., Cambridge, 1978-79; postdoctoral fellow Stanford U., 1984; staff scientist Creative Biomolecules, San Francisco, 1984-85, Invitron Corp., Redwood City, Calif., 1985-87; sr. scientist Invitron Corp., Redwood City, 1987-88; ind. cons. Comm-Tech Internat., Menlo Park, Calif., 1989; investment mgr. Advent Internat. Corp., Boston, 1990-92, ptnr., 1992-96; gen. ptnr. Walden Group, San Francisco, 1996—; membership sales and program advisor Summit Orgn., Foster City, Calif., 1987-88; cons. Stanford Bus. Sch. Alumni Consulting Team, 1993—. Contbr. articles to profl. jours. Presdl. scholar, 1975. Mem. AAAS. Democrat. Office: Walden Group 750 Battery St San Francisco CA 94111

HSU, JOHN YU-SHENG, computer scientist; b. Republic of China, Mar. 17, 1938; came to U.S., 1962; s. James and Margaret (Yen) H.; m. Sheryl L. Hsu, Dec. 18, 1965; children: Mary, David. BSEE, Nat. Taiwan U., 1959; MSEE, U. Calif., Berkeley, 1964, PhD, 1969. Cons. Ames Rsch. Ctr., Mountain View, Calif., 1973-74, Federic Electric/ITT, Vandenberg, Calif., 1971-79, Inst. for Info. Industry, Taipei, 1979-80, Control Data Corp., Campbell, Calif., 1981-82, IBM Corp., San Jose, Calif., 1987-89; prof. Calif. Poly., San Luis Obispo, Calif., 1970—. Author: Computer Networks: Architecture, Protocols and Software, 1996. Mem. IEEE (sr.), Assn. for Computing Machinery. Office: Calif Poly San Luis Obispo CA 93407

HSU, SHU-DEAN, hematologist, oncologist; b. Chiba, Japan, Feb. 21, 1943; came to U.S., 1972; s. Tetzu and Takako (Koo) Minoyama; m. San-San Hsu, Mar. 3, 1973; children: Deborah Te-Lan, Peter Jie-Te. MD, Taipei (Taiwan) Med. Coll., 1968. Diplomate Am. Bd. Internal Medicine, Am. Bd. Hematology, Am. Bd. Med. Oncology. Asst. in medicine Mt. Sinai Sch. Medicine, N.Y.C., 1975-77; asst. instr. medicine U. Tex., Galveston, 1977-78; lectr. in medicine Tex. A&M U., Temple, 1978-80; asst. prof. medicine U. Ark., Little Rock, 1980-83; practice medicine specializing in hematology-oncology Visalia (Calif.) Med. Clinic, 1983—; chief hematology and oncology VA Med. Ctr., Temple, Tex., 1978-80. Contbr. articles to profl. jours. Fellow ACP; mem. N.Y. Acad. Scis., Am. Soc. Clin. Oncology, Am. Soc. Hematology, Calif. Med. Assn., Tulare County Med. Soc. Club: Visalia Racquet. Home: 3500 W Hydeway Visalia CA 93291 Office: Visalia Med Clinic PO Box 3347 Olympic Valley CA 96146

HU, EDNA GERTRUDE FENSKE, pediatrics nurse; b. Arlington, S.D., June 11, 1922; d. Walter O. and Therese (Kautz) Fenske; m. Patrick P.C. Hu, Nov. 26, 1954; children: Lou Anne Hu Yee, Mark C., Lawrence P. BS in Nursing, U. Colo. Sch. Nursing, 1954. RN, Colo. Staff pediatrics nurse Colo. Gen. Hosp., Denver, 1954-63, night nursing supr., 1963-65; staff nurse alcohol withdrawal unit Denver Gen. Hosp., 1971-73; staff surg. nurse Fitzsimons Army Hosp., Denver, 1973-79; staff nurse VA Hosp., Allens Pk., Mich., 1979-81, Drug and Alcohol Withdrawal and Rehab. Ctr., Ft. Dodge, Iowa, 1981-83; researcher Ft. Collins, Colo., 1988—; researcher effects on memory following long term residence in another culture; instr. English, health care, Asia. Recipient Disting. Alumna award Class of 1954. Mem. ANA, Colo. Nurses Assn., Non-practicing and Part-time Nurses Assn. Home: 2518 Timber Ct Fort Collins CO 80521-3120

HU, GRACE, mayor. Mayor City of Cerritos, Calif. Office: City of Cerritos PO Box 3130 Cerritos CA 90703

HU, JOHN CHIH-AN, retired chemist, research engineer; b. Nanzhang, Hubei, China, July 12, 1922; came to U.S., 1954, naturalized, 1965; s. Qi-Qing and Zhao-Xian (Zeng) H.; BS in Chemistry, Nat. Central U., Nanjing, China, 1946; MS in Organic Chemistry, U. So. Calif., 1957, postgrad., 1957-61; PhD (hon.) Marquis Giuseppe Scicluna Internat. Univ. Foundation, 1985; m. Betty Siao-Yung Ho, Oct. 26, 1957; children: Arthur, Benjamin, Carl, David, Eileen, Franklin, George. Dir. rsch. dept. Plant 1, Taiwan Fertilizer Mfg. Co., Chilung, 1947-54; rsch. assoc. chemistry dept. U. So. Calif., L.A., 1957-61; rsch. chemist Chem Seal Corp. Am., Los Angeles, 1961-62; rsch. chemist Products Rsch. & Chem. Corp., Glendale, Calif., 1962-66; sr. rsch. engr., materials and tech. unit, Boeing Co., Seattle, 1966-71, specialist engr. Quality Assurance Labs., 1971-90, ret., 1990; cons. UN; lectr., China, profl. confs. Fellow Am. Inst. Chemists; mem. Am. Chem. Soc. (chmn. Puget Sound sect. 1988, councilor 1989-92), Royal Soc. Chemistry (London), N.Y. Acad. Sci., Phi Lambda Upsilon. Patentee Chromatopyrography; contbg. author: Analytical Approach, 1983, Advances in Chromotography, vol. 23, 1984; contbr. articles on analytical pyrolysis, gas chromatography, mass spectrometry, polymer characterization, chemistry and tech. of sealants and adhesives to profl. publs. in Chinese and English; editor Puget Sound Chemist, 1984-92; referee profl. jours. Analytical Chemistry, Analytica Chimica Acta, Am. Chem. Soc. short courses. Home: 2813 Whitworth Ave S Renton WA 98055-5008

HU, JOSEPH KAI MING, insurance company executive; b. Hong Kong, Oct. 3, 1953; came to the U.S., 1963; s. Hon Wai and Kwan Yee (Lau) H.; m. Donna Taeko Aihara, Mar. 31, 1984; 1 child, Jennifer Chiemi. BBA in Mktg., U. Hawaii, 1980. CPCU. Sales rep. Bankers Life Nebr., Honolulu, 1980-82; comml. lines mgr. Royal Ins. Agy., Honolulu, 1982-86; account exec. Frank B. Hall of Hawaii Inc., Honolulu, 1986-87, Jardine Ins. Brokers Inc., Honolulu, 1987-88; sr. v.p. Am. Ins. Agy. Inc., Honolulu, 1988—. Mem. Chartered Property and Casualty Underwriters (pres. Hawaii chpt. 1990-91, dir. Hawaii chpt. 1995—), Profl. Ins. Agts. Assn. (dir. Hawaii chpt. 1988—, pres. Hawaii chpt. 1993-94), Internat. Ins. Soc., Hong Kong Bus. Assn. Hawaii, Chinese Chamber Hawaii, Waikiki Rotary (treas. 1991-92). Office: Am Ins Agy Inc 900 Fort St Mall Ste 500 Honolulu HI 96813

HU, MARY LEE, artist, educator; b. Lakewood, Ohio, Apr. 13, 1943; d. Dana Willis and Virginia Haines (Bennett) Lee; m. Tah-Kai Hu, Sept. 9, 1967 (dec. May 1972). Student, Miami U., Oxford, Ohio, 1961-63; BFA, Cranbrook Acad. Arts, Bloomfield Hills, Mich., 1965; MFA, So. Ill. U., 1967. Instr. So. Ill. U., Carbondale, 1968-69; freelance artist various locations, 1969-75; lectr. U. Wis., Madison, 1976-77; asst. prof. art Mich. State U., East Lansing, 1977-80; assoc. prof. U. Wash., Seattle, 1980-86, prof., 1986—; vis. artist U. Iowa, Iowa City, fall 1975; instr. Kans. State U., Manhattan, summer 1976; dep. v.p. for North Am. World Crafts Coun., N.Y.C., 1982-84. Represented in permanent collections: Columbus (Ohio) Mus. Art, 1975, Am. Craft Mus., N.Y.C., 1985, Renwick Gallery, Washington, 1985, The Art Inst., Chgo., 1989, The Victoria & Albert Mus., London, 1991, Mus. Fine Arts, Boston, 1996. Bd. dirs. Wing Luke Asian Mus., Seattle, 1984-88. Fellow Nat. Endowment Arts, 1976, 84, 92. Fellow Am. Crafts Coun. (sec. 1982-83, trustee 1980-84); mem. Soc. N.Am. Goldsmiths (disting., v.p. 1976-77, pres. 1977-80), Artist Blacksmith Assn. N.Am., N.W. Designer Craftsmen, Seattle Metals Guild, N.W. Bead Soc., James Renwick Alliance. Office: U Wash Art-Box 353440 Seattle WA 98195-3440

HU, TEH-WEI, economics educator; b. Shanghai, Oct. 10, 1937; came to U.S., 1961; married. PhD, U. Wis., 1967. Statis. analyst World Bank, Washington, 1962-63; asst. prof. Pa. State U., University Park, 1966-70, assoc. prof., 1970-72, prof., 1972-86; prof. U. Calif., Berkeley, 1986—, chmn., 1990-93; cons. World Bank, 1985-93, Ford Found., 1983-88, Ministry of Health, People's Rep. of China, 1990—. Named Disting. in Social Svcs., Pa. State Alumni Assn., 1985, Disting. Alumni, Econs. Inst., U. Colo., 1992. Mem. Am. Econs. Assn., N.Am. Chinese Econs. Assn. (pres. 1987-89). Office: U Calif Sch Pub Health 412 Warren Hall Berkeley CA 94720

HU, YONG-YAN, performing company executive. Music dir. Lincoln Symphony Orch., Neb. Office: Lincoln Symphony Orch 825 M St Ste 214 Lincoln NE 68508*

HUANG, CHIEN CHANG, electrical engineer; b. Nanking, Peoples Republic of China, Feb. 16, 1931; came to U.S., 1957; s. Ling-Kuo Huang and Yi-Ching Liu; m. Li-May Tsai, June 2, 1962; children: Frederick G., Lewis G. BSEE, Taiwan Coll. Engring., Tainan, 1954; MSEE, U. Ill., 1959; postgrad., U. Pa., 1960-62. Engr. Burrough Corp., Paoli, Pa., 1960-64; sr. staff engr. Unisys Corp., San Diego, 1974—; sr. engr. Philco Ford Corp., Blue Bell, Pa., 1965-69; staff engr. Fairchild Semiconductor, Mountain View, Calif., 1969-71; sr. staff engr. Am. Micro Systems, Santa Clara, Calif., 1971-74. Contbr. articles to profl. jours. Home: 14481 Maplewood St Poway CA 92064-6446 Office: Unisys Corp 10850 Via Frontera San Diego CA 92127-1705

HUANG, FAN-H FRANK, materials scientist, researcher; b. Taiwan, May 13, 1940; came to U.S., 1966; BS, Taiwan Normal U., 1965; PhD, Rensselaer Poly. Inst., Troy, N.Y., 1973. Rsch. assoc. Cornell U., Ithaca, N.Y., 1973-77; prin. scientist Westinghouse Hanford Co., Richland, Wash., 1977-94, Kaiser Hanfor Co., Richland, 1994-96, Fluor Daniel N.W., Inc., Richland, 1996—. Author: Fracture Properties of Irradiated Alloys, 1995; contbr. articles to profl. jours. Mem. ASTM, Am. Nuclear Soc. Office: Fluor Daniel Northwest Inc PO Box 1050 X3-85 Richland WA 99352

HUANG, FRANCIS FU-TSE, mechanical engineering educator; b. Hong Kong, Aug. 27, 1922; came to U.S., 1945, naturalized, 1960; s. Kwong Set and Chen-Ho (Yee) H.; m. Fung-Yuen Fung, Apr. 10, 1954; children: Raymond, Stanley. BS, San Jose State Coll., 1951; MS, Stanford U., 1952; Profl. M.E., Columbia U., 1964; Cultural Doctorate in Energy Sci. (hon.), World U., Ariz., 1990. Design engr. M.W. Kellogg Co., N.Y.C., 1952-58; faculty San Jose (Calif.) State U., 1958—, assoc. prof. mech. engring., 1962-67, prof., 1967-91, prof. emeritus, 1991, chmn. dept., 1973-81; hon. prof. heat power engring. Taiyuan (People's Republic of China) U. Tech., 1981—. Author: Engineering Thermodynamics—Fundamentals and Applications, 1976, 2d edit., 1988. Capt. Chinese Army, 1943-45. Recipient Disting. Teaching award Calif. State Coll. System, 1968-69; named Outstanding Prof. of Yr., Tau Beta Pi, 1967, 76, Prof. of Yr., Pi Tau Sigma, 1985; NSF faculty fellow, 1962-64. Mem. AAAS, ASME, AIAA, AAUP, Am. Soc. Engring. Edn., N.Y. Acad. Scis., Sigma Xi. Home: 1259 Sierra Mar Dr San Jose CA 95118-1235 Office: San Jose State U Dept Mech Engring San Jose CA 95192

HUANG, KUN LIEN, software engineer, scientist; b. Nantou, Taiwan, Jan. 20, 1953; came to U.S., 1984; S. Chai-Chang and Fei-Chei (Chi) H.; m. Sue Hui Lee, Mar. 24, 1981; 1 child, Wayne. BS, Nat. Taipei Inst. Tech., Taiwan, 1973, N.D. State U., 1986; MS, U. Mo., 1988. Mech. engr. Ta Tung Aluminum Co., Taipei, 1975-76; rsch. mgr. Ta Tung Aluminum Co., Tapei, 1976-77, prodn. tech. mgr., 1977-79, quality control mgr., 1979-84; computer programmer U. Mo., Columbia, 1988; systems analyst, programmer NCR Corp., San Diego, 1989-92; database cons. Gamma-Metrics, 1992-93; software engr. Sci. Applications Internat. Corp., 1993-95; Unix adminstr. Gen. Instrument Corp., 1995—; cons. Computing Ctr., U. Mo., Columbia, 1987-88. Recipient Nat. scholarship Republic China Jaycees, Taipei, 1972. Mem. AAAS, San Diego Taiwanese Cultural Assn. Republican. Home: 8939 Adobe Bluffs Dr San Diego CA 92129-4400

HUANG, LINDA CHEN, plastic surgeon; b. Ithaca, N.Y., July 24, 1952. MD, StanfordU, 1979. Chmn. plastic surgery St. Joseph Hosp., Denver. Office: 1578 Humboldt St Denver CO 80218-1638

HUANG, SUNG-CHENG, electrical engineering educator; b. Canton, China, Oct. 26, 1944; came to U.S., 1967; s. Hip-chung Wong and Chung Huang; m. Caroline S. Soong, Sept. 4, 1971; children: Michael, Dennis. BSEE, Nat. Taiwan U., Taipei, 1966; DSc, Wash. U., 1973. Postdoctral rsch. assoc. Biomed. Computer Lab. Wash. U., St. Louis, 1973-74; project engr. Picker Corp., Cleve., 1974-77; asst. prof. Sch. Medicine UCLA, 1977-82, assoc. prof. Sch. Medicine, 1982-86, prof. Sch. Medicine, 1986—; Edward Farber lectr. U. Chgo., 1986. Mem. editorial bd. Jour. Cerebral Blood Flow, 1989-92, Jour. Nuclear Medicine, 1997—; dep. chief editor Jour. Cerebral Blood Flow and Metabolism, 1993—; contbr. more than 200 articles to scholarly and profl. jours. Recipient George Von Hevesy Prize World Congress of Nuclear Medicine and Biology, 1982; grantee U.S. Dept. Energy, 1977—, NIH, 1977—. Mem. AAAS, IEEE, Soc. Nuclear Medicine, Soc. Cerebral Blood Flow. Office: UCLA Sch Medicine Divsn Nuclear Medicine and Biophysics 10833 Le Conte Ave Los Angeles CA 90095-6948

HUANG, SUNGRUNG RON, engineer; b. Taipei, July 26, 1960; came to U.S., 1987; s. Wanliang and Cheh (Lee) H.; m. Tsaefen Yang, Sept. 7, 1983; children: Jeffrey, Vickie, Diane. BSEE, Nat. Taiwan U., Taipei, 1982, MSEE, 1985; PhDEE, U. Rochester, 1990. Ultrasound scientist Bio-Imaging Rsch. Inc., Lincolnshire, Ill., 1990-92; image analysis engr. Acuson Computed Sonography, Mountain View, Calif., 1992—. Inventor sonoelasticity imaging, blood loss monitoring system, needle tip position monitoring system. Mem. IEEE, Am. Inst. of Ultrasound, Acoustical Soc. of Am. Office: Acuson PO Box 7393 Mountain View CA 94039

HUANG, XUEDONG DAVID, senior reseacher; b. Wuhan, Hubei, China, Oct. 20, 1962; came to U.S., 1989; s. Heqing and Jiansong (Ling) H.; m. Yingzhi Zhou, Oct. 4, 1986; 1 child, Angela. BS, Hunan U., Chanagsha, China, 1982; MS, Tsinghua U., Beijing, 1984; PhD, U. Edinburgh, U.K., 1989. Rsch. assoc. Tsinghua U., Beijing, 1984-87; fellow, vis. scientist U. Edinburgh, 1987-89; rsch. computer scientist Carnegie Mellon U., Pitts., 1989-93; mgr., sr. rschr. Speech Rsch. group, Microsoft Corp., Redmond, Wash., 1993—. Author: Hidden Markov Models for Speech Recognition, 1990; inventor in field; assoc. editor IEEE Trans. on Speech and Audio Processing, 1992—. Mem. IEEE (sr. mem., Paper award 1994). Home: 20020 NE 121st St Woodinville WA 98072 Office: Microsoft Corp Redmond WA 98052

HUBBARD, DONALD, marine artist, writer; b. Bronx, N.Y., Jan. 15, 1926; s. Ernest Fortesque and Lilly Violet (Beck) H.; student Brown U., 1944-45; A.A., George Washington U., 1959, B.A., 1958; student Naval War Coll., 1965-66; m. Darlene Julia Huber, Dec. 13, 1957; children: Leslie Carol, Christopher Eric, Lauren Ivy, Carmeron C. McNall. Commd. ensign U.S. Navy, 1944, advanced through grades to comdr., 1965; served naval aviator, ret., 1967; founder Ocean Ventures Industries, Inc., Coronado, Calif., 1969, operator, 1969-77; marine artist; founder, operator Sea Eagle Pubs., Coronado, 1988; lectr. on marine art; SCUBA instr. Author: Ships-in-Bottles, 2d edition, 1988, A How to Guide to a Venerable Nautical Craft, 1971; Buddleschiffe: Wie Macht Man Sie, 1972; The Complete Book of Inflatable Boats, 1979; Where to Paddle in San Diego County and Nearby Mexico, 1992, Days of Yore: Rhymes & Other Writings, 1995, Neptunes Table: Cooking the Sea Food Exotics, 1997; editor: The Bottle Shipwright; works featured in Am. Artist of the Bookplate, 1970-90, Cambridge Bookplate Press, 1990; contbr. articles in field to publs. Decorated Air Medal. Mem. Ships-in-Bottles Assn. (pres. N.Am. div. 1982—), Nature Printing Soc., Am. Soc. Bookplate Collectors adn Designers, San Diego Watercolor Soc. (bd. dirs. 1981-82), Marine Hist. Soc., San Diego Maritime Assn. Home and Office: 1022 Park Pl Coronado CA 92118-2822

HUBBARD, GREGORY SCOTT, physicist; b. Lexington, Ky., Dec. 27, 1948; s. Robert Nicholas and Nancy Clay (Brown) H.; B.A., Vanderbilt U., 1970; postgrad. U. Calif., Berkeley, 1975-77; m. Susan Artimissa Ruggeri, Aug. 1, 1982. Lab. engr. physics dept. Vanderbilt U., Nashville, 1970-73; staff scientist Lawrence Berkeley Lab. Dept. Instrument Techniques, Berkeley, Calif., 1974-80; dir. research and devel. Canberra Industries, Inc., Detector Products Div., Novato, Calif., 1980-82; v.p., gen. mgr. Canberra Semicondr., Novato, Calif., 1982-85; cons., owner Hubbard Cons. Services, 1978—; cons. SRI Internat., Menlo Park, Calif., 1979-86, sr. rsch. physicist, 1986-87; div. staff scientist space exploration projects office Ames Rsch. Ctr., NASA, Moffett Field, Calif., 1987-90, chief space instrumentation and studies br., 1990-92; dep. chief space projects divsn., 1992-96, assoc. dir. space directorate, 1996—; lectr. in field. Recipient Founders Scholarship, Vanderbilt U., 1966, Exceptional Achievement medal NASA, 1994. Mem. AIAA, IEEE, Nuclear Sci. Soc., Am. Phys. Soc., Commonwealth Club Calif., Hon. Order Ky. Cols.

HUBBARD, RICHARD WARD, clinical biochemist; b. Battle Creek, Mich., Dec. 24, 1929; s. Ralph Martin and Myrtle (Ward) H.; m. Constance Mae Hubbard, Nov. 18, 1951; children: Robert John, Jeffrey Allen, Karen Ann. BA, Pacific Union Coll., 1951; MS, Purdue U., 1959, PhD, 1961. Analytical chemist Willard Storage Battery Co., East L.A., 1951-53; med. tech. trainee L.A. County Gen. Hosp., 1953-54; instr. biochemistry Dept. Dermatology, U. Mich., Ann Arbor, 1960-63; sr. rsch. chemist Spinco div. Beckman Instruments, Palo Alto, Calif., 1963-67; project leader biochemistry NASA/SRI, Biosatellite Primate Pr., Menlo Park, 1967-70; asst. prof. biochemistry Depts. Pathology and Biochemistry, Loma Linda (Calif.) U., 1970-73, assoc. prof. biochemistry, 1973-89, assoc. rsch. prof. pathology, 1989—; cons., tchr. Beckman Instruments, Palo Alto, 1967-69; cons. biochemistry NASA/Stanford Rsch. Inst., Menlo Park, Calif., 1978-79; scientific advisor Spinco div. Beckman Instruments, Palo Alto, 1986—, Nat. Registry in Clin. Chemistry, 1972. Author: Preservation of Biol. Sp., 1972; (with others) Amino Acid Connection, 1988, Monographs on Atherosclerosis, 1990, The Potential of Diet to Alter Disease Processes, 1994. Mem. Am. Inst. Nutrition, Am. Inst. Clin. Nutrition, Am. Assn. Clin. Chemists (sec. 1980-84), Am. Chem. Soc., Am. Soc. Med. Tech. (chpt. pres. 1983), N.Y. Acad. Sci., Phi Lambda Upsilon, Sigma Xi. Republican. Seventh-Day Adventist. Home: 1906 Verde Vista Dr Redlands CA 92373-7322

HUBBELL, ROBERT NEWELL, psychologist; b. Neenah, Wis., Oct. 23, 1931; s. Ralph Newell and Ruth Elizabeth (Lindsey) H.; m. Joann Marguerite Jansen, Aug. 14, 1954; children: Scott David, Brian Jansen. BS, Northwestern U., 1954; MA, U. Wis., 1961, PhD, 1964. Lic. psychologist, Colo. Dean of men, asst. prof. U. Iowa, 1964-67; Am. Coun. on Edn. intern U. Calif., Santa Barbara, 1967-68; assoc. prof., staff psychologist Colo. State U., Ft. Collins, 1968-72; coord. Community Counseling Ctr., Granby, Colo., 1972-76; coord. mental health svcs. West Cent. Mental Health Ctr., Canon City, Colo., 1976-77; pvt. practice clin. psychology Canon City, 1977—; behavioral sci. intern Nat. Tng. Labs., Bethel, Maine, summer 1968; cons. Pomona Coll., summer 1969, Luth. Ch. Am., 1969-70, Higher Edn. Assocs., 1970-72; adj. prof. Walden U., Naples, Fla., 1971—, Colo. State Penitentiary, 1977-79. Lt. (j.g.) USNR, 1954-57. Contbr. articles to profl. jours. Mem. APA, Biofeedback Soc. Am. (cert.), Am. Soc. Clin. Hypnosis, Nat. Register Health Svcs. Providers in Psychology, Colo. Psychol. Assn. Methodist. Home: 2317 Greenway Cir Canon City CO 81212-2036 Office: PO Box 687 Canon City CO 81215-0687

HUBBS, DONALD HARVEY, foundation executive; b. Kingman, Ariz., Jan. 3, 1918; s. Wayne and Grace Lillian (Hoose) H.; m. Flora Vincent, June 14, 1945; children: Donald Jr., Susan Tyner, Diane Schultz, Wayne, David, Adrienne Busk. BA in Edn., Ariz. State U., 1940; JD, Southwestern U., 1956. Bar: Calif., 1956; CPA. Acct. Wright and Hubbs, L.A., 1945-67; pvt. practice atty. L.A., 1956-81; pres., dir. Conrad N. Hilton Found., L.A., 1981—; bd. dirs. Trans World Airlines, 1977; regent Mt. St. Mary's Coll., 1983—; bd. councilors U. So. Calif. Law Sch., 1992—. 1st lt. (inf.) U.S. Army. Decorated Purple Heart. Mem. State Bar of Calif., So. Calif. Assn. for Philanthropy (pres. 1985-86), Riviera Country Club, L.A. Country Club. Home: 1658 San Onofre Dr Pacific Palisades CA 90272-2735 Office: Conrad N Hilton Found 10100 Santa Monica Blvd Ste 740 Los Angeles CA 90067-4011

HUBER, CLAYTON SHIRL, university dean; b. LaPoint, Utah, Feb. 28, 1938; s. LeRoy and Vera Johanna (Taylor) H.; m. Beth briggs, July 25, 1963; children: Kerry, Philip, LaNae, Douglas, LeAnn, Brad, Kevin. BS, Utah State U., 1962, MS, 1963; PhD, Purdue U., 1968. Lab. instr. Utah State U., Logan, 1962-63; rsch. asst. Purdue U., West Lafayette, Ind., 1965-68; sr. scientist Kraftco, Glenview, Ill., 1968; mgr. Technology Inc., Houston, 1968-75; scientist Am. Potato Co., Blackfoot, Idaho, 1975-76; dept. chair Brigham Young U., Provo, Utah, 1976-88, dean, 1988—; chmn. adv. com. NASA Ctr., Purdue U., West Lafayette, 1990-95; cons. to food industry, 1976—; mem. exec. com. Thrasher Rsch. Found., Salt Lake City, 1994—. Mem. editl. bd. Comtex Sci., 1982; contbr. articles to profl. jours.; patentee in field. Dist. chmn. Boy Scouts Am., Houston, 1974-75; voting dist. chmn. Rep. Party, Provo, 1979-82, county and state del. 1st lt. U.S. Army, 1963-65. Decorated Army Commendation medal; recipient Snoopy award Astronaut Office/NASA, 1970, NASA's Sci. and Tech award, 1971; named Virginia Cutler Lecture, Brigham Young U. Fellow Inst. Food Technologists (Tex. sect. chmn. 1972-73, chmn. Bonneville sect. 1980-81), Poultry Sci. Assn. (com. chmn. 1980-81). Republican. LDS. Home: 189 E 4380 N Provo UT 84604

HUBER, JOSEPH H., mayor; m.; 2 children. BA, U. Notre Dame; LLB, Stanford U. Councilman City of Palo Alto, Calif., 1991-96, mayor, 1997—; liaison City of Mountain View, Calif., 1994, Stanford U., 1993, 95, Neibors Abroad, 1996; del. Airport Land Use Commission Hearing Bd., 1994-97, Santa Clara County Bond Adv. Com., 1992-97, Santa Clara Valley Water Dist. Commn., 1992-93, 96, alt., 1994-95; alt. Palo Alto Child Care Task Force, 1992-93, Hist. Resources Bd., 1992-94, 97, Pub. Art Commn., 1993,

Sr. Coord. Coun., 1995-96, Santa Clara County Emergency Preparedness Coun., 1993-94, Santa Clara County Intergovtl. Coun., 1992; active Santa Clara County Paratransit Coord. Coun., 1992-95; policy adv. bd. Santa Clara County Traffic Authority, 1993-97; rep. Santa Clara Valley Water Dist.-N.W. Flood Control Zone Adv. Com., 1992-93, alt., 1994-97. Pres. Univ. Park Neighborhood Assn., 1977-87; bd. dirs. Palo Alto Adolescent Svcs., 1981-88, pres., 1983; chmn., troop com. mem. Boy Scouts Am. Mem. Santa Clara County Cities Assn. (del. 1997). Office: 250 Hamilton Ave Palo Alto CA 94301

HUBER, LINDA RUTH, non-commissioned officer; b. Stafford Springs, Conn., Aug. 3, 1955; d. Joseph Lawrence and Edith Viola (Plante) Young; m. Vernon R. Huber Jr., Dec. 26, 1981; children: James R., Brian D., Chad T., Nicole L., Christopher A. AA, C.C. of Air Force, 1986; student pre-edn. program, Ariz. U. Admission clk. St. Anthony Hosp., St. Petersburg, Fla., 1974-76; customer svc. rep. Zayre Dept. Stores, St. Petersburg, 1976-77; jet engine technician Fighter Interceptor Squadron, Griffiss AFB, N.Y., 1977-79, Logistics Support Squadron, Okinawa, Japan, 1979-81; asst. NCOIC outbound assignments Combat Support Group, McConnell AFB, Kans., 1981-82; jet engine specialist Consolidated Aircraft Maintenance Squadron, Altus AFB, Okla., 1982-84; NCOIC quick engine changes sect. 81 Component Repair Squadron, RAF Bentwaters, UK, 1984-88; NCOIC tech. adminstrn. 355 Component Repair Squadron, Davis-Monthan AFB, Tucson, 1988-92; NCOIC orderly room 355 Ops. Support Squadron, Davis-Monthan AFB, Tucson, 1992—; USAF disaster preparedness support team Combat Support Group, RAF Bentwaters, 1984-88; mem. Desert Shield/Desert Storm support Component Repair Squadron, Davis-Monthan AFB, 1990-91; tutor for AHDH and ADD diagnosed children, 1993—. Coach Pop Warner Mitey Mite Football, Tucson, 1989, Apache Little League Baseball, Tucson, 1988-92; coach (asst.) Pantano Soccer League, Tucson, 1989-92; fundraiser rep. Pop Warner Football, Tucson, 1990-92, U. Ariz. Soccer program, 1993—. Democrat. Lutheran. Office: 355 Ops Support Squadron Davis Monthan AFB Tucson AZ 85707

HUBER, WAYNE CHARLES, engineering educator; b. Shelby, Mont., Aug. 2, 1941; s. Hubert Henry and Lois Marion (Hendrickson) H.; m. Catherine Ann Forster, June 22, 1968; 1 child, Lydia Ann. BS, Calif. Inst. Tech., Pasadena, 1963; MS, MIT, 1965, PhD, 1968. Registered profl. engr., Fla. Asst. prof. dept. environ. engring. scis. U. Fla., Gainesville, 1968-73, assoc. prof. dept. environ. engring. scis., 1973-79, prof. dept. environ. engring. scis., 1979-91; prof., head dept. civil, constrn. and environ. engring. Oreg. State U., Covallis, 1991—; cons. Nat. Oceanic and Atmospheric Adminstrn., Rockville, Md., 1990-91, Internat. Inst. for Hydraulic and Environ. Engring., Delft, Netherlands, 1988-91, U.S. EPA, Washington, 1978-83. Co-author: Hydrology and Floodplain Analysis, 1992; contbr. articles to profl. jours. Recipient Lorenz G. Straub award U. Minn., 1969, Outstanding Tech. Achievement award Fla. Engring. Soc., 1985. Mem. ASCE (com. chair 1990-92, Hilgard Hydraulic prize 1973), Internat. Assn. for Hydraulic Rsch., Am. Geophys. Union, Am. Water Resources Assn., Sigma Xi, Tau Beta Pi. Democrat. Home: 3310 NW Crest Dr Corvallis OR 97330-1809 Office: Oreg State U Dept Civil Constrn and Environ Engring Corvallis OR 97331-2302

HUBERT, HELEN BETTY, epidemiologist; b. N.Y.C., Jan. 22, 1950; d. Leo and Ruth (Rosenbaum) H.; m. Carlos Barbaro Arostegui, Sept. 11, 1976 (div. May 1987); 1 child, Joshua Daniel Hubert. BA magna cum laude, Barnard Coll., 1970; MPH, Yale U., 1973, MPhil, 1976, PhD, 1978. Rsch. assoc. Yale U., New Haven, 1977-78; rsch. epidemiologist Nat. Heart, Lung and Blood Inst., Bethesda, Md., 1978-84; rsch. dir. Gen. Health, Inc., Washington, 1984-87; sr. rsch. scientist Stanford (Calif.) U., 1988—. Peer rev. Am. Jour. Epidemiology, Am. Jour. Pub. Health, Chest, Jour. AMA (JAMA), Archives Internal Medicine; contbr. articles to profl. jours., chpts. to books. Mem. Am. Heart Assn. (Coun. on Epidemiology), Am. Coll. Epidemiology, Soc. Epidemiol. Rsch., Assn. Rheumatology Health Profls., Phi Beta Kappa, Sigma Xi (grant-in-aid for rsch. 1978). Office: Stanford Univ Med Ctr Dept Health Rsch and Policy Rm T210 Stanford CA 94305

HUCHEL, FREDERICK M., historian, writer, consultant, speaker; b. Brigham City, Utah, Aug. 28, 1947; s. John L. and Mary L. (Andersen) H. BS, Brigham Young U., 1975. Dir. Railroad Village Mus., Corinne, Utah, 1965; asst. ch. history dept. Brigham Young U., Provo, Utah, 1970-75; translation exegesis specialist LDS Ch., Salt Lake City, 1975-76; dir. Brigham City Mus. Gallery, 1977-82; pres. Sequitur Computer Systems, Brigham City, 1983-91; asst. dir. for bus. rels. Utah State U. Bus. Coll., Logan, 1991-94; staff dir. Utah Biomed. Industry Coun., Salt Lake City, 1994-95; pres. FMH Cons. Svcs., Brigham City, 1995—; chmn. Brigham City Art Week, 1977-82, Beersheba Exhibit Com., 1979; site chmn. Utah Statehood Day, 1982; bd. dirs. Internat. Archaeol. Rsch. Inst., 1986; dir. Utah Internat. Med. Device Congress Steering Com., 1994-95; rsch. historian multi-vol. series The Work and the Glory, 1989—. Author: Utah State Centennial History of Box Elder County, 1996; editor Utah Internat. Med. Device Congress Proc., 1992-94; contbr. articles and revs. to hist. and profl. jours. and newspapers. Advisor Gov.'s Golden Spike Centennial Com., 1965-66; mem. Brigham City Comty. Theatre Bd., 1970; v.p. Golden Spike Assn.

HUCHTHAUSEN, DAVID RICHARD, sculptor, real estate developer; b. Wisconsin Rapids, Wis., Mar. 25, 1951; s. Richard Leeland and Irma Ruth (Fehrmann) H. BA, U. Wis., Wausau, 1972; BS, U. Wis., 1974; MFA, Ill. State U., 1977. Instr. Ill. State U., Bloomington, 1975-77, Royal Coll. Art, London, 1977; artist-in-residence J. and L. Lobmetr, Vienna, Austria, 1977-78; design dir. Milropa Studios, N.Y.C., 1979-80; prof. art Tenn. Tech. U., Cookeville, 1980-89; mng. ptnr. W/H Properties, Seattle, 1989—; pres. Somerset Properties Inc., Seattle, 1994—; curatorial cons. Woodson Art Mus., Wausau, Wis., 1976-90. One man shows include Habatat Galleries, Detroit, 1978, 83, 86, 90, 93, Miami, Fla., 1984, 88, Chgo., 1988, Boca Raton, Fla., 1990, 92, Pontiac Mich., 1995, Heller Gallery, N.Y.C., 1979, 82, 83, 85, 88, St. Louis Art Mus., 1984, Traver Sutton Gallery, Seattle, 1984, 87, William Traver Gallery, Seattle, 1990, 92, 95, Leo Kaplan Modern, 1992, 94, 96, Galerie L, Hamburg, Germany, 1994, 96; exhibited in group shows at Bloomingdales, N.Y.C., 1975, Mus. fur Kuntshandwerk, Frankfurt, West Germany, 1976, Huntington (W.Va.) Galleries, 1976, U. Wis., Madison, 1976, Habatat Galleries, Detroit, 1976-79, 80, 83, 86, 87, 88, 90, 91, U. Kans., Lawrence, 1977, Ill. State Mus., Springfield, 1977, Little Rock Art Ctr., 1978, J. & L. Lobmer Galleries, Vienna, Austria, 1980, Det. Inst. Art, 1981, 82, 87, Hastings (Nebr.) Coll., 1982, Huntsville (Ala.) Mus. Art, 1982, Am. Craft Mus., 1982, Heller Gallery, N.Y.C., 1984-88, Huntington Mus., 1984, 86, Boise (Idaho) Mus. Art, 1984, Nippon Gakki, Tokyo, 1984, Toledo Mus. Art, 1988, 92, Darmstadt Mus. Art, West Germany, 1988, Corning (N.Y.) Mus., 1988, 90, Bellevue (Wash.) Art Mus., 1991, Hokkaldo Mus. Art, Sapporo, Japan, 1991-92, Tamayo Mus., Mexico City, 1992, Marco Mus., Montreay, Mex., 1992; represented in permanent collections Met. Mus. Art N.Y.C., Smithsonian Inst., Washington, L.A. County Mus., High Mus., Atlanta, Corning Mus., Am. Craft Mus., N.Y.C., Hokkaido Mus. Art, Sapporo, Japan, Art Mus., Dusseldorf, Germany, Det. Inst. Art, Indpls. Mus. Art, Toledo Mus. Art, Mus. fur Kunst und Gerwerbe, Hamburg, Germany, Rockwell Mus., Corning, Huntington Mus. Art, Ill. State Mus., Normal, St. Louis Mus. Art, Mus. Decorative Arts, Prague, Czechoslovakia, JB Speed Mus., Louisville, Birmingham (Ala.) Mus. Art. Author: Americans in Glass, 1981, 84. Chair exec. com. North Duwamish Com., Seattle, 1995—; mem. South Downtown Bus. Group, Seattle, 1995—, Trust for Hist. Preservation. Rsch. grant Woodson Found., 1973-74; Stein fellowship Ill. State U., 1976; Fulbright scholar U. Applied Arts, 1977-78. Mem. Am. Craft Coun., Glass Art Soc., Classic Yacht Assn., Sodo Bus. Assn. (Seattle). Office: Somerset Properties Inc 3911 Airport Way Seattle WA 98108

HUCK, LARRY RALPH, manufacturers representative, sales consultant; b. Yakima, Wash., Aug. 10, 1942; s. Frank Joseph and Helen Barbara (Swalley) H.; 1 child, Larry Ralph II. Student Wash. Tech. Inst., 1965-66, Seattle Community Coll., 1966-68, Edmonds Community Coll., 1969-70. Salesman, Kirby Co., Seattle, 1964-68, sales mgr., 1968-69; saleman Sanico Chem. Co., Seattle, 1968-69; salesman Synkoloid Co., Seattle, 1970-71; tech. sales rep. Vis Queen div. Ethyl Corp., Seattle, 1971-75; Western sales mgr. B & K Films, Inc., Belmont, Calif., 1975-77; pres. N.W. Mfrs. Assocs., Inc., Bellevue, Wash., 1977-86; pres. combined sales group, 1984 ; nat. sales mgr. Gazelle, Inc., Tomah, Wis., 1979-81; dir. sales J.M.J. Mktg. E.Z. Frame div., 1984-85; pres. Combined Sales Group, Seattle, 1984; nat. accounts mgr. Upnorth Plastics, St. Paul, 1984-87; pres. Combined Sales Group, Inc., Redmond, Wash., 1987—. V.p. Bellevue Nat. Little League; basketball coord. Cath. Youth Orgn., Sacred Heart Ch.; head baseball coach Pierce Coll., Tacoma. With USMC, 1959-66. Mem. Nat. Coun. Salesmen's Orgns., Mfrs. Agts. Nat. Assn., Am. Hardware Mfrs. Assn., Northwest Mfrs. Assn. (pres.), Hardware Affiliated Reps., Inc., Door and Hardware Inst., Internal Conf. Bldg. Ofcls., Am. Baseball Coaches Assn., Marine Corps Assn., 1st Marine Div. Assn., 3d Marine Div. Assn. (life, v.p.). Roman Catholic. Office: 14925 NE 40th St Redmond WA 98052-5326

HUCKABEE, PHYLLIS, gas industry professional; b. Andrews, Tex., Aug. 11, 1963; d. Tommie Jack and Sylvia (Wingo) H. BBA in Fin., Tex. Tech U., 1984, MBA, 1986. Clk. loan escrow 1st Fed. Savs. Bank, Lubbock, Tex., 1984; mgmt. trainee El Paso (Tex.) Nat. Gas Co., 1986-87, analyst rate dept., 1987-88, specialist Calif. affairs, 1988-91, rep. Calif. affairs, 1991-92; asst. dir. Cambridge Energy Rsch. Assocs., Oakland, Calif., 1992-93; regulatory rels. mgr. Pacific Enterprises, San Francisco, 1994-96; dir. State Regulatory Rels., San Francisco, 1996—; mem. adj. faculty No. Calif. campus U. Phoenix, San Francisco, 1994—. Bd. dirs. El Paso Community Concert Assn., 1988, bd. dirs. Performing Arts Workshop, 1991-92, mem. adv. bd., 1992—; vol. Bus. Vols. for Arts, San Francisco, 1989, East Bay Habitat for Humanity, 1993; tutor, fundraiser Project Read, San Francisco, 1990. Mem. Women Energy Assocs. (bd. dirs. 1990—), Leadership Calif. (Class of 1996), Pacific Coast Gas Assn. Methodist. Democrat. Home: 615 Mayfield Ave Stanford CA 94305-8464

HUCKEBY, KAREN MARIE, graphic arts executive; b. San Diego, June 4, 1957; d. Floyd Riley and Georgette Laura (Wegimont) H. Student Coll. of Alameda, 1976; student 3-M dealer tng. program, St. Paul, 1975. Staff Huck's Press Service, Inc., Emeryville, Calif., 1968—, v.p., 1975—. Mem. Rep. Nat. Task Force, 1984—; bd. dirs. CitiArts Benefactors, Concord, Calif., 1990-93, v.p., treas., 1991-93. Recipient service award ARC, 1977. Mem. East Bay Club of Printing House Craftsman (treas. 1977-78), Oakland Mus. Soc., Nat. Trust Historic Preservation, Smithsonian Inst., San Francisco Mus. Soc., Internat. Platform Assn., Am. Film Inst., Commonwealth Club. Home: 1054 Hera Ct Hercules CA 94547 Office: Staff Huck's Press Svc Inc 691 S 31st St Richmond CA 94804-4022

HUD, NICHOLAS VINCENT, biophysicist; b. L.A., June 8, 1964; s. Joseph Anton and Helen Mary (Kern) H.; m. Mona Gonzalez, Oct. 5, 1987; children: Nicholas Xavier, Anton Alexander. BS in physics cum laude, Loyola Marymount U., 1986; MS in applied physics, U. Calif., Davis, 1988, PhD in applied physics, 1992. Physicist Lawrence Livermore Nat. Lab., Livermore, Calif., 1987-95; with dept. of chemistry UCLA, 1995—. Contbr. articles to profl. jours. Ahmanson Found. fellow, L.A., 1984-86, NIH postdoctoral fellowship, 1995—. Mem. Biophys. Soc. Office: U Calif Dept Chemistry Los Angeles CA 90095

HUDAK, PAUL ALEXANDER, retired engineer; b. Youngstown, Ohio, Oct. 8, 1930; s. Paul and Elizabeth (Hoffman) H.; m. Ingrid Gertrud Matzke, June 6, 1964; children: Frank, David, Greta. BS in Math., Youngstown U., 1958. Reliability/safety engr. N.Am. Aviation, L.A. and Downey, Calif., 1958-64, Douglas Aircraft, Long Beach, Calif., 1964-73, Chrysler Def., Sterling Heights, Mich., 1973-77, Boeing Airplane Co., Seattle and Everett, Wash., 1977-85, Mare Island Naval Shipyard, Vallejo, Calif., 1985-93; ret., 1993. Cpl. USMC, 1951-53. Mem. IEEE. Home: 220 Bluebell Pl Vallejo CA 94591-8086

HUDAK, THOMAS MICHAEL, plastic surgeon; b. Akron, Ohio, May 16, 1937; s. Rudolph Michael and Muriel (Creighton) H.; m. Anne Elizabeth Verhey, Aug. 11, 1963 (div.); m. Mary Louise Schmidt, Aug. 16, 1974; children: Michael, Stephen, Allison. BA, U. Mich., 1959, MD, 1963. Diplomate Am. Bd. Plastic Surgery. Intern U. Md. Hosp., Balt., 1963-64, resident gen. surgery, 1964-68; resident in plastic surgery U. Mich., Ann Arbor, 1968-70; pvt. practice Phoenix, 1970—. Mem. Phoenix Thunderbirds, 1976—, Ariz. Acad., 1991—; pres. The Heart Mus., Phoenix, 1989-91. Recipient Outstanding Paper award Nat. Residents' Conf., Salt Lake City, 1970. Mem. NCCJ (bd. dirs. 1983-88), Am. Soc. Plastic and Reconstructive Surgery, Am. Sc. Aesthetic Plastic Surgery, Reed O. Dingham Soc., Frederick A. Coller Soc., Am. Assn. Hand Surgery., Men's Art Coun., Phoenix Country Club. Republican. Roman Catholic. Address: 5219 N Casa Blanca Dr Paradise Valley AZ 85253-6999

HUDDLESTON, FOREST WILLIS, mental healing counselor; b. Kingsburg, Calif., Oct. 3, 1915; s. John Samuel and Myra Jennie (Beaver) H.; m. Allene Moore, June 3, 1944 (div. 1979); children: June M., Ralph Reed, Virginia Marie; m. Jacqueline Louise Barber, Sept. 3, 1986. Student, Redley (Calif.) City Coll., 1934-36, U. Puget Sound, 1936-38, Fresno State Coll., 1940-41, 47-48. Ordained to ministry Universal Life Ch., 1978. Mem. sales staff various furniture stores, Sacramento, 1959-70; research dir. Allied Research and Counseling, Sacramento, 1970-76, Huddleston Claibourne Counseling Ctr., Sacramento, 1983-84; ret., 1984. Developer Huddleston Method treatment for mental illness. Asst. dir. Oak Park Youth Band, Sacramento, 1968-70; active various community service orgns., Sacramento, 1958-. Sgt. USAF, 1942-45. Nominated Nobel Peace Prize, 1992. Home and Office: 5965 E Shields # 160 Fresno CA 93727

HUDGINS, CHRISTOPHER CHAPMAN, English educator; b. Richmond, Va., Mar. 22, 1947; s. William Jesse and Cathryn (Turner) H.; m. Marsha Lee Huffman, Aug. 22, 1970 (div. Dec. 1986); 1 child, Caitlin Crawford. AB, Davidson Coll., 1968; MA, Emory U., 1969, PhD, 1976. Univ. fellow Emory U., Atlanta, 1968-69; instr. English Old Dominion U., Norfolk, Va., 1969-71; teaching asst. Emory U., Atlanta, 1971-74, lectr., 1974-75; asst. prof. English U. Nev., Las Vegas, 1976-82; assoc. prof. English U. Nev., 1982—, chair English, 1984-93; cons. in field. Contbr. articles to profl. jours.; editorial bd. Harold Pinter Rev., 1986—. Dir., lectr. Humanities Com. and Allied Arts Coun., Las Vegas, 1980—; bd. dirs. faculty devel. seminars NEH, 1987, 88; gov.'s appointee and vice chmn., Nev. Humanities Commn., exec. bd. Mem. MLA, Soc. for Cinema Studies, Harold Pinter Soc. (v.p.), David Mamet Soc. (v.p., treas.). Office: U Nevada 4505 S Maryland Pky Las Vegas NV 89154-9900

HUDGINS, LOUANNE, pediatrician, educator; b. Leavenworth, Kans., Nov. 17, 1957. BA, U. Kans., 1980; MD, U. Kans., Kansas City, 1984. Diplomate Am. Bd. Pediatrics, Am. Bd. Med. Genetics. Asst. prof. pediatrics U. Ariz., Tucson, 1990-93, U. Wash., Seattle, 1993—. Fellow Am. Coll. Med. Genetics, Am. Acad. Pediatrics; mem. Am. Soc. Human Genetics. Office: Children's Hosp & Med Ctr 4800 Sand Point Way CH-25 Seattle WA 98105-0371

HUDSON, CHRISTOPHER JOHN, publisher; b. Watford, Eng., June 8, 1948; s. Joseph Edward and Gladys Jenny Patricia (Madgwick); m. Lois Jeanne Lyons, June 16, 1979; children: Thomas, Ellen, Ronald, Timothy. BA with honors, Cambridge U., Eng., 1969, MA with honors, 1972. Promotion mgr. Prentice-Hall Internat., Eng., 1969-70; area mgr. Prentice-Hall Internat., Eng., France, 1970-71; mktg. mgr. Prentice-Hall Internat., Englewood Cliffs, N.J., 1971-74, dir. mktg., 1974-76, asst. v.p., 1976; group internat. dir. I.T.T. Pub., N.Y.C., 1976-77; pres. Focal Press, Inc., N.Y.C., 1977-82; v.p., pub. Aperture Found. Inc., N.Y.C., 1983-86; head publs. J. Paul Getty Trust, L.A., 1986—. Author: Guide to International Book Fairs, 1976; pub. Aperture, 1983-86, J. Paul Getty Mus. Jour., 1986—. Mem. adv. coun. Nat. Heritage Village, Kioni, Greece; mem. trade with eastern Europe com. Assn. Am. Pubs., N.Y., 1976-79, internat. fairs com., 1986-88. Mem. Internat. Assn. Mus. Publs. (Frankfurt, Fed. Republic Germany, chmn. 1992-95), U.S. Mus. Publ. Group (chmn. 1989—), Internat. Pubs. Assn., Hellenic Soc. (London), Oxford & Cambridge Club (London), Internat. Assn. Scholarly Pubs. (sec.-gen. 1994-97, chmn. internat. contracts com.). Office: J Paul Getty Mus 1200 Getty Ctr Dr Ste 1000 Los Angeles CA 90049-1687

HUDSON, EDWARD VOYLE, linen supply company executive; b. Seymour, Mo., Apr. 3, 1915; s. Marion A. and Alma (Von Gonten) H.; student Bellingham (Wash.) Normal Coll., 1933-36, also U. Wash.; m. Margaret Carolyn Greely, Dec. 24, 1939; children—Edward G., Carolyn K. Asst. to mgr. Natural Hard Metal Co., Bellingham, 1935-37; partner Met. Laundry Co., Tacoma, 1938-39; propr., mgr. Peerless Laundry & Linen Supply Co., Tacoma, 1939—; propr. Independent Laundry & Everett Linen Supply Co., 1946-74, 99 Cleaners and Launderers Co., Tacoma, 1957-79; chmn. Tacoma Public Utilities, 1959-60; trustee United Mut. Savs. Bank; bd. dirs. Tacoma Better Bus. Bur., 1977—. Pres., Wash. Conf. on Unemployment Compensation, 1975-76; pres. Tacoma Boys' Club, 1970; v.p. Puget Sound USO, 1972-91; elder Emmanuel Presbyn. Ch., 1974—; past campaign mgr., pres. Tacoma-Pierce County United Good Neighbors. Recipient Disting. Citizen's cert. U.S. Air Force Mil. Airlift Com., 1977; U.S. Dept. Def. medal for outstanding public service, 1978. Mem. Tacoma Sales and Mktg. Execs. (pres. 1957-58), Pacific NW Laundry, Dry Cleaning and Linen Supply Assn. (pres. 1959, treas. 1965-75), Internat. Fabricare Inst. (dir. dist. 7 treas. 1979, pres. 1982), Am. Security Council Bd., Tacoma C. of C. (pres. 1965), Air Force Assn. (pres. Tacoma chpt. 1976-77, v.p. Wash. state 1983-84, pres. 1985-86), Navy League, Puget Sound Indsl. Devel. Council (chmn. 1967), Tacoma-Ft. Lewis-Olympia Army Assn. (past pres.) Republican. Clubs: Elks (vice chmn. bd. trustees 1984, chmn. 1985-86), Shriners (potentate 1979), Masons, Scottish Rite, Tacoma, Tacoma Country and Golf, Jesters, Rotary (pres. Tacoma chpt. 1967-68), Tacoma Knife and Fork (pres. 1964). Home: 3901 N 37th St Tacoma WA 98407-5636 Office: Peerless Laundry & Linen Supply Co 2902 S 12th St Tacoma WA 98405-2539

HUDSON, GARY MICHAEL, corporate executive; b. Lander, Wyo., July 28, 1946; s. Frank L. and Sarah Elizabeth (Jones) H.; m. Linda Ann Shaw, July 5, 1985; 1 child, Zachary Michael. BA, U. Wyo., 1968; MA, Western Ky. U., 1970. Tchr. Hopkinsville (Ky.) Pub. Schs., 1968-69; tchr., counselor Warren County Sch., Hadly, Ky., 1969-70; counselor, social worker Wyo. State Tng. Sch., Lander, 1970-72; counselor, adminstr. Cen. Wyo. Coll., Riverton, 1972-75; chief exec. officer Community Entry Svcs., Riverton, 1975—. Contbr. articles and revs. to profl. jours.; mem. editorial adv. bd. Sta. KTRZ-TV, Riverton, 1989-90. Mem. adv. bd. Cen. Wyo. Coll. Trades and Industry, Riverton, 1989—, Human Devel. Svcs. Program, 1990—, Wyo. Dept. Health, 1991—, Pineridge Hosp., Lander, 1986-88; chairperson employer com. Rocky Mountain Regional Head Injury Ctr., 1991—; chairperson Regional Svcs. Providers Wyo., 1990-92; bd. dirs. Riverton Bicentennial Com., 1976, Wyo. Assn. Retarded Citizens, Cheyenne, 1983-86, Nat. Assn. Devel. Disability Couns., Washington, 1980-81, Rocky Mountain Brain Injury Ctr., 1991—; sec. CES Found., Inc.; active Ctrl. Wyo. Boy Scouts. Recipient Regional Dir.'s award Region 8 HEW, 1977. Mem. Wyo. Assn. Rehab. Facilities (chmn. 1984-85, sec. 1985-87), Fremont County Assn. Retarded Citizens, Lions, Masons (master 1984-85), Hugh de Payne Commandry (comdr. 1985-86), Rotary of Lander. Republican. Episcopalian. Home: 2980 Sinks Canyon Rd Lander WY 82520-9714 Office: Community Entry Svcs 2441 Peck St Riverton WY 82501-2272

HUDSON, HEATHER ELIZABETH, telecommunications educator, consultant, lawyer; b. Vancouver, B.C., Can., Jan. 4, 1947; came to U.S., 1968; d. Bruce Earl and Beulah May (Ashton) Hudson. BA with honors, U. B.C., 1968; MA, Stanford U., 1969, PhD, 1974; JD, U. Tex., 1987. Bar: Calif. Cons. Can. Dept. Comms., Ottawa, Ont., 1970-74, State of Alaska, Anchorage, 1976-77; dir. telecomms. Acad. for Ednl. Devel., Washington, 1977-81; assoc. prof. U. Tex., Austin, 1981-87; prof., dir. telecomms. program McLaren Sch. Bus., U. San Francisco, 1987—; pres. Keewatin Comms., Ottawa, 1980—; gov. Internat. Coun. for Computer Comm., 1990—; mem. adv. bd. NRC, FCC, Washington, 1990—, Privacy Rights Clearinghouse, San Diego, 1992—. Author: When Telephones Reach the Village, 1984, Rural America in the Information Age, 1989, Communication Satellites, 1990, Electronic Byways, 1995, Global Connections, 1997; mem. editl. bd. Telecommunications Policy. Recipient Electronic Media Book of Yr. award Nat. Assn. Broadcasters, 1990; East-West Ctr. sr. fellow, Honolulu, 1991, CIRCIT sr. fellow, Melbourne, 1992, Asia-Pacific Disting. Lectureship Fulbright fellowship, Singapore, Malaysia, Hong Kong, Japan, 1996. Mem. ABA, Bar Assn. San Francisco, Internat. Comm. Assn., Internat. Inst. Comm., Soc. Satellite Profls. Internat., Pacific Telecomms. Coun., Telecom. Assn. Alliance for Pub. Tech., Bay Area Telecomms. Forum. Stanford Alumni Assn. (life), City Club of San Francisco, Sierra Club, Commonwealth Club, World Affairs Coun., Internat. Coun. Computer Comm. (gov. 1990—), Telecom. Assn. Office: U San Francisco 2130 Fulton St San Francisco CA 94117-1080

HUDSON, JERRY E., university president; b. Chattanooga, Mar. 3, 1938; s. Clarence E. and Laura (Campbell) H.; m. Myra Ann Jared, June 11, 1957; children: Judith, Laura, Janet, Angela. B.A., David Lipscomb Coll., 1959; M.A., Tulane U., 1961, Ph.D., 1965; LL.D. (hon.), Pepperdine U., 1983; D of Comm. (hon.), Tokyo Internat. U., 1997. Systems engr. IBM, Atlanta, 1961; prof. Coll. Arts and Scis., Pepperdine U., 1962-75; provost, dean Coll. Arts and Scis., Malibu Campus, Pepperdine U., 1971-75; pres. Hamline U., St. Paul, 1975-80, Willamette U., Salem, Oreg., 1980-97; exec. v.p. Collins Found., Portland, Oreg., 1997—; dir. Portland Gen. Co., E.I.I.A. Mem. Nat. Assn. Ind. Colls. (bd. dirs.), Phi Alpha Theta. Office: Willamette U Office of Pres 900 State St Salem OR 97301-3930

HUDSON, JOHN IRVIN, retired marine officer; b. Louisville, Oct. 12, 1932; s. Irvin Hudson and Elizabeth (Reid) Hudson Hornbeck; m. Zetta Ann Yates, June 27, 1954; children: Reid Irvin, Lori Ann, John Yates, Clark Ray. BS in Bus. Mgmt., Murray State U., 1971. Commd. 2nd lt. USMC, 1954, advanced through grades to lt. gen., 1987; comdg. officer Marine Fighter Attack Squadron 115, Vietnam, 1968, Marine Corps Air Sta., Yuma, Ariz., 1977-80; asst. wing comdr. 2nd Marine Air Wing, Cherry Point, N.C., 1980-81; comdg. gen. LFTCLANT 4th Marine Amphibious Brigade, Norfolk, Va., 1981-83, 3rd Marine Aircraft Wing, El Toro, Calif., 1985-87, IMAF, Campen, Calif., 1986-87; dep. chief staff for manpower Hdqrs. USMC, Washington, 1987-89; dir. U.S. Marine Corps Edn. Ctr., Quantico, Va., 1983-85; ret. active duty Hdqrs. USMC, Washington, 1989. Apptd. to Ariz. State Transp. Bd., 1994—. Decorated DFC, DSM, Bronze Star, Air medals, Silver Hawk; flew 308 combat missions in Vietnam in F-4 Phantom. Mem. VFW, Marine Corps Aviation Assn. (life), Marine Corps Assn., Marine Corps Hist. Soc., Order of Daedalians (life). Home: 12439 E Del Rico Yuma AZ 85367-7366

HUDSON, KATHERINE LEE, education association executive; b. Newport Beach, Calif., Aug. 2, 1966; d. Robert Lee and Jacqueline (Ross) Simonds; m. Timothy Roger Hudson, Dec. 28, 1991; children: Jeremy Blaze, Nicholas Clay. AA, Orange Coast C.C., Costa Mesa, Calif., 1987; BA, Calif. State U., Long Beach, 1989. Various positions to v.p. Nat. Assn. of Christian Educators, Irvine, Calif., 1983—; adv. bd. Ctrl. Orange County Regional Occupation Program, Santa Ana, Calif., 1989-92, Heritage Schoals, nat. adv. bd., 1993—. Author: Raising Kids God's Way, 1995; author, editor (newsletter) Education Newsline, 1989—, Family Building Blocks, 1995—. Republican. Office: Nat Assn Christian Educators 18092 Sky Park Cir Ste B Irvine CA 92614-6530

HUDSON, LEE (ARLENE HUDSON), environmental activist; b. Oakland, Calif., Apr. 17, 1936; d. Clyde Edward and Helen Therese McIrvin; m. James Joseph Coté, Mar. 28, 1958 (div. 1963); 1 child, Steven Michael. BA in Psychology, Calif. State U., Sacramento, 1976, postgrad., 1977-78. Exec. field dir. Dem. State Cen. Com., Sacramento, 1967-68; mem. staff Calif. Legis., Sacramento, 1967-72; founder, chmn., editor newsletter The Group for Alternatives to Spreading Poisons, Nevada City, Calif., 1983—; nonchem. advocate on adv. com. to Calif. Dept. Transp. Roadside Vegetation Mgmt. Com., 1993—. Vol. various state, fed. and local campaigns or initiatives, 1967—; founding mem. Toxics Coordinating Project, San Francisco, 1985-90; co-founder Calif. Coalition for Alternatives to Pesticides, Arcata and Eureka, 1983—, pres., chmn. bd. dirs., 1989—; mem. Com. for Sustainable Agriculture, 1986—, mem. mktg.-order subcom., 1986-89; bd. dirs. NW Coalition for Alternatives to Pesticides, Eugene, 1987-93; mem., chmn. tech. writing com. Nevada County Adv. Com. on Air Pollution, 1988-93; mem. Hazardous Waste Transfer Facility Siting Com. for Nevada County, 1989-90; mem. Nevada County Hazardous Waste Task Force, 1987-95, chair tech. sub-com., 1988-90; mem. Cen. Valley Hazardous Waste Minimization Com., 1990-91; mem. Nat. Coalition Against the Misuse of Pesticides, Nevada County Land Trust Cmty. Alliance with Family Farmers. Mem. Sierra Club (chmn. toxic subcom. Sierra Nevada group 1985-88), Amnesty Internat. Better World Soc., Cascade Holistic Econ. Cons., Coun. for Livable World, Nat. Peace Inst. Found., People's Med. Soc., Earth First, Nat. Resources Def. Coun., Nevada County C. of C., Greenpeace, Planning and Conservation League, Nevada County Greens Alliance, North Columbia Schoolhouse Cultural Ctr., South Yuba River Citizen's League, Siskiyou Mountains Resource Coun. (life), Rural Def. League, Beyond Pesticides, Environ. Protection Info. Ctr., Yuba Watershed Inst., Planet Drum. Mem. Universal Life Ch. Home and Office: Box 451 Nevada City CA 95959-8751

HUDSON, PATRICK A., plastic surgeon; b. Blickling, Eng., July 4, 1948; came to U.S., 1974; MD, London U., 1972. Diplomate Am. Bd. Plastic Surgery. Intern St. Stephens-Hillingdon, London, 1972-73; resident Danbury Hosp., 1973-74; resident U. N.Mex. Hosp., Albuquerque, 1974-78, fellow in hand surgery, 1978; with Presbyn. Hosp., St. Joseph Hosp., Albuquerque; pvt. practice; preceptor U. N.Mex. Author: Esthetics: Comprehensive Online Information About Cosmetic Plastic Surgery, 1996. Fellow ACS; mem. BMA, NMMS, Am. Assn. Hand Surgery, Am. Soc. Plastic and Reconstructive Surgeons. Office: # 100E 4273 Montgomery Blvd NE Albuquerque NM 87109-6746

HUDSON POMIJE, MAURA ANN, editor; b. Santa Monica, Calif., Apr. 3, 1970; d. Dirk Ludwig and Sharon Jean (Kuker) Hudson; m. Michael Pomije, July 30, 1994. BA in Newspaper Journalism, Calif. State U., Long Beach, 1993. Student asst. info. resources and tech. Chancellor's office Calif. State U., Los Alamitos, 1992-93; editor/writer Entrepreneur Mag. Group, Irvine, Calif., 1993-95; sr. editor/comm. specialist Am. Youth Soccer Orgn., Hawthorne, Calif., 1995—; freelance newspaper designer/freelance writer, Irvine. Contbg. editor: Small Business Advisor, 1995; author: (lesson plans for soccer coaches) Take Five Because Character Counts, 1995. Vol. Orange County Registrar of Voters, Lake Forest, Calif., 1994; vol. painter City of Orange Beautification Project, 1996, Habitat for Humanity, Venice, 1995. Recipient 1st place for investigative reporting Calif. Intercollegiate Press Assn., 1993; named Hamilton Writer of the Mo., Dept. of Journalism, Calif. State U.-Long Beach, 1992. Mem. Soc. Profl. Journalists, Am. Entrepreneurs Assn. Democrat.

HUELSBECK, JULIE MARIE, librarian; b. Appleton, Wis., Apr. 12, 1957; d. Richard John and Phyllis Jean (Flanagan) H. BA in Spanish, BA in Libr. Sci., U. Wis., Oshkosh, 1979; MLS, U. Wis., Milw., 1980. Info. libr. El Paso Pub. Libr., 1981-86; asst. coord., interlibr. loan libr. Tex. Trans-Pecos Libr. System, El Paso, 1986-92; libr. Mohave County Libr. Dist., Bullhead City, Ariz., 1992—; participant Internetworking Rural Librs. Inst., U. Wis.-Milw./Dept. Edn., 1994. Mem. Friends of the Bullhead City Libr., 1992—; sec. Workplace, Edn. and Literacy Coalition of Mohave County, 1994—; bd. rep. Mohave Libr. Alliance, 1994—. Mem. Ariz. State Libr. Assn. Roman Catholic. Office: Bullhead City Libr 1170 Hancock Rd Bullhead City AZ 86442-5903

HUFBAUER, KARL GEORGE, historian of science; b. San Diego, July 7, 1937; s. Clarence Clyde and Arabelle Maxwell (McKee) H.; m. Sarah Grant Brannon, Aug. 6, 1960; children: Sarah Beth, Benjamin Grant, Ruth Arabelle. BS in Engring. Sci., Stanford U., 1959; diploma in history and philos. sci., Oxford (Eng.) U., 1961; PhD in History of Sci., U. Calif., Berkeley, 1970. From asst. prof. to prof. dept. history U. Calif., Irvine, 1966—; chair dept. history U. Calif., Irvine, 1992-96; contract historian NASA, Washington, 1984-90. Author: Formation of German Chemical Community, 1982, Exploring the Sun, 1991 (Emme prize 1993). Co-presiding officer Stop Polluting Our Newport, Newport Beach, Calif., 1987-92. Mem. Green Party. Home: 20241 Bayview Ave Newport Beach CA 92660 Office: Dept History U Calif Irvine CA 92697

HUFF, DALE EUGENE, retired environmental services executive; b. Windsor, Colo., Nov. 1, 1930; s. Floyd Eugene and Katherine Oleva (Parsons) H.; m. Flossie Leone Moses, Nov. 18, 1951; children: Clifford Allen, Herbert Eugene, Dalene Faye, Linda Reneé. BA, Pacific Union Coll., 1963, MA, 1968. Tchr. Pleasant Hill (Calif.) Jr. Acad., 1963-66; prin. Ukiah (Calif.) Jr. Acad., 1966-71; tchr. Paradise (Calif.) Adventist Acad., 1971-80; acct. Loma Linda (Calif.) U., 1980-86, environ. svcs. exec., 1986-96; ret., 1996. With U.S. Army, 1946-49. Mem. Nat. Exec. Housekeeping Assn. (exec. bd. 1987-90). Republican. Home: 10961 Desert Lawn Dr # 145 Calimesa CA 92320-2242 Office: Loma Linda U Dept Environ Svcs Loma Linda CA 92350

HUFF, GARY D., lawyer; b. Seattle, May 9, 1950. BA cum laude, U. Wash., 1972, JD, 1975. Bar: Wash. 1975. Lawyer Karr Tuttle Campbell, Seattle. Mem. ABA, Wash. State Bar Assn., Seattle-King County Bar Assn., Phi Beta Kappa. Office: Karr Tuttle & Campbell 1201 3rd Ave Ste 2900 Seattle WA 98101-3028

HUFF, MARILYN L., federal judge; b. 1951. BA, Calvin Coll., Grand Rapids, Mich., 1972; JD, U. Mich., 1976. Assoc. Gray, Cary, Ames & Frye, 1976-83, ptnr., 1983-91; judge U.S. Dist. Ct. (so. dist.) Calif., San Diego, 1991—. Contbr. articles to profl. jours. Mem. adv. coun. Calif. LWV, 1987—, Am. Lung Assn.; bd. dirs. San Diego and Imperial Counties, 1989—; mem. LaJolla Presbyn. Ch. Named Legal Profl. of Yr. San Diego City Club and Jr. C. of C., 1990; recipient Superior Ct. Valuable Svc. award, 1982. Mem. ABA, San Diego Bar Found., San Diego Bar Assn. (bd. dirs. 1986-88, v.p. 1988, chmn. profl. edn. com. 1990, Svc. award to legal profession, 1989, Lawyer of Yr. 1990), Calif. State Bar Assn., Calif. Women Lawyers, Am. Bd. Trial Advs., Libel Def. Resource Ctr., Am. Inns of Ct. (master 1987—, exec. com. 1989—), Lawyers' Club San Diego (adv. bd. 1989-90, Belva Lockwood Svc. award 1987), Univ. Club, Aardvarks Lt. Office: US Dist Ct US Courthouse Rm 8 940 Front St San Diego CA 92101-8994*

HUFFEY, VINTON EARL, clergyman; b. Luana, Iowa, July 7, 1915; s. Walter Angus and Tilda Boleta (Olson) H.; m. Lillian Bertha Crouse, June 22, 1942; children: Naomi, Rhoda, Stephen, Deborah. Student, Ctrl. Bible Coll., Springfield, Mo., 1936-38, North Ctrl. Bible Coll., Mpls., 1938-40. Ordained to ministry Assemblies of God, 1942. Pastor Assemblies of God, Oelwein, Iowa, 1940-43, LeMars, Iowa, 1943-47; evangelist Assemblies of God, Iowa and Mo., 1947-48; pres. youth Assemblies of God, Iowa and North Mo., 1948-52, editor News of West Ctrl., 1948-52; pastor Assemblies of God, Ames, Iowa, 1952-58, Monrovia, Calif., 1958-78; crusader inner-city evangelism Assemblies of God, 1978-93; pastor Assemblies of God, South Pasadena, Calif., 1993-96; motivation lectr. Assemblies of God, 1980-92; originator inner-city revolving loan fund, mem. urban task force So. Calif. Dist. Assemblies of God, Irvine, Calif., Springfield, Mo., Gen. Counsel of the Assemblies of God, 1982. Author: (pamphlet) The Church and America's Inner-cities, 1981; author of poems. Mem. Think Am. Com. City Coun., Duarte, Calif., 1962, lit. rev. com., 1965; chmn. What About Duarte? L.A. County Dept. Human Rels. City of Hope, Duarte, 1963. Recipient Decade of Harvest award So. Calif. Dist. Coun. Assemblies of God, Irvine, Calif., 1994. Republican. Home and Office: 161 N Mayflower Ave Monrovia CA 91016-2000

HUFFMAN, DAVID GEORGE, electrical engineer; b. Fresno, Calif., Apr. 13, 1965; s. Fred Norman and Sharon (Richardson) H.; m. Johnnie Ann Valtierra, Sept. 21, 1991; children: Matthew Christopher Kenerly, Makenna Francisca-Elise. BSEE, Fresno State U., 1988. Field engr. Power Systems Testing Co., Fresno, Calif., 1988-93, dir. engring., 1993—, mgr., 1994—. Mem. Internat. Electronic and Electrical Engrs. Assn., Eta Kappa Nu. Office: Power Systems Testing Co 4688 W Jennifer Ave Ste 108 Fresno CA 93722-6418

HUFFMAN, NONA GAY, financial consultant, retirement planning specialist; b. Albuquerque, June 22, 1942; d. William Abraham and Opal Irene (Leaton) Crisp; m. Donald Clyde Williams, Oct. 20, 1961; children: Debra Gaylene, James Donald. Student pub. schs. Lawndale, Calif. Lic. ins., securities dealer, N.Mex. Sec. City of L.A., 1960, L.A. City Schs. 1960-62, Aerospace Corp., El Segundo, Calif., 1962-64, Albuquerque Pub. Schs., 1972-73, Pub. Service Co. N.Mex., Albuquerque, 1973; rep., fin. planner Waddell & Reed, Inc., Albuquerque, 1979-84; broker Rauscher Pierce Refsnes, Inc., 1984-85; rep., investment and retirement specialist Fin. Network Investment Corp., 1985-89, John Hancock Fin. Svcs., 1989-90; account exec. Eppler, Guerin & Turner, Inc., 1990-91, Fin. Network Investment Corp., Albuquerque, 1991—; instr. on-site corp. training of fin. strategies for retirement Philips Semi Conductors, Honeywell & Gulton Industries Office: Fin Network Investment Corp 8500 Menaul Blvd NE Ste 195B Albuquerque NM 87112-2243

HUFFMAN, THOMAS PATRICK, secondary education educator; b. Salem, Ind., Aug. 22, 1963; s. Patrick Henry and Patricia (Stewart) H.; m. Cynthia Densford, June 27, 1987; 1 child, Mackenzie Lucille. BA in Biosci., DePauw U., 1985; MA in Edn., U. Phoenix, 1997. Quality control mgr., asst. ops. mgr. Wayne Dairy Products, Richmond, Ind., 1985-86; acct. mgr. Klenzade Divsn. Ecolab Inc., St. Paul, 1986-88; realtor West USA Realty, Phoenix, 1988-94; secondary sci. educator Westview H.S., Avondale, Ariz., 1994—; athletic trainer Tolleson (Ariz.) H.S., 1994—. Named to Pres.'s Roundtable, Phoenix Assn. Realtors, 1993. Mem. Am. Mensa, Sigma Alpha Epsilon. Home: 19001 N 67th Dr Glendale AZ 85308 Office: Westview High Sch 9419 W Garden Lakes Pkwy Avondale AZ 85323

HUFFS, BOB, mayor. BA cum laude, Westmont Coll., 1975. Mayor City of Diamond Bar, Calif.; v.p. S.W. Mktg. Corp., Diamond Bar, 1975-83; owner Ray S. French Co., Diamond Bar, 1983—. Office: 21660 E Copley Dr Ste 100 Diamond Bar CA 91765

HUFSCHMIDT, MAYNARD MICHAEL, resources planning educator; b. Catawba, Wis., Sept. 28, 1912; s. John Jacob and Emma Lena (Von Arx) H.; m. Elizabeth Louise Leake, July 5, 1941; children: Emily Ann, Mark Andrew. BS, U. Ill., 1939; MPA, Harvard U., 1955, DPA, 1964. Planner Ill. State Planning Commn., Chgo., 1939-41; engr. U.S. Nat. Resources Planning Bd., Washington, 1941-43; budget examiner U.S. Bur. Budget, Washington, 1943-49; program staff mem. Office of Sec., Dept. Interior, Washington, 1949-55; research asso. Grad. Sch. Public Adminstrn., Harvard U., 1955-65; prof. depts. city and regional planning, environ. scis. and engring. U. N.C., Chapel Hill, 1965—; fellow Environ. and Policy Inst., East-West Center, Honolulu, 1979-85, acting dir., 1985-86, sr. cons., 1986-89, sr. fellow, 1990-94; cons. U.S. Bur. Budget, 1961, Council Econ. Advisers, 1965-67, Nat. Acad. Scis., 1967, 69-70, Pan-Am. Health Orgn., 1967, 70, WHO, 1970, 71, 76, 77, Resources for Future, 1955, 56, 72-74. Author: (with Arthur Maass and others) Design of Water-Resource Systems, 1962, (with Myron B. Fiering) Simulation Techniques for Design of Water-Resource Systems, 1966; Editor: Regional Planning—Challenge and Prospects, 1969; editor: (with Eric L. Hyman) Economic Approaches to Natural Resource and Environmental Quality Analysis, 1982, (with David E. James and others) Environment, Natural Systems and Development: An Economic Valuation Guide, 1983, (with John A. Dixon) Economic Valuation Techniques for the Environment, 1986, (with K. William Easter and John A. Dixon) Watershed Resources Management, 1986, (with Janusz Kindler) Approaches to Integrated Water Resources Management in Humid Tropical and Arid and Semiarid Zones in Developing Countries, 1991, (with Michael Bonell and John S. Gladwell) Hydrology and Water Management in the Humid Tropics, 1993. Recipient Clemens Herschel award Boston Soc. Civil Engrs., 1958, Pub. Svc. award U.S. Dept. Interior, 1994; named Friend of Univs. Coun. on Water Resources, 1990; sr. postdoctoral rsch. fellow NSF, 1971.

HUG, PROCTER RALPH, JR., federal judge; b. Reno, Mar. 11, 1931; s. Procter Ralph and Margaret (Beverly) H.; m. Barbara Van Meter, Apr. 4, 1954; children: Cheryl Ann, Procter James, Elyse Marie. B.S., U. Nev., 1953; LL.B., J.D., Stanford U., 1958. Bar: Nev. 1958. With firm Springer, McKissick & Hug, 1958-63, Woodburn, Wedge, Blakey, Folsom & Hug, Reno, 1963-77; U.S. judge 9th Circuit Ct. Appeals, Reno, 1977—, U.S. chief judge, 1996—; chmn. 9th Cir. Edn. Com., 1984-89, chmn. long range planning com., 1992-93; chmn. Nev. State Bar Com. on Jury Inst.; dep. atty. gen. State of Nev.; v.p. dir. Nev. Tel. & Tel. Co., 1958-77. V.p. Young Dems. Nev., 1960-61; chmn. bd. regents U. Nev.; bd. visitors Stanford Law Sch.; mem. Nev. Humanities Commn., 1988-94; vol. civilian aid sect. U.S. Army, 1977. Lt. USNR, 1953-55. Recipient Outstanding Alumnus award U. Nev., 1967, Disting. Nevadan citation, 1982; named Alumnus of Yr. U. Nev., 1988. Mem. ABA (bd. govs. 1976-78), Am. Judicare Soc. (bd. dirs. 1975-77), Nat. Judicial Coll. (bd. dirs. 1977-78), Nat. Assn. Coll. and Univ. Attys. (past mem. exec. bd.), U. Nev. Alumni Assn. (past pres.), Stanford Law Soc. Nev. (pres.). Office: US Ct Appeals 9th Cir US Courthouse Fed Bldg 400 S Virginia St # 708 Reno NV 89501

HUGGETT, MONICA, performing company executive. Artistic dir. Portland Baroque Orch., Oreg. Office: Portland Baroque Orch 610 SW Broadway Ste 602 Portland OR 97205*

HUGGINS, EARL MCCLURE, English language educator; b. Phila., Jan. 25, 1939; s. Horace Greely and Helen Marie (Keimer) H.; m. Alice Elizabeth Malia, June 23, 1962; children: Alice Lynn, Donna Marie. BS, So. Ill. U., 1979; MS, Nat. Univ., 1990. Cert. adult sch. tchr., Calif. Aviation electronics technician USN, 1957-81; tchr. San Diego C.C., 1981-84, Chula Vista (Calif.) Adult Sch., 1984—. Ret. sr. vol. San Diego Police Dept., 1991—. Recipient USN Expeditionary award, 1980, Humanitarian Svc. medal, 1980. Mem. Fleet Res. Assn. (parade coord.), Nat. Univ. Alumni Assn. (life), Phi Kappa Phi. Democrat. Home and Office: 2549 Caulfield Dr San Diego CA 92154

HUGHES, BRADLEY RICHARD, business executive; b. Detroit, Oct. 8, 1954; s. John Arthur and Nancy Irene (Middleton) H.; m. Linda McCants, Feb. 14, 1977; children: Bradley Richard Jr., Brian Jeffrey. AA, Oakland Coll., 1974; BS in Journalism, U. Colo., 1979, BJ, 1979, MBA in Fin. and Mktg., 1981, MS in Telecommunications, 1990. Cert. office automation profl., cert. systems profl. Buyer Joslins Co., Denver, 1979; mktg. adminstr. Mountain Bell, Denver, 1980-82; ch. cons. AT&T Info. Systems, mktg. exec. AT&T, Denver, 1983-86, acct. exec., 1986-87; mktg. mgr. U.S. West, Denver, 1987-95; dir. U. Colo. Coll. Engring., Denver, 1995—; exec.-on-loan U. Colo. Coll. Engring. Contbr. articles to bus. publs. Bd. dirs. Brandychase Assn.; state del., committeeman Republican Party Colo. Mem. IEEE, Assn. MBA Execs., U.S. Chess Fedn., Internat. Platform Assn., Mensa, Intertel, Assn. Telecommunications Profls., Am. Mgmt. Assn., Am. Mktg. Assn., Info. Industry Assn., Office Automation Soc. Internat., World Future Soc., Triple Nine Soc., Internat. Soc. Philos. Inquiry, Assn. Computing Machinery. Republican. Mem. Christian Reformed Ch. Home: 5759 S Jericho Way Aurora CO 80015-3653 Office: U Colo Coll Engring Campus Box 104 Denver CO 80217

HUGHES, EDWARD JOHN, artist; b. North Vancouver, B.C., Feb. 17, 1913; s. Edward Samuel Daniell and Katherine Mary (McLean) H.; m. Fern Rosabell Irvine Smith, Feb. 10, 1940 (dec. 1974). Grad., Vancouver Sch. Art, 1933; D Fine Art (hon.), U. Victoria, 1995. Exhbns. include retrospective, Vancouver Art Gallery, 1967, Surrey Art Gallery, Art Gallery of Greater Victoria, Edmonton Art Gallery, Calgary Glenbow Gallery, 1983-85, Nat. Gallery Can., Beaverbrook Gallery, Fredericton, 1983-85; represented in permanent collections, Nat. Gallery Can., Ottawa, Art Gallery Ont., Toronto, Vancouver Art Gallery, Montreal Mus. Fine Art, Greater Victoria Art Gallery; ofcl. Army war artist, 1942-46. Served with Can. Army, 1939-46. Recipient Can. Council grants, 1958, 63, 67, 70. Mem. Royal Can. Acad. Arts. Presbyterian. Address: 2449 Heather St, Duncan, BC Canada V9L 2Z6

HUGHES, EUGENE MORGAN, university president; b. Scottsbluff, Nebr., Apr. 3, 1934; s. Ruby Melvin and Hazel Marie (Griffith) H.; m. Margaret Ann Romeo; children: Deborah Kaye, Greg Eugene, Lisa Ann, Jeff, Mark, Christi. Diploma, Neb. Western Coll., 1954; BS in Math. magna cum laude, Chadron State Coll., 1956; MS in Math., Kans. State U., 1958; PhD in Math., George Peabody Coll. for Tchrs., Vanderbilt U., 1968. Grad. asst. dept. math. Kans. State U., Manhattan, 1956-57; instr. math. Nebr. State Tchrs. Coll. at Chadron, 1957-58; asst. prof. math., head dept. Chadron State Coll., 1958-66, assoc. prof., 1966-69, prof. math., 1969-70, dir. rsch., 1965-66, asst. to the pres., 1966-68, dean adminstrn., 1968-70; grad. asst. dept. math. George Peabody Coll. for Tchrs., Nashville, 1962-63, 64-65; asst. to undergrad. dean George Peabody Coll. for Tchrs., 1964, asst. to pres., 1964-65; instr. Peabody Demonstration Sch., 1963-64; prof. math. No. Ariz. U., Flagstaff, 1970-93; dean No. Ariz. U. (Coll. Arts and Scis.), 1970-71, provost univ. arts and sci. edn., 1971-72, acad. v.p., 1972-79, pres., 1979-93, pres. emeritus, 1993—; pres. Wichita State U., 1993—; cons. Nebr. Dept. Edn., 1966-70; mem. adv. bd. United Bank Ariz., 1980-82; mem. nat. adv. bd. Ctr. for Study of Sport in Society, 1990; bd. dirs. Ariz. Bank; mem. adv. bd. Bank IV, 1993—. Mem. staff bd. trustees Nebr. State Colls., Lincoln, 1969-70; co-dir. workshop tchr. edn. North Cen. Assn. U. Minn., 1968-70; officer fed. ednl. programs, Nebr., Ariz., 1966-93; mem. Ariz. Commn. Post-secondary Edn.; bd. fellows Am. Grad. Sch. Internat. Mgmt., 1980-93; mem. Gov.'s Com. Quality Edn., Chadron Housing Authority, 1968-70, Pres.' Commn. NCAA; pres. bd. dirs. Ariz. State Bd. Edn., 1991, Flagstaff Summer Festival, Ariz. Coun. Humanities and Pub. Policy, Mus. No. Ariz., Grand Canyon coun, Boy Scouts Am.; chair Ariz. Leadership Adv. Coun., 1990-93; mem. Ariz. Town Hall, 1991; commr. Western Interstate Commn. for Higher Edn., 1992-93; mem. Gov.'s Strategic Partnership for Econ. Devel., 1992; mem. Christopher Columbus Quincentenary Commn., 1990—; sec., mem. Wichita/Sedgwick Partnership for Growth, 1993—, Wichita/Sedgwick County Employment Tng. Bd., 1993—. Ariz. Acad. NSF fellow, 1963, 64; recipient Chief Manuelito award Navajo Tribe, 1976, Disting. Svc. award Chadron State Coll., 1982, Flagstaff Citizen of Yr., 1988, Disting. Math. Grad. award Kans. State U., 1990, Cmty. Svc. award, 1994; named Hon. Chmn. black Bd. Dirs., 1989. Mem. NEA, Am. Assn. State Colls.and Univs. (past chmn. & mem. com. on grad. studies 1979—, bd. dirs., mem. com. on accreditation, 1980—), Math. Assn. Am. (vis. lectr. secondary schs. Western Nebr. 1962), Ariz. Edn. Assn., North Cen. Assn. Colls. and Secondary Schs. (coord. 1968-72, cons./evaluator 1977—), Nat. Coun. Tchrs. of Math., Wichita Area C. of C., Flagstaff C. of C., Blue Key, Masons, Elks, Rotary (past pres.), Pi Mu Epsilon, Phi Delta Kappa, Kappa Mu Epsilon, Phi Kappa Phi. *

HUGHES, GETHIN B., bishop. Bishop Episcopal Diocese of San Diego, 1992—. Office: Episcopal Diocese of San Diego 2728 6th Ave San Diego CA 92103-6301*

HUGHES, HERBERT HOWARD, public administrator; b. Roy, N.Mex., Sept. 15, 1930; s. Herbert Perry and Katherine Ruth (Hill) H.; m. Nancy Wagner, Sept. 28, 1957; children: Katherine Ellen, H. W. Bryn. BS, U. N.Mex., 1956; MS, Fla. State U., 1958, PhD, 1960. Prof. U. No. Colo., Greeley, 1960-66; dir. N.Mex. edn. rsch. com. State of N.Mex., Santa Fe, 1966-67, state budget dir., 1967-68; prof. U. N.Mex., Albuquerque, 1968-70; health and edn. bus. cons. Albuquerque, 1970-73; v.p. Fidelity Nat. Bank, Albuquerque, 1973-75; state banking commr. State of N.Mex., Santa Fe, 1975-77; dir. evaluation N.Mex. cancer program U. N.Mex. Med. Sch., Albuquerque, 1977-78; mgr. adminstrn. BDM Corp., Albuquerque, 1978-80; dir. fin. and adminstrn., pub. safety and adminstrv. svcs. Bernalillo County, Albuquerque, 1980—; part-time city councillor City of Albuquerque, 1987—. Sr. author: (booklet) State Responsibility for Public Edn. in N.Mex., 1967. V.p. State Constl. Conv., State of N.Mex., 1969—; mem. steering com. Energy, Environment and Natural Resources, Nat. League of Cities, 1994, 95. Mem. APA, Am. Soc. Pub. Adminstrn. (pres. 1980—), Am. Edn. Rsch. Assn. (N.Mex. br. 1960—), Nat. Conf. State Bank Suprs., Assn. Mil. Surgeons U.S., Naval Res. Assn. Home: 7112 Lantern Rd NE Albuquerque NM 87109-2915 Office: City County Bldg 1 Civic Plz 10th Fl Albuquerque NM 87102

HUGHES, JAMES ARTHUR, electrical engineer; b. Wayne, Nebr., Feb. 15, 1939; s. James Wallace and Ruth Genevieve H.; m. Judy Lorraine Gaskins, July 18, 1967; children: Robert Linn, Benjamin Reed, Barnaby James. BSEE, U. Nebr., 1967. Electronic technician, space tech. labs. TRW, Redondo Beach, Calif., 1963-67, mem. tech. staff systems group, 1967-80, sect. mgr. electronics and def. div., 1980-82, systems engr. space and electronics group, 1982-93, sub-project mgr., 1993—. Designer solid state thermostat, pn generator. Deacon First Bapt. Ch. Lakewood, Long Beach, Calif., 1975-76, 78-80, 87-89; mem. exec. bd. parent-tchr. fellowship, Grace Sch., Rossmoor, Calif., 1981-87. With USN, 1959-63. Mem. AAAS, IEEE, Nat. Soc. Profl. Engrs. Republican. Office: TRW Space and Electronics Group 1 Space Park Blvd # 1869 Redondo Beach CA 90278-1001

HUGHES, LINDA J., newspaper publisher; b. Princeton, B.C., Can., Sept. 27, 1950; d. Edward Rees and Madge Preston (Bryan) H.; m. George Fredrick Ward, Dec. 16, 1978; children: Sean Ward, Kate Ward. BA, U. Victoria (B.C.), 1972. With Edmonton Jour., Alta., Can., 1976—, from reporter to asst. mng. editor, 1984-87, editor, 1987-92, pub., 1992—. Southam fellow U. Toronto, Ont., Can., 1977-78. Office: Edmonton Journal, 10006 101st St PO Box 2421, Edmonton, AB Canada T5J 2S6

HUGHES, MARGARET JANE, nurse; b. L.A., Sept. 13, 1950; d. John Lawarence and Etta May (Kenny) H. BSN, U. St. Thomas, Houston, 1984; ADN, Saddleback Coll., Mission Viejo, Calif., 1980; cert. in perfusion, Tex. Heart Inst., Houston, 1976. RN, Calif., Tex., Hawaii; CCRN; cert. BLS, ACLS, perfusionist. Nurse ICU Saddleback Hosp., Laguna Hills, Calif., 1974-76, 79-81; perfusionist Baylor Coll. Medicine, Houston, 1973-79, 81-86; nurse ICU VA Hosp., L.A., 1986-90; nurse, perfusionist Kay Med. Group, L.A., 1987-90; nurce ICU Hilo (Hawaii) Hosp., 1990-91; nurse recovery room King Khaled Eye Hosp., Riyadh, Saudi Arabia, 1992; clin. nurse specialist Kay Med. Group, L.A., 1992; nurse ICU and recovery room Kona (Hawaii) Hosp., 1992-94; clin. nurse specialist Sciemed Ltd., Cairo, 1994; nurse UCLA Dental Sch., 1994-95; nurse ICU, Whittier (Calif.) Hosp., 1995-96; resource nurse Glendale (Calif.) Meml. Hosp., 1996—. Vol. Am. Heart Assn., Kona, 1993, Diabetic Assn., Kona, 1993. Mem. AACN. Democrat. Roman Catholic. Home: 13496 Trumball St Whittier CA 90605-3331 Office: Glendale Mem Hosp Glendale CA 91204-2594

HUGHES, MARVIS JOCELYN, poet, photographer; b. Ft. Worth, May 17, 1942; d. Charles H. and Bobbye Etta (Harrell) H.; m. Rodolfo J. Broullon, May 1972 (div. 1980); 1 child (dec.). Student, UCLA, 1960-65, NYU, 1968-72. Poet-in-residence Brockman Gallery, L.A., 1980-81, Calif. State Mus. African-Am. Culture and History, L.A., 1984, William Grant Still Art Ctr., City of L.A., 1981-85; photographer, videographer Dept. HEW, Washington, 1971-72, 75-77, L.A., Miss., 1971-72, Ark., 1975-77; photography instr. Internat. children's Sch., L.A., 1980-81; media producer Broadcast Media Prodns., U. So. Calif., L.A., 1980; videographer, libr. L.A. Inst. Contemporary Art, 1979. Author: Vis-a-Vis and Other Poems, 1960s, The Time Traveller Variations, 1980s, Bones and Eyes, 1990s, (film) Ciné-Poém #1. . .n, 1970s. Named Golden Poet of Yr., World of Poetry, 1987, 91, 92; anthologized in Greatest Poems of the 20th Century, World of Poetry, 1979. Mem. PEN West, Calif. Poets in the Schs., L.A. Poetry Festival, Nat. Coun. Negro Women, Assn. for Study of African-Am. Life and History, NAACP. Methodist.

HUGHES, MARY KATHERINE, lawyer; b. Kodiak, Alaska, July 16, 1949; d. John Chamberlain and Marjorie (Anstey) H.; m. Andrew H. Eker, July 7, 1982. BBA cum laude, U. Alaska, 1971; JD, Willamette U., 1974; postgrad. Heriot-Watt U., Edinburgh, Scotland, 1971. Bar: Alaska 1975. Ptnr., Hughes, Thorsness, Gantz, Powell & Brundin, Anchorage, 1974-95, mem. mgmt. com., 1991-92; mcpl. atty. Municipality of Anchorage, 1995—. trustee Alaska Bar Found., pres., 1984—; bd. visitors Willamette U., Salem, Oreg., 1980—; bd. dirs. Alaska Repertory Theatre, 1986-88, pres., 1987-88; commr. Alaska Code Revision Commn., 1987-94; mem. U. Alaska Found., 1985—, trustee, 1990—; bd. vis. U. Alaska Fairbanks, 1994—; bd. dirs. Anchorage Econ. Devel. Corp., 1989—, chmn. 1994; mem. com. bd. Providence Health Sys., 1993—; lawyer rep. 9th Cir. Judicial Conf., 1995—. Fellow Am. Bar Found.; mem. Alaska Bar Assn. (bd. govs. 1981-84, pres. 1983-84), Anchorage Assn. Women Lawyers (pres. 1976-77), AAUW, Delta Theta Phi. Republican. Roman Catholic. Club: Soroptimists (v.p. 1986-87, pres. 1986-87). Home: 2240 Kissee Ct Anchorage AK 99517-1003 Office: Municipality Anchorage PO Box 196650 Anchorage AK 99519-6650

HUGHES, ROBERT EDWARD, elementary education educator; b. Lynn, Mass., Apr. 24, 1944; s. Frederick Ambrose and Frances Josephine (Martin) H.; m. Susan Martha Strang, Sept. 9, 1967; children: Lisa, Jayme, Shawna. BA in Elem. Edn., Ariz. State U., 1970, MA in Elem. Edn., 1974. Cert. tchr., Ariz. Tchr. Madison Sch. Dist., Phoenix, 1970—; mem. Sch. Site Base Mgmt. Team, Phoenix, 1992-94, Sch. Profl. Coun., Phoenix, 1990—, Dist. Math. and Social Studies Com., Phoenix, 1974-90, coach boys and girls athletic teams, Phoenix, 1970-90. With USAF, 1962-66. Mem. Madison Fedn. Tchrs. (v.p. 1975-78, pres. 1978-79). Office: Madison # 1 Sch 5525 N 16th St Phoenix AZ 85016-2901

HUGHES, ROBERT MERRILL, control system engineer; b. Glendale, Calif., Sept. 11, 1936; s. Fred P. and Gertrude G. (Merrill) H.; AA, Pasadena

City Coll., 1957; 1 child, Tammie Lynn Cobble. Engr. Aerojet Gen. Corp., Azusa, Calif., 1957-64, 66-74; pres. Automatic Electronics Corp., Sacramento, 1964-66; specialist Perkin Elmer Corp., Pomona, Calif., 1974-75; gen. mgr. Hughes Mining Inc., Covina, Calif., 1975-76; project mgr. L&A Water Treatment, City of Industry, Calif., 1976-79; dir. Hughes Industries Inc., Alta Loma, Calif., 1979—; pres. Hughes Devel. Corp., Carson City, Nev.; chmn. bd. Hughes Mining Inc., Hughes Video Corp. Registered profl. engr., Calif; lic. gen. bld. contractor. Mem. AIME, Nat. Soc. Profl. Engrs., Instrument Soc. Am., Am. Inst. Plant Engrs. Republican. Patentee in field. Home: 10009 Banyan St Alta Loma CA 91737-3603 Office: PO Box 915 Carson City NV 89702-0915

HUGHES, TRAVIS HUBERT, geologist; b. Rapid City, S.D., Feb. 21, 1937; s. Frank Lyon and Jane (Brown) H.; m. Suzy Hatcher, Dec. 22, 1957; children: Travis Jr., Tracy. BA, Vanderbilt U., Nashville, 1959, MS, 1960; PhD, U. Colo., 1967. Registered profl. geologist, Ind., Tenn., Ga., Fla., N.C., S.C., Ark., Wyo., Ky., Oreg., Alaska. Chief geologist Oman Constrn. Co., Nashville, 1960-62; prof. geology U. Ala., Tuscaloosa, 1966-82; v.p. P.E. LaMoreaux & Assocs., Inc., Tuscaloosa, 1982-92; prin. Hydraulic Cons., Inc., Lakewood, Colo., 1992—; chmn. dept. geology U. Ala., 1978-81; sr. staff scientist Environ. Inst. for Waste Mgmt. Studies, U. Ala., 1984-88; mem. sr. rev. group Waste Mgmt. of North Am.,; mem. com. on onshore oil and gas leasing Nat. Acad. Scis., 1989-90. Contbr. over 40 articles to profl. jours. Recipient Waldemar Lindgren award for excellence in rsch. Soc. Econ. Geologists,, 1968, NASA Citation for Innovative Rsch., 1978, Dist. Achievement in Earth Sci., Fedn. Lapidary and Mineralogical Socs., 1979. Mem. Geol. Soc. Am., Geochem. Soc., Am. Geol. Inst., Assn. Ground Water Scientists and Engrs., Am. Inst. Profl. Geologists (pres. 1986). Home: 512 N Jackson St Golden CO 80403-1326 Office: Hydrologic Consultants Inc 143 Union Blvd Ste 525 Lakewood CO 80228-1827

HUGHES, W. JAMES, optometrist; b. Shawnee, Okla., Oct. 15, 1944; s. Willis J. and Elizabeth Alice (Nimohoyah) H. B.A. in Anthropology, U. Okla., 1966, M.A. in Anthropology, 1972; O.D., U. Houston, 1976; M.P.H., U. Tex., 1977. Lic. Optometrist, Okla., Tex., W. Va. commd. med. officer USPHS, 1966; advanced through the grades to capt./optometrist, USPHS, 1993; physician's asst., Houston, Dallas, 1969-70; teaching asst. in clin. optics U. Houston, 1973-74, contact lens research asst., 1974; Wesley Jessen Contact Lens Rep., 1974-76; extern eye clinic Tuba City Indian Hosp., 1975; teaching fellow pub. health optometry U. Houston, 1975-76; Indian Health Service optometrist, Eagle Butte, S.D., 1976; optometrist vision care project Crockett Ind. Sch. Dist., 1977; vision care program dir. Bemidji Area Indian Health Service, 1977-78; optometrist Navajo Area Indian Health Service, Chinle Health Ctr., 1978-79; adj. prof. So. Calif. Coll. of Optometry, Los Angeles, U. Houston Coll. of Optometry, 1978—, So. Coll. Optometry, Memphis, 1980—; optometrist Shiprock USPHS Indian Hosp., 1979—; chief vision care program Northern Navajo Med. Ctr., 1994—; dir. eye clinic USPHS Northern Navajo Med. Ctr., Shiprock, N.Mex.; Navajo area Indian Health Service rep. to optometry career devel. com. USPHS. Sgt. U.S. Army, 1966-69, Capt. USPHS 1993—. Decorated Bronze Star, Purple Heart. Recipient House of Vision award 1974; Community Health Optometry award 1976; Better Vision scholar, 1973-76. Mem. Am. Pub. Health Assn., Am. Optometric Assn., Tex. Optometric Assn. Commd. Officers Soc., Assn. Am. Indian Physicians, Beta Sigma Kappa. Democrat. Roman Catholic. Contbr. articles to profl. jours.

HUGHS, MARY GERALDINE, accountant, social service specialist; b. Marshalltown, Iowa, Nov. 28, 1929; d. Don Harold, Sr., and Alice Dorothy (Keister) Shaw; A.A., Highline Community Coll., 1970; B.A., U. Wash., 1972; m. Charles G. Hughs, Jan. 31, 1949; children: Mark George, Deborah Kay, Juli Ann, Grant Wesley. Asst. controller Moduline Internat., Inc., Chehalis, Wash., 1972-73; controller Data Recall Corp., El Segundo, Calif., 1973-74; fin. adminstr., acct. Saturn Mfg. Corp., Torrance, Calif., 1974-77; sr. acct., adminstrv. asst. Van Camp Ins., San Pedro, Calif., 1977-78; asst. adminstr. Harbor Regional Ctr., Torrance, Calif., 1979-87; active bookkeeping svc., 1978—; instr. math. and acctg. South Bay Bus. Coll., 1976-77. Sec. Pacific N.W. Mycol. Soc., 1966-67; treas., bd. dirs. Harbor Employees Fed. Credit Union; mem. YMCA Club. Recipient award Am. Mgmt. Assn., 1979. Mem. Beta Alpha Psi. Republican. United Ch. of Christ. Author: Iowa Auto Dealers Assn. Title System, 1955; Harbor Regional Center Affirmative Action Plan, 1980; Harbor Regional Center - Financial Format, 1978—; Provider Audit System, 1979; Handling Client Funds, 1983. Home and Office: 32724 Coastsite Dr # 107 Rancho Palos Verdes CA 90275

HUGLE, LINDA JANE, gifted and talented educator; b. Cin., Mar. 21, 1954; d. William Bell and Frances Betty (Sarnat) H.; m. Scott E. Loomis, June 19, 1971; children: Jacob W. Loomis, Brandy M. Hugle-Loomis. Student, Santa Clara U., 1970-74; BA in Edn., So. Oreg. State Coll., 1978, MA in Edn., 1986. Cert. secondary tchr. and adminstrn. ESL/bilingual tchr. Phoenix (Oreg.)-Talent Sch. Dist., 1979-81; English tchr. Pacific U., Forest Grove, Oreg., 1982; Spanish/social sci. tchr. Illinois Valley H.S., Cave Junction, Oreg., 1982-88; econs. tchr., coll. guidance counselor Hidden Valley H.S., Murphy, Oreg., 1988-93; secondary talented and gifted coord. Three Rivers Sch. Dist., Murphy, 1993—; vol. ESL tchr. Del Rio Orchards, Gold Hill, Oreg., 1976-80; So. Oreg. mem. Title I-M State Adv. Bd., 1976-78; bd. mem. So. Oreg. Consortium, Ashland, 1989-91; trainer law related edn. Nat. Inst. Citizen Edn. in Law, Washington, 1991—; presenter, mem. Classroom Law Project Team, 1994—; curriculum developer content stds. Oreg. Dept. Edn., Salem, 1995-96. Vol., chair, bd. dirs. Women's Crisis Support Team, 1993—; bd. dirs. Rogue River (Oreg.) Sch. Dist., 1993-95, Cmty. Ptnrs. in Edn., Rogue River, 1994—; mem., bd. dirs. Teen Theatre, 1994—; pres. adv. coun. Ret. & Sr. Vol. Program, Grants Pass, Oreg., 1994—. Mem. Oreg. ACLU, Human Rights Alliance, Delta Kappa Gamma (rsch. chair 1987—). Democrat. Office: Three Rivers Sch Dist PO Box 160 Murphy OR 97533

HUGO, JOAN LYALL, academic administrator, art critic, curator; b. Weehawken, N.J., Jan. 12, 1930; d. Thomas Lyall and Bertha (Agnus) Dowey; m. Michel Hugo, May 2, 1952 (div.); children: Alan, Peter. BS in Libr. Sci., Simmons Coll., 1951. Libr. Am. Libr. Paris, 1952-53; cataloguer Bklyn. Mus. Libr., 1954; libr. dir. Otis Art Inst., L.A., 1957-80; So. Calif. editor Artweek, Oakland, Calif., 1980-90; westcoast editor New Art Examiner, Chgo., 1990-94; asst. to provost Calif. Inst. Arts, Valencia, 1990—; instr. Otis Art Inst., 1978-90, UCLA Ext., 1982-90; curator numerous exhbns. Contbr. reviews to profl. jours., catalogue essays. Bd. dirs. L.A. Contemporary Exhbns., L.A., 1980-84, Woman's Bldg., L.A., 1986-89, Cactus Found., L.A., 1988—; mem. bd. advisors Found. Art Resources, L.A., 1986-96. Recipient Vesta award Woman's Bldg., 1990. Mem. Coll. Art Assn., Art Table, Assn. Internat. des Critiques D'Art. Home: 2601 Waverly Dr Los Angeles CA 90039-2724 Office: Calif Inst Arts 24700 McBean Pkwy Valencia CA 91355-2340

HUI, KENNETH CHI-WAN, surgeon; b. Hong Kong, Dec. 22, 1955; s. Kenneth K.L. and Ada S.H. (Wong) H.; m. Anna Hui, Nov. 21, 1981; children: Kenneth Jr., Eric. MD, BS, U. London, England, 1979. Diplomate Am. Bd. Plastic Surgery. Intern St. Bartholomew's Hosp., London U., gen. surgery resident; gen. surgery resident U. Medicine and Dentistry N.J., Robert Wood Johnson U., New Brunswick; resident in plastic surgery Hershey Med. Ctr., Pa. State U.; fellow in microsurgery Ralph K. Dawes Med. Ctr., San Francisco; asst. prof. Stanford U. Med. Ctr., Palo Alto, Calif., 1991; staff surgeon VA Med. Ctr., Palo Alto, Calif., 1991, sect. chief divsn. plastic surgery, 1992—; chmn. care review com. Stanford U. Med. Ctr. Divsn. Plastic Surgery, Calif., 1992. Contbd. articles to profl. jours. Recipient Basic Sci. Rsch. prize N.J. Chpt. Am. Coll. Surgeons, 1987. Fellow Royal Coll. Surgeons, Am. Coll. Surgeons; mem. Stanford Asian Am. Med. Faculty Assn., Am. Soc. Plastic and Reconstructive Surgery, Calif. Soc. Plastic Surgeons, Am. Soc. for Reconstructive Microsurgey, Pan Pacific Surgical Assn. Office: Stanford U Med Ctr Divsn Plastic Surgery NC-104 Stanford CA 94305

HUIGENS, DANIEL DEAN, dentist; b. Osmond, Nebr., May 16, 1953; s. Mickey Helen (White) H.; m. Linda Sue Wilbourn, May 19, 1982 (div. 1991); 1 child, Matthew Blake. BA, U. LaVerne, 1975; BS, U. Okla., 1979, DDS with honors, 1982. EMT Community Ambulance Svc., San Dimas, Calif., 1971-74; emergency room technician San Dimas Community Hosp., San Dimas, Calif., 1974-77; physician assoc. Muskogee Bone and Joint Clinic, 1979-82; dentist Drs. Huigens and Hanawalt, LaVerne, Calif., 1986-94; pvt. practice LaVerne, 1994—; mem. part time staff UCLA Coll. Dentistry. Mem. ADA, Acad. Gen. Dentistry, Calif. Dental Assn., Tri County Dental Soc., Pomona Valley Amateur Astronomers Assn., LaVerne C. of C., Assn. Flying Dentists, Aircraft Owners and Pilots Assn., Omicron Kappa Upsilon. Office: 2187 Foothill Blvd Ste E La Verne CA 91750-2943

HULL, DENNIS JACQUES, counselor; b. Orange, N.J., June 8, 1945; s. Jacques Lionel and Ora May (Holdman) H.; m. Elizabeth Ann Martin, Sept. 7, 1969; 1 child, Jonathan. BA in Psychology, Calif. State Univ., Hayward, 1968, MS in Counseling, 1975. Cert. counselor Nat. Bd. Cert. Counselors, Inc. Counselor L.A. Harbor Coll., Wilmington, Calif., 1979-84; counselor Western Nev. C.C., Carson City, 1984-86, coord. counseling svcs., 1987-94, dir. counseling svcs., 1994—. With USAF, 1968-72. Mem. ACA, Calif. Assn. Counseling Devel., Calif. C.C. Counselors Assn. (bd. dirs., so. conf. chair 1983-84), Nev. Counselors Assn., Nev. Coll. Counselors Assn. Office: Western Nev Cmty Coll 2201 W College Pkwy Carson City NV 89703-7316

HULL, JANE DEE, state official, former state legislator; b. Kansas City, Mo., Aug. 8, 1935; d. Justin D. and Mildred (Swenson) Bowersock; m. Terrance Ward Hull, Feb. 12, 1954; children: Jeannette Shipley, Robin Hillebrand, Jeff, Mike. BS, U. Kans., 1957; postgrad., U. Ariz., 1972-78. Spkr. pro tem Ariz. Ho. of Reps., Phoenix, 1993, chmn. ethics com., chmn. econ. devel., 1993, mem. legis. coun., 1993, mem. gov.'s internat. trade and tourism adv. bd., 1993, mem. gov.'s strategic partnership for econ. devel., 1993, mem. gov.'s office of employement implementation task force, 1993, spkr. of house, 1989-93, house majority whip, 1987-88; now secretary of state State of Arizona, Phoenix. Bd. dirs. Morrison Inst. for Pub. Policy, Beatitudes D.O.A.R., 1992, Ariz. Town Hall, Ariz. Econs. Coun.; mem. dean's coun. Ariz. State U., 1989-92; assoc. mem. Heard Mus. Guild, Cactus Wren Rep. Women, ; mem. Maricopa Med. Aux., Ariz. State Med. Aux., Freedom Found., Valley Citizens League, Charter 100, North Phoenix Rep. Women, 1970, Trunk 'N Tusk Legis. Liaison Ariz. Rep. Party, 1993; Rep. candidate sec. of state, 1994. Recipient Econ. Devel. award Ariz. Innovation Network, 1993. Mem. Nat. Orgn. of Women Legislators, Am. Legis. Exch. Coun., Nat. Rep. Legislators Assn. (Nat. Legislator of Yr. award 1989), Soroptimists (hon.). Republican. Roman Catholic. Home: 10458 N 9th St Phoenix AZ 85020-1585 Address: Office of th Sec State State Capitol 1700 W Washington Phoenix AZ 85007-2888*

HULL, JOSEPH L., state senator; b. Ogden, Utah, Dec. 18, 1945; m. Sandra Glanville. BA, Weber State Coll.; MEd, Utah State U. Educator Utah State U.; mem. Utah State Senate, 1992—, asst. minority whip, 1995-96; mem. Utah Ho. of Reps., 1986-92; mem. various coms. including edn. and human svcs. Democrat. Office: 5250 W 4000 Hooper UT 84315

HULL, MAURY LANE, mechanical engineering educator; b. Washington, July 18, 1947; s. Maury Isaac and Marguerite Fern (Lane) H.; m. Karen Slakey, Sept. 15, 1984. BSME, Carnegie-Mellon U., 1969; MSME, U. Calif., Berkeley, 1970, PhD in Mech. Engring., 1975. Asst. specialist in mech. engring. U. Calif., Berkeley, 1975; from asst. prof. to assoc. prof. mech. engring. U. Calif., Davis, 1976-88, prof. mech. engring., 1988—, chair biomed. engring., 1993—; cons. Tyrolia Corp., Vienna, Austria, 1985—, Shimano Corp., Osaka, Japan, 1988—. Mem. editl. bd. Internat. Jour. Sport Biomechanics, 1989-92, Jour. Biomechanics, 1993—; contbr. numerous tech. articles to sci. jours. and procs. Fellow ASME; mem. Internat. Soc. Skiing Safety, Internat. Soc. Biomechanics, Am. Soc. Biomechanics (Giovanni Borelli award 1989), Orthopedic Rsch. Soc. Home: 8565 Olive School Ln Winters CA 95694-9652 Office: U Calif Dept Mech Engring Davis CA 95616

HULL, ROGER KERMIT, naval officer; b. Chattanooga, Tenn., Apr. 19, 1946; s. George Fletcher and Dorothy Helen (Suddarth) H.; m. Mary Alison Welter Hull, Dec. 21, 1981; children: Nathan Kyle, Rachel Rebecca. BS in Aviation Mgmt., Auburn U., Ala., 1968; MS in Ops. Rsch., Naval Postgrad. Sch., Monterey, Calif., 1977. Cert. flight instr. fixed wing and hot air balloon, airline transport pilot, designated acquisition profl., USN. Commd. ensign USN, 1968, advanced through grades to capt., 1989; flight student Naval Aviation Sch. Command, Pensacola, Fla., 1968-69; advanced jet flight instructor Naval Aviation Training Command, Kingsville, Tex., 1969-71; combat attack pilot Attack Squadron 146, Lemoore Calif., Vietnam, 1971-74; student Naval Postgrad. Sch., Monterey, Calif., 1974-77; competition parachutist U.S. Parachute Team, Pope Valley, Calif., 1977; dept. head Attack Squadron 56, Yokosuka, Japan, 1977-81; test and evaluation pilot, chief operation test dir. Air Test and Evaluation Squadron Five, China Lake, Calif., 1981-84; air ops. officer Cruiser Destroyer Group One, San Diego, 1984-87; program mgr. Space and Naval Warfare Systems Command, Washington, 1987-90; comdg. officer Naval Weapons Eval. Facility, Albuquerque, N.Mex., 1990-93; vice comdr. NAWC Weapons Divsn., China Lake/Point Mugu, Calif., 1993-95; small bus. owner "Copy To:", Hanford, Calif., 1975-77; cons. ops. analyst, San Diego, 1984-87. Author: United We Fall, 1977; contbr. articles to profl. jours. Capt., USN, 1968—. Recipient World Champion Parachutist, Fed. Aeronautics Internat., Gatton, Autralia, 1977; Indiv. Overall Nat. Champion Parachutist, U.S. Parachute Assn., Talequah, Okla., 1977; Proven Subspecialist Ops. Rsch., USN., 1981; Proven Subspecialist Command & Control, USN, 1988. Mem. Balloon Fedn. Am., Omicron Delta Kappa. Office: Space and Naval Warfare Sys Command PMW-171 San Diego CA 92152

HULL, TOD CHRISTOPHER, environmental consultant; b. Cleve., Nov. 4, 1953; s. Tracy Charles and Winifred Hull; m. Bridget Hull Collins, Oct. 4, 1986. BA in Botany, Miami U. Ohio, 1985. Vol. U.S. Peace Corps, Washington, 1983-85; resource analyst Kaibab Forest Products Co., Fredonia, Ariz., 1986-93; environ. cons. Applied Ecosys. Mgmt., Inc., Flagstaff, Ariz., 1993—; mem. adv. coun., past chmn. land com. Comm. on Ariz. Environ., Phoenix, 1988-96; breeding bird survey vol. U.S. Fish and Wildlife Svc., Washington, 1992—; mem. adv. bd. Ariz. Gov.'s Select Ecosys. Tech. Com., Phoenix, 1992-95. Vol. travelers aid ctr. and thrift store St. Vincent De Paul Soc., Flagstaff, 1992—; precinct committeeman Flagstaff Rep. Com., 1994—. Mem. Wildlife Soc., Am. Ornithol. Union. Roman Catholic. Home: 5161 E Hawthorne Dr Flagstaff AZ 86004 Office: Applied Ecosys Mgmt Inc 125 E Elm Ave Ste A Flagstaff AZ 86001

HULL, TOM ALLAN, mechanics educator; b. Centralia, Wash., Feb. 3, 1956; s. Royce Keith and Barbara (Peyton) H. BS in Indsl. Arts, Western Wash. U., Bellingham, 1984; MEd, Oreg. State U., 1987. Cert. Automtive Svc. Excellence master mechanic; indsl. mechanics vocat. tchg. cert.; lic. tchr., Oreg. Mailroom clk. Daily Chronicle, Centralia, 1970-74; cmty. antennae technician McCaw Comms., Wash., 1974-84; classroom tchr. South Umpqua H.S., Myrtle Creek, Oreg., 1984—; chmn. site coun. South Umpqua H.S., Myrtle Creek, 1994-96, mem. work exp. adv. bd., 1996—; past chmn., mem. South Umpqua Sch. Imp. Team, Myrtle Creek, 1992—; field worker Plastics Industry/Diesel Mech., Myrtle Creek, 1984-95. Editor, author: (newsletter) Quarter Inch Dr., 1993—; contbr. book revs. and tech. articles to profl. jours. Team teach plastics class PMC, Glendale, Oreg., 1995. Named Douglas County Educator of Yr., Masons, 1995, Oreg. Tech. Tchr. of Yr., Tech. Educators Oreg., 1996. Mem. Soc. Automotive Engrs., Soc. for History of Tech., Am. Truck Hist. Soc., Coun. Tech. Tchr. Edn., Soc. Indsl. Archaeology, Josephine County Pistol Club (pres., sec., treas. 1993—). Home: 319 Taylor Myrtle Creek OR 97457 Office: South Umpqua H S 501 Chadwick Ln Myrtle Creek OR 97457

HULLAR, THEODORE LEE, environmental educator; b. Mar. 19, 1935; m. Joan J. Miller, Aug. 2, 1958; children: Theodore W., Timothy E. BS with high distinction, U. Minn., 1957, PhD in Biochemistry, 1963. Asst. prof. medicinal chemistry SUNY, Buffalo, 1964-69, assoc. prof., 1969-75, assoc. dean grad. sch., 1969-71; dep. commr. programs and research N.Y. State Dept. Environ. Conservation, 1975-79; assoc. dir. Cornell U. Agrl. Experiment Sta., 1979-81, dir., 1981-84; assoc. dir. research N.Y. State Coll. Agriculture and Life Scis., Cornell U., 1979-81; dir. N.Y. State Coll. Agriculture and Life Scis. Cornell U., 1981-84; adj. prof. natural resources, prof. natural resources Cornell U., 1981-84; chancellor, prof. biochem. U. Calif., Riverside, 1985-87; prof. environ. toxicology U. Calif., Davis, 1987—, chancellor, 1985-94; chmn. hazardous waste mgmt. com. So. Calif. Assn. Govs., 1986-87, chmn. air quality task force, 1985-87, mem. regional adv. coun., 1985-87; chmn. con. on environment nat. Assn. State Univs. and Land Grant Colls., 1985-93, com. on biotech., 1982-88, chmn. program devel. subcom., 1982-88, coord. Agr. Rsch. Initiative; chn. Gov. Deukmejian's Task Force on Toxics, Waste and Tech., 1985-86; chmn. bd. agr. Nat. Rsch. Coun., 1988-93; co-founder, chmn. Calif. Coun. on Sci. and Tech., 1988-93; mem. gov. bd. Internat. Irrigation Mgmt. Inst., 1991—; bd. dirs. Boyce Thompson Inst. for Plant Rsch., 1985—; chair univ. rev. and accreditation coms., 1990—; lectr. various orgns. Contbr. articles to profl. jours. Commr. Environ. Quality Erie County, N.Y., 1974-75; alternate to Gov. N.Y. on Delaware and Susquehanna River Basin Commns., 1975-79; mem. N.Y. State Agrl. Resources Commn., 1974-75; mem. Arlington Heights Greenbelt Study Com., 1986-87; mem. Monday Morning Group, 1985-87; active various community orgns. NSF postdoctoral fellow SUNY Buffalo, 1963-64. Mem. Am. Chem. Soc., AAAS, Chem. Soc. London, Regional Inst. So. Calif., Greater Riverside C. of C., (bd. dirs. 1985-87), Sigma Xi. Home: PO Box 1606 Davis CA 95617-1606 Office: U Calif Environ Toxicology Davis CA 95616-8588

HULSE, RALPH ROBERT, management consultant; b. St. Joseph, Mo., Jan. 14, 1935; s. Ralph Raymond and Eva Laduska (Hatfield) H.; m. Gwen Lea Bartosh, May 21, 1956 (div. 1959); m. Jutta-Beaujean, Jan. 14, 1961. AB, Cen. Meth. Coll., 1957; MEd, U. Mo., 1965. Continuing edn. programmer U. Mo., Columbia, 1969-71; dir. edn. tng. North Kansas City (Mo.) Meml. Hosp., 1971-74; mgmt. cons. Lawrence-Leiter, Kansas City, 1974-77; adminstr. U.S. Congress, 6th dist., Mo., 1977-78; bus. cons. Hulse & Assocs., Kansas City, 1978-88; adminstr. Sales Tng. Inst. div. Mile Hi Bus. Coll., Denver, 1988-89; bus. cons., pres. Crystal Devel. Systems, Inc, Denver, 1989-95; agent Bankers Life & Casualty Ins., 1994—; founder, bd. dirs. Opportunity Industry Inc., St. Joseph, 1965-71; pres. State Adult Edn. Assn., Mo., 1978-79. Contbr. articles to profl. jours. (Nat. Pub. award 1974, 75). Served with U.S. Army, 1959-61. Mem. Colo. Cons. Assn. (founder, pres. 1985-87). Republican. Methodist. Home and Office: 5282 Union Ct #4 Arvada CO 80002-1946

HULTERSTROM, WILLIAM E., foundation executive; b. L.A., July 2, 1957; s. Walter K. and Betty (Richardson) H.; m. Tammy Anderson, July 9, 1987; 1 child, Andrew William. BA in Bus. Mgmt., Brigham Young U., 1981. Projects dir. Utah Spl. Olympics, Provo, Utah, 1981-83; assoc. exec. dir. United Way of Utah County, Provo, Utah, 1983-85; pres., exec. dir. United Way of Ctrl. and So. Utah, Provo, Utah, 1985—; trainer United Way of Am., Provo, 1984—, cons., 1986—; mentor Operation Spotlight, United Way, Helena, Mont., 1989-92. Contbr. articles to profl. jours. Vice chmn. Utah County Homeless Task Force, 1988—; mem. Mountainland Aging Adv. Com., 1985—, State Homeless Coordinating Com., 1988—, State Project Action Com.-Easter Seals, 1990-92. Mem. Kiwanis Club of Provo (bd. dir. 1987—, Citizen of the Yr. 1994), Provo/Orem C. of C. (bd. dirs. 1991—). Office: United Way of Utah County PO Box 135 Provo UT 84603

HUMBER, PHILIP RICHARD, plastic surgeon; b. Milw., Wis., Jan. 19, 1950. MD, Med. Coll. Wis., 1976. Plastic surgeon Scripps Encinitas Hosp., Calif.; also with Tri-City Med. Ctr., Calif. Office: 320 Santa Fe Dr Ste 107 Encinitas CA 92024-5139

HUME, DARREL J., retail executive; b. 1948. Student, U. Wash. With Nordstrom, Inc., Seattle, 1969—; gen. mgr. Nordstrom S.W. Nordstrom, Inc., Dallas, 1996—. Office: Nordstrom Inc 5220 Alpha Rd Dallas TX 75240

HUMES, CHARLES WARREN, counselor, educator; b. Cambridge, Mass.; s. Charles W. and Alice E. Humes; m. Marilyn A. Harper, Aug. 7, 1965; children: Rebecca Ellyn, Malinda Maye. MA, NYU, 1952; EdM, Springfield Coll., 1956; EdD, U. Mass., 1968. Lic. profl. counselor, Va.; cert. profl. counselor, Ariz. Sch. psychologist Westfield Pub. Schs. (Mass.), 1955-62; dir. guidance Westfield Pub. Schs. (Mass.), 1962-70; assoc. prof. Springfield Coll. (Mass.), 1968-70; dir. pupil svc. and spl. edn. Greenwich Pub. Schs. (Conn.), 1970-80; assoc. prof. No. Va. Grad. Ctr., Va. Tech. U., Falls Church, 1980-88, prof. 1988-93, prof. emeritus, 1993—; pvt. practice, Vienna, Va. and Phoenix, 1985—. V.p. Westfield Area Child Guidance Clinic, 1963-65, pres., 1965-66; mem. Greenwich Hosp. Nursing Coun., 1970-75. Mem. APA, ACA (cons.), SAR (registrar, genealogist Palo Verde chpt.), Conn. Assn. Counselor Edn. & Supervision (pres. 1979-80), Ariz. Counselors Assn., Nat. Geneal. Soc., Phi Delta Kappa (v.p. Va. Tech. 1982-83), Phi Kappa Phi. Author: Pupil Services: Development, Coordination, Administration, 1984; Contemporary Counseling: Services, Applications, Issues, 1987. Book rev. editor Sch. Counselor, 1984-93. Contbr. over 60 articles on counseling to profl. jours. Home and Office: 15038 E Palomino Blvd Fountain Hills AZ 85268

HUMMEL, FRED ERNEST, architect; b. Sheridan, Wyo., Jan. 10, 1927; s. Fred Edward and Glenna Ruth (Horton) H.; m. Sue Anne Estep, May 11, 1970; children: Jessica, Rebecca and Amber (triplets); children by previous marriage: Glenn, Mark, Shaun and Lindsay (twins). B.A., U. Calif.-Berkeley, 1951. Pvt. practice architecture Ventura, Calif., 1951-68, Sacramento, 1968-73; state architect, State of Calif., Sacramento, 1968-73; instr. architecture UCLA, 1966-67, Davis, 1974; mem. adv. panel for archtl. services GSA, 1974; cons. State of Ark. Capitol Outlay Study, 1975; chmn. Calif. Bldg. Standards Coordination Council, 1970-71; ex-officio mem. Calif. Bldg. Standards Commn., 1969-73, Field Act Adv. Group, 1968-72; archtl. cons. Mich. Gov.'s Commn. on Architecture, 1972; mem. Calif. Gov.'s Earthquake Council, 1972-73, Calif. Affirmative Action Implementation Com., 1971-72, Calif. Ad Hoc Commn. on Energy Conservation, 1973, Capitol Mall Adv. Planning Com., 1970-71, Calif. Gov.'s Task Force on Capitol Outlay Projects, 1970-71; mem. adv. com. on environ. design and urban studies to Calif. Coordinating Council for Higher Edn., 1970-71; mem. adv. group on engring. and earthquake scis. to Calif. Joint Legis. Com. on Seismic Safety, 1972-73; mem. Commn. of the Californias, 1972-82; mem. adv. bd. Nat. Park System, 1981-84; mem. Sacramento County Sheriff's Air Squadron, 1981; apptd. by Pres. Reagan to bd. dirs. Nat. Inst. Bldg. Scis., 1986-90; apptd. project mgr. Ronald Reagan Presdl. Library, 1986-91, Del Mar Racetrack, 1991-93; apptd. state architect, Calif., 1996—. Served to 1st lt. inf. U.S. Army, 1945-47, 51, Korea. Recipient award of honor Chico State U., 1974, Hon. award Cons. Engrs. Assn. of Calif., 1969, presentation Ann. Architects and Engrs. Forum, Los Angeles, 1969, Calif. Senate and Assembly resolutions of commendation, 1973. Fellow AIA (pres., dir. Santa Barbara, Calif. chpt. 1962, dir. Calif. council 1961-63, mem. Calif. profl. practice com. 1969, mem. exec. com. Calif. council, state treas. 1961-62, AIA Disting. Service Citation Calif. council 1973, v.p. edn. Calif. council 1978, mem. nat. govtl. relations com. 1974-76, nat. capitol com. 1973-74, dir. Central Valley chtp. 1973-74, mem. nat. architects in govt. com. 1971-72, chmn. Calif. council architects in govt. com. 1970-73, mem. Calif. govt. relations com. 1964-67, dir. Ventura County chpt. 1964-66, mem. Calif. evaluation bd. 1964). Republican. Home: 5007 Sugar Ln Carmichael CA 95608-3128 *Work hard, be honest, take time to smell the flowers, and trust in God.*

HUMMEL, JOSEPH WILLIAM, hospital administrator; b. Vinton, Iowa, Dec. 7, 1940; married. BA, Calif. State U., 1965; M Health Adminstrn., U Calif., 1966. Adminstrv. instr. Merrithew Meml. Hosp., Martinez, Calif., 1965; adminstrv. res. Mt. Zion Hosp. and Med. Ctr., San Francisco, 1966-67, adminstrv. pat. care, 1967-68, adminstrv. asst., 1968-70; assoc. adminstr. Valley Med. Ctr., Fresno, Calif., 1970-74; CEO Kern Med. Ctr., Bakersfield, Calif., 1974-86; adminstr. Kaiser Found. Hosp., L.A., 1987—, sr. v.p. area mng. Mem. Calif. Hosp. Assn. (bd. dirs. 1983-89). Home: 2050 Maginn St Glendale CA 91202-1128 Office: Kaiser Found Hosp 4747 W Sunset Blvd Los Angeles CA 90027-5969*

HUMMER-SHARPE, ELIZABETH ANASTASIA, genealogist, writer; b. Morristown, N.J., Dec. 15, 1931; d. Harold Arlington and Sophia Anastasia (Dombrowski) Hummer; divorced; children: Dean T., Dana E., Robert K., Jean F., Christopher K. Studetn, Santa Monica Coll., 1968-69. Cashier L. Bamberger Co., Morristown, 1949; telephone sales, asst. office mgr. L.A. Times, Santa Monica, 1968-69; unit sec. St. Johns Hosp., Santa Monica, 1969-75; telephone sales L.A. Times, Culver City, 1976-79; mktg. dir. Ramsgate Films, Santa Monica, 1976-78; sr. file clk. Crown Wholesale Co., L.A., 1979-80; telephone sales L.A. Times, Santa Monica, 1988-91. Bd. dirs. Desert Opera Theatre, Palmdale, Calif., 1994—. Mem. Internat. Platform Soc., Antelope Valley Geneal. Soc., Nat. Audubon Soc., Arbor Day Found., Planetary Soc. (charter mem.), UFD Soc. Roman Catholic.

HUMPHREY, JOHN JULIUS, university program director, historian, writer; b. Booneville, Miss., Jan. 22, 1926; s. George Duke and Josephine (Robertson) H.; m. Mary Margaret Ryan, Jan. 19, 1949; children: George Duke II, Laurie Ann. BS, Miss. State U., 1945; BA, U. Wyo., 1946, MA, 1964, postgrad., 1964-68; postgrad., U. Ariz., 1969-71. Pres. J.J. Humphrey Co. Inc., Laramie, Wyo., 1947-68; lectr. History U. Ariz., Tucson, 1969-71, asst. dir. placement, 1969-70, dir. scholarships, awards, 1970-72, dir. office of scholarships and fin. aid, 1972-84, dir. scholarship devel., 1970-91; asst. to pres. western area Cumberland Coll., Williamsburg, Ky., 1991; v.p. bus. affairs Tucson Coll. Arts and Scis., 1992. Sec. Baird Found., Tucson, 1970—; bd. dirs. Bendalin Fund, Phoenix, 1976—, Cacioppo Found., Tucson, 1986—; cons. DeMund Found., St. Louis, 1970—; mem. Pres. Club U. Ariz. Found.; mem. Ariz. Assn. Fin. Aid Officers, 1970-91, pres., 1973-74; pres. Ariz. Coll. & Univ. Faculty Assn., 1972-73. Ivinson Meml. Hosp. Bd., Laramie, 1964-68. Recipient Spl. award U. Ariz. Black Student Govt., 1983, Black Alumni, 1990; study grantee U. Ariz., 1993—. Mem. Am. Indian Alumni Assn. (Spl. Appreciation for Svc. in Scholarships Native Ams. award 1982), Mormon History Assn., Masons (32 degree, Knight York Cross of Honor), Shriners. Methodist. Home: 6901 E Potawatami Dr Tucson AZ 85715-3246

HUMPHREY, PHYLLIS A., writer; b. Oak Park, Ill., July 22, 1929; d. Richard William and Antoinette (Chalupa) Ashworth; m. Herbert A. Pihl, Sept. 13, 1946 (div. 1957); children: Christine Pihl Gibson, Gary Fraizer Pihl; m. Curtis H. Humphrey, June 21, 1965; 1 child, Marc. AA, Coll. San Mateo, Calif., 1972; postgrad., Northwestern U., 1945-47. Ptnr. Criterion House, Oceanside, Calif., 1972—. Author: Wall Street on $20 a Month, 1986, Golden Fire, 1986, Sweet Folly, 1990, Flying High, 1995; author radio scripts Am. Radio Theatre, 1983-84; contbr. short stories and articles to popular mags. Mem. Mensa. Republican. Christian Sci. Ch. Office: Criterion House PO Box 586295 Oceanside CA 92058-6295

HUMPHRIES, SANDRA LEE FORGER, artist, teacher; b. Norwalk, Conn., Dec. 1, 1946; d. Edmund Ernest and Grace Muriel (Seale) Forger; m. Stanley Humphries Jr., Aug. 10, 1968 (div. July 1992); children: Colin, Courtney. BFA, R.I. Sch. Design, 1968; MA, U. N.Mex., 1994. Studio artist Albuquerque, 1980—; instr. watercolor Sandra Humphries Fine Art, Albuquerque, 1992—; dir. Shows Gallery, Albuquerque, 1994-96, Sandra Humphries Gallery, Albuquerque, 1997—. Exhibited in group shows at Rocky Mountain Watermedia Exhbn., 1983, 86, 89, 90, 91, Western Fedn. Watercolor Socs., 1984, 86, 87, 90, Am. Watercolor Soc. Exhbn., 1985, Nat. Watercolor Soc. Exhbn., 1989, Artists of the West Invitational, 1993, 94, 95, 96. Mem. Nat. Watercolor Soc. (signature), Rocky Mountain Watermedia Soc. (signature), N.Mex. Watercolor Soc. (signature). Home: 3503 Berkeley Pl NE Albuquerque NM 87106

HUMPHRIES, STEPHEN EDWARD, writer; b. Camden, N.J., Oct. 14, 1950; s. Edward W. and Dolores (Weaver) H.; m. Elsa Schroeder, Oct. 30, 1977 (div. Oct. 1983); m. Ruth Ivy Frishman, Sept. 27, 1992. AA with honors, Broward Community Coll., 1970; student, U. Colo., 1972-74, Colo. Sch. Mines, 1981-84, Met. State Coll., 1986-88. Engring. tech., tech. writer Enviro-Test Ltd., Denver, 1975-77; asst. editor Am. Water Works Assn., Denver, 1977; assoc. project scientist TRC Environ. Cons., Denver, 1978-82; geol. asst., writer Colo. Sch. Mines, Golden, 1983-84; reporter, editor High Timber Times, Conifer, Colo., 1984-88; reporter Aspen (Colo.) Times/Times Daily, 1988-89; copy editor The Leader Newspapers, Houston, 1989; mng. editor S. Coast Community Newspapers, Santa Barbara, Calif., 1989-90; freelance writer Houston, 1989-91; editor Tahoe World, Tahoe City, Calif., 1991-93; freelance writer Truckee, Calif., 1993—. Trustee Tahoe Forest Hosp. Found., Truckee Donner Land Trust; vol. U.S. Geol. Survey; adv. bd. Tahoe Truckee Housing Devel. Corp. Recipient 2d place feature photography for weeklies award Colo. Press Assn., 1985, hon. mention news stories for weeklies, 1987, sweepstakes winner feature stories for weeklies, 1989; hon. mention serious columnist for weekly Nat. Newspaper Assn., 1987, hon. mention editorial pages for weeklies, 1989; award Met. Water Providers, 1987, Meritorious Svc. award VFW, 1988. Mem. Internat. Soc. Weekly Newspaper Editors, Soc. Profl. Journalists.

HUMPHRY, DEREK, association executive, writer; b. Bath, Somerset, Eng., Apr. 29, 1930; came to U.S., 1978; s. Royston Martin and Bettine (Duggan) H.; m. Jean Edna Crane, May 5, 1953 (dec. Mar. 1975); children: Edgar, Clive, Stephen; m. Ann Wickett Kooman, Feb. 16, 1976 (div. 1990); m. Gretchen Crocker, 1991. Student pub. schs. Reporter, Evening News, Manchester, Eng., 1951-55, Daily Mail, London, 1955-63; editor Havering Recorder, Essex, Eng., 1963-67; sr. reporter Sunday Times, London, 1967-78; spl. writer L.A. Times, 1978-79; founder, exec. dir. Hemlock Soc. N.Am., L.A., 1980-92, pres. 1988-90. Author: Because They're Black, 1971 (M.L. King award 1972), Police Power and Black People, 1972; Jean's Way, 1978, Let Me Die Before I Wake, 1982, The Right to Die, 1986, Final Exit, 1991, Dying With Dignity, 1992, Lawful Exit, 1993. With Brit. Army, 1948-50. Mem. World Fedn. Right-to-Die Socs. (newsletter editor 1979-84, 1992-94, sec.-treas. 1983-84, pres. 1988-90), Ams. Death with Dignity (v.p. 1993), Hemlock Soc. No. Calif. (v.p. 1994), Euthanasia Rsch. and Guidance Orgn. (pres. 1993—). Home: 24829 Norris Ln Junction City OR 97448-9559

HUNDAHL, SCOTT ALFRED, oncologic surgeon; b. Omaha, Jan. 2, 1956; s. Robert E. and Mariann Berg (Hundahl) Appley; m. Conchita Leilani Siri, May 13, 1986 (div. Dec. 1992). BA magna cum laude, Harvard U., 1977; MD, Yale U., 1981. Diplomate Am. Bd. Surgery, Am. Bd. Med. Examiners. Resident in general surgery U. Hawaii, Honolulu, 1981-86; fellow Meml. Sloan-Kettering Cancer Ctr., N.Y.C., 1986-88; asst. prof. surgery U. Hawaii, Honolulu, 1988-95, assoc. clin. prof. surgery, 1996—; rsch. staff Cancer Rsch. Ctr. Hawaii, Honolulu, 1993-96; mem. Commn. on Cancer, Chgo., 1993—; regional chmn. Commn. on Cancer Liaisons, 1993—; assoc. chief surgery Queen's Med. Ctr., Honolulu, 1993-95, chief of surgery, 1995—; pvt. practice surgical oncology, Honolulu, 1988—; co-founder, bd. dirs. Comprehensive Home Svcs. Hawaii, 1986-96, now Care Resource, 1996—. Pres. Honolulu unit Am. Cancer Soc., 1992-93, v.p. Hawaii-Pacific divsn., 1993-96; vice chair Nat. Cancer Data Com., 1994-96, Nat. Commn. on Cancer, 1996—. Recipient best presentation award WHO Collaborating Ctrs. for Gastric Cancer, Munich, Germany, 1993; named State Chmn. of the Yr., Commn. on Cancer, 1995. Fellow ACS (exec. com. Hawaii chpt. 1991—, state cancer liaison chmn. 1991—), Soc. Surg. Oncology; mem. AMA, AAAS, Pacific Club, Hawaii Wado Kai (pres. 1989—), Hawaii Med. Assn. (continuing med. edn. com. 1992-93, bd. councilors 1992-95), Hawaiian Surg. Assn., Honolulu County Med. Soc., Soc. Head and Neck Surgeons, Union Internat. Contre le Cancer (internat. cancer data com.). Republican. Episcopalian. Office: 1380 Lusitana St #410 Honolulu HI 96813

HUNDLEY, NORRIS CECIL, JR., history educator; b. Houston, Oct. 26, 1935; s. Norris Cecil and Helen Marie (Mundine) H.; m. Carol Marie Beckquist, June 8, 1957; children: Wendy Michelle Hundley Harris, Jacqueline Marie Hundley Reid. A.A., Mt. San Antonio Coll., 1956; A.B., Whittier Coll., 1958; Ph.D. (Univ. fellow), UCLA, 1963. Instr. U. Houston, 1963-64; asst. prof. Am. history UCLA, 1964-69, assoc. prof., 1969-73, prof., 1973—, chmn. exec. com. Inst. Am. Cultures, 1976-93, chmn. univ. program on Mex., 1981-94, acting dir. Latin Am. Ctr., 1989-90, dir. Latin Am. Ctr., 1990-94; mem. exec. com. U. Calif. Consortium on Mex. and the U.S., 1981-86; mem. adv. com. Calif. water atlas project Calif. Office Planning and Research, 1977-79. Author: Dividing the Waters: A Century of Controversy Between the United States and Mexico, 1966, Water and the West: The Colorado River Compact and the Politics of Water in the American West, 1975, The Great Thirst: Californians and Water 1770s-1990s, 1992; co-author: The Calif. Water Atlas, 1979, California: History of a Remarkable State, 1982; editor: The American Indian, 1974, The Chicano, 1975, The Asian American, 1976; co-editor: The American West: Frontier and Region, 1969, Golden State Series, 1978—; mng. editor Pacific Hist. Rev., 1968—; mem. bd. editors Jour. San Diego History, 1970—; mem. editorial bd. cons. Calif. Hist. Soc., 1980-89; contbr. articles to profl. jours. Bd. dirs. John and LaRee Caughey Found., 1983—, Henry J. Bruman Ednl. Found., 1983—, Forest History Soc., 1987-93. Recipient award of merit Calif. Hist. Soc., 1979; Am. Philos. Soc. grantee, 1964, 71, Ford Found. grantee, 1968-69, U. Calif. Water Resources Ctr. grantee, 1969-72, 91, Sourisseau Acad. grantee, 1972, NEH grantee, 1983-89, Hewlett Found. grantee, 1986-89, U. Calif. Regents faculty fellow in humanities, 1975, Guggenheim fellow, 1978-79, Hist. Soc. So. Calif. fellow, 1996—. Mem. Am. Hist. Assn. (exec. coun. Pacific Coast br. 1969—, v.p. 1993-94, pres. 1994-95), Western History Assn. (coun. 1985-88, 93-97, pres. 1994-95, Winther award 1973, 79), Orgn. Am. Historians. Office: UCLA Dept History Los Angeles CA 90095

HUNDLEY, RONNIE, academic administrator; b. Columbus, Ga., July 18, 1950; s. Jack and Gwendolyn B. (Sasser) Hawthorne; m. Kathy A. Marcure, Apr. 28, 1972; children: Noel, Rhonda, Maria. BSME in Engring., U. Wash., 1974; MSME, Navy Postgrad., 1982, Degree of Engr., 1984. Registered profl. engr., Wash. Dir. engring. tech. Henry Cogswell Coll., Kirkland, Wash., 1989-91, acad. dean, 1991-93, pres., 1993—. Comdr. USN, 1968-89. Mem. ASME, Am. Assn. Higher Edn., Rotary. Office: Henry Cogswell Coll 2808 Wetmore Ave Ste 100 Everett WA 98201

HUNG, SAMMY T., physician; b. Swatow, China; s. Phillip H. and Sou-Mui (Wong) H.; m. Patricia A. Hung, Aug. 22, 1970 (div. July 1988); children: Erick, Kevin, David, Mailee. BA, Amherst Coll., 1968; PhD, U. Calif., Berkeley, 1972; MD, U. Calif., San Francisco, 1976. Diplomate Am. Bd. Internal Medicine. Intern then resident VA Med. Ctr., Martinez, Calif., 1976-79, pulmonary fellow, 1979-81; med. dir. dept. cardiopulmonary St. Rose Hosp., Hayward, Calif., 1981—; cons. in field. Fellow Am. Coll. Chest Physicians; mem. ACP. Office: 27001 Calaroga Ave Ste 4 Hayward CA 94545-4345

HUNGERFORD, EDWARD ARTHUR, humanities professional educator; b. Bremerton, Wash., Sept. 24, 1921; s. Arthur and Mamie (Fredlund) H.; m. Sheila J. Lamar, June 3, 1950; children: Emily, Nancy. BA, U. Puget Sound, 1947; MA, Cornell U., 1948; PhD, NYU, 1960. Instr. English U. Puget Sound, Tacoma, 1949-50, U. Del., Newark, 1952-56; rep. textbook Houghton Mifflin Co., Boston, 1956-59; asst. prof. English Ctrl. Wash. U., Ellensburg, 1959-66; prof. English So. Oreg. U., Ashland, 1966-88; ret., 1988. Contbr. articles to profl. jours. Mem. Modern Lang. Assn., Virginia Woolf Soc. (founding).

HUNING, DEBORAH GRAY, actress, dancer, audiologist, photographer, video producer-editor; b. Evanston, Ill., Aug. 23, 1950; d. Hans Karl Otto and Angenette Dudley (Willard) H.; divorced; 1 child, Bree Alyeska. BS, No. Ill. U., 1981, MA, 1983. Actress, soloist, dancer, dir. various univ. and community theater depts., Bklyn., Chgo. and Cranbrook, B.C., Can., 1967—; ski instr. Winter Park (Colo.) Recreation Assn., 1975-79; house photographer C Lazy U Ranch, Granby, Colo., 1979; audiologist, ednl. programming cons. East Kootenay Ministry of Health, Cranbrook, 1985-89; ind. video prodn./asst., 1991—; owner Maxaroma Espresso and Incredible Edibles, 1993-95; pres. Pan Prodns., 1989—; writer, prodr., editor KTVZ, Bend, Oreg., 1996—; master of ceremonies East Kootenay Talent Showcase, EXPO '86, Vancouver B.C., Can., 1986; creator, workshop leader: A Hearing Impaired Child in the Classroom, 1986. Producer, writer, dir., editor (video) Down With Decibels, 1992; author: Living Well With Hearing Loss: A Guide for the Hearing-Impaired and Their Families, 1992. Sec., treas. Women for Wildlife, Cranbrook, 1985-86; assoc. mem. adv. bd. Grand County Community Coll., Winter Park, Colo., 1975-77; assoc. mem. bd. dirs. Boys and Girls Club of Can., Cranbrook, 1985. Mem. Internat. Marine Animal Trainers Assn.

HUNKINS, RAYMOND BREEDLOVE, lawyer, rancher; b. Culver City, Calif., Mar. 19, 1939; s. Charles F. and Louise (Breedlove) H.; m. Mary Deborah McBride, Dec. 12, 1968; children: Amanda, Blake, Ashley. BA, U. Wyo., 1966, JD, 1968. Ptnr. Jones, Jones, Vines & Hunkins, Wheatland, Wyo., 1968—; mem. local rules com. U.S. Dist. Ct., 1990—; spl. counsel U. Wyo., Laramie, State of Wyo., Cheyenne; mem. faculty Western Trial Adv. Inst., 1993—, Wyo. sect. Commn. Jud. Salary and Benefits, 1996—; owner Thunderhead Ranches, Albany and Platte Counties, Wyo.; gen. ptnr. Split Rock Land & Cattle Co.; spl. asst. atty. gen., Wyo. Chmn. Platte County Reps., Wheatland, 1972-74, mem. adv. coun. Coll. of Commerce and Industry, U. Wyo., 1978-79; bd. dirs. U. Wyo. Found., 1996—, Am. Heritage Ctr., 1995—; mem. Gov.'s Crime Commn., 1970-78; pres. Wyo. U. Alumni Assn., 1973-74, commr. Wyo. Aeronautics Commn., 1987—; moderator United Ch. Christ. With USMC, 1955-57. Fellow Am. Coll. Trial Lawyers, Internat. Soc. Barristers, Am. Bd. Trial Advs.; mem. ABA (aviation com. 1980-86, forum com. on constrn. industry litigation sect.), Wyo. Bar Assn. (chmn. grievance com. 1980-86, mem. com. on civil pattern jury instrns.), Wyo. Trial Lawyers Assn. (past pres.), Lions, Elks. Office: Jones Jones Vines & Hunkins PO Drawer 189 9th and Maple Wheatland WY 82201

HUNNICUTT, ROBERT WILLIAM, engineer; b. Pauls Valley, Okla., Aug. 12, 1954; s. James Warren Hunnicutt. BS, N.Mex. State U., 1980; postgrad., U. Ariz., 1996—. Sr. assoc. engr. IBM, Tucson, 1980-94. Mem. Liason officer, Collegiate Nat. Assn. of the Deaf, U. Ariz. Home: 8383 S Pistol Hill Rd Vail AZ 85641

HUNSAKER, FLOYD B., accountant; b. Collinston, Utah, Sept. 6, 1915; s. Allen G. and Mary Ann (Bowcutt) H.; grad. high sch.; m. Zella D. Hepworth, Mar. 3, 1943; children: Marcia (Mrs. Marvin Bahr), Charlene (Mrs. Abelino Ancira), Sonia (Mrs. Val Fisher), Rhonda (Mrs. Kim Veigel), Tamara (Mrs. Randy Beardall), Shelia (dec. 1945). Lic. ins. salesman, security dealer, notary pub., Lincoln County, Wyo. Owner, operator dairy farm, Bedford, Wyo., 1946-70; acct., Afton, Wyo., 1959—; owner Credit Bur. Star Valley, Afton, 1967-87; mcpl. judge Town of Afton, 1967-77; local office claimstaker Wyo. Unemployment Compensation Dept., 1975-85. Pres., Holdaway Sch. PTA, 1960; active Boy Scouts Am., 1946-49, 58-67; chmn. Cub Scouts com., 1987-95; bd. dirs. Star Valley Sr. Citizens, 1981-83, 84-88; pres. Lower Valley 4-H council, 1961-62, leader, 1959-63; chmn. Star Valley chpt. Am. Revolution Bicentennial Adminstrn., 1975-76, Star Valley chpt. ARC, 1976-96; hon. bd. dirs. Lincoln County Chpt. ARC; ward pres. Sunday Sch., 1985-87; mem. Wyo. Centennial Com., 1990; subdivider Fertile Acres 1981-88; archtl. designer Star Valley Vets. Meml. Monument, 1990; mem. Lincoln County Selective Svc. Bd., 1984-96. Pub. Star Valley Bus. Directory, 1990—. Recipient 50 Yr. Vol. award ARC, 1992, First Place award Farm Bur. Talent Contest; Floyd B. Hunsaker Day named in his honor, 1995. Served with Devils Brigade, 1941-45; ETO. Mem. Farm Bur. (exec. sec. Lincoln County 1961-66), Internat. Platform Assn., Afton C. of C. (dir. 1973-74), Star Valley C. of C. (dir. 1988—, exec. sec. 1989-90, treas. 1991—, Outstanding Cmty. Svc. award 1994), VFW (post svc. officer 1949—, post quartermaster 1959—, dist. comdr. Wyo. 1974-75, 77-78, state dept. jr. vice comdr. 1978-79, sr. vice comdr. 1979-80, state comdr. 1980-81, dist. comdr. 1982-83, 86-88, chmn. state audit com. 1985-94), Am. Legion (post svc. officer, adj. treas. 1975—). Mem. Ch. of Jesus Christ of Latter-day Saints. Home: PO Box 516 323 Adams St Afton WY 83110 Office: 498 Washington St Afton WY 83110

HUNSAKER, SCOTT LESLIE, gifted and talented education educator; b. Provo, Utah, Oct. 22, 1953; s. Melvin J and Ruth Lofthouse (Pulsipher) H.; m. Rebecca Naser, June 2, 1982; children: Adam Scott, Jacob Christian, Rachel Noelle. BA cum laude, Brigham Young U., 1977, MEd, 1982; PhD, U. Va., 1991. Classroom tchr. Alpine Sch. Dist., Orem, Utah, 1977-85; gifted coord. Alpine Sch. Dist., American Fork, Utah, 1986-87; rsch. asst. U. Va., Charlottesville, 1987-91; asst. prof. U. Ga., Athens, 1991-95, Utah State U., Logan, 1995—; presenter workshops and papers to internat., nat., state, and local confs. Co-author: Suggestions for Program Development in Gifted Education; contbr. articles to profl. jours. Mem. Mormon Tabernacle Choir. Governor's fellow U. Va., 1989. Mem. Am. Edn. Rsch. Assn., Nat. Assn. Gifted Children (bd. dirs. 1992—, creativity div. chair 1989-90, John C. Gowan Grad. Student award 1989, Early Leader award 1991), Coun. Exceptional Children/The Assn. for Gifted. LDS. Office: Dept Elem Edn Utah State Univ Logan UT 84322-2805

HUNSBERGER, CHARLES WESLEY, library director; b. Elkhart, Ind., Sept. 25, 1929; s. Charles August and Emma Edna (Zimmerman) H.; m. Hilda Carol Showalter, July 3, 1949 (div.); children: Jonathan Wesley, Jerald Wayne, Jane Wannette. BA, Bethel Coll., Mishawaka, Ind., 1952; MLS, Ind. U., 1967. Mem. Ft. Wayne (Ind.) Libr. Staff, 1960-62; dir. Columbia (Ind.) City Libr., 1962-64, Monroe County Libr., Bloomington, Ind., 1964-71, Clark County Libr. Dist., Las Vegas, Nev., 1971-93; owner Las Vegas Libr. Cons. Svcs., 1993—, Las Vegas, Nev. cons. sch., pub. librs., 1968-70; lectr. libr. schs. Ind. U., 1970-71, U. Ariz., 1974, U. Nev., Reno, 1976; mem. Nev. Coun. on Librs., 1973-81, chmn., 1980-81. Mem. Calif. Libr. Assn., ALA, Nev. Libr. Assn. (named Libr. of Yr. 1988), Internat. Assn. of Met. City Librs. (sec./treas., 1992-95), Rotary (pres. 1979-80, Las Vegas-Paradise chpt.). Democrat. Home: 52 Crestview Dr Las Vegas NV 89124-9135 Office: Las Vegas Libr Cons Svcs PO Box 73221 Las Vegas NV 89170-3221

HUNT, BARNABAS JOHN, priest, religious order administrator; b. Sayre, Pa., Jan. 6, 1937; s. Clarence Elmer and Margarite Frances (Bennett) H. BS in Edn., Pa. State U., 1958; postgrad., Elmira Coll., 1960-61, Portland (Oreg.) State U., 1969-70, Clackamas C.C., 1970-71, Mt. Hood Community Coll., 1973-74. Joined Soc. St. Paul, 1961, ordained priest Episcopal Ch. 1984. H.s. tchr. Pub. Schs., Candor, N.Y., 1958-61; headmaster St. Luke's Sch., Soc. St. Paul, Gresham, Oreg., 1961-64; lic. adminstr. St. Jude's Nursing Home, Inc., Portland and Sandy, Oreg., 1964-73; assoc. rector Soc. St. Paul, Palm Desert, Calif., 1975-89, rector, 1989—. Pres. adv. bd. The Carlotta, 1985-92. Mem. Tri-County Bd., Oreg. Agy. on Aging, 1971-76; pres. Sandy C. of C., 1972; mem. Sandy City Coun., 1975-76, candidate for City Coun., City of Palm Desert, 1986; pres. St. Jude's Home, Inc., Palm Desert, 1989—. Fellow Am. Coll. Health Care Adminstrs. (pres. Coll. Found. 1984-87); mem. Nat. Guild Churchmen (pres. 1982—), Conf. on Religious Life in Anglican Communion (v.p. 1992-97, archivist 1982—). Episcopalian. Home and Office: PO Box 14350 Palm Desert CA 92255-4350

HUNT, CHARLES AMOES, librarian; b. Montclair, N.J., Jan. 21, 1950; s. William Henry Hunt and Juliet Adele (Carter) Bey. Cert. computer programing, MTI Bus. Coll., 1968; BA in English Lit., tchg. cert., Doane Coll., 1973; MSLS, Syracuse U., 1975; postgrad., U. of the Pacific, 1997. Cert. in librarianship, pub. program mgmt. Asst. br. libr., br. libr. The Chgo. (Ill.) Pub. Libr., 1975-78; tech. libr. Atlantic Richfield Co., L.A., 1978-79; reference libr. Calif. State U., Fullerton, 1979; English tchr., libr. Kiddy Coll. English Sch., Mishima City, Japan, 1979-81; adult svcs. libr., br. libr. Stockton (Calif.)-San Joaquin County Pub. Libr., 1981-90, supervising libr., br. mgr., 1991—; cons. Office for Libr. Outreach Svcs. Adv. Com., ALA, Chgo., 1977-79. Editor: Information and Referral Promotional Samples, 1988. Judge Yosemite Forensic League, Stockton, 1986-88; fund distbn. reviewer, mem. recertification com. United Way of San Joaquin County, Stockton, 1994-95; sec. San Joaquin chpt. ACLU, 1995; chair Manteca Info. Tech. Task Force, 1995—. Scholar Turrell Fund, East Orange, N.J., Doane Coll., Crete, Nebr., 1969-73; fellow Syracuse (N.Y.) U., 1974-75. Mem. NAACP, ALA (com. chair, sect. pres.), Pub. Libr. Assn., Social Responsibilities Round Table, Black Caucus, Freedom to Read Found., Calif. Libr. Assn. (com. mem.), Calif. Librs. Black Caucus, Manteca (Calif.) Kiwanis (newsletter editor 1985-89). Democrat. Baptist. Home: 1209 W Downs St Stockton CA 95207-6913 Office: Manteca Libr Stockton-San Joaquin County Pub Libr 320 W Center St Manteca CA 95336

HUNT, DENNIS, public relations executive. BA in English, Notre Dame U.; MA in Edn. Adv. mgr., contbg. editor San Francisco Bus. Mag.; exec. v.p., gen. mgr. Deaver & Hannaford; mng. ptnr. Hunt/Marmillion Assocs., 1983-88; exec. v.p., gen. mgr. Ogilvy Adams &Rinehart, 1988-92; pres. Stoorza, Ziegaus, Metzger & Hunt, Sacramento, 1992—; adj. instr. Santa Monica (Calif.) Coll. Office: Stoorza Ziegaus Metzger & Hunt 555 Capitol Mall Ste 600 Sacramento CA 95814-4502

HUNT, GEORGE ANDREW, lawyer; b. Salina, Utah, Mar. 5, 1949; s. Loyd G. and Inez Hunt; m. Elizabeth Jean Brandise, July 28, 1973 (div.); children: Rachael, Rinaldo, Andrew, Geoffrey. BS in Internat. Relations cum laude, U. Utah, 1971, JD, 1974. Bar: Utah 1974, U.S. Dist. Ct. Utah 1974, U.S. Ct. Appeals (10th cir.) 1976, U.S. Supreme Ct. 1978, U.S. Ct. Appeals (9th cir.) 1984. Assoc. Snow, Christensen & Martineau, Salt Lake City, 1974-78, ptnr., 1978-90; founding ptnr. Williams & Hunt, Salt Lake City, 1991—. Pres. U. Utah Coll. of Law, Salt Lake City, 1974. Mem. Utah Bar Assn. (bar examiner 1976-80, chmn. constrn. law sect. 1985-88), Salt Lake County Bar Assn. (mem. exec. com. 1979-90, treas. 1984, sec. 1985, v.p. 1986-87, pres. 1987-88), U. Coll. of Law (bd. trustees 1993-96), Alta Club. Republican. Roman Catholic. Office: Williams & Hunt PO Box 45678 Salt Lake City UT 84145-0678

HUNT, GORDON, lawyer; b. L.A., Oct. 26, 1934; s. Howard Wilson and Esther Nita (Dempsey) H. BA in Polit. Sci, UCLA, 1956; JD, U. So. Calif., 1959. Bar: Calif. 1960. Law clk. Appellate Dept., Superior Ct. L.A. County, 1959-60; mem. firm Behymer & Hoffman, Los Angeles, 1960-65; partner firm Behymer, Hoffman & Hunt, Los Angeles, 1965-68; ptnr. firm Munns, Kofford, Hoffman, Hunt & Throckmorton, Pasadena, 1969-90, Hunt, Ortman, Blasco, Palffy & Rossell, Pasadena, 1990-95; mem. Hunt, Ortman, Blasco, Palffy & Rossell Inc., 1995—; lectr. UCLA, various yrs.; chmn. legal adv. com. Assoc. Gen. Contractors Calif., 1985; arbitrator L.A. Superior Ct., State of Calif. Author: Construction Surety and Bonding Handbook; co-author: California Construction Law, 15th edit.; contbr. numerous articles to legal jours. Mem. ABA, Calif. Bar Assn. (del. Conv. 1964-69), L.A. County Bar Assn. (real property com. 1965-66, exec. com. 1970-72, sec. 1972-73, vice chmn. 1972-75, chmn. real property sect. 1975-76, co-chmn. continuing edn. bar com. 1969-71), Am. Arbitration Assn. (arbitrator, mediator). Office: 301 N Lake Ave Fl 7 Pasadena CA 91101-4108

HUNT, JAMES L., lawyer; b. Chgo., Oct. 20, 1942. BA magna cum laude, DePauw U., 1964; JD, Northwestern U., 1967. Bar: Calif. 1967. Atty. McCutheon, Doyle, Brown & Enersen, San Francisco; atty. rep. 9th Cir. Jud. Conf., 1991—. Assoc. editor: Northwestern U. Law Rev., 1966-67. Bd. dirs. San Francisco Giants; bd. visitors Northwestern U. Law Sch., 1989—. Mem. Am. Coll. Trial Lawyers. Office: McCutchen Doyle Brown & Enersen 3 Embarcadero Ctr San Francisco CA 94111-4003

HUNT, JOHN JOSEPH, educational specialist; b. Miami, Fla., Sept. 10, 1952; s. John J. and Marjorie (Kern) H. BS in Social Studies Edn., Fla. Internat. U., 1977, MPA, 1991. Cert. profl. pub. buyer Nat. Inst. Govtl. Purchasing. Gen. mgr. Nat. Screen Mfg. Corp., Miami, 1975-81; asst. to utilities dir. City of North Miami Beach, Fla., 1982-93; grant coord. State of Hawaii Dept. Health, Lihue, 1993-95; ednl. specialist U. Hawaii Coll. Bus. Ctr. for Internat. Bus. Edn. and Rsch., Honolulu, 1996—; data processing com. City North Miami Beach, 1992-93. City councilman code enforcement Village El Portal, Fla., 1987, city councilman pub. safety, 1988. Recipient Resolution of Appreciation, Village Coun., Village of El Portal; Outstanding scholar Fla. Internat. U., Sch. Pub. Adminstrn., North Miami, 1992. Mem. Assn. for Info. and Imaging Mgmt., Fla. Water Polution Control Operators Assn. (co-editor Pipeline Mag. 1991-92), Miami Chpt. Nat. Inst. Govt. Purchasing, Deja-Brews Homebrew Club. Democrat. Home: PO Box 86 Anahola HI 96703-0086 Office: Univ Hawaii CIBER 2404 Maile Way C202 Honolulu HI 96822

HUNT, PETER ROGER, film director, writer, editor; b. London, Mar. 11, 1925; came to U.S., 1975; s. Arthur George and Elizabeth H.; widowed; 1 child, Nicholas Constantine. Student, London Sch. Music. Actor English Repertory Theater, London. Camera asst., asst. editor various documentaries; asst. editor various feature films. London Film Co.; scriptor various films; editor (films): Hill in Korea, Admirable Crichton, Next to No Time, Paradise Lagoon, Cry From the Streets, Greengage Summer (Am. title: Loss of Innocence), Ferry to Hong Kong, H.M.S. Defiant (Am. title: Damn the Defiant), Sink the Bismarck, Operation Snaffu; supervising editor, 2d unit dir.: Dr. No, Call Me Bwana, From Russia with Love, Goldfinger, Ibcress File, Thunderball, You Only Live Twice, Jigsaw Man, Desperate Hours; assoc. producer: Chitty Chitty Bang Bang; dir.: On Her Majesty's Secret Service, Gullivers Travels (film and animated), Gold, Shout at the Devil, Death Hunt, Wild Geese II, Assassination, Hyper Sapien, (TV episodes) Marlowe, Shirley's World, Persuaders; (NBC-TV movie) Beasts in the Streets, (ABC-TV mini-series) Last Days of Pompeii, (CBS-TV special) Eyes of a Witness. Mem. Assn. Cinematic Technicians Great Britain, Dirs. Guild of Am., Motion Picture Acad. Arts, Acad. Television. Office: 2337 Roscomare Rd #2-145 Los Angeles CA 90077-1851

HUNT, ROBERT WILLIAM, theatrical producer, data processing consultant; b. Seattle, June 8, 1947; s. William Roland and Margaret Anderson (Crowe) H.; m. Marcie Loomis, Aug. 24, 1968 (div. Dec. 1975); 1 child, Megan; m. Susan Moyer, June 17, 1989; children: Donovan, Jillian. BA, U. Wash., 1969. CPA, Wash. Data processing cons Arthur Andersen & Co., Seattle, 1968-78; owner, cons. Robert W. Hunt & Assocs., Seattle, 1978—; exec. producer Village Theatre, Issaquah, Wash., 1979—; developer Francis J. Gaudette Theatre, Issaquah, Wash., 1994; cons. San Francisco Mus.

Modern Art, 1981-90, Mus. of Flight, Seattle, 1983-90, Met. Mus. N.Y.C., 1984-85. Creator arts computer software; prodr. (mus.) Eleanor, 1987, Heidi, 1989, Charlie and the Chocolate Factory, 1989, Book of James, 1990, Funny Pages, 1991, Jungle Queen Debutante, 1991, Glimmerglass, 1995, City Kid, 1995, Bootlegger, 1996; creator, writer (pop group music and video) The Shrimps, 1984. Chmn. com. Seattle Arts Commn., 1975-78; treas. Arts Resource Svcs., Seattle, 1976-78; gen. mgr. Musicomedy Northwest, Seattle, 1977-79. Grantee Seattle Arts Commn., 1978-79, Wash. State Arts Commn., 1980—, King County Arts Commn., 1980—, Nat. Endowment for the Arts, 1992—. Mem. Wash. Soc. CPAs., Nat. Alliance of Mus. Theatre Producers (treas., bd. dirs.). Office: Village Theatre 303 Front St N Issaquah WA 98027-3234

HUNT, ROGER LEE, judge; b. Overton, Nev., Apr. 29, 1942; s. Ferlin Hansen and Verda (Peterson) H.; m. Mauna Sue Hawkes, July 20, 1965; children: Roger Todd (dec.), Rachelle, Kristina, Tyler, Melanee, Ryan. Student, Coll. So. Utah; BA, Brigham Young U., 1966; JD, George Washington U., 1970. Bar: Nev. 1970, U.S. Dist. Ct. Nev. 1970, U.S. Supreme Ct. 1977, U.S. Ct. Appeals 1980. Dep. dist. atty. Clark County Dist. Atty.'s Office, Las Vegas, Nev., 1971; assoc. Rose & Norwood, Las Vegas, 1971-73; sr. ptnr. Edwards, Hunt, Hale & Hansen, Las Vegas, 1973-92; U.S. magistrate judge U.S. Dist. Ct. Nev., Las Vegas, 1992—. Office: US Dist Ct Foley Fed Bldg #2300 300 Las Vegas Blvd S Las Vegas NV 89101-5833*

HUNT, STEVEN BRUCE, law educator; b. Dayton, Ohio, Nov. 12, 1946. BA, U. Denver, 1968; MA, U. Houston, 1970; PhD, U. Kans., 1973; JD, Lewis and Clark Coll., 1985. Prof. Lewis and Clark Coll., Portland, Oreg., 1973—; pres. Cross-Exam. Debate, 1995-96. Editor: PKD The Forensic, 1993-97. Capt. U.S. Army, 1970-73. Norton scholar Pi Kappa Delta, 1996. Office: Lewis and Clark Coll Dept Comm Portland OR 97219

HUNT, WILLIAM E., SR., state supreme court justice; b. 1923. BA, LLB, U. Mont., JD, 1955. Bar: 1955. Judge State Workers' Compensation Ct., 1975-81; justice Mont. Supreme Ct., Helena, 1984—. Office: Mont Supreme Ct 414 Justice Bldg 215 N Sanders St Helena MT 59601-4522

HUNT, WINSLOW ROBERT, psychiatrist; b. Detroit, July 2, 1928; s. Theodore Hall and Manya (Szarzynski) H.; m. Irmgard Albine Pfnür, Dec. 26, 1958 (div. 1978); children: Peter Alan, Karen Ingrid; m. Kathleen Marie King, Dec. 28, 1988. AB cum laude, U. Chgo., 1946, MA, 1950; postgrad., Columbia U., 1952-54, MD, 1958; grad., N.Y. Psychoanalytic Inst., 1970. Diplomate Am. Bd. Neurology and Psychiatry (bd. examiner 1986-95). Intern in medicine U. Calif. Hosps., San Francisco, 1958-59; resident in psychiatry N.Y. State Psychiat. Inst./Presbyn. Hosp., N.Y.C., 1959-62; pvt. practice N.Y.C., 1962-84, Pocatello, Idaho, 1984—; psychiat. cons. to Student Health Svc. and Counseling Ctr. Idaho State U., Pocatello, 1991—; psychiat. cons. Indian Health Svc., Ft. Hall, Idaho, 1984-95; attending physician Bannock Regional Med. Ctr., Pocatello, 1984—, Pocatello Regional Med. Ctr., 1984—; attending psychiatrist Aspen Crest Hosp., Pocatello, 1984-94, med. dir., pres. med. staff; psychiat. cons. to dean of students Coll. Physicians and Surgeons, Columbia U., 1973-84, instr. psychiatry, 1967-69, assoc. in psychiatry, 1970-71, asst. prof., 1971-77, assoc. prof., 1977-85; adminstrv./faculty positions out-patient dept. Presbyn. Hosp. of N.Y.C., 1962-84; psychiatrist Student Health Svc., NYU, 1962-64; psychologist Stevenson, Jordan and Harrison, Inc., Mgmt. Cons., N.Y.C., 1950-52. Contbr. articles to profl. jours. Fellow Am. Psychiat. Assn.; mem. AMA, APA, Am. Psychoanalytic Assn., Internat. Psychoanalytic Assn., S.E. Idaho Med. Assn. Office: 151 N 3d Ave Ste 106 Pocatello ID 83201

HUNTEN, DONALD MOUNT, planetary scientist, educator; b. Montreal, Mar. 1, 1925; came to U.S., 1963, naturalized, 1979; s. Kenneth William and Winnifred Binnmore (Mount) H.; m. Isobel Ann Rubenstein, Dec. 28, 1949 (div. Apr. 1995); children: Keith Atherton, Mark Ross; m. Ann Louise Sprague, May 21, 1995. B.Sc., U. Western Ont., 1946; Ph.D., McGill U., 1950. From research asso. to prof. physics U. Sask. (Can.), Saskatoon, 1950-63; physicist Kitt Peak Nat. Obs., Tucson, 1963-77; sci. adv. to asso. adminstr. for space sci. NASA, Washington, 1976-77; prof. planetary scis. U. Ariz., Tucson, 1977-88, Regents prof., 1988—; cons. NASA, 1964—. Author: Introduction to Electronics, 1964; (with J.W. Chamberlain) Theory of Planetary Atmospheres, 1987; contbr. articles to profl. jours. Recipient Pub. Svc. medal NASA, 1977, 85,96, medal for exceptional sci. achievement, 1980. Mem. Am. Phys. Soc., Can. Assn. Physicists (editor 1961-63), Am. Geophys. Union, Am. Astron. Soc. (chmn. div. planetary scis. 1977), Internat. Astron. Union, Internat. Union Geodesy and Geophysics, Internat. Assn. Geomagnetism and Aeronomy, AAAS, Nat. Acad. Scis., Explorers Club. Club: Cosmos (Washington). Home: 3445 W Foxes Den Dr Tucson AZ 85745-5102 Office: U Ariz Dept Planetary Scis Tucson AZ 85721

HUNTER, DUNCAN LEE, congressman; b. Riverside, Calif., May 31, 1948; m. Lynne Layh, 1973; children: Robert Samuel, Duncan Duane. J.D., Western State U., 1976. Bar: Calif. 1976. Practiced in San Diego; mem. 97th Congress from 42d Dist. Calif., 98th 105th Congresses from 45th Dist. Calif., 103rd Congress from 52nd Dist. Calif.; mem. nat. security com., subcom. mil. installations and facilities, chmn. subcom. on mil. procurement, subcom. on mil. pers. Served with U.S. Army, 1969-71, Vietnam. Decorated Air medal, Bronze Star. Mem. Navy League. Republican. Baptist. *

HUNTER, FRANK A., secondary education educator; b. Torrington, Wyo., May 9, 1936; s. Raymond S. and Lois B. (Sawyer) H. BA, Hastings (Nebr.) Coll., 1958; MA, U. Nebr., Lincoln, 1962. Cert. secondary tchr., Colo. Tchr. English, speech and theatre Gering (Nebr.) H.S., 1958-61; with scenery shop U. Nebr., Lincoln, 1961-62; tchr. speech and theatre Sterling (Colo.) H.S., 1965—, chair creative arts dept., 1966-89. Served with U.S. Army, 1962-65, Europe. Named Star Tchr., C. of C., 1980. Mem. NEA, Masons, Elks, Lions Internat. (sec. 1972-76), Am. Legion. Office: 400 W Broadway St Sterling CO 80751-3052

HUNTER, SCOTT WARREN, journalist; b. Fargo, N.D., Nov. 19, 1954; s. Lyol Murray and Helen Marie (Erickson) H.; m. Kathleen Esther Kellmer, Oct. 20, 1972 (div. Feb., 1986); children: Heather, Sara; m. Sheri Rae Edwards, Oct. 11, 1986. AA, Spokane Falls C.C., 1984. Reporter The Star, Grand Coulee, Wash., 1988-92; pub. The Star, Grand Coulee, 1992—. Treas. Coulee Med. Found., 1994—, pres., 1990. Mem. Wash. Newspaper Pub.'s Assn. (chmn. journalism edn. com. 1995-96, Best editorial award 1995), Nat. Newspaper Assn. (2d pl. Best Investigative Story award 1990), Rotary (pres.-elect Grand Coulee Dam club 1996-97).

HUNTINGTON, HILLARD GRISWOLD, economist; b. Boston, Apr. 10, 1944; s. Hillard Bell and Ruth Smedley (Wheeler) H.; m. Honor Mary Griffin, Sept. 30, 1972; children: Honora Redmond, Emma Anne Hillard. BS, Cornell U., 1967; MA, SUNY, Binghamton, 1972, PhD, 1974. Staff economist Fed. Energy Adminstrn., Washington, 1974-77; dir., sr. economist Data Resources, Inc., Washington, 1977-80; exec. dir. Energy Modeling Forum Stanford (Calif.) U., 1980—; vol. U.S. Peace Corps., Pub. Utilities Authority, Monrovia, Liberia, 1967-69; vis. rsch. assoc. Inst. Devel. Studies, U. Nairobi, Kenya, 1972-73; mem. joint U.S.-U.S.S.R. Nat. Acad. Sci. Panel on Energy Conservation, 1986-90; mem. peer rev. panel Nat. Acid Precipitation Assessment Program Task Force, Ctrs. for Excellence Govt. Can.; consultant to Argonne Nat. Lab., Electric Power Rsch. Inst., numerous others. Editor Macroeconomic Impacts of Energy Shocks, 1987, N. Am. Natural Gas Markets: selected tech. studies, 1989. Named Life Fellow, Clare Hall, U. Cambridge, Eng. Mem. Internat. Assn. Energy Econs. (v.p. publs. 1990-92, program chmn. N.Am. conf., program chmn. internat. conf.), Am. Statis. Assn. (com. on energy stats. 1992-94), Am. Econ. Assn., U.S. Assn. Energy Econs. (pres. 1997). Home: 305 Hermosa Way Menlo Park CA 94025-5821 Office: Stanford U 406 Terman Ctr Stanford CA 94305

HUNT-JENKINS, LORI EVELYN, education educator; b. Shelby, Mich., Sept. 18, 1954; d. Leonard Frank and Evelyn Gertrude (Ernst) H. BS in Health Edn., Cen. Mich. U., 1977; MS in Community Health, U. Wis., 1980; PhD in Health Edn., U. N.Mex., 1991. Phys. fitness specialist Sentry Ins. Co., Stevens Point, Wis., 1978-79; instr., dir. adult fitness program Cen. Mich. U., Mt. Pleasant, 1980-83; dir. sports medicine Muskegon (Mich.) Gen. Hosp., 1983-86; grad. coord. adult fitness program U. N.Mex., Albuquerque, 1986-88, cons. Wellness Ctr., 1988-89; instr. Newheart Cardiac Rehab. Program, Albuquerque, 1988-90; asst. prof. health promotions Okla. State U., Stillwater, 1990-94; asst. prof. exercise sci. Ft. Lewis Coll., Durango, Colo., 1994—; pvt. cons. in field. Author: Effects of Perceived Quality of Life Between Coronary Artery Bypass Graft and Heart Transplantation Patients with Regard to Cardiac Rehabilitation, 1991. First aid instr. ARC, Stillwater, 1990-94, Durango, Colo., 1994—. Mem. AAHPERD, Am. Jour. Health Promotion, Eta Sigma Gamma. Home: 650 County Rd 520 Bayfield CO 81122

HUNTLEY, MARK EDWARD, biological oceanographer; b. Seattle, May 7, 1950; s. James Robert Huntley and Patricia Mary (Barricklow) Kissel; m. Patricia Darlene McFarlane, June 21, 1973 (div. 1980); children: Seth, Timothy; m. Kimberly Batcheller Brown, Sept. 19, 1981 (div. 1992); children: Swan Fairchild, Flannery Elizabeth, Zara Edith, Fletcher Wells. BSC with honors, U. Victoria, B.C., Can., 1976; PhD, Dalhousie U., Halifax, N.S., Can., 1980. Postdoctoral fellow Inst. Marine Resources, Scripps Instn. Oceanography, U. Calif. San Diego, La Jolla, Calif., 1980-82, asst. rsch. biologist, 1982-84; adj. lecturer Scripps Instn. Oceanography, U. Calif. San Diego, La Jolla, 1984—; asst. rsch. biologist marine biology rsch. div. Scripps Instn. Oceanography, La Jolla, 1984-87, assoc. rsch. biologist, 1987—; pres. Aquasearch, Inc., San Diego, 1984-88, chief oper. officer, 1988-93, CEO, 1993—, also chmn. bd. dirs., 1988—; deputy coord. water rsch. project U. Calif. San Diego, La Jolla, 1988-90; chmn. bd. dirs. Aquasearch, Inc., San Diego, 1984—; chief scientist Rsch. Antarctic Coastal Ecosystem Rates, La Jolla, 1986-87, 89, 91-92; exec. and steering com. mem. Global Ocean Ecosystem Dynamics, Washington, 1989—. Editor: Biological Treatment of Agricultural Wastewater, 1989; inventor Aquasearch Growth Module, 1989. Grantee Nat. Sci. Found. Office Naval Rsch., 1980—. Mem. Am. Soc. Limnology and Oceanography, Oceangraphy Soc. Office: Scripps Instn Oceangraphy 0202 La Jolla CA 92093

HUNTSMAN, EDWARD LOYD, business consultant, marketing executive; b. Farmington, N.Mex., Dec. 19, 1951; s. Arral B and Ann McFarland (Viles) H.; m. Debbie J. Komadina, Aug. 21, 1976; 1 child, Steven Christopher. Student, U. N.Mex., 1973-75; BS in Bus. Adminstrn., Pacific Western U., L.A., 1991, MBA in Mgmt., 1993. Staff instr. U. N.Mex., Gallup, 1976-78; sta. mgr., staff mgr. Frontier Airlines, Denver and Durango, Colo., 1977-85; corp. sales mgr. Tamarron Inn and Country Club, Durango, 1985-86; dir. mktg. Royal West Airlines, Las Vegas, 1986-88; mgr. sales and svc. Am. West Vacations, Tempe, Ariz., 1988-91; bus. and mktg. cons. Total Resource Network, Tempe, 1991—; mktg. cons. Huntsman Graphic Design, Phoenix, 1988—; call ctr. dir. Maxserv, Inc., Scottsdale, Ariz., 1993-97. Photographer: Graphic Art Collateral, 1983. Bd. dirs. McKinley County United Way, Gallup, 1976-78; mem. exec. bd. Boy Scouts Am., Las Vegas, 1986-87; staff instr. Police Athletic League, Albuquerque, 1978-80; mem. Durango Area Mktg. Group, 1985-86; elder Presbyn. Ch. U.S.A., Durango, 1985. Sgt. U.S. Army, 1969-73, Viet Nam and Germany. Decorated Army Commendation medal; recipient Outstanding Leadership award Albuquerque Police Athletic League, 1976, Cert. of Merit for stopping a hijacking attempt Air Transp. Assn. Am./FAA, 1983; col., aide-de-camp to Gov. of N.Mex., 1976; named to Outstanding Young Men of Am., 1987. Office: Total Resource Network 2850 S Roosevelt St Tempe AZ 85282-2021

HUNTSMAN, JON M., chemical company executive; b. 1937. BS, U. Pa., 1959; MBA, U. So. Calif., 1970. With Olson Bros, Inc., North Hollywood, Calif., from 1961; assoc. adminstr. HEW, spl. asst. to the pres., 1971-92; with Huntsman Container Corp., Salt Lake City, 1972-83, Huntsman Chem. Corp, Salt Lake City, 1982—; chmn. bd. Huntsman Corp., Salt Lake City, 1996—. Pres. mission LDS Ch., Washington, 1980-83. Office: Huntsman Corp 500 Huntsman Way Salt Lake City UT 84108-1235

HUPP, HARRY L., federal judge; b. L.A., Apr. 5, 1929; s. Earl L. and Dorothy (Goodspeed) H.; m. Patricia Hupp, Sept. 13, 1953; children: Virginia, Karen, Keith, Brian. AB, Stanford U., 1953, LLB, 1955. Bar: Calif. 1956, U.S. Dist. Ct. (cen. dist.) Calif. 1956, U.S. Supreme Ct. Pvt. practice law Beardsley, Hufstedler and Kemble, L.A., 1955-72; judge Superior Ct. of Los Angeles, 1972-84; appointed fed. dist. judge U.S. Dist. Ct. (cen. dist.) Calif., L.A., 1984—. Served with U.S. Army, 1950-52. Mem. Calif. Bar Assn., Los Angeles County Bar Assn. (Trial Judge of Yr. 1983), Order of Coif, Phi Alpha Delta. Office: US Dist Ct 312 N Spring St Rm 218P Los Angeles CA 90012-4701*

HUPPERT, MERLE CECIL, mechanical engineer; b. Dysart, Iowa, June 29, 1917; s. Edwin Alvertis and Rosa (Gulick) H.; m. Leslie Barbara Little, June 17, 1942; children: Judith, Daniel, Frederick. BSME, Iowa State U., 1942; postgrad., Case Inst. Tech., 1944-47, UCLA, 1957, 62. Mech. engr. NASA Lewis Rsch. Ctr., Cleve., 1942-56, Rocketdyne divsn. Rockwell Internat., Caonga Park, Calif., 1956-70; mgr. turbopump analysis sect. Aerojet Nuclear Sys. Co., Sacramento, 1970-72; surface effects ship performance supr. Aerojet Gen. Corp., Tacoma, 1972-74; mem. R&D staff, mech. engr. Aerojet-Gen. Corp., Liquid Rocket Co., Sacramento, 1974-83; pvt. practice cons. El Dorado Hills, Calif., 1984 . Patentee in field; contbr. articles to profl. publs. Recipient Apollo Achievement award NASA, 1969. ASME (sr.), AIAA, Sons in Retirement. Home: 3535 Mesa Verdes Dr El Dorado Hills CA 95762-4552

HURABIELL, JOHN PHILIP, SR., lawyer; b. San Francisco, June 2, 1947; s. Emile John and Anna Beatrice (Blumenauer) H.; m. Judith Marie Hurabiell, June 7, 1969; children—Marie Louise, Michele, Heather, John Philip Jr. J.D., San Francisco Law Sch., 1976. Bar: Calif. 1977. Sole practice, San Francisco, 1977-86; ptnr. Huppert & Hurabiell, San Francisco, 1985—; pres. San Francisco S.A.F.E., Inc., 1983-88, pres. emeritus 1988—. Treas. Rep. election coms.; 1st v.p. Bling Babies Found., 1989-91, bd. dir., sec., 1995—; bd. dirs. Calif. State Mining and Mineral Mus., 1990-93. With USN, Vietnam. Decorated Navy Commendation Medal. Mem. Calif. Bar Assn., Assn. Trial Lawyers Am., San Francisco Trial Lawyers Assn., Lawyers Club San Francisco, St. Thomas More Soc., St. Francis Hook & Ladder Soc. (trustee). Roman Catholic. Clubs: The Family Ferrari Club Am. (pres. Pacific region 1997), Golden Gate Breakfast Club. Lodge: KC, Alhambra (organizing regional dir. 1983-85). Editor, primary author: C.A.L.U. Business Practices Guidelines, rev. edit., 1980. Avocation: racing vintage automobiles. Office: Huppert & Hurabiell 1390 Market St Ste 1201 San Francisco CA 94102-5306

HURD, JAMES DANIEL, software and product designer; b. Washington, Jan. 17, 1955; s. James Douglas and Nancy (Schwartz) H. BFA, George Washington U., 1981. Pres. Jim Hurd Design, Washington, 1982-85, San Francisco, 1986-93; pres. Up Software, San Francisco, 1993—. Author: Presents Alive, 1990, Software: Achieving Your Career, 1993; co-author software: Jumpstart Your Job Skills, 1994; designer, co-author: Skillsup, 1996. Recipient nat. graphic design awards in Am. Corp. Identity 5 and 8, Coll. Choice award Insider Mag., 1994, profl. resource award Career Planning & Adult Devel. Network, 1995. Democrat. Office: Up Software Inc 722 Lombard St Ste 204 San Francisco CA 94133-2300

HURD, PAUL GEMMILL, lawyer; b. Salt Lake City, Nov. 23, 1946; s. Melvin Erskine and Marjorie (Gemmill) H. BS, Portland State U., 1968; JD, Lewis and Clark Coll., 1976. Bar: Oreg. 1976, Wash. 1984, U.S. Dist. Ct. Oreg. 1980, U.S. Ct. Appeals (9th cir.) 1981, U.S. Supreme Ct. 1988. Sr. dep. dist. atty. Multnomah County Dist. Atty., Portland, Oreg., 1976-80; trial counsel Burlington No. R.R., Portland, 1980-84; asst. gen. counsel Freightliner Corp., Portland, 1984-89, assoc. gen. counsel, 1989—. Trustee Leukemia Assn. of Oreg., Portland, 1984-90. Mem. ABA, Oreg. Bar Assn., Wash. Bar Assn., Multnomah Bar Assn., Am. Corp. Counsel Assn. (bd. dirs. N.W. chpt.), Nat. Inst. for Trial Adv. (diplomate 1982). Republican. Presbyterian. Office: Freightliner Corp Legal Dept PO Box 3849 Portland OR 97208-3849

HURLEY, BRUCE PALMER, artist; b. Tacoma, May 9, 1944; s. Gerald Baynton and Donna Ray (Whealey) H.; m. Ivy Jane Partridge; 1 child, Paul George. BS in Edn., Oreg. Coll. Edn., 1968. Cert. secondary edn. tchr. One-man shows include Goldberg's, 1966, Hillsboro Pub. Libr., 1969, 71, Valley Art Assn., Forest Grove, 1971, 74; group shows include Portland Art Mus., 1970, Northwest Artist Workshop, 1979, Sun Bird Gallery, 1986, Sunriver Juried Show, 1986, 92, Beaverton Arts Showcase, 1990, 91, 92, 93, 94, 96; represented in permanent collections Oreg. Coll., Oriental Medicine, David Wheeler, D.C., Libr. of Am. Psychiat. Assn., D.C., Schools Med. Plz., Tigard, Oreg., Atty. Mark Olson, N.Y.C., others; author: Planet Ploob Vacation, 1992, Divine Soliloquy, 1994; inventor: numerous paintings, drawings and sculptures. Recipient Cmty. Svc. award Beaverton Arts Commn., 1993, Royal Patronage award Hutt River, Australia, 1995. Mem. Theosophical Soc. Home: 251 NW Bailey St Hillsboro OR 97124-2903

HURLEY, FRANCIS T., archbishop; b. San Francisco, Jan. 12, 1927. Ed., St. Patrick Sem., Menlo Park, Calif., Catholic U. Am. Ordained priest Roman Cath. Ch., 1951; with Nat. Cath. Welfare Conf., Washington, asst. sec., 1958-68; assoc. sec. Nat. Cath. Welfare Conf., now U.S. Cath. Conf., 1968-70; consecrated bishop, 1970; titular bishop Daimlaig and aux. bishop Diocese of Juneau, Alaska, 1970-71; bishop of Juneau, 1971-76, archbishop of Anchorage, 1976—. Office: Archdiocese of Anchorage Chancery Office 225 Cordova St Anchorage AK 99501-2409*

HURLEY, MARK JOSEPH, bishop; b. San Francisco, Dec. 13, 1919; s. Mark J. and Josephine (Keohane) H. Student, St. Joseph's Coll., Mountain View, Calif., 1939, St. Patrick's Sem., Menlo Park, Calif., 1944; postgrad., U. Calif., Berkeley, 1943-45; PhD, Cath. U. Am., 1947; JCB, Lateran U., Rome, 1963; LLD, U. Portland, 1971. Ordained to priest Roman Cath. Ch., 1944. Asst. supt. schs. Archdiocese, San Francisco, 1944-51; tchr. Serra High Sch., San Mateo, Calif., 1944; prin. Bishop O'Dowd High Sch., Oakland, Calif., 1951-58, Marin Cath. High Sch., Marin County, Calif., 1959-61; supt. schs. Diocese, Stockton, Calif., 1962-65; chancellor, diocesan counsultor Diocese, 1962-65; asst. chancellor Arcdiocese, San Francisco, 1965-67; vicar gen. Arcdiocese, 1967-69; titular bishop Thunusuda; aux. bishop Thunusuda, San Francisco, 1967-69; bishop Santa Rosa, Cal., 1969—; pastor St. Francis Assisi Ch., San Francisco, 1967—; prof. grad. schs. Loyola U., Balt., 1946, U. San Francisco, 1948, San Francisco Coll. Women, 1949, Dominican Coll., San Rafael, Calif., 1949, Cath. U. Am., 1954; prof. theology Beda Coll. Rome, 1987—, Angelicum U., Rome, 1989—; Del. Conf. Psychiatry and Religion, San Francisco, 1957; mem. bd. Calif. Com. on Study Edn., 1955-60; cons. Congregation for Cath. Edn., 1986—; del.-at-large Cal., White House Conf. on Youth, 1960; Cath. del., observer Nat. Council Chs., Columbus, Ohio, 1964; del. edn. conf. German and Am. educators, Nat. Cath. Edn. Assn., Munich, Germany, 1960; mem. commns. sems., univs. and schs. II Vatican Council, Rome, 1962-65; mem. commn. Christian formation U.S. Cath. Conf. Bishops, 1968; asst. archdiocesan coordinator Campaign on Taxation Schs. Calif., 1958, Rosary Crusade, 1961; adminstr. Cath. Sch. Purchasing Div., 1948-51, St. Eugene's Ch., Santa Rosa, Calif., 1959, St. John's Ch., San Francisco, 1961; mem. U.S. Bishops' Press Panel, Vatican Council, 1964-65, U.S. Bishops' Com. on Laity, 1964, U.S. Bishops' Com. Cath.-Jewish Relationships, 1965—, U.S. Bishops' Com. on Ecumenical and Interreligious Affairs, 1970, Conf. Maj. Superiors of Men, 1970; chmn. citizens Com. for San Francisco State Coll., 1968—; mem. adminstrn. bd. Nat. Council Cath. Bishops, 1970, mem. nominating com., 1971; mem. Internat. Secretariat for Non-Believers, Vatican, 1973; chmn. Secretariat for Human Values, Nat. Conf. Cath. Bishops, Washington, 1975; mem. Secretariat for Non-Believers, Vatican, 1986—; Vatican del. World Intellectual Properties Orgn., Washington, 1990; adj. prof. philosophy Grad. Theol. Union, Berkeley, Calif., 1994. Syndicated columnist San Francisco Monitor, Sacramento Herald, Oakland Voice, Yakima (Wash.) Our Times, Guam Diocesan Press, 1949-66, TV speaker and panelist, 1956-67; author: Church State Relationships in Education in California, 1948, Commentary on Declaration on Christian Education in Vatican II, 1966, Report on Education in Peru, 1965, The Church and Science, 1982, Blood on the Shamrock, 1989, The Unholy Ghost, 1992, Vatican Star, Star of David, 1996. Trustee N.Am. Coll., Rome, 1970, Cath. U. Am., 1978—, Cath. Relief Services, 1979; cons. Congregation for Edn.; mem. Secretariat for Non-Belief, Vatican City; bd. dirs. Overseas Blind Found., Ctr. for Theology and Natural Sci., Berkeley. Address: 273 Ulloa St San Francisco CA 94127-1226

HURLEY, REBECCA JOHNSON, marketing professional; b. East Moline, Ill., June 24, 1950; d. Raymond Harold and Alberta (Powell) Ifft; m. James Patrick Hurley, June 7, 1989. BA in Social Scis. cum laude, Colo. State U., 1972. Dir. pub. rels. Gates Land Co., Colorado Springs, Colo., 1977-88; dir. media rels. U.S. Space Found., Colorado Springs, 1988-89, Concept Comm., Inc., Colorado Springs, 1989-92; rsch. devel. dir. Colorado Springs Cablevision, Colorado Springs, 1992-94; regional mktg. devel. mgr. Century Comm. Corp., Colorado Springs, 1994—; mem. task force EDC Pub. Rels. and Comm., 1986-88, 94. Author: Everyone's Complete Astrology & Horoscope, 1971, Astrology for Men, 1972, Astrology For Women, 1972. Bd. dirs. El Paso County Fair, 1975-78, Pikes Peak Ctr. Bd., 1988-94; adv. bd. Colorado Springs Park and Recreation, 1979-82; active mem. Jr. League of Colorado Springs, 1981-87, Am. Cancer Soc., 1990-93. Recipient Women's Life Festival Woman of Spirit and Note award, 1990. Home: 1817 Pine Grove Ave Colorado Springs CO 80906-2929 Office: Century Comm Corp 100 E Saint Vrain St Ste 100 Colorado Springs CO 80903-1143

HURLOW, RANDAL THOMAS, communications executive; b. Tacoma, July 14, 1962; s. Edward James and Marilyn Ann (Fansler) H. BA in Speech Comms., Western Wash. U., 1986. APR accreditation, 1996. Comms. asst. Pub. Info. Office Western Wash. U., 1986-88, resident dir. Office Residence Life, 1986-88; dist. exec. dir. S.W. Area Office Am. Cancer Soc., 1986-90, media rels. coord. Washington divsn. Office, 1990-91, dir. comms. Washington divsn. Office, 1991-94; pub. rels. specialist Virginia Mason Med. Ctr., Seattle, 1994—. Mem. Pub. Rels. Soc. Am. (bd. dirs. Puget Sound chpt., chmn. pub. rels. primer seminar 1989, chmn. membership com. 1995, participant Totem Awards com., long range planning com., seminar for non-profits com., seminar non-profits, 2 Totem awards, Outstanding New Mem. of Yr. 1989), Kiwanis. Home: 1119 1st Ave 205 Seattle WA 98101-2934

HURST, RAYMOND THOMAS, special education facility administrator, educator; b. Porterville, Calif., Feb. 25, 1956; s. Harlan David and Violet Merle (Slay) Phipps; m. Sherri L. Henderson, Mar. 20, 1981; children: Manda L., Michael S., Crystal D., Adam T. AA, Porterville Coll., 1976; BA in Music, Calif. State U., Fresno, 1978; MEd in Sch. Adminstrn., U. La Verne, 1985. Cert. learning handicapped tchr., music tchr., cmty. coll. Tchr. San Jacinto (Calif.) Unified Sch. Dist., 1979-87; program dir. Advocate Schs., Grand Terrace, Calif., 1987-89; prin. Oak Grove Inst./Jack Weaver Sch., Murrieta, Calif., 1989—; instr. U. Calif., Riverside (Calif.) Extension, 1993—; adj. prof. Nat. Univ., Riverside, 1990-94. Mem. ASCD, Coun. Exceptional Children. Republican. Mormon. Office: Oak Grove Inst/Jack Weaver 24275 Jefferson Ave Murrieta CA 92562

HURT, ARLEN LEE, editor, retired public school principal; b. Kansas City, Mo., Jan. 16, 1935; s. Wilfield and Myrtle Victoria (Johnson) H.; m. Elisa Trujillo Banuelos, July 10, 1987; children: Karen, Wiley, Marissa. AB in Edn., San Diego State U., 1963, MA in Adminstrn., 1973; EdD in Adminstrn., No. Ariz. U., 1981. Cert. tchr., adminstr., Calif. Tchr. National City (Calif.) Sch. Dist., 1963-72; adult edn. tchr. San Diego Unified Sch. Dist., 1964-66; resource tchr. National City Sch. Dist., 1967-72, prin., 1971-92; instr. National University, San Diego, 1986-87; editor Toy Train Operating Soc., Pasadena, Calif., 1992—; econ. coord. Calif. Tchrs. Assn., L.A., 1966-73; dir. summer sch. National City Sch. Dist., 1985; mentor, devel. tng. San Diego County Edn. Ctr., 1989; assessor, assessment ctr. San Diego Edn. Ctr., 1983—. Owner, editor (weekly newspaper) The Julian Epitaph, 1973-78; editor (newsletter) The Main-Line, 1982-94, The Daylighter, 1992—, (mag.) The TTOS Bulletin, 1992— (plaque 1993, 94, 95). Sch. bd. candidate Julian, Calif., 1973, 74; editor, communicator Assn. Calif. Sch. Adminstrs., San Diego; editor, KU West, Kans. Univ. Alumni Assn., 1995, 96; precinct inspector San Diego County, 1995, 96. Yeoman 2d class USN, 1955-59. Recipient Cert. of Appreciation, Optimist Internat., National City, 1991, 92, 93. Mem. Dem. Nat. Com., Am. Flyer Collector Club, Am. Assn. Ret. Persons, All Gauge Toy Train Assn. (editor 1982-94), Toy Train Operating Soc. Home: 2120 Paseo Grande El Cajon CA 92019-3853 Office: Toy Train Operating Soc 25 W Walnut St Pasadena CA 91103-3634

HURT, CHARLIE DEUEL, III, library school director, educator; b. Charlottesville, Va., Sept. 20, 1950; s. Charlie Deuel Jr. and Timie Oletta (Young) H.; m. Susan Edith Scudamore, May 15, 1981. BA, U. Va., 1971; MLS, U. Ky., 1975; PhD, U. Wis., 1981. Engring. librarian U. Va.,

Charlottesville, 1975-78, automation librarian, 1977-78; asst. prof. McGill U., Montreal, Que., Can., 1981-84, assoc. prof., 1984; assoc. prof. Simmons Coll., Boston, 1984-86; dir., prof. lib. sch. U. Ariz., Tucson, 1986—; prin. Info. Prime, Montreal, 1984—; cons. Scudamore & Assocs. Montreal, 1984-85. Author: Information Sources in Science and Technology, 1994; co-author: Scientific and Technical Literature, 1990; contbr. articles to profl. jours. Hollowell grantee Simmons Coll., 1984. Mem. IEEE, Am. Math. Soc., Am. Soc. Info. Sci., Am. Mgmt. Assn., Am. Statis. Assn., N.Y. Acad. Sci. Home: 1820 W Wimbledon Way Tucson AZ 85737-9070 Office: U Ariz Sch Info Resources 1515 E 1st St Tucson AZ 85719-4505

HURVITZ, JAMES S., plastic surgeon; b. Santa Monica, Calif., Feb. 21, 1947. MD, U. So. Calif., 1973. Instr., plastic surgeon L.A. County U. So. Calif. Med. Ctr. Office: 724 E 2021 Santa Monica Blvd Santa Monica CA 90404-2208*

HURVITZ, S. ALLAN, thoracic and cardiovascular surgeon; b. Pitts., Dec. 19, 1929; s. Nathan N. and Belle S. (Gold) H.; m. Barbara Freed, Dec. 22, 1963; children: Nathan, Lawrence, Robert. BS, UCLA, 1951; MD, Boston U., 1955. Diplomate Am. Bd. Surgery, Am. Bd. Thoracic Surgery. Intern L.A. County Gen. Hosp., 1955-56; resident in gen. surgery L.A. County Harbor Gen. Hosp., Torrance, Calif., 1956-60; resident in thoracic surgery VA Hosp., West L.A., 1962-64, thoracic surgery resident, 1962-64; pvt. practice thoracic surgery L.A., 1964—. Contbr. articles to profl. jours. Lt. cmmdr. USN, 1960-62. Fellow Am. Coll. Angiology; mem. Soc. for Neurovascular Surgery, Soc. of Thoracic Surgeons, Western Thoracic Surgical Assn. Office: S Allan Hurvitz MD 1801 Ave Of Stars Ste 640 Los Angeles CA 90067-5908

HUSKEY, HARRY DOUGLAS, information and computer science educator; b. Whittier, N.C., Jan. 19, 1916; s. Cornelius and Myrtle (Cunningham) H.; m. Velma Elizabeth Roeth, Jan. 2, 1939 (dec. Jan. 1991); children: Carolyn, Roxanne, Harry Douglas, Linda; m. Nancy Grindstaff, Sept. 10, 1994. BS, U. Idaho, 1937; student, Ohio U., 1937-38; MA, Ohio State U., 1940, PhD, 1943. Temp. prin. sci. officer Nat. Phys. Labs., Eng., 1947; head machine devel. lab. Nat. Bur. Standards, 1948; asst. dir. Inst. Numerical Analysis, 1948-54; asso. dir. computation lab. Wayne U., Detroit, 1952-53; asso. prof. U. Calif., Berkeley, 1954-58, prof., 1958-68, vice chmn. elec. engring., 1965-66; prof. info. and computer sci. U. Calif., Santa Cruz, 1968-85, prof. emeritus, 1985—; dir. Computer Center, 1968-77, chmn. bd. info. sci., 1976-79, 82-83; vis. prof. Indian Inst. Tech., Kanpur; (Indo-Am. program), 1963-64, 71, Delhi U., 1971; cons. computer div. Bendix, 1954-63; vis. prof. M.I.T., 1966; mem. computer sci. panel NSF, Naval Research Adv. Com.; cons. on computers for developing countries UN, 1969-71; chmn. com. to advise Brazil on computer sci. edn. NAS, 1970-72; project coord. UNESCO/Burma contract, 1973-79; mem. adv. com. on use microcomputers in developing countries NRC, 1983-85. Co-editor: Computer Handbook, 1962. Recipient Disting. Alumni award Idaho State U., 1978, Pioneer award Nat. Computer Conf., 1978, IEEE Computer Soc., 1982; U.S. sr.scientist awardee Fulbright-Alexander von Humboldt Found., Mathematisches Institut der Tech. U. Munich, 1974-75, 25th Ann. medal ENIAC; inducted into U. Idaho Alumni Hall of Fame, 1989. Fellow AAAS, ACM, IEEE (edit. bd., editor-in-chief computer group 1965-71, Centennial award 1984), Brit. Computer Soc.; mem. Am. Math. Soc., Math. Assn. Am., Assn. Computing Machinery (pres. 1960-62), Am. Fedn. Info. Processing Socs. (governing bd. 1961-63), Sigma Xi. Home: 10 Devant Ln Bluffton SC 29910 Office: U Calif Computer & Info Sci Santa Cruz CA 95064

HUSTON, HARRIETTE IRENE OTWELL (REE HUSTON), retired county official; d. Harry C. Otwell and Fannie (Mitchell) Otwell Geffert; m. Dan E. Huston, Jan. 21, 1951; children: Terry Dane, Dale Curtis, Ronald William, Randall Philip. BS, Kans. State Coll., 1951. Cert. life & health ins. agt., Wash.; cert. wastewater operator in tng., Wash. Tchr. Kans., Ill., 1955-68; assoc. home economist McCall's Patterns Co., N.Y.C., 1959-62; counselor, owner Dunhill of Seattle Personnel, 1968-75; enrollment officer, trainer, adminstrv. sec. Teller Tng. Insts., Seattle, 1975-76; life and health ins. agt. Lincoln Nat. Sales, Seattle, 1976-77; office mgr., adminstrv. sec. ARA Transp. Group, Seattle, 1977-78; asst. to the pres. Pryde Corp., Bellevue, Wash., 1978-80; sr. sec. Municipality of Met. Seattle, 1980-92, project asst., 1992-93; adminstrv. specialist II King County Dept. Met. Svcs. (formerly Municipality of Met. Seattle, 1993-95; primary and secondary substitute tchr. Sequim (Wash.) Pub. Schs., 1996—. Co-author: Homemaking textbook, 1956; contbr. articles to profl. jours.. Sec. exec., mem. gen. bd. Bellevue Christian Ch., Disciples of Christ, 1976-77, 86-87, chmn. flowers com., 1978-83, elder, 1978, deacon, 1987; bd. dirs., sec. Surrey Downs Cmty. Club, Bellevue, 1983-85; mem. choir Sequim Presbyn. Ch., 1994—, elder, 1996—, chair congl. life com., 1996—; vol. leader, coord. Linking Home and Sch. Through the Workplace, 1992-93. Recipient Clothing award check McCall's Patterns Co., N.Y.C., 1962, Certs. of Merit Metro Hdqrs., Seattle, 1981, 82, 83, 86, 89. Mem. Bellevue Bridge Club. Home: 1783 E Sequim Bay Rd Sequim WA 98382-8675

HUSTON, MARK LOUIS, economics educator; b. San Francisco, Dec. 5, 1951; s. Arthur Robert and Doris June (Crouch) H.; m. Anne Beyer (div. 1980); 1 child, Lauren Suzanne; m. Edel Corla Savage, Sept. 30, 1982 (div. Feb. 1996); 1 child, Mardel Leyland. BA in Bus., U. San Francisco, 1977; MA in Econs., U. Pitts., 1979; MBA in Bus. Adminstrn., Calif. Coast U., 1987, PhD in Bus. Adminstrn., 1994. Med. adminstrn. specialist USAF, 1970-74; supr. data processing Pacific Mut. Ins. Co., Corte Madera, Calif., 1974-77; asst. fellow U. Pitts., 1977-79; sr. forecast analyst General Tire & Rubber, Akron, Ohio, 1979-81; supr., mgmt. cons. Arabian Bechtel, Jubail, Saudi Arabia, 1981-83; sr. cons., pres. Bus. and Econ. Svcs., San Rafael, Calif., 1983-89; regional v.p. IMPAC, Litchfield, Calif., 1989-90; prof. econs. San Diego-Mesa Coll., San Diego, 1990—. Author: Executive Computer Literacy, 1986, Drug Abuse-Clinet-Pay Programs; Insurance Billing Intake and Billing Handbook, 1986, Economic Principles and Course Notes, 1st edit., 1992, 2d edit., 1993, 3d edit., 1996; producer World War II Film series, 1993. Sgt. USAF, 1970-74. Mem. Am. Fedn. Tchr., Am. Legion. Republican. Home: 2423 Morena Blvd San Diego CA 92110-4139 Office: Mesa Coll 7520 Mesa College Dr San Diego CA 92111-5000

HUSZCZUK VEL HUSZCZA, ANDREW RICHARD, physiologist; b. Wilno, Poland, Oct. 7, 1939; came to U.S., 1979; s. Leon and Jadwiga (Oladowska) H.; m. Teresa Lada, June 7, 1973 (div. June 1983); 1 child, Paulina; m. Beata Brzezinski, July 21, 1990; 1 child, Agata. MSc, Warsaw (Poland) Poly., 1964; PhD, Polish Acad. Scis., Warsaw, Poland, 1972. Rsch. asst. Polish Acad. Scis., Warsaw, Poland, 1964-66, sr. rsch. asst., 1967-69, chief designer, 1970-72, asst. prof., 1973-79; vis. scientist Harbor-UCLA Med. Ctr., Torrance, Calif., 1979-82, rsch. assoc., 1982-88, assoc. rschr., 1988-93; dir. R & D Vacumetrics, Ventura, Calif., 1993—; vol. rsch. prof. Calif. State U., Long Beach, 1993—; rsch. fellow U. Oxford, U.K., 1968-69; dir. Medipan Sci. Instruments, Warsaw, 1972-73; postdoctoral rsch. fellow Charring Cross Hosp. Med. Sch., London, 1973-74. Contbr. numerous articles to Jour. of Physiology, Jour. of Applied Physiology and others; patentee in field. Recipient Sci. award of the Yr., Polish Acad. Scis., 1970; grantee Am. Lung Assn., 1982-83, Am. Heart Assn., 1982-84, NIH, 1985-88. Mem. Am. Physiol. Soc., Am. Heart Assn. Office: Vacumetrics 4483 Mcgrath St Ventura CA 93003-7737

HUTCHENS, JOHN GREGORY, engineering and management consultant; b. Denver, June 16, 1960; s. John Raymond and Delores Marie (Schoepf) H.; m. Carol Lynn Zanmiller, Aug. 10, 1991; children: Zoe Elizabeth, Tia Noelle. BS in Electronic Engring. Tech., DeVry Tech. Inst., 1982; MS in Mgmt., Boston U., 1991. Registered profl. engr., Colo. Mem. tech. staff Hughes Aircraft Space and Comm., Elsegundo, Calif., 1982-88; sr. rsch. engr. Lockheed Missiles and Space, Eng., 1988-94; assoc., cons. Booz-Allen & Hamilton, Colorado Springs, Colo., 1994—. Mem. IEEE. Home: 3940 Regency Dr Colorado Springs CO 80906-4319 Office: Booz Allen & Hamilton 1050 S Academy Blvd Colorado Springs CO 80910-3924

HUTCHERSON, CHRISTOPHER ALFRED, marketing and recruiting and educational consultant; b. Memphis, June 13, 1950; s. Alfred Wayne Hutcherson and Loretta (Morris) Kindsfather; m. Glenda Ann Champ, May 22, 1971 (dec. 1995). BS, U. Houston, 1972, MA in Adminstrn., 1977, postgrad., 1977-79. Cert. tchr. and adminstr., Tex. Pvt. music instr. Spring Br. and Pasadena Ind. Sch. Dists., Tex., 1968-75; jr. high and high sch. band dir. Deer Park (Tex.) Ind. Schs., 1972-80; recruiter M. David Lowe Personnel, Houston, 1981; sales dir. Instl. Financing Svcs., Benicia, Calif., 1982-85; sales mgr. Instl. Financing Svcs., Benicia, 1985-87; nat. tng. dir. Champion Products and Svcs., San Diego, 1987-88, west coast and midwest sales mgr., 1988-89; pres. Camelot, Inc., Auburn, Calif., 1989-91; pres., CEO Camelot Telephone Assistance Program, Inc., Folsom, Calif., 1991-92; nat. dir. sales and mktg. edn. and devel. Nat. Scrip Ctr., Inc., Santa Rosa, Calif., 1992-95; exec. v.p. Scrip Plus Inc., Fresno, Calif., 1995-96; chmn., CEO Children's Heros, Inc., L.A., 1996—; fund raising cons. non-profit orgns., 1982—; speaker in field. Judge Tex. jr. high and high sch. bands, 1974-81, regional band chmn., 1973-77; choir dir. St. Hyacinth Ch., Deer Park, 1979-81; vice chmn. Ch. Coun. St. Hyacinth Ch., 1980; founder Tex. Region XIX Jr. High Band Competition, 1973 (Spl. Achievement award 1979); 1st chair clarinet Tex. All-State Band, 1968; founder Glenda Hutcherson Heroes Found., 1996—; creator Loyaltycard Smart Card Program, 1996—. Mem. Kappa Kappa Psi (v.p. Outstanding Mem. award 1970). Republican. Roman Catholic. Home: 14105 Lodestar Dr Grass Valley CA 95949-8362

HUTCHESON, JERRY DEE, manufacturing company executive; b. Hammon, Okla., Oct. 31, 1932; s. Radford Andrew and Ethel Mae (Boulware) H.; B.S. in Physics, Eastern N. Mex. U., 1959; postgrad. Temple U., 1961-62, U. N.Mex., 1964-65; m. Lynda Lou Weber, Mar. 6, 1953; children—Gerald Dan, Lisa Marie, Vicki Lynn. Research engr. RCA, 1959-62; sect. head Motorola, 1962-63; research physicist Dikewood Corp., 1963-66; sr. mem. tech. staff Signetics Corp., 1966-69; engring. mgr. Litton Systems, Sunnyvale, Calif., 1969-70; engring. mgr. Fairchild Semiconductor, Mountain View, Calif., 1971; equipment engr., group mgr. Teledyne Semiconductor, Mountain View, 1971-74; dir. engring. DCA Reliability Labs., Sunnyvale, 1974-75; founder, prin. Tech. Ventures, San Jose, Calif., 1975—; chief exec. officer VLSI Research, Inc., 1981—. Democratic precinct committeeman, Albuquerque, 1964-66. Served with USAF, 1951-55. Registered profl. engr., Calif. Mem. Nat. Soc. Profl. Engrs., Profl. Engrs. Pvt. Practice, Calif. Soc. Profl. Engrs., Semiconductor Equipment and Materials Inst., Soc. Photo-Optical Instrumentation Engrs., Am. Soc. Test Engrs., Presbyterian. Club: Masons. Contbr. articles to profl. jours. Home: 5950 Vista Loop San Jose CA 95124-6562 Office: VSLI Rsch 1754 Technology Dr Ste 117 San Jose CA 95110-1308

HUTCHINS, JAMES LEIGH, quality assurance professional; b. Bangor, Maine, Aug. 11, 1950; s. Elbridge Leland and Harret Alice (Johnson) H.; m. Dolores Jean Sweezey; children: Sandra Kay, Alice Elizbeth. BS in Electronics Tech., Chapman Coll., Orange, Calif., 1981. Quality assurance engr. McDonnell Douglas Astronautics, Monrovia, Calif., 1983-84; sr. quality assurance engr. Comarco Weapons Sys. Divsn., Ridgecrest, Calif., 1985-86, Endevco, San Juan Capistrano, Calif., 1986; sr. reliability engr. Los Alamos Tech. Assocs., Albuquerque, 1986-88; software product assurance specialist Northrop-Grumman, Palmdale, Calif., 1988—. Vice chair L.A. Dem. Ctrl. Com., Region 1, 1994-95; 36th Assembly Dist. coord., Calif. Dem. Party, 1993. Sgt. USMC, 1969-78. Named Man of Yr. 36th Assembly Dist. L.A. County Dem. Ctrl. Com., 1993. Mem. Am. Soc. Quality Control, Elks, Masons, Shriners. Democrat. Home: 2219 Rosewood Ave Lancaster CA 93535-5610

HUTCHINS, JEFFREY CARLTON, protective services official; b. Coronado, Calif., May 28, 1959; s. Carlton Leroy and Lucille (Cash) H.; m. Patricia Lynn Palmer, Feb. 16, 1980; children: Ashleigh Lynne, Emily Erin, Glenell Renee, Kendall Marie. AS in Criminal Justice, Southwestern Calif. Coll., Chula Vista, 1983. Dispatcher City of Coronado Police Dept., 1977-80, police officer, 1980-86, police investigator, 1986-89, police sgt., 1989—; rep. City of San Diego County Disaster Coun., 1986-89; mem. So. Calif. Emergency Svcs. Assn., 1986-89. Cons.: (book) Emergency Planning Guidelines for Local Law Enforcement, 1989. Mem. Calif. Police Officers Assn., Coronado Police Officers Assn. (sec., treas. 1977-80), Fraternal Order of Police, Amateur Radio League, Coronado Kiwanis. Republican. Methodist. Office: Coronado Police Dept 700 Orange Ave Coronado CA 92118-1827

HUTCHINSON, ANN, development director; b. East Stroudsburg, Pa., May 15, 1950; d. David Ellis and Susie (Ingalls) H.; m. Paul Harrison McAllister, Jan. 2, 1986. BS in Vocat. Edn., Fla. Internat. U., 1985; MBA, Pepperdine U., 1990. Cert. advanced vocat. tchr., Fla. Motorcycle technician Ft. Lauderdale, Fla., 1973-78, machinist, 1978-79; instr., motorcycle tech. Sheridan Vocat. Tech. Sch., Hollywood, Fla., 1979-85; adminstr., tng. program Am. Honda Motorcycle Div., Torrance, Calif., 1985-86, curriculum developer motorcycles svc. tech., 1986-90, coll. program coord., 1990-94; ednl. devel. dir. Clinton Tech. Inst., Phoenix, 1994-96; tng. officer II Ariz. State Dept. Econ. Security, Phoenix, 1996—; chmn. high tech. acad. steering coms. Pasadena (Calif.) United Sch. Dist., 1991-94; ednl. cons. Ctr. for Occupation R&D Sch.-to-Work Awards, 1994-97. Examiner for Gov.'s Award for Excellence, 1997; mem. Ams. with disabilities act com. Ariz. Dept. Econ. Security, 1995—. Recipient State of Ky. Colonel award, 1990, A2 State Quality award. Mem. Am. Motorcycle Assn., Am. Vocat. Assn., ASTD, Vocat. Indsl. Clubs Am. (co-chmn. motorcycle tech. com. 1988-90, 94—, automotive nat. tech. com. 1990-94, adv. Hollywood, Fla. 1979-85), Toastmasters Internat. (Zenger Miller cert. 1996—). Office: Ariz Dept Econ Security Office Orgn and Mgmt Devel 1140 E Washington Rm 206 Phoenix AZ 85034

HUTCHINSON, CHARLES SMITH, JR., book publisher; b. Topeka, Oct. 17, 1930; s. Charles S. and Cecil Marguerite (Weidenhamer) H.; m. Elizabeth Dunbar Hall, June 16, 1956; children: Amy Elizabeth, Todd Charles. BA, Principia Coll., 1952. Editor-in-chief, sec., dir. Burgess Pub. Co., Mpls., 1955-65; editor-in-chief coll. and profl. books, dir. Reinhold Book Corp., N.Y.C., 1965-68; editor-in-chief profl. and reference books Van Nostrand Reinhold Co., N.Y.C., 1968-70; pres., chmn. bd. dirs. Dowden, Hutchinson and Ross, Inc., Stroudsburg, Pa., 1970-78, v.p., sec., 1978-80; v.p. Hutchinson Ross Pub. Co., Stroudsburg, 1980-83; sci. pub. Van Nostrand Reinhold Co., N.Y.C., 1984-86; mng. dir. Hutchinson Assocs., Prescott, Ariz., 1987-91; pres. Geosci. Press, Inc., Tucson, 1989—, Harbinger House, Inc., Tucson, 1992-94; mng. ptnr. Picacho Peak Press, L.L.C., Tucson, 1994—. Bd. dirs. Hist. Farms Assn., Stroudsburg, 1980-86, pres., 1985-86. With C.E., U.S. Army, 1952-55. Recipient NuJay award Mpls. Jaycees, 1957. Fellow Geol. Soc. Am.; mem. Rocky Mountain Books Pubs. Assn., Kiwanis (treas. Stroudsburg chpt. 1977-78, v.p. 1978-80, pres. 1980-81, Disting. Pres. award 1981). Home: 5520 N Camino Arenosa Tucson AZ 85718-5416

HUTCHINSON, DEBRA ANN, school psychologist; b. Denver, Sept. 13, 1951; d. Joseph D. and Ruth W. (Jameson) Weddel; m. Thomas H. Hutchinson, Aug. 18, 1973; children: Justin, Matthew, Travis. BS, Colo. State U., 1973; MA, U. Colo., 1975. Lic. sch. psychologist. Sch. psychologist Boulder (Colo.) Valley Pub. Sch., 1977-78; univ. rsc. asst. U. Colo., Boulder, 1982-84; sch. psychologist St. Vrain Valley Sch. Dist., Longmont, Colo., 1987-96, tchr. gifted and talented, 1989-93, 94-96; gifted Edn., coord. St Vrain Valley Sch. Dist., 1996—; parent mem., vice chair Gifted/Talented Adv. Bd., Longmont. Author: (poem) The Seedling, 1995. Mem. ASCD, Colo. Soc. Sch. Psychologists, Colo. Assn. Gifted/Talented, St. Vrain Valley Edn. Assn. Office: 395 S Pratt Pkwy Longmont CO 80501

HUTCHINSON, DONALD WILSON, state commissioner of financial institutions; b. Seattle, Dec. 29, 1936. BS in Bus. and Edn., Mont. State U., 1960; Grad. Degree in Banking, Pacific Coast Banking Sch., Seattle, 1979. With First Nat. Bank, Bozeman, Mont., 1963-69, Owatonna, Minn., 1969-71; with First Security Bank, Livingston, Mont., 1971-82; v.p. Bank of Sheridan, Mont., 1983-84; gen. mgr., cons. Pryor Creek Devel. Co., Billings, Mont., 1984-85; chief lending officer Valley Bank of Belgrade, Mont., 1986-90; commr. State of Mont. Divsn. Banking and Fin. Instns., Helena, 1990—. Dir. Livingston (Mont.) Meml. Hosp., Livingston Alcohol & Drug Abuse Ctr., Gallatin County (Mont.) Big Bros. and Big Sisters; mem. Belgrade City/County Planning Bd.; treas., bd. trustees, Paul Clark Home/McDonald's Family Place, Butte, Mont. Mem. Livingston Rotary Club (past pres.). Office: Montana Divsn Banking Lee Metcalf Bldg 1520 E 6th St Rm 50 Helena MT 59620

HUTCHINSON, EDWARD PAUL, city official; b. Tucson, May 19, 1961; s. Willard Lafayette and Dorothy Jean (Ellis) H. AAS in Security Adminstrn., C.C. of the Air Force, Montgomery, Ala., 1989; AAS in Electronic Sys. Tech., C.C. of the Air Force, 1994. Cert. peace officer, Ariz.; emergency med. technician; cert. field tng. officer. Enlisted U.S. Air Force, 1978, served in U.S., Europe, Asia, Africa, 1978-95; Elite Guard flight chief 7001st Spl. Security Squadron, Ramstein Air Base, West Germany, 1983-86; non-commd. officer in charge secure communication 53d Combat Communications Squadron, Robins AFB, Ga., 1987-90; aircraft security flight chief 836th Security Police Squadron, Davis-Monthan AFB, Ariz., 1990-91, non-commd. officer in charge, confinement, 1991; shift comdr. 355th Security Police Squadron, Davis-Monthan AFB, 1991-95; ret. USAF, 1995; quality advisor, 1992-95; adult probation surveillance officer Pima County, Tucson, 1996-97; res. officer Tucson Police Dept., 1991-94, South Tucson Police Dept., 1996—; mil. customs insp. U.S. Customs Svc., Nogales, Ariz., 1991-95. Troop comm. mem. Boy Scouts Am., Robins AFB, 1988-89; vol. emergency med. technician USAF Clinic, Spangdahlem Air Base, West Germany, 1982-83. Decorated Air Force Commendation medal, two Air Force Achievement medals, Air Force Meritorious Svc. medal; named to Outstanding Young Men in Am., 1987. Christian. Office: Pima County Adult Probation 2695 E Ajo Way Tucson AZ 85713

HUTCHINSON, JOSEPH CANDLER, retired foreign language educator; b. Hazelhurst, Ga., Jan. 10, 1920; s. George Washington and Lillie Arizona (Rowan) H.; m. June Cruce O'Shields, Aug. 12, 1950 (div. 1980); children: Junie O'Shields, Joseph Candler. BA, Emory U., 1940, MA, 1941; PhD, U. N.C., 1950; postgrad. U. Paris, summers 1951, 53. Tchr., Tech. High Sch., Atlanta, 1941-42; instr. French, German, Italian, Emory U., Atlanta, 1946-47; instr. U. N.C., Chapel Hill, 1947-50, asst. prof., 1954, assoc. prof., to 1957; asst. prof. Sweet Briar (Va.) Coll., 1950-51, 53-54; assoc. prof. Tulane U., New Orleans, 1957-59; fgn. lang. specialist U.S. Office Edn., Washington, 1959-64; acad. adv. hdqrs. Def. Lang. Inst., Washington, 1964-74, Monterey, 1974-77, dir. tng. devel. Def. Lang. Inst. Fgn. Lang. Ctr., Monterey, Calif., 1977-82, asst. acad. dean, 1982-85; dean of policy, from 1985-88; vis. prof. U. Va., Charlottesville, 1966, Arlington, 1970, Georgetown U., 1968, Am. U., 1971; cons. Council of Chief State Sch. Officers, 1960, U. Del., 1966, U. Colo., 1968, U. Ill., 1968; U.S. del. Bur. Internat. Lang. Coordination, NATO, 1964-79, 81-82, 86-87. Author: Using the Language Laboratory Effectively: School Executive's Guide, 1964, The Language Laboratory: Equipment and Utilization in Trends in Language Teaching, 1966, others; editor Dialog on Language Instruction, 1986-88; contbr. articles to profl. jours. Served with U.S. Army, 1942-46, 51-53. Decorated Bronze Star. Mem. Am. Council on Edn. (task force on internat. edn. 1973), NEA (sec. dept. fgn. langs. 1961-64), AARP/VOTE (17th Congl. dist. team), Higher Edn. Assn. Monterey Peninsula, Am. Council on Teaching of Fgn. Lang., MLA, Am. Mgmt. Assn., Am. Soc. Tng. and Devel., Nat. Assn. Ret. Fed. Employees (v.p. Monterey chpt. 1990, pres. 1991-92), Monterey Choral Soc., Camerata Singers, Washington Linguistics Club (v.p. 1970-72). Episcopalian.

HUTCHISON, DAVID EASTON, surgeon, educator; b. Denver, Nov. 3, 1936; s. James Easton and Helen (Bryant) H.; m. Judy H. Hutchison, June 15, 1963; children: Kathryn Louise Heissenbattle, Suzann Louise, Helen Marie. BA, Lafayette Coll., Easton, Pa., 1958; MD, U. Colo., Denver, 1963. Rotating intern Phila. Gen. Hosp., 1963-64; resident in gen. surgery U. Colo. Health Sci. Ctr., Denver, 1964-66, fellow in transplant surgery, 1966-67; sr. registrar St. Bartholomew's Hosp., London, 1968-69; chief resident in gen. surgery U. Colo., Denver, 1969-70; pvt. practice Denver; pres. med. staff Mercy (St. Anthony's) Hosp., Denver, 1991-93; clin. prof. surgery U. Colo. Health Sci. Ctr., Denver, 1996—. Comdr. USNR, 1969-71. Mem. Am. Bd. Surgery (bd. dirs. 1996—), Am. Bd. Thoracic Surgery (bd. dirs. 1997—), Southwestern Surg. Soc. (bd. dirs. 1986-88, 95—), Denver Acad. Surgeons (pres. 1988), Denver Med. Soc. (pres. 1996). Home: 250 S Clemont Denver CO 80222 Office: Associated Surgeons 4200 W Conejos Pl Denver CO 80204-1333

HUTCHISON, JAMES DONALD, retired engineer, historian; b. Lafayette, Colo., Jan. 15, 1921; s. John Porter and Hazel Jane (Hood) H.; m. Elizabeth May Marion, Dec. 9, 1945; children: John William, Daniel James, Janet May (Mrs. Gerald Lee Morrell), Ronald Raymond. Student, U. Colo.; BA, U. No. Colo., 1974. Registered profl. engr., Colo.; land surveyor, Colo. Telegraph operator Colo. and So. R.R., Denver, 1945-46; rodman Colo. Dept. Hwys., Denver, 1949-51; cryogenic technician Cambridge Corp., Boulder, 1953-54; project engr. Colo. Dept. Hwys., Boulder, 1954-82; engr. cons. Lafayette, Colo., 1982—; mus. dir. Lafayette Miner's Mus., 1987—. Author: Survey and Settlement Lafayette Colorado, 1994; editor: The War Years 50th Anniversary Album Lafayette Colorado, 1994. Unit leader Boy Scouts Am., Lafayette, 1956-82; dir. Lafayette Centennial History Book, 1990. With USMC, 1942-45. Recipient Silver Beaver award Long Peak Coun. Boy Scouts Am., 1968, Person of the Yr. award Lafayette News, 1990. Mem. VFW (life), Lafayette Hist. Soc. (life), Assn. No. Front Range Mus. Assn., Lafayette Lions Club (pres. 1993-94, zone chmn. 1994-95), Scottish Clan Donald (Colo. eastern convener 1995—). Methodist. Home: 778 Applewood Dr Lafayette CO 80026-8908

HUTCHISON, LOYAL DWAYNE, pharmacist; b. Stockton, Calif., Jan. 3, 1933; s. Lester and Muriel (Van Nortwick) H.; m. Jean E. McColl, Jan. 26, 1961; children: Michael, Donald. BS in Pharmacy, U. Pacific, 1966. Pharmacist Fifth St. Pharmacy, Stockton, 1966-76, prin., 1976—; prin. Hutchison Pharmacies Inc., Stockton, 1976—, McKinley Pharmacy, Stockton, 1976—, Lathrop (Calif.) Pharmacy, 1976—. Served with U.S. Army, 1957-59. Fellow Am. Coll. Apothecary; mem. Calif. Pharmacists Assn. (Pac Silver Circle), Am. Pharmacists Assn. Home: PO Box 1737 Stockton CA 95201-1737 Office: Hutchison Pharmacies Inc 1839 S El Dorado St Stockton CA 95206-2025

HUTCHISON, MERRILL DEAN, recreation facility professional; b. Pocatello, Idaho, Jan. 28, 1948; s. William Merrill and Cleo Jean (Flint) H.; m. Erma LuDean Young, July 14, 1973; children: Merrill, Daniel, David, Janae, Mark, Bryan, Brent. BS, Brigham Young U., 1971. Maintenance worker I Provo (Utah) City Parks, 1974-78, maintenance worker II, 1978-82, park maintenance supr., 1982-93, project mgr., 1993—; master gardener USU Exention Svc., 1988—. Hunter safety instr. Utah State Divsn. of Wildlife Resource, Provo, 1982—; scoutmaster Boy Scouts Am., Provo, 1991—; del. to state polit. conv. Rep. Party, Provo, 1984, 94, 95. Mem. NRA, Pacific State Rifle Club (treas. 1974-97), Utah State Rifle and Pistol Assn. (chmn. rifle chpt. 1982-89). Office: Provo City Parks/Recreation 351 W Center St Provo UT 84601-4338

HUTCHISON, RICHARD LOUIS, plastic surgeon; b. Elgin, Ill, Jan. 31, 1956. MD, U. Chgo., 1983. Plastic surgeon Fairbanks Meml. Hosp., Fairbanks, Ak., 1994—. Office: 1919 Lathrop St Fairbanks AK 99701-5930

HUTNER, HERBERT L., financial consultant, lawyer; b. N.Y.C.; s. Nathan M. and Ethel (Helhor) H.; m. Juli Reding, Nov. 28, 1969; children by previous marriage: Jeffrey J., Lynn M. Colwell; 1 stepson, Christopher D. Taylor. B.A., Columbia U., 1928, J.D., 1931. Bar: N.Y. 1932. Ptnr., Osterman & Hutner, mem. N.Y. Stock Exch., N.Y.C., 1945-57; successively pres. N.E. Life Insurance Co., N.Y.C.; chmn. bd. Sleight & Hellmuth Inc., N.Y.C.; chmn. bd. Pressed Metals of Am., Port Huron, Mich.; chmn. bd. Struthers Wells Corp., Warren, Pa., Plateau Mining Co. Inc., Oak Ridge, Tenn.; investor, cons., L.A., 1963—; dir. United Artists Communications, Inc., 1965-87, Todd AO-Glen Glen, 1987—, L.A. Rams, 1972-75, mem. adv. bd., 1991—; chmn. bd. Cellvent, Inc., 1991—. Chmn. pres.'s adv. com. on arts, Kennedy Ctr., 1982-90; founder L.A. Music Ctr.; chmn. profl. sports com. United Way; corporator Schepens Eye Rsch. Inst., Boston; mem. internat. adv. com. Up With People. Decorated title DATO, Sultan of Johore, Malaysia, Highest Order of the Crown, 1981. Mem. ASCAP, Deepdale Golf Club (Manhasset, N.Y.). Composer: The Super Bowl Song, Go Rams Go, others.

HUXLEY, MARY ATSUKO, artist; b. Stockton, Calif., Mar. 5, 1930; d. Henry K. and Kiku H. (Kisanuki) Taniguchi; m. Harold Daniels Huxley, 1957. Student, San Francisco Art Inst., 1968; studied with, Thomas C. Leighton, 1970-75. Solo shows include Artists' Coop., San Francisco, 1973, 75, 76, The Univ. Club, San Francisco, 1976, I. Magnin, San Mateo, 1976, Palo Alto Med. Found., 1992, Galerie Genese, San Mateo, 1993; exhibited in group shows at Catharine Lorillard Wolf Art Club, N.Y.C., 1979, Knickerbocker Artists of Am., N.Y.C., 1979, Salmagundi Club Ann., N.Y.C., 1981, Butler Inst. Am. Art, Youngstown, Ohio, 1982, Am. Artists Profl.

League, N.Y.C., 1982, 83, 86, 87, 88, Oil Painters of Am. Ann., Ill., 1993, 94, Taos, N.Mex., 1997, also San Francisco Ann. Art Festival, Renaissance Gallery, Santa Rosa, Paramount Theater, Oakland, Met. Club Invitational, San Francisco, Marin Soc. Artists Ann., Soc. Western Artists Ann., San Francisco, Peninsula Art Assn. Ann., Belmont, Calif., Fresno Fashion Fair Ann., numerous others; represented in more than 200 pvt. and corp. collections in U.S., Europe and the Far East. Recipient Marjorie Walter Spl. award San Mateo County Exhbn., 1975, Gold medallion and 1st award San Mateo County Fair Fine Arts Exhbn., 1976, numerous others. Fellow Am. Artists Profl. League; mem. Soc. Western Artists (trustee 1986—, bd. dirs. 1972-75, chmn. juried exhbns.), Am. Soc. Classical Realism, Oil Painters Am., Allied Artists Am., Marin Soc. Artists, Palo Alto Cultural Ctr. Studio: PO Box 5467 San Mateo CA 94402-0467

HUYGHEBAERT, JAMES E., state official; b. Chgo., June 7, 1947; s. Alfons Eugene and Mary (Magno) H.; m. Linda Janet Geoglein, Sept. 2, 1992. BA in Econs., No. Ill. U., 1969, MA in Econs., 1971; postgrad., Colo. State U., 1980-84. Economist U.S. Dept. Commerce, Washington, 1971-75, Internat. Monetary Fund, Washington, 1975-80, Utah State Tax Commn., Salt Lake City, 1984-86, Ariz. State U., Tempe, 1986-87; dir. tax analysis Colo. Dept. Revenue, Denver, 1987—. Mem. citizen adv. budget com. City of Aurora, Colo., 1995. Mem. Phi Beta Kappa. Republican. Home: 1350 S Idalia St Unit C Aurora CO 80017 Office: Colorado Dept Revenue Tax Analysis Rm 422 1375 Sherman St Denver CO 80261

HWANG, CORDELIA JONG, chemist; b. N.Y.C., July 14, 1942; d. Goddard and Lily (Fung) Jong; m. Warren C. Hwang, Mar. 29, 1969; 1 child, Kevin. Student Alfred U., 1960-62; BA, Barnard Coll., 1964; M.S., SUNY-Stony Brook, 1969. Rsch. asst. Columbia U., N.Y.C., 1964-66; analytical chemist Veritron West Inc., Chatsworth, Calif., 1969-70; asst. lab. dir., chief chemist Pomeroy, Johnston & Bailey Environ. Engrs., Pasadena, Calif., 1970-76; chemist Met. Water Dist. So. Calif., Los Angeles, 1976-79, rsch. chemist 1980-91, sr. chemist 1992—; mem. Joint Task Group on Instrumental Identification of Taste and Odor Compounds, 1983-85, instr. Citrus Coll., 1974-76; chair Joint Task Group on Disinfection by-products: chlorine, 1990. Mem. Am. Chem. Soc., Am. Water Works Assn. (cert. water quality analyst level 3, Calif.-Nev.), Am. Soc. for Mass Spectometry. Office: Met Water Dist So Calif 700 Moreno Ave La Verne CA 91750-3303

HWANG, DAVID GENPAI, ophthalmologist, educator; b. Carbondale, Ill., Aug. 22, 1963. Student, Northwestern U., 1978-80; BS, U. Calif., San Francisco, 1982, MD, 1984. Diplomate Am. Bd. Ophthalmology, Nat. Bd. Med. Examiners; cert. physician and surgeon, Calif. Intern U. Calif. San Franciso Hosps., 1984-86, resident in internal medicine, 1985-86, resident in ophthalmology, 1986-89; fellow in cornea, external disease and uveitis U. So. Calif./Doheny Eye Inst., L.A., 1989-90; clin. instr. ophthalmology U. So. Calif. Sch. Medicine, L.A., 1989-90; asst. prof. ophthalmology U. Calif. San Francisco Sch. Medicine, 1990-95, assoc. prof. ophthalmology, 1995—; co-dir. cornea svc. U. Calif., San Franisco, 1990-95, co-dir. cornea and refractive surg. svcs., 1995—, Vision Correction Ctr., 1995—, med. dir. Eye Bank, 1990—, rsch. assoc. Francis I. Proctor Found., 1992—. Contbr. numerous articles to profl. jours. Heed fellow, 1989-90; NIH grantee, 1989, others. Fellow ACS, Am. Acad. Ophthalmology; mem. AAAS, AMA, Calif. Med. Assn., Contact Lens Assn. Ophthalmologists, Assn. for Rsch. in Vision and Ophthalmology, Am. Soc. Cataract and Refractive Surgery, Internat. Soc. Refractive Keratoplasty, Am. Soc. Microbiology, Paton Soc., Alpha Omega Alpha. Office: U Calif San Francisco Dept Ophthalmology 10 Kirkham St Rm K301 San Francisco CA 94122-3815

HYAMS, HAROLD, lawyer; b. Bklyn., May 19, 1943; s. Frank Charles and Celia (Silverstein) H.; m. Simone Elkeharrat, Nov. 18, 1973; children: Gabriel, Galite, Emilie, Jonathan. BA, U. Vt., 1965; MA in Latin Am. Studies, Georgetown U., 1966; JD, Syracuse U., 1970. Bar: N.Y. 1971, Ariz. 1974, U.S. Dist. Ct. Ariz. 1974, U.S. Ct. Appeals (9th cir.) 1974. Asst. to the gen. counsel Am. Express Co., N.Y.C., 1970-72; atty. Legal Aid Soc., Bklyn., 1973; ptnr. Harold Hyams and Assocs., Tucson, 1974—; mem. panel of arbitrators Am. Arbitration Assn., N.Y.C., 1971-73. Bd. dirs. Chafetz Chaim Congregation, Tucson, 1985-90, Tucson Hebrew Acad., 1985-86; mem. Commn. on Ariz. Environ., 1988. Mem. Am. Bd. Trial Advs., Ariz. Trial Lawyers Assn., Pima County Bar Assn., Assn. Trial Lawyers Am. (adv. bd. trial advocates 1990, cert. specialist in personal injury and wrongful death 1991). Home: 3175 N Elena Maria Tucson AZ 85715-2915 Office: 680 S Craycroft Rd Tucson AZ 85711-7108

HYATT, DAN RICHARD, lawyer; b. Seattle, Nov. 23, 1949; s. Edward and Laura (Hopkins) H.; m. Robin L. Hinkle, Dec. 20, 1973 (div. 1988); m. Karen A. Schneider, Dec. 20, 1988; children: Casey, Dorianne, Jordan, David. BA in English, U. Oreg., 1975; JD, Lewis & Clark Coll., Eugene, Oreg., 1978. Bar: Oreg. 1978, U.S. Dist. Ct. Oreg. 1978, U.S. Ct. Mil. Appeals 1984, U.S. Ct. Appeals (9th cir.) 1985, U.S. Ct. Fed. Claims 1986, U.S. Supreme Ct. 1993. Ptnr. Hyatt, Jackson & Vause, Portland, Oreg., 1978-82; sr. def. counsel USN, Guam, 1983-84; spl. asst. U.S. atty. Dept. Justice, Seattle, 1984-85; pvt. practice, Portland, 1985—; lawyer's chair MOMS, Frederick, Md., 1991—; nat. counsel Am. Fighter Aces Assn., Mesa, Ariz., 1994—, Nat. Spiritualist Assn., Lilydale, N.Y., 1990-94. Elder Westminster Presbyn. Ch., Portland, 1986-89. Comdr. USNR, 1984—. Mem. Oreg. State Bar Assn. (counsel to bar-ethics 1993—, chair mil. and vets. sect. 1995—, bd. govs. (ex-officio 1995—), Judge Advocates Assn., Am. Legion, Am. Fighter Aces Mus. Found. (counsel 1994—), False Memory Syndrome Found. Office: 1500 S W 1st Ave Ste 330 Portland OR 97201

HYATT, LAURA, healthcare company executive; b. L.A.. bd. dirs. Ctr. for Healthy Aging; mayoral appointee L.A. City Coun. on Aging; mem. adv. panel Nat. Stroke Assn.; presenter nat. confs.; guest on radio and TV programs. Author: Redefining Healthcare, 1995; contbr. articles and columns to profl. jours.; mem. editl. bd. 11 health pubs. Presdl. del. to White House Conf. on Aging, 1995. Recipient Golden Advocate award Healthcare Pub. Rels. and Mktg. Assn., 1990, 1995 Woman of the Yr. Nat. Coun. on Aging, Visionary award Bill Comms., 1996.

HYBL, WILLIAM JOSEPH, lawyer, foundation executive; b. Des Moines, July 16, 1942; s. Joseph A. and Geraldine (Evans) H.; m. Kathleen Horrigan, June 6, 1967; children: William J. Jr., Kyle Horrigan. BA, Colo. Coll., 1964; JD, U. Colo., 1967. Bar: Colo. 1967. Asst. dist. atty. 4th Jud. Dist., El Paso and Teller Counties, 1970-72; pres., exec. v.p., dir. Garden City Co., 1973—; dir. Broadmoor Hotel, Inc., 1973—, also vice-chmn., 1987—; chmn., CEO, trustee El Pomar Found, Colorado Springs, Colo., 1973—; pres. U.S. Olympic Com. 1991-92, 96—, 1991-92; bd. dirs. USAA, San Antonio, KN Energy Inc., Lakewood, Colo., FirstBank Holding Co. of Colo., Lakewood; mem. Colo. Ho. Reps., 1972-73; spl. counsel The White House, Washington, 1981. Trustee, vice chmn. Colo. Coll., 1978-94; pres., trustee Air Force Acad. Found.; sec., dir. Nat. Jr. Achievement; vice chmn. bd. U.S. Adv. Commn. on Pub. Diplomacy, 1990—; civilian aide to sec. of army, 1986—. Capt. U.S. Army, 1967-69. Republican.

HYLKO, JAMES MARK, health physicist; b. Detroit, Sept. 11, 1961; s. James John and Frances Rose (Gorski) H. BS in Biochemistry, Ea. Mich. U., 1984; MPH in Health Physics, U. Mich., 1986. Cert. quality auditor. Lab. tech. dept. chemistry Ea. Mich. U., Ypsilanti, 1980-84; environ. radiochemist Argonne (Ill.) Nat. Lab., 1984; radiochemist U. Mich., Ann Arbor, 1984-86; health physics tech. Monticello (Minn.) Nuclear Sta., 1985; rsch. scientist/grad. asst. U. Va., Charlottesville, 1986-88; health physicist Fluor Daniel Inc., Chgo., 1988-92, Roy F. Weston, Inc., Albuquerque, 1992—; instr. dept. chem. and nuclear engring. U. N.Mex., 1993, 94, 95, 96; guest lectr. Purdue U., 1991; invited spkr. Inst. Atomic Energy, Swierk-Otwock, Poland, 1991. Contbr. over 40 articles to various peer-reviewed jours.; tech. reviewer Jour. Radiation Protection Mgmt., Nuclear Tech.; book reviewer Jour. Health Physics, and Sci. Books and Films. Judge N.Mex. Regional and State Sci. and Engring. Fair, 1993, 94, 95, 96, 97. Fellow Inst. Nuclear Power Ops., 1986. Mem. Health Physics Soc. (history com., Rio Grande chpt. exec. bd., treas., chair 1999 Midyear Planning com., co-chair 1999 Midyear Symposium), Am.Nuclear Soc., Am. Soc. Quality Control (cert.), Toastmasters (pres. Fluor Daniel chpt. 1990). Home: 10800 Lowe NE Albuquerque NM 87111-6192 Office: Roy F Weston Inc 6501 Americas Pkwy NE Ste 800 Albuquerque NM 87110-8120

HYMAN, HARVEY ANDREW, lawyer; b. N.Y.C., Nov. 4, 1956; s. Julian Bennett and Elaine (Lubart) H.; m. Lael Irene Carlson, Dec. 22, 1985; 1 child, Simone Carlson. BA in Philosophy summa cum laude, Yale U., 1978; JD, Georgetown U., 1981. Pvt. practice San Francisco, 1986—. Lectr. on prevention of traumatic brain injury at pub. high schs., No. Calif., 1996. Mem. ATLA, Bar Assn. San Francisco, Nat. Brain Injury Assn., Calif. Brain Injury Assn., Phi Beta Kappa. Democrat. Jewish. Office: 22 Battery St # 333 San Francisco CA 94111

HYNEK, FREDERICK JAMES, architect; b. Minot, N.D., May 24, 1944; s. Frederick Frank and Esther Irene (Hermanson) H.; m. Jane Rebecca Lowitz, June 9, 1966; children: Tyler James, Scott Anthony. BArch, N.D. State U., 1967. Intern archtl. firms in Bismarck, N.D., 1967-72; architect Gerald W. Deines, Architect, Casper and Cody, Wyo., 1972-73; v.p. Gerald Deines and Assos., 1973-77; propr. Fred J. Hynek, AIA/Architect, Cody, 1977-80; pres. Design Group, P.C., Architects/Planners, Cody, 1980-86; pres. CHD Architects, Cody, 1986-94; CEO Cathexes, Inc., Reno, 1994-95; project mgr. Merrick and Co., Denver, 1995—; mem. cert. of need rev. bd. State of Wyo., 1984-87, selection com. for archtl. students for Western Interstate Commn. for Higher Edn. Profl. Student Exchange Program, U. Wyo., 1979-94; chmn. archtl. adv. commn. City of Cody. Bd. dirs. Cody Stampede, Inc., 1977-82, Cody Nordic Ski Found., Park County Libr. Found.; chmn. Cody Econ. Devel. Council, 1982-84; coach Absaroka Ski Assn., Bill Koch Youth Ski League, 1990-94. Served with USAR, 1967-68. Mem. AIA (dir. Wyo. chpt. 1976-83, pres. 1980, 81, sec./treas., 1990-91; conf. chmn. Western Mountain region 1977, mem. awards jury 1981, 92, treas. 1982-86; chmn. design awards jury N.D. 1981, 2 awards for Excellence in Archtl. Design Wyo. chpt.), U.S. Ski Assn., U.S. Ski Coaches Assn., Cody County C. of C. (dir., pres. 1982). Republican. Presbyterian. Clubs: Cody Country Amb. (Amb. of Yr. 1990). Mem. editorial adv. bd. Symposia mag., 1981-82. Home: 17614 Peyton Dr Parker CO 80134 Office: 2450 S Peoria St Aurora CO 80014-1896

HYSLOP, ROSANN ROSS, psychotherapist, educator; b. Chgo., May 2, 1956; d. Joseph Charles Ross and Dolores Ann (Horan) Allgaier. BA, U. No. Colo., 1991, MA, 1994. Nat. cert. counselor Nat. Bd. Cert. Counselors; lic. profl. counselor State of Colo. Psychotherapist Counseling Clinic, Greeley, Colo., 1994-96; instr. U. No. Colo., Greeley, 1995—; mental health therapist Weld Mental Health, Greeley, 1996—; group facilitator No. Colo. AIDS Project, Ft. Collins, Colo., 1995-96. Vol. therapist Pro Bono of Weld County, Greeley, 1994-96. Mem. ACA. Office: Univ Northern Colo Dept Psychology Greeley CO 80639

IACANGELO, PETER AUGUST, actor; b. Bklyn., Aug. 13, 1948; s. Peter and Mary Rose (Bordini) I.; m. Melody Rose Marzola, Apr. 5, 1975; children: Peter August III, Perique Ashly, Paxton Aaires. AA in Marine Biology, Suffolk County Community Coll., 1968; BFA, Hofstra U., 1971. Actor South Bronx (N.Y.) Repertory Co., 1971, The Fifteen Cent Token Improvisation, N.Y.C., 1971; actor off-Broadway One Flew Over The Cuckoo's Nest, 1972, Moon Children, 1972-74; actor off-Broadway and N.Y. Shakespeare Festival Comedy of Errors, 1975; actor on-Broadway Three Penny Opera, 1976-77; actor Blood Brothers Warner Bros., N.Y.C. and Hollywood, Calif., 1977; actor Hoodlums Nai Bonet Entertainment, N.Y.C., 1977; ind. actor, 1978—; actor on Broadway Filumena, N.Y.C., 1979-80, Passione, N.Y.C., 1980; tchr. Upward Bound Program, Brunswick, Maine, 1968; owner, tchr., coach Conflict Workshop, N.Y.C., 1971-74; tchr., acting coach Learning Tree U., Northridge, Calif., 1985-86. Contbr. short stories and poems to various mags., 1965—; appeared in prodns. incl. Tattoo, 1978, Times Square, 1979, Spittoon, 1980-81, Hanky Panky, 1981, Hero at Large, 1979, Archie Bunkers Place, 1981, Hill Street Blues, 1981, St. Elsewhere, 1981, The A Team, 1981, 86, Taxi, 1981-82, Cagney & Lacey, 1982, Over Here, Mr. President, 1982, The Jeffersons, 1982, 85, Carpool, 1982, Gimmie a Break, 1982, Hardcastle & McCormick, 1983, The Phoenix, Falcon Crest, 1983, Masquerade, 1984, Cheers, 1984, Night Court, 1984, The Fall Guy, 1984, Knots Landing, 1985, Amazing Stories, Who's the Boss, 1985, Our Family Honor, 1985, The Return of Mickey Spillane's Mike Hammer, 1986, The New Mike Hammer, 1986, Easy Street, 1986, The Tortellis, 1986, Santa Barbara, 1986, On The Edge, 1987, Amen, 1987, Valerie's Family, 1988, Over the Edge, 1988, Nitti, 1988, Killer Instinct, 1989, Gangsters, 1989, Freddy's Nightmares, 1989, Brothers, 1989, Alf, 1989, Mr. Belvedere, 1989, Wolf, 1989, Capital News, 1990, Singer & Sons, 1990, Best Intentions, 1990, Strong Man's Weak Child at L.A.T.C., 1990; (TV) They Came From Outer Space, 1991, Babes, 1991, Life Goes On, 1991, Murphy Brown, 1991, Dream On, 1991, Dear John, 1991, Good & Evil, 1991, Walter & Emily, 1991, Quantum Leap, 1992, Down the Shore, 1992, Good Advice, 1992, Love and War, 1993, Wild Oats, 1994, Simon, 1995, The Faculty, 1995, Ink, 1996, Malcom and Eddie, 1996, Caroline in the City, 1997, The Drew Carrey Show, 1997 (feature films) We're Talking Serious Money, 1991, Addams Family II, 1993, The Night of the Running Man, 1994, Fighting Gravity, 1996, Two Bits, 1996. Vol. Better Horizons Program, Selden, N.Y., 1967-68, Nat. Fedn. of the Blind, N.Y.C., 1971-73, Spl. Olympics, So. Calif., 1981—; actor benefit performance for N.Y.C. and Mayor John V. Lindsey, 1972; celebrity participant St. Jude's Children's Hosp. Fun Shoot. Recipient certificate Mayor John V. Lindsey, 1972. Mem. AFTRA, NRA, SAG, Actors Equity Assn., Actors Fund Am. (life), West Coast Ind. Chess Masters (pres.), The Universal Coterie of Pipe Smokers, Pipe Collectors Internat. (life). Roman Catholic.

IAFRATE, GERALD CARL, motion picture company executive, lawyer; b. Denver, Aug. 17, 1951; s. Vincenzo and Anita M. (Iacobelli) I.; m. Linda S. Hartzell, June 26, 1980 (div. Jan. 1983); 1 child, Mario J.; m. Jennine Saltzman, Dec. 10, 1992 (dec. May 1994). BS in Anthropology, NYU, 1971; DC, Cleve. Chiropractic Coll., Kansas City, Mo., 1975; JD, U. San Francisco, 1988. Bar: Calif., 1988, N.Y., 1988; diplomate Nat. Bd. Chiropractic Examiners, 1975; lic. chiropractor Mo., 1975. Pvt. practice, ptnr. Midwest Chiropractic Clinics, Inc., Cameron, Mo., 1976-83; legal affairs commnr. USPHS, Washington, 1989-94; dep. insp. gen., Atlantic Maritime Adminstrn., Washington and London, 1991-92; admiralty law counsel U.S. Naval Inst., Annapolis, Md., 1992—; pres. Ilex-Ryder Corp., Beverly Hills, Calif., 1995—. Contbr. treatise Columbia Internat. Law Rev., 1988. Mem. Emissary Assembly World Jewish Congress, N.Y.C., 1991—. Rear admiral USPHS, 1989-94. Diplomate Command Staff Coll., Ft. Leavenworth, Kans., 1990. Mem. ABA, Res. Officers Assn., Am. Legion (Honor award 1996), Brit. Royal Anthropol. Soc., Beverly Hills Rotary Club. Republican. Jewish. Office: Ilex-Ryder Corp 240 N Canon Dr Beverly Hills CA 90210-5302

IAMELE, RICHARD THOMAS, law librarian; b. Newark, Jan. 29, 1942; s. Armando Anthony and Evelyn (Coladonato) I.; m. Marilyn Ann Berutto, Aug. 21, 1965; children: Thomas, Ann Marie. BA, Loyola U., L.A., 1963; MSLS, U. So. Calif., 1967; JD, Southwestern U., L.A., 1976. Bar: Calif. 1977. Cataloger U. So. Calif., L.A., 1967-71; asst. cataloger L.A. County Law Libr., 1971-77, asst. ref. libr., 1977-78, asst. libr., 1978-80, libr. dir., 1980—. Mem. ABA, Am. Assn. Law Librs., Calif. Libr. Assn., So. Calif. Assn. Law Librs., Coun. Calif. County Law Librs. (pres. 1981-82, 88-90). Office: Los Angeles County Law Libr 301 W 1st St Los Angeles CA 90012-3140

IANZITI, ADELBERT JOHN, industrial designer; b. Napa, Calif., Oct. 10, 1927; s. John and Mary Lucy (Lecair) I.; student Napa Jr. Coll., 1947, 48-49; m. Doris Moore, Aug. 31, 1952; children: Barbara Ann Ream, Susan Therese Shifflett, Joanne Lynn Lely, Jonathan Peter, Janet Carolyn Kroyer. AA, Fullerton Jr. Coll., 1950; student UCLA, 1950, Santa Monica Community Coll., 1950-51. Design draftsman Basalt Rock Co. Inc. div. Dillingham Heavy Constrn., Napa, 1951-66, chief draftsman plant engring., 1966-68, process designer, 1968-82, pres. employees assn., 1967; now self-employed indsl. design cons. V.p., Justin-Siena Parent-Tchr. Group, 1967. Mem. Aggregates and Concrete Assn. No. Calif. (vice-chmn. environ. subcom. 1976-77), Constrn. Specifications Inst., Native Sons of the Golden West, Nat. Italian Am. Found., World Affairs Coun. No. Calif., Internat. Platform Assn., Commonwealth of Calif. Club. Republican. Roman Catholic. Home and Office: 2650 Dorset St Napa CA 94558-6110

IBARRA, JOSE, city council. BA in Mexican-Am. studies, U. Ariz., 1994. Campaign mgr. Mayor George Miller, 1991; with Border Vol. Corps., 1991-94; aide County Supv. Raul Grijalva, 1994; city coun. Tucson, 1995—. Office: 940 W Alameda Tucson AZ 85745

IBASITAS, JAN WONG, special education educator; b. San Francisco, Jan. 11, 1966; d. Chung Sum and King Ying (Ng) Wong; m. Arnel Mabunga Ibasitas, Aug. 28, 1993. BA in Human Devel., BA in Sociology, U. Calif., Riverside, 1988; MS in Edn., Calif. State U., Fullerton, 1996. Cert. tchr. learning handicapped. Tchr. Riverside Unified S.D., Riverside, 1989-91; chpt. one tchr. Westminster (Calif.) Sch. Dist., 1993-94; tchr. spl. edn. Garden Grove (Calif.) Unified Sch. Dist., 1994—. Office: Garden Grove Sch Dist Morningside Elem Sch 10521 Morningside Dr Garden Grove CA 92843-4810

ICE, RICHARD EUGENE, retired minister, retirement housing company executive; b. Ft. Lewis, Wash., Sept. 25, 1930; s. Shirley and Nellie Rebecca (Pedersen) I.; m. Pearl Lucille Daniels, July 17, 1955 (dec. June 7, 1992); children: Lorinda Susan, Diana Laurene, Julianne Adele. AA, Centralia Coll., 1950; BA, Linfield Coll., 1952, LHD (hon.), 1978; MA, Berkeley Bapt. Div. Sch., 1959, DD (hon.), 1995; grad. advanced mgmt. program Harvard U., 1971. Ordained to ministry Am. Bapt. Ch., 1954; pastor Ridgecrest Community Bapt. Ch., Seattle, 1955-59; dir. ch. extension Wash. Bapt. Conv., 1959-61; dir. loans Am. Bapt. Extension Corp., Valley Forge, Pa., 1961-64; assoc. exec. minister Am. Bapt. Chs. of West, Oakland, Calif., 1964-67; dep. exec. sec., treas. Am. Bapt. Home Mission Socs., Valley Forge, 1967-72; pres. Am. Bapt. Homes of the West, Oakland, 1972-95, pres. emeritus, 1995—; dir. Minister's Life Ins. Co., Mpls., 1975-87, chmn. bd. dirs. 1986-87; bd. dir. Bapt. Life Assn., Buffalo, 1988—; pres. Am. Bapt. Homes and Hosps. Assn., 1978-81. v.p. Am. Bapt. Chs. U.S.A., 1990-91; Ministers and Missionaries Benefit Bd., 1982-89; mem. Bapt. Joint Com. on Pub. Affairs; trustee Linfield Coll., 1972—, chmn. bd. trustees, 1994—; trustee Calif./Nev. Methodist Homes, 1975—, Bacone Coll., 1968-77, Grad. Theol. Union, Berkeley, Calif., 1982—; trustee Am. Bapt. Sem. of West, Berkeley, 1975—, chmn. bd. trustees, 1987-95. Recipient Disting. Baconian award Bacone Coll., 1977, Disting. Alumnus award Centralia Coll., 1981, Meritorious Service award Am. Assn. Homes for Aging, 1982, Merit citation Am. Bapt. Homes and Hosp. Assn., 1985, Award of Honor Calif. Assn. Homes for the Aging, 1988. Mem. U.S. Assn. for UN, Am. Assn. Homes and Svcs. for Aging (Award of Honor 1994), Calif. Assn. Homes for Aging, The Oakland 100, Pi Gamma Mu. Democrat. Clubs: Harvard of San Francisco, Bellevue, Oakland. Office: Am Baptist Homes of West 400 Roland Way Oakland CA 94621-2012

ICENOGLE, RONALD DEAN, physical chemist, plastics engineer, writer, educator; b. Bismarck, N.D., May 5, 1951; s. Grover Donald and Mary Adeline (Parks) I.; m. Maria Cecilia Co., Apr. 26, 1987; children: Paul Steven, James Andrew. BS, Mich. State U., 1974; MS, Cornell U., 1977, PhD, 1981; BA in Edn., Ea. Washington U., 1996. Lab. technician N.D. State U., Fargo, 1974-75; tchg. asst. Cornell U., Ithaca, N.Y., 1975-77; rsch. chemist Shell Devel. Co., Houston, 1980-85; writer on philosophy and sci. Spokane, Wash., 1985-87; sr. devel. engr. Teknor Apex Co., Pawtucket, R.I., 1987-89; writer Spokane, Wash., 1990-96; agt. N.Y. Life Ins. Co., Spokane, 1991; ind. ins. mktg. agt. Spokane, 1991-92; registrar Ind. Order Foresters, Spokane, Wash., 1992; tchr. Olympia (Wash.) Sch. Dist., 1996—. Author: Science and Moral Choice, 1996; co-inventor, 5 U.S. patents low-smoke polypropylene insulation compounds, also fgn. patents granted; contbr. articles to profl. jours. Mem. NEA, Wash. Edn. Assn., Olympia Edn. Assn., Am. Chem. Soc., N.Y. Acad. Scis., Internat. Platform Assn., Phi Beta Kappa, Phi Kappa Phi, Kappa Delta Pi. Republican. Roman Catholic. Home: 5639 Ipsut Ct SE Lacey WA 98503-5168 Office: Olympia HS 1302 North St Olympia WA 98501-3697

ICHELSON, DAVID LEON, physician; b. San Francisco, Oct. 12, 1921; s. Maury Moses and Selene Diane (Jones) I.; m. Jean Pearch, June 14, 1946 (div.); m. Patricia Badali, Sept. 26, 1958; children: Suzanne, Kathryn, David Jr., Nancy, Mary Jane, Beth Ann; m. Katherine E. Shippey, Dec. 26, 1981. AB, Stanford U., 1943; MD, Bowman Gray U., 1950. Intern L.A. County Hosp., 1950-51; resident Tulare County Hosp., 1951-53; pvt. practice Calif., 1953-86, Sacramento, 1986—; chmn. gen. practice dept. Stanford Hosp., Palokto, Calif., 1976, Sequoia Hosp., Redwood City, Calif., 1979; chief staff Corning (Calif.) Meml. Hosp., 1987. Patent on athletic bra and hair clip for repairing scalp lacerations. Inf. U.S. Army, 1944-46. Mem. Am. Acad. Family Practice. Home: 6825 Steamboat Way Sacramento CA 95831-2513

IDEMAN, JAMES M., federal judge; b. Rockford, Ill., Apr. 2, 1931; s. Joseph and Natalie Ideman; m. Gertraud Erika Ideman, June 1, 1971. BA, The Citadel, 1953; JD, U. So. Calif., 1963. Bar: Calif. 1964, U.S. Dist. Ct. (cen. dist.) Calif. 1964, U.S. Ct. Mil. Appeals 1967, U.S. Supreme Ct. 1967. Dep. dist. atty. Los Angeles County, 1964-79; judge Los Angeles County Superior Ct., 1979-84; appointed judge U.S. Dist. Ct. (Cen. Dist.) Calif., Los Angeles, 1984—. Served to 1st lt. U.S. Army, 1953-56, col. AUS Ret. Republican. Office: US Dist Ct 312 N Spring St Rm 218J Los Angeles CA 90012-4701*

IDOURAINE, AHMED, nutritionist, food chemist; b. Souk El-Had, Algiers, Algeria, Jan. 22, 1948; came to U.S., 1983; s. Mohamed Idouraine and Fatma Kennoud; 1 child, Melissa-Sara. BS in Food Tech., Nat. Inst. Agronomy, Algiers, 1977; MS in Food Scis., U. Ariz., 1987, PhD in Nutritional Scis., 1993. Rsch. team leader Sonatrach, Algiers, 1977-81; instr. food sci. dept. Nat. Inst. Light Industries, Boumerdes, Algeria, 1981-83; rsch./tchg. asst. dept. nutrition & food sci. U. Ariz., Tucson, 1985-93; rsch. assoc. Harrington Arthritis Rsch. Ctr., Phoenix, 1994—. Contbr. numerous articles to profl. jours., also numerous abstracts and presentations. McClelland scholar U. Ariz., 1991, Food Sci. scholar, 1992, Sonatrach scholar, 1983-87. Mem. Inst. Food Technologists, Am. Assn. Cereal Chemists, Ariz. Soc. Food Technologists, N.Y. Acad. Scis., Sigma Xi, Gamma Sigma Delta. Office: Harrington Arthritis Rsch Ctr 300 N 18th Stren St Phoenix AZ 85006

IDURY, RAMANA MURTHY, computer scientist; b. Bhimavaram, India, Jan. 24, 1962; s. Kesavarama Murthy and Savitri Devi (Kallakuri) I.; m. Radha Modukuri, Aug. 15, 1988; 1 child, Ramya Mala. B of Tech., Indian Inst. Tech., 1984, M of Tech., 1985; MS in Computer Sci., Rice U., 1992, PhD in Computer Sci., 1993. Rsch. asst. I.I.T., India, 1985; teaching asst. Rice U., Houston, 1988-90, rsch. asst., 1990-92; systems engr. rsch. & devel. CMC Ltd., India, 1986-88; researcher Keck Ctr., Houston, 1992; rsch. assoc. in computational biology U. So. Calif., L.A., 1993-95; biocomputational scientist Sequana Therapeutics, Inc., San Diego, 1995—; presenter in field. Contbr. articles to profl. jours. W.M. Keck Found. fellow; Nat. Merit scholar. Mem. Assn. Computing Machinery, Am. Soc. Human Genetics.

IKEDA, CLYDE JUNICHI, plastic and reconstructive surgeon; b. Kobe, Japan, 1951; s. Paul Tamotsu and Kazu Ikeda. BA, SUNY, Binghamton, 1973; MD, N.Y. Med. Coll., Valhalla, 1979. Chmn. residency tng. program St. Francis Meml. Hosp., San Francisco, 1991—, med. dir. burn ctr., 1992—, med. examiner, 1993—, med. dir. wound healing ctr., 1994—. Fellow Am. Coll. Surgeons. Office: 1199 Bush St Ste 640 San Francisco CA 94109-5999

IKEDA, DONNA RIKA, former state senator; b. Honolulu, Aug. 31, 1939; d. William G. and Lillian (Kim) Yoshida; div.; children: Rika, Aaron, Julie. BA in Speech, U. Hawaii. Substitute tchr., 1969-71; legis. rschr. Hawaii Rep. Rsch. Office, 1971-74; asst. v.p. Grand Pacific Life Ins. Ltd., Honolulu, 1989—; mem. Hawaii Ho. of Reps., 1974-86, Hawaii Senate, 1987-96. *

IKEDA, MOSS MARCUS MASANOBU, retired state education official, lecturer, consultant; b. L.A., Sept. 11, 1931; s. Masao Eugene and Masako (Yamashina) I.; m. Shirley Yaeko Okimoto; children: Cynthia Cecile Ikeda Tamashiro, Mark Eugene, Matthew Albert. BE, U. Hawaii, 1960, MEd, 1962; postgrad. Stanford U., 1961-62; M in Mil. Art and Sci., U.S. Army Command and Gen. Staff Coll., 1975; grad. U.S. Army War Coll., 1976; EdD, U. Hawaii, 1986. Tchr., Farrington H.S., Honolulu, 1962-64; vice-prin. Kailua Intermediate Sch. 1964-65; adminstrv. intern Central Intermediate Sch., Honolulu, 1965-66; vice-prin. Kaimuki H.S., Honolulu, 1966-67; prin. Kawananakoa Intermediate Sch., Honolulu, 1967-68, Kailua H.S., 1969-71, Kalaheo H.S., Kailua, 1972-77; ednl. specialist Hawaii Dept.

Edn., Honolulu, 1977-79, ednl. adminstr., 1979-95, ret., 1995; frequent spkr. on edn.; lectr. U. Hawaii, 1987—. Served with AUS, 1951-57, 68-69, col. U.S. Army ret. Decorated Legion of Merit, Army Commendation medal. Mem. Nat. Assn. Secondary Sch. Prins., Western Assn. Schs. and Colls. (past bd. dirs., pres., chair), Accrediting Commn. for Schs. (chair, commr. 1992-94), Network for Outcome-Based Schs., Commonwealth Coun. for Ednl. Adminstrn., Assn. U.S. Army, Res. Officers Assn., Go For Broke Assn., Army War Coll. Alumni Assn., Hawaii Govt. Employees Assn., Hawaii Assn. Ind. Schs. (bd. dirs. emeritus), Phi Delta Kappa, Phi Kappa Phi. Home and Office: 47-494 Apoalewa Pl Kaneohe HI 96744-4565

IKEDA, TSUGUO (IKE IKEDA), social services center administrator, consultant; b. Portland, Oreg., Aug. 15, 1924; s. Tom Minoru and Tomoe Ikeda; m. Sumiko Hara, Sept. 2, 1951; children: Wanda Amy, Helen Mari, Julie Ann, Patricia Kiyo. BA, Lewis & Clark Coll., 1949; MSW, U. Wash., 1951. Social group worker Neighborhood House, Seattle, 1951-53; exec. dir. Atlantic St. Ctr., Seattle, 1953-86; pres. Urban Partnerships, Seattle, 1986-88, Tsuguo "Ike" Ikeda and Assoc., Seattle, 1988—; cons. Seattle, 1988—; cons. Commn. on Religion and Race, Washington, 1973, North Northeast Mental Health Ctr., Portland, 1985; affirmative action cons. NASW, Washington, 1977; cons./trainer various other orgns.; conf. coord. Beyond the Mask of Denial Wash. State Conf. on Drug/Alcohol/Substance Abuse in the Asian/Pacific Islander Cmtys., 1993; coord. Minority Mental Health Colloquium in Wash., 1994-95; coord. Asian Pacific Islander Coming Home Together Summit-95, Tacoma, Asian Pacific Bi-Ann. Leadership Conf., 1995-96; Tsuguo "Ike" Ikeda, Pub. Svc. ann. award established in 1987. Mem. Nat. Task Force to develop standards and goals for juv. delinquency, 1976; mem. Gov.'s Select Panel for social and health svcs., Olympia, Wash., 1977; chmn. Asian Am. Task Force, Community Coll., Seattle dist., 1982, King County Coordinated Health Care Initiative Client Edn., Mktg. Subcom., 1993; div. chmn. social agys. Seattle United Way campaign, 1985; vice-chmn. Wash. State Com. on Vocat. Edn., Olympia, 1985-86, chmn. 1986-87; chmn. regional adv. com. Dept. Social and Health Svcs., 1990-91; mem. Gov. Mike Lawry's Commn. on Ethics Govt., Campaign Practices, 1993—; mem. exec. task force King County Dept. Youth Svcs., 1996-97. With Mil. Intelligence Lang. Sch., 1945-46. Recipient cert. appreciation U.S. Dept. Justice, Washington, 1975-76, Am. Dream award C.c. Dist., Seattle, 1984, Asian Counseling & Referral Svc., 1991, 95, Wing Lake Mus., 1991-92, Atlantic St. Ctr., 1992, Seattle Chinese Post, 1992, Bishop's award PNW Conf., U. Meth. Ch., Tacoma, Wash., 1984, cmty. svc. award Seattle Rotary Club, 1985, Outstanding Citizen award Mcpl. League, Seattle and King County, 1986, Outstanding Leadership award Dept. Social and Health Svcs., 1993, cmty. award South Pacific Islander Program Seattle Pub. Schs., 1993, Pasasalmat award Filipino Youth Activities, 1993, Tsuguo "Ike" Ikeda Park, 1995, Brass Ring award Asian Am. Polit. Alliance, 1993, Cmty. award South Pacific Islander, 1993, Comm. Svc. award Asian Counseling and Referral Svc., 1994, Disting. Alumnus award Multicultural Alumni Partnership U. Wash. Alumni Assn., 1996; award Gen. Bd. Global Ministies, United Meth. Ch., 1995; recognized as Community Treasure, United Way of King County, 1996. Mem. NASW (chpt. pres., Social Worker of Yr. 1971, Social Work Pioneer 1995), Vol. Agy. Exec. Coalition (pres., Outstanding Cmty. Svc. award 1979), Ethnic Minority Mental Health Consortium (chmn., Outstanding Leader 1992, David E. "Ned" Skinner Cmty. Svc. award 1990), Minority Exec. Dirs. Coalition (organizer, mem. chmn. 1980-86). Democrat. Methodist.

ILANIT, TAMAR, psychologist; b. Tel Aviv, May 5, 1929; d. Aharon and Ada (Berman) Pougatch; came to U.S., 1950, naturalized, 1970; grad. Levinski Tchr. Sem., 1949; Ph.D., U. So. Calif., 1959; m. Apr. 15, 1948; children—Rona, Gill. Research dir. United Cerebral Palsy Assn., Los Angeles, 1959-61; instr. Pepperdine U., Los Angeles, 1962-64; spl. cons. White Meml. Med. Center, Los Angeles; pvt. practice clin. psychology, Los Angeles, 1963—; mem. disability evaluation panel Social Security Adminstrn., 1961-85. Mem. Am. Psychol. Assn., Los Angeles County Psychol. Assn., Sigma Xi, Phi Beta Kappa, Phi Kappa Phi. Jewish. Contbr. articles to profl. jours. Office: 1964 Westwood Blvd Ste 430 Los Angeles CA 90025-4651

ILES, EILEEN MARIE, bank executive, controller; b. Highland Park, Ill., Sept. 29, 1965; d. Dennis Jay and Ida Sigrid (Calderelli) Connolly; m. Kenneth Robert Iles, Dec. 14, 1985; children: Kevin Andrew, Eric Robert. Student, U. Ill., Chgo., 1983-85; BBA in Acctg. and Mktg. Mgmt., U. N.Mex., 1988, M in Acctg., 1992. Acct. Charter Bank for Savs., Albuquerque, 1989-90, bank acctg. supr., 1990-91, asst. contr., 1991—, asst. v.p., 1992—; instr. acctg. U. N.Mex., Albuquerque, 1994—; cons. in field. Mem. Inst. Mgmt. Accts.

ILKIW, JANET ELIZABETH, veterinary science educator; b. Wahroonga, NSW, Australia, June 14, 1949; d. Albert George and Laura Margheritta (Kerz) Wright; m. William John Ilkiw, 1970 (div.). BVS, U. Sydney, 1972, PhD, 1980. Diplomate Bd. of Veterinary Surgeons, NSW. Tutor, vet anaesthetist U. Sydney/Vet. Clin. Studies, NSW, 1976-79, lectr., 1979-82, sr. lectr., head dept., 1983-87; asst. prof. dept. surgery U. Calif., Davis, 1987-91, assoc. prof., 1992—, assoc. prof, head dept. surgery, 1994—. Mem. Assn. Vet. Anaesthetists, Australian Coll. Vet. Surgeons. Office: Univ Calif Davis CA 95616

ILLK, SERENA PEARL, accountant; b. San Angelo, Tex., July 26, 1951; d. Paul Jacob and Goldie Alberta (Crippen) I.; m. Harry Daniel McCormack, June 20, 1984 (dec. Jan., 1990). BA in Acctg., Albertson's Coll. of Idaho, 1973. CPA, Alaska, Wash. From asst. supr. to supr. spl. funds. acctg. dept. Multnomah Sch. Dist., Portland, Oreg., 1974-75; payroll dept. acct. Alyeska pipeline Fluer Alaska, Inc., Valdez, Alaska, 1976-77; various temporary positions in acctg. Seattle, 1978-80; staff acct. Peasley, Tugby & Co., CPAs, Seattle, 1981-83; sr. acct. Boyle & Assocs., CPAs, Anchorage, Alaska, 1984-86; sr. acct. Minkemann & Assocs., CPAs, Anchorage, 1987-90, ptnr., 1991—. Vol. panel mem. KTVA Channel 11, Alaska TV answering tax questions for Alaskan taxpayers, Anchorage, 1991. Mem. AICPA, Alaska Soc. CPAs, Wash. Soc. CPAs. Office: Minkemann & Assocs CPAs 4300 B St Ste 308 Anchorage AK 99503-5933

ILSTAD, GEIR ARE, venture capitalist; b. Norway, Mar. 19, 1955; s. Johan Julius and Ronnaug Synnove (Kristensen) I.; children: Bergen Burnett, Alexandra Burnett. Degree in Econs., U. Fribourg, Switzerland, 1980; BS, Menlo Sch. Bus., Atherton, Calif., 1982, MBA, 1982. Prin. Ilstad Group, Menlo Park, 1981; mgr. Bergen Bank A/S, Oslo, 1982-85; ptnr. SØR Invest A/S, 1984; project mgr. corp. fin. A.S. Factoring Finans, Oslo, 1985-86; pres., chmn. Prudent Mgmt., Inc., Menlo Park, 1986—. Mem. Nesodden Speed Skating Club, 1969-75, Unge Høyre, Nesodden, Norway, 1971. Served with paratroopers Norwegian Army, 1975-76. Mem. Norwegian Bus. Forum (bd. dirs.). Home and Office: Prudent Mgmt Inc PO Box 275 Los Altos CA 94023-0275

IMAMURA, EUGENE HACHIRO, osteopathic physician, surgeon; b. Waipahu, Hawaii. BS, U. Hawaii, 1943; DO, Kansas City Coll. Osteopath, 1953. Intern Waldo Gen. Hosp., Seattle, 1953-54; pvt. practice Seattle, 1955-86, Terrace, 1986—; pres. of staff Waldo Gen. Hosp., Seattle, 1957-58. Contbr. articles to profl. jours. Life patron Edmonds Art Festival. With U.S. Army, 1944-46. Mem. Am. Osteo Assn. (life mem.), UHS Coll. of Osteo. Med., Wash. Osteo. Med. Assn. (life), Am. Coll. Gen. Practitioners, Am. Coll. Osteo. Family Physicians. Home: 16024 75th Pl W Edmonds WA 98026-4524 Office: 5707 244th St SW Mountlake Terrace WA 98043-5449

IMANA, JORGE GARRON, artist; b. Sucre, Bolivia, Sept. 20, 1930; s. Juan S. and Lola (Garron) I.; grad. Fine Arts Acad., U. San Francisco Xavier, 1950; cert. Nat. Sch. for Tchrs., Bolivia, 1952; came to U.S., 1964, naturalized, 1974; m. Cristina Imana; children—George, Ivan. Prof. art Nat. Sch. Tchrs., Sucre, 1954-56; prof. biology Padilla Coll., Sucre, 1956-60; head dept. art Inst. Normal Simon Bolivar, La Paz, Bolivia, 1961-62; propr., mgr. The Artists Showroom, San Diego, 1973—. Over 90 one-man shows of paintings in U.S., S. Am. and Europe, 1952—, including: Gallery Banet, La Paz, 1965, Artists Showroom, San Diego, 1964, 66, 68, 74, 76, 77, San Diego Art Inst., 1966, 68, 72, 73, Contrast Gallery, Chula Vista, Calif., 1966, Central Public Library, San Diego, 1969, Universidad de Zulia, Maracaibo, Venezuela, 1969, Spanish Village Art Center, San Diego, 1974, 75, 76, La Jolla Art Assn. Gallery, 1969, 72-93, Internat. Gallery, Washington, 1976, Galeria de Arte L'Atelier, La Paz, 1977, Museo Nacional, La Paz, 1987, Casa del Arte, La Jolla, Calif., 1987, Museo Nacional, La Paz, Bolivia, 1988, Simon Patino Found., Bolivia, 1994; numerous group shows including: Fine Arts Gallery, San Diego, 1964, Mus. of Modern Art, Paris, 1973, exhibits in galleries of Budapest (Hungary), 1975, Moscow (USSR), 1975, Warsaw (Poland), 1976; represented in permanent collections: Museo Nacional, La Paz, Bolivia, Museo de la Universidad de Potosi, Bolivia, Muse Nacional de Bogota, Colombia, S. Am., Ministerio de Edn., Managua, Nicaragua, Bolivian embassy, Moscow and Washington, also pvt. collections in U.S., Europe and Latin Am.; executed many murals including: Colegio Padilla, Sucre, Bolivia, 1958, Colegio Junin, Sucre, Bolivia, 1959, Sindicato de Construccion Civil, Lima, Peru, 1960. Hon. consul of Bolivia, So. Calif., 1969-73. Served to lt. Bolivian Army, 1953. Recipient Mcpl. award Sucre, Bolivia, 1958. Mem. San Diego Art Inst., San Diego Watercolor Soc., Internat. Fine Arts Guild, La Jolla Art Assn. Home: 3357 Caminito Gandara La Jolla CA 92037-2907

IMBROGNO, CYNTHIA, judge. BA, Ind. Univ. of Pa., 1970; JD cum laude, Gonzaga Univ. Sch. of Law, 1979. Law clk. to Hon. Justin L. Quackenbush U.S. Dist. Ct. (Wash. ea. dist.), 1979-80, 1980-83; law clk. Wash. State Ct. of Appeals, 1984; civil rights staff atty. Ea. Dist. of Wash., 1984-85, complex litigation staff atty., 1986-88; with Preston, Thorgrimson, Shidler, Gates & Ellis, 1988-90, Perkins Coie, 1990-91; magistrate judge U.S. Dist. Ct. (Wash. ea. dist.), 9th circuit, Spokane, 1991—. Office: US Courthouse PO Box 263 920 Riverside Ave W 7th Fl Spokane WA 99210

IMLAY, GORDON LAKE, development consultant; b. Fairmont, W.Va., Oct. 12, 1937; s. Julian Mortimer and Fredricka Jane (Harveycutter) I.; m. Margaret Julia Rodina, Aug. 31, 1958; children: Jane Ellen Imlay Skeen, James Elliot. BA, Mo. Valley Coll., 1959; MS, San Jose State U., 1977; EdD, U. Pacific, 1980. Registered recreator; cert. fund raising exec. Dist. scout exec. Boy Scouts Am., Bloomington, Ind., 1959-63; dist. scout exec. Boy Scouts Am., Detroit, 1963-68, field dir., 1968-72; exec. dir. Am. Humanics, Marshall, Mo., 1972-74, Stockton, Calif., 1974-81; v.p. YMCA of Metro Los Angeles, 1981-84; exec. dir. East Valley Family YMCA, No. Hollywood, Calif., 1984-87; exec. v.p. Netzel Assocs., Culver City, Calif., 1987—; cons. Western Wash. U., Bellingham, 1995-97, Idaho Commn. Arts, Boise, 1982; faculty mem. YMCA Nat. Staff Tng., Foster City, Calif., 1982-84; nat. cons. Boy Scouts Am., Dallas, 1974-81; chmn. nat. teen task force YMCA U.S.A., Chgo., 1981-85. Author: Identifying the Community Power Structure, 1977; editor: YMCA Leadership Development with Teens, 1983; contbr. articles to profl. jours. Mem. Nat. Soc. Fundraising Execs. (bd. dirs. Wash. chpt. 1995—, pres.-elect 1997), YMCA Assn. Profl. Dirs. (acad. cert. 1986). Republican. Presbyterian. Club: Wing PT Country (Bainbridge Island, Wash.), Rancho Las Palmas Country (Rancho Mirage, Calif.). Lodges: Rotary (program chmn. No. Hollywood, Calif. chpt. 1987, sec. Redford Twp., Mich. chpt. 1965), Lions (key mem. Martinsville, Ind. chpt. 1960). Home: Ste 3A 470 Wood Ave SW Bainbridge Island WA 98110 Office: Netzel Assocs 9696 Culver Blvd Ste 204 Culver City CA 90232-2753

IMRE, JOHN VANARSDALE, quality improvement consultant; b. N.Y.C., Sept. 23, 1937; s. Raymond Paul and Elisabeth (Muir) I. B in Elec. Engring., Cornell U., 1962; BA in English Lit., U. Wash., 1975, MA in English Lit., 1979; MA in Whole Sys. Design, Antioch U., 1990. Quality improvement pubs. cons., author Volt Tech. Boeing Aerospace, Seattle, 1984-86; author, editor, writer, instr. Quality Improvement Ctr. Boeing Commercial Airplane Group, Renton, Wash., 1986-88; process improvement methods cons., mgr. Everett (Wash.) Divsn. Boeing Commercial Airplane Group, 1988-95, airplane investigation teaming cons., 1996—; instr. South Puget Sound C.C., 1996—, Tacoma C.C., 1996—; adj. faculty City U., Renton, Wash., 1996; cons. and presenter in field. AUthor: Canyon Racer's Pocket Guide, 1983, Managing Quality Guide, 1985 (Excellence award Soc. Tech. Comm. 1986), Guide to Total Quality, 1987; co-author: Total Quality Improvement, 1987 (Disting. award Soc. Tech. Comm. 1988); contbr. newsletters. Recipient Achievement award Soc. Tech. Comm., 1987, Merit award Internat. Assn. Bus. Communicators, 1988. Mem. ASTD (chpt. bd. dirs. 1990-92), Enological Soc. (Seattle chpt. bd., regional bd. sec. 1990-94, chmn. many coms.), Profl. Ski Instrs. Am. (cert. level 3), Orgnl. Devel. Network (chpt. bd. dirs., mktg. chmn., conf. editor 1995, conf. 1994—), Assn. Quality and Participation, Mensa. Home: 344 18th Ave E Seattle WA 98112-5109

INAMA, CHRISTOPHER ROY, lawyer, educator; b. Burbank, Calif., Apr. 4, 1952; s. Leo H. Inama and Jeanne (Bauer) Truax; m. Colleen J. Deal, Dec. 30, 1986. BA, U. Calif., Santa Barbara, 1974; JD, U. Calif., San Francisco, 1977; MA in Econs., Calif. State U., Hayward, 1996. Bar: Calif. 1977, U.S. Dist. Ct. (no. dist.) Calif. 1977. Pvt. practice Law Office of Christopher R. Inama, Redwood City, Calif., 1978—; chief of security San Francisco Giants, 1974-89; adj. prof. econs. U. Phoenix, 1996—, Golden Gate U., 1996—. County chair Calif. Libertarian Party, San Mateo County, 1990-92; candidate Calif. State Assembly, Dist. 21, 1990, 96, Calif. State Senate, Dist. 11, 1992. Chief warrant officer USCGR, 1987—. Mem. Mensa, Hastings Old Boys Rugby Club, St. Thomas More Soc., Native Sons of Golden West #66. Libertarian. Roman Catholic. Office: 399 Bradford St Ste 102 Redwood City CA 94063

INDIEK, VICTOR HENRY, finance corporation executive; b. Spearville, Kans., Nov. 15, 1937; s. Ben W. and Helen Ann (Schreck) I.; m. Marlene Gould, June 2, 1962; children: Kathy, Kevin. Student, U. Nebr., 1955-57; BS in Bus., U. Kans., 1959; postgrad., U. Nebr., 1955-57. CPA, Kans. Audit mgr. Arthur Andersen & Co., Kansas City, Mo., 1961-70; pres., chief exec. officer Fed. Home Loan Mortgage Corp., Washington, 1970-77; pres., dir. Builders Capital Corp., Los Angeles, 1977-84; chief fin. officer, exec. v.p. Fin. Corp. of Am., Irvine, Calif., 1984-88; pres., chief exec. officer FarWest Savs. and Loan Assn., Newport Beach, Calif., 1988—; with Kennedy Wilson; v.p. and pres. regional Assn. Small Businesses Investment Cos., 1979-81, bd. govs. nat. assn., 1982. Mem. Selective Service Bd., Santa Monica, Calif., 1978; capt. United Fund, Kansas City, 1968. Served with USN, 1959-61. Republican. Roman Catholic. Office: Kennedy Wilson 30011 Ive Glenn Ste 224 Laguna Beach CA 92677-1822*

INGALLS, JEREMY, poet, educator; b. Gloucester, Mass., Apr. 2, 1911; d. Charles A. and May E. (Dodge) Ingalls. AB, Tufts Coll., 1932, AM, 1933; student, U. Chgo., 1938-39; LHD, Rockford Coll., 1960; LittD, Tufts U., 1965. Asst. prof. English Lit. Western Coll., Oxford, Ohio, 1941-43; resident poet, asst. prof. English lit. Rockford (Ill.) Coll., 1948-50, successively assoc. prof. English and Asian studies, prof., chmn. div. arts, chmn. English dept., 1950-60; Fulbright prof. Am. lit., Japan, 1957; Rockefeller Found. lectr. Kyoto Am. Studies seminar, 1958. Author: A Book of Legends, 1941, The Metaphysical Sword, 1941, Tahl, 1945, The Galilean Way, 1953, The Woman from the Island, 1958, These Islands Also, 1959, This Stubborn Quantum, 1983, Summer Liturgy, 1985, The Epic Tradition and Related Essays, 1989; translator (from Chinese) A Political History of China, 1840-1928 (Li Chien-Nung), 1956, The Malice of Empire (Yao Hsin-Nung), 1970, (from Japanese) Tenno Yugao (Nakagawa), 1975. Recipient Yale Series of Younger Poets prize, 1941, Shelley Meml. award, 1950, and other awards for poetry; apptd. hon. epic poet laureate United Poets Laureate Internat., 1965; Guggenheim fellow, 1943, Chinese classics rsch. fellow Republic of China, 1945, 46, Am. Acad. Arts and Letters grantee, 1944, Ford Found. fellow Asian studies, 1952, 53. Fellow Internat. Inst. Arts and Letters; mem. MLA (chmn. Oriental-western lit. rels. conf.), Assn. Asian Studies (life), Authors Guild, Poetry Soc. Am., New Eng. Poetry Soc., Dante Soc. Am. (life), Phi Beta Kappa, Chi Omega. Episcopalian. Home: 6269 E Rosewood St Tucson AZ 85711-1638

INGERMAN, MICHAEL LEIGH, realtor; b. N.Y.C., Nov. 30, 1937; s. Charles Stryker and Ernestine (Leigh) I.; m. Madeleine Edison Sloane; Nov. 24, 1984; children by previous marriage: Shawn Marie, Jenifer Lyn. BS, George Washington U., 1963. Health planner, Marin County, Calif., 1969-72; regional cons. Bay Area Comprehensive Health Coun., San Francisco, 1972-73; hosp. cons. Booz, Allen & Hamilton, San Francisco, 1974; health planning coord. Peralta Hosp., Oakland, Calif., 1975-76; pres. Discern, Inc., mgmt. cons., Nicasio, Calif., 1976-93; prin. Human Resources Mgmt. Group, San Francisco, 1991-93; broker assoc. Frank Howard Allen Realtors, Greenbrae, Calif., 1993—; broker assoc. Alaska Pacific Realty, Sitka, 1995-97; instr. Golden Gate U., 1981-88. Bd. dirs. Nicasio Land Owners Assn., 1989-91, pres., 1990; coord. Nicasio Disaster Com., 1988-89; nat. bd. dirs. Am. Friends Svc. Com., 1980-81, bd. dirs. John Woolman Sch., 1980-87, 90-94, bd. chmn., 1991, Hospice of Marin, 1983-89, pres. bd. dirs., 1988-89; bd. dirs. Vol. Ctr. Marin, 1991—, Friends Assn. Svc. for the Elderly, 1984-89, pres. 1988-89; mem. Marin County Civil Grand Jury, 1977-78, Nicasio Design Rev. Com., 1979-83; mem. allocation com. Marin County United Way, 1993-96, campaign com., 1994-96. Office: Frank Howard Allen Realtors 505 Sir Francis Drake Blvd Greenbrae CA 94904-2305

INGERSOLL, ANDREW PERRY, planetary science educator; b. Chgo., Jan. 2, 1940; s. Jeremiah Crary and Minneola (Perry) I.; m. Sarah Morin, Aug. 27, 1961; children: Jeremiah, Ruth Ingersoll Wood, Marion, Minneola, George. BA, Amherst Coll., 1960; PhD, Harvard U., 1965. Rsch. fellow Harvard U., Cambridge, Mass., 1965-66; mem. staff summer study program Woods Hole (Mass.) Oceanographic Inst., 1965, 70-73, Pasadena, 1976, 80, 92; asst. prof. Calif. Inst. Tech., Pasadena, 1966-71, assoc. prof., 1971-76, prof., 1976—; prin. investigator Pioneer Saturn Infrared Radiometer Team, NASA; mem. Voyager Imaging Team, NASA, Cassini Imaging Team; interdisciplinary scientist, Mars Global Surveyor Project, Galileo Project, NASA. Bd. trustees Poly. Sch., Pasadena. Fellow AAAS, Am. Geophys. Union; mem. Am. Astron. Soc. (vice chmn. div. planetary sci. 1988-89, chmn. 1989-90). Office: Calif Inst Tech # 150-21 Pasadena CA 91125

INGERSOLL, JOHN GREGORY, physicist, energy specialist, educator; b. Athens, Greece, July 25, 1948; came to U.S., 1971; s. Gregory and Catherine (Asteris) I.; m. Sally Lynn Roberts, Apr. 7, 1984. BS, Nat. Tech. U., Athens, 1970; MS, Syracuse U., 1973; PhD, U. Calif., Berkeley, 1978. Instr. physics U. Calif., 1974-75, research asst. Lawrence Berkeley Lab., 1975-77, from asst. research prof. to assoc. research prof. Lawrence Berkeley Lab., 1978-82; sr. staff scientist Hughes Aircraft Co., Los Angeles, 1983—; staff mem., advisor USN Energy Office, Washington, 1988—; founder, pres. Helios Internat., 1991—; cons. Calif. Energy Commn., Sacramento, 1981-82, U.S. Dept. Energy, Washington, 1981-83, Bldg. Industry, N.Y. and Calif., 1982—, local govts. on alternative fuels; prin. investigator Energy Tech. Group UCLA, 1983—; mem. tech. team for devel. of a comml. passenger electric vehicle GM, 1990-93. Author: Natural Gas Vehicles, 1996; contbr. over 80 articles on nuclear sci., renewable energy sources, indoor air quality, efficient utilization of energy in bldgs., passive solar systems and solar elec. energy to profl. jours.; author one book on natural gas vehicles and contbg. author to three books on energy mgmt. in bldgs.; patentee heat pipe devels., non-freon low power air conditioner for electric vehicles and buses. Mem. Rep. Presdl. Task Force, Calif., 1981-83. Served as lt. USNR, 1982—. Recipient 2d Pl. award Edison Electric Inst., Gen. Motors, and Dept. Energy, 1993, 1st Pl. award Smithsonian Inst., AIA, 1996, 1st Pl. award Smithsonian Inst./AIA/Nat. Renewable Energy Lab.-Dept. Energy, 1996; fellow Democritus Nuclear Research Ctr., Athens, 1970, Syracuse U., 1972, Rockefeller Found., 1974. Mem. Gen. Motors team (tasked with development, production, mktg. of passenger electric vehicle). Presbyterian. Home: 21315 Lighthill Dr Topanga CA 90290-4442 Office: Helios Internat Inc 3601 W Empire Ave Burbank CA 91505-1115

INGHAM, CHARLES ANDREW, English language educator; b. Manchester, Eng., Aug. 6, 1952; came to U.S., 1982; s. Alan Roy and Jean (Fox) I.; m. Elaine Elizabeth Jones, Sept. 28, 1974; 1 child, Lewis Alexander. BA in Lit. with Honors, U. Essex, U.K., 1976; MPhil in Lit., U. Essex, 1985. Lectr. San Diego State U., 1982-91, U. San Diego, 1983-85; assoc. prof. English Palomar Coll., San Marcos, Calif., 1991—. Co-editor Ochre Mag., 1976-80; contbr. concert and record revs. to Melody Maker; author short stories and poems. Recipient Gavel award Alpha Gamma Sigma, 1994, Nat. Inst. Staff and Orgnl. Devel. Excellence award U. Tex. at Austin, 1995; grantee Dept. Edn. and Sci., 1976, travel grantee, 1978.

INGHAM, EDWARD A., career officer; b. Seattle, June 30, 1962; s. Edward Alfred and Norma Marie (Arnegaard) I.; m. Renee Franceschi, Apr. 13, 1985; children: Connan Edward, Dillon James. BS in Engring. Scis., USAF Acad., 1984; MS in Syss. Engring., Air Force Inst. Tech., 1993, PhD, 1996. Cert. sr. pilot USAF. Commd. USAF, advanced through grades to maj., 1980; T-37 instr. pilot USAF, Phoenix, Ariz., 1984-89, F-16 pilot, 1996—; F-16 instr. pilot USAF, Misawa AFB, Japan, 1989-92; T-37 flight examiner USAF, Phoenix, 1988-89, mission comdr., Misawa AFB, 1992. Mem. Order Daedalians, Assn. Grads. USAF Acad., Tau Beta Pi, Eta Kappa Nu. Roman Catholic. Home: 1345 Meadowlands Dr Fairborn OH 45324

INGLE, MARY SVETZ, preschool educator; b. Streator, Ill., June 18, 1948; d. Robert George and Clara Louella (Clark) Svetz; m. Arthur Joseph Ingle, Aug. 19, 1972; children: Nicholas M., Christopher B. BA, Ill. State U., 1970; MEd, Ariz. State U., 1992. Cert. tchr., Ariz. Substitute tchr. Chandler (Ariz.) Unified Sch. Dist., 1991-93; presch. tchr. Suriya Montessori Presch., Tempe, Ariz., 1993—; participant Project Wild, Advanced Project Wild, Tempe and Phoenix. Author: (children's book) Lindsey's Postcards, 1992. Vol. edn. dept. Phoenix Zoo, 1988-93; cubmaster, day camp staff mem., den leader, leader coach, merit counselor Boy Scouts Am., Lancaster, Pa. and Mesa, Ariz., 1985-91. Recipient 250 Hour Pin, Phoenix Zoo, 1993. Office: Suriya Montessori Presch 11th St Tempe AZ 85281

INGLE, ROBERT D., newspaper editor, newspaper executive; b. Sioux City, Iowa, Apr. 29, 1939; s. Walter J. and Thelma L (McCoy) I.; m. Martha N. Nelson, Sept. 12, 1964 (div. 1984); 1 child, Julia L.; m. Sandra R. Reed, Mar. 2, 1985. B.A. in Journalism and Polit. Sci., U. Iowa, 1962. Various positions Miami Herald, 1962-75, asst. mng. editor, 1975-77, mng. editor, 1977-81; exec. editor San Jose (Calif.) Mercury News, 1981-93, pres., exec. editor, 1993-95; v.p. new media Knight-Ridder Inc., San Jose, Calif., 1995—, pres. Pres. Calif. First Amendment Coalition, 1990-92. Mem. AP Mng. Editors Assn., Am. Soc. Newspaper Editors. Office: Knight Ridder New Media Ctr 50 W San Fernando St Ste 700 San Jose CA 95113*

INGRAM, ARTONYON S., mental health professional, therapist; b. Fremont, N.C., Dec. 2, 1962; s. Gliffie and Doris Ingram. BS, Atlantic Christian Coll., 1985; cert. in drugs and alcohol abuse, Pierce Coll., Steilacoom, Wash., 1993, AA, 1993; MEd, City U., Bellevue, Wash., 1995; cert. parent educator, Clover Pk. Tech. Coll., 1995. Teaching parent Onslow Mental Health Ctr., Jacksonville, N.C., 1987-89; social svcs. asst. Rainer Vista Health Care, Puyallup, Wash., 1990-91, Lakewood Health Care, Tacoma, Wash., 1990-91; group life counselor Jessie Dyslin Boys Ranch, Tacoma, Wash., 1991-92; case mgr. Puget Sound Ctr., Tacoma, Wash., 1991; counselor intern Dotters Counseling Ctr., Puyallup, Wash., 1992-93, Cross Rd. Treatment Ctr., Tacoma, 1993; instr. Clover Pk. Tech. Coll., Tacoma, 1993—. Counselor First Bapt. Ch., Jacksonville, N.C. With USNG, 1981-88. Army Nat. Guard scholar, 1978-81, L.N. Forbes scholar, Boeing Engring. scholar, 1993. Mem. Nat. Assn. Alcoholism and Drug Abuse Counselors, Chem. Dependency Profls. Home: 3910 B 70th Ave NW Gig Harbor WA 98335 Office: Lincoln HS 701 S 37th St Tacoma WA 98408

INGRAM, JUDITH ELIZABETH, counselor; b. Alameda, Calif., May 6, 1951; d. William Ralph and Elizabeth (Lelis) Madler; m. Frank David Ingram, Sept. 4, 1971; 1 child, Melanie Anne. AA, Chabot Coll., Hayward, Calif., 1972; BS in Biology summa cum laude, Calif. State U., Hayward, 1978; MA in Counseling, St. Mary's Coll. of Calif., Moraga, 1996. Tech. writer Tech. Writing Svcs., Dublin, Calif., 1990-93; counselor trainee Valley Christian Counseling, Dublin, 1995-96, counselor, dir. devel., 1996—. Mem. ACA, Western Assn. for Counselor Edn. and Supervision (bd. officer, newsletter editor), Calif. Assn. Marriage and Family Therapists, Am. Assn. Christian Counselors, Assn. for Spiritual, Ethical and Religious Values in Counseling. Presbyterian. Home: 8724 Augusta Ct Dublin CA 94568-1063

INGRAM, PEGGY JOYCE, secondary education educator; b. Wichita Falls, Tex., Feb. 15, 1943; d. Albert Cronjie and Esther (Wiist) Weiss; m. Darwin Keith Ingram, Aug. 19, 1972; 1 child, Lindsey Michelle. Student, Midwestern U., 1961-62; BS, West Tex. State U., 1966; MNS, U. Okla., 1972; postgrad., Ea. N.Mex. U., 1975. Cert. secondary sci. tchr. Tchr. Palo Duro High Sch., Amarillo, Tex., 1966-72, Texico (N.Mex.) High Sch., 1972-73; tchr., chair sci. dept. Clovis High Sch., 1973—; tchr. Ea. N.Mex. U., Clovis, 1981-82; participant NASA Honors Workshop, Jet Propulsion Lab., 1990; part-time instr. Clovis C.C., 1991—. Mem. NEA, Clovis Edn. Assn., Nat. Sci. Tchrs. Assn., N.Mex. Acad. of Sci., Delta Kappa Gamma. Democrat. Methodist. Home: 2501 Williams Ave Clovis NM 88101-3330 Office: Clovis High Sch 1900 N Thornton St Clovis NM 88101-4555

INGRAM, ROBERT M., communications company executive; b. Hattiesburg, Miss., Nov. 23, 1950; s. Harold V. and Mattie Louise I.; m. Betty L. DeVolp, June 7, 1975. BA in Comm., U. So. Miss., 1972; MA in Linguistics, Brown U., 1985. Dir. cmty. svcs. Detroit Hearing & Speech ctr., 1972-74; instr., curriculum specialist Madonna U., Livonia, Mich., 1979-80; pres., CEO Am. Sign Lang. Assocs., Hayward, Calif., 1975-85; mgr. intercultural tng. Applied Materials Japan, Tokyo, 1985-87; diversity program mgr. Hewlett-Packard Co., Palo Alto, Calif., 1987-94; mgr. human resource, adminstrn. Air Touch Internat., Seoul, Korea, 1994-95; pres., CEO Ingram Comms., Union City, Calif., 1994—. Author/pub.: (booklet) The ADA and Reasonable Accommodations for People with Psychiatric Disabilities, 1995; author: Principles and Procedures of Teaching Sign Languages, 1977. Adv. bd. Ctr. for Study of Lang. and Info., Stanford U., 1981—; spl. advisor Pres.'s Com. on Employment of People with Disabilities, Washington, 1987-94; mem. Ariz. Coun. for the Deaf, Phoenix, 1978-79; founder Silicon Valley Diversity Roundtable, 1988—. Named Toastmaster of the Yr., Toastmasters Internat., 1989; George C. Marshall fellow Marshall Found., Copenhagen, 1976-77. Fellow Linguistic Soc. Am.; mem. ASTD, Nat. Spkrs. Assn., Internat. Soc. of Sign Lang. Interpreters (chmn. 1976-83). Democrat. Office: Ingram Communications 33717 Second St Union City CA 94587

INLOW, RUSH OSBORNE, chemist; b. Seattle, July 10, 1944; s. Edgar Burke and Marigale (Osborne) I.; BS, U. Wash., 1966; PhD, Vanderbilt U., 1975; m. Gloria Elisa Duran, June 7, 1980. Chemist, sect. chief U.S. Dept. Energy, New Brunswick Lab., Argonne, Ill., 1975-78, chief nuclear safeguards br. Albuquerque ops., 1978-82, sr. program engr. Cruise missile systems, 1983-84, program mgr. Navy Strategic Systems, 1984-85, dir. weapon programs div., 1985-88, dir. prodn. ops. div., 1988-90, asst. mgr. safeguards and security, 1990-94, asst. mgr. nat. def. programs, 1994-96, deputy mgr. 1996—; apptd. Fed. Sr. Exec. Svc., 1985. Served with USN, 1966-71. Tenn. Eastman fellow, 1974-75; recipient Pres. Meritorious Exec. award The White House, Pres. Clinton, 1994. Mem. Am. Chem. Soc., Sigma Xi. Republican. Episcopalian. Contbr. articles to profl. jours.

INMAN, JAMES RUSSELL, claims consultant; b. Tucson, May 24, 1936; s. Claude Colbert and Myra Eugenia (Langdon) I.; m. Charleen M. Bowman, Feb. 22, 1964 (div. 1977). Student, Pomona Coll., Claremont, Calif., 1954-60. Supr. res. dept. Honnold Libr., Claremont Coll., 1959-60; supr. casualty claims CNA Ins., L.A., 1961-70; asst. mgr., head entertainment claims Firemen's Fund, L.A., Beverly Hills, 1970-83; pres. Wilnor Corp., L.A., 1982—; claims auditor dirs. and officers claims Harbor/Continental Ins., L.A., 1984-86; claims mgr. Advent Mgmt., L.A., 1987, Completion Bond Co., Century City, Calif., 1988; asst. to pres., claims specialist Am. Multiline Corp., L.A., 1988-92; sr. claims specialist Reliance Ins. Co., Glendale, Calif., 1992-94; expert witness in field. Mem. First Century Families: Calif.; mem. com. Baldwin Hills Dam Disaster, 1968-72; pres. Alcohol Info. Ctr., L.A., 1983-85. Mem. L.A. Athletic Club, Wilshire Country Club. Republican. Home: 623 S Arden Blvd Los Angeles CA 90005

INNES, KENNETH FREDERICK, III, lawyer; b. San Francisco, May 15, 1950; s. Kenneth F. Jr. and Jean I.; m. Patricia Ann Graboyes, May 12, 1973; children: Kenneth F. IV, Julia Christine. BA, San Francisco State U., 1972, JD, 1984. Bar: Calif. 1984, U.S. Dist. Ct. (no. dist.) Calif. 1987, U.S. Dist. Ct. (ea. dist.) Calif. 1988. Tchr. secondary schs. Red Bluff, Calif., 1973-74; postal clk. U.S. Postal Svc., Vallejo, Calif., 1977-84; postal insp. U.S. Postal Svc., Denver, 1984-87; regional atty. U.S. Postal Inspection Svc., Memphis, 1987-90, fin. auditor, 1990-92; regional atty. U.S. Postal Inspection Svc., San Francisco, 1992—. Capt. USMCR, 1974-77. Mem. ABA, Calif. Bar Assn., Mensa, Elks. Democrat. Roman Catholic. Home: 157 Heartwood Ct Vallejo CA 94591-5638 Office: US Postal Insp Svc PO Box 882528 San Francisco CA 94188-2528

INOUE, MICHAEL SHIGERU, industrial engineer, electrical engineer; b. Tokyo, June 27, 1936; came to U.S., 1956; s. Takajiro and Kazu (Morimoto) I.; m. Mary Louise Shuhart, Sept. 23, 1965; children: Stephen M., Rosanne E., Marcus S., Joanne K., Suzanne T. BSEE magna cum laude, U. Dayton, 1959; MS, Oreg. State U., 1963, PhD, 1967. Registered profl. engr., Oreg., Calif.; cert. data processor. Sr. rsch. engr. Black and Decker Mfg. Co., Towson, Md., 1960-62; prof. Oreg. State U., Corvallis, 1966-82; v.p. Kyocera Internat., Inc., San Diego, 1982—; exec. com. corp. assocs. U. San Diego; adv. bd. Ahlers Ctr for Internat. Bus. Co-author: Introduction to Operation Research & Management Science, 1975, Circulo de Qualidad, 1982, Pacific Saury, 1971. Mem. exec. com. Japan Soc. San Diego and Tijuana, Corp. Assocs., U. San Diego; mem. adv. bd. Ahlers Ctr. Internat. Bus. Recipient Grad. Rsch. award IBM, 1965. Mem. Inst. Indsl. Engrs. (sr. mem., Oreg. IE of Yr. award 1976), Am. Cer. Soc., Inst. Mgmt. Scis., Japan Soc. of San Diego and Tijuana (exec. com.). Republican. Roman Catholic. Home: 5154 Via Playa Los Santos San Diego CA 92124-1555 Office: Kyocera International Inc 8611 Balboa Ave San Diego CA 92123-1501

INOUYE, DANIEL KEN, senator; b. Honolulu, Sept. 7, 1924; s. Hyotaro I. and Kame Imanaga; m. Margaret Shinobu Awamura, June 12, 1949; 1 child, Daniel Ken. A.B., U. Hawaii, 1950; J.D., George Washington U., 1952. Bar: Hawaii 1953. Asst. pub. prosecutor Honolulu, 1953-54, pvt. practice, 1954—; majority leader Territorial Ho. of Reps., 1954-58, Senate, 1958-59; mem. 86th-87th U.S. Congresses from Hawaii, U.S. Senate from Hawaii, 1962—; sec. Senate Dem. Conf., 1978-88; chmn. Dem. Steering Com., Senate Com. on Appropriations; chmn. subcom. def., mem. Commerce Com.; chmn. subcom. on communications Select Com. on Intelligence, 1976-77, ranking mem. subcom. budget authorizations, 1979-84; former chmn. Select Com. Indian Affairs; mem. Select Com. on Presdl. Campaign Activities, 1973-74; chmn. Sen. select com. Secret Mil. Assistance to Iran and Nicaraguan Opposition, 1987; ranking minority mem. Appropriations subcom. on defense, Commerce, Sci., & Transp. subcom on surface transp. & merchant marine; mem. Indian Affairs Com., Rules & Adminstrn. Com. Joint Com. on the Libr. & Congl. Intern Program, Dem. Steering & Coordination Com. Author: Journey to Washington. Active YMCA, Boy Scouts Am. Keynoter; temporary chmn. Dem. Nat. Conv., 1968, rules com. chmn., 1980, co-chmn. conv., 1984. Pvt. to capt. AUS, 1943-47. Decorated D.S.C., Bronze Star, Purple Heart with cluster; named 1 of 10 Outstanding Young Men of Yr. U.S. Jr. C. of C., 1960; recipient Splendid Am. award Thomas A. Dooley Found., 1967 Golden Plate award Am. Acad. Achievement, 1968. Mem. DAV (past comdr. Hawaii), Honolulu C. of C., Am. Legion (Nat. Comdr.'s award 1973). Methodist. Clubs: Lion. (Hawaii), 442d Veterans (Hawaii). Home: 469 Ena Rd Honolulu HI 96815-1749 Office: US Senate 722 Hart Senate Bldg Washington DC 20510

INTRIERE, ANTHONY DONALD, physician; b. Greenwich, Conn., May 9, 1920; s. Rocco and Angelina (Belcastro) I.; m. Carol A. Yarmey, Aug. 1, 1945; children: Sherry Shoemaker, Michael, Nancy M., Lisa A. MD, U. Mich., 1944. Intern, New Rochelle (N.Y.) Hosp., 1944-45; pvt. practice, Greenwich, Conn., 1947-53, Olney, Ill., 1956-61, Granite City, Ill., 1961-74, San Diego, 1975—; fellow in internal medicine Cleve. Clinic, 1953-55; fellow in gastroenterology Lahey Clinic, Boston, 1955-56. Capt. M.C., AUS, 1945-47. Fellow Am. Coll. Gastroenterology (assoc.); mem. AMA, ACP (assoc.), Am. Soc. Internal Medicine, Fifty Yr. Club Ill. State Med. Soc. Home: 9981 Caminito Chirimolla San Diego CA 92131-2001

INTRILIGATOR, DEVRIE SHAPIRO, physicist; b. N.Y.C.; d. Carl and Lillian Shapiro; m. Michael Intriligator; children: Kenneth, James, William, Robert. BS in Physics, MIT, 1962, MS, 1964; PhD in Planetary and Space Physics, UCLA, 1967. NRC-NASA rsch. assoc. NASA, Ames, Calif., 1967-69; rsch. fellow in physics Calif. Inst. Tech., Pasadena, 1969-72, vis. assoc., 1972-73; asst. prof. U. So. Calif., 1972-80; mem. Space Scis. Ctr., 1978-83; sr. rsch. physicist Carmel Rsch. Ctr., Santa Monica, Calif., 1979—; dir. Space Plasma Lab., 1980—; cons. NASA, NOAA, Jet Propulsion Lab.; chmn. NAS-NRC com. on solar-terrestrial rsch., 1983-86, exec. com. bd. atmospheric sci. and climate, 1983-86, geophysics study com., 1983-86; U.S. nat. rep. Sci. Com. on Solar-Terrestrial Physics, 1983-86; mem. adv. com. NSF Divsn. Atmospheric Sci. Co-editor: Exploration of the Outer Solar System, 1976; contbr. articles to profl. jours. Recipient 3 Achievement awards NASA, Calif. Resolution of Commendation, 1982. Mem. AAAS, Am. Phys. Soc., Am. Geophys. Union, Cosmos Club. Home: 140 Foxtail Dr Santa Monica CA 90402-2048 Office: Carmel Rsch Ctr PO Box 1732 Santa Monica CA 90406-1732

INVERSO, MARLENE JOY, optometrist; b. Los Angeles, May 10, 1942; d. Elmer Encel Wood and Sally Marie (Sample) Hirons; m. John S. Inverso, Dec. 16, 1962; 1 child, Christopher Edward. BA, Calif. State U., Northridge, 1964; MS, SUNY, Potsdam, 1975; OD, Pacific U., 1981. Cert. doctor optometry, Wash., Oreg. English tchr. Chatsworth (Calif.) High Sch., 1964-68, Nelson A. Boylen Second Sch., Toronto, Ont., Can., 1968-70, Gouverneur (N.Y.) Jr.-Sr. High Sch., 1970-74, 76-77; reading resource room tchr. Parishville (N.Y.) Hopkinton Sch., 1974-75; coordinator learning disability clinic SUNY, Potsdam, 1975-77; optometrist and vision therapist Am. Family Vision Clinics, Olympia, Wash., 1982—; mem. adv. com. Sunshine House St. Peter Hosp., Olympia, 1984-86, Pacific U. Coll. Optometry, Forest Grove, Oreg. 1986. Contbr. articles to profl. jours. Mem. Altrusa Svc. Club, Olympia, 1982-86; tchr. Ch. Living Water, Olympia, 1983-88, Olympia-Lacey Ch. of God, 1989—, sec. women's bd., 1990; bd. advisors Crisis Pregnancy Ctr., Olympia, 1987-89; den mother Cub Scouts Am. Pack 202, Lacey, Wash., 1987-88; vol. World Vision Countertop ptnr., 1986—. Fellow Coll. Optometrists in Optometric Devel.; mem. Am. Optometric Assn. (sec. 1983-84), Assn. Children and Adults with Learning Disabilities, Optometric Extension Program, Sigma Xi, Beta Sigma Kappa. Home: 4336 Libby Rd NE Olympia WA 98506

IPSEN, GRANT RUEL, insurance and investments professional; b. Malad, Idaho, Nov. 6, 1932; s. Nephi Ruel and Ada (Hughes) I.; m. Edna Wayne Hughes, July 27, 1956; children: Edna Gaye, LeAnn, Garin Grant, Shawna Lee, Wayne Ruel. BA, Brigham Young U., 1961. CPA, CLU, ChFC. Acct. Ernst & Ernst, Boise, Idaho, 1961-64; with sales dept. Mut. of N.Y., Boise, 1964—; mem. Idaho State Senate, 1992—. Active Boy Scouts Am., 1945—; co-convener Boise Religious Freedom Com., 1991-94. With U.S. Army, 1956-58. Named Agt. of Yr., Boise Assn. Life Underwriters, 1978, Man of Yr., Mut. of N.Y., 1982. Mem. Million Dollar Round Table (life), Brigham Young Univ. Alumni (bd. dirs. 1987-93). Republican. LDS.

IRAGUI-MADOZ, VICENTE J., neurologist, neurosciences educator; b. Pamplona, Spain, Oct. 27, 1946; s. Miguel and Marce (Madoz) Iragui; m. Evelyn S. Tecoma, July 4, 1992. MD, U. Navarra, Pamplona, Spain, 1969; PhD, U. Calif., San Diego, 1977. Intern U. Hosp., Pamplona, Spain, 1969-70, resident neurology, 1971-72; intern U. Calif. Med. Ctr., San Diego, 1976-77, resident neurology, 1977-80; instr. in neurology Sch. Medicine, U. Navarra, Spain, 1972-73; instr. neuroanatomy Sch. Medicine, U. Calif., San Diego, 1973-75; staff neurologist U. Calif. and VA Med. Ctr., San Diego, 1980—, dir. clin. neurophysiology, 1982—; dir. Epilepsy Ctr. U. Calif., San Diego, 1984—, prof. dept. neuroscis., 1992—; cons. Speech, Health and Neurosensory Ctr., Children's Hosp., San Diego, 1981-84. Fulbright fellow, 1973-75, Ministry Fgn. Affairs fellow French Govt., 1973, A.P. Sloan Found. fellow U. Calif., 1975-76. Mem. Am. Neurol. Assn., Am. Acad. Neurology, Am. Electroencephalographic Soc., Am. Epilepsy Soc., San Diego Neurol. Soc., Sociedad Española de Neurologia, Western EEG Soc. (pres. 1989-90). Office: U Calif Med Ctr Mail Code 8740 200 W Arbor Dr San Diego CA 92103-1911

IRANI, MEHRABOON S., pathologist; b. Bombay, Nov. 12, 1958; came to U.S., 1984; s. Shapoor Ardeshir and Khorshed S. (Panthaki) I. BA, Cambridge U., 1980, MB BChir, 1982, MA, 1984. Diplomate in anat. pathology, clin. pathology, blood banking hematopathology Am. Bd. Pathology. Resident in anat. and clin. pathology Baylor Coll. Medicine, Houston, 1984-88, fellow in hematopathology, 1989-90; fellow in transfusion medicine U. Ariz., Tucson, 1988-89; physician-in-charge Hematology/blood bank VA Med. Ctr., Houston, 1990-93; pathologist Pathology Assocs. of Albuquerque, 1993—; pathologist, dir. coagulation lab. Presbyn. Hosp., Albuquerque/. Fellow Coll. Am. Pathologists, Am. Soc. Clin. Pathologists; mem. AMA, Am. Assn. Blood Banks. Parsee (Zoroastrian). Office: Presbyn Hosp Lab 1100 Central SE Albuquerque NM 87106

IRANI, RAY R., oil and gas and chemical company executive; b. Beirut, Lebanon, Jan. 15, 1935; came to U.S., 1953, naturalized, 1956; s. Rida and Naz I.; children: Glenn R., Lillian M., Martin R. BS in Chemistry, Am. U. Beirut, 1953; PhD in Phys. Chemistry, U. So. Calif., 1957. Rsch. scientist, then sr. rsch. scientist Monsanto Co., 1957-67; assoc. dir. new products, then dir. research Diamond Shamrock Corp., 1967-73; with Olin Corp., 1973-83, pres. chems. group, 1978-80; corp. pres., dir. Olin Corp., Stamford, Conn., 1980-83, COO, 1981-83; chmn. Occidental Petroleum Corp. subs. Occidental Chem. Corp., Dallas, 1983-94; CEO Occidental Petroleum Corp., subs. Occidental Chem. Corp., Dallas, 1983-91; chmn. Can. Occidental Petroleum Corp. Ltd., Calgary, 1987—; exec. v.p. Occidental Petroleum Corp., L.A., 1983-84, pres., COO, 1984-91, pres., 1991-96, chmn., CEO, 1991—, also bd. dirs.; bd. dirs. Am. Petroleum Inst., Oxy Oil and Gas USA Inc., Occidental Oil and Gas Corp., Occidental Petroleum Investment Corp. Author: Particle Size; also author papers in field; numerous patents in field. Trustee U. So. Calif., Am. U. Beirut, St. John's Hosp. and Health Ctr. Found., Natural History Mus. Los Angeles County; bd. govs. Los Angeles Town Hall, Los Angeles World Affairs Coun. Mem. Nat. Petroleum Coun., Am. Inst. Chemists, Am. Chem. Soc., Sci. Rsch. Soc. Am., Indsl. Rsch. Inst., The Conf. Bd., The CEO Roundtable, Nat. Assn. Mfrs. (bd. dirs.), Am. Petroleum Inst. (bd. dirs.), U.S.-Russian Bus. Coun. Office: 10889 Wilshire Blvd Los Angeles CA 90024-4201

IRELAND, BARBARA ALICE, film producer, director, writer; b. Seattle, Mar. 8, 1963; d. Joseph L. Ireland and Evelyn E. (Stocker) Daly. Student, U. Wash., 1981-83; BFA cum laude, NYU, 1986; prodr.'s diploma, Hollywood Film Inst., 1995. Script asst. Lionel Rogosin, N.Y.C., 1985-86, Scratch 'n" Sniff Prodns., N.Y.C., 1988; video prodr., dir. Dream Prodns., Seattle, 1989-90; fl. dir. Sta. KING-TV (NBC), Seattle, 1990-91, assoc. prodr., 1991-93; pres. Filmus Maximus, Inc., Seattle, 1993—; mem. adv. bd. Seattle Film Soc., 1981-82. Dir., writer: (film) Secrets, 1986 (3 awards 1987), (trailer) Divine Madness, 1996, (documentary video) Cirque de Soleil, 1990, (music video) Sky Cries Mary—Every Iceberg Is Afire, 1994 (Winning Film award 1994). Grantee Artist Trust, 1995. Fellow Internat. Documentary Assn. Home: 1815 N 43rd St Seattle WA 98103 Office: Filmus Maximus Inc Ste 412 603 Stewart St Seattle WA 98101

IRIS (SILVERSTEIN), BONNIE, artist, writer, educator; b. N.Y.C., Aug. 15, 1941; d. Bernard and Hannah Libbey Kramer; m. Richard Harold Silverstein, May 27, 1967 (div. Oct. 1987). BA, Queens Coll., 1962; MA, NYU, 1963. Asst. editor IEEE, N.Y.C., 1963-68; prodn. mgr. AIAA, N.Y.C., 1973-75; assoc. editor Watson-Guptill Publs., N.Y.C., 1975-82, devel. editor, 1979-82, sr. editor, 1982-88; acquisitions editor North Light Books, Cin., 1988-90; contbg. writer Watercolor Mag., Am. Artist, Step-by-Step Graphics, N.Y.C., 1993—; art workshop tchr. Step-by-Step Graphics, Peoria, Ill., 1995—; art workshop tchr. Rocky Mountain Nat. Park, Foothills Art Ctr., Golden, Colo., Skinner H.S., Denver, 1996—; represented by Arts of Georgetown and Arts of Silver Plume, Foothills II, Golden, Chautauqua Gift Cottage, Boulder; juror art shows Lonmont Art Club, 1996, Depot Art Group, Littleton, Colo., 1996. One woman show at Delectable Egg Restaurant, Denver, 1995, NCAR Gallery, 1996; group shows include Art Students League of N.Y. Gallery, 1970-92, Nat. Arts Club, N.Y.C, 1990, 91, Salmagundi Club, N.Y.C., 1992, Creede Repertory Theatre, 1993-95, Genre Gallery, Inaugural Colo. Sr. Art Show, 1994 (2d prize opaque), Boulder Art Assn. Show, 1993, Foothills Art Ctr., 1994 (merit award 1996), Hildebrandt Gallery, Littleton, Colo., 1994, Faces of Women Show, Las Vegas, N.Mex., 1995, Thompson Valley Art League (3d pl. portraits), This is Colo. Exhbn., Littleton, 1995 (3d pl. award), 97, Longmont Artists Guild, 1995 (Hon. Mention), Louisville Arts Festival, 1995 (Merit award), 96, Glenwood Springs Ann. Fall Festival, 1994 (3rd pl., hon. mention), 96 (hon. mention), East Boulder Recreation Ctr., 1996, others; contbr. articles, illustrations to Artists Mag., Art of the West, others; work featured in several art mags. Mem. Art Students League N.Y. (life), Foothills Art Ctr., Boulder Art Assn. (program dir. 1994—), Allied Artists (assoc.), Knickerbocker Artists, others. Home and Studio: 4500 19th St # 124 Boulder CO 80304-0615

IRISH, THOMAS JUDSON, plastic surgeon; b. Forest City, Iowa, May 23, 1936; m. Sandra Rudolph. BS, Iowa State Coll., 1958; MD, State U. of Iowa, 1962. Intern King County Hosp. (now Harborview Hosp.), Seattle, 1962-63; pvt. practice Forest City, Iowa, 1963-66; resident in gen. surgery U. Colo. Med. Ctr., Denver, 1966-70; resident in plastic surgery Norfolk Gen. Hosp. & Kings Daughters Children's Hosp., Va., 1970-72; pvt. practice Plastic Surgeons NW, Tacoma, Wash., 1972—; fellow in plastic surgery Canniesburn Hosp., Glasgow, Scotland, 1971. Fellow ACS; mem. Am. Soc. Plastic and Reconstructive Surgery, Alpha Omega Alpha. Office: Plastic Surgeons NW 1802 S Yakima Ave Ste 208 Tacoma WA 98405-5304

IRONS, GEORGE BENTON, plastic surgeon; b. Lewisburg, W.Va., Oct. 14, 1933; s. George Benton Sr. and Anna Ruth (Christie) I.; m. Sudelle Kiser, June 6, 1958; children: Andrew, Susan, Stesha. BA, W.Va. U., 1954, BS, 1956; MD, Med. Coll. Va., 1958. Head divsn. plastic surgery Mayo Clinic, Scottsdale, Ariz., 1987—. Office: Mayo Clinic Scottsdale 13400 E Shea Blvd Scottsdale AZ 85259-5404*

IRVINE, VERNON BRUCE, accounting educator, administrator; b. Regina, Sask., Can., May 31, 1943; s. Joseph Vern and Anna Francis (Phillip) I.; m. Marilyn Ann Craik, Apr. 29, 1967; children: Lee-Ann, Cameron, Sandra. B. Commerce, U. Sask., 1965; MBA, U. Chgo., 1967; PhD, U. Minn., 1977. Cert. mgmt. acct. Researcher, Sask. Royal Commn. on Taxation, Regina, 1964; lectr. acctg. Coll. Commerce, U. Sask., Saskatoon, 1967-69, asst. prof., 1969-74, assoc. prof., 1974-79, prof., 1979—, head dept. acctg., 1981-84; profl. program lectr. Inst. Chartered Accts., Regina, 1982-84, Soc. Mgmt. Accts., Saskatoon, 1982-84, 94-95. Co-author: A Practical Approach to the Appraisal of Capital Expenditures, 1981; Intermediate Accounting: Canadian Edition, 1982, 4th edit., 1994; contbr. articles to acctg. jours. Grantee John Wiley & Sons, Ltd., 1981, 85, 87, 88, 92, 93, 96, Soc. Mgmt. Accts. Can., 1979, Pres.'s Fund, U. Sask., 1978, Nelson Can. grantee, 1990. Bd. dirs. Big Sisters of Sask., 1987-90. Fellow Soc. Mgmt. Accts. Can. (bd. dirs. 1979-82, 85-87, 89-92, chmn. Nat. Edn. Svcs. com.); mem. Can. Acad. Acctg. Assn. (pres. 1994-95, pres.- elect 1993-94, sec. 1992-93, exec. com., chmn. mem. com. 1989-91), Internat. Acctg. Standards Com. (Can. rep. 1984-87, 96-97), Internat. Fedn. Accts. Council (tech. advisor 1988-90), Soc. of Mgmt. Accts. of Sask. (pres. 1980-81). Clubs: Sutherland Curling (treas. 1979-83), Saskatoon Golf and Country (bd. dirs. 1988-90). Home: 45 Cantlon Crescent, Saskatoon, SK Canada S7J 2T2 Office: U Sask, Commerce Bldg 25 Campus Dr, Saskatoon, SK Canada S7N 5A7

IRWIN, CHARLES DENNIS, JR., geological consultant; b. Rushville, Nebr., Oct. 10, 1930; s. Charles Dennis and Elsie Gladys (Prell) I.; m. Patricia Jean Riley, Apr. 18, 1959; children: Laurie, Christy, David. BA, U. Colo., 1952; PhD, U. N.Mex., 1969. Jr. computer analyst Robert H. Ray Co., Dickinson, N.D., 1952; jr. geologist Gulf Oil Co., Salt Lake City, 1955, Ardmore, Okla., 1956; project geologist Carter Oil Co., Durango, Colo., 1957-60; project and dist. geologist Tenneco Oil Co., Durango, Casper, Colo., Wyo, 1960-66; area exploration mgr. Wolf Ridge Minerals Corp., Albuquerque, 1968-69; regional explorationist Walter Duncan Oil Properties, Denver, 1970-73; cons. geologist Boulder, Colo., 1973—. Editor: Geological Cross-Sections of Colorado, 1977; contbr. articles to profl. jours. With USN, 1953-54, Korea. Mem. Am. Assn. Petroleum Geologists (adv. coun. 1994—, sec. ho. of dels. 1981-82), Rocky Mountain Assn. Geologists (pres. 1990, councilor 1987, 2 v.p. 1984, sec. 1976), Four Corners Geol. Soc. (1st v.p. 1965, sec. 1960-61), Wyo. Geol. Assn., Computer Oriented Geol. Scientists, Assn. Petroleum Geochem. Explorationists, Soc. Ind. Profl. Earth Scientists. Presbyterian. Home and Office: 220 Cimmaron Way Boulder CO 80303-4204

IRWIN, MILDRED LORINE WARRICK, library consultant, civic worker; b. Kellerton, Iowa, June 21, 1917; d. Webie Arthur and Bonnie Lorine (Hyatt) DeVries; m. Carl Wesley Warrick, Feb. 11, 1937 (dec. June 1983); children: Carl Dwayne, Arthur Will; m. John B. Irwin, Feb. 1, 1994 (dec. Apr. 10, 1997). BS in Edn., Drake U., 1959; M of Librarianship, Kans. State Tchrs. Coll., 1970. Cert. tchr., libr., Iowa. Elem. tchr. Monroe Ctr. Rural Sch., Kellerton, Iowa, 1935-37, Denham Rural Sch., Grand River, Iowa, 1945-48, Grand River Ind. Sch., 1948-52, Woodmansee Rural Sch., Decatur, Iowa, 1952-55, Centennial Rural Sch., Decatur, 1955-56; elem. tchr., acting libr. Cen. Decatur Sch., Leon, Iowa, 1956-71, media libr. jr. and sr. high sch., 1971-79; libr. Northminster Presbyn. Ch., Tucson, 1984-93, advisor, 1994—; media resource instr. Graceland Coll., Lamoni, Iowa, 1971-72; lit. dir. S.W. Iowa Assn. Classroom Tchrs., 1965-69. Editor (media packet) Mini History and Quilt Blocks, 1976, Grandma Lori's Nourishing Nuggets for Body and Soul, 1985, As I Recall (Loren Drake), 1989, Foland Family Supplement III, 1983; author: (with Quentin Oiler) Van Der Vlugt Family Record, 1976; compiler, editor Abigail Specials, 1991, Abigail Assemblage, 1996; compiler Tribute to Ferm Mills 1911-1992, 1992; co-editor: (with Dorothy Heitlinger) Milestones and Touchstones, 1993; contbr. articles to publs. Leader Grand River 4-H Club for Girls, 1954-58; sec. South Ctrl. Iowa Quarter Horse Assn., Chariton, 1967-68; chmn. Decatur County Dems., 1981-83, del., 1970-83; pianist Salvation Army Amphi League of Mercy Rhythm Noters, 1984-90; pianist, dir. Joymakers, 1990—; Sunday Sch. tchr. Decatur United Meth. Ch., 1945-54, 80-83, lay speaker, 1981-83, dir. vacation Bible sch., 1982, 83. Named Classroom Tchr. of Iowa Classroom Tchrs. Assn., 1962, Woman of Yr., Leon Bus. and Profl. Women, 1978, Northminster Presbyn. Ch. Women, 1990; named to Internat. Profl. and Bus. Women Hall of Fame for outstanding achievements in field of edn. and libr. sci., 1995; English and reading grantee Nat. Dept. Edn., 1966. Mem. NEA (life), AAUW (chmn. Tucson creative writing/cultural interests 1986-87, 89-93, historian, 1994—, Honoree award for ednl. found. programs Tucson br., Svc. award 1991), Internat. Reading Assn. (pres. Clarke-Ring-gold-Decatur chpts. 1967-68), Cen. Cmty. Tchrs. Assn. (pres. 1961-62), Pima County Ret. Tchrs. Assn. (pres. 1989-90), Decatur County Assn. (pres. 1961-63), Decatur County Ret. Tchrs. Assn. (historian 1980-83), Iowa Edn. Assn. (life), Presbyn. Women (hon. life 1990—), Luth. Ch. Libr. Assn. (historian Tucson area chpt. 1991-92, v.p. 1993-94, pres. 1994-95), Delta Kappa Gamma (pres. Iowa Beta XI chpt. 1974-76, sec. 1984-85, historian Ariz. Alpha Gamma chpt. 1986-89). Democrat. Presbyterian. Home: 2879 E Presidio Rd Tucson AZ 85716-1539

IRWIN, R. ROBERT, lawyer; b. Denver, July 27, 1933; s. Royal Robert and Mildred Mary (Wilson) I.; m. Sue Ann Scott, Dec. 16, 1956; children—Lori, Stacy, Kristi, Amy. Student U. Colo., 1951-54, B.S.L., U. Denver, 1955, LL.B., 1957. Bar: Colo. 1957, Wyo. 1967. Asst. atty. gen. State of Colo., 1958-66; asst. div. atty. Mobil Oil Corp., Casper, Wyo. 1966-70; prin. atty. No. Natural Gas Co., Omaha 1970-72; sr. atty. Coastal Oil & Gas Corp., Denver 1972-83, asst. sec. 1972-83; ptnr. Baker & Hostetler, 1983-87; pvt. practice 1987—. Mem. Colo. Bar Assn., Arapahoe County Bar Assn., Rocky Mountain Oil and Gas Assn. Republican. Clubs: Los Verdes Golf, Petroleum, Denver Law (Denver). Office: 650 S Alton Way 4-D Denver CO 80231

ISAAC, ROBERT MICHAEL, past mayor; b. Colorado Springs, Colo., Jan. 27, 1928; married; 5 children. Student, U. Colo., 1945-46; BS, U.S. Mil. Acad., 1951; JD, U. So. Calif., 1962. Bar: Colo. 1962, Calif. 1962. Sales engr. The Trane Co., L.A., 1957-62; pvt. practice Colorado Springs, 1962-69; ptnr. Trott, Kunstle, Isaac and Hughes, Colorado Springs, 1969-72, Isaac, Johnson and Alpern, 1972-88; dep. city atty. City of Colorado Springs, 1962-64; asst. dist. atty. 4th Jud. Dist., Colo., 1965-66; mcpl. judge City of Colorado Springs, 1966-69; mem. Colorado Springs City Coun., 1975-79; mayor Colorado Springs, 1979-97; mem. adv. bd. U.S. Conf. Mayors, 1984-85, bd. trustees, 1986-88, chmn. adv. bd., 1988, v.p., 1989, pres., 1990; bd. dirs. Nat. League Cities, 1982-84, adv. bd., 1985—; mem. Adv. Commn. on Intergovtl. Rels., 1987-95; pres. Nat. Conf. Rep. Mayors and Mcpl. Elected Ofcls., 1983-84; guest lectr. on honor code USAF. Bd. trustees Harry S. Truman Scholarship Found., 1984-88; mem. Gov.'s Met. Water Roundtable, State Energy Impact Assistance Adv. Com., 1983-92; bd. dirs. Colo. Mcpl. League, 1981-95; chmn. Pikes Peak Area Coun. Govts., 1975-78; mem. nat. coun. USO, 1969; past pres. Pikes Peak region West Point Soc., 1962—; pres. Pikes Peak Y, 1969-70; pres. YMCA, 1966-69, El Paso County Soc. for Crippled Children and Adults, 1964-67. With U.S. Army, 1946-57. Recipient Outstanding Pub. Svc. award Water for Colo., 1986. Office: PO Box 1575 Mail Code 410 Colorado Springs CO 80901-1575

ISAACSON, GENE LESTER, fine arts educator; b. Rugby, N.D., June 14, 1936; s. Lester O. and Sybil J. (Strandness) I. BA in Art and Music, Concordia Coll., Moorhead, Minn., 1958; MFA, U. No. Colo., 1962. Lic. tchr., Calif., Oreg., Iowa, Minn. Supr. art Mt. Pleasant (Iowa) Pub. Schs., 1960-62; chmn. dept. art Willamette U., Salem, Oreg., 1962-64; art historian, chair Rancho Santiago Coll., Santa Ana, Calif., 1964—, Orange Coast Coll., Costa Mesa, Calif., 1975—; asst. prof. art history Chapman Coll., 1970-71;

advisor/cons. City Arts Programs, Calif.; art/archtl. advisor various orgns. Editor Art Forum Newsletter, 1982-92; contbr. articles to profl. jours. Bd. trustees Orange County Ctr. for Contemporary Art, Santa Ana, 1984-94; advisor High Sch. Performing Arts, Calif., 1989-93. Lutheran. Home: PO Box 6157 Huntington Beach CA 92646-6157 Office: Rancho Santiago Coll 17th & Bristol Sts Santa Ana CA 92706

ISAACSON, JOSEPH MORRIS, rheumatologist; b. Omaha, May 10, 1949. MD, U. Mich., 1975. Diplomate Am. Bd. Internal Medicine, Am. Bd. Rheumatology, Am. Bd. Allery and Immunology. Rheumatologist Good Samaritan Hosp., San Jose, Calif., 1981—; with Cmty. Hosp., Los Gatos, Calif., 1982—; rheumatologist O'Connor Hosp., 1993—; clin. assoc. prof. Stanford U., 1985—. Fellow ACP. Office: 3002 Leigh Ave San Jose CA 95124-2222

ISAACSON, ROBERT LOUIS, investment company executive; b. Chgo., Apr. 21, 1944; s. Abe B. and Laverne (Skolka) I. BS, Mich. State U., 1966. Mktg. mgr. Florasynth, Inc., San Francisco, 1966-69; br. mgr. Florasynth, Inc., Lincolnwood and Palo Alto, Calif., 1969-72; br. office mgr. Geldermann, Palo Alto, 1972-76; founder, pres. Commodity Investment Cons., Los Altos, Calif., 1976—, Future Funding Cons., Menlo Park, Calif., 1976—; co-founder, co-chmn. Nat. Assn. Futures Trading Advisors; bd. dirs. Futures Industry Assn. Edn. and Tng., Williams & Clarissa, Inc.; bd. dirs., exec. com., membership com. Nat. Futures Assn.; membership Nat. Futures Assn. Regional Bus. Conduct Com.; v.p. Lind-Waldock Co., Chgo.; pres. Interalliance U.S.A. Contbr. articles to mags and profl. jours. Founder Fun for Lunch Bunch. With U.S. Mil., 1966-72. Recipient Doncheon award Managed Accounts Report, 1984. Mem. San Francisco Futures Soc., Managed Futures Assn. (past co-chmn., bd. dirs.), Asian Pacific Managed Futures Assn. (bd. dirs., founding mem.), World Trading Day CARE (exec. com.), Peninsula Commodities Club, Elks, Kiwanis. Home: 380 La Questa Way Woodside CA 94062-2428 Office: Commodity Investment Cons Future Funding Cons 380 La Questa Way Woodside CA 94062-2428

ISAUTIER, BERNARD FRANÇOIS, business executive; b. Tours, France, Sept. 19, 1942; s. Francois and Genevieve (Roy) I.; m. Charlotte Roche, July 22, 1968; children: Anne-Caroline, Armelle, Francois. Grad., Ecole Polytechnique, Paris, 1963, Ecole des Mines, Paris, 1966, Institute d'Etudes Politiques, Paris, 1968. Uranium advisor Rep. of Niger, 1968-70; energy and minerals advisor to min. industry and energy Govt. France, Paris, 1970-75; gen. mgr. ops. Elf-Aquitaine Group, Tunis, Tunisia, 1976-78; pres., CEO Aquitaine Co. of Can. Ltd., Calgary, Can., 1978-81, Canterra Energy, Calgary, 1981-85, Polysar Energy & Chem. Corp., Toronto, Ont., 1986-88; chmn., CEO Thomson Consumer Electronics, Paris, 190-92; CEO Can. Occidental Petroleum, Calgary, Can., 1993-95; bd. dirs. Archer Resources, Calgary, Can. FracMaster, Ltd., Calgary, Chauvco Resources, Calgary, Credit Lyonnais, Montreal, Firan Corp., Toronto, Gronarctic Energy, Calgary, Hurricane Hydrocarbons, Calgary, Lafarge, Paris, Wilan Co.. Served to lt. Res. Army of France, 1961-64. Decorated Order of Nat. Meite.

ISBELL, HAROLD M(AX), writer, investor; b. Maquoketa, Iowa, Sept. 20, 1936; s. H. Max and Marcella E. I.; BA cum laude (scholar), Loras Coll., 1959; MA (fellow), U. Notre Dame, 1962; grad. U. Mich. Grad. Sch. Bank Mgmt., 1982; m. Mary Carolyn Cosgriff, June 15, 1963; children: Walter Harold, Susan Elizabeth, David Harold, Alice Kathleen. Instr., U. Notre Dame, South Bend, Ind., 1963-64; assoc. prof. St. Mary's Coll., 1969-72; asst. prof. San Francisco Coll. for Women, 1964-69; with Continental Bank & Trust Co., Salt Lake City, 1972-83, v.p., 1977-83, comml. credit officer, 1978-83, also dir. Trustee Judge Meml. Cath. High Sch., Salt Lake City, 1977-84; mem. Utah Coun. for Handicapped and Developmentally Disabled Persons, 1980-81; bd. dirs. Ballet West, 1983-90, emeritus, 1990—, Story Line Press, 1994—, Smuin Ballets, San Francisco, 1994—; founder Cath. Found. Utah, pres. 1984-86, trustee, 1984-89. Mem. MLA, Mediaeval Acad. Am., Am. Assn. for the Advancement of Sci. Democrat. Roman Catholic. Club: Alta. Editor and translator: The Last Poets of Imperial Rome, 1971, Ovid: Heroides, 1990; contbr. to publs. in field of classical Latin lit. and contemporary Am. Lit.

ISELY, BARBARA J., sociologist, consultant; b. Winfield, Kans., Dec. 28, 1941; d. Lyman S. and S. Elise (Isely) Johnson; m. Charles C. Langford, 1968. BM, Southwestern Coll., 1964; M in Music Edn., North Tex. State U., 1967; MA in Sociology, U. Oreg., 1975, PhD in Sociology, 1981. Asst. prof. sociology Oreg. State U., 1980-90, adminstr. women in internat. devel. coord., 1984-85; affiliated rschr. Gandhigram Rural U. and Tamil U., India, 1987-93; sociologist PKM Campus, Kathamandu, Nepal, 1993; lectr. in field; cons. on World Bank funded projects, Lagos, Nigeria, 1995, in Ghana, 1995, 96, 97. Contbr. articles to profl. jours. Vol. condr. profl. devel. workshops for faculty members various univs. and colls., India, 1991-95; vol. Christian Med. Coll., Vellore, India, 1996. Recipient Servant Leadership award Southwestern Coll., Winfield, 1993. Mem. APHA, Am. Sociol. Assn., Internat. Fedn. for Women in Agr. (founding), Rural Sociol. Soc., Assn. for Women in Devel., Population Assn. Am., Women in Soc. of the Internat. Sociol. Assn. (rsch. com.).

ISEMAN, MICHAEL DEE, medical educator; b. St. Paul, Mar. 3, 1939; s. Manuel Wessel and Eileen Catherine (Croghan) I.; m. Joan Marie Christensen, Aug. 31, 1963; children: Thomas Michael, Matthew Charles. BA in History, Princeton U., 1961; MD, Columbia U., 1965. Intern, jr. resident in medicine Columbia Svc., Bellevue Hosp., N.Y.C., 1965-67; sr. resident in medicine Columbia Svc., Harlem Hosp., N.Y.C., 1969-70; fellow pulmonary medicine Harlem Hosp., N.Y.C., 1970-72; assoc. dir. pulmonary svc. Denver Gen. Hosp., 1972-82; chief clin. mycobacteriology svc. Nat. Jewish Ctr. for Immunology and Respiratory Medicine, Denver, 1982—; asst. prof. medicine U. Colo. Sch. Medicine, Denver, 1973-79, assoc. prof. medicine, 1979-89, prof., 1989—. Assoc. editor Am. Rev. Respiratory Diseases, N.Y., 1984-89; editor-in-chief Tubercle and Lung Diseases, 1995—. Pres. Am. Lung Assn. Colo., Denver, 1982-83; alumni trustee Princeton U., 1981-85. Lt. comdr. USN, 1967-69. Prin. investigator devel. and evaluation of drugs for treatment of mycobacterium avium in AIDS, NIH, 1984-1992. Fellow ACP, Am. Coll. Chest Physicians; mem. Am. Thoracic Soc. (v.p. 1983-84). Presbyterian. Office: Nat Jewish Ctr Immunology & Respiratory Medicine 1400 Jackson St Denver CO 80206-2761

ISHII, CLYDE HIDEO, plastic surgeon; b. Lihue, Hawaii, Mar. 29, 1952. MD, Jefferson Med. Coll., 1978. Diplomate Am. Bd. Surgery, Am. Bd. Plastic Surgery. Chief plastic surgery Queens Med. Ctr., Honolulu, Shriners Hosp., Honolulu, 1993—. Office: 1329 Lusitana St Ste 502 Honolulu HI 96813-2449

ISHIMATSU, EIJI, investment company executive; b. 1951. With Hazama-Gumi Ltd., Tokyo, 1972-87; pres., sec. Hazama USA Corp., Gardena, Calif., 1987—. Office: Hazama USA Corp 1045 W Redondo Beach Blvd Ste 400 Gardena CA 90247-4128*

ISIDORO, EDITH ANNETTE, horticulturist; b. Albuquerque, Oct. 14, 1957; d. Robert Joseph and Marion Elizabeth (Miller) I. BS in Horticulture, N.Mex. State U., 1981, MS in Horticulture, 1984; postgrad., U. Nev., Reno, 1992—. Range conservationist Soil Conservation Service, Estancia, Grants, N.Mex., 1980-82; lab. aide N.Mex. State U. Dept. Horticulture, Las Cruces, 1982, 83-84; technician N.Mex. State U. Coop. Extension Service, Las Cruces, 1983-84, county agrl. extension agt., 1985; area extension agr. U. Nev., Reno, Fallon, 1985—; hay tester Nev. Agrl. Services, Fallon, 1988-92. Mem. AAUW, Am. Soc. Hort. Sci., Am. Horticulture Soc., Am. Botany Soc., Am. Horticulture Therapy Assn., Alpha Zeta, Pi Alpha Psi. Home: 3900 Sheckler Rd Fallon NV 89406-8202 Office: Churchill County Coop Extension 1450 Mclean Rd Fallon NV 89406-8880

ISRAEL, JOAN, social worker; b. Bklyn., July 19, 1943; d. Joseph Israel and Irene (Solon) Kansey; m. Ronald Jerome Janesh, June 28, 1980 (div. Feb. 1985); 1 child, Ariel Naomi. BA, Bklyn. Coll., 1965; MSW, U. Mich., 1974. Lic. clin. social worker, Nev. Social worker Alameda County Welfare Dept., Oakland, Calif., 1965-72; group therapist Pacific Ctr. for Human Growth, Berkeley, Calif., 1975-77; individual and group therapist, bd. dir. Bi-Ctr., San Francisco, 1976-78; clin. social worker, supr. Audrey L. Smith Devel. Ctr., San Francisco, 1977-78; psychiat. social worker South Nev. Adult Mental Health Dept., Las Vegas, 1978-84, part-time clin. social worker, 1988—; pvt. practice clin. social worker Las Vegas, 1984—. Contbr. articles to profl. publs. Organizer Drug/Alcohol Abuse Task Force, Las Vegas, 1983-84, Task Force on AIDS, Las Vegas, 1985-86. Mem. NASW (chair nominating com. 1978-80, 82-84, sec. 1984-86, chair com. on inquiry 1988—, legis. chair 1982-84, diplomate clin. social work), Sierra Club. Democrat. Jewish. Office: 3180 W Sahara Ave Ste 25C Las Vegas NV 89102-6005

ISRAEL, MARK A., pediatrics and neurological surgery educator; b. Newburgh, N.Y., Aug. 12, 1946; m. Susan Jean Israel; children: Joshua, Rebecca, Samuel. BA, Hamilton Coll., 1968; MD, Yeshiva U., 1973. Intern, resident Children's Hosp., Boston, 1973-75; postdoctoral fellow Nat. Inst. Allergy and Infectious Disease, Bethesda, Md., 1975-77; fellow in pediatric oncology Nat. Cancer Inst., Bethesda, 1978-82, investigator, 1982-84, chief molecular genetic sect., 1984-89; prof. pediatrics and neurol. surgery U. Calif., San Francisco, 1989—. Editor: Molecular Biology of Cancer, 1994; assoc. editor: Cancer Rsch.; contbr. over 175 articles to profl. jours. Trustee Marin Acad., San Raphael, Calif., 1992—; mem. citizens adv. com. San Quentin (Calif.) Prison, 1993—. With USPHS, 1975-89. Recipient USPHS commendation, 1985, 87, Heinz Karger Found. award, Geneva, 1988. Mem. Am. Soc. Clin. Investigation, Soc. Pediat. Rsch., Am. Assn. Cancer Rsch., Am. Assn. Clin. Oncologists, Alpha Omega Alpha. Office: U Calif 513 Parnassus Ave Rm Hse722 San Francisco CA 94122-2722

ISRAEL, PAUL NEAL, computer design engineer, author; b. Balt., Apr. 22, 1959; s. Sheldon Leonard and Sheila Lee (Goldmacher) I. BS in EECS, U. Calif., Berkeley, 1981. Project mgr. computer sci. dept. U. Calif., Berkeley, 1981-82; design engr. Electronic Signature Lock Corp., Berkeley, 1983; staff engr. Qantel Bus. Systems, Hayward, Calif., 1983-89; sr. hardware design engr. SBE, Inc., Concord, Calif., 1989-90; engring. contractor Renegade Systems, Sunnyvale, Calif., 1990-92; prin. engr. Unisys Corp., San Jose, Calif., 1992-95; sr. design engr. Network Virtual Systems, Inc., San Jose, 1995—. Mem. IEEE, Assn. Computing Machinery, Bay Area Sci. Fiction Assn. Office: Network Virtual Systems Inc 2077 Gateway Pl Ste 220 San Jose CA 95110

ISRAEL, RICHARD STANLEY, investment banker; b. Oakland, Calif., Sept. 27, 1931; s. Sybil Noble, July 29, 1962; children: Richard Lee, Lynne, Lawrence. BA, U. Calif., Berkeley, 1953, MA, 1953. Copy editor San Francisco Chronicle, 1953-59; publicist CBS TV Network, L.A., 1959-62; sr. v.p. Rogers & Cowan, Beverly Hills, Calif., 1962-69; v.p. Cantor, Fitzgerald, Beverly Hills, 1969-73; pres. Sponsored Cons. Svcs., L.A., 1973—; bd. dirs. Hurst Labeling Systems. Pres. North Beverly Dr. Homeowners Assn., Beverly Hills, 1986-88; v.p. Temple Emanuel, Beverly Hills, 1988-93, L.A. chpt. Juvenile Diabetes Found. Internat, 1987—. With U.S. Army, 1956-58. Recipient Alumni citation U. Calif. Alumni Assn., Berkeley, 1984. Mem. L.A. Venture Assn. (pres. 1987), Assn. for Corp. Growth (v.p. bd. dirs. L.A. chpt.). Democrat. Office: Sponsored Cons Svcs 8929 Wilshire Blvd Ste 214 Beverly Hills CA 90211-1951

ISSARI, M(OHAMMAD) ALI, film producer, educator, consultant; b. Esfahan, Iran, Oct. 3, 1921; s. Abbas Bek and Qamar (Soltan) I.; m. Joan Gura Aamodt, 1953; children: Scheherezade, Katayoun, Roxana. B.A., U. Tehran, Iran, 1963; M.A., U. So. Calif., 1968; Ph.D., 1979. Films officer Brit. Embassy, Brit. Council Joint Film Div., Tehran, 1944-50; asst. motion picture officer USIS, Tehran, 1950-65; cons. to various Iranian Govt. ministries on film and TV devels., 1950-77; liaison officer Am. and Iranian govt. ofcls., 1950-65; prof. cinema Coll. Communication Arts and Scis. Mich. State U., East Lansing, 1969-81; also dir. instructional film and multimedia prodn. Mich. State U., 1969-78; mass media cons., 1981—; pres. Multimedia Prodn. Svcs., Thousand Oaks, Calif., 1989—; film, public relations adviser to Iranian Oil Operating Cos. in, Iran, 1963-65; spl. cons. on edn. and instructional TV Saudi Arabian Ministry of Info., 1972; tchr. Persian lang. Iran-Am. Soc., Tehran, 1949-59; introduced audio-visual edn. in Iran, 1951; established first film festivals in Iran; pres. House of Iran, Inc. Producer, dir. over 1000 ednl., instructional and documentary films, 1956-78; freelance film reporter: Telenews, UPI, Iran, 1959-61; project dir., exec. producer: Ancient Iran Film Series, 1974-78; dir. film prodn. workshops, Cranbrook Inst., Detroit, 1973-74; author: (with Doris A. Paul) A Picture of Persia, 1977, What is Cinema Vérité?, 1979, Cinema in Iran, 1900-1979, 1989; contbr. articles on ednl. communication and audio-visual instruction to periodicals and profl. jours. Founder, exec. sec. Youth Orgn. of Iran, 1951-52; v.p. Rugby Football Fedn., Iran, 1952-53, pres., 1954-55. Decorated Order of Magnum Cap Ord: S.F. Danaie M. Sigillum (Denmark), Order of Cavalieres (Italy), Order of Oranje Nassau (The Netherlands), 1959, Orders of Kooshesh and Pas (Iran), Order of Esteghlal (Jordan), Order of Ordinis Sancti Silvestri Papae (The Vatican); recipient Meritorious Honor award USIA, 1965, Golden Eagle award Coun. for Internat. Non-Theatrical Events, 1975. Mem. Anglo-Iranian Dramatic Soc. (bd. dirs. 1943-50), Mich. Film Assn. (co-founder 1972, bd. dirs. 1972-73), Mid. East Studies Assn., N.Am. Soc. Motion Picture and TV Engrs. (life), Ancient Studies Inst. (co-founder, pres. 1991, 97—), Assn. Ednl. Comm. and Tech., Delta Kappa Alpha (v.p. 1967). *Man will achieve his goals through honesty, hard work and perseverence. The goals worth pursuing are in the service of mankind.*

ITTNER, PERRY MARTIN, sales and marketing consultant; b. Anaheim, Calif., June 14, 1961; s. Franklin Glenn and Delina (Martin) I.; m. Sylvia Marie Garcia, May 16, 1987; children: Kristina Nicole, Amber Delayne. Student, Cerritos Coll., 1979-82. Purchasing agt. Shield Healthcare, Inc., Van Nuys, Calif., 1979-85; gen. mgr. Propak div. of Devco Med. Co., Santa Fe Springs, Calif., 1985-86; materials mgr. Reliable Med. Supply, Brea, Calif., 1986-87; dir. sales and mktg. Telesis Rsch. Group, La Crescenta, Calif., 1985-90; mktg. product specialist Interhealth Corp., Whittier, Calif., 1988-89; pres. PSI Healthcare Assocs., Inc., Santa Fe Springs, Calif., 1990—. Mem. Health Industry Reps. Assn., The Planetary Soc., Nat. Assn. Self Employed, Nat. Fedn. Ind. Bus. Office: PSI Healthcare Assocs Inc 12035 Slauson Ave Ste J Santa Fe Springs CA 90670

IVERSON, RONALD E., plastic surgeon; b. Hailey, Idaho, 1938. MD, UCLA, 1965. Diplomate Am. Bd. Plastic Surgery. Plastic surgeon Eden Hosp., Castro Valley, Calif.; clin. prof. Stanford U. Office: Plas Surg Ctr 1387 Santa Rita Rd Pleasanton CA 94566-5643

IVESTER, VICKY JO, sales professional; b. Atlanta, July 27, 1951; d. Thomas Bryan and Duane (Neureuther) I. BBA, U. Ga., 1973; MBA, Ga. State U., 1982. Lic. real estate broker. Mgmt. trainee Citizens and So. Nat. Bank, Atlanta, 1973-75; sales merchandiser Chesebrough-Ponds, Inc., Atlanta, 1975; sales rep., key accounts Clairol, Inc., Macon and Atlanta, Ga., 1975-81; account mgr. Pepperidge Farm, Atlanta, 1982-84; dist. sales mgr., account mgr., mktg. mgr. Coca-Cola USA, Atlanta, Albuquerque,, Dallas and, St. Louis, 1984-88; real estate broker CAMCO Realty, Albuquerque, 1989-91; registered sales asst. Prudential Securities, Inc., Albuquerque, 1991-92; area sales mgr. Nordic Track, Inc., Albuquerque, 1992-93; inside sales mgr. Kyser Co., Inc., Albuquerque, 1993-94; pres., owner Melon Rags, Inc., Albuquerque, 1994—. Pres. and founder Acad. Ridge East Neighborhood Assn., Albuquerque, 1989-91; founder U. Ga. Alumni Group, Albuquerque, 1989-92. Mem. Am. Mktg. Assn. (bd. dirs. 1983-84), NAFE. Presbyterian. Home: 10817 Malagueña Ln NE Albuquerque NM 87111 Office: Melon Rags Inc 5850 Eubank Blvd NE Ste B49 Albuquerque NM 87111-6111

IVEY-SMITH, JANICE ROSS, clergy, author; b. Tulsa, Apr. 17, 1937; d. William Thomas and Gethsemane Jesse (Mays) Ross; m. Vincent Thomas Keith Ivey (dec.); 1 child, Stuart Antonio Ivey. Student, Fresno State U., 1958, San Francisco U., U. Philippines, Bagio, 1968; AA, Christian Life Coll., Stockton, Calif., 1989, BA, 1990; postgrad., Western Sem., Sacramento, 1996—. Lic. minister United Pentecostal Ch. Internat., 1993. Assoc. pastor Christian Life Ministries, Stockton, 1991—; pastor Christian Life Ctr., Stockton, 1991—, pub. rels. officer, 1994—, dir. Home Bible Study Ministry, 1990—; vocalist San Quentin Prison. Author: How to Teach Home Bible Studies, 1987, What Happens When Someone Dies?, 1994, (poetry) I Am Not a Hireling, 1995, Confidence, 1990, The Silence of Women, 1990. Bd. dirs. Foster Grandparents, Stockton, 1994—, World Missions, Stockton, 1997; guest Commn. on Aging, 1995—; chaplain various hosps., 1994—. Mem. Concerned Women of Am. Democrat. Apostolic. Office: Christian Life Ministries 9025 N West Ln Stockton CA 95210

IVY, EDWARD EVERETT, entomologist, consultant; b. Hollis, Okla., Sept. 24, 1913; s. James Thomas and Betty (Minnear) I.; m. Elizabeth Alberta Slater, Feb. 23, 1935 (dec. Mar. 1981); children: James, Betty. BS, Okla State U., 1934; PhD, Tex. A&M U., 1951. Registered profl. entomologist, all 50 states, Can., Mex. Research entomologist USDA, College Station, Tex., 1940-55; salesman pesticides Mich. Chem. Corp., St. Louis, Mich., 1955-63; research entomologist Pennwalt Corp., Phila., 1963-75; cons. in pesticide devel. various nations, 1975—. Contbr. numerous articles to profl. jours. Recipient AR100 award for invention of Penncap M, 1973. Mem. Entomol. Soc. Am., Am. Registry Profl. Entomologists, Sigma Xi. Presbyterian. Home and Office: 1771 Broadway St Apt 217 Concord CA 94520-2639

IWASAKI, KOUICHI, molecular geneticist; b. Yokosuka, Kanagawa, Japan, Jan. 10, 1961; came to U.S., 1986; s. Yukio and Mayako Iwasaki. BS, Kyoto (Japan) U., 1984, MS, 1986; PhD, U. Wis., 1991. Rsch. assoc. Washington U., St. Louis, 1991-94, U. Wash., Seattle, 1994—. Contbr. articles to profl. jours. Recipient Keck award W. Keck Found., 1992. Mem. AAAS, Soc. for Neurosci., N.Y. Acad. Scis. Office: U Wash Dept Genetics Mail Box 357360 Seattle WA 98195

IZAC, SUZETTE MARIE, retired air force officer; b. Coronado, Calif., Nov. 8, 1950; d. Edouard V. M. Jr. and Betty Ross (Allen) I.; m. Gregory F. Howell, Apr. 8, 1971 (div. 1974); 1 child, Roxanne Elizabeth Howell-Izac. BA in English, Calif. State U., Fullerton, 1977; MS in Pub. Adminstrn., Troy State U., 1982; student, Squadron Officer Sch., 1983, 84, Air Command & Staff Coll., 1987, Orange Coast Coll., 1996—, Newport Ballet Acad., DeFore Studio, 1996—. Commd. 2d lt. USAF, 1979, advanced through grades to maj., 1991; asst. chief ctrl. base adminstrn. USAF, Aviano Air Base, Italy, 1979-80, asst. exec. officer, group commdr., 1980, exec./adminstrv. support officer for dep. commdr. for ops., 1980-82; chief base adminstrn. divsn. Tempelhof Ctrl. Airport USAF, West Berlin, Germany, 1982-85; ops. officer Milw. mil. entrance processing sta. USAF, 1988-91; wing exec. officer 319th bombardment wing USAF, Grand Forks, N.D., 1991, chief wing exercises 319 air refueling wing, dep. wing insp., 1991-92; asst. prof. aerospace studies AFROTC detachment 845 Tex. Christian U., Ft. Worth, 1985-88. Treas., bd. dirs. North Valley Arts Assn., Grand Forks, 1992-94; dancer Bowman Sch. of Dance, 1994-95. Mem. Air Force Assn. (life), Zeta Tau Alpha (life). Address: 1201 W Curie Ave Santa Ana CA 92707-3838

IZZO, HERBERT JOHN, language and linguistics educator, researcher; b. Saginaw, Mich., July 17, 1928; s. Joseph Anthony and Eleanor Bertha (Karau) I.; m. Barbara Suzanne McLaughlin, Sept. 22, 1958 (div); children: Victoria Sue, Alexander John, Sylvia Rachel, Daniel Stanley; m. Olga Frances Koutna, Dec. 30, 1989. BA in Spanish, U. Mich., 1950, MA in Spanish and Italian, 1951, BS in Chemistry, 1953, PhD in Linguistics, 1965. Asst. prof. fgn. langs. Mansfield (Pa.) State Coll., 1957; chargé de cours Huê (Vietnam) U., 1958-59; instr. Spanish U. Ariz., Tucson, 1960-61; instr. Spanish and linguistics Stanford (Calif.) U., 1961-64; asst. prof. Spanish San Jose (Calif.) State U., 1964-68; from assoc. to prof. linguistics U. Calgary, Alberta, Can., 1968—, prof. emeritus, 1988—; vis. prof. Romance linguistics U. Mich., Ann Arbor, 1977-78, 93-94; vis. prof. linguistics U. Bucharest, Romania, 1975-76; vis. prof. Italian, Stanford U., 1990-91; mem. adv. bd. Quaderni d'Italianistica, Can., 1979—. Author: Tuscan and Etruscan, 1972; editor: The Sixth LACUS Forum, 1980, Italic and Romance, 1985; editor for linguistics Can. Jour. of Italian Studies, 1988—. Bd. dirs. Fathers Alberta, Calgary, 1986-87. Recipient grad. fellowship U. N.Mex., 1953, Award for Advanced Study, Am. Coun. Learned Socs., 1963, Fulbright-Hays award U.S. Dept. State, 1966, 75. Mem. Am. Assn. Italian Studies, Linguistic Assn. Can. of U.S. (conf. organizer 1978), N.Am. Assn. for History of Lang. Scis. (v.p. 1977-80), Am. Assn. Tchrs. of Italian (life), Linguistic Soc. Am. (life), Am. Assn. Tchrs. of Spanish and Portuguese (life), Can. Soc. Italian Studies (nominating com. 1977-78, adv. bd. 1974-80), Phi Beta Kappa. Libertarian. Office: Univ Calgary Dept Linguistics, University Dr, Calgary, AB Canada T2N 1N4 also: 101 Lumbard St Hillsdale MI 49242-1412

IZZO, MARY ALICE, real estate broker; b. Mesa, Ariz., Aug. 5, 1953; d. Edward Lee and Evangeline Lauda (Gorraiz) Meeker; m. Michael David Izzo, Dec. 26, 1971; children: Michael Wade, Clinton Jarred, Antoinette Marie. Student, Pioneer Coll., 1977, Yavapai Coll., 1984-93. Cert. realtor, Ariz. Sales agt. Babbit Bros., Flagstaff, Ariz., 1970-76; owner Cottonwood (Ariz.) Tees, 1978-84; realtor Weston Realty, Cottonwood, 1985-86, Coldwell Banker Mabery Real Estate, Cottonwood, 1986-89; sales agent, assoc. broker The Glenarm Land Co., Cottonwood, 1989—; office mgr., sec. Izzo & Sons Contracting, 1985—, Wilhoit Water Co., 1991-93; sales assoc. Walmart, 1995-96, asst. regional commr., 1996—; office mgr., sec. Gonzales & Sons Electric, 1996—. Auhtor: Current Customer Cook Book, 1984. Bd. dirs. cub scouts Boy Scouts Am., 1984, 87; bd. dirs. AYSO Soccer, Verde Valley, Ariz., 1984-87, 92—, coach tournament all girls' traveling team, 1993-95, also pub. dir., asst. regional commn., 1996—; leader youth group, Cottonwood. Democrat. Roman Catholic. Home: 649 E Elm St Cottonwood AZ 86326-2002 Office: The Glenarm Land Co 408 S Main St Cottonwood AZ 86326-3903

JABARA, MICHAEL DEAN, investment banker; b. Sioux Falls, S.D., Oct. 26, 1952; s. James M. and Jean Marie (Swiden) J.; m. Gundula Beate Dietz, Aug. 26, 1984; children: James Michael, Jenna Mariel. Student, Mich. Tech. U., 1970-72; BSBA, U. Calif., Berkeley, 1974; MBA, Pepperdine U., 1979. Mgr. original Sprint project team So. Pacific Communications Corp., 1976-78; network product mgr. ROLM Corp., 1978-81; cons. McGraw Hill Co., Hamburg (Fed. Republic of Germany) and London, 1982-83; founder, chief exec. officer Friend Techs. Inc. (merger VoiceCom Systems, Inc.), San Francisco, 1984-88; pres. VoiceCom Ventures, San Francisco, 1988-93; mng. dir. Telecom, EMS Group Ltd., London, 1993-95; owner Jabara & Co., Glenbrook, Nev., 1993—; chmn. bd., COO Bingo Card Minder Corp., Stateline, Nev., 1996. Patentee in field. Active Tahoe-Douglas C. of C.; chmn. Tahoe Citizens Com., 1995—. Mem. Infor. Industry Assn. (conf. program chair 1995), Assn. for Corp. Growth, Caribbean Cable TV Assn., Satellite Broadcasters & Comms. Assn., Pepperdine Bus. Alumni, U. Calif. Berkeley Bus. Alumni, Mich. Tech Alumni Assn., The Classic Cars of the Candy Store, Reno Jaguar Club, Tahoe-Douglas Rotary, Lighting W Ranch Golf Club. Office: Jabara & Co PO Box 568 Glenbrook NV 89413-0568

JABLECKI, CHARLES K., clinical neurologist; b. Providence, Dec. 17, 1943; m. Elizabeth; 1 child, Michael. BA magna cum laude, Harvard U., 1965, MD cum laude, 1969. Bd. cert. Am. Bd. Psychiatry and Neurology, Am. Bd. Electrodiagnostic Medicine. Intern internal medicine Presbyn. St. Luke's Hosp., Chgo., 1969-70; resident clin. neurology Mayo Grad. Sch., Mayo Clinic, Rochester, Minn., 1972-76; instr. in neurology Mayo Med. Sch., U. Minn., Rochester, 1975-76; asst. clin. prof. neurosciences U. Calif., San Diego, 1976-82, assoc. clin. prof. neurosciences, 1982-96, clin. prof. neurosci., 1997—; co-dir. Clin. Neurophysiology Lab. U. Calif. Med. Ctr., San Diego, 1978-82, dir. Neurology Outpatient Clinics, 1979-82; staff assoc. Lab. of Neurochemistry, NIMH, Bethesda, Md., 1970-72; neurology cons. U. Hosp., San Diego, 1976—, Sharp Hosp., San Diego, 1982—, Mercy Hosp., San Diego, 1982—; cons. Muscular Dystrophy Assn., San Diego, 1978—; cons. electromyographer EMG Lab., Children's Hosp., San Diego, 1978—; examiner Am. Assn. Electromyography and Electrodiagnosis, 1979-89, Am. Bd. Psychiatry and Neurology, 1982—, Am. Bd. Electrodiagnostic Medicine, 1990—; qualified med. evaluator State of Calif., 1992—. Contbr. chpts. to books and articles to profl. jours. Asst. surgeon USPHS, 1970-72. Scholar Harvard Coll., 1961-65, Charles H. Smith scholar Harvard Med. Sch., 1965-69. Fellow Am. Acad. Neurology, Am. Assn. Electrodiagnostic Medicine (pres. 1995-96, nomenclature com. 1975-76, chair membership com. 1976-80, equipment and material com. 1978-80, bd. dirs. 1979-82, profl. standards com., others), Am. Acad. Disability Evaluating Physicians; mem. AMA, San Diego Neurol. Assn. (sec.-treas. 1992-95, pres. 1995—). Office: 550 Washington St Ste 221 San Diego CA 92103-2227

JACISIN, JOHN JAMES, psychiatrist; b. Ironwood, Mich., June 30, 1942; s. Frank Anthony and Amelia Lucy J.; m. Hoa Thi Hyunh, Feb. 27, 1971; children: Ann, Tina, Kim. Student Mich. Tech. U., 1960-61; BS in

Psychology, U. Mich., 1964, MD, 1968. Intern, Mt. Carmel Hosp., Columbus, Ohio, 1968-69; resident in psychiatry U., Mich., Ann Arbor, 1971-74; dir. inpatient psychiatry Riverwood Cmty. Mental Health Ctr., St. Joseph, Mich., 1974-75; dir. psychiat. inpatient svcs. Henry Ford Hosp., Detroit, 1975-81, acting dept. chmn., 1976-77, dir. psychiat. residency tng. program., 1977-87, dept. vice chmn., 1984-87, dir. psychiat. services Fairlane Ctr., 1981-84; clin. instr. U. Mich. Med. Sch., 1977-87; dir. inpatient svc., Modesto Psychiat. Ctr., Calif., 1987-91, assoc. med. dir., 1991-93; Psychiat. Med. Group, Modesto, 1987—; mem. adj. faculty U. Pacific, 1991-94. Served to capt. USAF, 1969-71. Decorated Bronze star. Fellow Am. Psychiat. Assn.; mem. AMA, Am. Bd. Psychiatry and Neurology (cert. in psychitry 1977, geriat. psychiatry 1996), Am. Coll. Clin. Psychiatrists, Anxiety Disorder Assn. Am., Ctrl. Calif. Psychiat. Soc. (pres. Yosemite chpt. 1995-96), Obsessive Compulsive Disorder Found. Office: Psychiat Med Group 3425 Coffee Rd Ste 2A Modesto CA 95355-1582

JACKLIN, DOYLE, food products executive. With Vaughan Jacklin Corp., Coeur d'Alene, Idaho, 1965-83; v.p. Jacklin Seed Co., Post Falls, Idaho, 1983—. With USN, 1962-65. Office: Jacklin Seed Co 5300 W Riverbend Rd Post Falls ID 83854-9456*

JACKLIN, DUANE, agricultural products executive; b. 1945. With Vaughan Jackin Corp., Coeur d'Alene, Idaho, 1968-83; pres., treas. Jacklin Seed Co., Post Falls, Idaho, 1983—. With USN, 1966-68. Office: Jacklin Seed Co 5300 W Riverbend Rd Post Falls ID 83854-9456*

JACKMAN, JAY M., psychiatrist; b. Bklyn., June 4, 1939; s. James Jeremiah and Dora (Emmer) J.; m. Judith Gail Meisels, Nov. 23, 1963 (div. Sept. 1987); children: Tenaya, Rashi, Jason Scott; m. Myra Hoffenberg Strober, Oct. 21, 1990. BA, Columbia U., 1960; MD, Harvard U., 1964; postgrad., U. Calif., San Francisco, 1966—. Diplomate Am. Bd. Psychiatry and Neurology. Rotating intern San Francisco County Gen. Hosp., 1965; psychiat. resident Stanford U., 1969; asst. dir. community psychiatry Mt. Zion Hosp., San Francisco, 1969-70; dir. drug treatment programs Westside Community Mental Health Ctr., San Francisco, 1970-74; pvt. practice San Francisco, 1969-74; dir. Lanakila Clinic Kalihi-Palama Community Mental Health Ctr., Honolulu, 1974-75; pvt. practice specializing in forensic psychiatry, Honolulu, 1975-90, Stanford, Calif., 1990—; cons. Salvation Army Addiction Treatment Facility, Honolulu, 1974-81; chmn. Task Force on Drugs, Nat. Coun. Community Mental Health Ctrs., 1971-75; chmn. no. sect. Calif. Assn. Methodone Programs, 1973-74. Contbr. articles on substance abuse to profl. jours. Trustee Foothill-DeAnza C.C. Bd., 1993—; active Mayor's Adv. Com. on Drug Abuse, Honolulu, 1975-77. Mem. Am. Psychiat. Assn. (commn. on drugs 1973-77), Am. Acad. Psychiatry and Law, Am. Coll. Forensic Psychiatrists, No. Calif. Psychiat. Soc., Santa Clara County Bar Assn. (vol., lay mem. fee arbitration com. 1992), Calif. Attys. for Criminal Justice. Democrat. Jewish.

JACKS, ROGER LARRY, secondary education educator; b. Oskaloosa, Iowa, May 24, 1942; s. Roger Melvin and Sue May (Howard) J.; m. Joan R. Cates, June 20, 1992. BA in Social Studies, U. No. Colo., 1966; MA in Sociology, Pepperdine U., 1977; MS in Ednl. Leadership, Nova U., 1996. Cert. social studies secondary edn., Nev.; cert. adminstrn. secondary edn., Nev. Commd. 2d lt. USAF, 1966, advanced through grades to col., 1986; B-52 aircrew USAF, Loring AFB, Maine, 1968-72; SR-71 aircrew USAF, Beale AFB, Calif., 1972-77; air staff USAF, Norton AFB, Calif., 1977-81; flight test staff USAF, Edwards AFB, Calif., 1981-85; Base comdr. USAF, Arnold AFB, Tenn., 1985-88, Beale AFB, 1988-90; aerospace prof. USAF-U. Ariz., 1990-92; N.W. Region comdr. USAF, Peterson AFB, Colo., 1992-93; tchr. student activities Rancho H.S., Las Vegas, Nev., 1993-95; magnet sch. coord. Rancho H.S., Las Vegas, 1995—. Contbr. articles to profl. jours. Mem. mil. com. Marysville (Calif.) C. of C., 1988-90; mem. exec. coun. Boy Scouts Am., Sutter Butte, Marysville, 1988-90; mem. Youth in Aviation, Las Vegas, 1995—. Mem. NEA, ASCD, Air Force Assn. (Thunderbird chpt., medal of merit 1996), Nellis Officers Club, Ret. Officers Assn. Office: Rancho High Sch 1900 E Owens Ave North Las Vegas NV 89030-7045

JACKSON, ALLEN KEITH, museum administrator; b. Rocky Ford, Colo., July 22, 1932; s. Monford L. and Leliah Jean (Hipp) J.; m. Barbara May Hollard, June 13, 1954; children: Cary Vincent, Deborah Kay and Edward Keith (twins), Fredrick James. B.A., U. Denver, 1954; postgrad., Cambridge (Eng.) U., 1955; Th.M. (Elizabeth Iliff Warren fellow), Iliff Sch. Theology, 1958; Ph.D., Emory U., 1960. Meth. student minister Erie, Colo., 1955-58; ordained elder Meth. Ch., 1958; instr. sociology Emory U., 1958-60; chaplain, asst. prof. religion and sociology Morningside Coll., Sioux City, Iowa, 1960-62; dean coll. Morningside Coll., 1962-67; pres. Huntingdon Coll., Montgomery, Ala., 1968-93; dir. Idaho Mus. Natural History, Idaho State U., Pocatello, 1993—. Contbr. articles to profl. jours. Past pres. Montgomery Area United Appeal. Fulbright scholar Cambridge U., 1955; honor fellow Emory U., 1960. Mem. Ala. Assn. Ind. Colls. and Univs. (pres. 1969-71), Ala. Council Advancement Pvt. Colls. (pres. 1975-81), Phi Beta Kappa, Omicron Delta Kappa, Beta Theta Pi. Club: Rotarian. Home: 6353 Old Ranch Rd Pocatello ID 83204-3841 Office: Mus Natural History Idaho State U Pocatello ID 83204 *A worthy aim it seems to me, is to seek the Truth and to share the truths you find.*

JACKSON, BEVERLEY JOY JACOBSON, columnist, lecturer; b. L.A., Nov. 20, 1928; d. Phillip and Dorothy Jacobson; student U. So. Calif., UCLA; m. Robert David Jackson (div. Aug. 1964); 1 child, Tracey Dee. Daily columnist Santa Barbara (Calif.) News Press, 1968-92, Santa Barbara Independent, 1992-94; nat. lectr. Santa Barbara History, History of China Recreated, Chinese Footbinding, Shoes for Bound Feet, China Today; free lance writer, fgn. corr. Bd. dirs. Santa Barbara br. Am. Cancer Soc., 1963—; mem. art mus. coun. L.A. Mus. Art, 1959—, mem. costume coun., 1983—; docent L.A. Mus. Art, 1962-64; mem. exec. bd. Channel City Club (formerly Channel City Women's Forum), 1969—; mem. adv. bd. Santa Barbara Mus. Natural History, Coun. of Christmas Cheer, Women's Shelter Bldg., Direct Relief Internat., Nat. Coun. Drug and Alcohol Abuse, Am. Oceans Campaign; mem adv. bd. Hospice of Santa Barbara, 1981—, Stop AIDS Coun., Arthritis Found.; bd. dirs. So. Calif. Com. for Shakespear's Globe Theatre; chmn. Santa Barbara Com. for Visit Queen Elizabeth II, 1982—; founder costume guild Santa Barbara Hist. Soc.; curator Chinese collections Santa Barbara Hist. Mus.; adv. bd. Santa Barbara Choral Soc.; hon. bd. Santa Barbara Salvation Army, Ensemble Theatre Santa Barbara; adv. bd. Storyteller Sch. Homeless Children. Author: Dolls and Doll Houses of Spain, 1970, (with others) I'm Just Wild About Harry, 1979, Spendid Slippers: The History of Chinese Footbinding and Lotus Shoes, 1997. Home: PO Box 5118 Santa Barbara CA 93150-5118

JACKSON, BO (VINCENT EDWARD JACKSON), professional baseball, former football player; b. Bessemer, Ala., Nov. 30, 1962; m. Linda Jackson. PhD in Counseling Psychology, Auburn U., 1995. Baseball player Kansas City Royals, 1986-91; football player L.A. Raiders, 1987-90; baseball player Chicago White Sox, 1991-93, California Angels, 1994-95. Recipient Heisman Trophy, 1985, All-Star Game MVP, 1989; mem. NFL Pro Bowl Team, 1990; mem. A.L. All-StarTeam, 1989, named Comeback Player of Yr., Sporting News, 1993. Address: care Becky Daniel 1765 Old Shell Rd Mobile AL 36604-1335

JACKSON, CYNTHIA L., lawyer; b. Houston, May 6, 1954. BA, Stanford U., 1976; JD, U. Tex., 1979. Bar: Tex. 1979, Calif. 1980. Mem. Heller, Ehrman, White & McAuliffe, Palo Alto, Calif. Mem. ABA. Office: Heller Ehrman White & McAuliffe 525 University Ave Ste 1100 Palo Alto CA 94301-1908

JACKSON, DAVID ROBERT, school system administrator; b. Long Beach, Calif., Jan. 15, 1945; s. Harlan Leroy and Helen Louise (Worthen) J.; m. Stacey Ann Bryan, Nov. 13, 1971; children: David, Daniel, Chad, Loren, Darcy. Student, Fullerton Coll., 1963-64, Brigham Young U., 1965-67, Santa Ana Coll., 1977, Orange Coast Coll., 1977-78. Mgr. trainee Carl Karcher Enterprizes, Fullerton, Calif., 1964; asst. mgr. Household Fin. Co., Santa Ana., Calif., 1964-65; pres. Areo Wash Co., Santa Ana., Calif., 1970-79; mgr. Chateau Apres Lodge, Park City, Utah, 1965-69; pres. Areo Wash Co., Santa Ana., Calif., 1970-79; exec. dir. Fairmont Schs. Inc., Anaheim, Calif., 1979—. Former leader Boy Scouts Am.; bishop LDS Ch., Corona, 1990-96; chmn. Orange County 2000, Calif., 1991-93, also bd. dirs. Mem. Nat. Ind. Pvt. Sch. Assn. (bd. dirs. 1981—, founding mem., pres. 1993—), Calif. Assn. Nationally Recognized Schs. (founder, pres. 1992-93), Orange County Pvt. Sch. Assn. (pres. 1990-93, founder). Republican. Office: Fairmont Sch 1557 W Mable St Anaheim CA 92802-1021

JACKSON, DAWNA DARLENE, mental health counselor, educator; b. Livingston, Mont., July 14, 1946; d. Donald William and Eva Mae (Boyer) Nelson; m. Gary F. Jackson, Aug. 9, 1969. BA, Idaho State U., 1969, M of Counseling, 1982. Lic. profl. counselor, Idaho; cert. secondary sch. tchr., Idaho. Sch. tchr. phys. edn. Sch. Dist. # 55, Blackfoot, Idaho, 1968-70; juvenile probation officer Ada County Juvenile Ctr., Boise, Idaho, 1971-77, 81-82; clinic dir. Weight Loss Clinic of Am., Boise, 1978-81; facility dir. Idaho Youth Ranch, Boise, 1983-85; psychotherapist, pvt. practice Family Comm. Counseling Boise, 1983—; mem. adj. faculty Albertson Coll. of Idaho, Caldwell, 1988-95; mental health cons. Malheur County Head Start Program, Ont., Oreg., 1992—; cons. Migrant Indian Coalition, Ont. and Hermaston, Oreg., 1992-93; active Idaho Lic. Profl. Counselors Licensing Bd., 1994—, pres., 1995—. Bd. dirs. Parents and Youth Against Drug Abuse, Boise, 1986-88; pres., bd. dirs. Idaho Arthritis Found., Boise, 1987-89; active Shepherd of the Valley Luth. Ch., Boise. Mem. ACA, Idaho Counselors Assn. (Disting. Svc. award 1989), Idaho Mental Health Counselors Assn. (Counselor of Yr. 1988-89), Internat. Assn. Marriage & Family Counselors. Home: 3900 Genesee Dr Boise ID 83709-4523 Office: Family Comm Counseling 1084 N Cole Rd Boise ID 83704-8642

JACKSON, DILLON EDWARD, lawyer; b. Washington, Apr. 18, 1945; s. Paul David and Virginia (Dillon) J.; children: David I., Anne E.; m. Misha Halvarsson, Aug. 19, 1989. BA, Middlebury (Vt.) Coll., 1967; JD, U. Wash., 1970. Bar: Wash. 1970, U.S. Dist. Ct. (we. and ea. dists.) Wash. 1970, U.S. Ct. Appeals (9th cir.) 1970, U.S. Dist. Ct. Ariz. 1991. Assoc. Kleist & Helmick, Seattle, 1971-73, Powell Livengood & Silvernale, Kirkland, Wash., 1973-75; ptnr. Keller Jacobsen Jackson & Snodgrass, Bellevue, Wash., 1975-85, Hatch & Leslie, Seattle, 1985-91, Foster Pepper & Shefelman, Seattle, 1991—; chairperson creditor rights and bankruptcy dept. Am. Bankruptcy Bd. Cert.; mem. adv. bd. Applied Environ. Tech., Seattle, 1992—; bd. mem. Consumer Credit Counseling, Seattle, 1975-79; chmn. publs. com. Am. Bankruptcy Inst. Co-author: Commercial Law Desk Book, 1995; contbg. author: Advance Chapter 11 Bankruptcy Practice, 1989-95. Pres. Dox Coop., Seattle, 1989-91. Fellow Am. Coll. Bankruptcy, 1990. Mem. ABA, Wash. State Trial Lawyers Assn., Wash. State Bar Assn. (creditor-debtitor sect., chairperson 1984-88), Continuing Legal Edn. Bd. (chairperson 1991-92). Office: Foster Pepper & Shefelman 1111 3rd Ave Ste 3400 Seattle WA 98101-3299

JACKSON, EDWARD MILTON, toxicologist, researcher, business executive; b. Wheeling, W.Va., June 4, 1938; s. Ralph Edward and Anna (Timcho) J.; m. Rosemarie Cook, Aug. 28, 1976. BA in Philosophy, Cath. U. Am., 1961, MS in Biology, 1964, PhD in Cell Physiology and Biochemistry, 1973. Rsch. and teaching asst. Cath. U. Am., Washington, 1970-73; assoc. prof. biology No. Va. C.C., Annapolis, 1974-77; dir. rsch. svcs. dept. Noxell Corp., Hunt Valley, Md., 1977-90; dir. rsch. svcs. and quality assurance Andrew Jergens Co., Cin., 1990-92; founder, CEO, pres. Jackson Rsch. Assocs., Inc., Sumner, Wash., 1992—; adj. assoc. prof. pharms. U. Md., Balt., 1986-94; clin. asst. prof. dermatology U. Cin., 1992-95; affiliate prof. ophthalmology U. Oreg. Health Scis., Portland, 1995—. Editor: Irritant Contact Dermatitis, 1990; founder, editor Jour. Cutaneous and Ocular Toxicology, 1982—. Chmn. Harford Hospice Found., Bel Air, Md., 1988-90. Roman Catholic. Office: Jackson Rsch Assocs Inc 20203 121st Street Ct E Sumner WA 98390-7442

JACKSON, ELIZABETH RIDDLE, writer, translator, educator; b. Boston, May 13, 1926; m. Matthew Casey and Katharine (Kerr) Riddle; m. Gabriel Jackson, Dec. 1949 (div. Sept. 1969); children: Katharine, Rachel. BA, Reed Coll., 1947; MA, Wellesley Coll., 1959; Doctorat de l'Université, Sorbonne U., Paris, 1963. Statistician Nat. Bur. Econ. Rsch., N.Y.C., 1947-48; tchr. math. Putney (Vt.) Sch., 1948-49; tutor French Goddard Coll., Plainsfield, Vt., 1953-55; lectr. in French Knox Coll., Galesburg, Ill., 1963-65; assoc. humanities U. Calif. San Diego, La Jolla, 1965-66; prof. French San Diego State U., 1969-87; cons. Toronto (Can.) U. Press, PMLA; mem. rev. panel NEH, Washington, 1977; mem. screening com. Fulbright Study Abroad, 1981-92. Author: L'Evolution de la Mémoire Involontaire dans l'oeuvre de Marcel Proust, 1966, Worlds Apart: Structural Parallels in the Poetry of Paul Valéry, Saint-John Perse, Benjamin Péret and René Charr, 1976, Secrets Observateurs...: la Poéesie d'André Chénier, 1993; translator: A Marvelous World: Poems by Benjamin Péret, 1985, Meidosems (by Henry Michaux), 1993. Grantee French Govt., 1960-61, Fulbright Found., 1960-61, Ctr. Nat. Rsch. Sci., France, 1965. Mem. Amnesty Internat., So. Oreg. Learning in Retirement (curriculum com.). Home: 1122 Tolman Creek Rd Ashland OR 97520

JACKSON, GARY LYNN, osteopath, internist, pulmonologist; b. Sept. 9, 1949; m. Vickie S. Williams, 1982; children: Heather L., Elizabeth M. BA, U. Kans., 1971; BS, Pittsburg State U., 1973; DO, U. Health Scis. Coll. Osteo., Kansas City, Mo., 1978. Diplomate Nat. Bd. Osteo. Med. Examiners, Am. Bd. Internal Medicine. Intern U. Hosp.-Coll. Osteo. Medicine, Kansas City, Mo., 1978-79; pvt. practice Blue Valley Med. Group Corp. Offices, Overland Pk., Kans., 1979-82; gen. med. officer gen. med. clinic Fitzsimons Army Med. Ctr., Aurora, Colo., 1982-83; resident in internal medicine Fitzsimons Army Med. Ctr., 1983-86, fellow in pulmonary disease svc., 1986-88; dir. med. intensive care unit, chief pulmonary disease svc. William Beaumont Army Med. Ctr., El Paso, Tex., 1989-90; pvt. practice Alamogordo, N.M., 1990—; vice chief profl. staff Lincoln County Med. Ctr., Ruidoso, N.M., 1992, 93, pulmonary cons. to med. staff dir. of cardiopulmonary svcs., 1990—; dir. cardio-pulmonary svcs. Gerald Champion Meml. Hosp., Alamogordo, 1993—; pulmonary cons. Eastern N.M. Med. Ctr., Roswell, 1990-92; presenter in field. Contbr. articles to profl. jours. Maj. U.S. Army, 1982-90, res., 1990—. Fellow Am. Coll. Chest Physicians (assoc.); mem. ACP, Am. Osteo. Assn. (alt. ho. dels. 1988, del. 1989), Assn. Mil. Osteo. Physicians and Surgeons (program chmn. continuing med. edn. 1989, v.p. 1989-90), N.M. Soc. Med. Assts. (physician cons. 1994—), Beta Beta Beta, Alpha Chi Sigma, Theta Chi, Rho Sigma Chi. Home: PO Drawer 3535 HS 208 Mountain Shadow Rd Ruidoso NM 88345 Office: 923 9th St Ste A Alamogordo NM 88310-6467

JACKSON, HARRY ANDREW, artist; b. Chgo., Apr. 18, 1924; s. Harry and Ellen Grace J.; m. Theodora Rehard DuBois, 1946 (div.); m. Grace Hartigan, 1948 (div.); m. Claire Rodgers, 1950 (div.); m. Joan Hunt, 1951 (div.); m. Sarah Mason, Sept. 10, 1962 (div.); children: Matthew, Molly; m. Tina Lear, Aug. 11, 1973 (div.); children: Jesse, Luke, Chloe. Diploma, H.S., 1945; LLD (hon.), U. Wyo., 1986. Founder fine art foundry Camaiore, Italy, 1964—, Wyo. Foundry Studios di Harry Jackson, Italy, 1965—; CEO Harry Jackson Studios (formerly Wyo. Foundry Studios, Inc.), Cody, Wyo., 1971—; founder Western Arts Found., 1974—; foundry ptnr. Jackson-Mariani Fine Art Foundry, Camaiore, Italy, 1985—; founder Harry Jackson Art Mus., Cody, Wyo., 1994. Author: Lost Wax Bronze Casting, 1972; one man exhbns. include Ninth St. Show, N.Y.C., 1951, Tibor de Nagy Gallery, N.Y.C., 1952, 53, Martha Jackson Gallery, N.Y.C., 1956, M. Knoedler & Co., N.Y.C., 1960, Amon Carter Mus., Fort Worth, 1961, 68, Kennedy Galleries, N.Y.C., 1964, 68, Smithsonian Instn., Washington, 1964, Whitney Gallery Western Art, Cody, 1964, 81, Mont. Hist. Soc., 1964, NAD, 1965, 68, Nat. Cowboy Hall of Fame, Oklahoma City, 1966, XVII Mostra Internazionale d'Arte, Premio del Fiorino, Florence, Italy, 1966, Pennational Artists Ann., Pa., 1967, Mostra de Arte Moderna, Convento di S. Lazzaro, Camaiore, 1968, Am. Artists Profl. League, N.Y., 1968, Cowboy Artists Am., 1971-76, S.W. Mus., L.A., 1979, Smith Gallery, N.Y.C., 1981, 85; major retrospective exhbns. include Buffalo Bill Hist. Ctr., 1981, Palm Springs Desert Mus., 1981, Mpls. Inst. Art, 1982, Camaiore, Italy, 1985, Met. Mus. Art, N.Y.C., 1987; represented in permanent collections Met. Mus. Art, NAD, Nat. Mus. Am. Art, Nat. Portrait Gallery, Washington, Her Majesty Queen Elizabeth II, Sandringam Castle, Eng., Am. Mus. of Gt. Britain, Bath, Eng., U.S. State Dept., Washington, Lyndon Baines Johnson Meml. Libr., Austin, Tex., Ronald Reagan Meml. Libr., Santa Barbara, Calif., Whitney Gallery Western Art, Plains Indian Mus., Buffalo Bill Hist. Ctr., Cody, Wyo., Wadsworth Atheneum, Hartford, Conn., Alberta Glenbow Mus., Calgary, Can., Univ. So. Calif., Stanford (Calif.) Univ., Love Libr. Univ. Nebr., Lincoln, Portsmouth (R.I.) Abbey, S.W. Mus., Gene Autrey Mus., L.A., Nat. Cowboy Hall of Fame, Oklahoma City, Gilcrease Mus., Tulsa, Fort Pitts Mus., Pitts., Amon Carter Mus., Pro Rodeo Cowboy Hall of Fame, Colorado Springs, Colo., Eiteljorg Mus., Indpls., Shelburne (Vt.) Mus., Columbus (Ga.) Mus. Arts & Scis., Oreg. Hist. Soc., Portland, Salt Lake City Art Ctr., Norfolk (Nebr.) Arts Ctr., Aspen (Colo.) Art Mus., Woolaroc Mus., Bartlesville, Okla., U. Wyo. Art Mus., Laramie, Mont. Hist. Soc., Helena, Norton Mus., Shreveport, La., Columbia U., N.Y.C., Trout Gallery Dickinson Coll., Carlisle, Pa., Ctrl. Wyo. Coll., Riverton, N.W. C.C., Powell, Wyo., Baylor Sch., Chattanooga, Orme Sch., Mayer, Ariz., others; commd. works include (sculpture) William R. Coe Commn., 1959, 60, Fort Pitt Mus., 1964, 73, Plains Indian Mus., Cody, Wyo., Ctrl. Wyo. Coll., Riverton, 1978, 81, Piazza della Chiesa, Capezzano, Pianore, Italy, 1985, Great Western Savs. & Loan, Santa Barbara, Calif., 1985, John Wayne monumental sculpture Beverly Hills, Calif, 1981, 84, (portrait busts) Met. Mus. Trustees, C. Douglas Dillon, 1985, 87, (portrait) "John Wayne" TIME cover, Aug. 8, 1969 (Nat. Best Cover Art award Am. Inst. Graphic Arts 1969), (paintings) Whitney Gallery Western Art, Cody, 1960, 66, (mural) R.K. Mellon. Served with USMC, 1942-45. Decorated Purple Heart with gold star; recipient Gold medal NAD, 1968; grantee Fulbright, 1954, Italian Govt., 1956, 57. Fellow NAD (academician), RISD, Nat. Acad. Western Art, Nat. Sculpture Soc., Am. Artists League; mem. Bohemian Club (San Francisco). Office: PO Box 2836 Cody WY 82414-2836 also: Via Montegiori, 55040 Camaiore Lucca, Italy

JACKSON, ISAIAH, conductor; b. Richmond, Va., Jan. 22, 1945; s. Isaiah Allen and Alma Alverta (Norris) J.; m. Helen Tuntland, Aug. 6, 1977; children: Benjamin, Katharine, Caroline. BA cum laude, Harvard U., 1966; MA, Stanford U., 1967; MS, Juilliard Sch. Music, 1969, DMA, 1973. Founder, condr. Juilliard String Ensemble, N.Y.C., 1970-71; asst. condr. Am. Symphony Orch., N.Y.C., 1970-71, Balt. Symphony Orch., 1971-73; assoc. condr. Rochester (N.Y.) Philharmonic Orch., 1973-87; music dir. Dayton (Ohio) Philharm. Orch., 1987-95, 1987-95; prin. condr. Royal Ballet, Covent Garden, London, 1986, music dir., 1987-90; prin. guest condr. Queensland (Australia) Symphony Orch., 1993—; music dir. Youngstown (Ohio) Symphony, 1996—; guest condr. N.Y. Philharm. Orch., 1978, Boston Pops Orch., 1983, 90-94, Detroit Symphony Orch., 1983, 85, San Francisco Symphony, 1984, Toronto Symphony, 1984, 90, Orch. de la Suisse Romande, 1985, 88, BBC Concert Orch., 1987, Berlin Symp hony, 1989-95, Dallas Symphony, 1993, Royal Liverpool Philharm., 1995, Houston Symphony, 1995; numerous recordings for Koch, Australian Broadcasting Corp. Recipient First Gov.'s award for arts in Va., Commonwealth Va., 1979, Signet Soc. medal for the arts Harvard U., 1991. Office: care United Arts 3906 Sunbeam Dr Los Angeles CA 90065-3551

JACKSON, JANE W., interior designer; b. Asheville, N.C., Aug. 5, 1944; d. James and Willie Mae (Stoner) Harris; m. Bruce G. Jackson; children: Yvette, Scott. Student, Boston U., 1964; BA, Leslie Coll., 1967; postgrad., Artisan Sch. Interior Design, 1980-82. Tchr. Montessori, Brookline, Mass., 1969-72; interior designer, owner Nettle Creek Shop, Honolulu, 1980-88; owner Wellesley Interiors, Honolulu, 1988—. Active Mayor's Com. for Small Bus., Honolulu, 1984. Mem. Honolulu Club. Democrat. Office: Wellesley Interiors PO Box 1622 Kaneohe HI 96744

JACKSON, JESS S., vintner. JD, U. Calif. Practice San Francisco; now pres. Kendall-Jackson Winery Ltd., Santa Rosa, Calif., chmn. bd. dirs. Mem. Calif. Bar Assn. Office: Kendall-Jackson Winery Ltd 421 Aviation Blvd Santa Rosa CA 95403-1069

JACKSON, JEWEL, retired state youth authority executive; b. Shreveport, La., June 3, 1942; d. Willie Burghardt and Bernice Jewel (Mayberry) Norton; children: Steven, June Kelly, Michael, Anthony. With Calif. Youth Authority, 1965-91, group supr., San Andreas and Santa Rosa, 1965-67, youth counselor, Ventura, 1967-78, sr. youth counselor, Stockton, 1978-81, parole agt., 1986, treatment team supr., program mgr., Whittier and Ione, 1981-91; retired, 1991; pres. Valley Paralegal Svc., Stockton. Avocations: reading, horseback riding, interior design, fabric painting, stamp collecting. Home and Office: 2416 Hall Ave Stockton CA 95205-8422

JACKSON, JOHN JAY, clergyman, denomination administrator; b. Chula Vista, Calif., July 13, 1961; s. E. Marvin and Mildred L. Jackson; m. Pamela Harrison, Aug. 18, 1979; children: Jennifer, Dena, Rachel, Joshua. BA in Religion, Chapman U., 1981; MA in Theology, Fuller Theol. Sem., 1983; MA in Ednl. Adminstrn., U. Calif., Santa Barbara, 1984, PhD in Ednl. Adminstrn., 1986. Youth dir. First Bapt. Ch., Buena Park, Calif., 1979-81; min. of youth Oxnard (Calif.) First Bapt., 1981-83, min. of edn., 1983-84, assoc. pastor, 1984-87, sr. pastor, 1988-92; exec. min. Am.-Bapt. Chs. Pacific S.W., Covina, Calif., 1993-97; pastor Carson Valley Christian Ctr., Minden, Nev., 1997—. Bd. dirs. Am. Bapt. Homes of the West, Oakland, Calif., 1993-97, Atherton Bapt. Homes, 1993-97; chair integration adv. com. Oxnard Sch. Dist., 1990-92. Recipient Disting. Svc. award Oxnard Sch. Dist., 1992. Mem. Christian Mgmt. Assn., Oxnard C. of C. (leadership com. 1991, chair edn. com. 1988-90). Office: Carson Valley Christian Ctr PO Box 892 Minden NV 89423-0892

JACKSON, KEITH DOUGLAS, police captain; b. Vallejo, Calif., Sept. 19, 1950; s. Douglas Eugene and Lavada (Wallace) J.; m. Carolyn Lee Mangione, Dec. 30, 1972; children: Jeffrey Keith, Kevin Joseph. BS, San Jose State U., 1972; MS, Calif. State Poly. U.-Pomona, 1991. Police officer Fremont (Calif.) Police Dept., 1975-80, police detective, 1980-82, police sgt., 1982-83, police lt., 1983-88, police capt., 1988—. Bd. dirs. Am. Heart Assn., Alameda County, Calif., 1991. Capt. USMC, 1969-79. Recipient Leatherneck award USMC, 1969. Mem. Calif. Peace Officers Assn., Command Coll. Alumni Assn., Marine Corps Res. Officers Assn., Rotary (pres. Club of Mission San Jose 1987—). Republican. Office: Fremont Police Dept 2000 Stevenson Blvd Fremont CA 94538-2359

JACKSON, MICHAEL VINCENT, physician, medical educator; b. Buffalo, N.Y., May 10, 1952; s. Vincent S. and Joan Marie (Guest) J.; m. Virginia Marie Hanson; children: Brian, Christopher. BS, Boston Coll., 1974; MD, Tufts U., 1978. Cert. internal medicine, pulmonary medicine and critical care Am. Bd. Internal Medicine. Intern and resident in internal medicine U. Mich., Ann Arbor, 1978-81; fellow in pulmonary and critical care medicine U. Pa., Phila., 1981-83; physician Pulmonary Medicine Assocs., Reno, 1983—; pres., CEO Pulmonary Medicine Assocs., Reno, Nev., 1995—; assoc. clin. prof. U. Nev., Reno, 1983—; co-dir. ICU, Washoe Med. Ctr., Reno, 1992—, chief pulmonary sect., 1995—; dir. ICU No. Nev. Med. Ctr., Sparks, Nev., 1993—, vice chief staff, 1997—. Fellow Am. Coll. Chest Physicians; mem. ACP, AMA, Am. Thoracic Soc., Soc. for Critical Care Medicine, Nev. State Med. Soc., Nev. Soc. for Repiratory Care (med. dir. 1992—), Med. Group Mgmt. Assn., Soc. Physicians in Adminstrn. Office: Pulmonary Medicine Assocs 236 W 6th St Ste 100 Reno NV 89503-4549

JACKSON, PATRICK JOSEPH, insurance executive; b. Minn., Mar. 31, 1942; s. Paul Arthur and Lucille Margaret (Cummings) J.; m. Barbara Ann Simpson, July 19, 1964 (div. Apr. 1980); m. Shirley Ann Wellman, Sept. 12, 1982; children: Patricia Ann, Laura Kathleen, Katherine Lucille, Stacy Lynn. BS, Portland State U., 1968. Bank loan officer First Nat. Bank of Oreg., Portland, 1964-68; credit mgr. Meier & Frank Corp., Portland, 1968-70; agt., mgr. Aetna Life, San Jose, Calif., 1970-75; dist. mgr. Calif. Casualty, San Jose, 1975-78; gen. agt. Great So. Life, San Jose, 1978-82; account agt., agy. mgr. Allstate Ins., San Jose, 1982—; instr. Santa Clara (Calif.) U., 1974-76. Author: (monograph) The Affairs of, 1978; newspaper columnist, 1978-82. Mem. ins. subcom. Calif. State Senate, 1978; officer Los Gatos (Calif.) Police Res., 1970-78, treas., 1974-78; mem. Sch. Site Coun., Saratoga, Calif., 1978-80; mem. City Coun., Discovery Bay, Calif., 1991-95, mayor, 1993-94. Named Man of Yr., Los Gatos Youth Unltd., 1978. Mem. San Jose Life Underwriters (bd. dirs. 1974-76), No. Calif. Tollycraft Assn. (sec. 1995—), Discovery Bay Yacht Club. Republican. Lutheran. Office: Allstate Ins Co 2923 The Villages Pky San Jose CA 95135-1442

JACKSON, PETER VORIOUS, III, retired association executive; b. Butte, Mont., May 18, 1927; s. Peter V. and Besse Portia (McLean) J.; m. Johnneta Pierce, Apr. 29, 1949; children: Ward, Michelle (Mrs. Jerry Vanhour), Johnathan. Wheat and cattle rancher, 1949—; mem. Mont. Ho. of Reps., 1971-72; chief Grass Conservation bur. Mont. Dept. Natural Resources, Helena, 1972-74; supr. Conservation Dist. Madison County, Ennis, Mont., from 1957; past exec. dir. Western Environ. Trade Assn., Helena.; exec. v.p. Soc. for Range Mgmt., Denver, 1983-92; ret., 1992; vol. to develop and implement grazing lands conservation initiative Soil Conservation Soc. USDA, 1992—; mem. Nat. Steering Com. of Grazing Land Conservation Initiative, 1993-97. Author: Montana Rangeland Resources Program, 1970. Mem. Madison County Fair Bd.; pres. Grazing Lands Forum, 1988. Recipient Renner award Soc. Range Mgmt., 1971, Conservation award Mont. Wildlife Fedn., 1966. Mem. Nat. Assn. Conservation Dists. (bd. dirs.), Mont. Assn. Conservation Dists. (exec. v.p. 1974), Soc. for Range Mgmt. (nat. pres., spl. award for outstanding achievement 1992). Lodges: Masons, Elks. Home and Office: PO Box 86 Harrison MT 59735-0086

JACKSON, ROGERNALD DOUGLAS, county tax collector; b. Austin, Tex., July 19, 1952; s. Rogernald Paul and Essie Marie (Morris) J.; m. Tamara Yvonne Hodge, Feb. 14, 1988; children: Rogernald Paul III, Randall James. BS in Polit. Sci., U. San Francisco, 1975; MPA, Golden Gate U., 1979. Profl. baseball players Seattle Rainiers, Seattle, 1974-75; urban employment analyst City of Oakland (Calif.), 1977-79; presdl. mgmt. intern U.S. Dept. Transp., Washington, 1979-81; chief staff to mayor City of Oakland, 1981-86; pres. Sight and Sound Co., Oakland, 1983—; cons. to treas. Alameda County, Oakland, 1987-92, chief of staff to treas., 1992—; chair combined fed. campaign Martin L. King. Jr. Ctr. for Nonviolence, 1983—, pub. rels. cons., Atlanta, 1996. Exec. producer (documentary video) A Step to the Presidency, 1983; assoc. producer (pub. rels. video) Richmond Quit Smoking, 1986. Bd. dirs. East Oakland Youth Devel. Ctr., Oakland, 1982, 83, 84, Selective Svc. Sys., Oakland, 1986-89. Mem. Govt.'s Fin. Officers Assn., Calif. Assn. of County Treas.'s/Tax Collectors, Calif. Mcpl. Bus. Tax Assn., Assn. of Black Pub. Adminstrs., Alpha Phi Alpha Fraternity. Democrat. Baptist. Office: Alameda County Office Treas and Tax Collector 1221 Oak St Oakland CA 94612-4222

JACKSON, SALLY, location casting director; b. Lubbock, Tex., June 2, 1950; d. Francis Marion and Dorothy (Kelly) J. Location casting dir.: (films) Koyannisqatsi, 1975, Red Dawn, 1983, Silverado, 1985, The Milagro Beanfield War, 1986, Young Guns, 1988, Indiana Jones and the Last Crusade, 1988, Young Guns II, 1990, City Slickers, 1990, Twins, 1990, White Sands, 1991, Natural Born Killers, 1993, Wyatt Earp, 1993, Selena, 1996, The Postman, 1997, others, (TV) Dress Gray, 1986, Gambler III, 1987, Desperado II and III, 1987, The Hunters, 1989, Unsolved Mysteries, 1990, To Save a Child, 1991, America's Most Wanted, 1992, Revenge on the Highway (Overdrive), 1992; set prodn. coord. Silverado, 1985. Coun. mem. moving image arts adv. coun. Coll. Santa Fe, 1993-94. Mem. SAG. Home: 286 Calle Loma Norte Santa Fe NM 87501

JACKSON, SAMUEL JOHN, scuba diving industry executive; b. Toronto, Ont., Can., Dec. 30, 1947; s. Walter James and Joyce (Thomson) J.; m. Mary Ann Edwards, Sep. 14, 1974; xhildren: Daniel Edwards, David Samuel. BA, York U., Toronto, 1983; MBA, Claremont Grad. Sch., 1997. Mgr. advt. and promotion Prentice-Hall, Scarborough, Ont., 1971-75; dir. comm. Seneca Coll., North York, Ont., 1975-83; dir. mktg. AES Data, Mississanga, Ont., 1983-87; exec. dir. Nat. Assn. Underwater Instructions, Montclair, Calif., 1987-95, Diving Equipment & Mktg. Assn., Anaheim, Calif., 1995—; mem. supervisory com. San Bernardino Cmty. Credit Union, 1988—. Columnist Sources, 1987-95. Bd. dirs. Outdoor Recreation Coalition of Am., Boulder, Colo., 1989-96. Presbyterian. Office: DEMA 2050 S Santa Cruz St Anaheim CA 92805-6816

JACKSON, STU, professional sports team executive, former university basketball coach; b. Reading, Pa., Dec. 11, 1955; m. Dr. Janet Taylor; four daughters. BA, business administration and management, Seattle U., 1978. Grad. asst. coach U. Oregon, 1981-82, asst. coach, 1982-83; asst. coach Wash. State U., 1983-85; assoc. coach Providence Coll., 1985-87; asst. coach N.Y. Knicks, 1987-89, head coach, 1989-91; dir. basketball ops. NBA, N.Y.C., 1991-92; head coach Univ. Wisc., Madison, 1992-94; pres., gen. mgr. basketball ops. NBA Vancouver expansion team, B.C., Canada, 1994—. Office: Vancouver Grizzlies, 800 Griffiths Way, Vancouver, BC Canada V6B 6G1

JACKSON, THIRSTON HENRY, JR., retired adult education educator; b. Camden, N.J., Mar. 28, 1913; s. Thirston Henry and Elizabeth Loraine (Keck) J.; m. Grace Roberta Ballard, Sept. 26, 1934 (dec. Dec. 1993); 1 child, Diane Jackson Bove. BSEE, Duke U., 1934; MA in Edn., Calif. Luth. U., 1984. Registered profl. engr., Calif.; registered tchr., Calif. Physicist Hughes Aircraft, Hawthorne, Calif., 1932-40; radio engr. Northrop Aviation, Hawthorne, 1940-50; electronic engr. N.Am. Aviation, Inglewood, Calif., 1950-60; sr. design engr. N.Am. Aviation, Downey, Calif., 1960-72; asst. chief engr. Marquardt Aircraft, Van Nuys, Calif., 1972-79; exec. v.p. 21st Century Tech., L.A., 1979-82; tchr. electronics Simi Adult Sch., Simi Valley, Calif., 1982-90; ret., 1990. Patentee automatic navigation device; developer missile navigation heat seeker. Scoutmaster Boy Scouts Am., N.J., 1929-32, N.C., 1932-33, L.A., 1933-54. Mem. Nat. Eagle Scout Assn. (sr.). Home: 6694 Tremont Cir Simi Valley CA 93063

JACKSON, TOM, mayor. Mayor Huntington Pk., Calif. Address: 6550 Miles Ave Huntington Park CA 90255

JACKSON, WILFRIED, banker; b. Lima, Peru, Feb. 15, 1955; came to U.S., 1970; s. Jack and Beni (Rivera) J.; m. Lina Belkis Leon, June 18, 1981 (div. June 1984); m. Linda Sue Matheney, Aug. 31, 1985; children: Nichole Brooke, Blake Wilfried. AS, Miami Dade C.C., 1977; BSEE, Fla. Internat. U., South Miami, 1980, BSIE, 1981. Prodn. ops. ACR Electronics, Hollywood, Fla., 1979-80; mgr. field svcs. ops. Modems Plus, Miami Lakes, Fla., 1980-82; mgr. complex sys. integration Timeplex-Unisys, Tampa, Fla., 1982-84; mgr. advanced Telecomm. sys. Bank of Am.-Internat., Miami, 1984-86; mgr. C.I.O. consumer bank Citibank N.A., Ft. Lauderdale, Fla., 1986-95; pres., CEO Citibank Nev., The Lakes, 1995—; bd. dirs. Nev. Devel. Authority, Las Vegas; mem. adv. bd. Nev. Capital Devel. Corp., Las Vegas, 1995—. Contbr. articles to profl. jours. Mem. Nev. Bankers Assn. (bd. dirs. 1996—). Republican. Presbyterian. Home: 8309 Opal Cove Dr Las Vegas NV 89128 Office: Citibank (Nev) NA 8725 W Sahara Las Vegas NV 89117

JACOBS, ARTHUR DIETRICH, educator, researcher, health services executive; b. Bklyn., Feb. 4, 1933; s. Lambert Dietrich and Paula Sophia (Knissel) J.; m. Viva Jane Sims, Mar. 24, 1952; children: Archie (dec.), David L., Dwayne C., Dianna K. Hatfield. BBA, Ariz. State U., 1962, MBA, 1966. Enlisted USAF, 1951, commd. 2d lt., 1962, advanced through grades to maj., 1972, ret., 1973; indsl. engr. Motorola, Phoenix, 1973-74; mgmt. cons. state of Ariz., 1974-76; mgmt. cons. Productivity Internat., Tempe, Ariz., 1976-79; faculty assoc. Coll. Bus. Adminstrn., Ariz. State U., Tempe, 1977-94, sr. lectr., 1995, ret. 1996; productivity advisor Scottsdale (Ariz.) Meml. Health Services Co., 1979-84; researcher U.S. internment of European-Am. aliens and citizens of European ancestry during World War II. Bd. dirs. United Way of Tempe, 1979-85. Mem. Am. Soc. Quality Control, Ariz. State U. Alumni Assn. (bd. dirs. 1973-79, pres. 1978-79), Inst. Indsl. Engrs. (pres. Central Ariz. chpt. 1984-85), Ops. Research Soc. Am., Sigma Iota Epsilon, Beta Gamma Sigma, Delta Sigma Pi. Club: Optimist (life) (Tempe). Co-editor: The World War Two Experience-The Internment of German-Americans: Documents, vol. IV; contbr. articles to profl. jours.

JACOBS, BOB, mayor. Mayor Olympia, Wash. Address: 900 Plum St Olympia WA 98507

JACOBS, BRUCE MARRIN, lawyer; b. Oakland, Calif., July 21, 1926; s. Allen Walter and Celia Teresa (Marrin) J.; m. Jane Gray, June 26, 1954; children: Tracy Ann, Brian G., Nancy C. Fleming. AB, U. Calif., Berkeley, 1947; JD, U. San Francisco, 1953. Bar: Calif. 1953. Assoc. Law Office Robert K. Byers, Gilroy, Calif., 1953-56; ptnr. Byers & Jacobs, Gilroy, 1957-67, Jacobs & Biafore, Gilroy, 1967-74, Jacobs & McDonald, Gilroy, 1974-95; retired, 1995; dir. Nat. Fiberglass, Gilroy. Bd. pres. Gavilan Community Coll., Gilroy, 1963, trustee, 1963-73; city atty. City of Gilroy, 1968-91. Lt. (j.g.) USN, 1944-49, PTO. Mem. State Bar Calif., Gilroy C. of C. (pres. 1958), Gilroy Rotary (pres. 1957, 59), Gilroy Elks. Republican. Presbyterian. Home: 7820 Santa Theresa Dr Gilroy CA 95020-4923

JACOBS, HENRY STEPHEN, computer engineer; b. N.Y.C., Oct. 9, 1950; s. Leonard Irving and Shirley Ruth J.; m. Phylis Lee Papurt, Aug. 12, 1979; children: Sabrina, Rebecca. BS in Systems Engring., Case Western Reserve U., 1972; MS in Systems Engring., UCLA, 1976. Mem. tech. staff TRW Defense & Space Systems, Redondo Beach, Calif., 1972-74; rsch. asst. UCLA-Biotech. Lab., L.A., 1974-76; sr. microprocessor engr. Beckman Instruments, Inc., Fullerton, Calif., 1976-84; sr. software engr. Comtal Divsn. 3M, Pasadena, Calif., 1984-87, Archive Corp., Costa Mesa, Calif., 1987-91; prin. software engr. CalComp, Anaheim, Calif., 1991-96; cons. Jacobs Rsch., 1996—. Mem. Acad. Magical Arts, Inc., Toastmasters Internat. Home and Office: 17 Whistling Isle Irvine CA 92614-5459

JACOBS, IRVIN HERBERT, physician, social services consultant; b. Ambridge, Pa., Feb. 9, 1937; s. Martin Walter and Pauline (Martin) J.; m. Jacqueline Rotman Lerner, Apr. 3, 1963; children: Karl Monte, Kenneth Allan. BS, MD, U. Pitts., 1961; postgrad. Grad. Sch. Pub. Health, San Diego U. Diplomate Am. Bd. Internal Medicine. Resident in internal medicine Dallas VA Hosp., 1961-63, U. N.Mex., Albuquerque, 1965-67; fellow infectious diseases L.A. VA Hosp., 1967-68; internist Alvarado Internal Medicine Group, San Diego, 1968-81; dir. Continuity Med. Edn. College Park Hosp., San Diego, 1979-82; cons. Calif. Dept. Social Svcs., San Diego, 1981—; chief of medicine Grossmont Hosp., La Mesa, Calif., 1971-72, Alvarado Hosp. Med. Ctr., San Diego, 1974-75; chief of staff College Park Hosp., 1975. Mem. spkrs. bur. Am. Jewish Com., San Diego, 1990—, bd. sec., 1994—. Capt. U.S. Army Med. Corps, 1963-65. Republican. Home: 2064 Carmel Valley Rd Del Mar CA 92014-3615 Office: Dept Social Svcs PO Box 85326 San Diego CA 92186

JACOBS, JOANNE LEE, journalist; b. Chgo., Mar. 31, 1952; d. Alan Joseph and Phyllis (Leaf) Jacobs; m. Colin Bowman Hunter, June 18, 1977 (div. 1985); 1 child, Allison Sarah Hunter. BA in English and Creative Writing, Stanford U., 1974. Copy editor, reporter Suburban Newspapers, Cupertino, Calif., 1974-76; assoc. editor Super 8 Filmaker, San Francisco, 1976-78; copy editor San Jose (Calif.) Mercury News, 1978-80, editorial writer, 1980-84, columnist, editorial writer, 1984—; bd. dirs. Stanford Daily. Bd. dirs. Women's Freedom Network, Washington, 1993—. Mich. Journalism fellow U. Mich., 1991-92.

JACOBS, JOHN HOWARD, professional society administrator; b. Phila., June 7, 1925; s. Howard Elias and Elizabeth Pauline (Dresel) J.; m. Shirley Elizabeth Salini, Apr. 21, 1960. BS in Econs., N.Mex. State U., 1950; LLD (hon.), Golden Gate U., 1985. Adminstrv. officer U.S. Fgn. Service (NATO), London, Paris, 1951-53; gen. mgr. Vis-a-Pack Corp., Beverly, N.J., 1953-58; exec. dir. Red. Agy., City of Stockton, Calif., 1958-66, San Francisco Planning and Urban Research, 1966-81; exec. dir. San Francisco C. of C., 1981-88, pres., 1988-89; chmn. Pacific Region Nat. Assn. Housing and Redevel. Ofcls., Stockton, 1965-66, mem. nat. bd. govs., San Francisco, 1966-70. Trustee emeritus Fine Arts Mus. San Francisco; bd. dirs. Point Reyes Bird Obs., San Francisco, World Affairs Coun. No. Calif., San Francisco State U. Found.; chmn. pres.'s adv. coun. San Francisco State U.; v.p. San Francisco Devel. Fund. Home: 2823 Octavia St San Francisco CA 94123-4305

JACOBS, KENT FREDERICK, dermatologist; b. El Paso, Tex., Feb. 13, 1938; s. Carl Frederick and Mercedes D. (Johns) J.; m. Sallie Ritter, Apr. 13, 1971. BS, N.Mex. State U., 1960; MD, Northwestern U., 1964; postgrad. U. Colo., 1967-70. Dir. service unit USPHS, Laguna, N.Mex., 1966-67; pvt. practice specializing in dermatology Las Cruces, N.Mex., 1970—; cons. U.S. Army, San Francisco, 1968-70, cons. NIH, Washington, 1983, Holloman AFB, 1972-77; research assoc. VA Hosp., Denver, 1969-70; preceptor U. Tex., Galveston, 1976-77; mem. clin. staff Tex. Tech U., Lubbock, 1977—; asst. clin. prof. U. N.Mex., Albuquerque, 1972—; bd. dirs. First Nat. Bank of Dona Ana County, Las Cruces, N.Mex., 1987—. Author: Breckkan, 1996; contbr. articles to profl. jours. and popular mags. Trustee Mus. N.Mex. Found., 1987—, mem. bd. regents, 1987—, pres., 1989-91, 95—; bd. dirs. Dona Ana Arts Coun., 1992-93, Border Book Festival, 1996—, N.Mex. State U. Found., 1993—. Invitational scholar Oreg. Primate Ctr., 1968; Acad. Dermatology Found. fellow, 1969; named Disting. Alumnus N.Mex. State U., 1985. Fellow Am. Acad. Dermatology, Royal Soc. Medicine, Soc. Investigative Dermatology; mem. AMA, Fedn. State Med. Bds. (bd. dirs. 1984-86), N.Mex. Med. Soc., N.Mex. Bd. Med. Examiners (pres. 1983-84, N.Mex. State U. Alumni Assn. (bd. dirs. 1975-79), Mil Gracias Club (pres. 1972-74) Pres.'s Assocs., Univ. Ambs., Rotary, Phi Beta Kappa, Beta Beta Beta. Democrat. Presbyterian. Home: 3610 Southwind Rd Las Cruces NM 88005-5556 Office: 2525 S Telshor Blvd # 15-106 Las Cruces NM 88011-9148 also: Mus NM PO Box 2087 Santa Fe NM 87504-2087

JACOBS, PETER ALAN, artist, educator; b. N.Y.C., Jan. 31, 1939; s. Peter A. and Elsie Katherine (Hirchi) J.; m. Nanci Gardner, Apr. 1, 1961; children: Christopher P.D., Cathi Kottenstette. BS, SUNY, New Paltz, 1960, MS, 1962; EdD, Vanderbilt U., 1965. Assoc. prof. art SUNY, New Paltz, 1961-62; prof. art and dept. chair U. Wis., Whitewater, 1965-70, No. Ariz. U., Flagstaff, 1970-74, Ctrl. Mich. U., Mt. Pleasant, 1975-76; prof. art and dept. chair Colo. State U., Ft. Collins, 1976-86, prof. art, 1988—; vis. prof. and dept. head U. Wyo., Laramie, 1987-88; founder, 1st pres. Nat. Coun. Art Adminstrs., 1972; pres. The Douglas Soc., Native Arts Dept.; pres. Denver Art Mus., 1994-95, bd. dirs., 1993—. Over 65 one-artist exhbns. in 14 states including Nicolaysen Art Mus., Casper, Wyo., 1991, Wyo. State Mus., Cheyenne, 1991, Julliet Denious Gallery, Carnegie Ctr. for Arts, Dodge City, Kans., 1990, Banares Hindu U., Varanasi, India, Gallery Bog, Boulder, Colo., Scottsdale (Ariz.) Fine Arts Ctr., Port Huron (Mich.) Mus. of Art, Ohio State U., Columbus, Northwestern U., Evanston, Ill.; exhbns. in Italy, India, Poland, Germany, Can., Bulgaria; numerous juried exhbns. Bd. dirs. Nightwalker Enterprises, Ft. Collins, Colo., 1985—, One-West Contemporary Art Ctr., Ft. Collins, 1979-86, Artists' Adv. Com., 1994-95, No. Colo. Intertribal Pow-wow Assn. Fulbright scholar, India, 1981-82. Mem. Coll. Art Assn., Native Am. Art Study Assn., Artist Adv. Coun. One-West Contemporary Art Ctr. Lutheran. Office: Colo State U Dept Art Fort Collins CO 80523

JACOBS, RALPH, JR., artist; b. El Centro, Calif., May 22, 1940; s. Ralph and Julia Vahe (Kirkorian) J. Paintings appeared in: Prize Winning Art (3 awards), 1964, 65, 66, and New Woman Mag., 1975; one man shows and exhbns. Villa Montalvo, Calif., Stanford Rsch. Inst., Calif., Fresno Art Ctr., Calif., de Young Meml. Mus., Calif., Rosicrucian Mus., Calif., Cunningham Meml. Gallery, Calif., 40th Ann. Nat. Art Exhibit, Utah, Nat. Exhbn. Coun. of Am. Artists Socs., N.Y.C., Am. Artists Profl. League Show, Armenian Allied Arts, Calif., Monterey Peninsula Mus. Art, Calif. Recipient 1st place award Statewide Annual Santa Cruz Art League Gallery, 1963, 64; 2nd place award Soc. Western Artists Ann. M.H. de Young Mus., 1964; A.E. Klumpkey Meml. award, 1965. Address: PO Box 5906 Carmel CA 93921-5906

JACOBS, RANDALL BRIAN, lawyer; b. N.Y.C., July 8, 1951; s. John and Evelyn Jacobs; 1 child, Jillian. BA, Coll. of Idaho, 1972; JD, U. West L.A., 1978. Bar: Calif., D.C., Wis. Lawyer B. Randall Jacobs Law Corp., Brentwood, Calif., 1978—; real estate broker Morgan Reed & Co., Brentwood, 1979—; pvt. investigator Randy Brian Assocs., Brentwood, 1976—. Reserve deputy sheriff, L.A. County Sheriff, L.A., 1979—. Mem. Shom Rim Soc., Nat. Rifle Assn., Masons, Shriners. Office: Law Offices R B Jacobs 522 S Sepulveda Blvd Ste 110 Los Angeles CA 90049-3539

JACOBS, ROBERT COOPER, political scientist, consultant; b. N.Y.C., Jan. 23, 1939; s. Max and Paula (Glotzer) J.; m. Barbara Linda Lax (div.); children: Michael, Deborah; m. Mollie Jenks Edson; children: Elliot, Madeleine, Eleanor. AB, CCNY, 1959; AM, Columbia U., 1961, PhD, 1970. Instr. Colby Coll., Waterville, Maine, 1965-68, asst. prof., 1968-70; from asst. prof. to prof. Cen. Wash. U., Ellensburg, 1970—, dir. law and justice, 1974-88, prof., 1982—; vis. prof. criminal justice Temple U., 1988-89. Contbr. articles to profl. jours. and encyclopedias. Mem. Kittitas County Juvenile Accountability Bd., Ellensburg, 1975-79; trustee Ellensburg Pub. Libr., 1994—, chmn., 1996. N.Y. State Regents scholar, 1955-59; State of N.Y. teaching fellow, 1962-63. Mem. Am. Polit. Sci. Assn., Wash. Assn. Criminal Justice Educators (past pres.), Supreme Ct. Hist. Soc. Democrat. Home: 111 E 10th Ave Ellensburg WA 98926-2909 Office: Cen Wash U Dept Polit Sci Ellensburg WA 98926

JACOBS, WILBUR RIPLEY, writer, history educator; b. Chgo.; s. Walter Ripley and Nona Isabel (Deutsch) J.; divorced; children: Elizabeth Shirley Jacobs Hayden, Catherine Elaine,; m. Priscilla Beth Dehmel, Dec. 20, 1982; children: William Ripley, Emily Marilyn. BA with honors, UCLA, MA with honors, PhD; postgrad., Johns Hopkins U. Prof. history U. Calif., Santa Barbara, 1965-88, chmn., dean of students; apt. rsch. scholar Huntington Libr., San Marino, Calif., 1989—; vis. prof. U. Calif., Berkeley, Claremont Grad. Sch., UCLA, Ind. U., U. Mich.; Fulbright prof. Australian Nat. U., Canberra; Am. studies lectr. U. Sidney, Melbourne U., U. Papua New Guinea, U. Queensland; lectr. U. Calif. Alumni Camps; U.S. Dept. State Cultural Exch. Program Yugoslavia, rep. for vis. historians from USSR; lectr. Gene Autry Mus. Western Heritage, 1997. Author: Wilderness Politics and Indian Gifts, 1968 (Pacific Coast Am.-Hist. Assn. prize), The Historical World of Frederick Jackson Turner, 1968, Dispossessing the American Indian, 1985, Francis Parkman, The Historian As Hero, 1991, On the Trail of Turner, 100 Years of Writing Western History, 1994, The Fatal Confrontation, Historical Studies on Indians and the Environment, 1996; co-author: Turner Bolton and Webb, Three Historians of The Frontier, 1965, Survey of American History, 1949; editor: The Paxton Riots and the Frontier Theory, 1958, Letters of Francis Parkman, 1960 (runner up Pulitzer prize in history 1961), Indians of the Southern Colonial Frontier, 1969, Benjamin Franklin, Philosopher-Statesman of Materialist, 1972, Frederick Jackson Turner's Legacy, 1965; writer, narrator A&E TV Biography Series, 1995—; cons., narrator A&E TV Biography Series; contbr. numerous articles, essays to profl. jours., newspapers, Ency. Britannica. Mem. exec. bd. dirs. Econ. Roundtable of So. Calif., Get Oil Out, Santa Barbara, Throop Unitarian Ch. Grantee Stanford U., Rockefeller Found., Ford Found., Am. Philos. Soc., Huntington Libr. Mem. Am. Hist. Assn. (Pacific coast br., pres.), Am. Soc. Ethnohistory (pres.), Am. Soc. Environ. History (pres.), Am. Studies Assn. (pres. Calif. br.), Humane Soc. U.S. (nat. bd.), Assocs. Calif. Inst. Tech., Mass. Hist. Soc., Soc. of Fellows Huntington Libr.

JACOBSEN, LAREN, programmer, analyst; b. Salt Lake City, June 15, 1937; s. Joseph Smith and Marian (Thomas) J.; B.S., U. Utah, 1963; m. Audrey Bartlett, July 29, 1970 (div.); children—Andrea, Cecily, Julian. Programmer, IBM Corp., 1963-70; systems programmer Xerox Computer Services, 1970-79; pres. Prescient Investments Co., 1975-82; sr. systems analyst Quotron Systems, Los Angeles, 1979-86; programmer/analyst Great Western Bank, 1987-92. Served with USAR, 1961. Mem. Am. Guild Organists (dean San Jose chpt. 1967), Mensa. Home: PO Box 91174 Los Angeles CA 90009-1174

JACOBSEN, MICHAEL ANTHONY, art historian, educator; b. Pasadena, Calif., June 4, 1942; s. Lars P. and Dorothy (Stuart) J.; m. Rebecca Hanson, Sept. 25, 1970; 1 child, Leif Peter. BA, U. Calif., Santa Barbara, 1965, MA, 1970; PhD, Columbia U., 1976. Asst. prof. Cleve. State U., 1973-77; assoc. prof., chair art history dept. U. Ga., Athens, 1979-86; vis. assoc. prof. Stanford U., Palo Alto, Calif., 1987, U. Calif., Riverside, 1988; lectr. Calif. State Poly. U., Pomona, 1989—. Contbr. articles to profl. publs. Rsch. grantee, 1968-82; S. H. Kress Found. fellow, 1971-72. Mem. Coll. Art Assn., So. Calif. Art Historians. Office: Calif State Poly U 3801 W Temple Ave Pomona CA 91768-2557

JACOBSEN, RICHARD T., mechanical engineering educator; b. Pocatello, Idaho, Nov. 12, 1941; s. Thorleif (dec.), and Edith Emily (Gladwin) J.; m. Vicki Belle Hopkins, July 16, 1959 (div. Mar. 1973); children: Pamela Sue, Richard T., Eric Ernest; m. Bonnie Lee Stewart, Oct. 19, 1973; 1 child, Jay Michael; stepchild: Erik David Lustig. BSME, U. Idaho, 1963, MSME, 1965; PhD in Engring. Sci., Wash. State U., 1972. Registered profl. engr., Idaho. Instr. U. Idaho, 1964-66, asst. prof. mech. engring., 1966-72, assoc. prof., 1972-77, prof., 1977—, chmn. dept. mech. engring., 1980-85, assoc. dean engring., 1985-90, assoc. dir. Ctr. for Applied Thermodynamic Studies, 1975-86, dir., 1986—, dean engring., 1990—. Author: International Union of Pure and Applied Chemistry, Nitrogen-International Thermodynamic Tables of the Fluid State-6, 1979; Oxygen-International Thermodynamic Tables of the Fluid State-9, 1987, Ethylene-International Thermodynamic Tables of the Fluid State-10, 1988, ASHRAE Thermodynamic Properties of Refrigerants (2 vols.), 1986, (monograph series) Thermodynamic Properties of Cryogenic Fluids, 1997; numerous reports on thermodynamic properties of fluids, 1971—; contbr. articles to profl. jours. NSF sci. faculty fellow, 1968-69; NSF rsch. and travel grantee, 1976-83; Nat. Inst. Standards and Tech. grantee, 1974-91, 95-96, Gas Rsch. Inst. grantee, 1986-91, 1992-95, Dept. Energy grantee, 1991-95. Fellow ASME (faculty advisor 1972-75, 78-84, chmn. region VIII dept. heads com. 1983-85, honors and awards chmn. 1985-91, K-7 tech. com. thermophys. properties 1985—, chmn. 1986-89, 92-95, rsch. tech. com. on water and steam in thermal power systems, 1988—, gen. awards com. 1985-91, chmn. 1988-91, com. on honors 1988—, vice chmn. 1995-96—, mem. bd. on profl. practice and ethics, 1991—), N.W. Coll. and Univ. Assn. for Sci. (bd. dirs. 1990-93), Idaho Rsch. Found. (bd. dirs. 1991—), Soc. Automotive Engrs. (Ralph R. Teetor Edn. award, Detroit 1968), ASHRAE (co-recipient Best Tech. Paper award 1984), International. Energy Agy. (Annex 18 thermophys. properties environ. acceptable refrigerants 1991—), Sigma Xi, Tau Beta Pi, Phi Kappa Phi (Disting. Faculty award 1989). Office: U Idaho Coll Engring Office of Dean Janssen Engring Bldg 125 Moscow ID 83844

JACOBSMEYER, JAY MICHAEL, electrical engineer; b. Okaloosa County, Fla., Mar. 13, 1959; s. John Henry and Patricia Ann (McDonough) J.; m. Joyce Ann Deem, June 20, 1981; children: Abigail Ann, Brian James. BS magna cum laude, Va. Poly. Inst. & State U., 1981; MS, Cornell U., 1987. Registered profl. engr., Colo. Commd. 2nd lt. USAF, 1981-90, advanced through grades to capt., 1985; elec. engr. 3397 Tech. Tng. Squadron, Biloxi, Miss., 1981-82; comm. engr. 1st Combat Comm. Group, Wiesbaden, Germany, 1982-85; communications engr. HQ Air Force Space Command, Colorado Springs, 1987-90; resigned USAF, 1990; staff engr. ENSCO, Inc., Colorado Springs, 1990-91, sr. staff engr., 1991-93; co-founder, chief tech. officer Pericle Comm. Co., 1992—. Patent pending wireless data modem; contbr. articles to profl. publs. Maj. USAFR. Decorated Meritorious Svc. medal, Air Force Commendation medal; named Man of Yr., Va. Poly. Inst. and State U., 1981; rsch. grantee, NSF, USN. Mem. IEEE (sr.), Armed Forces Comm. and Electronics Assn. (v.p. 1989-90), Air Force Assn., Omicron Delta Kappa, Eta Kappa Nu. Home: 2475 Edenderry Dr Colorado Springs CO 80919-3876

JACOBSON, ALBERT DALE, pediatrician, accountant; b. Portland, Oreg., Mar. 28, 1942; s. Leonard Dale and Allice Cleo (Wiesendanger) J.; m. Donna Marie Shaw, Aug. 8, 1964; children: Heidi, Craig, Bryan and Chad. BS in acctg., Ariz. State U., 1964; MD, U. Oreg., Portland, 1969. CPA, Oreg.; diplomate Am. Bd. Pediatrics, Am. Bd. Nephrology. Pub. acct. Winn & Co., Eugene, Oreg., 1964-65; intern Good Samaritan Hosp., Phoenix, Ariz., 1970; residency in pediatrics and pediatric nephrology fellowship Naval Hosp., San Diego, 1972, U. Calif., San Diego, 1972; chief pediatrics Naval Regional Med. Clinic, Pearl Harbor, Hawaii, 1972-75; sect. chief pediatric nephrology Tripler Army Hosp., Honolulu, 1972-75; attending staff pediatrician, clin. asst. prof. pediatrics U. Hawaii Med. Sch., Honolulu, 1972-75; pediatrician Health Maintenance Assocs., Phoenix, Ariz., 1975-77; v.p. Health Maintenance Assocs., Inc., Phoenix, Ariz., 1976-77; adminstrv. staff pediatrician, sect. head pediatric nephrology Maricopa County Gen. Hosp., 1977-78; chief pediatric rehab. Barrows Neurological Institution, 1986-88, Children's Med. Ctr., St. Joseph's Hosp., 1986-88; pvt. practice Pediatric Assocs., P.C., Phoenix, Ariz., 1977—; divsn. chmn. Emergency Dept. Children's Hosp., Honolulu, 1972-75; cons. Waimano State Institution for the Retarded, 1972-75, Children's Hosp., Honolulu, 1972-75; advisor Poision Contro Ctr. State of Hawaii, 1972-75; chief of pediatrics Naval Regional Med. Clinics, 1972-75; navy chmn. child abuse com. Tripler Army Hosp., 1972-75; mem. gov.'s adv. bd. Child Protection Soc., 1972-75; media rep., TV appearances on children's health Phoenix Pediatric, 1981-92; host weekly radio program, KTAR Speaking of Kids, 1982-84. Contbr. to profl. jours. Coach Phoenix Little League, 1975-93. Comdr. U.S. Navy, 1970-75. Recipient Best Doctor award Phoenix Mag., 1994; Oreg. State Heart Assn. fellow, 1966; Nat. Pharm. and Drug Mfg. Rsch. fellow, 1968. Fellow Am. Acad. Pediatrics (tech. advisor third party payments, 1972-75, state chmn. child health planning com., 1975-77, sec. Ariz. chpt. 1980-82, advisor com. of pediatric practice, 1983-92, chmn. child health finance, 1986-89, exec. com. sect. on adminstrn. and practice mgmt. 1993—, mem. nat. com. on practice and ambulatory medicine 1993—, mem. nat. com. RBRUS 1995—), Am. Spinal Injury Assn.; mem. AMA, Internat. Soc. Pediatrics, Honolulu and State Hawaii Pediatric Soc. (state chmn. on third party payments), Phoenix Pediatric Soc. (pres. 1996-97), Ariz. Med. Assn., Maricopa County Med. Assn., Maricopa County Pediatric Soc. (pres. elect. 1981-82, pres. 1982-83, com. for the formation of Phoenix Children's Hosp., 1979-83). Office: Pediatric Assocs PC Pointe Corridor Ctr II 7600 N 15th St Ste 130 Phoenix AZ 85020-4330

JACOBSON, EDWIN JAMES, medical educator; b. Chgo., June 27, 1947; s. Edwin Julius and Rose Josephine (Jirinec) J.; m. Martha Shanks; 1 child, Emily. BA, U. So. Calif., 1969; MD, UCLA, 1976. Diplomate Nat. Bd. Med. Examiners, Am. Bd. Internal Medicine; lic. physician, Calif. Intern in medicine UCLA Hosp., 1976-77, resident in medicine, 1977-79, fellow in nephrology, 1979-81, chief resident in medicine, 1979-81; asst. clin. prof. of medicine UCLA, 1981-88, assoc. clin. prof. medicine, 1988-94, clin. prof. medicine, 1994—; adj. asst. prof. medicine, UCLA, 1980-81; mem. med. sch. admissions com. UCLA, 1981—, med. staff credentials com., 1984—, med.staff exec. com., 1990-94, med. staff/hosp. adminstrn. liaison com. 1991-94, hosp./med. sch. faculty rels. com., 1991—, nat. kidney found., 1991—, med. adv. bd., 1991—; prin. investigator A/M Group Grant, UCLA Med. Ctr., 1993, Peter Langer Meml. Fund Award, 1993; lectr. in field. Author: Medical Diagnosis: An Algorithmic Approach, 1989; co-author: (with P. Healy) Il Proceso Decisionale nella Diagnosi Medica, 1992; manuscript rev. bd.: Bone Marrow Transplantation, 1988—, Jour. Am. Geriatrics Soc., 1989—; editor for symposia in field; contbr. articles to profl. jours.; editor book chpts. Recipient Upjohn Achievement award, 1977. Mem. ACP, Alpha Omega Alpha. Office: UCLA 100 UCLA Medical Plz Ste 690 Los Angeles CA 90024-6970

JACOBSON, GORDON R., architect; b. Provo, Utah, Dec. 13, 1961; s. Jeston O. and Maurine (Meservy) J.; m. Suzanne Porcaro, Apr. 12, 1984; children: Kraig, Breanna, Kyle, Kevin, Annecia. AS in Design, Utah Valley State Coll., 1986, AS in Acctg., 1990; BS in Acctg., U. Utah, 1992. Registered arch., Utah. Designer Talbot & Wells Architects, St. George, Utah, 1986-89, L&T Constrn., Orem, Utah, 1989-92; prin. Design Originals, Orem, 1992-94, Terra Firma Architecture, Orem, 1994—; cons. Terra Firma Architecture, 1995-96. Prin. works include Troon Towers, White residence (Best Custom award 1995), numerous other comml. and residential projects. Office: Terra Firma Architecture PO Box 2122 Orem UT 84059

JACOBSON, JACOB G., psychoanalyst; b. N.Y.C., June 17, 1928; s. Max and Jeanne (Schatz) J.; married; children: Carol Wright, Beth Smith, Matthew Jacobson. BS in Psychology, U. Mich., 1948, MD, 1952. Diplomate Am. Bd. Psychiatry and Neurology. Clin. asst. prof. to assoc. prof. psychiatry U. Colo., Denver, 1958-86, clin. prof., 1986—; faculty Denver Inst. Psychoanalysis, 1972—, tng. and supr. analyst, 1977—. Contbr. articles to profl. jours. Life fellow APA. Mem. Am. Psychoanalytic Assn. (chmn. com. on insts. 1986-91). Office: 1636 16th St Boulder CO 80302-6356

JACOBSON, JAY ANDREW, physician; b. Spartanburg, S.C., Sept. 19, 1945; s. Abraham Irving and Doris (Barbanell) J.; m. Julie Evelyn Taylor, May 4, 1969; 1 son, Aaron Robert. BS in Chemistry, U. Mich., 1967; MD with honors, U. Fla., 1971. Diplomate Am. Bd. Internal Medicine, sub-bd. infectious diseases. Resident in internal medicine U. Fla., Gainesville, 1971-73; epidemiologist CDC, Atlanta, 1974-75; fellow in infectious diseases U. Utah, Salt Lake City, 1976-78, mem. faculty, 1978—, prof. internal medicine, 1990—; chief div. med. ethics, mem. div. infectious diseases LDS Hosp./U. Utah Sch. Medicine, Salt Lake City, 1989—; vis. scholar U. Chgo. Ctr. for Clin. Med. Ethics, 1988-89; chmn. instl. rev. bd. U. Utah Sch. Medicine, 1994—. Contbr. articles to med. jours. Pres. Congregation Kol Ami, Salt Lake City, 1990-92. Lt. comdr. USPHS, 1974-76. Fellow ACP, Infectious Diseases Soc. Am.; mem. Soc. for Health and Human Values, Am. Soc. for Law, Medicine and Ethics, Utah Med. Assn. (task force of HIV/AIDS 1987-95, Disting. Svc. award 1990). Democrat. Office: LDS Hosp Divsn Med Ethics 8th Ave And C St Salt Lake City UT 84143

JACOBSON, LOWELL STEVEN (JAKE JACOBSON), railroad executive; b. Riley, Kans., Sept. 17, 1940; s. Myron A. and Irene (Anderson) J.; m. Patricia L. Boyce, Feb. 2, 1963; children: Michael W., Jacqulin D. Steel bridge worker Union Pacific R.R., Frankfort, Kans., 1958-64; indsl. foreman Union Pacific R.R., Salina, Kans., 1964-69; indsl. supt. Union Pacific R.R., Kansas City, Mo., 1969-73; trainmaster Union Pacific R.R., Topeka, 1973-85; supt. Union Pacific R.R., Kans., Nebr., Mo., Colo., 1985; railroad cons. S.W. U.S., 1986-87; gen. supt., gen. mgr., v.p. Copper Basin Ry., Hayden, Ariz., 1987—. Sgt. USAF, 1963-66. Named Railroader of the Yr., Rlwy. Age Mag., 1994. Office: Copper Basin Ry Highway 177 Hayden AZ 85235

JACOBSON, RAYMOND EARL, electronics company entrepreneur and executive; b. St. Paul, May 25, 1922; s. Albert H. and Gertrude W. (Anderson) J.; BE with high honors, Yale U., 1944; MBA with distinction, Harvard U., 1948; B.A. (Rhodes scholar), Oxford U., 1950, M.A., 1954; m. Margaret Maxine Meadows, Dec. 22, 1959 (div. 1986); children: Michael David, Karl Raymond, Christopher Eric. Asst. to gen. mgr. PRD Electronics, Inc., Bklyn., 1951-55; sales mgr. Curtiss-Wright Electronics Div., Carlstadt, N.J., 1955-57; dir. mktg. TRW Computers Co., Los Angeles, 1957-60; v.p. ops. Electro-Sci. Investors, Dallas, 1960-63; pres. Whitehall Electronics, Inc., Dallas, 1961-63, dir., 1961-63; chmn. bd. Gen. Electronic Control, Inc., Mpls., 1961-63, Staco, Inc., Dayton, Ohio, 1961-63; pres. Maxson Electronics Corp., Gt. River, N.Y., 1963-64, Jacobson Assocs., San Jose, Calif., 1964-67; co-founder, pres., chmn., chief exec. officer Anderson Jacobson, Inc., San Jose, 1967-88; chmn. Anderson Jacobson, SA, Paris, 1974-88; chmn. Anderson Jacobson, Ltd., London, 1975-85; chmn. Anderson Jacobson Can., Ltd./Ltée, Toronto, 1975-85, Anderson Jacobson, GmbH, Cologne, 1978-83, CXR Corp., San Jose, 1988-94; bd. dirs. Tamar Electronics, Inc., L.A., Rawco Instruments, Inc., Dallas, 1960-63, Micro Radionics, Inc., L.A., 1964-67; lectr. engring., UCLA, 1958-60; mem. underwriting Lloyd's London, 1975—. Eagle Scout Boy Scouts Am., 1935, committeeman 1968-80. Lt. (j.g.) USNR, 1943-46. Mem. Assn. Am. Rhodes Scholars, Harvard Bus. Sch. Assn., Oxford Soc., Yale Club, Sigma Xi, Tau Beta Pi. Republican. Lutheran. Clubs: Courtside Tennis, Seascape Swim and Racquet. Home: 1247 Montcourse Ln San Jose CA 95131-2420

JACOBSON, STUART NEIL, biotechnology company executive, consultant; b. N.Y.C., Aug. 28, 1953; s. Roy and Shirley (Roth) J.; m. Gretchen Marion Haupt, June 5, 1977; children: Jesse, Eli, Taimi. BS, CCNY, 1974; MS, Cornell U., 1978, PhD, 1981. Rsch. technician Sloan Kettering Inst., N.Y.C., 1974-75; sci. script cons. Chris Jeans Prodns., N.Y.C., 1980; owner, mgr. The Upper Crust, Salt Lake City, 1982-88; founder, mgr. S. J. Biologics, Camarillo, Calif., 1989—; microbiol. cons. various orgns., 1986—.

JACOBSON, SVERRE THEODORE, retired minister; b. Loreburn, Sask., Can., Sept. 20, 1922; s. Sverre and Aline Tomina (Joel) J.; m. Phyllis Lorraine Sylte, Sept. 14, 1948; children—Katherine Ann, Paul Theodore. B.A., U. Sask., 1946; B.D., Luther Theol. Sem., Sask., 1947; postgrad., Luther Theol. Sem., St. Paul, Minn., 1952-53; Th.D., Princeton Theol. Sem., 1959. Ordained to ministry Evang. Luth. Ch., 1947. Pastor Lomond, Alta., 1947-53; lectr. Luther Theol. Sem., Saskatoon, Sask., 1956-57; pastor Torquay, Sask., 1958-63; asst. to pres. Evang. Luth. Ch. Can., Saskatoon, 1963-70; pres. Evang. Luth. Ch. Can., 1970-85; interim parish pastor Calgary, Alta., Saskatoon, Weyburn, Elbow and Loreburn, Sask., 1987—; lectr. Luth. Theol. Sem., Saskatoon, 1987-88. Home: 53 Moxon Crescent, Saskatoon, SK Canada S7H 3B8

JADVAR, HOSSEIN, physician, biomedical engineer; b. Tehran, Iran, Apr. 6, 1961; came to U.S., 1978, naturalized, 1995; s. Ramezan Ali and Fatemeh (Afzal) J. BS, Iowa State U., 1982; MS, U. Wis., 1984, U. Mich., Ann Arbor, 1986; PhD, U. Mich., Ann Arbor, 1988; MD, U. Chgo., 1993. Rsch. asst. dept. human oncology U. Wis., Madison, 1983-84; rsch. asst. dept. elec. engring. U. Mich., Ann Arbor, 1984-88; sr. rsch. engr. Arzco Med. Electronics, Inc., Chgo., 1988-89; sr. rsch. assoc. Pritzker Inst., Ill. Inst. Tech., Chgo., 1989-92; med. intern U. Calif., San Francisco, 1993-94; resident in radiology Stanford (Calif.) U., 1994-96, resident in nuc. medicine, 1996—; reviewer study sect. small bus. innovative rsch. program NIH, 1989; session chmn. IEEE/EMBS 11th Ann. Conf., Seattle, 1989. Contbr. articles to profl. jours., chpts. to books. Recipient Resident Rsch. award NIH, 1994, Roentgen Rsch. award Radiol. Soc. of N.Am., 1997, Roentgen Resident/FellowRsch. award RSNA, 1997. Mem. AMA, IEEE, Am. Roetgeon Ray Soc., Am. Coll. Radiology, Radiol. Soc. N.Am., Assn. for Advancement of Med. Instrumentation, Biomed Engring. Soc., Soc. Nuclear Medicine, Computers in Cardiology (local organizing com. mem. 1990), Tau Beta Pi, Sigma Xi, Eta Kappa Nu. Home: 1170 Welch Rd # 734 Palo Alto CA 94304-9999 Office: Stanford Univ Med Ctr Dept Radiology Divsn Nuc Medicine 300 Pasteur Dr Rm H0101 Stanford CA 94305-5105

JAEGER, SHARON ANN, chiropractor; b. Adrian, Mich., Feb. 9, 1952; d. Fredrick Adolf and Jean Mary (Theby) J. Student, Western Mich. U., 1970-73; BS, Nat. Coll. Chiropractic, 1975, D in Chiropractic, 1976. Diplomate Am. Chiropractic Bd. of Radiology; lic. chiropractor, Calif., Ill., Ky. Instr. L.A. Coll. Chiropractic, 1978-80; prof. Cleve. Chiropractic Coll., L.A., 1980-81, 1992-94; cons. Philip C. Runsten Chiropractic, Canoga Park, Calif., 1980-84, Radiology Cons., Chatsworth, Calif., 1984—; pvt. practice North Hollywood, Calif., 1989—. Author: Atlas of Radiographic Positioning, Normal Anatomy and Developmental Variants, 1988; co-author: Case Studies in Chiropractic Radiology, 1990; mem. editl. bd. The Journal of Chiropractic Research, Study of Clinical Investigation, radiology section Journal of Neuromusculoskeletal Sys., Topics in Diagonostic Imaging and the ACA Press; contbr. articles to jours. Mem. Patrons of Children Support Group L.A. Police Dept. Juvenile Disvn., bd. dirs., sec., 1989-92, v.p., 1992-96. Western Mich. U. scholar, Mich. State Chiropractic Aux. scholar, Buccholtz scholar, Springwall scholar; grantee Coun. Roengenology grantee Found. Chiropractic Edn. and Rsch. Fellow Internat. Coll. of Chiropractors; mem. APHA (sec. Radiological Health Sect. 1987-90, sect. coun. 1990-92, Governing coun. 1993-95), Nat. Coll. Chiropractic Alumni Assn., Am. Coll. Chiropractic Radiologists (bd. mem. 1985-91, v.p. 1987-88, pres. 1988-90), Am. Chiropractic Assn., Calif. Chiropractic Assn., Ky. Chiropractic Assn., San Fernando Valley Chiropractic Assn. (2d v.p. 1982-83, edn. chmn. 1984-85, sec. 1988-89), Radiologic Tech. Cert. Com., Coun. Diagnostic Imaging, FCER (bd. dirs. 1991—, sec., treas., bd. regents, LACC 1993-97), Sigma Chi Psi, Delta Tau Alpha. Office: 4426 Lankershim Blvd North Hollywood CA 91602

JAEGER-KEENAN, GERALYN MARIE, medical/surgical and women's health nurse; b. Spokane, Wash., May 4, 1960; d. Thomas Charles and Rose Maureen (LaCoste) Jaeger; m. H. Bill Keenan, Jr.; children: Kaylah Marie, Matthew Thomas. Assoc. Degree, Spokane C.C., 1983; BSN, Georgetown U.; MS, U. Portland. Cert. primary health care, women's health care, addiction medicine. Staff nurse Holy Family Hosp., Spokane, 1981-83; charge nurse/staff nurse Deaconess Med. Ctr., Spokane, 1983-89; advanced nurse practitioner Native Am. Cmty. Health Svcs., Spokane, 1989—, Downtown Homeless Clinic/Dr. Dan Phillips, Spokane Urban Indian Health. Mem. Wash. State Nurses Assn., Nurses Assn. of Am. Coll. Obgyn. Office: # 515 W801 5th Spokane WA 99204

JAFFE, CHARLES J., allergist; b. Phila., Feb. 3, 1946. MD, Duke U., 1971, PhD, 1972. Allergist Scripps Meml. Hosp., Encinitas, Calif.; prof. allergy and immunology U. Calif., San Diego. Mem. ACAAI (chmn. computer com). Office: 477 N El Camino Real Ste A308 Encinitas CA 92024-1329

JAFFE, EDWARD A., lawyer; b. Chgo., Sept. 17, 1945; s. Julius C. and Esther R. (Cohen) J.; m. Marlene E. Epstein, June 16, 1968; children: Kimberly A., Jonathan S. BA, Drake Univ., 1967; JD cum laude, Northwestern Univ., 1970. Bar: Ill. 1970, Hawaii 1971, U.s. Dist. Ct. Hawaii 1971, U.S. Ct. Appeals (9th cir.) 1972, (2d cir.) 1979, U.S. Supreme Ct. 1984. Assoc. Cades, Schutte, Fleming & Wright, Honolulu, 1970-75, ptnr., 1976-88; sr. ptnr. Torkildson, Katz, Fonseca, Jaffe, Moore & Hetherington, Honolulu, 1988—; facualty Nat. Inst. Trail Advocacy, Honolulu, 1985—, Univ. Hawaii Col. Continuing Edn., Honolulu, 1973—; arbitrator Am. Arbitration Assn., Honolulu, 1973—, Ct. Annexed Arbitration Program, Honolulu, 1987—. pres. Temple Emanu-El, Honolulu, 1989-91, bd. trustees, 1980-93. Office: Torkildson Katz Fonseca Jaffe Moore Hetherington 700 Bishop Ste 15th Flr Honolulu HI 96813-4187

JAFFE, F. FILMORE, judge; b. Chgo., May 4, 1918; s. Jacob Isadore and Goldie (Rabinowitz) J.; m. Mary Main, Nov. 7, 1942; children: Jo Anne, Jay. Student, Southwestern U., 1936-39; J.D., Pacific Coast U., 1940. Bar: Calif. 1945, U.S. Supreme Ct. 1964. Practiced law Los Angeles, 1945-91; ptnr. Bernard & Jaffe, Los Angeles, 1947-74, Jaffe & Jaffe, Los Angeles, 1975-91; apptd. referee Superior Ct. of Los Angeles County, 1991-97, apptd. judge pro tem, 1991-97; mem. L.A. Traffic Commn., 1947-48; arbitrator Am. Arbitration Assn., 1968-91; chmn. pro bono com. Superior Ct. Calif., County of Los Angeles, 1980-86; lectr. on paternity. Served to capt. inf. AUS, 1942-45. Decorated Purple Heart, Croix de Guerre with Silver Star, Bronze Star with oak leaf cluster; honored Human Rights Commn. Los Angeles, Los Angeles County Bd. Suprs.; recipient Pro Bono award State Bar Calif., commendation State Bar Calif., 1983. Mem. ABA, Los Angeles County Bar (honored by family law sect. 1983), Los Angeles Criminal Ct. Bar Assn. (charter mem.), U.S. Supreme Ct. Bar Assn., Masons, Shriners. Office: Superior Ct LA County 600 S Commonwealth Ave Los Angeles CA 90005

JAFFE, ROBERT S., lawyer; b. Walla Walla, Wash., May 16, 1946. BA, U. Wash., 1968, JD, 1972. Bar: Wash. 1972. Atty. Preston Gates & Ellis, L.L.P., Seattle. Mem. ABA (mem. corp., banking and bus. law sect., mem. small bus. com. 1982-92), Order of Coif. Office: Preston Gates & Ellis LLP 5000 Columbia Seafirst Ctr 701 5th Ave Seattle WA 98104-7016

JAFFE, ROSS ALLAN, physician; b. Suffolk, Va., Sept. 12, 1958. AB, Dartmouth Coll., 1980; MD, Johns Hopkins U., 1985; MBA, Stanford U., 1990. Rsch. assoc. Lewin & Assocs., Washington, 1980-81; resident U. Calif. Med. Ctr., San Francisco, 1985-88; physician Redwood Med. Clinic, Redwood City, Calif., 1988-89; clin. instr., attending physician U. Calif. Med. Ctr., 1988-90, 92-95, U. Calif., Irvine, 1990-92; gen. ptnr. Brentwood Assocs., Menlo Park, Calif., 1990—; cons. in field. Contbr. articles to profl. jours. Com. mem. Blue Cross Adv. com. Peninsula Cmty. Found., San Mateo, Calif., 1995—. Office: Brentwood Venture Capital Ste 260 3000 Sand Hill Rd Bldg 1 Menlo Park CA 94025

JAFFER, ADRIAN MICHAEL, physician; b. Cape Town, S. Africa, Aug. 24, 1943; came to U.S., 1969; s. George Daniel Jaffer and Theresa (Kourie) Binsted; children: Brendan, Terence. MBChB, U. Cape Town Med. Sch., 1966. Diplomate Am. Coll. Physicians. Intern Loyola Univ. Hosp., Maywood, Ill., 1969-70; resident Northwestern U., Chgo., 1970-72; fellow Harvard U., Boston, 1972-73, Scapps Clinic & Rsch., LaJolla, Calif., 1973-75, Northwestern U., Chgo., 1975-76; pvt. practice LaJolla, 1976—; assoc. clin. prof. U. Calif. San Diego, LaJolla, 1976—. Contbr. articles to profl. jours. Mem. AMA, Am. Coll. Rheumatology, Am. Acad. Allergy. Office: 9850 Genesee Ave Ste 860 La Jolla CA 92037-1219

JAGER, MERLE LEROY, aerospace engineer; b. Eugene, Oreg., Sept. 22, 1942; s. Earl Christian and Alma Marie (Jensen) J.; m. Shannon Kay Jacobsen, Mar. 18, 1967; children: Holly, Peter, Melanie, Marissa. BS in Mech. Engring., Oreg. State U., 1965; MS in Aeronautical Engring., U. So. Calif., 1967. Aerodynamicist Lockheed-Calif. Co., Burbank, 1965-68; rsch. engr. The Boeing Co., Seattle, 1968-70; aerodynamics engr. Gates Learjet Corp., Torrance, Calif., 1970; project engr. Irvin Industries, Inc., Gardena, Calif., 1971-73; aerodynamics mgr. Northrop Corp., Hawthorne, Calif., 1973-91; mgr. flight mechanics Northrop Corp., Pico Rivera, Calif., 1991-95; aerodynamics mgr. McDonnell Douglas Corp., Long Beach, Calif., 1995—. Patentee in field. Treas. Goldenwest Assn., Westminster, Calif., 1976-78; tribal chief YMCA Indian Princesses Program, Huntington Beach, Calif., 1986-87; bishopric counselor Mormon Ch., Westminster, 1986-95. Mem. AIAA, Tau Beta Pi, Pi Tau Sigma, Sigma Tau. Republican. Home: 6771 Findley Cir Huntington Beach CA 92648-3075 Office: McDonnell Douglas Corp Long Beach CA 90810

JAGNOW, DAVID HENRY, petroleum geologist; b. Dubuque, Iowa, Nov. 24, 1947; s. Albert August and Ardath Helen (Goettsch) J.; divorced; children: Daniel David, Robert Carl, Beth Laura. BA in Geology, U. Iowa, 1970; MS in Geology, U. N.Mex., 1977. Exploration geologist Shell Oil Co., Houston, 1973-77; staff geologist Energy Reserves Group, Denver, 1977-78; exploration mgr. Donald C. Slawson Oil Prodr., Oklahoma City, 1978-82; cons. geologist pvt. practice, Edmond, Okla., 1982-87, Los Alamos, N.Mex., 1987—; venture capitalist Venture Calital Info., Edmond, 1986-87, Los Alamos, 1987—; v.p. RDS Devel., Tempe, Ariz., 1996—; conservation chair Nat. Speleological Soc., 1995—; dir. Project Underground VA, 1995—; dir. Diversified Ventures, Inc., Nev.; mem. caves and karst task force Bur. Land Mgmt., Carlsbad, N.Mex., 1991-93, Guadalupe caverns geology panel Nat. Park Svc., Carlsbad, 1993. Author: Cavern Development in the Guadalupe Mountains, 1979, Stories From Stones, 1992. Conservation chair, v.p. Pajarito Grotto, Los Alamos, 1993-94. Recipient Gov.'s Dist. Svc. award Gov. Iowa, 1970, W.A. Tarr award Sigma Gamma Epsilon, 1970, Lowden prize Geology U. Iowa, 1970. Fellow Nat. Speleological Soc. (Conservation award 1995); mem. Am. Assn. Petroleum Geologists, N.Mex. Entrepreneurs Assn. (bd. dirs. 1988-89), Cave Rsch. Found. (chief scientist 1988-89), Omicron Delta Kappa. Lutheran. Home: 1300 Iris St Apt 103 Los Alamos NM 87544-3140 Office: Venture Capital Info Inc 901 18th St # 11300 Los Alamos NM 87544-4001

JAGODZINSKI, RUTH CLARK, nursing administrator; b. N.Y.C., Feb. 24, 1938; d. John Kirkland and Ruth Fishwick Clark; m. Thomas John Jagodzinski, Nov. 1962 (div. 1974); children: Christine Ruth, James Clark. Diploma, Roosevelt Hosp. Sch. Nursing, 1959. Cert. substance abuse counselor and program adminstrn.; RN, Nev., N.Y. Head nurse drug/alcohol detox Sunrise Hosp., Las Vegas, Nev., 1973-75; program coord. careunit North Las Vegas (Nev.) Hosp., 1975-77; co-owner, adminstr. Sunrise Home Health, Las Vegas, 1983-89; dir. pers. PRN Home Health, Las Vegas, 1990-91; dir. home health svcs. Med. Pers. Pool, Las Vegas, 1990-92; dir. profl. svc. Olsten Kimberly Quality Care, Las Vegas, 1992-95; adminstr. Valley Home Health, Las Vegas, 1995-97; dir. regional ops. IHS Mgmt. Svcs., Brunswick, Ga., 1997—; mem. Nev. State Cert. Bd. Substance Abuse Counselors and Program Adminstrs., 1976-86, 90-97, pres., 1980-86. Mem. Nev. Gov.'s Adv. Bd. for Alcohol and Drugs; bd. dirs. We Care Found., 1974—; trustee Community Referral Svcs., 1975-80; bd. dirs. Alcohol Program So. Nev., 1975-85; mem. In-Home Care Svcs. Clark County, 1978-83; bd. dirs. So. Nev. Girls Clubs, 1984-86; mem. adv. bd. Nathan Adelson Hospice, Las Vegas, 1977-89; chmn. nursing subcom. profl. ednn. div. So. Nev. chpt. Am. Cancer Soc., 1989-90, mem. Nev. Bd. Com. on Occupational Excellence, 1989-90. Recipient Community Svc. award Alcohol Program So. Nev., 1978, Svc. award We Care Found., 1989. Mem. Home Health Care Assns. Nev. (v.p. 1984-86, 94-95, pres. 1995—). Home: 4573 Royal Ridge Way Las Vegas NV 89103-5034 Office: Valley Home Health 620 Shadow Ln Ste G Las Vegas NV 89106

JAHN, E. MARK, research specialist; b. Evanston, Ill., Apr. 24, 1955; s. Richard G. and Lois (Koenig) J.; children: Jenna P., Janelle A. AAS, Harper Coll., Palatine, Ill., 1978; BS, Calif. Poly. State U., 1982; MA, San Diego State U., 1992. Mfg. engr. Storage Tech., Louisville, 1982-84; mfg. rsch. engr. rohr Inc., Chula Vista, Calif., 1984-86; sr. quality engr. Info. Magnetics, San Diego, 1986-87; engring. supr. Johnson & Johnson, ACO, San Diego, 1987-89; rsch. specialist Rohr, Inc., Chula Vista, Calif., 1990-95; sr. devel. engr. Composite Optics Inc., San Diego, 1996—; prin. Mfg. Methods Cons., Jamul, Calif., 1989—; adj. prof. mech. engring. San Diego State U., 1987-90. Inventor method of mfg. laminated plastic tooling. Advisor Nat. U., San Diego, 1987-88. Mem. Soc. for the Advancement of Material and Process Engring. (ednl. chair, dir. San Diego County chpt. 1996-97). Home: PO Box 1036 Jamul CA 91935-1036 Office: Composite Optics Inc 9617 Distribution Ave San Diego CA 92121

JAIN, JAWAHAR, computer scientist, engineer, researcher; b. Bhopal, M.P., India, Apr. 14, 1965; came to U.S., 1986; s. Chadra Kant and Chandra Kumari (Kothari) J.; m. Jayshree Banthia, Jan. 23, 1994; 1 child, Lakshya. BEE, Bhopal U., M.P., India, 1986; MEE and Computer Engring., U. Tex., 1989, PhD in Elec. Engring. and Computer Engring., 1993. Rsch. scientist asst. Ctr. Trans. Rsch. U. Tex., Austin, 1988; summer intern Microelectronics and Computer Tech. Corp., Austin, 1991; rsch. asst. Computer Engring. Rsch. Ctr. U. Tex., Austin, 1989-92, postdoctoral fellow Computer Engring. Rsch. Ctr., 1992-93, 93-94; rsch. assoc. dept. computer sci. Tex. A & M. U., 1992-93; mem. rsch. staff Fujitsu Labs. Am., San Jose, Calif., 1994—; cons. Fault-Tolerant Computing Group Dept. Computer Sci., Tex. A & M U., 1993-94; spkr. in field; referee Internat. Conf. CAD, Design Automation Conf., European Design and Test Conf., Very Large Scale Integrated Circuits Design and Test. Contbr. articles to profl. jours. Mem. Assn. for Computing Machinery, IEEE (referee Transactions on Computers, Transactions on CAD). Home: 3500 Granada Ave Apt 164 Santa Clara CA 95051-3317 Office: Fujitsu Labs Am 3350 Scott Blvd Bldg # 34 Santa Clara CA 95054

JAIVIN, JONATHAN STEVEN, orthopedic surgeon; b. New London, Conn., May 7, 1958; s. Lewis Stanley and Naomi (Dorsky) J.; m. Ann Melissa Halverstadt, Sept. 4, 1988. ScB with honors in Biology, Brown U., 1980; MD, U. Conn., 1985. Diplomate Am. Bd. Orthopedic Surgery, Nat. Bd. Med. Examiners; qualified med. examiner, Calif.; lic. physician, Calif. Intern in gen. surgery Hartford (Conn.) Hosp., 1985-86, resident in gen. surgery, 1986-87; resident in orthop. surgery U. Conn. Combined Program, Farmington, 1987-90; fellow in foot and ankle surgery Baylor Coll. Medicine, Houston, 1990-91; attending surgeon So. Calif. Orthop. Inst., Van Nuys, 1991—; chmn. dept. orthop. surgery Valley Presbyn. Hosp., Van Nuys, 1994—; provisional staff Henry Mayo Newhall Hosp., Valencia, Calif., Motion Picture Hosp., Woodland Hills, Calif., West Hills Med. Ctr., West Hills; lectr. in field. Contbr. articles to profl. jours. Fellow Am. Acad. Orthop. Surgeons; mem. Am. Orthop. Foot and Ankle Soc. Office: So Calif Orthop Inst 6815 Noble Ave Van Nuys CA 91405-3794

JAKUBANIS, BETH, advertising executive; b. Chgo., Mar. 19, 1970; d. Theodore Francis and Barbera (Mays) J. BA in Comm. cum laude, Wash. State Univ., 1992. Extra Gen. Hosp., Hollywood, Calif., 1988-92; prodn. asst. Acad. Awards, Hollywood, 1990-92; advt. exec. KDAR Radio, Ventura, Calif., 1992-94, KEYT TV, Santa Barbara, Calif., 1994-95, KKLA Radio, L.A., 1995, Seltel Inc., 1997. Counselor Camp Cherith Pioneer Girls, Angelus Oaks, Calif., 1986-96; big sister YMCA, Pullman, Wash., 1991-92; missionary Calvary Cmty. Ch., Ensenada, Mex., 1995-96. Mem. Phi Beta Kappa. Home: 2731 Erringer Rd # 82 Simi Valley CA 93065-5751

JALAL, MAHBUBUL A.F., research chemist; b. Sylhet, Bangladesh, Dec. 31, 1948; came to U.S., 1982; s. Muhammad Nasibur Rahman and Kamrun Nesa Khanam; m. Ayesha Shirin Majumdar, Jan. 4, 1973; children: Adib Adnan, Niaz Ahsan, Sahel Afsan. BS with honors, U. Dhaka, Bangladesh, 1968, MS, 1969; PhD, U. Liverpool, Eng., 1977; MIBiol., CBiol. (hon.), Inst. of Biology, London, 1981. Chartered biologist, Eng. Lectr. plant scis. U. Dhaka, 1970-73, U. Chittagong, Bangladesh, 1973; postdoctoral assoc. dept. chemistry U. Glasgow, Scotland, 1977-78; postdoctoral assoc. depts. chemistry and botany U. Sheffield, Eng., 1978-82; rsch. scientist dept. chemistry U. Okla., Norman, 1982-88; scientist Plant Cell Rsch. Inst., Dublin, Calif., 1988-91; sr. rsch. chemist Pan-Agrl. Labs., Madera, Calif., 1991-94; rsch. chemist Valent USA Corp., 1995—. Contbr. chpts. to books, more than 30 articles to profl. jours.; patentee microbial method. Mem. Am. Chem. Soc., Inst. of Biology (London). Home: 7036 Lancaster Ct Dublin CA 94568-2111 Office: Valent USA Corp 6560 Trinity Ct Dublin CA 94568-2628 Address: 7036 Lancaster Ct Dublin CA 94568-2111

JALLINS, RICHARD DAVID, lawyer; b. L.A., Mar. 21, 1957; s. Walter Joshua and Elaine Beatrice (Youngerman) J.; m. Katherine Sue Pfeiffer, June 12, 1982; children: Stephen David, Rachel Marie. BA, U. Calif., Santa Barbara, 1978; JD, Calif. Western Sch. Law, 1981. Bar: Calif. 1988, U.S. Dist. Ct. (so. dist.) Calif. 1988. Panel atty. Bd. Prison Terms, Sacramento, 1989-96, Appellate Defenders, Inc., San Diego, 1989-91, Calif. Dept. Corrections, Parole Hearings Divsn., Sacramento, 1992-94; dep. commr. Bd. Prison Terms, 1996—. Mem. ABA, San Diego County Bar Assn., Phi Alpha Delta.

JAMES, CHARLES E., JR., lawyer; b. Pontiac, Mich., Sept. 19, 1948. BA, Occidental Coll., 1970; JD with highest distinction, U. Ariz. Bar: Ariz. 1973. Ptnr. Snell & Wilmer, Phoenix. Mem. ABA, Nat. Assn. Bond Lawyers. Office: Snell & Wilmer 1 Arizona Ctr Phoenix AZ 85004

JAMES, DARYL NORMAN, environmental engineer; b. Culver City, Calif., Feb. 2, 1946; s. Warren and Alayne (Meistral) Smith; m. June Alice

McClow, June 24, 1978; children: Matthew Dwayne, Andrew David. A of Engring., El Camino Coll., 1966; BSME, Calif. State U., Long Beach, 1969. Registered profl. engr., Nev., Calif. Structural design engr. Northrup Corp., Hawthorne, Calif., 1969-70; mech. engr. Long Beach (Calif.) Naval Shipyard, 1970-73; recreation supr. City of Manhattan Beach, Calif., 1975-79; engring. technician Spink Corp., Reno, 1979-80; civil engr. Nev. Dept. Transp., Carson City, 1980-86, prin. engr., 1986-92, chief environ. svcs., 1992—. Appointed mem. Parks & Recreation Commn., Carson City, Nev., 1993-94. Home: 3782 Prospect Dr Carson City NV 89703-7529 Office: Nev Dept Transp 1263 S Stewart St Carson City NV 89701-5229

JAMES, FRANKLIN JOSEPH, JR., public policy educator; b. Tampa, Fla., Nov. 11, 1946; s. Franklin Joseph Sr. and Eve (Keene) J.; m. Melanie Anne Lee, Sept. 9, 1967 (dec. Dec. 1987); children: Charles, Philip. BA in Econs. with honors, U. Ga., 1967; MPhil in Econs., Columbia U., 1976, PhD in Econs., 1976. Rsch. asst. Nat. Bur. Econ. Rsch., N.Y.C., 1969-71; sr. rsch. economist Rutgers U., Ctr. for Urban Policy, New Brunswick, N.J., 1971-74; rsch. assoc. The Urban Inst., Washington, 1974-77; dir. urban policy staff U.S. Dept. Housing and Urban Devel., Washington, 1977-81; prof. pub. policy U. Colo., Denver, 1981—; dir. doctoral studies U. Colo. Grad. Sch. Pub. Affairs, Denver; mem. rsch. adv. com. Fed. Nat. Mortgage Assn., Washington; mem. adv. com. Ctr. Cmty. Devel., N.Y.C. Co-author: President's National Urban Policy Report, 1980, Minorities in the Sunbelt, 1984; co-editor: Future of National Urban Policy, 1990. Staff dir. Colo. Pub. Pvt. Housing State Task Force, Denver; rsch. Gov.'s Task Force on the Homeless, Denver; mem. Mayor's Disbursement Com. for Ryan White Fund, Denver. Mem. Phi Beta Kappa. Democrat. Episcopalian. Home: 546 E Nichols Dr Littleton CO 80122-2838

JAMES, FREBURN LEROY, pathologist, retired; b. Battle Creek, Mich., Mar. 11, 1921; s. Freburn Watson and Aelola Adelaide (Clark) J.; m. Nina Wilanna Johnson, Apr. 11, 1946; children: Cherelyn Yvette, Karyl Susan, Donald Freburn. BA, W.Va. U., 1944; MD, Loma Linda U., 1949. Diplomate Am. Bd. Pathology. Instr. pathology for nurses Glendale Sanitarium and Hosp., 1948-50; instr. histology extension course Camp Roberts U. Calif., Santa Barbara, 1952; pathologist, dir. labs. Boulder Colo. Sanitarium and Hosp., 1953-55; pathologist Boulder County Hosp., 1953-54; instr. pathology U. Colo. Med. Sch., Denver, 1954-55; asst. pathologist, dir. sch. of med. tech. St. Joseph's Hosp., Denver, 1955; pathologist, dir. labs., dir. sch. med. tech. Port Huron (Mich.) Hosp., 1955-62; pathologist, dir. labs. Westminster (Calif.) Community Hosp., 1962-67; dir. Clin. Lab. Freburn L. James, M.D., Huntington Beach, Calif., 1963-69; pathologist Orange (Calif.) County Med. Ctr., 1967-69; asst. clin. prof. pathology U. Calif., Irvine, 1969, Grand Valley State Coll., Allendale, Mich., 1982-83; pathologist, dir. various labs. ICN Med. Labs. (formerly United Med. Labs.), Portland, Oreg., 1969-80; pathologist, dir. Reese-James Pathology Lab., Portland, 1969-75, Officer Histology Assocs. Lab., P.C., Portland, 1975-80, Heritage Hosp. Lab., Muskegon Heights, Mich., 1980-86, Visitors Hosp. (formerly Unity Hosp. Lab.), Buchanan, Mich., 1981-87, Continental Bio-Clin. Lab. Svcs., Inc., Grand Rapids, Mich., 1980-88, Reed City (Mich.) Hosp. Lab., 1986-88, Three Rivers (Mich.) Area Hosp. Lab., 1986-88; locum tenens, pathologist Kennewick (Wash.) Gen. Hosp., 1990-95, Sunnyside (Wash.) Hosp., 1990—, Our Lady of Lourdes Hosp., Pasco, Wash., 1990—, Western Labs., Yakima, Wash., 1990-95; part-time worker Reed City Hosp. Lab., Three Rivers Area Hosp. Lab., Bio-Clin. Lab. Svcs., Inc., 1988-89. Capt., USAR, 1951-53. Fellow Am. Soc. Clin. Pathology, Coll. Am. Pathologists; mem. AMA, Am. Soc. Cytology.

JAMES, GEORGE BARKER, II, apparel industry executive; b. Haverhill, Mass., May 25, 1937; s. Paul Withington and Ruth (Burns) J.; m. Beverly A. Burch, Sept. 22, 1962; children: Alexander, Christopher, Geoffrey, Matthew. AB, Harvard U., 1959; MBA, Stanford U., 1962. Fiscal dir. E.G. & G. Inc., Bedford, Mass., 1963-67; fin. exec. Am. Brands Inc., N.Y.C., 1967-69; v.p. Pepsico, Inc., N.Y.C., 1969-72; sr. v.p., chief fin. officer Arcata Corp., Menlo Park, Calif., 1972-82; exec. v.p. Crown Zellerbach Corp., San Francisco, 1982-85; sr. v.p., chief fin. officer Levi Strauss & Co., San Francisco, 1985—; bd. dirs. Pacific States Industries, Inc., Basic Vegetable Products, Inc., Fibreboard Corp., Crown Vantage Corp. Author: Industrial Development in the Ohio Valley, 1962. Mem. Andover (Mass.) Town Com., 1965-67; mem. Select Congl. Com. on World Hunger; mem. adv. coun. Calif. State Employees Pension Fund; chmn. bd. dirs. Towle Trust Fund; trustee Nat. Corp. Fund for the Dance, Cate Sch., Levi Strauss Found., Stern Grove Festival Assn., Zellerbach Family Fund, San Francisco Ballet Assn., Com. for Econ. Devel.; bd. dirs. Stanford U. Hosp.; vice-chmn. World Affairs Coun.; mem. San Francisco Com. on Fgn. Rels. With AUS, 1960-61. Mem. Pacific Union Club, Bohemian Club, Menlo Circus Club, Harvard Club, N.Y. Athletic Club. Home: 207 Walnut St San Francisco CA 94118-2012 Office: Levi Strauss & Co Levi's Plz 1155 Battery St San Francisco CA 94111-1230

JAMES, GEORGE LEROY, broadcasting executive; b. Colorado Springs, Colo., June 10, 1942; s. Cecil H. and Madeline (Dillon) J.; m. Joanne P. James, Aug. 18, 1986; children from previous marriage, Kevin, Brandon James. Student, Pueblo Jr. Coll. Former gen. mgr., owner KPIK, Colorado Springs, announcer, chief engr., sales, mktg. and pub. rels. staff; mktg. dir. Security Pacific Indsl. Bank, 1980; v.p. engring. and devel. KIQX Radio Sta., Durango, Colo., 1982-85; announcer personality KKCS Radio Sta., Colorado Springs, 1985; owner, operator motel bus. Dillon Motel, Manitou Springs, 1987—; part-time co-host talk show Kvor Radio Sta., Colorado Springs, 1989-91. Mem. Fiesta and Rodeo Com., Snowdown Com.; mem. Manitou Springs Park and Recreation Adv. Bd., 1991; mem. Ambassadors Com., Mktg. Com., Manitou Springs; chmn. Accommodations Com. and Intergovtl. Affairs Com., Manitou Springs; mem. Colo. Springs City Coun., 1977-81; chmn. Ambulance Svc. Tech. Adv. Bd., Colorado Springs; mem. regional plumbing com. Regional Bldg. Dept.; bd. dirs. Nat. Little Britches Rodeo; mem. Pikes Peak Area Coun. Govts., 1977-81; chmn. gov. front range project El Paso County. Mem. Manitou Springs C. of C. (bd. dirs. 1993). Home and Office: 134 Manitou Ave Manitou Springs CO 80829-2427

JAMES, HELEN ANN, plastic surgeon; b. Palmerston North, New Zealand, May 5, 1940; came to U.S., 1977; d. George Headley and Betty Beatrice (McDonald) J.; married (dec. Apr. 1993). MB, ChB, U. Otago, Dunedin, New Zealand, 1964; Fellow, Royal Coll. Surgeons, London, England, 1972. Diplomate Am. Bd. Plastic Surgery. Internship Palmerston North Hosp., New Zealand, 1965-66; residency plastic surgery Brdg Earn Hosp., Perthshire, England, 1973-74, St. Lukes Hosp., Bradford, England, 1975-77; fellow plastic surgery Mount Sinai Med. Ctr., Miami Beach, 1977-79; residency plastic surgery N.C. Meml. Med. Ctr., Chapel Hill, 1979-81; St. Joseph Hosp., Bellingham, Wash.; pvt. practice Bellingham, Wash. Mem. AMA, Am. Soc. Plastic and Reconstructive Surgeons, Wash. State Med. Assn. Office: 3001 Squalicum Pky Ste 5 Bellingham WA 98225-1932

JAMES, HERB MARK (JAY JAMES), foundation and insurance executive, free trade consultant; b. Trail, B.C., Can., Jan. 30, 1936; s. George William and Violet Ethyl (Corbin) J. Student, bus. adminstrn. Simon Fraser U., 1965-69; m. Patricia Helen Boyd, Nov. 1, 1958; 1 child, Brad Mark. Founder Internat. Sound Found., Ottawa, Can., 1967—, Blaine, Wash., 1975—; cons. Fed. Bus. Dev. Bank; mem. bus. adv. bd. U.S. Senate, 1981—; pres. Bus. Navigator Svcs.; cons. Can. Internat. Devel. Agy.; founder Better Hearing Better Life projects, Fiji, Kenya, Cayman Islands, Nepal, Costa Rica, Pakistan, Guatemala, Mex., Canassist Mazatlan, Mex., 1995—. Musician B. Pops Orch., South Pacific N.G.O. Group, Ctrl. European Enterprise Devel. Group, North-South Free Trade Adjustment Group; pres. N.W. NAFTA Trade Assn. Govt. of Can. grantee, 1973-83. Mem. Christian Bus. Men's Assn., Can.-Philippines Soc. (co-founder), Conbrio Soc. (hon. dir.), Blaine C. of C., Masons, Shriners, Demolay. Office: Am Bldg PO Box 1587 Blaine WA 98231-1587 also: Columbia Sq 105-1005 Columbia St New Westchester BC

JAMES, MARION RAY, magazine founder, editor; b. Bellmont, Ill., Dec. 6, 1940; s. Francis Miller and Lorraine A. (Wylie) J.; m. Janet Sue Tennis, June 16, 1960; children: Jeffrey Glenn, David Ray, Daniel Scott, Cheryl Lynne. BS, Oakland City Coll., Ind., 1964; MS, St. Francis Coll., Fort Wayne, Ind., 1978. Sports and city editor Daily Clarion, Princeton, Ind., 1963-65; English tchr. Jac-Cen-Del High Sch., Osgood, Ind., 1965-66; indsl. editor Whirlpool Corp., Evansville and LaPorte, Ind., 1966-68, Magnavox Govt. and Indsl. Electronics Co., Fort Wayne, 1968-79; editor, pub., founder Bowhunter mag., Fort Wayne, Ind., 1971-88; editor Bowhunter mag., Kalispell, Mont., 1989—; instr. Ind.-Purdue U., Ft. Wayne, 1980-88. Author: Bowhunting for Whitetail and Mule Deer, 1975, Successful Bowhunting, 1985, My Place, 1991, The Bowhunter's Handbook, 1997; editor: Pope and Young Book World Records, 1975, 4th edit., 1993, Bowhunting Adventures, 1977. Recipient Best Editorial award United Community Svc. Publs., 1970-72; named Alumnus of Yr., Oakland City Coll., 1982, to Hall of Fame, Mt. Carmel High Sch., Ill., 1983. Mem. Outdoor Writers Assn. Am., Fort Wayne Assn. Bus. Editors (Fort Wayne Bus. Editor of Yr. 1969, pres. 1975-76), Toastmasters (Able Toastmaster award), Alpha Phi Gamma, Alpha Psi Omega, Mu Tau Kappa. Home: 2325 Wolftail Pnes Whitefish MT 59937-8099 *Read! Being a good reader is the key to good thinking. Develop and expand your mind through active use of the printed word and you will discover a wide world of unlimited possibilities - and ultimate success that comes with self-discovery.*

JAMES, MARK WILLIAM, camera operator; b. L.A., Nov. 10, 1954; s. William Dean J. and Barbara Elizabeth (Lyon) Harrison; m. Christine Marie McGarry, Mar 3, 1990; 1 child, William Scott. BA in Anthropology, Claif. State U., L.A., 1978; postgrad., UCLA, 1987. Freelance cameraman KNBC-TV, KTLA-TV, 1987—; judge ATAS nat. and local Emmy, ACE awards. Mem. Nat. Press Club (Golden Mike & Emmy awards 1995), Nat. Press Photographers Assb., L.A. Press Club (cert. merit 1992), L.A. Press Photographers Assn. Home: 2420 Los Olivos Ln La Crescenta CA 91214-3130

JAMES, NORMAN JOHN, plastic and reconstructive hand surgeon; b. Milw., Nov. 25, 1938. BA, Lawrence Coll., 1960; MD, U. Chgo., 1964. cert. gen. surgery, plastic surgery, hand surgery. Office: 235 E Rowan Ave Ste 206 Spokane WA 99207-1239*

JAMES, ROSEMARIE, mayor. Mayor Hesperia, Calif. Address: 15776 Main St Ste 10 Hesperia CA 92345

JAMES, WAYNE EDWARD, electrical engineer; b. Racine, Wis., Apr. 2, 1950; s. Ronald Dean James and Arlene Joyce (Mickelsen) Dawson; m. Edith Yvonne Cone, Apr. 6, 1997; children: Terry Scott, Kevin Arthur. BS in Electronic Engring. Tech., U. So. Colo., 1976; MS in Computer Sci., Colo. U., 1996. Electronic technician Lawrence Livermore (Calif.) Nat. Lab., 1976-80; electronic technician Inmos Corp., Colorado Springs, Colo., 1980-86, CAD engr., 1986-87; CAD engr. United Techs. Microelectronics Ctr., Colorado Springs, 1988—. Sec.-treas. Stratmoor Hills Vol. Fire Dept., Colorado Springs, 1983, 84, lt., 1985, capt., 1986. Served with USN, 1968-72. Named Fireman of Yr., Stratmoor Hills Vol. Fire Dept., 1983. Lutheran. Office: UTMC Microelectronic Systems 4350 Centennial Blvd Colorado Springs CO 80907-3415

JAMES, WILLIAM LANGFORD, aerospace engineer; b. Southampton, Va., Jan. 13, 1939; s. Leroy and Worthie (Murphy) J.; m. Elaine Cecilia Reed; children: William Jr., Terri Lynne. Student, Va. State Coll., 1956, Hampton Inst., 1958; BS, Calif. State U., Los Angeles, 1962, MS, 1964; postgrad., U. Nev., Reno, 1984; spl. engring. studies, UCLA, 1970-82. Rsch. engr. non-metallic materials lab. N.Am. Aviation, L.A., 1960-67; rsch. analyst tech. staff The Aerospace Corp., El Segundo, 1967-75, materials engr., 1975-85; project engr. program mgmt. office space launch ops. The Aerospace Corp., El Segundo, Calif., 1985-96. Contbr. numerous articles and reports to profl. publs.; patentee in field. Recipient numerous awards for USAF space contributions. Mem. AAAS, Soc. Advancement Material and Process Engring. (vice-chmn. 1987-89). Home: PO Box 19735 Los Angeles CA 90019-0735 Office: Aerospace Corp M5 712 Los Angeles CA 90009

JAMESON, PATRICIA MARIAN, government agency administrator; b. Pitts., Mar. 17, 1945; d. Vernon L. and Dorothy Leam (Wilson) J.; B.A., Northwestern U., 1967; M.A., Ohio State U., 1969, with HUD, 1970—, project mgr., Detroit, 1976-77, acting dir. housing mgmt., 1978, dep. area mgr. Milw. Area Office, 1978-85, acting area mgr., 1979-80, 82, regional dir. adminstrn. Chgo. Regional Office, 1985-95, dir. adminstrv. svc. ctr., Denver, 1995—. Mem. Chgo. Council on Fgn. Relations. Recipient Quality Performance award HUD, 1973, 75, 80, Outstanding Performance award, 1980, 85, 87, 88, 90, 91, 92, 94, 96, Disting. Svc. award 1992; NDEA fellow, 1967-69. Mem. Nat. Assn. Female Execs., NOW, Fed. Execs. Inst. Alumni Assn., Phi Beta Kappa, Pi Sigma Alpha. Office: 633 17th St Denver CO 80202-3660

JAMIESON, DALE WALTER, philosophy and biology educator; b. Sioux City, Iowa, Oct. 21, 1947; s. Dale Walter and Betty Jo (Smith) J.; m. Toby Carlin Jacober, Sept. 23, 1988. BA, San Francisco State U., 1970; MA, U. N.C., 1972, PhD, 1976. Instr., asst. prof. N.C. State U., Raleigh, 1975-78; asst. prof. SUNY, Fredonia, 1978-80; asst. prof. U. Colo., Boulder, 1980-85, assoc. prof., 1985-92, prof. environmental philosophy and philosophy biology, 1992—. Co-editor: Interpretation and Explanation in the Study of Animal Behavior, 1990, Reflecting on Nature, 1994, Readings in Animal Cognition. Office: U Colorado Dept Philosophy CB 232 Boulder CO 80309

JAMIESON, JAMES BRADSHAW, foundation administrator; b. L.A., June 10, 1931; s. Charles Cameron and Ruth (Bradshaw) J.; m. Perry McNaughton, Dec. 27, 1959; children: Jeffrey McNaughton, Dalton Charles. AA, Citrus Coll., 1950; BA, Claremont Men's Coll., 1955; MA, Claremont Grad. Sch., 1958; PhD, Brown U., 1966. Assoc. prof. polit. studies Pitzer Coll. and Claremont Grad. Sch., 1968-75; rsch. polit. scientist UCLA, 1972-73; v.p. for devel. Pitzer Coll., 1968-72, v.p., 1973-78, prof. polit. studies, 1975-83, exec. v.p., 1979-83, acting pres., 1978-79; prof. govt. Claremont Grad. Sch., 1975-87; v.p. for rsch. Claremont McKenna Coll., 1983-87; exec. dir. Found. for Performing Art Ctr., San Luis Obispo, Calif., 1987—; commr. Calif. Postsecondary Edn. Commn., Sacramento, 1987-92; dir. Global Village, Seattle, 1989—. Contbr. articles to profl. jours. Staff, sec. Ctrl. Coast Performing Arts Ctr. Commn., San Luis Obispo, 1993—. Sgt. USAF, 1950-52. Fellow Brown U., 1960, 63, tchg. fellow, 1962, fellow Resources for the Future, 1964; rsch. grantee U.S. Dept. Interior, 1972-73. Mem. Santa Lucia Flyfishers (bd. dirs. 1988—), Trout Unltd. (bd. dirs. Calif. coun. 1989-94, bd. dirs. nat. bd. 1986-90), Marine's Meml. Club. Office: Found for Performing Arts PO 12843 San Luis Obispo CA 93406-2843

JAMIESON NICHOLS, JILL, journalist; b. Denver, Sept. 20, 1956; d. Paul Clark Jr. and Dorothy Marie (Pulley) Jamieson; m. Kevin Shawn Nichols, July 9, 1953; 1 child, Holly Marie Nichols. BA in Mass Comms., U. So. Colo., 1979. Reporter, photographer Bent County Democrat, Las Animas, Colo., 1979-81, Valley Courier, Alamosa, Colo., 1981-83; assoc. editor Canyon Courier, Evergreen, Colo., 1983-87; assoc. editor Golden (Colo.) Transcript, 1987-96, editor, 1996; staff reporter Colo. Real Estate Jour., 1996—. Mem. Jeffco Local Emergency Planning Com., Golden, 1988-89; bd. dirs. Jefferson Symphony Orch., 1996—. Recipient Cmty. Svc. award Colo. Press Assn., 1986, 94, Sweepstakes Best News Story award, 1989, Shining Star award, 1993, Best Feature Story award, 1994, Best Serious Column award, 1995. Republican. Home: 2014 Washington Cir Golden CO 80401-2363 Office: Golden Transcript 1000 10th St Golden CO 80401-1028

JAMIN, MATTHEW DANIEL, lawyer, magistrate judge; b. New Brunswick, N.J., Nov. 29, 1947; s. Matthew Bernard and Frances Marie (Newburg) J.; m. Christine Frances Bjorkman, June 28, 1969; children: Rebecca, Erica. BA, Colgate U., 1969; JD, Harvard U., 1974. Bar: Alaska 1974, U.S. Dist. Ct. Alaska 1974, U.S. Ct. Appeals (9th cir.) 1980. Staff atty. Alaska Legal Svcs., Anchorage, 1974-75; supervising atty. Alaska Legal Svcs., Kodiak, Alaska, 1975-81; contract atty. Pub. Defender's Office State of Alaska, Kodiak, 1976-82; prin. Matthew D. Jamin, Atty., Kodiak, 1982; ptnr. Jamin & Bolger, Kodiak, 1982-85, Jamin, Ebell, Bolger & Gentry, Kodiak, 1985—; part-time magistrate judge U.S. Cts., Kodiak, 1984—. Part-time instr. U. Alaska Kodiak Coll., 1975—; active Threshhold Svcs., Inc., Kodiak, 1985—, pres., 1985-92, 95-96. Mem. Alaska Bar Assn. (Professionalism award 1988), Kodiak Bar Assn. Office: US Dist Ct 323 Carolyn Ave Kodiak AK 99615-6348

JAMISON, WARREN, writer, lecturer, publisher, literary agent; b. Mitchell, S.D., Aug. 12, 1924; s. Robert William J.; m. Kitty Sue Wilkerson, Oct. 7, 1961; children: Cynthia Sue, Brian Erik. Co-author: (with Danielle Kennedy) How to List and Sell Real Estate in the 90s, 1991; (with Ed McMahon) Ed McMahon's Superselling, 1989, (Literary Guild Selection); (with others) Screw: The Truth About Walpole Prison by the Guard Who Lived It, 1989, (Conservative Book Club Selection), (with Brian Jamison and Josh Gold) Electronic Selling: 23 Steps to E-Selling Profits, 1997; editor: (books) Ed McMahon's The Art of Public Speaking, 1986, How to Master the Art of Selling, Tom Hopkins, 1980, 2d rev. edition, 1982, The Official Guide to Success, 1983, Tom Hopkins, Guide to Greatness in Sales, Tom Hopkins, 1992, Toughness Training for Life, Dr. James E. Loehr, 1993, The New Toughness Training for Sports, Dr. James E Loehr, 1994, The Anti-Diet Book, Jack Groppel, 1995. Mem. Authors Guild, Am. Soc. Journalists and Authors. Home and Office: 2201 S Palm Canyon #202 Palm Springs CA 92264-9341

JAMPLIS, ROBERT WARREN, surgeon, medical foundation executive; b. Chgo., Apr. 1, 1920; s. Mark and Janet (McKenna) J.; m. Roberta Cecelia Prior, Sept. 5, 1947; children: Mark Prior, Elizabeth Ann Jamplis Bluestone. B.S., U. Chgo., 1941, M.D., 1944; M.S., U. Minn., 1951. Diplomate Am. Bd. Surgery, Am. Bd. Thoracic Surgery. Asst. resident in surgery U. Chgo., 1946-47; fellow in thoracic surgery Mayo Clinic, Rochester, Minn., 1947-52; chief thoracic surgery Palo Alto (Calif.) Med. Clinic, 1958-81, exec. dir., 1965-81; clin. prof. surgery Stanford U. Sch. Medicine, 1958—; mem. council SRI Internat.; chmn. bd. TakeCare Corp.; charter mem., bd. regents Am. Coll. Physician Execs.; mem. staff Stanford Univ. Hosp., Santa Clara Valley Med. Center, San Jose, VA Hosp., Palo Alto, Sequoia Hosp., Redwood City, Calif., El Camino Hosp., Mountain View, Calif., Harold D. Chope Community Hosp., San Mateo, Calif.; pres., chief exec. officer Palo Alto Med. Found.; past chmn. Fedn. Am. Clinics; dir. Blue Cross Calif.; varsity football team physician Stanford U. Author: (with G.A. Lillington) A Diagnostic Approach to Chest Diseases, 1965, 2d edit., 1979; contbr. numerous articles to profl. jours. Trustee Santa Barbara Med. Found. Clinic; past pres. Calif. div. Am. Cancer Soc.; past chmn. bd. Group Practice Polit. Action Com.; past mem. athletic bd. Stanford U.; past mem. cabinet U. Chgo.; bd. dirs. Herbert Hoover Boys' Club; past trustee No. Calif. Cancer Program; past bd. dirs. Core Communications in Health, Community Blood Res., others. Served to lt. USNR, 1944-46, 52-54. Recipient Alumni citation U. Chgo., 1968, Nat. Divsn. award Am. Cancer Soc., 1979, Med. Exec. award Am. Coll. Med. Group Adminstrs., 1981, Russel V. Lee award lectr. Am. Group Practice Assn., 1982, Mayo Disting. Alumnus award, 1991. Mem. Inst. Medicine of Nat. Acad. Scis., ACS, Am. Assn. Thoracic Surgery, Am. Surg. Assn., Soc. Thoracic Surgeons (past pres.), Western Thoracic Surg. Assn. (past pres.), Western Surg. Assn., Pacific Coast Surg. Assn., San Francisco Surg. Soc. (past pres.), Portland Surg. Soc. (hon.), Doctors Mayo Soc., Am. Coll. Chest Physicians (bd. govs.), Calif. Acad. Medicine, Am. Fedn. Clin. Research, Am. Group Practice Assn. (past pres.), AMA, Calif. Med. Assn., Santa Clara County Med. Assn., Sigma Xi. Republican. Roman Catholic. Clubs: Bohemian, Pacific Union, Commonwealth of California (San Francisco); Menlo Country (Woodside, (Calif.); Menlo Circus (Atherton, Calif.); Stanford (Calif.) Golf; Rancheros Visitadores (Santa Barbara, Calif.). Office: 300 Homer Ave Palo Alto CA 94301-2726

JAMPOL, JEFFREY, music industry executive; b. L.A., Sept. 16, 1958; s. Richard Alan and Sylvia X. (Levine) J. Student, Sonoma State U., 1974-76; BA, San Francisco State U., 1978. Retail mgmt. CBS, Inc., San Francisco, 1976-78; local promotion CBS, Inc. Epic Records, San Francisco, 1978-79, WEA, Inc. Atlantic Records, San Francisco, 1979-81; exec. producer Polymedia, Inc., Beverly Hills, Calif., 1981-83; nat. advt./promotion mgr. Music Connection Mag., Hollywood, Calif., 1983-84; nat. advt. dir. Gold Trade Publ., Inc., Encino, Calif., 1984-89; v.p., assoc. publisher Coast Media, Inc., Culver City, Calif., 1990-94; sr. v.p., ptnr. Brentwood News Group, Inc., Westwood, Calif., 1990; prin. Jampol Artist Mgmt., L.A., 1993—. Mem. Nat. Acad. Rec. Arts and Scis. (bd. dirs. L.A. chpt. 1983-85, voting mem. 1985—), Westchester/LAX C. of C. (bd. dirs. 1992-93), Culver City Jaycees, Santa Monica Jaycees. Democrat. Office: 2546 Westwood Blvd Los Angeles CA 90064-3240

JANES, ROBERT ROY, museum executive, archaeologist; b. Rochester, Minn., Apr. 23, 1948; m. Priscilla Bickel; children: Erica Helen, Peter Bickel. Student, Lawrence U., 1966-68, BA in Anthropology cum laude, 1970; student, U. of the Ams., Mexico City, 1968, U. Calif., Berkeley, 1968-69; PhD in Archaeology, U. Calgary, Alta., Can., 1976. Postdoctoral fellow Arctic Inst. N.Am., U. Calgary, 1981-82; adj. prof. archaeology U. Calgary, 1990—; founding dir. Prince of Wales No. Heritage Centre, Yellowknife, N.W.T., 1976-86, project dir. Dealy Island Archaeol. and Conservation Project, 1977-82; founding exec. dir. Sci. Inst. of N.W.T.; sci. advisor Govt. of N.W.T., Yellowknife, 1986-89; exec. dir., pres., CEO Glenbow Mus. Art Gallery Libr. and Archives, Calgary, 1989—; adj. prof. archaeology U. Calgary, 1990—. Author book, manuscripts, monographs, book chpts.; ontbr. articles to profl. jours. mem. First Nations/CMA Task Force on Mus. and First Peoples, 1989-92. Recipient Nat. Pks. Centennial award Environment Can., 1985, Can. Studies Writing award Assn. Can. Studies, 1989, Disting. Alumni award Alumni Assn. of U. Calgary, 1989, L.R. Briggs Disting. Achievement award Lawrence U., 1991; Can. Coun. doctoral fellow, 1973-76; rsch. grantee Govt. of Can., 1974, Social Scis. and Humanities Rsch. Coun. Can., 1988-89. Fellow Arctic Inst. N.Am. (bd. dirs. 1983-90, vice-chmn. bd. 1985-89, hon. rsch. assoc. 1983-84, chmn. priorities and planning com. 1983-84, exec. com. 1984-86, assoc. editor Arctic jour. 1987—), Am. Anthrop. Assn. (fgn. fellow); mem. Soc. for Am. Archaeology, Can. Archaeol. Assn. (v.p. 1980-82, pres. 1984-86, co-chmn. fed. heritage policy com. 1986-88), Current Anthropology (assoc.), Can. Mus. Assn. (hon. life mem., cert accreditation 1982, Outstanding award in Mus. Mgmt., Outstanding Achievement award for publ. 1996), Internat. Coun. Mus., Can. Art Mus. Dirs. Orgn. (mem.-at-large bd. dirs.), Mus. West (bd. dirs.), Alberta Mus. Assn. (moderator seminars 1990, Merit award 1992, Merit award for Museums and the Paradox of Change 1996), Ranchmens Club, Calgary Philharmonic Soc., Sigma Xi. Home: Box 32 Site 32, RR 12, Calgary, AB Canada T3E 6W3 Office: Glenbow Mus-AB Inst, 130 9 Ave SE, Calgary, AB Canada T2G 0P3

JANIGIAN, BRUCE JASPER, lawyer, educator; b. San Francisco, Oct. 21, 1950; s. Michael D. Janigian and Stella (Minasian) Amerian; m. Susan Elizabeth Frye, Oct. 4, 1986; children: Alan Michael, Alison Elizabeth. AB, U. Calif., Berkeley, 1972; JD, U. Calif., San Francisco, 1975; LLM, George Washington U., 1982. Bar: Calif. 1975, U.S. Supreme Ct. 1979, D.C. 1981. Dir. Hastings Rsch. Svcs., Inc., San Francisco, 1973-75; judge adv. in Spain, 1976-78; commr. U.S. Navy and Marine Corps Ct. Mil. Rev., 1978-79; atty. advisor AID U.S. State Dept., Washington, 1979-84; dep. dir., gen. counsel Calif. Employment Devel. Dept., Sacramento, 1984-89; Fulbright scholar, vis. prof. law U. Salzburg, Austria, 1989-90; chmn. Calif. Agrl. Labor Rels. Bd., 1990-95; v.p. Europe, resident dir. Salzburg (Austria) Seminar, 1995-96; U.S. legate European Acad. Scis. and Art, 1996—; Rapporteur World Economic Forum, 1996—; prof. law McGeorge Sch. Law, U. Pacific, Sacramento, 1986—, Inst. on Internat. Legal Studies, Salzburg, summer 1987, London Inst. on Comml. Law, summers 1989, 92, 93; vis. scholar Hoover Inst. War, Revolution and Peace, Stanford U., 1991-92; dir. Vienna-Budapest East/West Trade Inst., 1993; vis. prof. law U. Salzburg, 1995-96. Editor: Financing International Trade and Development, 1986, 87, 89, International Business Transactions, 1989, 92, International Trade Law, 1993, 94. Coord. fund raiser March of Dimes, Sacramento, 1987. Capt. USNR, JAGC, 1976-79, mem. Res. Fulbright scholar, 1989-90; decorated Meritorious Achievement medal; recipeint USAID Meritorious Honor award. Mem. Calif. Bar Assn., D.C. Bar Assn., Sacamento Bar Assn. (exec. com. taxation sect. 1988-89), Sacramento Met. C. of C. (award for program contbns. and cmty. enrichment 1989), European Acad. Scis. and Art, World Art Forum, Austro-Am. Soc. (v.p. 1996), Naval Res. Officers Assn., Marine Meml. Assn., Fulbright Assoc. (life), Knights of Vartan, Phi Beta Kappa. Home and Office: 1631 12th Ave Sacramento CA 95818-4146

JANIGRO, DAMIR, physiologist, educator; b. Zagreb, Croatia, Mar. 16, 1957; came to the U.S., 1984; s. Antonio and Neda (Cihlar) J.; m. Kim Ann Conklin, Dec. 20, 1989; 1 child, Mattia Antonio. PhD, U. Milan, Italy, 1982. Project leader FIDIA Rsch. Labs., Abano, Italy, 1982-84; postdoctoral assoc. U. Wash., Seattle, 1984-87; rsch. assoc. U. Milan, Italy, 1987-89; asst. prof. U. Wash., Seattle, 1990-96, assoc. prof., 1996—.

Recipient First award NIH, 1994. Mem. Am. Heart Assn., A. Physiol. Soc., Internat. Brain Rsch. Orgn., Soc. for Neurosci.

JANIS, KENNETH M., physician; b. Bklyn., Aug. 12, 1939; s. Robert and Ida (Sonis) J.; m. Judy Byrnes, Oct. 3, 1994. BA, Colgate U., 1960; MD, NYU, 1964. Intern Boston City Hosp., 1964-65; resident Mass. Gen. Hosp., 1965-67; fellow Stanford (Calif.) U., 1967-68; asst. prof. Harvard U./Mass. Gen. Hosp., Boston, 1972-74; clin. prof. U. Calif., Irvine, 1976-92; assoc. prof. anesthesiology U. N.Mex., Albuquerque, 1992—. Capt. USAF, 1968-70. Office: Univ NMex Anesthesiology Sch of Medicine Albuquerque NM 87131-5216

JANIS, SHARON LEAH, film and television editor and producer, author; b. Detroit, Oct. 21, 1959; d. Melvin and Eva (Gant) J. Editor, producer Disney KCAL-TV, 1990-92; editor, co-producer feature film Beretta's Island, 1992-93; editor Power Rangers TV Show, 1993-95; editor, assoc. producer X-Men TV Show, 1993-95. Author: Never to Return: Stories and Insights on the Path of Conscious Evolution, 1996; editor NBC network promos; producer/dir./editor music video Desert to the Sea. Recipient Best TV Enterprise award AP, 1991, Silver medal N.Y. FEstivals, 1992, 1st place for video editing L.A. Press Club, 1991. Mem. Acad. TV Arts and Scis. (Emmy 1991).

JANKOVITZ, JOSEPH EDWARD, psychologist, educator, nurse; b. N.Y.C., Oct. 24, 1943; s. Joseph George and Theresa (Wrbal) J.; m. Joann Coulbourn O'Boyle, Aug. 6, 1976; children: Joseph G., Robert O'Boyle, Suzan O'Boyle, Joseph K. O'Boyle. AA in Nursing, Glendale C.C., 1972; BS in Rehab. Counseling, U. Ariz., 1974, MEd in Counseling, 1975; PhD in Clin. Psychology, La Jolla U., 1992. RN, Ariz.; cert. in clin. and med. Ericksonian hypnosis, substance abuse counseling, neuro linguistic programming (master practitioner and trainer), eye movement desensitization and reprocessing. Staff nurse U. Ariz. Hosp., Tucson, 1972-73; charge nurse psychiat. unit St. Mary's Hosp. and Health Ctr., Tucson, 1973-74, Pima County Hosp., Tucson, 1974-77; owner, clin. dir. Horizons Unltd Counseling Svcs., Tucson, 1977-80; charge nurse Posada Del Sol, Tucson, 1980-81; asst. DON Desert Hosp., Palm Springs, Calif., 1981-83; assoc. DON Indio (Calif.) Cmty. Hosp., 1983; mental health unit supr. Victor Valley Hosp., Victorville, Calif., 1984-86; clin. intern, psychiat. RN Horizons Unlimited Counseling Svc., Joshua Tree, 1986-91; post-doctoral intern, clin. therapist Dept. Mental Health San Bernadino County, 1993-95; clin. dir. Oasis Mental Health Treatment Hosp., Indio, Calif., 1995—; adj. prof. psychology Chapman U., Copper Mountain Campus of Coll. of Desert. Bd. dirs. Joshua Basin Water Dist., 1986-90. With USN, 1960-68, Vietnam. Decorated Cross of Galantry (Vietnam). Mem. Masters and Wardens Assn. (pres. 1979), Masons (32d degree, master 1979), Shriners, Kappa Delta Pi, Phi Delta Kappa.

JANKOWSKA, MARIA ANNA, librarian; b. Jarocin, Poland, Aug. 12, 1952; d. Tadeusz and Aleksandra (Ruszkowska) Nocun; m. Piotr L. Jankowski, Jan. 14, 1978; children: Pawel Pat, Marta Maja. MA, Sch. Econs., Poznan, Poland, 1975, PhD, 1983; M Libr. Info. Sci., U. Calif., Berkeley, 1989. Rsch. and tchg. asst. Sch. Econs., Poznan, 1976-83, asst. prof., 1983-85; catalog libr., asst. prof. U. Idaho, Moscow, 1989-94, network resources libr., assoc. prof., 1995—. Author: Electronic Guide to Polish Research and University Libraries, 1996; founding editor Green Libr. Jour., 1991-94; gen. editor Electronic Green Jour., 1994—. Guest scholar Smithsonian Inst., Woodrow Wilson Internat. Ctr., Washington, 1985; fellow U Calif., Berkeley Sch. Libr. and Info. Studies, 1989; grantee Rsch. Coun. Grant, U. Idaho, 1990, 95, Internat. Rsch. and Exchs. Bd., Washington, 1995. Mem. ALA (chair task force on environ. 1993-95, Idaho Libr. Assn., Beta Phi Mu. Office: U Idaho Libr Rayburn St Moscow ID 83844-2350

JANKOWSKI, THEODORE ANDREW, artist; b. New Brunswick, N.J., Dec. 14, 1946; s. Theodore Andrew and Lois (Amarescu) J.; m. Rebecca Buck, July 23, 1983; 1 child, Tito Henry. Student, McMurrough Sch. Art, Indialantic, Fla., 1956-58, 74-75, R.I. Sch. Design, 1972, Cape Sch. of Art, Provincetown, Mass., 1975-76, 79-87, Cen. Fla. U., 1976-77. One-man shows include Eye of Horus Gallery, Provincetown, 1985; exhibited in group shows at Provincetown Art Assn. Mus., 1984, Bethlehem (Pa.) City Hall, 1988, Michael Ingbar Gallery, N.Y.C., 1988, 91; represented in permanent collections at State Mus. at Palace of Peter the Gt., Leningrad, USSR, Mishkan Olemanut Mus. Art, Israel, CIGNA Mus., Phila., Johns Hopkins U., Balt., Holyoke (Mass.) Mus. Art, McGill U., Montreal, Que., Can., Downey (Calif.) Mus. Art, Ark. Art Ctr., Little Rock, others. Mem. Copley Soc. Boston, Internat. Platform Assn. Home: PO Box 791 Kapaau HI 96755-0791

JANOS, LEO HERBERT, writer; b. N.Y.C., Feb. 3, 1933; s. Seymour and Lucille (Roth) J.; m. Bonnie Parker, July 23, 1955; children: Karen, Linda, Steven. BA in English, Park Coll., 1955; MA in Comm., U. Chgo., 1956. Pub. rels. asst. Peace Corps, Washington, 1962-64; editor U.S. Info. Agy., Washington, 1964-65; speech writer White House, Washington, 1965-68; journalist Time Mag., Washington, Houston & LA, 1968-78; pvt. practice writer L.A., 1978—; author's cons. UCLA Writer's Program, 1993—, instr., 1993, 94. Author: Crime of Passion, 1983, Yeager, 1985, Skunk Works, 1995. With U.S. Army, 1957-59. Recipient Writing award U.S. Steel Found. Am. Inst. Physics Sci., Balt., 1981. Mem. PEN, Author's Guild.

JANOTA, DEBILYN MARIE, school principal; b. Portland, Oreg., Apr. 25, 1953; d. Art Philip and LaVeta Marie (Dozler) Christiansen; m. Joseph Edward Janota III, June 10, 1972; children: Gia Ann, Joseph Ernest IV. BA in Music Edn. K-12, Oreg. Coll. Edn., Monmouth, 1975. Cert. K-12 music specialist. Tchr. Regis H.S., Stayton, Oreg., 1975-77, St. Mary Grade Sch., Stayton, 1978-94; prin. Queen of Peace, Salem, Oreg., 1994—. Chair Chemeketa Cmty. Schs. Kids Track, Stayton, 1983-94. Recipient Support-Cooperation award YMCA, Salem, 1995. Mem. ASCD, AAUW, Archdiocese of Portland in Oreg. Edn., Nat. Cath. Ednl. Assn. (Disting. Grad. 1994), DARE (nat. and county), Willamette Valley Devel. Officers, Salem Area C. of C. Home: 11632 Shaff Rd SE Aumsville OR 97325-9726 Office: Queen of Peace Sch 4227 Lone Oak Rd SE Salem OR 97302-5750

JANOWSKI, KARYN ANN, artist; b. Milw., Aug. 15, 1958; d. Robert Arthur and Evelyn Rose (Spanbauer) J. BS in Art, U. Wis., 1984. Dir., founder Warehouse Studio for Visual Artists and Musicians, Madison, 1984-86, 88-89; tchg. asst. art therapy seminar U. Wis., 1983; artist assoc. San Francisco Women Artists Gallery, 1990-91. Muralist Whitewater (Wis.) Hist. Soc., 1980, Mifflin St. Cmty. Coop Mural, Madison, 1987; contbr. artwork/biography to American Artists, an Illustrated Survey of Leading Contemporaries, The California Art Rev., Art Comm. Internat. Curated Collection I; scenic artist: The Wind in the Willows; works in permanent collections at Tralfamadore Coop, Archive of Wis. Regional Primate Rsch. Ctr., Dynamic Resources, Inc., Soc. of Haight-Ashbury Charade, San Francisco, Niels and faith Ingwersen, Jeff Scott Olson, Esq; exhbns. include: Wis. Ctr., Madison, Firehouse 7, DAS Club, The Cannery Bldg., San Francisco, L.A. Mcpl. Art Gallery. Mem. L.A. Cultural Affairs Slide Registry, 1996—. Mem. Art Access. Democrat. Home and Office: 1775 N Orange Dr #202 Los Angeles CA 90028

JANSEN, ALLAN W., lawyer; b. Oak Park, Ill., July 22, 1948. BS in Aerospace Engring., U. Ill., 1971; JD, John Marshall Law Sch., 1978. Bar: Calif. 1978, U.S. Dist. Ct. (cen. dist.) Calif. 1978, U.S. Ct. Appeals (9th cir.) 1978, U.S. Patent Office. Ptnr. Lyon & Lyon, L.A. Mem. editorial bd. John Marshall Jour. Practice & Procedure, 1977-78. Mem. ABA, Am. Intellectual Property Law Assn., State Bar Calif., L.A. County Bar Assn., L.A. Intellectual Property Law Assn., Phi Delta Phi. Office: Lyon & Lyon 34th Fl 611 W 6th St Fl 34 Los Angeles CA 90017-3101

JANSON, RICHARD ANTHONY, plastic surgeon; b. Passaic, N.J., Nov. 30, 1945; m. Mary Ann Janson, 1971; children: Sarah, Matthew. BA, Rice U., 1967; MD, Med. Coll. Wis., 1971. Diplomate Am. Bd. Plastic Surgery. Intern St. Joseph Hosp., Denver, 1971-72, resident in gen. surgery, 1972-76; resident in plastic surgery U. Tex. Med. Branch, Galveston, 1976-79; pvt. practice Grand Junction, Colo., 1979—. Fellow ACS, Am. Soc. Plastic & Reconstructive Surgeons; mem. Colo. Soc. Plastic & Reconstructive Surgeons. Office: 1120 Wellington Ave Grand Junction CO 81501-6129

JANSSEN, JAMES ROBERT, consulting software engineer; b. Frederick, Md., June 14, 1959; s. Robert James and Kathryn Doris (Randolph) J.; m. Deborah June Dellwo, Mar. 15, 1986 (div. Sept. 20, 1988). BSEE, Stanford U., 1981, MSEE, 1982. Simulation technician Varian Assocs., Palo Alto, Calif., 1981; hardware design engr. Fairchild Test Systems, San Jose, Calif., 1982-86, Factron Test Systems, Latham, N.Y., 1986-87; software, sys. designer Schlumberger Technologies Labs., Palo Alto, 1988; software engr. Photon Dynamics, Inc., San Jose, 1989-90, ADAC Labs., Milpitas, Calif., 1990-92; software, system designer ADAC Labs., Aalborg, Denmark, 1992, Milpitas, 1992-94; consulting software engr. self-employed, Sunnyvale, Calif., 1994-96; mem. tech. staff Netscape Comms. Corp., Mountain View, Calif., 1996—; pres., founder Digital Studio Systems, Inc., Sunnyvale, 1990-93. Patentee multiple timing signal generator. Civic vol. City of Sunnyvale, 1993. Mem. Tau Beta Pi. Home and Office: 2028 Lockhart Gulch Rd Scotts Valley CA 95066-2923

JANSSER, ROLLS, mayor. Mayor City of Bell, Calif. Office: City of Bell 6330 Pine Ave Bell CA 90201

JANTZEN, J(OHN) MARC, retired education educator; b. Hillsboro, Kans., July 30, 1908; s. John D. and Louise (Janzen) J.; m. Ruth Patton, June 9, 1935; children: John Marc, Myron Patton, Karen Louise. A.B., Bethel Coll., Newton, Kans., 1934; A.M., U. Kans., 1937, Ph.D., 1940. Elementary sch. tchr. Marion County, Kans., 1927-30, Hillsboro, Kan., 1930-31; high sch. tchr., 1934-36; instr. sch. edn. U. Kans., 1936-40; asst. prof. Sch. Edn., U. of Pacific, Stockton, Calif., 1940-42; assoc. prof. Sch. Edn., U. of Pacific, 1942-44, prof., 1944-78, prof. emeritus, 1978—, also dean sch. edn., 1944-74, emeritus, 1974—, dir. summer sessions, 1940-72; condr. overseas seminars; mem., chmn. commn. equal opportunities in edn. Calif. Dept. Edn., 1959-69; mem., chmn. Commn. Tchr. Edn. Calif. Tchrs. Assn., 1956-62; mem. Nat. Coun. for Accreditation Tchr. Edn., 1969-72. Bd. dirs. Ednl. Travel Inst., 1965-89. Recipient hon. svd. award Calif. Congress Parents and Tchrs., 1982, McCaffrey disting. Svc. award in recognition of leadership in higher edn., cmty. relationships and internat. svc. San Joaquin Delta Coll., 1996. Mem. NEA, Am. Edn. Rsch. Assn., Calif. Edn. Rsch. Assn. (past pres. 1954-55), Calif. Coun. for Edn. Tchrs., Calif. Assn. of Colls. for Tchr. Edn. (sec., treas. 1975-85), Rotary (Outstanding Rotarian of Yr. award North Stockton 1990, Paul Harris fellow 1980), Phi Delta Kappa. Methodist. Home: 117 W Euclid Ave Stockton CA 95204-3122 *I maintain that my success in life is a result of multiple factors, among which the most important are a supportive home environment on a Kansas family farm; a wife who shared her husband's ambitions and supported him fully, often at considerable personal sacrifice; an attempt to serve others through a "power with" attitude rather than a "power over" struggle; and a conviction that one's life transcends the immediacy of the here and now.*

JANZEN, TIMOTHY PAUL, family practice physician; b. Salem, Oreg., Dec. 3, 1960; s. Robert Lee and Betty Maude (Youngman) J.; m. Rachel Ann Sauter, Sept. 7, 1985; children: Paul, Marilee, Andrew, Bethany. BS in Chemistry, George Fox Coll., 1983; MD, Oreg. Health Scis. U., 1987. Intern, then resident in family practice Scottsdale (Ariz.) Meml. Hosp., 1987-90; family practice physician South Tabor Family Physicians, Portland, Oreg., 1990—. Co-author: The Peters Family Genealogy, 1995; contbr. articles to profl. publs. Bd. dirs. United Health Network, Portland, 1996. Benson scholar, 1979-83. Fellow Am. Acad. Family Physicians; mem. Christian Med. Soc., Am. Hist. Soc. Germans from Russia, Am. Birding Assn., Oreg. Field Ornithologists. Republican. Baptist. Office: South Tabor Family Physicians 10803 SE Cherry Blossom Dr Portland OR 97216

JAOUEN, RICHARD MATTHIE, plastic surgeon. MD, U. Autonoma de Guadalajara, Jalisco, Mexico, 1975. Intern St. Joseph Hosp., Denver, 1976-77, surgeon, 1977-81; plastic surgeon Ind. U. Med. Sch., Indpls., 1981-83, North Colo. Med. Ctr., Greeley, Colo., 1983—. Office: 1640 25th Ave Greeley CO 80631-4957

JAQUITH, GEORGE OAKES, ophthalmologist; b. Caldwell, Idaho, July 29, 1916; s. Gail Belmont and Myrtle (Burch) J.; BA, Coll. Idaho, 1938; MB, Northwestern U., 1942, MD, 1943; m. Pearl Elizabeth Taylor, Nov. 30, 1939; children: Patricia Ann Jaquith Mueller, George, Michele Eugenie Jaquith Smith. Intern, Wesley Meml. Hosp., Chgo., 1942-43; resident ophthalmology U.S. Naval Hosp., San Diego, 1946-48; pvt. practice medicine, specializing in ophthalmology, Brawley, Calif., 1948—; pres. Pioneers Meml. Hosp. staff, Brawley, 1953; dir., exec. com. Calif. Med. Eye Council, 1960—; v.p. Calif. Med. Eye Found., 1976—. Sponsor Anza council Boy Scouts Am., 1966—. Gold card holder Rep. Assocs., Imperial County, Calif., 1967-68. Served with USMC, USN, 1943-47; PTO. Mem. Imperial County Med. Soc. (pres. 1961), Calif. Med. Assn. (del. 1961—), Nat., So. Calif. (dir. 1966—, chmn. med. adv. com. 1968-69) Soc. Prevention Blindness, Calif. Assn. Ophthalmology (treas. 1976—), San Diego, L.A. Ophthal. Socs., L.A. Rsch. Study Club, Nathan Smith Davis Soc., Coll. Idaho Associates, Am. Legion, VFW, Res. Officers Assn., Basenji Assn., Nat. Geneal. Soc., Cuyamaca Club (San Diego), Elks, Phi Beta Pi, Lambda Chi Alpha (Hall of Fame). Presbyterian (elder). Office: PO Box 511 665 S Western Brawley CA 92227-0511

JARAMILLO, DEBBIE, mayor. Mayor City of Santa Fe, 1994—; lectr. in field. Debbie Jaramillo award named in her honor Am. Fedn. State, County and Mcpl. Employees; recipient Affordable Housing Champion award Neighborhood Housing Svcs. Santa Fe, Women in Govt. award Santa Fe Bus. and Profl. Women, Recognition award Nat. Safety Orgn., U. N.Mex. Womens Studies Program. Democrat. Office: PO Box 909 Santa Fe NM 87504

JARMAN, DONALD RAY, retired public relations professional, minister; b. Benton Harbor, Mich., May 6, 1928; s. Ray Charles and Grace Marie (Timanus) J.; m. Bo Dee Foster, July 7, 1950 (div. 1985); children: Mark, Katharine Law, Luanne Miller; m. Sharon Lee Becker, Feb. 16, 1991. BA, Chapman U., 1950; MDiv, Lexington Theol. Sem., 1953; DMin, Sch. of Theology, Claremont, 1970. Ordained min. Disciples of Christ, 1950; cert. fundraising exec. Nat. Soc. Fundraising Execs., 1980-89. Pastor Sharpsberg (Ky.) Christian, 1950-53, First Christian Ch., Santa Maria, Calif., 1953-58, St. Claire St. Ch. of Christ, Kirkcaldy, Scotland, 1958-61, So. Bay Christian, Redondo Beach, Calif., 1961-71; dir. human value in health care Eskaton, Charmichael, Calif., 1971-73; exec. dir. Northwestern NBA Svc., Portland, Oreg., 1973-85; dir. pub. relations and mktg. Retirement Housing Found., Long Beach, Calif., 1985-89; part time minister Pico Rivera Christian Ch., 1986-87; dir. community rels. Coscan Davidson Homes, Signal Hill, Calif., 1989-96; interim min. Southgate First Christian Ch., 1994-95; pres. So. Calif. Mins., 1967; chmn. Pacific S.W. Region Christian Ch., 1968; mem. gen. bd. Disciples of Christ, 1969-70; exec. dir. Signal Hill Econ. Devel. Bd., 1992-96. Editor: Reachout, 1973-84, Hill Street News, 1992-95; editor-in-chief: December Rose, 1985-89; columnist NW Senior News, 1980-84. Pres. Signal Hill C. of C., 1992-93; treas. Hist. Soc., Signal Hill, 1990-94; commr. L.A. County Commn. on Aging, 1994—, Signal Hill Commn. Pks. and Recreation, 1996—. Recipient Master Make-up Technician award Portland Opera, 1983, Outstanding Older American award City of Signal Hill, Calif., 1993. Mem. Rotary (pres. Progress, Oreg. 1983-84, pres. Signal Hill 1993-94, Paul Harris fellow), Chapman U. Alumni Assn. (pres. 1994-95, trustee 1994-96), Los Alamitos Cmty. Art League, So. Calif. Pastel Soc., Lakewood Artist Guild, Masons. Democrat. Home: 1923 Molino Ave Unit 101 Signal Hill CA 90804-1028

JARMON, LAWRENCE, developmental communications educator; b. L.A., Nov. 7, 1946; s. Robert and Movella (Young) J. BA, Calif. State U., 1969, MA in Adminstrn. Health and Safety, 1988; MS, U. Wash., 1972; EdD in Edn. Adminstrn., Wash. State U., 1975; MA, Calif. State U., L.A., 1988. Cert. alcohol and drug problems specialist. Athletic dir., instr. dept. phys. edn. L.A. SW Coll., 1975-85, agy. dir. summer programfor disadvantaged youth, 1975-94, asst. dean instruction, 1976, project adminstr. NCAA, 1977-79; instr. health edn. Golden West Coll., Huntington Beach, Calif., 1978; instr. dept. English Calif. State U., L.A., 1986; instr. dept. edn. Nat. U., L.A., 1986-88; prof. developmental comm. L.A. S.W. Coll., 1988-92, prof. dept. devel. comm., staff devel. coord. and dir., dir. nat. youth sports program, 1993—. Author numerous booklets, manuscripts and manuals on sports programs and edn. qualifications and policies. Bd. advisors Scholastic Placement Orgn. for Student Athlete, Mount Laurel, N.J.; bd. dirs. Black Edn. Commn., L.A. Unified Sch. Dist., Calif. State U., L.A. Alumni Assn., Involvement for Young Achievers, L.A., L.A. Police Dept. Football Centurions, Paradise Ch. Found., Inc., L.A., Pop Warner Little Scholars, Inc., Phila.; employee assistance program liaison officer L.A. Cmty. Dist. Named one of Outstanding Young Men of Am., 1980, 81. Mem. Am. Alliance Health, Phys. Edn. and Recreation, Am. Alliance Health Edn., Am. Assn. Sch. Adminstrs., Calif. State Alumni Assn., U. Wash. Alumni Assn., Wash. State Alumni Assn., Calif. Assn. Health, Phys. Edn. and Recreation, Calif. State Athletic Dirs. Assn., L.A. Jr. C. of C., Kappa Alpha Psi, Nat. Interscholastic Athletic Adminstrs. Assn., Phi Delta Kappa. Office: LA SW Coll 1600 W Imperial Hwy Los Angeles CA 90047-4810

JARNAGIN, DAVID RICHARD, real estate appraiser, real estate executive; b. Waco, Tex., Nov. 2, 1958; s. Leondas Colton Jarnagin and Aliene (Belluzzi) Hardesty; m. Cynthia Lynne Tucker, May 25, 1991; children: Corrine, Jacob. BS in Real Estate, Ariz. State U., 1982. Cert. residential appraiser, Ariz. Owner, appraiser Jarnagin Appraisal, Ltd., Phoenix, 1989—; pres. CD Assets, Ltd., Phoenix, 1992—; pres., dir. Jarnagin and Jarnagin, Inc., Phoenix, 1992—. Mem. Nat. Assn. Realtors (appraisal sect., RAA 1994), dir., Realtors Land Insts., dist. 3, Ariz. chapt. Republican. Office: Jarnagin Appraisal 729 E Hatcher Rd # 102 Phoenix AZ 85020-2506

JAROS, DEAN, university official; b. Racine, Wis., Aug. 23, 1938; s. Joseph and Emma (Kotas) J. B.A., Lawrence Coll., Appleton, Wis., 1960; M.A., Vanderbilt U., 1962, Ph.D., 1966. Asst. prof. polit. sci. Wayne State U., Detroit, 1963-66; from asst. prof. to prof. polit. sci. U. Ky., 1966-78, assoc. dean Grad. Sch., 1978-80; dean Grad. Sch. No. Ill. U., DeKalb, 1980-84; dean Grad. Sch. Colo. State U., Ft. Collins, 1984-91, assoc. provost, 1991—. Author: Socialization to Politics, 1973, Political Behavior: Choices and Perspectives, 1974, Heroes Without Legacy, 1993, also articles.; Mem. editorial bds. profl. jours. Mem. Exptl. Aircraft Assn. Office: Colo State U Grad Sch Fort Collins CO 80523

JARRELL, WESLEY MICHAEL, soil and ecosystem science educator, researcher, consultant; b. Forest Grove, Oreg., May 23, 1948; s. Burl Omer and Edith LaVerne (Sahnow) J.; m. Linda Ann Illig, June 24, 1972; children: Benjamin George, Emily Theresa. BA, Stanford U., 1970; MS, Oreg. State U., 1974, PhD, 1976. Grad. rsch. asst. Oreg. State U., 1971-76; asst. prof. soil sci. U. Calif., Riverside, 1976-83, assoc. prof., 1983-88; dir. Dry Lands Res. Inst., 1985-88; assoc. prof. Oreg. Grad. Inst., Portland, 1988-91, prof., 1991—; dept. head, internat. cons. agr., 1992-94; internat. cons. agr. environ. Mem. AAAS, Soil Sci. Soc. Am., Am. Soc. Agronomy. Democrat. Lutheran. Contbr. articles to profl. jours. Home: 1920 NW 110th Ct Portland OR 97229-4852 Office: Oreg Grad Inst Environ Sci Engring PO Box 91000 Portland OR 97291-1000

JARRETT, RONALD DOUGLAS, lawyer, nurse; b. Oceanside, Calif., Oct. 31, 1952; s. W. Douglas and Francia Elizabeth (Ladd) J.; m. Lois Ellen Shurmaster, Dec. 26, 1984; 1 child, Emily Rose. AA, AS in Nursing, Cabrillo Coll., Aptos, Calif., 1981; student Nursing Sci., NYU, 1982-89; JD, Lincoln Law Sch., Sacramento, Calif., 1993. Bar: Calif. 1993, U.S. Dist. Ct. (ea. dist.) Calif. 1993, U.S. Dist. Ct. (no. dist.) Calif. 1994. Law clk. CIGNA Counsel, Sacramento, 1992-94; sole practitioner Sacramento, 1994—; med., legal record rev., pvt. practice, Sacramento, 1992—; computer cons. for lawyers, 1994—. With USN, 1970-73. Mem. ABA, ATLA, Consumer Lawyers Calif., Sacramento County Bar Assn. Office: PO Box 277682 Sacramento CA 95827

JARVIE, LARS N., protective services official. Chief of police Mesa, Ariz. Office: 130 N Robson St Mesa AZ 85201

JARVIK, GAIL PAIRITZ, medical geneticist; b. Evanston, Ill., Feb. 8, 1959; d. Lawrence Alan and Lenore Mae P.; m. Jeffrey Gil Jarvik, Aug. 22, 1992. PhD in Human Genetics, U. Mich., 1986; MD, U. Iowa, 1987. Sr. rsch. fellow U. Wash., Seattle, 1992-95, asst. prof. medicine, divsn. med. genetics, 1995—; affiliate mem. Fred Hutchinson Cancer Rsch. Ctr., Seattle, 1994—. Contbr. to profl. jours. Howard Hughes Rsch. fellow, 1992-95. Mem. Am. Soc. Human Genetics, Internat. Genetic Epidemiology Soc.

JARVIS, DONALD BERTRAM, judge; b. Newark, N.J., Dec. 14, 1928; s. Benjamin and Esther (Golden) J.; BA, Rutgers U., 1949; JD, Stanford U., 1952; m. Rosalind C. Chodorcove, June 13, 1954; children: Nancie, Brian, Joanne. Bar: Calif. 1953. Law clk. Justice John W. Shenk, Calif. Supreme Ct., 1953-54; assoc. Erskine, Erskine & Tulley, 1955; assoc. Aaron N. Cohen, 1955-56; law clk. Dist. Ct. Appeal, 1956; assoc. Carl Hoppe, 1956-57; adminstrv. law judge Calif. Pub. Utilities Commn., San Francisco, 1957-91, U.S. Dept. of Labor, 1992—. mem. exec. com. Nat. Conf. Adminstrv. Law Judges, 1986-88, sec. 1988-89, vice-chair, 1990-91, chair-elect, 1991-92, chair 1992-93; pres. Calif. Adminstrv. Law Judges Coun., 1978-84; mem. faculty Nat. Jud. Coll., U. Nev., 1977, 78, 80. Chmn. pack Boy Scouts Am., 1967-69, chmn. troop, 1972; class chmn. Stanford Law Sch. Fund, 1959, mem. nat. com., 1963-65; dir. Forest Hill Assn., 1970-71. Served to col. USAF Res., 1949-79. Decorated Legion of Merit. Mem. ABA (mem. ho. of dels. 1993—), State Bar Calif., Bar Assn. San Francisco, Calif. Conf. Pub. Utility Counsel (pres. 1980-81), Air Force Assn., Res. Officers Assn., Ret. Officers Assn., De Young Museum Soc. and Patrons Art and Music, San Francisco Gem and Mineral Soc., Stanford Alumni Assn., Rutgers Alumni Assn., Phi Beta Kappa (pres. No. Calif. 1973-74), Tau Kappa Alpha, Phi Alpha Theta, Phi Alpha Delta. Home: 530 Dewey Blvd San Francisco CA 94116-1427 Office: 50 Fremont St San Francisco CA 94105-2230

JARVIS, LOVELL STUBER, economist, educator; b. Halstead, Kans., June 18, 1941; s. Laurence Fredonia and Virginia Francis (Moore) J.; m. Nancy Anne Beall, June 10, 1968 (div. Dec. 1975); 1 child, Hope Oriana; m. Maria Isabel Rivas, Dec. 29, 1979; children: Lucas Sebastian, Daniel Christopher, Amalia Pilar. BA in Econs., U. Kans., 1964; PhD in Econs., MIT, 1969. Rsch. assoc. Guayana Project Harvard-MIT Joint Ctr. for Urban Studies, Caracas, Venezuela, 1965; vis. rschr. Ctr. for Econ. Rsch., Torcuato Di Tella Inst., Buenos Aires, 1968; asst. prof. dept. econs. U. Calif., Berkeley, 1969-77, vis. lectr. dept. econs., 1978-83; prof. dept. agrl. econs. U. Calif., Davis, 1984—, chair grad. program internat. agrl. devel., 1987-90, 95—; program advisor in econs. The Ford Found., Santiago, 1972-73; vis. prof. dept. industry Faculty of Phys. Scis. and Math., U. Chile, 1973; cons. The World Bank, 1974—, Ministry Agriculture and Fisheries, Uruguay, 1976, 77, Programa Regional del Empleo para Am. Latina y el Caribe, Santiago, Chile, 1978, 79, others; vis. prof. Corporacion de Investigaciones Econs. para Latinoamerica, Santiago, 1991-92. Contbg. editor: Handbook for Latin American Studies, 1974-75; editorial adv. bd.: East Africa Economic Review, 1985—; contbr. book revs. and articles to profl. jours. Recipient Fulbright award for rsch., 1991, Social Sci. Rsch. Coun. award, 1991-92. Office: U Calif Dept Agrl Econs Davis CA 95616

JARVIS, PETER R., lawyer; b. N.Y.C., July 19, 1950. BA in Econs. magna cum laude, Harvard U., 1972; MA in Econs., Yale U., 1976, JD, 1976. Bar: Oreg. 1976, U.S. Dist. Ct. Oreg. 1976, U.S. Ct. Appeals (9th cir.) 1977, Wash. 1983, U.S. Dist. Ct. (we. dist.) Wash. 1983, U.S. Dist. Ct. (ea. dist.) Wash. 1985, U.S. Tax Ct. 1991. Mem. Stowl Rives LLP, Portland, Oreg. Author: (with others) Roles of Oregon Professional Responsibility (updated annually); editor, author: (with others) The Ethical Oregon Lawyer, 1991, 94. Mem. ALI, Phi Beta Kappa. Office: Stoel Rives Boley Jones & Grey 900 SW 5th Ave Ste 2300 Portland OR 97204-1232

JARVIS, RICHARD S., academic administrator; b. Nottingham, Eng., Feb. 13, 1949; came to U.S., 1974; s. John Leslie and Mary Margaret (Dodman) J.; m. Marilou Thompson, Nov. 7, 1986; stepchildren: Kimberly Nipko, Christopher Healey. BA in Geography, Cambridge (Eng.) U., 1970, MA, 1974, PhD in Geography, 1975. Lectr. Durham (Eng.) U., 1973-74; assoc. prof. SUNY, Buffalo, 1975-87, asst. to pres., 1986-87; v.p. acad. SUNY, Fredonia, 1987-90, prof. geoscis., 1987-90; vice provost SUNY Sys., Albany, 1990-94; chancellor Univ. and C.C. Sys. Nev., Reno and Las Vegas, 1994—; mem. adv. bd. Bechtel Nev., Las Vegas, 1995-97, NTS Devel. Corp., Las Vegas, 1997, INC, Las Vegas, 1997. Editor: River Networks, 1983; contbr. articles to profl. jours. Trustee United Way, Reno, 1996—, EDAWN, Reno, 1996—. Office: Univ and CC Sys Nev 2601 Enterprise Rd Reno NV 89512

JARVIS, STEVEN L., technology director; b. Herkimer, N.Y., July 11, 1949; s. Alexander Bruce Jarvis and Lucille (Rankin) Ladd; m. Cynthia S. Turner, June 12, 1971; 1 child, Christopher. BSEE, SUNY, Buffalo, 1973; MBA, U. N.Mex., 1982. Rsch. engr. TRW Tech. Divsn., Redondo Beach, Calif., 1973-77; mktg. mgr. TRW Dist. Office, Albuquerque, 1978-83; strategic planning mgr. TRW Space & Electricity, Redondo Beach, 1984-88; tech. devel. dir. TRW Electicity Sys. Group, Redondo Beach, 1989-92; tech. office dir. State of Calif. Commerce Agy., Sacramento, 1993—; dir. bd. Commerce Net, Menlo Park, Calif., 1994-96; pres. So. Calif. Corp. Planners Assn., L.A., 1985-87; mem. tech. adv. com. GTC & Tech. Expo, Sacramento, 1994—. Contbr. numerous articles to profl. publs. Treas. TRW Employee Charity Orgn., Redondo Beach, 1988-90; commodore Sea Exploring Cluster, L.A. coun. Boy Scouts Am., 1995—, asst. scoutmaster troop 966, Torrance, Calif., 1988—, mate ship 618, Redondo Beach, 1994—, active brotherhood Order of Arrow, 1994—. Office: Calif Commerce Agy of Strat Tech # 204 200 E Del Mar Pasadena CA 91105

JASNOW, EDWARD JAY, subcontracts manager; b. N.Y.C., Nov. 13, 1941; s. Martin and Lillian (Stolzberg) J.; m. Marlyn Turner, June 25, 1967 (div. Nov. 1977); children: Shari Jasnow Simmons, Todd; m. Mona Townson, Feb. 17, 1979. BA, Rutgers U., 1963; MA, U. Md., 1970. Contract negotiator NASA-Goddard Space Ctr., Greenbelt, Md., 1966-68; contracting officer Dept. of Navy, Washington, 1968-70; contract adminstr. Washington Metro Transit Authority, 1970-80; mgr. ops. security Jet Propulsion Lab., Pasadena, Calif., 1980-95; subcontracts mgr. Calif. Inst. Tech., Pasadena, 1995—. Fellow Nat. Contract Mgmt. Assn. (pres. San Gabriel Valley chpt. 1987-88); mem. Rotary Internat. (pres. Altadena chpt. 1995-96). Office: Calif Inst Tech M/C 51-33 1200 E California Blvd Pasadena CA 91125

JASON, DEBRA ANN, copywriter; b. Flushing, N.Y., Dec. 1, 1954. BA, Queens Coll., 1975; MA, U. Colo., 1977. Prodn. dir., copywriter Krupp Mail Order, Boulder, Colo., 1983-87; prodn. mgr. Mellow Mail, N.Y.C., 1987-88; acct. coord., jr. copywriter Grey Direct, N.Y.C., 1988; owner, copywriter The Write Direction, Boulder, Colo., 1989—; tchr. continuing edn. program U. Colo., Boulder; presenter seminar Boulder County Bus. Expo., 1993. Contbr. articles to bus. publs. Participant Leadership Boulder XI, 1991-92; bd. dirs. YWCA, Boulder, 1992-93. Recipient Outstanding Accomplishment citation Boulder C. of C. and City of Boulder, 1991. Mem. Denver Advt. Fedn. (pub. rels. com. 1991-92), Boulder C. of C. (chair bus. women's leadership group 1991-92, program com. 1992-93, small bus. support coun. 1993-94, bd. dirs. 1994—, Vol. of Yr. 1993), Rocky Mt. Direct Mktg. Assn. (newsletter editor 1993-95, bd. dirs. 1995—), Art Dirs. Club of Denver (newsletter editor 1990-91, Bronze award of excellence 1991). Office: The Write Direction 1920 13th St Ste B Boulder CO 80302-5205

JASON, SONYA, recording artist; b. Wayne, Nebr., Jan. 10, 1963; d. Glen Arthur and Janice Marie (Anderson) Rathgeber. Student, Mills Coll., 1981-83; BMus summa cum laude, Berklee Coll. Music, Boston, 1985. Owner, mgr., prodr. Saja Prodns., Phoenix, 1985-91, L.A., 1991—; clinician Yamaha Corp., L.A., 1993—; rec. artist Warner Discovery Music, L.A., 1992-94. Artist, composer, prodr.: Secret Lover, 1989, Tigress, 1993, Goddess, 1994. Recipient Outstanding Musicianship award Nat. Assn. Jazz Educators, Calif., 1981, 83, Phil Woods scholarship Berklee Coll. Music, Boston, 1983. Mem. ASCAP, Nat. Acad. Rec. Arts and Scis. Office: Saja Prodns 2633 Lincoln Blvd # 500 Santa Monica CA 90405-4656

JAUME, JUAN CARLOS, physician, educator; b. Buenos Aires, Dec. 27, 1959; came to U.S., 1986; s. Juan Antonio and Hebe Teresa J.; m. Maria Alejandra Alfonso, June 1, 1987. MD, Nat. U. Buenos Aires, Buenos Aires, 1985. Intern U. Hosp. Nat. U. Buenos Aires, 1985-86; vis. postdoctorate in Surgery SUNY, Stony Brook, 1986-87, resident in Surgery, 1987-88; resident in Internal Medicine Albert Einstein Coll. of Medicine, Bronx, 1988-91; fellow in endocrinology/metabolism U. Calif., San Francisco, 1991-94, asst. prof. medicine, endocrinology and metabolism, 1994—. Contbr. articles to profl. jours. Office: VA Med Ctr U Calif Thyroid Molecular Biology Unit 4150 Clement St San Francisco CA 94121-1545

JAUNDALDERIS, JULIA LEE, software engineer; b. Neubrüke, Germany, Nov. 28, 1961; came to U.S., 1963; d. Imants and Virginia Lee (Wine) J. BS in Computer Sci., We. Wash. U., Bellingham, 1984; MS, U. Wash., 1991. Cert. nat. note investor. Analyst Pacific N.W. Bell, Bellevue, Wash., 1984-87; software engr. U.S. West Comms., Bellevue, 1987-94; sr. software engr. GTE, Bothell, Wash., 1994—; stained glass designer; real estate investor. Athletes' Village liaison 1990 Goodwill Games, Seattle, 1990; v.p. Wash. State Coun. for Self-Esteem, Bothell, 1993-94, Northwest chpt. U.S. Amateur Ballroom Dancers Assn., 1996. Mem. U.S. Ballroom Dancers Assn. (NW chpt. v.p.). Home: PO Box 1605 Bothell WA 98041-1605

JAWAD, SAID TAYEB (SAID TAYEB DJAWAD), political commentator, writer; b. Kandahr, Afghanistan, Feb. 27, 1958; came to U.S., 1986; s. Mir Hussain and zakia Shah; m. Shamin Rahman, Nov. 16, 1986. Student, Kabul (Afghanistan) U., 1976-80, Wilhelms U., Muenster, Germany, 1984-86, Long Island U., 1986. Paralegal Lehnardt & Bauman, N.Y.C., 1988-89, Steefel, Levitt & Weiss, San Francisco, 1989—; polit. commentator various newspapers, radio and TV stas. including BBC. Editor weekly newspaper OMAID, 1992-95; pub. Substratum of Human Rights Violations in Afghanistan, Modern Dictatorship, Occupation of Wakhan, Soviets Expansion to the South, Fundamentalism in Central Asia; contbr. articles to BBC World Reports (London) and to profl. jours. throughout world. Bd. dirs. Afghanistan Cultural Soc., San Francisco, 1990-92; mem. Internat. Soc. for Human Rights, Frankfort, Germany, 1983-86; mem. nat. adv. bd. Info. Am., Atlanta, 1991-94; active Amnesty Internat., N.Y.C., 1987—. Home: 4279 Merced Cir Antioch CA 94509-8227

JAY, DAVID JAKUBOWICZ, management consultant; b. Danzig, Poland, Dec. 7, 1925; s. Mendel and Gladys Gitta (Zalc) Jakubowicz; came to U.S., 1938, naturalized, 1944; BS, Wayne State U., 1948; MS, U. Mich., 1949, postgrad., 1956-57; postgrad. U. Cin., 1951-53, MIT, 1957; m. Shirley Anne Shapiro, Sept. 7, 1947; children: Melvin Maurice, Evelyn Deborah. Supr. man-made diamonds GE Corp., Detroit, 1951-56; instr. U. Detroit, 1948-51; asst. to v.p. engring. Ford Motor Co., Dearborn, Mich., 1956-63; project mgr. Apollo environ. control radiators N.Am. Rockwell, Downey, Calif., 1963-68; staff to v.p. corporate planning Aerospace Corp., El Segundo, Calif., 1968-70; founder, pres. PBM Systems Inc., 1970-83; pres. Cal-Best Hydrofarms Coop., Los Alamitos, 1972-77; cons. in field, 1983—. Pres., Community Design Corp., Los Alamitos, 1971-75; life master Am. Contract Bridge League. Served with USNR, 1944-46. Registered profl. engr., Calif., Mich., Ohio. Fellow Inst. Advancement Engring.; mem. Art Stamp and Stencil Dealers Assn. (pres. 1993—), Inst. Mgmt. Sci. (chmn. 1961-62), Western Greenhouse Vegetable Growers Assn. (sec.-treas. 1972-75), Tau Beta Pi. Jewish. Patentee in air supported ground vehicle, others. Home: 13441 Roane Santa Ana CA 92705-2271 Office: 13882 Newport Ave Ste E Tustin CA 92780-4666

JAY, MARTIN EVAN, historian, educator; b. N.Y.C., May 4, 1944; s. Edward and Sari Toby (Sidel) J.; m. M. Catherine Gallagher, July 6, 1974; 1 child, Rebecca Erin; 1 stepchild, Margaret Shana Gallagher. BA, Union Coll., Schenectady, N.Y., 1965; PhD, Harvard U., 1971. Prof. history U. Calif., Berkeley, 1971-97, Sidney Hellman ehrman prof., 1997—. Author: The Dialectical Imagination, 1973, Marxism and Totality, 1984, Adorno, 1984, Downcast Eyes, 1993, Force Fields, 1993, Cultural Semantics, 1997; sr. editor Theory and Society, 1977—; columnist Salmagundi, Saratoga Springs, N.Y., 1987—; editor Cultural Critique, Berkeley, 1990—. Guggenheim fellow, 1973; NEH fellow, 1979; Rockefeller Found. fellow, 1984; Am. Coun. Learned Socs. fellow, 1989. Fellow Am. Acad. Arts and Scis.; mem. Am. Hist. Assn. Home: 718 Contra Costa Ave Berkeley CA 94707-1918 Office: U Calif Dept History Berkeley CA 94720

JAY, ROY, corporate executive; b. Portland, Oreg., July 22, 1947. Announcer Sta. KGAR, Vancouver, Wash., 1970-72; gen. mgr. Sta. KQIV-FM, Portland, 1972-76; v.p. Underwood-McLean Assoc., Portland, 1976-78; nat. mgr. regional ops. Mutual Credit/SNTCOR, Portland, 1978—; pres. Trade-Mark Bus. Svcs. Corp., Portland, 1980—; pres., chief exec. officer Oreg. Bus. Network, Portland; pres., founder Data-Chek Corp., Portland, 1982—; chief exec. officer, investigator, collector Law-One, Inc., 1985—; chief exec. officer Trade-Mark Legal Adminstrs., 1985—; owner Trade-Mark Computer Sales, 1985—; ptnr. Trade-Mark Express Printing, Trade-Mark Telecommunications, 1985—; pres. Celebrity Limousine, Limousine At Your Call, All Star Limousine. Bd. dirs. Greater Portland Vis. and Conv. Assn., 1985-92, chmn. mem. com., 1988-90; bd. dirs. Girls Scouts of U.S.A., Columbia Pacific Region, 1986-93, chmn. nominating com., 1988; bd. dirs. Mainstream Youth Program, 1985-91; mem. Multnomah County Justice Coordinating Coun., 1987-92; exec. dir. Oreg. Conv. and Vis. Svcs. Network, Portland, 1988—; coord. Miss Oreg. U.S.A. Pageants, 1988-95; bd. mem. Resolutions N.W. Youth Intervention Program. Mem. Nat. Assn. Black Journalists (mem. Pres. Club), Oreg. Soc. Assn. Execs., Oreg. Lodging Assn., Tri-County Lodging Assn., Pre-paid Legal Svcs. Inst., Southwest Bus. Mchts. Assn., Oreg. Legal Assts. Assn., Black Profl. Network, Oreg. Assn. Minority Entreprenurs, African Am. C. of C. of Oreg. (pres.), Hispanic C. of C. of Oreg., Oreg. Bus. Network (exec. dir.), Washington County Visitors Assn. (treas. 1995—), Nat. Coalition Black Meeeting Planners, African Am. Conv. and Tourism (nat. pres. elect), Limousine Owners and Operators Oreg. (pres. 1992—), Portland Rose Festival Assn.

JEBENS, ARTHUR BERTRAM, management consultant, lawyer; b. Davenport, Iowa, Mar. 30, 1916; s. Gus and Anna Marie (Bertram) J.; m. Genett Herrick, June 25, 1940; children: Jennifer Herrick, Arthur Herrick, Holly Ann Herrick. BA, U. Iowa, 1937, JD, 1939; MA in pub. adminstr., U. Minn., 1941. Mcpl. analyst U. Minn., Mpls., 1940-41; rsch. asst. Am. Mcpl. Assn., Chgo., 1941; legislative rsch. analyst Dept. Agri., Washington, 1942-47; adminstrn. analyst Fed. Pub. Housing, Washington, 1942-47; mgmt. analyst Office of Sec. Interior Dept., Washington, 1947-52; dir. mgmt. rsch. U.S. Dept. Interior, Washington, 1952-70; vice chancelor adminstrn. U. Calif., Riverside, 1970-73; mgmt. cons. U. Calif., San Diego, 1973-76; cons. U.S. Bureau of Budget, Washington, 1968; awards com. U.S. Dept. Interior, Washington, 1952-70. Contbr. articles to profl. jours. Pres. Parent Teachers Assn., Bethesda, Md., 1954, Mohican Hills Civic Assn., Bethesda, 1956, Interagency Mgmt. Analyst Assn., Washington, 1962. With U.S. Army, 1943-45, Germany. Decorated Bronze Star, POW medal, Combat Infatryman badge, U.S. Army; Rockefellow grant Stillman Found., U. Minn., 1939-40, congressional fellow Am. Pol. Sci. Assn., Washington, 1966. Mem. Am. Assn. Advancement Sci., Audubon Soc., Wilderness Soc., Iowa Bar, Am. Soc. Pub. Adminstrn. (v.p. 1965). Democrat. Home: 956 Santa Queta Solana Beach CA 92075-1527

JEFFERSON, PAUL, police chief. AA in Edn., L.A. City Coll., 1976; BS in Pub. Mgmt., Pepperdine U., 1979; MA, John F. Kennedy U., 1990. cert. tchr. Calif., 1977. Police officer L.A. Police Dept., 1968-73, detective of police, 1973-77, sgt. of police, 1977-80, police lt., 1981-90, capt. of police, 1990-92; chief of police Modesto Police Dept., Calif., 1992—; chair Com. of Bar Examiners of the State Bar of Calif. Author: Rock Cocaine, 1985. Bd. dirs. Modesto YMCA, Region IV United Way, Gould Med. Found., Modesto Doctors Med. Ctr., The Haven, Modesto Police Activities League, Modesto Salvation Army; chair com. of bar examiners State Bar Calif. Mem. Internat. Assn. Chiefs of Police, Calif. Police Chiefs Assn., Nat. Orgn. Black Law Enforcement Execs., Calif. Police Officers Assn., Stanislaus County Chief's, Sheriff's and Dist. Atty's Assn., FBI Nat. Acad. Associates, Black on Black Crime Inst., Assn. Black Law Enforcement Execs. (past pres.), Oscar Joel Bryant Assn., Black Police Officer Assn., Calif. Peace Officers Standards and Training (mem. adv. com. on cmty. based policing, cultural awareness training and sexual harassment), Modesto Downtown Rotary. Office: 601 11th St Modesto CA 95354

JEFFERY, JAMES NELS, protective services official; b. Torrance, Calif., May 16, 1944; s. Daryl Fredrick and Mildred Evelyn (Sogard) J. AA, Long Beach City Coll., 1964; student, Calif. State U., Long Beach, 1964-65, Calif. State U., Sacramento, 1979-80. Capt., firefighter L.A. Fire Dept., 1965-87; dir. Long Beach (Calif.) Search & Rescue Unit, 1968—; asst. chief fire div. Calif. Office Emergency Svcs., Riverside, 1987—; rep. Firescope Communications, Riverside, 1979—. Co-author emergency plans. Chmn. svc. com. Boy Scouts Am., Long Beach, 1979-81, tng. com., 1982—; bd. dirs. Long Beach Community Episepsy Clinic, 1971-72. Recipient Disting. Svc. award Long Beach Jaycees, 1977, Community Svc. award Long Beach Fire Dept., 1978, Silver Beaver award Boy Scouts Am., 1983, Commendation Mayor City of L.A., 1985. Mem. Calif. State Firemen's Assn., Calif. Fire Chiefs Assn., Nat. Coord. Coun. on Emergency Mgmt., Nat. Eagle Scout Assn., So. Calif. Assn. Foresters and Fire Wardens, Lions, Elks. Republican. Lutheran. Home: 3916 Cerritos Ave Long Beach CA 90807-3608 Office: Office Emergency Svcs PO Box 92257 Long Beach CA 90809-2257

JEFFREDO, JOHN VICTOR, aerospace engineer, manufacturing company executive, inventor; b. Los Angeles, Nov. 5, 1927; s. John Edward and Pauline Matilda (Whitten) J.; m. Elma Jean Nesmith (div. 1958); children: Joyce Jean Jeffredo Ryder, Michael John; m. Doris Louise Hinz, (div. 1980); children: John Victor, Louise Victoria Jeffredo-Warden; m. Gerda Adelheid Pillich, 1980. Grad. in Aeronautical Engring. Cal-Aero Tech. Inst., 1948; AA in Machine Design, Pasadena City Coll., 1951; grad. in Electronics The Ordnance Sch. U.S. Army, 1951; postgrad. U. So. Calif., 1955-58, Palomar Coll., 1977-96; MBA, La Jolla U., 1980, PhD in Human Rels., 1984. Design engr. Douglas Aircraft Co., Long Beach and Santa Monica, Calif., 1955-58; devel. engr. Honeywell Ordnance Corp., Duarte, Calif., 1958-62; cons. Honeywell devel. labs., Seattle, 1962-65; supr. mech. engring. dept. aerospace divsn. Control Data Corp., Pasadena, Calif., 1965-68; project engr. Cubic Corp., San Diego, 1968-70; supr. mech. engring. dept. Babcock Electronics Co., Costa Mesa, Calif., 1970-72; owner, operator Jeffredo Gunsight Co., Fallbrook, Calif., 1971-81; chief engr. Western Designs, Inc., Fallbrook, 1972-81, exec. dir., 1981-88, CEO, 1988-96; owner, operator Western Designs, Fallbrook, 1981-87, Western Design Concepts, Inc., 1987-94; exec. dir. JXJ, Inc., San Marcos, Calif., 1981-88, CEO, 1988—; mgr. Jeffredo Gunsight divsn., 1981-94; chief engr. JXJ, Inc., 1987-92 (merger JXJ, Inc. and Western Design Concepts, Fallbrook, Calif.), prin., 1992—; owner, mgr. Energy Assocs., San Diego, 1982-86; pres. Jeffredo Internat., 1984-88; founder, CEO John-Victor Internat., San Marcos, Calif., Frankfurt, Fed. Republic Germany, 1988—, The Jeffredo Solution, Fallbrook, 1996—; engring. cons. Action Intruments Co., Inc., Gen. Dynamics, Alcyon Corp., Systems Exploration, Inc. (all San Diego), Hughes Aircraft Co., El Segundo, Allied-Bendix, San Marcos; bd. dirs. Indian World Corp., JXJ, Inc., John-Victor Internat. Author: Gabrieleño. The Ocean People, Wildcatting; contbr. articles to trade jours. and mags.; guest editl. writer Town Hall, San Diego Union; narrator: (film) The Sacred Desert, 1994; spkr. in field; patentee agrl. frost control, vehicle off-road drive system, recoil absorbing system for firearms, telescope sight mounting system for firearms, breech mech. sporting firearm, elec. switch activating system, 37 others, others pending. Mem. San Diego County Border Task Force on Undocumented Aliens, 1979-80, 81-82; mgr., rep. Island Gabrieleno Group, NAGPRA repatriation project, 1995—; spokesman Island Shoshone, 1995—; chmn. Native Californian Coalition, 1982—; bd. dirs. Nat. Geog. Soc., 1968. With U.S. Army, 1951-53. Recipient Superior Svc. Commendation award U.S. Naval Ordnance Test Sta., Pasadena, 1959. Mem. AIAA (sr.), NRA (life), Soc. Automotive Engrs., San Diego Zool. Soc., Sierra Club (life), The Wilderness Soc., Pechanga Band of Luiseno Indians (life), Escondido Sculpture Guild, North County Scots. Avocations: chess, music, archaeology, conservation, travel. Home: 1629 Via Monserate Fallbrook CA 92028-9305 Office: PO Box 669 San Marcos CA 92079-0669

JEFFREY, JOHN ORVAL, lawyer; b. Portsmouth, Va., Aug. 6, 1963; s. Orval L. and Mary L. (Coakley) J. BA, U. Dayton (Ohio), 1985; diploma internat. legal studies, U. San Diego, Paris, 1987; JD, Southwestern U., L.A., 1988. Bar: Calif. 1988, U.S. Dist. Ct. (cen. dist.) Calif. 1988. Assoc. Shield & Smith, L.A., 1989-90, Hewitt, Kaldor & Prout, L.A., 1990-93; mgr. bus. and legal affairs fx subs. Fox TV. Campaign worker John Glenn Campaign for Pres., N.H., 1984; vol. Amnesty Internat. Mem. ABA (internat. law sect., litigation sect., entertainment/sports law sect.), Internat. Bar Assn., Los Angeles County Bar Assn. (mem. evaluation profl. standards com., mem. legis. activity com., mem. artists and the law com.), Phi Alpha Delta, Alpha Nu Omega. Democrat. *

JEFFRIES, RUSSELL MORDEN, communications company official; b. Carmel, Calif., July 15, 1935; s. Herman M. and Louise (Morden) J.; m. Barbara Jean Borcovich, Nov. 24, 1962; 1 child, Lynne Louise. AA, Hartnell Coll., 1971. Sr. communications technician AT&T, Salinas, Calif., 1955-91; mayor City of Salinas, 1987-91. Pres. El Gabilan Sch. PTA, Salinas, 1971-74, Salinas Valley Council PTA, 1975-76; mem. Salinas City Sch. Bd., 1975-81; mem. Salinas City Council, 1981-87; bd. dirs. Community Hosp. Salinas Found., 1987—, Salinas-Kushikino Sister City, 1987—, pres. 1992-93, John Steinbeck Ctr. Found., 1987-96, Food Bank for Monterey County, 1992-96; hon. bd. dirs. Monterey Film Festival, 1987-96, Calif. Rodeo Assn., 1987; mem. ctrl. bd. Calif. Regional Water Quality, 1992—; commr. Moss Landing Harbor, 1996. Recipient hon. service award PTA, Salinas, 1976; cert. of appreciation Calif. Dept. Edn., 1980, Salinas City Sch. Dist., 1981, Calif. Sch. Bds. Assn., 1981, Steinbeck Kiwanis, Salinas, 1987; named hon. mem. Filipino community Salinas Valley, 1988. Mem. Salinas C. of C., Native Sons Golden West, K.C., Rotary, Moose. Republican. Roman Catholic. Home: 204 E Curtis St Salinas CA 93906-2804

JEFFRYES, MARK ALLEN, elementary school educator, administrator; b. Wakefield, Nebr., Nov. 10, 1953; s. James A. Jeffryes and Martha G. Wright. BA, U. Colo., 1977; MA in Curriculum and Instrn., U. Colo., Denver, 1991; grad., Nat. Geographic Inst., 1992. Cert. tchr., Colo. Elem. tchr. Jefferson County Schs., Lakewood, Colo., 1990—; presenter Midwest Regional Geography Conf., Greeley, Colo., 1993; dean of students/sch. tech. coord., 1995—. Vol. tutor Denver Pub. Schs., 1987. Profl. Alternative Consortium for Tchrs. intern fellow U. Colo., Denver, 1990-91. Mem. ASCD, NEA, Colo. Geographic Alliance (tchr. cons. 1992—, grad. Summer Geography Inst. 1992), Internat. Tech. Edn. Assn. Democrat. Home: 8801 W Mississippi Ave Lakewood CO 80226-4262 Office: Westgate Elem Sch 8550 W Vassar Dr Denver CO 80227-3111

JEKOWSKY, BARRY, conductor, music director. MusB and MusM, Juilliard Sch. Founder, music dir. Calif. Symphony Orch.; assoc. condr. Nat. Symphony Orch., Washington, 1994—. Numerous orch. appearances throughout N.Am. and Europe including London Phila. Orch., Halle Orch. Recipient Leopold Stokowski Conducting prize. Office: Calif Symphony Orch PO Box 596 Orinda CA 94563*

JELLINEK, ROGER, editor; b. Mexico City, Jan. 16, 1938; came to U.S., 1961; s. Frank Louis Mark and Marguerite Lilla Donne (Lewis) J.; m. Margherita DiCenzo, Dec. 22, 1963 (div. 1984); children: Andrew Mark, Claire; m. Eden-Lee Murray, 1984; 1 child, Everett Peter Murray. Student, Bryanston Sch., Dorset, Eng., 1951-56; MA, Cambridge U., Eng., 1961. Assoc. editor Random House, 1963-64; editor Walker & Co., 1964-65; editor N.Y. Times Book Rev., 1966-70, dep. editor, 1970-73; editor in chief Times Books, Quadrangle/N.Y. Times Book Co., 1974-78, sr. editor, 1978-81, editor Lamont newsletter and yearbook, 1981-91; pres. Clairemark, Ltd., 1981—, Jellinek & Murray Literary Agy. Editor Atlantic Realm Project, 1983-93; publisher Hawaii map series. Pres. Art Maps Ltd., 1996—. With Royal Marines, 1956-57; 2d lt. Brit. Intelligence Corps., 1957-58. Mellon fellow Yale, 1961-63. Home and Office: 980 Kaahue St Honolulu HI 96825-1341

JENES, THEODORE GEORGE, JR., retired military officer; b. Portland, Oreg., Feb. 21, 1930; s. Theodore George and Mabel Marie (Moon) J.; m. Beverly Lorraine Knutson, Jan. 29, 1953; children—Ted, Mark. BS, U. Ga., 1956; MS, Auburn U., 1969; grad., Army Command and Gen. Staff Coll., Armed Forces Staff Coll., Air War Coll.; LLD (hon.), U. Akron, 1986. Enlisted U.S. Army, 1951, commd. 2d lt., 1953, advanced through grades to lt. gen., 1984, various assignments, 1953-75; comdr. 3d Brigade, 2d Inf. Div., Republic of Korea, 1975-76, 172d Inf. Brigade, Ft. Richardson, Alaska, 1978-81; dep. commdg. gen. U.S. Army Tng. Ctr., Ft. Dix, N.J., 1976-78; comdr. 4th Inf. Div., Ft. Carson, Colo., 1982-84; dep. commdg. gen. U.S. Army Combined Arms Combat Devel. Activity, Ft. Leavenworth, Kans., 1981-82; comdg. gen. 3d U.S. Army, Ft. McPherson, Ga., 1984-87; commander U.S. Army Forces Ctrl. Command, Ft. McPherson, Ga., 1984-87; dep. comdg. gen. hdqrs. U.S. Army Forces Command, Ft. McPherson, Ga., 1984-87, ret., 1987; cons. Burdeshaw and Assocs., 1987-88; gen. mgr. Seattle Tennis Club, 1988-94. Decorated D.S.M., Legion of Merit, Bronze Star, Meritorious Service medal, Air medal, Army Commendation medal, Vietnamese Cross of Gallantry with Silver Star. Mem. Assn. of U.S. Army, Rotary. United Methodist. Home: 809 169th Pl SW Lynnwood WA 98037-3307

JENKINS, BRUCE, sportswriter; b. Oct. 4, 1948; s. Gordon Jenkins; m. Martha Jane Stanton; 2 children. Degree in Journalism, U. Calif., Berkeley, 1971. With San Francisco Chronicle, 1973—, sports columnist, 1989—. Author: Life After Saberhagen, 1986, North Shore Chronicles, 1990. Recipient nat. awards AP, UPI, Basketball Writers Assn.; nominated Pulitzer Prize for columns Barcelona Olympics, 1992. Office: San Francisco Chronicle 901 Mission St San Francisco CA 94103-2905*

JENKINS, BRUCE STERLING, federal judge; b. Salt Lake City, Utah, May 27, 1927; s. Joseph and Bessie Pearl (Iverson) J.; m. Margaret Watkins, Sept. 19, 1952; children—Judith Margaret, David Bruce, Michael Glen, Carol Alice. B.A. with high honors, U. Utah, 1949, LL.B., 1952, J.D., 1952. Bar: Utah 1952, U.S. Dist. Ct. 1952, U.S. Supreme Ct. 1962, U.S. Circuit Ct. Appeals 1962. Pvt. practice law Salt Lake City, 1952-59; assoc. firm George McMillan, 1959-65; asst. atty. gen. State of Utah, 1952; dep. county atty. Salt Lake County, 1954-58; bankruptcy judge U.S. Dist. Ct., Dist. of Utah, 1965-78; judge U.S. Dist. Ct. of Utah, 1978—, chief judge, 1984-93; adj. prof. U. Utah, 1987-88, 96—. Research, publs. in field; contbr. essays to Law jours.; bd. editors: Utah Law Rev, 1951-52. Mem. Utah Senate, 1959-65, minority leader, 1963, pres. senate, 1965, vice chmn. commn. on orgn. exec. br. of Utah Govt., 1965-66; Mem. adv. com. Utah Tech. Coll., 1967-72; mem. instl. council Utah State U., 1976. Served with USN, 1945-46. Recipient Alumnus of Yr. award Coll. Law Univ. Utah, 1985, Admiration and Appreciation award Utah State Bar, 1995. Fellow Am. Bar Found.; mem. ABA, Am. Inn Ct., Utah State Bar Assn. (Judge of Yr. 1993), Salt Lake County Bar Assn., Fed. Bar Assn. (Disting. Jud. Svc. awrd Utah chpt. 1993), Order of Coif, Phi Beta Kappa, Phi Kappa Phi, Phi Eta Sigma, Phi Sigma Alpha, Tau Kappa Alpha. Democrat. Mormon. Office: US Dist Ct 251 US Courthouse 350 S Main St Salt Lake City UT 84101-2106

JENKINS, CAROL ANNE, educator; b. Kearny, N.J., Mar. 1, 1945; d. Lawrence Augustine and Sara (Ball) J. BA, Malone Coll., 1968; MA in Religious Edn., Chgo. Grad.Sch. Theology, 1969; MA in Sociology, Western Mich. U., 1972; PhD in Sociology, Kans. State U., 1986. Asst. prof., program dir. various orgns., Grand Rapids and Livonia, Mich., 1970-73; asst. prof. Judson Coll., Elgin, Ill., 1973-74, No. State Coll., Aberdeen, S.D., 1974-75, Henry Ford Community Coll., Dearborn, Mich., 1975-76, Wheeling (W.Va.) Coll., 1976-78, Tabor Coll., Hillsboro, Kans., 1978-82; instr. Kans. State U., Manhattan, 1982-85; assoc. prof. Biola U., La Mirada, Calif., 1985-92; prof. Glendale (Ariz.) C.C., 1992—; bd. dirs., chairwoman bd. Faculty Student Union, La Mirada, Christian Conciliation Svcs. of Orange County, Calif.; chair Maricopa C. C. Dist. Sociology Instructional Coun., 1992-93; cons. in field. Author: Thanatology: Discussions On Death & Dying, 1986, Social Problems: Issues and Their Opposing Viewpoints, 1987, Toward An Understanding of Social Thought, 1987, Toward an Understanding of Sociological Theory, 1989; contbr. chpts. to books and articles to profl. jours. Vol. umpire Hillsboro Recreation Dept., 1980-82; speaker Kiwanis, Hillsboro, 1981, Marquette High Sch., 1982; vol. Cedar Hill Mobile Country Club, Fullerton, Calif., 1986-92. Instnl. Rsch. grantee, 1990-91, 91-92. Mem. Am. Sociol. Assn. (exec. coun., awards chair, sect. undergrad. edn. 1993-96, com. on sociology in elem. and sec. schs. 1996—), Pacific Sociol. Assn. (program chair 1988), Midwest Sociol. Assn. (undergrad. edn. com. 1982-85, 96—), Rural Sociol. Soc. (membership com. 1996—, task force on futures 1996—), Assn. Christians Tchg. Sociology (nat. program chair 1981, 92, 90), Religious Edn. Assn., AAUW, Nat. Assn. Ethnic Studies, William Lock Singers Players, Alpha Kappa Delta. Mennonite. Home: 19502 N 98th Ave Peoria AZ 85382-4113

JENKINS, GENI LOUISE EVANS, home health nurse; b. Chula Vista, Calif., Sept. 26, 1954; d. Howard Eugene and Gladys Louise (Phinney) Evans; children: Gretchen Dawn, Thomas Glenn. ADN, Walla Walla (Wash.) C.C., 1984; BSN, Lewis Clark State Coll., 1992. RN, Wash., Idaho, Oreg., Calif.; cert. home health nurse ANA. Staff oncol. nurse St. Joseph's Regional Med. Ctr., Lewiston, Idaho, 1984-86; office nurse Southway Internists, Lewiston, 1986-90; office urol. nurse D.A. Shrader, MD, Lewiston, 1990-91; home health nurse St. Joseph's Regional Med. Ctr., Lewiston, 1991-

93; DON Able Home Health Svcs., Inc., Lewiston, 1993-96; dir. profl. svcs. South Coast Home Health Svcs., Lakewood, Calif., 1996—; speaker in field. Mem. ANA, Idaho Nurses Assn., Nat. League of Nursing. Home: 420 Lake St # 301 Huntington Beach CA 92648

JENKINS, KEVIN J., airline company executive; b. Edmonton, Alta., Can.; m. Helen Jenkins; 3 children. Law degree, U. Alta.; MBA, Harvard U. Ptnr. law firm Can Airlines, Edmonton, Alta., 1980s; with fin. dept. Can. Airlines, Calgary, Alta., 1985, various positions including CFO, pres., 1991—, pres., CEO, 1994—; also bd. dirs.; pres. Wardair; bd. govs. Internat. Air Transport Assn.; mem. exec. com. Can. Tourism Commn.; mem. Bus. Coun. on Nat. Issues; bd. dirs. Japan Soc.; chmn. Air Transport Assn. of Can., 1992-93, Can. Quality Month, 1995. Mem. bus. adv. coun. Faculty of Bus., U. Alta.; mem. Young Pres.'s Orgn.; bd. dirs. Young Life of Can. Office: Can Airlines, 700 2nd St SW # 2800, Calgary, AB Canada T2P 2W2

JENKINS, ROYAL GREGORY, manufacturing executive; b. Springville, Utah, Dec. 11, 1936; s. Chester W. and Sarah E. (Finch) J.; m. Donna Jeanne Jones, Aug. 3, 1957; children: Brad, Kent. BS in Engring., San Jose State U., 1959; MBA, U. Santa Clara, 1968. With Lockheed Corp., Sunnyvale, Calif., 1959-64; contr. ICORE Industries, Sunnyvale, 1964-68; div. v.p. fin. Dart Industries, Los Angeles, 1968-74; dir. planning, div. v.p. Avery Label Group, Avery Internat., Los Angeles, 1974-81, group v.p. Materials Group, Painesville, Ohio, 1981-87, sr. v.p. tech. and planning, Pasadena, Calif., 1987-88, sr. v.p. fin., 1988—; CFO, Avery Dennison Corp. Republican. Avocation: golf. Office: Avery Dennison 150 N Orange Grove Blvd Pasadena CA 91103-3534

JENKINS, SPEIGHT, opera company executive, writer; b. Dallas, Jan. 31, 1937; s. Speight and Sara (Baird) J.; m. Linda Ann Sands, Sept. 6, 1966; children: Linda Leonie, Speight. B.A., U. Tex.-Austin, 1957; LL.B., Columbia U., 1961; DMus (hon.), U. Puget Sound, 1992; HHD, Seattle U., 1992. News and reports editor Opera News, N.Y.C., 1967-73; music critic N.Y. Post, N.Y.C., 1973-81; TV host Live From the Met, Met. Opera, N.Y.C., 1981-83; gen. dir. Seattle Opera, 1983—; classical music editor Record World, N.Y.C., 1973-81; contbg. editor Ovation Mag., N.Y.C., 1980—, Opera Quar., Los Angeles, 1982—. Served to capt. U.S. Army, 1961-66. Recipient Emmy award for Met. Opera telecast La Boheme TV Acad. Arts and Scis., 1982. Mem. Phi Beta Kappa Assocs. Presbyterian. Home: 903 Harvard Ave E Seattle WA 98102-4561 Office: Seattle Opera Assn PO Box 9248 Seattle WA 98109-0248

JENKS, TOM, writer; b. Temple, Tex., Aug. 23, 1950; s. Edwin Riley and Ouida (Baxter) J.; m. Carol Louise Edgarian, Aug. 21, 1993; children: Richard, Anne Riley, Lucy Honor. BA magna cum laude, U. Va., 1980; MFA, Columbia U., 1983. Contbg. editor The Paris Rev., N.Y.C., 1980—; assoc. fiction editor Esquire mag., N.Y.C., 1983-85; sr. editor Scribners, N.Y.C., 1985-87; lit. editor GQ mag., N.Y.C., 1987-91; vis. lectr. Iowa Writer's Workshop, Iowa City, 1989; Hurst prof. Washington U., St. Louis, 1990; vis. prof. U. Calif., Davis, 1990-93; editor Writer Nights Lincoln Ctr., N.Y.C., 1986-88. Author: Our Happiness, 1990; editor: American Short Story Masterpieces, 1987; editor: Hemingway's The Garden of Eden, 1986, (with Carol Edgarian) The Writer's Life, 1997. Mem. Poets Editors Novelists Am.

JENNER, MIKE, newspaper editor. Reporter, photographer Hattiesburg (Miss.) Am.; editing positions The Phila. Inquirer, Columbia (Mo.) Tribune, Coffeyville (Kans.) Jour.; asst. mng. editor Hartford (Conn.) Courant, mng. editor; ind. newspaper cons.; mng. editor The Bakersfield Californian, 1993—. Office: The Bakersfield Californian 1707 Eye St Bakersfield CA 93301

JENNERICH, ELAINE, librarian; b. New Castle, Pa., Apr. 17, 1947; d. C. Paul and Regina Anna (Wajert) Zaremba; m. Edward John Jennerich, May 27, 1972; children: Ethan Edward, Emily Elaine. AB, Syracuse U., 1968; MSLS, Drexel U., 1970; PhD, U. Pitts., 1974. Ref. libr. CarLow Coll., Pitts., 1971-74; head ref. svc. Baylor U., Waco, Tex., 1974-83; libr. bond investment Aetna Life and Casualty, Hartford, Conn., 1983-84; ref./media libr. Va. Intermont Coll., Bristol, Va., 1984-85; libr. dir. Emory & Henry Coll., Emory, Va., 1985-87; circulation libr. U. Wash., Seattle, 1988-89; constrn. coord. U. Wash. Librs., Seattle, 1989-91, staff devel. coord., 1991—. Co-author: Reference Interview As Creative Art, 1997. Mem. ALA, Phi Beta Mu, Chi Omega. Roman Catholic. Office: Univ of Washington Suzzallo Libr Box 352900 Seattle WA 98195

JENNERJAHN, WARREN P., artist, educator; b. Milw., June 15, 1922; s. Ervin Henry and Helen (Krewshewski) J.; m. Elizabeth M. Schmitt, Mar. 14, 1947; children: Hans, Ann. BS in Art Edn., Milw. State Tchrs. Coll., 1946; MS in Art Edn., U. Wis., 1947. Instr. Black Mountain (N.C.) Coll., 1949-51, Cooper Union, N.Y.C., 1952-54, Hunter Coll., N.Y.C., 1953; prof. Adelphi U., Garden City, N.Y., 1954-87; instr. Sedona (Ariz.) Art Ctr., 1990—; instr. art Elderhostel program No. Ariz. U., 1995—. Illustrator: (album cover) Choral Music From Five Centuries, 1973, (books) Respect for Life, 1974, Laboratory Investigations in Human Physiology, 1978. Active Sedona (Ariz.) Art Ctr., 1991—. 1st lt. U.S. Army Air Corps, 1941-45, ETO. Grantee Louis Comfort Tiffany grant, N.Y.C., 1952, Adelphi U., Garden City, 1961-87. Home: 707 Rainbow Trl Sedona AZ 86351-9204

JENNETT, SHIRLEY SHIMMICK, home care management executive, nurse; b. Jennings, Kans., May 1, 1937; d. William and Mabel C. (Mowry) Shimmick; m. Nelson K. Jennett, Aug. 20, 1960 (div. 1972); children: Jon W., Cheryl L.; m. Albert J. Kukral, Apr. 16, 1977 (div. 1990). Diploma, Rsch. Hosp. Sch. Nursing, Kansas City, Mo., 1958. RN, Mo., Colo., Tex., Ill. Staff nurse, head nurse Rsch. Hosp., 1958-60; head nurse Penrose Hosp., Colorado Springs, Colo., 1960-62, Hotel Dieu Hosp., El Paso, Tex., 1962-63; staff nurse Oak Park (Ill.) Hosp., 1963-64, NcNeal Hosp., Berwyn, Ill., 1964-65, St. Anthony Hosp., Denver, 1968-69; staff nurse, head nurse, nurse recruiter Luth. Hosp., Wheat Ridge, Colo., 1969-79; owner, mgr. Med. Placement Svcs., Lakewood, Colo., 1980-84; vol., primary care nurse, admissions coord., team mgr. Hospice of Metro Denver, 1984-88, dir. patient and family svcs., 1988, exec. dir., 1988-94; pres. Care Mgmt. & Resources, Inc., Denver, 1996—. Mem. NAFE, Nat. Women Bus. Owners Assn., Nat. Hospice Orgn. (bd. dirs. emeritus1992-95), Nat. Orgn. Profl. Geriatric Care Mgrs., Denver Bus. Women's Network. Mem. Ch. of Religious Sci. Office: Care Mgmt & Resources Inc 820 S Monaco Pkwy # 250 Denver CO 80224

JENNINGS, CHARLES RAYMOND, music educator, bands director; b. Oakland, Calif., Oct. 21, 1955; s. Charles Raymond and Ann V. Jennings; m. Heather Lane Owen, June 20, 1987; children: Emily Ann, Catherine Michelle, Robert Weston. AA, Santa Rosa (Calif.) Jr. Coll., 1975; BA in Music, Calif. State U., Chico, 1976, MA in Music, 1983; D of Mus. Arts, U. So. Calif., 1995. Music tchr., dir. bands, chmn. dept. Sonoma Valley H.S., Sonoma, Calif., 1978-85; music instr., acting dir. bands Santa Rosa Jr. Coll., 1985-86, Modesto (Calif.) Jr. Coll., 1986-87; music instr. Kings River C.C., Reedley, Calif., 1987-88; music tchr., dir. instrumental music, dist. arts facilitator Tamalpais Union H.S. Dist., Mill Valley, Calif., 1989—; prof. music, dir. bands San Joaquin Delta Coll., Stockton, Calif., 1989—. Condr. various honor bands in Calif. Mem. NEA, Internat. Assn. Jazz Educators, Music Educators Nat. Conf., Coll. Band Dirs. Nat. Assn., Music Assn. Calif. C.C.s (pres. 1992-94), Pi Kappa Lambda. Democrat. Lutheran. Office: San Joaquin Delta Coll Dept Music 5151 Pacific Ave Stockton CA 95207-6304

JENNINGS, IRMENGARD KATHARINA, academic administrator; b. L.A., May 20, 1957; d. Walter Heinrich and Annemarie (Bauer) Brandes; m. Grant Andrew Jennings, May 25, 1979 (dec. May 1991); 1 child, Marcus Joseph. MusB, U. Redlands, 1979, MusM, 1994. Sales clk. Sliger's Music, Redlands, Calif., 1979-81; tchr. music Montessori in Redlands, 1983; sec. cmty. sch. music & arts U. Redlands, 1984-88, sec. sch. music, 1984-95, asst. to dir. sch. music, dir. cmty. sch. music & arts, 1995—; assoc. dir. Cmty. Chorus Redlands, 1984—, U. Redlands Choir, 1984—. Interim organist Trinity United Meth. Ch., Pomona, Calif., 1983-84; dir. music United Meth. Ch., Yucaipa, Calif., 1984-88; sec. Ch. of Christ, Redlands, 1983-84; dir. handbells, assoc. dir. music Trinity Episcopal Ch., Redlands, 1988—. Mem. Sigma Alpha Iota (scholastic award 1978), Pi Kappa Lambda. Office: U Redlands Sch Music PO Box 3080 1200 E Colton Ave Redlands CA 92374

JENNINGS, JUDITH MADRONE, city official; b. Teaneck, N.J., May 21, 1949; d. Frank Gouverneur and Ethel Kathleen (Richards) J. BA, CUNY, N.Y.C., 1971. Cert. elec. inspector. Electrician Internat. Brotherhood of Elec. Workers, Oakland, Calif., 1978-86; elec. inspector City of Oakland, Calif., 1986—. Mem. Internat. Assn. Elec. Inspectors (cert.), Internat. Brotherhood of Elec. Workers. Office: City of Oakland 1330 Broadway Oakland CA 94612-2503

JENNINGS, MARCELLA GRADY, rancher, investor; b. Springfield, Ill., Mar. 4, 1920; d. William Francis and Magdalene Mary (Spies) Grady; student pub. schs.; m. Leo J. Jennings, Dec. 16, 1950 (dec.). Pub. relations Econolite Corp., Los Angeles, 1958-61; v.p., asst. mgr. LJ Quarter Circle Ranch, Inc., Polson, Mont., 1961-73, pres., gen. mgr., owner, 1973—; dir. Giselle's Travel Inc., Sacramento; fin. advisor to Allentown, Inc., Charlo, Mont.; sales cons. to Amie's Jumpin' Jacks and Jills, Garland, Tex. Investor. Mem. Internat. Charolais Assn., Los Angeles County Apt. Assn. Republican. Roman Catholic. Home and Office: 509 Mount Holyoke Ave Pacific Palisades CA 90272-4328

JENNINGS, MARK RUSSELL, biologist; b. Santa Paula, Calif., May 25, 1956; s. Roy Fay and Helen virginia (Sowers) J. AA in Life Scis., Ventura (Calif.) Coll., 1976; BS in Fisheries, Humboldt State U., 1978, MA in Natural Resources, 1981; PhD in Wildlife and Fisheries Sci., U. Ariz., 1986. Fisheries staff Humboldt State U., Arcata, Calif., 1979-81; grad. student asst. Calif. Dept. Fish & Game, Red bluff, Calif., 1981; rsch. assoc. U. Ariz., Tucson, 1982-86; rsch. fishery biologist U.S. Fish and Wildlife Svc., Dixon, Calif., 1986-90; rsch. fish and wildlife biologist U.S. Fish and Wildlife Svc., San Simeon, Calif., 1992-93, Nat. Biol. Svc., San Simeon, 1993-96, U.S. Geol. Survey, San Simeon, 1996—; rsch. assoc. Calif. Acad. Sci., San Francisco, 1987—, Calif. Poly. State U., San Luis Obispo, 1994—; asst. adj. prof. U. Calif., Santa Barbara, 1993—; asst. in agrl. experiment sta. U. Calif., Davis, 1995—. Contbr. articles to profl. jours. Bank of Am. Award winner, 1974; recipient Spl. Achievement award for superior svc. U.S. Fish and Wildlife Svc., 1987, Conservation award Southwestern Herpetologists Soc., 1991, Spl. Achievement award for superior svc. Nat. Biol. Svc., 1994. Mem. Am. Fisheries Soc. (cert. fisheries scientist, newsletter co-editor 1978—), Am. Soc. Ichthyologists and Herpetologists (soc. historian 1978—), Soc. for Study of Amphibians and Reptiles, Herpetologists League, Am. Inst. of Fishery Rsch. Biologists, The Wildlife Soc. Office: US Geological Survey Biol Resources Divsn PO Box 70 San Simeon CA 93452-0070

JENNINGS, NANCY PATRICIA, publications and communications executive; b. Oakland, Calif., Aug. 31, 1963; d. Amos Charles Sudler III and Vicki Lynn (Barr) Jennings. BA, Calif. State U., Hayward, 1985. Corporate comm. asst. Crocker Nat. Bank, San Francisco, 1985-86; publs. assoc. Calif. Bankers Assn., San Francisco, 1986-89; dir. mktg. and comm. Western Independent Bankers, San Francisco, 1989—; freelance computer cons., desktop pub. cons. Editor newsletter Newsline, 1989—. Mem. Nat. Assn. Desktop Publishers. Office: Western Independent Bankers 100 Spear St Ste 1505 San Francisco CA 94105-1527

JENNINGS, PAUL CHRISTIAN, civil engineering educator, academic administrator; b. Brigham City, Utah, May 21, 1936; s. Robert Webb and Elva S. (Simonsen) J.; m. Millicent Marie Bachman, Aug. 28, 1981; m. Barbara Elaine Morgan, Sept. 3, 1960 (div. 1981); children: Kathryn Diane, Margaret Ann. BSCE, Colo. State U., 1958; MSCE, Calif. Inst. Tech., 1960, PhD, 1963. Prof. civil engring., applied mechanics Calif. Inst. Tech., Pasadena, 1966—; chmn. divsn. engring. Calif. Tech. Inst., Pasadena, 1985-89, v.p., provost, 1989-95, acting v.p. for bus. and fin., 1995; mem. faculty bd. Calif. Tech. Inst., 1974-76, steering com., 1974-76, chmn. nominating com., 1975, grad. studies com., 1978-80; cons. in field. Author: (with others) Earthquake Design Criteria. Contbr. numerous articles to profl. jours. 1st lt. USAF, 1965-66. Recipient Honor Alumnus award Colo. State U., 1992, Achievement in Academia award Coll. Engring., 1992; Erskine fellow U. Canterbury, New Zealand, 1970, 85. Fellow AAAS, New Zealand Soc. Earthquake Engring.; mem. ASCE (Walter Huber award 1973, Newmark medal 1992), Seismol. Soc. Am. (pres. 1980), Earthquake Engring. Rsch. Inst. (pres. 1981-83), Athenaeum Club. Home: 640 S Grand Ave Pasadena CA 91105-2423 Office: Calif Inst Tech Mail Code 104-44 Pasadena CA 91125

JENNINGS, THOMAS E., mayor; b. Roswell, N.Mex., Sept. 4, 1950; m. Miandra Van Aswegan; 1 child, Jacqueline. Prin. Oil and Gas Landman, 1992—; mayor City of Roswell, 1994—. Coun. mem. City of Roswell, 1985-94, coun. pres., 1991-92, chmn. parks and recreation com.; chmn. Chaves County Extraterritorial Zoning Authority; treas. Dem. Party, Chaves County, 1984-93, N.Mex. Landmans Assn., 1992-93, v.p., 1993-94. Home: 800 N Kentucky Ave Roswell NM 22801 Office: PO Box 1838 425 N Richardson Roswell NM 88202-1838

JENNISON, BRIAN L., environmental specialist; b. Chelsea, Mass., June 13, 1950; s. Lewis L. and Myra S. (Piper) J. BA, U. N.H., 1972; PhD, U. Calif., Berkeley, 1977; cert. hazardous materials mgr., U. Calif., Davis, 1986. Teaching, rsch. asst. U. Calif., Berkeley, 1972-77; staff rsch. assoc. Dept. of Molecular Biology, Berkeley, 1978-80; instr. dept. biology Calif. State U., Hayward, 1977; sr. biologist San Francisco Bay Marine Rsch. Ctr., Emeryville, Calif., 1980-81; inspector I Bay Area Air Quality Mgmt.Dist., San Francisco, 1981-83, inspector II, 1983-88; enforcement program specialist Bay Area Air Quality Mgmt. Dist., San Francisco, 1988-92; dir. air quality mgmt. div. Washoe County Dist. Health Dept., Reno, Nev., 1992—; cons. U.S. Army Corps of Engrs., L.A., 1980, San Francisco, 1981; instr. U. Calif., Berkeley ext., 1990-93, Assoc. Bay Area Govs., 1990-92; adj. prof. U. Nev., Reno, 1994—. Contbr. articles to profl. jours. Sustaining mem. Rep. Nat. Com., Washington. Postdoctoral fellow, Harbor Br. Found., 1977-78. Mem. AAAS, Air and Waste Mgmt. Assn. (chmn. Ea. Sierra chpt. 1994—), Navy League of U.S. (life), Phi Beta Kappa. Republican. Office: Washoe County Dist Health Dept PO Box 11130 Reno NV 89520

JENSEN, CAROLYN JEAN, public relations executive; b. Visalia, Calif., Nov. 7, 1947; d. Charles Thomas and Bette Jean (Williamson) Madden; m. Robert Laurits Jensen, Apr. 6, 1968 (div. Dec. 1980); children: Francene Ann, Christene Ann, Jeanne Marie. AA, Coastline Coll., 1978, cert, 1982; BSBA in mktg., fin., U. Phoenix, 1992, MA in Orgnl. Mgmt., 1995. Conservation rep. Southern Calif. Edison, Santa Ana, 1978-80; conservation, load mgmt. cons. Southern Calif. Edison, Rosemead, Calif., 1980-81; energy svcs. cons. Southern Calif. Edison, Santa Ana, 1981-89, sales and mktg. mgr., 1989-91; product mgr. Southern Calif. Edison, Rosemead, 1991-92, program mgr., 1992-93, adminstr., 1993-94; mktg. dir. K.L. Geans Co., 1994—; v.p. mktg. Millennium Techs., 1996—; corp. speaker Southern Calif. Edison; tech. cons. Urban Rail, Orange County Urban Trail, 1992. Contb. articles to profl. jours. Adv. Rails for Trails, Laguna Beach, 1992-94, Urban Design for Mass Transit, Orange County, 1991-93; exec. com. Parent Teacher Orgns. 1980-90, exec. vol. 1985. Recipient Nat. Maglev Initiative award, Fed. Railroad Adminstrn, Washington, 1992, Mktg. award Edison Elec. Inst., Washington, 1988, 89, Exemplary Vol. award Carnation Co. and Vol. Ctr. for Orange County, 1985, 86. Mem. NAFE, ASHRAE (tech. energy com. 1993-94, govt. affairs com. 1990-91, Energy award 1989, 90, 91), Wycliffe Assocs. (Cornerstone award 1986, 87), Women in Engring. Program Advocates Network. Republican. Presbyterian. Office: Millennium 15491 Pasadena Ste 2 Tustin CA 92780

JENSEN, CHERRYL KAY, college public relations director; b. Maquoketa, Iowa, Dec. 27, 1949; d. Lewis Leroy and Mary Virginia (Rowan) J.; 1 child, Aschleigh Farynn Jensen-Eldridge. BA in English Lit., U. Iowa, 1972; MA in Journalism, Ctrl. Mich. U., 1981. Editorial asst. U. Iowa, Iowa City, 1972-73; writer Ctrl. Mich. U., Mt. Pleasant, 1973-79, news bur. dir., 1979-84; asst. dir. pub. rels. Mich. State U., East Lansing, 1984-90; dir. univ. rels. Iowa State U., Ames, 1990-94; dir. comm. Heritage Coll., Toppenish, Wash., 1994—; mem. adv. bd. N.W. Pub. Radio, Washington, 1996—. Mem. Coun. for the Advancement and Support of Edn. (chair instnl. rels. track dist. V conf. 1987, conf. program chair dist. VI 1994). Office: Heritage Coll 3240 Fort Rd Toppenish WA 98948

JENSEN, D. LOWELL, federal judge, lawyer, government official; b. Brigham, Utah, June 3, 1928; s. Wendell and Elnora (Hatch) J.; m. Barbara Cowin, Apr. 20, 1951; children: Peter, Marcia, Thomas. A.B. in Econs, U. Calif.-Berkeley, 1949, LL.B., 1952. Bar: Calif. 1952. Dep. dist. atty. Alameda County, 1955-66, asst. dist. atty., 1966-69, dist. atty., 1969-81; asst. atty. gen. criminal div. Dept. Justice, Washington, 1981-83, assoc. atty. gen., 1983-85, dep. atty. gen., 1985-86; judge U.S. Dist. Ct. (no. dist.) Calif., Oakland, 1986—; mem. Calif. Council on Criminal Justice, 1974-81; past pres. Calif. Dist. Atty.'s Assn. Served with U.S. Army, 1952-54. Fellow Am. Coll. Trial Lawyers; mem. Nat. Dist. Atty.'s Assn. (victim/witness commn. 1974-81), Boalt Hall Alumni Assn. (past pres.). Office: US Dist Ct 1301 Clay St Rm 490C Oakland CA 94612-5212*

JENSEN, EDMUND PAUL, bank holding company executive; b. Oakland, Calif., Apr. 13, 1937; s. Edmund and Olive E. (Kessell) J.; m. Marilyn Norris, Nov. 14, 1959; children: Juliana L., Annika M. BA, U. Wash., 1959; postgrad., U. Santa Clara, Stanford U., 1981. Lic. real estate broker, Oreg., Calif. Mgr. fin. plan and evaluation Technicolor, Inc., Los Angeles, 1967-69; group v.p. Nat. Industries & Subs, Louisville, 1969-72; v.p. fin. Wedgewood Homes, Portland, 1972-74; various mgmt. positions U.S. Bancorp, Portland, 1974-83; pres., COO U.S. Bancorp, Inc., Portland, 1983-93; vice chmn., COO U.S. Bancorp, Inc., Portland, 1993-94; pres., CEO Visa Internat., 1994—; bd. dirs. U.S. Nat. Bank of Oreg., U.S. Bank Washington. Chmn. United Way, 1986, N.W. Bus. Coalition, 1987; bd. dirs. Saturday Acad., Portland, 1984—, Visa U.S.A., Visa Internat., Marylhurst Coll., Oreg. Bus. Coun., Oreg. Downtown Devel. Assn., Oreg. Ind. Coll. Found., 1983—, treas., 1986—, chmn., 1988—; bd. dirs. Portland Art Mus., 1983—, vice chmn., 1989—. Mem. Portland C. of C. (bd. dirs. 1981—, chmn. 1987), Assn. Res. City Bankers, Assn. for Portland Progress (pres. 1988), Waverly Country Club, Multnomah Athletic Club, Arlington Club. Office: US Bancorp PO Box 8837 Portland OR 97208-8837

JENSEN, HELEN, musical artists management company executive; b. Seattle, June 30, 1919; d. Frank and Sophia (Kantosky) Leponis; student pub. schs., Seattle; m. Ernest Jensen, Dec. 2, 1939; children: Ernest, Ronald Lee. Co-chmn., Seattle Community Concert Assn., 1957-62; sec. family concerts Seattle Symphony Orch., 1959-61; hostess radio program Timely Topics, 1959-60; gen. mgr. Western Opera Co., Seattle, 1962-64, pres. 1963-64; v.p., dir., mgr. pub. rels. Seattle Opera Assn., 1964-83, preview artists coord., 1981-84; bus. mgr. Portland (Oreg.) Opera Co., 1968, cons., 1967-69; owner, mgr. Helen Jensen Artists Mgmt., Seattle, 1970-92. First v.p. Music and Art Found., 1981-84, pres. 1984-85. Recipient Cert., Women in Bus in the Field of Art, 1973, award Seattle Opera Assn., 1974, Outstanding Svc. award Music and Art Found., 1984, Women of Achievement award Women in Communications, 1992. Mem. Am. Guild Mus. Artists, Music and Art Found. (life), Seattle Opera Guild (life, bd. dirs. 1988-92, pres., award of distinction 1983, parliamentarian 1987-89), Ballard Symphony League (sec.), Portland Opera Assn., Portland Opera Guild, Seattle Civic Opera Assn. (pres. 1981—), 200 Plus One, Aria Preview, Lyric Preview Group (chmn. 1988-92), Past Pres. Assembly (pres. 1977-79, parliamentarian 1987-89), Pres.'s Forum (1st v.p. 1990-91, program vice chmn. 1987-88, pres. 1991-92), North Shore Performing Arts Assn. (pres. 1981), Women of Achievement (past pres's. assembly, chmn.), Pres.'s Forum (pres. 1991-92), Woman's Century Club (chmn. art, drama, music dept. 1992-93, 92-97), Helen Jensen Hiking Club. Home: 19029 56th Ln NE Seattle WA 98155-3156

JENSEN, JAKKI RENEE, retail company executive; b. Eugene, Oreg., Mar. 1, 1959; d. Philip William Jensen and Mary Katherine (Sommers) Henderson; m. Johnny Claiborne Hawthorne, May 7, 1983 (div. Dec. 1996). Student, Oreg. State U., 1977-78; student (hon.), Portland State U., 1978-81. With Nordstrom Inc., Beaverton, Oreg., 1981—; mgr. cosmetics Nordstrom Inc., Beaverton, 1984; mgr. cosmetics Nordstrom Inc., Walnut Creek, Calif., 1984-86, buyer cosmetics, 1986-88; buyer cosmetics Nordstrom Inc., San Francisco, 1988-93; area mdse. mgr. Nordstrom Own Product, San Francisco, 1993—. Affiliate, vol. San Francisco Soc. for Prevention of Cruelty to Animals, 1990—. Mem. I/SPA, No. Calif. Cosmetic Assn., Exec. Women of Am. Republican. Home: 724 16th Ave # 4 San Francisco CA 94118 Office: 865 Market St San Francisco CA 94103-1900

JENSEN, JOHN MICHAEL, mathematics educator, consultant; b. Bklyn., Feb. 4, 1949; s. John Adolph and Katherine Mary (O'Sullivan) J.; m. Joyce Ann Janiga, Jan. 3, 1981. BA, Fordham U., 1970; MA, Ariz. State U., 1978. Math. tchr. Shea Mid. Sch., Phoenix, 1971-73, Paradise Valley High Sch., Phoenix, 1973-74; math. tchr., dept. head Shadow Mountain High Sch., Phoenix, 1974-80, Horizon High Sch., Scottsdale, Ariz., 1980—; cons. The Coll. Bd., San Jose, Calif., 1988—; adj. instr. Ottawa U., Phoenix, 1987-91, Maricopa County C.C., Phoenix, 1978-93. Woodrow Wilson Inst. fellow Princeton U., 1985; named Tchr. of Yr. Ariz. Assn. Engr. & Sci. Soc., 1987; recipient Presdl. Award in Math., Pres. of U.S., 1987. Mem. NEA, Ariz. Edn. Assn., Paradise Valley Edn. Assn. (treas. 1976), Nat. Coun. Tchrs. Math., Mensa.

JENSEN, MARK KEVIN, foreign language educator; b. Bethesda, Md., Aug. 13, 1951; s. Harold Boyd and Annabelle Bertha (Johnson) J.; m. Agnès Guichard, Dec. 20, 1976; 1 child, Gregory. BA, Princeton U., 1974; MA, U. Calif., Berkeley, 1983, PhD, 1989. Asst. prof. French, Pacific Luth. U., Tacoma, 1989—. Co-author: The Traveler in the Life and Works of George Sand, 1994, Mélanges sur L'Oeuvre de Paul Bénichou, 1995; translator: Émile Zola's J'Accuse, 1992; contbr. articles to profl. jours. Pres. Cercle Français de Tacoma, 1993-95; co-founder, v.p. Anna Comstock Dinner Club and Literary Union, 1993—. Mem. MLA, AAUP, Am. Assn. Tchrs. French, Assn. Internat. des Etudes Françaises, Assn. des Amis D'Alfred de Vigny, Washington Assn. Fng. Lang. Tchrs. Home: 3110 N 31st St Tacoma WA 98407-6411 Office: Pacific Luth U Dept Langs and Lits Tacoma WA 98447

JENSEN, PAUL EDWARD TYSON, business educator, consultant; b. New Orleans, Apr. 27, 1926; s. Paul Christian and Nena Laura (Robertson) J.; m. Jule Valerie Geisenhofer, Jan. 10, 1953; children: Christian, Elena, Constance. BS in Physics, Tulane U., 1947, BBA, 1949; MBA, Golden Gate U., 1976. Asst. mgr. Cuban Atlantic Sugar Co., Lugareño, Cuba, 1952-55; sr. engring. specialist GTE, Mountain View, Calif., 1955-82; sr. staff engr. TRW, Inc., Sunnyvale, Calif., 1982-92; assoc. prof. Northwestern Poly. U., Fremont, Calif., 1988—, also bd. dirs.; cons. geog. info. sys. TRW, Inc., Sunnyvale, 1993-94. Capt. USMCR, 1945-61, WWII, Korea. Fellow Soc. Tech. Comm. (assoc.); mem. IEEE (life and sr. mem.), Am. Phys. Soc., Soc. Computer Simulation, World Future Soc., Assn. Old Crows. Presbyterian. Home: 8033 Regency Dr Pleasanton CA 94588 Office: Northwestern Poly U 117 Fourier Ave Fremont CA 94539

JENTZSCH, RICHARD ALLEN, city manager; b. Salt Lake City, Utah, Oct. 4, 1938; s. Carl Eugene and Garda (Webb) J.; m. Gale Patricia Hammond, Dec. 15, 1967; 1 child, Charles Edward. Student adult edn., Salt Lake City Pub. Schs., 1958-60; student, U. Utah, 1960-61, Portland State U., 1971, Chemeketa Community Coll., 1971. Asst. county planner/surveyor Davis County Planning and Engring. Depts., Farmington, Utah, 1957-65; planner Lorain County Regional Planning Commn., Elyria, Ohio, 1965-68; prin. planner Ind. State Planning Svcs. Agy., Indpls., 1968-70; local govt. coord. Intergovernmental Rels. div. Exec. Dept. State of Oreg., Salem, 1970-77, acting asst. adminstr., 1974-75, acting adminstr., 1975; exec. dir. Lincoln-Uinta Assn. Govts., Kemmerer, Wyo., 1977-79, Ind. Heartland Coord. Commn., Indpls., 1979-81; city adminstr. City of Myrtle Point, Oreg., 1981-83; exec. dir. Mid-Columbia Coun. Govts., The Dalles, Oreg., 1983-89; planning and devel. dir. City of Page, Ariz., 1989-90; asst. city mgr. for planning and devel. CIty of Page, Ariz., 1990—. Mem. Jefferson City (Oreg.) Planning Commn. and Budget Com., elected to city coun., 1977, chmn. coun. fin. com., ex-officio mem. planning commn.; sec. Myrtle Point (Oreg.) C. of C. Devel. Com., 1981-83; mem. The Dalles C. of C., 1984-88, mem. child care task force, 1988; mem. Wasco County Jail Task Force, 1987-88; mem. Page/Lake Powell C. of C., 1989—. Mem. Internat. City Mgmt. Assn., Am. Planning Assn., No. Ariz. Coun. Govts. (regional coun. 1992—, transp. tech. sub-comn. 1989—, transp. com. 1992—, co-chair overall econ. devel. dist. adv. com. 1992—, 208 water quality com. 1996—), Rural Ariz. Econ. Devel. Adv. Com., Cocopai RC&D. Home: PO Box 484 Page AZ 86040-0484 Office: City of Page Box 1180 Page AZ 86040

JEPPESEN, M. K., university administrator; b. Logan, Utah, Dec. 31, 1935; s. Moses A. and Afton (Hillyard) J.; m. Carol Jenkins, June 10, 1955 (dec. Nov. 1963); children: Steven, Juliane, Karen, Jennifer; m. Ellen Rae

Burtenshaw, July 14, 1966; children: Christine, Craig, David, Nanette. BS, Utah State U., 1957, MBA, 1971. Cert. profl. contracts mgr., rsch. adminstr. Mgr. bus. Utah Sci. Found., 1958-60; rep. controllers Utah State U., Logan, 1960-69, dir. contracts/grants, 1972—, mem. patent com., investment adv. com., research council, 1978-94; auditor Peat Marwick Main, Salt Lake City, 1969-71; adj. prof. acctg. Utah State U., Logan, 1989—; CFO, treas. Utah State Found., 1987—; pres. Nat. Calibration Co., Logan, 1978-87; cons. and lectr. in field; condr. seminars, workshops in field; mem. exec. com. fin. and budget Nat. Coun. Univ. Rsch. Adminstrs. Trustee Utah State U. Found., 1987-94. Lt. U.S. Army, 1957-63. Fellow Nat. Contracts Mgmt. Assn. (cert. chmn. program com. 1983-84); mem. Soc. Rsch. Adminstrs. (pres. western sect. 1986-87, mountain chpt 1983-85, nat. nominating com. 1987-88, publs. com. 1988-90), Nat. Coun. Univ. Rsch. Adminstrs. (profl. devel. com. 1982-85, mem. nominating com. 1987-88, nat. chmn. budget and fin. com. 1992—), Nat. Assn. Coll. and Univ. Bus. Officers, Western Assn. Coll and Univ. Bus. Officers, Soc. Pub. Accts., Cache C. of C., Logan Country Club. Republican. Mormon. Home: 2628 N 800 E North Logan UT 84341 Office: Utah State U Umc # 1415 Logan UT 84322

JERMINI, ELLEN, educational administrator, philosopher; b. Krefeld, Germany, Aug. 25, 1939; came to U.S., 1986.; d. Maximilian and Mathilde (Wachtberger) Wilms; m. Helios Jermini, 1961 (div. June 1989); children: Mariella Arnoldi, Diego Jermini. PhB, U. Healing, 1984, M in Healing Sci., 1985, PhD, 1986; PhB, U. Philosophy, 1992. Sec. Germany, Switzerland, 1962; pub. translator, 1984—; seminar organizer Europe, 1983—; dir. U. Philosophy/European Found., 1986—; pres. U. Healing, Campo, Calif., 1986—, U. Philosophy, Campo, 1986—; abbot Absolute Monastery, Campo, 1986—. Editor: (newsletter in Italian) Absolute, (newsletter in German) Absolute. Spkr. various univs. and orgns. in Calif. and N.Y., 1989-92, St. Petersburg, Moscow, 1991, Africa, 1994, Egypt, 1995, various seminars and workshops, Ghana, Nigeria. Mem. Toastmasters Internat. (Competent Toastmaster). Home and Office: Univ of Healing 1101 Far Valley Rd Campo CA 91906-3213

JERNIGAN, EARL WESLEY, archaeologist, museum director; b. Alhambra, Calif., June 1, 1940; s. Harvey Richard and Jeanne Jernigan; m. Gisela Evelyn Brashear, June 8, 1968; children: Marcus, Kevin, Thomas, Alan. BA, U. Ariz., 1968, MA, 1970, PhD, 1973. Asst. prof. anthropology U. Ariz., Tucson, 1978-86; sign designer various Tucson firms, 1986-89; dir. mus. Ea. Ariz. Coll., Thatcher, 1989—. Author: Jewelry of the Prehistoric Southwest, 1978, White Metal Universe, 1980; illustrator: (children's) One Green Mesquite Tree (Best Juvenile Book of Yr. 1988), Agave Blooms Just Once (co-recipient Author of Yr. 1990). Office: Ea Ariz Coll Mus Anthropology Thatcher AZ 85552-0769

JERRITTS, STEPHEN G., computer company executive; b. New Brunswick, N.J., Sept. 14, 1925; s. Steve and Anna (Kovacs) J.; m. Audrey Virginia Smith, June 1948; children: Marsha Carol, Robert Stephen, Linda Ann; m. 2d, Ewa Elizabet Rydell-Vejlens, Nov. 5, 1966; 1 son, Carl Stephen. Student, Union Coll., 1943-44; B.M.E., Rensselaer Poly. Inst., 1947, M.S. Mgmt., 1948. With IBM, various locations, 1949-58, IBM World Trade, N.Y.C., 1958-67, Bull Gen. Electric div. Gen. Electric, France, 1967-70, merged into Honeywell Bull, 1970-74; v.p., mng. dir. Honeywell Info. Systems Ltd., London, 1974-76; group v.p. Honeywell U.S. Info. Systems, Boston, 1977-80; pres., chief operating officer Honeywell Info. Systems, 1980-82, also bd. dirs.; pres., chief exec. officer Lee Data Corp., 1983-85; with Storage Tech. Corp., 1985-88, pres., chief operating officer, 1985-87, also bd. dirs., vice-chmn. bd. dirs., 1988; pres., chief exec. officer NBI Corp., 1988-92, also bd. dirs.; corp. sr. v.p., pres. Latin Am., bd. dirs. Wang Labs. Inc.; bd. dirs. High Ground Sys., Inc., PubNetics, Inc., Wang Labs., Inc., PubNetics, Inc.; cons. mgmt. corp. turnarounds. Bd. dirs. Guthrie Theatre, 1980-83, Charles Babbage Inst., 1980-92, Minn. Orch., 1980-85; trustee Rensselaer Poly. Inst., 1980-85, mem. adv. bd. Lally Sch. Mgmt., 1994—. With USNR, 1943-46. Mem. Computer Bus. Equipment Mfrs. (dir. exec. com. 1979-82), Assoc. Industries Mass. (dir. 1978-80). Home and Office: 650 College Ave Boulder CO 80302-7136

JERRYTONE, SAMUEL JOSEPH, trade school executive; b. Pittston, Pa., Mar. 21, 1947; s. Sebastian and Susan Teresa (Chiampi) J.; children: Sandra, Cheryl, Samuel, Sebastian. Assoc. in Bus., Scranton (Pa.) Lackawanna Jr. Coll., 1966. Mgr. House of Jerrytone Beauty Salon, West Pittston, Pa., 1967-68; regional sales dir. United Republic Life Ins., Harrisburg, Pa., 1970-76; night instr. Wilkes-Barre (Pa.) Vo-Tech High Sch., 1976-78; spl. sales agt. Franklin Life Ins. Co., Wilkes-Barre, 1978-80; instr. Jerrytone Beauty Sch., Pittston, Pa., 1968-69, supr., 1969-95; prof. sch. evaluator Nat. Accrediting Com. Arts and Scis., 1974-95; mem. adv. craft com. Wiles-Barre Vo-Tech H.S., 1988—. Mem. com. Rep. Presdl. Task Force, Washington, 1984. Mem. Pa. Hairdressers Assn., Nat. Accrediting Com. Cosmetology, Am. Coun. Cosmetology Educators, Masons (3d degree award 1983, 32d degree award Lodge Coun. chpt. consistory 1984), Shriners (Irem temple). Roman Catholic.

JERVIS, JANE LISE, college official, science historian; b. Newark, N.J., June 14, 1938; d. Ernest Robert and Helen Jenny (Roland) J.; m. Kenneth Albert Pruett, June 20, 1959 (div. 1974); children: Holly Jane Pruett, Cynthia Lorraine Pruett; m. Norman Joseph Chonacky, Dec. 26, 1981; children: Philip Joseph Chonacky, Joseph Norman Chonacky. AB, Radcliffe Coll., 1959; MA, Yale U., 1974, MPhil, 1975, PhD in History of Sci., 1978. Freelance sci. editor and writer, 1962-72; lectr. in history Rensselaer Poly. Inst., 1977-78; dean Davenport Coll., lectr. in history of sci. Yale U., 1978-82; dean students., assoc. prof. history Hamilton Coll., 1982-87; dean coll., lectr. in history Bowdoin Coll., 1988-92; pres. Evergreen State Coll., Olympia, Wash., 1992—. Author: Cometary Theory in 15th Century Europe; contbr. articles to profl. jours.; book reviewer; presenter in field. Trustee Maine Hist. Assn., 1991-92, Stonehill Coll., 1996—; chair Maine selection com. Rhodes Scholarship Trust, 1990-92, chair N.W. selection com., 1992-93; commr. N.W. Assn. Schs. and Colls. Commn. on Colls., 1994—. Office: Evergreen State Coll Office of President Olympia WA 98505

JERVIS, WILLIAM HORACE, JR., plastic and reconstructive surgeon; b. Vicksburg, Miss., Dec. 7, 1934; s. William H. Sr. and Margaret Elizabeth (Bates) J.; children: Vincent H., Helga J., Hans W. BA, Occidental Coll., 1957; MD, McGill U., Montreal, Can., 1961. Diplomate Am. Bd. Plastic Surgery, Nat. Bd. Med. Examiners; lic. physician and surgeon, Calif. Internship L.A. County Gen. Hosp., 1961-62; flight surgeon Brooks AFB, San Antonio, 1963; capt. Evreux (France) AFB and Lockbourne AFB, 1963-65; gen. surgery Pacific Med. Ctr., San Francisco, 1965-66, Kaiser Found. Hosp., Oakland, Calif., 1969-71; gen. practice residency Contra Costa County Hosp., Martinez, Calif., 1968-69; plastic surgery residency U. Tex. Southwestern Med. Sch., Dallas, 1972-74; pvt. practice plastic and reconstructive surgery Walnut Creek, Calif., 1974—; vol. reconstructive surgery La Familia Found. Hosp., Nuevo Progresso, Guatemala, 1983, 84, 85, 86, 87, 88, 89, 90, 93; clin. instr. plastic surgery Sch. of Medicine U. Calif., Davis, 1979-92; chief sect. plastic surgery John Muir Med. Ctr., Walnut Creek, 1982-85. Contbr. articles to profl. jours. Fellow ACS; mem. AMA, Calif. Med. Assn., Alameda-Contra Costa Med. Soc., Am. Soc. Plastic and Reconstructive Surgeons, Calif. Soc. Plastic Surgeons, Am. Soc. for Aesthetic Plastic Surgery, Lipolyis Soc. N.Am. Office: William Jervis MD Inc 1844 San Miguel Dr Ste 109 Walnut Creek CA 94596-4913

JESKE, KEITH WILLIAM, real estate and mortgage executive; b. Milw., June 16, 1950; s. Gilbert F. and Betty A. (Langdon) J.; children: KC William, Camie Sloan; m. Christy Sue Bynum, Feb. 12, 1993. AA, San Bernardino Valley Coll., 1971; BA, Point Loma, San Diego, 1973; JD, U. West Los Angeles, 1976. Chmn. bd., CEO Keith Jeske Realty, Las Vegas, Nev., 1976—; CEO Levin Mortgage, Las Vegas, 1991—; pres., CEO Echelon Group, 1994—; pres. Fred Sands Las Vegas Properties, 1995—; CEO Nat. Home Funding Corp., 1996; cons. Consumer Credit Counselors, L.A., 1974-78, Culver City (Calif.) Planning Commn., 1975-77. Author: Goal Mind, 1988; contbr. articles to profl. jours. Mediator Community Mediation of San Diego, 1990; educator, arbitrator Alternative Dispute Resolutions, Las Vegas, 1992. Named Sales Person of Yr., Beverly Hills, 1973, Mgr. of Yr., Bd. of Realtors, L.A., 1979. Mem. Nat. Assn. Realtors, Calif. Assn. Realtors, L.A. Bd. Realtors, Culver City Bd. Realtors, Las Vegas Bd. Realtors, Mortgage Brokers Assn., Mortgage Bankers Assn. Home: 1101 Broadmoor Ave Las Vegas NV 89109-1556

JESSUP, W. EDGAR, JR., lawyer; b. L.A., Sept. 9, 1922; s. Walter E. and Marian (Moses) J.; m. Audrey B. Vail; children: Bryn W., Holden D. ScB in Engring. magna cum laude, Brown U., 1943; JD, U. So. Calif., L.A., 1949. Bar: Calif. 1950, U.S. Dist. Ct. (cen. dist.) Calif. 1950, U.S. Claims Ct. 1976, U.S. Tax Ct., 1952. Founding ptnr. Ervin, Cohen & Jessup, Beverly Hills, Calif., 1953—; lectr. Sch. Engring. U. So. Calif., 1950-58, Sch. Law, 1965-76; bd. dirs. Logicon, Inc., L.A., Magnetika, Inc., L.A., Software Techs. Corp., L.A. Author: Law & Specifications for Engineers & Scientists, 1963; contbr. articles to profl. jours. Bd. dirs. Assn. Alumni Brown U., Providence, 1985-89; chmn. bd. dirs. Westside Family YMCA, West Los Angeles, Calif., 1988-93, chmn. 1988-93; bd. dirs. Brentwood (Calif.) Westwood Symphony, 1953-93; bd. mgrs. L.A. Metro YMCA, 1984-93. Lt. USNR, 1943-46, ETO, PTO. Mem. ABA, State Bar Calif., L.A. Bar Assn., Beverly Hills Bar Assn., Brown U. Club So. Calif. (pres. 1984-91), Calif. Yacht Club (former flag officer), Order of Coif, Tau Beta Pi, Phi Kappa Phi, Phi Alpha Delta. Office: Ervin Cohen & Jessup 9401 Wilshire Blvd Beverly Hills CA 90212-2928

JIMENEZ, JOSEPHINE SANTOS, portfolio manager; b. Lucena, Quezon, Philippines, June 6, 1954; came to U.S., 1972; d. Jose Hirang and Virginia Villapando (Santos) J. BS, NYU, 1979; MS, MIT, 1981. Securities analyst Mass. Mut. Life Ins. Co., Springfield, 1982-83; investment officer One Fed. Asset Mgmt., Boston, 1984-87; sr. analyst, portfolio mgr. Emerging Markets Investors Corp., Washington, 1988-91; mng. dir., portfolio mgr. Montgomery Asset Mgmt., San Francisco, 1991—; founding ptnr. Montgomery Emerging Markets Fund; trustee M.I.T. Corp. Trustee MIT Corp. Mem. Inst. Chartered Fin. Analysts. Office: Montgomery Asset Mgmt 101 California St San Francisco CA 94111-5802

JIMENEZ, LUIS ALFONSO, JR., sculptor; b. El Paso, Tex., July 30, 1940; s. Luis Alfonso and Alicia (Franco) J.; m. Susan Brockman; children: Elisa Victoria, Luis Adan, Juan Orion, Sarah Alicia Xochil. B.S. in Art and Architecture, U. Tex., Austin, 1964; postgrad., Ciudad U., Mexico City, 1964. Exhibited in one-man shows, including, Graham Gallery, N.Y.C., 1969-70, O.K. Harris Works of Art, N.Y.C., 1972-75, Contemporary Arts Mus., Houston, 1974, Mus. of N.Mex., Santa Fe, 1980, Frumkin Struve, Chgo., 1981, Adeliza's Candy Store Gallery, Folsom, Calif., 1982, Phyllis Kind Gallery, N.Y.C., 1984, Moody Gallery, Houston, 1987, 95, Scottsdale Cultural Arts Ctr., Nat. Mus. Am. Art, Washington, 1994, Marsha Mateyka Gallery, Washington, 1994, Adair Margo Gallery, El Paso, Tex., 1995, A.C.A. Galleries, N.Y.C., 1995, Dallas Mus. Art, 1997; exhibited in group shows, including, Human Concern Personal Torment, Whitney Mus., N.Y., 1969, Nat. Mus. Am. Art, Washington, 1980, Albuquerque Mus., 1980, Edinburgh (Scotland) Festival, 1980, Walker Art Center, Mpls., 1980, U. Minn., Mpls., 1981, Roswell Mus. and Art Ctr., N. Mex., 1984, Albright-Knox Art Mus., Buffalo, N.Y., Hirshhorn Mus. and Sculpture Garden, Smithsonian Instn., Washington, Hispanic Art in the U.S., 1988, Hispanic Arts in the U.S. traveling show, 1987-89, Latin Am. Spirit in the U.S., 1989, Committed To Print, Mus. Modern Art, N.Y.C., 1989, Whitney Biennial, N.Y.C., 1991, New Mus., N.Y.C., Art of the Other Mex. traveling exhibit, 1993, 20 Yrs. of Landfall Prints, Whitney Mus., 1997; represented in permanent collections, Nat. Mus. Am. Art, Witte Mus., San Antonio, Long Beach (Calif.) Mus., New Orleans Mus. Art, Roswell (N. Mex.) Mus. and Art Center, Sheldon Meml. Gallery, Lincoln, Nebr., Art Inst. Chgo., Met. Mus. Art, N.Y.C., Smithsonian Instn., Mus. Modern Art, Albuquerque Mus. Art, Fed. Reserve Bank, Dallas, others, also pvt. collections; works include Vaquero Sculpture, Moody Park, Houston, 1977; Nat. Endowment for Arts and City Housing Authority commn. Sodbuster sculpture, Fargo, N.D., 1977; Southwest Pietà, Nat. Endowment for Arts commn. Art in Pub. Places, City of Albuquerque, 1981; Steel Worker, Nat. Endowment for Arts, La Salle Sta., Buffalo, N.Y.; Niagara Frontier, Transp. Authority Commn., VA Hosp., 1982; Flag Raising, Oklahoma City Sculpture Commn.; Howl, Wichita State U., Kans., 1983; Border Crossing, Otis Art Inst. of Parsons Sch. Design, Los Angeles, 1984; Fiesta Dancers, Gen. Services Adminstrn., Otay Mesa, Calif., 1986; sculpture commn. NEA and City of El Paso, 1986, Fountain Project, Omni Hotel, San Diego, 1986, City of Las Vegas, 1989, New Denver Airport, 1991, City of N.Y. Cultural Affairs, Hunt's Point Market, Bronx, N.Y., Firefighter, Cleve., 1996. Recipient Steuben Glass award 1972, Hassam Fund award Am. Acad. Arts and Letters, 1977, awards in visual arts, 1985, Greenburger Found. award, 1987, Showhegan sculpture award, 1989, Gov.'s award State of N.Mex., 1993, Award of Distinction Nat. Coun. of Art Adminstrs., 1995; named goodwill amb. City of Houston, 1993; fellow Nat. Endowment Arts, 1987, 88, Am. Acad. in Rome, 1979, La Napoule Art Found. and Nat. Endowment Arts residency fellow, 1990. *I am a traditional artist in the sense that I give form to my culture's icons. I work with folk sources; the popular culture and mythology, and a popular material; fiberglass, shiny finishes, metal flake, and at times with neon and illuminated. In the past the important icons were religious, now they are secular.*

JIMENEZ, WALTER ANTHONY, air force officer; b. Long Beach, Calif., Oct. 1, 1970; s. Minor Manuel and Ruth Anna (Hohl) J. BS in Aviation Bus. Adminstrn., Embry-Riddle Aerospace U., 1992; M of Criminal Justice Adminstrn., U. Great Falls, 1996. Commd. 2d lt. USAF, 1992, advanced through grades to 1st lt., 1994; capt., 1996—. Sustaining mem. Rep. Nat. Com., Washington, 1996. Recipient Nat. Defense medal, Combat Readiness medal. Mem. NRA, N.Am. Hunting Club. Roman Catholic. Home: 3408 Coyote Ln Great Falls MT 59404-3832 Office: 12 Missile Squadron 341 Missile Wing Bldg 500 Malmstrom AFB Great Falls MT 59402

JIMMINK, GLENDA LEE, retired elementary school educator; b. Lamar, Colo., Feb. 13, 1935; d. Harold Dale and Ruth Grace (Ellenberger) Fasnacht; m. Gary Jimmink, Oct. 24, 1964 (div. 1984); 1 child, Erik Gerard. BA, U. LaVerne, Calif., 1955. Tchr. elem. grades Pomona (Calif.) Unified Sch. Dist., 1955-61, Palo Alto (Calif.) Unified Sch. Dist., 1961-65, San Rafael (Calif.) Sch. Dist., 1966-95; ret.; mem. curriculum coun. San Rafael Sch. Dist., 1983-90, 94-95, mentor tchr., 1989-90, mem. social studies steering com., 1990-95; charter mem. Marin County Curriculum Connection, 1991-95. Artist, pub. (calendar) Dry Creek Valley, 1987; author: World Geography Resource Handbook for Tchrs., 1990, others. Mem. Marin Arts Coun., San Rafael, 1988-95, Big Bros.-Big Sisters, San Rafael, 1986-93, Earthwatch, 1990—. Mem. Colored Pencil Soc. Am., Mendocino Art Assn., Nat. Wildlife Soc., Richmond Art Ctr., Sierra Club, Gualala Arts Assn., Berkeley Art Ctr/.

JINDRICH, ERVIN JAMES, municipal government official; b. Chgo., June 5, 1939; s. Ervin James and Lydia Renata (Ahrens) J.; m. Denise Lobeth Fowler, Mar. 4, 1970; children: Devin Logan, Antonia Elizabeth. Student, U. Ill., 1960; BS, MD, Northwestern U., 1964. Resident in anatomic and clin. pathology Kaiser Hosp., San Francisco, 1968-72; fellow in forensic pathology U. Calif., San Francisco, 1972-73; coroner City and County of San Francisco, 1973-74, County of Marin, Calif., 1975—; pvt. practice as medico-legal cons., Mill Valley, Calif., 1975—. Contbr. articles to Jour. Forensic Scis., Jour. Analytical Toxicology. Bd. dirs. Marin Suicide Prevention Ctr. and Grief Counseling Svcs., Marin, 1977-96. Capt. U.S. Army, 1965-67. Decorated Cert. of Achievement. Fellow Am. Acad. Forensic Scis.; mem. Nat. Assn. Med. Examiners. Home: 9 Heuters Ln Mill Valley CA 94941-2701 Office: County of Marin Civic Ctr Rm 241 San Rafael CA 94903

JIRAUCH, CHARLES W., lawyer; b. St. Louis, Apr. 27, 1944; s. Mary K. (Horan) J.; m. Sally J. Costello, June 1, 1968 (div. Mar. 1977); m. Dana K. Bowen; children: Melissa, Mathew, Kathleen. BS, Washington U., 1966; JD, Georgetown U., 1970. Bar: Ill. 1971, Ariz. 1975, Nev. 1991, , Calif. 1993, Colo. 1993, U.S. Patent Office 1970, U.S. Supreme Ct. 1978. Atty. Leydig, Voit & Mayer, Chgo., 1970-71, McDermott, Will & Emery, Chgo., 1971-75, Streich Lang, Phoenix, 1975—. Mem. ABA, Ariz. Bar Found., Maricopa County Bar Found., Am. Judicature Soc., Am. Intellectual Property Assn., Ariz. Dem. Coun., Ariz. Civil Liberties Union. Democrat. Roman Catholic. Office: Streich Lang 2 N Central Ave Phoenix AZ 85004-2322

JOANS, BARBARA, museum director. Dir. Merritt Mus. of Anthropology, Oakland, Calif. Office: Merritt Mus of Anthropology 12500 Campus Dr Oakland CA 94619

JOAQUIM, RICHARD RALPH, hotel executive; b. Cambridge, Mass., July 28, 1936; s. Manuel and Mary (Marrano) J.; m. Nancy Phyllis Reis, Oct. 22, 1960; 1 child, Vanessa Reis. BFA, Boston U., 1955, MusB, 1959. Social dir., coord. summer resort, Wolfeboro, N.H., 1957-59; concert soloist N.H. Symphony Orch., Vt. Choral Soc., Choral Arts Soc., Schenectady Chamber Orch., 1957-60; coord. performance functions, mgr. theatre Boston U., 1959-60, asst. program dir., 1963-64, dir. univ. programs, 1964-70; gen. mgr. Harrison House of Glen Cove; dir. Conf. Svc. Corp., Glen Cove, N.Y., 1970-74, sr. v.p., dir. design and devel.; v.p. Arltec, also mng. dir. Sheraton Internat. Conf. Ctr., 1975-76; v.p., mng. dir. Scottsdale (Ariz.) Conf. Ctr. and Resort Hotel, 1976—; pres. Internat. Conf. Resorts, Inc., 1977, chmn. bd., 1977—; pres. Western Conf. Resorts; concert solist U.S. Army Field Band, Washington, 1960-62. Creative arts cons., editorial cons., concert mgr. Commr. recreation Watertown, Mass., 1967—; mem. Spl. Study Com. Watertown, 1967—, Glen Cove Mayor's Urban Renewal Com., Nat. Com. for Performing Arts Ctr. at Boston U., Jacob K. Javits Fellows Program Fellowship Bd. Bd. dirs. Nat. Entertainment Conf.; trustee Boston U., 1983—, Hotel and Food Adminstrn. Program Adv. Bd., Boston U., 1986—, Ariz. Opera Co. With AUS, 1960-62. Recipient Disting. Alumni award Boston U., 1991. Mem. Assn. Coll. and Univ. Concert Mgrs., Am. Symphonic League, Am. Fedn. Film Socs., Assn. Am. Artists, Am. Pers. and Guidance Assn., La Chaine des Rotisseurs, Knights of the Vine, Order of St. John, Nat. Alumni Council Boston U. Clubs: The Lotos (N.Y.). Office: Scottsdale Conf Ctr & Resort Hotel 7700 E Mccormick Pky Scottsdale AZ 85258-3431

JOFFE, BARBARA LYNNE, computer project manager; b. Bklyn., Apr. 12, 1951; d. Lester L. and Julia (Schuelke) J.; m. James K. Whitney, Aug. 25, 1990; 1 child, Nichole. BA, U. Oreg., 1975; MFA, U. Mont., 1982. Applications engr., software developer So. Pacific Transp., San Francisco, 1986-93; computer fine artist Barbara Joffe Assocs., San Francisco, Englewood, Colo., 1988—; instr. computer graphics Ohlone Coll., Fremont, Calif., 1990-91; adv. programmer, project mgr.-client/server Integrated Sys. Solutions Corp./ IBM Global Svcs. So. Pacific/Union Pacific Railroads, Denver, 1994—. Artwork included in exhibits at Calif. Crafts XIII, Crocker Art Mus., Sacramento, 1983, Rara Avis Gallery, Sacramento, 1984, Redding (Calif.) Mus. and Art Ctr., 1985, Euphrat Gallery, Cupertino, Calif., 1988, Computer Mus., Boston, 1989, Siggraph Traveling Art Shown, Europe and Australia, 1990, 91, 4th and 7th Nat. Computer Art Invitational, Cheney, Wash., 1991, 94, Visual Arts Mus., N.Y.C., 1994, 96. Mem. Assn. Computing Machinery, Project Mgmt. Inst. Home: 7271 S Jersey Ct Englewood CO 80112-1512

JOFFE, BENJAMIN, mechanical engineer; b. Riga, Latvia, Feb. 23, 1931; came to U.S., 1980, naturalized, 1985; s. Alexander and Mery (Levenson) J.; m. Frida Erenshteyn, Aug. 6, 1960; children: Alexander, Helena. ASME, Mech. Tech. Sch., Kransnoyarsk, USSR, 1951; BSME, Polytechnic Inst. Moscow, 1959; MSME, Polytechnic Inst. Riga, 1961; PhD, Acad. Scis., Riga, 1969. Design engr. Electromachine Mfg. Corp., Riga, 1955-59, head engring. dept., 1959-62; sr. design engr. Acad. Scis., Riga, 1962-67; sr. scientist Inst. Physics, Riga, 1967-78; chief design engr. Main Design Bur., Riga, 1978-80; sr. design engr. Elec-Trol, Inc., Saugus, Calif., 1980-81; sr. design engr. VSI Aerospace div. Fairchild, Chatsworth, Calif., 1981-85; mech. engring. mgr. Am. Semiconductor Equipment Tech., Woodland Hills, Calif., 1985-90; mem. tech. staff Jet Propulsion Lab. Calif. Inst. Tech., Pasadena, 1991-97; staff scientist aerospace/comm. divsn. ITT, Ft. Wayne, Ind., 1997—. Author 5 sci. engring. books; contbr. numerous articles to profl. jours. Recipient Honored Inventor award Latvian Republic, Riga, 1967, 1st prize Latvian Acad. Scis., 1972, Latvian State award in engring. scis., 1974. Mem. ASME (dir. exec. bd.). Republican. Office: ITT Aerospace/Comm Divsn 1919 W Cook Rd PO Box 3700 Fort Wayne IN 46801

JOHANOS, DONALD, orchestra conductor; b. Cedar Rapids, Iowa, Feb. 10, 1928; s. Gregory Hedges and Doris (Nelson) J.; m. Thelma Trimble, Aug. 27, 1950; children—Jennifer Claire, Thea Christine, Gregory Bruce (dec.), Andrew Mark, Eve Marie; m. Corinne Rutledge, Sept. 28, 1985. Mus.B., Eastman Sch. Music, 1950, Mus.M., 1952; D.F.A. (hon.), Coe Coll., 1962. Tchr. Pa. State U., 1953-55, So. Meth. U., 1958-62, Hockaday Sch., 1962-65; now condr. laureate Honolulu Symphony Orch. Mus. dir., Altoona (Pa.) Symphony, 1953-56, Johnstown (Pa.) Symphony, 1955-56, asso. condr., Dallas Symphony Orch., 1957-61, resident condr., 1961-62, mus. dir., 1962-70, assoc. condr., Pitts. Symphony, 1970-79, mus. dir., Honolulu Symphony Orch., 1979—, artistic dir., Hawaii Opera Theater, 1979-83, guest condr., Phila. Orch., Amsterdam Concertgebouw Orch., Pitts. Symphony, Rochester Philharm., New Orleans Philharm., Denver Symphony, Vancouver Symphony, Chgo. Symphony, San Francisco Symphony, Netherlands Radio Philharm., Swiss Radio Orch., Mpls. Symphony, Paris Opera, Boston Symphony, San Antonio Symphony, Orchestre Nat. de Lyon, others; recordings for Marco Polo, Naxos, Turnabout, Candide, others. Advanced study grantee Am. Symphony Orch. League and Rockefeller Found., 1955-58. Mem. Am. Fedn. Musicians Internat. Congress of Strings (dir.). Office: Schofer/Gold 50 Riverside Dr New York NY 10024*

JOHANSON, DONALD CARL, physical anthropologist; b. Chgo., June 28, 1943; s. Carl Torsten and Sally Eugenia (Johnson) J. ; m. Lenora Carey, 1988; 1 child, Tesfaye Meles. BA, U. Ill., 1966; MA, U. Chgo., 1970, PhD, 1974; DSc (hon.), John Carroll U., 1979; D.Sc. (hon.), Coll. of Wooster, 1985. Mem. dept. phys. anthropology Cleve. Mus. Natural History, 1972-81, curator, 1974-81; pres. Inst. Human Origins, Berkeley, Calif., 1981—; prof. anthropology Stanford U., 1983-89; adj. prof. Case Western Res. U., 1978-81, Kent State U., 1978-81. Co-author: (with M.A. Edey) Lucy: The Beginnings of Humankind, 1981 (Am. Book award 1982), Blueprints: Solving the Mystery of Evolution, 1989, (with James Shreeve) Lucy's Child: Discovering a Human Ancestor, 1989, (with Kevin O'Farrell) Journey from the Dawn: Life with the World's First Family, 1990, (with Lenora Johanson and Blake Edgar) Ancestors: In Search of Human Origins, 1994, (with Blake Edgar) From Lucy to Language, 1997; host PBS Natures Series; prodr. (film) Lucy in Disguise, 1982; host, narrator NOVA series In Search of Human Origins, 1994 (Emmy nomination 1995); contbr. numerous articles to profl. jours. Recipient Jared Potter Kirtland award for outstanding sci. achievement Cleve. Mus. Natural History, 1979, Profl. Achievement award U. Chgo., 1980, Gold Mercury Internat. ad personem award Ethiopia, 1982, Humanist Laureate award Acad. of Humanism, 1983, Disting. Svc. award Am. Humanist Assn., 1983, San Francisco Exploratorium award, 1986, Internat. Premio Fregene award, 1987, Alumni Achievement award U. Ill., 1995; grantee Wenner-Gren Found., NSF, Nat. Geog. Soc., L.S.B. Leakey Found., Cleve. Found., George Gund Found., Roush Found. Fellow AAAS, Calif. Acad. Scis., Rochester (N.Y.) Mus., Royal Geog. Soc.; mem. Am. Assn. Phys. Anthropologists, Internat. Assn. Dental Research, Internat. Assn. Human Biologists, Am. Assn. Africanist Archaeologists, Soc. Vertebrate Paleontology, Soc. Study of Human Biology, Societe de l'Anthropologie de Paris, Centro Studi Ricerche Ligabue (Venice), Founders' Coun., Chgo. Field Mus. Natural History (hon.), Assn. Internationale pour l'etude de Paleontologie Humaine, Mus. Nat. d'Histoire Naturelle de Paris (corr.), Explorers Club (hon. dir.), Nat. Ctr. Sci. Edn. (supporting scientist). Office: Inst Human Origins 1288 9th St Berkeley CA 94710-1501

JOHNS, DAVID M., conservationist; b. Portland, Oreg., Mar. 26, 1951; m. Carol E. Jones, 1992. BS, Portland State U., 1976; MA, Columbia U., 1978, JD, 1981. Bar: N.Y. Asst. downtown planning and devel. Office of Mayor, City of Portland, 1975-76; atty. advisor Office of Sec., U.S. Dept. Transp., 1980-81; asst. mgr. Portland Bur. Gen. Svcs., 1981-85; mgr. urban svcs. program, legis. affairs Portland Bur. Water Works, 1985-92; with reforestation project Inst. Forestry and Natural Resources, Nicaragua, 1987; advisor Environ. Law Ctr., Can., Can. Fed. Govt. Environ. and External Affairs Dept., 1990-91; pres., exec. dir. The Wildlands Project, 1992-96, sec.-treas., 1996—; vis. instr. Inst. Policy Studies, 1981; vis. prof. polit. sci. Oreg. State U., 1989; adj. asst. prof. polit. sci. Portland State U., 1981—; bd. dirs. Wild Earth Mag., edit. advisor, 1990—; mem. bd. Yellowstone to Yukon Biodiversity Strategy, 1995—. Contbr. articles to profl. jours. Internat. fellow Columbia U.; Harlan Fiske Stone scholar Columbia Law Sch., Portland U. scholar. Mem. N.Y. State Bar Assn., Soc. Ecological Restoration and Mgmt., Soc. Conservation Biology. Office: The Wildlands Project PO Box 725 Mcminnville OR 97128 also: 1955 W Grant Rd Ste 148 Tucson AZ 85745

JOHNS, KAREN LOUISE, nurse, psychotherapist; b. Chgo., Jan. 21, 1942; d. John Leonard and Virginia Selma (Kliner) J. Diploma in Nursing, St.

Elizabeth Hosp., Chgo., 1962; BSN, Loyola U., Chgo., 1967; MSN, Calif. State U., L.A., 1972; MA in Psychology, Immaculate Heart Coll., L.A., 1978. RN, Calif.; registered marriage, family and child counselor; cert. clin. specialist in psychiat./mental health nursing; registered poetry therapist; lic. marriage, family, child counselor. Staff nurse Luth. Gen. Hosp., Park Ridge, Ill., 1962-63; staff nurse, insvc. edn. coord. Holy Family Hosp., Des Plaines, Ill., 1963-67; instr. St. Vincent's Coll. of Nursing, L.A., 1967-72; assoc. prof. L.A. Valley Coll., Van Nuys, Calif., 1972-76; nurse Brotman Med. Ctr., Culver City, Calif., 1976-77, St. John's Hosp., Santa Monica, Calif., 1977-78, VA Med. Ctr., L.A., 1982—; counselor Kedren Cmty. Mental Health Ctr., L.A., 1980-81. Mem. Nat. Assn. Poetry Therapy (bd. dirs. 1989-91). Office: WLA VA Med Ctr 11301 Wilshire Blvd Los Angeles CA 90073-1003

JOHNS, ROY (BUD JOHNS), publisher, author; b. Detroit, July 9, 1929; s. Roy and Isabel Johns; m. Judith Spector Clancy, 1971 (dec. 1990); m. Frances Moreland, 1992. BA in English and Econs., Albion (Mich.) Coll., 1951. Various editorial positions Mich. and Calif. daily newspapers, 1942-60; bur. chief Fairchild Pubs., 1960-69; dir. corp. communications Levi Strauss & Co., 1969-81, corp. v.p., 1979-81; pres. Synergistic Press, Inc., San Francisco, 1968—; bd. dirs. Apple-Wood Books, Bedford, Mass.; founder, ptnr. Apple Trees Press, Flint, Mich., 1954-55; cons. on comms., pub., and related areas. Author: The Ombibulous Mr. Mencken, 1968, What is This Madness?, 1985; co-editor, author: Bastard in the Ragged Suit, 1977; scriptwriter, exec. producer: What is This Madness?, 1976; exec. producer: The Best You Can Be, 1979 (CINE Golden Eagle award 1980); editor: Old Dogs Remembered, 1993; free-lance writer numerous mag. articles. Mem. Nat. Coun. of Mus. of Am. Indian, N.Y.C., 1980-90; dir. The San Francisco Contemporary Music Players, 1981—, Greenbelt Alliance, San Francisco, 1982—, pres., 1990-95; dir. Save San Francisco Bay Assn., 1996—. Home and Office: 3965 Sacramento St San Francisco CA 94118-1627

JOHNSON, ALAN BOND, federal judge; b. 1939. BA, Vanderbilt U., 1961; JD, U. Wyo., 1964. Pvt. practice law Cheyenne, Wyo., 1968-71; assoc. Hanes, Carmichael, Johnson, Gage & Speight P.C., Cheyenne, 1971-74; judge Wyo. Dist. Ct., 1974-85; judge U.S. Dist. Ct. Wyo., 1986—, chief judge; part-time fed. magistrate U.S. Dist. Ct. Wyo., 1971-74; substitute judge Mcpl. Ct., Cheyenne, 1973-74. Served to capt. USAF, 1964-67, to col. Wyo. Air N.G., 1973-90. Mem. ABA, Wyo. State Bar, Laramie County Bar Assn. (sec.-treas. 1968-70), Wyo. Jud. Conf. (sec. 1977-78, chmn. 1979), Wyo. Jud. Council. Office: O'Mahoney Fed Ctr Rm 2242 2120 Capitol Ave Ste 2242 Cheyenne WY 82001-3666*

JOHNSON, ALICE ELAINE, retired academic administrator; b. Janesville, Wis., Oct. 9, 1929; d. Floyd C. and Alma M. (Walthers) Chester; m. Richard C. Johnson, Sept. 25, 1948 (div. 1974); children: Randall S., Nile C., Linnea E. BA, U. Colo., 1968. Pres., administrator Pikes Peak Inst. Med. Tech., Colorado Springs, Colo., 1968-88; mem. adv. com. to Colo. Commn. on Higher Edn., 1979-80, State Adv. Coun. on Pvt. Occupational Schs., Denver, 1978-86; mem. tech. adv. com. State Health Occupations, 1986-88; bd. dirs. All Souls Unitarian Ch., Colorado Springs, 1990—, mem. celebration team, 1990-91, pres. bd. trustees, 1991-93. Mem. Colo. Pvt. Sch. Assn. (pres. 1981-82, bd. dirs. 1976-88, Outstanding Mem. 1978, 80), Phi Beta Kappa. Democrat. Unitarian. *We must review and renew our committment, as a nation, to true freedom of religion, and resist current tendencies to mix church and state.*

JOHNSON, ARTHUR WILLIAM, JR., planetarium executive; b. Steubenville, Ohio, Jan. 8, 1949; s. Arthur William and Carol (Gilcrest) J.; B.Mus., U. So. Calif., 1973. Lectr., Griffith Obs. and Planetarium, 1969-73; planetarium writer, lectr. Mt. San Antonio Coll. Planetarium, Walnut, Calif., 1970-73; dir. Fleischmann Planetarium, U. Nev., Reno, 1973—. Organist, choirmaster Trinity Episcopal Ch., Reno, 1980—; bd. dirs. Reno Chamber Orch. Assn., 1981-87 , 1st v.p., 1984-85. Nev. Humanities Com., Inc. grantee, 1979-83; apptd. Nev. state coord. N.S.T.A./NASA Space Sci. Student Involvement Program, 1994. Mem. Am. Guild Organists (dean No. Nev. chpt. 1984-85, 96-97), Internat. Planetarium Soc., Cinema 360 (treas. 1985-90, pres. 1990—), Pacific Planetarium Assn. (pres. 1980), Lions (pres. Reno Host Club 1991-92), Large Format Cinema Assn. (v.p. 1996—). Republican. Episcopalian. Writer, producer films: (with Donald G. Potter) Beautiful Nevada, 1978, Riches: The Story of Nevada Mining, 1984. Office: Fleischmann Plantarium U Nev 1650 N Virginia St Reno NV 89503-1738

JOHNSON, AUSTON G., auditor; m. Mary Johnson; 3 children. BS, Utah State U. CPA, Utah. Auditor State of Utah, Salt Lake City, 1976—; acctg. adv. bd. U. Utah Sch. Acctg., 1993; sch. accountancy adv. coun. Utah State U., 1994—. With USN, 1969-73. Mem. AICPA (Outstanding Discussion Leader 1993), Utah Assn. CPAs (vice-chmn. state and local govt. com. 1987-88). Office: Office Utah State Auditor 211 State Capitol Bldg Salt Lake City UT 84114

JOHNSON, BRIAN KEITH, electrical engineering educator; b. Madison, Wis., Mar. 11, 1965; s. Alton Cornelius and Virginia Rae (Kroener) J. BS, U. Wis., 1987, MS, 1989, PhD, 1992. Registered profl. engr., Wis., Idaho. Teaching asst. U. Wis., Madison, 1988, rsch. asst., 1988-92; engr. Lawrence Livermore Nat. Labs., Livermore, Calif., 1989; asst. prof. U. Idaho, Moscow, 1992-97, assoc. prof., 1997—; instr. Coll. Engring. Tchg. Asst. Tng., U. Wis., Madison, 1988, Engring. profl. devel., 1992; advisor Iron Cross Leadership Soc., Madison, 1988-92, U. Idaho IEEE Student Chpt.; dir. Western Virtual Engring. Lodge chief Order of the Arrow, Boy Scouts Am., 1982-84, dir. Brownsea Double 2Course, Madison, 1987, advisor, 1990-92. Recipient Vigil Hon. Membership, Order of the Arrow, Boy Scouts Am., 1988, Leadership award, Exploring Boy Scouts Am., 1986, Outstanding Young Faculty award U. Idaho Coll. Engring., 1985. Mem. IEEE, Nat. Soc. Profl. Engrs., Am. Soc. Engring. Edn., Wilderness Soc. Lutheran. Office: U Idaho Dept Elec Engring Moscow ID 83844

JOHNSON, BROOKS, publishing executive. Pres., publ. The Sun, San Bernardino, Calif. Office: The Sun 399 North D St San Bernardino CA 92666

JOHNSON, BYRON JERALD, state supreme court judge; b. Boise, Idaho, Aug. 2, 1937; s. Arlie Johnson and V. Bronell (Dunten) J.; children: Matthew, Ethan, Elaine, Laura; m. Paticia G. Young, 1984. AB, Harvard U., 1959, LLB, 1962. Bar: Idaho, 1962. Justice Idaho Supreme Ct., Boise, 1988—. Office: Supreme Ct Idaho PO Box 83720 Boise ID 83720-0002*

JOHNSON, CAROL LYNN, secondary school counselor; b. Wooster, Ohio, Dec. 17, 1951; d. John K. and Marge M. (Reese) Coffey; m. Robert B. Johnson, June 19, 1950; children: Katie Johnson, Russell Johnson. BS in Edn., U. Akron, 1973; MA in Edn., Colo. State U., 1982, PhD in Edn., 1995. Cert. tchr., Colo. Tchr. North Ctrl. Sch. Dist., Creston, Ohio, 1972-78; tchr./counselor Estes Park (Colo.) H.S. Park R-3 Sch. Dist., 1978—. Mem. AAUW, ASCD, Colo. Assn. Sch. Execs., Delta Kappa Gamma, Phi Delta Kappa. Home: 169 1/2 Stanley Circle Dr Estes Park CO 80517 Office: Estes Park HS 1600 Manford Ave Estes Park CO 80517

JOHNSON, CAROLYN EVERALL, poet, secondary school educator; b. San Diego, Dec. 17, 1949. BA in English cum laude, Calif. State U., San Diego, 1972; MA in Edn., Smith Coll., 1973, R.I. Sch. design, 1988. Cert. tchr. English, Calif. Adminstrv. asst. Royal Albert Hall, London, 1976-77; dir. edn. Hopkins Ctr. for Performing Arts/Hood Mus. Art Dartmouth Coll., Hanover, N.H., 1988-90; chmn. dept. English Marian H.S., San Diego, 1992-94; tchr. English lit. Santa Margarita H.S., Rancho Santa Margarita, Calif., 1995—. Contbr. poetry to various literary mags. (Grand prize winner N.Am. Open Poetry Competition); co-editor: Getty Center Museum Education Curriculum Handbook, 1995. Home: 7301 Alicante Rd Carlsbad CA 92009

JOHNSON, CHARLES BARTLETT, mutual fund executive; b. Montclair, N.J., Jan. 6, 1933; s. Rupert Harris and Florence (Endler) J.; m. Ann Demarest Lutes, Mar. 26, 1955; children: Charles E., Holly, Sarah, Gregory, William, Jennifer, Mary (dec.). BA, Yale U., 1954. With R.H. Johnson & Co., N.Y.C., 1954-55; pres. Franklin Distbrs., Inc., N.Y.C., 1957—; pres., ceo Franklin Resources, Inc., 1969-90; bd. dirs. Gen. Host Corp. and various Franklin and Templeton Mut. Funds; bd. govs. Investment Co. Inst., 1973-88. Trustee Crystal Springs Uplands Sch., 1984-92; bd. dirs. Peninsula Cmty. Found., 1986-96, San Francisco Symphony, 1984—, NASD, 1990-92, 96—, chmn., 1992; bd. overseers Hoover Instn., 1993—. Mem. Nat. Assn. Securities Dirs. (bd. govs. 1990-92, chmn. 1992), Burlingame Country Club, Pacific Union Club (San Francisco), Commonwealth Club of Calif. (bd. dirs.). Office: Franklin Resources 777 Mariners Island Blvd San Mateo CA 94404-1584*

JOHNSON, CHARLES WILLIAM, justice; b. Tacoma, Wash., Mar. 16, 1951. BA in Econs., U. Wash., 1973; JD, U. Puget Sound, 1976. Bar: Wash. 1977. Justice Wash. Supreme Ct., 1991—; mem. Wash. State Minority and Justice Commn. Bd. dirs. Wash. Assn. Children and Parents; mem. vis. com. U. Wash. Sch. Social Work; bd. visitors Seattle U. Sch. Law, mem. Washington State Courthouse Sec. Task Force. Mem. Wash. State Bar Assn., Tacoma-Pierce County Bar Assn. (Liberty Bell award young lawyers sect. 1994). Office: Wash State Supreme Ct Temple of Justice PO Box 40929 Olympia WA 98504-0929*

JOHNSON, CHRISTOPHER GARDNER, technology educator; b. Akron, Ohio, Aug. 18, 1954; s. Francis McWhorter and Ann (Gardner) J.; m. Ingrid Novodvorsky, Dec. 1, 1990. BA in Secondary Edn., U. Ariz., 1976, MEd in Edn. Media, 1978, PhD in Secondary Edn., 1987. Cert. tchr. cmty. coll. Programmer Coll. of Nursing U. Ariz., Tucson, 1977-78, project coord. physics dept., 1978-85, assoc. site dir. lab. for computer based instrn., 1980-85, dir. humanities computing and tech., 1985—; assoc. faculty Pima Cmty. Coll., Tucson, 1978; cons. Control Data Corp., Mpls., 1983, 86, Apple Computer Inc., Cuppertino, Calif., 1991-94; adj. lectr. humanities U. Ariz., Tucson, 1987—, adj. asst. prof. ednl. psychology, 1995—, adj. asst. prof. ednl. leadership, 1996—, process improvement facilitator/quality focal point, 1995—, CORE ptnr. Office of Continuous Orgnl. Renewal, 1995—. Project coord.: (computer software) Lower Division Engineering Curriculum, 1984, 86; contbr. articles to profl. jours. Track and field, basketball, team handball and floor hockey coach Ariz. Spl. Olympics, Tucson, 1989-92, basketball, team handball and floor hockey ofcl., 1991—, sec. bd. dirs., Phoenix, 1992-93 (Chmn's award 1993). Recipient Group award Carnation Cmty. Svcs., Tucson, 1991. Mem. ASCD, Ariz. Ednl. Media Assn. (S.E. regional dir. 1994-96, pres.-elect 1996, 1992 Spl. Svc. award 1992), Tucson Area Coun. for Tech. (chair 1994—). Office: Univ Ariz Humanities Computing & Tech Modern Lang 345 Tucson AZ 85721-0067

JOHNSON, CIRI DIANE, graphic design firm owner; b. Ann Arbor, Mich., Aug. 19, 1956; d. Paul Christian and Genevieve Ruth J. Student, U. Ariz., 1974-76, U. Oreg., 1976-78; BFA, San Francisco Art Inst., 1980; MA, NYU, 1982. Artist asst. Lucio Pozzi, N.Y.C., 1983-85; editor, art dir. New Observations Mag., N.Y.C., 1985-91; owner Ciri Johnson Design, Bklyn, 1988-91, Tucson, 1991—; asst. tchr. Parson's Sch. Design, N.Y.C., 1985-86; instr. NYU, 1982. Prin. works published in The National Poetry Magazine of Lower East Side, 1988-90; designed promotional piece for Elisa Monte Dance Co. chosen for reproduction in 1991 Artist's Market. Mem. Resources for Women, Tucson Ad Club (Bronze Addy award for mag. advt. campaign, Merit cert. 1992, 94, 95, Gold Addy award for art exhbn. catalog, Bronze Addy for self-promotion 1993, Bronze Addy award for poster and Bronze Addy award for pub. svc. brochure 1995). Democrat. Office: PO Box 18608 Tucson AZ 85731

JOHNSON, CURTIS LEE, real estate executive and broker; b. Medford, Oreg., Oct. 20, 1956; s. Edward Lee and Anne Virginia (Christensen) J.; m. Bonita Sue Maddox, May 22, 1982 (June 1987); m. Karen Jean MacLauchlan, Apr. 29, 1989; children: Jamie Lyn, Justin Robert. BS, Oreg. State U., 1978. Cert. realtor. Chief lobbyist Assoc. Students of Oreg. State U., Salem, 1977-78, Mont. Student Lobby, Helena, 1979-80; real estate owner, mgr. Jackson County Fed. Savs. and Loan Assn., Medford, Oreg., 1980-87; real estate mgr. Eugene F. Burrill Lumber Co., Medford, Oreg., 1987—; v.p., broker Burrill Real Estate Co., Medford, Oreg., 1988—; mem. adv. bd. Bear Creek Valley Sanitary, Medford, 1990—, Jackson County Urban Renewal, White City, 1992—; mem. 2050 Medford Water Commn., 1992—. Bd. dirs. United Way of Jackson County, Medford, 1985; bd. dirs., pres. Kiwanis Club and Found., Medford, 1988-86; bd. dirs., treas. Rogue Coun. Campfire, Medford, 1986. Mem. Medford/Jackson County C. of C. (bd. dirs.), Rogue Valley Country Club, Moose. Home: 1528 Ridge Way Medford OR 97504-6681 Office: Burrill Real Estate Co 1322 E Mcandrews Rd Ste 201 Medford OR 97504-6177

JOHNSON, DANIEL LEON, aeronautical engineer; b. Manistee, Mich., Jan. 24, 1936; s. Malcolm Storer and Viola Johanna (Hinkle) J.; m. Dorothy Gwynn Chandler, Sept. 22, 1963; children: Romer D., Olin M., Daniela D., Wenona B., Conrad C., Garrett H. BS, U.S. Mil. Acad., West Point, N.Y., 1958; MS in Aero. Engring., U. Mich., 1960, MS in Instrumentation Engring., 1960; PhD in Aero. Engring., U. Colo., 1971. Comd. 2d lt. USAF, 1958, advanced through grades to col., 1978; engr. Material Command, Beale AFB, Calif., 1960-62; engr., chief missle test Logistics Command, Hill AFB, Utah, 1963-67, engr., liason Logistics Command, Vietnam, 1967-68; engr. Aerospace Med. Rsch. Lab., Wright-Patterson AFB, Ohio, 1971-78, chief tech. svcs. divsn., 1978-84; chief scientist Larson-Davis Labs., Provo, Utah, 1984-89; dir. biophysics ops. EG&G MSI, Kirtland AFB, N.Mex., 1989—; mem. phys. agts. TLV com. Am. Conf. Govtl. Indsl. Hygienists, 1992—; mem. com. on hearing, bioacoustics and biomechanics steering com. NRC, 1990-93. Contbr. over 80 articles to profl. jours., chpts. to books. Decorated Bronze Star, Legion of Merit; recipient Harry G. Armstrong award Aerospace Med. Rsch. Lab., 1977. Fellow Acoustical Soc. Am. (chmn. noise com. 1992-94, vice chmn. com. on stds. 1993-97, dir. 1997—, chmn. ANSI S1 and S12 coms. 1984-96), mem. Soc. Automotive Engrs., Nat. Hearing Conservation Assn., Inst. Noise Control Engring. Home: 3020 Camino de la Sierra Albuquerque NM 87111 Office: EG&G MSI PO Box 9100 2450 Alamo Albuquerque NM 87119

JOHNSON, DAVID ELLSWORTH, pediatrician, medical educator; b. Mpls., June 26, 1943; s. Orville Martin and E. Marian (Wallin) J.; m. Kathleen Lou Kuhn, Aug. 5, 1967 (div. June 1983); children: Jenna Ann, Elizabeth Kathleen Marie; m. Jennifer Lynn Green, June 18, 1984; children: Lindsay Mary Anne Christine, Rachel Lynn Marie. BA, Bethel Coll., St. Paul, 1965; MD, U. Minn., 1969. Diplomate Am. Bd. Pediat. Intern in medicine, pediat. U. Rochester, N.Y., 1969-70; gen. med. officer USPHS-IHS, Ketchikan, Alaska, 1970-72; resident in pediat. U. Wash., Seattle, 1972-74; physician Ketchikan Med. Clinic, 1974—; clin. instr. family practice U. Wash. Med. Sch., Seattle, 1978-86, clin. asst. prof. family practice, 1986—. Lt. comdr. USPHS, 1972-74. Fellow Am. Acad. Pediat.; mem. AMA, Alaska State Med. Assn. (pres. 1980-81, alt. del. to AMA 1984—, Physician of Yr. 1985), North Pacific Pediat. Soc. Methodist. Home: PO Box 6852 Ketchikan AK 99901 Office: Ketchikan Med Clinic 3612 Tongass Ave Ketchikan AK 99901

JOHNSON, DAVID GEORGE, Chinese history educator; b. Webster, S.D., July 15, 1938; s. George Andrew and Elizabeth Caroline (Herrlinger) J.; m. In Ja Rhee, June 6, 1976; 1 child, Caroline. AB, Harvard U., 1960; PhD, U. Calif., Berkeley, 1970. Asst. prof. dept. East Asian langs. and cultures Columbia U., N.Y.C., 1970-79; assoc. prof. dept. history U. Calif., Berkeley, 1983-87, prof., 1987—; dir. Chinese Popular Culture Project, Berkeley, 1987—; mem. Am. Coun. Learned Socs.-Social Sci. Rsch. Coun. Joint Com. on Chinese Studies, N.Y.C., 1984-89. Author: Medieval Chinese Oligarchy, 1977, (with others) Domesticated Deities and Auspicious Emblems, 1992; editor, contbr.: Ritual Opera, Operatic Ritual, 1989, Ritual and Scripture in Chinese Popular Religion, 1995; co-editor, contbr. Popular Culture in Late Imperial China, 1987; mem. edit. bd. Studies in Chinese Ritual, Theatre and Folklore. Grantee ACLS, 1978, 81, 93, NEH, 1987-91, Rockefeller Found., 1987-91, Com. on Scholarly Comm. with the Peoples Republic of China, 1984. Mem. Assn. for Asian Studies (China and Inner Asia Coun. 1988-91). Office: U Calif Dept History Dwinelle Hall Berkeley CA 94720

JOHNSON, DAVID MITCHELL, architect, artist; b. Moorhead, Minn., Aug. 22, 1960; s. A.T. and Irene (Rost) J.; m. Karen J. Koenig, June 1, 1985. B Arch. with hons., U. Ariz., Tucson, 1987. Registered profl. architect, Calif. Designer Kaplan, McLaughlin, Diaz, Architects, San Francisco, 1987-88; architect, assoc. Cesar Pelli & Assocs., New Haven, Conn., 1988-95, Hellmuth, Obata & Kassabaum, Inc., San Francisco, 1995—. Mem. AIA. Office: Hellmuth Obata & Kassabaum Inc 71 Stevenson St San Francisco CA 94105-2934

JOHNSON, DAVID SELLIE, civil engineer; b. Mpls., Apr. 10, 1935; s. Milton Edward and Helen M. (Sellie) J. BS, Mont. Coll. Mineral Sci. Tech., 1958. Registered profl. engr., Mont. Trainee Mont. Dept. Hwys., Helena, 1958-59, designer, 1959-66, asst. preconstrn. engr., 1966-68, regional engr., 1968-72, engring. specialities supr., 1972-89, preconstrn. chief, 1989-93, forensic engr., 1965—, traffic accident reconstructionist, 1978—; consulting engr., 1985—. Contbr. articles on hwy. safety to profl. jours. Adv. bd. mem. Helena Vocat.-Tech. Edn., 1972-73. Fellow Inst. Transp. Engrs. (expert witness coun.); mem. NSPE, Nat. Acad. Forensic Engrs. (diplomate), Mont. Soc. Profl. Engrs., Transp. Rsch. Bd. (geometric design com., tort liability com.), Wash. Assn. Tech. Accident Investigators, Corvette Club, Treasure State Club (pres. Helena 1972-78, sec. 1979-82), Shriners. Home and Office: 1921 E 6th Ave Helena MT 59601-4766

JOHNSON, DORIS ANN, educational administrator; b. Marinette, Wis., Dec. 4, 1950; d. Jerome Louis and Jean Fern (Henry) La Plant; m. Daniel Lee Leonard, June 10, 1972 (div. June 1987); children: Jeremiah Daniel, Erica Leigh, Wesley Cyril; m. Paul Robert Johnson, Oct. 21, 1989; stepchildren: Kindra Michelle, Tanya Mari. Student, U. Wis., Oshkosh, 1969-70; BA in Edn., U. Wis., Eau Claire, 1973; MS in Edn., U. Wis., Whitewater, 1975; postgrad., Oreg. State U., 1988—. Reading specialist Brookfield (Wis.) Cen. High Sch., 1975-79; lead instr. N.E. Wis. Tech. Coll., Marinette, 1979-87; dir. adult basic edn. Umpqua C.C., Roseburg, Oreg., 1987-95, dir. developmental edn., 1995—; founding bd. dirs. Project Literacy, Umpqua Region, Roseburg, 1989—; mem. adv. bd. Umpqua Cmty. Action Network, Roseburg, 1987-94; mem. State Dirs. of Adult Edn., Oreg., 1987—, vice chair, 1992-93, chair, 1993-94; mem. Adminstrn. Assn., Roseburg, 1989—, chair, 1993-94, 94-95; bd. dirs. Greater Douglas United Way, 1994—; adv. bd. Oreg. Litaracy Line, 1994-96. Co-author literacy module Communication Skills, 1988; author ednl. curriculum. Founding mem., bd. dirs. St. Joseph Maternity Home, Roseburg, 1987-90; mem. Literacy Theater, Roseburg, 1988-95; bd. dirs. Greater Douglas United Way, 1994—; mem. Project Leadership, Roseburg, 1988-89; mem. adv. bd. Oreg. Literacy Line, 1994-96; mem. Roseburg Valley Rep. Women, 1994—. State legalizatoin assistance grantee Fed. Govt., 1988-93, homeless literacy grantee Fed. Govt., 1990-91, family literacy grantee Fed. Govt., 1991-93, intergenerational literacy grantee State of Oreg., 1991, literacy expansion grantee Fed. Govt., 1992-95, literacy outreach grantee Fed. Govt., 1992—, staff devel. spl. projects grantee Fed. Govt., 1992-93. Fellow TESOL, Inst. Inst. Leadership Devel., Am. Assn. Adult and Continuing Edn., Oreg. Assn. Disabled Students, Oreg. Developmental Edn. Studies, Oreg. Assn. for Children with Learning Disabilities, Western Coll. Reading and Learning Assn., Am. Assn. Women in Coll. and Jr. Coll., Roseburg Valley Rep. Women, Altrusa Internat. Club of Roseburg (chair literacy com. 1993-97), Rep. Women. Republican. Lutheran. Home: 761 Garden Grove Roseburg OR 97470-9511 Office: Umpqua CC PO Box 967 Roseburg OR 97470

JOHNSON, DOUGLAS WALTER, artist; b. Portland, Oreg., July 8, 1946; s. Herbert Walter Johnson and Barbara Elizabeth (Speer) Hall. Student, San Jose (Calif.) State Coll. Artist Jamison Gallery, Santa Fe, 1971-77, Horwich Gallery, Santa Fe, 1977-86, Gerald Peters Corp., Santa Fe, 1986-96, Nedra Matteucci's Fenn Gallery, Santa Fe, 1996—, Parks Gallery, Taos, N.Mex., 1996—. Executed mural El Dorado Hotel, 1986; exhibited in numerous group shows.

JOHNSON, DUANE P., academic administrator; b. Wadena, Minn., Mar. 19, 1937; s. Julian C. and Lillian M. (petri) J.; m. Mary E., Oct. 22, 1960; children: Michael D., Gregory P. BS, Iowa State U., 1959; MEd, Colo. State U., 1970. County extension agt. 4-H Oreg. State U., Gresham, 1959-70; ext. specialist 4-H and youth devel. Oreg. State U., Corvallis, 1970-80, state leader 4-H, 1980-94, prof. adult edn., ext. specialist program devel., 1994—. Contbr. numerous articles to profl. jours. Mem. Nat. Assn. Ext. 4-H Agts., Assn. Vol. Adminstrn., ASCD, Oreg. State U. Ext. Assn. Office: Oreg State U Ballard Extension Hall Rm 105 Corvallis OR 97331-3608

JOHNSON, E. ERIC, insurance executive; b. Chgo., Feb. 7, 1927; s. Edwin Eric and Xenia Alice (Waisanen) J.; m. Elizabeth Dewar Brass, Sept. 3, 1949; children: Christal L. Johnson Neal, Craig R. BA, Stanford U., 1948. Dir. group annuities Equitable Life Assurance Soc., San Francisco, 1950-54; div. mgr. Equitable Life Assurance Soc., L.A., 1955-59; v.p. Johnson & Higgins of Calif., L.A., 1960-67, dir., 1968-87, chmn., 1986-87; chmn. TBG Fin., L.A., 1988—; bd. dirs. Am. Mutual Fund; exec. v.p. Johnson & Higgins, N.Y.C., 1984-87. Bd. dirs. Sta. KCET, pub. TV, L.A., 1977-95, chmn., 1992-94; mem. adv. bd. UCLA Med. Ctr., 1983—, chmn. 1995—; bd. dirs. Jonsson Comprehensive Cancer Ctr., UCLA, 1985—, Stanford U. Grad Sch. Bus., 1986-91; trustee Nuclear Decommissioning Trust, Rosemead, Calif., 1986-94. Mem. Calif. Club, L.A. Country Club, Vintage Club, Riviera Tennis Club, Links Club N.Y.C., Beach Club, So. Calif. Tennis Assn. (treas.). Office: TBG Fin 2029 Century Park E Los Angeles CA 90067-2901

JOHNSON, EARVIN (MAGIC JOHNSON), professional sports team executive, former professional basketball coach; b. Lansing, Mich., Aug. 14, 1959; s. Earvin and Christine Johnson; m. Cookie Kelly; 1 son, Earvin. Student, Mich. State U., 1976-79. Basketball player L.A. Lakers, 1979-91, 95-96; sportscaster NBC-TV, 1993-94; head coach L.A. Lakers, 1994, v.p., co-owner, 1994—; gold medalist, U.S. Olympic Basketball Team, 1992. Author: (autobiography) Magic, 1983; (autobiography, with Roy S. Johnson) Magic's Touch, 1989; What You Can Do to Avoid AIDS, 1992; My Life, 1992. Recipient Citizenship award, 1992, All-Around Contbns. to Team Success award IDM, 1984; mem. NCAA Championship Team, 1979, NBA All-Star Team, 1980, 82-92, MVP NBA All-Star Game, 1990, 92, NBA Championship Team, 1980, 82, 85, 87, 88; named MVP NBA Playoffs, 1980, 82, 87, NBA, 1987, 89, 90, All-Star Game, 1990, 92, Player of the Year, Sporting News, 1987; recipient Schick Pivotal Player award, 1984; named to All-NBA first team, 1983-91, second team, 1982, NBA All-Rookie Team, 1980. Office: Great Western Forum PO Box 32 Inglewood CA 90312-0032*

JOHNSON, ELIZABETH HILL, foundation administrator; b. Ft. Wayne, Ind., Aug. 21, 1913; d. Harry W. and Lydia (Buechner) Hill; m. Samuel Spencer Johnson, Oct. 7, 1944 (dec. 1984); children: Elizabeth Katharine, Patricia Caroline. BS summa cum laude, Miami U., Oxford, Ohio, 1935; MA in English Lit., Wellesley Coll., 1937; postgrad., U. Chgo., 1936. Cert. tchr., Ohio. Pres., co-founder S.S. Johnson Found., Calif. Corp., San Francisco, 1947—. Mem. Oreg. State Bd. Higher Edn., Eugene, 1962-75, Oreg. State Edn. Coord. Com., Salem, 1975-82, Assn. Governing Bds., Washington, 1970-80, chairperson, 1975-76; mem. Oreg. State Tchr. Standards and Practices Commn., Salem, 1982-89; bd. dirs. Lewis and Clark Coll., Portland, Oreg., 1985—, Pacific U., Forest Grove, Oreg., 1982—, Sunriver Prep. Sch., 1983-92, Oreg. Hist. Soc., Portland, 1985—, Cen. Oreg. Dist. Hosp., Redmond, 1982—, Oreg. High Desert Mus., 1984—, Bend, Oreg., Health Decisions, 1986-92, Ctrl. Oreg. Coun. Aging, 1991—; Deschutes County Hist. Soc., 1996—. Lt. USNR, 1943-46. Named Honoree March of Dimes White Rose Luncheon, 1984; recipient Aubrey Watzek award Lewis and Clark Coll., 1984, Cen. Oreg. 1st Citizen award, Abrams award Emanuel Hosp., 1982, Pres. award Marylhurst Coll., 1991, Thomas Jefferson award Oregon Historical Soc., 1993, Pres.'s award Remond C. of C., 1996. Mem. Am. Assn. Higher Edn., Am. Assn. Jr. Colls., ASCD, Soroptimists (hon.), Francisca Club, Town Club, Univ. Club, Waverley Club, Beta Sigma Phi, Phi Beta Kappa, Phi Delta Kappa, Delta Gamma. Republican. Lutheran. Home: 415 SW Canyon Dr Redmond OR 97756-2028 Office: S S Johnson Found 441 SW Canyon Dr Redmond OR 97756-2028

JOHNSON, ELLWOOD GERD, English language educator; b. McCall, Idaho, Nov. 4, 1924; s. Orlando Bennett and Hilkea (Jenssen) J.; m. Diane Louise Ostrom, Aug. 25, 1983; children: Wendy, Helen, Karen, Michael. PhD in English, U. Wash., 1969. Prof. Am. lit. Western Wash. U., Bellingham, 1963—. Contbr. articles to profl. jours. Mem. Modern Lang. Assn. Office: Western Wash U Dept English Bellingham WA 98226

JOHNSON, F. MICHAEL, electrical and automation systems professional; b. Sacramento, Jan. 14, 1953; s. Carroll Loren and Constance (Latterell) J.; m. Donna Louise Hamilton, June 28, 1975; children: Bryan J., Cassandra

L. BSChemE, U. Calif., Davis, 1975. Registered profl. control systems engr., Calif. Field engr., instrumentation Universal Oil Products, 1975-80; project engr. and leader Atkinson System Techs. Co., 1980-85; control systems project leader, system mgr. spl. project Stearns-Roger, Denver, 1985-87; digital sys. engr., mgr. spl. software applications CH2M HILL, Denver, 1987-91; dept. mgr., sr. project leader software & instrumentation CH2M HILL, Milw., 1991-94; sr. cons. project mgr. for automation and info. sys. CH2M HILL, Calif., 1994—. Recipient Top Cat award Atkinson Systems Tech. Co., 1985. Mem. Am. Chem. Soc., Instrument Soc. Am., Toastmasters. Office: CH2M HILL 1994 Ste 200 3 Hutton Center Dr Santa Ana CA 92707

JOHNSON, FRANK, retired state official, educator; b. Ogden, Utah, Mar. 12, 1928; s. Clarence Budd and Arline (Parry) J.; m. Maralyn Brewer, Aug. 15, 1950; children: Scott, Arline, Laurie, Kelly, Edward. BS, U. Utah, 1955; MS, U. Ill., 1958, PhD, 1960. Instr. U. N.D., Grand Forks, 1955-56; teaching asst. U. Ill., Urbana, 1956-59; rsch. asst. prof. U. Del., Newark, 1959-60; prof. U. Utah, Salt Lake City, 1960-93, assoc. dean, 1970-77, dir. divsn. pub. utilities State of Utah, Salt Lake City, 1989-95; cons. Gen. Foods, Sears, Magnavox, Albertsons, Zion Bank, Nat. Food Brokers Assn., others; owner, part-owner Old Post Office Bldg., Ogden, Utah, Seventeenth St. Storage. Legis. Utah House of Reps., Salt Lake City, 1982-88. Republican. Home: 2373 E Dayspring Ln Salt Lake City UT 84124

JOHNSON, FRANK EDWARD, former newspaper editor; b. Pekin, Ill., July 1, 1920; s. Frank Ellis and Margaret (Pitner) J.; m. Louise Marguerite Beall, Sept. 16, 1945; children—Frank Edgar, Christia Louise Gibbons, John Jeffrey (dec.). U. Ariz., Tucson, 1946-47. Reporter Galion Inquirer, Galion, Ohio, 1945; reporter News-Journal, Mansfield, OH, 1945; reporter Ariz. Daily Star, Tucson, 1946-47, city editor, 1948-61, asst. mng. editor, 1961-67, mng. editor, 1967-82, exec. editor, 1983-85; contbg. editor Ariz. Daily Star, 1986-87, ret., 1987. Bd. dirs. Fan Kane Fund for Brain-Damaged Children, Tucson, 1950-91, Ariz. Daily Star Sportsman's Fund, Tucson, 1966—. Served as 1st sgt. U.S. Army, 1940-45. Named Tucson's Newsman of Yr., Tucson Press Club, 1966; recipient Disting. Service to Journalism award, Ariz. Press Club, 1981. Mem. Am. Soc. Newspaper Editors, AP Mng. Editors Assn. (bd. dirs. 1981-83, regent 1985—), Ariz. Newspapers Assn. (pres. 1976-77, Master Editor-Pub. award 1982,, Hall of Fame 1996), Soc. Profl. Journalists (Freedom of Info. award Valley of Sun chpt. 1986), Tucson Press Club (pres. 1969).

JOHNSON, GARY EARL, governor; b. Minot, N.D., Jan. 1, 1953; s. Earl W. and Lorraine B. (Bostow) J.; m. Dee Simms, Nov. 27, 1976; children: Seah, Erik. BA in Polit. Sch., U. N.Mex., 1975. Pres., CEO Big J Enterprises, Albuquerque, 1976—; gov. State of N.Mex., 1995—. Bd. dirs. Entrepreneurship Studies at U. N.Mex., 1993-95. Named to list of Big 50 Remodelers in the USA, 1987; named Entrepreneur of Yr., 1995. Mem. LWV, C. of C. Albuquerque (bd. dirs. 1993-95). Republican. Lutheran. Office: Office of Gov State Capitol Santa Fe NM 87503

JOHNSON, GARY KENT, management education company executive; b. Provo, Utah, Apr. 16, 1936; s. Clyde LeRoy and Ruth Laie (Taylor) J.; m. Mary Joyce Crowther, Aug. 26, 1955; children: Mary Ann Johnson Harvey, Gary Kent, Brent James, Jeremy Clyde. Student Brigham Young U., 1954-55, U. Utah, 1955-58, 60-61, U. Calif.-Berkeley, 1962. Sales rep. Roche Labs., Salt Lake City, 1958-61, sales trainer, Denver, 1962, sales trainer, Oakland, Calif., 1962, div. mgr., Seattle, 1962-69; sec.-treas. Western Mgmt. Inst., Seattle, 1969-71; pres. WMI Corp., Bellevue, Wash., 1971-96, pres. GKJ Corp., 1996—, Provisor Corp., 1983-86; speaker, cons. various nat. orgns. Bd. dirs. Big Bros.; del. King County Republican Com. Served with U.S. N.G., 1953-61. Walgreen scholar, 1955-58; Bristol scholar, 1958. Mem. Am. Soc. Tng. and Devel., Internat. Platform Assn., Bellevue Athletic Club. Phi Sigma Epsilon. Mem. LDS Ch. Author: Select the Best, 1976; Antitrust Untangled, 1977; The Utilities Management Series, 1979; Performance Appraisal, A Program for Improving Productivity, 1981, QSE Quality Service Everytime, 1990, Continuous Performance Improvement, 1993. Office: GKJ Corp 1416 W Lake Sammamish Pkwy SE Bellevue WA 98008-5218

JOHNSON, GORDON JAMES, artistic director, conductor; b. St. Paul, 1949. BS, Bemidji State U., 1971; MS, Northwestern U., 1977; D in Mus. Arts, U. Oreg.; studied with Leonard Bernstein, Erich Leinsdorf, Herbert Blomstedt. Music dir., condr. Great Falls (Mont.) Symphony Assn., 1981—, Glacier Orch. and Chorale, Mont., 1982-97; artistic dir., condr. Flathead Music Festival, Mont., 1987-96; music dir., condr. Mesa (Ariz.) Symphony Orch., 1997—; grad. teaching fellow U. Oreg., 1979-81; artist in residence Condr's Guild Inst., W.Va. U., condr. orch., 1984; condr. Spokane Symphony at The Festival at Sandpoint; guest condr. St. Paul Chamber Orch., 1971, Spokane Symphony, 1983, 86, Dubuque (Iowa) Symphony, 1985, Charlotte (N.C.) Symphony, 1985, Lethbridge (Alberta, Can.) Symphony, 1986, Cheyenne (Wyo.) Symphony, 1986, West Shore (Mich.) Symphony, 1988, Bozeman (Mont.) Symphony, 1989, Kumamoto Symphony (Kyshu, Japan), 1991, Kankakee (Ill.) Symphony, 1993, Toulon (France) Symphonies, 1994, Guam Symphony, 1995, Tokyo Lumiere Orch., 1995, Fort Collins (Colo.) Symphony, 1995, Wilmslow (Eng.) Symphony Orch., 1997; guest ballet condr. Alberta Ballet, 1986, Oakland (Calif.) Ballet, 1988, Eugene (Oreg.) Ballet, 1993, David Taylor Ballet, Colo., 1994, St. Petersburg (Russia) Ballet, 1995, Western Ballet Theater, Oreg., 1996; spkr. regional conf. Am. Symphony Orch. League, 1987, nat. conf., 1988; mem. adj. faculty U. Great Falls, 1981—, U. Mont., 1996—; lectr. U. Guam, 1995; condr. seminars L.A. Philharmonic Inst., 1983, Condr.'s Guild Inst., 1984, Festival at Sandpoint, Condr.'s Program, 1986, Am. Symphony Orch. League's Am. Condr.'s Program, N.Y. Philharmonic, 1987, Condr.'s Guild "Bruckner Seminar", Chgo. Symphony Orch., 1989, Carnegie Hall Tng. Program for Condrs., Cleve. Orch., 1993. Philharmonic Condr.'s scholar St. Paul Chamber Orch., 1971; L.A. Philharmonic Inst. fellow, 1983; named to Highland Park High Sch. Hall of Fame, St. Paul, 1997. Mem. ASCAP. Office: Great Falls Symphony Assn PO Box 1078 Great Falls MT 59403

JOHNSON, GWENAVERE ANELISA, artist; b. Newark, S.D., Oct. 16, 1909; d. Arthur E. and Susie Ellen (King) Nelson; m. John Wendell Johnson, Dec. 17, 1937; 1 child, John Forrest. Student, Mpsl. Sch. Art, 1930; BA, U. Minn., 1937; MA, San Jose State U., 1957. Cert. gen. elem., secondary, art tchr., Calif. Art tchr., supr. Austin (Minn.) Schs., 1937-38; art tchr. Hillbrook Sch., Los Gatos, Calif., 1947-52; art tchr., supr. Santa Clara (Calif.) Pub. Schs., 1952-55; art tchr., dept. chmn. San Jose (Calif.) Unified Schs., 1955-75; owner Tree Tops studio, San Jose, 1975—. Juried shows: Los Gatos Art Assn., 1976-79, 85-88, Artist of Yr., 1988 (1st and 2d awards), 83, 84 (Best of Show awards), Treeside gallery, 1991, Los Gatos, 1980, 81 (1st awards); Livermore Art Assn., 1977 (2d award), Los Gatos Art Mus., 1981 (1st award), 82 (2d award), 91 (best of show award), Rosicrucean Mus., 1983, Centre d'Art Contemporian, Paris, 1983; creator Overfelt portrait Alexian Bros. Hosp., San Jose, Calif., 1977; exhibited in group shows ann. Garden Art Show, 1981-95, Triton Art Mus., 1983-95. Named People's Choice, Triton Art Mus., 1975; recipient Golden Centaur award Acad. Italia, 1982, Golden Album of prize winning Artists, 1984, Golden Flame award Academia Italia, 1986, others. Mem. San Jose Art League, Santa Clara Art Assn., Los Gatos Art Assn. (Artist of Yr. 1988, 2d, 3d awards), Santa Clara Art Assn. (Artist of Yr. 1983, 3 First awards 1989, 2d award in spl. merit achiever's exhbn. 1992, 3 First awards in merit achiever's exhbn. 1993), Soc. Western Artists, Nat. League Am. Penwomen (corr. sec., Merit Achiever award), Los gatos Art Assn., Santa Clara Art Assn., San Jose Art League. Home and Office: 2054 Booksin Ave San Jose CA 95125-4909

JOHNSON, HEIDI SMITH, science educator; b. Mpls., June 1, 1946; d. Russell Ward and Eva Ninette (Holmquist) Smith; m. Alan C. Sweeney, Dec. 21, 1968 (div. 1977); m. Robert Allen Johnson, July 17, 1981. BA, U. Calif., Riverside, 1969; MA, No. Ariz. U., 1992. Park ranger U.S. Nat. Parks Svc., Pinnacles Nat. Monument, 1972-73; aide Petrified Forest Mus. Assn., Ariz., 1973-75; dispatcher police dept. U. Ariz., Tucson, 1975-76; communications operator II dept. ops. City of Tucson, 1976-78; dispatcher Tucson Police Dept., 1978-82, communications supr., 1982-85, communications coord., 1985; substitute tchr. Bisbee (Ariz.) Pub. Schs., 1985-91; instr. English Cochise Community Coll., Douglas, Ariz., 1990-92; tchr. English/creative writing Bisbee H.S., 1992-93; tchr. phys. sci. and geology Lowell Mid. Sch., Bisbee, 1993—; GEd tchr. Cochise County Jail, 1988-89; owner Johnson's Antiques and Books, Bisbee, 1990—. Trustee Bisbee Coun. on Arts and Humanities, 1986-88; pres. Cooper Queen Libr. Bd., Bisbee, 1988-91; book sales chmn. Shattuck Libr., Bisbee Mining Mus., 1987-92; founder Riverside (Calif.) chpt. Zero Population Growth, 1968. Mem. Mid-Am. Paleontol. Soc., Paleontol. Soc., So. Calif. Paleontol. Soc., Sierra Club (mem. nat. wilderness study com. 1969-72, wilderness survey leader 1969-72), Paleontol. Soc., Nat. Ctr. Sci. Edn. Roman Catholic. Home: PO Box 1221 Bisbee AZ 85603-2221

JOHNSON, HOLLY ROUILLARD, public relations executive; b. Norwood, Mass., Dec. 19, 1960; d. Lawrence Hadley Rouillard and Carol Hyde (Sreenan) Rouillard-Wolff; m. Perry Brian Johnson, Nov. 28, 1960. BS, U. Denver, 1983. Asst. dir. pub. rels. Colo. Ski Country USA, Denver, 1983-87; news bur. mgr. Colo. Tourism Bd., Denver, 1987-90; group mgr. travel, tourism, consumer mktg. JohnstonWells Group, Denver, 1990-94; pres. Johnson Comms., 1994—; mem. tourism adv. coun. Denver Conv. and Visitors Bur., 1993—; mem. mktg. adv. coun. Downtown Denver Partnership, 1991—. Mem. N.Am. Ski Journalists Assn., Colo. Hotel and Lodging Assn. Democrat. Episcopalian. Home: 4098 Surrey Ct Lafayette CO 80026 Office: Johnson Comms 730 Burbank St Broomfield CO 80020-1658

JOHNSON, J. V., financial analyst; b. Denver, Aug. 19, 1966; m. Kristina Mae Johnson. BS in Fin., Ariz. State U., 1988; MS in Fin., U. Colo., 1993. Chartered fin. analyst. CFO Pentastic Sys., Denver, 1995—. Mem. Assn. Investment Mgmt. and Rsch., Denver Soc. Security Analysts (chair edn. com. 1995—). Home: 3040 Jay St Denver CO 80214

JOHNSON, JAMES DANIEL, theoretical physicist; b. Toledo, Mar. 21, 1944; s. James Elmer and Gwendolin (Dale) J.; m. Suzanne Darling, June 11, 1966; 1 child, Ian Christopher. B.S., Case Inst. Tech., 1966; M.A., SUNY-Stony Brook, 1968, Ph.D., 1972. Research assoc. Rockefeller U., N.Y.C., 1972-74; research assoc. Los Alamos Nat. Lab., Los Alamos, N.Mex., 1974-76, staff mem., 1976-89, acting head Sesame Library, 1982-85, project mgr. carbon project, 1984-89, dep. group leader, 1989—; head Sesame Libr., 1989—. Contbr. articles to profl. jours. Adult advisor Gt. S.W. Area council Boy Scouts Am., 1980-83; adult advisor sr. high youth group United Ch. of Los Alamos, 1982-85; active Los Alamos Light Opera Orgn., Los Alamos Little Theater; mem. U.S. Del. to Nuclear Testing Talks, 1988-89. Recipient Disting. Performance award Los Alamos Nat. Lab, 1988; NSF fellow 1966-71; Air Force grantee, 1980-82. Mem. Am. Phys. Soc., AAAS. Democrat. Club: Los Alamos Ski. Home: 321 Manhattan Loop Los Alamos NM 87544-2918 Office: Los Alamos Nat Lab T-1 MS B221 Los Alamos NM 87545

JOHNSON, JAMES DAVID, concert pianist, organist, educator; b. Greenville, S.C., Aug. 7, 1948; s. Theron David and Lucile (Pearson) J.; m. Karen Elizabeth Jacobson, Feb. 1, 1975. MusB, U. Ariz., 1970, MusM, 1972, D of Mus. Arts, 1976; MusM, Westminster Choir Coll., 1986. Concert pianist, organist Pianists Found. Am., Boston Pops Orch., Royal Philharm., Nat. Symphony Orch., Leningrad Philharmonic, Victoria Symphony, others, 1961—; organist, choirmaster St. Paul's Episcopal Ch., Tucson, 1968-74, First United Meth. Ch., Fairbanks, Alaska, 1974-89, All Saints Episc. Ch., Omaha, 1995—; prof. music U. Alaska, Fairbanks, 1974-91, chair music dept., 1991; Isaacson prof. of music U. Nebr., Omaha, 1994—; organist, choirmaster All Sts. Episcopal Ch., Omaha, 1995—. Recordings include Moszkowski Etudes, 1973, Works of Chaminade Dohnanyi, 1977, Mendelssohn Concerti, 1978, Beethoven First Concerto, 1980, Beethoven, Reinecke, Ireland Trios with Alaska Chamber Ensemble, 1988, Kabalevsky Third Concerto, Muczynski Concerto, Muczynski Suite, 1990, Beethoven Third Concerto, 1993. Recipient Record of Month award Mus. Heritage Soc., 1979, 80; finalist mus. amb. program USIA, 1983. Mem. Music Tchrs. Nat. Assn., Phi Kappa Phi, Pi Kappa Lambda. Episcopalian. Office: U Nebr Dept Music Omaha NE 68182

JOHNSON, JAMES GIBSON, JR., community recycling specialist; b. Flagstaff, Ariz., Feb. 26, 1938; s. James Gibson and Inga Anette J.; m. Faye Bodian, Aug. 23, 1973; children: Jill Johnson, Ginger Johnson, Jonathan Johnson. BA, U. Colo., 1960. Editor, pub. Town and Country Rev., Boulder, Colo., 1963-78; owner James G. Johnson and Assocs., Boulder, Colo., 1978-87; exec. dir. Eco Cycle Recycling, Boulder, Colo., 1987-89; community recycling specialist Office of Energy Conservation, State of Colo., Denver, 1989—. Mem. Open Space Bd. Trustees, Boulder, 1980-85, chmn., 1984-85; mem. Boulder County Pks. and Open Space Bd., 1985-93; chmn., 1987-89; mem. Boulder County Planning Commn., 1993—. Democrat. Home: 630 Northstar Ct Boulder CO 80304-1021 Office: Colo Office of Energy Conservation 1675 Broadway Ste 1300 Denver CO 80202-4675

JOHNSON, JANICE SUSAN GALLIK, finance executive; b. Akron, Ohio; d. Emil John and Antoinette Mary (Verdi) G.; children: Thomas Butowicz II, Elizabeth Henshaw; m. Michael F. Johnson. BS cum laude, U. Akron, 1965; postgrad., St. Francis Coll., 1978; MS, Ind. U., 1981; EdD, Seattle U., 1988. Mng. ptnr., treas., dir. pub. rels. Buckeye Group, Inc., Orion Inc., 1977-81; contr. D.S. Willett, Inc., 1982-85; mgr. acctg. G. Raden & Sons, Inc., 1986-89; cons. J. Gallik & Assocs., 1985—; controller Merit Steamship Agy., Inc., 1988-91; dir. adminstrv. svcs. Seattle Children's Home, 1991—; adj. faculty Seattle Pacific U. Contbr. articles to profl. jours. Trustee, bd. dirs. Columbus 500 Com., 1989—; bd. dirs. Lit. Ctr., 1988-89; bus./community rels. Bellevue Art Mus., 1983-85; bd. dirs., com. mem., dir. pub. rels. Ft. Wayne Philharmonic, 1978-81; treas., pres. Aboite River Women's Club, 1980-81; bd. dirs. Izaak Walton's League, 1980; area rep. Girl Scouts Am.; bd. dirs., pres. Zelienople Jr. Women, 1974-76; med. team search com. Zelienople, Pa., 1976. Scholl scholarship St. Francis, 1978; rsch. grant NYU Ctr. for Entrepreneurship, 1986. Mem. Seattle C. of C., Acad. Mgmt., Seattle U. Alumni Assn. (bd. govs.), Phi Delta Kappa, Alpha Delta Pi. Office: Seattle Children's Home 2142 10th Ave W Seattle WA 98119-2845

JOHNSON, JEFFREY PAUL, systems engineer; b. Columbus, Ohio, Jan. 10, 1945; s. Samuel and Joyce Eileen (Lockary) J.; m. Rita Rae Rapino, Dec. 1, 1973; children: Jeffrey Paul Jr., Margaret Joyce. BS in Physics, Ohio U., 1967; MS in Sys. Engring., Wright State U., 1978. Nuclear rsch. officer air force weapons lab. USAF, Kirtland AFB, Ohio, 1967-69; optical physics fgn. tech. divsn. USAF, Wright-Patterson AFB, Ohio, 1971-73; dep. missile combat crew cmdr. USAF, McConnell AFB, Kans., 1973-74; rsch. physicist Sys. Rsch. Labs., Dayton, Ohio, 1974-79; tech. staff Rockwell Internat., Anaheim, Calif., 1979-84; sr. staff scientist Photon Rsch. Assocs., Albuquerque, 1984—. Mem. Internat. Soc. Optical Enring. Optical Soc. Am. Home: 1209 Sierra Larga Dr NE Albuquerque NM 87112-6510 Office: Photon Rsch Assocs Albuquerque NM 87110

JOHNSON, JENNIFER LUCKY, psychotherapist; b. Paso, Wash., Oct. 22, 1938; d. Carl Eilert Leslie and Doris Christine (Westby) Lucky; m. Robert Eugene Johnson, Aug. 11, 1962; children: Nathan Robert, Douglas Eugene, Jeffrey Carl. BSN, St. Olaf Coll., 1960; M in Pastoral Ministry, Seattle U., 1990. RN, Wash.; cert. advanced nurse practitioner; cert. clin. specialist in adult mental health/psychiat. nursing. Staff nurse ICU U. Minn., Mpls., 1960-61, U. Wash., Seattle, 1961-62; psychiat. nurse Am. Lake VA Hosp., Tacoma, Wash., 1962; Indian pub. health nurse U.S. Pub. Health Hosp., Harlem, Mont., 1963-66; geriatric nurse Christian Rest Home, Lynden, Wash., 1983-93; dir. social svcs. and psychiat. cons. Christian Rest Home, Lynden, 1988-93; pvt. practice therapist Bellingham, Wash., 1992—; prescribing psychiat. nurse Whatcom Counseling and Psychiat. Clinic, Bellingham, 1994—; adj. faculty Seattle U., 1996—; chair social svcs. forum Wash. Assn. Homes for the Aging, Seattle, 1992-94; mem. adv. bd. Wash. Dept. Health and Social Svcs., Mental Health and Aging, Olympia, 1993; dementia trainer in field. Co-author: (tng. manual for profls.) Prosthetic Care for the Person with Dementia: A Holistic Approach, 1993. Bd. mem. Whatcom Symphony, Bellingham, 1984-85, Mt. Baker Meadows, Ferndale, Wash., 1990-92. Recipient Light of Love award Alzheimer's Soc. Wash., Bellingham, 1993. Mem. Wash. State Nurses Assn., Coalition Mental Health Profls. and Consumers. Lutheran. Office: 1909 Broadway Bellingham WA 98225-3237

JOHNSON, JEROME LINNÉ, cardiologist; b. Rockford, Ill., June 19, 1929; s. Thomas Arthur and Myrtle Elizabeth (Swanson) J.; m. Molly Ann Rideout, June 27, 1953; children: Susan Johnson Nowels, William Rideout. BA, U. Chgo., 1951; BS, Northwestern U., 1952, MD, 1955. Diplomate Nat. Bd. Med. Examiners. Intern U. Chgo. Clinics, 1955-56; resident Northwestern U., Chgo., 1958-61; chief resident Chgo. Wesley Meml. Hosp., 1960-61; mem., v.p. Hauch Med. Clinic, Pomona, Calif., 1961-88; pvt. practice cardiology and internal medicine Pomona, 1988—; clin. assoc. prof. medicine, U. So. Calif., L.A., 1961—; mem. staff Pomona Valley Hosp. Med. Ctr., chmn. coronary care com. 1967-77; mem. staff L.A. County Hosp. Citizen ambassador, People to People; mem. Town Hall of Calif., L.A. World Affairs Coun. Lt. USNR, 1956-58; bd. dirs. Claremont chpt. ARC, 1993—; bd. dirs., health com. Mt. San Antonio Gardens Retirement Home, 1993—. Fellow Am. Coll. Cardiology, Am. Geriatrics Soc., Royal Soc. Health; mem. Galileo Soc., Am. Heart Assn. (bd. dirs. L.A. County div. 1967-84, San Gabriel div. 1963-89), Am. Soc. Internal Medicine, Inland Soc. Internal Medicine, Pomona Host Lions. Home: 648 Delaware Dr Claremont CA 91711-3457

JOHNSON, JIM CHARLES, clinical psychologist; b. San Francisco, July 25, 1949; s. George L. and Dorothy Fern Johnson; m. Merrily J. Rockwell, Sept. 15, 1974; children: Collier, Anelissa, William. BA, Walla Walla Coll., 1972, MA, 1975; PhD, Calif. Sch. Profl. Psychology, Fresno, 1979. Diplomate Am. Bd. Med. Psychotherapists, Am. Bd. Disability Analysts. Psychol. technician VA Hosp., Walla Walla, Wash., 1975-76, Gresham (Oreg.) Psychologists/NW Med. Psychologists, 1980-87; dir. psychol. svc. Pioneer Trail Adolescent Treatment Ctr., Gresham, 1990-93; clin. dir. N.W. Med. Psychologists, Gresham, 1987-93, Adventist Health Systems West, Portland, Oreg., 1986-88; cons. psychologist Portland Adventist Med. Ctr., 1980-88; asst. chief of profl. staff Pioneer Trails Adolescent Ctr., Gresham, 1990-93. Author: Metaphores of Hope, 1982. Mem. Portland Psychol. Assn. (pres. 1991), Provider in Med. Care (pres. 1990—), Fulcrum Behavioral Health (pres. 1994—). Mem. Seventh-Day Adventist. Office: 516 SE 71st St Portland OR 97215

JOHNSON, JOAN BRAY, insurance company consultant; b. Kennett, Mo., Nov. 19, 1926; d. Ples Green and Mary Scott (Williams) Bray; m. Frank Johnson Jr., Nov. 6, 1955; 1 child, Victor Kent. Student, Drury Coll., 1949-51, Cen. Bible Inst. and Coll., 1946-49. Staff writer Gospel Pub. Co., Springfield, Mo., 1949-51; sec. Kennett Sch. Dist. Bd. Edn., 1951-58; spl. features corr. Memphis Press-Scimitar, 1959-60; sec. to v.p. Cotton Exchange Bank, Kennett, Mo., 1959-60; proposal analyst Aetna Life Ins. Co., El Paso, Tex., 1960-64, pension adminstr., 1964-71; office mgr. Brokerage div. Aetna Life Ins. Co., Denver, 1971-78; office adminstr. Life Consol. div. Aetna Life Ins. Co., Oakland, Calif., 1979-82; office adminstr. PFSD div. Aetna Life Ins. Co., Walnut Creek, Calif., 1983-86; office adminstr. PFSD-Health Mktg. div. Aetna Life Ins. Co., Sacramento, Calif., 1986-89; regional adminstr. Aetna Life Ins. Co., Hartford, Conn., 1989-91; cons. Aetna Life Ins. Co., Santa Ana, Calif., 1991—. Officer local PTA, 1964-71; prs. Wesley Svc. Guild, 1968-71; den mother Boy Scouts Am.; fin. sec. Green Valley United Meth. Ch., 1992—. Recipient Tex. Life Svc. award PTA, 1970. Fellow Life Office Mgmt. Assn. (instr. classes); mem. DAR (regent Silver State Nev. chpt. 1994-96, treas. 1996-98, bd. dirs. Nev. 1996-98), Assn. Bus. and Profl. Women, Life Underwriters Assn., Clark County Heritage Mus., Last Monday Club, Opti-Mrs., Allied Arts Club. Democrat. Home: 2415 La Estrella St Henderson NV 89014-3608 Office: 1677 N Main St Ste 250 Santa Ana CA 92701-2324

JOHNSON, JOHN H., publisher, consumer products executive; b. Arkansas City, Ark., Jan. 19, 1918; m. Eunice Johnson; children: John Harold (dec.), Linda Johnson Rice. Student, U. Chgo., Northwestern U., Howard U.; LL.D., Central State Coll., Shaw U., N.C. Coll., Benedict Coll., Carnegie-Mellon Inst., Morehouse Coll., N.C. A. and T. State U., Syracuse U., Eastern Mich. U., Hamilton Coll., Lincoln U., Malcolm X Coll., Upper Iowa Coll., Wayne State U., Pratt Inst., Chgo. State U., Northeastern U. Pub., chmn. chief exec. officer Johnson Pub. Co., Inc., Chgo. N.Y.C., L.A., Washington, 1942—; pub., editor Ebony, Jet, EM-Ebony Man (mags.); pres. Sta. WJPC-AM-FM, Chgo., Sta. WLOU, Louisville, Fashion Fair Cosmetics, Chgo., Eboné Cosmetics, Supreme Beauty Products; chmn., chief exec. officer Supreme Life Ins. Co., Chgo.; bd. dirs. Greyhound Corp., Dillard Dept. Stores, Inc. Author: Succeeding Against the Odds, 1989. Trustee Art Inst., Chgo. Named Outstanding Young Man U.S. Jaycees, 1951, Communicator of Yr. U. Chgo. Alumni Assn., 1974, Chicagoan of Yr., Chgo. Boys Club, 1983; recipient Horatio Alger award, 1966; John Russwurm award Nat. Newspaper Pubs. Assn., 1966, Spingarn medal NAACP, 1966, Henry Johnson Fisher award Mag. Pubs. Assn., 1971,Columbia Journalism award, 1974, Honors Disting. Accomplishment United Negro Coll. Fund, 1983, Robie award Jackie Robinson Found., 1985, Disting. Contbrn. to Journalism award Nat. Press Found., 1986; named to Acad. Disting. Entrepreneurs Babson Coll., 1979; Chgo. Bus. Hall of Fame, 1983; named to Entrepreneur of Decade Black Enterprise Mag., 1987; inducted into Black Press Hall of Fame, 1987, Pub. Hall of Fame Folio Ednl. Trust Inc., 1987, Ill. Bus. Hall of Fame, 1989, Nat. Sales Hall of Fame, 1989, Chgo. Journalism Hall of Fame, 1990; recipient Harold H. Hines Jr. Benefactors' award United Negro Coll. Fund, 1988, Excel award Internat. Assn. Bus. communicators, Founders award NCCJ, 1989, Disting. Svc. award Harvard U. Grad. Sch. Bus. Adminstrn., 1991, Salute to the Media award Impact Publs., Africa's Future award UNICEF, 1992, Booker T. Washington Speaker's award Booker T. Washington Bus. Assn., Heritage award Exec. Leadership Coun., 1992, Dow Jones Entrepreneurial Excellence award Dow Jones and the Wall Street Jour., 1993. Fellow Sigma Delta Chi; mem. U.S. C. of C. (dir.), Mag. Pubs. Assn. Office: 1270 Avenue Of The Americas New York NY 10020 also: 1750 Pennsylvania Ave NW Washington DC 20006-4502*

JOHNSON, JOHN PHILIP, geneticist, researcher; b. Wabash, Ind., June 6, 1949; s. Melvin Leroy and Cleo Pauline (Aldrich) J.; m. Sheryl Kay Kennedy, June 3, 1978; children: Craig Eric, Lindsay Sara. BS, U. Mich., 1971, MD, 1975. Diplomate Am. Bd. Pediatrics, Am. Bd. Med. Genetics. Intern, 2d-yr. resident Children's Hosp. Los Angeles, 1975-77; 3d yr. resident in pediatrics U. Utah, Salt Lake City, 1977-78, fellow in genetics, 1980-82, asst. prof. pediatrics, 1982-85; pediatrician Family Health Program, Salt Lake City, 1978-80; assoc. dir. med. genetics, attending/active staff physician Children's Hosp. Oakland, Calif., 1985-92; dir. med. genetics, attending/active staff physician Children's Hosp., Oakland, 1992-94; dir. med. genetics Shodair Children's Hosp., Helena, Mont., 1994—, active mem. staff, 1995—; clinic physician Utah State Tng. Sch., American Fork, 1982-85; attending and staff physician Primary Children's Med. Ctr., Salt Lake City, 1978-80. Assoc. editor Am. Jour. Med. Genetics, 1995-97; contbr. articles to med. jours. Recipient William J. Branstrom award U. Mich., 1967. Fellow Am. Acad. Pediatrics; mem. Am. Soc. Human Genetics, Soc. for Pediatric Rsch., Alpha Omega Alpha. Home: 2604 Gold Rush Ave Helena MT 59601-5625 Office: Shodair Children's Hosp PO Box 5539 Helena MT 59604-5539

JOHNSON, KEITH LIDDELL, chemical company executive; b. Darlington, U.K., July 22, 1939; came to U.S., 1948, naturalized, 1958; s. Arthur Henry and Beatrice (Liddell) J.; m. Margaret Elaine Meston, Aug. 29, 1959; children: Leslie Margaret, Kevin Liddell, Gregory Norman, Kathleen Elaine; 1 ward, Ann Louise Warwick. BA, U. Mich., 1960. Chem. technician Ajem Labs., Livonia, Mich., 1956-60; research chemist labs Swift & Co., Chgo., 1960-63, project mgr., 1963-67, group leader research and devel. ctr., Oak Brook, Ill., 1967-71, adminstrv. asst. to exec. v.p., Chgo., 1971-72, quality assurance dir., 1974-78, group mgr. plant quality assurance, 1978-82; quality assurance mgr. refinery div. Swift Edible Oil Co. subs. Swift & Co., Chgo., 1972-73, corp. quality assurance mgr., 1973-74; tech. dir. Norman Fox & Co., L.A., 1982-83, br. mgr., 1983-88, gen. mgr., 1988—, exec. v.p., dir. 1989—, pres., 1993—; bd. dirs. Lexard Corp., L.A., v.p., 1990—; mem. Chgo. Manpower Area Planning Com., 1971; mem. industry adv. bd. South Coast Air Quality Mgmt. Dist., Calif., 1982-84. Contbr. articles to profl. jours. Holder 17 U.S. and 25 fgn. patents. V.p., dir. St. Martha's Senior Care Ctr., West Covina, Calif., 1993—, chmn. bd., 1995—; vestry St. Martha's Episcopal Ch., 1991-96, sr. warden, 1992-96. Mem. Chgo. Chemists Club, Chem. Arts Forum Chgo. (v.p. 1980, pres. 1981), Am. Chem. Soc., Soc. Cosmetic Chemists (membership chmn. Bay area chpt., 1985, chmn. 1987-88), Am. Oil Chemists Soc., Jr. Assn. Commerce and Industry (dir. 1968, v.p. 1969, exec. v.p. 1970, pres. 1971), Chem. Mktg. Assn. So. Calif., U.S. Jr. C. of C. (dir. 1972), Ill. Jr. C. of C. (v.p. 1972). Episcopalian. Home: 342 Amberwood Dr Walnut CA 91789-2473 Office: PO Box 58727 Los Angeles CA 90058-0727

JOHNSON, KENNETH F., lawyer; b. Ft. Bragg, Calif., June 10, 1938. BSCE, U. Calif., Berkeley, 1962; JD, U. Calif., 1969. Bar: Calif. 1970. Atty. Crosby, Heafey, Roach & May, Oakland, Calif. Note and comment editor: Hastings Law Jour., 1968-69. Mem. ABA, State Bar Calif., Alameda County Bar Assn., Order of Coif. Office: Crosby Heafey Roach & May 1999 Harrison St Oakland CA 94612-3517

JOHNSON, KENNETH LOUIS, education marketing specialist; b. Blackfoot, Idaho, Dec. 22, 1957; s. Stuart Paul and Afton (Dance) J.; m. Stacy Rae Siirila, Sept. 29, 1989; children: Rachel Garrett, Patrick Garrett, Lisa Johnson. BA cum laude, Brigham Young U., 1982; MBA in Health Svcs. Adminstrn., U. Utah, 1988, postgrad., 1995—. Dir. pub. rels. Bingham Meml. Hosp., Blackfoot, Idaho, 1982; pub. rels. specialist U. Utah Health Scis., Salt Lake City, 1982-89; dir. mktg. Lakeview Hosp., Bountiful, Utah, 1989-90, asst. adminstr., 1990-92; mktg. adminstr. Weber State U., Ogden, Utah, 1992-95, dir. rsch. and ann. fund, 1995-96; mgr. spl. medicine clinic Univ. Utah Hosps. and Clinics, Salt Lake City, 1996—; mktg. cons. Sport Cove Scuba Diving, Salt Lake City, 1984-88, U. Utah Small Bus., Salt Lake City, 1986; pub. rels. cons. Springville (Utah) World Folkfest, 1986. Cub master, den leader, explorer advisor Boy Scouts Am., Utah, 1986—; coun. mem. United Way, Davis County, Utah, 1990-91; mem. Ogden/Weber Leadership Acad., 1994. Mem. Internat. Assn. Bus. Communicators, Am. Coll. Healthcare Execs., Utah Soc. for Hosp. Planning, Mktg. & Pub. Rels. (pres. 1990-91, past pres. 1991-92), Rotary Internat. (Layton, Utah). LDS. Home: 3090 N 1150 E Ogden UT 84414-1894 Office: U Utah Hosp Clinic 1-2-3 Salt Lake City UT 84132

JOHNSON, KENNETH RUSSELL, medical educator; b. Superior, Wis., Dec. 14, 1945; m. Cathy Woest; children: Todd, Kellie, Stacy, Mark. BS, Wis. State U., Superior, 1968; MD, U. Wis., Madison, 1972. Diplomate Am. Bd. Surgery; lic. physician, Ariz. Resident in gen. surgery UCLA, 1972-74, Tucson Hosps., 1975-77; asst. clin. prof. surgery U. Ariz., Tucson, 1979—; mem. med. staff St. Elizabeth's Hungary Clinic, Tucson, 1977—, Tucson Med. Ctr., St. Joseph's Hosp., Tucson, St. Mary's Hosp., Tucson, El Dorado Med. Ctr., Tucson, Univ. Hosp., Tucson, N.W. Hosp., Tucson. Contbr. articles to profl. jours. Mem. contract maintenance citizen's panel Pima County Transp. and Flood Control Dist., 1984; mem. profl. adv. group Olsten Quality Care (formerly Kimberly Home Health Svcs.), Tucson, 1987—. Recipient Thomas Leonard award, 1969, Eben J. Carey award, 1969, Michael J. Carey Sr. Svc. award, 1972; Phillip's scholar, 1971. Fellow ACS; mem. AMA, Am. Trauma Soc. (founder), Am. Soc. Gen. Surgeons, Wis. med. Alumni Assn., Calif. med. Assn., Ariz. Med. Assn. L.A. County Med. Assn., Pima County Med. Soc., Tucson Surg. Soc., Student Am. Med. Assn., Student Health Orgn., Med. Student's Assn., U. Assn. Emergency Med. Svcs., Southwestern Surg. Congress, Elks, Sigma Sigma, Alpha Omega Alpha, Phi Chi. Home: 5155 Camino Alisa Tucson AZ 85718 Office: Thomas-Davis Med Ctrs 630 N Alvernon Way Tucson AZ 85711-1808

JOHNSON, KEVIN MAURICE, professional basketball player; b. Sacramento, Mar. 4, 1966. Student, U. Calif. Basketball player Cleveland Cavaliers, 1987-88, Phoenix Suns, 1988—. Named to Dream Team II, 1994, NBA Most Improved Player, 1989, All-NBA Second Team, 1989-91, 94, All-NBA Third Team, 1992. Office: care Phoenix Suns 201 E Jefferson St Phoenix AZ 85004-2412

JOHNSON, LAWRENCE M., banker; b. 1940. Student, U. Hawaii. With Bank of Hawaii, Honolulu, 1963—, exec. v.p., 1980-84, vice chmn., 1984-89, pres., 1989—, now chmn. bd., CEO; pres. Bancorp Hawaii, Inc. Office: Bancorp Hawaii Inc 130 Merchant St PO Box 2900 Honolulu HI 96846 Office: Bancorp Hawaii Inc 130 Merchant St Honolulu HI 96813*

JOHNSON, LEONA MINDELL, librarian, educator; b. Bremerton, Wash., Sept. 18, 1946; d. Edward and Adene Mindell (Lynum) Vig; m. James David Selin, Nov. 27, 1969 (div. 1977); 1 child: Korin Nicole; m. Paul Wallace Johnson, May 21, 1977; children: Gunnar, Turi, Ole-Paul. BA in Psychology, Western Wash. U., 1969; forest technician cert., Peninsula Coll., 1975; MEd, Central Wash. U., 1994. Cert. tchr. K-8, Wash. Forest engr. Crown Zellerbach, Sekiu, Wash., 1975-77; forest tech. U.S. Forest Svc., Cle Elum, Wash., 1978; libr. Roslyn (Wash.) Pub. Libr., 1978—, Carpenter Meml. Libr., Cle Elum, 1980-81; libr. II Clallam Bay (Wash.) Correctional Ctr., 1990; grad. asst. Ctrl. Wash. U., Ellensburg, Wash., 1992-93, libr. specialist, 1996—; substitute tchr. Cle Elum (Wash.)-Roslyn Sch., 1994-96. Scholar AAUW, 1992. Mem. Internat. Reading Assn., Kappa Delta Pi, Psi Chi. Office: Cen Wash U Library Ellensburg WA 98926

JOHNSON, LEONIDAS ALEXANDER, optometrist, minister; b. Chgo., Jan. 16, 1959; s. Leon and Dolores J.; m. Crystal Dwaun Ellington, June 23, 1990. BA in Biology, Ill. Wesleyan U., 1981; BS in Visual Sci., So. Calif. Coll. of Optometry, Fullerton, 1983, OD, 1985; student, Grace Theol. Sem., Long Beach, Calif., 1986-89; MA in Specialized Ministry, Biola U., La Mirada, Calif., 1997. Optometrist Larry Gotlieb, O.D., Redondo Beach, Calif., 1985-86, James Moses, O.D., Inglewood, Calif., 1986-87, Eyecare U.S.A., Montclair, Calif., 1987-89, Pearle Visioncare, Brea, Calif., 1989-94, Montebello Med. Eye Ctr., Calif., 1994-95, Watts Health Found., Inc., L.A., 1994—; chief vision care svcs. Watt's Health Found., Inc., L.A., 1996—; mem. quality assurance com. Eyecare U.S.A., 1988-89, Watts Health Ctr., 1996—, United Health Plan, 1996—; investigator Ocular Hypertension Treatment Study. Co-author: What Is This Thing Called Preaching? An Authentic Collection of Sermons by Rev. Leon Johnson, Vol. One, 1996, Vol. Two, 1997; contbr. articles to profl. jours. Min., deacon Friendship Bapt. Ch., Yorba Linda, Calif. Fellow Am. Acad. Optometry; mem. Am. Optometric Assn., Calif. Optometric Assn., Nat. Optometric Assn. Home: PO Box 4434 Diamond Bar CA 91765-0434 Office: Watts Health Ctr 10300 Compton Ave Los Angeles CA 90002-3628

JOHNSON, LEROY F., chemist; b. Seattle, Feb. 4, 1933; s. LeRoy F. and Anna C. (Amdahl) J.; m. Margaret L. Lindsley, Sept. 8, 1956; children: Noel, Brett. BS, Oreg. State U., 1954, MS, 1956. NMR applications chemist Varian Assocs., Palo Alto, Calif., 1957-72; v.p. rsch. Nicolet Magnetics Corp., Mountain View, Calif., 1972-83; sr. scientist NMR Instruments div. GE, Fremont, Calif., 1983-92; analytical NMR mgr. Bruker Instruments, Fremont, 1992-94; NMR cons. Cupertino, Calif., 1994—; tchr. NMR short course, Am. Chem. Soc., 1966—. Author: Carbon 13 NMR Spectra, 1972; contbr. numerous articles to profl. jours. Mem. Am. Chem. Soc., Internat. Soc. Magnetic Resonance.

JOHNSON, LINDA DUNLAVY, principal; b. Wentachee, Wash., Nov. 17, 1950; d. Don Churchill and Anna Bernice (Pond) Dunlavy; m. Richard Lynn Johnson, Nov. 17, 1973; children: Guy, Orv. BA in Music Edn., U. No. Colo., 1973; MA in Edn., Chadron State Coll., 1995, Chadron State Coll., 1996. Cert. counselor, prin., music instructor. Music/dance instr. Goshen County Schs., Torrington, Wyo., 1973-93; sch. counselor intern Chadron (Nebr.) Schs., 1995-96; sch. prin. Red Cloud Indian Sch., Pine Ridge, S.D., 1996—. choreographer numerous musicals and choirs, 1974—; guest conductor numerous bands and wind ensembles, 1993—. French hornist Panhandle Symphony/Band, Scotts Bluff, Nebr., 1974-93, Chadron State Coll., 1993-95; dance/drill team dir. City Schs., Torrington, Wyo., 1975-88; adjudicator Rocky Mountain Drill/Dance, Salt Lake City, 1978-88, Miss Drill Team USA, Santa Monica, Calif., 1983-88; motivational speaker, Wyo., Nebr., and Colo., 1985—; co-dir. Jr. Miss, Torrington, 1993-95. mem. Am. Counseling Assn., Am. Sch. Counseling Assn., Nat. Assn. Secondary Sch. Prins., Music Educators Nat. Conf., Nebr. Counseling Assn., Chi Sigma Iota. Home: Rte 1 Box 523 Torrington WY 82240

JOHNSON, LLOYD P., surgeon, educator; b. Yakima, Wash., Nov. 6, 1931; s. Philip Samuel and Harriet Evangeline (Danielson) J.; m. Joann Nordale; children: Cynthia, Lloyd Philip Jr., Douglas; m. Kathleen Elizabeth Gates; 1 stepchild, Anthony. BS, U. Wash., 1953, MD, 1956. Diplomate Am. Bd. Surgery. Intern San Francisco Hosp./U. Calif. Svc., 1956-57; resident in surgery U. Wash., 1959-64, sr. rsch. fellow in surgery, 1964-65; prof. surgery Pub. Health Coll. Haile Selassi I U., Gondar, Ethiopia, 1965-67; pvt. practice Seattle Surg. Group; clin. asst. prof. surgery U. Wash., Seattle, 1972-77, clin. assoc. prof. surgery, 1978-89, clin. prof. surgery, 1989-96; exec. dir. Scientific Tech. and Lang. Inst., Seattle, 1996—; pres. bd. dirs. Logoc Bookstore, Seattle, 1970-80; prof. surgery Haile Selassie U., Gondar, Ethiopia, 1965-68; mem. lung com. S.W. Oncology Group, 1957—, mem. surg. exec. com., 1975-80, lung cancer study group, 1978-89. Contbr. articles to med. jours.; developer intra-tracheal oxygen catheter. Vis. surgeon World Med. Mission, Mercy Corps., Sci. Tech. and Lang. Inst., India, 1978, Kenya, 1982, Pakistan, 1990, Kyrgystan, 1993. Capt., flight surgeon USAF, 1957-59. Fellow ACS; mem. AMA, Seattle Surg. Soc. (pres. 1991), King County Med. Soc., Wash. State Med. Assn., North Pacific Surg. Assn. (sec.-treas. 1989-95), Pacific Coast Surg. Assn., Sigma Xi, Alpha Epsilon Delta. Presbyterian. Home: 5600 Ann Arbor Ave NE Seattle WA 98105-2116 Office: Scientific Tech and Lang Inst 1833 N 105th St Seattle WA 98133-8973

JOHNSON, LYNN DOUGLAS, psychologist; b. St. George, Utah, Aug. 23, 1946; s. Grant Douglas and Lorriane (Mason) J.; m. Carol Sue Edson, Feb. 7, 1976; children: Christopher, Jeffrey, Catherine, Stephen. BS, Brigham Young U., 1970; MS, U. Utah, 1974, PhD, 1976. Lic. psychologist, Utah. Pvt. practice psychology Salt Lake City, 1977—; dir. Brief Therapy Ctr., Salt Lake City, 1984—; cons. Aetna/Human Affairs Internat., Salt Lake City, 1988—. Author: Psychotherapy in the Age of Accountability, 1995. Mem. APA, Am. Soc. Clin. Hypnosis, Utah Soc. Clin. Hypnosis (pres. 1970-72), Internat. Assn. Near-Data Studies (dir. Utah chpt. 1993—). Office: Brief Therapy Ctr 166 E 5900 S B-108 Salt Lake City UT 84107

JOHNSON, MAGIC See JOHNSON, EARVIN

JOHNSON, MARIAN ILENE, education educator; b. Hawarden, Iowa, Oct. 3, 1929; d. Henry Richard and Wilhelmina Anna (Schmidt) Stoltenberg; m. Paul Irving Jones, June 14, 1958 (dec. Feb. 1985); m. William Andrew Johnson, Oct. 3, 1991. BA, U La Verne, 1959; MA, Claremont Grad. Sch., 1962; PhD, Ariz. State U., 1971. Cert. tchr., Iowa, Calif. Elem. tchr. Cherokee (Iowa) Sch. Dist., 1949-52, Sioux City (Iowa) Sch. Dist., 1952-56, Ontario (Calif.) Pub. Schs., 1956-61, Reed Union Sch. Dist., Belvedere-Tiburon, Calif., 1962-65, Columbia (Calif.) Union Sch. Dist., 1965-68; prof. edn. Calif. State U., Chico, 1972-91. Home: 26437 S Lakewood Dr Sun Lakes AZ 85248-7246

JOHNSON, MARK STEVEN, community health facility administrator; b. Rockford, Ill., July 18, 1949; s. Mark F. and Rita M. (Petersen) J.; m. Deborah K. Nelson/Gill, Dec. 22, 1969 (div. Dec. 1983); m. Betty J. Johnson, May 7, 1988; stepchildren: Shannon C. Sexton, Cramer M. Sexton. BA, No. Ill. U., 1971; MPA, U. Alaska S.E., Juneau, 1987. Substitute tchr. Harlem Sch. Dist., Rockford, 1971-72; caseworker Ill. Dept. Pub. Aid, Rockford, 1972-74; EMS health planner Comprehensive Health Planning of N.W. Ill., Rockford, 1974-78; EMS coord. Physicians Svcs. of Fairbanks, Alsaks, 1978-79; chief emergency med. svcs. sect. Alaska Dept. Health and Social Svc., Juneau, 1979-95, chief cmty. health and EMS, 1996—; dir. EMS for Children project, dir. Injury Prevention project Alaska Dept. Health and Social Svcs., 1990—. Mem. editorial bd. Prehosp. and Disaster Medicine, 1993—; author book chpt. and articles. Named EMS Adminstr. of Yr., Gov. Hickel and Alaska Coun. on EMS, 1993. Mem. Nat. Assn. State EMS Dirs. (exec. bd. 1985-88), Am. Soc. for Circumpolar Health, Alaska Pub. Health Assn. (exec. bd. 1988, Barbara Berger award 1995), State and Terr. Injury Prevention Dirs. (v.p. 1996), Alaska State Emergency REsponse Commn. Home: 10726 Horizon Dr Juneau AK 99801 Office: Cmty Health and EMS Dept Health and Social Svcs 432 N Franklin St Juneau AK 88711-0616

JOHNSON, MARTIN CLIFTON, physician; b. Santa Fe, Nov. 16, 1933; s. Henry J. and Dorothy (Clifton) J.; AB, Stanford, 1955, MD, 1959; Diplomate Am. Bd. Neurol. Surgery, Am. Bd. Pediat. Neurosurgery, Am. Bd. Forensic Examiners, Am. Bd. Forensic Medicine; m. Priscilla Bollam, June 13, 1959; children: Martin Clifton II, Kurt B., Kirsten L., Katharine E. Intern, Palo Alto Stanford U. Hosp., 1959-60; fellow in neurosurgery Mayo Found., Rochester, Minn., 1960-61; asst. resident gen. surgery Presbyn. Med. Ctr., San Francisco, 1963-64; asst. resident, resident, sr. resident, chief resident in neurosurgery U. Cin., 1964-68; pvt. practice medicine specializing in neurosurgery, with spl. interest in pediatric neurosurgery, Portland, Oreg., 1968—; mem. staff Emanuel Hosp., Meridian Park Hosp., St. Vincent's Providence Hosp., Providence Med. Ctr.; neurosurg. cons. Shriners Hosp. for Crippled Children. Col. M.C., USAR. Fellow ACS, Am. Acad. Pediats.; mem. Multnomah County, Oreg. med. socs., AMA, Congress Neurol. Surgeons, Am. Assn. Neurol. Surgeons, Pan Pacific Surg. Assn., Portland Surg. Soc., Soc. Critical Care Medicine, N.W. Pediatric Soc., North Pacific Soc. Neurology and Psychiatry, Oreg. Neurosurg. Soc., Internat. Soc. for Pediatric Neurol. Surgery, Portland Acad. Pediatrics, Airplane Owners and Pilots Assn., Flying Physicians Assn. Clubs: Multnomah Athletic, Columbia Aviation. Home: 31870 SW Country View Ln Wilsonville OR 97070-7476 Office: Pacific Northwest Neurol Assocs PC Ste 350 501 N Graham St Portland OR 97227-1643

JOHNSON, MARY, museum director. Acting dir. Dept. Libr. and Pub. Records, Phoenix. Office: Dept Libr Archives and Pub Records 1700 W Washington Ste 200 Phoenix AZ 85007

JOHNSON, MARY ELIZABETH, retired elementary education educator; b. St. Louis, Sept. 17, 1943; d. Richard William Blayney and Alice Bonjean (Taylor) Blayney Needham; m. Clyde Robert Johnson, Aug. 31, 1963; children: Brian (dec. 1991), Elizabeth Johnson Meyer, David. BS cum laude, U. Ill., 1966; MA, Maryville U., 1990; postgrad., So. Ill. U., 1990. Cert. elem. tchr., Ill., Mo. Tchr. Hazelwood Sch. Dist., Florissant, Mo., 1971-93, positive intervention tchr., 1989-91; Author play: Say No to Drugs, 1991. Author: Secret Study Skills for Third Graders, 1990. Mem. Hazelwood Schs. Music Boosters, 1980-88; mem. coms. Townsend PTA, Florissant, 1976—; contbr. Schlarship Run-Walk, 1982—; mem. Children's United Rsch. Effort in Cancer, 1986—; vol. Spl. Love, Inc., camp for children with cancer, 1986—; active The Children's Inn, Bethesda, Md., 1990—, Bailey Scholarship Fund, U. Ill., 1994—. Fred S. Bailey scholar, 1962-66, Edmund J. James scholar, 1964-65; named Townsend Tchr. of Yr., 1989-90. Mem. NEA, Internat. Platform Assn., Kappa Delta Pi, Alpha Lambda Delta, Phi Kappa Phi. Baptist. Home: 12 Shamblin Rd Florissant MO 63034-1354 also: 5230 E Brown Rd Apt 114 Mesa AZ 85205-4364

JOHNSON, MARY KATHERINE, elementary education educator; b. Prescott, Wis., June 12, 1945; d. Walter Frank and Mary Jane (Larson) Johnson; m. William F. Hilton, June 23, 1968 (div. 1985); children: Bradley Eric, Karin Louise. BA, Mich. State U., 1967, MA, 1970; postgrad., U. Calif., Berkeley, 1970—. Cert. elem. tchr., Calif. Tchr. East Lansing (Mich.) Pub. Schs., 1967-68, Hall's Crossroads Sch., Aberdeen, Md., 1968-69, Oakland (Calif.) Pub. Schs., 1970-82; tchr., cons. Bay Area Writing Project, Berkeley, 1978—; cons. Child Devel. Project, San Ramon, Calif., 1985; tchr. Berkeley Unified Sch. Dist., 1986-96; coord. pub. programs, math. edn. program Lawrence Hall of Sci., U. Calif., Berkeley, 1996—; mem. MATHTEQ U. Calif., Berkeley, 1987-90; mem. com. of credentials Commn. for Tchr. Preparation and Licensing, Sacramento, 1974-76; spkr. Asilomar Math. Conf., 1991, 94, 95, 96, program com. Asilomar Math. conf., 1995; spkr. Wine Country Math. Conf., 1992, Cal-TASH Conf., 1992, 94, 97, TASH Internat. Conf., 1993, Supported Life Conf., 1992; rep. No. Regional Spl. Edn. Local Plan Area Com., Region III Full Inclusion Task Force for State of Calif., 1994—; participant Calif. Rsch. Inst., 1992; mem. adv. task force on tchr. preparation in mainstreaming Calif. Commn. on Tchr. Credentialling, 1996. Contbg. author: Portfolio Assessment in Mathematics, 1990, Teacher Handbook on Homework, C.M.C. Communicator, 1993. Coord. children's coun. Epworth Meth. Ch., Berkeley, 1985-88, 96—, Youth Coun., 1993-95; cert. lay spkr. Bay View dist. Calif.-Nev. United Meth. Ch., Berkeley, 1989—, bd. trustees, 1994-96; pres. bd. trustees Maya's Music Therapy Fund, 1994—. Named Math. Tchr. of Yr. Alameda/Contra Costa Counties Math. Educators, 1996; Berkeley Pub. Edn. Found. grantee, 1988, 89, 90, 92, 94, 95, In Dulce Jullibo Inc. grantee, 1989, 90, 92, 94, 95, BAMP grantee, 1995, Calif. Math. Coun. grantee, 1995; Bay Area Math. Project fellow, 1994. Fellow Oakland/Bay Area Writing Project, Bay Area Writing Project; mem. P.E.O. Sisterhood, Nat. Coun. Tchrs. English, Nat. Coun. Tchrs. Math., Calif. English Coun., Calif. Math. Coun. Democrat. Home: 1016 Keeler Ave Berkeley CA 94708-1404 Office: U Calif Math Edn Program Lawrence Hall Sci Berkeley CA 94720

JOHNSON, MARY PERRINE, musician, educator; b. Centralia, Ill., Apr. 21, 1929; d. David bates and Fanny Eliza (French) Perrine; m. Robert Royce Johnson, Dec. 30, 1953; children: Perrine Johnson Anderson, Royce W., Allegra F. Johnson Pitera. BS, Cornell U., 1951. Rsch. asst. Harvard U., Cambridge, Mass., 1951-52, Calif. Inst. Tech., Pasadena, 1952-55; mem. Recorders Court, Detroit, 1966-80, Good Company, Detroit, 1979-87, Musica Reservata of Utah, Logan, 1988—; workshop faculty Mideast Workshop, Pitts., 1980—; workshop leader various recorder socs., Mich., N.Y., Utah; artist in edn. Utah Arts Coun., Salt Lake City, 1990-94. Reviewer Music Rev., 1996—. Music dir. Salt Lake Recorder Soc., 1988—; breast cancer awareness com., vol. Am. Cancer Soc., Salt Lake City, 1993—. Mem. Am. Recorder Soc. (cert. tchr.), Viola da Gamba Soc. Am., PEO, Univ. of Utah Women's Club (pres. 1990-91), Sigma Xi. Home: 3857 S Eagle Point Dr Salt Lake City UT 84109-3822

JOHNSON, MARYANN ELAINE, educational administrator; b. Franklin Twp., Pa., Nov. 1, 1943; d. Mary I. Sollick; BS in Elementary Edn., Mansfield State U., Pa., 1964; MS in Elementary Edn., U. Alaska, College 1973; EdD, Wash. State U., Pullman, 1981; married. Tchr. Nayatt Sch., Barrington, R.I., 1964-66, North Sch., North Chicago, Ill., 1966-67, Kodiak (Alaska) On-Base Sch., 1967-71, Eastmont Sch. Dist., 1971-74, reading coord., East Wenatchee, Wash., 1974-77, adminstrv. asst., 1977-82, asst. supt. Sec. Parent Advisory Com., 1982-93; asst. supt. South Kitsap Sch. Dist., Port Orchard, Wash., 1993-95; curriculum dir. Clarkston Sch. Dist., Wash., 1995-96, asst. supt., 1996—; chair Wash. State Discover Card Scholarship, 1993—. Active Ctrl. Wash. Hosp. Bd., 1991-93, Ctrl. Wash. Hosp. Found. Bd., 1993—. Mem. Assn. Supervision and Curriculum Devel. (review coun. 1993-99), Wash. State Assn. Supervision and Curriculum Devel. (bd. dirs. 1986-89, pres. elect 1989-90, pres. 1990-91, Educator of Yr. 1981), NEA, Wash. Assn. Sch. Adminstrs. (bd. dirs., chmn. curriculum and instrn. Job-Alike, profl. devel. com., Project Leadership, pres. elect 1986-87, pres. 1987-88, leadership award, 1986, award of merit, 1992, Exec. Educator 100 1988, 93, chmn. WASA 21st century scholarship com. 1988—, leadership acad. 1993), Am. Assn. Sch. Adminstrs. (resolutions com. 1988-89, com. for advancement of sch. adminstrs. 1989-92), East Wenatchee C. of C. (bd. dirs. 1990-93, chair edn. com. 1990-91), Delta Kappa Gamma (pres. 1982-84), Phi Delta Kappa, Phi Kappa Phi. Named Eastmont Tchr. of the Yr., 1973-74. Office: Clarkston Sch Dist 847 5th St PO Box 70 Clarkston WA 99403-0070

JOHNSON, MICHAEL EDWARD, communication consultant, magician; b. Escondido, Calif., Jan. 14, 1959; s. Harold W. and Joan C. (Donkin) J.; m. Cynthia Lee Tunget, Sept. 3, 1994. AA in Liberal Scis., Palomar Coll., San Marcos, Calif., 1979; BA in Speech Comm., San Diego State U., 1981. Journalist cons. Aztec Shops Ltd., San Diego, 1979-83; mktg. rep. Commuter Computer, San Diego, 1984-86; ridesharing coord. Assn. Monterey Bay Area Govts., Monterey, Calif., 1986-89; editor Paul Kagan Assocs., Inc., Carmel, Calif., 1989-91; account exec. Commuter Computer, San Diego, 1991-92; pub. info. specialist Air Pollution Control Dist., San Diego, 1992-93; pres. Michael E. Johnson & Assocs., San Diego, 1993—; chmn. Telecommuting Strategic Planning team, San Diego, 1994; vice chair Commute Mgmt. Adv. Com., Sacramento, 1989. Editor jour. The Astrophile, 1995-97; editor newsletters Autograph Rsch., 1991—, Space Autograph News, 1993—, Celebrity Home Adress Newsletter, 1995—. Recipient Bronze medal Aviacion y Espacio, 1996, 1st place high jump Mt. San Antonio Relays, 1979. Mem. Soc. Am. Magicians, Universal Autograph Collectors Club. Office: Michael E Johnson & Assocs 862 Thomas Ave San Diego CA 92109-3940

JOHNSON, MILDRED GRACE MASH, investment company executive; b. Castle Rock, Wash., Mar. 3, 1922; d. Percival and Hilda C. (Nyberg) M.; widowed, 1988; children: John, Joy, Judy, Chris, Steven. Student, U. Wash. V.p. Johnson Constrn. Co., Seattle, 1950-58, pres., 1988-91; v.p. Johnson Investment Co., Seattle, 1950-58, pres., 1988—. Deacon U. Presbyn. Ch., Seattle, 1981—. Mem. Am. Bus. Women's Assn. (v.p. 1979-89, Woman of Yr. 1981), Apt. Assn., Master Builders, Daus. Nile, Order of Ea. Star. Republican. Home: 3812 E Mcgilvra St Seattle WA 98112-2427

JOHNSON, MORGAN BURTON, artist, writer; b. Santa Monica, Calif., Nov. 25, 1952; s. Arnold and Roma (Burton) J. BA in Psychology, U. Calif., San Diego, 1974; Cert. Fgn. Studies, Lycee du Universite, Dijon, France, 1968. Mgr. Coronet Stores, Las Vegas, Nev., 1975; mgr., chef Diver's Cove Restaurant, Long Beach, Calif., 1977-80; prodn. control asst. Century Plastics, Compton, Calif., 1980; prodn. supr. Analytichem Internat., Harbor City, Calif., 1980-81; sr. planner Sci. Mfg./Am. Hosp., Emeryville, Calif., 1982-85; materials mgr. Applied Biosys. (Perkin-Elmer), Foster City, Calif., 1985-90; owner, pres. Two Bears Restoration, 1990—. Exhibited in group shows at Medford (Oreg.) Ctr., 1993, Mills House Art Gallery, Garden Grove, Calif., 1979, San Bernardino Mus. Art, 1980-81, Calif. Poly. State U., San Luis Obispo, 1985, West Coast Biennial, Pacific Grove Art Ctr., 1985, Cunningham Meml. Art Show, Bakersfield, Calif., 1985, The Rogue Gallery, Medford, 1984, 85, 90, 91, C. Erickson Gallery, Half Moon Bay, Calif., 1986-90, Britt Music Festival, Jacksonville, Oreg., 1994; solo shows include Daleo Farms, Sams Valley, Oreg., 1995, Cache Salon, Walnut Creek, 1996, First Congl. Ch., Long Beach, 1996; included in pvt. collections; author: Trees of Other Colors, 1994, Condemned to a Life of Painting Pretty Pictures, 1994, Circle of the White Buffalo, 1996. Mem. So. Oreg. Arts Coun., Medford, 1990—, San Francisco Artist's Coop, 1980-83; fin. sec. Long Beach Art Assn., 1978-79; hanging com. mem. San Diego Art Inst., 1974-76. Recipient 1st prize Recreation and Parks Dept., L.A., 1965, 66, Long Beach Art Assn., 1977, 3d pl. award Downey Mus. Art. Home and Office: 4521 Beagle Rd White City OR 97503-9590

JOHNSON, P. ANNA, publishing executive; b. Niagara Falls, N.Y., July 18, 1938; d. Walter Sherman and Laura Ann (Wiseman) J.; children: Arlo Eugene Rodieck, Jorma Leonard Rodieck. BA, Colby Coll., 1960; postgrad., Nat. Art Sch., Sydney, Australia, 1963-64, George Washington U., 1983. Counselor Boston Ctr. for Blind Children, 1960-61; dance tchr. Pennshurst Girls High Sch., Sydney, 1962; rsch. asst. Sydney U., 1963; artist, potter Sydney, 1966-78; pub. Open Hand Pub. Inc., Seattle, 1981-83, Washington, 1983-88, Seattle, 1988—; bd. dirs. Multicultural Pubs. Exch., Madison Wis., Book Pubs. N.W., 1991-93. Pub., editor: Habari Gani? What's the News, 1992; pub.: The Black West, 1985, High Tide of Black Resistance, 1994, Stone on Stone/Piedra sobre Piedra, 1994. Bd. dirs. Kinma Sch., Sydney, 1974-78; sec. Unemployed and Poverty Action Coun., Washington, 1984-87. Grantee Nat. Coun. for Arts, Australia, 1975, Nat. Endowment for the Arts, 1994. Office: Open Hand Pub Inc PO Box 22048 Seattle WA 98122-0048

JOHNSON, PAM, newspaper editor. Mng. editor Ariz. Republic, Phoenix. Office: Ariz Republic PO Box 1950 Phoenix AZ 85001

JOHNSON, PETER FINK, prosthodontist, educator, consultant; b. Richmond, Va., July 30, 1945; s. Joel Benjamine and Emma Elizabeth (Fink) J.; m. Marie Bernadette Betts, Oct. 29, 1988; 1 child, Neil Wesley. AB, Princeton U., 1967; DMD, U. Pa., 1971; cert. in prosthodontics, U. So. Calif., 1977. Diplomate Am. Bd. Prosthodontists. Commd. 1st lt. USN, 1971, advanced through grades to capt., 1987; dir. Area Dental Lab. USN, San Diego, 1986-91; ret., 1991; pvt. practice, La Mesa, Calif., 1991—; former asst. prof. Naval Dental Sch., Bethesda, Md.; professorial lectr. Georgetown U., Washington, 1982-87; asst. prof. U. So. Calif. Sch. Dentistry, L.A., 1988-96, assoc. prof., 1996—. Contbr. articles to dental jours. Fellow Am. Coll. Prosthodontists (bd. dirs. 1988—, pres. 1993-94), Internat. Coll. Prosthodontists, Internat. Coll. Dentists; mem. ADA, Calif. Dental Assn., Pacific Coast Soc. Prosthodontists, Omicron Kappa Upsilon. Office: Ste 1-110 5565 Grossmont Center Dr La Mesa CA 91942-3020

JOHNSON, PHILIP LESLIE, lawyer; b. Beloit, Wis., Jan. 24, 1939; s. James Philip and Christabel (Williams) J.; m. Kathleen Rose Westover, May 12, 1979; children: Celeste Marie, Nicole Michelle. AB, Princeton U., 1961; JD, U. South Calif., 1973. Bar: Calif. 1973, U.S. Ct. Appeals (9th cir.) 1975, U.S. Ct. of Military Appeals, 1978, U.S. Supreme Ct. 1980. Pilot U.S. Marine Corps., 1961-70; assoc. Law Office Wm. G. Tucker, L.A., 1973-78; ptnr. Engstrom, Lipscomb & Lack, L.A., 1978-92, Johnson & Nelson, L.A., 1992-93, Lillick & Charles, Long Beach, Calif., 1993—; chmn. aerospace law com. Def. Rsch. Inst. Contbr. articles to profl. jours. Pres., bd. dirs. U. So. Calif. Legion Lex, 1992-93; chmn. com. to nom. alumni trustees Princeton U., mem. alumni coun. Mem. ABA, (aviation & space law com., torts & ins. practice section), Calif. State Bar Ct. (judge pro tem. 1990-95), Princeton Club (So. Calif., bd. dirs.). Home: 5340 Valley View Rd Rancho Palos CA

90275-5089 Office: Lillick & Charles One World Trade Ctr # 950 Long Beach CA 90831

JOHNSON, QULAN ADRIAN, software engineer; b. Great Falls, Mont., Sept. 17, 1942; s. Raymond Eugene and Bertha Marie (Nagengast) J.; m. Helen Louise Pocha, July 24, 1965; children—Brenda Marie, Douglas Paul, Scot Paul, Mathew James. B.A. in Psychology, Coll. Gt. Falls, 1964. Lead operator 1st Computer Corp., Helena, Mont., 1966-67; v.p., sec.-treas. Computer Corp. of Mt., Great Falls, 1967-76, dir., 1971-76; sr. systems analyst Mont. Dept. Revenue, Helena, 1976-78; software engr. Mont. Systems Devel. Co., Helena, 1978-80; programmer/analyst III info. systems div. Mont. Dept. Adminstrn., Helena, 1980-82; systems analyst centralized services Dept. Social and Rehab. Services State of Mont., 1982-87, systems and programming mgr. info systems, Blue Cross and Blue Shield of Montana, Helena. Mem. World Future Soc., Mensa, Assn. Info. Tech. Profls. Home: 2231 8th Ave Helena MT 59601-4841 Office: Blue Cross & Blue Shield Info Systems 404 Fuller Ave Helena MT 59601-5006

JOHNSON, RANDALL DAVID (RANDY JOHNSON), professional baseball player; b. Walnut Creek, Calif., Sept. 10, 1963. Student, U. So. Calif. With Montreal (Can.) Expos, 1985-89; pitcher Seattle Mariners, 1989—. Named to All-Star Team, 1990, 93-95; recipient Cy Young award, 1995; named Pitcher of Yr. Sporting News, 1995; Am. League strikeout leader, 1995. Office: Seattle Mariners 411 1st Ave S PO Box 4100 Seattle WA 98104-2860*

JOHNSON, RAYMOND BRUCE, medical educator; b. Sheridan, Wyo., Aug. 25, 1946; s. Charles Raymond and Dorothy Alberta (Fowler) J.; m. Judith Elaine Fisher, Aug. 31, 1968; children: Kristi, Erica. BS, Chadron State Coll., 1968; B of Med. Sci., Emory U., 1973. Lic. physician asst., Wyo. Med. tech. intern. St. John's Hosp., Rapid City, S.D., 1968-69, med. technologist, 1968-70, lab. supr., 1969-70; physician asst. Dr. Mary Fisher Clinic, Pagosa Springs, Colo., 1973-79; asst. prof. family practice, asst. dir. adminstrn. affairs family practice residency program U. Wyo., Casper, 1979—; mem. adv. bd. Wyo. Bd. Medicine, 1980-94; acting dir. Area Health Edn. Ctr., Wyo., 1994—. Contbr. articles to profl. jours. Coroner Archuleta County, Pagosa Springs, 1978-79. Recipient Hernan Alvarez Meml. award Wyo. Heart Assn., 1987; named EMS Profl. of Decade 1980-90 Wyo. Office Emergency Med. Svcs. Fellow Am. Acad. Physician Assts. (Nat. Phys. Asst. of Yr. 1987, profl. practice coun. 1987-94), Wyo. Assn. of Physician Assts. (Physician Asst. of Yr. 1984, 87, pres. 1985-86, v.p. 1983-84, sec. 1982-83). Home: 4036 Bretton Casper WY 82609 Office: U Wyo Family Practice Residency 1522 E A St Casper WY 82601-2217

JOHNSON, RICHARD GREENE, physician, psychiatrist, psychoanalyst; b. Louisville, June 3, 1921; s. Greene Johnson and Anne Wood Stout; m. Agnes Campbell Johnson, Nov. 2, 1945; children: Carole, Richard Jr., Craig, Holly. Student, Centre Coll. Ky.; BA, U. Louisville, 1943, MD, 1946; PhD, So. Calif. Psychoanalytic Inst., 1956. Diplomate Am. Bd. Psychiatry and Neurology. Rotating internship Met. Hosp. N.Y.C. Dept. Hosp., 1946-47; residency Emory U./Walter Reed Army Hosp.; pvt. practice, 1955—; clin. faculty dept. psychiatry UCLA, 1954—; asst. clin. prof. dept. psychiatry UCLA; cons. dept. dermatology UCLA; organizer, med. dir., chmn. bd. dirs. Westwood Psychiatric Hosp., 1959-70; organizer Mental Health Clinic Westwood Cmty. Meth. Ch., 1955; cons. LA County Dept. Mental Health, 1968-73, LA Protestant Cmty. Svcs., 1957-73; area chmn. Acad. of Religion and Mental Health; mem. rsch. com. Nat. Assn. Psychiatric Hosps., 1964. Capt. U.S. Army, 1948-54. Mem. L.A. County Med. Assn. (pres. sect. on psychiatry com. on mental health and clergy), So. Calif. Psychiat. Soc. (pres. 1980, Disting. Svc. award 1990), Calif. Psychiat. Assn., Am. Group Psychotherapy Assn., Am. Psychiat. Assn., Am. Psychoanalytic Assn. Republican. Office: 12301 Wilshire Blvd Ste 310 Los Angeles CA 90025-1023

JOHNSON, RICHARD KARL, hospitality company executive; b. Gaylord, Minn., May 27, 1947; s. Karl S. and Mildred (Tollefson) J.; m. Eva Margaret Wick, Oct. 12, 1973; children: Michelle, Richard, Ryan. BA, Gustavus Adolphus U., St. Peter, Minn., 1969. Gen. mgr. Green Giant Restaurants, Inc., Mpls., 1969-71, Mpls. Elks Club, Mpls., 1971-73; dir. concept devel. Internat. Multifoods, Mpls., 1972-75; v.p. concept devel. A&WFood Svcs. Can., North Vancouver, B.C., 1975-81; dir. food and beverages Ramada, Reno, 1981-82; pres., owner R.K. Johnson & Assoc., Reno, 1981—; owner D.J. Mgmt., 1990—; asst. gen. mgr. Gold Dust West Casino, Reno, 1983-85; gen. mgr. P&M Corp., Reno, 1985-86; v.p. ops. C.P.S.W. Inc., Reno and Tempe, Ariz., 1986-87, Lincoln Fairview, Reno, 1987-89; v.p. corp. affairs Myers Realty, 1991—. Mem. Aircraft Owners and Pilots Assn., Nat. Restaurant Assn., Nev. Realtor, Elks Club. Lutheran. Home and Office: RK Johnson & Assoc 825 Meadow Springs Dr Reno NV 89509-5913

JOHNSON, RICHARD VERNON, artist, educator; b. Glenwood, Minn., Sept. 21, 1905; s. Benjamin and Ida Josephine (Thompson) J.; m. Bertha Maude Abel, Sept. 6, 1930 (dec. Mar. 1970); m. Dorothy Alice Baldwin, Apr. 18, 1987. Student, Univ. Mont., 1927; cert. in Aircraft Engring., Calif. Tech., Douglas Aircraft, Long Beach, Calif., 1945. Cert. tchr., Calif.; lic. pvt. pilot. Advt. illustrator Foster and Klieser, Long Beach, 1930-40, pictorial painter, 1946-52; art tchr. Orange Coast Coll., Costa Mesa, 1951-76; founding faculty Costa Mesa (Calif.) C.C., 1976-82; retired, 1982; freelance advt. illustrator, N.Y.C., 1940-41; ptnr., art supr. Assoc. Outdoor, Long Beach, 1952-60; artist, tchr. Traditional Artists' Guild, Paramount, Calif. Exhibited one-man and group shows; works represented in permanent collection Long Beach Naval Sta., Superstition Mt. Hist. Mus., Apache Junction, Ariz., Sanctuary Grace United Meth. Ch., Long Beach.; patentee in field. With USAF, 1942-45. Recipient Best of Show, Crescent City Hall Dedication, others. Mem. Laguna Beach Art Assn. (life), Am. Water Color Assn., Pelican Bay Art Assn. Republican. Home: 849 Brookhaven Dr Brookings OR 97415

JOHNSON, ROBERT HERSEL, journalist; b. Colorado City, Tex., May 28, 1923; s. Robert Hersel and Leah (Sikes) J.; m. Luise Putcamp, Jr., Feb. 24, 1945; children: Robert Hersel, III, Luise Robin, Jan Leah, Stephanie Neale, Jennifer Anne, Ann Tapia. B.S. in Journalism, So. Methodist U., 1947. Reporter Phoenix Gazette, 1940-42; asst. sports editor Ariz. Republic, Phoenix, 1942-43; newscast writer Sta. KOY, Phoenix, 1943; reporter Dallas Times-Herald, 1946; with AP, 1946-88, Utah-Idaho bur. chief, 1954-59, Ind. bur. chief, 1959-62, Tex. bur. chief, 1962-69, gen. sports editor, 1969-73, mng. editor, 1973-77, asst. gen. mgr., spl. asst. to pres., 1977-84, N.Mex. bureau chief, 1984-88; prof. journalism N.Mex. State U., Las Cruces, 1988, U. N.Mex., Albuquerque, 1989; exec. dir. N.Mex. Found. for Open Govt., Albuquerque, 1989—; mem. Newspaper Readership Coun., 1977-82. Mem. N. Mex. Hist. Records Adv. Bd., 1993—. Capt. USMCR, 1943-46, 51-52. Home: 2740 Tramway Cir NE Albuquerque NM 87122-1205 *The kind of journalism that is likely to bring about change for the better is journalism that is painfully honest, painfully clear, that illuminates large issues with small details, and in which the reporter is not a participant or an advocate but a dispassionate observer who keeps his own emotions at bay until the story is told.*

JOHNSON, ROBERT LELAND, lawyer; b. Denver, May 1, 1933; m. Pamela Gay Stearns, June 6, 1964; children: Mary Morris (dec.), Anthony Morris. BA, Yale U., 1955; JD, U. Denver, 1958, BA in English, 1962. Bar: Colo. 1959, U.S. Dist. Ct. Colo. 1959, U.S. Ct. Appeals (10th cir.), 1959, U.S. Supreme Ct. 1959. Pvt. practice law Denver, 1962—; asst. regional svcs. counsel region 8 U.S. Gen. Svcs. Adminstrn.; law clk. Colo. Supreme Ct.; lectr. U. Colo., 1978-83. Author: The Newspaper Accounts of B.F. Wright, Esq., and Others of Louisa County, Iowa, 1967, Trial Handbook for Colorado Torts Lawyers, 1967, Matrimonial Practice in Colorado Courts, 1969, The American Heritage of James Norman Hall, 1970, Colorado Mechanic's Liens, 1970, A Geneaological Excursion Through Historic Philadelphia, 1976 (with Pamela Gay Johnson) A Mother's Love, 1977, Letters to Glenn Doman: A Story on Enriched and Accelerated Childhood Development, 1980, Super Babies, 1982, Super Kids & Their Parents, 1986, The Ancestry of Anthony Morris Johnson, vols. 1 and 2, 1989, vol. 3, 1991, vol. 4, 1994, vol. 5, 1995, vol. 6, 1996, Corriegenda to Ancestry of Anthony Morris Johnson vol. 3, 1991, The King Arthur Book or Second Corriegenda to Supplement to Ancestry of Anthony Morris Johnson vol. 3, 1991. Mem. ABA, Am. Judicature Soc., Colo. Trial Lawyers Assn., Denver Bar Assn. (legal aid and pub. defender com., family law com., interprofl. com.). Democrat. Mem. Soc. of Friends. Home: 9751 Melody Dr Denver CO 80221 Office: 705 W 8th Ave Denver CO 80204-4329

JOHNSON, RODNEY DALE, law enforcement officer, photographer; b. Montebello, Calif., May 14, 1944; s. Albert Gottfreid and Maxine Elliot (Rogers) J.; m. Karen Rae Van Antwerp, May 18, 1968; 1 child, Tiffany Nicole. AA, Ela Community Coll., 1973; postgrad. Law Enforcement Spl., FBI, Acad., 1976; BA, U. of La Verne, 1978. Cert. tchr. police sci., Calif. Dep., Los Angeles County Sheriff, 1969-75, dep. IV, 1976-78, sgt., 1978—; fire arms inst., Hacienda Heights, Calif., 1975-94; photographer Weddings and Portraits, 1983-94; photography instr., Hacienda Heights, 1983-94; pres. Wheelhouse Enterprises, Inc., Whittier, 1971-86; instr. State Sheriff's Civil Procedural Sch. Los Medanos Coll., Concord, Calif., 1985-88. Creator and actor, Cap'n Andy, 1973-80; song writer for Cap'n Andy theme, 1972. Sgt. USMC, 1965-69, Vietnam, master gunnery sgt. Res., 1969-94, ret.; intelligence chief, Persian Gulf. Recipient Service award Trinity Broadcasting Network, 1979. Mem. Profl. Peace Officers Assn., Sheriff's Relief Assn., Assoc. Photographers Internat., Marine Corps. Intelligence Assn., Inc. Republican. Mem. Assembly of God. Club: Faithbuilders (pres. 1981-87), (Pomona).

JOHNSON, RONALD DOUGLAS, business executive; b. Klamath Falls, Oreg., Sept. 16, 1949; s. Clifford Douglas and Anna Elizabeth (Fine) J.; m. Wendi Susan Brown, Aug. 20, 1972; children: Bryan Douglas, Timothy Christopher, Michael Casey. BA in Polit. Sci., Wash. State U., 1975, MA in Pub. Adminstrn., 1976, MA in Agrl. Econs., 1981. Rsch. asst. Wash. Water Rsch. Ctr., Pullman, 1974-75; mgmt. trainee Potlatch Corp., 1971-74; intern Gov. Daniel J. Evans, Olympia, Wash., 1975; rsch. asst. Wash. State U., Pullman, 1976-79; asst. mgr. Reardan Grain Gowers Assn., Wash., 1980-82; gen. mgr. Bean Growers Warehouse Assn., Twin Falls, Idaho, 1982-84; dry bean group mgr. Rogers NK Seed Co., Boise, Idaho, 1984-95; owner Agraplus, Inc., 1995—; cons. Rogers Seed Co., Basic Am. Foods, Sunspiced Inc., 1994—; bd. dirs. Consolidated Agrl. Inc., Twin Falls. With U.S. Army, 1968-70, Viet Nam. Commn. Econ. Assistance grantee Oreg. State U., 1978, Washington Water Rsch. grantee, Wash. State U., 1976. Home: 4190 N Jones Ave Boise ID 83704-2700 Office: Rogers Seed Co 600 N Armstrong Pl Boise ID 83704

JOHNSON, ROY RAGNAR, electrical engineer; b. Chgo., Jan. 23, 1932; s. Ragnar Anders and Ann Viktoria (Lundquist) J.; m. Martha Ann Mattson, June 21, 1963; children: Linnea Marit, Kaisa Ann. B.S. in Elec. Engring, U. Minn., 1954, M.S., 1956, Ph.D., 1959. Research fellow U. Minn., 1957-59; from rsch. engr. to sr. basic rsch. scientist Boeing Sci. Research Labs., Seattle, 1959-72; prin. scientist KMS Fusion, Inc., Ann Arbor, Mich., 1972-74; dir. fusion expts. KMS Fusion, Inc., 1974-78, tech. dir., 1978-91, dept. head for fusion and plasmas, 1985-88; tech. dir. Innovation Assocs., Inc., Ann Arbor, 1992; inertial confinement fusion classification/records mgr. Lawrence Livermore Nat. Lab., 1992—; vis. lectr. U. Wash., Seattle, 1959-60; vis. scientist Royal Inst. Tech., Stockholm, 1963-64; cons. Dept. Edn., Washington, 1995. Author: Nonlinear Effects in Plasmas, 1969, Plasma Physics, 1977, Research Trends in Physics, 1992; contbr. articles to profl. pubis.; patentee in field. Bd. advisors Rose-Hulman Inst. Tech., 1982—. Decorated chevalier Order of St. George; comdr. Order of Holy Cross of Jerusalem. Fellow Am. Phys. Soc.; mem. AAAS, AIAA, IEEE (life), Nuclear Plasma Scis. Soc. of IEEE (exec. com. 1972-75), N.Y. Acad. Scis., Am. Def. Preparedness Assn., Assn. of Old Crows, Vasa Order Am., Am. Swedish Inst., Torpar Riddar Orden, Swedish Pioneer Hist. Soc., Swedish Coun. Am., Detroit Swedish Coun., Swedish Club of Detroit, Swedish Am. Hist. Soc., Eta Kappa Nu, Gamma Alpha. Lutheran. Home: 1141 Concannon Blvd Livermore CA 94550-6451 Office: Livermore Nat Lab PO Box 808 Livermore CA 94551-0808

JOHNSON, RUPERT HARRIS, finance company executive. Grad., Washington and Lee U. With Franklin Resources, Inc., San Mateo, Calif., 1965—, exec. v.p., chief investment officer, dir.; sr. v.p., asst. sec. Franklin Templeton Distbrs., Inc.; pres. Franklin Advisers, Inc.; mem. exec. com., bd. govs. Investment Co. Inst.; trustee Santa Clara U., Washington and Lee U.; chmn. bd. dirs. Franklin Mgmt., Inc.; exec. v.p., sr. investment officer Franklin Trust Co.; dir. various Franklin Templeton funds; portfolio mgr. Franklin DynaTech Fund. With USMC. Mem. Nat. Assn. Securities Dealers (dist. conduct com.). Office: Franklin Resources Inc 777 Mariners Island Blvd San Mateo CA 94404

JOHNSON, RUTH EILEEN, dietitian, researcher, home economics educator; b. Hot Springs, S.D., July 23, 1927; d. George Ernest and Eva Mae Lebo; m. James H. Johnson Jr., Aug. 7, 1948; children: Kenneth L., Gary S. BS, U. Nebr., 1947, postgrad., 1950-51; MA, Calif. State U., 1971. Rsch. asst. food and nutrition rsch. dept. U. Nebr., Lincoln, 1947-51; rsch. technician Scripps Coll., Claremont, Calif., 1969; instr., collaborating investigator men's phys. edn. Calif. State U.-Long Beach, 1969-71, instr. home econs., 1970-72; asst. prof. home econs. Calif. State U.-Los Angeles, 1971-75; chief nutritionist Mr. Fit Ctr., U. So. Calif. Sch. Medicine, 1974-79; sr. nutritionist, clin. coord. atherosclerosis rsch. U. So. Calif. Sch. Medicine, 1979-87, asst. clin. prof. medicine, 1987—; cons. in field. Author, co-author numerous text and reference materials. Editor Calif. Home Economist, 1964-75. Founding com. mem. Meals on Wheels, Whittier, Calif., 1969; Calif. Congress Parents and Tchrs., 1961-72; pres. Lowell High Sch., 1968-69; Dental health chmn. Macy and Starbuck Schs., 1962-68. Mem. Am. Heart Assn. Nat. Ctr. mem. corp. rel. review com., chair product review panel, (fellow council of epidemiology, mem. adv. com. and orgn., planning and devel. com., Los Angeles Affiliate Vol. of Yr. 1981-82, Heart of Gold award, 1991, Nat. Ctr. Meritorious Achievement award 1995), Am. Assn. Family and Consumer Scientists, Calif. Assn. Assn. Family and Consumer Scientists (Outstanding Home Economist 1979, 83), Am. Dietetics Assn., Calif. Dietetics Assn., Nutrition Today Soc. Am. Soc. Testing and Materials, Greater Los Angeles Nutrition Council, Calif. Nutrition Council, Orange County Nutrition Council, AAUW (Las Distinguidas award 1985), Iota Sigma Pi, Phi Delta Gamma, Kappa Omicron Nu. Avocations: needlepoint, piano, bridge, travel. Home: 10110 Pounds Ave Whittier CA 90603-1649

JOHNSON, RUTH FLOYD, university educator, consultant; b. Plateau, Ala., Apr. 19, 1935; d. Nathan Daniel and Ora Anna (Ellis) Floyd; children: Anthony, Walter, Camille. Student, Tuskegee Inst., 1951-53; BS in History, Bowie (Md.) State U., 1970; MEd in Counseling, U. Md., 1977; PhD in Human Svcs. Adminstrn., Univ. for Humanistic Studies, San Diego, 1982. Cert. tchr., counselor. Radio personality Sta. WMOZ, 1953-56; owner, dir. Azalea Sch. Dance, 1954-56; numerous posts for fed. govt., 1957-69; tchr., adminstr. Pub. Schs. of Prince George's County, Md., 1970-78; tchr.-counselor Dunbar S.T.A.Y. Sch., Washington, 1974-75; instr. child and youth study divsn. U. Md., 1977-78; CEO Diametron Corp., 1979-81; tchr. L.A. Unified Sch. Dist., 1980-82, Pasadena (Calif.) Unified Sch. Dist., 1982-83, Rialto (Calif.) Unified Sch. Dist., 1984—; profl. devel. coord. Calif. State Polytech. U., 1995—. Author: Remediating Mass Poverty: Development of a Model Program, 1982, Pep Squad handbook, 1991, (with others: Government/Contemporary Issues: A Curriculum Guide, 1976. Active PTAs; mem. organizing com. Peppermill Village Civic Assn., 1966; vol. Boy Scouts Am., 1968-72, Sr. Citizens of Prince George's County, 1974-76; bd. dirs.Mill Point Improvement Assn., 1975-78, Combined Communities in Action, 1976-78; mem. Prince George's County Hosp. Commn., 1978; mem. Altadena Town Coun., 1983; founder Rialto Freedom and Cultural Soc., 1988; mem. Calif. 36th Dist. Bicentennial Adv. Com., 1989; mem. exec. com. Rialto Police/Community Rels. Team, 1993. Recipient Outstanding Svc. to Children and Yourh award Md. Congress PTA, 1969, Services to Boy Scouts Am. award, 1969, Svcs. to Sr. Citizens award, 1975, Community Svc. award Rialto Freedom and Cultural Soc., 1993, others. Mem. NEA, NAACP, Nat. Assn. Univ. Women, Nat. Coun. Negro Women, Zeta Phi Beta, Gamma Phi Delta. Home: PO Box 1946 Rialto CA 92377-1946

JOHNSON, STEWART WILLARD, civil engineer; b. Mitchell, S.D., Aug. 17, 1933; s. James Elmer Johnson and Grace Mahala (Erwin) Johnson Parsons; m. Mary Anis Giddings, June 24, 1956; children: Janelle Chiemi, Gregory Stewart, Eric Willard. BSCE, S.D. State U., 1956; BA in Bus. Adminstrn. and Polit. Sci., U. Md., 1960; MSCE, PhD, U. Ill., 1964. Registered profl. engr., Ohio. Commd. 2d lt. USAF, 1956, advanced through grades to lt. col.; prof. mechs. and civil engring. Air Force Inst. Tech. USAF, Dayton, Ohio, 1964-75; dir. civil engring. USAF, Seoul, Republic of Korea, 1976-77; chief civil engring. research div. USAF, Kirtland AFB, N.Mex., 1977-80; ret. USAF, 1980; prin. engr. BDM Corp., Albuquerque, 1980-94, Johnson and Assocs., Albuquerque, 1994—; cons. in site surveys, found. design, constrn. of ground stas. for satellite comm. sys., 1992—; cons. space sci. and lunar basing NASA, U. N.Mex., N.Mex. State U., Los Alamos Nat. Labs., 1986—; adj. prof. civil engring. U. N.Mex., 1987—; prin. investigator devel. concepts for lunar astron. obs. U. N.Mex., N.Mex. State U., NASA, 1987—; tech. chmn. Space '88, Space '90, Space '94 and Space '96 Internat. Confs., Albuquerque; vis. lectr. Internat. Space U., Japan, 1992, Huntsville, Ala., 1993, Barcelona, Spain, 1994, Stockholm, 1995; mem. panel on siting lunar base European Space Agy., 1994; gen. chair Space 96 and RCEII Conf., Albuquerque, 1996. Editor Engineering, Construction, and Operations in Space, I, 1988. II, 90, V, 96; contbr. articles to profl. jours. Pres. ch. coun. Ch. of Good Shepherd United Ch. of Christ, Albuquerque, 1983-85, chmn. bd. deacons, 1991-93, moderator, 1996—; S.W. Conf. (United Ch. Christ) del. to Gen. Synod XIX, St. Louis, 1993, Gen. Synod XX, Oakland, Calif., 1995; trustee Lunar Geotech. Inst., 1990—; mem. adv. bd. Lab. for Extraterrestrial Structures Rsch., Rutgers U., 1990—. Fellow Nat. Acad. Scis. NRC, 1970-71; recipient World Bar Assn. Space Humanitarian award, 1996. Mem. AIAA (space logistics com., Engr. of Yr. region IV 1990), ASCE (chmn. exec. com. aerospace divsn. 1979, tech. activities com. 1984, chmn. com space engring. and constrn. 1987—, mem. nat. space policy com. 1988—, chmn. 1990—, Outstanding News Corr. award 1981, Aerospace Scis. and Tech. Applications award 1985, 90, Edmund Friedman Profl. Recognition award 1989), Soc. Am. Mil. Engrs., Am. Geophys. Union, Soc. Am. Milit. Engrs., Sigma Xi, Pi Sigma Alpha. Republican. Mem. United Ch. of Christ.

JOHNSON, SYLVIA SUE, university administrator, educator; b. Abiline, Tex., Aug. 10, 1940; d. SE Boyd and Margaret MacGillivray (Withington) Smith; m. William Ruel Johnson; children: Margaret Ruth, Laura Jane, Catherine Withington. BA, U. Calif., Riverside, 1962; postgrad., U. Hawaii, 1963. Elem. edn. credential, 1962. Mem. bd. regents U. Calif.; mem. steering com. Citizens Univ. Com., chmn., 1978-79; bd. dirs., charter mem. U. Calif.-Riverside Found., chmn. nominating com., 1983—; pres., bd. dirs. Friends of the Mission Inn, 1969-72, 73-76, Mission Inn Found., 1977—, Calif. Bapt. Coll. Citiznes Com., 1980—; bd. dirs. Riverside Comty. Hosp., 1980—, Riverside Jr. League, 1976-77, Nat. Charity League, 1984-85; mem. chancellors blue ribbon com., devel. com. Calif. Mus. Photography. Named Woman of Yr., State of Calif. Legislature, 1989, 91, Citizen of Yr., C. of C., 1989. Mem. U. Calif.-Riverside Alumni Assn. (bd. dirs. 1966-68, v.p. 1968-70).

JOHNSON, THOMAS EUGENE, biology educator; b. Denver, June 19, 1948; s. Albert L. Johnson and Barbara J. (Bickle) Lloyd; m. Victoria J. Simpson, Apr. 24, 1982; children: Ariel Rene, Paul Andrew, Katherine Elizabeth. BS, MIT, 1970; PhD, U. Wash., 1975. Research assoc. Cornell U., Ithaca, N.Y., 1975-77, U. Colo., Boulder, 1977-82; fellow Inst. Behavioral Genetics U. Colo., Denver, 1981-82; asst. prof. U. Calif., Irvine, 1982-88; assoc. prof. U. Colo., Boulder, 1988-96, prof., 1996—; organizer UCLA Symposium on Molecular Biology of Aging, 1989, Keystone Symposium on Molecular Biology of Aging, 1988, 91; chair Gordon Conf. on Biology on Aging, 1997. Editor: Handbook of the Biology of Aging; assoc. editor Jour. of Gerontology Biol. Sci. Grantee USPHS, Washington, 1978, 85, 88, 91, 92, 95, 96, NSF, Washington, 1982; USPHS fellow, 1977, AFAR, 1986, 87; recipient Busse award for biomed. gerontology, 1993, Nathan Shock award Gerontology Rsch. Ctr., 1995. Fellow Gerontology Soc. of Am. (chair biol. sci. 1991-92), Am. Fedn. for Aging Rsch.; mem. AAAS, Rsch. Soc. on Alcoholism, Genetics, Soc. Am., Am. Aging Assn. (bd. dirs. 1990-95), Nat. Inst. Health (biological and clin. aging rev. subcom. A 1992-96). Democrat. Unitarian. Office: U Colo Inst Behavioral Genetics PO Box 447 Boulder CO 80309-0447

JOHNSON, TINA, elementary education educator; b. Denver, Apr. 2, 1947; d. Ernest Harold and Hildegard (Kranefeld) J. BA, Trinity U., San Antonio, 1969; MA, U. Colo., 1980. Colo. profl. tchr. license. Tchr. Jefferson County Schs., Arvada, Colo., 1969—; mem. master tchr. program Jefferson County Schs., Arvada, 1982-85, mem. peer coaching program, 1984-85, mentor tchr. induction program, 1996; off campus coll. instr. Colo. State U., Arvada, 1992—. Co-author: Around the World in 180 School Days, 1994, Geography Too, 1994. Active Holy Cross Luth. Ch., Wheatridge, Colo., 1958—. Recipient Honorable Mention Colo. Tchr. of Yr., Colo. Dept. Edn. and Colo. State Bd. Edn., 1985; Colo. Venture grantee Jefferson Found., 1990-91; Delta Kappa Action Rsch. grantee for geography, 1990-91. Mem. NEA, Colo. Edn. Assn., Jefferson County Edn. Assn., Colo. Geog. Alliance, Delta Kappa Gamma, Phi Delta Kappa. Home: 8255 Iris St Arvada CO 80005 Office: Weber Elem 8725 W 81st Pl Arvada CO 80005-2414

JOHNSON, TORRENCE VAINO, astronomer; b. Rockville Centre, N.Y., Dec. 1, 1944; s. Vaino Oliver and Priscilla Welch (Sneed) J.; m. Mary Eleanor Zachman, Mar. 31, 1967; children: Aaron Torrence, Eleanor Nancy. BS with honors, Washington U., St. Louis, 1966; PhD, Calif. Inst. Tech., 1970; Laurea Honoris Causa in Astronomy, U. Padua, Italy, 1997. Research assoc. Planetary Astronomy Lab., MIT, 1969-71; resident research assoc. NRC, Jet Propulsion Lab., Pasadena, 1971-73, sr. scientist, mem. tech. staff, 1973-74; group supr. Optical Astronomy Group, 1974-85, project scientist Project Galileo, 1977—, research scientist, 1980-81, sr. research scientist, 1981—; vis. assoc. prof. Calif. Inst. Tech., 1981-83; cons. Jet Propulsion Lab., Pasadena, 1971. NASA trainee Calif. Inst. Tech., 1966-69, Exceptional Svc. medal NASA, 1991; recipient Exceptional Achievement medal NASA, 1980, 81. Fellow Explorers Club, Am. Geophys. Union (pres. planetology sect. 1990-92); mem. AAAS, Am. Astron. Soc. (sec.-treas. divsn. planetary sci. 1977-80), Internat. Astron. Union, Planetary Soc. (founding mem.), Internat. Acad. Astronautics (corres.), Sigma Xi. Office: California Inst Tech 183-501 Jet Propulsion Lab 4800 Oak Grove Dr Pasadena CA 91109-8001 *A major Theme in my life has been curiosity. My parents encouraged this trait, as did a variety of schools around the United States, and I have been fortunate to be allowed to satisfy my curiosity professionally, and occasionally to get paid for it. To date, one of the greatest fullfillments in my life has been the opportunity to participate in the Voyager mission, which has opened our eyes to worlds which I had previously only glimpsed dimly, through earth bound telescopes as a boy and a young astronomer.*

JOHNSON, WALTER EARL, geophysicist; b. Denver, Dec. 16, 1942; s. Earl S. and Helen F. (Llewellyn) J.; Geophys. Engr., Colo. Sch. Mines, 1966; m. Ramey Kandice Kayes, Aug. 6, 1967; children—Gretchen, Roger, Aniela. Geophysicist, Pan. Am. Petroleum Corp., 1966-73; seismic processing supr. Amoco Prodn. Co., Denver, 1973-74, marine tech. supr., 1974-76, div. processing cons., 1976-79, geophys. supr. No. Thrust Belt, 1979-80; chief geophysicist Husky Oil Co., 1981-82, exploration mgr. Rocky Mountain and Gulf Coast div., 1982-84; geophys. mgr. ANR Prodn. Co., 1985—; pres. Sch. Lateral Ditch Co.; cons. engr. Bd. dirs. Rocky Mountain Residence, nursing home. Registered profl. engr., cert. geologist, Colo. Mem. Denver Geophys. Soc., Soc. Exploration Geophysicists. Republican. Baptist. Office: 600 17th St Ste 800 Denver CO 80202-5402

JOHNSON, WARREN LYLE, secondary education educator; b. Mpls., Oct. 14, 1939; s. Paul A. and Irene (Lazorik) Wilson; m. Lana-Jean Cole, June 24, 1967; 1 child, Kenneth Lee. BS, Ea. N.Mex., 1962; MA, Boston U., 1984; postgrad., Air War Coll., 1976; diploma, Def. Systems Coll., 1989; student, Royal Mil. Coll., Swindon, Eng., 1989. Polit. intern State of N.Mex., Santa Fe, 1962-63; commd. 2d lt. USAF, 1964, advanced through grades to major, 1976, ret., 1984; educator State of N.H., Concord, 1984-85; analyst U.S. Govt., Boston, 1985-86, U.S. Govt., U.S. Embassy, Bonn, Germany, 1986-88; reQ officer U.S. Govt., USAF Hqrs. Europe, 1988-90; educator Albuquerque Pub. Sch., 1991—; head negotiator U.S. Govt., Germany, 1986-90, with spl. projects, Washington, 1990; selected to work with Josephson Inst. of Ethics in Character Issues in Pub. Edn., 1994; established 1st U.S. Civil Air Patrol Cadet in Pub. Schs. in U.S., 1994. Editor concept paper. V.p. Shenandoah Neighborhood Assn., Albuquerque, 1991—; mem. Mayors Adv. Bd. ram, Albuquerque, 1991-92; vol. Mexi 10 Mutual Assistance Refugee Soc. Decorated Cross of Gallantry, Bronze Star, Meritorious Svc., Commendation medal; NAS grantee, 1993-94. Mem. Am. Polit. Sci. Soc., Ret. Officers Assn., U.S. Naval Inst. and Nimitz Mus., Air

Force Assn., Confederate Airforce, Vietnam Vets. Am. (state rep. 1986-94, v.p. 1994-95, state edn. chmn.), DAV, Masons (32d degree). Democrat. Lutheran.

JOHNSON, WAYNE EATON, writer, editor, former drama critic; b. Phoenix, May 9, 1930; s. Roscoe and Marion (Eaton) J.; children: Katherine, Jeffrey. BA, U. Colo., 1952; postgrad., Duke U., 1952-53; postgrad. (KLM polit. reporting fellow 1957), U. Vienna, Austria, 1955-56; MA, UCLA, 1957. Reporter Internat. News Service, Des Moines, 1958, Wheat Ridge (Colo.) Advocate, 1957, Pueblo (Colo.) Chieftain, 1959; reporter Denver Post, 1960, editorial writer, music critic, 1961-65; arts and entertainment editor Seattle Times, 1965-82, drama critic, 1980-92; instr. journalism Colo. Woman's Coll., 1962. Author: Show: A Concert Program for Actor and Orchestra, 1971, America! A Concert of American Images, Words and Music, 1973, From Where the Sun Now Stands: The Indian Experience, 1973; editor, co-pub.: Secrets of Warmth, 1992, Footprints on the Peaks, 1995, The Burgess Book of Lies, 1995. Served with CIC AUS, 1953-55, Korea. Home: 11303 Durland Pl NE Seattle WA 98125-5926

JOHNSON, WAYNE HAROLD, librarian, county official; b. El Paso, Tex., May 2, 1942; s. Earl Harold and Cathryn Louise (Greeno) J.; m. Patricia Ann Froedge, June 15, 1973; children: Meredith Jessica (dec.), Alexandra Noëlle Victoria. BS, Utah State U., 1968; MPA, U. Colo., 1970; MLS, U. Okla., 1972. Circulation libr. Utah State U., Logan, 1968, adminstrv. asst. libr., 1969; with rsch. dept. Okla. Mgmt. and Engring. Cons., Norman, 1972; chief adminstrv. svcs. Wyo. State Libr., Cheyenne, 1973-76, chief bus. officer libr. archives and hist. dept., 1976-78, state libr., 1978-89; county grants mgr. Laramie County, Wyo., 1989—. Trustee Bibliog. Ctr. for Rsch., Denver, pres., 1983, 84; mem. Cheyenne dist. Longs Park coun. Boy Scouts Am., 1982-86; active Cheyenne Frontier Days, 1975—; mem. admissions and allocation com. United Way, 1991-94; mem. Ho. of Reps., Wyo. Legislature, 1993—. Served with USCG, 1960-64. Mem. Aircraft Owners and Pilots Assn., Cheyenne C. of C. (chmn. transp. com. 1982, 83, military affairs com. 1994—), Am. Legion. Republican. Presbyterian. Club: No. Colo. Yacht. Lodges: Masons, Kiwanis (bd. dirs. 1986, 87). Office: 309 W 20th St Cheyenne WY 82001-3601

JOHNSON, WESLEY ORIN, statistics educator; b. Spokane, Wash., Apr. 27, 1948; s. Orin L. and Elizabeth (Carr) Johnson. BS, U. Wash., 1972; MS, Calif. State U., Hayward, 1974; PhD, U. Minn., 1979. Asst. prof., then assoc. prof. stats. U. Calif., Davis, 1979-93, prof., 1993—. Office: U Calif Divsn Stats Davis CA 95616

JOHNSON, WILLIAM HARRY, international management consultant; b. Ridley Park, Pa., Oct. 1, 1941; s. Harry Brown and Florence Lydia (Round) J.; m. Anna Marie Castellanos, Oct. 19, 1984. BS, Drexel U., Phila., 1963; MBA, Drexel U., 1967. Mgmt. exec. DuPont Co., Wilmington, Del., 1963-69; bus. analysis mgr. Imperial Chem. Ind., Wilmington, 1970-76; mgr. analysis and acquisitions Fluor Daniel Corp., Irvine, Calif., 1976-78; fin. analysis mgr. Alexander Proudfoot, Chgo., 1978-79; exec. v.p., chief fin. officer Sego Internat., Niagara Falls, Ont., Can., 1980-82; exec. v.p., gen. mgr. Sci. Mgmt. Corp., Basking Ridge, N.J., 1982-87; exec. mgr. McDonnell Douglas Corp., Long Beach, Calif., 1987—; bd. dirs. A.M.T. Inc., Pierrefonds, Que., Can., CRA, Inc., Clariton, Pa., Madden Assocs., Buffalo Grove, Ill., KABB Inc., El Segundo, Calif., Sego Internat., Productivity Cons., Inc., Montreal, Commonwealth Cos., London. Author: Explosives Distributors, 1967, Maintenance Productivity - It Can Be Achieved, 1988, Facilities Work Order Guide, 1989, Participative Management in Facilities Operations, 1991; contbr. articles to profl. jours. Mem. Rep. Nat. Com., Washington, El Segundo Residents Assn. Recipient Presdl. Achievement award, Rep. Nat. Com., 1988, Outstanding Achievement award, Sego Internat., 1981. Mem. Inst. Indsl. Engrs., Am. Mgmt. Assn., Nat. Productivity Assn. of Can. (dir. 1980-85), Nat. Assn. Accts., Nat. Petroleum Refinery Assn., Am. Mktg. Assn., Internat. Productivity Orgn., Drexel U. Alumni Assn. (bd. dirs.), Highlander Clan, Lions (Kowloon, Hong Kong), K & C Clans Assn. (Hong Kong), Internat. Bus. Assocs. (Sydney, Australia). Republican. Presbyterian. Home: 807 Hillcrest St El Segundo CA 90245-2025 Office: McDonnell Douglas Transport Aircraft (ONEC) 2401 E Wardlow Rd Long Beach CA 90807-5309

JOHNSON, WILLIAM HUGH, JR., hospital administrator; b. N.Y.C., Oct. 29, 1935; s. William H. and Florence P. (Seinsoth) J.; m. Gloria C. Stube, Jan. 23, 1960; children: Karen A., William H. III. B.A., Hofstra U., 1957; M.Ed., U. Hawaii, 1969. Commd. 2d lt. U.S. Army, 1957, advanced through grades to lt. col., 1972, health adminstr., world wide, 1957-77, health adminstr., world wide, ret., 1977; chief exec. officer U. N. Mex. Hosp., Albuquerque, 1977-96; asst. prof. U.S. Mil. Acad., West Point, N.Y., 1962-65; mem. clin. faculty U. Minn., Mpls., 1980-83; preceptor Ariz. State U., Tempe, 1982-83; pres. Albuquerque Area Hosp. Council, 1980; v.p. strategic alliances U. N.Mex. Health Scis. Ctr.; bd. dirs. Bank Am. of N.Mex., Tri West, Inc. Mem. exec. bd. Albuquerque Com. on Devel.; v.p. Vis. Nurse Svc., Albuquerque, 1979; pres. Magnifico Arts Fiesta; bd. dirs. Goodwill N.Mex.; bd. dirs. Albuqueque Conv. and Visitors Bur., mem. exec. com., 1994—. Decorated Army Commendation Medal with 2 oak leaf clusters, Order of Merit (Rep. of Vietnam), Legion of Merit. Mem. Am. Hosp. Assn. (governing bd. met. hosp. sect. 1982-86, chmn. com. AIDS, mem. regional policy bd. 1982-86, 88—), Am. Coll. Hosp. Adminstrs., Coun. Tchg. Hosps. (bd. dirs.), N.Mex. Hosp. Assn. (bd. dirs. 1983, chmn. 1995—), Nat. Assn. Pub. Hosps. (bd. dirs. Tri West Inc., Vita S.W.), Greater Albuquerque C. of C. (bd. dirs., econ. planning coun., v.p.), N.Mex. Assn. Commerce and Industry (treas.), Albuquerque Conv. and Visitors Bur. (bd. dirs.). Roman Catholic. Home: 7920 Sartan Way NE Albuquerque NM 87109-3128 Office: Univ N Mex Hosp 2211 Lomas Blvd NE Albuquerque NM 87106-2745

JOHNSON, WILLIAM LEWIS, information science eduator; b. Ft. Worth, June 8, 1957; s. Larry Claud and Rhoda Ann (Brown) J.; m. Kimberly Gallaway Hale, Jan. 2, 1982. AB in Linguistics summa cum laude, Princeton U., 1978; MS in Computer Sci., Yale U., 1980, PhD in Computer Sci., 1985. Rsch. scientist Info. Scis. Inst., U. So. Calif., Marina del Rey, 1985—, project leader, rsch. asst. prof., 1987-95, rsch. assoc. prof., 1995—; chmn. First Internat. Conf. on Autonomous Agts. Editor-in-chief Automated Software Engring.; contbr. numerous articles to profl. publs. Mem. Special Interest Group for Artificial Intelligence (chmn. 1995—conf. chair 7th Knowledge-Based Software Engring. Conf., also several program coms.), Soc. Artificial Intellingence in Edn. (exec. com., Soc. Artificial Intelligence in Edn. 93 tutorial/workshop chair-world conf. on artificial intelligence edn., also steering and program coms.), Am. Assn. for Artificial Intelligence (chair automating software design workshop, co-chair 1991 spring symposium on design composite systems, program com. AAAI-88);. Office: U So Calif Info Scis Inst 4676 Admiralty Way Marina Del Rey CA 90292-6601

JOHNSON, WILLIAM POTTER, newspaper publisher; b. Peoria, Ill., May 4, 1935; s. William Zweigle and Helen Marr (Potter) J.; m. Pauline Ruth Rowe, May 18, 1968; children: Darragh Elizabeth, William Potter. AB, U. Mich., 1957. Gen. mgr. Bureau County Rep., Inc., Princeton, Ill., 1961-72; pres. Johnson Newspapers, Inc., Sebastopol, Calif., 1972-75, Evergreen, Colo., 1974-86, Canyon Commons Investment, Evergreen, 1974—; pres., chmn. bd. dirs. Johnson Media, Inc., Granby, Colo., 1987—. Author: How the Michigan Betas Built a $1,000,000 Chapter House in the '80s. Alt. del. Rep. Nat. Conv., 1968. Lt. USNR, 1958-61. Mem. Colo. Press Assn., Nat. Newspaper Assn., Maple Bluff Country Club, Madison Club, Bishops Bay Country Club, Bal Harbour Club, Beta Theta Pi. Home: 5302 Lighthouse Bay Dr Madison WI 53704-1114 Office: PO Box 409 Granby CO 80446-0409

JOHNSON, WILLIAM R., JR., minister; b. Quincy, Fla., July 4, 1935; s. William R. Sr. and Mable Elaine (Robinson) J.; m. Eleanor Finch, April 4, 1943; children: Raymond Patrice, Malcolm Maurice.; BA, Lane Coll., 1957; MA, Columbia U., 1960; MDiv, Interdenominational Theol. Cert., Atlanta, 1968; MST, Princeton Theol. Sem., 1970; D of Ministry, Vanderbilt U., 1977; DD (hon.), Miles Coll., 1975. Pub. rels. rep. N.Y.C. Housing Auth., 1959-60; dir. youth and student activities Gen. Bd. Christian Edn. Christian Meth. Episcopal Ch., Chgo., 1960-62; adminstrv. and editl. asst. Gen. Bd. Christian Edn. Christian Meth. Episcopal Ch., Memphis, 1962-64, dir. div. higher edn., 1971-74, gen. sec., 1974-86; instr. and dorm counselor Clark Coll., Atlanta, 1964-65; pastor (while student) St. Mark Christian Meth. Episcopal, Birmingham, Ala., 1966-68, Mount Olive Christian Meth. Episcopal Ch., Camden, N.J., 1969-71; pastor Washington Chapel Christian Meth. Episcopal Ch., Memphis, 1980-83, Curry Temple Christian Meth. Episcopal Ch., Compton, Calif., 1986—. Author: Developing the Educational Ministry of Local Church, 1977, Beliefs that Make a Difference, 1984, Discipling Children and Youth the Mandate of the Church, 1995. Pres. Urban League, Memphis, 1975-78; pres. NAACP, Memphis, 1980-81; bd. dirs. Memphis O.I.C., 1977-83, mem. Comm. on Race Rels., Memphis, 1972-75; Founder: Cmty. Dev. Corp. Mem. Lane Coll. Alumni Orgn., Masons (Prince Hall Affiliate), Mystic Order of the Shrine, Alpha Phi Alpha Fraternity. Home: 16615 Estella Ave Cerritos CA 90703 Office: Curry Temple Box 5509 Compton CA 90224-5509

JOHNSON, WILLIAM THEODORE, school system administrator; b. Detroit, Jan. 12, 1951; s. Theodore Hamilton and Gloria May (Remy) J.; m. Debra Shoshana Lipner, Nov. 27, 1982; children: Amanda, Emily, Alex. BS in Natural Resources Mgmt., Calif. Poly. State U., San Luis Obispo, 1974; MA in Counseling Psychology, U. Calif., Santa Barbara, 1984; MA in Ednl. Adminstrn., Calif. State U., L.A., 1990. Nat. cert. sch. psychologist Nat. Crisis Prevention Inst., Inc. Cons. environ. edn. San Luis Obispo (Calif.) County Office Edn., 1974-77; tchr. Paso Robles (Calif.) Union Sch. Dist., 1978-82; sch. psychologist Baldwin Park (Calif.) Unified Sch. Dist., 1985-96; coord. spl. edn. Santa Barbara County Edn., 1996—; assoc. instr. Nat. Crisis Prevention Inst., Baldwin Park, 1995—. Coach Ctrl. Altadena (Calif.) Little League, 1994, 96. Mem. ASCD, Assn. Calif. Sch. Adminstrs., Baldwin Park Orgn. Suprs. and Adminstrs. (v.p. membership 1993-94, v.p. programs 1994-95, pres. 1995-96).

JOHNSON, WILLIE DAN, lawyer; b. Senatobia, Miss., Mar. 26, 1948; s. Beauregard and Geraldine J.; m. Marilyn Ann Stamps, Jan. 4, 1967; children: Renita Annette, Jamaal Curtis, Courtnay Erin. BA, UCLA, 1973, JD, 1977. Bar: Calif. 1978, U.S. Dist. Ct. (cen.) Dist. Calif. 1978. Lawyer, sole practice L.A. Sgt. USAF, 1966-70. Mem. ABA, ATLA, Consumer Atty. Assn. Calif., Consumer Atty. Assn. L.A. Office: Law Offices of Willie Dan Johnson 3500 S Figueroa St Ste 217 Los Angeles CA 90007-4363

JOHNSTON, ANDREA RUTH, writer, educator; b. N.Y.C., Nov. 25, 1944; d. Stephen Emul and Kathryn Mary (Countis) Senecka; m. William R. Johnston, Feb. 29, 1972 (div. Apr. 1984); 1 child, Jesse William. BA, CUNY, 1966; JD, Empire Coll., 1984. Cert. tchr., N.Y., Calif. Tchr. N.Y.C. Bd. Edn., 1964-72; founding pres. Nat. Assn. for Edn. Young Children, N.J., 1973-75; founding dir. R.R. Rainbow Sch., Guerneville, Calif., 1978-83; founding owner The Learning Tree, Sussex, N.J., 1973-76; writer, critic The Paper, Freestone, Calif., 1981-94, The Independent, Santa Rosa, Calif., 1994; tchr. Sonoma County Office of Edn., Santa Rosa, 1984-94; convenor Nat. Young Girls Coalition, Guerneville, Calif., 1995—, 1st Nat. Girls Conf., 1997; co-founder (with Gloria Steinem) Girls Speak Out, nationwide project on consciousness raising and feminism for young girls, 1994; cons. Ga. Campaign for Adolescent Pregnancy Prevention, 1997—. Author: Living on the Farm, 1976, Girls Speak Out: Finding Your True Self, 1997; theatre reviews, 1992. Mem. NEA, Nat. Assn. for Gifted (Calif. bd. dirs. 1988-92). Democrat. Home: 18200 Sweetwater Springs Rd Guerneville CA 95446-8915 Office: Girls Speak Out 18200 Sweetwater Springs Rd Guerneville CA 95446

JOHNSTON, BERNARD FOX, foundation executive; b. Taft, Calif., Nov. 19, 1934; s. Bernard Lowe and Georgia Victoria (Fox) J.; m. Audrey Rhoades, June 9, 1956 (div. Sept. 1963); 1 child, Sheldon Bernard. BA in Creative Arts, San Francisco State U., 1957, MA in World Lit., 1958. Lectr. philosophy Coll. of Marin, Kentfield, Calif., 1957-58; lectr. humanities San Francisco State U., 1957-58, 67-68; instr. English Contra Costa Coll., San Pablo, Calif., 1958-63; Knowles Found. philosophy fellow, 1962; fellow Syracuse (N.Y.) U., 1964-66; freelance writer Piedmont, Calif., 1968-77; pres. Cinema Repertory, Inc., Point Richmond, Calif., 1978-89; pres., exec. dir. Athena Found., Tiburon-Truckee, Calif., 1990—; exec. prodr. (TV series) The Heroes of Time, (TV documentary) The Shudder of Awe. Author: (screenplay) Point Exeter, 1979, Ascent Allowed, 1988 (award); author, editor: Issues in Education: An Anthology of Controversy, 1964, The Literature of Learning, 1971. Mem. Coun. for Basic Edn., Wilson Ctr. Assocs., Smithsonian Instn., Donner Land Trust, San Francisco State Alumni Assn., Commonwealth Club of Calif. Office: Athena Found 11679 Mougle Ln Truckee CA 96161-6117

JOHNSTON, BETTY, editor; b. El Paso, Tex., Sept. 19, 1925; d. Robert Blaine and Mary Augusta (Schmidt) Anderson; m. E.M. Johnston, Mar. 18, 1956; stepchildren: Jess, Mark. BA, U. Ariz., 1947. Copywriter Radio Sta. KOPO, Tucson, 1947-49, San Francisco, 1949-50; sales copy writer Sta. K60-TV, San Francisco, 1950-52; dir. advt. and publicity Paramount Picture Theatres Corp., L.A., 1952-57; writer, office mgr., casting dir. Flagg Films, L.A., 1957-62; lifestyle editor Laguna Beach (Calif.) News Post, 1967-70; reporter, editor The Vista (Calif.) Press, 1970-86; village life editor The Enterprise, Fallbrook, Calif., 1986-91, editor, 1991—; zone editor N.C. Times, San Diego, 1995—. Mem. Friends of Fallbrook Libr., Fallbrook Hist. Soc. Mem. Angel Soc. Republican. Office: Fallbrook Enterprise 232 S Main St Fallbrook CA 92028-2850

JOHNSTON, CHARLES, protective services official. BA in Law Enforcement Adminstrn., San Jose State U.; MPA, U. No. Colo.; grad., Nat. Acad. FBI; attended, Harvard U., Northwestern U., U. Denver, U. Colo. Police officer Salinas (Calif.) Police Dept.; police officer Lakewood (Calif.) Police Dept., 1970-80, acting chief of police, 1980-81, chief of police, 1981—; active Colo. Peace Officer Stds. and Tng. Bd., Justice Assistance Act Adv. Bd. Mem. Jefferson County coun. ARC; chmn. steering com. Law Enforcement Torch Run; active Colo. Spl. Olympics. Decorated Bronze star (4), Purple Heart, Army Air medal; recipient Man of Yr. award Lakewood Sentinel, 1984, Hall of Fame award Lakewood/South Jefferson County C. of C., 1989; named Vol. of Yr., Colo. Spl. Olympics Hall of Fame, 1990. Office: Lakewood Police Dept 445 S Allison Pkwy Lakewood CO 80226-3106*

JOHNSTON, DAVID RITCHEY, construction company executive; b. Highland Park, Ill., Nov. 7, 1950; Sherman and Vivian (Ritchey) J. BS, So. Ill. U., 1976. Owner Survival Systems Constrn., Bath, Maine, 1976-77; cons. Nat. Rec. and Parks Assn., Rosslyn, Va., 1977-78, Planning Research Corp., McLean, Va., 1978-79; v.p. Potomac Energy Group, Alexandria, Va., 1979-83; pres. Passive Solar Industries Council, Alexandria, Va., 1981-83, Lightworks Constrn., Inc., Bethesda, Md., 1983-91, What's Working, Boulder, Colo., 1991—; bd. dirs. Whole Systems Design, Inc., Lorton, Va., Potomac Energy Group, Inc., Bus. Crafters, New Alternative in Pub., Retailing & Advt., Big Horn Builders, Boulder Energy Conservation Ctr., Boulder C. of C. Author: Technical Solar Field Guide, 1979; exec. producer (film) Sunbuilders, 1980. Pres. Cabin John (Md.) Citizens Assn., 1986; bd. dirs. Renewable Energy Inst., 1982-83, STAR Found., Portland, Maine, 1979-89. Named to Remodeling Industry Hall of Fame, 1989. Mem. Nat. Assn. Remodeling Industry (bd. dirs.), Entrepreneurs Group of Washington, D.C. (pres.), Excellence Group, Bus. Crafters (bd. dirs. 1991—), New Age Pubs. and Retailers Assn., Home Builders Assn. Home: 57 Acorn Ln Boulder CO 80304-0402

JOHNSTON, GWINAVERE ADAMS, public relations consultant; b. Casper, Wyo., Jan. 6, 1943; d. Donald Milton Adams and Gwinavere Marie (Newell) Quillen; m. H.R. Johnston, Sept. 26, 1963 (div. 1973); children: Gwinavere G., Gabrielle Suzanne; m. Donald Charles Cannalte, Apr. 4, 1981. BS in Journalism, U. Wyo., 1966; postgrad., Denver U., 1968-69. Editor, reporter Laramie (Wyo.) Daily Boomerang, 1965-66; account exec. William Kostka Assocs., Denver, 1966-71, v.p., 1969-71; exec. v.p. Slottow, McKinlay & Johnston, Denver, 1971-74; pres. The Johnston Group, Denver, 1974-92; chair, CEO JohnstonWells Pub. Rels., Denver, 1992—; adj. faculty U. Colo. Sch. Journalism, 1988-90. Bd. dirs. Leadership Denver Assn., 1975-77, 83-86, Mile High United Way, 1989-95, Denver's 2% Club, Spring Inst., 1997—, Lower Downtown Denver, Inc.; bd. dirs. Colo. Jud. Inst., 1991—, chair, 1996—. Fellow Am. Pub. Rels. Soc. (pres. Colo. chpt. 1978-79, bd. dirs. 1975-80, 83-86, nat. exec. com. Counselor's Acad. 1988-93, sec.-treas. 1994, pres.-elect 1995, pres. 1996, profl. award Disting. Svc. award 1992); mem. Colo. Women's Forum, Rocky Mountain Pub. Rels. Group (founder), Denver Athletic Club, Denver Press Club. Republican. Home: 717 Monaco Pky Denver CO 80220-6040 Office: JohnstonWells Pub Rels 1512 Larimer St Ste 720 Denver CO 80202-1610

JOHNSTON, MARY ELLEN, nursing educator; b. Roswell, N.Mex., June 4, 1951; d. E. Bernard and Jane (Shugart) J. BSN, Baylor U., 1973; MSN, Oral Roberts U., 1982. Staff nurse crit. care dept. Tucson Med. Ctr., 1973-74; charge nurse med. unit St. Mary's Hosp., Roswell, 1975; instr. nursing Ea. N.Mex. U., Roswell, 1975—. Mem. ANA (cert. med.-surg. nurse), N.Mex. Nurses Assn. (past pres. dist. V), Baylor U. Nurses Alumni Assn., Philanthropic and Ednl. Orgn., Daus. of Am. Colonists, Altrusa Club Roswell, DAR, Sigma Theta Tau. Republican. Methodist. Home: 2715 N Kentucky Ave Apt 16 Roswell NM 88201-5868 Office: Ea NMex U PO Box 6000 Roswell NM 88202-6000

JOHNSTON, PATRICIA KATHLEEN, college dean; b. Seattle, May 21, 1936; d. Robert Leonard and Dorothy Evelyn (Crow) Pearson; m. Edward Paul Johnston, Sept. 3, 1955; children: Linda Suzanne Johnston Murosako, Martin Edward. BA, Walla Walla Coll., 1958; MPH, Loma Linda U., 1978; MS, U. Wash., 1979; DrPH, UCLA, 1987. Registered dietitian. Instr. Loma Linda (Calif.) U., 1979-81, asst. prof., 1981-88, assoc. prof., 1988-94, prof., 1994—, dir. DrPH program, 1987-90, chmn. nutrition dept., 1990-96, assoc. dean Sch. Pub. Health, 1990—; chmn. program 2d Internat. Congress on Vegetarian Nutrition, Washington, 1992, 3d, Loma Linda, Calif., 1997, editor proc.; speaker in field. Contbr. articles to profl. jours.; editor jour. Vibrant Life, 1988-95. Recipient Danforth Found. award Auburn Acad., 1953, Honored Student award L.A. Nutrition Coun., 1985, G. Emmerson award UCLA, 1985, Excellence in Edn. award, , CDA, 1996. Mem. APHA, Am. Dietetic Assn., Am. Soc. Bone and Mineral Rsch., Calif. Nutrition Coun., Soc. Nutrition Edn., Assn. Grad. Faculties in Pub. Health Nutrition, Calif. Dietetic Assn. (v.p. 1993-95), Omicron Nu, Delta Omega (nat. merit award 1981). Seventh Day Adventist. Office: Loma Linda U Sch Pub Health Loma Linda CA 92350

JOHNSTON, RICHARD C., newspaper editor. BS, Portland State U., 1965. Reporter The Oregonian, Portland, 1965-66, asst. city editor, 1966-79, Washington corr., 1979-82, asst. mng. editor, 1982-94, asst. to the editor, 1994—. Office: The Oregonian 1320 SW Broadway Portland OR 97201

JOHNSTON, ROBERT JAKE, federal magistrate judge; b. Denver, Sept. 30, 1947; m. Julie Ann Black; children: Jennifer, Robert, Jr., Michelle. BS, Brigham Young U., 1973; JD, U. Pacific, 1977. Bar: Nev. 1977, U.S. Dist. Ct. Nev. 1978, U.S. Ct. Appeals (9th cir.) 1984. Law clk. to Hon. Merlyn Hoyt Nev. 7th Judicial Dist., Ely, 1977-78; dist. atty. White Pine County, Ely, 1979-82; pvt. practice Johnston & Fairman, Ely, 1979-82; deputy dist. atty. Office Clark County Dist. Atty., Las Vegas, Nev., 1983-84; asst. U.S. atty. Office U.S. Atty., Las Vegas, 1984-87; chief civil div. Office U.S. Atty., 1986-87; U.S. magistrate judge U.S. Dist. Ct., Las Vegas, 1987—. Dir. Boy Scouts Am. Boulder Dam Area Coun., Las Vegas. With U.S. Army, 1967-70. Mem. Nev. Bar Assn., Clark County Bar Assn., Fed. Magistrate Judicial Assn. (dir. 1990-92), Las Vegas Track Club. Office: US Dist Ct 300 Las Vegas Blvd S Las Vegas NV 89101

JOHNSTON, THOMAS ALIX, artist, educator; b. Oklahoma City, June 4, 1941; s. Elmer Arthur and Madelyn Leona (Norton) J.; m. Kathleen Lord, Feb. 17, 1962 (div. 1971); children: Steven Thomas, Scott Randall; m. Ann Gail Friedman, Sept. 27, 1980. AA, San Diego City Coll., 1963; BA, San Diego State U., 1965; MFA, U. Calif., Santa Barbara, 1967. Prof. art Western Wash. U., Bellingham, 1967—; dir. Western Gallery Western Wash. U., 1983-87; artist Atelier Lacourière et Frélaut, Paris, 1981, 82, 88, 93, Atelier Rudolf Broulim, Zwijndrecht, Belgium, 1988, Santa Reparata Graphic Arts Ctr., Florence, Italy, 1981, Atelier 17, Paris, 1980; artist in residence Chateau Suduiraut, Preignac, France, 1993. Numerous one-man and group shows, including Galerie Jean-Claude Riedel, Paris, 1989, Tacoma Art Mus., 1990, Ctr. on Contemporary Art, Seattle, 1990, Dart Gallery, Chgo., 1992, Seattle Art Mus., 1992, Davidson Galleries, Seattle, 1993, Louisa McIntosh Gallery, Atlanta, 1993, SAGA, Paris, 1993, Chateau Suduiraut, 1994, Atelier Lacourière, Frèlaut, 1994; represented in permanent collections, including Beaufour Collection, Paris. Office: Western Wash U 518 High St Bellingham WA 98225-5946

JOHNSTON, VIRGINIA EVELYN, editor; b. Spokane, Wash., Apr. 26, 1933; d. Edwin and Emma Lucile (Munroe) Rowe; student Portland C.C., 1964, Portland State U., 1966, 78-79; m. Alan Paul Beckley, Dec. 26, 1974; children: Chris, Denise, Rex. Proofreader, The Oregonian, Portland, 1960-62, teletypesetter operator, 1962-66, operator Photon 200, 1966-68, copy editor, asst. women's editor, 1968-80; spl. sects. editor (UPDATE), 1981-83, 88-95; editor FOODday, 1982—; pres. Matrix Assos., Inc., Portland, 1975—, chmn. bd., 1979—; past pres. Bones & Brew Inc., treas.; bd. dir. Computer Tools Inc. Cons. Dem. Party Oreg., 1969, Portland Sch. Dist. No. 1, 1978. Mem. Eating and Drinking Soc. Oreg. (past pres.), We. Culinary Inst. (mem. adv. bd.), Internat. Food Media Conf. (mem. adv. bd.). Democrat. Editor Principles of Computer Systems for Newspaper Mgmt., 1975-76. Home: 4140 NE 137th Ave Portland OR 97230 2624 Office: Oregonian Pub Co 1320 SW Broadway Portland OR 97201-3411

JOHNSTONE, CLINT, electric power industry executive. Sr. v.p., bd. dirs. Bechtel Nat. Inc., San Francisco. Office: Bechtel Nat Inc 50 Beale St # 3965 San Francisco CA 94105-1813*

JOHNSTONE, KENNETH ERNEST, electronics and business consultant; b. L.A., Sept. 13, 1929; s. John Ernest and Lorena Hayes (Patterson) J.; m. Edna Mae Iverson, Aug. 20, 1950; children: Bruce, Kent, Anita, Christian, Daniel, Carol, Karen. BSEE, U. Wash., 1966. Registered profl. engr., Wash. Electronics technician The Boeing Co., Seattle, 1955-66, engr., 1966-75; engring. mgr. Boeing Aerosystems Internat., Seattle, 1975-85; ptnr. North Creek Engring., Lynnwood, Wash., 1985-87; pres. SensorLink Corp., Lynnwood, 1987-90; electronics and bus. cons. Bellingham, Wash., 1991—; internat. cons., lectr. in field. Mem. IEEE (sr.), Tau Beta Pi. Home and Office: 3765 E Smith Rd Bellingham WA 98226-9573

JOLLES, BERNARD, lawyer; b. N.Y.C., Oct. 5, 1928; s. Harry and Dora (Hirschorn) J.; m. Lenore Madison Jolles, Oct. 11, 1953 (div. Jan. 1984); children: Abbe, Jacqueline, Caroline. BA, N.Y.U., 1951; LLB, Lewis & Clark Coll., 1961. Bar: Oreg. 1963, U.S. Dist. Ct. Oreg. 1964, U.S. Dist. Ct. (no. dist.) Miss. 1968, U.S. Ct. Appeals (9th cir.) 1965, U.S. Supreme Ct. 1979. Assoc. Anderson Franklin Jones & Olsen, Portland, Oreg., 1963-68; ptnr. Franklin Olsen Bennett & Desbarsay, Portland, Oreg., 1968-79, Jolles Bernstein & Garone and predecessor firms Jolles Sokol & Bernstein, Portland, Oreg., 1979—. Editor: Damages, 1974. Bd. dirs. ACLU, Portland, Oreg., 1975—. Fellow Am. Coll. Trial Lawyers; mem. Oreg. State Bar Assn. (pres. 1986-87), Am. Inns of Ct. (sr. barrister 1985—). Office: Jolles Bernstein & Garone 721 SW Oak St Portland OR 97205-3712

JOLOVICH-MOTES, SONDRA LEA, principal; b. Wheatridge, Colo., July 3, 1965; d. Donald Joseph and Judith Anne (Baker) Jolovich; m. Brian William Motes, Aug. 5, 1989; children: Brian William Jr., Xena Diana. BS, Weber State U., 1989; M. in Edn. Adminstrn., U. Utah, 1992. Cert. tchr. math., sci.; cert. adminstr. Utah. Phys. sci./math. tchr. Salt Lake City Sch. Dist., 1989-91; adminstrv. intern Granite Sch. Dist., Salt Lake City, 1991-92, asst. prin. jr. high, 1992-94; asst. prin. mid. sch. Ogden (Utah) Sch. Dist., 1994-96; prin. Mountain View Elem. Sch., Ogden, 1996—; co-chmn. sch. cmty. coun. Ogden Sch. Dist., 1995-96, mem. dist. site-based decision-making com., 1994-95, mem. dist. testing com., 1995-96. Vol. fundraiser Big Bros./Big Sisters, Jr. League, Ogden, 1996; coach AYSO Soccer, 1997. Mem. Utah Edn. Assn., Nat. Assn. Secondary Sch. Prins., Nat. Assn. Elem. Sch. Prins., Phi Delta Kappa. Democrat. Roman Catholic. Office: Mountain View Elementary School 170 15th St Ogden UT 84404-5661

JONAITIS, ALDONA CLAIRE, museum administrator, art historian; b. N.Y.C., Nov. 27, 1948; d. Thomas and Demie (Genaitis) J. BA, SUNY, Stony Brook, 1969; MA, Columbia U., 1972, PhD, 1977. Chair art dept. SUNY, Stony Brook, 1983-85, assoc. provost, 1985-86, vice provost undergrad. studies, 1986-89; v.p. for pub. programs Am. Mus. Natural History, N.Y.C., 1989-93; dir. U. Alaska, Fairbanks, 1993—. Author: From the Land of the Totem Poles, 1988;editor, author: Chiefly Feasts: The Enduring

Kwakiutl Potlatch, 1991; editor: A Wealth of Thought: Franz Boas on Native American Art History, 1995. Mem. Native Am. Art Studies Assn. (bd. dirs. 1985-95). Office: U Alaska Mus 907 Yukon Dr Fairbanks AK 99775

JONES, A. DURAND, park administrator. CEO Rocky Mountain Nat. Park, Estes Park, Colo. Office: Rocky Mountain Nat Park Estes Park CO 80517*

JONES, ALAN C., grocery company executive; b. 1942; married. BS, Portland State U., 1967. Computer operator United Grocers Inc., Portland, Oreg., 1964-66, buyer, 1966-72, inventory control mgr., 1972-74, mktg. dept. mgr., 1974-82, asst. gen. mgr., 1982-83, pres., 1983—, formerly chief exec. officer, sec., treas. Served with USAF, 1960-64. Office: United Grocers Inc PO Box 22187 6433 SE Lake Rd Portland OR 97269-2136*

JONES, AMELIA GWEN, art history educator, curator; b. Durham, N.C., July 14, 1961; d. Edward Ellsworth and Virginia (Sweetnam) J.; m. Anthony Joseph Sherin, Mar. 7, 1987; 1 child, Evan Ellsworth Sherin-Jones.. BA, Harvard U., 1983; MA, U. Pa., 1987; PhD, UCLA, 1991. Curator Univ. Art Gallery, Riverside, Calif., 1991-92, Calif. Mus. Photography, Riverside, Calif., 1993-94, UCLA/Hammer Mus., 1993-96; art writer Art Forum, Art Issues, N.Y., L.A., 1987-96; instr., advisor Art Cen. Coll. Design, Pasadena, Calif., 1990-91; art history, art instr. U. Southern Calif., L.A., 1992; art history prof. U. Calif., Riverside, 1991—; adv. Workshop on Visual Culture U. Calif., Irvine, 1994-95; cons. J. Paul Getty Mus., Malibu, Calif., 1986. Author: Postmodernism and the En-Gendering of Marcel Duchamp, 1994; editor, co-author: Sexual Politics, 1996; contbr. articles to profl. jours. Bd. dirs. L.A. Cen. of Photographic Studies, 1994—, Teachers for a Dem. Culture, 1993—, Women's Action Coalition, 1992-93. Recipient Disting. Humanist Achievement award U. Calif., 1994, postdoctoral fellowship Am. Coun. of Learned Societies, N.Y., 1994-95, Dickson fellowship UCLA, 1989-91, Dean's fellowship U. Pa., 1986-87, Harvard Coll. fellowship Harvard U., 1980-82. Mem. Coll. Art Assn., Internat. Assn. of Art Critics. Home: 339 S Orange Dr Los Angeles CA 90036-3008 Office: U Calif Dept Art History Riverside CA 92521

JONES, ANN AKRIDGE, construction company executive; b. Dallas, June 1, 1945; d. Frank O. and Mary Virginia (Touchstone) Akridge; m. M. Douglas Jones Jr., May 25, 1968; children: Monica Akridge, Tobin Laurence. BA, U. Tex., 1967; MA, U. Colo., 1971, PhD, 1977. From spl. asst. to pres. to v.p. planning and devel. Johns Hopkins Hosp., Balt., 1979-84; v.p. ops. Zamoiski Co., Balt., 1984-85; adminstr. Johns Hopkins Med. Inst., Balt., 1986-89; exec. dir. Spiegel & McDiarmid, Washington, 1989-90; asst. vice chancellor U. Colo. Health Sci. Ctr., Denver, 1990-91; assoc. v.p. facilities Univ. Hosp., Denver, 1991-95; pres. Jonescorp., 1996—; cons. St. Vincent's Hosp., N.Y.C., 1982—. Contbr. articles to profl. jours. Advisor Kempe Children's Found., 1996—; active pub. affairs com. Planned Parenthood, Denver, 1994; bd. dirs. Md. Com. for Children, 1985-89, Balt. City Ct. Appointed Spl. Advocates, 1990, Colo. Children's Campaign, Denver, 1994-96. Recipient Gov. citation State of Md., 1982, Leadership award House of Ruth, 1984, Recognition cert., 1985, Citizen citation Balt. Mayor's Task Force, 1987. Mem. Am. Soc. Hosp. Engrs., Am. Assn. Med. Colls. Home: PO Box 3275 Evergreen CO 80437-3275

JONES, ARTHUR FRANCIS, surgeon; b. Utica, N.Y., May 13, 1946; s. Arthur Hywel and Ellen Joanna (Burke) J.; m. Patricia Ann Barton, Aug. 24, 1968 (div. Apr. 1981); children: David A., Eric W.; m. Wanda Lea Stewart, June 4, 1983; 1 child, Christopher. AB, Hamilton Coll., 1967; MD cum laude, Yale U., 1971. Diplomate Am. Bd. Surgery. Intern U. Colo., Denver, 1971-72, resident in surgery, 1972-73, 75-79; ptnr., surgeon Foothills Surg. Assocs., Wheat Ridge, Colo., 1979—; chmn. dept. surgery Luth. Med. Ctr., Wheat Ridge, 1989-90. Maj. U.S. Army, 1973-75. Fellow ACS (pres. Colo. chpt. 1991); mem. Denver Acad. Surgery (program dir. 1994-95, pres.-elect 1995-96, pres. 1996-97), Southwestern Surg. Soc., Alpha Omega Alpha, Beta Gamma Sigma, Western Surg. Assn. Unitarian. Office: Foothills Surg Assocs 8550 W 38th Ave Ste 308 Wheat Ridge CO 80033-4355

JONES, CHARLES E., state chief justice. BA, Brigham Young U., 1959; JD, Stanford U., 1962. Bar: Calif. 1962, U.S. Dist. Ct. Ariz. 1963, U.S. Ct. Appeals (9th cir.) 1963, Ariz. 1964, U.S. Ct. Appeals (10th cir.) 1974, U.S. Supreme Ct. 1979. Law clk. to Hon. Richard H. Chambers U.S. Ct. Appeals (9th cir.), 1962-63; ptnr. Jennings, Strouss & Salmon, Phoenix, Ariz., 1963-96; apptd. justice Ariz. Supreme Ct., Phoenix, 1996, vice chief justice, 1997—. Bd. visitors Brigham Young U. Law Sch., 1973-81, chmn., 1978-81. Named Avocat du Consulat-Gen. de France, 1981—; recipient Alumni Disting. Svc. award Brigham Young U., 1982. Mem. State Bar Ariz., Fed. Bar Assn. (pres. Ariz. chpt. 1971-73), J. Reuben Clark Law Soc. (nat. chmn. 1994—), Maricopa County Bar Assn., Pi Sigma Alpha.

JONES, CHARLES IRVING, bishop; b. El Paso, Tex., Sept. 13, 1943; s. Charles I. Jr. and Helen A. (Heyward) J.; m. Ashby MacArthur, June 18, 1966; children: Charles I. IV, Courtney M., Frederic M., Keith A. BS, The Citadel, 1965; MBA, U. N.C., 1966; MDiv, U. of the South, 1977, DD, 1989. CPA. Pub. acctg. D.E. Gatewood and Co., Winston-Salem, N.C., 1966-72; dir. devel. Chatham (Va.) Hall, 1972-74; instr. acctg. U. of the South, Sewanee, Tenn., 1974-77; coll. chaplain Western Ky. U., Bowling Green, 1977-81; vicar Trinity Episcopal Ch., Russelville, Ky., 1977-85; archdeacon Diocese of Ky., Louisville, 1981-86; bishop Episcopal Diocese of Mont., Helena, 1986—; bd. dirs. New Directions Ministries, Inc., N.Y.C.; mem. standing com. Joint Commn. on Chs. in Small Communities, 1988-91, Program, Budget and Fin., 1991-94; v.p. province VI Episcopal Ch., 1991-94, mem. Presiding Bishop's Coun. Advice, 1991-94. Author: Mission Strategy in the 21st Century, 1989, Total Ministry: A Practical Approach, 1993; bd. editors Grass Roots, Luling, Tex., 1985-90; contbr. articles to profl. jours. Founder Concerned Citizens for Children, Russelville, 1981; bd. dirs. St. Peter's Hosp., Helena, 1986—; bd. dirs. Christian Ministry in Nat. Parks, 1992—. With USMCR, 1961-65. Mem. Aircraft Owners and Pilots Assn. Office: Diocese Mont 515 N Park Ave Helena MT 59601-2703

JONES, CHARLES J., consultant; b. Marshfield, Oreg., Jan. 29, 1940; s. Charles J. Cotter and Lois C. (Smith) Meltebeke; m. Sharon S. Madsen, Mar. 29, 1969; children: Mary E., Judith A., Kari C., April M., Autumn C. AS in Fire Sci. Tech., Portland Community Coll., 1974; BS in Fire Adminstrn., Eastern Oreg. State Coll., 1983; diploma, Nat. Fire Acad., 1983, 85; MPA, Lewis and Clark Coll., 1989. Cert. class VI fire officer, Oreg., hazardous materials instr., fire instr. I; lic. real estate agt., Oreg. From firefighter to capt. Washington County Fire Dist., Aloha, Oreg., 1964-74, battalion chief, 1974-81, dir. comms., dir. research and devel., 1981-85, dir. strategic planning, 1986-88; cons. Tualatin Valley Fire & Rescue, Aloha, 1989-90; pres., CEO Jones Transp., 1989—; basic and advanced 1st aid instr. ARC, 1965-80; cons. Washington County Consol. Communications Agy., 1983-86, chmn. 9-1-1 mgmt. bd., 1982-83; mem. adv. bd. Washington County Emergency Med. Svcs., 1981-83; owner/instr. Internat. Vocat. Inst. and Family Tree Learning Ctrs. Jones Internat., Ltd., 1990-95. Editor local newsletter Internat. Assn. Firefighters, 1970; contbr. articles on fire dept. mgmt. to jours. Active Community Planning Orgn., Washington County, 1979-90, chmn. 1988-89. With USAF, 1957-59. Mem. Oreg. Fire Chiefs Assn. (chmn. seminar com. 1982-83, 89, co-chmn. 1981, 84, 86, 87, 88). Republican. Mem. Infinity Universal Ch. Office: Jones Transp PO Box 7206 Aloha OR 97007-7206

JONES, CLAIRE BURTCHAELL, artist, teacher, writer; b. Oakland, Calif.; d. Clarence Samuel and Florence Mallett (Hinchman) Burtchaell; m. E.C. Jones; children: Holland Mallett, Lela Claire, S. Evan. AB, Stanford U.; postgrad. Laguna Beach Sch. Art, 1972-73, San Diego Art Acad., 1980-82. Freelance art tchr., Park Ridge, Ill., 1967; tchr. Jade Fon Group, Pacific Grove, Calif., 1972-73, Merced Coll., Sierra Mountains, Calif., 1973; freelance pvt. workshop, painting for commns. and galleries, Calif., 1973—. Author: First The Blade (ann. collection), 1939; Arrows in the Air, 1947-51; Utah Sings, 1953. Editor: Watercolor West Newsletter, 1978-83. Contbr. articles to profl. jours. Recipient numerous awards for artwork. Mem. Nat. Mus. Women in the Arts (founding mem.), Assn. Western Artists (bd. dirs. 1970-71), Watercolor West (bd. dirs. 1978-81, 86—, membership chmn. 1988-96), Stanford Alumni Assn., Literati West (founder, sec.-treas. 1994—).

JONES, CLEON BOYD, research engineer; b. Norwalk, Calif., Nov. 9, 1961; s. Cleon Earl and Marjorie Helen (McDade) J. BS in Math., Biola U., 1983. Rsch. libr. Christian Rsch. Inst., San Juan Capistrano, Calif., 1981-84; flight control engr. Leading Systems, Inc., Irvine, Calif., 1984-90; rsch. engr. Dynamic Rsch., Inc., Torrance, Calif., 1990—. Recipient NASA Group Achievement award Pilot Project Team, 1994. Republican. Home: 12464 Fallcreek Ln Cerritos CA 90703-2075

JONES, D. MICHAEL, banker; b. Tacoma, June 25, 1942; s. Delbert Edward and Marilyn Maurine (Myers) J.; m. Linda R. Lavigne, June 7, 1964; 1 child, Karee Michele. BA in Econs., Wash. State U., 1964. CPA, Wash. Acct. Deloitte Haskins & Sells, Seattle, 1964-68, princ., 1968-72; treas. Old Nat. Bancorp., Spokane, Wash., 1973-76, exec. v.p., 1976-81, pres., 1982-87; pres. Moore Fin. Group Inc. (now West One Bancorp), Boise, ID, 1987-1996; pres., ceo Source Capitol Corp., Spokane, Wa, 1996; bd. dirs. Columbia Paint Co., Spokane. Bd. dirs. Spokane City Libraries, 1974-78, Leadership Spokane, 1982-84; sec. treas., bd. dirs. Spokane Unltd., 1980-86. Recipient Outstanding Alumnus award, Wash. State U., 1986. Mem. Am. Inst. CPA's, Wash. Soc. CPA's, Spokane C. of C. (sec. treas. 1985-86). Episcopalian. Clubs: Spokane (pres. 1984-85); Hayden Lake (Idaho) Country (pres. 1982-83). Office: Source Capitol Corporation 1825 N Hutchinson Rd Spokane WA 99212-2444*

JONES, DANIEL EDWIN, JR., bishop; b. Westcliffe, Colo., Jan. 31, 1942; s. Daniel Edwin and Vivian Mary (Falkenberg) J. BA, Carroll Coll., Helena, Mont., 1964; MA, Am. Coll., Louvain, Belgium, 1968. Ordained priest Roman Cath. Ch., 1968; ordained to ministry Ch. of Jesus Christ, 1994. Parish priest Diocese of Pueblo, Colo., 1968-72; itinerant mission priest Traditional Cath. Movement, Westcliffe, Colo., 1972-93; itinerant bishop Ch. of Jesus Christ, St. Jovite, Que., Can., 1994—. Editor/pub. Sangre de Cristo Newsnotes, 1973—. Mem. Order of the Magnificat of the Mother of God (3d order mem.). Office: Sangre de Cristo Newsnotes PO Box 89 Westcliffe CO 81252

JONES, DANIEL LEE, software development company executive; b. Sterling, Colo., Feb. 17, 1954; s. Gerald Dean and Joyce Elaine (Pyle) J.; m. Laurie Elaine Ganong, Sept. 6, 1975; 1 child, Jonathon Alexander. AB cum laude, Dartmouth Coll., 1976; MA in Physics, U. Calif., Davis, 1977, PhD in Physics, 1979. Assoc. in physics U. Calif., Davis, 1976-79; physicist Argonne (Ill.) Nat. Lab., 1979-82; mem. tech. staff TRW, Inc., Redondo Beach, Calif., 1982-84; chief scientist, co-founder Affine Scis. Corp., Newport Beach, Calif., 1984-85; chief scientist Peripheral Systems, Inc., Van Nuys, Calif., 1985-89; dir. info. systems Jones & Jones, Sterling, Colo., 1989—; v.p., co-founder Jones Techs. Inc., Sterling, 1991-92, also bd. dirs.; chief scientist Sykes Enterprises, Inc., Sterling, 1992—; sec. Jones Techs. Inc., Sterling, 1991-92; cons. Davis Polk & Wardwell, N.Y.C., 1987-91. Author (newspaper column) Your Computer, 1991-93; contbr. articles to profl. jours. Dist. accountability com. RE-1 Valley Schs., Sterling, 1991-94, dist. tech. com., 1991-94; mem. Northwestern Jr. Coll. Found. Bd., 1995—. Recipient Rufus Choate scholar Dartmouth Coll., 1972, Outstanding Contbrn. Inst. of Internal Auditors, 1987-88; tech. transfer grantee TRW, Inc., 1982. Mem. IEEE, IEEE Computer Soc., Assn. for Computing Machinery, Soc. for Indsl. and Applied Math., Uni-Forum. Republican. Methodist. Home: 510 Glenora St Sterling CO 80751-4642 Office: Sykes Enterprises Inc 777 N 4th St Sterling CO 80751-3244

JONES, DARCY GLEN ALAN, land use planner, consultant; b. Vancouver, B.C., Can., June 23, 1959; came to U.S., 1962; s. Harry Patrick and Margery Meta (Tierney) J.; m. Amy Lynne Baron, Sept. 30, 1995. BA in Geography, Ctrl. Wash. U., 1982; MS in Regional Planning, Western Wash. U., 1986. Lic. land surveyor, Calif. Land survey technician Jones Assocs., Bellevue, Wash., 1976-85; project planner Stevens Planning Group, San Diego, 1986-87, VTN S.W., San Diego, 1987-88; pres. Jones Engrs. Inc., San Diego, 1988—; legis. adv. County San Diego, 1990—. Den leader Boy Scouts Am., La Mesa, Calif., 1992-94. Mem. Am. Inst. Cert. Planners (cert. land planner), Am. Planning Assn., Calif. Assn. Subdivsn. Cons., Calif. Land Surveyors Assn., Bldg. Industry Assn., Alamo Ct. Homeowners Assn. (pres. 1992—). Home: 6767 Alamo Ct La Mesa CA 91941

JONES, DAVID, artist; b. Columbus, Ohio, Feb. 26, 1948. Student, Ohio State U., 1967; BFA, Kansas City Art Inst., 1970; MA, U. Calif., Berkeley, 1971, MFA, 1973. One-man shows include Braunstein/Quay Gallery, 1984, 87, 91-92, San Jose State U., 1971, Daniel Weinberg Gallery, 1973, Michael Walls Gallery, 1975; exhibited in group shows at San Diego State U., 1971, U. Santa Clara, 1971, San Francisco Art Festival, 1971-72, Pasadena Mus. Art, 1972, San Francisco Art Inst., 1973, 75, Whitney Mus. Am. Art, 1975, Huntsville Mus. Art, 1977, San Francisco Mus. Modern Art, 1976, Nat. Collection Fine Arts Smithsonian Instn., 1976, Art Inst. and Calif. State U., 1982, Richard/Bennett Gallery, 1989, Chgo. Internat. Art Exposition, 1989, Oakland Mus., 1994, U. Calif., Berkeley, 1994, MIT Mus., 1996. Recipient Eisner prize U. Calif., Berkeley, 1971, 1st Painting prize Richmond Art Ctr., 1971, Group Show award Oakland Mus., 1971, Purchase award San Francisco Art Festival, 1971; Nat. Endowment for Arts Artists grantee, 1974, Soc. for Encouragement of Contemporary Art Artists grantee, 1974; Marian Davies fellow U. Calif., Berkeley, 1972. Home: PO Box 8872 Emeryville CA 94662-8872

JONES, DONALD RAY, entrepreneur; b. Phoenix, July 19, 1947; m. Rose Fryer, Nov. 15, 1969; children: Duryea, Tramar. Student, Phoenix Coll., 1972-74. Sales rep. Consumer Product Co., 1973-81; dir. mktg. maj. auto dealer, 1983-84; founder, pres. DRJ & Assocs., Inc., Phoenix, 1984—. Mem. adv. bd. Sta. KPNX Broadcasting, South Mountain Cmty. Coll., Foster Care Rev. Bd., Pvt. Practice Industry Coun. With U.S. Army, 1967-69, Vietnam. Office: DRJ & Assocs PO Box 2314 Phoenix AZ 85002-2314

JONES, DONNA MARILYN, real estate broker, legislator; b. Brush, Colo., Jan. 14, 1939; d. Virgil Dale and Margaret Elizabeth (McDaniel) Wolfe; m. Donald Eugene Jones, June 9, 1956; children: Dawn Richter, Lisa Shira, Stuart. Student, Treasure Valley Community Coll., 1981-82; grad., Realtors Inst. Cert. residential specialist. Co-owner Parts, Inc., Payette, Idaho, 1967-79; dept. mgr., buyer Lloyd's Dept. Store, Payette, Idaho, 1979-80; sales assoc. Idaho-Oreg. Realty, Payette, Idaho, 1981-82; mem. dist. 13 Idaho Ho. of Reps., Boise, 1987-90, mem. dist. 10, 1990-94, mem. dist. 9, 1995—; assoc. broker Classic Properties Inc., Payette, 1983-91; owner, broker ERA Preferred Properities Inc., 1991—; mem. dist. 9 Idaho Ho. of Reps., 1992—. Co-chmn. Apple Blossom Parade, 1982; mem. Payette Civic League, 1968-84, pres. 1972; mem. Payette County Planning and Zoning Commn., 1985-88, vice-chmn. 1987; field coordinator Idaho Rep. Party Second Congl. Dist., 1986; mem. Payette County Rep. Cen. Com. 1978—; precinct II com. person, 1978-79, state committeewoman, 1980-84, chmn. 1984-87, outstanding county chmn. region III Idaho Rep. Party Regional Hall of Fame, 1985-86; mem. Payette County Rep. Women's Fedn., 1988—, bd. dirs., 1990-92; mem. Idaho Hispanic Commn., 1989-92, Idaho State Permanent Bldg. Adv. Coun., 1990—; bd. dirs. Payette Edn. Found., 1993-96, Western Treasure Valley Cultural Ctr., 1993-96; nat. bd. dirs. Am. Legis. Exchange Coun., 1993—; mem. legis. adv. coun. Idaho Housing Agy., 1992-97; committeeperson Payette County Cen.; chmn. Ways and Means Idaho House of Reps., 1993-97, House Revenue & Taxation Com., 1997—; mem. Multi-State Tax Compact, 1997—; Idaho chmn. Am. Legis. Exchange Coun., 1991-95. Recipient White Rose award Idaho March of Dimes, 1988; named Payette/Washington County Realtor of Yr., 1987. Mem. Idaho Assn. Realtors (legis. com. 1984-87, chmn. 1986, realtors active in politics com. 1982—, polit. action com. 1986, polit. affairs com. 1986-88, chmn. 1987, bd. dirs. 1984-88), Payette/Washington County Bd. Realtors (v.p. 1981, state dir. 1984-88, bd. dirs 1983-88, sec. 1983), Bus. and Profl. Women (Woman of Progress award 1988, 90, treas. 1988), Payette C. of C., Fruitland C. of C., Wiesr C. of C.. Republican. Home: 1911 1st Ave S Payette ID 83661-3003 Office: ERA Preferred Properties 1610 6th Ave S Payette ID 83661-3348

JONES, DOUGLAS CLYDE, author; b. Winslow, Ark., Dec. 6, 1924; s. Marvin Clyde and Bethel Mae (Stockburger) J.; m. Mary Arnold, Jan. 1, 1949; children: Mary Glenn, Martha Claire, Kathryn Greer, Douglas Eben. B.A. in Journalism, U. Ark., 1949; M.S. in Mass Communications, U. Wis., Madison, 1962. Commd. U.S. Army, 1949, advanced through grades to lt. col., 1968; service in W. Ger. and Korea; chief armed forces news br. Dept. Def., 1966-68, ret., 1968; prof. U. Wis. Sch. Journalism, Madison, 1968-74. Painter of plains Indians, 1974-75; novelist, 1976—; author: Treaty of Medicine Lodge, 1966, Court Martial of G.A. Custer, 1976 (Spur award Western Writers Am. 1976), Arrest Sitting Bull, 1977, Creek Called Wounded Knee, 1978, Winding Stair, 1979, Elkhorn Tavern, 1980 (Friends of Am. Writers Award 1980), Weedy Rough, 1981, The Barefoot Brigade, 1982, Season of Yellow Leaf, 1983, Gone the Dreams and Dancing, 1984 (Spur award 1986), Roman (Spur award WWA 1985); (short stories) Hickory Cured, 1987, Remember Santiago, 1988, Come Winter, 1989, The Search for Temperance Moon, 1991, This Savage Race, 1993, Shadow of the Moon, 1995, A Spider for Loco Shoat, 1997. Served with U.S. Army, 1943-45, World War II, PTO. Decorated Commendation medal (3) Legion of Merit. Recipient Chancellor's award U. Wis., 1987, Owen Wister award for body of work Western Writers Am., 1993. Home: 1424 Harold St Fayetteville AR 72703-3823

JONES, DOUGLAS MICHAEL, pastor; b. Omar, W.Va., July 25, 1945; s. Douglas George and Phyllis Lee (Jones) J.; m. Janet Lorraine Spoelstra, Jan. 7, 1967; children: Kimberlee Anne, Michael Paul, Susan Reneé. BA, Biola U., 1972; MA, Internat. Coll., Honolulu, 1984, D in Ministry, 1990. Youth pastor Sunkist Bapt. Ch., Anaheim, Calif., 1970-72; assoc. pastor Ind. Bible Ch., Port Angeles, Wash., 1974-75, sr. pastor, 1975—; bd dirs N.W. Ind. Ch. Ext., Tacoma, 1976-86, Western Sem., Seattle, 1994-97; pres. and founder Pac Rim Bible Coll., Port Angeles, 1992-95. Bd. dirs. Clallam County Mental Health, Port Angeles, 1978. Sgt. USAF, 1966-70. Recipient Christian Leadership award The Am. Christian Leadership Coun., 1989. Charter mem. Am. Assn. Christian Counselors. Republican. Home: 1114 W 9th St Port Angeles WA 98363 Office: Ind Bible Ch 112 N Lincoln Port Angeles WA 98362

JONES, EDWARD LOUIS, historian, educator; b. Georgetown, Tex., Jan. 15, 1922; s. Henry Horace and Elizabeth (Steen) J.; m. Dorothy M. Showers, Mar. 1, 1952 (div. Sept. 1963); children: Cynthia, Frances, Edward Lawrence; Lynne Ann McGreevy, Oct. 7, 1963; children Christopher Louis, Teresa Lynne. BA in Philosophy, U. Wash., 1952, BA in Far East, 1952, BA in Speech, 1955, postgrad., 1952-54; JD, Gonzaga U., 1967. Social worker Los Angeles Pub. Assistance, 1956-57; producer, dir. Little Theatre, Hollywood, Calif. and Seattle, 1956-60; research analyst, cons. to Office of Atty. Gen., Olympia and Seattle, Wash., 1963-66; coordinator of counseling SOIC, Seattle, 1966-68; lectr., advisor, asst. to dean U. Wash., Seattle, 1968—; instr. Gonzaga U., Spokane, Wash., 1961-62, Seattle Community Coll., 1967-68; dir. drama workshop, Driftwood Players, Edmonds, Wash., 1975-76. Author: The Black Diaspora: Colonization of Colored People, 1988, Tutankhamon: Son of the Sun, King of Upper and Lower Egypt, 1978, Black Orators' Workbook, 1982, Black Zeus, 1972, Profiles in African Heritage, 1972, From Rulers of the World to Slavery, 1990, President Zachary Taylor and Senator Hamlin: Union or Death, 1991, Why Colored Americans Need an Abraham Lincoln in 1992, Forty Acres and a Mule: The Rape of Colored Americans, 1994; editor pub. NACADA Jour. Nat. Acad. Advising Assn., more. V.p. Wash. Com. on Consumer Interests, Seattle, 1966-68. Served to 2d lt. Fr. Army, 1940-45. Recipient Outstanding Teaching award U. Wash., 1986, Tyee Inst. Yr. U. Wash., 1987, appreciation award Office Minority Affairs, 1987, acad. excellence award Nat. Soc. Black Engrs., 1987, Appreciation award Fla. chpt. Nat. Bar Assn., 1990; Frederick Douglass scholar Nat. Coun. Black Studies, 1985, 86. Mem. Nat. Assn. Student Personnel Adminstrs., Smithsonian Inst. (assoc.), Am. Acad. Polit. and Social Sci., Nat. Acad. Advising Assn. (bd. dirs. 1979-82, Cert. of Appreciation 1982, editor Jour. 1981—, award for Excellence 1985), Western Polit. Sci. Assn. Democrat. Baptist. Office: Univ Wash Ethnic Cultural Ctr Seattle WA 98195

JONES, GAIL KATHLEEN, educational administrator; b. Oklahoma City, June 28, 1935; d. Lloyd Clifton Jones and Cleo Kathleen (Shackelford) Ahlstedt; m. Jerry Lynn Jones, Aug. 8, 1954; children: Kathleen DeVaughan, Jerry Clifton, Gregory Taylor. BA in English, Cen. Wash. U., 1971. Coordinator outreach program Ellensburg City Library, Wash., 1971-77; dir. alumni affairs and community rels. Cen. Wash. U., Ellensburg, 1977-95, ret., 1995, now disting. emeriti adminstr.; Pub. newsletter Central Today, 1977—. Mem. Wash. Gov.'s com. for Handicapped, 1978-83; officer United Way Bd., Ellensburg, 1982-86; mem. Beautification Commn., Ellensburg, 1980-83, Distributive Edn. Adv. Council, Ellensburg, 1978-82, chair, Ctrl. Wash. U. Centennial, 1990-92. Mem. Council Advancement and Support Edn., AAUW, LWV, Ellensburg C. of C. Presbyterian. Lodge: Soroptimists (charter pres. Kittitas County (Wash.) club 1986-88, dist. dir. 1990-92). Home: 405 N Anderson St Ellensburg WA 98926-3145

JONES, GALEN RAY, physician assistant; b. Salt Lake City, Feb. 1, 1948; s. Leonard Ray and Veda (Whitehead) J.; m. Patricia Ann Poulson, Jan. 21, 1972; children: Brian, Marci, Natalie. Grad., Med. Field Svc. Sch. Ft. Sam Houston, San Antonio, 1971; BS, U. Utah, 1982. Missionary Ch. of Jesus Christ of Latter Day Saints, Alta., Sask., Can., 1967-69; asst. mgr. Cowan's Frostop Hamburger Stand, Salt Lake City, 1969-70; with Safeway Stores, Inc., Salt Lake City, 1970; o.r. tech. Latter Day Saint Hosp., Salt Lake City, 1973-75; physician asst. Lovell Clinic Inc., Lovell, Wyo., 1975-77, Family Health Care, Inc., Tooele, Utah, 1977-86, West Dermatology and Surgery Med. Grp., Redlands, Calif., 1986-95; with blood and marrow transplant program Univ. Hosp. and Primary Childrens Med. Ctr. U. Utah, 1996—; maturation lectr. Tooele Sch. Dist., 1978-86; course dir., instr. EMT, North Big Horn County Search and Rescue, 1976; instr. EMT, Grantsville Ambulance Inc., 1979-85; lectr. on skin care and changes to sr. citizen groups, hosp. auxs., health fairs, 1986—; high sch. sophomore sem. tchr. religion, 1991-96; owner Adventureland and TopHat Video, Magna, Utah. Author: (with others) The P.A. Medical Handbook, 1995. Chmn. County Health Teen Pregnancy Prevention Project, Tooele, 1980-81; adv. bd. State Dept. Health-Rural Health Network, Salt Lake City, 1985-86; health lectr. County Health & Edn. Dept. Progs., Tooele, 1977-86; mormon bishop/pastor Lakeview Ward, Latter Day Saints Ch., Tooele, 1982-86; mem. Utah Acad. Physician Assts. (pres. 1980-81, editor newsletter 1979-80). With U.S. Army, 1971-73. U. Utah grantee, 1966, 67, 69. Fellow Am. Acad. Physician Assts., Calif. Acad. Physicians Assts. Republican. Mem. LDS Ch. Home: 2670 E Willowwick Dr Sandy UT 84093

JONES, GAYLE CLAUSSE, secretary; b. Ogden, Utah, June 22, 1947; d. Joseph James and Helen Jean (Blackinton) Clausse; m. Robert Scott Jones, May 22, 1971 (div. Oct. 1979); 1 child, Marie Jones. BBA, Steven Henagers Bus. Coll., 1969; AS, Weber State U., 1991, BS, 1993. Sec. Ogden Iron Works, 1970-75, Weber County Sch. Dist., 1977—. Sec.-treas. Daus. of Utah Pioneers; mem. Utah Hist. Soc., Weber County Hist. Soc. Mem. Utah Geneal. Assn. Mem. LDS Ch.

JONES, GEORGIA ANN, publisher; b. Ogden, Utah, July 6, 1946; d. Sam Oliveto and Edythe June Murphy; m. Lowell David Jones; children: Lowell Scott, Curtis Todd. Journalist, 1968-72; appraiser real property Profl. Real Estate Appraisal, San Carlos, Calif., 1980-95; owner, pub. Ladybug Press, San Carlos, 1996—; workshop leader Women's Wire, 1994—. Author: A Garden of Weedin', 1997; sculptor, 1965-78; patentee Scruples-tag, 1980; editor, pub. Women on a Wire, 1996. Office: Ladybug Press 751 Laurel St #223 San Carlos CA 94070

JONES, GERRE LYLE, marketing and public relations consultant; b. Kansas City, Mo., June 22, 1926; s. Eugene Riley and Carolyn (Newell) J.; m. Charlotte Mae Reinhold, Oct. 30, 1948; children: Beverly Anne Jones Putnam, Wendy S. Jones Stout. BJ, U. Mo., 1948, postgrad., 1953-54. Exec. sec. Effingham (Ill.) C. of C., 1948-50; field rep. Nat. Found. Infantile Paralysis, N.Y.C., 1950-57; dir. pub. relations Inst. Logopedics, Wichita, Kans., 1957-58; owner Gerre Jones & Assocs., Pub. Relations, Kansas City, Mo., 1958-63; info. officer Radio Free Europe Fund, Munich, Federal Republic of Germany, 1963-65, spl. asst. to dir. pub. relations, 1965-66; exec. asst. pub. affairs Edward Durell Stone, 1967-68; dir. mktg. and communications Vincent G. Kling & Ptnrs., Phila., 1969-71; mktg. cons. Ellerbe Architects, Washington, 1972; v.p. Gaio Assocs., Ltd., Washington, 1972-73, exec. v.p., 1973-76; exec. v.p. Bldg. Industry Devel. Services, Washington, 1973-76; pres. Gerre Jones Assocs. Inc., Albuquerque, 1976-89, ret., 1989; sr. v.p. Barlow Assocs., Inc., Washington, 1977-78; lectr. numerous colls. and univs. Author: How to Market Professional Design Services, 1973, 2d edit., 1983, How to Prepare Professional Design Brochures, 1976, (with Stuart H. Rose) How to Find and Win New Business, 1976, Public Relations for the

Design Professional, 1980; contbr. articles to profl. jours. Served with USAAF, 1944-45, maj. USAF (ret.). Mem. Nat. Assn. Sci. Writers, AIA (hon.), Sigma Delta Chi, Alpha Delta Sigma, Phi Delta Phi, Overseas Press Club, Masons. Republican.

JONES, GREGORY TAYLOR, human resources risk manager; b. Fayetteville, Ark., July 21, 1962; s. Jerry Lynn and Gail Kathleen J.; m. Wendes RE Johnson, Apr. 5, 1982 (div. June 1994); children: G. Taylor, Romanda K. Parker L. BSBA, Ctrl. Wash. U., 1983; MPA, Calif. State U., Hayward, 1997. Personnel analyst City of Concord (Calif.), 1990-93, sr. personnel analyst, 1993-95, risk mgr., 1996—; bd. dirs. Contra Costa County Risk Mgmt., Walnut Creek, Calif. Capt. USAF, 1983-90. Mem. Internat. Personnel Mgrs. Assn., Pub. Agy. Risk Mgrs. Assn. Democrat. Office: City of Concord 1950 Parkside Dr Concord CA 94519-2526

JONES, J. GILBERT, research consultant; b. San Francisco, June 1, 1922; s. Enoch Roscoe L. Sr. and Remedios (Ponce de Leon) J.; student U.S. Mcht. Marine Acad., 1942-44, San Francisco City Coll., 1942-44, 46-47; AB, U. Calif., Berkeley, 1949, MA, 1952. Lic. pvt. investigator. Ins. insp. Ins. Cos. Insp. Bur., San Francisco, 1959-62; pub. rels. cons., San Francisco, 1962-67; ins. insp. Am. Svc. Bur., San Francisco, 1967-72; propr., mgr. Dawn Universal Internat. San Francisco, 1972—, Dawn Universal Security Svc., San Francisco, 1983—. Mem. SAR, Libr. of Congress Assocs., Sons. Spanish-Am. War Vets. Soc., World Affairs Coun. N. Calif., U. Calif. Alumni Assn., Commonwealth Club of Calif. Republican. Office: PO Box 424057 San Francisco CA 94142-4057

JONES, J. SORTON, lawyer; b. Llandudno, Wales, 1941. BSc, U. St. Andrews, Scotland, 1964; JD, U. Calif., Berkeley, 1973. Bar: Calif. 1973, N.Y. 1975; Registered Civil Engr. Calif. 1969. Mem. Carroll, Burdick & McDonough, San Francisco. Fellow Chartered Inst. of Arbitrators London; mem. ABA (internat. law sect.), Corp. Counsel Com., Am. Arbitration Assn., Inst. Civil Engrs. London (assoc.). Office: Carroll Burdick & McDonough 44 Montgomery St Ste 400 San Francisco CA 94104-4706

JONES, JAMES DAVID, health care executive; b. Harrison, Ark., Jan. 14, 1948; s. James Andrew and Thelma (Rogers) J.; m. Judith Ann Salzman, Feb. 10, 1968 (div. Apr. 1983); 1 child, Kirk Anthony; m. Cherryl Lynn Walker, Mar. 3, 1984; 1 child, Callie Ann. BBA, Nat. U., 1985. Pro. lt. USCG, 1977, retired, 1987; exec. dir. Big Valley Med. Ctr., Bieber, Calif., 1987—; instr. Lassen C.C., Susanville, Calif., 1990—; mem. exec. com. primary care clinics adv. com. State of Calif., Sacramento, 1988-91; pres. Associated Calif. Health Ctrs. Benefit Trust, Sacramento, 1989-92; bd. dirs. No. Sierra Rural Health Network, 1996—. Treas. Big Valley Sports Assn., 1992—; sports announcer Big Valley High Sch., 1990—. Named Honorary Okie Gov. Okla., Oklahoma City, 1978. Mem. Nat. Rural Health Assn., Calif. Primary Care Assn., Bieber C. of C., Fall River Golf & Country Club. Republican. Office: Big Valley Med Ctr 554-850 Med Ctr Dr Bieber CA 96009

JONES, JAMES EDWARD, editor, publisher; b. Dearborn, Mich., July 22, 1929; s. Frank Thomas and Henrieta Ann (Ziel) J.; m. Margaret Elizabeth Wilton, Aug. 26, 1950; children: Becky Lynn, James Kevin. AA, Henry Ford C.C., Dearborn, 1949. Profl. photographer. Supr. Burroughs Corp., Detroit; pub. rels. mgr. Henry Ford Mus., Dearborn, 1953-62; dir. St. Louis Tourism Bur., 1963-70; exec. dir. San Mateo County Convention Tourist Bureau, Calif., 1970-75; pub. rels. dir. Calif. Assn. Health Facilities, Sacramento, 1976-86; editor, publisher Gold River (Calif.) News, 1987—; cons. Sacramento County Sheriff, 1995-96, Sacramento Mcpl. Utility Dist., 1987-90; feature writer Senior Spectrum, Sacramento, 1987-89. Author, photographer Story of Flight, 1959, The Engineer, 1960. Bd. dirs. Vol. Ctr. Sacramento, 1991—, Kinglsey Art Club, Sacramento, 1995—; v.p. Internat. Footprint, Sacramento, 1970—. Named Editor of Yr. Calif. Newspaper Publs. Assn., Sacramento, 1995. Mem. Optimist Internat. (life, pres. 1993—, Optimist of Yr. 1994), Sacramento Press Club (bd. dirs. 1986—). Republican. Home and Office: 6231 Center Mall Way # 1 Sacramento CA 95823-2709

JONES, JAMES HENRY, physiology educator, researcher; b. Phoenix, Oct. 23, 1952; s. Loyal Herbert and Marjorie Lois (McHenry) J. BS, BA, U. Ariz., 1974, MS, 1976; PhD, Duke U., 1979; DVM, Colo. State U., 1983. Park ranger, naturalist U.S. Natural Park Svc., Yellowstone Nat. Park, 1973-76, Glacier Nat. Park, 1981-82; sr. rsch. officer U. Cape Town, South Africa, 1980; biology lectr. Dept. Organismic and Evolutionary Biology Harvard U., Cambridge, Mass., 1983-86; asst. assoc. prof. Sch. Vet. Medicine U. Calif., Davis, 1986-96, chair physiology grad. group, 1992—, chair animal use and care com., 1993—, prof. Sch. Vet. Medicine, 1996—; vis. prof. anatomy U. Berne, Switzerland, 1986; vis. prof. physiology U. São Paulo, 1990, vis. prof. organismic and evolutionary biology, Harvard U., 1995-96. Author, editor: Comparative Vertebrate Exercise Physiology, Vols. A and B, 1994; contbr. articles to profl. jours. With USN, 1970-72. Grantee NIH, 1987, NASA, 1989, Am. Heart Assn., 1992. Mem. Am. Physiol. Soc. (Scholander award 1986), Am. Soc. Zoologists. Office: U Calif Sch Vet Medicine Dept Surgery and Radiol Scis Davis CA 95616

JONES, JAN LAVERTY, mayor. Grad. Stanford Univ. Mayor, City of Las Vegas. Office: Office of Mayor City Hall 10th Fl 400 Stewart Ave Las Vegas NV 89101-2942

JONES, JEFFREY DEAN, interior designer; b. L.A., May 12, 1960; s. Philip Brent and Karin Myrial (Kavelin) J.; m. Sharon Kay Wanerus, Feb. 29, 1992; 1 child, Casey Matthew. BFA with honors, Chapman U., 1992. Cert. interior designer, Calif. Pres. Brentwood Contract Interiors, Palm Desert, Calif., 1994—. Contbr.: The Desert Sun, 1994; contbr. articles to profl. pubis. Recipient Cert. Merit Lightolier, 1988. Mem. AIA (affiliate), Am. Soc. Interior Designers (exec. bd. 1991-97, pres. 1997, Presdl. Citation 1992), Internat. Interior Design Assn., Internat. Soc. Interior Designers (profl. mem.), Internat. Soc. Lighting Designers (assoc.); media spokesperson for Calif. Coun. for Interior Design Cert.

JONES, JERVE MALDWYN, construction company executive; b. L.A., Sept. 21, 1918; s. Oliver Cromwell and Zola (Hill) J.; m. Alice Castle Holcomb, Apr. 12, 1942; children—Jay Gregory, Janey Lee Matt, Joel Kevin. B.S. in Civil Engring., U. So. Calif., 1939. Registered profl. engr., Calif. Stress analyst Northrop Aircraft, L.A., 1940-43; ptnr. Jones Bros. Constrn. Co., Beverly Hills, Calif., 1946-56; pres., chief exec. officer Peck/Jones Constrn. Corp. (formerly Jones Bros. Constrn. Co.), Beverly Hills, Calif., 1956—; cons. Jerve M. Jones Assocs., Beverly Hills, 1970—; chmn. Jones Constrn. Mgmt., Beverly Hills, 1983—. Bd. dirs. Huntington Library, San Marino, Calif., 1984—, Pepperdine U., Malibu, Calif., Boy Scouts Am., L.A., Santa Monica Hosp. Found., YMCA Met. L.A.; chmn. L.A. Music Ctr., United Fund Campaign; life mem. Town Hall Calif., L.A., adv. bd. UCLA Med. Ctr.; mem. State Calif. Strong Motion Instrumentation Program, Dept. Mines and Geology. With USNR, 1943-46, PTO. Recipient Civil Engring. Alumnus of Yr. award U. So. Calif., 1985, Bronze Hat award United Contractors Assn., 1985, Disting. Scout award, 1989. Mem. Constrn. Mgmt. Assn. Am. (nat. pres. 1984, Founders award 1985), Archtl. Guild, Archimedes Circle, Constrn. Industry Commn. (chmn. 1980-84), Assoc. Gen. Contractors Am., Los Angeles Area C. of C. (dir.). Republican. Episcopalian. Clubs: Los Angeles Country, California. Lodge: Rotary (dir. 1962-68). Office: Peck/Jones Constrn Corp 10866 Wilshire Blvd Fl 7 Los Angeles CA 90024-4300

JONES, JEWEL, social services administrator. BA, Langston Coll., 1962; MA, U. Alaska, 1974. Dir. Social Svcs. Dept., Anchorage, 1970-85, Health and Human Svcs. Dept., Anchorage, 1985-88; mgr. social svcs. divsn. health and human svcs. dept. Muncipality of Anchorage, 1988—. Office: Bd Dirs 520 E 34th Ave Anchorage AK 99503

JONES, JOEL MACKEY, educational administrator; b. Millersburg, Ohio, Aug. 11, 1937; s. Theodore R. and Edna Mae (Mackey) Jones; children: Carolyn Mae, Jocelyn Corinne. BA, Yale U., 1960; MA, Miami U., Oxford, Ohio, 1962; PhD, U. N.Mex., 1966. Dir. Am. studies U. Md., Balt., 1966-69; chmn. Am. studies U. N.Mex., Albuquerque, 1969-73, asst. v.p. acad. affairs, 1973-77, dean faculties, assoc. provost, prof. Am. studies, 1977-85, v.p. adminstrn., 1985-88; pres. Ft. Lewis Coll., Durango, Colo., 1988—. Contbr. numerous essays, articles and chpts. to books. Founder Rio Grande Nature Preserve Soc., Albuquerque, 1974—; bd. dirs., mem. exec. com., United Way, Albuquerque, 1980-83; nat. bd. cons. NEH, 1978—; bd. dirs. Mercy Hosp., 1990-94, 1st Nat. Bank; mem. ACE Commn. on Leadership. Farwell scholar Yale U., New Haven, 1960; Sr. fellow NEH, 1972, Adminstrv. fellow Am. Coun. Edn., Washington, 1972-73. Mem. Am. Studies Assn., Am. Assn. Higher Edn., Am. Assn. State Colls. and Univs. (chair com. on cultural diversity, Colo. state rep., 1994—). Home: 35 Lewis Mountain Ln Durango CO 81301-6531 Office: Ft Lewis Coll Office of Pres Durango CO 81301-3999*

JONES, JOHN HARDING, photographer; b. Pitts., Apr. 28, 1923; s. John F. and Emma Eleanor (West) J.; divorced; 1 child, Blair Harding. BFA, Rochester Inst. Tech., 1949; MBA, Pepperdine U., 1978; PhD, U. London, 1983; M in Photography (hon.), Brantridge Forest, Eng.; DLitt (hon.), Ky. Christian U.; EdD, St. John's U. Seaman U.S. Naval Air, 1940, advanced through grades to comdr., 1948; ret., 1963; chief photographer U.S. Steel Corp., Pitts.; mgr. art & photo dept. Magnavox Corp., Urbana, Ill.; chief photographer rehab. medicine sect. U.S. Vet. Adminstrn., L.A.; coord. rehab. medicine domiciliary sect. Wadsworth VA Hosp., L.A.; tchr. Carnegie Mellon Inst., Pitts., Earl Wheeler Schs., Pitts., Seattle U., Art Inst. Pitts.; dir., owner The Little Studio, Panorama City, Calif., 1989—, The Little Studio West, Panorama City, 1994—. Author: Photography, 1972, The Correspondence Educational Directory, 1976, 79, 84, 94, Correspondence Courses for High School Credit & GED Preparation, 1994. Comdr. USNR, ret. Recipient award Writers Guild, 1977, Merit award Cooking, 1986; elected to Am. Police Hall of Fame, 1996. Mem. Profl. Photographers Am., Masons, Shriners, Order of the Eastern Star (worthy patron 1986). Presbyn. Office: Ste 305 10050 Sepulveda Blvd Mission Hills CA 91345

JONES, JOHN WESLEY, entrepreneur; b. Wenatchee, Wash., Nov. 15, 1942; s. Richard F. and Hazel F. (Hendrix) J.; m. Melissa L. Meyer, June 22, 1968 (div. 1982); children: John E., Jennifer L.; m. Deborah G. Matthews, Apr. 24, 1993. BA in Bus./Econs., Western Wash. U., Bellingham, 1966. Trainee Jones Bldg., Seattle, 1967-69; mgr. Jones Bldg., 1969-78; owner/mgr. N.W. Inboards, Bellevue, Wash., 1974-78, Jones Bldg., Seattle, 1978-86; pvt. investor Bellevue, 1987—; owner/mgr. J. Jones Enterprises, 1994—; trustee BOMA Health & Welfare Trust, 1982-86, chmn. 1986; mem. Seattle Fire Code Adv. Bd., 1979-86. With USMCR, 1966-72. Mem. Seattle Bldg. Owners and Mgrs. Assn. (trustee 1979-86), Bldg. Owners and Mgrs. Internat., N.W. Marine Trade Assn., Am. Assn. Individual Investors, Composite Fabricators Assn., Soc. Naval Architects and Marine Engrs., Boat U.S., Seattle Yacht Club, NRA, Internat. Show Car Assn., Nat. Street Rod Assn., Specialty Equipment Mktg. Assn. Republican. Home: 61 Skagit Key Bellevue WA 98006-1021 Office: 12819 SE 38th St # 288 Bellevue WA 98006-1395

JONES, JOHNPAUL, architect. BArch, U. Oreg., 1967. Registered architect, Wash., Calif., Oreg., Idaho, Hawaii, Ariz., N.Mex., Fla.; nat. cert. architect, NCARB. With Paul Thiry, Architect, Seattle, Oda/McCarty Architects, Hilo, Hawaii; sr. prin. Jones & Jones, Architects and Landscape Architects, Seattle, 1972—; lectr. in field. Prin. works include Cedar River Visitor Facility, Seattle, Dea'ht Tribal Elders Ctr., Neah Bay, Wash., Edn. Pavilion and Children's Zoo, Honolulu, Longhouse Cultural Edn. Ctr., Olympia, Washington, Mercer Slough Nature Ctr., Bellevue, Wash., Overlake Blueberry Farm, Bellevue, Seattle Children's Mus., Stimson Green Hist. Gardens, Seattle, Ctr. Urban Horticulture Bldgs. and Douglas Rsch. Conservatory U. Wash., Seattle, rsch. lab. and support greenhouses U. Alaska, Fairbanks, Tilikum Pl. Urban Pub. Sq., Seattle, Eagle Island State Pk. Bldgs., Boise, Idaho, Gene Coulon Meml. Beach Pk. Bldgs., Renton, Washington (Honor award AIA 1982, 1st Honor award Am. Steel Assn. 1982, Excellence on the Water Honor award Waterfront Ctr. 1987, The Inhabited Landscape award Archtl. League N.Y. Exhbn. 1987), Newcastle Beach Pk. Bldgs., Bellevue (Merit award AIA 1988, Best Design of 1988 Times Mag., Excellence on the Water Honor award Waterfront Ctr. 1988, Honor award regional AIA 1990), Newhalem ranger sta. and campground bldg. North Cascades Nat. Pk., Washington (1st Honor award Am. Wood Coun. 1981), Nat. Pk. Svc. Skagway (Alaska) Maintenance Facility, Hertz Adminstrn. Maintenance and Regional Facility, SeaTac Airport, Washington, others, (landscape designs) Zool. Soc. San Diego, Woodland Pk. Zoo and Zool. Gardens (Pres.'s Award of Excellence Am. Soc. Landscape Architects 1980), Seattle, City of Honolulu Dept. Pks. and Recreation, N.Mex. State Pks., Carlsbad, Dallas Zoo, Point Defiance Zoo & Aquarium (Merit award Wash. chpt. Am. Soc. Landscape Architects 1981), Tacoma, Ariz.-Sonora Desert Mus., Tucson, San Diego Zoo (Best Exhibit award Am. Assn. Zool. Pks. & Aquariums 1989), others, (historic preservation) Icicle Canyon Arts Ctr., Leavenworth, Washington, Icicle Canyon Guest Lodges, Klondike Goldrush Nat. Hist. Pk. Maintenance Facility, Skagway. Chmn. Pioneer Sq. Hist. Preservation Bd., Seattle; former bd. dirs. King County United Way. Fellow AIA (mem. Seattle chpt.); mem. Nat. Assn. Indian Architects & Engrs. Office: Jones & Jones 105 S Main St 4th Flr Seattle WA 98104-2535*

JONES, JOSEPHINE A., poet; b. Salina, Kans., Sept. 7, 1955; d. Grover Norman and Melba June (Kindall) J.; 1 child, Sarah; m. Jeffrey S. Conger, Sept. 24, 1994; 1 child, Amoreena Whitteker. BA in Writing, Boise State U., 1986, MA in English, 1989. Writer, poet Boise, Idaho, 1970—; lectr. Mont. Humanities Coun., 1990, Idaho Humanities Coun., 1990—; prodr., performer Sagebrush Writers Series, Boise, 1986-91, Speakeasy Prodns., Boise, 1994—, Growl Prodns., Boise, 1995—; performer Earthfest '96, Boise, 1996. Contbr. poems to profl. jours. Home: 1016 N 13th Boise ID 83702

JONES, KENNETH MERLE, rehabilitation services professional; b. Glenns Ferry, Idaho, May 9, 1937; s. Frank Cassius and C. Virginia (Parker) J.; m. N. Jeannette Sutton, Sept. 30, 1962. BS in Edn., U. Idaho, 1969, MEd, 1975; cert., U. San Francisco, 1972. Lic. profl. counselor, Idaho. Vocat. trainer Idaho State Sch. and Hosp., Nampa, Idaho, 1969-72; exec. dir. Vocat. Devel. ctr., Boise, Idaho, 1972-73; facility supr. Idaho Vocat. Rehab., Boise, 1973-76, chief field svcs., 1976-86, chief mgmt. svc., 1986—; cons. Com. on Acreditation Rehab. Facilities, Tucson, 1972-74; bd. dirs. Devel. Disabilities Coun., Boise, 1976-80; apptd. by gov. state dir. Internat. Yr. of Disabled, Boise, 1980. Pres. Mayors Com. on Employment of Persons with Disabilities, Boise, 1989-90, 94, 95; Boise liaison Nat. Orgn. Disability, 1989-93; nat. bd. dirs. U. Idaho Vandal Boosters. With U.S. Army, 1959-62. Mem. Nat. Rehab. Assn. (pres. local chpt. 1983, 89, pres. pacific region 1992), NRA Adminstrn. Assn. (nat. bd. dirs. 1995-97, Profl. of Yr. 1989, Meritorious Svc. award 1996). Home: 4400 E Goldenrod Ave Meridian ID 83642-5604 Office: Idaho Div Vocat Rehab Lbj 650 W State # 150 Boise ID 83720

JONES, LORETTA LUCEK, chemistry educator, writer; b. Rockford, Ill., Apr. 26, 1943; d. Walter Joseph and Magdalen Mary (Kazunas) Lucek; m. J.T. Jones, Oct. 4, 1964 (div. 1976); 1 child, Lara Mayet. BS with hons., Loyola U., 1964; MS, U. Chgo., 1968; PhD, D.A., U. Ill., 1979. Sec., treas. Sonicraft, Inc., Chgo., 1968-74; vis. asst. prof. U. Ill., Urbana, 1979-82, asst. dir. gen. chemistry program, lectr., 1982-85, assoc. dir., 1985-92; asst. prof. U. No. Colo., Greeley, 1992-93, assoc. prof., 1993-97; cons. scholar Acad. Info. Syss. IBM Corp., Milford, Conn., 1987-88; mem. adv. bd. Mid-Atlantic Dicovery Project Franklin and Marshall Coll., 1994-96; co-prin. investigator Rocky Mtn. Tchr. Edn. Collaborative, Greeley, Colo., 1994-96; prin. investigator Chemistry for the Info. Age, Greeley, 1995-96. Author: (videotape series) Lecture Demonstrations, 1980 (award Amoco, 1981); co-author: (videotape courses) Chemistry 101, 102, 1980-92, (software) Exploring Chemistry, 1988-94 (Educom award 1987, 89), (textbook) Chemistry: Molecules, Matter and Change, 1997. Fellow AAAS; mem. ACS (councilor 1992—), AAUW, Nat. Assn. Rsch. in Sci. Tchg., Examinations Inst. (bd. trustees). Office: U No Colo Dept Chemistry & Biochem 501 20th St Greeley CO 80639

JONES, LUCIA JEAN, physical education educator; b. Racine, Wis., Apr. 24, 1942; d. Lawrence E. and Laura (Westphall) J. BS, U. Ariz., 1964; MS, Ariz. State U., 1967. Cert. tchr., Ariz. Tchr., chair women's phys. edn., coach Leysin (Switzerland) Am. Sch., 1964-65; prof., coach U. Ariz., Tucson, 1965-66; chair, coach phys. edn. dept. Hohokam Elem. Sch., Scottsdale, Ariz., 1967-68; instr. phys. edn., coach Alhambra High Sch., Phoenix, 1968-83; instr. phys. edn., health Trevor Browne High Sch., Phoenix, 1983-89; instr. physical edn. Alhambra High Sch., Phoenix, 1989-91, physical edn., health dept. chair, 1992-95; delegate citizen amb. to Russia and Belarus, Temple Univ., 1993; program head golf profl. Ogontz White Mountain Resort, Lisbon, N.H., 1962-65; instr. Swiss Ski Sch., Leysin, 1964-65; tennis teaching profl. Top Seed Tennis Club, Phoenix, 1974-78; bd. dirs. Phoenix Dist. Tennis Assn., 1974-82; dir. European Study Tours, 1981-83; tennis coach Phoenix Coll., 1983-86; Jr. Wightman Cup coach Phoenix Dist. Tennis Assn., 1979-80. Contbr. articles to profl. publs.; author curriculum materials. Tchr. golf Scottsdale YWCA, 1967-71; bd. dirs. Ariz. Interscholastic Assn., Phoenix, 1968-92; cons. Phoenix Rackets Profl. Tennis Team, 1973-76; cons., bd. dirs. Phoenix Dist. Tennis Assn., 1973-92. Recipient Championship Recognition award Phoenix Union H.S. Sys., 1979-81, AIA Svc. award, 1993; named Wonder Woman Coach Tennis West Publications, 1979, Phoenix Metro Coach of Yr. softball Metro Phoenix Coaches Assn., 1981. Mem. NEA, AAHPERD, Ariz. AAHPERD (Secondary Phys. Edn. Tchr. of Yr. 1990), Phoenix Futures Forum, U.S. Tennis Assn. Umpires Coun., Ariz. Edn. Assn., Ariz. Interscholastic Assn. (Earl McCullar award 1979), Delta Psi Kappa. Republican. Home: 7108 N 15th Dr Phoenix AZ 85021-8506 Office: Alhambra High Sch 3839 W Camelback Rd Phoenix AZ 85019-2512

JONES, MARK ALAN, broadcast technician; b. San Francisco, 1957; m. Stephanie Phillips, 1983. BA in Communication Studies, Calif. State U., 1979. Chief operator Sta. KXPR, Sacramento, 1979-80, with ops./prodn.dept., 1980—. Recipient pub. radio program award for Excellence, Corp. Pub. Broadcasting, 1981. Office: Stas KXPR/KXJZ Inc 3416 American River Dr Ste B Sacramento CA 95864-5715

JONES, MARK LOGAN, educational association executive, educator; b. Provo, Utah, Dec. 16, 1950; s. Edward Evans and Doris (Logan) J. BS, Ea. Mont. Coll., 1975; postgrad. in labor rels., Cornell U.; postgrad., SUNY, Buffalo. Narcotics detective Yellowstone County Sheriff's Dept., Billings, Mont., 1972-74; math tchr. Billings (Mont.) Pub. Schs., 1975-87; rep. Nat. Edn. Assn. of N.Y., Buffalo, Jamestown, 1987-91, Nat. Edn. Assn. Alaska, Anchorage, 1991—. Photographs featured in 1991 N.Y. Art Rev. and Am. Artist. Committeeman Yellowstone Dem. Party, Billings, 1984-87; exec. com. Dem. Cen. Com., Billings, 1985-87; bd. dirs. Billings Community Ctr., 1975-87; concert chmn. Billings Community Concert Assn., 1980-87; bd. dirs. Chautauqua County Arts Coun.; bd. dirs. Big Brothers and Big Sisters Anchorage. With U.S. Army, 1970-72. Recipient Distinguished Svc. award, Billings Edn. Assn., 1985, Mont. Edn. Assn., 1987. Mem. Billings Edn. Assn. (bd. dirs. 1980-82, negotiator 1981-87, pres. 1982-87), Mont. Edn. Assn. (bd. dirs. 1982-87), Ea. Mont. Coll. Tchr. Edn. Project, Accreditation Reviewer Team Mont. Office Pub. Edn., Big Sky Orchard, Masonic, Scottish Rite. Home: PO Box 102904 Anchorage AK 99510-2904 Office: Nat Edn Assn Alaska 1840 S Bragaw St Ste 103 Anchorage AK 99508-3463

JONES, NATHANIEL, bishop. Bishop Ch. of God in Christ, Barstow, Calif. Office: Ch of God in Christ 630 Chateau Way Barstow CA 92311-5721*

JONES, NEIL FORD, surgeon; b. Merthyr Tydvil, Wales, Nov. 30, 1947; s. John Robert and Kathleen Mary (Ford) J.; m. Barbara Rose Unterman, Feb. 18, 1978; 1 child, Nicholas Huw. B of Medicine, B of Surgery, MA, Oxford (Eng.) U., 1975. Registrar N.E. Thames Regional Plastic Surgery Centre, Billericay, Eng., 1982; fellow in hand surgery and microsurgery Mass. Gen. Hosp. Harvard U., Boston, 1983; asst. prof. surgery U. Pitts., 1984-89, assoc. prof. surgery, 1989-93, dir. hand and microsurgery fellowship, 1987-93; prof., chief of hand surgery UCLA Med. Ctr. dept. orthopedic surgery divsn. plastic and reconstructive surgery, 1993—. Contbr. articles to profl. jours. Fellow Royal Coll. Surgeons Eng., Am. Coll. Surgeons; mem. Am. Soc. Plastic and Reconstructive Surgeons, Am. Soc. Surgery of the Hand, Am. Soc. Reconstructive Microsurgery, Internat. Soc. Reconstructive Microsurgery. Home: 532 N Bonhill Rd Los Angeles CA 90049-2326 Office: UCLA Med Ctr 200 UCLA Med Plz # 140 Los Angeles CA 90024-6977

JONES, PENN HOLTER, advertising executive; b. Dallas, Dec. 18, 1961; s. Gordon Lee Jr. and Marilyn Christine (Holter) J.; m. Erin Gail Dettling, May 30, 1987; 1 child, Hayley McConnell. Student, U. So. Calif., 1979-84. Press box intern L.A. Express/U.S. Football League, 1983; mid-day news intern KTTV, Hollywood, Calif., 1983; intern L.A. (Calif.) Dodgers, 1984, asst. pub. rels. staff, 1984-86; affiliate rels. mgr. Harmon Cove Prodns./Dodgervision, Hollywood, 1986-87; account exec. Popular Mechanics/Hearst Corp., Santa Monica, Calif., 1987-88; account exec. Cosmopolitan/Hearst Corp., Santa Monica, 1988-89, L.A. mgr., 1989-90, west coast mgr., 1990-94; west coast advt. dir. Time/In Style, L.A., 1994—. Bd. dirs. U. So. Calif. Cardinal & Gold, life mem. Mem. Jr. C. of C. (dir. L.A. open, traffic control 1988-90, Best Performance award 1989), Sigma Alpha Epsilon (pres., Order of Phoenix award 1982-83). Home: 2260 24th St Santa Monica CA 90405-1811

JONES, PETER F., lawyer; b. Hanover, N.H., Jan. 3, 1944; s. J. Franklin Jr. and Elizabeth Anne (Dunning) J.; m. Anne M. Jones, Apr. 17, 1971; children: David, Philip. BA, Ripon Coll., 1967; JD, U. Denver, 1970. Bar: Colo. 1971, U.S. Dist. Ct. Colo. 1971. Assoc. Duane O. Littell, Denver, 1971-76; assoc. Hall & Evans, Denver, 1976-78, ptnr., 1978—. Office: Hall & Evans 1200 17th St Ste 1700 Denver CO 80202-5835

JONES, RICHARD ARTHUR, retired community college president, educator; b. Santa Ana, Calif., Sept. 1, 1932; s. Arthur Kincaid and Gladys Dorothy (Peden) J.; m. Mary Louise Miller, June 20, 1959; children: Richard Arthur, Patricia Louise Jones Cowan, Geoffrey Scott, Susan Elizabeth. AA, San Bernardino Valley Coll., 1953; BA, San Jose State U., 1955, MA, 1958; EdD, UCLA, 1970. Tchr. La Habra (Calif.) H.S., 1956-58; tchr., counselor, residence hall adminstr. Bakersfield (Calif.) Coll., 1958-66; dean Desert Campus Bakersfield Coll., Ridgecrest, Calif., 1966-73; founding pres. Cerro Coso C.C., Ridgecrest, 1970-75; pres. Clark Coll., Vancouver, Wash., 1975-81; chancellor San Bernardo C.C. Dist., 1981-88; prof.English Crafton Hills Coll., Yucaipa, Calif., 1988-92; interim dean instr. and student svcs. San Jose City Coll., 1989-90, interim pres., 1990-91; interim pres. Coll. San Mateo, Calif., 1991-92, DeAnza Coll., Cupertino, Calif., 1992-93. Author: Upward Mobility of Disadvantaged Community College Students, 1970. Chair exec. com. Vancouver (Wash.) Ctrl. Park, 1979-81; bd. dirs. Met. YMCA, San Bernardino, 1982-88; mem. adv. coun. and site selection task force City Arts and Conf. Ctr., Vancouver, 1979-81. Lt. comdr. USCGR, 1948-52, 59-66. Kellogg fellow, 1963, 66; Newspaper Guild scholar, 1954. Mem. Assn. Calif. C.C. Adminstrs., Rotary Club of Redlands, Vancouver C. of C. (bd. dirs. 1978-81). Presbyterian. Home: 9758 Azurite St Yucaipa CA 92399

JONES, ROBBIE RENE, farmer; b. Portales, N.Mex., Apr. 14, 1963; d. Robert Lee and Edith Irene (Davis) Jones; m. Robert Burdean Atchley, July 26, 1986 (div. 1994); m. Greg Kendal Smith, Nov. 26, 1994 (div. 1995). BS, N.Mex. State U., 1985. With ins. mktg. dept. Bob Jones State Farm, Corrales, N.Mex., 1986-90; farmer Clovis, N.Mex., 1990—. Mem. Altrusa (treas., bd. dirs. Clovis chpt. 1993—), Cattle Capital Cowbelles. Republican. Methodist. Home and Office: 1898 Sr 311 Clovis NM 88101-1249

JONES, ROBERT ALONZO, economist; b. Evanston, Ill., Mar. 15, 1937; s. Robert Vernon and Elsie Pierce (Brown) J.; m. Ina Turner Jones; children: Lindsay Rae, Robert Pierce, Gregory Alan, William Kenneth. AB, Middlebury Coll., 1959; MBA, Northwestern U., 1961, LLD (hon.) Middlebury (Vt.) Coll., 1992. Economist Hahn, Wise & Assoc., San Carlos, Calif., 1966-69; sr. rsch. officer Bank of Am., San Francisco, 1969-74; v.p., dir. fin. forecasting Chase Econometrics, San Francisco, 1974-76; chmn. bd. Money Market Svcs., Inc., Belmont, Calif., 1974-86; chmn. bd. MMS Internat., Redwood City, Calif., 1986-89, chmn. emeritus, 1989—; chmn. bd. dirs. Market News Svc., N.Y.C.; chmn. emeritus Geonomics Inst., Middlebury, 1995—, chmn. bd., 1986-95; chmn. bd. Jones Internat., 1989—; chmn. bd. Market News Svc., Inc., N.Y.C., 1993—; chmn. bd. Market Broadcasting Corp., Incline Village, N.Y.; dean coun. Harvard U. Div. Sch., Cambridge, Mass., 1991—; mem. Kellogg Alumni Adv. Bd., Northwestern U., 1993—; instr. money and banking, Am. Inst. Banking, San Francisco, 1971, 72; councilman, City of Belmont (Calif.), 1970-77, mayor, 1971, 72, 75, 76; dir. San Mateo County Transit Dist., 1975-77; chmn. San Mateo County Coun. of Mayors, 1975-76; trustee Incline Village Gen. Improvement Dist., Nev., 1984-85, trustee, Carlmont United Meth. Ch., 1978-81. Author: U.S.

Financial System and the Federal Reserve, 1974, Power of Coinage, 1987. 1st lt. USAR, 1961-68. Named Hon. Life Mem. Calif. PTA, ordo honorum Kappa Delta Rho Nat. Fraternity; recipient Ernst & Young Entrepreneur of the Yr. award, 1986; John Harvard fellow Harvard U., 1996, Stanton Recognition award North Shore Country Day Sch., 1996. Mem. Nat. Assn. Bus. Economists, San Francisco Bond Club. Republican. Methodist. Office: Jones Internat Inc PO Box 7498 Incline Village NV 89452-7498 *The entrepreneurial spirit is distinguished by passion, creativity, and the fulfillment of mission through other people.*

JONES, ROBERT EDWARD, federal judge; b. Portland, Oreg., July 5, 1927; s. Howard C. and Leita (Hendricks) J.; m. Pearl F. Jensen, May 29, 1948; children—Jeffrey Scott, Julie Lynn. BA, U. Hawaii, 1949; JD, Lewis and Clark Coll., 1953, LHD (hon.), 1995; LLD (hon.), City U., Seattle, 1984, Lewis and Clark Coll., 1995. Bar: Oreg. Trial atty. Portland, Oreg., 1953-63; judge Oreg. Circuit Ct., Portland, 1963-83; justice Oreg. Supreme Ct., Salem, 1983-90; judge U.S. Dist. Ct. Oreg., Portland, 1990—; mem. faculty Nat. Jud. Coll., Am. Acad. Jud. Edn., ABA Appellate Judges Seminars; former mem. Oreg. Evidence Revision Commn., Oreg. Ho. of Reps.; former chmn. Oreg. Commn. Prison Terms and Parole Stds.; adj. prof. Northwestern Sch. Law, Lewis and Clark Coll., 1963—, Willamette Law Sch., 1988—. Bd. overseers Lewis and Clark Coll. Served to capt. JAGC, USNR. Recipient merit award Multnomah Bar Assn., 1979; Citizen award NCCJ, Legal Citizen of the Yr. award Law Related Edn. Project, 1988; Service to Mankind award Sertoma Club Oreg.; James Madison award Sigma Delta Chi; named Disting. Grad., Northwestern Sch. Law. Mem. State Bar Oreg. (past chmn. Continuing Legal Edn.), Oregon Circuit Judges Assn. (pres. 1967—), Oreg. Trial Lawyers Assn. (pres. 1959, chair 9th cir. edn. com. 1996-97). Office: US Dist Ct House 620 SW Main St Portland OR 97205-3037

JONES, ROGER CLYDE, retired electrical engineering educator; b. Lake Andes, S.D., Aug. 17, 1919; s. Robert Clyde and Martha (Albertson) J.; m. Katherine M. Tucker, June 7, 1952; children: Linda Lee, Vonnie Lynette. B.S., U. Nebr., 1949; M.S., U. Md., 1953; Ph.D. U. Md., 1963. With U.S. Naval Research Lab., Washington, 1949-57; staff sr. engr. to chief engr. Melpar, Inc., Falls Church, Va., 1957-58; cons. project engr. Melpar, Inc., 1958-59, sect. head physics, 1959-64, chief scientist for physics, 1964; prof. dept. elec. engring. U. Ariz., Tucson, 1964-89; dir. quantum electronics lab. U. Ariz., 1968-88, adj. prof. radiology, 1978-86, adj. prof. radiation-oncology, 1986-88, prof. of radiation-oncology, 1988-89, prof. emeritus, 1989—; guest prof. in exptl. oncology Inst. Cancer Research, Aarhus, Denmark, 1982-83; tech. dir. H.S.C. and A. El Paso, El Paso, 1989-96. Patentee in field. Served with AUS, 1942-45. Mem. Am. Phys. Soc., Optical Soc. Am., Internat. Soc. Optical Engring., Bioelectromagnetics Soc., IEEE, AAAS, NSPE, Am. Congress on Surveying and Mapping, Eta Kappa Nu, Pi Mu Epsilon, N.Mex. Acad. Sci. Home: 5809 E 3rd St Tucson AZ 85711-1519

JONES, ROGER WAYNE, electronics executive; b. Riverside, Calif., Nov. 21, 1939; s. Virgil Elsworth and Beulah (Mills) J.; m. Sherill Lee Bottjer, Dec. 28, 1975; children: Jerrod Wayne, Jordan Anthony. BS in Engring., San Diego State U., 1962. Br. sales mgr. Bourns, Inc., Riverside, 1962-68; sales and mktg. mgr. Spectrol Electronics, Industry, Calif., 1968-77, v.p. mktg., 1979-81; mng. dir. Spectrol Reliance, Ltd., Swindon, England, 1977-79; sr. v.p. S.W. group Kierulff Electronics Corp., L.A., 1981-83; v.p. sales and mktg. worldwide electronic techs. div. Beckman Instruments, Fullerton, Calif., 1983-86; pres., ptnr. Jones & McGeoy Sales, Inc., Newport Beach, Calif., 1986—. Author: The History of Villa Rockledge, A National Treasure in Laguna Beach, 1991. Republican. Home: 4 Roma Ct Newport Beach CA 92657-1531 Office: 5100 Campus Dr Newport Beach CA 92660-2101

JONES, RONALD H., computer information systems executive; b. San Diego, Feb. 11, 1938; s. Henry G. and Geneva H. (Hodges) J.; m. Carol Sue Carmichael, Dec. 9, 1967. BS, San Diego State Coll., 1959, MS, 1961. Project mgr. UNIVAC, San Diego, 1961-67, Computer Scis. Corp., San Diego, 1967-75; v.p. Interactive, Inc., San Diego, 1975-92; owner Consulting Co., San Diego, 1992—; ind. cons., programmer various mfg. & distbg. cos., San Diego, 1992—. Contbr. articles to profl. jours; tech. advisor to Internat. Spectrum Mag. Advisor San Diego State Univ.; Rep. nat. committeeman, 1979—. Mem. AARP, Am. Prodn. and Inventory Control Soc., Assn. for Computing Machinery, Calpirg and Ucan. Presbyterian. Home and Office: 2484 Pine St San Diego CA 92103-1042 Office: Ron Jones Cons PO Box 370083 San Diego CA 92137-0083

JONES, STANLEY BELMONT, counselor; b. Newport News, Va., Aug. 7, 1961; s. Stanley Brown and Irma Virginia (Owens) J.; m. LaRita Yvonne Ross, June 21, 1986; 1 child, Alanah Yvonne. BA in Speech Comm., U. Richmond, 1983; MEd in Guidance and Counseling, City U., 1995. Commd. officer U.S. Army, 1983, advanced through grades to capt., 1988; various positions 542nd Maintenace Co., Ft. Lewis, Wash., 1984-87; plans and policy officer 593rd Area Support Group, Ft. Lewis, 1987-88; logistics officer 1st Maintenance Battalion, Boblingen, Germany, 1989-90; co. comdr. 22nd Maintenance Co., Heilbronn, Germany, 1990-91; maintenance officer 44th Support Bat., Ft. Lewis, 1992; ret. U.S. Army, 1992; counselor, football coach A.G. Hudtloff Jr. H.S., Tacoma, 1993-96, Clover Park High Sch., Lakewood Center, Wash., 1996—; planner earthquake preparedness A.G. Hudtloff Jr. H.S., Tacoma, 1993—, cons. sch. adv. bd., 1993—, dir. student conflict mediation program, 1993—. Named Outstanding Young Men in Am., 1984. Mem. ACA, NEA, Wash. Edn. Assn., Phi Beta Sigma (sec. Mu Omicron chpt. 1981-82, v.p., 1982-83), Phi Beta Sigma (Epsilon Epsilon Sigma chpt.). Baptist. Office: Clover Park High Sch Lakewood Center WA 98499

JONES, STANLEY R., government contracts business consultant; b. Bozeman, Mont., Jan. 13, 1939; s. James Alford and Rose Opal (Bohna) J.; m. Pamela Lynn Ray, Sept. 13, 1980. BS, Mont. State U., 1961; MBA, Ariz. State U., 1970. Cert. profl. contract mgr. Dir. Mid-East Ops. Telemedia, Inc., Chgo., 1974-76; cons. Bellevue, Wash., 1976-80; dir. project mgmt. Tacoma (Wash.) Boat Bldg. Co., 1980-82; pres. Yesterday's Rent-A-Car, Seattle, 1982-88; cons. Price-Waterhouse, Bellvue, 1988-90, Renton, Wash., 1990—. Lt. Col. USAF, 1961-74. Fellow Nat. Contract Mgmt. Assn. (chpt. v.p. edn. 1988-90, chpt. pres. 1990-92). Office: Stan Jones Assocs 15 S Grady Way Ste 421 Renton WA 98055

JONES, STANTON WILLIAM, management consultant; b. New Orleans, May 24, 1939; s. Albert DeWitt and Clara Arimenta (Stanton) J.; m. Helen Marie Trice, May 23, 1964 (div. Aug. 1972); 1 child, Ellen Marie; m. Gladys Marina Caceres, Aug. 21, 1990; children: Hazel Nathalye, Albert Stanton. BS, Embry-Riddle Aero. U., Daytona Beach, Fla., 1973; MBA, Syracuse (N.Y.) U., 1977. Cert. internal auditor. Commd. 2d lt. U.S. Army, 1963, advanced through grades to lt. col., 1979; fixed wing pilot U.S. Army, Ft. Rucker, Ala., 1965-72, rotary wing pilot, 1972; mgmt. cons. Stanton W. Jones & Assocs., San Francisco, 1987—; joint venture ptnr. Budget Analyst to Bd. Suprs., San Francisco, 1988—. Treas. Hunter's Point Boys & Girls Club, San Francisco, 1987-93. Decorated Meritorious Svc. medal. Mem. Alpha Phi Alpha (pres. 1988-90). Roman Catholic. Home: 1948 Cortereal Ave Oakland CA 94611-2632 Office: Stanton W Jones & Assocs 57 Post St Ste 713 San Francisco CA 94104-5025

JONES, STEPHANIE LEE, biologist, ornithologist, botanist; b. Salt Lake City, Nov. 17, 1954; d. Lamar Spenser Jones and Marian Frances (Schoular) Robinson. BA, San Francisco State U., 1978; MA, San Jose (Calif.) State U., 1988. Clk. U.S. Geol. Survey, Menlo Pk., Calif., 1985-88; dist. biologist U.S. Forest Svc., Weaverville, Calif., 1989-91; nongame bird biologist U.S. Fish and Wildlife Svc., Denver, 1992—. Author: Canyon Wren, 1995. Recipient Merit Achievement award Ptnrs. in Flight, Estes Pk., Colo., 1992. Mem. Am. Ornithol. Soc., Soc. Western Botany, Wilson Ornithol. Soc., Cooper Ornithol. Soc. (mem. membership com. 1988—). Office: US Fish and Wildlife Svc PO Box 25486 DFC Denver CO 80225

JONES, THOMAS ROBERT, social worker; b. Escanaba, Mich., Jan. 3, 1950; s. Gene Milton and Alica Una (Mattson) J.; m. Joy Sedlock. BA, U. Laverne, 1977; MSW, U. Hawaii, 1979. Social work assoc. Continuing Care Svcs., Camarillo, Calif., 1973-78; psychiat. social worker Camarillo State Hosp., 1980-84; psychotherapist Terkensha Child Treatment Ctr., Sacramento, Calif., 1984-86; psychiat. social worker Napa (Calif.) State Hosp., 1986-87, Vets. Home Calif., Yountville, 1987—. Mem. Nat. Assn. Social Workers, Soc. Clin. Social Work, Am. Orthopsychiat. Assn., Acad. Cert. Social Workers, Assn. for Advancement Behavior Therapy. Home: PO Box 1095 Yountville CA 94599-1095 Office: Vets Home Calif Yountville CA 94599

JONES, THOMAS WILLIAM, artist; b. Lakewood, Ohio, Aug. 13, 1942; s. Robert W. and Roberta P. Jones; m. Carrie Pemberton, July 21, 1973. Diploma of Art, Cleve. Inst. Art, 1964. Selected exhbns. include Hubbard Mus., Ruidoso Downs, N.Mex. (Art Award of Excellence), Colo. Heritage Ctr. Mus., Denver, Henry Gallery Invitation, Seattle, Nat. Acad. Western Art, Oklahoma City, 154th Nat. Acad. Design, N.Y.C., Springfield (Mo.) Art Mus., Butler Inst. Am. Art, Youngstown, Ohio, Seattle Art Mus., Frye Art Mus., Seattle; commd. to paint ofcl. White House Christmas card for Pres. and Mrs. Ronald Reagan, 1985-88. Works in permanent collections at Frye Art Mus., Seattle, Gen. Telephone Co. of N.W., Seattle First Nat. Bank, Western Internat. Hotels, Carlton House, Pitts., St. Francis Hotel, San Francisco, Eddie Bauer, Inc., Redmond, Wash., Wash. Mut. Savs. Bank, Seattle, City of Seattle Selects II, Safeco, Seattle, Pacific Car and Foundry, Seattle, USN, Rainier Bank, Seattle, Reed, McClure, Moceri and Thonn, P.S., Seattle; contbr. articles to profl. jours. Recipient Ted Kautzky Meml. award Am. Watercolor Soc. 108th Ann., 1975, 112th Ann. Bronze Medal, 1979, Nat. Acad. Western Art Gold Medal, 1987, Silver Medal, 1984, 93, others. Mem. Nat. Acad. Western Art, Fedn. Can. Artists (hon.).

JONES, THORNTON KEITH, research chemist; b. Brawley, Calif., Dec. 17, 1923; s. Alfred George and Madge Jones; m. Evalee Vestal, July 4, 1965; children: Brian Keith, Donna Eileen. BS, U. Calif., Berkeley, 1949, postgrad., 1951-52. Research chemist Griffin Chem. Co., Richmond, Calif., 1949-55; western product devel. and improvement mgr. Nopco Chem. Co., Richmond, Calif., 1955; research chemist Chevron Research Co., Richmond, 1956-65, research chemist in spl. products research and devel., 1965-1982; product quality mgr. Chevron USA, Inc., San Francisco, 1982-87, ret. Patentee in field. Vol. fireman and officer, Terra Linda, Calif., 1957-64; mem. adv. com. Terra Linda Dixie Elem. Sch. Dist., 1960-64. Served with Signal Corps, U.S. Army, 1943-46. Mem. Am. Chem. Soc., Forest Products Research Soc., Am. Wood Preservers Assn., Alpha Chi Sigma. Republican. Presbyterian.

JONES, VERNON QUENTIN, surveyor; b. Sioux City, Iowa, May 6, 1930; s. Vernon Boyd and Winnifred Rhoda (Bremmer) J.; student UCLA, 1948-50; m. Rebeca Buckovecz, Oct. 1981; children: Steven Vernon, Gregory Richard, Stanley Alan, Lynn Sue. Draftsman III Pasadena (Calif.) city engr., 1950-53; sr. civil engring. asst. L.A. County engr., L.A., 1953-55; v.p. Treadwell Engring. Corp., Arcadia, Calif., 1955-61, pres., 1961-64; pres. Hillcrest Engring. Corp., Arcadia, 1961-64; dep. county surveyor, Ventura, Calif., 1964-78; propr. Vernon Jones Land Surveyor, Riviera, Ariz., 1978—; city engr. Needles (Calif.), 1980-87; instr. Mohave Community Coll., 1987—. Chmn. graphic tech. com. Ventura Unified Sch. Dist., 1972-78, mem. career adv. com., 1972-74; mem. engring. adv. com. Pierce Coll., 1973; pres. Mgmt. Employees of Ventura County, 1974. V.p. Young Reps. of Ventura County, 1965. Pres., Marina Pacifica Homeowners Assn., 1973. Mem. League Calif. Surveying Orgns. (pres. 1975), Am. Congress on Surveying and Mapping (chmn. So. Calif. sect. 1976), Am. Soc. Photogrammetry, Am. Pub. Works Assn., County Engr. Assn. Calif. Home: 913E San Juan Ct Bullhead City AZ 86442-5618

JONES, WAYNE ROSS, agronomist; b. Chenoa, Ill., July 14, 1925; s. Everett Elmer and Martha Elizabeth (Falkingham) J.; m. Myrtle (Dolly) Geissler Jones, Apr. 26, 1947; children: Kathy, Keith, Connie. Grad., Arrowsmith (Ill.) H.S., 1944. Supt. tool design ITT Canon Electric, Santa Ana, Calif., 1959-68; mgr. ops. RDS Labs., Exeter, Calif., 1970-73; engring. and mfg. cons. Upright Harvester, Selma, Calif., 1974-75; owner, operator Sci. Agrl. Svcs., Inc., Napa, Calif., 1975—. Mem. NRA, Am. Soc. Agronomy, Am. Quarter Horse Assn., Crop Sci. Soc. Am., Soil Sci. Soc. Am. Republican. Office: Sci Agrl Svcs Inc 3393 Atlas Peak Rd Napa CA 94558

JONES, WILLIAM LEON, state legislator, rancher; b. Coalinga, Calif., Dec. 20, 1949; s. C.W. and Cora Jones; m. Maurine Abramson, Aug. 29, 1971; children: Wendy, Andrea. BS in Agribus. and Plant Sci., Calif. State U., Fresno, 1971. Ptnr. ranch, nr. Firebaugh, Calif.; mem. Calif. Assembly, Sacramento, 1983—, Rep. leader, 1991—; now Sec. of State State of California. Former chmn. Fresno County Rep. Cen. Com. Named Outstanding Young Farmer, Fresno C. of C. Mem. Fresno County and City C. of C. (past bd. dirs.). Methodist. Home: 2254 W Dovewood Ln Fresno CA 93711-2810 Office: Office Sec State 1500 11th St Sacramento CA 95814-5701*

JONES-EDDY, JULIE MARGARET, librarian; b. Hayden, Colo., Feb. 20, 1942; d. Hugh A. and Margaret E. (Tagert) J.; m. John H. Eddy Jr., June 3, 1965; 1 child, Mark. BA, U. Colo., 1964; MLS, U. Okla., 1976. Cert. libr. Art tchr. Fort Collins (Colo.) Pub. Schs., 1964-65, Gunnison (Colo.) Pub. Schs., 1965-66; govt. documents libr. Tutt Libr., Colo. Coll., Colorado Springs, 1977—; presenter in field of oral history project on women, 1984—. Author: (videotape) Women of Northwestern Colorado, 1890-1940: Glimpses of Our Lives, 1984; author: Homesteading Women: An Oral History of Colorado, 1890-1950, 1992. Grantee Colo. Endowment for the Humanities, 1984, 89. Mem. ALA, Colo. Libr. Assn., Oral History Assn. Office: Colorado Coll Tutt Library 1021 N Cascade Ave Colorado Springs CO 80903-3252

JONGEWARD, GEORGE RONALD, retired systems analyst; b. Yakima, Wash., Aug. 9, 1934; s. George Ira and Dorothy Marie (Cronk) J.; m. Janet Jeanne Williams, July 15, 1955; children: Mary Jeanne, Dona Lee, Karen Anne. BA, Whitworth Coll., 1957; postgrad., Utah State U., 1961. Sr. systems analyst Computer Scis. Corp., Honolulu, 1969-71; cons. in field Honolulu, 1972-76; prin. The Hobby Co., Honolulu, 1977-81; sr. systems analyst Computer Systems Internat., Honolulu, 1981-96, asst. v.p., 1994-96; instr. EDP Hawaii Pacific U., Honolulu, 1982-90. Mem. car show com. Easter Seal Soc., Honolulu. 1977-82; active Variety Club, Honolulu, 1978-81. Mem. Mensa (Hawaii pres. 1967-69), Triple-9. Republican. Presbyterian. Home: 4108 Avalanche Ave Yakima WA 98908

JONKER, PETER EMILE, gas company executive; b. The Hague, The Netherlands, Sept. 15, 1948; came to U.S., 1966, naturalized, 1985; s. Jacob and Jurrina (Wories) J.; m. Janet Lynn Gotfredson, Sept. 6, 1974; children: Jeffrey, Annelies. BSChemE cum laude, U. So. Calif., 1971, MSChemE, 1972; JD with honors, Western State U., Fullerton, Calif., 1979. Bar: Calif. 1979. Research engr. Union Oil Co., Los Angeles, 1972-75; regulations coordinator Union Oil Co., L.A., 1975-79, atty., 1979; mgr. govtl. and pub. affairs Western Liquefied Nat. Gas, L.A., 1979-81; mgr. environ. permitting Tosco Corp., L.A., 1981-83; mgr. regional pub. affairs So. Calif. Gas. Co., L.A., 1983-85, mgr. rate design, demand forecast and analysis, 1986-88, mgr. fed. energy affairs, 1988-90, mgr. support svcs., 1990-92; mgr. policy and planning So. Calif. Gas Co., L.A., 1992-94, mgr. external affairs, 1994-95, dir. govtl. affairs, 1995—; mem. So. Coast Air Quality Mgmt. Dist. Adv. Coun., L.A., 1983-85; mem. Fed. Clean Air Act Adv. Com.; dir. Calif. Coun. for Environ. and Econ. Balance, 1994—. Editor Western State Law Rev., 1976-79; contbr. articles to profl. jours. Trustee, deacon San Marino (Calif.) Presbyn. Community Ch., 1980—; councilman U. So. Calif. Engring. Student Council, Los Angeles, 1971-72, dir. Engring. Alumni Assn., 1971-72; fgn. del. White House Conf., Washington, 1971. Mem. Am. Gas Assn., Air and Waste Mgmt. Assn. (v.p. West Coast chpt. 1984, 85, dir. West Coast sect. 1993—), Fed. Energy Bar Assn., Pacific Coast Gas Assn., Tau Beta Pi (pres., v.p. Calif. Delta chpt. 1970-71). Republican. Home: 2796 Heritage Dr Pasadena CA 91107-5915 Office: So Calif Gas Co 555 W 5th St Los Angeles CA 90013-1010

JONSSON-DEVILLERS, EDITH, foreign language educator; b. Marseille, France; came to U.S., 1969; married: Erik Jonsson, Mar. 29, 1959; children: Sylvia, Irline. Diploma of English Studies, Cambridge (U.K.) U., 1954; Lic. in Letters, The Sorbonne, Paris, 1957; PhD in Comparative Lit., U. Calif., San Diego, 1976. Cert. interpreter Spanish/French, Calif. Free-lance interpreter, 1960—; free-lance translator San Diego, 1970—, ct. interpreter, 1986—; asst. prof. U. Calif., San Diego, 1970-76, 87—, Occidental Coll., L.A., 1976-79; lectr. U. San Diego, 1969-70, 82-86, San Diego State U., 1981-87, 91; founding dir. Alliance Francaise Sch., San Diego, 1989-93. Contbr. articles to profl. jours. Fulbright travel grantee, 1954-55; U. Calif.-San Diego Dissertation fellow, 1975. Mem. MLA, Am. Lit. Translators Assn., Calif. Ct. Interpreters Assn. (v.p. 1994—), Am. Translators Assn., U.S. Mexico Border Health Assn. Instituto Internacional de Literatura Iberoamericana.

JOOST-GAUGIER, CHRISTIANE LOUISE, art history educator; b. Ste. Maxime, France; d. Louis Clair and Agnes Larsen Gaugier; children: Leonarda A. Joost, Nathalie P. Joost. BA, Radcliffe Coll., 1955; MA, Harvard U., 1959, PhD, 1973. Lectr. U. Mich., Ann Arbor, 1960; asst. prof. Mich. State U., East Lansing, 1961-62, Tufts U., Medford, Mass., 1968-73; assoc. prof. to prof., dept. chmn. N.Mex. State U., Las Cruces, 1975-85; prof., dept. chmn. U. N.Mex., Albuquerque, 1985-87, prof. art history, 1987—; bd. dirs. Nat. Coun. Art Adminstrs. Author: Selected Drawings of Jacopo Bellini, 1980; contbr. articles to profl. jours. Grantee Delmas, Am. Philos. Soc.; Fulbright fellow, ACLS fellow, Vassie James Hill fellow AAUW. Mem. Coll. Art Assn. Am. (bd. dirs.), Renaissance Soc. Am. (bd. dirs.), Internat. Soc. for the Classical Tradition, Am. Assn. for Italian Studies, The Sixteenth Century Soc. Office: Univ NMex Dept Art & Art History Albuquerque NM 87131

JORAJURIA, ELSIE JEAN, elementary education educator; b. Flagstaff, Ariz., June 28, 1946; d. Frank Y. and Elsie (Barreres) Auza; m. Ramon Jorajuria, June 23, 1973; children: Tonya, Nina. BS in Edn., No. Ariz. U., 1971, MA in Elem. Edn., 1975. Cert. elem. edn., Ariz. First grade tchr. Kinsey Sch., Flagstaff, Ariz., 1971-73; third grade tchr. Mohawk Valley Sch., Roll, Ariz., 1973-77, migrant edn. coord., 1980-83, second lang. English Kindergarten tchr., 1983-84, first grade tchr., 1984—; tchr. ESL Ariz. Wester Coll., Yuma, Ariz., 1987. Cheerleader sponsor, Roll, Ariz., 1984-97; vol. 4-H, Roll, 1986-97, project leader, 1990-97, cmty. leader, 1994-97, sponsor Student Coun., Roll, 1994-95. Named Tchr. of Yr., Mohawk Valley Sch., 1987-88, 88-89, 95-96, Woman of the Yr., Bus. Profl. Woman, 1994. Mem. NEA, Ariz. Edn. Assn., Mohawk Valley Tchr. Assn. (pres. 1992-94), Ariz. Wool Growers Assn. Democrat. Roman Catholic. Home: PO Box 485 40154 Colorado Ave Tacna AZ 85352 Office: Mohawk Valley Sch PO Box 67 Roll AZ 85347

JORDAHL, GEIR ARILD, photographer, educator; b. Kristiansund, Norway, Jan. 27, 1957; came to U.S., 1961; s. Sigurd and Solveig Ingvarda (Pedersen) J.; m. Kathleen Patricia O'Grady, Sept. 24, 1983. BA, Calif. State U., Hayward, 1979; MFA, Ohio U., 1983. Life C.C. teaching credential, Calif. Teaching assoc. Ohio U., Athens, 1980-82; instr. photography Chabot Coll., Hayward, Calif., 1983—; owner, mgr. Geir & Kate Jordahl, Photography, Hayward, 1983—; ind. curator, Hayward, 1984—; coord. PhotoCen. Photography Programs, Hayward, 1983—; artist-in-residence Yosemite (Calif.) Nat. Park, 1993; mem. curatorial com. Hayward Forum for Arts/Sun Gallery, 1992. Exhibited in numerous shows including Kansas City (Mo.) Art Inst., 1987, Ohio State Art Gallery, Newark, 1987, Mus. Art U. Oreg., Eugene, 1988, Mus. for Photography, Braunschweig, Germany, 1988, Ansel Adams Gallery, Yosemite, 1989, Mus. Modern Art, Tampere, Finland, 1989, Trenton (N.J.) Mus. Art, 1991, Ansel Adams Ctr. for Photography, San Francisco, 1990, Photo Forum Gallery, Pitts., 1993, Yosemite Nat. Park Mus., 1994, Ansel Adams Gallery, 1995, Yosemite Nat. Park Visitor Ctr., 1996, Bibliotheque Nat. de France, and other pvt. and pub. collections; contbr. to profl. publs.; photographer various catalogues. Precinct capt. Hayward Dem. Com., 1992. Recipient purchase award Hayward Area Forum Arts, 1986, Ohio State U., 1987, Yosemite Nat. Park and Curry Co., 1992, award of excellence Calif. State Fair, 1987, 89, One of Top 100 New Photographers award Maine Photog. Workshops and Kodak Corp., 1987, Innovative New Program award Calif. Parks and Recreation Soc., 1990; scholar Calif. State U., 1975, Ohio U., 1981, Oslo Internat. Summer Sch., 1982, exch. scholar U. Trondheim, Norway, 1983, Peder P. Johnsen scholar Sons of Norway, 1983. Mem. Soc. Photog. Edn., Internat. Assn. Panoramic Photographers, Friends of Photography, San Francisco Camerawork. Home and Studio: PO Box 3998 144 Medford Ave Hayward CA 94540

JORDAHL, KATHLEEN PATRICIA (KATE JORDAHL), photographer, educator; b. Summit, N.J., Aug. 23, 1959; d. Martin Patrick and Marie Pauline (Quinn) O'Grady; m. Geir Arild Jordahl, Sept. 24, 1983. BA in Art & Art History magna cum laude with distinction, U. Del., 1980; MFA in Photography, Ohio U., 1982. Lifetime credential in art and design, Calif. Teaching assoc. Sch. Art Ohio U., Athens, 1980-82; adminstrv. asst. A.D. Coleman, S.I., N.Y., 1981; placement asst. career planning & placement U. Calif., Berkeley, 1983; instr. Coll. for Kids, Hayward, Calif., 1987-88; supr. student/alumni employment office Chabot Coll., Hayward, 1983-87, tchr. photography, 1987—; workshop coord. Friends of Photography, San Francisco, 1990; instr., workshop leader, coord. PhotoCen. Photography Programs, Hayward, 1983—; mem., co-coord., publ. evaluation accreditation com. Chabot Coll., Hayward, 1984, instrnl. skills workshop facilitator, 1994, speaker opening day, 1986, coord. ann. classified staff devel. workshop, 1985; workshop leader Ansel Adams Gallery, Yosemite, Calif., 1991, 92, artist-in-residence Yosemite Nat. Park Mus., 1993; ind. curator numerous exhbns., 1984—; coord., curator Women's Photography Workshop & Exhbn., 1993—. Exhibited in group shows Parts Gallery, Minn., 1992, The Alameda Arts Commn. Gallery, Oakland, 1992, Panoramic Invitational, Tampere, Finland, 1992, Photo Forum, Pitts., 1992, Photo Metro Gallery, San Francisco, 1993, Ansel Adams Gallery, Yosemite, 1994, Yosemite Mus., 1994, Vision Gallery, San Francisco, 1994, 95, San Francisco Mus. Modern Art Rental Gallery, 1994; represented in permanent collections Muse Gallery, Phila., 1982, Ohio U. Libr. Rare Books Collection, Athens, 1982, Yosemite Mus., 1994, Bibliotheque Nationale de France, Paris; contbr. photos and articles to photography mags. and publs. Recipient Innovative New Program award Calif. Parks and Recreation Soc., 1990; Sons of Norway scholar U. Oslo, summer 1996. Mem. Internat. Assn. Panoramic Photographers, Soc. Photographic Edn., Friends of Photography, Sun Gallery, Phi Beta Kappa. Democrat. Office: PO Box 3998 Hayward CA 94540-3998

JORDAN, CHARLES MORRELL, retired automotive designer; b. Whittier, Calif., Oct. 21, 1927; s. Charles L. and Bernice May (Letts) J.; m. Sally Irene Mericle, Mar. 8, 1951; children: Debra, Mark, Melissa. BS, MIT, 1949; grad. advanced mgmt. program, Harvard U., 1979; Doctorate (hon.), Art Ctr. Coll. Design, 1992. With GM, Warren, Mich., 1949—, chief designer Cadillac Studio, 1957-61, group chief designer, 1961-62, exec. in charge automotive design, 1962-67, dir. styling Adam Opel A.G., 1967-70, exec. in charge Cadillac, Oldsmobile, Buick Studios, 1970-73, exec. in charge Chevrolet, Pontiac and Comml. Vehicle Studios, 1973-77, dir. design, 1977-86, v.p. design staff, 1986-92; retired, 1992. 1st lt. USAF, 1952-53. Recipient First Nat. award Fisher Body Craftsman's Guild, 1947, disting. svc. citation Automotive Hall of Fame, 1993; named Hon. Judge, Pebble Beach Concours d'Elegance, 1970—. Mem. Calif. Scholastic Fedn. (life), Ferrari Club Am. Address: PO Box 8330 Rancho Santa Fe CA 92067-8330

JORDAN, EDWARD GEORGE, business investor, former college president, former railroad executive; b. Oakland, Cal., Nov. 13, 1929; s. Edward A. and Alice (Smith) J.; m. Nancy Phyllis Schmidt, June 20, 1954; children: Susan Gail, Kathryn Claire, Jonathan Edward, Christopher Austin. B.A. in Econs. with honors, U. Calif. at Berkeley, 1951; M.B.A., Stanford U., 1953. Pres. Pinehurst Corp. (ins. and pension plans), Los Angeles, 1973-74, U.S. Ry. Assn., Washington, 1974-75; chmn., chief exec. officer Consol. Rail Corp., 1975-80, cons. to chmn., 1981; dean Cornell U. Grad. Sch. Bus. and Public Adminstrn., Ithaca, N.Y., 1981; exec. v.p. U. Pa., 1981-82; pres. Am. Coll., Bryn Mawr, Pa., 1982-87; bd. dirs. Aramark Corp., Cambridge Energy Rsch. Assocs., Acme Metals Co. Chmn. Calif. Transp. Commn. Mem. Merion Golf Club, Univ. Club N.Y., Monterey Peninsula Country Club. Home: 26162 Ladera Dr Carmel CA 93923-9207

JORDAN, GLENN, director; b. San Antonio, Apr. 5, 1936. B.A., Harvard U., 1957; postgrad., Yale U. Drama Sch., 1957-58. Dir. regional and stock theatre, including Cafe La Mama, late 1950s; N.Y. directorial debut with Another Evening With Harry Stoones, 1961; other plays include A Taste of Honey, 1968; Rosencrantz and Guildenstern Are Dead, 1969, A Streetcar Named Desire at Cin. Playhouse in the Park, 1973, All My Sons at Huntington Hartford Theatre, 1975; founder, N.Y. TV Theater, 1965, dir. various plays, including Paradise Lost and Hogan's Goat; dir. mini-series Benjamin Franklin, CBS, 1974 (Emmy award 1975, Peabody award); Family, ABC-TV series, 1976-77, including segment Rights of Friendship (Dirs. Guild Am. award); numerous TV plays for public TV, including Eccentricities of a Nightingale, 1976; The Displaced Person, 1976; TV movies including Shell Game, 1975, One Of My Wives Is Missing, 1975, Delta County U.S.A, 1977, In The Matter of Karen Ann Quinlan, 1977, Sunshine Christmas, 1977, Les Miserables, 1978, Son-Rise, A Miracle of Love, 1979, The Family Man, 1979, The Women's Room, 1980, Lois Gibbs and the Love Canal, 1982, Heartsounds, 1984 (Peabody award), Toughlove, 1985, Dress Gray, 1986, Something in Common, 1986, Promise, 1986 (2 Emmy awards for producing, directing, Peabody award, Golden Globe award), Echoes in the Darkness, 1987, Jesse, 1988, Home Fires Burning, 1988, Challenger, 1989, The Boys, 1990, Sarah Plain and Tall, 1990, Aftermath, 1990, O Pioneers!, 1991, Barbarians at the Gate, 1992 (Emmy award Outstanding Made for TV Movie, 1993, Golden Globe award, Best Mini-series or movie made for TV, 1994), To Dance with the White Dog, 1994, Jane's House, 1994, My Brother's Keeper, 1994, A Streetcar Named Desire, 1995, Jake's Women (Neil Simon), 1996, After Jimmy, 1996, Mary and Tim, 1996; dir: feature film Only When I Laugh (Neil Simon), 1981, The Buddy System, 1983, Mass Appeal, 1984. Recipient Emmy awards for N.Y. TV Theater Plays, 1970, Actors Choice, 1970. Office: Creative Artists Agy 9830 Wilshire Blvd Beverly Hills CA 90212-1804 also: 9401 Wilshire Blvd Ste 700 Beverly Hills CA 90212-2920

JORDAN, ISOLDE JAHNCKE, Spanish and Portuguese language educator; b. Lisbon, Sept. 16, 1942; came to U.S., 1982; d. Bernhard and Grete (Durholt) Jahncke; m. William Thomas Warren III, July 7, 1967 (div. Feb. 1973); children: Alex Warren, John Warren; m. Sandoe Quarton Jordan, Feb. 2, 1987. Cert. in teaching, U. Bonn, Germany, 1965; PhD, U. Paris, 1966; PhD in Spanish, U. Colo., 1987. Lectr. Portuguese U. Ill., Urbana, 1967-69, U. Freiburg, Germany, 1972-73; lectr. Spanish and Portuguese U. Colo., Boulder, 1987-94, sr. instr., 1994—. Author: Introduccion al analisis linguistico del discurso, 1994, Cohesion y retorica en la conversacion, 1997; editor: El inmovilismo existencial en la narrativa de Julio Ricci; contbr. articles to profl. jours. Mem. MLA, Am. Assn. Tchrs. Spanish and Portuguese. Home: 3243 4th St Boulder CO 80304-2155 Office: U Colo Dept Spanish CB278 Boulder CO 80309

JORDAN, JAMES DOUGLAS, JR., chemical dependency consultant; b. Bklyn., Oct. 1, 1965; s. James Douglas Sr. and Vergia (Kemp) J. BS, Coll. of Notre Dame, Belmont, Calif., 1987, MA in Psychology, 1993. Leadership devel. specialist Regional Leadership, Menlo Park, Calif., 1986-88; counselor Community Living Ctrs., Redwood City, Calif., 1987-89, client program coord., 1989-90; juvenile group supr. San Mateo Probation Dept., Belmont, Calif., 1988-93; supervising case mgr. Community Living Ctrs., Redwood City, 1990-92; exec. cons. Chem. Dependency Cons. and Mktg. Group, San Jose, Calif., 1992—. Author papers. Rschr. Congl. Election Com., Sunnyvale, Calif., 1988-91; dir. pub. rels. Omega Youth Club, East Palo Alto, Calif., 1991—. Mem. Coll. of Notre Dame Alumni Assn. (bd. dirs. 1988-91), Delta Epsilon Sigma, Kappa Gamma Pi. Office: Chem Dependency Consulting & Mktg Group 5339 Prospect Rd # 409 San Jose CA 95129-5033

JORDAN, JEFFREY GUY, marketing and marketing research consultant; b. Oshkosh, Wis., May 21, 1950; s. Berwin Russell and Delores Suzanne (Tomlitz) J. BS, U. Wis., Oshkosh, 1973; postgrad., UCLA, 1978. Analyst corp. planning and rsch. May Co. Dept. Store, L.A., 1973-77; dir. mktg. svcs. DJMC Advt., L.A., 1977-80; dir. mktg. Wienerschnitzel, Internat., Newport Beach, Calif., 1980-84, York Steakhouse Restaurants (Gen. Mills), Columbus, Ohio, 1984-85, Paragon Restaurant Group, San Diego, 1985-87; v.p. mktg. Paragon Steakhouse Restaurants, Inc., San Diego, 1987-94; owner, pres. 1-on-One Mktg. Assocs., 1994—; cons., presenter U.S. Internat. U., San Diego, 1989. Mem. Conv. and Visitors Bur., San Diego; vol. Boys' Club of Am., Oshkosh, 1973-74; fundraising coord. Am. Cancer Soc., L.A., 1976. Mem. Am. Mktg. Assn. (treas., bd. dirs. 1996-97), Multi Unit Foodservice Operators Assn., San Diego Advt. Assn. (creative exec. 1986-88), San Diego C. of C. Republican. Lutheran.

JORDAN, KARIN BALTEN-BABKOWSKI, health facility administrator; b. Hannover, Germany, July 26, 1958; came to U.S., 1979; d. Ekkehard and Liselotte (Pache) Babkowski; m. Wayne Donald Jordan, June 13, 1981. BA in Biology cum laude, Colo. Christian Coll., Denver, 1987; MA in Counseling, Rollins Coll., Winter Park, Fla., 1989; PhD in Child and Family Devel., U. Ga., 1992. RN; lic. marriage and family therapist, Colo.; cert. kindergarten tchr., Germany. Intern in counseling Hope and Help Ctr., Orlando, Fla., 1989; intern in marriage and family therapy McPhaul Ctr., Athens, 1990-91; asst. clin. dir. Cross Keys Counseling Ctr., Atlanta, 1991-93; practicum supr. U. Colo., Denver, 1993, clin. dir., faculty, 1994—; rsch. asst. dept. child and family devel. U. Ga., Athens, 1989-91; bd. dirs., counselor Sun Valley Family Hope Counseling Ctr., Denver, 1996—. Contbr. articles to profl. jours. Mem. mental health com. 9News Health Fair, Denver, 1995 ; mem. com. Colo. Okla. Resource Coun., Denver, 1996—. Mem. APA (divsn. 16 com. children, youth, families 1996—), Am. Assn. Marriage Family Therapy (cert. therapist, supr.), Colo. Assn. Marriage Family Therapy (pub. rels. com. 1996—, v.p.), Colo. Counseling Assn., Internat. Assn. Marriage Family Counselors, Nat. Acad. Cert. Family Therapist. Office: Univ Colo Sch Edn Campus Box 106 PO Box 173364 Denver CO 80217

JORDAN, LOYD EDWARD, county sheriff; b. Ft. Collins, Colo., July 15, 1950; s. Lloyd Ross and Norma Shirleen (Tuescher) J.; children: Loyd Ross II, Andrew Trenton Jordan, Claire Careen. BA, U. Northern Colo., 1972. Laborer Western States Constrn., Loveland, Colo., 1972-73; adjuster Gen. Adjustment Bur., Stochton, Calif., 1972-76; dep. sheriff Weld County (Colo.) Sheriff's Office, Greeley, 1976-87, sheriff, 1987—. founding mem. Weld Svc. Abuse Team, Greeley, 1979-84; mem. Colo. Juvenile Justice and Delinquency Council, Denver, 1987—; dist. capt. Weld County Rep. Party, Greeley, 1980-86. Mem. County Sheriff's of Colo., Am. Jail Assn., Nat. Sheriff's Assn., Norteastern Colo. Peace Assn., Colo. State Sheriff's Posse Assn., Shriner (2d v.p. 1988), South Platte Lions, Masons. Office: Weld County Sheriff's Office 910 10th Ave # 759 Greeley CO 80631-3873

JORDAN, MARIANNE WALLACE, nursing administrator, educator; b. Abington, Pa., July 10, 1950; d. Ambrose Culver and Gertrude Kimber (Clark) M. Diploma in Nursing, Madison (Wis.) Gen. Hosp., 1974; BS, UCLA, 1984. Cert. emergency nurse, flight RN, basic life support instr., ACLS instr., pediatric advanced life support instr., advanced trauma life support, flight nurse advanced trauma. Staff nurse Brotman Hosp., Culver City, Calif., 1975-78, Torrance (Calif.) Meml. Hosp., 1978-79; rsch. assoc. UCLA, 1983-85; rsch. technician U. So. Calif., L.A., 1987-88; critical care transport nurse Schaeffer Ambulance, L.A., 1986-88; staff murse Emergency Med. Ctr., UCLA, 1979-88; med. crew coord. Sierra Med-Evac, Mammoth Lakes, Calif., 1992-93; chief flight nurse Sierra Life Flight, Bishop, Calif., 1993-94; supr./instr. Centinela Mammoth Hosp., Mammoth Lakes, 1988-96; ACLS instr.-cons. Centinela Mammoth Hosp., 1989-96; EMT instr., cons. Lake Tahoe (Calif.) C.C., 1992—; flight nurse Golden Empire Air Rescue, Bakersfield, Calif., 1995-96, Valley Children's Hosp., Fresno, Calif., 1996—, chief flight nurse, Columbia Alaska, regional flight nurse, Anchorage Ark., 1996—; inst. Alaska Med. Course. Author: ACLS Study Guide, 1992, 94; reviewer Air Medical jour. Chmn. Task Force on Pre-Hosp. Care, Mono County, Calif., 1994. Mem. Emergency Nurses Assn., Nat. Flight Nurses Assn., Aircraft Owners and Pilots Assn., Assn. of Air Med. Svcs., Post Anesthesia Nurse Assn. of Calif., Alpha Lambda Delta. Home and Office: 733 W 4th Ave #758 Anchorage AK 99501

JORDAN, MICHAEL AYTCH, accounts manager; b. Lewiston, Idaho, July 22, 1948; s. Aytch Jordan and Betty Jean (Petrie) Jordan Nestor; m. Nancy Loraine Lewis, sept. 27, 1972 (div. June 1990); m. Betsy Jane Conant, Dec. 27, 1990; children: Leatha, Sarah, Joshua, Michael. BBA magna cum laude, Nat. U., 1978, MBA, 1979. Human resource rep. Westinghouse, Richland, Wash., 1980; wardrobe cons. S.L. Sterling, Kennewick, Wash., 1980-84; area account mgr. Wyeth-A-Lerst Labs., Phila., 1984—; study adv. bd. N.W. Pharmacy Rsch. Network, Seattle, 1993—. With USN, 1968-79, Vietnam. Mem. Nat. Bus. Womens Assn. Home: 23620 219th Pl SE Maple Valley WA 98038-8593

JORDAN, ROBERT LEON, lawyer, educator; b. Reading, Pa., Feb. 27, 1928; s. Anthony and Carmela (Votto) J.; m. Evelyn Allen Willard, Feb. 15, 1958; children—John Willard, David Anthony. BA, Pa. State U., 1948; LLB, Harvard U., 1951. Bar: N.Y. 1952. Assoc. White & Case, N.Y.C., 1953-59; prof. law UCLA, 1959-70, 75-91, prof. law emeritus, 1991—, assoc. dean Sch. Law, 1968-69; vis. prof. law Cornell U., Ithaca, N.Y., 1962-63; co-reporter Uniform Consumer Credit Code, 1964-70, Uniform Comml. Code Articles 3, 4, 4A, 1985-90; Fulbright lectr. U. Pisa, Italy, 1967-68. Co-author: (with W.D. Warren) Commercial Law, 1983, 3d edit., 1992, 4th edit., 1997, Bankruptcy, 1985, 3d edit., 1993, 4th edit., 1995. Lt. USAF, 1951-53. Office: UCLA Sch Law 405 Hilgard Ave Los Angeles CA 90024-1301

JORDAN, THOMAS VINCENT, advertising educator, consultant; b. Washington, Aug. 8, 1941; s. Vincent Joseph and Elizabeth (Quinlan) J.; m. Barbara S. Faulkner, Apr. 1, 1967 (div. Apr. 1988); 1 child, Shannon Ann. AA, San Francisco City Coll., 1968; BA, San Francisco State U., 1970, MA, 1971. Freight agt. United Airlines, San Francisco, 1967-71; pub. rels. rep. United Airlines, Chgo., 1971-73; copywriter Leo Burnett Co., Chgo., 1973-76; sr. copywriter Sieber & McIntyre, Chgo., 1976-77; product mgr. Honeywell Info. Systems, Phoenix, 1977-80, mgr. communications, 1980-85; pvt. practice mktg. communications cons. Phoenix and San Jose, Calif., 1986—; prof. San Jose State U., 1987-94; chair Santa Clara Arts and Culture Commn., 1991-94; panelist Women in Communication, Phoenix, 1984; fellow Gannett Seminar on Advt., Chapel Hill, N.C., 1988, Creative Workshop, Chgo., 1990, Direct Mktg. Edn. Found., L.A. and San Francisco, 1990. Contbrs. articles to profl. jours. Speaker Alliance for Bus., Phoenix, 1982-84; vol. Consumer Affairs, Santa Clara, Calif., 1987-88; publicist Sun City Ret. Citizens, Phoenix, 1983-85; pres. bd. dirs. Pate House-Recovery for Men, San Jose, Calif., 1993-94; chair libr. bd. City of Santa Clara, 1994-96; mem. alcohol anc drug abuse adv. bd. Santa Clara County, 1994-96. With USAF, 1959-63, Korea. Hon. Librarian, City of Chgo., 1975. Mem. ACLU (supporting mem.), Bus. Mktg. Assn. (internat. spkr.'s bur. 1984-85, v.p. acad. rels. 1991), Calif. Faculty Assn. (mem. comms. com. 1989-90, treas. San Jose chpt. 1989-93, acad. senator San Jose State Univ. 1993-96), Am. Acad. Advt. (accreditation com. 1988-91, industry rels. com. 1992—), Western Mktg. Educators Assn., Mensa, Intertel, World Future Soc. Internat. Home: 1700 Civic Center Dr Apt 602 Santa Clara CA 95050-4116 Office: San Jose State U One Washington Sq San Jose CA 95192-0055

JORGENSEN, ERIK HOLGER, lawyer; b. Copenhagen, July 19, 1916; s. Holger and Karla (Andersen) J.; children: Jette Friis, Lone Olesen, John, Jean Ann. JD, San Francisco Law Sch., 1960. Bar: Calif. 1961. Pvt. practice law, 1961-70; ptnr. Hersh, Hadfield, Jorgensen & Fried, San Francisco, 1970-76, Hadfield & Jorgensen, San Francisco, 1976-88 . Pres. Aldersly, Danish Retirement Home, San Rafael, Calif., 1974-77, Rebild Park Soc. Bay Area chpt., 1974-77. Fellow Scandinavian Am. Found. (hon.); mem. ABA, San Francisco Lawyers Club, Bar Assn. of San Francisco, Calif. Assn. Realtors (hon. life bd. dirs.). Author: Master Forms Guide for Successful Real Estate Agreements, Successful Real Estate Sales Agreements, 1991; contbr. articles on law and real estate law to profl. jours.

JORGENSEN, GORDON DAVID, engineering company executive; b. Chgo., Apr. 29, 1921; s. Jacob and Marie (Jensen) J.; BS in Elec. Engring., U. Wash., 1948, postgrad. in bus. and mgmt., 1956-59; m. Nadina Anita Peters, Dec. 17, 1948 (div. Aug. 1971); children: Karen Ann, David William, Susan Marie; m. Barbara Noel, Feb. 10, 1972 (div. July 1976); m. Ruth Barnes Chalmers, June 15, 1990. With R.W. Beck & Assos., Cons. Engrs., Phoenix, 1948—, ptnr., 1954-86; pres. Beck Internat., Phoenix, 1971—. Served to lt. (j.g.) U.S. Maritime Service, 1942-45. Recipient Outstanding Service award Phoenix Tennis Assn., 1967; Commendation, Govt. Honduras, 1970. Registered profl. engr., Alaska, Ariz., Calif., Colo., Nev., N.Mex., N.D., Utah, Wash., Wyo. Mem. IEEE (chmn. Wash.-Alaska sect. 1959-60), Nat. Soc. Profl. Engrs., Am. Soc. Appraisers (sr. mem.), Ariz. Cons. Engrs. Assn., Ariz. Soc. Profl. Engrs., Internat. Assn. Assessing Officers, Southwestern Tennis Assn. (past pres.), U.S. Tennis Assn. (pres. 1987-88, chmn. U.S. Open com.); chmn. U.S. Davis Cup com.; chmn. Internat. Tennis Fed., Davis Cup com. Presbyterian (elder). Project mgr. for mgmt., operation studies and reorgn. study Honduras power system, 1969-70. Home: 74-574 Palo Verde Dr Indian Wells CA 92210-7314 Office: RW Beck & Assocs 3003 N Central Ave Phoenix AZ 85012-2902

JORGENSEN, JUDITH ANN, psychiatrist; b. Parris Island, S.C.; d. George Emil and Margaret Georgia Jorgensen; BA, Stanford U., 1963; MD, U. Calif., 1968; m. Ronald Francis Crown, July 11, 1970 (dec. Oct. 1996). Intern, Meml. Hosp., Long Beach, 1969-70; resident County Mental Health Services, San Diego, 1970-73; staff psychiatrist Children and Adolescent Services, San Diego, 1973-78; practice medicine specializing in psychiatry, La Jolla, Calif., 1973—; staff psychiatrist County Mental Health Services of San Diego, 1973-78, San Diego State U. Health Services, 1985-87; psychiat. cons. San Diego City Coll., 1973-78, 85-86; asst. prof. dept. psychiatry U. Calif., 1978-91, assoc. prof. dept. psychiatry, 1991-96; chmn. med. quality rev. com. Dist. XIV, State of Calif., 1982-83. Mem. Am. Psychiat. Assn., San Diego Psychiat. Soc. (chmn. membership com. 1976-78, v.p. 1978-80, fed. legis. rep. 1985-87, fellowship com. 1989—), Am. Soc. Adolescent Psychiatry, San Diego Soc. Adolescent Psychiatry (pres. 1981-82), Calif. Med. Assn. (former alternate del.), Soc. Sci. Study of Sex, San Diego Soc. Sex Therapy and Edn. (cert. sex therapist), San Diego County Med. Soc. (credentials com. 1982-84). Club: Rowing. Office: 470 Nautilus St Ste 211 La Jolla CA 92037-5970

JORGENSEN, LOU ANN BIRKBECK, social worker; b. Park City, Utah, May 14, 1931; d. Robert John and Lillian Pearl (Langford) Birkbeck; student Westminster Coll., 1949-51; B.S., U. Utah, 1953, M.S.W., 1972, D.S.W., 1979; grad. Harvard Inst. Ednl. Mgmt., 1983; m. Howard Arnold Jorgensen, June 9, 1954; children: Gregory Arnold, Blake John, Paul Clayton. Social work adminstr. nursing home demonstration project, dept. family and community medicine U. Utah Med. Ctr., Salt Lake City, 1972-74; mental health ednl. specialist Grad. Sch. Social Work, U. Utah, 1974-77, 77-80, asst. prof., 1974-80, assoc. prof., 1980-94, prof., 1994—, dir. doctoral program, 1984-89, assoc. dean, 1986-94; regional mental health cons. Bd. dirs. Info. and Referral Ctr., 1975-82, United Way of Utah, 1976-82, Pioneer Trail Parks, 1977-83, Rowland Hall-St. Marks Sch., 1980-86; Salt Lake County housing commr., 1980-86, Utah State Health Facilities Bd., 1991—, chair, 1994; pres. Human Svcs. Conf. for Utah, 1979-80; bd. dirs. Alzheimer Assn., Utah chpt., 1990—, Salt Lake County Coalition Bus. and Human Svcs., 1990-94, Town Club 1990-93, bd.; mem. Valley Mental Health Bd., 1990—. Mem. Coun. on Social Work Edn., Commn. Women in High Edn., Nat. Assn. Social Workers (pres. Utah chpt. 1978-79), Adminstrs. of Public Agys. Assn., Human Svcs. Assn. Utah, Jr. League of Salt Lake City, Phi Kappa Phi. Republican. Episcopalian. Clubs: Town. Author: Explorations in Living, 1978, Social Work in Business and Industry, 1979; Handbook of the Social Services, 1981; contbr. articles to profl. jours. Home: 1458 Kristianna Cir Salt Lake City UT 84103-4221 Office: U Utah Grad Sch Social Work Social Work Bldg 324 Salt Lake City UT 84112-1182

JOSEPH, EZEKIEL (ED JOSEPH), manufacturing company executive; b. Rangoon, Burma, June 24, 1938; s. Joe E. Joseph and Rachel Levi; m. Sheila G. Rabinovitch, Feb. 17, 1963; children: Renah, Heather, Jerald. Mktg. mgr. Gen. Electric Corp., Waynesboro, Va., 1968-75; dir. Actron div. McDonnell Douglas Corp., Monrovia, Calif., 1975-78; pres. Joseph Machinery Inc., Huntington Beach, Calif., 1978-84, Xtalite Display Systems Inc.), Huntington Beach, 1985-88, Secure Optical Systems Inc., Anaheim, Calif., 1992—; pres. Retract-a-Roof Inc., Huntington Beach. Pres. Temple Beth David, Huntington Beach, 1990-93. Mem. Austin Healey Assoc. Democrat. Home: 16242 Typhoon Ln Huntington Beach CA 92649-2542 Office: Chemtek Co & Magic Machinery Co 16835 Algonquin St Ste 366 Huntington Beach CA 92649-3810

JOSEPH, JAMES EDWARD, engineering technician; b. Napa, Calif., Sept. 24, 1946; s. Wilbur Raymond and Lois Grace (Pouget) J.; m. Deborah Dianne Horvath, June 5, 1971; children: Brian Christopher, Stacy Lynn Joseph Holster. Diploma, N. Am. Sch. Drafting, 1974, hon. grad. cert., 1977; AA, Napa Valley Coll., 1976; BS, So. Ill. U., 1986. Basic instr. tng. cert., 1993. Naval archtl. aide Mare Island Naval Shipyard, Vallejo, 1967-70; naval archtl. technician Mare Island Naval Shipyard, Vallejo, Calif., 1974-77, 77-89; naval architect tech. supr. Mare Island Naval Shipyard, Vallejo, 1989-91, project leader, 1991-92, material control mgr., 1992-94, engring. technician, 1994—; refinery operator Union Oil Co. Calif., 1971-74; designer, draftsman Morris Guralnick Assocs., Inc., 1974, propulsion technician, 1977; designer, draftsman, owner, operator Joseph's Drafting & Design Svc., 1984-88; mech. engring. technician Puget Sound Naval Shipyard, Bremerton, Wash., 1994—; designer, draftsman Napa Babe Ruth Baseball League, 1986. Author: Work Control of Critical System Pipe Hangers, 1987, Steering and Diving Hydraulic Cylinder Foundation, Inspection, Removal, Repair and Installation, 1987 (material control program) Navyshipydmareinst, 1993, Desk Notes for Ocean Engineering Subsafe Re-Entry Control Group, 1994. Chair citizen adv. panel Dept. Motor Vehicles, Napa; bd. dirs. Youth Adv. Bd. Oleum Fed. Credit Union, Rodeo, Calif., 1971-74; coach Young Am. Bowling Assn., Napa, 1980-83, 93-94, T-Ball and Babe Ruth Baseball, 1979-80, 85-86; auditor West Park Elem. Sch. PTA, 1994, parent vol., outdoor edn. vol. trips; key person for C/124-Puget Sound Naval Shipyard, Combined Fed. Campaign, 1994. With USNR, 1966-72. Mem. AARP, Internat. Platform Assn., Am. Bowling Congress, Olympic Philatelic Soc., Am. Diabetes Assn. Republican. Home: 12699 Plateau Cir NW Silverdale WA 98383-8014 Office: Puget Sound Naval Shipyard Engring Code 126 Bremerton WA 98314-5000

JOSEPH, JUDY, business administration and health educator; b. Upland, Calif., Sept. 14, 1962; d. Pedro H. and Mary A. (Lopez) Juarez; m. Keith M. Joseph, Aug. 15, 1987; children: Shunté, Sirbrina, Keith Jr., Kevin. AA, Coll. of Sequoias, 1994. Health record tech. Meth. Hosp., New Orleans, 1980-83; health record analyst Humana Corp., New Orleans, 1983-91, Delano (Calif.) Med. Ctr., 1991-93, St. Agnes Med. Ctr., Fresno, Calif., 1993-96; instr. allied health divsn. Fresno City C.C., 1995—; instr. bus. adminstrn. San Joaquin Valley Coll., Visalia, Calif., 1996—. Mem. AHIMA (cert.). Home: 1841 E Stockham Ave Tulare CA 93274

JOSEPH, MICHELE BETH, special education educator, educational therapist; b. Newark, July 17, 1964; d. Allan Irwin Whitman and Carole Dee (Ratner) Chillscyzn; m. Bartlett T. Joseph, Dec. 16, 1990. BA, U. Calif., Irvine, 1985; credentials Multiple Subject, Spl. Edn., Calif. State U., Northridge, 1987, MA, 1989. Cert. spl. edn. tchr., Calif. Spl. edn. educator Newhall (Calif.) Sch. Dist., 1987-88, Simi Valley (Calif.) Unified Sch. Dist., 1988-95, Saugus (Calif.) Union Sch. Dist., 1995—; master tchr. Simi Valley Unified Sch. Dist., 1990. Mem. NEA, Coun. for Exceptional Children, Calif. Tchrs. Assn. Office: 23109 Conde Dr Valencia CA 91354-2310

JOSEPHINE, HELEN BOWDEN, librarian; b. Chgo., Dec. 13, 1948; d. John Newton Bowden and Florence L. (Barker) Hackel; m. Allan J. Dyson, Nov. 28, 1973 (div. Mar. 1979); m. Dale L. Callaway, Dec. 28, 1983; children: Alanna A., Kevin P., Darren E. AB, Monmouth (Ill.) Coll., 1972; MLS, U. Calif., Berkeley, 1974. Ref. libr. Solano County Pub. Libr., Vallejo, Calif., 1976-78; dir. rsch. Info. on Demand, Berkeley, 1978-79; ref. libr. Ariz. State U., Tempe, 1985-87, info. mgr., 1988-93; program dir. U. Hawaii, Honolulu, 1993-96; collections libr. Menlo Coll., Atherton, Calif., 1996—. Contbr. articles to profl. jours., chpts. to books. Recipient McKinley Prize in English, Monmouth Coll., 1971, 72; Whitney Fund grantee ALA, 1982. Mem. AAUW, ALA (editor RQ ref. and adult svcs. divsn. 1979-80), Hawaii Libr. Assn. Home: PO Box 724 Ben Lomond CA 95005-0724 Office: Bowman Libr Menlo Coll 1000 El Camino Real Menlo Park CA 94027

JOSEPHS, ALICE RUTH, retired executive secretary; b. Dvinsk, Latvia, Oct. 19, 1912; came to U.S., 1912; d. Benjamin Solomon and Sarah (Kuritzky) Hodes; m. Ben Gardner, May 10, 1932 (dec. Oct. 1944); 1 child, Steven Robert; m. Fred Josephs, Dec. 8, 1952; children: Susan, Cynthia, David. BA in Journalism, Radio, TV, Film, Calif. State U., Northridge, 1979. Exec. sec. astronomy dept. UCLA, 1965-71; exec. sec. Boy Scouts Am., Van Nuys, Calif., 1988-93. Playwright Night of Broken Glass. Sec. bd. dirs. Synthaxis Theatre Co., North Hollywood, Calif., 1979-96; bd. dirs. Valley Cities Jewish Comty. Ctr., Van Nuys, 1964, 65, 66, 67-68, pres. women's club, 1967-68; leader Camp Fire Girls, Van Nuys, 1962, 63, 65. Playwright: A Woman's Place, Stars in Her Eyes, Window Panes, Failure Is Impossible—Susan B. Anthony; asst. editor: (mag.) Journalism History, 1977, 78, 79. Mem. AAUW, Am. Assn. Ret. Persons, Nat. Writers Assn., Gold Star Wives Am. (historian). Home: # 3 14341 Chandler Van Nuys CA 91401

JOSEPHSON, HAROLD ALLAN, real estate developer; b. Montreal, Que., Can., July 21, 1944; s. Joseph and Edith (Marco) J.; m. Sheila Gloria Laing, July 4, 1966 (div. July 1976); children: Daniel, Robert.; MBA with distinction, Harvard U., 1971. V.p. Marcil Mortgage Corp., Montreal, 1976-78; prin. Josephson Properties, Montreal, 1978-83, Los Angeles, 1983—. Mem. Urban Land Inst., Nat. Assn. Indsl. and Office Parks, Internat. Council Shopping Ctrs. Jewish. Office: 2029 Century Park E Ste 1200 Los Angeles CA 90067-2913

JOSHI, JANARDAN SHANTILAL, surgeon; b. Ahmedabad, Gujarat, India, Oct. 19, 1931; came to U.S., 1977; s. Shantilal Jatashanker and Ramlaxmi S. Joshi; m. Hansa Janardan, May 14, 1954; children: Mukesh J., Chetana K. MB BChir, Med. Coll., Baroda, India, 1955; Diploma in Laryngology and Otology, M.S. U., Baroda, 1957. Bd. cert. Am. Bd. Otolaryngology. Prof., head ear, nose and throat dept. NHL Mcpl. Med. Coll. and KM Sch. Postgrad. Medicine/Rsch., Ahmedabad, 1964-76; pvt. practice Ahmedabad, 1966-76, San Jose, Calif., 1983—. Fellow Royal Coll. Surgeons Edinburgh, Am. Acad. Otolaryngology-Head and Neck Surgery Inc.; mem. Am. Acad. Facial Plastic and Reconstructive Surgery. Office: Ste 201 244 N Jackson Ave San Jose CA 95116

JOSSELSON, FRANK, lawyer; b. Cin., Sept. 27, 1944; s. Jack Bernard and Beatrice Elaine (Lichtenstein) J.; m. Linda Mae Mustard, 1968 (div. 1986); children: Laura, David. Bar: Ohio 1969, Oreg. 1973, U.S. Dist. Ct. (so. dist.) Oreg., U.S. Ct. Appeals (6th and 9th cirs.). Law clk. to Hon. Anthony J. Celebrezze U.S. Ct. Appeals (6th cir.) Ohio, 1969-71; asst. atty. gen. Office Atty. Gen. Ohio, Columbus, 1971-73; assoc. Stoel, Rives, Portland, Oreg., 1973-75; ptnr. Griffith, Bittner, Abbott & Roberts, Portland, 1975-83, Josselson, Potter & Roberts, Portland, 1983—. Editor: Oreg. Land Use Bd. Appeals Decisions, 1981-82, Oreg. Land Conservation & Devel. Commn. Decisions, 1981; assoc. editor, editor-in-chief Oreg. Real Estate & Land Use Digest, 1978-88; recent case editor Cin. Law Rev., 1968-69. Mem. Met. Svc. Dist. charter com., 1991-92. Mem. ABA, Oreg. State Bar (exec. com., real estate and land use sect.), Ohio State Bar, Multnomah County Bar Assn. Office: Josselson Potter & Roberts 53 SW Yamhill St Portland OR 97204-3310

JOW, PAT See KAGEMOTO, PATRICIA JOW

JOY, CARLA MARIE, history educator; b. Denver, Sept. 5, 1945; d. Carl P. and Theresa M. (Lotito) J. AB cum laude, Loretto Heights Coll., 1967; MA, U. Denver, 1969, postgrad., 1984—. Instr. history Community Coll. Denver; prof. history Red Rocks Community Coll., Lakewood, Colo., 1970—; cons. for innovative ednl. programs; reviewer fed. grants, 1983-89; mem. adv. panel Colo. Endowment for Humanities, 1985-89. Contbr. articles to profl. publs. Instr. vocat. edn. Mile High United Way, Jefferson County, 1975; participant Jefferson County Sch. System R-1 Dist., 1983-88; active Red Rocks Community Coll. Speakers Bur., 1972-89, strategic planning com., 1992—; chair history discipline Colo. Gen. Edn. Core Transfer Consortium, 1986-96; mem. history, geography, civics stds. and geography frameworks adv. com. Colo. Dept. Edn., 1995-96; steering com. Ctr. Teaching Excellence, 1991-92, 1996-97; with North Ctrl. Self-Study Process, 1972-73, 80-81, 86-88, 96—; with K-16 Linkages Colo. Commn. for Higher Ed., 1997—. Cert. in vocat. edn. Colo. State Bd. Community Colls. and Occupational Edn., 1975; mem. evaluation team for Colo. Awards, edn. and civic achievement for Widefield Sch. Dist. #3, 1989; mem. Red Rocks Community Coll.-Clear Creek Sch. System Articulation Team, 1990-91; mem Statue of Liberty-Ellis Island Found. Inc. Ford Found. fellow, 1969; recipient cert. of appreciation Kiwanis Club, 1981, Cert. of Appreciation Telecommunication Coop. for Colo's. Community Colls., 1990-92; Master Tchr. award U. Tex. at Austin, 1982. Mem. Am. Hist. Assn., Am. Assn. Higher Edn., Nat. Council for Social Studies, Nat. Geog. Soc., Omohundro Inst. Early Am. History and Culture, Nat. Edn. Assn., Colo. Edn. Assn., Colo. Council for Social Studies, The Smithsonian Nat. Assocs., Denver Art Mus., Denver Mus. of Nat. Hist., Community Coll. Humanities Assn., Orgn. Am. Historians, The Colo. Hist. Soc., Colo. Endowment for the Humanities,

Colo. Geographic Alliance, Soc. History Edn., Phi Alpha Theta. Home: 1849 S Lee St Apt D Lakewood CO 80232-6252 Office: Red Rocks C C 13300 W 6th Ave Lakewood CO 80228-1255

JOYCE, ROSEMARY ALEXANDRIA, anthropology educator; b. Lackawanna, N.Y., Apr. 7, 1956; d. Thomas Robert and Joanne Hannah (Poth) J.; m. Russell Nicholas Sheptak, Jan. 7, 1984. BA, Cornell U., 1978; PhD, U. Ill., 1985. Instr. Jackson (Mich.) Community Coll., 1983; lectr. U. Ill., Urbana, 1984-85; asst. curator Peabody Mus., Harvard U., Cambridge, Mass., 1985-86, asst. dir., 1986-89; asst. prof. anthropology Harvard U., Cambridge, Mass., 1989-91, assoc. prof. anthropology, 1991—. Author: Cerro Palenque, 1991; contbr. articles to profl. jours. NSF grantee, 1989, NEH grantee, 1985, 86; Fulbright fellow, 1981-82. Mem. Soc. for Am. Archaeology, Am. Anthropol. Assn., New Eng. Mus. Office: U Calif Phoebe Apperson Hearst Mus Anthropology 103 Kroeber Hall Berkeley CA 94720-3712*

JOYCE, STEPHEN MICHAEL, lawyer; b. Los Angeles, Mar. 19, 1945; s. John Rowland and Elizabeth Rose (Rahe) J.; m. Bernadette Anne Novey, Aug. 18, 1973; children: Natalie Elizabeth, Vanessa Anne. BS, Calif. State U., Los Angeles, 1970; JD, U. LaVerne, 1976. Bar: Calif. 1976, U.S. Dist. Ct. (cen. dist.) Calif. 1977, U.S. Ct. Claims 1981. Pvt. practice Beverly Hills, Calif., 1976-93; ptnr. Gold & Joyce, Beverly Hills, 1982-84; personal atty. to Stevie Wonder and various other celebrities, 1977—. Contbr. articles to profl. jours. Served to pvt. USAR, 1963-69. Mem. ABA, Calif. Bar Assn., Los Angeles County Bar Assn., Beverly Hills Bar Assn., Los Angeles Trial Lawyers Assn., San Fernando Valley Bar Assn., Calabasas Athletic Club. Democrat. Roman Catholic. Home: 4724 Barcelona Ct Calabasas CA 91302-1403 Office: 15260 Ventura Blvd Ste 640 Sherman Oaks CA 91403-5340

JUAREZ, MARETTA LIYA CALIMPONG, social worker; b. Gilroy, Calif., Feb. 14, 1958; d. Sulpicio Magsalay and Pelagia Lagotom (Viacrusis) Calimpong; m. Henry Juarez, Mar. 24, 1984. BA, U. Calif., Berkeley, 1979; MSW, San Jose State U., 1983. Lic. clin. social worker; cert. in eye movement desensitization and reprocessing. Mgr. Pacific Bell, San Jose, Calif., 1983-84; revenue officer IRS, Salinas, Calif., 1984-85; social worker Santa Cruz (Calif.) County, 1985, Santa Clara County, San Jose, 1985—; co-chair Inter-Agy. Coun. of South Santa Clara County. Recipient award Am. Legion, 1972. Mem. NASW, Nat. Coun. on Alcoholism, Assn. Play Therapists, No. Calif. Sandplay Soc., EMDR Network, Sandplay Therapists Am., South County Multidisciplinary Team (co-founder), Calif. Alumni, U. Calif. Club of Santa Clara County. Democrat. Roman Catholic.

JUBERG, RICHARD KENT, mathematician, educator; b. Cooperstown, N.D., May 14, 1929; s. Palmer and Hattie Noreen (Nelson) J.; m. Janet Elisabeth Witchell, Mar. 17, 1956 (div.); children: Alison K., Kevin A., Hilary N., Ian C.T.; m. Sandra Jean Vakerics, July 8, 1989. BS, U. Minn., 1952, PhD, 1958. Asst. prof. U. Minn., Mpls., 1958-65; sci. faculty fellow Univerista di Pisa, Italy, 1965-66; assoc. prof. U. Calif., Irvine, 1966-72, U. Sussex, Eng., 1972-73; prof. U. Calif., Irvine, 1974-91, prof. emeritus, 1991—; vis. prof. U. Goteborg, Sweden, 1981; mem. Courant Inst. Math. Scis., NYU, 1957-58. Contbr. articles to profl. jours. With USN, 1946-48, Guam. NSF Faculty fellow, Univ. Pisa, Italy, 1965-66. Mem. Am. Math. Soc., Tau Beta Pi. Democrat. Office: U Calif Math Dept Irvine CA 92717

JUDD, BRUCE DIVEN, architect; b. Pasadena, Calif., Sept. 28, 1947; s. David Lockhart and Martha Leah (Brown) J.; m. Diane Reinbolt, Feb. 4, 1976 (div. Oct. 1985); 1 child, Ian David. BArch, U. Calif., Berkeley, 1970, MArch, 1971. Registered arch., Calif., Nev.; cert. Nat. Coun. Archtl. Registration Bds. Designer Ribera and Sue Landscape Archs., Oakland, Calif., 1968-70, Page Clowdsley & Baleix, San Francisco, 1971-75; v.p. Charles Hall Page Assocs., San Francisco, 1975-80; ptnr. Archtl. Resources Group, San Francisco, 1980—; mem. adv. bd. fed. rehab. guidelines program Nat. Inst. Bldg. Scis., HUD, 1979-80; mem. city-wide survey planning com. City of Oakland, Calif., 1979-80; cons. Nat. Main St. Program, Washington. Bd. dirs., co-founder Oakland Heritage Alliance, 1980-85; mem. Calif. Hist. Resources Commn., 1982-86, chmn., 1983-85; bd. dirs. Preservation Action, Washington, 1982-85, 90—, Friends of Terra Cotta, 1981-86, Berkeley Archtl. Heritage Assn., 1993—; mem. bd. advisors Nat. Trust for Hist. Preservation, Washington, 1981-90, advisor emeritus, 1990—; bd. trustees Calif. Preservation Found., San Francisco, 1985—, v.p., 1990-92, trustee, 1990—; active Calif. State Hist. Bldg. Safety Bd., 1991-93, also others. Recipient Excellence Honor award State of Calif., Excellence award in archtl. conservation, Spl. Restoration award Sunset Mag.; named Preservationist of Yr., Calif. Preservation Found., 1993. Fellow AIA (preservation officer No. Calif. chpt. 1978-81, hist. resources com. Calif. coun. 1979-80, nat. hist. resources com. 1981—, chmn. 1981-82); mem. Internat. Assn. for Preservation Tech. (bd. dirs. 1983-85), Park Hills Homes Assn. (chmn. archtl. com. 1992—), U.S./Internat. Coun. Monuments and Sites. Office: Archtl Resources Group Pier 9 The Embarcadero San Francisco CA 94111*

JUDD, DENNIS L., lawyer; b. Provo, Utah, June 27, 1954; s. Derrel Wesley and Leila (Lundquist) J.; m. Carol Lynne Chilberg, May 6, 1977; children: Lynne Marie, Amy Jo, Tiffany Ann, Andrew, Jacquelyn Nicole. BA in Polit. Sci. summa cum laude, Brigham Young U., 1978, JD, 1981. Bar: Utah 1981, U.S. Dist. Ct. Utah 1981. Assoc. Nielson & Senior, Salt Lake City and Vernal, Utah, 1981-83; dep. county atty. Uintah County, Vernal, 1982-84; ptnr. Bennett & Judd, Vernal, 1983-88; county atty. Daggett County, Utah, 1985-89, 91—; pvt. practice Vernal, 1988—; county atty. Daggett County, 1991—; prosecutor City of Naples, Naples, 1996—; legal counsel Uintah County Sch. Dist., 1996—; mem. governing bd. Uintah Basin applied Tech. Ctr., 1991-95, v.p., 1993-94, pres., 1994-95. Chmn. bd. adjustment Zoning and Planning Bd., Naples, 1982-91, 94—; mem. Naples City Coun., 1982-91; mayor pro tem City of Naples, 1983-91; legis. v.p. Naples PTA, 1988-90; v.p. Uintah Dist. PTA Coun., 1990-92; mem. resolution com. Utah League Cities and Towns, 1985-86, small cities com., 1985-86; trustee Uintah Sch. Dist. Found., 1988—, vice chmn., 1991-93; mem. Uintah County Sch. Dist. Bd. Edn., 1991-95, v.p., 1991-92, pres., 1992-95. Hinkley scholar Brigham Young U., 1977. Mem. Utah Bar Assn., Uintah Basin Bar Assn., Statewide Assn. Prosecutors, Vernal C. of C. Republican. Mormon. Home: 402 E 1500 S Vernal UT 84078-4471 Office: 461 West 200 South Vernal UT 84078-2517

JUDD, THOMAS ELI, electrical engineer; b. Salt Lake City, Apr. 12, 1927; s. Henry Eli Judd and Jennie Meibos; m. Mary Lu Edman, June 21, 1948; children: Shauna, Kirk E., Blake E., Lisa. BSEE, U. Utah, 1950. Registered profl. engr., Utah. Mech. engr. Utah Power & Light Co., Salt Lake City, 1950-55; chief engr. Electronic Motor Car Corp., Salt Lake City, 1955-56, Equi-Tech Corp., Salt Lake City, 1978-79; hydraulic devel. engr. Galigher Co., Salt Lake City, 1956-58; pres. Toran Corp., Salt Lake City, 1958-71, T M Industries, Salt Lake City, 1971-78; chief exec. officer, mgr. Ramos Corp., Salt Lake City, 1979—; project cons. Eimco Corp., Salt Lake City, 1966; design cons. to tech. cos. Patentee in field in U.S. and fgn. countries; contbr. editor U.S. Rail News, 1982—. Cons. Nat. Fedn. Ind. Bus., 1983—. With USNR, 1945-46, PTO. Mem. Tau Beta Pi. Republican. Mormon. Home: 956 Elm Ave Salt Lake City UT 84106-2330 Office: Ramos Corp 956 Elm Ave Salt Lake City UT 84106-2330

JUDGE, GEORGE GARRETT, economics educator; b. Carlisle, Ky., May 2, 1925; s. William Everett and Etna (Perkins) J.; m. Sue Dunkle, Mar. 17, 1950; children: Lisa C., Laura S.; m. Margaret C. Copeland, Oct. 8, 1976. BS, U. Ky., 1948; MS, Iowa State U., 1949, PhD, 1952; Asst. prof. U. Conn., Storrs, 1951-55; prof. U. Okla., Stillwater, 1955-58; vis. prof. Yale U., New Haven, 1958-59; prof. econs. U. Ill., Urbana, 1959-86; prof. U. Calif., Berkeley, 1986—; vis. disting. prof. U. Ga., 1977-79; cons. Internat. Wool Secretariat, London, 1976-77. Author: Maximum Entropy Econometrics, 1996, Learning and Practicing Econometrics, 1993, Improved Methods of Inference, 1986, Introduction to the Theory and Practice of Econometrics, 1982, 88, Theory and Practice of Econometrics, 1980, 85, Pre-Test and Stein Rule Estimators, 1978, Allocation Over Space and Time, 1975, Spatial Equilibrium, 1972; Markov Processes, 1970. Served with USAAF, 1943-45; PTO. Fellow Social Sci. Research Council, 1958-59, NSF, 1965-66; NSF grantee, 1976-87. Fellow Econometric Soc.; mem. Am. Statis. Assn., Am. Econ. Assn. Club: Dial. Avocations: golf, sailing. Office: U Calif 207 Giannini Hall Berkeley CA 94720-3311

JUDSON, CHERYL JEAN, college administrator, management consultant; b. Mpls., Mar. 6, 1947; d. Peter Joseph and Eileen Clair (Smith) Lynch; divorced. BA, U. Minn., Duluth, 1969; MA, Mich. State U., 1972; PhD, Oreg. State U., 1981. Dir. admissions St. Martins Acad., Rapid City, S.D., 1972-75; vets. coord. Oreg. Inst. Tech., Klamath Falls, 1975-77; asst. dir. fin. aid Oreg. State U., Corvallis, 1978-84; dir. fin. aid Met. State Coll. of Denver, 1984-92, asst. v.p. fin. aid, 1993-95; exporter Am. Cowboy Outfitters, Westminster, Colo., 1995—; mem. nat. adv. bd. Am. Coll. Testing, Iowa City, Iowa, 1987-89, mem. regional adv. bd., 1984-87. Author monograph. Title IX coord. LWV, Klamath Falls, Oreg., 1975. Named to Outstanding Young Women of Am., 1982. Mem. Nat. Assn. Fin. Aid Adminstrs. (editorial bd. 1981-88, assoc. editor 1988-89), Colo. Assn. Fin. Aid Adminstrs., Rocky Mt. Assn. Student Affairs Adminstrs., Rocky Mountain Dressage Soc. (treas. 1990-92), N.Am. Trail Ride Conf. Home: 10955 Gray Cir Westminster CO 80030 Office: American Cowboy Outfitters 10955 Gray Cir Westminster CO 80030

JUHLIN, NILS FREDERICK, engineering company executive, consultant; b. Lund, Sweden, Oct. 21, 1958; came to U.S., 1960; s. Einar Axel and Britta Margareta (Angvert) J.; m. Nikki Jann Broto, Aug. 3, 1985; children: Annika Alisa, Ilsa Victoria Daniela. BS in Mech. Engring., Boston U., 1980; MS in Mech. Engring., U. Wash., 1983, PhD, 1991. Registered profl. engr., Wash. Engr. Boeing Aerospace Co., Kent, Wash., 1983-87; pres. NovaComp Engring., Inc., Seattle, 1990—. Mem. ASME. Office: NovaComp Engring Inc 1101 N Northlake Way Ste 2 Seattle WA 98103-8948

JUKKOLA, GEORGE DUANE, obstetrician, gynecologist; b. Aliquippa, Pa., Feb. 28, 1945; s. Waino Helmer and Bedelia (Pyle) J.; m. Gretchen Louise Strom, Feb. 14, 1970 (div. 1984); children: David, Jeffrey; m. Wendee Leigh Bookhart, Apr. 23, 1988 (div. 1993). BA in Psychology, U. Calif., Berkeley, 1970; MD, U. Pitts., 1975. Diplomate Am. Bd. Ob-Gyn., Am. Bd. Quality Assurance Utilization Rev. Physicians. Caseworker Pa. Dept. Welfare, Rochester, 1971; resident in ob.-gyn. Akron (Ohio) Med. Ctr., 1975-78; pvt. practice Riverside, Calif., 1978—; co-founder Family Birthing Ctr., Riverside, 1981-87; v.p. Inland Physicians Med. Group, 1987-88; mng. ptnr. Parkview Profl. Ctr., Riveside, 1984-93; chief dept. ob-gyn. Parkview Cmty. Hosp., Riverside, 1986-91, vice-chief of staff, 1992-93, chief of staff, 1994-96; chmn. ob-gyn dept. Moreno Valley Med. Ctr., 1991-93, dir. perinatal svcs., 1992-94, mem.-at-large exec. com., 1996-97, mem. CMA survey team, 1992—; guest lectr. Riverside Cmty. Coll., 1984, 85; health care adv. com. 43d Congl. Dist., Calif., 1994—; mem. Riverside County Fetal-Infant Mortality Com., 1994—; founder, chmn. bd. dirs. Inland Empire OBG IPA. With USAF, 1965-69. Decorated Air medal with 4 oak leaf clusters. Fellow ACOG; mem. AMA, Am. Coll. Physician Execs., Calif. Med. Assn., Riverside County Med. Assn., Am. Assn. Individual Investors, Victoria Club Riverside, Mensa. Republican. Unitarian-Universalist. Home: 10252 Victoria Ave Riverside CA 92503-6100 Office: 3900 Sherman Sr Ste F Riverside CA 92503-4062

JUMAO-AS, ALEX BARONDA, civil engineer; b. Surigao City, The Philippines, June 12, 1961; came to U.S., 1982; s. Gaudencio Tamosa and Adelaida (Baronda) J.; m. Remedios Panoncillo, Jan. 28, 1981; children: Real James, Rylan Justin. BS in Indsl. Engring. with high honors, U. San Jose Recoletos, Cebu City, Philippines, 1982; grad. mech. and elec. tech. with high honors, U. Alaska, 1988, AAS in Archtl. and Engring. with honors, 1989, BS in Civil Engring. with high hons., 1989. Drafter Dept. Interior Bur. Land Mgmt., Anchorage, 1983-84, Raj Bhargava Assocs., Anchorage, 1984; asst. engr., drafter Unicom, Inc., Anchorage, 1984-93; civil engr. Raytheon Svc. Co., Anchorage, 1993-96, Anchorage Water and Wastewater Utility, Anchorage, 1996—; adj. instr. U. Alaska, 1989-91; v.p. Unicom, Inc. Anchorage Employee Svc. Assn., 1985-86. Mem. Metro Cebu Jaycees, Am. Inst. Design and Drafting, Pundok Bisaya (Cebuano Filipino Assn. Alaska) (v.p.), Bisayans of Alaska (mem. bd. dirs. 1993-94), Filipino-Bisayans of Alaska Inc. (pres. 1996—). Roman Catholic. Home: 8412 Barnett Dr Anchorage AK 99518-2900 Office: Anchorage Water and Wastewater Utility 3000 Arctic Blvd Anchorage AK 99503

JUMONVILLE, FELIX JOSEPH, JR., physical education educator, realtor; b. Crowley, La., Nov. 20, 1920; s. Felix Joseph and Mabel (Rogers) J.; m. Mary Louise Hoke, Jan. 11, 1952; children: Carol, Susan. BS, La. State U., 1942; MS, U. So. Calif., 1948, EdD, 1952. Assoc. prof. phys. edn. Los Angeles State Coll., 1948-60; prof. phys. edn. Calif. State U., Northridge, 1960-87, emeritus prof. phys. edn., 1987—; owner Felix Jumonville Realty, Northridge, 1974-82, Big Valley Realty, Inc., 1982-83, Century 21 Lamb Realtors, 1983-86, Cardinal Realtors, 1986-87; varsity track and cross-country head coach L.A. State Coll., 1952-60, Calif. State U., Northridge, 1960-71. Served with USCGR, 1942-46. Mem. Assn. Calif. State Univ. Profs., AAHPER, Pi Tau Pi, Phi Epsilon Kappa. Home: 2001 E Camino Parocela Apt 98N Palm Springs CA 92264-8283

JUN, JONG SUP, public administration educator; b. Sunsan, Korea, July 26, 1936; s. Myung D. and Jeum S. (Pai) J.; m. Soon Y. Jun, Sept. 16, 1964; children: Eugene, Amy. LLB, Yeungnam U., Taegu, Korea, 1960; MA, U. Oreg., 1964; PhD, U. So. Calif., 1969. Prof. Calif. State U., Hayward, 1968—; vis. prof. Hosei U., Tokyo, 1992-93; coord. Pub. Adminstrn.Theory Network, 1993—; coord. The Pub. Adminstrn. Theory Network. Author: Public Administration: Design and Problem Solving, 1986, Philosophy of Administration, 1994; editor: Development in the Asia Pacific, 1994; editor: Administrative Theory and Praxis, editor Internat. Rev. Adminstrv. Sci., 1991; co-editor Adminstrn.Theory and Praxis, 1993—, Globalization and Decentralization, 1996. Recipient Rsch. Grant award Social Rsch.Coun., N.Y., 1979, Outstanding Acad. Achievement award Am. Soc. Pub. Adminstrn., San Francisco, 1982; Fulbright scholar Yonsei U., Korea. Fellow Nat. Acad. Public Adminstrn. Home: 18698 Mount Lassen Ct Castro Valley CA 94552-1955 Office: Calif State U Hayward CA 94552

JUNE, ROY ETHIEL, lawyer; b. Forsyth, Mont., Aug. 12, 1922; s. Charles E. and Elizabeth F. (Newnes) J.; m. Laura Brautigam, June 20, 1949; children—Patricia June, Richard Tyler. B.A., U. Mont., 1948, B.A. in Law, 1951, LL.B., 1952. Bar: Mont. 1952, Calif. 1961. Sole practice, Billings, Mont., 1952-57, Sanders and June, 1953-57; real estate developer, Orange County, Calif., 1957-61; ptnr. Dugan, Tobias, Tornay & June, Costa Mesa, Calif., 1961-62; city prosecutor, Costa Mesa, 1962-63, asst. city atty., 1963-67, city atty., 1967-78; sole practice, Costa Mesa, 1962—. Atty., founder, dir. Citizens Bank of Costa Mesa, 1972-92; atty. Costa Mesa Hist. Soc., Costa Mesa Playhouse Patron's Assn., Red Barons Orange County, Costa Mesa Meml. Hosp. Aux., Harbor Key, Child Guidance Ctr. Orange County, Fairview State Hosp. Therapeutic Pool Vols., Inc.; active Eagle Scout evaluation team, Harbor Area Boy Scouts Am., YMCA; atty. United Fund/Community Chest Costa Mesa and Newport Beach; bd. dirs. Boys' Club Harbor Area, bd. dirs. Mardan Ctr. Ednl. Therapy, United Cerebral Palsy Found. Orange County. Served with USAF, World War II. Decorated Air medal with oak leaf cluster, D.F.C. Mem. Mont. Bar Assn., Calif. Bar Assn., Orange County Bar Assn., Harbor Bar Assn., Costa Mesa C. of C. (bd. dirs.). Clubs: Masons, Scottish Rite, Shriners, Santa Ana Country, Amigos Viejos, Los Fiestadores.

JUNG, HENRY HUNG, mechanical engineer; b. Hong Kong, Aug. 3, 1957; s. Cheuk-Sun and Siu-Kuen (Ma) J.; m. Mi-Ying Miranda, Mar. 28, 1986. BS MechE, Ariz. State U., 1980; MS MechE, U. Ill., 1983; MBA, Santa Clara U., 1994. Engr. Lockheed Aircraft, Burbank, Calif., 1981-82; researcher U. Ill., Champaign-Urbana, 1982-83; engr. Pratt & Whitney Aircraft, West Palm Beach, Fla., 1983-84; sr. scientist Lockheed Missiles & Space Co., Palo Alto, Calif., 1984-94; sr. mfg. engr. Sun Microsystems Co., Mountain View, Calif., 1994-96; sr. supplies engr. Apple Computer, Cupertino, Calif., 1996—. Mem. ASME, AIAA, N.Y. Acad. Scis., Sigma Xi, Tau Beta Pi, Pi Tau Sigma. Home: 21486 Holly Oak Dr Cupertino CA 95014-4928 Office: Apple Computer Cupertino CA 95014

JUNG, KWAN YEE, artist; b. Toisun, Kwang Tung, China, Nov. 25, 1932; came to U.S., 1963; s. Fred Hing and Shun Tong (Lee) J.; m. Yee Wah Yip, Sept. 10, 1962; children: Jeanne, Kathy, Laura. BA, New Asia Coll., Hong Kong, 1961. Comml. artist advt. dept. Hong Kong Soy Bean Products Co., 1961-63; owner Jung's Gallery, La Jolla, Calif., 1976-78; freelance artist, instr., demonstrator San Diego, 1978—; jury panelist African-Am. Mus. Art, San Diego, 1994—. Exhibited in group shows including 170th ann. exhbn. NAD, 1995, Am. Fine Art Connection Poway Ctr. for Performing Arts, Calif., 1995, Water to Women Margaret Cross Gallery, Old Pasadena, Calif., 1995, May Snow Kim's Art Gallery, Rowland Heights, Calif., 1995, Co-art Internat. Gallery, Vancouver, B.C., Can., 1996, Kruglak Gallery, Mira Costa Coll., Oceanside, Calif., 1997. Recipient First Place award San Diego Watercolor Soc., 1973, Best of Show award Sumi-E Soc. Am., 1974, Purchase award Springville Mus. Art, 1974. Mem. Nat. Acad. Design (Merit award 1992, nat. academician), Am. Watercolor Soc., Nat. Watercolor Soc., Asiatic Art Guild (pres. 1992—). Home: 5468 Bloch St San Diego CA 92122-4010

JUNG, TIMOTHY TAE KUN, otolaryngologist; b. Seoul, Korea, Dec. 1, 1943; came to U.S., 1969; s. Yoon Yong and Helen Chung-Hyuk (Im) J.; m. Lucy Moon Young, Sept. 10, 1972; children: David, Michael, Karen. BS, Seoul Nat. U., 1966, Loma Linda U., 1971; MD, Loma Linda U., 1974; PhD, U. Minn., 1980. Diplomate, Am. Bd. Otolaryngology. Med. intern Loma Linda (Calif.) U. Med. Ctr., 1974-75; resident in surgery U. Minn. Med. Sch., Mpls., 1975-76; resident in otolaryngology U. Minn. Med. Sch., 1976-80, asst. prof. otolaryngology, 1980-84, clin. asst. prof., dir. prostaglandin lab., 1984-85; assoc. prof., dir. otolaryngology rsch. Loma Linda U., 1985-90, prof., dir. otolaryngology rsch., 1990-92, clin. prof., assoc. dir. otolaryngology rsch., 1992—; mem. deafness and communications disroders rev. com. Nat. Inst. Deafness and Communications, NIH, 1989-92. Bd. editors Annals of Otology, Rhinology & Laryngology, 1994—; contbr. numerous chpts. to med. books, over 100 articles and abstracts to med. jours. Sgt. Korean army, 1966-69. Recipient Edmund Price Fowler award. Fellow ACS, Triological Soc., Am. Acad. Otolaryngology (honor award 1990); mem. AMA, Am. Otol. Soc., Am. Neurotol. Soc., Soc. Univ. Otolaryngologists, Assn. Rsch. in Otolaryngology, Centurions, Collegium Otorhinolaryngogicum Amicetiae Sacrum, N.Am. Skull Base Soc., Alpha Omega Alpha. Seventh-day Adventist. Home: 11790 Pecan Way Loma Linda CA 92354-3452 Office: 3975 Jackson St Ste 202 Riverside CA 92503-3947

JUNG, YEE WAH, artist; b. Canton, Quangdong, China, Sept. 4, 1936; came to U.S., 1963; d. Yeun Tsin and Shiu Fung (Poon) Yip; m. Kwan Yee Jung, Sept. 10, 1962; children: Jeanne, Kathy, Laura. Student, Chung Nam Art Sch., Wupei, China, 1954-58, New Asia Coll., Hong Kong, 1958-62. Art instr. Shiu Fung Art Studio, Hong Kong, 1958-63; art tchr. Chi-Ching Mid. Sch., Hong Kong, 1962-63; freelance artist San Diego, 1963—; owner Jung's Gallery, La Jolla, Calif., 1976-78; solo juror Clairemont Art Guild Annual, San Diego, 1989, So. Calif. Expo Art, 1996. Exhbns. include Am. Fine Art Connection Exhbn., Poway (Calif.) Ctr. for the Performing Atts, 1995, Watercolor USA, Knoxville (Tenn.) Mus. of Art, 1995, Co-Art Gallery, Vancouver, B.C., Can., 1996. Recipient First prize So. Calif. Expo, 1970, Watercolor USA Cash award Calif. Nat. Watercolor Soc., 1973, First Place award 25th Annual Art Festival, San Diego, 1989, Three King award Advent Fine Art 7th Annual, San Diego, 1990. Mem. Nat. Watercolor Soc., Watercolor Honor Soc., Asiatic Art Guild (panel juror 1993). Home: 5468 Bloch St San Diego CA 92122-4010

JUNGBLUTH, CONNIE CARLSON, tax manager; b. Cheyenne, Wyo., June 20, 1955; d. Charles Marion and Janice Yvonne (Keldsen) Carlson; m. Kirk E. Jungbluth, Feb. 5, 1977; children: Tyler, Ryan. BS, Colo. State U., 1976. CPA, Colo. Sr. acct. Rhode Scripter & Assoc., Boulder, Colo., 1977-81; mng. acct. Arthur Young, Denver, 1981-85; asst. v.p. Dain Bosworth, Denver, 1985-87; v.p. George K. Baum & Co., Denver, 1987-91; acct. Ariz. Luth. Acad., 1994-95; sr. tax acct. Ernst & Young, LLP, Phoenix, 1995-96; tax mgr. McGladrey & Pullen, LLP, Phoenix, 1996—. Active Denver Estate Planning Coun., 1981-85, Ctrl. Ariz. Estate Planning Coun., 1997—; organizer Little People Am., Rocky Mountain Med. Clinic and Symposium, Denver, 1986; adv. bd. Children's Home Health, Denver, 1986-89; fin. adv. bd. Gail Shoettler for State Treas., Denver, 1986; campaign chmn. Kathi Williams for Colo. State Legislature, 1986; mem. Sch. dist. 12 Colo. Edn. Found. Bd., 1991, Napa Sch. Dist. Elem. Site com., 1992-94. Named one of 50 to watch, Denver mag., 1988. Mem. AICPA, Colo. Soc. CPAs (strategic planning com. 1987-89, instr. bank 1983, trustee 1984-87, pres. bd. trustees 1986-87, bd. dirs. 1987-89, chmn. career edn. com. 1982-83, pub. svc. award 1985-87), Little People of Am., Colo. Mcpl. Bond Dealers, Ariz. Herb Assn., Ctrl. Ariz. Estate Planning Coun., Metro North C. of C. (bd. dirs. 1987-90), Denver City Club (bd. dirs. 1987-88), Phi Beta Phi. Office: McGladrey & Pullen LLP Ste 315 2231 E Camelback Rd Phoenix AZ 85016

JUNGBLUTH, KIRK E., real estate appraiser, mortgage banking executive; b. Lima, Ohio, Apr. 5, 1949; s. Harold A. and Marjorie J. (Brown) J.; m. Connie Carlson, Feb. 5, 1977; children: Tyler, Ryan. Student, Mesa Coll., Grand Junction, Colo., Regis Coll., Denver. Cert. Gen. real estate appraiser, Calif., Ariz. Loan officer, real estate appraiser Home Fed. Savs. & Loan, Ft. Collins, Colo., 1973-76; real estate appraiser Jungbluth & Assocs., Ft. Collins, 1976-83; pres., bd. dirs. Security Diamond Corp., Denver, 1982-90; nat. sales dir. InfoAm. Computers, Denver, 1982-90; chmn. bd. dirs., CEO U.S. Capital Lending Corp., Denver, 1987-91; ct.-appointed receiver Dist. Ct. State of Colo., 1990; mgr. real estate appraisal World Savs. & Loan Assn., Walnut Creek, 1992—, Pleasanton, Calif., 1992—. Sec.-treas. St. Peters Luth. Ch., Ft. Collins, Colo., 1980-81, pres., 1982-84. Sgt. USMC, 1969-71. Republican.

JUNGKIND, WALTER, design educator, writer, consultant; b. Zurich, Switzerland, Mar. 9, 1923; came to Can., 1968; s. Oskar and Frieda (Leuthold) J.; m. Jenny Voskamp, 1953; children—Christine, Stefan, Brigit. Nat diploma, Kunstgewerbeschule, Zurich, 1943; nat diploma, Regent Street Poly tech., London, 1953. Freelance designer London, 1955-68; lectr. London Coll. Printing and Graphic Arts, 1960-65, sr. lectr., 1965-68; assoc. prof. dept. art and design U. Alta., Edmonton, Can., 1968-72, prof., 1972-90, prof. emeritus, 1990—; Design cons. pub. works Province of Alta., 1972-75; chmn. Canadian Adv. Com. Standards Council Can., 1978—. Initiator and curator internat. exhbn. Graphic Design for Pub. Service, 1972, Language Made Visible, 1973. Recipient Design Can. award Nat. Design Council Can., 1979, 1984; Chmns. award Nat. Design Council Can., 1982. Fellow Soc. Chartered Designers Gt. Britain, Soc. Graphic Designers Can. (pres. 1978-82); mem. Internat Coun. Graphic Design Assns. (pres. 1974-76, Design for Edn. award 1972.). Home: 6304-109th Ave, Edmonton, AB Canada T6A 1S2

JUNGREN, JON ERIK, civil engineer; b. Malmo, Sweden, Oct. 19, 1927; came to U.S., 1966; s. Axel Bernhard and Lilly Ottonie (Eliasson) Ljungren; m. Elaine Berry, May 13, 1977. BS, Chalmers Inst. Technology, Gothenburg, Sweden, 1951; MS, Chalmers Inst. Technology, 1952; BA, Royal Inst. Technology, Stockholm, Sweden, 1954; PhD, Columbia Pacific U., 1985. Registered civil engr., Calif., Ariz. Br. mgr. Jacobsen & Widmark, Lund, Sweden, 1954-59; pres., owner Civilingnjoren SVR Jan Ljunggren AB, Lund, 1959-66; supervising engr. Bechtel Corp., San Francisco, 1966-74; engring. mgr. Morrison Knudsen, Holland, U.S.A., 1974-83; chmn. Jungren & Duran, Inc., Corona, Calif., 1983—; cons. engr. Assn. of Calif. Legis. Com., 1987-90. Contbr. articles to profl. jours. Recipient Archtl. award, 1959, 66. Mem. ASCE, Am. Cons. Engrs. Coun., Cons. Engrs. Assn. Calif., Am. Concrete Inst., Internat. Conf. Bldg. Ofcls., Masons, Mensa. Democrat. Home: 1185 W Grand Blvd Corona CA 91720-4354 Office: Jungren & Duran Inc 1175 W Grand Blvd Corona CA 91720-4354

JUNKER, HOWARD HENRY, periodical editor; b. Port Washington, N.Y., Oct. 8, 1940; s. Howard Ralph Junker and Evelyn Pott; m. Rozanne Enerson, Nov. 23, 1985; 1 child, Madison. BA, Amherst Coll., 1961; MA, U. San Francisco, 1978. Editor ZYZZYVA, San Francisco, 1985—. Editor: (anthologies) Roots and Branches, 1991, The Writer's Notebook, 1995, Strange Attraction, 1995. With U.S. Naval Air Res., 1964-66. Office: ZYZZYVA 41 Sutter St Ste 1400 San Francisco CA 94104-4903

JURA, DEBRA DOWELL, bilingual educator; b. Modesto, Calif., Feb. 20, 1952; d. Charles Hubert and Peggy Sue (Hittle) Dowell; divorced; children: Aaron Vincent, Amanda Lael. Cert. tchr., Calif. State U., Fresno, 1986, BS, 1994; M Lang. Devel., Pacific Coll., 1995. Cert. lang. devel. specialist, Calif., cert. reading recovery tchr. Bilingual tchr. Selma (Calif.) Unified Sch. Dist., 1986—, mentor tchr. drug prevention edn., 1989-93, mentor tchr. health edn., 1993—, mentor tchr. lang. devel. and early literacy, 1996—, staff developer, 1996-97; project D.A.T.E. coord. Selma Unified Sch. Dist.,

1989—, chair Healthy Kids Healty Calif. task force, 1990—, parent educator, 1992—; mem. adv. bd. Gang Task Force, Selma, 1993—; mem. English Lang. Arts Curriculum Com., 1990—, Health Curriculum Com., 1993—; mentor tchr. Early Literacy, 1996-97; mem. coordinating com. G.A.T.E., 1996, mem. adv. bd., 1996. Author: Mostly Magnets, 1990, Supplemental Guide to HLAY 200, 1995, other curriculum materials; co-author: Gang Curriculum 1993. Mem. El Concilio, Fresno, 1993-94, Fresno Zool. Soc., 1980—, Selma Pub. Edn. Found. Grantee Selma Unified Sch. Dist., 1987, Selma Pub. Edn. Found., 1994, S. USD Pub. Edn. Found., 1996. Mem. NEA, Calif. Tchrs. Assn., Nat. Coun. Tchrs. Edn., C.U.E. Democrat. Methodist. Home: 2051 Oak St Selma CA 93662-2443

JUSTESEN, ELAINE TOOMER, genealogist; b. Billings, Mont., June 2, 1929; d. Thomas Henry and Margaret (Stevens) Toomer; m. Glade Clifford Justesen, Aug. 4, 1947; children: Gary, Kirby, Kimball, Thomas, Rick, Brian. Student tech. genealogy, Brigham Young U., Salt Lake City, 1966. Accredited genealogist, Utah. Self-employed profl. genealogist Salt Lake City, 1966-93; editor Geneal. Jour. Utah Geneal. Assn., Salt Lake City, 1994—. Compiler, rschr.: Ancestry of James M. Williams, 1982, 21 family histories, 1982-95. Mem. Nat. Geneal. Soc. (local arrangements chair 1984-85), Assn. Profl. Genealogists, Utah Geneal. Assn. (v.p. 1983-87, bd. dirs. 1974-84). Republican. Mem. Latter-day Saints Ch. Office: Utah Geneal Assn PO Box 1144 Salt Lake City UT 84110-1144

JUSTICE, JAMES WALCOTT, physician, research scientist; b. N.Y.C., Dec. 16, 1932; s. Frederick Emerson and Eleanor Gertrude (Haddock) J.; m. M. Ann Haight, Feb. 11, 1961; children: Sean, Wade, Kathleen, Scott. BA, Bucknell U., 1954; MD, N.Y. Med. Coll., 1958; MPH, Johns Hopkins U., 1962. Diplomate gen. preventive medicine Am. Bd. Preventive Medicine and Pub. Health. Intern Stanford U., San Francisco, 1958-59; resident pub. health U. Okla., Oklahoma City, 1963-65; commd. officer USPHS, 1959-85; med. dir. State Alaska Dept. Corrections, Anchorage, 1985-87; rsch. scientist Native Am. Rsch. and Tng. Ctr. Ariz. Health Sci. Ctr. U. Ariz., Tucson, 1987—. Author: Bibliography Health and Disease Native America, 1988; contbr. chpts. to books and articles to profl. jours. Pres. Family/Faculty Assn., Tucson, 1974-75; chmn. Home Owner's Assn., Tucson, 1975, 89-90. Col. USPHS, 1959-85. Decorated Meritorious medal USPHS-DHHS, 1973; recipient Group Achievement award NASA, 1977, Fgn. Svc. award USPHS-DHHS, 1981, Nat. Recognition award Nat. Indian Health Bd., 1982. Fellow Am. Coll. Preventive Medicine; mem. APHA, Ariz. Pub. Health Assn., Physicians for Social Responsibility, Ctr. for Creative Photography, So. Ariz. Water Color Guild. Office: U Ariz Native Am Rsch Ctr 1642 E Helen St Tucson AZ 85719

JUSTISS, BARBARA HARRIS, hospital foundation executive; b. Union County, Ark., Jan. 31, 1941; d. Oliver Graden and Nettie Evelyn (Jolley) Harris; m. Lewis G. Justiss, June, 1960; 1 child, Jeffrey Lewis. Student, U. Ark., 1958-60, U. Wis., 1981-82, U. So. Ark., 1983-84, Duke U., 1984. Exec. dir. fund devel. & mktg. Med. Ctr. So. Ark., El Dorado, 1976-89; v.p., exec. dir. St. Rose Dominican Health Found., Henderson, Nev., 1990—. Author: NAHD Journal, 1989. Lay minister Univ. United Meth. Ch., Las Vegas, 1996. Mem. Nat. Soc. Fund Raising Execs. (chpt. bd. dirs., com.chair 1992), Assn. Health Philatherapy (regional com. 1989). Office: St Rose Dominican Health Found 102 ELake Mead Dr Henderson NV 89015

JUTILA, GEORGE ARMAS, surgeon; b. Nevada City, Calif., May 17, 1935; s. Armas Einor and Marrian Ruth (Anderson) J.; m. Sylvia Fisher, June 30, 1958; children: Jennifer, Janice, Jill, James, Jerron. BS, U. Wis., Superior, 1956; MD, U. Utah, 1961. Rotating intern St. Luke's Hosp., Duluth, Minn., 1961-62; pvt. practice, Fortuna, Calif., 1964—; chief staff Redwood Meml. Hosp., Fortuna, 1972, 74. Capt. USAF, 1962-64. Mem. ACS (pres. Humboldt Del Norte br. 1976), Calif. Med. Assn., Humboldt Del Norte County Med. Soc. (pres. 1975), Rotary (charter, pres. Fortuna 1992-93). Home: PO Box 606 Fortuna CA 95540-0606 Office: Fortuna Family Medical Group Inc 874 Main St Fortuna CA 95540-1926

JUVET, RICHARD SPALDING, JR., chemistry educator; b. Los Angeles, Aug. 8, 1930; s. Richard Spalding and Marion Elizabeth (Dalton) J.; m. Martha Joy Myers, Jan. 29, 1955 (div. Nov. 1978); children: Victoria, David, Stephen, Richard P.; m. Evelyn Raeburn Elthon, July 1, 1984. B.S., UCLA, 1952, Ph.D., 1955. Research chemist Dupont, 1955; instr. U. Ill., 1955-57, asst. prof., 1957-61, assoc. prof., 1961-70; prof. analytical chemistry Ariz. State U., Tempe, 1970-95, prof. emeritus, 1995—; vis. prof. UCLA, 1960, U. Cambridge, Eng., 1964-65, Nat. Taiwan U., 1968, Ecole Polytechnique, France, 1976-77, U. Vienna, Austria, 1989-90; mem. air pollution chemistry and physics adv. com. EPA, HEW, 1969-72; mem. adv. panel on advanced chem. alarm tech., devel. and enging. directorate, def. sys. divsn. Edgewood Arsenal, 1975; mem. adv. panel on postdoctoral associateships NAS-NRC, 1991-94. Author: Gas-Liquid Chromatography, Theory and Practice, 1962, Russian edit., 1966; editl. advisor Jour. Chromatographic Sci., 1969-85, Jour. Gas Chromatography, 1963-68, Analytica Chimica Acta, 1972-74, Analytical Chemistry, 1974-77; biennial reviewer for gas chromatography lit. Analytical Chemistry, 1962-76. NSF sr. postdoctoral fellow, 1964-65; recipient Sci. Exch. Agreement award to Czechoslovakia, Hungary, Romania and Yugoslavia, 1977. Fellow Am. Inst. Chemists; mem. AAAS, Am. Chem. Soc. (nat. chmn. divsn. analytical chemistry 1972-73, nat. sec.-treas. 1969-71, divsn. com. on chem. edn., subcom. on grad. edn. 1988—, councilor 1978-89, coun. com. analytical reagents 1985-95, co-author Reagent Chemicals, 7th edit. 1986, 8th edit. 1993, chmn. U. Ill. sect. 1968-69, sec. 1962-63, directorate divsn. officers' caucus 1987-90), Internat. Union Pure and Applied Chemistry, Internat. Platform Assn., Am. Radio Relay League (Amateur-Extra lic.), Sigma Xi, Phi Lambda Upsilon, Alpha Chi Sigma (profl. rep.-at-large 1989-94, chmn. expansion com. 1990-92, nat. v.p. grand collegiate alchemist 1994-96). Presbyterian (deacon 1960—, ruling elder 1972—, commr. Grand Canyon Presbytery 1974-76). Home: 4821 E Calle Tuberia Phoenix AZ 85018-2932 Office: Ariz State U Dept Chem and Biochem Tempe AZ 85287-1604

KABALIN, JOHN NICHOLAS, urologist; b. L.A., Dec. 23, 1958; s. Nicholas Augustin and Mary Jane (Engleman) K.; m. Pamela Grace White, July 11, 1981. BS, Stanford U., 1980; MD, Johns Hopkins U., 1984. Diplomate Am. Bd. Urology. Intern in surgery Stanford U. Med. Ctr., 1984-85, resident in surgery, 1985-86, resident in urology, 1986-90, chief resident in urology, 1989-90; chief urology sect. Va Med. Ctr., Palo Alto, Calif., 1990—; asst. prof. urology Stanford (Calif.) U., 1990—. Contbr. over 75 articles to profl. jours., 12 chpts. in books. Fellow ACS; mem. AMA, Am. Urol. Assn., Am. Soc. for Laser Medicine and Surgery, Soc. Urologic Oncology, Soc. Univ. Urologists, Phi Beta Kappa, Alpha Omega Alpha. Roman Catholic. Office: VA Medical Center 3801 Miranda Ave Palo Alto CA 94304-1207

KADDEN, BRUCE JAY, rabbi; b. Berkeley, Calif., Nov. 7, 1954; s. Paul Emanuel and Shirley Janice (Hertzberg) K.; m. Barbara Ellen Binder, Sept. 2, 1978; children: Alana Sharon, Micah Benjamin. AB in Religious Studies, Stanford (Calif.) U., 1976; MA in Hebrew Letters, Hebrew Union Coll., L.A., 1979. Ordained rabbi, 1981. Rabbi Mount Zion Temple, St. Paul, 1981-84; Jewish chaplain Correctional Tng. Facility, Soledad, Calif., 1987-96; rabbi Temple Beth El, Salinas, Calif., 1984—. Co-author: Teaching Tefilah: Insights and Activities on Prayer, 1994, Teaching Mitzvot: Concepts, Values and Activities, 1988, Teaching Jewish Life Cycles: Insights and Activities, 1997. Bd. dirs. Ctr. for Community Advocacy, Salinas, 1993—, Planned Parenthood, Monterey County, 1985-92, Franciscan Workers of Junipero Serra, Salinas, 1995—. Mem. Pacific Asn. of Reform Rabbis. Democrat. Office: Temple Beth El 1212 Riker St Salinas CA 93901-2111

KADNER, CARL GEORGE, biology educator emeritus; b. Oakland, Calif., May 23, 1911; s. Adolph L. and Otilia (Pecht) K.; m. Mary Elizabeth Moran, June 24, 1939; children: Robert, Grace Wickersham, Carl L. BS, U. San Francisco, 1933; MS, U. Calif., Berkeley, 1936, PhD, 1941. Prof. biology Loyola Marymount U., Los Angeles, 1936-78, prof. emeritus, 1978—; trustee Loyola U., Los Angeles, 1970-73. Served to maj. U.S. Army, 1943-46. Mem. Entomol. Soc. Am. (emeritus), Sigma Xi, Alpha Sigma Nu. Republican. Roman Catholic. Home: 8100 Loyola Blvd Los Angeles CA 90045-2639

KADOHIRO, JANE KAY, diabetes nurse educator, consultant; b. Lima, Ohio, July 20, 1947; d. Howard M. and Betty J. (Johoske) Keller; m. Howard M. Kadohiro, Dec. 27, 1969; children: Christopher, Jennifer. BA in Sociology and Edn., U. Hawaii, 1969; BS in Nursing, U. Hawaii, Honolulu, 1977, MPH, 1990; MS, U. Hawaii, 1994, DrPHC, 1996, postgrad., 1994—. Staff nurse Children's Hosp., Honolulu, 1977-78; staff pub. health nurse Hawaii State Dept. Health, Honolulu, 1978-80, coord. hypertension and diabetes, 1980-85, projects adminstr., 1985-89, chief chronic diseases, 1989-91; office mgr. Hanalei Trends, Honolulu, 1985-89; clin. nurse specialist Queen's Med. Ctr., Honolulu, 1991-94; cons. Aiea, Hawaii, 1991—; nurse investigator Honolulu Heart Program, 1991-95; instr. U. Hawaii at Manoa, Honolulu, 1991—; mem. diabetes project Office Hawaiian Affairs, Honolulu, 1993-95. Leader, advisor, life mem. Girl Scouts U.S., Honolulu, 1978-90; mem. nat. programs com. Nat. Youth Congress, 1993-96; steering com. Internat. Diabetes Camping Program, 1989—. Named Disting. Alumni U. Hawaii Sch. Nursing, 1987; one of Hawaii's Unsung Heroes, Honolulu Star Bull., 1993. Mem. ANA (polit. action com. 1994—), APHA, Hawaii Nurses Assn. (Excellence in Clin. Practice award 1995), Am. Diabetes Assn. (vol., founding bd. dirs. 1978—, cano nurse and camp dir. 1982—, past pres. 1986, nat. programs com. nat. youth congress 1993-95, outstanding contbns. to diabetes and camping award 1994), Hawaii Diabetes Assn., Hawaii Pub. Health Assn., Am. Assn. Diabetes Educators, Hawaii Assn. Diabetes Educators (founding mem., bd. dirs. 1989—, pres. 1996—, state legis. coord. 1996—, treas. 1994-95, pub. affairs chair 1996—, diabetes camp edn. award 1995), Internat. Diabetes Fedn., Internat. Soc. Pediat. and Adolescent Diabetes, Am. Heart Assn. (mem. cardiovascular nursing coun. 1985—), Sigma Theta Tau (founding mem., chair nominating com. 1995— Gamma Psi chpt., chmn. recognition com. 1986-89). Home: 98 1773 Kaahumanu St # C Aiea HI 96701 Office: Univ Hawaii at Manoa 2528 The Mall/Webster Honolulu HI 96822

KAEMPFER, WILLIAM HUTCHISON, economics educator; b. West Chester, Pa., Mar. 4, 1951; s. John Henry and Jane McFarlane (Hutchison) K.; m. Suzanne Hearne, July 17, 1976 (div. Mar. 1983); m. Mary Gerilyn Arnberg Pecchio, Dec. 30, 1992; 1 child, Jenna Marie. BA, Coll. Wooster, 1973; MA, Duke U., 1975, PhD, 1979. Instr. Coll. Wooster, Ohio, 1975-76; asst. prof. U. N.C., Greensboro, 1978-79, U. Wash., Seattle, 1979-81; asst. prof. U. Colo., Boulder, 1981-88, assoc. prof., 1988-94, prof., 1994—; asst. prof. Claremont (Calif.) McKenna Coll., 1985-88; assoc. prof. Claremont Grad. Sch., 1990. Author: International Economic Sanctions, 1992; contbr. articles to profl. jours. Mem. Am. Economic Assn. Office: Univ Colo PO Box 256 Boulder CO 80309-0256

KAFOURY, ANN GRAHAM, psychotherapist; b. Spokane, Wash., Mar. 27, 1945; d. William Matheson and Gladys Irene (Swift) Graham; m. David Kafoury; children: Trevor, Kenan, Stephanie. BA, U. Oreg., 1967; MAT, Portland State U., 1976; MA in Counseling and Psychology, Lewis and Clark Coll., 1982. Tchr. U.S. Peace Corps, Ghana, West Africa, 1967-69, Tigard (Oreg.) Sr. H.S., 1970-74, Portland (Oreg.) C.C., 1976-79; cons. Oreg. Fitness & Health Ctr., Good Samaritan Hosp., Portland, 1982-83; alcohol and drug counselor, co-dependency group leader Cedar Hills Hosp., Portland, 1989-93, outpatient coord., 1990-93; pvt. practice psychotherapist Portland, 1982—; Oreg. network coord. Eye Movement Desensitization and Reprocessing, Portland, 1992—; intensive family therapist, Portland, 1993—. Chairperson Hillside Park Bd., Portland, 1977-80; mem. Friends of West Women's Hotel, Portland, 1983-88; officer, bd. mem. Burnside Cmty. Coun., Portland, 1984-87; sponsor Oreg. Counselors Polit. Action Com., Oreg., 1988—. Mem. ACA, Oreg. Counseling Assn., Nat. Bd. Cert. Counselors. Home: 804 NW Culpepper Ter Portland OR 97210-3125 Office: 10490 SW Eastridge St Ste 130 Portland OR 97225-5030

KAGAN, MARTIN I., arts administrator; b. Ft. William, Ont., Can., Dec. 30, 1946; came to U.S., 1977; s. John David and Sadie Kagan. BA with honors, Waterloo Luth. U., 1969; M. in Environ. Studies, York U., 1972; diploma in arts adminstrn., Harvard U., 1972. Arts planner Cadillac-Fairview Corp., Toronto, Ont., 1972-74; gen. mgr. Anna Wyman Dancers, Vancouver, B.C., Can., 1974-76, Centaur Theatre, Montreal, Que., Can., 1976-77, Dennis Wayne Dancers, N.Y.C., 1977-78, Jacobs Pillow Dance Festival, Washington, 1978-80; exec. dir. OPERA Am., Washington, 1980-90; pres., chief exec. officer The Dance Gallery, L.A., 1990-92; v.p. Music Ctr. L.A. County, 1994-95; exec. dir. Alex Theatre, 1995—; mem. adv. bd. Madison Nat. Bank, Washington, 1985-90; bd. dirs. Am. Guild Mus. Artists Pension and Health Funds, N.Y.C., 1980-87. Home: 1815 Monterey Rd South Pasadena CA 91030-3933 Office: Alex Theatre 216 N Brand Blvd Glendale CA 91203-2610

KAGEMOTO, PATRICIA JOW (PAT JOW), artist, printmaker; b. N.Y.C., Feb. 20, 1952; d. Tong Fook and Toy Kuen (Lee) Jow; m. Haro Kagemoto, Sept. 21, 1991. BFA, SUNY, New Paltz, 1975. Printmaking workshop asst. SUNY, New Paltz, 1974-75, print shop asst., 1975; printmaking cons. Comm. Village, Ltd., Kingston, N.Y., 1975-84; arts and crafts tchr. Neighborhood Svc. Orgn., Poughkeepsie, N.Y., 1976; printmaking instr., adminstrv. asst. Comm. Village, Ltd., Kingston, 1977-79; exhbn. auditor N.Y. State Coun. on Arts, N.Y.C., 1984-87; gallery asst. Watermark/Cargo Gallery, Kingston, 1988-91; vis. artist N.Y. State Summer Sch. of Visual Arts, Fredonia, 1978, SUNY, New Paltz, 1983-84; cons. printer Printmaking Workshop, N.Y.C., 1984; children's printmaking workshop dir. Woodstock (N.Y.) Libr., 1989. One-woman shows Woodstock Libr., 1989, Watermark/Cargo Gallery, 1991, also others; 2-person shows Catherine Street Gallery, N.Y.C., 1983, 84, Cinque Gallery, N.Y.C., 1984, Watermark/Cargo Gallery, 1989; exhibited in numerous group shows, including Schenectady Mus., 1977, Albany (N.Y.) Inst. History and Art, 1978, Aaron Faber Gallery, N.Y.C., 1984, Printmaking Workshop, N.Y.C., 1984, Woodstock Artists' Assn., 1985, 91, Watermark/Cargo Gallery, 1989. Recipient grant Am. the Beautiful Fund, 1976, Ulster County Decentralization grant N.Y. State Coun. on Arts, 1989. Studio: 2806 Truman Ave Oakland CA 94605-4847

KAGIWADA, REYNOLD SHIGERU, advanced technology manager; b. L.A., July 8, 1938; s. Harry Yoshifusa and Helen Kinue (Imura) K.; m. Harriet Hatsune Natsuyama, Aug. 19, 1961; children: Julia, Conan. BS in Physics, UCLA, 1960, MS in Physics, 1962, PhD in Physics, 1966. Asst. prof. in residence physics UCLA, 1966-69; asst. prof. physics U. So. Calif., 1969-72; mem. tech. staff TRW, Redondo Beach, Calif., 1972-75, scientist, sect. head, 1975-77, sr. scientist, dept. mgr., 1977-83, lab. mgr., 1984-87, project mgr., 1987-88, MIMIC chief scientist, 1988-89, asst. program mgr., 1989-90; advanced technology mgr. TRW, Redondo Beach, 1990—. Presenter papers at numerous profl. meetings, co-author more than 41 articles; patentee eight solid state devices. Recipient Gold Medal award TRW, 1985, Ramo Tech. award, 1985, Transfer award, IEEE MTT-S N. Walter Cox award, 1997. Fellow IEEE (v.p. IEEE MTT-S Adminstrn. Com. 1991, IEEE MTT-S N. Walter Cox 1997, pres. 1992); mem. Assn. Old Crows, Sigma Pi Sigma, Sigma Xi. Home: 3117 Malcolm Ave Los Angeles CA 90034-3406 Office: TRW-SEG Bldg M5 Rm 1470 One Space Park Bldg Redondo Beach CA 90278

KAHAN, SHELDON JEREMIAH, musician, singer; b. Honolulu, Mar. 5, 1948; s. Aaron Kahan and Marianne (Royjiczek) Sann. Student, Tel Aviv U., 1967-69, Merritt Coll., 1972-74. Guitarist The Grim Reapers, Miami Beach, Fla., 1965-66; bassist The Electric Stage, Jerusalem, 1969-71; music dir., musician Fanfare, L.A., 1974-75, Jean Paul Vignon & 1st Love, L.A., 1975-76; musician Jenny Jones & Co., L.A., 1976; musician, vocalist Fantasy, L.A., 1977-79; leader, musician, vocalist Fortune, L.A., 1980-83; bassist Johnny Tillotson Show, Nev., 1983; ptnr., musician, vocalist Heartlight, L.A., 1983-84; leader, musician, vocalist The Boogie Bros., L.A., 1984—; arranger, conductor L.A. Rock Chorus, 1988; musician, vocalist Jeremiah Kahan, L.A., 1988; bass player LIX, L.A., 1990—; solo act Sheldon Kahan, L.A., 1990—; spokesman Moore Oldsmobile & Cadillac, Valencia, Calif., 1987. Compiled musical work copyrighted in Libr. Congress: Sheldon Jeremiah Kahan The Early Years-Vol. I; prodr., disk jockey Kaleidoscope Radio Mag., Am. Radio Ntwork; one-man show El Caapitan, Irvine, Calif., 1990, Sagebrush Cantina, Calabassas, Calif., 1990, Don Jose, Artesia, Calif., Pineapple Hill, Tustin, Calif., 1991, The Fling, Tustin, 1992, Beverly Garland, North Hollywood, Calif., Brian Patch, Garden Grove, Calif., Sugar Suite, Granada Hills, Calif., 1993, The Blarney Stone, Fountain Valley, Calif., 1994, Sunset Lounge, Fullerton, Calif., Rembrandts, Placentia, Calif., 1995, Chez Lynn, Orange, Calif., 1996, Maxwells, Anaheim Hills, Calif., Royal Crown, Fullerton, Calif., 1997, The Oasis, Garden Grove, Calif., 1997; albums include Out of the Shadows, 1992, City Lights, 1993. Mem. AFTRA, Am. Fedn. Musicians. Democrat. Jewish. Home: 3915 1/2 Fredonia Dr Los Angeles CA 90068-1213

KAHIKINA, MICHAEL PUAMAMO, social services administrator, state legislator; b. Honolulu, Jan. 16, 1950; m. Naomi Abigail Barros; children: Puamamo, Kealoha, Kaua'i, Kanoe. AA, Leeward C.C., Pearl City, Hawaii, 1988; BS in Pub. Adminstrn., U. Hawaii-West Oahu, 1990. Utility electrician U.S. Navy Exch., Pearl Harbor, Hawaii, 1972-74; electrician City & County of Honolulu, 1974-75; outreach counselor Waianae Rap Ctr., 1975-79; social worker II Queen Liliuokalani Ctr., Nanakuli, Hawaii, 1979-85; agrl. specialist Honolulu Cmty. Action Program, Waianae, 1985-87; cmty. outreach . Hale Ola Ho'opakolea, Nanakuli, 1987-90; unit dir. Boys & Girls Club-Waianae, 1990—. Mem. State Ho. Reps. (Dist. 43), 1994-96; bd. dirs. Neighborhood Bd.-Waianae, 1988-92; mem. Tchr. Retention Task Force, Waianae, 1987, Sch. Cmty. Based Mgmt. Task Force, Honolulu, 1988. Sgt. USAF, 1968-72. Democrat. Home: 89-416 Nanakuli Ave Nanakuli HI 96792 Office: Ho Reps State Capitol 435 S Beretania St Honolulu HI 96813

KAHN, ARLENE JUDY MILLER, nurse, educator; b. Chgo., Dec. 16, 1940; d. Fred and Sophie (Schelbe) Miller; RN, AB, U. Ill., Chgo., 1963, MSN, 1970; EdD, U. San Francisco, 1986; m. Roy M. Kahn, Oct. 25, 1968; 1 child, Jennifer M. Head nurse psychiat. unit Grant Hosp., Chgo., 1966; supervising nurse Ill. Psychiat. Inst., Chgo., 1967; instr. psychiat. nursing Calif. State U., San Francisco, 1968-70; mem. faculty Calif. State U., Hayward, 1974—, assoc. prof. nursing, 1980-86, prof., 1986—, chair dept. nursing and health scis. Sch. Sci., 1992—; cons. in field. Research grantee Calif. State U., Hayward, 1980-81. Fellow Am. Assn. Psychiat. Nursing; mem. United Profs. Calif., Calif. Assn. Colls. of Nursing (treas. 1996—), Calif. Nursing Assn., Bay Area Nursing Diagnosis Assn. (officer 1986—), Sigma Theta Tau. Author articles in field. Home: 95 Sonia St Oakland CA 94618-2548 Office: Hayward State U School of Science Hayward CA 94542

KAHN, EARL LESTER, market research executive; b. Kansas City, Mo., May 30, 1919; s. Samuel and Sarah (Kaufman) K. BA, Harvard U., 1940; MA, U. Chgo., 1947. Pres. Social Research, Inc., Chgo., 1946-74; chmn. bd. KPR Assocs., Inc., Scottsdale, Ariz., 1974-88. Contbr. articles to profl. jour. Served to capt. USAF, 1942-46. Mem. Am. Mktg. Assn, Am. Sociol. Assn. Home: 5608 N Scottsdale Rd Paradise Valley AZ 85253-5912

KAHN, EDWIN S., lawyer; b. N.Y.C., Jan. 22, 1938; m. Cynthia Chutter, May 30, 1966; children—David, Jonathan, Jennifer. B.A., U. Colo., 1958; J.D., Harvard U., 1965. Bar: Colo. 1965, U.S. Dist. Ct. (Colo.) 1965, U.S. Ct. Appeals (10th cir.) 1965, U.S. Supreme Ct. 1968. Assoc. Holland & Hart, Denver, 1965-70, ptnr., 1970-77; ptnr., shareholder, Kelly/Haglund/Garnsey & Kahn, LLC, Denver, 1978—. Served as 1st lt. USAF, 1959-62, Eng. Fellow Am. Coll. Trial Lawyers: mem. Denver Bar Assn. (pres. 1984-85). Home: 2345 Leyden St Denver CO 80207-3441 Office: Kelly Haglund Garnsey & Kahn LLC 1441 18th St Ste 300 Denver CO 80202-1255

KAHN, IRWIN WILLIAM, industrial engineer; b. N.Y.C., Feb. 3, 1923; s. Milton and Clara (Clark) K.; BS, U. Calif.-Berkeley, 1949; student Cath. U., 1943-44; m. Mildred Cross, May 14, 1946 (dec. May 1966); children: Steven Edward, Michael William, Evelyn Ruth, Joanne Susan; m. 2d, Marajayne Smith, Oct. 9, 1979. Chief indsl. engr. Malsbary Mfg. Co., Oakland, Calif., 1953-57, Yale & Towne Mfg. Co., San Leandro, Calif., 1957-60; sr. indsl. engr. Eitel McCulloch, San Carlos, Calif., 1961-62, Lockheed, Sunnyvale, Calif., 1962-69; v.p. Performance Investors, Inc., Palo Alto, 1969-74; with Kaiser-Permanente Svcs., Oakland, 1974-76; nat. mgr. material handling Cutter Labs., Berkeley, Calif., 1976-83; sr. mgmt. engr. Children's Hosp. Med. Ctr., Oakland, 1983; sr. indsl. engr. Naval Air Rework Facility, Alameda, Calif., 1983-85, Naval Supply Ctr., Oakland, 1985-88; vis. lectr. U. Calif., Berkeley, 1986; tchr. indsl. engring. Laney Coll., Oakland, 1967—, Chabot Coll., Hayward, Calif.; pres. East Bay Table Pad Co., 1990. Chmn. Alameda County Libr. Adv. Commn., 1965—. Served with AUS, 1943-46. Registered profl. engr., Calif. Mem. Am. Inst. Indsl. Engrs. (chpt. pres. 1963-64, chmn. conf. 1967 nat. publ. dir. aerospace div. 1968-69), Calif. Soc. Profl. Engrs. (pres. chpt.). Club: Toastmasters (dist. gov. 1960-61).

KAHN, KEVIN COMERFORD, software engineering executive; b. N.Y.C., Dec. 8, 1950; s. Arthur L. and Eileen M. (Comerford) K.; m. Suzanne Louise Schmitt, May 22, 1976. BS in Math., Manhattan Coll., 1972; MS in Computer Sci., Purdue U., 1973, PhD in Computer Sci., 1976. Sr. software engr. Intel Corp., Santa Clara, Calif., 1976-77, Aloha, Oreg., 1977-79, software project leader, 1979-82, dept. mgr., Hillsboro, Oreg., 1982-83, software enging. mgr., 1983-86, enging. mgr., 1986—, dir. systems architecture BiiN, Hillsboro, 1988—, lab. mgr., 1990-93; Intel fellow, dir. Software Arch., 1994-95, dir. comm. architecture lab., 1995—. Contbr. articles to profl. jours. Patentee in field. NSF fellow, 1972. Mem. Assn. Computer Machinery, Spl. Interest Group Operating Systems (sec., treas. 1983-85), Phi Beta Kappa. Home: 3324 SW Sherwood Pl Portland OR 97201-1461 Office: Intel Corp JF3-206 5200 NE Elam Young Pky Hillsboro OR 97124-6463

KAHN, LINDA MCCLURE, maritime industry executive; b. Jacksonville, Fla.; d. George Calvin and Myrtice Louise (Boggs) McClure; m. Paul Markham Kahn, May 20, 1968. BS with high honors, U. Fla.; MS, U. Mich., 1964. Actuarial trainee N.Y. Life Ins. Co., N.Y.C., 1964-66, actuarial asst., 1966-69, asst. actuary, 1969-71; v.p., actuary US Life Ins., Pasadena, Calif., 1972-74; mgr. Coopers & Lybrand, Los Angeles, 1974-76, sr. cons., San Francisco, 1976-82; dir. program mgmt. Pacific Maritime Assn., San Francisco, 1982—. Bd. dirs. Pacific Heights Residents Assn., sec.-treas., 1981; trustee ILWU-PMA Welfare Plan, SIU-PD-PMA Pension and Supplemental Benefits Plans, 1982-90, Seafarers Med. Ctr., 1982-90, others. Fellow Soc. Actuaries (chmn. com. on minority recruiting 1988-91, chmn. actuary of future sect. 1993-95), Conf. Consulting Actuaries; mem. Internat. Actuarial Assn., Internat. Assn. Cons. Actuaries, Actuarial Studies Non-Life Ins., Am. Acad. Actuaries (enrolled actuary), Western Pension and Benefits Conf. (newsletter editor 1983-85, sec. 1985-88, treas. 1989-90), Actuarial Club Pacific States, San Francisco Actuarial Club (pres. 1981), Met. Club, Commonwealth Club, Soroptimists Club (v.p. 1973-74). Home: 2430 Pacific Ave San Francisco CA 94115-1238 Office: Pacific Maritime Assn Sacramento St Tower 550 California St San Francisco CA 94104-1006

KAHN, MARIO SANTAMARIA, international marketing executive; b. Manila, Jan. 16, 1956; came to U.S., 1980; s. Rene L. and Dolores (Santamaria) K.; m. Maria Victoria Legaspi, Dec. 28, 1987; 1 child, Marc Daniel. AB in Mktg. & Comm., De La Salle U., Manila, 1977; MA in Comm. Mgmt. cum laude, U. So. Calif., 1982; postgrad., Stanford U., 1989. Account mgr. McCann-Erickson, Manila, 1977-80; teaching asst. U. So. Calif., L.A., 1980-82; ops. mgr. Dayton-Hudson Corp., Mpls., 1982-85; sr. mgr. Asia Sunkist Growers, Ontario, Calif., 1986—; bd. dirs. Sunkist Soft Drink Internat. Mem. Am. Mktg. Assn., Am. Mgmt. Assn., Stanford Alumni Assn., Annenberg Alumni Assn., De La Salle Alumni Assn. Office: Sunkist Growers Inc 720 E Sunkist St Ontario CA 91761-1861

KAHN, MARTIN JEROME, art gallery owner; b. Paterson, N.J., July 11, 1946; s. Macwell C. and Doris (Altman) K.; m. Carole Magagnoli, Nov. 7, 1976; children: Lisa, Maya, Sol. BA in Art History, Rutgers U., 1968. Tchr., 1968-72; owner Kahn Sandals, St. Croix, U.S. V.I., Kauai Leather, Hawaii, 1975-79, Kauai Gold Ltd., Hawaii, 1979-84; pres. Kahn Galleries, Hawaii, 1984—. Past pres. Jewish Cmty. Kauai, Rotary of Kapaa. Office: Kahn Galleries 4569 Kukui St Kauai HI 96746

KAHN, PAUL MARKHAM, actuary; b. San Francisco, May 8, 1935; s. Sigmund Max and Alexandrina K. (Strauch) K.; m. Linda P. McClure, May 20, 1968. BS, Stanford U., 1956; MA, U. Mich., 1957, PhD, 1961. Asst. actuary Equitable Life Assurance Soc., N.Y.C., 1961-71; v.p., life actuary Beneficial Std. Life, L.A., 1971-75; v.p., actuary Am. Express Life Ins. Co., San Rafael, Calif., 1975-77, P.M. Kahn & Assocs., 1977—; adj. prof. actuarial math. San Fransisco State U.; imperial actuary, 1995. Editor Dictionary of Actuarial and Life Ins. Terms, 1972, 2d edit., 1983, Credibility: Theory and Practice, 1975, Computational Probability, 1980. Fellow Soc. Actuaries (Triennial prize 1961-64), Can. Inst. Actuaries, Conf. of Cons.

Actuaries; mem. Am. Acad. Actuaries, Internat. Actuarial Assn., Inst. Actuaries (Eng.), Spanish Actuarial Inst., Swiss Actuarial Assn., German Actuarial Assn., Italian Actuarial Inst., Am. Antiquarian Soc., Grolier Club (N.Y.C.) Zamorano Club (L.A.), Roxburghe Club, Concordia-Argonaut Club (San Francisco), Pacific Club (Honolulu). Address: 2430 Pacific Ave San Francisco CA 94115-1238

KAHN, SEYMOUR, air transportation executive; b. 1927. Student, UCLA, Southwest U. Prin. Seymour Kahn, Westwood, Calif., 1947-66; asst. to pres. Bell Electronics Corp., Gardena, Calif., 1966-69; pres. IPM Tech. Inc., L.A., 1969—, Mercury Airgroup Inc. (formerly Maytag Aircraft Corp.). Office: Maytag Aircraft Corp 6145 Lehman Dr Ste 300 Colorado Springs CO 80918-3440*

KAHN, VIVIAN, urban planner; b. N.Y., Mar. 16, 1944; d. Elmer Albert and Lillian (Kahn) Neumann; m. Robert Tim Brown, Aug. 23, 1963 (div. Nov. 1968); m. Larry J. Mortimer, April 1, 1986; 1 child, Aaron C. Kahn-Mortimer. BA, CUNY, 1965; attended, Pratt Inst. Sch. Architecture, 1969-71, Columbia U. Sch. Journalism, 1965-66. Reporter Ridgewood (N.J.) Newspapers, 1966-67, N.Y. Times, 1967-69; sr. planner Assn. Bay Area Govts., Oakland, Calif., 1972-76; chief cmty. assist. State Office of Planning and Rsch., Sacramento, Calif., 1976-78; exec. dir. No. Calif. Assn. Non-Profit Housing, San Francisco, 1983-84; prin., ptnr. Kahn/Mortimer Assocs., Oakland, Calif., 1979—; planning mgr., zoning officer City of Berkeley, Calif., 1987-95; mem. bd. dirs. Jubilee West, Inc., Oakland, 1993—, Am. Planning Assn., Washington, 1994—; adj. instr. U. Calif., Berkeley ext., 1995—. Mem. edit. adv. bd. Jour. Am. Planning Assn., 1996—; contbr. articles to profl. jours. Trustee Calif. Preservation Found., Oakland, 1987-90; pres., mem bd. dirs. Metro-Greater Oakland Dem. Club, 1989—; chair 37th Dist. Dem., Seattle, 1982-83; treas. Seattle Housing Resources Group, 1980-83. Recipient Alumni scholar Columbia U. Sch. Journalism, N.Y., 1965. Mem. AICP, Phi Beta Kappa. Home: 4623 Davenport Ave Oakland CA 94619-2916

KAIDA, TAMARRA, art and photography educator; b. Lienz, Austria, July 6, 1946; came to U.S., 1950; d. Ivan and Matrona (Bratasuk) K.; m. Paul S. Knapp; 1 child, Krister. BA, Goddard Coll., 1974; MFA, SUNY, Buffalo, 1979. Tutor photography Empire State Coll., 1977-79; asst. dir. dept. edn. Internat. Mus. Photography, George Eastman House, 1976-79; vis. lectr. Ariz. State U., Tempe, 1979-80, asst. prof., 1980-85, assoc. prof., 1985-92, prof., 1992—; represented by Etherton Gallery, Tucson, Califia Books, San Francisco; mem. faculty Internat. Sommerakademie fur Bildende Kunst, Salzburg, Austria, 1985, Friends of Photography Summer Workshop, Carmel, Calif., 1989, vis. photographers program R.I. Sch. Design, 1989, guest artist lecture and lazer print transfer demonstration Photography Studies in France, Paris, 1991; panelist NEA S.W. Regional Photogaphy Task Force, 1980; juror nat. photography competition Calif. Inst. Arts, Valencia, 1981; curator, lectr., cons. in field. Author: (with Rita Dove) The Other Side of the House, 1988; Tremors from the Faultline, 1989; contbr. articles to profl. jours.; author short stories; many one-woman shows including Scottsdale (Ariz.) Ctr. Arts, 1987, Fine Arts Gallery RISD, 1989, OPSIS Found. Gallery, N.Y.C., 1990, Fyerweather Gallery U. Va., Charlottesville, 1991, Photography Gallery, Fine Art Ctr., U. R.I., Kingston, R.I., 1992, Kharkov (Ukraine) Regional Mus. Art, 1993, Sky Harbor Airport, Phoenix, Ariz., 1994; numerous nat. and internat. group shows including Coconino Ctr. Arts, Flagstaff, Ariz., 1985, Frankfurt Art Soc., Germany, 1985, Mus. Art and Trade, Hamburg, Germany, 1985, Boulder (Colo.) Ctr. Visual Arts, 1985, Art Inst. Chgo., Mpls. Coll. Art & Design, 1986, Hood Mus. Art Dartmouth Coll., Hanover, N.H., 1987, Lawrence (Kans.) Art Ctr., 1987, Miller's Studio, Zurich, Switzerland, 1987, Palazzo Braschi, Rome, 1987, Sante Fe Ctr. Photography, 1987, Dinnerware Gallery, Tucson, 1987, Sante Fe Ctr. Arts (purchase award), 1987, Rockwell Mus., Corning, N.Y., 1987, Grand Canyon Coll., Phoenix, 1987, Tucson Mus. Art, 1988, Halsey Gallery Coll. of Charleston, S.C., 1988, Long Beach (Calif.) Coll. Fine Arts, 1988, Atrium Gallery U. Conn. Storrs, 1988, Gallery of Kans. City (Mo.) Artists Coalition (1st prize, fellowship award) 1989, Lieberman and Saul Gallery, N.Y.C., 1989, Downey (Calif.) Mus. Art, 1989, Anderson Ranch Arts Ctr., Aspen, Colo., 1989, San Francisco Camerawork, 1990, Phoenix Mus. Art, 1990, Ctr. for Photography, Cin., 1991, Mus. Art U. Okla., 1991, Rockford (Ill.) Coll., 1991, Ctr. for Creative Photography, Tucson, 1991-92; Huntington Gallery, Mass. Coll. Art, Boston, 1992, Ariz. State Capital, Phoenix, 1992, Barbara Zusman Art and Antiques Gallery, Santa Fe, N.Mex., 1992; internat. traveling exhbns.; represented in permanent collections Union Russian Art Photography, Moscow, U. Calif. Santa Cruz, Kennedy Ctr. Performing Arts, Washington, L.A. County Mus. Art, Internat. Mus. Photography George Eastman House, Rochester, N.Y., N.Y. Pub. Libr., SUNY Buffalo, Libr. Congress, Polaroid Corp., Cambridge, Mass., Sante Fe Mus. Fine Arts, Scottsdale Ctr. Art, Snell and Wilmer, Phoenix, Valley Nat. Bank, Phoenix, others; photographs featured various works. Judge spring art show Scottsdale C.C., 1980; organizer Artist Against Hunger money and food drive Ariz. State U. Sch. Art, 1984; juror New Times Newspaper, 1985, Tempe Fine Arts Ctr., 1989, Yavapai Coll., Prescott, Ariz., 1989. Recipient Faculty Grant-in-Aid, 1982, 85, 93, Current Works 1989 Excellence award Soc. Contemporary Photography, Visual Artists fellowship grant Nat. Endowment for Arts, 1986, rsch. grant Coll. Fine Arts, 1987, 93, grant Arts/Social Svcs./Humanities, 1989, Sch. Art Assistance to Faculty, 1990, Visual Arts fellowship grant Ariz. Commn. Arts, 1989-90, Inst. for Studies in Arts, 1992, materials grant Polaroid Corp., 1992, Gov.'s Arts award, 1992, Women's Studies Summer Rsch. award., 1992. Mem. Coll. Arts Assn., Soc. Photographic Edn. (co-chair, organizer West/S.W. Regional Conf. 1983), Friends of Photography (Ferguson award 1983). Democrat. Russian Orthodox. Home: 534 N Orange Mesa AZ 85201-5609

KAIL, JOSEPH GERARD, communications sales and marketing executive; b. Cin., Dec. 23, 1946; s. Henry Thomas and Cosma (Contadino) K.; m. Patricia Lynne Riedel, June 28, 1969; children: Robert, Daniel, Joseph. BS, Xavier U., Cin., 1969, MEd, 1973. Tchr., athletic coach Alter High Sch., Kettering, Ohio, 1969-77; sales rep. Philips Bus. Systems, Inc., Cin., 1977-78, Hewlett-Packard Co., Dayton, 1978-81; dist. sales mgr. Hewlett-Packard Co., Pitts., 1981-83; sales mgr. Rocky Mountain area Hewlett-Packard Co., Denver, 1983-87, western regional sales mgr. bus. computer systems, 1988-91, western regional mktg. mgr. computer systems, 1991-92, am. mktg. mgr. computer systems organization, 1992-93, nat. sales mgr., home products, 1994-96, nat. sales mgr. comm., 1996—. Com. mem. troop 986, Boy Scouts Am., Denver, 1984-88, Highlands Ranch High Sch. Boosters, Denver, 1988. Republican. Roman Catholic. Office: Hewlett-Packard Co 24 Inverness Dr E Englewood CO 80112-5624

KAIL, KONRAD, physician; b. Iowa City, July 7, 1949; s. Joseph Andrew Kail and Jean Lucille (Peterson) Tienan; m. Jane Marie Petersen, Jan. 5, 1973. BS in Biology, U. Houston, 1974; BS in Medicine, Baylor Coll. Medicine, 1976; ND, Nat. Coll. Naturopathic, Medicine, 1983; DACNFM, Am. Coll. Naturopathic Family, Medicine, 1995. Lic. naturopathic physician. Cardiac-catherization technician St. Luke's/Tex. Children's Hosp., Houston, 1972-75; physician's asst. various clinics, Silver City, N.Mex., 1976-80; dir. Naturopathic Wheeling and Healing Around Country Bike Tour, 1983-84; chmn. bd. dirs. U.S. Complementary Health, Inc., Phoenix, 1995—; dean postgrad. med. edn. S.W. Coll. of Naturopathic Medicine, Phoenix, 1996—; owner, operator Naturopathic Family Care, Phoenix, 1990—; cons. Ins. Cos., Nutrient Supplement Cos., Govt. Agys., 1985—. Editor: Alternative Medicine, 1994; contbr. articles to profl. jours. Mem. adv. bd. Inst. for Natural Medicine. With USN Res., 1971-76. Fellow Am. Assn. Naturopathic Physicians (chmn. scientific affil. 1986-97, pres. 1992-94), Am. Coll. Naturopathic Family Practice (chmn., pres. 1995—). Green Party. Office: Naturopathic Family Care 13832 N 32nd St Ste C2-4 Phoenix AZ 85032-5616

KAISCH, KENNETH BURTON, psychologist, priest; b. Detroit, Aug. 29, 1948; s. Kenneth R. Kaisch and Marjorie F. (Howe) Bourke; m. Suzanne Carol LePrevost, Aug. 31, 1969; 1 child, Samuel. BA, San Francisco State U., 1972; MDiv, Ch. Divinity Sch. Pacific, 1976; MS, Utah State U., 1983, PhD in Clin. Psychology, 1986. Ordained deacon Episcopal Ch., 1976, priest, 1977; lic. clin. psychologist, Calif. Intern local parish, 1973-76; ordinand tng. program Ch. of the Good Shepherd, Ogden, Utah, 1976-77; pastor St. Francis' Episc. Ch., Moab, Utah, 1977-80, St. John's Episc. Ch., Logan, Utah, 1980-84; psychol. asst. Peter Ebersole, Ph.D., Fullerton, Calif., 1984-86; intern in clin. psychology Patton State Hosp., Calif., 1985-86; psychol. asst. Ronald Wong Jue, Ph.D., Fullerton and Newport Beach, Calif., 1986-88; pvt. practice clin. psychologist Calif., 1988—; clin. dir. Anxiety Clinic, Fullerton, 1993—; exec. dir. Contemplative Congress, Fullerton, 1988-91, Inner Peace Conf., 1995—; founder, pres. OneHeart, 1986—, Contemplative Visions, Fullerton, 1990—; supply priest Episc. Diocese of L.A.; invited lectr. Acad. Sch. Profl. Psychology, Moscow, 1992, 93. Co-author: Fundamentals of Psychotherapy, 1984; author: Finding God: A Handbook of Christian Mediation, 1994: contbr. numerous articles to profl. jours. Mem. St. Andrew's Episc. Ch., Fullerton. Mem. APA, Calif. Psychol. Assn., Anxiety Disorders Assn. Am., Nat. Register of Health Svc. Providers in Psychology, Phi Kappa Phi, Rotary (bd. dirs., past officer). Episcopalian. Office: 2555 E Chapman Ave Ste 617 Fullerton CA 92831

KAISER, JAMES RUSSELL, insurance agent, retired police officer; b. L.A., Nov. 8, 1948; s. Morris A. and Sara (Ornelas) K.; m. Wendy Hauk Kaiser, Sept. 20, 1987; children: Mike, Jill, Carrie, Thomas. BS, Calif. State U., L.A., 1975; postgrad., Coll. of Redwoods, Eureka, Calif. Std. advanced post cert.; cabinet making cert. Patrol office L.A. Police Dept., 1972-93; ins. agt. Farmers Ins. Co., Eureka, 1996—; guest spkr. Lions Club, 1996, Kiwanis Club, 1996, Humboldt State U., 1996. Author: 21 Years Los Angeles Police Department, 1996. Rescue police officer City of Blue Lake, Calif., 1994. Sgt. USAF, 1967-72. Republican. Home: 2865 Little Pond St Mckinleyville CA 95519-9111 Office: Farmers Ins 428 C St Eureka CA 95501-0356

KAISER, NINA IRENE, health facility administrator; b. San Diego, Nov. 29, 1953; d. Louis Frederick and Mary Elizabeth (Wright) K.; m. N. Klimist, Aug. 27, 1987; children: Kellen Anne Kaiser, Ethan Andrew Kaiser-Klimist. BSN, BA in Women Studies, San Francisco State U., 1980. RN, Calif. RN Calif. Pacific Med. Ctr., San Francisco, 1980-81, Ralph K. Davies Med. Ctr., San Francisco, 1982-85, Planned Parenthood, San Francisco, 1985-86, Visiting Nurses and Hospice, San Francisco, 1986-88; RN supr. St. Mary's Home Care, San Francisco, 1991-93; RN dir. St. Vincent's Homecare and Hospice, Fremont, Calif., 1993-94, Home Health Link, San Leandro, Calif., 1994—. Pres. Daus. of Bilitis, San Francisco, 1977-78; founding mem. Buena Vista Lesbian and Gay Parents Assn., San Francisco, 1985; treas., bd. dirs. Holladay Ave. Homeowners Assn., San Francisco, 1984-96; bd. dirs. Midrasha High Sch., Berkeley, Calif., 1996. With USN, 1971-74.

KAISER, ROBERT BLAIR, journalist; b. Detroit, Dec. 3, 1930; s. Robert Pisar and Olive Grace (Blair) Hungate; m. Susan Ann Mulcahey, Nov. 26, 1959 (div. July 7, 1964); m. Karen McCaffery, June 7, 1966 (div. Feb. 7, 1972); children: Margaret Anne, John Gustave, William Grant. BA, Gonzaga U., 1954, MA, 1955. Reporter Arizona Republic, Phoenix, 1958-61; corr. Time mag., N.Y.C., 1961-66; reporter New York Times, N.Y.C., 1979-81; prof., chmn. dept. journalism U. Nev., Reno, 1981-84; columnist The Tribune, San Diego, 1984-86; freelance journalist Phoenix, 1966—. Author: Pope, Council and World, 1963, R.F.K. Must Die!, 1970, Melvin Belli: My Life on Trial, 1976, Pat Haden: My Rookie Season with the Los Angeles Rams, 1977, The Politics of Sex and Religion, 1985, Life Is Too Short, 1991, Just Farr Fun, 1994, The Search for Sonny Skies, 1994, Homosexuality A Freedom Too Far, 1995. Bd. dirs. Assn. for Rights of Caths. in the Ch., 1996—. Mem. Overseas Press Club (Best Mag. Reporting of Fgn. Affairs 1963), Soc. of Profl. Journalists. Office: PO Box 33698 Phoenix AZ 85067

KAISER, SUE, school administrator; b. Colorado Springs, Colo., Nov. 26, 1956; d. James Byron McClure and Billie (Richmond) Ortega; m. Gregory John Kaiser, Dec. 11, 1982; children: Timothy David, Matthew John, Carolyn Beth, Christopher Mark. BA, U. LaVerne, Calif., 1979; MA, Calif. State U., Pomona, 1984. Tchr. Evergreen Sch., Diamond Bar, Calif., 1982-91; asst. prin. Walnut (Calif.) Elem. Sch., 1991-92; admin. state and fed. programs Walnut Sch. Dist., 1992—; adv. bd. Mt. Sac Sch. to Career, Walnut, 1995—. Mem.(Assn. of Curriculum Devel.), Assn. of Calif. Adminstrs. Office: Walnut V Unified Sch Dis 880 S Lemon Ave Walnut CA 91789-2931

KAISER-BOTSAI, SHARON KAY, early chilhood educator; b. Waterloo, Iowa, Aug. 9, 1941; d. Peter A. Ley and Lorraine (Worthington) Burton; m. Hugh W. Kaiser, Aug. 28, 1968 (div. 1981); 1 child, Kiana; m. Elmer E. Botsai, Dec. 5, 1981; children: Kiana, Don, Kurt. BSBA, U. Ariz., 1963; MEd, U. Hawaii, Honolulu, 1970; postgrad., Hawaii Loa Coll., 1971, U. Hawaii, 1972-88. Cert. elem. edn. tchr., Hawaii. Sec. Donald M. Drake, San Francisco, 1964-66; tchr. St. Mark's Kindergarten, Honolulu, 1966-73; head tchr. Cen. Union Preschool, Honolulu, 1967-77; tchr. Waiokeola Preschool, Honolulu, 1974-76, 77-88; tchr. staff instruction Honolulu Dist. Dept. of Edn., 1989-90; tchr. students of ltd. English proficiency Kaahumanu Sch., Honolulu, 1990-94; tchr. kindergarten Palolo Sch., Honolulu, 1991—; pvt. instr. in Hawaiian dance, 1977-79; workshop leader marine sea crafts Sea Grant Inst. for Marine Educators, 1977, HAEYC Conf., 1979, 82, 84, 85, 86, chair workshops in music and creative drama, 1977, drama workshop, 1994; speaker Celebration of Life Sta. KHON-TV, 1979; workshop leader MECAP Conf., 1985; mem. com. Improvement Symphony Performance for Preschoolers, 1977; art advisor, coord. Sunday sch. program Waiokeola Ch., 1973, speaker creative communication, 1984; validator accreditation program Nat. Acad. for Edn. of Young Children, 1986—; asst. to co-chair conf. Hawaii Assn. for Edn. Young Children, 1987-88; Hawaii State Tchrs. Assn. rep. Palolo Sch., 1993. Author: Creative Dramatics, 1990; co-author: Preschool Activities, 1990. Actress Presido Playhouse, San Francisco, 1962, Little Theatre, Honolulu Zoo, 1976; instr. spl. edn. students Kaneohe YWCA, 1967; troop co-leader Girl Scouts U.S.A., 1981-84; bd. dirs. Zoo Hui, 1984-86; trustee, stewardship chmn. Waiokeola Ch., 1986-88. Mem. Hawaii Assn. for Edn. of Young Children (First recipient Phyllis Loveless Excellence in Teaching award 1979), Delta Delta Delta. Lutheran. Home: 321 Wailupe Cir Honolulu HI 96821-1524

KAISERSHOT, EDWARD JOSEPH, elementary education educator, coach; b. Dickinson, N.D., Dec. 24, 1956; s. Edward A. and Margaret M. (Ridl) K.; children: Derrik E., David J. BS in Elem. Edn. and Physical Edn., Dickinson State U., 1979; certificate of edn. computing, Calif State Univ., San Bernardino, 1992. Elem. tchr., track-baksetball coach, asst. football coach New England (N.D.) Pub. Sch., 1979-80; equipment operator, western region chemist Dowell div. Dow Chem. Co., Dickinson, 1980-83; tchr., track and basketball coach Tioga (N.D.) Pub. Schs., 1983-86; elem. tchr. phys. edn., basketball coach El Camino Real Acad. WBT/SIL, Bogota, Colombia, 1986-88; elem. tchr. phys. edn. Del Rosa Christian Sch., San Bernardino, Calif., 1988-89; tchr. kindergarten San Bernarndino City Unified Sch. Dist., 1989—; asst. track coach Dickinson State Univ., 1983—; tech. liaison for sch. site San Bernardino City Unified Sch. Dist. 1992—, sch. site sci. fair coord., 1991—; bd. dirs. Computer Using Educators, San Bernardino and Riverside Counties, Calif., 1995—. Camp counselor Child Evangelism Fellowship, N.D., 1984-85, bd. dirs. So. Calif., 1995—; judge Inland Empire Sci. and Engring. Fair, San Bernardino, 1994; bd. dirs., trustee Temple Bapt. Sch., Redlands, Calif., 1995—; leader Children's Bible Club, N.D., Bogota, 1983-88, Calif., 1990—; trustee 1st Bapt. Ch. Tioga, 1984-86; vol. Tioga Community Nursing Home and Hosp., 1983-86; coach N. D. Spl. Olympics; vol. San Bernardino Spl. Olympics, 1995—. Office: San Bernardino City Unified Schs 777 N F St San Bernardino CA 92410-3017

KAKUGAWA, TERRI ETSUMI, osteopath; b. Honolulu, Sept. 16, 1965; d. Paul Katsumi and Ruby Yetsuko (Oshiro) K. BA, U. Hawaii, 1987; DO, Kirksville Coll. Osteo. Medicine, 1992. Diplomate Am. Bd. Osteo. Family Physicians. Intern Cmty. Health Ctr., Branch County, Coldwater, Mich., 1992-93, resident in family medicine, 1993-95; group practice Waianae, Hawaii, 1995—. Mem. Am. Osteo. Assn., Am. Coll. Osteo. Family Physicians, Hawaii Assn. Osteo. Physicians and Surgeons. Democrat. Office: Waianae Coast Comprehensive Health Ctr 87-2070 Farrington Hwy Waianae HI 96792-3757

KALB, BENJAMIN STUART, television producer, director; b. L.A., Mar. 17, 1948; s. Marcus and Charlotte K. BS in Journalism, U. Oreg., 1969. Sportswriter, Honolulu Advertiser, 1971-76; traveled with tennis profl. Ilie Nastase; contbr. articles N.Y. Times, Sport Mag. and Tennis U.S.A., 1976; editor Racquetball Illustrated, 1978-82; segment producer PM Mag. and Hollywood Close-Up, 1983-86; exec. producer Ben Kalb Prodns., 1986—; instr. sports in soc. U. Hawaii, 1974-75. Producer (video) The Natural Way to Meet the Right Person, 1987; producer, dir. (video) Casting Call: Director's Choice, 1987, The Natural Way to Meet The Right Person (Best Home Videos of Yr. L.A. Times), (TV pilot and home video) Bizarro, 1988, (infomercial) How To Start Your Own Million Dollar Business, 1990, The Nucelle Promise, 1993-94; prodr.-dir. (infomercials) Banamex USA Credit Card, 1995, Slimaster Exerciser, 1996, Koolatron Companion, 1997, (short feature film) Against the Ropes, 1996; segment dir. (home video) Movie Magic, 1990, (TV show) Totally Hidden Video; writer-segment dir. (home video) Making of The American Dream Calendar Girl, 1991; producer, host (cable TV show) Delicious Sports, 1987-88; segment dir. Totally Hidden Video (Fox TV Network), 1991-92; prodr., dir. short feature film Love Match, 1995. Served with Hawaii Army N.G., 1970-75. Named Outstanding Male Grad. in Journalism, U. Oreg., 1969. Mem. Sigma Delta Chi (chpt. pres. 1968). Democrat. Jewish. Contbr. articles to mags. and newspapers. Home: 1429 S Bundy Dr # 4 Los Angeles CA 90025-2108 Office: Ben Kalb Prodns 1541 Ocean Ave Ste 200 Santa Monica CA 90401-2104

KALB, RONALD GARY, public relations executive; b. L.A., Feb. 10, 1944; s. Frederick Augustus and Yola Lillian (Weiner) K.; m. Lynda Jane Moyer, Dec. 3, 1982; children: Lisa Christine, Darren Frederick. Bachelor's degree, San Francisco State U., 1966, lifetime tchg. credential, 1967; postgrad., San Jose State U., 1978-79. Mgmt. cert. U. of the Pacific. Tchr. English, journalism James Logan H.S., Union City, Calif., 1967-78; v.p. Russom & Co., San Francisco, 1979-87; sr. v.p., gen. mgr. Porter/Novelli Public Rels., San Francisco, 1987-88; v.p., group mgr., sr. cons. Burson-Marsteller, San Francisco, 1988-90; news bur. mgr. Lawrence Livermore Nat. Lab., Livermore, Calif., 1990-93, dep. dir. pub. affairs, 1993—. Contbr. music revs. and articles to mags. Bd. dirs. San Francisco Coun. on Entertainment, 1986-89. Recipient Bay Area Best award Internat. Assn. Bus. Communicators, 1983, Joey award San Jose Advt. Club, 1983. Mem. Pub. Rels. Soc. Am. (mem. San Francisco chpt. 1979—, Compass award 1988), Pub. Rels. Round Table, Pub. Affairs Coun., Livermore C. of C., Pleasanton C. of C., San Ramon Valley C. of C., Tracy C. of C., Kappa Tau Alpha. Republican. Office: Lawrence Livermore Nat Lab L-404 PO Box 808 Livermore CA 94551-0808

KALIHER, MICHAEL DENNIS, historian, book seller; b. Santa Monica, Calif., Nov. 7, 1947; s. Eugene Charles and Phyllis Joan (McCrary) K. BA, U. Ariz., 1990. Pres. Klamath County (Oreg.) Hist. Soc., 1985; founder Native Am. History Week, Klamath County Mus., 1985-86. Contbr. articles to various hist. jours. Mem. Thoreau Soc., Pi Lambda Theta, Phi Alpha Theta. Roman Catholic. Home: PO Box 634 Winslow AZ 86047-0634

KALINA, ROBERT EDWARD, physician, educator; b. New Prague, Minn., Nov. 13, 1936; s. Edward Robert and Grace Susan (Hess) K.; m. Janet Jessie Larsen, July 18, 1959; children: Paul Edward, Lynne Janet. B.A. magna cum laude, U. Minn., 1957, B.S., 1960, M.D., 1960. Diplomate Am. Bd. Ophthalmology (dir. 1981-89). Intern U. Oreg. Med. Sch. Hosp., Portland, 1960-61; resident in ophthalmology U. Oreg. Med. Sch. Hosp., 1961-62, 63-66; asst. in retina surgery Children's Hosp., San Francisco, 1966-67; Nat. Inst. Neurol. Diseases and Blindness Spl. fellow Mass. Eye and Ear Infirmary, Boston, 1967; instr. ophthalmology U. Wash., 1967-69, asst. prof., 1969-71, acting chmn. dept. ophthalmology, 1970-71, asso. prof., 1971-72, chmn. dept. ophthalmology, 1971-96, prof., 1972—; mem. staffs Univ. Hosp., Harborview Hosp., Children's Hosp., Seattle; cons. VA Hosp., Seattle, Pacific Med. Ctr., Seattle, Madigan Hosp., Tacoma; assoc. head divsn. ophthalmology dept. surgery Children's Hosp., Seattle, 1975-86; pres. U. Wash. Physicians, 1990-93. Contbr. author: Introduction to Clinical Pediatrics, 1972, Ophthalmology Study Guide for Medical Students, 1975; contbr. numerous articles to profl. publs. Served to capt., M.C. USAF, 1962-63. Fellow ACS, Am. Acad. Ophthalmology (Sr. Honor award 1989); mem. AMA, Assn. Univ. Profs. Ophthalmology (pres. 1983-84, exec. v.p. 1989-94), Assn. Rsch. in Vision and Ophthalmology, Pacific Coast Oto-Ophthalmol. Soc. (councilor 1972-74), King County Med. Soc., Wash. State Acad. Ophthalmology, Phi Beta Kappa. Home: 2627 96th Ave NE Bellevue WA 98004-2107 Office: U Wash Dept Ophthalmology Box 356485 1959 NE Pacific St Seattle WA 98195-6485

KALIS, MURRAY, advertising agency executive, writer; s. Bernard and Bernis Kalis. BS in Comm., U. Ill.; MFA in Printmaking, Drake U., U. Iowa. Former chmn. art dept. Midwestern Coll., Denison, Iowa; creative dir., v.p. Leo Burnett Advt., Chgo.; exec. creative dir., sr. v.p. Young & Rubicam Advt. Joint Ventures, L.A.; pres. Coen/Kalis Advt., L.A., 1989-95; chmn. Kalis & Savage Advt., 1995—. 1st lt. U.S. Army. Recipient cert. of merit N.Y. Art Dirs. One Show; Bronze Lion, Cannes Festival, gold medal Chgo. Film Festival, Clio award, Best in West, Belding, Spl. award UN for Pub. Svc. Advt., intaglio art in permanent collection Phila. Mus. Art. Author: Candida by Amy Voltaire, 1979; Love in Paris, 1980; Are You Experienced? The Jimi Hendrix Story, 1984, (play) Single Scene, 1989. Clubs: Creative, Los Angeles Advt. Office: Kalis & Savage Advt 17383 W Sunset Blvd # 450 Pacific Palisades CA 90272-4138

KALISH, NANCY, psychology educator, writer; b. Long Branch, N.J.. BA, Douglass Coll./Rutgers U., 1969; PhD, CUNY, 1973. Asst. prof. Monmouth U., West Long Branch, N.J., 1972-73, Loyola U., Chgo., 1973-74; assoc. prof. Calif. State U., Sacramento, 1974-78, prof., 1978—. Author (nonfiction) Lost and Found Lovers, 1997; contbr. articles to profl. jours. Mem. APA (divsn. 46), Am. Psych. Soc. Office: Calif State Univ Dept Psychology 6000 J St Sacramento CA 95819-2605

KALLA, ALEC KARL, writer, rancher; b. Pitts., Feb. 7, 1950; s. Milton Miklos and Marion Dorothy Kalla. Attended, Boston U., 1968-72. Rancher Conifer, Colo., 1977—; v.p. Health Care Assocs., Evergreen, Colo., 1989; freelance writer Conifer, 1990—; guest author, panelist Rocky Mountain Book Fesitval, Denver, 1993-95. Author: Velvet, 1993; patentee in field, 1984. Mem. Mystery Writers Am. Home and Office: PO Box 85 Conifer CO 80433

KALLA, KRISTIN ANNE, genetic counselor; b. San Diego, Nov. 6, 1960; d. Joseph M. and Janice A. Kalla. BS, U. Calif., Davis, 1982; MS, U. Calif., Irvine, 1996. Cert. Am. Bd. Genetics Counseling. Rsch. asst. Scripps Clinic & Rsch. Found., San Diego, 1982-83; assoc. chemist Behring Diagnostics, San Diego, 1984-86; technician, mgr. transgenics & embryonic stem cell facility Howard Hughes Med. Inst., San Diego, 1986-94; genetic counselor Children's Hosp., San Diego, 1996—. Contbr. rsch. articles to profl. publs. Mem. Nat. Soc. Genetic Counselors. Office: Children's Hosp 8010 Frost St San Diego CA 92023

KALLAY, MICHAEL FRANK, II, medical devices company official; b. Painesville, Ohio, Aug. 24, 1944; s. Michael Frank and Marie Francis (Sage) K.; BBA, Ohio U., 1967; m. Irma Yolanda Corona, Aug. 30, 1975; 1 son, William Albert. Salesman, Howmedica, Inc., Rutherford, N.J., 1972-75, Biochem. Procedures/Metpath, North Hollywood, Calif., 1975-76; surg. specialist USCI div. C. R. Bard, Inc., Billerica, Mass., 1976-78; western and central regional mgr. ARCO Med. Products Co., Phila., 1978-80; Midwest regional mgr. Intermedics, Inc., Freeport, Tex., 1980-82; Western U.S. mgr. Renal Systems, Inc., Mpls., 1982—; pres. Kall-Med, Inc., Anaheim Hills, Calif., 1982—. Mem. Am. Mgmt. Assn., Phi Kappa Sigma. Home and Office: PO Box 17248 7539 E Bridgewood Dr Anaheim CA 92817-7248

KALLENBERG, JOHN KENNETH, librarian; b. Anderson, Ind., June 10, 1942; s. Herbert A. and Helen S. K.; m. Ruth Barrett, Aug. 19, 1965; children: Jennifer Anne, Gregory John. A.B., Ind. U., 1964, M.L.S., 1969. With Fresno County Library, Fresno, Calif., 1965-70, dir., 1976—; librarian Fig Garden Pub. Library br., 1968-70; asst. dir. Santa Barbara (Calif.) Pub. Library, 1970-76; mem. Calif. Libr. Svcs. bd., 1990—, v.p., 1992-95, pres., 1996-97; Beth Ann Harnish lectr. com., 1988-91, chmn., 1989-90. Mem. Calif. Libr. Assn. (councilor 1976-77, v.p., pres. 1987), Calif. County Librs. Assn. (pres. 1977), Calif. Libr. Authority for Sys. and Svcs. (chmn. authority adv. coun. 1978-80), Kiwanis (pres. Fresno 1981-82, lt. gov. divsn. 5 1991-92, co-editor Cal-Nev-Ha News 1993-94, 95-96). Presbyterian. Office: Fresno County Free Libr 2420 Mariposa St Fresno CA 93721-2204

KALMANSOHN, ROBERT BRUCE, physician, consultant, lecturer; b. Sioux City, Iowa, June 20, 1924. Student, Creighton U., 1942-43, U. Vt., 1943-44, Washington U., St. Louis, 1943-45; MD, U. Nebr., 1948. Diplomate Am. Bd. Internal Medicine. Intern Mt. Zion Hosp., San Francisco, 1948-49, resident in cardiology, 1949-50; fellow in cardiology Harvard Med. Svc., Beth Israel Hosp., Boston, 1950-51; pvt. practice internal medicine and cardiology, 1953—; attending cardiologist VA; attending physician in cardiology Cedars Sinai Med. Ctr.; assoc. clin. prof. medicine UCLA Med. Sch.; cardiac cons. L.A. City Sch. System, State of Calif., Dept. Vocat. Rehab.; mem. speakers bur. Los Angeles County Heart Assn.; lectr. in field. Mem. editorial staff Circulation, Exec. Health Letter; sr. editor, mem. editorial staff, editor-in-chief Jour. of Angiology; contbr. numerous articles to profl. jours. Chair subcom. on lit. and films Los Angeles County Heart Assn. Served to 1st lt. M.C., U.S. Army, 1951-53. Fellow ACP, Am. Coll. Cardiology, Am. Coll. Angiology (pres.), Am. Coll. Chest Physicians, Internat. Coll. Angiology; mem. AMA, Calif. Med. Assn., Am. Heart Assn., L.A. County Med. Assn., Alpha Omega Alpha. Jewish. Office: Kalmansohn Med Corp 852 S Robertson Blvd Los Angeles CA 90035

KAM, THOMAS KWOCK YUNG, accountant educator; b. Honolulu, Nov. 12, 1955; s. William Kwock Yung and Mae S. M. (Yee) K.; m. Sally Ben Huai, July 9, 1983; children: Tiffany L. M., Stephen C. M. BBA, U. Hawaii, 1975, MBA, 1978, postgrad., 1993—. CPA, Hawaii; CMA. Intern Coopers & Lybrand, Honolulu, 1975-76; instr. Beckers CPA Rev. Course, Honolulu, 1982-83; statis. asst. Hawaiian Elec. Co., Inc., Honolulu, 1976-78, assoc. budget analyst, 1978-86; adult edn. tchr. Farrington Cmty. Sch., Honolulu, 1978-84, McKinley Cmty. Sch., Honolulu, 1978-86; lectr. West Oahu Coll., Honolulu, 1986; asst. prof. acctg. and fin. Hawaii Pacific U., Honolulu, 1984—. Mem. Neighborhood Bd. (Liliha-Kapalama), 1980-83; treas., fin. com. chmn. Neighborhood Bd. (Pearl City), 1985-88, vice chair health, edn. and welfare com. 1985, chmn., 1988-93, chmn. devel., planning and zoning com. 93—; auditor Kams' Soc., 1984-89, 3d v.p., 1990-91, 2d v.p., 1992-93, 1st v.p., 1994-95, pres., 1996—; mem. loan com. Native Hawaiian Revolving Loan Fund, 1989-91; co-facilitator Pearl City Highlands Elem. Sch. SCBM Coun., 1992-93, 95-96; dir. Pearl City Highlands Elem. Sch., Kokua Hui, 1992-93, treas., 1993—; chmn. Leeward Dist. Sch. Adv. Coun., 1995—. Named Co-Adult Edn. Tchr. of Yr., Hawaii Adult Edn. Assn., 1988. Mem. AICPA, Hawaii Adult Edn. Assn. (dir. 1978-79, treas. 1979-81, pres. 1981-83), Hawaii Bus. Educators Assn., Inst. Mgmt. Accts., Hui Luna Club (dir. 1978, 85, auditor 1979, treas. 1980, 81), Friends of the Libr. of Hawaii, Toastmasters (Kam 720 Club treas. 1981, 82, Disting. Toastmaster 1985, Dist. 49 audit com. chmn. 1981-82, treas. 1982-84, speechcraft chmn. 1984-85). Office: Hawaii Pacific Univ 1188 Fort Street Mall Ste 252 Honolulu HI 96813-2713

KAM, VERNON TAM SIU, accounting educator; b. Honolulu, Sept. 2, 1933; s. Henry K.F. and Maizie Y.C. (Ching) K.; m. Alice T. Takizawa, Aug. 15, 1965; children: Carolyn, Garret. BA, U. Hawaii, 1955; MBA, U. Calif., Berkeley, 1959, PhD, 1968. CPA, Ill. Auditor L.A. County, 1959-60; asst. prof. U. Ill., Chgo., 1965-69; prof. Calif. State U., Hayward, 1969-87, chair dept., 1987—. Author: Accounting Theory, 1986, 2d edit., 1990, Consolidation of Financial Statements, 1981, 2d edit., 1991, 3d edit., 1996; co-author: Financial Accounting, 1995; contbr. articles to profl. jours. 1st lt. U.S. Army, 1955-57, Korea. Mem. AICPA, Am. Acctg. Assn. Office: Calif State U Dept Acctg Hayward CA 94542

KAMADA, ALAN KATSUKI, pharmacology educator; b. Sacramento, Sept. 22, 1964; s. Kenneth Katsuki and Hazel Masae (Hayase) K. D in Pharmacy, U. So. Calif., 1988. Lic. pharmacist, Calif., Colo., Nev. Intern in pharmacy Medi-Val Drugs, Lomita, Calif., 1985-88; resident in pharmacy VA Med. Ctr., Denver, 1988-89; clin. pharmacy fellow Nat. Jewish Ctr. Immunology and Repiratory Medicine, Denver, 1989-92, asst. prof. clin. pharmacology, 1993—; adj. asst. prof. pharmacy practice U. Colo. Health Scis. Ctr.; staff pharmacist Dept. VA Med. Ctr., Denver, 1989; lectr. in field. Author: (with others) Handbook of Pediatrics, 17th edit., 1993, Asthma and Rhinitis, 1994; mem. editoril bd. Annals of Pharmacotherapy, 1994—; ad hoc reviewer jours.; contbr. numerous articles and abstracts to profl. jours. Grantee Miles, Inc., 1989, Upjohn Co., 1989, 91, Muro Pharm., 1992. Mem. Am. Acad. Allergy and Immunology, Am. Coll. Clin. Pharmacy (grantee 1991), Colo. Soc. Hosp. Pharmacists. Office: Nat Jewish Med & Rsch Ctr 1400 Jackson St Denver CO 80206-2762

KAMEGAI, MINAO, physicist, consultant; b. Koshu, Korea, July 7, 1932; came to U.S., 1952; s. Kuwasaburo and Cho (Kaneko) K.; children: Stephanie Marie, Sharon Akemi; m. Meera McCuaig Blattner, June 22, 1985. BA, U. Hawaii, 1957; MS, U. Chgo., 1960, PhD, 1963. Lic. tech. transfer and commercialization specialist. Sr. physicist Knolls Atomic Power Lab., Schenectady, N.Y., 1963-66, Lawrence Livermore (Calif.) Nat. Lab., 1966-93; cons. Kamegai and Assocs., Livermore, 1994—. Bd. dirs. U. Chgo. Alumni Assn., San Francisco, 1980-92, Livermore-Yotsukaido Sister City Orgn., Livermore, 1988-90. Mem. World Affairs Coun. No. Calif., Japan Soc. No. Calif., Keizai Soc., Tech. Transfer Soc. No. Calif., Sigma Xi, Phi Beta Kappa. Home and Office: Kamegai and Assocs 908 Florence Rd Livermore CA 94550-5541

KAMEMOTO, GARETT HIROSHI, reporter; b. Honolulu, Oct. 30, 1966; s. Fred I. and Alice T. (Asayama) K. BA, U. Hawaii, 1989. Reporter Sta. KHVH, Honolulu, 1989-92, 93-94; Sta. KGMB-TV, Honolulu, 1992-93, 94—. Home: 3664 Waaloa Way Honolulu HI 96822-1151 Office: Sta KGMB-TV 1534 Kapiolani Blvd Honolulu HI 96814-3715

KAMILLI, ROBERT JOSEPH, geologist; b. Phila., June 14, 1947; s. Joseph George and Marie Emma (Clauss) K.; m. Diana Ferguson Chapman, June 28, 1969; children: Ann Chapman, Robert Chapman. BA summa cum laude, Rutgers U., 1969; AM, Harvard U., 1971, PhD, 1976. Geologist Climax Molybdenum Co., Empire, Colo., 1976-79, asst. resident geologist, 1979-80; project geologist Climax Molybdenum Co., Golden, Colo., 1980-83; geologist U.S. Geol. Survey, Saudi Arabian Mission, Jeddah, 1983-87, mission chief geologist, 1987-89; rsch. geologist, project chief U.S. Geol. Survey, Tucson, Ariz., 1989-96, scientist-in-charge, 1996—; adj. prof. U. Colo., Boulder, 1981-83, U. Ariz., Tucson, 1997—. Mem. editorial bd. Econ. Geology; contbr. articles to profl. jours. Henry Rutgers scholar Rutgers U., 1968-69. Fellow Geol. Soc. Am., Soc. Econ. Geologists; mem. Ariz. Geol. Soc. (v.p. 1995-97), Phi Beta Kappa, Sigma Xi. Home: 5050 N Siesta Dr Tucson AZ 85750-9652 Office: US Geol Survey SW Field Office Ste 355 520 N Park Ave Tucson AZ 85719

KAMIN, AVIVA, sports association administrator. BS in Phys. Edn. and Health Edn. & Psychology, U. Ariz., 1954; MA in Clin. Psychology, Calif. State U., 1963; PhD in Clin. Psychology, Human Behavior, Higher Edn. Leadership, U.S. Internat. U., San Diego, 1976. Phys. edn. instr., coach El Camino Coll., 1961-70, athletic dir., 1968-72, coord. student activities, 1970-72, dean of students, 1972-76; pres. Matchmaker Realty, Inc., Long Beach, Calif., 1980—; commr. Western State Athletic Conf., 1981—; chair of grants and project com. Beach Cities Health Dist., 1992—, pres. bd. dirs., 1994—. Named to Athletic Hall of Fame U. Ariz., 1985, Commr. of the Yr. City Manhattan Beach Parks and Recreation Commn., 1992-93, Hall of Fame El Camino Coll., 1994, State Athletic Hall of Fame Adminstrv. Divsn. Cmty. Coll., 1995. Office: Western State Conf 812 6th St Manhattan Beach CA 90266-5821*

KAMIN, SCOTT ALLAN, lawyer; b. Portland, July 1, 1948; s. Lloyd F. and Edith G. (Goldstein) K.; m. Susan Jo Whitlock, Mar. 12, 1978; children: Sarah R., Leah R. BS, U. Oreg., 1971; JD, Lewis & Clark Coll., 1976. Bar: Oreg. 1976, U.S. Dist. Ct. Oreg. 1976, U.S. Tax Ct. 1976. Assoc. atty. Douglas H. Stearns, P.C., Portland, Oreg., 1976-79; atty., ptnr. Weatherhead & Kamin, Portland, 1979-81; atty., shareholder Scott A. Kamin, P.C., Portland, 1981—; IRS liaison Oreg. State Bar, Lake Oswego, 1989—, tax sect. seminar, 1992. Mem. Mensa. Office: 1020 SW Taylor St Ste 550 Portland OR 97205-2510

KAMINE, BERNARD SAMUEL, lawyer; m. Marcia Phyllis Haber; children: Jorge Hershel, Benjamin Haber, Tovy Haber. BA, U. Denver, 1965; JD, Harvard U., 1968. Bar: Calif. 1969, Colo. 1969. Dep. atty. gen. Calif. Dept. Justice, L.A., 1969-72; asst. atty. gen. Colo. Dept. Law, Denver, 1972-74; assoc. Shapiro & Maguire, Beverly Hills, Calif., 1974-76; ptnr. Kamine, Steiner & Ungerer (and predecessor firms), L.A., Calif., 1976—; instr. Glendale (Calif.) U. Coll. Law, 1971-72; judge pro tem Mcpl. Ct., 1974—, Superior Ct., 1989—; bd. dirs., sec. Pub. Works Stds., Inc., 1996—; arbitrator Calif. Pub. Works Contract Arbitration Com., 1990—, Am. Arbitration Assn., 1976—; mem. adv. com. legal forms Calif. Jud. Coun., 1978-82. Author: Public Works Construction Manual: A Legal Guide for California, 1996; contbr. chpts. to legal texts, articles to profl. jours. Mem. L.A. County Dem. Cen. Com., 1982-85; mem. Anti-Defamation League, assoc. nat. commr., 1995—, Pacific Southwest Regional Bd., 1982—, chair bd. exec. com., 1996—. Col. USAR, 1969—. Mem. ABA, Calif. State Bar Assn. (chair conf. dels. calendar coordinating com. 1991-92), L.A. County Bar Assn. (chair Superior Cts. com. 1977-79, chair constrn. law subsect. of real property sect. 1981-83), Engring. Contractors' Assn. (bd. dirs. 1985—, affiliate chair 1992-93, affiliate DIG award 1996), Assoc. Gen. Contractors Calif. (L.A. dist. bd. dirs. 1995—), Am. Constrn. Insps. Assn. (bd. registered constrn. inspectors 1990—), Res. Officers Assn. (pres. chpt. 1977-78), Omicron Delta Kappa. Office: 350 S Figueroa St Ste 250 Los Angeles CA 90071-1201

KAMINS, PHILIP E., diversified manufacturing company executive; b. 1936. Salesman H. Muehlstein, 1957-62; founder Kamco Plastics Inc., Sun Valley, Calif., 1965-71; pres., CEO PMC Inc., Sun Valley, Calif., also bd. dirs. Office: PMC Inc PO Box 1367 Sun Valley CA 91353

KAMINSKI, CHARLES ANTHONY, portfolio manager; b. Norwich, Conn.; m. Elizabeth Carbery Wick, Oct. 19, 1985; children: Catherine, Ian, Charles. BEE, MIT, 1970, MEE, 1972; MBA, Harvard U., 1974. Chartered fin. analyst. Assoc. John Barry and Assocs., Newport Beach, Calif., 1974-75; sales mgr. N.Am. Video, Acton, Mass., 1975-79; v.p. mktg. Creare Innovations, Hanover, N.H., 1979-82; pres. Commtech, Cambridge, Mass., 1982-84; group mktg. mgr. Instrumentation Lab. (Allied), Lexington, Mass., 1983-84; dir., portfolio mgr. Baring Am. Asset Mgmt., Boston, 1984-92; sr. v.p. investments Consumer Savs. & Ins. Group, GE Capital, Seattle, 1992—; bd. dirs. Wash. State Investment Bd., GE Capital Assurance Co., Gt. No. Insured Annuity Corp., First GNA Life Ins. Co., Fed. Home Life Ins. Co. Mem. Inst. CFA, Boston Econ. Club, Sigma Xi, Eta Kappa Nu, Tau Beta Pi. Home: 7224 W Mercer Way Mercer Island WA 98040-5534 Office: GNA Two Union Square Seattle WA 98101

KAMM, HERBERT, journalist; b. Long Branch, N.J., Apr. 1, 1917; s. Louis and Rose (Cohen) K.; m. Phyllis I. Silberblatt, Dec. 6, 1936; children: Laurence R., Lewis R., Robert H. Reporter, sports editor Asbury Park (N.J.) Press, 1935-42; with AP, 1942-43; with N.Y. World-Telegram and Sun, 1943-66, successively rewrite man, picture editor, asst. city editor, feature editor, mag. editor, 1943-63, asst. mng. editor, 1963, mng. editor, 1963-66; exec. editor N.Y. World Jour. Tribune, 1966-67; editorial cons. Scripps Howard Newspapers, 1967-69; assoc. editor Cleve. Press, 1969-80, editor, 1980-82, editor emeritus, 1982; edit. dir. Sta. WJW-TV, Cleve., 1982-85; instr. journalism Case Western Res. U., 1972-75, Calif. Poly., San Luis Obispo, 1991—. Radio and TV news commentator and panelist, 1950-85, TV talk show host, 1974-85; freelance writer, 1985—; author: A Candle for Popsy, 1953; editor: Junior Illustrated Encyclopedia of Sports, 1960. Bd. overseers Case Western Res. U., 1974-78. Herb Kamm scholarship in journalism established Kent State U., 1983, Calif. Poly., 1995; inducted Cleve. Journalism Hall of Fame, 1986. Mem. AFTRA, Soc. Profl. Journalists (pres. Calif. Missions chpt. 1986-87). Clubs: City of Cleve. (pres. 1982), Silurians. Home: 147 River View Dr Avila Beach CA 93424-2307
Journalism lifed a poor boy with a limited formal education into a world of learning, excitement and fulfillment. But none of this could have been possible without a devoted wife of more than 60 years.

KAMM, JACQUELINE ANN, elementary reading specialist; b. Santa Monica, Calif., Aug. 22, 1958; d. Philip Schuyler Jr. and Juanita (Jones) K. BA in History, U. Calif., L.A., 1980; MS in Edn., Curriculum and Instrn., U. So. Calif., 1987, postgrad., 1989—. Cert. instr. multiple subjects, reading specialist, Calif. Tchr. 1st grade Bonner Sch., L.A., 1981-82, Curtis Sch., L.A., 1982-88; reading specialist Culver City (Calif.) Unified Sch. Dist., 1988—, mentor tchr., 1995—; adj. prof. Grad. Sch. Edn. and Psychology, Pepperdine U., Culver City, 1994-96; tchr. cons. writing project U. So. Calif., 1996—. Dir. St. Matthew's Summer Day Camp, Pacific Palisades, Calif., 1989-94; mem. Strategic Planning Task Force I, Curriculum, Culver City, 1989—; active Jr. Charity League. Culver City Edn. Found. grantee, 1990, 92, 93, 94, 95, 96. Mem. ASCD, Internat. Reading Assn., Santa Monica Bay Area Reading Assn. (pres.), Coronets of Nat. Charity League, Grad. Sch. Edn. Alumni Assn. (charter), Phi Kappa Phi, Phi Delta Kappa. Home: 500 Lombard Ave Pacific Palisades CA 90272-4347 Office: La Ballona Sch 10915 Washington Blvd Culver City CA 90232-4045

KAMPFER, JOHN BRENNAN, data processing administrator; b. Albany, N.Y., May 10, 1939; s. Franklyn Fredrick and Jeanne Marie (Fleming) K.; m. Joyce Elizabeth Boiser, Dec. 6, 1963 (div. Feb., 1990); children: Valerie (dec.), Robert, Regina, Elizabeth. BS, U.S. Military Acad., 1961; MS Computer Systems Mgmt., U.S. Naval Postgrad. Sch., 1969; MBA, U. S. Fla., 1976. Cert. CDP, CSP, Inst. for Certification of Computer Profls. Commd. 2d. lt. U.S. Army, 1961, adv. through ranks to Lt. Col., 1977; 25th Inf. Divsn. U.S. Army, Hawaii, 1962-66; 3d Bde 25th Inf. Divsn., 4th Inf. Divsn. U.S. Army, 1967-68, Hdqs. DA, 1969-71; mgr. pers. actions divsn. U.S. Army, Long Binh, Vietnam, 1971-72; data processing staff officer U.S. Readiness Command, Tampa, Fla., 1972-76; mgr. programming 25th Data Processing Unit Persinscom., Heidelberg, Germany, 1976-78; mgr. computer ops. 25th Data Processing Unit Persinscom., Heidelberg, 1978-79, mgr. plans and devel., 1979-80; data processing mgr. Rapid Deployment Joint Task Force (ctrl. command), Tampa, 1979-80; from mgr. planning to asst. mgr. facilities, data security Data Processing Divsn. Bank of Hawaii, Honolulu, 1981-87; mgr. facilities, data security Data Processing Divsn. Bank Hawaii, Honolulu, 1987-96;. Elected mem. Wahiawa Neighborhood Bd., 1985—, chmn. 1992—; mem. ctrl. com. Hawaii Dems., 1986—, treas., 1990-94; mem. Hawaii election adv. com., Honolulu, 1987-94; pres. catechetical bd. Our Lady of Sorrows Ch., 1994—. Decorated Bronze Star medal (2), U.S. Army; recipient Honolulu Diocese Our Lady of Peace award, 1995. Mem. Data Processing Mgmt. Assn. (v.p., exec. v.p., pres. Hawaii chpt.), Info. Systems Security Assn. (founding pres. 1990-96), Lions Club (v.p., bd. dirs., pres. Wahiawa chpt., Dist. 50 zone chmn. 1992-93, region chmn. 1993-94), Serra Club of Honolulu (v.p., trustee, pres. 1996—). Office: Bank of Hawaii IS 309 PO Box 2900 Honolulu HI 96846

KAMRANY, NAKE MOHAMMAD, economics and law educator, lawyer; b. Kabul, Afghanistan, Aug. 29, 1934; came to U.S., 1955; s. Shair M. Kamrany and Farukh (Sultan) Sidiqi; m. Barbara Helen Gehlke, Dec., 1957 (div.); children: Michael Shair John, Lily Joy; m. Sajia Walizada, Nov. 12, 1978; children: Dennis Wali, Michelle Nazo. BS, UCLA, 1959; MA, U. So. Calif., L.A., 1962, PhD, 1962; JD, U. West L.A., Culver City, 1981. Bar: Calif. 1993. Sr. economist Battelle Inst., Columbus, Ohio, 1962-65, System Devel. Corp., Santa Monica, Calif., 1965-69; country economist World Bank, Washington, 1969-71; chief economist Info. Scis. Inst. U. So. Calif., L.A., 1971-73; dir., rsch. assoc. Ctr. for Policy Alternative, MIT, Cambridge, Mass., 1973-76; dir. program in law and econs. Dept. Econs. U. So. Calif., 1976—, prof., sr. lectr., 1976—; econ. cons. for law firms, 1986—; expert economist UN, Lebanon, 1980-82; bd. dirs. Ocean Towers Corp., Santa Monica, 1989-94. Author: Internat. Econ. Reform, 1977, Econ. Issues of the Eighties, 1979, The New Economics of Less Developed Countries, 1978; editor Econ. Directions, 1989-95; contbr. numerous articles to learned jours. Active numerous community organizations. Grantee Advanced Project Agy., NSF, Sloan Found., Agy. for Internat. Devel. for Sahel Project; recipient Assocs. award U. So. Calif. Mem. Am. Econ. Assn., Soc. for Internat. Devel., Newport Found. (bd. dirs.), Afghanistan Studies Assn. (founder), Calif Bar. Home: 1106 Kagawa St Pacific Palisades CA 90272-3837 Office: U So Calif Dept Econs Los Angeles CA 90089

KAMSTRA, BETTYE MAURICE, secondary education educator; b. Merkel, Tex., June 26, 1941; d. Eldon Maurice and Susie Grace (Burk) Reeves; m. L. Duane Kamstra, Aug. 25, 1966. BS, Hardin-Simmon U., 1965; MS, Calif. State U., Northridge, 1979; postgrad., Ariz. State U., U. Calif., Santa Barbara. Tchr. South Kern Unified Schs., Rosamond, Calif. Mem. NEA, Nat. Bus. Edn. Assn., Nat. Coun. Tchrs. of English (assembly lit. for adolescents), Calif. Assn. Tchrs. of English, Southland Coun. Tchrs. of English, Western Bus. Edn. Assn.

KANANEN, MARVIN JOHN, English educator, author; b. Laurium, Mich.; s. E. John and Nelma A. (Kangas) K.; m. Jean E.C. Wahlstrom, Apr. 7, 1990. AA, Suomi Coll., Hancock, Mich., 1966; BA, Pacific Luth. U., 1968; MA, Oakland U., 1975; DD (hon.), Christian Family of God Coll., Auburn, Wash., 1984. Tchr. North Beach Schs., Moclips, Wash.; pastor Bethel Chapel, Arlington, Wash., 1987-90; prof. English Luth. Bible Inst., Issaquah, Wash., 1992—; missionary ELCA Arusha, Tanzania, 1992-93. Author: (6 vols. puzzles) Bible Word Crosswords, 1990-96, (biography) Escape from Bondage, 1984; also plays, bible studies. Mem. adv. bd. United Way, Luth. Brotherhood, CSAC; chmn., dir. Granite Falls Food Bank, 1984—; tchr. St. Andrews Luth. Ch., 1991—. Home: 1609 149th Pl SE #3 Bellevue WA 98007

KANAVALOV, MARIA JOSE, small business owner; b. San Salvador, El Salvador, Jan. 8, 1956; came to U.S., 1981; Student, Met. Kill Ctr., L.A., 1988-89, L.A. C.C., 1990-93. Lic. life and health ins. agt.; cert. tax preparer. Nurse asst. Country Villa Convalescent Ctr., Long Beach, Calif., 1982-84; ctrl. supply clk. Brier Oaks Convalescent Ctr., L.A., 1984-86; med. records staff Cedar Glen Convalescent Ctr., El Monte, Calif., 1986-88, Daniel Freeman Med. Ctr., Inglewood, Calif., 1988-89; computer operator White Meml. Med. Ctr., L.A., 1989-93; med. biller Scheffer's Ambulance Svc., L.A., 1993-95; owner GDC Ctr., L.A., 1995—; notary pub. instr. L.A. C.C., 1994—; computer usage instr. Computer User's Club, L.A., 1996—; pub., graphic designer, translator L.A. City Newsletter, 1996—. Founder L.A. Small Bus. Owner's Assn./Independently United, L.A., 1996. Mem. Nat. Assn. Notary Pub., Nat. Assn. Self-Employed, Desktop Pub. Club, High tech Times Club. Home: PO Box 291363 Los Angeles CA 90029

KANCHIER, CAROLE, psychologist; b. Winnipeg, Manitoba, Can.; came to U.S., 1993; d. Michael and Mary (Dyma) K. BA in Social Scis., U. Manitoba, Winnipeg, Can., BEd in Guidance and Counseling, MEd in Guidance and Counseling; PhD in Counseling Psychology, U. Calgary, Alberta, Can., 1981. Registered psychologist; cert. tchr. Dir. arts and crafts Winnipeg Parks Bd.; dir. women's phys. edn. Daniel McIntyre Collegiate, Winnipeg; dir. publicity Royal Winnipeg Ballet; dir. guidance and counseling Kelvin H.S., Winnipeg; dir. rsch. Thomson and Lightstone, Calgary, 1981-82; instr. edn. psychology U. Calgary, 1981-82; edn. and psychology cons. Vogue Bus. Svcs., Calgary, 1981-82; faculty edn. psychology and adult edn. U. Alta., Edmonton, 1983-92; prin. Questers Consulting, Mountain View, Calif., 1983—; postdoctoral scholar Inst. Transpersonal Psychology, Palo Alto, Calif., 1990; chair career change Nat. Career Devel. Assn., Alexandria, Va., 1989-93; exec. bd. Life Plan Ctr., San Francisco, 1993-96; instr., advisor adult edn. credentialing program U. Calif, Santa Cruz, 1994-96. Author: Dare to Change Your Job -- And Your Life, 1996 (Best Can. popular book 1989); contbr. articles to profl. jours. including Ency. of Career Decisions and Work Issues, The Career Devel. Quarterly, Internat. Jour. for Advancement of Counseling, Wall St. Jour., Your Money, Am. Counselor, etc. Mem. ASTD, APA, ACA, NAFE, Nat. Career Devel. Assn., Inst. Noetic Scis., Can. Assn. Adult Edn., Canadian Psychol. Assn. Home and Office: # S206 555 W Middlefield Rd Mountain View CA 94043-3543

KANDANES, ANDREW, recording industry executive, percussionist; b. Paterson, N.J., Aug. 6, 1947; s. Anthony and Elmyra Kandanes; m. Denise Kandanes; children: Ace Pothier, Diella, Alexis. Student, USAF Acad., Santa Rosa Jr. Coll.; BA, Coll. of the Redwoods, 1970. Music prodr., pub. Andrew Kandanes & Assocs. Prodr. and arranger (rec.) Firebyrd, 1980; arranger, producer, percussionist (rec.) Not Alone, 1985, This Byrd Has Flown, 1997, 3 Byrds Land in London, 1997; composer: The Rain Song, Rodeo Rider, 1980. Home: PO Box 618 Cobb CA 95426-0618

KANDLER, JOSEPH RUDOLPH, financial executive; b. Vienna, Austria, Dec. 13, 1921; came to Can., 1952; s. Franz and Maria Franziska (Stanzel) K.; m. Lubomyra-Melitta Melnechuk, June 15, 1963. D.Rerum Commercialium, Sch. Econs., Vienna, 1949; Chartered Acct., Inst. Chartered Accts. Alta., 1965. Sales exec. Philips, Vienna, 1951; acct. Brown & Root, Ltd. Edmonton, Alta., Can., 1952-54, 56, chief acct., 1957-64; v.p. fin. Healy Ford Ctr. and Assoc. Cos., Edmonton, 1964-89; pres. Sentha Investments, Ltd., Edmonton, 1978—. Bd. dirs. Edmonton Symphony, 1969-72, Alta. Cultural Heritage Council, 1973-81, Edmonton Opera, 1982-84, Tri-Bach Festival, 1982-84; founder Johann Strauss Found., Alta., bd. dirs. 1975-84, pres. 1975-78, founder, pres. B.C. chpt., 1985—; bd. govs. U. Alta., 1982-86, mem. senate, 1973-79, 82-86; mem. adv. com. on cultural and convention ctr. City of Edmonton, 1974-78, vice-chmn., 1976-78. Recipient Achievement award for svc. to community Govt. Alta., 1975, Johann Strauss medal in gold Vienna Tourist Bd., 1989, Knight's Cross of Honor 1st Class Republic of Austria, 1990, Golden Emblem of Honor City of Vienna, 1991, Golden Emblem of Honor Sch. Econs., Vienna, 1995. Mem. Inst. Chartered Accts. Alta. Address: Sentha Investments Ltd, 392 Langs Rd, Salt Spring Island, BC Canada V8K 1N3

KANDO, THOMAS MATTHEW, sociology educator, author; b. Budapest, Hungary, Apr. 8, 1941; came to U.S., 1965; s. Jules and Ata Edith (Gorog) K.; m. Anita Chris Costa, June 30, 1973; children—Danielle, Leah. Student Union Coll., 1960-61; B.S., U. Amsterdam (Netherlands), 1965; M.A., U. Minn., 1967, Ph.D., 1969. Asst. prof. sociology U. Wis.-Stout, Menomonie, 1968-69; cons. Calif. Dept. Parks and Recreation, Sacramento, 1969-70; asst. prof. Calif. State U.-Sacramento, 1969-72, U. Calif.-Riverside, 1972-73; assoc. prof. Calif. State U.-Sacramento, 1973-77; assoc. prof. recreation and parks Pa. State U., 1978-79, prof. sociology and criminal justice Calif. State U.-Sacramento, 1979—. U. Amsterdam fellow, 1962-65; U. Minn. fellow, 1967; Fulbright fellow, 1960-61. Mem. AAUP (pres. local chpt. 1974—, pres. statewide 1976-78), Am. Sociol Assn., Internat. Sociol. Assn., Internat. Com. Leisure Research, Nat. Recreation and Parks Assn., Pacific Sociol. Assn., Popular Culture Assn., Internat. Com. on Sports Sociology, Athletic Congress, Phi Sigma Kappa. Republican. Author: Sex Change: The Achievement of Gender Identity Among Feminized Transsexuals, 1973; Leisure and Popular Culture in Transition, 1975, 80; Social Interaction, 1977; Sexual Behavior and Family Life in Transition, 1978; assoc. editor Pacific Sociol. Rev., 1973-78; Readings in Criminology, 1995, Contemporary Sociology, 1975-79; contbr. numerous articles to profl. jours, popular mags. Home: 11671 Prospect Hill Dr Gold River CA 95670-8247 Office: Calif State U Dept Sociology 6000 J St Sacramento CA 95819-2605

KANDUS, RICHARD JAY, adult education educator; b. L.A., May 25, 1952; s. Irving and Anita June Cohen; m. Colleen Nagel Kandus, June 11, 1988; 1 child, Julia Tenaya. BA, UCLA, 1974; MA, Humboldt State U., 1979. Instr. Humboldt State U., Arcata, Calif., 1979—, Coll. Redwoods, Eureka, Calif., 1980—; dir. Biofeedback Ctr., Arcata, 1980—; libr. liason Coll. Redwoods, Eureka, 1995—, rep. Acad. Senate, 1989-92. Author: Daily Health and Stress Scale, 1986, 1995; (with others) Personal Growth, 1994. Docent Audubon Soc., Arcata, 1996. Mem. AAUP, APA. Office: College of the Redwoods Dept Psychology Eureka CA 95501

KANE, BARTHOLOMEW ALOYSIUS, state librarian; b. Pitts., Nov. 2, 1945; s. Bartholomew A. and Ruth M. (Loerlein) K.; m. Elaine Murphy; 1 child, Leah. BA in Journalism, Pa. State U., 1967; MLS, U. Pitts., 1971; cert., Modern Archives Inst., 1987. Cert. Preservation Inst. Nat. Archives, 1990. Dir. Bradford Meml. Library, El Dorado, Kans., 1972-74; researcher Hawaii Dept. Planning and Econ. Devel., Honolulu, 1974-75, state librarian, 1982—; librarian Hawaii State Library System, Lanai City, 1975-79, Honolulu, 1979-82; adj. faculty mem. U. Hawaii, Manoa, 1986, 88, 92. Mem. Gov.'s Coun. on Literacy, 1985—. Hazel McCoy fellow Friends of Library of Hawaii, 1971. Mem. ALA, Hawaii Libr. Assn. Democrat. Home: 44-130 Puuohalai Pl Kaneohe HI 96744-2545 Office: Hawaii State Pub Libr System 465 S King St Rm B-1 Honolulu HI 96813-2911

KANE, KAREN MARIE, public affairs consultant; b. Colorado Springs, Colo., Mar. 7, 1947; d. Bernard Francis and Adeline Marie (Logan) K. Student, Mills Coll., Oakland, Calif., 1965-66; BA, U. Wash., 1970, MA, 1973, PhC, 1977, postgrad. Pub. affairs cons., housing subcom. Seattle Ret. Tchrs. Assn., 1981-84; pub. affairs cons. 1st U.S. Women's Olympic Marathon Trials, 1982-83, Seattle, 1985—. Contbr. articles to newsletters and mags. Vol. various polit. campaigns, Seattle; bd. dirs. Showboat Theatre

Found./Bravo (formerly Showboat Theatre Found.), 1984—; chmn. hist. preservation LWV, Seattle, 1989—; mem. Allied Arts of Seattle, trustee, 1987-96, past chmn. hist. preservation com., sec. bd. trustees, mem. exec. com., 1987-96; mem. Mayor's Landmark Theatre Adv. Group, 1991-93; mayoral appointee as commr. on Pike Pl. Hist. Commn., Seattle, 1992—, commn. chair, 1997—. Recipient Award of Honor Wash. Trust for Hist. Preservation, 1990, Recognition award Found. for Hist. Preservation and Adaptive Reuse, Seattle, 1991; Am. Found. grantee, 1989, 91. Mem. Am. Assn. Univ. Women, Mills Coll. Alumnae Assn., U. Wash. Alumni Assn., Nat. Trust for Hist. Preservation, Hist. Hawai'i Found., Found. for San Francisco's Archtl. Heritage, Internat. Platform Assn., Wash. Trust for Hist. Preservation. Office: Allied Arts of Seattle 105 S Main St Seattle WA 98104-2535

KANE, THOMAS JAY, III, orthopaedic surgeon, educator; b. Merced, Calif., Sept. 2, 1951; s. Thomas J. Jr. and Kathryn (Hassler) K.; m. Marie Rose Van Emmerik, Oct. 10, 1987; children: Thomas Keola, Travis Reid, Samantha Marie. BA in History, U. Santa Clara, 1973; MD, U. Calif., Davis, 1977. Diplomate Am. Bd. Orthopaedic Surgery. Intern U. Calif. Davis Sacramento Med. Ctr., 1977-78, resident in surgery, 1978-81; resident in orthopaedic surgery U. Hawaii, 1987-91; fellowship adult joint reconstruction Rancho Los Amigos Med. Ctr., 1991-92; ptnr. Orthop. Assocs. of Hawaii, Inc., Honolulu, 1992—; asst. prof. surgery U. Hawaii, Honolulu, 1993—, chief divsn. implant surgery, 1993—. Contbr. articles to profl. jours. Mem. AMA, Hawaii Med. Assn., Hawaii Orthop. Assn., Am. Acad. Orthop. Surgery, Western Orthopedic Assn., Alpha Omega Alpha, Phi Kappa Phi. Office: Orthopaedic Assocs Hawaii 1380 Lusitana St Ste 608 Honolulu HI 96813-2442

KANEDA, DAVID KEN, electrical engineering company executive; b. Norristown, Pa., May 13, 1958; s. Ben and Sumako Florence Kaneda; m. Stephania Wong, Nov. 16, 1993. B Archtl. Engring., Pa. State U., 1981; MBA, U. London Bus. Sch., 1993. Registered profl. engr., Ill., Calif.; registered architect, Wis.; chartered engr., U.K., European Engr. Tech. instr. Internat. Edn. Svcs., Tokyo, 1981-82; assoc. Skidmore, Owings & Merrill, Chgo., 1982-87, London, 1987-91, L.A., 1991; regional mgr. Elliptipar Inc., New Haven, 1993-95; prin. Am. Cons. Engrs. Inc., Santa Clara, Calif., 1995—; cons. Pinniger & Ptnr./Franz Sill, Gmbh, London and Berlin, 1992, ECS Lighting Controls Ltd., London, 1993. Recipient Edison award GE, 1987, achievement award Pa. Electric Assn., 1981, award of merit Chgo. Lighting Inst., 1987, design award Santa Clara Valley AIA, 1996. Mem. AIA, Chartered Inst. Bldg. Svcs. Engrs. U.K., Engring. Coun. U.K., European Fedn. Nat. Engring. Assns., Illuminating Engring. Soc. N.Am. (E.F. Guth award of merit 1987, design award 1987), Nat. Coun. Examiners for Engring. and Surveying, Nat. Assn. Asian Am. Profls. (bd. dirs. 1986-87), Alpha Phi Omega (pres. Alpha Beta chpt. 1979-80). Office: Am Cons Engrs Inc 2005 De La Cruz Blvd Ste 111 Santa Clara CA 95050-3030

KANEHIRO, KENNETH KENJI, insurance educator, risk analyst, consultant; b. Honolulu, May 10, 1934; s. Charles Yutaka and Betty Misako (Hoshino) K.; m. Eiko Asari, June 23, 1962; 1 child, Everett Peter. B in Counseling Psychology, U. Hawaii, 1956, grad. cert. in Counseling Psychology, 1957; grad. cert. in ins., The Am. Inst., 1971. CPCU; cert. continuing profl. devel. cert. Claims adjustor Cooke Trust Co., Honolulu, 1959-62, underwriter, 1962-66; account supr. Alexander & Baldwin, Honolulu, 1966-68; spl. risk exec. Hawaiian Ins. & Guaranty, Honolulu, 1968-71; br. mgr. Hawaiian Ins. & Guaranty, Hilo, Hawaii, 1971-72, Marsh & McLennan, Inc., Hilo, 1972-78; sr. mktg. rep. Occidental Underwriters, Honolulu, 1978-87; pvt. practice Honolulu, 1987—; coord. Ins. Sch. of Pacific, Honolulu, 1978—; lectr. ins. Hawaii Dist. Cts., 1986—; cons. Dai Tokyo Royal State Ins. Co., 1992—; mem. arbitration panel, ct. observer panel Hawaii Family Ct., 1993-96, Hawaii Criminal Ct., 1994—; proctor Hawaii State Bar Exam., 1994—; ins. expert witness, 1995—; instr. ins. agt.'s lic. course, 1995—. Adult leader Boy Scouts Am., Hilo and Honolulu, 1956—, risk mgr. Aloha coun., Honolulu, 1980—; edn. chmn. Gen. Ins. Assn., Hawaii, Hilo, 1971-77; ins. cons. Arcadia Retirement Residence, Honolulu, 1987—; bd. govs. U. Hawaii Founders Alumni Assn., Honolulu, 1993—, scholarship chmn., 1993—. With U.S. Army, 1957-59. Recipient First Lady's Outstanding Vol. award First Lady/State of Hawaii, 1990. Mem. Soc. CPCU (pres. 1986-87, nat. publs. com., 1996—, contbr. jour.), Soc. Ins. Trainers and Educators. Home: 1128 Ala Napunani St Apt 705 Honolulu HI 96818-1606

KANENAKA, REBECCA YAE, microbiologist; b. Wailuku, Hawaii, Jan. 9, 1958; d. Masakazu Robert and Takako (Oka) Fujimoto; m. Brian Ken Kanenaka, Nov. 10, 1989; children: Kent Masakazu, Kym Sachiko. Student, U. Hawaii, Manoa, 1976-77; BS, Colo. State U., 1980. Lab. asst. Colo. State U., Ft. Collins, 1979-80; microbiologist Foster Farms, Livingston, Calif., 1980-81; microbiologist Hawaii Dept. Health, Lihue, 1981-86, Honolulu, 1986—. Mem. Am. Soc. Microbiology (Hawaii chpt.), Nat. Registry of Microbiologists, Am. Soc. Microbiology, Brown Bag Club (Lihue, pres. 1985-86), Golden Ripples (4-H leader), Clover Kids (4-H leader). Home: 1520 Liholiho St Apt 502 Honolulu HI 96822-4093 Office: Hawaii Dept Health Lab 2725 Waimano Home Rd Pearl City HI 96782-1401

KANER, CEM, lawyer, computer software consultant; b. Detroit, July 8, 1953; s. Harry and Wilma Kaner; 1 child, Virginia Rose. Student, U. Windsor (Ont., Can.), 1971-72; BA, Brock U., St. Catharines, Ont., 1974; postgrad., York U., Toronto, Ont., 1975-76; PhD, McMaster U., Hamilton, Ont., 1984; JD, Golden Gate U., 1993. Cert. quality engr.; Bar: Calif., 1993. Asst. mgr. Gallenkamp Shoes, Toronto, 1975; systems analyst Kaners and 1 plus 1, Windsor, 1981-83; lectr. McMaster U., 1981-83; software testing supr. MicroPro (WordStar), San Rafael, Calif., 1983-84; human factors analyst, software engr. Telenova, Los Gatos, Calif., 1984-88; software testing mgr. creativity div. Electronic Arts, San Mateo, Calif., 1988; software devel. mgr., documentation group mgr., dir. of documentation and software testing Power Up Software, San Mateo, 1989-94; pvt. practice Calif., 1994—; sr. assoc. Psylomar Orgn. Devel., San Francisco, 1983-85; spkr. in field. Author: Testing Computer Software, 1988, (with Jack Falk and Hung Q Nguyen) Testing Computer Software, 2d edit., 1993 (award for excellence No. Calif. Tech. Publ. Competition 1993), (video course) Testing Computer Software, 1995; columnist Software QA; contbr. articles to profl. publs. Cons. Dundas (Ont.) Pub. Library, 1982-83; vol. Santa Clara County Dept. Consumer Affairs, San Jose, 1987-88; alt. mem. San Mateo County Dem. Central Com., 1988-89; chmn. Foster City Dem Club, 1989; vol. dep. dist. atty. County of Santa Clara, Calif., 1994; grievance handler, intellectual property, book contract advisor Nat. Writers Union, San Francisco, Calif., 1994—; bd. dir. No. Calif. Hemophilia Found., Oakland, Calif., 1995-97; advisor NCCUSL drafting com. for UCC article 2B. Scholar, Can. Nat. Rsch. Coun., 1977-78, Can. Natural Scis. and Engring. Rsch. Coun., 1979, Golden Gate U. Tuition scholar, 1989-93. Mem. ABA, ATLA, APA, ACLU, Assn. for Computing Machinery, Assn. Support Profls., Am. Soc. Quality Control, Consumer Attys. Assn. Calif., Human Factors and Ergonomics Soc., Soc. for Tech. Comm. Jewish. Office: PO Box 1200 Santa Clara CA 95052-1200

KANG, ISAMU YONG, nuclear medicine physician; b. Osaka, Japan, Aug. 27, 1939; came to U.S., 1966; s. Chi-Chieh and Ichi (Morita) K.; m. Midori Ishibashi, Mar. 15, 1971; children: Rika Florence, Hiroshi Frederick. MD, Kyushu U., Fukuoka, Japan, 1965. Diplomate Am. Bd. Pathology, Am. Bd. Nuc. Medicine. Intern Grad. Hosp. U. Pa., Phila., 1967-68; resident in pathology U. Calif., San Diego, 1972-74, Letterman Army Med. Ctr., San Francisco, 1974-76; fellow in nuclear medicine Walter Reed Army Med Ctr., Washington, 1976-78; asst. chief nuclear medicine Walter Reed Army Med. Ctr., Washington, 1978-80; co-dir. clin. lab. Kaiser Permanente Med. Ctr., Oakland, Calif., 1980-86; chief nuclear medicine Kaiser Permanente Med. Ctr., Walnut Creek, Calif., 1986—, radiation safety officer, 1986—. Lt. col. U.S. Army, 1969-80, Vietnam. Mem. Soc. Nuc. Medicine, Calif. Med. Assn. Buddhist. Home: 3554 Via Los Colorados Lafayette CA 94549-5332 Office: Kaiser Permanente Med Ctr 1425 S Main St Walnut Creek CA 94596

KANIECKI, MICHAEL JOSEPH, bishop; b. Detroit, Apr. 13, 1935; s. Stanley Joseph and Julia Marie (Konjora) K. BA, Gonzaga U., 1958, MA in Philosophy, 1960; MA in Theology, St. Mary's, Halifax, Can., 1966. Ordained priest, 1965; consecrated bishop, 1984. Missionary Alaska, 1960-83; coadjutor bishop Diocese of Fairbanks, Alaska, 1984-85, bishop, 1985—. Address: 1316 Peger Rd Fairbanks AK 99709-5168*

KANNENBERG, IDA MARGUERITE, writer; b. West Liberty, Iowa, Oct. 28, 1914; d. Ernest John and Vera Ella (Smith) Green; m. David Harold Murdach, Nov. 30, 1934 (div. Aug. 1956); 1 child, Lee Rae Murdach Kirk; m. William Paul Kannenberg, June 26, 1969 (dec. Mar. 1988). Student, Multnomah C.C. Sec. various civil svc. and legal orgns. Portland, Oreg., 1955-69; owner antique shops Eugene and Portland, Oreg., 1969-89. Author: UFOs and the Psychic Factor, 1992, Alien Book of Truth, 1993, Project Earth From The E.T. Perspective, 1995. Mem. Soc. for Investigation of The Unexplained, Mensa. Home and Office: Hartmut Jager Art Ltd 415 Brae Burn Dr Eugene OR 97405-4941

KANNER, EDWIN BENJAMIN, electrical manufacturing company executive; b. N.Y.C., July 2, 1922; s. Charles and Grace (Edelson) K.; m. S. Barbara Penenberg, Aug. 3, 1944; children: Jaimie Sue, Richard, Keith. BBA, CCNY, 1943; MBA, Harvard U., 1947. Asst. West Coast mgr. Fairchild Publs., N.Y.C. and L.A., 1948-50; gen. mgr. Dible Enterprises, L.A., 1951-53; sales mgr., gen. mgr., prs. Western Insulated Wire Co. div. Teledyne, L.A., 1954-68; pres. Carol Cable Co. West div. Avnet, L.A., 1969-79; exec. v.p., COO Avnet Inc., N.Y.C., 1980-83; pres. Pacific Electricord and Am. Ins. Wire Co., L.A., also Providence, 1948—. Lt. comdr. USNR, 1943-47, PTO. Office: Pacific Electricord 747 W Redondo Beach Blvd Gardena CA 90247-4203

KANNER, GIDEON, lawyer; b. Lwów, Poland, Apr. 15, 1930; came to U.S., 1947; s. Stanley and Claire (Roth) K.; children: Jonathan, Jesse. B of Mech. Engring., The Cooper Union, 1954; JD, U. So. Calif., 1961. Bar: Calif. 1962, U.S. Supreme Ct. 1967. Rocket engr. USN, N.J., 1954-55, Rocketdyne, Calif., 1955-64; lawyer Fadem & Kanner, L.S., 1964-74; law prof. Loyola Law Sch., L.S., 1974-90; lawyer Crosby, Heafey, Roach & May, L.S., 1990-95, Berger & Norton, Santa Monica, Calif., 1995—; cons. Calif. Law Revision Commn., 1968-77. Co-editor: Nichols in Eminent Domain, Compensation for Expropriation-A Comparative Study, Vol. II, 1990, After Lucas: Land Use Regulation and the Taking of Property Without Compensation, 1993; editor, pub. Just Compensation, 1974—; contbr. articles and revs. to profl. law jours. Recipient Shattuck prize Am. Inst. Real Estate Appraisers. Home: PO Box 1741 Burbank CA 91507-1741 Office: Berger & Norton 1620 26th St Ste 200 Sout Santa Monica CA 90404-4013

KANNER, RICHARD ELLIOT, physician, educator; b. Bklyn., Oct. 1, 1935; s. William W. and Elsie Alice (Karpf) K. AB, U. Mich., 1958; MD, SUNY, Bklyn., 1962. Diplomate Am. Bd. Internal Medicine, sub-bd. pulmonary disease. Intern then resident in internal medicine U. Utah Hosps., Salt Lake City, 1962-65; fellow pulmonary medicine Columbia Presbyn. Med. Ctr., N.Y.C., 1965-66, U. Utah Med. Ctr., 1968-70; from instr. to prof. medicine U. Utah Sch. Medicine, Salt Lake City, 1970-91, instr. medicine, 1970-71, asst. prof. medicine, 1971-77, assoc. prof. medicine, 1977-91, prof. medicine, 1991—; vis. assoc. prof. medicine Harvard Med. Sch., Boston, 1980-81. Mem. air quality bd. Dept. Environ. Quality, State of Utah, 1988-97, chmn., 1995-97. Served to lt. comdr. USNR, 1966-68, Vietnam. Fellow Am. Coll. Chest Physicians (chmn. coun. of govs. 1991), mem. Am. Thoracic Soc. Office: U Utah Sch Medicine 701 Wintrobe Bldg Salt Lake City UT 84132

KANNER, STEVEN BRIAN, immunologist; b. Miami, Fla., Oct. 2, 1958; s. Ben and Sylvia Ruth (Naness) K. BA, U. Calif., Berkeley, 1980; PhD, U. Miami, 1986. Post-doctoral fellow U. Va., Charlottesville, 1986-90; sr. scientist Bristol-Myers Squibb, Seattle, 1990-93, sr. rsch. investigator, 1993-97, prin. scientist, 1997—. Contbr. articles to profl. jours. Recipient Presdl. scholarship U. Miami, 1981-86, post-doctoral fellowship NIH, 1987-90. Mem. Am. Soc. Microbiology, Am. Assn. Immunologists.

KANODE, CAROLYN KERRIGAN, school nurse, pediatric nurse practitioner; b. Trenton, N.J., July 2, 1937; d. Lawrence Stephen and Louise (Welde) Kerrigan; m. Irwin Kanode, Aug. 26, 1960; children: Cathy, Barbara, Teresa. BS cum laude, Calif. State U., Long Beach, 1976; MS, Pepperdine U., Malibu, Calif., 1984. RN, Calif.; cert. pediatric nurse practitioner. Staff nurse Bellevue Hosp., N.Y.C., 1958-60; charge nurse Westside Hosp., L.A., 1960; office nurse Dr. Lenahan, Fullerton, Calif., 1960-64; sch. nurse Oceanview Sch. Dist., Huntington Beach, Calif., 1977—. Trustee Ocean View Sch. Dist., Huntington Beach, Calif., 1990—; co-founder Huntington Youth Shelter, Huntington Beach, 1987, pres., 1987-90; chair, subcom. Family Resource Ctr., 1995—. Recipient Humanitarian award Soroptomists, Human Svcs. award City of Huntington Beach, 1995; named Woman of Yr., Calif. Assembly, 1994. Mem. Calif. Sch. Nurses Assn. (legis. chair, Calif. Sch. Nurse of Yr. 1990), Am. Assn Univ. Women, Orange County Sch. Nurse Orgn. (past pres.), Dream Catchers Guild, Orange County Sch. Bd. Assn. (editor newsletter 1992—). Home: 17382 Alta Vista Cir Huntington Beach CA 92647-6130

KANTOR, IGO, film and television producer; b. Vienna, Austria, Aug. 18, 1930; came to U.S., 1947; s. Samuel and Miriam (Sommerfreund) K.; m. Enid Lois Dershewitz, June 24, 1962; children: Loren, Mark, Lisa. AA, UCLA, 1950, BS, 1952, MS in Polit. Sci., 1954. Fgn. corr. Portuguese Mag. Flama, L.A., 1949-57; music supr., editor Screen Gems, Columbia, L.A., 1954-63; post-prodn. supr. various ind. cos. L.A., 1963-64; music supr.-editor Universal-MCA, L.A., 1964-66; pres., film editor Synchrofilm, Inc., L.A., 1966-74; pres., producer Duque Films, Inc., L.A., 1971-78; ind. producer Jerry Lewis Films, Film Ventures, L.A., 1979-84; pres., producer Laurelwood Prodns. Inc., L.A., 1984-87, Major Arts Corp., L.A., 1987—; pres. Jubilee Holding Co., L.A., 1988—. Producer Legends of the West with Jack Palance (TV spl. series), 1992, United We Stand, 1988, Act of Piracy, 1987, The Golden Eagle Awards, 1986, It's A Wonderful World, 1986, The Grand Tour, 1985, Shaker Run, 1984, From Hawaii with Love, 1983, Night Shadows, 1983, Kill and Kill Again, 1981, Hardly Working, 1980, Good Luck, Miss Wyckoff, 1979, Holiday Classic Cartoons, 1994, Mom USA, 1996, many others. Named Emmy nominee, 1967, 68, 69, 70. Mem. Acad. Motion Picture Arts & Scis. (exec. sound bd. 1969-71), Dirs. Guild Am. (assoc. dir.). Democrat. Jewish. Office: Major Arts Corp 9171 Wilshire Blvd Beverly Hills CA 90210 Address: PO Box 1340 Studio City CA 91614

KAO, CHENG CHI, electronics executive; b. Taipei, Taiwan, Republic of China, Aug. 3, 1941; s. Chin Wu and Su Chin (Wu) K.; m. Susan Lin, July 4, 1970; children: Antonia Hueilan, Albert Chengwei, Helen Siaolan. BS, Taiwan U., 1963; AM, Harvard U., 1965, PhD, 1969. Research fellow Harvard U., Cambridge, Mass., 1969-70; scientist Xerox Corp., Webster, N.Y., 1970-75; mgr. Internat. Materials Research, Inc., Santa Clara, Calif., 1976-78; exec. v.p. President Enterprises Corp., Tainan, Taiwan, 1979-85; pres. Kolyn Enterprises Corp., Los Altos, Calif., 1979—. Contbr. articles to profl. jours. Bd. dirs. Taipei Am. Sch., 1980-82. Mem. IEEE, Chinese Inst. Elec. Engring. (bd. dirs. 1982-85), Sigma Xi. Club: Am. in China (Taipei), Palo Alto Hills Golf and Country. Office: Kolyn Enterprises Corp 4962 El Camino Real Ste 119 Los Altos CA 94022-1410

KAO, LILY CHING-CHIUNG, neonatologist; b. Hong Kong, Hong Kong, Aug. 4, 1951; came to U.S., 1970; d. Eugene Wei-yu and Yun-Ling (Chiang) K.; m. Wen Hsien Hsu, July 2, 1983; children: Davina, Christina, Sarena, Edmund. BA, Temple U., 1974; MD, U. Pa., 1978. Intern, resident in pediat. Pitts. Children's Hosp., 1978-81; neonatology and respiratory disease fellow L.A. Children's Hosp., 1981-82; neonatologist Children's Hosp., Oakland, Calif., 1983—. Fellow Am. Acad. Pediat.; mem. Western Soc. Pediat. Rsch., Soc. Pediat. Rsch. Office: Children's Hosp Oakland CA 94609

KAPELOVITZ, LEONARD HERMAN, psychiatrist; b. Dickinson, N.D., Aug. 22, 1939; s. Ignace and Ethel Rose (Grouse) K.; m. Abbey Carol Poze, June 10, 1965; children: Mara Ilise, Daniel Ignace. SB, U. Chgo., 1961; MD, Harvard U., 1965; grad., Denver Psychoanalytic Inst., 1980. Diplomate Am. Bd. Psychiatry and Neurology. Chief resident in psychiatry U. Colo., Denver, 1968-69; asst. prof. psychiatry U. Colo. Med. Sch., Denver, 1971-75, clin. asst. prof. psychiatry, 1975—; pvt. practice psychiatry and psychoanalysis Englewood, Colo., 1975—; med. dir. psychiatry St. Anthony Hosp, Westminster, Colo., 1991—; vice chair psychiatry Provenant Health Systems, Denver, 1993—; mem. faculty tng. and supervising psychoanalyst Colo. Soc. for Psychology and Psychoanalysis, Denver, 1990—; mem. continuing med. edn. faculty Denver Psychoanalytic Soc., 1990—, Denver Psychoanalytic Inst., 1990—. Author: To Love and To Work, 1976, 2d edit., 1987; contbr. articles to profl. jours. Pres. bd. dirs. Denver Mental Health Ctr., 1983-85; candidate Colo. Ho. of Reps., 1972. Served as capt. USAF, 1969-71. Fellow Am. Psychiat. Assn.; mem. Colo. Psychiat. Soc., Denver Psychoanalytic Soc., Colo. Soc. for Psychology and Psychoanalysis, Maimonides Soc. Democrat. Jewish. Office: 8095 E Prentice Ave Englewood CO 80111-2705

KAPERICK, JOHN ANTHONY, information specialist; b. Tacoma, Wash., July 11, 1964; s. Victor Raymond and Billie Ann (Carlson) K.; m. Dawn Marie Canfield, Aug. 5, 1989; 1 child, Amanda Jeanne Kaperick. Cert., Bates Vocat. Tech. Inst., Tacoma, Wash., 1985; cert., Boeing Computer Svcs., Seattle, 1990. Apprentice cabinetmaker Custom Craft Fixtures, Tacoma, 1986-87; computer operator Vic's Enterprises, Tacoma, 1987-90; info. specialist NOAA (U.S. Dept. Commerce), Seattle, 1990—. Mem. Spl. Librs. Assn., Environment and Resource Mgmt. Divsn. Office: NOAA Hazmat 7600 Sand Point Way NE Seattle WA 98115-6349

KAPLAN, BARRY MARTIN, lawyer; b. N.Y.C., Nov. 9, 1950; s. Stanley Seymour and Lillian (Schner) K.; m. Erica Green, July 26, 1981; children: Matthew Aaron, Elizabeth Rose, Andrew Nathan. BA, Colgate U., 1973; JD cum laude, U. Mich., 1976. Bar: Mich. 1976, Wash., 1978, U.S. Dist. (ea. dist.) Mich. 1976, U.S. Dist. Ct. (we. dist.) Wash. 1978, U.S. Dist. Ct. (ea. dist.) Wash. 1986, U.S. Tax Ct. 1983, U.S. Ct. Appeals (9th cir.) 1990. Law clk. to Hon. Charles W. Joiner U.S. Dist. Ct. (ea. dist.) Mich., Detroit, 1976-78; assoc. Perkins Coie, Seattle, 1978-85, ptnr., 1985—; spkr. in field. Author: Washington Corporation Law and Practice, 1991; contbr. articles to legal jours. and procs. Mem. ABA (litigation sect., securities litigation com., bus. law sect., bus. and corp. litigation com., subcom. chmn. on control transactions 1993), Wash. State Bar Assn. (CLE spkr., bus. law sect., securities com., subcom. chair on dir.'s liability 1993), Wash. Athletic Club. Office: Perkins Coie 40th Fl 1201 3rd Ave Fl 40 Seattle WA 98101-3099

KAPLAN, DONALD SHELDON, real estate developer and rehabilitator, property management company executive; b. L.A., Aug. 1, 1938; s. Adolph Iven and Ruth Janet (Rose) K.; m. Marsha Lynn Le Van, June 12, 1960 (div. July 1980); children: Lisa Ann, Drew Jason; m. Joanne Natalie Cossu, Apr. 19, 1981; children: Alyson Ilene, Tara Ruth. Student, L.A. City Coll., 1957-58, Pacific State U., 1959-60. Pres. DSK Devel. Co., Inc., 1964--, Assured Maintenance Corp., Inc., 1974--, DSK Mgmt. Co., Inc., 1983--, New Renaissance Investments, Inc., 1986--, Kaplan Enterprises, Inc., L.A., 1986--; pres. Telephony Worldwide Enterprises, 1989—, Voice Telephone Co., 1993—, Fin. Svcs. of Am., 1993—, Western Fin. Investments, 1992—. Home and Office: Kaplan Enterprises Inc 5699 Kanan Rd Apt 234 Agoura Hills CA 91301-3358

KAPLAN, DONNA ELAINE, artist, educator; b. South Amboy, N.J., Dec. 30, 1942; d. Oscar Ivan and Otta Theora (Hamilton) Olsen; m. Barnett Morris Kaplan, Sept. 20, 1975; children: William, Ivan, Benjamin. Diploma in profl. nursing, Chaffey Coll., Alta Loma, Calif., 1964; BS in Occupl. Therapy, U. Puget Sound, Tacoma, 1972; student, Factory of Visual Arts, Seattle, 1977-79. RN, Wash.; cert. psychiat. nurse, Calif.; registered occupl. therapist. Shift charge nurse rsch. unit Langley Porter Neuropsychiat. Inst., San Francisco, 1967-70; supr. nursing Western State Hosp., Steilacoom, Wash., 1972-73; instr. in-svc. edn. Inst. Pa. Hosp., Phila., 1974-75; owner DK Design Studio, North Bend, Wash., 1984—; juror No. Calif. Reg. Fiber Show, Sacramento, Calif., 1993; guest curator Northwest Gallery, 1994; nat. touring guest arts instr. 1987—. Co-author: Beads as Warp and Weft, 1996; contbr. articles to art jours.; exhibitions include: Tacoma Art Mus., Wash., 1980, Window Gallery of Fine Art, Alaska, 1989, Craft Alliance Gallery, St. Louis, 1989, Tohomo Chul Park Gallery, Ariz., 1995, Whatcom Mus. History and Art, Wash., 1995, Bellevue Art Mus., Wash., 1982, 89, 96, Contemporary Crafts Ctr., Seattle, 1996, Raindance Gallery, Oreg., 1996. Recipient Best Creative Use of Materials award Absolutely Beads Show/Beads and Beyond, Bellevue, Wash., 1994, Mus. Purchase award Edmonds (Wash.) Art Festival Mus., 1994, 1st pl. award Art Splash, City of Redmond, Wash., 1995. Mem. Seattle Weavers' Guild (corr. sec. 1982-83, Peoples Choice award 1986, Art D award 1995), N.W. Designer Craftsmen, N.W. Craft Alliance (v.p., bd. dirs. 1994-96), N.W. Bead Soc., Fiber Art Profls., Friends of Fiber Art Internat. Studio: DK Design Studio 43406 SE 88th St North Bend WA 98045

KAPLAN, DOUGLAS ALLEN, county official; b. L.A., Aug. 14, 1956; s. Martin and Sally Kaplan. BA in Pub. Svc./Polit. Sci., U. Calif., Davis, 1978; cert., Solano (Calif.) Fire Acad., 1979. Cert. Calif. Pub. Guardians Assn., Nat. Guardianship Assn. Fire safety supr. Davis & Winter Fire Dept., 1979-80; asst. manpower analyst Yolo County, Woodland, Calif., 1980, voter outreach coord., 1980-82, pub. guardian, adminstr., 1983—; tchr. U. Calif. Ext., 1992—; chair conservatorship adv. com. Am. River Coll., Sacramento, 1989-90. Mem. exec. bd. Calif. Dem. Party, Sacramento, 1987-88, 93-94, state ctrl. com., 1985—; bd. mem. N.C.A. Ombudsman Adv. Bd., Sacramento, 1996—. Recipient Grassroots Activism award Nat. Jewish Dem. Coun., Washington, 1993. Mem. Nat. Guardianship Assn. (legis. chair, bd. mem. 1988—, pres. 1994-96), Calif. Pub. Guardian Assn. (pres. 1988-89), Calif. State Bar (planning, probate and trust sect. com. 1995—). Jewish. Office: Yolo County Pub Guardian/Adminstr PO Box 2265 Woodland CA 95776

KAPLAN, GARY, executive recruiter; b. Phila., Aug. 14, 1939; s. Morris and Minnie (Leve) K.; m. Linda Ann Wilson, May 30, 1968; children: Michael Warren, Marc Jonathan, Jeffrey Russell. BA in Polit. Sci., Pa. State U., 1961. Tchr. biology N.E. High Sch., Phila., 1962-63; coll. employment rep. Bell Telephone Labs., Murray Hill, N.J., 1966-67; supr. recruitment and placement Unisys, Blue Bell, Pa., 1967-69; pres. Electronic Systems Personnel, Phila., 1969-70; staff selection rep. Booz, Allen & Hamilton, N.Y.C., 1970-72; mgr. exec. recruitment M&T Chems., Rahway, N.J., 1972-74; dir. exec. recruitment IU Internat. Mgmt. Corp., Phila., 1974-78; v.p. personnel Crocker Bank, Los Angeles, 1978-79; mng. v.p. ptnr. western region Korn-Ferry Internat., Los Angeles, 1979-85; pres. Gary Kaplan & Assocs., Pasadena, Calif., 1985—; bd. dirs. Vis. Nurses Assn., L.A., Home Pharmacy of Calif.; mem. Pa. State U. Indsl./Orgnl. Psychology Adv. Bd. Mgmt. columnist, Radio and Records newspaper, 1984-85. Chmn. bd. dirs. Vis. Nurse Assn., L.A., 1985-87; bd. dirs. The Wellness Cmty.-Nat., Home Pharmacy of Calif.; mem. indsl./orgnl. psychology adv. bd. Pa. State U. Capt. Adj. Gen. Corps., U.S. Army, 1963-66. Mem. Am. Compensation Assn. Home: 1735 Fairmont Ave La Canada Flintridge CA 91011-1632 Office: Gary Kaplan & Assocs 201 S Lake Ave Pasadena CA 91101-3004

KAPLAN, JERROLD MARVIN, internist; b. Chgo., Nov. 17, 1938; s. Meyer and Edith (Maltz) K.; m. Henrietta Carolyn Appel, Aug. 19, 1962; children: David P., Brian H. BS, U. Ill., 1960; MD, U. Ill., Chgo., 1963. Diplomate Nat. Bd. Med. Examiners, Am. Bd. Internal Medicine. Intern Letterman Gen. Army Hosp., San Francisco, 1963-64, resident in medicine, 1964-66, sr. resident in medicine, chief med. resident, 1966-67; fellow in cardiology Cedars Sinai Med. Ctr., L.A., 1970-71; pvt. practice internal medicine, cardiology San Bruno (Calif.) Internists Group, 1971—; attending physician cardiology clinic Stanford (Calif.) U. Sch. Medicine, 1972; active staff mem. Peninsula Hosp. and Med. Ctr., Burlingame, Calif., 1971—, instr. physical diagnosis, 1975-87; clin. asst. prof., vol. clin. faculty mem. Stanford U. Sch. Medicine, 1984-87; physician cons. Jour. AMA, 1965-67. Contbr. articles to med. jours. With U.S. Army Med. Corps, 1963-70. Fellow ACP; mem. Am. Soc. Internal Medicine, Calif. Med. Assn., San Mateo County Med. Assn., Alpha Omega Alpha. Office: Unified Med Clinics 1001 Sneath Ln Ste 300 San Bruno CA 94066-2349

KAPLAN, JONATHAN, psychiatrist, educator; b. N.Y.C., Sept. 5, 1943; s. Milton A. and Marian W. Kaplan; m. Lynna M. Gay, Oct. 25, 1980; 1 child, Daniel Aaron. BA, Swarthmore Coll., 1964; MD, U. Pa., 1968. Diplomate Am. Bd. Psychiatry and Neurology. Straight med. intern U. Wis. Hosp., Madison, 1968-69; resident in psychiatry U. Pa. Hosp., Phila., 1969-72; sr. investigator NIMH, Washington, 1971-74; unit chief VA Hosp., Palo Alto, Calif., 1974-78; pvt. practice Menlo Park, Calif., 1979—; clin. assoc. prof. dept. psychiatry Stanford (Calif.) U., 1980—. Contbr. articles to profl. jours.

Surgeon USPHS, 1971-74. Mem. Am. Psychiat. Assn., No. Calif. Psychiat. Assn. Office: 1225 Crane St Ste 106 Menlo Park CA 94025-4253

KAPLAN, MARC J., lawyer; b. Phila., Mar. 12, 1957; s. Ronald L. Kaplan and Syvia B. (Meyers) Price; m. Mary J. Dulacki, Sept. 16, 1984; children: Alexandra Zoe, Rini Isadora. BA, Duke U., 1979; JD, U. Denver, 1983. Bar: Colo. 1984, U.S. Dist. Ct. Colo. 1984, U.S. Ct. Appeals (10th cir.) 1984. Asst. for polit. ops. Dem. Nat. Com., Washington, 1979-80; asst. to spl. asst. to pres. White House, Washington, 1980-81; atty. Aisenberg & Kaplan, Denver, 1984-94, Rossi, Cox, Kiker & Inderwish, P.C., Denver, 1994—; polit. cons. Washington, 1981, lawyering process adj. prof. U. Denver Coll. of Law, 1990-92, faculty basic civil litig. skills continuing legal edn. of Denver, 1990-92, Colo, Supreme Ct. Greivance Com. Hearing Bd., Denver, 1993—. Contbr. Colo. Auto Litigator's Handbook. Pres. Duke Club of Denver, 1990-92, chmn. Children of Violence Com., Denver, 1993-94. Named Young Polit. Leader U.S. State Dept., Washington, 1979. Mem. ATLA, Colo. Bar Assn. (gov. 1990-93, Pro Bono award 1993), Colo. Trial Lawyers Assn. (dir. 1986—, officer 1995—), Denver and Arapahoe Bar Assn., Thompson G. Marsh Inn of Ct., Fed. Employers' Liability Act. Office: Rossi Cox Kiker & Inderwish PC 12203 E 2nd Ave Aurora CO 80011-8302

KAPLAN, MARTIN HAROLD, writer, producer; b. Newark, N.J., Aug. 21, 1950; m. Susan R. Estrich, Nov. 26, 1986; children: Isabel, James. AB summa cum laude, Harvard Coll., 1971; MA, Cambridge (Eng.) U., 1973; PhD, Stanford (Calif.) U., 1975. Program exec. Aspen (Colo.) Inst. for Humanistic Studies, 1975-76; exec. asst. to the commr. U.S. Office of Edn., HEW, Washington, 1977-78; chief speechwriter to the v.p. The White House, Washington, 1978-80; columnist, editor Washington Star, 1981; guest scholar Brookings Instn., Washington, 1982; dep. campaign mgr., chief speechwriter Mondale Presdl. campaign, Washington, 1983-84; v.p. prodn. Walt Disney Studios, Burbank, Calif., 1985-88, writer, producer, 1989—. Screenwriter Noises Off, 1992; screenwriter, exec. prodr. The Distinguished Gentleman, 1992 (Environ. Media award). Marshall scholar Brit. Govt., 1971; Danforth fellow Danforth Found., 1973. Office: 444 N Larchmont Blvd Los Angeles CA 90004

KAPLAN, MARTIN NATHAN, electrical and electronic engineer; b. Beloit, Wis., Nov. 14, 1916; s. Abraham Louis and Eva (Schomer) K.; m. Florence Helen Grumet (div. 1956); 1 child, Kathy Sue; m. Sylvia Greif, Dec. 7, 1963. BSEE, U. Wis., 1942. Sr. electronics engr. Convair, San Diego, 1951-56; rsch. engr. AMF/Sunstrand, Pacoima, Calif., 1956-59; sr. rsch. engr. Ryan Electronics, San Diego, 1959-63; sr. design engr. N.Am. Aviation, Downey, Calif., 1963-66; rsch. specialist Lockheed, Burbank, Calif., 1966-70; mem. tech. staff Aerospace Corp., El Segundo, Calif., 1980-82; rsch. scientist Motorotor, North Hollywood, Calif., 1983—. Lt. (j.g.) USNR, 1943-46. Mem. IEEE (life), Am. Phys. Soc. (life). Home and Office: Motorotor 11610 Cantlay St North Hollywood CA 91605-3940

KAPLAN, MIKE, film and video producer, director, and distributor, marketing executive; b. Providence, Mar. 16, 1943; s. Julius and Ida (Rabinovitz) k. BA, U. R.I., 1964. Assoc. editor Ind. Film Jour., N.Y.C., 1964-65; publicist MGM, N.Y.C., 1965-68, publicity coord., 1968, nat. publicity dir., 1968-71; v.p. Polaris Prodns. (Stanley Kubrick), London, 1971-73; internat mkgt. exec. Warner Bros., L.A., London, 1973-74; pres. Circle Assocs. Ltd., U.S., London, 1973—, Lion's Gate Distbn., 1975-80; mktg. v.p. Lion's Gate Films (Robert Altman), 1975-80; producer, pres. Circle Assoc. Ltd., L.A., 1978—; v.p. mktg. Northstar Internat., Hal Ashby, L.A., 1981-83; pres. mktg. Alive Films, L.A., 1985-87. Producer: (Film) The Whales of August, 1987; (video) Oak Grove Sch., 1988; assoc. prodr.; (film) Short Cuts, 1992; prodr., dir. (documentary) Luck, Trust and Ketchup: Robert Altman in Carver Country, 1994; actor: Buffalo Bill and The Indians, Welcome To L.A., Choose Me, The Player. Recipient Best Film award Nat. Media Awards, Retirement Rsch. Found., 1987, Key Art award Hollywood Reporter, 1976, 87. Mem. Acad. Motion Picture Arts and Scis., Screen Actors Guild, Publicists Guild. Office: Circle Assocs PO Box 5730 Santa Monica CA 90409-5730

KAPLAN, OZER BENJAMIN, environmental health specialist, consultant; b. Santiago, Chile, Jan. 3, 1940; naturalized U.S. citizen, 1969; s. David and Raquel (Klorman) K.; m. Adele M. Brandt, Jan. 12, 1974 (div. 1993);m. Janna Mirkh, Nov. 20, 1994. Student, U. Chile, 1958-59; BS, Calif. Polytech. U., 1964; MS, U. Calif., Davis, 1966, PhD, 1969; MPH, UCLA, 1973. Teaching and rsch. asst. U. Calif., Davis, 1968-69; assoc. prof. soil sci. N.C. A & T State U., Greensboro, 1969-70; assoc. prof. biology Morris Coll., Sumter, S.C., 1970-71; ind. cost/benefit cons. L.A., 1971-72; mem. environ. health task force Inland Counties Health Systems Agy., San Bernardino, Calif., 1974-76; environ. health planning coord. San Bernardino County, Calif., 1974-80; ind. cons. environ. health San Bernardino, 1987—. Author: Septic Systems Handbook, 1986, 2d edit. 1990. V.p. Citizens Against Pass Area Prisons, Riverside County, Calif., 1982-86, Pass Citizens for Sound Planning, Riverside County, 1986-91. Mem. Soil Sci. Soc. Am. (emeritus), Am. Botanical Coun./Herb Rsch. Found., Calif. Environ. Health Assn. (chmn. land use com., chmn. environ. health sect., Cert. of Appreciation, 1976, 77), Sigma Xi. Home and Office: 24641 Santa Clara Ave Dana Point CA 92629-3044

KAPLAN, ROBERT B., linguistics educator, consultant, researcher; b. N.Y.C., Sept. 20, 1929; s. Emanuel B. and Natalie K.; m. Audrey A. Lien, Apr. 21, 1951; children—Robin Ann Kaplan Gibson, Lisa Kaplan Morris, Robert Allen. Student, Champlain Coll., 1947-48, Syracuse U., 1948-49; B.A., Willamette U., 1952; M.A., U. So. Calif., 1957, Ph.D., 1962. Teaching asst. U. So. Calif., Los Angeles, 1955-57, instr. coordinator, asst. prof. English communication program for fgn. students, 1965-72, assoc. prof., dir. English communication program for fgn. students, 1972-76, assoc. dean continuing edn., 1973-76, prof. applied linguistics, 1976-95, prof. emeritus, 1995—, dir. Am. Lang. Inst., 1986-91; instr. U. Oreg., 1957-60; cons. field service program Nat. Assn. Fgn. Student Affairs, 1964-84; pres.-elect faculty senate U. So. Calif., 1988-89, pres., 1989-90; adv. bd. internat. comparability study of standardized lang. exams. U. Cambridge Local Exams. Syndicate. Author: Reading and Rhetoric: A Reader, 1963; (with V. Tufte, P. Cook and J. Aurbach) Transformational Grammar: A Guide for Teachers, 1968; (with R.D. Schoesler) Learning English Through Typewriting, 1969; The Anatomy of Rhetoric: Prolegomena to a Functional Theory of Rhetoric, 1971; On the Scope of Applied Linguistics, 1980; The Language Needs of Migrant Workers, 1980; (with P. Shaw) Exploring Academic English, 1984; (with U. Connor) Writing Across Languages: Analysis of L2 Text, 1987; (with W. Grabe) Introduction To Applied Linguistics, 1991, Writing Around the Pacific Rim, 1995, (with W. Grabe) Theory and Practice of Writing: An Applied Linguistics Perspective, 1996—, (with R.B. Baldauf) Language Policy from Practice to Theory, 1997; editl. bd. Jour. Asian Pacific Comm., Internat. Educator, BBC English Dictionary, Second Lang. Instruction/Acquisition Abstracts, Jour. of Second Lang. Writing, Forensic Linguistics, Jour. Multilingual and Multicultural Devels., Asian Jour. of English Lang. Tchg.; contbr. articles to profl. jours., U.S. Australia, Brazil, Can., Chile, Germany, Holland, Japan, Mexico, N.Z., Philippines and Singapore; mem. editorial bd. Oxford Internat. Encyclopedia Linguistics; editor in chief Ann. Rev. Applied Linguistics, 1980-91, editorial bd., 1991—; contbr. notes, revs. to profl. jours. U.S. and abroad. Bd. dirs. Internat. Bilingual Sch. L.A., 1986-91, Internat. Edn. Rsch. Found., 1986-94. Served with inf. U.S. Army, Korea. Fulbright sr. scholar, Australia, 1978, Hong Kong, 1986, New Zealand, 1992. Mem. Am. Anthrop. Assn., AAAS, Am. Assn. Applied Linguistics (v.p., pres. 1992-94), AAUP, Assn. Internationale de Linguistique Applique, Assn. Internationale Pour La Researche et La Diffusion Des Methodes Audio-Visuelles et Structuro-Globales, Assn. Tchrs. English as Second Lang. (chmn. 1968-69), Calif. Assn. Tchrs. English to Speakers Other Langs. (pres. 1970-71), Can. Council Tchrs. English, Nat. Assn. Fgn. Student Affairs (nat. pres. 1983-84), Linguistics Soc. Am., Tchrs. English to Speakers of Other Langs. (1st v.p., pres. 1989-91).

KAPLAN, SANDRA LEE, artist; b. Cin., May 23, 1943; d. Howard and Helen (Katz) K.; m. Stanley Joseph Dragul, 1964 (div. 1974); 1 child, Sacha; m. Robert Lawrence Denerstein, 1986. Student, Art Acad. Cin., 1960-61; BFA with honors, Pratt Inst., Bklyn., 1965; student, CUNY, 1968-70. Illustrator Christian Sci. Monitor, Boston, 1991-94; drawing instr. Denver C.C., 1991-92; antique dealer Wazee Deco, Denver, 1992—; com. mem. Arvada Ctr. for the Arts, 1994-96. Sole exhibits in various galleries including Dubins Gallery, L.A., 1988, Ventana Gallery, Santa Fe, 1985-90, Land-Escapes in Aruada Ctr. for the Arts, Arvada, Colo., 1991, Human and or Nature in Nicolaysen Mus., Casper, Wyo., 1992, Rule Modern & Contemporary, Denver, 1993, 96, Land-Escape in Wave Hill, Riverdale, N.Y., 1995, Boulder (Colo.) Mus. Contemporary Art, 1997, Indigo Gallery, Boca Raton, Fla., 1997; commd. works Hong Kong Marriott Hotel, 1988, Gt. West Life Assurance Co., 1991, Arvada City Hall, 1993, Sch. Pharmacy U. Colo., 1994. Yaddo Corp. fellow, 1985; Ludwig Vogelstein grantee, 1986, Covisions grantee Colo. Coun. of Arts, 1992. Mem. Arapahoe Acres Design Rev. Democrat. Jewish. Office: St Francis Sch 235 S Sherman St Denver CO 80209-1620

KAPLINSKI, BUFFALO, artist; b. Chgo., May 25, 1943; s. Jacob Kaplinski and Genevive Stryczek; m. Vicky Jeanine Smith, June 10, 1944; 1 child, Tiaja Karenina. Student, Chgo. Art Inst., 1964, Am. Acad. Art, 1965. lectr. Foothills Art Ctr., Golden, Colo., Denver Art Mus., Jewish Comty. Ctr., Denver; master instr. Art Students League, Denver. One-man shows include Am. Water Color Soc., N.Y.C., Nat. Acad. Design, N.Y.C., U. Portland, Oreg., Berger Sandzen Mus., Lindsberg, Kans., Southwestern Biennial-Mus. N.Mex., Santa Fe, Denver Art Mus., Mus. Natural History, Denver, Contemporary S.W., Potsdam (N.Y.) Coll.; exhibited in group shows Denver Art Mus., 1993, Nat. Cowboy Hall of Fame, Oklahoma City, 1993, Pioneer Mus., Colorado Springs, Colo., 1993, Pikes Peak Ctr., Colorado Springs, 1993, Opicka Gallery, Denver, 1994, Loveland (Colo.) Mus., 1994, Colo. Essence Gallery, Breckenridge, 1995, Foothills Art Ctr., Golden, Colo., 1996; represented in pvt. and pub. collections. Home: PO Box 44 Elizabeth CO 80107-0044

KAPLOWITZ, KAREN (JILL), lawyer; b. New Haven, Nov. 27, 1946; d. Charles Cohen and Estelle (Gerber) K.; m. Alan George Cohen, Aug. 17, 1980; children: Benjamin, Elizabeth. BA cum laude, Barnard Coll., 1968; JD, U. Chgo., 1971. Bar: Calif. 1971, U.S. Dist. Ct. (cen. dist.) Calif. 1971. Assoc. O'Melveny & Myers, L.A., 1971-74; ptnr. Bardeen, Bersch & Kaplowitz, L.A., 1974-80, Alschuler, Grossman & Pines, L.A., 1980—. Contbr. articles to profl. jours. Mem. vis. com. U. Chgo. Law Sch., 1990-93. Mem. ABA (chmn. employer-employee rels. com. of tors and ins. practice sect.), Assn. Bus. Trial Lawyers (pres.), Calif. Women Lawyers (Fay Stender award 1982), Women Lawyers Assn. L.A. Home: 244 Euclid St Santa Monica CA 90402-2116 Office: Alschuler Grossman & Pines 2049 Century Park E # 39 Los Angeles CA 90067-3101

KAPOOR, SANDRA A., restaurant management educator; b. Madison, S.D., Sept. 10, 1952; d. Curt and Harriette (Ochs) Kaiser; m. Tarun Kapoor. BS in Nutrition and Food Sci., S.D. State U., 1974; M. Pub. Health Nutrition, U. Minn., 1976, PhD, 1986. Food svc. dir./chef Project Newgate, St. Paul, 1974-75; cons. dietitian Tracy (Minn.) Hosp., 1978-79; instr. Culinary Inst. Am., Hyde Park, N.Y., 1979-80; coord. continuing edn. programs and adj. faculty instr. Dept. of Vocat. and Tech. Edn., U. Minn., St. Paul, 1981-83; cons./seminar dir./trainer Pomona, Calif., 1976—; assoc. prof. hotel, restaurant and instnl. mgmt. S.W. State U., Marshall, Minn., 1976-86; owner/operator Kebabi Restaurant and Bar, Kebabi Cafe, The Caterers, Mpls., 1984-91; asst. prof. hotel, restaurant and instnl. mgmt. Mich. State U., East Lansing, 1986-88; prof. Sch. Hotel and Restaurant Mgmt. Calif. State Poly. U., Pomona, 1988—; cook SAGA Foodsvc., Brookings, S.D., 1970-74; food svc. dir./chef Elks Youth Camp, Brainerd, Minn., summers 1974-75; gen. mgr., exec. chef Minnesouri Club and Resort, Alexandria, Minn., summers 1976-77; dir. nutrition Weight Reduction Resort, Camp Camelot, South Hampton, N.Y., summer 1980; lectr. in field. Author: Bulimia: A Program for Friends and Family Members, 1988, Professional Healthy Cooking, 1995, Healthy & Delicious: 400 Professional Recipes, 1996; contbr. numerous articles to profl. jours. Named to Outstanding Young Women in Am., 1981; grantee S.W. State U., 1977, 78, 79, 84, 85, Calif. State Poly. U., 1988, 89, 90, 91, Calif. Restaurant Assn., 1991; Maternal and Child Health fellow Dept. Pub. Health, U. Minn., Mpls., 1975-76, Nat. Inst. Foodsvc. Industry fellow, 1983. Mem. Am. Dietetic Assn. (registered), Calif. Dietetic Assn., Am. Culinary Fedn., Chefs de Cuisine, Nat. restaurant Assn., Calif. Restaurant Assn., Hospitality and Tourism Educators, Pacific Hospitality and Tourism Educators, Roundtable for Women in Foodsvc. (Pace Setter award 1991). Office: Calif Poly State Univ Sch Hotel/Restaurant Mgmt 3801 W Temple Ave Pomona CA 91768-2557

KAPP, ELEANOR JEANNE, impressionistic artist, writer, researcher; b. Hagerstown, Md., Oct. 16, 1933; d. James Norman and Nellie Belle (Welty) Weagley; m. Alan Howard Kapp, Sept. 25, 1972. Cert., L.A. Interior Design, 1969; student, U. Utah, 1976-82. Artist Farmers Ins. Group, L.A., 1960-63; interior designer W&J Sloane, Beverly Hills, Calif., 1965-70; ski resort exec. Snowpine Lodge, Alta, Utah, 1970-84; dir. mktg. and pub. rels. Alta Resort Assn., 1979-84; free-lance photographer Alta, 1979—; bus. owner Creative Art Enterprises, Sandy, Utah, 1984-85; artist-resident Collector's Corner Art Gallery, San Ramon, Calif., 1991—; owner Art of Jeanne Kapp, Lafayette, Calif., 1985—; artist-resident St. Germain Gallery, Tiburon, Calif., 1993—, Regional Art Ctr. Gift Store, Walnut Creek, Calif., 1994—, Valley Art Ctr., Walnut Creek, 1995—. Author, pub.: The American Connection, 1985, 91; author, prodr. (documentary) A Look at China Today, 1981; photographer: Best of the West, 1983. Promotion liaison Alta Town Coun., 1980-84; floral decorator Coun. State Govts., Snowbird, Utah, 1976; photographer Utah Dems., Salt Lake City, 1981; exhibit curator Salt Lake County Libr. System, 1982, founder Alta Br. Libr., 1982; fundraiser Friends of Libr., Alta, 1982; mem. Alta Town-Libr. Adv. Bd., 1983. Recipient Cert. of Appreciation, Salt Lake County Libr. System, 1981, Cert. of Recognition, Gov. Cal Rampton, Salt Lake City, 1972-74, Calendar Cover award Utah Travel Coun., 1981, Internat. Invitational Art Exhibit, Centre Internat. D'Art Contemporain, Paris, 1983. Mem. Internat. Platform Assn., Diablo Art Assn. (pub. rels. chmn. 1987, Hon. Mention award 1989), Concord Art Assn. (qst pl. award 1991), Alamo and Danville Artist's Soc. (cir. leader 1990—, hon. Mention award 1991, chmn. art exhbn. 1993, chmn. art program 1994), Las Junas Artist Assn. (juror's asst. 1992, 2d pl. award 1992, curator art exhbn., vol. Contra Costa County, Calif. Libr.-Main Br., 1995—, Ann. 1st pl. award 1995). Home: 411 Donegal Way Lafayette CA 94549-1707

KAPPY, MICHAEL STEVEN, pediatrics educator; b. Bklyn., Feb. 8, 1940; s. Jack and Lilyan (Banchefsky) K.; children: Douglas Bruce, Gregory Louis. BA, Johns Hopkins U., 1961; MD, PhD, U. Wis., 1967. Asst. prof. U. Ariz. Med. Sch., Tucson, 1975-78; fellow pediatric endocrinology Johns Hopkins Hosp., Balt., 1978-80; assoc. prof. U. Fla. Med. Sch., Gainesville, 1980-85; clin. prof. U. Ariz. Med. Sch., Tucson, 1985-94; med. dir. Children's Health Ctr., Phoenix, 1985-94; prof. pediatrics U. Colo. Health Sci. Ctr., Denver, 1994—; chief pediatric endocrinology The Children's Hosp., Denver, 1994—. Editor: (jour.) Today's Child, 1985, (book) Wilkins-The Diagnosis and Treatment of Endocrine Disorders in Children and Adolescents, 1994. Med. advisor Am. Diabetes Assn., Phoenix, 1985-94; bd. dirs. Ronald McDonald House, Phoenix, 1987-94. Mem. Assn. Pediatric Program Dirs. (pres. 1992-94), Soc. for Pediatric Rsch., Endocrine Soc., Am. Acad. Pediatrics, Physicians for Social Responsibility, Alpha Omega Alpha. Home: 483 Josephine St Denver CO 80206-4208 Office: The Childrens Hosp 1056 E 19th Ave # B-265 Denver CO 80218-1007

KARABAY, ADNAN SAMI, artist; b. Ankara, Turkey, Jan. 4, 1957; came to the U.S., 1960; s. Vecihi and Sylvia (Catala) K. BA in Econs., UCLA, 1976. Tchr. Am. Acad. Interior Design, Seattle, 1979-82; interior designer L'Ermitage Hotels Internat., L.A., 1985-92; costume designer Noel Taylor, L.A., 1986-94; pvt. practice artist L.A., 1990—. Works exhibited 8 times in Tiffany & Co. window displays, at Entre-Nous Gallery, Vancouver, B.C., Can., 1992, Dyansen Gallery, Beverly Hills, Calif., 1992, C.F. M. Gallery, N.Y.C., 1993-95, Stricoff Fine Arts, N.Y.C., 1994, Edith Lambert Gallery, Santa Fe, 1995, Mus. of Miniatures, L.A., Rosalie Whyel Mus. Doll Art, Seattle, Demi Moore Mus. Doll Art, Sun Valley, Utah, Santa Barbara Mus. Art, Musée de Neuilly, Paris; subject of numerous articles on doll art. Named Boy of the Yr., YMCA, Manhattan, 1967. Mem. Am. Soc. Interior Design (cert.). Home and Office: 1414 N Fairfax Ave Apt 204 Los Angeles CA 90046-3928

KARABELA, LEDA, public relations and fund raising executive; b. Thessaloniki, Greece, Dec. 8, 1957; came to U.S., 1980; children: Thano, Julie. LLB in Jurisprudence, Aristotelian U. Law Sch., Greece, 1970; MS in Pub. Rels. with honors, Boston U., 1988; negotiation program for sr. execs., Inter U. Consortium, Harvard, MIT, Tufts U., 1991. Dir. alumni rels. Anatolia Coll. Office of Trustees, Boston, 1983-87; cons. to dir. mktg., client rels. Sullivan & Worcester Law Office, Boston, 1987-88; dir. ops. BBB, Inc., Boston, 1988-89; account exec. BBK Advt., Pub. Rels., Chestnut Hill, Mass., 1989-95; dir. mktg., comms., major gifts Alta Bates Med. Ctr. Found., Berkeley, Calif., 1990-96; dir. comm. Stanford computer industry project Stanford (Calif.) U., 1996—. Mem. Pub. Rels. Soc. Am. (accredited pub. relations professional). Nat. Soc. Fund Raising Execs. (cert.), Assn. of Healthcare Philantrophy. Office: Stanford University Stanford Computer Ind Proj Grad Sch of Business Stanford CA 94305-5015

KARAKEY, SHERRY JOANNE, financial and real estate investment company executive, interior designer; b. Wendall, Idaho, Apr. 16, 1942; d. John Donald and Vera Ella (Frost) Kingery; children: Artist Roxanne, Buddy (George II), Kami JoAnne, Launi JoElla. Student, Ariz. State U., 1960. Corp. sec., treas. Karbel Metals Co., Phoenix, 1963-67; sec. to pub. Scottsdale (Ariz.) Daily Progress, 1969-72; with D-Velco Mfg. of Ariz., Phoenix, 1959-62, dir., exec. v.p., sec., treas., 1972-87; mng. ptnr. Karitage, Ltd., Scottsdale, 1987—.

KARALIS, JOHN PETER, computer company executive, lawyer; b. Mpls., July 6, 1938; s. Peter John and Vivian (Deckas) K.; m. Mary Curtis, Sept. 7, 1963; children: Amy Curtis, Theodore Curtis. BA, U. Minn., 1960, JD, 1963. Bar: Minn. 1963, Mass. 1972, Ariz. 1983, N.Y. 1986, Pa. 1986. Pvt. practice Mpls., 1963-70; assoc. gen. counsel Honeywell Inc., Mpls., 1970-83, v.p., 1982-83; pvt. practice Phoenix, 1983-85; sr. v.p., gen. counsel Sperry Corp., N.Y.C., 1985-87; v.p. gen. counsel Apple Computer Inc., Cupertino, Calif., 1987-89; of counsel Brown and Bain, Phoenix, 1989-92; sr. v.p. corp. devel. Tektronix, Inc., Portland, 1992—; bd. dirs. Sony/Tektronix Corp., Merix Corp.; mem. bd. advisors Ctr. for Study of Law, Sci. and Tech., Ariz. State U. Coll. Law, Tempe, 1983—, adj. prof., 1990-91. Author: International Joint Ventures, A Practical Guide, 1992. Recipient Disting. Achievement award Ariz. State U., Tempe, 1985. Mem. Met. Club (N.Y.C.), Gainey Ranch Golf Club.

KARAS, GENE ARTHUR, secondary education educator; b. Lamar, Colo., July 2, 1931; s. Arthur and Hazel Irene (Wilson) K.; m. Ruth Louise Newman, Dec. 15, 1951; children: David Lee, Daniel Gene, Alexandria. BA, U. No. Colo., Greeley, 1958, MA, 1966; Adminstr., U. No. Ill., 1973. Cert. tchr. Tchr. Lakewood (Colo.) Jr. H.S., 1958-59, Cottonwood (Ariz.) Children's Home, 1959-60, Mapleton Sch. Dist., Thorton, Colo., 1960-67; ednl. trainer Uni-Royal Corp., Joliet, Ill., 1967-68; tchr. Glenbard Sch. Dist., Glen Ellyn, Ill., 1968-77, Union City (Calif.) H.S., 1980-82, West Samona County Union H.S. Dist., Sebastopol, Calif., 1985—; salesman Envirotherm, San Rafael, CAlif., 1977-80; owner Tidy Car, San Rafael, 1980-81. Co-author: (math. text) Beginning Math, 1981. Sgt. 1st Class USAF, 1950-51. Named Coord. of Yr., Ill. Dept. Edn., 1977, Outstanding Tech. Tcrh. Calif. Dept. Edn., Sacramento, 1989. Mem. Calif. Indsl. and Tech. Edn. Assn. (pres. N.W. sect. 1995-96, Classroom Tchr. of Yr. 1995), Internat. Tech. Edn. Assn. (Classroom Tchr. of Yr. 1996), Sonoma County Bus. Edn. Roundtable, Calif.-Vocat. Indsl. Clubs Am. (Ill. State dir., 1973-76), Calif., Regional Coord., 1994—. Home: 27 Yosemite Rd San Rafael CA 94903-2275 Office: Sonoma County Office Edn 5340 Skylane Blvd Santa Rosa CA 95403-1082

KARASA, NORMAN LUKAS, home builder, developer, geologist; b. Balt., June 10, 1951; s. Norman and Ona K.; m. Lois J. Hansen, Jan. 4, 1974; children: Andrew, Jane. AB in Geology, Rutgers Coll., 1973; MS in Geophysics, U. Wyo., 1976; MBA in Fin., U. Colo., Colorado Springs, 1990. Systems mgr. Brit. Petroleum, N.Y.C., 1973-74; seismic processing leader Phillips Petroleum, Bartlesville, Okla., 1976-79; geophysicist Phillips Petroleum, Houston, 1979-80; internat. spl. project geophysicist Marathon Oil, Findlay, Ohio, 1980-82; internat. exploration geophysicist Marathon Oil, Houston, 1982-85, internat. reservoir geologist/geophysicist, 1985-86; home builder, designer, owner D'signer Inc., Monument Homes, Colo., 1986—, developer, hydrologist, 1992—; owner Tri-Lakes Montessori Sch.; lic. stock broker, ins. advisor Prin. Group, Colo., 1987—; realtor ReMax. Active Boy Scouts Am., Colo., 1987—. Mem. Home Builder Assocs. Presbyterian. Office: Monument Homes PO Box 1423 Monument CO 80132-1423

KARATZ, BRUCE E., business executive; b. Chgo., Oct. 10, 1945; s. Robert Harry and Naomi Rae (Goldstein) K.; m. Janet Louise Dreisen, July 28, 1968; children: Elizabeth, Matthew, Theodore. BA, Boston U., 1967; JD, U. So. Calif., 1970. Bar: Calif. 1971. Assoc. Keatinge & Sterling, Los Angeles, 1970-72; assoc. corp. counsel Kaufman and Broad, Inc., Los Angeles, 1972-73; dir. forward planning Kaufman and Broad, Inc., Irvine, Calif., 1973-74; pres. Kaufman and Broad Provence, Aix-en-Provence, France, 1974-76, Kaufman and Broad France, Paris, 1976-80, Kaufman and Broad Devel. Group, Los Angeles, 1980-86; pres., chief exec. officer Kaufman and Broad Home Corp., Los Angeles, 1985—, also bd. dirs., also chmn. bd. dirs., 1993; bd. dirs. Nat. Golf Properties, Inc., Honeywell Inc.; trustee Rand Corp., Nat. Park Found. Founder Mus. Contemporary Art, L.A., 1981; trustee Pitzer Coll., Claremont, Calif., 1983—; bd. councilors U. So. Calif. Law Ctr. Mem. Young Pres.' Orgn., Calif. Bus. Roundtable, Coun. on Fgn. Rels., Pacific Coun. on Internat. Policy. Democrat. Office: Kaufman & Broad Home Corp 10990 Wilshire Blvd 7th Flr Los Angeles CA 90024-3913*

KARCZEWSKI, RAYMOND RONALD, writer, philosopher; b. Chgo., Sept. 23, 1937; s. Raymond Joseph and Esther Loretta (Nawracaj) K.; m. Anita Louise Graves, Oct. 25, 1958; children: Kathryn Lynne, Lisa Lynne, David Michael. AA in Liberal Arts, Skyline Coll., San Bruno, Calif., 1970. Police officer Pacifica (Calif.) Police Dept., 1962-65, sgt., patrol shift commdr., 1965-68, sgt., investigator, 1968-70; owner, mgr. Pacific Coast Investigations and Security, Pacifica, 1970-82; ret., 1982; represented by Ark Enterprises Pub., Cave Junction, Oreg., 1993—; arms instr., range officer Pacifica Police Dept. Author: (books) Journey Beyond Thought, 1993, Christs with Amnesia, 1995. Bd. dirs., chmn. citizen's adv. bd., Youth Svc. Bur. 1969; advisor Police Explorer Scouts, Boy Scouts Am. With U.S. Army, 1956-57, Korea. Office: Ark Enterprises Pub PO Box 1870 Cave Junction OR 97523

KARDINAL, ROYCE ANN, hotel executive; b. Long Beach, Calif., May 17, 1944; d. Roy Perry and Betty Lois (Randolph) Coxwell; m. Glenn Roy Kardinal, Aug. 17, 1965; children: Kimberly, Kristan, Kelsea. AA in Interior Design, Woodbury Coll., L.A., 1966. Cert. hotel adminstrn. Gen. mgr. Great Western Hosts, Wickenburg, Ariz., 1966-79; mng. ptnr. Best Western Rancho Grande, Wickenburg, 1979—. Co-author: The Rightside Up Town on the Upside Down River, 1974. Trustee Ariz. Hotel Found., Phoenix, 1993—; chmn. bd. Desert Caballeros Mus., Wickenburg, 1990-91; pres., bd. trustees Wickenburg Sch. Bd., 1989—; pres. Las Senoras de Socorro, Wickenburg, 1974, 95; chmn. bd. Wickenburg Film Commn.; co-chmn. Tourism Authority, 1996—; trustee Wickenburg Found. Ednl. Enrichment, 1990-96; adult advisor Internat. Order Rainbow Girls, 1980-95; mem. steering com. Wickenburg Town Forum, 1996; mem. Las Damas, 1968—. Recipient Silver Spur, Desert Caballeros, 1995, Harry T. Needham award Desert Caballeros Western Mus., 1992; named Citizen of the Yr., Wickenburg C. of C., 1991, Woman of the Yr., Bus. and Profl. Women, 1985. Mem. Ariz. Hotel/Motel Assn. (pres. 1992-93), Best Western Internat. (dist. gov. 1992—), Am. Hotel/Motel Assn. (ho. of dels. 1995—). Episcopalian. Home: One Redbird Hill Wickenburg AZ 85390 Office: Best Western Rancho Grande 293 E Wickenburg Way Wickenburg AZ 85390

KARELITZ, RAYMOND, secondary school educator and writer; b. Fontainebleau, France, Nov. 11, 1952; came to U.S., 1957; s. Mitchell and Gabriella (Kaiser) K. BA cum laude, U. Hawaii, 1974, MA, 1975, Profl. Diploma, 1992. Tchr. St. Louis Sch., Honolulu, 1984-85, 89-90, 1994—; tchr. Farrington High Sch., Honolulu, 1990—; pres., instr. Verbal and Math (SAT) Program, Honolulu, 1986—; pub. Hi-Lite Pub. Co., Honolulu, 1991—; pres. Golden Memories Cookies, Inc., Honolulu, 1983-84, Goin' Back Enterprises, Honolulu, 1976-84; lectr. Leeward C.C., Honolulu, 1976-78; tutor Verbal and Math Enrichment Program, Honolulu, 1984-93; condr. workshops in field. Author: Understanding the SAT in 10 Easy Lessons,

1991, Rock Lyrics Trivia Quiz Book, 1993, Hi-Lite Series Vocabulary Program, 1993, The New SAT in 10 Easy Steps, 1994, Rock Lyrics Quiz Book, 1994, Karelitz Dictionary of One-Word Definitions, 1994, (novels) Fear None But the Innocent, From the Other Side, Even Odds, 1994. Office: Hi-Lite Publishing Co PO Box 240161 Honolulu HI 96824-0161

KARI, DAVEN MICHAEL, religion educator; b. Hot Springs, S.D., Sept. 24, 1953; s. John Nelson and Corinna Nicolls (Morse) K.; m. Priya Perianayakam, Apr. 4, 1988; children: David Prem, Daniel Michael, Dante Gabriel. BA in English, Bibl. Studies, History, Fresno Pacific Coll., 1975, BA in Music, 1977; MA in English, Baylor U., 1983; MA, PhD in English, Purdue U., 1985, 86; MDiv, PhD, So. Bapt. Theol. Sem., 1988, 91. Lic. to ministry So. Bapt. Ch., 1971, ordained to ministry, 1996. Photography studio technician Johnson's Studio, Manteca, Calif., 1975-77; grad. teaching asst. Baylor U., Waco, Tex., 1978-79; minister of music Calvary Bapt. Ch., West Lafayette, Ind., 1984-85; grad. teaching asst. Purdue U., West Lafayette, Ind., 1979-85; lectr. in English Jefferson C.C., Louisville, 1987-90, Spalding U., Louisville, 1986-90, U. Louisville, 1986-90; asst. prof. English Mo. Bapt. Coll., St. Louis, 1991; assoc. prof. Christian ministry and fine arts, dir. Christian Ministry Ctr., Calif. Bapt. Coll., Riverside, 1991—. Author: T. S. Eliot's Dramatic Pilgrimage, 1990, Bibliography of Sources in Christianity and the Arts, 1995; co-editor: Learning from Beauty: Baptist Reflections on Christianity and the Arts, 1997. Founder, co-dir. local Boys Brigade, Linden, Calif., 1969-71; asst. pastor Linden (Calif.) First Bapt. Ch., 1971; chair transp. com. Calvary Bapt. Ch., West Lafayette, 1982-83, dir. singles ministry, 1983-85; moderator Scholar's Bowl Quiz Contest, Riverside, 1993-94. Recipient Lit. Criticism award Purdue U., 1983; named to Outstanding Young Men Am., 1985; named Faculty Mem. of Yr., Calif. Bapt. Coll., 1993. Mem. Nat. Coun. Tchrs. English, Am. Acad. Religion, Conf. on Christianity and Lit., Conf. Coll. Composition and Comm. Democrat. Baptist. Home: 23878 Bouquet Canyon Pl Moreno Valley CA 92557-2956

KARIMI, SIMIN, linguist, educator; b. Tehran. BA in German Lang. and Lit., U. Tehran, 1973, MA in Gen. Linguistics, 1976; PhD in Linguistics, U. Wash., 1989. Asst. prof. U. Ariz., 1990—; mem. cognitive sci. program, linguistics and anthropology joint degree program U. Ariz., Tucson, 1991—; mem. numerous acad. coms.; lectr. and cons. in field; presenter workshops. Contbr. articles to profl. publs. Recipient scholarship Ministry of Higher Edn. in Iran, 1976, Grad. Sch. Tuition scholar U. Wash., 1986, SBS Rsch. Professorship, 1994; Travel grantee U. Ariz., 1993. Mem. Soc. Iranian Studies, Linguistic Soc. Am., MId. Ea. Studies Assn. Office: Dept Linguistics Univ Ariz Tucson AZ 85721

KARL, GEORGE, professional basketball coach; b. Penn Hills, Pa., May 12, 1951; m. Cathy Karl; children—Kelci Ryanne, Coby Joseph. Grad., U. N.C., 1973. Guard San Antonio Spurs, NBA, 1973-78, asst. coach, head scout, 1978-80; coach Mont. Golden Nuggets, Continental Basketball Assn., 1980-83; dir. player acquisition Cleve. Cavaliers, 1983-84, coach, 1984-86; head coach Golden State Warriors, Oakland, Calif., from 1986, Albany (N.Y.) Patrons, 1988-89, 90-91, Real Madrid, Spain, 1991-92, Seattle Supersonics, 1992—. Named Coach of Yr., Continental Basketball Assn., 1981, 83. Mem. Continental Basketball Assn. Office: care Seattle Supersonics 190 Queen Anne Ave N Ste 200 Seattle WA 98109-4926*

KARLEN, PETER HURD, lawyer, writer; b. N.Y.C., Feb. 22, 1949; s. S. H. and Jean Karlen; m. Lynette Ann Thwaites, Dec. 22, 1978. BA in History, U. Calif., Berkeley, 1971; JD, U. Calif., Hastings, 1974; MS in Law and Soc., U. Denver, 1976. Bar: Calif. 1974, Hawaii 1989, Colo. 1991, U.S. Dist. Ct. (so. dist.) Calif. 1976, U.S. Dist. Ct. (no. dist.) Calif. 1983, U.S. Dist. Ct. (Hawaii) 1989, U.S. Supreme Ct. 1990. Assoc. Sankary & Sankary, San Diego, 1976; teaching fellow Coll. of Law U. Denver, 1974-75; lectr. Sch. of Law U. Warwick, United Kingdon, 1976-78; pvt. practice La Jolla, Calif., 1979-86; prin. Peter H. Karlen, P.C., La Jolla, 1986—; adj. prof. U. San Diego Sch. of Law, 1979-84; mem. adj. faculty Western State U. Coll. of Law, San Diego, 1976, 79-80, 88, 92. Contbg. editor Artweek, 1979-95, Art Calendar, 1989—, Art Cellar Exch. mag., 1989-92; mem. editl. bd. Copyright World, 1988—, IP World, 1997—; contbr. numerous articles to profl. jours. Mem. Am. Soc. for Aesthetics, Brit. Soc. Aesthetics. Office: 1205 Prospect St Ste 400 La Jolla CA 92037-3613

KARLTON, LAWRENCE K., federal judge; b. Bklyn., May 28, 1935; s. Aaron Katz and Sylvia (Meltzer) K.; m. Mychelle Stiebel, Sept. 7, 1958 (dec.). Student, Washington Sq. Coll., 1952-54; LL.B., Columbia U., 1958. Bar: Fla. 1958, Calif. 1962. Acting legal officer Sacramento Army Depot, Dept. Army, Sacramento, 1958-60; civilian legal officer Sacramento Army Depot, Dept. Army, 1960-62; individual practice law Sacramento, 1962-64; mem. firm Abbott, Karlton & White, 1964, Karlton & Blease, 1964-71, Karlton, Blease & Vanderlaan, 1971-76; judge Calif. Superior Ct. for Sacramento County, 1976-79, U.S. Dist. Ct. (ea. dist.) Calif., Sacramento, 1979—; formerly chief judge U.S. Dist. Ct., Sacramento, 1983-90. Co-chmn. Central Calif. council B'nai B'rith Anit-Defamation League Commn., 1964-65; treas. Sacramento Jewish Community Relations Council, chmn., 1967-68; chmn. Vol. Lawyers Commn. Sun Valley ACLU, 1964-76. Mem. Am. Bar Assn., Sacramento County Bar Assn., Calif. Bar Assn., Fed. Bar Assn., Fed. Judges Assn., 9th Cir. Judges Assn. Club: B'nai B'rith (past pres.). Office: US Dist Ct 2012 US Courthouse 650 Capitol Mall Sacramento CA 95814-4708

KARPELES, DAVID, museum director; b. Santa Barbara, Calif., Jan. 26, 1936; s. Leon and Betty (Friedman) K.; m. Marsha Mirsky, June 29, 1958; children: Mark, Leslie, Cheryl, Jason. BS, U. Minn., 1956, postgrad., 1956-59; MA, San Diego State U., 1962; postgrad., U. Calif., Santa Barbara, 1965-69. Founder Karpeles Manuscript Libr. Mus., Montecito, Calif., 1983—; dir., founder Karpeles Manuscript Libr. Mus., Santa Barbara, Calif., 1988—, N.Y.C., 1990—, Tacoma, Wash., 1991—, Jacksonville, Fla., 1992—, Duluth, Minn., 1993—, Charleston, S.C., 1995—, Buffalo, 1995—; founder, dir. 102 mini-museums throughout U.S. and Can.; established the 1st cultural literacy program, presented to schs. by respective mus. staffs, 1993—. Creator program to provide ownership of homes to low-income families, 1981. Recipient Affordable Housing Competition award Gov. Edmund G. Brown Jr., State of Calif., Dept. Housing and Community Devel., 1981. Jewish. Home: 465 Hot Springs Rd Santa Barbara CA 93108-2029

KARPENKO, VICTOR NICHOLAS, mechanical engineer; b. Harbin, China, Jan. 23, 1922; s. Nicholas Stephan and Sophia Andrea (Kootas) K.; came to U.S., 1941, naturalized, 1943; student San Francisco State Coll., 1941-42, Oreg. State Coll., 1943; B.S. in Mech. Engring., U. Calif., Berkeley, 1948; m. Lydia Kamotsky, June 23, 1950; children—Victor, Mark, Alexandra. Staff engr. Atomic Products Equipment div. Gen. Electric Co., San Jose, Calif., 1956-57; project engr. nuclear explosives engring. Lawrence Livermore (Calif.) Lab., 1957-65, sect. leader nuclear explosives engring., 1965-66, div. leader Nuclear Test Engring. div., 1966-76, project mgr. Mirror Fusion Test Facility, 1976-85; div. head Magnet System Superconducting Super Collider, Univ. Research Assn., Berkeley, Calif., 1986-87, cons. tech. and mgmt., 1987—; ptnr. devel. cryogenic equipment PHPK Tech. Inc., Columbus, Ohio, 1992—; mem. fusion reactor safety com. Dept. Energy; mem. Containment Evaluation Panel, ERDA. Dist. chmn. U. Calif. Alumni Scholarship Program, 1976-80; com. mem. U. Calif. Alumni Scholarship Program, 1972-76; pres. San Ramon AAU Swim Club, 1964. Served with AUS, 1943-46. Registered profl. mech. and nuclear engr., Calif. Mem. Am. Nuclear Soc., Calif. Alumni Assn. Republican. Greek Orthodox. Home: 613 Bradford Pl Danville CA 94526-2357

KARPILOW, CRAIG, physician; b. San Francisco, Oct. 23, 1947; s. David and Babette (David) K.; BSc, U. Alta. (Can.), 1967; MA, U. So. Calif., 1970; MD, Dalhousie U., 1974. Diplomate Canadian Coll. of Family Practice. Intern, Dalhousie U., Halifax, N.S., Can., 1974-75; resident in family practice medicine Meml. U. Nfld., St. John's, 1975-77; practice medicine specializing in family medicine and occupational medicine, 1978-95; practice occupational medicine, Snohomish, Wash., 1981-83; med. health officer Storey County, Nev., 1978-80; med. dir. Med. Ctr., Dayton, 1978-81; pres. Internat. Profl. Assocs. Ltd., 1978—; med. dir./clin. N.W. Occupational Health Ctrs., Seattle, 1983-84; ptnr. physician, co-dir. CHEC Med. Ctr., Seattle, 1984-85; head dept. occupational and diagnostic medicine St. Cabrini Hosp., Seattle, 1984-86; med. dir. N.W. Indsl. Health Svcs., 1985-86, Queen Anne Med. Ctr., Seattle, 1985-95, Travel Med. and Immunization Clinic of Seattle, 1986-94; ptnr. Clin. Assocs., 1990-95. Diplomate Am. Bd. Family Practice; licenciate Med. Coll. Can. Author: Occupational Medicine in The International Workplace, 1991, Handbook of Occupational Medicine, 1994. Fellow Am. Acad. Family Practice, Am. Coll. Occupational & Environmental Medicine, Royal Soc. Tropical Medicine, Am. Coll. Occupational Medicine (recorder Ho. of Dels./bd. dirs. 1990-91); mem. AMA, Am. Soc. Tropical Medicine and Hygiene, Wash. State Med. Assn. King County Med. Soc., Wash. Acad. Family Physicians (rsch. collaborative, Com. on Rsch.), Am. Coll. Occupational and Environ. Medicine (chmn. internat. occupational medicine sect.), N.W. Occupational Med. Assn. (bd. dirs. 1985-92, 95—, pres. 1990-91), Can. Soc. for Internat. Health, Can. Pub. Health Assn., Am. Com. Clin., Tropical and Travel Medicine, Can. Soc. of Northwest, Marimed Found. Pacific N.W. (adv. bd.), Seattle Swiss Soc., Finnish Soc., Corinthian Yacht Club, Nature Conservancy, Rotary (bd. dirs., chmn. internat. rels. com., chmn. Hepatis Project, chmn. Malaria Project), U. So. Calif. Alumni assn., Kappa Sigma.

KARPISEK, MARIAN ELLEN, librarian; b. Dover, Ohio, May 8, 1938; d. Samuel C. and Ruth E. (Meese) Ream; m. Robert L. Karpisek, Aug. 13, 1960; children: Kristine L., Jennifer L. Karpisek Storie. BS in Elem. Edn., Miami U., 1960; MS in Edn., U. Utah, 1975, adminstrv. cert., 1984. Cert. tchr. 3rd grade tchr. Lower Twp. Consolidated Schs., Cape May, N.J., 1960-61; 1st grade tchr. Denver Pub. Schs., 1961-64; 6th grade tchr. Mayfield Hts. (Ohio) Sch. Dist., 1968-69; libr. media specialist Riley Elem. Sch., Salt Lake City, Utah, 1970-72, E. High Sch., Salt Lake City, 1972-81; supr. libr. media svcs. Salt Lake City Sch. Dist., 1981-95; cons., script writer, author Pahrump, Nev., 1995—; adj. faculty Brigham Young U., 1985-92; mem. Utah Libr. Svcs. and Constrn. Act Bd., 1985-92, Utah Govs. Conf. on Libr. and Info. Svcs., 1990-91; grant reviewer Coll. Libr. Tech. and Coop. Grants Program, 1988-91, 93. Contbr. Utah sect. Reading for Young People, 1980, Making Self-Teaching Kits for Library Skills, 1983, Policy Making for School Library Media Programs, 1989; contbr. articles to profl. jours. Recipient Ralph D. Thomson scholarship U. Utah, 1975, USIA/ALA Libr. fellow in Trinidad and Tobago, 1996. Mem. Am. Libr. Assn. (active numerous coms. Am. Assn. Sch. Librs., John Cotton Dana Libr. Pub. Rels. award 1984), Utah Libr. Assn. (pres. 1993-94, Libr. of Yr. 1991), Utah Libr. Media Suprs. Assn. (chair 1986-89, 93-94), Utah Ednl. Libr. Media Assn. (Disting. Svc., award 1990), Phi Delta Kappa (treas. 1984-88, Outstanding Svc. award 1988). Home and Office: Apt 2168 6301 S Squaw Valley Rd Pahrump NV 89048-7949

KARPMAN, ROBERT RONALD, orthopedic surgeon; b. Phila., Nov. 18, 1952; s. Sol H. and Tillie C. (Ginsburg) K.; m. Laurel Ann Brody, May 29, 1977; children: Hannah Elizabeth, Jodi Gayle. BA magna cum laude, LaSalle Coll., Phila., 1973; MD, U. Pa., Phila., 1977; MBA, U. Phoenix, 1992. Diplomate Am. Bd. Orthopedic Surgeons. Intern U. Ariz. Health Scis. Ctr., Tucson, 1977-78, resident in orthopedic surgery, 1978-81; gen. surgery intern U. Ariz., Tucson, 1977-78; pvt. practice Phoenix, 1981-86; resident in orthopedic surgery U. Ariz., Tucson, 1978-81; dir. acad. affairs Maricopa Med. Ctr., Phoenix, 1992—; assoc. prof. dept. orthopedic surgery Med. Sch. Mayo; adj. prof. dept. biomed. engring. Ariz. State U., Phoenix, 1991—; clin. prof. surgery Coll. Medicine U. Ariz., Tucson, 1989-95, clin. prof. surgery, 1995—. Editor: Musculoskeletal Disorders in Aging, 1989; contbr. 30 articles to profl. jours., 1981. Fellow ACS, Royal Soc. Medicine, Am. Acad. Orthopedic Surgeons; mem. Am. Orthopedic Foot and Ankle Soc., Gerontol. Soc. Am., Acad. Orthopedic Soc. (pres.), Ariz. Geriatrics Soc. (pres. 1990-91). Jewish. Office: Maricopa Med Ctr 2601 E Roosevelt St Phoenix AZ 85008-4973

KARR, DAVID DEAN, lawyer; b. Denver, Sept. 3, 1953; s. Dean Speece and Jean (Ransbottom) K.; m. Laura A. Foster, Apr. 10, 1982; children: Emily Ann, Bradley Foster. BA, U. Puget Sound, 1975; JD, Loyola U., 1979. Bar: Colo. 1979, U.S. Dist. Ct. 1979, U.S. Ct. Appeals (10th cir.) 1981, U.S. Supreme Ct. 1983. Assoc. Pryor Carney & Johnson, P.C., Englewood, Colo., 1979-84, ptnr., 1984-95; ptnr. Pryor, Johnson, Montoya, Carney and Karr, P.C., Englewood, Colo., 1995—. Mem. ABA (lead atty. pro bono team death penalty project Tex. chpt. 1988—), Colo. Bar Assn. (interprofl. com. 1990—), Arapahoe County Bar Assn.. Denver Bar Assn. Home: 5474 E Hinsdale Cir Littleton CO 80122-2538 Office: Pryor Johnson Montoya Carney and Karr PC Ste 1313 6400 S Fiddlers Green Cir Englewood CO 80111-4741

KARR, MARIE ALINE CHRISTENSEN, executive; b. L.A., Oct. 28, 1952; d. William Doane and Lois Aline (Christensen) K. BA, Sonoma State U., 1975; MA, San Francisco State U., 1982. Editor city desk L.A. Times, 1975-78; free-lance journalist San Francisco & L.A., 1978—; tchr. L.A. Unified Sch. Dist., 1985-88, San Bernardino (Calif.) SanCLASS, 1989-93; dir. ComputED LearningLabs, Cardiff, Calif., 1993—; pres. San Diego Ctr. for Ednl. Tech., Cardiff, 1996—; chair lang. arts com. SanCLASS, San Bernardino, 1989-93, chair tech. com., 1990-93, mentor tchr., 1991-93; cons. in field. Contbr. articles to profl. jours. Chair Learning Labs. Office: ComputED/San Diego Ctr Ednl Tech 2611 S Highway 101 Ste 103 Cardiff By The Sea CA 92007-2112

KARRAS, DONALD GEORGE, tax administrator; b. Sioux City, Iowa, Dec. 23, 1953; s. George D. and Mary T. (Kyriakos) K.; m. Donna Lynn Ciripompa, Mar. 6, 1982; children: Dane Anthony, Dillon James. BA, Augustana Coll., 1977; MBA, U. S.D., 1980, JD, 1981. CPA, S.D. Bar: S.D. 1981. Instr. U. S.D. Sch. Bus., Vermillion, 1980-81; tax sr. acct. Deloitte Haskins & Sells, Denver, 1981-84; tax mgr. The Anschutz Corp., Denver, 1984-87; dir. taxes Kennecott Corp., Salt Lake City, 1988-92; v.p. taxes Newmont Mining Corp., Denver, 1992—. Mem. Colo. Pub. Expenditure Coun. Mem. ABA, S.D. Bar Assn., Tax Execs. Inst., Nat. Mining Assn. (fin. com.), Rocky Mountain Mineral Law Found., Colo. Mining Assn., Internat. Fiscal Assn., Nev. Mining Assn. Republican. Home: 7100 W Princeton Ave Denver CO 80235-3036 Office: Newmont Mining Corp One Norwest Ctr 1700 Lincoln St Denver CO 80203-4501

KARSTAEDT, ARTHUR R., III, lawyer; b. Madison, Wis., Sept. 15, 1951. BA, U. Wis., 1972; JD, U. Denver, 1975. Bar: Colo. 1976. Formerly lawyer Hall & Evans, Denver; ptnr. Harris, Karstaedt, Jamison & Powers, P.C., Englewood, Colo., 1995—. Office: Harris Karstaedt Jamison & Powers PC 5299 Dtc Blvd Ste 1130 Englewood CO 80111-3305

KASAMA, HIDETO PETER, accountant, advisor, real estate consultant; b. Tokyo, Nov. 21, 1946; came to U.S., 1969; s. Toshiyoshi and Hamako (Yoshioka) K.; m. Evelyn Patricia Cruz (div. Apr. 1990); children: Jennifer, Nicole, Leona; m. Heidi W. Snare, June 29, 1991; 1 child, Serena. BABA, Seattle U., 1971, MBA, 1973. CPA. Mgmt. trainee Security Pacific Bank, Seattle, 1972-74; audit supr. Ernst & Young, Seattle, 1974-79; pres. KASPAC Corp., Seattle, 1979-89; mng. ptnr. Kasama & Co., Seattle, 1980—. Contbr. articles to newspapers. Mem. AICPA, Wash. Soc. CPA's, Columbia Tower Club (founder). Home: 725 9th Ave S Edmonds WA 98020-3311 Office: Kasama & Co 3147 Fairview Ave E Ste 110 Seattle WA 98102-3041

KASAMATSU, ROBERT KEN, podiatric physician, surgeon, educator; b. L.A., June 16, 1962; s. Takao and Lillian (Yuriko) K.; m. Nancy Tam, Aug. 3, 1959. BS in Biology, UCLA, 1985; D of Podiatric Medicine, Ohio Coll. Podiatric Medicine, 1989; MS, Calif. Coll. Podiatric Medicine, 1990. Diplomate Am. Bd. Podiatric Orthopedic, Am. Acad. Pain Mgmt. Resident so. campus program Calif. Coll. of Podiatric Medicine, USC Med. Ctr., 1989-90; podiatry clinic dir. Century Freeway Med. Group, L.A., 1991—; owner Nursing Home Svcs., La Puente, Calif., 1991—, Coast Foot and Ankle, Inglewood, Calif., 1991—; podiatrist Extended Care Podiatry Group, Laguna Hills, Calif., 1995—; asst. prof., mem. staff Martin Luther King Jr. Hosp.; mem. staff Robert F. Kennedy Med. Ctr., 1995—, Hawthorne Hosp., 1992—, Surgictr. of South Bay, 1995—; asst. prof. Martin Luther King Jr. Hosp., 19996—. Recipient Recognition award Calif. State Senate, 1990, Recognition award Am. Acad. Family Physicians. Mem. Am. Bd. Podiatric Orthopedics and Primary Podiatric Medicine, Am. Acad. Pain Mgmt., Asian Am. Physicians Assn., Hawthorne Rotary (internat. svc. dir. 1995—). Democrat. Office: Coast Foot and Ankle 330 E Hillcrest Blvd Inglewood CA 90301-2406

KASARI, LEONARD SAMUEL, quality control professional, concrete consultant; b. Los Angeles, Sept. 22, 1924; s. Kustaa Adolph and Impi (Sikio) K.; m. Elizabeth P. Keplinger, Aug. 25, 1956; children: Lorraine Carol, Lance Eric. Student, Compton Coll., 1942-43, UCLA, 1964-70. Registered profl. engr., Calif. Gen. construction Los Angeles, 1946-61; supr. inspection service Osborne Labs., Los Angeles, 1961-64; mgr. customer service Lightweight Processing, Los Angeles, 1965-77; dir. tech. service Crestlite Aggregates, San Clemente, Calif., 1977-78; quality control mgr. Standard Concrete, Santa Ana, Calif., 1978-92. Camp dir. Torrance YMCA, High Sierras, Calif., 1969-80, mem. bd. mgrs., 1970—. Served with USN, 1943-46. Recipient Sam Hobbs Svc. award ACI-So. Calif., 1992; named Hon. Life Mem. Calif. PTA, 1983. Mem. Am. Concrete Inst., So. Calif. Structural Engrs. Assn. Democrat. Lutheran. Office: 2450 W 233rd St Torrance CA 90501-5730

KASBERGER-MAHONEY, ELVERA A., educational administrator; b. Oak Park, Ill., July 2, 1952; d. Lawrence and Aura Louise (Rutledge) Petrongelli; m. Daniel Mahoney, July 14, 1988. BA, Northeastern Ill. U., 1974, MA, 1978; grad., Calif. Sch. Leadership Acad., 1990. Tchr. Social Emotionally Disturbed Children Warren Twp. High Sch., Gurnee, Ill.; dean of students Adlai Stevenson High Sch., Prairie View, Ill.; asst. prin. Hesperia (Calif.) Unified Sch. Dist.; prin., supt. schs. San Bernardino County, 1988-90; asst. prin. Elsinore High Sch., Lake Elsinore, Calif., 1990-95, Temescal Canyon H.S., Elsinore, 1995-96; asst. prin. of student svcs. Jurupa Valley H.S., Jurupa Unified Sch. Dist., Mira Loma, Calif., 1996—. Chpt. I grantee; Job Tng. Partnership grantee. Mem. ASCD, Assn. Calif. Sch. Adminstrs., Coun. for Exceptional Children.

KASPER, CATHERINE LOUISE, poet, editor. BA with highest distinction, U. Ill., 1982; MA, U. Ill., Chgo., 1995; postgrad., U. Denver, 1995—. Pvt. pilot's lic., Ill. Mgr. Galway Bay Cottages Ltd., Galway, Ireland, 1982; store buyer, mgr. Prairie Ave. Bookstore, Chgo., 1985-88; mktg. dir. Schroeder, Murchie, Laya, Chgo., 1988-93; mktg. cons. Chgo., 1992-95; tchg. asst. U. Ill., Chgo., 1993-95, U. Denver, 1995-96; mng. editor Denver Quar., 1996—; book reviewer AIA, Chgo., 1988-93; cons. Gale Rsch., Detroit, 1996; mem. unit. textbook com. U. Ill., St. Martins Press, Bedford, Chgo. and Denver, 1995. Author/editor: (poetry chapbook) Poems, 1988; poetry pubs. Mid-Am. Rev., 1996. Vol. in constrn. Oz Park/City Park for Children, Chgo., 1992; co-designer doghouse for the blind Guidedogs for the Blind, 1988. Recipient Charles Goodnow award U. Ill.-Chgo., 1994; Colo. fellow U. Denver, 1995-96; James scholar U. Ill., 1981-82. Mem. MLA, Acad. Am. Poets, AWP. Office: Denver Quarterly Univ of Denver 422 Pioneer Hall Denver CO 80208

KASS, JEROME ALLAN, writer; b. Chgo., Apr. 21, 1937; s. Sidney J. and Celia (Gorman) K.; children from previous marriage: Julie, Adam; m. Delia Ephron, May 21, 1982. BA, NYU, 1958, MA, 1959. Playwright: Monopoly, 1965, Saturday Night, 1968, (mus.) Ballroom, 1978 (Tony nomination), (TV) A Brand New Life, 1973, Queen of the Stardust Ballroom, 1975 (Writers Guild Am. award, Emmy nomination), My Old Man, 1979, The Fighter, 1982, Scorned and Swindled, 1984, Crossing to Freedom (aka Pied Piper), 1989, Last Wish, 1991, The Only Way Out, 1993, Secrets, 1995; screenwriter: The Black Stallion Returns, 1981, (miniseries) Evergreen, 1985; author: Four Short Plays by Jerome Kass, 1966, Saturday Night, 1969. Mem. Dramatists Guild, Writers Guild Am., Phi Beta Kappa.

KASS, PHILIP HOWARD, epidemiology educator; b. L.A., Aug. 19, 1958; s. Leonard and Zita (Dunn) K.; m. Jan Carmikle, Oct. 14, 1961; children: Lauren, Alexander. DVM, U. Calif., Davis, 1983, M of Preventive Veterinary Medicine, 1984, MS in Stats., 1988, PhD in Epidemiology, 1990. Asst. prof. epidemiology U. Calif., Davis, 1990-95, assoc. prof. epidemiology, 1995—. Mem. Am. Coll. Vet. Preventive Medicine (sec. epidemiology specialty 1993-95), Am. Statis. Assn., Biometrics Soc., Am. Vet. Med. Assn., Soc. Epidemiologic Rsch., Calif. Acad. Vet. Medicine (bd. dirs. 1994-96). Home: 2760 Ottowa Ave Davis CA 95616-2928 Office: U Calif Sch Vet Medicine Sect Biometrics/Prev Med Dept Population Health Davis CA 95616

KASSAN, STUART S., rheumatologist; b. White Plains, N.Y., Nov. 19, 1946; s. Robert Jacob and Rosalind (Suchin) K.; m. Gail Karesh, Apr. 4, 1971; children: Michael Andrew, Merrill Alissa. BA, Case Western Res., 1968; MD, George Washington U., 1972. Diplomate Am. Bd. Internal Medicine, Am. Bd. Rheumatology, Am. Bd. Geriatrics. Intern and resident Grady Meml. Hosp., Altanta, 1972-74; clin. fellow NIH, Bethesda, Md., 1974-76; fellow Hosp. for Spl. Surgery, Cornell Med. Ctr., N.Y.C., 1976-78; head rheumatology clinic VA Med. Ctr., Denver, 1978-80; asst. clin. prof. medicine U. Colo. Health Scis. Ctr., Denver, 1978-84, assoc. clin. prof. medicine, 1984-94, clin. prof. medicine, 1994—; med. dir. rehab unit. Luth. Med. Ctr., Wheatridge, Colo., 1983-87; med. dir. rehab. unit St. Anthony Hosp., Denver, 1987-93; cons. Annals Internal Medicine, Phila., 1986—, Arthritis and Rheumatism, Atlanta, 1995—, Jour. of Rheumatology, 1996—; vis. alumni scholar George Washington U. Sch. Medicine, 1986; chmn. med. adv. bd. Sjögren's Syndrome Found., Jerico, N.Y., 1996—, bd. dirs, 1996—. Co-editor: Sjögren's Syndrome, 1987; contbr. over 25 articles to profl. jours. Bd. dirs. Rocky Mountain chpt. Arthritis Found., Denver, 1978-80, Polachek fellow, 1976-77; bd. dirs. Lupus Found. Colo., v.p., 1995-96, pres., 1996—; bd. dirs. Sjofer Syndrome Found., 1996—. With USPHS, 1974-76. Fellow ACP, Am. Coll. Rheumatology (network physician 1989); mem. Harvey Soc. Jewish. Office: Colo Arthritis Assoc 4200 W Conejos Pl Ste 314 Denver CO 80204-1311

KASSEBAUM, GENE GIRARD, sociology educator; b. St. Louis, June 24, 1929; s. John G. and Flora (Girard) K.; m. Gayathri Rajapur, Aug. 1966; 1 child, Krishna. AB, U. Mo., 1951; MA, Harvard U., 1955, PhD, 1958. Rsch. asst. Harvard U., Cambridge, Mass., 1954-57; rsch. assoc. Cornell U. Med. Ctr., N.Y. Hosp., N.Y.C., 1957-60, Sch. Pub. Health, UCLA, L.A., 1960-65; assoc. prof. Am. U. in Cairo, Egypt, 1965-68; prof. sociology U. Hawaii, Honolulu, 1968—, dir. ctr. youth rsch., 1993-95. Author: Delinquency and Social Policy, 1974; co-author: Women's Prison, 1965, Prison Treatment Parole Survival, 1971; contbr. articles to profl. jours. Cpl. U.S. Army, 1951-53. Sr. Fulbright scholar U.S. Dept. State, India, 1974, 81. Mem. Am. Soc. Criminology, Am. Sociol. Assn., Phi Beta Kappa. Office: Univ Hawaii 2424 Maile Way Honolulu HI 96822-2223

KASSNER, JAY EDWARD, small business owner; b. San Diego, July 6, 1943; s. Ewald George and Thelma Marie (Ernster) K.; m. Mary Lou Ness, Dec. 10, 1963; 1 child, Adam Wayne; m. Tammy Lynn Peden, Dec. 31, 1982; children: Brittany Michelle, Courtney Marie. BA in Bus. Adminstrn., U. Wash., 1971. Cert. mgmt. specialist, Wash. Acct. Sites & Co., Inc., Seattle, 1971-73; ptnr. Arctic World Ltd., Anchorage, 1972-75; owner Kassner & Assocs., Anchorage, 1976—; pres. Alaska Fishing Charters, Inc., Anchorage, 1990—; v.p. Interior Plant Designs, Inc., Anchorage, 1982—; pres. Norton Sound Constrn., Inc., Anchorage, 1992—; chmn., CEO K & R Enterprises, Inc., Anchorage, 1981—; bd. dirs. Trans-Pacific North, Inc., Kenai, Alaska, TLC Flooring, Inc., Anchorage. Editor: Who's Available, 1969; newspaper editor Jet City News, 1969. 1st lt. inf. U.S. Army, 1966-69; Vietnam. Decorated Bronze Star, Purple Heart; NSF scholar, 1960. Mem. Am. Legion, Elks, Eagles, Moose, Amvets, Mil. Order of Purple Heart. Republican. Lutheran.

KASSNER, MICHAEL ERNEST, materials science educator, researcher; b. Osaka, Japan, Nov. 22, 1950; (parents Am. citizens); s. Ernest and Clara (Christa) K.; m. Marcia J. Wright, Aug. 19, 1972 (div. Dec. 1976). BS, Northwestern U., 1972; MS, Stanford U., 1979, PhD, 1981. Metallurgist Sargent and Lundy Engrs., Chgo., 1977; metallurgist Lawrence Livermore (Calif.) Nat. Lab., 1981-90, head phys. metallurgy and joining sect., 1988-90; lectr. San Francisco State U., 1983; prof. Naval Postgrad. Sch., Monterey, Calif., 1984-86; prof., dir. grad. program in materials sci. Oreg. State U., Corvallis, 1990—, Chevron endowed prof., 1996; temporary assignment as project mgr. Office Basic Energy Scis., U.S. Dept. Energy, 1991-96; head DOE Ctr. for Excellence Synthesis and Processing of Materials, 1996—; vis. scholar dept. physics U. Groningen, Netherlands, 1985-87; vis. scholar dept. materials, sci. and engring. Stanford U., 1981-83; vis. prof. U. Calif., San Diego, 1997—. Author over 110 articles; author book on binary phase diagrams; editor various sci. jours. Lt. USN, 1972-76; lt. comdr. USNR, 1976-81. Fulbright scholar, The Netherlands. Mem. ASME, Am. Soc. Metals, The Metall. Soc., Materials Research Soc., Sigma Xi. Roman Catholic. Home: PO Box 269 Otter Rock OR 97369-0269

KASSOUF, ESTHER KAY, middle school education educator; b. Kinston, N.C., Apr. 19, 1950; d. William Gid and Josephine (Smith) Holland; m. John Michael Kassouf Jr., May 8, 1976. AS, Mt. Olive (N.C.) Jr. Coll., 1970; BS, Atlantic Christian Coll., 1972; MEd, U. Nev., 1990. Tchr. 6th grade Kinston City Pub. Schs., 1972-76; tchr. 5th, 7th, 8th grades Clark County Sch. Dist., Las Vegas, Nev., 1976—. Office: Clark County Sch Dist Helen Cannon Mid Sch Las Vegas NV 89121

KAST, BARRY, state agency administrator. Adminstr. mental health, DD divsn. Dept. Human Resources, Salem, Oreg., 1995—. Office: Dept Human Resources 2575 Bittern St NE Salem OR 97310

KASTELIC, FAY BARR, city official; b. Bowie, Tex., Feb. 28, 1918; d. Jim Martin and Manisa Pearlee Barr; m. Frank R. Kastelic, May 29, 1946 (dec. Dec. 15, 1975); children: Phillip M., Ted, Brien F. Student, U. Tex., 1939-42; BA, U. So. Colo., 1965; MEd, U. Colo., 1973. Tchr. Sch. Dist. #70, Pueblo, Colo., 1939-42, elem. sch. prin., 1974-81, dir. instrn., 1981-90; pres. Pueblo City Coun., 1992-96. Pres. Pueblo County Bd. for Devel. Disabilities, 1981—. Fulbright scholar, 1977; U. Tel Aviv travel grantee, 1978; Edward W. Hazen fellow Hazen Found., 1979; named FED PAC Outstanding Adminstr. for Children, State Dept. Edn., Denver, 1989. Mem. So. Colo. Alumni Assn. (Outstanding Svc. to Community award 1993), Colo. Mcpl. League (policy com. 1991—), Kiwanis (chair 1987), Beta Sigma Phi (pres.), Phi Delta Kappa (pres. 1981). Democrat. Baptist. Home: 841 Beulah Ave Pueblo CO 81004-1703 Office: City of Pueblo City Coun 1 City Hall Pl Pueblo CO 81003-4201*

KASTRUL, JEROME JOE, geriatrician; b. Chgo., Dec. 14, 1934; s. Sam and Gladys (Lipschitz) K.; m. May 19, 1967 (dec. June 1996); children: Sterling, Jenifer, Stephen, Patrick, Tamara, Michelle, David, Lisa. AB, U. Chgo., 1954; MD, Northwestern U., 1958. Diplomate Am. Bd. Internal Medicine. Med. dir. Phoenix (Ariz.) Geriatric Inst., 1964-93; staff physician Family and Sr. Care, Peoria, Ariz., 1993—; med. dir. Kivel Geriatric Ctr., Phoenix, 1982-90, Nova Home Health Care, Phoenix, 1989-93, Tempe (Ariz.) Adult Day Health Ctr., 1991—, Glendale (Ariz.) Adult Day Health Ctr., 1992—. Mem. Gov.'s Adv. Coun. on Aging, Phoenix, 1989-93, Gov.'s Alzheimer Adv. Com., Phoenix, 1991-93. Mem. ACP, Am. Geriatrics Soc., Ariz. Med. Soc. Home: 12014 N 60th Ave Glendale AZ 85304 Office: Family & Sr Care Peoria C-2 13660 N 94th Dr Peoria AZ 85381-4836

KASULKA, LARRY HERMAN, management consultant; b. Wagner, S.D., Apr. 5, 1940; s. Alfred E. and Lillian J. (Gasper) K.; m. Susan A. Smart, Sept. 8, 1962; children: Shawn L., Christine A. BS in Electronics, Northrop U., 1961; grad. cert. in bus. adminstrn., UCLA, 1969; grad. cert., Brookings Inst., 1986, Harvard U., 1989; PhD in Bus. Adminstrn., LaSalle U., 1995. Registered profl. engr., Calif. Electronic engr. Douglas Aircraft Co., 1962-77; unit chief avionics McDonnell Douglas Astronautics Co., 1977-81, br. chief avionics, 1981-84; dir. design engr. McDonnell Douglas Electronic Systems Co., 1984-87, dir. program mgmt., 1987-89, dir. new bus., 1989-91; spl. asst. U.S. Dept. Commerce, Office of the Dep. Sec., 1990-91; v.p., dep. gen. mgr. Kennedy Space Ctr. McDonnell Douglas Space Systems Co., 1991-93; v.p., gen. mgr. McDonnell Douglas Aerospace N.Mex. Ops., 1993-94; program mgr. McDonnell Douglas Aerospace, Huntingron Beach, Calif., 1994-96; mgmt. cons. L.H. Kasulka & Assocs., 1996—; presenter in field. Contbr. articles to profl. jours. Bd. dirs. Brevard Achievement Ctr., Rockledge, Fla., 1991-93; mentor Sci. Engrin. and Rsch. Career Help; mem. Pres. Commn. Exec. Exch. Alumni U. Calif.-L.A. Alumni. Recipient Dir.'s Safety award NASA KSC Ctr., 1992, Group Achievement award NASA JSC Ctr., 1995, Sr. Exec. Svc. award Dept. Commerce, 1990, commendation Inst. Soc. Am., 1983, White House Pres. Bush, 1990; named Outstanding Cadet, CAP-Internat. Aviation Cadet Exch.; named to Hon. Order Ky. Cols. Assoc. fellow AIAA; mem. Armed Forces and Comm. Elec. Assn., Nat. Man. Assn., Assn for Quality Participation, Am. Soc. Quality Control, UCLA Alumni Assn. (mem. Goal/9PC Pres.' Commn. on Exec. Exch. Alumni).

KASZNIAK, ALFRED WAYNE, neuropsychologist; b. Chgo., June 2, 1949; s. Alfred H. and Ann Virginia (Simonsen) K.; B.S. with honors, U. Ill., 1970, M.A., 1973, Ph.D., 1976; m. Mary Ellen Beaurain, Aug. 26, 1973; children: Jesse, Elizabeth. Instr. dept. psychology Rush Med. Coll., Chgo., 1974-76, asst. prof. dept. psychology, 1976-79; from asst. prof. to assoc. prof. dept. psychiatry U. Ariz. Coll. Medicine, Tucson, 1979-82, assoc. prof. dept. psychology and psychiatry, 1982-87; prof. depts. psychology, neurology and psychiatry, 1987—; chmn. U. Ariz. Commn. on Gerontology, 1990-93, acting head U. Ariz. dept. psychology, 1992-93; dir. U. Ariz. Clin. Psychology Program, U. Ariz. Coordinated Clin. Neuropsychology Program; dir. staff psychologist Presbyn.-St. Luke's Hosp., Chgo., 1976-79, Univ. Hosp., Tucson, 1979—; mem. human devel. and aging study sect. div. research grants NIH, 1981-86. Trustee So. Ariz. chpt. Nat. Multiple Sclerosis Soc., 1980-82; mem. med. and sci. adv. bd. Nat. Alzheimer's Disease and Related Disorders Assn., 1981-84; mem. VA Geriatrics and Gerontology Adv. Com., 1986-89, Ariz. Gov.'s Adv. Com. on Alzheimer's Disease, 1988-92; mem. med. adv. bd. Fan Kane Fund for Brain-Injured Children, Tucson, 1980-92. Grantee Nat. Inst. Aging, 1978-83, 89-94, NIMH, 1984-94, Robert Wood Johnson Found., 1986-89, Fetzer Inst., 1997—. Fellow Am. Psychol. Assn. (Disting. Contbr. award div. 20 1978, pres. clin. geropsychology sect. 1995), Am. Psychol. Soc.; mem. Internat. Neuropsychol. Soc., (bd gov's., 1994—), Gerontol. Soc. (rsch. fellow 1980). Author 3 books; mem. editorial bd. Psychology and Aging, 1984-87; The Clin. Neuropsychologist, 1986-96, Clin. Geropsychology, 1994—, Jour. Clin. and Exp. Neuropsychol., 1987-90, Jour Gerontology, 1988-92, Neuropsychology, 1992-93; contbr. articles to profl. jours. Home: 2327 E Hawthorne St Tucson AZ 85719-4944 Office: U Ariz Dept Psychology Tucson AZ 85721

KATCHUR, MARLENE MARTHA, nursing administrator; b. Belleville, Ill., Dec. 20, 1946; d. Elmer E. and Hilda B. (Gutherz) Wilde; m. Raymond J. Katchur, Feb. 22, 1969; 1 child, Nickolas Phillip. BSN, So. Ill. U., 1968; MS in Health Care Adminstrn., Calif. State U., L.A., 1982. RN; cert. critical care nurse. Staff nurse, head nurse, nursing supr. U. So. Calif Med. Ctr. LA County, 1968-81, assoc. dir. nursing, internal medicine nursing, 1981-83, internal medicine nursing info. systems coord., 1983-89, patient-centered info. systems cons., 1989-90, nursing info. systems cons. for pediatrics, psychiatry and ICU, 1990-92, psychiat. nursing svcs. human resources and info. systems, 1992-94; nursing supr. adminstrv. nursing office, 1994-95; nurse mgr. Gen. Hosp., 1995—. Mem. Sheriff's Relief Assn. Mem. AACCN, NAFE, AAUW, Nat. Critical Care Inst. Edn., Am. Heart Assn., So. Ill. U. Alumni Assn. (life), Health Svcs. Mgmt. Forum, Orgn. Nurse Execs. Calif. (membership com.), Am. Soc. Profl. and Exec. Women, Soc. Clin. Data Mgmt. Systems (bd. dirs. 1990-91), Soc. Med. Computer Observers (charter), Am. Legion Aux., Nat. Hist. Soc., Job's Daus. (past honor queen). Office: LA County U So Calif Med Ct 1200 N State St Los Angeles CA 90033-4525

KATEMOPOULOS, MILDRED JOSEPHINE, executive secretary; b. Shanghai, China, Apr. 29, 1925; came to the U.S., 1977; d. James Jeremiah and Camille Helmana (Barradas) O'Leary; m. Theodore Demetrius Katemopoulos, Apr. 29, 1946; children: Maureen, Eileen, Kathryn, Paul, Anne-Marie. Grad., Loretto H.S., Shanghai. Pvt. sec. Royal Netherlands Embassy, Shanghai, 1946-49; sec. to mng. dir. Dairy Farm Co., Hong Kong, 1949-58; confidential sec. H.K. Land Co., Hong Kong, 1958-66; writer Children's Page H.K. Sunday Std., Hong Kong, 1966-71; pub. rels. staff Mandarin Hotel, Hong Kong, 1970-73; asst. to CEO Regent Internat. Hotels, Hong Kong, 1974-77; sr. sec. Stanford Rsch. Inst., Menlo Park, Calif., 1977-79; asst. to CEO Cath. Charities, San Jose, Calif., 1981-89, Econ. and Social Opportunities, San Jose, 1989-94; adminstrv. asst. Christ United Presbyn. Ch., San Jose, 1995—; Author: Loretto School, 1990, Born in Shanghai, 1996, (book of poems) When Silver Turns to Gold, 1996. Chmn. Loretto Internat. in the Far East, Hong Kong, 1966-77; founder, pres. Tuesday Club of Hong Kong, 1970-77; pres. Little Flower Club, Hong Kong, 1972-77. Recipient resolution for decade of svc. to Cath. Charities, Bishop of San Jose, 1989. Roman Catholic.

KATH, VIKKI, public relations coordinator, writer; b. Raleigh, N.C., June 9, 1944; m. Robert Kinmont, Oct. 6, 1962 (div. Oct. 1, 1981); children: Ben, Anna McNamara, Seth. Grad., Ont. Coll. of Art, 1971; student, Sonoma State U., 1981, Santa Rosa (Calif.) Jr. Coll., 1991. Co-founder Coyote Fine Arts, Bishop, Calif., 1975-79; asst. to dean of faculty Carleton Coll., Northfield, Minn., 1986-90; ednl. ctr. coord. Glen Ellen Winery, Sonoma, Calif., 1991-93; non-profit devel. coord. Vine Village, Inc., Napa, Calif., 1995—; edn. cons. and dev. cons., Sonoma, 1993S. Author: Simple Foods for the Pack, 1972, rev. edit., 1986. Home: PO Box 81 Glen Ellen CA 95442-0081

KATHER, GERHARD, retired air force base administrator; b. Allenstein, Germany, Jan. 30, 1939; came to U.S., 1952, naturalized, 1959; s. Ernst and Maria (Kempa) K.; m. Carol Anne Knutsen, Aug. 18, 1962; children: Scott T., Cynthia M., Tracey S., Chris A.; m. Mary Elsie Frank, Oct. 25, 1980. BA in Govt., U. Ariz., 1964; MPA, U. So. Calif., 1971; cert. in personnel adminstrn., U. N.Mex., 1987. Tchr. social studies, Covina, Calif., 1965-67; tng. officer Civil Personnel, Ft. MacArthur, Calif., 1967-70; chief employee tng. and devel. Corps Engrs., L.A., 1970-72; chief employee tng. and devel. Frankfurt Area Army Personnel Office, 1972-73; chief employee rels. and tng. brs. Corps Engrs., L.A., 1973-74; chief employee devel. and tng. Kirtland AFB, N.Mex., 1974-87; labor relations officer, Kirtland AFB and detachments in 13 U.S. cities, 1987-90; project coord., adv. Protection and Advocacy System, 1991-96, ret., 1996. Mem. adv. com. Albuquerque Tech.-Vocat. Inst., 1982-92, U. N.Mex. Valencia Campus, 1985-92; mem. Coalition for Disability Rights, 1988-96; chmn. Comprehensive Accessibility Network, 1990-96; adv. coun. N.Mex. Disability Prevention, 1992-96; recording sec. N.Mex. Commn. Blind State Rehab. Adv. Coun., 1993-96. Served with USAF, 1958-64. Named Prominent Tng. and Devel. Profl., H. Whitney McMillan Co., 1984; Outstanding Handicapped Fed. Employee of Yr., all fed. agys., 1984; recipient Govt. Employees Ins. Co. GEICO Pub. Svc. award for work in phys. rehab., 1988. Mem. Am. Soc. Tng. and Devel. (treas. chpt. 1984-85), Paralyzed Vets. Am. (bd. dirs. 1986-87, pres. local chpt. 1986-87, 1990-92), Toastmasters Internat. (chpt. treas., v.p., pres. 1967-70), Vietnam Vets. of Am., Phi Delta Kappa. Democrat. Roman Catholic. Office: 1720 Louisiana Blvd NE Ste 204 Albuquerque NM 87110-7070

KATHKA, DAVID ARLIN, director educational services; b. Columbus, Nebr.; s. Arlin Arthur and Edith Ferne (Wilcox) K.; m. Anne Condon Butler, Aug. 15, 1965. BA, Wayne (Nebr.) State Coll., 1964, MA, 1966; PhD in History, U. Mo., 1976. Tchr. Ravenna (Nebr.) Pub. Schs., 1964-65; instr. Midwestern Coll., Denison, Iowa, 1966-68; prof. history Western Wyo. Coll., Rock Springs, 1972-87, dean acad. affairs, 1980-84, interim pres., 1984-85, v.p. acad. affairs, 1985-87; dir. State Parks and Cultural Resources Div., State of Wyo., Cheyenne, 1987-94, Sweetwater Bd. Coop. Ednl. Svcs., Wyo., 1994—; adj. prof. U. Wyo., Laramie, 1976—, adj. prof. history Western Wyo. Coll., 1996—; vis. instr. U. Mo., St. Louis, 1971-72; cons. various Wyo. govt. agys.; mem. gov.'s Blue ribbon Task Force on Cultural Resources, Wyo. Trails adv. com. Author hist. papers; contbr. hist. articles to mags. Bd. dirs. Sweetwater Mus. Found., Wyo. Territorial Park, 1987-94, Tracks Across Wyo., Wyo. Hist. Found., Rock Springs Area Cmty. Found.; mem. Wyo. Centennial Commn., 1986-87, Rock Springs Libr. Bd.,1 984-87, Gov.'s Com. on Hist. Preservation, 1982; v.p. Rocky Mountain Region Kidney Found., Denver, 1976-77. Recipient Wyo. Humanities award for exemplary svc., 1990. Mem. Orgn. Am. Historians, Wyo. State Hist. Soc. (pres. 1984-85), Wyo. Assn. Profl. Historians (v.p. 1994-96, pres. 1996—). Democrat. Office: Sweetwater Bd Coop Ednl Svcs Box 428 Rock Springs WY 82902-0428

KATHOL, ANTHONY LOUIS, finance executive; b. San Diego, June 12, 1964; s. Cletus Louis and Regina Antoinette (Ellrott) K.; m. Kathleen Marie Moore, Jan. 23, 1988; children: Nicole Kathleen, Natalie Antoinette, Holly Rose. BS, U. So. Calif., 1986; MBA, U. San Diego, 1988. Fin. aid analyst U. San Diego, 1986-87; bookkeeper Golden Lion Tavern, San Diego, 1987-88; fin. and budget coord. Santa Fe Pacific Realty Corp. (name now Catellus Devel. Corp.), Brea, Calif., 1988-91; mgr. fin. analysis SW U.S. Catellus Devel. Corp., Anaheim, Calif., 1992-93; mgr. leasing Pacific Design Ctr., West Hollywood, Calif., 1994-95, dir. fin. and policy, 1995-96, v.p. asset mgmt., 1996—. Calif. Bldg. Industry Assn. fellow, 1986, U. San Diego fellow, 1987. Mem. U. San Diego Grad. Bus. Students Assn., K.C. (fin. sec. 1990-91), Tau Kappa Epsilon. Republican. Roman Catholic. Home: 3805 Maxon Ln Chino CA 91710-2073 Office: Pacific Design Ctr #M-60 8687 Melrose Ave West Hollywood CA 90069-5701

KATKIN, KEN, lawyer; b. Buffalo, Jan. 30, 1966; s. Edward Samuel and Wendy Sue (Freedman) K.; m. Linda Marie Dynan, Feb. 21, 1992; 1 child, Nathan. AB, Princeton U., 1987; JD magna cum laude, Northwestern U., 1996. Bar: N.Y. 1997. Actuarial asst. Ins. Svcs. Office, N.Y.C., 1987-90; artists and repertoire dir. Homestead Records, Rockville Centre, N.Y., 1990-92, Safe House Records, N.Y.C., 1992-93; law clk. to Hon. David M. Ebel U.S. Ct. Appeals (10th cir.), Denver, 1996-97; vol. radio disc jockey/announcer, 1983-96. Editor Northwestern U. Law Rev., 1994-96; writer short stories and essays. Mem. Order of Coif.

KATO, BRUCE, curator. Curator Alaska State Mus., Juneau, 1987—. Office: Alaska State Mus 395 Whittier Juneau AK 99801-1718

KATO, NORMAN SCOTT, cardiac surgeon, educational administrator; b. Chgo., Dec. 30, 1955; s. Walter Yoneo and Anna Chieko (Kurata) K.; m. Nancy Jane Douts, July 20, 1985; children: Nicole Anna-Marie, Natalie Gene Yoneko. BA with distinction, Swarthmore Coll., 1977; MD, U. Pa., 1981. Diplomate Am. Bd. Med. Examiners, Am. Bd. Surgery with sub-specialty in surg. critical care, Am. Bd. Thoracic Surgery. Intern in surgery U. Pa. Hosp., Phila., 1981-82, resident in surgery, 1982-86, chief resident in surgery, 1986-87; postdoctoral fellow in physiology U. Pa., Phila., 1987-89; resident in cardiothoracic surgery NYU, 1989-90, chief resident in cardiothoracic surgery, 1990-91; asst. prof. surgery UCLA Med. Ctr., 1991—; dir. GHCH/UCLA Heart Ctr., Granada Hills, 1993—; cons. Interqual, Boston, 1994-96, RAND, Santa Monica, Calif., 1995—; cons. Pacific Bus. Group on Health, 1995—. Contbr. articles to profl. jours. Pfizer postdoctoral fellow Pfizer Pharms., 1987; grantee Am. Heart Assn., 1993. Fellow ACS, Am. Coll. Cardiology, Am. Coll. chest Physicians; mem. Phi Beta Kappa, Alpha Omega Alpha. Home: 10218 Briarwood Dr Los Angeles CA 90077-2522 Office: UCLA Med Ctr Divsn Cardiothoracic Surgery 10833 Le Conte Ave Los Angeles CA 90024

KATO, TERRI EMI, special education educator; b. Gardena, Calif., Sept. 1, 1953; d. Shunji James and Ruby Miyo (Sumi) K. BA, Calif. State U., Long Beach, 1976; MA, U.S. Internat. U., 1987. Cert. tchr. multiple subjects, learning handicapped, severely handicapped, resource specialist, lang. devel. specialist, c.c.'s, Calif. Learning disabled group specialist Montebello (Calif.) Unified Sch. Dist., 1979-81; resource specialist ABC Unified Sch. Dist., Cerritos, Calif., 1981-82; spl. day class tchr. Santa Ana (Calif.) Unified Sch. Dist., 1982—; math. resource tchr., 1990—; 1st and 2nd grade tchr. Santa Anna (Calif.) Unified Sch. Dist., 1996—. Mem. NEA, Calif. Tchrs. Assn., Santa Ana Educators Assn. (spl. edn. task force rules and election com., bldg. rep. 1992—, supt.'s cabinet 1995—), Coun. for Exceptional Children, Orange County Math. Coun. Office: James Monroe Elem 417 E Central Ave Santa Ana CA 92707-3501

KATONA, ROBERT ROY, artist, sculptor; b. Athens, Ohio, Mar. 16, 1947; s. Arthur and Verna (Wendelin) K.; m. Jo Laverne Bell, 1980; children: Katherine Day, John Darren. Student, U. Colo., 1965. Numerous one-man shows, including Gallery One, Denver, 1985, 90, 91, Grace Harkin Gallery, N.Y., 1989, Chabot Gallery, San Jose, Calif., 1990, 93, C. Anthony Gallery, Dallas, 1990, 91, Fillmore Plaza Gallery, Denver, 1993; exhibited in group shows Denver Art Mus., 1968, 73-74, Munich Mus. Art, 1982, Taipei Mus. Fine Arts, 1983, Arabian Internat. Art Exhbn., 1982-85, Salmagundi Club, N.Y.C., 1983, Fine Arts Mus. of Long Island, N.Y., 1989, New Yorkers in Barcelona, Spain, 1990, also others; represented in permanent collections USAF Acad., also corp. and pvt. collections. Recipient Jenkins award Gilpin County Arts Assn., 1970, 74, 1st prize for book illustration Soc. Illustrators, 1976, 1st prize for graphics Grolla D'Oro Internat., Treviso, Italy, 1982.

KATZ, ALAN ROY, public health educator; b. Pitts., Aug. 21, 1954; s. Leon B. and Bernice Sonia (Glass) K.; m. Donna Marie Crandall, Jan. 19, 1986; 1 child, Sarah Elizabeth. BA, U. Calif., San Diego, 1976; MD, U. Calif., Irvine, 1980; MPH, U. Hawaii, 1987; postgrad., U. So. Calif., 1980-81, U. Hawaii, 1982-83. Staff physician emergency medicine L.A. County U. So. Calif. Med. Ctr., 1981-82; staff physician, med. dir. Waikiki Health Ctr., Honolulu, 1983-87; dir. AIDS/STD prevention program Hawaii State Dept. of Health, Honolulu, 1987-88; asst. prof. dept. pub. health scis. U. Hawaii, Honolulu, 1988-94, assoc. prof., 1994—, dir. preventive medicine residency program, 1994—; bd. dirs. Hawaii AIDS Task Group; mem. Chlamydia control workgroup USPHS, 1985-87. Contbr. articles to profl. jours. Me. Leptospirosis ad hoc com. Hawaii State Dept. Health, Honolulu, 1988—, mem. prenatal screening adv. com., 1992—; mem. com. human subjects U. Hawaii, 1989—. USPHS Chlamydia Prevalence Survey grantee, Hawaii, 1986, Tuberculosis Survey grantee U. Hawaii, 1991; recipient presdl. citation for meritorious teaching, U. Hawaii, 1989, regents medal excellence in teaching U. Hawaii, 1992. Fellow Am. Coll. Preventive Medicine; mem. Am. Pub. Health Assn., Soc. Epidemiologic Rsch., Delta Omega. Office: U Hawaii Sch Pub Health Dept Pub Health Sci 1960 E West Rd Honolulu HI 96822-2319

KATZ, CHARLES J., JR., lawyer; b. San Antonio, Mar. 25, 1948. AB, Stanford U., 1969; MA, N.Y.U., 1973; JD, U. Tex., 1976. Book review editor Tex. Law Review, 1975-76; mem. Perkins Coie, Seattle. Mem. Order of the Coif. Office: Perkins Coie 1201 3rd Ave Fl 40 Seattle WA 98101-3099

KATZ, ILLANA PAULETTE, writer; b. N.Y.C., May 30, 1946; d. Emanuel and Alice (Reich) Schear; m. David Arthur Katz, July 31, 1966; children: Heather, Todd, Ethan, Seth. BA in Anthropology summa cum laude, Calif. State U., 1977, postgrad. Owner, pres., pub. Real Life Storybooks, West Hills, Calif., 1992—; social facilitation cons. Yellen and Assoc., Inc., Granada Hills, Calif., 1996—; mini-course instr. L.A. Unified Sch. Dist., 1985, 93; lectr. State Autism Conv., 1994, Nat. Autism Conv., 1994. Author: Joey and Sam, 1993 (award 1994), Show Me Where It Hurts, 1993, Uncle Jimmy, 1994, Sarah, 1994, Hungry Mind-Hungry Body, 1995; (audio-cassette) Was Einstein Autistic?, 1994. Head of Israeli affairs United Synagogue, Beverly Hills, 1988; aliyah councelor Jewish Fedn., L.A., 1991—. Mem. Authors and Celebrities Forum (award of excellence 1994), Soc. of Children's Book Writers, Book Publicists Assn. (nominated non-fiction children's book award, 1996), Pub. Mktg. Assn. Home and Office: 8370 Kentland Ave West Hills CA 91304-3329

KATZ, JEANNE LYN, counselor, educator; b. Pitts.; d. Paul and Geraldine (Roth) K. Student, Ohio U., Athens, 1966-68; BS, U. Pitts., 1970; MA, Mich. State U., 1973. Cert. Nat. Bd. Cert. Counselors; lic. profl. counselor; cert. bereavement facilitator. Vol. coord. El Paso County Dept. of Social Svcs., Colorado Springs, Colo., 1973-74; mental health therapist Pikes Peak Mental Health Ctr., Colorado Springs, 1974-76; coll. instr. Pikes Peak C.C., Colorado Springs, 1976-81; med. social worker and supr. Penrose-St. Francis Healthcare, Colorado Springs, 1979-95; instr. Colo. Free U., Colorado Springs, 1995—; facilitator wellness workshop Ind. Contractor, Colorado Springs, 1980—; coord. social work and bereavement Hospice of the Comforter, Colorado Springs, 1994—. Vol. Spanish Peaks Mental Health Ctr. VISTA, Pueblo, Colo., 1970; vol. bereavement coord. Pikes Peak Hospice, Colorado Springs, 1980. Mem. Life Found. Sch. of Therapeutics (Am. rep. U.K.; Earth Star award 1994), Integral Yoga Inst. (instr.), So. Colo. Assn. of Lic. Profl. Counselors, Am. Counseling Assn., Assn. for Death Edn. and Counseling. Home: 5004 Sunsuite Trail S Colorado Springs CO 80917

KATZ, JERRY PAUL, corporate executive; b. L.A., Jan. 24, 1944; s. Samuel and Dorothy Rose (Solovay) K.; m. Judy Simmering, Sept. 10, 1985 (div. 1988); m. Julie Stacey, Aug. 26, 1990; 1 child, Brandon Louis. AA, East L.A. Coll., 1964; BS, BA, Calif. State U., 1970. Registered sanitarian, Calif. Sanitarian L.A. County Health Dept., L.A., 1971-73; dir. Compton (Calif.) Model Cities Vector Control, 1973-74; health officer Lynwood (Calif.) City, 1974-76; pres., chief exec. officer Associated Industries, L.A., 1976—; cons., bd. dirs. All Am. Fire Protection, L.A., 1987—. Founding mem. Moore St. Homeowners Assn., Monterey Park, Calif., 1989—; mem. Nature Conservancy, World Wildlife Fund. Recipient World Record (2) hang gliding Nat. Assn. Aeronautics, 1977; named for Distance-Altitude Gain, Guinness Book of World Records, London, 1977. Mem. Native Am. Rights Fund, Green Peace, Surfrider Found., U.S. Hangliding Assn., Sea Shepard Soc. Office: Associated Industries 5140 Via Corona St Los Angeles CA 90022-2007

KATZ, JOHN W., lawyer, state official; b. Balt., June 3, 1943; s. Leonard Wallach and Jean W. (Kane) K.; m. Joan Katz, June 11, 1969 (div. 1982); 1 child, Kimberly Erin. BA, Johns Hopkins U., 1965; JD, U. Calif., Berkeley, 1969; DDL (hon.) U. Alaska, 1994. Bar: Alaska, Pa., U.S. Dist. Ct. D.C. 1971, U.S. Ct. Appeals (D.C. cir.), U.S. Tax Ct., U.S. Ct. Claims, U.S. Ct. Mil. Justice, U.S. Supreme Ct. Legis. and adminstrv. asst. to Congressman Howard W. Pollock of Alaska, Washington, 1969-70; legis. asst. to U.S. Senator Ted Stevens of Alaska, Washington, 1971; assoc. McGrath and Flint, Anchorage, 1972; gen. counsel Joint Fed. State Land Use Planning Commn. for Alaska, Anchorage, 1972-79; spl. counsel to Gov. Jay S. Hammond of Alaska, Anchorage and Washington, 1979-81; commr. Alaska Dept. Natural Resources, Juneau, 1981-83; dir. state fed. relations and spl. counsel to Gov. Bill Sheffield of Alaska, Washington and Juneau, 1983-86; dir. state-fed. relations, spl. counsel to Gov. Steve Cowper of Alaska, Washington, 1986-90, Gov. Walter J. Hickel of Alaska, Washington, 1990-94, Gov. Tony Knowles, 1994—; mem. Alaska Power Survey Exec. Adv. Com. of FPC, Anchorage, 1972-74; mem. spl. com. hard rock minerals Govs. Council of Sci. and Tech., Anchorage, 1979-80; guest lectr. on natural resources U. Alaska, U. Denver. Contbr. articles to profl. jours.; columnist Anchorage Times until 1991. Acad. supr. Alaska Externship Program, U. Denver Coll. Law, 1976-79; mem. Reagan-Bush transition team for U.S. Dept. Justice, 1980. Recipient Superior Sustained Performance award Joint Fed. State Land Use Planning Commn. for Alaska, 1978, Resolution of Commendation award Alaska Legis., 1988. Republican. Office: State of Alaska Office of Gov 444 N Capitol St NW # 336 Washington DC 20001-1512

KATZ, LEW, advertising executive. Fin. dir. Team One Advertising, El Segundo, Calif. Office: 1960 E Grand Ave Ste 700 El Segundo CA 90245*

KATZ, MICHAEL JEFFERY, lawyer; b. Detroit, May 11, 1950; s. Wilfred Lester and Bernice (Ackerman) K. BE with honors, U. Mich., 1972; JD, U. Colo., 1976; cert. mgmt., U. Denver, 1985, cert. fin. mgmt., 1990. Bar: Colo. 1978. Rsch. atty., immigration specialist Colo. Rural Legal Svcs., Denver, 1976-77, supervising atty. migrant farm lab., 1977-78; ind. contractor Colo. Sch. Fin., Denver, 1978-79; sole practice Denver, 1978-86; assoc. Levine and Pitler, P.C., Denver, 1986-88; gen. counsel, sec. Grease Monkey Internat., Inc., Denver, 1988-92; prin. Katz & Co., Denver, 1992—; exec. v.p. Nat. Network Exchange, Inc., Denver, 1992—; lectr. on incorporating small bus. and real estate purchase agreements Front Range Coll., 1986—, condr. various seminars on real estate and landlord/tenant law, 1980—; of counsel Levine and Pitler, P.C., Englewood, Colo., 1985—. Contbr. Action Line column Rocky Mountain News; contbr. articles to profl. jours. Mem. Assn. Trial Lawyers Am., Am. Arbitration Assn. (mem. panel of arbitrators 1989), Denver Bar Assn. (mem. law day com. 1985—, mem. real estate com. 1980—, mem. pro bono svcs. com. 1984—), U.S. Yacht Racing Assn., Dillon Yacht Club. Office: 6053 S Quebec St Ste 200 Greenwood Village CO 80111

KATZ, ROGER, pediatrician, educator; b. Menominee, Mich., Feb. 23, 1938; s. Peter W. and Mae C. (Chudacoff) K.; m. Barbara Morguelan, Feb. 6, 1966; children: Carl, Gary, Robyn. BS, U. Wis., 1960; MD, U. Louisville, 1965. Diplomate Am. Bd. Allergy and Immunology, Am. Bd. Pediatric Allergy, Am. Bd. Pediatrics. Clin. prof. pediatrics UCLA, 1978—; spkr. in field; expert legal evaluator. Author and editor sci. books and manuscripts. Maj. U.S. Army, 1970-72. Fellow Am. Acad. Allergy, Asthma and Immunology, Am. Coll. Allergy, Asthma and Immunology (bd. regents 1990-93), Am. Acad. Pediat., Am. Coll. Chest Physicians, Joint Coun. Allergy, Asthma and Immunology (pres. 1986-90). Office: 100 UCLA Medical Plz Ste 550 Los Angeles CA 90024-6970

KATZ, STEVEN JOSEPH, school counselor; b. Springfield, Ohio, June 2, 1946; s. Robert and Mildred (Popov) K. BA in Econs., Oberlin Coll., 1968; MEd in Elem. Edn., Antioch Coll., Yellow Springs, Ohio, 1971; MS in Anthropology, U. Oreg., 1979, MS in Counseling, 1980. Cert. Nat. Bd. Cert Counselors, Nat. Bd. Cert. Sch. Counselors. Psychiat. aide Lincoln (Nebr.) State Hosp., 1967; elem. tchr. Phila. Pub. Schs., 1979-72; firefighter U.S. Forest Svc., Trout Lake, Wash., 1975-77; cultural resource archaeologist U.S. Forest Svc./Bur. Land Mgmt., Oreg., 1978-87; elem. sch. counselor, tchr.

Bethel Sch. Dist., Eugene, Oreg., 1986—; mem. at risk team Bethel Sch. Dist., Eugene, 1986-89, mem., chair counselor adv. com., 1990-94, co-founder family advocacy cmty. team, 1993-94, mem. leadership team, 1992-94. Co-author: An Assessment of Mental Health Svcs. for Native Americans in Aouthwest Oregon SW Oreg. Indian Health Project & Oreg. State Dept. Human Resources, 1981, (presentation) Effective Classroom, Group and Individual Guidance, 1994; program host KLCC-FM, Eugene, 1979—. Mem. Oreg. Tuba Ensemble Oreg. Tuba Assn., Eugene, 1979—; bd. mem. Eugene Symphonic Band, Eugene, 1991-94. Mem. ACA, Oreg. Counseling Assn., Oreg. Soc. Individual Psychology. Office: Bethel Sch Dist 4640 Barger Dr Eugene OR 97402-1239

KATZ, TONNIE, newspaper editor. BA, Barnard Coll., 1966; MSc, Columbia U., 1967. Editor, reporter newspapers including The Quincy Patriot Ledger, Boston Herald Am., Boston Globe; Sunday/projects editor Newsday; mng. editor Balt. News Am., 1983-86, The Sun, San Bernardino, Calif., 1986-88; asst. mng. editor for news The Orange County Register, Santa Ana, Calif., 1988-89, mng. editor, 1989-92, editor, v.p., 1992—. Office: Freedom Newspapers Inc Orange County Register 625 N Grand Ave Santa Ana CA 92701-4347

KATZ, VERA, mayor, former college administrator, state legislator; b. Dusseldorf, Germany, Aug. 3, 1933; came to U.S., 1940; d. Lazar Pistrak and Raissa Goodman; m. Mel Katz (div. 1985); 1 child, Jesse. BA, Bklyn. Coll., 1955, postgrad., 1955-57. Market research analyst TIMEX, B.T. Babbitt, N.Y.C., 1957-62; mem. Oreg. Ho. of Reps., Salem; former dir. devel. Portland Community Coll., from 1982; mayor City of Portland, Oreg., 1993—; mem. Gov.'s Council on Alcohol and Drug Abuse Programs, Oreg. Legis., Salem, 1985—; mem. adv. com. Gov.'s Council on Health, Fitness and Sports, Oreg. Legis., 1985—; mem. Gov.'s Commn. on Sch. Funding Reform; mem. Carnegie task Force on Teaching as Profession, Washington, 1985-87; vice-chair assembly Nat. Conf. State Legis., Denver, 1986—. Recipient Abigail Scott Duniway award Women in Communications, Inc., Portland, 1985, Jeanette Rankin First Woman award Oreg. Women's Polit. Caucus, Portland, 1985, Leadership award The Neighborhood newspaper Portland, 1985, Woman of Achievement award Commn. for Women, 1985, Outstanding Legis. Advocacy award Oreg. Primary Care Assn., 1985, Service to Portland Pub. Sch. Children award Portland Pub. Schs., 1985. Fellow Am. Leadership Forum (founder Oreg. chpt.); mem. Dem. Legis. Leaders Assn., Nat. Bd. for Profl. Teaching Standards. Democrat. Jewish. Office: Office of the Mayor City Hall Rm 303 1220 SW 5th Ave Portland OR 97204-1913*

KATZBECK, KAREN LYNN, accounting executive; b. Chgo., Aug. 11, 1951; d. Frank A. and Lorraine S. (Williams) K.; m. Carl A. Petersen, June 17, 1972 (div. June 1975); m. Jack L. Shishido, Dec. 10, 1982 (div. Oct. 1991). BS, U. Ill.-Chgo., 1976. CPA. Mem. tax staff Price Waterhouse, Chgo., 1977-78, tax sr./mgr., Tokyo, 1978-82, tax mgr., L.A., 1982-83, sr. mgr., 1984-85; mgr. internat. tax Walt Disney Co., Burbank, Calif., 1985-88; chief fin. officer Santiago Air Conditioning, 1988-89; v.p. fin., adminstrn. Houlihan, Lokey, Howard & Zukin, Inc., L.A., 1989-93; exec. dir. Cox, Castle and Nicholson, L.A., 1993, pvt. practice, 1994—. Active Asia Pacific Coun. Am. Chambers, Tokyo, 1979-82. Recipient Pres.'s Leadership award Am. C. of C. in Japan, 1980. Mem. AICPA, Calif. CPA Soc., Am. Soc. Women CPAs (treas. 1995-97), Japan-Am. Soc., Glendale C. of C. Office: 2041 Parkmount Dr Ste 201 Glendale CA 91206-1746

KATZEN, MOLLIE, writer, artist; b. Rochester, N.Y., Oct. 13, 1950; d. Leon and Betty (Heller) K.; m. Jeffrey David Black, June 26, 1983 (div. Oct. 1985); 1 child, Samuel Katzen Black; m. Carl Shames, Dec. 12, 1986. BFA, San Francisco Art Inst., 1972. Author, illustrator: Mossewood Cookbook, 1977, Enchanted Broccoli Forest, 1982, Still Life with Menu, 1988. Recipient Graphic Arts award Arnot Art Gallery, 1976, Cert. of Commendation, Calif. State Assembly, 1989. Jewish.

KATZMAN, RICHARD ALAN, lawyer, judicial arbitrator; b. N.Y.C., N.Y., Sept. 3, 1953; s. George and Ellen Delyse (Shure) K.; 1 child, Braden Michael Harris Katzman. AA, Miami-Dade Jr. Coll., 1972; BA, Fla. Internat. U., 1973; JD, U. Miami, 1976; MA, U. So. Calif., 1981. Bar: Fla. 1976, N.J. 1977, Calif. 1980, U.S. Dist. Ct. (so. dist.) Fla. 1976, U.S. Dist. Ct. N.J. 1977, U.S. Dist. Ct. (cent. dist.) Calif. 1980, U.S. Ct. Appeals (9th cir.) 1980, U.S. Ct. Appeals (5th and 11th cirs.) 1981, U.S. Supreme Ct. 1979. Of counsel Black and Denaro, Miami, 1976-78; rsch. atty. 3d Dist. Ct. Appeal, Miami, 1978; labor atty. Pomona (Calif.) divsn. Gen. Dynamics, 1980-82; assoc. atty. Balowitz & Wolf, Santa Ana, Calif., 1982-84; sr. assoc. Petersen & Ferguson, Santa Ana, Calif., 1984-86; sr. litig. L.A. County Met. Transp. Authority, L.A., 1986-94; prin. dep. county counsel County of L.A., L.A., 1994-96; asst. gen. counsel Santa Clara Valley Transp. Authority, 1996—; jud. arbitrator L.A. County Superior Ct., 1986-96, Orange County Superior Ct., Santa Ana, Calif., 1988-96. Judge Pro Tempore West Orange County Mun. Ct., Westminster, Calif., 1985-96. Mem. Amer. Coll. of Legal Medicine (assoc.-in-law). Home: 310 N 1st St Apt 2 Campbell CA 95008-1341 Office: 3331 N 1st St Fl 2 San Jose CA 95134-1906

KATZUNG, BERTRAM GEORGE, pharmacologist; b. Mineola, N.Y., June 11, 1932; m. Alice V. Camp; children: Katharine Blanche, Brian Lee. BA, Syracuse U., 1953; MD, SUNY, Syracuse, 1957; PhD, U. Calif., San Francisco, 1962. Prof. U. Calif., San Francisco, 1958—. Author: Drug Therapy, 1991, Basic and Clinical Pharmacology, 1995, Pharmacology, Examination and Board Review, 1995; contbr. to profl. jours. Markle scholar. Mem. AAAS, AAUP, Am. Soc. Pharmacology and Exptl. Therapeutics, Biophysical Soc., Fed. Am. Scientists, Internat. Soc. Heart Rsch., Soc. Gen. Physiologists, Western Pharmacology Soc., N.Y. Acad. Sci., Phi Beta Kappa, Alpha Omega Alpha, Golden Gate Computer Soc. Office: UCSF Dept Pharmacology PO Box 0450 San Francisco CA 94143

KAUFFMAN, GEORGE BERNARD, chemistry educator; b. Phila., Sept. 4, 1930; s. Philip Joseph and Laura (Fisher) K.; m. Ingeborg Salomon, June 5, 1952 (div. Dec. 1969); children: Ruth Deborah (Mrs. Martin H. Bryskier), Judith Miriam (Mrs. Mario L. Reposo); m. Laurie Marks Papazian, Dec. 21, 1969; stepchildren: Stanley Robert Papazian, Teresa Lynn Papazian Baron, Mary Ellen Papazian Yoder. BA with honors, U. Pa., 1951; PhD, U. Fla., 1956. Grad. asst. U. Fla., 1951-55; rsch. participant Oak Ridge Nat. Lab., 1955; instr. U. Tex., Austin, 1955-56; rsch. chemist Humble Oil & Refining Co., Baytown, Tex., 1956, GE, Cin., 1957, 59; asst. prof. chemistry Calif. State U., Fresno, 1956-61; assoc. prof. Calif. State U., 1961-66, prof., 1966—; guest lectr. coop. lecture tours Am. Chem. Soc., 1971; vis. scholar U. Calif., Berkeley, 1976, U. Puget Sound, 1978; dir. undergrad. rsch. participation program NSF, 1972. Author: Alfred Werner—Founder of Coordination Chemistry, 1966, Classics in Coordination Chemistry, Part I, 1968, Part II, 1976, Part III, 1978, Werner Centennial, 1967, Teaching the History of Chemistry, 1971, Coordination Chemistry: Its History through the Time of Werner, 1977, Inorganic Coordination Compounds, 1981, The Central Science: Essays on the Uses of Chemistry, 1984, Frederick Soddy (1877-1956): Early Pioneer in Radiochemistry, 1986, Aleksandr Porfirevich Borodin: A Chemist's Biography, 1988, Coordination Chemistry: A Century of Progress, 1994, Classics in Coordination Chemistry, 1995, Metal and Nonmetal Biguanide Complexes, 1997; contbr. numerous articles to profl. publs.; contbg. editor: Jour. Coll. Sci. Teaching, 1973—, The Hexagon, 1980—, Polyhedron, 1983-85, Industrial Chemist, 1985-88, Jour. Chem. Edn., 1987—, Today's Chemist, 1989-91, The Chemical Intelligencer, 1994—, Today's Chemist at Work, 1995—, Chemical Heritage, 1996—; guest editor: Coodination Chemistry Centennial Symposium (C3S) issue, Polyhedron, 1994; editor tape lecture series: Am. Chem. Soc, 1975-81. Named Outstanding Prof. Calif. State U. and Colls. System, 1973; recipient Exceptional Merit Svc. award, 1984, Meritorious Performance and Profl. Promise award, 1986-87, 88-89; recipient Coll. Chemistry Tchr. Excellence award Mfg. Chemists Assn., 1976, Chugaev medal, 1976, Kurnakov medal, 1990, Chernyaev medal, 1991, USSR Acad. Sci., George C. Pimentel award in Chemical Education, Am. Chemical Soc., 1993, Dexter award in History of Chemistry, 1978, Marc-Auguste Pictet medal Société de Physique et d'Histoire Naturelle de Genève, 1992, Pres.'s medal of Distinction Calif. State U., Fresno, 1994; Research Corp. grantee, 1956-57, 57-59, 59-61, Am. Chem. Soc. Petroleum Research Fund grantee, 1962-64, 65-69, Am. Philos. Soc. grantee, 1963-64, 69-70, NSF grantee, 1960-61, 63-64, 67-69, 76-77, NEH grantee, 1982-83; John Simon Guggenheim Meml. Found. fellow, 1972-73; grantee, 1975; Strindberg fellow Swedish Inst., Stockholm, 1983. Mem. AAAS, AAUP, Assn. Univ. Pa. Chemists, History of Sci. Soc., Soc. History Alchemy and Chemistry, Am. Chem. Soc. (chmn. divsn. history of chemistry 1969, mem. exec. com. 1970, councilor 1976-78, George C. Pimentel award in Chem. Edn., 1993), Mensa, Sigma Xi, Phi Lambda Upsilon, Phi Kappa Phi, Alpha Chi Sigma, Gamma Sigma Epsilon. Home: 1609 E Quincy Ave Fresno CA 93720-2309 Office: Calif State U Dept Chemistry Fresno CA 93740

KAUFMAN, ALBERT I., lawyer; b. N.Y.C., Oct. 2, 1936; s. Israel and Pauline (Pardes) K.; m. Ruth Feldman, Jan. 25, 1959; 1 son, Michael Paul. AA, L.A. City Coll., 1957; BA, U. San Fernando Valley, 1964, JD, 1966. Bar: Calif. 1967, U.S. Ct. Appeals (9th cir.) 1968, U.S. Supreme Ct. 1971, U.S. Dist. Ct. (cen. dist.) Calif. 1967, U.S. Tax Ct. 1971, U.S. Ct. Internat. Trade 1981. Sole practice, Encino, Calif., 1967—; judge pro tem L.A. Mcpl. Ct., 1980—, L.A. Superior Ct., 1991—; family law mediator L.A. Superior Ct., 1980—. Mem. Pacific S.W. regional bd. Anti-Defamation league of B'nai B'rith, 1970-91. Served with USAF, 1959-65, to col. CAP, 1956—. Recipient Disting. Svc. award B'nai B'rith, 1969; Exceptional Svc. award CAP, 1977, 95. Mem. ABA, L.A. County Bar Assn., San Fernando Valley Bar Assn., Consumer Atty. of Calif., Consumer Atty. Assn. L.A. Republican. Clubs: Toastmasters, Westerners 1117 (pres. 1969), B'nai B'rith (pres. 1971-72), Santa Monica Yacht (judge adv.) Office: 17609 Ventura Blvd Ste 201 Encino CA 91316-3825

KAUFMAN, CHARLES DAVID, controller; b. N.Y.C., Apr. 17, 1931; s. M. Laurence and Anna (Goldberg) K.; m. Elvira Sampere Camps, Mar. 1, 1955; children: John, Janet. BS, Northwestern U., 1952; MBA, NYU, 1958. CPA, N.Y. Fin. analyst Nestle Co., Stamford, Conn., 1958-61; area contr. IBM World Trade Corp., Mexico City, 1967-69; dir. fin. controls ITT Corp., Brussels and N.Y.C., 1974-85, controller's dept., 1985-94; ret., 1994. Active Scottsdale League for The Arts; vol. cons. Exec. Svc. Corps Ariz., Svc. Corps Ret. Execs. Cpl. U.S. Army, 1952-54. Mem. AICPAs, N.Y. Soc. CPAs, Ariz. Soc. CPAs.

KAUFMAN, CHARLOTTE KING, artist, retired educational administrator; b. Balt., Dec. 5, 1920; d. Ben and Belle (Turow) King; A.B., Goucher Coll., 1969; M.P.H., Johns Hopkins U., 1972, M.Ed., 1976; m. Albert Kaufman, July 22, 1945; children—Matthew King, Ezra King. Dir. public relations Balt. Jewish Community Center, 1962-67; research and editor Johns Hopkins U. Sch. Hygiene and Public Health, Balt., 1969-72, admissions officer, 1972-74, dir. admissions and registrar, 1974-86, dir. study cons. program undergraduates, 1986-89, pub. health acad. adviser, 1989-95. Mem. Am. Pub. Health Assn., Am. Assn. for Higher Edn., Am. Assn. Collegiate Registrars and Admissions Officers, Artists Equity Assn. (v.p. Md. chpt. 1988-90), Md. Printmakers (exec. bd. 1989-94), Delta Omega. Democrat. Jewish. Home: Monterey Country Club 159 Las Lomas Palm Desert CA 92260-2153

KAUFMAN, EDWARD REDDING, psychiatrist, educator. BA, Temple U., 1956; MD, Jefferson Med. Coll., 1960. Intern L.A. County Hosp., 1960-61; resident N.Y. State Psychiat. Inst., Columbia Presbyn. Med. Ctr., N.Y.C., 1961-64; med. dir. chem. dependency progrm Capistrano by the Sea Hosp., Dana Point, Calif., 1991-96; psychiatrist N.Y. State Psychiat. Inst., 1966-67, St. Lukes Hosp., 1967-70; dir. N.Y.C. Prison Mental Health Svcs., 1970-72; pvt. practice N.Y.C., 1972-77, Irvine, Calif., 1977—; clin. prof. U. Calif., Irvine, 1992—; med. dir. chem. dependency program South Coast Hosp., South Laguna, Calif., 1996—; examiner Am. Bd. Psychiatry and Neurology, 1980—; E. Pumpian-Mindlin Ann. Vis. professorship U. Okla., 1988. Author: Substance Abuse and Family Therapy, 1985; author: (with others) Substance Abuse: Clin. Problems and Perspectives, 1981, Adolescent and Family Therapy: A Handbook of Theory and Practice, 1985, Alcohol Abuse Treatment Research, 1985, Psychotherapy of Addicted Persons, 1994; editor-in-chief Am. Jour. Drug and Alcohol Abuse, 1974—; exec. editor: Internat. Jour. Addictions, 1980—; editorial bd. Advances in Alcohol and Substance Abuse, 1980—, Clin. Textbook of Addictive Disorders, 1990; editor: Drug Abuse: Modern Trends, Issues and Perspective, 1978, Critical Concerns in the Field of Drug Abuse, 1979, Family Therapy of Drug and Alcohol Abuse, 1979, 2d edit. 1992, Encyclopedic Handbook of Alcoholism, 1982, Familientherpie Bei Alkohol und Drogenabhaniegkeit, 1983, Power to Change: Family Case Studies in The Treatment of Alcoholism, 1984; contbr. articles to profl. jours. Fellow USPHS, 1959; grantee NIH, 1965, Van Ameringen Found., 1968-70, Lower East Side Svc. Ctr., 1972-76, U. Calif., Irvine, 1980-94, NIMH, 1983-86, Calif. Dept. Mental Health, 1985-88, Beverly Lowry Rsch. Endowment, 1986. Fellow Am. Psychiat. Assn. Home: 31105 Holly Dr Laguna Beach CA 92677-2620 Office: 33971 Selva Rd Ste 125 Dana Point CA 92629

KAUFMAN, HERBERT MARK, finance educator; b. Bronx, N.Y., Nov. 1, 1946; s. Henry and Betty (Fried) K.; m. Helen Laurie Fox, July 23, 1967; 1 child, Jonathan Hart. BA, SUNY, Binghamton, 1967; PhD, Pa. State U., 1972. Economist Fed. Nat. Mortgage Assn., Washington, 1972-73; asst. prof. Ariz. State U., Tempe, 1973-76; econs. prof. Ariz. State U., 1980-88; fin. prof. Ariz. State U., Tempe, 1988—, chair dept. fin., 1991—; exec. dir. Ctr. for Fin. System Ariz. State U., 1988—; cons. World Bank, Washington, 1985-86, Gen. Acctg. Office, Washington, 1985, Congl. Budget Office, Washington, 1980, N.Y. Stock Exch., 1995—. Author: Financial Markets, Financial Institutions and Money, 1983, (with others) The Political Economy of Policy Making, 1979, Money and Banking, 1991; contbr. articles to profl. jours. Mem. Am. Econ. Assn., Am. Fin. Assn., Nat. Assn. of Bus. Economists. Home: 1847 E Calle De Caballos Tempe AZ 85284-2505 Office: Ariz State U Dept Fin Tempe AZ 85287

KAUFMAN, IRVING, retired engineering educator; b. Geinsheim, Germany, Jan. 11, 1925; came to US., 1938, naturalized, 1945; s. Albert and Hedwig Kaufmann; m. Ruby Lee Dordek, Sept. 10, 1950; children—Eve Deborah, Sharon Anne, Julie Ellen. B.E., Vanderbilt U., 1945; M.S., U. Ill., 1949, Ph.D., 1957. Engr. RCA Victor, Indpls., Ind. and Camden, N.J., 1945-48; instr., research assoc. U. Ill., Urbana, 1949-56; sr. mem. tech. staff Ramo-Wooldridge & Space Tech. Labs., Calif., 1957-64; prof. engring. Ariz. State U., 1965-94, ret., 1994; founder, dir. Solid State Research Lab., 1968-78; collaborator Los Alamos Nat. Lab., 1989, 91; vis. scientist Consiglio Nazionale delle Ricerche, Italy, 1973-74; vis. prof. U. Auckland, N.Z., 1974; liaison scientist U.S. Office Naval Rsch., London, 1978-80; lectr. and cons. elec. engring. Contbr. articles to profl. jours. and encys. Recipient Disting. Research award Ariz. State U. Grad. Coll., 1986-87; Sr. Fulbright research fellow Italy, 1964-65, 73-74, Am. Soc. for Engring. Edn./Naval Rsch. Lab. fellow, 1988. Fellow IEEE (life, Phoenix sect. leadership award 1994); mem. Electromagnetics Acad., Gold Key (hon.), Sigma Xi, Tau Beta Pi, Eta Kappa Nu, Pi Mu Epsilon. Jewish. Office: Ariz State U Dept Elec And Engring Tempe AZ 85287-5706

KAUFMAN, JUDITH DIANE, English language educator, consultant; b. Boston, Feb. 10, 1947; d. David G. and Shirley Bernice (Goodman) K. BA in Russian Lang. and Lit., U. Chgo., 1970, MA in Russian Lit., 1972, PhD in Comparative Lit., 1978. Editl. asst. Acta Cytologica, Chgo., 1977-79; vis. asst. prof. English Eastern Wash. U., Cheney, 1979-82, dir. tech. comm. program, 1980—, asst. prof. English, 1982-85, assoc. prof. English, 1985-92, prof. English, 1992—, asst. chair English, 1996—; cons. tech. writing, editing St. Martin's Press, N.Y.C., 1983-85, Little, Brown, Boston, 1986, Holt, Rinehart & Winston, N.Y.C., 1986, Harper & Row, N.Y.C., 1988, Scott, Foresman, Glenview, Ill., 1989-90, Intercollegiate Ctr. Nursing Edn., Spokane, Wash., 1990-92, Blair Press, Boston, 1991, Harper Collins, N.Y.C., 1992, Harcourt Brace Jovanovich, Ft. Worth, 1992-93, Oxford U. Press, N.Y.C., 1996. Assoc. editor: Differential Social Impacts of Rural Resource Development, 1986; contbr. articles to profl. jours. Mem. planning com. Wash. Ctr. for Improving the Quality of Undergrad. Edn., 1992-96. Woodrow Wilson fellow, 1970-71, Nat. Def. Edn. Act Title VI fellow, 1972-74, Josephine de Karman fellow, 1974-75. Mem. AAUP, MLA, Nat. Coun. Tchrs. English, Soc. Tech. Comm. (sr., chpt. employment mgr. 1990—), Assn. Tchrs. Tech. Writing, Coun. Programs in Tech. and Sci. Comm., Rocky Mountain Modern Lang. Assn., U. Chgo. Alumni (schs. com.), Phi Beta Kappa. Jewish. Office: Eastern Wash U MS-25 526 5th St Cheney WA 99004-1619

KAUFMAN, JULIAN MORTIMER, broadcasting company executive, consultant; b. Detroit, Apr. 3, 1918; s. Anton and Fannie (Newman) K.; m. Katherine LaVerne Likins, May 6, 1942; children: Nikki, Keith Anthony. Grad. high sch., Newark. Pub. Elizabeth (N.J.) Sunday Sun, Inc., 1937-39; account exec. Tolle Advt. Agy., San Diego, 1947-49; pub. Tucson Shopper, 1948-50; account exec. ABC, San Francisco, 1949-50; mgr. Sta. KPHO-TV, Phoenix, 1950-52; gen. mgr., v.p. Bay City TV Corp., San Diego, 1952-85; v.p. Jai Alai Films, Inc., San Diego, 1961—; TV cons. Julian Kaufman, Inc., San Diego, 1985—; dir. Spanish Internat. Broadcasting, Inc., L.A.; chmn. bd. dirs. Bay City TV Inc. Contbr. articles to profl. jours.; producer (TV show) Pick a Winner. Mem. Gov.'s adv. bd., Mental Health Assn., 1958—; bd. dirs. Francis Parker Sch., San Diego Better Bus. Bur., 1979-84, San Diego Conv. and Visitors Bur., World Affairs Coun., Pala Indian Mission. Served with USAAF, 1942-46. Recipient Peabody award, 1975, Emmy award, 1980. Mem. San Diego C. of C., Advt. and Sales Club, Sigma Delta Chi. Republican. Clubs: San Diego Press, University (San Diego). Home: 3125 Montesano Rd Escondido CA 92029-7302 Office: Ste 210 7677 Ronson Rd San Diego CA 92111-2004

KAUFMAN, STEVEN MICHAEL, lawyer; b. Spokane, Wash., July 2, 1951; s. Gordon Leonard and Terri (Thal) K.; m. Connie Hoopes, June 7, 1973; children: Kristopher, Shana. BS magna cum laude, U. Utah, 1973; JD cum laude, Gonzaga U., 1977. Bar: Utah 1977, U.S. Dist. Ct. Utah, 1977, U.S. Ct. Appeals (10th cir.) 1977, U.S. Supreme Ct. 1985. Founding ptnr. Farr, Kaufman, Hamilton, Phillips, Sullivan, Gorman & Perkins, Ogden, Utah, 1979—; mng. ptnr. Farr, Kaufman, Sullivan, Gorman, Jensen, Nichols, Medsker & Perkins, 1979—; judge pro tem, 1981—, bar commr., 1991—. Chmn. Commn. on Pub. Defenders, Ogden, 1984. Mem. ATLA, ABA, Utah State Bar Assn. (pres. elect, 1995-96, pres., 1996-97), Weber County Bar Assn. (pres. 1981-82). Jewish. Home: 5878 S 1050 E South Ogden UT 84405 Office: Farr Kaufman Sullivan Gorman Jensen Nichols Medsker & Perkins 205 26th St Ste 34 Ogden UT 84401-3194

KAUNE, JAMES EDWARD, ship repair company executive, former naval officer; b. Santa Fe, N.Mex., Mar. 4, 1927; s. Henry Eugene and Lucile (Carter) K.; B.S., U.S. Naval Acad., 1950; Naval Engr. degree Mass. Inst. Tech., 1955; B.S. in Metallurgy, Carnegie-Mellon U., 1960; m. Pauline Stamatos, June 24, 1956; children: Bradford Scott, Audrey Lynn, Jason Douglas. Commd. ensign U.S. Navy, 1950, advanced through grades to capt., 1970; asst. gunnery officer U.S.S. Floyd B. Parks, 1950-52; project officer U.S.S. Gyatt, Boston Naval Shipyard, 1955-57; main propulsion officer U.S.S. Tarawa, 1957-58; asst. planning officer Her Majesty's Canadian Dockyard, Halifax, N.S., Can., 1960-62; repair officer U.S.S. Cadmus, 1962-64; fleet maintenance officer Naval Boiler and Turbine Lab., 1964-68; various shipyard assignments, 1968-70, material staff officer U.S. Naval Air Forces Atlantic Fleet, 1971-74; production officer Phila. Naval Shipyard, 1974-79; comdr. Long Beach Naval Shipyard, Calif.; exec. v.p. Am. Metal Bearing Co., Garden Grove, Calif., from 1979; gen. mgr. San Francisco div. Topp Shipyards, Alameda, Calif., v.p. engring. Point Richmond Shipyard, Calif., 1983-84; v.p. engring., mktg. Service Engring. Corp, San Francisco, 1984-92; CEO Am. Modular Power Systems, San Francisco, 1992—. Mem. Am. Soc. Naval Engrs., Am. Soc. Quality Control, Soc. Naval Architects and Marine Engrs., U.S. Naval Inst., Am. Soc. Metals. Episcopalian. Club: Masons. Contbr. articles to profl. jours. Home: 403 Camino Sobrante Orinda CA 94563-1844 Office: Am Modular Power Sys 2101 3d St San Francisco CA 94107

KAUNITZ, JONATHAN DAVIDSON, physician; b. N.Y.C., Nov. 6, 1950; s. Paul Ehrlich and Rita (Davidson) K.; m. Christine Lee, July 31, 1983; children: Justin Lee, Genevieve Jung. BA in Molecular Biology, Columbia Coll., 1972, MD, 1976. Diplomate Am. Bd. Internal Medicine, Am. Bd. Gastroenterology. Intern in medicine Presbyn. Hosp., N.Y.C., 1976-77, resident in medicine, 1977-79; gastroenterology fellow U. Calif., San Francisco, 1979-80, gastrointestinal rsch. fellow, 1980-81; gastrointestinal rsch. fellow U. Calif., L.A., 1981-82; asst. prof. medicine U. Calif. L.A. Sch. Medicine, 1983-91; assoc. investigator VA Career Devel. Series, 1984-85, rsch. assoc., 1985-88, clin. investigator, 1990-95; assoc. dir. UCLA Integrated Tng. Program in Digestive Diseases, 1986-90, co-dir., 1996—; assoc. prof. dept. medicine Sch. Medicine UCLA, 1991—; assoc. chief med. svc. gastrointestinal sect. Wadsworth VA Med. Ctr., 1993—; mem. legis. assembly UCLA, 1991-94, com. on appointments and promotions, 1991—; mem. gastrointestinal bd. Med. Rsch. Svc., Dept. Vet. Affairs, 1993-96, chair, 1995, mem. coun., 1996. Editl. bd. Am. Jour. of Physiology. Recipient numerous rsch. grants. Mem. Am. Gastroenterol. Assn., Am. Physiol. Soc., Columbia Coll. Physicians and Surgeons (alumni dir. 1976—), Soc. for Auditory Integration Tng. (bd. dirs. 1993—, v.p. 1994-95), Cure Autism Now (sci. adv. group 1995—, chair 1996—), West Coast Salt and Water Club (program chmn. 1989, treas. 1989—), Alpha Omega Alpha.

KAUPINS, GUNDARS EGONS, education educator; b. Mpls., Dec. 29, 1956; s. Alfreds and Skaidrite (Akots) K. BA, Wartburg Coll., 1979; MBA, U. No. Iowa, 1981; PhD, U. Iowa, 1986. Sr. prof. in human resources. Grad. asst. U. No. Iowa, Cedar Falls, 1979-81; employee rels. asst. Norand Corp., Cedar Rapids, 1983; grad. asst. Univ. Iowa, Iowa City, 1981-86; assoc. prof. Boise (Idaho) State U., 1986—; cons. in field. Contbr. articles to profl. jours. Recipient rsch. grants Boise State U., 1987-89, Ponder scholarship U. Iowa, 1983-85; named Adv. of the Yr., Boise State U., 1989. Mem. Soc. for Human Resource Mgmt. (sec., v.p. 1982-83), ASTD (sec. 1989), Assn. of Mgmt., Acad. of Mgmt., Am. Psychol. Assn. Home: 1368 E Monterey Dr Boise ID 83706 Office: Boise State U Dept Mgmt Boise ID 83725

KAUSER, FAZAL BAKHSH, aerospace engineer, educator; b. Multan, Panjab, Pakistan, Nov. 15, 1943; came to U.S., 1980; s. Haji Khuda Bakhsh and Bagh Begum; m. Qamar, May 29, 1969; children: Hina Kauser, Shella Kauser. BSc in Physics and Math., Panjab U., 1961; BSc (hons.) in aero engring., Loughborough U., 1966, diploma in indsl. studies, 1966; MS in Aero. Engring., Air Force Inst. Tech., Wright-Patterson AFB, Ohio, 1976. Registered profl. engr., aerospace engr., Fla., mech. engr., Calif. Dir. wind tunnels labs. Pakistan Air Force Engring. Acad., Karachi, 1966-76, head aerodynamic divs., 1977-80; rsch. asst. Pa. State U., College Park, Pa., 1980-82; asst. prof. Embry Riddle Aeronautical U., Daytona Beach, Fla., 1982-86; assoc. prof. Calif. State Polytechnic U., Pomona, 1986—; car Calif. Poly. State U., Pomona, 1986-96; prof. airbreathing propulsion and advanced aerodyns. Calif. Poly. Inst., Pomona, 1995; cons. Lockheed Aeronautical Systems Co., Burbank, Calif., 1988, NASA Jet Propulsion Lab, Pasadena; reviewer Delmar Pub. Co., N.Y., 1989-90; prin. investigator rsch. projects in field, 1978-90. Contbr. articles to profl. jours. Squadron leader Pakistan Air Force, 1966-80. Fellow NASA/ASEE Summer Faculty Program, 1996. Fellow AIAA (assoc., mem. airbreathing propulsion com.); mem. ASME (pub. sub. com.), Am. Soc. Engring. Edn., Tau Alpha Pi, Tau Beta Pi. Office: Calif State Poly Tech U 3801 W Temple Ave Pomona CA 91768-2557

KAWACHIKA, JAMES AKIO, lawyer; b. Honolulu, Dec. 5, 1947; s. Shinichi and Tsuyuko (Murashige) K.; m. Karen Keiko Takahashi, Sept. 1, 1973; 1 child, Robyn Mari. BA, U. Hawaii, Honolulu, 1969; JD, U. Calif., Berkeley, 1973. Bar: Hawaii 1973, U.S. Dist. Ct. Hawaii 1973, U.S. Ct. Appeals (9th cir.) 1974, U.S. Supreme Ct. 1992. Dep. atty. gen. Office of Atty. Gen. State of Hawaii, Honolulu, 1973-74; assoc. Padgett, Greeley & Marumoto, Honolulu, 1974-75, Law Office of Frank D. Padgett, Honolulu, 1975-77, Kobayashi, Watanabe, Sugita & Kawashima, Honolulu, 1977-82; ptnr. Carlsmith, Wichman, Case, Mukai & Ichiki, Honolulu, 1982-86, Bays, Deaver, Hiatt, Kawachika & Lezak, Honolulu, 1986-95; propr. Law Offices of James A. Kawachika, Honolulu, 1996—; mem. Hawaii Bd. of Bar Examiners, Honolulu; arbitrator Cir. Ct. Arbitration Program State of Hawaii, Honolulu, 1986—. Chmn. Disciplinary Bd. Hawaii Supreme Ct., 1991—; mem. U.S. dist. Ct. Adv. Com. on the Civil Justice Reform Act of 1990, 1991—. Mem. ABA, ATLA, Hawaii Bar Assn. (bd. dirs. Honolulu chpt. 1975-76, young lawyers sect. 1983-84, 92-93, treas. 1987-88, v.p./pres.-elect 1997-98), 9th Crct. Jud. Conf. (lawyer rep., Honolulu chpt. 1988-90). Office: Grosvenor Ctr Mauka Tower 737 Bishop St Ste 2750 Honolulu HI 96813

KAWAI, ERNEST GORDON, higher education director; b. Altadena, Calif., Nov. 8, 1946; s. Nobu T. and Miye (Fujioka) K.; m. Sandra Kimiko Taba, Aug. 31, 1973; 1 child, Julie K. BS, Calif. State U., L.A., 1969. Cert. store profl. Adminstrv. asst. County of San Diego, 1973-78; adminstr. Calif. Poly. Pomona Found., 1978-81, dir. bookstores, 1982—; dir.-at-large Calif. Assn. Coll. Stores, La Mesa, 1990-91, v.p., 1992, pres., 1993. 1st lt. U.S.

Army, 1969-72. Mem. Assistance League of Upland (patron). Office: Bronco Bookstore 3801 W Temple Ave Pomona CA 91768-2557

KAWAMOTO, HENRY K., plastic surgeon; b. Long Beach, Calif., 1937. Intern U. Calif. Hosp., L.A., 1965; resident Columbia Presbyn. Med. Ctr., N.Y., 1969-71; resident plastic surgery NYU, 1971-73; fellow cranofacial surgery Dr. Paul Tessier, Paris, 1973-74; clin. prof. plastic surgery U. Calif., L.A. Mem. Am. Assn. Plastic Surgery, Am. Soc. Plastic and Reconstructive Surgery, ASMS, AOA. Office: 1301 20th St # 460 Santa Monica CA 90404-2050

KAWASAKI, LILLIAN YURIKO, city general manager environmental affairs; b. Denver, Sept. 17, 1950. BS in Zoology, Calif. State L.A., 1974, MS in Biology, 1980. Dir. environ. mgmt. L.A. City Harbor, 1988-90; instr. part-time UCLA, 1990—; gen. mgr. City of L.A. Environ. Affairs, 1990—. Mem. U.S. EPA Nat. Environ. Justice Adv. Coun., U.S. EPA Local Govt. Adv. Com.; bd. dirs. Calif. State U. Found., 1993—. Recipient Disting. Alumni award Calif. State L.A., 1992, Pres.'s award Asian-Am. Architects/Engrs., 1992, Inaugural Environ. award Pat Brown Inst., 1996, Environ. Leadership award Calif. League Conservation, 1996. Office: City of LA Environ Affairs Dept 201 N Figueroa St Ste 200 Los Angeles CA 90012-2625

KAWESKI, SUSAN, plastic surgeon, naval officer; b. Oil City, Pa., Jan. 27, 1955; d. Richard Francis and Lottie Ann (Malek) K.; m. Henry Nicholas Ernecoff, Aug. 7, 1983. BA, Washington and Jefferson Coll., 1976; MA, SUNY, Buffalo, 1979; MD, Pa. State U., 1983. Diplomate Am. Bd. Surgery, Am. Bd. Plastic Surgery. Commd. lt. USN, 1983, advanced through grades to comdr., 1993; intern in gen. surgery Naval Hosp., San Diego, 1983-84; head med. dept. USN, 1984-85; resident in gen. surgery Naval Hosp., San Diego, 1985-89; resident in plastic surgery Pa. State U., Hershey, 1989-91; staff plastic surgeon Naval Med. Ctr., San Diego, 1991-95; head divsn. plastic surgery, surgeon gen. advisor USN, 1994-95; craniofacial fellow Dr. Ian T. Jackson, Mich., 1995-96; head cleft palate/craniofacial team Naval Med. Ctr., 1996—; chmn. Cleft Palate/Craniofacial Bd., San Diego; plastic surgery advisor to surgeon gen. USN, 1994-95; presenter in field. Author chpt. to book. Recipient Ernest Witebsky Meml. award for proficiency in microbiology SUNY at Buffalo, 1978. Fellow ACS (assoc., 1st Place Rsch. award 1991); mem. Am. Assn. Plastic and Reconstructive Surgeons, Am. Cleft Palate Assn., Am. Assn. Women Surgeons, Am. Med. Women's Assn., Assn. Mil. Surgeons U.S., Univ. Club. Republican. Roman Catholic. Home: 1158 Barcelona Dr San Diego CA 92107-4151 Office: Divsn Plastic Surgery Naval Med Ctr Bob Wilson Dr San Diego CA 92134

KAY, ALAN COOKE, federal judge; b. 1932; s. Harold Thomas and Ann (Cooke) K. BA, Princeton U., 1957; LLB, U. Calif., Berkeley, 1960. Assoc. Case, Kay & Lynch, Honolulu, 1960-64, ptnr., 1965-86; judge U.S. Dist. Ct. Hawaii, Honolulu, 1986—, chief judge; bd. regents Internat. Coll. and Grad. Sch., 1994—. Mem. steering com. Fuller Theol. Sem. Hawaii, 1985-86; pres., trustee Hawaii Mission Children's Soc., Honolulu, 1980-86; bd. dirs. Good News Mission, 1980-86, Econ. Devel. Corp. Honolulu, 1985-86, Legal Aid Soc., Honolulu, 1968-71. Mem. ABA, Hawaii Bar Assn. (exec. com. 1972-73, bd. dirs. real estate sect. 1983-86), Fed. Judges Assn. (9th cir. jud. coun. 1994—, 9th cir. Pacific Islands com. 1994—), Am. Inns of Ct. (counselor Aloha Inn 1987—). Republican. Office: US Dist Ct PO Box 50128 Honolulu HI 96850-0001*

KAY, HERMA HILL, law educator; b. Orangeburg, S.C., Aug. 18, 1934; d. Charles Esdorn and Herma Lee (Crawford) Hill. BA, So. Meth. U., 1956; JD, U. Chgo., 1959. Bar: Calif. 1960, U.S. Supreme Ct. 1978. Law clk. to Justice Roger Traynor, Calif. Supreme Ct., 1959-60; asst. prof. law U. Calif., Berkeley, 1960-62; assoc. prof. U. Calif., 1962, prof., 1963, dir. family law project, 1964-67, Jennings prof., 1987-96, dean, 1992—; Armstrong prof., 1996—; co-reporter uniform marriage and div. act Nat. Conf. Commrs. on Uniform State Laws, 1968-70; vis. prof. U. Manchester, Eng., 1972, Harvard U., 1976; mem. Gov.'s Commn. on Family, 1966. Author: (with Martha S. West) Text Cases and Materials on Sex-based Discrimination, 4th edit., 1996, (with R. Cramton, D. Currie and L. Kramer) Conflict of Laws: Cases, Comments, Questions, 5th edit., 1993; contbr. articles to profl. jours. Trustee Russell Sage Found., N.Y., 1972-87, chmn. bd., 1980-84; trustee, bd. dirs. Equal Rights Advs. Calif., 1976—, chmn., 1976-83; pres. bd. dirs. Rosenberg Found., Calif., 1987-88, bd. dirs. 1978—. Recipient rsch. award Am. Bar Found., 1990, award ABA Commn. Women in Profession, 1992, Marshall-Wythe medal, 1995; fellow Ctr. Advanced Study in Behavioral Sci., Palo Alto, Calif., 1963. Mem. Calif. Bar Assn., Bar U.S. Supreme Ct., Calif. Women Lawyers (bd. govs. 1975-77), Am. Law Inst. (mem. coun. 1985-), Assn. Am. Law Schs. (exec. com. 1986-87, pres.-elect 1988, pres. 1989, past pres. 1990), Am. Acad. Arts and Scis., Order of Coif (nat. pres. 1983-85). Democrat. Office: U Calif Law Sch Boalt Hall Berkeley CA 94720

KAYALAR, SELAHATTIN, electrical engineer; b. Dinar, Turkey, Feb. 11, 1954; came to U.S., 1979; s. Salih and Ülfet (Taskoparan) K.; m. Lena Fazelian, Aug. 11, 1987; 1 child, Yasemin. BSEE, Boğaziçi U., Istanbul, Turkey, 1977; MSEE, Purdue U., 1981; MS in Engring., Johns Hopkins U., 1983, PhD in EE, 1987. Rsch. asst. Philips Rsch. Lab., Eindhoven, The Netherlands, 1978-79, Johns Hopkins U., Balt., 1981-87; vis. lectr. Ind. U. Purdue U., Indpls., 1979-81, asst. prof., 1987-91; mem. tech. staff Jet Propulsion Lab., Pasadena, Calif., 1991—. Recipient Tech. Achievement award NASA, 1993. Mem. IEEE, IEEE Comms. Soc., IEEE Control Engring. Soc. Muslim. Home: 45 Southwind Aliso Viejo CA 92656-1385 Office: Jet Propulsion Lab 4800 Oak Grove Dr Pasadena CA 91109-8001

KAYATE, ETHEL MAE, physician assistant; b. Albuquerque, Nov. 9, 1939; d. John and Lucy (Kiro) K. Diploma, Regina Sch. Nursing, 1960; AA, U. N.Mex., 1976. Staff nurse St. Joseph Hosp., Albuquerque, 1960-61, USPHS Indian Health Svc. Gallup (N.Mex.) Indian Med Ctr., 1969-71; physician asst. Gallup Indian Med. Ctr., 1974-95. Native Am. Tribal Affiliation: Pueblo of Laguna, N.Mex.; dir. religious edn. St. John Vianney, Gallup, 1995-96. Lt. col. USAF, 1962-69, 72-87. Fellow Am. Acad. Physician Assts., N.Mex. Physician Assts. Roman Catholic. Home: 3610 Zia Dr Gallup NM 87301

KAYE, BRIAN RANDALL, rheumatologist, educator; b. Detroit, Dec. 13, 1957; s. Ronald Lee and Tobye Faye (Davidson) K.; m. Fran Alice Tannenbaum, Apr. 30, 1983; children: Naomi Shoshana, Joshua Hillel. AB summa cum laude, Princeton U., 1979; MD, Baylor Coll. Medicine, 1983. Diplomate Am. Bd. Internal Medicine, Am. Bd. Rheumatology. Resident in internal medicine Santa Clara Valley Med. Ctr., San Jose, Calif., 1983-86; fellow in rheumatology Stanford U., Palo Alto, Calif., 1986-88, clin. asst. prof. medicine, 1992—; pvt. practice, Oakland, San Leandro, Calif., 1988-91, Berkeley, Calif., 1992—; attending physician Highland Gen. Hosp., Oakland, Calif., 1988—; clin. asst. prof. medicine U. Calif., San Francisco, 1989—; manuscript reviewer Arthritis and Rheumatism, Atlanta, 1990—, Jour. Rheumatology, Toronto, Ont., Can., 1990—. Contbr. articles to med. jours. Mem. alumni schs. com. Princeton U., Castro Valley, Calif., 1983—, bd. dirs.; chmn. adult edn. and youth coms. Beth Jacob Congregation, Oakland, 1993—; pres., sec., bd. dirs. Oakland Hebrew Day Sch. Sr. thesis rsch. grantee Princeton U., 1978; Wexner Found. fellow, 1995—. Fellow ACP, Am. Coll. Rheumatology; mem. AMA, Calif. Med. Assn., Alameda-Contra Costa Med. Assn., No. Calif. Rheumatism Soc. (program chair 1988-90, sec.-treas. 1992-94, pres. 1994-96). Office: The Arthritis Ctr 3010 Colby St Ste 118 Berkeley CA 94705-2059

KAYE, CAROLE, museum director and curator; b. Somerville, N.J., Apr. 24, 1933; d. Harry and Grace (Schwartz) Golison; m. Paul Littman, June 29, 1952 (dec. Apr. 1960); children: Fern, Alan; m. Barry Kaye; children: Howard. Student, Syracuse U., 1951. With Barry Kaye Assocs., L.A.; owner, curator Carole and Barry Kaye Mus. Miniatures, L.A.; v.p. Barry Kaye Assocs. Mus., 1994—. Past pres. Hadassah, Beverly Hills, Calif.; founder Music Ctr., Cedars-Sinai Hosp., L.A.; mem. Jewish Fedn. Mem. Friends of Ben Gurion U. Office: Carole & Barry Kaye Mus Miniatures 5900 Wilshire Blvd Los Angeles CA 90036-5013

KAYE, MICHAEL DUNCAN, physician, gastroenterologist, consultant; b. Coventry, Eng., July 26, 1939; came to U.S., 1969; s. Duncan Kaye and Rotha Valerie (Jones) Tyndall; m. Marina Sakellarides, July 26, 1962 (div. Sept. 8, 1987); children: Lydia Sophia, Delia Rosalind Julia, Duncan Edmund Alexander. BA, Oxford (Eng.) U., 1960, MA, BM, BCh, 1963, DM, 1970. House physician, surgeon Radcliffe Infirmary, Oxford, 1964-65; sr. house officer, registrar Sully Hosp. Penarth, South Wales, 1965-67; professorial unit registrar Cardiff Royal Infirmary, South Wales, 1967-69; fellow in gastroenterology Med. Sch. U. Colo., Denver, 1969-72, asst. prof. medicine, 1972-74; assoc. prof. medicine U. Vt., Burlington, 1974-80, prof. medicine, 1980-87; cons. in gastroenterology Fronk Clinic, Honolulu, 1987-90, Straub Clinic and Hospital, Honolulu, 1990—. Contbr. more than 50 articles to profl. jours. Grantee NIH, 1972—. Fellow Royal Coll. Physicians (London); mem. Hawaii Gastroenterol. Assn. (pres.), Am. Gastroenterol. Soc., Am. Assn. for the Study of Liver Diseases, Brit. Soc. Gastroenterology, Honolulu Club, Oahu Country Club. Office: Straub Clinic 888 S King St Honolulu HI 96813-3009

KAYE, PETER FREDERIC, television editor; b. Chgo., Mar. 8, 1928; s. Ralph A. and Sara Corson (Philipson) K.; m. Martha Louise Wood, Mar. 20, 1955; children: Loren, Terry, Adam. BA in Govt., Pomona Coll., 1949. Reporter Alhambra (Calif.) Post-Advocate, 1950-53; reporter, editorial writer, polit. writer The San Diego Union, 1953-68; news and pub. affairs dir. KPBS-TV, San Diego State Coll., 1968-72; corr., producer Nat. Pub. Affairs Ctr. for TV, Washington, 1972-74; comm. dir. So. Calif. First Nat. Bank, San Diego, 1974-75; press sec. The Pres. Ford Com., Washington, 1975-76; mgr. Copley Videotex, San Diego, 1982-84; assoc. editor The San Diego Union, 1976-94; editl. dir. KNSD, San Diego, 1996—; freelance TV producer programs KPBS, PBS, BBC; San Diego corr. Newsweek, 1968-71, McGraw-Hill, 1959-67; lectr. comm. U. Calif., San Diego, 1971; copywriter Washburn-Justice Advt., San Diego, 1959-70. Producer 10 TV programs including including Jacob Bronowski: Life and Legacy, Twenty-Five Years of Presidency, The Presidency, The Press and the People. Press asst. Eisenhower-Nixon Campaign, L.A., 1952; asst. press sec. Richard Nixon Presdl. Campaign, Washington, 1960; dir. Pete Wilson for Mayor Campaign, San Diego, 1971; comm. dir. Flournoy for Gov. Campaign, Beverly Hills, Calif., 1974. With U.S. Mcht. Marines, 1945, U.S. Army, 1950-52. Jefferson fellow East-West Ctr., Honolulu, 1987; recipient Golden Mike awards So. Calif. TV News Dirs. Assn., 1969, 70, 71, Best Pub. Affairs Program award Nat. Ednl. TV, 1970, Best Local TV Series award Radio-TV Mirror, 1971, Nat. Emmy award Spl. Events Reporter, Watergate Coverage, 1973-74, Best Editorial awards Copley Newspapers Ring of Truth, 1979, Sigma Delta Chi, 1985, Calif. Newspaper Pubs. Assn., 1985; San Diego Emmy awards, 1985, 87, 91. Mem. NATAS, State Bar Calif. (bd. govs. 1991—, v.p. 1993-94, 96-97), Sigma Delta Chi. Republican. Home: 240 Ocean View Ave Del Mar CA 92014-3322

KAYFETZ, VICTOR JOEL, writer, editor, translator; b. N.Y.C., July 20, 1945; s. Daniel Osler and Selma Harriet (Walowitz) K.; BA, Columbia U., 1966; postgrad. U. Stockholm (Sweden), 1966-67; MA in History, U. Calif.-Berkeley, 1969. Teaching asst. in Swedish, U. Calif., Berkeley, 1969-70; tchr., adminstr. Swedish adult edn. programs, 1970-75; corr. Reuters, Stockholm, 1975-78; sub-editor Reuters World Ser., London, 1978; corr. London Fin. Times, Stockholm, 1979-80; free lance translator Swedish, Danish, Norwegian, 1967—; free lance editor Swedish and Am. mags., 1980—. Henry Evans traveling fellow, 1966-67; Nat. Def. Fgn. Lang. fellow, 1967-69; Thord Gray fellow Am.-Scandinavian Found., 1970. Mem. Swedish Am. C. of C., Soc. Advancement Scandinavian Study, Am. Scandinavian Found., Swedish Assn. Profl. Translators, World Affairs Council No. Calif., Sierra Club, Phi Beta Kappa. Author: Sweden in Brief, 1974, 80; Invest in Sweden, 1984, Skanska, the First Century, 1987; editor, translator numerous books, ann. reports, mags. for Swedish govt. agys. interest orgns., univs., indsl. corps., banks. Office: Scan Edit 760 Market St Ste 1067 San Francisco CA 94102-2305

KAYLAN, HOWARD LAWRENCE, musical entertainer, composer; b. N.Y.C., June 22, 1947; s. Sidney and Sally Joyce (Berlin) K.; m. Mary Melita Pepper, June 10, 1967 (div. Sept. 1971); 1 child, Emily Anne; m. Susan Karen Olsen, Apr. 18, 1982 (div. June 1996); 1 child, Alexandra Leigh. Student, UCLA. Lead singer rock group The Turtles, Los Angeles, 1965-70, Mothers of Invention, Los Angeles, 1970-72, Flo and Eddie, 1972—; radio, TV, recording entertainer various broadcast organizations, Los Angeles, 1972—; screenwriter Larry Gelbart, Carl Gotleib prodns., Los Angeles, 1979-85; producer children's records Kidstuff Records, Hollywood, Fla., 1980—; singer, producer rock band Flo and Eddie, Los Angeles, 1976—; singer, producer The Turtles (reunion of original band), Los Angeles, 1980—; actor, TV and film Screen Actors Guild, Los Angeles, 1983—; background vocalist various albums for numerous performers; syndicated talk show host Unistar Radio Network, 1989—; radio personality Sta. WXRK-FM, N.Y.C., 1990-91, KLOU, St. Louis, 1993, WGRR, Cin., 1995-96. Author: Hi Bob, 1995, The Energy Pals, 1995; contbr. articles to Creem mag., L.A. Free Press, Rockit mag., Phonograph Record; screenwriter: (film) Death Masque, 1985; actor: (film) Get Crazy, 1985, General Hospital; performed at the White House, 1970. Recipient 10 Gold and Platinum LP album awards while lead singer, 1965—, Fine Arts award, Bank of Am., L.A., 1965, Spl. Billboard Mag. award, 1992; recorded numerous top ten hit songs with Turtles, Bruce Springstein, The Ramones, Duran Duran, T. Rex, John Lennon and others. Mem. AFTRA, Screen Actors Guild, Am. Fedn. Musicians, AGVA.

KAYLOR, ANDREA LYNN, secondary school counselor; b. L.A., May 19, 1946; d. Kenneth D. and Florence R. (Berkman) Cooper; m. Stephan A. Kaylor, Dec. 4, 1983; children: Gavin Chandler, Kiley Chandler. AA, Diablo Valley Coll., Pleasant Hill, Calif., 1971; BS, U. Nev., Reno, 1983, MA in Counseling, 1989. Cert. dental hygiene, teaching cert.; cert. sch. counselor. Registered dental hygienist Davis, Calif., 1971-73, L.A., 1973-78, Reno, 1978-80; elem. tchr. Rita Cannon Sch., Reno, 1984-88, Alice Maxwell Sch., Sparks, Nev., 1989-90; high sch. counselor McQueen High Sch., Reno, 1990—; tchr. trainer Math Cadre Washoe County Sch. Dist., Reno, 1987-89; presenter WC Math Assn. Biannual Conf., Reno, 1985-89. Del. Democratic County Conv., Reno, 1988; campaign mgr. Mcpl. Judge Race, Reno, 1980; treas., state conv. del. PTA, Reno, 1985-89; tchr. rep. Alice Maxwell PTA, Sparks, 1989-90. Recipient Nat. Sallie Mae Tchr. Award for Outstanding 1st Yr. Tchrs., Sallie Mae Found., 1985; Mary Sartor Meml. scholar for acad. excellence, Dept. Edn. U. Nev. Reno, 1982. Mem. NEA, ACA, Nev. State Edn. Assn., Greater Nev. Sch. Counselors Assn. (past pres., state of Nev. liaison), Am. Sch. Counselor Assn. Democrat. Home: PO Box 696 Verdi NV 89439-0696 Office: McQueen High Sch 6055 Lancer St Reno NV 89523-1208

KAYTON, MYRON, engineering company executive; b. N.Y.C., Apr. 26, 1934; s. Albert Louis and Rae (Danoff) K.; m. Paula Erde, Sept. 5, 1954; children: Elizabeth Kayton Kerns, Susan Kayton Barclay. BS, The Cooper Union, 1955; MS, Harvard U., 1956; PhD, MIT, 1960. Registered engr., Calif. Sect. head Litton Industries, Woodland Hills, Calif., 1960-65; dep. mgr. NASA, Houston, 1965-69; mem. sr. staff TRW, Inc., Redondo Beach, Calif., 1969-81; pres. Kayton Engring. Co., Inc., Santa Monica, Calif., 1981—; chmn. bd. dirs. WINCON Conf., L.A., 1985-92; founding dir. Caltech-MIT Enterprise Forum, Pasadena, Calif., 1984—; tchr. tech. courses UCLA Extension, 1969-88. Author: Avionic Navigation Systems, 1966, 2d edit., 1997, Navigation: Land, Sea, Air and Space, 1990, MSS, 1997; contbr. numerous articles on engring., econs. and other profl. subjects. Founding dir. UCLA Friends of Humanities, 1971-75; West coast chmn. Cooper Union Fund Campaign, 1989-93. Fellow NSF, Washington, 1956-57, 58-60; recipient Gano Dunn medal The Cooper Union, N.Y.C., 1975. Fellow IEEE (corp. bd. dirs. 1996-97, pres. aerospace 1993-94, exec. v.p. aerospace 1991-92, v.p. tech. ops. 1988-90, nat. bd. govs. 1983—, vice-chmn. L.A. coun. 1983-84, M.B. Carlton award 1988, Disting. lectr.); mem. ASME, Harvard Grad. Soc. (coun. mem. chmn. nominating com. 1988-91, Inst. Navigation, Soc. Automotive Engr., Harvard Club So. Calif. (pres. 1979-80), MIT Club (L.A.). Office: Kayton Engring Co PO Box 802 Santa Monica CA 90406-0802

KAZLE, ELYNMARIE, producer; b. St. Paul, June 22, 1958; d. Victor Anton and Marylu (Gardner) K. BFA, U. Minn., Duluth, 1982; MFA, Ohio U., 1984. Prodn. mgr. Great Lakes Shakespeare, Cleve., 1983; prodn. stage mgr. San Diego (Calif.) Opera, 1984, PCPA Theaterfest, Santa Maria, Calif., 1986-87; stage mgr. Bklyn. Acad. Music, 1987; assoc. producer Assn. Am. Theater Actors, N.Y.C., 1988-89; prodn. stage mgr. Time Flies When You're Alive, West Hollywood, Calif., 1988—; asst. advt. display Wall St. Jour., L.A., 1988-89; West Coast adminstr. Soc. Stage Dirs. and Choreographers, 1991-93; assoc. mng. dir. Actors Alley, North Hollywood, Calif., 1993—; assoc. mag. dir., Actors Alley, 1993-96; mng. ptnr., AIW Prodns., 1997—. Editor, pub. The Ohio Network newsletter, 1984-90; prodr. Santa Monica Playhouse, 1988-94; assoc. mng. dir. Actors Alley Repertory Theater, North Hollywood Calif., 1993-96. Trustee Theatre/L.A., 1992-94. Mem. Stage Mgrs. Assn., Stage Mgrs. Assn. L.A., U.S. Inst. for Theatre Tech. (bd. dirs. 1990—), Actors Equity Assn., North Hollywood/Universal City C. of C. (bd. dirs. 1994-96), Phi Kappa Phi, Delta Chi Omega (past pres. 1978). Office: Actors Alley PO Box 8500 Van Nuys CA 91409-8500

KEA, JONATHAN GUY, instrumental music educator; b. Honolulu, June 2, 1960; s. Gilbert Halemano and Goldie Lee Gum (Chun) K. BMus, cert. teaching, Coe Coll., Cedar Rapids, Iowa, 1982. Band dir. James Campbell High Sch., Ewa Beach, Hawaii, 1982—; asst. condr. Honolulu Cmty. Band, 1988-94; dir. Honolulu Cmty. Jazz Band, 1993—. Mem. NEA, Oahu Band Dirs. Assn., Hawaii Music Educators Assn., Music Educators Nat. Conf., Phi Mu Alpha. Office: James Campbell High Sch 91-980 North Rd Ewa Beach HI 96706-2746

KEALIINOHOMOKU, JOANN WHEELER, anthropologist, dance ethnologist, educator; b. Kansas City, Mo., May 20, 1930; d. George V. and Leona Lavena (Moore) Wheeler; 1 child, Halla K. BSS, Northwestern U., 1955, MA, 1965; PhD, Ind. U., 1976. Mem. faculty No. Ariz. U., Flagstaff, 1970-72, 75-87, assoc. prof. anthropology, 1980-87, emeritus prof. anthropology, 1987; sr. rsch. assoc. Ctr. for Colo. Plateau Studies No. Ariz. U., 1987-92, ind. scholar, 1987—; mem. faculty World Campus Afloat, fall 1972, 73, Semester-at-Sea, 1989; resident scholar Sch. Am. Research, Santa Fe, 1974-75; vis. faculty U. Hawaii, Hilo, spring 1973, summer 1973, 74, U. Hawaii-Manoa, fall 1981, spring, 1991, NYU, summer 1980, 84, U. N.C., Greensboro, summer 1990, Tex. Woman's U., summer 1992, summer Inst. Hawaiian and Polynesian Studies U. Hawaii, Windword Cmty. Coll., 1993. Bd. dirs. Native Americans for Community Action, Flagstaff Indian Center, 1977-82, sec., 1980-82. Grantee, Am. Philos. Soc., 1966, 69-70, Wenner Gren Found., Ariz. Humanities Coun., 1991; Weatherhead fellow Sch. Am. Research, 1974-75; research fellow East-West Center, 1981; NEH grantee, 1986; recipient Disting. Pub. Scholar award Ariz. Humanities Coun., 1996. Fellow Current Anthropology; mem. Soc. Ethnomusicology (councilor; co founder Southwestern chpt.), Dance Research Center (charter), Congress on Research in Dance (bd. dirs. 1974-79, award in recognition of outstanding contbn. to dance rsch.), Cross-Cultural Dance Resources (co-founder 1981). Contbr. articles to profl. jours.

KEANE, KEVIN PATRICK, philosopher, consultant; b. N.Y.C., June 7, 1944; s. William Arthur and Geraldine Ann (Maher) K.; m. Joan Wilhelmina Kelly, Aug. 30, 1970; children: Brigid Anne, Padraic Kevin. AB in Philosophy magna cum laude, Rockhurst Coll., 1967; MA in Theology & Religion, Fordham U., 1969, PhD in Philosophy & Religion, 1978. Lectr. in philosophy Nassau C.C., Garden City, N.Y., 1968-70; lectr. religion Good Counsel Coll., Pace U., White Plains, N.Y., 1968-70; lectr. philosophy Dowling Coll., Oakdale, N.Y., 1972-73; instr. depts. philosophy and fgn. langs. Colo. State U., 1973-77, dir. inter-disciplinary program in religion, 1975-76; cons. Robert Panero Assocs., N.Y.C., 1977-79; founder, dir. Presidents' Seminar No. Colo. Exec. Forum/Denver Exec. Forum, 1979—; mem. affiliate faculty dept. philosophy Colo. State U., 1986—, dir. ethics and professionalism, 1989—; invited participant Liberty Fund Conf., Big Sky, Mont., 1991, South Woodstock, Vt., 1992, Jackson, Wyo., 1993. Mem. Bd. Editorial Contributors, Rocky Mountain News, 1991—; contbr. articles and essays to profl. publs. Recipient Elliott prize Mediaeval Acad. Am., 1977; fellow/specialist in philosophy Aspen Exec. Seminar, 1979. Mem. Alpha Sigma Nu. Roman Catholic. Home and Office: 4106 Attleboro Ct Fort Collins CO 80525-3445

KEANE, MELISSA, museum director. Pres., bd. trustees Phoenix Mus. History. Office: Phoenix Mus History 105 N 5th St Phoenix AZ 85004-4404

KEANE, PETER GERALD, lawyer, educator, broadcaster; b. N.Y.C., Feb. 8, 1943; s. John Martin and Mary Veronica (Neville) K.; m. Nancy Anne Ellsworth, Sept. 6, 1968; children: Lauren Alexandra, Heather Elizabeth. BA, CCNY, 1965; JD, So. Meth. U., 1968. Bar: Tex. 1968, Calif. 1970, U.S. Dist. Ct. (no. dist.) Tex. 1968, U.S. Ct. Appeals (5th cir.) 1968, U.S. Dist. Ct. (no. dist.) Calif. 1970, U.S. Dist. Ct. (cen. dist.) Calif. 1975, U.S. Dist. Ct. (we. dist.) Wash. 1977, U.S. Ct. Appeals (9th cir.) 1970, U.S. Supreme Ct. 1973. Chief atty. San Francisco Pub. Defender's Office, 1979—; asst. prof. law U. Calif. Hastings Coll. Law, San Francisco, 1981—; adj. prof. law Golden Gate Coll., San Francisco, 1987—; chair bd. dirs. 1st Appellate Dist. Project, 1986-92; legal analyst Sta. KPIX-TV, 1994—, Sta. KPIX-Radio, 1994—; broadcaster host "Keane on the Law", Sta. KPIX-Radio, San Francisco, 1994—. Mem. San Francisco Bar Assn. (pres. 1989), Calif. State Bar (chair criminal law adv. com. 1985-88, exec. com. criminal law sect. 1990-92, bd. govs. 1992-95, vice pres. 1995), Commn. on Future of Legal Profession. Democrat. Office: 555 7th St Rm 308 San Francisco CA 94103-4732

KEARNEY, JOSEPH LAURENCE, retired athletic conference administrator; b. Pitts., Apr. 28, 1927; s. Joseph L. and Iva M. (Nikirk) K.; m. Dorothea Hurst, May 13, 1950; children: Jan Marie, Kevin Robert, Erin Lynn, Shawn Alane, Robin James. B.A., Seattle Pacific U., 1952, LL.D., 1979; M.A., San Jose State U., 1964; Ed.D., U. Wash., 1970. Tchr., coach Paradise (Calif.) High Sch., 1952-53; asst. basketball coach U. Wash., 1953-54; coach, tchr. Sunnyside (Wash.) High Sch., 1954-57; prin. high sch., coach Onalaska (Wash.) High Sch., 1957-61; prin. Tumwater (Wash.) High Sch., 1961-63; asst. dir. Wash. High Sch. Activities Assn., 1963-64; athletic dir., assoc. dir. U. Wash., 1964-76; athletic dir. intercollegiate athletics Mich. State U., East Lansing, 1976-80, Ariz. State U., Tempe, 1980; commr. Western Athletic Conf., Denver, 1980-95; hon. chmn. Holiday Bowl, 1994, commr. emeritus, 1994. Pres. Cmty. Devel. Assn., 1957-61; bd. dirs. U.S. Olympic Com., 1985-94, chmn. games preparation com., 1985—. Recipient Disting. Service award Mich. Assn. Professions, 1979, Citation for Disting. Svc., Colo. Sports Hall of Fame, U.S. Olympic Com. Order of Olympic Shield, 1996. Mem. Nat. Football Found. (ct. of honors com.), Nat. Collegiate Athletic Assn., Nat. Assn. Collegiate Dirs. Athletics (Corbett award 1991, Adminstr. Excellence award), Collegiate Commrs. Assn. (pres.). Home: 2810 W Magee Rd Tucson AZ 85741-1500

KEARNS, HOMER H., school system administrator. AA in Spanish, West Hills Coll., Coalinga, Calif., 1962; BA in Spanish and Life Sci., Calif. State U., Fresno, 1964, MA in Adminstrn., 1970; PhD in Adminstrn. Higher Edn. and Sociology, Mich. State U., 1971. Tchr., head tchr., prin. Clovis (Calif.) Unified Sch. Dist, 1964-70; asst. prof. edn. dept. curriculum and instrn. coll. edn., assoc. dir. Northwest Cmty. Edn. Devel. Ctr. U. Oreg., Eugene, 1971-72; supt. schs. Sisters (Oreg.) Sch. Dist., 1972-75, Redmond (Oreg.) Sch. Dist., 1975-81; county supt. schs. Deschutes County Edn. Svc. Dist., Bend, Oreg., 1978-81; assoc., dep. supt. Salem-Keizer Pub. Schs., Salem, Oreg., 1981-86, supt. schs., 1986—; mem. exec. com. Coalition for Equitable Sch. Funding, 1988-91; bd. dirs. Marion & Polk Schs. Credit Union, 1992-94, Salem Econ. Devel. corp., Northwest Regional Ednl. Lab., chair bd. equity com. Bd. dirs. Salem Family YMCA, 3rd Century Edn. Found.; past bd. dirs. Oreg. Congl. Awards Coun., Cascade Child Treatment Ctr.; bd. dirs. Salem Sch. Found.; active Oreg. 2000 Com., United Way, County Planning Commn., Econ. Devel. Strategic Planning Group; mem. panel Gannet Found. Named Supt of Yr., Oreg. Counseling Assn., 1988, Outstanding Adminstr. Oreg. Multicultural Edn. Assn., 1994. Mem. Am. Assn. Sch. Adminstrs. (chair suburban supts. adv. com. 1990, exec. com. 1992-94, pres. elect 1994-95, pres. 1995-96, immediate past pres. 1996), Oreg. Assn. Sch. Execs. (bd. dirs., pres. 1990, chair sch. funding coalition 1992, Supt. of Yr. award with Am. Assn. Sch. Adminstrs. 1990), Rotary Internat. Office: Salem/Keizer SD 24J PO Box 12024 Salem OR 97309-0024

KEARSE, DAVID GRIER, stage and screen writer, journalist; b. Annapolis, Md., June 24, 1937; s. Francis Grier and Esther Carlisle (McCusker) K. BA, U. Miami, 1959; postgrad., Columbia U., 1959-60, NYU, 1988-89. Reporter, editor Capital Gazette Press, Annapolis, 1961-67; critic, copy editor The Balt. Sun, 1967-78; creative dept. Young and Rubicam Advtg.,

N.Y.C., 1978-83; with pub. rels. dept. Stephen W. Brener Assoc., N.Y.C., 1985-89; ind. screenwriter Hollywood, Calif., 1989—. Author: (musical) Miranda, 1991; author, dir. (play) Once Bitten, 1978; author: (screenplay) Alfredo's Sunset, 1991; dir.: The Winter's Tale, 1978, Playformers, 1989. Co-founder Annapolis Fine Arts Festival, 1963; AIDS vol. Roosevelt Hosp., N.Y.C., 1988-89; mem. Spiritual Adv. Com. AIDS Project L.A.; assoc. Episcopal Order Holy Cross. Mem. The Dramatists Guild, Writers Guild Am. (assoc.), Westwood Village Rotary Club. Democrat.

KEATING, DAVID, photographer; b. Rye, N.Y., Sept. 5, 1962. BA in Philosophy, Yale U., 1985; MA in Studio Art with distinction, U. N.Mex., 1991; student, Calif. Inst. Arts, Santa Clarita, 1992; MFA in Studio Art with distinction, U. N.Mex., 1994. Solo exhbns. include U. N.Mex., 1990 (traveled to Pace U., N.Y.C., Nat. Coun. Alcoholism Conf. of Affiliates, Nashville), 91, Calif. Inst. Arts, 1992, Graham Gallery, Albuquerque, 1994, Univ. Art Mus. Downtown, Albuquerque, 1995, Internat. Mus. Photography and Film, Rochester, N.Y., 1996, others; group exhbns. include Raw Space Gallery, Albuquerque, 1990, Betty Rymer Gallery, Sch. Art Inst. Chgo., 1991, 92, Randolph St. Gallery, Chgo., 1992, Atlanta Gallery Photography, 1992, San Jose (Calif.) Inst. Contemporary Art, 1992, Univ. Art Mus., Albuquerque, 1993, Ctr. African Am. History and Culture, Smithsonian Instn., Washington, 1994, Mus. Photographic Arts, San Diego, 1996, others; represented in pub. collections, including Univ. Art Mus., Albuquerque; subject of various articles and catalogs, 1992—. NEA Visual Artists fellow in photography, 1994, Van Deren Coke fellow, U. N.Mex., 1991; recipient award Photographers and Friends United Against AIDS/Art Matters Inc., 1992. Home: 1410 Central Ave SW#30 Albuquerque NM 87104

KEATINGE, CORNELIA WYMA, architectural preservationist consultant, lawyer; b. Poughkeepsie, N.Y., July 22, 1952; d. Edwin R. and Josephine B. (Brazis) Wyma; m. Robert Reed Keatinge, Aug. 21, 1982; 1 child, Courtney Elizabeth. BArch, U. Ky., 1974; MA in History and Theory of Architecture, U. Essex, Colchester, Eng., 1976; JD, U. Denver, 1982. Bar: Colo. 1982. Archtl. historian Kans. State Hist. Soc., Topeka, 1975-77; hist. architect Nat. Park Service, Denver, 1977-79; assoc. Richard E. Young, Denver, 1982-84; hist. architect Colo. Hist.Soc., Denver, 1984-86; sole practice, cons. architecture Denver, 1986; hist. preservation specialist Adv. Council Hist. Preservation, Golden, Colo., 1986—. Vol. Denver Art Mus., 1980—, Jr. League Denver, 1983—. Rotary fellow, 1974-75; recipient Spl. Achievement award, Nat. Park Service, 1980. Mem. ABA. Home: 460 S Marion Pky # 1904 Denver CO 80209-2544 Office: 12136 W Bayaud Ave Ste 330 Lakewood CO 80226

KEATINGE, ROBERT REED, lawyer; b. Berkeley, Calif., Apr. 22, 1948; s. Gerald Robert and Elizabeth Jean (Benedict) K.; m. Katherine Lou Carr, Feb. 1, 1969 (div. Dec. 1981); 1 child, Michael Towne; m. Cornelia Elizabeth Wyma, Aug. 21, 1982; 1 child, Courtney Elizabeth. BA, U. Colo., 1970; JD, U. Denver, 1973, LLM, 1982. Bar: Colo. 1974, U.S. Dist. Ct. Colo. 1974, U.S. Ct. Appeals (10th cir.) 1977, U.S. Tax Ct. 1980. Ptnr. Kubie & Keatinge, Denver, 1974-76; pvt. practice Denver, 1976; assoc. Richard Young, Denver, 1977-86; counsel Durham & Assoc. P.C., Denver, 1986-89, Durham & Baron, Denver, 1989-90; project editor taxation Shepard's/McGraw-Hill, Colorado Springs, Colo., 1990-96; of counsel Holland & Hart, LLP, Denver, 1992—; lectr. law U. Denver, 1982-92, adj. prof. grad. tax program, 1983—. Author, cons. (CD-ROM) Entity Expert, 1996; co-author: Ribstein and Keatinge on Limited Liability Companies, 1992; contbr. articles to profl. jours. and treatises. Spkr. to profl. socs. and univs. including AICPA, ALI-ABA, U. TEx., 1984—. Recipient Law Week award U. Denver Bur. Nat. Affairs, 1974. Mem. ABA (chmn. subcom. ltd. liability cos. of com. on partnerships 1990-95, chmn. com. on taxation 1995—, mem. ho. of dels. 1996—), Colo. Bar Assn. (corp. code revision com., co-chmn. ltd. liability co. revision com., taxation sect. exec. coun. 1988-94, sec.-treas. 1991-92, chmn. 1993-94), Denver Bar Assn. Home: 460 S Marion Pky # 1904 Denver CO 80209-2544

KEATON, SUSAN CAMILLE, editor; b. Nashville, Sept. 1, 1960; d. William Capelle and Belma Ree (Wallace) K.; m. Steven Nelson Koppes, May 18, 1984. BA in Comm., Stephens Coll., 1981. Reporter The Morning Sun, Pittsburg, Kans., 1981-83, The Gastonia (N.C.) Gazette, 1983-84; info. specialist Ariz. State U., Tempe, 1984; reporter, news editor Scottsdale (Ariz.) Progress, 1984-89; asst. metro editor Tribune Newspapers, Mesa, Ariz., 1989-92; bus. editor Tribune Newspapers, 1992-93; editor Chandler (Ariz.) Arizonan Tribune, 1993—. Freelance writer rsch. mag. Ariz. State U., 1991-92. Mem. Soc. Profl. Journalists, Stephens Coll. Alumnae Assn. (active pub. rels. Phoenix chpt. 1989-91, active membership 1991-92, v.p. 1992-93, pres. 1993-95, bd. dirs. 1993-95, exec. v.p. 1995—), Soroptimist Internat. (newsletter editor, program chair 1994—). Methodist. Office: Chandler Arizonan Tribune 25 S Arizona Pl #565 Chandler AZ 85225

KECECIOGLU, DIMITRI BASIL, reliability engineering educator, consultant; b. Istanbul, Turkey, Dec. 26, 1922; came to U.S., 1946, naturalized, 1956; s. Basil C. and Mary (Melayios) K.; m. Lorene June Legan, Dec. 22, 1951; children: Zoe Diana Kececioglu Draelos, John Dimitri. BS, Robert Coll., Istanbul, 1942; MS, Purdue U., 1948, PhD, 1953. Asst. instr. Purdue U., Lafayette, Ind., 1943-47; instr. Purdue U., 1947-52; engrng. scientist in charge mech. research labs. Allis-Chalmers Mfg. Co., Milw., 1952-57; asst. to dir. mech. engrng. industries group Allis-Chalmers Mfg. Co., 1957-60, cons. engr. industries group, 1960-63, dir. corp. reliability program, 1960-63; prof. aerospace and mech. engrng. U. Ariz., Tucson, 1963—; reliability and maintainability engrng. cons., Tucson, 1963—; dir. Reliability Engrng. and Mgmt. Inst., 1963—, Reliability Testing Inst., 1975—; applied reliability cons. Northrop Space Labs., Gen. Elec. Co., Center for Mgmt. and Indsl. Devel., Rotterdam, Netherlands, Delco Radio div. Gen. Motors Corp., Aerojet-Gen. Corp., Westinghouse Elec. Co., U.S. Army Mgmt. Engrng. Tng. Agy., Allied Signal, Data General, Polaroid, Storage Tek, Motorola, Digital Equipment, ITT, B.F. Goodrich, Gen. Dynamics, Xerox, Ford, JPL, Bendix, Cummins Engine, MOOG, Copeland, Eastman Kodak, Allied Chem. and many others; Fulbright lectr. Nat. Tech. U., Athens, 1971-72; sr. extension tchr. UCLA, 1983; hon. prof. Shanghai U. Tech., 1984. Author: Bibliography on Plasticity, 1950, Introduction to Probabilistic Design for Reliability, 1975, Manual of Product Assurance Films and Videotapes, 1980, Reliability Engineering Handbook, Vols. 1-2, 1991, 5th printing, 1996, The 1992-94 Reliability Maintainability and Availability Software Handbook, 1992, Reliability and Life Testing Handbook, Vols. 1-2, 1993, 94, Environmental Stress Screening, 1995, Burn-in Testing, 1997, Maintainability, Availability and Operational Readiness Engineering Handbook Vol. 1, 1995; contbr. over 130 articles to profl. jours. Founder, fund raiser Dr. Dimitri Basil Kececioglu Reliability Engrng. Rsch. Fellowships Endowment Fund, 1987. Recipient Presidency award Milw. Tech. Coun., 1962, Automotive Industries Author award, 1963, Ralph E. Teetor Outstanding Engrng. Educator award Soc. Automotive Engrs., 1977, Anderson prize U. Ariz., 1983, U. Ariz. Scholarship Devel. Office award, 1991, Acad. of Achievement award in edn. Am. Hellenic Ednl. Progressive Assn., 1991-92. Fellow Soc. Automotive Engrs.; mem. ASME (chmn. Milw. sect. 1960), IEEE, Soc. Exptl. Stress Analysis (chmn. Milw. sect. 1957), Am. Hellenic Ednl. Progressive Assn. (Adac. Achievement award in edn. 1992), Am. Soc. Engrng. Edn., Am. Soc. Quality Control (Reliability Edn. Advancement award 1980, Allen Chop award for outstanding contbns. to reliability 1981), Soc. Reliability Engrs. (founder, pres. Tucson chpt. 1974-77), Hellenic Ops. Rsch. Soc. Greece, Phi Beta Kappa (hon.), Sigma Xi (pres. Univ. chpt. 1990-91), Tau Beta Pi, Phi Kappa Phi (pres. U. Ariz. chpt. 1988-89), Nat. Golden Key Soc. (hon.). Home: 7340 N La Oesta Ave Tucson AZ 85704-3119

KECHICHIAN, JOSEPH ALBERT, political scientist, educator; b. Bourj-Hammoud, Lebanon, Mar. 15, 1954; came to U.S., 1974; s. Albert and Josephine (Seraydarian) K.; m. Ritta Bardakjian, Oct. 1, 1994. BA, Immaculate Heart Coll., 1977; MA, Monterey Inst. 1980; PhD, U. Va., 1985. Lectr. Coll. William & Mary, Williamsburg, Va., 1985-86, U. Va., Charlottesville, 1986-89; assoc. polit. scientist Rand Corp., Santa Monica, Calif., 1989-96; lectr. history UCLA, 1990-96; cons. FBI Acad., Quantico, Va., 1986—; mem. adv. bd. Middle East Policy, Washington, 1994—; pres. K2 Assocs. Author: Political Dynamics and Security in The Persian Gulf Through the 1990s, 1993, Oman and the World: The Emergence of an Independent Foreign Policy, 1995; contbr. articles to profl. jours. Gulbenkian fellow U. Va., 1982-83, Kaprielian fellow, 1983-84, Hoover fellow U.S. State Dept., 1989. Mem. Middle East Inst., Middle East Studies Assn. (life), Soc. Armenian Studies (bd. dirs. 1989-92, pres. 1996-97), Soc. Arab Gulf Studies. Armenian Catholic.

KEEGAN, JOHN E., lawyer; b. Spokane, Wash., Apr. 29, 1943. BA, Gonzaga U., 1965; LLB, Harvard U., 1968. Bar: Wash. 1968, U.S. Ct. Appeals (9th cir.) 1976, U.S. Supreme Ct. Gen. counsel Dept. Housing and Urban Devel., Washington, 1968-70; instr. in bus. sch. and inst. environ. studies U. Wash., 1973-76, instr. land use and environ. law, 1976-78; now ptnr. Davis, Wright & Tremaine, Seattle. Office: Davis Wright Tremaine 2600 Century Sq 1501 4th Ave Seattle WA 98101-1662

KEELE, ALAN FRANK, adult education educator; b. Provo, Utah, Nov. 17, 1942; s. Frank Alonzo and Lasca Taft (Smith) K.; m. Linda Kay Sellers, Jan. 29, 1966; children: Kamron, Heather, Kristopher, Brandon, Celeste, Jeremy. Student, U. Utah, 1960-61; BA, Brigham Young U., 1967; PhD, Princeton U., 1971. Prof. Brigham Young U., Provo, 1971—. Author: Paul Schallück, 1972, The Apocalyptic Vision, 1982, Understanding Günter Grass, 1990, When Truth was Treason, 1996. Democrat. Mem. LDS Ch. Office: Brigham Young U 4096 JKHB Provo UT 84602

KEELEY, MICHAEL GLENN, risk management analyst; b. Memphis, Jan. 8, 1953; s. Lerman and Benneta (Thompson) K.; m. Sandra Virginia Hughes, Oct. 6, 1978 (div. Aug. 1992); m. Karen Bonner, Dec. 31, 1993; 1 child, Kim. BA, UCLA, 1975; JD, U. Calif., Hastings, 1978. Negotiator for NFL players Profl. Sports Mgmt. Inc., 1979-81; sr. rep. Employers Benefits Ins., 1981-85; claims supr. Claims Mgmt. Svcs., 1985-86; sr. litigation specialist Reliance/United Pacific Ins Co, Rancho Cordova, Calif., 1986-96; ptnr. JKP Mgmt. Svcs. Inc., Sacramento, 1996—; cons. to 3rd party adminstr. in workers' compensation, casualty and auto claims. Mem. Black Ins. Profls. Assn. (pres. 1991-92, student mentor program 1991-93, LINK program 1991), Charles Houston Bar Assn. Office: JKP Mgmt Svcs Inc PO Box 255708 Sacramento CA 95865

KEEN, DERL WALTER, child development educator; b. Leonard, Tex., July 18, 1932; s. Willard Francis and Ora Edda (Martin) K.; m. Shirley Marie Smith, Nov. 14, 1954; children—Deborha, Gregory, Karen, Cynthia. B.S., U. Calif.-Davis, 1954; M.A., Calif. State U.-Fresno, 1973; Ed.D., U. So. Calif., 1978. Cotton gin mgr. Anderson Clayton & Co., Tulare, Calif., 1956-60, farm mgr., Mendota, Calif., 1960-69; owner, operator Liquor Market Country Store, Chatsworth, Calif., 1969-70; owner, operator Keen's Day Sch., Fresno, Calif., 1970-75; instr. child devel., Fresno City Coll., 1975—; mem. Agr. Adv. Council, U. Calif., Berkeley, 1968-72, West Side Field Sta. Adv. Council, U. Calif., Five Points, 1962-72; dir. Calif. Tomato Growers Assn., Stockton, 1964-70; mem. Calif. State Articulation Council Early Childhood Edn., 1975-85, chmn., 1984-85. Served to 1st lt. U.S. Army, 1955-56.Mem. Calif. Assn. for Edn. Young Children (scholarship chmn. 1981-83), World Orgn. for Edn. Young Children. Republican. Methodist. Office: Fresno City Coll 1101 E University Ave Fresno CA 93704-6219

KEEN, RONALD LEE, career officer; b. Abilene, Tex., Jan. 28, 1959; s. Larry Lee and Betty Louise (Lesser) K.; Cindy Kaye Smedley, June 17, 1978; children: Cristina, Jordon, Brian. AA in Communication Mgmt., Community Coll. of USAF, 1983; BA in Applied Arts and Sci., Southwest Tex. S. U., 1986; MS in Aero. Sci., Embry Riddle A.U., 1991. Enlisted USAF, 1979, advanced through grades to capt., 1990; sr. group comm. analyst 6920 ESG USAF, Misawa AB, Japan, 1980-83; Intel rsch. analyst HQ electronic securiry CMD USAF, Kelly AFB, Tex., 1983-86; instr. crew ICBM 44 Strategic Missile Wing USAF, Ellsworth AFB, S.D., 1986-88, commdr. crew ICBM 68 Strategic Missile Squad, 1988-89, commdr. alt CMD post ICBM 68 Strategic Missile Squad, 1989-90, evaluator ICBM crew 44 Strategic Missile Wing, 1990-91; officer squad activation HQ Air Force Space Command USAF, Peterson AFB, Colo., 1991-92; officer space ops. evaluator 4 Space Ops. Squad USAF, Falcon AFB, Colo., 1992-94; chief base plans and programs officer 35 Civil Engr. Squadon USAF, Misawa AFB, Japan, 1994-96; chief war plans officer 21 Space Wing USAF, Peterson AFB, Colo., 1996—; ops. officer SELM 90-1 44 Strategic Missile Wing, Ellsworth AFB, 1990. Commr. youth baseball and soccer leagues Ellsworth Youth Sports Assn., 1988-91; coach Rapid City (S.D.) Youth Sports Assn., 1989-91, Colorado Springs Youth Sports, 1991-94, Colo. Springs Parks and Recreation, 1994; coach Misawa Youth Sports Assn., 1994-96; offensive coach Edgren H.S., Misawa Air Base, Japan, 1996; cubmaster Boy Scouts Am., Ellsworth AFB, 1990-91, Misawa Air Base, Japan, 1996. asst. cubmaster, Colorado Springs, 1991-93, chmn. pack com., 1992-93, scoutmaster, Misawa Air Base, Japan, 1996. Decorated Commendation medal with 2 oak leaf clusters, Meritorious Svc. medal with 1 oak leaf cluster, Air Force Achievement medal with 4 oak leaf clusters. Mem. Air Force Assn., Nat. Eagle Scout Assn., Air Force Assn. Misslers, Nat. Youth Sports Coaches Assn. Republican. Home: 8140 Mainsail Ct Colorado Springs CO 80920

KEENAN, RETHA ELLEN VORNHOLT, retired nurse, educator; b. Solon, Iowa, Aug. 15, 1934; d. Charles Elias and Helen Maurine (Konicek) Vornholt; BSN, State U. Iowa, 1955; MSN, Calif. State U., Long Beach, 1978; m. David James Iverson, June 17, 1956; children: Scott, Craig ; m. Roy Vincent Keenan, Jan. 5, 1980. Publ. health nurse City of Long Beach, 1970-73, 94-96, ret., 1996; pub. health nurse Hosp. Home Care, Torrance, Calif., 1973-75; patient care coord. Hillhaven, L.A., 1975-76; mental health cons. InterCity Home Health, L.A., 1978-79; instr. Community Coll. Dist., L.A., 1979-87; instr. nursing El Camino Coll., Torrance, 1981-86; instr. nursing Chapman Coll., Orange, Calif., 1982, Mt. Saint Mary's Coll., 1986-87; cons., pvt. practice, Rancho Palos Verdes, Calif., 1987-89. Contbg. author: American Journal of Nursing Question and Answer Book for Nursing Boards Review, 1984, Nursing Care Planning Guides for Psychiatric and Mental Health Care, 1987-88, Nursing Care Planning Guides for Children, 1987, Nursing Care Planning Guides for Adults, 1988, Nursing Care Planning Guides for Critically Ill Adults, 1988. Cert. nurse practitioner adult and mental health, 1979; mem. Assistance League of San Pedro, Palos Verdes, Calif. NIMH grantee, 1977-78. Mem. Sigma Theta Tau, Phi Kappa Phi, Delta Zeta. Republican. Lutheran. Avocations: travel, writing, reading. Home: 27849 Longhill Dr Rancho Palos Verdes CA 90275

KEENAN, ROBERT, architect; b. Rochester, N.Y., Jan. 8, 1950; s. John Lawrence and Frances (Hartigan) K.; m. Marianne Julia Janko, Sept. 9, 1989; 1 child, Robert John. BA, Fordham U., 1971; MArch, Harvard U., 1976. Registered architect, Mass., Calif.; cert. nat. coun. archtl. registration bds. Project architect Archtl. Resources Cambridge Inc., Cambridge, Mass., 1977-79; architect Hoskins, Scott, Taylor & Ptnrs., Boston, 1979-81; project architect Harry Weese & Assocs., Chgo., 1981-89, v.p., 1983-89; sr. resident architect Singapore Mass Rapid Transit Project, 1982-84; chief architect Metro Rail Transit Cons., 1986-89; architect, engrng. mgr., urban designer Bechtel Corp., San Francisco, 1989—; chief architect Bay Area Transit Cons., 1989-91, Athens Metro, 1991-94; dir. facility engrng. Light Rail Transit, Kuala Lumpur, Malaysia, 1994-95; project architect We. Corridor Ry. Feasibility Study Kowloon-Canton Ry. Corp., Hong Kong, 1995; chief architect West Rail Divsn. Kowloon Canton Ry. Corp., Hong Kong, 1996—; speaker, session chmn. Internat. Conf. on Tall Bldgs., Singapore, 1984. Prin. works include Regis Coll. Athletic Facility, Weston, Mass., Singapore Mass Rapid Transit Sys., So. Calif. Red Line Metro Rail, L.A., Bay Area Rapid Transit Sys., San Francisco, Attiko Metro, Athens, Kuala Lumpur (Malaysia) LRT 2, KCRC/West Rail Project, Hong Kong. Mem. AIA. Republican. Roman Catholic. Office: Bechtel Corp PO Box 193965 50 Beale St San Francisco CA 94119-3965

KEENAN, ROBERT JOSEPH, trade association executive; b. San Francisco, May 25, 1946; s. Lawrence Alexander and Elma Patricia (Frenor) K.; m. Hildegard I. Gerlitz, Aug. 22, 1969; children: Michael Alexander, Patrick Sean. BS in Pub. Rels., Armstrong Coll., Berkeley, Calif., 1971; cert. in orgnl. mgmt., U. Santa Clara, 1975. Asst. mgr. Redwood City (Calif.) C. of C., 1971-73; exec. v.p. Lancaster (Calif.) C. of C., 1973-76, Montclair (Calif.) C. of C., 1976-79, Calif. Electric Sign Assn., Claremont, 1979-91, Bldg. Industry Assn. Tulare/Kings Counties, Visalia, Calif., 1991—; chmn. Lancaster Inc. Com., 1974-76; dir., mktg. chair Workforce Coalition, Visalia, 1995-96; mem. select com. unlicensed contractors Calif. State Assembly, 1987-92. Author city incorp. game, 1974 (Congl. record 1975). Author chpt. 2.5 Calif. Bus. and Profl. Code, 1987-88, Calif. Electric Sign Assn., Claremont, 1989-90; author AB2823 Bldg. Industry Assn., Visalia, 1996. With U.S. Army, 1966-69. Republican. Roman Catholic. Office: Bldg Industry Assn 315 W Oak Ave Visalia CA 93291-4928

KEENEY, EDMUND LUDLOW, physician; b. Shelbyville, Ind., Aug. 11, 1908; s. Bayard G. and Ethel (Adams) K.; m. Esther Cox Loney Wight, Mar. 14, 1950; children: Edmund Ludlow, Eleanor Seymour (Mrs. Cameron Leroy Smith). A.B., Ind. U., 1930; M.D., Johns Hopkins U., 1934. Diplomate Am. Bd. Internal Medicine. Intern Johns Hopkins Hosp., 1934-37, vis. physician, instr. internal medicine, 1940-48; practice medicine, specializing internal medicine San Diego, 1948- 55; dir. Scripps Clinic and Research Found., La Jolla, 1955-67; pres. Scripps Clinic and Research Found., 1967-77, pres. emeritus, 1977—; dir. rsch. on fungus infections OSRD, 1942-46. Author: Practical Medical Mycology, 1955, Medical Advice for International Travel; contbr. articles on allergy, immunology and mycology to med. jours. Bd. dirs. U. San Diego, Allergy Found. Am. Fellow A.C.P.; mem. A.M.A., Am. Soc. Clin. Investigation, Am. Acad. Allergy (pres. 1964), Western Assn. Physicians, Calif. Med. Assn., Western Soc. Clin. Research, Phi Beta Kappa, Alpha Omega Alpha, Beta Theta Pi. Republican. Presbyterian. Home: 338 Via Del Norte La Jolla CA 92037-6539 Office: 10666 N Torrey Pines Rd La Jolla CA 92037-1027 *The great use of a lifetime is to spend it for something that outlives it.*

KEEP, JUDITH N., federal judge; b. Omaha, Mar. 24, 1944. B.A., Scripps Coll., 1966; J.D., U. San Diego, 1970. Bar: Calif. 1971. Atty. Defenders Inc., San Diego, 1971-73; pvt. practice law, 1973-76; asst. U.S. atty. U.S. Dept. Justice, 1976; judge Mcpl. Ct., San Diego, 1976-80; judge U.S. Dist. Ct. (so. dist.) Calif., San Diego, 1980—, chief judge, 1991—. Office: US Dist Ct 940 Front St Rm 16 San Diego CA 92101-8994

KEGLEY, JACQUELYN ANN, philosophy educator; b. Conneaut, Ohio, July 18, 1938; d. Steven Paul and Gertrude Evelyn (Frank) Kovacevic; m. Charles William Kegley, June 12, 1964; children: Jacquelyn Ann, Stephen Lincoln Luther. BA cum laude, Allegheny Coll., 1960; MA summa cum laude, Rice U., 1964; PhD, Columbia U., 1971. Asst. prof. philosophy Calif. State U., Bakersfield, 1973-77, assoc. prof., 1977-81, prof., 1981—; vis. prof. U. Philippines, Quezon City, 1966-68; grant project dir. Calif. Council Humanities, 1977, project dir. 1980, 82; mem. work group on ethics Am. Colls. of Nursing, Washington, 1984-86; mem. Am. Bd. Forensic Examiners. Author: Introduction to Logic, 1978, Genuine Individuals and Genuine Communities, 1996; editor: Humanistic Delivery of Services to Families, 1982, Education for the Handicaped, 1982; mem. editl. bd. Jour. Philosophy in Lit., 1979-84; contbr. articles to profl. jours. Bd. dirs. Bakersfield Mental Health Assn., 1982-84, Citizens for Betterment of Community. Recipinet Outstanding Prof. award Calif. State U., 1989-90, Golden Roadrunner award Bakersfield Community, 1991. Mem. Philosophy of Sci. Assn., Soc. Advancement Am. Phil. soc. (chmn. Pacific div. 1979-83, nat. exec. com. 1974-79), Philosophy Soc., Soc. Interdisciplinary Study of Mind, Am. Philosophical Assn., Dorian Soc., Phi Beta Kappa. Democrat. Lutheran. Home: 7312 Kroll Way Bakersfield CA 93309-2336 Office: Calif State U Dept Philosophy Bakersfield CA 93311

KEGLEY, JOSEPH EDWARD, realtor; b. Red Bank, N.J., Dec. 4, 1942; m. Mary F. Blair, Jan. 31, 1942; children: Joseph, Jerry, Kimberley, Laura, Tracey. Grad. h.s. Cert. residential specialist, cert. investment specialist. Franchise owner Southland Corp., N.J., Ariz. and Nev., 1964-85; realtor Century 21 Personal Choice, Mesa, Ariz., 1985—. Mem. Nat. Assn. Realtors, Ariz. Assn. Realtors, Multi-Million Dollar Club. Home: 16533 E Tremaine Gilbert AZ 85234 Office: Century 21 Personal Choice # 115 2815 S Alma Sch Mesa AZ 85210

KEHL, RANDALL HERMAN, investment company executive, consultant; b. Furstenfeldbruck, Fed. Republic of Germany, May 18, 1954; came to U.S., 1955; s. Raymond Herman and Annabelle (Fair) K.; m. Sharon Kay Barnes; children: Lindsey Elizabeth, Jessica Anne, Austin Randall. BS, USAF Acad., 1976; MBA, U. N.D., 1980; JD, Pepperdine U., 1983. Bar: N.D. 1983, D.C. 1988, U.S. Supreme Ct. 1990. Commd. 2d lt. USAF, 1976, advanced through grades to maj., 1986, chief civil law, 1983-84, chief criminal law, 1984-85; squadron commdr. Alaska Air Command, Anchorage, 1985, chief def. counsel, 1985-86; dep. base atty. Kirtland AFB, Albuquerque, 1986-89; spl. asst. U.S. atty. U.S. Dept. Justice, Albuquerque, 1986-89; chief energy litigation Office of USAF JAG, Washington, 1989-90; White House fellow, 1990-91; chmn., CEO POD Assocs., Inc., 1991-96; cons., counsel to DESA-office of sec. of def. U.S. Dept. Def., Albuquerque, 1993; prin. Randall H. Kehl Consulting, Albuquerque, 1993—; chmn. RHK Capital Group Internat., San Antonio, 1997—; mem. staff Pres.'s Coun. on Competiveness, 1990-91; vice-chmn. White House Working group on Commercialization of Fed. Lab. Tech., 1991; chmn. Candeli, Ltd., Kerorioni, Ltd., Rep. of Georgia, 1992-96; adj. instr. law U. Alaska, 1985-86; bd. dirs., counsel Kirtland Fed. Credit Union, Albuquerque; bd. dirs., sec. Triad Communications, Inc., Albuquerque; chmn. bd. POD Assocs., Inc., 1988-90. Asst. scoutmaster Boy Scouts Am., Minot, N.D., 1977-80; tchr. Officers Christian Fellowship, Minot, 1977-80; civic arbitrator Mediation and Conciliation Svc., 1983-86; mem. pvt. sch. bd. Anchorage, 1984-85; mem. Gov.'s Task Force for Utility Corp. Restructuring, 1987; vice-chmn. N.Mex. Gov.-Elect Transition Team, 1994, Gov.'s Bus. Adv. Coun., 1995—; mem. steering com. Rep. Campaigns, 1995—; co-chmn. N. Mex. Character Counts in the Workplace, 1996—; bd. dirs. Kirtland Partnership Com., 1995—; mem. Tax and Fiscal Policy Network, 1996—, Econ. Forum, 1995—; chmn. Dole/Kemp '96 Campaign, Congrl. Dist. 1 and Bernalillo County, N.Mex., 1996. Mem. ABA, Albuquerque Acad. Capital Devel. Coun. and Assoc. Trustee, The Forman Sch. (capital devel. com.), Phi Delta Phi. Republican. Presbyterian. Office: Ste 415 5100 John D Ryan Blvd San Antonio TX 78245-4259

KEHLER, DOROTHEA FAITH, English educator; b. N.Y.C., Apr. 21, 1936; d. Nathan and Minnie (Coopersmith) Gutwill; (widowed 1981); children: Paul Dolid, Eve Boyd, Jessica, Ted. BA, CCNY, 1956; MA, Ohio U., 1967, PhD, 1969. Instr. MacMurray Coll., Ill., 1964-65; instr. Ohio U., Athens, 1965-66, teaching fellow, 1966-68; lectr. San Diego State U., 1969-70, asst. prof., 1970-85, assoc. prof., 1985-88, prof., 1988—. Author: Problems in Literary Research, 1975, 2d edit., 1981, 3d edit., 1987, 4th edit., 1997; editor: In Another Country: Feminist Perspectives on Renaissance Drama, 1991. Nat. Endowment for the Humanities fellow Harvard U., 1983; Folger Libr. Inst. grantee, 1988; San Diego State U. scholar, 1990—. Mem. Internat. Shakespeare Assn., Rocky Mountain Modern Lang. Assn., Southeastern Renaissance Conf., Renaissance Conf. So. Calif., Shakespeare Assn. Am., Amnesty Internat., Pacific Ancient and Modern Lang. Assn., Phi Beta Kappa (hon.). Democrat. Office: San Diego State U English Dept San Diego CA 92182

KEHLMANN, ROBERT, artist, critic; b. Bklyn., Mar. 9, 1942. BA, Antioch Coll., 1963; MA, U. Calif., Berkeley, 1966. One-man shows include: Richmond Art Ctr., Calif., 1976, William Sawyer Gallery, San Francisco, 1978, 82, 86, Galerie M, Kassel, Fed. Republic Germany, 1985, Anne O'Brien Gallery, Washington, 1988, 90, Dorothy Weiss Gallery, San Francisco, 1993, Hearst Art Gallery, Moraga, 1996; group shows include: Am. Craft Mus., N.Y.C., 1978, 86, Corning (N.Y.) Mus. Glass, 1979, Tucson Mus. of Art, 1983, Kulturhuset, Stockholm, Sweden, 1985; represented in permanent collections at Corning Mus. Glass, Leigh Yawkey Woodson Art Mus., Hessisches Landes Mus., W.Ger., Bank of Am. World Hdqrs., San Francisco, Toledo Mus. Art, Hokkaido Mus. Modern Art, Sapporo, Japan, Huntington Mus. of Art, W.Va., Am. Craft Mus., N.Y.C., Musée des Arts Décoratifs, Lausanne, Switzerland; instr. glass design Calif. Coll. Arts and Crafts, Oakland, 1978-80, 91, Pilchuck Glass Ctr., Stanwood, Wash., 1978-80. Author: Twentieth Century Stained Glass: A New Definition, 1992; contbg. editor: New Glass Work mag., 1988-89; editor: Glass Art Soc. Jour., 1981-84. NEA grantee, 1977-78. Chmn. Landmarks Preservation Commn., Berkeley, 1995-97. Mem. Glass Art Soc. (bd. dirs. 1980-84, 89-92, hon. life mem.). Office: Dorothy Weiss Gallery 256 Sutter St San Francisco CA 94108-4409

KEHOE, JAMES WILLIAM, JR., marketing manager; b. Sacramento, June 27, 1949; s. James William and Margaret Louise (Kennedy) K.; m. Brenda Lynn Magee, July 28, 1978; children: Michael Herrin Troyer, Aaron Max Troyer. BA in Geography, U. Colo., 1972; postgrad., No. Ariz. U., 1978-79. Mfg. rep. James Kehoe Co., San Francisco, 1976-78; divsn. head

Hillsdale Sash & Door Co., Inc., Portland, Oreg., 1979-81, sales rep., 1981-86, sales mgr., 1986-94; dir. Am. Inst. Bldg. Design, Portland, 1985-86. Lt. USN, 1972-76, PTO. Office: Hillsdale Sash & Door Co PO Box 629 Wilsonville OR 97070-0629

KEHOE, VINCENT JEFFRÉ-ROUX, photographer, author, cosmetic company executive; b. Bklyn., N.Y., Sept. 12, 1921; s. John James and Bertha Florence (Roux) K.; m. Gena Irene Marino, Nov. 2, 1966. Student, MIT, 1940-41, Lowell Technol. Inst., 1941-42, Boston U., 1942; BFA in Motion Picture and TV Prodn., Columbia U., 1957. Dir. make-up dept. CBS-TV, N.Y.C., 1948-49, NBC Hallmark Hall of Fame series, 1951-53; make-up artist in charge of make-up for numerous film, TV and stage prodns., 1942—; dir. make-up Turner Hall Corp., 1959-61, Internat. Beauty Show, 1962-66; pres., dir. research Research Council of Make-up Artists, Inc., 1963—; chief press officer at Spanish Pavilion, N.Y. World's Fair, 1965; free-lance photographer, 1956—. Contbr. photographs to numerous mags. including Time, Life, Sports Illustrated, Argosy, Popular Photography; author: The Technique of Film and Television Make-up for Color, 1970, The Make-up Artist in the Beauty Salon, 1969, We Were There: April 19, 1775, 1974, A Military Guide, 1974, 2d rev. edit., 1993, The Re-Created Officer's Guide, 1996, The Technique of the Professional Makeup Artist, 1985, 2nd edit., 1995, Special Make-up Effects, 1991; author-photographer bullfighting books: Aficionado! (N.Y. Art Dirs. Club award 1960), Wine, Women and Toros! (N.Y. Art Dirs. award 1962); producer: (documentary color film) Matador de Toros, 1959. Served with inf. U.S. Army, World War II, ETO. Decorated Purple Heart, Bronze Star, CIB; recipient Torch award Council of 13 Original States, 1979. Fellow Co. Mil. Historians; mem. Tenth Foot Royal Lincolnshire Regimental Assn. (life; Hon. Col. 1968), Soc. Motion Picture and TV Engrs. (life), Acad. TV Arts and Scis., Soc. for Army Hist. Research (Eng.) (life), Brit. Officers Club New England (life), 10th Mountain Div. Assn. (life), 70th Inf. Div. (life), DAV (life), Nat. Rifle Assn. (life), Eagle Scout Assn. (life). Home and Office: PO Box 850 Somis CA 93066-0850

KEIM, MICHAEL RAY, dentist; b. Sabetha, Kans., June 8, 1951; s. Milton Leroy and Dorothy Juanita (Stover) K.; m. Christine Anne Lorenzen, Nov. 20, 1971; children: Michael Scott, Dawn Marie, Erik Alan. Student, U. Utah, 1969-72; DDS, Creighton U., 1976. Pvt. practice Casper, Wyo., 1976—. Mem. organizing bd. dirs. Ctrl. Wyo. Soccer Assn., 1976-77; mem. Casper Mountain Ski Patrol, Nat. Ski Patrol Sys., 1980—, avalanche and ski mountaineering advisor No. Divsn. Region III, 1992-96; 1st asst. patrol dir. Nat. Ski Patrol Sys., 1996—; bd. dirs., dep. commr. for fast pitch Wyo. Amateur Softball Assn., 1980-84; bd. dirs. Ctrl. Wyo. Softball Assn., 1980-84; pres. Wyo. Spl. Smiles Found., 1995-96; mem. organizing com. Prevent Abuse & Neglect thru Dental Awareness Coalition, Wyo., 1996; mem. adv. com. Natrona County Headstart, 1985—. Recipient Purple Merit Star for Saving a Life, 1992. Mem.. ADA, Fedn. Dentaire Internat., Pierre Fauchard Acad., Wyo. Acad. Gen. Dentristry (sec.-treas. 1980-82, pres. 1982-87), Wyo. Dental Assn. (bd. dirs. 1992—, chmn. conv. 1993, ADA alt. del. 1994-95, v.p. 1993-94, pres.-elect 1994-95, pres. 1995-96, editor 1997—), Wyo. Dental Polit. Action Com. (sec.-treas. 1985—), Ctrl. Wyo. Dental Assn. (sec.-treas. 1981-82, pres. 1982-83), Wyo. Dental Hist. Assn. (bd. dirs. 1989-95), Wyo. Donated Dental Svcs. (organizing bd. dirs. 1994, pres. 1995-96), Kiwanis (v.p. Casper club 1988-89, bd. dirs. 1986-96, pres.-elect 1989-90, pres. 1990-91, internat. del. 1989-91, chmn. internat. rels. com. 1992—), Creighton Club (pres. 1982-84). Methodist. Home: 58 Jonquil St Casper WY 82604-3863 Office: 1749 S Boxelder St Casper WY 82604-3538

KEIMIG, ALAN CHARLES, architect; b. Torrington, Wyo., Oct. 9, 1942; s. Edwin Jack and Eunice Adaline (Goddard) K.; m. Judith Ann Hodgson, Mary Jane Polack (div.); children: Randall James, Angela Jane, John Joseph, Christina Carol, Jené Marie; m. Carol R. Nedderman. BS, U. Wyo., 1968. Engring. technician U.S. Soil Conservation, Casper, Wyo., 1961-63; surveying asst. U.S. Forest Svc., Laramie, Wyo., 1964; designer J. T. Banner & Assocs., Laramie, 1964-66; undergrad. asst. U. Wyo., Laramie, 1966-68; planner The Boeing Co., Auburn, Wash., 1968; project mgr. Thompson/Hansen Architects, Federal Way, Wash., 1968-71, Ronald E. Thompson, Federal Way, 1971-73; owner, arch., planner The Keimig Assocs., Auburn, Wash., 1973—; bd. mem. Gov.'s Adv. Bd. on Indian Affairs, State of Wash., 1974-75; v.p. exec. com., steering com., chairperson econ. restructuring, mem. Design Com., Auburn Downtown Assn., 1993—; disting. spkr. Indian Affairs U.S. Govt., 1972. Coord. Am. Civil Liberties, South King County, 1970. Recipient Disting. Alumni Scholarship, 1966, James Kramlich award for outstanding committment and svc., 1994. Mem. Airlines of Am. (bd. dirs. 1995), City of Auburn Landmarks and Heritage Commn., Auburn C. of C. (EDC com., named Citizen of the Month of Oct., 1996). Democrat. Office: The Keimig Assocs 216 A St NW Auburn WA 98001-4927

KEIPER, MARILYN MORRISON, elementary education educator; b. South Gate, Calif., June 12, 1930; d. David Cline and Matilda Ruth (Pearce) M.; m. Edward E. Keiper, June 18, 1962; children: Becky S. Swickard, Edward M. BA, Calif. State U., L.A., 1954; postgrad., UCLA, 1968. Elem. tchr. Rosemead (Calif.) Sch. Dist., 1954—; recreation leader L.A. County, 1951-62, 2d reader 1st Ch. Christ Scientist, Arcadia, Calif., 1991-94; mem. cons. Janson Adv. Group, Rosemead, 1985—; bd. dirs. Janson PTA, Rosemead, 1985—; participant Sta. KNBC Spirit of Edn., 1990-92. Participant Sta. KNBC Spirit of Edn., 1990-92. Named Tchr. of the Yr., L.A. County, 1983-84; recipient Recognition award for outstanding service to children, Theta Kappa Chpt. Delta Kappa Gamma, 1996. Fellow Rosemead Tchrs. Assn., Delta Kappa Gamma.

KEIR, GERALD JANES, banker; b. Ludlow, Mass., Aug. 22, 1943; s. Alexander J. and Evelyn M. (Buckley) K.; m. Karen Mary Devine, July 22, 1972; children: Matthew J., Katherine B., Megan E. BA, Mich. State U., 1964, MA, 1966. Reporter Honolulu Advertiser, 1968-74, city editor, 1974-86, mng. editor, 1986-89, editor, 1989-95; sr. v.p. corp. comms. First Hawaiian Bank, Honolulu, 1995—. Co-author text: Advanced Reporting: Beyond News Events, 1985, Advanced Reporting: Discovering Patterns in News Events. Bd. dirs. Aloha United Way; bd. govs. Hawaii Comty. Found. Recipient Nat. Reporting award Am. Polit. Sci. Assn., 1971, Benjamin Fine Nat. award Am. Assn. Secondary Sch. Prins., 1981; John Ben Snow fellow, 1983, NEH fellow, 1973. Mem. Am. Soc. Newspaper Editors, Assoc. Press Mng. Editors, Am. Assn. Pub. Opinion Rsch. Soc. Profl. Journalists, Asian-Am. Journalists Assn., Social Sci. Assn., Pacific Club. Office: First Hawaiian Bank PO Box 3200 Honolulu HI 96847

KEISER, MEGAN MARIE, neuroscience nurse specialist; b. Ann Arbor, Mich., Aug. 22, 1964; d. Franklin Delano McDonald and Mary Patricia (Ranere) Currier; m. Edward Vincent Keiser, Aug. 3, 1991; children: Johnathan Joseph, Kristi Marie, Patricia Ruthanne. BSN, U. Mich., 1986, MS in Med.-Surg. Nursing, 1990; cert. nurse practitioner, Calif. State U., Long Beach, 1996. RN, Mich., Calif.; cert. BCLS, ACLS, clin. specialist in med.-surg. nursing; cert. neurosci. RN. Nursing asst. in neurosciss. U. Mich. Hosp., Ann Arbor, 1984-86, staff nurse neurosciss., 1986-90; clin. nurse specialist in neurosurgery Detroit Receiving Hosp., 1990-92; clin. nurse specialist Comprehensive Epilepsy Program, L.A., 1993-94; edn. coord. St. Jude Med. Ctr., Fullerton, Calif., 1995-96; neuro/ortho outcomes mgr. St. Jude Med. Ctr., Fullerton, 1996—; BLS instr. Am. Heart Assn., 1990. Mem. AACN, ANA, Am. Assn. Neurosci. Nurses, Epi Found. of Am., Case Mgmt. Soc. Am. Roman Catholic.

KEISLING, PHILLIP ANDREW, state official; b. Portland, Oreg., June 23, 1955; s. Les and Ione Keisling; m. Pam Wiley, Sept. 4, 1988. BA, Yale U., 1977. Speech writer Gov. Tom McCall, Salem, Oreg., 1978; reporter Willamette Week, Portland, 1978-81; editor Washington Monthly mag., 1982-84; sr. legis asst. Oreg. Speakers of the Ho., Salem, 1985-88; mem. Oreg. Ho. of Reps., Salem, 1989-91; sec. of state State of Oreg., Salem, 1991—; mem. State Land Bd., Salem, 1991—, Hanford Waste Bd., Portland, 1991—. Chmn. Brooklyn Neighborhood Assn., Portland, 1986-88. Office: Office Sec of State State Capitol Rm 136 Salem OR 97310

KEISTER, JEAN CLARE, lawyer; b. Warren, Ohio, Aug. 28, 1931; d. John R. Keister and Anna Helen Brennan. JD, Southwestern U., 1966. Bar: Calif. 1967, U.S. Supreme Ct. 1972, U.S. Dist. Ct. (so. dist.) Calif. 1988. Legal writer Gilbert Law Summaries, L.A., 1967; instr. Glendale (Calif.) Coll. Law, 1968; pvt. practice Glendale, 1967-70, L.A., Calif., 1970-80, Burbank, Calif., 1987—, Lancaster, Calif., 1992—. Mem. Themis Soc., 1989-96. Recipient Golden Poet award World of Poetry. Mem. Burbank Bar Assn. (sec. 1993), Antelope Valley Bar Assn.

KEITH, BRUCE EDGAR, political analyst, genealogist; b. Curtis, Nebr., Feb. 17, 1918; s. Edgar L. and Corinne E. (Marsteller) K.; m. Evelyn E. Johnston, Oct. 29, 1944; children: Mona Louise, Kent Marsteller, Melanie Ann. AB with high distinction, Nebr. Wesleyan U., 1940; MA, Stanford U., 1952; grad. Command and Staff, Marine Corps Schs., 1958, Sr. Resident Sch., Naval War Coll., 1962; PhD, U. Calif.-Berkeley, 1982. Commd. 2d lt. U.S. Marine Corps, 1942, advanced through grades to col., 1962, ret., 1971. OinC Marine Corps Nat. Media, N.Y.C., 1946-49, support arms coord. 1st Marines, Seoul, Chosin, Korea, 1950, comdg. officer 3d Bn., 11th Marines, 1958-59, ops. officer, Pres. Dwight D. Eisenhower visit to Okinawa, 1960, G-3 ops. officer Fleet Marine Force, Pacific, Cuban Missile Crisis, 1962, mem. U.S. del. SEATO, Planning Conf., Bangkok, Thailand, 1964, G-3, Fleet Marine Force, Pacific, 1964-65, head Strategic Planning Study Dept., Naval War Coll., 1966-68, genealogist, 1967—, exec. officer Hdqrs. Marine Corps programs, Washington, 1968-71; election analyst Inst. Govtl. Studies, U. Calif.-Berkeley, 1974-86, polit. analyst, 1986—; teaching asst. U. Calif.-Berkeley, 1973-74. Bd. dirs., Bay Area Funeral Soc., 1980-83, v.p., 1981-83. Decorated Bronze Star, Navy Commendation medal, Presdl. Unit citation with 3 bronze stars. Recipient Phi Kappa Phi Silver medal Nebr. Wesleyan U., 1940, Alumni award, 1964. Mem. Am. Polit. Sci. Assn., Acad. Polit. Sci., Am. Acad. Polit. and Social Sci., World Affairs Coun. No. Calif., Marine Corps Assn., Ret. Officers Assn. Phi Kappa Phi, Pi Gamma Mu. Republican. Unitarian. Clubs: Commonwealth of Calif. (San Francisco), Marines' Meml. (San Francisco). Lodge: Masons. Contbg. author: The Descendants of Daniel and Elizabeth (Disbrow) Keith, 1979-81; History of Curtis, Nebraska-The First Hundred Years, 1984; author: A Comparison of the House Armed Services Coms. in the 91st and 94th Congresses: How They Differed and Why, 1982; The Johnstons of Morning Sun, 1979; The Marstellers of Arrellton, 1978; The Morris Family of Brookville, 1977; Japan-the Key to America's Future in the Far East, 1962; A United States General Staff: A Must or a Monster?, 1950; co-author: California Votes, 1960-72, 1974; The Myth of the Independent Voter, 1992; Further Evidence on the Partisan Affinities of Independent " Leaners," 1983. Address: PO Box 156 El Cerrito CA 94530-0156

KEITH, KATHRYN MARIE, editor, systems operator; b. Needham, Mass., Feb. 14, 1969; d. Robert Roy and Margaret Beaton Keith. BA in Lit., Am. U., 1991; MA in Journalism, U. Memphis, 1994. Editor, sys. operator Wash. Newspaper Pubs. Assn., Seattle, 1995—. With USN, 1991-94. Mem. Soc. Profl. Journalists (profl. mem.). Republican. Home: # 203 1535 NW 52d Seattle WA 98107 Office: Wash Newspaper Pubs Assn 3838 Stone Way N Seattle WA 98103

KEITH, KENT MARSTELLER, academic administrator, corporate executive, government official, lawyer; b. N.Y.C., May 22, 1948; s. Bruce Edgar and Evelyn E. (Johnston) K.; m. Elizabeth Misao Carlson, Aug. 22, 1976. BA in Govt., Harvard U., 1970; BA in Politics and Philosophy, Oxford U., Eng., 1972, MA, 1977; JD, U. Hawaii, 1977; Ed.D., U. So. Calif., 1996. Bar: Hawaii 1977, D.C. 1979. Assoc. Cades, Schutte, Fleming & Wright, Honolulu, 1977-79; coord. Hawaii Dept. Planning and Econ. Devel., Honolulu, 1979-81, dep. dir., 1981-83, dir., 1983-86; energy resources coord. State of Hawaii, Honolulu, 1983-86, chmn. State Policy Coun., 1983-86; chmn. Aloha Tower Devel. Corp., 1983-86; project mgr. Mililani Tech. Park Castle and Cooke Properties Inc., 1986-88, v.p. pub. rels. and bus. devel., 1988-89, pres. Chaminade U. Honolulu, 1989-95; bd. dirs. Grove Farm Co., Inc., 1990-93. Author: Jobs for Hawaii's People: Fundamental Issues in Economic Development, 1985, Hawaii: Looking Back from the Year 2050, 1987, For the Love of Students, 1992; contbr. articles on ocean law to law jours. Pres. Manoa Valley Ch., Honolulu, 1976-78; mem. platform com., Hawaii Dem. Conv., 1982, 84, 86; trustee Hawaii Loa Coll., 1986-89, vice chmn. 1987-89; mem. Diocesan Bd. Edn., 1990-95, chmn. 1990-93; bd. dirs. St. Louis Sch., 1990-95, Hanahauoli Sch., 1990—; chmn. Manoa Neighborhood Bd., 1989-91. Rhodes scholar, 1970; Named one of 10 Outstanding Young Men of Am., U.S. Jaycees, 1984; recipient Disting. Alumni award, 1993. Mem. Am. Assn. Rhodes Scholars, Internat. House of Japan, Nature Conservancy, Pla. Club, Pacific Club, Harvard Club of Hawaii (Honolulu, bd. dirs. 1974-78, sec. 1974-76), Rotary (Honolulu). Home: 2626 Hillside Ave Honolulu HI 96822-1716

KEITH, NORMAN THOMAS, aerospace company administrator; b. Antioch, Calif., Jan. 12, 1936; s. Dean Theodore and Edna Margaret (Doty) K.; m. Marla Mildred Osten, Sept. 9, 1962. B of Tech., Tex. State Tech. Inst. Cert. profl. mgr. Field service engr. Gen. Dynamics Corp., San Diego, 1955-66, supr. Data Ctr., 1966-76, chief data systems, 1976-81, chief property adminstrn., 1981-83, motivational mgr., 1983-86, sr. program adminstr., 1986-90, mgr. total quality mgmt.Convair divsn., 1990—. Contbr. articles to profl. jours. Mem. mil. adv. bd. congressman Ron Packard, 1983-86; sgt. Res. Dep. Sheriff's Office, San Diego County; bd. dirs. San Dieguito Boys/Girls Clubs, Encinitas, 1966-69, loaned exec. United Way, San Diego, 1980-81. Mem. Nat. Mgmt. Assn. (bd. dirs., pres.), Nat. U. Alumni Assn. (life), Woodbury Coll. Alumni Assn., San Diego State U. Alumni Assn., Hon. Dep. Sheriff's Assn. (bd. dirs.). Republican. Lutheran. Lodges: Lions (sec. 1962-63), Elks. Home: 620 Cole Ranch Rd Encinitas CA 92024-6522 Office: Gen Dynamics Convair Div 5001 Kearny Villa Rd San Diego CA 92123-1407

KEITH, PAULINE MARY, artist, illustrator, writer; b. Fairfield, Nebr., July 21, 1924; d. Siebelt Ralph and Pauline Alethia (Garrison) Goldenstein; m. Everett B. Keith, Feb. 14, 1957; 1 child, Nathan Ralph. Student, George Fox Coll., 1947-48, Oreg. State U., 1955. Illustrator Merlin Press, San Jose, Calif., 1980-81; artist, illustrator, watercolorist Corvallis, Oreg., 1980—. Author 5 chapbooks, 1980-85; editor: Four Generations of Verse, 1979; contbr. poems to anthologies and mags. and articles to mags.; one-woman shows include Roger's Meml. Libr., Forest Grove, Oreg., 1959, Corvallis Art Ctr., 1960, Human Resources Bldg., Corvallis, 1959-61, Chintimini Sr. Ctr., 1994—, Corvallis Parteral Counseling Ctr., 1992-94, 96, Hall Gallery, Sr. Ctr., 1993, 94, Consumer Power, Philomath, Oreg., 1994, Art, Etc., Newburg, Oreg., 1995, 96; exhibited in group shows at Hewlett-Packard Co., 1984-85, Corvallis Art Ctr., 1992, Chintimini Sr. Ctr., 1992, Hall Gallery, Corvallis, 1995, 96, Art Etc., Newberg, 1995-96. Co-elder First Christian Ch. (Disciples of Christ), Corvallis, 1988-89, co-deacon, 1980-83, elder, 1991-93; sec. Hostess Club of Chintimini Sr. Ctr., Corvallis, 1987, pres., 1988-89, v.p., 1992-94. Recipient Watercolor 1st price Benton County Fair, 1982, 83, 88, 89, 91, 2d prize, 1987, 91, 3d prize, 1984, 90, 92. Mem. Oreg. Assn. Christian Writers, Internat. Assn. Women Mins., Am. Legion Aux. (elected poet post II Corvallis chpt. 1989-90, elected sec. 1991-92, chaplain 1992-93, 94-95, v.p. 1994-95), Chintimine Artists, Corvallis Art Guild. Republican. Office: 304 S College St Newberg OR 97132-3114

KELEN, JOYCE ARLENE, social worker; b. N.Y.C., Dec. 5, 1949; d. Samuel and Rebecca (Rochman) Green; m. Leslie George Kelen, Jan. 31, 1971; children: David, Jonathan. BA, Lehman Coll., 1970; MSW, Univ. Utah, 1974, DSW, 1980. Recreation dir. N.Y.C. Housing Authority, Bronx, 1970-72; cottage supr. Kennedy Home, Bronx, 1974; sch. social worker Davis County Sch. Dist., Farmington, Utah, 1976-86; clin. asst. prof. U. Utah., Salt Lake City, 1976—; sch. social worker Salt Lake City Sch. Dist., 1986—; cons. in field, Salt Lake City, 1981—. Editor: To Whom Are We Beautiful As We Go?, 1979; contbr. articles to profl. jours. Utah Coll. of Nursing grantee, 1985. Mem. Nat. Assn. Social Workers (chairperson Gerontology Council, 1983-84, Utah Sch. Social Worker of Yr., 1977), NEA, Utah Edn. Assn., Davis Edn. Assn. Democrat. Jewish. Home: 128 M St Salt Lake City UT 84103-3854 Office: Franklin Elem Sch 1100 W 400 S Salt Lake City UT 84104-2334

KELIN, DANIEL ALLEN, II, theater director, writer, storyteller; b. Walnut Creek, Calif., Apr. 2, 1961; s. Daniel Allen and Ruth Noreen (Johnson) K. BA, U. Vt., 1983; postgrad., U. Miss., 1984; MFA, U. Hawaii, 1987. Dir. edn. Honolulu Theatre for Youth, 1986—; assoc. artist Very Spl. Arts Hawaii, Honolulu, 1987-92; dir. theatre Jodrikdrik Nan Jodrikdrik, Majuro, Marshall Islands, 1991—; storyteller Hawaii State Libr., Honolulu, 1992—. Contbg. author: American Theatrical Company, 1986; contbr. articles and stories to jours.; playwright: He'e Nalu, 1994. Grantee Theatre Comms. Group, 1994, Rockefeller Found., 1993, 95. Mem. Am. Alliance for Theatre and Edn. (com. chair 1993—, network coun. 1993—), Hawaii Alliance for Arts Edn., Soc. for Children's Book Writers, Hawaii Lit. Arts Coun., Children's Lit. Hawaii (scholar cons.). Home: 226 Kaimuohema Pl # A Honolulu HI 96817-1145

KELLAM, NORMA DAWN, medical, surgical nurse; b. Benton Harbor, Mich., June 13, 1938; d. Edgar Arnold and Bernice (Cronk) K. AA, San Bernardino Valley Coll., 1958; student, Calif. State Coll., Long Beach, 1961-1964, 1965, 1966, 1967; BS, San Diego State Coll., 1961; MS, Calif. State U., Fresno, 1972. Nursing instr. Porterville (Calif.) State Hosp., 1968-69; staff nurse Northside Psychiat. Hosp., Fresno, 1969-72; nursing instr. Pasadena (Calif.) City Coll., 1972-73; night shift lead Fairview Devel. Ctr., Costa Mesa, Calif., 1973-96; freelance writer, 1996—. Contbr. articles to newspapers. Vol. Spanish translator for Interstitial Cystitis Assn. Recipient Cert. of Appreciation for vol. work Interstitial Cystitis Assn. Mem. Calif. Nurses Assn., Soc. Urologic Nurses and Assocs., Inc., Phi Kappa Phi.

KELLAR, WILLIAM OWEN, business owner, writer; b. Omaha, Jan. 3, 1922; s. Clyde Amos and Agnes (Conolly) K.; widowed; children: Juan, Carmen, Philip, William. BS, U.S. Naval Acad., 1944; MA, U. So. Calif., 1946; PhD, U. Mo. Unity Campus, 1978. Commd. ensign USN, 1944, advanced through grades to vice adm., 1994, ret., 1975; pres. Kelco Internat. Inc., Ashland, Oreg., 1979—. Decorated Congressional medal of honor, 2 Navy Cross, Silver Star, Bronze Star, 4 Purple Hearts. Home: 804 Hillview Dr Ashland OR 97520-3518

KELLEHER, RICHARD CORNELIUS, marketing and communications executive; b. Buffalo, Nov. 21, 1949; s. Cornelius and Lucile Norma (White) K.; m. Sherri Fae Anderson, Mar. 17, 1981 (div. 1991); children: Erin Marie, Shawn Michael. BA, U. New Mex., 1975; MBA, U. Phoenix, 1984. Reporter, photographer Daily Lobo, Albuquerque, 1973-75; mgn. editor News Bulletin, Belen, New Mex., 1975-77; various corp. mktg. titles AT&T Mountain Bell, Denver, 1978-84; exec. editor Dairy Mag., Denver, 1984-86; communications dir. Am. Heart Assn., Phoenix, 1987-90; cons. Kelleher Communications & Mktg., Phoenix, 1990—; spl. writer Denver Post, 1977-82, Denver Corr. Billboard Mag., 1977-82. Mem. Gov.'s Roundtable on Employee Productivity, Gov. of Ariz., 1990-91; vol. communications Am. Cancer Soc., 1990-92. Recipient Harvey Communications Study award, 1986. Mem. Pub. Rels. Soc. Am., Toastmasters.

KELLER, ARTHUR MICHAEL, computer science researcher; b. N.Y.C., Jan. 14, 1957; s. David and Luba K. BS summa cum laude with honors, Bklyn. Coll., 1977; MS, Stanford U., 1979, PhD, 1985. Instr. computer sci. Stanford (Calif.) U., 1979-81, rsch. asst., 1977-85, acting asst. chmn. dept. computer sci., 1982, rsch. assoc., 1985, 89-91, vis. asst. prof., 1987-89, rsch. scientist, 1991-92, sr. rsch. scientist, 1992—; sr. rsch. scientist Advanced Decision Systems, Mountain View, Calif., 1989-92; chief tech. advisor Persistence Software, San Mateo, Calif., 1991—; CFO, COO Epistemics, Inc., Palo Alto, Calif., 1996—; bd. dirs. Persistence Software, Epistemics, Inc.; sys. analyst Bklyn. Coll. Computer Ctr., 1974-77; summer rsch. asst. IBM, Thomas J. Watson Rsch. Ctr., Yorktown Heights, N.Y., 1980; acad. assoc. IBM San Jose Rsch. Lab., 1981; asst. prof. U. Tex., Austin, 1985-88, adj. asst. prof., 1988-89; mem. program com. Internat. Conf. on Data Engring., L.A., 1986, 87, 89, Internat. Conf. on Very Large Data Bases, Amsterdam, The Netherlands, 1989; mem. program com. Internat. Workshop on Advanced Transaction Models & Architectures, Goa, India, 1996, Internat. Conf. on Info. & Knowledge Mgmt., Rockville, Md., 1996. Author: A First Course in Computer Programming Using Pascal, 1982. Bd. dirs. Congregation Kol Emeth, Palo Alto. Mem. IEEE (vice chmn. com. database engring. Computer Soc. 1986-87), Assn. Computing Machinery, TeX Users Group (fin. com. 1983-85, internat. coord. 1985-87), Chai Soc. (communications officer 1987-89, v.p. publicity 1989-90). Home: 3881 Corina Way Palo Alto CA 94303-4507 Office: Stanford U Dept Computer Sci Gates Bldg 2A Stanford CA 94305-9020 also: 1720 S Amphlett Blvd Ste 300 San Mateo CA 94402-2717

KELLER, BARBARA LYNN, special education educator, reading teacher; b. Great Falls, Mont., July 18, 1941; d. Edward Jerome and Alvina Elizabeth (Kampsnider) Daly; m. Ray B. Keller, Dec. 28, 1961; 1 child, Forest Ry. Student, Ea. Mont. Coll., 1967-69; BA, U. Mont., 1976; MEd., Mont. State U., 1996; postgrad., No. Mont. Coll., 1989-91; MEd, Mont. State U., 1996. Tchr. grades 1-4 Pub. Schs. Birch Creek Hutterite Colony, Dupuyer, Mont., 1962-63; tchr. grade 2 Pub. Sch. Blackfeet Indian Reservation, Heart Butte, Mont., 1963-64; tchr. reading remediation Pub. Sch., Fort Benton, Mont., 1967-68; tchr. emotionally disturbed Manzanita Ranch Residential Sch., Hyompom, Calif., 1968-69; tchr. reading remediation Pub. Schs., Bigfork, Mont., 1975-78; tchr. ESL Flathead C.C., Kalispell, Mont., 1978-82; pvt. practice tchr. reading, ESL, emotionally disturbed Bigfork, 1982-85; tchr. spl. edn. Pub. Schs. Blackfeet Indian Reservation, Browning, Mont., 1985-94; tchr. study skills and reading, coord. Parents' Ctr. Browning (Mont.) H.S., 1994—, Parents' Ctr. coord.; pres. Eagle's View Publs., Bigfork, 1989—; author-in-residence Am. Edn. Inst., 1994—; cons. adult edn. Author: Reading Pals—A Handbook for Volunteers, 1990, Reading Pals—A Teacher's Manual, 1990, The Parents' Guide—Studying Made Easy, 1991, Gifts of Love and Literacy—A Parent's Guide to Raising Children Who Love to Read, 1993, Read With Your Child—Make a Difference, 1994; (edn. program) Studying Made Easy—The Complete Program, 1992, The Students' Guide—Studying Made Easy, 1996, Teachers Manual Studying Made Easy. Reading cons. Personal Vol. Svc., Bigfork, 1970—, Browning, Mont., 1985—. Recipient Author of Yr. award Am. Edn. Inst., 1993. Mem. ASCD, Internat. Reading Assn., Am. Fedn. Tchrs., Literacy Vols. Am., Mont. Counseling Assn., Learning Disabilities Assn., SPAN (Small Publs. Assn. No. Am.). Home: PO Box 1814 Browning MT 59417-1814 Office: Eagle's View Publs 750 Cascade Ave Bigfork MT 59911-3625

KELLER, GEORGE MATTHEW, retired oil company executive; b. Kansas City, Mo., Dec. 3, 1923; s. George Matthew and Edna Louise (Mathews) K.; m. Adelaide McCague, Dec. 27, 1946; children: William G., Robert A., Barry R. BSChemE, MIT, 1948. Engr. Std. Oil Calif. (now Chevron Corp.), San Francisco, 1948-63, fgn. ops. staff, 1963-67, asst. v.p., asst. to pres., 1967-69, v.p., 1969-74, dir., 1970-88, vice-chmn., 1974-81, chmn., chief exec. officer, 1981-88; bd. dirs. SRI Internat., Chronicle Pub. Co. Trustee Notre Dame Coll., Belmont, Calif. Served to 1st lt. USAAF, 1943-46. Mem. Bus. Coun. Office: Chevron Corp 555 Market St San Francisco CA 94105-2801

KELLER, JAMES WARREN, college administrator; b. San Francisco, June 28, 1950; s. Ralph Waldo and Jane (Kephart) K.; m. Joan Hardie McIlhiney, June 5, 1976; children: Christina Elizabeth, Kathryn Michelle. AB in Econs., Stanford U., 1972; MBA, Santa Clara U., 1977. Ops. officer Bank of Am., Mt. View, Calif., 1972-73; bus. mgr. Palo Alto (Calif.) Unified Sch. Dist., 1973-89; asst. vice chancellor West Valley-Mission Coll., Saratoga, Calif., 1989-91; chief bus. officer Foothill-De Anza Coll., Los Altos Hills, Calif., 1991—. Mem. Assn. Calif. C.C. Bus. Ofcls. (dir. 1993—). Home: 12412 Titus Ave Saratoga CA 95070-4030 Office: Foothill-De Anza Coll 12345 El Monte Ave Los Altos CA 94022-4504

KELLER, J(AMES) WESLEY, credit union executive; b. Jonesboro, Ark., Jan. 6, 1958; s. Norman Grady and Norma Lee (Ridgeway) Patrick; m. Patricia Maria Delavan, July 7, 1979. Student, U. Miss., 1976-78; BS in Bus. and Mgmt., Redlands U., 1991, MBA, 1994. Sr. collector Rodkwell Fed. Credit Union, Downey, Calif., 1978-79; acct. Lucky Fed. Credit Union, Buena Park, Calif., 1979-84; pres., chief exec. officer Long Beach (Calif.) State Employees Credit Union, 1984—. Mem. Credit Union Exec. Soc., Calif. Credit Union League (bd. govs. Long Beach chpt., treas. 1985-86), So. Calif. Credit Union Mgrs. Assn., U. Redlands Whitehead Leadership Soc., Nat. Assn. State Charted Credit Unions (chmn. 1995—), Kiwanis. Republican. Baptist. Office: Long Beach State Employees Credit Union 3840 N Long Beach Blvd Long Beach CA 90807-3312

KELLER, KENT EUGENE, advertising and public relations executive; b. Oil City, Pa., Oct. 5, 1941; s. George W. and Lois (Wallace) K.; divorced; children: Eric Trent, Todd Jason. BA, Kent State U., 1963; cert., Chrysler Inst., Detroit, 1968, UCLA, 1973. Editor Oil City (Pa.) Derrick, 1959-60; various mgmt. positions Chrysler Corp., Twinsburg, Ohio, 1960-64, prodn.

cont. mgr., 1964-67; group mgr. Chrysler Corp. AMG, Detroit, 1967-69; dir. advt. and pub. rels. Zero Corp., Burbank, Calif., 1969-75; exec. v.p. Basso & Assocs. Inc., Newport Beach, Calif., 1975-80; pres. Jason Trent & Co., Inc., North Tustin, Calif., 1980—; pub. rels. counsel Electronic Convs. Inc., L.A., 1980-85; bd. dirs. Neurosci. Tech. Inc., Tarzana, Calif.; cons. Global Engrng., Irvine, Calif., 1989—; co-founder Strategic Concepts, Fountain Valley, Calif., 1990. Editor (industry report) TOLD Report, 1985—, (mag.) Zero Dimensions, 1969-75. Mem. Town Hall of Calif., L.A., 1980—. Mem. Bus. & Profl. Advt. Assn., Pub. Rels. Soc. Am., Back Bay Club. Republican. Presbyterian. Home: 18072 Darmel Pl Santa Ana CA 92705-1916 Office: Ste 4D 1440 S State College Blvd Anaheim CA 92806

KELLER, MICHAEL CROSLEY, correctional facilities official; b. Salem, Oreg., Aug. 3, 1949; s. John L. and E. Ruth (Simmons) K.; m. Renée L. Romanko, June 30, 1975 (dec.Apr. 1984); m. Edie Ann Cannon, Mar. 25, 1989; children: Aaron Crosley, Alexis Catherine. BS, Western Oreg. State Coll., 1978; postgrad., Sonoma State U., 1978-84. Substitute tchr. Apache County Schs., Ganado, Ariz., 1972; correctional officer San Quentin (Calif.) State Prison, 1978-80, correctional sgt., 1980-82, correctional counselor, 1982-84, employee rels. officer, 1984-85; watch comdr., lt. Correctional Tng. Facility, Soledad, Calif., 1988-93; capt. North Kern State Prison, Delano, Calif., 1993-95; acad. adminstr. Correctional Training Acad., Galt, Calif., 1995—; asst. negotiator Dept. of Pers. Adminstrn., Sacramento, 1985. With U.S. Army, 1973-76, Korea. Republican. Office: Correctional Training Ctr 9850 Twin Cities Rd Galt CA 95632-8821

KELLER, PETER CHARLES, museum director, mineralogist; b. Allentown, Pa., Aug. 16, 1947; s. Charles Donald and Barbara Jean (Miller) K.; children: Bret Charles, Elizabeth Austin. BA, George Washington U., 1972; MA, U. Tex., 1974, PhD, 1977. Grad. gemologist, 1980. Curator mineralogy L.A. County Mus., Los Angeles, 1976-80; dir. edn. Gemological Inst. Am., Santa Monica, Calif., 1980-84; lectr. geology U. So. Calif., L.A., 1980-87; assoc. dirs. L.A. County Mus. Natural History, 1987-91; exec. dir. Bowers Mus. of Cultural Art, Santa Ana, Calif., 1991—. Assoc. editor: Gems and Gemology, 1980-91; contbr. articles in field to profl. jours. Trustee, Natural History Mus. Found., 1980-84; treas. Mineral Mus. Adv. Council, 1984. Fellow Leakey Found., Explorers Club; mem. Internat. Commn. Mus., Am. Assn. Mus., Mineral. Soc. Am., Gemol. Assn. Gt. Britain, Internat. Mineral. Assn. (U.S. rep. for mus.), Geol. Soc. Am., Mineral. Soc. Gt. Britain, Sigma Xi, Phi Kappa Phi. Home: 401 Seaward Rd Corona Del Mar CA 92625-2670 Office: Bowers Mus Cultural Art 2002 N Main St Santa Ana CA 92706-2731*

KELLER, ROBERT M., bishop. Bishop Evang. Luth. Ch. in Am., Spokane, Wash. Office: Synod of E Washington-Idaho 314 S Spruce St Ste A Spokane WA 99204-1098

KELLER, SHIRLEY INEZ, accountant; b. Ferguson, Iowa, Sept. 15, 1930; d. Adelbert Leslie and Inez Marie (Abbey) Hilsabeck; m. Earl Wilson Keller, Feb. 2, 1957 (dec. 1987); children: Earl William, Cynthia Marie, Eric Walter, Kenneth Paul. Student, U. Iowa, 1949-51; AS, Cameron U., 1971, BS, 1973; postgrad., Arapahoe Community Coll., 1986. High speed radio operator U.S. Army Signal Corps, N.Y.C., Japan, 1951-57; auditor U.S. Dept. Justice, Washington, 1973-76, U.S. Dept. Energy, Oklahoma City, 1976-83, U.S. Dept. Interior, Albuquerque, 1983-86; acct. U.S. Dept. Interior, Denver, 1986-95, ret., 1995; seminar instr. U.S. Dept. Interior, Denver, other cities, 1989-94. Author: Oil and Gas Payor Handbook, 1993. Scorekeeper Boy's Baseball, Lawton, Okla., 1964-72; den mother Boy Scouts Am., Lawton, 1965-66. Sgt. U.S. Army, 1951-57. Decorated Merit Unit Commendation, U.N. Commendation, Korean Svc. medal. Mem. Toastmasters Internat. (sec. Buffalo chpt. 1991, sgt.-at-arms Buffalo chpt. 1992, Competent Toastmaster 1993). Democrat. Roman Catholic. Home: PO Box 280535 Lakewood CO 80228-0535

KELLER, SUSAN AGNES, insurance executive; b. Moline, Ill., July 12, 1952; d. Kenneth Francis and Ethel Louise (Odendahl) Hulsbrink. Grad. in Pub. Relations, Patricia Stevens Career Coll., 1971; grad. in Gen. Ins., Ins. Inst. Am., 1986. CPCU; lic. ins. and real estate agt.; notary public. Comml. lines rater Bitiminous Casualty Corp., Rock Island, Ill., 1973-78; with Roadway Express, Inc., Rock Island, 1978-81; front line supr. Yellow Freight System, Inc., Denver, 1982-83; supr. plumbing and sheet metal prodn. Bell Plumbing and Heating, Denver, 1983-84; v.p. underwriting farm/ranch dept. Golden Eagle Ins. Co., San Diego, 1985—; cons. real estate foreclosure County Records Svc., San Diego, 1986-89; tchr. Ins. Inst. of Am., 1991. Vol. DAV, San Diego, 1985—; tchr. IEA and CPCU courses. Mem. Soc. CPCU (pres., bd. dirs.), Profl. Women in Ins., NAFE. Roman Catholic. Home: 891 Mountainview Rd El Cajon CA 92021-7818 Office: Golden Eagle Ins Co 7175 Navajo Rd PO Box 85826 San Diego CA 92119-1642

KELLER, WILLIAM D., federal judge; b. 1934. BS, U. Calif., Berkeley, 1956; LLB, UCLA, 1960. Asst. U.S. atty. U.S. Dist. Ct. (so. dist.) Calif., 1961-64; assoc. Dryden, Harrington, Horgan & Swartz, Calif., 1964-72; U.S. atty. U.S. Dist. Ct. (cen. dist.) Calif., Los Angeles, 1972-77; ptnr. Rosenfeld, Meyer & Susman, 1977-78; solo practice, 1978-81; ptnr. Mahm & Cazier, 1981-84; judge U.S. Dist. Ct. (cen. dist.) Calif., Los Angeles, 1984—; ptnr. Rosenfeld, Meyer & Susman, Calif., 1977-78; pvt. practice law Calif., 1978-81; ptnr. Hahn & Cazier, Calif., 1981-84. Office: US Dist Ct 312 N Spring St Ste 1653 Los Angeles CA 90012-4718

KELLER-HOM, KIMBERLY S., marketing professional, researcher, editor; b. Flint, Mich., July 16, 1965; d. Bob V. and Carolyn L. K.; m. Reagan J. Hom, Aug. 31, 1989. Diploma in graphic design, Platt Coll., 1990. Bookkeeper III Los Angeles County Bd. Suprs., Alhambra, Calif., 1988-92; co-owner, bookkeeper A.E. Mobile Syss., Alhambra, Calif., 1994-96; owner, editor, publ., market rschr., info. broker K.H. Enterprises, South Pasadena, Calif., 1996—. Author, pub.: (booklet) The Secret Shopper, 1996; pub., editor: (newsletter) The Prudent Saver, 1996. Office: KH Enterprises 1107 Fair Oaks Ave #322 South Pasadena CA 91030

KELLERMAN, FAYE MARDER, novelist, dentist; b. St. Louis, July 31, 1952; d. Oscar and Anne (Steinberg) Marder; m. Jonathan Seth Kellerman, July 23, 1972; children: Jesse Oren, Rachel Diana, Ilana Judith, Aliza Celeste. AB in Math., UCLA, 1974, DDS, 1978. Author: The Ritual Bath, 1986 (Macavity award best 1st novel 1986), Sacred and Profane, 1987, The Quality of Mercy, 1989, Milk and Honey, 1990, Day of Atonement, 1991, False Prophet, 1992, Grievous Sin, 1993, Sanctuary, 1994, Justice, 1995, Prayers for the Dead, 1996, Serpent's Tooth, 1997; contbr. short stories to Sisters in Crime vols. 1 and 3, Ellery Queen Mag., A Woman's Eye, Women of Mystery, the year's 2d finest crime: mystery stories, The Year's 25 Finest Mystery and Crime Stories, A Modern Treasury of Great Detective and Murder Mysteries, Mothers, Murder for Love. UCLA rsch. fellow, 1978. Mem. Mystery Writers of Am. (So. Calif. bd. dirs.), Womens' Israeli Polit. Action Com., Sisters in Crime. Jewish.

KELLEY, BRUCE DUTTON, pharmacist; b. Hartford, Conn., Jan. 4, 1957; s. Roger Weston and Elizabeth Morrill (Atwood) K.; m. DawnReneé Cinocco, Jan. 19, 1990. Student, U. Hartford, 1975-77; BS in Pharmacy, U. Colo., 1985; diplomas in Russian, Moscow U., Moscow, 1993, 95; BA in Russian, U. Colo., 1995. RPh, Colo. Pharmacist King Soopers, Inc., Boulder, Colo., 1990—; asst. tour leader in Russia U. Tex., El Paso, 1991; Russia asst. guide, U. Ariz., Tucson, 1992 (summer). Vol. Warderburg Student Health Ctr., U. Colo., Boulder, 1981-83, Am. Diabetes Assn. Mem. Elks, Nat. Eagle Scout Assn., Am. Legion. Republican. Home: 6152 Willow Ln Boulder CO 80301-5356 Office: King Soopers Inc 6550 Lookout Rd Boulder CO 80301-3303

KELLEY, HAROLD EDWARD, metallurgical engineer; b. Butte, Mont., Sept. 8, 1960; s. Harold Arthur and Dorothy Gene (Barnes) K.; m. Kristine Marie Ganzer, Jan. 9, 1988; children: Tiffany Michelle, Harold Andrew. BS in Material Sci. and Engring., U. Utah, 1982; MS in Metall. Engring., Mont. Tech. U., 1984. Rsch. asst. Mont. Tech., Butte, 1982-84; mem. tech. staff Rockwell Internat., Anaheim, Calif., 1985-88; metall. engr. Kennametal, Inc., Fallon, Nev., 1988-93, sr. metall. engr., 1993—. Patentee arc hardfacing rod. Youth advisor Anaheim Meth. Ch., 1985-88; mem. Ptnrs. in Edn., Fallon, 1992—; CPR and first aid instr. ARC, Fallon, 1992-95, soccer coach, 1995—. Mem. Am. Soc. Metals Internat. (exec. com. Orange county chpt. 1985-88), The Metall. Soc. Methodist. Home: 521 Michael Dr Fallon NV 89406-5725 Office: Kennametal Inc 347 N Taylor St Fallon NV 89406-5730

KELLEY, KEVIN PATRICK, security, safety, risk management administrator; b. Indpls., Apr. 21, 1954; s. Everett Lee and Emily Louise (Bottoms) K.; m. Kathie Jo Fluegeman, Oct. 13, 1984. BS, Calif. State U., Long Beach, 1984; cert. mgmt. supervision, UCLA, 1984. Mgmt. asst. FBI, Los Angeles, 1973-79; security/safety supr. U. Calif., 1979-82; security/safety adminstr. Micom Systems, Inc., Chatsworth, Calif., 1982-83; loss prevention, safety auditor Joseph Magnin, Inc., San Francisco, 1983-84; loss prevention, safety adminstr. Wherehouse Entertainment, Inc., Gardena, Calif., 1984-86; risk control cons. Indsl. Indemnity Co., Los Angeles, 1986-87, Kemper Group, City of Industry, Calif., 1987-90; account mgr. loss control engring. Tokio Marine Mgmt. Inc., Pasadena, Calif., 1990-97; risk mgmt. cons., 1997—; commr. pub. safety City of Norwalk, Calif., 1984-86. Mem. security com. Los Angeles Olympic Organizing Com., 1984. Mem. Am. Soc. Indsl. Security (cert., Peter Updike Meml. scholar 1985), Am. Soc. Safety Engrs., Chief Spl. Agts. Assn., Risk Ins. Mgmt. Soc., Nat. Safety Mgmt. Soc. (sec. 1985-86), Am. Heart Assn. (governing bd. chmn. 1986-88), Ins. Inst. Am. (cert.). Republican. Roman Catholic. Lodges: Rotary, Kiwanis.

KELLEY, LISA STONE, public guardian, conservator; b. Sacramento, Calif., Mar. 10, 1947; d. John William and Coral Frances (Roberts) Stone; m. Charles B. Kelley, Oct. 7, 1967 (div. Feb. 1987); children: Brian Christopher, Darren Matthew. Student, Sacramento City Coll., 1965-67, AA in Social Sci., 1978; BA in Social Work with honors, Calif. State U., Sacramento, 1982, MSW with honors, 1985; postgrad. in Psychology, Calif. Coast U., 1994—. Lic. clin. social worker, Calif. Pharmacy clerk S. Sacramento Pharmacy, 1966-68; temp. med. asst. Sacramento, 1978-80; adv., counselor El Dorado Women's Info. Ctr., Placerville, Calif., 1982; dep. patients rights adv. Sacramento County Office Patients Rights, 1983-84; sch. social worker Elk Grove (Calif.) Unified Sch. Dist., 1984-85; mental health counselor Sacramento Mental Health Ctr., 1986; dep. pub. guardian/conservator Sacramento County, 1986—. Mem. NASW, Sacramento County Employees Orgn., Am. Orthopsychiat. Assn., Menninger Found., Calif. Soc. for Clin. Social Work, Am. Rabbit Breeders Assn., Calif. State U. Alumni Assn., Calif. Coast U. Alumni Assn., Holland Lop Rabbit Specialty Club, Phi Kappa Phi. Democrat. Office: Sacramento County Pub Guardian/Conservator 4875 Broadway Ste I Sacramento CA 95820-1500

KELLEY, LOUANNA ELAINE, newspaper columnist, researcher; b. Denver, Oct. 17, 1920; d. John Earl and Violet May (Griffin) Richards; m. George Vanstavoren Kelley, Dec. 1942 (dec. Oct. 1975); children: William Richard, John Henry; stepchild, Joan Fenicle; m. Glen Russell Fenicle, Jan. 1984 (dec. Apr. 1996). Student in Dental Tng., Emily Griffith Sch., 1960-61; Student in Bus., Red Rocks Coll., 1976-77. Dental asst. Colo. Dental, Denver, 1961-70; columnist Front Range Jour., Idaho Springs, Colo., 1975-80; reporter Colo. Transcript, Golden, Colo., 1975-82; columnist, reporter Clear Creek Courant, Idaho Springs, Colo., 1980-88, Mountain Messenger, Idaho Springs, Colo., 1988—; researcher Nat. Mining Hall of Fame, Leadville, Colo. 1987—, lectr. Colo. Sch. Mines, Golden, 1977, Jefferson County Schs., Golden, 1975-84; bd. dirs. Vetco Credit Union, Denver. Author: Take Your Pick And Strike It Rich, 1988; contbr. articles to profl. jours. Historian Clear Creek County and Jefferson County, Colo. Mem. Social Ethics (v.p. 1986—), Colo. Fedn. Women's. Republican. Lutheran. Home: 12790 W 6th Pl Golden CO 80401-4674 Office: Mountain Messenger Box 2090 Idaho Springs CO 80452

KELLEY, ROBERT SUMA, systems analyst; b. Chgo., July 2, 1961; s. Jerry Dean and Jean (Laine) K. BA in Philosophy, Western Md. Coll., 1985; MBA in MIS, Ind. U., 1989. Human resource specialist Marriott Corp., Gaithersburg, Md., 1985-86; mgr. in tng. Courtyard by Marriott, Fairfax, Va., 1986-87; sys. analyst Hewlett-Packard, Palo Alto, Calif., 1989—; mem. adv. com. for implementation of Calif. Assembly bill for improving edn. opportunities for learning disabled children, 1991-94. counselor Camp Allen for the Physically Handicapped, Manchester, N.H., 1977; track coach for disadvantaged youth Rockville (Md.) Recreation, 1980. Home: 408 Grant Ave Apt 306 Palo Alto CA 94306-1813 Office: Hewlett-Packard 3000 Hanover St # 20bj Palo Alto CA 94304-1112

KELLEY, WILLIAM, author, screenwriter; b. Staten Island, N.Y., May 27, 1929; s. Edward Thomas and Alethea Waldegrave (Mulligan) K.; m. Cornelia Ann Chamberlin, Sept. 18, 1954; children: Maura Alethea Kelley Deering, Shawn Kelley Jahshan. AB, Brown U., 1955; AM, Harvard U., 1957. West Coast editor Doubleday & Co., N.Y.C., 1958-61; fiction editor McGraw Hill Co., N.Y.C., 1961-62. Author: Gemini, 1959, The God Hunter, 1965, The Tyree Legend, 1979, (feature film) Witness, 1985 (Academy Award 1986). Sgt. USAF, 1947-50. Recipient Edgar award Mystery Writers Assn., 1986, Best Script award for Witness, W.G.A., 1986, Western Writers, 1972, 77. Home: Rocking K Ranch 30 Running Iron Rd Bishop CA 93514

KELLNER, RICHARD GEORGE, mathematician, computer scientist; b. Cleve., July 10, 1943; s. George Ernst and Wanda Julia (Lapinski) K.; BS, Case Inst. Tech., 1965; MS, Stanford U., 1968, PhD, 1969; m. Charlene Ann Zajc, June 26, 1965; children: Michael Richard, David George. Staff mem. Los Alamos (N.M.) Scientific Lab., 1969-79, Los Alamos Nat. Lab., 1983-88; co-owner, dir. software devel. KMP Computer Systems, Inc., Los Alamos, 1979-84; mgr. spl. projects KMP Computer Systems div. 1st Data Resources Inc., Los Alamos, 1984-87; with microcomputer div., 1988; owner CompuSpeed, 1986—; co-owner Computer-Aided Communications, 1982-84; v.p. Applied Computing Systems Inc., 1988—; cons., 1979—. Recipient Commendation award for outstanding support of operation Desert Storm. Mem. IEEE, Assn. Computing Machinery, Math. Assn. Am., Soc. Indsl. and Applied Math., Am. Math. Soc. Home: 4496 Ridgeway Dr Los Alamos NM 87544-1960 Office: Applied Computing Systems Inc 120 Longview Dr Los Alamos NM 87544-3728

KELLOGG, DONALD RAY, surgeon, plastic surgeon; b. Hot Lake, Oreg., 1938. MD, Loma Linda U., 1965. Diplomate Am. Bd. Surgery; Am. Bd. Plastic Surgery. Intern Henry Ford Hosp., Detroit, 1965-66; residentgen. surgery Loma Linda Hosps., 1966-70; resident plastic surgery Washington U., St. Louis, 1970-72; resident Salinas Valley (Calif.) Meml. Hosp. Mem. AMA. Office: 242 E Romie Ln Salinas CA 93901-3128

KELLOGG, FREDERICK, historian; b. Boston, Dec. 9, 1929; s. Frederick Floyd and Stella Harriet (Plummer) K.; m. Patricia Kay Hanbery, Aug. 21, 1954 (dec. 1975); 1 child, Kristine Marie Calvert. AB, Stanford U., 1952; MA, U. So. Calif., 1958; PhD, Ind. U., 1969. Instr., Boise State U., 1962-64, asst. prof., 1964-65; vis. asst. prof. U. Idaho, 1965; asso. prof. Boise State U., 1966-67; instr. history U. Ariz., 1967-68, asst. prof., 1968-71, asso. prof., 1971—. Founder, chmn. Idaho Hist. Conf., 1964. U.S.-Romania Cultural Exchange Research scholar, 1960-61; Sr. Fulbright-Hays Research scholar, Romania, 1969-70. Recipient Am. Council Learned Socs. Research grant, 1970-71; Internat. Research and Exchanges Bd. Sr. Research grant, 1973-74. Mem. Am. Hist. Assn., Am. Assn. Advancement Slavic Studies, Am. Assn. Southeast European Studies. Author: A History of Romanian Historical Writing, 1990, The Road to Romanian Independence, 1995, O istorie a istoriografiei romane, 1996; mng. editor Southeastern Europe, 1974—; contbr. articles to academic publs. Office: U Ariz Dept History Tucson AZ 85721

KELLOGG, GEORGE WILLIAM, psychiatrist; m. Betty L. BS in Chemistry, La. State U., 1963, MD, 1967; JD, U. Chgo., 1975; MBA, Golden Gate U., 1982. Intern Letterman Hosp., San Francisco, 1967-68; resident Walter Redd Hosp., Washington, 1968-71; psychiatrist pvt. practice, Salinas, Calif., 1974—. Maj. U.S. Army, 1966-74, Vietnam. Office: 11 Maple St Ste A Salinas CA 93901-3249

KELLOGG, KENYON P., lawyer; b. Dubuque, Iowa, Aug. 5, 1946; s. Kenyon P. and Maleta (Fleege) K.; m. Carolyn Jo Dick, July 18, 1970; children: Andrew P., Kenyon P., Jonathan P. BSBA summa cum laude, Creighton U., 1968; JD cum laude, U. Mich., 1971. Bar: U.S. Dist. Ct. (we. dist.) Wash. 1971, U.S. Tax Ct. 1980; CPA, Wash. With Arthur Andersen & Co., Omaha and Detroit, 1968-71; assoc. Lane Powell Spears Lubersky, Seattle, 1971-78, ptnr., 1978—. Bd. regents Seattle U., 1989—, dean's coun. Alber's Sch. Bus. and Econs., 1992—; mem. nat. alumni bd. Creighton U., 1995—; trustee Naval Undersea Mus. Found., 1995—; mem. FALES com. USN Acad., 1995—. Capt. USAR, 1968-77. Mem. AICPAs, Wash. Soc. CPAs, Seattle Rotary, Seattle Yacht Club (trustee), Cruising Club of Am., Naval Acad. Sailing Squadron. Office: Lane Powell Spears Lubersky 1420 5th Ave Ste 4100 Seattle WA 98101-2333

KELLOUGH, RICHARD DEAN, educator; b. Jamestown, Ohio, Oct. 31, 1935; s. Stanley Eugene and Mayme Elizabeth (Stephens) K. BS, Wilmington Coll., 1956; MAT in Botany, Miami U., 1959; EdD, Oreg. State U., 1967. Tchr. Clinton County Schs., Martinsville, Ohio, 1956-59, San Juan Unified Sch. Dist., Carmichael, Calif., 1960-61, Davis (Calif.) Sr. H.S., 1961-69; asst. prof. tchr. edn. Calif. State U., Sacramento, 1969-73, assoc. prof., 1973-77, prof., 1977—; rsch. asst. Kettering Found., Yellow Springs, Ohio, 1957-58; lab. tch. II U. Calif., Davis, 1959-61; NSF rsch. fellow U. Calif., Davis, 1962. Author numerous textbooks including Science for the Elementary School, 1997, Middle School Teaching: A Guide to Methods and Resources, 1996, A Resource Guide for Teaching: K-12, 1997. Office: Calif State Univ 6000 J St Sacramento CA 95819-2605

KELLY, BETH, writer, songwriter; b. Miami, Fla., Sept. 24, 1953. BA, UCLA, 1976. Owner Once and Future Glass; reporter Glendale (Calif.) News Press. Author essays, articles, poetry, reviews, short stories; composer songs. Recipient Editor's Choice award Nat. Poetry Soc., 1995. Mem. Soc. Children's Lit. Home: PO Box 330 Topanga CA 90290

KELLY, BRETT, fundraiser; b. Santa Barbara, Calif., Sept. 8, 1962; s. William B. Kelly and Barbara F. (Goodridge) Tracy. BA, San Diego State U., 1989. Bus. mgr. KCR Radio, San Diego, 1981-83; gen. mgr. KCR Radio, 1983-84, radio announcer, 1983-85; supr. TV ops. KPBS-TV, San Diego, 1985-91; dir. fundraising KPBS-TV, 1991—; freelance lighting designer, San Diego, 1990—. Bd. dirs. GLAAD, San Diego, 1995-96. Democrat. Office: KPBS-TV 5200 Campanile Dr San Diego CA 92182-1901

KELLY, BRIAN MATTHEW, industrial hygienist; b. Ogdensburg, N.Y., June 16, 1956; s. Lauris F. and Catherine M. (McEvoy) K. BA, SUNY, Oswego, 1978; BS, Clarkson U., 1981; MS in Indsl. Safety, Cen. Mo. State U., 1990. Cert. indsl. hygienist Am. Bd. Indsl. Hygiene; cert. accident investigator U.S. Dept. Energy, NASA and Nuclear Regulatory Commn. Maintenance engr. Kelly Sales Corp., Madrid, N.Y., 1978-80, carpenter, 1981-82; hygienist indsl. hygiene and toxicology ES&H assessments program office Sandia Nat. Labs., Albuquerque, 1983—; mem. tech. adv. bd. Albuquerque (N.Mex.) Tech. Vocat. Inst., 1989—. Mem. Am. Inst. Chemists, Am. Indsl. Hygienists Assn., N.Y. Acad. Scis., Am. Conf. Govtl. Indls. Hygienists, Am. Soc. Safety Engrs., Am. Acad. Indsl. Hygiene, Gamma Sigma Epsilon, Phi Kappa Phi. Republican. Roman Catholic. Home: 1455 Beall St Bosque Farms NM 87068-9109 Office: Sandia Nat Labs ES&H Assess Prog Ofc 12870 1515 Eubank Blvd SE Albuquerque NM 87185-0346

KELLY, CAROLYN SUE, newspaper executive; b. Pasco, Wash., Oct. 25, 1952; d. Jerald Davin and Margaret Helen (Nibler) K. BBA, Gonzaga U., 1974; MBA, Seattle U., 1985. CPA, Wash. Acct. Brajcich & Loeffler, Spokane, Wash., 1972-74; auditor Peat, Marwick, Mitchell & Co., Seattle, 1974-77; fin. analyst Seattle Times, 1977-81, asst. circulation mgr., 1981-83, spl. project advt. mgr., 1983-86, dir. mktg. and new bus., 1986-89, v.p., chief fin. officer, 1989—. Bd. dirs. Econ. Devel. Coun., Seattle, 1992, Campfire, Artists Unltd. Mem. Fin. Execs. Office: Seattle Times PO Box 70 Seattle WA 98111-0070*

KELLY, CHRISTINE ELISE, city planner; b. Hollywood, Calif., Nov. 22, 1952; d. Lorenzo Iral Alcott and Louise Jean Paule Ressier; children: Ryan, Jacqueline, Michael. BA, Calif. State U., Long Beach, 1978, MPA, 1986. Dir. cmty. devel. City of Cypress, Calif. Mem. Am. Planning Assn., Urban Land Inst., Comty. Redevel. Assn., Orange County Planning Dires. Assn. (v.p. 1986, pres. 1987). Office: City of Cypress 5275 Orange Ave Cypress CA 90630-2957

KELLY, DENNIS RAY, sales executive; b. Olympia, Wash., Aug. 20, 1948; s. William E. and Irene (Lewis) K.; m. Pamela Jo Kresevich, Mar. 16, 1974. BA, Cen. Wash. U., 1972; postgrad., U. Wash., 1977-78. Sales rep. Bumble Bee Sea Foods, Seattle, 1972-74; retail sales mgr. Pacific Pearl Sea Foods, Seattle, 1974-76; regional sales mgr. Castle & Cooke Foods, Seattle, Phila., and N.Y.C., 1976-80; v.p. sales mktg. Frances Andrew Ltd., Seattle, 1980-82; regional sales mgr. Tenneco West, Seattle, 1982-85; sales and mktg. mgr. for western U.S. David Oppenheimer, Seattle, 1985—. Alumni advisor Ctrl. Wash. U., Ellensburg, 1979-87, alumni bd. dirs., 1986—, fund drive chmn., 1988, mem. sch. cmty. group bd.; bd. dirs. Bay Vista Tower Assn., v.p.; mem. Statue of Liberty Ellis Island Found.; chmn. ann. fund drive Ctrl. Wash. U., bd. dirs., 1992. Mem. New Zealand-Am. Soc., Mfrs. Reps. Club Wash. (bd. dirs.). Republican. Home: 2821 2nd Ave Apt 1204 Seattle WA 98121-1249

KELLY, EMMA JANE, veterinarian; b. Liverpool, Eng., July 16, 1965. AS, Wayne C.C., Goldsboro, N.C., 1983; BS in Animal Sci. summa cum laude, N.C. State U., 1985, DVM, 1989; MS in Bioveterinary Sci., Utah State U., 1992. Extern Liverpool U. Vet. Sch., 1988; clin. vet. resident Utah State U., Provo, 1989-91, asst. vet. diagnostician, 1991-94, diagnostician, 1994—; lectr. in field. Contbr. articles to profl. jours. Recipient Radiology award N.C. State U.-CVM, 1989; Winslow Found. scholar, 1982-83. Mem. Phi Kappa Phi, Phi Zeta, Gamma Sigma Delta, Phi Theta Kappa. Office: Utah State Univ Veterinary Diagnostic Lab 2031 S State St Provo UT 84606-6552

KELLY, J. MICHAEL, lawyer; b. Hattiesburg, Miss., Dec. 5, 1943. BA, Emory U., 1966; LLB, U. Va., 1969. Bar: Ga. 1969, U.S. Supreme Ct. 1978, D.C. 1980, Utah 1982, Calif. 1988. Law clerk to Judge Griffin B. Bell (5th cir.) U.S. Ct. Appeals, Atlanta, 1969-70; ptnr. Alston & Bird (formerly Alston, Miller & Gaines), Atlanta, 1970-77, 81-82; counselor to atty. gen. U.S. Dept. Justice, Washington, 1977-79; counselor to sec. U.S. Dept. Energy, Washington, 1979-81; ptnr., shareholder, dir. Ray, Quinney & Nebeker, Salt Lake City, 1982-87; ptnr. Cooley Godward LLP, San Francisco, 1987—. Mem. Omicron Delta Kappa, Phi Alpha Delta. Office: Cooley Godward LLP 20th Fl 1 Maritime Plz San Francisco CA 94111-3580

KELLY, JEROME BERNARD, insurance company executive; b. Kankakee, Ill., Oct. 4, 1954; s. Joseph B. and Mary J. (Demerly) K.; m. Barbara Fawcett, June 21, 1986; children: Anna, Sarah. BA, Regis Coll., 1980; MBA, U. Phoenix, 1989. V.p. Shearson Hayden Stone, Denver, 1977-83, E.F. Hutton, Denver, 1983-85; portfolio mgr. 17th St. Fin. Mgmt., Denver, 1985-87; stockbroker Dain Bosworth, Denver, 1987-88; owner J.B. Kelly Ins. Agy., Denver, 1988—. Bd. dirs. United Cerebral Palsy Assn. Denver, 1987-90; mem. selection com. Cultural Facilities Tax Dist., Denver, 1995—. Mem. Colo. Bus. Sch. Club (pres. 1988-89), Trout Unltd., Nat. Assn. of Securities Dealers (bd. arbitration 1987—), Am. Arbitration Assn. (panel arbitrators 1990—). Office: JB Kelly Ins Agy 1863 S Pearl St Denver CO 80210-3136

KELLY, JOHN J., prosecutor. U.S. atty. for N.Mex. U.S. Dept. Justice, Albuquerque. Office: US Atty for Dist NMex 625 Silver Ave SW PO Box 607 Albuquerque NM 87103*

KELLY, KATHLEEN SUZANNE, marketing professional; b. Inglewood, Calif., Dec. 20, 1966; d. Robert Duane and Anne Margaret (Halpin) K. BS, U. So. Calif., L.A., 1989. Asst. media buyer Kelly, Scott & Madison, Chgo., 1989-90; pub. rels. rep. In-N-Out Burger, Baldwin Park, Calif., 1990-91, interim mktg. dir., 1991-92, advt. and pub. rels. adminstr., 1992-93; project mgr. L.A. Unified Sch. Dist., 1993-97; cons. in field. Pres. bd. dirs. Haven House, 1995-97. Mem. NAFE, AAUW, Pub. Rels. Soc. Am., Am. Mgmt. Assn., Trojan Jr. Aux., San Gabriel Valley Trojan Club (bd. dirs.), U. So. Calif. Trojan Club-SGV. Republican. Roman Catholic. Home and Office: 62 5th Ave Shalimar FL 32579-1820

KELLY, KEVIN FRANCIS, lawyer; b. New Orleans, Apr. 27, 1949; s. Frank J. and Dorothy P. (Paige) K.; m. Jean A. Friedhoff, Dec. 27, 1969; children: Bryan F., Eric W. BA, Gonzaga U., 1970; JD, U. Calif. Berkeley, 1973. Bar: Wash. 1973. Law clk. to Hon. Eugene A. Wright U.S. Ct. Appeals, 9th Cir., Seattle, 1973-74; assoc. Davis, Wright, Todd, Riese & Jones, Seattle, 1974-76; ptnr. Wickwire, Goldmark & Schorr, Seattle, 1976-88, Heller, Ehrman, White & McAuliffe, Seattle, 1988—. Bd. dirs. Big Bros. King County, Seattle, 1985-95, v.p., 1991, pres., 1992; bd. trustees Legal Found. Wash., Seattle, 1994-97, pres., 1997. Mem. Wash. Biotechnology and Biomedical Assn. (bd. dirs. 1996—), Wash. Soc. Hosp. Lawyers, Order of Coif. Home: 4040 55th Ave NE Seattle WA 98105-4957

KELLY, PAUL JOSEPH, JR., judge; b. Freeport, N.Y., Dec. 6, 1940; s. Paul J. and Jacqueline M. (Nolan) K.; BBA, U. Notre Dame, 1963; JD, Fordham U., 1967; m. Ruth Ellen Dowling, June 27, 1964; children—Johanna, Paul Edwin, Thomas Martin, Christopher Mark, Heather Marie. Bar: N.Mex. 1967. Law clk. Cravath, Swaine & Moore, N.Y.C., 1964-67; assoc. firm Hinkle, Cox, Eaton, Coffield & Hensley, Roswell, N.Mex., 1967-71, ptnr., 1971-92; judge U.S. Ct. Appeals (10th cir.), Santa Fe, 1992—; mem. N.Mex. Bd. Bar Examiners, 1982-85; mem. N.Mex. Ho. of Reps., 1976-81, chmn. consumer and public affairs com., mem. judiciary com. Mem. N.Mex. Pub. Defender Bd.; bd. of visitors, Fordham U. Sch. of Law, 1992—; pres. No. N.M. Am. Inn of Ct., 1993—; pres. Roswell Drug Abuse Com., 1970-71; mem. Appellate Judges Nominating Commn., 1989-92. Pres. Chaves County Young Reps., 1971-72; vice chmn. N.Mex. Young Reps., 1969-71, treas., 1968-69; mem. bd. dirs. Zia council Girl Scouts Am., Roswell Girls Club, Chaves County Mental Health Assn., 1974-77; bd. dirs. Santa Fe Orch., 1992-93, Roswell Symphony Orch. Soc., 1969-82, treas., 1970-73, pres., 1973-75; mem. Eastern N.Mex. State Fair Bd., 1978-83. Mem. ABA, Fed. Bar Assn., State Bar N.Mex. (v.p. young lawyers sect. 1969, co-chmn. ins. sub-com. 1972-73, mem. continuing legal edn. com. 1970-73). Roman Catholic (pres. parish council 1971-76). K.C. Office: US Court Appeals 10th Circuit Federal Courthouse PO Box 10113 Santa Fe NM 87504-6113

KELLY, PETER BERNARD, chemistry educator, researcher; b. Seneca Falls, N.Y., Sept. 10, 1954; s. Glenn Bernard and Ruth Margret (Larsen) K. AB, Dartmouth Coll., 1976; PhD, Pa. State U., State College, 1981. Postdoctoral assoc. Princeton (N.J.) U., 1981-83, U. Oreg., Eugene, 1983-86; asst. prof. U. Calif., Davis, 1986-93, assoc. prof., 1993-94; vis. assoc. prof. Rice U., Houston, 1994-95. Contbr. articles to profl. jours. Mem. Am. Chem. Soc., Am. Optical Soc., Western Spectroscopy Assn. Methodist. Office: U Calif Chemistry Dept Davis CA 95616

KELLY, ROBERT EDWARD, engineer, educator; b. Abington, Pa., Oct. 20, 1934; s. Bernard Joseph and Rose Monica (Lautenschlager) K.; m. Karin Elizabeth Lampert, Aug. 15, 1964; children: Nicholas, Jennifer. BA, Franklin & Marshall Coll., 1957; BS, Rensselaer Poly. Inst., 1957; MS in Aero. Engring., MIT, 1959, ScD, 1964. Asst. prof. UCLA, 1967-70, assoc. prof., 1970-75, prof. dept. mech. and aerospace engring., 1975—, vice chair grad. affairs, 1976, 94—; sr. vis. fellow Imperial Coll. Sci. and Tech., London, 1974; vis. prof. Northwestern U., Evanston, Ill., 1985, U. Manchester, Eng., 1994; vis. scientist Japan Atomic Energy Rsch. Inst., Tokai-mura, 1991; cons. Hughes Aircraft Co., El Segundo, Calif., 1976-83. Assoc. editor Physics of Fluids, 1981-83, 92—; mem. editorial bd. Phys. Rev. E, 1990-96; contbr. over 60 articles to profl. jours. Fellow Am. Phys. Soc. (chmn. divsn. fluid dynamics 1980-81), ASME, mem. AIAA. Office: MAE Dept UCLA Los Angeles CA 90095-1597

KELLY, RYAN JOSEPH, newspaper editor, writer, pilot; b. Cheyenne, Wyo., Dec. 19, 1968; s. Peter Mullane and Lynn Patricia (McLaughlin) K. BS in Mktg., U. Wyo., 1992. Chief copywriter Kelly Comm., Littleton, Colo., 1992—; reporter Jefferson Sentinel Newspapers, Lakewood, Colo., 1995, sports editor, 1995—. 1st lt. USAR, 1992—. Recipient award Marshall Found., 1995. Mem. Nat. Writers Assn. Office: Jefferson Sentinel Newspapers 1220 Wadsworth Blvd Lakewood CO 80215

KELLY, THOMAS J., sports association executive; b. Madison, Wis.; m. Carole Kelly. BA in Journalism, U. Wis., 1974. Photographer Madison's daily newspapers; sports editor weekly newspaper; pub. rels. dir. midwestern ski resort, 1977; asst. nat. nordic dir. U.S. Ski Assn., 1988-95; dir. comms. U.S. Skiing, 1988—, dir. ops., 1995—, v.p. communication svcs.; mem. bd. dirs. Ski Utah. Mem. Rotary. Office: US Ski Team PO Box 100 Park City UT 84060-0100*

KELLY, THOMAS LLOYD, II, investment firm executive; b. New Haven, Nov. 24, 1958; s. Arthur Lloyd Kelly and Cynthia Alexander Williams; m. Wendy Lynn Anderson, June 10, 1989. BA in Econs. magna cum laude, Yale U., 1980, BS in Adminstrv. Sciences with honors, 1980; MBA, Harvard U., 1984. Fin. analyst Morgan Stanley & Co., Inc., N.Y.C., 1980-82; ptnr. Bass Bros. Enterprises, Ft. Worth, 1984-86, Pacific Asset Holdings, L.P., L.A., 1986-87, Rainwater, Inc., Ft. Worth, 1987-94; gen. ptnr. CHB Capital Ptnrs., Denver, 1994 ; bd. dirs. ENSCO, Dallas, Drilltec, Houston, Trussway, Ltd., Houston. Home: 511 16th St Ste 600 Denver CO 80202 Office: 51 E 16th Ave Ste 600 Denver CO 80202-5108

KELLY, TIMOTHY DONAHUE, state senator; b. Sacramento, Aug. 15, 1944; m. Lisa B. Nelson, Jan. 1, 1994; children: Ingrid Brose, Theodore Ambrose. Former legis. aide to Calif. and Nev. Legislatures; mortgage banker; mem. Alaska Ho. of Reps., 1976-78, Alaska Senate, 1978—, senate pres., 1989-90. With USMCR, Alaska Air NG. Office: State Capitol Juneau AK 99801-1182

KELLY, WILLIAM BRET, insurance executive; b. Rocky Ford, Colo., Sept. 28, 1922; s. William Andrew and Florence Gail (Yant) K.; m. Patricia Ruth Ducy, Mar. 25, 1944; children: Eric Damian, Kathryn Gail Kelly Schweitzer. BA cum laude, U. Colo., 1947. CPCU. With Steel City Agys., Inc., and predecessor, Pueblo, Colo., 1946—, pres., 1961-76, chmn. bd., 1977—; dir. United Bank Pueblo, 1963-94, chmn. bd., 1983-88; mem. Pub. Expenditure Coun., 1984—; v.p. Colo. Ins. Edn. Found., 1981, pres., 1982. Mem. Pueblo Area Coun. Govts., 1971-73, Colo. Forum 1985—, trustee Pueblo Bd. Water Works, 1966-80, pres., 1970-71; pres. Pueblo Single Fund Plan, 1960-61, Pueblo Heart Coun., 1962, Family Svc. Soc. Pueblo, 1963; mem. 10th Jud. Dist. Nominating Com., 1967-71; trustee U. So. Colo. Found., 1967—, v.p., 1991, 92, 93, 94, 95; trustee Jackson Found., 1972—, Farley Found., 1979—, Roselawn Cemetery Assn., 1982—, Kelly-Ducy Found., 1983—; hon. parade marshall Colo. State Fair, 1991. With inf. AUS, 1943-45. Decorated Silver Star, Bronze Star with oak leaf cluster, Purple Heart with oak leaf cluster; recipient Disting. Svc. award U. Colo., 1992; honored for cmty. svc. Parkview Episcopal Med. Ctr., 1992; named to Pueblo Hall of Fame, 1995. Mem. Soc. CPCU's, Pueblo C. of C. (past pres.), Pueblo Kiwanis (past pres.), Pueblo Country Club (treas. 1964-66), So. Colo. Press Club (Outstanding Community Svc. award 1991), Phi Beta Kappa. Democrat. Home: 264 S Sifford Ct Pueblo West CO 81007-2843 Office: 1414 W 4th St Pueblo CO 81004-1205

KELMAN, BRUCE JERRY, toxicologist, consultant; b. Chgo., July 1, 1947; s. LeRoy Rayfield and Louise (Rosen) K.; m. Jacqueline Anne Clark, Feb. 5, 1972; children: Aaron Wayne, Diantha Renee, Coreyanne Louise. BS, U. Ill., 1969, MS, 1971, PhD, 1975. Diplomate Am. Bd. Toxicology. Postdoctoral rsch. assoc. U. Tenn., Oak Ridge, 1974-76, asst. prof., leader prenatal toxicology group, 1976-79; mgr. devel. toxicology sect. Battelle NW, Richland, Wash., 1980-84, assoc. mgr. biology and chemistry dept., 1984-85, mgr., 1985-89, mgr. new products devel. Life Scis. Ctr., 1989-90; mgr. Internat. Toxicology Office, Battelle Meml. Inst., Richland, 1986-89; mng. scientist, mgr. toxicology dept. Failure Analysis Assocs., Inc., Menlo Park, Calif., 1990-93; mgr. toxicology and risk assessment Golder Assocs. Inc., Redmond, Wash., 1993; nat. dir. health and environ. scis., 1994—; mem. Nation Rsch. Coun. com. on possible effects of electromagnetic fields on biologic sys., 1993-96; adj. prof. N.Mex. State U., Las Cruces, 1983—. Co-editor: Interactions of Biological Systems with Static and ELF Electric and Magnetic Fields, 1987; mem. editorial bd. Trophoblast Rsch., 1983—, Biological Effects of Heavy Metals, 1990. Mem. adv. coun. Seattle Fire Dept., 1988-90; mem. Wash. Gov.'s Biotech. Targeted Sector Adv. Com., 1989-90. Fellow Am. Acad. Vet. and Comparative Toxicology; mem. Soc. Toxicology (founding pres. molecular biology splty. sect. 1988-89, pres. metals splty. sect. 1985-86, cert. of recognition 1989), Am. Soc. for Exptl. Pharmacology and Therapeutics, Soc. for Exptl. Biology and Medicine (award of merit 1980), Teratology Soc., Wash. State Biotech. Assn. (bd. dirs. 1989-90). Office: Golder Assocs Inc 4104 148th Ave NE Redmond WA 98052-5164

KELSEY, EDITH JEANINE, psychotherapist, consultant; b. Freeport, Ill., Oct. 15, 1937; d. John Melvin and Florence Lucille (Ewald) Anderson; divorced; children: Steven Craig, Kevin John. Student, Pasadena Coll., 1955-58; BA in Psychology, Calif. State U., San Jose, 1980; MA in Counseling Psychology, Santa Clara U., 1984. Lic. marriage, family and child counselor. Counselor, cons., cert. trainer Values Tech., Santa Cruz, Calif., 1981—, dir. research, 1982-84; intern in counseling Sr. Residential Services, San Jose, 1983-84; psychotherapist Process Therapy Inst., Los Gatos, Calif., 1983-86, Sexual Abuse Treatment Ctr., San Jose, 1984-87; cons. in field, Santa Clara Valley, 1982—; trainer, cons. Omega Assoc., 1987-88; teaching asst. Santa Clara U., 1987-88, supr. interns counseling high-risk students, 1997—; pvt. practice psychotherapy, cons., tng., 1987—. Contbr. articles to profl. jours. Vol. Parental Stress Hotline, Palo Alto, Calif., 1980-85. Mem. Am. Assn. Marriage and Family Therapists, Am. Soc. Aging, Calif. Assn. Marriage and Family Therapists (clin.), Palo Alto C. of C. Democrat. Presbyterian. Home: 431 Casita Ct Los Altos CA 94022-1736 Office: 153 Forest Ave Palo Alto CA 94301-1615

KELSEY, MICHAEL LOYAL, geography educator; b. Greeley, Colo., Dec. 15, 1953; s. Loyal Lee and Luwanda Marie (Steffens) K. BS, Salisbury State U., 1976; MA in Geography, U. Northern Colo., 1988; PhD in Geography, Kent State U., 1993. Founder, mgr. Salisbury (Md.) State U. Book Co-op., 1975-76; mgmt. trainee J.C. Penney Co., Inc., Salisbury, 1976-77; cost acctg. and time study mgr. W.D. Byron & Sons, Inc., Williamsport, Md., 1978-83; corp. inventory controller Stuart McGuire Co., Inc., Salem, Va., 1983-84; owner, mgr. New Century Ribbon Co., Greeley, Colo., 1984-88; instr., doctoral teaching fellow Kent (Ohio) State U., 1988-91; instr. Montgomery Coll., Rockville, Md., 1991-93; prof., chmn. geography and econs. dept. Aims Coll., Greeley, 1993—; officer, bd. dirs. Seagulf Concepts, Inc., Salisbury, Md., 1975-76; cons. Laserhead Graphics, Greeley, 1993—. Dir. Internat. Ctr. Recipient top bus. student award Rotary Internat., Salisbury, 1975, grad. fellowship U. No. Colo., Greeley, 1986-87, grant IBM Corp., Rockville, Md., 1992, award for tchg. excellence, 1996, Sam W. Walton Free Enterprise fellow and Free Enterprise Educator award, 1996. Mem. Assn. Am. Geographers, Nat. Coun. for Geographic Edn., Gamma Theta Upsilon (pres. U. No. Colo. 1987-89), Phi Kappa Phi, Omicron Delta Kappa. Home: 4040 W 12th St Apt 6 Greeley CO 80634 Office: Aims CC 5401 W 20th St Greeley CO 80634

KELSO, DAVID WILLIAM, fine arts publishing executive, artist; b. Van Nuys, Calif., Jan. 29, 1948; s. William Joseph and Elsa Estra (Scipione) K.; m. Christine Barone Mehling, June 19, 1983. Student, U. Calif., Riverside, 1969; BA, U. Calif., Berkeley, 1970. Printer El Dorado Press, Berkeley, 1972-78, Crown Point Press, Oakland, Calif., 1978-79; dir., printer Made in California Editions, Oakland, Calif., 1980—. Recipient Purchase award NW Internat. Small Format Print Ex., Seattle, 1978, Juror's award Berkeley (Calif.) Art Ctr., 1991. Mem. Rutgers Archives for Printmaking Studios, Vicente Dance Club. Office: Made in Calif Intaglio Editions 3246 Ettie St # 16 Oakland CA 94608-4016

KELSO, MARY JEAN, author; b. Eugene, Oreg., Nov. 27, 1938; d. Thomas Jasper and Eula Ethel (Warren) Williams; m. Byron Eugene Kelso Sr., June 30, 1956; children: Byron Jr., Bryon, Wendy Lynne Whiteman, Byron III. Editorial asst. Aster Pub., Springfield, Oreg., 1983-84; customer svcs. rep. El Jay divsn. Cedarapids Inc., Eugene, Oreg., 1984-95. Author, illustrator: Mystery of Virginia City, 1984, Abducted, 1986, Sierra Summer, 1992, A Virginia City Mystery, 1992; pub. Goodbye, Bodie, 1988. Address: PO Box 134 Springfield OR 97477

KELTON, ARTHUR MARVIN, JR., real estate developer; b. Bennington, Vt., Sept. 12, 1939; s. Arthur Marvin and Lorraine (Millington) K.; m. Elaine White, Nov. 1, 1986; 1 child, Ashley. BA, Dartmouth Coll., 1961. Ptnr. Kelton and Assocs., Vail, Colo., 1966-77; pres. Kelton, Garton and Assocs. Inc., Vail, 1977-84, Kelton, Garton, Kendall, Vail, 1984-93, Christopher, Denton, Kelton, Kendall, Vail, 1993—. Head agt. Dartmouth Alumni Fund, Hanover, N.H., 1985-90, class pres., 1990-96; Dartmouth Alumni Coun., 1996—; pres. Vail Valley Med. Ctr. Found., 1991—. Republican. Congregationalist. Home: 1034 Homestake Cir Vail CO 81657-5111 Office: Christopher Denton Kelton Kendall 288 Bridge St Vail CO 81657-4523

KEMERY, WILLIAM ELSWORTH, psychotherapist, hypnotherapist; b. Portland, Oreg., Apr. 16, 1929; s. William Elsworth Jr. and Charlotte Francis (Leydic) K.; m. Norma Mae Ishmael, Nov. 22, 1963 (div. May 1972); children: William M., Robert Z.; m. Marlene Agnes Kwiatkowski, Dec. 15, 1983; children: William E., William M., Robert Z., Bradley E. DD, Episcopal Sem., Balt., 1953; BA, Fresno State U., 1954; PhD (hon.), Hamilton State, 1973; Masters, Newport Internat. U., 1976, PhD, 1979. Cert. psychotherapist, hypnotherapist, sex therapist. Psychotherapist Chula Vista, Calif., 1967—; founding dir. Calif. Hypnotists Examining Coun., L.A., 1974; pres., fellow Acad. Sci. Hypnotherapy, San Diego, 1974—; bishop Holy Episcopal Ch., Chula Vista, 1978—; dir. Assn. of Spiritual Psychology, San Diego, 1968—. Contbr. articles to profl. jours. Named Hon. Mayor, Chula Vist C. of C., 1967, Knight of Grace, Order of St. John of Jerusalem, 1981. Fellow Nutrition and Preventive Medicine Assn.; mem. Internat. Assn. Clin. Hypnotherapy (life), Acad. Orthomolecular Psychiatry, Assn. Humanistic Psychology, Internat. New Thought Alliance, Am. Guild Hypnotherapists, Am. Mental Health Counselors Assn., Am. Assn. Sex Educators, Counselors and Therapists. Republican. Home and Office: 379 G St Chula Vista CA 91910

KEMMER, MICHELLE MARIE, music merchandiser, bookkeeper; b. Bemidji, Minn., Mar. 24, 1969; d. Roger Raymond and Barbara (Falk) K. AA in Fashion Design, Brooks Coll., Long Beach, Calif., 1989; student, Glendale (Calif.) Coll., 1994—. Receptionist William Morris Agy., Beverly Hills, Calif., 1989-90; bookkeeper Gladstones 4 Fish, Pacific Palisades, Calif., 1989-92; exec. asst. Borman Entertainment, L.A., 1990-92; bookkeeper L.A. To Go, 1994—; asst. to dir. merchandising Warner Bros. Records, Burbank, Calif., 1993—. Mentor, L.A. Unified Sch. Dist., 1995-96; vol. AIDS Project L.A., 1995. Mem. Alpha Gamma Sigma. Democrat.

KEMMIS, DANIEL ORRA, cultural organization administrator, author; b. Fairview, Mont., Dec. 5, 1945; s. Orra Raymond and Lilly Samantha (Shidler) K.; m. Jeanne Marie Koester, June 9, 1978; children: Abraham, Samuel; children by previous marriage: Deva, John. BA, Harvard U., 1968; JD, U. Mont., 1978. Bar: Mont. 1978. State rep. Mont. Ho. of Reps., Helena, 1975-84, minority leader, 1981-82, Speaker of House, 1983-84; ptnr. Morrison, Jonkel, Kemmis & Rossbach, Missoula, 1978-80, Jonkel & Kemmis, 1981-84; mayor City of Missoula, Mont., 1990-96; dir. ctr. rocky mountain west Univ. Mont., Missoula, 1996—; cons. No. Lights Inst., Missoula, Mont., 1985-89. Author: Community and the Politics of Place, 1990, The Good City and the Good life, 1995; contbr. articles to profl. jours. Candidate for chief justice Mont. Supreme Ct.; mem. adv. bd. Nat. Civic League, Pew Partnership for Civic Change; chmn. leadership tng. coun. Nat. League Cities, 1992-94; bd. dirs. Charles F. Kettering Found.; fellow Dallas Inst. for Humanities & Culture. Named Disting. Young Alumnus U. Mont., 1981, 100 Visionaries, Utne Reader, 1995; recipient Charles Frankel prize NEH, 1997. Democrat. Home: 521 Hartman Ct #10 Missoula MT 59802 Office: Ctr Rocky Mountain West Univ Mont Missoula MT 59812-1205

KEMP, ANTHONY MAYNARD, English educator; b. London, Apr. 14, 1956; came to U.S., 1976; s. Frederick George and Margaret (Heald) K. BA in Religious Studies and Philosophy, Northeastern Coll., 1978; MA in English Lit., Drew U., 1981; MPhil in English and Comparative Lit., Columbia U., 1984, PhD in English and Comparative Lit., 1989. Tutor, reader, rsch. asst. Columbia U., N.Y.C., 1981-83; editl. asst. Columbia U. Press, N.Y.C., 1981-82; rsch. assoc. Libr. of Am., N.Y.C., 1983-85; adj. instr. Pace U., N.Y.C., 1994; tchg. asst. Harvard U., Cambridge, Mass., 1984-88; asst. prof. U. So. Calif., L.A., 1988-94, assoc. prof. English, 1994—; lectr. in field. Author: the Estrangement of the Past: A Study in the Origins of Modern Historical Consciousness, 1991; contbr. articles, revs., poems and translations to profl. publs. Mem. MLA, Am. Comparative Lit. Assn. Office: U So Calif Taper Hall Rm 420 Los Angeles CA 90089-0354

KEMP, SHAWN T., professional basketball player; b. Elkhart, Ind., Nov. 26, 1969. Student, U. Ky., Trinity Valley C.C., 1988-89. Basketball player Seattle Supersonics, 1989—. Named to NBA All-Star team, 1993, Dream Team II, 1994, All-NBA Second Team, 1994.

KEMPF, MARTINE, voice control device manufacturing company executive; b. Strasbourg, France, Dec. 9, 1958; came to U.S., 1985; d. Jean-Pierre and Brigitte Marguerite (Klockenbring) K. Student in Astronomy, Friedrich Wilhelm U., Bonn, Fed. Republic of Germany, 1981-83. Owner, mgr. Kempf, Sunnyvale, Calif., 1985—. Inventor Comeldir Multiplex Handicapped Driving Systems (Goldenes Lenkrad Axel Springer Verlag 1981), Katalavox speech recognition control system (Oscar, World Almanac Inventions 1984, Prix Grand Siecle, Comite Couronne Francaise 1985). Recipient Medal for Service to Humanity Spinal Cord Soc., 1986; street named in honor in Dossenheim-Kochersberg, Alsace, France, 1987; named Citizen of Honor City of Dossenheim-Kochersberg, 1985, Outstanding Businessperson of Yr. City of Sunnyvale, 1990. Office: 1080 E Duane Ave Ste E Sunnyvale CA 94086-2628

KEMPTHORNE, DIRK ARTHUR, senator; b. San Diego, Oct. 29, 1951; s. James Henry and Maxine Jesse (Gustason) K.; m. Patricia Jean Merrill, Sept. 18, 1977; children: Heather Patricia, Jeffrey Dirk. BS in Polit. Sci., U. Idaho, 1975. Exec. asst. to dir. Idaho Dept. Lands, Boise, 1975-78; exec. v.p. Idaho Home Builders Assn., Boise, 1978-81; campaign mgr. Batt for Gov., Boise, 1981-82; lic. securities rep. Swanson Investments, Boise, 1983; Idaho pub. affairs mgr. FMC Corp., Boise, 1983-86; mayor Boise, 1986-93; U.S. Senator from Idaho, 1993—; 1st v.p. Assn. of Idaho Cities, 1990-93; chmn. U.S. Conf. of Mayors Standing Com. on Energy and Environment, 1991-93, mem. adv. bd., 1991-93 ; sec. Nat. Conf. of Rep. Mayors and Mcpl. Elected Officials, 1991-93; mem. Senate Armed Svcs. Com., 1993—, Senate Small Bus. Com., 1993—, Senate Environ. and Pub. Works Com., 1993—, Nat. Rep. Senatorial Com., 1993—; chmn. Senate Drinking Water, Fisheries and Wildlife Subcommittee, 1995—, mem. advisory commn. on Intergovernmental Rels., 1995-96; chmn. Armed Svcs Personnel Subcommittee, 1996—. Pres. Associated Students U. Idaho, Moscow, 1975; chmn. bd. dirs. Wesleyan Presch., Boise, 1982-85; mem. magistrate commn. 4th Jud. Dist., Boise, 1986-93; mem. task force Nat. League of Cities Election, 1988; bd. dirs. Parents and Youth Against Drug Abuse, 1987—; mem. bd. vis. USAF Acad., 1994—; chmn. Idaho Working Ptnrs. Ltd., 1993—; hon. chmn. Idaho Congressional Award, 1994—. Named Idaho Citizen of Yr. The Idaho Statesman, 1988, Legislator of the Year Nat. Assn. Counties, 1995, State Legislator of the Year Nat. Assn. of Towns and Townships, 1995; recipient U.S. Conference of Mayor's Nat. Legis. Leadership award, 1994, Disting. Svc. award Nat. Conf. State Legislatures, 1995, Disting. Congressional award Nat. League of Cities, 1995, Guardian of Freedom award Council of State Governments, 1995. Republican. Methodist. Office: US Senate 367 Dirksen Senate Office Bldg Washington DC 20510-1204

KENAGY, JOHN WARNER, surgeon; b. Lincoln, Nebr., May 28, 1945; s. Wyman Black and Sylvia (Adams) K.; m. Barbara Penterman, Feb. 1968 (div. 1975); 1 child, Jennifer; m. Jonell Day, Apr. 21, 1978; children: Susanne, Emma, John Wyman. BS, U. Nebr., 1967, MD, U. Nebr., Omaha, 1971. Diplomate Am. Bd. Surgery; splty. cert. in gen. vascular surgery. Intern, Hosps. of U. Wash., Seattle, 1971-72, resident in surgery, 1971-76; surgeon Longview Surgical Group, Longview, Wash., 1976—; clin. instr. surgery U. Wash., Seattle, 1979-82, clin. asst. prof. surgery, 1982-89, clin. assoc. prof., 1989—; dir. peripheral vascular svcs. St. Johns Hosp., Longview, 1979-88, chmn. credentials com., 1989-90; dir. trauma svcs. St. Johns Med. Ctr., 1990-92; regional v.p. bus. devel. Lower Columbia Regional Health System; regional v.p. med. divsn. Peace Health, 1995—, regional v.p., med. divsn., 1995-96, regional v.p. bus. sect., 1996—. Editor current concepts in vascular diagnosis St. Johns Vascular Lab., Longview, 1979-88; contbr. articles to profl. jours. Chmn. bd. dirs. Cowlitz Med. Service, Longview, 1985-86. Regents scholar U. Nebr., Lincoln, 1963-67. Fellow ACS, Henry Harkins Surg. Soc. (trustee 1983-84), Seattle Surg. Soc.; mem. Internat. Cardiovascular Soc., Pacific N.W. Vascular Soc. (pres.-elect 1986-87, pres. 1987-88, chmn. com. on standards 1989-91), North Pacific Surg. Soc., Med. Group Mgmt. Assn., Am. Coll. Physician Execs., Alpha Omega Alpha, Theta Nu, Phi Gamma Delta. Republican. Office: Peace Health Regional Office 329 17th Ave Longview WA 98632

KENDALL, HARRY OVID, internist; b. Eugene, Oreg., Nov. 29, 1929; s. Edward Lee and Jessie Avis (Giem) K.; m. Katherine Alexander, June 20, 1951 (div. 1957); 1 child, Jessica Gail Gress; m. Barbara Ann Matt, Jan. 21, 1961 (div. June 1, 1977); children: David Lee, Brian Padraic; m. Wanda Eve Helmer, July 2, 1993. AB, U. Redlands, 1952; MD, Yale U., 1955. Diplomate Am. Bd. Internal Medicine, Am. Bd. Pulmonary Disease. Intern in internal medicine UCLA Med. Ctr., 1955-57; resident in internal medicine West L.A. VA Med. Ctr., 1957-59; staff physician U.S. Naval Regional Med. Ctr., San Diego, 1959-62, Tulare-Kings Counties Hosp., Springville, Calif., 1962-63; staff physician, ptnr. So. Calif. Permanente Med. Group, Fontana, Calif., 1963-67, Kaiser Hosp. and So. Calif. Permanente Med. Group, San Diego, 1967—; dir. respiratory care Kaiser Hosp., San Diego, 1967—; attending physician San Bernardino County Hosp., 1964-67; asst. clin. prof. medicine U. Calif. San Diego Med. Ctr., 1976—; com. mem. numerous hosps. and med. clinics. Mem. NAACP, Amnesty Internat., ACLU. Lt. USNR, 1954-56, lt. comdr. 1961, comdr. 1973. Mem. Am. Thoracic Soc., cAlif. Thoracic Soc., San Diego Pulmonary Soc.

KENDALL, ROBERT DANIEL, priest, theology educator; b. Miami, Ariz., Jan. 11, 1939; s. Robert Daniel and Loretto Agnes (Jakle) K. BA, Gonzaga U., 1963, MA, 1964; ThM, Santa Clara U., 1971; SSL, Pontifical Bibl. Inst., Rome, 1973; STD, Gregorian U., Rome, 1975. Tchr. Brophy Coll. Prep., Phoenix, 1964-67; asst. prof. Gonzaga U., Spokane, Wash., 1975-79; from asst. prof. to assoc. prof. U. San Francisco, 1979-90, prof., 1990—. Author: Focus on Jesus, 1996, The Resurrection, 1997, The Bible for Theology, 1997. Mem. Soc. Jesus, Cath. Bibl. Assn. Home: 650 Parker Ave San Francisco CA 94118

KENDLER, HOWARD H(ARVARD), psychologist, educator; b. N.Y.C., June 9, 1919; s. Harry H. and Sylvia (Rosenberg) K.; m. Tracy Seedman, Sept. 20, 1941; children—Joel Harlan, Kenneth Seedman. A.B., Bklyn. Coll., 1940; M.A., U. Iowa, 1941, Ph.D., 1943. Instr. U. Iowa, 1943; research psychologist OSRD, 1944; asst. prof. U. Colo., 1946-48; assoc. prof. NYU, 1948-51, prof., 1951-63; chmn. dept. Univ. Coll., 1951-61; prof. U. Calif., Santa Barbara, 1963-89, prof. emeritus, 1989—, chmn. dept. psychology, 1965-66; project dir. Office Naval Rsch., 1950-68; prin. investigator NSF, 1953-65, USAAF, 1951-53; mem. adv. panel psychobiology NSF, 1960-62; tng. com. Nat. Inst. Child Health and Human Devel., 1963-66; cons. Dept. Def., Smithsonian Instn., 1959-60, Human Resources Rsch. Office, George Washington U., 1960; vis. prof. U. Calif., Berkeley, 1960-61, Hebrew U., Jerusalem, 1974-75, Tel Aviv U., 1990; chief clin. psychologist Walter Reed Gen. Hosp., 1945-46. Author: Basic Psychology, 1963, 2d edit., 1968, 3d edit., 1974, Basic Psychology: Brief Version, 1977, Psychology: A Science in Conflict, 1981, Historical Foundations of Modern Psychology, 1987; co-author: Basic Psychology: Brief Edition, 1970; co-editor: Essays in Neobehaviorism: A Memorial Volume to Kenneth W. Spence; assoc. editor Jour. Exptl. Psychology, 1963-65; contbr. to profl. jours., books. Served as 1st lt. AUS. Fellow Center for Advanced Studies in Behavioral Scis., Stanford, Calif., 1969-70; NSF grantee, 1954-76. Mem. Am. Psychol. Assn. (pres. div. exptl. psychology 1964-65, pres. div. gen. psychology 1967-68), Western Psychol. Assn. (pres. 1970-71), Soc. Exptl. Psychologists (exec. com. 1971-73), Psychonomic Soc. (governing bd. 1963-69, chmn. 1968-69), Sigma Xi. Home and Office: 4596 Camino Molinero Santa Barbara CA 93110-1040

KENISON, LYNN T., chemist; b. Provo, Utah, Feb. 20, 1943; s. John Silves and Grace (Thacker) K.; m. Daralyn Wold, June 10, 1969; children: Marlene, Mark, Evan, Guy, Amy, Suzanne. BS in Chemistry, Brigham Young U., 1968, MS in Chemistry, 1971. Tchr. Weber County Sch. Dist., Ogden, Utah, 1968-69; bench chemist (drugs) Salt Lake City/County Health Dept., 1971-74; chemist U.S. Dept. Labor, OSHA Salt Lake Tech. Ctr., 1974—, bench chemist, 1974-77, supr., br. chief, 1977-84, sr. chemist,

1984—; tech. writer OSHA. Editor: Review Methods and Analytical Papers Before Publication, 1984—; tech. writer, 1984—. Councilman West Bountiful City, Utah, 1980-83, 85-89; scouting coord. Boy Scouts Am., cubmaster local pack, 1990-94; full-time missionary LDS Ch., Ark., Mo., Ill., 1962-64; vol. spkr. in local pub. schs., 1988—. Mem. Am. Indsl. Hygiene Assn., Fed. Exec. Assn. (Disting. Svc. award, Jr. Award for Outstanding Fed. and Cmty. Svc. 1980), Toastmasters Internat. (treas. Salt Lake City chpt. 1987-91). Home: 1745 N 600 W West Bountiful UT 84087-1150 Office: US Dept of Labor OSHA Salt Lake Tech Ctr 1781 S 300 W Salt Lake City UT 84115-1802

KENNARD, JOYCE L., judge. Former judge L.A. Mcpl. Ct., Superior Ct., Ct. Appeal, Calif.; assoc. justice Calif. Supreme Ct., San Francisco, 1989—. Office: Calif Supreme Ct South Tower 303 2nd St San Francisco CA 94107-1366

KENNEDY, CHARLENE FARRINGTON, librarian; b. Cin., Sept. 17, 1947; d. Charles Winifred and Margaret Irene (Hurd) Farrington; m. Timothy Louis Kennedy, May 12, 1977 (div. 1981). BS in Sociology, U. Wis., 1969, MLS, 1971. Libr. intern Milw. Cen. Libr., 1969-71; reference libr. Atkinson Br. Libr., Milw., 1972-73; reference libr. sci. and bus. dept. Milw. Cen. Libr., 1973-78; reference libr., coord. on-line svcs. City of Carlsbad, Calif., 1978-85, head reference svcs., 1985-95, head of adult svcs., 1995—. Contbr. articles to profl. jours. Mem. Soroptimist Internat., Carlsbad, 1987. Mem. Palomar Libr. Assn., San Diego On-Line Users Group, North San Diego County Genealogical Soc., Bus. and Profl. Women (pres. Carlsbad chpt. 1983). Office: Carlsbad City Libr 1250 Carlsbad Village Dr Carlsbad CA 92008-1949

KENNEDY, CHARLES JOHN, marketing company executive; b. Phoenix, Nov. 18, 1928; s. Charles Ambrose and Katherine Anne K.; m. Millicent B. Russell; 6 children. BS in English, Loyola U., 1953. Tech. writer Hughes Aircraft, Culver City, Calif., 1951-53; sales advt. L.A. Times, 1953-55; sales dist. mgr. Chrysler Corp., L.A., 1955-62; sales, mgr., pres. Motor Parts Depot, L.A., 1962-89; pres. Kennedy Mktg., Whittier, Calif., 1991-96; pres. Calif. Automotive Wholesalers, Sacramento, 1987, So. Calif. Jobbers, L.A., 1976, 84, Pacific Automotive Show, Anaheim, Calif., 1986. Author (sales column) Booster Mag., 1991-94. With USNR. Republican. Roman Catholic. Home and Office: Kennedy Mktg 11122 Valley View Ave Whittier CA 90604-1726

KENNEDY, CHRISTOPHER ROBBINS, credit union executive; b. Salt Lake City, June 24, 1959; s. Edwin John and Suzanne (Robbins) K.; m. Linda Joyce Horne, July 13, 1982; children: Christopher Robbins II, Amber Chanel, Alexandra. BS, U. Utah, 1985; MBA, Nat. U., San Diego, 1987; PhD, Calif. Coast U., 1996. Asst. v.p. Beneficial Fin., San Diego, 1987-88, Great Western Bank, Salt Lake City, 1988-90; pres., chief exec. officer SLP Credit Union, Salt Lake City, 1990-94; exec. v.p. Hawthorne (Nev.) Credit Union, 1995—. Del. Rep. Cen. Com., Salt Lake City, 1992. Recipient Life Saving award Am. Trauma Soc., 1979. Mem. Sons Utah Pioneers (life), Kiwanis, Golden Key. Mormon. Address: PO Box 2355 Hawthorne NV 89415-2355 Office: Hawthorne Credit Union 895 Sierra Way Box 2288 Hawthorne NV 89415-2288

KENNEDY, DEBRA JOYCE, marketing professional; b. Covina, Calif., July 9, 1955; d. John Nathan and Drea Hannah (Lancaster) Ward; m. John William Kennedy, Sept. 3, 1977 (div.); children: Drea, Noelle. BS in Communications, Calif. State Poly. U., 1977. Pub. rels. coord. Whittier (Calif.) Hosp., 1978-79, pub. relations mgr., 1980; pub. rels. dir. San Clemente (Calif.) Hosp., 1979-80; dir. pub. rels. Garfield Med. Ctr., Monterey Park, Calif., 1980-82; dir. mktg. and community rels. Charter Oak Hosp., Covina, 1983-85; mktg. dir. CPC Horizon Hosp., Pomona, 1985-89; dir. mktg. Sierra Royale Hosp., Azusa, 1989-90; mktg. rep. PacifiCare, Cypress, 1990-92; regional medicare mgr. Health Net, Woodland Hills, Calif., 1992-95; dist. sales mgr. Kaiser Permante Health Plan, Pasadena, Calif., 1995—. Mem. Am. Soc. Hosp. Pub. Rels., Healthcare Mktg. Assn., Healthcare Pub. Rels. and Mktg. Assn., Covina and Covina West C. of C., West Covina Jaycees. Republican. Methodist. Club: Soroptimist. Contbr. articles to profl. jours.

KENNEDY, DENNIS L., lawyer; b. Tacoma, Oct. 28, 1950. BA, U. Wash., 1972, JD, 1975. Bar: Nev. 1975. With Lionel Sawyer & Collins, Las Vegas, Nev. Bd. editors Washington Law Review, 1974-75. Fellow Am. Coll. Trial Lawyers; mem. ABA (administrv. law sect., antitrust law sect., forum com. health law 1980—), Am. Acad. Hosp. Attys., Am. Soc. Law and Medicine, Internat. Assn. Gaming Attys., Nat. Health Lawyers Assn., State Bar Nev. (mem. disciplinary comm. 1988—),. Office: Lionel Sawyer & Collins 1700 Bank Am Plz 300 S 4th St Las Vegas NV 89101-6014

KENNEDY, DONALD, environmental science educator, former academic administrator; b. N.Y.C., Aug. 18, 1931; s. William Dorsey and Barbara (Bean) K.; children: Laura Page, Julia Hale; m. Robin Beth Wiseman, Nov. 27, 1987; stepchildren: Cameron Rachel, Jamie Christopher. AB, Harvard U., 1952, AM, 1954, PhD, 1956; DSc (hon.), Columbia U., Williams Coll., U. Mich., U. Ariz., U. Rochester, Reed Coll., Whitman Coll. Mem. faculty Stanford (Calif.) U., 1960-77, prof. biol. scis., 1965-77, chmn. dept., 1965-72, sr. cons. sci. and tech. policy Exec. Office of Pres., 1976, commr. FDA, 1977-79, provost, 1979-80, pres., 1980-92; prof. emeritus, Bing prof. environ. sci. Stanford U., 1992—; bd. overseers Harvard U., 1970-76; bd. dirs. Health Effects Inst., Nat. Commn. on Pub. Svc., Carnegie Commn. on Sci., Tech. and Govt. Mem. editorial bd. Jour. Comparative Physiology, 1965-76, Jour. Neurophysiology, 1969-75, Science, 1973-77; contbr. articles to profl. jours. Bd. dirs. Carnegie Endowment for Internat. Peace. Fellow AAAS, Am. Acad. Arts and Scis.; mem. NAS, Am. Philos. Soc. Office: Stanford U Inst for Internat Studies Encina Hall 201 Stanford CA 94305

KENNEDY, GWENDOLYN DEBRA, film animator, parapsychologist, artist, play and film writer; b. Daly City, Calif., Nov. 18, 1960; d. Adolphus Brooks and Ella (Robinson) K.; children: Gwendolyn Fincher, Edward James, Jr. Diploma, U. San Francisco, 1987, M in Film and Theater, 1992. Dir. film animation Walt Disney, Buena Vista, Calif., 1994—; pres., owner Black Panther Party Press, 1993—; owner mail order co. La Chateau D'Gwendolyn Kennedy Co., 1991—. Author: Dorothy Dandrige Collection, 1993, Kane Kut Murder Trial, 1993, Poetic Justice, 1994, No Struggle No Progress, 1995, Nyami the Sky God, 1996; (authored two screen plays) Nat Turner, The Pied Piper, 1997; patentee musical boudoir cache. Min. info. Black Panther Party, San Francisco, 1993, leader, comdr., 1993—. Recipient Journalist of Yr. award City News Svc., Mo., 1995. Lutheran. Home: 285 Bellevue Ave Daly City CA 94014-1305 Office: PO Box 135 Daly City CA 94016-0135

KENNEDY, JACK LELAND, lawyer; b. Portland, Oreg., Jan. 30, 1924; s. Ernest E. and Lera M. (Talley) K.; m. Clara C. Hagans, June 5, 1948; children: James M., John C. Student, U.S. Maritime Commn. Acad., Southwestern U., L.A.; JD, Lewis and Clark Coll., 1951. Bar: Oreg. 1951. Pvt. practice Portland; ptnr. Kennedy & King, Portland, 1971-77, Kennedy, King & McClurg, Portland, 1977-82, Kennedy, King & Zimmer, Portland, 1982—; trustee Northwestern Coll. Law, Portland; dir. Profl. Liability Fund, 1979-82. Contbr. articles to legal jours. Mem. bd. visitors Lewis and Clark Coll. With USNR, 1942-46. Recipient Disting. Grad. award Lewis and Clark Coll., 1983. Fellow Am. Coll. Trial Lawyers, Am. Bar Found. (life), Oreg. Bar Found. (charter); mem. ABA (ho. of dels. 1984-88), Oreg. State Bar (bd. govs. 1976-79, pres. 1978-79), Multnomah Bar Assn., City Club, Columbia River Yacht Club. Republican. Office: Kennedy King & Zimmer 1211 SW 5th Ave Ste 2600 Portland OR 97204-3726

KENNEDY, JAMES WILLIAM, JR. (SARGE KENNEDY), special education administrator, consultant; b. Santa Rosa, Calif., Oct. 6, 1940; s. James William and Kay Jean (Eaton) K.; m. Lorene Adele Dunaway, May 12, 1962 (div. Sept. 1971); children: Sean, Erin, Mark; m. Carolyn Judith Nighsonger, Mar. 30, 1972 (div. Dec. 1979); m. Patricia Carter Critchlow, Nov. 5, 1988; 1 stepchild, Joy. BA, San Francisco State U., 1964, MA, 1970. Tchr., prin., coord. spl. edn., dir. spl. edn. local plan area Napa County (Calif.) Schs., 1968-83; spl. edn. compliance cons. overseas dependent schs. Mediterranean region Dept. Def., 1983-84; adminstr. spl. edn. local plan area and dir. spl. programs Tehama County Dept. Edn., Red Bluff, Calif., 1985—. Editor Calif. Fed. Coun. Exceptional Children Jour. 1971-77, 81-83. Mem. Wilson Riles Spl. Edn. Task Force, Calif., 1981-82, Spl. Edn. Fiscal Task Force, Calif., 1987-89. Mem. Coun. for Adminstrs. Spl. Edn., SELPA Adminstrs. Assn. Calif., Coun. for Exceptional Children (sgt.-at-arms 1980-95), Calif. Fedn. Coun. for Exceptional Children (treas. 1990—), Profl. Football rschrs. Assn., San Francisco State Alumni Assn., Phi Delta Kappa. Democrat. Office: Tehama County Dept Edn PO Box 689 Red Bluff CA 96080-0689

KENNEDY, JOHN EDWARD, art dealer, appraiser, curator; b. Glens Falls, N.Y., Apr. 21, 1930; s. John Edward and Veronica Irene (Young) K.; m. Katherine Joan Donovan, July 14, 1956 (div. June 1973); m. Blake Hale Whitney, Dec. 24, 1995. AB with hons., Boston Coll., 1951; JD, Harvard U., 1956; grad., U.S. Army Command and Gen. Staff Coll., 1964. Bar: Mass. 1956. Asst. counsel New England Mut. Life Ins., Boston, 1956-64; counsel Pa. Life Ins. Co., Beverly Hills, Calif., 1964-68; investment banker Smith Barney and Co., L.A. and N.Y.C., 1968-70; real estate developer Calif. and Hawaii, 1970-80; v.p. Galerie De Tours, Carmel, Calif., 1980-88; curator Gallery Americana, Carmel, 1988-92; patron Monterey Peninsula Mus. of Art., 1988—, Carmel Art Assn., 1985—. Trustee Harrison Meml. Libr., Carmel, 1986-88; commr. Planning commn., Carmel, 1988-94, chmn., 1992-94. With U.S. Army, 1952-53, Korea, Lt. Col., U.S. Army Res., 1969. Decorated Bronze Star for Valor, Purple Heart with cluster; recipient Disting. Mil. Svc. medal Republic of Korea, 1953. Mem. Am. Soc. of Appraisers (cert.), New England Appraisers Assn. (cert.), Am. Planning Assn., Marines Meml. Club. Republican. Episcopalian. Home: PO Box 1844 Carmel CA 93921-1844 Office: New Masters Gallery Dolores 7th Carmel CA 93921

KENNEDY, JOHN HARVEY, chemistry educator; b. Oak Park, Ill., Apr. 24, 1933; s. John Harvey and Margaret Helen (Drenthe) K.; m. Joan Corinne Hipsky, June 9, 1956 (div. Mar. 1969); children: Bruce Laurence, Bryan Donald, Brent Peter, Jill Amy.; m. Victoria Jane Matthew, July 2, 1970; 1 child, Karen Anne. BS, UCLA, 1954; AM, Harvard U., 1956, PhD, 1957. Sr. research chemist E.I. du Pont de Nemours, Wilmington, Del., 1957-61; asst. prof. chemistry U. Calif., Santa Barbara, 1961-63, 67-69, assoc. prof., 1969-76, prof., 1976-93, prof. emeritus, 1993—, chmn. dept., 1982-85; assoc. prof. Boston Coll., Chestnut Hill, 1963-64; head inorganic chemistry Gen. Motors, Santa Barbara, 1964-67; cons. Eveready Battery Co., Cleve., 1983—; vis. prof. U. N.C., Chapel Hill, 1980-81, Japan Soc. Promotion of Sci., Nagoya, 1974-75, Leningrad State U., 1989, China Acad. Scis., 1990. Author: Analytical Chemistry, Principles, 1990, Analytical Chemistry, Practice, 1990; contbr. articles to profl. jours.; patentee in field. Mus. dir. Christ the King Episcopal Ch., Santa Barbara, 1982—. Mem. Am. Chem. Soc., Electrochem. Soc. Democrat. Home: 5357 Agana Dr Santa Barbara CA 93111-1601 Office: U Calif Dept Chemistry Santa Barbara CA 93106

KENNEDY, ORIN, film company executive; b. N.Y.C., May 24, 1939; s. Solomon Fuchs and Gertrude Krex. BFA, N.Y. Sch. Interior Design, 1963. Prodn. assoc. Fries Entertainment, Los Angeles, 1976-84; exec. location mgr. Metro-Goldwyn-Mayer subs. United Artists Entertainment, Culver City, Calif., 1984-85; exec. location mgr. The Twilight Zone TV series CBS Entertainment, Los Angeles, 1985-86; exec. location mgr. LA Law TV series 20th Century Fox Film Corp., Los Angeles, 1986-94, exec. location mgr. Picket Fences TV series, 1991-96; Chicago Hope TV series, 1994—.

KENNEDY, RICHARD JEROME, writer; b. Jefferson City, Mo., Dec. 23, 1932; s. Donald and Mary Louise (O'Keefe) K.; m. Lillian Elsie Nance, Aug. 3, 1960; children: Joseph Troy, Matthew Cook. BS, Portland State U., 1958. Author: (novel) Amy's Eye, 1985 (Internat. Rattenfanger Lit. prize, Fed. Republic Germany 1988), also 18 children's books including Richard Kennedy: Collected Stories, 1988 and 3 musicals; inclusion of stories in: The Oxford Book of Modern Fairy Tales, 1993, The Oxford Book of Children's Stories, 1993. With USAF, 1951-54. Home and Office: 415 W Olive St Newport OR 97365-3716

KENNEDY, RICK ALAN, history educator; b. Olathe, Kans., Mar. 22, 1958; s. George Robert and Donna Jean (Barber) K.; m. Susan Elizabeth Barbaria, Dec. 15, 1979; children: Matthew David, Steven Crawford, Elizabeth Joy. BA in History, U. Calif., Santa Barbara, 1980, MA in History, 1983, PhD in History, 1987. Asst. prof. history Ind. U. S.E., New Albany, 1987-93, assoc. prof. history, 1993-95; assoc. prof. history Point Loma Nazarene Coll., San Diego, 1995—. Contbr. articles to profl. jours. Presbyterian. Office: Point Loma Nazarene Coll 618 Savoy St San Diego CA 92106

KENNEDY, SANDRA DENISE, state representative; b. Oklahoma City, Dec. 25, 1957; d. Leland and Doll B. (Alford) K.; 1 child, Mahogany Renee Cherry. Student, Phoenix Coll., 1975-76, So. Mountain Community Coll. and Ariz. State U., 1976-86. Acct. Kennedy and Assocs., Phoenix, 1983—; state rep. Ariz. Ho. of Reps., Phoenix, 1986—; del. Fgn. Relations Conf. Am. Council Young Polit. Leaders, Washington, 1987, alternate del. Commn. Internat. Trade State Fed. Assembly, Washington, 1987. Bd. dirs. Ariz. Cactus Pine Girl Scouts, Phoenix, 1987—. Mem. Nat. Conf. State Legislators, Nat. Black Caucus State Legislators, Order Women Legislators, Nat. Assn. Exec. Women Inc. Baptist. Home: 2333 E Wier Ave Phoenix AZ 85040-2657 Office: Ariz State Sen State Cap Senate Wing 1700 W Washington Phoenix AZ 85007*

KENNEDY-MINOTT, RODNEY, international relations educator, former ambassador; b. Portland, Oreg.; s. Joseph Albert and Gainor (Baird) Minott; children: Katharine Pardow, Rodney Glisan, Polly Berry. AB, Stanford U., 1953, MA, 1956, PhD, 1960. Instr. history Stanford U., 1960-61, asst. prof., asst. dir. history of western civilization program, 1961-62, asst. dir. summer session, 1962-63, dir. summer session, 1963-65; assoc. prof. Portland State U., 1965-66; assoc. prof., assoc. dean instrn. Calif. State U., Hayward, 1966-67, prof., 1967-77, head div. humanities, 1967-69; ambassador to Sweden and chmn. Swedish Fulbright Com., 1977-80; adj. prof. Monterey Inst. Internat. Studies, Calif., 1981; exec. v.p. Direction Internat., Washington, 1982-83; sr. research fellow Hoover Instn., 1981-82, 85—; chmn. Alpha Internat., Washington, 1983-85; sr. fellow Ctr. Internat. Rels., UCLA, 1986-90; prof. nat. security affairs tng., U.S. Naval Postgrad. Sch., Monterey, Calif., 1990—, acad. assoc. for area studies, 1995—, asst. provist for external affairs, 1995—. Author: Peerless Patriots: The Organized Veterans and the Spirit of Americanism, 1962, The Fortress That Never Was: The Myth of Hitler's Bavarian Stronghold, 1964, The Sinking of the Lollipop: Shirley Temple v. Pete McCloskey, 1968, Regional Force Application: The Maritime Strategy and Its Affect on Nordic Stability, 1988, Tension in the North: Sweden and Nordic Security, 1989, Lonely Path to Follow: Non-aligned Sweden, United States/NATO, and the U.S.S.R., 1990. Mem. adv. bd. Ctr. for the Pacific Rim U. San Francisco, 1988-93. With U.S. Army, 1946-48, USAR, 1948-54. Mem. Am. Hist. Assn., Orgn. Am. Historians, World Affairs Coun. No. Calif., Am. Fgn. Svc. Assn. (assoc.), Marines Meml. Assn. (San Francisco), Stanford U. Faculty Club. Office: Dept Nat Security Affairs US Naval Postgrad Sch Monterey CA 93943

KENNEL, JAMES OTTO, marketing professional; b. Bloomington, Ill., Jan. 23, 1952; s. Shirley C. and Alice Irene (Culp) K.; m. Pamela Kay Murray, Dec. 23, 1987; children: Forrest, Emily. BS in Acctg., U. Ill., 1975. Lic. Colo. real estate broker. Planning Franklin Life Ins., Springfield, Ill., 1975-76; field underwriter Horace Mann Ins., Springfield, 1976-77; asst. group dir. Horace Mann Ins., Atlanta, 1977-78; mktg. dir. Horace Mann Ins., Denver, 1978-80; pres. Kennel & Assocs., Denver, 1981—, Atlas Properties, Inc., Denver, 1988—, Direct Mktg. Excellence, Inc., Denver, 1991—. Home: 7503 E Sunset Trail Parker CO 80134 Office: Direct Mktg Excellence Inc Ste 400 6795 E Tennessee Ave Denver CO 80224-1649

KENNELLY, SISTER KAREN MARGARET, college administrator; b. Graceville, Minn., Aug. 4, 1933; d. Walter John Kennelly and Clara Stella Eastman. BA, Coll. St. Catherine, St. Paul, 1956; MA, Cath. U. Am., 1958; PhD, U. Calif., Berkeley, 1962. Joined Sisters of St. Joseph of Carondelet, Roman Cath. Ch., 1954. Prof. history Coll. St. Catherine, 1962-71, acad. dean, 1971-79; exec. dir. Nat. Fedn. Carondelet Colls., U.S., 1979-82; province dir. Sisters of St. Joseph of Carondelet, St. Paul, 1982-88; pres. Mt. St. Mary's Coll., L.A., 1989—; cons. N. Cen. Accreditation Assn., Chgo., 1974-84, Ohio Bd. Regents, Columbus, 1983-89; trustee colls., hosps., Minn., Wis., Calif., 1972—; chmn. Sisters St. Joseph Coll. Consortium, 1989-93. Editor, co author: American Catholic Women, 1989; author: (with others) Women of Minnesota, 1977. Bd. dirs. Am. Coun. on Edn., 1997—, Nat. Assn. Ind. Colls. and Univs., 1997—, Assn. Cath. Colls. and Univs., 1996—. Fulbright fellow, 1964, Am. Coun. Learned Socs. fellow, 1964-65. Mem. Am. Hist. Soc., Am. Cath. Hist. Soc., Medieval Acad., Am. Assn. Rsch. Historians on Medieval Spain, Nat. Assn. of Ind. Colls. and Univs. (bd. dirs. 1997—), Am. Coun. on Edn. (bd. dirs. 1997—), Assn. of Cath. Colls. and Univs. (exec. bd. 1996—). Roman Catholic. Home and Office: Mt St Marys Coll 12001 Chalon Rd Los Angeles CA 90049-1526

KENNER, RONALD W., writer, editor; b. Chgo., Apr. 21, 1935; s. Jack Morris and Sandra Cohan Kenner; m. Mary Abbott, Feb. 29, 1964. BA in English Lit., Calif. State U., L.A., 1975, postgrad., 1975-76. World news editor, deskman, staff writer Daily Pilot, Costa Mesa, Calif., 1960-61; editor Humboldt Star, Winnemucca, Nev., 1961-62; corr. No. Nev. United Press, 1961-62; deskman, staff writer The Register, Santa Ana, Calif., 1962-64; corr. Orange County (Calif.) Assoc. Press, 1962-64; writing cons. book editing Mexico City, 1964-65; reporter, staff writer L.A. Times, Metro, L.A., 1965-66; editor ctrl. desk Call-Enterprise Newspapers, Bellflower, Calif., 1966-67; mng. editor Norwalk Call, 1966-67; co-editor press & pub. rels. bur. News Features, Internat. & Kenner Press Features, Copenhagen, 1967-69; metro reporter, staff writer L.A. Times, 1969-70; v.p. pub. rels., press dir. Compu-Transit Corp., L.A., 1970-73; supr. publs. Santa Fe Internat. Corp., Orange, Calif., 1977-78; author, book editor, freelance, publs. rels. publicity dir. Kenner Press Features, L.A., 1978-89, News Features Internat., Copenhagen, 1978-89; author, book editor, editorial cons. L.A., 1990-95; guest lectr. writing classes UCLA, Calif. State U., Northridge, Northbridge H.S. Author: (biography) Max the Butcher, 1982; co-author: The Garbage People, 1971, 1995; editor numerous biographies; editl. cons.: Those Who Dared and Rescued, 1995, Anne Frank in Historical Perspective: A Teaching Guide for Secondary Schools, 1995; contbr. articles to profl. jours. Recipient John Swett award Calif. State Tchrs. Assn., 1967, Spl. Recognition award Nat. Assn. Adult Educators; co-recipient Pulitzer prize with 35-man L.A. Times metro staff for Watts Riot coverage, 1965. Mem. Pen Ctr. USA West. Home: 1900 Vine St Los Angeles CA 90068-3972

KENNERKNECHT, RICHARD EUGENE, marketing executive; b. Glendale, Calif., Apr. 29, 1961; s. Richard and Sharon Mavis (Zane) K. V.p. Def. Tech. Corp. Am., 1993-96; pres. Rocky Mountain divsn. Nat. Telecom. Group, Casper, Wyo., 1996—; pres. FDC Inc., Lost Hills, Calif., 1989-91; profl. sporting clays shooter, exhbn. shooter. Mem. U.S. Sporting Assn. (mem. team U.S.A. 1988, 89, all-Am. team 1988, 89, 90, winner gold medal U.S.-French Profl. Invitational 1990, 91), U.S. Sporting Clays Assn. (mem. rules and ethics com., capt. team Perazzi), Verdugo Hills Ducks Unltd. (founding mem.), Nat. Sporting Clays Assn. (mem. nat. adv. coun. 1991-92), Olin Winchester (adv. coun. 1991-93), Calif. Waterfowl Assn. (shooting sports dir. 1992-93), Western Outdoor News (outdoor columnist 1992-93). Republican. Episcoplian. Home: PO Box 1180 Mills WY 82644 Office: Nat Telecom Group PO Box 1180 Mills WY 82644

KENNETT, E. ALAN, agricultural products executive; b. 1944. Pres., gen. mgr. Gay & Robinson Inc., Kaumakani, Hawaii. With U.S. Coast Guard, 1965-70. Office: Gay & Robinson Inc 1 Kaumakani Ave Kaumakani HI 96747

KENNETTE, JENNIE LAURA FAKES, medical and surgical nurse; b. Hanston, Kans., Jan. 16, 1935; d. Jack Delmont and Bertha Mabel (Law) Fakes; m. Leslie Cleland Koontz, Dec. 4 1958 (dec.); children: Kim, Lynn, Gay, Jan, Jay, Lee; m. Robert Ray Hamill, Oct. 21, 1979 (div.); m. Russell T. Kennette Jr., Nov. 17, 1990. ADN, Barton County Community Coll., 1971; BSN, U. Wyo., 1988. RN; cert. med.-surg. nurse, gerontol. nurse. Staff nurse clin. level III Laramie County Hosp., Cheyenne, Wyo.; asst. head nurse DePaul Hosp., Cheyenne, 1981-87; charge nurse St. Catherine's Hosp., Garden City, Kans., 1979-81; DON Spearville (Kans.) Dist. Hosp., 1973-78; charge nurse Meml. Hosp. Laramie County, Cheyenne, 1987-91, Laramie County Hosp., Cheyenne, Wyo., 1987-91; supr. Wyo. Retirement Ctr., 1991-96; contract nurse Q.S. Nursing Corp., Colorado Springs, Colo., 1996—; GIMC Beds Clinic, Gallup, N.Mex., 1996—. Mem. ANA, Barton County C.C. Alumni Assn. Home: PO Box 841 Basin WY 82410-0841 Office: 862 N 6th St Basin WY 82410

KENNEY, WILLIAM FITZGERALD, lawyer; b. San Francisco, Nov. 4, 1935; s. Lionel Fitzgerald and Ethel Constance (Brennan) K.; m. Susan Elizabeth Langfitt, May 5, 1962; children: Anne, Carol, James. BA, U. Calif.-Berkeley, 1957, JD, 1960. Bar: Calif. 1961. Assoc. Miller, Osborne Miller & Bartlett, San Mateo, Calif., 1962-64; ptnr. Tormey, Kenney & Cotchett, San Mateo, 1965-67; pres. William F. Kenney, Inc., San Mateo, 1968—; gen. ptnr. All Am. Self Storage, 1985—, Second St. Self Storage, 1990-96, Cochrane Road Self Storage, 1996—. Trustee San Mateo City Sch. Dist., 1971-79, pres., 1972-74; pres. March of Dimes, 1972-73; bd. dirs. Boys Club of San Mateo, 1972-90, Samaritan House, 1989—, Lesley Found., 1992—. With U.S. Army, 1960-62. Mem. State Bar of Calif. (taxation com. 1973-76), San Mateo County Bar Assn. (bd. dir. 1973-75), Calif. Assn. Realtors (legal affairs com. 1978—), San Mateo C. of C. (bd. dirs. 1987-93), Self Storage Assn. (we. region, pres. 1989-90, nat. bd. dirs. 1990—, nat. v.p. 1994-95, pres. 1996-97), Rotary (pres. 1978-79, Elks (exalted ruler 1974-75). Republican. Roman Catholic. Home: 221 Clark Dr San Mateo CA 94402-1004 Office: William F Kenney Inc 120 N El Camino Real San Mateo CA 94401-2705

KENNICOTT, JAMES W., lawyer; b. Latrobe, Pa., Feb. 14, 1945; s. W.L. and Alice (Hayes) K.; m. Margot Barnes, Aug. 19, 1975 (div. 1977); m. Lynne Dratler Finney, July 1, 1984 (div. 1989). AB, Syracuse (N.Y.) U., 1967; JD, U. Wyo., 1979. Bar: Utah 1979. Prin. Ski Cons., Park City, Utah, 1969—; pvt. practice Park City, 1979-87, 89—; ptnr. Kennicott & Finney, Park City, 1987-89; pvt. practice Park City, 1989—; cons. Destination Sports Specialists, Park City, 1984—; judge pro tem Utah 3d Dist. Ct., Park City, 1988—; arbitrator Am. Arbitration Assn., 1989—. Chmn. Park City Libr. Bd. 1987; bd. dirs. Park City Libr., 1985-91, Park City Handicapped Sports, 1988-94, The Counseling Inst., 1993—, chmn., 1994-95, treas. 1995-96, mem. program com. Gov.'s Commn. on Librs. and Info. Svcs., 1990-91. Mem. Utah Bar Assn., Am. Arbitration Assn. Home and Office: PO Box 2339 Park City UT 84060-2339

KENNY, RAY, geology and geochemistry educator, researcher; b. Chgo., June 13, 1955; m. Kerrie E. Neet, Sept. 19, 1992. BS, Northeastern Ill. U., Chgo., 1983; MS, Ariz. State U., 1986, PhD, 1991. Registered geologist, Mo. Rsch. assoc. U. Colo., Boulder, 1991-93; prof. N.Mex. Highlands U., Las Vegas, 1993—. Contbr. articles to profl. jours. Mem. AAUP, Nat. Assn. Geology Tchrs., Geol. Soc. Am., Am. Geophys. Union. Office: NMex Highlands U Dept Geology National Ave Las Vegas NV 87701

KENT, BETTY DICKINSON, horsemanship educator; b. Flagstaff, Ariz., July 17, 1924; d. Walter E. Dickinson and Margaret Opal (Smith) Langdon; m. Walter Kent, Mar. 4, 1943; children: Sherry Lee DeVillier, W. Norman, Charles H., Daniel W. Grad. pub. sch., 1942. Owner, operator Come by Chance Riding Acad., Flagstaff, 1945-65; owner, mgr. San Francisco Peaks Riding & Hunt Club, Flagstaff, 1965-75; mem. horsemanship tchg. staff No. Ariz. U., Flagstaff, 1966-75; cert. tchr. Yavapai C.C., Clarkdale, Ariz., 1979—. Contbr. articles to Western Horseman mag.; reporter, columnist The Verde Ind., Verde View. Pres. Camp Verde (Ariz.) Hist. Soc., 1990—.

KENT, GAYLON MARK, broadcasting executive, reporter; b. L.A., Nov. 4, 1965; s. Gaylon Hammond and Gloria Regina (Aranda) K. Grad. h.s., L.A. Qualified in submarines USN. Announcer Sta. KXO, El Centro, Calif., 1988-95; reporter Imperial Valley Press, El Centro, 1995—; founder, chmn., CEO Pro Com Radio Sports, El Centro, 1994—. Author: Sam Rider, Private Detective, 1992. 3d class quartermaster USN, 1983-87. Office: Pro Com Radio Sports PO Box 1671 El Centro CA 92244

KENT, JEFFREY DONALD, lawyer; b. Whittier, Calif., Apr. 30, 1967; s. Michael Floyd and Cheryl Ann (Gautsche) K. BA in Econs., U. Calif., Irvine, 1989, BA in Polit. Sci., 1989; JD, Western State U., 1992. Bar: Calif. 1992, U.S. Dist. Ct. (ctrl. and ea. dists.) Calif. 1993, U.S. Dist. Ct. (so. dist.) Calif. 1995, U.S. Ct. Appeals (9th cir.) 1995, U.S. Supreme Ct. 1996. Law clk. Orange County Pub. Defender, Santa Ana, Calif., 1990-91, Orange

County Dist. Atty., Santa Ana, 1991-92; substitute tchr. East Whittier Sch. Dist., 1992-93; assoc. Bridgman, Mordkin, Gould & Shapiro, Fountain Valley, Calif., 1993-95, Law Offices Michael R. McDonnell, Inc., La Habra, Calif., 1995—. Mem. ACLU, Orange County Bar Assn., State Bar Calif., Calif. Pub. Defenders Assn., Assn. Fed. Def. Attys., Calif. Attys. for Criminal Justice, Calif. Deuce Defenders Assn., Nat. Assn. Criminal Def. Lawyers. Democrat. Office: 440 E La Habra Blvd La Habra CA 90631

KENT, LISA, writer; b. Sept. 13, 1942; d. Francis and Agnes (Coutts) Loughlin; m. Edward Krones (div.); m. Larry Kent, June 25, 1985; children: Leah Barr Becker, Mark Krones. Student, Columbia U., The New Sch., N.Y.C., UCLA; diploma, Finch Jr. Coll. Author: Love is Always There, 1993, Hilde Knows: Someone Cries for the Children, 1994, The Thirteenth Sign, 1997; screenwriter: Hot Dogs. Home: 28315 Ridgehaven Ct Rancho Palos Verdes CA 90275

KENT, MOLLIE, writer, publishing executive, editor; b. Abilene, Tex., July 21, 1933; d. Henry Lee and Clyde Radia (Free) Summers; m. Paul Raymond Kintzinger, June 5, 1954 (div. July 1982); children: Katrina, Alice, Sarah. Student, Tulsa (Okla.) U., 1962-64; U. N.Mex., 1970-72. Lic. insurance and real estate broker, N.Mex. Owner, pub. Jemez Pub. Co., Jemez Springs, N.Mex., 1976-81, Albuquerque and Bernalillo, N.Mex., 1976-81; owner Kent Enterprises, La Plata, N.Mex., 1990—. Pub., editor: (newspapers) Jemez Mountain Views, 1976-80, Sandoval County Rev., 1977-80, Sandia Sun, 1979-81; assoc. editor, advertising mgr.: The Aztec (N.Mex.) Local News, 1993—. Republican. Home: PO Box 360 La Plata NM 87418 Office: The Aztec Local News PO Box 275 Aztec NM 87410

KENT, SUSAN GOLDBERG, library director, consultant; b. N.Y.C., Mar. 18, 1944; d. Elias and Minnie (Barnett) Solomon; m. Eric Goldberg, Mar. 27, 1966 (div. Mar. 1991); children: Evan, Jessica, Joanna; m. Rolly Kent, Dec. 20, 1991. BA in English Lit. with honors, SUNY, 1965; MS, Columbia U., 1966. Libr., sr. libr. N.Y. Pub. Libr., 1965-67, br. mgr. Donnell Art Libr., 1967-68; reference libr. Paedergaat br. Bklyn. Pub. Libr., 1971-72; reference libr. Finkelstein Meml. Libr., Spring Valley, N.Y., 1974-76; coord. adult and young adult svcs. Tucson Pub. Libr., 1977-80, acting libr. dir., 1982, dep. libr. dir., 1980-87; mng. dir. Ariz. Theatre Co., Tucson and Phoenix, 1987-89; dir. Mpls. Pub. Libr. and Info. Ctr., 1990-95; city libr. L.A. Pub. Libr., 1995—; tchr. Pima C.C., Tucson, 1978, grad. libr. sch. U. Ariz., Tucson, 1978, 79; panelist Ariz. Commn. Arts, 1981-85; reviewer pub. programs NEH, 1985, 89, panelist challenge grants, 1986-89, panelist state programs, 1988; cons. to librs. and nonprofit instns., 1989-90, 92—; mem. bd. devel. and fundraising Child's Play, Phoenix, 1983; bd. dirs., mem. organizing devel. and fundraising com. Flagstaff (Ariz.) Symphony Orch., 1988; cons., presenter workshops Young Adult Svcs. divsn. ALA, 1986-88; presenter in field. Contbr. articles to profl. jours. Chair arts and culture com. Tucson Tomorrow, 1981-85; bd. dirs., v.p. Ariz. Dance Theatre, 1984-86; bd. dirs. women's studies adv. coun. U. Ariz., 1985-90, Arizonans for Cultural Devel., 1987-89, YWCA Mpls., 1991-92; commr. Ariz. Commn. on Arts, 1983-87; participant Leadership Mpls., 1990-91. Fellow Sch. Libr. Sci., Columbia U., 1965-66. Mem. ALA (membership com. S.W. regional chair 1983-86, com. on appts. 1986-87, planning and budget assembly del. 1991-93, gov. coun. 1990—, chair conf. com. 1996—), Pub. Libr. Assn. (nominating com. 1980-82, v.p. 1986-87, pres. 1987-88, chair pubs. assembly 1988-89, chair nat. conf. 1994, chair legis. com. 1994-95), Calif. Libr. Assn., Urban Librs. Coun. (exec. bd. 1994—, treas. 1996—), Libr. Adminstrn. and Mgmt. Assn. (John Cotton Dana Award com. 1994-95). Office: LA Pub Libr 630 W 5th St Los Angeles CA 90071-2002

KENT, THEODORE CHARLES, psychologist; m. Shirley, June 7, 1948; children: Donald, Susan, Steven. BA, Yale U., 1935, MA, Columbia U., 1940, MA, Mills Coll., 1953, PhD, U. So. Calif., 1951; Dr. Rerum Naturalium, Johannes Gutenberg U., Mainz, Germany, 1960. Diplomate in clin. psychology. Clin. psychologist, behavioral scientist USAF, 1951-65, chief psychologist, Europe, 1956-60; head dept. behavioral sci. U. So. Colo., Pueblo, 1965-78, emeritus, 1978—; staff psychologist Yuma Behavioral Health, Ariz., 1978-82, chief profl. svcs., 1982-83; dir. psychol. svcs. Rio Colo. Health Systems, Yuma, 1983-85; clin. psychologist, dir. mental health Ft. Yuma (Calif.) Indian Health Svc., USPHS, 1985-88; exec. dir. Human Sci. Ctr., San Diego, 1982—. Columnist Yuma Daily Sun, 1982-86. Author (tests) symbol arrangement test, 1952, internat. culture free non-verbal intelligence, 1957, self-other location chart, 1970, test of suffering, 1982; (books) Skills in Living Together, 1983, Conflict Resolution, 1986, A Psychologist Answers Your Questions, 1987, Behind The Therapsist's Notes, 1993, Mapping the Human Genome—Reality, Morality and Diety, 1995, Poems For Living, 1995, Genetic Engineering, Yes, No or Maybe - A look At What's Ahead, 1997; plays and video Three Warriors Against Substance Abuse. Named Outstanding prof. U. So. Colo., 1977. Fellow APA (disting. visitor undergrad. edn. program); mem. AAAS, Deutsche Gesellschaft fur Antropologie, Internat. Assn. Study of Symbols (founder, 1st pres. 1957-61), Japanese Soc. Study KTSA (hon. pres.), Home and Office: PO Box 270169 San Diego CA 92198-2169

KENTFIELD, JOHN ALAN, mechanical engineering educator; b. Hitchin, Eng., Mar. 4, 1930; s. William George and Cecile Lillian (Blackmore) K.; m. Amelia Elizabeth Emmerson, July 9, 1966. BS, U. Southhampton (Eng.), 1959; diploma of Imperial Coll., U. London, PhD, 1963. Registered prof. engr., Alta., Can. Trainee CVA-Kearney and Trecker, Ltd., Brighton, Eng., 1950-52; asst. tester Ricardo and Co., Shoreham, Eng., 1952-56; asst. lectr. Imperial Coll., U. London, 1962-63; project engr. Curtiss-Wright Corp., Woodridge, N.J., 1963-66; lectr. Imperial Coll., U. London, 1966-70; assoc. prof. U. Calgary (Alta., Can.), 1970-78, prof., 1978—; cons. several U.S. and Can. corps., 1976—; mem. assoc. com. on propulsion Nat. Rsch. Coun., Ottawa, Ont., Can., 1983-90; mem. wind-energy tech. adv. com. Energy Mines and Resources, Ottawa, 1985-87. Author: (reference/textbook) Nonsteady 1D, Internal Compressible Flows, 1993, (reference book) The Fundamentals of Wind-Driven Water Pumpers, 1996; contbr.: Canadian Ency., 1985; contbr. 158 articles to profl. publs., including SAE Trans., ASME Jour. Engring., AIAA Jour. Aircraft. Killiam Resident fellow U. Calgary, 1980; rsch. operating grantee Nat. Scis. and Engring. Rsch. Coun., Ottawa, 1990, 93, 96; recipient Ordinary Nat. Cert. prize Brighton (Eng.) Tech. Coll., 1953, Higher Nat. Cert. prize Brighton Tech. Coll., 1955. Mem. ASME, AIAA, Am. Wind Energy Assn., Can. Wind Energy Assn. (R.J. Templin award 1992). Home: 1222 Bowness Rd NW #301, Calgary, AB Canada T2N 3J7 Office: Dept Mech Engring, U Calgary Faculty Engring, Calgary, AB Canada T2N 1N4

KENVIN, ROGER LEE, writer, retired English educator; b. N.Y.C., May 26, 1926; s. James Marion and Gladys Irene (Macdonald) K.; m. Verna Rudd Trimble, Apr. 5, 1952; children: Brooke Trimble Kenvin Goldstein, Heather Trimble Kenvin Hietala. BA, Bowdoin Coll., 1949; MA, Harvard U., 1956; MFA, Yale U., 1959, DFA, 1961. Copywriter Crowell-Collier Pub., N.Y.C., 1950-53; tchr. Le Rosey, Rolle, Switzerland, 1953-55; prof. English, Mary Washington Coll., Fredericksburg, Va., 1959-68; chmn. dept. drama Mary Washington Coll., Fredericksburg, Md., 1970-82; prof., chmn. dept. speech and drama U. Notre Dame and St. Mary's Coll., South Bend, Ind., 1968-70; prof., chmn. dept. theatre and dance Calif. Poly. State U., San Luis Obispo, 1983-88. Author: (play) Krishnalight, 1976, (short stories) The Gaffer and Seven Fables, 1987, Harpo's Garden, 1997; contbr. short stories to lit. publs. With USN, 1944-46. Mem. Phi Beta Kappa. Home: 575 Fairview Ave Arcadia CA 91007

KENWORTHY, ELDON GORDON (BUD KENWORTHY), political science educator; b. Pasadena, Calif., May 27, 1935; s. Luther Clifford and Evangeline (Blohm) K.; m. Cynthia Witman, Aug., 1989; 1 child, Lauren. AB in History, Oberlin Coll., 1956; PhD in Polit. Sci., Yale U., 1970. From asst. prof. to assoc. prof. Cornell U., Ithaca, N.Y., 1966-90; assoc. prof. Whitman Coll., Walla Walla, Wash., 1990-93, prof., 1994—. Author: America/Américas, 1995; contbr. articles and book chpts. to profl. publs. Ptnr. Tropical Forestry Initiative, Costa Rica, 1992—. Office: Whitman Coll Boyer Ave Walla Walla WA 99362

KENYON, CARLETON WELLER, librarian; b. Lafayette, N.Y., Oct. 7, 1923; s. Herbert Abram and Esther Elizabeth (Weller) K.; m. Dora Marie Kallander, May 21, 1948; children: Garnet Eileen, Harmon Clark, Kay Adelle. A.B., Yankton Coll., 1947; M.A., U. S.D., 1950, J.D., 1950; A.M. in L.S, U. Mich., 1951. Bar: S.D. 1950. Asst. law librarian, head catalog librarian U. Nebr., 1951-52; asst. reference librarian Los Angeles County Law Library, 1952-54, head catalog librarian, 1954-60; law librarian State of Calif., Sacramento, 1960-69; became cons. Library of Congress, Washington, 1963; asso. law librarian Library of Congress, 1969-71, law librarian, 1971-89; cons. county law libraries; lectr. legal bibliography and research. Author: California County Law Library Basic List Handbook and Information of New Materials, 1967; compiler: Calif. Library Laws; assisted in compiling checklists of basic: Am. publs. and subject headings; contbr. articles and book revs. to law revs., library jours. Served with USAAC, 1943-46. Mem. ABA, State Bar S.D., Am. Assn. Law Librarians (chmn. com. on cataloging and classification 1969-71, mem. staff Law Library Inst. 1969, 71), Law Librarians Soc. Washington. Home: 4239 44th Ct NE Salem OR 97305-2117

KENYON, DAVID LLOYD, architect, architectural firm executive; b. Lockport, N.Y., Sept. 9, 1952; s. F. Robert and Betty Jane (Reviere) K.; m. Susan Clair Doyle, Jan. 6, 1990; children: Sean Phillip Kenyon, Colin Doyle Kenyon. A in Civil Tech., SUNY, Utica, 1972; BArch, Syracuse U., 1975. Lic. architect, N.Y., Pa., Ariz., Calif. Oreg., Ill., Washington. Assoc. The Myrus Group, Syracuse, N.Y., 1973-79; assoc. dir. design Chase Archtl. Assocs., Syracuse, N.Y., 1978-80; prin. Kenyon Archtl. Group, Phoenix, Ariz., 1980—; cons. Nat. Trust for Historic Preservation, Washington, 1978; faculty assoc. Ariz. State U. Coll. Architecture, Tempe, Ariz., 1983-89; with nat. solar study USAID, Morocco, 1991; with mission to Malta and Morocco, OPEC, Washington, 1991-92; lectr. Assn. Construction Inspectors, 1993. Author: (textbook) A Hands on Approach to Construction Inspection, 1992. Recipient Energy Innovation award U.S. Dept. Energy, 1988, Environmental Excellence award Crescordia Valley Forward, 1991, Western Regional Design award Am. Inst. Architects, 1991, CAC Honor award, 1992. Fellow Ariz. Acad.; mem. Nat. Trust for Historic Preservation, Soc. Archtl. Historians, Internat. Conference Bldg. Officials. Office: Kenyon Archtl Group 398 S Mill Ave Tempe AZ 85281-2819

KENYON, DAVID V., federal judge; b. 1930; m. Mary Cramer; children: George Cramer, John Clark. B.A., U. Calif.-Berkeley, 1952; J.D., U. So. Calif., 1957. Law clk. presiding justice U.S. Dist. Ct. (cen. dist.) Calif., 1957-58; house counsel Metro-Goldwyn-Mayer, 1959-60, Nat. Theatres and TV Inc., 1960-61; pvt. practice law, 1961-71; judge Mcpl. Ct. L.A., 1971-72, L.A. Superior Ct., 1972-80; judge U.S. Dist. Ct. (cen. dist.) Calif., L.A., 1980—, sr. judge. Office: US Dist Ct 312 N Spring St Rm 2445 Los Angeles CA 90012-4701*

KEOGH, HEIDI HELEN DAKE, publishing executive; b. Saratoga, N.Y., July 12, 1950; d. Charles Starks and Phyllis Sylvia (Edmunds) Dake; m. Randall Frank Keogh, Nov. 3, 1973; children: Tyler Cameron, Kelly Dake. Student, U. Colo., 1972. Reception, promotions Sta. KLAK, KJAE, Lakewood, Colo., 1972-73; account exec. Mixed Media Advt. Agy., Denver, 1973-75; writer, mktg. Jr. League Cookbook Devel., Denver, 1986-88; chmn., coordinator Colorado Cache & Creme de Colorado Cookbooks, 1988-90; speakers bur. Mile High Transplant Bank, Denver, 1983-84, Writer's Inst., U. Denver, 1988; bd. dirs. Stewart's Ice Cream Co., Inc., Jr. League, Denver. Contbr. 6 articles to profl. jours. Fiscal officer, bd. dirs. Mile High Transplant Bank; blockworker Heart Fund and Am. Cancer Soc., Littleton, Colo., 1978—, Littleton Rep. Com., 1980-84; fundraising vol. Littleton Pub. Schs., 1980—; vol. Gathering Place, bd. dirs., 1996—, chmn. Brown Bag benefit, 1996; vol. Hearts for Life, 1991—, Oneday, 1992, Denver Ballet Guild, 1992—, Denver Ctr. Alliance, 1993—, Newborn Hope, 1980—. Mem. Jr. League Denver (pub. rels. bd., v.p. ways and means 1989-90, planning coun./ad hoc 1990-92, sustainer spl. events 1993-94), Community Emergency Fund (chair 1991-92), Jon D. Williams Cotillion at Columbine (chmn. 1991-93), Columbine Country Club, Gamma Alpha Chi, Pi Beta Phi Alumnae Club (pres. Denver chpt. 1984-85, 93-94, alumnae adv. com. U. Colo. chpt. 1997—). Episcopalian. Home: 63 Fairway Ln Littleton CO 80123-6648

KEPHART, FLOYD W., corporate strategist; b. Ft. Oglethorpe, Ga., May 16, 1942; s. Floyd William Kephart and Zada (Whaley) Lindsay; m. Jean Waters, 1993. BA, Mid. Tenn. State U., 1965. Rsch. asst. Kennedy staff White House, Washington, 1961-63; budget dir. Dept. Transp. Gov.'s Office, Tenn., 1963-68; assoc. prof. polit. sci. Mid. Tenn. State U., Murfreesboro, 1968-70; polit. analyst NBC, Nashville, 1970-80; chmn., CEO So. States Corp., Nashville, 1980-83; CEO, chmn. McDowell Corp., Nashville, 1983-84; chmn. Artists & Entertainment, Inc., Nashville, 1988—; chmn., CEO Insight Mktg. Corp., L.A., 1992—; chmn. Solutions Corp. of America; cons. Head Start, Washington, 1963-73; exec. dir. Fiscal Rev. Com., Nashville, 1967. Cons. Dem. Nat. Com., Washington, 1968-84; community spokesperson Boy Scouts Am., Nashville, 1971-73. Home: 890 Curtiswood Ln Nashville TN 37204-4317

KEPLER, CHARLES GEORGE, lawyer; b. Salina, Kans., July 13, 1922; s. Forrest Miller and Berniece Eleanor (Stivers) K.; m. Ursula L. Manewal, Apr. 26, 1944; 1 child, Loretta Berniece. BS, U. Wyo., 1949, JD, 1948; LLM, U. Mich., 1950. Prof. bus. law U. Wyo., Laramie, 1948-49; asst. prof. law U. Okla., Norman, 1950-52; mem. legal dept. Husky Oil, Cody, Wyo., 1952-60; mem. Simpson, Kepler & Edwards, Cody, 1960—. Mem. Wyo. Jud. Nominating Commn., 1973-77; mem., chmn. State Bd. Bar Examiners, Wyo., 1976-80; bd. dirs. The Salk Inst., La Jolla, Calif., 1986-95. Capt. inf. U.S. Army, 1942-46. Mem. Am. Judicature Soc., Am. Bar Found., Am. Coll. Trust & Estate Counsel. Republican. Methodist. Home: 1213 Sunshine Ave Cody WY 82414

KEPNER, JANE ELLEN, psychotherapist, educator, minister; b. Lancaster, Pa., July 13, 1948; d. Richard Darlington and Miriam (Harclerode) K.; m. Raymond Earl Sparks Jr., July 23, 1969 (div. Apr. 1978); 1 child, Heather Elizabeth. AB, CCNY, 1975; MDiv, Harvard Divinity Sch., 1985. Vol. Vista, Auburn, Ala., 1967-69; creative drama tchr. East Harlem Day Care, N.Y.C., 1972-76; editl. asst. Bantam Books, Inc., N.Y.C., 1976-78; rschr. Theseus Prodns., Greenwich, Conn., 1978-82; homeless advocate Harvard Sq. Chs., Cambridge, Mass., 1984-85; cmty. organizer So. Middlesex Opportunity Coun., Marlboro, Mass., 1985-88; emergency psychiat. clinician Advocates, Inc., Framingham, Mass., 1988-89; assoc. prof. Curry Coll., Milton, Mass., 1989-90; psychologist, mental health advocate Portland (Oreg.) Health Svc., 1991-95, bd. advisors, 1992-94. Organizer emergency food pantry Marlboro City Coun., 1987; tenants rights and housing rights advocates Tenants Action Com., Marlboro, 1985-87. Pfeiffer fellow Harvard U. Div. Sch., 1983. Mem. Am. Counseling Assn., Oreg. Friends of C.G. Jung, Club 53 (bd. dirs. 1992-94), Amnesty Internat., Oreg. Coalition to Abolish the Death Penalty.

KERBS, WAYNE ALLAN, transportation executive; b. Hoisington, Kans., Mar. 21, 1930; s. Emanuel and Mattie (Brack) K.; m. Patricia Ann Aitchison, Dec. 5, 1953; chidlren: Jacqueline Lee Kerbs Kepler, Robert Wayne. BSEE, U. Kans., 1952; MSEE, Ohio State U., 1960; M in Engring., UCLA, 1968. Test engr. Mpls.-Honeywell, 1952-54; sr. engr. Booz Allen & Hamilton, Dayton, Ohio, 1957-60; program mgr. Hughes Aircraft Co., L.A., 1960-74; pres., bd. dirs. Kerbs Industries, Inc., Los Alamitos, Calif., 1975—. Developer spacecraft devel. surveyor, 1960's, transit plan, 1996; patentee in field. Vol. PTA, Boy Scouts Am., Meth. Ch., 1952—; organizer Am. Mature Vols., L.a., 1994—; active Orange County Transp. Authority, 1994—. Lt. USN, 1954-57. Mem. Soc. Automotive Engrs. (sec.), Elec. Automobile Assn., Advanced Transit Assn., Transp. Rsch. Bd., Am. Legion, Sigma Tau, Eta Kappa Nu. Republican.

KERMAN, BARRY MARTIN, ophthalmologist, educator; b. Chgo., Mar. 31, 1945; s. Harvey Nathan and Evelyn (Bialis) K.; B.S., U. Ill., 1967, M.D. with high honors, 1970. Diplomate Am. Bd. Ophthalmology; children: Gregory Jason, Jeremy Adam. Intern in medicine Harbor Gen. Hosp., Torrance, Calif., 1970-71; resident in ophthalmology Wadsworth VA Hosp., L.A., 1971-74; fellow in diseases of the retina, vitreous and choroid Jules Stein Eye Inst. UCLA, 1974-75; fellow in ophthalmic ultrasonography Edward S. Harkness Eye Inst., Columbia U., N.Y.C. and U. Iowa Hosps., Iowa City, 1975; asst. prof. ophthalmology UCLA, 1976-78, Harbor Gen. Hosp., 1976-78; asst. clin. prof. ophthalmology UCLA, 1978-83, assoc. clin. prof., 1983-95, clin. prof., 1995—, dir. ophthalmic ultrasonography lab., 1976—; cons. ophthalmologist, L.A., 1976—; mem. exec. bd. Am. Registry Diagnostic Med. Sonographers, 1981-87. With USAFR, 1971-77. Fellow Am. Acad. Ophthalmology; mem. Am. Soc. Cataract and Refractive Surgery, L.A. Soc. Ophthalmology, Am. Soc. Ophthalmic Ultrasound, Am. Assn. Ophthalmic Standardized Echography, Societas Internat. Pro Diagnostica Ultrasonica in Ophthalmic, Western Retina Study Club. Contbr. articles to profl. jours. Office: 2080 Century Park E Ste 800 Los Angeles CA 90067-2011

KERN, DONALD MICHAEL, internist; b. Belleville, Ill., Nov. 21, 1951; s. Donald Milton and Dolores Olivia (Rust) K. BS in Biology, Tulane U., 1973; MD magna cum laude, U. Brussels, 1983. ECFMG cert.; lic. Calif. Intern in surgery Berkshire Med. Ctr., Pittsfield, Mass., 1983-84; intern in psychiatry Tufts New England Med. Ctr., Boston, 1984-85; resident in internal medicine Kaiser Found. Hosp., San Francisco, 1985-87; with assoc. staff internal medicine Kaiser Permanente Med. Group, Inc., San Francisco, 1987-89; assoc. investigator AIDS Clin. Trial Unit Kaiser Permanente Med. Ctr., Stanford U., Nat. Inst. Allergy & Infectious Disease, San Francisco, 1988-90; mem. staff internal medicine Kaiser Permanente Med. Group, South San Francisco, 1989-96; mem. staff Desert Med. Group, Palm Springs, Calif., 1996—. Democrat. Roman Catholic.

KERN, PAUL ALFRED, advertising company executive, research consultant, realtor; b. Hackensack, N.J., Mar. 17, 1958; s. Paul Julian and Edith Helen (Colten) K. BS in Commerce, U. Va., 1980; MBA, U. So. Calif., 1983. Sales rep. Procter & Gamble, Cin., 1980-81; rsch. svcs. mgr. Opinion Rsch., Long Beach, Calif., 1984; consumer planning supr. Dentsu, Young & Rubicam, L.A., 1984-85; rsch. exec. DJMC Advt., Inc., L.A., 1986; realtor assoc. Tarbell Realtors, Santa Ana, Calif., 1988-89; corp. pres. Jennskore, Inc., Torrance, Calif., 1989-93, also bd. dirs.; bd. dirs. Applicon, Inc., Hillsdale, N.J., Kernokopia, Hillsdale; cons. Venture Six Enterprises, Encino, Calif., 1985-87, DFS/Dorland, Torrance, 1986, IMI Machinery Inc., Charleston, S.C., 1987—. Coach, supr. Little League Football, Alexandria, Va., 1981; active Surf and Sun Softball League (1987 champions). Recipient Most Calls Per Day award Procter and Gamble, 1980. Mem. Profl. Research Assn., Am. Mktg. Assn., Am. Film Inst., Internat. Platform Assn., U.S. Tennis Assn. (Michelob Light 4.5 Team Championship 1982), U. Va. Alumni Assn, Nat. Assn. Realtors, Calif. Assn. of Realtors, S. Bay Rd. of Realtors (Torrance-Lomita), Carson Bd. of Realtors. Club: Alta Vista Racquet. Home and Office: 48-253 Silver Spur Trl Palm Desert CA 92260-6611

KERNER, ROBERT FRED, packaging company executive; b. Fresno, Calif., Apr. 17, 1936; s. Fred George and Katherine (Borgardt) K.; m. Anne Carolyn Lackey, Nov. 29, 1960 (div. Jan. 1976); children: Robert Fred Jr., Katherine Anne, Susan Ruth, Carolyn Margaret. BS in Printing Engring., Calif. State U., San Luis Obispo, 1959. Graphics mgr. Am. Can Co., Greenwich, Conn., 1960-77, Envases Venzolanos, Caracas, Venezuela, 1977-81; dir. mfg. Packaging Industries, San Leandro, Calif., 1981-93; plant mgr. Gaylord Graphics, Livermore, Calif., 1993—. Sgt. Air N.G., 1958-64. Mem. Pacific Metal Deco Assn. (treas. 1963-66), Masons, Delta Sigma Phi. Home: 5265 Canyon Crest Dr San Ramon CA 94583 Office: Gaylord Graphics 7041-A Las Positas Rd Livermore CA 94550

KERNODLE, UNA MAE, home economics curriculum specialist, retired secondary education educator; b. Jackson, Tenn., Mar. 4, 1947; d. James G. and Mary E. (McLemore) Sikes. B.S. in Home Econs., U. Tenn., 1969; M.Edn., U. Alaska, 1974. Tchr., head dept. vocat. edn. and electives Chugiak High Sch., Anchorage, ret.; home econs. curriculum specialist King Career Ctr., Anchorage; edn. cons. State of Alaska, Anchorage Talent Bank; presenter Gov.'s Conf. on Child Abuse, Alaska Vocat. Edn. Assn. Conf., Alaska Home Econs. Inst., 1989; state officer Alaska Home Econs. Recipient Gruening award, 1989. Mem. Am. Home Econs. Assn., Anchorage Assn. Edn. Young Children, NEA, Am. Vocat. Assn. Democrat. Baptist. Office: Office of Career Tech 2650 E Northern Lights Blvd Anchorage AK 99508-4119

KERR, FORREST DAVID, actor, writer, producer; b. Burnet, Tex., Jan. 25, 1949; s. Forrest and Dorothy Web (Dennis) K.; m. Kathleen Mable Keller, Dec. 6, 1969 (div. Mar. 1975). Student, C.C. Balt., 1970-71; AS in Bus. Adminstrn., Austin C.C., 1980; postgrad., St. Edwards U., Austin, 1980-81, Am. Acad. Dramatic Arts, Pasadena, Calif., 1990, UCLA, 1992. Control clk. Social Security Adminstrn., Balt., 1970-71; assoc. br. mgr. Fin. Am., Smyrna, Del., 1971-75; br. mgr. Investors Loan Corp., Alexandria, Va., 1865-77; mgr.-in-tng. Gt. Western Fin., Austin, 1977-78; leasing agt. Safty Kleen Corp., Austin, 1979-80; tech. staff asst. Austin C.C., 1982; mgr. main br. Jim Walter Homes Corp., Corpus Christi, Tex., 1983-84; dir. sales Royal T Homes Corp., Houston, 1985-87; gen. mgr. Conner Home Sales Corp., Houston, 1987-88, Times Manufactured Housing and Tomball (Tex.) Mobile Homes, 1988-89; asst. mgr. Florsheim Thayer McNiel, Northridge, Calif., 1990-91; apprentice editor Concorde/New Horizon Films, Venice, Calif., 1991-92; freelance writer and prodr., Thorne Pictures, Palos Verdes, Calif., 1993—; cons. Am. Cons. League, Houston, 1988-90; copy editor Fieldings Worldwide Travel Guides, Redondo Beach, Calif., 1994. Author: (screen plays) Unlikely Angel, 1990, Thunderbirds, 1992; appeared in (plays) Mousetrap, My Sister Eileen, (films) Sudden Death, Melrose Place, Man of Her Dreams, Sheriff Garrett, 1992, Graveyard Man, 1992, Chauffer, 1993, Feathered Detective, 1994, Ken Osborn, 1996; assoc. prodr. (films) Thornes of Fate, 1993; (videos) Elinor Rigby, 1991, Hard Luck Woman, 1992; writer, prodr., dir. (play) The Way It Wasn't, 1989. Mem. ind. feature project, Santa Monica, Calif., 1993—; vol. Book Pals, SAG Found., L.A., 1995. With USCG, 1966-70. Mem. SAG (Screen Actors Guild awards, nominating com. L.A. 1996, conservatory 1995—), Phi Theta Kappa.

KERR, KLEON HARDING, former state senator, educator; b. Plain City, Utah, Apr. 26, 1911; s. William A. and Rosemond (Harding) K.; m. Katherine Abbott, Mar. 15, 1941; children: Kathleen, William A., Rebecca Rae. AS, Weber Coll., 1936; BA, George Washington U., 1939; MS, Utah State U., Logan, 1946. Tchr., Bear River High Sch., Tremonton, Utah, 1940-56, prin. jr. high sch., 1956-60, prin. Bear River High Sch., 1960-71; city justice Tremonton, 1941-46; sec. to Senator Arthur V. Watkins, 1947. Mayor, Tremonton City, 1948-53; mem. Utah Local Govt. Survey Commn., 1954-55; mem. Utah Ho. of Reps., 1953-56; mem. Utah State Senate, 1957-64, chmn. appropriation com., 1959—, majority leader, 1963; mem. Utah Legis. Council. Author: (poetry) Open My Eyes, 1983, We Remember, 1983, Trouble in the Amen Corner, 1985, Past Imperfect, 1988, A Helping Hand, 1990, Sound of Silence, 1991, Power Behind the Throne, 1992, Unreachable Goal?, 1993, The Only Difference, 1994, Please Boss, 1995, Beach Comber, 1995; (history) Those Who Served Box Elder County, 1984, Those Who Served Tremonton City, 1985, Diamond in the Rough, 1987, Facts of Life, 1987, Gettin' and Givin', 1989. Dist. dir. vocat. edn. Box Elder Sch. Dist. Recipient Alpha Delta Kappa award for outstanding contbn. to edn., 1982, award for outstanding contbrs. to edn. and govt. Theta Chpt. Alpha Beta Kappa, 1982, Excellence Achieved in Promotion of Tourism award, Allied Category award Utah Travel Counc., 1988, Merit award, 1993, Andy Ryting Community Svc. award, 1991; named Tourism Ambassador of Month, 1986. Mem. NEA, Utah, Box Elder edn. assns., Nat., Utah secondary schs. prins. assns., Utah Sheriff's Assn. (hon.), Bear River Valley. C. of C. (sec., mgr. 1955-58), Lions, Kiwanis, Phi Delta Kappa. Mem. Ch. of Jesus Christ of Latter-day Saints. Home: PO Box 246 Tremonton UT 84337-0246

KERR, NANCY KAROLYN, pastor, mental health consultant; b. Ottumwa, Iowa, July 10, 1934; d. Owen W. and Iris Irene (Israel) K. Student Boston U., 1953; AA, U. Bridgeport, 1966; BA, Hofstra U., 1967; postgrad. in clin. psychology Adelphi U. Inst. Advanced Psychol. Studies, 1968-73; MDiv Associated Mennonite Bibl. Sems., 1986; m. Richard Clayton Williams, June 28, 1953 (div.); children: Richard Charles, Donna Louise. Ordained pastor Mennonite Ch., 1987; apptd. pastor Kamloops Presbytery Ch., Can., 1987. Pastoral counselor Nat. Council Chs., Jackson, Miss., 1964; dir. teen program Waterbury (Conn.) YWCA, 1966-67; intern in psychology N.Y. Med. Coll., 1971-72; rsch. cons., 1972-73; coord. home svcs., psychologist City and County of Denver, 1972-75; cons. Mennonite Mental Health Svcs., Denver, 1975-78; asst. prof. psychology Messiah Coll., 1978-79; mental health cons., 1979-81; called to ministry Mennonite Ch., 1981, pastor Cin. Mennonite Fellowship, 1981-83, coord. campus peace evangelism, 1981-83, mem. Gen. Conf. Peace and Justice Reference Council, 1983-85; instr. Associated Mennonite Bibl. Sems., 1985; teaching elder Assembly Mennonite Ch., 1985-86; pastor Pulaski Mennonite Ch., 1986-89; v.p. Davis County Mins.' Assn., 1988-89; exec. dir., pastoral counselor Bethesda Counseling

Svcs., Prince George B.C., 1989—; bd. dirs. Tri-County Counselling Clinic, Memphis, Mo., 1980-81; spl. ch. curriculum Nat. Council Chs., 1981; mem. Cen. Dist. Conf. Peace and Justice Com., 1981-89; mem. exec. bd. People for Peace, 1981-83. Mem. Waterbury Planned Parenthood Bd., 1964-67; mem. MW Children's Home Bd., 1974-75; bd. dirs. Boulder (Colo.) ARC, 1977-78, PLURA, B.C. Synod, 1995—; elder St. Giles Presbyn. Ch., 1996—; mem. Mennonite Disabilities Respite Care Bd., 1981-86; P.G. Children's Svcs. com., 1992-94; bd. dirs. Prince George Neighborlink, 1995—; adv. com. Prince George Planning, 1995. Mem. APA (assoc.), Can. Psychol. Assn., Soc. Psychologists for Study of Social Issues, Christian Assn. Psychol. Studies, Davis County Mins. Assn. (v.p. 1988-89), Prince George Ministerial Assn. (chmn. edn. and Airport chapel coms. 1990-92), Soc. Bib. Lit. & Exegesis. Office: 575 Quebec St, Prince George, BC Canada V2L 1W6

KERR, ROBERT JAMES, mediator, educational consultant; b. Wichita, Kans., Aug. 31, 1952; s. James Winton and Lorna Marie (Griffith) Kerr. BA in Lit., Wichita State U., 1975; MEd, Colo. State U., 1977. Cert. mediator, COR Assocs., 1995. Coord. Greek affairs Drake U., Des Moines, 1977-80; asst. dir. alumni rels. U. Colo., Boulder, 1981-84; v.p. adminstrn. Youmans & Assocs., Denver, 1984-87; sr. cons. The Midas Group, Denver, 1987-90; instr. Ctr. for Legal Studies, Golden, Colo., 1995—; sr. cons. Firstep, Golden, Colo., 1990—; cons. Leading Edge Comm., 1990, Adams Sch. Dist. 14, 1992, Mountain Solutions, 1993, The Quick Co., 1993, Western Mus. Mining and Industry, 1993, NOVA, 1993; workshop designer, facilitator Cmty. Problem Solving, U. Denver, 1992, Strategic Planning, Utah State U., 1992, Risk Mgmt., Regional Leadership Conf., Kans. City, 1993, Philanthropy and Cmty. Action, Front Range Conf., U. N.C., 1993, Planning for Academic Success, 1993, Orgnl. Planning, U. No. Colo., 1993, Goal Setting, Colo. Sch. Mines, 1993, Vol. Tng. and Goal Setting, NOVA, 1993, Strategic Planning and Goal Setting, Western Mus. Mining and Industry, 1993, Regional Mentor Program, U. Wyo., 1995, Implementing Change, Colo. Sch. Mines, 1995; coord. Greek Life U. No. Colo., 1996—. Contbr. articles and other writings to mags. and fraternity jours.; author: So You Wanna Go to College—A Guide on How to Get There, 1992, (screenplay) Second Season, 1996. Mediator Jefferson County (Colo.) Mediation Svcs., 1995; mem. steering com. Leadership Golden, 1990-92, Buffalo Bill Days Festival, 1989; mem. Resource Bank Cmty. Leadership Program, 1991—; bd. dirs. Cmty. Shares of Colo., 1992-93; coord. Greek life U. Ctr., U. No. Colo., Greeley. Recipient Cert. of Dedication Kans. Boys State program, 1969-77, Recipient of the Jefferson Cup, disting. svc. Dist. Gov. Mem. bd. gov's., Phi Kappa Delta, Omicron Delta Kappa, Sigma Phi Epsilon. Democrat. Home and Office: 3750 W 24th St 1-201 Greeley CO 80634

KERR, THOMAS ANDREW, advisory engineer, scientist; b. Seattle, Feb. 26, 1953; s. Gerald Dale and Maureen Eilish (Doherty) K.; m. Susan Myra Kellogg, May 18, 1980. BS in Corp. Tng., Idaho State U., 1994. Tng. supr. Chem-Nuclear Systems, Inc., Barnwell, S.C., 1977-84; assoc. instr. Duke Power Co., Charlotte, N.C., 1984-87; chief low level radioactive waste mgmt. Ill. Dept. Nuclear Safety, Springfield, 1987-90; adv. engr., scientist nat. low level radioactive waste mgmt. Idaho Nat. Engring. Lab., Idaho Falls, 1990—. Contbr. articles to N.Y. Acad. Medicine Bulletin, 1988, Waste Mgmt., 1989, ASME Internat. Waste Mgmt. Conf., 1991, 95. With USN, 1973-77. Mem. Am. Nuclear Soc., Nat. Environ. Tng. Assn. (cert. environ. trainer). Home: 9673 S Ammon Rd Idaho Falls ID 83406-8311 Office: Idaho Nat Engring Lab PO Box 1625 Idaho Falls ID 83415-0001

KERRICK, DAVID ELLSWORTH, lawyer; b. Caldwell, Idaho, Jan. 15, 1951; s. Charles Ellsworth and Patria (Olesen) K.; m. Juneal Casper, May 24, 1980; children: Peter Ellsworth, Beth Anne, George Ellis, Katherine Leigh. Student, Coll. of Idaho, 1969-71; BA, U. Wash., 1972; JD, U. Idaho, 1980. Bar: Idaho 1980, U.S. Dist. Ct. Idaho 1980, U.S. Ct. Appeals (9th cir.) 1981. Mem. Idaho Senate, 1990-96, majority caucus chmn., 1992-94, majority leader, 1994-96. Mem. S.W. Idaho Estate Planning Coun. Mem. ABA, Assn. Trial Lawyers Am., Idaho Bar Assn. (3d dist. pres. 1985-86), Idaho Trial Lawyers Assn., Canyon County Lawyers Assn. (pres. 1985). Republican. Presbyterian. Lodge: Elks. Office: PO Box 44 Caldwell ID 83606

KERSCHNER, LEE R(ONALD), academic administrator, political science educator; b. May 31, 1931; m. Helga Koller, June 22, 1958; children: David, Gabriel, Riza. B.A. in Polit. Sci. (Univ. fellow), Rutgers U., 1953; M.A. in Internat. Relations (Univ. fellow), Johns Hopkins U., 1958; Ph.D. in Polit. Sci. (Univ. fellow), Georgetown U., 1964. From instr. to prof. polit. sci. Calif. State U., Fullerton, 1961-69, prof., 1988—; state univ. dean Calif. State Univs. and Colls. Hdqrs., Long Beach, 1969-71, asst. exec. vice chancellor, 1971-76, vice chancellor for adminstrv. affairs, 1976-77, vice chancellor acad. affairs, 1987-92; exec. dir. Colo. Commn. on Higher Edn., Denver, 1977-83, Nat. Assn. Trade and Tech. Schs., 1983-85, Calif. Commn. on Master Plan for Higher Edn., 1985-87; interim pres. Calif. State U., Stanislaus, 1992-94, spl. asst. to the chancellor, 1994—; exec. vice chancellor Minn. State Colls. and Univs., St. Paul, 1996—; mem. Calif. Student Aid Commn., 1993-96; cons. in field. Mem. exec. com. Am. Jewish Com., Denver, 1978-83; internat. bd. dirs. Amigos de las Americas, 1982-88 (chmn. 1985-87). Served with USAF, 1954-58; col. Res., ret. Home: PO Box 748 Weimar CA 95736-0748 Office: Minn State Colls and Univs Apt 16D 740 Mississippi Rover Blvd Saint Paul MN 55116

KERSEY, TERRY L(EE), astronautical engineer; b. San Francisco, June 9, 1947; s. Ida Helen (Schmeichel) K. Houseman, orderly Mills Meml. Hosp., San Mateo, Calif., 1965-68; security guard Lawrence Security, San Francisco, 1973-74; electronic engr. and technician engring. research and devel. dept. McCulloch Corp., L.A., 1977; warehouseman C.C.H. Computax Co., Redondo Beach, Calif., 1977-78; with material ops. and planning customer support dept. Allied-Signal Aerospace Co., Torrance, Calif., 1978-91; security guard Guardsmark Inc., L.A., 1993; electronic technician J.W. Griffin, Venice, Calif., 1993-96. Participant 9th Space Simulation conf., Los Angeles, 1977, 31st Internat. Astronautical Fedn. Congress., Tokyo, 1980, Unispace 1982 for the U.N., Vienna. Sgt. USAF, 1968-72, Vietnam. Decorated Vietnam Svc. medal with 2 bronze stars, Republic of Vietnam Campaign medal, Air Force commendation medal for Vietnam campaign Svc. Mem. AAAS, AIAA (sr., mem. space sys. tech. com. 1981—, mem. aerodynamics com. 1980—, mem. Wright Flyer Project Aerodynamics com. 1980—, mem. pub. policy com. 1989—), Nat. Space Inst., Am. Astronautical Soc., The Planetary Soc. (vol. NASA CD-rom project for Cassini mission to planet Saturn 1996-97), Internat. L5 Soc., Ind. Space Rsch. Group, Computer Soc. of IEEE, Space Studies Inst. (sr. assoc.). Zen Buddhist.

KERSHNER, IVAN HARRY, principal; b. Buffalo, Wyo., Apr. 20, 1948; s. Charles Howard and Shirley May (Branaman) K.; m. Vikki I. Fortune (div. 1988); 1 child, Kristopher; m. Lynn Voliter, Dec. 1991; children: Kimberly, Tyler. BS, Chadron State Coll., 1970, MS, 1974; EdS, Kearney State Coll., 1985. Tchr. Douglas (Wyo.) High Sch., 1970-77; prin. Polk (Nebr.) Pub. Schs., 1977-79; vice-prin. North Platte (Nebr.) High Sch., 1979-84, asst. supt., 1984-86, prin., 1986-90; prin. Eagle Valley High Sch., Gypsum, Colo., 1990—. Recipient Cert. of Award Countdown 2001, 1989, Miliken Nat. Educator award, 1995. Unitarian Universalist. Home: PO Box 178 Edwards CO 81632-0178 Office: Eagle Valley High Sch Box 188 Gypsum CO 81637-9714

KERTZ, MARSHA HELENE, accountant, educator; b. Palo Alto, Calif., May 29, 1946; d. Joe and Ruth (Lazear) K. BSBA in Acctg., San Jose State U., 1976, MBA, 1977. CPA, Calif., cert. tax profl. Staff acct. Steven Kroff & Co., CPA's, Palo Alto, 1968-71, 73-74; contr. Rand Teleprocessing Corp., San Francisco, 1972; auditor, sr. acct. Ben F. Priest Accountancy Corp., Mountain View, Calif., 1974-83; tchr. San Jose Unified Regional Occupation Program, San Jose, 1977; pvt. practice accounting San Jose, 1977—; lectr. San Jose State U., 1977—. Mem. AICPA, Nat. Soc. of Tax Profls., Am. Inst. Tax Studies, Am. Acctg. Assn., Calif. Soc. CPAs, Beta Alpha Psi, Beta Gamma Sigma. Democrat. Jewish. Home: 4544 Strawberry Park Dr San Jose CA 95129-2213 Office: San Jose State U Acctg & Fin Dept San Jose CA 95192

KERVER, THOMAS JOSEPH, editor, consultant; b. Cleve., Nov. 9, 1934; s. William F. and Hope M. (Roberts) K.; m. Elizabeth G. Galloway, Apr. 12, 1969 (div. Apr. 1990); children: Kenneth, Stephen, Suzanne, Sarah. BA, Xavier U., 1956; M of Mil. Arts and Scis., U.S. Army Gen. Staff Coll., 1966; MA in Polit. Sci., U. Wis., 1972, MA in Journalism, 1972. Commd. 2d lt. U.S. Army, 1956, advanced through grades to lt. col., 1976; pres. Kerver People, Ft. Collins, Colo., 1976-80; dir. communications, publicity Colo. Bankers Assn., Denver, 1980-82; sr. editor Cardiff Pub. Co., Englewood, Colo., 1982-90; bus. editor Cablevision Mag., Denver, 1990—; prof. journalism Colo. State U., Ft. Collins, 1978-80; vice chmn. Larimer County Budget Adv. Com., Ft. Collins, 1978-79; chmn. Larimer Conty Pvt. Industry Coun., Ft. Collins, 1979-80; adv. bd. Nat. Cable TV Mus. Inst. Contbr. articles to profl. jours. Organizer Larimer County Dem. Party, Ft. Collins, 1976-80; cons. Nat. Urban Indian Coun., Denver, 1980-81; organizer, affiliate Clinton for Pres. Campaign, Denver, 1992. Decorated Bronze Star (4), Legion of Merit (2); recipient Presdl. Citation award Pres. Jimmy Carter, 1980, Cert. of Distinction award Nat. Alliance Bus., 1980, Morton Margolin award Disting. Nat. Bus. Reporting, 1993, 94, 1st prize Best Editl. Dept., Chilton Publs., 2nd prize Assn. Bus. Press Editors, 1996. Mem. Cable/Satellite Broadcasters Assn. Asia (chartered), Soc. Satellite Profls. Roman Catholic. Home: 7652 E Nassau Ave Denver CO 80237-2135 Office: Chilton Comm 600 S Cherry St Ste 400 Denver CO 80222-1706

KERWIN, WILLIAM JAMES, electrical engineering educator, consultant; b. Portage, Wis., Sept. 27, 1922; s. James William and Nina Elizabeth (Haight) K.; m. Madolyn Lee Lyons, Aug. 31, 1947; children: Dorothy E., Deborah K., David W. B.S., U Redlands, 1948; M.S., Stanford U., 1954, Ph.D., 1967. Aero. research scientist NACA, Moffett Field, Calif., 1948-59; chief measurements research br. NASA, Moffett Field, Calif., 1959-62, chief space tech. br., 1962-64, chief electronics research br., 1964-70; head electronics dept. Stanford Linear Accelerator Ctr., 1962; prof. elec. engring. U. Ariz., Tucson, 1969-85, prof. emeritus, 1986—. Author: (with others) Active Filters, 1970, Handbook Measurement Science, 1982, Instrumentation and Control, 1990, Handbook of Electrical Engineering, 1993; contbr. articles to profl. jours.; patentee in field. Served to capt. USAAF, 1942-46. Recipient Invention NASA, 1969, 70; recipient fellow NASA, 1966-67. Fellow IEEE (Centennial medal 1984). Home: 1981 W Shalimar Way Tucson AZ 85704-1250 Office: U Ariz Dept Elec and Computer Engring Tucson AZ 85721

KESEY, KEN, writer; b. La Hunta, Colo., Sept. 17, 1935; s. Fred and Geneva (Smith) K.; m. Norma Faye Haxby, May 20, 1956; children: Shannon, Zane, Jed (dec. 1984) Sunshine. B.S., U. Oreg., 1957; postgrad., Stanford U., 1958-60. Pres. Intrepid Trips, Inc., 1964; editor, pub. mag. Spit in the Ocean, 1974—. Author: One Flew Over the Cuckoo's Nest, 1962, Sometimes a Great Notion, 1964, Garage Sale, 1973, Demon Box, 1986, Little Trickler the Squirrel Meets Big Double the Bear, 1988, (co-author) Caverns, 1989, The Further Inquiry, 1990, The Sea Lion, 1991, Sailor Song, 1992, (with Ken Babbs) Last Go Round: a Real Western, 1994; author, prodr.: (play) Twister, 1995. Address: 85829 Ridgeway Rd Pleasant Hill OR 97455-9627

KESSELHEIM, A. DONN, environmental education educator; b. Billings, Mont., June 2, 1927; s. Bernhard and Bernice (Allen) K.; m. Chelsea Robbins, June 22, 1949; children: Alan Stanton, Craig, Ann Noel. BA in Econs., Stanford U., 1948; MA in Social Studies and History, U. Northern Colo., Greeley, 1951; EdD in Ednl. Adminstrn., Harvard, 1964. Assoc. dir., head sci. dept. Tarsus Coll., Tarsus, Turkey, 1952-57; physics tchr. Newton High Sch., Newtonville, Mass., 1957-59, housemaster, 1959-61; tchr. Newton Pub. Schs., Newton, Mass., 1957-61; prin. New Trier Twp. High Sch., 1963-65; with New Trier Twp. Pub. Schs., Winnetka, Ill., 1963-68; prin. New Trier High Sch. West, 1965-68; corp. planner Gen. Learning Corp., N.Y.C., 1967-68; coord. tng. Nat. Alliance of Businessmen, Gen. Learning Corp, Chgo., 1968; prof. Sch. Edn. U. Mass., Amherst, Mass., 1970-74; dep. supr. El Paso County Sch. Dist. 11, Colorado Springs, Colo., 1974-76; staff dir. Colo. Mt. Trail Found., Englewood, Colo., 1976-77; acting prin. Tarsus Am. Sch., Tarsus, Turkey, 1978-79; headmaster Woodstock Sch., Mussoorie, India, 1979-81, Robert Coll., Turkey, 1982-84; sr. cons. Turkey Devel. Found., Ankara, Turkey, 1984-85; dir edn. Wyoming Outdoor Coun., Lander, Wyo., 1985-94, Wyo. Riparian Assn., 1994—; dir. Antelope Retreat Ctr., Savery, Wyo., 1993—. Contbr. to profl. jours. With U.S. Navy, 1945-46. Mem. Phi Delta Kappa (delegate pres. 1992-94). Democrat. Mem. Soc. of Friends. Home and Office: 22 Pheasant Run Dr Lander WY 82520-9783

KESSLER, KEITH LEON, lawyer; b. Seattle, July 18, 1947; s. Robert Lawrence and Priscilla Ellen (Allbee) K.; m. Lynn Elizabeth Eisen, Dec. 24, 1980; children: William Moore, Christopher Moore, Bradley Moore, Jamie Kessler. BA in Philosophy, U. Wash., 1969, JD, 1972. Bar: Wash. 1972, U.S. Dist. Ct. (we. dist.) Wash. 1973, U.S. Dist. Ct. (ea. dist. 1992); U.S. Ct. Appeals (9th cir.) 1973, U.S. Supreme Ct. 1975. Law clk. to Hon. Robert Finley Wash. Supreme Ct., Olympia, Wash., 1972-73; ptnr. Kessler, Tegland & Urmston, Seattle, 1973-75, Kessler & Urmston, Seattle, 1975-76, Kessler, Urmston & Sever, Seattle, 1976-77, Kessler & Sever, Seattle, 1977-79; assoc. Stritmatter & Stritmatter, Hoquiam, Wash., 1980-83; ptnr. Stritmatter, Kessler & McCauley, Hoquiam, Wash., 1983-93, Stritmatter Kessler, Hoquiam, Wash., 1993—; chmn. LAW PAC, Seattle, 1991-93. Editor: Trial Evidence, 1996, author: (with others) Motor Vehicle Accident Litigation Desk Book, 1988, 1995. Pres. Kairos Ctr., Aberdeen, Wash., 1984-86; co-founder Grays Harbor Support Group; bd. dir. Wash. State Head Injury Found., Bellevue, Wash., 1993—. Recipient Founders award Wash. State Head Injury, 1990, Silver award United Way, 1992; Named Trial Lawyer of the Year Wash. State Trial Lawyers, 1994. Mem. Am. Bd. Trial Advocates, (pres. Wash. chpt. 1996), Wash. State Trial Lawyers Assn. (pres. 1990-91), Damage Attys. Round Table, Wash. Trial Attys. Political Forum (chmn. 1993-95), Trial Lawyers for Public Justice (exec. com. 1994—). Office: Stritmatter Kessler 407 8th St Hoquiam WA 98550-3607

KESSLER, PETER BERNARD, computer scientist, researcher; b. N.Y.C., Apr. 5, 1952; s. Richard Howard and Marian Judith (Singer) K.; m. Monica Elaine McHenney, Dec. 27, 1984; children: Jacob Mitchell, Samuel Morris, Ryan Michael. BS, Yale Coll., 1973; MS, U. Calif., Berkeley, 1980, PhD, 1984. Mem. rsch. staff Xerox Palo Alto (Calif.) Rsch. Ctr., 1985-90; staff engr. Sun Microsystems Labs., Inc., Mountain View, Calif., 1990-94; sr. staff engr. Sun Soft, Mountain View, Calif., 1994-95, Java Soft, Cupertino, Calif., 1995—. Reviewer various confs. and jours.; contbr. articles to profl. jours. Judge paper airplanes Palo Alto Jr. Mus., 1990-94. Mem. IEEE, Assn. for Computing Machinery, Computer Profls. for Social Responsibility. Office: Sun Microsystems Inc 2550 Garcia Ave Mountain View CA 94043-1100

KESSLER, ROBERT ALLEN, data processing executive; b. N.Y.C., Feb. 2, 1940; s. Henry and Caroline Catherine (Axinger) K.; m. Marie Therese Anton, Mar. 17, 1967; children: Susanne, Mark. BA in Math., CUNY, 1961; postgrad., UCLA, 1963-64. EDP analyst Boeing Aircraft, Seattle, 1961-62; computer specialist System Devel. Corp., Santa Monica, Calif., 1962-66; mem. tech. staff Computer Scis. Corp., El Segundo, Calif., 1966-67, sr. mem. tech. staff, 1971-72, computer scientist, 1974-81; systems mgr. Xerox Data Systems, L.A., 1967-71; prin. scientist Digital Resources, Algiers, Algeria, 1972-74; sr. systems cons. Atlantic Richfield, L.A., 1981-94; computer cons., 1994—. Mem. Big. Bros. L.A., 1962-66; precinct capt. Goldwater for Pres., Santa Monica, 1964; mem. L.A. Conservancy, 1987. Mem. Assn. Computing Machinery. Home: 6138 W 75th Pl Los Angeles CA 90045-1634 Office: ARCO 515 S Flower St Los Angeles CA 90071-2201

KESSLER, STEPHEN JAMES, writer, editor; b. L.A., Jan. 12, 1947; s. Jack and Nina (Ifland) K.; 1 child, Claire Kessler-Bradner. BA, Bard Coll., 1968; MA, U. Calif., Santa Cruz, 1969. Editor Green Horse Press, Santa Cruz, 1973-79; editor, pub. Alcatraz Edits., Santa Cruz, 1979-85, The Sun, Santa Cruz, 1986-89; editor OutLook, Mendocino, Calif., 1994; freelance poet, translator, essayist, journalist, 1972—. Author: (translation) Destruction or Love, 1976; author: Beauty Fatigue, 1978; editor mag./anthology Alcatraz, 1979-85; contbr. essays to Poetry Flash, 1985-96.

KESTNER, ROBERT RICHARD, II, engineering psychologist; b. Ft. Belvoir, Va., Oct. 18, 1948; s. Robert Richard and Mary Eunice (Wooten) K.; m. Durema Joyce Hall, Dec. 27, 1970; children: James Michael, Jacob Paul. AB in Edn., U. N.C., 1970; MS in Human Sys., Fla. State U., 1975. Cert. lay spkr. United Meth. Ch. Dir. halfway house Leon County Mental Health Ctr., Tallahassee, Fla., 1973-75; dir. Crossroads Drug Treatment Program, Fayetteville, N.C., 1975-76; edn. officer 7th Army Tng. Command U.S. Army, Vilseck, Germany, 1976-78; dir. mental health ctr. 3d Squadron/2 Armed Cavalry Regiment U.S. Army, Amberg, Germany, 1979-80; chief human factors lab. Tropic Test Ctr. U.S. Army, Republic of Panama, 1985-87; engring. psychologist, project engr. U.S. Army, White Sands Missile Range, N.Mex., 1980-85, 87-96. Author/co-author test reports. Dist. commr., mem. Boy Scouts Am., Alamogordo, N.Mex., 1995-96; mayor White Sands Missile Range, N.Mex., 1981-83. With USN, 1971-73. Recipient Cross and Flame, United Meth. Ch., 1993. Mem. Human Factors Soc. (pres. Rio Grande chpt. 1983-84). Office: White Sands Missile Range Box 88 White Sands Missile Range NM 88002

KESZTHELYI, LASZLO P., volcanologist, geologist; b. Tokyo, Aug. 21, 1968; came to U.S., 1969; s. Csaba P. and Kikuko M. (Kawachi) K. BS, U. Tex., Austin, 1987, U. Tex., Austin, 1988; MS, Calif. Inst. of Tech., 1993, PhD, 1994. Post doctoral fellow NSF, Honolulu, 1994—. Vol. U.S. Geol. Survey Hawaii Nat. Park, 1991—, Nat. Park Svc. 1994; assoc. rsch. U. Hawaii, 1996—. Office: Hawaii Volcano Obs USGS Hawaii Nat Pk PO Box 51 Hawaii National Park HI 96718

KETCHEL, STEVEN J., internist; b. Cleve., May 5, 1946; s. Bertram J. and Ruth Sydney (Kavanau) K.; m. Marta Lee Fingado, May 29, 1972; children: Aron, Alana. AB, Stanford U., 1967; MD, U. Ariz., 1972. Diplomate Am. Bd. Internal Medicine. Intern and resident in internal medicine U. Ariz. Affiliated Hosps., Tucson, 1972-75; fellow in med. oncology M.D. Anderson Hosp., Houston, 1975-77; pvt. practice, Tucson, 1977—; trustee El Dorado Hosp., Tucson, 1992-95, chief of staff, 1993-95. Bd. dirs. Pima County unit Am. Cancer Soc., Tucson, 1990—, vice chmn. 1994-96, chmn., 1996—. Fellow ACP; mem. AMA, Am. Soc. Internal Medicine, Am. Soc. Clin. Oncology. Office: Hematology-Oncology Physicians PC 2625 N Craycroft Rd Ste 200 Tucson AZ 85712-2254

KETCHERSID, WAYNE LESTER, JR., medical technologist; b. Seattle, Oct. 16, 1946; s. Wayne Lester and Hazel May (Greene) K.; m. Wilette LaVerne Mautz, Oct. 6, 1972; 1 son, William Les. BS in Biology, Pacific Luth. U., 1976, BS in Med. Tech., 1978; MS in Adminstrn., Ctrl. Mich. U., 1990; postgrad. Kennedy Western U., 1996—. Cert. med. technologist; cert. clin. lab. dir. Nat. Cert. Agy. for Med. Lab. Pers. Staff technologist Tacoma Gen. Hosp., 1978-79, chemistry supr., 1979-81, head chemistry, 1981-83; head chemistry Multicare Med. Ctr., 1984-86, mgr., 1986-93, clin. lab. scientist, 1993—. Mem. Nat. Rep. Com. With U.S. Army, 1966-68. William E. Slaughter Found. scholar, 1975-76. Mem. Am. Soc. Clin. Lab. Sci. (cert., chmn. region IX adminstrn. 1984-94, nat. del. 1984—, vice chmn. govt. affairs com. 1991-92, chmn. 1992-93, vice chair, 1993-94, bd. trustees polit. action com. 1991-97, treas. 1994-97, nat. licensure coord. 1996—, sec./treas. bd. dirs. 1996—, nominee Mem. of Yr. 1992, Bd. Dirs. award 1994, Mendelson award 1994, Pres. award 1996), Wash. State Soc. Clin. Lab. Sci. (chmn. biochemistry sect. 1983-86, dist. pres. 1986—, co-chair ann. meeting 1996, cert. merit 1983, 84, 86, 88, pres. 1988-89, 89-90, mem. of the yr., 1990, chmn. govt. affairs com. 1991-92, chmn. 1992—, Pres.'s award 1996), Am. Soc. Clin. Pathologists (med. technolgist), N.W. Med. lab. Symposium (chmn. 1986-88, 90, 92), Alpha Mu Tau. Lutheran. Contbr. articles to profl. jours. Office: 2906 S 274th Pl Auburn WA 98001-1803

KETCHUM, MILO SMITH, civil engineer; b. Denver, Mar. 8, 1910; s. Milo Smith and Esther (Beatty) K.; m. Gretchen Allenbach, Feb. 28, 1944 (dec. Dec. 21, 1990); children: David Milo, Marcia Anne, Matthew Phillip, Mark Allen. B.S., U. Ill., 1931, M.S., 1932; D.Sc. (hon.), U. Colo., 1976. Asst. prof. Case Sch. Applied Sci., Cleve., 1937-44; engr. F.G. Browne, Marion, Ohio, 1944-45; owner, operator Milo S. Ketchum, Cons. Engrs., Denver, 1945-52; partner, prin. Ketchum, Konkel, Barrett, Nickel & Austin, Cons. Engrs. and predecessor firm, Denver, 1952—; prof. civil engring. U. Conn., Storrs, 1967-78; emeritus U. Conn., 1978—; mem. Progressive Architecture Design Awards Jury, 1958, Am. Inst. Steel Constrn. Design Awards Jury, 1975, James F. Lincoln Arc Welding Found. Design Awards Jury, 1977; Stanton Walker lectr. U. Md., 1966. Author: Handbook of Standard Structural Details for Buildings, 1956; editor-in-chief Structural Engineering Practice, 1981-84; contbr. engring. articles to tech. mags. and jours. Recipient Disting. Alumnus award U. Ill., 1979. Mem. Am. Concrete Inst. (hon., bd. dirs., Turner medal 1966), ASCE (hon., pres. Colo. sect.), Am. Cons. Engrs. Coun., Nat. Acad. Engring., Am. Engring. Edn., Structural Engrs. Assn. Colo. (pres.), Cons. Engrs. Coun. Colo. (pres.), Sigma Xi, Tau Beta Ph, Chi Epsilon, Phi Kappa Phi, Alpha Delta Phi. *Everyone makes mistakes. The more you do, the more mistakes you make. The important thing is what you do with your mistakes. If you disregard them and say they do not exist, then you are in trouble. You must follow through until the problem caused by the mistake is solved.*

KETCHUM, ROBERT GEORGE, college administrator; b. Spokane, Wash., Feb. 21, 1951; s. Robert Harris and Mary Catherine (Bach) K.; m. Heather Dawn Matheson, Feb. 17, 1985; 1 child, Tiernan Robert. BA, Ea. Wash. U., 1973, MEd, 1976; PhD in Edn., Wash. State U., 1985; postgrad., Maharishi European Rsch. U., 1976-77. Indsl. arts tchr. Sandy (Oreg.) Elem. Schs., 1973-75; instr. indsl. tech. dept. Ea. Wash. U., Cheney, 1977-78; dir. Spokane office Am. Fedn. for Sci. of Creative Intelligence, 1978-80; instr. tech. tng. program Maharishi Internat. U., Fairfield, Iowa, 1980-81, dir. tech. tng. program, 1981-82, dir. tech. tng. programs, asst. prof. tech. tng., 1985-90; assoc. dean instrn., workforce tng. and cmty. edn. North Idaho Coll., Coeur d'Alene, 1990—. Mem. ASCD, ASTD, Am. Vocat. Assn., Epsilon Pi Tau, Phi Delta Kappa. Home: 1376 Circle Dr Hayden ID 83835-9503 Office: North Idaho Coll Workforce Tng Ctr 525 W Clear Water Loop Post Falls ID 83854-9400

KETTEMBOROUGH, CLIFFORD RUSSELL, computer scientist, consultant, manager; b. Pitesti, Arges, Romania, June 8, 1953; came to U.S., 1983; s. Petre and Constanta (Dascalu) I. MS in Math., U. Bucharest, Romania, 1976; MS in Computer Sci., West Coast U., L.A., 1985; MS in Mgmt. Info. System, West Coast U., Los Angeles, 1986; PhD in Computer and Info. Sci., Pacific We. U., 1988; MBA, U. LaVerne, 1992; PhD in Bus. Adminstrn., U. Santa Barbara, 1996. Lic. mathematician. Mathematician, programmer Nat. Dept. Chemistry, Bucharest, 1976-80; sr. programmer, analyst Nat. Dept. Metallurgy, Bucharest, 1980-82; sr. software engr. Xerox Corp., El Segundo, Calif., 1983-88; computer and info. scientist Jet Propulsion Lab. NASA, Pasadena, Calif., 1988-89; task mgr. Rockwell Internat., Canoga Park, Calif., 1989-91, cons., 1991-93; mgr. micro devel. Transam. Corp., L.A., 1993-95; MIS dir. Maxicare Health Plans, L.A., 1995—; adj., asst. prof. W. Coast U., Chapman U., U. Redlands, Nat. U., U. Phoenix, Union Inst., 1991—. Contbr. articles to profl. jours. Sec. Romanian Nat. Body Bldg. Com., Bucharest, 1980-82; pres., chmn. Bucharest Mcpl. Body Bldg. Com., 1978-82. Served to lt. Romanian Army, 1978. Mem. IEEE, Assn. for Computing Machinery. Republican. Home: 6004 N Walnut Grove Ave San Gabriel CA 91775-2530

KEVANE, RAYMOND A., career consultant, management consultant; b. Rembrandt, Iowa, Dec. 18, 1928; s. Michael and Sarah A. (Distel) K.; m. Lillian A. Schiltz, July 26, 1972; children: Karen, Mark, Mary. B.A., Loras Coll., Dubuque, Iowa, 1950; S.T.L., Gregorian U., Rome, 1954; Doctorate, Lateran U., Rome, 1957. Adminstr. social programs and assistance to disadvantaged projects, 1957-71; chief cons., assoc. dir. J. Frederick Marcy & Assocs., Portland, Oreg., 1972-78; pres., chief cons. R.A. Kevane & Assocs., Inc., Portland and Seattle, 1978-91; pres., CEO R.A. Kevane & Assocs., Seattle, 1990—; founder, creator The Self Directed Career. Served to capt. Army N.G., 1959-61. Mem. Am. Counselling Assn., Seattle C. of C., Nat. Career Devel. Assn. Author: Career Development Manual, 1979, Business Procedure Manual, 1982, Employment Power: Take Control of Your Career, 1994, Career Consultants Manual, 1995. Office: Ste 160 11201 SE 8th St Bellevue WA 98004

KEVLES, DANIEL JEROME, history educator, writer; b. Phila., Mar. 2, 1939; s. David and Anne (Rothstein) K.; m. Bettyann Holtzmann, May 18, 1961; children: Beth Carolyn, Jonathan David. BA in Physics, Princeton U., 1960; postgrad., Oxford U., 1960-61; PhD in History, Princeton U., 1964. From asst. to full prof. of history Calif. Inst. Tech., Pasadena, 1964-86, Koepfli prof. humanities, 1986—, head program in sci., ethics, and pub. policy, 1987—; vis. rsch. fellow U. Sussex, Brighton, Eng., 1976; vis. prof. U. Pa., Phila., 1979; dir. studies Ecole des Hautes Etudes en Sciences Sociales, Paris, 1991; chmn. of faculty, Calif. Inst. Tech., Pasadena, 1995-97. Author: The Physicists, 1978 (Nat. Hist. Soc. prize 1979), In the Name of Eugenics, 1985; (mag. series) Annals of Eugenics (Page One award 1985); co-editor:

The Code of Codes, 1992; contbr. articles to The New Yorker, N.Y. Rev. Books, other mags. Charles Warren fellow Harvard U., 1981-82, Ctr. for Advanced Study Behavorial Scis. fellow, 1986-87, Nat. Endowment for Humanities sr. fellow, 1981-82, Guggenheim fellow, 1983. Fellow AAAS (chmn. sect. L 1983-85); mem. PEN, Author's Guild, Am. Acad. Arts and Scis., Orgn. Am. Historians, Am. Hist. Assn., History Sci. Soc. (coun 1980-82, com. publ. 1984-88, Sarton lectr. 1985), Am. Philos. Soc., Princeton Club (N.Y.C.), Century Assn., Phi Beta Kappa. Democrat. Office: Calif Inst Tech 1200 E California Blvd Pasadena CA 91125-0001

KEY, JACK DAYTON, librarian; b. Enid, Okla., Feb. 24, 1934; s. Ernest Dayton and Janie (Haldeman) K.; m. Virgie Ruth Richardson, Aug. 12, 1956; children—Toni, Scot, Todd. B.A., Phillips U., Enid, Okla., 1958; M.A., U. N.Mex., 1960; M.S., U. Ill., 1962. Staff supr. Grad. Library U. Ill., 1960-62; pharmacy librarian U. Iowa, 1962-64; med. librarian Lovelace Found. for Med. Edn. and Research, Albuquerque, 1965-70; dir. Mayo Med. Ctr. Librs., Rochester, Minn., 1970-94, dir. emeritus, 1994—; prof. emeritus biomed. comm. Mayo Med. Sch.; cons. in field; participant Naval War Coll. Conf., 1979; Alberta A. Brown lectr. Western Mich. U., 1979. Author: The Origin of the Vaccine Inoculation by Edward Jenner, 1977, William Alexander Hammond (1828-1900), 1979; editor: Library Automation: The Orient and South Pacific, 1975, Automated Activities in Health Sciences Libraries, 1975-78, Classics and Other Selected Readings in Medical Librarianship, 1980, Journal of a Quest for the Elusive Doctor Arthur Conan Doyle, 1982, Medical Vanities, 1982, William A. Hammond, M.D., 1828-1900: The Publications of an American Neurologist, 1983, Classics in Cardiology, Vol. 3, 1983, Vol. 4, 1989, Medical Casebook of Dr. Arthur Conan Doyle from Practitioner to Sherlock Holmes and Beyond, 1984, Medicine, Literature and Eponyms: An Encyclopedia of Medical Eponyms Derived from Literary Characters, 1989, Conan Doyle's Tales of Medical Humanism and Values, 1992; contbr. articles to profl. jours. Served with USN, 1952-55. U. N.Mex. fellow, 1958-59; N.Mex. Library Assn. Marion Dorroh Meml. scholar, 1960; Rotary Paul Harris fellow, 1979; recipient Outstanding Hist. Writing award Minn. Medicine, 1980, Spl. Svc. award Am. Acad. Dermatology, 1992, Farthing award Baker St. Jour., 1993; decorated knight Icelandic Order of Falcon; named to Phillips U. Hall Fame, 1988; named Hall of Fame Phillips U., 1988. Mem. Med. Library Assn., Am. Inst. History Pharmacy, Am. Assn. History Medicine, Am. Med. Writers Assn., Am. Osler Soc. (pres. 1990-91), Mystery Writers of Am., Alcuin Soc., Ampersand Club, Sigma Xi (cert. of recognition 1982). Mem. Christian Ch. (Disciples of Christ). Home: PO Box 231 54 Skyline Dr Sandia Park NM 87047 Office: Mayo Clinic Rochester MN 55905

KEY, JACK ROLLIN, contracting officer; b. Battle Creek, Mich., Jan. 7, 1946; s. Shirly and Emma Lee (Jefferies) K.; m. Yvonne Kay Goodman, Oct. 7, 1995. Grad., Western Mich. U., 1971-75. Contracting officer U.S. Army Elex Command, Ft. Monmouth, N.J., 1978-85, U.S. Army Contracting Command, Heidelberg, Germany, 1985-89, C.E., Riyadh, Saudi Arabia, 1989-92, NATO Base, Keflavic, Iceland, 1992-94, USMC, Oceanside, Calif., 1994—. Office: USMC Contracting Office PO Box 1609 Oceanside CA 92051

KEY, MARY RITCHIE (MRS. AUDLEY E. PATTON), linguist, author, educator; b. San Diego, Mar. 19, 1924; d. George Lawrence and Iris (Lyons) Ritchie; children: Mary Helen Key Ellis, Harold Hayden Key (dec.), Thomas George Key. Student, U. Chgo., summer 1954, U. Mich., 1959; M.A., U. Tex., 1960, Ph.D., 1963; postgrad., UCLA, 1966. Asst. prof. linguistics Chapman Coll., Orange, Calif., 1963-66; asst. prof. linguistics U. Calif., Irvine, 1966-71; assoc. prof. U. Calif., 1971-78, prof., 1978—, chmn. program linguistics, 1969-71, 75-77, 87—; cons. Am. Indian langs., Spanish, in Mexico, 1946-55, S.Am., 1955-62, English dialects, 1968-74, Easter Island, 1975, Calif. Dept. Edn., 1966, 70-75, Center Applied Linguistics, Washington, 1967, 69; lectr. in field. Author: Comparative Tacanan Phonology, 1968, Male/Female Language, 1975, 2d edit., 1996, Paralanguage and Kinesics, 1975, Nonverbal Communication, 1977, The Grouping of South American Indian Languages, 1979, The Relationship of Verbal and Nonverbal Communication, 1980, Catherine the Great's Linguistic Contribution, 1980, Polynesian and American Linguistic Connections, 1984, Comparative Linguistics of South American Indian Languages, 1987, General and Amerindian Ethnolinguistics, 1989, Language Change in South American Indian Languages, 1991; founder, editor: newsletter Nonverbal Components of Communication, 1972-76; mem. editoral bd. Forum Linguisticum, 1976—, Lang. Scis., 1978—, La Linguistique, 1979—, Multilingua, 1987—; contbr. articles to profl. jours. Recipient Friends of Libr. Book award, 1976, hon. mention, Rolex awards for Enterprise, project Computerizing the Languages of the World, 1990; U. Calif. Regent's grantee, 1974, Fulbright-Hays grantee, 1975; faculty rsch. fellow, 1984-85. Mem. Linguistic Soc. Am., Am. Dialect Soc. (exec. council; regional sec. 1974-83), Internat. Reading Assn. (dir. 1968-72), Delta Kappa Gamma (local pres. 1974-76). Office: U Calif-Irvine Dept Linguistics Irvine CA 92697-5100

KEYLER, ROBERT GORDON, material handling company executive; b. Elgin, Ill., May 9, 1958; s. Robert Dean and Lois Jean (Hobbs) K.; m. Linda Jane Mendes, Sept. 21, 1988 (div. Jan. 1993). Grad., Morris County Vo-Tech., 1980. Mgr. Gardentown Ctr., Rockaway, N.J., 1976-80, Genuine Parts-NAPA, Albuquerque, 1980-88; owner G&B Enterprises, Albuquerque, 1988-91; sales rep. Parts Plus of Albuquerque, 1989-91; v.p. sales and purchasing Material Handling Specialists, Albuquerque, 1991—; cons. in field. Sponsor Youth of Unity, Albuquerque, 1980—; bd. dirs. Unity Ch., Albuquerque, 1986—, pres., 1987. Home: 11 Constellation Dr Tijeras NM 87059 Office: Material Handling Specialists 3214 Los Arboles NE Albuquerque NM 87107

KEYSTON, STEPHANI ANN, small business owner; b. Baytown, Tex., Aug. 6, 1955; d. Herbert Howard and Janice Faye (Stowe) Cruickshank; m. George Keyston III, Oct. 8, 1983; children: Jeremy George, Kristopher Samuel. AA with honors, Merced Coll., Merced, Calif., 1975; BA in Journalism with distinction, San Jose State U., 1976. Reporter, Fresno (Calif.) Bee, 1974-75; reporter, photographer Merced (Calif.) Sun-Star, 1974-77; pub. info. officer Fresno City Coll. (Calif.), 1977-80; dir. comms. Aerojet Tactical Sys. Co., Sacramento, 1980-83; co-owner, v.p. Keyco Landscape Contractor Inc., Loomis, Calif., 1984—. Co-coord. Aerojet United Way Campaign, 1981; Aerojet Tactical Sys. Co. coord. West Coast Nat. Derby Rallies, 1981-83; co-founder, pres. Calif. Lion Awareness. Mem. Internat. Assn. Bus. Communicators (dir. Sacramento chpt. 1983), Citrus Heights C. of C. (v.p. 1983). Republican. Home: 13399 Lakeview Pl Auburn CA 95602-8920 Office: Keyco Landscape Contractor Inc 3350 Swetzer Rd Loomis CA 95650-9584

KHACHATOURIANS, GEORGE GHARADAGHI, microbiology educator; b. Nov. 21, 1940; s. Sumbat and Mariam (Ghazarian) K.; m. Lorraine M. McGrath, Oct. 14, 1974; 1 child, Ariane K. BA, Calif. State U., San Francisco, 1966, MA, 1969; PhD, U. B.C., Vancouver, 1971. Postdoctoral fellow Biol. Div. Oak Ridge (Tenn.) Nat. Lab., 1971-73; rsch. assoc. U. Mass. Med. Sch., Worcester, 1973-74; asst. prof. microbiology dept. U. Saskatchewan, Sask., Can., 1974-77, assoc. prof., 1977-80, prof., 1980-81, prof. applied microbiology and food sci., 1981—; mem. Gov. of Can. Fed. Task Force on Biotech., Ottawa, Ont., Can., 1980-81, Operating Grants Panel, Can. Agr., 1981-84, Biomed. Grants Panel, Sask. Health Rsch., 1988—; bd. dirs. PhilomBios Inc., Biolin Rsch. Inc.; pres. Khachatourians Enterprises Inc.; founding dir. BioInsecticide Rsch. Labs., U. Sask, 1982—; vis. prof. U. B.C., Vancouver, 1992. Contbg. author ency. chpts.; co-editor: (book series) Food Biotechnology-Microorganisms, 1995. Recipient Golden Wheel award Rotary Internat., 1996; grantee Nat. Sci. Engring. Coun., Ottawa, 1974-92, Sask. Agr. Rsch. Found., 1981-85, NRC, 1977-78, Agrl. Devel. Found., Regina, 1985—. Mem. Am. Soc. Microbiology, Can. Soc. Microbiology, Soc. Indsl. Microbiology, Am. Entomol. Soc., Soc. Invertabrate Pathology, Internat. Soc. Toxicology. Home: 1125 13th St East, Saskatoon, SK Canada S7H 0C1 Office: U Sask, Applied Micro-Food Sci Dept, Saskatoon, SK Canada S7N 5A8

KHAIAT, LAURENT E., film producer; b. Tel Aviv, Israel, May 25, 1968; came to U.S., 1983; s. Alain Victor and Anna Michelle (Riczker) K.; m. Akemi Nakata, June 2, 1997. Exec. prodr. Los Caminantes en Vivo, L.A., 1989; prodr. The Right Way, L.A., 1990, Death Penalty, L.A., 1994; assoc. prodr. Dark Secret, L.A., 1995, Death Game, Vancouver, B.C., 1996; co-prodr. La Perra de la Frontera, L.A., 1990, Gipsy, L.A., 1990, Killing American Style, L.A., 1991, Samurai Cop, N.Y.C., 1991, Eliminator, L.A., 1992; prodr., dir. Kiss of Steel, 1989; tv prodr. Little Pain, 1995. Recipient Golden Star Halo award So. Calif. Motion Picture Counsel, 1989, Lifetime Membership award, 1989, Jeanie Golden Halo Eagle award, 1989. Office: Motion Pictures Internat 421 N Rodeo Dr #15100 Beverly Hills CA 90210

KHAN, AHMED MOHIUDDIN, finance, insurance executive; b. Hyderabad, Andhra Pradesh, India, Nov. 14, 1955; s. Mohammad Mominuddin and Mehar-Unnisa Begum Hyderabad; m. Marjorie L. Klein-Khan, Mar. 31, 1983; 1 child, Yosuf F. MBA, U. Palm Beach, 1975; doctoral studies, Calif. Coast U. Inventory auditor RGIS, Inc., Chgo., 1975-78; staff acct. Sommerset, Inc., Chgo., 1979-84; fin. cons. Provident Mutual Fin. Svc., Inc., Phoenix, 1985-91; regional mgr. fin. svcs. US Life/Old Line Life Ins. Co. of Am., Phoenix, 1992—; pres. Khan and Assocs., Fin./Ins. Svcs., Phoenix, 1993—. Named to Execs. Hall of Fame, 1991. Mem. India Assn., U.S.A., Assn. MBA Execs., Nat. Assn. Life Underwriters, Ariz. Assn. Life Underwriters, Millon Dollar Round Table. Democrat. Islam. Home and Office: 4643 E Grandview Rd Phoenix AZ 85032-3416

KHAN, KHALID SAIFULLAH, engineering executive; b. Calcutta, India, Sept. 19, 1949; arrived in Can., 1974; s. Tahir Ali and Fatima (Bibi) K.; m. Jamila Bibi, Apr. 20, 1982; children: M. Tariq, Kamron. BEE, Osmania U., 1973; MEE, Concordia U., Montreal, Can., 1978. Asst. exec. engr. Teleglobe Can., Montreal, 1978-80; R&D engr. GTE Internat., Waltham, Mass., 1980-82; sr. engr. Aydin Corp., San Jose, Calif., 1982-84; project engring. mgr. FMC Corp., Dallas, 1984-86; tech. mktg. mgr. Dalsat Inc., Plano, Tex., 1986-89; system engr. Andrew Corp., Richardson, Tex., 1989-90; mgr. SATCOM engring. MCI Telecomm., Richardson, 1990-96; dir. Lockheed Martin Missiles and Space, Sunnyvale, Calif., 1996, Century Telephone Enterprises, Monroe, La., 1996—; tchr. U. Dallas, Tex., 1988-91; seminar presenter in field. Contbr. articles to profl. jours. Mem. IEEE, Order of Engr. of Que., Can. Home: PO Box 6068 Monroe LA 71211 Office: CTE PO Box 4065 Monroe LA 71211

KHANDEKAR, SHEKHAR DINKAR, electrical engineer; b. Indore, India, Aug. 28, 1956; came to U.S., 1982; s. Dinkar N. and Sulochana D. (Dhavale) K.; m. Sandhya C. Bhave, July 22, 1982; children: Kunal, Kavita. BSEE, U. Indore, India, 1979; MSEE, Northwestern U., 1984. Electronics engr. Naidunia, Indore, 1980-81, Indian Express, Bombay, 1981-82; failure analysis engr. Tex. Instruments, Houston and Dallas, 1984-88; sr. component engr. Allen Bradley Co., Milw., 1988; mgr. device analysis Compaq Computer Corp., Houston, 1988-93; mgr. reliability assurance Level One Comms., Sacramento, 1993—. Author: Failure Analysis Handbook, 1993; author conf. papers. Mem. organizing com. Houston Marathi Mandal, 1985-86. Mem. IEEE (mem. tech. com. internat. reliability physics symposium 1992—, publs. chair 1997—, chair tech. subcom. 1995), ASM Internat. (organizing com. internat. symposium on test and failure analysis 1990—, vice chair 1996—). Democrat. Hindu. Office: Level One Comm 9750 Goethe Rd Sacramento CA 95827-3500

KHANJIAN, ARA, economics educator; b. Beirut, Lebanon, Apr. 2, 1956; came to U.S., 1976; BA in Econs., U. British Columbia, 1981; MA in Econs., Queen's U., 1982; PhD in Econs., The New Sch. for Social Rsch., N.Y.C., 1989. Econ. instr. St. John's U., N.Y.C., 1984-85, N.Y.U., 1985-88; prof. econs. Ventura (Calif.) Coll., 1989—; econ. instr. Hofstra U., Hempstead, N.Y., 1986-87; prof. econs. L.A. Harbor Coll., 1989; cons., researcher The Econ. Inst. of Ministry of Economy, Yerevan, Armenia, 1991. Rsch. fellow Govt. Can., 1981. Mem. Am. Econ. Assn., Assn. for Comparative Econ. Studies. Office: Ventura Coll 4667 Telegraph Rd Ventura CA 93003-3872

KHATAIN, KENNETH GEORGE, psychiatrist, former air force officer; b. Seattle, Oct. 11, 1953; s. Edward and LaVerne Mae (Bender) K.; m. Marla Dee Morgan, Aug. 12, 1978; children: Alanna E., Larissa E. AAS, Edmonds Community Coll., Lynnwood, Wash., 1976; BS in Molecular and Cellular Biology, U. Wash., 1978; MD, Wayne State U., 1986. Diplomate Am. Bd. Psychiatry and Neurology with qualifications in geriatric psychiatry, Nat. Bd. Med. Examiners. Resident in psychiatry Wright State U., Dayton, Ohio, 1986-90; commd. capt. USAF, 1986; advanced through grades to maj., 1992; chief inpatient psychiatry mental health svcs. Wilford Hall Med. Ctr., Lackland AFB, Tex., 1990-94; chief inpatient psychiatry VA Med. Ctr., Boise, Idaho, 1994—; guest reviewer AIDS articles Psychiat. Svcs., 1988—; clin. cons. Nat. Tng. Lab. Inst., Bethel, Maine, 1989; workshop presenter, guest speaker in field. Mem. adult edn. com. Westminster Presbyn. Ch., Dayton, 1989. Recipient physician recognition award AMA, 1989, Arnold Allen outstanding resident award Wright State U., 1990. Mem. Am. Psychiat. Assn., Tex. Soc. Psychiat. Physicians, Bexar County Psychiat. Soc., Phi Beta Kappa, Phi Theta Kappa. Office: VA Med Ctr 500 W Fort St Boise ID 83702-4501

KHOO, ROBERT E.H., colon and rectal surgeon; b. Sydney, New South Wales, Australia, Nov. 21, 1956; came to the U.S., 1992.; s. Anthony and Patricia (Lim) K.; m. Sheryl Ann Khoo, Oct. 9, 1982; children: Justin, Jonathan. BS, U. British Columbia, 1978; MD, U. Calgary, Can., 1981. Diplomate Am. Bd. Surgery, Am. Bd. Colon and Rectal Surgery. Staff surgeon Calgary Dist. Hosp. Group, 1987-92, Rose Med. Hosp., Denver, 1992—; asst. clin. prof. surgery U. Colo., Denver, 1994—. Contbr. articles to profl. jours. Fellow ACS, Royal Coll. Physicians and Surgeons Can., Am. Soc. Colon and Rectal Surgeons. Office: 4600 Hale Pkwy Ste 400 Denver CO 80220

KHOSLA, VED MITTER, oral and maxillofacial surgeon, educator; b. Nairobi, Kenya, Jan. 13, 1926; s. Jagdish Rai and Tara V. K.; m. Santosh Ved Chabra, Oct. 11, 1952; children: Ashok M., Siddarth M. Student, U. Cambridge, 1945; L.D.S., Edinburgh Dental Hosp. and Sch., 1950, Coll. Dental Surgeons, Sask., Can., 1962. Prof. oral surgery, dir. postdoctoral studies in oral surgery Sch. Dentistry U. Calif., San Francisco, 1968—; chief oral surgery San Francisco Gen. Hosp.; lectr. oral surgery U. of Pacific, VA Hosp.; vis. cons. Fresno County Hosp. Dental Clinic.; Mem. planning com., exec. med. com. San Francisco Gen. Hosp. Contbr. articles to profl. jours. Examiner in photography and gardening Boy Scouts Am., 1971-73, Guatemala Clinic, 1972. Granted personal coat of arms by H.M. Queen Elizabeth II, 1959. Fellow Royal Coll. Surgeons (Edinburgh), Internat. Assn. Oral Surgeons, Internat. Coll. Applied Nutrition, Internat. Coll. Dentists, Royal Soc. Health, AAAS, Am. Coll. Dentists; mem. Brit. Assn. Oral Surgeons, Am. Soc. Oral Surgeons, Am. Dental Soc. Anesthesiology, Am. Acad. Dental Radiology, Omicron Kappa Upsilon. Club: Masons. Home: 1525 Lakeview Dr Hillsborough CA 94010-7330 Office: U Calif Sch Dentistry Oral Surgery Div 3D Parnassus Ave San Francisco CA 94117-4342 *It is part of the cure to wish to be cured. With God all things are possible.*

KIANG, ASSUMPTA (AMY KIANG), brokerage house executive; b. Beijing, Aug. 15, 1939; came to U.S., 1962; d. Pei-yu and Yu-Jean (Liu) Chao; m. Wan-lin Kiang, Aug. 14, 1965; 1 child, Eliot Y. BA, Nat. Taiwan U., 1960; MS, Marywood Coll., Scranton, Pa., 1964; MBA, Calif. State U., Long Beach, 1977. Data programmer IBM World Trade, N.Y.C., 1963; libr. East Cleve. Pub. Libr., 1964-68; lectr. Nat. Taiwan U., Taipei, 1971-73; with reference dept. U.S. Info. Svc., Taipei, 1971-74; v.p. Merrill Lynch, Santa Ana, Calif., 1977-96; v.p., sr. fin. cons. Merrill Lynch, Costa Mesa, Calif., 1996—. Author numerous rsch. reports in field. Founder Pan Pacific Performing Arts Inc., Orange County, Calif., 1987; treas. women league Calif. State U., Long Beach, 1980-82. Mem. AAUW (treas. Newport-Costa Mesa br. 1996—), Chinese Bus. Assn. Soc. Calif. (chmn. 1987—, v.p. 1986-87), Chinese Am. Profl. Women's League (treas. 1993, pres. 1997—), Pacific Rim Investment and trade Assn. (vice-chair 1994-96), U.C.I. Chancellor's Club, Old Ranch Country Club. Democrat. Roman Catholic. Office: Merrill Lynch 650 Town Center Dr Ste 500 Costa Mesa CA 92626

KIBBLE, EDWARD BRUCE, insurance-investment advisory company executive; b. Seattle, May 11, 1940; s. Francis Bruce and Doris Kibble; m. Carol Kibble, July 8, 1961; 3 children. BA, U. Wash., 1972. CLU. Agt. Equitable of Iowa, Seattle, 1962-72; co-founder, co-chmn. Kibble & Prentice, Inc., Seattle, 1972—; bd. dirs. Seattle Best Coffee, Kibble & Prentice/KPI-Western Ins., Seattle, Drug Emporium, Bellevue, Wash., Northwestern Trust. Contbr. articles to profl. jours. Bd. dirs. Jr. Achievement Greater Puget Sound, Seattle Pacific Found. Mem. Assn. for Advanced Life Underwriting, Nat. Assn. Life Underwriters (Seattle Life Underwriter of Yr. award), Million Dollar Round Table, Estate Planning Coun. Seattle (past pres.), Wash. Athletic Club, Columbia Tower Club, Rainier Club, Seattle Yacht Club, Rotary (bd. dirs. Seattle). Republican. Office: 600 Stewart St Ste 1000 Seattle WA 98101-1217

KICKERT, JULIANA ARLENE, private investor; b. Blue Island, Ill., Sept. 1, 1943; d. Robert J. and Delia (Vander Giessen) K.; m. Durwood Perry Long, July 14, 1973 (div. Oct. 1974). AA, U. Fla., 1963, BS, 1965; MS, Ind. U., 1971. Registered real estate sales, Ill., Chgo. Instr. Chgo. Bd. Edn., 1965-71; dir. legal office program Sauk Area Career Ctr., Crestwood, Ill., 1973-76; real estate sales Kahn Kaplan Realty, Inc., Chgo., 1977-86; pvt. investor Sedona, Ariz. Apptd. Yavapai County Mounted Posse Search and Rescue Team, 1994—. Recipient Life Time Coop. Sales award North Side Real Estate Bd., Chgo., 1984, Top 20 Residential Salesperson award Condex Info. Svcs., 1984, 86; named Ariz. Horsewoman of Yr. Bridle & Bit Newspaper, 1990. Mem. Verde Valley Horsemen's Coun., Sedona Saddle Club (founding mem., pres. 1990-92, bd. dirs. 1993-94), Mensa, Delta Pi Epsilon. Republican. Home and Office: PO Box 459 Placerville CO 81430

KIDD, REUBEN PROCTOR, management engineer; b. Bedford, Va., Feb. 18, 1913; s. Oscar Kibbler and Estelle (Johnson) K.; B.S., Va. Poly. Inst., 1936; m. Margaret Jerome, June 23, 1952. Pres., Frito Corp. of Roanoke (Va.), 1947-49; indsl. engr. USAF, Sacramento, 1956-73; chmn. bd. USDR, Inc., Sacramento, 1961-69, MEN Internat., Inc., Mpls., 1977—; owner The Kidd Cos., operator Precision Tune-Up, Sacramento, 1974—. Served to capt. U.S. Army, 1942-46, to maj., 1949-51. Decorated Silver Star; registered profl. engr., Calif. Republican. Presbyterian. Home: 5809 Northgrove Way Citrus Heights CA 95610-6522 Office: Precision Tune-Up 6241 Spruce Ave Sacramento CA 95841-2052

KIDDE, ANDREW JUDSON, sales executive, consultant; b. N.Y.C., Nov. 6, 1948; s. Fred Judson and Ellice (Welch) K.; m. Monica Bertell (div. 1981); m. Linda Jean Olsen, Feb. 24, 1983; children: Judson F., Briana P. BA in History, Polic. Sci., Hawthorne Coll., 1971; AA in Hotel Adminstrn., LaSalle U., 1993. Banquet mgr. Sheraton Hotel, Manchester, N.H., 1967-71; asst. dir. sales Hilton Hotel Corp., N.Y.C., 1971-75; regional dir. sales Ramada Inns, Detroit, 1975-77; regional sales mgr. Westin Hotels, Inc., Detroit, 1977-79; pres. Kidde & Assocs., San Diego, 1979-82; nat. sales mgr. Las Vegas (Nev.) Hilton, 1982-85; dir. sales, mktg. Madison Hotels, Washington, 1986-89; sr. nat. sales mgr. Walt Disney Resorts, Anaheim, Calif., 1989-93; sr. sales mgr. Hilton Hotel Corp., Anaheim, Calif., 1993-96; v.p. sales Solidarity Meeting Mgmt. Co., Rancho Santa Margarita, Calif., 1996—. Recipient Nat. Hotel Sales award Guiness Book, 1985, 86. Mem. Greater Washington D.C. Soc. of Assn. Execs. (assoc.), Am. Soc. Assn. Execs. (assoc.), Profl. Conv. Mgmt. Assn. (assoc.). Republican. Home: 30 Charca Rancho Santa Margarita CA 92688-2703 Office: Solidarity Meeting Mgmt Co PO Box 80638 Rancho Santa Margarita CA 92688

KIDDE, JOHN EDGAR, food company executive; b. Kansas City, Mo., May 4, 1946; s. Gustave E. and Mary Sloan (Orear) K.; m. Donna C. Peterson, Aug. 4, 1973; children: Kari Lauren, Laurie Catherine, Kellie Ann. BA, Stanford U., 1968; MBA, Northwestern U., 1971. Corp. banking officer First Interstate Bank, L.A., 1971-73; v.p. ops. Colony Foods, Inc., Newport Beach, Calif., 1973-78; pres. Western Host Food Svcs., Inc., Newport Beach, 1978-81, Giuliano's Delicatessen & Bakery,Inc., Carson, Calif., 1981-90; pres., chief exec. officer Sona & Hollen Foods, Inc., Los Alamitos, Calif., 1990—, bd. dirs. Mem. adv. bd. Restaurant Institutions mag., 1975-78. Trustee Harbor Day Sch., 1990-96; mem. alumni admissions com. Phillips Acad., 1981—. 1st lt. U.S. Army, 1969-70. Mem. Stanford Club Orange County, Stanford Buck Club, Los Alamitos C. of C. Republican. Episcopalian. Home: 3907 Inlet Isle Dr Corona Del Mar CA 92625-1605 Office: Sona & Hollen Foods Inc 3712 Cerritos Ave Los Alamitos CA 90720-2419

KIEFER, RENATA GERTRUD, pediatrician, epidemiologist, economist, international health consultant; b. Lorrach, Baden, Germany, July 4, 1946; came to U.S., 1970; d. Friedrich W. and Gertrud Anna (Keller) K.; m. James C. Bridgman. BA, Stanford U., 1963; MA, U. Calif., Berkeley, 1967; MD, U. Geneva, Switzerland, 1982; MPH, U. Calif., Berkeley, 1990. Diplomate Am. Bd. Pediatrics; cert. in environ. health, Germany. Asst. instr. dissection lab. dept. morphology U. Geneva Sch. of Medicine, Switzerland, 1979-80; interim resident dept. diagnostic radiology Univ. Hosp., Geneva, 1980, intern physician, 1982-83; clin. fellow in pediatrics Harvard Med. Sch., Boston, 1983-85; resident physician Mass. Gen. Hosp., Boston, 1983-85; sr. resident dept. pediatrics U. Calif., San Francisco, 1985-86; attending physician emergency dept. Children's Hosp. Med. Ctr., Oakland, Calif., 1986-94; fellow dept. epidemiology and internat. health U. Calif., San Francisco, 1988-90; German tech. cooperation expert tropical medicine & internat. health Inst. for Health Sci. Rsch., Asuncion, Paraguay, 1990-94, vis. prof. epidemiol. and preventive medicine, 1992—; sci. methods advisor Nat. U. Asuncion, 1994—; chief adv. rsch. and human resource devel. Health Strategies Internat.; rep. of IICS/Internat. Orgns., cons. and presenter in field. Contbr. numerous articles to profl. jours. Co-winner nat. sci. prize Paraguay Parliament, 1994; ASSU scholar Stanford U., 1962-63, Fulbright scholar, 1962-64, Internat. scholar Swedish Inst., 1968, Internat. Health scholar U. Calif., 1990; fellow AAUW, 1968; recipient award USPHS Nat. Rsch. Svc., 1989-90. Address: 6 Locksley Ave San Francisco CA 94122-3854

KIEFER, ROBERT HARRY, real estate broker; b. Tonopah, Nev., Apr. 25, 1945; s. Martin Leon and Anne Alice (Abrahamson) K.; m. Nancy Lynn Resnick, June 19, 1966; children: Courtney Martine, Reed Martin, Tyler Robert. BA in Journalism, U. Minn., 1967. V.p. mktg. Minnetonka Inc., Chaska, Minn., 1972-75; CEO Merchandising's Mktg. Inc., Mpls., 1975-79, Vet. Derm Products Inc., Mission Viejo, Calif., 1979-87; v.p., regional mgr. Calmark Devel., L.A., Las Vegas, Nev., 1987-90; prin., broker Western New Home Sales, Anaheim, Calif., 1990-94; v.p. Real Estate Dimensions, Irvine, Calif., 1994-95; prin., broker Kiefer Tract Sales & Mktg., Irvine, 1995—; mem. sales and mktg. coun. BIA, So. Calif., 1992—. Author: By Word of Mouth..., 1971. Mem. Youth Task Force South Orange County Cmty. Svc. Coun., San Clemente, Calif., 1996; mem. steering com. Surfrider Found., San Clemente, 1996; bd. dirs., mem. Jewish Cmty. Ctr., Orange County, 1996. Mem. Bldg. Industry Assn. (judge 1995-96), San Onofre Surfing Club (v.p. 1991-93), Simon Wiesenthal ctr, Anti Defamation League.

KIEHL, KATHLEEN SUZANNE, English language educator; b. La Grange, Ill., June 4, 1958; d. James Ogden and Barbara JoAnn (Andersen) K.; m. Dennis John Moberg, July 4, 1985; children: Christiaan Anders, Annalise Alleen. BA, San Jose State U., 1981, MA, 1989. C.C. cert., Calif. Adminstrv. asst. Kaiser Electronics, San Jose, Calif., 1978-83; dir. adminstrv. svcs. Leavey Sch. Bus. Santa Clara (Calif.) U., 1983-89; English instr. Cabrillo Coll., Aptos, Calif., 1989—; mem. writing awards com. and composition com. Cabrillo Coll., Aptos, 1994—; reader, presenter Porter Gulch Rev., Aptos, 1994-96. Author poetry and short fiction. Newsletter editor Glen Arbor Sch., Ben Lomond, Calif., 1992—; parent class rep. Quail Hollow Sch., Ben Lomond, 1993—; team mother San Lorenzo Valley Little League, Ben Lomond, 1994. Mem. MLA, Nat. Coun. Tchrs. English. Office: Cabrillo Coll 6500 Soquel Dr Aptos CA 95003-3119

KIEHN, ARTHUR JOHN, chemist, educator; b. Chgo., Nov. 1, 1944; s. Edgar Henry and Emma (Ritter) K.; m. Joan S. Stoltenberg, Aug. 9, 1980; 1 child, Katherine M. BS in Chemistry, U. Wash., 1968, BA in Edn.istry, 1974, MS in Meteorology, 1974. Chemist Bardhal Mfg., Seattle, 1968-74, chief chemist, 1975-84, dir. tech. svcs., 1984-96, v.p. R&D, 1996—; sci. tchr. Seattle Sch. Dist., 1974-75. Contbr. articles to profl. jours.; patentee in field. Mem. Soc. Tribologists and Lubrication Engrs. (co-chair edn. 1986-94), Am. Chem. Soc., Soc. of Automotive Engrs. Office: Bardahl Mfg PO Box 70607 Seattle WA 98107

KIEHN, MOGENS HANS, aviation engineer, consultant; b. Copenhagen, July 30, 1918; came to U.S., 1957; s. Hans-Christian and Lydia-Thea-Constans (Theill-Burban de Parmer) K.; m. Ase Rasmusen, Apr. 28, 1942; children: Marianne, Hans, Lars. BS, ME, PE, U. Tech. Engring., Copenhagen, 1940; MS, Copenhagen U., 1942; degree in Army Intelligence, Def. Indsl. Security Inst., 1972. Registered profl. engr., Ariz. Pres. Hamo Engring., Copenhagen, 1939-49, Evanston, Ill., 1958-78; engr. Sundstrand,

Rockford, Ill., 1957-58; pres. Kiehn Internat. Engring., Phoenix, 1980—; chmn., pres. ETO Internat. Engring., Phoenix, 1980—; tech. engring. cons. Scandinavian Airlines, Sundstrand Engring., McDonnell Douglas, Ford, GM, Chrysler, Honeywell, Motorola, Gen. Electric, Hughes Aircraft; chmn. bd. Internat. Tech. Engring. Recipient 32 patents including rehab. hosp. lighting for highmast, drafting machine, tooling machinery, parts for aircraft, garbage and pollution machine, optical coupler, also others. With Finnish Army, 1939, Danish Underground, 1940-45, Morocco French Fgn. Legion, 1948-53, Vietnam. Mem. AIII, NSPE, Soc. Illuminating Engrs., Nat. Geog. Soc., Am. Fedn. Police, East Africa Wildlife Soc., Internat. Intelligence and Organized Crime Orgn., Adventures Club Denmarkk, Honors Club Internat. Office: Internat Tech Engring PO Box 1561 Scottsdale AZ 85252-1561

KIEHN, RUBEN LEWIS, construction cost estimator; b. Woodland, Calif., Dec. 25, 1941; s. Ruben and Ruby Elaine (Condrey) K.; m. Barbara Elaine Hilton, Dec. 2, 1968; children: Kenneth, Shannon, Jeffrey. BA in Econs., Calif. State U., Sacramento, 1981; Bechtel bus. cert., Golden Gate U., 1985. Estimator, project mgr. Woodland Electric Co., Inc., Yuba City, Calif., 1965-81; sr. cost engr. Bechtel Nuclear Fuel Ops., San Francisco, 1981-83; project cost engr. Bechtel Advanced Tech. Divsn., San Francisco, 1983-85; cost engring. supr. Office of the State Arch., Sacramento, 1985-93; mgr. cost control Divsn. of the State Arch., Sacramento, 1993—. Author: The Walls Family of Delaware, 1988, (computer program) Alta Vista Constrn. Estimator, 1993. With U.S. Army, 1961-64. Mem. Am. Assn. Cost Engrs., Del. Hist. Soc., Calif. State U. Sacramento Alumni Assn. Republican. Office: Divsn of the State Arch 8th Fl 1300 I St Fl 8 Sacramento CA 95814-2913

KIELAROWSKI, HENRY EDWARD, marketing executive; b. Pitts., Dec. 29, 1946; s. Henry Andrew Kielarowski and Evelyn Marie Kline Boileau; m. Lynda Blair Powell, Aug. 1971 (div. 1976); children: Amorette, Blair. BA, Duquesne U., Pitts., 1969; MA, Duquesne U., 1974, PhD, 1974. Pres. Communicators, Inc., Pitts., 1974-76; mktg. specialist McGraw-Hill, Inc., N.Y.C., 1976-81; mktg. dir. Fidelity S.A., Allison Park, Pa., 1981-86; exec. v.p. ARC Systems, Inc., Pitts., 1986-88; v.p. mktg. Providian Bancorp, San Francisco, 1988—. Author: Microcomputer Consulting in the CPA Environment, 1987; contbr. articles to profl. jours. Mem. Am. Mktg. Assn. (mktg. excellence award 1988), Direct Mktg. Assn. Democrat. Home: 107 Lyon St San Francisco CA 94117-2112

KIELHORN, RICHARD WERNER, chemist; b. Berlin, Germany, June 17, 1931; s. Richard H. and Auguste (Lammek) K.; m. Anneliese Heinrich, Aug. 9, 1952; children: Anita, Margit. BS, Chem. Tech. Sch., Berlin, 1953. Lab. tech. Zoellner Werke, Berlin, 1950-57, Montrose Chem. Corp., Henderson, Nev., 1957-78; chief chemist Stauffer Chem. Corp., Henderson, 1978-88, Pioneer Chlor Alkali Co., Henderson, 1988-92; tax. cons. H&R Block, Las Vegas, Nev., 1972-96, Exec. Tax Svc., instr., 1978-95. Mem. ASTM, Am. Chem. Soc., Am. Soc. Quality Control, Nat. Soc. Tax Profls., Nat. Assn. Tax Practitioners. Home: 1047 Westminster Ave Las Vegas NV 89119-1825

KIELSMEIER, CATHERINE JANE, school system administrator; b. San Jose, Calif; d. Frank Delos and Catherine Doris (Sellar) MacGowan; M.S., U. So. Calif., 1964, Ph.D., 1971; m. Milton Kielsmeier; children: Catherine Louise, Barry Delos. Tchr. pub. schs. Maricopa, Calif.; sch. psychologist Campbell (Calif.) Union Sch Dist., 1961-66; asst. prof. edn. and psychology Western Oreg. State Coll., Monmouth, 1966-67, 70; asst. research prof. Oreg. System Higher Edn., Monmouth, 1967-70; dir. spl. services Pub. Schs., Santa Rosa, Calif., 1971-91; cons., 1991—. Mem. Sonoma County Council Community Services, 1974-84, bd. dirs. 1976-82, Sonoma County Orgn. for Retarded/Becoming Independent, 1978-84, bd. dirs. 1978-82; bd. dirs. Gold Ridge Sangha, 1994-97, Hosp. Chaplaincy Svcs., 1996—. Office: 7495 Poplar Dr Forestville CA 95436-9671

KIENHOLZ, LYN SHEARER, international arts projects coordinator; b. Chgo.; d. Mitchell W. and Lucille M. (Hock) Shearer; student Sullins Coll., Md. Coll. Women. Assoc. producer Kurt Simon Prodns., Beverly Hills, Calif., 1963-65; owner, mgr. Vuokko Boutique, Beverly Hills, 1969-75; bd. dirs. L.A. Inst. Contemporary Art, 1976-79, Fellows of Contemporary Art, 1977-79, Internat. Network for Arts, 1979-89, L.A. Contemporary Exhbns., 1980-82; exec. sec., bd. dirs. Beaubourg Found. (now George Pompidou Art and Culture Found.), 1977-81; visual arts adv. Performing Arts Coun., L.A. Music Ctr., 1980-89; bd. govs. Calif. Inst. Tech. Baxter Art Gallery, 1980-85; adv. bd. dirs. Fine Arts Communications, pub. Images & Issues mag., 1981-85; founder, chmn. bd. Calif./Internat. Arts Found., 1981—; bd. dirs., western chmn. ArtTable 1983-89; bd. dirs. Galef Inst., 1992—; exec. bd. Sovereign Fund, 1981-93; exec. bd. dirs. Scandinavia Today, 1982-83, Art L.A., 1987, 88, 89; mem. adv. bd. Otis/Parsons Sch. Design, 1983-85, U. So. Calif. dept. fine arts, 1983-85; bd. dirs. UK/LA Festival of Britain, 1986-88, 92-94; hon. bd. dirs. L'Ensemble des Deux Mondes, Paris, 1986-91; mem. Comité Internat. pour les Musées d'Art Moderne, 1985—, bd. dirs., 1991—; mem. adv. bd. Cyber Studios, 1996—; Bd. dirs. Arts, Inc., 1987-89. Mem. adv. bd. dirs. CyberStudios, 1996—. Co-host nat. pub. radio program ARTS/L.A., 1987-91; contbg. editor Calif. mag., 1984-89. Address: 2737 Outpost Dr Los Angeles CA 90068-2061

KIERSCH, GEORGE ALFRED, geological consultant, retired educator; b. Lodi, Calif., Apr. 15, 1918; s. Adolph Theodore and Viola Elizabeth (Bahmeier) K.; m. Jane J. Keith, Nov. 29, 1942; children—Dana Elizabeth Kiersch Haycock, Mary Annan, George Keith, Nancy McCandless Kiersch Bohnett. Student, Modesto Jr. Coll., 1936-37; B.S. in Geol. Engring., Colo. Sch. Mines, 1942; Ph.D. in Geology, U. Ariz., 1947. Geologist 79 Mining Co., Ariz., 1946-47; geologist underground explosion tests and Folsom Dam-Reservoir Project U.S. C.E., Calif., 1948-50; supervising geologist Internat. Boundary and Water Commn., U.S.-Mex., 1950-51; asst. prof. geology U. Ariz., Tucson, 1951-55, dir. Mineral Resources Survey Navajo-Hopi Indian Reservation, 1952-55; exploration mgr. resources survey So. Pacific Co., San Francisco, 1955-60; assoc. prof. geol. sci. Cornell U., Ithaca, N.Y., 1960-63, prof., 1963-78, prof. emeritus, 1978—, chmn. dept. geol. scis., 1965-71; geol. cons., Ithaca, 1960-78, Tucson, 1978—; chmn. coordinating com. on environment and natural hazards, Internat. Lithosphere Program, 1986-1991. Author: Engineering Geology, 1955, Mineral Resources of Navajo-Hopi Indian Reservations, 3 vols., 1955, Geothermal Steam-A World Wide Assessment, 1964; author: (with others) Advanced Dam Engineering, 1988; editor/author: Heritage of Engineering Geology--First Hundred Years 1888-1988 (vol. of Geol. Soc. Am.), 1991; editor: Case Histories in Engineering Geology, 4 vols., 1963-69; mem. editorial bd. Engring. Geology/Amsterdam, 1965—. Mem. adv. coun. to bd. trustees Colo. Sch. Mines, 1962-71, pres. coms., 1990—; mem. nine coms. NAE/NAS, 1966-90; reporter coordinating com. 1 CCI Nat. Hazards U.S. GeoDynamics Com., 1985-90. Capt. C.E., U.S. Army, 1942-45. NSF sr. postdoctoral fellow Tech. U. Vienna, 1963-64; recipient award for best article Indsl. Mktg. Mag., 1964. Fellow ASCE, Geol. Soc. Am. (chmn. div. engring. geology 1960-61, mem. U.S. nat. com. on rock mechanics 1980-86, Disting. Practice award 1986, Burwell award 1992); mem. Soc. Econ. Geologists, U.S. Com. on Large Dams, Internat. Soc. Rock Mechanics, Internat. Assn. Engring. Geologists (U.S. com. 1980-86, chmn. com. 1983-87, v.p. N.Am. 1986-90), Assn. Engring. Geologists (1st receipient Claire P. Holdredge award 1965, 93, hon. mem. 1985), Cornell Club (N.Y.C.), Statler Club, Tower Club (Ithaca), Mining Club of Southwest (Tucson). Republican. Episcopalian. Home and Office: 4750 N Camino Luz Tucson AZ 85718-5819

KIESECKER, ROBERT, retired military officer, educator; b. Glen Cove, N.Y., June 2, 1935; s. John and Helen (Smith) K.; m. Sept. 28, 1958; children: Robert Jr., Peter J., Diana M. AA, Mesa C.C., 1976; BA in Ind. Edn., Ariz. State U., 1978. Cert. fed. insp. OSHA. Maintenance technician Motorola, Ariz., 1974, Garratt, Phoenix, 1980; tech., elec. and electronics tchr. Westwood H.S., Mesa, Ariz., 1978-90, Kino Jr. H.S., Mesa, 1990-95; owner R&R TV Svc., 1976-90; ret., 1995. With USAF, 1953-66, U.S. Army, 1966-74. Mem. KC (grand knight 1977, dist. dep. 1978-86, state program dir. 1986-88, faithful navigator 1986, marshall 1986-90, master 1990-95), VFW (quartermaster), DAV, Life mem. OSHA Occupl. Safety and Health Inspector. Democrat. Roman Catholic. Home: 1865 W 5th Pl Mesa AZ 85201

KIEST, ALAN SCOTT, social services administrator; b. Portland, Oreg., May 14, 1949; s. Roger M. and Ellen Kiest; m. Heather L. Griffin; 1 child, Jennifer S. BA in Polit. Sci., U. Puget Sound, Tacoma, 1970; MPA, U. Wash., 1979. Welfare eligibility examiner Wash. Dept. Social and Health Services, Seattle, 1970-72, caseworker, 1972-76, service delivery coordinator, 1976-82; community svcs. office adminstr. Wash. Dept. Social and Health Svcs., Seattle, 1982—; planning commr. City of Lake Forest Park, 1989, mem. city coun., 1990—, chair city fin. com., 1992—; mem. King County Mangaged Health Care Oversight Com., 1993-95; mem. King County Human Svcs. Roundtable, 1995—. Mem. Suburban Cities Assn., Met. King County Coun. Reg. Policy Com. Home: 18810 26th Ave NE Lake Forest Park WA 98155 Office: Wash Dept Social & Health Svcs 14360 SE Eastgate Way Bellevue WA 98007

KILBOURN, ALDEAN GAE, secondary educator; b. Olympia, Wash., Apr. 27, 1951; d. Alfred Richard and Alda Jane (Gabel) Lewis; m. David Charles Kilbourn, June 24, 1972; children: Benjamin Lee, Adam Richard, Peter David. BA in Polit. Sci., U. Wash., 1972; teaching cert., U. Alaska, 1974. Tchr. fgn. lang. and social studies West Valley H.S., North Star Borough Sch. Dist., Fairbanks, Alaska, 1981-86; tchr. fgn. lang., social studies, reading North Pole Mid. Sch., Fairbanks, 1987-97; tchr. social studies, English, reading Ryan Mid. Sch., Fairbanks, 1997—; mem. social studies curriculum com. Fairbanks North Star Borough Sch. Dist., 1990—; presenter dist. and statewide confs./insvc. for sch. dist. on various social studies and computer related topics, 1985—. Bd. mem. Cmty. Rsch. Ctr., Fairbanks, 1984-95. Mem. AAUW, Nat. Mid. Sch. Assn., Alaska Coun. Social Studies (bd. dirs. 1989-93), Fairbanks Coun. Social Studies (pres. 1992-96). Republican. Home: 3217 Riverview Dr Fairbanks AK 99709-4741 Office: North Pole Mid Sch 300 E 8th Ave North Pole AK 99705-7664

KILBOURN, LEE FERRIS, architect, specifications writer; b. L.A., Mar. 9, 1936; s. Lewis Whitman and Kathryn Mae (Lee) K.; m. Joan Priscilla Payne, June 11, 1961; children: Laurie Jane, Ellen Mae. BS in Gen. Sci., Oreg. State U., 1963; BS in Architecture, U. Oreg., 1965. Registered architect, Oreg. Specifier Wolff Zimmer Assocs., Portland, Oreg., 1965-75; specifier, assoc. Wolff Zimmer Gunsul Frasca, Portland, 1975-77; specifier, assoc. Zimmer Gunsul Frasca Partnership, Portland, 1977-81, specifier, assoc. ptnr., 1981—. Jr. warden, then sr. warden St. Stephen's Episcopal Parish, Portland. With U.S. Army, 1959-60. Fellow AIA (mem. master spec. rev. com. 1976-78, mem. documents com. 1981-89), Constrn. Specifications Inst. (mem. participating tech. documents com. 1976-78, cert. com. 1980-82, Al Hansen Meml. award Portland chpt. 1987, Frank Stanton Meml. award N.W. region 1987, chpt. pres. 1979-80); mem. Internat. Conf. Bldg. Ofcls. Home: 3178 SW Fairmount Blvd Portland OR 97201-1468 Office: Zimmer Gunsul Frasca Partnership 320 SW Oak St Ste 500 Portland OR 97204-2735

KILBURN, KAYE HATCH, medical educator; b. Logan, Utah, Sept. 20, 1931; d. H. Parley and Winona (Hatch) K.; m. Gerrie Griffin, June 7, 1954; children: Ann Louise, Scott Kaye, Jean Marie. BS, U. Utah, 1951, MD, 1954. Diplomate Am. Bd. Internal Medicine, Am. Bd. Preventive Medicine. Asst. prof. Med. Sch. Washington U., St. Louis, 1960-62; assoc. prof., chief of medicine Durham (N.C.) VA Hosp., 1962-69; prof., dir. environ. medicine Duke Med. Ctr., Durham, 1969-73; prof. medicine and environ. medicine U. Mo., Columbia, 1973-77; prof. medicine and cmty. medicine CUNY Mt. Siai Med. Sch., 1977-80; Ralph Edgington prof. medicine U. So. Calif. Sch. Medicine, L.A., 1980—; pres. Neurotest Inc., 1988—; pres. Workers Disease Detection Svc. Inc., 1986-95. Author: Chemical Brain Injury, 1997; editor-in-chief Archives of Environ. Health, 1986—; editor Jour. Applied Physiology, 1970-80, Environ. Rsch., 1975—, Am. Jour. Indsl. Medicine, 1980—; contbr. more than 200 articles to profl. jours. Capt. M.C., U.S. Army, 1958-60. Home: 3250 Mesaloa Ln Pasadena CA 91107-1129 Office: U So Calif Sch Medicine 2025 Zonal Ave Los Angeles CA 90033-4526

KILEY, ROBERT RALPH, governmental affairs consultant; b. Honolulu, Apr. 21, 1948; s. Kenneth John and Dorothy Irene (Ambrozich) K.; m. Barbara Lynn Weber, Mar. 1985; children: Tiryn Marie, Kristin Leigh. AA, Fullerton Coll., 1971; BA, U. So. Calif., 1975. Adminstrv. aide Hon. Robert H. Finch for U.S. Senate, Fullerton, 1975-76; field supr. Rep. Nat. Com., Washington, 1976; exec. dir. Rep. Party Orange County, Orange, Calif., 1976-80; pres., cons. Robert Kiley & Assocs., Yorba Linda, Calif., 1980—; lead advancement Pres. and Mrs. Ronald Reagan, Washington, 1984-88. Bd. dirs. Bd. Psychology, Sacramento, 1984-92; chmn. legis. com. Sacramento, 1986-92; co-founder Save Our State-Proposition 1987; pres. Cmty. West Devel. Corp. Named One of Outstanding Young Men Am., 1977-81; recipient Cert. Appreciation Anaheim Lions Club, 1987, Calif.-Nev. Lions Internat., 1988. Mem. U. So. Calif. Alumni Assn. (life). Office: 5028 Vista Montana Yorba Linda CA 92886-4594

KILEY, THOMAS, rehabilitation counselor; b. Mpls., Aug. 18, 1937; s. Gerald Sidney and Veronica (Kennedy) K.; m. Jane Virginia Butler, Aug. 25, 1989; children: Martin, Truman, Tami, Brian. BA in English, UCLA, 1959; MS in Rehab. Counseling, San Francisco State U., 1989. Cert. rehab counselor, nat. and Hawaii. Former rsch. profl., businessman various S.E. Asian cos.; sr. social worker Episcopal Sanctuary, San Francisco, 1986-88; dir. social svcs. Hamilton Family Ctr., San Francisco, 1988-89; rehab. specialist Intracorp, Honolulu, 1989-91; pres. Heritage Counselling Svc., Honolulu, 1991—; pres. Hunter Employment Svcs., Yuma, Ariz., Brawley and Salinas, Calif., 1995—. Mem. Am. Counseling Assn., Nat. Assn. Rehab. Profls. in Pvt. Sector, Am. Rehab. Counselors Assn. (profl.), Nat. Rehab. Assn., Rehab. Assn. Hawaii, Rotary, Phi Delta Kappa. Office: Heritage Counselling Svcs PO Box 3098 Mililani HI 96789-0098 also: 2450 S 4th Ave # 306 Yuma AZ 85364

KILLEAN, CATHERINE LOUISE, psychotherapist, psychiatric nursing specialist; b. Chgo., July 17, 1945; d. Louis Kiel and Irene (Piwinski) Accorsi; m. James Edward Killean, Jan. 21, 1967; children: Lou, Cathy, Jim, David, Michael. BSN, Loyola U., Chgo., 1967; MA, Bradley U., 1979. Therapist Human Svc. Ctr., Peoria, Ill., 1978-86; pvt. practice Casper, Wyo., 1986-90; instr. U. Wyo., Casper, 1990-95. Chair Natrona County Dems., Casper, 1995-96. Mem. ANA, Am. Orthopsychiat. Assn., Wyo. Counselling Assn., Internat. Women's Writers Guild (regional rep. Wyo. 1990-96). Home: 5138 Alcova Box 3 Casper WY 82604

KILLEBREW, ELLEN JANE (MRS. EDWARD S. GRAVES), cardiologist; b. Tiffin, Ohio, Oct. 8, 1937; d. Joseph Arthur and Stephanie (Beriont) K.; BS in Biology, Bucknell U., 1959; MD, N.J. Coll. Medicine, 1965; m. Edward S. Graves, Sept. 12, 1970. Intern, U. Colo., 1965-66, resident 1966-68; cardiology fellow Pacific Med. Center, San Francisco, 1968-70; dir. coronary care, Permanent Med. Group, Richmond, Calif., 1970-83; asst. prof. U. Calif. Med. Center, San Francisco, 1970-83, assoc. prof., 1983-93, clin. prof. medicine, Univ. Calif., San Francisco, 1992—. Contbr. chpt. to book. Robert C. Kirkwood Meml. scholar in cardiology, 1970; recipient Physician's Recognition award continuing med. edn., Lowell Beal award excellence in teaching, Permante Med. Group/House Staff Assn., 1992. Diplomate in cardiovascular disease Am. Bd. Internal Medicine. Fellow ACP, Am. Coll. Cardiology: mem. Fedn. Clin. Rsch., Am. Heart Assn. (rsch. chmn. Contra Costa chpt. 1975—, v.p. 1980, pres. chpt. 1981-82, chm. CPR com. Alameda chpt. 1984, pres. Oakland Piedmont br. 1995—, bd. dirs. Calif. affiliate). Home: 30 Redding Ct Belvedere Tiburon CA 94920-1318 Office: 280 W Macarthur Blvd Oakland CA 94611-5642

KILLIAN, GEORGE ERNEST, educational association administrator; b. Valley Stream, N.Y., Apr. 6, 1924; s. George and Reina (Moeller) K.; m. Janice E. Bachert, May 26, 1951 (dec.); children: Susan E., Sandra J.; m. Marilyn R. Killian, Sept. 1, 1984. BS in Edn., Ohio No. U., 1949; EdM, U. Buffalo, 1954; PhD in Phys. Scis., Ohio Northern U., 1989. Tchr.-coach Wharton (Ohio) High Sch., 1949-51; insp. USN, Buffalo, 1951-54; dir. athletics Erie County (N.Y.) Tech. Inst., Buffalo, 1954-69; asst. prof. health, phys. edn., recreation Erie County (N.Y.) Tech. Inst., 1954-60, asso. prof., 1960-62, prof., 1962-69; exec. dir. Nat. Jr. Coll. Athletic Assn., Colorado Springs, Colo., 1969—. Editor: Juco Rev., 1960—. Served with AUS, 1943-45. Recipient Bd. Trustees award Hudson Valley C. of C., 1969, Erie County Tech. Inst., 1969, Service award Ohio No. U. Alumni, 1972, Service award Lysle Rishel Post, Am. Legion, 1982; named to Ohio No. U. Hall of Fame, 1979, Olympic Order, IOC, 1996. Mem. U.S. Olympic Com. (dir.), Internat. Olympic Com., Am. Legion, Internat. Basketball Fedn. (pres. 1990—), Internat. U. Sports Fedn. (1st v.p. 1995), Phi Delta Kappa, Delta Sigma Phi. Clubs: Masons, Rotary. Home: 325 Rangely Dr Colorado Springs CO 80921-2655 Office: Nat Jr Coll Athletic Assn PO Box 7305 Colorado Springs CO 80933-7305

KILLIAN, MARK, state legislator. Mem., spkr. dist. 30 Ariz. Ho. of Reps., Phoenix, 1983—. Office: Ariz Ho of Reps 1700 W Washington Rm 223 Phoenix AZ 85007

KILLIAN, RICHARD M., library director; b. Buffalo, Jan. 13, 1942; m. Nancy Killian; children from previous marriage: Tessa, Lee Ann. BA, SUNY, Buffalo, 1964; MA, Western Mich. U., 1965; grad. advanced mgmt. library adminstrn., Miami U., Oxford, Ohio, 1981; grad. library adminstrn. devel. program, U. Md., 1985. Various positions Buffalo and Erie County Pub. Libraries, 1963-74, asst. dep. dir., personnel officer, 1979-80; dir. Town of Tonawanda (N.Y.) Pub. Library, 1974-78; asst. city librarian, dir. pub. svcs. Denver Pub. Library, 1978-79; exec. dir. Nioga Library System, Buffalo, 1980-87; library dir. Sacramento (Calif.) Pub. Library, 1987—. Mem. ALA, Calif. Library Assn., Rotary. Home: 3501 H St Sacramento CA 95816-4501 Office: Sacramento Pub Libr Adminstrn Ctr 828 I St Sacramento CA 95814-2508*

KILLINGSWORTH, KATHLEEN NOLA, artist, photographer, company executive; b. Eglin AFB, Fla., Sept. 5, 1952; d. Marlin Donald Evans and Winnifred Irene (Pelton) Yow; m. Thomas Marion, Dec. 31, 1973 (div. Feb. 1976). Grad. high sch., Myrtle Point, Oreg. Food svc. Internat. Trade Club, Mobile, Ala., 1970-73; food and beverage Gussies Restaurant and Night Club, Coos Bay, Oreg., 1973-77, Libr. Buttery and Pub, Las Vegas, Nev., 1977-79; beverage dir. Laughlin's (Nev.) Riverside Resort, 1979-80; food and beverage Hyatt Regency Maui, Lahaina, Hawaii, 1980-92; realtor assoc. Wailea (Hawaii) Properties, 1990; sole propr. K N Killingsworth Enterprises, Lahaina, 1990—; assoc. Kona Coast Resort II, 1992—; vol. Lahaina Arts Soc., 1992—; mem. Hui No'eau Visual Arts Ctr., Makawao, Maui, Hawaii, 1992—. Artist numerous watercolor and acrylic paintings; photographer nature greeting cards; pub. Photo Jour. Maui I, 1996. Vol. The Word For Today, Lahaina, 1983-87, Kumalani Chapel, Kapalua, Hawaii, 1983-87, Maui Special Olympics, 1993—; founding mem. & vol. Maui Community Arts & Cultural Ctr.; supporter Teen Challenge, Lahaina, 1987—. Mem. Lahina Arts Soc., 1992—. Republican. Office: K N Killingsworth Enterprises PO Box 5369 Lahaina HI 96761-5369

KILMER, JOSEPH CHARLES, secondary school educator; b. Omaha, Nov. 21, 1942; s. Randall Delmore and Helen June (Barber) K.; m. Marietta Josée van Eek, Dec. 21, 1963; children: Jason Robert, Ryan Patrick, Derek Christian. BS, U. Wash., 1965, MA, 1970. Cert. secondary tchr., Wash. Tchr. Sch. Dist. # 121, Port Angeles, Wash., 1965-95; ret., 1995; coach various sports Sch. Dist. #121, Port Angeles, 1966-78; computer lab./rsch. ctr. supr. Chrysalis Sch. for Ind. Study, Woodinville, Wash., 1996—; bldg. rep. Port Angeles Edn. Assn., 1966-68, 88-90, treas., 1968-69; tchr. assistance program mentor Olympic Endl. Svc. Dist., 1992-93; curriculum and instrn. cons. with Sch. Dist. # 121, 1995-96; enrichment class instr. for N.W. Svcs. P)vt. Industry Coun., summers, 1992-96. Active Port Angeles Children's Theatre, 1982-85, Port Angeles Cmty. Players, 1987-95; mem. exec. bd. Port Angeles YMCA, 1968-71, v.p. bd., 1969, pres. bd., 1970; cubmaster Port Angeles coun. Boy Scouts Am., 1979-84, exec. coun. Mt. Olympus dist., 1979-84; coach YBA youth soccer and basketball, 1979-86; precinct com. person Dem. Com., 1988-96; pres. Clallam County Dem. Club, 1993-96; mem. Friends of the Fine Arts Ctr., Friends of the Libr. Active Port Angeles Children's Theatre, 1982-85, Port Angeles Community Players, 1987-95; mem. exec. bd. Port Angeles YMCA, 1968-71, v.p. bd., 1969, pres. bd., 1970; cubmaster Port Angeles coun. Boy Scouts Am., 1979-84, exec. coun. Mt. Olympus dist., 1979-84; coach YBA youth soccer and basketball, 1979-86; precinct com. person Dem. Com., 1988-96, pres. Clallam County Dem. Club, 1993-96; mem. Friends of the Fine Arts Ctr., Friends of the Libr. Recipient Cubmaster of Yr. award Boy Scouts Am., 1982, Mt. Olympus Dist. Extra Mile award, 1982, Profl. Excellence award Northwest Svcs./Pvt. Industry Coun., 1993. Mem. NEA, Port Angeles Edn. Assn., Wash. Edn. Assn. (500-Hour Service award 1969), Princeton Parents Assn. Nat. Com., Phi Delta Kappa.

KILMER, MAURICE DOUGLAS, marketing executive; b. Flint, Mich., Sept. 14, 1928; s. John Jennings and Eleanor Minnie (Gerholz) K.; m. Vera May Passino, Mar. 30, 1950; children: Brad Douglas, Mark David, Brian John, David Scott, Karen Sue. B of Indsl. Engring., Gen. Motors Inst., 1951; MBA, U. Minn., 1969. Quality svcs. mgr. ordnance div. Honeywell, Hopkins, Minn., 1964-69; product assurance dir. peripheral ops. Honeywell, San Diego, 1969-71; pres. Convenience Systems, Inc., San Diego, 1972-75; salesman real estate Forest E. Olson Coldwell Banker, La Mesa, Calif., 1976-77; resident mgr. Forest E. Olson Coldwell Banker, Huntington Beach, Calif., 1977-78; mgmt. cons. Century 21 of the Pacific, Santa Ana, Calif., 1978-83; dir. broker svcs. Century 21 of the Pacific, Anaheim, Calif., 1983-85; exec. dir. Century 21 of S.W., Phoenix, 1985-86; sales assoc. Century 21 Rattan Realtors, San Diego, 1986-88; mgr. Rattan Realtors, San Diego, 1988-92, relocation dir., 1993—. With U.S. Army, 1951-52. Mem. Am. Soc. for Quality Control, San Diego Bd. Realtors. Republican. Home: 29450 Circle R Greens Dr Escondido CA 92026-5910 Office: Rattan Realtors 2878 Camino del Rio Ste 100 San Diego CA 92108-3846

KILMER, NEAL HAROLD, software engineer; b. Orange, Tex., Apr. 24, 1943; s. Harold Norval and Luella Alice (Sharp) K. BS in Chemistry and Math., Northwestern Okla. State U., 1964; MS in Chemistry, Okla. State U., 1971; PhD in Chemistry, Mich. State U., 1979. Rsch. assoc. N.Mex. Petroleum Recovery Rsch. Ctr. N.Mex. Inst. Mining & Tech., Socorro, 1979-81, rsch. chemist, 1981-85, lectr. I geol. engring., 1984, asst. prof. mining engring., 1985-86; phys. scientist Phys. Sci. Lab. N.Mex. State U., Las Cruces, 1986-96; software engr. AlliedSignal Tech. Svcs. Corp., Las Cruces, N.Mex., 1996—. Contbr. articles to profl. jours. Mem. Am. Chem. Soc., Am. Inst. Physics, Soc. Photo-Optical Instrumentation Engrs., Optical Soc. Am., Sigma Xi, Pi Mu Epsilon, Phi Lambda Upsilon. Presbyterian. Home: 2200 Corley Dr Apt 14G Las Cruces NM 88001-5827 Office: Software Maintenance & Tng Facility PO Box 9000 Las Cruces NM 88004

KILPATRICK, ANITA See STAUB, ANITA

KILPATRICK, FRANK STANTON, television commercial product strategy consultant; b. San Jose, Calif., Dec. 2, 1950; s. Frank George and Marian (Polk) K.; AB in Polit. Sci., U. Calif., Berkeley, 1975, postgrad., 1976; student U. Wis., 1968-71. Successively writer, advt. sales rep., Midwest regional mgr., Western mktg. mgr. 13-30 Corp. (Whittle Comm.), 1970-74; with Grey Advt., 1977; mktg. mgr. East/West Network, 1978-79; mktg. dir. Calif. Bus. mag., Los Angeles, 1979-81; v.p. mktg. Harlequin Mags, 1981; gen. mgr. new venture devel. Knapp Comm. Corp. Corp., 1981-96; gen. ptnr. Pacific Cellular, 1982-86; gen. ptnr. Calif. Coast Comm., 1981-84; dir., pres. Pasadena Media Inc., 1984-85; mgmt. cons. Kilpatrick & Assocs., L.A., 1984—; lectr. entrepreneur program U. So. Calif. Sch. Bus. Adminstrn., 1984-85, UCLA Extension, 1989—; pres. Capital Equity Group, 1986-87, WaterMate Tech Corp., 1991-93, Stanford Multi Media Tech. Group, 1991-94, HomeTown Television, 1993—. Vol. counselor 1736 Teen Crisis Ctr., Hermosa Beach, Calif., 1989-90. Mem. L.A. Advt. Club (Belding award 1980), Direct Mktg. Club So. Calif., Western Publs. Assn., World Affairs Counsel, Town Hall Calif., U. Calif. Alumni Assn., Stanford Grad. Bus. Sch. Alumni Assn. (sec. 1985-86, v.p. events 1986-87, dir. 1987-90, pres. 1990-92), Stanford Entrepreneurial Forum (founder), L.A. Venture Assn. (charter mem. 1985—).

KIM, CHAN-HIE, educator, clergyman; b. Hoeryung, Korea, June 7, 1935; came to U.S., 1961; s. Chong-Jin and Kansung (Moon) K.; m. Sook-Chung Kim, Sept. 9, 1962; 1 child, Alexis Hangin. BA, Yonsei U., Seoul, 1958; BD, Vanderbilt U., 1964, PhD, 1970. Ordained deacon United Methodist Ch., 1965, ordained elder, 1967. Acad. instr. Air Command and Staff Coll., Korean Air Force, 1958-60; asst. prof. religion Yonsei U., 1971-72; staff Bd. of Discipleship, United Meth. Ch., Nashville, 1974-77; dir. Ctr. for Asian-Am. Ministries, Claremont, Calif., 1977-87; affiliate prof. N.T. Claremont Sch. of Theology, 1977-87, prof. N.T., 1987—; prof. religion Claremont Grad. Sch., 1987—; bd. dirs. U. So. Calif. Korean Heritage Libr., L.A., 1990—, Ctr. for Pacific-Asian Am. Ministries, Claremont, 1987—. Author: Form and Structure of Familiar Greek Letter of Recommendation, 1970. Bd. dirs. Korean Heritage Libr., USC, 1994—; rschr. Korean-Am. Rsch.

Inst., L.A., 1994—. Mem. Soc. Bibl. Lit., Am. Acad. Religion. Office: Claremont Sch of Theology 1325 N College Ave Claremont CA 91711-3154

KIM, EDWARD WILLIAM, ophthalmic surgeon; b. Seoul, Korea, Nov. 25, 1949; came to U.S., 1957; s. Shoon Kul and Pok Chu (Kim) K.; m. Carole Sachi Takemoto, July 24, 1976; children: Brian, Ashley. BA, Occidental Coll., Los Angeles, 1971; postgrad. Calif. Inst. Tech., 1971; MD, U. Calif.-San Francisco, 1975; MPH, U. Calif.-Berkley, 1975. Diplomate Nat. Bd. Med. Examiners, Am. Bd. Ophthalmology. Intern, San Francisco Gen. Hosp., 1975-76; resident in ophthalmology Harvard U.-Mass. Eye and Ear Infirmary, Boston, 1977-79; clin. fellow in ophthalmology Harvard U., 1977-79; clin. fellow in retina Harvard, 1980; practice medicine in ophthalmic surgery, South Laguna and San Clemente, Calif., 1980—; vol. ophthalmologist Eye Care Inc., Ecole St. Vincent's, Haiti, 1980, Liga, Mex., 1989; chief staff, South Coast Med. Ctr., 1988-89; assoc. clin. prof. dept. ophthalmology, U. Calif., Irvine. Founding mem. Orange County Ctr. for Performing Arts, Calif., 1982, dir. at large, 1991; pres. Laguna Beach Summer Music Festival, Calif., 1984. Reinhart scholar U. Calif.-San Francisco, 1972-73; R. Taussig scholar, 1974-75. Fellow ACS, Am. Acad. Ophthalmology, Royal Soc. Medicine, Internat. Coll. Surgeons; mem. Calif. Med. Assn., Keratorefractive Soc., Orange County Med. Assn., Mensa, Expts. in Art and Tech. Office: Harvard Eye Assocs 665 Camino De Los Mares Ste 102 San Clemente CA 92673-2840

KIM, HAN PYONG, dentist, researcher; b. Seoul, Korea, May 2, 1945; s. Koe Jin and Jung Bok (Park) K.; m. Young Sook Yoon, Apr. 27, 1974; 1 child, Sung Mo. MA, DDS, Seoul Nat. U., 1975; PhD, Yonsei U., Seoul, 1982; MA, Monterey Inst. Internat. Study, 1996. Prof. Yonsei U., Seoul, 1977-84; vis. scholar UCLA, 1982; project rschr. for health care sys. Korea Dental Assn., Seoul, 1988-92; mem. bd. health ins. Nat. HIC, Seoul, 1990-92. Mem. Pres.'s Leadership Circle, Washington, 1995. Home: PO Box 3854 Carmel CA 93921-3854

KIM, JAY, congressman; b. Korea, 1939; m. June, 1961; children: Richard, Kathy, Eugene. BS, U. So. Calif., MCE; MPA, Calif. State U. Mem. City Coun. city of Diamond Bar, Calif., 1990, mayor, 1991; mem. 103rd Congress from 41st dist. Calif., 1993—; pres., founder Jaykim Engrs. Inc. Recipient Outstanding Achievement in Bus. and Community Devel. award, Engr. of Yr. award, Caballero de Distinction award, Engr. Bus. of the Yr. award, others. Republican. Methodist. Office: US Ho of Reps 435 Cannon Washington DC 20515

KIM, JOUNG-IM, communication educator, consultant; b. Taejon, Choongnam, Republic of Korea, May 8, 1947; came to U.S., 1975; d. Yong-Kap Kim and Im-Soon Nam; m. James Andrew Palmore, Jr., Jan. 21, 1989 (div. Nov. 1993). BA in Libr. Sci., Yonsei U., Seoul, Korea, 1970, postgrad., 1974-75; postgrad., U. Hawaii at Manoa, 1975, MA in Sociology, 1978; PhD in Comm., Stanford U., 1986. Rschr. Korean Inst. Family Planning, Seoul, 1974-75; spl. resource person UN/East-West Ctr., Honolulu, 1976; rsch. asst. East-West Ctr., Honolulu, 1977-78; rsch., teaching asst. Stanford (Calif.) U., 1979-83, instr., 1984; asst. prof. U. Hawaii at Manoa, Honolulu, 1984-95, assoc. prof., 1995—; cons. UN Econ. and Social Commn. for Asia and Pacific, Bangkok, 1979, 84-86, 89, 90-92; cons. UN Devel. Program, Devel. Tng. Comm. Planning, Bangkok, 1984, UN Population Funds, N.Y.C., 1991, 92; mem. faculty communication and info. scis. doctoral program U. Hawaii at Manoa, Honolulu, mem. faculty Ctr. Korean Studies. Contbr. articles to profl. jours., monographs, and chpts. to books. Grantee East-West Ctr., 1972, 75-78; Population Libr. fellow U. N.C., 1973; Stanford U. fellow, 1978-79, 83, 84. Mem. Internat. Comm. Assn., Internat. Network for Social Network Analysis. Office: U Hawaii at Manoa 2560 Campus Rd # 336 Honolulu HI 96822-2217

KIM, KARL EUJUNG, urban planning educator; b. Junction City, Kans., Sept. 5, 1957; s. Yee Sik and Young Soon (Lee) K.; m. Shilla K.H. Yoon, Mar. 25, 1989; children: Kelly Hosue, Kenneth Taysoo. AB, Brown U., 1979; PhD, MIT, 1987. Asst. prof. urban and regional planning U. Hawaii Manoa, Honolulu, 1987-91, assoc. prof., 1991—; pres. Progressive Analytics, Inc., Honolulu, 1993. Mem. editl. bd. Korean Studies, 1989— mem. editl. bd. Accident Analysis and Prevention, 1995—; contbr. articles to profl. publs. Commr. Rental Housing Trust Fund, Honolulu, 1992-93; mem. exec. bd. dirs. Common Cause Hawaii, 1993-94; elected to Manoa Neighborhood Bd., 1993. Fulbright fellow, Korea, 1991; scholar-in-residence Western Govs. Assn., Denver, 1990; grantee Hawaii CODES project U.S. Dept. of Transp./Nat. Hwy. Traffic Safety Adminstrn., 1992. Mem. Am. Planning Assn. (pub. issues chairperson 1991), Nat. Rsch. Coun. (mem. transp. rsch. bd. 1990-94), Nat. Safety Coun. (mem. traffic records com. 1990-94). Office: Univ Hawaii Manoa Porteus Hall 107 2424 Maile Way Honolulu HI 96822-2223

KIM, MARK CHRISTOPHER, prosecutor; b. Santa Barbara, Calif., May 11, 1962; s. Dong K. and Soon J. Kim; m. Sunmin Park, Mar. 10, 1990. BA, U. Calif., Berkeley, 1985; JD, Cornell U., 1988. Bar: Calif. 1989, Ill. 1990. Assoc. McKenna, Conner, Cuneo, L.A., 1988-90; dept. dist. atty. L.A. County Dist. Atty.'s Office, 1990—. Mem. ABA, Korean Am. Bar Assn., Calif. Dist. Atty.'s Assn., Phi Beta Kappa. Republican. Home: 18 Aspen Way Rolling Hills CA 90274 Office: LA County Dist Atty 210 W Temple St Fl 17 Los Angeles CA 90012

KIM, SANG U., gastroenterologist; b. South Korea, Aug. 16, 1963. BSEE, U. Wash., 1986, MD, 1990. Diplomate Am. Bd. Internal Medicine, sub-bd. Gastroenterology. Resident in internal medicine U. Wash. Med. Ctr., Seattle, 1990-93, fellow in gastroenterology, 1993-95; pvt. practice Gastrointestinal and Liver Clinic of Edmonds, Wash., 1995—. Office: Gastrointestinal & Liver Clinic Edmonds 21616 76th Ave W Ste 207 Edmonds WA 98026

KIM, YONGMIN, electrical engineering educator; b. Cheju, Korea, May 19, 1953, came to U.S., 1976; s. Ki-Whan and Yang-Whi (Kim) K.; m. Eunai Yoo, May 21, 1976; children: Janice, Christine, Daniel. BEE, Seoul Nat. U., Republic of Korea, 1975; MEE, U. Wis., Madison, 1979, PhD, 1982. Asst. prof. U. Wash., Seattle, 1982-86, assoc. prof., 1986-90, prof., 1990—; bd. dirs. Optimedx, Precision Digital Images, Redmond, Wash.; cons. MITRE Corp., McLean, Va., 1990, Lotte-Canon, Seoul, 1991, Seattle Silicon, Bellevue, Wash., 1990-93, U.S. Army, 1989-96, Neopath, Inc., Bellevue, Wash., 1989-90, Trinius Ptnrs., Seattle, 1989-91, Samsung Advanced Inst. Tech., Suwon, Republic of Korea, 1989-92, Daewoo Telecom Co., Seoul, 1989-91, Intel Corp., Santa Clara, 1992, Aptec Systems, Portland, Oreg., 1992-93, Optimedx, Seattle, 1992-96, Precision Digital Images, Redmond, Wash., 1994-96, Micro Vision, Seattle, 1994-96, Hitachi, Tokyo, 1995—, Fujitsu, Tokyo, 1995—; bd. dirs. Image Computing Systems Lab., 1984—, Ctr. for Imaging Systems Optimization, 1991, Optimedx, 1993-96, U. Wash. Image Computing Libr. Consortium, 1995—; program evaluator Accreditation Bd. for Engring. and Tech., 1992—. Contbr. numerous articles to profl. jours., chpts. in books; editor Proceedings of the Annual International Conference of the IEEE EMBS, vol. 11, 1989, Proceedings of the SPIE Medical Imaging Conferences, vol. 1232, 1990, vol. 1444, 1991, vol. 1653, 1992, vol. 1897, 1993, vol. 2164, 1994, vol. 2431, 1995, vol. 2707, 1996, vol. 3031, 1997; mem. numerous editl. bds.; inventor in field. Mem. various nat. coms., chmn. steering com. IEEE TMI; chmn. numerous confs. Recipient Career Devel. award Physio Control Corp., 1982; grantee NIH, 1984—, NSF, 1984—, U.S. Army, 1986—, USN, 1986—; Whitaker Found. biomed. engring. grantee, 1986. Fellow Am. Inst. Med. and Biological Engring., IEEE (Early Career Achievement award 1988, Disting. Speaker 1991); mem. Assn. Computing Machinery, Soc Photo-Optical Instrumentation Engrs., Tau Beta Pi, Eta Kappa Nu. Presbyterian. Subspecialties: computer engring., multimedia, high-performance image computing workstations, image processing, computer graphics, medical imaging, and virtual reality. Home: 4431 NE 189th Pl Seattle WA 98155-2814

KIMBALL, RICHARD WILSON, reporter, copy editor; b. Nashua, N.H., Aug. 14, 1938; s. Rowe Wilson and Helen Louise (Thompson) K.; m. Barbara Helen Adams, Apr. 8, 1961 (div. Sept. 1975); children: Richard Michael, Daniel Wilson; m. Veronica Lucille McGovern/Barnes, Nov. 21, 1992. BA, U. N.Mex., 1976; Cert. mag. pub., NYU, 1978. Concession mgr. Benson's Wild Animal Farm, Hudson, N.H., 1953-59; typesetter Ray's Typesetting, Inc., Nashua, N.H., 1960-66; photo compositor U. N.Mex., Albuquerque, 1966-76; sr. VDT writer Westinghouse Electric Corp., Albuquerque, 1980-83; tech. writer Tiguex Editorial Svcs., Albuquerque, 1985-88; editor, reporter Chino Valley (Ariz.) Rev., 1988-92; reporter Prescott (Ariz.) Daily Courier, 1992—; editorial advisor Corrales Village Press, Corrales, N.Mex., 1975-76. Newsletter editor Distant Drums, 1985-86; inventor bd. game Patolli, the game of the Aztecs, 1986; pub., writer more than 100 limited edit. hist. booklets, 1980—. With USCG, 1977-79. Democrat. Buddhist. Home: 39 Woodside Dr Prescott AZ 86301-5092 Office: Prescott Daily Courier 147 N Cortez St Prescott AZ 86301-3015

KIMBALL, SPENCER LEVAN, lawyer, educator; b. Thatcher, Ariz., Aug. 26, 1918; s. Spencer Woolley and Camilla (Eyring) K.; m. Kathryn Ann Murphy, June 12, 1939; children: Barbara Jean (Mrs. Thomas Sherman), Judith Ann (Mrs. William Stillion), Kathleen Louise, Spencer David, Kent Douglas, Timothy Jay. BS, U. Ariz., 1940; postgrad., U. Utah, 1946-47; BCL, Oxford (Eng.) U., 1949; SJD, U. Wis., 1958. Bar: Utah 1950, Mich. 1965, Wis. 1968, U.S. Dist. Ct. (we. dist.) Wis. 1968, U.S. Supreme Ct. 1982, U.S. Ct. Appeals (9th cir.) 1986. Assoc. prof. U. Utah Coll. Law, Salt Lake City, 1949-50, dean, 1950-54, prof., 1954-57, rsch. prof., 1993—; prof. U. Mich., 1957-68, dir. legal research Law Sch., 1962-67; staff dir. Wis. Ins. Law Revision Project, 1966-79; prof. law, dean U. Wis. Law Sch., 1968-72; exec. dir. Am. Bar Found., Chgo., 1972-82; prof. law U. Chgo., 1972-88, Seymour Logan prof., 1978-88, Seymour Logan prof. emeritus, 1988—. Lt. USNR, 1943-46. Fellow Am. Bar Found.; mem. ABA, Mich. State Bar, Utah State Bar, Wis. State Bar, Internat. Assn. Ins. Law (hon pres., past pres. U.S. chpt., mem. presdl. council), Phi Beta Kappa, Phi Kappa Phi. Author: Insurance and Public Policy (Elizur Wright award), 1960, Rsch. award Am. Bar Found., Fellow Outstanding Rsch. in Law and Gov't, 1984, Am. Bar Assn. Section of Torts and Ins. Practice, Robert B. Mckay award Lifetime contrubutions to Ins. and Tort Law, 1991; Introduction to the Legal System, 1966; Essays in Insurance Regulation, 1966, Cases and Materials on Insurance Law, 1992; (with Werner Pfenningstorf) The Regulation of Insurance Companies in the United States and the European Communities: A Comparative Study, 1981; co-editor with Werner & Fennigstorf: Insurance, Government and Social Policy, 1969, Legal Service Plans, 1977; bd. editors: Jour. Ins. Regulation, Internat. Jour. Ins. Law; contbr. articles to profl. jours. Home: 241 N Vine #100 1-W Salt Lake City UT 84103 Office: U Utah Coll Law Salt Lake City UT 84112

KIMBERLEY, A. G., industrial products factory representative, management executive; b. Portland, Oreg., Oct. 29, 1939; s. A. Gurney and Meta (Horgan) K.; m. M. Susan Solie, Sept. 15, 1949 (div.); children: John Langton, Thea Ness; m. Roxanne Johannesen, Mar. 26, 1952. BS, Lewis & Clark Coll., 1959-62; postgrad., U. Oreg., 1963. Mgr. meat and dairy div. Hudson House Co., Portland, 1963-64; pres. Wall-Western Inc., Portland, 1964-92, Kimberley Indsl., Portland, 1982-92; owner Kimberley Boxwood Farm, Wilsonville, Oreg., 1987—, A. G. Kimberley & Co., 1992—; factory rep. to industry including Finale Internat., 1980, Avery Abrasive, 1980, Tape Master Tool Co., 1980, Tifco Spline Inc., 1983, Nachi Corp., 1983, Midwest Press Brake Dies, 1985, Nordic Saw & Tool Co., 1993, Coast to Coast Indsl., 1993, Taurus Tool & Engring., 1995, Greenleaf Corp., 1995, Gen. Indsl. Diamond, 1995, Dianamic Abrasive, 1995, Rsch. Abrasive, 1995. Republican. Episcopalian. Home: 16720 SW Wilsonville Rd Wilsonville OR 97070-7544

KIMBRELL, GRADY NED, author, educator; b. Tallant, Okla., Apr. 6, 1933; s. Virgil Leroy Kimbrell and La Veria Dee Underwood; m. Marilyn Louise King, May 30, 1953 (div.); m. Mary Ellen Cunningham, Apr. 11, 1973; children: Mark Leroy, Lisa Christine, Joni Lynne. BA, Southwestern Coll., Winfield, Kans., 1956; MA, Colo. State Coll., 1958. Cert. tchr. (life), Calif., Colo.; cert. adminstr., Calif. Bus. tchr. Peabody (Kans.) High Sch., 1956-58; bus. tchr. Santa Barbara (Calif.) High Sch., 1958-65, coordinator work edn., 1965-75, dir. research and evaluation, 1975-88; cons., textbook researcher and author. Author: Introduction of Business and Office Careers, 1974, The World of Work Career Interest Survey, 1986; co-author: Succeeding in the World of Work, 1970, 5th rev. edit., 1992, Entering the World of Work, 1974, 3rd rev. edit., 1988, The Savvy Consumer, 1984, Marketing Essentials, 1991, 2d edit., 1996, Office Skills for the 1990's, 1992, Advancing in the World of Work, 1992, Exploring Business and Computer Careers, 1992, Employment Skills for Office Careers, 1995. With U.S. Army, 1953-55. Mem. NEA, Calif. Assn. Work Experience Educators (life, v.p. 1968-70), Nat. Work Experience Edn. Assn., Calif. Tchrs. Assn., Coop. Work Experience Assn. Republican.

KIMBRELL, LEONARD BUELL, retired art history educator, art appraiser; b. Archibald, La., Aug. 3, 1922; s. Lee Baines and Jessie Mae (Wilson) K.; m. Betty Evelyn Davis, Dec. 30, 1942; children: Anna Kathryn, Rebecca Lynn Bogorad. BA, La. State No. Coll., Natchitoches, 1942; MS, U. Oreg., 1950, MFA, 1954; PhD, State U. Iowa, 1965. Tchr. Roseburg (Oreg.) H.S., 1946-48, Parkrose H.S., Portland, Oreg., 1952-54; asst. prof. art history Eastern Oreg. Coll., LaGrande, 1955-61; prof. art history Portland State U., 1961-93, prof. emeritus, 1993—; art appraiser Portland, 1991—. Co-author: McCosh, 1985; contbr. articles to Artweek Northwest Mag., and other publs.; paintings and lithographs in collections at U. Oreg. Mus. and Portland Art Mus. Sgt. U.S. Army, 1942-46, ETO. Recipient rsch. grant Kress Found., Pacific Northwest, 1968. Democrat. Home: 1785 SW Montgomery Dr Portland OR 97201-2482

KIMBROUGH, LORELEI, elementary education educator; b. Chgo.; d. Paul and Lina (Higgs) Bobbett; children: Denise, Devi, Paul, Jeri Lynn. BS in Edn., Ill. State U., 1947; postgrad., DePaul U., Chgo. U., others. Cert. tchr., Ill. Tchr. of Latin and English Greensboro (N.C.) Pub. Schs.; spl. edn. tchr. Chgo. State Hosp./Reed Zone Ctr., Chgo., Jewish Children's Bur., Chgo.; elem. tchr. Chgo. Bd. of Edn., Pasadena (Calif.) High Sch.; English tchr. Malala H.S., Madang, 1993-94; tchr. jr. h.s. Cathedral Chapel Cath. Sch., 1995-96; tutor to fgn. students. Missionary worker L.A. Archdiocese, Papua New Guinea; vol. ARC, Solheim Luth. Home, Glendale Meml. Hosp. Recipient four-year scholarship State of Ill., Chgo. Musical Coll. award. Mem. Nat. Coun. Tchrs. of English, Ill. Coun. of Social Studies, Nat. Coun. Social Studies.

KIMME, ERNEST GODFREY, communications engineer; b. Long Beach, Calif., June 7, 1929; s. Ernest Godfrey and Lura Elizabeth (Dake) K.; BA cum laude, Pomona Coll., 1952; MA, U. Minn., 1954, PhD, 1955; m. Margaret Jeanne Bolen, Dec. 10, 1978; children by previous marriage: Ernest G., Elizabeth E., Karl Frederick. Mem. grad. faculty Oreg. State U., Corvallis, 1955-57; mem. tech. staff Bell Telephone Labs., Murray Hill, N.J., 1957-65, supr. mobile radio rsch. lab., 1962-65; head applied sci. dept. Collins Radio Co., Newport Beach, Calif., 1965-72; rsch. engr. Northrop Electronics, Hawthorne, Calif., 1972-74; sr. staff engr. Interstate Electronics Corp., Anaheim, Calif., 1974-79; dir. advanced systems, dir. advanced comm. systems, tech. dir. spl. comm. programs Gould Navcomm Systems, El Monte, Calif., 1979-82; pres. Cobit, Inc, 1982-84; tech. staff Gen. Rsch. Corp., Santa Barbara, 1984-87; v.p. engring. Starfind, Inc., Laguna Niguel, Calif., 1987-88; dir. engring. R&D Unit Instruments, Orange, Calif., 1988-89; staff scientist Brunswick Def. Systems, Costa Mesa, Calif., 1989-90; v.p. engring. Redband Techs., Inc., 1990-96; prin. assoc. Ameta Cons. Technologists; v.p. A.S. Johnston Drilling Corp., Woodland Hills, Calif.; adj. prof. U. Redlands, Golden Gate Univ., 1989—; adj. faculty math. U. Redlands Whitehead Coll., 1990—. Contbr. articles to profl. jours. Mem. AAAS, Aircraft Owners and Pilots Assn., Exptl. Aircraft Assn., Phi Beta Kappa, Sigma Xi. Home: 301 N Starfire St Anaheim CA 92807-2928

KIMMICH, JON BRADFORD, computer science program executive; b. Lancaster, Pa., Aug. 8, 1964; s. John Howard and Alice (Ingram) K. BS in Computer Sci., Ind. U. Pa., 1986; MS in Computer Sci., Ohio State U., 1988; MBA, Seattle U., 1993. Developer Microsoft, Redmond, Wash., 1988-93, lead program mgr., sr. producer, 1993—. Contbr. articles to profl. jours. Mem. IEEE (Computer Soc.), Assn. for Computing Machinery, Acad. Interactive Arts and Scis., Internat. Interactive Comms. Soc., Am. Film Inst. Home: 1442 W Lake Sammamish Pkwy SE Bellevue WA 98008 Office: Microsoft Corp 1 Microsoft Way Redmond WA 98052-8300

KIMMICH, ROBERT ANDRÉ, psychiatrist; b. Indpls., Nov. 2, 1920; s. John Martin and Renée Marie (Baron) K.; m. Nancy Earle Smith, 1944 (div. 1952); children: Robert, John, Nancy. BS, Ind. U., 1940, MD, 1943. Diplomate Am. Bd. Psychiatry and Neurology; lic. physician, Calif. Intern St. Vincent's Hosp., Indpls., 1943-44; resident in psychiatry Inst. Pa. Hosp., Phila., 1944-45, U.S. Army Hosp., Phoenixville, Pa., 1945-47; chief male psychiat. div. Worcester (Mass.) State Hosp., 1947-48; resident in psychiatry Harvard Advanced Study Mental Health Ctr., Boston, 1948; asst. prof., asst. chief outpatient dept. Yale U. Sch. Medicine, 1949-51; chief psychosomatic svc. VA Hosp., Newington, Conn., 1949-51; med. dir. Territorial Psychiat. Hosp., Kaneohe, Hawaii, 1951-58; clin. dir. Ill. State Psychiat. Inst., Chgo., 1958-59; chief profl. edn. Stockton (Calif.) State Hosp., 1959-60; chief mental health program and svcs. City of San Francisco, 1960-64; dir. dept. mental health State of Mich., 1964-68; chmn. dept. psychiatry Children's Hosp., San Francisco, 1968-76; pvt. practice San Francisco, 1970—; asst. prof. psychiatry Yale U. Med. Sch., 1948-51; assoc. prof. Northwestern U. Med. Sch., 1958-59; asst. clin. prof. U. Calif., San Francisco, 1960-64; assoc. clin. prof. U. Mich. Med. Sch., Ann Arbor, 1964-68, Stanford U. Med. Sch., 1967-80; lectr. U. Hawaii, 1952-58; pres., founder San Francisco Coordinating Coun. on Mental Retardation, 1961-64; com. on psychiat. tng. State of Calif., 1963-64; chair adv. bd. Mich. Mental Health and Mental Retardation, 1964-67; cons. on mental retardation White House, 1965; exec. com. Children's Hosp., San Francisco, 1967-76; pres. Western Inst. for Rsch. in Mental Health, 1962-64, v.p., 1964-67; ind. med. examiner Calif. Bd. Indsl. Accidents, 1984—; bd. dirs. Children's Physicians Assocs. Editor Northern California Psychiatric Physician, 1985-94. Bd. dirs., chmn., fin. com. mem. Nat. Assn. State Mental Health, 1965-66; chmn., managed care com. No. Calif. Psychiat. Soc., 1991-93; bd. dirs. Westside Mental Health Ctr., San Francisco, 1967-77. Capt. M.C., U.S. Army, 1945-47. Fellow Am. Psychiat. Assn. (life, pres. Hawaii dist. br. 1954-55, rep. to nat. assembly 1986—, task force on ethics 1989-90, com. on procedures 1990—, commn. psychotherapy 1996—, com. on stds. 1966, spl. com. on prepayment health ins. 1965, com. on mental hosps. 1965), Am. Hosp. Assn. (liaison 1964, nominating com. 1993—); mem. AMA, Mich. State Med. Soc., Calif. Med. Assn., San Francisco Med. Soc., No. Calif. Psychiat. Soc. (pres. elect 1991-93, pres. 1993-95, coun. mem. 1984—, editor 1984-94), San Francisco Psychiat. Soc. (pres. 1984-85), Calif. Pacific Medicine Assn., Inc. (pres. 1997—). Office: 341 Spruce St San Francisco CA 94118-1830

KIMPTON, DAVID RAYMOND, natural resource consultant, writer; b. Twin Falls, Idaho, Feb. 19, 1942; s. Lloyd and Retura (Robins) K.; m. Joanna Peak, June 2, 1984; foster children: Donnie, Derrick, Dustin. BS in Forestry, U. Idaho, 1964. Forester U.S. Forest Svc., Panguitch, Utah, 1966-68; with dept. interdisciplinary natural resources U.S. Forest Svc., Ely, Nev., 1968-71; with dept. interdisciplinary natural resources U.S. Forest Svc., Stanley, Idaho, 1971-72, dist. ranger, 1972-78; dist. ranger U.S. Forest Svc., Mountain City, Nev., 1978-84; natural resource cons. Idaho, 1984-92; range conservationist U.S. Forest Svc., Stanley, Idaho, 1992-93; program mgr. natural resources Sawtooth Nat. Recreation Area, Stanley, Idaho, 1993—; incident comdr. U.S. Forest Svc., Western States, 1978-86; botanist pvt. and govtl., Idaho, Nev., 1985-92; naturalist schs., pvt., govt., Idaho, Nev., 1988—; bd. dirs. Salmon River Emergency Med. Clinic, Stanley, Idaho, 1984-86, v.p., 1987-92; bd. dirs., v.p. Idaho Mountain Health Clinics, Boise, 1985-92. Author Mining Law jour., 1990; author Life Saving Rescue mag., 1989. Pres. Meth. Youth Found., Twin Falls, 1960—; treas., v.p. Chrisman Bd. Dirs., Moscow, Idaho, 1960-63; bd. dirs. Vol. Fire Dept., Ely, 1968-71, Sawtooth Valley Meditation Chapel, 1974-76, Stanley Cmty. Bldg., 1977-78; mem. Sawtooth Valley Assn, Stanley, 1971-72, Vol. Fire Dept. Stanley, 1975-78, Mountain Search and Rescue, Stanley, 1972-78, Coalition of Taxpayers, Stanley, 1990-95. With U.S. Army, 1965-66, Vietnam. Named Outstanding Young Men Am., Bd. Nat. Advs., 1971, Outstanding Mem., White Pine Jaycees, 1969. Mem. Idaho Wildlife, Sawtooth Wildlife Coun. Mem. Christian Ch. Home: PO Box 32 Stanley ID 83278-0032

KIMURA, JOAN ALEXANDRA, artist, educator; b. L.A., July 10, 1934; children: Carey Tadao, Devin Isamu. Cert., Art Ctr. Coll. Design, 1955; BFA, U. Alaska, 1979; MFA, Syracuse U., 1984. Illustrator James Eng Assocs. and Sudler and Hennesey, N.Y.C., 1955-57; freelance illustrator N.Y.C., 1955-71; tchr. Anchorage C.C., 1976-87; prof. art U. Alaska, Anchorage, 1987-93; adj. instr. art Anchorage C.C., 1973-76; workshop leader Anchorage Mus. History and Art, 1988, Fairbanks Art Festival, 1989-91. One-woman shows include Chas. Z. Mann Gallery, N.Y.C., 1969, Anchorage Mus. History and Art, 1975, 83, 88, Westbroadway Gallery, Alternate Space, N.Y.C., 1981, 83, others; exhibited in group shows Nat. Soc. Painters in Casein and Acrylic, N.Y.C., 1968, Nat. Acad. Design, N.Y.C., 1969, Conn. Acad. Fine Arts, 1968, 71, 72, 74, 77, Audubon Artists, N.Y.C., 1968, 81, Art Ctr. Coll. Design Alumni Show, 1973, 74, 75, 76, 78, 80, 81, Visual Arts Ctr. Alaska, 1984, 8, Anchorage (Alaska) Mus. History, 1988-89, 90-91, numerous others; represented in permanent collections Alaska State Mus., Fairbanks, Juneau, Anchorage Mus. History and Art, Alaska State Coun. on Arts, Rainier Bank of Alaska, Atlantic Richfield Co.; reviewer Arts Mag., 1969, Artspeak, 1983; reviewer (book) Painting in the North, 1993. Grants panelist Alaska State Coun. Arts, 1984-87; bd. dirs. Anchorage Mus. History and Art, 1981-88, acquisition com., 1988-94; active Conn. Acad. Fine Art, 1971-94. Recipient Sage Allen award Conn. Acad. Fine Art, 1971, Mel Kohler award All Alaska Juried Show, 1972, Fine Art award Art Ctr. Coll. Design, 1973, Juror's Choice Anch Mus. of History & Art, 1974, Best of Show award All Alaska Juried Show, 1976, 1st prize Pacific N.W. Figure Drawing Competition, 1986, Painting award All Alaska Juried Show, 1988; travel grantee Alaska State Coun. Art, 1983, 90, fellowship grantee, 1984. Home: 15000 Stevens Rd SE Olalla WA 98359-9428

KINCAID, JUDITH WELLS, electronics company executive; b. Tampa, Fla., July 1, 1944; d. George Redfield and Louise Wells (Brodt) K.; B.A., Stanford U., 1966, M.S. in Indsl. Engring., 1978; 1 dau., Jennifer Wells Maben. Scientific programmer med. research Stanford (Calif.) U., 1972-77; info. systems mgr. Hewlett Packard Corp., Palo Alto, Calif., 1978-84, mgr. strategic systems, 1985-91; direct mktg. mgr., 1991—, worldwide customer info. mgr., 1995—. Mem. Inst. Indsl. Engrs., Dir. Mktg. Assn. Office: Hewlett Packard Corp 3495 Deer Creek Rd Palo Alto CA 94304-1316

KINCHELOE, WILLIAM ROBERTSON, JR., electrical engineering educator; b. Little Rock, June 17, 1926; s. William Robertson and Genevieve (Skinner) K.; m. Helen Joan Wehrly, Nov. 2, 1956 (div. 1993); children: Karen Lee, Robert Wallace, Wylliam Carl, John Stuart. BSEE, U. Okla., 1946, MIT, 1947; MSEE, Stanford U., 1951, PhD, 1962. Radio engr. Sta. WNAD, Norman, 1943-44; rsch. engr., prof. Stanford (Calif.) U., 1951-91; cons. Kincheloe Engring., Los Altos Hills, Calif., 1981-91. Lt. USN, 1947-50. Mem. IEEE (sr.), Tau Beta Pi, Sigma Xi. Home: Winslow Cohousing Group 353 Wallace Way NE Apt 5 Bainbridge Island WA 98110-2828

KIND, ANNE WILSON, engineer; b. Carmel, Calif., Dec. 1, 1958; d. Patrick Wayne and Mary Elaine (Bryan) Wilson; m. David Lee Kind, June 5, 1992; 1 child, Vivian Elaine Wilson. AAS in Music, Everett C.C., 1981; BSME, Calif. State U., Long Beach, 1987. Lic. pilot, FAA. Engr. Rockwell-Aircraft Divsn., El Segundo, Calif., 1983-86, Rockwell-Satellite Divsn., Seal Beach, Calif., 1986-89; Engr. Rockwell-Space Divsn., Downey, Calif., 1989, Northrop B-2 Divsn., Pico Rivera, Calif., 1989-91, McDonnell Douglas-Space Sta., Huntington Beach, Calif., 1991-94. Pianist Ridgecrest Christian Ch., Albuquerque, 1982-83. Mem. Soaring Soc. Am. (Symons Wave meml. award 1993), Orange County Soaring Assn. (editor 1991-95, v.p. 1993, pres. 1994-95), Pres. award 1993), United Radio Amateur Club. Republican. Home and Office: PO Box 1347 Sugarloaf CA 92386-1347

KIND, KENNETH WAYNE, lawyer, real estate broker; b. Missoula, Mont., Apr. 1, 1948; s. Joseph Bruce and Elinor Joy (Smith) K.; m. Diane Lucille Jozaitis, Aug. 28, 1971; children: Kirstin Amber, Kenneth Warner. BA, Calif. State U.-Northridge, 1973; JD, Calif. Western U., 1976. Bar: Calif. 1976, U.S. Dist. Ct. (ea., so., no. dists.) Calif., 1976, U.S. Cir. Ct. Appeals (9th cir.); lic. NASCAR driver, 1987. Mem. celebrity security staff Brownstone Am., Beverly Hills, Calif., 1970-76; tchr. Army and Navy Acad., Carlsbad, Calif., 1975-76; real estate broker, Bakersfield, Calif., 1978—; sole practice, Bakersfield, 1976—; lectr. mechanic's lien laws, Calif., 1983—. Staff writer Calif. Western Law Jour., 1975. Sgt. U.S. Army, 1967-70. Mem. ABA, VFW, Nat. Order Barristers. Libertarian. Office: 4540 California Ave Ste 210 Bakersfield CA 93309-7019

KINDER, RALPH EUGENE, military officer; b. Tulsa, Okla., Apr. 17, 1959; s. Ralph R. Kinder and Mary F. (Green) Milam; m. Petrice Le-Ann

Davidson, Dec. 22, 1990; children: Ashleigh Rene, Garrett Ray. BS in Civil Engring., Okla. State U., 1982; MS in Acquisition Mgmt., Fla. Tech., 1994; diploma in environ. engring., Colo. Sch. Mines, Golden, 1996. Commd. 2d lt. U.S. Army, 1982, advanced through grades to maj., 1994; instr. U.S. Army Logistics Mgmt. Coll., 1993-95, environ. engr., advanced degree program, 1996—. Major USMC, 1982—. Decorated Navy Achievement medal, Meritorious Svc. medal. Mem.Tau Beta Pi. Home: 8894 W Ontario Ave Littleton CO 80123

KINDRED, RAMONA GENITH, publishing company executive, management consultant; b. Detroit, Jan. 19, 1958; d. Horace Percy and Mary Catherine (Rhodes) Clark; divorced; children: Kenya Kareen Milton, Chané Jamil Milton. Grad. high sch., Compton, Calif., 1975. Mgmt. devel. rep. McDonnell Douglas, Monrovia, Calif., 1990-91; profl. asst. II ARCO, L.A., 1991-94; owner A-hG Publs., Temecula, Calif., 1993—; founder, CEO, pres. A-hG Prodns. Co., Temecula, 1993—, A-hG Mgmt. Devel. Svcs., Temecula, 1996—. Author (poetry): Collective Works of RGK, 1984; Angel-Armoured, 1994; Angel-heart, 1994; Heart Felt, 1996. Bd. dirs. Duarte Youth Athletic Assn., press rels. 1993-94. Office: A-hG Prodns/A-hG Mgmt Devel Svcs PO Box 655 Temecula CA 92593

KING, ALONZO, artistic director, choreographer. Student, Sch. Am. Ballet, Am. ballet theatre Sch., Harkness House Ballet Arts. Founder Lines Contemporary Ballet, San Francisco, 1982—; master tchr. working with Les Ballets de Monte-Carlo, London's Ballet Rambert, Nat. Ballet of Can., N.C. Sch. of Arts, San Francisco Ballet; inaugurator San Francisco Inst. Choreography, 1982; performer Honolulu City Ballet, Santa Barbara Ballet, DTH. Commd. to create and stage ballets for The Joffrey Ballet, Dance Theatre of Harlem; ballets in repertoires of Frankfurt Ballet, Dresden Ballet, BalletMet, Washington Ballet, Hong Kong Ballet; choreographer for Les Ballets de Monte-Carlo; choreogrpaher for prima ballerine Natalia Makarova, Patrick Swazye; original works choreographed include Ocean (3 Isadora Duncan Dance award 1994 for outstanding achievement in choreography, original score and co. performance)), Rock, 1995, Signs and Wonders, Rain Dreaming, Stealing Light, Without Wax, 1990, others. Mem. panels Nat. Endowment for Arts, Calif. Arts Coun., City of Columbus Arts Coun., Lila Wallace-Reader's Digest Arts Ptnrs. Program; former art commr. City and County of San Francisco. Nat. Endowment for Arts Chroeographer's fellow. Office: Lines Contemporary Ballet 50 Oak St 4th Fl San Francisco CA 94102

KING, CHARLES LYNN, librarian; b. Olney, Ill., Oct. 31, 1949; s. Bernard DeWitt and Mary Catherine (Potts) K.; m. Esther Fukiko Fukui, May 16, 1987. AS Health Care Adminstrn., George Washington U., 1976; BS Health Care Adminstrn., So. Ill. U., 1977; MA in Mgmt., Webster Coll., 1978; M in Libr. and Info. Studies, U. Hawaii Manoa, 1992. Cert. health care exec. Pub. health adminstr. Ctrl. Oahu Mental Health, Pearl City, Hawaii, 1993; libr. Hawaii State Libr., Honolulu, 1993—. Lt. USN, 1970-91. Mem. ALA, Ret. Officers Assn., Hawaii Libr. Assn. Home: 98-1369 Koaheahe Pl Apt 89 Pearl City HI 96782-3091 Office: Hawaii State Libr 478 S King St Honolulu HI 96813-2901

KING, CHAROLETTE ELAINE, retired administrative officer; b. Baker, Oreg., Apr. 10, 1945; d. Melvin Howard and Rella Maxine (Gwilliam) Wright; m. Craig Seldon King, April 14, 1965; children: Andrea Karen, Diana Susan. Clerical positions various firms, Idaho, Va., Conn., 1964-71; nursing sec. VA, San Diego, 1974-77; sec. USN, Agana, Guam, 1972-73; procurement clk. USN, Bremerton, Wash., 1977-80; procurement clk. USN, San Diego, 1980, support svcs. supr., 1980-83, div. dir., 1983-87, program analyst, 1987-93, adminstrv. officer, 1993-96, mgmt. analyst, 1996. Recipient Model Agy. cup USN, San Diego, 1986. Republican.

KING, DAVID BURNETT, history educator; b. Phila., Jan. 31, 1930; s. Karl Burnett and Edith (Loveless) K.; m. Mary Brownson, Mar., 1952 (div. 1962); children: Laura, Bonnie, Thomas; m. Paula Richter, Mar., 1963 (div. 1967); 1 child, Stephen; m. Juanita Parot, Sept. 3, 1974; 1 child, Hannah. BA, Hamilton Coll., 1951; MA, Rutgers U., 1955; postgrad., U. Heidelberg, 1957-58; PhD, Cornell U., 1962. Vis. instr. Culver (Ind.) Mil. Acad., 1964-65; from instr. to asst. prof. history Oreg. State U., Corvallis, 1962-64, from assoc. to prof. history, 1965-97, prof. emeritus, 1997; head honors program Oreg. State U., 1967-68. Author: The Crisis of Our Time: Reflections on the Course of Western Civilization, 1988. 1st lt. U.S. Army, 1951-54. Schurman fellow Heidelberg U., 1957-58, Andrew White fellow Cornell U., 1958-59; Fulbright grantee Bonn, 1981. Mem. German Studies Assn., AAUP (v.p. Corvallis chpt. 1966-67). Home: 7950 NW Oxbow Dr Corvallis OR 97330-2830 Office: Oreg State U History Dept Corvallis OR 97331

KING, ELIZABETH ANN, writer; b. Malden, Mass., May 9, 1938; d. Richard H. Sheldon and Jane I. (Cotton) Killoran; m. Richard William King, 1965 (div.); children: Kathy Ann, Richard Eric. AA, Moorpark Coll., 1977; BA, Calif. State U., Northridge, 1978. Adminstrv. sec., 1981-86, freelance writer, 1987—. Author: Corridors, Winter Solstice, (with Sam Kane (Giancana)) Tales of the Vanguard: The Announcer; author of short stories; contbr. poetry to anthologies; lyricist: I Believe in Heroes, 1987, Journey's End, 1988. Home: 1021 Scandia Ave Apt 4 Ventura CA 93004-2465

KING, ELLEN MCGINTY, lawyer; b. San Francisco, Mar. 1, 1946. AB, U. Calif., Berkeley, 1968; MSJ, Northwestern U., 1971; JD, Stanford U., 1976. Bar: Calif. 1976. Ptnr. Jackson, Tufts, Cole & Black, San Francisco, San Jose, 1976—; mem. faculty fed. practice program U.S. Dist. Ct. (no. dist.) Calif., 1986-89; faculty mem. fed. case mgmt. program U.S. Dist. Ct. (no. dist.) Calif., 1995; panelist Calif. Continuing Edn. for Bar, 1992. Mem. ABA (litigation sect.), Santa Clara County Bar Assn. (panelist 1984, 90), Bar Assn. San Francisco, Phi Beta Kappa. Office: Jackson Tufts Cole & Black LLP 60 S Market St Fl 10 San Jose CA 95113

KING, FRANK WILLIAM, writer; b. Port Huron, Mich., Oct. 1, 1922; s. William Ernest and Catherine Theresa (Smith) K.; student U. Utah, 1963-65, Santa Monica City Coll., 1941, 48-49; BA, Marylhurst Coll., 1979; MA, U. Portland, 1982; m. Carma Morrison Sellers, Sept. 16, 1961; children: Rosanne, Jeanine Nell, Melanie, Lisa June; one stepson, Michael Sellers. Air traffic contr. FAA, Salt Lake City, Albuquerque and Boise, Idaho; 1949-65, info. officer Western Region, L.A., 1965-68; pub. affairs officer L.A. Dist. C.E., U.S. Army, 1968-69, Walla Walla (Wash.), 1969-77, N. Pacific div., Portland, Oreg., 1977-79; dir. pub. rels. U. Portland, 1979-80; adj. asst. prof. comm. U. Portland, 1982-83; instr. Portland (Oreg.) C.C., 1980-87; freelance writer, 1960—. Exec. asst. L.A. Fed. Exec. Bd., 1965-67; chmn. Walla Walla County Alcoholism Adminstrv. Bd., 1974-75; vice-chmn. Walla Walla County Human Services Adminstrv. Bd., 1976-78, chmn., 1977-78. Served with USMCR, 1942-45. Decorated Air medal; William Randolph Hearst scholar, 1965. Mem. Soc. Profl. Journalists, Pub. Relations Soc. Am. (accredited), Kappa Tau Alpha. Democrat. Roman Catholic. Home and Office: 310 N Fawn Dr Otis OR 97368-9323

KING, FREDERIC, health services management executive, educator; b. N.Y.C., N.Y., May 9, 1937; s. Benjamin and Jeanne (Fritz) K.; m. Linda Ann Udell, Mar. 17, 1976; children by previous marriage—Coby Allen, Allison Beth, Lisa Robyn, Daniel Seth. B.B.A. cum laude, Bernard M. Baruch Sch. Bus. and Public Adminstrn., CUNY, 1958. Dir. adminstrn. Albert Einstein Coll. Medicine, Bronx, N.Y., 1970-72; assoc. v.p. health affairs Tulane Med. Ctr., New Orleans, 1972-77; dir. fin. Mt. Sinai Med. Ctr., N.Y.C., 1977-78; v.p. fin. Cedars-Sinai Med. Ctr., Los Angeles, 1978-82; pres. Vascular Diagnostic Services, Inc., Woodland Hills, Calif., 1982-84; exec. dir. South Bay Ind. Physicians Med. Group Inc., Torrance, Calif., 1984—; assoc. adj. prof. Tulane U. Sch. Pub. Health; asst. prof. Mt. Sinai Med. Ctr.; instr. Pierce Coll., Los Angeles. Bd. dirs Ohr Eliyahu Acad., chmn.; bd. dirs. AMHO Pacific Region, Torah Learning Ctr. Served with U.S. Army, 1959-62. Mem. Healthcare Forum, Am. Hosp. Assn., Pres.'s Assn., Calif. Assn. Hosps. and Health Systems. Republican. Jewish. Home: 1116 Rose Ave Venice CA 90291-2835

KING, GARY CURTIS, author, lecturer; b. Bonne Terre, Mo., Jan. 26, 1954; s. Curtis H. and Eunice C. (Veith) K.; m. Teresita Uson Engles, Mar. 5, 1983; children: Kirsten Nicole, Sarah Tiffany. Grad. high sch., Portland, Oreg. Freelance author, 1980—; lectr. Friends of Mystery, Portland, Oreg., 1993—. Author: Blood Lust: Portrait of a Serial Sex Killer, 1992 (featured selection True Crime Book Club 1992), Driven to Kill, 1993 (featured selection True Crime Book Club 1993), Web of Deceit, 1994 (featured selection True Crime Book Club 1994), Blind Rage, 1995, Savage Vengeance, 1996; contbr. over 400 stories to crime mags., recognized internat. authority on serial murders and emergence of sociopathy in the twentieth century. With USAF, 1972-76. Mem. Authors Guild, Authors League Am., Internat. Assn. Crime Writers, Mystery Writers Am., Nat. Press Club, Pacific N.W. Writers Conf. (lectr. 1993—), Willamette Writers (lectr. 1995—). Roman Catholic. Home: #106 1027 S Rainbow Blvd Las Vegas NV 89128

KING, GUNDAR JULIAN, retired university dean; b. Riga, Latvia, Apr. 19, 1926; came to U.S., 1950, naturalized, 1954; s. Attis K. and Austra (Dale) Kenins: m. Valda K. Andersons, Sept. 18, 1954; children: John T., Marita A. Student, J.W. Goethe U., Frankfurt, Germany, 1946-48; BBA, U. Oreg., 1956; MBA, Stanford U., 1958, PhD, 1964; DSc (hon.), Riga Tech. U., 1991; D Habil. Oecon., Latvian Sci. Coun., 1992. Asst. field supr. Internat. Refugee Orgn., Frankfurt, 1948-50; br. office mfr. Williams Form Engring. Corp., Portland, Oreg., 1952-54; project mgr. Market Rsch. Assocs., Palo Alto, Calif., 1958-60; asst. prof., assoc. prof. Pacific Luth. U., 1960-66, prof., 1966—, dean Sch. Bus. Adminstrn., 1970-90; vis. prof. mgmt. U.S. Naval Postgrad. Sch., 1971-72, San Francisco State U., 1980, 1987-88; internat. econ. mem. Latvian Acad. Scis., 1990—; regent Estonian Bus. Sch., 1991—; vis. prof. Riga Tech. U., 1993—. Author: Economic Policies in Occupied Latvia, 1965; contbr. articles to profl. publs. Mem. Gov.'s Com. on Reorgn. Wash. State Govt., 1965-88; mem. study group on pricing U.S. Commn. Govt. Procurement, 1971-72; pres. N.W. Univs. Bus. Adminstrn. Conf., 1965-66. With AUS, 1950-52. Fulbright-Hayes scholar, Thailand, 1988, Fulbright scholar, Latvia, 1993-94. Mem. AAUP (past chpt. pres.), Am. Mktg. Assn. (past chpt. pres.), Assn. Advancement Baltic Studies (pres. 1970), Western Assn. Collegiate Schs. Bus. (pres. 1971), Latvian Acad. Scis., Alpha Kappa Psi, Beta Gamma Sigma. Home: PO Box 44401 Tacoma WA 98444-0401 Office: Pacific Luth U Tacoma WA 98447

KING, HARRY ALDEN, author; b. Juneau, Alaska, Apr. 3, 1928; s. Walter Bradley and Lillian Lucile K.; m. Anga Burt, Oct. 4, 1952. BSChemE, U. Colo., 1949; postgrad., MIT, 1950, U. Calif., 1951, U. Md., 1953. Tech. svc. dir. Nat. Starch Products, San Francisco, 1949-55; head rsch., composites divsn. Aerojet-Gen. Corp., Azusa, Calif., 1955-60, program mgr., 1962-68; tech. dir. Western Backing Corp., Culver City, Calif., 1960-62; mgr. rsch. & engring. Narmco/Whittaker Corp., Costa Mesa, Calif., 1968-70; pres. King Rsch., Yorba Linda, Calif., 1970-78; dir. rsch. Amicon/W.R. Grace, Lexington, Mass., 1978-90; pres. Spirit House Press, Tucson, 1993—; cons. King Rsch., 1960-90; featured spkr. and lectr. at many univs. and confs.; chmn. many tech. symposiums. Featured spkr. PBS TV program Innovations, 1967; author 25 tech. papers on variety of subjects, 1966-90; patentee in field; author: (Pure, Golden Light of Love, 1993; extensive article on tech. work L.A. Times, 1966. Aviation cadet USN, 1945-46; with Chem. Corps, U.S. Army, 1952-53. Office: Spirit House Press PO Box 37163 Tucson AZ 85740-7163

KING, INDLE GIFFORD, industrial designer, educator; b. Seattle, Oct. 23, 1934; s. Indle Frank and Phyllis (Kenney) K.; m. Rosalie Rosso, Sept. 10, 1960; children: Indle Gifford Jr., Paige Phyllis. BA, U. Wash., 1960, MA, 1968. Indsl. designer Hewlett-Packard, Palo Alto, Calif., 1961-63; mgr. indsl. design Sanborn Co., Boston, 1963-65; mgr. corp. design Fluke Corp., Everett, Wash., 1965—; prof. indsl. design Western Wash. U., Bellingham, 1985—; judge nat. and. internat. competitions; cons. in field. Contbr. articles to profl. jours.; designer patents in field. Coach Mercer Island (Wash.) Boys' Soccer Assn., 1972-77; pres. Mercer Island PTA, 1973; advisor Jr. Achievement, Seattle, 1975-78. Mem. Idsl. Design Soc. Am. (Alcoa award 1965, v.p. Seattle chpt. 1986-88), Mercer Island Country Club. Office: Fluke Corp 6920 Seaway Blvd Everett WA 98203-5829

KING, JACK A., lawyer; b. Lafayette, Ind., July 29, 1936; s. Noah C. and Mabel E. (Pierce) K.; m. Mary S. King, Dec. 10, 1960; children: Jeffrey A., Janice D., Julie D. BS in Fin., Ind. U., 1958, JD, 1961. Bar: Ind. 1961. Ptnr. Ball, Eggleston, King & Bumbleburg, Lafayette, 1961-70; judge Superior Ct. 2 of Tippecanoe County (Ind.), 1970-78; assoc. gen. counsel Dairyland Ins. Co., 1978, v.p. and assoc. gen. counsel, 1979, v.p., gen. counsel and asst. sec., 1980-85; v.p. and counsel Sentry Ctr. West, 1981-85; asst. gen. counsel Sentry Corp., 1979-85; v.p., gen. counsel, and asst. sec. Gt. S.W. Fire Ins. Co., 1980-85, Gt. S.W. Surplus Lines Ins. Co., 1981-85; v.p and gen. counsel Dairyland County Mut. Ins. Co. Tex., 1980-85; v.p. legal and. asst. sec. Scottsdale Ins. Co., 1985-95; asst. sec. Nat. Casualty Co. 1985-95; v.p.-legal and asst. sec. Scottsdale Indemnity Co., 1992-95, sr. v.p., gen. coun. Tig Excess & Surplus Lines, Inc., 1995-96, also bd. dirs., 1995-96; bd. dirs. Countrywide Ins. Co.; v.p. bd. dirs. Ariz. Ins. Info. Assn., 1988-96; cons., mediator and arbitrator, 1996—; bd. dirs. Ariz. Joint Underwriting Plan, 1978-81, mem. exec. com., 1980-81; mem. Ariz. Property & Casualty Ins. Commn., 1985-86, vice chmn., 1986; mem. Ariz. Study Commn. on Ins., 1986-87; mem. Ariz. task force on Ct. Orgn. and Adminstrn., 1988-89; mem. adv. com. Ariz. Ho. Rep. Majority Leaders, 1989, Ariz. Dept. Ins. Fraud Unit, 1997-97. Bd. dirs. Scottsdale (Ariz.) Art Ctr. Assn., 1981-84. Mem. ABA, Ind. Bar Assn., Maricopa County Bar Assn. Contbr. The Law of Competitive Business Practices, 2d edit. Office: 2141 E Highland Ave Phoenix AZ 85016

KING, JANE CUDLIP COBLENTZ, volunteer educator; b. Iron Mountain, Mich., May 4, 1922; d. William Stacey and Mary Elva (Martin) Cudlip; m. George Samuel Coblentz, June 8, 1942 (dec. June 1989); children: Bruce Harper, Keith George, Nancy Allison Coblentz Patch; m. James E. King, August 23, 1991 (dec. Jan. 1994). BA, Mills Coll., 1942. Mem. Sch. Resource and Career Guidance Vols., Inc., Atherton, Calif., 1965-69, pres., CEO, 1969—; part-time exec. asst. to dean of admissions Mills Coll., 1994—. Proofreader, contbr., campus liaison Mills Coll. Quarterly mag. Life gov. Royal Children's Hosp., Melbourne, Australia, 1963—; pres. United Menlo Park (Calif.) Homeowner's Assn., 1994—; nat. pres. Mills Coll. Alumnae Assn., 1969-73, bd. trustees, 1975-83. Named Vol. of Yr., Sequoia Union H.S. Dist., 1988, Golden Acorn award for Outstanding Svc., Menlo Park C. of C., 1991. Mem. AAUW (Menlo-Atherton branch pres. 1994-96, v.p. programs 1996-97), Atherlons, Palo Alto (Calif.) Area Mills Coll. Club (pres. 1986), Phi Beta Kappa. Episcopalian. Office: Menlo-Atherton HS Resource-Career Guid Vols 555 Middlefield Rd Atherton CA 94027

KING, JANE LOUISE, artist; b. South Bend, Ind., Aug. 9, 1951; d. Bill and Anne Luciel (Hopkins) Berta; m. Gerald William King Jr., July 7, 1973; children: Kelly Anne, Dinah Jolene. Student, Ind. U., South Bend, 1969-70, Ind. U., 1970-71; BFA, Ohio State U., 1973. Ind. artist Colo., 1974—; instr. Sangre de Cristo Art Ctr., Pueblo, Colo., 1982, Art Studio, Longmont, Colo., 1989. Exhibited oil and pastel paintings in numerous group shows including 5th Ann. Internat. Exhibit Kans. Pastel Soc., 10th and 22nd Ann. Pastel Soc. Am., N.Y., Colo. State Fairs, Poudre Valley Art League; prin. works represented in numerous pvt. collections; contbr. poems to At Days End, 1994. Leader 4-H Club, Longmont, 1986—; sec. Longmont Artists Guild Gallery, 1988-89, bd. dirs., 1989; supt. 1st Bapt. Ch., Longmont, 1990-91. Mem. Colo. Artists Assn. (area 1 rep. 1994), Longmont Artists Guild (Grumbacher award 1992), Longmont Arts Coun., Knickerbocker Artists N.Y, Audubon Artists N.Y. Republican. Home: 1508 Kempton Ct Longmont CO 80501-6716

KING, JANET FELLAND, family nurse practitioner; b. Ann Arbor, Mich., May 5, 1947; d. Robert Marcy and Marjorie Marie (Sherman) Felland; m. William Curtis Runyon, May 20, 1967 (div. May 8, 1972); m. Robert Allen King, Oct. 26, 1974; 1 child, Stephen Tremain King. Student, U. Mich., 1965-67, Earlham Coll., 1968-69; BSN, Ball State U., 1971; MNSc, U. Ark., 1976. RN, Idaho. Med. surg. nurse Meml. Hosp., Oxford, Ohio, 1971-72; migrant health nurse Colo. Dept. Health, Lamar, 1972-74; pub. health nurse City Health Dept., Little Rock, 1974-75; family nurse practitioner Idaho Migrant Coun., Burley, 1976-81; pub. health nurse South Ctrl. Dist. Health, Burley, 1981-82; family nurse practitioner Family Health Svcs., Burley, 1982—; treas. Mini Cassia Child Protection Team, Burley, 1982—; mem. Idaho Health Profl. Loan Repayment Bd., Pocatello, 1992—. Vol., nurse and deacon Diocese of Honduras, Roatan, 1990; archdeacon Diocese of Idaho, 1990—; trustee Episcopal Camp & Conf. Bd., 1991—. Named Woman of Progress, Bus. and Profl. Women, 1981-82; recipient Outstanding Clinician Achievement award N.W. Primary Care Assn., 1984-92. Mem. Idaho Nurses Assn. (regional rep. 1982-84), Sigma Theta Tau. Episcopalian. Home: 678 E 400 N Rupert ID 83350-9414 Office: Family Health Svcs 2311 Park Ave Ste 11 Burley ID 83318-2170

KING, LEA ANN, community volunteer and leader; b. Elkhart, Ind., July 26, 1941; d. Lloyd Emerson and Mildred Salome (Hostetler) Hartzler; children: Thomas Ellsworth III, Alden Elizabeth. BA in History, DePauw U., 1963. Participant in Intensive Workshop in Intercultural Comm. U. Calif., Irvine, 1993, Study Tour of Ethnic Minorites of China, UCLA Extension, 1990; audited The Ethics of War and Peace, Ethikon Inst., Jerusalem, 1993; attended Three Intercultural Colloquia of Family Life, Cultural Diversity and Human Values, Ethikon Inst., 1989. Producer, hostess Pub. Access cable TV programs; travel writer, photographer. Bd. dirs., chair The Ethikon Inst. for Study of Ethical Diversity and Intercultural Rels.; pres. Vol. Ctr. S. Bay-Harbor-Long Beach, 1993-95; v.p. Cmty. Assn. of the Peninsula, chair multicultural com., chair PV 2000; sec. Planned Parenthood L.A., 1991—; past pres. Jr. League L.A.; past chair San Pedro Peninsula Hosp. Found.; founding chair Forward-Looking Strategies for Women Coalition, 1985; co-chair United Way System Wide Admissions Com.; mem. Nordstrom's Com. for Salute to Cultural Diversity, L.A., 1993-95, diversity com. Planned Parenthood Fedn. We. Region, 1996. Named Woman of Yr. Nat. Women's Polit. Caucus, San Fernando Valley, 1986, South Bay YWCA; recipient John Anson Ford award L.A. County Commn. on Human Rels., 1992, Spirit of Volunteerism award Jr. League L.A., 1991, Founders award Vol. Ctrs. Calif., 1996, commendations from L.A. Mayor Tom Bradley, L.A. County Bd. Suprs., Calif. State Sen. Robert Beverly, Congressmen Dana Rohrabcher and Howard Berman; mem. Los Angeles County Commn. on Human Rels., 1993, 96, pres., 1997. Home and Office: 49 Strawberry Ln Rolling Hills Estates CA 90274-4111

KING, RHETA BARON, disability management consultant; b. L.A., Dec. 15, 1935; d. Albert James and Marietta (Malcomson) Baron; m. Stuart Alan Walling, June, 11, 1956 (div. July 1968); children: S. Alan, Lynne Heather; m. Kenneth Bruce King, Oct. 11, 1968 (div. Apr. 1983). AB cum laude, Occidental Coll., 1957; postgrad., Calif. State U., Los Angeles, 1960-68, Calif. State U., Long Beach, 1963-64. Cert. rehab. counselor, cert. disability mgmt. specialist, social security vocat. expert. Counselor Calif. Dept. Rehab., Burbank, 1972-74; coordinator staff devel. Los Angeles, 1974, program supr., 1975-78; nat. dir. staff devel. Comprehensive Rehab. Services, Inc., Arcadia, Calif., 1978-80; dir. comprehensive rehab. ctr. Daniel Freeman Meml. Hosp., Inglewood, Calif., 1981-83, dir. vocat. programs, 1984-86; pvt. practice rehab. cons. Pasadena, Calif., 1981—; tech. advisor Devel. Disabilities Area Bd., L.A., 1978; cons. Social Security Office Hearings and Appeals, Pasadena and L.A., 1981—, Am. Coll. Neurology, 1986, Nat. Multiple Sclerosis Soc., 1986—, Calif. Applicants' Attys. Assn., Internat. Pers. Mgmt. Assn. Assessment Coun., Calif. State U., L.A.; rsch. scientist Human Interaction Rsch. Inst., L.A., 1986—. Author graphic model, 1980. Mem. exec. bd. Calif. Gov.'s Com. for People With Disabilities, 1983-94, Calif. Health Care Plan Adv. Com., 1990-91; mem. L.A. Long-Term Care Task Force, 1987; advisor, counselor edn. program Calif. State U., L.A., 1989—; mem. vestry Episc. Ch. of the Ascension, Sierra Madre, 1994-97; commr. Certification of Disability Mgmt. Specialists Commn., 1992—. Elizabeth Woods fellow, 1964; recipient Outstanding Svc. award Pasadena Mayor's Com., 1993. Mem. AAUW, ACA, Gov.'s Women Appointees Coun., Nat. Assn. Rehab. Profls. in Pvt. Sector, Am. Rehab. Counseling Assn., Occidental Coll. Alumni Assn. (bd. govs. 1983-86). Republican. Episcopalian. Home and Office: 515 S Oakland Ave Apt 5 Pasadena CA 91101-3358

KING, RO, psychotherapist, educator; b. New York City, May 25, 1941; d. George and Selma King. BS cum laude, Pa. State U., 1963; MS in Sch. Psychology, CUNY, 1970; PhD, Am. Commonwealth U., 1987. Lic. clin. mental health counselor, N.Mex.; cert. sch. psychologist, N.Y., human capacities practitioner. Psychologist NYU Reading Inst., 1969-73; with gen. studies NYU, 1971-73; psychotherapist Richmond Coll. CUNY, N.Y.C., 1973-75; workshop leader Ctr. Experiential Psychotherapy, N.Y.C., 1970—; supr. Ctr. Human Potential, Identy House, N.Y.C., 1970—; pvt. practice psychotherapy N.Y., N.Mex., 1970—; psychology educator NYU, CCNY, Soc. Ethical Culture, 1971—; guest lectr. New Sch. Social Rsch.; leader, mem. Therapist Networking, Santa Fe, 1995—. Leade, mem. People for Peace, Santa Fe, 1991-94; organizer Multicultural exch., Santa Fe, 1992; mem. various women's orgns., N.Y.C., 1969—; leader Women's Action Coun., Santa Fe, 1993. Mem. Am. Counseling Assn., Helix Profl. Devel. Group, Associated Psychotherapists (salon leader 1978-89). Home: 2 Camino Peralta Santa Fe NM 87501

KING, ROBERT EUGENE, economic development consultant; b. Abilene, Kans., Jan. 8, 1935; s. Clarence Leroy and Margaret (Swift) K.; B.A., Kans. Wesleyan U., 1961; postgrad. U. Fla., 1963-64; m. Marilyn Jean Watts, May 17, 1977; children—Robert Eugene, Brian Stewart. Dir. indsl. devel. Kans. Dept. Econ. Devel., Topeka, 1973-77; dir. econ. devel. N.W. Kans. Econ. Devel. Dist., Hill City, 1977-80; dir. Econ. Devel. Council, Springfield, Ill., 1980-83; exec. dir. Econ. Devel. Commn., Midwest City, Okla., 1983-87; with Clark County Cmty Resources, Las Vegas, Nev., 1987-95; cons. King & Assocs., Henderson, Nev., 1995—. Sec.-treas. Great Lakes Area Devel. Council, 1980-81. Served with USN, 1954-58. Mem. Am. Econ. Devel. Council (dir.), Ill. Devel. Council, So. Indsl. Devel. Council, Nat. Assn. Rev. Appraisers, Indsl. Devel. Research Council, Methodist. Club: Elks. Office: King & Assocs 1952 Flagstone Ranch Ln Henderson NV 89016-0386

KING, ROBERT LEONARD, warehousing executive; b. Seattle, Feb. 20, 1938; s. Robert Leonard and Phoebe Easley (Edmunds) K.; m. Helen Blair Lewis, Sept. 11, 1959; children: Robert E., David B., Elizabeth S., Victoria C. BA, Dartmouth coll., 1959, MBA, 1960; LLB, LaSalle Coll., 1964. CPA, Wash. Acct. Haskins & Sells, Seattle, 1960-63; trader Marshall & Meyer, Seattle, 1963-64; pres. Herron Northwest, Inc., Seattle, 1964-73; v.p. Piper Jaffray & Hopwood, Mpls., 1973-74; pres. Klamath Fin. Services, Klamath Falls, Oreg., 1974-76, Seafirst Investment Advs., Seattle, 1975-80; v.p. Prudential Bache Securities, Seattle, 1980-85; pres. Rainier Cold Storage & Ice, Seattle, 1985—. Trustee, treas. Lakeside Sch., Seattle, 1966-72, Virginia Mason Med. Found., 1976-81; trustee, pres. St. Thomas Day Sch., Bellevue, 1976-81; trustee, pres., chmn. Seattle Repertory Theater, 1970—. Mem. AICPA, Wash. Soc. CPAs, Internat. Assn. Refrigerated Warehouses, Nat. Fisheries Inst., Useless Bay Golf and Country Club. Office: Rainier Cold Storage & Ice 6004 Airport Way S Seattle WA 98108-2716

KING, ROSEMARY ANN, air force officer; b. Erie, Pa., Dec. 2, 1966; d. Thomas Leonard and Dolores Ann (Sikora) King. BS, U.S. Air Force Acad., 1988; MLA, Harvard Extension Sch., 1992; postgrad., Ariz. State U., 1997—. Commd. 2d lt. U.S. Air Force, 1988, advanced through grades to capt., 1995; aquisition officer Onizuka Air Stn. U.S. Air Force, Sunnyvale, Calif., 1995—. Asst. editor War, Lit. and Arts, 1992-95; book reviewer; author conf. papers. Participant, asst. Spl. Olympics, Colo., 1993-94; mem. Citizen's Project, Colo., 1992-95; child sponsor Children's Internat., Calif., 1992—; vol. Ann. Art/Wine Festival, Calif., 1995—. Recipient Amelia Earhart award USAF, 1996; Fulbright Hays scholar, 1994; Air Force grantee, 1993. Mem. Assn. Grads., Virginia Woolf Soc., Air Force Assn. Democrat. Unitarian Universalist.

KING, SAMUEL PAILTHORPE, federal judge; b. Hankow, China, Apr. 13, 1916; s. Samuel W. and Pauline (Evans) K.; m. Anne Van Patten Grilk, July 8, 1944; children—Samuel Pailthorpe, Louise Van Patten, Charlotte Lelepoki. B.S., Yale, 1937, LL.B., 1940. Bar: D.C., Hawaii bars 1940. Practiced law Honolulu, 1941-42, 46-61, 70-72, Washington, 1942; atty. King & McGregor, 1947-53, King & Myhre, 1957-61; judge 1st Circuit Ct. Hawaii, 1961-70, Family Ct., 1966-70; judge U.S. Dist. Ct. for Hawaii, 1972—, chief judge, 1974-84; Faculty Nat. Coll. State Judiciary, 1968-73, Nat. Inst. Trial Advocacy, 1976, U. Hawaii Law Sch., 1980-84. Co-translator, co-editor: (O. Korschelt) The Theory and Practice of Go, 1965. Served with USNR, 1941-46; capt. Res. ret. Fellow Am. Bar Found.; mem. ABA, Hawaii Bar Assn. (pres. 1953), Order of Coif. Republican (chmn. Hawaii central com. 1953-55, nat. com. 1971-72). Episcopalian. Home: 1717 Mott-smith Dr Apt 2814 Honolulu HI 96822-2850 Office: US Dist Ct Box 50128 Honolulu HI 96850

KING, TERESA HOWARD, special education educator, consultant; b. Clovis, N.Mex., Nov. 28, 1949; children: Heather, Matthew. BS, Ea. N.Mex. U., 1974, MA, 1981. Cert. elem. tchr., spl. edn. tchr. Tchr. 4th grade Clovis (N.Mex.) Mcpl. Schs., Clovis, N.Mex., 1975-76; tchr. 3d grade Clovis (N.Mex.) Mcpl. Schs., 1976-80, tchr. 5th grade, 1980-87, tchr. spl. edn., 1987-93, facilitator enriched learning program, 1994, ednl. diagnostician, 1994—; co-owner TD Enterprises, Clovis, N.Mex., 1994—. Co-author (computer software) Diagnostic Report Writer, 1995, R/2/4/KIDZ, 1995. Artists in Residency grantee N.Mex. Arts Divsn., 1992. Mem. Phi Delta Kappa. Home: 2301 Miller St Clovis NM 88101

KING, TODD ALLEN, programmer, analyst; b. Downey, Calif., Feb. 15, 1959; s. John Flago and Audrey K.; children: Garreth Merlin, Brendon Galen. BS in applied geophysics, UCLA, 1985. Programmer, analyst Inst. Geophysics and Planetary Physics, L.A., 1982—; cons. Space Environment Corp., Provo, Utah, 1992-94, Ctr. for Digital Innovation UCLA, 1996-97. Author: Dynamic Data Structures: Theory and Applications, 1993. Recipient Group Achievement award NASA, 1991, Adminstrn. and Profl. Devel. award UCLA, 1989, 91. Mem. IEEE, Assn. Computing Machines. Office: IGPP UCLA 5881 Slichter Hall Los Angeles CA 90024

KING, W. DAVID, professional hockey coach; b. North Battleford, Sask., Can., Dec. 22, 1947. Head coach Team Can. Internat. League, 1984-92; head coach Calgary (Can.) Flames, 1992-97, Montreal, Can., 1997—. Office: 1260 De la Gauchetiere W, Montreal, PQ Canada H3B 5V8*

KINGMAN, DONG, artist, educator; b. Oakland, Calif., Apr. 1, 1911; s. Dong Chuan-Fee and Lew Shee K.; m. Wong Shee, Sept. 1929 (dec. June 1954); children—Eddie, Dong Kingman Jr.; m. Helena Kuo, Sept. 1956. Student, Lingnan, Hong Kong, 1924-26; LHD (hon.), Acad. Art Coll., San Franciso, 1987. Tchr. art San Diego Art Gallery, 1941-43; tchr. Famous Artists Schs., Westport, Conn., Columbia U., Hunter Coll.; Lectr. tour around world sponsored by internat. cultural exchange program Dept. State, 1954. Represented in permanent collections, Whitney Mus. Am. Art, Am. Acad. Arts and Letters, Bklyn. Mus., Toledo Mus. Art, Joslyn Art Mus., Omaha, Mus. Fine Arts, Boston, Met. Mus. Art, Mus. Modern Art, N.Y.C., U. Nebr., Wadsworth Atheneum, Bloomington (Ill.) Art Assn., San Francisco Mus., Mills Coll., De Young Mus., Albert Bender Collection, Eleanor Roosevelt Collection, Chgo. Art Inst., N.Y. State Tchrs. Coll., Springfield (Ill.) Art Assn., Cranbrook Acad. Art, Butler Art Inst., Ft. Wayne Mus., Addison Gallery, U.S. Dept. State, many others; executed murals, Bank of Calif., San Francisco, N.Y. Hilton Hotel, R.H. Macy & Co., Franklin Sq., N.Y., Boca Raton Hotel, Fla., Hyatt Regency Hotel, Hong Kong, Ambassador Hotel, Kowloon, Hong Kong, Lincoln Savs. Bank, N.Y.C.; illustrator: The Bamboo Gate (Vanya Oakes), 1946, China's Story (Enid LaMonte Meadowcroft), 1946, Nightingale (Andersen), 1948, Johnny Hong in Chinatown (Clyde Robert Bulla), 1952, Caen's and Kingman's San Francisco (Herb Caen), 1964, City on the Golden Hill (Herb Caen), 1967; author: (with Helena Kuo Kingman) Dong Kingman's Watercolors, 1980, Paint the Yellow Tiger, 1991; Painted: (with Helena Kuo Kingman) title paintings for 55 Days at Peking, movie title paints for Flower Drum Song, 1964, movie poster Universal Studio Tour. Served in U.S. Army. Recipient award Chgo. Internat. Watercolor Exhbn., 1944, Gold medal of honor Audubon Artists Exhbn. 1946, award, 1956; Joseph Pennel Meml. medal Phila. Watercolor Club, 1950, award, 1968; Watercolor prize Pa. Acad., 1953, Am. Watercolor Soc. award, 1956, 60, 62-65, 67, 72, High Wings Medal award, 1973, V.K. McCracken Young award, 1976, Ford-Times award, 1978, Barse Miller Meml. award, 1979, Dolphin Medal award, 1987; 150th Anniversary Gold Medal award Nat. Acad. Design, 1975, Walter Bigg Meml. award, 1977; Key to City of Omaha, 1980, Key to City of Cin., 1980; San Diego Watercolor Soc. prize, 1984, 1st prize for Ch. No. 1, San Francisco Art Assn., 1936; named Hon. Admiral of Navy, Omaha, 1979, Hon. Citizen of Louisville, 1980, Hon. Capt. of Belle of Louisville, 1980, Man of Yr. Chinatown Planning Coun., N.Y.C., 1981, Man of Yr. Oakland (Calif.) Chinese Community Coun., 1985, Man of Yr. Rotary Club 1991, Man of Yr. Chinese Affirmative Action, San Francisco, 1991, Guest of Honor for Opening Internat. Book Fair, Hong Kong, 1991, judge Miss Universe and Miss U.S.A., 1963-85; Guggenheim fellow, 1942-43. Home: 21 W 58th St New York NY 10019 Office: care Stary Sheet Gallery 14988 Sand Canyon Ave Irvine CA 92618-2107

KINGMAN, ELIZABETH YELM, anthropologist; b. Lafayette, Ind., Oct. 15, 1911; d. Charles Walter and Mary Irene (Weakley) Yelm; m. Eugene Kingman, June 10, 1939; children—Mixie Kingman Eddy, Elizabeth Anne Kingman. BA U. Denver, 1933, MA, 1935. Asst. in anthropology U. Denver, 1932-34; mus. asst. Ranger Naturalist Staff, Mesa Verde Nat. Park, Colo., 1934-38; asst. to husband in curatorial work, Indian art exhibits Philbrook Art Ctr., Tulsa, 1939-42, Joslyn Art Mus., Omaha, 1947-69; tutor humanities dept. U. Omaha, 1947-50; chmn. bd. govs. Pi Beta Phi Settlement Sch., Gatlinburg, Tenn., 1969-72; asst. to husband in exhibit design mus. of Tex. Tech. U., 1970-75, bibliographer Internat. Ctr. Arid and Semi-Arid Land Studies, 1974-75; librarian Sch. Am. Research, Santa Fe, 1978-86; research assoc., 1986—; v.p. Santa Fe Corral of the Westerners, 1985-86. Mem. AAUW, LWV, Archeol. Inst. Am. (v.p. Santa Fe chpt. 1981-83), Santa Fe Hist. Soc. (sec. 1981-83). Home: 604 Sunset St Santa Fe NM 87501-1118 Office: Sch Am Rsch 660 Garcia St Santa Fe NM 87501-2858

KINGORE, EDITH LOUISE, retired geriatrics and rehabilitation nurse; b. Parsons, Kans., Nov. 18, 1922; d. George Richard and Josephine (Martin) K. Diploma, Mo. Meth. Hosp., St. Joseph, 1955. RN. Staff nurse El Cerrito Hosp., Long Beach, Calif., 1966-69; nurse Alamitos-Belmont Convalescent Hosp., Long Beach, 1973-75; staff nurse Freeman Hosp., Joplin, Mo., 1975-76, Oak Hill Osteo. Hosp., Joplin, 1976-77; surg. care and rehab. nurse St. Francis Med. Ctr., Cape Guiardo, Mo., 1977-78; psychiat. nurse Western Mo. Mental Health Ctr., Kansas City, Mo., 1978; pvt. duty nurse, 1978-83. Historian South Coast Ecumenical Coun., 1993-94. Home: 3333 Pacific Pl Apt 108 Long Beach CA 90806-1245

KINGSHILL, KONRAD, social sciences educator; b. Burgstädt, Saxony, Germany, June 22, 1923; naturalized U.S. citizen, 1944; s. William and Gertrude (Sachs) K.; m. Carolyn Ryberg; children: Christina, Kim Andrew, Kenneth Paul. BA magna cum laude, Hastings Coll., 1944; MS in Physics, U. Chgo., 1944; PhD in Anthropology, Cornell U., 1957; LHD (hon.), Hastings Coll., 1971. Instr. physics Morgan Pk. Jr. Coll., Chgo., 1946-47; instr. math., physics and English Prince Royal's Coll., Chiang Mai, Thailand, 1947-50, head univ. prep. divsn., 1953-63; head secondary divsn. Bangkok Christian Coll., 1963-68; cons., instr. Nan (Thailand) Christian Sch., 1968-70; supt. of schs. Ch. of Christ in Thailand, various locations, 1966-74; v.p. Payap U., Chiang Mai, 1974-83, acting pres., then sr. v.p., 1984-88, hon. prof. sociology and anthropology, 1987, prof. emeritus, pres.'s rep. overseas, 1988—; vis. lectr. anthropology Hastings (Nebr.) Coll., 1970-71; advisor, mem. planning and devel. com. Christian Coll., Bangkok, 1993—. Author: Ku-Daeng -- The Red Tomb, A Village Study in Northern Thailand, A.D. 1954-64, 2nd edit., 1965, Ku Daeng - Thirty Years Later, NIU Ctr. for S.E. Asian Studies, 1991; contbr. or co-contbr. articles to profl. publs. Bd. dirs., chmn. acad. adv. bd. Chiang Mai Internat. Sch., 1984-88; mem. bd. edn. Ch. of Christ in Thailand, 1966-84, chmn. bd. edn., 1983-84, advisor to bd. edn., 1984-86, cons. welfare program, 1976-78, dir. bd. welfare, 1981-88, mem. commn. on structural orgn., 1977-88; chmn. bd. dirs. Chiang Mai Co-Ednl. Ctr., 1974-81; mem. founding bd. Payap Coll., 1971-74; mem. Foothill Master Chorale, 1989-91, Claremont (Calif.) Chorale, 1992—; treas. CROP Walk, Pomona Inland Valley Coun. of Chs., 1993-94; various positions Presbytery of San Gabriel, Synod of So. Calif. & Hawaii, Shepherd of the Valley Presbyn. Ch., Hacienda Heights, Calif., Claremont Presbyn. Ch. With USN, 1944-46. Named to Most Exalted Order of White Elephant, 3rd Class, King Bhumibol Adulyadej, Thailand, 1990. Mem. Siam Soc. (life). Home: 680 Avery Rd Claremont CA 91711-4222

KINNEY, BRIAN MALTBIE, plastic surgeon; b. Baton Rouge, Apr. 28, 1954; s. Kenneth Lee and Louise Estelle (Walker) K.; m. Laureen Alida McGillis, Aug. 29, 1980 (div. Jan. 1984). SB in Mechanical Engring., Mass. Inst. Tech., 1976, SM, 1980; MD, Tulane U., 1982. Intern, residency gen. surgery UCLA Med. Ctr., L.A., 1982-86, chief residency gen. surgery, 1987, resident divsn. plastic surgery, 1988, chief resident plastic surgery, 1989; pvt. practice L.A., 1989—; cons. An. Hosp. Supply Corp., 1978-80, Ingene Corp., Santa Monica, Calif., 1984—. Author: Lymphatic Drainage in Early and Chronic Lymphedema, 1984, Revascularization and the Pattern of Regeneration and Fibrosis in Free Muscle Grafts, 1984, Studies in Free Muscle Grafting, 1984-88. Treas. Tulane Med. Sch., 1986; vol. plastic reconstructive surgeon Mexican Red Cross, Los Mochis, Mexico, 1987-89; chief plastic surgeon Operation 2nd Chance, Croatia-Bosnia, 1992—. Walter C. Teagle Found. scholar, 1972-76, 76-78, 80-82, Grad. Rsch. Assistantship scholar, 1978-80; recipient Postdoctoral Scholar Rsch. award, 1983-84. Mem. AMA, IEEE, Am. Soc. Plastic & Reconstructive Surgeons. Am. Inst. Physics, Am. Soc. Mech. Engring., Calif. Med. Assn. Office: 2080 Century Park E Ste 1110 Los Angeles CA 90067-2014*

KINNEY, PAUL WILLIAM, investment company executive; b. Denver, Nov. 3, 1952; s. Thomas Grayson and Margaret Jane Kinney; children: Lauren, Michele, Hope, Elizabeth. AB, Occidental Coll., L.A., 1975; MPA, U. Colo., Denver, 1978. 1st v.p. investments Dean Witter Reynolds Inc., Glendale, Calif., 1978—. Pres. bd. dirs. Glendale (Calif.) Symphony Orch. Assn., 1995—; bd. dirs. Glendale Cmty. Found., 1995—, cfo. Mem. Investment Mgmt. Cons. Assn., Pi Alpha Alpha. Office: Dean Witter 801 N Brand Blvd Ste 908 Glendale CA 91203

KINNEY, RALEIGH EARL, artist; b. Brainerd, Minn., Mar. 11, 1938; s. Earl Martin and Nancy Ann (Wolleat) K.; m. Darlene Joyce Fox, Sept. 12, 1964; children: Rodney Eric, Aaron Weston. BS, St. Cloud (Minn.) State U., 1965, MA, 1968. Cert. tchr. Art tchr. St. Cloud Jr. High Sch., 1965-70; art tchr., dept. chmn. St. Cloud Sr. High Sch., 1970-80; ind. instr. watercolor workshop, 1980—. Contbg. artist North Light Pub., 1993, 94. Served with USN, 1957-61. Named Artist of Yr. Phoenix C. of C., 1987. Mem. Ariz. Watercolor Soc. (signature), Midwest Watercolor Soc. (v.p. 1976-77, signature), Plein Air Painters Am. Republican. Home: 506 W Pebble Beach Dr Tempe AZ 85282-5815

KINNISON, HARRY AUSTIN, transportation engineer; b. Springfield, Ohio, Oct. 2, 1935; s. Errett Lowell and Audrey Muriel (Smith) K. BSEE, U. Wyo., 1964; M. in Transp. Engring., Seattle U., 1983; PhD in Civil Engring., U. Tenn., 1987. Enlisted USAF, 1958, commd. 2d lt., 1964, advanced through grades to capt., 1968, released from active duty, 1968; electronics engr. 1839th Electronics Installation Group, Keesler AFB, Biloxi, Miss., 1972-77; staff engr. Casper (Wyo.) Air Facilities Sector FAA, 1977; test engr. Boeing Aerospace Co., Seattle, 1977-81; grad. rsch. engr. U. Tenn. Transp. Ctr., Knoxville, 1983-87; avionics engr. Boeing Comml. Airplane Co., Seattle, 1981-83, 87-90, maintenance programs engr. customer svcs. div., 1990—. Mem. Inst. Transp. Engrs. (assoc.), Transp. Rsch. Bd. (assoc.). Republican. Mem. Christian Ch. Home: 11630 SE 219th Pl Kent WA 98031-3922 Office: Boeing Comml Airplane Group M/S 2J-21 PO Box 3707 Seattle WA 98124

KINNISON, ROBERT WHEELOCK, retired accountant; b. Des Moines, Sept. 17, 1914; s. Virgil R. and Sopha J. (Jackson) K.; m. Randi Hjelle, Oct. 28, 1971; children—Paul F., Hazel Jo Huff. B.S. in Acctg., U. Wyo., 1940. C.P.A., Wyo., Colo. Ptnr. 24 hour auto service, Laramie, Wyo., 1945-59; pvt. practice acctg., Laramie, Wyo., 1963-71, Las Vegas, Nev., 1972-74, Westminster, Colo., 1974-76, Ft. Collins, Colo., 1976-97; ret., 1997. Served with U.S. Army, 1941-45; PTO. Mem. Wyo. Soc. C.P.A.s, Am. Legion (past comdr.), Laramie Soc. C.P.A.s (pres. 1966), VFW. Clubs: Laramie Optimist (pres. 1950), Sertoma. Home: PO Box 168 Fort Collins CO 80522-0168

KINSLER, BRUCE WHITNEY, air traffic controller, consultant, air traffic control engineer, air defense engineer; b. Ukiah, Calif., Jan. 11, 1947; s. John Arthur and Mary Helen (Hudson) K.; m. Mickey Kinsler, Apr. 1, 1969 (div. Nov. 1976); 1 child, Arthur Todd; m. Segundina L. Pangilinan, May 27, 1978; 1 stepchild, Stephanie Camalig. AA, El Camino Coll., 1979; BA, Calif. State U., Long Beach, 1984. Air traffic controller FAA, various locations, 1971-81; cen. sta. mgr. Times Mirror Security Communications, Irvine, Calif., 1982-84; supr. office services Law Offices Paul, Hastings, Janofsky & Walker, L.A., 1984-85; air traffic control cons. Hughes Aircraft Co., Fullerton, Calif., 1985-88; engr., scientist space sta. div. McDonnell Douglas, Huntington Beach, Calif., 1989-90; ATC/ADGE sr. syss. engr. Hughes Aircraft Co., Fullerton, Calif., 1990—; mem. citizens adv. com. Calif. Dept. Transp., Sacramento, 1982—. Author air traffic control tng. manuals, air def. manuals. Res. dep. sheriff Orange County. With USNR, 1986—. Mem. Nat. Air Traffic Com. (nat. com.), Air Traffic Control Assn., Human Factors Soc. (pres. Orange County chpt.). Republican. Home: Unit 66809 Box 816 APO AE 09858-6809

KINSMAN, ROBERT PRESTON, biomedical plastics engineer; b. Cambridge, Mass., July 25, 1949; s. Fred Nelson and Myra Roxanne (Preston) K. BS in Plastics Engring., U. Mass., Lowell, 1971; MBA, Pepperdine U., Malibu, Calif., 1982. Cert. biomed. engr., Calif.; lic. real estate sales person, Calif. Product devel. engr., plastics divsn. Gen. Tire Corp., Lawrence, Mass., 1976-77; mfg. engr. Am. Edwards Labs. divsn. Am. Hosp. Supply Corp., Irvine, Calif., 1978-80, sr. engr., 1981-82; mfg. engring. mgr. Edwards Labs., Inc. subs. Am. Hosp. Supply Corp., Añasco, P.R., 1983; project mgr. Baxter Edwards Critical Care divsn. Baxter Healthcare Corp., Irvine, 1984-87, engring. and prodn. mgr., 1987-93; pres. Kinsman & Assocs., Irvine, Calif., 1993—; expert/auditor Med. Device Certification GmbH, Memmingen, Germany, 1995—; mem. mgmt. adv. panel Modern Plastics mag., N.Y.C., 1979-80; elected Nat. Hon. Soc., 1967. Vol. worker VA, Bedford, Mass., 1967-71; instr. first aid ARC, N.D., Mass., Calif., 1971-82; pres., bd. dirs. Lakes Homeowners Assn., Irvine, 1985-91; chmn., bd. dirs., newsletter editor Paradise Park Owners Assn., Las Vegas, Nev., 1988—; chmn. bd. dirs. Orange County (Calif.) divsn. Am. Heart Assn., 1991—, chmn. devel. com., 1993-95, v.p. bd. dirs., 1993-94, chmn.-elect bd. dirs., 1994-95, chmn. bd. dirs., 1995-96, adv. coun. rep., 1994-96, immediate past chmn. bd. dirs., 1996-97; mem. steering com. Heart and Sole Classic fundraiser, 1988—, event chmn., 1991-92, mem. devel. com. Calif. affiliate, 1993-95. Capt. USAF, 1971-75, USAFR, 1975-81. Recipient Cert. of Appreciation, VA, 1971, Am. Heart Assn., 1991-95, Outstanding Svc. award., 1996; selected Comty. Hero Torchbearer 1996 Olympic Games, United Way Am. and Atlanta Com. for Olympic Games. Baxter/Allegiance Found. Comty. Svc. grantee, Deerfield, Ill., 1992, 93. Mem. Soc. Mfg. Engrs. (sr.), Soc. Plastics Engrs. (sr., Mem. of Month So. Calif. sect. 1989), Am. Mgmt. Assn., Arnold Air Soc. (comptr. 1969, pledge tng. officer 1970), Plastics Acad., Demolay, Profl. Ski Instrs. Am., Mensa, Am. Legion, Elks, Phi Gamma Psi. Office: Kinsman & Assocs 4790 Irvine Blvd Ste 105-289 Irvine CA 92620-1973

KINSMAN, ROBERT WARREN, emergency management consultant; b. Palo Alto, Calif., Mar. 18, 1943; s. Karl Kenneth and Vera Evelyn (Romwall) K.; m. Susan Mary Hurtig, Oct. 26, 1968; 1 child, Erik Karl. BA, Calif. State U., San Francisco, 1965. Cert. secondary tchr., Calif., community coll.; registered environ. assessor, Calif. Probation officer San Mateo County Probation Dept., Redwood City, Calif., 1963-82; pub. edn. coord. San Mateo County Office of Emergency Svc., Redwood City, 1982-83, asst. area coord., 1983-90; emergency mgmt. cons. Emergency Mgmt. Assocs., Half Moon Bay, Calif., 1988—; project mgr. Indsl. Emergency Coun., San Carlos, Calif., 1992—. Author: Radiological Incident Management, 1990; contbr. articles to profl. jours. Bd. dirs. ARC Bay Area, San Mateo, 1988—, Coastside Emergency Coun., Half Moon Bay, 1975—, Bay Area March of Dimes, 1975-88, walk chmn.; coun. pres., treas. Coastside Luth. Ch., 1988-92. Recipient People Who Care award San Mateo County Bd. of Supr., 1981, Vol. of Yr. City of Half Moon Bay, 1979. Mem. Radiol. Emergency Mgmt. Soc. (state pres. 1983-88, Citation 1986), Nat. Coordinating Coun. on Emergency Mgmt., Internat. Soc. to Emergency/Diaster Medicine, Calif. Emergency Svcs. Assn. (industry rels. bd. 1983—, Citation 1990), Assn. of Profl. Emergency Planners. Republican. Lutheran. Home: 413 Casa Del Mar Dr Half Moon Bay CA 94019-1413 Office: Emergency Mgmt Assocs PO Box 3181 Half Moon Bay CA 94019-3181

KINT, ARNE TONIS, industrial engineer, mechanical engineer; b. Tallinn, Harjumaa, Estonia, Nov. 2, 1932; came to U.S., 1957; s. Tõnis Kint and Salme (Redlich) K.; m. Saima Kärp, Aug. 30, 1964. BS in Mech. Engring., Stockholm Tekniska Inst., 1954; BS in Indsl. Engring., Ga. Tech., 1960; MS in Indsl. Engring., U. Calif., 1963. Registered profl. indsl. engr., Calif.; cert. profl. materials handling and mgmt., Mich. Mech. engr. Philips Neon Co., Stockholm, 1954-57; student indsl. engr. Weirton (W. Va.) Steel Co., 1959; plant, foundry engr. H.C. McCaulay Foundry, Inc., Berkeley, Calif., 1960-67; indsl. engring. project leader Matson Navigation Co., San Francisco, 1967-69; area indsl. engr. Interpace Corp., Pitts., 1969-72; cons. indsl. engr. Oakland, Calif., 1972-73; work design, analysis supr. Truck Divsn. Internat. Harvester Co., Inc., San Leandro, Calif., 1973-75; project mgr., sr. syss. project engr. Engineered Syss. and Devel. Corp., Santa Clara and San Jose, Calif., 1975-89; cons. ind. engr. Applied Engring. and Design, Inc., San Jose, Calif., 1989-90; project engr. Jacobs Engring. Group, Martinez, Calif., 1990-92; cons. ind. engr. Indsl. Engring. USA, Oakland, Calif., 1992—. Bd. dirs. Estonian Info. Ctr., Stockholm, 1946-75; pres. Estonian League of Liberation, San Francisco, 1968-73. Decorated Gold Svc. medal Estonian Nat. Found., 1971. Mem. Estonian Soc. San Francisco (pres. 1962, 63), Swedish Am. C. of C., Estonian Ski Club. Home: 312 Alta Vista Ave Oakland CA 94610-1941 Office: Indsl Engring USA 312 Alta Vista Ave Oakland CA 94610-1941

KINZELL, LA MOYNE B., school health services administrator, educator; b. Melstone, Mont., May 4, 1930; d. William Edward and Iro Millicent (Keeton) Berger; m. Les Kieth Kinzell, Sept. 18, 1954; children: Yvette Li Goins, Anitra Elise Chew, Antony Mikhail Kinzell. BS, Mont. State U., 1954; MA, Calif. State U., 1982. RN, Calif. Instr. surg. nursing Mont. Deaconess Hosp., Great Falls, 1954-55; instr. nursing arts St. Patrick's Hosp., Missoula, Mont., 1957-59; instr. sci. Palmdale (Calif.) Sch. Dist., 1966-86, dir. health svcs., 1986—; adv. bd. facilitator Palmdale Healthy Start, 1992—; com. mem. Am. Cancer Soc., 1986—, United Way, 1991—. Mem. Citizen Amb. Sch. Nursing Del. to Europe, 1994; treas. campaign sch. bd. mem., Palmdale, 1989, 93. Recipient Tchr. of Yr. award Palmdale, 1985-86, L.A. County Sheriffs Dept. award, 1985, Nat. Every Child by Two, Immunization Ptnrs. award, 1995; grantee Drug, Alcohol and Tobacco Edn., 1987, Healthy Start Planning, 1994, 95, Healthy Start Operational award, 1996. Mem. Am. Lung Assn. (chair edn. 1988-94), Calif. Sch. Nurse Orgn. (sec. 1992-95), Phi Kappa Phi, Alpha Tau Delta, Sigma Theta Tau, Delta Kappa Gamma (chair legislature 1993-95, area IX dir. 1995-97, mem. Chi state expansion com.). Democrat. Episcopalian. Home: 38817 2nd St E Palmdale CA 93550-3201 Office: Palmdale Sch Dist 39139 10th St E Palmdale CA 93550-3419

KIPPUR, MERRIE MARGOLIN, lawyer; b. Denver, July 24, 1962; d. Morton Leonard and Bonnie (Seldin) Margolin; m. Bruce R. Kippur, Sept. 7, 1986. BA, Colo. Coll., 1983; JD, U. Colo., 1986. Bar: Colo. 1986, U.S. Dist. Ct. Colo. 1986, U.S. Ct. Appeals (10th cir.) 1987. Assoc. Sterling & Miller, Denver, 1985-88, McKenna & Cuneo, Denver, 1989-94; sr. v.p., gen. counsel, dir. First United Bank, Denver, 1994-96; prin. Merrie Margolin Kippur Assocs., P.C., Denver, 1997—; lectr. trial practice, bankruptcy, article 4, uniform comml. code, estate planning, others. Author: Student Improvement in the 1980's, 1984, (with others) Ethical Considerations in Bankruptcy, 1985, Partnership Bankruptcy, 1986, Colorado Methods of Practise, 1988, others. Contract liaison Jr. League Denver, 1992-94; bd. dirs. Bylaws Parliamentarian, 1994-95, mem. planning coun., 1995-96, mem. nominating com., 1996-97, facilitator, 1996-97, facilitator co-chair, 1997—. Mem. ABA, Nat. Network Estate Planning Attys., Colo. Bar Assn., Denver Bar Assn., Am. Judicature Soc., Gamma Phi Beta, Phi Delta Phi, Pi Gamma Mu. Democrat.

KIRBY, ORVILLE EDWARD, potter, painter, sculptor; b. Wichita, Kans., Jan. 31, 1912; s. Charlie and Elizabeth J. (Sage) K. Student, U. Utah, 1935-36, U. So. Calif., L.A., 1934-35, St. Paul Sch. Fine Art, 1933-34. Owner Orville Kirby Pottery, L.A., 1941-47; owner Sleepy Hollow Pottery, Laguna Beach, Calif., 1948-54, Monroe, Utah, 1955—. Republican. Mormon. Home and Office: 95 W Center St Monroe UT 84754-4159

KIRBY, THOMAS PAUL, artist; b. San Francisco, June 10, 1926; s. Edward Thomas and Alice Madeline (Flood) K.; m. Virginia Gay Christianson, May 17, 1963 (div. Jan. 1984); children: Dawn, Paul, Alice, Steven, Thomas; m. Joan D. Truman, 1985. Student, Calif. Coll. Arts and Crafts, 1946-47, San Francisco Art Inst., 1948. Curator exhbns. dept. Mus. N.Mex., Santa Fe, 1970-74; concert hall and tour mgr. Santa Fe Chamber Music Festival, 1973. One man shows at East-West Gallery, San Francisco, 1954, 55, Lucien Labaudt Gallery, San Francisco, 1957, San Francisco Mus. Modern Art, 1964, Anchorage (Alaska) Fine Arts Mus., 1969, West Gallery, Santa Fe, 1970, Hill's Gallery, Santa Fe, 1972, 74, Hartnell Coll. Gallery, Salinas, Calif., 1980, Monterey (Calif.) Peninsula Mus. Art, 1981, Bay Window Gallery, Mendocino, Calif., 1987; group exhbns. include Bratta Gallery, N.Y.C., San Francisco Art Inst. Annual Exhbns. and Traveling Exhbns., 1959-62, Zellerbach Bldg., San Francisco, 1963, The deYoung Mus., San Francisco, 1963, Highlands U., Las Vegas, 1973, Roswell Mus. Fall Invitational, 1973, Francis McGray Gallery, Silver City, N.Mex; represented in permanent collections The Monterey (Calif.) Peninsula Mus. Art, The Mus. Fine Arts, Anchorage, The Fine Arts Mus., Santa Fe, The Roswell Mus. and Art Ctr., IBM Corp., ITEL, Torrance, Calif., SSI Corp., San Francisco, Mobil Oil Co., Denver, Kona Surf Hotel, Hawaii, Rosewood Hotel, Tex., The Fairmount, Tex., The Peabody Hotel, Orlando, Fla., Touche Ross & Co., San Jose, Calif. With USN, 1944-46. Mem. San Francisco Art Inst. Alumni. Home and Studio: 118 Willow St Salinas CA 93901-3227

KIRCH, PATRICK VINTON, anthropology educator; b. Honolulu, July 7, 1950; s. Harold William and Barbara Ver (MacGarvin) K.; m. Debra Connelly, Mar. 3, 1979 (div. 1990); m. Therese Babineau, Feb. 6, 1994. BA, U. Pa., 1971; MPhil, Yale U., 1974, PhD, 1975. Assoc. anthropologist Bishop Mus., Honolulu, 1975-76, anthropologist, 1976-82, head archaeology div., 1982-84, asst. chmn. anthropology, 1983-84, dir., assoc. prof. Burke Mus. U. Wash., Seattle, 1984-87, prof., 1987-89; prof. U. Calif., Berkeley, 1989—; curator Hearst Mus. Anthropology, 1989—; adj. faculty U. Hawaii, Honolulu, 1979-84; mem. lasting legacy com. Wash. State Centennial Commn., 1986-88; pres. Soc. Hawaiian Archaeology, 1980-81. Author: The Anthropology of History in the Kingdom of Hawaii, 1992, Feathered Gods and Fishhooks, 1985, Evolution of the Polynesian Chiefdoms, 1984, The Wet and the Dry, 1994, The Lapita Peoples, 1996, Legacy of the Landscape, 1996; editor: Island Societies, 1986; contbr. articles to profl. pubs. Grantee NSF, 1974, 76, 77, 82, 87, 88, 89, 93, 96, NEA, 1985, NEH, 1988, Hawaii Com. for Humanities, 1981; Rsch. grantee Nat. Geographic Soc., 1986, 89, 96. Fellow NAS, Am. Acad. Arts and Scis., Am. Anthrop. Assn., Am. Assn. Advancement Sci.; mem. Assn. Field Archaeology, Polynesian Soc., Seattle C. of C., Sigma Xi. Democrat. Office: U Calif Dept Anthropology Berkeley CA 94720

KIRCHER, ANNE CATHERINE, communications consultant; b. Portland, Oreg., Dec. 27, 1962; d. John Lawrence and Helen (Morris) K. Student, U. N.Mex., 1981-83. Planning and rsch. clk. Albuquerque Pub. Schs., 1985-89, desktop publisher, designer, 1989-90; pub. info. and comm. cons. Presbyn. Healthcare Svcs., Albuquerque, 1990—. Mem. N.Mex. Soc. Healthcare Mktg. and Pub. Rels. (sec. 1994-95, v.p. 1995). Home: 1405 San Carlos Dr SW # 2 Albuquerque NM 87104-1060 Office: Presbyn Healthcare Svcs 5901 Harper Dr NE Albuquerque NM 87109-3587

KIRK, CARMEN ZETLER, data processing executive; b. Altoona, Pa., May 22, 1941; d. Paul Alan and Mary Evelyn (Pearce) Zetler. BA, Pa. State U., 1959-63; MBA, St. Mary's Coll. Calif., 1977. Cert. in data processing. Pub. sch. tchr. State Ga., 1965-66; systems analyst U.S. Govt. Dept. Army, Oakland, Calif., 1967-70; programmer analyst Contra Costa County, Martinez, Calif., 1970-76; applications mgr. Stanford (Calif.) U., 1976-79; pres. Zetler Assocs., Inc., Palo Alto, Calif., 1979—; cons. State Calif., Sacramento, 1985-88. Office: Zetler Assocs Inc PO Box 50395 Palo Alto CA 94303-0395

KIRK, CASSIUS LAMB, JR., lawyer, investor; b. Bozeman, Mont., June 8, 1929; s. Cassius Lamb and Gertrude Violet (McCarthy) K.; AB, Stanford U., 1951; JD, U. Calif., Berkeley, 1954. Bar: Calif. 1955. Assoc. firm Cooley, Godward, Castro, Huddleson & Tatum, San Francisco, 1956-60; staff counsel for bus. affairs Stanford U., 1960-78; chief bus. officer, staff counsel Menlo Sch. and Coll., Atherton, Calif., 1978-81; chmn. Eberli-Kirk Properties, Inc. (doing bus. as Just Closets), Menlo Park, 1981-94; mem. summer faculty Coll. Bus. Adminstrn. U. Calif., Santa Barbara, 1967-73; past mem. adv. bd. Allied Arts Guild, Menlo Park; past nat. vice chmn. Stanford U. Annual Fund; past v.p. Palo Alto C. of C. With U.S. Army, 1954-56. Mem. Stanford Assocs., Order of Coif, Phi Alpha Delta. Republican. Club:

Stanford Faculty. Home and Office: 1330 University Dr Apt 52 Menlo Park CA 94025-4241

KIRK, HENRY PORT, academic administrator; b. Clearfield, Pa., Dec. 20, 1935; s. Henry P. and Ann (H.) K.; m. Mattie F., Feb. 11, 1956; children: Timothy, Mary Ann, Rebecca. BA, Geneva Coll., 1958; MA, U. Denver, 1963; EdD, U. Southern Calif., 1973. Counselor, ednl. Columbia Coll., Columbia, Mo., 1963-65; dean Huron (S.D.) Coll., 1965-66; assoc. dean Calif. State U., L.A., 1966-70; dean El Camino Coll., Torrance, Calif., 1970-81; v.p. Pasadena (Calif.) City Coll., 1981-86; pres. Centralia (Wash.) Coll., 1986—. Contbr. articles to profl. jours. Mem. hist. commn., City Chehalis, 1990, pres. econ. devel. coun., 1992; campaign chmn., United Way, Centralia, 1989-90. Recipient PTK Bennett Disting. Pres. award, 1990; Exemplary Contbn. to Resource Devel. award Nat. Coun. Resource Devel., 1993. Mem. Wash. Assn. Community Colls., Torrance Rotary Club (pres. 1987-88), Centralia Rotary Club (pres. 1990-91), Phi Theta Kappa, Phi Delta Kappa. Presbyterian. Office: Centralia Coll 600 W Locust St Centralia WA 98531-4035

KIRK, JANET BROWN, artist, educator, art gallery owner; b. Cisco, Tex., Oct. 3, 1929; d. Olen Benjamin Brown and Evelyn (White) Pitman; m. Glenn L. Kirk, Aug. 5, 1949; children: David Patrick, Dennis Paul, Steven Lloyd, Lisa Evelyn Nave. Student, U. Colo., 1973, 74, 76, Metro State Coll., 1978, 80, Rocky Mountain Sch. Art., 1982. instr. art classes and workshops, Wyo., Colo., 1982—; gallery affiliations Cornerstone Gallery, Longmont, 1970-92, Wild Basin Gallery, Allenspark, Colo., 1988-91, Eastin Gallery, Allenspark, 1992—, Profl. Galleries, St. Cloud, Minn., 1989—, J. Michaels Gallery, Edina, Minn., 1989—, San Juan Art Ctr., Ridgeway, Colo., 1992, Gwendolyn's Art Gallery Ltd., Lake City, Colo., 1993—, Estes Park (Colo.) Art Ctr., 1996—. Exhibited in one person shows Niwot (Colo.) Art Gallery, 1982, Santa Fe Gallery, Odessa, Tex., 1984, Cornerstone Gallery, Longmont, Colo., 1988; exhibited in group shows The COORS Show, Golden, Colo., 1988, Colo. Artists ABS Shows, Loveland, 1988, 89, Denver, 1991, Colo. Watercolor Soc. Show, Botanical Gardens, Denver, 1992-96, 97, Colo. Artists Guild State Hist. Mus. Show, Denver, 1992, New England Art Inst. State of the Arts 1993, Boston, 1993, Colo. Watercolor Soc. State Show, 1996, Artists of Colo. State Show, 1996-97; represented in permanent collections Citi-Corp., USA, Energy Div., Denver, John Cox Drilling Co., Midland, others. Bd. mem. Longmont (Colo.) Coun. for the Arts, 1990-91; speaker and demonstrator in field. Recipient Purchase award Glenwood Springs (Colo.) Art Show, 1992. Mem. Am. Watercolor Soc. (assoc.), Nat. Watercolor Soc. (assoc.), Southwest Watercolor Soc. (assoc.), Colo. Watercolor Soc. (qualified signature membership 1995), Western Colo. Watercolor Soc., Colo. Art Guild, Coun. on Arts and Humanities (bd. mem. 1990-92), Colo. Artists Assn. (regional rep. 1982-86, exec. bd. mem. 1986—, Juror's Choice award State Conv. 1991, Spl. Merit award State Conv. 1992, 95, 96). Home: 719 3rd Ave Longmont CO 80501-5926

KIRK, REA HELENE (REA HELENE GLAZER), special education educator; b. N.Y.C., Nov. 17, 1944; d. Benjamin and Lillian (Kellis) Glazer; 3 stepdaughters. BA, UCLA, 1966; MA, Eastern Mont. Coll., 1981; EdD U. So. Calif., 1995. Life cert. spl. edn. tchr., Calif., Mont. Spl. edn. tchr., L.A., 1966-73; clin. sec. speech and lang. clinic, Missoula, Mont., 1973-75; spl. edn. tchr., Missoula and Gt. Falls, Mont., 1975-82; br. mgr. YWCA of L.A., Beverly Hills, Calif., 1989-91; sch. adminstrn., ednl. coord. Adv. Schs. of Calif., 1991-94; dir. Woman's Resource Ctr., Gt. Falls, Mont., 1981-82; dir. Battered Woman's Shelter, Rock Springs, Wyo., 1982-84; dir. Battered Victims Program Sweetwater County, Wyo., 1984-88, Battered Woman's Program, San Gabriel Valley, Calif., 1988, Spl. Edn., Pasadena, 1994-96, prin., 1995; instr. U. Wis., Platteville, 1996—; mem. Wyo. Commn. on Aging, Rock Springs; mem. Community Action Bd. City of L.A. Pres., bd. dirs. battered woman's shelter, Gt. Falls, Woman's Resource Ctr., Gt. Falls; founder, advisor Rape Action Line, Gt. Falls; founder Jewish religious svcs., Missoula; 4-H leader; hostess Friendship Force; Friendship Force ambassador, Wyo., Fed. Republic Germany, Italy; mem. YWCA Mont. and Wyo. Recipient Gladys Byron scholar U. So. Calif., 1993, Dept. Edn. scholar U. So. Calif., 1994, honors Missoula 4-H; recognized as significant Wyo. woman as social justice reformer and peace activist Sweetwater County, Wyo.; nominated Wyo. Woman of the Yr., 1981, 82; honored by L.A. Mayor Bradley for Anti-Poverty work. Mem. Council for Exceptional Children (v.p. Gt. Falls 1981-82), Assn. for Children with Learning Disabilities (Named Oustanding Mem. 1982), Phi Delta Kappa, Delta Kappa Gamma, Psi Chi, Pi Lamda Theta. Democrat. Jewish.

KIRK, SAMUEL ALEXANDER, psychologist, educator; b. Rugby, N.D., Sept. 1, 1904; s. Richard B. and Nellie (Boussard) K.; m. Winifred Eloise Day, June 25, 1933; children: Jerome Richard, Nancy Lorraine. Ph.B., U. Chgo., 1929, M.S., 1931; Ph.D., U. Mich., 1935; L.H.D., Lesley Coll., 1969; D.L., U. Ill., 1983. Research psychologist Wayne Country Tng. Sch., Northville, Mich., 1931-34, mental hygienist, 1934-35; dir. div. edn. for exceptional children State Tchrs. Coll., Milw., 1935-42, 46; chmn. grad. sch. vis. lectr. U. Mich, 1942; prof. edn. and psychology U. Ill., 1947-68, prof. emeritus, 1968—; dir. Inst. Research Exceptional Children, 1952-68; prof. spl. edn. U. Ariz., Tucson, 1968-86. Author: (with Hegge and W.D. Kirk) Remedial Reading Drills, 1936, Teaching Reading to Slow-Learning Children, 1940, (with Johnson) Educating the Retarded Child, 1951, (with Karnes and Kirk) You and Your Retarded Child, 1955, Early Education of the Mentally Retarded, 1958, Educating Exceptional Children, 1962, 2d edit, 1972, (with Gallagher) Educating Exceptional Children, 1979, 83, 86, 89, (with Gallagher and Anastasiow) Educating Exceptional Children, 1993, (with Wiener) Behavioral Research on Exceptional Children, 1964, (with J.J. McCarthy and Kirk) The Illinois Test of Psycholinguistic Abilities, rev. edit., 1968, (with Kirk) Psycholinguistic Learning Disabilities, 1971, (with Lord) Exceptional Children: Resources and Perspectives, 1974, (with J.M. McCarthy) Learning Disabilities, 1975, (with Kleibahn and Lerner) Teaching Reading to Slow and Disabled Readers, 1978, (with Chalfant) Academic and Developmental Learning Disabilities, 1984, (with Kirk and Minskoff) Phonic Remedial Reading Lessons, 1985, The Foundations of Special Education: Selected Papers and Speeches of Samuel A. Kirk, 1993; contbr. articles to profl. publs. Served as maj. AUS, 1942-46. Recipient 1st internat. award for profl. service in mental retardation Joseph P. Kennedy Jr. Found., 1962, J.E. Wallace Wallin ann. award Council for Exceptional Children, 1966, recognition award for early childhood edn., 1981, ann. award Assn. Children with Learning Disabilities, 1966, ann. award Caritas Soc., 1966, Internat. Milestone award Internat. Fedn. Learning Disabilities, 1975, Disting. Service award Am. Assn. Speech and Hearing, 1976, Disting. Citizen award U. Ariz. Alumni Assn., 1977, award for outstanding leadership Ill. Council Exceptional Children, 1980, recognition award Pa. Assn. Children with Learning Disabilities, 1980, Ariz. Div. Devel. Disability, 1980, Helen T. Devereaux Meml. award, 1981. Fellow Am. Psychol. Assn. (Edgar Bell award 1980); Am. Assn. for Mental Deficiency (award 1969); mem. Internat. Council Exceptional Children (pres. 1941-43), Nat. Soc. Study Edn. (chmn. 1950 yearbook com), Brit. Assn. Spl. Edn. (hon. v.p. 1962), Sigma Xi. Home: 7500 N Calle Sin Envidia Tucson AZ 85718-7300 *The satisfaction derived from service to mankind is a manifestation of the idealism of America.*

KIRKMAN, ROY C., mining executive; b. Hackensack, N.J., Mar. 26, 1944; s. William Christian Kirkman and Emily Elenor Frazer; m. Sharon Lee Rounds, June 14, 1969; children: David, John. PCE, Colo. Sch. Mines, 1966, MS in Mineral Econs., 1976; cert. real estate, U. Colo. Lic. real estate broker, Colo. Property adminstr. and project geologist USA C.E., Buffalo, 1968-69; geolo. and mining engr. U.S. AEC, Grand Junction, Colo., 1969-74; pres. and chmn. bd. Kirkman Energy Resources Corp., Boulder, Colo., 1975—; pres. Artificial Exploration Intelligence Sys, 1995. Inventor: Probabilistic Risk Analysis of Fund Resources. Co-founder Colo. chpt. Nat. Taxpayers Union; treas. Boy Scouts Am.; chmn. Boulder chpt. ACM, 1978-81; mem. bd. deacons St. Andrews Presbyn., 1981. With U.S. Army, 1967-69. Mem. AIME, Colo. Mining Assn. Republican. Episcopalian. Home: 2320 Hillsdale Way Boulder CO 80303 Office: Kirkman Energy Resources Corp PO Box 3271 Boulder CO 80307

KIRKORIAN, DONALD GEORGE, college official, management consultant; b. San Mateo, Calif., Nov. 30, 1938; s. George and Alice (Sergius) K. BA, San Jose State U., 1961, MA, 1966, postgrad., 1968; postgrad., Stanford U., 1961, U. So. Calif., 1966; PhD, Northwestern U., 1972. Producer Sta. KNTV, San Jose, Calif., 1961; tchr. L.A. City Schs., 1963; instrnl. TV coord. Fremont Union High Sch. Dist., Sunnyvale, Calif., 1963-73; assoc. dean instrn. learning resources Solano C.C., Suisun City, Calif., 1973-85, dean instrnl. services, 1985-89, dean learning resources and staff devel., 1989—; owner, pres. Kirkorian and Assocs., Suisun City; field cons. Nat. Assn. Edn. Broadcasters, 1966-68; adj. faculty San Jose State U., 1968-69, U. Calif., Santa Cruz, 1970-73, U. Calif., Davis, 1973-76; chmn. Bay Area TV Consortium, 1976-77, 86-87; mem. adv. panel Speech Comm. Assn./Am. Theater Assn. tchr. preparation in speech., comm., theater and media, N.Y.C., 1973-77. Author: Staffing Information Handbook, 1990, National Learning Resources Directory, 1991, 93; editor: Media Memo, 1973-80, Intercom: The Newsletter for Calif. Community Coll. Librs., 1974-75, Update, 1980-90, Exploring the Benicia State Recreation Area, 1977, California History Resource Materials, 1977, Time Management, 1980; contbr. articles to profl. jours. Chmn. Solano County Media Adv. Com., 1974-76; bd. dirs. Napa-Solano United Way, 1980-82; mem. adv. bd. Calif. Youth Authority, 1986-93. Mem. Nat. Assn. Ednl. Broadcasters, Assn. for Edn. Comm. and Tech., Broadcast Edn. Assn., Calif. Assn. Ednl. Media and Tech. (treas.), Western Ednl. Soc. for Telecomm. (bd. dirs. 1973-75, pres. 1976-77, State Chancellor's com. on Telecomm. 1982-86), Learning Resources Assn. Calif. Comm. Colls. (exec. dir. 1976—, sec.-treas., pres.), Assn. Calif. C.C. Adminstrs. (bd. dirs. 1985-91), Cmty. Coll. Instrnl. Network. Home: 1655 Rockville Rd Suisun City CA 94585-1373 Office: Solano CC 4000 Suisun Valley Rd Suisun City CA 94585-4017

KIRKPATRICK, DAVID TEAL, archaelogist; b. Sacramento, Jan. 11, 1949; s. Charles T. and Phyllis (Shaw) K.; m. Meliha Sue Duran, May 31, 1974; 1 child, Leyla Duran. BA in Anthropology, Univ. Calf., Santa Barbara, 1971; MA in Anthropology, Wash. State Univ., 1975, PhD in Anthropology, 1986. Archaeologist N.M. State Univ., Las Cruces, 1977-83; assoc. dir. Human Sys. Rsch., Las Cruces, 1983—. Trustee Dona Ana County Hist. Soc., 1990-95. Mem. N.M. Archaeology Coun. (pres.-elect 1988, pres. 1989), Archaeol. Soc. N.M. (trustee 1987-95, co-editor 1988—, Achievement award 1992), El Paso Archaeol. Soc. (1st v.p. 1994), Soc. Am. Archaeology. Home: 3201 Linden Las Cruces NM 88005 Office: Human Sys Rsch 317 S Main St Las Cruces NM 88001-1203

KIRKPATRICK, RICHARD ALAN, internist; b. Rochester, Minn., Jan. 17, 1947; s. Neal R. and Ethel C. (Hull) K.; m. Susan Baxter; children: James N., Ronald S., David B., Mary J., Scott B., Christina Marie. BA in Chemistry with honors, U. Wash., 1968, BS in Psychology, 1968, MD, 1972. Diplomate Am. Bd. Internal Medicine. Intern, resident in internal medicine Mayo Grad. Sch., Rochester, 1972-76, spl. resident in biomed. communications, 1974-75; pvt. practice specializing in internal medicine Longview, Wash., 1976—; founding ptnr. Internal Medicine Clinic of Longview, 1996, Kirkpatrick Family Care, Longview, 1996; mem. clin. faculty U. Wash.; dir. cardiac rehab. program St. John's Hosp.; sec. The Physicians Alliance. Editor: Drug Therapy Abstracts, Wash. Internists; mem. editorial adv. bd. Your Patient and Cancer, Primary Care and Cancer; weekly med. TV talk show host, 1978—; contbr. articles to med. jours. Bd. dirs., v.p. Columbia Theatre for Performing Arts; mem. City Coun., Longview; mem. S.W. Wash. Symphony; bd. dirs. S.W. Wash. Youth Symphony; pres., bd. dirs. Sta. KLTV. Named to Hall of Fame, Lower Columbia Coll., 1996. Fellow ACP (gov.'s coun., sec. Washington chpt.); mem. Wash. State Soc. Internal Medicine (trustee, past pres.), Am. Geriatrics Soc., Am. Soc. Echocardiography, Am. Soc. Internal Medicine, Wash. Med. Assn. (mem. com.), Am. Cancer Soc. (local bd. dirs.), Am. Soc. Clin. Oncology, AMA, Am. Med. Writers Assn. Office: Washington Way at Civic Ctr Longview WA 98632

KIRKPATRICK, WILLIS F., state banking and securities administrator; b. Caldwell, Idaho; m. Phyllis Galloway; 3 children. Grad., Coll. Idaho, 1957; postgrad., U. Oreg., 1957-59. Dist. mgr. Chrysler Corp., Dodge Divsn., Spokane, Wash.; staff Walston & Co. Investment Brokers, Spokane, Wash.; examiner State of Alaska Divsn. Banking, Securities and Corps., Juneau, 1969-73, dir., 1973, 81—; mgr. Juneau offices Alaska Fed. Savings and Loan, 1974-81; apptd. acting commr. dept. commerce and econ. devel., State of Alaska, during 3 gov. transitions, 1981—. Past pres. Juneau Children's Receiving Home, Southeast Alaska Coun. Boy Scouts Am. Mem. Juneau Downtown Rotary Club (pres. 1978-79, cmty. svc. chmn. Alaska-Whitehorse dist.). Office: State of Alaska Dept Commerce Divsn Banking PO Box 110807 Juneau AK 99811-0807

KIRSCHENMAN, KARL AARON, editor; b. Ridgecrest, Calif., Apr. 27, 1969; s. Karl Lewis Kirschenman and Carol Elaine (Spargo) Reid. BS, No. Ariz. U., Flagstaff, 1994. Editor The Post Group, Hollywood, Calif., 1992—; supr. comml. prodn. KNAZ-TV, Flagstaff, 1992-93; prodn. mgr., editor Envision Prodns., Sedona, Ariz., 1993-95; freelance editor Studio City, Calif., 1995-96. Office: The Post Group 6335 Homewood Ave Hollywood CA 90028

KIRSCHNER, BRUCE HERBERT, federal official, political science educator; b. N.Y.C., Aug. 13, 1953; s. Arthur S. and Miriam (Edelman) K.; m. Janet P. Lowe, Aug. 16, 1978; children: Aron, Paul, Sam. BA English, Polit. Sci. magna cum laude, SUNY, Buffalo, 1975; MPA, U. New Mex., 1977; PhD in Pub. Adminstrn., U. Colo., Denver, 1990. Rsch. asst. Cmty. Planning Assitance Ctr. Western N.Y., Buffalo, 1974-75, N.Y. State Senate Com. on Consumer Protection, Albany, 1975-76, Divsn. Pub. Adminstrn. U. New Mex., Albuquerque, 1976-77; program specialist Inst. for Applied Rsch. Svcs. U. New Mex., Albuquerque, 1978; mgmt. analyst Office Nuclear Reactor Regulation U.S. Nuclear Reg. Commn., Bethesda, Md., 1978-79; program analyst Asst. Sec. for Conservation, Solar Energy U.S. Dept Energy, Washington, 1979-81, Western Area Power Adminstrn. U.S. Dept. Energy, Golden, Colo., 1981—; speaker various govt. sponsored panels and tech. orgn. confs.; adj. prof. polit. sci. & pub. adminstrn. U. Colo., Denver. Contbr. articles to profl. jours. Co-founder Boulder Cmty. Network. Named one of Outstanding Young Men of Am., U.S. Jaycees, 1977. Mem. Alliance for Pub. Tech., The Electronic Frontier Found., The World Future Soc., Am. Soc. for Pub. Adminstrn.; Phi Beta Kappa, Pi Alpha Alpha. Office: Western Area Power Adminstrn 1627 Cole Blvd Golden CO 80401-3305

KIRSCHNER, MELVIN HENRY, physician; b. N.Y.C., Aug. 13, 1926; s. Philip S. and Belle (Lobel) K.; m. Geraldine Lee Williams, Dec. 30, 1961; children: Darin Markley, Corey Alan, Todd Andrew. BA, UCLA, 1948, BS, 1949; MPH, U. Calif., Berkeley, 1955; MD, U. So. Calif., 1960. Sanitarian Tulare (Calif.) County Health Dept., 1949-51, Oakland (Calif.) City Health Dept., 1951-52, 55; cons. pub. health sanitarian Calif. State Health Dept., Berkeley, 1952-54; sanitary engr. Calif. State Health Dept., 1956-59; intern L.A. County Hosp., 1960-61; pvt. family practice Van Nuys, Calif., 1961—; mem., past chmn. Unihealth Bioethics Inst.; med. dir. San Fernando Valley Home Health Agy., Encino, Calif., 1968-71, Sheraton Convalescent Hosp., Sepulveda, Calif., 1968—, Beverly Manor Convalscent Hosp., Panorama City, Calif., 1967—; dir. biomed. ethics Valley Hosp. Med. Ctr., Van Nuys, 1986—, Panorama Hosp. Med. Ctr., 1982-91; chmn. family practice com. Valley Presbyn. Hosp., 1992, Bioethics Mission Cmty. Hosp., Panorama City, 1993—. With USN, 1944-46. Mem. AMA, APHA, Am. Acad. Family Physicians (diplomate), Nat. Coun. Against Health Fraud, Calif. Med. Assn., Calif. Acad. Family Practice, L.A. County Med. Assn. (co-chmn. biomed. ethics com.). Office: 14411 Gilmore St Van Nuys CA 91401-1430

KIRSCHNER, RICHARD MICHAEL, naturopathic physician, speaker, author; b. Cin., Sept. 27, 1949; s. Alan George and Lois (Dickey) K.; 1 child, Aden Netanya; m. Lindea Bowe. BS in Human Biology, Kans. Newman Coll., 1979; D in Naturopathic Medicine, Nat. Coll. Naturopathic Medicine, 1981. Vice pres. D. Kirschner & Son, Inc., Newport, Ky., 1974-77; co-owner, mgr. Sunshine Ranch Arabian Horses, Melbourne, Ky., 1975-77; pvt. practice Portland, Oreg., 1981-83, Ashland, Oreg., 1983—; seminar leader, trainer Inst. for Meta-Linguistics, Portland, 1981-84; cons. Nat. Elec. Contractors Assn., So. Oreg., 1985-86, United Telephone N.W., 1986; spkr. Ford Motor Co., Blue Cross-Blue Shield, Balfour Corp., NEA, AT&T, Triad Sys., Supercuts, 1986-89, Hewlett-Packard, Pepsi Co., George Bush Co., 1990-91, Goodwill Industries Am., Motorola, 1992, The Homestead T.V.A., Federated Ambulatory Surg. Assn., V.H.A. Satellite Broadcast, 1993, Oreg. Dept. Edn., Anaheim Meml. Hosp., 1994, Inc. 500 Conf., U.S. C. of C., Inst. Indsl. Engrs., 1995, EDS, ASFSA, Safeco Ins., Fairfax County, Va.; spkr., trainer Careertrack Seminars, Boulder, Colo., 1986-93; owner, spkr., trainer R & R Prodns., Ashland, Oreg., 1984—. Co-author: audio tape seminar How to Deal with Difficult People, 1987, video tape seminar, 1988; author: (audio tape seminar) How to Find and Keep a Mate, 1988, (videotape seminar) How to Find a Mate, 1990, The Happiness of Pursuit, 1994, (videotape seminar) How to Deal with Difficult People, Vol. II, 1992, (book) Dealing With People You Can't Stand, 1994, Digital Publishing on e World, Discussions of Problem People and Happiness, 1995. Spokesman Rogue Valley PBS, 1986, 87. Mem. Am. Assn. Naturopathic Physicians (bd. dirs., chmn. pub. affairs 1989-93), Wilderness Soc., Internat. Platform Assn. Republican. Office: R&R Prodns PO Box 896 Ashland OR 97520-0030

KIRSHBAUM, HOWARD M., arbiter, judge; b. Oberlin, Ohio, Sept. 19, 1938; s. Joseph and Gertrude (Morris) K.; m. Priscilla Joy Parmakian, Aug. 15, 1964; children—Audra Lee, Andrew William. B.A., Yale U., 1960; A.B., Cambridge U., 1962, M.A., 1966; LL.B., Harvard U., 1965. Ptnr. Zarlengo and Kirshbaum, Denver, 1969-75; judge Denver Dist. Ct., Denver, 1975-80, Colo. Ct. Appeals, Denver, 1980-83; justice Colo. Supreme Ct., Denver, 1983-97; arbiter Jud. Arbiter Group, Inc., Denver, 1997—, sr. judge, 1997—; adj. prof. law U. Denver, 1970—; dir. Am. Law Inst. Phila., Am. Judicature Soc., Chgo., 1983-85, Colo. Jud. Inst. Denver, 1979-89; pres. Colo. Legal Care Soc., Denver, 1974-75. Bd. dirs. Young Artists Orch., Denver, 1976-85; pres. Community Arts Symphony, Englewood, Colo., 1972-74; dir. Denver Opportunity, Inc., Denver, 1972-74; vice-chmn. Denver Council on Arts and Humanities, 1969. Mem. ABA (com. on coll. and univ. legal studies), Colo. Bar Assn., Denver Bar Assn. (trustee 1981-83), Am. Judicature Soc., Soc. Profls. in Dispute Resolution. Office: Jud Arbiter Group Inc 1601 Blake St Ste 400 Denver CO 80202-1328

KIRSHBAUM, JACK D., pathologist; b. Chgo., Dec. 31, 1902; s. David and Rebecca (Uno) K.; m. Florence R. Kirshbaum, Dec. 27, 1931; children: Gerald, Robert, Richard. MD, U. Ill., 1929, MS, 1934. Inter Cook County Hosp., Chgo., 1929-30, intern in pathology, 1932-41; instr. medicine U. Ill., 1932-34; prof. pathology, head dept. Chog. Med. Sch., 1946-47; sr. pathologist Nagasaki, Japan, 1968-70, Atomic Bomb Casualty Commn.; asst. prof. pathology Loma Linda, 1949-59; sr. pathologist Hadassah Hosp., Israel, 1978-79; mem. staff Emeritus Desert Hosp. Comdr. Jewish War Vets., Calif., 1947-48. Col. U.S. Army, 1942-45. Fellow ACP, Coll. Am. Pathologists; mem. U.S. Acad. Pathology, Can. Acad. Pathology, L.A. County Med. Assn., L.A. Pathology Soc., Calif. Pathology Soc., Am. Bd. Pathologists, Colo. Assn. Sch. Execs., Soc. Clin. Pathologists, Israel Red Cross Magen David (life), Hadassah (life fellow, assoc.), B'Nai Brith, Sigma Xi. Home: 24441 Calle Sonora Apt 250 Laguna Hills CA 92653-7705

KIRSNER, ROBERT SHNEIDER, Dutch and Afrikaans educator; b. Chgo., Oct. 18, 1941; s. Joseph B. and Minnie (Shneider) K.; married, July 14, 1968; children: Rachel, Daniel. BA in Chemistry with honors, Oberlin Coll., 1962; MA in Gen. Linguistics, Columbia U., 1968, PhD in Gen. Linguistics with distinction, 1972. Preceptor linguistics Columbia U., N.Y.C., 1970-71; from asst. prof. to assoc. prof. Dutch and Afrikaans UCLA, 1972-89, prof., 1989—; lectr. in linguistics Columbia U., N.Y.C., 1971-72; pres. Netherlandic studies program UCLA, chair dept. curriculum com., mem. departmental com. Germanic lang. instrn., mem. acad. senate faculty welfare com., mem. undergraduate courses and curricula, mem. libr. com. Editor: Low Countries and Beyond, 1993; mem. editl. bd. Tydskrif vir Nederlands en Afrikaans, Publications of the American Association for Netherlandic Studies, Tijdschrift voor Nederlands en Afrikaans; mem. adv. bd. Functions of Language; mem. adv. bd. linguistics Algemene Nederlandse Spraakkunst. Fulbright Fellow, 1968-69; Colubia U. Pres.'s fellow, 1969-70; U. Calif. Regents' Faculty fellow, 1974; fellow-in-residence Netherlands Inst. Advanced Study Humanities and Social Scis., 1979-80; NSF grantee, 1980-83; Sr. Fulbright Rsch. scholar, 1984; Visitor's fellow Netherlands Orgn. Advancement Pure Rsch., 1984; vis. scholarNetherlands Inst. Advanced Study, 1984; Am. Philos. Soc. grantee, 1988; Visitor's fellow South African Coun. Humanities Rsch., 1992; Visitor's fellow Netherlands Orgn. Sci. Rsch., 1995. Mem. Internat. Assn. Dutch Studies, Internat. Cognitive Linguistics Assn., Internat. Pragmatics Assn., So. African Assn. Dutch Studies, Linguistic Soc. Netherlands, Am. Assn. Netherlandic Studies, Linguistic Soc. Am. Office: UCLA Dept Germanic Langs Box 951539 2326 Murphy Hall Los Angeles CA 90095-1539

KISCHER, CLAYTON WARD, embryologist, educator; b. Des Moines, Mar. 2, 1930; s. Frank August and Bessie Erma (Sawtell) K.; m.Linda Sese Espejo, Nov. 7. 1964; children: Eric Armine, Frank Henry. BS in Edn., U. Omaha, 1953; MS, Iowa State U., 1960, PhD, 1962. Asst. prof. biology Ill. State U., 1962-63; rsch. assoc. Argonne (Ill.) Nat. Lab., 1963; asst. prof. zoology Iowa State U., 1963-64; NIH postdoctoral fellow in biochemistry M.D. Anderson Hosp, Houston, 1964-66; chief sect. electron microscopy S.W. Found. Rsch. and Edn., San Antonio, 1966-67; assoc. prof. anatomy U. Tex. Med. Br., Galveston, 1967-77; assoc. prof. anatomy U. Ariz. Coll. Medicine, Tucson, 1977-92, prof. emeritus, 1993—; dir. Scanning electron microscopy lab. Shrine Burns Inst., Galveston, 1969-73, cons. right to life groups. Author sci. and pub. policy; contbr. articles to profl. jours. Cubmaster pack 107 Island Dist., Galveston, 1974-76; bd. dirs. YMCA. With USN, 1947-49. NIH Rsch. grantee, 1968-89; Morrison Trust grantee, 1975-76. Mem. SAR, Galveston Rsch. Soc. (pres. 1971-72), Am. Soc. Cell Biology, Electron Microscopy Soc. Am., Am. Assn. Anatomists, Tex. Soc. Electron Microscopy (hon.) (editor newsletter 1969-73, pres. 1975-76), Ariz. Soc. Electron Microscopy (pres. 1980-81), Gamma Pi Sigma. Home: 6249 N Camino Miraval Tucson AZ 85718-3024 Office: U Ariz Coll Medicine Dept Anatomy Tucson AZ 85724

KISER, ROBERTA KATHERINE, medical administrator, education educator; b. Alton, Ill., Aug. 13, 1938; d. Stephen Robert and Virginia Elizabeth (Lasher) Golden; m. James Robert Crisman, sept. 6, 1958 (div. May 1971); 1 child, Robert Glenn; m. James Earl Kiser, Dec. 19, 1971; 1 child, James Jacob. BEd, So. Ill. U., 1960. Cert. tchr., Ill., Calif. Librarian Oaklawn (Ill.) Elem. Sch., 1960-62, Alsip (Ill.) Elem. Sch., 1966-69; tchr. Desert Sands Unified Sch. Dist., Indio, Calif., 1969-79; prin. Mothercare Infant Sch., Rancho Mirage, Calif., 1980-89; substitute tchr. Greater Coachella Valley Sch., Calif., 1989-91; med. acct. Desert Health Care, Bermuda Dunes, Calif., 1990-92; mentor tchr., computing, typing skils Wilde Woode Children's Ctr., Palm Springs, Calif., 1990-92; chiropractic asst. Rapp Chiropractic Health Ctr, Palm Desert, Calif., 1992-93; sr. med. records clk. Eisenhower Med. Ctr., Rancho Mirage, 1993—. V.p. Palm Desert (Calif.) Community Ch. Montessori Sch. Bd., 1982-85. Republican. Presbyterian. Home: 39-575 Keenan Dr Rancho Mirage CA 92270-3610 Office: Eisenhower Med Ctr 39000 Bob Hope Dr Rancho Mirage CA 92270-3221

KISER, STEPHEN, artist, educator; b. Koloa, Hawaii, Feb. 4, 1944; s. Mary A. Kiser; m. Kathleen A. Cahill, Jan. 14, 1973; children: Lisa, Kari. Cert., Brooks Inst. Photography, 1965; BA, San Jose State U., 1976, MA, 1978. Freelance photojournalist, 1964-66, 72-74; photographer Pace Publs., L.A. and N.Y.C., 1966-68; exec. and artistic dir. Tidewater Young Performers, Norfolk, Va., 1968-69; owner Steve Kiser Prodns., Orange, Calif., 1970-72; coord. dir. Ctr. for Creative Arts and Scis., San Francisco, 1976-78; owner Steve Kiser Studios, Palo Alto, Calif., 1995—; assoc. prof. Foothill Coll., Los Altos Hills, Calif., 1996—; trustee Am. Indian Contemporary Arts, San Francisco, 1988—. Exhibiting artist with numerous one man and group shows, 1970—. Event coord. Calif. Winter Spl. Olympics, Momouth, Calif., 1975-80; v.p. Hands Across the Water, U.S./Indonesia, 1984-93; advisor Leadership Palo Alto, 1995. With USN, 1968-69. Fellow Rotary, Brazil, 1970; Arts fellow for Contemporary Native Am. Artist, Ednl. Found. Am., 1996. Mem. Am. Soc. Media. Photographers, Internat. Sculpture Assn., Soc. for Photog. Edn., Coll. Art Assn., Hale Naua III. Home: 3302 Vernon Ter Palo Alto CA 94303-4203 Office: 4000 Middlefield Rd # 3 Palo Alto CA 94303-4739

KISKADDEN, ROBERT MORGAN, artist, educator; b. Tulsa, Dec. 6, 1918; s. William Walter and Irene Sylvia (Price) K.; m. Barbara Jane Meyer, Dec. 23, 1948; children: Kathryn Ann Kiskadden McMurray, Jayne Ann Kiskadden Bechtel. BFA, U. Kans., 1947; MA, Ohio Wesleyan U., 1949. Tchg. fellow Ohio Wesleyan U., Delaware, 1947-49; asst. prof. art Wichita (Kans.) Mcpl. U., 1949-57; assoc. prof. art Wichita State U., 1958-66, prof. art, 1967-68, prof. and acting chmn., 1969, prof., chmn. dept. art, 1970, asst. dean divsn. art, 1971-84, prof., asst. dean emeritus, 1984—. One man shows include Ohio Wesleyan, Delaware, 1949, Estes Park, Colo., 1950, 51, Wichita

State U., 1958, Petroleum Club, Wichita, 1958, Hutchinson (Kans.) Art Assn., 1961, 77, Studio Gallery, Topeka, 1962, Wichita Art Mus., 1965, Melody Art Mart, Paducah, Ky., 1966, Wichita State Bank, 1967, Hays (Kans.) State Coll., 1967, Wichita Art Assn., 1972, 84, Bethel Coll., Newton, Kans., 1974, Ellington Gallery, Wichita, 1979, Carmel (Calif.) Fine Art Gallery, 1988, Mus. of the S.W., Midland, Tex., 1993; exhibited in group shows at U. Wichita Gallery, 1949, 60, William Rockhill Nelson Gallery, Kansas City, 1952-55, 57, 59, 63, Wichita Art Mus., 1953-70, Mulvane Art Mus., 1957, 72, 74, Blue Door Gallery, Taos, N.Mex., 1958, Mus. N.Mex., Santa Fe, 1959, Springfield (Mo.) Art Mus., 1965, U. Tex.-El Paso, 1969, Sacred Heart Coll., 1969, So. State Coll., Springfield, S.D., 1971, Birger Sandzen Meml. Gallery, Lindsborg, 1981, McFarland Gallery, Wichita, 1969, Raven Art Gallery, Wichita, 1972, Ulrich Mus., 1977, 79, Ellington Gallery Oils and Watercolors, Wichita, 1979, annually Wichita Art Assn., Wichita State U., others; works in permanent collections Am. Embassy, Cairo, Peking U., others; contbr., worked on Joan Miro Mosaic Project facade of Ulrich Mus. Art, 1976-78. Chmn. bdlg. com. McKnight Art Ctr., Wichita, 1974; ex-officio mem. Wichita Art Mus., Wichita Art Assn.; adv. coun. Kans. Cultural Arts Commn., Topeka, 1969, 75. Sgt. C.E. U.S. Army, 1942-45. Recipient numerous awards of merit, best of show, cash, purchase awards, popular, hon. mention, 1st, 2d, 3rd prizes, 1949-93; named to Nat. Cowboy Hall of Fame; Kiskadden Scholarship for Studio Art Majors established by Wichata State U., 1984—. Mem. Srs. in Retirement, Chisholm Trail Antique Gun Assn. (life), Wichita Art Assn. (adv. bd.), Wichita Artist Guild (past pres., bd. dirs.), Kans. Watercolor Soc. (charter), Kans. Acad. Oil Painters (charter), Nat. Assn. Mus., Sigma Alpha Epsilon.

KITADA, SHINICHI, biochemist; b. Osaka, Japan, Dec. 9, 1948; came to U.S., 1975; s. Koichi and Asako Kitada. MD, Kyoto U., 1973; MS in Biol. Chemistry, UCLA, 1977, PhD, 1979. Intern Kyoto U. Hosp., Japan, 1973-74; resident physician Chest Disease Research Inst., 1974-75; rsch. scholar lab. nuclear medicine and radiation biology UCLA, 1979-87, rsch. scholar Jules Stein Eye Inst., 1988-91; rsch. biochemist La Jolla (Calif.) Cancer Rsch. Found., 1992—. Author papers in field. Japan Soc. Promotion Sci. fellow 1975-76. Mem. Am. Oil Chemists Soc., N.Y. Acad. Scis., Sigma Xi. Home: 920 Kline St Ste 301 La Jolla CA 92037-4320 Office: The Burnham Inst 10901 N Torrey Pines Rd La Jolla CA 92037-1005

KITAGAWA, JOE, food products executive; b. 1945; s. Kiyoko Kitagawa. Pres. Y.K. Packing Co. (Inc.), Thermal, Calif., 1962—, Kitagawa & Sons, Inc., Thermal, 1967—, Golden Acres Farms. Office: Golden Acres Farms PO Box 371 87770 Ave 62 Thermal CA 92274*

KITAGAWA, KIYOKO, food products executive; b. 1924; m. Yeji Kitagawa (dec.). Sec.-treas. Kitagawa & Sons, Inc., Thermal, Calif., 1949—, Y.K. Packing Co., Inc., Thermal, 1962—; with Golden Acres Farm, 1972—. Office: Golden Acres Farms PO Box 371 87770 Ave 62 Thermal CA 92274*

KITANO, MASAMI, neurologist; b. Tokyo, Nov. 3, 1930; came to U.S., 1969; s. Rokuro and Teruyo (Yamaguchi) K.; m. Hiroko Umeda, June 6, 1966; children: Soichiro, Mariko. Grad. pre-med. sch., Keio U., Tokyo, 1950, MD, 1954, DMS, 1959. Intern/resident in Surgery Keio U. Hosp., Tokyo, 1954-59; resident in Surgery and Anesthesiology Jewish Hosp., St. Louis, 1959-62; rsch. fellow in Neurology UCLA, 1962-66; staff physician Keio U., Tokyo, 1966-68; resident in Neurology VA Hosp. UCLA, 1969-71, rsch. assoc., adj. asst. prof. Neurology, 1972-73; pvt. practice in Neurology Torrance, Calif., 1974—. contbr. 27 articles to profl. jours.; lectr. in field. V.p., bd. dirs. Japanese Am. Cultural Cmty. Ctr., L.A., 1987—. Mem. AMA, Japanese Med. Assn. (L.A.), Calif. Med. Assn., L.A. County Med. Assn., L.A. Soc. Neurosci., Am. Acad. Neurology. Office: 23441 Madison St Ste 280 Torrance CA 90505-4734

KITCHEN, JOHN MARTIN, historian, educator; b. Nottingham, Eng., Dec. 21, 1936; s. John Sutherland and Margaret Helen (Pearson) K. BA with honors, U. London, 1963, PhD, 1966. Mem. Cambridge Group Population Studies, Eng., 1965-66; mem. faculty Simon Fraser U., Burnaby, B.C., Can., 1966—. Author: The German Officer Corps 1890-1914, 1968, A Military History of Germany, 1975, Fascism, 1976, The Silent Dictatorship, 1976, The Political Economy of Germany 1815-1914, 1979, The Coming of Austrian Fascism, 1980, Germany in the Age of Total War, 1981, British Policy Towards the Soviet Union During the Second World War, 1986, The Origins of the Cold War in Comparative Perspective, 1988, Europe Between the Wars, 1988, A World in Flames, 1990, Empire and After: A Short History of the British Empire and Commonwealth, 1994, Nazi Germany at War, 1994, The Cambridge Illustrated History of Germany, 1996, Empire and Commonwealth, 1996. Fellow Inter-Univ. Seminar on Armed Forces and Soc. Fellow Royal Hist. Soc., Royal Soc. Can. Office: Simon Fraser U, Dept History, Burnaby, BC Canada V5A 1S6

KITTO, FRANKLIN CURTIS, computer systems specialist; b. Salt Lake City, Nov. 18, 1954; s. Curtis Eugene and Margaret (Ipson) K.; m. Collette Madsen, Sept. 16, 1982; children: Melissa Erin, Heather Elise, Stephen Curtis. BA, Brigham Young U., 1978, MA, 1980. Tv sta. operator Sta. KBYU-TV, Provo, Utah, 1973-78; grad. teaching asst. Brigham Young Univ., 1978-80; cable TV system operator Instructional Media U. Utah, Salt Lake City, 1980-82, data processing mgr., 1982-83, media supr., 1983-85, bus. mgr., 1985-87; dir. computer systems tng. MegaWest Systems, Inc., Salt Lake City, 1987-90, dir. new product devel., 1990-91, mgr. tng. and installation, 1991-93, mgr. rsch. and devel., 1993; tng. and installation mgr. Total Solutions, American Fork, Utah, 1993-95, tng., support and installation mgr., 1995; EDI programmer Megawest Systems, Inc., 1996, EDI supervisor, 1996—. Recipient Kiwanis Freedom Leadership award, Salt Lake City, 1970, Golden Microphone award Brigham Young U., 1978. Mem. Assn. Ednl. Communications and Tech., Utah Pick Users Group (sec. 1983-87, pres. 1987-89, treas. 1989-90), Am. Soc. Tng. and Devel., Assn. for Computer Tng. and Support, Phi Eta Sigma, Kappa Tau Alpha. Mormon. Home: 10931 S Avila Dr Sandy UT 84094-5965 Office: Mega West Sys Inc 345 Bearcat Dr Salt Lake City UT 84115

KITTREDGE, JOHN RUSSELL, physician; b. Ellsworth, Maine, Apr. 17, 1950; s. Russell Millard and Florence Elizabeth (Davis) K.; divorced; children: Crichton, Russa, Olivia, Clare, Clive. AB in Biology cum laude, Boston U., 1972; MD, Albany Med. Coll. Union U., 1976. Resident Overlook Hosp., Summit, N.J., 1976-79; staff physician Indian Health Svc., Shawnee, Okla., 1979-80, clin. dir., 1980-89; clin. dir. Indian Health Svc., Tucson, Ariz., 1989-92, coord. med. contracts, 1992—, acting chief med. officer, 1993—, acting dep. assoc. dir., 1996—. Capt. USPHS, 1979—. Mem. Am. Acad. Family Practice, Ariz. Acad. Family Practice, Officers Assn. USPHS, Soc. Tchrs. Family Medicine. Independent. Home: 1009 E Windsor St Tucson AZ 85719-1840 Office: Indian Health Svc 7900 S J Stock Rd Tucson AZ 85746-7012

KITZHABER, JOHN ALBERT, governor, physician, former state senator; b. Colfax, Wash., Mar. 5, 1947; s. Albert Raymond and Annabel Reed (Wetzel) K. BA, Dartmouth Coll., 1969; MD, U. Oreg., 1973. Intern Gen. Rose Meml. Hosp., Denver, 1976-77; Emergency physician Mercy Hosp., Roseburg, Oreg., 1974-75; mem. Oreg. Ho. of Reps., 1979-81; mem. Oreg. Senate, 1981-95, pres., 1985, 87, 89, 91; gov. State of Oregon, 1995—; assoc. prof. Oreg. Health Sci. U., 1986—. Mem. Am. Coll. Emergency Physicians, Douglas County Med. Soc., Physicians for Social Responsibility, Am. Council Young Polit. Leaders, Oreg. Trout. Democrat. Office: Office of the Gov State Capitol Bldg Rm 254 Salem OR 97310*

KIVELSON, MARGARET GALLAND, physicist; b. N.Y.C., Oct. 21, 1928; d. Walter Isaac and Madeleine (Wiener) Galland; m. Daniel Kivelson, Aug. 15, 1949; children: Steven Allan, Valerie Ann. AB, Radcliffe Coll., 1950, AM, 1951, PhD, 1957. Cons. Rand Corp., Santa Monica, Calif., 1956-69; asst. to geophysicist UCLA, 1967-83, prof., 1983—, also chmn. dept. earth and space scis., 1984-87; prin. investigator of magnetometer, Galileo Mission, Jet Propulsion Lab., Pasadena, Calif., 1977—; overseer Harvard Coll., 1977-83; mem. adv. coun. NASA, 1987-93; chair atmospheric adv. com. NSF, 1986-89, Com. Solar and Space Physics, 1977-86, com. planetary exploration, 1986-87, com. solar terrestial phys., 1989-92; mem. adv. com. geoscis. NSF. Editor: The Solar System: Observations and Interpretations, 1986; co-editor: Introduction to Space Physics, 1995; contbr. articels to profl. jours. Named Woman of Yr., L.A. Mus. Sci. and Industry, 1979, Woman of Sci., UCLA, 1984; recipient Grad. Soc. medal Radcliffe Coll., 1983, 350th Anniversary Alumni medal Harvard U. Fellow AAAS, Am. Geophysics Union; mem. Am. Phys. Soc., Am. Astron. Soc., Internat. Inst. Astronautics (corr. mem.). Office: UCLA Dept Earth & Space Scis 6847 Slichter Los Angeles CA 90095-1567

KIVENSON, GILBERT, engineering consultant, patent agent; b. Pitts., Dec. 5, 1920; s. Samuel and Anne (Bortnicker) K. BSChemE, Carnegie Mellon U., 1942; MSChemE, U. Pitts., 1947. Registered profl. engr., Calif. Fellow Mellon Inst. Indsl. Rsch., Pitts., 1944-54; engr. Westinghouse Electric Co., Pitts., 1955-68; sr. engr. Rockwell North Am. Aviation, L.A, 1971-73, 76-79, J.B. Lansing, L.A, 1980-81; cons., patent agent L.A., 1980—. Author: Industrial Stroboscopy, 1965, Durability & Reliability In Engine Design, 1971, Art & Science of Inventing, 1977, 2d edit., 1982. Home: 22030 Wyandotte St Canoga Park CA 91303

KIYOTA, HEIDE PAULINE, clinical psychologist; b. Bamberg, Fed. Republic Germany, July 6, 1942; came to U.S., 1970; d. Fritz and Marcella (Schropfer) S.; m. Ronald Masaki Kiyota, Dec. 26, 1982; children: Heather E., Catherine M., Michelle H. BS, U. Md., 1975, MA, 1979; PhD, U. Hawaii, 1986. Lic. psychologist, Hawaii; cert. Hypnotherapist, 1997. Counselor-trainee Regional Inst. for Children & Adolescents, Balt., 1976-77; supr.-counselor Multiple Offender Alcoholism Program, Balt., 1977-80; therapist-intern VA, Honolulu, 1983-84; clin. psychologist Kalihi-Palama Counseling Svcs., Honolulu, 1987-89; pvt. practice psychologist Honolulu, 1988—; presenter in field. Contbr. articles to profl. jours. Mem. Am. Psychol. Assn., Hawaii Psychol. Assn., Phi Kappa Phi. Home: 1812 Nahenahe Pl Wahiawa HI 96786-2627 Office: Heritage Counseling Clinic 95-390 Kuahelani Ave Bldg 2F Mililani HI 96789-1182

KIZZIAR, JANET WRIGHT, psychologist, author, lecturer; b. Independence, Kans.; d. John L. and Thelma (Rooks) Wright; m. Mark Kizziar. BA, U. Tulsa, 1961, MA, 1964, EdD, 1969. Sch. psychologist Tulsa Pub. Schs.; pvt. practice psychology Tulsa, 1969-78, Bartlesville, Okla., 1978-88; lectr. univs., corps., health spas, 1989—. Co-host: Psychologists' Corner program, Sta. KOTV, Tulsa.; author: (with Judy W. Hagedorn) Gemini: The Psychology and Phenomena of Twins, 1975, Search for Acceptance: The Adolescent and Self Esteem, 1979. Sponsor Youth Crisis Intervention Telephone Center, 1972-74; bd. dirs. March of Dimes, Child Protection Team, Women and Children in Crisis, United Fund, YMCA Fund, Mental Health of Washington County, Alternative H.S.; edn. dir. appt. Gov.'s commn. on Violence Against Women Public Awarness Com., 1996, Women's Found. Fresh Start, 1995. Named Disting. Alumni U. Tulsa, Outstanding Young Woman of Okla. Mem. APA, NOW, Internat. Twins Assn. (pres. 1976-77). Home: 9427 N 87th Way Scottsdale AZ 85258-1913 Office: PO Box 5227 Scottsdale AZ 85261-5227

KJELLBERG, BETTY J., association administrator; b. Lynwood, Calif., Sept. 24, 1947; d. Albert Ray Ferguson and Virginia Louise (Kanavos) Wanderman; m. T.H. Kjellberg, Dec. 8, 1973. BA, Calif. State Coll., L.A., 1969; MS in LS, U. So. Calif., 1971; MBA, Ariz. State U., 1982; M of Aviation Mgmt., Embry Riddle Aero. U., Daytona Beach, Fla., 1990. Cert. assn. exec.; lic. pvt. pilot. Dir. health sci. libr. Good Samaritan Med. Ctr., Phoenix, 1971-83; adminstrv. dir. Greater Phoenix Cmty. Clin. Oncology Program, Phoenix, 1983-85; med. staff svcs. adminstr. Good Samaritan Regional Med. Ctr., Phoenix, 1985-88; exec. dir. Ariz. Psychol. Assn., Scottsdale, 1989—; chair Coun. of Execs. of State and Provincial Psychol. Assns., Washington, 1995-96, mem. exec. com., 1993-96. Bd. dirs. Scottsdale Leadership Inc., 1995—, treas., 1996—; precinct committeeman Rep. Party, Scottsdale, 1986-90; mem. City of Scottsdale Airport Adv. Commn., 1994—; pub. mem. Good Samaritan Regional Med. Ctr. Instnl. Rev. Bd., Phoenix, 1994—, Ariz. Supreme Ct. Jud. Performance Rev. Team, Phoenix, 1994-95; mem. adv. com. City of Scottsdale CityShape 2020, 1995. Mem. Am. Soc. Assn. Execs., Ariz. Soc. Assn. Execs., Ariz. Pilots Assn. (bd. dirs. 1986-94), Soroptimist Internat. of Phoenix, Las Rancheras Rep. Women, Am. Assoc. U. Women, (Scottsdale Br.). Office: Ariz Psychol Assn 6210 E Thomas Rd Ste 209 Scottsdale AZ 85251-7003

KLAKEG, CLAYTON HAROLD, cardiologist; b. Big Woods, Minn., Mar. 31, 1920; s. Knute O. and Agnes (Folvik) K.; student Concordia Coll., Moorhead, Minn., 1938-40; BS, N.D. State U., 1942; BS in Medicine, N.D. U., 1943; M.D., Temple U., 1945; MS in Medicine and Physiology, U. Minn.-Mayo Found., 1954; children: Julie Ann, Robert Clayton, Richard Scott. Intern, Med. Ctr., Jersey City, 1945-46; mem. staff VA Hosp., Fargo, N.D., 1948-51; fellow in medicine and cardiology Mayo Found., Rochester, Minn., 1951-55; internist, cardiologist Sansum Med. Clinic Inc., Santa Barbara, Calif., 1955—; mem. staff Cottage Hosp., St. Francis Hosp. Bd. dirs. Sansum Med. Rsch. Found., pres., 1990. Served to capt. M.C., USAF, 1946-48. Diplomate Am. Bd. Internal Medicine. Fellow ACP, Am. Coll. Cardiology, Am. Coll. Chest Physicians, Am. Heart Assn. (mem. council on clin. cardiology); mem. Calif. Heart Assn. (pres. 1971-72, Meritorious Service award 1968, Disting. Service award 1977, Disting. Achievement award 1975), Santa Barbara County Heart Assn. (pres. 1959-60, Disting. Service award 1958, Disting. Achievement award 1971), Calif. Med. Assn., Los Angeles Acad. Medicine, Santa Barbara County Med. Assn., Mayo Clinic Alumni Assn., Santa Barbara Soc. Internal Medicine (pres. 1963), Sigma Xi, Phi Beta Pi. Republican. Lutheran. Club: Channel City. Contbr. articles to profl. jours. Home: 5956 Trudi Dr Santa Barbara CA 93117-2175 Office: Sansum Med Clinic Inc PO Box 1239 Santa Barbara CA 93102-1239

KLAMMER, JOSEPH FRANCIS, management consultant; b. Omaha, Mar. 25, 1925; s. Aloys Arcadius and Sophie (Nadolny) K.; BS, Creighton U., 1948; MBA, Stanford, 1950; cert. in polit. econs. Grad. Inst. Internat. Studies, U. Geneva, 1951. cert. mgmt. cons. Adminstrv. analyst Chevron Corp., San Francisco, 1952-53; staff asst. Enron Corp., Omaha, 1953-57; mgmt. cons., bd. dirs. Cresap, McCormick and Paget, Inc., N.Y.C., 1957-75, v.p., mgr. San Francisco region, 1968-75; mgmt. cons., prin. J.F. Klammer Assocs., San Francisco, 1975—. CEO, pres. Isabelle Towers Homeowners Assn., 1993-94, bd. dirs., 1993-94, mem. fin. com., 1994-95, mem. rules com., 1995-96, mem. fin. com., 1996—; past bd. dirs. Conard House. Apptd. and attended U.S. Mil. Acad., West Point, N.Y.; served to 1st lt. USAAF, 1943-46; lt. col. USAF (ret.). Rotary Found. fellow, 1950-51; recipient Sovereign Mil. Hospitaller Order of St. John of Jerusalem of Rhodes and of Malta. Mem. Omaha Club, Knights of Malta, Alpha Sigma Nu. Republican. Roman Catholic. Home: 1998 Broadway San Francisco CA 94109-2281 Office: 1850 Union St Ste 1226 San Francisco CA 94123-4309

KLAPHAKE, RONALD LAWRENCE, non-profit executive; b. St. Cloud, Minn., Sept. 24, 1945; s. Frank Bernard and Alvina H. (Welle) K.; m. Dec. 31, 1968; children: Karena Beth, Kiel Franz. BA, St. Cloud State U., 1967; MPA, Am. U., 1972, U. So. Calif., 1995. Disbursing officer USS Henry B. Wilson, San Francisco, 1968-70, Naval Rsch. Lab., Washington, 1970-72; asst. to mayor St. Cloud, 1972-73; city mgr. Morris, Minn., 1973-81; city adminstr. River Falls, Wis., 1977-81; exec. dir. St. Cloud Downtown Devel., 1981-86; pres., CEO Missoula (Mont) Area Econ. Devel. Corp., 1986—. Bd. dirs. Missoula Area United Way, 1986-89, Missoula Children's Theatre, Inc., Missoula, 1988—, Internat. Choral Festival, Missoula, 1990—, Nat. Forest Svc. Mus., Missoula, 1993—. Mem. ASPA, Am. Econ. Devel. Coun., Pacific N.W. Econ. Devel. Coun., VFW, Rotary, Missoula Mendelssohn Club (pres. 1987—), Pi Sigma Alpha. Office: Missoula Area Econ Devel Corp Ste 216 127 E Front Missoula MT 59802

KLATSKY, ARTHUR LOUIS, cardiologist, epidemiologist; b. N.Y.C., Oct. 24, 1929; s. Martin Max and Rose M. (Hurwitz) K.; m. Eileen Selma Rohrberg, June 21, 1953; children: Jennifer Ann Klatsky Ferrer, Benjamin Paul. BA, Yale U., 1950; MD, Harvard U., 1954. Diplomate Am. Bd. Internal Medicine, Am. Bd. Cardiovascular Disease. Intern in medicine Boston City Hosp., 1954-56; resident in internal medicine and cardiology Boston VA Hosp., 1958-60; trainee in cardiology U. Calif., San Francisco, 1960-61; clin. instr. in medicine U. Calif. Med. Ctr., San Francisco, 1961-68, asst. clin. prof. medicine, 1968-80; staff physician internal medicine and cardiology Kaiser Found. Hosp., Oakland, Calif., 1961-80, sub-chief dept. medicine, 1973, chief divsn. cardiology, 1978-94; assoc. divsn. rsch. Kaiser Permanente Med. Care Program, Oakland, 1975—; sr. cons. in Cardiology, 1995—; mem. med. adv. coun. Wine Inst., San Francisco, 1978—. Contbr. articles to profl. jours., chpts. to books. Mem. profl. edn. com. Alameda County Heart Assn., 1969—. With Med. Corps, 1956-58. Fellow Am. Heart Assn. Coun. on Epidemiology, 1975—; recipient rsch. award Med. Friends of Wine, 1984, 1st Thomas Turner award for Excellence in Alcohol Rsch., Alcoholic Beverage Med. Rsch. Found., 1992. Fellow ACP, Am. Coll. Cardiology; mem. Am. Wine Alliance for Rsch. and Edn. (bd. dirs. 1989—), Disting. Practioner in Medicine, Nat. Acad. of Practice. Office: Kaiser Found Hosp 280 W Macarthur Blvd Oakland CA 94611-5642

KLATT, CAROL, mayor. Mayor City of Daly City, Calif. Office: 333 90th St Daly City CA 94015

KLAUS, MARION, biologist, educator; b. Vicksburg, Miss., Nov. 6, 1949; d. Sylvain Wolff Klaus and Florence Charlotte (Goodsell) Schell; m. Larry Mehlhaff, June 16, 1990. BS with honors, U. Wyo., Laramie, 1970, MS, 1973, MA, 1978; PhD, Mont. State U. Mem. faculty dept. biology No. Wyo. Cmty. Coll. Dist., Sheridan, 1977—. Contbr. articles to profl. jours. Choreographer coll. prodns. The Fantasticks, 1995, Ahmal and the Night Visitors, 1996. Named Wyo. Career Woman of Yr., Bus. and Profl. Women, Sheridan, 1980. Mem. AAAS, Soc. for Conservation Biology, Wyo. Native Plant Soc., Wyo. Assn. for Environ. Edn., Sierra Club, Phi Beta Kappa. Democrat. Unitarian. Office: NWCCD-Sheridan Coll 3059 Coffeen Ave Sheridan WY 82801

KLAUSNER, JACK DANIEL, lawyer; b. N.Y.C., July 31, 1945; s. Burt and Marjory (Brown) K.; m. Dale Arlene Kreis, July 1, 1968; children: Andrew Russell, Mark Raymond. BS in Bus., Miami U., Oxford, Ohio, 1967; JD, U. Fla., 1969. Bar: N.Y. 1971, Ariz. 1975, U.S. Dist. Ct. Ariz. 1975, U.S. Ct. Appeals (9th cir.) 1975, U.S. Supreme Ct. 1975. Assoc. counsel John P. McGuire & Co., Inc., N.Y.C., 1970-71; assoc. atty. Hahn & Hessen, N.Y.C., 1971-72; gen. counsel Equilease Corp., N.Y.C., 1972-74; assoc. Burch & Cracchiolo, Phoenix, 1974-78; ptnr. Burch & Cracchiolo, 1978—; judge pro tem Maricopa County Superior Ct., 1990—, Ariz. Ct. Appeals, 1992—. Bd. dirs. Santos Soccer Club, Phoenix, 1989-90; bd. dirs., pres. south Bank Soccer Club, Tempe, 1987-88. Home: 1390 W Island Cir Chandler AZ 85248-3700 Office: Burch & Cracchiolo 702 E Osborn Rd Phoenix AZ 85014-5241

KLAUSS, KENNETH KARL, composer, educator; b. Parkston, S.D., Apr. 8, 1923; s. Christian and Paulina (Engel) K. *Kenneth Klauss's family has a music tradition. His maternal uncle, violinist Carl Engel, taught at Union College, Lincoln, Nebraska. Engel Hall, on campus, is a music building dedicated to his memory. His sister, pianist Mabel Klauss Anderson, toured in the early 1920s with a Chatauqua group out of Lincoln which was under the leadership of Thurlow Lieurance, an early researcher of the music of Native Americans.* MusB in Composition, U. So. Calif., 1946. Tchr. composition and piano L.A., 1946-50; composer Lester Horton Theater, L.A., 1949-50; tchr. music San Francisco, 1950-61; composer, educator L.A., 1961—; lectr. in music for dance Idyllwild (Calif.) Sch. Music and Arts, 1967-74; lectr. in music history So. Calif. Inst. Architecture, Santa Monica, 1970-76; composer in residence Perry/Mansfield Camp, Steamboat Springs, Colo., 1966; guest performer, composer, lectr. Libr. Congress, Am. U., Washington, 1996. Composer: (opera) Fall of the House of Usher, 1952; author, composer: (poetry/music orchestration) Story of the World Volumes I to VIII, 1952-86, 86-96. Founder, patron Klauss/James Archive and Art Mus., Parkston, 1995—. Recipient hon. mention opera competition Ohio U., Athens, 1954. Democrat. Home: 440 Wren Dr Los Angeles CA 90065-5040 *The Klauss Archive will serve as a reference source for the universities and colleges of southeastern South Dakota. It consists of an extended collection of manuscripts, memorabilia, recordings, scores, and technical and historical books dealing with music and art. The James Art Museum displays an impressive collection of the paintings of Bernard James, a native of Dayton, Tennessee. Both the Archive and the Museum are housed in an historic (1904) building, First and Main Streets, Parkston.*

KLEBAN, CHERYL CHRISTINE, insurance company executive; b. Irvington, N.J., Nov. 12, 1955; d. Kenneth Howard and Wanda Faye (Simmons) Fuller; m. Daniel Albert Kleban, Mar. 12, 1983. BA, U. Calif., Santa Barbara, 1976. CLU, CPCU. Dept. mgr. Mervyns, Oxnard, Calif., 1976-77; underwriter State Farm, Westlake Village, Calif., 1977-81, underwriting supr., 1981-86, underwriting, ops. supt., 1986—; ins. educator Soc. CPCU, Ins. Inst. of Am., Westlake Village, 1981—. Mem. CPCU (v.p. L.A. chpt. 1989-90, treas. 1988-89, bd. dirs. 1985-88, pres. elect 1990-91, pres. 1991-92), Omicron Delta Epsilon. Republican. Presbyterian. Office: State Farm Ins 31303 Agoura Rd Westlake Village CA 91363-0001

KLEEMAN, NANCY GRAY ERVIN, special education educator; b. Boston, Feb. 19, 1946; d. John Wesley and Harriet Elizabeth (Teuchert) Ervin; m. Brian Carlton Kleeman, June 27, 1969. BA, Calif. State U., Northridge, 1969; MS, Calif. State U., Long Beach, 1976, Calif. State U., Long Beach, 1976; cert. resource specialist, Calif. State U., Long Beach, 1982. Cert. spl. edn., learning disabilities and resource specialist tchr., Calif. Tchr. spl. edn., resource specialist Downey (Calif.) Unified Sch. Dist., 1972-86; tchr. spl. day class Irvine (Calif.) Sch. Dist., 1986—; tutor in field; spkr. Commn. for Handicapped, L.A., 1975; advisor Com. to Downey Unified Sch. Dist., 1976-82; owner ISIS Design Publs. Author: Rhyme Your Times, 1990; author numerous greeting cards. Vol. sec. UN, L.A., 1980-83; vol. coord., art dir., educator Sierra Vista Mid. Sch., Irvine, 1986-88; liaison Tustin (Calif.) Manor Convalscent Home and Regents Point Retirement Home, Irvine, 1988—; fundraiser Ronald McDonald House, Orange, Calif.; mem. Nat. Young Svc., Washington; vol. Sr. Cheer Project, 1984—, Vets. Cheer Project, 1996—. Recipient award Concerned Students Orgn., Downey, 1984; named Tchr. Yr. Sierra Vista Middle Sch., 1988. Mem. NEA, Irvine Tchrs. Assn., Calif. Tchrs. Assn., Dogs for the Blind, Nat. Hist. Soc. Office: Irvine Unified Sch Dist 2 Liberty Irvine CA 92720-2536

KLEEMANN, GARY LEWIS, university official; b. Pasadena, Calif., June 8, 1945; s. Ernest W. Kleemann and Martha May (Lewis) Grant; m. Balvina Sotelo, Sept. 12, 1970; children: Robert Franklin, Michael Patrick. BA, San Jose (Calif.) State U., 1968; MS, Oreg. State U., 1973; PhD, Ariz. State U., 1984. Dir. student activities Boise (Idaho) State U., 1970-72; asst. dean U. Calif., Irvine, 1973-74; dir. univ. ctr. U. of the Pacific, Stockton, Calif., 1974-79; exec. coord. assoc. students program Ariz. State U., Tempe, 1979-93, sr. mgmt. rsch. analyst, 1990-91, cons. Student Health Ctr., 1993; coord. mgmt. rsch. Ariz. State U.-East, Mesa, 1993-95, assoc. dir. student affairs, 1995-96, dir. campus life svcs., 1995—, mem. adj. faculty, 1988—; pres. GarVi Associates, Inc., Tempe, 1982—. Contbr. numerous articles to profl. jours. Lt. USN, 1968-70, Vietnam. Calif. State scholar, 1963-67; recipient La Torre Svc. award, 1966. Mem. Am. Assn. Higher Edn., Am. Coll. Pers. Assn., Am. Ednl. Rsch. Assn., Ariz. Coll. Pers. Assn., Assn. for Study Higher Edn., Assn. Coll. Unions Internat., Nat. Assn. Student Pers. Adminstrs. (editl. bd. Jour. 1989-93, 94-97, exec. com. Ariz. chpt.), Blue Key. Home: 1831 E Cornell Dr Tempe AZ 85283-2256 Office: Ariz State Univ East Campus Life Svcs 6001 S Power Rd Mesa AZ 85206-0999

KLEESE, WILLIAM CARL, genealogy research consultant; b. Williamsport, Pa., Jan. 20, 1940; s. Donald Raymond and Helen Alice (Mulberger) K.; m. Vivian Ann Yeager, June 12, 1958; children: Scott, Jolene, Mark, Troy, Brett, Kecia, Lance. BS in Wildlife Biology, U. Ariz., 1975, MS in Animal Physiology, 1979, PhD in Animal Physiology, 1981. Sales rep. Terminix Co., Tucson, 1971-72; pest control operator, 1973-75; fire fighter Douglas Ranger Dist. Coronado Nat. Forest U.S. Forest Svc., 1975, biol. technician Santa Catalina ranger dist., 1975-76; lab. technician dept. animal scis. U. Ariz., 1977-78, rsch. technician dept. pharmacology and toxicology, 1978, rsch. asst. dept. biochemistry, 1979-81, rsch. specialist muscle biology group, 1981—; genealogy rsch. cons. Tucson, 1988—. Author: Introduction to Genealogy, 1988, Introduction to Genealogical Research, 1989, The Genealogical Researcher, Neophyte to Graduate, 1992, Genealogical Research in the British Isles, 1991; contbr. numerous articles to profl. jours. Chaplain Ariz. State Prisons, Tucson, 1988—. Mem. Ariz. Geneaolgy Adv. Bd. (com. chmn. 1990-92), Herpetologists League, Lycoming County Geneal. Soc., Nat. Geneal. Soc., Nat. Wildlife Fedn., Pa. Geneal. Soc., Soc. for the Study of Amphibians and Reptiles, Soc. of Vertebrate Paleontology, Ariz. State Geneal. Soc. (pres. 1990-93). Republican. Mem. LDS Ch. Home: 6521 E Fayette St Tucson AZ 85730-2220 Office: 6061 E Broadway Blvd Ste 128 Tucson AZ 85711-4020

KLEHN, HENRY, JR., engineering company executive; b. 1936. BS in Geol. Engring., U. Calif., MS in Engring. Sci. With Dames & Moore, L.A., 1960—. Office: Dames & Moore 911 Wilshire Blvd Ste 700 Los Angeles CA 90017-3436*

KLEIMAN, VIVIAN ABBE, filmmaker; b. Phila., Oct. 11, 1950; d. Philip and Hilda (Kramer) K. BA, U. Calif., 1974. Filmmaker; lectr. Grad. Program in Documentary Film Prodn. Stanford U., 1995, 96, 97; bd. dirs. Cultural Rsch. and Comm., Berkeley, Calif., Catticus Corp., Berkeley; founding dir. Jewish Film Festival, Berkeley, 1981-85, Frameline, San Francisco, 1985—; pres. Signifyin' Works, Berkeley, 1991—; v.p. Film Arts Found., San Francisco, 1983-93; cinematographer Tongues Untied, 1989. Producer, dir. films including Judy Chicago: The Birth Project, 1985, Ein Stehaufmannchen, 1991, My Body's My Business, 1992; producer films including Routes of Exile: A Moroccan Jewish Odyssey, 1982, California Gold, 1984, Color Adjustment, 1992, Roam Sweet Home, 1996, The Fire This Time, 1997; assoc. producer The Disney Channel, 1982-83; rschr. for various films including A Woman Named Golda, 1982. Recipient George Foster Peabody award Sundance Film Festival, Outstanding Achievement award Internat. Documentary Assn., Nat. Emmy award nominee, The Eric Barnouw awards Orgn. Am. Historians, Red ribbon Am. Film and Video Festival, Best of Festival award Black Maria Festival, Black Internat. Cinema Berlin, Gold Plaque, Social/Polit. Documentary Chgo. Internat. Film Festival, N.C. Silver Juror's prize. Mem. Bay Area Video Coalition, Film Arts Found., Internat. Documentary Assn. Office: 2600 10th St Berkeley CA 94710-2522

KLEIN, ARNOLD WILLIAM, dermatologist; b. Mt. Clemens, Mich., Feb. 27, 1945; s. David Klein; m. Malvina Kraemer. BA, U. Pa., 1967, MD, 1971. Intern Cedars-Sinai Med. Ctr., Los Angeles, 1971-72; resident in dermatology Hosp. U. Pa., Phila., 1972-73, U. Calif., Los Angeles, 1973-75; pvt. practice dermatology Berverly Hills, Calif., 1975—; assoc. clin. prof. dermatology/medicine U. Calif. Ctr. for Health Scis; mem. med. staff Cedars-Sinai Med. Ctr.; asst. clin. prof. dermatology Stanford U., 1982-89; asst. clin. prof. to assoc. clin. prof. dermatology/medicine, UCLA; Calif. state commr., 1983-89; med. adv. bd. Skin Cancer Found., Lupus Found. Am., Collagen Corp.; presenter seminars in field. Reviewer Jour. Dermatologic Surgery and Oncology, Jour. Sexually Transmitted Diseases, Jour. Am. Acad. Dermatology; mem. editorial bd. Men's Fitness mag., Shape mag., Jour. Dermatologic Surgery and Oncology; contbr. numerous articles to med. jours. Mem. AMA, Calif. Med. Assn., Am. Soc. Dermatologic Surgery, Internat. Soc. Dermatologic Surgery, Calif. Soc. Specialty Plastic Surgery, Am. Assn. Cosmetic Surgeons, Assn. Sci. Advisors, Los Angeles Med. Assn., Am. Coll. Chemosurgery, Met. Dermatology Soc., Am. Acad. Dermatology, Dermatology Found., Scleroderma Found., Internat. Psoriasis Found., Lupus Found., Am. Venereal Disease Assn., Soc. Cosmetic Chemists, AFTRA, Los Angeles Mus. Contemporary Art (founder), Dance Gallery Los Angeles (founder), Am. Found. AIDS Research (founder, dir.), Friars Club, Phi Beta Kappa, Sigma Tau Sigma, Delphos. Office: 435 N Roxbury Dr Ste 204 Beverly Hills CA 90210-5004 *The sincerest form of respect is trust. Being a Physician is all about serving this trust. Also, it is about dedication, observation, obsession and creative intelligence. Who and what I am...where I begin and where I end...is all about being a physician.*

KLEIN, CORNELIS, geology educator; b. Haarlem, The Netherlands, Sept. 4, 1937; came to U.S., 1960; s. Cornelis and Wilhelmina (van'tHoen) K.; m. Angela M. Nobbs, Sept. 14, 1960 (dec. 1996); children: Marc Alexander, Stephanie Wilhelmina. BS in Geology with honors, McGill U., Montreal, Que., Can., 1958, MS in Geology, 1960; PhD in Geology, Harvard U., 1965. Lectr. in mineralogy Harvard U., Cambridge, Mass., 1965-69, assoc. prof., 1969-72, asst. dean, 1966-70; prof. mineralogy Ind. U., Bloomington, 1972-84; prof. geology U. N.Mex., Albuquerque, 1984—. Author: (with C.S. Hurlbut) Manual of Mineralogy, 21st edit., 1993, Minerals and Rocks: Exercises in Crystallography, Mineralogy, and Hand Specimen Pathology, 2d rev. edit., 1994; author (with S.M. Stoller Co.) Mineralogy Tutorials, interactive instrn. on CD-ROM, 1995; contbr. articles to profl. jours. Parker fellow Harvard U. fellow, 1962-63, Guggenheim fellow, 1978, Presdl. Tchg. fellow U. N.Mex., 1995—; recipient Faculty Achievement award Burlington Resources, U. N.Mex., 1991, Carnegie Mineralogical award, 1997. Fellow Mineral. Soc. Am., Geol. Soc. Am., AAAS; mem. Soc. Econ. Goelogists, Mineral. Assn. Can. Home: 736 Val Verde Dr SE Albuquerque NM 87108-3468 Office: U NMex Dept Earth Planetary Sci 200 Yale Blvd SE Albuquerque NM 87106-4014

KLEIN, EDITH MILLER, lawyer, former state senator; b. Wallace, Idaho, Aug. 4, 1915; d. Fred L.B. and Edith (Gallup) Miller; m. Sandor S. Klein (dec. 1970). BS in Bus., U. Idaho, 1935; teaching fellowship, Wash. State U., 1935-36; JD, George Washington U., 1946, LLM, 1954. Bar: D.C. 1946, Idaho 1947, N.Y. 1955, U.S. Supreme Ct. 1954. Pers. spec. Labor and War Depts., Wash., 1942-46; practice law Boise, Idaho, 1947—; judge Mcpl. Ct., Boise, 1947-49; mem. Idaho Ho. Reps., 1948-50, 64-68, Idaho Senate, 1968-82; atty. FCC Wash., 1953-54; FHA N.Y.C., 1955-56. Chmn. Idaho Gov.'s Commn. Status Women, 1964-72, mem., 1965-79, 82-92; mem. Idaho Gov.'s Coun. Comprehensive Health Planning, 1969-76, Idaho Law Enforcement Planning Commn., 1972-82, Nat. Adv. Commn. Regional Med. Programs, 1974-76, Idaho Endowment Investment Bd., 1979-82; trustee Boise State U. Found., Ind., 1973-95; pres. Boise Music Week, 1991-94; bd. dirs. Harry W. Morison Found. Ind., 1978—, St. Alphonsus Regional Med. Ctr. Found., 1982-96; past pres. bd. dirs. Boise Philharm. Assn., Opera Idaho. Named Woman of Yr. Boise Altrusa Club, 1966, Boise C. of C., 1970, Disting. Citizen, Idaho Statesman 1970, Woman of Progress, Idaho Bus. Prof. Women, 1978; recipient Women Helping Women award Soroptimist Club, 1980, Stein Meml. award Y.M.C.A., 1983, Silver and Gold award for Outstanding Svc., U. Idaho, 1985, March of Dimes award to Honor Outstanding Women, 1987, Cert. of Appreciation by Boise Br., AAUW, 1990, Morrison Ctr. Hall of Fame award, 1990, Disting. Cmty. Svc. award Boise Area C. of C., 1995. Mem. DAR (regent Pioneer chpt. 1991-93). Republican. Congregationalist. Home: 1588 Lenz Lane PO Box 475 Boise ID 83701 Office: 1400 US Bank Plaza PO Box 2527 Boise ID 83701

KLEIN, (MARY) ELEANOR, retired clinical social worker; b. Luzon, Philippines, Dec. 13, 1919; came to U.S., 1921; (parents Am. citizens); d. Roy Edgar and Edith Lillian Hay; m. Edward George Klein, June 24, 1955. BA, Pacific Union Coll., 1946; MSW, U. So. Calif., 1953. Lic. clin. social worker. Social worker White Meml. Hosp., Los Angeles, 1948-56; clin. social worker UCLA Hosp. Clinics, 1956-65, supr. social worker, 1965-67, assoc. dir., 1967-73, dir., 1973-82. Bd. dirs., treas. Los Amigos de la Humanidad, U. So. Calif. Sch. Social Work; hon. life mem. bd. dirs. Calif. div. Am. Cancer Soc., mem. vol. bd. Calif. div., 1964—, del. nat. dir., 1980-84, chmn. residential crusade for Orange County (Calif.) unit, 1985-86; bd. dirs. Vol. Exchange, 1988—, sec., 1991-96, v.p., 1996-97; v.p. Dem. Club West Orange County, 1996—. Recipient Disting. Alumni award Los Amigos de la Humanidad, 1984, Outstanding Performance award UCLA Hosp., 1968, various service awards Am. Cancer Soc., 1972-88. Fellow Soc. Clin. Social Work; mem. Nat. Assn. Social Workers (charter), Am. Hosp. Assn., Soc. Social Work Administrs. in Health Care (formerly Soc. Hosp. Social Work Dirs.) (nat. pres. 1981, bd. dirs. 1978-82, life mem. local chpt.), Am. Pub. Health Assn. Democrat. Unitarian. Home: 1661 Texas Cir Costa Mesa CA 92626-2238

KLEIN, FREDA, retired state agency administrator; b. Seattle, May 17, 1920; d. Joseph and Julia (Caplan) Vinikow; m. Jerry Jerome Klein, Oct. 20, 1946; children: Jan Susan Klein Waples, Kerry Joseph, Robin Jo Klein. BA, U. Wash., 1942; MS, U. Nev., Las Vega, 1969, EdD, 1978. Owner, mgr. Smart Shop, Provo, Utah, 1958-60, Small Fry Shop, Las Vegas, 1961-66; vocat. counselor, test adminstr. Nev. Employment Security Dept., Las Vegas, 1966-77, local office mgr., 1978-95; ret., 1995. Contbr. articles to profl. jours. Exec. bd. Pvt. Industry Coun., Las Vegas, 1988—, Interstate Conf. on Employment Security Agys., Nev., 1988-90, Area Coordinating Com. for Econ. Devel., Las Vegas, 1988—. Recipient Achievement award Nev. Bus. Svc., 1990, Cert. of Spl. Congl. Recognition, 1992; named Outstanding Woman, Goodwill Industries sci. and rsch. divsn., 1977. Mem. AAUW, Internat. Assn. Pers. in Employment Security, U. Nev. Las Vegas Alumni Assn., Henderson C. of C. (exec. bd. 1986—), Soroptimist Internat. (pres. 1987-88), Phi Kappa Phi (scholastic hon.). Home: 2830 Phoenix St Las Vegas NV 89121-1312

KLEIN, HENRY, architect; b. Cham, Germany, Sept. 6, 1920; came to U.S., 1939; s. Fred and Hedwig (Weiskopf) K.; m. Phyllis Harvey, Dec. 27, 1952; children: Vincent, Paul, David. Student, Inst. Rauch, Lausanne, Switzerland, 1936-38; BArch, Cornell U., 1943. Registered architect, Oreg., Wash. Designer Office of Pietro Belluschi, Architect, Portland, Oreg., 1948-51; architect Henry Klein Partnership, Architects, Mt. Vernon, Wash., 1952—. Bd. dirs. Wash. Pks. Found., Seattle, 1977—, Mus. N.W. Art, 1988—. With U.S. Army, 1943-46. Recipient Louis Sullivan award Internat. Union Bricklayers and Allied Craftsmen, 1981; Presdl. Design award Nat. Endowment Arts, 1988; George A. and Eliza Howard Found. fellow. Fellow AIA (Seattle chpt. medal 1995). Jewish. Home: 1957 Little Mountain Rd Mount Vernon WA 98274-8311 Office: Henry Klein Partnership 3/4 Pine St Mount Vernon WA 98273

KLEIN, JAMES MIKEL, music educator; b. Greenville, S.C., Aug. 27, 1953; s. Rubin Harry Klein and Billie (Mikel) Newton. BM, U. Tex., 1975, MM, 1977; MusD, U. Cincinnati, 1981. Prin. trombone player Austin (Tex.) Symphony Orch., 1973-77; conducting asst. U. Tex., Austin, 1975-77, U. Cin., 1977-78; dir. instrumental music Valparaiso (Ind.) U., 1978-84; prof. music Calif. State U. Stanislaus, Turlock, 1984—, spkr. of faculty, 1997—; mem. faculty Nat. Luth. Music Camp, Lincoln, Nebr., 1985-86, 95-97; guest conductor, clinician, adjudicator various states, internationally, 1978—; trombone player Modesto (Calif.) Symphony Orch., 1984—; conductor Stanislaus Youth Symphony, Modesto, 1985; music dir. Modesto Symphony Youth Orch., 1986—; site adminstr. Nat. Honors Orch., Anaheim, Calif., 1986, Indpls., 1988, Cin., 1992, asst. condr., Kansas City, 1996; faculty, coord. instrumental music Calif. State Summer Sch. of Arts, 1987-88. Pres. Turlock Arts Fund for Youth, 1986-88; mem. internat. Friendship Com., subcom., City of Modesto, 1990-92; vol. Big Bros. Am. Recipient Meritorious Prof. award Calif. State U., Stanislaus, 1988, Outstanding Young Man Am. award, 1990. Mem. Music Educators Nat. Assn., Nat. Sch. Orch. Assn. (pub. rels. chair 1994-96), Am. Fedn. Musicians (local 1), Condrs. Guild, Am. Symphony Orch. League, Calif. Orch. Dir.'s Assn. (pres.-elect 1988-90, pres. 1990-92, Orch. Dir. of the Year, 1994). Home: 565 N Daubenberger Rd Turlock CA 95380 Office: Calif State U Dept Music 801 W Monte Vista Ave Turlock CA 95382-0256

KLEIN, JEFFREY HOWARD, oncologist, internist; b. Cleve., Jan. 24, 1943; s. Joseph Bart and Tillie Alice Klein; m. Nancy Klein, June 5, 1971; 1 child, Bart Edward. BS in Medicine, Northwestern U., 1966, MD, 1968. Diplomate Am. Bd. Internal Medicine, Am. Bd. Med. Oncology. Intern Cleve. Met. Gen. Hosp., 1968-69, resident, 1969-70; resident Rush-Presbyn. St. Luke's Med. Ctr., Chgo., 1970-71, Am. Cancer Soc. clin. fellow, 1971-72; pvt. practice internist, oncologist Lombard Med. Group, Thousand Oaks, Calif., 1974—; also bd. dirs. Lombard Med. Group, Thousand Oaks; chief of medicine Los Robles Regional Med. Ctr., Thousand Oaks, 1976-77, chief of staff, 1979-81; trustee Columbia/Los Robles Med. Ctr., Thousand Oaks, 1995—. Maj. USAF, 1972-74. Mem. Am. Soc. Clin. Oncology, So. Calif. Acad. Clin. Oncology (charter), Phi Beta Kappa, Pi Kappa Epsilon, Alpha Omega Alpha. Office: Lombard Med Group Inc 2230 Lynn Rd Thousand Oaks CA 91360-1901

KLEIN, LOUIS, physical therapist; b. Balt., May 17, 1948; s. Hyman Klein and Shirley Kramer; m. Elizabeth Ellen Cauldwell, May 31, 1976; children: Adam Sherman, Tamara Arielle, David Jared. BA in Biology, U. Md., Balt., 1970; MA in Phys. Therapy, NYU, 1978. Cert. hand therapist; cert. disability specialist; cert. work capacity evaluator; lic. phys. therapist, N.Y., Calif.; cert. instr. basic CPR; cert. scuba diver. Phys. therapist NYU Inst. Rehab. Medicine, N.Y.C., 1972-74, Kaiser Found. Hosps., Santa Clara, Calif., 1974-75, Calif. Coll. Podiatric Medicine, San Francisco, 1975-77; owner, operator Hand Rehab. Clinic, San Francisco, 1977-88; owner, operator Hand Rehab. Assocs., Oakland, Calif., 1979-89, Concord, Calif., 1981—, Pleasanton, Calif., 1986—; owner, operator Calif. Athletic and Rehab. Medicine, Oakland, 1989—; cons. Calif. Golden Seals hockey team, Oakland, 1975, Men's Phys. Edn. Dept. El Camino H.S., Daly City, Calif., 1975, student adv. and asst. dept. U. Calif. Berkeley Health Sci. Career Fair, 1977, 78—, St. Mary's H.S., 1979-80, Blue Cross, Calif., 1991; spkr., presenter confs. in field. Paramedic Forest Hills (N.Y.) Vol. Ambulance Corps, 1971-74, crew chief, 1972; instr. CPR San Francisco Bay Area Heart Assn., 1983-86; vol. umpire Dist. 5 Clayton Valley Little League, 1985-89; vol. emergency med. treatment La Morinda Soccer League, 1990-91. With U.S. Army N.G., 1971-74; major USAR, 1974-89. Mem. Am. Phys. Therapy Assn. (sports medicine sect. 1972—, orthop. and pvt. practice sects. 1976—, Bay Area dirs. forum 1976—, sect. on adminstrn. 1976—, sect. on hand rehab. 1976—, rsch. sect. 1976—, continuing edn. com. Golden Gate dist. 1976, program coord. total shoulder replacement 1976, project coord. burn course for phys. therapists 1976, sports medicine coord. for phys. therapists 1976, coord. mobilization course 1977, coord. EMG instrn. Bay Area Golden Gate dist. 1977), Nat. Athletic Trainers Assn., Am. Congress Rehab. Medicine, Am. Coll. Rehab. Medicine, Am. Soc. Hand Therapists (chair continuing edn. subcom. 1980-82, chair nominating com. 1981-82, liaison continuing edn. com. 1982-84, bd. dirs. at large exec. bd. 1983-85, 84-88), Am. Orthop. Soc. for Sports Medicine, Am. Acad. Phys. Medicine and Rehab., Am. Back Soc., Am. Bd. Profl. Disability Consultants, Com. of Cert. of Work Adjustment and Vocat. Evaluation Specialty, Nat. Strengthening and Conditioning Assn., Am. Assn. Hand Surgery, Calif. Assn. Rehab. Profls., Ctr. for Chinese Medicine, Rehab. R & D Svc. VA, Career Resources Devel. Ctr. Democrat. Jewish. Home: 615 Murray Ln Lafayette CA 94549 Office: Premier Healthcare Mgmt Inc 5175 Johnson Dr Pleasanton CA 94588

KLEIN, MARC S., newspaper editor and publisher; b. Feb. 16, 1949; married; 2 children. BA in Journalism, Pa. State U., 1970. Bur. chief Courier-Post, Camden, N.J., 1970-75; asst. mng. editor Phila. Bull., 1975-81; editor Jewish Exponent, Phila., 1981-83; editor, pub. Jewish Bull. of No. Calif., San Francisco, 1984—. Past pres. Temple Israel, Alameda; former bd. dirs. Oakland-Piedmont Jewish Community Ctr. Recipient 1st place awards Phila. Press Assn., 1973, 1st place award N.J. Press Assn., 1973; Wall St. Jour. Newspaper Fund intern, fellow, 1969. Mem. Am. Jewish Press Assn. (past pres.), Soc. Profl. Journalists (past bd. dirs.). Office: 225 Bush St # 1480 San Francisco CA 94104-4207

KLEIN, M(ARY) A(LICE), fiber artist; b. Berwyn, Ill., Oct. 21, 1930; d. Ralph Logie and Dorothy (Tuttle) Low; m. Fred Arthur Hanson, Aug. 21, 1954 (div. 1974); children: Carol-Lynn, Kathryn, Susan, Linda; m. Charles Keith Klein, July 7, 1974; adopted children: Ellen, Elizabeth, Mary, Charles Jr. BA in Recreational Therapy, U. Calif., Berkeley, 1952; postgrad., Stanford U., 1954; degree Fine Arts, Famous Artists Sch., Westport, Conn., 1958-62. Recreational therapist Langley Porter Clinic, U. Calif. Hosp., San Francisco, 1952-53; exec. dir. Children's HomeSoc., San Francisco, 1954-55; designer, owner Hanson Handcrafts, Burlingame, Calif., 1968-74, Sunbow, Albuquerque, N. Mex., 1974-76, Monterey Bay Needleworks, Monterey, Calif., 1976-79; creator, owner M.A. Klein Design, Calif., 1980—; owner, mgr. M.A. Klein Co., Placerville, Portola Valley, Calif., 1991—; bd. dir. Calif. Needlework Assn., San Francisco, 1973-75; craftsmen's advisory bd. Goodfellow Craft Enterprises and Western Exhibitors, San Francisco, 1984; site nat. planner Nat. Standards Coun. of Am. Embroiders, Northbrook, Ill., 1989-91. Author: Stitchery Booklets with Slide Presentations, 1987-90; group shows include: Great Am. Needlework Show, Saratoga, Calif., 1982 (judges award 3 first prizes), Nat. Standards Coun. of Am. Embroiderers, Pitts. (best of show) 1985, Carmel Merchants Assn., Carmel, Calif. (best of show, purchase award), 1982, Art Quilt Internat. and Fiber Expression I, Mt. View, Calif. (selected as poster piece), 1994; prin. works include: (Wallhangings) Horizon Corp. Toronto, Can., St. Timothy's Ch., Danville, Calif., Libr. of Congress, Washington. Mem. Am. Crafts Assn., Coun. Am. Embroiderers (tchr. lectr. 1980—), Sacramento Ctr. Textile Arts (tchr. lectr. 1989—), Contemporary Quilters Fiber Artists (resource dir. 1994—), Pacific Art League, No. Calif. Artists Assn., Sacramento Fin Art Ctr. Episcopalian.

KLEIN, PERRY ANDREW, counselor; b. L.I., N.Y., May 4, 1964; s., Philip Donald and Estelle (Truman) K.; m. Patricia Louise Hanson, Dec. 23, 1994. AA, Seminole Cmty. Coll., Sanford, Fla., 1985; BA in Psychology, U. Ctrl. Fla., 1987; MC, U. Phoenix, 1996. Sr. case mgr. Mental Health Svcs. of Orange County, Orlando, Fla., 1987-90; case mgr. Temporary Living Ctr., Apopka, Fla., 1990-91; behavioral sci. specialist U.S. Army, Ft. Huachuca, Ariz., 1991-94; case mgr. Ariz. Ctr. for Clin. Mgmt., Tucson, 1994-95; counselor Southeastern Ariz. Behavioral Health Svcs.; cons. regarding clin. assessment and diagnosis, counseling Specialist U.S. Army, 1991-94; mem. Ariz. N.G., 1994-95. Decorated Expert Badge/M-16 Rifle, Army Achievemetn medal. Mem. Am. Counseling Assn., Am. Mental Health Counselors Assn., Golden Key Nat. Honor Soc. Home: 8617 E Ellsworth Ln Hereford AZ 85615-2733

KLEIN, R. KENT, lawyer; b. Richmond, Mo., Feb. 11, 1944. BA with distinction, U. Ariz., 1965, JD, 1968. Bar: Ariz. 1968. Atty. State Compensation Fund Ariz., 1968-74, Lewis & Roca, Phoenix. Mem. State Bar Ariz. Office: Lewis & Roca 40 N Central Ave Phoenix AZ 85004-4429

KLEIN, RALPH, premier of Alberta; b. Calgary, Alta., Can.; ; m. 2nd, Colleen, 1972; 5 children. Dir. pub. rels. Alta. div. Red Cross; dir. pub. rels. Calgary United Way Fund, 1966-69; with CFCN, 1969-80; newsreader radio div., later television reporter, 1969-80; mayor City of Calgary, 1980-89; legislator Calgary-Elbow constituency Alta. Legislature, Edmonton, 1989—; minister of environment Alta. Legislature, 1992—. Office: Office of the Premier, 10800 97 Ave #307, Edmonton, AB Canada T5K 2B6*

KLEIN, ROBERT GORDON, judge; b. Honolulu, Nov. 11, 1947; s. Gordon Ernest Klein and Clara (Cutter) Elliot; m. Aleta Elizabeth Webb, July 27, 1986; children: Kurt William, Erik Robert. BA, Stanford U., 1969; JD, U. Oreg., 1972. Dep. atty. gen. State of Hawaii, 1973, with state campaign spening commn., 1974, with state dept regulatory agys., 1975-78; judge State Dist. Ct. Hawaii, 1978-84; judge cir. ct. State of Hawaii, 1984-92, supreme ct. justice, 1992—. Office: Supreme Ct 417 S King St Honolulu HI 96813-2902

KLEIN, SNIRA L(UBOVSKY), Hebrew language and literature educator; came to U.S., 1959, naturalized, 1974; d. Avraham and Devora (Unger) Lubovsky; m. Earl H. Klein, Dec. 25, 1975. Tchr. cert., Tchrs. Seminar, Netanya, Israel, 1956; B. Rel. Edn., U. Judaism, 1961, M in Hebrew Lit., 1963; BA, Calif. State U., Northridge, 1966; MA, UCLA, 1971, PhD, 1983. Tchg. asst. UCLA, 1969-71; instr., continuing edn. U. Judaism, L.A., 1971-76, 94—, instr., 1975-84; vis. lectr. UCLA, 1985-91; adj. asst. prof. U. Judaism, 1984-94. Mem. Assn. for Jewish Studies, Nat. Assn. of Profs. of Hebrew, World Union of Jewish Studies. Jewish. Office: U Judaism 15600 Mulholland Dr Los Angeles CA 90077-1519

KLEIN, STEPHEN PAUL, engineering and mathematics educator; b. L.A., Jan. 16, 1947; s. Paul Eugene and Frances (Lewis) K.; m. Cheryl Anne Harvey, June 14, 1968 (div. Aug. 1981); 1 child, Paul William; m. Lauren Ellin Syda, Aug. 11, 1984. BSME, U. Calif., Davis, 1968, postgrad., 1987; MSE, U. Mich., 1969; MS in Oceanography, U. Calif., San Diego, 1974. Rsch. asst. Scripps Instn. of Oceanography, La Jolla, Calif., 1969-73; test engr. Offshore Tech. Corp., Escondido, Calif., 1971-73; rsch. engr. Oreg. State U., Corvallis, 1974-76; instr. engring. U. Calif., Davis, 1980-81; tenured prof. math, computer sci. and engring. depts. Yuba Coll., Marysville, Calif., 1976—; participant NASA Space Tech. Summer Inst., U. So. Calif., 1967, Energy Summer Inst., U. Calif., Davis, 1978, NASA KC135 Zero G Rsch. Flight, Ellington AFB, Tex., 1987. Contbr. articles to profl. jours. Pres. Corvallis Velo Club, 1974-76. Mem. AAUP, Am. Soc. Engring. Edn., Yuba Sutter Bicycle Club (pres. 1977-80). Office: Yuba Coll 2088 N Beale Rd Marysville CA 95901-7605

KLEIN, WILLIAM MCKINLEY JR., museum director. CEO, pres., exec. dir. Nat. Tropical Botanical Garden, Lawai, Hawaii. Office: Nat Tropical Botanical Garden PO Box 340 Lawai HI 96765

KLEINBERG, JAMES P., lawyer; b. Pitts., Mar. 28, 1943. BA, U. Pitts., 1964; JD, U. Mich., 1967. Bar: Calif. 1968. Trial atty. antitrust divsn. Dept. Justice, 1967-68; ptnr. McCutchen, Doyle, Brown & Enersen, San Francisco and San Jose, Calif.; atty. rep. 9th Cir. Jud. Conf. No. Dist. Calif., 1984-84, mem. exec. com., 1984-87; mem. adv. group No. Dist. Calif., 1990—; mem. civil trial advocacy consulting group Bd. Legal Specialization, 1979-90, mem. com. adminstrn. justice, 1984-87; panelist Ann. Fed. Practice Insts., 1992—. Mem. visitors com. U. Mich. Law Sch., 1985—. Fellow Am. Bar Found. Office: McCutchen Doyle Brown & Enersen Market Post Tower 3 Embarcadero Ctr Ste 1500 San Francisco CA 94111-4038

KLEINBERG, JUDITH G., lawyer, children's advocate; b. Hartford, Conn., Jan. 28, 1946; d. Burleigh B. and Ruth (Leven) Greenberg; m. James Paul Kleinberg, Aug. 30, 1970; children: Alexander, Lauren. BA cum laude, U. Mich., 1968; JD, U. Calif., Berkeley, 1971. Atty. pvt. practice, San Francisco, 1971-74; legal affairs reporter comml. and pub. TV, San Francisco, 1974-76; prof. law Mills Coll., Oakland, Calif., 1977-84; chief of staff The Global Fund for Women, Los Altos, Calif., 1987-88; pub. interest atty., non-profit corp. law/orgn. specialist alternative dispute resolution Palo Alto, Calif., 1988-94; exec. dir. Kids in Common: A Children & Families Collaborative, San Jose, Calif., 1994—; arbitrator/mediator, legal adv. for abortion rights, women and children's rights and environ. groups, Santa Clara County and Calif., 1980—; speaker in field. Mem. bd. editors Calif. Law Rev., 1969-71. Mem. steering com. lawyers coun. No. Calif. sect. ACLU, bd. dirs., 1990-92; founder, chairperson No. Calif. Friends of Pediat. AIDS Found.; past pres. Com. for Green Foothills; mem. legis. and steering coms. Calif. Coalition for Childhood Immunization, 1995—; mem. Calif. Children's Advs. Roundtable, 1995—; bd. dirs. Palo Alto SAFE, Support Network for Battered Women, 1990-92, Palo Alto Coun. PTAs, Leadership Midpeninsula, 1994-96; pres. Palo Alto Stanford divsn. Am. Heart Assn., 1994-95; v.p. Assn. for Sr. Day Health, 1994-95; founder Safer Summer Project; pres., legal counsel Calif. Abortion and Reproductive Rights Action League, 1980-86. Recipient Calif. Pks. and Recreation Soc. Merit award, 1995, World of People award Girl Scouts Am., Santa Clara County, 1996. Mem. Nat. Assn. Child Advocates, Calif. Women Lawyers (v.p. 1986-88).

KLEINDIENST, WILLIAM, mayor. Mayor Palm Springs, Calif. Address: 3200 E Tahquitz-McCallum Way Palm Springs CA 92262

KLEINER, KATHLEEN ALLEN, psychology educator; b. Phila., Nov. 12, 1958; d. William Anton and Marjorie Anne (Fine) K.; m. Roy Owen Gathercoal, Aug. 9, 1988; 1 child, Glen William Gathercoal. AB, Franklin & Marshall Coll., Lancaster, Pa., 1981; MA, PhD, Case Western Res. U., 1985. Teaching asst. Frankln & Marshall Coll., 1980-81; rsch. asst. Case Western Res. U., Cleve., 1981-85; researcher U. Calif., Berkeley, 1985-87; asst. prof. psychology Ind. U.-Purdue U., Indpls., 1987-93; assoc. prof. psychology, chair dept. psychology George Fox Coll., Newberg, Oreg., 1993—; summer faculty fellow Ind. U., Bloomington, 1988. Contbr. articles to profl. jours. Evaluation mem. Campaign for Healthy Babies, Indpls., 1990-92; active Yamhill County Commn. on Children and Families. Nat. Inst. Child Health and Human Devel. predoctoral fellow, 1981-85; Case Western Res. U. grad. alumni grantee, 1984, Project Devel. Program Interdisciplinary grantee Ind. U.-Purdue U., 1990, Intercampus Rsch. Funds, Ind. U., 1991. Mem. Mem. APA, Western Psychol. Assn., Soc. Rsch. in Child Devel., Internat. Soc. Infant Studies, Psi Chi. Mem. Soc. of Friends. Home: 2504 Haworth Ave Newberg OR 97132-1951 Office: George Fox Coll 414 N Meridian St Newberg OR 97132-2625

KLEINFELD, ANDREW JAY, federal judge; b. 1945. BA magna cum laude, Wesleyan U., 1966; JD cum laude, Harvard U., 1969. Law clk. Alaska Supreme Ct., 1969-71; U.S. magistrate U.S. Dist. Ct. Alaska, Fairbanks, 1971-74; pvt. practice law Fairbanks, 1971-86; judge U.S. Dist. Ct. Alaska, Anchorage, 1986-91, U.S. Ct. Appeals (9th cir.), San Francisco, 1991—. Contbr. articles to profl. jours. Mem. Alaska Bar Assn. (pres. 1982-83, bd. govs. 1981-84), Tanana Valley Bar Assn. (pres. 1974-75), Phi Beta Kappa. Republican. Office: US Ct Appeals 9th Cir Courthouse Sq 250 Cushman St Ste 3-a Fairbanks AK 99701-4640

KLEINSMITH, BRUCE JOHN See NUTZLE, FUTZIE

KLEITMAN, JOSEPH, mayor. Mayor City of Mountain View, Calif. Office: 444 Castro St Mountain View CA 94039

KLEMENTIEV, ALEXANDRE ALEXANDROVICH, computer scientist, consultant, educator; b. Moscow, July 1, 1942; came to U.S., 1992; s. Alexandre Dmitrievich and Vera Petrovna (Bakoulina) K.; m. Tamara Dmitrievna Polyakova, Mar. 7, 1964; children, Dmitry, Alexandre. MSEE, Moscow Physico-Tech. Inst., 1966, PhD in Applied Maths., 1971; PhD Math. Epidemiology, Inst. Cybernetics, Kiev, Ukraine, 1991. Engr. Inst. Control Scis. Russian Acad. Scis., Moscow, 1966-71, sr. rsch. scientist Inst. Control Scis., 1973-75, leading rsch. scientist Inst. Control Scis., 1978-92; head lab. syss. analysis Moscow City Coun. Rsch. Computing Ctr., 1971-73; rsch. scholar Internat. Inst. Applied Sys. Analysis/Bio-Med. Project, Vienna, 1975-78; sr. rsch. scientist NeuRobotics, Inc., Puyallup, Wash., 1992-94; cons. Tom H. Foulds and Assoc. Counsel, Seattle, 1996—; instr. automation and remote control Moscow Inst. Automation and Computer Tech., 1980-81, sys. modeling Moscow Power Inst., 1981-82, computer modeling in health field Moscow Inst. Physics and Tech., 1984-92, bus. data processing, operating syss., programming visual basic Tacoma (Wash.) C.C., 1996—; cons. regional Health Ministry Computer Ctrs., Stavropol, Moscow, Novosibirsk, Tbilishi. Author: Quantitative Models Developement for Solving the Health Control Problems, 1985; contbr. 2 monographs, over 50 articles to scientific jours.

KLEPINGER, JOHN WILLIAM, trailer manufacturing company executive; b. Lafayette, Ind., Feb. 7, 1945; s. John Franklin and R. Wanda (North) K.; m. Mary Patricia Duffy, May 1, 1976; 1 child, Nicholas Patrick. BS, Ball State U., 1967, MA, 1968. Sales engr. CTS Corp., Elkhart, Ind., 1969-70; exec. v.p. Woodlawn Products Corp., Elkhart, 1970-78; v.p. Period Ind., Henderson, Ky., 1976-78, Sotebeer Constrn. Co., Inc., Elkhart, 1978-81; gen. mgr. Wells Industries Inc., Ogden, Utah, 1981—, Wells Cargo, Inc., Phoenix, 1995—; regional dir. Zion's First Nat. Bank, Ogden, 1986—. Bd. dirs. St. Benedict's Hosp., Ogden, 1986-94, chmn., 1987-94; bd. dirs. Weber County Indsl. Devel. Corp., Nat. Job Tng. Partnership Inc., 1986-89; mem. Weber-Morgan Pvt. Industry Coun., 1983-96, Utah Job Tng. Coordinating Coun., 1988-96, chmn. 1993-94. Named Ogden Bus. Man of Yr., Weber County Sch. Dist., 1984. Mem. Nat. Assn. Trailer Mfrs. (bd. dirs., vice chmn. 1994-95, chmn. 1995-97), Weber County Prodn. Mgrs. Assn. (pres. 1984-85, 92-93), Nat. Assn. Pvt. Industry Couns. (bd. dirs. 1986-96, pres. 1988-92), Nat. Alliance Bus. (bd. dirs. 1987-90), Ogden Area C. of C. (bd. dirs. 1986-96, treas. 1986-89), Phoenix C. of C., Exch. Club (bd. dirs. Ogden 1984-86). Roman Catholic. Home: 5181 Aztec Dr Ogden UT 84403-4606 Office: Wells Industries Inc PO Box 1619 Ogden UT 84402-1619

KLEPPE, SHIRLEY R. KLEIN, artist; b. Sedalia, Mo., Sept. 29, 1946; d. Benjamin Eades Klein and Clara Louise Shirley; m. Stephen Douglas Kleppe, Nov. 22, 1968; children: Clinton Douglas, Nicole Lynne. BS in Edn., Ctrl. Mo. State U., 1967; postgrad., Ariz. State U., 1988. Art tchr. Benton County R#1 Sch. Dist., Cole Camp, Mo., 1967-68, Turner (Kans.) Unified Sch. Dist., 1968-69; graphic designer Menorah Med. Ctr., Kansas City, Mo., 1969-70; freelance graphic designer, illustrator Kansas City, 1970-75; advt. dir. Gorges Wholesale Meats, inc., Harlingen, Tex., 1975-76; art instr. City of Phoenix, 1979-82; sponsor vis. artist program Ctrl. Mo. State U., Warrensburg, 1993—; pres. Outrageous Red Inc., Scottsdale, Ariz., 1994—. Exhibited in shows at Western Fedn. Watercolor Socs., El Cajon, Calif., 1990 (Best of Show), Salmagundi Club, N.Y.C., 1990 (Thomas Moran award for watercolor), Rocky Mountain Nat. Watermedia, Golden, Colo., 1994 (3d Pl. award), Ky. Watercolor Soc., 1995 (Top award for watercolor); contbr. watercolor painting articles to profl. publs. Pres. Edmond (Okla.) Iris Soc., 1986-87. Mem. Nat. Watercolor Soc. (2d pl. award 1997), Watercolor West, Pa. Watercolor Soc., Ky. Watercolor Soc., Western Fedn. Watercolor Socs., Ariz. Watercolor Soc. (Royal Scorpion mem.), Ariz. Artists Guild (v.p. membership 1983-84, scholarship chmn. 1990-95). Home and Office: 8210 E Tether Tr Scottsdale AZ 85255

KLEPPER, CAROL HERDMAN, mental health therapist; b. Wagner, S.D., July 17, 1933; d. Forrest Glenwood and Augusta Wilhamina (Mills) Herdman; m. Albert Raymond Klepper, May 14, 1955; children: James David, Leesa Lynn, Krista Patrice. BS in Psychology cum laude, S. Oreg. State Coll., 1987; MS in Counseling, Oreg. State U., 1989. Nat. cert. counselor, lic. profl. counselor. Dir. counseling Klamath Hospice, Klamath Falls, Oreg., 1990-91; staff therapist Klamath Mental Health Ctr., 1991-94; in-house counselor Wednesday's Child, 1995—, title 19 adminstr., 1996—; data rschr. Rich Pickett and Co., Klamath Falls, 1986-90; pre-commitment investigator Klamath Mental Health Ctr., 1991-94; EPSDT coord. County of Klamath, 1991-94. Mem. youth svcs. team local mid-schs., Klamath Falls, 1992-94; juv. fire-setters network Klamath Falls Fire Dist. #1, 1992-95; head start health bd., Klamath Falls, 1991—, RAPP Team Mem., 1995—. Mem. Psi Chi. Home and Office: 8926 Hwy 66 Klamath Falls OR 97601-9538

KLEVAN, ROBERT BRUCE, music educator; b. Lodi, Calif., May 12, 1953; s. Stanley P. and Mary C. (Canepa) K.; m. Norma D. Taylor, May 26, 1974; children: Rebecca, Roxanne, Anthony. MusB summa cum laude, U. Pacific, 1975, MusM, 1981; PhD in Music, U. Tex., 1993. Cert. tchr. music, Calif. Dir. mus. Marysville (Calif.) H.S., 1975-77, Robert Louis Stevenson Sch., Pebble Beach, Calif., 1977—; instr. Monterey (Calif.) Peninsula Coll., 1994—; fine arts chmn. Robert Louis Stevenson Sch., Pebble Beach, 1986—, summer camp dir., 1995—. Contbr. articles to profl. jours. Founding mem. Monterey Jazz Festival Edn. Com., 1983; bd. dirs. Chamber Music Soc., Carmel, Calif., 1992-94. Recipient Youth Leadership award Elks, Stockton, Calif., 1971. Mem. Ctrl. Coast Section Music Educators (bd. dirs., chmn. medals com. 1994—), Calif. Orch. Dirs. Assn. (pres. 1994-96), Internat. Assn. Jazz Educators, Am. Choral Dirs. Assn., Calif. Music Educators Assn. (Outstanding Music Educator award 1993), Music Educators Nat. Conf. Office: Robert Louis Stevenson Sch Box 657 Pebble Beach CA 93953

KLEVIT, ALAN BARRE, publishing executive, motivational speaker, writer; b. Balt., June 25, 1935; s. Robert and Minnie (Goodman) K.; m. Marilyn Rosenthal, Nov. 26, 1955; children: Mindy Faith, Lawrence Michael, Richard Steven. BS in Econs., Georgetown U., 1956, MA in Econs., 1960; MA in Pub. Adminstrn. and Urban Affairs, Am. U., 1970. Asst. mgr. AS Beck Shoe Co., Washington, 1956-57; stat., economist Commerce Dept., Washington, 1957-60; securities analyst, rsch. dir. T.J. McDonald & Co., Washington, 1960-62; mgmt. analyst, div. chief Fed. Aviation Adminstrn., Washington, 1962-73; CEO Art Fair, Inc., Silver Spring, Md., 1974-90; founder, dir. Klevit Fine Art, Internat., Silver Spring and Malibu, Calif., 1987—; founder, exec. officer Robert Klevit Found. for Humanitarianism, Silver Spring and Malibu, Calif., 1987—; dir. Stardust Pub., Malibu, 1990—; co-founder, dir. Charity Editions, Silver Spring and Malibu, 1987; mem. faculty Mgmt. by Objectives Fed. Exec. Sch., Charlottesville, Va., 1969-71; motivational speaker, Malibu, 1988—. Author: Three Days in Sedona, 1990, How to Make Your Dreams Come True, 1991, Follow the Rainbow, 1991, (book and audiocassette) Pass the Pickles, Please and Other Stories, 1995; (video) Journey Within, 1993; host radio show: Today's Art World with Alan Klevit, 1983-84, (TV Show) Off the Beaten Path with Alan Klevit, 1992—; contbr. articles to mags. and newspapers including regular contbns. to Malibu Mag.; writer, prodr., featured performer tv commls., 1994—. Bd. dirs. Summer Opera, Washington, 1987—, Marine & Mountain Wildlife Rescue, Malibu, 1991—; mem. Hammer Mus. Mem. Inst. for Econometric Rsch., World Wildlife Fedn., Inst. for Noetic Scis., Planetary Soc., Malibu C. of C., Masons. Office: Stardust Pub PO Box 6356 Malibu CA 90265-6356

KLIEGER, PAUL CHRISTIAAN, anthropologist, researcher; b. Great Falls, Mont., July 27, 1951; s. Samuel and Charlotte E. (Odegard) K. BA, U. Mont., 1973; MA in Asian Religions, U. Hawaii, 1980, MA in Anthropology, 1985, PhD, 1989. Lectr. Chaminade U., Honolulu, 1985-88, U. Hawaii, Honolulu, 1988; vis. lectr. U. Pitts., 1989; acting dir. Tibetan Cultural Ctr., Missoula, Mont., 1990; assoc. anthropologist Bishop Mus., Honolulu, 1991—; dir. Tibetan-U.S. resettlement Com., 1990-91, advisor, 1991-93; bd. dirs. Friends of Moku'ula, Lahaina, Hawaii, 1994. Author: Tibetan Nationalism, 1992, Na Maka o Halawa, 1995; entries in Asian Am. Encyclopedia, 1994; contbr. articles to anthrop. publs. Cons. U.S.-Tibet Com., Missoula, Mont., 1990-91, Mus. of Internat. Folk Art, Santa Fe. Recipient Maui Hist. Soc. Hist. Preservation award, 1995; Pacific-Asian scholar U. Hawaii, Honolulu, 1985-86; grantee Lahaina (Maui, Hawaii) Restoration Found., 1993, Native Hawaiian Culture and Arts Program, Honolulu, 1994. Mem. Am. Anthrop. Assn. (com. on refugee issues 1989—, coun. on human rights 1989—), Soc. for Hawaiian Archaeology (sec. 1996—), Hawaiian Anthrop. Assn. (v.p. 1983, editor 1989), Hawaiian Hist. Soc., Sigma Xi. Buddhist. Office: Bishop Mus Dept Anthropology 1525 Bernice St Honolulu HI 96817-2704

KLIEN, WOLFGANG JOSEF, architect; b. Hollabrunn, Austria, Sept. 29, 1942; s. Josef and Maria (Kainz) K.; Dipl. Ing., Vienna Tech. U., 1967; m. Jean M. Klien; children: Christina Olga, Angelika Maria. Designer, E. Donau, Architect, Vienna, 1968; with C. Nitschke & Assos., Architects, Columbus, Ohio, 1968-71; project architect GSAS Architects, Phoenix, 1971-75, 77-78; prodn. architect Harry Glueck, Vienna, 1976-77; v.p. architecture Am. Indian Engring. Inc., Phoenix, 1978-81; pres. S.W. Estate Group, Inc., real estate devel., San Diego, 1980-82; pres., tech. dir., branch mgr. Ariz. br. office SEG-S.W. Estate Group, Inc., Phoenix, 1982-86; prin. Klien & Assoc., Architecture, Planning, Devel. Cons., Phoenix, 1986—, Atlantic-Pacific Trading Corp., Internat. Trade, Phoenix, 1986-88; pres., gen. mgr. Polybau, Inc., Hayward, Calif., 1988-90; pres. Libra Cons., INc., Phoenix, 1989—; ptnr. Heart Devel. Co., LLC, dBa Heart Homes, 1993-96; v.p. Sunrise Custom Homes, Inc., 1995—. Recipient Great Silver Medal of Merit, Republic of Austria, 1993. Mem. AIA, Austro-Am. Council West, Austrian Soc. Ariz. (founder 1985, v.p. 1985-86, pres. 1987—). Roman Catholic. Home and Office: 4524 S Willow Dr Tempe AZ 85282-7365

KLIMA, ROGER R., physiatrist; b. Prague, Czechoslovakia; came to U.S., 1982, naturalized, 1988; s. Josef and Radka Klima. BA, Zatlanka Coll., Prague, 1971; MD, Charles U., Prague, 1978. Diplomate Am. Bd. Phys. Medicine and Rehab., Am. Bd. Electrodiagnostic Medicine. Resident in surgery Charles U., 1978-79, resident in orthopedic surgery, 1979-81; fellow, clin. clk. Beverly Hills Med. Ctr. and Cedars-Sinai Med. Ctr., L.A., 1984-86; resident in surgery U. Medicine and Dentistry-N.J. Med. Sch., Newark, 1986-87; resident in phys. medicine and rehab. U. Medicine and Dentistry-N.J. Med. Sch./Kessler Inst., Newark and West Orange, 1987-90; mem. phys. medicine and rehab. faculty Stanford (Calif.) U. and affiliated hosps., 1990—; dir. phys. medicine and rehab. outpatient svcs. Palo Alto (Calif.) VA Health Care Sys., 1992—, also co-dir. comprehensive pain mgmt.; clin. instr. in phys. medicine and rehab. U. Medicine and Dentistry-N.J.Med. Sch., 1989-90; clin. instr. in phys., medicine and rehab. Stanford U. Sch. Medicine, 1990-96, asst. prof., 1996—. Contbr. articles to profl. jours. Recipient first ann. Thompson Humanitarian award Stanford U. Phys. Medicine and Rehab., 1994. Mem. Am. Acad. Phys. Medicine and Rehab. (liaison resident physician coun. 1989-90), Assn. Acad. Physiatrists, Am. Assn. Electrodiagnostic Medicine. Office: Stanford U Med Ctr Divsn Phys Medicine and Rehab Rm NC 104 Stanford CA 94305

KLINE, FRED WALTER, retired communications company executive; b. Oakland, Calif., May 17, 1918; s. Walter E. and Jean M. Kline; m. Verna Marie Taylor, Dec. 27, 1952; children—Kathleen, Nora, Fred Walter. B.A. in Calif. History, U. Calif.-Berkeley, 1940. With Walter E. Kline & Assocs. and successor Fred Kline Agy., Inc., from 1937; chmn. bd., pres. Kline Communications Corp., Los Angeles, 1956-96, ret., 1996; pres. Capitol News Service. Commr. Los Angeles County Fire Services Commn., Calif. Motion Picture Devel. Council; cons., advisor Calif. Film Commn.; former fed. civil def. liaison; developer state-wide paramedic rescue program; Calif. chmn. Office of Asst. Sec. Def.; mem. Calif. Com. for Employer Support of Guard and Res.; mem. Los Angeles Film Com. Served with USAAF, World War II; brig. gen. Calif. Mil. Dept. Recipient Inter-Racial award City of Los Angeles, 1963, named Man of Yr., 1964. Mem. Acad. Motion Picture Arts and Scis., Radio and TV News Assn. So. Calif., Pub. Relations Soc. Am., Calif. Newspaper Pubs. Assn., Cath. Press Council (founding mem.), Pacific Pioneer Broadcasters, Footprinters Internat., Am. Mil. Govt. Assn. (past pres.), Navy League, Calif. State Police Officers Assn., Internat. Assn. Profl. Firefighters (hon. life), Peace Officers Assn. Los Angeles County (life), Internat. Assn. Chiefs of Police, Internat. Assn. Fire Chiefs, Calif. Fire Chiefs Assn., Fire Marshals Assn. N.Am., Nat. Fire Protection Assn., Nat. Fin. Writers Assn., Hollywood C. of C., Nat. Fire Sci. Acad., Calif. State Mil. Forces, Calif. Pubs. Assn., So. Calif. Cable Club. Sigma Delta Chi. Clubs: Greater Los Angeles Press, Media (Los Angeles), Sacramento Press. Columnist Calif. newspapers. Office: 1180 Weber Way Sacramento CA 95822-1840

KLINE, HOWARD JAY, cardiologist; b. White Plains, N.Y., Nov. 5, 1932; s. Raymond Kline and Rose Plane; divorced; children: Michael, Ethan; m. Ellen Sawamura, June 13, 1987; 1 child, Christopher. BA, Dickinson Coll., 1954; MD, N.Y. Med. Coll., 1958. Intern San Francisco Gen. Hosp., 1958-59; resident Mt. Sinai Hosp., N.Y.C., 1959-61; sr. resident U. Calif. Med. Ctr., San Francisco, 1961-62; cardiology fellow Mt. Sinai Hosp., N.Y.C., 1962-64; dir. cardiology training program St. Mary's Hosp., San Francisco, 1970-90, Calif. Pacific Med. Ctr., San Francisco, 1992—; clin. prof. medicine U. Calif. Med. Ctr., San Francisco, 1984—; vis. prof. Nihon U., Tokyo, 1986. Editor (jours.) Hosp. Practice, Cardiology, 1992—; contbr. articles to Hosp. Practice. Lt. col. U.S. Med. Corps, 1967-69. Fellow ACP, Am. Heart Assn., Am. Coll. Cardiology, Am. Coll. Chest Physicians; mem. Burkes Tennis Club. Office: 2100 Webster St Ste 518 San Francisco CA 94115-2382

KLINE, NATASHA CALE, biologist; b. Montclair, N.J., Sept. 20, 1959; d. Arland Theodore and Gail (Hulslander) K.; m. Victor William Brown, Jun 13, 1986; 1 child, Zoë Bailey Brown. BS in Zoology, U. Calif., Davis, 1982; MS in Biology, U. Miami, 1987. Biol. technician U.S. Fish and Wildlife Svc., Adak, Alaska, 1982-84; biol. technician U.S. Nat. Park Svc., Everglades Nat. Park, Fla., 1986-88, Grand Canyon Nat. Park, Ariz., 1990-91; nat. resource program mgr. USAF, Phoenix, 1991-93; wildlife biologist U.S. Nat. Park Svc., Tucson, Ariz., 1993—; regl. rep. Ptnrs. in Flight, USAF, Phoenix, 1992-93; cons. biologist U.S. Nat. Park Svc., Page, Ariz., 1990. Contbr. articles to profl. jours. Recipient Nat. Resource Response award U.S. Dept. Interior, Washington, 1989, Teagle Found. scholarship Exxon Corp., 1985, Maytag fellowship U. Miami, Coral Gables, Fla., 1984-86; rsch. grantee Tropical Audubon Soc., Miami, 1985. Office: Saguaro Nat Park Nat Park Svc 3693 S Old Spanish Trl Tucson AZ 85730-5601

KLINGENSMITH, ARTHUR PAUL, relocation and redevelopment consultant; b. L.A., May 23, 1949; s. Paul Arthur and Hermine Elinore K.; m. Donna J. Bellucci, Apr. 26, 1976 (div. Jan. 1981). AA in Social Sci., Indian Valley Jr. Coll., 1976; BA in Indsl. Psychology, San Francisco State U., 1979; MA in Indsl. Psychology, Columbia Pacific U., 1980. Enlisted USAF, Biloxi, Miss.; advanced through grades to staff sgt. USAF; instr. radio ops. USAF, Biloxi, 1968-72; air traffic control operator USAF, Hamilton AFB Novato, Calif., 1972-74; resigned USAF, 1974; elec. technician Calif. Dept. Transp., Oakland, 1975-78; right of way agt. Calif. Dept. Transp., San Francisco, 1978-85; sr. right of way agt. Calif. Dept. Transp., Sacramento, 1985-87, computer researcher, 1985-87; v.p., cons. Associated Right of Way Svcs., Inc., 1989-92; pvt. practice relocation and redevel. cons., 1987-96, bus. and pers. devel. cons., 1996—. V.p. bd. dirs. PAST Found. Mem. Am. Pres. Assn., Internat. Right of Way Assn. (instr. 1982—), Am. Arbitration Assn., Assn. Humanistic Psychology, Inst. Noetic Scis., Am. Planning Assn. Republican. Home and Office: Arthur P Klingensmith & Assocs PO Box 574 Sausalito CA 94966-0574

KLINGER, PAUL ANTHONY, educational therapist, administrator; b. Cleve., Jan. 3, 1941; s. Tobias Gilbert and Olga Gertrude (Jacobson) K. BA in Psychology, UCLA, 1963, cert. in elem. teaching, 1966, MA in Spl. Edn., 1968, EdD in Spl. Edn., 1976. Pvt. tutor L.A., 1962-72; itinerant tutor Countryside Preparatory Sch., Northridge, Calif., 1985-89; dir., owner Granada Hills (Calif.) One to One Reading and Ednl. Ctr., 1972—. Mem. Assn. Ednl. Therapists (cert., treas. 1980-86), Orton Dyslexia Soc., Coun. Exceptional Children. Democrat. Office: Granada Hills One To One Reading & Ednl Ctr 10324 Woodley Ave Granada Hills CA 91344-6916

KLINGER, WAYNE JULIUS, secondary education educator; b. Chgo., Dec. 2, 1934; s. Walter Otto and Katherine Veronica (Murtha) K.; m. Dona Larene Sandkuhl, Sept. 26, 1967 (div. 1980); m. Ellen Jane Lawseth, July 7, 1991 (div. Mar. 1996); children: Susan Jackson-Woods, David. BA, Villanova U., 1957; MS, Cath. U. Am., 1963. Cert. tchr., Ill., Mich., Calif., Oreg., Minn. Tchr. Order St. Augustine, Rockford, Ill., 1961-62, Detroit, 1962-63; tchr., dir. studies Order St. Augustine, Chgo., 1963-66; tchr., activity dir. Order St. Augustine, Holland, Mich., 1966-67; tchr. Palo Alto (Calif.) Unified Sch. Dist., 1967-72, Salem (Oreg.) Pub. Schs., 1972-77, Stockton (Calif.) Unified Sch. Dist., 1986—; NSF inst. participant Ill. Inst. Tech., 1963-64, Harvard Project Physics, Santa Clara, Calif., 1969, geology practicum We. Wash. State U., 1971, laser inst. San Jose State U., 1990; participant Woodrow Wilson Found. Physics Inst., U. Calif.-Santa Cruz, 1988, 89, 92, 93, Physics Tchrs. Resource Agts., 1995-95; pres. Sch. Site Coun., 1991-92; participant numerous workshops. Founder, dir. Cardboard Boat Regatta, Stockton, 1988-96. Mem. NEA, Nat. Sci. Tchrs. Assn., Am. Assn. Physics Tchrs., Calif. Sci. Tchrs. Assn., Valley Assn. Sci. Tchrs., Stockton Tchrs. Assn. Democrat. Roman Catholic. Home: 1309 Havenhill Way Stockton CA 95209-1410 Office: Edison H S 1425 S Center St Stockton CA 95206-2016

KLINK, PAUL LEO, business executive; b. Auburn, N.Y., July 28, 1965; s. Charles Lawrence and Regina Joyce (Maniscalco) K. Student, SUNY, Cayuga, 1979-95. Pres., CEO Klink, Inc., Honolulu, 1979—; pres. http://www hawaiian com/ Inc., 1995—; chmn. Ad 2 Honolulu; bd. dirs. First Night Honolulu. Contbr. and edited articles for profl. jours. Co-chmn. direct mktg. com. Aloha United Way, Honolulu, 1988—; active computer affairs Friends of Congressman O'Shiro, Ewa Beach, Hawaii, 1988—, Friends of Gov. Cayetano, Honolulu, 1988—, Friends of Mayor Harris, Honolulu, 1988—; bd. dirs. Postal Customer Coun., 1992—; founder Rock 'n Vote; co-founder Live Aloha: attendee inauguration of U.S. Pres. William J. Clinton and U.S. V.p. Albert Gore, 1993, 97. Mem. Ad 2 (pres. 1995-96, chmn. bd. dirs. 1996-97), Japanese C. of C. (strategic planning officer, mem. steering com.), Puu
aloa Rifel and Pistol Club, Mensa, Pacific Club, Rotary, La Mariana Sailing Club, Nat. Press Club, Havana Pacific Club, Georgetown Club, Honolulu Zool. Soc. Office: Klink Inc Box 8578 330 Saratoga Rd Honolulu HI 96830-0578

KLINT, RONALD V., math educator, financial consultant; b. Chgo., Feb. 11, 1939; s. Charles W. and Claire P. (Buente) K.; m. Carol L. Rodningen, Oct. 13, 1984; children: Matthew, Andrew. AA, Glendale (Calif.) C.C., 1958; BA, UCLA, 1960; MA, Calif. State U., L.A., 1964. Cert. tchr. and admin., Calif. Math instr. Glendale Schs., 1961—; pres. Prof. Edn. of Glendale (Calif.), 1967-70; mentor tchr. Glendale Schs., 1988-92. Vol. Glendale Rep. Party, various time. Mem. Foothill Math. Coun., Calif. Math Coun. Home: 4400 Ramsdell Ave La Crescenta CA 91214

KLIPPING, ROBERT SAMUEL, geophysicist; b. Glaston, N.D., Dec. 5, 1928; s. Roy Samuel and Marie (Peterson) K.; m. Gayle Cleone Swanson, Sept. 29, 1951; children: Barbara, Sharon, Joan. BS in Geology, Colo. Coll., Colorado Springs, 1953. Geophys. computer scientist Gen. Geophys. Co., Denver, 1953-57; geophys. supr. Mandrel Indsl. Inc., Denver, 1957-65, area mgr., 1965-69; geophys. Pennzoil Co., Denver, 1969-72, exploration mgr., 1972-78; geophys. cons., owner Klipping & Assocs., Denver, 1978—. Author: American Association of Petroleum Geologists, 1976, Montana Geological Society, 1978. Staff sgt. U.S. Army, 1946-48. Mem. Am. Assn. Petroleum Geologists, Soc. Exploration Geophysicists, Denver Geophys. Soc. (treas. 1972-73, sec. 1973-74). Republican. Methodist. Home: 14645 Sterling Rd Colorado Springs CO 80921-2618 Office: Klipping & Assocs 518 17th St Denver CO 80202

KLOBE, TOM, art gallery director; b. Mpls., Nov. 26, 1940; s. Charles S. and Lorna (Effertz) K.; m. Delmarie Pauline Motta, June 21, 1975. BFA, U. Hawaii, 1964, MFA, 1968; postgrad., UCLA, 1972-73. Vol. peace corps Alang, Iran, 1964-66; tchr. Calif. State U., Fullerton, 1969-72, Santa Ana (Calif.) Coll., 1972-77, Orange Coast Coll., Costa Mesa, Calif., 1974-77, Golden West Coll., Huntington Beach, Calif., 1976-77; art gallery dir. U. Hawaii, Honolulu, 1977—; acting dir. Downey (Calif.) Mus. Art, 1976; cons. Judiciary History Mus., Honolulu, 1982-96, Maui (Hawaii) Arts and Cultural Ctr., 1984-94, curator Kāia Wai Ola: This Living Water, 1994; exhibit designer Inst. for Astronomy, Honolulu, 1983-86; exhibit design cons. Japanese Cultural Ctr. Hawaii, 1993—; juror Print Casebooks; project coord. Crossings '97, France, Hawaii. Recipient Best in Exhbn. Design award Print Casebooks, 1984, 86, 88, Vol. Svc. award City of Downey, 1977; Exhbn. grantee NEA, 1979—, State Found. Culture and the Arts, 1977—. Mem. Hawaii Mus. Assn., Nat. Assn. Mus. Exhbn. Roman Catholic. Office: U Hawaii Art Gallery 2535 The Mall Honolulu HI 96822-2233 *Personal philosophy: Nothing is impossible. Believe in yourself and in each other. Each of us has the ability to shape our destiny.*

KLOEPFER, CLARENCE VICTOR, oil company executive; b. Calgary, AB, Can., May 24, 1933; s. Arthur Thomas and Philomena Agnes (Gilker) K.; m. Olive Mary Sultan, Apr. 27, 1957; children: Susan M., Jay V., Anthony J. BS, U. Okla., 1954. Cert. profl. engr., Alta. Engr. Husky Oil, Ltd., Calgary; engring. group supr. Pan Am. Petroleum Corp/AMOCO, Calgary; chief engr. Banff Oil, Ltd., Calgary; mgr. engring. Aquitaine Co. of Can., Calgary; pres. Kloepfer & Assocs., Ltd., Calgary, Permez Petroleums, Ltd., Calgary and Vancouver; bd. dirs. Westley Technologies Ltd., Vancouver, Enertec Geophys. Svcs., Calgary, Computolog, Ltd., Calgary, Ancilla Techs. Inc., Vancouver, Purchase Oil and Gas Inc., Calgary, Westcastle Energy Trust, Acanthus Energy Trust, Calgary. Mem. Can. Inst. of Mining (Disting. Svc. award 1981), APEGGA, Rotary, SPE. Roman Catholic. Home: 2328 Mathers Ave, West Vancouver, BC Canada V7V 2H6

KLOHS, MURLE WILLIAM, chemist, consultant; b. Aberdeen, S.D., Dec. 24, 1920; s. William Henry and Lowell (Lewis) K.; m. Dolores Catherine Borm, June 16, 1946; children: Wendy C., Linda L. Student Westmar Coll., 1938-40; BSc, U. Notre Dame, 1947. Jr. chemist Harrower Lab., Glendale, Calif., 1947, Rexall Drug Co., L.A., 1947-49; sr. chemist Riker Labs., Inc., L.A., 1949-57, dir. medicinal chemistry, Northridge, Calif., 1957-69, mgr. chem rsch. dept., 1969-72, mgr. pharm. devel. dept., 1972-73, mgr. tech. liaison and comml. devel., 1973-82; cons. chemist, 1982—. Contbr. articles to profl. jours. Served to lt. USNR, 1943-46. Riker fellow Harvard U., 1950. Mem. Am. Chem. Soc., Am. Pharm. Assn., Adventures Club (L.A.). Home and Office: Lake Wildwood 19831 Echo Blue Dr Penn Valley CA 95946

KLONTZ, JAMES MATHIAS, architect; b. Kent, Wash., May 3, 1920; s. George John and Mary Ellen (Lavin) K.; m. Angie Mary Gomes, Jan. 15, 1949; children: Melinda, Marsha, Nancy, Karen, Joyce. BArch, U. Wash., 1943. Registered arch., Wash., Alaska. Assoc. arch. Bliss Moore Jr. & Assoc., Seattle, 1946-51; prin. arch. Klontz & Assocs., Seattle, 1951—. Capt. U.S. Army, 1943-46, ETO. Mem. AIA. Office: Klontz & Assocs 4000 Aurora Ave N Seattle WA 98103-7853

KLOPFLEISCH, STEPHANIE SQUANCE, social services agency administrator; b. Rupert, Idaho, Dec. 21, 1940; d. William Jaynes and Elizabeth (Cunningham) Squance; B.A., Pomona Coll., 1962; M.S.W., UCLA, 1966; m. Randall Klopfleisch, June 27, 1970; children—Elizabeth, Jennifer, Matthew. Social worker, Los Angeles County, 1963-67; program dir. day care, vol. services Los Angeles County, 1968-71; div. chief children's services Dept. Public Social Services, Los Angeles County, 1971-73, dir. bur. of social services, 1973-79; chief dep. dir. Dept. Community Services, Los Angeles County, 1979-95; interim dir. Cmty. & Sr. Svcs., Los Angeles County, 1996—; with Area 10 Devel. Disabilities, 1981-82; bd. dirs. Los Angeles Fed. Emergency Mgmt. Act, 1985-91, pres., 1987; bd. dirs. Los Angeles Shelter Partnership, Pomona Coll. Assocs., 1988—. Mem. Calif. Commn. on Family Planning, 1976-79; mem. Los Angeles Commn. Children's Instns., 1977-78; bd. dirs. United Way Info., 1978-79; chmn. Los Angeles County Internat. Yr. of Child Commn., 1978-79; bd. govs. Sch. Social Welfare, UCLA, 1981-84. Mem. Nat. Assn. Social Workers, Am. Soc. Pub. Adminstrn., L.A. Philhamonic Affiliates, 1995, Soroptimist Internat. (bd. dirs. 1989—, pres. L.A. chpt. 1993).

KLOSINSKI, LEONARD FRANK, mathematics educator; b. Michigan City, Ind., July 16, 1938; s. Frank and Helen (Podgorna) K.:. BS, U. Santa Clara, 1961; MA, Oreg. State U., 1963. Programmer NASA Ames Rsch. Ctr., Mountain View, Calif., 1963; instr. math. Santa Clara (Calif.) U., 1964-68, asst. prof., 1968-76, assoc. prof., 1976—; dir. Nat. Sci. Found. Insts., 1969-74; mng. editor, treas. Fibonacci Assn., 1975-80; dir. William Lowell Putnam Math. Competition, 1978—. Author: Santa Clara Silver Anniversary Contest Book/ Problems and Solutions of the University of Santa Clara High School Mathematics Contests, 1985, Students' Solutions Manual to Accompany Lynn E. Garner's Calculus and Analytical Geometry, 1988; editor: William Lowell Putnam Mathematical Competition Problems and

Solutions , 1965-84, 1985; contbr. articles to profl. jours. Mem. Math. Assn. Am. (coun. on competitions 1992—, Putnam prize com. 1975—, adv. bd. Math. Horizons 1993—, sec.-treas. No. Calif. sect. 1979—). Democrat. Roman Catholic. Office: Santa Clara U Math Dept Santa Clara CA 95053

KLOTZ, SUZANNE RUTH, artist; b. Shawno, Wis., Oct. 15, 1944; d. Arthur Paul and Margaret Ruth (Pollard) K. BFA, Kansas City Art Inst., 1966; secondary art teaching cert., U. Mo., Kansas City, 1967; MFA, Tex. Tech U., 1972. tchr. art pub. secondary schs. and univs. in Ariz., Tex. and Calif.; vis. artist, Israel, 1990-91; art cons., South Austrailia, 1991; guest artist Mishkenot Sha'ananim, Jerusalem, 1992; vis. assoc. prof. U. Utah, Salt Lake City, 1992-93. Prin. works exhibited in numerous one-woman and group shows including Phoenix Art Mus., Mus. South Tex., Corpus Christi, Spencer Art Mus., Lawrence, Kans., Y. Tex., San Antonio, Schneider Mus. Art, Ashland, Oreg., Mesa Centennial Conf. Ctr.; childrens art unity workshops Senegal and Burkino Faso, 1995, Taipei, Taiwan, 1995; works represented in numerous collections including Nat. Mus. Am. Art, Smithsonian Instn., Baha'i World Ctr., Haifa, Israel, Minn. Mus. Art, St. Paul, many others. Craftsman fellow Nat. Endowment for Arts, 1975, 78, NEA fellow for performance and dance, 1983. Baha'i.

KLUCK, CLARENCE JOSEPH, physician; b. Stevens Point, Wis., June 20, 1929; s. Joseph Bernard and Mildred Lorraine (Helminiak) K.; divorced; children: Paul Bernard, Annette Louise Kluck Winston, David John, Maureen Ellen. BS in Med. Sci., U. Wis., 1951, MD, 1954. Resident San Joaquin Hosp., French Camp, Calif., 1955-56; asst. instr. medicine Ohio State U., Columbus, 1958-60; physician, chief of medicine Redford Med. Ctr., Detroit, 1960-69; practice medicine specializing in internal medicine Denver, 1969-83; med. dir. Atlantic Richfield Co., Denver, 1983-85; corp. med. dir. Cyprus Minerals Co., Englewood, Colo., 1985-92; pres. Kluck Med. Assocs., Englewood, 1992—; bd. dirs. Climbo Catering, Detroit, 1967-69, Met. Labs., Denver, 1970-81, Provost, Inc., Denver, 1985-92; pres., CEO, chmn. bd. Corpcare, Inc., Englewood, 1992—; CEO, pres. Corpcare Med. Assocs., P.C., 1992—; pres. Denver Occupational and Aviation Medicine Clinic, P.C., 1995—. Contbr. articles to profl. jours. Served to capt. U.S. Army, 1956-58. Recipient Century Club award Boy Scouts Am., 1972. Fellow Am. Occupational Med. Assn., Am. Coll. Occupational and Environ. Medicine, Am. Coll. Occupational Medicine; mem. Am. Acad. Occupational Medicine, Rocky Mountain Acad. Occupational Medicine (bd. dirs. 1985-88), Arapahoe County Med. Soc., Denver Med. Soc. (bd. dirs. 1973-74, council mem. 1981-87), Colo. Med. Soc. (del. 1973-74, 81-87), Am. Mining Congress Health Commn., Am. Soc. Internal Medicine, Colo. Soc. Internal Medicine. Roman Catholic. Clubs: Flatirons (Boulder, Colo.); Metropolitan. Office: 3700 Havana St Ste 200 Denver CO 80239-3242

KLUG, JOHN JOSEPH, secondary education educator, director of dramatics; b. Denver, Apr. 27, 1948; s. John Joseph Sr. and Dorthea Virginia (Feely) Carlyle. BA in English, U. N.C., 1974; MA in Theatre, U. Colo., 1984. Tchr. Carmody Jr. High Sch., Lakewood, Colo., 1976-78; tchr. Golden (Colo.) High Sch., 1978—, dir. of dramatics, 1978—; producer, dir. Children's Theatre Tours, 1978—; theatrical cons., 1983—; improvisational workshop leader, 1983—. Playwright, editor: Children's Theatre scripts, 1982—; producer, dir. Denver Theatre Sports, 1993—. Recipient Bravo/TCI Theatre award, 1995. Home: 4565 King St Denver CO 80211-1357 Office: Golden High Sch 701 24th St Golden CO 80401-2379

KLUGE, ARTHUR J., engineering company executive; b. 1937. BS in Physics and Math., Manhattan Coll., 1959; postgrad., U. Calif., 1960-64. With N. Am. Rockwell Corp., Downey, Calif., 1964-68; sr. rsch. engr. Gen. Rsch. Corp., Santa Barbara, Calif., 1968-74; chmn. bd. Tecolote Rsch. Inc., Santa Barbara, Calif., 1989—. Office: Tecolote Research Inc 5290 Overpass Rd Bldg D Santa Barbara CA 93111-3011*

KLUGER, MATTHEW JAY, physiologist, educator; b. Bklyn., Dec. 14, 1946; s. Morris and Gladys (Feit) K.; m. Susan Lepold, Sept. 3, 1967; children: Sharon, Hilary. BS, Cornell U., 1967; MS, U. Ill., 1969, PhD, 1970; postgrad., U. N.Mex. Postdoctoral fellow Yale U., New Haven, 1970-72; asst. prof. U. Mich. Med. Sch., Ann Arbor, 1972-76, assoc. prof., 1976-81, prof. physiology, 1981-93; dir. inst. basic & applied med. rsch. The Lovelace Insts., Albuquerque, N.Mex., 1993-96; dir. pathophysiology Lovelace Respiratory Rsch. Inst., Albuquerque, 1996—; vis. prof. St. Thomas' Hosp., London, 1979, U. Witwatersrand, South Africa, 1992; vis. scientist Cetus Corp., Palo Alto, Calif., 1986-87. Author: Fever: Its Biology, Evolution and Function, 1979; editl. bd. Jour. Thermal Biology, 1991—, Cytokine, 1991—, Am. Jour. Physiology, 1992—, Med. Sci. Sports Exercises, 1994—, NeuroImmuno Modulation, 1995—; author workbooks; co-editor text books. Grantee NIH, other agys. Mem. Am. Physiol. Soc., Am. Assn. Immunologists. Home: 6103 Blue Bird Ln NE Albuquerque NM 87122-1817 Office: Lovelace Respiratory Rsch Inst 2425 Ridgecrest Dr SE Albuquerque NM 87108-5129

KLUGER, STEVE, writer, scriptwriter; b. Balt., June 24, 1952; s. Alan Charles and Florence Pearl (Shapiro) K. Student, U. So. Calif., 1970-71. Novelist, freelance scriptwriter and journalist, 1983—. Author: (novels) Changing Pitches, 1984, Bullpen, 1990, Bye Bye Brooklyn, 1997; (nonfiction) Lawyers Say the Darndest Things, 1990, Yank: World War II From the Guys Who Brought You Victory, 1991; scriptwriter films including: Once Upon a Crime, 1992, Bye Bye Brooklyn, 1997; (plays) Bullpen, 1984, Cafe 50's, 1988, James Dean Slept Here, 1989, Jukebox Saturday Night, 1990, Pilots of the Purple Twilight, 1991; (TV prodns.) Baseball, 1994, Yankee Doodle Boys, 1995. Democrat. Jewish. Office: care Gail Hochman Brandt & Brandt 1501 Broadway Ste 2130 New York NY 10036

KLUNGNESS, ELIZABETH JANE, publisher, writer, retired accountant; b. Indpls., Apr. 25, 1924; d. Robert Andrew and Mary (Van Gorder) Butler; m. Walter James Hicks, Aug. 24, 1946 (div. Jan. 1970); children: Pamela K. Hicks, Jerry L. Hicks; m. James Gregory Klungness, July 10, 1971. Student, Arthur Jordon Conservatory, Indpls., 1942-44, Butler U., Indpls., 1945-48. Clk. Eli Lilly, William H. Block Dept. Store, Bridgeport Brass, Indpls., 1943-48; pub. acct. Ind., Tex., Wash., Oreg., 1948-67; agt. IRS, Longview, Wash., 1967-72; pvt. practice Tower Acctg., Castle Rock, Wash., 1973-75; writer, editor Tower Enterprises, Yuma, Ariz., 1975-89; pub. Tower Enterprises, Vista, Calif., 1989—; book reviewer Bremerton (Wash.) Sun, 1957-60, Yuma Sun, 1981-83; instr. Chehalis (Wash.) Jr. Coll., 1970-71, Ariz. Western U., 1983-84; spkr. in field. Author: Prisoners in Petticoats, 1993; author, pub.: Century House Cookbook, 1981, Non-Golfer's Cookbook, 1982, Tax Tips for Writers, 1994, 95, 96, Grandma, I Want to Write, 1994; contbr. articles to jours.; editor, pub.: Writer's News, 1994—. Recipient 1st pl. fiction award Coun. for Arts, Carlsbad, Calif., 1993, 1st pl. award PEN/Dorothy Daniels, 1993. Mem. Philanthropic Ednl. Orgn., Nat. Writers Assn., Sisters in Crime, Soc. S.W. Authors, Pi Bet Phi. Home and Office: 2130 Sunset Dr Apt 47 Vista CA 92083

KLYCINSKI, FREDERICK ALLEN See ALLEN, RICK

KMET, REBECCA EUGENIA PATTERSON, pharmacist; b. Ellisville, Miss., June 17, 1948; d. Eugene Roberts and Ruth Winn (Pettis) Patterson; m. Joseph Paul Kmet, Mar. 29, 1969. BS in Pharmacy, U. Ariz., 1971; MBA, Nat. U., 1981. Pharmacist Santa Monica (Calif.) Bldg. Profl. Pharmacy, 1972-73, Vets. Hosp., West Los Angeles, Calif., 1973-74, Kaiser Med. Ctr., San Diego, 1979-82, Farmersville Drug Store, Farmersville, Calif., 1991-95. Community svc. vol. Lt. USN, 1975-78. Recipient Presdl. Achievement award Rep. Party Nat. Congl. com. Mem. DAR, Navy League, Naval Hist. Found., Marine Corps Hist. Soc., U.S. English, Am. Immigration Control Fedn., Rho Chi, Kappa Epsilon. Independent. Episcopalian. Home: 2912 No Wilson Tucson AZ 85719

KMETOVICZ, RONALD EUGENE, new product development educator, engineer, writer; b. May 31, 1947; m. Suzanne Marie Daley (div.); children: Kristyn, Cherisa; m. Gayle Anselmo. BSEE, Pa. State U., 1969; MSEE, Santa Clara U., 1978. Radio frequency/microwave engr. Goodyear Aerospace, Phoenix, 1969-72; hardware and software engr. Hewlett-Packard, Palo Alto, Calif., 1972-78, engring. mgr., 1978-88; founder, pres. Time to Market Assocs., Verdi, Nev., 1988—; cons. Sematech, Austin, 1988—; bus. advisor high tech. cos., 1988—. Author: New Product Development, 1992, It's About Time, 1994; author (column) Kmet's Korner in Elec. Design mag., 1990—; contbr. articles to mags. Mem. IEEE. Office: Time to Market Assocs PO Box 1070 Verdi NV 89439-1070

KNAPP, DONALD EUGENE, gastroenterologist; b. Burlington, Iowa, Aug. 17, 1931. Grad., Western Ill. U., 1955-58; MD, U. So. Calif., 1962. Diplomate Am. Bd. Internal Medicine, Am. Bd. Gastroenterology. Intern Valley Med. Ctr., Fresno, Calif., 1962-63, resident in internal medicine, 1963-65, chief med. resident, 1965-66; fellow in gastroenterology Valley Med. Ctr. and Mt. Sinai Hosp., Fresno and L.A., 1966-67; chmn. dept. medicine Valley Med. Ctr., Fresno, 1972-88, pres. attending staff, 1976-78, mem. active tchg. staff, 1967—; instr. of medicine UCLA, 1970-74; from asst. to assoc. clin. prof. medicine U. Calif., San Francisco, 1976-82; gastroenterologist Digestive Disease Cons. Corp., Fresno; mem. active staff St. Agnes Hosp. and Med. Ctr., 1967—, Fresno Cmty. Hosp. and Med. Ctr., 1967—. Trustee Cmty. Hosps. of Ctrl. Calif., 1988—; bd. med. quality assurance, chmn. Ninth Dist. Med. Quality Rev. Com., 1976-85; bd. dirs. Valley Med. Ctr. Found., 1971-80, Fresno Found. for Med. Care, 1975-80, Fresno-Madera PSRO, 1977-80, Fresno Cmty. Hosp. and Med. Ctr., 1987; v.p. Ctrl. Calif. Blood Bank, 1976—, pres. 1995. With USN, 1951-55. Mem. AMA, ACP, Am. Gastroent. Assn., Am. Soc. for Gastroent. Endoscopy, Calif. Med. Assn. (del. 1975-87, jud. commn. 1982-87), Fresno-Madera Med. Soc. (pres. 1974, chmn. prof. rels. com. 1982-87), Am. Soc. Internal Medicine, Calif. Soc. Internal Medicine, Fresno Soc. Internal Medicine (pres. 1981-83). Office: Digestive Disease Cons 1187 E Herndon Ste 106 Fresno CA 93720

KNAPP, LONNIE TROY, elementary education educator; b. Charles City, Iowa, Dec. 2, 1948; s. Troy Leroy and Anna Mildred (Conner) K.; m. Nancy Maureen Godfrey, Aug. 19, 1972; children: Eric Lonnie, Jamie Troy, Dusty Mack. BA, U. No. Iowa, 1972. Elem. tchr. Clear Lake, Iowa, 1972-92, Palm Springs (Calif.) Unified Sch. Dist., 1992—. Contbr. articles to profl. jours. Recipient Outstanding Tchr. award, Conservation Tchr. award, Iowa, North Cen. U.S. Mem. NEA, Iowa Edn. Assn., Calif. Tchrs. Assn., Clear Lake Edn. Assn. (various offices).

KNAPP, THOMAS EDWIN, sculptor, painter; b. Gillette, Wyo., Sept. 28, 1925; s. Chester M. and Georgia Mabel (Blankenship) K.; m. Dorothy Wellborn; children: Gordon, Kathy, Dan, Kent, Keith. Student, Santa Rosa Jr. Coll., 1952-53; A.A., Calif. Coll. Arts and Crafts, 1953-54; student, Art Ctr. Sch., Los Angeles, 1954-55. Animation artist Walt Disney Studios, Burbank, Calif., 1954-56, Portrait & Hobby Camera Shops, WyoFoto Studies, Cody, Wyo., 1956-64; owner Rocky Mountain Land Devel. Corp., Cody, Wyo., 1965-66; comml. artist Mountain States Telephone Co., Albuquerque, 1966-69; lectr. at art seminars. Exhibited one-man shows, Cody County Art League, 1968, Jamison Gallery, Santa Fe, 1969, Mesilla Gallery, 1971, Inn of Mountain Gods, Mescalero Apache Reservation, N.Mex., Mountain Oyster Club, Tucson, joint shows, Rosquist Gallery, Tucson, (with Michael Coleman), Zantman Gallery, Palm Desert Calif.; one and two person shows nationally with Dorothy Bell Knapp through 1988; group shows, Saddleback Inn, Santa Ana, Calif., Zantman Gallery, Carmel, Calif., Borglum Meml. Sculpture Exhbn. Nat. Cowboy Hall of Fame, Oklahoma City, 1975-76, Maxwell Gallery, San Francisco, 1975; represented permanent collections, Whitney Gallery Western Art, Cody, Senator Quinn Meml. Auditorium, Spencer, Mass., Heritage Mus., Anchorage, Indpls. Mus. Art, Mescalero Tribe, N.Mex.; works include Dance of the Mountain Spirits (Blue Ribbon award 1976), Laguna Eagle dancer (spl. award 1974, Blue Ribbon Los Angeles Indian Art Show, 1975-76), Santa Clara Buffalo dancer (Spl. award San Antonio Indian Nat. show 1974, Spl. award Los Angeles Indian show 1976), Mandan chieftan (Spl. award San Diego Indian show 1974, Spl. award Los Angeles Indian show 1976); commd. to sculpt bronze statue of Tex. ranger Capt. Bill McMurrey, now in Tex. Ranger Mus., San Antonio, bronze Giant Galapagos Tortoise in collection of Gladys Porter Zoo, Brownsville, Tex., Meijer Found., Grand Rapids, Mich., El Paso Mus. of Art, Mus. of Native Am. Cultures, Spokane, Wash., Cherokee Nat. Hist. Mus., Talequah, Okla., Diamond M. Found. Mus., Snyder, Tex., Buffalo Bill Hist. Ctr., Cody, Wyoming; Tex. Ranger (horseback) in bronze installed El Paso Mus. Art, 1989; commissioned giant Galapagos Tortoise in bronze for installation Sculpture Pk., Loveland, Colo., 1990, 13-foot bronze endangered salt water crocodile for Gladys Porter Zoo, Brownsville, Tex., 1990, heroic size bronze commd. for Rose Bowl, Tournament of Roses, 1992, heroic size Cahuilla Indian woman The Reed Gatherer, Waring Plaza, Palm Desert, Calif. Active Boy Scouts Am., 1947-68, World Wildlife Fund. Served with USN, World War II, Korea. Decorated Air medal; recipient Order Arrow award Boy Scout Am., 1968. Mem. Mensa, N.Y. Zool. Soc. Home and Office: PO Box 430144 Laredo TX 78043

KNAUFF, HANS GEORG, physician, educator; b. Bad Hersfeld, Germany, July 8, 1927; s. Friedrich and Sophie (Sauer) K.; student U. Erlangen, 1947-49, U. Freiburg, 1949, U. Basel, 1949-51, U. Heidelberg, 1951-52; Dr. Med., U. Heidelberg, 1953; m. Sigrid W. Keppner, Aug. 28, 1956; children—Ursula v. Wrangel, Barbara K. Asst., pharmacology dept. Heidelberg (W. Ger.) U., 1953; with pharmacology dept. Univ. Coll., London, 1953, Royal Coll. Surgeons, London, 1954; with Pathol. Inst., Heidelberg U., 1955, Med. Clinic, U. Munchen, 1955-63; privat dozent for internal medizin München and Marburg, 1961-67; prof. internal medizin, 1967; prof. Med. Clinic, U. Marburg (W. Ger.), 1967-83. Served with German Air Force, 1943-45. Mem. Deutsche Gesellschaft für Innere Medizin, Gesellschaft für Verdauungs und Stoffwechselkrankheiten. Mem. Luth. Ch. Contbr. articles to sci. jours. Home: 2155 Westhill Wynd, West Vancouver, BC Canada V7S 2Z3

KNAUSS, THOMAS ALVIN, pediatric neurologist; b. Buffalo, Nov. 24, 1940; s. Alvin C. and Dolores E. Knauss; children: Pam, Janet. BA, Knox Coll., 1961; PhD, UCLA, 1966, MD, 1969. Diplomate Am. Bd. Neurology, Am. Bd. Child Neurology. Med. intern UCLA, 1969-70; resident in pediatrics U. Wash., Seattle, 1970-71, resident in neurology, 1971-74, asst. prof. pediatrics, 1974-77, asst. clin. prof. pediatrics, 1977—, assoc. clin. prof. pediatrics, 1985—; neurologist Group Health of Puget Sound, Seattle, 1977—.

KNECHT, BEN HARROLD, surgeon; b. Rapid City, S.D., May 3, 1938; s. Ben and Ona K.; m. Jane Bowles, Aug. 27, 1961; children: John, Janelle. BA, U. S.D., 1960; MD, U. Iowa, 1964. Diplomate Am. Bd. Surgery. Intern Los Angeles County Gen. Hosp., 1964-65; resident in surgery U. Iowa Sch. Medicine, Iowa City, 1968-72; surgeon Wenatchee (Wash.) Valley Clinic, 1972—; dir. emergency rm. Ctrl. Wash. Hosp., Wenatchee, 1972-79, chief surgery, 1983-86; chmn. claims rev. panel Wash. State Med. Assn., Seattle, 1979-82, prof. liability com. risk mgmt., 1985-90; clin. assoc. prof. surgery U. Wash.; mem. adv. risk mgmt. com. Wash. State Physicians Ins. Subscribers, 1990—, regional adv. com. Nat. Libr. Medicine, 1991-93. Fundraiser Cen. Wash. Hosp. Found., 1987; del. Gov.'s Conf. on Librs., 1991. Lt. comdr. USN, 1965-68, Vietnam. Mem. AMA (alt. del. 1985-87, del. 1988—, surg. caucus exec. com. 1991-94), ACS (bd. dirs. Wash. chpt. 1981-84), North Pacific Surg. Assn., Wash. State Med. Assn. (trustee 1980—), Chelan-Douglas County Med. Soc., Am. Soc. Gen. Surgery (founding bd. 1994—, bd. dir.1992—), Rotary (chmn. youth com. 1976-78). Office: Wenatchee Valley Clinic 820 N Chelan Ave Wenatchee WA 98801-2028

KNEE, RICHARD ALAN, journalist; b. Chgo., Apr. 8, 1946; s. Aaron David Knee and Eva (Wolff) Sachs; m. Carolyn Becker, Sept. 17, 1988. BA in Journalism, Calif. State U., Northridge, 1972. Cert. C.C. tchr., Calif. Reporter Valley News, Van Nuys, Calif., 1969-73; pub. info. officer L.A. Harbor Coll., Wilmington, Calif., 1973-75; pub. rels. instr. East L.A. Coll., Monterey Park, Calif., 1975-78; copy editor Valley News, Van Nuys, 1978-80, Daily Rev., Hayward, Calif., 1980-81; mng. editor Daily Comml. News, San Francisco, 1981-84; assoc. editor Am. Shipper, San Francisco, 1984-97; freelance writer, editor, 1997—. Bd. dirs. San Francisco Press Club, 1986-88. With U.S. Army, 1964. Mem. Soc. Profl. Journalists (bd. dirs. No. Calif. chpt., v.p. 1990-91, pres. 1991-93). Office: Am Shipper 5 3rd St Ste 1114 San Francisco CA 94103-3210

KNEESE, GEORGE VERNON, city manager; b. Fallon, Nev., June 9, 1944; s. George August and Lavern Mervel (Walton) K.; m. Susan Jane Kneese, Dec. 28, 1968; children: Alyce Lowenstein, Shepheard B. Glass. Student, Portland C.C., 1988, 89. Storm and sanitary sewer sys. foreman Granite Constrn. Co., Gardnerville, Nev., 1968-70; pipe crew supr. Boise Cascade Constrn. Co., Hayward, Calif., 1970-7; sewer-storm pipe crew laborer-foreman McSween Constrn. Co., Lake Tahoe, Nev., 1977-83; sewer maintenance supr. Dept. Pub. Works City of Hillsboro, 1983—; presenter Hillsboro City Hall, 1989, , City of Hillsboro, 1992-93, Am. Pub. Works Assn., Wilsonville, 1990-93, Oreg. Waste Water Collection Pers. Sect., North Bend, 1991, Roseburg, 1990, Clackamas C.C., 1993, 94; mem. regional steering com., command sys., ops. ICS, 1995; instr. basic skills course II & III, FEMA, 1994-95, exercise design course Earthquake Mgmt. Course, 1994. Mem. Oreg. Coun. on Alcoholism and Drug Addiction, 1984—; pres. Wash. County Boosters Club, 1992; v.p. Wash. County Rodeo Bd., 1990-91. Mem. Am. Pub. Works Assn., Am. Water Works Assn., Water Environment Fedn., Pacific N.W. Pollution Control Assn., Profl. Rodeo Cowboys Assn. Republican. Office: City of Hillsboro 123 W Main St Hillsboro OR 97123

KNIERIM, ROBERT VALENTINE, electrical engineer, consultant; b. Oakland, Calif., Sept. 27, 1916; s. Otto Valentine and Edith May (Bell) K.; m. Esther Perry Bateman, July 10, 1954; children: Kathleen Dianne, David Lyell, Daniel Goddard. BS, U. Calif., Berkeley, 1941; postgrad., U. Pitts., 1942, U. Colo., 1944-45, Raytheon Field Engring Sch, 1945. Registered profl. elec. engr., Calif. Student engr. Westinghouse Corp., East Pittsburgh, Pa., 1942; marine elec. engr. U.S. Maritime Commn., Oakland, 1943-44; elec. engr. U.S. Bur. Reclamation, Denver, 1944-45, Sacramento, 1945-48; field engr. Raytheon Corp., Waltham, Mass., 1945; electronics engr. Sacramento Signal Depot, 1948-49; assoc. elec. engr. Calif. Office Architecture and Constrn., 1949-57, sr. elec. engr., 1957-76; cons. engring., 1976. Mem. Century Club of Golden Empire Coun. Boy Scouts Am., 1969-87, instnl. rep. 1948-54, dist. chmn., camping and activities com. 1951-54; mem. Cascade Pacific Coun. Boy Scouts of Am. 1987—. Recipient James E. West Fellowship award Boy Scouts of Am., 1994. Mem. Sacramento Engrs. Club (charter), IEEE (sr., life), Nat. Rifle Assn. (life), Sierra Club (life, chpt. treas. 1962-65), Nat. Assn. Corrosion Engrs. (life), Calif. Alumni Assn. (life), Eta Kappa Nu, Alpha Phi Omega (life). Republican. Congregationalist. Lodge: Masons. Home and Office: Cons Elec Engring 10325 SW Ashton Circle Wilsonville OR 97070-9532

KNIGHT, ANDREW KONG, visual artist, educator; b. Seattle, July 5, 1964; s. Richard Ivan Cook and Clara Kun Nai Kong; m. Julie Anne McLean, Feb. 2, 1991. Student, Calif. Coll. Arts and Crafts, 1978; BFA, San Francisco Art Inst., 1986; postgrad., Nat. U., 1996. Cert. tchr., Calif. Staff illustrator Western Ind. Bankers, Oakland, Calif., 1984-88, Western assn. Equipment Lessors, Oakland, 1989-94; art educator Kenneth C. Aikin Cmty. Ctr., Castro Valley, Calif., 1986-96; art educator, mural supr. Hayward (Calif.) Unified Sch. Dist., 1992—; freelance illustrator Miller Freeman Pubs., San Francisco, Hewlett Packard, Palo Alto, Calif., New United Motor Co., Fremont, Calif., 1983—; guest lectr. Stanford U., Palo Alto, 1996, Calif. State U., Hayward, 1992-96; spkr. in field. Exhibited in at Art of Calif., 1993, 94 (Silver award 1993, Gold award 1994), Am. Illustration 13, 1994 (award), Airbrush-Action Mag. (1st Pl. Fine Art award 1993), 3 Dimensional Art Dirs. and Illustrators Awards Show, 1996 (Gold award). Mem. adv. Hayward Arts Coun., 1994-95. Mem. NEA, Nat. Assn. Artists' Orgns., Calif. Tchrs. Assn., Precita Eyes Muralists. Home: 21095 Gary Dr Ste 309 Hayward CA 94546

KNIGHT, CAROL BELL, author, lecturer, clergyperson; b. Girard, Kans., June 14, 1924; d. August William and Ethel Marie (Knight) Vilmure; m. William Porter Kinney, June 12, 1953 (div. 1971); children: David, Paul, Sheina. BA, Kans. State Tchrs. Coll., Pittsburg, 1947; DD, Kans. Meth. Sem., Topeka, 1950. Ordained to ministry United Ch. of Religious Sci., 1983. Founding dir. The Forum Found., Santa Fe, 1979—; minister The Forum Celebration, Santa Fe, 1990-93; world seminars with the Forum Found., Eng., Sweden, Denmark, Norway, Switzerland, Ireland, Can., U.S., 1990—; planner New Alexandrian Libr. Author: Passing the Torch, 1985, Thought Has Wings, 1990, Saturation: A Prosperity Manual, 1993, The Holy Place, 1994, Vortex of Fire, 1996. Mem. Inst. of Noetic Scis., Internat. New Thought Alliance. Office: The Forum Found PO Box 5915 Santa Fe NM 87502

KNIGHT, CONSTANCE BRACKEN, writer, realtor, corporate executive; b. Detroit, Oct. 30, 1937; d. Thomas Francis and Margaret (Kearney) Bracken; m. James Edwards Knight, June 14, 1958 (div. Feb. 1968); children: Constance Lynne Knight Campbell, James Seaton, Keith Bracken. Student, Barry Coll., 1955-56, Fla. State U., 1958-60; AA, Marymount Coll., 1957. Columnist, feature writer Miami Herald, Ft. Lauderdale, Fla., 1954-55, 79-80; pub. rels. dir. Lauderdale Beach Hotel, 1965-67; columnist, feature writer Ft. Lauderdale News/Sun-Sentinel, 1980-81; owner Connie Knight and Assoc. Pub. Rels., Ft. Lauderdale, 1981-85; editor, pub. Vail (Colo.) Mag., 1986-89, contbg. freelance writer, 1989—; editorial cons. Vail Valley Mag., 1993; pres. Knight Enterprises, Vail, 1994—; instr. Colo. Mountain Coll., Vail, 1979; copywriter Colo. Ski Mus., Vail, 1986—. Mem. Planning and Environ. Commn., Vail, 1990-92, Vail Licensing Authority, 1995—. Mem. Soc. Profl. Journalists, N.Am. Ski Journalists (treas. 1990-93). Office: 5197 Black Gore Dr Vail CO 81657-5453

KNIGHT, FRANK JAMES, pharmaceutical marketing professional; b. L.A., July 17, 1947; s. George Orlando Jr. and Virginia Clarabelle (Seig) K.; m. Mary Jane Vargo, Aug. 7, 1977 (div. July 1989); children: Cheryl Lynne, Michael Scott; m. Barbara Lorrene Garlick, June 19, 1993. BS, Okla. State U., 1970. Mktg. rep. Mobil Oil Corp., N.Y.C., 1971-73; sales rep. Monarch Crown Corp., N.Y.C., 1974-78; territory mgr. V.H. Monette, Inc., Smithfield, Va., 1978-81; profl. rep. Dermik Labs., Blue Bell, Pa., 1981-83; sr. profl. oncology specialist Novartis Oncology, East Hanover, N.J., 1983—. Capt. U.S. Army, 1970. Mem. Harley Owners Group. Home: 8768 Banyan Alta Loma CA 91701 Office: Novartis Pharms 59 State Route 10 East Hanover NJ 07936-1011

KNIGHT, JEFFREY RICHARD, small business owner; b. Salt Lake City, Apr. 22, 1962; s. Richard M. and Donna H. (Hallman) K.; m. Carrie Lyn Jackson. BBA, Calif. State Poly. Inst. U., 1984, MBA, 1986. owner KD Enterprises, 1995—; pres. Lockheed Martin Activities Coordinating Com., Camarillo, 1991-93. With Lockheed Martin, Camarillo, Calif., 1985-96; prin. engr. DirecTV, quality assurance mgr., 1996—; owner, KD Enterprises, pres. Co. Activities Coordinating Com., Camarillo, 1991-93. Treas. Hillcrest Park Home Owners Assn., 1990-92, pres., 1992-93; chmn. Calif. State Poly. Inst. U. Rose Float Com., 1984-85. Mem. Thailand Darts Assn., Rose Float Alumni Assn. (treas. 1985-86, bd. dirs. 1987-88, pres. 1991-93, historian/archivist 1994—, chmn. 50th float activities com.), Nat. Employee Svcs. and Recreation Assn. (pres. Gold Coast chpt. 1994-95), Toastmasters Internat. (chpt. treas. 1996, v.p. pub. rels. 1996, Competent Toastmaster award 1996). Republican. Home: 2143 Saxe Ct Thousand Oaks CA 91360-3148

KNIGHT, PHILIP H(AMPSON), shoe manufacturing company executive; b. Portland, Oreg., Feb. 24, 1938; s. William W. and Lota (Hatfield) K.; m. Penelope Parks, Sept. 13, 1968; children: Matthew, Travis. B.B.A., U. Oreg.; M.B.A., Stanford U. C.P.A., Oreg. Chmn., chief exec. officer, past pres. Nike, Inc., Beaverton, Oreg., 1967—. Bd. dirs. U.S.-Asian Bus. Coun., Washington, 1st lt. AUS, 1959-60. Named Oreg. Businessman of Yr., 1982, One of 1988's Best Mgrs., Bus. Week Magazine. Mem. AICPA. Republican. Episcopalian. Office: Nike Inc 1 SW Bowerman Dr Beaverton OR 97005-0979*

KNIGHT, ROBERT EDWARD, banker; b. Alliance, Nebr., Nov. 27, 1941; s. Edward McKean and Ruth (McDuffee) K.; m. Eva Sophia Youngstom, Aug. 12, 1966. BA, Yale U., 1963; MA, Harvard U., 1965, PhD, 1968. Asst. prof. U.S. Naval Acad., Annapolis, Md., 1966-68; lectr. U. Md., 1967-68; fin. economist Fed. Res. Bank of Kansas City (Mo.), 1968-70, research officer, economist, 1971-76, asst. v.p., sec., 1977, v.p., sec., 1978-79; pres. Alliance (Nebr.) Nat. Bank, 1979-94, also chmn., 1983-94; pres. Robert Knight Assocs., banking and econ. cons., Cheyenne, 1979—; vis. prof., chair banking and fin. E. Tenn. State U., Johnson City, 1988; mem. faculty Stonier Grad. Sch. Banking, 1972—, Colo. Grad. Sch. Banking, 1975-82, Am. Inst. Banking, U. Mo., Kansas City, 1971-79, Prochnow Grad. Sch. Banking, U. Wis.; mem. extended learning faculty Park Coll., 1996—; mem. Coun. for Excellence for Bur. Bus. Rsch. U. Nebr., Lincoln, 1991-94, mem. Grad. Sch. Arts & Scis Coun., Harvard, 1994—; chmn. Taxable Mcpl. Bondholders Protective Com., 1991-94. Trustee, 1984-85, Knox Presbyn. Ch., Overland Park, Kans., 1965-69; bd. regents Nat. Comml. Lending Sch., 1980-83; mem.

Downtown Improvement Com., Alliance, 1981-94; trustee U. Nebr. Found.; bd. dirs. Stonier Grad. Sch. Banking, Box Butte County Devel. Commn., Nebr. Com. for Humanities, 1986-90; mem. fin. com. United Meth. Ch., Alliance, 1982-85, trustee, 1990-93; Box Butte County Indsl. Devel. Bd., 1987-94; mem. Nebr. Com. for the Humanities, 1986-90; amb. Nebr. Diplomats. Woodrow Wilson fellow, 1963-64. Mem. Am. Econ. Assn., Am. Fin. Assn., So. Econ. Assn., Nebr. Bankers Assn. (com. state legis. 1980-81, com. comml. loans and investments 1986-87), Am. Inst. Banking (state com. for Nebr. 1980-83), Am. Bankers Assn. (econ. adv. com. 1980-83, cmty. bank leadership coun.), Western Econ. Assn., Econometric Soc., Rotary, Masons. Contbr. articles to profl. jours. Home and Office: 429 W Fifth Ave Cheyenne WY 82001-1249

KNIGHT, THOMAS JOSEPH, history educator; b. Denton, Tex., Aug. 5, 1937; s. Thomas Daniel Knight and Laura Jo (Savage) Knight Myrick; m. Barbara Lorraine Jones, Dec. 29, 1955; children: Russell Alan, Karen Jeanne. BA, North Tex. State U., Denton, 1959; postgrad., U. Minn., 1959-61; PhD, U. Tex., 1967. Instr. history U. Nebr., Lincoln, 1964-65; asst. prof. humanities Mich. State U., East Lansing, 1966-68; asst. prof., then assoc. prof. Pa. State U., Harrisburg, 1968-76; assoc. dean, prof. social scis. Pa. State U., University Park, 1976-82; dean, prof. history U. W.Va., Morgantown, 1982-86, Colo. State U., Ft. Collins, 1986—; cons. Orgn. Econ. Coop. and Devel., Paris, 1982. Author: Latin America Comes of Age, 1979, Technology's Future, 1982. Trustee Univ. Press Colo., Niwot, 1989-95. Mem. World History Assn., Nat. Assn. Sci., Tech. and Society, Am. Acad. Polit. and Social Sci., Phi Alpha Theta. Democrat. Unitarian. Home: 2006 Brookwood Dr Fort Collins CO 80525-1212 Office: Colo State U Dept History Fort Collins CO 80523

KNIGHT, VICK, JR. (RALPH KNIGHT), dean, education educator, counselor; b. Lakewood, Ohio, Apr. 6, 1928; s. Vick Ralph and Janice (Higgins) K. BS, U. So. Calif., 1952; MA, L.S. State Coll., 1956; postgrad. Whittier Coll., 1959-61, Long Beach State Coll., 1960-61, Calif. State Coll.-Fullerton, 1961-64, Claremont U., 1963-65; EdD, Calif. Coast U., 1991; m. Beverly Joyce McKeighan, Apr. 14, 1949 (div. 1973); children: Stephen Foster, Mary Ann; m. Carolyn Schlee, June 6, 1981; children: Kathy, Meri. Producer-dir. Here Comes Tom Harmon radio series ABC, Hollywood, Calif., 1947-50; tchr., vice-prin. Ranchito Sch. Dist., Pico Rivera, Calif., 1952-59; prin. Kraemer Intermediate Sch., Placentia, Calif., 1959-64; dir. instructional svcs. Placentia Unified Sch. Dist., 1964-65, asst. supt., 1965-71; program dir. World Vista Travel Svcs., 1970-72; bd. dir. grad. extension La Verne Coll., 1971-73; v.p. Nat. Gen. West Investments, 1971-74; bd. dir. community rels. and devel. Childrens Hosp. of Orange County (Calif.), 1974-84; sr. dir. curriculum and edn. svcs. Elsinore Union High Sch. Dist., Lake Elsinore, Calif., 1985-88; exec. dir. Elsinore Valley Community Devel. Corp., 1989-92; dean Sch. Edn. Newport U., Newport Beach, Calif., 1992—; pres. Aristan Assocs.; bd. dirs. Key Records, Hollywood. Dist. chmn. Valencia Coun. Boy Scouts Am.; chmn. Cancer Soc. Ptnrs. of Ams., also chmn. Sister City Com.; chmn. Community Chest Drives; chmn. adv. com. Esperenza Hosp.; mem. Educare; hon. life mem. Calif. PTA. Bd. dirs. U. Calif.-Irvine Friends of Library, pres., 1975-77; bd. trustees Lake Elsinore Unified Sch. Dist., 1991, pres. 1993-97; bd. dirs. Muckenthaler Cultural Groups Found.; chmn. bd. William Claude Fields Found. Club With USN, 1946-48. Recipient Disting. Citizen award Whittier Coll., 1960; Educator of Yr. award Orange County Press Club, 1971, Author and Book award U. Calif., 1973, Children's Lit. award Calif. State U.-Fullerton, 1979, Bronze Pelican award Boy Scouts Am.; named Canyon Lake Man of the Yr., 1994. Mem. Nat. Sch. Pub. Rels. Assn. (regional v.p.), U.S. Jr. C. of C. (bd. dir., Young Man of Calif. 1959), Calif. Jr. C. of C. (state v.p.), Pico Rivera Jr. C. of C. (pres.), Audubon Soc., Western Soc. Naturalists, Calif. Tchrs. Assn., NEA, Internat. Platform Assn., ASCAP, Soc. Children's Book Writers, Authors Guild, Authors League Am., Anti-Slubberdegullion Soc., Bank Dicks, Assn. Hosp. Devel., Art Experience, Good Bears of World, Los Compadres con Libros, Blue Key, Skull and Dagger, Les Amis du Vin, Phi Sigma Kappa, Alpha Delta Sigma, E Clampus Vitus, Theta Nu Epsilon, Kiwanian (pres.), Mason, Canyon Lake Home Owners Club (pres. 1989-91), West Atwood Yacht (commodore) Club. Writer weekly Nature Notebook newspaper columns, 1957—, wine columnist Riverside Press-Enterprise, 1991—; fine arts editor Placentia Courier; editor curriculum guides: New Math., Lang. Arts, Social Scis., Pub. Rels., Biol. Sci. Substitute Tchrs; author: (ecology textbooks) It's Our World; It's Our Future; It's Our Choice, Snakes of Hawaii, Earle the Squirrel, Night the Crayons Talked; My Word!; Send for Haym Salomon!. Joby and the Wishing Well; Twilight of the Animal Kingdom; A Tale of Twos, Who's Zoo, A Navel Salute, Friend or Enema?, John Sevier: Citizen Soldier, Toasting Temecula Wines, also math. instrn. units; contbr. articles to various jours. Home: 22597 Canyon Lake Dr S Canyon Lake CA 92587-7595

KNIGHTON, GWENDOLYN LAYVONEE, advocate; b. Cuthbert, Ga., Sept. 27, 1955; d. Willie James and Mendell (Wilburn) K.; m. John L. Wesley, Oct. 3, 1980 (div. Nov. 1992); 1 child, Matthew J. BA, Trinity Coll., 1978; M in Health Svcs., Fla. Internat. U., 1995. Legis. asst. U.S. Congress, Washington, 1978-82; regulatory analyst U.S. Fed. Govt., Washington, 1986-92; dir. mktg. Red Rocks Health, Denver, 1995-96, program coord. Colo. Coalition Against Sexual Assault, Denver, 1996-97. Mem. Am. Assn. Healthcare Execs., Internat. Assn. Forensic Nurses. Democrat. Roman Catholic. Home: 343 Van Gordon St 17-508 Denver CO 80228

KNITTLE, WILLIAM JOSEPH, JR., media executive, psychologist, religious leader, management and marketing consultant; b. Santa Monica, Calif., June 11, 1945; s. William Joseph Knittle and Lahlee (Duggins) Morrell; m. Linda Catherine Black, Apr. 19, 1969 (div. Aug. 1977); 1 child, Kristen Elizabeth; m. Alexis Carrell Upton, Sept. 30, 1977 (div. Aug. 1996); 1 child, Jonathan Kynan. Student, Inst. for Japanese Culture, 1960, Am. Nat. Theater and Acad., 1962-64; BA in English, Loyola U., L.A., 1966, MA in Communication Arts, 1970, MA in Counseling Psychology, 1973; PhD in Communication Theory and Social Psychology, Lawrence U., Santa Barbara, Calif., 1976; D of Dharma in Asian Religion and Philosophy, U. Oriental Studies, 1980; MBA, U. La Verne, 1983; grad., Grantsmanship Ctr., L.A., 1980. Ordained Sramanera, Buddhist monk, 1976; ordained Bikkhu, Vietnamese lineage, 1977, Chinese lineage, 1977; ordained Zen Master and High Tchr. in all Buddhist Traditions, Fo Kuang Shan Monastery, Taiwan, 1977. Assoc. editor Black Belt mag., 1960-65; asst. news dir., pub. affairs/continuity acceptance coord. Sta. KHJ-TV, L.A., 1966-67; news editor Sta. KFWB Radio, L.A., 1967-69; dir. news and media rels. Loyola Marymount U., L.A., 1969-75; pvt. therapist L.A., 1974—; gen. mgr., dir. televised studies Media Five Film and TV Prodns., L.A., 1976-79, v.p., 1981-83; assoc. dir. divsn. of continuing edn. U. La Verne, Calif., 1979-81; pres. Western News Assocs., L.A., 1983—; adj. prof. U. La Verne, Calif., 1980—; chmn. East-West psychology dept. U. Oriental Studies, L.A., 1979-83; asst. to dean UCLA Sch. Medicine, 1985-86; advt./mktg. dir. summer sessions UCLA, 1986—; prof. Coll. Buddhist Studies, L.A., 1991—; pvt. therapist L.A., 1974—; cons. Asian psychology U.S. State Dept. and USMC, 1977-80; cons. Libbey Lithography, 1980; chief instr. martial arts Loyola Marymount U., 1963-74; lectr. L.A. Police Dept., 1978; cons. Purex Corp., 1980; founder Realization Therapy, 1976; host Campus report, KHJ-AM/KRTH-FM, L.A., 1973-74, At Your Leisure program KXLU-FM, L.A., 1972-76; dir. film segments KCOP-TV, L.A., 1966; tech. dir. Quien Lo Sabe program KMEX-TV, L.A., 1964; instr. systematic theology and sacred scripture L.A. Archdiocese, 1969-72. Author: Survival Strategies for the Classroom Teacher, 1982; syndicated columnist various newspapers, mags., 1970—; Hollywood corr. Columbia mag., 1974-87; contbr. articles to profl. jours.; writer/cinematographer On Campus series KNBC-TV, L.A., 1974; tech. dir. Quien Lo Sabe, KMEX-TV, L.A., 1963-64; dir. film segments KCOP-TV, L.A., 1966; host At Your Leisure, KXLU-FM, L.A., 1972-76; host Campus Report, KHJ-AM/KRTH-FM, L.A., 1973-74; speechwriter Chinese Freedom Dissidents, 1996—. Media spokesman Am. Cancer Soc., 1960-62; media teenage coord. Los Angeles County March of Dimes, 1961-68; assoc. dir. Pasadena/San Gabriel Valley Counseling Ctr., Pasadena, 1973-74; asst. abbot Internat. Buddhist Med. Ctr., L.A., 1976-81; bd. dirs. Dharma Vijaya Buddhist Vihara, L.A., 1985—; mem. So. Calif. Buddhist Sangha Coun., L.A. Buddhist Union, So. Calif. Interreligious Coun.; host, announcer 3d Internat. Karate Championship Tournament, 1975, 5th ann. open Am. Tae KwonDo-Kung Fu Championship Tournament, 1976. Recipient Martial Arts Pioneer award Am. Tae Kwon Do-Kung Fu Assn., 1976, Nat. Headliners award Wash. Press Club, 1968, Internat. Journalism award Sigma Delta Chi, 1968. Mem. AAAS, NATAS, Assn. for Transpersonal Psychology, Inst. for Holistic Edn., Soc. Interdisciplinary Study of Mind, Internat. Brotherhood of Magicians, Internat. Imagery Assn., Am. Soc. Tng. and Devel., Nat. Book Critics Circle, Investigative Reporters and Editors, Am. Fedn. Police (chaplain 1985—), Nat. Police Acad., Nat. Acad. TV Arts and Scis. Home and Office: Western News Assocs PO Box 24130 Los Angeles CA 90024-0130

KNOEPFLER, GAYLE STEWART, sex therapist; b. Bottineou, N.D., Mar. 8, 1934; d. Alfred Earnest and Lois (Stewart) Kurth; m. Peter Tamas Knoepfler, July 3, 1960; children: David, Daniel, Paul. MS, Yeshiva U., 1960; PhB, U. N.D., 1957. Cert. sex therapist, mental health counselor, Wash. Caseworker ARC, St. Louis, Wichita Falls, Tex., Colorado Springs, Colo., 1957-59; copy writer KTRN, Wichita Falls; high sch. history tchr. A.B. Davis High Sch., Mt. Vernon, N.Y., 1959-61; sex educator Planned Parenthood, Seattle and Bellevue, Wash., 1972-82; sex educator, pvt. practice Bellevue, 1975—, sex therapist, 1975—, group therapist, 1975—; co-founder sex info. telephone line, Planned Parenthood, Seattle/King Co., 1979-81. Contbr. articles to profl. jours. State bd. dirs. LWV, Utah, 1968, eastside bd. dirs., Washington, 1971-72; chmn. bd. dirs., dean Unitarian/Eliot Inst., Pacific N.W. Dist., 1973, 89, 92; east shore ch. bd. mem. Unitarian Ch., Bellevue, 1993-95; chmn. Puget Sound Unitarian Coun., Seattle, 1980-82; precinct chmn. 41st Dist. Dem. Party. Vol. of Yr. Planned Parenthood Seattle, 1980. Mem. Am. Assn. Sex Education Therapists (chmn. dist. conv. 1983), Soc. for Scientific Study of Sex (conv. co-chair 1993). Unitarian. Office: 1201 116 St NE Ste 9 Bellevue WA 98004

KNOLL, JAMES LEWIS, lawyer; b. Chgo., Oct. 5, 1942. AB, Brown U., 1964; JD, U. Chgo., 1967. Bar: Ill. 1967, Oreg. 1971, Wash. 1984, Alaska 1993. Mediator, arbitrator Portland, Oreg.; adj. prof. law Northwestern Sc. Law, Lewis and Clark Coll., 1982-91. Mem. ABA (mem. TIPS coun. 1989-92, chair property ins. com. 1984-85, mem. fidelity surety com., chair comml. tort com. 1985-86), Oreg. State Bar (editor 2 vol. text on ins. 1983, 96), Wash. State Bar, Oreg. Assn. Def. Coun. (pres. 1984), Def. Rsch. and Trial Lawyers Assn. Office: 1500 SW Taylor St Portland OR 97205

KNOLL, WILLIAM LEE, animation director; b. Long Beach, Calif., July 9, 1948; s. Robert B. aned Virginia M. (Humphrey) K.; m. Susan D. Spafford Johnson, May 28, 1971 (div. Dec. 1976); m. Linda L. Gill, July 18, 1981; 1 child, Tracy Lynn. BA, San Diego State U., 1974. Mem. Motion Picture Screen Cartoonists, North Hollywood, Calif., 1976—; asst. animator DePatie-Freleng, Van Nuys, Calif., 1976-80, Hanna-Barbera, North Hollywood, 1980-86; FX animator Boss Films, Marina del Rey, Calif., 1986; dir. Marvel Prodns., Van Nuys, 1986-87; timing dir. D.I.C., Burbank, Calif., 1988-91, Warner Bros. Animation, Sherman Oaks, Calif., 1991-96, Dreamworks, Inc., Encino, Calif., 1996—; mem. adv. com. for animation devel. Mt. San Antonio Coll., 1996—. Animator: (animated program) Ziggy's Gift, 1982 (Emmy award 1982-83); dir.: (animated program) Muppet Babies, 1986 (Emmy award 1986-87); timing dir.: (animated program) Animaniacs, 1995 (Emmy award 1995-96), (children's program) Animaniacs, 1995 (Emmy award 1995-96). Chmn. Animal Control Commn., South Pasadena, 1983-84; v.p. Booster's Club, South Pasadena, 1983-84; pres. Covina (Calif.) Am. Little League, 1989, 90; candidate Covina Unified Sch. Dist. Sch. Bd., 1995. Recipient Certs. of Appreciation, City of South Pasadena, 1984, Covina Firefighters, 1996, Cert. of Recognition City of Covina, 1995. Mem. NATAS, Aztec Athletic Found., Covina Breakfast Lions (pres. 1988—, Lion of Yr. 1995), Lions Internat. Youth Exch. (dist. chmn. 1991-94, govenor 1993), Lambda Chi Alpha Alumni. Home: 2412 E Rio Verde Dr West Covina CA 91791-2140 Office: Dreamworks Inc 16030 Ventura Blvd Fl 4 Encino CA 91436-2778

KNOLLER, GUY DAVID, lawyer; b. N.Y.C., July 23, 1946; s. Charles and Odette Knoller; children: Jennifer Judy, Geoffrey David. BA cum laude, Bloomfield (N.J.) Coll., 1968; JD cum laude, Ariz. State U., 1971. Bar: Ariz. 1971, U.S. Dist. Ct. Ariz. 1971, U.S. Sup. Ct. 1976. Trial atty. atty. gen.'s honor program Dept. Justice, 1971-72; atty., adv., NLRB, 1972-73, field atty. region 28, Phoenix, 1972-74; assoc. Powers, Ehrenreich, Boutell & Kurn, Phoenix, 1974-79; ptnr. Froimson & Knoller, Phoenix, 1979-81; sole practice, Phoenix, 1981-84; ptnr. Fannin, Terry & Hay, P.A., 1984-85; sole practice, Phoenix, 1985—; of counsel Burns & Burns. Mem. bd. visitors Ariz. State U. Coll. Law, 1975-76; pres. Ariz. Theatre Guild, 1990, 91. Fellow Ariz. Bar Found.; mem. ABA, State Bar Ariz. (chmn. labor relations sect. 1977-78), Ariz. State U. Coll. Law Alumni Assn. (pres. 1977). Office: 3550 N Central Ave Ste 1401 Phoenix AZ 85012-2112

KNOOP, VERN THOMAS, civil engineer, consultant; b. Paola, Kans., Nov. 19, 1932; s. Vernon Thomas and Nancy Alice (Christian) K. Student, Kans. U., 1953-54; BSCE, Kans. State U., 1959. Registered profl. engr., Calif. Surveyor James L. Bell, Surveyors and Engrs., Overland Park, Kans., 1954; engr. asst. to county engr. Miami County Hwy. Dept., Paola, 1955; engr. State of Calif. Dept. Water Resources, L.A., 1959-85, sr. engr., 1986-88; chief, water supply evaluations sect. State of Calif. Dept. Water Resources, L.A., Glendale, 1989—; hydrology tchr. State of Calif. Dept. Water Resources, L.A., 1984; mem. Interagency Drought Task Force, Sacramento, 1988-91. Mem. Jefferson Ednl. Found., Washington, 1988-91, Heritage Found., Washington, 1988—, Nat. Rep. Senatorial Com., Washington, 1990—, Rep. Presdl. Task Force, Washington, 1990-91. With U.S. Army, 1956-57. Decorated Good Conduct medal U.S. Army, Germany, 1957. Mem. ASCE (life, dir. L.A. sect. hydraulics/water resources mgmt. tech. group 1985-86, chmn. 1984-85), Profl. Engrs. Calif. Govt. (dist. suprs. rep. 1986—), Am. Assn. Individual Investors (life), L.A. World Affairs Coun., Singles Internat. Baptist. Home: 116 N Berendo St Los Angeles CA 90004-4711 Office: State of Calif Dept Water Resources 770 Fairmont Ave Glendale CA 91203-1035

KNOTT, WILLIAM ALAN, library director, library management and building consultant; b. Muscatine, Iowa, Oct. 4, 1942; s. Edward Marlan and Dorothy Mae (Holzhauer) K.; m. Mary Farrell, Aug. 23, 1969; children: Andrew Jerome, Sarah Louise. BA in English, U. Iowa, 1967, MA in L.S., 1968. Asst. dir. Ottumwa (Iowa) Pub. Libr., 1968-69; libr. cons. Iowa State Libr., Des Moines, 1968-69; dir. Hutchinson (Kans.) Pub. Libr. and S. Cen. Kans. Libr. System, Hutchinson, 1969-71; dir. Jefferson County Pub. Libr., Lakewood, Colo., 1971—. Served with U.S. Army, 1965-67. Mem. ALA, Colo. Libr. Assn. Author: Books by Mail: A Guide, 1973; co-author: A Phased Approach to Library Automation, 1969; editor: Conservation Catalog, 1982. Office: Jefferson County Pub Libr 10200 W 20th Ave Lakewood CO 80215-1402

KNOWLES, JAMES KENYON, applied mechanics educator; b. Cleve., Apr. 14, 1931; s. Newton Talbot and Allyan (Gray) K.; m. Jacqueline De Bolt, Nov. 26, 1952; children: John Kenyon, Jeffrey Gray, James Talbot. SB in Math., MIT, 1952, PhD, 1957; DSc (hon.), Nat. U. Ireland, 1985. Instr. math. MIT, Cambridge, 1957-58; asst. prof. applied mechanics Calif. Inst. Tech., Pasadena, 1958-61, assoc. prof., 1961-65, prof. applied mechanics, 1965—, William R. Kenan Jr. prof., 1991—, William R. Kenan Jr. prof. emeritus, 1996—; vis. prof. MIT, 1993-94; cons. in field. Contbr. articles to profl. jours. Recipient Eringen medal Soc. Engring. Sci., 1991. Fellow ASME, AAAS, Am. Acad. Mechanics. Home: 522 Michillinda Way Sierra Madre CA 91024-1066 Office: Calif Inst Tech Div Engring & Applied Sci 104-44 1201 E California Pasadena CA 91125-0001

KNOWLES, TONY, governor; b. Tulsa, Jan. 1, 1943; m. Susan Morris; children: Devon, Lucas, Sara. BA in Econs., Yale U., 1968. Owner, mgr. The Works, Anchorage, 1968—, Downtown Deli, Anchorage, 1978—; mayor Municipality of Anchorage, 1981-87; now gov. State of Alaska, 1994—. Mem. citizen's com. to develop comprehensive plan for growth and devel., Anchorage, 1972; mem. Borough Assembly, Anchorage, 1975-79; bd. dirs. Fairview Cmty. Ctr., March of Dimes, Pub. TV Sta. KAKM, numerous sports facilities coms. Served with U.S. Army, 1961-65, Vietnam. Mem. Anchorage C. of C. (bd. dirs.). Office: Office of the Governor PO Box 110001 Juneau AK 99811-0001*

KNUDSEN, LINDA, special education educator; b. Provo, Utah, Apr. 18, 1968; d. Kent Burch and Charlotte Elaine (Smith) K. AA, AS, Ricks Coll., 1968; BA, Brigham Young U., 1994. Cert. tchr. of Spanish and English. Undergrad. rsch. asst., Edn. Psychol. Dept. Brigham Young, U., Provo, 1994-96; ESL tchr. Meridian (Idaho) Sch. Dist., 1994—; ESL vol. tutor Provo Adult Edn., 1993-94; ESL cons. Meridian Sch. Dist., 1996. Mem. TESOL Horizons Reading Coun., Multicultural Issues Com. Mem. LDS Ch. Office: Eagle High School 579 N Park Lane Eagle ID 83616-4513

KNUDSON, MELVIN ROBERT, management consultant, business executive; b. Libby, Mont., Oct. 27, 1917; s. John and Serina (Bakken) K.; BS in Wood Chemistry, Oreg. State U., 1942; m. Melba Irene Joice, Mar. 5, 1946; children—Mark Bradley, Kevin Marie, Kari Lynne. Mgr. quality control J. Neils Lumber Co., Libby, Mont., 1946-55; mgr. research and devel. St. Regis Paper Co., Libby, 1955-65, div. dir. tech. devel., Tacoma, Wash., 1965-69, div. dir. short and long-range planning, 1969-70; exec. v.p. Property Holding and Devel. Co., Tacoma, 1970-75; exec. v.p. and gen. mgr. U.S. Computers, Inc., Tacoma, 1975-79; corp. mgmt., orgn., univ. governance and adminstrn. cons., 1979—; owner Knudson Travel, Tacoma, 1981—; bd. dirs., special cons., incorporator Larex Internat. Corp. Mem. adv. bd. Coll. Engring., Wash. State U., 1967—, chmn., 1971-73; trustee 1st Luth. Ch., Libby, 1948-56, chmn., 1954-56; trustee Sch. Dist. # 4, Libby, 1964-65; trustee Christ Luth. Ch., Tacoma, 1966-71, com. chmn.; trustee Greater Lakes Mental Health Clinic, 1969-73, com. chmn., 1970-73; bd. regents Pacific Luth. U., Tacoma, 1969—, chmn., 1976-81; mem. Steilacoom Improvement Com., 1971-73; chmn. Pacific Luth. U. Pres. Search Com., 1974-75; dir. Wauna Dance Club, 1976-79; dir. Pacific Luth. Univ. "Q" Club, 1976-86; bd. dirs. Tenzler Library, Tacoma, 1980-83, Crime Stoppers, 1981-84, Operation Night Watch, 1989. Served to lt. col. F.A., Paratroops, U.S. Army, 1941-46. Recipient Disting. Service award Pacific Luth. U., 1986. Mem. Wash. Realtors Assn., Wash. Securities Sales, Am. Governing Bds., Center for Study of Democratic Institutions. Republican. Clubs: Tacoma Country and Golf, Normana Male Chorus (Norwegian Singers Assn. Am.). Patentee high-temperature wood-drying process, patentee Ultrarefined Arabinogalactan product; developer domestic natural gum. Home: 6928 100th St SW Tacoma WA 98499-1819 Office: 1103 A St Ste 200 Tacoma WA 98438-1301

KNUDSON, THOMAS JEFFERY, journalist; b. Manning, Iowa, July 6, 1953; s. Melvin Jake and Coreen Rose (Nickum) K. B.A. in Journalism, Iowa State U., 1980. Reporter/intern Wall Street Jour., Chgo., summer 1979; staff writer Des Moines Register, 1980—. Author: (series) A Harvest of Harm: The Farm Health Crisis, 1984 (Pulitzer Prize 1985); (series) Majesty and Tragedy; The Sierra in Peril, 1991 (Pulitzer Prize 1992). Recipient James W. Schwartz award Iowa State U., 1985, Nat. Press Club Robert Kozik award, 1992. Office: Sacramento Bee PO Box 15779 21st and Q Sts Sacramento CA 95852*

KNUTSON, STANLEY, software professional; b. Kenosha, Wis., Aug. 19, 1954; s. Norman and Nettie Knutson. BS in Computer Sci., MIT, 1976, MSME, 1978. Prin. engr. Butler Automatic, Canton, Mass., 1977-78; dir. software SAC Inc., Hingham, Mass., 1978-79; v.p. software DAC Tech., Peabody, Mass., 1979-89; chief engr. ICAD Inc., Cambridge, Mass., 1989—, Concentra Corp., Cambridge, 1989—; cons. Lambda Rsch., Littleton, Mass., 1993—. Mem. ACM, ASME, IEEE. Home: PO Box 1270 Menlo Park CA 94026 Office: Concentra Corp 7th Fl 21 North Ave Burlington MA

KO, DENNY R. S., research & development executive; b. 1939. PhD, Calif. Inst. Tech., 1968. With TRW Sys., Redondo Beach, Calif., 1969-72, Dynatech Devel. Corp., Torrance, Calif., 1972—; v.p., gen. mgr. Flow Industries, Seattle, 1972-75; r & d Physical Dynamics, Inc., La Jolla, Calif., 1975-76; with Dynamics Tech., Inc., 1976—, now pres., CEO. Office: Dynamics Tech Inc 21311 Hawthorne Blvd Ste 300 Torrance CA 90503-5610*

KO, KATHLEEN LIM, health administrator; b. Shaker Heights, Ohio, Apr. 26, 1958; d. Wen Hsiung Ko and Christina Chen; m. Maurice Lim Miller, Mar. 29, 1986; children: Alicia Berta Lim, Nicholas Hilario Lim. BA, Stanford U., 1980; MS, Harvard U., 1984. Youth program coord. YWCA, San Francisco, 1979; instr. English Fudan U., Shanghai, China, 1980; asst. clinic mgr. Planned Parenthood, San Francisco, 1981; rsch. intern Inst. Health Policy Studies, U. Calif., San Francisco, 1981-82; analyst dept ob-gyn. San Francisco Gen. Hosp., 1983; ops. dir. Asian Health Svcs., Oakland, Calif., 1984-89, program planning and devel. officer, 1989-92, assoc. dir., 1993-97; bd. dirs., mem., pres. Bay Area Asian Health Alliance, Oakland, 1982—. Producer: (film/video) Impossible choices, 1993—. Bd. dirs. Asian Women's Shelter, San Francisco, 1987-94, pres., 1989-93; v.p. Arts Sch. PTA, Oakland, 1994-95; bd. dirs. Californians United, San Francisco, 1986. Recipient Cmty. Svc. award Stanford Asian Pacifc Alumni Assn., 1993, Woman Warrior award health & human svcs. Pacific Asian Am. Women Bay Area Coalition, 1996. Mem. Am. Pub. Health Assn., Asian Pacific Island Am. Health Forum, Oakland Chinatown C. of C. (bd. dirs. 1997—). Democrat. Office: Asian Health Svcs 818 Webster St Oakland CA 94607-4253

KOBAYASHI, ANN H., state legislator; b. Honolulu, Apr. 10, 1937; m.; 3 children. Student Pembroke Coll., Northwestern U. Officer family corp.; former legis. aide, adminstrv. asst. Hawaii Senate, now mem. Senate from 14th Dist. Republican. Home: 3657 Waaloa Way Honolulu HI 96822-1150*

KOBY, THOMAS, protective services official. Chief of police Boulder, Colo. Office: 1805 33d St Boulder CO 80301

KOBZA, DENNIS JEROME, architect; b. Ullysses, Nebr., Sept. 30, 1933; s. Jerry Frank and Agnes Elizabeth (Lavicky) K.; B.S., Healds Archtl. Engring., 1959; m. Doris Mae Riemann, Dec. 26, 1953; children—Dennis Jerome, Diana Jill, David John. Draftsman, designer B.L. Schroder, Palo Alto, Calif., 1959-60; sr. draftsman, designer Ned Abrams, Architect, Sunnyvale, Calif., 1960-61, Kenneth Elvin, Architect, Los Altos, Calif., 1961-62; partner B.L. Schroder, Architect, Palo Alto, 1962-66; pvt. practice architecture, Mountain View, Calif., 1966—. Served with USAF, 1952-56. Recipient Solar PAL award, Palo Alto, 1983, Mountain View Mayoral award, 1979. Mem. C. of C. (dir. 1977-79, Archtl. Excellence award Hayward chpt. 1985, Outstanding Indsl. Devel. award Sacramento chpt., 1980), AIA (chpt. dir. 1973), Constrn. Specifications Inst. (dir. 1967-68), Am. Inst. Plant Engrs., Nat. Fedn. Ind. Bus. Orgn. Club: Rotary (dir. 1978-79, pres. 1986-87). Home: 3840 May Ct Palo Alto CA 94303-4545 Office: 2083 Old Middlefield Way Mountain View CA 94043-2401

KOCAOGLU, DUNDAR F., engineering management educator, industrial and civil engineer; b. Turkey, June 1, 1939; came to U.S., 1960; s. Irfan and Meliha (Uzay) K.; m. Alev Baysak, Oct. 17, 1968; 1 child, Timur. BSCE, Robert Coll., Istanbul, Turkey, 1960; MSCE, Lehigh U., 1962; MS in Indsl. Engring., U. Pitts., 1972, PhD in Ops. Rsch., 1976. Registered profl. engr., Pa., Oreg. Design engr. Modjeski & Masters, Harrisburg, Pa., 1962-64; ptnr. TEKSER Engring. Co., Istanbul, 1966-69; project engr. United Engrs., Phila., 1964-71; rsch. asst. U. Pitts., 1972-74, vis. asst. prof., 1974-76, assoc. prof. indsl. engring., dir. engring. mgmt., 1976-87; prof., dir. engring. mgmt. program, Portland State U., 1987—; pres. TMA-Tech. Mgmt. Assocs., Portland, Oreg., 1973—, pres. Portland Internat. Conf. Mgmt. Engring. and Tech., 1990—. Co-author: Engineering Management, 1981; editor: Management of R&D and Engineering, 1992; co-editor: Technology Management—The New International Language, 1991; series editor Wiley Series in Engring. and Tech. Mgmt.; contbr. articles on tech. mgmt. to profl. jours. Lt. C.E., Turkish Army, 1966-68. Fellow IEEE (Centennial medal 1984, editor-in-chief trans. on engring. mgmt. 1986—); mem. Informs (chmn. Coll. Engring. Mgmt. 1979-81), Am. Soc. Engring. Edn. (chmn. engring. mgmt. div. 1982-83), IEEE Engring. Mgmt. Soc. (fellow, publs. dir. 1982-85), ASCE (mem. engring. mgmt. bd. govs. 1988—), Muhendis, Ilim Adamlari ve Mimarlar Dernegi Soc. Turkish Engrs. and Scientists (hon.), Am. Soc. Engring. Mgmt. (dir. 1981-86), Omega Rho (pres. 1984-86). Office: Portland State U Engring Mgmt Program PO Box 751 Portland OR 97207-0751

KOCEN, LORRAINE AYRAL, accountant; b. Levittown, N.Y., July 20, 1956; d. Edward Joseph and Joan Dorothy (Destefanis) Ayral; m. Ross Kocen, Oct. 4, 1981; 1 child, Daniel. BS, Hofstra U., 1978; MBA, U. Minn., 1985. Engr. Sperry Systems Mgmt., Great Neck, N.Y., 1978-81; fin. analyst ITT Consumer Fin. Corp., Mpls., 1981-84; cost acct. Mercy Med. Ctr., Mpls., 1984-85, contr., 1985-86; bus. segments acct. GTE, Thousand Oaks, Calif., 1986-88, Cerritos project acct., 1988-90, Cerritos project adminstr., 1990-92, fin. adminstr., 1992-93, sr. sales adminstr., 1993-94, adminstr. mobile comms., 1994-96; fin. mgr. Blue Cross of Calif., Newbury Park, 1996—. Asst. editor newsletter Healthcare Fin. Mgmt. Assn., Mpls., 1985-86. Mem. archtl. com. Foxmoor Hills Homeowners Assn., Westlake, Calif., 1989. Office: GTE 2000 Corporate Dr Newbury Park CA 91320

KOCH, WILLIAM FREDERICK, paleontologist; b. Paterson, N.J., Sept. 24, 1949; s. William F. and Lucille May (Gamberton) K. BA in Geology, Rutgers Coll., 1971; MS in Geology, U. Mich., 1973; PhD in Geology, Oreg. State U., 1979. Vis. asst. prof. geology Portland (Oreg.) State U., 1980, St. Lawrence U., Canton, N.Y., 1980-81; asst. prof. geology Waynesburg (Pa.) Coll., 1981-83; rsch. assoc. zoology Oreg. State U., Corvallis, 1983—; cons. in field. Contbr. articles to profl. jours. Chmn. Waynesburg Food Coop., 1981-83; bd. trustees Odd Fellows Mgmt. Trust, Off Fellows Relief Trust. Mem. AAAS, Paleontol. Soc., Cactus and Succulent Soc., Odd Fellows, Sigma Xi. Democrat. Unitarian. Home and Office: 3140 NW Grant Ave Corvallis OR 97330-2335

KOCHER, CHARLES RODNEY, journalist; b. Portland, Oreg., Apr. 9, 1952; s. Kenneth Wilson and Kathlyn Elizabeth (Adams) K.; m. Gerry Kay Livingston, Apr. 18, 1981; children: KayLee Jean, Morgan Harris. BS in Journalism, Northwestern U., Evanston, Ill., 1974. Staff writer, copy editor The Idaho Statesman, Boise, 1973-75; city editor, staff writer The World Newspaper, Coos Bay, Oreg., 1975-82, mng. editor, 1982-95; econ. devel. specialist, grant writer Coquille Econ. Devel. Corp., North Bend, Oreg., 1995-96; pub. Curry Costal Pilot Newspaper, Brookings, Oreg., 1996—. Bd. dirs., vol. Helpline of the S. Coast, Coos Bay, 1976—; bd. dirs. Oreg. Geographic Names Bd., Portland, 1980—, Pacific Child Ctr., North Bend, Oreg., 1988-96, Oreg. Coast Music Assn., Coos Bay, 1980-90, Friends of Shore Acres, 1992-96. Recipient several state, regional and nat. writing and editing awards. Mem. Rotary (Brookings Harbor club, com. chmn.). Home: PO Box 6878 Brookings OR 97415 Office: Curry Coastal Pilot PO Box 700 Brookings OR 97415

KOEHLER, CHRISTOPHER JOSEPH, non-profit company executive, consultant; b. Oceanside, N.Y., Mar. 19, 1962; s. John Joseph and Catherine Veronica (Hammer) K.; m. Lisa Gail Fraser, May 20, 1995. BA in Polit. Sci., SUNY, Cortland, 1984; MA in Internat. Adminstrn., Sch. Internat. Tng., Brattleboro, Vt., 1996. Vol. Peace Corps, Guatemala, 1985-87; activities dir. Brookwood Court, Chapel Hill and Buckley Nursing Homes, Holyoke, Mass., 1987-90; cons. Koehler & White, Brattleboro, Vt., 1990-95; program dir. St. James ESL Program, Seattle, 1993—; cons. Koehler, Fraser & Assocs., Seattle, 1995—. Mediator DRC of Snohomish County, Everett, Wash., 1993-96; pres. bd. dirs. King County Literacy Coalition, Seattle, 1995-97. Office: St James ESL Program 804 9th Ave Seattle WA 98104-1265

KOEHLER, JAMES, tapestry artist; b. Detroit, Apr. 14, 1952; s. James Gerald and Maybelle Ralph (Thomas) K. BA, U. Mich., 1974. Benedictine monk Monastery of Christ in the Desert, Abiquiu, N.Mex., 1977-87; tapestry artist, 1987—; weaving tchr. Taos (N.Mex.) Inst. Arts, 1991-93. Exhibited in one/two person shows at Weaving S.W., Taos, 1992, Kent Galleries, Sante Fe, 1993, 95, Bentley Gallery, Scottsdale, Ariz., 1995; group shows include Wayrich Gallery, Albuquerque, 1986, Wichita Nat. All Media Crafts Exhibit, 1988, Santa Fe Festival of Arts, 1988, Taos Fall Arts Celebration, 1988, N.Mex. Arts and Crafts Fair, Albuquerque, 1986, 87, 88, 89, 90, 91, Stables Art Ctr., Taos, 1991, Am. Crafts Mus., N.Y., 1991, S.W. Arts and Crafts Festival, Albuquerque, 1987, 89, 90, 91, Mus. Fine Arts, Santa Fe, 1993, 96, Nat. Tapestry Invitational Exhibit, Ohio State U., 1994, Contemporary Concepts IV, Los Carlos Mus., Corrales, N.Mex., 1994, Fiber Celebrated, Tucson Mus. Art, 1995, Am. Tapestry Biennial, Oak Ridge, Tenn., Carbondale, Ill., Greenville, N.C., Golden, Colo., 1996—, Loveland (Colo.) Mus., 1996. Home: PO Box 549 Ranchos De Taos NM 87557-0549 Studio: PO Box 279 Santa Fe NM 87504-0279

KOEL, BRUCE EDWARD, chemistry educator; b. Norton, Kans., June 30, 1955. BS in Chemistry with highest honors, Emporia State U., 1976, MS in Chemistry, 1978; PhD in Chemistry, U. Tex., 1981. Miller Inst. postdoctoral fellow U. Calif., Berkeley, 1981-83; asst. prof. chemistry and biochemistry U. Colo., Boulder, 1983-89, assoc. prof. chemistry and biochemistry, 1989, fellow Coop. Inst. for Rsch. in Environ. Scis., 1983-89; assoc. prof. chemistry U. So. Calif., L.A., 1990-93, prof. chemistry, 1993—; cons. Chemistry and Laser Scis.-2 Los Alamos Nat. Lab., 1984-92, Hewlett-Packard, 1985-89, J&A Assocs., 1986, Chemistry and Laser Scis.-1 Los Alamos Nat. Lab., 1992-94, Burge and Assocs., 1992-95, Chem Alert Corp., 1993-95; reviewer for proposals to Am. Chem. Soc.-Petroleum Rsch. Fund, Army Rsch. Office, Dept. Energy, ISF, NSF; lectr., spkr. in field. Mem. editorial adv. bd.: Langmuir; referee Applied Surface Sci., Catalysis Letters, Chemistry of Materials, Internat. Conf. on Metall. Coatings and Thin Films, Jour. Catalysis, Jour. Chem. Physics, Jour. Electron Spectroscopy and Related Phenomena, Jour. Phys. Chemistry, Jour. Am. Chem. Soc., Jour. Vacuum Sci. and Tech., Langmuir, Sci., Surface Sci.; contbr. articles to profl. jours. Recipient Dreyfus Found. grant for New Faculty, 1983, Exxon Edn. Found. award, 1987, Union Carbide Innovation Rsch. awards, 1990, 91; U. fellow U. Tex., Austin, 1978, NSF Energy Related trainee, 1978, Alfred P. Sloan Rsch. fellow, 1990. Mem. Am. Chem. Soc. (divsn. colloid and surface chemistry Proctor and Gamble fellowship 1980, various com. positions), Am. Phys. Soc., Am. Vacuum Soc., Materials Rsch. Soc. Office: Univ So Calif Dept Chemistry Los Angeles CA 90089-0482

KOELMEL, LORNA LEE, data processing executive; b. Denver, May 15, 1936; d. George Bannister and Gladys Lee (Henshall) Steuart; m. Herbert Howard Nelson, Sept. 9, 1956 (div. Mar. 1967); children: Karen Dianne, Phillip Dean, Lois Lynn; m. Robert Darrel Koelmel, May 12, 1981; stepchildren: Kim, Cheryl, Dawn, Debbie. BA in English, U. Colo., 1967. Cert. secondary English tchr. Substitute English tchr. Jefferson County Schs., Lakewood, Colo., 1967-68; sec. specialist IBM Corp., Denver, 1968-75, pers. administr., 1975-82, asst. ctr. coord., 1982-85, office systems specialist, 1985-87, backup computer operator, 1987—; computer instr. Barnes Bus. Coll., Denver, 1987-92; owner, mgr. Lorna's Precision Word Processing and Desktop Pub., Denver, 1987-89; computer cons. Denver, 1990—. Editor newsletter Colo. Nat. Campers and Hikers Assn., 1992-94. Organist Christian Sci. Soc., Buena Vista, Colo., 1963-66, 1st Ch. Christ Scientists Thornton-Westminster, Thornton, Colo., 1994—; chmn. bd. dirs., 1979-80. Mem. NAFE, Nat. Secs. Assn. (retirement ctr. chair 1977-78, newsletter chair 1979-80, v.p. 1980-81), Am. Guild Organists, U. Colo. Alumni Assn., Alpha Chi Omega (publicity com. 1986-88). Republican. Club: Nat. Writers. Lodge: Job's Daus. (recorder 1953-54).

KOENIG, GINA LEE, microbiologist; b. Scranton, Pa., July 3, 1962; d. Leon Henry Koenig and Carmela Ann (Romolo) Koenigsberg; m. John Henry Carter III, Feb. 11, 1989 (div. 1995). BS, Pa. State U., 1984; MA with honors, San Francisco State U., 1993. Rsch. asst. Ctr. for Air Environ. Studies, State College, Pa., 1983-84; fisheries biologist Nat. Marine Fisheries Svc., Seattle, 1984-85; rsch. asst. Monterey Mushrooms, Watsonville, Calif., 1985-87; microbiologist Genencor, Internat., South San Francisco, 1987-92; rsch. scientist, curator culture collection dept. Roche Molecular Sys., Alameda, Calif., 1992-96, mem. instnl. biol. safety com., 1992—, sr. scientist, 1996—. Contbr. articles to profl. jours. Recipient 1st pl. award Calif. State U. Biology Student Rsch. Competition, 1992. Mem. Am. Soc. Microbiology (com. for symposium convener 1997, com. for culture collections 1994—), Soc. for Cryobiology, U.S. Fedn. Culture Collections (program com. 1992, chmn. publicity com. 1992-94, exec. bd. dirs.-at-large 1993-96, v.p. 1996-97, pres. 1998—), World Fedn. Culture Collections (program com. 1996), Toastmasters Internat. (v.p. edn. 1996, Competent Toastmaster 1996), Mycological Soc. Am., Mycological Soc. San Francisco, Pa. State U. Alumni Assn., Soc. for Indsl. Microbiology (convener symposium 1997). Democrat. Mem. Christian Ch. Office: Roche Molecular Systems Inc 1145 Atlantic Ave Alameda CA 94501-1145

KOENIG, JAMES WILLIAM, opera singer, writer; b. Little Rock, Mar. 6, 1953; s. Wilbert Henry and Viola Anna Marie (Haag) K. MusB, Northwestern U., Evanston, Ill., 1973; MusM, Northwestern U., 1975; advanced cert., Goethe INst., Donaueschingen, Germany, 1970, 81; postgrad., Inst. dell'Opera Italiana, Asolo, Italy, 1984. Author: And the Meter is Running, 1995; writer, performer: (one-man shows) Calll It a Love Song, 1992, There's Always One, N.Y.C., 1993; N.Y. operatic debut as L'Emir in Verdi's Jerusalem, N.Y. Grand Opera at Carnegie Hall, N.Y.C., 1994; N.Y. solo recital debut at St. Peter's Ch., N.Y.C.; appeared in I Pagliacci, Pine Mountain Festival, Mich., Un Giorno di Regno, N.Y. Grand Opera Ctrl. Pk. Summer Stage, St. John Passion, L.A. Bach Festival, 1992, Mystical Songs, Requiem, Carolina Symphony, An Evening with Stephen Sondheim, Spokane Symphony, Tosca, Ariz. Opera, Rigoletto, Baton Rouge Opera, La Traviata, Riverside Opera, Der Vampyr, Cosi fan tutte, Amahl and the Night Visitors, L.A. Music Ctr., The Juggler of Notre Dame, New Music Settings Ensemble, Tosca, Laguna Festival, The Rape of Lucretia, USC Opera, Torrance Symphony, Falstaff, Music Acad. of the West, L.A. County Mus. of Art, Kosciuszko Found., N.Y., Pasadena-Järvempää Sister City 10th Anniversary Recital, Finnish Concerts Tour, Am. Scandinavian Found. recitals. Active AIDS Outpatient Lunch Program, St. Thomas the Apostle Ch. Opera study grantee Pillsbury Found., 1974; recipient Finlandia award Suomi Coll, Hancock, Mich., 1995; medalist Internat. Vocal Competition, Italy, 1984. Mem. Am. Scandinavian Found. of L.A. (bd. dirs., pres. 1992-93, program dir. 1994-96, chmn. scholarships 1995-96), Nat. Acad. Poetry, Nat. Libr. Poetry (2d prize nat. competition 1995, Editor's Choice award 1996). Home: 3445 Winslow Dr Los Angeles CA 90026-6213 Office: 345 E 52d St Apt 2-C New York NY 10022

KOEP, LAWRENCE JAMES, surgeon; b. Pasadena, Calif., May 6, 1944; s. Ambrose Urban and Loma Mary (Riordan) K.; m. Jennifer Leigh James, FEb. 4, 1982 (div. Jan. 1992); children: Alexander, Erik, Lauren. BS, Johns Hopkins U., 1966, MD, 1970. Diplomate Am. Bd. Surgery. Intern Johns Hopkins Hosp., Balt., 1970-71, resident, 1971-76; assoc. prof. U. Colo., Denver, 1976-81; pvt. practice Phoenix, 1981—; bd. dirs. Donor Network Ariz. Mem. ACS, Am. Soc. Transplant Surgeons, Western Surg. Assn. Home: 3729 E Rancho Dr Paradise Valley AZ 85253-5022 Office: 1410 N 3rd St Phoenix AZ 85004-1608

KOEPPEL, GARY MERLE, publisher, art gallery owner, writer ; b. Albany, Oreg., Jan 20, 1938; s. Carl Melvin and Barbara Emma (Adams) K.; m. Emma Katerina Koeppel, May 20, 1984. BA, Portland State U., 1961; MFA, State U. Iowa, 1963. Writing instr. State U. Iowa, Iowa City, 1963-64; guest prof. English, U. P.R. San Juan, 1964-65; assoc. prof. creative writing Portland (Oreg.) State U., 1965-68; owner, operator Coast Gallery, Big Sur, 1971—, Pebble Beach, Calif., 1986—, Maui, Hawaii, 1985—, Hana, Hawaii, 1991—, Lahaina, Hawaii, 1992; owner Coast Pub. Co., Coast Seri Graphics, 1991—; editor, pub. Big Sur Gazette, 1978-81; producer, sponsor Maui Marine Art Expo., 1984-95, Calif. Marine Art Expo., Paris Marine Art Expo., Hawaiian Cultural Arts Expo., 1993; founder The Blue Movement, 1994; founder, pres. Global Art Expos, 1994, Planet Big Sur, 1996. Author: Sculptured Sandcast Candles, 1974, Henry Miller, The Paintings, 1991. Founder Big Sur Vol. Fire Brigade, 1975; chmn. coordinating com. Big Sur Area Planning, 1972-75; chmn. Big Sur Citizens Adv. Com., 1975-78. Mem. Internat. Soc. Appraisers, Am. Soc. Appraisers, Big Sur C. of C. (pres. 1974-75, 82-84), Big Sur Grange, Audubon Soc., Cousteau Soc., Phi Gamma Delta, Alpha Delta Sigma. Address: Coast Gallery PO Box 223519 Carmel CA 93922-3519

KOERBER, JOHN ROBERT, computer programmer; b. L.A., Aug. 17, 1955; s. Thomas Joseph and Betty (Turner) Koerber; m. Kimberly Sue Rider, Mar. 15, 1986. BS, Yale U., 1977. Computer technician Tech Mart, Tarzana, Calif., 1977-79; programmer, ptnr. J&J Computer Svc., Northridge, Calif., 1979-80; sr. programmer Mitec Computer Bus. Systems, Chartsworth, Calif., 1980-87; sr. software engr. Dracon div. Harris Corp., Camarillo, Calif., 1987-88; programmer, cons. SALING Computer Systems, Chatsworth, 1988—. Mem. IEEE (affiliate, Commns. Soc.), Assn. for Computing Machinery. Democrat. Home: 6657 Franrivers Ave West Hills CA 91307-2816 Office: SALING Computer Systems 10258 Glade Ave Chatsworth CA 91311-2812

KOERBER, LINDA RENÉ GWÉNS, educator, counselor; b. Seattle, Mar. 9, 1948; d. david and Gladys (Hall) Givens; children: Andre, Dominic, Kendra Corr. AA, Ctrl. seattle Coll., 1973; BA, U. Wash., 1975; MEd, City U. Seattle, 1996. Tchrs. aid Seattle Sch. Dist., 1970-73, tchr., 1975—, counselor, 1976—; tchr. King County Juvenile Ct., 1977-82; trainer strengthening multi ethnic families and comtys. Vol. Ctrl. Area Youth Club, Seattle, 1971, Ctrl. Area Sch. Coun., Seattle, 1972-73, Black Prisoners Forum, Seattle, 1970—; mem. Mayor's Commn. on Children and Youth, Seattle, 1994-95; foster parent Dept. Social and Health Svcs., Seattle, 1996, Casey Family Found. Mem. Am. Fedn. Tchrs. (chpt. organizer 1971). Baptist. Home: 7705 S Mission Dr Seattle WA 98178-3143

KOESTEL, MARK ALFRED, geologist, photographer, consultant; b. Cleve., Jan. 1, 1951; s. Alfred and Lucille (Kemeny) K.; children: Jennifer Rose, Bonnie Leigh. BS, U. Ariz., 1978. Registered profl. geologist Wyo., Alaska, Ind.; registered environ. assessor, Calif. Sr. geologist Union Oil Co. of Calif., Tucson and Denver, 1978-86; mgr. geology Harmsworth Assocs., Laguna Hills, Calif., 1986-88; sr. project mgr. Applied GeoSystems, Irvine, Calif., 1988-90; cons. geologist, photographer Adventures in Geology/Outdoor Images, Laguna Hills, Calif., Phillips Ranch, Calif., 1990—. Contbr. articles and photographs to profl. jours. and mags. N.Mex. state rep. Minerals Exploration Coalition, Tucson and Denver, 1982. Sci. Found. scholarship No. Ariz. U., 1969, Acad. Achievement scholarship, 1970, Disting. Scholastic Achievement scholarship, 1971. Mem. Am. Inst. of Profl. Geologists (cert.), Soc. of Mining Engrs., Aircraft Owners and Pilots Assn., Geol. Soc. of Am., Nat. Geographic Soc. Home and Office: 45 Brownfield Ln Phillips Ranch CA 91766-6641

KOESTER, BERTHOLD KARL, lawyer, law educator, retired honorary consul; b. Aachen, Germany, June 30, 1931; s. Wilhelm P. and Margarethe A. (Witteler) K.; m. Hildegard Maria Buettner, June 30, 1961; children: Georg W., Wolfgang J., Reinhard B. JD, U. Muenster, Fed. Republic Germany, 1957. Cert. Real Estate Broker, Ariz. Asst. prof. civil and internat. law U. Muenster, 1957-60; atty. Cts. of Duesseldorf, Fed. Republic Germany, 1960-82; v.p. Bank J. H. Vogeler & Co., Duesseldorf, 1960-64; pres. Bremer Tank-u., Kuehlschiffahrtsges.m.b.H., 1964-72; atty., trustee internat. corps., Duesseldorf and Phoenix, 1973-82, Phoenix, 1983—; of counsel Tancer Law Offices, Phoenix, 1978-86; prof. internat. bus. law Am. Grad. Sch. Internat. Mgmt., Glendale, Ariz., 1978-81; with Applewhite, Laflin & Lewis, Real Estate Investments, Phoenix, 1981-86, ptnr., 1982-86, Beucler Real Estate Investments, 1986-88, Scottsdale, Ariz.; chief exec. officer, chmn. bd. German Consultants in Real Estate Investments, Phoenix, 1989—; hon. consul Fed. Republic of Germany for Ariz., 1982-92; prof. internat. bus. law Western Internat. U., Phoenix, 1996—; chmn., CEO Arimpex Hi-Tec, Inc., Phoenix, 1981—; bd. dirs. Ariz. Ptnrship for Air Transp., 1988-92; chmn. Finvest Corp., Phoenix, 1990—. Contbr. articles to profl. jours. Pres. Parents Assn. Humboldt Gymnasium, Duesseldorf, 1971-78; active German Red Cross, from 1977. Mem. Duesseldorf Chamber of Lawyers, Bochum (Fed. Republic Germany) Assn. Tax Lawyers, Bonn German-Saudi Arabian Assn. (pres. 1976-79), Bonn German-Korean Assn., Assn. for German-Korean Econ. Devel. (pres. 1974-78), Ariz. Consular Corps (sec., treas. 1988-89), German-Am. C. of C., Phoenix Met. C. of C., Rotary (Scottsdale, Ariz.). Home: 6201 E Cactus Rd Scottsdale AZ 85254-4409 Office: PO Box 15674 Phoenix AZ 85060-5674

KOETSER, DAVID, export company executive; b. Amsterdam, The Netherlands, July 22, 1906; came to U.S., 1939; s. Joseph and Mathilda Pauline (Hollander) K. Grad., Lyceum, Amsterdam, 1926. Owner Music Pub. Co., Amsterdam, 1935-39; exec. sec. The Netherlands C. of C., 1947-56; owner D.K. Co., Inc., San Francisco, 1957-84. Contbr. articles to profl. jours. Moderator U.S. Small Bus. Adminstrn., Score workshops, San Francisco, 1987—. Staff sgt. CIC, 1942-45, ETO. Mem. Holland Am. Soc. (treas. 1950—), World Trade Club (entertainment com. 1960—), Internat. Exporters Assn. (pres. 1965, recipient Pres. E award). Home and Office: 100 Thorndale Dr Apt 341 San Rafael CA 94903-4574

KOFAHL, ROBERT EUGENE, science and education consultant; b. Taft, Calif., Oct. 5, 1924; s. Lynn Hosey and Beatrice (Cotteral) K. BS in Chemistry, Calif. Inst. Tech., 1949, PhD in Chemistry, 1954. From instr. to prof. Highland Coll., Pasadena, Calif., 1950-71, pres., 1957-71; rsch. scientist Carter Rsch. Lab., Pasadena, 1955-57; sci. coord. Creation-Sci. Rsch. Ctr., San Diego, 1972—. Sr. author: The Creation Explanation, 1975; author: Handy Dandy Evolution Refuter, 1977, 92. Bd. dirs. Westminster Acad. Christian Day Sch., L.A., 1953—. With U.S. Army, 1943-46. Mem. AAAS, Creation Rsch. Soc. Republican. Presbyterian. Home: 1322 E Wilson Ave Glendale CA 91206-4632 Office: Creation-Sci Rsch Ctr PO Box 421007 San Diego CA 92142

KOFF, ROBERT LOUIS, insurance executive; b. Phila., Nov. 5, 1943; s. Harry Nathaniel and Ida Sarah (Lurge) K.; children: Betsy Lynn, Richard Howard, Alexa Lynsay, Randall Leigh, Austin Harry. BA in English, Calif. State U., Northridge, 1966; postgrad., San Fernando Valley Coll. Law, 1966-68. Registered health underwriter. Mgr. Harry N. Koff Agy. Inc., L.A., 1966-68, v.p., 1968-78, pres., chief exec. officer, 1978-91, chmn., 1991—; field v.p. Chubb Life Am., L.A., 1993-95; chmn. Prof Asset Prof Corp, 1993—; chmn. Strat. Assur. Svcs. Inc., 1996—; chmn. nat. adv. coun. Mass. Casualty Ins. Co., Boston, 1986-87; mem. faculty Davidson Ctr. for Continuing Edn. U. So. Calif.; appointee Senate Adv. Commn. on Life and Health Ins., Calif., 1989—, Small Bus. Adv. Com., 1994-96, Farfill Commn., 1996—; Landfill Commn., L.A., 1996—; inaugural mem. Chubb Life Am. Underwriting Field Coun., 1995—. Mem. Starlight Found., L.A., 1987—; bd. dirs. United Cerebral Palsy, L.A., 1974-79, L.A. Children's Film Inst., 1983; mem. exec. com. Shaare Zedek Hosp., Jerusalem. Mem. Internat. Assn. Health Underwriters (Health Ins. Quality award 1978), Internat. Assn. Fin. Planners, Variety Club Internat. Republican. Jewish. Office: 28230 Agoura Rd # 1 Agoura Hills CA 91301-2490

KOGA, ROKUTARO, astrophysicist; b. Nagoya, Japan, Aug. 18, 1942; came to U.S., 1961, naturalized, 1966; s. Toyoki and Emiko (Shinra) K.; m. Cordula Rosow, May 5, 1981; children: Evan A., Nicole A. B.A., U. Calif.-Berkeley, 1966; Ph.D., U. Calif.-Riverside, 1974. Research fellow U. Calif.-Riverside, 1974-75; research physicist Case Western Res U., Cleve., 1975-79, asst. prof., 1979-81; physicist Aerospace Corp., Los Angeles, 1981—. Mem. Am. Phys. Soc., Am. Geophys. Union, IEEE, N.Y. Acad. Scis., Sigma Xi. Contbr. articles to profl. confs.; research on gamma-ray astronomy, solar neutron observation, space scis., charged particles in space and the effect of cosmic rays on microcircuits in space. Home: 7325 Oglesby Ave Los Angeles CA 90045-1356 Office: Aerospace Corp Space Scis Labs Los Angeles CA 90009

KOH, EUSEBIO LEGARDA, mathematics educator; b. Manila, Oct. 4, 1931; s. Enrique Legarda and Felisa Un (Makabuhay) K.; m. Donelita Mesina Viardo, Feb. 21, 1958; children—Eudonette, Elizabeth, Ethel, Denise. B.S. in Mech. Engring. cum laude, U. Philippines, Quezon City, 1954; M.S. in Mech. Engring., Purdue U., 1956; M.S., Birmingham, 1961; Ph.D., SUNY-Stony Brook, 1967. Research engr. Internat. Harvester Co., Chgo., 1956-57; asst. prof. mech. engring. U. Philippines, 1959-64, head dept., 1963-64; assoc. prof. math. U. Regina, Sask., Can., 1970-75, prof., 1975—, head dept. math., 1977-79; guest prof. math. Techn. Hochschule, Darmstadt, Fed. Republic Germany, 1975-76; prof. math. U. Petroleum/Minerals, Dhahran, Saudi Arabia, 1979-81. Contbr. research papers to profl. jours. Pres., Philippine Assn. Sask., 1971, bd. dirs., 1984; editor: Philippine Newsletter, 1985. Colombo Plan scholar Brit. Council, 1960; Travel fellow Nat. Research Council, Fed. Republic Germany, 1975; research grantee Nat. Sci. and Engring. Research Council, 1971—; named Outstanding Prof., U. Philippines Student Union, 1962, Outstanding Filipino-Can. in Edn., The Pinoy Digest, 1990. Mem. Soc. Indsl. and Applied Math., Am. Math. Soc., Math. Assn. Am., Can. Applied Math. Soc., Philippine Am. Acad. Sci. and Engring. (founding). Avocations: chess, bridge, tennis, golf. Office: U of Regina, Dept Math & Stats, Regina, SK Canada S4S 0A2

KOHAN, DENNIS LYNN, international trade educator, consultant; b. Kankakee, Ill., Nov. 22, 1945; s. Leon Stanley and Nellie (Foster) K.; m. Julianne Johnson, Feb. 14, 1976 (dec. Sept. 1985); children: Toni, Bart, Elyse; m. Betsy Burns, Mar. 8, 1986; 1 child, David. BA, Ill. Wesleyan U., 1967; MPA, Gov.'s State U., 1975; postgrad., John. Marshall Law Sch., 1971-74. Police officer Kankakee County, 1967-75; loan counselor, security officer Kankakee Fed. Savs. & Loan, Kankakee, 1975-76; mgr. Bank Western, Denver, 1976-85; mgr. real estate lending dept. Cen. Savs., San Diego, 1985-87; maj. loan work-out officer Imperial Savs., San Diego, 1987-88; cons. Equity Assurance Holding Corp., Newport Beach, Calif., 1987-88; compliance officer Am. Real Estate Group and New West Fed. Savs. and Loan, Irvine, Calif., 1988-90; co-founder Consortium-Real Estate Asset Cons., Costa Mesa, Calif., 1990-91; investigator, criminal coord. Resolution Trust Corp., Newport Beach, Calif., 1991-94; instr. Inst. for Internat. Trade Anhui Inst. Fin. and Trade, Bengbu, People's Republic of China, 1994-95; instr. Gungnthou Inst. Fgn. Trade, People's Republic of China, 1995—; instr. U. No. Colo. Coll. Bus., Greeley, 1981-85; chmn. bd. North Colo. Med. Ctr., Greeley, 1983-85; pres. bd. Normedco, Greeley, 1984-85; bus. cons., expert witness, 1995—. Vol. cons., chmn. ARC, Colo., 1979-85; campaign mgr. Donley Senatorial campaign, Colo., 1982, Kinkade City Coun. campaign, Colo., 1983; chmn. Weld County Housing Authority, 1981. Staff sgt. U.S. Army, 1969-71, Vietnam. Mem. Nat. Assn. Realtors, Shriners, Kiwanis.

KOHI, SUSAN, bilingual educator, translator; b. San Francisco, Nov. 28, 1948; d. Maurice Winkler Levinson and Fay Patricia (Lacey) Krier; m. Mahmoud Kohi, Mar. 24, 1973 (div. May 1993); children: Kamila, Samir, Kelly. BA, Holy Names Coll., 1970; MA, Middlebury Coll., 1973. Cert. secondary bilingual tchr., Ariz. Tchr. fgn. lang. Marin Cath. H.S., Greenbrae, Calif., 1970-71; tchr. English Ecole Breguet, Paris, 1971-72; fgn. exch. teller Bank of Am., Paris, 1972-73; tchr. fgn. lang. Scottsdale (Ariz.) C.C., 1974-75; translator Nat. Semiconductor Corp., Sidi-Bel-Abbes, Algeria, 1976-77; tchr. English Société Informatique, Aix-en-Provence, France, 1992; tchr. ESL Greenway Mid. Sch., Phoenix, 1994—. Recipient scholarship Pi Delta Phi. Mem. NEA, Nat. Assn. for Bilingual Edn., Ariz. Tchrs. of ESL. Home: 15449 N 38th Pl Phoenix AZ 85032

KOHL, JEANNE ELIZABETH, state senator, sociologist, educator; b. Madison, Wis., Oct. 19, 1942; d. Lloyd Jr. and Elizabeth Anne (Sinness) K.; m. Kenneth D. Jenkins, Apr. 15, 1973; children: Randall Hill, Brennan Hill, Terra Jenkins, Kyle Jenkins, Devon Jenkins; m. Alexander Sumner Welles, Nov. 10, 1985. BA, Calif. State U., Northridge, 1965, MA, 1970; MA, UCLA, 1973, PhD, 1974. Tchr. L.A. Sch. Dist., 1965-68; lectr. Calif. State U., Long Beach, 1973-85; vis. asst. prof. U. Calif., Irvine, 1974-77; So. Calif. mgr. Project Equity/U.S. Dept. Edn., 1978-84; asst. dean, coord. women's programs U. Calif., Irvine, 1979-82; lectr. Calif. State U., Fullerton, 1982-85, U. Wash., Seattle, 1985—; asst. prof. Pacific Luth. U., Tacoma, Wash., 1986-88; state legislator from 36th dist. Wash. Ho. of Reps., Olympia, 1992-94, majority whip, 1993-94; mem. Wash. Senate, Olympia, 1994—. Author: Explorations in Social Research, 1993, Student Study Guide-Marriage and the Family, 1993, 94, 95, 97; contbr. articles to profl. jours. Bd. dirs. Com. for Children, Seattle, 1986-91, Queen Anne Cmty. Coun., Seattle, 1988-93, Stop Youth Violence, Wash., 1993—, Queen Anne Helpline, Seattle, 1992—, Youth Care, 1996—; mem. Wash. State Sentencing Guidelines Commn., 1995—, Wash. State Child Care Coord. Com., 1995—; mem. Gov.'s Task Force on Higher Edn., 1995-96, Youth Care Bd. Grantee U.S. Dept. Edn., 1988-89, 90-91. Home: 301 W Kinnear Pl Seattle WA 98119-3732 Office: Wash State Senate PO Box 40436 Olympia WA 98504-0436

KOHLER, DOLORES MARIE, gallery owner; b. Rochester, N.Y., June 26, 1928; d. Thomas Beranda and Kathryn (Held) White; m. Reuel S. Kohler, June 27, 1946; children: Richard, Kathryn Kohler Farnsworth, Linda Kohler Barnes, Pamela Kohler Conners. BMus, U. Utah, 1976. Lic. real estate broker, lic. cert. gen. real estate appraiser. Broker Kohler Investment Realty, Bountiful, Utah, 1962—; registered rep. Frank D. Richards, Salt Lake City, 1986-93, Internmountain Fin. Svcs. Corp., Salt Lake City, 1996—; appraiser FHA/HUD, 1962—; owner Marble House Gallery, Salt Lake City, 1987—; owner Sandcastle Theaters, Bountiful, 1976—. Composer songs, 1973—. Music chmn. N. Canyon Stake LDS Ch., Bountiful, 1989-93, sec. North Canyon 3d Ward Sunday Sch., 1993—, music dir. Relief Soc., 1996—. Mem. Inst. Real Estate Mgmt. (pres. 1984), Salt Lake Bd. Realtors, Salt Lake Art Dealers Assn. (v.p. 1988-90, pres. 1990-91), U. Utah Coll. Fine Arts Alumni Assn. (coun. 1995—, sec. 1997), Composers Guild, Mu Phi Epsilon. Home: 2891 S 650 E Bountiful UT 84010-4455 Office: Marble House Gallery 44 Exchange Pl Salt Lake City UT 84111-2713

KOHLER, ERIC DAVE, history educator; b. Cin., Oct. 24, 1943; s. Walter Joseph and Irmgard (Marx) K.; m. Kathryn D. K. Kohler, June 22, 1968. AB, Brown U., 1965; MA, Stanford U., 1967, PhD, 1971. Vis. asst.

prof. history Calif. State U., Humboldt, 1970-71; asst. prof. U. Wyo., Laramie, 1971-78, assoc. prof., 1978—, acting head history dept., 1989-90. Chair Ivinson Hosp. La Grande Fleur Charity Ball, 1993. Recipient Deutcher Akademischer Austauchdienst award, 1968, U. Wyo. Faculty Devel. award, 1972. Mem. Am. Cath. Hist. Assn., Am. Hist. Assn., Am. Assn. for History of Medicine, German Studies Assn. (program dir. 1989). Club: Laramie Country. Office: U Wyo Dept History PO Box 3198 Laramie WY 82071-3198

KOHLER, WILLIAM CURTIS, sleep specialist, neurologist; b. Wharton, N.J., May 22, 1942; s. Walter Henry and Elizabeth (Curtis) K.; m. Barbara Bauman, Sept. 1, 1962; children: Jonathan, Kristina, Elizabeth. AB, Oberlin Coll., 1964; MD, U. Fla., 1968. Diplomate Am. Bd. Pediats., Am. Bd. Neurology with spl. competence in child neurology, Am. Bd. Electroencephalography and Neurophysiology, Am. Bd. Sleep Medicine. Asst. prof. pediatrics U. Fla., Gainesville, 1973-76; neurologist Tallahassee Neurol. Clinic, 1976-94, Billings (Mont.) Clinic, 1994-96, The Sleep Ctr. of Mont., Billings, 1996—; med. dir. The Sleep Ctr. at St. Vincent, 1996—; staff neurologist Wilford Hall Med. Ctr., USAF, San Antonio, 1973-75; from clin. asst. to clin. assoc. prof. pediatric neurology U. Tex., San Antonio, 1973-75; cons. child neurology Divsn. Children's Med. Svcs. Fla., Tallahassee, 1973-94; med. dir. Lancaster Youth Devel. Ctr., Trenton, Fla., 1975-76. Bd. dirs. United Cerebral Palsy Assn., 1977-84, Big Bend Epilepsy Assn., 1977-92. Recipient Humanitarian Svc. award United Cerebral Palsy Assn. Fellow Am. Acad. Pediatrics, Am. Acad. Neurology, Am. Sleep Disorders Assn.; mem. Am. Med. EEG Assn., Am. Epilepsy Soc., AMA (physician's recognition award). Office: The Sleep Ctr of Montana 2900 12th Ave N # 34 Billings MT 59101-7506

KOHLHASE, CHARLES EMILE, JR., mission architect; b. Knoxville, Tenn., Aug. 15, 1935; s. Charles Emile Sr. and Beverly Brock (Baumann) K.; m. Sonia Monica Walter, Mar. 25, 1959 (div. 1970); children: Elizabeth Alison Kohlhase Richards, Carolyn Wendy. BS in Physics, Ga. Tech., 1957; M in Engring., UCLA, 1968. Engr. traj. design and deep space navigation Caltech Jet Propulsion Lab., Pasadena, 1959-64, project engr. Mariner Mars 1969 mission, 1965-69, group supr. mission analysis and navigation groups, 1970-74, mission design mgr. Voyager Project, 1975-89, sci. and mission mgr. The Cassini Program, 1990—; rev. bd. mem. NASA and Jet Propulsion Lab., Pasadena, 1975—; seminar leader SUNY, Binghamton, 1982-86; space cons., author Time-Life Books, Washington, 1986-88; co-chair NASA Space Sta., Washington, 1988. Author, editor: Voyager Neptune Travel Guide, 1989; editor Encyclopedia of Applied Physics, 1991; author (computer program) Wilderness, 1984-85 (Best of 1985, 1986); World Leading Designer of Unmanned deep space missions: (Spaceflight Mag. 1992); contbr. articles to profl. jours. Lt. (j.g.) USN, 1957-59. Mem. Sierra Club, Green Peace, The Planetary Soc., Tau Bet Pi (pres. 1957). Office: Caltech Jet Propulsion Lab 4800 Oak Grove Dr Pasadena CA 91109

KOHN, GERHARD, psychologist, educator; b. Neisse, Germany, Nov. 18, 1921; s. Erich and Marie (Prager) K.; m. Irena M. Billinger, Feb. 9, 1947; children: Mary, Eric. B.S., Northwestern U., 1948, M.A., 1949, Ph.D., 1952; postgrad. U. So. Calif., 1960. Diplomate Am. Bd. Forensic Examiners (fellow), forensic psychology. Instr., Northwestern U., 1947-49; instr., counselor, dir. pub. relations Kendall Coll., Evanston, Ill., 1947-51; psychologist, counselor Jewish Vocat. Services, Los Angeles, 1951-53, Long Beach Unified Sch. Dist., Calif., 1953-61; instr. Long Beach City Coll., 1955-61; asst. prof. psychology Long Beach State U., 1955-56; counselor, instr. Santa Ana Coll., Calif., 1961-65; prof. Calif. State U., Fullerton, 1971-72; lectr. Orange Coast Coll., 1972-75; asst. clin. prof. psychiatry U. Calif.-Irvine; dir. Reading Devel. Ctr., Long Beach, 1958-88, Gerhard Kohn Sch. Ednl. Therapy, 1967-85; exec. dir. Young Horizons; pvt. practice psychology, 1958—; for juvenile diversion program Long Beach Area, 1982—; cons. HEW, Bur. Hearing and Appeals, Social Security Adminstrn., Long Beach/Orange County B'nai B'rith Career and Counseling Svcs. (cons. to Long Beach Coun.), Long Beach Coun. of Parent Coop. Nursery Sch., Orange County Headstart, Orange County Coop. Pre-Schs.; mem. police complaint commn. City of Long Beach; commr. Long Beach Coalition Police Complaint Commn. With AUS, 1942-47. Mem. NEA, Am. Pers. and Guidance Assn., Nat. Vocat. Guidance Assn., Am. Psychol. Assn., Calif. Psychol. Assn. (dir. 1976-79, 91-94, sec. 1980-81), Orange County Psychol. Assn. (dir., pres. 1974), Long Beach Psychol. Assn. (pres. 1985, 86, 93, 94, 95, sec. 1989, treas. 1991, chmn. govtl. affairs com., dir. 1996), L.A. County Psychol. Assn. (treas., sec.), Calif. Assn. Sch. Psychologists, Elks, Kiwanis, Phi Delta Kappa, Psi Chi. Office: 320 Pine Ave Ste 308 Long Beach CA 90802-2307

KOHN, ROBERT SAMUEL, JR., real estate investment consultant; b. Denver, Jan. 7, 1949; s. Robert Samuel and Miriam Lackner (Neusteter) K.; m. Eleanor B. Kohn; children: Joseph Robert, Randall Stanton, Andrea Rene. BS, U. Ariz., 1971. Asst. buyer Robinson's Dept. Store, L.A., 1971; agt. Neusteter Realty Co., Denver, 1972-73, exec. v.p., 1973-76; pres. Project Devel. Svcs., Denver, 1976-78, pres., CEO, 1978-83; pres. Kohn and Assocs., Inc., 1979-83; pres. The Burke Co., Inc., Irvine, Calif., 1983-84, ptnr., 1984-91; sr. mktg. assoc. Iliff, Phoenix, 1992-94; owner RSKJ, Inc., 1992- . Mem. Bldg. Owners and Mgrs. Assn. (pres. 1977-78, dir. 1972-78, dir. S.W. Conf. Bd. 1977-78), Denver Art Mus., Denver U. Libr. Assn., Central City Opera House Assn., Inst. Real Estate Mgmt., Newport Beach Tennis Club. Republican. Jewish.

KOHN, ROGER ALAN, surgeon; b. Chgo., May 1, 1946; s. Arthur Jerome and Sylvia Lee (Karlen) K.; m. Barbara Helene, Mar. 30, 1974; children: Bradley, Allison. BA, U. Ill., 1967; MD, Northwestern U., 1971. Diplomate Am. Bd. Ophthalmology. Internship UCLA, 1971-72; residency Northwestern U., Chgo., 1972-75, fellowship U. Ala., Birmingham, 1975, Harvard Med. Sch., Boston, 1975-76; chmn. dept. ophthalmology Kern Med. Ctr., Bakersfield, Calif., 1978-87; asst. prof. UCLA Med. Sch., 1978-82, assoc. prof., 1982-86, prof., 1986—. Author: Textbook of Ophthalmic Plastic and Reconstructive Surgery, 1988; contbr. numerous articles to profl. jours.; author chpts. in 16 additional textbooks; patentee in field. Bd. dirs. Santa Barbara (Calif.) Symphony, 1990—. Capt. USAR, 1971-77. Name applied to med. syndrome Kohn-Romano Syndrome. Mem. Am. Soc. Ophthalmic Plastic and Reconstuctive Surgery (cert.), Pacific Coast Ophthal. Soc. (bd. dirs. 1986—, 1st v.p. 1990). Jewish. Office: 525 E Micheltorena St Ste 201 Santa Barbara CA 93103-2254

KOHRING, VIC, state legislator, construction company executive; b. Waukegan, Ill., Aug. 2, 1958; s. Heinz H. and Dolores E. Kohring. AAS, Matanuska-Susitna C.C., Palmer, Alaska, 1985; BA, Alaska Pacific U., 1987, MBA, 1989. Owner South Ctrl. Bldg. Maintenance, Wasilla, Alaska, 1994—; state legislator Ho. of Reps., Wasilla, 1994—. Bd. dirs. Alaska Housing Fin. Corp., Anchorage, 1991-94; mem. Wasilla Planning & Utilities Commn., 1991-94, Mat-Su Borough Econ. Devel. Commn., Palmer, 1993-94; mem. Iditarod Trail Com. Mem. NRA (life), Wasilla Hist. Soc., Greater Wasilla C. of C., Chugiak-Eagle River C. of C. Republican. Home: PO Box 870515 Wasilla AK 99687 Office: Alaska House of Representatives 600 E Railroad Ave Wasilla AK 99654

KOJAC, JEFFREY STANLEY, military officer; b. L.A., Nov. 30, 1967. BA, St. John's Coll., Annapolis, Md., 1989; cert., Amphibious Warfare Sch., 1992. Commd. 2d lt. USMC, 1989, advanced through grades to capt., 1994; instr. Marine Corps Comm.-Electronics Sch., 1993-96; comdr. Tactical Air Ops. Ctr., 1997—. Contbr. articles, revs. to Procs. Marine Corps Gazette, Naval War Coll. Rev., Joint Force Quar. Participant Pacific Coun. on Internat. Policy, L.A., 1995-96. Recipient Navy Commendation medal, USMC, 1996. Mem. U.S. Naval Inst., U.S. Strategic Inst., Marine Corps Assn.

KOKALJ, JAMES EDWARD, retired aerospace administrator; b. Chgo., Oct. 29, 1933; s. John and Antoinette (Zabukovec) K. AA in Engring., El Camino Coll., Torrance, Calif., 1953. Dynomometer lab. technician U.S. Electric Motors, L.A., 1953-54; devel. lab. technician AiResearch divsn. Garrett, L.A., 1956-59; tech. rep. McCulloch, L.A., 1959-65; dist. mgr. Yamaha Internat., Montebello, Calif., 1965-67; salesman Vasek Polak BMW, Manhattan Beach, Calif., 1967-68; sr. svc. rep. Stratos-We. div. Fairchild, Manhattan Beach, 1968-70; asst. regional mgr. we. states J.B.E. Olson div. Grumman, L.A., 1970-71; gen. mgr. Internat. Kart Fedn., Glendora, Calif., 1971-73; logistics support data specialist Mil. Aircraft divsn. Northrop Grumman, Hawthorne, Calif., 1974-95; ret., 1995. Author: Technical Inspection Handbook, 1972; contbr. articles to profl. jours. With USN, 1954-56. Mem. U.S. Naval Inst., Internat. Naval Rsch. Orgn., Nat. Maritime Hist. Soc., So. Calif. Hist. Aircraft Found. Republican. Roman Catholic. Home: 805 Bayview Dr Hermosa Beach CA 90254-4147

KOKANOVICH, JON DOUGLAS, crime laboratory director, forensic chemist; b. Phoenix, Sept. 11, 1951; s. Dan and Doris (Schupbach) K.; m. Nancy Anne Freed, Apr. 14, 1974; children: Mark, Heidi, Holly, Tim. Student, Mesa (Ariz.) C.C., 1969-71; BA in Edn., Ariz. State U., 1973, MA in Edn., 1976. Sci. tchr. Paradise Valley High Sch., Phoenix, 1973-76; criminalist Ariz. Dept. Pub. Safety Crime Lab. System, 1977-80; criminalist, crime lab dir. Mesa Police Dept. Crime Lab., 1980—. Contbr. articles to profl. jours. Lay min. Apostolic Christian Ch., Phoenix, 1981. Mem. Am. Acad. Forensic Scis., Am. Soc. Crime Lab. Dirs., Assn. Firearms and Toolmark Examiners, Southwestern Assn. Forensic Scientists, Calif. Assn. Criminalists. Office: Mesa Police Crime Lab 130 N Robson Mesa AZ 85201-6609

KOLANOSKI, THOMAS EDWIN, financial company executive; b. San Francisco, Mar. 1, 1937; s. Theodore Thaddeus and Mary J. (Luczynski) K.; m. Sheila O'Brien, Dec. 26, 1960; children: Kenneth John, Thomas Patrick, Michael Sean. BS, U. San Francisco, 1959, MA, 1965. Cert. fin. planner; registered rep. Educator, counselor, administr. San Francisco Unified Sch. Dist.; adminstr. Huntington Beach (Calif.) Union, 1969-79; v.p. fin. svcs. Waddell & Reed, Inc., Ariz., Nev., Utah, So. Calif., 1979-94; retired Waddell & Reed, Inc., 1994; personal fin. planner. Fellow NDEA, 1965. Mem. Nat. Assn. Secondary Sch. Prins., Internat. Assn. of Fin. Planners, Nat. Assn. Securities Dealers. Republican. Roman Catholic. Home: 1783 Panay Cir Costa Mesa CA 92626-2348

KOLAROV, KRASIMIR DOBROMIROV, computer scientist, researcher; b. Sofia, Bulgaria, Oct. 16, 1961; came to the U.S., 1987; s. Dobromir Krastev and Margarita Georgieva (Kurukafova) K.; m. Janet Louise Barba, July 4, 1990; children: April, Kathryn, Sonia, Elena. BS in Math. with honors, U. Sofia, Bulgaria, 1981, MS in Ops. Rsch. with honors, 1982, MA in English, 1982; MS in Mech. Engring., Stanford U., 1990, PhD in Mech. Engring., 1993. Rschr. Bulgarian Acad. Scis., Sofia, 1982-83; rsch. assoc., vis. prof. Inst. Mechanics and Biomechanics, Bulgarian Acad. Scis., Sofia, 1983-87; tchg. asst. Stanford (Calif.) U., 1988-92; mem. rsch. staff Interval Rsch. Corp., Palo Alto, Calif., 1992—; vis. prof. Inst. for Civil Engring., Sofia, 1983-86; lectr. H.S. U., Sofia, 1985; reviewer Jour. Robotic Sys., Palo Alto, 1991—, others. Contbr. articles to profl. jours. Mem. IEEE, Assn. for Computing Machinery, Soc. for Indsl. and Applied Math. Office: Interval Rsch Corp 1801 Page Mill Rd # C Palo Alto CA 94304-1216

KOLB, DOROTHY GONG, elementary education educator; b. San Jose, Calif.; d. Jack and Lucille (Chinn) Gong; m. William Harris Kolb, Mar. 22, 1970. BA (with highest honors), San Jose State U., 1964; postgrad., U. Hawaii, Calif. State U., L.A.; MA in Ednl. Tech., Pepperdine U., 1992. Cert. life elem. educator, mentally retarded educator K-12, learning handicapped pre-sch., K-12, adult classes. Tchr. Cambrian Sch. Dist., San Jose, Calif., 1964-66, Cen. Oahu (Hawaii) Sch. Dist., Wahiawa, 1966-68, Montebello (Calif.) Unified Sch. Dist., 1968—. Named to Pi Lambda Theta, Kappa Delta Pi, Pi Tau Sigma, Tau Beta Pi; recipient Walter Bachrodt Meml. scholar.

KOLB, KEITH ROBERT, architect, educator; b. Billings, Mont., Feb. 9, 1922; s. Percy Fletcher and Josephine (Randolph) K.; m. Jacqueline Cecile Jump, June 18, 1947; children: Brooks Robin, Bliss Richards. Grad. basic engring., US Army Specialized Training Rutgers U., 1944; BArch cum laude, U. Wash., 1947; MArch, Harvard U., 1950. Registered architect, Wash., Mont., Idaho, Calif., Oreg., Nat. Council Archtl. Registration Bds. Draftsman, designer various archtl. firms Seattle, 1946-54; draftsman, designer Walter Gropius and Architects Collaborative, Cambridge, Mass., 1950-52; prin. Keith R. Kolb, Architect, Seattle, 1954-64, Keith R. Kolb Architect & Assocs., Seattle, 1964-66; ptnr. Decker, Kolb & Stansfield, Seattle, 1966-71, Kolb & Stansfield AIA Architects, Seattle, 1971-89; pvt. practice Keith R. Kolb FAIA Architects, Seattle, 1989—; instr. Mont. State Coll., Bozeman, 1947-49; asst. prof. arch. U. Wash., Seattle, 1952-60, assoc. prof., 1960-82, prof., 1982-90, prof. emeritus, 1990—. Design architect Dist. II Hdqrs. and Comm. Ctr., Wash. State Patrol, Bellevue, 1970 (Exhbn. award Seattle chpt. AIA), Hampson residence, 1970 (nat. AIA 1st honor 1973, citation Seattle chpt. AIA 1980), Acute Gen. Stevens Meml. Hosp., 1973, Redmond Pub. Libr., 1975 (jury selection Wash. coun. AIA 1980), Tolstedt residence, Helena, Mont., 1976, Herbert L. Eastlick Biol. Scis. Lab. bldg. Wash. State U., 1977, Redmond Svc. Ctr., Puget Sound Power and Light Co., 1979, Computer and Mgmt. Svcs. Ctr., Paccar Inc., 1981 (curatorial team selection Mus. History and Industry exhbn. 100th anniversary of AIA 1994), Seattle Town House, 1960 (curatorial team selection Mus. History and Industry exhbn. 100th anniversary of AIA 1994), Comm. Tower, Pacific N.W. Bell, 1981 (nat. J.F. Lincoln bronze), Forks br. Seattle 1st Nat. Bank, 1981 (commendation award Seattle chpt. AIA 1981, nat. jury selection Am. Architecture, The State of the Art in the '80's 1985, regional citation Am. Wood Coun. 1981), Reg. ops. Control Ctr. Sacramento Dist. Corps Engrs. McChord AFB, Wash., 1982, Puget Sound Blood Ctr., 1983-88, expansion vis./dining/recreation facilities Wash. State Reformatory, Monroe, 1983, Univ. Sta. P.O., U.S. Postal Svc., Seattle, 1983, Guard Towers, McNeil Island Corrections Ctr. Wash., 1983, Magnolia Queen Anne Carrier Annex, U.S. Postal Svc., Seattle, 1986, Tolstedt residence, Seattle, 1987, Maxim residence, Camano Island, Wash., 1991, Carmean residence alterations/additions, Seattle, 1995, 96. Pres. Laurelhurst Community Club, Seattle, 1966. Served with U.S. Army, 1943-45, ETO. Decorated Bronze Star medal ETO; recipient Alpha Rho Chi medal; selected Am. Architects, Facts on File, inc., 1989. Fellow AIA (dir. Seattle chpt. 1970-71, sec. Seattle chpt. 1972, Wash. state coun. 1973, pres. sr. coun. Seattle chpt. 1994-96, trustee Seattle Archtl. Found. 1994-96, Citation award Seattle chpt. for a Seattle 1960 Town House, 1990); mem. U. Wash. Archtl. Alumni Assn. (pres. 1958-59), Phi Beta Kappa, Tau Sigma Delta. Home and Office: 3379 47th Ave NE Seattle WA 98105-5326

KOLB, KEN LLOYD, writer; b. Portland, Oreg., July 14, 1926; s. Frederick Von and Ella May (Bay) K.; m. Emma LaVada Sanford, June 7, 1952; children: Kevin, Lauren, Kimrie. BA in English with honors, U. Calif., Berkeley, 1950; MA with honors, San Francisco State U., 1953. Cert. jr. coll. English tchr. Freelance fiction writer various nat. mags., N.Y.C., 1951-56; freelance screenwriter various film and TV studios, Los Angeles, 1956-81; freelance novelist Chilton, Random House, Playboy Press, N.Y.C., 1967—; instr. creative writing Feather River Coll., Quincy Calif., 1969; minister Universal Life Ch. Author: (teleplay) She Walks in Beauty, 1956 (Writers Guild award 1956), (feature films) Seventh Voyage of Sinbad, 1957, Snow Job, 1972, (novels) Getting Straight, 1967 (made into feature film), The Couch Trip, 1970 (made into feature film), Night Crossing, 1974; contbr. fiction and humor to nat. mags. and anthologies. Foreman Plumas County Grand Jury, Quincy, 1970; chmn. Region C Criminal Justice Planning commn., Oroville, Calif., 1975-77; film commr. Plumas County, 1986-87. Served with USNR, 1944-46. Establishment Ken Kolb Collection (Boston U. Library 1969). Mem. Writers Guild Am. West, Authors Guild, Mensa, Phi Beta Kappa, Theta Chi. Democrat. Club: Plumas Ski (pres. 1977-78). Home and Office: PO Box 30022 Cromberg CA 96103-2022 *The true measure of success is not the attainment of great wealth or a position of power over others, but the quality of one's own life. I'm grateful for the money and honors I've had from writing, but more important to me is my ongoing love affair with my wife and the loving friendship of my grown children. I believe in God and a sense of humor as guiding principles, but I can't explain either one.*

KOLBE, JAMES THOMAS, congressman; b. Evanston, Ill., June 28, 1942; s. Walter William and Helen (Reed) K. BA in Polit. Sci., Northwestern U., 1965; MBA in Econs., Stanford U., 1967. Asst. to coordinating architect Ill. Bldg. Authority, Chgo., 1970-72; spl. asst. to Gov. Richard Ogilvie Chgo., 1972-73; v.p. Wood Canyon Corp., Tucson, 1973-80; mem. Ariz. Senate, 1977-83, majority whip, 1979-81; cons. Tucson, 1983-85; mem. 99th-105th Congresses from 5th dist. Ariz., 1985—; mem. appropriations com., 1987—, mem. budget com. Trustee Embry-Riddle Aero. U., Daytona Beach, Fla.; bd. dirs. Community Food Bank, Tucson; Republican precinct committeeman, Tucson, 1974—. Served as lt. USNR, 1977-79, Vietnam. Mem. Am. Legion, VFW. Republican. Methodist. Office: US Ho of Reps 205 Cannon HOB Washington DC 20515-0305*

KOLBECK, SISTER ANN LAWRENCE, school principal; b. Salem, S.D., Jan. 10, 1935; d. Lawrence Bernard and Nora Jeannette (Dunn) K. BA in Sociology, Cardinal Stritch Coll., Milw., 1973; MA in Adminstrn., Loyola Marymount U., L.A., 1987. Tchr. for mentally retarded St. Coletta Sch., Jefferson, Wis., 1956-74; tchr. Hanna Boys Ctr., Sonoma, Calif., 1975-77, St. Benedict Sch., Montebello, Calif., 1978-84; prin. St. Benedict Sch., 1985—. Office: St Benedict Sch 217 N 10th St Montebello CA 90640-4604

KOLBESON, MARILYN HOPF, holistic practioner, educator, artist, retired advertising executive; b. Cin., June 9, 1930; d. Henry Dilg and Carolyn Josephine (Brown) Hopf; children: Michael Llen, Kenneth Ray, Patrick James, Pamela Sue Kolbeson Lang, James Allan. Student U. Cin., 1947, 48, 50. Sales and mktg. mgr. Cox Patrick United Van Lines, 1977-80; sales mktg. mgr. Creative Incentives, Houston, 1980-81; pres. Ad Sense, Inc., Houston, 1981-87, M.H. Kolbeson & Assocs., Houston, 1987, Seattle, 1987—, The Phoenix Books, Seattle, 1987-90; cons. N.L.P. Communications; holographic memory release practitioner, 1996—; lectr., cons. in field. Mem. adv. bd. Alief Ind. Sch. Dist., 1981-87, pres., 1983-84; bd. dirs. Santa Maria Hostel, 1983-86, v.p., 1983-84; founder, pres. Mind Force, Houston, 1978-87 and Seattle, 1987-95; founder META Group, Seattle, 1991—, Meta-Self Healing Ministries, Seattle, 1997—. Pub.: You Make the Difference in the Nat. Lit. Poetry Anthonology, Morning Song, 1996; originator Heart Button Technique, 1995. Mem. citizen's adv. bd. Arcola (Ill.) Sch. Bd., 1966-67; mem. Greater Houston Conv. and Visitors Coun., loaned exec., 1986-87; mem. adv. bd. Am. Inst. Achievement, 1986-87; vol. Seattle Pub. Schs., 1992—; charter mem. Rep. Task Force. Mem. Internat. Platform Assn., Houston Advt. Splty. Assn. (bd. dirs. 1984-87, treas. 1985, v.p. 1986-87), Inst. Noetic Scis. (charter), Galleria Area C. of C. (bd. dirs. 1986-87), Toastmasters (area gov. 1978), Grand Club (v.p. 1986), Lakewood Seward Park Community Club (bd. dirs. 1992—), Fair and Tender Ladies Book Group. Republican. Christian Scientist. Office: 5247 S Brandon St Seattle WA 98118-2522

KOLDE, BERT, professional basketball team executive. Vice chmn. Portland Trail Blazers. Office: Portland Trail Blazers One Center Ct Ste 200 Portland OR 97232

KOLDING, LAURA ALICE, artist, educator; b. San Francisco, June 3, 1963; d. Oliver Herbert and Helen Laura (Tainter) Shaffer; m. Joseph Daniel Kolding, Dec. 2, 1986; children: Heidi, Kyle, Isaac. Student, Cen. Oreg. C.C., 1990. Artist Prineville, Oreg., 1985—; tchr. drawing Ctrl. Oreg. C.C. One person shows include Cafe Paradiso, Bend, Oreg., 1995, 96, Mirror Pond Gallery, Bend, 1996; exhibited in group show at Portland (Oreg.) Art Mus. Sales & Rental Gallerys, 1997; represented in permanent personal collections. Comdr. Royal Rangers, Prineville, 1996. Mem. Cen. Oreg. Arts Assn. (area rep. 1996—). Pentecostal. Home: 8000 S Davis Loop Prineville OR 97754

KOLETTY, STEPHEN RONALD, geographer, educator; b. Jan. 17, 1949; s. John William and Margaret C. (Ford) K.; m. Yuhaniz Anang, Aug. 15, 1981; children: Manoah Koa'e, Gio Helaku. AA in Geology, L.A. Harbor Coll., 1969; BA in Geography/Earth & Space Sci., Calif. State U., Dominguez Hills, 1974; MA in Geography/Resource Mgmt., cert. Pacific Urban Studies and Planning, U. Hawaii at Manoa, 1983; postgrad., U. So. Calif., 1992—. Cert. c.c. instr., Calif. Evening coord. Office Student Affairs Calif. State U., Dominguez Hills, 1974-76, counselor, coord. internat. programs Office Student Devel., 1978—; rsch. asst., teaching asst. geography dept. U. So. Calif., L.A., 1993—; lectr. Calif. State U., Dominguez Hills, 1980, 81, 82, 85, 87, 89, 90, 91, 92, 93, asst. prof., summer 1982, 83, 86, 95, 96, instr., fall 1986, 87, 88, 89, 90, faculty pers. com. reappointment, tenure, promotion subcom. acad. senate, 1984-86, faculty advisor Polynesian Club, 1982-92, nat. student exch. del., 1988-92; instr. Fullerton Coll., spring 1989, Cypress Coll., spring 1990, El Camino Coll., 1990—, Long Beach City Coll., 1995, 96; presenter in field. Mem. Assn. Am. Geographers, Assn. Pacific Coast Geographers, Calif. Geographic Soc., Calif. Coll. Pers. Assn., The Mongolia Soc. Home: 241 S Walker Ave San Pedro CA 90732-3245 Office: U So Calif Dept Geography Los Angeles CA 90089-0255

KOLKEY, DANIEL MILES, lawyer; b. Chgo., Apr. 21, 1952; s. Eugene Louis and Gilda Penelope (Cowan) K.; m. Donna Lynn Christie, May 15, 1982; children: Eugene, William, Christopher, Jonathan. BA, Stanford U., 1974; JD, Harvard U., 1977. Bar: Calif. 1977, U.S. Dist. Ct. (cen. dist.) Calif. 1979, U.S. Dist. Ct. (no. dist.) Calif. 1980, U.S. Dist. Ct. (ea. dist.) Calif. 1978, U.S. Dist. Ct. (so. dist.) Calif. 1994, U.S. Dist. Ct. Ariz. 1992, U.S. Ct. Appeals (9th cir.) 1979, U.S. Supreme Ct., 1983. Law clk. U.S. Dist. Ct. judge, N.Y.C., 1977-78; assoc. Gibson Dunn & Crutcher, L.A., 1978-84, ptnr., 1985-94; counsel to Gov. and legal affairs sec. to Calif. Gov. Pete Wilson, 1995—; arbitrator bi-nat. panel for U.S.-Can. Free Trade Agreement, 1990-94; commr. Calif. Law Revision Commn., 1992-94, vice chair, 1993-94, chair, 1994; mem. Blue Ribbon Commn. on Jury Sys. Improvement, 1996. Contbr. articles to profl. publs. Co-chmn. internat. rels. sect. Town Hall of Calif., L.A., 1981-90; chmn. internat. trade legis. subcom., internat. commerce steering com. L.A. Area C. of C., 1983-91 (mem. law & justice com., 1993-94); mem. adv. coun. and exec. com. Asia Pacific Ctr. for Resolution of Internat. Bus. Disputes, 1991-94; bd. dirs., L.A. Ctr. for Internat. Comml. Arbitration, 1986-94, treas., 1986-88, v.p. 1988-90, pres., 1990-94; assoc. mem. ctrl. com. Calif. Rep. Party, 1983-94, mem. ctrl. com., 1995—, dep. gen. coun. credentials com., Republican Nat. Convention, 1992, alt. Calif. Delegation, 1992, Calif. del., 1996; mem. L.A. Com. on Fgn. Rels., 1983-95; gen. counsel Citizens Rsch. Found., 1990-94. Master Kennedy Inns of Ct.; mem. Am. Arbitration Assn. (panel of arbitrators, arbitrator large complex case dispute resolution program, 1993—), Chartered Inst. Arbitrators, London (assoc.), Anthony Kennedy Inns Ct. (master), Friends of Wilton Park So. Calif. (chmn. exec. com. 1986-94, exec. com. 1986—). Jewish. Office: Gov's Office State Capitol Sacramento CA 95814-4906

KOLLITZ, JANICE ARLENE, English literature educator, freelance writer; b. Stockton, Calif., Sept. 8, 1937; d. Charles Millard and Anna Henrietta (Neidhardt) Morris; m. Richard LeRoy Hollenbeck (div. 1971); children: Richard Gordon Hollenbeck, John Morgan Hollenbeck, Margaret Joy Hollenbeck Stepe; m. Gerhard Kollitz. AA, Riverside (Calif.) C.C., 1986; BA, Calif. State U., San Bernardino, 1987, MA, 1989; PhD, Union Insts., Cincinnati, 1997. Cert. cmty. coll. tchr., Calif. V.p. Concept Now, Inc., City of Commerce, Calif., 1971-72; owner wholesale giftwares co. GJK Enterprises, Riverside, Calif., 1972-85; art editor Elan Mag., Colton, Calif., 1987-90; prof. English Riverside C.C., 1988—; adj. instr. Chaffee Coll., Rancho Cucamonga, Calif., 1988-90, Valley Coll., San Bernardino, 1988-90, Crafton Hills Coll., Yucaipa, Calif., 1988-90; adj. lectr. Calif. State U., San Bernardino, 1989—; advisor Muse Lit. Mag., Riverside, 1992—; mem. editorial staff Pacific Rev., San Bernardino, 1987-88. Ghost writer: (biography) Machine Gun Kelly: To Right a Wrong, 1992; co-author: (hist. novel) Madagh, 1993; contbr. articles to Elan mag. Active in Republican politics, 1956, 64. Named Tchr. of Distinction, Latter Day Saints Student Orgn., 1994, 95, Most Influential Instr., Riverside C.C. Disabled Students, 1991, 93, 94, Tchr. of Yr. Assoc. Students Riverside C.C., 1991, 93, 95, 96. Mem. MLA. Mem. Reformed Ch. in Am. Office: Riverside CC 4800 Magnolia Ave Riverside CA 92506-1242

KOLODNY, STEPHEN ARTHUR, lawyer; b. Monticello, N.Y., June 25, 1940; s. H. Lewis and Ida K.; children: Jeffery, Lee. BA in Bus. Adminstrn., Boston U., 1963, JD, 1965. Bar: Calif. 1966, U.S. Dist. Ct. (cen. dist.) Calif. 1966; cert. family law specialist. Sole practice L.A., 1966-95; with Kolodny & Anteau, L.A., 1995—; lectr. on family law subjects. Co-author: Divorce Practice Handbook, 1994; author: Evidence ABA Advocate, 1996. Mem. ABA (family law sect., author ABA Advocate), Internat. Acad. Matrimonial Lawyers (bd. govs., pres. USA chpt.), Calif. State Bar Assn. (cert. family law specialist, lectr. State Bar panel, CEB programs, mem. family law sect.), Los Angeles County Bar Assn. (lectr., mem. & past chmn. family law sect.), Beverly Hills Bar Assn. (lectr., mem. family law sect.).

KOLPAS, SIDNEY, mathematician, educator; b. Chgo., Oct. 19, 1947; s. Irving and Molly Lou (Lubin) K.; m. Laurie Ann Puhn, June 27, 1971;

children: Allison, Jamie. BA magna cum laude, Calif. State U., Northridge, 1969, MS, 1971; EdD, U. So. Calif., L.A., 1979. Tchr. Luther Burbank (Calif.) Jr. High Sch., 1971-79; tchr., author Tandy Corp., L.A., 1979-85; tchr. John Burroughs High Sch., Burbank, 1979-90; adj. instr. Coll. of the Canyons, Valencia, Calif., 1985-90; ind. cons. L.A., 1979—; instr. Glendale (Calif.) Coll., 1990—; statis. cons. U. So. Calif., L.A.; math. and computer sci. mentor Burbank Unified Sch. Dist., 1985-89; tchr. math. Korean Coll. Prep. Sch., 1989; instr. Moorpark (Calif.) Coll., 1990; tchr. computer programming L.A. Valley Jr. Coll., 1976-77. Author: Topics in Mathematics, 1971, A Theory of Motivation in Mathematics, 1972, Model 3 TRSDOS and Disk Basic, 1979, Computer Applications in Patient Care, 1986, Quest for James Coffin, 1990, The Pythagorean Theorem: 8 Classic Proofs, 1991; contbr. articles to profl. jours. Recipient Teaching award McLuhen Found., L.A., 1984, Honors Teaching award NASA/Nat. Coun. Tchrs. Math., 1987, teaching commendation L.A. County, 1992, Disting. Prof. award Glendale Coll. chpt. Alpha Gamma Sigma, 1993; named Outstanding Tchr., Kiwanis, 1985, Woodrow Wilson Master Tchr., Woodrow Wilson Nat. Fellowship Found., Princeton, 1988, Ministerial and Burbank Tchr. of Yr., 1992. Mem. Nat. Coun. Tchrs. Math., Calif. Math. Coun. (com. chmn. 1985—), Foothill Math. Coun. (pres. 1989-90, 92-93), L.A. County Math. Tchrs. Assn. (bd. dirs. 1985-87), Phi Delta Kappa, Phi Eta Sigma, Alpha Mu Gamma. Democrat. Jewish. Office: Glendale Coll 1500 N Verdugo Rd Glendale CA 91208-2809

KOLSRUD, HENRY GERALD, dentist; b. Minnewaukan, N.D., Aug. 12, 1923; s. Henry G. and Anna Naomi (Moen) K.; m. Loretta Dorothy Cooper, Sept. 3, 1945; children—Gerald Roger, Charles Cooper. Student Concordia Coll., 1941-44; DDS, U. Minn., 1947. Gen. practice dentistry, Spokane, Wash., 1953—. Bd. dirs. Spokane County Rep. Com., United Crusade, Spokane; at-large-del. Republican Planning Com.; mem. Republican Presdl. Task Force. Capt. USAF, 1950-52. Recipient Employer of the Yr. award Lilac City Bus. and Profl. Women, 1994. Mem. ADA, Wash. State Dental Assn., Spokane Dist. Dental Soc. Lutheran. Clubs: Spokane Country, Spokane, Empire. Lodges: Masons, Shriners. Home: 2107 W Waikiki Rd Spokane WA 99218-2780 Office: 3718 N Monroe St Spokane WA 99205-2850

KOLSTAD, CHARLES DURGIN, economics and environmental studies educator; b. Warehan, Mass., Apr. 30, 1948; s. George Andrew and Christine Joyce (Stillman) K.; m. Dorothy Valerie Thompson, July 8, 1972; children: Jonathan, Kate. BS, Bates Coll., 1969; MA, U. Rochester, N.Y., 1973; PhD, Stanford U., 1982. Staff mem. Los Alamos (N. Mex.) Nat. Lab., 1974-83; asst. prof. econs. and environ. studies U. Ill., Urbana, 1983-88, assoc. prof., 1988-92, prof., 1992-94; vis. prof. econs. U. Calif., Santa Barbara, 1992, prof. econs. and environ. studies, 1993-96, prof. environ. sci. and mgmt., 1997—; vis. scholar Norwegian Sch. Econs., Bergen, 1985; vis. asst. prof. MIT, Cambridge, 1986-87; vis. prof. Cath. U. Louvain, Belgium, 1993; pres. Resource Econs. Corp., Urbana, 1984—; mem. sci. adv. bd. U.S. EPA, 1992—; mem. bd. energy and environ. systems NRC/NAS. Editor: Resource and Energy Economics; assoc. editor Jour. Environ. Econs. and Mgmt., 1992-93; contbr. articles to profl. jours. Named Univ. Scholar, U. Ill., 1988. Mem. Assn. for Environ. and Resource Econs. (bd. dirs.), Am. Econ. Assn., Econometric Soc. Office: U Calif Dept Econs Santa Barbara CA 93106-9210

KOLSTAD, ROBERT BRUCE, computer scientist; b. Montevideo, Minn., Aug. 21, 1953; s. Clayton Robert and Joanne Marie (Peterson) K. B in Applied Sci., So. Meth. U., 1974; MSEE, U. Notre Dame, 1976; PhD, U. Ill., 1982. Sr. engr., mgr. Convex Computer Corp., Dallas, 1982-88; sr. software engr. Prisma, Inc., Colorado Springs, 1988-89, v.p. software, 1989; sr. staff engr. Sun Micro Systems, Colorado Springs, 1989-91; pres. Berkeley Software Design, Inc., Colorado Springs, 1991—; sec., bd. officer USENIX, Berkeley, 1986-92. Patentee in field. Recipient Orange County Community Svc. award, 1989, UNIX Personality of the Yr. award, 1988; named to Guiness Book of World Records. Home: 7759 Delmonico Dr Colorado Springs CO 80919-1050 Office: 5575 Tech Center Dr Ste 110 Colorado Springs CO 80919-2349

KOLTAI, STEPHEN MIKLOS, mechanical engineer, consultant, economist, writer, educator; b. Ujpest, Hungary, Nov. 5, 1922; came to U.S., 1963; s. Maximilian and Elisabeth (Rado) K.; m. Franciska Gabor, Sept. 14, 1948; children: Eva, Susy. MS in Mech. Enging., U. Budapest, Hungary, 1948, MS in Econs., MS, BA, 1955. Engr. Hungarian Govt., 1943-49; cons. engr. and diplomatic service various European countries, 1950-62; cons. engr. Pan Bus. Cons. Corp., Switzerland and U.S., 1963-77, Palm Springs, Calif., 1977—. Patentee in field. Charter mem. Rep. Presdl. task force, Washington, 1984—.

KOMATER, CHRISTOPHER JOHN, artist; b. South Bend, Ind., Nov. 16, 1965; s. Rudolph Andrew and Mary Frances (Napolitan) K. BFA, San Francisco Art Inst., 1987. Curator exhbn. Millenium Coming: The New Degenerate Art Show, 1995; one-man show 509 Cultural Ctr., San Francisco, 1997; exhibited in group shows Haines Gallery, San Francisco, 1991, Jan Kesner Gallery, L.A., 1994, Oliver Art Ctr., CCAC, Oakland, Calif., 1994, Capp Street Project, San Francisco, 1996, Refusalon, San Francisco, 1997. pres. bd. dirs. The Lab Gallery, San Francisco, 1995—, mem. curatorial com., 1994—; bd. dirs. Secession Gallery, San Francisco, 1990-95, mem. adv. bd., 1995—. Regional Visual Arts fellow Western States Art Fedn./Nat. Endowment Arts, 1994; recipient artist residency award Villa Montalvo Ctr. for Arts, 1994. Home and Studio: 4303 20th St San Francisco CA 94114

KOMDAT, JOHN RAYMOND, data processing consultant; b. Brownsville, Tex., Apr. 29, 1943; s. John William and Sara Grace (Williams) K.; m. Linda Jean Garrette, Aug. 26, 1965 (div.); m. Barbara Milroy O'Cain, Sept. 27, 1986; children: Philip August, John William. Student U. Tex., 1961-65. Sr. systems analyst Mass. Blue Cross, Boston, 1970-74; pvt. practice data processing cons., San Francisco, 1974-80, Denver, 1981—; prin. sys. analyst mgmt. info. svcs. divsn. Dept. of Revenue, State of Colo., 1986-89; prin. sys. analyst Info. Mgmt. Commn. Staff Dept. Adminstrn. State Colo., 1989—; mem. Mus. Modern Art, CODASYL End User Facilities Com., 1974-76, funds distbn. com. Mile High United Way. Served with U.S. Army, 1966-70. Mem. IEEE, AAAS, ACLU, Colo. Info. Mgrs. Assn., Assn. Computing Machinery, Denver Art Mus., Friend of Pub. Radio, Friend of Denver Pub. Libr., Colo. State Mgrs. Assn, Nature Conservancy, Sierra Club, Common Cause, Trout Unlimited. Democrat. Office: PO Box 9757 Denver CO 80209-0757

KOMENICH, KIM, photographer; b. Laramie, Wyo., Oct. 15, 1956; s. Milo and Juanita Mary (Beggs) K. BA in Journalism, San Jose State U., 1979. Reporter/photographer Manteca (Calif.) Bull., 1976-77; staff photographer Contra Costa Times, Walnut Creek, Calif., 1979-82, San Francisco Examiner, 1982—; lectr. San Francisco Acad. Art. John S. Knight fellow Stanford U., 1993-94; recipient 1st Pl. award UPI, 1982, 85, Nat. Headliner award, 1983, 88, 87 1st Pl. award World Press Photo Awards, 1983, 1st Pl. award AP, 1985, 87, Disting. Svc. award Sigma Delta Xi, 1986, Pulitzer prize, 1987, others. Office: San Francisco Examiner 110 5th St San Francisco CA 94103-2918

KOMISAR, JEROME BERTRAM, university administrator; b. Bklyn., Jan. 31, 1937; s. Harry and Fanny (Neumann) K.; m. Natalie Rosenberg, Sept. 8, 1957; children: Harriet, Wade, Frances, Aurenna. BS, NYU, 1957; MA, Columbia U., 1959, PhD, 1968. Asst. prof. econs. Hamilton Coll., Clinton, N.Y., 1961-66; asst. prof., then assoc. prof. mgmt. SUNY, Binghamton, 1966-74, asst. to pres., 1971-74; vice chancellor faculty and staff rels. SUNY System, 1974-81, provost, 1982-85, pres. Rsch. Found., 1982-90, exec. vice chancellor, 1985-90, acting chancellor, 1987-88; acting pres. SUNY, New Paltz, 1979-80, prof. econs. and adminstrn., 1988-90; pres. U. Alaska System, Fairbanks, 1990—; regents prof. U. Alaska, 1990—; Alaska commr. We. Interstate Commn. for Higher Edn., 1990—; chmn. Alaska Aerospace Devel. Corp., 1991—. Author: Work Scheduling in the Wholesale Trades in Manhattan's Central Business District, 1962, Social Legislation and Labor Force Behavior, 1968; co-author: (with John S. Gambs) Economics and Man, 1964. Bd. dirs. Sta. WAMC-FM, Albany, 1982-90; chair bd. overseers Rockefeller Inst., 1987-88. Office: U Alaska System 202 Butrovich Bldg 910 Yukon Dr Fairbanks AK 99775

KOMISSARCHIK, EDWARD A., computer scientist; b. Moscow, Russia, July 5, 1949; came to U.S., 1990; s. Alexander and Riva (Zilberstein) K.; m. Stella Mnatsakanian, Sept. 5, 1969; 1 child, Julia. M in Math., Lomonosov U., Moscow, 1971; PhD of Computer Sci., Inst. Cybernetics, Russia, 1978. Rsch. scientist Inst. Control Scis., Acad. Scis., Moscow, 1971-77, Inst. Sys. Studies, Acad. Scis., Moscow, 1977-90; assoc. prof. computer sci. Inst. Radio Electronics and Automation, Moscow, 1978-90; pres., chief tech. officer Accent, Inc., San Francisco, 1993—. Contbr. articles to profl. jours. Mem. IEEE, ACM, N.Y. Acad. Scis., Russian Math. Soc., Scientists Club. Home: 2452 Melendy Dr San Carlos CA 94070 Office: Accent Inc 200 Rome St San Francisco CA 94112

KOMPALA, DHINAKAR SATHYANATHAN, chemical engineering educator, biochemical engineering researcher; b. Madras, India, Nov. 20, 1958; came to U.S., 1979; s. Sathyanathan and Sulochana Kompala; m. Sushila Viswamurthy Rudramuniappa, Nov. 18, 1983; children: Tejaswi Dina, Chytanya Robby. BTech., Indian Inst. Tech., Madras, 1979; MS, Purdue U., 1982, PhD, 1984. Asst. prof. chem. engring. U. Colo., Boulder, 1985-91, assoc. prof., 1991—; vis. assoc. chem. enging. Calif. Inst. Tech., 1991-92. Editor Cell Separation Sci. and Tech., 1991; contbr. articles to profl. jours. Recipient NSF Presdl. Young Investigators award, 1988-93; NSF Biotech. Rsch. grantee, 1986-89, 89-92, 95—; Dept. Commerce rsch. grantee, 1988; The Whitaker Found. grantee, 1990-93. Mem. Am. Inst. Chem. Engrs., Am. Chem. Soc. (program chair biochem. tech. divsn. 1993). Office: U Colo PO Box 424 Boulder CO 80309-0424

KONDA, VENKAT, computer scientist, lecturer; b. Tenali, India, June 30, 1966; came to U.S., 1988; s. Siva Reddy and Raja Kumari (Jonnala) K.; m. Santhi Sompalli, Dec. 14, 1987. BTech in Elec. Engring., Nagarjuna U., Vijaywada, India, 1986; MTech in Elec. Engring., Indian Inst. Tech., Kharagpur, 1987; PhD in Computer Sci., U. Louisville, 1992. Staff scientist NCUBE Corp., Foster City, Calif., 1992-95; adj. lectr. computer engring. dept. Santa Clara (Calif.) U., 1994—; sr. mem. tech. staff Mitsubishi Electric ITA, Sunnvale (Calif.) R&D Lab., 1995-97; sr. engring. mgr. VSIS Inc., Sunnyvale, 1997—; referee tech. confs. and jours. Mem. IEEE, Assn. Computing Machinery. Home: 6278 Grand Oak Way San Jose CA 95135 Office: VSIS Inc 1060 East Arques Ave Sunnyvale CA 94086

KONDRASUK, JACK N. (JOHN KONDRASUK), business educator; b. Eau Claire, Wis., Jan. 23, 1942; s. Frank Mathew and Ruth (Norton) K. Student, Coll. St. Thomas, 1960-61; BS, U. Wis., Eau Claire, 1964; MA, U. Minn., 1966, PhD, 1972. Pers. adminstr. Honeywell, Inc., Mpls., 1967-68; instr. U. Minn., Mpls., 1969; mgmt. edn. specialist Control Data Corp., Mpls., 1969-71; mgmt. cons. J.N. Kondrasuk Co., Mpls., 1971-73; psychologist Persona Corp., Portland, Oreg., 1973; cons. Rohrer, Hibler & Repogle, Inc. (now called RHR Internat.), Portland, Oreg., 1973-74; asst. to pres. U. Portland, 1980-81, asst./assoc. prof., 1975—; vis. prof. Novgorod (Russia) Poly. Inst., 1993, Wroslav (Poland), 1994, Oaxaca (Mexico), 1996. Contbr. articles to profl. jours. Mem. adv. group City of Portland, 1978, State of Oreg., Salem, 1987-88; mem. Clackamas County Econ. Devel. Commn., 1992-94; mem. Clark County Transp. Futures Com., 1995-96, Clark County Planning Commn., 1996—. Mem. ASTD (pres. 1987, nat. coms. 1987—, dir. HRD Cons. Network, regional conf. chair 1984-86), Soc. Human Resource Mgmt. (sr. profl. in human resources, tng. com. 1988—), N.W. Human Resource Mgmt. Assn. (chair 1979), Acad. of Mgmt. (div. newsletter editor 1982), Am. Psychol. Soc., Soc. Indsl. Orgn. Psychology. Office: U Portland Sch Bus 5000 N Willamette Blvd Portland OR 97203-5743

KONG, LAURA S. L., geophysicist; b. Honolulu, July 23, 1961; d. Albert T.S. and Cordelia (Seu) K.; m. Kevin T.M. Johnson, Mar. 3, 1990. ScB, Brown U., 1983; PhD, MIT/Woods Hole Oceanog. Inst., 1990. Grad. rschr. Woods Hole (Mass.) Oceanog. Instn., 1984-90; postdoctoral fellow U. Tokyo, 1990-91; geophysicist Pacific Tsunami Warning Ctr., Ewa Beach, Hawaii, 1991-93; seismologist U.S. Geol. Survey Hawaiian Volcano Obs., 1993-95; rschr. U. Hawaii, Honolulu, 1996—; mem. Hawaii State Earthquake adv. bd., 1994—; mem. equal opportunity adv. bd. Nat. Earth Svc. Pacific Region, Honolulu, 1992-93, Asin-Am./Pacific Islander spl. emphasis program mgr., 1992-93. Contbr. articles to profl. jours.; spkr., editl. reviewer in field. Rsch. fellow Japan Govt.-Japan Soc. for Promotion of Sci., 1990; recipient Young Investigator grant Japan Soc. for Promotion of Sci., 1990. Mem. Am. Geophys. Union, Seismol. Soc. Am., Hawaii Ctr. for Volcanology, Assn. Women in Sci., Sigma Xi. Office: U Hawaii Hawaii Inst Geophysics 2525 Correa Rd Honolulu HI 96822

KONING, HENDRIK, architect; came to the U.S., 1979; BArch, U. Melbourne, Australia, 1978; MArch II, UCLA, 1981. Lic. architect Calif., 1982, contractor, 1984; registered architect, Australia; cert. Nat. Coun. Archtl. Registration Bds. Prin. in charge of tech., code, and prodn. issues Koning Eizenberg Architecture, 1981—; instr. UCLA, U. B.C., Harvard U., MIT; lectr. in field. Exhbns. incl. "House Rules" Wexner Ctr., 1994, "The Architect's Dream Houses for the Next Millenium", The Contemporary Arts Ctr., 1993, " Angels & Franciscans", Gagosian Gallery, 1992, "Conceptual Drawings by Architects", Bannatyne Gallery, 1991, Koning and Eizenberg Projects Grad. Sch. Architecture & Urban Planning UCLA, 1990, others; prin. works include Digital Domain renovation and screening rm., Santa Monica, Lightstorm Entertainment offices and THX theater, Santa Monica, Gilmore Bank addition and remodel, L.A., 1548-1550 Studios, Santa Monica, (with RTA) Materials Rsch. Lab. U. Calif., Santa Barbara, Ken. Edwards Ctr. Cmty. Svcs., Santa Monica, Peck Park Cmty. Ctr. Gymnasium, San Pedro, Calif., Sepulveda Recreation Ctr. Gymnasium, L.A., (Nat. Concrete /Masonry award 1996, AIA Calif. Coun. Honor award 1996, L.A. Bus. Coun. Beautification awrd 1996, AIA/SFV Design award 1995), PS# 1 Elem. Sch., Santa Monica, Famers Market additions and master plan, L.A. (Westside Urban Forum prize 1991), Stage Deli, L.A., Simone Hotel, L.A. (Nat. Honor award AIA 1994), Boyd Hotel, L.A. Cmty. Corp. Santa Monica Housing Projects, 5th St. Family Housing, Santa Monica, St. John's Hosp. Replacement Housing Program, Santa Monica, Liffman Ho., Santa Monica, (with Glenn Erikson) Electric Artblock, Venice (Beautification award L.A. Bus. Coun. 1993), 6th St. Condominiums, Santa Monica, Hollywood Duplex, Hollywood Hills (Record Houses Archtl. Record 1988), Calif. Ave. Duplex, Santa Monica, Tarzana Ho. (Merit award L.A. chpt. AIA 1991, Sunset Western Home awards 1993-94), 909 Ho., Santa Monica (Merit award L.A. chpt. AIA 1991), 31st St. Ho., Santa Monica (Honor award AIACC 1994, Record House 1995, Nat. AIA Honor award 1996), others. Recipient 1st award Progressive Architecture, 1987; named one of Domino's Top 30 Architects, 1989. Fellow AIA (juror San Diego design awards 1992, panelist honor awards 1994, Calif. coun. spl. awards 1997, nat. interior design awards 1997), Royal Australian Inst. Archs.; mem. Nat. Trust for Hist. Preservation, So. Calif. Assn. Non-Profit Housing, L.A. Conservancy. Office: Koning Eizenberg Architecture 1548 18th St Santa Monica CA 90404-3404

KONOLD, ELIZABETH KAY, university administrator; b. Pasadena, Calif., Apr. 7, 1937; d. A. Ewing and Hazel (Bragg) K.; children: James H. Ewing, Julia K. Earls. Student, Stanford U., Palo Alto, Calif.; BA, Occidental Coll., Glendale, Calif., 1958; M Internat. Mgmt., Am. Grad. Sch. Internat. Mgmt., Glendale, Ariz., 1979; cert. Sch. Mgmt., Oxford U. Real estate broker Frank Howard Allen & Co., Greenbrae, Calif., 1973-78; dir. devel. svcs. Am. Grad. Sch. Internat. Mgmt., Glendale, 1979-82; dir. ann. fund U. Redlands, Calif., 1982-86; dir. ann. Pacific Fund U. Pacific, Stockton, Calif., 1986-94; exec. dir. alumni affairs U. Calif. Davis Sch. Medicine, Sacramento, 1994—. Pres., sec. Stanford Women of San Joaquin County, Stockton, 1988-94. Mem. Zonta Internat. (sec., v.p. 1982-86), Rotary Internat. Home: 608 Elmhurst Cir Sacramento CA 95825-6640 Office: U Calif Davis Sch Med 2315 Stockton Blvd Sacramento CA 95817-2201

KONTNY, VINCENT L., rancher, engineering executive; b. Chappell, Nebr., July 19, 1937; s. Edward James and Ruth Regina (Schumann) K.; m. Joan Dashwood FitzGibbon, Feb. 20, 1970; children: Natascha Marie, Michael Christian, Amber Brooke. BSCE, U. Colo., 1958, DSc honoris causa, 1991. Operator heavy equipment, grade foreman Peter Kiewit Son's Co., Denver, 1958-59; project mgr. Utah Constrn. and Mining Co., Western Australia, 1965-69, Fluor Australia, Queensland, Australia, 1969-72; sr. project mgr. Fluor Utah, San Mateo, Calif., 1972-73; sr. v.p. Holmes & Narver, Inc., Orange, Calif., 1973-79; mng. dir. Fluor Australia, Melbourne, 1979-82; group v.p. Fluor Engrs., Inc., Irvine, Calif., 1982-85, pres., chief exec. officer, 1985-87; group pres. Fluor Daniel, Irvine, Calif., 1987-88, pres., 1988-94; pres. Fluor Corp., Irvine, 1990-94, vice chmn., 1994; ret., 1994; purchased Last Dollar Ranch, Ridgway Co. 1989, Centennial Ranch, Colona Co., 1992, owner Double Shoe Cattle Co. Contbr. articles to profl. jours. Mem. engring. devel. coun., U. Colo.; mem. engring. adv. coun., Stanford U. Lt. USN, 1959-65. Republican. Roman Catholic. Club: Cet. (Costa Mesa, Calif.).

KONWIN, THOR WARNER, financial executive; b. Berwyn, Ill., Aug. 17, 1943; s. Frank and Alice S. (Johnson) K.; m. Carol A. Svitak, Aug. 2, 1967 (div. Feb. 1990); 1 child, Christopher Vernon; m. Virginia Colburn, May 21, 1993. AA, Morton Jr. Coll., 1966; BS, No. Ill. U., 1967; MS, Roosevelt U., 1971. Acct. Beckerman & Terrill, CPA's, Chgo., 1967-68; cost acct. Sunbeam Corp., Chgo., 1968-72; controller Gen. Molded Products, Inc., Chgo., 1972-75, Sunbeam Appliance Co., Chgo., 1975-81; chief fin. officer Bear Med. System, Inc., Riverside, Calif., 1981-84, Bird Products Corp., Palm Springs, Calif., 1984—; gen. ptnr., 1985—; pres. B&B Ventures Ltd., Riverside, 1987—; chief exec. officer Med One Fin. Group, Salt Lake City; pres. Tags Antiques, Inc., Palm Springs; bd. dris. Bird Med. Techs., Inc., Palm Springs, Bird Products Corp., Palm Springs, Bird Internat., Inc., Riverside, B&B Ventures, Inc., Riverside, Equilink, Inc. Riverside, Stackhouse, Inc., Riverside, Med One Fin. Group, Salt Lake City; CEO Equitable Inc., Palm Springs, Calif., 1990—; adv. coun. U. Calif. Grad. Bus. Sch., Riverside, 1988—; CEO Entertainment Leader Inc., Cathedral City, Calif., 1995—. Served with U.S. Army, 1969-71. Home: 45500 Verde Santa Palm Desert CA 92260 Office: 68845 Perez Rd Ste 30 Cathedral City CA 92234-7254

KOON, RAY HAROLD, management and security consultant; b. Little Mountain, S.C., Nov. 19, 1934; s. Harold Clay and Jessie Rae (Epting) K.; m. Bertha Mae Gardner, Aug. 19, 1958; children: Shari Madilyn Koon Goode, Schyler Michele Koon Richards, Kamela Suzanne Koon Scott. BSBA, Old Dominion U., 1957; postgrad., Columbia (S.C.) Coll., 1957-58. Lic. pvt. pilot. Supr. office svcs. FBI, Norfolk, Va., 1953-61, Las Vegas, Nev., 1961-62; agt. State Gaming Control Bd., Carson City, Nev., 1962-64, coord., 1967-80, chief of investigations, 1980-83; prodn. control mgr. Colite Industries, Inc., West Columbia, S.C., 1964-67; pres. Assoc. Gaming Consultants, Las Vegas, 1983; dir. gaming surveillance Hilton Hotels Corp., Beverly Hills, Calif., 1983-86; pres. JRJ Enterprises, Las Vegas, 1986-88, Assoc. Cons. Enterprises, Las Vegas, 1983—; pres. Assoc. Gaming Cons., Las Vegas, 1983—, CEO, 1990—; past sec. Sta. KNIS-FM; bd. dirs. Casino Mgmt. Internat., Carson City. Editor, pub. Ray Koon's Gaming Gram, 1986—; columnist Casino Gaming Internat., 1990-92. Chief vols. Warren Engine Co. 1, Carson City Fire Dept., 1962-83; mem. Carson City Sheriff's Aero Squadron, 1983—, past comdr.; past mem. exec. bd. Nev. Bapt. Conv. With U.S. Army, 1957-59. Mem. Nev. Arbitration Assn. (bd. dirs. 1986-90), Las Vegas C. of C. (mem. commerce crime prevention and legis. action coms. 1989-90), Zelzah Shrine Aviation Club (past comdr.), Nat. Intelligence and Counterintelligence Assn. (bd. dirs. 1995—), Assn. Former Intelligence Officers, Toastmasters, Masons. Republican. Office: Assoc Cons Enterprises 3271 S Highland Dr Ste 705A Las Vegas NV 89109-1051

KOONCE, JOHN PETER, investment company executive; b. Coronado, Calif., Jan. 8, 1932; s. Allen Clark and Elizabeth (Webb) K.; B.S., U.S. Naval Acad., 1954; postgrad. U. So. Calif., 1957, U. Alaska, 1961, U. Ill., 1968-69; M.S. in Ops. Research, Fla. Inst. Tech., 1970; postgrad. Claremont Grad. Sch., 1970; m. Marilyn Rose Campbell, Sept. 21, 1952; children—Stephen Allen, William Clark, Peter Marshall. Indsl. engr. Aluminum Co. Am. Lafayette, Ind., 1954-56; electronic research engr. Autonetics Div. N.Am. Aviation, Downey, Calif., 1956-57; systems field engr. Remington Rand Univac, Fayetteville, N.C., 1957-59; project engr. RCA Service Co., Cheyenne, Wyo., 1959-60, project supr., Clear, Alaska, 1960-62, project supr., Yorkshire, Eng., 1962-64, re-entry signature analyst, Patrick AFB, Fla., 1964-66; mem. tech. staff TRW Systems Group, Washington, 1966-68; mgr. ops research systems analysis Magnavox Co., Urbana, Ill., 1968-69; tech. advisor, EDP, to USAF, Aerojet Electro Systems Co., Azusa, Calif., Woomera, Australia, 1969-72; investment exec. Shearson Hammill, Los Angeles, 1972-74; investment exec. Reynolds Securities, Los Angeles, 1974-75; v.p. investments Shearson Hayden Stone, Glendale, Calif., 1975-77; v.p. accounts Paine, Webber, Jackson & Curtis Inc., Los Angeles, 1977-82; pres. Argo Fin. Corp., Santa Monica, Calif., 1982-83, Fin. Packaging Corp., Flintridge, Calif., 1983—; fin. lectr. cruise ship Island Princess; tchr. investments Citrus Coll., Azusa, Calif., Claremont (Calif.) Evening Sch. Vice pres. Claremont Republican Club, 1973, pres., 1974. Chmn., Verdugo Hosp. Assos., 1979. Recipient Merit certificate RCA, 1966. Mem. Nat. Assn. Security Dealers, Internat. Assn. Fin. Planners, L.A. Philharmonic Bus. and Profl. Com., Navy League U.S., Naval Acad. Alumni Assn. Clubs: Masons (master 1987, pres. dist. officers assn., 32d degree), Shriner (Al Malaikin Temple), Kiwanis (pres. La Canada chpt. 1995-96), Marbella Golf & Country. Host, commentator, Sta. KWHY-TV, Los Angeles, (weekly) West of Wall Street, 1986-87; contbr. articles to bus. jours. Home: 5228 Escalante Dr La Canada Flintridge CA 91011-1326 Office: 2909 Community Ave La Crescenta CA 91214-3408

KOPEL, GERALD HENRY, retired state legislator; b. Balt., June 16, 1928; m. Dolores Blanke, June 16, 1952; children: David, Stephen (dec.). BA, U. Colo., 1952; LLB cum laude, U. Denver, 1958. Bar: Colo. 1958. Asst. atty. gen. State of Colo., 1959-61; mem. Colo. Ho. of Reps., 1965-67, 71-77, 1979-93; chmn. ho. jud. com., 1975-77, legal svc. com., 1976-77, statutory revision com., 1981-85, Gov.'s adv. com. on consumer credit, 1976-93, asst. minority leader, 1983-89; advisor, 1993-95; mem. Ho.-Senate Sunrise-Sunset Com., 1983-93; commr. uniform state laws, 1975-77; mem. health facilities rev. com., 1977-80; Legis. Columnist Colo. Statesman Newspaper, 1993—; commr. Denver election, 1995. With AUS, 1946-48. Recipient Civil Rights award Anti.-Def. League, 1991, Disting. Legislator award ACLU, 1992, Nat. Legislator award CLEAR, 1992, awards for columns Colo. Press Assn., 1993, 95. Democrat. Home: 1755 Glencoe St Denver CO 80220-1342 Office: 1535 Grant St Ste 280 Denver CO 80203-1843

KOPETSKI, MIKE, former congressman; b. Oreg., Oct. 27, 1949; 1 child, Matthew. BA, Am. U.; JD, Lewis & Clark Coll. Congl. aide Senate Watergate Com., Washington, 1973-74; del. Dem. Nat. Conv., 1976; adminstr. coms. Oreg. State Legis., 1977-79, 81, state rep., 1985-89; cons. labor, mgmt. and edn.; community organizer Oreg. Law Related Edn. Project, 1986; v.p. Currier-McCormick Communications, 1989-90; mem. 102nd-103rd Congresses from 5th Oreg. dist., Washington, D.C., 1991-94, Ways and Means Com., Washington, D.C.; pres. House of Reps. 1st term Dem. class, 1992; pvt. practice internat. trade cons., 1995—; v.p. Ho. Reps. 1st term Dem. Class, 1991. Address: 517 Colecroft Ct Alexandria VA 22314

KOPLIN, DONALD LEROY, health products executive, consumer advocate; b. Greenleaf, Kans., Dec. 31, 1932; s. Henry G. Koplin and Edith Mary Stevens; m. Patricia Joynes, June 2, 1962 (div. Aug. 1974); children: Marie Claire, Marie Joelle (adopted). Student, U. San Diego, 1956-59, 67-68. Electronics test insp. Gen. Dynamics, San Diego, 1956-59; cryptographer Dept. of State, Washington, 1959-67; communications program officer Dept. of State, France, Angola, Madagascar, Qatar, India, Oman, Benin and the Bahamas, 1977-86; tech. writer Ryan Aero. Corp., San Diego, 1967-68; comml. dir., tech. advisor, pub. rels. officer Societe AGM, San Francisco, Athens, Greece, Antananarivo and Morondava, Dem. Republic of Madagascar, 1968-72; founder, dir. Soc. Bells, Cyclone & Akai, Antananarivo, 1972-74; founder, ptnr., assoc. editor Angola Report, Luanda, 1974-75; polit. reporter Angola Report, Reuters, AP, UPI Corr., BBC, Luanda; supr. Tex. Instruments, Lubbock, 1976-77; exec. Dial A Contact Lens, Inc., La Jolla, Calif., 1986-90, Assn. for Retarded Citizens, San Diego, 1992-94, Club Med, Copper Mountain, Colo., 1992-94; CEO Vient Inc., 1994—, Koplin Kollection Fine Arts Gallery, La Jolla, Calif., 1996—. Active San Diego Zool. Soc. With USN, 1951-55, Korea. Mem. Am. Fgn. Svc. Assn. Republican. Roman Catholic. Home: 6718 Evergreen Ave Oakland CA 94611-1518 Office: Koplin Kollection Gallery 1298 Prospect St 2G La Jolla CA 92037

KOPP, CLAIRE JOAN BERNSTEIN, psychologist, educator; b. N.Y.C., July 8, 1931; d. Gerson Jerome and Martha Jane (Stavisky) Bernstein; m. Eugene Howard Kopp, Aug. 31, 1950; children: Carolyn, Michael, Paul. BS, NYU, 1951; MS, U. So. Calif., 1961; PhD, Claremont Grad. Sch., 1970. Cert. psychologist, Calif. Teaching staff UCLA, 1970-77, mem.

faculty, 1977-95; mem. faculty Claremont (Calif.) Grad. Sch., 1995—. Fellow APA (sec., treas. div. 7 1985-88, pres. 1993-94), Am. Occupational Therapy Assn.; mem. AAAS, Soc. Rsch. in Child Devel. (editor newsletter 1991—), Internat. Orgn. 99s (chmn. San Gabriel Valley chpt. 1985-86), Internat. Soc. for the Study of Behavioral Devel. (treas., membership sec. 1994-95). Office: Claremont Grad Sch Claremont CA 91711-3955

KOPP, DAVID EUGENE, manufacturing company executive; b. St. Louis, Apr. 21, 1951; s. Doyle Eugene and Irene Audrey (Gloyeske) K. BA in English, U. South Fla., 1975. Supr. Titleist Golf Co., Escondido, Calif., 1979-80; supr. Imed Corp., San Diego, 1980-82, process engr., 1982-83, sr. process engr., 1983-85; area mgr. Husky Injection Molding Systems Inc., Newport Beach, Calif., 1985-91; dir. sales Tech C.B.I. Inc., Scottsdale, Ariz., 1991-93; exec. v.p. Top-Seal Corp., Phoenix, 1993—. Mem. Soc. Plastic Engrs. (affiliate, bd. dirs., student liaison person Canoga Park, 1985-87). Republican. Roman Catholic. Home: 9980 N 106th St Scottsdale AZ 85258-9203 Office: Top-Seal Corp 2236 E University Dr Phoenix AZ 85034-6823

KOPP, HARRIET GREEN, communication specialist; b. N.Y.C., June 18, 1917; m. George A. Kopp, 1948 (dec. 1968); m. Kurt Friedrich, 1972 (dec. 1996). MA, Bklyn. Coll., 1939; diploma in edn. of deaf, Columbia U., 1939, PhD, 1962. Scientist Bell Telephone Labs., 1943-46; mem. faculty Eastern Mich. U., 1946-48; adj. prof. Wayne State U., Detroit, 1948-70; dir. communication clinics Rehab. Inst. Met. Detroit, 1955-59; dir. programs deaf and aphasic Detroit Bd. Edn., 1959-70; prof., chmn. communication disorders San Diego State U., 1970-80; acting dean Coll. Human Svcs., 1980-83; prof. emerita San Diego State U., 1983—; mem. Nat. Adv. Com. on Deaf, 1965-72, chmn., 1970-72; mem. Nat. Adv. Com. on Handicapped, 1972-73; adv., rev. panels Bur. Educationally Handicapped, HEW, 1963-83. Author: (with R. Potter, G.A. Kopp) Visible Speech, 1948, 68, Some Applications of Phonetic Principles, 1948, 65, 62, 68, 70, 78, 85, 86; editor: Curriculum, Cognition and Content, 1968, 75, Reading: Cognitive Input and Output, 49th Claremont Reading Conf. Yearbook, 1982, Bilingual Problems of the Hispanic Deaf, 1984. Chair quality of life bd. City of San Diego, 1978-92. Recipient Outstanding Faculty award San Diego State U., 1983. Fellow Am. Speech and Hearing Assn.; mem. AAAS, A.G. Bell Assn. (dir. 1964-68, chmn. edit. bd. 1966-75), Calif. Speech and Hearing Assn., Phi Kappa Phi. Address: 6711 Golfcrest Dr San Diego CA 92119-2427 *My career has been dedicated to scientific inquiry, clinical practice and the development of theoretical models underlying clinical and educational practice in order to prepare university graduates to assist infants, children and adults with communicative disorders. Research and publications have been focused on these areas as has the administration of hospital, research and public education programs.*

KOPPES, STEVEN NELSON, public information officer, science writer; b. Manhattan, Kans., Aug. 28, 1957; s. Ralph James and Mary Louise (Nelson) K.; m. Susan Camille Keaton, May 18, 1984. BS in Anthropology cum laude, Kans. State U., 1978; MS in Journalism, Kans. U., 1982. Rsch. asst. dept. anthropology Kans. State U., Manhattan, 1979; reporter The Morning Sun, Pittsburg, Kans., 1981-83; co-mgr. Doc's B.R. Others Restaurant, Tempe, Ariz., 1983-85; info. specialist Ariz. State U. New Bur., Tempe, 1985-87, asst. dir., 1987-96, interim dir., 1996—; cons. Ariz. Sci. Ctr., 1995-96. Contbr. to Ariz. State U. Rsch. Mag., 1984—; contbr. articles to various publs. Bd. dirs. Children's Mus. of Metro Phoenix, 1988. Recipient award of excellence Internat. Assn. Bus. Communicators, 1991-92, award of merit, 1989-93, Disting. Tech. Comm. award Soc. Tech. Comm. Phoenix Chpt., 1994-95. Mem. Nat. Assn. Sci. Writers, Ariz. Archaeol. Soc. (bd. dirs. Phoenix chpt. 1987-88), Rio Salado Rowing Club (charter mem. 1995—). Office: Ariz State U New Bur Tempe AZ 85287

KORAN, DENNIS HOWARD, publisher; b. L.A., May 21, 1947; s. Aaron Baer and Shirley Mildred (Kassan) K.; m. Roslynn Ruth Cohen, Apr. 6, 1979; 1 child, Michael; stepchildren: Jeff, Beth, Judy. Student, U. Leeds, Eng., 1966-67, UCLA, 1979-80; BA, U. Calif., Berkeley, 1980; postgrad., Loyola U., L.A., 1982-84, 86-89. Co-founder, co-editor Cloud Marauder Press, Berkeley, 1969-72, Panjandrum/Aris Books, San Francisco, 1973-81; founder, editor Panjandrum Books, San Francisco, 1971—, Panjandrum Press, Inc., San Francisco, 1971—; co-dir. poetry reading series Panjandrum Books, 1972-76. Author: (book of poetry) Vacancies, 1975, After All, 1993; editor Panjandrum Poetry Jour., 1971—; co-editor Cloud Marauder, 1969-72; author poetry pub. various jours. Liaison between U.S. Govt. and Seminole Indians VISTA, Sasakwa, Okla., 1969-70. Nat. Endowment for Arts Lit. Pub. grantee, 1974, 76, 79, 81, 82, 84, Coord. Coun. for Lit. Mags., 1971-80. Mem. Lovers of the Stinking Rose, Poets and Writers. Office: Panjandrum Books 6156 Wilkinson Ave North Hollywood CA 91606-4518

KORB, LAWRENCE JOHN, metallurgist; b. Warren, Pa., Apr. 28, 1930; s. Stanley Curtis and Dagna (Pedersen) K.; B.Chem.Engring., Rensselaer Poly. Inst., Troy, N.Y., 1952; m. Janet Davis, Mar. 30, 1957; children: James, William, Jeanine. Sales engr. Alcoa, Buffalo, 1955-59; metall. engr. N. Am. Rockwell Co., Downey, Calif., 1959-62; engring. supr. metallurgy Apollo program Rockwell Internat. Co., Downey, 1962-66, engring. supr. advanced materials, 1966-72, engring. supr. metals and ceramics space shuttle program, 1972-88; cons., 1988—; mem. tech. adv. com. metallurgy Cerritos Coll., 1969-74. Served with USNR, 1952-55. Registered profl. engr., Calif. Fellow Am. Soc. Metals (chmn. aerospace activity com. 1971-76, judge materials application competition 1969, handbook com. 1978-83, chmn. handbook com. 1983, chmn. publs. coun. 1984). Republican. Author articles, chpts. in books. Home: 251 S Violet Ln Orange CA 92869-3740

KORB, ROBERT WILLIAM, former materials and processes engineer; b. Warren, Pa., Mar. 12, 1929; s. Dallas Weigand and Evelyn Eleanor (Peterson) K.; m. Diane Marie Anderson, Oct. 14, 1964 (div. 1972); 1 child, Karen; m. Setsu Campbell, Aug. 9, 1980; children: Theresa Campbell, Mark Campbell, Laura Campbell. BS in Chemistry, U. Nev., 1951. Chemist Rezolin, Inc., Santa Monica, Calif., 1956-57; mem. tech. staff Hughes Aircraft Co., Culver City, Calif., 1957-64; mem. tech. staff Hughes Aircraft Co., Fullerton, Calif., 1971-74, group head materials engring., 1974-79, sect. head materials and processes engring., 1979-93; mem. tech. staff TRW Systems, Redondo Beach, Calif., 1964-71; ret., 1993. Contbr. articles to profl. jours.; patentee flexible cable process. 1st lt. USAF, 1951-56. Mem. Inst. for Interconnecting and Packaging Electronic Circuits (co. rep.), Soc. for Advancement Materials and Process Engring. Republican. Home: 12 Palmatum Irvine CA 92620-1862

KORELOV, NIKOLAI, artist; b. Kursk, USSR, Feb. 7, 1963; came to U.S., 1993; Red Diploma (with high honors), S. Samokish Coll., 1981; student, Kiev Acad. Art, Ukraine. Exhibited in group shows at St. Petersburg, Moscow, Kiev, Prague, Warsaw and Belgrade, internat. exhibit, Poland; pvt. collections include bus. and art galleries in Italy, Germany, Holland, France, U.S., and former Soviet Union. Studio: 1069 S Hayworth Ave Los Angeles CA 90035-2601

KORENEK, STEPHEN DUANE, state agency official; b. Smithville, Tex., Sept. 7, 1946; s. Clayton Edward and Doris June (Wansley) K.; m. Rebecca Ann Rogers, June 3, 1968; children: Meridith June, Stephanie Deanne, Elizabeth Marie, Andrea Kay. BA in Journalism, Tex. A&M U., 1968. Cmty. corrections officer State of Alaska, Fairbanks, 1975-82; cmty. corrections dist. supr. State of Alaska, Nome, 1982—; chmn. Alaska Cmty. Corrections Policy and Procedure Com., Anchorage, 1995—. Vol. instr. water safety ARC, 1985—; vol. instr. Am. Heart Assn., 1996—. With U.S. Army, 1968-75; BG Alaska Army N.G., 1976—. Decorated Bronze Star medal; named Fairbanks Peace Officer of the Yr., Alaska Peace Officers Assn., 1982. Mem. Soc. Profl. Journalists, Assn. U.S. Army, Am. Rifle Assn., Ducks Unltd. (dist. chmn. 1995—). Episcopalian. Home: 993 E 5th St Nome AK 99762

KORF, LEONARD LEE, theater arts educator; b. Chgo., Jan. 31, 1917; s. William Milton and Eva (Lewin) K.; m. Claire Jean Prinz, Aug. 15, 1949; children: William Milton II, Kerry Lee, Geoffrey Leonard. BA, UCLA, 1949; diploma, Harvard U., 1945; MA, UCLA, 1957, PhD, 1972; diploma, Harvard U. Lifetime tchg. credential, Calif. Prof. theatre arts, chmn. dept. Fullerton (Calif.) Coll., 1952-56, Cerritos (Calif.) Coll., 1956-82; CEO Korfco, Inc., Whittier, Calif., 1983—. Screen writer The AAF Comes of Age, 1945, The Lifemaker, 1956; exec. editor Ednl. Theatre News, 1956-93; book and theatre reviewer L.A. Times, 1972-73; rev. editor Calif. Ednl. Theatre Assn., L.A., 1993—; lead actor Space Chase. Maj. USAF, 1941-46. Decorated Disting. Flying Cross with two clusters USAF, 1943-44, Air medal with 5 clusters USAF, 1943-44. Fellow Am. Theatre Fellow Kennedy Ctr. (life); mem. Am. Theatre Assn. (bd. mem., pub. rels. dir. 1970-71), So. Calif. Ednl. Theatre Assn. (pres. 1975-76). Democrat. Agnostic. Home and Office: Korfco Inc 9811 Pounds Ave Whittier CA 90603-1616

KORGE, PAAVO, cell physiologist; b. Tartu, Estonia, Sept. 6, 1943; came to U.S., 1989; s. Kuno and Elsa (Ruus) K.; m. Sirje Kipper, Dec. 26, 1964; children: Indrek, Kristjan. PhD in Physiology, Tartu U., 1969, DSc in Physiology, 1974. From jr. scientist to assoc. prof. Tartu U., 1967-76, prof., 1978-89; asst. prof. Washington State U., Pullman, 1989-92, prof., 1992—; vis. scientist Copenhagen U., 1976-78; sci. bd. dirs. Tartu U., 1976-89; chmn. all union conf. on hormonal regulation phys. activity, 1973, 77, 82, 87. Author: Molecular Mechanism of Glucocorticoid Action, 1981, Hormons and Physical Fitness, 1983, Glucocorticoids in the Regulation of Heart Function and Metabolism, 1984; contbr. articles to profl. jours. Grantee USSR Sports Com., 1978-82, Inst. Aviation, Leningrad, USSR, 1983-88; USSR Ministry Higher Edn. scholar, 1976; recipient Young Scientist award Estonian Govt., 1978. Mem. N.Y. Acad. Scis. Home: S 1718 Ogden Dr Los Angeles CA 90019 Office: UCLA Sch Medicine Cardiovascular Rsch Labs MRL Bldg R3-645 675 Cir Dr So Los Angeles CA 90024-1760

KORIAT, RAPHAEL, manufacturing company executive; b. Meknes, Morocco, Mar. 18, 1947; came to U.S., 1979; s. Shlomo and Rivka (Adery) K.; m. Shimria Sobel, Aug. 11, 1971; children: Ravit, Dori, Sharon. BSME, Technion Inst. of Tech., Haifa, Israel, 1972; MSME, Drexel U., 1975; grad. exec. MBA program, Stanford U., Palo Alto, Calif., 1991. Chief engr. Kulso Ltd., Haifa, 1975-80; dir. bus. divsn. Kulicke & Soffa Ind., Willow Grove, Pa., 1985-88, dir. engring. and tech., 1989-90; corp. v.p. engring. tech. Kulicke & Soffa Ind., Willow Grove, 1990-92; gen. mgr. AG Assocs., Sunnyvale, Calif., 1992-94; pres. AGI Inc., San Jose, Calif., 1994—. Contbr. articles to profl. jours. Mem. Mech. Engring. Soc., AEA Orgn., Entrepreneur Com. Home: 74 Ester Rabin St, Haifa 34789, Israel Office: AGI Inc 4425 Fortran Dr San Jose CA 95134-2300

KORKUNIS, TONY WILLIAM, consumer products executive; b. L.A., Nov. 3, 1954; s. William Anthony and Christine (Raptis) K.; m. Deborah Maria Frederic, Oct. 24, 1984 (div. June 1990); 1 child, Amanda Christine; m. Kristin Kellogg Dutton, July 13, 1991; 1 child, Grace Kellogg. BS in Math., Harvey Mudd Coll., 1977; MA in Ops. Rsch., Claremont (Calif.) Grad. Sch., 1977; MBA, UCLA, 1989. Ops. rsch. analyst to retail mktg. specialist Products Co., Atlantic Richfield Co., L.A., 1977-80; economist Coun. on Wage and Price Stability, Office of the Pres., Washington, 1980; analyst Congrl. Budget Office, U.S. Congress, Washington, 1981-82; supr. sales forecasting to supr. ops. planning Mars, Inc., Kal Kan Foods, Inc., Vernon, Calif., 1982-85, mgr. bus. sys., 1985-87, mgr. customer svc., 1987-89, mgr. svc. and fin., 1989-91; cons. bus. strategy Toranago Technologies, Calsbad, Calif., 1991-92; mgr. sales planning Buena Vista Home Video, Burbank, Calif., 1992-93, dir. forecasting, space planning, 1993—; bd. dirs. Lodestone Pacific, Anaheim; cons. Young Pres. Orgn. of Orange County, Newport Beach, Calif., 1994. Office: Walt Disney Co Buena Vista Home Video 350 S Buena Vista St Burbank CA 91505-4807

KORMONDY, EDWARD JOHN, university official, biology educator; b. Beacon, N.Y., June 10, 1926; s. Anthony and Frances (Glover) K.; m. Peggy Virginia Hedrick, June 5, 1950 (div. 1989); children: Lynn Ellen, Eric Paul, Mark Hedrick. BA in Biology summa cum laude, Tusculum Coll., 1950; MS in Zoology, U. Mich., 1951, PhD in Zoology, 1955. Teaching fellow U. Mich., 1952-55; instr. zoology, curator insects Mus. Zoology, 1955-57; asst. prof. Oberlin (Ohio) Coll., 1957-63, assoc. prof., 1963-67, prof., 1967-69, acting assoc. dean, 1966-67; dir. Commn. Undergrad. Edn. in Biol. Scis., Washington, 1968-72; dir. Office Biol. Edn., Am. Inst. Biol. Scis., Washington, 1968-71; mem. faculty Evergreen State Coll., Olympia, Wash., 1971-79, interim acting dean, 1972-73, v.p., provost, 1973-78; sr. profl. assoc., directorate sci. edn. NSF, 1979; provost, prof. biology U. So. Maine, Portland, 1979-82; v.p. acad. affairs, prof. biology Calif. State U., Los Angeles, 1982-86; sr. v.p., chancellor, prof. biology U. Hawaii, Hilo/West Oahu, 1986-93; pres. U. West L.A., 1995—. Author: Concepts of Ecology, 1969, 76, 83, 96, General Biology: The Integrity and Natural History of Organisms, 1977, Handbook of Contemporary World Developments in Ecology, 1981, International Handbook of Pollution Control, 1989, ; (h.s. textbook) Biology, 1984, 88; contbr. articles to profl. jours. Served with USN, 1944-46. U. Ga. postdoctoral fellow radiation ecology, 1963-64; vis. research fellow Center for Bioethics, Georgetown U., 1978-79; research grantee Nat. Acad. Scis., Am. Philos. Soc., NSF, Sigma Xi. Fellow AAAS; mem. Ecol. Soc. Am. (sec. 1976-78), Nat. Assn. Biology Tchrs. (pres. 1981), Soc. Calif. Acad. Scis. (bd. dirs. 1985-86, 93-97, v.p. 1995-96), Sigma Xi, Phi Kappa Phi.

KORN, WALTER, writer; b. Prague, Czechoslovakia, May 22, 1908; came to U.S., 1950, naturalized, 1956; s. Bernard and Clara (Deutsch) K.; m. Herta Klemperer, Dec. 24, 1933. Dr.Comm., Charles U., Prague, 1938; postgrad. London Sch. Econs., 1949-50; cert. systems and procedures Wayne State U., 1957; cert. polit. sci. New Sch., N.Y.C., 1972-73. Dir. mktg. Kosmos Works, Prague, 1934-39; contract mgr. Cantie Switches, Chester, Eng., 1941-44; dir. UN Relief and Rehab. Adminstrn., U.S. Zone Occupation, Germany, 1945-47; country dir. Orgn. for Rehab. and Tng., Geneva, 1948-49; contract mgr. Royal Metal Mfg. Co., N.Y.C., 1951-55; bus. mgr. J. Cmty. Ctr., Detroit, 1956-59; dir. adminstrn. Am. Joint Distbn. Com., Tel Aviv, 1960-64; exec. asst. Self Help/United Help, N.Y.C., 1965-69; housing mgmt. cons. Exec. Dept. Divsn. Housing and Cmty. Renewal, State N.Y., N.Y.C., 1970-76; lectr. housing for aged and housing fin., 1958-74; lectr. Brit. Allied Council, Liverpool, Eng., 1942-44. Nat. field rep. United Jewish Appeal, 1968—; mem. Vols. for Internat. Tech. Assistance, 1968-71. Capt. Czechoslovakian Army, 1938. Mem. Acad. Polit. Sci., Acad. Polit and Social Sci., Am. Judicature Soc., Amnesty Internat., World Affairs Coun., Princeton Club of N.Y., Commonwealth Club of Calif., Press Club (San Francisco), Masons. Author: On Hobbies, 1936, Earn as You Learn, 1948, Learn As You Earn, 1949, The Brilliant Touch, 1950, Modern Chess Openings, 14th edit., 1997, America's Chess Heritage, 1978, American Chess Art, 1975, Moderne Schach Eroeffnungen I and II, 1968, 91, The Art of Chess Composition, 1995, 2d edit., 1996; contbr. essay on chess to Ency. Britannica, 1974. Home: 816 N Delaware St Apt 207 San Mateo CA 94401-1543

KORNBERG, ARTHUR, biochemist; b. N.Y.C., N.Y., Mar. 3, 1918; s. Joseph and Lena (Katz) K.; m. Sylvy R. Levy, Nov. 21, 1943 (dec. 1986); children: Roger, Thomas Bill, Kenneth Andrew; m. Charlene Walsh Levering, 1988 (dec. 1995). BS, CCNY, 1937, LLD (hon.), 1960; MD, U. Rochester, 1941, DSc (hon.), 1962; DSc (hon.), U. Pa., U. Notre Dame, 1965, Washington U., 1968, Princeton U., 1970, Colby Coll., 1970; LHD (hon.), Yeshiva U., 1963; MD honoris causa, U. Barcelona, Spain, 1970. Intern in medicine Strong Meml. Hosp., Rochester, N.Y., 1941-42; commd. officer USPHS, 1942, advanced through grades to med. dir., 1951; mem. staff NIH, Bethesda, Md., 1942-52, nutrition sect., div. physiology, 1942-45; chief sect. enzymes and metabolism Nat. Inst. Arthritis and Metabolic Diseases, 1947-52; guest research worker depts. chemistry and pharmacology coll. medicine NYU, 1946; dept. biol. chemistry med. sch. Washington U., 1947; dept. plant biochemistry U. Calif., 1951; prof., head dept. microbiology, med. sch. Washington U., St. Louis, 1953-59; prof. biochemistry Stanford U. Sch. Medicine, 1959—, chmn. dept., 1959-69, prof. emeritus dept. biochemistry, 1988—; Mem. sci. adv. bd. Mass. Gen. Hosp., 1964-67; bd. govs. Weizmann Inst., Israel. Author: For the Love of Enzymes, 1989; contbr. sci. articles to profl. jours. Served lt. (j.g.), med. officer USCGR, 1942. Recipient Paul-Lewis award in enzyme chemistry, 1951; co-recipient of Nobel prize in medicine, 1959; recipient Max Berg award prolonging human life, 1968, Sci. Achievement award AMA, 1968, Lucy Wortham James award James Ewing Soc., 1968, Borden award Am. Assn. Med. Colls., 1968, Nat. medal of sci., 1979. Gairdner Foundation International Awards, 1995. Mem. Am. Soc. Biol. Chemists (pres. 1965), Am. Chem. Soc., Harvey Soc., Am. Acad. Arts and Scis., Royal Soc., Nat. Acad. Scis. (mem. council 1963-66), Am. Philos. Soc., Phi Beta Kappa, Sigma Xi, Alpha Omega Alpha. Office: Stanford U Sch of Med Dept Biochemistry Beckman Ctr Rm B400 Stanford CA 94305-5307*

KORNELLY, IRENE LOUISE, state government affairs consultant; b. Chgo., Nov. 16, 1945; d. Raymond Mauritz and Hazel Marie (Whalen) Ring; m. Donald Elmer Kornelly, July 6, 1968 (div. Nov. 1987); 1 child, Sharon Irene. BA in Music History and Lit. cum laude, St. Olaf Coll., 1968; MM in Vocal Performance, Am. Conservatory of Music, Chgo., 1970; AB in Paralegal Sci., Southland U., Pasadena, Calif., 1983. Music assoc. First Presbyn. Ch., Colorado Springs, Colo., 1973-75; pvt. music instr. Colorado Springs, 1975-79; instr. music Geelong (Victoria, Australia) Coll., 1979-80; staff asst. U.S. Senator Gary Hart, 1981-85; coord. victim/witness program Office of Dist. Atty., 4th Jud. Dist., 1985-89; staff asst. U.S. Senator Timothy E. Wirth, 1989-93; cons. The Jefferson Group, Denver, 1993-94; dir. Office of Statewide Def. Initiatives, State of Colo., 1994—. Mem. State of Colo. Electoral Coll., 1992; mem. exec. com. Colo. Dem. Party, 1985-93, mem. rules com., 1995—; chair 5th Congl. Dem. Com., 1982-93; sec. El Paso County Dem. Com., 1977-79; mem. Colo. Capitol Adv. Com., 1993; pres. bd. Pikes Peak Community Action Agy.; mem. Exec. Clemency Adv. Bd. for State of Colo., 1987; mem. Citizens Goals Leadership 2000 Class, 1982; mem. Colo. Office of Space Advocacy; mem. Chem. Weapons Demilitarization Citizens Adv. Com., 1996—. Mem. AAUW, LWV, Common Cause, Nat. Women's Polit. Caucus, Colorado Springs World Affairs Coun.

KORNEY, ELLEN LEMER, interior designer; b. N.Y.C., Dec. 27, 1943; d. Gerald J. and Gladys (Rosenberg) Halbreich; m. Albert Lemer, Apr. 16, 1969 (div. Jan. 1982); 1 child, Alison Hope; m. Michael Stanley Korney, Dec. 25, 1988. BA, Hofstra U., 1965; cert., N.Y. Sch. Interior Design, 1970-71. Asst. Virginia F. Frankel Interiors, N.Y.C., 1971; pres. Ellen Terry Lemer Ltd., N.Y.C., 1971-89; owner Ellen Lemer Korney Assocs., L.A., 1989—; instr. UCLA Extension, 1989, Parsons Sch. of Design, N.Y.C., 1987; guest lectr. Marymount Manhattan, N.Y.C., 1986. Contbr. articles to: Showcase of Interior Design, 1992, 96, Very Small Spaces, 1988, Designing with Comfort, Interior Designer's Showcase of Color; contbr. articles to profl. jours. Mem. Bd. of Trade, Mus. of Modern Art N.Y.C., Mus. Contemporary Art L.A., Met. Mus., L.A. County Mus. Art, Armand Hammer Mus., Am. Soc. Interior Designers (profl. mem., treas. 1993-94, bd. dirs. L.A. 1990-93, N.Y.C. 1986-89, 1st place award design competition residential L.A., 1991, Presdl. Citation 1991). Republican. Office: Ellen Lemer Korney Assocs 10170 Culver Blvd Culver City CA 90232-3152

KORNFELD, JUDITH R., product marketing consultant; b. Oklahoma City, July 31, 1948; d. Samuel and Ida (Charetsky) K. BA in Linguistics, U. Chgo., 1969; PhD in Linguistics/Psychology, MIT, 1974. Sr. systems engr. SofTech, Inc., Waltham, Mass., 1978-81, Higher Order Software, Cambridge, Mass., 1978-81; mem. tech. staff AT&T Bell Labs., Short Hills, N.J., 1981-84; project mgr. ALPHATECH, Burlington, Mass., 1984-85; product mgr. Fed. Systems Group Mktg. Symbolics, Inc., Cambridge, 1985-87; product mgr. fed. sys. mktg. Sun Microsystems, Mountain View, Calif., 1987; ind. cons. in product mktg. Menlo Park, Calif., 1987—. Mem. ACM, Sigchi, Bay Area Human Factors Soc. Home and Office: 967 Menlo Ave Menlo Park CA 94025-4606

KORNFELD, PETER, internist; b. Vienna, Austria, Mar. 16, 1925; came to U.S., 1939; s. Otto and Rosa (Weitzmann) K. BA summa cum laude, U. Buffalo, 1948; MD, Columbia U., 1952. Diplomate Am. Bd. Internal Medicine. Intern Mt. Sinai Hosp., N.Y.C., 1952-53, asst. resident, then chief resident in internal medicine, 1955-56; postdoctoral fellow cardiovascular physiology, physician Nat. Heart Inst. at Columbia U./Presbyn. Hosp., N.Y.C., 1953-54; pvt. practice, N.Y., N.J., 1956-88; clin. prof. medicine, attending physician Stanford (Calif.) U. Hosp., 1991—; attending physician Mt. Sinai Hosp., N.Y.C., Hackensack (N.J.) Hosp.; mem. nat. med. adv. bd. Myasthenia Gravis Found., 1970-91; cons. physician N.Y. State Bur. Disability Determination, 1960-87; attending physician, dir. Myasthenia Gravis Clinic, Englewood Hosp., 1965-91; clin. prof. Mt. Sinai Sch. Medicine, CUNY, 1968-92. Contbr. numerous articles to med. jours. Grantee, NIH, 1966-70, Hoffman-LaRoche, Inc., 1966-73, Muscular Dystrophy Assn., 1978-81, 81-82, Rosenstiel Found., 1979-82; recipient Globus award, Mt. Sinai Jour. Medicine, 1976-77. Fellow ACP, ACA (assoc.), Am. Coll. Cardiology (assoc.), N.Y. Acad. Scis., N.Y. Acad. Medicine, Calif. Acad. Medicine; mem. AMA, Am. Fedn. Exptl. Biology, Am. Fedn. Clin. Rsch., Harvey Soc., Am. Diabetes Assn., Am. Heart Assn., Phi Beta Kappa, Alpha Omega Alpha, Sigma Xi.

KORSON, GERALD MICHAEL, newspaper editor; b. Riverside, Calif., Oct. 19, 1960; s. Paul Joseph and Maryann (Eisenbart) K.; m. Christina Cecilia Bohner, June 23, 1984; children: Michael Allan, Monica Mary, Catherine Ruth, Raymond Paul, Sophia Rose, Adrienne Marie, Mark Vincent. BA, U. San Diego, 1981; MA, St. Mary's Coll., Moraga, Calif., 1987. Prodn. mgr. So. Cross newspaper Cath. Diocese of San Diego, 1979-82; owner, operator Korson Pub. Co., Oakland, Calif., 1984-88; editor The Mont. Cath. newspaper, dir. comm. Cath. Diocese of Helena, Mont., 1988—. Mem. Fellowship of Cath. Scholars, Cath. Press Assn., Unda-U.S.A., Mont. Broadcasters Assn., Mont. Newspaper Assn. Republican. Roman Catholic. Office: Diocese of Helena PO Box 1729 Helena MT 59624

KORSTEN, MARY ANN, subcontract administrator, buyer; b. Oxnard, Calif., May 9, 1957; d. John Jacob and Lorene Mary (Moyer) K. BS in Bus. Mgmt., U. LaVerne, 1985; MBA in Mgmt., Golden Gate U., 1988. Salesperson Sears, Roebuck & Co., Santa Maria, Calif., 1976-79; casher, credit adminstr. Montgomery Wards, Santa Maria, 1979-81; adminstr., clk. ITT Fed. Svcs. Corp., Vandenberg AFB, Calif., 1981-86, subcontract adminstr., buyer, 1986-93; procurement and contract adminstr. ITT Fed. Svcs. Corp., Colorado Springs, Colo., 1993—. Mem. NAFE, Am. Legion Aux (pres. 1982-83), Nat. Contract Mgmt. Assn. Roman Catholic. Office: ITT Fed Svcs Corp 1330 Inverness Dr Colorado Springs CO 80910

KORY, MICHAEL A., 3D computer animator; b. L.A., May 8, 1959; s. Irving L. and Shirley (Kahan) K. Student, U. Calif., San Diego, 1976-79; BA, UCLA, 1983. Tech. dir. Digital Prodns., L.A., 1983-84, Omnibus, L.A., 1984-87; creative tech. dir. Homer & Assocs., L.A., 1987-94, Wunder Film Design, L.A., 1994-96, Cine Site, L.A., 1996—; instr. Am. Film Inst., L.A., 1997. Dir., designer animated short: Why Do You Think They Call Him Dope, 1990 (1st Pl. Montreal Animation Film Festival, 1st Pl. Truevision Competition). Recipient Emmy award, 1996, 4 Emmy award nominations, 1996. Mem. L.A. SIGGRAPH. Address: 2055 Gramercy Pl Los Angeles CA 90068-3616

KORZEC, PATRICIA ANN, museum administrator; b. Ware, Mass., Sept. 9, 1953; d. Edward and Bertha (Broton) Sablak. BA, Anna Maria Coll., Paxton, Mass., 1975. Cert. museum programmer. Dir. gallery Xanadu Gallery Folk Art Internat., San Francisco, 1990-92; dir. Bowers Kidseum, Santa Ana, Calif., 1992-96; docent MH De Young Mus., San Francisco, 1988-93; storyteller. Author (short story) The Magic Moment, 1995. Bd. dirs., adv. Bowers Singles for the Arts, 1995—. Recipient Earthwatch Folk Art Bali award Arensberg Found., 1995. Mem. Bead Soc. Orange County (founding com.), Collector's Coun. Democrat. Roman Catholic. Home: 1555 Mesa Verde Dr E Apt 57 K Costa Mesa CA 92626-5235

KOSHALEK, RICHARD, museum director, consultant; b. Wausau, Wis., Sept. 20, 1941; s. H. Martin and Ethel A. (Hochtritt) K.; m. Elizabeth J. Briar, July 1, 1967; 1 child, Anne Elizabeth. Student, U. Wis., 1960-61, MA, 1965-67; BA, U. Minn., 1965. Curator Walker Art Ctr., Mpls., 1967-72; asst. dir. NEA, Washington, 1972-74; dir. Ft. Worth Art Mus., 1974-76, Hudson River Mus., Westchester, N.Y., 1976-80, Mus. Contemporary Art, L.A., 1980—; mem. Pres.' Coun. on Arts, Yale U., New Haven, Conn., 1989-94; mem. internat. bd. Biennale di Venezia, Italy, 1992-93; mem. internat. adv. bd. Wexner Ctr., Ohio State U., Columbus, 1990—; mem. com. of assesors The Tate Gallery of Art, London; mem. internat. jury Philip Morris Art award, 1996; commr. Kwangju Biennale, 1997; mem. screening com. Osaka Triennale, 1997; cons. in field. Co-curator (exhibitions and books) Panza Collection, 1986, Ad Reinhardt, 1991, Arata Isozaki, 1991, Louis I. Kahn, 1992, Robert Irwin, 1993. Mem. Chase Manhattan Bank Art Com., N.Y.C., 1986—; chmn. architect selection Walt Disney Concert Hall, L.A., 1988-90; mem. adv. Neighborhood Revitalization Bd. for Pres. Clinton, Little Rock, Ark., 1993; bd. dirs. Am. Ctr. in Paris, 1993—. Recipient Parkinson Spirit of Urbanism award U. So. Calif. Archtl. Guild, 1996; NEA fellow, 1972, Durfee Found. fellow, 1992, Design fellow IBM, 1984. Mem.

Am. Assn. Mus. Dirs. Office: Mus Contemporary Art Calif Plz 250 S Grand Ave Los Angeles CA 90012

KOSHLAND, CATHERINE PRESTON, mechanical engineer, educator; b. Phila., May 11, 1950; d. Edmond III and Elizabeth Miriam (Johnston) Preston; m. James Marcus Koshland, May 17, 1975; children: Sarah, Margrethe, Jacob. Student, Smith Coll., Northampton, Mass., 1968-70; BA in Fine Arts, Haverford (Pa.) Coll., 1972; MS in Mech. Engring., Stanford U., Palo Alto, Calif., 1978, PhD in Mech. Engring., 1985. Asst. prof. U. Calif., Berkeley, 1985—, assoc. prof., 1992—, Wood-Calvert chair in Engring., 1995—; mem. Bay Area Air Quality Mgmt. Dist. Adv. Coun., San Francisco, 1988-94, chair, 1991-92; bd. mgrs. Haverford (Pa.) Coll., 1994—. Co-editor: Incineration of Hazardous Waste 1 and 2, 1992, 94; contbr. over 40 articles to profl. jours. Recipient base rsch. award Nat. Inst. Environ. Health Sci., 1988—. Mem. Combustion Inst. (dir. 1994—, sec. 1996—, mem. exec. bd. Western states sect. 1988—), Am. Chem. Soc. Office: U Calif 140 Warren Hall Berkeley CA 94720-7361

KOSICH, DOROTHY YVONNE, editor, general manager, journalist; b. Reno, Nev., Nov. 25, 1953; d. Radoslav and Bosilka Rose (Ragonovich) K. BA in Journalism, U. Nev., Reno, 1974, MA in Journalism, 1981, MPA in Pub. Policy, 1991. Reporter, producer KTVNTV News, Reno, Nev., 1974-77; pub. involvement coord. Dept Regional Planning, Reno, 1977-79; reporter Nev. Appeal, Carson City, 1979-86, Donrey Capital Bur., Carson City, 1986-88; asst. exec. dir. Nev. Mining Assn., Reno, 1988-89; mng. editor Mining World News, Reno, editor, 1993-96; editor, gen. mgr. N.Am. Mining, Reno, 1997—; adj. prof. U. Nev., 1984-88. Lector Our Lady of Wisdom Cath. Ch., Reno; past pres. Nev. chpt. Soc. Profl. Journalists, dep. regional dir. Nat. Soc., 1985. Mem. Soc. Am. Bus. Editors and Writers, Pi Sigma Alpha. Office: N Am Mining 100 W Grove St Ste 240 Reno NV 89509-4027

KOSKI, CHARLENE WEBER, social worker; b. Phila., Mar. 2, 1943; d. Walter Gotlieb and Dorothy (Peart) W.; m. Billy Mack Carroll, Oct. 3, 1959 (div. Sept. 1974); children: Dorothy Patricia, Robert Walter, Lydia Baker, Billy Bob, Elizabeth Louise; m. John Edward Thomaston, Sept. 26, 1974 (div. July 1986); m. Stan Koski, Dec. 31, 1994. BSW with honors, Coll. Santa Fe, 1983; MSW, N.Mex. Highlands U., 1988. Client service agt. I Social Svcs. div. Dept. Human Svcs., Albuquerque, 1975-78, client service agt. IV, 1978-83; social worker II Social Svcs. div. Dept. Human Svcs., Bernalillo, N.Mex., 1983, social worker III, 1983—. Mem. Nat. Assn. Social Workers, N.Mex. Council on Crime and Deliquency, Albuquerque Retarded Assn., Child Welfare League. Democrat. Home: 72 Umber Ct NE Albuquerque NM 87124-2454 Office: New Mexico Dept Human Svcs Div Social Svcs PO Box 820 Bernalillo NM 87004-0820

KOSKI, DONNA FAITH, poet; b. Wildwood, N.J., Aug. 18, 1935; d. Sebastian and Mildred (Shastany) Rossitto; m. Paul A. Koski, May 5, 1968 (div. June 1982); children: Danita Joy, Darla Jean, Deanna Rene, Deena Marie, Charles Ray. Student, San Diego Jr. Coll., 1955-58, Mesa Jr. Coll, San Diego, 1993. With Pacific Telephone, San Diego, 1954-68; credit clk. Norwich (Conn.) Gas & Lights, 1968-70; clk. Navy Exch., New London, Conn., 1969-70; front desk clk. Del Webb's, San Diego, 1971-72; payroll clk. U.S.I.U., San Diego, 1974-76; facility mgr. Price Costco, San Diego, 1978-94, Price Enterprises, Inc., San Diego, 1994—. Author poetry: The Power of Love, 1995, Nights in Sedona, 1995, Faces in the Clouds, 1994. Vol. Nat. Multiple Sclerosis Soc., San Diego, 1995, React-Telecom. Emergency, San Diego, 1985-93, Perot Hdqrs., San Diego, 1992, 96, Social Svcs., San Diego, 1980-82. Recipient Editor's Choice award Nat. Libr. of Poetry, 1995, Accomplishment of Merit, Creative Arts and Sci., 1994. Mem. Internat. Soc. Poets, Internat. Soc. Authors and Artists, Nat. Autor's registry, Being Fit Health Club, Moose Lodge. Unity Ch. Home: 5025 Park Rim Dr San Diego CA 92117 Office: Price Enterprises Inc 4649 Morena Blvd San Diego CA 92117

KOST, GERALD JOSEPH, physician, scientist; b. Sacramento, July 12, 1945; s. Edward William and Ora Imogene K.; m. Angela Louise Baldo, Sept. 9, 1972; children: Christopher Murray, Laurie Elizabeth. BS in Engring., Stanford U., 1967, MS in Engring.-Econ. Systems, 1968; PhD in Bioengring., U. Calif., San Diego, 1977; MD, U. Calif., San Francisco, 1978. Diplomate Nat. Bd. Med. Examiners, Am. Bd. Pathology. Resident dept. medicine UCLA, 1978-79, resident dept. neurology, 1979-80; resident dept. lab. medicine U. Wash., Seattle, 1980-81, chief resident dept. lab. medicine, 1981-82, cardiopulmonary-bioengring. and clin. chemistry researcher, 1982-83; asst. prof. pathology U. Calif., Davis, 1983-87, assoc. prof., 1987-93, prof., dir. clin. chemistry, faculty biomed. engring., 1993—; vis. prof. and Lilly scholar, 1990; numerous sci. cons., nat. and internat. speaker, invited lectr. Author: Handbook of Clinical Automation Robotics and Optimization, 1996; contbr. numerous articles to profl. and sci. jours.; editor, author various monographs, video and audio prodns. Recipient awards, honors and rsch. grants including Bank Am. Fine Arts award, 1963, Millberry Art award, 1970, Nat. Rsch. Svc. award Nat. Heart, Lung and Blood Inst., 1972-77, Young Investigator award Acad. Clin. Lab. Physicians and Scientists, 1982, 83, Nuclear Magnetic Resonance award U. Calif., Davis, 1984-88; S.A. Pepper Collegiate scholar, 1963; fellow Stanford U., 1967-68, Internat. scholar MOP, Venezuela, 1967, NIH, 1970, Highest Honor Calif. Scholarship Fedn.; grantee Am. Heart Assn., U. Calif., Davis, Lawrence Livermore Nat. Lab., others. Mem. Sigma Xi, Phi Kappa Phi, Mu Alpha Theta.

KOSTOULAS, IOANNIS GEORGIOU, physicist; b. Petra, Pierias, Greece, Sept. 12, 1936; came to U.S., 1965, naturalized, 1984; s. Georgios Ioannou and Panagiota (Zarogiannis) K.; m. Katina Sioras Kay, June 23, 1979; 1 child, Alexandra. Diploma in Physics U. Thessoloniki, Greece, 1963; MA, U. Rochester, 1969, PhD, 1972; MS, U. Ala., 1977, Instr. U. Thessaloniki, 1963-65; teaching asst. U. Ala., 1966-67, U. Rochester, 1967-68; guest jr. research assoc. Brookhaven Nat. Lab., Upton, N.Y., 1968-72; research physicist, lectr. UCLA, U. Calif.-San Diego, 1972-76; sr. research assoc. Mich. State U., East Lansing, 1976-78, Fermi Nat. Accelerator Lab., Betavia, Ill., 1976-78; research staff mem. MIT, Cambridge, 1978-80; sr. system engr., physicist Hughes Aircraft Co., El Segundo, Calif., 1980-86; sr. physicist electro-optics and space sensors Rockwell Internat. Corp., Downey, Calif., 1986—. Contbr. articles to profl. jours. Served with Greek Army, 1961-63. Research grantee U. Rochester, 1968-72. Mem. Am. Phys. Soc., Los Alamos Sci. Lab. Exptl. Users Group, Fermi Nat. Accelerator Lab. Users Group, High Energy Discussion Group of Brookhaven Nat. Lab., Pan Macedonian Assn., Save Cyprus Council Los Angeles, Sigma Pi Sigma. Club: Hellenic U. Lodge: Ahepa. Home: 2404 Marshallfield Ln # B Redondo Beach CA 90278-4406 Office: Rockwell Internat Co MC FD27 Space System Div 12214 Lakewood Blvd Downey CA 90242-2655

KOSTRIKIN, MARYBETH ELAINE, excavating company executive; b. Clarkston, Wash., Nov. 22, 1954; d. William Bruce and Rachel Ann (Osborn) Hodgson; m. David Kostrikin, Jan. 6, 1983; children: Troy James Pierson, Rachel Anne. Student, U. Idaho, 1972-75, Clackamas C.C., Oregon City, Oreg., 1976, 77. Meter reader, energy specialist Canby (Oreg.) Utility Bd., 1978-84; sec. Kostco Landscape Mgmt., Canby, 1983-91; v.p. KLM Excavating, Inc., Canby, 1991—. Mem. Nat. Fedn. Ind. Bus. Republican. Baptist.

KOTANSKY, ROY D., ancient languages, religion and culture educator; b. Montreal, Que., Can., Feb. 3, 1953; s. Daniel Joseph Kotansky and Jo-Anne (Dexter) Kells; m. Jeanne Marie Miller, Feb. 8, 1992. BA with honors, Westmont Coll., 1975; MA, Fuller Theol. Sem., 1977; PhD, U. Chgo., 1988. Samuel Sandmel Rsch. fellow in Hellenistic Judaism U. Chgo., 1980-81, rsch. specialist Corpus Hellenisticum Project, 1981-83; rsch. fellowship Alexander von Humboldt-Stiftung U. Cologne, Germany, 1990-91, 92-93. Author, editor: A Lex Sacra from Selinous, 1993, Greek Magical Amulets, 1994; consulting editor Greek Magical Papyri in Translation, 1981-83; contbr. articles to profl. jours. Recipient Noyes-Cutter Greek prize U. Chgo., 1980; fellow in antiquities, J. Paul Getty Mus., 1983-84. Mem. Am. Soc. Papyrologists, Nat. Assn. Profs. of Hebrew, Inst. Biblical Rsch., Soc. Biblical Lit. Home: 902 Idaho Ave Santa Monica CA 90403-2904

KOTLER, RICHARD LEE, lawyer; b. L.A., Apr. 13, 1952; s. Allen S. Kotler and Marcella (Fromberg) Swartz; m. Cindy Jasik, Dec. 9, 1990; children: Kelsey Elizabeth, Charles Max. BA, Sonoma State Coll., 1976; JD, Southwestern U., 1979. Bar: Calif. 1980, U.S. Dist. Ct. (cen. dist.) Cal. 1980; cert. family law specialist. Sole practice Newhall, Calif., 1980-83, 88—; sr. ptnr. Kotler & Hann, Newhall, 1983-88; pvt. practice Law Offices of Richard L. Kotler, Newhall, 1984-86; judge pro temp Municipal Ct., 1981-84, Superior Ct., 1985—. Chmn. Santa Clarita Valley Battered Women's Assn., Newhall, 1983-87; bd. dirs. Santa Clarita Valley Hotline, Newhall, 1981-83. Recipient Commendation award L.A. County, 1983; named SCV Paintball champion. Mem. Santa Clarita Valley Bar Assn. (v.p. 1985—), Los Angeles Astronomy Soc., Newhall Astronomy Club. Office: 23942 Lyons Ave Ste 202 Santa Clarita CA 91321-2444

KOTTKAMP, JOHN HARLAN, lawyer; b. Portland, Oreg., Oct. 19, 1930; s. John Henry and Anna Margaret (Schnell) K.; m. Elizabeth Ann Lawrence, July 10, 1954; children: Elizabeth, Andrew, Molly, Jennifer, Carrie. B.S., U. Oreg., 1952, LL.B., 1957. Bar: Oreg. 1957, U.S. Dist. Ct. Oreg. 1957, U.S. Supreme Ct. 1971. Assoc. Kilkenny & Fabre, Pendleton, Oreg., 1957-59, Fabre, Collins & Kottkamp, Pendleton, 1959-61; pvt. practice, Pendleton, 1961-64; ptnr. Kottkamp & O'Rourke, Pendleton, Oreg., 1964—. Served with U.S. Army, 1952-54. Fellow Am. Bar Found., Am. Coll. Trial Lawyers. Republican. Club: Pendleton Country. Lodge: Elks. Office: Kottkamp & O'Rourke LLP 331 SE 2nd St Pendleton OR 97801-2224

KOTTLER, DENNIS BRUCE, physician; b. Newark, N.J., May 19, 1949; married; 2 children. BA cum laude, Yale U., 1971; MD, Cornell U., 1975. Diplomate Am. Bd. Psychiatry and Neurology. Intern Med. Coll. Pa., Phila., 1976-77; resident N.Y. Hosp., N.Y.C., 1976-79; pvt. practice Westlake Village, Calif., 1979—; instr. Yale U., 1969; asst. dir. Payne Whitney Clinic, N.Y.C., 1979; assoc. med. dir. Pacific Shores Hosp., Oxnard, Calif., 1989-90; clin. dir. adult inpatient svcs. Woodview Calabasas (Calif.) Hosp., 1990—, med. dir., 1992—. Editor jour. Yale Daily News, 1970; contbr. articles to profl. jours. Mem. Am. Psychiatric Assn., So. Calif. Psychiatric Assn., L.A. County Med. Assn. Home: 31822 Village Center Rd Ste 203 Westlake Village CA 91361-4316

KOTTLOWSKI, FRANK EDWARD, geologist; b. Indpls., Apr. 11, 1921; s. Frank Charles and Adella (Markworth) K.; m. Florence Jean Chriscoe, Sept. 15, 1945; children: Karen, Janet, Diane. Student, Butler U., 1939-42; AB, Ind. U., 1947, MA, 1949, PhD, 1951. Party chief Ind. Geology Survey, Bloomington, summers 1948-50; fellow Ind. U., 1947-51, instr. geology, 1950; adj. prof. N.Mex. Inst. Mining and Tech., Socorro, 1970—; econ. geologist N.Mex. Bur. Mines and Mineral Resources, 1951-66, asst. dir., 1966-68, 70-74, acting dir., 1968-70, dir., 1974-91, state geologist, 1989—, dir. emeritus, 1991—; geologic cons. Sandia Corp., 1966-72. Contbr. articles on mineral resources, stratigraphy and areal geology to tech. jours. Mem. Planning Commn. Socorro, 1960-68, 71-78, chmn., 86-90; mem. N.Mex. Energy Resources Bd.; chmn. N.Mex. Coal Surface Mining Commn.; sec. Socorro County Democratic Party, 1964-68. Served to 1st lt. USAAF, 1942-45. Decorated D.F.C., Air medal; recipient Richard Owen Disting. Alumni award in Govt. and Industry, U. Ind., 1987. Fellow AAAS, Geol. Soc. Am. (councilor 1979-82, mem. exec. com. 1981-82, Disting. Svc. award coal geology divsn., Cady Coal Geology award 1996); mem. AIME, Am. Assn. Petroleum Geologists (hon.; dist. rep. 1965-68, editor 1971-75, pres. energy minerals divsn. 1987-88, Disting. Svc. award), Assn. Am. State Geologists (pres. 1985-86), Soc. Econ. Geologists, Am. Inst. Profl. Geologists (Pub. Svc. award 1986), Am. Commn. Statigraphic Nomenclature (past sec., chmn.), Cosmos Club, Rotary Internat. (Paul Harris fellow), Sigma Xi. Home: 703 Sunset St Socorro NM 87801-4657 Office: NMex Bur Mines NMex Tech 801 Leroy Pl Socorro NM 87801-4796

KOUNALAKIS, MARKOS, foreign correspondent; b. San Francisco, Dec. 1, 1956; s. Antonios Markos and Vasiliki (Rozakis) K. BA in Polit. Sci. with honors, U. Calif., Berkeley, 1978; student, U. Stockholm, 1980; MS in Journalism, Columbia U., 1988; cert., U. So. Calif., 1996. Reporter, anchor Radio Sweden Internat., Stockholm, 1980-82; producer Spotlight on World Affairs, San Francisco, 1982-84; founder, ptnr. Earwax Prodns., San Francisco, 1984—; journalism fellow Robert Bosch Found., Germany, 1988-89; East European reporter Newsweek Mag., 1989-91; Moscow corr. NBC-Mut. News Network, Russia, 1991-92; creative dir. Visible Interactive Corp., San Francisco, 1994-95; sr. comm. cons. Silicon Graphics, 1997. Author: (book) Defying Gravity: The Making of Newton, 1993 (Gold award 1994). Fellow Ctr. for Internat. Journalism U. So. Calif. and El Colegio de Mex., L.A. and Mexico City, 1995-96.

KOURLIS, REBECCA LOVE, judge; b. Colorado Springs, Colo., Nov. 11, 1952; d. John Arthur and Ann (Daniels) Love; m. Thomas Aristithis Kourlis, Aug. 19, 1978; children: Stacy Ann, Katherine Love. BA with distinction in English, Stanford U., 1973, JD, 1976. Bar: Colo. 1976, D.C. 1979, U.S. Dist. Ct. Colo. 1976, U.S. Ct. Appeals (10th cir.) 1976, Colo. Supreme Ct., U.S. Ct. Appeals (D.C. cir.), U.S. Claims Ct., U.S. Supreme Ct. Assoc. Davis, Graham & Stubbs, Denver, 1976-78; sole practice, Craig, Colo., 1978-87; assoc. Gibson, Dunn & Crutcher, Denver, part time 1981-87; judge 14th Jud. Dist. Ct., 1987-94; arbiter Jud. Arbiter Group, Inc., 1994-95; justice Colo. Supreme Ct., 1995—; water judge Divsn. 6, 1987-94; lectr. to profl. groups. Contbr. articles to profl. jours. Chmn. Moffat County Arts and Humanities, Craig, 1979; mem. Colo. Commn. on Higher Edn., Denver, 1980-81; mem. adv. bd. Colo. Divsn. Youth Svcs., 1988-91; mem. com. adminstrv. restructure Colo. Supreme Ct., 1992, mem. com. civil jury instructions, 1990-95, standing com. gender & justice, 1994—; mem. state ct. adminstr. selection com., 1992; mem. long range planning com. Moffat County Sch., 1990; bd. visitors Stanford U., 1989-94; mem. Colo. Commn. Higher Edn., 1980-81. Fellow Am. Bar Found., Colo. Bar Found.; mem. Rocky Mountain Mineral Found., Colo. Bar Assn. (bd. govs. 1983-85, mineral law sect. bd. dirs. 1985, sr. v.p. 1987-88), Dist. Ct. Judges' Assn. (pres. 1993-94), N.W. Colo. Bar Assn. (Cmty. Svc. award 1993-94), Denver Bar Assn. Republican. Greek Orthodox. Office: State Jud Bldg 2 E 14th Ave Rm 415 Denver CO 80203-2115

KOUYMJIAN, DICKRAN, art historian, Orientalist, educator; b. Tulcea, Romania, June 6, 1934; came to U.S. (parents Am. citizens), 1939; s. Toros S. and Zabelle I. (Calusdian) K.; m. Angèle Kapoïan, Sept. 16, 1967. BS in European Cultural History, U. Wis., 1957; MA in Arab Studies, Am. U., Beirut, 1961; PhD in Near East Lang. and Culture, Columbia U., 1969. Instr. English Columbia U., N.Y.C., 1961-64; dir. Am. Authors, Inc., N.Y.C., 1965-67; asst. prof. and asst. dir. Ctr. for Arabic Studies Am. U., Cairo, 1967-71; assoc. prof. history Am. U. Beirut, 1971-75; prof. art history Am. U., Paris, 1976-77; prof. history and art, dir. Armenian Studies program Calif. State U., Fresno, 1977—; dir. Sarkis and Meline Kalfayan Ctr. for Armenian Studies, Calif. State U., Fresno, 1990—; Fulbright disting. lectr., prof. Armenian and Am. Lit., Yerevan (Armenia, USSR), 1987; cons. archaeology UNESCO, Paris, 1976; prof., chairholder Armenian Sect., Inst. Nat. des Langs. et Civilisations Orientales, U. Paris, 1988-91; 1st incumbent Haig & Isabel Berberian endowed chair Armenian Studies Calif. State U., Fresno, 1989—, 2nd incumbent William Saroyan endowed chair of Armenian studies U. Calif., Berkeley, 1996-97. Author: Index of Armenian Art, part I, 1977, part II, 1979, The Armenian History of Ghazar P'arpetzi, 1986, Arts of Armenia, 1992; co-author: (with A. Kapoïan) The Splendor of Egypt, 1975; author and editor: William Saroyan: An Armenian Trilogy, 1986, William Saroyan: Warsaw Visitor and Tales of the Vienna Streets, 1990; editor: (books) Near Eastern Numistatics, Iconography, Epigraphy and History, 1974, Essays in Armenian Numismatics in Honor of C. Sibilian, 1981, Armenian Studies: In Memoriam Haïg Berbèrian, 1986; editl. bd. Armenian Rev., 1974—, Ararat Lit. mag., 1975—, Revue des Etudes Arménniennes, 1978—, NAASR Jour. Armenian Studies, Jour. of the Soc. for Armenian Studies, 1995—; contbr. articles to profl. jours. Served with U.S. Army, 1957. Recipient St. Sahaq and St. Mesrob medal His Holiness Karekin I, Catholics of All Armenians, 1996, Outstanding Prof. award Am. U., Cairo, 1968-69, 69-70, Outstanding Prof. of Yr. award Calif. State U., 1985-86, Hagop Kevorkian Disting. Lectureship in Near Eastern Art and Civilization, NYU, 1979; Fulbright fellow, USSR, 1986-87; grantee NEH, Paris, 1980-81, 95, Bertha & John Garabedian Charitable Found., 1994-96. Mem. Am. Oriental Soc., Am. Numismatic Soc., Mid. East Studies Assn. (charter), Coll. Arts Assn., Soc. Armenian Studies (charter, pres. 1985-86, 92-94), Société asiatique (Paris), Medieval Acad. Internat. Assn. of Armenian Studies, Mid. East Medievalist. Home: 30 rue Chevert, 75007 Paris France Office: Calif State U Armenian Studies Program Fresno CA 93740-0004

KOVACH, THOMAS ALLEN, educator; b. Providence, Oct. 22, 1949; s. George Paul and Madeline Elizabeth (Besnyö) K.; divorced; children: Leah Beth; 1 step-child, Sarah Shanti Stein. BA in German magna cum laude, Columbia U., 1971; PhD in Comparative Lit., Princeton (N.J.) U., 1978. Asst. prof. Dept. Langs. U. Utah, Salt Lake City, 1978-85; assoc. prof. Dept. Langs. and Lit., U. Utah, Salt Lake City, 1985-90; assoc. prof., dept. chair Dept. German and Russian, U. Ala., Tuscaloosa, 1990-94; assoc. prof., dept. head German studies U. Ariz., Tucson, 1994—. Author: Hofmannsthal and Symbolism, 1985; contbr. articles to profl. jours. Recipient Deutscher Verein Prize Columbia U., 1971; Fulbright-Hays Grad. fellowship, 1974-75; Fulbright-Hays faculty grant, 1983. Mem. MLA, AATG, German Studies Assn., Am. Comparative Lit. Assn., Phi Beta Kappa. Jewish. Home: 701 N Palo Verde Blvd Tucson AZ 85716-4615 Office: U Ariz Dept German Studies 571 Modern Langs Bldg Tucson AZ 85721

KOVACHY, EDWARD MIKLOS, JR., psychiatrist; b. Cleve., Dec. 3, 1946; s. Edward Miklos and Evelyn Amelia (Palenscar) K.; m. Susan Eileen Light, June 21, 1981; children: Timothy Light, Benjamin Light. BA, Harvard U., 1968, JD, 1972, MBA, 1972; MD, Case Western Reserve U., 1977. Diplomate Nat. Bd. Med. Examiners. Resident in psychiatry Stanford U. Med. Ctr., Stanford, Calif., 1977-81; pvt. practice psychiatry mediator mgmt. cons. Menlo Park, Calif., 1981—; mediator, mgmt. cons. Columnist The Peninsula Times Tribune, 1983-85. Bd. trustees Mid Peninsula H.S., Palo Alto, Calif., 1990—; mem. gift com. Harvard Coll. Class of 1968, 25th reunion chmn. participation, San Francisco, 1993. Mem. Am. Psychiat. Assn., Physicians for Social Responsibility, Assn. Family and Conciliation Cts., No. Calif. Psychiat. Soc., San Francisco Acad. Hypnosis. Presbyterian. Office: 1187 University Dr Menlo Park CA 94025-4423

KOVARIK, JOSEPH LEWIS, surgeon; b. Omaha, Sept. 16, 1927; m. Delores Marie Casey, June 20, 1953; children: Jane Ann, Joseph Edward, Patricia Marie, James John, Karen Rose, Kenneth Michael. Student, Creighton U., 1944, Ctrl. Mo. State U., Warrensburg, 1945, Brown U., 1945-46; MD, U. Nebr., 1950. Diplomate Am. Bd. Surgery, Am. Bd. Thoracic Surgery; lic. physician Nebr., Ill., Colo. Intern U. Ill. Rsch. and Ednl. Hosps., Chgo., 1950-51; resident in gen. surgery St. Francis Hosp., Peoria, Ill., 1951-53, Presbyn. Hosp., Chgo., 1953-55; resident in thoracic surgery Chgo. State Tuberculosis Sanitarium, 1955, VA Hosp., Hines, Ill., 1956; fellow in thoracic and cardiovascular surgery Rush-Presbyn.-St. Luke's Med. Ctr., Chgo., 1957; pvt. practice surgery Englewood, Colo.; active staff Presbyn.-St. Luke's Med. Ctr., Denver; staff St. Joseph Hosp., Denver; cons. in thoracic surgery VA Hosp., Albuquerque, 1961-66; cons. in surgery Colo. State Hosp., Pueblo, Colo., 1960-80; attending in thoracic surgery VA Hosp., Denver, 1959-85; asst. clin. prof. surgery U. Colo. Health Scis. Ctr., Denver, 1965-76, assoc. clin. prof., 1976-87, clin. prof. surgery, 1987—; staff surgeon Gates Med. Clinic, Denver, 1973-93. Contbr. numerous articles to profl. jours.; mem. physician's adv. panel Med. World News, 1980. Pres. Colo. divsn. Am. Cancer Soc., 1981-83, adv. com., 1986—, exec. com., 1965-86); bd. dirs., chmn. profl. adv. com. Cmty. Homemaker Svc., Denver, 1964-68; v.p., chmn. med. adv. com. Colo. Cystic Fibrosis Assn., 1964-69; surg. rev. com. Blue Cross/Blue Shield of Colo., 1981-88, cons., 1988—; bd. govs. QuaLife Wellness Cmty., Denver, 1988-91; bd. dirs. Denver Boys, Inc., 1992-93; health care adminstrv. adv. bd. Denver Tech. Coll., 1993—; physician advisor Colo. Found. Med. Care, 1988—. With U.S. Naval Air Corps, 1945-46. Mem. ACS (bd. govs. 1979-85, Colo. chpt. pres. 1976-77), AMA, Southwestern Surg. Congress (pres. 1986-87), Denver Med. Soc. (pres. 1969-70, chmn. bd. trustees 1970-71), Colo. Med. Soc. (del. 1982-85), Rush Surg. Soc. (pres. 1989-90), Western Thoracic Surg. Assn., Am. Assn. for Thoracic Surgery, Western Surg. Assn., Am. Coll. Chest Physicians, Colo. Trudeau Soc., Am. Thoracic Soc., Denver Acad. Surgery (bd. dirs. 1985-86), Rotary. Home and Office: 6189 E Princeton Cir Englewood CO 80111-1040

KOVTYNOVICH, DAN, civil engineer; b. Eugene, Oreg., May 17, 1952; s. John and Elva Lano (Robie) K. BCE, Oreg. State U., 1975, BBA, 1976. Registered profl. engr., Calif., Oreg. V.p. Kovtynovich, Inc., Contractors and Engrs., Eugene, 1976-80, pres., chief exec. officer, 1980—. Apptd. to State of Oreg. Bldg. Codes and Structures Bd., 1996—. Fellow ASCE; mem. Am. Arbitration Assn. (arbitrator 1979—), N.W. China Coun., Navy League of U.S., Eugene Asian Coun. Republican. Office: Kovtynovich Inc PO Box 898 910 A Avenue Lake Oswego OR 97034

KOWALSKI, KAZIMIERZ, computer science educator, researcher; b. Turek, Poland, Nov. 7, 1946; came to U.S., 1986; naturalized, 1994; s. Waclaw and Helena (Wisniewska) K.; m. Eugenia Zajaczkowska, Aug. 5, 1972. MSc, Wroclaw (Poland) U. Tech., 1970, PhD, 1974. Asst. prof. Wroclaw U. Tech., 1970-76, assoc. prof., 1976-86; assoc. prof. Pan Am. U., Edinburg, Tex., 1987-88; prof. computer sci. Calif. State U.-Dominguez Hills, Carson, 1988—; lectr. U. Basrah, Iraq, 1981-85; cons. XXCal, Inc., L.A., 1987-91; conf. presenter in field; rsch. fellow Power Inst. Moscow, USSR, 1978; info. sys. tng. UNESCO, Paris, 1978. Co-author: Principles of Computer Science, 1975, Organization and Programming of Computers, 1976; also articles. Recipient Bronze Merit Cross, Govt. of Poland, 1980. Mem. IEEE Computer Soc., The N.Y. Acad. Scis., Assn. for Computing Machinery, Am. Assn. for Artificial Intelligence, Mensa, Sigma Xi. Home: 3836 Weston Pl Long Beach CA 90807-3317 Office: Calif State U 1000 E Victoria St Carson CA 90747-0001

KOWALSKI, SUSAN DOLORES, critical care nurse, educator; b. Aurora, Ill., Dec. 20, 1944; d. George Bernard and Dolores Ida (Smith) Bockman; m. Edgar Peter Kowalski, July 9, 1988. BSN, No. Ill. U., 1971; MSN, Boston Coll., 1976; MBA, Rockford Coll., 1987; PhD, Tex. Woman's U., 1994. Staff nurse ICU St. Joseph Hosp., Bloomington, Ill., 1971-72, St. Francis Hosp., Peoria, Ill., 1972-73; nursing instr. St. Francis Hosp. Sch. Nursing, Peoria, 1973-75, St. Anthony Med. Ctr. Sch. Nursing, Rockford, 1976-85; staff nurse ICU St. Joseph Hosp., South Bend, Ind., 1986-89; clin. instr. Ind. Vocat. Tech. Coll., South Bend, 1986-89; asst. prof. St. Mary's Coll., Notre Dame, Ind., 1987-89; sr. lectr. U. Tex., Tyler, 1990-94; asst. prof. U. Nev., Las Vegas, 1994—; mem. respiratory therapy adv. bd. Rock Valley Coll., Rockford, 1978-81. Contbr. articles to nursing jours. Crisis intervention counselor Contact Crisis Intervention Line, Rockford, 1978-84. Recipient Cert. of Achievement Leadership, YMCA, 1985. Mem. Nat. League Nursing, Sigma Theta Tau. Republican. Roman Catholic. Home: 7736 Rye Canyon Dr Las Vegas NV 89123-0752 Office: U Nev 4505 S Maryland Pky Las Vegas NV 89154-9900

KOWDLEY, KRIS V., gastroenterologist, hepatologist, educator; s. V. S. and Geetha (Iyer) K.; m. Bonnie Dixit. AB, Columbia U., 1981; MD, Mount Sinai, N.Y.C., 1985. Diplomate Am. Bd. Gastroenterology. Intern Oreg. Health Sci. U., Portland, 1985-86, resident in internal medicine, 1986-88; gastrointestinal fellow New Eng. Med. Ctr., Boston, 1989-91; asst. prof. Case Western U., Cleve., 1991-93, U. Wash., Seattle, 1993—. Author: Collagen Diseases of Liver, 1993, Difficult Decisions in Digestive Disease, 1994; contbr. articles to Gastroenterology and Hepatology. Mem. Am. Gastroenterology Assn., Am. Assn. Study Liver Diseases, Am. Soc. Gastroenterology Endoscopy, Am. Coll. Gastroenterologists. Office: U Wash Box 356424 Seattle WA 98195

KOZAREK, RICHARD ANTHONY, gastroenterologist, educator; b. Duluth, Minn., Apr. 22, 1947; s. Clarence Edward and Patricia Ann (Koors) K.; m. Linda Jane Cooper, June 9, 1973; children: Katherine, Ellen. BA in Philosophy, U. Wis., 1969, MD, 1973. Diplomate Am. Bd. Internal Medicine; bd. cert. internal medicine and gastroenterology. Intern Dalhousie U., Halifax, N.S., Can., 1973-74; resident Good Samaritan Hosp., Phoenix, Ariz., 1974-76; fellow U. Ariz.-Phoenix VA Med. Ctr., Tucson, 1976-78; asst. chief gastroenterology Phoenix VA Med. Ctr., Tucson, 1978-83; asst. clin. prof. medicine U. Wash., Seattle, 1978-83; with sect. gastroenterology Virginia Mason Med. Ctr., Seattle, 1983—; chief gastroenterology Va. Mason Med. Ctr., Seattle, 1989—; clin. prof. medicine U. Wash., Seattle, 1990—. Author 4 books, 50 book chpts., numerous sci. articles. Recipient Eddy D. Palmer award William Beaumont Soc., 1982. Fellow ACP, Am. Coll. Gastroenterology; mem. Am. Gastroenterology Assn., Soc. for Gastrointestinal Endoscopy (gov. bd. 1990-95, pres.-elect 1996-97), Pacific N.W. Gastroenterology Soc. (sec. 1990, pres. 1991). Office: Virgina Mason Med Ctr 1100 9th Ave Seattle WA 98101-2756

KOZINSKI, ALEX, federal judge; b. Bucharest, Romania, July 23, 1950; came to U.S., 1962; s. Moses and Sabine (Zapler) K.; m. Marcy J. Tiffany, July 9, 1977; children: Yale Tiffany, Wyatt Tiffany, Clayton Tiffany. AB in Econs. cum laude, UCLA, 1972, JD, 1975. Bar: Calif. 1975, D.C., 1978. Law clk. to Hon. Anthony M. Kennedy U.S. Ct. Appeals (9th cir.), 1975-76; law clk. to Chief Justice Warren E. Burger U.S. Supreme Ct., 1976-77; assoc. Covington & Burling, Washington, 1979-81; asst. counsel Office of Counsel to Pres., White House, Washington, 1981; spl. counsel Merit Systems Protection Bd., Washington, 1981-82; chief judge U.S. Claims Ct., Washington, 1982-85; judge U.S. Ct. Appeals (9th cir.), 1985—; lectr. law U. So. Calif., 1992. Office: US Ct Appeals PO Box 91510 125 S Grand Ave Ste 200 Pasadena CA 91109-1510*

KRACHT, THEODORE ANDREW, air force officer; b. Wooster, Ohio, Mar. 15, 1967; s. William and Edna Lucille (Radcliffe) K. BS in History, USAF Acad., 1989; MA in History, U. Ala., 1996. Commd. 2d lt. USAF, 1989, advanced through grades to capt., 1993, comdr. for missle crews, 1990-93, instr., 1993-94, exec. officer Air Command and Staff Coll., 1994-96; instr. history USAF Acad., Colorado Springs, 1997—. Recipient 20th Air Force Crewmember Excellence award 20th Air Force and USAF Space Command, 1993; named one of Outstanding Young Men of Am., 1992. Mem. Am. Hist. Assn., Air Force Assn., Assn. Grad.-USAF Acad., Soc. for Mil. History. Roman Catholic. Home: 2835 Lennox Pl #7 Colorado Springs CO 80920

KRAEMER, KENNETH LEO, architect, urban planner, educator; b. Plain, Wis., Oct. 29, 1936; s. Leo Adam and Lucy Rose (Bauer) K.; m. Norine Florence, June 13, 1959; children: Kurt Randall, Kim Rene. BArch, U. Notre Dame, 1959; MS in City and Regional Planning, U. So. Calif., 1964, M of Pub. Adminstrn., 1965, PhD, 1967. From instr. to asst. prof. U. So. Calif., Los Angeles, 1965-67; asst. prof. U. Calif., Irvine, 1967-71, assoc. prof., 1971-78, prof., 1978—, dir. Pub. Policy Research Orgn., 1974-92, dir. Ctr. for Rsch. on Info. Tech. and Orgns., 1992—; cons. Office of Tech. Assessment, Washington, 1980, 84-85; pres. Irvine Research Corp., 1978—. Author: Management of Information Systems, 1980, Computers and Politics, 1982, Dynamics of Computing, 1983, People and Computers, 1985, Modeling as Negotiating, 1986, Data Wars, 1987, Wired Cities, 1987, Managing Information Systems, 1989. Mem. Blue Ribbon Data Processing Com., Orange County, Calif., 1973, 79-80, Telecomm. Adv. Bd., Sacramento, 1987-92. Mem. Am. Soc. for Pub. Adminstrn. (Disting. Research award 1985), Internat. Conf. on Info. Systems, Am. Planning Assn., Assn. for Computing Machinery. Democrat. Roman Catholic. Club: Notre Dame. Office: U Calif Ctr Rsch Info Tech & Orgns Berkley Pl N Ste 3200 Irvine CA 92697

KRAFT, GEORGE HOWARD, physician, educator; b. Columbus, Ohio, Sept. 27, 1936; s. Glen Homer and Helen Winner (Howard) K.; children: Jonathan Ashbrook, Susannah Mary. AB, Harvard U., 1958; MD, Ohio State U., 1963, MS, 1967. Cert. Am. Bd. Phys. Medicine and Rehab., Am. Bd. Electrodiagnostic Medicine. Intern U. Calif. Hosp., San Francisco, 1963-64, resident, 1964-65; resident Ohio State U., Columbus, 1965-67; assoc. U. Pa. Med. Sch., Phila., 1968-69; asst. prof. U. Wash., Seattle, 1969-72, assoc. prof., 1972-76, prof., 1976—, chief of staff Med. Ctr., 1993-95; dir. electrodiagnostic medicine U. Wash. Hosp., 1987—, dir. Multiple Sclerosis Clin. Ctr., 1982—; co-dir. Muscular Dystrophy Clinic, 1974—; assoc. dir. rehab. medicine Overlake Hosp., Bellevue, Wash., 1989—; bd. dirs. Am. Bd. Electrodiagnostic Medicine, 1993—, chmn., 1996—. Co-author: Chronic Disease and Disability, 1994, Living with Multiple Sclerosis: A Wellness Approach, 1996; cons. editor: Phys. Medicine and Rehab. Clinics, 1990—, EEG and Clin. Neurophysiology, 1992-96; assoc. editor Jour. Neurol. Rehab., 1988—; contbr. articles to profl. jours. Sci. peer rev. com. C Nat. Multiple Sclerosis Soc., N.Y.C., 1990-96, chmn., 1993-96, med. adv. bd., exec. com. med. adv. bd., 1991—; bd. sponsors Wash. Physicians for Social Responsibility, Seattle, 1986—. Rsch. grantee Rehab. Svcs. Adminstrn., 1978-81, NEW, 1976-79, Nat. Inst. Handicapped Rsch., 1984-88, Nat. Multiple Sclerosis Soc., 1990-92, 94-95. Fellow Am. Acad. Phys. Medicine and Rehab. (pres. 1984-85, Zeiter award 1991); mem. Am. Assn. Electrodiagnostic Medicine (cert., pres. 1982-83), Assn. Acad. Physiatrists (pres. 1980-81), Am. Acad. Clin. Neurophysiology (pres. 1995-97), Am. Acad. Neurology, Internat. Rehab. Medicine Assn. Episcopalian. Office: U Wash Dept Rehab PO Box 356490 Seattle WA 98195-0004

KRAFT, RICHARD JOE, sales executive; b. Toppenish, Wash., Apr. 20, 1944; s. Joseph Nian and Rose Goldie (Merrick) K.; m. Karolyn Idell Keyes, Oct. 9, 1963 (div. 1982); children: Craig J., Jeffrey Eugene; m. Margaret Celeste Porter, Apr. 9, 1983. Student, Yakima Valley Coll., 1962-63; student, U. Wash., 1964-70. Project engr. Gray & Osborne Consulting Engrs., Seattle, 1965-76; project engr., constrn. cons. Pool Engring., Ketchikan, Alaska, 1976-81; project mgr. Cape Fox Corp., Ketchikan, 1982; project engr. Buno Constrn., Woodinville, Wash., 1983, Straiger Engring. Svcs., Ketchikan, Sitka, Alaska, 1984; owner Kraft Constrn. Svcs., Kirkland, Wash., 1984-85; dir. mcpl. projects ESM, Inc., Renton, Wash., 1985-86; estimator Active Constrn., Inc., Gig Harbor, Wash., 1987; sr. sales engr. Advanced Drainage Systems, Inc., Woodinville, 1987-93; with Ty-Matt, Inc., Ketchikan, 1993-94; owner Kraft Constrn. Svcs., Ketchikan, 1994—; storm sewer/sanitary specification subcom. Am. Pub. Works Assn., Wash. state chpt., 1985-93. Pres. Snohomish (Wash.) Camp, Gideons Internat., 1990-91; pres. exec. com. Maltby (Wash.) Congl. Ch. Mem. Utility Contractors Assn. Wash. (bd. dirs. 1990-92). Mem. Christian Ch. Home and Office: PO Box 6384 Ketchikan AK 99901-1384

KRAFT, SCOTT COREY, correspondent; b. Kansas City, Mo., Mar. 31, 1955; s. Marvin Emanuel and Patricia (Kirk) K.; m. Elizabeth Brown, May 1, 1982; children: Kate, Kevin. BS, Kans. State U., 1977. Staff writer AP, Jefferson City, Mo., 1976-77, Kansas City, 1977-79; corr. AP, Wichita, Kans., 1979-80; nat. writer AP, N.Y.C., 1980-84; nat. corr. L.A. Times, Chgo., 1984-86; bur. chief L.A. Times, Nairobi, Kenya, 1986-88, Johannesburg, South Africa, 1988-93, Paris, 1993-96; dep. fgn. editor L.A. Times, 1996—. Recipient Disting. Reporting in a Specialized Field award Soc. of the Silurians, 1982, Peter Lisagor award Headline Club Chgo., 1985, Feature Writing finalist Pulitzer Prize Bd., 1985, Sigma Delta Chi award, 1993. Office: LA Times Foreign Desk Times Mirror Square Los Angeles CA 90053

KRAFT, SCOTT WALLACE, writer, actor; b. Cambridge, Mass., July 30, 1960; s. Robert Alan and Carol Louise (Wallace) K.; m. Nadine Marie van der Velde, Oct. 28, 1990. Student, Am. Coll. in Paris, 1980; BA in English Lit., U. Pa., 1983; student, Padua Hills Playwrights Conf., L.A., 1988. Writer CBS, HBO, Viacom, others, L.A., 1988—; actor BCS, ABC, NBC, NFB, others, L.A., 1982—; playwright Essential Stage, Wilton Project, L.A., 1986—; lit. advisor Audrey Skirall-Kenis Theater, L.A., 1990-92; founding mem. Wilton Project Theater Co., L.A., 1991—; book reviewer L.A. Times, 1992—; theater reviewer Biztravel.Com, 1996—. Author: (plays) The Big One Shot, 1992, Narcissus in the Second Millenium, 1996; co-author: (film) The Silencer, 1993; actor (film) For the Moment, 1993, (plays) Hurleyburley, 1989, Genie, 1994 (nominated Best Supporting Actor 1994, Blizzard, 1995 (nominated Best Supporting Actor 1995). Mem. PEN, SAG, Writers Guild Am., Alliance of Can. Cinema, TV and Radio Artists, Writers Guild Can. Office: care The Artists Agy 10000 Santa Monica Blvd Los Angeles CA 90067 also: Great North Artists, 350 Dupont St, Toronto, ON Canada M5R 1U9

KRAFT, WILLIAM ARMSTRONG, retired priest; b. Rochester, N.Y., Apr. 13, 1926; s. William Andrew and Elizabeth Ruth (Armstrong) K. BA, St. Bernard Coll., 1947; ThM, Immaculate Heart Theol. Coll., 1951; D of Ministry, Claremont Sch. of Theology, 1981. Ordained priest Roman Cath. Ch., 1951. Dir. and founder of Newman Apostolate Diocese of San Diego, Calif., 1951-63; dir. of pub. rels. Diocese of San Diego, 1956-63, dir. of cemeteries, 1964-70, exec. dir. of devel., 1979-91; founding pastor St. Therese of Child Jesus Parish, San Diego, 1956-70, Good Shepherd Parish, San Diego, 1970-77; pastor St. Charles Borromeo Parish, San Diego, 1977-79; bd. dirs. Cath. Charities, San Diego; bd. of consultors Diocese of San Diego, 1985-91, mem. Presbyteral Coun., 1985-91, mem. bldg. commn., 1977-91. Bd. dirs. Am. Nat. Red Cross, San Diego, 1956-63, Legal Aid Soc., San Diego, 1956-65, Travelers' Aid Soc., San Diego, 1956-65; mem. Presdl. Task Force, Washington, 1984—; spl. dep. San Diego County Sheriff, 1964—. Named Prelate of Honor to Pope, Pope John Paul II, Vatican City, 1985, Knight Comdr. of Equestrian, Order of The Holy Sepulchre, Latin Patriarcii, Jerusalem, 1984, Knights of Columbus 4th degree. Mem. Benevolent and Protective Order of Elks, Univ. Club Atop Symphony Towers, Nat. Cath. Conf. for Total Stewardship (bd. dirs.), Nat. Cath. Devel. Conf., Nat. Soc. Fund Raising Execs. (cert.). Republican. Home: 6910 Cibola Rd San Diego CA 92120-1709

KRAG, OLGA, interior designer; b. St. Louis, Nov. 27, 1937; d. Jovica Todor and Milka (Slijepcevic) Golubovic. AA, U. Mo., 1958; cert. interior design UCLA, 1979. Interior designer William L. Pereira Assocs., L.A., 1977-80; assoc. Reel/Grobman Assocs., L.A., 1980-81; project mgr. Kaneko/Laff Assocs., L.A., 1982; project mgr. Stuart Laff Assocs., L.A., 1983-85; restaurateur The Edge, St. Louis, 1983-84; pvt. practice comml. interior design, L.A., 1981—, pres., R.I., 1989—. Mem. invitation and ticket com. Calif. Chamber Symphony Soc., 1980-81; vol. Westside Rep. Coun., Proposition 1, 1971; asst. inaugural presentation Mus. of Childhood, L.A., 1985. Recipient Carole Eichen design award U. Calif., 1979. Mem. Am. Soc. Interior Designers, Inst. Bus. Designers, Phi Chi Theta, Beta Sigma Phi. Republican. Serbian Orthodox. Home and Office: 700 Levering Ave Apt 10 Los Angeles CA 90024-2797

KRAHMER, DONALD L., JR., financial services company executive; b. Hillsboro, Oreg., Nov. 11, 1957; s. Donald L. and Joan Elizabeth (Karns) K.; m. Suzanne M. Blanchard, Aug. 16, 1986; children: Hillary, Zachary. BS, Willamette U., 1981, MM, 1987, JD, 1987. Bar: Oreg. 1988. Fin. analyst U.S. Bancorp, Portland, 1977-87; intern U.S. Senator Mark Hatfield, 1978; legis. aide State Sen. Jeannette Hamby, Hillsboro, Oreg., 1981-83, State Rep. Delna Jones, Beaverton, Oreg., 1983; bus. analyst Pacificorp, Portland, 1987; mgr. mergers/acquisitions Pacificorp Fin. Svcs., Portland, 1988-89; dir. Pacificorp Fin. Svcs., 1990; CEO, pres. Atkinson Group, Portland, 1991—; ptnr. Black Helterline, Portland, 1991—; bd. dirs., sec. Marathon Fin. Assocs., Portland, 1989; bd. dirs. Self-Enhancement, Inc.; chmn. Willamette Forum; chmn.-elect bd. dirs., chmn. adv. bd., editor Oreg. Enterprise Forum, 1991—; bd. dirs. Concordia Univ. Found. Treas. Com. to Re-Elect Jeannette Hamby, 1986; bd. dirs. fin. com./devel. com. Am. Diabetes Assn., Portland, 1990-96; founder Needle Bros., 1994; chmn. Atkinson Grad. Sch. Devel. Com., Salem, 1989-92; founder Conf. of Entrepreneurship, Salem, 1984, chmn. Entrepreneurship Breakfast Forum, Portland, 1993; chmn., founder Oreg. Conf. on Entrepreneurship and Awards Dinner, 1994-97. Recipient Pub.'s award Oreg. Bus. Mag., 1987, Founders award Willamette U., 1987, award Scripps Found., 1980, Bus. Jour. 40 Under 40 award, 1996. Mem. ABA, Oreg. Bar Assn. (chmn. exec. com., fin. instns. com. sec., exec. com., bus. law sect.), Multnomah County Bar Assn., Washington County Bar Assn., Portland Soc. Fin. Analysts, Japan-Am. Soc. Oreg., Assn. Investment Mgmt. and Rsch., City Club. Republican. Lutheran. Home: 16230 SW Copper Creek Dr Portland OR 97224-6500 Office: Black Helterline 1200 Bank of Calif Tower 707 SW Washington St Portland OR 97205-3536

KRAHN, THOMAS FRANK, photographer; b. Racine, Wis., Feb. 14, 1941; s. Marvin Carl and Marie Mattie (Myers) K. Diploma, Control Data Inst., 1972; Doctorate (hon.), United World Assembly, 1984. Pres. Puget Sound Pub. Group, Everett, Wash.; photographer Arcturus Studio, Everett, Student Foto Supply, Everett. Author: (novels) Atkar, The Norseman, Adventure at Whiterood, (novellas) The Boy on the Horse, 1994, The Naked Prey, 1994, Die Wolfenkindern, Vols. 1-3, 1994, The Indian Affair, The Dry Creek Canyon Incident, Something Lives Under the Porch, (non-fiction) Gay Ethics, Vols. 1 and 2, Vessels of Silver and Gold, 1994, Children and Chicanery, A Biblical Approach to Modern Gay Living, 1989, The Complete Number Line and Introduction to the Algebraic Celestial Sphere, (booklets) The Seven Days of Wonder, 1996, How Do I Love Thee, 1996, (plays) The Doughnut, The Dumpster, Witness for the Defense, Oz-Mosis (Oz Twenty Years Later), The Mystery of Edmund O'Shay, Every Man's Folly, also stories, poems; composer various works for piano, organ, vocal ensembles and solo works. Pres. First All-Everett Foto Flea Market, 1996-97. Recipient Cert. of Appreciation KCTS 9 TV Sta., 1991, award Exec. Coun. Selection Com., Everett C.C., 1988-89. Mem. Hist. Everett Theater Soc., Everet Photo Club (pres. 1996-97), Tau Alpha Epsilon. Home: 3401 Rucker E Ste Everett WA 98201 Office: Student Foto Supply 2531 Broadway Ste D-11 Everett WA 98201

KRAKEL, DEAN, museum administrator, consultant, historian; b. Ault, Colo., July 3, 1923; s. Eldon A. and Gretta (Cross) K.; m. Iris Lesh, June, 1947 (div. 1994); children—Ira Dean, Jennie L., Jack R. B.A., No. Colo. U., 1950; M.A. in History, U. Denver, 1952; D.H.L. (hon.), U. Colo., 1976. Asst. curator Colo. State Hist. Soc., Denver, 1950-52; dir., archivist U. Wyo. Library, Laramie, 1952-56; dep. dir. Mus. and Fine Arts Program, U.S. Air Force Acad., Colo., 1956-61; exec. dir. Thomas Gilcrage Inst., Tulsa, 1961-64; dir., exec. v.p. Nat. Cowboy Hall of Fame, Oklahoma City, 1964-85; dir. Anti Metric Soc., 1976—. Author: South Platte Country, 1952, Saga of Tom Horn, 1952, James Boren: A Study in Discipline, 1968, Tom Ryan, 1971, End of The Trail: The Odyessey of a Statue, 1973, Adventures In Western Art, 1977, Mitch: On the Tail End of the Old West, 1981, Schwering: Painting On the Square, 1981, Dear Mr. Remington, 1991. Served with USN, 1943-46. Recipient Am. Heritage award No. Colo. U., 1978; Gari Melcher Medal for Arts N.Y. Art Soc., 1985. Mem. Nat. Cowboy Hall of Fame (Gold Buckle Rodeo award 1974, trustees' gold medal award, 1975). Avocation: art appraisal. Home: 1615 Tanque Verde Loop Rd Tucson AZ 85749

KRAMARSIC, ROMAN JOSEPH, engineering consultant; b. Mokronog, Slovenia, Feb. 15, 1926; came to U.S., 1957; s. Roman and Josipina (Bucar) K; m. Joanna B. Ruffo, Oct. 29, 1964; children: Joannine M., Roman III. Student, U. Bologna, Italy, 1947-48, BS, U. Toronto, Can., 1954, MS, 1956; PhD, U. So. Calif., 1973. Registered profl. engr., Ont., Can. Rsch. engr. Chrysler Rsch., Detroit, 1957-58; chief design engr. Annin Corp., Montebello, Calif., 1959-60; mgr. Plasmadyne Corp., Santa Ana, Calif., 1960-62; sr. rsch. engr. NESCO, Pasadena, Calif., 1962-64; asst. prof. U. So. Calif., L.A., 1971-77; mgr. engring. div. MERDI, Butte, Mont., 1977-78; sr. rsch. engr. RDA, Albuquerque, 1978-85; sr. staff mem. BDM, Albuquerque, 1985-90; owner Dr. R. J. Kramarsic's Engring. Svcs., Laguna Beach, Calif., 1985—; cons. various tech. cos., So. Calif., 1964—; mem. various govt. coms. evaluating high power lasers. Author tech. presentations; contbr. articles to profl. jours. Violinist Albuquerque Civic Light Opera, 1980-85. Mem. ASME (sr.), AIAA (sr.), ASM Internat., Nat. Ski Patrol (aux. leader 1990-94). Roman Catholic. Office: Kramarsic's Engring Svcs PO Box 608 Laguna Beach CA 92652-0608

KRAMER, ALEXANDER GOTTLIEB, financial director; b. DesPlaines, Ill., Sept. 21, 1964; s. Gottlieb G. and Norma L. Kramer. BA in Econ. Devel. and Internat. Rels., Lake Forest Coll., 1987; M in Internat. Fin., Am. Grad. Sch. Internat. Mgmt., Glendale, Ariz., 1990. Asst. to dir. parliamentary affairs Spanish Parliament, Madrid, 1985-87; intern to chief polit. consular U.S. Dept. State, Rabat, Morocco, 1987-88; project mgr. H. Shapiro & Assocs., Inc., Chgo., 1988-90; dir. fin. and logistics Pacific Inter-Trade Corp., Westlake Village, Calif., 1990-93; fin. dir. Export SBDC Sr. Counsel Internat., L.A., 1993-95; head trade fin. group Am. Honda Motor Co., Torrance, Calif., 1995—; prof. internat. fin., West Coast U., L.A., 1991—; mem. adv. bd. Bestone Group, Hong Kong and Shanghai; bd. dirs. Export Mgrs. Assn. Calif. Mem. Fgn. Trade Assn., Peruvian Arts Soc., Phi Sigma Iota. Home: # 185 1603 W Pacific Coast Hwy Wilmington CA 90744 Office: Am Honda Motor Co 100-2W-SE 1919 Torrance Blvd Torrance CA 90501

KRAMER, BARRY ALAN, psychiatrist; b. Phila., Sept. 9, 1948; s. Morris and Harriet (Greenberg) K.; m. Paulie Hoffman, June 9, 1974; children—Daniel Mark, Steven Philip. B.A. in Chemistry, NYU, 1970; M.D., Hahnemann Med. Coll., 1974. Resident in psychiatry Montefiore Hosp. and Med. Ctr., Bronx, N.Y., 1974-77; practice medicine specializing in psychiatry, N.Y.C., 1977-82; staff psychiatrist L.I. Jewish-Hillside Med. Ctr., Glen Oaks, N.Y., 1977-82; asst. prof. SUNY, Stony Brook, 1978-82; practice medicine specializing in psychiatry, L.A., 1982—; asst. prof. psychiatry U. So. Calif., 1982-89, assoc. prof. clin. psychiatry, 1989-94, prof. clin. psychiatry U. So. Calif. U. Hosp., 1994—; ward chief Los Angeles County/U. So. Calif. Med. Ctr., 1982—; mem. med. staff USC U. Hosp., Cedars Sinai Hosp.; cons. Little Neck Nursing Home (N.Y.), 1979-82, L.I. Nursing Home, 1980-82; dir. ECT U. So. Calif. Sch. Medicine, 1990. Reviewer: Am. Jour. Psychiatry, Hospital and Community Psychiatry; mem. editorial bd. Convulsive Therapy; contbr. articles to profl. jours., papers to sci. meetings. NIMH grantee, 1979-80; fellow UCLA/U. So. Calif. Long-Term Gerontology Ctr., 1985-86. Fellow Am. Psychiat. Assoc.; mem. AMA, Assn. Convulsive Therapy (editorial bd.), Soc. Biol. Psychiatry, Calif. Med. Assn., L.A. Med. Assn., Am. Assn. Geriatric Psychiatry, Gerontol. Soc. Am., So. Calif. Psychiat. Soc. (chair ETC com.). Jewish. Office: U So Calif U Hosp 1510 San Pablo St Ste 600 Los Angeles CA 90033-4586 also: PO Box 5792 Beverly Hills CA 90209-5792

KRAMER, DONOVAN MERSHON, SR., newspaper publisher; b. Galesburg, Ill., Oct. 24, 1925; s. Verle V. and Sybil (Mershon) K.; m. Ruth A. Heins, Apr. 3, 1949; children: Donovan M. Jr., Diana Sue, Kara J. Kramer Cooper, Eric H. BS in Journalism, Pub. Mgmt., U. Ill., 1948. Editor, publisher, ptnr. Fairbury (Ill.) Blade, 1948-63, Forrest (Ill.) News, 1953-63; ptnr. Gibson City (Ill.) Courier, 1952-63; pres., publisher, editor Casa Grande (Ariz.) Valley Newspapers, Inc., 1963—; mng. ptnr. White Mt. Pub. Co., Show Low, Ariz., 1978—. Wrote, edited numerous articles and newspaper stories. Many award-winners including Sweepstakes award in Ill. and Ariz. Mem., chmn. Econ. Planning and Devel. Bd. State of Ariz., Phoenix, 1976-81; pres. Indsl. Devel. Authority of Casa Grande, 1977—; founding pres. Greater Casa Grande Econ. Devel. Found., bd. dirs., 1982-97 (Lifetime Achievement award 1994); gov. apptd. bd. mem. Ariz. Dept. Transp., 1992—, chmn., 1997. Recipient Econ. Devel. plaque City of Casa Grande, 1982, Lifetime Achievement award Greater Casa Grande Econ. Devel. Found., 1994. Mem. Ariz. Newspapers Assn. (pres. 1980, Master Editor-Pub. 1977), Cmty. Newspapers Ariz. (pres. 1970-71), Inland Newspapers Assn., Newspapers Assn. Am., Ctrl. Ariz. Project Assn., Nat. Newspapers Assn., Greater Casa Grande C. of C. (pres. 1981-82, Hall of Fame 1991), Soc. Profl. Journalists. Republican. Lutheran. Home: PO Box 15002 1125 E Cottonwood Ln Casa Grande AZ 85230-5002

KRAMER, GEORGE H., historic preservation consultant; b. Mayfield Heights, Ohio, Sept. 21, 1958; s. Allen Kramer and Jean Shirley (Hirsch) Mains; m. Joyce Van Anne, May 28, 1981; children: Benjamin Allen, Noah Ruysbroek. BA in History, Sonoma State U., 1980; MS in Hist. Preservation, U. Oreg., 1989. Hist. preservation cons. Ashland, Oreg., 1989—; hist. cons. City of Talent, Oreg., 1993—, City of Grants Pass, Oreg., 1992, City of Medford, Oreg., 1994—, Anchorage Hist. Property, 1988, City of Jacksonville (Oreg.), 1995—. Author: Camp White: City in the Agate Desert, 1992. Chmn. Ashland Hist. Commn., 1984-87, Jackson City Hist. Adv. Com., Medford, 1993—; bd. dirs. Hist. Preservation League Org., Ashland, 1989—, Nat. Alliance of Preservation Commns., 1994—; mem. bd. advisors Nat. Trust for Hist. Preservation, Washington, 1993—. Named Preservationist of Yr., City of Ashland, 1992. Mem. Soc. for Comml. Archeology, N.W. Pacific Coast chpt. Soc. Archtl. Historians, Siskiyou Pioneer Sites Found. (sec. 1989—, v.p. 1994—). Democrat. Home and Office: 386 N Laurel St Ashland OR 97520-1154

KRAMER, GORDON, mechanical engineer; b. Bklyn., Aug. 1937; s. Joseph and Etta (Grossberg) K.; m. Ruth Ellen Harter, Mar. 5, 1967 (div. June 1986); children: Samuel Maurice, Leah Marie; m. Eve Burstein, Dec. 17, 1988. BS Cooper Union, 1959; MS, Calif. Inst. Tech., 1960. With Hughes Aircraft Co., Malibu, Calif., 1959-63; sr. scientist Avco Corp., Norman, Okla., 1963-64; asst. div. head Batelle Meml. Inst., Columbus, Ohio, 1964-67; sr. scientist Aerojet Electrosystems, Azusa, Calif., 1967-75; chief engr. Beckman Instrument Co., Fullerton, Calif., 1975-82; prin. scientist McDonnell Douglas Microelectronics Co., 1982-83, Kramer and Assocs., 1983-85; program mgr. Hughes Aircraft Co., 1985-96; ret., 1996—; cons. Korea Inst. Tech. NSF fellow, 1959-60. Mem. IEEE. Democrat. Jewish. Home: 153 Lake Shore Dr Rancho Mirage CA 92270-4055

KRAMER, GORDON EDWARD, manufacturing executive; b. San Mateo, Calif., June 22, 1946; s. Roy Charles and Bernice Jeanne (Rones) K.; BS in Aero. Engring., San Jose State Coll., 1970; m. Christina Hodges, Feb. 14, 1970; children: Roy Charles, Charlena. Purchasing agent Am. Racing Equipment, Brisbane, Calif., 1970-71, asst. to v.p. mktg., 1971-72; founder, pres. Safety Direct Inc., hearing protection equipment, Sparks, Nev., 1972—; dir. Hodges Transp., Condor Inc.; mem. adv. bd. to pres. Truckee Meadows Community Coll., 1991—. Named Nev. Small Businessperson of Yr., Nev. Small Bus. Adminstrn., 1987, Bus. Person of Yr. Sparks Community C. of C., 1987. Mem. Am. Soc. Safety Engrs., Safety Equipment Distributors Assn., Indsl. Safety Equipment Assn., Nat. Assn. Sporting Goods Wholesalers, Nat. Sporting Goods Assn., Nev. State Amature Trapshooting Assn. (dir. 1978-79), Pacific Internat. Trapshooting Assn. (Nev. pres. 1979-80, 80-81), Nev. Mfrs. Assn. (dir. 1992—), Advanced Soccer Club (pres.1985-86). Republican. Methodist. Rotary Club (pres. Spark Club 1988-89). Office: Safety Direct Inc 56 Coney Island Dr Sparks NV 89431-6335

KRAMER, JAMES JOSEPH, artist, painter; b. Columbus, OH, Oct. 24, 1927; s. James Joseph and Louise Julia (Eireman) K.; m. Barbara Peters, Apr. 11, 1959; children: Susan Kramer Erickson, Joan Kramer Busick. Student, OH State U., 1950, Cleve. Sch. of Art, Cleve., 1949. Archtl. Lic. Exhibited w/ Ohio Watercolor Soc., Columbus, OH, 1948-50; pvt. archtl. practice Columbus, OH, 1950-57; architect Hertzka and Knowles, Arch., San Francisco, CA, 1957-59; assoc. Burde, Shaw and Assoc., Arch., Carmel, CA, 1959-70; retired from arch. Carmel, CA, 1970-76; artist, painter Santa Fe, N.Mex., 1976-95, Albuquerque, 1995—; instr. Valdes Art Workshop, Santa Fe, N.Mex., 1985—, Scottsdale Artists Sch., Scottsdale Ariz., 1986-88, Ghost Ranch Workshop, Abiquiu, N.Mex., 1980, Mont. Art Edn., Assn., Great Falls, Mont., 1974. Exhibited in group shows at Royal Watercolor Soc., London, Taiwan Mus., N.Mex. Mus. Fine art, Santa Fe, Mus. Western Art, Denver, Gilcrease Mus., Tulsa, Millicent Rogers Mus., Taos, N.Mex., Albuquerque Mus., Colo. Heritage Ctr. Mus., Denver, others; represented in permanent collections at Monterey Peninsula Mus. Art, Calif., Georgetown Hist. Soc., Colo., U. Nev., Reno, Colo. Heritage Ctr. Mus., Mus. Western Art. Recipient Silver Medal, Nat. Acad. of West Art, Okla. City, 1989, Frederic Remington award for artistic merit, 1991, Calif. Art Club, L.A., 1974, Gold Medal, 1973, Best of Show, Mother Lode Art Assn., Sonora, Calif., 1971.

KRAMER, LORNE C., protective services official. BA in Pub. Mgmt., U. Redlands, 1977; MPA with honors, U. So. Calif., 1979; Advanced Exec. Cert., Calif. Law Enforcement Coll., 1987; grad., Nat. Exec. Inst., 1993. Comdr. L.A. Police Dept., 1963-91; chief police Colorado Springs (Colo.) Police Dept., 1991—; Cons., instr. drugs and gangs Nat. Inst. Justice, Office Juvenile Justice U.S. Dept. Justice. Active Colo. State DARE Adv. Bd.; bd. dirs. Ctr. Prevention Domestic Violence, Pikes Peak Mental Health. Mem. Colo. Assn. Chiefs Police (bd. dirs., major cities rep.), Internat. Assn. Chiefs Police (juvenile justice com.), Police Exec. Rsch. Forum. Office: PO Box 2169 Colorado Springs CO 80901

KRAMER, MELANY BETH, lawyer; b. Pueblo, Colo., Apr. 30, 1954; d. George David and Grace Rita (Sherwood) K. BA in Lit. and Humanities, Pepperdine U., 1975; JD, U. of the Pacific, 1978. Assoc. Ramsey, Morrison & Keddy, Sacramento, 1980-83, Cooper & Schafer, Sacramento, 1983-85, Barrett, Penney & Byrd, Sacramento, 1985-87, Dummit, Faber & Brown, Sacramento and L.A., 1987-90; cmty. activist and cons., 1990—. Vol. Sta. KVIE, Channel 6, Sacramento, 1980-85, Sta. KXPR-FM, Sacramento, 1986—, Workout For Hope, 1992—, Lukemia Soc., 1995—,Sta. KQED-FM, 1996—. Mem. State Bar Calif. Democrat. Baptist.

KRAMER, REMI THOMAS, film director; b. L.A., Mar. 7, 1935; s. Justina Magdelene Kramer; m. Agnes Marie Gallagher, Feb. 1, 1969; children: Matthew, Christiana, Timothy, Ian, Vincent, Brigitte, Danika. BA, UCLA, 1956; MA, Calif. State U., L.A., 1963. Art dir. Doyle, Dane, Bernbach Advt., L.A., 1965-66, N.W. Ayer Advt., N.Y.C., 1966-67; dir. John Urie & Assocs. Haboush Co., Hollywood, Calif., 1967-69, Columbia-Screen Gems, Hollywood, 1969-76, 79-81, 1st Asian Films, Hollywood and Manila, 1976-77, Peterson Co., Hollywood, 1977-79; freelance film dir. Hollywood, 1981-85; founder Oz Enterprises, Inc., Sandpoint, Idaho, 1985—. Author: The Legend of Lonestar Bear Series, 1988—, How Lonestar Got His Name, 1988, Soaring with Eagles, 1989, The Mystery of the Walking Cactus, 1990 (The 100 Best Products of the Yr. 1990, Best Illustration: Creativity 90, 1990); author, illustrator: Klondike Ike, 1992; writer, dir. film High Velocity, 1976; patentee children's pacifier toy; designer Lonestar Bear plush animal collection. With U.S. Army, 1958-60. Recipient Clio award, 1971, 1st Internat. Broadcast awards, 1973, Cine Golden Eagle award, 1976, The Golden Teddy award, 1990, 91. Mem. Dirs. Guild Am., Writers Guild Am. Roman Catholic. Office: PO Box 637 Sandpoint ID 83864-0637

KRAMER, STEVEN G., ophthalmologist; b. Chgo., Feb. 28, 1941; s. Paul and Maria Kramer; m. Anne Crystal Kramer, Dec. 26, 1961 (div.); children: Janice Lynn, Kenneth David; m. Bernadette E. Coatar, June 30, 1974 (div.); children: Daniel Steven, Susan Mary; m. Susan E. Garrett, Jan. 17, 1997. BA in Biology, U. Chgo., 1967; MD, Case Western Res. U., 1965; PhD, U. Chgo., 1971. Cert. assoc. examiner Am. Bd. Ophthalmology; lic. ophthalmologist, Calif., Wash. Instr. ophthalmology U. Chgo., 1968-71; chief of ophthalmology Madigan Army Med. Ctr., Tacoma, 1971-73; chief of ophathlmology VA Med. Ctr., San Francisco, 1973-75; prof. ophthalmology, chmn. U. Calif., San Francisco, 1975—, dir. Beckman Vision Ctr., 1988—; mem. various coms. VA Hosp., San Francisco, 1973—; mem. exec. med. bd. sch. medicine U. Calif., 1975—, mem./chmn. various coms., 1975—, mem. clin. dept. chmn. group, 1975—, mem. governing bd. continuing med. edn. program, 1984-85, mem. clin. rev. working group, 1985-86, pres.-elect med. staff, 1985, pres., 1986-88, mem. chancellor's governance group, 1986—, mem. adv. group devel. spine svcs., 1992—; v.p. That Man May See, Inc., 1975—, bd. trustees, 1975—, campaign cabinet mem. for Vision Rsch. Ctr., 1983—; sec., bd. govs. Francis Proctor Found. for Rsch. in Opthalmology, 1975—; mem. Rsch. to Prevent Blindness, Inc., N.Y., 1976—, ad hoc adv. com., 1976-77; NIH mem. vision rsch. program com. NEI, 1978-82, chmn., 1980-82; site visit chmn. U. Wash., Seattle, 1979, Mass. Eye and Ear Infirmary, Boston, 1980, dept. neurobiology Harvard Med. Sch., Boston, 1980; mem. joint program and planning bd. sch. medicine U. Calif./Mt. Zion, 1985-88; mem. courtesy staff San Francisco Gen. Hosp.; lectr. in field. Editor, editl. bd. therapeutics rev. sect. Survey of Ophthalmology, 1977-84, diagnostic and surg. techniques sect., 1984—; sci. referee Am. Jour. Ophthalmology, 1967-81, editl. bd., 1981—; editl. bd. Ophthalmic Soc.; sci. referee Life Scis.; editor CMA Ophthalmology Epitomes, Western Jour. Medicine, 1976-77; med. adv. bd. Nat. Soc. to Prevent Blindness, 1979—; editor sect. cornea and sclera Yearbook of Ophthalmology, 1982. Mem. legis. com. for State of Calif., 1977; bd. dirs. Found. for Glaucoma Rsch., 1980—. Maj. U.S. Army, 1971-73. USPHS Spl. fellow in ophthalmologic rsch., 1970; VA Hosp. Rsch. Program grantee; NIH grantee, That Man May See grantee. Mem. AMA, ACS, Am. Acad. Ophthalmology, Am. Intra-Ocular Implant Soc., Assn. for Rsch. in Vision and Ophthalmology, Pacific Coast Oto-Ophthalmology Soc., Frederick C. Cordes Eye Soc., Calif. Med. Assn. (sci. adv. panel 1974—, adv. panel on ophthalmology subcom. for accreditation 1976-77, 78), Calif. Assn. Ophthalmology (adv. cons.), Assn. Univ. Profs. of Ophthalmology (chmn. resident placement svc. com., mem. ophthalmology resident and fellowship edn. com.), No. Calif. Soc. to Prevent Blindness (med. adv. bd.), Pan Am. Assn. Ophthalmology, Am. Congress, San Francisco Ophthal. Round Table, Rsch. to Prevent Blindness, Inc., Retinitis Pigmentosa Internat. Soc. (founding mem., sci. adv. bd.), Castroviejo Corneal Soc., Internat. Cornea Soc., Internat. Soc. Refractive Keratoplasty, Calif. Cornea Club, Ophthalmologic Hon. Soc. of Am. Ophthal. Soc., Phi Beta Kappa, Alpha Omega Alpha, Sigma Xi. Office: U Calif 10 Kirkham St # K-301 San Francisco CA 94122-3815

KRANAK, PETER VAL, geologist; b. Pasadena, Calif., Oct. 7, 1951; s. Andrew Anthony and Virginia (Wherritt) K.; m. Margaret Fitting, Dec. 29, 1973; children: Virginia Meghan, Joseph Anthony. BS, U. Wash., 1974; MS, Okla. State U., 1978; MBA, U. Denver, 1991. Computer programmer Call Computer, Palo Alto, Calif., 1967-71; mineral explorationist Conoco, Reno, Nev., 1975-76; rsch. asst. Okla. State U., Stillwater, 1977-78; mineral explorationist Texaco, Corpus Christi, Tex., 1979-82; petroleum geologist Texaco, Midland, Tex., 1982-84; petroleum geologist Texaco, Denver, 1984-90, exploration risk specialist, 1990-92, planning mgr.-exploration, 1992-94, sr. fin. planner, 1994—. Mem. Am. Assn. Petroleum Geologists (jr.). Office: Texaco USA PO Box 2100 Denver CO 80201-2100

KRANCE, CHARLES ANDREW, literature educator; b. Paris, Oct. 7, 1937; came to U.S., 1941; s. Casimir and Felicia (Lilpop) K.; m. Mary Ann Ramsey, Aug. 29, 1961 (div. Mar. 1988; m. Marie-Florine Bruneau, Nov. 11, 1989; 1 child, Andrea Michele Hansen. BA, U. Wis., 1961, PhD, 1970; MA, Middlebury Coll., 1962. Instr. Ripon (Wis.) Coll., 1961-62, Moorhead (Minn.) State Coll., 1964, Lawrence U., Appleton, Wis., 1966-69; asst. prof., assoc. prof. U. Chgo., 1969-94, ret., 1995. Author: L.-F. Céline: The I of the Storm, 1992; editor bilingual variorum edit. of Samuel Beckett's Company and A Piece of Monologue, 1993, Ill Seen Ill Heard, 1996; editor (series) Bilingual Beckett Editions. Grantee ACLS, 1986, NEH, 1988, 91, Fulbright Found., 1990, Am. Philos. Soc., 1993. Mem. Am. Assn. Tchrs. French, Modern Lang. Assn., Fulbright Assn., Soc. des Etudes Céliniennes, Samuel Beckett Soc., Midwest Modern Lang. Assn. Home: 2049 Barry Ave West Los Angeles CA 90025

KRASNEY, MARTIN, writer, organization executive, educator; b. Phila., Apr. 2, 1945; s. Leonard and Sarah (Allen) K.; m. Pamela Parker Sanderson, Aug. 10, 1984; children: Samantha Sanderson, Parker Leonard Krasney. AB, Princeton U., 1967; MA, U. Mich., 1968; postgrad., Stanford U., 1968-69; MBA, Harvard U., 1975. Asst. to dir. Nat. Humanities Series/Woodrow Wilson Nat. Fellowship Found., Princeton, N.J., 1969-70, program dir., 1970-73; asst. to pres. Aspen Inst., N.Y.C., 1975-76, dir. exec. seminars, 1976-81; mgr. exec. devel. Atlantic Richfield Co., L.A., 1981-82; pres. Am. Leadership Forum, Houston, 1982-83; dir. pub. affairs Levi Strauss & Co., San Francisco, 1983-85; pres. Ctr. for the Twenty-First Century, San Francisco, 1986—; exec. dir. Coalition for the Presidio Pacific Ctr., San Francisco, 1991-96; sr. fellow Commonweal, 1995—; con. to found., ednl. orgns. and corps. Editor Aspen Institute Readings, 1976-81. Bd. dirs. Calif. Tomorrow, 1988—; trustee Marin Country Day Sch., 1992—; mem. adv. bd. Commonweal, Global Fund for Women. Home: 122 Santa Rosa Ave Sausalito CA 94965-2035 Office: 220 Sansome St Ste 1300 San Francisco CA 94104-2728

KRASSA, KATHY BOLTREK, molecular biologist; b. N.Y.C., Dec. 6, 1946; d. Henry and Gloria Beatrice (Poliakoff) Boltrek; m. Robert Frederick Taylor Krassa; children: Josh Boltrek, Vicky Krassa. BS, Cornell U., 1968; postgrad., L.I. U., 1973-74; PhD, U. Colo., 1987. Lab. tech. U. Colo., Boulder, 1968-70; teaching asst. C.W. Post Coll., L.I. U., Glen Cove, N.Y., 1973-74; rsch. assoc. Nassau County Med. Ctr., East Meadow, N.Y., 1975-79; teaching asst. U. Colo., Boulder, 1980-81, rsch. asst., 1981-87, postdoctoral rschr., 1988-91; CEO Molecular Jeanetics, Boulder, 1991—. Author: Structure and Function of the Single-Stranded DNA Binding Protein of the Bacteriophage T4, 1987; contbr. articles to profl. jours. NIH grantee, 1974, 82, Am. Cancer Soc. rsch. grantee, 1988, 89.

KRATKA, ILENE, artist, sculptor; b. Bridgeton, N.J., May 31, 1941; d. William Herbert Kratka and Zelda Verna Osdin; companion Lawrence A. Healey, Oct. 15, 1983. BA, American U., 1965; postgrad., Corcoran Sch. Art, 1968-71. Presch. tchr. Headstart Program, Washington, 1963-65; pottery tchr. Centering, Cambridge, Mass., 1971-77, Hui Noeau, Maui, Hawaii, 1977-78. Exhibited in group shows including Hawaii Craftsman, 1979, Art Maui, 1989, Lahaina Arts Soc., 1985, Hui Noeau, 1987, Viewpoints Gallery, 1990, 93, 94, 95; in collections of H.M.S. Assocs., San Francisco, The Willkinsburg Drop-In Ctr., Pitts., County of Maui. Mem. Centering Pottery Coop., Cambridge, Mass., 1970-77. Mem. Centering Pottery (co-founder), Maui Crafts Guild (bd. dirs., display chairperson), Viewpoints Artists Collective (bd. dirs. and installations, pres. 1997). Office: Viewpoints Artists Collective 3620 Baldwin Ave Makawao HI 96768-9500

KRATZER, CINDY CARSON, religious organization administrator; b. King City, Calif., Oct. 6, 1959; d. Warren Bradford and Susan (Chakmakjian) Carson; m. Hank A. Kratzer IV, Apr. 14, 1989. MusB, Univ. Pacific, 1981; MEd, UCLA, 1991, PhD, 1996. Cert. tchr., Calif. Tchr. World Impact, Inc., L.A., 1981-90, human resource mgr., 1990-92, coord. staff and curriculum devel., 1996—; asst. prin. World Impact, Inc., L.A., 1989-91. Mem. bd. dirs. L.A. Christian Sch., 1992—. Office: World Impact Inc 2001 S Vermont Ave Los Angeles CA 90007-1256

KRAUS, JOE, editor and publisher, writer; b. Portland, Oreg., Sept. 8, 1939; s. Joseph Kraus and Ethel Riggs; m. Karren Kraus, Apr. 10, 1968; children: Heidi, Peter, Becky. Student, Citrus Coll., Azusa, Calif., 1966-68. Mng. editor Prescott (Ariz.) Evening Courier, 1970-72, Banning (Calif.) Daily Record, 1973-75, Daily Ledger-Gazette, Lancaster, Calif., 1976-85; editor, pub. Autograph Collector Mag., 1986-92, Child Stars Mag., 1992—. Author: Alive in the Desert, 1978; author more than 300 nat. mag. articles in more than 60 publs. Scoutmaster, Boy Scouts Am., 12 yrs. Served with USN, 1961-63. Democrat. Mormon. Home and Office: PO Box 55328 Stockton CA 95205-8828

KRAUS, JOHN WALTER, former aerospace engineering company executive; b. N.Y.C., Feb. 5, 1918; s. Walter Max Kraus and Marian Florance (Nathan) Sandor; m. Janice Edna Utter, June 21, 1947 (dec. Feb. 1981); children: Melinda Jean Kraus Peters, Kim Kohl Kraus; m. Jean Curtis, Aug. 27, 1983. BS, MIT, 1941; MBA, U. So. Calif., 1972. Registered indsl. engr., Calif. From indsl. engr. to indsl. engring. mgr. TRW, Inc., Cleve., 1941-61; spl. asst. Atomics Internat., Chatsworth, Calif., 1961-65; br. chief McDonnell Douglas Astronautics Co., Huntington Beach, Calif., 1966-74; sr. mgr. McDonnell Douglas Space Systems Co., Huntington Beach, Calif., 1983-93; pres. Kraus and DuVall, Inc., Santa Ana, Calif., 1975-83; retired, 1993; cons. Tech. Assocs. So. Calif., Santa Ana, 1974-75. Author: (handbook) Handbook of Reliability Engineering and Management, 1988. Mem. Am. Def. Preparedness Assn. (life, chmn. tech. div. 1954-57), Nat. Soc. Profl. Engrs. (life), Oasis Sailing Club (commodore 1996—). Republican. Home: 2001 Commodore Rd Newport Beach CA 92660-4307

KRAUS, PANSY DAEGLING, gemology consultant, editor, writer; b. Santa Paula, Calif., Sept. 21, 1916; d. Arthur David and Elsie (Pardee) Daegling; m. Charles Frederick Kraus, Mar. 1, 1941 (div. Nov. 1961). AA, San Bernardino Valley Jr. Coll., 1938; student Longmeyer's Bus. Coll., 1940; grad. gemologist diploma Gemological Assn. Gt. Britain, 1960, Gemological Inst. Am., 1966. Clk. Convair, San Diego, 1943-48; clk. San Diego County Schs. Publs., 1948-57; mgr. Rogers and Boblet Art-Craft, San Diego, 1958-64; part-time editorial asst. Lapidary Jour., San Diego, 1963-64, assoc. editor, 1964-69, editor, 1970-94, sr. editor, 1984-85; pvt. practice cons., San Diego, 1985—; lectr. gems, gemology local gem, mineral groups; gem & mineral club bull. editor groups. Mem. San Diego Mineral & Gem Soc., Gemol. Soc. San Diego, Gemol. Assn. Great Britain, Mineral. Soc. Am., Gemological Inst. Am., Epsilon Sigma Alpha. Author: Introduction to Lapidary, 1987; editor, layout dir.: Gem Cutting Shop Helps, 1964, The Fundamentals of Gemstone Carving, 1967, Appalachian Mineral and Gem Trails, 1968, Practical Gem Knowledge for the Amateur, 1969, Southwest Mineral and Gem Trails, 1972, Introduction to Lapidary, 1987; revision editor Gemcraft (Quick and Leiper), 1977; contbr. articles to Lapidary jour., Keystone Mktg. catalog. Home and Office: PO Box 600908 San Diego CA 92160-0908

KRAUSE, LAWRENCE BERLE, economics educator; b. Detroit, Dec. 8, 1929; s. Paul Henry and Lena (Blair) K.; m. Sallye Kirstein, Dec. 20, 1953; children: Leonard, Jason. BA, U. Mich., 1951, MA, 1952; PhD, Harvard U., 1958. Instr. Yale U., New Haven, 1957-58, asst. prof., 1958-63; sr. fellow The Brookings Instn., Washington, 1963-67, 69-86; sr. staff Coun. of Econ. Advisers, Washington, 1967-69; prof. econs., dir. Korea-Pacific Program U. Calif., San Diego, 1986-90, Pacific Econ. Coop. prof., chair, dir. Korea Pacific Program, 1990-97, prof. emeritus, dir. Korea-Pacific program, APEC Studies Ctr., 1997—; mem. editorial bd. Calif. Mgmt. Rev., 1988—; coord. Pacific econ. outlook project Pacific Econ. Coop. Coun., 1988—; mem. com. on U.S.-Republic of Korea Rels., 1989—; bd. advisors U.S.-Korea Found., 1991—; mem. adv. com. Robert A. Scalapino Program for Edn. on Korea, The Asia Soc., 1992—; mem. internat. adv. panel East-West Ctr., 1993—; hon. adviser Inst. for High Intelligence Edn., Hong Kong, 1996—. Author: U.S. Economic Policy Toward Association of S.E. Asian Nations: Meeting the Japanese Challenge, 1982, The Singapore Economy Reconsidered, 1987; co-editor: Trade and Growth of the Advanced Developing Countries in Pacific Basin, 1981, The Australian Economy, A View from the North, 1984, Liberalization in the Process of Economic Development, 1991, Social Issues in Korea: A Korean and American Perspective, 1993; mem. editl. adv. bd. Singapore Econ. Rev., 1994—, Hong Kong Bank of Can. Papers on Asia., 1994—. Endowed chair Pacific Econ. Cooperation U. Calif., San Diego, 1990; 1st lt. USMC, 1954-56. Disting vis. fellow Korea Devel. Inst., 1984; Disting fellow internat. banking and fin. Inst. of SE Asian Studies, 1986; fellow Social Sci. Rsch. Coun., 1961-62, fellow Brookings Instn., 1961-62. Home: 13941 Nob Ave Del Mar CA 92014-3063 Office: U Calif-San Diego Grad Sch Internat Rels & Pacific Studies Gilman Dr La Jolla CA 92093-0519

KRAUSE, THOMAS EVANS, record promotion consultant; b. Mpls., Dec. 17, 1951; s. Donald Bernhard and Betty Ann (Nokleby) K.; m. Barbara Ann Kaufman, Aug. 17, 1974 (div. Apr. 1978); m. Nicole Michelle Purkerson, Aug. 13, 1988; children: Andrew Todd Evans, Allison Michelle. Student, Augsburg Coll., 1969-73; BA, Hastings Coll., 1975. Lic. 3d class with broadcast endorsement FCC. Air personality Sta. KHAS Radio, Hastings, Nebr., 1974-75; air personality, news dir. Sta. KWSL Radio, Sioux City, Iowa, 1975-76; asst. program dir. Sta. KISD Radio, Sioux Falls, S.D., 1976-78; music dir. Sta. KVOX Radio, Fargo, N.D., 1978; program dir. Sta. KPRQ Radio, Salt Lake City, 1978-79; air personality Sta. KIOA Radio, Des Moines, 1980; program dir., ops. mgr. Sta. KKSS Radio, Sioux Falls, 1981-83; program dir. Stas. KIYS/KBBK Radio, Boise, Idaho, 1983-87; program dir., ops. mgr. Sta. WSRZ AM/FM Radio, Sarasota, Fla., 1988-90; owner, cons. Tom Evans Mktg., Seattle, 1990—; editor, pub. Northwest Log, Seattle, 1991-96; mgr. neverMAN, 1994—; co-founder Sta. KCMR Radio, Augsburg Coll., Mpls., 1973; TV show coord./host Z-106 Hottraxx, Sarasota, 1988-90; air personality/guest disc jockey various radio stas., Pacific N.W., 1990—; host Am. Music Report. Sta. KIX-106 Radio, Canberra, Australia, 1992; instr. Sta. KGRG-FM and KENU-AM, Green River Coll., Auburn, Wash., 1994—. Contbr. articles to various trade publs., mags. Bd. judges Loyola U. Marconi Awards, Chgo., 1992-93; bd. dirs. Habitat for Humanity, Snohomish County, Wash., 1992-96, Martin Luther King Day Celebration, Sarasota County, Fla., 1989-90, Shoreline/So. County YMCA, 1992-95; dist. coord. Carter for Pres., Nebr. 1st Dist., 1975-76; hon. chairperson March of Dimes Walk Am., Sioux Falls, 1977; media vol., MC or spokesperson M.S. Soc., MDA, Am. Diabetes Assn., Human Soc., others. Mem. Free Methodist Ch. Office: Tom Evans Mktg 16426 65th Ave W Lynnwood WA 98037-2710

KRAVETZ, NATHAN, educator, author; b. N.Y.C., Feb. 11, 1921; s. Louis and Anna (Thau) K. m. Evelyn Cottan, Dec. 10, 1944; children: Deborah Ruth, Daniel. BEd with hons., UCLA, 1941, MA, 1949, EdD, 1954. Cert. tchg., adminstrn., Calif. Tchr. Walnut Creek (Calif.) Elem Sch., 1941-42; tchr., prin. L.A. Unified Sch. Dist., 1946-64; prof. Hunter/Lehman Coll., CUNY, N.Y.C., 1964-76; prof. internat. and gifted edn., dean Calif. State U., San Bernardino, 1976-84; fgn. svc. officer U.S. Dept. State, Lima, Peru, 1958-60; staff officer UNESCO, Paris, 1969-72, cons. Venezuela, 1968; cons. Ford Found., Chile, 1964, UN Devel. Program, S.Am., 1973-74; cons. U.S. AID, Pakistan and Indonesia, 1974-75, Benin, 1977, Guatemala, 1992. Author 9 children's books. Mem. Am. Jewish Com., L.A. With USAAF, 1942-46. Univ. fellow Harvard U., 1951-52; grantee Fulbright Found., Argentina, 1980.

KRAVITZ, ELLEN KING, musicologist, educator; b. Fords, N.J., May 25, 1929; d. Walter J. and Frances M. (Prybylowski) Kokowicz; m. Hilard L. Kravitz, Jan. 9, 1972; 1 child, Julie Frances; stepchildren: Kent, Kerry, Jay. BA, Georgian Ct. Coll., 1964; MM, U. So. Calif., 1966, PhD, 1970. Tchr. 7th and 8th grade music Mt. St. Mary Acad., North Plainfield, N.J., 1949-50; cloistered nun Carmelite Monastery, Lafayette, La., 1950-61; instr. Loyola U., L.A., 1967; asst. prof. music Calif. State U., L.A., 1967-71, assoc. prof., 1971-74, prof., 1974—; founder Friends of Music at Calif. State U., L.A., 1976. Author: Music in Our Culture, 1996; Jour. Arnold Schoenberg Inst., L.A.; jour. editor Vol I, No. 3, 1977, Vol II, No. 3, 1978; author (with others) Catalog of Schoenberg's Paintings, Drawings and Sketches; mem. editl. adv. bd. Jour. Arnold Schoenberg Inst., 1977-87. Mem. Schoenberg Centennial Com., 1974, guest lectr., 1969—. Recipient award for masters thesis U. So. Calif., 1966. Mem. Am. Musicol. Soc. (treas. Pacific S.W. chpt. 1994—), L.A. County Mus. Art, L.A. Music Ctr., Mu Phi Epsilon, Pi Kappa Lambda. Home: PO Box 5360 Beverly Hills CA 90209-5360

KRAVITZ, HILARD L(EONARD), physician; b. Dayton, Ohio, June 26, 1917; s. Philip and Ethel (Charek) K.; divorced; children: Kent C., Kerry, Jay; m. Ellen King, Jan. 9, 1972; 1 child, Julie Frances. BA, U. Cin., 1939, MD, 1943. Lic. physician, Calif., Ohio. Resident in internal medicine Miami Valley Hosp., VA Hosp., Dayton, 1946-49; practice medicine specializing in internal medicine Dayton, 1950-54, Beverly Hills and Los Angeles, Calif., 1955—; practice medicine specializing in internal medicine and cardiology Los Angeles, 1955—; attending physician Cedars-Sinai Med. Ctr., 1955—; cons., med. dir. Adolph's Ltd., Los Angeles, 1955-74; mem. exec. com. Reiss-Davis Clinic, Los Angeles, 1966-70; chmn. pharmacy and therapeutic com. Cent City Hosp., Los Angeles, 1974-79; mem. pain commn. service Dept. Health and Human Services, Washington, 1985-86. Patentee sugar substitute, 1959, mineral-based salt, 1978. V.p. Friends of Music Calif. State U., Los Angeles, 1979-81. Served to capt. U.S. Army, 1944-46, ETO. Decorated Bronze Star with oak leaf cluster; Fourragere (France). Mem. AMA, Calif. Med. Assn., Los Angeles County Med. Assn., Am. Soc. Internal Medicine, Calif. Soc. Internal Medicine (del. 1974). Jewish. Office: 436 N Bedford Dr Ste 211 Beverly Hills CA 90210-4312

KRAVITZ, LENNY, singer, guitarist. Albums: Let Love Rule, 1989, Mama Said, 1991, Are You Gonna Go My Way, 1993 (2 Grammy nominations), Circus, 1995. Office: care CAA 9830 Wilshire Blvd Beverly Hills CA 90212-1804 also: Virgin Records 550 Madison Ave New York NY 10019*

KRAVJANSKY, MIKULAS, artist; b. Rudnany, Slovakia, May 3, 1928; came to U.S., 1978; s. Imrich and Anna (Kubicekova) K.; m. Ruzena Horvath, Jan. 4, 1958; 1 child, Vladimir. Magister, Acad. Muzas Arts, Czechoslovakia, 1957. Scenographer State Theatre of J.Z., Czechoslovakia, 1957-62, Nat. Theatre Czechoslovakia, Bratislava, 1958-68; head of art and design Czechoslovakian Tel., Bratislava, 1962-68; asst. master Humber Coll., Toronto, Ont., Can., 1969-75; creator, dir. Black Box Theatre Can., Toronto, 1969-78; pres. Kravjansky Arts Inc., Pampano Beach, Fla., 1978-88, Napa, Calif., 1988—; asst. prof. Acad. of Muzas Art, Bratislava, 1962-68. Bd. dirs. Assn. Slovak Artists, Bratislava, 1965-68. Recipient Golden medal Bienale of Art, Sao Paulo, 1958. Mem. Kiwanis Internat. (bd. dirs. 1989-90). Home: 23 Newport Dr Napa CA 94559-4819

KRAW, GEORGE MARTIN, lawyer, essayist; b. Oakland, Calif., June 17, 1949; s. George and Pauline Dorothy (Herceg) K.; m. Sarah Lee Kenyon, Sept. 3, 1983. BA, U. Calif.-Santa Cruz, 1971; student, Lenin Inst., Moscow, 1971; MA, U. Calif.-Berkeley, 1974, JD, 1976. Bar: Calif. 1976, U.S. Dist. Ct. (no. dist.) Calif. 1976, U.S. Supreme Ct. 1980, D.C., 1992. Pvt. practice, 1976—; ptnr. Kraw & Kraw, San Jose, 1988—; Mem. ABA, Am. Soc. Law, Medicine and Ethics, Nat. Assn. Health Lawyers, Inter-Am. Bar Assn., Union Internationale des Avocats, Internat. Bar Assn. Office: Kraw & Kraw 333 W San Carlos St Ste 1050 San Jose CA 95110-2711

KREBS, EDWIN GERHARD, biochemistry educator; b. Lansing, Iowa, June 6, 1918; s. William Carl and Louise Helena (Stegeman) K.; m. Virginia Frech, Mar. 10, 1945; children: Sally, Robert, Martha. AB in Chemistry, U. Ill., 1940; MD, Washington U., St. Louis, 1943, DSc (hon.), 1995; DSc honoris causa, U. Geneva, 1979; hon. degree, Med. Coll. Ohio, 1993; DSc (hon.), U. Ind., 1993, U. Ill., 1995; D honoris causa, U. Nat. De Cuyo, 1993. Intern, asst. resident Barnes Hosp., St. Louis, 1944-45; rsch. fellow biol. chemistry Wash. U., St. Louis, 1946-48; prof., chmn. dept. biol. chemistry Sch. Medicine U. Calif., Davis, 1968-76; from asst. prof. to prof. biochemistry U. Wash., Seattle, 1948-66, prof., chmn. dept. pharmacology, 1977-83, prof. biochemistry and pharmacology, 1984-91; investigator, sr. investigator Howard Hughes Med. Inst., Seattle, 1983-90, sr. investigator emeritus, 1991—; mem. Phys. Chemistry Study Sect. NIH, 1963-68, Biochemistry Test Com. Nat. Bd. Med. Examiners, 1968-71, rsch. com. Am. Heart Assn., 1970-74, bd. sci. counselors Nat. Inst. Arthritis, Metabolism and Digestive Diseases, NIH, 1979-84, Internat. Bd. Rev., Alberta Heritage Found. for Med. Rsch., 1986, external adv. com. Weis Ctr. for Rsch., 1987-91; mem. subgroup interconvertible enzymes IUB Spl. Interest Group Metabolic Regulation; internat. adv. bd. Advances in Second Messenger Phosphoprotein Rsch.; external adv. com. Cell Therapeutics Inc., Seattle; adv. bd. Kinetek, Vancouver, B.C. Mem. editorial bd. Jour. Biol. Chemistry, 1965-70; mem. editorial adv. bd. Biochemistry, 1971-76; mem. editorial and adv. bd. Molecular Pharmacology, 1972-77; assoc. editor Jour. Biol. Chemistry, 1971-93; mem. internat. adv. bd. Advances in Cyclic Nucleotide Rsch., 1972—; editorial advisor Molecular and Cellular Biochemistry, 1987—. Recipient Nobel Prize in Medicine or Physiology, 1992, Gairdner Found. award, Toronto, 1978, J.J. Berzelius lectureship, Karolinska Institutet, 1982, George W. Thorn award for sci. excellence, 1983, Sir Frederick Hopkins Meml. lectureship, London, 1984, Rsch. Achievement award Am. Heart Assn., Anaheim, Calif., 1987, 3M Life Scis. award FASEB, New Orleans, 1989, Albert Lasker Basic Med. Rsch. award, 1989, CIBA-GEIGY-Drew award Drew U., 1991, Steven C. Beering award, Ind. U., 1991, Welch award in chemistry Welch Found., 1991, Louisa Gross Horwitz award Columbia U., 1989, Alumni Achievement award Coll. Liberal Arts and Scis. U. Ill., 1992, Kaul Found. award for excellence, 1996; John Simon Guggenheim fellow, 1959, 66. Mem. NAS, Am. Soc. Biol. Chemists (pres. 1986, ednl. affairs com. 1965-68, councillor 1975-78), Am. Acad. Arts and Scis., Am. Soc. Pharmacology and Exptl. Therapeutics. Office: U Wash Dept Pharmacology Box 357370 Seattle WA 98195

KREBS, NINA BOYD, psychologist; b. Phoenix, Sept. 9, 1938; d. Hugh Lewis and Elizabeth Bevette (Burleson) Boyd; m. Richard Lee Schafer, Aug. 13, 1960 (div. 1969); children: Erica Schafer, Karen Fleming; m. David O. Krebs, Aug. 27, 1973. BA in Edn., Ariz. State U., 1960, MA in Edn., 1964; EdD in Counseling and Guidance, Ball State U., Muncie, Ind., 1971. Lic. psychologist, Calif. Counseling psychologist Calif. State U., Sacramento, 1971-76; ptnr. Ctr. for Family, Individual and Orgnl. Devel., Sacramento, 1976-83; pvt. practice psychology Sacramento, 1976—; psychology examiner Calif. State Bd. of Med. Quality Assurance, 1978-93; ind. contractor U.S. Bur. Reclamation, Mid-Pacific Region, 1979; cons. in field; presenter workshops in field; lectr. in field, creator, presenter 7-session workshop series, Feminine Power at Work, 1990—. Author: Changing Woman Changing Work, 1993; co-author: (with Robert Allen) Psychotheatrics, the New Art of Self-Transformation, 1979; contbr. articles to profl. jours. Mem. Sacramento Valley Psychol. Assn. (divsn. 1 pres. 1991-92), Orgn. of Calif. Counseling Ctr. Dirs. in Higher Edn., Calif. Pers. Assn. (statewide chair counseling ctr., 1974-75). Office: 2200 L St Sacramento CA 95816-4927

KREBS, SHERRY LYNN, elementary education educator; b. Seattle, May 26, 1951; d. Donald Eugene and Ailene Leda (Wine) Barngrover; m. Kenneth Marvin Krebs, Aug. 25, 1950; children: Camille Kathleen, Karl Josef. BA, Whitworth Coll., Spokane, Wash., 1973; MEd, Lesley Coll., Cambridge, Mass., 1996. Tchr. jr. high sch. phys. edn. Wenatchee (Wash.) Pub. Schs., 1973-80; bus. mgr. Wenatchee Valley Symphony, 1980-88; tchr. elem. music Wenatchee (Wash.) Pub. Schs., 1989—. Prodr./artist: (cassette tape music) Woodside: Dances and Dreams, 1994. Actor, musician, condr. Music Theater of Wenatchee, 1975—; music dir. Short Shakespeareans, Wenatchee, 1986-92. Recipient Christa MacAulliff Excellence in Edn. award State of Wash. Legis., 1994, Excellence in Edn. award North Ctrl. Wash. E.S.D., 1994; Barbara Thomas Meml. scholar, 1993. Mem. NEA, ASCD, Wash. Edn. Assn., Wenatchee Edn. Assn. Home: 1520 9th St Wenatchee WA 98801 Office: Lincoln Elem Sch 1224 Methow St Wenatchee WA 98801

KREDLO, THOMAS ANDREW, real estate appraiser; b. East Chicago, Ind., Jan. 27, 1952; s. Raymond Vincent and Mary Maude (Smith) K. BS, Ind. U., 1977. Loan officer Michigan City (Ind.) Savs. and Loan, 1978-81; assoc. appraiser Meyer & Assocs., Hillsboro, Oreg., 1981-85, Lamb, Hanson, Lamb, Seattle, 1985-93; staff appraiser Strategic Mortgage Svcs., Denver, 1993-96. Author of short stories. Mem. Ptarmigan Mountaineering Club. Democrat. Mem. Ch. of God in Christ.

KREGER, MELVIN JOSEPH, lawyer; b. Buffalo, Feb. 21, 1937; s. Philip and Bernice (Gerstman) K.; m. Patricia Anderson, July 1, 1955 (div. 1963); children: Beth Barbour, Arlene Roux; m. Renate Hochleitner, Aug. 15, 1975. JD, Mid-valley Coll. Law, 1978; LLM in Taxation, U. San Diego, 1988. Bar: Calif. 1978, U.S. Dist. Ct. (cen. dist.) Calif. 1979, U.S. Tax Ct. 1979, U.S. Supreme Ct. 1995; cert. specialist in probate law, trust law and estate planning law, Calif., cert. specialist in taxation law, Calif. Life underwriter Met. Life Ins. Co., Buffalo, 1958-63; bus. mgr. M. Kreger Bus. Mgmt., Sherman Oaks, Calif., 1963-78;, 1971—; sole practice North Hollywood, Calif., 1978—. Mem. Nat. Assn. Enrolled Agts., Calif. Soc. Enrolled Agts., State Bar Calif., L.A. Bar Assn., San Fernando Valley Bar Assn. (probate sect., tax sect.). Jewish. Office: 11424 Burbank Blvd North Hollywood CA 91601-2301

KREIL, CURTIS LEE, research chemist; b. Milw., Aug. 22, 1955; s. Hugo Harvey and Sofia (Patelski) K. AA, U. Wis. Ctr., West Bend, 1975; BS in Chemistry, U. Wis., Madison, 1977; PhD in Chemistry, U. Calif., Los Angeles, 1983. Tech. prodn. asst. DIMAT Inc., Cedarburg, Wis., 1973-75; rsch. asst. U. Wis., Madison, 1975-77; rsch. fellow Columbia U., N.Y.C., 1976; rsch. asst. U. Calif., L.A., 1977-82; sr. rsch. chemist 3M, St. Paul, 1983-86; quality assurance supr. 3M, Camarillo, Calif., 1986-90, tech. mgr., 1990-92, tech. specialist, 1993-96; tech. specialist Imation Enterprises Corp., White City, Oreg., 1996—; chmn. photochemistry chpt. 3M Tech. Forum, St. Paul, 1984-85; chmn. 3M Tech. Forum, Camarillo, 1989-90. Contbr. articles to profl. jours.; inventor electron beam adhesion-promoting treatment of polyester film base for silicone release liners, electron beam adhesion promoting treatment of polyester film base. 1st lt. CAP. Recipient Merck Index award Merck & Co., 1977; grad. fellow NSF, 1977-80. Mem. Am. Chem. Soc., Aircraft Owners and Pilots Assn., Exptl. Aircraft Assn. (v.p. 1991), 3M Aviation Club (pres. 1985-86), Phi Beta Kappa. Office: Imation Enterprises Inc 8124 Pacific Ave White City OR 97503

KREINBERG, PENELOPE PETTIT, counselor; b. N.Y.C., Aug. 3, 1946; d. William Dutton and Carole (Earle) P.; m. Robert Lee Kreinberg, July 4, 1968; children: Joshua Adam, Patricia Dawn, Sarah Lynn. BA in Psychology/Sociology/Anthropology, Cornell U., 1968; MA in Counseling Psychology, Lewis & Clark Coll., 1993. Portland (Oreg.) chair Candlelighters for Children, 1982, 87, Oreg. pres., 1988-90; instr., counselor Clackama C.C., Portland, 1993—; pvt. practice counselor Portland, 1994-96; bd. dirs. Candlelighters for Children, Oreg., 1984-96; bd. dirs. Candlelighters Childhood Cancer Found., Washington, 1990-96. Bd. dirs. Camp Ukandu, Am. Cancer Found., Portland, 1985-89, mem. adv. bd. svc. and rehab. com., 1987-89; mem. local sch. adv. com. Grant H.S. PTA, Portland, 1984-88, 92-96; vol. U.S. Peace Corps, Colombia, 1968-70; vol. facilitator Dougy Ctr. for Grieving Children, Portland, 1994-96; vol. Ronald McDonald House, Portland, 1988-89; People to People Citizen Ambassador to South Africa, 1996. Recipient Cmty. Svc. award J. C. Penney, 1990, Met. Family Svc. award City of Portland, 1988. Mem. Nat. Counseling Assn., Oreg. Counseling Assn., Am. Assn. Mental Health Counselors, Oreg. Assn. Aging and Devel., Assn. for Psychol. Type, Am. Assn. Women in C.C.s, Oreg. Career Devel. Assn., Phi Beta Kappa, Delta Gamma. Democrat. Episcopalian. Home: 3145 NE 20th Ave Portland OR 97212-2410

KREISSMAN, STARRETT, librarian; b. N.Y.C., Jan. 4, 1946; d. Bernard and Shirley (Relis) K.; m. David Dolan, Apr. 13, 1985; 1 child, Sonya. BA, Grinnell Coll., 1967; MLS, Columbia U., 1968. Asst. circulation libr. Columbia U., N.Y.C., 1968-70; sci. libr. N.Y. Pub. Libr., N.Y.C., 1970-71; outreach libr. Stanislaus County Free Libr., Modesto, Calif., 1971-73, Oakdale libr., 1974-79, acquisitions libr., 1979-85, br. supr., 1985-92, county libr., 1992—. Writer book revs. Stanislaus County Commn. on Women. Mem. ALA, Pub. Libr. Assn., Calif. Libr. Assn. (legis. com. 1993-95), Rotary. Office: Stanislaus County Free Libr 1500 I St Modesto CA 95354-1120

KREITENBERG, ARTHUR, orthopedic surgeon, consultant; b. L.A., Apr. 24, 1957; s. Sam and Irene Dina (Deutsch) K.; m. Melissa Carr, Sept. 4, 1988; children: Elliot Moses, Zoe Rachel. B of Math. magna cum laude, UCLA, 1978; MD, U. Calif., San Diego, 1982; cert. bioengr., U. Calif., Irvine, 1984. Diplomate Am. Bd. Orthopedic Surgeons. Summer intern NASA, Houston, 1979; resident U. Calif., Irvine, 1982-87, chief resident, 1987-88, asst. clin. prof., 1989—; pvt. practice Beverly Hills, Calif., 1989—; expert med. reviewer Med. Bd. Calif., Sacramento, 1991—; med. examiner State of Calif., San Francisco, 1993—. Contbr. articles to profl. jours.; patentee in field. Bd. dirs., past pres. Calif. Handicapped Skiers, Big Bear, Calif., 1992—; med. officer Nat. Disaster Med. Systems, San Diego, 1994—. Astronaut selection finalist NASA, 1992, 94. Fellow ACS, Am. Acad. Orthopedic Surgeons; mem. AIAA. Office: 436 N Roxbury Dr Ste 202 Beverly Hills CA 90210-5017

KREITZBERG, FRED CHARLES, construction management company executive; b. Paterson, N.J., June 1, 1934; s. William and Ella (Bohen) K.; m. Barbara Braun, June 9, 1957; children: Kim, Caroline, Allison, Bruce, Catherine. BSCE, Norwich U., 1957, DS in Bus. Adminstrn. (hon.), 1994. Registered profl. engr., Ala., Alaska, Ariz., Ark., Calif., Colo., Del., D.C., Fla., Ga., Idaho, Ill., Ind., Iowa, Kans., Ky., Md., Mass., Minn., Miss., Mo., Nebr., Nev., N.H., N.J., N.Mex., N.Y., Ohio, Okla., Oreg., S.C., S.D., Tenn., Va., Vt., Wash., W.Va., Wis., Wyo. Asst. supt. Turner Constrn. Co., N.Y.C., 1957; project mgr. Project Mercury RCA, N.J., 1958-63; schedule cost mgr. Catalytic Constrn. Co., Pa., 1963-65, 65—; cons. Meridien Engring., 1965-68; prin. MDC Systems Corp., 1968-72; chmn., CEO O'Brien-Kreitzberg Inc., San Francisco, 1972—; lectr. Stanford (Calif.) U., U. Calif., Berkeley. Author: Crit. Path Method Scheduling for Contractor's Mgmt. Handbook, 1971; tech. editor Constrn. Inspection Handbook, 1972; contbr. articles to profl. jours. Bd. dirs. Partridge Soc.; chmn. bd. trustees Norwich U. 2d lt. C.E., U.S. Army, 1957-58. Recipient Disting. Alumnus award Norwich U., 1987; named Boss of Yr., Nat. Assn. Women in Constrn., 1987, Crystal Vision award, 1997; named in his honor Kreitzberg Amphitheatre, 1987, Kreitzberg Libr. at Norwich U., 1992; Bay Area Discovery Mus.-Birthday rm. and snack bar named in honor of Kreitzberg family, 1989. Fellow ASCE (Constrn. Mgr. of Yr. 1982); mem. Am. Arbitration Assn., Constrn. Mgmt. Assn. Am. (founding, bd. dirs.), Soc. Am. Value Engrs., Community Field Assn., Ross Hist. Soc., N.J. Soc. Civil Engrs., N.J. Soc. Profl. Planners, Project Mgmt. Inst., Constrn. Industry Pres. Forum. Home: 19 Spring Rd PO Box 1200 Ross CA 94957-1200 Office: OBrien-Kreitzberg Inc 50 Fremont St 24th Fl San Francisco CA 94105

KREJCI, ROBERT HARRY, non-profit organizations development consultant; b. Chgo., June 4, 1913; s. John and Johanna (Tischer) K.; m. Marian Hallock, Mar. 28, 1941 (dec. Aug. 1986); 1 child, Susan Ann Krejci Stevens. BS in Forestry with honors, Mich. State U., 1940. Dist. exec. Boy Scouts Am., Chgo., 1940-48, asst. scout exec., 1948-50; scout exec. Boy Scouts Am., Herrin, Ill., Huntington, W.Va., 1950-65; devel. cons. The Cumerford Corp., Kansas City, 1965-73; dir. western divsn. The Cumerford Corp., Ft. Lauderdale, Fla., 1974-78; devel. cons. in pvt. practice, San Diego, 1978-90; co-founder, pres. Philanthropy Coun., San Diego, 1987-93; dir. World War II Farm Labor Camp, State of Ill., 1942, 43. Author: How to Succeed in Fund Raising For Your Non-Profit Organization, 1989. Vol. organizer United Way, various cities, Ill., 1955, 56. Recipient George Washington medal Freedoms Found. at Valley Forge, 1953; named Vol. of Yr. Philanthropy Coun., 1996, Exemplar, Rancho Bernardo Rotary Found., 1995. Mem. Rotary Internat. (Paul Harris fellow). Home: 16566 Casero Rd San Diego CA 92128

KREJCI, ROBERT HENRY, aerospace engineer; b. Shenandoah, Iowa, Nov. 15, 1943; s. Henry and Marie Josephine (Kubicek) K.; m. Carolyn R. Meyer, Aug. 21, 1967; children—Christopher S., Ryan D. B.S. with honors in Aerospace Engring., Iowa State U., Ames, 1967, M.Aerospace Engring., 1971. Commd. 2d lt. U.S. Air Force, 1968, advanced through grades to capt., 1978; lt. col. Res.; served with systems command Space Launch Vehicles Systems Program Office, Advanced ICBM program officer; research assoc. U.S. Dept. Energy Lawrence Livermore lab.; dept. mgr. advanced tech. programs Strategic div. Thiokol Corp., 1978-84, mgr. space programs, 1984-85, mgr. Navy spl. projects, 1986—. Decorated A.F. commendation medal, Nat. Def. Service medal, Meritorious Svc. medal. Fellow AIAA. Home: 885 N 300 E Brigham City UT 84302-1310 Office: Thiokol Corp PO Box 689 Brigham City UT 84302-0689

KREMERS, CAROLYN SUE, writer, musician, educator; b. Denver, Nov. 2, 1951; d. Richard Treakle and Patricia Sue (Willson) K. BA in English & Humanities with honors, Stanford U., 1973; BA in Flute Performance, Met. State Coll., 1981; MFA in Creative Writing, U. Alaska, 1991. Cert. secondary English lang. arts tchr., Alaska. Tchr. music and English various schs., Ill., Colo., Alaska, 1974-88; vis. asst. prof. English U. Alaska Fairbanks, 1991-92; asst. prof. devel. studies U. Alaska Fairbanks, Bethel, 1992-93; instr. English U. Alaska Fairbanks, 1993—; cons. Alaska State Writing Consortium, 1990—. Author: Place of the Pretend People: Gifts from a Yup'ik Eskimo Village, 1996; author numerous essays and poems. Individual Artist fellow Alaska State Coun. Arts, 1992. Home: PO Box 84231 Fairbanks AK 99708

KREMPEL, RALF HUGO BERNHARD, author, artist, art gallery owner; b. Groitzsch, Saxony, Germany, June 5, 1935; came to U.S., 1964; s. Curt Bernhard and Liesbeth Anna Margarete (Franz) K.; m. Barbara von Eberhardt, Dec. 21, 1967 (div. 1985); 1 child, Karma. Student, Wood and Steel Constrn. Coll., Leipzig, German Democratic Republic, 1955. Steel constructor worldwide, 1955-73; co-owner San Francisco Pvt. Mint, 1973-81; prin. artist San Francisco Painter Magnate, 1982—; dir. Stadtgalerie Wiprechtsburg Groitzsch, Germany, 1991—, Museumsgalerie am Markt, Groitzsch, 1994—. Exhbns. Centre Internat. d'Art Contemporain, 1985, Art Contemporain Cabinet des Dessins, 1986, Galerie Salammbo-Atlante, 1987 and others, Retrospective Mus.-gallery Borna, 1993; inventor, designer Visual Communication System, utilizing colors instead of letters to depict and transmit messages; 5 order of the universe registrations Libr. of Congress, Washington, 1991—. Home: 2400 Pacific Ave San Francisco CA 94115-1280 Office: San Francisco Painter Magnate Rincon Ctr San Francisco CA 94119-3368 also: Brühl 2, 04539 Groitzsch Germany

KREMPEL, ROGER ERNEST, public works management consultant; b. Waukesha, Wis., Oct. 8, 1926; s. Henry and Clara K.; m. Shirley Ann Gray, June 16, 1948; children: John, Sara, Peter. Student Ripon Coll., 1944, Stanford U., 1945; BCE, U. Wis.-Madison, 1950. Registered profl. engr., Wis., Colo.; registered land surveyor, Wis. Asst. city engr., Manitowoc, Wis., 1950-51; city engr. dir. pub. works, Janesville, Wis., 1951-75; dir. water utilities, pub. works Ft. Collins, Colo., 1975-84, dir. natural resources, streets and stormwater utilities, Ft. Collins, 1984-88; pub. works mgmt. cons., 1988—; lectr. various univ., coll., nat. confs. and seminars. Contbr. articles to profl. pubs. Past pres. bd. Janesville YMCA. Served with U.S. Army, 1944-46. Recipient numerous tech. and profl. awards, Distin. Svc. citation U. Wis. Coll. Engring., 1989. Fellow ASCE (life, Gov. Civil Engr. award 1984); mem. NSPE, AWWA (life), Am. Pub. Works Assn. (life mem., past pres. Colo. and Wis. chpts., past mem. rsch. found., Man of Yr. 1971, Nichols award 1984, Swearingen award 1988), Pub. Works Hist. Soc. (pres. 1993-95), Wis. Soc. Profl. Engrs. (past pres.), Am. Acad. Environ. Engrs. (diplomate, 1982-91), Colo. Engrs. Coun. (pres. 1990-91, honor award 1989), Am. Soc. Civil Engrs. (mgmt. award 1990)

KRENDL, CATHY STRICKLIN, lawyer; b. Paris, Tex., Mar. 14, 1945; d. Louis and Margaret Helen (Young) S.; m. James R. Krendl, July 5, 1969; children: Peggy, Susan, Anne. BA summa cum laude, North Tex. State U., 1967; JD cum laude, Harvard U., 1970. Bar: Alaska 1970, Colo. 1972. Atty. Hughes, Thorsness, Lowe Gantz & Clark, Anchorage, 1970-71; adj. prof. U. Colo. Denver Ctr., 1972-73; from asst. prof. to prof. law, dir. bus planning program U. Denver, 1973-83; ptnr. Krendl, Horowitz & Krendl, Denver, 1983—. Author: Business Organizations, 1997, Colorado Business Corporation Act Deskbook, 1997; editor: Colorado Methods of Practice, vols. 1983-97, Closely Held Corporations in Colorado, vols. 1-3, 1981; contbr. articles to profl jours. Named Disting. Alumna North Tex. State U., 1985. Mem. Colo. Bar Assn. (bd. govs. 1982-86, 88-91, chmn. securities subsect. 1986, bus. law sect. 1988-89), Denver Bar Assn. (pres. 1989-90). Office: Krendl Horowitz & Krendl 370 E 17th Ave Ste 5350 Denver CO 80203-1274

KREPS, DAVID MARC, economist, educator; b. N.Y.C., Oct. 18, 1950; s. Saul Ian and Sarah (Kaskin) Kreps; m. Anat Ruth Admati, Jan. 4, 1984; children: Tamar, Oren, Auner. AB, Dartmouth Coll., 1972; MA, PhD, Stanford U., 1975. Asst. prof. Stanford U., 1975-78, assoc. prof., 1978-80, prof., 1980-84, Holden prof., 1984—; rsch. officer U. Cambridge, Eng., 1978-79, fellow commoner Churchill Coll., Cambridge, 1978-79; vis. prof. Yale U., New Haven, 1982, Harvard U., Cambridge, Mass., 1983, U. Paris, 1985; vis. prof. U. Tel Aviv, 1989-90, sr. prof. by spl. apppintment, 1991—. Author: Notes on the Theory of Choice, 1988, A Course in Microeconomic Theory, 1990, Game Theory and Economic Modelling, 1990; co-editor Econometrica, 1984-88. Alfred P. Sloan Found. fellow, 1983, John S. Guggenheim fellow, 1988. Fellow Econometric Soc.; mem. Am. Econ. Assn. (J.B. Clark medal 1989), Am. Acad. Arts and Scis. Office: Stanford U Grad Sch of Bus Stanford CA 94305-5015

KRESA, KENT, aerospace executive; b. N.Y.C., Mar. 24, 1938; s. Helmy and Marjorie (Boutelle) K.; m. Joyce Anne McBride, Nov. 4, 1961; 1 child, Kiren. BSAA, MIT, 1959, MSAA, 1961, EAA, 1966. Sr. scientist research and advanced devel. div. AVCO, Wilmington, Mass., 1959-61; staff mem. MIT Lincoln Lab., Lexington, Mass., 1961-68; dep. dir. strategic tech. office Def. Advanced Research Projects Agy., Washington, 1968-73; dir. tactical tech. office Def. Advanced Research Project Agy., Washington, 1973-75; v.p., mgr. Research & Tech. Ctr. Northrop Corp., Hawthorne, Calif., 1975-76; v.p., gen. mgr. Ventura div. Northrop Corp., Newbury Park, Calif., 1976-82; group v.p. Aircraft Group Northrop Corp., L.A., 1982-86, sr. v.p. tech. devel. and planning, 1986-87, pres., COO, 1987-90; chmn. bd., pres., CEO Northrop Grumman Corp., L.A., 1990—; bd. dirs. John Tracy Clinic.; mem. Chief of Naval Ops. exec. panel Washington, Def. Sci. Bd., Washington, DNA New Alternatives Working Group, L.A., Dept. Aeronautics and Astronautics Corp. Vis. Com. MIT. Bd. dirs. John Tracy Clinic for the Hearing-Impaired, W.M. Keck Found., L.A. World Affairs Coun.; bd. govs. L.A. Music Ctr. Recipient Henry Webb Salsbury award MIT, 1959, Arthur D. Flemming award, 1975, Calif. Industrialist of Yr. Calif. Mus. of Sci. and Industry and the Calif. Mus. Found., 1996, Bob Hope Disting. Citizen award Nat. Security Indsl. Assn., 1996; Sec. of Def. Meritorious Civilian Service medal, 1975, USN Meritorious Pub. Service citation, 1975, Exceptional Civilian Service award USAF, 1987. Fellow AIAA; mem. Aerospace Industries Assn. (past bd. govs.), Naval Aviation Mus. Found., Navy League U.S., Soc. Flight Test Engrs., Assn. U.S. Army, Nat. Space Club, Am. Def. Preparedness Assn., L.A. Country Club. Office: Northrop Grumman Corp 1840 Century Park E Los Angeles CA 90067-2101

KREUTEL, RANDALL WILLIAM, JR., electrical engineer; b. Norwood, Mass., May 3, 1934; s. Randall William Sr. and Dorothy Elizabeth (Reynolds) K.; m. Kay Irene Dadmun, Oct. 19, 1958 (div. Nov. 1973); children: John William, James Thomas, Karen Irene, Robert Steven; m. Alice Jean Guillory, June 26, 1975. BSEE, Northea. U., 1961, MSEE, 1964; DSc, George Washington U., 1978. Rsch. engr. Sylvania Electronic System, Waltham, Mass., 1957-66; tech. staff Comsat Corp., Washington, 1966-68; dept. mgr. antenna dept. Comsat Corp., Clarksburg, Md., 1968-77, dir. optics lab., 1977-81, div. dir. devel. engr., 1981-84; div. dir. System Planning Corp., Arlington, Va., 1984-87; mgr. Sci.-Atlanta Corp., 1987-89; prin. engr. Electromagnetic Scis., Inc., Norcross, Ga., 1989-92; tech. staff mem. Motorola Satcom Div., Chandler, Ariz., 1992—. Contbr. McGraw-Hill Encyclopedia of Science and Technology, 6th, 7th editions; patentee in field; contbr. articles to profl. jours. Bd. dirs. System Planning Antenna Corp., 1986-88. Fellow AIAA (assoc.); mem. IEEE (sr.), Internat. Union Radio Sci., Antenna and Propagation Soc. (vice chmn. Washington and no. Va. chpt. 1986-87, chmn. 1987-880, Sigma Xi, Eta Kappa Nu. Home: 2005 E Granite View Dr Phoenix AZ 85048-4503 Office: Motorola Satcom 2501 S Price Rd Chandler AZ 85248-2802

KREUTZBERG, DAVID W., lawyer; b. Edwardsville, Ill., May 20, 1953. BA summa cum laude, Ariz. State U., 1975, JD magna cum laude, 1978. Bar: Ariz. 1978, U.S. Dist. Ct. (Ariz. dist.) 1978. Law clk. to Hon. William E. Eubank Ariz. Ct. Appeals, Phoenix, 1978-79; ptnr. Squire, Sanders & Dempsey LLP, Phoenix. Mem. ABA (mem. bus. law sect.), State Bar Ariz., Maricopa County Bar Assn., Phi Beta Kappa. Office: Squire Sanders & Dempsey LLP Two Renaissance Sq 40 N Central Ave Ste 2700 Phoenix AZ 85004-4424

KREVANS, JULIUS RICHARD, university administrator, physician; b. N.Y.C., May 1, 1924; s. Sol and Anita (Makovetsky) K.; m. Patricia N. Abrams, May 28, 1950; children: Nita, Julius R., Rachel, Sarah, Nora Kate. B.S. Arts and Scis, N.Y. U., 1943, M.D., 1946. Diplomate: Am. Bd. Internal Med. Intern, then resident Johns Hopkins Med. Sch. Hosp., mem. faculty, until 1970, dean acad. affairs, 1969-70; physician in chief Balt. City Hosp., 1963-69; prof. medicine U. Calif., San Francisco, 1970—, dean Sch. Medicine, 1971-82, chancellor, 1982-93, chancellor emeritus, 1993—. Contbr. articles on hematology, internal med. profl. jours. Served with M.C. AUS, 1948-50. Mem. A.C.P., Assn. Am. Physicians. Office: U Calif San Francisco Sch Medicine San Francisco CA 94143-0296

KRICH, KENNETH L., computer dealer executive; b. L.A., May 19, 1946; s. Percy and Rita (Shane) K.; m. Nancy Leahong, Dec. 12, 1982. BA, U. Chgo., 1967; MBA, U. Calif., Berkeley, 1983. V.p., gen. mgr. Westbrae Nat. Foods, Berkeley, Calif., 1974-79; ptnr. Bear Valley Foods, Berkeley, 1979-81; fin. analyst Harris Farinon, San Carlos, Calif., 1983-84; mgr. fin. planning internat. divsn. Computerland, Oakland, Calif., 1984-85; dir. ops. GTL divsn. Computerland, Hayward, Calif., 1985-87; exec. v.p., gen. mgr. Jasmine Techs., San Francisco, 1987-88; v.p. ops. Computerware, Palo Alto, Calif., 1988-91, pres., CEO, 1991—. Office: ComputerWare 605 W California Ave Sunnyvale CA 94086

KRICHELS, TED, public television station executive; b. Pittsfield, Mass., Sept. 15, 1948; m. Patricia Howard; children: Alexander, Hayley. BA, U. Pa., 1970; MA, Naropa Inst., Boulder, Colo., 1977. Counselor Pine St. Recovery Ctr., Boulder, 1976-77; vol. coord. KBDI-TV Channel 12, Denver, 1979-80, program dir., 1980-82, dir. programming and prodn., 1982-84, gen. mgr., 1984—; exec. dir. Denver Cmty. TV, Denver, 1989-96; mem. pub. TV task force Corp. for Pub. Broadcasting, Washington, 1994—; mem. task force onprogram and pricing policy Pub. Broadcasting Svc., Washington, 1994—. Recipient Emmy award Nat. Acad. TV Arts and Scis., 1985; named Broadcast Citizen of Yr., Colo. Broadcasters Assn., 1995. Office: KBDI-TV Channel 12 2900 Welton St # 100 Denver CO 80205-3022

KRICHMAR, LEE, information systems executive; b. Santa Ana, Calif., May 26, 1965; d. Sidney and Jeanette (York) K. BS, DeVry Inst. Tech., Calif., 1986; postgrad., Claremont (Calif.) Coll., 1996. Ops. mgr. GTECH Corp., Whittier, Calif., 1986-90; ops. supr. Pacific States Casualty Co., Chino, Calif., 1990-93; info. sys. mgr. VNA Home Health Systems, Orange, Calif., 1993—. Republican. Jewish. Home: 201 N Wayfield Apt 10 Orange CA 92856 Office: VNA Home Health Systems 1337 W Braden Ct Orange CA 92868-1123

KRIEGEL, ARLYN ALVIN, accounting company executive; b. Clovis, N.Mex., Mar. 26, 1931; s. Alvin E. and Eleonora H. (Schwede) K.; m. Elizabeth A. Kallsen, Jan. 26, 1958; children: Joan L., Beth A. BBA in Acctg., Tex. Tech U., 1954. CPA, Tex., N.Mex. Mem. staff Neff & Co., Albuquerque, 1958-62; ptnr. Neff & Co., Las Cruces, N.Mex., 1963-78; pres. Kriegel & Co. Ltd., Las Cruces, 1978—; sec. bd. dirs. First Nat. Bank of Dona Ana County. Bd. dirs. N.Mex. State Found., 1970-90, pres., 1989-90; bd. dirs. Mem. Med. Ctr. Found., 1989-91. 1st lt. USAF, 1954-58. Mem. AICPAs, N.Mex. Soc. CPAs (pres. Dona Ana chpt. 1974), Las Cruces C. of C. Las Cruces Rotary. Presbyterian. Home: 2955 Sundance Cir Las Cruces NM 88011-4609

KRIEGER, WILLIAM CARL, English language educator; b. Seattle, Mar. 21, 1946; s. Robert Irving Krieger and Mary (McKibben) Durfee; m. Patricia Kathleen Callow, Aug. 20, 1966; children: Richard William, Robert Irving III, Kathleen Elizabeth. BA in English, Pacific Luth. U., 1968, MA in Humanities, 1973; PhD in Am. Studies, Wash. State U., 1986. Instr. Pierce Coll., Tacoma, 1969—; ombudsman, 1995—; chmn. English dept. Pierce Coll., Tacoma, 1973-79, 81-84, 95—, chmn. humanities divsn., 1979-81, prof. English, 1969—; adj. prof. hist. and English Cen. Wash. State U., 1980; vis. prof. hist. and English So. Ill. U., Carbondale, 1981-84, Pacific Luth. U., Tacoma, 1981-84; head coach Gig Harbor H.S. Wrestling, 1990-95; bd. dirs. Thoreau Cabin Project, Tacoma, 1979—; project dir. Campus Wash. Centennial Project, Tacoma, 1984-89; spl. cons. Clover Park Sch. Dist., Tacoma, 1985; lang. arts cons. Inst. for Citizen Edn. in Law, U. Puget Sound Law Sch., 1990. Apptd. Wash. State Centennial Commn., Constns. Com., Pierce Couny Centennial Com.; mem. bd. dirs. Tacoma Symphony; choir dir. Rosendale Ch.; mem. Peninsula Comty. Chorus, 1993-97, pres., 1995; dir. Peninsula Madrigal Singers, 1995-97. Recipient Disting. Achievement award Wash. State Centennial Commn., 1989, Outstanding Achievement award Pierce County Centennial Commn., 1989, Centennial Alumni recognition Pacific Luth. U., 1990; named Outstanding Tchr. Nat. Inst. Staff and Orgnl. Devel., 1992; NEH rsch. fellow Johns Hopkins U. and Peabody Conservatory of Music, 1994. Mem. Thoreau Soc. (life), Community Coll. Humanities Assn. (standing com. 1982-83), Am. Studies Assn., Wash. Community Coll. Humanities Assn. (bd. dirs. 1982-84, grantee, 1984), Western Wash. Ofcls. Assn. Home: 4415 68th Street Ct NW Gig Harbor WA 98335-8312 Office: Pierce Coll 9401 Farwest Dr SW Tacoma WA 98498-1919

KRIENKE, CAROL BELLE MANIKOWSKE (MRS. OLIVER KENNETH KRIENKE), realtor; b. Oakland, Calif., June 19, 1917; d. George and Ethel (Purdon) Manikowske; student U. Mo., 1937; BS, U. Minn., 1940; postgrad. UCLA, 1949; m. Oliver Kenneth Krienke, June 4, 1941 (dec. Dec. 1988); children: Diane (Mrs. Robert Denny), Judith (Mrs. Kenneth A. Giss), Debra Louise (Mrs. Ed Paul Davalos). Demonstrator, Gen. Foods Corp., Mpls., 1940; youth leadership State of Minn. Congl. Conf., U. Minn., Mpls. 1940-41; war prodn. worker Airesearch Mfg. Co., Los Angeles, 1944; tchr. L.A. City Schs., 1945-49, realtor DBA Ethel Purdon, Manhattan Beach, Calif., 1949; buyer Purdon Furniture & Appliances, Manhattan Beach, 1950-58; realtor O.K. Krienke Realty, Manhattan Beach, 1958—. Manhattan Beach bd. rep. Community Chest for Girl Scouts U.S., 1957; bd. dirs. South Bay council Girl Scouts U.S.A., 1957-62, mem. Manhattan Beach Coordinating Coun., 1956-68, South Coast Botanic Garden Found., 1989—; v.p. Long Beach Area Childrens Home Soc., 1967-68, pres. 1979; charter mem. Beach Pixies, 1957-93, pres. 1967; chmn. United Way, 1967; sponsor Beach Cities Symphony, 1953—, Little League Umpires, 1981-91. Recipient Longstanding Local Bus. award City of Manhattan Beach, 1993. Mem. DAR (life, citizenship chmn. 1972-73, v.p. 1979, 83—), Calif. Retired Tchrs. Assn. (life), Colonial Dames XVII Century (charter mem. Jared Eliot chpt. 1977, v.p., pres. 1979-81, 83-84), Friends of Library, South Bay Assn. of Realtors, Nat. Soc. New England Women (life, Calif. Poppy Colony), Internat. Platform Assn., Soc. Descs. of Founders of Hartford (life), Friends of Banning Mus., Hist. Soc. of Centinela Valley, Manhattan Beach Hist. Soc., Manhattan Beach C. of C. (Rose and Scroll award 1985), U. Minn. Alumni (life). Republican. Mem. Community Ch. (pres. Women's Fellowship 1970-71). Home: 924 Highview Ave Manhattan Beach CA 90266-5813 Office: OK Krienke Realty 1716 Manhattan Beach Blvd Manhattan Beach CA 90266-6220

KRIKEN, JOHN LUND, architect; b. Calif., July 5, 1938; s. John Erik Nord and Ragnhild (Lund) K.; m. Anne Girard (div.); m. Katherine Koelsch, Aug. 8, 1988. BArch, U. Calif., Berkeley, 1961; MArch, Harvard U., 1968. Ptnr. Skidmore, Owings and Merrill, San Francisco, 1970—; tchr. Washington U., St. Louis, 1968, U. Calif., Berkeley, 1972, Rice U., Houston, 1979; design advisor, chief architect Ho Chi Minh City, Vietnam, 1994—; mem. design rev. bd. Port San Francisco, 1995—. Mem. Bay Conservation and Devel. Commn., Calif., 1984—; mem. Arts Commn. City and County of San Francisco, 1989-95; mem. design rev. bd. Berkeley campus U. Calif., 1986-92; bd. dirs. San Francisco Planning and Rsch., 1995—. Fellow AIA; mem. Am. Inst. Cert. Planners, Sunday Afternoon Watercolor Soc. (founding mem.), Lambda Alpha Internat. Office: Skimore Owings & Merrill 1 Front St San Francisco CA 94111

KRINSKY, IRA WALTER, executive search consultant; b. Long Beach, N.Y., Jan. 15, 1949; s. Rubin and Lillian Evelyn (Tucker) K.; m. Susan Lois Paul, June 6, 1971 (div. July 15, 1989); 1 child, Brian Paul. BA, Hofstra U., 1971; MA, NYU, 1974; EdD, Harvard U., 1979. Tchr. Monticello (N.Y.) Pub. Schs., 1971-72; tchr., adminstr. Huntington (N.Y.) Pub. Schs., 1972-75; asst. supt. Levittown (N.Y.) Pub. Schs., 1978-79; dep. supt. Pomona (Calif.) Unified Sch. Dist., 1979-82; mng. v.p. Korn/Ferry Internat., L.A., 1982-88, 92—; pres. Ira W. Krinsky and Assoc., L.A., 1988-92; mem. adv. bd. Supts. Prepared, Washington, 1992—. Mem. editorial adv. bd. Interant. Jour. of Edn. Reform, Lancaster, Pa., 1992—; author: The Careers Makers, 1990, 92, 94; contbr. articles to profl. jours. Trustee Southwestern U. Sch. of Law, 1985—. With U.S. Army, 1966-69, Vietnam. Mem. Am. Philat. Soc., Am. Air Mail Soc., Phi Delta Kappa. Office: Korn/Ferry Internat 1800 Century Park E Ste 900 Los Angeles CA 90067-1512

KRIPPAEHNE, MARION CAROLYN, physician; b. Missoula, Mont., June 22, 1923; d. Martin Isadore and Mathilda (Johansen) Larsen; m.

William wonn Krippaehne, Nov. 17, 1949; children: William Jr., Thomas, Joanne, Carol, Richard, Suzanne, Robert. BS, U. Wash., 1944; MD, U. Oreg., Portland, 1948. Lic. physician, Oreg. Intern, then resident Emanuel Hosp., Portland, 1948-50; resident, then fellow exptl. medicine divsn. U. Oreg., Portland, 1950-52; from clin. instr. to prof. medicine Oreg. Health Scis. U., 1953-88, prof. medicine emeritus, 1988—.

KRIPPNER, STANLEY CURTIS, psychologist; b. Edgerton, Wis., Oct. 4, 1932; s. Carroll Porter and Ruth Genevieve (Volenberg) K.; m. Lelie Anne Harris, June 25, 1966; stepchildren: Caron, Robert. BS, U. Wis., 1954; MA, Northwestern U., 1957, PhD, 1961; PhD (hon.), U. Humanistic Studies, San Diego, 1982. Diplomate Am. Bd. Sexology. Speech therapist Warren Pub. Schs. (Ill.), 1954-55, Richmond Pub. Schs. (Va.), 1955-56; dir. Child Study Ctr. Kent (Ohio) State U., 1961-64; dir. dream lab. Maimonides Med. Ctr., Bklyn., 1964-73; prof. of psychology Saybrook Inst., San Francisco, 1973—; adj. prof. psychology Calif. Inst. Human Sci., 1994—; vis. prof. U. P.R., 1972, Sonoma State U., 1972-73, U. Life Scis., Bogota, Colombia, 1974, Inst. for Psychodrama and Humanistic Psychology, Caracas, Venezuela, 1975, West Ga. Coll., 1976, John F. Kennedy U., 1980-82, Inst. for Rsch. in Biopsychophysics, Curitiba, Brazil, 1990; adj. prof. Calif. Inst. Integral Studies, 1991—; lectr. Acad. Pedagogical Scis., Moscow, 1971, Acad. Scis., Beijing, 1981, Minas Gerais U., Belo Horizonte, Brazil, 1986-87. Author: (with Montague Ullman) Dream Telepathy, 1973, rev. edit., 1989, Song of the Siren: A Parapsychological Odyssey, 1975; (with Alberto Villoldo) The Realms of Healing, 1976, rev. edit., 1987, Human Possibilities, 1980, (with Alberto Villoldo) Healing States, 1987; (with Jerry Solfvin) La Science et les Pouvoirs Psychiques de l'Homme, 1986, (with Joseph Dillard) Dreamworking, 1988, (with David Feinstein) Personal Mythology, 1988, (with Patrick Welch) Spiritual Dimensions of Healing, 1992, (with Dennis Thong and Bruce Carpenter) A Psychiatrist in Paradise, 1993, (with David Feinstein) The Mystic Path, 1997; editor: Advances in Parapsychological Research, Vol. 1, 1977, Vol. 2, 1978, Vol. 3, 1982, Vol. 4, 1984, Vol. 5, 1987, Vol. 6, 1990, Vol. 7, 1994, Psychoenergetic Systems, 1979; co-editor: Galaxies of Life, 1973, The Kirlian Aura, 1974, The Energies of Consciousness, 1975, Future Science, 1977, Dreamtime and Dreamwork, 1990; mem. editl. bd. Alternative Therapies in Health and Medicine, Jour. Humanistic Psychology, Jour. Transpersonal Psychology, Jour. Indian Psychology, Dream Network, Humanistic Psychologist; contbr. 500 articles to profl. jours. Bd. dirs., adv. bd. Acad. Religion and Phys. Rsch., Survival Rsch. Found., Hartley Film Found., Inst. for Multilevel Learning, Humanistic Psychology Ctr. N.Y., Joseph Plan Found. Recipient Svc. to Youth award YMCA, 1959, Citation of Merit Nat. Assn. Creative Children and Adults, 1975, Cert. Recognition Office Gifted and Talented, U.S. Office Edn., 1976, Volker medal South Africa Soc. Psychical Rsch., 1980, Bicentennial medal U. Ga., 1985, Charlotte Bühler award, 1992, Dan Overlade Meml. award, 1994, Humanist of Yr. award Ch. of Humanism, 1996. Fellow APA (pres. divsn. 32, 1980, divsn. 30, 1997), Am. Soc. Clin. Hypnosis, Am. Psychol. Soc., Soc. Sci. Study Religion, Soc. Sci. Study Sexuality, Western Psychol. Assn.; mem. AAAS, Am. Soc. Psychical Rsch., Am. Ednl. Rsch. Assn., Am. Counseling Assn., Internat. Council Psychologists, Assn. for Study of Dreams (pres. 1993-94), Soc. for the Anthropology Consciousness, Com. for Study Anomalistic Rsch., Inter-Am. Psychol. Assn., Assn. Humanistic Psychology (pres. 1974-75), Assn. Transpersonal Psychology, Internat. Soc. Hypnosis, Internat. Soc. for Study of Dissociation, Nat. Assn. for Gifted Children, Sleep Rsch. Soc., Soc. Sci. Exploration, Biofeedback Soc. Am., Coun. Exceptional Children, Soc. Accelerative Learning and Tchg., Soc. Gen. Sys. Rsch., Swedish Soc. Clin. and Exptl. Hypnosis, Western Psychol. Assn., Internat. Soc. Gen. Semantics, Menninger Found., Nat. Soc. Study of Edn., Parapsychol. Assn. (pres. 1983), Soc. Clin. and Exptl. Hypnosis, World Future Soc. Home: 79 Woodland Rd Fairfax CA 94930-2153 Office: Saybrook Inst 450 Pacific Ave # 300 San Francisco CA 94133-4640

KRISKOVICH, JOE, human resources specialist; b. Butte, Mont., May 21, 1960; s. Ronald John and Marlene May (Malyvec) K.; m. Tracy Fennessy Kriskovich, June 29, 1985; children: Tanner, Nikki. BA in Biology/Psychology, Carroll Coll., 1982; MBA, U. Phoenix, 1996. Designated assoc. safety profl. Workforce planning mgr. United Parcel Svc., Oakland, Calif., 1991, health and safety mgr., 1992—. Mem. Am. Soc. Safety Engrs., Soc. for Human Resource Mgmt., Nat. Safety Coun., Elks Club. Republican. Roman Catholic. Office: United Parcel Svc 8400 Pardee Dr Oakland CA 94621-1412

KRISTIANSEN, MICHAEL SIGURD, botanical gardens director; b. Durban, Natal, Republic of South Africa, Apr. 27, 1942; came to U.S., 1978; s. Sigurd and Claire (Reed) K.; m. Terry Ellen O'Reilly; children: Matt, Erik Colin. BSc in Landscape Architecture, Calif. State Poly. U., 1970. Cert. park adminstr. and ornamental horticulturist Inst. Park Adminstrn. Durban, 1966, cert arborist. Landscape draftsman Keith French Assocs., L.A., 1970-72; landscape architecture planning Kristiansen Assoc., Johannesburg, 1972-78; horticultural cons. Kristiansen Assoc., 1979—; instr. horticulture Dept. Arts UCLA, 1979-89; instr. landscape architecture Dept. of Scis., UCLA, 1979-89; instr. horticulture West Valley Occupational Ctr., L.A., 1980-89; exec. dir. The Virginia Robinson Gardens, Beverly Hills, 1996—; mentor tchr., 1985-89. Mem. Mayor's Com. on Graffitti Tech. Resource, L.A., 1988-89, Wahiawa (Hawaii) Task Force, 1994-96, Am. the Beautiful, Honolulu, 1992-96, Hawaii Job Corps Adv. Com., 1990-96. William Poulton scholar City of Durban (2) 1966, (1) 1967. Home: 1682 San Onofre Dr Pacific Palisades CA 90272 Office: Honolulu Botanical Gardens 50 N Vineyard Blvd Honolulu HI 96817-3759 Office: The Virginia Robinson Gardens 1008 Elden Way Beverly Hills CA 90210

KRISTY, JAMES E., financial management consultant; b. Kenosha, Wis., Sept. 3, 1929; s. Eugene H. and Ann T. Kristy; BS in Econs., U. Wis., 1951; MBA in Fin., U. So. Calif., 1964; postgrad. Claremont (Calif.) Grad. Sch.; PhD in Mgmt. and Edn., Columbia-Pacific U., 1981; m. Edith L. Reid, Feb. 19, 1955; children: James R., Ann E., Robert E. V.p., Lloyds Bank Calif., L.A., 1969-71; chief treasury officer Computer Machinery Corp., L.A., 1971-75; sr. v.p., chief fin. officer Century Bank, L.A., 1979; vis. prof. Chapman U., 1995—; self-employed cons., writer, and lectr., Buena Park, Calif., 1975-78, 80—; seminar leader Frost & Sullivan, London, CEL Ltd., Hong Kong, U. Calif., U. Hawaii, U. Colo., Temple U., Rutgers U., Tulane U.; past dir. Grycner Motors Corp., Madera Mfg. Co. 1st lt. U.S. Army, 1951-53; Korea. Recipient Pub. Svc. award SBA, 1971. Author: Analyzing Financial Statements: Quick and Clean, 5th edit., 1991, Price Deflator Software, 1997, Handbook of Budgeting, 1992; (with others) Finance Without Fear, 1983, Commercial Credit Matrix Software, 1994. Address: PO Box 113 Buena Park CA 90621-0113

KRIVE, IRWIN, new products development company executive; b. Bklyn., Nov. 12, 1929; m. Sylvia Stall; children: Taryn, Risa, Lance. BS, NYU, 1951, MA, 1957. Cert. chief sch. adminstr., secondary sch. prin., vocat. and indsl. arts tchr., N.Y. Tchr. Port Washington (N.Y.) Unified Free Dist. 4, asst. supt., coord. redesign; prin. H.S., Oceanside (N.Y.) Bd. Edn.; dir. tech. tng. Plainedge (N.Y.) Bd. Edn.; pres., founder Heartfelt Products Co., West Hills, Calif. Patentee muscle mimicry exerciser for ski industry. Former asst. scoutmaster troop 181 Boy Scouts Am., Bklyn. With U.S. Army, 1951-53. Home and Office: 6720 Capistrano Ave West Hills CA 91307-3733

KRIVIS, SCOTT ALAN, accountant, limousine company executive; b. L.A., Sept. 21, 1959; s. Gene Howard and Ruth (Lewinstein) K.; m. Kimberly Louise LaVally, July 17, 1983; children: Shayna, Shelea, Shelby. BSBA, Calif. State U., Northridge, 1982. CPA, Calif. Staff acct. Weber, Lipshie & Co., Beverly Hills, Calif., 1982-87; owner, mgr. Scott Krivis & Co., Tarzana, Calif., 1987—; pres. Straightline Transp. Svcs., Inc., Van Nuys, Calif., 1991—. Treas. Temple Beth Ami, Reseda, Calif., 1992-94, Blue Grass Homeowners Assn., Chatsworth, Calif., 1996—. Mem. Calif. Soc. CPA's, Zeta Beta Tau (trustee Northridge 1984—). Home: 20331 Celtic St Chatsworth CA 91311 Office: 18757 Burbank Blvd Ste 120 Tarzana CA 91356

KRMPOTICH, FRANK ZVONKO, fiberglass company executive, consultant; b. Zagreb, Croatia, Feb. 17, 1948; came to U.S., 1983; s. Franjo and Anica (Pavlich) K.; m. Jana Snjezana Fabjanovich, May 25, 1973; children: Kris, Tomi. BSME, U. Zagreb, 1978; Degree in Arctic Engring. (hon.), U. Anchorage, 1985. Design engr. Fiberglass Fabricator, Zagreb, 1976-79; sr. design engr. Mech. Engring. Inst., Zagreb, 1979-84; prin. engr. Alaska Engring., Anchorage, 1984-87; sr. design engr. Test Co., Anchorage, 1987-89, Ershigs, Bellingham, Wash., 1989-90, Chemetics Internat., Vancouver, B.C., Can., 1991-93; sr. design cons. engr. Fiberglass Cons. Engring., Bellingham, 1990-91, CEO, 1994—; cons. engr., Bellingham, 1990—. Author: FRP Equipment Design, 1994. Pres. Croatian Bus. Assn., Zagreb-Seattle, 1991. Mem. ASME, NSPE, Nat. Assn. Corrosion Engrs., Soc. Plastic Industry. Republican. Roman Catholic. Home: 3111 Crestline Dr Bellingham WA 98226-4206

KROEGER, TERRY J., newspaper publisher; b. Omaha, June 18, 1962; m. Jackie Kroeger; children: Molly, Maggie, Ellie. Degree in fin. and econ., U. Nebr., 1984. Asst. purchasing agt., bldg. mgr. The Omaha World-Herald Co., 1985, v.p., bd. dirs.; pres. Rapid Press, Inc.; pres. World Newspapers, Inc., 1991-94, also bd. dirs.; pub. The Record, Stockton, Calif., 1994—; pres., CEO, Stockton Newspapers Inc.; bd. dirs. World Cos., Inc., World Investments, Inc., Inland Press Assn., Inland Press Found., San Joaquin County Bus. Coun., San Joaquin Partnership. Mem. adv. bd. U. Pacific; bd. dirs. YMCA San Joaquin County, United Way of San Joaquin County, San Joaquin County Acad. Decathalon, U. Pacific Athletic Found., No. Californians for Nebr.; chmn. United Way campaign, 1996. Mem. Ch. of the Presentation. Office: The Record 530 E Market St Stockton CA 95202

KROEKER, JOANNE ELIZABETH, missionary, writer; b. Vanga, Kwilu, Zaire, Mar. 23, 1942; came to U.S., 1993; d. Abraham Franklin and Mary Rose (Neufeld) K. BA, Biola U., La Mirada, Calif., 1962. Sec. cultural adaptation of transl., in-house writer Editeurs de Litterature Biblique, Brussels, 1962-93; with Bibl. Lit. Fellowship; cultural adaptations writer Sunday sch. materials Scripture Press, 1962-89. Author: Shiny Shore on Dusty Paths, 1995, Vol. 2, 1996; contbr. articles to profl. jours. Office: Grow Books International PO Box 95 Palo Cedro CA 96073

KROHN, KENNETH ALBERT, radiology educator; b. Stevens Point, Wis., June 19, 1945; s. Albert William and Erma Belle (Cornwell) K.; 1 child, Galen. BA in Chemistry, Andrews U., 1966; PhD in Chemistry, U. Calif., 1971. Acting assoc. prof. U. Wash., Seattle, 1981-84, assoc. prof. radiology, 1984-86, prof. radiology and radiation oncology, 1986—, adj. prof. chemistry, 1986—; guest scientist Donner Lab. Lawrence Berkeley (Calif.) Lab., 1980-81; radiochemist, VA Med. Ctr., Seattle, 1982—. Contbr. numerous articles to profl. jours.; patentee in field. NDEA fellow. Fellow AAAS; mem. Am. Chem. Soc., Radiation Rsch. Soc., Soc. Nuclear Medicine, Acad. Coun., Sigma Xi. Home: NE550 Lake Ridge Dr Belfair WA 98528 Office: U Washington Imaging Rsch Lab Box 356004 Seattle WA 98195-6004

KROKENBERGER, LINDA ROSE, chemist, environmental analyst; b. Ridley Park, Pa., July 17, 1954; d. Roy Frank and Rose Marie (Kraffert) K. BS in Chemistry, Syracuse U., 1976; postgrad., Life Chiropractic Coll. West, San Lorenzo, Calif., 1995—. Radiopharm. chemist Upstate Med. Ctr., SUNY, Syracuse, 1976-78; chemist, asst. mgr. lab. IT Corp., Cerritos, Calif., 1978-86; mgr. data control Enseco-Cal Lab., West Sacramento, Calif., 1987; asst. mgr. lab. Sci. Applications Internat. Corp., San Diego, 1987-89; ind. cons. in environ. compliance and analytical chemistry Poway, Calif., 1989-95. Recipient Citizenship award DAR, 1972. Republican. Methodist. Home and Office: 724 Lewelling Blvd Apt 341 San Leandro CA 94579-2455

KROLICKI, BRIAN KEITH, state official; b. Providence, Dec. 31, 1960; s. Thadeus James Krolicki and Gail Carolyn (Gourdeau) Jacus; m. Kelly Lea DiGiusto, May 21, 1994. BA in Polit. Sci., Stanford U., 1983. Cert. gov. fin. mgr.; lic. securities dealer. Assoc. banker Bankers Trust Co., N.Y.C., 1984-85; sr. account exec. First Commodity Boston, Zephyr Cove, Nev., 1985-86; account exec. Smith Barney, San Francisco, 1986-87; investment banker Smith Barney, Manama, Bahrain, 1987-89; pres. Inter Am. Mktg. Corp., Reno, London, 1989-91; chief dep. state treas. and sec. state bd. fin. State Nev., Carson City, 1991—; sec. Nev. Master Lease Corp., Carson City, 1992—. Mem. Rep. State Ctrl. Com., Nev., 1990—; vice chmn. planning commn. Douglas County, Minden, Nev., 1991—; chmn. support svcs. Am. Cancer Soc., Nev., 1993-96; bd. dirs. found. Lake Tahoe (Calif.) C.C., 1996—. Mem. Nev. Govt. Fin. Officer Assn. Home: PO Box 7033 Stateline NV 89449 Office: State Treasurers Office Capitol Complex Carson City NV 89710

KROLL, JAMES XAVIER, librarian; b. Michigan City, Ind., July 9, 1951; s. John Stephen and Clara Marie (Widelski) K.; m. Joan Marie Spadacene, Aug. 6, 1977; children: Michael James, John Xavier, Benjamin Edward. BA, Gannon U., 1973; MS, U. Denver, 1979; MLS, Emporia State U., 1993. Libr. Denver Pub. Libr., 1980-86, sr. libr., 1986-88, mgr. humanities dept., 1989-94, mgr. gen. reference and nonfiction dept., 1995—. 1st lt. U.S. Army, 1973-79. Mem. Colo. Geneaol. Soc. (pres. 1984-88). Home: 2307 Ivy St Denver CO 80207-3410 Office: Denver Pub Libr 10 W 14th Avenue Pkwy Denver CO 80204-2749

KROLL, MARK WILLIAM, electrical engineer; b. Mpls., July 11, 1952; s. William H.O. and Irene Claudia Kroll; m. Lori Carolyn Palm, Sept. 6, 1975; children: Braden, Mollie, Ryan, Chase. BS in Math., U. Minn., 1975, MSEE, 1983, PhDEE, 1987; MBA, U. St. Thomas, St. Paul, 1990. Circuit designer Medtronic, Fridley, Minn., 1970-72; teaching asst. U. Minn., Mpls., 1973-78; v.p. R & D Intercomp, Plymouth, Minn., 1978-84; v.p. of rsch. and devel. Cherne Med. Co., Edina, Minn., 1985-90; v.p. rsch. Angeion, Plymouth, 1991-95; v.p. Tachycardia Bus. Unit Pacesetter, 1995=97; v.p. and chief sci. officer St. Jude Med., Inc., 1997—; bd. dirs. Surviva-Link, Plymouth, Creative Toy Co., Mpls. Co-editor: Implantable Cardioverter Defibrilator Therapy, 1996; contbr. over 55 papers to profl. publs. Bd. dirs. St. Peter's Luth. Sch., Edina, 1990-93. Alfred P. Sloan fellow, 1971. Mem. IEEE, Am. Heart Assn. (coun. on clin. cardiology). Office: Pacesetter 15900 Valley View Ct Sylmar CA 91392

KROLL, PAUL BENEDICT, auditor; b. Ft. Ord, Calif., Oct. 24, 1954; s. Harry Gardner and Jane Ellen (Cornwell) K.; 1 child, Dane Garcia. BA, Kans. Wesleyan U., 1977; MS, Emporia State U., 1979, MBA, 1983; cert. tchr., Washburn U., 1990. Cert. tchr., Kans. Pension adminstr. Kansas City (Mo.) Life Ins., 1980-82; actuary Victory Life Ins. Co., Topeka, 1983-85; actuarial analyst Security Trust Life Ins., Macon, Ga., 1985-87; policy examiner Kans. Ins. Dept., Topeka, 1987-88; adj. instr. math. Highland (Kans.) C.C., 1991-93; premium auditor Mountain States Mus. Cos., Albuquerque, 1993—. Author: The Student's T Distribution, 1979. Home and Office: 7516 Pecos Tr NW Albuquerque NM 87120-2877

KRONENBERG, JACALYN (JACKI KRONENBERG), nurse administrator; b. N.Y.C., July 21, 1949; d. Martin Jerome and Joyce (Weinberg) Jacobs; m. Robert Kronenberg, Jan. 23, 1971 (div.); 1 child, Joshua Louis. BA, William Paterson Coll. of N.J., 1971; ADN, Phoenix Coll., 1977. RN, Calif.; cert. IV nurse, chemo, ACLS, PALS. Asst. charge nurse Phoenix Gen. Hosp.; nurse Ariz. State Crippled Children's Hosp., Tempe; maternal, child nurse Desert Samaritan Hosp., Mesa, Ariz.; nurse mgr. PPS Inc., Phoenix, Med-Pro 2000, Phoenix; clin. nurse II Phoenix Children's Hosp.; nurse mgr. adolescent unit Shriners Hosp., L.A.; nurse mgr. pediatrics, oncology, gynecology, med./surg. Santa Monica (Calif.) Hosp. Med. Ctr., 1993-94; dir. nurses, dir. patient care svcs. NMC Homecare, Anaheim, Calif., 1994; dir. med./surg. svcs. and staffing, nursing office/supr. Midway Hosp. Med. Ctr., L.A., 1995, mgr. nursing office, urgent care clinic, 1995; dir. patient care svcs., dir. nursing edn. Infusion Svcs. & Pediatrics, L.A., 1995-96; with Children's Home Care, 1996—; dir. patient care svcs. Nurse Providers Home Care, Inc., L.A., 1996—, L.A. Home Care, L.A., 1996—; mem. joint rsch. project on pediatric cystic fibrosis and human growth factor U. Calif., Irvine; rschr. in field. Nursing Lab. Tech. scholar, 1976. Mem. Oncology Nursing Soc., IV Nursing Soc., Pediatric Nursing Soc. Office: 3250 Wilshire Blvd # 1308 Los Angeles CA 90010

KROPOTOFF, GEORGE ALEX, civil engineer; b. Sofia, Bulgaria, Dec. 6, 1921; s. Alex S. and Anna A. (Kurat) K.; came to Brazil, 1948, to U.S., 1952, naturalized, 1958; BS in Engring., Inst. Tech., Sofia, 1941; postgrad. in computer sci. U. Calif., 1968; Registered profl. engr., Calif.; m. Helen P., July 23, 1972. With Standard Eletrica S.A., Rio de Janeiro, 1948-52, Pacific Car & Foundry Co., Seattle, 1952-64, T.G. Atkinson Assocs., Structural Engrs., San Diego, 1960-62, Tucker, Sadler & Bennett A-E, San Diego, 1964-74, Gen. Dynamics-Astronautics, San Diego, 1967-68, Engring. Sci., Inc., Arcadia, Calif., 1975-76, Incomtel, Rio de Janeiro, Brazil, 1976, Bennett Engrs., structural cons., San Diego, 1976-82; project structural engr. Hope Cons. Group, San Diego and Saudi Arabia, 1982-84; cons. structural engr. Pioneered engring. computer software. Warrant officer U.S. Army, 1945-46. Fellow ASCE; mem. Structural Engrs. Assn. San Diego (assoc.), Soc. Am. Mil. Engrs., Soc. Profl. Engrs. Brazil. Republican. Russian Orthodox. Home: Apt E 7430 Park Ridge Blvd San Diego CA 92120

KROTKI, KAROL JOZEF, sociology educator, demographer; b. Cieszyn, Poland, May 15, 1922; emigrated to Can., 1964; s. Karol Stanislaw and Anna Elzbieta (Skrzywanek) K.; m. Joanna Patkowski, July 12, 1947; children—Karol Peter, Jan Jozef, Filip Karol. B.A. (hons.), Cambridge (Eng.) U., 1948, M.A., 1952; M.A., Princeton U., 1959, Ph.D., 1960. Civil ser. Eng., 1948-49; dep. dir. stats. Sudan, 1949-58; vis. fellow Princeton U., 1958-60; research adviser Pakistan Inst. Devel. Econs., 1960-64; asst. dir. census research Dominion Bur. Stats., Can., 1964-68; prof. sociology U. Alta., 1968-83, univ. prof., 1983-91, univ. prof. emeritus, 1991—; vis. prof. U. Calif., Berkeley, 1967, U. N.C., 1970-73, U. Mich., 1975, U. Costa Rica, 1993; coord. program socio-econ. rsch. Province Alta., 1969-71; cons. in field. Author 14 books and monographs; contbr. numerous articles to profl. jours. Served with Polish, French and Brit. Armed Forces, 1939-46. Decorated 9 wartime medals; recipient Achievement award Province of Alta, 1970, Commemorative medal for 125th Ann. of Can., 1992; hon. citizen Gizalki, Poland, 1994; grantee in field. Fellow Am. Statis Assn., Royal Soc. Can. (v.p. 1986-88), Acad. Humanities and Social Scis. (v.p. 1984-86, pres. 1986-88); mem. Fedn. Can. Demographers (v.p. 1977-82, pres. 1982-84), Can. Population Soc., Assn. des Demographes du Que., Soc. Edmonton Demographers (founder, pres. 1990-96), Ctrl. and E. European Studies Soc. (pres. 1986-88), Population Assn. Am., Internat. Union Sci. Study Population, Assn. Internat. des Demographes de Langue Francaise, Internat. Statis. Inst., Royal Statis. Soc. Roman Catholic. Home: 10137 Clifton Pl, 10137 Clifton Pl, Edmonton, AB Canada T5N 3H9 Office: U Alta, Dept Sociology, Dept Sociology, Edmonton, AB Canada T6G 2H4

KROUSE, ERIKA DAWN, technical writer; b. Yonkers, N.Y., Mar. 28, 1969; d. Harold Mark and Carolyn Adele (Robert) K. BA, Grinnell Coll., 1991; MA, U. Colo., 1996. Tech. writer Physician Reimbursement Sys., Denver; English instr. U. Colo., Boulder, 1994-96; editor Sniper Logic, Boulder, 1995-96; tech. publ. writer Cencorp, Boulder, 1996—. Author: (poetry) Calamity Jane, 1996. Democrat.

KROUT, BOYD MERRILL, psychiatrist; b. Oakland, Calif., Jan. 31, 1931; s. Boyd Merrill and Phoebe Lenore (Colby) K.; m. Helena Luise Keel, Aug. 25, 1965. AB, Stanford U., 1951, MD, 1955. Diplomate Am. Bd. Psychiatry and Neurology. Intern San Francisco Hosp., 1954-55; resident Boston U. Hosps., 1958-60, Boston Va Hosp., 1960-61; asst. to clin. prof. UCLA Sch. Medicine, 1961-95, vis. prof., 1995—; chief physician Harbor/UCLA Med. Ctr., Torrance, 1961-95. Capt. USAF, 1955-58. Fellow Am. Psychiat. Assn., So. Calif. Psychiat. Soc. (councillor 1988-91), Am. Psychiat. Soc.; mem. L.A. County Med. Soc. Republican. Office: Harbor/UCLA Med Ctr PO Box 8 Torrance CA 90509-2910

KROZEL, JIMMY ALAN, research scientist, artist; b. Morton Grove, Ill., Dec. 13, 1963; s. Walter A. and Irene (Bogard) K. AS, Purdue U., W. Lafayette, Ind., 1984; BS, 1985, MA, 1988, PhD, 1992. Rsch. scientist Hughes Info. Scis. Lab., Malibu, Calif., 1987-95; sr. rsch. engr. Seagull Technology, Inc., Cupertino, Calif., 1995—. Contbr. articles to profl. jours. Recipient Am. Inst. Aeronautics and Astronautics scholarship Washington, 1984; Ames Rsch. Ctr. fellowship NASA, Moffett Field, Calif., 1985; Hughes Doctoral fellowship Hughes Aircraft Co., L.A., 1987. Home: 1494 McKendrie St San Jose CA 95126 Office: Seagull Technology Inc 16400 Lark Ave Los Gatos CA 95032

KRUEGER, CANDICE JAE, assistant principal; b. Milw., Jan. 24, 1946; d. William Elmer and June Marie (Nelson) K. BA in English, U. No. Colo., 1967; MA in Edn. Curriculum and Instrn., Boise State U., 1989; Ednl. Specialist, U. Idaho, 1994. Tchr. English Grant Joint Union Sch. Dist., Sacramento, 1967-69, Sch. Dist. #11, Colorado Springs, Colo., 1969-74, Meridian (Idaho) Sch. Dist. #2, 1974-94, Sch. Dist. #422, Cascade, Idaho, 1994-95; asst. prin. Mountain Home (Idaho) Sch. Dist. #193, 1995—. Newsletter editor Idaho Coun. Tchrs. English, 1990-93; contbr. poetry to profl. jours. Vol., race coord. Ronald McDonald House, Boise, 1989—; vol. Idaho Women's Fitness Celebration, Boise, 1996, Hallando House, Cath. Diocese of Denver, Colorado Springs, 1970-74; coach Little League, Boise, 1990-92. Mem. ASCD, N.W. Women in Edn. (mem.-at-large). Republican. Episcopalian. Home: 2310 Smith Ave Boise ID 83702 Office: Mountain Home High School 300 S 11th E Mountain Home ID 83647-3235

KRUEGER, JAMES, lawyer; b. N.Y.C., Oct. 27, 1938; s. Carl and Ida (Levey) K.; m. Merry Michael Hill, July 5, 1967; children—Melissa Carlton, James Michael. BA, UCLA, 1960; LLB, Loyola U., L.A., 1965. Bar: Hawaii 1966, U.S. Dist. Ct. Hawaii 1966, U.S. Ct. Appeals (9th cir.) 1967, U.S. Tax Ct. 1974, U.S. Supreme Ct. 1982, Colo. 1996. Assoc. firm Padgett, Greeley, Marumoto & Akinaka, Honolulu, 1967-72; atty. Krueger & Cahill, Attys. at Law, Wailuku, Maui, Hawaii, 1973—; mem. Hawaii com. Pattern Jury Instrns., 1992-93. Contbr. articles to profl. jours. Co-founder Nat. Bd. of Trial Advocacy, Hawaii Acad. of Plaintiffs Attys.; Gold Trustee Thomas F. Lambert Chair; mem. Commn. Hawaii Ct. Annexed Arbitration, Hawaii State Commn. on Lawyer Professionalism, 1988-90, Hawaii State Commn. on Solicitation and Advt.; del. Hawaii Jud. Conf., 1986-88, Fed. Jud. Conf., 1989. Fellow Internat. Soc. Barristers, Internat. Acad. Trial Lawyers; mem. ABA (trial techniques com. 1974-76, com. medicine and law, nat. vice-chmn. sect. on tort and ins. practice 1977-81), Assn. Trial Lawyers Am. (gov. 1976-82, state committeeman 1975-76, constl. revisions com. 1977-78, nat. exec. com. 1981-82, amicus curiae com. 1979-80, fed. liaison com. 1980-81, nat. vice chmn. profl. rsch. and devel. com. 1980-81, nat. vice-chmn. publs. dept. 1982-83, nat. vice chmn. edn. policy bd. 1983-84, chmn. Nat. Midwinter Convs., 1988, 91, chmn. Nat. Pub. Rels. Com. 1986-88), Hawaii Bar Assn., Fed. Bar Assn., Maui County Bar Assn. (pres. 1975), Melvin M. Belli Soc. (trustee), Am. Coll. Legal Medicine, Am. Soc. Hosp. Attys., Am. Bd. Profl. Liability Attys., Western Trial Lawyers Assn. (pres. 1978-79, v.p. 1977-78, bd. govs. 1982—), Calif. Trial Lawyers Assn., N.Y. Trial Lawyers Assn., Pa. Trial Lawyers Assn., Tex. Trial Lawyers Assn., Colo. Trial Lawyers Assn., NITA Advocates Assn., Hawaii Inst. Cont. Legal End. (pres. 1994), Consumer Lawyers of Hawaii (pres. 1995-96, bd. govs., lifetime), Million Dollar Advocates Forum, Olympic Club, Phi Alpha Delta. Jewish. Clubs: Outrigger Canoe, Oahu (Honolulu); Olympic Club (San Francisco); Transpacific Yacht (Los Angeles); Maui Country; Maui Ocean Swim. Office: 2065 Main St PO Box 1460 Wailuku HI 96793

KRUEGER, KURT ARNOLD, sports psychologist, institute administrator; b. L.A., Jan. 29, 1946; s. Charles H. and Adlaide M. Krueger; m. Teresa Anne Krueger, May 10, 1992; children: Keith Charles, Narayan Francis. AA in History, L.A. Valley Coll., 1967; BA in History, Classics and Phys. Edn., U. Colo., 1969; MS in Edn., Mt. St. Mary's Coll., L.A., 1972. Cert. Calif. Std. secondary tchr.; cert. mediation and yoga instr. Tchr. social studies Belvedere Jr. High Sch. L.A. Unified Sch. Dist., 1969; tchr. social studies and phys. edn. Torrance (Calif.) Unified Sch. Dists., 1969-71; tchr. social studies Berendo Jr. High Sch. L.A. Unified Sch. Dist., 1971-76, tchr. social studies Crenshaw High Sch., 1977-81, tchr. phys. edn. Webster Jr. High Sch., 1984, tchr. social studies and phys. edn. Pastuer Jr. High Sch., 1984-87, tchr. social studies Palms Jr. High Sch., 1987-91, substitute secondary tchr., 1992-93; tchr. social studies and phys. edn. Van Nuys (Calif.) Mid. Sch., 1993—; mem. faculty phys. edn. and psychology Calif. State U., L.A., 1978-81, 93, phys. edn. Glendale Coll., 1979-81; tchr. Calif. State U. at L.A., Long Beach and Dominguez Hills, 1978-81, 93, Stockholm U., 1983, Calif. State U., L.A., Nat. Inst. Sports, India, 1982; condr. workshops in stress mgmt., peak performance, yoga, meditation, winning ways, practical sports psychology, 1975—; dir., instr., co-founder Inst. Sports Psychology, Bombay and L.A., 1982—; tchr. stress mgmt. or succes systems. Author: Japan Hijack, 1978; (audio tapes) Winning Ways: The Neuropsychology of Sports Excellence, 1988; contbr. articles to profl. jours. and mags.; appearances on TV KNBC, Everywhere Show, 1981, Theta Cable You Are That, 1981, Century Cable, 1988, KCAL Weekend Gallery, 1988, KCBS Barbara De Angeles Show on Twins, 1992, radio KABC Tom Hall Program, 1981, KMDY, 1987, KGIL HealthChoice, 1988, others. Recipient Sr.

Olypmic Swim Championship medals, 1979, 80, 81, 84, 85. Mem. Assn. for Advancement of Applied Sports Psychology, Internat. Soc. Sport Psychology, Calif. Assn. Health, Phys. Edn. and Recreation and Dance, Parent, Tchr., Student Assn. Home and Office: 13339 Sylvan St Van Nuys CA 91401-2414

KRUEGER, KURT DONN, lawyer; b. Worthington, Minn., May 8, 1952; s. Donn Kurt and Lola (Lueck) K.; m. Kim Short, Jan. 2, 1983; children: Krista Marie, Kurt Derrick. BA in Gov., Mont. State U., 1974; JD, George Mason U., 1978. Bar: Va. 1978, U.S. Dist. Ct. (ea. dist.) Va. 1979, U.S. Ct. Appeals (4th and D.C. cirs.) 1979, Mont. 1980, U.S. Dist. Ct. Mont. 1980, U.S. Ct. Appeals (9th cir.) 1985, U.S. Supreme Ct. 1990. Law clk. to superior ct. judge Washington, 1978-80; staff atty. Mont. Legal Svcs. Assn., Butte, 1980-83; pvt. practice Butte, 1984—; bd. dirs Mont. Legal Svcs. Assn., Helena, 1984—, pres., 1988-89. State rep. Mont. State Legis., Helena, 1985-87; bd. dirs. Big Bros. and Big Sisters, Butte, 1985-88, Butte Silver Bow Zoning Bd. Adjustment, 1989-92; adv. bd. vigilante dist. Boy Scouts Am., 1989—. Mem. Va. Bar Assn., Mont. Bar Assn., Butte Silver Bar Assn., Assn. Trial Lawyers Am., Mont. Trial Lawyers Assn., Trout Unlimited, Ducks Unlimited, Skyline Sportsman (bd. dirs. 1997—). Democrat. Methodist. Office: 66 W Park St Ste 211 Butte MT 59701-1714

KRUEGER, KURT EDWARD, appliance manufacturing company official; b. Santa Monica, Calif., June 24, 1952; s. Richard L. and Peggy J. (Cisler) K.; m. Maureen S. Catland, Aug. 4, 1973; children: Corey Edward, Brendan Kurt, Alyssa Marie. BA in Biology, Calif. State U., Northridge, 1978, MS in Environ. and Occupational Health & Safety, 1980; MBA, Pepperdine U., 1988. Registered environ. health specialist. Regional health and safety coord. Internat. Tech. Corp., Wilmington, Calif., 1979-82, mgr. emergency response program, 1982-85, ops. mgr., 1985-88, gen. mgr., 1988-89; dir. health and safety Internat. Tech. Corp., Torrance, Calif., 1989-97; mgr. health and safety GE, Fairfield, Conn., 1997—. Mem. Am. Soc. Safety Engrs., Am. Indsl. Hygiene Assn. (cert.), Nat. Fire Protection Assn., Nat. Safety Mgmt. Soc., Hazardous Waste Action Coalition (chmn. health and safety subcom. 1996-97), Masons. Office: GE 3135 Easton Turnpike Fairfield CT 06431

KRUEGER, ROBERT EDWARD, manufacturing executive, mechanical engineer; b. L.A., Mar. 26, 1922; s. Edward Jr. and Ida Viola (Herren) K.; m. Elizabeth Westerfors, Sept. 10, 1949; children: Karen Elizabeth, Clarence Frederick (dec.), Roger Carl (dec.), Bruce Wayne, Glen Herren. Student, L.A. City Coll., 1939-40, Calif. Inst. Tech., 1940-43, 46-47, Yale U., Harvard U., MIT, AETC, 1943-44; BSME, Stanford U., 1950, MBA, 1952. Lic. fed. firearms dealer and ammunition mfr. Trainee Douglas Aircraft Co., Santa Monica, Calif., summers 1941-43; mem. staff Los Alamos (N.Mex.) Sci. Lab., 1947-49; chief engr. Rutishauser Corp., Pasadena, Calif., 1952-53; asst. to pres. Unitek Corp., El Monte, Calif., 1953-55; sales mgr. Donner Sci. Co., Concord, Calif., 1955-57, Shand & Jurs divsn. GPE, Berkeley, 1957-58; v.p. sales Advanced Instruments, Richmond, Calif., 1958-60; sales mgr. Gilliland Instruments, Oakland, Calif., 1960-62; ptnr. Krueger & Smith, Berkeley, 1969-72; founder, pres. Tetra Valves, Inc., Berkeley, 1972-78; owner, propr. Krueger Mfg.-Engring., Lafayette, Calif., 1962—. Author or co-author books, manuals, other works; patentee in field. Donor portraits of U.S. Pres. George Bush and Barbara Bush, White Ho., Washington, 1995, portrait of U.S. Pres. George Bush, Nat. Portrait Gallery, Washington, 1995; v.p. Calif. Rep. Assembly, 1983-84. With USAAF, 1942-47; with USAFR, 1947-53. Mem. IEEE (life), AAAS, ASTM, NRA (life, endowment), Am. Soc. for Metals, Inc. (life), Am. Def. Preparedness Assn. (life), James Smithson Soc./Smithsonian Instn. (Patron award Benefactors Cir. 1991), Nat. Mus. Am. Indian (charter), Colonial Williamsburg Found. (assoc.), Calif. Rifle and Pistol Assn. (life). Pantheist. Home: 1084 Via Roble Lafayette CA 94549 Office: Krueger Mfg-Engring 1084 Via Roble Lafayette CA 94549

KRUG, DONNA REBECCA DONDES, history educator, small business owner; b. Decatur, Ga., Feb. 17, 1947; d. Aaron and Gladys (Lynch) Dondes; m. John A. Krug, Nov. 30, 1968. BA in History summa cum laude, Calif. State U., Northridge, 1980; MA in Am. History, U. Calif., Irvine, 1983, PhD in History, 1990. Student rsch. asst. Calif. State U., Northridge, 1979-80; teaching asst., teaching assoc. U. Calif., Irvine, 1982-88, rsch. asst., 1988-90; asst. prof. history Va. State U., Petersburg, 1990-93; owner Donna's Korner Kollectibles, Orange, Calif., 1984—; instr. summer sch. U. Calif., Irvine, 1989; adj. history instr. Rancho Santiago Cmty. Coll., Santa Ana, 1990. Contbr. articles to jours. Active mem. Orange County Bd. Electors. Regents Dissertation fellow U. Calif., Irvine, 1987. Mem. Am. Hist. Assn., Orgn. Am. Historians, So. Hist. Assn., So. Hist. Assn. Women Historians, Phi Kappa Phi, Phi Alpha Theta. Home and Office: 2689 N Galley St Orange CA 92865-2420

KRUGER, KENNETH CHARLES, architect; b. Santa Barbara, Calif., Aug. 19, 1930; s. Thomas Albin and Chleople (Gaines) K.; m. Patricia Kathryn Rasey, Aug. 21, 1955; children: David, Eric. B.Arch., U. So. Calif., 1953. Registered architect, Calif. Pres. Kruger Bensen Ziemer, Santa Barbara, 1960-90; part-time instr. architecture dept. Calif. Poly., San Luis Obispo, 1993-95; part-time architect, 1993—. Bd. dirs. United Boys & Girls Club. Fellow AIA; mem. Archtl. Found. Santa Barbara (pres. 1987-89). Democrat. Unitarian. Home: 1255 Ferrelo Rd Santa Barbara CA 93103-2101

KRUGER, LAWRENCE, neuroscientist; b. New Brunswick, N.J., Aug. 15, 1929; s. Jacob C. and Kate M. (Newman) K.; m. Virginia Findlay, Sept. 30, 1960; children: Erika, Paula. PhD, Yale U., 1954. Postdoctoral fellow Johns Hopkins U., Balt., 1955-58, Coll. de France, Paris, 1958, Oxford (Eng.) U., 1958-59; asst. prof. anatomy UCLA, 1960-62, assoc. prof., 1962-65, prof., 1966—; Wellcome vis. prof., Albany (N.Y.) Med. Coll., 1981. Founding editor Somatosensory and Motor Research. Recipient Lederle Med. Faculty award, 1964-67, Javits Neurosci. Investigator award, 1984, 91; Fogarty Sr. Internat. Scholar, St. Mary's Hosp. Med. Sch., London, 1977, U. Verona, 1989-90. Mem. Internat. Brain Rsch. Orgn., Internat. Assn. for Study of Pain, Am. Assn. Anatomists, Am. Physiol. Soc., Soc. Neurosci. Office: UCLA Dept Neurobiology 10833 Le Conte Ave Los Angeles CA 90095

KRUGER, PAUL ROBERT, insurance broker; b. Ft. Dodge, Iowa, Nov. 16, 1957; s. Robert Wayne and Corinne Maxine (Wierson) K.; m. Lisa Diane Rouselle, June 9, 1990; children: Whitney Katherine, Austin Jacob and Garrett Jackson (twins). BSBA in Fin. and Mktg., Iowa State U., 1980. Claims rep. IMT Ins. Co., Des Moines, 1981-82; sales mgr. JCPenney Fin. Svcs., Plano, Tex., 1982-89, GranTree Furniture Rental, Aurora, Colo., 1989-90; sales rep. Sentry Ins., Denver, 1990—; with Preferred Risk Ins., Englewood, Colo., 1991—; ins. broker The Urman Co., Englewood, 1992—. Mem. Life Underwriting Tng. Coun., Boulder C. of C., Apt. Assn. Met. Denver (social com. 1989-90, amb. club 1989-90, trade show com. 1989-90), Boulder Jaycees (bd. dirs. 1983-84), Phi Kappa Tau (song leader 1979-80, pledge trainer 1977-78, asst. treas. 1978-79). Republican. Mem. Ch. of Nazarene. Home: 21224 E Belleview Pl Aurora CO 80015

KRUGGEL, JOHN LOUIS, plastic surgeon; b. Lake Mills, Iowa, Jan. 27, 1931; s. August and Elizabeth (Gleitz) K.; m. Kathleen Ann Lawson, June 1958 (div. 1972); children: Deborah, Natalie, Victoria, Pamela, Michael; m. Donna Marie Koerner, Mar. 2, 1978; 1 child, Matthew. AS, Waldorf Coll., 1951; MD, U. Iowa, 1957. Diplomate Am. Bd. Plastic Surgery, Am. Bd. Surgery. Intern Mercy Hosp., San Diego; resident Orange Meml. Hosp., Orlando, Fla., Mercy Hosp., San Diego, U. Calif., San Francisco; pvt. practice in plastic surgery San Diego, 1966—. Capt. USAF, 1959-61. Mem. Am. Soc. Plastic and Reconstructive Surgery, Calif. Soc. Plastic and Reconstructive Surgery, Calif. Med. Soc., San Diego County Med. Soc. (del. to Calif. Med. Assn.). Office: 4060 4th Ave Ste 120 San Diego CA 92103-2120

KRULAK, VICTOR HAROLD, newspaper executive; b. Denver, Jan. 7, 1913; s. Morris and Besse M. (Ball) K.; m. Amy Chandler, June 1, 1936; children: Victor Harold Jr., William Morris, Charles Chandler. B.S., U.S. Naval Acad., 1934; LL.D., U. San Diego. Commd. 2d lt. USMC, 1934; advanced through grades to lt. gen.; service in China, at sea, with USMC (Fleet Marine Forces), 1935-39; staff officer, also bn. regimental and divsn. comdr. World War II, World War II; chief staff (1st Marine Div. Korea); formerly comdg. gen. (Marine Corps Recruit Depot), San Diego; formerly spl asst. to dir., joint staff counterinsurgency and spl. activities (Office Joint Chiefs Staff); comdg. gen. Fleet Marine Force Pacific, Pacific, 1964-68; ret., 1968; v.p. Copley Newspaper Corp., 1968-79; pres. Words Ltd. Corp., San Diego. Trustee Zool. Soc. San Diego. Decorated D.S.M., Navy Cross, Legion of Merit with 3 oak leaf clusters, Bronze Star, Air medal, Purple Heart (2) U.S.; Cross of Gallantry; Medal of Merit Vietnam; Distinguished Service medal (Korea), Order of Cloud and Banner, Republic of China. Mem. U.S. Naval Inst., U.S. Marine Corps Assn., Am. Soc. Newspaper Editors, InterAm. Press Assn., U.S. Strategic Inst. (vice chmn.). Home: 3665 Carleton St San Diego CA 92106-2163 Office: Words Ltd 3045 Rosecrans St San Diego CA 92110-4827

KRUMPE, PETER E., medical educator; b. Jamaica, N.Y., July 26, 1943; s. Edward George K.; m. Jo Anne Krumpe, Nov. 24, 1990; children: Katherine, Kara, Stephanie, Stephen. BA, Vanderbitl U., 1965; MD, Emory U., 1969. Resident New Eng. Med. Ctr., Boston, 1969-71; fellow pulmonary medicine McGill U., Montreal, 1973-75; asst. assoc. prof. U. Calif., Davis, 1975-91; prof. medicine U. Nev. Sch. Medicine, Reno, 1991—. Contbr. chpts. to books. Lt. comdr. USNR, 1973-75. Fellow Am. Coll. Chest Physicians, Am. Coll. Physicians; mem. Am. Heart Assn., Am. Lung Assn. Home: 3715 Brighton Way Reno NV 89509-6800 Office: Reno VA Med Ctr 1000 Locust St Reno NV 89520-0102

KRUPP, EDWIN CHARLES, astronomer; b. Chgo., Nov. 18, 1944; s. Edwin Frederick and Florence Ann (Olander) K.; m. Robin Suzanne Rector, Dec. 31, 1968; 1 son, Ethan Hembree. BA, Pomona Coll., 1966; MA, UCLA, 1968, PhD (NDEA fellow, 1970-71), 1972. Astronomer Griffith Obs., Los Angeles Dept. Recreation and Parks, 1972—, dir., 1976—; mem. faculty El Camino Coll., U. So. Calif., extension divs. U. Calif.; cons. in ednl. TV Community Colls. Consortium; host teleseries Project: Universe. Author: Echoes of the Ancient Skies, 1983, The Comet and You, 1986 (Best Sci. Writing award Am. Inst. Physics 1986), The Big Dipper and You, 1989, Beyond the Blue Horizon, 1991, The Moon and You, 1993, Skywatchers, Shamans & Kings, 1996; editor, co-author: In Search of Ancient Astronomies, 1978 (Am. Inst. Physics-U.S. Steel Found. award for Best Sci. Writing 1978), Archaeoastronomy and the Roots of Science; editor-in-chief Griffith Obs., 1984—; contbg. editor Sky & Telescope, 1993—. Mem. Am. Astron. Soc. (past chmn. hist. astronomy divsn.), Astron. Soc. Pacific (past dir., recipient Klumpke-Roberts outstanding contbns. to the public understanding and appreciation of astronomy award 1989, G. Bruce Blair medal for contbns. to Pub. Astronomy 1996), Internat. Astron. Union, Explorers Club, Sigma Xi. Office: Griffith Observatory 2800 E Observatory Ave Los Angeles CA 90027-1255

KRUSE, KATHARINE ANN, women's health nurse; b. Brownwood, Tex., Oct. 29, 1960; d. Eugene and Audrey Ann (Johnson) K. Cert. in emergency med. tech., U. Mo., 1982; BSN, U. No. Colo., 1988. RN, Colo.; cert. EMT. Paramedic Sweet Springs (Mo.) Ambulance Dist., 1982; clin. technician drug and alcohol rehab. Harmony Found., Estes Park, Colo., 1984; camp nurse Sanborn Western Camps, Florissant, Colo., 1988; staff nurse labor/delivery unit Humana Hosp. of Lake Charles, La., 1989-90; cmty. health nurse II, pub. health nurse, adminstr. Lincoln County Nursing Svc., Hugo, Colo., 1990—; childbirth educator Lincoln County, Colo. Cancer Fedn. scholar. Home: PO Box 34 Agate CO 80101 Office: Lincoln County Nursing Svc PO Box 125 Hugo CO 80821

KSICINSKI, JOYCE MARY, education specialist; b. Milw., Jan. 29, 1945; d. Marcellus Joseph and Stefania (Serocuk) K.; m. Rex Sinclair, Apr. 1, 1979. BA in Art History, U. Wis., Milw., 1968; MA in Art History, U. Wis., 1972, MA in Bus., 1976. Bus. mgr. Honolulu Theatre for Youth, 1977-79; mng. dir. Manoa Valley Theatre, Honolulu, 1979-80; cmty. rels. coord. Waikiki Aquarium U. Hawaii, Honolulu, 1984-85; devel. dir. Maui (Hawaii) Acad. Performing Arts, 1986-89; resource devel. specialist Coll. of the Redwoods, Eureka, Calif., 1991—. Fellow William H. Donnor Found., 1968, Ford Found., 1969, Nat. Endowment for Arts, 1976. Mem. Nat. Coun. for Resource Devel., Am. Assn. for Higher Edn., Beta Gamma Sigma. Office: Coll of the Redwoods 7351 Tompkins Hill Rd Eureka CA 95501-9302

KUBIAS, CRAIG OWEN, philosophy educator; b. St. Louis, Apr. 6, 1955; m. Karen Scott, Sept. 23, 1995. B in Gen. Studies, Ohio U., 1978; MDiv, Louisville Presbyn. Theol., 1982; PhD in Philosophy of Religion, U. Denver, 1991. Ordained min. Presbyn. Ch. Adj. prof. religion and culture Teikyo Loretto Heights U., Denver, 1992-93; adj. prof. philosophy Coll. of St. Francis, Denver, 1993—, Met. State Coll., Denver, 1993—, Red Rocks C.C., Denver, 1995—, U. Phoenix, Denver, 1995—. Author: Love and Other Neat Stuff, 1996. Office: Red Rocks CC 13300 W 6th Ave Golden CO 80401-5357

KUBOTA, GAYLORD, museum director. Exec. dir. Alexander and Baldwin Sugar Mus., Puunene, Hawaii. Office: Alexander and Baldwin Sugar Mus 3957 Hansen Rd Puunene HI 96784

KUCERA, GREGORY MICHAEL, art dealer; b. Seattle, May 6, 1956; life ptnr. Larry W. Yocom, 1985. BA in Art, U. Wash., 1980. Art dealer Greg Kucera Gallery, Seattle. Pres. Seattle (Wash.) Art Dealers Assn., 1990-92, 94-96. Democrat. Office: Greg Kucera Gallery 608 2nd Ave Seattle WA 98104-2204

KUCHAR, THEODORE, conductor, academic administrator, musician; b. N.Y.C.. Music dir., condr. Boulder (Colo.) Philharm. Orch., 1987—; prin. violist leading orchs. Cleve. and Helsinki, Finland; soloist, chamber musician Australia, Europe, New Zealand, U.S., Russia, festivals including Blossom, Edinburgh, Kuhmo, Tanglewood, others; dir. orchestral studies U. Colo., 1996—; artistic dir., prin. condr. Nat. Symphony Orch. Ukraine; artistic dir. Australian Festival Chamber Music, 1990—; past music dir. Queensland Philharm. Orch., Brisbane, Australia, W. Australian Ballet, Perth. Muscian Penderecki's String Trio, N.Y.C., 1994; music dir., condr. recordings with Nat. Symphony Orch. and Ukrainian Chamber Orch. including Lyatoshynsky's Symphonies Nos. 2 and 3 (Best Internat. Recording of Yr. 1994), others; music dir., condr. worldwide tours. Paul Fromm fellow, 1980; recipient bronze medal for his work in promoting that country's music Finnish Govt., 1989. Office: Boulder Philharm Orch 2590 Walnut St Ste 6 Boulder CO 80302*

KUDENOV, JERRY DAVID, zoology educator; b. Lynwood, Calif., Dec. 19, 1946; s. William and Marion Kudenov; m. Kathryn Anne Brown, May 30, 1969; children: Peter Alexander, Michael William. BA, U. Calif., San Diego, 1968; MS, U. Pacific, 1970; PhD, U. Ariz., 1974. Research scientist Ministry for Conservation, Melbourne, Australia, 1974-79; asst. prof. zoology U. Alaska, Anchorage, 1980-82, assoc. prof., 1982-86, prof., 1987—, chmn. dept. biol. sci., 1986-90; vis. asst. prof. U. So. Calif., Los Angeles, 1979-80. Assoc. editor Am. Geophys. Union Antarctic Rsch. Series, 1994—. Mem. AAAS, Am. Soc. Zoologists, Sci. Research Soc. N. Am., Biol. Soc. Wash., So. Calif. Acad. Scis. (bd. dirs. 1980), Internat. Polychaete Assn. Home: 3930 Alitak Bay Cir Anchorage AK 99515-2366 Office: U Alaska Anchorage Dept Biol Scis 3211 Providence Dr Anchorage AK 99508-4614

KUDO, EMIKO IWASHITA, former state official; b. Kona, Hawaii, June 5, 1923; s. Tetsuzo and Kuma (Koga) Iwashita; BS, U. Hawaii, 1944; MS in Vocational Edn., Pa. State U., 1950; postgrad. U. Hawaii, U. Ore., others; m. Thomas Mitsugi Kudo, Aug. 21, 1951; children: Guy J.T., Scott K., Candace F. Tchr. jr. and sr. high sch., Hawaii, 1945-51; instr. home econs. edn. U. Hawaii Tchrs. Coll., Honolulu, 1948-51, Pa. State U., State College, 1949-50; with Hawaii Dept. Edn., Honolulu, 1951-82, supr. sch. lunch svc., 1951-64, home econ. edn., 1951-64, dir. home econ. edn., 1964-68, adminstr. vocat.-tech. edn., 1968-76, asst. supt. instructional svcs., 1976-78, dep. supt. State Dept. Edn., 1978-82; cons. Am. Samoa vocat. edn. state plan devel., 1970-71, vocat. edn. U. Hawaii, 1986, internat. secondary program devel. Ashiya Ednl. System, Japan, 1986-91, cons. to atty. gen. mental health svcs. for children and adolescents State of Hawaii, 1994; chief planner devel. State of Hawaii Children & Adolescents Mental Health Svcs. Implementation Plan, 1994-95; state coord. industry-labor-edn., 1972-76; mem. nat. task force edn. and tng. for minority bus. enterprise, 1972-73; steering com. Career Info. Ctr. Project, 1973-78; co-dir. Hawaii Career Devel. Continuum project, 1971-74; mem. Nat Accreditation and Instl. Eligibility Adv. Council, 1974-77, cons., 1977-78; mem. panel Internat. Conf. Vocat. Guidance, 1978, 80, 82, 86, 88; state commr. edn. commn. of the states, 1982-90; mem. Hawaii edn. coun., 1982-90; dir. Dept. Parks and Recreation, City and County of Honolulu, 1982-84; bd. dirs. Honolulu Neighborhood Housing Svcs., 1991—. Exec. bd. Aloha council Boy Scouts Am., 1978-88. Japan Found. Cultural grantee, 1977; Pa. State U. Alumni fellow, 1982; bd. trustees St. Louis High Sch., 1988-95; mem. Gov.'s Commn. on Sesquicentennial Observance of Pub. Edn. In Hawaii, 1990-91; mem. Commn. State Rental Housing Trust Fund, 1992—; mem. steering com. Hawaii Long Term Care Coalition, 1992—. Mem. Am. Assn. Retired Persons (mem. state legis. com. 1990-92), Pa. State U. Disting. Alumni, Western Assn. Schs. and Colls. (accreditation team mem. Ch. Coll. of Hawaii 1972-73), Am. Vocat. Assn., Hawaii Vocat. Assn., NEA, Hawaii Edn. Assn. (trustee 1992—), Hawaii State Ednl. Officers Assn. (Konawaena H.S. Hall of Fame 1997), Am., Hawaii Family Consumer Sci. Assn., Nat., Hawaii assns. for supervision and curriculum devel., Am. Tech. Edn. Assn., Hawaii Recreation and Park Assn., Omicron Nu, Pi Lambda Theta, Phi Delta Kappa, Delta Kappa Gamma. Author handbooks and pamphlets in field. Home and Office: 217 Nenue St Honolulu HI 96821-1811

KUDZA, SARAH MARIE, human services administrator; b. Flint, Mich.. BBA in Pub. Adminstrn., Coll. Santa Fe, 1987. Asst. to dean of students Coll. Santa Fe, 1987-88; eligibility worker II State of N.Mex.-Human Svcs., Santa Fe, 1988-89, quality control reviewer, 1989-94, mgmt. analyst III, 1994-95, mgmt. analyst IV, 1995-96, program compliance bur. chief, 1996—. Office: Human Svcs Dept-Office Inspector Gen Program Compliance Bur PO Box 2348 Pollon Plz Santa Fe NM 87502

KUEBLER, RICHARD ARTHUR, theater educator, consultant; b. Lincoln, Nebr., July 31, 1947; s. Richard Arthur Sr. and Phyllis Darlene (Belka) K. BA, Wayne (Nebr.) State Coll., 1970; MFA, U. Nebr., 1980, postgrad., 1980-81. Dir., actor Nettlecreek Players, Inc., Hagerstown, Ind., summers 1975-76; dir. of theatre Kearney (Nebr.) Pub. Schs., 1971-78; dir., actor Kearney Pks. & Recreation, summers 1973-77; workshop and tour dir. U. Nebr., Lincoln, 1978-80, teaching asst., 1979-80; scenic supr. Doane Coll., Crete, Nebr., 1980-81; dir. theatre Northeastern Jr. Coll., Sterling, Colo., 1981—; state festival chmn., adjudicator Colo. Community Theatre Coalition, Sterling, 1989-90, dir. all-state prodn., 1996, 97; regional adjudicator Am. Coll. Theatre Festival; state theatre chmn. Colo. Community Coll./Occupational Edn. System, Denver, 1988-89; drama chmn. Sterling Arts Coun., 1990—; mem. theatre grant rev. panel Colo. Coun. on the Arts and Humanities, 1990—, community theatre liaison to the organizational assistance program; U.S. rep. The Enniskillen (No. Ireland) Internat. Community Theatre Festival, 1990, The Dundalk (Republic Ireland) Internat. Amateur Theatre Festival, 1990; mem. community theatre liaison Alliance for Colo. Acts; mem. coll./univ. adv. panel to the Denver Ctr. Theatre Comp.; guest dir. U. Wyo., summer 1993, Backstage Theatre, summer 1996, Bas Bleu Theatre, summer 1996; dir. RMTA Showcase, 1997. Dir. (play) Luann Hampton Laverty Oberlander, 1980 (Best Dir.), Vanities, 1989 (Best Dir. 1989), The Shadow Box, 1990 (Best Dir.). Pres. Prairie Players, Sterling, 1986—; bd. dirs. Colo. Cmty. Theatre Coalition, 1989—, state ajudicator, 1989—, pres., 1992—, all state prodn. dir., 1996; bd. dirs. Sterling Arts Coun., 1988—; sponsor Northeastern Jr. Coll. Players, 1981—. Recipient All State Co. Directing award Colo. Cmty. Theatre Coalition, 1995, Bd. Mem. of Yr. award, 1990, Higher Edn. Theatre Educator of Yr., Alliance of Colo. Theatre award, 1992; Formfit-Rogers scholar, 1965, Knights of Ak-Sar-Ben scholar. Mem. Am. Assn. Community Theatre (rep. region VII 1989-95, 96—, Colo. state rep. 1995-96), Rocky Mountain Theatre Assn. (bd. trustees 1992—, pres. elect 1995-97, pres. 1997—, showcase dir. 1997). Home: 705 S 6th Ave Sterling CO 80751-3616 Office: Northeastern Jr Coll ES French Hall Sterling CO 80751

KUECHLE, ROLAND KOERNER, architect; b. Columbus, Ohio, Aug. 4, 1916; s. Theodore Frederick and Josephine (Koerner) K.; m. Nayaulderson Webb, July 13, 1940; children: Richard Roland, Joel Frederick. BArch, Ohio State U., 1940. Registered architect, Calif. Assoc. engr. Applachian Electric Power Co., Huntington, W.Va., 1939-41; archtectural draftsman Ohio State U. Architect, Columbus, 1941, Basic magnesium, Inc., Henderson, Nev., 1941-43, Corlet & Anderson, Ponsford & Price, Oakland, Calif., 1943-45; assoc. architect Confer & Willis, Oakland, 1945-55; architect Rosener Engring., Inc., San Francisco, 1955-58, Roland K. Kuechle, Architect, Oakland, 1950-61; engr./architect Lawrence Livermore (Calif.) Nat. Labs., 1961-85, engr./architect indeterminate, 1985—. Photographer (recipient Photo/Travel Slide of Yr. award No. Calif. Coun. of Camera Clubs 1982); architectural designer residence (Hon. mention Rich's Progressive Architecture Mag. competition 1946), naval supply depot (Meritorious Civilian Svc. medal 1945). Recipient sch. medal AIA, Ohio State U., 1940. Mem. East Bay Assn. Architects (treas. 1946-52), Rossmoor Camera Club (pres. 1987-88, numerous awards), No. Calif. Coun. of Camera Clubs (assoc., rep. 1991-93). Republican. Presbyterian. Home: 3100 Rossmoor Pky Apt 2 Walnut Creek CA 94595-3327

KUEHN, CARL PETER, information technology consultant, statistician; b. Neenah, Wis., May 16, 1966; s. Hasso Manfred and Alide (Koppenstein) K.; m. JoDee Stahlecker, Aug. 13, 1994. BS, U. Wis., 1988; postgrad., George Washington U., 1989-91; MS, Am. U., 1993. Statistician Bur. Labor Stats./U.S. Dept. Labor, Washington, 1989-94; bus. sys. cons. Am. Mgmt. Systems, Inc., Golden, Colo., 1994—, recruiter, 1995—. Patron Close UP Washington, Westminster, Colo., 1997; group Bible study leader Gethsemane Luth. Ch., 1995—. Office: Am Mgmt Sys 14033 Denver West Pkwy Golden CO 80401

KUEHN, JODEE STAHLECKER, information technology consultant; b. Thornton, Colo., Aug. 25, 1966; d. Robert James Stahlecker; m. Carl Kuehn, Aug. 13, 1994. BS, U. Denver, 1988; MBA, U. Ariz., 1993. Tech. trainer Info. Found., Denver, 1988-90, programmer/analyst, 1990-91; bus. systems cons. Am. Mgmt. Systems, Inc., Golden, Colo., 1993—. Big sister Big Sisters Colo., Denver, 1989-91; nursing hostess vol. Humana Mountain View Hosp., Thornton, 1989-90. Hornbeck scholar U. Denver, 1984-85. Mem. Golden Key, Pi Mu Epsilon. Office: Am Mgmt Sys 14033 Denver West Pkwy Golden CO 80401

KUEHN, KLAUS KARL ALBERT, ophthalmologist; b. Breslau, Germany, Apr. 1, 1938; came to U.S., 1956, naturalized, 1971; s. Max and Anneliese (Hecht) K.; m. Eileen L. Nordgaard, June 22, 1961 (div. 1972); children: Stephan Eric, Kristina Annette; m. Lynda O. Hubbs, Oct. 2, 1974. Student, St. Olaf Coll., 1956-57; BA, BS, U. Minn., 1961; MD, 1963. Diplomate Am. Bd. Ophthalmology. Resident in ophthalmology UCLA Affiliated Hosps., 1968-71; practice medicine specializing in ophthalmology, San Bernardino, Calif., 1971—; chief ophthalmology dept. San Bernardino County Med. Ctr., 1979-80; assoc. clin. prof. ophthalmology Jules Stein Eye Inst. and UCLA Med. Ctr., 1978-81. Served to capt. U.S. Army, 1963-64. Fellow Am. Acad. Ophthalmology; mem. AMA, Calif. Med. Assn., Calif. Assn. Ophthalmology (bd. dirs.). Office: 902 E Highland Ave San Bernardino CA 92404-4007

KUGA, MARK WAYNE, economist; b. Renton, Wash., Oct. 5, 1959; s. Henry S. and O. Lavonne (Ninnemann) K.; m. Nanette K. Starr, Apr. 27, 1990. BA in Econs., U. Wash., 1982; MA, UCLA, 1984, PhD, 1989. Econ. Lexecon, Inc., Chgo., 1987-89; sr. econ. Econ. Analysis Corp., L.A., 1989-93; prin. Willamette Mgmt. Assocs., Portland, Oreg., 1993-95; pres. Delta Econ. Cons. Corp., Tualatin, Oreg., 1996—; adj. instr. Portland State U., 1993—. Rsch. fellow Alfred P. Sloan Found., 1984-87. Mem. Am. Econ. Assn., Am. Acad. Econ. and Fin. Experts, Am. Arbitration Assn. (nat. panel of comml. arbitrators), Nat. Assn. Bus. Econs., Nat. Assn. Forensic Econs, So. Econ. Assn., Western Econ. Assn. Office: Delta Econ Cons Corp 7451 SW Coho Ct Ste 107 Tualatin OR 97062

KUH, ERNEST SHIU-JEN, electrical engineering educator; b. Peking, China, Oct. 2, 1928; came to U.S., 1948, naturalized, 1960; s. Zone Shung and Tsia (Chu) K.; m. Bettine Chow, Aug. 4, 1957; children: Anthony, Theodore. BS, U. Mich., 1949; MS, MIT, 1950; PhD, Stanford U., 1952. Mem. tech. staff Bell Tel. Labs., Murray Hill, N.J., 1952-56; assoc. prof. elec. engring. U. Calif., Berkeley, 1956-62, prof., 1962—, Miller rsch. prof., 1965-66, William S. Floyd Jr. prof. engring., 1990—, William S. Floyd Jr. prof. engring. emeritus, 1993—, chmn. dept. elec. engring. and computer sci., 1968-72, dean Coll. Engring., 1973-80; cons. IBM Rsch. Lab., San Jose,

Calif., 1957-62, NSF, 1975-84; mem. panel Nat. Bur. Stds., 1975-80; vis. com. Gen. Motors Inst., 1975-79, dept. elec. engring. and computer scis. MIT, 1986-91; mem. adv. coun. elec. engring. dept. Princeton (N.J.) U., 1986—; mem. bd. councilors sch. engring. U. So. Calif., 1986-91; mem. sci. adv. bd. Mills Coll., 1976-80. Co-author: Principles of Circuit Synthesis, 1959, Basic Circuit Theory, 1967, Theory of Linear Active Network, 1967; Linear and Nonlinear Circuits, 1987. Recipient Alexander von Humboldt award, 1980, Lamme medal Am. Soc. Endring. Edn., 1981, U. Mich. Disting. Alumnus award, 1970, Berkeley citation, 1993, C & C prize Japanese Found. for Computers and Comm. Promotion, 1996; Brit. Soc. Engring. and Rsch. fellow, 1982. Fellow IEEE (Edn. medal 1981, Centenial medal 1984, Circuits and Systems Soc. award. 1988), AAAS; mem. NAE, Acad. Sinica, Sigma Xi, Phi Kappa Phi. Office: U Calif Elec Engring & Computer Sci Depts Berkeley CA 94720

KUHL, RONALD WEBSTER, marketing executive; b. Chgo., Dec. 12, 1938; s. Robert Emerson and Kathleen (Webster) K.; m. Mary Walls, Sept. 28, 1968; children: David Douglas, Kevin Lathrop. BS in Econs., U. Pa., 1960; MBA, Harvard U., 1964. Account exec. Young & Rubicam Advt., N.Y.C., 1964-71; v.p. mgmt. supr. Young & Rubicam Advt., San Francisco, 1988-90; mgr. promotion and design The First Ch. of Christ Scientist, Boston, 1971-75; account exec. BBDO Advt., San Francisco, 1975-77; acct. supr. Ketchum Communications, San Francisco, 1977-80; dir. mktg. ComputerLand Corp., Hayward, Calif., 1985-88; v.p. mktg. communications Ventura Software Inc., San Diego, 1990-92; v.p. mktg. Castelle, Santa Clara, Calif., 1992-94; v.p. advt. and mktg. svcs. Interactive Video Enterprises, San Ramon, Calif., 1994-96; v.p. mktg. and svcs. NetSoft, Irvine, Calif., 1996—. 1st lt. U.S. Army, 1960-62. Office: NetSoft Enterprises 31 Technology Dr Irvine CA 92618

KUHLMAN, WALTER EGEL, artist, educator; b. St. Paul, Nov. 16, 1918; s. Peter and Marie (Jensen) K.; m. Nora McCants; 1 son, Christopher; m. Tulip Chestman, April 9, 1979. Student, St. Paul Sch. Art; BS, U. Minn., 1941; postgrad., Tulane U., Academiè de la Grand Chaumierè, Paris, Calif. Sch. Fine Arts. mem. faculty U. Calif. Sch. Fine Arts, Stanford, U. Mich., Santa Clara (Calif.) U., U. N.Mex., Sonoma State U., Rohnert Park, Calif., (prof. emeritus, 1988—). One person shows include U. N.Mex., Walker Art Center, Mpls., The Berkshire Museum, Mass., La Jolla Museum of Contemporary Art, Calif., Santa Barbara Mus. of Art, Calif., San Francisco Mus. of Modern Art, 1958, New Arts Gallery, Houston, 1959-61, Roswell Mus. Palace of Legion of Honor, Calif., 1956, 59, 61, 62, 64, San Francisco Mus. Art, De Saisset Mus., Jonson Gallery U. N.Mex., 1963, 64, 65, Charles Campbell Gallery, San Francisco, 1981, 83, 85, Djurovich Gallery, Sacramento, The Carlson Gallery, San Francisco, 1989, Gump's Gallery, San Francisco, 1976, 1992, University Gallery, Sonoma State U., Natsoulis Gallery Davis, Calif., Albuquerque Mus. Fine Arts, 1994, George Krevsky Fine Arts, San Francisco, 1994, 96, Robert Green Gallery, Mill Valley, Calif.; group shows include N.Y. World's Fair, St. Paul Gallery, WPA Exhibition, Lawson Galleries, San Francisco, A 1948 Portfolio: 16 Lithographs (Diebenkorn, Lobdell, Hultberg), All Annual Invitational Exhibitions, San Francisco Mus. Modern Art, 1948-58, Petit Palais Mus., Paris, San Francisco Mus. Modern Art, III Biennial of Sao Paulo, Museo de Arte Moderna, Brazil, L.A. County Mus., Mus. Modern Art, Rio de Janiero, San Francisco Mus. Modern Art, 1955, 57, 66, 76, 96, Graham Found., Chgo, L.A. County Mus., Calif. Palace of the Legion of Honor, Virginia Mus. Fine Arts, Richmond, Stanford U., Gallery, Roswell Mus., 1961, 62, Univ. Art Mus., Austin, Texas Santa Fe Mus. Fine Arts, NM, Ca. Palace of Legion of Honor, Richard L. Nelson Gallery, UC Davis, Natsoulis Gallery, Northern California Figuration Expositions Art USA, 1992, 93, 94, George Krevsky Fine Art, San Francisco, Art Mus. Santa Cruz, Calif., 1993, Pasquale Ianetti Art Galleries, San Francisco, 1994, Robert Green Fine Arts, Mill Valley, Calif. 1994, 95, Acad. Arts and Letters, N.Y. 1995; permanent Collections include: The Phillips Collection, Washington, Nat. Gallery Am. Art, Washington, Walker Art Ctr., Washington, San Francisco Mus. Modern Art, Brit. Mus., Met. Mus. Art, NAD, N.Y., others. Recipient Maestro award Calif. Arts Coun., Outstanding Calif. Working Artist and Tchr. award; fellow Tiffany Found., Graham Found., Cummington Found. Mem. Nat. Acad. Design N.Y. Studio: Indsl Ctr Bldg Studio 335 480 Gate 5 Rd Sausalito CA 94965-1430

KUHN, DONALD MARSHALL, marketing professional; b. Miami, Fla., Nov. 2, 1922; s. Paul Carlton Kuhn and Helen (Merrick) Bond; m. Jane Emma Williams, Dec. 24, 1948 (dec. 1988); children: Marshall Merrick, Richard Williams, Diane Joan, Paul Willard; m. Kay Bardsley, Feb. 25, 1990. BA in Journalism and Drama, U. Miami, 1949. Cert. fundraising executive. Advt. copywriter Sears Roebuck and Co., Chgo., 1949-50; dir. pub. relations Tb Inst. Chgo. and Cook County, 1950-54; dir. fundraising Dade County Tb Assn., Miami, 1955-59, Minn. Tb and Health Assn., St. Paul, 1959-60, Mich. Lung Assn., Lansing, 1960-68, Am. Lung Assn., N.Y.C., 1966-78; nat. founder, dir. regional fin. program Rep. Nat. Com., Washington, 1978-79; exec. v.p., dir. fundraising div. Walter Karl, Inc., Armonk, N.Y., 1979-90, cons., 1990-93; cons. May Devel. Svcs., Greenwich, Conn., 1993—; mem. direct mktg. task force Am. Red Cross, Washington, 1983-84; mem. direct mail task force Am. Heart Assn., Dallas, 1982. Editor: Non-profit Council Info. Exchange, 1987-90; contbr. articles to Fundraising Mgmt. Mag. Bd. dirs. Isadora Duncan Internat. Inst., N.Y.C., 1987—. Mem. Nat. Soc. Fundraising Execs. (bd. dirs. 1978-80), Direct Mktg. Assn. (mem. operating com., non-profit coun. 1987-90, recipient non-profit coun. fundraising achievement award 1991). Republican. Congregational. Home and Office: 6305 S Geneva Cir Englewood CO 80111-5437

KUHN, HOLLY HUNT, elementary education educator; b. Mesa, Ariz., July 24, 1963; d. Albert Lufkin and Mary Louise (Schneider) H. BA in Edn., No. Ariz. U., 1987. Cert. spl. edn. and elem. tchr., Ariz. Elem. tchr. Deer Valley Pub. Schs., Phoenix, 1988—; reading specialist Chpt. One, Phoenix, 1993-94. Mem. LDS Ch. Office: Desert Winds Elem Sch 19825 N 15th Ave Phoenix AZ 85027-4305

KUHN, ROBERT FREDERICK (BOB KUHN), artist, illustrator; b. Buffalo, Jan. 28, 1920; s. Edward George and Marie W. (Trapp) K.; m. Elizabeth Jane Casey, July 26, 1941; children: Robert Casey, Karen Elizabeth, Julie Ann. Student, Pratt Inst., 1937-40. Writer, illustrator: The Animal Art of Bob Kuhn, 1973; represented in permanent collections Gilcrease Mus., Tulsa, Nat. Cowboy Hall of Fame, Oklahoma City, Genesee County Mus., Rochester, N.Y., Nat. Mus. Wildlife Art, Jackson, Wyo. With USMS, 1943-45. Recipient numerous awards including Prix de West, 1991, Gold medal (2), Silver medal, Award of Merit (5) Soc. Animal Artists, Rungius medal Nat. Mus. Wildlife Art, 1989, Disting. Wildlife Artist award Liegh Yauxey Woodson Art Mus., 1990.

KUHN, ROBERT LAWRENCE, investment banker, corporate financier, strategist, author, educator; b. N.Y.C., Nov. 6, 1944; s. Louis and Lee (Kahn) K.; m. Dora Elana Serviarian, June 23, 1967; children: Aaron, Adam, Daniella. AB in Human Biology, Johns Hopkins U., 1964; PhD in Brain Sci., UCLA, 1968; MS in Mgmt., MIT, 1980. Investment banker, fin adv. representing various firms, N.Y.C., L.A., Beijing, Tokyo, 1980—; cons. corp. strategy and fin., N.Y.C., L.A., Beijing, Tokyo, 1980—; pres. The Geneva Cos., Irvine, Calif, 1991—; adj. prof. Grad. Sch. Bus. Adminstrn., NYU, 1981-89; exec.-in-residence U. So. Calif., 1990; bd. advisors, U. So. Calif. Sch. Bus., 1992—; internat. adviser in fin. and high tech. to govts. U.S., Israel, Fed. Republic Germany, China, 1984—; vice chmn. bd. dirs. Data Software and Systems; bd. dirs. Tower Semiconductor, N.Y.C.; cons. and lectr. in field. Author: Mid-Sized Firms: Success Strategies and Methodology, 1982, Creativity and Strategy in Mid-Sized Firms, 1988, (with George Geis) The Firm Bond: Linking Meaning and Mission in Business and Religion, 1984, Micromanaging: Transforming Business Leaders with Personal Computers, 1987, To Flourish Among Giants: Creative Management for Mid-Sized Firms, 1985 (Japanese translation, 1986, Macmillan Book Club main selection), (with Arie Lavie) Industrial Research and Development in Israel, 1986, Dealmaker: All the Negotiating Skills and Secrets You Need, 1988, Investment Banking: The Art and Science of High-Stakes Dealmaking, 1989, Japanese translation, 1990, Chinese translation, 1995, (with Don Gamache) The Creativity Infusion, 1989; editor: Commercializing Defense-Related Technology, 1984; (with Raymond Smilor) Corporate Creativity: Robust Companies and the Entrepreneurial Spirit, 1984; (with Margaret Maxey) Regulatory Reform: Private Enterprise and Risk Assessment, 1985; (with Eugene Konecci) Technology Venturing: American Innovation and Risk Taking, 1985; (with Raymond Smilor) Managing Take-Off in Fast Growth Companies, 1985; Frontiers in Creative and Innovative Management, 1985; (with Yuji Ijiri) New Directions in Creative and Innovative Management, 1988; Medical Information Sciences, 1988; Commercializing Strategic Defense Technologies, 1986, Commercializing SDI Technologies (with Stewart Nozette, 1987). Editor-in-chief: Handbook for Creative and Innovative Managers, 1987, Libr. of Investment Banking, 7 vols., 1990; contbg. editor, columnist Jour. Bus. Strategy, 1984-90. Sloan fellow MIT, Cambridge, 1979; sr. research fellow in creative and innovative mgmt. IC2 Inst., U. Tex., Austin, 1983—. Mem. Phi Beta Kappa. Avocations: weight-lifting, table tennis, chess, classical music. Office: The Geneva Coms 5 Park Plz Irvine CA 92614-5995

KUHN, RONALD GREG, education corporation executive; b. Lusk, Wyo., Sept. 5, 1943; s. Greg Kuhn and Adelaide Kennelly Kuhn Abbey; m. Phyllis Ruth Antonelli, Sept. 30, 1989; children: Ronald Andrew, Christopher John, Jill Susan. Student, U. N.D.; BS, Bemidji (Minn.) State U., 1965; MS, Mankato (Minn.) State U., 1969; DMA, U. Wash., 1979. Cert. tchr., Minn., Mont., Wash. Elem. music tchr. pub. schs., Ely, Minn., 1966-68; dir. choral music Great Falls (Mont.) H.S., 1969-72; dir. music Univ. Congl. Ch., Seattle, 1974-80; pres., CEO Keys to Excellence, Inc., Scottsdale, Ariz., 1980—; adj. prof. Mont. State U., Bozeman, 1985-88. Author, presenter video curricula including Keys to Excellence for Youth, 1983; co-author: (with Phyllis R. Antonelli) Keys to Innervision, 1990, Keys to Innervisions-Possibility Parenting, 1993. Pres. Puget Sound Choral Condrs. Guild, Seattle, 1975-76. Mem. Scottsdale C. of C. Mem. Unity Ch.

KUHNS, CRAIG SHAFFER, business educator; b. Spokane, Wash., Apr. 14, 1928; s. Theodore Lewis and Audrey Grace (Shaffer) K. BS, U. Calif., Berkeley, 1950, BA, 1954, MBA, 1955. Analyst Standard Oil Co. of Calif., San Francisco, 1955-57; bus. educator U. Calif./San Jose State U., 1958-63, City Coll. of San Francisco, 1963—; adj. faculty U. San Francisco, 1977-90. 1st lt. U.S. Army, 1951-52, col. Mil. Intelligence USAR, 1953-80, col. AUS, ret. Mem. Calif. Alumni Assn., U.S. Army War Coll. Alumni Assn., Res. Officers Assn., Japan Soc. Republican. Home: 8 Locksley Ave Apt 8A San Francisco CA 94122-3850 Office: City Coll of San Francisco 50 Phelan Ave San Francisco CA 94112-1821

KUIVINEN, NED ALLAN, pathologist; b. Mt. Vernon, Ohio, May 19, 1936; s. Thomas Oscar and Pauline Ruthella (Pealer) K.; m. Deborah Berle Miller, Feb. 5, 1972; children: David Joseph, Matthew Thomas. BS, Ohio State U., 1958, MD, 1962. Diplomate Am. Bd. Pathology. Pathologist St. Joseph's Hosp., Phoenix, 1969—; dir. clin. lab. W. O. Boswell Meml. Hosp., Sun City, Ariz., 1970—; pathologist D. E. Webb Meml. Hosp., Sun City, Ariz., 1988—; dir. clin. lab. Vencor Hosp. Phoenix, Youngtown, Ariz., 1990-92. Lt. comdr. U.S. Navy, 1966-68. Fellow Am. Soc. Clin. Pathology, Coll. Am. Pathology; mem. Ariz. Med. Assn., Ariz. Soc. Pathologists (pres. 1993-95). Home: 5835 N 2nd Ave Phoenix AZ 85013-1535 Office: Pathology Assocs Ltd 555 W Catalina Dr Ste 12 Phoenix AZ 85013-4427

KUKLIN, JEFFREY PETER, lawyer, talent agency executive; b. N.Y.C., Dec. 13, 1935; s. Norman Bennett and Deane (Cable) K.; m. Jensina Olson, Nov. 18, 1960; 1 son, Andrew Bennett; m. 2d, Ronia Levene, June 22, 1969; children: Adam Blake, Jensena Lynne, Jeremy Brett. AB, Columbia U., 1957, JD, 1960. Bar: N.Y. 1962, U.S. Supreme Ct. 1965, Calif. 1973. Atty., TV sales adminstrn. NBC-TV, N.Y.C., 1966-67; asst. to dir. bus. affairs CBS News, N.Y.C., 1967-69; atty., assoc. dir. contracts ABC-TV, N.Y.C. and Los Angeles, 1969-73; v.p. bus. affairs and law Tomorrow Entertainment, Inc., Los Angeles, 1973-75; v.p. legal and bus. affairs Billy Jack Enterprises, Inc., Los Angeles, 1975-76; atty., bus. affairs exec. William Morris Agy., Inc., Beverly Hills, Calif., 1976-79, head TV bus. affairs, 1979-93, v.p., 1981-97. Mem. ABA, Acad. TV Arts and Scis. Home: 5465 White Oak Ave Encino CA 91316-2400

KULATILAKE, PINNADUWA H.S.W., mining and geological engineering educator; b. Colombo, Sri Lanka, Sept. 21, 1953; came to U.S., 1978; s. Samee De Silva and Koruwage Theadora (Wijewardane) K.; m. Thili Nayana Chandradasa Kulatilake; 1 child, Roy Sheyhan Kulatilake. BS in Civil Engring. with honors, U. Sri Lanka, Peradeniya, Sri Lanka, 1976; MEng in Soil Engring., Asian Inst. of Techol., Bangkok, Thailand, 1978; PhD in Civil Engring., Ohio State U., 1981. Registered Civil Engr., Calif. Chief instr. in geotechnical lab. U. Sri Lanka, Peradeniya, Sri Lanka, 1976; grad. scholar, teaching assoc. Geotechnical Engring. Dept. of Civil Engring. U. Calgary, Calgary, Alberta, Can., 1978; grad. rsch. assoc. Geotechnical Engring. Dept. of Civil Engring. Ohio State U., Columbus, 1978-81, sr. rsch. assoc., 1981; grad. teaching assoc. mathematics Dept. of Mathematics Ohio State U., Columbus, 1980-81; asst. prof. Geotechnical Engring. Dept. of Mining and Geological Engring. U. Ariz., Tucson, 1981-88, assoc. prof., 1988—; vis. rsch. fellow Norwegian Geotechnical Inst., 1988; vis. rsch. prof. Lulea U. of Technol., 1988-89, 1990; civil engr. Dept. of Nat. Housing, Colombo, Sri Lanka, U.N. Gunasekara & Co., Sri Lanka, Water Supply & Drainage Bd., Sri Lanka; short-course lectr. Reviewer 10 jours.; contbr. articles to profl. jours.; invited speaker in field. Exxon Ednl. Fdn. awards, 1982-85. Mem. ASCE (control group mem. geotech. safety and reliability com., EMD divsn. properties of materials com.), ASTM (head com. stability, erosion control and damage mitigation of mine slopes geotech. divsn.), Am. Soc. of Mining Engrs., Internat. Assn. for Civil Engring. Reliability and Risk Analysis, Internat. Assn. for Computer Methods and Advances in Geomechanics, Internat. Soc. for Soil Mechanics and Fdn. Engring., Internat. Soc. for Rock Mechanics, Internat. Assn. for Mathematical Geology, Phi Kappa Phi. Home: 5277 W Peridot St Tucson AZ 85742 Office: U Ariz Dept Mining & Geological Engring Tucson AZ 85721

KULKOSKY, PAUL JOSEPH, psychology educator; b. Newark, N.J., Mar. 3, 1949; s. Peter Francis and Rose Mary (Leonetti) K.; m. Tanya Marie Weightman, Sept. 16, 1978. BA, Columbia U., N.Y.C., 1971, MA, 1972; PhD, U. Wash., 1975. Research assoc. Cornell U., White Plains, N.Y., 1980-81, instr. psychiatry, 1981-82; asst. prof. psychology U. So. Colo., Pueblo, 1982-86, assoc. prof., 1986-89, chmn. dept. psychology, 1988-91, prof., 1989—; bd. advisors Pueblo Zool. Soc., 1984-85, 1988-91, bd. dirs., 1985-88; editorial cons. to pubs. Contbr. chpts. to books, articles to profl. jours.; referee psychol. jours. Liaison Rocky Mountain region Coun. Undergrad. Psychology Programs, 1990-91. Named Hon. Affiliate Prof. Am. U., Washington, 1977; rsch. grantee NIH, 1984—; staff fellow Nat. Inst. Alcohol Abuse and Alcoholism, 1976-80. Mem. AAAS (vice chmn. psychol. scis. sect. Southwestern and Rocky Mountain divsn. 1990-91, chmn. 1991-92, exec. com. Colo. rep. 1991-94, pres.-elect 1994-95, pres. 1995-96, past pres. 1996—), Consortium Aquariums, Univs. and Zoos, N.Y. Acad. Scis., Internat. Brain Rsch. Orgn., Soc. for Neurosci., Internat. Soc. Biomed. Rsch. on Alcoholism (charter), Psychonomic Soc., Soc. for Study Ingestive Behavior (charter), Colo.-Wyo. Acad. Sci. (exec. com. 1997—), U. So. Colo. Club, Sigma Xi (treas. 1986-96), Phi Kappa Phi, also others. Home: 417 Tyler St Pueblo CO 81004-1405 Office: U Soc Colo 2200 Bonforte Blvd Pueblo CO 81001-4901

KULONGOSKI, THEODORE R., state supreme court justice; b. St. Francois County, Mo., Nov. 5, 1940; married; 3 children. Grad., U. Mo., law degree, 1970. Ptnr. Kulongoski, Durham, Drummonds, and Colombo, Portland, Oreg., 1974-87; dir., Oreg. ins. commr., Oreg. corp. commr., dir. Oreg. fin. institutions, dir. Oreg. workers' compensation program Oreg. Dept. Ins. and Fin., 1987-91; exec. dir. Met. Family Svcs., 1991-92; atty. gen. State of Oreg., 1993-97; justice Oreg. Supreme Ct., Salem, 1997—; gen. counsel Oreg. AFL-CIO; mem. Oreg. legis., 1975-83; chair Ho., Senate labor coms., senate banking and ins. com., mem. Ho. and Senate jud. coms., environ. and energy coms., agriculture and forestry coms. Dem. Party nominee Gov. Oreg., 1982. With USMC. Office: 1163 State St NE Salem OR 97310

KUMAGAI, STACEY, broadcast executive. Student, Acad. Radio Broadcasting, Orange Coast Coll.; cert., U. Calif., Irvine. Broadcast studio counselor Acad. Radio Broadcasting, Huntington Beach, Calif., 1987; quality control dir. sta. KDOC-TV, Anaheim, Calif., 1987-88; mktg. promotional graphics sales Blue White Ind., Westminster, Calif., 1989-92; mktg., promotions rep. sta. KIIS-FM, L.A., 1992-93; on-camera talent, voiceover artist Berzon Talent Agy., Costa Mesa, Calif.; broadcast media coord. Jill Lloyd & Assocs., Costa Mesa, Calif.; v.p. Audio-dition, Inc., Fountain Valley, Calif., 1993-94; dir. broadcast affiliate rels. Who Did That Music?, L.A., 1994-96; dir. broadcast media rels. Back State West Mag. Actorfest, 1997; ptnr., pres. What If. . .Inc., 1997—; pres., sole proprietor Media Monster Comm., 1986—; mktg./acct. exec. Boot Music Advt., Irvine; sales mgr. MSC, Westminster ; assoc. prodr., writer Larger Than Life, Century Cable, Santa Monica, Calif.; mktg. cons. Infotrex Network Sys., Westminster; mktg. promotions asst. O'Brien & Shore Broadcast Enterprises, Downey, Calif.; reporter BNN-BournsNews Network Pilot, Orange, Calif.; co-host JCET Ednl. Network Spl., Huntington Beach, Calif.; host, writer Local Cable Update, Garden Grove, Calif.; radio personality Sta. KBCH-FM, Huntington Beach. Writer, pub.: Doing Business in California, 1997. Mem. Women in Comms., Unity Media Access Project, Am. Women in Radio and TV (broadcast media judge Gracie Allen Commendation awards So. Calif. chpt. 1997). Office: 11684 Ventura Blvd Ste 662 Studio City CA 91604

KUMAR, ANIL, nuclear engineer; b. Agra, India, Aug. 3, 1952; came to U.S., 1988; s. Vedprakash and Satyawati (Sudhir) Parashar; m. Geeta Sharma, Nov. 29, 1979; 1 child, Amitabh. MSc in Physics, Agra U., 1973; PhD in Nuclear Engring., U. Bombay, India, 1981. Sci. officer Bhabha Atomic Rsch. Ctr., Bombay, 1974-81; sr. researcher Ecole Poly. Fed. Lausanne, Switzerland, 1982-88; devel. engr. UCLA, 1988-90, sr. devel. engr., 1990—. Contbr. articles to Jour. Fusion Energy, Nuclear Sci. and Engring., Fusion Tech., Fusion Engring. and Design, Atom Kern Energie, proc. internat. confs. and symposia. Mem. Am. Nuclear Soc., Am. Phys. Soc., Soc. Indsl. and Applied Math. Office: UCLA 43-133 Eng IV 405 Hilgard Ave Los Angeles CA 90024-1301

KUMAR, RAJENDRA, electrical engineering educator; b. Amroha, India, Aug. 22, 1948; came to U.S., 1980; s. Satya Pal Agarwal and Kailash Vati Agarwal; m. Pushpa Agarwal, Feb. 16, 1971; children: Anshu, Shipra. BS in Math. and Sci., Meerut Coll., 1964; BEE, Indian Inst. Tech., Kanpur, 1969, MEE, 1977; PhD in Electrical Engring., U. New Castle, NSW, Australia, 1981. Mem. tech. staff Electronis and Radar Devel., Bangalore, India, 1969-72; rsch. engr. Indian Inst. Tech., Kanpur, 1972-77; asst. prof. Calif. State U., Fullerton, 1981-83, Brown U., Providence, 1980-81; prof. Calif. State U., Long Beach, 1983—; cons. Jet Propulsion Lab., Pasadena, Calif., 1984-91. Contbr. numerous articles to profl. jours.; patentee; efficient detection and signal parameter estimation with applications to high dynamic GPS receivers; multistage estimation of received carrier signal parameters under very high dynamic conditions of the receiver; fast frequency acquisition via adaptive least squares algorithms. Recipient Best Paper award Internat. Telemetering Conf., Las Vegas, 1986, 10 New Technology awards NASA, Washington, 1987-91. Mem. IEEE (sr.), NEA, AAUP, Calif. Faculty Assn., Auto Club So. Calif. (Cerritos), Sigma Xi, Eta Kappa Nu, Tau Beta Pi (eminent mem.). Home: 13910 Rose St Cerritos CA 90703-9043 Office: Calif State U 1250 N Bellflower Blvd Long Beach CA 90840-0006

KUMMER, GLENN F., manufactured housing executive; b. Park City, Utah, 1933. B.S., U. Utah, 1961. Sr. acct. Ernst & Ernst, 1961-65; trainee Fleetwood Enterprises Inc., Riverside, Calif., 1965-67, purchasing mgr., 1967-68, plant mgr., 1968-70, gen. mgr. recreational vehicle div., 1970-71, asst. v.p. ops., 1971-72, sr. v.p. ops., 1972-77, exec. v.p. ops., 1977-82, pres., 1982—, dir., 1983—. Office: Fleetwood Enterprises Inc PO Box 7638 3125 Myers St Riverside CA 92503-5527

KUNDU, SMRITI KANA, biomedical scientist; b. Asansol, India, Mar. 5, 1959; came to U.S., 1989; d. Mrityunjoy and Uma (Mondal) K.; m. Siba P. Raychaudhuri, June 7, 1987; children: Suravi Raychaudhuri, Sanchita Raychaudhuri. MD, All India Inst. Med. Scis., New Delhi, 1987. Postdoctoral fellow Stanford (Calif.) U. Med. Ctr., 1989-92, rsch. assoc., 1992-94, sr. rsch. assoc., 1995—; mem. AIDS clin. trials unit NIH, Bethesda, Md., 1989—; mem. sci. rev. bd. FDA, 1995. Contbr. articles to profl. jours. Mem. Am. Assn. Immunologists, New Acad. Scis., N.Y. Acad. Scis., Am. Soc. for Microbiologists. Home: 510 Ashton Ave Palo Alto CA 94306-3607 Office: Stanford U Med Ctr Divsn Infectious Diseases 300 Pasteur Dr Rm S-156 Palo Alto CA 94305-5107

KUNEY, GARY WALLACE, elementary school educator, real estate agent; b. Gridley, Calif., July 30, 1951; s. W. Loren and Tawana Jo (Yadon) K.; m. Nancy Ellen Borden, Aug. 22, 1974. BS with honors, Portland State U., 1980, MS in Tchg., 1983. Cert. tchr., Oreg., Wash. Adaptive specialist Beaverton (Oreg.) Sch. Dist., 1979-80; phys. edn. specialist Gresham (Oreg.) Grade Dist., 1980-81, Damascus (Oreg.) Union Dist., 1981-82; self def. instr. Clackamas Cmty. Coll., Milwaukie, 1983; phys. edn. specialist North Clackamas Dist., Milwaukie, 1982-83, Damascus Union Dist., 1983-86; grad. instr. Portland State Continuing Edn., 1991; instr. Portland Parks Bur., 1988-93; phys. edn. specialist Portland Pub. Schs., 1986—; U.S. fitness del. Citizen's Amb. Program, Hungary and Russia, 1991; wellness dir. Woodmere and Woodlawn Schs., Portland, 1986—; volleyball coach, 1980-86. Author: Fitness Success for Everyone, 1985 (Impact II award 1990), Body and Mind: The WRITE WAY, 1986 (Impact II award 1989); co-author: School Wide Daily Sports Math, 1989 (Impact II award 1991), (with others) Goals and Strategies for Teaching Physical Education by Dr. Hellison, 1985. With U.S. Army, 1969-76. Mem. AAHPERD (chair com. '95 conv. 1994-95), Masons (32 degree, line officer lodge 55, sr. warden 1991—, pub. sch. employee outstanding svc. award 1991), Scottish Rite (line officer Rose Croix, wise master). Republican. Home: 3208 SW Binford Ave Gresham OR 97080-9572

KUNG, FRANK F. C., medical products executive; b. 1948. BS, Nat. Tsing Hwa Univ., Taiwan, 1970; MBA, U. Calif., Berkeley, 1983, PhD in Molecular Biology, 1976. Post doctoral rsch. scientist Univ. Calif., Berkeley, 1976-77; rsch. dir. Clin. Bio-Rsch., Emeryville, Calif., 1977-79; scientist, asst. to pres. Cetus Immune Corp. (subs. of Cetus Corp.), Berkeley, Calif., 1979-81; dir. Cetus Immune Corp. (subs. of Cetus Corp.), Palo Alto, Calif., 1980-84; pres., CEO Genelabs Techs., Inc., Redwood City, Calif., 1984-95, chmn., 1984-96; chmn. Bio Asia Investments, Menlo Park, Calif, 1996—; pres. Bio Asia Investments, Palo Alto, Calif., 1996—. Office: Bio Asia Investment 575 High St Ste 201 Palo Alto CA 94301*

KUNKEE, RALPH EDWARD, viticulture and enology educator; b. San Fernando, Calif., July 30, 1927; s. Azor Frederick and Edith Electa (Engle) K. AB, U. Calif., Berkeley, 1950, PhD, 1955. Research biochemist E.I. Du Pont De Nemours, Wilmington, Del., 1955-60; prof. enology U. Calif., Davis, 1963-91, prof. emeritus, 1991; cons. UNFAO, Bangalore, India, 1986. Co-author: Technology of Winemaking, 1971, Principles and Practices of Winemaking, 1996. Fulbright fellow, Mainz, Fed. Republic Germany, 1970-71, France fellow, Montpellier, France, 1977-78. Fellow AAAS; mem. Am. Chem. Soc., Am. Soc. Microbiology, Am. Soc. Enology and Viticulture (sec./treas. 1983-85), Soc. Wine Educators. Home: 820 Radcliffe Dr Davis CA 95616-0941 Office: U Calif Dept Viniculture & Enology Davis CA 95616

KUNKEL, GEORGIE MYRTIA, writer, retired school counselor; b. Chehalis, Wash.; d. George Riley and Myrtia (McLaughlin) Bright; m. Norman C. Kunkel, Apr. 25, 1946; children: N. Joseph D.C., Stephen Gregory, Susan Ann, Kimberly Jane Waligorska. BA in Edn., Western Wash. U., 1944; MEd, U. Wash., 1968. Typist, clk. FHA, Seattle, 1940; tchr. pub. schs. Vader, Centralia, Wash., Seattle, 1941-67; pvt. cons., Seattle, 1970—; counselor Highline Pub. Schs., Seattle, 1967-82; sch. counselor rep. State of Art Conf., Balt., 1980. Editor Women and Girls in Edn., 1972-75. Author (under pseudonym Dorothy Bright): My Sex Secrets, 1989, How Do You Know You're Dying, 1991, Grandma's Holiday Greetings, 1992; contbr. articles to profl. jours. Organizer Women and Girls in Edn., Wash. state, 1971; pres. Wash. State NOW, 1973; mem. West Seattle Community Council, 1980. Grantee Women Adminstrs. Wash. State, 1971, Edn. Service Dist., Seattle, 1980. Mem. NEA (sec. pub. relations), Am. Assn. Counseling and Devel. (pres. state br. 1982-83), Am. Sch. Counseling Assn. (pres. state divsn. 1980-81), Seattle Counselors Assn. (organizer, past pres. office exec., Counselor of Yr. 1990), Holmes Harbor Homeowners Assn. (organizer and pres.), West Seattle C. of C., Past Pres. Assembly, West Seattle Dem. Women's Club (pres.). Unitarian Universalist. Avocation: singing with "Raging Grannies", an activist group. Home and Office: 3409 SW Trenton St Seattle WA 98126-3743

KUNKEL, SCOTT WILLIAM, strategic management and entrepreneurship educator; b. St. Louis, May 26, 1945; s. Robert Scott and Mary (Muldowney) K.; n. Cindy Jones; children: Mary Charlotte, Deborah Ann. BBA in Accountancy, Memphis State U., 1974, MS in Finance, 1979; PhD in Bus. Adminstrn., U. Ga., 1991. Asst. v.p., controller First Fed. Savs. & Loan, Memphis, 1976-79; v.p. Maury County Fed. Savs. & Loan, Columbia, Tenn., 1979-81, Great Southern Fed. Savs. & Loan, Gainesville, Ga., 1981-82; assoc. prof. Brenau U., Gainesville, 1982-88; asst. prof. U. Nev., Reno, 1988-92; assoc. prof., dir. Family Bus. Inst. U. San Diego, 1992—. Mem. U.S. Assn. Small Bus. and Entrepreneurship, Acad. Mgmt., Internat. Family Bus. Program Assn., Family Firm Inst., Acad. Entrepreneurship, Internat. Coun. Sm. Bus. Republican. Roman Catholic. Office: U San Diego Sch Bus San Diego CA 92110-2492

KUNZ, CHARLES ALAN, computer consultant; b. St. Louis, May 16, 1945; s. Glennon Charles and Lillian Margaret (Nies) K.; m. Teresa Anne Klutenkamper, Oct. 8, 1966; children: Leanne Teresa, Karl Thomas, Alicia Marie, Andrew Conrad. Diploma in Nursing, St. Louis City Hosp., 1966; BS, Regis Coll., 1985; MA in Computer Resource Mgmt., Webster U., 1989; Cert. in Anesthesia, Wilford Hall USAF Med. Ctr., San Antonio, 1980. RN. Commd. 2d lt. USAF, 1966, advanced through ranks to lt. col., 1966; operating room nurse Bethesda Gen. Hosp., St. Louis, 1986; gen. duty nurse USAF, Amarillo, Tex., 1967-68; flight nurse USAF DaNang AB, Vietnam, 1968-69; oper. room nurse USAF Hosp., Wiesbaden, Fed. Republic Germany, 1970-73; oper. room supr. USAF Altus AFB, Okla., 1974-77; staff nurse anesthetist USAF Hosp., Lakenheath, Eng., 1980-83; chief nurse anesthetist USAF Acad., Colorado Springs, 1983-88; nursing systems coord. Keesler AFB, Biloxi, Miss., 1988-91; chief clin. systems Keesler AFB, Biloxi, 1991-92; program mgr. Loral Tng. & Tech. Svcs., Colorado Springs, Colo., 1992-94, Las Vegas, Nev., 1994-96; sr. cons., clin. systems analyst J.R. O'Pry Cons., Virgina Beach, Va., 1996—; cons. in nurse anesthesia to USAF Surgeon Gen., 1982-83, cons. med. systems, 1989-92. Asst. scoutmaster Boy Scouts Am., Ocean Springs, Miss., 1988-92; mem. CAP, 1990-92. Recipient Agatha Hodgins Meml. award to Outstanding Grad., Am. Assn. Nurse Anesthetists, 1980, Wall Street Jour. Student Achievement award, 1985. Mem. Nat. Model R.R. Assn. (life), Keesler Amateur Radio Club (pres. 1990-92), Pikes Peak Computer Applications Soc. (pres. 1988), Ret. Officers' Assn. (life), Am. Radio Relay League (life). Home: 7573 Lorinda Ave Las Vegas NV 89128-0213 Office: JR O'Pry Cons 7573 Lorinda Ave Las Vegas NV 89128-0213

KUNZ, PHILLIP RAY, sociologist, educator; b. Bern, Idaho, July 19, 1936; s. Parley P. and Hilda Irene (Stoor) K.; m. Joyce Sheffield, Mar. 18, 1960; children: Jay, Jenifer, Jody, Johnathan, Jana. B.S., Brigham Young U., 1961, M.S. cum laude, 1962; Ph.D. (fellow), U. Mich., 1967. Instr. Eastern Mich. U., Ypsilanti, 1964, U. Mich., Ann Arbor, 1965-67; asst. prof. sociology U. Wyo., Laramie, 1967-68; prof. sociology Brigham Young U., Provo, Utah, 1968—; acting dept. chmn. Brigham Young U., 1973; dir. Inst. Geneal. Studies, 1972-74; cons. various edn1. and research instns., 1968—; missionary Ch. Jesus Christ LDS, Ga. and S.C., 1956-58, mem. high coun., 1969-70, bishop; mission pres. La. Baton Rouge Mission, 1990-93. Author: (book) 10 Critical Keys for Highly Effective Families and other books; contbr. articles on social orgn., family rels. and deviant behavior to profl. jours. Housing commr. City of Provo, 1984—. Served with AUS, 1954-56. Recipient Karl G. Maeser research award, 1977. Mem. Am. Sociol. Assn., Rocky Mountain Social Sci. Assn., Am. Council Family Relations, Rural Sociol. Soc., Am. Soc. Criminology, Soc. Sci. Study of Religion, Religious Research Assn., Sigma Xi, Phi Kappa Phi, Alpha Kappa Delta. Democrat. Home: 3040 Navajo Ln Provo UT 84604-4820 Office: Brigham Young Univ Dept Sociology Provo UT 84602

KUO, FRANKLIN F., computer scientist, electrical engineer; b. Apr. 22, 1934; came to U.S., 1950, naturalized, 1961; s. Steven C. and Grace C. (Huang) K.; m. Dora Lee, Aug. 30, 1958; children: Jennifer, Douglas. BS, U. Ill., 1955, MS, 1956, PhD, 1958. Asst. prof. dept. elec. engring. Poly. Inst. Bklyn., 1958-60; mem. tech. staff Bell Telephone Labs., Murray Hill, N.J., 1960-66; prof. elec. engring. U. Hawaii, Honolulu, 1966-82; exec. dir. SRI Internat., Menlo Park, Calif., 1982-94; v.p. Gen. Wireless Comm. Corp., 1994—; dir. info. systems Office Sec. of Def., 1976-77; liason scientist U.S. Office Naval Research, London, 1971-72; cons. prof. elec. engring. Stanford U., Calif., 1982—; vis. prof. U. Mannheim, Germany, 1995-96; mem. exec. panel Chief of Naval Ops., 1980-85. Author: Network Analysis and Synthesis, 1962, (2d edit.), 1966, Linear Circuits and Computations, 1973; co-author: System Analysis by Digital Computer, 1966, Computer Oriented Circuit Design, 1969, Computer Communications Networks, 1973, Protocols and Techniques in Data Communication Networks, 1981; cons. editor, Prentice-Hall Inc., 1967—; mem. editorial bd. Future Generations Computer Systems; contbr. articles to profl. jours.; developer Alohanet packet broadcast radio network. Mem. Pres. coun. U. Ill.; adv. bd. Beckman Inst. Recipient Alexander von Humboldt Found. Rsch. award, 1994. Fellow IEEE; mem. The Internet Soc., Tau Beta Pi, Eta Kappa Nu. Home: 824 La Mesa Dr Portola Valley CA 94028-7421

KUO, PING-CHIA, historian, educator; b. Yangshe, Kiangsu, China, Nov. 27, 1908; s. Chu-sen and Hsiao-kuan (Hsu) K.; m. Anita H. Bradley, Aug. 8, 1946. A.M., Harvard U., 1930, Ph.D., 1933. Prof. modern history and Far Eastern internat. relations Nat. Wuhan U., Wuchang, China, 1933-38; editor China Forum, Hankow and Chungking, 1938-40; counsellor Nat. Mil. Council, Chungking, China, 1940-46, Ministry Fgn. Affairs, 1943-46; participated in Cairo Conf. as spl. polit. asst. to Generalissimo Chiang Kai-shek, 1943; during war yrs. in Chungking, also served Chinese Govt. concurrently in following capacities: mem. fgn. affairs com. Nat. Supreme Def. Council, 1939-46; chief, editorial and pubs. dept. Ministry Information, 1940-42, mem. central planning bd., 1941-45; tech. expert to Chinese delegation San Francisco Conf., 1945; chief trusteeship sect. secretariat UN, London; (exec. com. prep. commn. and gen. assembly), 1945-46; top-ranking dir. Dept. Security Council Affairs, UN, 1946-48; vis. prof. Chinese history San Francisco State Coll., summers 1954, 58; assoc. prof. history So. Ill. U., 1959-63, prof. history, 1963-72, chmn. dept. history, 1967-71, prof. emeritus, 1972—; sr. fellow Nat. Endowment for Humanities, 1973-74; Pres. Midwest Conf. Asian Studies, 1964. Author: A Critical Study of the First Anglo-Chinese War, with Documents, 1935, Modern Far Eastern Diplomatic History (in Chinese), 1937, China: New Age and New Outlook, 1960, China, in the Modern World Series, 1970; Contbr. to Am. hist. pubs. and various mags. in China and Ency. Brit. Decorated Kwang Hua medal A-1 grade Nat. Mil. Council, Chungking, 1941; Auspicious Star medal Nat. Govt., Chungking, 1944; Victory medal, 1945. Mem. Am. Hist. Assn., Assn. Asian Studies. Club: Commonwealth (San Francisco). Home: 8661 Don Carol Dr El Cerrito CA 94530-2752

KUPEL, DOUGLAS EDWARD, historian; b. Long Beach, Calif., July 18, 1956; s. Frederick John and Nancy Kathryn (Eubank) K.; m. Maria Carmen Olivas, Nov. 27, 1991; 1 child, John Carlos. BA, U. Oreg., 1979; MA, U. Ariz., 1986; PhD, Ariz. State U., 1995. Archaeologist Regional Environ. Cons., San Diego, 1979-81, Calif. Dept. Transp., San Diego, 1981-84; historian Ariz. State Parks, Phoenix, 1986-88, City of Phoenix, 1988—; cons. historian Ryden Architects, Phoenix, 1990—; history instr. Maricopa County C.C. Dist., Phoenix, 1996—. Author: Indian and American Military Conflict, 1996. Pres. bd. dirs. Ariz. Preservation Found., Phoenix, 1988-94; fundraising capt. Phoenix Boys' Choir, 1994—. Recipient Recognition award Ariz. Hist. Sites Rev. Commn., 1995. Mem. Ariz. Hist. Soc. (James E. Officer award 1994), Soc. Profl. Archaeologists (cert.), Nat. Coun. for Public History, Soc. Hist. Archaeology, Nat. Trust for Hist. Preservation. Democrat. Office: City of Phoenix Law Dept 200 W Washington Phoenix AZ 85803

KUPFERMAN, DAVID JAN, accountant, internet and multimedia consultant; b. Morristown, N.J., Jan. 26, 1957; s. Kurt and Shirley (Sakrin) K.; m. Flora Helen Burger, Dec. 23, 1984; children: Elana, Shoshana. BS in Internat. Trade & Transport, San Francisco State U., 1978. CPA, Calif. Asst. to chmn. Latin Am./India Shipping Conf., San Francisco, 1978-84; logistical analyst GTE Govt. Systems, Mountain View, Calif., 1984-85; contr. ADVAN, San Francisco, 1985; CPA, auditor KPMG Peat Marwick, San Francisco, 1987-90; asst. contr. CMI, San Francisco, 1990-91; contr. Clubsource, Club One, and Sports Club at City Ctr., San Francisco, 1991-95; prin. David J. Kupferman, CPA, San Francisco, 1995—; chmn., founder Nat. Club Contr.'s Forum, San Francisco, 1993; bd. dirs., fgn. analyst Am. Assn. Ethiopian Jews, 1984. Bd. mem.-at-large United Jewish Community Ctr. No. Calif., 1993, chmn. audit com., 1994; neighborhood activist Group to Save Noe Valley Libr., San Francisco, 1991. Mem. City Club San Francisco, Multimedia Devel. Group, Nat. Assn. Health Clubs. Jewish. Home: 149 Warren Dr San Francisco CA 94131-1030

KUPPERMAN, HENRY JOHN, lawyer; b. N.Y.C., May 18, 1957; s. Ben J. and Roma M. (Ash) K.; m. Rebecca Beauchamp, 1990; 1 child, Jonathan Andrew. BA, Johns Hopkins U., 1978; JD, St. John's U., 1982. Bar: N.Y. 1983, U.S. Ct. Appeals (3d cir.) 1983, Pa. 1984, Calif. 1987, U.S. Ct. Appeals (9th cir.) 1987, U.S. Supreme Ct. 1988; cert. fraud examiner. Student law clk. to judge U.S. Dist. Ct., N.Y.C., 1981-82; law clk. to chief judge U.S. Dist. Ct., Wilmington, Del., 1982-83; assoc. Drinker, Biddle & Reath, Phila., 1984-86; assoc. Brobeck, Phleger & Harrison, L.A., 1986-89, ptnr., 1990-93; gen. counsel, dir. West Coast ops. The Investigative Group, Inc., L.A., 1994—. Mem. ABA (co-chmn. subcom. on fed. local procedure 1986-88), Calif. Bar Assn. L.A. Bar Assn., Beverly Hills Bar Assn. Jewish. Office: The Investigative Group Inc 725 S Figueroa St Ste 2400 Los Angeles CA 90017-5425

KURAISHI, AKARI LUKE, real estate company executive; b. Nagano, Japan, July 29, 1959; came to U.S. 1984; s. Atsushi and Kuniko (Tomita) K.; m. Hiromi Lydia Hatae, Oct. 10, 1987; children: Katrina Ayumi, Kristin Kasumi. BA, Nat. Def. Acad., Yokosuka, Japan, 1982; MBA, U. Dallas, 1986. Registered internat. mem. Internat. Real Estate Inst., real estate broker, Calif. Mgr. Gateway Travel & Tours, Dallas, 1985-87; with portfolio investments dept. Mitsui Real Estate Sales USA Co., Ltd., L.A., 1987-90; mgr., 1990-91; asst. v.p. Mitsui Real Estate Sales USA Co., Ltd., L.A., 1991-95, v.p., broker/officer, 1995—; dir. ALKALY Inc., Orange, Calif., 1991—; v.p. Santa Ana (Calif.) Corp., 1992—, Santa Ana Mgmt. Corp., 1992—; sec. MI Ptnrs. LA Co., Ltd., 1993—. Mem. NRA, Colt Collectors Assn., Orange County Japanese Am. Assn. (bd. dirs. 1994—, treas. 1996—), Japanese-Am. Network (charter mem., bd. dirs. 1997—), U. Dallas Alumni Assn., Greater So. Calif. CCIM (L.A. chpt.), Lake Elsinore Sportman Assn. Home: 2348 E Trenton Ave Orange CA 92867-4454 Office: Mitsui Real Estate Sales USA Co Ltd 601 S Figueroa St Fl 4600 Los Angeles CA 90017-5751

KURIMSKY, CAROL GRAY, marketing executive; b. Wilmington, Del., June 9, 1959; d. Linsley Shepard and Lois Gray; m. Troy Wayne Kurimsky, May 23, 1992. BS in Bus., Ind. U., 1981; M.Mgmt., Northwestern U., 1986. Sales rep. Alcoa, Chgo., 1981-84; brand asst. Procter & Gamble, Cin., 1986-87, asst. brand mgr., 1987-89, brand mgr., 1989-90; mktg. mgr. Pizza Hut Internat., Wichita, Kans., 1990-91, dir. mktg., 1991-93; dir. mktg. Quaker Oats, Pleasanton, Calif., 1993-96, Hunt-Wesson, Fullerton, Calif., 1996-97; v.p. mktg. Hunt-Wesson, Fullerton, 1997—, dir. mktg., 1996—. Mem. Union Bd. Alumni Assn. (Whittenberger Soc.) (bd. dirs. 1989—), Northwestern Alumni Club (pres. 1989-90), Mortar Bd., Beta Gamma Sigma.

KURLINSKI, JOHN PARKER, physician; b. Buchanon, W.Va., Jan. 17, 1948; s. John Peter and Jean (Holloway) K.; m. Claire Sawyer, June 12, 1971; children: Joshua John, Ryan Edward, Seth Parker. AB cum laude, Williams Coll., 1970; MD, Johns Hopkins Sch. Medicine, 1974. Intern, then resident Johns Hopkins Hosp., Baltimore, 1974-77; fellowship neonatal/perinatal medicine U. Calif., San Diego, 1977-79; chief resident pediatrician Johns Hopkins Hosp., 1979-80; clin. assoc. prof. pediatrics U. Nev. Sch. Medicine, Reno, 1994—; vice chief of staff Sunrise Children's Hosp., Las Vegas, 1989-90, chief of staff, 1990-95; pediatrician, co-dir. neonatology S.W. Regional Neonatal Ctr. at Sunrise Hosp. and Med. Ctr., Las Vegas, 1980-93; vice chief pediatrics Sunrise Hosp., Las Vegas, 1983-90; dir. NICU Sunrise Children's Hosp., 1994—; bd. dirs. S.W. Regional Neonatal Ctr. Edn. Found.; chmn. bd. dirs. Sunrise Children's Hosp. Found.; mem. Med.-Legal Screening Panel, Nev., 1986—; many hosp. coms., 1980—. Bd. dirs. So Nev. chpt. March of Dimes, Las. Vegas, 1984—. Mem. AMA, Am. Acad. Pediatrics (v.p. Nev. chpt. 1987-90, pres. 1990-93, coun. mem. dist. VIII sect. on perinatal pediatrics), Clark County Med. Soc., Las Vegas Pediatric Soc. (founding), Phi Beta Kappa. Home: 3322 Beam Dr Las Vegas NV 89139-5902 Office: Sunrise Childrens Hosp 3186 S Maryland Pky Las Vegas NV 89109-2317

KURSEWICZ, LEE Z., marketing consultant; b. Chgo., Oct. 26, 1916; s. Antoni and Henryka (Sulkowska) K.; ed. Chgo. and Bata ind. schs.; m. Ruth Elizabeth Venzke, Jan. 31, 1940; 1 son, Dennis. With Bata Shoe Co., Inc., 1936-78, plant mgr., Salem, Ind., 1963-65, v.p., mng. dir., Batawa, Ont., Can., 1965-71; v.p., dir. Bata Industries, Batawa, 1965-71, plant mgr., Salem, 1971-76; pres. Bata Shoe Co., Inc., Belcamp, Md., 1976-77, sr. v.p., dir., 1977-79; gen. mgr. Harford Insulated Panel Systems div. Hazleton Industries, 1981-82. City mgr. City of Batawa, 1965-71; vice chmn. Trenton (Ont.) Meml. Hosp., 1970-71; pres. Priestford Hills Community Assn., 1979-80; chmn. adv. bd. Phoenix Festival Theatre, Hartford County Community Coll., 81; vice chmn. Harford County chpt. ARC, 1980-81, chmn., 1982-83; chmn. Harford County Econ. Devel. Adv. Bd., 1983 85; mem. Susquehanna Region Pvt. Industry Council, 1983-85. Mem. Am. Mgmt. Assn. Clubs: Rotary, Bush River Yacht (commodore 1956), Bush River Power Squadron (comdr. 1957), Western Hills Country of Salem (pres. 1975), Trenton Country (pres. 1968-69), Md. Country. Home and Office: 31382 Abanita Way Laguna Niguel CA 92677-2725

KURTZ, KARL THEODORE, government executive; b. Oberlin, Ohio, Nov. 28, 1945; s. John W. and Edith M. (Davis) K.; m. Cecile C. Kurtz, June 7, 1967 (div. Sept. 1982); children: Eric J., Sarah C.; m. Janet L. Beardsley, Aug. 29, 1987; children: Emily L., Andrew S. AB, Oberlin Coll., 1967; PhD, Washington U., St. Louis, 1972. Congl. fellow Am. Polit. Sci. Assn., Washington, 1970-71; vis. prof. U. Ga., Athens, 1971-72; asst. dir. Nat. Legis. Conf., Lexington, Ky., 1972-74; dir. Nat. Conf. State Legislatures, Denver, 1975—. Contbr. articles to profl. jours. Regional selection panel Truman Scholarship Found., Denver, 1977—; mem., chair Bd. Adjustment, Boulder County, Colo., 1993-95; mem. Planning Commn., Boulder County, 1996—. Home and Office: Nat Conf State Legislatures 1560 Broadway # 700 Denver CO 80202

KURTZ, MAXINE, personnel consultant, lawyer; b. Mpls., Oct. 17, 1921; d. Jack Isadore and Beatrice (Cohen) K. BA, U. Minn., 1942; MS in Govt. Mgmt., U. Denver, 1945, JD, 1962; postdoctoral student, U. Calif., San Diego, 1978. Bar: Colo. 1962; U.S. Dist. Ct., Colo., 1992. Analyst Tri-County Regional Planning, Denver, 1945-47; chief rsch. and spl. projects Planning Office, City and County of Denver, 1947-66, dir. tech. and evaluation Model Cities Program, 1966-71; pers. rsch. officer Denver Career Service Auth., 1972-86, dir. pers. svcs., 1986-88, sr. pers. specialist, 1988-90; pub. sector pers. cons., 1990-95, atty., 1990—, pers. and human resources cons., 1996—; expert witness nat. com. on urban problems U.S. Ho. of Reps., U.S. Senate. Author: Law of Planning and Land Use Regulations in Colorado, 1966; co-author: Care and Feeding of Witnesses, Expert and Otherwise, 1974; bd. editors: Pub. Adminstrn. Rev., Washington, 1980-83, 88-92; editorial adv. bd. Internat. Pers. Mgmt. Assn.; prin. investigator: Employment: An American Enigma, 1979. Active Women's Forum of Colo.; Denver Dem. Com.; chair Colo. adv. com. to U.S. Civil Rights Commn., 1985-89, mem. 1989—. Sloan fellow, U. Denver, 1944-45; recipient Outstanding Achievement award U. Minn., 1971, Alumni of Notable Achievement award, 1994. Mem. ABA, Am. Inst. Planners (sec. treas. 1968-70, bd. govs. 1972-75), Am. Soc. Pub. Adminstrn. (nat. council 1978-81, Donald Stone award), Colo. Bar Assn., Denver Bar Assn., Order St. Ives., Pi Alpha Alpha. Jewish. Home and Office: 2361 Monaco Pky Denver CO 80207-3453

KURTZIG, SANDRA L., software company executive; b. Chgo., Oct. 21, 1946; d. Barney and Marian (Boruck) Brody; children: Andrew Paul, Kenneth Alan; BS in Math., UCLA, 1968; MS in aeronaut. engring., Stanford U., 1968. Math analyst TRW Systems, 1967-68; mktg. rep., Gen. Electric Co., 1969-72; chmn. bd., CEO, pres. ASK Computer Systems, Mountain View, Calif., 1972-85, chmn. bd., 1986-89; founder The ASK Group, 1972—, chmn., pres., CEO, 1989-93; chmn. emeritus, 1993—, chmn. E-Benefits, 1996—. bd. dirs. Hoover Instn., Harvard Bus. Sch., Stanford Sch. of Engring., UCLA Anderson Grad. Sch. Mgmt. Author: CEO: Building a $400 Million Company from the Ground Up, 1991, 94. Cited one of 50 most influential bus. people in Am., Bus. Week, 1985. Office: 2420 Sand Hill Rd Ste 201 Menlo Park CA 94025-6948

KURTZMAN, RALPH HAROLD, retired biochemist, researcher, consultant; b. Mpls., Feb. 21, 1933; s. Ralph Harold, Sr. and Susie Marie (Elwell) K.; m. Nancy Virginia Leussler, Aug. 27, 1955; children: Steven Paul, Sue. BS, U. Minn., 1955; MS, U. Wis., 1958, PhD, 1959. Asst. prof. U. R.I., Kingston, 1959-62, U. Minn., Morris, 1962-65; biochemist U.S. Dept. Agriculture, Albany, Calif., 1965-97; instr. U. Calif., Berkeley, 1981-82; cons. Bliss Valley Farms, Twin Falls, Idaho, 1983-84; pres. Santa Clara Valley Tex. Instrument PC Users' Group, 1991-92, editor, 1993—; cons. in field. Editor Internat. Jour. Mushroom Scis., 1995—; inventor mushroom substrate (compost) preparation, 1982, decaffeination of beverages, 1973; contbr. articles to profl. jours. Chmn. Berkeley YMCA Camp Program Com., 1971-72; official Amateur Athletic Union (swimming), San Francisco, 1973-80; treas. Calif. Native Plant Soc., 1970. Mem. Am. Mushroom Inst., Mycological Soc. Am., Mycological Soc. Japan, Sigma Xi. Home: 445 Vassar Ave Berkeley CA 94708-1215

KUS, JAMES STEDRY, geography educator, archaeologist; b. Cleve., Jan. 11, 1944; s. Alfred Otto and Dorothea Elizabeth (Sieferd) K.; m. Barbara Ann Roecker, Aug. 21, 1969 (div. Feb. 1985); children: James Alan, Elizabeth Ann; m. Claudia Ann Mader, July 18, 1989. BA, Case Western Res. U., 1965; MA, Mich. State U., 1965; PhD, UCLA, 1972. Prof. geography Calif. State U., Fresno, 1970—; prin. James S. Kus & Assocs., Clovis, Calif., 1986—. Contbr. articles to profl. jours. Mem. Fresno County Archaeol. Soc. (pres. 1990-92, editor 1993-97, v.p. 1994-97). Home: 10528 E Sierra Clovis CA 93611 Office: Calif State U Fresno CA 93740

KUSAKA, MARYANNE W., mayor. Mayor City of Lihue, Hawaii. Office: City of Lihue 5396 Rice St Ste 101 Lihue HI 96766

KUSSMAN, ELEANOR (ELLIE KUSSMAN), retired educational superintendent; b. Bklyn., Mar. 17, 1934; d. Mortimer Joseph and Eleanor Mary (O'Brien) Gleeson; m. Karl Kussman, June 30, 1956 (dec. Oct. 1988); children: Katherine Ann, Kristine Sue. BA, Wheaton Coll., Norton, Mass., 1955; MS, LaVerne Coll., Claremont, Calif., 1974. Cert. tchr. K-C.C., cert. in pupil pers. and adminstrn., Calif. Tchr. sci. and math. Norwood (Mass.) Jr. High Sch., 1955-56; tchr. phys. edn. Brawley (Calif.) Union High Sch., 1956-58; tchr. phys. edn. Ctrl. Union High Sch., El Centro, Calif., 1958-74, tchr. health careers, 1974-80, state and fed. project dir., 1980-85; instr. horse husbandry and equitation Imperial Valley Coll., Imperial, Calif., 1974-76; supr. Imperial Valley (Calif.) Regional Occupational Program, 1985-95; cons. E.E. Kussman Cons., El Centro, 1992—, Calif. Joint Gender Equity Com., Sacramento, 1991—, State of Calif. Gender Equity, Sacramento, 1986—; instr. program in counseling and guidance U.Calif., Redlands, 1989. Mem. fin. com. United Way, El Centro, 1987-93; sec.-treas. Pvt. Industry Coun., El Centro, 1985-95; past sec.-treas. Calif. Regional Occupational Ctrs./Programs, 1986-88. Named Educator of Yr. Imperial Valley Chpt. Phi Delta Kappa, 1995. Mem. AAUW, ASCD, Assn. Calif. Sch. Adminstrs. (past local and regional officer), Rotary Internat. (bd. dirs. 1994—). Home and Office: PO Box 83 El Centro CA 92244-0083

KUSTER, ROBERT KENNETH, scientist; b. Los Angeles, July 11, 1932; s. Arthur Rollo Kuster and Ermine Rosebud (Prittchett) Woodward. AS, Gavilan Coll., 1974, AA in Humanities, 1981; student, San Jose State U., 1955, 1974-76, UCLA, 1977. Installer Western Electric Co., Inc., Corpus Christi, Tex., 1951-52, 1955, San Jose, Calif., 1957-58, 1960-83; ptnr., scientist, cons. WE-Woodward's Enterprises, Morgan Hill, Calif., 1975—; technician AT&T Tech., Inc., San Jose, 1983-85; scientist pvt. practice, Gilroy, 1978—. Served to sgt. U.S. Army Corps Engrs., 1952-54. Mem. AAAS, Astron. Soc. Pacific, Calif. Acad. Scis., N.Y. Acad. Scis., Am. Legion, VFW. Baptist. Lodge: Elks. Home: 17506 Hoot Owl Way Morgan Hill CA 95037-6524 Office: Woodward's Enterprises 179 Bender Cir Morgan Hill CA 95037-3533

KUTER, KAY E., writer, actor; b. L.A., Apr. 25, 1925; s. Leo E. and Evelyn Belle (Edler) K. Student, Pomona Coll.; BFA in Drama, Carnegie Inst. Tech., 1949, BFA, 1949. Radio actor NBC, 1944; actor, 1944—. Actor in 198 musicals, off-Broadway, stock, repertory, touring, and Shakespearean stage prodns.; 45 feature films; more than 400 TV shows, including 7 yrs. as a series regular (Newt Kiley) in Green Acres and Petticoat Junction; voice-over actor for cartoon series Aladdin, The Little Mermaid, Prince Valiant, Biker Mice From Mars, Fantastic Four; in cartoon spls. Olympic Mascot Izzy, Annabelle's Wish; in CD-ROMS The Beast Within, Ultima 9, Grim Fandango: The Curse of Monkey Island; author: Carmen Incarnate, 1946, Ships That Never Sailed, 1994, Hollywood Houdini, Picture Perfect World, 1995; voiceover spokesman Hershey's Kisses, 1989—; editor: The Jester, 1956-60, The Jester 35th Anniversary, 1976; contbr. to Nat. Libr. Poetry anthologies, 1995, 96, 97; dir. more than 50 stage prodns. Bd. dirs. Family Svc. of L.A., 1950-70. Mem. SAG (bd. dirs. 1970-73), AEA, AFTRA, ACLU, NOW, NARAL, Internat. Platform Assn., Book Publicists of So. Calif., Nat. Soc. Hist. Preservation, Smithsonian, Carnegie Mellon U. Westcoast Drama Alumni Clan (founding mem., officer, bd. dirs. 1968-80), Ephebian Soc., Internat. Soc. Poets (disting. mem.), Albert C. May soc., Acad. Am. Poets, Andrew Carnegie Soc., Pacific Pioneer Broadcasters, Carnegie Mellon U. Alumni Assn. (regional v.p. 1976-79, Svc. award 1979), Masquers Club (bd. dirs. 1953-75, rec. sec. 1956-70, corr. sec. 1957-69. v.p. 1971-75), Actors' Fund of Am. (life mem.), others. Democrat. Home: 6207 Satsuma Ave North Hollywood CA 91606-3819

KUTINAC, JOHN GEORGE, JR., psychologist; b. Chgo., Dec. 26, 1947; s. John G. Sr. and Ann (Michalec) K.; m. Linda S. Derrico, Aug. 3, 1968; children: John Eric, Jason Edward, Erin Elizabeth. BA, Avila Coll., 1978; MA, N.Mex. State U., 1980. Program dir. Open Door Ctr., Las Cruces, N.Mex., 1978-81; counselor Las Cruces Pub. Sch., 1981-90; psychologist pvt. practice, Las Cruces, 1990—. Bd. dirs., pres. Shalom Family Svcs., Las Cruces, 1990—; v.p. Trinity Luth. Ch. Coun., Las Cruces, 1987-90. With U.S. Army, 1968-70, Vietnam. Mem. APA, ACA, Am. Mental Health Counseling Assn. Office: 715 E Idaho Ave Ste 1D Las Cruces NM 88001-3793

KUTTNER, DONNA HOLBERG, health education specialist; b. Houston, Sept. 14, 1945; d. L.R. and Melba Holberg; m. Charles H. Kuttner, Jan. 22, 1971; 1 child, Arwen Eve. MusB, U. Houston, 1968; EdM, Oreg. State U., 1988, MS, 1992, PhD, 1995. Cert. health edn. specialist. Tchr. elem. sch. Galveston (Tex.) Ind. Sch. Dist., 1968-70, Hitchcock (Tex.) Ind. Sch. Dist., 1970-73; tchr. music in pvt. practice San Francisco, 1973-76, Corvallis, Oreg., 1977-85; tchr. dept. edn. Oreg. State U., Corvallis, 1986-87, tchr. dept. pub. health, 1993, 95; cons. editor mental health divsn. State of Oreg., Salem, 1988-89; instrnl. designer Oreg. State Hosp., 1987-88; cons. health edn. Corvallis, 1996—; sec.-treas. Oreg. Alliance for Health Edn., 1996—. Editor Oreg. jour. of Oreg. Alliance for Health PE recreation and dance, 1992—; contbr. articles to profl. jours., (Corvallis Macintosh User Group newsletter) Mouse Droppings, 1990—. Bd. dirs. Corvallis Macintosh User Group, Corvallis, 1995-97. Mem. Am. Alliance for Health Physical Edn., Recreation and Dance, Am. Assn. Health Edn., Internat. Soc. for HIV/AIDS Edn. & Prevention, Music Tchr. Nat. Assn.

KUTVIRT, DUDA CHYTILOVA (RUZENA), scientific translator; b. Pilsen, Czechoslovakia, Sept. 17, 1919; came to U.S., 1949; d. Frantisek and Ruzena (Vitousek) Chytil; m. Otakar Kutvirt, July 10, 1942 (dec.); children: Thomas (dec.), Daniel. BA, Smith Coll., 1940; MA, Mills Coll., 1942. Rsch. asst. U. Rochester Med. Sch., 1942-44; scientific translator Eastman Kodak Rsch. Labs., Rochester, 1944-45, 61-78. Voter registrar LWV, Albuquerque, 1980—, Rochester, 1955-70; vol. U. N.Mex. Hosp. Svc. League, Albuquerque, 1979—; mem. Albuquerque com. for fgn. affairs. Home: 5 Pool St NW Albuquerque NM 87120-1809

KUWABARA, DENNIS MATSUICHI, optometrist; b. Honolulu, July 20, 1945; s. Robert Tokuichi and Toshiko (Nakashima) K.; m. Judith Naomi Tokumaru, June 28, 1970; children: Jennifer Tomiko, Susan Kazuko. BS, So. Calif. Coll. Optometry, 1968, OD cum laude, 1970. Pvt. practice optometry Waipahu, Honolulu, Hawaii, 1972—; pres. 1st Study Club for Optometrists, Honolulu, 1982-83; chmn. Bd. Examiners in Optometry,

Honolulu, 1982-90; state dir. Optometric Extension Found., Honolulu, 1980-88. Served to lt. Med. Service Corps, USN, 1970-72. Named Outstanding Young Person of Hawaii, Hawaii State Jaycees, 1979. Fellow Am. Acad. Optometry (diplomate cornea and contact lens sect. 1991); mem. Hawaii Optometric Assn. (pres. 1979-80, Man of Yr. award 1976, Optometrist of Yr. 1983), Am. Optometric Assn., Armed Forces Optometric Soc. Home: 94-447 Holaniku St Mililani HI 96789-1710 Office: 94-748 Hikimoe St Waipahu HI 96797-3350 also: 1441 Kapiolani Blvd #1520 Honolulu HI 96814-4404

KUWABARA, JAMES SHIGERU, research hydrologist; b. Honolulu, Apr. 26, 1953; s. Donald Shigeyuki and Setsue (Ogawa) K.; m. Rie Rita Kimura, June 6, 1982; children: Sara Mie, Annie Mako. BSCE, U. Hawaii, 1975; MS in Environ. Engring., Calif. Inst. Tech., 1976, PhD in Environ. Engring., 1980. Computer operator Computer Info. Svcs., Honolulu, 1971; engring. rschr. U. Hawaii, Honolulu, 1971-73; aquacultural rschr. Sea Grants Program, Honolulu, 1973-75; grad. rsch. fellow NSF, Pasadena, Calif., 1975-78; grad. rsch. asst. Calif. Inst. Tech., Pasadena, Calif., 1978-80; postdoctoral rsch. fellow Nat. Rsch. Coun., Menlo Park, Calif., 1980-82; rsch. hydrologist U.S. Geol. Survey, Menlo Park, Calif., 1982—; conf. chmn. West Coast Water Chem. Workshop, Stanford, 1986; final rev. panel Water Res. Rsch. Grants, Reston, Va., 1988-89; session organizer Estuarine Rsch. Conf., San Francisco, 1991; session moderator Am. Chem. Soc., Washington, 1992. Editor Estuaries, 1993; contbr. chpts. to books; contbr. numerous articles to Jour. of Phycology, Limnology and Oceanography, Science, and other profl. jours. Eagle scout rev. bd. Boy Scouts of Am., Honolulu, 1974-75. Hawaii State Acad. scholar U. Hawaii, 1972; recipient NSF Grad. fellowship Calif. Inst. Tech., 1975; Nat. Rsch. Coun. postdoctoral rsch. assoc. U.S. Geol. Survey, 1980. Mem. ASCE, Am. Inst. Chemists, Estuarine Rsch. Fedn., Phycological Soc. Am. Office: US Geol Survey 345 Middlefield Rd # MS/439 Menlo Park CA 94025-3561

KUWAYAMA, GEORGE, curator; b. N.Y.C., Feb. 25, 1925; s. Senzo and Fumiko Kuwayama; m. Lillian Yetsuko Yamashita, Dec. 5, 1961; children: Holly, Mark, Jeremy. B.A., Williams Coll., 1948; postgrad., NYU, 1948-54; M.A., U. Mich., 1956. Curator Oriental art L.A. County Mus. Art, L.A., 1959-70, sr. curator Far Ea. art, 1970—; lectr. U. So. Calif., UCLA; organizer spl. exhbns. Author: Far Eastern Lacquer, 1980, Shippo: The Art of Enameling in Japan, 1980, Chinese Ceramics in Colonial Mexico, 1997; author, editor: Japanese Ink Painting, 1983, The Quest for Eternity, 1987, Ancient Mortuary Traditions of China, 1991, New Perspective on the Art of Ceramics in China, 1992; author, co-editor: Imperial Taste, 1989; editor, author: The Great Bronze Age of China: A Symposium, 1983. Served with parachute inf. U.S. Army, 1944-46. Charles Freer scholar U. Mich., 1955-56; Inter-Univ. fellow Ford Found., 1957-58; rsch. travel grantee Nat. Endowment for Arts, 1974, 88. Mem. Assn. for Asian Studies, Am. Oriental Soc. (Louise Hackney fellow 1956), Coll. Art Assn., Japan Soc., Internat. House Japan, China Colloquium, Far Ea. Art Coun. Democrat. Methodist. Home: 1417 Comstock Ave Los Angeles CA 90024-5316 Office: LA County Mus Art 5905 Wilshire Blvd Los Angeles CA 90036-4523

KUZMA, GEORGE MARTIN, bishop; b. Windber, Pa., July 24, 1925; s. Ambrose and Anne (Marton) K. Student, Benedictine Coll., Lisle, Ill.; BA, Duquesne U., postgrad.; postgrad., U. Mich.; grad., SS Cyril and Methodius Byzantine Cath. Sem. Ordained priest Byzantine Cath. Ch., 1955. Asst. pastor SS Peter and Paul Ch., Braddock, Pa., 1955-57; pastor Holy Ghost Ch., Charleroi, Pa., 1957-65, St. Michael Ch., Flint, Mich., 1965-70, St. Eugene Ch., Bedford, Ohio, 1970-72, Annunciation Ch., Anaheim, Calif., 1970-86; rev. monsignor Byzantine Cath. Ch., 1984, titular bishop, 1986, consecrated bishop, 1987; aux. bishop Byzantine Cath. Diocese of Passaic, N.J., 1987-90; bishop Van Nuys, Calif., 1991—; judge matrimonial tribunal, mem. religious edn. commn., mem. commn. orthodox rels. Diocese of Pitts., 1955-69; judge matrimonial tribunal, vicar for religious Diocese of Parma, 1969-82; treas., bd. dirs., chmn. liturgical commn., mem. clergy & seminarian rev. bd., liaison to ea. Cath. dirs. religious edn., bd. dirs. diocesan credit union, chmn. diocesan heritage bd., chmn. diocesan ecumenical commn. Diocese of Van Nuys, 1982-86; vicar gen. Diocese of Passaic; episcopal vicar for Ea. Pa.; chmn. Diocesan Retirement Plan Bd.; pres. Father Walter Cizsek Prayer League; chaplain Byzantine Carmelite Monastery, Sugarloaf, Pa. Assoc. editor Byzantine Cath. World; editor The Apostle. With USN, 1943-46, PTO. Address: Byzantine Rite 8131 N 16th St Phoenix AZ 85020-3901*

KVAMME, MARK D., marketing professional. Programmer Apple Computer; founding mem., then internat. product mgr. in U.S. Apple France; founder, pres., CEO Internat. Solutions; dir. internat. mktg. Wyse Tech.; pres., CEO CKS Group, Cupertino, Calif. Office: 10443 Brandley Dr Cupertino CA 95014

KVENVOLDEN, KEITH ARTHUR, geochemist; b. Cheyenne, Wyo., July 16, 1930; s. Owen Arthur and Agnes B. Kvenvolden; m. Mary Ann Lawrence, Nov. 7, 1959; children: Joan Agnes, Jon William. Geophys. Engr., Colo. Sch. Mines, 1952; MS, Stanford U., 1958, PhD, 1961. Registered geologist, Calif. Jr. geologist Socony Mobil Oil Co., Caracas, Venezuela, 1952-54; sr. rsch. technologist Mobil Oil Corp., Dallas, 1961-65; rsch. sci. Ames Rsch. Ctr. NASA, Mountain View, Calif., 1965-75, br. chief Ames Rsch. Ctr., 1971-75, div. chief Ames Rsch. Ctr., 1974-75; geologist U.S. Geol. Survey, Menlo Park, Calif., 1975-92, sr. scientist, 1992—; cons. prof. geology Stanford (Calif.) U., 1967—; courtesy prof. oceanography Oreg. State U., Corvallis, 1988—. Editor: Geochemistry and the Origin of Life, 1974, Geochemistry of Organic Molecules, 1980; contbr. articles to profl. jours. With U.S. Army, 1952-54. Gilbert fellow U.S. Geol. Survey, 1989; recipient Meritorious Svc. award U.S. Dept. of Interior, Disting. Svc. award. Fellow AAAS, Geol. Soc. Am., Explorers Club, Am. Geophys. Union; mem. Am. Assn. Petroleum Geologists, Geochem. Soc. (chmn. Organic Geochemical div., Best Paper award 1971). Office: US Geol Survey M/S 999 M 345 Middlefield Rd Menlo Park CA 94025-3561

KWAAN, JACK HAU MING, retired physician; b. Hong Kong, Apr. 9, 1928; came to U.S., 1953; s. Y.K. and Rose W. Kwaan; m. Min K. Ho, Feb. 11, 1973; children: Mary, Peter, Rebecca, Nicholas. MD, U. Hong Kong, 1952. Diplomate Am. Bd. Radiology, Am. Bd. Surgery, Am. Bd. Thoracic Surgery. Resident in radiology Roswell Park Meml. Inst., 1955-56; chief resident Peter Bent Brigham Hosp., 1956-57; rsch. fellow in radiology Harvard Med. Sch., Boston, 1956-57; sr. cancer rsch. radiol. therapist Roswell Park Meml. Inst., Buffalo, 1958-59; asst. prof. radiology U. Ky., Lexington, 1963-65; resident in surgery U. Calif., Irvine, 1965-68; rsch. fellow oncologic surgery M.D. Anderson Hosp., Houston, 1968-69; resident in thoracic U. Calif., Irvine, 1969-71, chief resident thoracic surgery, 1970, asst. prof. surgery, 1972-73; chief vascular surgery sect., co-dir. vascular surgery tng. program U. Calif. Irvine/Long Beach VA Med. Ctr., 1974-87; prof. surgery U. Calif., Irvine, 1983-87; sr. resident in thoracic surgery U. So. Calif./L.A. County Med. Ctr., 1971; staff thoracic cardiovasc. surgeon Long Beach VA Hosp., 1972-73; asst. chief surgery Valley Med. Ctr., Fresno, Calif., 1973-74; prof. surgery U. Okla., Tulsa, 1987-93; ret., 1993; chief dept. surgery Valley Med. Ctr., Fresno, Calif., 1973-74; chief vascular surgery sect. Long Beach VA Med. Ctr., 1974-87; surgical cons. Kaiser Permanente Hosp. Contbr. articles to profl. jours. Fellow Am. Coll. Surgeons; mem. Brit. Med. Assn., Gen. Med. Coun. London (registrant), Assn. Mil. Surgeons of U.S. (life), Assn. VA Surgeons, Internat. Cardiovascular Soc. Home: PO Box 50183 Long Beach CA 90815

KWAN, BENJAMIN CHING KEE, ophthalmologist; b. Hong Kong, July 12, 1940; came to U.S., 1959; s. Shun Ming and Lurk Ming (Lai) K.; m. Catherine Ning, Aug. 29, 1964; children: Susan San, David Daiwai. MD, Wash. U., St. Louis, 1967. Diplomate Am. Bd. Ophthalmology. Ptnr. So. Calif. Permanente Med. Ctr., Harbor City, 1976—, chief of svc. ophthalmology, 1976-88; clin. prof. dept. ophthalmology UCLA, 1995—. Chmn. winter blossom ball Chinese Am. Debutante's Guild, 1993. Capt. U.S. Army, 1969-71. Recipient Svc. award Asian Am. Sr. Citizens Svc. Ctr., 1993, Proclamation award Calif. Sec. of State, 1993, Svc. award East L.A. Chinese Everspring Sr. Assn., 1994. Fellow Am. Acad. Ophthalmology; mem. Chinese Am. Ophthal. Soc. (pres. elect 1997—, Svc. award 1994), Chinese Physician's Soc. So. Calif. (bd. dirs., pres. 1983—, Svc. award 1983, 89), Orgn. Chinese Ams. (pres. L.A. chpt. 1986-87). Roman Catholic. Home: 6327 Tarragon Rd Rancho Palos Verdes CA 90275 Office: 1050 W Pacific Coast Hwy Harbor City CA 90710

KWAN, MARCUS R., surgeon; b. L.A., Dec. 14, 1941. BS in Med. Sci., U. Calif., San Francisco, 1963, MD, 1967. Diplomate Am. Bd. Surgery. Intern Bronx (N.Y.) Mcpl. Hosp. Ctr., 1967-68; resident in surgery Albert Einstein Coll. Medicine, Bronx, 1968-70, Ariz. Med. Ctr./U. Ariz., Tucson, 1972-74; NIH fellow in acad. surgery U. Calif., Berkeley, 1970-72; pvt. practice surgery Santa Cruz, Calif., 1977—; mem. staff Watsonville (Calif.) Cmty. Hosp., Dominican-Santa Cruz Hosp., Santa Cruz Surgery Ctr. Commr. Bd. Parks and Recreation, Santa Cruz County, 1990-94. Lt. comdr. U.S. Army, 1973-77. Fellow ACS; mem. Santa Cruz County Med. Assn., Calif. Med. Assn. Office: 1595 Soquel Dr Ste 340 Santa Cruz CA 95065-1717

KWOK, REGINALD YIN-WANG, urban planning and development educator, architect; b. Hong Kong, Hong Kong, Jan. 24, 1937; came to U.S., 1967; s. On and Yee Fong (Pun) K.; m. Annette Holmes, Aug. 29, 1964; 1 child, Zoe Song-Yi. Diploma in architecture, Poly., London, 1963; Diploma in tropical studies, Archtl. Assn., London, 1967; MS in Architecture, MS in Urban Planning, Colombia U., N.Y.C., 1969, PhD in Urban Planning, 1973. Asst. architect Chamberlin Powell and Bon, London, 1960-61; architect Denys Lasdun and Ptnrs., London, 1963-64, 65-66, Palmer and Turner, Hong Kong, 1965; ind. architect London, 1971; rschr. Inst. Urban Environment, 1968-69; asst. prof. divsn. urban planning Columbia U., 1972-76, assoc. prof., 1976-80, assoc. East Asian Inst., 1975-80; prof. Ctr. Urban Studies and Planning, U. Hong Kong, 1980-89; prof. Sch. Hawaiian/Asian/Pacific Studies, Coll. Social Sci. U. Hawaii at Manoa, Honolulu, 1989—; vis. prof., Zhongshan (China) U., 1983—, Tsinghua (China) U., 1985—, Wuhan (China) Acad. Urban Constrn., 1985—; vis. fellow Princeton U., 1986, Inst. Urgan and Regional Devel. U. Calif., Berkeley, 1987; adv. prof. Tongji U., Shanghai, 1987—; dir. planning program for developing nations Columbia U., 1976-80; dir. Ctr. Urban Studies and Urban Planning U. Hong Kong, 1980-89; chairperson internat. affairs planning coun. U. Hawaii at Manoa, 1990-93, advisor MA in Asian Studies program; vis. scholar Fairbank Ctr. for East Asian Rsch., Harvard U., 1996-97. Author: General Theories of Urban Planning (transl. and edited by H. Chen), 1992, (with M. Castells and L. Goh) The Shek Kip Mei Syndrome: Economic Development and Public Housing in Hong Kong and Singapore, 1990; editor: (with W.L. Parish and A.G.O. Yeh) Chinese Urban Reforms: What Model Now?, 1990, (with Alvin Y. So) The Hong Kong-Guangdong Link, 1996. Mem. bldg. com. Hong Kong Housing Authority, 1982-83, mem. mgmt. com., 1983-88; mem. planning bd. Lands and Works Br., 1985-89; mem. met. study steering group Hong Kong, 1987-89; mem. spl. econ. zone Shenzhen (China) City Planning Com., 1986—; bd. dirs. Chinatown Planning Coun., N.Y.C., 1976-80; mem. adv. com. to borough pres. Manhattan Overall Econ. Devel. Program, N.Y.C., 1978-80; mem., sec. econ. devel. com., Chinatown Improvement Com., N.Y., 1975-76. Rsch. and study grantee, most recently Min. des Affaires Etranges, France, and Consulat Gen. de France, Hong Kong, 1988, Hawaii Com. of Humanities, 1990, Eu Tong Sen Endowment, 1992-93. Mem. Am. Planning Assn., Archtl. Assn. (U.K.), Assn. Asian Studies, Internat. Fedn. Housing and Planning, Pacific Sci. Assn., Archtl. Soc. China (hon. mem. coun. 1983—), Royal Inst. Brit. Architects (assoc.), Ea. Regional Orgn. Planning and Housing (mem. coun., mem. exec. com. Kuala Lumpur 1984—, dep. pres. 1984-86, hon. pres. 1986—), Hong Kong Inst. Architects, Internat. Sociol. Assn., Nat. Com. U.S.-China Rels., Regional Sci. Assn., Regional Studies Assn. (U.K.), Geog. Soc. China. Office: Univ Hawaii at Manoa Porteus Hall 107 Honolulu HI 96822

KWOK, SUN, astronomer; b. Hong Kong, Sept. 15, 1949; arrived in Canada, 1967.; s. Chuen-Poon and Pui-Ling (Chan) K.; m. Shiu-Tseng Emily Yu, June 16, 1973; children: Roberta Wing-Yue, Kelly Wing-Hang. BSc, McMaster U., Hamilton, Ont., Can., 1970; MSc, U. Minn., Mpls., 1972, PhD, 1974. Postdoctoral fellow U. British Columbia, Vancouver, Can., 1974-76; asst. prof. U. Minn., Duluth, 1976-77; rsch. assoc. Centre for Rsch. in Exptl. Space Sci., Toronto, Ont., Can., 1977-78, Herzberg Inst. of Astrophysics, Ottawa, Ont., Can., 1978-83; asst. prof. U. Calgary, Calgary, Alta., Can., 1983-85, assoc. prof., 1985-88, prof., 1988—; vis. fellow Joint Inst. Lab. Astrophysics, Boulder, Colo., 1989-90; project specialist Internat. Adv. Panel, World Bank, 1984; mem. grant selection com. Natural Sci. and Engring. Rsch. Coun., Ottawa, Can., 1985-88; mem. Nat. Facilities Bd. Nat. Rsch. Coun., Ottawa, 1986-89; prin. investigator Odin Satellite project, 1994—. Editor: Late Stages of Stellar Evolution, 1987, Astronomical Infrared Spectroscopy: Future Observational Directions, 1993; contbr. over 140 articles to scholarly and profl. jours. Natural Sci. and Engring. Rsch. Coun. grantee, 1984—, NASA grantee, 1990; Nat. Inst. for Standards and Tech. vis. fellowship, 1989-90. Mem. Internat. Astron. Union, Can. Astron. Soc., Am. Astron. Soc. Home: 139 Edgeland Rd NW, Calgary, AB Canada T3A 2Y3 Office: Univ of Calgary, Dept Physics & Astronomy, Calgary, AB Canada T2N 1N4

KWONG, ALVIN LIN-PIK, financial controller; b. Hong Kong, Oct. 28, 1955; s. Heung Ting and Lai Han (Wong) K. BS, Nat. Taiwan Normal U., 1980; MBA, San Francisco State U., 1991. CPA, Md., CMA, CDP, cert. internal auditor. Sci. panel chmn., tchr. Christian Faith Coll., Hong Kong, 1980-86; staff acct. Blue Star (N.A.) Ltd., Calif., 1992-93, fin. analyst, 1993-95; staff technician KPMG Peat Marwick LLP, Calif., 1995-96; fin. controller Satchi Group, Hong Kong, 1996—. Mem. Inst. Mgmt. Accts., Info. Systems Audit and Control Assn., AICPAs, Hong Kong Soc. Accts. (assoc.). Home: Flat A 30/F Block 40, City One Shatin, Shatin, Hong Kong Hong Kong Office: Satchi Group 11/F Block A Marvel, Industrial Bldg 25-31 Kwai Fung, Crescent Kwai Chung Hong Kong Hong Kong

KWONG, DANIEL WAI-KIN, business consultant, educator, songwriter, poet; b. Hong Kong, Aug. 1, 1958; came to U.S., 1978; s. Moon Kwok and Fung Ha (Leung) K.; m. Oriana Bao-er Ou, Sept. 2, 1985 (div. Mar. 1993); 1 child, Cassandra Anthea. AA, East L.A. Coll., 1980; BA, Calif. State U., L.A., 1982; postgrad., Am. Grad. Sch. Internat. Mgmt., 1983; JD, Thomas Jefferson Coll. Law, 1993. Chmn. Global Investment & Mgmt. Inst., Inc., Monterey Park, Calif., 1996—, Shen Zhen Star River Indust. Corp., China, 1996—; chmn., CEO, Golden Harvest Holdings, Ltd., 1997—; translator, Monterey Park, 1989—; h.s. guest tchr. L.A. County, 1989—; law book cons., critic Glansville Pubs., Dobbs Ferry, N.Y., 1986—; prof., faculty advisor LaSalle U., Slidell, La., 1994—; mem. Pres.'s Club League Women Voters, Team 1000, Washington; bd. dirs. Americ Asia Media Inc.; mem. China Seminar, 1996; Calif. regional coord. Fgn. Policy Assn.'s 1996 Great Decisions Program; world peace promoter; bd. advisor Acad. Med. Ctr U.S., Am. Mil. Univ., 1996; pub. rels. adv. Ctr. for Modern China, Princeton, N.J., 1996—; chmn. & pres. Global Investment & Mgmt. Inst., Inc., 1996—; chmn. Shen Zhen Star River Indsl. Corp., 1996; invited mem. Nat. Com. on U.S.-China Rels. Author: A Hidden Tool, 1990; translator: (from Chinese to English) The Tales of Marsh-Land, 1990; critic, cons. various law and polit. books; contbr. book critic to New Asia Rev., 1994—; author poem: Cassandra; songwriter: (with Richard Gardner) Cassandra, (with Ramsey Kearney) Cass' Story; editl. adv. bd. Scis. of Traditional Chinese Medicine Mo. Jour. Hon. chmn. House Spkr.'s Victory Circle, 1996; founder Bob Dole Comm. Ctr., Washington, 1996; mem. steering com. Asian Coalition (Dole/Kemp), 1996; founding life mem., chmn.'s coun. Rep. Nat. Com., 1992—, Rep. Presdl. Task Force, trustee 1991, honor roll, 1991, ofcl. del., 1994, campaign advisor, 1996; mem. Free Enterprise Coun., 1993—; founding mem. U.S. Holocaust Mus., Washington, 1992, Monday Morning; consul-gen. Holy See of Antioch, U.K., 1994; assoc. State Ctrl. Com., Calif. Rep. Party, 1992—, founding mem. Victory Fund, 1993; founding ptnr. Competitiveness Ctr. Hudson Inst., 1993—; founding mem. Rep. Presdl. Trust, 1992—, Rep. Nat. Candidate Trust, 1992—; presdl. election com. Bush-Quayle, 1992; at-large del. Rep. Platform Planning Com., 1992—; sponsor Nat. Rep. Congrl. com., 1992—, Population Comm. Internat., 1993—; mem. Rep. Senatorial Inner Circle, 1993—, Rep. Fund for the 90s, 1993—, Heritage Found., 1993—; mem. adv. bd. Oliver North for U.S. Senate Com.; mem. campaign team Matt Fong for State Treas. Com.-Calif.; mem. Bush for Tex. Gov. Com., Jeb Bush for Fla. Gov. Com., Sen. Orrin Hatch Com., Sen. Daniel Moynihan Com., Mike Huffington for U.S. Senate Com., Gov. Pete Wilson Com.-Calif.; mem. Pub. Concern Found., U.S. Justice Found., Ctr. Marine Conservation, Sino Charity Found., Inc., Am. Conservative Union; del., lobbyist, activist Calif. Coun. Internat. Trade; invited Rep. Presdl. Roundtable summer policy forum, Washington, 1994; founding nat. mem. U.S. Libr. Congress; chair blingual adv. coun., Repetto Sch., Alhambra Sch. Dist., Calif., 1994—, mem site coun., 1994—; founding mem. invited by House Speaker Gingrich The Speaker's Citizen Task Force, 1995—; mem. exploratory com. 250 Club of Dole, 1995—; co-sponsor Nat. Tax Limitation Com., 1994—; mem. Coll. Rep. Nat. Com., 1994—; commr. Congl. Platform Commn.; nat. campaign advisor Nat. Rep. Senatorial Com., 1996, Rep. Presdl. Task Force, 1996; trustee Idaho Inst. Arts and Tech., 1996; Christian counselor Am. Assn. Christian Counselors, 1996—; pub. rels. advisor Ctr. Modern China, Princeton, N.J., 1996—; founder Bob Dole Comm. Ctr., Nat. Naxpayer Union Bldg.; hon. chrmn. House Speaker's Victory Circle, 1996, Steering Comm. mem. Asian Coalition (Dole/Kemp '96) California. Recipient Presdl. award Rep. Presdl. Legion Merit, 1994, presdl. honor roll, 1993, Cert. Commendation, U.S. Vice Pres. Dan Quayle, 1992, Presdl. EleYr. recognition Rep. Nat. Com., 1992, Cert. Appreciation, Order of Liberty, Nat. Rep. Congl. Com., 1993, Ronald Reagan Flame of Freedom award Republican Presdl. Task Force, 1994, Congressional Order of Freedom, 1995, Wall of Honor Inscription Ronald Reagan Calif. Rep. Ctr., 1996; named VIP guest del. Rep. Nat. Conv., 1992; Knight Grand Cross, Order Golden Fleece, The Holy See of Antioch, 1994, Hon. Consul Genl., Holy See of Antioch, 1994, Hereditary Marshal, Baronies of Athenry & Fermoy (Ireland), 1994, Order Golden Seraphim, 1994, Man of the Year award by American Biographical Inst., 1996, Knight Commander, Order of Sword of England (KCS), 1996. Mem. ASCAP, AAAS, N.Y. Acad. Scis., Chinese Assn. Internat. Trade, Ctr. Modern China (rschr. 1992—), Asia Soc., Hong Kong Assn. So. Calif., Pres.'s Club, Orgn. Chinese Ams., L.A.-Quangzhou Sister City Assn., Internat. Churchill Soc., Monterey Park Rep. Club, Songwriter's Club Am. (life), Acad. Polit. Sci., Poet's Guild, Ripon Soc., Acad. Polit. Sci., Am. Biographical Inst. N.C. (editl. adv. bd., rsch. bd.), Nat. Authors Registry, Internat. Platform Assn. (elected), Citizens Sound Economy, Am. Soc. Composers, Authors and Pubsl., Gospel Music Assn, fellow (elect.) Acad. Pol. Sci. (1996). Home: 601 Cecil St Monterey Park CA 91755-3909

KWONG, DONALD, purchasing agent, consultant; b. Sacramento, Calif., Feb. 10, 1968; s. Dewey and Wai Ying (Chin) K. BA, U. Calif., Santa Cruz, 1991; DD, Universal Life Ch., 1996. Purchasing agt. U.S. Dept. Energy, Sacramento, 1991-93; procurement specialist PRC Environ. Mgmt., San Francisco, 1993-95; cons. San Jose MBDC, 1995-96; subcontract adminstr. Aerotherm Corp., Mountain View, Calif., 1996—; mem. Industry Coun. for Small Bus. Devel., 1996—, Dept. of Def. Small Bus. Coun., 1996—. Editor: (literary jour.) Seaweed Soup, 1990-91. No. sec. Asian Pacific Caucus, Calif. Dem. Party, 1995-96; treas. Asian Pacific Dem. Club, San Francisco, 1995. Mem. Nat. Contract Mgmt. (chpt. v.p. 1994-95), Alumni Assn. U. Calif. Santa Cruz (life), Orgn. Chinese Ams. (bd. dirs. 1996—). Democrat. Office: Aerotherm Corp 580 Clyde Ave Mountain View CA 94043

KYD, MARILYN GRATTON, writer, editor; b. Wichita, Kans., Jan. 26, 1948; d. Robert and Celia (Goldman) Gratton; m. Charles W. Kyd, Mar. 25, 1984. AA, Pasadena City Coll., 1967; BA in English, UCLA, 1969. Cert. secondary tchr., Calif. Tchr. English Glendora (Calif.) High Sch., 1970-72; tchr. English and creative writing Hueneme High Sch., Oxnard, Calif., 1972-76; employment counselor Snelling & Snelling, Oxnard, 1976-77; ptnr., mgr. MG Pers. Agy., Santa Monica, Calif., 1977-78; tech. writer, editor Stanwick Corp., Ventura, Calif., 1978-80; engring. writer Northrop Corp., Newbury Park, Calif., 1980; logistics analyst Automation Industries, Vitro Labs., Oxnard, 1980-81; mgr. documentation Computer Data Corp., Westlake Village, Calif., 1981-82; dir. mktg. Kiely Profl. Svcs., Westlake Village, 1983-84; pres., owner CashMaster Bus. Systems, Inc., Seattle, 1984—; owner, operator profl. resume preparation bus.; free-lance tech. writer and editor. Author: It's A Good Thing I'm Not Married, 1975; contbr. articles to profl. jours. Named Young Careerist Bus. Profl. Women, 1975; recipient 3rd pl. Nat. Writers Club articles contest, 1976, 2nd pl. for photography Port Hueneme Harbor Days, 1976, Honorable mention Writer's Digest Articles Contest, 1987. Mem. Nat. Writers Club, UCLA Alumni Assn., Mensa (columnist 1978).

KYL, JON, senator; b. Oakland, Nebr., Apr. 25, 1942; s. John and Arlene (Griffith) K.; m. Caryll Louise Collins, June 5, 1964; children: Kristine Kyl Gavin, John Jeffry. BA, U. Ariz., 1964, LLB, 1966. Atty. Jennings, Strouss & Salmon, Phoenix, 1966-86; mem. 100th-103rd Congresses from 4th Ariz. dist., 1987-94; senator Ariz., 1995—; mem. Energy & Natural Resources Com., Jud. Com., select com. on Intelligence. Past chmn. Phoenix C. of C.; founding dir. Crime Victim Found., Phoenix Econ. Growth Corp.; past bd. dirs. Ariz. Acad.; past chmn. Young Rep.; gen. coun. Ariz. Rep. Party. Mem. Ariz. State Bar Assn. Office: 702 Hart Senate Bldg Washington DC 20515-0302*

KYLE, CHESTER RICHARD, mechanical engineer; b. L.A., Nov. 18, 1927; s. Chester Raymond and Lorena Dale (Olson) K.; m. Joyce Sylvia; children: Scott D., Kelley L., Cova-Lee, Chester W. BSME, U. Ariz., 1951; MS in Engring., UCLA, 1964, PhD, 1969. Registered profl. engr., Calif. Prodn. engr. Shell Oil Co., Long Beach, Calif., 1951-57; prodn. supt. Internat. Petroleum Co., Talara, Peru, 1957-59; prof., mech. engr. Calif. State U., Long Beach, 1959-84; dir. Sports Equipment Rsch. Assocs., Weed, Calif., 1989—; pub., editor Cycling Sci., Mt. Shasta, Calif., 1989-91; bicycle design coord. U.S. Olympic Cycling Team, 1994-96; mem. sports equipment and tech. com. U.S. Olympic Com., Colorado Springs, Colo., 1984-88; cons. on solar cars U.S. DOE, 1993. Sci. editor Bicycling, 1987-91; mem. editorial bd. Internat. Jour. Sports Biomechanics, 1988-92; contbr. articles to Sci. Am., Smithsonian, other profl. jours.; contbg. author/author books and publs. in field. Named Faculty fellow in sci. NSF, UCLA, 1967, Rsch. fellow U.S. Olympic Com., Long Beach, 1982-88, Fulbright prof., Lima, Peru, 1964-65; recipient Paul Dudley White award League Am. Wheelmen, 1993. Fellow Explorers Club (N.Y.); mem. Internat. Human Powered Vehicle Assn. (founder, bd. dirs. 1975—), L.A. Adventurer's Club (pres. 1986). Home and Office: 9539 N Old Stage Rd Weed CA 96094-9516

KYRIAKOPOULOS, STEVE GEORGE, song writer; b. San Francisco, Aug. 26, 1950; s. Steve James and Eva Michele (Diamond) K. BS, San Mateo Coll., 1971. Studio musician Arch Angel Prodn., Hollywood, Calif., 1979—; sound engr. Neil Diamond Prodn., Hollywood, Calif., 1980—. With U.S. Army, 1972-79.

KYTE, LYDIANE, botanist; b. L.A., Jan. 6, 1919; d. Aurele and Helen Scott (Douglas) Vermeulen; m. Robert McClung Kyte, June 2, 1939; children: Katherine Liu, Bobbin Cave, William Robert Kyte. BS, U. Wash., 1964. Supt. Weyerhaeuser Co., Rochester, Wash., 1972-77; lab mgr. Briggs Nursery, Olympia, Wash., 1977-80; owner Cedar Valley Nursery, Centralia, Wash., 1980—; cons. Internat. Exec. Service Corps, Brazil, 1987, Egypt, 1990. Author: Plants From Test Tubes: An Introduction to Micropropagation, 1983, 2d rev. edit., 1988, 3d edit., 1996. Mem. Internat. Plant Propagators' Soc., Tissue Culture Assn., Internat. Assn. Plant Tissue Culture, Am. Assn. for Hort. Sci., Am. Assn. Univ. Women. Home and Office: Cedar Valley Nursery 3833 Mcelfresh Rd SW Centralia WA 98531-9510

LAALY, HESHMAT OLLAH, chemist, roofing materials executive, consultant; b. Kermanshah, Iran, June 23, 1927; came to Germany, 1951, Can., 1967, U.S., 1984; s. Jacob and Saltanat (Afshani) L.; m. Parvaneh Modarai, Oct. 7, 1963; (div. 1971); children: Ramesh, Edmond S.; m. Parivash M. Farahmand, Feb. 7, 1982. BS in Chemistry, U. Stuttgart, Germany, 1955; MS in Chemistry, U. Stuttgart, Republic of Germany, 1958, PhD in Chemistry, 1962. Chief chemist Kress Sohne, Krefeld, Germany, 1963-67; analytical chemist Gulf Oil Research Ctr., Montreal, Que., Can., 1967-70; material scientist Bell-Northern Research, Ottawa, Ont., Can., 1970-71; research officer NRC of Can., Ottawa, 1972-84; pres. Roofing Materials Sci. and Tech., L.A., 1984—; Patentee in field. Author: The Science and Technology of Traditional and Modern Roofing Systems, 1992 (World Lifetime Achievement award Am. Biog. Inst. 1992); patentee bi-functional photovoltaic single ply roofing membrane. Mem. ASTM, Inst. Roofing and Waterproofing Cons., Single-Ply Roofing Inst., Assn. Profl. Engrs. Ontario, Am. Chem. Soc., Internat. Union of Testing and Rsch. Labs. for Material and Structures (tech. com. 75), Constrn. Specifications Inst., Nat. Roofing Contractors Assn., UN Indsl. Devels. Orgn., Internat. Conf. Bldg. Ofcls., Roofing Cons. Inst., Inst. for Roofing and Waterproofing Cons., Can. Standard Assn., Can. Gen. Standards Bd., The Engineered Wood Assn. Office: Roofing Materials Sci & Tech 9037 Monte Mar Dr Los Angeles CA 90035-4235

LAANANEN, DAVID HORTON, mechanical engineer, educator; b. Winchester, Mass., Nov. 11, 1942; s. Joseph and Helen Katherine (Horton) L.; m. Mary Ellen Storck, Sept. 9, 1967 (div. 1981); children: Gregg David,

Robin Kaye; m. Delores Ann Talbert, May 21, 1988. BS in Mech. Engring., Worcester Poly. Inst., 1964; MS, Northeastern U., 1965, PhD, 1968. Project engr. Dynamic Sci., Phoenix, 1972-74; asst. prof. Pa. State U., State College, 1974-78; mgr. R&D Simula Inc., Phoenix, 1978-83; assoc. prof. Ariz. State U., Tempe, 1983—, dir. aerospace rsch. ctr., 1992—. Referee: Jour. Aircraft, Jour. Mech. Design; contbr. articles to Jour. Aircraft, Jour. Am. Helicopter Soc., Jour. Safety Rsch., Jour. Thermoplastic Composite Materials, Composites Sci. and Tech. Fellow AIAA (assoc.; design engring. tech. com.); mem. ASME, Am. Helicopter Soc., Sigma Xi, Sigma Gamma Tau, Pi Tau Sigma. Democrat. Office: Ariz State U Dept Mech Aerospace En Tempe AZ 85287

LABA, MARVIN, management consultant; b. Newark, Mar. 17, 1928; s. Joseph Abraham and Jean Cecil (Saunders) L.; m. Sandra Seltzer, Apr. 16, 1961 (div. May 1974); children: Stuart Michael, Jonathan Todd; m. Elizabeth Luger, June 11, 1974 (div. 1979). BBA, Ind. U., 1951. Buyer Bamberger's (Macy's N.J.), Newark, 1951-67; v.p., mdse. adminstr. Macy's N.Y., 1967-73; v.p., gen. mdse. mgr. Howland/Steinback, White Plains, N.Y., 1973-75, Pomeroy's, Levittown, Pa., 1975-76; v.p., gen. mdse. mgr., sr. v.p., exec. v.p. May Co. Calif., North Hollywood, 1976-79; pres., chief exec. officer G. Fox & Co. (div. of the May dept. stores), Hartford, Conn., 1979-82; pres. Richard Theobald & Asocs., L.A., 1983; pres., chief exec. officer Marvin Laba & Assocs., L.A., 1983—. With U.S. Army, 1946-48. Office: Marvin Laba & Assoc 6255 W Sunset Blvd Ste 617 Los Angeles CA 90028-7407

LABAGH, RICHARD EDWARD, commercial real estate appraiser; b. Sacramento, July 17, 1959; s. Richard Edward and Dolores Julia (Coffey) L. BSBA, U. San Francisco, 1988, MBA, 1990. Fin. analyst QED Rsch., Palo Alto, Calif., 1992; comml. real estate appraiser The Reitman Group, Palo Alto, 1993—. Author computer software: The Teacher's Pet, 1991, The Financial Calculator, 1992. McClaren Rsch. fellow, 1988-89. Mem. Beta Gamma Sigma. Republican. Home: 1594 16th Ave San Francisco CA 94122-3525

LABAYEN, LOUIE ANTHONY LOPEZ, information analyst, consultant; b. Manila, Jan. 17, 1960; came to U.S., 1976; s. Wilfredo Lizares and Rose Jocelyn Ocampo (Lopez) L.; m. Rosalinda Maglonzo Torres, June 6, 1987; children: John Gustav Torres, James Daniel Torres. BA, De La Salle U., Manila, 1981; MusM, U. No. Colo., 1986. Mgr. Network Mgmt. Corp., Kansas City, Mo., 1988-90; sr. analyst Blue Cross Blue Shield, Kansas City, Mo., 1990-94; v.p. Patriot Mortgage Co., 1994; team leader Tapestry Computing, 1994-95; sr. cons. Oracle Corp., 1995; devel. mgr. Uniband, Inc., 1995-96; prin. cons. Paladin Data Sys., Inc., 1996—; lectr. Mt. Carmel Coll., Baler, Philippines, 1982-83; project leader Blue Cross Blue Shield, 1991-94. Mem. Am. Symphony Orch. League, 1985—. Mem. IEEE, Mu Phi Epsilon, Rotary (exch. student Antwerp, Ohio 1976). Home and Office: 11225 19th Ave SE Apt E104 Everett WA 98208-5139

LABBE, ARMAND JOSEPH, museum curator, anthropologist; b. Lawrence, Mass., June 13, 1944; s. Armand Henri and Gertrude Marie (Martineau) L.; m. Denise Marie Scott, Jan. 17, 1969 (div. 1972). BA in Anthropology, Univ. Mass., 1969; MA in Anthropology, Calif. State U., 1986; lifetime instr. credential in anthropology, State Calif. Curator collections Bowers Mus., Santa Ana, Calif., 1978-79, curator anthropology, 1979-86, chief curator, 1986—, dir. rsch. and collections, 1991—; instr. prof. Santa Ana Coll., 1981-86, U. Calif., Irvine, 1983, 87, 91, 93, Chapman U., 1996, Calif. State U., Fullerton, 1982, 83, 88, 97, rsch. assoc. dept. anthropology, 1997—; trustee Balboa Arts Conservation Ctr., San Diego, 1989—, Ams. Found., Greenfield, Mass., 1985-94, Quintcentenary Festival Discovery, Orange County, Calif., 1990-91, Mingei Internat. Mus., La Jolla, Calif., 1993—, treas. bd. dirs. 1996—; mem. adv. bd. Elan Internat., Newport Beach, Calif., 1992-95; inaugural guest lectr. Friends of Ethnic Art, San Francisco, 1988; hon. bd. dirs. Ethnic Arts Coun., L.A. Author: Man and Cosmos, 1982, Ban Chiang, 1985, Colombia Before Columbus, 1986 (1st prize 1987), Leigh Wiener: Portraits, 1987, Colombia Antes de Colón, 1988 (honored at Gold Mus. Bogotá, Colombia, 1988), Images of Power: Master Works of the Bowers Museum of Cultural Art, 1992; co-author Tribute to The Gods: Treasures of the Museo del Oro, Bogotá, 1992, Guardians of the Life Stream: Shamans, Art and Power In Prehispanic Central Panama, 1995. Hon. bd. dirs. Ethnic Arts Coun. L.A.; cons. Orange County Coun. on History and Art, Santa Ana, 1981-85; mem. Task Force on County Cultural Resources, Orange County, 1979; cons., interviewer TV prodn. The Human Journey, Fullerton, 1986-89; treas., bd. trustees Mingei Internat. Mus., San Diego, 1996—. With USAF, 1963-67. Recipient cert. of Recognition Orange County Bd. Suprs., 1982, award for outstanding scholarship Colombian Community, 1987; honored for authorship Friends of Libr., 1987, 88. Fellow Am. Anthrop. Assn.; mem. AAAS, Am. Assn. Mus., N.Y. Acad. Scis., S.W. Anthrop. Assn. Home: 2854 Royal Palm Dr Apt C Costa Mesa CA 92626-3828

LABBY, DANIEL HARVEY, medical educator, psychiatry educator; b. Portland, Oreg., Sept. 1, 1914; s. Harry A. and Sonia (Goldfarb) L.; m. Margaret Selling, Dec. 28, 1940; children: Joan, David, Louise. BA, Reed Coll., 1935; MD, U. Oreg., 1939. Intern Johns Hopkins Hosp., Balt., 1939-40; resident medicine N.Y. Hosp., N.Y.C., 1943-45; fellow psychiatry Tavistock Inst. for Human Rels., London, Eng., 1970-71, 77-78; prof. medicine Oreg. Health Sci. U., Portland, 1948—, prof. psychiatry, 1978—; asst. The Rockefeller Inst., N.Y.C., 1945-48; vis. prof. medicine Med. Coll. Va., 1958, U. Strasbourg, France, 1960-61, U. Colo. Med. Sch., 1964; sr. scholar Ctr. for Ethics in Health Care, Oreg. Health Sci. Ctr., 1989—. Contbr. articles to profl. jours. Capt. USMC, 1941-44. Noble Wiley Jones fellow in pathology U. Oreg. Med. Sch., 1937-38, A Blaine Brower fellow Ames Coll., 1953, Commonwealth fellow, 1960-61, Disting. Svc. award Reed Coll., 1995; named Alumnus of Yr. Oreg. Health Sci. Ctr., 1991. Mem. Sigma Xi, Alpha Omega Alpha. Home: 5931 SW Hamilton St Portland OR 97221-1231 Office: Oreg Health Scis Univ Health Scis Ctr 3181 SW Sam Jackson Park Rd Portland OR 97201-3011

LABINER, GERALD WILK, physician, medical educator; b. N.Y.C., Nov. 7, 1923; s. Benjamin and Mollie (Wilk) L.; m. Suzanne Solov, May 3, 1953; children: Caroline Moser, Charles. BS, Rutgers U., 1944; MD, Ind. U., 1949. Intern. Phila. Gen. Hosp., 1949-51, resident, 1951-52; sr. asst. surgeon USPHS, Washington, 1951-53; fellow Lahey Clinic, Boston, 1953-55; pvt. practice Beverly Hills, Calif., 1955—. Lt. j.g., USN, 1944-45; with USPHS, 1951-53. Fellow ACP, Am. Geriat. Soc., Contemporary Art Soc.; mem. Aescolapi Assn., Far Eastern Coun. (pres. 1964-65), Alpha Omega Alpha. Office: 8920 Wilshire Blvd Beverly Hills CA 90211

LABOVITZ, EARL A., allergist; b. Cleveland, Miss., June 12, 1949. MD, U Miss, 1975. Allergist Desert Samaritan Hosp., Mesa, Ariz. Office: Mesa-Tempe Allergy & Asthma Clinic Ste B-300 2451 E Baseline Rd Gilbert AZ 85234

LACEY, HENRY BERNARD, lawyer; b. Aurora, Colo., Nov. 30, 1963; s. Leonard Joseph and Colleen Trece (Ryan) L. BS, Ariz. State U., 1988, JD, 1991. Bar: Ariz. 1991, Oreg. 1996; U.S. Dist. Ct. Ariz. 1991, U.S. Ct. Appeals (9th cir.) 1992. Jud. law clk. to Hon. Cecil F. Poole U.S. Ct. Appeals 9th Cir., San Francisco, 1991-92; assoc. Kimball & Curry, P.C., Phoenix, 1992-93; atty. Law Office of Henry B. Lacey, Scottsdale, Ariz., 1993-94; vis. fellow Natural Resources Law Inst. Northwestern Sch. Law, Lewis & Clark Coll., Portland, Oreg., 1994-95; freelance writer Lake Oswego, Oreg., 1995-96; atty. Wilenchik & Bartness P.C., Phoenix, Ariz., 1996—; counsel/environ. group adv. bd. dirs. Coalition to Reform the Ctrl. Ariz. Project, Phoenix, 1993; vol. lawyer/Ariz. bd. dirs. Land and Water Fund of the Rockies, Boulder, Colo., 1993—; vol. lawyer Portland Audubon Soc., 1996—. Gen. counsel Maricopa County, Ariz. Dem. Party, 1992-94; counsel Carol Cure for Congress Campaign, Phoenix, 1994; vol. Ariz. for Clinton-Gore '92, 1992. Mem. ABA (young lawyers divsn. 1991—, sec. on natural resources, energy and environ. law, 1991—, sec. on litigation 1994—), Ariz. State Bar (environ. and natural resources law sec., 1991—, trial practice sec. 1996—), Maricopa County Bar Assn. (environ. law com. 1993—), Environ. Law Inst., Am. Inns of Ct. (McFarland chpt. 1994—), Order of the Coif, Phi Delta Phi. Roman Catholic. Office: 13th Flr 2828 N Central Ave Phoenix AZ 85004

LACHEMANN, MARCEL, professional baseball manager; b. L.A., June 13, 1941. BSBA, U. So. Calif., 1962. Former player Kansas City A's (moved to Oakland); pitching coach Calif. Angels (now Anaheim Angels), 1983-92, mgr., head coach, 1994-96; pitching coach Anaheim Angels, 1996—, Fla. Marlins, 1992-94. Office: Anaheim Angels 2000 Gene Autry Way Anaheim CA 92806-6100

LACKEY, MARCIA ANN, writer; b. Seattle, Feb. 24, 1952; d. Herbert Earl Larrick and Blanche Elsie (Brumley) Cannon. Dipl., San Diego State U., 1992. Pub. rels. exec. Viejas Indian Sch., Alpine, Calif., til 1995; dir. art gallery Michael McCormick Presents, Taos, N.Mex., til 1996; freelance writer Taos, 1996—. Author, poet: Fiction International, 1991; author: (anthologies) Earth Song/Sky Spirit, 1993 (Oakland Josephine Miles award 1994), Worlds of Difference, 1996. Democrat. Roman Catholic. Home and Office: PO Box 2301 Ranchos De Taos NM 87557

LACOM, WAYNE CARL, artist, writer; b. Glendale, Calif., Oct. 11, 1922; s. Ferdinand and Blanche Charlotte (Heinmiller) LaC.; m. Diana Crystal Strode LaCom, Aug. 27, 1949; children: Lawrence Carl, Laura Diane, Eric Wayne. Student, Art Ctr. Sch., L.A., 1942-43, Chouinard Art Inst., L.A., 1943-45, Jepson Art Inst., L.A., 1945-47. Cert. Dept. Edn., Calif. Artist Conners-Joyce, L.A., N.Y.C., 1943-45; freelance artist pvt. practice, L.A., 1946-47; artist, tchr. L.A. Unified Sch. Dist., 1948-78; artist, graphic designer Emerson Gallery, Encino, Tarzana, Calif., 1964-84; owner, dir., pres. Internat. Art Svcs., Inc., Encino, Calif., 1975—; in-svc. tng. cons. L.A. Unified Sch. Dist., 1950-63; treas. Artists for Ednl. Action, L.A., 1972-75. 100 one man shows Watercolor Painting, 1943—; TV demos, 1960-65; designer: Sculputre and Stained Glass, 1964—; publisher: over 300 edits., 1975—; paintings reproduced in numerous art books including The California Style and The California Romantics. Recipient various Juried Shows awards, 1949—; named 1st Place Catalina Art Assn., 1989, Best of Show Lahainatown Poster Comp, Hawaii, 1993. Mem. Nat. Watercolor Soc. (past pres.). Home: 16703 Alginet Pl Encino CA 91436-4119 Office: International Art Services 16703 Alginet Pl Encino CA 91436-4119

LACROSSE, PATRICK, museum administrator. CEO, pres. Oreg. Mus. of Sci. & Industry, Portland, Oreg. Office: Oreg Mus Sci. and Industry 1945 SE Water Ave Portland OR 97214*

LACY, CAROLYN JEAN, elementary education educator, secondary education educator; b. Marshall, Ark., Apr. 6, 1944; d. Charles Ira Bolch and Edna Rebecca Cherry; 1 child, Kelli Jean. AA with distinction, Riverside City Coll., 1980; BA, U. Calif., Riverside, 1982, postgrad., 1983; MEd, U.S. Internat. U., 1993. Cert. social sci. tchr., Calif. Educator Perris (Calif.) Elem. Sch. Dist., 1984-89, Rialto (Calif.) Unified Sch. Dist., 1989—; instr. Developing Capable People, Riverside, Calif., 1986-89; presenter, lectr. Jurupa Unified Sch. Dist., Riverside, 1990, Rialto Unified Sch. Dist., 1990; developer peer tutor program Perris Elem. Sch. Dist., 1989; dir. chess club Dollahan Elem. Sch., 1995, computer chmn., 1995—. Editor: (newsletter) Perris Lights, 1989. Active Students in Environ. Action, Riverside, 1978; mem. Riverside County Task Force for Self-Esteem. Named Mentor Tchr. State of Calif., 1988. Mem. AAUW, NEA, Calif. Tchrs. Assn., Internat. Reading Assn., U. Calif. Alumni Assn., Phi Delta Kappa, Alpha Gamma Sigma. Democrat. Mem. LDS Ch. Home: 4044 Wallace St Riverside CA 92509-6809

LACY, JOHN R., lawyer; b. Dallas, Dec. 15, 1942. BS, San Diego State U., 1966; MS, U. So. Calif., 1971; JD, U. Calif., 1973. Bar: Calif. 1973, Hawaii 1974. Atty. Goodsill Anderson Quinn & Stifel, Honolulu; arbitrator Ct. Annexed Arbitration Program, 1986—. Comment editor Hastings Law Jour., 1972-73. Mem. ABA, Hawaii Bar Assn., State Bar Calif., Am. Bd. Trial Advs., Maritime Law Assn. U.S., Thurston Soc., Order of Coif. Office: Goodsill Anderson Quinn & Stifel PO Box 3196 1800 Alii Pl 1099 Alakea St Honolulu HI 96813-4500

LADEHOFF, ROBERT LOUIS, bishop; b. Feb. 19, 1932; m. Jean Arthur Burcham (dec. Feb. 1992); 1 child, Robert Louis Jr. Grad., Duke U., 1954, Gen. Theol. Sem., 1957, Va. Theol. Sem., 1980. Ordained deacon, priest The Episcopal Ch., 1957;. Priest in charge N.C. parishes, 1957-60; rector St. Christopher's Ch., Charlotte, N.C., 1960-74, St. John's Ch., Fayetteville, 1974-85; bishop, co-adjutor of Oreg., 1985, bishop, 1986—. Office: Diocese of Oreg PO Box 467 Lake Oswego OR 97034-0467

LADNER, ALAN ROBERT, secondary school educator; b. Ft. Fairfield, Maine, June 14, 1953; s. Montford Charles and Arlene Mae (Williams) L.; m. Naomi Ruth Peters, Aug. 18, 1972; children: Carol, Sarah, Sharon. BA summa cum laude, So. Calif. Coll., 1975; MA in Edn., Fresno Pacific Coll., 1987. Cert. tchr., Calif. Math/sci. tchr. Modesto (Calif.) Christian Sch., 1975-77; math. tchr. Maranatha H.S., Sierra Madre, Calif., 1977—; adj. prof. So. Calif. Coll., Costa Mesa, 1995—; seminar leader Assn. of Christian Schs. Internat., Whittier, Calif., 1982—, Calif. Math Coun., 1983-86, L.A. City Tchrs. of Math. Assn., 1982-84, also bd. dirs. Author: (textbook) Adventures in Geometry, 1994. Mem. Hillside Adv. Bd., City of Monrovia, 1991—; bd. dirs. Foothill Christian Ctr., Glendora, Calif., 1990-92, 96—. Mem. Calif. Math. Coun. Republican. Assemblies of God. Home: 325 N Alta Vista Ave Monrovia CA 91016-1614

LAFERRIERE, GAIL KAREN, college administrator; b. Mpls., Dec. 16, 1956; d. Orel Richard Leferriere and Alvina Clara (Wimmer) Hanson; m. Stephen Mark Kane, May 6, 1978 (div. Dec. 1984); m. Roger Dale Bacon, July 5, 1987. BA in Psychology, Kalamazoo (Mich.) Coll., 1979. Vocat. counselor United Rehab. Svcs., Portland, Oreg., 1986-88; career devel. specialist Clackamas C.C., Oregon City, Oreg., 1988-93, North Idaho Coll., Coeur D'Alene, 1994—; membership chair, bd. mem. Oreg. Career Devel. Assn., 1991-93; Oreg. leader Am. Assn. for Women in Cmty Colleges, Oreg. Leadership Inst., 1992; career adv. profl. study group State Task Force Oreg. Edn. Reform Legislation, Portland, 1992. Mem. ACA, Nat. Career Devel. Assn., Career Planning and Adult Devel. Network, Nat. Assn. Colls. and Employers, Idaho Career Devel. Assn., Idaho Counseling Assn. Office: North Idaho Coll 1000 W Garden Ave Coeur D Alene ID 83814-2161

LAFF, NED SCOTT, English educator, university administrator; b. Chgo., May 17, 1949; s. Milton M. and Bertha (Ruder) L.; children: Rachel, Rebecca, Elanor. BA in English, U. Ill., 1971, PhD in English Edn., 1983; MA in English, U. Wyo., 1973. Instr. English U. Wyo., Laramie, 1972-73; instr. rhetoric U. Ill., Urbana, 1977-80, adminstr. advisor/grad. asst. advisor, 1979-81, adminstrv. asst. Office of Dean Coll. of Edn., 1980-83, asst. dir. acad. programs Unit 1 Divsn. of Housing, 1983-85; asst. dean for freshmen, lectr. dept. edn. St. Lawrence U., Canton, N.Y., 1985-87; adj. asst. prof., asst. dir. for acad. advising U. No. Colo., Greeley, 1987-89; asst. dir. for acad. advising U. No. Colo., 1987-89; dir. acad. support svcs. Coll. Liberal Arts Fla. Atlantic U., Davie, 1991-93; adj. asst. prof. English Fla. Atlantic U., 1992—, asst. dean Coll. Liberal Arts, 1993—; adj. asst. prof. English Weber State U., Ogden, Utah, 1995—; dir. univ. advising Weber State U., 1995—; grad. asst. to asst. and assoc. deans Coll. Liberal Arts and Scis., U. Ill., 1977-80; mem. numerous univ. coms.; cons. Title III advising/retention program Roosevelt U., Chgo., 1990, advising and retention audit U. Ind., 1993; presenter in field. Contbr. numerous articles, revs. to profl. jours. Mem. MLA (nominee exec. com. divsn. on tchg. of lit. 1986), Am. Assn. Higher Edn., Assn. Gen. and Liberal Studies, Nat. Acad. Advising Assn. (cons., editl. bd. jour.), Coll. English Assn., Nat. Conf. Tchrs. of English, Conf. on Coll. Composition and Comm., Phi Kappa Phi. Home: 625 S 1300 E Salt Lake City UT 84102 Office: Weber State U Ogden UT 84408

LAFFERTON, MACKIE V. (MAKKI V. LAFFERTON), artist; b. Gallina, N.Mex., Dec. 11, 1933; d. Jose Melquiades and Maria Ruperta (Serrano) Valdez; m. Henry Imre Lafferton, July 31, 1959 (div. Dec. 1983); children: Sandra Marie, Henry James, Jacqueline Margit. Student, N.Mex. State U., 1977, 82, San Juan Coll., 1983, 84, Art Masters Acad., Albuquerque, N. Mex., 1995—. Owner, mgr. Bloomfield (N.Mex.) Plumbing and Heating, Inc., 1971-83, Central Apts., Bloomfield, 1981-93, Fine Arts By Makki, Albuquerque, 1995—; mem., fundraiser Bloomfield C. of C., 1972-84. Tailor, designer ready-made clothing (numerous awards 1971-80); artist: represented in private and pub. collections throughout the U.S. and abroad; in permanent collections: Multi-Cultural Ctr. of Bloomfield, N. Mex., Cath. Social Svcs. of Albuquerque, Casa Esperanza, Inc., Albuquerque, Salmon Ruins Mus., Bloomfield; exhbns. and awards include: Portraiture and figurative painting and drawings: 1st prize, Farmington, N. Mex., 1987, numerous shows at the Civic Ctr. of Farmington, N. Mex., 1993, People's Choice award, N. Mex. Art League, Albuquerque, 1995, Hon. Mention Marco Polo Art Exhibit, Nairobi, Kenya, 1995, Jurors Selection award of recognition Minature Arts Bardean, Albuquerque, 1996, 25th Nat. Small Painting Exhibition Jurors Selection N. Mex. Art League, Albuquerque, 1996. Mem. N.Mex. Watercolor Soc., N.Mex. Art League, Knickerbocker Artists, Pastel Soc. N.Mex. Republican. Roman Catholic. Home and Studio: Fine Arts By Makki 6128 Alderman Dr NW Albuquerque NM 87120-5415

LAFLEUR, KAREN JAMIE, psychologist; b. Pembrooke, Ont., Can., Feb. 28, 1955; d. Gerald Nelson and Ruth (Buchannan) Coe; m. Martin J. LaFleur, Mar. 5, 1993. BSc in Sci. and Biology, Brock U., 1974, BA with honors in Psychology, 1975; MA in Adult Psychology, Guelph U., 1976; PhD in Clin. Psychology, U. Calgary, 1979. Registered psychologist, Alta. Sr. cons. Orgn. Resource Cons., Calgary, Alta., Can., 1982-84; sr. practice cons. Thorne Stephenson & Kellogg, Calgary and Vancouver, B.C., 1984-86; mgr. planning devel. and recruitment Gulf Can. Resources, Calgary, 1986-88; mgr. corp. planning NOVA Corp., Calgary, 1988-90; assoc. search cons. O'Callaghan-Honey & Assoc., Calgary, 1990-93; dir. Elite Bur. Investigations, Calgary, 1993—; pres. Talkworks Inc., Calgary, 1994—, Lafleur & Co. Internat. Inc., Calgary, 1993—; sr. clin. psychologist Calgary Gen. Hosp., 1978-79. Mem. Can. Psychol. Assn., Psychol. Assoc. Alta., Calgary C. of C. Office: 1500 400 3d Ave SW, Calgary, AB Canada T2P 4H2

LA FLEUR, WALTER J., engineering executive; b. Carrizozo, N.Mex., July 22, 1933; s. Walter J. and Mariam Evelyn (Grumbles) La F.; m. Vera Jean Scott Shupe, Dec. 20, 1953 (div. Mar. 1970); children: Walter IV, Ian; m. Mary Lee Johenning, May 6, 1972 (dec. Dec. 1994). BS in Physics, N.Mex. State U., 1955, MS in Electronic Engring., 1960. Assoc. physicist Phys. Sci. Lab. N.Mex. State U., University Park, 1956-60; dir. Bermuda Sta. NASA, Goddard Space Flight Ctr., 1961-67; chief tracking and data systems br. NASA, Goddard Space Flight Ctr., Greenbelt, Md., 1967-70, assoc. chief support divsn., 1971, chief ops. divsn., 1972-78, dep. dir. networks, 1980-84; asst. assoc. adminstr., tech. NASA, Office Tracking and Data Acquisition, Washington, 1979; dep. dir. tech. ops. Voice of Am., Washington, 1984-88; dir. engring. Voice of Am. and Worldnet, Washington, 1989-93; chmn. bd. Marconi Comm., Inc., Reston, Va., 1994-96. Recipient Rank of Meritorious Exec. Pres. Bush, Washington, 1989, Rank of Disting. Exec. Pres. Bush, Washington, 1991. Fellow Radio Club Am.; mem. IEEE, Nat. Assn. Radio and TV Engrs. (sr.), Am. Radio Relay League. Home and Office: PO Box 1029 Silver City NM 88062-1029

LA FORCE, JAMES CLAYBURN, JR., economist, educator; b. San Diego, Dec. 28, 1928; s. James Clayburn and Beatrice Maureen (Boyd) La F.; m. Barbara Lea Latham, Sept. 23, 1952; children: Jessica, Allison, Joseph. BA, San Diego State Coll., 1951; MA, UCLA, 1958, PhD, 1962. Asst. prof. econs. UCLA, 1962-66, assoc. prof., 1967-70, prof., 1971-93, prof. emeritus, 1993—, chmn. dept. econs., 1969-78, dean Anderson Sch. Mgmt., 1978-93; acting dean Hong Kong U. Sci. & Tech., 1991-93; bd. dirs. Rockwell Internat., Eli Lilly & Co., Jacobs Engring. Group Inc., The Timken Co., The Black Rock Funds, Imperial Credit Industries, Inc., Payden & Rygel Investment Trust, Providence Investment Coun. Mut. Funds; chmn. adv. com. Calif. Workmen's Compensation. Author: The Development of the Spanish Textile Industry 1750-1800, 1965, (with Warren C. Scoville) The Economic Development of Western Europe, vols. 1-5, 1969-70. Bd. dirs. Nat. Bur. Econ. Rsch., 1975-88, Found. Francisco Marroquin, Lynde and Harry Bradley Found., Pacific Legal Found., 1981-86; trustee Found. for Rsch. in Econs. and Edn., 1970—, chmn., 1977—; mem. bd. overseers Hoover Inst. on War, Revolution and Peace, 1979-85, 86-93; mem. nat. coun. on humanities NEH, 1981-88; chmn. Pres.'s Task Force on Food Assistance, 1983-84. Social Sci. Research Council research tng. fellow, 1958-60; Fulbright sr. research grantee, 1965-66; Am. Philos. Soc. grantee, 1965-66. Mem. Econ. History Assn., Mont Pelerin Soc., Phi Beta Kappa. Office: UCLA Anderson Grad Sch Mgmt 405 Hilgard Ave Los Angeles CA 90024-1301

LAFRANCHI, STEPHEN HENRY, pediatric endocrinologist, educator, researcher; b. St. Helena, Calif., Aug. 26, 1943; s. Edward Henry and Marion Blanche (Holcomb) LaF.; m. Pamela Ann Fisher; children: Christopher, Alexander. BA in Biology, U. So. Calif., 1965; MD, UCLA, 1969. Resident in pediat. UCLA, 1969-72, fellow in pediat. endocrinology, 1972-75; asst. prof. pediat. Oreg. Health Scis. U., Portland, 1975-80, assoc. prof. pediat., 1980-85, prof. pediat., 1985—; vis. prof. Chiba Children's Hosp., Okinawa, 1987, U. Ariz., Phoenix, 1987. Contbr. numerous articles and abstracts to med. jours. Mem. Physicians for Social Responsibility, 1975—. Fogarty Sr. Internat. fellow NIH, Zurich, Switzerland, 1982-83. Fellow Am. Acad. Pediat. (exec. com. endocrine sect. 1994—); mem. Am. Acad. Pediat., Lawson Wilkins Pediat. Endocrine Soc. (treas. 1988-93), The Endocrine Soc., Am. Thyroid Assn., Portland Acad. Pediat. (pres. 1991), European Soc. Pediat. Rsch. Office: Oregon Health Svcs Univ Dept of Pediatrics (NRC-5) 3181 SW Sam Jackson Park Rd Portland OR 97201-3011

LAGASSE, BRUCE KENNETH, structural engineer; b. Bklyn., Feb. 1, 1940; s. Joseph F. Lagasse and Dora S. Gould. BSME, U. Calif., Berkeley, 1964. Structures engr. Rockwell Internat., Canoga Park, Calif., 1964-69; mem. tech. staff Hughes Aircraft Co., Los Angeles, 1969-70; scientist/engr. Hughes Aircraft Co., El Segundo, Calif., 1972—; sr. engr. Litton Ship Systems, Los Angeles, 1971-72; lectr., tech. edn. class coord. Hughes Aircraft Co., El Segundo, 1980—; cons. in field, Van Nuys, Calif., 1979—. Libertarian state chmn., L.A., 1977-79, nat. committeeman, Washington, 1979-81. Mem. ASME. Home: 7247 Balboa Blvd Van Nuys CA 91406-2702

LAGER, DOUGLAS ROY, property tax consultant; b. Eau Claire, Wis., Dec. 10, 1947; m. Barbara Joyce Johnston, Oct. 5, 1985; 1 child, Jeffrey D. BSBA in Acctg., Rockhurst Coll., Kansas City, Mo., 1971. Cert. gen. appraiser, Colo. Head dept. personal property Jackson County Assessor, Kansas City, Mo., 1971-74; property assessment specialist Wis. Dept. Revenue, Madison, 1974-80; property tax cons. Property Tax Svc., Mpls., 1980-84, Denver, 1984-87; property tax cons. Avtax, Inc., Denver, 1987—. Home: 9 White Alder Littleton CO 80127-3598 Office: Avtax Inc 5555 Dtc Pkwy Ste C-3300 Englewood CO 80111-3005

LAGERBERG, RANDALL ERLAND, mental health specialist; b. Seattle, June 1, 1959; s. Floyd R. and Rose M. (Nixon) L. AA, Shoreline C.C., Seattle, 1988; BA in Comms., U. Wash., 1991. Registered councelor. Customer svc. rep. Speakerlab, Inc., Seattle, 1978-82; svc. rep. Linde Homecare, Redmond, Wash., 1984-88; mng. editor The Ebbtide, Seattle, 1988; reporter The Daily, Seattle, 1989-91; staff reporter North Seattle Press, 1991; mental health specialist N.W. E&T, Seattle, 1991—. Photographer: Spindrift, 1988, 2d edit., 1989; author mag. Seafair, 1991. Vol. Audubon Soc.

LAGOMARSINI, GEORGE CAESAR, engineering and mathematics educator, consultant; b. Bklyn., June 22, 1924; s. Charles Henry and Josephine (Re) L.; m. Mildred Pierne, Dec. 23, 1949; 1 child, Roberta. BSEE, U. N.Mex., 1950; MSEE, Calif. State U., L.A., 1975; MBA, Claremont (Calif.) Grad. Sch., 1982. Registered profl. engr. Rsch. asst. Columbia U., N.Y.C., 1942-47; rsch. engr. U. Calif., Los Alamos, N.Mex., 1947-53; chief engr. Telecomputing Corp., North Hollywood, Calif., 1953-62; engring. project mgr. CARY/Varian Assocs., Monrovia, Calif., 1962-73; asst. prof. Calif. State U., L.A., 1976-83; asst. prof. Jet Propulsion Lab., Calif. Inst. Tech., Pasadena, 1973-87; instr. Victor Valley Coll., Victorville, Calif., 1995—; engring. cons., Alphius Systems, Rancho Cucamonga, Calif., 1992-95, Jet Propulsion Lab., Pasadena, Calif., 1989-95. Author, prodr. (tutor training play) 12-Teps to Independence, 1995; author, dir. (tutor training play) Windmills, 1995; author (book of poems) The Bridge, 1996. Vol. leader Campfire Girls, Glendale, Calif., 1968-74; vol. tutor, programmer Victor Valley Coll., 1994—. Recipient Von Nardoff Sci. medal, Styvesant H.S., N.Y.C., 1942. Mem. IEEE (life), Am. Philatelic Soc., Tau Beta Pi (life), Phi Theta Kappa. Office: Victor Valley College 18422 Bear Valley Rd Victorville CA 92392

LAGORIA, GEORGIANNA MARIE, curator, writer, editor, visual art consultant; b. Oakland, Calif., Nov. 3, 1953; d. Charles Wilson and Margaret

Claire (Vella) L.; m. David Joseph de la Torre, May 15, 1982; 1 child, Mateo Joseph. BA in Philosophy, Santa Clara U., 1975; MA in Museology, U. San Francisco, 1978. Exhbn. coordinator Allrich Gallery, San Francisco, 1977-78; asst. registrar Fine Arts Mus., San Francisco, 1978-79; gallery coordinator de Saisset Mus., Santa Clara, Calif., 1979-80, asst. dir., 1980-83, dir., 1983-86; dir. Palo Alto (Calif.) Cultural Ctr., 1986-91; ind. writer, editor and cons. mus. and visual arts orgns., Hawaii, 1991-95; dir. The Contemporary Mus., Honolulu, 1995—; V.p. Non-Profit Gallery Assn., San Francisco, 1980-82; bd. dirs. Fiberworks, Berkeley, Calif., 1981-85; field reviewer Inst. Mus. Services, Washington, 1985-87; adv. bd. Hearst Art Gallery, Moraga, Calif., 1986-89, Womens Caucus for Art, San Francisco, 1987—; mem. adv. bd. Weigand Art Gallery, Notre Dame Coll., Belmont, Calif. Curator exhbns. The Candy Store Gallery, 1980, Fiber '81, 1981; curator, author exhbn. catalogue Contemporary Hand Colored Photographs, 1981, Northern Calif. Art of the Sixties, 1982, The Artist and the Machine: 1910-1940, 1986; author catalogue, guide Persis Collection of Contemporary Art at Honolulu Advertiser, 1993; co-author: The Little Hawaiian Cookbook, 1994; coord. exhbn. selections Laila and Thurston Twigg-Smith Collection and Toshiko Takaezu ceramics for Hui No'eau Visual Arts Ctr., Maui, 1993; editor Nuhou (newsletter Hawaii State Mus. Assn.), 1991-94; spl. exhbn. coord. Honolulu Acad. Arts, 1995; dir. The Contemporary Mus., Honolulu, 1995—. Mem. Arts Adv. Alliance, Santa Clara County, 1985-86; grant panelist Santa Clara County Arts Council, 1987. Exhbn. grantee Ahmanson Found., 1981, NEA, 1984, Calif. Arts Coun., 1985-89. Mem. Am. Assn. Mus., ArtTable, 1983—, Calif. Assn. Mus. (bd. dirs. 1987-89), Hawaiian Craftsmen (bd. dirs. 1994-95), Honolulu Jr. League, Key Project (bd. dirs. 1993-94). Democrat. Roman Catholic. Home and Office: 47-665 Mapele Rd Kaneohe HI 96744-4918

LAGREEN, ALAN LENNART, public relations executive, radio personality; b. Burbank, Calif., May 20, 1951; s. Lennart Franklin and Mary (Cassara) LaG.; m. Wendy Diane Gilmaker, June 28, 1975; 1 child, Cara Diane. BA, U. So. Calif., L.A., 1972. Pub. rels. asst. Dames & Moore, L.A., 1972-75; asst. pub. Orange County Illustrated, Newport Beach, Calif., 1975; asst. exec. dir. Toastmasters Internat., Santa Ana, Calif., 1975-86; meetings and conv. mgr. Fluor Corp., Irvine, Calif., 1986-87; v.p. Pacific Bldg. Investors, Inc., Santa Ana, Calif., 1987—; reporter Airtraffic Comm., Tustin, Calif., 1997—; morning radio personality Sta. KSBR-FM Jazz Radio, Mission Viejo, Calif. Home: 591 N Turnberry Dr Orange CA 92869-2576

LAGUERRE, MICHEL SATURNIN, anthropology educator; b. Lascahobas, Haiti; came to U.S., 1971; s. Magloire Laguerre and Anilia Roseau. BA in Philosophy, U. Quebec, 1971; MA in Sociology, Roosevelt U., 1973; PhD in Social Anthropology, U. Ill., 1976. Asst. prof. sociology Fordham U., N.Y.C., 1977-78; asst. prof. anthropology and African-Am. studies U. Calif., Berkeley, 1978-82, assoc. prof., 1982-90, prof., 1990—; vis. prof./scholar Harvard U., 1991-92; trustee Refugee Policy Group, Washington, 1982-90; Barbara Weinstock lectureship U. Calif., Berkeley, 1994-95. Author: American Odyssey: Haitians in N.Y.C., 1984, Urban Poverty in the Caribbean, 1990, The Military and Society in Haiti, 1993, The Informal City, 1994, Diasporic Citizenship: Haitian Americans in Transitional America, 1997; co-editor Am. Anthropologist, 1990-94. Fellow Am. Anthrop. Assn.; mem. Am. Sociol. Assn. Roman Catholic. Office: U Calif Dept Anthropology Berkeley CA 94720

LAHAY, DAVID GEORGE MICHAEL, ballet company director; b. Barrie, Ont., Can., July 15, 1949; s. George Anthony and Edna Alice (Silverberg) LaH. B.A., Trent U., Peterborough, Ont., 1971; B.F.A. with honors, York U., Toronto, 1973. Prin. dancer Les Grands Ballets Canadiens, Montreal, 1978-87, asst. ballet master, 1987-91; prin. dancer Atlanta Ballet, 1978; ballet master Ottawa Ballet, 1991; ballet pedagogue, choreographer The Banff (Alta.) Ctr., 1993-96. Choreographer Canadian Heritage Festival, 1989, 90, 91, The Banff Ctr., 1993-96; balletmaster Alberta Ballet. Ont. scholar, 1968; Can Council grantee, 1973, 75, 78. Office: Alberta Ballet Nat Christie Ctr, 141 18th Ave, Calgary, AB Canada T2S 0B8

LAHEY, CAROLYN BAKER, foundation administrator, realtor; b. Corona, Calif., Sept. 4, 1953; d. Earl Ross and Mary Louise (Stanley) Baker; m. Michael J. Laurella, Mar. 4, 1973 (div. Sept. 1982); children: Jaime Ann, Samuel Earl; m. Thomas W. Lahey, Aug. 23, 1991. BS in Phys. Edn., Ariz. State U., 1981, MA in Human Rels., 1988. Lic. realtor, Ariz. Mem. faculty Rio Salado C.C., Phoenix, 1981-92; dir. Wickenburg (Ariz.) Regional Healthcare Found., 1988—; owner RE/MAX of Wickenburg, 1995—. Composer lyrics and music (song) Home Remedy, 1995; musician (mandolin and vocals) Daughters of the Purple Sage, Wickenburg, 1996. Cons. Wickenburg Bd. Edn., 1995; commr. Wickenburg Revitalization Adv. Commn., 1996. Mem. Ariz. Assn. Healthcare Philanthropy, Wickenburg Bus. and Profl. Women. Home: PO Box 408 Wickenburg AZ 85358 Office: RE/MAX of Wickenburg 186 N Tegner St Wickenburg AZ 85390

LAI, LIWEN, molecular geneticist, educator; b. Taipei, Taiwan, 1957; d. Kwan-Long Lai. BS, Nat. Taiwan U., 1980; MS, U. Calif., San Francisco, 1983; PhD, U. Tex., Dallas, 1987. Diplomate Am. Coll. Med. Genetics. Postdoctoral fellow NIH, Bethesda, Md., 1987-89; asst. rsch. sci. U. Ariz., Tuscon, 1990-94, asst. dir. Molecular Diagnostic Lab., 1992—, rsch. asst. prof., 1995—. Rsch. grantee Elks, 1994-96, Dialysis Clinic Inc., 1994-96, So. Ariz. Found., 1996—, NIH, 1997—. Mem. Am. Soc. Human Genetics, Am. Soc. Gene Therapy. Office: U Ariz Dept Pediatrics 1501 N Campbell Ave Tucson AZ 85724-0001

LAI, WAIHANG, art educator; b. Hong Kong, Jan. 7, 1939; s. Sing and Yu-ching L.; came to U.S., 1964; BA, Chinese U. Hong Kong, 1964; MA, Claremont Grad. Sch., 1967; m. Celia Cheung, Aug. 13, 1966. Asst. prof. art Maunaolu Coll., Maui, Hawaii, 1968-70; prof. art Kauai (Hawaii) Community Coll., 1970—. Vis. prof. art Ariz. State U., Tempe, summer 1967. Recipient Excellence in Teaching award U. Hawaii, 1992, Nat. Inst. Staff and Orgnl. Devel. Excellence award U. Tex., 1993. Mem. Kauai (pres. 1974—) Watercolor Socs., Phila. Watercolor Club, Hawaii Computer Art Soc., Kauai Oriental Art Soc. (pres. 1981—), AM. Watercolor Soc. Author: The Chinese Landscape Paintings of Waihang Lai, 1966, The Watercolors of Waihang Lai, 1967; illustrator: The Tao of Practice Success, 1991, Advertisements for Acupuncturists, 1992. Home: PO Box 363 Lihue HI 96766-0363 Office: Kauai Community Coll Lihue HI 96766

LAIDIG, ELDON LINDLEY, financial planner; b. Oberlin, Kans., Jan. 20, 1932; s. Ira Lawless and Minnie Lorene (Williams) L.; m. Mary Jane Urban, Feb. 13, 1953 (dec. June 1981); 1 child, Larry Wayne; m. Lois Audrey Davey Cameron, Feb. 11, 1983. BS, Ft. Hay Kans. State U., 1954, MS, U. Tex., 1960, PhD, 1967. CFP. Jr. high prin. Jefferson County Pub. Schs., Arvada, Colo., 1963-88; pvt. practice fin. planner Personal Benefit Svcs., Arvada, 1988—. Author: The Influence of Situational Factors on Administrative Behavior, 1967, An Organizational Manual, 1979; editor various local and state newsletters; contbr. fin. column Arvada Cmty. News. Bd. dirs. Highlander's Inc., Denver, 1978-83, Arvada Coun. for the Arts and Humanities, 1982, chmn., 1988-93; pres. Jefferson County Sch. Adminstrs., Lakewood, Colo., 1971-72; elder Arvada Presbyn., 1964—; v.p. Arvada Sister Cities Internat., 1992—. Named as Comdg. Officer of Outstanding Coast Guard Unit, 2nd Coast Guard Dist., 1968; recipient Disting. Svc. citation U.S. Dept. of Def., 1974, Unit citation Def. Civil Preparedness Agy., 1974, Don Kemp award for outstanding fundraising Arvada Ctr. for the Arts & Humanities, 1983. Mem. Arvada Hist. Soc. (v.p. 1983-85), Res. Officers Assn. (pres. Denver chpt. 1974, pres. Dept. of Colo., nat. councilman 1979), Arvada Sentinal and N.W. Metro C. of C. (Arvada Man of Yr. 1990), Rotary (bd. dirs. Arvada chpt. 1989-96), Friendship Force of Greater Denver (pres. 1997). Home: 7038 Ammons St Arvada CO 80004-1849 Office: Personal Benefit Svcs 5400 Ward Rd Arvada CO 80002-1819

LAIDLAW, HARRY HYDE, JR., entomology educator; b. Houston, Apr. 12, 1907; s. Harry Hyde and Elizabeth Louisa (Quinn) L.; BS, La. State U., 1933, MS, 1934; PhD (Univ. fellow, Genetics fellow, Wis. Dormitory fellow, Wis. Alumni Rsch. Found. fellow), U. Wis., 1939; m. Ruth Grant Collins, Oct. 26, 1946; 1 child, Barbara Scott Laidlaw Murphy. Teaching asst. La. State U., 1933-34, rsch. asst., 1934-35; prof. biol. sci. Oakland City (Ind.) Coll., 1939-41; state apiarist Ala. Dept. Agr. and Industries, Montgomery, 1941-42; entomologist First Army, N.Y.C., 1946-47; asst. prof. entomology, asst. apiculturist U. Calif.-Davis, 1947-53, assoc. prof. entomology, assoc. apiculturist, 1953-59, prof. entomology, apiculturist, 1959-74, asso. dean Coll. Agr., 1960-64, chair agr. faculty, staff, 1965-66, prof. entomology emeritus, apiculturist emeritus, 1974—; coord. U. Calif.-Egypt Agrl. Devel. Program, AID, 1979-83. Rockefeller Found. grantee, Brazil, 1954-55, Sudan, 1967; honored guest Tamagawa U., Tokyo, 1980. Trustee, Yolo County (Calif.) Med. Soc. Scholarship Com., 1965-83. Served to capt. AUS, 1942-46. Recipient Cert. of Merit Am. Bee Jour., 1957, Spl. Merit award U. Calif.-Davis, 1959, Merit award Calif. Central Valley Bee Club, 1974, Merit award Western Apicultural Soc., 1980, Gold Merit award Internat. Fedn. Beekeepers' Assns., 1986; recipient Disting. Svc. award Ariz. Beekeepers Assn., 1988. Cert. of Appreciation Calif. State Beekeepers' Assn., 1987, award Alan Clemson Meml. Found., 1989: NIH grantee, 1963-66; NSF grantee, 1966-74. Fellow AAAS, Entomol. Soc. Am. (honoree spl. symposium 1990, C.W. Woodworth award Pacific br. 1981); mem. Am. Inst. Biol. Scis., Am. Soc. Naturalists, Am. Soc. Integrative Biology, Nat. Assn. Uniformed Svcs., Ret. Officers Assn. (2d v.p. Sacramento chpt. 1984-86), Scabbard and Blade, Sigma Xi (treas. Davis chpt. 1959-60, v.p. chpt. 1966-67), Alpha Gamma Rho (pres. La. chpt. 1933-34, counsellor Western Province 1960-66). Democrat. Presbyterian. Author books including Instrumental Insemination of Honey Bee Queens, 1977; Contemporary Queen Rearing, 1979, Queen Rearing and Bee Breeding, 1997; author slide set: Instrumental Insemination of Queen Honey Bees, 1976. Achievements include determination of cause of failure of attempts to artificially inseminate queen honey bees; invention of instruments and procedures to consistently accomplish same; elucidation of genetic relationships of individuals of polyandrous honey bee colonies; design of genetic procedures for behavioral study and breeding of honey bees for general and specific uses. Home: 761 Sycamore Ln Davis CA 95616-3432 Office: U Calif Dept Entomology Davis CA 95616

LAIDLAW, VICTOR D., construction executive; b. 1946. Officer Moran Cons., Alhambra, Calif., 1968-88; pres. Koll Cons., 1988—. Office: Koll Cons 4343 Van Carmen Ave Newport Beach CA 92660*

LAING-MALCOLMSON, SALLY ANNE, enrolled tax agent, tax consultant; b. Seattle, Sept. 25, 1957; d. Ian Laing-Malcolmson and Frances Rutherford (Arold) Cook; children: Rhiannon Ethel Quandt, Peter Eugene Stone, Benjamin Elliott Stone. AS in Bus., SUNY, 1989. With accounts payable dept. King County Airport, Seattle, 1984-86; bookkeeper Driftmeir Architects, P.S., Kirkland, Wash., 1986; pvt. practice tax cons. Bellevue, Wash., 1987—; tax specialist Puget Sound Nat. Bank, Tacoma, 1990-92; bookkeeper Papillon, Inc.; sec. Washington State Tax Cons., Bellevue, 1991—, Am. Bus. Women's Assn., Bellevue, 1992—; tax specialist Barbara Pulley, CPA, Missoula, Mont. Newsletter editor PTA, 1991—. Mem. Pentecostal Ch. Home and Office: 3170 Kinsler Ln Stevensville MT 59870-6967

LAIRD, JOHN SCOTT, government analyst; b. Santa Rosa, Calif., Mar. 29, 1950; s. Ralph Jr. and Dorothy Jean (Ofstedahl) L. AB in Politics with honors, U. Calif., Santa Cruz, 1972; coll. fellow, Merrill Coll., 1991. Congl. asst. Rep. Jerome Waldie, Martinez, Calif., 1972-74; govt. analyst Santa Cruz Co., 1975-91, 95—; exec. dir. Santa Cruz AIDS Project, 1991-93; network developer Handsnet, Inc., Cupertino, Calif., 1993-95. Author editl. page column Santa Cruz Sentinel, 1991-93; columnist Lavendar Reader, 1986—; commentator KZSC, 1990—; contbr. chpt. to book. Mem. State Dem. Ctrl. Com., Sacramento, 1976—; dir., chair Santa Cruz Metro Transit Dist., 1981-90; dir., pres. Assn. Monterey Bay Area Govts., 1981-83, 88-90; commr., chair Santa Clara County Regional Transp. Commn., 1981-90; mayor City of Santa Cruz, 1983-84, City coun., 1981-90; presdl. elector Electoral Coll., 1992, 96; county chair Dem. party, Santa Cruz, 1994—; trustee Cabrillo Coll., Aptos, Calif., 1994—. Named Person of Yr. Santa Cruz Cunty Child Care Coun., 1988, John Laird Day, Mayor of Santa Cruz, 1984, 88. Home: 1214 King St Santa Cruz CA 95060-2417

LAIRD, MARY See WOOD, LARRY

LAIRD, WILBUR DAVID, JR., bookseller, editor; b. Kansas City, Mo., Mar. 15, 1937; s. Wilbur David and Alma Blanche (Turner) L.; children: Wendy, Cynthia, Brian Andrew, David Alexander; m. Helen M. Ingram, July 12, 1984. Student, U. Wichita, 1959-60; BA, UCLA, 1965, MLS, 1966. Reference libr. U. Calif., Davis, 1966-67; acquisitions libr. U. Utah, 1967-70, asst. dir. for tech. svcs., 1970-71, assoc. dir., 1971-72; univ. libr. U. Ariz., Tucson, 1972-90; pres. Books West S.W., Tucson, 1990—. Author: Hopi Bibliography, 1977; editor: Books of the Southwest, 1977-97. Bd. dirs. Westerners Internat., 1974-87, Tucson Civic Ballet, 1975-76, S.W. Pks. and Mon. Assn., 1993—. With USN, 1955-59. Mem. ALA, Ariz. State Libr. Assn. (pres. 1978-79), Western History Assn., Western Lit. Assn., Guild Ariz. Antiquarian Booksellers. Office: Books West Southwest Inc 14 Whitman Ct Irvine CA 92612

LAITONE, EDMUND VICTOR, mechanical engineer; b. San Francisco, Sept. 6, 1915; s. Victor S. L.; m. Dorothy Bishop, Sept. 1, 1951; children: Victoria, Jonathan A. BSME, U. Calif., Berkeley, 1938; PhD in Applied Mechanics, Stanford U., 1960. Aero. engr. Nat. Adv. Com. for Aeros., Langley Field, Va., 1938-45; sect. head, flight engr. Cornell Aero. Lab., Buffalo, 1945-47; prof. U. Calif., Berkeley, 1947—; cons. aero. engr. Hughes Aircraft & Douglas Aircraft, 1948-78; U.S. acad. rep. to flight mechanics AGARD/NATO, 1984-88; chmn. engring. dept. U. Calif. Extension, Berkeley, 1979-96. Author: Surface Waves, 1960; author, editor: Integrated Design of Advanced Fighter Aircraft, 1987; contbr. articles to Jour. Aero. Scis., Aircraft and Math. Jour. Named Miller Rsch. prof., 1960, U.S. Exch. prof., Moscow, 1964; vis. fellow Balliol Coll., 1968; vis. prof. Northwestern Poly. Inst., Xian, China, 1980. Fellow AIAA (San Francisco region chmn. 1960-61, assoc. fellow 1964-88); mem. Am. Math Soc., Am. Soc. for Engring. Edn. Home: 6915 Wilson Way El Cerrito CA 94530-1853 Office: U of Calif Dept Mech Engring Berkeley CA 94720

LAKE, DAVID S., publisher, lawyer; b. Youngstown, Ohio, July 17, 1938; s. Frank and Charlotte (Stahl) L.; m. Sandra J. Levin, Dec. 18, 1960 (div. Aug. 14, 1987); children: Joshua Seth, Jonathan Daniel. B.A. in Math, Youngstown State U., 1960; J.D. cum laude, Cleve. State U., 1965. Bar: Ohio 1965, D.C. 1970, U.S. Supreme Ct. 1969. Gen. counsel World Pub. Co., Cleve., 1965-68; dir. devel. Cath. U. Am., Washington, 1968-69; v.p., gen. counsel Microform Pub. Corp., Washington, 1969-70; dir. spl. projects Library Resources, Inc., Chgo., 1970-72; gen. mgr., partner Nat. Textbook Co., Skokie, Ill., 1972-76; pres. David S. Lake Pubs., Belmont, Calif., 1976-89, pres, owner, 1984-89; owner Lake Pub Co., Belmont, 1989—. Contbr. to: Cleve. Marshall Law Rev, 1964. Served with USMC, 1960-62. Jewish. Office: Lake Pub Co 67 W Shore Rd Belvedere CA 94920

LAKE, MOLLY ANNE, state official; b. Eureka, Calif., Feb. 26, 1957. Cert. crime scene investigator. Rsch. bibliographer UCLA, 1988-91; dep. dir. Office Gov. State Calif., L.A., 1991-95; pub. safety liaison Office Gov. State Calif., 1995—; organizer Gov.'s 1994 Crime Summit, L.A., 1994, Gov.'s Calif. Focus on Fathers Summit, Burbank, 1995; pub. safety lobbyist, 1994-96; mem. Gov.'s Econ. Red Team; lectr. Calif. State Univ., Northridge, 1996—. Author various legis. Campaign vol. 3 Strikes/1 Strike, L.A., 1994, Proposition 172 Pub. Safety, L.A., 1994; exec. v.p. SafeHaven Family Violence Shelter, Glendale, Calif., 1995—; exec. dir. juvenile impact program L.A. Police Dept., 1995—, mem. citizen police adv. bd., 1996; mem. exec. com. Citizen Police Acad., Pasadena, 1996—; commr. pub. safety, South Pasadena, 1996—; bd. dirs. Police Activities League Pasadena Police Dept., 1997. Recipient commendation South Pasadena C. of C., 1995, City of Alhambra, Calif., 1995, proclamation City of Covina, Calif., 1995, 96; Chief's Spl. award Pasadena Police Dept. Mem. Los Angeles County Police Chief's Assn. (hon.), Calif. Criminal Justice Legal Found., Calif. Gang Investigators Assn. Office: Office of Gov 16th Fl South Tower 300 S Spring St Los Angeles CA 90013

LAKE, STANLEY JAMES, security consulting company executive, motel chain executive, locksmith; b. Oklahoma City, June 3, 1926; s. Clyde Edward Lake and Helene Frances (Herndon) Hunnicut; m. Lila Marguerite Mosley, Mar 29, 1947 (div. Aug. 1952); children: Katherine, Marilyn, Stanley James II; m. Norma Jean Phelps, Jan. 21, 1960. Student, Mont. State U., 1946-48. Owner, mgr. Lake Oil Co., Glendive, Mont., 1949-53, Lake Mining Co., Salt Lake City, 1954-57, Lake Realty Co., Denver, 1958-63, Stanlake Corp., Denver, 1964—, Stanlake Luxury Budget Motels, Denver, 1979—, Lake's Security and Lock Svc., Englewood, Colo., 1979—; co-owner, instr. Colo. Karate Assn., Denver, 1965-73, 2d degree black belt. Originator modular budget motel concept, 1963. Chmn. bd. for karate Rocky Mountain region AAU, 1972-73. With USAAC, 1945-46. Recipient Presdl. award for teaching karate to disadvantaged and civic orgns., 1972, numerous others. Mem. Assn. Locksmiths Am. (cert. master locksmith), Rocky Mountain Locksmiths Assn., Japan Karate Assn. Rocky Mountain Area (chmn. bd. 1970-73), Masons, Shriners. Republican. Methodist. Home: 6026 S Elizabeth Way Littleton CO 80121-2816 Office: Lake's Security & Lock Svc 6200 S Syracuse Way Ste 125 Englewood CO 80111-4738

LA LANDE, JEFFREY MAX, historian; b. Troy, N.Y., Nov. 14, 1947; s. Albert Max and Georgia Louise (Vogel) LaL.; m. Judith Kay Vantil, Apr. 23, 1988; 1 child, Daniel Ethan. BS, Georgetown U., 1969; MA, Oreg. State U., 1981; PhD, U. Oreg., 1993. Historian and writer-editor Rogue River Nat. Forest, Medford, Oreg., 1976-79; archaeol. rsch. asst. Oreg. State U., Corvallis, 1979-80; tchg. fellow U. Oreg., Eugene, 1991-92; archaeologist U.S. Forest Svc., Medford, Oreg., 1980—; hist. rsch. cons. and writer Ashland, Oreg., 1978—; adj. prof. history So. Oreg. State Coll., Ashland, 1985—. Author: (books) First Over the Siskiyous: Peter Ogden, 1987, Medford Corporation: A History, 1979, (monograph) The Indians of Southwestern Oregon, 1991; contbr. articles to hist. jours. Trustee So. Oreg. Hist. Soc., Jacksonville, 1980-83; bd. dirs. City Hist. Commn., Ashland, 1977-79. Recipient certs. of merit USDA, 1980-92, Regional Forester's Archaeology award U.S. Forest Svc., 1994. Mem. Orgn. of Am. Historians, Pacific Coast Br./Am. Hist. Assn., Soc. for Am. Archaeology, Oreg. Hist. Soc., Wash. State Hist. Soc. (Charles Gates award 1993), Forest and Conservation History Soc. Democrat. Roman Catholic. Home: 1110 Hillview Dr Ashland OR 97520-3574 Office: US Forest Svc Rogue River PO Box 520 Medford OR 97501

LALLY, NORMA ROSS, federal agency administrator, retired; b. Crawford, Nebr., Aug. 10, 1932; d. Roy Anderson and Alma Leona (Barber) Lively; m. Robert Edward Lally, Dec. 4, 1953 (div. Mar. 1986); children: Robyn Carol Murch, Jeffrey Alan, Gregory Roy. BA, Boise (Idaho) State U., 1974, MA, 1976; postgrad., Columbia Pacific U., 1988—. With grad. admissions Boise State U., 1971-74; with officer programs USN Recruiting, Boise, 1974; pub. affairs officer IRS, Boise and Las Vegas, 1975-94; ret., 1994; speaker in field, Boise and Las Vegas, 1977—. Contbr. articles to newspapers. Mem. task force Clark County Sch. Dist., Las Vegas. Staff sgt. USAF, 1950-54. Mem. NAFE, Internat. Assn. Bus. Communicators, Women in Mil. Svc. Am., Mensa, Toastmasters (Las Vegas), Marine's Meml. Club (life), Am. Legion. Home: 3013 Hawksdale Dr Las Vegas NV 89134-8967

LA LUZERNE-OI, SALLY ANN, humanities educator; b. Green Bay, Wis., Nov. 21, 1953; d. Bernard Joseph and Bernice Lucille (Mommaerts) La L.; m. Sadaji Oi, July 25, 1987. BS in French and Spanish, U. Wis., Green Bay, 1976; MA in ESL, U. Ariz., 1983. Cert. tchr. French and Spanish, Wis. Tchr. English as Fgn. Lang./French Inst. de la Salle, Querétaro, Mexico, 1977; migrant tchr. Coop. Ednl. Svc. Agy., Hartford, Wis., 1977; instr. ESL Systran Corp., Oshkosh, Wis., 1978; tchr. French St. Joseph Acad., Green Bay, Wis., 1978-80, Colegio Internat. de Caracas, Venezuela, 1980-82; instr. English as Fgn. Lang. Interlingua Instituto de Linguas, Lagos, Portugal, 1983-84, Trident Coll., Nagoya, Japan, 1984-87; ESL instr., asst. coord. spl. English programs U. Hawaii, Manoa, 1988; instr. ESL, French Hawaii Pacific U., Honolulu, 1989—; tchr. trainer, Ukraine, summers 1994, 95, 96; conf. presenter Kyoto, Japan, Nagoya, Japan, Honolulu, Hong Kong, Long Beach, Calif., Odessa, Ukraine. Author: (with Cynthia McKeag Tsukamoto) (text) Tell Me About It!, (instrs. manual) Tell Me About It!, (Cassette) Tell Me About It!, 1993. Lectr. Sacred Heart Parish, Honolulu, 1992-95. Recipient Profl. Devel. Funding award Hawaii Pacific U., Honolulu, 1993, 95; Fulbright scholar Ukraine, 1995-96. Mem. TESOL, Hawaii TESOL, Hawaii Coun. Tchrs. English, Hawaii Assn. Lang. Tchrs. Roman Catholic. Office: Hawaii Pacific U 1188 Fort Street Mall Honolulu HI 96813-2713

LAM, CHEUNG-WEI, electrical engineer; b. Hong Kong, Mar. 5, 1965; came to U.S., 1987; s. Yeung-Tak and Sau-Jin (Wong) L.; m. Hoi-Man Sarah Hui, May 29, 1993; 1 child, Isaac Samuel. BS, Chinese U. Hong Kong, 1987; MS, MIT, 1989, PhD, 1993. Rsch. asst. MIT, Cambridge, 1988-93; rschr. Schlumberger-Doll Rsch, Ridgefield, Conn., 1990; mem. tech. staff Quad Design Tech., Camarillo, Calif., 1993—; mem. com. Soc. Automotive Engrs./Electromagnetic Compatibility Modeling Task Force, 1994—. Contbr. articles to Jour. Superconductivity, IEEE, Jour. Electromagnetic Waves and Applications. Bank of Am. scholar, 1985, Du Pont scholar, 1986. Mem. IEEE (prize 1987), Sigma Xi. Home: 1395 La Culebra Cir Camarillo CA 93012-5551 Office: Quad Design Tech 1385 Del Norte Rd Camarillo CA 93010-8437

LAM, KIT SANG, medical educator; b. Hong Kong, Jan. 10, 1954; came to U.S., 1972; s. Kang To Lam and Chuen Fong But; m. Bonita M.S. Soohoo; 1 child, Reina Y.H. BA in Microbiology, U. Tex., 1975; PhD in Oncology, U. Wis., 1980; MD, Stanford U., 1984. Intern in internal medicine U. Ariz., Tucson, 1984-85, resident in internal medicine, 1985-87, fellow in med. oncology, 1987-89, asst. prof. medicine, 1989-94; assoc. prof., 1994—; founding scientist Selectide Corp., Tucson, 1990, chief cons. scientist, 1990—. Leukemia spl. fellow Leukemia Soc. Am., 1989-92, leukemia scholar, 1992—. Mem. AAAS, Am. Assn. Cancer Rsch., Am. Chem. Soc., Am. Peptide Soc., Am. Soc. Clin. Oncology, Soc. Chinese Bioscientists in Am. Office: Ariz Cancer Ctr 1501 N Campbell Ave Tucson AZ 85724-0001

LAM, LUI, physicist; b. Lianxian, China, Nov. 17, 1944; came to U.S., 1966; s. Lap-Chung and Lai-Jane (Wong) L.; m. Heung-Mee Lee, July 1, 1972; 1 child, Charlene. B.S., U. Hong Kong, 1965; M.S., U. of B.C., 1968; M.A., Columbia U., 1969, Ph.D., 1973. Research assoc. City Coll. CUNY, 1972-75; research scientist U. Instelling Antwerpen, Belgium, 1975-76, U. Saarlandes, Saarbrucken, Fed. Republic Germany, 1976-77; assoc. research prof. Inst. Physics, Academia Sinica, Beijing, China, 1978-83, adj. prof., 1984—, City Coll.; assoc. prof. Queensborough Community Coll., CUNY, 1984-87; prof., San Jose State U., 1987—; founder, co-editor Springer Series on Partially Ordered Systems, 1987—, Woodward Conf. Series, 1988—; elected mem. planning and steering com. Internat. Liquid Crystal Conf., 1984-90. Editor and co-editor: Wave Phenomena, 1989, Nonlinear Structures in Physical Systems, 1990, Solitons in Liquid Crystals, 1992, Modeling Complex Phenomena, 1992, Liquid Crystalline and Mesomorphic Polymers, 1994, Novel Laser Sources and Applications, 1994, Nonlinear Physics for Beginners, 1997, Introduction to Nonlinear Physics, 1997; assoc. editor Jour. Molecular Crystal and Liquid Crystals, 1981-93; editorial mem. Liquid Crystals, 1986-90. Li Po Kwai scholar U. Hong Kong, 1963-65; Eugene Higgins fellow Columbia U., 1966-67, Nordita fellow, 1976. Mem. Am. Phys. Soc., Internat. Liquid Crystal Soc. (founder, bd. dir., chmn. conf. com. 1990-94). Office: San Jose State U Dept Physics San Jose CA 95192-0106

LAMAR, SHARON ANN, special and gifted education educator, consultant; b. Mattoon, Ill., Mar. 19, 1953; d. Ambrose B. and Stella (Deters) Probst; m. Steve E. Lamar, June 5, 1976; children: Annie, Lucas,. BS in Edn., Ea. Ill. U., Charleston, 1974; MA in Edn., Murray (Ky.) State U., 1980. Chpt. I reading tchr. Rosiclare (Ill.) High Sch., 1975-76, Hellgate High Sch., Missoula, Mont., 1976-78; elem. classroom tchr. Swan Valley Elem. Sch., Condon, Mont., 1978-79; spl. edn. tchr. Missoula Spl. Edn. Coop., Missoula, Mont., 1982-93; gifted edn. tchr. Swan Valley Elem. Sch., Condon, Mont., 1986-93; spl. edn. tchr. Bigfork Elem. Sch., 1993—, gifted edn. facilitator, 1994—; chairperson Swan Valley Gifted/Talented Adv. Com., Condon, Mont., 1986-93; mem. Bd. Dir. Mont. Future Problem Solving Program, Butte, 1990—; Nat. and State Evaluator Future Problem Solving Program, Butte, Mont., 1989—; mem. Bigfork Elem. Adn. Coun. Mem. Swan Valley Hist. Soc., Condon. Mont., 1989; wilderness walks leader Mont. Wilderness Assn., 1990; mem. Swan Valley Earth Day Com., 1990; recorder Swan Valley Citizen's Com., 1990; mem. Swan Valley Prforming Arts Com., 1989; mgmt. com. Swan Valley Linkage Zone, 1994—. Recipient Project Excellence in the Dissemination of Gifted Edn., Mont. Assn. Gifted and Talented Edn., 1990. Mem. Mont. Edn. Assn., Mont. Assn. Gifted and Talented Edn. (bd. dirs.), Coun. for Exceptional Children, Swan Valley Tchr.'s Assn. (pres. 1993). Office: Bigfork Elem School PO Box 188 Bigfork MT 59911

LAMB, BERTON LEE, II, policy analyst, researcher; b. Torrance, Calif., July 4, 1945; s. Berton Lee and Phyllis Jean (Schultz) L.; m. Susan Elizabeth Snow, June 22, 1968; 1 child, Kara Lee. BA, Calif. Luth. U., 1967; MA in Internat. Polits., San Francisco State U., 1970; PhD in Polit. Sci., Wash. State U., 1976. Instr. polit. sci. George Fox Coll., Newberg, Oreg., 1969-72; rsch. asst. Water Rsch. Ctr. Wash. State U., Pullman, 1974-75; asst. prof. polit. sci. Ea. Ky. U., Richmond, 1975-76; water res. policy specialist U.S. Fish and Wildlife Svc., Ft. Collins, Colo., 1976-79, policy analyst Nat. Ecology Rsch. Ctr., 1979-86, leader water resources analysis sect., Nat. Ecology Rsch. Ctr., 1986-90; project leader Nat. Ecology Rsch. Ctr., Ft. Collins, Colo., 1990-93; sect. leader Midcontinent Ecol. Sci. Ctr. Nat. Biol. Svc., Ft. Collins, 1993-96, US Geol. Svc., Ft. Collins, 1996—. Editor: Water Quality Administration, 1980; co-editor: Water Resources Administration. Symposium in Public Administration Review, 1976; bd. editors P.A. Times, 1988-91, Soc. and Natural Resources, 1995—; author chpts. in Instream Flow Protection in the West, 2d edit., 1993, Inland Fisheries Management, 1993, At the Nexus: Science Policy, 1996, Global Environmental Policy and Administration, 1997; contbr. articles to profl. jours. Pres. Trinity Luth. Ch. Coun., Ft. Collins, 1981-82. Future faculty fellow Am. Luth. Ch., 1973; faculty devel. grantee George Fox Coll., 1972; scholar, diplomat Internat. Studies Assn.-Dept. of State, 1973; rsch. fellow Nat. Resources Law Ctr., Sch. of Law, U. Colo., 1990. Mem. Am. Soc. Pub. Administrn. Western Social Sci. Assn. (exec. coun. 1989-92, pres.-elect 1995-96, pres. 1996—), Western Polit. Sci. Assn., Glacier View Meadows Road and Recreation Assn. (bd. dirs. 1995—). Lutheran. Office: US Geol Svc Midcontinent Ecol Sci Ctr 4512 Mcmurray Ave Fort Collins CO 80525-3400

LAMB, DARLIS CAROL, sculptor; b. Wausa, Nebr.; d. Lindor Soren and June Berniece (Skalberg) Nelson; m. James Robert Lamb; children: Sherry Lamb Sobh, Michael, Mitchell. BA in Fine Arts, Columbia Pacific U., San Rafael, Calif., 1988; MA in Fine Arts, Columbia Pacific U., 1989. Exhibited in group shows at Nat. Arts Club, N.Y.C., 1983, 85, 89, 91, 92, 93, 95, 96 (Catherine Lorillard Wolfe award sculpture 1983, C.L. Wolfe Horse's Head award 1994, Anna Hyatt Huntington cash award 1995, honorable mention 1996), N.Am. Sculpture Exhibit, Foothills Art Ctr., Golden, Colo., 1983-84, 86-87, 90-91 (Pub. Svc. Co. of Colo. sculpture award 1990), Nat. Acad. of Design, 1986, Nat. Sculpture Soc., 1985, 91, 95 (C. Percival Dietch Sculpture prize 1991), Loveland Mus. and Gallery, 1990-91, Audubon Artists, 1991, Allied Artists Am., 1992, 95, Pen and Brush, 1993, 95-96 (Roman Bronze award 1995), Colorado Springs Fine Arts Mus., 1996, others; represented in permanent collections in Nebr. Hist. Soc., Am. Lung Assn. of Colo., Benson Park Sculpture Garden, Loveland, U.S. Space Found., others. Mem. Catherine Lorillard Wolfe Art Club, N.Am. Sculpture Soc. Office: PO Box 9043 Englewood CO 80111-0301

LAMB, ELIZABETH SEARLE, freelance writer, poet; b. Topeka, Jan. 22, 1917; d. Howard Sanford and Helen Baker (Shaver) Searle; m. F. Bruce Lamb, Dec. 11 1941 (dec. Dec. 1992); 1 child, Carolyn. BA, U. Kans., Lawrence, 1939, BMus, 1940. Canon City corr. Pueblo (Colo.) Chieftan, 1957-59; editor Frogpond: Quar. Haiku Jour./Haiku Soc. Am., N.Y.C., 1984-91, 94. Author: Today and Every Day, 1970, in this blaze of sun, 1975, Picasso's Bust of Sylvette, 1977 (HSA Merit Book award), 39 Blossoms, 1982 (HSA Merit Book award), Casting into a Cloud: Southwest Haiku, 1985 (HSA Merit Book award), Lines for my mothr, dying, 1988, (in Chinese) The Light of Elizabeth Lamb: 100 American Haiku, 1993, (juvenile book) Inside Me, Outside Me, 1974; assoc. editor Haiku S.W., Santa Fe, 1993; poems printed in more than 30 anthologies; haiku and longer poems pub. in more than 250 mags. and newspapers in Can., Eng., New Zealand, Australia, Japan, China, Germany, Poland, Romania; contbr. critical essays and book revs. to haiku mags. Bd. dirs. Pub. Libr., Canon City, 1957-58; sec. Friends of the Pub. Libr., Santa Fe, 1979-82; 1st hon. curator Am. Haiku Archive, Calif. State Libr., Sacramento, 1996. Recipient 2d place award Ruben Dario Meml. Poetry Contest, OAS, 1967, awards Nat. League Am. Pen Women, Haiku Soc. Am., Mus. Haiku Lit., Tokyo, Mainichi Daily News, Tokyo, Poetry Soc. Japan, numerous others. Mem. Haiku Soc. Am. (pres. 1971), Poetry Soc. Am., Haiku Internat. Assn. (Japan), Assn. Internat. Renku (Japan), Haiku Can. Democrat. Christian. Home: 970 Acequia Madre Santa Fe NM 87501

LAMB, H. RICHARD, psychiatry educator; b. Phila., Sept. 18, 1929; s. Julius R. and Lillian (Beerman) L.; m. Doris Murial Koehn, Feb. 10, 1969; children: Jonathan Howard, Carolyn Elizabeth, Thomas Warren. BA, U. Pa., 1950; MD, Yale U., 1954. Diplomate Am. Bd. Psychiatry and Neurology. Chief rehab. svcs. San Mateo (Calif.) County Mental Health Svcs., 1960-76; prof. psychiatry U. So. Calif. Sch. Medicine, L.A., 1976—; vis. prof. U. Wales, Coll. Medicine, Cardiff, 1991; chmn. Hosp. & Cmty. Psychiatry Inst. Program Planning Com., 1990—. Editor: New Directions for Mental Health Services, 1979—; mem. editl. bd.: Hosp. & Cmty. Psychiatry, 1981-90, 96—, Psychosocial Rehab. Jour., 1982—, Internat. Jour. Social Psychiatry, 1988—; author 6 books; contbr. chpts. to books, articles to profl. jours. Capt. U.S. Army, 1958-60. Named Exemplary Psychiatrist, Nat. Alliance for Mentally Ill, 1992. Fellow Am. Psychiat. Assn. (chmn. task force on homeless mentally ill 1983-84, Presdl. Commendation 1985, coun. on psychiat. svcs. 1996—), Am. Coll. Psychiatrists. Office: U So Calif Dept Psychiatry 1934 Hospital Pl Los Angeles CA 90033-1071

LAMB, PHILIP, museum administrator. Pres. Pacific Northwest Mus. of Natural History, Ashland, Oreg. Office: Pacific Northwest Mus Natural History 1500 E Main St Ashland OR 97520*

LAMB, RONALD ALFRED, editor; b. Seattle, Mar. 17, 1948; s. Lowell Rendall and Esther Irene (Fischer) L.; m. Nancy Sandine, Apr. 20, 1973; children: Braden Daniel, Kirsten Marie. AA, Highline Coll., 1968; BA, U. Wash., 1970. Sports writer Federal Way/Des Moines (Wash.) News, 1972-74; sports writer Skagit Valley Herald, Mt. Vernon, Wash., 1975-77, reporter, 1977-79; reporter Bremerton (Wash.) Sun, 1979-84; editor Microsoft Press, Bellevue and Redmond, Wash., 1984—. Editor: Command Performance: Microsoft Excel, 1986 (Achievement award Puget Sound chpt. Soc. Tech. Comm. 1986), Computer Lib/Dream Machines, 1987 (Non-fiction Computer Book of Yr. award Computer Press Assn. 1988), Variations in C, 2d edit., 1989 (Merit award Puget Sound chpt. Soc. Tech. Comm. 1989), Inside OLE 2, 1994 (Merit award Puget Sound chpt. Soc. Tech. Comm. 1994), Word 6 for Windows Companion, 1994 (Excellence award Puget Sound chpt. Soc. Tech. Comm. 1994), The Ultimate Windows 95 Book, 1995 (Disting. award Puget Sound Chpt. Soc. Tech. Comm. 1995-96, Achievement award Internat. Tech. Pubs. Competition 1996; Official Microsoft Internet Explorer Book, 1996 (Merit award Puget Sound chpt. Soc. Tech. Comm. 1996-97); contbg. author: Tukwila: Community at the Crossroads, 1991 (1st place non-fiction books history Wash. Press Assn., 1992). Del. to state conv. Wash. State Dem. Party, Tacoma, 1984; sec. South Ctrl. Schs. Adv. Coun., Tukwila, 1987-88; mem. Foster Friends of Libr., Tukwila, 1988—; chmn. South Ctrl. 2000 Com., Tukwila, 1987-89, Foster Annexation Com., Tukwila, 1988-89; bd. dirs. South Ctrl. Sch. Dist., Tukwila, 1989-93, chmn. bd. dirs., 1991-93. Mem. Soc. Profl. Journalists, King County Dirs. Assn. (bd. dirs. 1992-93), Wash. State Sch. Dirs. Assn. (urban schs. com. 1993). Democrat. Home: 4251 S 139th St Tukwila WA 98168-3260 Office: Microsoft Press 1 Microsoft Way Redmond WA 98052-8300

LAMB, WILLIS EUGENE, JR., physicist, educator; b. L.A., July 12, 1913; s. Willis Eugene and Marie Helen (Metcalf) L.; m. Ursula Schaefer, June 5, 1939 (dec. Aug. 1996); m. Bruria Kaufman, Nov. 29, 1996. BS, U. Calif., 1934, PhD, 1938; DSc (hon.), U. Pa., 1953, Gustavus Adolphus Coll., 1975, Columbia U., 1990; MA (hon.), Oxford (Eng.) U., 1956, Yale, 1961; LHD (hon.), Yeshiva U., 1965. Mem. faculty Columbia U., 1938-52, prof. physics, 1948-52; prof. physics Stanford U., 1951-56; Wykeham prof. physics and fellow New Coll., Oxford U., 1956-62; Henry Ford 2d prof. physics Yale U., 1962-72, J. Willard Gibbs prof. physics, 1972-74; prof. physics and optical scis. U. Ariz., Tucson, 1974—, Regents prof., 1990—; Morris Loeb lectr. Harvard U., 1953-54; Gordon Shrum lectr. Simon Fraser U., 1972; cons. Philips Labs., Bell Telephone Labs., Perkin-Elmer, NASA; vis. com. Brookhaven Nat. Lab. Recipient (with P. Kusch) Nobel prize in physics, 1955, Rumford premium Am. Acad. Arts and Scis., 1953; award Rsch. Corp., 1954, Yeshiva award, 1962; Guggenheim fellow, 1960-61, sr. Alexander von Humboldt fellow, 1992-94. Fellow Am. Phys. Soc., N.Y. Acad. Scis.; hon. fellow Inst. Physics and Phys. Soc. (Guthrie lectr. 1958), Royal Soc. Edinburgh (fgn. mem.); mem. Nat. Acad. Scis., Phi Beta Kappa, Sigma Xi. Office: U Ariz Optical Scis Ctr PO Box 210094 Tucson AZ 85721-0094

LAMBERT, KATHY L., elementary educator, legislator; b. Calif., Feb. 24, 1953; d. Andrew M. and Jacqueline V. Kristensen; m. D. Lambert. AA, Coll. of Marin, Kentfield, Calif., 1975; BA, U. Wash., 1984; postgrad., Seattle Pacific U. Cert. tchr., Wash. Officer Bank of Am., Petaluma, Calif., 1972-75, 80-82; store owner Petaluma, 1975-79; tchr. Monroe (Wash.) Pub. Schs., 1985—; legislator Ho. of Reps., Olympia, Wash., 1995—, asst. majority floor leader, 1995—; mem. law and justice com. Am. Legis. Exch. Coun., 1995—. Author: (Life of) Martin Luther King, Jr., 1993. Bd. dirs. Multi-Svcs. Ctr. East King County, Redmond; mem. indigent def. and pension policy com. Olympia, 1995-97; precinct officer, area chairperson 45th Dist. Rep. Party, 1993-95; co-counselor Marriage Enrichment seminars; counseling staff mem. Residential Drug Treatment Ctr.; advisor At-Risk Youth Program; participant Redmond Forum; active PTA; merit badge counselor Boy Scout Am.; mem. Redmond Blockwatch; scorekeeper Redmond Little League, Hawks Football League, numerous others. Named Profl. of the Yr., Family Law sect. Wash. Bar assn., 1996. Home: PO Box 1138 Woodinville WA 98072 Office: House of Representatives 428 John L O'Brien Bldg Olympia WA 98504

LAMBERT, LINDA LOU, educator; b. Chgo., June 19; d. John William and Lucretia Mae (Lashmet) Todd; m. James L. Green, Dec. 20, 1959 (div. Dec. 1980); children: April R. Smock, Tod Taylor; m. Morgan D. Lambert, Aug. 22, 1981. BA, Washburn U., 1966; EdD, U. San Francisco, 1984. Social worker City of Kansas City and City of Topeka, 1964-66; tchr. various schs., 1967-76; prin. Novato (Calif.) Unified Schs., 1980-84; dir. Marin County Office of Edn., San Rafael, Calif., 1984-87; prof. ednl. leadership Calif. State U., Hayward, 1987—; staff devel. expert, cons. Ministry of Edn., Cairo, Egypt, 1989-91; dir., chair Ctr. for Ednl. Leadership, Hayward, 1991—. Lead author: The Constructivist Leader, 1995, Who Will Save Our Schools?, 1996; contbr. chpts. to books and articles to profl. jours. Rep. USAID/Mexican Govt., 1992, 95; mem. Oakland (Calif.) Mayor's Edn. Cabinet, 1996—. Hewlett Found. grantee, Palo Alto, Calif., 1995-96. Mem. Assn. Calif. Schs. (assoc.), Calif. Collaborative for Edn. (co-chair 1994—). Democrat. Office: Calif State Univ Dept Education Hayward CA 94542-3080

LAMBERT, THOMAS P., lawyer; b. Kankakee, Ill., Oct. 14, 1946. BA, Loyola U., L.A., 1968; JD, UCLA, 1971. Bar: Calif. 1971. Atty. Mitchell, Silberberg & Knupp, L.A. Note and comment editor UCLA Law Rev., 1970-71. Mem. ABA (antitrust law sect., litigation sect.), State Bar Calif., Beverly Hills Bar Assn., L.A. County Bar Assn. Office: Mitchell Silberberg & Knupp 11377 W Olympic Blvd Los Angeles CA 90064-1625

LAMBERT, WILLIAM JESSE, III, writer; b. Spokane, Wash., May 22, 1942; s. William Jesse Jr. and Olive Nellie Mae (Brown) L. BA in Bus. Adminstrn., Wash. State U., 1964. Free-lance writer Spokane, Wash., 1965—. Author: Adonis, 1969, Adonis at Actum, 1970, Adonis at Bomasa, 1970, Five Roads to Tlen, 1970, Maneaters of Malibu, 1971, Their Husbands are at War, 1971, Starship Intercourse, 1971, Faculty Wife, 1971, Too Beautiful, 1972, Big Guns, 1972, Sex Intrigue, 1972, Dog-Collar Boys, 1972, Male Sex Idol, 1972, The Erection, 1972, Blackballed, 1972, Mountain Men, 1972, Joint Hunger, 1973, Making the Jock, 1973, E-Mission, 1974, Beat the Man Down, 1975, Bugger Boy, 1975, Trucker Sucker, 1975, Stud Maker, 1975, Bondage Boy, 1976, Leather Bound, 1976, Brother in Bondage, 1976, B&D Boys, 1976, Strung and Hung, 1976, Boy in Bondage, 1977, Hotel Hustlers, 1977, The Secret of the Phallic Stone, 1977, In the Hole, 1977, Animal Man, 1978, Incestuous Summer, 1978, Lessons for Mother, 1978, The Gang-Ravaged Teacher, 1978, Love's Courage, 1979, Hung Father, 1979, Oil-Rig Boys, 1979, Enlisted Man, 1979, Love's Emerald Flame, 1980, Vanessa in White Marble, 1980, House of Brave Bulls, 1980, The Last Galaxy Game, 1980, Voyage of the Trigon, 1981, The Galactic Arena, 1981, Michael: The Master, 1981, Well-Hung Hustler, 1981, Heavy Cruisers, 1982, Masters and Slaves, 1982, In Stocks and Bondage, 1982, Golden Shower Slave, 1982, Love's Golden Spell, 1983, Emerald-Silk Intrigue, 1987, Jungle-Quest Intrique, 1987, Moon-Stone Intrigue, 1988, numerous others; contbr. articles to various publs. With U.S. Army, 1964-67. Mem. Northwest Playwrights Guild.

LAMBERTI, JOHN JOSEPH, cardiovascular surgeon; b. Yonkers, N.Y., Jan. 4, 1942; s. John Joseph and Gertrude Margaret (Dean) L.; m. Maureen Estelle McCarthy, June 17, 1967 (div. Dec. 1989); children: Andrea, Amy. BS, Mass. Inst. Tech., 1963; MD, U. Pitts., 1967. Diplomate Am. Bd. Surgery, Am. Bd. Thoracic Surgery. Surgical intern Peter Bent Brigham Hosp., Boston, 1967-68, surgical resident, 1968-72, chief resident cardiac and thoracic surgery, 1972-73; chief resident cardiac surgery Children's Hosp. Medical Ctr., Boston, 1973; asst. in surgery Peter Bent Brigham Hosp., 1973-74, jr. assoc. in surgery, 1974; instr. in surgery Harvard Medical Sch., Boston, 1974; asst. prof. surgery The Univ. Chgo., 1974-77, assoc. prof. surgery, 1977-78; assoc. clinical prof. cardiothoracic surgery U. Calif., San Diego, 1980; dir. cardiovascular surgery Children's Hosp. and Health Ctr., San Diego, 1981-88, 90-95, chmn. dept. surgery, 1989-95, dir. cardiovascular inst., 1990—; attending physician Donald N. Sharp Meml. Hosp., Children's Hosp. and Health Ctr., Scripps Clinic and Rsch. Found., 1978—. Contbr. numerous articles to profl. jours. Actice Am. Heart Assn. Recipient Pa. Heart Assn. Rsch. award, 1967. Fellow Am. Coll. Surgeons, Am. Coll. Cardiology, Am. Coll. Chest Physicians; mem. Assn. Acad. Surgery, Am. Fedn. Clinical Rsch., Soc. Thoracic Surgeons, Am. Soc. Artificial Internal Organs, Am. Assn. Thoracic Surgery, Western Thoracic Surgical Soc., Pacific Coast Surgical Soc., Calif. Soc. Pediatric Cardiology. Office: 3030 Childrens Way Ste 310 San Diego CA 92123-4228

LAMBORN, W. JOHN, bank executive; b. Ithaca, N.Y., Oct. 28, 1945; s. Ellis W. and Ruth A. (Dutson) L.; m. Sara A. Wilhelm Smith, June 1968 (div. 1976); children: Michael, Scott; m. Kathryn A. Bramble, Jan. 27, 1978; 1 child, Chad. BS in Econs. magna cum laude, U. Utah, 1970. Cert. Trust and Fin. Advisor, Inst. Cert. Bankers, 1992; Trust Cert., Pacific Coast Banking Sch., U. Washington, 1977. V.p. and trust officer, trust divsn. First Security Bank, Salt Lake City, 1971-87, v.p. and mgr., charitable trusts and founds. dept., 1987—; trustee, treas. Salt Lake Acting Co., Salt Lake City, 1990—, Utah Children, Salt Lake City, 1992—; trustee, co-founder Utah Planned Giving Round Table, Salt Lake City, 1992—; bd. mgrs. Dee Founds., Salt Lake City, 1990—. Author Planned Giving Concept, Utah Planned Giving Roundtable, 1996, spkr. 1994-96. Trustee com. Salt Lake (City) Found., 1986—; advisor legacy commn. Am. Cancer Soc., Salt Lake City, 1992-94; dir., chair Salt Lake Exch. Club Found., 1988—; advisor critical issues, Salt Lake City C. of C., 1990—. Mem. Amateur Trapshooting Assn. (Champion 1988), Eaglewood Golf Club Men's Assn. Office: First Security Bank 61 S Main St Salt Lake City UT 84111-1909

LAMBRECHT, FRANK LAURENT, medical entomologist, parasitology researcher; b. Glamorgan, Wales, Aug. 30, 1915; came to U.S., 1959; s. Franciscus Josephus and Maria Theresa (Vroome) L.; m. Dora Johanna Mangin, Nov. 22, 1938; children: Winifred, Jessica, Richard. BA in Chemistry, Tech. Coll., Antwerp, Belgium, 1932; diploma in tropical medicine and hygiene, Inst. Tropical Medicine, Antwerp, 1943; MA in Biology, U. San Francisco, 1964. Rsch. chemist J. Thienpont Chems., Antwerp, 1933-41, Inst. Tropical Medicine, Antwerp, 1942-45; health officer Congo Red Cross, Pawa, Belgian Congo, 1945-49; rschr. Inst. Sci. Rsch. Ctrl. Africa, Belgian Congo, 1949-59; assoc. rschr., prof. U. Calif., San Francisco, 1960-66; scientist, biologist WHO, Africa, 1966-76; prof. U. Ariz., Tucson, 1970-78; prin. rschr. Internat. Ctr. Insect Physiology & Ecology, Kenya, 1978-80; rsch. assoc. U. Calif., Irvine and Santa Barbara, 1985-93, rsch. assoc. emeritus, 1993—. Author: Where the Mopane Bloom, 1991, In the Shade of an Acacia Tree, 1992, PAWA: A Memoir from the Belgian Congo, 1994; contbr. articles to profl. jours. With inf. Belgian Army, 1935-36. Grantee Nat. Geog. Soc., 1981. Home: 333 Old Mill Rd 80 Santa Barbara CA 93110 Office: U Calif Dept Biol Scis Santa Barbara CA 93106

LAMEIRO, GERARD FRANCIS, research institute director; b. Paterson, N.J., Oct. 3, 1949; s. Frank Raymond and Beatrice Cecilia (Donley) L.; BS, Colo. State U., 1971, MS, 1973, PhD, 1977. Sr. scientist Solar Energy Rsch. Inst., Golden, Colo., 1977-78; asst. prof. mgmt. sci. and info. systems Colo. State U., Fort Collins, 1978-83, mem. editorial bd. energy engring., 1978-82, editorial bd. energy econs. policy and mgmt., 1981-82, lectr. dept. computer sci., 1983, lectr. dept. mgmt., 1983; pres. Successful Automated Office Systems, Inc., Fort Collins, 1982-84; product mgr. Hewlett Packard, 1984-88; computer networking cons., 1988-89, Ft. Collins.; mem. editorial bd. The HP Chronicle, 1986-88, columnist, 1988, mgmt. strategist, 1988-91; dir. Lameiro Rsch. Inst., 1991—, sr. rsch. fellow, dir., 1993—; mkt. developer Hewlett-Packard Co., 1996—. Author: Campaign Code of Ethics, 1988, Ten Laws for Winning Presidential Elections, 1992, Ten Laws for Creating Wealthy Nations, 1994; mem. editorial bd. Hp Chronicle, 1986-88, Energy Engring., Policy and Mgmt., 1981-82, Energy Engring., 1978-82; developer LRI Presdl. Electoral Outlook Model, 1992, LRI Gold Model for Projecting Presdl. Elections, 1996. Mem. Presdl. Electoral Coll., 1980. Recipient nat. Disting. Svc. award Assn. Energy Engrs., 1981, Honors Prof. award Colo. State U., 1982; Colo. Energy Rsch. Inst. fellow 1976; NSF Postdoctoral fellow 1977. Mem. Assn. for Computing Machinery, Assn. Energy Engrs. (pres. 1980, Nat. Distinguish Service award 1981, internat. bd. dirs. 1980-81), Am. Mgmt. Assn., Am. Soc. for Tng. and Devel., Am. Mktg. Assn. (exec.), Am. Soc. For Quality Control, IEEE Computer Soc., Inst. Indsl. Engrs., U.S. C. of C., Crystal Cathedral Golden Eagles Club, The Heritage Found., Sigma Xi, Phi Kappa Phi, Beta Gamma Sigma, Kappa Mu Epsilon. Roman Catholic. Author: Ten Laws for Winning Presidential Elections, 1992, Campaign Code of Ethics, 1988, Ten Laws for Creating Wealthy Nations, 1994; contbr. articles in mgmt. and tech. areas to profl. jours. Home: PO Box 9580 Fort Collins CO 80525-0500 Office: 3313 Downing Ct Fort Collins CO 80526-2315

LAMENDOLA, WALTER FRANKLIN, human services, information technology consultant; b. Donora, Pa., Jan. 29, 1943. BA in English, St. Vincent Coll., 1964; MSWin Community Orgn., U. Pitts., 1966; diploma in Sociology and Social Welfare, U. Stockholm, 1970; PhD in Social Work, U. Minn., 1976. Cmty. svcs. dir. Ariz. tng. programs State Dept. Mental Retardation, Tucson, 1970-73; assoc. prof. social welfare adminstrn. Fla. State U., 1976-77; pres., CEO Minn. Rsch. and Tech., Inc., 1977-81; assoc. prof., dir. Allied Health Computer Lab. East Carolina U., 1981-84; prof., dir. info. tech. ctr. Grad. Sch. Social Work U. Denver, 1984-87; cons. info. tech., rsch. human svcs., 1987-90; v.p. rsch. Colo. Trust, Denver, 1990-93, info. tech. and rsch. cons., 1993—; cons. European Network Info. Tech. & Human Svcs.; mem. rebldg. cmtys. initiative PODER project Casey Found., 1996-97; mem. adv. bd. ctr. human svcs. U. Southampton, Brit. Rsch. Coun. Univs., Human Svc. Info. Tech. Applications, CREON Found., The Netherlands; lectr. conf., symposia, univs. U.S., Europe; mem. nat. adv. bd. Native Elder Health Resource Ctr., 1994-96; co-founder Denver Free Net, 1993—; info. tech. cons. Healthy Nations Program Robert Wood Johnson Found, 1993-96; evaluator Nat. Libr. Rsch. Program, Access Colo. grant, 1994, Nat. Info. Infrastructure grant Colo. State Libr.; cons. set up on the Internet for U.S. Cts.-Ct. for Mental Health Svcs., NIH, Frontier Mental Health Svcs. Network grant; collaborating investigator SBIR award Computerized Advance Directives, tech. plan San Mateo County and Seattle Dist. Cts.; keynote spkr. conf. Human Svc. Info. Tech. Applications, Finland, 1996. Co-author: Choices for Colorado's Future, 1993, The Integrity of Intelligence: A Bill of Rights for the Information Age, 1992, Choices for Colorado's Future: Executive Summary, 1991, Choices for Colorado's Future: Regional Summaries, 1991; co-editor: A Casebook of Computer Applications in Health and Social Services, 1989; contbr. numerous articles to profl. jours. Capt. U.S. Army, 1966-69. Recipient Innovative Computer Application award Internat. Fedn. Info. Processing Socs., 1979; Nat. Lib. Rsch. Evaluator grantee, Colo., 1994—, Nat. Info. Infrastructure grantee Dept. Edn., State Libr. and Adult Literacy, 1994-95; Funds & Couns. Tng. scholar United Way Am., 1964-66, Donaldson Fund scholar, 1965-66, NIMH scholar, 1964-66, 73-76, St. Vincent Coll. Benedictine Soc. scholar, 1963-64; vis. fellow U. Southampton. Office: 4098 Field Dr Wheat Ridge CO 80033-4358

LAMM, JULE DAVID, optometrist; b. L.A.; s. Joseph and Rose Lilly (Dachis) L.; m. Judy A. Bernstein, Dec. 15, 1956; children: Randy J., Brett K., Wendy S. AA, UCLA, 1946; BS, OD, No. Ill. Coll. Optometry, Chgo., 1950. Lic. optometrist. Optometrist L.A., 1950—. V.p., bd. mem. Venice Family Clinic, 1950—; chmn. Citizens Transp. Commn., L.A., 1967-73; long range planning com. City of Santa Monica, Calif., 1976; chmn. Airport Commn., Santa Monica, 1988—. 1st lt. USAAF, 1943-46. Named Citizen of Yr. Brentwood Chamber and City Coun., L.A., 1992. Mem. Los Angeles County Optometric Assn. (pres. 1950-64, Rotary (bd. dirs. Brentwood 1986—), Liga. Home: 212 16th St Santa Monica CA 90402-2216

LAMONA, THOMAS ADRIAN, consulting engineer; b. L.A., Aug. 19, 1925; s. Thomas Adrian and Joy A. (Kirkman) L.; m. Jeanne Muse, May 21, 1953 (div. 1958); m. Joyce Maurer, Dec. 12, 1971. Student San Fernando Valley Jr. Coll., 1945-46, UCLA, 1948, U. So. Calif., 1955. Various positions 1943-54; sales engr. Everlube Corp., North Hollywood, Calif., 1954-57; cons. engring., Newport Beach, Calif., 1957-67, 1973—; sales engr. Lubeco, Compton, Calif., 1967-73; pres. Thomas A. Lamona & Assocs. Inc., Newport Beach, 1979—; exec. v.p./sec., bd. dirs. Innovative Coatings Tech. Corp., Mojave, Calif., 1992—; v.p., bd. dirs. Coating Tech. Corp., Glen Ellyn, Ill., 1986-88. With U.S. Army, 1951. Recipient Spl. Svc. citation Soc. Mfg. Engrs., region VII, 1979. Mem. Standards Engring. Soc. (L.A. sect., mem. chmn. 1975-77, program dir. 1977-78, treas. 1978-81, chmn. 1981-82, Spl. Service citation 1978, cert. in standards engring. 1979, Outstanding Sect. Mem. 1984), Porsche Owner's Club, Calif. Sports Car Club Am. (Los Angeles) (press relations com. 1955-63).

LAMONICA, JOHN, food executive; b. Bklyn., Apr. 26, 1954; s. Lou and Alda (Merola) L. BS in Acctg., Bklyn. Coll., 1977. With N.S.L. Enterprises, 1982—; with Aniellos Pizza, 1979—, Lamonicas N.Y. Pizza, 1980—; restaurant cons. Developer of new pizzas. Republican. Mem. Beverly Hills Gun Club, Shelby Am. Club. Office: 1066 Gayley Ave Los Angeles CA 90024-3402

LAMONT, SANDERS HICKEY, journalist; b. Atlanta, Nov. 9, 1940; s. Louis Earnest and Dorothy Rebecca (Strickland) LaM.; m. Patricia Jean Taylor, Aug. 5, 1966; children—Patricia Ruth, Zachary Taylor. A.A., Marion Mil. Inst., Ala., 1960; B.A. in Journalism, U. Ala., 1962; postgrad. U. Mich., 1977-78. Reporter, bur. chief Gannett News Service, various locations, 1961-74; mng. editor Ft. Myers News Press, Fla., 1974-77; exec. editor Marietta Times, Ohio, 1978-80, Modesto Bee, Calif., 1980—; chmn. AP News Execs. Council, Calif., 1984-85. NEH journalism fellow, U. Mich., 1977-78; Pulitzer prize juror, 1984-85. Served to 1st lt. U.S. Army, 1963-65. Mem. Am. Soc. Newspaper Editors, AP Mng. Editors, Soc. Profl. Journalists . Methodist. Office: The Modesto Bee PO Box 5256 Modesto CA 95352-5256

LA MONT-WELLS, TAWANA FAYE, camera operator, video director; b. Ft. Worth, May 12, 1948; d. Jerry James and Roberta Ann (Wilkinson) La M. AA, Antelope Coll., 1979; BA in Anthropology, UCLA, 1982. Forest technician, trail constrn. supr. Angeles Nat. Forest, Region 9 U.S. Forest Svc., Pear Blossom, Calif., 1974-79; trail constrn. supr., maintenance asst. Calif. State Parks, 1979-81; cable TV installer Sammons Comm., Glendale, Calif., 1981-83, camera operator, 1983-87; video studio and ENG remotes dir., mgr., program mgr. channel 6 Sammons Cable, Glendale, Calif., 1981-97; video studio and ENG remotes dir., mgr., program mgr. channel 21 Marcus Cable, Glendale, Calif., 1981-97; video dir., prodr. LBW & Assocs. Internat., Ltd., 1988—; pres., CEO Chamblee Found., Ltd., 1995—; mem. ednl. access channel satellite program evaluation com., Glendale and Burbank, 1990-92; mem. Foothill Cmty. TV Network, Glendale and Burbank, 1987-97. Prodr., dir. (homeless video) Bittersweet Streets, 1988; cameraperson Rockin in A Hard Place, 1988-93; dir., editor over 1000 videos. Active Glendale Hist. Soc., 1992-97; bd. dirs. Am. Heart Assn., 1992-96, comms. chair; bd. dirs. ARC, 1993—, mem. disaster svcs. team, cultural diversity chair, 1994-95; mem. mktg. com. Burbank YMCA, 1994-96; bd. dirs. Glendale Rose Float Assn., 1995-96. Recipient award of appreciation LBW and Assocs. Internat., 1988, Bur. Census, 1990, USMC, 1991, Verdugo Disaster Recovery Project, 1995, ARC, 1995, ARC Spl. citation for exceptional vol. svc., 1995, award of outstanding pub. svc. Social Security Adminstrn. HHS, 1989, dedicated svc. award Am. Heart Assn., 1992, cert. of appreciation, 1994, 95. Mem. NAFE, NRA, Internat. Alliance Theatrical Stage Employees, Moving Picture Technicians, Artists and Allied Crafts, Internat. Photographer's Guild, Am. Women in Radio and TV, Am. Bus. Women Assn., UCLA Alumni Assn. (life), Wildlife Waystation, Alpha Gamma. Democrat. Office: PO Box 142 Lake Hughes CA 93532

LAMOUREUX, CHARLES HARRINGTON, botanist, arboretum administrator; b. West Greenwich, R.I., Sept. 14, 1933; s. Emile and Cora May (Harrington) L.; m. Florence May Kettelle, Aug. 28, 1954; children: Mark Harrington, Anne Maile. BS in Botany, U. R.I., 1953; MS in Botany, U. Hawaii, 1955; PhD in Botany, U. Calif., Davis, 1961. From asst. to assoc. prof. botany U. Hawaii, Honolulu, 1959-71, prof., 1971—, chair dept. botany, 1962-65, 76-78, acting assoc. dean curriculum coll. arts and scis., 1976-77, 83, project coord. instrnl. assistance unit, 1977-79, assoc. dean acad. affairs coll. arts and scis., 1985-91; dir. Harold L. Lyon Arboretum, U. Hawaii, Honolulu, 1992—; rsch. assoc. botany Bernice P. Bishop Mus., Honolulu, 1963—; vis. asst. prof. botany U. B.C., Can., summer 1963; vis. colleague dept. botany Canterbury U., Christchurch, New Zealand, 1965-66; mem. sci. adv. com. Pacific Tropical Bot. Garden (name changed to Nat. Tropical Bot. Garden), 1967-94; dir. summer inst. sci. amd math. tchrs. U.S. children Far East NSF, Chofu, Japan, 1968-71, reviewer, mem. various rev. panels; faculty mem. ctr. Pacific islands studies U. Hawaii, 1971—; guest sci. Nat. Biol. Inst. Indonesia, Bogor, 1972-73, 79-80; mem. adv. com. plants and animals quarantine br. Hawaii State Dept. Agr., 1973-79, 89—; study lectr./leader Smithsonian Assocs. Study Tours S.E. Asia, 1985, 86, 88-95, Melanesia, 1987; report reviewer U.S. Congl. Office Tech. Assessment; rschr. in field; bot. and ecol. cons. to various businesses and agys. including State Hawaii Dept. Bus. and Econ. Devel., UNESCO, UN Devel. Programme. Author: Trailside Plants of Hawaii's National Parks, 1976, (U.S. Nat. Pk. Svc. Dir.'s award 1977, Nat. Pks. Coop. Assn. Award of Excellence 1977-78), rev. edits., 1982, 96; bd. editors Pacific Sci., 1965—, editor-in-chief, 1985-86; mem. editorial com. Allertonia, 1977-90; manuscript reviewer for various jours. and presses; contbr. articles to profl. jours. Active Hawaii Audubon Soc., 1959—, past pres., 1st v.p., Hawaiian Bot. Gardens Found., 1959-67, 1st v.p.; life mem. Conservation Coun. Hawaii, 1959—, state bd. dirs., mem. com. flora conservation, Hawaiian Bot. Soc., 1959—, trustee endowment fund, past pres., v.p., sec., treas., newsletter editor; mem. adv. com. Hawai'i Earth Day, 1990; bd. dirs. Friends Honolulu Bot. Garden, 1992—. Mem. Bot. Soc. Am., Am. Assn. Bot. Gardens and Arboreta, Hawaiian Acad. Sci. (councillor 1991-93, pres.-elect 1993, pres. 1994-95), Pacific Sci. Assn. (life, standing com. botany 1971—), Internat. Assn. Plant Taxonomists, Internat. Assn. Wood Anatomists. Home: 3426 Oahu Ave Honolulu HI 96822-1254 Office: Harold L Lyon Arboretum 3860 Manoa Rd Honolulu HI 96822-1180

LAMPERT, ELEANOR VERNA, retired human resources specialist; b. Porterville, Calif., Mar. 23; d. Ernest Samuel and Violet Edna (Watkins) Wilson; student in bus., fin. Porterville Jr. Coll., 1977-78; grad. Anthony Real Estate Sch., 1971; student Laguna Sch. of Art, 1972, U. Calif.-Santa Cruz, 1981; m. Robert Mathew Lampert, Aug. 21, 1935; children—Sally Lu Winton, Lary Lampert, Carol R. John. Bookkeeper, Porterville (Calif.) Hosp., 1956-71; real estate sales staff Ray Realty, Porterville, 1973; sec. Employment Devel. Dept., State of Calif., Porterville, 1973-83, orientation and tng. specialist CETA employees, 1976-80. Author: Black Bloomers and Han-Ga-Ber, 1986. Sec., Employer Adv. Group, 1973-80, 81—; mem. U.S. Senatorial Bus. Adv. Bd., 1981-84; charter mem. Presdl. Republican Task Force, 1981—; mem. Rep. Nat. Congl. Com., 1982-88; pres. Sierra View Hosp. Vol. League, 1988-89 ; vol. Calif. Hosp. Assn., 1983-89, Calif. Spl. Olympics Spirit Team. Recipient Merit Cert., Gov. Pat Brown, State of Calif., 1968. Mem. Lindsay Olive Growers, Sunkist Orange Growers, Am. Kennel Club, Internat. Assn. Personnel in Employment Security, Calif. State Employees Assn. (emeritus Nat. Wildlife Fedn., NRA, Friends of Porterville Library, Heritage Found., DAR (Kaweah chpt. rec. sec. 1988—), Internat. Platform Assn., Dist. Fedn. Women's Clubs (recording sec. Calif. chpt. 1988—), Ky. Hist. Soc., Women's Club of Calif. (pres. Porterville chpt. 1988-89, dist. rec. sec. 1987-89), Mo. Rep. Women of Taney County, Internat. Sporting and Leisure Club, Ladies Aux. VFW (No. 5168 Forsyth, Mo.), Ozark Walkers League.

LAMPHERE, LOUISE, anthropology and women's studies educator; b. St. Louis, Oct. 4, 1940; d. Harold and Miriam (Bretschneider) L.; 1 child, Peter Bret. BA, Stanford U., 1962; MA, Harvard U., 1966, PhD, 1968. Asst. prof. Brown U., Providence, 1972-75, assoc. prof., 1979-85; assoc. prof. U. N.Mex., Albuquerque, 1976-79, adj. prof., 1979-85; fellow Wellesley (Mass.) Coll., 1981; prof. anthropology Brown U., Providence, 1985-88; prof. anthropology U. N.Mex., Albuquerque, 1986—, acting dir. women studies, 1993-95. Author: From Working Daughters to Working, 1987, (with others) Sunbelt Working Mothers, 1993; editor: Structuring Diversity, 1992, Newcomers in the Workplace, 1993, (with others) Woman, Culture and Society, 1974, Situated Lives: Gender and Culture in Everyday Life, 1996; editor Frontiers: A Jour. of Women Studies, Albuquerque, 1990-93. Recipient Conrad Arensberg award Soc. for Anthropology of Work, 1994; grantee NSF, 1981-83, Russell Sage Found., 1985-86, Ford Found., 1987-90. Mem. Am. Ethnological Soc. (counsellor 1981-84, pres.-elect 1987, pres. 1987-89), Am. Anthropol. Soc. (exec. com. 1987-89), Assn. for Feminist Anthropology (bd. dirs. 1989-91, pres.-elect 1993-95, pres. 1995—). Office: U New Mex Dept Anthropology Albuquerque NM 87131

LAMPPU, JUDY SONIA, composer, writer; b. L.A., June 5, 1942; d. David Wolf and Evelyn (Gross) Berman; m. David Allen Russell, Feb., 1961 (div. Apr. 1964); 1 child, Elaina Anne; m. Peter Thomas Lamppu, June 4, 1972 (dec. Dec. 1995). Student, L.A. City Coll., 1960-61, Valley Coll., Van Nuys, Calif., 1973-74, Sta. KIIS Radio, L.A., 1975-76. Lic. broadcast endorsement FCC. Author: (screenplay) Caution Murder Can Be Hazardous to your Health (for Columbo, Universal TV), 1990; lyricist: (songs) Nobody, 1970, Lulu, 1971, Miracle, 1975. Recipient award for best essay Am. Legion, 1956. Mem. ASCAP, NARAS, Writers Guild Am. West, L.A. Women in Music. Democrat.

LAMSON, KRISTIN ANNE, finance company executive; b. Providence, Jan. 31, 1963; m. W. Scott Lamson, June, 1989; children: Nicholas, Katherine. BS, Santa Clara (Calif.) U., 1985; MBA, San Jose (Calif.) State U., 1992. V.p., asst. mgr. Union Bank, San Jose, 1985-94; v.p. real estate loans Housing Capital Co., San Mateo, Calif., 1994—. Vice chmn. ARC, Santa Clara County, 1992—. Mem. Jr. League. Office: Housing Capital Co 1825 S Grant St Ste 630 San Mateo CA 95032

LAMSON, ROBERT WOODROW, retired school system administrator; b. L.A., Dec. 28, 1917; s. Ernest K. and Mabel (Mahoney) L.; m. Jeannette Juett, July 22, 1949; children: Robert Woodrow Jr., Nancy Virginia, Kathleen Patricia. BA, Occidental Coll., 1940; MA, U. So. Calif., 1955. Cert. tchr., prin., supt., Calif. Tchr. El Monte (Calif.) Sch. Dist., 1940-43; tchr. L.A. City Sch. Dist., 1945-49, prin., 1949-55, supr., 1955-57, adminstrv. asst., 1957-59, area supt., 1959-78; ret., 1978; agt. Keilholtz Realtors, La Canada, Calif.; instr. various colls. and univs. so. Calif.; a founder, v.p., bd. dirs. U.S. Acad. Decathlon, Cerritos, Calif., 1981-86. Bd. dirs. 10th Dist. PTA, L.A., 1965-70; chmn. Scout-O-Rama, Gt. Western coun. Boy Scouts Am., 1980. Lt. comdr. USNR, 1943-46, mem. Res. ret. Mem. Am. Assn. Sch. Adminstrs., Assn. Adminstrs. L.A., Alumni Occidental Coll. in Edn. (a founder, past pres., bd. dirs.), Town Hall, Nat. PTA (hon. life), Calif. PTA (hon. life, bd. dirs. 1978-80), 31st Dist. PTA (hon. life, bd. dirs. 1965-78, auditorium named in his honor 1978), Phi Beta Kappa, Alpha Tau Omega. Republican. Home: 4911 Vineta Ave La Canada Flintridge CA 91011-2624 Office: Richard Keilholtz Realtors 727 Foothill Blvd La Canada Flintridge CA 91011-3405

LANAHAN, DANIEL JOSEPH, lawyer; b. Bklyn., Jan. 13, 1940. Attended, L.I. U., Temple U.; JD, San Francisco Law Sch., 1969. Bar: Calif. 1970. Dir. Ropers, Majeski, Kohn & Bentley, P.C., Santa Rosa, Calif., 1970-96; mng. ptnr. Lanahan & Reilley L.L.P., Santa Rosa, 1997—. Mem. State Bar Calif., San Mateo Bar Assn., Internat. Assn. Def. Counsel, Assn. Def. Counsel. Office: Lanahan & Reilley LLP 3558 Round Barn Blvd Santa Rosa CA 95403-1768

LANCASTER, KIMBERLY MEIRON (KC LANCASTER), artist; b. D.C., Jan. 28, 1965; d. James Edward and Donna Jeanne (Wilmot) Chase; m. William Christopher Rolls Lancaster, Apr. 21, 1990. Line worker Teledyne Waterpik, Ft. Collins, Colo., 1983-84; key operator Miracle Printer, Ft. Collins, 1984-85, Kwik Kopy, Lakewood, Colo., 1985-86, Copy Boy, Denver, 1986-87; supr. Kinko's Copies, Boulder, Colo., 1988-95; owner, operator Kirin Graphics, Northglenn, Colo., 1995—; artist White Mountain (Colo.) Souvenir Co., 1996-97; art dir., artist Alderac Entertainment Group, Inc., 1997—. Author, artist: Night Shade, Ltd., 1996. Mem. Soc. Creative Anachronism (illuminator-chronicler Ft. Collins, Denver 1982-84, craftsperson 1984-94), Internat. Fantasy Gaming Soc. Democrat. Office: Kirin Graphics PO Box 33516 Northglenn CO 80233

LANCE, ALAN GEORGE, lawyer, legislator, attorney general; b. McComb, Ohio, Apr. 27, 1949; s. Cloyce Lowell and Clara Rose (Wilhelm) L.; m. Sheryl C. Holden, May 31, 1969; children: Lisa, Alan Jr., Luke. BA, S.D. State U., 1971; JD, U. Toledo, 1973. Bar: Ohio 1974, U.S. Dist. Ct. (no. dist.) Ohio 1974, U.S. Ct. Mil. Appeals 1974, Idaho 1978, U.S. Supreme Ct. 1996. Asst. pros. atty. Fulton County, Wauseon, Ohio, 1973-74; ptnr. Foley and Lance, Chartered, Meridian, Idaho, 1978-90; prin. Alan G. Lance, Meridian, Idaho, 1990-94; rep. Idaho Ho. of Reps., Boise, 1990-94, majority caucus chmn., 1992-94; atty. gen. State of Idaho, 1995—. Capt. AUS, 1974-78. Mem. ABA, Nat. Assn. Attys. Gen. (exec. com. conf. western attys. gen.), Ohio Bar Assn., Idaho Bar Assn., Idaho Trial Lawyers Assn., Meridian C. of C. (pres. 1983), Am. Legion (judge adv. 1981-90, state comdr. 1988-89, alt. nat. exec. com. 1992-94, nat. exec. com. 1994-96, chmn. nat. fgn. rels. commn. 1996—, ex-officio mem. N.H. POW/MIA com. 1996—), Elks. Republican. Home: 1370 Eggers Pl Meridian ID 83642-6528 Office: PO Box 83720 Statehouse Rm 210 Boise ID 83720-0010

LAND, KEITH, councilman; b. Stockton, Calif., Oct. 13, 1950; m. Marcia Land; children: Tim, Ken, Stephanie, Trevor, Tami Sr. AA, Delta Coll., 1975. Councilman City of Lodi, Calif., 1996—. Active United Math. Ch., Lodi Grape Festival, San Joaquin Parks & Recreation, Friends of Lodi Libr., Lodi High Found.; commr. Lodi Parks & Recreation, 1994-96; pres. Lodi C. of C., 1987, bd. dirs., 1985-90, Lodi Boys and Girls Club, 1987, Lodi Sister City Com., 1992-93; vol. fire fighter City of Lodi, 1982-84; team leader United Way, Lodi, 1988; steering com. Leadership Lodi, 1990. Mem. VFW, Am. Legion, Elks (exalted ruler 1993), Kiwanis. Office: PO Box 3006 Lodi CA 95241

LAND, KENNETH DEAN, test and balance agency executive, energy and environmental consultant; b. Central City, Nebr., Oct. 5, 1931; s. Adrew Kenneth Land and Marie Eveline (Weaver) Gehrke. Grad., El Camino Coll., Gardena, Calif., 1954-56; student, Long Beach City Coll., 1958, Calif. State Coll., Long Beach, 1959. Cert. quality assurance inspector for smoke removal and life safety systems. Gen. mgr. Air Heat Engrs., Inc., Santa Fe Springs, Calif., 1956-61; sales and estimating engr. Thermodyne Corp., Los Alamitos, Calif., 1962-64; pres., founder Air Check Co., Inc., Santa Ana, Calif., 1964-69; chief engring. technician Nat. Air Balance Co., Los Angeles, 1969-73; gen. mgr. B&M Air Balance Co., South El Monte, Calif., 1973-78; chief exec. officer, founder Land Air Balance Tech. (LABTECH), Las Vegas, Nev., 1978—; bd. dirs. Energy Resources and Mgmt., Inc., San-I-Pac, Internat., Inc., Energy Equities Group, Inc.; founder, pres. Utility Connection, 1990—. Active Las Vegas Founders Club-Las Vegas Invitational PGA Tournament, 1983—, player, 1992; former trustee Assoc. Air Balance Coun.-Sheet Metal Workers Internat. Apprenticeship Tng. Fund; mem. Citizens Against Govt. Waste, 1990—, YNOT Night for YMCA, 1987—; co-founder The Golf Com., operators charity golf tournament for Am. Cancer Soc., 1990, 91, Am. Diabetes Assn., 1992, Nev. Child Seekers, 1992— . With USN, 1951-54, journalist. Mem. ASHRAE (pres. so. Nev. chpt. 1983-84, editor chpt. bull. 1979-89, Citizen of Yr. 1989), CSI (co-founder Las Vegas chpt., pres. 1989-90, editor, founder chpt. bull. 1987-90, S.W. regional mem. chmn. 1990-91), Assn. Energy Engrs., Am. Soc. Profl. Cons., Associated Air Balance Coun. (cert. test and balance engr. 1966—, internat. pres. 1988-89, bd. dirs. 1982-90, mem. numerous coms.), Sheet Metal Workers Internat. Tng. Fund, Internat. Conf. Bldg. Officials, Internat. Assn. Plumbing and Mech. Officials, Nat. Fedn. Ind. Businessmen, Rotary (So. El Monte Calif. Club 1977-78, Las Vegas S.W. Nev. Club 1978-94, bd. dirs. 1983-85, 88-90, photographer 1987-90, chmn. internat. svc., 4 Paul Harris fellowships, charter mem. Las Vegas West Club, Nev., 1994—), Citizens for Pvt. Enterprise, Nev. Taxpayers Assn., UNLV Golf Found., UNLV Presdl. Assocs. Group, Nev. Devel. Assn., Nev. Nuclear Waste Study Com. adv. coun., Sheet Metal and Air Conditioning Contractors Assn. (nat. and so. Nev. chpt. bd. dirs.), Associated Gen. Contractors (nat. and Las Vegas chpt.), Nat. Energy Mgmt. Inst. (cert., co-chmn. Nev. adv. coun., instr. Energy Mgmt. Tng. 1991), Nev. Energy Resources Assn., Las Vegas C. of C., Nat. Inst. Bldg. Scis., Nev. Assn. Ind. Businessman, Nat. Fire Protection Assn., Am. Soc. Hosp. Engrs., Nev. Profl. Facility Mgrs. Assn., 1992—, Las Vegas Country Club.

LANDAR, HERBERT JAY, linguistics educator, author; b. N.Y.C., Dec. 7, 1927; s. Leo and Mildred (Mann) L.; m. Muriel Anne Epstein; children: Clifford, Nancy, Stephen. BA, Queens Coll., 1949; MA, Yale U., 1955, PhD, 1960. Instr. Reed Coll., Portland, Oreg., 1957-59; prof. linguistics Calif. State U., L.A., 1960-91, prof. emeritus, 1991—; vis. prof. Ind. U., Bloomington, 1976-77, Université Blaise Pascal, Clermont-Ferrand, France, 1987-88. Author: Language and Culture, 1966, (in Japanese) Kotoba-To Bunka, 1977; contbr. numerous articles to profl. jours. Cpl. U.S. Army, 1950-52. Guggenheim Found. fellow, 1967-68; Fulbright Commn. grantee, 1987-88. Home: 220 San Anselmo Ave San Francisco CA 94127-2030

LANDAU, JOSEPH WHITE, dermatologist; b. Buffalo, N.Y., May 23, 1930; s. Fred and Carolyn (White) L.; children: Brenda, Kenneth, Jason. BA, Cornell U., 1951, MD, 1955. Diplomate Am. Bd. Pediatrics, Am. Bd. Dermatology; spl. competence cert. in dermatopathology. Intern Gen. Hosp., Buffalo, 1955-56; pediatric resident Children's Hosp., Buffalo, 1956, Boston, 1959-60; pediatric resident UCLA, 1960-61; pediatric hematology trainee Children's Hosp., L.A., 1961-62; postdoctoral trainee in mycology UCLA, 1962-63, asst. rsch. dermatologist, 1964, asst. prof. medicine-dermatology, 1964-68, assoc. prof. medicine-dermatology, 1968-74, assoc. clin. prof. medicine-dermatology, 1974—. Contbr. articles to profl. jours. Comdr. USNR, 1957-59. Mem. AAAS, Am. Soc. Dermatopathology, San Fernando Valley Dermatologic Soc., L.A. Dermatologic Soc., Am. Acad. Dermatology, Soc. for Pediatric Dermatology, L.A. Pediatric Soc., Soc. for Investigative Dermatology, Alpha Omega Alpha, Phi Beta Kappa, Alpha Epsilon Delta. Office: 2428 Santa Monica Blvd Ste 401 Santa Monica CA 90404-2047

LANDERS, VERNETTE TROSPER, writer, educator, association executive; b. Lawton, Okla., May 3, 1912; d. Fred Gilbert and LaVerne Hamilton (Stevens) Trosper; m. Paul Albert Lum, Aug. 29, 1952 (dec. May 1955); 1 child, William Tappan; m. 2d, Newlin Landers, May 2, 1959 (dec. Apr. 1990); children: Lawrence, Marlin. AB with honors, UCLA, 1933, MA, 1935, EdD, 1953; Cultural doctorate (hon.) Lit. World U., Tucson, 1985. Tchr. secondary schs., Montebello, Calif., 1935-45, 48-50, 51-59; prof. Long Beach City Coll., 1946-47; asst. prof. Los Angeles State Coll., 1950; dean girls Twenty Nine Palms (Calif.) High Sch., 1960-65; dist. counselor Morongo (Calif.) Unified Sch. Dist., 1965-72, coordinator adult edn., 1965-67, guidance project dir., 1967; clk.-in-charge Landers (Calif.) Post Office, 1962-82; ret., 1982. V.p., sec. Landers Assn., 1965—; sec. Landers Vol. Fire Dept., 1972—; life mem. Hi-Desert Playhouse Guild, Hi-Desert Meml. Hosp. Guild; bd. friends Copper Mountain Coll., 1990-91; bd. dirs., sec. Desert Emergency Radio Service; mem. Rep. Senatorial Inner Circle, 1990-92, Regent Nat. Fedn. Rep. Women, 1990-92, Nat. Rep. Congl. Com., 1990-91, Presdsl. Task Force, 1990-92; lifetime mem. Girl Scouts U.S., 1991. Recipient internat. diploma of honor for community service, 1973; Creativity award Internat. Personnel Research Assn., 1972, award Goat Mt. Grange No. 818, 1987; cert. of merit for disting. svc. to edn., 1973; Order of Rose, 1978, Order of Pearl, 1989, Alpha Xi Delta; poet laureate Center of Internat. Studies and Exchanges, 1981; diploma of merit in letters U. Arts, Parma, Italy, 1982; Golden Yr. Bruin UCLA, 1983; World Culture prize Nat. Ctr. for Studies and Research, Italian Acad., 1984; Golden Palm Diploma of Honor in poetry Leonardo Da Vinci Acad., 1984; Diploma of Merit and titular mem. internat. com. Internat. Ctr. Studies and Exchanges, Rome, 1984; Recognition award San Gorgonio council Girl Scouts U.S., 1984—; Cert. of appreciation Morongo Unified Sch. Dist., 1984, 89; plaque for contribution to postal service and community U.S. Postal Service, 1984; Biographee of Yr. award for outstanding achievement in the field of edn. and service to community Hist. Preservations of Am.; named Princess of Poetry of Internat. Ctr. Cultural Studies and Exchange, Italy, 1985; community dinner held in her honor for achievement and service to Community, 1984; Star of Contemporary Poetry Masters of Contemporary Poetry, Internat. Ctr. Cultural Studies and Exchanges, Italy, 1984; named to honor list of leaders of contemporary art and lit. and apptd. titular mem. of Internat. High Com. for World Culture & Arts Leonardo Da Vinci Acad., 1987; named to honor list Foremost Women 20th Century for Outstanding Contbn. to Rsch., IBC, 1987; Presdl. Order of Merit Pres. George Bush-Exec. Coun. of Nat. Rep. Senatorial Com., Congl. cert. of Appreciation U.S. Ho. of Reps.; other awards and certs. Life fellow Internat. Acad. Poets, World Lit. Acad.; mem. Am. Personnel and Guidance Assn., Internat. Platform Assn., Nat. Ret. Tchrs. Assn., Calif. and Nat. Assn. for Counseling and Devel., Am. Assn. for Counseling and Devel. (25 yr. membership pin 1991), Nat. Assn. Women Deans and Adminstrs., Montebello Bus. and Profl. Women's Club (pres.), Nat. League Am. Pen Women (sec. 1985-86), Leonardo Da Vinci Acad. Internat. Winged Glory diploma of honor in letters 1982), Landers Area C. of C. (sec. 1985-86, Presdl. award for outstanding service, Internat. Honors Cup 1992-93), Desert Nature Mus., Phi Beta Kappa, Pi Lambda Theta (Mortar Bd., Prytanean UCLA, UCLA Golden Yr. Bruin 1983), Sigma Delta Pi, Pi Delta Phi. Clubs: Whittier Toastmistress (Calif.) (pres. 1957); Homestead Valley Women's (Landers). Lodge: Soroptimists (sec. 29 Palms chpt. 1962, life mem. 1983, Soroptimist of Yr. local chpt. 1967, Woman of Distinction local chpt. 1987-88). Author: Impy, 1974, Talkie, 1975, Impy's Children, 1975; Nineteen O Four, 1976, Little Brown Bat, 1976; Slo-Go, 1977; Owls Who and Who Who, 1978; Sandy, The Coydog, 1979; The Kit Fox and the Walking Stick, 1980; contbr. articles to profl. jours., poems to anthologies. Guest of honor ground breaking ceremony Landers Elem. Sch., 1989, dedication ceremony, 1991. Home: 632 N Landers Ln PO Box 3839 Landers CA 92285

LANDING, BENJAMIN HARRISON, pathologist, educator; b. Buffalo, Sept. 11, 1920; s. Benjamin Harrison Sr. and Margaret Catherine (Crohen) L.; m. Dorothy Jean Hallas; children: Benjamin H., Susan L. Phillips, William M., David A. AB, Harvard U., 1942, MD, 1945. Diplomate Am. Bd. Pathology (anatomic pathology and pediatric pathology). Intern pathology Children's Hosp., Boston, 1945-46, asst. resident, then resident pathology, 1948-49; resident pathology Boston Lying-in Hosp., 1949, Free Hosp. for Women, Brookline, Mass., 1949; pathologist Children's Med. Ctr., Boston, 1950-53, Cin., 1953-61; pathologist-in-chief Children's Hosp., L.A., 1961-88, rsch. pathologist, 1988—; asst. pathologist Harvard U. Med. Sch., Boston, 1950-53; from asst. prof. to assoc. prof. U. Cin. Coll. Medicine, 1953-61; prof. pathology and pediatrics U. So. Calif. Sch. Medicine, L.A., 1961-91, prof. emeritus, 1991—. Author: Butterfly Color/Behavior Patterns, 1984; author chpts. in books; contbr. articles to profl. jours. Chmn. Pacific S.W. Dist. Unitarian-Universalist Assn., 1968-70; pres. Burbank (Calif.) Unitarian Fellowship, 1964-66. Capt. Med. Corps AUS, 1946-48. Mem. Soc. for Pediatric Pathology (pres. 1973-74), Internat. Pediatric Pathology Soc. (pres. 1980). Democrat. Unitarian-Universalist. Home: 4513 Deanwood Dr Woodland Hills CA 91364-5622 Office: Childrens Hosp LA Box 103 4650 W Sunset Blvd Los Angeles CA 90027-6062

LANDIS, RICHARD GORDON, retired food company executive; b. Davenport, Okla., Apr. 5, 1920; s. John William and Venna Marie (Perrin) L.; m. Beth Throne, Nov. 6, 1943; children: Gary Perrin, Dennis, Michael, Kay Ellen. BA, U. LaVerne, 1942; postgrad., Claremont Grad. Sch., 1947; LLD (hon.), U. LaVerne, 1981. Mgmt. Delmonte Corp, San Francisco, 1942-83, pres., 1971-77, pres. & chief exec. officer, 1977-78, chmn. & chief exec. officer, 1978-81; pres. Pacific div. R.J. Reynolds, Inc., San Francisco, 1981-83; former chancellor U. LaVerne, Calif.; bd. dirs. Oregon Steel, Portland, Stanford Rsch. Internat., Menlo Park, Calif. Mem. Commn. of Calif., 1984—; chmn. Pacific Basin Econ. Coun., 1975-83; officer Boy Scouts Am., 1946—, Invest in Am.; Lt. USAF, 1942-46. Mem. Pacific Union Club, Bohemian Club, Peachtree C. of C. Republican. Office: 120 Montgomery St Ste 1880 San Francisco CA 94104-4321

LANDIS, RICHARD PRESTON, corporate executive; b. Yakima, Wash., July 12, 1946; s. Richard Paul and Louise Beverly (Fletcher) L.; m. Diane Susan Hathaway, Apr. 8, 1972. AA in Law Enforcement, Ariz. Western Coll., 1978; BSBA, St. Mary's Coll. of Calif., 1979. Divsn. comdr./state police officer Ariz. Dept. Pub. Safety, Phoenix, 1971-91; assoc. adminstr. for motor carriers Fed. Hwy. Adminstrn./U.S. Dept. Transp., Washington, 1985-93; pres., CEO Heavy Vehicle Electronic Lic. Plate, Inc., Phoenix, 1993—; transp. specialist Nat. Hwy. Traffice Safety Adminstr., U.S. Dept. Transp., 1979-80. With USNR, 1965-68, Vietnam. Mem. Am. Soc. Assn. Execs., Its America, Rotary (bd. dirs. Estrella club 1993-94), Intelligent Transp. Soc. Am. (chmn. commercial vehicle ops. tech. com.). Republican. Home: 608 N La Loma Ave Litchfield Park AZ 85340-4324 Office: Help Inc 40 N Central Ave Ste 2250 Phoenix AZ 85004-4451

LANDON, JOJENE BABBITT, special education educator; b. Boise, Idaho, Feb. 7, 1940; d. Clarence Ray and Mary (McHenry) Babbitt; m. James Wallace Landon, Dec. 8, 1963; children: Sharon Jene, John Charles, Franklin Thomas, Jonathan Kennette. BA in Far Ea. History, U. Md., 1968; MEd in Spl. Edn., Bowie (Md.) State Coll., 1974; MS in Reading, Johns Hopkins U., 1978; postgrad., Calif. State U., Sacramento, 1987-92. Cert. tchr. for severely handicapped and learning handicapped, also reading specialsit, resource specialist multiple subject and social sci., Calif. Spl. edn. resource tchr. Anne Arundel County, Glen Burnie, Md., 1974-80; tchr. severely emotionally disturbed Leeward Dist., Ewa Beach, Hawaii, 1980-84, North Valley Schs. Inc., Stockton, Calif., 1984-85, Stockton Unified Sch.Dist., 1985-87, Serene Community Sch., Sacramento, 1987-90; tchr. spl. edn. Sacramento Unified Sch. Dist., 1990; tchr. spl. edn., dept. chair Rio Tierra Jr. High Sch., Sacramento, 1990—; developer, presenter project Ho'okoho U. Hawaii and Hawaii Dept. Edn., Honolulu, 1982-84. Supt. protestant Sunday schs. Pearl Harbor (Hawaii) Naval Sta. Chapel, 1983; lay speaker United Meth. Ch., 1989—. With U.S. Army, 1961-64. Named Grit. Dist. Tchr. of Yr., 1997. Mem. Coun. Exceptional Children. Republican. Home: 8941 Lake Grove Ct Elk Grove CA 95624-2722

LANDOVSKY, ROSEMARY REID, figure skating school director, coach; b. Chgo., July 26, 1933; d. Samuel Stuart and Audrey Todd (Lyons) Reid; m. John Indulis Landovsky, Feb. 20, 1960; children: David John, Linette. BA in Psychology, Colo. Coll., 1956. Profl. skater Holiday on Ice Touring Show, U.S., Mex., Cuba, 1956-58; skating dir. and coach Paradice Arena, Birmingham, 1958-62, Les Patineurs, Huntsville, Ala., 1960-62; coach competitive (Ice Skating Inst. Am., U.S. Figure Skating Assn.) Michael Kirby and Assocs., River Forest, Chgo., Ill., 1962-63; rink mgr., skating dir. Lake Meadows Ice Arena, Chgo., 1963-68; coach (ISIA, USFSA) Rainbo Arena, Chgo., 1968-73; skating dir. Northwestern U. Skating Sch., Evanston, Ill., 1968-73, Robert Crown Ice Ctr., Evanston, 1973-75; dir. instl. programs Skokie (Ill.) Park Dist., 1975-87; competition dir. ISIA All America Competition, 1985-86. Dir., producer, choreographer Ice Show: Nutcracker Ballet, 1973, Ice Extravaganza III, 1985, Ice Lights '86, '87. Election judge, worker, Ind. Dems., Chgo., 1964-68. Mem. Profl. Skaters Guild, Ice Skating Inst. Am., Coll. Coll. Alumni Assn. (mem. Chgo. area com.), Gamma Phi Beta.

LANDRE, DEBRA ANN, mathematics educator; b. Quantico, Va., Sept. 15, 1955; d. Thomas F. and Joy L. (Carstens) L. BA in French and Math., Bradley U., 1976, MS in Edn., 1977; MS in Math., Ill. State U., 1979. Math. instr. Bradley U., Peoria, Ill., 1977-79, Ill. Valley Community Coll., Peru, 1980, Ill. Wesleyan U., Bloomington, 1981; computer sci. instr. Lincoln Coll., Bloomington, 1981-85; math. instr. Ill. State U., Normal, 1979-85; pres. Quality Input Inc., Normal, 1983-85; dir. acad. computing San Joaquin Delta Coll., Stockton, Calif., 1985-88; math. instr. San Joaquin Delta Coll., Stockton, 1988—. Author: Explorations in Elementary Algebra, 1992, Explorations in Intermediate Algebra, 1992, Explorations in College Algebra, 1992, Explorations in Statistics and Probability, 1992, Amusements in Algebra, 1994; co-author: Mathematics: Theory into Practice, 1980, Microprocessor-Based Operations: Systems Software, 1985, Data Acquisition, 1985; contbr. articles to profl. jours. Treas. Acad. Senate Calif. C.C., 1996—. Mem. Am. Statis. Assn., Calif. Assn. Dirs. Acad. Computing (pres. 1988-90), Calif. Ednl. Computer Consortium (bd. dirs. 1987-90, editor 1988-90), No. Calif. C.C. Computer Consortium (sec./editor 1986-91), Calif. Math. Coun. (editor exec. bd. 1990—, pres. elect 1991-93, pres. 1994-95, past pres. 1995—), Am. Math. Assn. of Two Yr. Colls. (del. 1993—, editor 1994—), Calif. Tchrs. Assn. (pres.-elect 1994-95, pres. 1995-96), Calif. Assn. Women in Edn. and Rsch., C.C. Assn. (dist. dir. 1995—). Office: San Joaquin Delta Coll 5151 Pacific Ave Stockton CA 95207-6304

LANDRUM, LARRY JAMES, computer engineer; b. Santa Rita, N.Mex., May 29, 1943; s. Floyd Joseph and Jewel Helen (Andreska) L.; m. Ann Marie Hartman, Aug. 25, 1963 (div.); children: Larry James, David Wayne, Andrei Mikhail, Donal Wymore; m. 2d, Mary Kathleen Turner, July 27, 1980. Student N.Mex. Inst. Mining and Tech., 1961-62, N. Mex. State U., 1963-65; AA in Data Processing, Ea. Ariz. Coll., 1971; BA in Computer Sci., U. Tex., 1978. Tech. svc. rep. Nat. Cash Register, 1966-73; with ASC super-computer project Tex. Instruments, Austin, 1973-80, computer technician, 1973-75, tech. instr., 1975-76, product engr., 1976-78, operating sys. programmer, 1978-80; computer engr. Ariz. Pub. Svc., Phoenix, 1980-84, sr. computer engr., 1984-87, lead computer engr., 1987-88, sr. computer engr., 1988-90, sr. control sys. engr., 1990-94; software engr. CDI Corp., 1996—; pres., chmn. bd. dirs. Glendale Cmty. Housing Devel. Orgn., 1993; software engr. CDI Corp., Pitts., 1996—; instr. computer fundamentals Ea. Ariz. Coll., 1972-73, Rio Salado C.C., Phoenix, 1985-86; mem. bd. trustees Epworth United Meth. Ch., 1987-89, chmn. 1988; mem. cmty. devel. adv. com. City of Glendale (Ariz.), 1988-90, chmn., 1991-92; local arrangements chmn. Conf. on Software Maintenance, 1988. Mem. IEEE Computer Soc., Assn. Computing Machinery, Mensa, Phi Kappa Phi. Methodist. Home: 6025 W Medlock Dr Glendale AZ 85301-7321

LANDRY, WILLIAM FRANCIS, counselor, teacher; b. Beverly, Mass., Feb. 12, 1966; s. William Francis Landry and Nancy Marie (Lauzon) Dewester; m. Tani Bennett. BA in Edn., Western Wash. U., 1991; MEd, City U. Bellingham, 1995. Cert. continuing tchr., ednl. staff assoc. Tchr., counselor Arlington (Wash.) Sch. Dist., 1991—. Diversion vol. Wash. Correctional System, Marysville, 1993-96. Mem. NEA, Wash. Edn. Assn., Am. Counseling Assn., Wash. Counseling Assn. Home: 1504 90th Dr NE Everett WA 98205-1468 Office: 1220 E 5th St Arlington WA 98223

LAND-WEBER, ELLEN, photography educator; b. Rochester, N.Y., Mar. 16, 1943; d. David and Florence (Miller) Epstein; 1 child, Julia. BA, U. Iowa, 1965, MFA, 1968. Faculty mem. UCLA Extension, 1970-74, Orange Coast Coll., Costa Mesa, Calif., 1973, U. Nebr., Lincoln, 1974; asst. prof. photography Humboldt State U., Arcata, Calif., 1974-79, assoc. prof., 1979-83, prof., 1983—; photographer Seagram's Bicentennial Courthouse Project, 1976-77, Nat. Trust for Hist. Preservation/Soc. Photographic Edn., 1987. Author: The Passionate Collector, 1980, To Save a Life: Stories of Jewish Rescue; contbr. sects. to books; photographs pub. in numerous books and jours. Nat. Endowment for Arts fellow, 1974, 79, 82; Artist's support grantee Unicolor Corp., 1982, Polaroid 20X24 Artist's support grantee, 1990, 93-94; Fulbright sr. fellow, 1993-94. Mem. Soc. for Photog. Edn. (exec. bd. 1979-82, treas. 1979-81, sec. 1981-83). Office: Humboldt State U Art Dept Arcata CA 95521

LANE, GLORIA JULIAN, foundation administrator; b. Chgo., Oct. 6, 1932; d. Coy Berry and Katherine (McDowell) Julian; m. William Gordon Lane (div. Oct. 1958); 1 child, Julie Kay Rosewood. BS in Edn., Cen. Mo. State U., 1958; MA, Bowling Green State U., 1959; PhD, No. Ill. U., 1972. Cert. tchr. Assoc. prof. William Jewell Coll., Liberty, Mo., 1959-60; chair forensic div. Coral Gables (Fla.) High Sch., 1960-64; assoc. prof. No. Ill. U., DeKalb, 1964-70; prof. Elgin (Ill.) Community Coll., 1970-72; owner, pub. Lane and Assocs, Inc., San Diego, 1972-78; prof. Nat. U., San Diego, 1978-90; pres., chief exec. officer Women's Internat. Ctr., San Diego, 1982—; founder, dir. Living Legacy Awards, San Diego, 1984—. Author: Project Text for Effective Communications, 1972, Project Text for Executive Communication, 1980, Positive Concepts for Success, 1983; editor Who's Who Among San Diego Women, 1984, 85, 86, 90—, Systems and Structure, 1984. Named Woman of Accomplishment, Soroptimist Internat., 1985, Pres.'s Coun. San Diego, 1986, Center City Assn., 1986, Bus. and Profl. Women, San Diego, 1991, Woman of Yr., Girls' Clubs San Diego, 1986, Woman of Vision, Women's Internat. Ctr., 1990, Wonderwoman 2000 Women's Times Newspaper, 1991; recipient Independence award Ctr. for Disabled, 1986, Founder's award Children's Hosp. Internat., Washington, 1986. Home and Office: 6202 Friars Rd Apt 311 San Diego CA 92108-1008

LANE, JAMES F., software engineer; b. Jersey City, Nov. 6, 1953; s. Francis Robert and Margaret Ellen Lane. BS in Computer Sci., Worcester Poly. Inst., 1971-75; postgrad., U. Colo., 1978. Software engr. LFE Corp., Waltham, Mass., 1975-76, Martin Maretta, Waterton, Colo., 1976-77; sr. software engr. Digital Group, Denver, 1977; systems analyst Johns-Manville, Littleton, Colo., 1977-78; systems software designer, project leader Microsoft, Redmond, Wash., 1978-85; pres. Elvyn Software, Inc., Redmond, Wash., 1985-87; mgr. PDL group, mgr. software engring. dept. Hanzon Data Inc., Bothell, Wash., 1985-90; owner Novelty Hill Software, Inc., Redmond, 1987—. Vol. Seattle Folklife Fest., 1986-97. Home: 22006 NE 114th St Redmond WA 98053-5701 Office: Novelty Hill Software Inc Redmond WA 98053

LANE, JAMES FREDERICK, IV, publishing executive; b. Seattle, July 6, 1963; s. James F. III and Sharon Louise (Dugan) L.; m. Ann Colyer Rodewig, June 20, 1992; 1 child, Isabel Colyer. BA with distinction, U. Wash., 1985. Account rep. Harper's Mag., N.Y.C., 1986-89; circulation mgr. Fairfield Pub. Inc., N.Y.C., 1989; assoc. pub. LINKS mag., Hilton Head Island, S.C., 1989-92; v.p. spl. projects LINKS mag., Hilton Head Island, 1992-95; editor-in-chief, COO JSA Pub., Santa Monica, Calif., 1995—. Author: The Complete Golfer's Almanac, 1995, Peterson's Guide to Golf Schools and Resorts, 1995, The Complete Golfer's Almanac, 1996; editor-in-chief Incredible Innovations mag., 1996-97; editor-en-jefe Mundo Deportivo revista, 1995-97, Hogarama revista, 1995-97; supervising editor: The Endless Fairway, 4 vols., 1992-94, LINKS Mag. Property Lines, 1995; contbr. writer The East Village Eye, 1986-87, Bomb Mag., 1987, Capell's Circulation Report, 1989, Westways, 1994, iGOLF, 1995-96; host Southern Links, WHHI-TV, 1992-93; exec. prodr. Copa Nacional Mundo Deportivo, 1995; pub. Golfing Mag., 1997—. Mem. Beaufort (S.C.) County 2000 Edn. Task Force, 1994. Recipient Ala. Travel Writer award State of Ala., 1993. Mem. Old Sydneians Union, Psi Upsilon. Methodist. Office: JSA Pub 1658 10th St Santa Monica CA 90404-3706 also: Peterson Pub LLC 6420 Wilshire Blvd Los Angeles CA 90048

LANE, JOHN GERHART, orthopedic surgeon; b. Topeka, Kans., Dec. 31, 1955; s. Robert Gerhart and Mary Elaine (Griffith) L.; m. Allison Elizabeth Sundberg, Nov. 25, 1989; children: Christian, Katherine, Elizabeth. BS, U. So. Calif., 1978; MD, Yale U., 1984. Diplomate Am. Bd. Orthopedic Surgery. Physician San Diego Ctr. Sports Medicine, 1991—; clin. instr. U. Calif., San Diego, 1989—; adj. prof. San Diego State U., 1995—. Fellow Am. Acad. Orthopedic Surgeons; mem. Am. Orthopedic Soc. Sports Medicine, Arthroscopy Assn. N.Am. (grantee 1996). Office: 8010 Frost St Ste 510 San Diego CA 92123-4284

LANE, LARRY K., air industry service executive; b. 1948. BS in Social Scis., Oreg. Coll. Edn., 1974. With Evergreen Aviation Ground Logistics, 1967-78, 1984—, now chmn.; regional sales rep. Skyline Mobile Home Mfr., McMinnville, Oreg., 1978-84; pres. Evergreen Internat. Airlines, Inc., 1992—; bd. dirs. Evergreen Internat. Aviation. With USAR, 1969-75. Office: Evergeen Internat Airlines Inc 3850 Three Mile Ln Mcminnville OR 97128

LANE, LINDA PATRICIA, scriptwriter; b. L.A.; m. Warder Ray Harrison, 1981 (div. 1983); 1 child, Lucy Lane; m. Gunnar Magg, 1983 (div. 1986). BA, U. So. Calif., 1976. Screenwriter Writer's Guild Am., L.A., 1974—; screenwriter Warner Bros., Burbank, Calif., 1979-80; interactive writer Hands of Time Animation and Design, L.A., 1994. Co-author: Malibu 90265, 1990, (with Hermien Lee) The Spot Reducing Diet: How to Lose Weight Where You Want, 1983; screenwriter (movie) Crosstalk, 1982, (TV) Full House, 1994.

LANE, PATRICIA BAUMGARTNER, medical office manager; b. Scottsbluff, Nebr., Mar. 15, 1927; d. Casper and Myrtice A. (Edwards) Baumgartner; m. James A. Lane, Sept. 4, 1949; children: Leann Keller, Rene Rickabaugh. BBA, U. Denver, 1949. Sec. Edwin Shields Hewitt & Assocs., Chgo., 1949-51, C. of C., Newcastle, Wyo., 1951, Newcastle Sch. Dist., 1952-53; office mgr. Dr. James A. Lane, Newcastle, 1970—, optometric technician, 1980—. Pres. Wyo. Assn. Retarded Citizens, 1976-77; nat. bd. mem. Assn. Retarded Citizens, 1978-80, regional nat. v.p., 1980-84; bd. mem. United Fund of Weston County, Wyo., 1976-78; bd. trustees United Meth. Ch., Newcastle. Named Vol. of Yr. Assn. Retarded Citizens, Wyo., 1977. Mem. PEO Sisterhood, Wyo. Optometric Aux. (pres. 1960), 20th Century Club (treas. 1976—), Order Eastern Star. Republican. Home: 204 E Warwick St Newcastle WY 82701-2235

LANE, PEGGY LEE, educator; b. Ferndale, Mich., Jan. 13, 1948; d. Otto Gustave and Ruth Geraldine (Keyser) Kleve; m. Mark Lane, Sept. 7, 1978 (dec. June 1989). BA, Ctrl. Mich. U., 1972, MA, 1969; postgrad., U. North. Colo., 1991—. Tchr. Potterville (Mich.) Schs., 1969-76, Alpena (Mich.) Pub. Schs., 1976-78, 87-89, Anchor Bay Schs., New Baltimore, Mich., 1978-79; owner Park Lane Jewelry, Glasgow, Mont., 1979-87; county supt. Valley County, Glasgow, Mont., 1987; tchr. Littleton (Colo.) Pub. Schs., 1990—. Mem. ASCD, APS, Am. Edn. Rsch. Assn. Democrat. Unitarian. Home: 2905 S Clermont Dr Denver CO 80272

LANE, SYLVIA, economist, educator; b. N.Y.C.; m. Benjamin Lane, Sept. 2, 1939; children: Leonard, Reese, Nancy. A.B., U. Calif., Berkeley, 1934, M.A., 1936; postgrad., Columbia U., 1937; Ph.D., U. So. Calif., 1957. Lectr., asst. prof. U. So. Calif., Los Angeles, 1947-60; asso. prof. econs. San Diego State U., 1961-65; assoc. prof. finance, assoc. dir. Ctr. for Econ. Edn. Calif. State U., Fullerton, 1965-69, chmn. dept. fin., 1967-69; prof. agrl. econs. U. Calif., Davis, 1969-82, prof. emerita, 1982—; prof. emerita and economist Giannini Found., U. Calif.-Berkeley, 1982—; vis. scholar Stanford U., 1975-76; cons. Calif. Adv. Commn. Tax Reform, 1963, Office Consumer Affairs, Exec. Office of Pres., 1972-77, FAO, UN, 1983. Author: (with E. Bryant Phillips) Personal Finance, 1963, rev. edit., 1979, The Insurance Tax, 1965, California's Income Tax Conformity and Withholding, 1968, (with Irma Adelman) The Balance Between Industry and Agriculture in Economic Development, 1989; editl. bd. Agrl. Econs., 1986-92; also articles, reports in field. Project economist Los Angeles County Welfare Planning Coun., 1956-59; del. White House Conf. on Food and Nutrition, 1969, Pres.'s Summit Con. on Inflation, 1974; mem. adv. com. Ctr. for Bldg. Tech., Nat. Bur. Stds., 1975-79; bd. dirs. Am. Coun. Consumer Interests, 1972-74; exec. bd. Am. Agr. Econ. Assn. 1976-79. Ford Found. fellow UCLA, 1963; Ford Found. fellow U. Chgo., 1965; fellow U. Chgo., 1968. Fellow Am. Agrl. Econ. Assn. (life, Sylvia Lane Fellowship Fund 1993); mem. Am. Econ. Assn., Am. Coun. Consumer Interests, Omicron Delta Epsilon (pres. 1973-75, trustee 1975-83, chmn. bd. trustees 1982-84). Home: 1241 Grizzly Peak Blvd Berkeley CA 94708-2127 Office: U Calif Dept Agrl & Resource Econs Berkeley CA 94720 *Select goals carefully . . .*

LANE, THOMAS JAMES, business analyst, investment consultant; b. Seattle, Oct. 6, 1960; s. Edward Robert and Laura Louise L. BA in Humanities, Seattle U., 1980, BBA in Fin. and Econs., 1981; MBA in Fin. Mgmt., City U., Bellevue, Wash., 1992. Cost acct. Lockheed Marine, Seattle, 1982-83; bus. analyst Boeing Co., Seattle, 1984—. Home: 13035 39th NE Seattle WA 98125

LANE, WILLIAM KENNETH, physician; b. Butte, Mont., Nov. 5, 1922; s. John Patrick and Elizabeth Marie (Murphy) L.; m. Gilda Antoinette Parision, Aug. 21, 1954; children: William S., Francine Deirdre. Student, U. Mont., 1940-41, Mt. St. Charles Coll., 1941-43; MD, Marquette U., 1946; postgrad., Med. Coll. Wis. Intern Queen of Angels Hosp., L.A., 1946-47, resident physician, 1954-56; pvt. practice internal medicine San Francisco, 1947-51; resident in urology VA Hosp., Long Beach, Calif., 1956-58; physician VA Hosp., Long Beach, Oakland and Palo Alto, Calif., 1958—; lectr. on psychology of the elderly Foothill Coll., Los Altos, 1972-74; rschr. in field. Bd. dirs., mem. No. Cheyenne Indian Sch.; mem. Josef Meier's Black Hills Theatrical Group, S.D., 1940. With U.S. Army, 1943-46, ETO, lt. USN, 1951-54, Korea. Mem. AMA, Am. Geriatrics Soc., Nat. Assn. VA Physicians, San Francisco County Med. Soc., Woodrow Wilson Ctr. (assoc.), St. Vincent de Paul Soc., Cupertino Landscape Artists (past pres.), Audubon Soc., Stanford Hist. Soc., San Jose Movie/Video Club, San Jose Camera Club, Sierra Club. Roman Catholic. Home: 18926 Sara Park Cir Saratoga CA 95070-4164 Office: Stanford VA Med Ctr 3801 Miranda Ave # 171 Palo Alto CA 94304-1207

LANEY, LEROY OLAN, economist, banker; b. Atlanta, Mar. 20, 1943; s. Lee Edwin and Paula Izlar (Bishop) L.; m. Sandra Elaine Prescott, Sept. 3, 1966; children: Prescott Edwin, Lee Olan III. B Indsl. Engring., Ga. Inst. Tech., 1965; MBA in Fin., Emory U., 1967; MA in Econs., U. Colo., 1974, PhD in Econs., 1976. Budget analyst Martin-Marietta Corp., Denver, 1971-72; economist Coun. Econ. Advisers, Washington, 1974-75; internat. economist U.S. Treasury Dept., Washington, 1975-78; sr. economist Fed. Res. Bank Dallas, 1978-88; prof. econs., chmn. dept. Butler U., Indpls., 1989-90; sr. v.p. 1st Hawaiian Bank, Honolulu, 1990—; chmn. Fed. Res. Com. on Internat. Rsch., Washington, 1981-83; vis. prof. U. Tex., Arlington and Dallas, 1978-85; adj. prof. So. Meth. U., Dallas, 1982-85. Editor bank periodicals, 1975-88; contbr. articles to profl. jours. Mem. Internat. Fin. Symposium, Dallas, 1982-85; Hawaii Coun. on Revenues. Lt. USN, 1967-71. Scholar Ga. Inst. Tech., 1961; rsch. fellow Emory U., 1965-67, teaching fellow U. Colo., 1972-73; rsch. grantee Butler U., 1989-90. Mem. Am. Econ. Assn., Western Econ. Assn., Indpls. Econ. Forum, Plaza Club, Honolulu Rotary, Omicron Delta Epsilon, Lambda Alpha, Kappa Sigma. Office: 1st Hawaiian Bank Rsch Dept PO Box 3200 Honolulu HI 96847-0001

LANG, BRIAN JOSEPH, museum curator; b. Cleve., June 1, 1969; s. Joseph Francis and Marjorie (Ford) L.; m. Jennifer Noel Cervantes, May 28, 1994. BA, Beloit Coll., 1991; MA, U. Denver, 1997. Exhibits preparator Beloit (Wis.) Coll. Mus., 1987-91; intern New World dept. Denver Art Mus., 1991-93, adminstrv. asst. New World dept., 1993-94, security officer, 1994-95; curator Hiwan Homestead Mus., Evergreen, Colo., 1995—. Mem. Am. Assn. Mus., Soc. for Am. Archaeology, Jefferson County Hist. Soc., Assn. No. Front Range Mus. (sec.-treas. 1997—). Home: 2550 S University Blvd #203 Denver CO 80210 Office: Hiwan Homestead Mus 4208 S Timbervale Dr Evergreen CO 80439

LANG, GEORGE FRANK, insurance executive, consultant, lawyer; b. Orange, N.J., Aug. 21, 1937; s. Frank W. and Hilda I. (Pierson) L.; m. Grace B. Preisler, Jan. 30, 1960; children: Christine, Gregg, Cynthia; m. Valerie J. Hanson, Nov. 24, 1978. BS, Ill. Wesleyan U., 1960; JD, Ill. Inst. Tech., 1968. Account exec. Scarborough & Co., Chgo., 1960-67; dir. fin. inst. George F. Brown & Sons, Chgo., 1967-69; v.p., dir. Fin. Ins. Svc., Schaumburg, Ill., 1969-79; pres. City Ins. Svc., Elizabeth, N.J., 1980-84; mng. dir. Res. Fin. Mgmt., Miami, Fla., 1984-85; v.p. Beneficial Ins. Group, Newport Beach, Calif., 1985-86; v.p. Ask Ins. Svc., Irvine, Calif., 1986-89, cons. product ctr. sales, 1989; cons. Nat. Dealer Ins. Systems, 1989, New Liberty Adminstrn., 1990—, Home Crest Ins., 1991—, Great Western Ins. Agy., 1992—, Dana Harbor Ins. Svcs., Inc., 1995—; cons. in field. Bd. dirs. Woodview Civic Assn., Mt. Prospect, Ill., 1964-70, pres., bd. dirs., 1969; bd. dirs. Chippendale Assn., Barrington, Ill., 1972-76, v.p., bd. dirs., 1976. Home: 173 Ave de Poniente San Clemente CA 92672 Office: 24921 Dana Point Harbor Dr Dana Point CA 92629-2933

LANG, KURT, sociologist, educator, writer; b. Berlin, Jan. 25, 1924; came to U.S., 1936; s. Ernst and Ilse (Kass) L; m. Gladys Engel, June 9, 1950; children: Glenna Engel, Kevin Engel. BA, U. Chgo., 1949, MA, 1852, PhD, 1953. Rsch. analyst Office of U.S. Milit. Govt., Berlin, 1945-47; asst. prof. U. Miami, Fla., 1953-54; rsch. sociologist Can. Broadcasting Corp., Ottawa, Ont., 1954-56; from asst. to assoc. prof. Queens Coll. CUNY, Flushing, N.Y., 1956-62, assoc. prof., chair, 1963-64; prof. SUNY, Stony Brook, 1964-84, chair, 1965-68; prof. U. Wash., Seattle, 1984-93, prof. emeritus, 1993—, dir. Sch. Comm., 1984-87; vis. assoc. prof. U. Calif., Berkeley, 1962-63; vis. prof. Free U., Berlin, 1992; cons. CBS, N.Y.C., 1964-65, Nat. Adv. Commn. Civil Disorder, Washington, 1967. Author: Collective Dynamic, 1961, Television and Politics, 1968, 84, Battle for Public Opinion, 1983, Etched in Memory, 1990. U.S. Army Rsch. Inst. grantee, 1975-78, NEH fellow, 1971, Woodrow Wilson Ctr. fellow, 1978-79, Nat. Humanities Ctr. fellow, 1983-84, Sr. Fullbright fellow, 1994. Mem. Am. Polit. Sci. Assn. (Disting. Career award in polit. comm. 1994), Am. Assn. Pub. Opinion Rsch. (coun. 1975-77, Disting. Contbn. award 1989), Am. Sociol. Assn. (Edward L. Bernays award 1952), Internat. Inst. Comm. Democrat. Home: 1249 20th Ave E Seattle WA 98112-3530 Office: U Washington Dept Sociology Seattle WA 98195

LANG, MARGO TERZIAN, artist; b. Fresno, Calif.; d. Nishan and Araxie (Kazarosian) Terzian; m. Nov. 29, 1942; children: Sandra J. (Mrs. Ronald L. Carr), Roger Mark, Timothy Scott. Student, Fresno State U., 1939-42, Stanford U., 1948-50, Prado Mus., Madrid, 1957-59, Ariz. State U., 1960-61; workshops with, Dong Kingman, Ed Whitney, Rex Brandt, Millard Sheets, George Post. Maj. exhbns. include, Guadalajara, Mex., Brussels, N.Y.C., San Francisco, Chgo., Phoenix, Corcoran Gallery Art, Washington, internat. watercolor exhbn., Los Angeles, Bicentennial shows, Hammer Galleries, N.Y.C., spl. exhbn. aboard, S.S. France, others, over 50 paintings in various Am. embassies throughout world; represented in permanent collections, Nat. Collection Fine Arts Mus., Smithsonian Instn.; lectr., juror art shows; condr. workshops.; interviews and broadcasts on Radio Liberty, Voice of Am. Bd. dirs. Phoenix Symphony Assn., 1965-69, Phoenix Musical Theater, 1965-69. Recipient award for spl. achievements Symphony Assn., 1966, 67, 68, 72, spl. awards State of Ariz., silver medal of excellence Internat. Platform Assn., 1971; honoree U.S. Dept. State celebration of 25 yrs. of exhbn. of paintings in embassies worldwide, 1989. Mem. Internat. Platform Assn., Ariz. Watercolor Assn., Nat. Soc. Arts and Letters (nat. dir. 1971-72, nat. art chmn. 1974-76), Nat. Soc. Lit. and Arts, Phoenix Art Mus., Friends of Mexican Art, Am. Artists Profl. League, English-Speaking Union, Musical Theater Guild, Ariz. Costume Inst., Phoenix Art Mus., Scottsdale Art Ctr., Ariz. Arts Commn. (fine arts panel 1990-91). Home: 6127 E Calle Del Paisano Scottsdale AZ 85251-4212 *As a romantic impressionist I feel a tremendous exhilaration at being able to communicate my philosophy through my paintings. I look for God's beauty and mystery in all things, and as an artist, I feel very fortunate that I can eliminate the ugliness and the negatives and concentrate on the wonders of the universe around us.*

LANG, MARTIN T., mathematics educator; b. Yokohama, Japan, May 7, 1936; came to U.S., 1954; s. Ernst Friedrich and Dorothea M. (Bartsch) L.; m. Barbara Jane Parks, June 19, 1985; children: Rebecca E. Santos, Ruth E., Jonathan P. BA, North Ctrl. Coll., Naperville, Ill., 1959; MA, U. Kans., 1963; PhD, U. Tex., 1973. Asst. prof. San Diego State U., 1964-69; from asst. prof. to assoc. prof. Calif. Poly. State U., San Luis Obispo, 1969-78, prof., 1978—; site dir. Math Diagnostic Testing Project, Santa Barbara, San Luis Obispo, Monterey Counties, Calif., 1985—. Woodrow Wilson Nat. Fellowship Found. fellow, 1959; NDEA fellow, 1959. Mem. Nat. Coun. Tchrs. Math., Math. Assn. Am., Phi Beta Kappa. Methodist. Home: 1444 Tanglewood Ct San Luis Obispo CA 93401 Office: Calif Poly State Univ Math Dept San Luis Obispo CA 93407

LANG, NORMA ELLEN, art educator; b. Newton, Iowa, Mar. 11, 1931; d. Roger Hesser and Norma (Davis) Hostetler; m. Archibald Barrie Lang, Mar. 17, 1951; children: Stephanie, Christopher, Kimberly, Tracy. BA, Calif. State U., Northridge, 1973; BFA, Otis Art Inst., 1974, MFA, 1976. Cert. community coll. instr., Calif. Art instr. Coll. of the Redwoods, Crescent City, Calif., 1977-91, Southwestern Oreg. Community Coll., Coos Bay, 1979—; mem. Mayors Study Com. on the Arts, Glendale, Calif., 1972-76. Mem. budget com. Dist. 17C Sch. Dist., Brookings, Oreg., 1978-79, mem., chmn. sch. bd., 1979-84; mem. adv. coun. Libr. Bd., Brookings, 1990-93; vol. tax preparer AARP, Brookings Sr. Ctr., 1991-93; chmn. county safety campaign Curry County (Oreg.) Vol. Fire Assn., 1992. Mem. PEO, DAR (auditor), LWV (sec., treas. 1980—, cand. forum moderator 1984—). Home: PO Box 1859 Brookings OR 97415-0060

LANG, RICHARD ARTHUR, mayor, educator; b. Modesto, Calif., June 22, 1937; s. Frank Herbert and Joyce C. (Crowell) L.; m. Judith Karen Haertling, June 29, 1957; children: Susan Diane, Richard Arthur Jr., Julie Diane. BA in Polit. Sci., Calif. State U., Fresno, 1959; MA in Mgmt. Sys., Chapman Coll., 1973. Cert. tchr., Calif., cert. adminstr., Calif. Vice prin. Roosevelt Jr. H.S., 1974-77, La Loma Jr. H.S., 1977-79; asst. prin. in charge of student pers. svcs. Downey H.S., 1980; prin. Modesto (Calif.) H.S., 1980-90; govt. tchr. Downey H.S., Modesto, 1990—; mayor City of Modesto, 1991—. Elected to City Coun., City of Modesto, 1977, 81, 85, 89, vice mayor, 1981, chmn. citizen housing and comty. devel. com., 1983-92, chmn. solid waste com., 1984-92, chmn. downtown renaissance com., 1986—, chmn. econ. devel., comty. & intergovtl. rels. com., transp. policy com., utility svcs. & franchise com., pub. projects, budget and Stanislaus County solid waste adv. coms.; mem. Presdl. Mayors Task Force on Urban Affairs, 1992—; chmn. Modesto Bi-Centennial Com.; bd. dirs. Stanislaus chpt. ARC, 1992—, Assn. Retarded Citizens, Hanot Found., United Way, Family Tree. Named Man of Yr., VFW, 1992, Friend of the Chamber, Hispanic C. of C., 1991. Mem. Nat. Assn. Secondary Sch. Prins., Assn. Calif. Sch. Adminstrs., Modesto Rotary Club, Moose (lodge # 675), Phi Delta Kappa. Republican. Methodist. Home: 2705 Stafford Way Modesto CA 95350-2235 Office: PO Box 642 Modesto CA 95353

LANG, THOMPSON HUGHES, publishing company executive; b. Albuquerque, Dec. 12, 1946; s. Cornelius Thompson and Margaret Miller (Hughes) L. Student, U. N.Mex., 1965-68, U. Americas, Mexico City, 1968-69. Advt. salesman Albuquerque Pub. Co., 1969-70, pres., treas., gen. mgr., dir., 1971—; pub., pres., treas., dir. Jour. Pub. Co., 1971—; pres., dir. Masthead, Internat., 1971—; pres. Magnum Systems, Inc., 1973—; pres., treas., dir. Jour. Ctr. Corp., 1979—; chmn. bd., dir. Starline Printing, Inc., 1985—; chmn. bd. dirs. Corp. Security and Investigation, Inc., 1986—; pres., bd. dirs. Eagle Systems, Inc., 1986—. Mem. HOW Orgn., Sigma Delta Chi. Home: 8643 Rio Grande Blvd NW Albuquerque NM 87114-1301 Office: Albuquerque Pub Co PO Drawer JT(87103) 7777 Jefferson St NE Albuquerque NM 87109-4343

LANG, WENDY FRANCES, artist, photographer; b. Cleve., Feb. 15, 1938; d. H. Jack and Frances (Wise) L. BA, Antioch Coll., 1961; MA, Stanford U., 1963; student, Colegio de Mex., Mexico City, 1962, Inst. des Hautes Etudes, Paris, 1964-65. Assoc. film producer Richard Kaplan Prodns., Inc., N.Y.C., 1966; human resource specialist Community Devel. Agy., Project Head Start, N.Y.C., 1966-68; adminstrv. assoc. Model Cities Com., Office of Mayor, N.Y.C., 1968; tech. asst. Volt Tech. Corp., N.Y.C., 1968-69; photographer self-employed, N.Y.C., 1969-79; tchr. photography L.A. City Coll. Community Svcs., 1979-82; coord. The Photography Mus., L.A., 1980-81; interpreter Pasadena City Coll. Hearing Impaired Program, 1981-83; freelance interpreter L.A., 1984—; freelance photographer Nonstock, N.Y.C., 1984—; bd. dirs. Cameravision, chair grants com. 1976-77, activities com. (artists' hotseat), 1978-79; bd. dirs. L.A. Ctr. for Photographic Studies, 1979-82; bd. dirs., coord. Internat. Theatre Festival XV World Games for the Deaf, L.A., 1983-85; bd. dirs., 2d v.p. So. Calif. Recreation Assn. of the Deaf, 1983-87; bd. dirs., sec.-treas. Self-Actualization Inst. for the Deaf, 1983—, bd. dirs., treas. Damien Project, L.A., 1990-91. Exhibited works in one-person show at Cleve. Playhouse Gallery; group exhbns. include Soho/Cameraworks, L.A., Friends of Photography, Carmel, Steps into Space, L.A., Butler Inst. Am. Art, Youngstown, Ohio, Status Gallery, L.A., Clarence Kennedy Gallery, Cambridge, Mss., others; works featured in publs. including Wolf Mag. of Letters, Minolta Contact Sheet, Hispanic Am. Report, Worldmark Ency.; (rec. album) Communication Arts, 1974. Mem. Soc. for Photog. Edn., Friends of Photography, Ctr. for Creative Photography, Internat. Ctr. for Photography (N.Y.C.), Mus. of Photography. Home: 1231 Kipling Ave Los Angeles CA 90041-1616

LANG, WILLIAM EDWARD, mathematics educator; b. Salisbury, Md., Oct. 22, 1952; s. Woodrow Wilson and Clara T. L. BA, Carleton Coll., 1974; MS, Yale U., 1975; PhD, Harvard U., 1978. Vis. mem. Inst. for Advanced Study, Princeton, N.J., 1978-79; exch. prof. Universite de Paris, Orsay, 1980; C.L.E. Moore instr. MIT, Cambridge, 1980-82; asst. prof. U. Minn., Mpls., 1982-83, assoc. prof., 1983-89; vis. assoc. prof. Brigham Young U., Provo, Utah, 1988-89, prof., 1989—. Contbr. articles to profl. jours. Fellow NSF 1974-77, 79-80. Mem. Am. Math. Soc., Math. Assn. Am., Math. Scis. Rsch. Inst., Sigma Xi. Republican. Office: Brigham Young Univ Dept Math Provo UT 84602

LANGAGER, CRAIG T., artist; b. Seattle, July 5, 1946; s. Clarence John and Maybelle (Sandve) L.; m. Sarah Clark, 1979. BS in Art, Minn. State U., Bemidji, 1971; MFA, U. Oreg., 1974. Guest artist U. Minn., Mpls., 1975, Dartington (Eng.) Coll. Arts, 1977; chmn., tchr. coord. spl. events gallery Cornish Inst., Seattle, 1976-78; coord. Earthworks: Land Reclamation as Sculpture King County Arts Commn., Seattle, 1978-79; vis. sculptor Syracuse (N.Y.) U., 1982, U. Colo., Boulder, 1985. One-man shows include Foster/White Gallery, Seattle, 1975, 77, 79, Susan Caldwell, Inc., N.Y.C., 1980, 81, 83, 84, Inst. Contemporary Art, Boston, 1982, Winnipeg (Man.) Art Gallery, 1984, Ruth Siegel Ltd., N.Y.C., 1986, Bemidji (Minn.) State U.,

1986, Edith Baker Gallery, Dallas, 1987, William Traver Gallery, Seattle, 1991, Security Pacific Gallery, Seattle, 1991-92; exhibited in group shows at Foster/White Gallery, Seattle, 1973, 74, 76, Seattle Art Mus., 1975, 77, 87, Cornish Inst., Seattle, 1978, Goddard-Riverside Cmty. Ctr., N.Y.C., 1981, Wave Hill, Bronx, N.Y., 1981, Met. Mus. and Art Ctr., Coral Gables, Fla., 1982-83, Indpls. Mus. Art, 1982, 86, Contemporary Arts Ctr., Cin., 1985, Susan Caldwell Inc., N.Y.C., 1982, 83, 84, Siegel Contemporary Art, N.Y.C., 1983, Contemporary Arts Ctr., Cin., 1985-87, Ruth Siegel Ltd., N.Y.C., 1986, 87, 89, Edith Baker Gallery, Dallas, 1988, Colo. U. Art Galleries, 1992, U. Hawaii Art Gallery, Honolulu, 1994, many others; represented in permanent collections at Bklyn. Mus. Art, Denver Art Mus., Met. Mus. Art, N.Y.C., Mus. Art, U. Oreg., Eugene, Seattle Arts Commn., Seattle Art Mus., U. Colo. Galleries, Winnipeg Art Gallery, Can.; commd. by Niagara Frontier Transp. Authority Buffalo, Utica Station, 1982-83. Minn. State Arts grantee Minn. Coun. Arts, Mpls., 1975, Whitney Found. grantee, 1977.

LANGDELL, TIM, software company executive; b. Oxford, Eng., Jan. 1, 1953; came to U.S., 1972; s. Edgar George and Sybil Langdell; m. Cheri Colby Davis, Mar. 31, 1980; children: Melissa, Sebastian. BSc in Physics, Electronics, Psychology, Leicester (Eng.) U., 1975; MA in Psychology, Nottingham (Eng.) U., 1979; PhD in Psychology, U. Coll. London, 1981. Rsch. officer Nat. Phys. Lab., Twickenham, Eng., 1974; postdoctoral rsch. fellow U. Tilberg, Holland, 1977, UCLA Neuropsychiat. Inst., L.A., 1979; rsch. fellow, prof. Inst. Psychiatry, London, 1979-81; adj. prof. U. So. Calif. Film Sch., L.A., 1992-95; lectr. UCLA Ext., L.A., 1994—; CEO, chmn. Edge Interactive Media Ltd., London, 1982—; CEO Edge Interactive Media Inc., Pasadena, Calif., 1990—; cons. Sinclair Rsch., Cambridge, Eng., 1981-86; advisor, prodr. BBC Micro Live, London, 1983-86; chmn. Guild of Software Houses, London, 1983-85; bd. mem. Acad. Interactive Arts and Svcs., L.A., 1994—. Author: The Spectrum Handbook, 1982, Dragon 32, 1983, The New Hollywood, 1997. Recipient psychiat. fellowship Med. Rsch. Coun., London, 1980. Office: Edge Interactive Media 140 S Lake Ave # 206 Pasadena CA 91101

LANGDON, PAUL RUSSELL, retired accountant; b. Columbus, Ohio, Feb. 17, 1914; s. Waren Elmore and Ethel Hulda (Cowgill) L.; m. Marjorie Clark, Nov. 28, 1935; children: Larry R., Robert C. BSc, Ohio State U., 1935; postgrad., Am. U., Northwestern U. CPA, Ohio. Pub. acct. W.E. Langdon & Sons, Columbus, 1935-39, 47-48; dir. fin. U.S. R.R. Retirement Bd., Chgo., 1939-46; procedures analyst Nationwide Ins. Co., Columbus, 1948-49; asst. treas. Battelle Meml. Inst., Columbus, 1949-79. Mem. Columbus Sch. Bd., 1953-83, pres., 1958, 63, 65, 78; pres. Ohio Sch. Bds. Assn., Westerville, 1971; chmn. exec. com. Billy Graham Ctrl. Ohio Crusade, Columbus, 1964; trustee, sec. Malone Coll., Canton, Ohio, 1955-75; trustee mem. Columbus Tech. Inst., 1966-69. Recipient Spl. award for vocat. gidance Columbus Kiwanis, 1983, Emmerling Mgmt. award Adminstrv. Mgmt. Soc., 1960, Bronze Leadership award Jr. Achievement, Columbus, 1983. Mem. Ohio Soc. CPAs (life), PTA (life), Fin. Execs. Inst. (life). Republican. Presbyterian. Home: 2140 Santa Cruz Ave # C102 Menlo Park CA 94025

LANGE, GARY DAVID, periodontist; b. Mpls., Dec. 13, 1936; s. Emil and Esther Catherine (Schwartzkopf) L.; m. Donna Lynn Hall, Mar. 23, 1969; 1 child: Christian Elizabeth. BA, Augsburg Coll., Mpls., 1959; BS, U. Minn., 1961, DDS, 1963, MSD, 1971. Lic. periodontist. Dental intern U. S. Army Dental Corps, Tacoma, 1963-64; staff dentist and comdg. officer U. S. Army Dental Sect., Fulda, Fed. Republic of Germany, 1964-67; staff dentist U. S. Army Dental Corps, Ft. Bragg, N.C., 1967-69; periodontal resident U. Minn., Mpls., 1969-71; pvt. practice Rochester, Minn., 1971-74; staff periodontist VA, St. Petersburg, Fla., 1974-83, dir. gen. practice residency, 1983-86; chief dental svcs. VA, Columbia, Mo., 1986-92; chief dental svc. VA Med. Ctr., Prescott, Ariz., 1992—; asst. prof. Sch. Dentistry U. Minn., 1971-73, Kansas City Dental Sch., divsn. Grad Periodontics, U. Mo., 1987-92. Maj. U.S. Army, 1963-69. Mem. ADA, Am. Acad. Periodontology, Rotary Internat. Independent. Home: 2069 Meadowbrook Rd Prescott AZ 86303-5696

LANGE, GERALD WILLIAM, book artist, typographer; b. Green Bay, Wis., June 30, 1946; s. Carl Frederick and Harriet May (Miller) L. BA in Lit. and Lang., U. Wis., Green Bay, 1970; MLS in Libr. and Info. Sci., U. Wis., 1975. Propr. The Bieler Press, Marina Del Ray, Calif., 1975—; master printer U. So. Calif. Fine Arts Press, L.A., 1986-93. Editor (jours.) Coranto 1987-92, Abracadabra, 1990-96. Recipient certs. of excellence Am. Inst. Graphic Arts, N.Y.C., 1981, 82, 84, 86; certs. of typographic excellence Type Dirs. Club, N.Y.C., 1984, 92, Carl Hertzog award for excellence in book design, U. Tex., El Paso, 1991. Mem. Alliance for Contemporary Book Arts (founder, mng. editor, 1987—), Ampersand Club (printing officer, publishing officer 1982-86), Am. Printing Hist. Assn. (charter mem.), Pacific Ctr. for Book Arts (charter mem.), Rounce and Coffin Club. Office: The Bieler Press 4216 1/4 Glencoe Ave Marina Del Rey CA 90292

LANGE-OTSUKA, PATRICIA ANN, nursing educator; b. Sandusky, Ohio, June 25, 1959; d. James Henry and Elaine Elnora (Wiedeman) Lange; m. Lewis Masao Otsuka, Mar. 29, 1994; 1 stepchild, Katrina. Diploma in nursing, Providence Hosp. Sch. Nursing, 1981; BSN, Bowling Green State U., 1984; MSN in Cmty. Health, Med. Coll. Ohio Sch. Nursing, 1991; postgrad., Nova Southeastern U., 1994—. Cert. med.-surg. nurse, clin. specialist in cmty. health, ANA; CCRN, AACN. RN Providence Hosp., Sandusky, Ohio, 1981-91; grad. tchg. asst. Med. Coll. Ohio, Huron, 1989-91; nursing supr. Bellevue (Ohio) Hosp., 1991; asst. prof. nursing Hawaii Loa Coll., Kaneohe, 1991-92; nursing instr. U. Phoenix-Hawaii campus, 1992-93; asst. prof. nursing Hawaii Pacific U., Kaneohe, 1992—, acad. coord., 1993—; NCLEX rev. provider Med. Coll. Pa., Honolulu, 1993, Stanley Kaplan Corp., Honolulu, 1994, LBJ Tropical Med. Ctr., Pago Pago, 1996; freelance edn. cons., Hawaii, 1991—. Recipient Svc. awards Am. Diabetes Assn. Ohio Affiliate, Columbus and Sandusky, 1990. Mem. Providence Hosp. Sch. Nursing Alumnae Assn. (pres.-elect, pres. 1988-89), Sigma Theta Tau (Gamma Psi at large, counselor 1993—). Office: Hawaii Pacific Univ 45-045 Kamehameha Hwy Kaneohe HI 96749

LANGER, GLENN ARTHUR, cellular physiologist, educator; b. Nyack, N.Y., May 5, 1928; s. Adolph Arthur and Marie Catherine (Doscher) L.; m. Beverly Joyce Brawley, June 5, 1954 (dec. Nov. 1976); 1 child, Andrea; m. Marianne Phister, Oct. 12, 1977. BA, Colgate U., 1950; MD, Columbia U., N.Y.C., 1954. Diplomate Am. Bd. Internal Medicine. Asst. prof. medicine Columbia U. Coll. Physicians and Surgeons, N.Y.C., 1963-66; assoc. prof. medicine and physiology UCLA Sch. Medicine, 1966-69, prof., 1969—, Castera prof. cardiology, 1978—, assoc. dean rsch., 1986-91, dir. cardiovascular rsch. lab., 1987—; Griffith vis. prof. Am. Heart Assn., L.A., 1979; cons. Acad. Press, N.Y.C., 1989-97. Editor: The Mammalian Myocardium, 1974, 2d edit., 1997, Calcium and the Heart, 1990; mem. editorial bd. Circulation Rsch., 1971-76, Am. Jour. Physiology, 1971-76, Jour. Molecular Cell Cardiology, 1974-97; contbr. over 175 articles to profl. jours. Capt. U.S. Army, 1955-57. Recipient Disting. Achievement award Am. Heart Assn. Sci. Coun., 1982, Heart of Gold award, 1984, Cybulski medal Polish Physiol. Soc., Krakow, 1990, Pasarow Found. award for Cardiovascular Sci., 1993; Macy scholar Josiah Macy Found., 1979-80. Fellow AAAS, Am. Coll. Cardiology; mem. Am. Soc. Clin. Investigation, Am. Assn. Physicians.

LANGER, RICHARD CHARLES, minister; b. Chgo., Sept. 23, 1957; s. Gerhard and Ann Mae L.; m. Shari Lynn Langer, June 19, 1982; children: Crystal, Mark. BS, Colo. State U., 1979; MDiv, Talbot Sch. Theology, La Mirada, Calif., 1985; MA, U. Calif., Riverside, 1987, PhD, 1990. Ordained to ministry Evang. Free Ch. of Am. Pastor Trinity Ch., Redlands, Calif., 1985—; lectr. U. Calif., Riverside, 1990—; bio-ethicist Smart Practice, Phoenix, Ariz., 1994-96; mem. instnl. rev. bd. Loma Linda (Calif.) U., 1993—, southwest dist. bd. Evang. Free Ch. of Am., Mpls., 1996—. Contbr. articles to profl. jours. Active Bldg. a Generation task force United Way, Redlands, 1995—. Mem. Am. Philos. Assn., Soc. Christian Philosophers, Ministerial Assn. Evang. Free Ch. Office: Trinity Ch 1551 Reservoir Rd Redlands CA 92374

LANGER, STEPHEN MARC, clinical psychologist; b. Richland, Wash., May 22, 1955; s. Otto Heinrich and Erdmute Johanna (Heidtman) L.; m. Donna Marie Mendenhall; 1 child, Anneliese Mendenhall. BS magna cum laude, U. Wash., 1977; MA, U. Mont., 1980, PhD, 1983. Lic. psychologist, Wash.; cert. biofeedback Biofeedback Cert. Inst. Am., cert. health svc. provider in psychology Nat. Register Health Svc. Providers in Psychology. Counselor Mercer Inn Psychiat. Half-way House for Women, Seattle, 1976-77; psychology trainee level I psychology svc. VA Hosp., Battle Creek, Mich., 1978; instr. divsn. continuing edn. U. Mont., 1979, teaching asst. psychology dept., 1980-81, practicum asst. Clin. Psychology Ctr., 1980-81; psychology trainee level II psychology svc. VA Med. Ctr., Richmond, Va., 1980; intern psychology svc. VA Med. Ctr., Pitts., 1981-82; staff psychologist Behavioral Medicine Clinic, Olympia, Wash., 1982-86; psychologist Olympia, 1983—; part-time student psychologist Mont. State Prison, Deer Lodge, 1977-78, 81; part-time extern Children's Hosp., Pitts., 1982; staff psychologist St. Peter Hosp., Olympia, 1985-88; expert Madigan Army Med. Ctr., Tacoma, 1986-96; staff privileges St. Peter Hosp., Olympia, Madigan Army Med. Ctr., Tacoma; mem. Thurston-Mason County Mental Health Adv. Bd., 1985-88; dir. N.W. Brief Therapy Tng. Ctr., 1994—. Contbr. articles to profl. jours. Chmn. Henderson Inlet Watershed Coun., Thurston County, 1989—; vol. counselor phone crisis intervention Open Door Clinic, Seattle, 1975-77. Honors scholar U. Wash., 1975, 76, 77. Mem. APA (assoc.), Assn. for Advancement of Behavior Therapy, Assn. for Applied Psychophysiology and Biofeedback, Internat. Coun. Psychologists, Soc. for Clin. and Exptl. Hypnosis (assoc.), Wash. State Psychol. Assn., Biofeedback Soc. Wash. (past pres.), Deschutes Psychol. Assn. (past pres.), Phi Beta Kappa. Home: 3238 Lindell Rd NE Olympia WA 98506-3628 Office: 1021 Legion Way SE Olympia WA 98501-1522

LANGEVIN, MICHAEL PETER, publisher, author; b. Lawrence, Mass., Dec. 30, 1952; s. Louis Loyde and Eileen Winiferd (Gibbons) L.; m. Deborah Genito, July 7, 1989; children: Henry, Sophia. AA, No. Essex Coll., Haverhill, Mass., 1973; BS in Polit. Sci., U. Mass., 1975; M.English, San Francisco State U., 1982. Pub. Poor Farm Rev., Methuen, Mass., 1975-77, Shot in the Dark, Cambridge, Mass., 1977-78, Magical Blend, Chico, Calif., 1979—. Editor, co-author: A Magical Universe, 1976. Green Party. Office: Magical Blend 133-1/2 Broadway Chico CA 95928

LANGFORD, ROBERT BRUCE, chemistry educator; b. San Francisco, Mar. 7, 1919; s. Stephen George and Carrie Anna (Williams) L.; m. Wilma Ruth Ostrander, Feb. 1, 1957. BS in Chemistry, UCLA, 1948; MS in Chemistry, U. So. Calif., L.A., 1963, PhD in Pharm. Chemistry, 1972. Registered U.S. Patent Agt. Analytical chemist So. Pacific Co., L.A., 1949-54; rsch. chemist Stauffer Chem. Co., Torrance, Calif., 1954-58; prodn. mgr. Cyclo Chem. Corp., L.A., 1958-61; chemistry educator Marshall High Sch., L.A., 1961-64; prof. chemistry E. L.A. Coll., Monterey Park, Calif., 1964-86; prof. chemistry, emeritus E. L.A. Coll., Monterey Park, 1986—, head chemistry dept., 1968-74; adj. prof. chemistry L.A. Pierce Coll., Woodland Hills, Calif., 1992—. Patentee in field; contbr. articles to profl. jours. Staff sgt. USAF, 1941-45. Mem. Am. Chem. Soc., Masonic Lodge, Elks Lodge, Sigma Xi. Home: 644 Haverkamp Dr Glendale CA 91206-3117

LANGGUTH, EARL LEONARD, clergyman, writer, poet; b. San Diego, Apr. 7, 1927; s. Earl Chester and Kathleen Dakyne (Webster) l.; m. Mary Lu Langguth, Dec. 28, 1952; 1 child, Robert Leonard. AB, San Diego State U., 1951; postgrad., Columbia U., 1952-53; MDiv cum laude, Pacific Sch. Religion, Berkeley, Calif., 1956. Ordained minister Meth. Ch., 1956. Youth pastor Laurel Meth. Ch., Oakland, Calif., 1953-54; pastor Elverta (Calif.) Meth. Ch., 1954-56, Kings Beach (Calif.) Meth. Ch., 1956-60; pastor First Meth. Ch., Livingston, Calif., 1960-64, Dinuba, Calif., 1964-74; pastor Palm United Meth. Ch., Dinuba, 1970-74, Grass Valley (Calif.) United Meth. Ch., 1974-83, Faith United Meth. Ch., Sacramento, 1983-89, Montclair United Meth. Ch., Oakland, 1989-93, Laurel United Meth. Ch., Oakland, 1993—; assoc. statistician Cali.f-Nev. Conf., Dinuba, 1964-68, conf. statistician, 1968-88. Editor Bay View Rev., Oakland, 1991-97. Mem. Montclair Lions Club (pres.). Home: 4254 Detroit Ave Oakland CA 94619-1602 Office: Laurel United Meth Ch 3525 Kansas St Oakland CA 94619-1415

LANGLEY, MICHAEL DOUGLAS, secondary education educator; b. Martinez, Calif., Aug. 24, 1949; s. Harrold Lloyd and June Celeste (Lindstrom) Cline; m. Claudia Jane Neumann, July 20, 1974; children: Jennifer Jessen, Nicole Suzanne. BA in History cum laude, Calif. State U., Hayward, 1988. Tchg. credential in social studies. Sheet metal worker Prescolite, San Leandro, Calif., 1973-74; prodn. scheduler Prescolite, San Leandro, 1974-75; tchr. U.S. history El Dorado Middle Sch., Concord, Calif., 1989—; social studies dept. chair El Dorado Middle Sch., Concord, 1992—; interdisciplinary team leader El Dorado Middle Sch., Concord, 1992-93. Staff sgt. U.S. Army, 1976-84. Decorated Army Commendation medal with two oak leaf clusters, Joint Svc. Commendation medal Dept. Def., 1984; recipient Single Computer in Classroom grant Mt. Diablo Unified Sch. Dist., 1990; named Mid. Sch. History Tchr. of 1994, DAR, 1994. Mem. Nat. Assn. Mid. Schs., Calif. Tchrs. Assn. Democrat. Home: 3829 Chatworth Pittsburg CA 94565-5709 Office: El Dorado Middle Sch 1750 West St Concord CA 94521-1008

LANGLEY, PAMELA JANE, association executive; b. Havre, Mont., Mar. 11, 1947; d. Clarence James and Ruth Evine Patrick; m. Gary Alfred Langley, Oct. 22, 1972 (separated Oct. 1995); children: Jeff, Kari. BA in Home Econs., U. Mont., 1969, BA in Journalism, 1969, MA, 1980; postgrad., Carroll Coll., Helena, Mont. Tchr. journalism, home econs. Lincoln County H.S., Eureka, Mont., 1969-71; grad. asst. U. Mont. Sch. Journalism, Missoula, 1971-72; reporter Daily Interlake, Kalispell, Mont., summer 1971, U.S. West, Helena, 1972-73; pub. rels U.S. West (now Mountain Bell), Helena, 1973-74; tchr. journalism, English Helena H.S., 1974-81; exec. dir. Profl. Ins. Agts. Mont., Helena, 1981-84, 87-91, Mont. Agrl. Bus. Assn., Helena, 1987—; exec. sec. Mont. Grain Elevator Assn., Helena, 1993—. State committeewoman Mont. Rep. Ctrl. Com., Helena, 1970-71; trustee Helena Sch. Dist. #1, 1985-92; dir. bd. trustees Mont. Sch. Bd. Assn., 1990-92. Recipient Journalism Achievement award The Newspaper Fund, Princeton, N.J., 1977-78, Medal of Merit Journalsim Edn. Assn., 1982, North Star award Western Crop Protection Assn., 1992, Nat. Newsletter award State Agr. Chem. & Fertilizer, 1992, Marvin Heintz award Mont. Sch. Bds. Assn., 1991. Mem. Am. Soc. Assn. Execs., Mont. Soc. Assn. Execs., Nat. Journalism Edn. Assn. (v.p. 1978-81), Mont. Journalism Edn. Assn. (pres. 1976-77), Last Chance Press Club (pres. 1976). Republican. Lutheran. Office: Mont Grain Elevator Assn Mont Agr Bus Assn 1806 Capitol Ave Helena MT 59601

LANGLEY, ROCKY D., agricultural business executive; b. Albuquerque, Oct. 14, 1953; s. Ralph L. and Selia D. (Francis) L.; m. Debra Houston, May 17, 1975; children: Kristy K., Steven P. BS, N.Mex. State U., 1975. Asst. country supr. Farmers Home Adminstrn., Taos, N.Mex., 1975-77; acctg. mgr. Price's Valley Gold Dairies, Inc., Bernalillo, N.Mex., 1977-79, gen. mgr., sr. v.p., 1979—. Leathercraft leader 4-H, Bernalillo, 1993-97, dairy team leader, 1994-95; mem. N.Mex. State Engr. Water Conservancy Group, Sante Fe, 1992-93, Water Adv. Bd.-Torrance County, Estancia, N.Mex., 1994-97. Mem. Middle Rio Grande Dairy Herd Improvement Assn. (pres. 1987), Dairy Prodrs. N.Mex. (v.p. 1993-97). Republican. Home: 618 Hwy 528 Box 10862 Bernalillo NM 87004 Office: Price's Valley Gold Dairies PO Box 850 Bernalillo NM 87004

LANGLOIS, DONNA LEE, beauty trade school administrator; b. Harvey, Ill., Nov. 1, 1936; d. Leonard Clay and Mildred Anna (Seibert) Hampton; m. Robert Marvin Langlois, Oct. 15, 1974; children—Renee A. Holsen, Scott C. Farrand. Student U. Chgo., 1955-57, Art Inst. Chgo., 1956-58. Office mgr. Luth. Brotherhood Life Ins. Co., Chgo., 1959-72; sales dir. Mary Kay Cosmetics, Dallas, 1972-76; exec. sec. to pres. and chmn. bd. Talal Abu-Ghazaleh & Co., Kuwait, 1976-77; area mgr. Luzier Cosmetics Co., Kansas City, Kans., 1977-78; nat. dir. home mktg. div. Yves Roche Internat., Northbrook, Ill., 1979-81; regional v.p., Wilfred Am. Edn1. Corp., N.Y.C., 1981-90, ednl. exec. cons., Avon; Recipient various sales awards. Mem. Assn. Women Bus. Owners, Nat. Assn. Female Execs. Lutheran. Avocations: professional organist; reading; golfing. Home: PO Box 10410 Zephyr Cove NV 89448 Office: PO Box 1670 Zephyr Cove NV 89448

LANGMAN, ALAN WAYNE, physician; b. Phila., Feb. 28, 1956. BA, Temple U., 1978; MD, Hahnemann U., 1982. Diplomate Am. Bd. Otolaryngology. Resident in otolaryngology U. Calif., San Francisco, 1983-89; fellow U. Mich., Ann Arbor, 1989-90; staff physician Virginia Mason Med. Ctr., Seattle, 1990—. Contbr. articles to profl. jours. Fellow Am. Acad. Otolaryngology-Head and Neck Surgery, Am. Neurotology Soc. (assoc.); mem. Seattle Surg. Soc. Office: Virginia Mason Med Ctr 1100 9th Ave Seattle WA 98101-2756

LANGONI, RICHARD ALLEN, civil engineer; b. Trinidad, Colo., Aug. 7, 1945; s. Domenic and Josephine (Maria) L.; A of Applied Sci., Trinidad State Jr. Coll., 1966; BSCE Colo. State U., 1968; MA, U. No. Colo., 1978; m. Pamela Jill Stansberry, Aug. 19, 1972; children: Kristi, Kerri. Civil engr. Dow Chem. Co., Golden, Colo., 1968-71; city engr., dir. public works City of Trinidad, 1971-74; civil engr. Clement Bros. Constrn. Co., 1974-75; instr. Trinidad State Jr. Coll., 1975-78; city engr., dir. public works City of Durango (Colo.), 1978-82; region traffic engr. Colo. Dept. Transp., Durango, 1982—. Recipient Meritorious Svc. award City of Durango; registered profl. engr. Colo., N.Mex. Mem. Nat. Soc. Profl. Engrs., ASCE, Am. Public Works Assn., Water Pollution Control Fedn., Profl. Engrs. Colo., Durango C. of C., Nat. Ski Patrol (Purgatory and Wolf Creek), Phi Theta Kappa, Chi Epsilon. Home: 30 Moenkopi Dr Durango CO 81301-8599

LANG-PERALTA, LINDA ANN, English language educator; b. Coronado, Calif., July 13, 1953; d. William Harper and Catherine Margaret (Ray) Lang; m. Timothy Peralta, Apr. 2, 1982. BA in English, Calif. State U., Long Beach, 1980, MA in Comparative Lit., 1983; PhD in Comparative Lit., U. Calif., Irvine, 1991. Tchg. asst./assoc. U. Calif., Irvine, 1983-88, lectr. humanities, 1991-94; instr. humanities U. Redlands, Calif., 1991-94, Irvine (Calif.) Valley Coll., 1992-94; lectr. English U. Nev., Las Vegas, 1994—. Editor: Visions of Peace, 1982. Mem. MLA, Am. Lang. Assn., Am. Soc. for 18th Century Studies, Am. Conf. on Romanticism, Popular Culture Assn., Can. Soc. for 18th Century Studies, Phi Delta Gamma, Phi Kappa Phi. Office: U Nev Las Vegas Dept English PO Box 455011 4505 S Maryland Pky Las Vegas NV 89154-9900

LANGS, TED CHARLES, aerospace company executive; b. Orlando, Fla., July 20, 1954; s. Theodore Charles and Katherine Elizabeth (Willette) L.; m. Lois Ann Grimaldi, July 22, 1978; children: Eric Christopher, Samantha Ann. Student, Bryant Coll., 1973-76, U. R.I., 1976-78, Mira Mesa Coll., 1981-82, U. Phoenix, 1994—. Cert. telecomm. I. Br. supr., loan officer Columbus Nat. Bank, Providence, 1977-82; sr. analyst Travelodge-Trusthouse/Forte Hotels, 1982-86; chief fin. analyst/strategist Radelow/Gittins, San Diego, 1986-92; v.p. Arrow Aviation Spares, Oceanside, Calif., 1993—; Prin. Langs. and Assoc. Bus. Cons., Oceanside, 1992—; cons. World Bank, Inter Am. Devel. Bank. CRP instr., co-author new instrn. methods ARC, San Diego chpt.; commr. econ. devel., 1994—; bd. dirs., mktg. dir. Leadership 2000. Mem. Am. Hotel Motel Assn., Am. Bankers Assn., Profl. Assn. Diving Instrs., Oceanside C. of C. (bd. dirs., chair travel and tourism), San Diego C. of C., World Trade Assn. Irvine.

LANGTON, DANIEL JOSEPH, English, writing educator, poet; b. Paterson, N.J., Sept. 6, 1927; s. Daniel Patrick and Martha Langton; m. Eva Heymann, Feb. 1, 1949; 1 child, Mark. BA, San Francisco State U., 1952, MA, 1954; PhD, U. Calif., Berkeley, 1970. Lifetime tchg. credential, Calif. Tchr. San Rafael (Calif.) H.S., 1963-67; from asst. prof. to prof. English and creative writing San Francisco State U., 1967—. Author: Querenica, 1976 (Devins award 1976), The Hogarth-Selkirk Letters, 1985, The Inheritance, 1990, Life Forms, 1995. Mem. ACLU. Mem. Poetry Soc. Am., Internat. Poetry Soc., Am. Acad. Poets. Democrat. Home: 1673 Oak St San Francisco CA 94117 Office: San Francisco State Univ Coll Humanities San Francisco CA 94132

LANIER, WILLIAM JOSEPH, college program director; b. Great Falls, Mont., Dec. 20, 1963; s. Bolder Lanue and Nancy Jo (Kiszczak) L. AS, No. Mont. Coll., 1985, B Tech., 1987, MEd, 1989. Drafting intern Columbus Hosp., Great Falls, 1985-87; grad. asst. No. Mont. Coll., Havre, 1987-89; dir. student life Mont. State U. -No. (formerly No. Mont. Coll.), Havre, 1989-95, 1995—. Bd. dirs. Havre Encourages Long Range Prevention, 1992—, Hill County Crimestoppers, 1991-93; adv. bd. No. Ctrl. Mont. Upward Bound, Harlem, 1992—; mem. Nat. Eagle Scout Assn., Irving, Tex., 1991—. Recipient Golden N award student senate No. Mont. Coll., 1992. Mem. Am. Counseling Assn., Am. Coll. Pers. Assn., Nat. Assn. Student Pers. Adminstrs., No. Mont. Coll. Alumni Assn. (bd. dirs 1990—). Home: MacKenzie Hall Havre MT 59501 Office: Mont State U - No Box 7751 Havre MT 59501

LANKFORD, DUANE GAIL, investment banker, mountaineer; b. Ft. Collins, Colo., July 18, 1932; s. William Oliver and Mary Martha (Lago) L.; m. Eleanor Polly, June 18, 1955 (div. 1983); children: Scott, Kurt Edwin, Rebecca Ann; m. Jariyaporn Ekkanasing, Nov. 8, 1991. Student, Colo. State Coll. of Edn., 1950-51, Denver U., 1952-55. Lic. stockbroker over 40 states security commns. and all U.S. exchs. Mgr. Dial Fin., Denver, 1953-59; mgr. investment banking Peters Writer & Christianson, Denver, 1959-60, E.I. DuPont De Nemours, Denver, 1960; mgr. mcpl. investment banking Bache & Co., Denver, L.A., N.Y.C., 1961-68; v.p. sales Fin. Programs, Inc., San Francisco, 1968-69; fin. advisor Lankford & Co., Denver, 1969; mgr. muni bonds W.E. Hutton & Co., Denver, 1969-71; owner/operator Lankford & Co., Denver, 1972—, The Wilderness Inst./Lankford Mountain Guides, Denver, 1978—; chmn. Denver Lenders Exch., 1957-58; cons. advisor numerous cities, towns, states and corps.; expert witness in investment banking and mountaineering; cons. numerous legal firms; cons./advisor numerous fed. agys. Contbr. articles to profl. jours. Worldwide mountaineer numerous maj. peaks. Mem. Am. Alpine Club, Pioneers. Republican.

LANPHIER, SCOTT MATTHEW, transportation engineer; b. Chula Vista, Calif., June 22, 1963; s. Vernard Alaucios and Penny Larue (Anderson) L. BSCE, U. Colo., 1991. Sr. transp. engr. Korve Engring., Sacramento, 1991-95, Fehr & Peers Assocs., 1996—. With USMC, 1981-84. Mem. Inst. Transp. Engrs. (No. Calif. legis. chair 1992-93), N.Y. Acad. Scis. Republican. Home: 4152 Donald Dr Marysville CA 95901-9334

LANS, CARL GUSTAV, architect, economist; b. Gothenburg, Sweden, Oct. 19, 1907; came to U.S., 1916; s. Carl and Ida Carolina (Schon) L.; m. Gwynne Iris Meyer, Dec. 21, 1935; children: Douglas C., C. Randolph. Student, CCNY, 1925-26, Sch. Architecture, Columbia U., 1926-30. Registered architect, Calif. Architect with Harry T. Lindeberg N.Y.C., 1930-32; architect Borgia Bros. Ecclesiastical Marble, N.Y.C., 1932-34; with architects Paist & Stewart, Miami, Fla., 1934-35; chief engr. insp. Dept. Agr., 1936-38; asst. tech. dir. FHA, 1938-48; tech. dir. Nat. Assn. Home Builders, Washington, 1948-52; with Earl W. Smith Orgn., Berkeley, Calif., 1952-56; architect, economist Huntington Beach, Calif., 1956—; ptnr. John Hans Graham & Assocs. Architects, Washington, 1947-55; spl. adviser Pres. Rhee, Republic of Korea, 1955-56; guest lectr. various univs., 1949-52. Author: Earthquake Construction, 1954. Chmn. bd. edn. adv. com., Arlington, Va., 1948. Recipient Outstanding and Meritorious Svcs. citation Republic of Korea, 1956. Mem. AIA (citation), Nat. Acad. Scis. (bldg. rsch. adv. bd. dirs.), S.W. Rsch. Inst., Seismol. Soc. Am., Prestressed Concrete Inst., Urban Land Inst., Nat. Press Club. Home and Office: 21821 Fairlane Cir Huntington Beach CA 92646-7902

LANSDOWNE, WILLIAM M., police chief; b. May 10, 1944; s. Leonard M. and Grace (Dabuque) L.; m. Sharon L. Young, June 12, 1994; children: Greg, Erik. BS in Law Enforcement, San Jose State U., 1971. Asst. chief San Jose (Calif.) Police Dept., 1966-94; chief Richmond (Calif.) Police Dept., 1994—; bd. dirs. Los Medanos Coll. Law Enforcement, Pittsburgh, Calif. bd. dirs. Christmas in April, Richmond, YMCA. Mem. Internat. Assn. Chiefs of Police, Calif. Police Chiefs Assn., Rotary. Office: Richmond Police Dept 401 27th St Richmond CA 94804-1769

LANTER, SEAN KEITH, software engineer; b. Los Alamos, N.Mex., May 8, 1953; s. Robert Jackson and Norma Esther (Jonas) L.; m. Lauri Jane Willand, July 16, 1977; children: Tully Erik, Sarah Elizabeth, Rachel Erin. BA in Physics, U. Utah, 1974, MS in Mech. Engring., 1977. Registered profl. engr. Wash. Sr. engr. Boeing Comml. Airplane Co., Seattle, 1977-82; systems analyst Internat. Submarine Tech. Ltd., Redmond, Wash., 1982-83; engr. software Advanced Tech. Labs., Bellevue, Wash., 1983-84; engr. contract Rho Co., Redmond, 1984-85; sr. mem. tech. staff Cedar Software Inc., Redmond, 1985-87; pres. Connexions Engring. and Software, Woodinville, Wash., 1987-88; pres., chief engr. Connexions Engring., Inc., Woodinville,

1990-95; sys. engr. Microrim Software, Inc., Bellevue, Wash., 1995-96; cons., contract programmer, 1990—. Contbr. articles to profl. jours. Mem. Assn. Computing Machinery, NSPE. Lutheran. Office: Connexions Engring PO Box 3007 Woodinville WA 98072-3007

LANTING, FRANS MARTEN, photographer, writer; b. Rotterdam, The Netherlands, July 13, 1951; came to U.S., 1978; s. Frans Lanting and Geertruida Stravers. MS in Econs., Erasmus U., 1977. Ind. photographer, writer Nat. Geographic Mag., 1987—; roving editor Nat. Wildlife Fedn., Washington, 1992. Author: Madagascar: A World Out of Time, 1990, Okavango: Africa's Last Eden, 1993, Peace on Earth, 1993; co-author: Forgotten Edens, 1993, Bonobo, The Forgotten Ape, 1997, Eye to Eye, 1997; columnist: Outdoor Photographer Mag., 1994—. Recipient 1st prize World Press Photo, 1988-89, 1st prize Nat. Press Photographers Assn., 1994; named Wildlife Photographer of Yr., BBC Wildlife, 1991. Mem. Am. Soc. Media Photographers (mem. adv. bd. N.C. chpt. 1993—), N.Am. Nature Photography Assn. (bd. dirs. 1993—), World Wildlife Fund Holland (councillor 1995, editl. cons. 1993—). Home and Office: Frans Lanting Photography 1985 Smith Grade Santa Cruz CA 95060-9758

LANTOS, THOMAS PETER, congressman; b. Budapest, Hungary, Feb. 1, 1928; m. Annette Tillemann; children: Annette, Katrina. B.A., U. Washington, 1949, M.A., 1950; Ph.D., U. Calif.-Berkeley, 1953. Mem. faculty U. Wash., San Francisco State U., 1950-83; TV news analyst, commentator, sr. econ. and fgn. policy adviser to several U.S. senators; mem. Presdl. Task Force on Def. and Fgn. Policy, 97th-104th Congresses from 11th (now 12th) Calif dist., 1981—; ranking minority mem., internat. rels. subcom. on internat. ops. and human rels., internat. rels. subcom. on western hemisphere, mem. gov. reform and oversight com.; founder study abroad program Calif. State U. and Coll. System. Mem. Millbrae Bd. Edn., 1950-66. Democrat. Office: US Ho of Reps 2217 Rayburn HOB Washington DC 20515-0512*

LANTZ, NORMAN FOSTER, electrical engineer; b. Pekin, Ill., June 8, 1937; s. Norman Gough and Lenore (Elsbury) L.; m. Donnis Maureen Ballinger, Sept. 7, 1958 (div. Aug. 1991); children: Katherine, Deborah, Norman Daniel; m. Judith Eliane Peach, Dec. 7, 1991. BSEE, Purdue U., 1959, MSEE, 1961. System engr. GE Co., Phila., 1961-72; mem. tech. staff The Aerospace Corp., El Segundo, Calif., 1972-75, mgr., 1975-79, dir., 1979-83, prin. dir., 1983-90, sr. project engr., 1991—; dir. Internat. Found. for Telemetering, Woodland Hills, Calif., 1985—. 2d lt. U.S. Army, 1960-61. Mem. AIAA (sr.), IEEE, Am. Mgmt. Assn. Office: The Aerospace Corp Sr Project Engineer El Segundo CA 90245-4691

LAPAGE, ROGER, film producer; b. Southend on Sea, Eng., July 27, 1939; came to U.S., 1959; s. Norman George and Joyce (Heard) LaP.; m. Maureen Quinn, May 8, 1982; children: Jonathan Baratt, Kimberly Beth. Student, Dunraven Sch., London, Legat Sch., Tunbridge, Eng. Prodr. films Chicago Song, Rodeo Girl, The Blessing, Dealy Force, Hambone and Hilly, Hot Resort, Amazon Women on the Moon, Verne Miller, Out on A Whim, Living Right, Angel Town, Past Tense, The Good Bad Guy, 52 Pickup, Girls Just Wanna Have Fun, Transylvania 6 5000, Lion Heart, Mannequin 2, Barber Shop Wars, Blue Movie Blue/Wild Orchid 2, Red Shoe Diaries, Lost in Africa, Love Cheat and Steal, Shelf Life, Viper, Fishing With George, Red Line, (TV pilot) Love is Strange; co-prodr. Paint It Black; also numerous comml‍s. With U.S. Army, 1962-64. Mem. SAG, Dir. Guild Am. Democrat. Home: 5940 Donna Ave Tarzana CA 91356

LAPENA, FRANK RAYMOND, art educator; b. San Francisco, Oct. 5, 1937; s. Henry and Evelyn Gladys (Towndolly) LaP.; m. Catherine Alice Sell Skinner, Aug. 19, 1966 (div. Apr. 1984); children: Kari Renee, Vincent Craig; stepchildren: Ivy, Peggy, Dan, Paul, Nancy. Student, Calif. State U., Chico, 1956-65; secondary cert., San Francisco State Coll., 1968; MA in Ethnography, Calif. State U., Sacramento, 1978. Cert. silversmith, 1977, secondary teacher. Instr. Shasta Jr. Coll., Redding, Calif., 1969-71; from instr. to asst. prof. art Calif. State U., Sacramento, 1971-73, dir. Nat. Am. Studies, 1974—; instr. Pena-Adobe, Vacaville, Calif., 1970, U. Alberta, Leithbridge, Can., 1974; dir. HEW Designegration Project D.Q. U., Davis, Calif., 1972; rsch. assoc. U.S. Dept. Interior, Fair Oaks, Calif., 1984; cons. Calif. Arts Coun., Sacramento, 1980—. Author, illustrator: (poems) Singing of Earth, 1993, The Sound of Rattles and Clappers, 1994, Commemoration, 1995; cover artist: Keeping Slug Woman Alive, 1993; co-author, artist: California Indian Shamanism, 1992; co-editor, artist: Smithsonian Nat. Mus. Am. Indian, 1991-94; numerous one-man shows and group exhibits. Grantee Smithsonian Inst., 1976; recipient People On the Move award YMCA, 1975, Order of the Hornet and Disting. Svc. award Calif. State U. Alumni Assn., 1995. Office: Calif State Univ 6000 J St Sacramento CA 95819-2605

LAPHAM, SANDRA C., research scientist, physician; b. Detroit, Sept. 2, 1948; d. Wendell E. and Eva E. L.; m. Gary L. Simpson, Feb. 22, 1983; children: Cassandra A., Courtney M. BA in Psychology, U. Mich., 1970; MD, Wayne State U., 1975; MPH, Harvard U., 1978. Cert. in treatment of alcoholism and other drug dependencies, records review officer. Internship Mount Auburn Hosp., Cambridge, Mass., 1975-76, residency dept. of medicine, 1976-78; emergency med. staff Amesbury (Mass.) Hosp., 1978, asst. clin. prof. dept. Preventive Medicine U. Colo. Sch. of Medicine, 1979-80; E.I.S. officer Epidemic Intelligence Svc. Ctrs. for Disease Control, Atlanta, 1979-81; clin. assoc. Dept. Family, Cmty. and Emergency Medicine U. N.Mex. Sch. of Medicine, Albuquerque, 1981—; environ. epidemiologist Environ. Improvement divsn. Health and Environment Dept., 1981-84; co-ptnr. Placitas Consulting Group, 1984—; epidemiologist Clin. Studies Divsn. The Lovelace Insts., Albuquerque, 1986-88, dir. substance abuse rsch. program, 1989—; resource persons network Office of Minority Health Resource Ctr., 1989; editorial rev. bd. Jour. of Human Lactation, 1988-92; editorial reviewer Family of Medicine, 1993; peer rev. cons. NIH/ADAMHA, 1993; lectr. in field. Contbr. numerous articles to profl. publs., chpts. to books. Mem. N.Mex. Alcohol Issues Consortium, 1989—, N.Mex. Prenatal Care Network, 1989-92; mem. substance abuse adv. com. Health Care for the Homeless, 1991—; mem. task force on DWI, N.Mex. Atty. Gen., 1992—. Robert Wood Johnson fellow, 1976, AID grantee, 1977, Fogerty Sr. Internat. fellow, 1995. Mem. APHA, Am. Soc. Addiction Medicine, Am. Coll. Physicians, Rsch. Soc. on Alcoholism. Office: The Lovelace Insts 1650 University Blvd NE Ste 302 Albuquerque NM 87102-1732

LAPIROFF, JERRY, secondary school educator; b. Bklyn., Feb. 11, 1947; s. Harry and Betty (Klein) L.; m. Helen Chu, July 24, 1988; children: Harris, Mariah. Tchr. John F. Kennedy High Sch.; Fulbright exch. tchr., 1992-93; coord. Virtual H.S. Project. Named Spl. Recognition advisor Journalism, 1989, Disting. advisor Dow Jones Newspaper Fund, 1992. Office: 39999 Blacow Rd Fremont CA 94538-1913

LAPOTA, DAVID, oceanographer, marine biologist; b. L.A., June 1, 1949; s. M.H. and J.E. (Cassell) L.; m. Jeannette Harward, June 28, 1975. BS in Zoology, San Diego State U., 1973, MA in Geography, 1982; postgrad., U. Calif., Santa Barbara, 1992—. Data analyst San Diego State Found., 1974-79; biologist Naval Ocean Systems Ctr., San Diego, 1979-82, scientist, 1982—. Patentee in field; contbr. articles and abstracts to profl. jours. and chpts. to books. With USAR, 1969-75. Fellow Explorers Club; mem. Am. Geophys. Union, Biol. Soc. Washington, Oceanography Soc., AAAS. Home: 6678 Hemingway Dr San Diego CA 92120-1616 Office: Naval Command Control Ocean Surveillance Ctr Marine Environ Br Code D362 San Diego CA 92152-5000

LAPSLEY, JAMES NORVELL, JR., minister, pastoral theology educator; b. Clarksville, Tenn., Mar. 16, 1930; s. James Norvell and Evangeline (Winn) L.; m. Brenda Ann Weakley, June 4, 1953 (dec. May 1989); children: Joseph William, Jacqueline Evangeline; m. Helen Joan Winter, Feb. 24, 1990. BA, Rhodes Coll., 1952; BD, Union Theol. Sem., 1955; PhD (Div. Sch. fellow, Rockefeller fellow), U. Chgo., 1961. Ordained to ministry Presbyn. Ch., 1955; asst. min. Gentilly Presbyn. Ch., New Orleans, 1955-57; instr. Princeton (N.J.) Theol. Sem., 1961-63, asst. prof., 1963-67, assoc. prof., 1967-76, prof. pastoral theology, 1976-80, Carl and Helen Egner prof. pastoral theology, 1980-92, acad. dean, 1984-89, prof. emeritus, 1992—; mem. editl. bd. Jour. Pastoral Care, 1966-69, 91—; bd. dirs. N.W. Maricopa UN Assn., 1994—, v.p., 1995-96, pres., 1997; pres. Critical Issues Coun. of Sun Cities, 1996-97. Editor: The Concept of Willing, 1967, Salvation and Health, 1972, Renewal in Late Life Through Pastoral Counseling, 1992; editor: (with B.H. Childs, D.W. Waanders), Festschrift: The Treasure of Earthen Vessels, 1994; chmn. editl. bd. Pastoral Psychology Jour., 1975-84. Bd. dirs. Westminster Found., Princeton U., 1970-76. Danforth fellow Menninger Found., 1960-61. Mem. Am. Acad. Religion, Phi Beta Kappa. Presbyterian. Home: 16610 N Meadow Park Dr Sun City AZ 85351-1758

LAPSLEY, ROBERT CHARLES, state official; b. Berwyn, Ill., Sept. 21, 1959; s. Donald Gilbert and Marian Louise (Wentz) L.; m. Linda Christine Rao, Sept. 23, 1995. BS in Biology, Ill. State U., 1985, BS in Polit. Sci., 1985. Adminstrv. asst. San Francisco Supr. Tom Hsieh, 1986-87; legis. asst., chief of staff Assemblyman Chuck Quackenbush, Sacramento, 1987-91; polit. dir. Minority Leader Bill Jones, Sacramento, 1991-92; legis. dir. CAL/EPA, Sacramento, 1992-94; cons., campaign mgr. Joe Shumate & Assoc., Sacramento, 1994; undersec. Sec. of State, Sacramento, 1995—. Mem. River City Reps., Sacramento, 1991—. With USAF, 1977-81. Mem. Nat. Assn. Sec. State. Office: State Calif Secretary of State 1500 11th St Sacramento CA 95814

LARA, ADAIR, columnist, writer; b. San Francisco, Jan. 3, 1952; d. Eugene Thomas and Lee Louise (Hanley) Daly; m. James Lee Heig, June 18, 1976 (div. 1989); children: Morgan, Patrick; m. William Murdock LeBlond, Nov. 2, 1991. BA in English, San Francisco State U., 1976. Reader Coll. of Marin, Kentfield, Calif., 1976-83; freelance editor, 1983-86; mng. editor San Francisco Focus mag., 1986-89; exec. editor San Francisco mag., 1988-89; columnist San Francisco Chronicle, 1989—. Author: History of Petaluma: A California River Town, 1982, Welcome to Earth, Mom, 1992, Slowing Down in a Speeded-up World, 1994, At Adair's House, More Columns by America's Funniest Formerly Single Man, 1995; contbr. articles to profl. publs. Recipient Best Calif. Columnist award AP, 1990. Democrat. Office: San Francisco Chronicle 901 Mission St San Francisco CA 94103-2905

LARBALESTRIER, DEBORAH ELIZABETH, writer; b. Pitts., July 17, 1934; d. Theron Benjamin and Granetha Elizabeth (Crenshaw) Cowherd; m. Dec. 25, 1969 (div.). AB, Storer Coll., 1954; student, Robert H. Terrell Law Coll., 1954-58, Woodbury Coll., 1959-60; certs., Univ. W. Los Angeles, 1971-73. Cert. legal asst., paralegal specialist. Author Prentice-Hall Inc., Englewood Cliffs, N.J., 1975—; prof. Southland Career Inst., L.A., 1985—; paralegal mgr. Lynberg & Watkins, L.A., 1988-95; ret., 1995; bd. dirs. Am. Paralegal Assn., Los Angeles, 1975-80, exec. dir., 1980—; nat. chmn. Am. Inmate Paralegal Assn., 1984—; cons. Fed. Bur. Prisons, 1983—. Mem. Los Angeles Police Dept. (Wilshire div.) Community Police Council, 1985—, Harbor Human Relations Council, Wilmington, Calif., 1985—; vol., crime prevention specialist Los Angeles Police Dept. (Wilshire div.), 1985—; mem. adv. bd. U. West Los angeles, 1980, 88, trustee, 1994—. Recipient gold plaque Am. Paralegal Assn. Chpt. Pres., Los Angeles, 1975, Nat. Notary Assn., Hawaii, 1979, cert. of acknowledgment Los Angeles Police Dept., 1985, Humanitarian Award of Spl. Merit, So. Calif. Motion Picture Council, 1987, Disting. Alumni award U. West Los Angeles, 1996. Mem. Am. Paralegal Assn. (exec. dir. 1975), Am. Inmate Assn. (nat. chmn. 1983), U. W. Los Angeles Paralegal Alumni Assn. (Disting. Alumni award 1996). Republican. Jewish. Home: 1321-1/2s Sycamore Ave Los Angeles CA 90019

LAREAU, VIRGINIA RUTH, counselor; b. Big Beaver, Mich., Sept. 3, 1921; d. Leslie John and Celista Jane (Jones) McKinley; (div.); 1 child, Natalie Celista (dec. 1982). BA, Marylhurst Coll., 1992, postgrad., 1993—. Clk. Mich. Bell Tel., Detroit, 1941-54, TRW, Redondo Beach, Calif., 1955-84; counselor 1st Bapt. Ch., Oregon City, Oreg., 1994—. Mem. ACA. Republican. Office: First Bapt Ch 9th and John Adams Oregon City OR 97045

LARIZADEH, M(OHAMMED) R(EZA), business educator; b. Tehran, Iran, Apr. 14, 1947; came to U.S., 1966; s. Hassan and Nosrat (Saremi) L.; m. Dianne Ellen Pincus, Mar. 25, 1973; children: Dariush, Darya Anna. BA in Econs., Bus., UCLA, 1972, cert. in acctg., 1974. Cert. colls. teaching credential, Calif. (life); lic. real estate agent, Calif. Auditor Peat, Marwick & Mitchell, Los Angeles, 1972-74; controller Petromain Constrn. Co., Tehran, 1975-77; v.p. fin. Pilary Marine Shipping Co., Tehran, 1977-79; prof. Iranian Inst. Banking, Tehran, 1975-78; pres. Audicount Acctg. and Auditing Group, L.A., 1984—; prof. bus. and acctg. East L.A. Coll., 1980-87, vice-chmn. dept. bus. and acctg., 1987—, chmn. dept. bus. adminstrn., 1988—; prof. acctg. Santa Monica (Calif.) Coll., 1987—; mgmt. cons. L.P. Assocs. Mfg. Co., Los Angeles, 1981—; mng. dir. Barrington Enterprises, Los Angeles; prof. Santa Monica (Calif.) Coll., 1987. Author/translator: Accounting/Auditing, 1975. Mem. NEA, Internat. Fedn. Bus. Edn., Am. Mgmt. Assn., Am. Acctg. Assn., Faculty Assn. Calif. C.C.s, Am. Fedn. Tchrs., Calif. Tchrs. Assn., Am. Entrepreneur Assn., Nat. Assn. Realtors, Am. Assn. Pub. Accts., Calif. Assn. Bus. Educators, Calif. Assn. Realtors, Nat. Soc. Pub. Accts., Calif. Bus. Edn. Assn., Internat. Fedn. Bus. Edn., Inst. Mgmt. Accts., UCLA Alumni Assn. (life), Alpha Kappa Psi.

LARK, M. ANN, management consultant, strategic planner, naturalist; b. Denver, Feb. 28, 1952, d. Carl Eugene and Arlena Elizabeth (Bashor) Epperson; m. Larry S. Lark, Apr. 1, 1972 (div. 1979). Asst. corp. sec., savs. dir. Imperial Corp. dba Silver State Savs. & Loan, Denver, 1972-75; client svcs. mgr. 1st Fin. Mgmt. Corp., Englewood, Colo., 1977-81; regional account mgr. Ericsson Info. Systems, Chatsworth, Calif., 1981-82; ind. cons. Denver, 1982-84; regional account mgr. InnerLine/Am. Banker, Chgo., 1984-85; chief info. officer Security Pacific Credit Corp., San Diego, 1985-88; prin. The Genessee Group, Thousand Oaks, Calif., 1988—. Home and Office: 1144 El Monte Dr Thousand Oaks CA 91362-2117

LARK, RAYMOND, artist, art scholar; b. Phila., June 16, 1939; s. Thomas and Bertha (Lark) Crawford. Student, Phila. Mus. Sch. Art, 1948-51, Los Angeles Trade Tech. Coll., 1961-62; B.S., Temple U., 1961; L.H.D., U. Colo., 1985. Ednl. dir. Victor Bus. Sch., Los Angeles, 1969-71; public relations exec. Western States Service Co., Los Angeles, 1968-70; owner, mgr. Raymond Lark's House of Fine Foods, Los Angeles, 1962-67; exec. sec. to v.p. Physicians Drug and Supply Co., Phila., 1957-61; lectr. L.A. Trade Tech. Coll., 1973, Compton (Calif.) Coll., 1972, Nat. Secs. Assn., Hollywood, Calif., UCLA, U. Utah, Salt Lake City, 1993, numerous others. One-man shows include, Dalzell Hatfield Galleries, Los Angeles, 1970-86, Arthur's Gallery Masterpieces and Jewels, Beverly Hills, Calif., 1971, Dorothy Chandler Pavillion Music Center, L.A., 1974, Honolulu Acad. Arts, 1975, UCLA, 1983, U. Colo. Mus., 1984, Albany State Coll. Art Gallery, Albany, Ga., 1988, Utah Mus. Fine Arts, Salt Lake City, 1989, Mind's Art Gallery, Dickinson U., Dickinson, N.D., 1989, Trinton Mus. Art, Santa Clara, Calif., Greenville (N.C.) Mus. of Art, 1993, Springfield (Mo.) Art Mus., 1995, Washington County Museum of Fine Arts, Hagerstown, Md., 1996; The Peninisula Fine Arts Center, Newport News, Va. others; group exhbns. include, Smithsonian Instn., 1971, N.J. State Mus., Trenton, 1971, Guggenheim Mus., N.Y.C., 1975, Met. Mus. Art, 1976, La Galerie Mauffe, Paris, 1977, Portsmouth (Va.) Mus., 1979, Ava Dorog Galleries, Munich, W. Ger., 1979, Accademia Italia, Parma, 1980, Ames Art Galleries and Auctioneers, Beverly Hills, 1980, Le Salon des Nations at Centre International d'Art Contemporain, Paris, 1983; represented in permanent collections, Library of Congress, Ont. Coll. Art, Toronto, Mus. African and African Am. Art and Antiquities, Buffalo, Carnegie Inst., numerous others; art commns. for TV and film studios include, All in the Family, Carol Burnett Show, Maude, The Young and the Restless, Universal City Studios, Palace of the Living Arts, Movie Land Wax Mus.; author works in field; author and contbr. more than 50 scholarly treatises on art, edn. and the hist. devel. of Black Ams., chpts. to encyclopedias and textbooks, articles to jours., introductions to mus. exhbn. catalogues. Recipient gold medal Acad. Italia, 1980, also numerous gold medals and best of show awards, 3 presdl. proclamations; award Internat. Platform Assn.; Dr. Raymond Lark Day proclaimed by State of Md., 1994; grantee Nat. Endowment Arts, ARCO Found., Colo. Humanities Program, Adolph Coors Beer Found. Mem. Art West Assn. (pres. 1968-70). Address: PO Box 76169 Los Angeles CA 90076-0169 *I was telling people that I was Black, proud, and beautiful long before it became fashionable to be very dark. I never felt, "I am the greatest." However, I never had an inferiority complex. I always knew that I had God-given talent, character, and good common sense. In addition, I have always had great confidence in God and in myself. While I am not a soothsayer and never will be a braggart, I knew my art would be recognized. For whatever recognition I have received, I have worked extremely hard and have paid my dues.*

LARKIN, DIXON F., state insurance commissioner; b. Ogden, Utah; m. Carol Larkin; 4 children. Student, Weber State Coll.; MD with honors, U. Utah, 1974; JD, Brigham Young U., 1983. Diplomate Am. Coll. Radiology. Bar: Utah. Surg. intern U. Utah Affil. Hosps., 1974-75; asst. dir. Emergency Med. Svcs., Utah State Health Dept., 1975-76; resident and fellow in radiation oncology U. Utah Affil. Hosps., 1976-79; pvt. practice Appleton, Wis.; with Jones Waldo Holbrook & McDonough, Salt Lake City; v.p., legal counsel Blue Cross/Blue Shield of Utah, 1989; of counsel GTE Health Systems, 1993; deputy commr. Utah Inst. Dept., 1993—; assoc. prof. Gore Coll. Bus.-Westminster Coll.; adj. prof. law Brigham Young U.; comml. pilot.; flight instr. Active local and nat. health care reform. Office: Utah Ins Commr 3110 State Office Bldg Salt Lake City UT 84114

LARKIN, EDWARD COLBY, securities analyst, financial services company executive; b. Evanston, Ill., Jan. 6, 1951; s. Edward Tyrus and Ethel (Colby) L.; m. Teresa Mary Berger, Apr. 21, 1978; children: Sean, Brian, Trent. BS, U. Colo., 1973; MBA, U. Denver, 1974. Fin. analyst, supr. Nat. Assn. Securities Dealers, Denver, 1975-80; v.p. corp. fin. Wall Street West, Englewood, Colo., 1980-86, Richard Christman Lavigne, Inc., Seattle, 1986-87; exec. v.p., dir. rsch., chief fin. officer Cohig & Assocs., Denver, 1987—, pres., 1995—. Office: Cohig & Assocs 6300 S Syracuse Way Ste 430 Englewood CO 80111-6724

LARKIN, NELLE JEAN, computer programmer, analyst; b. Ralston, Okla., July 4, 1925; d. Charles Eugene and Jennivea Pearl (Lane) Reed; m. Burr Oakley Larkin, Dec. 28, 1948 (div. Aug. 1969); children: John Timothy, Kenneth James, Donald Jerome, Valerie Jean Larkin Rouse. Student, UCLA, 1944, El Camino Jr. Coll., 1946-49, San Jose (Calif.) City Coll., 1961-62. Sr. programmer, analyst III Santa Clara County, San Jose, Calif., 1963-69; sr. analyst, programmer Blue Cross of No. Calif., Oakland, 1971-73; sr. programmer, analyst Optimum Systems, Inc., Santa Clara, Calif., 1973-75, Crocker Bank, San Francisco, 1975-77, Greyhound Fin. Service, San Francisco, 1977-78; analyst, programmer TRW, Mountain View, Calif., 1978-79; sr. programer analyst Memorex, Santa Clara, 1979-80; staff mgmt. cons. Am. Mgmt. System, Foster City, Calif., 1980-82; sr. programmer, analyst, project leader Tymeshare, Cupertino, Calif., 1982-83; sr. programmer, analyst Beckman Instruments, Palo Alto, Calif., 1983-89; analyst, programmer U.S. Postal Svc., San Mateo, Calif., 1989—. Mem. Calif. Scholarship Fedn. (life mem. 1943), Alpha Sigma Gamma. Home: 3493 Londonderry Dr Santa Clara CA 95050-6632 Office: US Postal Svc 2700 Campus Dr San Mateo CA 94497-0001

LARNER, DANIEL M., theater educator, playwright, author; b. Olean, N.Y., Apr. 15, 1939; s. Martin L. and Clara Bronstein) L.; m. Margaret Dreher, Mar. 22, 1964 (div. May 1991); children: Eve Larner Bohn, Benjamin; m. Pandora Michael, Mar. 21, 1992; children: Richard Parkes, Elizabeth Parkes. AB in History and Sci., Harvard U., 1960; MS in History of sci., U. Wis., 1962, PhD in Speech in Theatre, 1968. Tutor St. John's Coll., Annapolis, Md., 1962-65; asst./assoc. prof. English, Speech, Theatre Western Wash. U., Bellingham, 1968-81, prof. theatre, 1981—, acting chmn. dept. theatre, 1980-81, dir. grad. study in theatre, 1976-82, founding dir. new playwrights theater, 1973-82, dean Fairhaven Coll., 1982-89; cons. R.F. McCann & Co., Architects Theatre, Seattle, 1983. Author: (plays) The Death of Christopher Marlowe, 1973, War Dance, 1978; contbr. numerous articles to profl. jours.; assoc. editor Religion and Theatre, 1980. Chmn. facilities/bldg. com. Mt. Baker Theatre Ctr., Bellingham, 1984-91, bd. dirs., 1984-94; bd. dirs. ACLU of Wash., Seattle, 1969-80, 89—. Recipient Mayor's Arts award City of Bellingham, 1987; numerous grants Nat. Endowment for the Arts, Wash. Arts Commn., Matsushita Found., Wash. Ctr. for Improvement of Undergrad. Edn., Western Wash. U., others. Mem. Assn. for Theatre in Higher Edn., Dramatists Guild (assocs.), Am. Soc. for Theatre Rsch., Popular Culture Assn. (nat. theatre area chmn. 1980-83), Theatre Comms. Group, Deutsche Shakespeare Gesellschaft, Wash. Athletic Club. Office: Western Washington Univ Fairhaven Coll MS-9118 Bellingham WA 98225-9118

LAROCK, BRUCE EDWARD, civil engineering educator; b. Berkeley, Calif., Dec. 24, 1940; s. Ralph W. and Hazel M. (Lambert) L.; m. Susan E. Gardner, June 17, 1968; children: Lynne M., Jean E. BS in Civil Engring., Stanford U., 1962, MS in Civil Engring., 1963, PhD, 1966. Registered profl. engr., Calif. Asst. prof. U. Calif., Davis, 1966-72, assoc. prof., 1972-79, prof., 1979—; sr. vis. fellow U. Wales, Swansea, 1972-73; U.S. sr. scientist Tech. U., Aachen, Germany, 1986-87. Author: (with D. Newnan) Engineer-in-Training Examination Review, 3d edit., 1991; contbr. over 75 tech. articles to profl. jours. Mem. ASCE, Sigma Xi, Tau Beta Pi. Lutheran. Office: U Calif Davis Dept Civil & Environ Engrin Davis CA 95616-5294

LAROCQUE, MARILYN ROSS ONDERDONK, writer, public relations consultant; b. Weehawken, N.J., Oct. 14, 1934; d. Chester Douglas and Marion (Ross) Onderdonk; B.A. cum laude, Mt. Holyoke Coll., 1956; postgrad. N.Y. U., 1956-57; M. Journalism, U. Calif. at Berkeley, 1965; m. Bernard Dean Benz, Oct. 5, 1957 (div. Sept. 1971); children: Mark Douglas, Dean Griffith; m. 2d, Rodney C. LaRocque, Feb. 10, 1973. Jr. exec. Bonwit Teller, N.Y.C., 1956; personnel asst. Warner-Lambert Pharm. Co., Morris Plains, N.J., 1957; editorial asst. Silver Burdett Co., Morristown, 1958; self-employed as pub. rels. cons., Moraga, Calif., 1963-71, 73-77; pub. rels. mgr. Shaklee Corp., Hayward, 1971-73; pub. rels. dir. Fidelity Savs., 1977-78; exec. dir. No. Calif. chpt. Nat. Multiple Sclerosis Soc., 1978-80; v.p. pub. rels. Cambridge Plan Internat., Monterey, Calif., 1980-81; sr. account exec. Hoefer-Amidei Assocs., San Francisco, 1981-82; dir. corp. comms., dir. spl. projects, asst. to chmn. Cambridge Plan Internat., Monterey, Calif., 1982-84; dir. comms. Buena Vista Winery, Sonoma, Calif., 1984-86, asst. v.p. comms. and market support, 1986-87; dir. comms. Rutherford Hill Winery, St. Helena, Calif., 1987-88; pres. LaRocque Pub. Rels. and Pub. Affairs, Napa, Calif., 1988-91; pres. LaRocque Profl. Svcs., Inc., 1991-95; writer, pub. rels. cons., 1996—; instr. pub. rels. U. Calif. Extension, San Francisco, 1977-79. Mem. exec. bd., rep-at-large Oakland (Calif.) Symphony Guild, 1968-69, Napa County Landmarks, Inc.; co-chmn. pub. rels. com. Oakland Mus. Assn., 1974-75; cabinet mem. Lincoln Child Ctr., Oakland, 1967-71, pres. membership cabinet, 1970-71, 2d v.p. bd. dirs., 1970-71; bd. dirs. Calif. Spring Garden and Home Show, 1971-77, 1st Agrl. Dist., 1971-77, Dunsmuir House and Gardens, 1976-77; mem. Calif. State Rep. Cen. Com., 1964-66; v.p. Piedmont coun. Boy Scouts Am., 1977. Mem. U. Calif. Alumni Assn., Pub. Rels. Soc. Am. (chpt. dir. 1980-82; accredited), Sonoma Valley Vintners Assn. (dir. 1984-87), Internat. Wine and Food Soc. (Marin chpt.), San Francisco Mus. Soc., Smithsonian Assocs., Sonoma Valley C. of C. (bd. dirs. 1984-87), Napa County Landmarks Inc. (bd. dirs. 1993-94, mem. di Rosa Preserve vol. coun. 1997—), Am. Assn. Univ. Women (Napa Valley chpt.), Napa Valley Republican Women, Knights of the Vine (master lady 1985-90), Mount Holyoke Coll. Alumnae Club, Silverado Country Club, DAR (vineyard trails chpt.). Office: LaRocque Profl Svcs Inc 1800 Soscol Ave Napa CA 94559-1345

LA ROSA, FRANCISCO GUILLERMO, pathologist, researcher, educator; b. Lima, Peru, Jan. 17, 1949; came to U.S., 1981; s. Anibal and Carmen (de la Pascua) La R.; m. Clara Ann Duffícy, May 21, 1989; children: David, Anamaria, Joseph. MD, U. Nacional Federico Villarreal, Lima, 1975. cert. (AP/CP), 1995. Instr. U. Nacional Federico Villarreal, Lima, 1973-79, asst. prof., 1979-81; resident in clin. pathology U. de San Marcos, Lima, 1977-79; postdoctoral fellow in immunology U. Colo., Denver, 1981-85, instr., 1985-87, asst. prof., 1987-94, resident in pathology, 1992-95, fellow in molecular pathology, 1995-96; lab. dir. Miners Colfax Med. Ctr., Raton, NM, 1996—; clin. asst. prof. dept path., immunology Webb-Waring Inst. for BioMed. Rsch., 1996—; pathologist Sterling Regional Med. Ctr., 1996—; pres. Pathology Conss., PC, 1995—; cons. Ortho Pharm., Lima, 1979-81, Reaads Med. Products, Inc., Denver, 1991. Contbr. chpts. to books, revs. and articles to profl. jours. Krock Found. fellow, 1985-86, Juvenile Diabetes Found. fellow, 1985-86; NIH grantee, 1988-91; recipient Enrique Leon Garcia Best MD Thesis award Peruvian Pediat. Soc., Lima, 1975, award Diabetes Rsch. and Edn. Found., 1987-88. Mem. AMA, The Transplantation Soc., Soc. Española Immunologia, Am. Assn. Immunologists, Coll. Am. Pathologists, Am. Soc. Clin. Pathologists, Peruvian Soc. Clin. Pathology, Peruvian Soc. Immunology and Allergy, Colo Med. Soc., N.Mex. Med. Soc.

Roman Catholic. Home: 2663 S Nelson Ct Lakewood CO 80227 Office: Univ of Colo HSC 4200 E 9th Ave # C321 Denver CO 80262

LAROSA, GIANNI, aerospace industry administrator; b. S. Biagio Platani, Italy, Jan. 22, 1937; came to U.S., 1954; s. Alfonso and Santa (Marino) LaR.; m. Maria Cappello, Jan. 6, 1958; children: Alfonso, Sandra, Claudio, Julio. Student, Cass Tech., 1962; diploma in art, Musée de Art Modern, Tonneins, France, 1993. Owner indsl./comml. food svc. equipment mfg. business Detroit, 1970-74; supr. aerospace industry, 1985—; presenter in field. Exhbns. include San Bernardino County (Calif.) Mus., 1992, San Clemente (Calif.) Art Fest, 1992, Paris City Hall, 1993, Modern Art Mus. Unet, Tonneins, France, 1993, Soho Internat. Art Competition, N.Y.C., 1993, Wirtz Gallery, Miami, 1993, Bower Mus., Orange County, Calif., 1995; represented in permanent collection at Modern Art du Unet, Bordeaux, France; discovery and write theory on the illusion of color perception. Recipient award Fine Arts Inst., 1992, award Soho Internat. Competition, 1993, award Mayor of Paris, Internat. Art Competition, 1993, Gold medal Musee Des D'Beux Arts D'Unet, France, 1996; named Disting. Vis., Mayor of Miami, Fla., 1994. Home: 26641 Domingo Dr Mission Viejo CA 92692-4114

LARSEN, AILEEN, principal; b. Spring City, Utah, Mar. 9, 1942; d. Soren Gottfred and Etta Marie (Johansen) L. AA, Snow Coll., Ephraim, Utah, 1962; BEd, Utah State U., 1964; MEd, Idaho State U., 1996. Cert. tchr. Utah, Idaho. Tchr. Salt Lake City Sch. Dist., 1964-65, So. Fremont Sch. Dist., St. Anthony, Idaho, 1965-67, North Gem Sch. Dist., Bancroft, Idaho, 1967-95; prin. North Gem Sch. Dist., Bancroft, 1995—. Named Tchr. of Yr. North Gem Sch. Dist., Bancroft, Idaho, 1992, Fan of the Yr. North Gem H.S. Student Body, Bancroft, 1992. Mem. Phi Kappa Phi. Home: 263 W 3rd S Bancroft ID 83217 Office: N Gem Sch Dist 322 S Main St Bancroft ID 83217

LARSEN, GWYNNE E., computer information systems educator; b. Omaha, Sept. 10, 1934; d. Melvin and Vernetta (Allen) Bannister; m. John M. Larsen, June 8, 1958; children: Bradley Allen, Blair Kevin, Randall Lawrence. A in Bus. Adminstrn., Denver U., 1956, MBA, 1975, PhD, 1979; BS, Met. State Coll., 1971. Instr. Met. State Coll. Denver, 1979-81, asst. prof., 1981-85, assoc. prof., 1985-88, prof., 1989—, acting chair computer dept., 1991-92; book reviewer McGraw Hill, 1991, Harcourt Brace Jovanovich, 1991, Macmillan Pub. Co., 1993, Southwestern Pub. Co., 1993; presenter Mountain Plains Mgmt. conf., Denver, 1982, Rocky Mountain Bus. Expo, Denver, 1982, Red Rocks C.C., 1984, Colo.-Wyo. Acad. Sci. conf., 1985, Boulder, 1986, Colorado Springs, 1987; local coord. John Wiley & Sons, Denver, 1982, 83; panel chmn. on office automation Assn. for Computing Machinery, Denver, 1985; spkr. ASTD, 1986, Am. Pub. Works Assn., 1986; participant numerous presentations and confs. Author: (with others) Computerized Business Information Systems Workbook, 1983, Collegiate Microcomputer, 1992, (with Verlene Leeberg) Word Processing: Using WordPerfect 5.0, 1989, Word Processing: Using WordPerfect 5.1, 1991, First Look at WordPerfect 5.1, 1991, First Look at DOS, 1991, First Look at NetWare, 1992, Using WordPerfect for Windows, 1993, (with Marold and Shaw) Using Microsoft Works: An Introduction to Computing, 1993, Using Microsoft Works, An Introduction to Computing, 1993, First Look at WordPerfect 6.0 for Windows, 1994, Using WordPerfect 6.0 for Windows, 1994, Using Microsoft Works for Windows, An Introduction to Computing, 1996, Beyond the Internet, 1996, (with Marold) Using Microsoft Works 4.0, 1997; apptd. editl. bd. Jour. Mgmt. Sys., 1988, Jour. Microcomputer Sys. Mgmt., 1989, Info. Resources Mgmt. Jour., 1991; mem. editl. rev. bd. Jour. Info. Resources Mgmt. Sys., 1985—, Jour. Mgmt. Info. Sys., 1986—, Jour. Database Mgmt. Sys., Jour. Database Mgmt. Sys., 1987—, Jour. End User Computing, 1990—; contbr. articles to profl. jours. Mem. Info. Resources Mgmt. Assn., Colo.-Wyo. Acad. Scis., Office Automation Soc. Internat., Internat. Acad. for Info. Mgmt., panel part., 1995. Home: 8083 S Adams Way Littleton CO 80122 Office: Met State Coll Denver Campus Box 45 PO Box 173362 Denver CO 80217-3362

LARSEN, JANICE CASEY, financial analyst; b. Ames, Iowa, July 23, 1954; d. Donald J. and LaDeane (Olser) C.; m. Craig L. Larsen, Apr. 6, 1991. BA, Iowa State U., 1976; postgrad., Ariz. State U., 1984-86, Coll. Fin. Planning, 1987-89. Cert. fin. planner. Sales rep. Vet. Sales Ancom Norden, Smithe-Kline, Phoenix, 1976-77; sales mgr. D.V.M. Inc., Los Angeles, 1977-78; regional cons. mgr. Hospitex, San Jose, Calif., 1978-79; dir. mktg. Incentive Journeys, San Jose, 1979-83; leasing agt., gen. mgr., advt. dir. Granada Mktg. Mgmt., Phoenix, 1983-86; adminstrv. asst. fin. planner McCarthy & Assocs. Anchor Nat. Fin. Services, Inc., Phoenix, 1986-89; mgr. Sun State Fin. Svcs. Corp., Phoenix, 1989; dir. broker, dealer svcs., contractor H.J. Tessier & Co., Phoenix, 1989; investment officer Security Pacific Bank Investments, Phoenix, 1990-91, The Bank of Calif., Seattle, 1991-93, U.S. Bancorp, Seattle, 1994; v.p., sales trainer Laughlin Group, Portland, Oreg., 1994—. Vocal soloist Maria Goretti Cath. Ch., Scottsdale, Ariz., 1987-91, All Saints Ch., Federal Way, Wash., 1992-94. Mem. Internat. Assn. Fin. Planners, Internat. Assn. Cert. Fin. Planners, Nat. Assn. Securities Dealers (registered rep., prin. ins., real estate). Office: Laughlin Group of Cos 8305 SW Creekside Pl Beaverton OR 97008-7104

LARSEN, KENNETH MARSHALL, art and human services advocate, consultant; b. San Francisco, June 5, 1946; s. Frank and Klara Margaret (Ashman) L. BA, Antioch Coll., 1968; postgrad., U. Calif., Davis, 1976. Lectr. U. Calif., Davis, 1976-78; assoc. pres. Hooper Billstein & Assocs., Oakland, Calif., 1978-80; dir. Rural Arts Svcs., Mendocino, Calif., 1980-88; assoc. dir. Calif. Confedn. of the Arts, Sacramento, 1988-96; adj. lectr. Golden Gate U., San Francisco, 1996—; dir. legislation Friends' Com. on Legislation, Sacramento, 1997—; cultural planner City and County of Sacramento, 1995; cultural planning advisor 15 Calif. cities and counties; book rev. editor Ridge Rev., Mendocino, 1980—. Editor mags. ARC: The Rural Arts Newsletter, 1980-88, Radius: Resources for Local Arts, 1985-91, Calif. Arts Advocate, 1990-94, Sacramento Arts Reporter, 1996—; contbr. articles to state and nat. trade publs. Mem. cultural awards panel Sacramento Arts Commn., 1995—; mem. interarts grants panel Nat. Endowment for the Arts, 1988-91; mem. grants orgn. Calif. Arts coun., 1981-86. Recipient Statewide Svc. awrd Arts-in-Corrections, 1993, Enabled Artists United, 1992. Mem. Calif. Assn. Nonprofits (bd. dirs. 1995—), Nonprofit Policy Coun. (bd. dirs. 1996—), Inst. for Cultural Democracy (bd. dirs. 1990—), Calif Lawyers for the Arts (arbitration and mediation svc. bd. 1996—). Office: Friends Com Legis 926 J St Ste 707 Sacramento CA 95814

LARSEN, KIMBERT E., journalist; b. Boulder, Colo., June 14, 1941; s. Junius and Dorothy May (Cavanaugh) Larsen. AA, Idaho State U., 1963. Bur. reporter Deseret News, Salt Lake City, 1959-60, Salt Lake Tribune, Salt Lake City, 1960-63; assoc. editor Register Sys. of Newspapers, Denver, 1963-64, Denver, 1966-69; city hall reporter Ind.-Record, Helena, Mont., 1964; editor Western Mont. Register, 1965-66; nat. affairs staff writer Nat. Cath. News Svc., Washington, 1969-70; Billings (Mont.) Gazette, Billings, 1970-90; freelance writer Billings, 1990—. Author: The Case for Rimrocks National Monument, 1970; contr. Ecotage!, 1972; mem. editl. bd. The Billings Gazette, 1983-85. Pres. Idaho Young Dems., Pocatello, Idaho, 1963; chmn. Diocesan Pastoral Coun., diocese of Great Falls-Billings, 1995—, Parish Pastoral Coun. of Holy Rosary Ch. in Billings, 1994—; mem. Billings Coalition for Human Rights. Travel grant, Norwegian Royal Ministry of Fgn. Affairs, Oslo, 1980. Mem. Yellowstone Valley Audubon Soc. Democrat. Roman Catholic. Home: 2451 Cascade Ave Billings MT 59102-0535

LARSEN, MICHAEL JOHN, research mycologist; b. London, Apr. 27, 1938; came to U.S., 1949; s. J. Futter and Nancy (Stevens) L.; m. Audrey Helen Sutherland, Jan. 4, 1970 (dec. 1977); children: Emily, Caitlin; m. Nancy Jo Onsager, Jan. 14, 1982; children: Scott, John, Anne, Christopher, Steven, Jaime. BS, Syracuse U., 1960; MS, N.Y. State Coll. Forestry, 1963, PhD, 1967. Rsch. scientist Canadian Forestry Svc. So. Rsch. Sta., Maple, Ontario, Canada, 1966-67, Great Lakes Forest Rsch. Ctr. Canadian Forestry Svc., Sault St. Marie, Ontario, Canada, 1967-70; rsch. mycologist U.S. Forest Svc., Ctr. for Forest Mycology Rsch., Madison, Wis., 1971-92, Forestry Scis. Lab., Moscow, Idaho, 1993—; adj. prof. Plant Pathology Dept., U. Wis., 1974-92, Dept. Forestry, Mich. Tech. U., Houghton, 1976—; adj. assoc. prof. Dept. Forest Scis., U. Idaho. Author: Tomentelloid Fungi of NA, 1968, A Contribution to the Taxonomy of the Genus Tomentella, 1974, The Genus Phellinus - A World Survey, 1990; contbr. numberous articles to profl. jours. Mem. Lodi (Wis.) Plan Commn., 1989-93, Lodi Land Use Planning Commn., 1989-93. Recipient Grad. Student honorarium N.Y. State Mus. Sci. Svc., 1964; NSF fellow, 1963-66. Mem. Mycol. Soc. Am. (counselor 1978-80, chmn. nomenclature com. 1988-90), Am. Inst. Biol. Sci. Internat. Mycol. Assocs. Home: 1580 Highway 99 Troy ID 83871-9606 Office: USDA Forest Svc 1221 S Main St Moscow ID 83843-4211

LARSEN, PAUL EDWARD, lawyer; b. Rock Springs, Wyo., Jan. 5, 1964; s. Otto E. and Linda K. (Wright) L.; m. Dawn Jannette Griffin, June 25, 1986; 1 child, Quinne Caitlin. BA, U. Oreg., 1986, JD, 1989. Bar: Nev. 1989, U.S. Dist. Ct. Nev. 1989, U.S. Ct. Appeals (9th cir.) 1994. Atty. Lionel, Sawyer & Collins, Las Vegas, Nev., 1989—, chmn. land use and planning divsn., 1995—; gen. counsel Nev. State Democrats, 1996, corp. for solar tech. and renewable resources, 1995-96. Author, editor: Nevada Environmental Law Handbook, 1991, 1st edit., 2d edit., 3rd edit.; contbg. author: Nevada Gaming Law, 2d edit., 1995; contbr. articles to profl. jours. Pres., dir. Desert Creek Homeowners Assn., Las Vegas, 1994-95; atty. Clark County Pro-Bono Project, Las Vegas, 1989-95, Nev. Dem. Party, Las Vegas, 1994. Mem. ABA (vice chair com. natural resources pub. lands sect. 1993-95, bd. dirs. young lawyers divsn. natural resources com. 1992-95, atty. young lawyers divsn. program 1989-90), Nev.-Am. Inns of Ct., Nev. Assn. Gaming Attys., Internat. Assn. Gaming Attys. Office: Lionel Sawyer and Collins 300 S 4th St Ste 1700 Las Vegas NV 89101-6014

LARSEN, RICHARD LEE, former mayor and city manager, business, municipal and labor relations consultant, arbitrator; b. Jackson, Miss., Apr. 16, 1934; s. Homer Thorsten and Mae Cordelia (Amidon) L.; m. Virginia Fay Alley, June 25, 1955; children: Karla, Daniel, Thomas (dec.), Krista, Lisa. B.S. in Econs. and Bus. Adminstrn, Westminster Coll., Fulton, Mo., 1959; postgrad., U. Kans., 1959-61. Fin. dir. Village of Northbrook, Ill., 1961-63; city mgr. Munising, Mich., 1963-66, Sault Ste. Marie, Mich., 1966-72, Ogden, Utah, 1972-77, Billings, Mont., 1977-79; mcpl. cons., 1979—, pub./pvt. sector labor relations cons., arbitrator, 1979—; mayor City of Billings, Mont., 1990-95; dep. gen. chmn. Greater Mich. Found., 1968. Bd. dirs. Central Weber Sewer Dist., 1972-77; chmn. labor com. Utah League Cities and Towns, 1973-77, Mont. League Cities and Towns, 1977-79; bd. dirs., coach Ogden Hockey Assn., 1972-77, Weber Sheltered Workshop, 1974-77, Billings YMCA, 1980-86, Rimrock Found., 1980-86; chmn. community relations council Weber Basin Job Corps Center, 1973-77. Served with USCG, 1953-57. Recipient Cmty. Devel. Disting. Achievement awards Munising, 1964, Cmty. Devel. Disting. Achievement awards Sault Ste. Marie, 1966-70, Citizen award Dept. of Interior, 1977, Alumni Achievement award Westminster Coll., 1990, Dist. award of merit Boy Scouts Am., 1993, Silver Beaver award Boy Scouts Am., 1994; named Utah Adminstr. of Yr., 1976. Mem. Internat. City Mgmt. Assn. (L.P. Cookingham career devel. award 1974, Clarence Ridley in-service tng. award 1979), Utah City Mgrs. Assn. (pres. 1972-74), Greater Ogden C. of C. (dir.), Rotary (pres. Billings 1997-98), Phi Gamma Delta. Mem. LDS Ch. Club: Rotary. Home and Office: 1733 Parkhill Dr Billings MT 59102-2358

LARSEN, ROBERT RAY, healthcare executive, surgeon; b. Cushing, Nebr., May 11, 1935; s. Almus Olvier and Margaret Evelyn (Christensen) L.; m. Norma Ruth Fry Fulkerson, June 20, 1962 (div. 1978); m. Rebecca Yasuko Takahashi, Aug. 29, 1982; chlidren: Micaela Brown, Kamala Evora, Karolee Mathison. BA in Biology, Bucknell U., 1956; MD, Temple U., 1960; postgrad., U. Calif., Irvine, 1987. Cert. in med. mgmt.; lic. physician, Calif., Colo. Med. supt. Nekursini (India) Christ Hosp., 1963-68; chief of surgery Platte Valley Med. Ctr., Brighton, Colo., 1971-85; chief of staff, surgeon FHP Hosp., Fountain Valley, Calif., 1985-86; med. dir. FHP Healthcare, Fountain Valley, 1986-94, v.p. med. affairs, 1994-96; v.p. managed care svcs. McGraw Hill Pub., Mpls., 1996—; CEO, pres. Interim Physician Execs., Fountain Valley, 1996—; assoc. prof. U. Calif., Irvine, 1986—; trustee U. Sioux Falls, S.D., 1990—, HealthReform Action Plan, Santa Ana, Calif., 1996—. Contbr. chpt. to book, articles to profl. jours. Group leader St. Andrews Presbyn. Ch., Newport Beach, Calif., 1991—; med. advisor GHAA, Washington, 1993-95, Inst. of Medicine, Washington, 1994. Named Med. Staff Exec. of Yr., Am. Coll. Med. Staff Execs., Atlanta, 1994. Fellow ACS, Southwestern Surg. Congress, Am. Coll. Physician Execs., Healthcare Info. Mgmt. Soc.; me. AMa, Nat. Assn. Managed Care Physicians. Home: 21772 Tahoe Ln Lake Forest CA 92708

LARSON, BRENT T., broadcasting executive; b. Ogden, Utah, Sept. 23, 1942; s. George Theodore and Doris (Peterson) L.; m. Tracy Ann Taylor; children: Michelle, Brent Todd, Lindsey. Student, pub. schs., Los Angeles; diploma in radio operational engring., Burbank, Calif., 1962. Owner, mgr. Sta. KAIN, Boise, Idaho, 1969-77; owner, operator Sta. KXA Radio, Seattle, 1975-83, Sta. KYYX Radio, Seattle, 1980-83, Sta. KGA Radio, Spokane, Wash., 1978-84, Sta. KUUZ Radio, Boise, 1976-82, Sta. KOOS Radio, North Bend, Oreg., 1980-81, Sta. KODL Radio, The Dalles, Oreg., 1974-80, Sta. KKWZ Radio, Richfield, Utah, 1980-94, Sta. KSVC Radio, Richfield, 1980-94; v.p. Casey Larson Fast Food Co., Oreg. and Idaho, 1976-94, Imperial Broadcasting Corp., Idaho, 1970—, KSOS Am & KLZX FM, 1983—; pres. First Nat. Broadcasting Corp., 1970—; v.p. Larson-Wynn Corp., 1974—, Brentwood Properties, Ogden, 1977—; pres. Sta. KSIT Broadcasting, Rock Springs, Wyo., 1980-90, Gold Coast Communications Corp., Oreg., 1980-81, Sevier Valley Broadcasting Co., Inc., Utah, 1980-94, Brent Larson Group Stas., Western U.S., 1969—; v.p. mktg. Internat. Foods Corp., Boise, 1969-81; ptnr. Larson Tours and Travel, Burley, Idaho, 1977-87; v.p. Harrison Square Inc., 1995—; founder 1st Nat. TV Div., 1990; bd. dirs. Casey-Larson Foods Co., La Grande, Oreg., Studio City Entertainment (Nev. L.C.), 1996—. Bd. dirs. Met. Sch., 1981-93, Children's Aid Soc., 1991-94; chmn. bd. ZLX Limited Libility Co., 1995—. Mem. Am. Advt. Fedn., Nat. Assn. Broadcasters, Nat. Radio Broadcasters Assn., Wash. Broadcasters Assn., Oreg. Broadcasters Assn., Idaho Broadcasters Assn., Utah Broadcasters Assn., Citizens for Responsible Broadcasting (bd. dirs.). Republican. Mem. LDS Ch. Home: 2613 Seashore Dr Las Vegas NV 89128 Office: First Nat Broadcasting Corp 4455 S 5500 W Ogden UT 84315-9650

LARSON, DOROTHY ANN, business educator; b. Nekoosa, Wis., Feb. 27, 1934; d. Edwin E. and Ruby E. (Burch) L.; children: Jean Marie Harkey, Kenneth Lee Fitz, Cynthia Ann Anderson. BS with high distinction in Bus. and English, No. Ariz. U., 1969; MA in English, 1971; EdD in Bus., Ariz. State U., 1980. Tchr. English, Cottonwood (Ariz.) Oak Creek Elem. Sch., 1969-70; tchr. bus. and English, Mingus Union High Sch., Cottonwood, 1970-79, dir. vocat. edn., 1976-79; mem. faculty dept. bus. adminstrn. Yavapai Coll., 1979-94, chairperson bus. divsn., 1981-86, prep. coord. Yavapai Tech., 1994-95; cons. Ariz. Dept. Edn.; curriculum specialist Northern Ariz. U., 1995—; mem. adv. coun. Gov's. Coun. Practitioners. Mem. Ariz. Bus. Edn. Assn. (pres. 1980-81), Nat. Bus. Edn. Assn., Am. Vocat. Assn., Ariz. Edn. Assn., NEA, Nat. Tech. Prep. Network, Pi Omega Pi, Delta Pi Epsilon, Phi Kappa Phi, Alpha Delta Kappa, Phi Delta Kappa. Republican. Editor Ariz. Bus. Edn. Newsletter, 1972-74. Home: 542 S Marina Dr Gilbert AZ 85233

LARSON, ELSIE J., writer; b. Salem, Oreg., June 4, 1929; d. John William and Annabel (Wagner) Douglas; m. Richard E. Larson, Mar. 3, 1949; children: Robin R., Paul R., Diane P. Larson Linden. Student, Willamette U., 1948-50. Dental lab. tech. Office of Drs. Wagoner & Quinn, Beaverton, Oreg., 1970-86; freelance writer, 1985—. Author: Matthias, 1990, Dawn's Early Light, 1996; contbr. stories to popular mags. (Favorite Story award Reader's Digets 1993). Mem. Oreg. Christian Writers (life, corr. sec. 1986-90, pres. 1990-92, publicist 1992-96, bd. advisors 1992-96, Writer of Yr. award 1992). Home: 1541 SW Pleasant View Dr Gresham OR 97080

LARSON, ERIC HUGH, public health scientist; b. Mpls., Mar. 19, 1957; s. Marvin Claire and Jean Elizabeth (Firmage) L.; m. Mary Alice Hausladen, Aug. 13, 1987; children: Sarah Elizabeth, Benjamin Hugh. BA in Geography, U. Minn., 1980; MS, U. Calgary, 1985; PhD in Geography, U. Wash., 1995. Grad. rsch. asst. dept. geography U. Calgary, Alberta, Canada, 1984; teaching asst. dept. geography U. Wash., Seattle, 1988, rsch. asst., scientific programmer rural health rsch. ctr., 1988-89, rsch. scientist, 1990-91, assoc. dir. rsch., 1991—; presenter in field. Contbr. articles to profl. jours. Mem. Am. Pub. Health Assn., Assn. Am. Geographers, Can. Assn. Geographers, Nat. Rural Health Assn., Wash. Rural Health Assn. Office: U Wash Dept Family Medicine Box 354795 Seattle WA 98195

LARSON, GALE KJELSHUS, English language educator, consultant; b. Ekalaka, Mont., Aug. 31, 1937; s. Roland Walter and Hazel Annette (Kjelshus) L.; m. Cathy Frances Sechser, Aug. 11, 1962; 1 child, Michael Dale. BA, Carroll Coll., 1960; MA, Creighton U., 1963; PhD, U. Nebr., 1968. Prof. English Calif. State U., Northridge, 1967—, dir. freshman composition, 1969-71, asst. chmn. dept. English, 1971-72, acting assoc. dean Sch. Letters and Scis., 1972-73, assoc. dean Sch. Humanities, 1973-83, acting assoc. v.p. acad. program, 1983-84, chmn. dept. English, 1985-91, coord. writing proficiency exam., 1980-87, 91—; coord. London semester Calif. State U., Northridge, 1982—; pres. Calif. State U. English Coun., Calif. State U. Sys., 1986-90, v.p. English Coun., 1994—. Editor: Caesar and Cleopatra (Bernard Shaw), 1974; contbg. author: (bibliography) Annotated Bibliography of Bernard Shaw, vol. III, 1986. Mem. MLA, Nat. Coun. Tchrs. of English, Shaw Soc. of Am. (London), Sigma Tau Delta, Phi Beta Delta. Democrat. Roman Catholic. Home: 10965 Bluffside Dr Apt 39 Studio City CA 91604-4418 Office: Calif State U 18111 Nordhoff Northridge CA 91330

LARSON, GERALD LEE, auditor; b. Billings, Mont., Apr. 18, 1937; s. Phillip Antone and Eunice (LaPoint) L. Student, U. Nev., 1955-59; AS, Western Nev. U., 1975. Mil. pers. mgr. Nev. Air NG, Reno, 1973-81; mgr. employee rels. Nev. Mil. Dept., Carson City, 1981-82, mil. pers. mgr., 1982-88; auditor Nev. State Indsl. Ins., Reno, 1989-92; sr. auditor Nev. State Indsl. Ins., Carson City, 1992—. State pres. Nev. Enlisted NG Assn., Carson City, 1983-87; nat. conf. chmn. Enlisted Assn. NG U.S., Reno, 1989; project chmn. 40th ann. book Nev. Air NG, 1988. CM Sgt. Nev. Air NG, USAF, 1955-88. Named Outstanding Sr. Non-Commissioned Officer of Yr., Nev. Air NG, 1979. Office: State Indsl Ins System 515 E Musser St Carson City NV 89701-4262

LARSON, JAMES LEE, Scandinavian languages educator; b. Newport, Wash., Sept. 17, 1931; s. Lars W. and Norma (Newburn) L. PhD, U. Calif., Berkeley, 1965; PhD honors cause, Uppsala U., Sweden, 1983. Asst. prof. U. Pa., Phila., 1965-67, U. Calif., Berkeley, 1967-72; assoc. prof. U. Calif., 1972-79, prof. Scandinavian lang., 1979—. Author: Reason and Experience, 1971, Songs of Something, 1982, Interpreting Nature, 1994; editor/translator: Linnaeus, 1983, Gothic Renaissance, 1991. With U.S. Army, 1953-55. Mem. Am. Soc. 18th Century Studies, Western Soc. 18th Century Studies, History of Sci. Soc. Home: 2451 Ashby Ave Berkeley CA 94705-2034 Office: U Calif Dept Scandinavian Berkeley CA 94720

LARSON, KENNETH GERARD, real estate professional; b. Bklyn., Apr. 6, 1949; s. Lawrence Joseph and Agnes Lucy (Hannon) L.; m. Diane Marie D'Amico, May 24, 1980. BSBA, Pfeiffer Coll., 1971. Lic. real estate broker, Colo. Real estate salesman Van Schaack & Co., Denver, 1979-80; real estate broker Perry & Butler Realty, Denver, 1980-87, Re/Max Internat., Denver, 1987-90; owner, broker Profl. Relocation Assocs. Realty, Broomfield, Colo., 1993—; relocation counselor Relocation Resources, Inc., Norwell, Mass., 1991—. Contbr. articles to profl. jours. Mem. ethics com. Jeffco Bd. Realtors, Lakewood, Colo., 1985-87; task force mem. Denver Ctr. for Performing Arts, Denver, 1993-94. Mem. Colo. Archaeol. Soc. (v.p. 1993-94, dir. 1995—), Native Am. Rights Fund, Nat. Mus. of the Am. Indian (Cert. of Appreciation 1995). Republican. Office: Relocation Resources Inc 1099 18th St Ste 1900 Denver CO 80202-1908

LARSON, KIRK DAVID, pomologist and extension specialist; b. Pasadena, Calif., July 1, 1953; s. David and Martha Louise (Munn) L.; m. Katherine Ann Whitson, June 29, 1985; children: Kyle Galen, Kaelyn Ann. BS with high honors, U. Calif., Davis, 1980, MS, 1984; PhD, U. Fla., 1991. Horticulturist Aponte Farms, Peñuelas, P.R., 1971-75; vol. horticulturist Guatemalan Agrl. Project, San Juan Comalapa, Guatemala, 1977-78; agronomist IRI Rsch. Inst., Tinaco, Venezuela, 1980; orchard prodn. mgr. Pike Mt. Apples, North San Juan, Calif., 1981; rsch., teaching asst. Dept. of Pomology U. Calif., Davis, 1982-84; fruit crops ext. agt. Dade County Coop. Ext. Svc., Homestead, Fla., 1985-86; orchard prodn. mgr. J. R. Brooks & Son, Inc., Homestead, Fla., 1986-88; rsch. and teaching asst. Dept. Fruit Crops U. Fla., Gainesville, 1988-91; pomologist, ext. specialist U. Calif., Davis, 1991—; horticultural cons. U.S. Agri. Svc., Miami, Fla., 1989-91, Agridec, Inc., Miami, 1990, U. Malaga, Andalucia, Spain, 1995, Spanish Strawberry Nursery Industry, Seville, 1995, El Monte, Caja de Huelva y Sevilla, Huelva, Spain, 1995. Contbr. articles to profl. jours. and chpt. to book. Recipient citation for Outstanding Achievement in Internat. Agrl. Devel., U. Calif. Davis, 1979; grantee Calif. Strawberry Commn., 1992—, USDA, 1994—. Mem. Am. Soc. for Horticultural Sci., N.Am. Strawberry Growers Assn., Fla. State Horticultural Soc., Phi Kappa Phi, Gamma Sigma Delta. Office: U Calif South Coast Rsch Ctr 7601 Irvine Blvd Irvine CA 92718-1201

LARSON, LARS KRISTOPHER, broadcast executive; b. Taipei, Taiwan, Mar. 6, 1959; came to U.S., 1960; s. Waldo Henry Gust and Harriett Maxine (Mills) L.; m. Debb Ann Janes, Feb. 9, 1991 (div. Dec. 1995). Student, U. Oreg., 1977-79. Radio staff announcer Sta. KTIL, Tillamook, Oreg., 1976-78, Sta. KWAX, Eugene, Oreg., 1977-78; radio news dir. Sta. KATR, Eugene, 1977-78; intern writer Sta. KEZI-TV, Eugene, 1977-78; intern anchor/reporter Sta. KPNW, Eugene, 1978; radio news dir., reporter/anchor Stas. KBDF/KZEL, Eugene, 1978-79; radio reporter, anchor Sta. KJRB, Spokane, Wash., 1979-80; radio anchor, reporter, assignment editor Sta. KXL, Portland, Oreg., 1980-83; investigative reporter, anchor/prodr. Sta. KVAL-TV, Eugene, 1983-85; investigative reporter, prodr./anchor 10 o'Clock News KPTV, Portland, 1985—; Sunday radio talk show host Sta. KEX, Portland, 1988-89; radio talk show host Sta. KGW, Portland, 1989-91; former mem. Oreg. Bar/Press Com.; appeared as guest on: Larry King Live, Town Hall, various radio stas. Contbr. articles to profl. jours. including OMNI mag., Eugene Register Guard, Pacific N.W. Mag.; prodr. Northwest Reports. Recipient Oreg. Assoc. Press Best Radio News Program award, 1981, 82, best documentary award, 1986, Tom McCall award, 1988, 89, best continuing coverage award, 1991, Bruce Baer Spl. Recognition award, 1986, N.Y. Internat. Film Festival Bronze medal, 1988, AP Best Investigative Report award, 1988, Nat. Press Club Consumer Journalism award, 1988, Wash. Mo. Mag. Journalism award, 1989, Bruce Baer Spl. Recognition award, 1989, Women in Comm. Tom McCall Freedom of Info. award, 1990, N.Y. Internat. Film Festival bronze medal, 1990, Peabody award, 1990, Ohio State award, 1991, Soc. Profl. Journalists Investigative Reporting award, 1991, Emmy award, 1991, ABA Silver Gavel award, 1992, AP Best Investigative Reporting award, 1994, Regional Emmy for best investigative reporting, 1994, numerous others. Mem. Investigative Reporters and Editors, Soc. Profl. Journalists, Oreg. Assoc. Press (bd. dirs.). Republican. Office: KPTV Oregons News 12 211 SE Caruthers Portland OR 97214

LARSON, MAUREEN INEZ, rehabilitation consultant; b. Madison, Minn., Mar. 10, 1955; d. Alvin John and Leona B. (Bornhorst) L.; m. Michael Earl Klemetsrud, July 7, 1979 (div. Sept. 1988); m. Kenneth Bell, Dec., 1993. BA in Psychology cum laude, U. Minn., 1977; MA in Counseling, U. N.D., 1978. Cert. rehab. counselor, ins. specialist. Employment counselor II, coordinator spl. programs Employment Security div. State of Wyo., Rawlins, 1978-80; employment interviewer Employment Security div. State of Wash., Tacoma, 1980; lead counselor Comprehensive Rehab. Counseling, Tacoma, 1980-81; dir. counseling Cascade Rehab. Counseling, Tacoma, 1981-87, dist. mgr., 1987-90; regional mgr. Rainier Case Mgmt., Tacoma, 1991-92; owner Maureen Larson and Assocs., Gig Harbor, Wash., 1992—; state capt. legis. div. Provisions Project Am. Personnel and Guidance Assn., 1980. Advocate Grand Forks (N.D.) Rape Crisis Ctr., 1977-78; mem. Pierce County YMCA; bd. dirs. Boys and Girls Clubs of Tacoma, chairperson sustaining drive, 1991, sec.-treas., 1992-93, pres., 1994, auction com. and spl. events com. State of Minn. scholar, 1973-77; recipient Alice Tweed Tuohy award U. Minn., 1977, Nat. Disting. Svcs. Registry award Libr. of Congress, 1987; named bd. mem. vol. of Yr. Boys and Girls Clubs of Tacoma, 1992. Mem. Nat. Fedn. Bus. and Profl. Women (rec. sec. 1978-80, runner-up Young Careerists' Program 1980), Nat. Rehab. Assn. (bd. dirs. Olympic chpt. 1988-97, pres. 1990-91, chairperson state conf. planning com. 1990, 93, 96), Nat. Rehab. Counseling Assn. (bd. dirs. 1993, State of Wash. Counselor of Yr. 1991, Pacific Region Counselor of Yr. 1992), Nat. Rehab. Adminstrs. Assn. (bd. dirs. 1993), Women in Workers Compensation Orgn., Washington Self-Insured Assn., Nat. Assn. Rehab. Profls. in Pvt. Sector, Pi Gamma Mu. Office: M Larson & Assocs 13504 82nd Ave NW Gig Harbor WA 98329-8642

LARSON, PAUL MARTIN, lawyer; b. Tacoma, June 8, 1949; s. Charles Philip and Margeret (Kobervig) L.; m. Kristina Simonson, June 19, 1971; children: Kristin Ilene, Paul Philip, Erika Louise. AB, Stanford U., 1971; JD, Gonzaga U., 1974. Bar: Wash. 1975, U.S. Dist. Ct. (we. dist.) Wash. 1975, U.S. Dist. Ct. (ea. dist.) Wash. 1978, U.S. Ct. Appeals (9th cir.) 1981. Assoc. Hoff & Cross, Tacoma, 1975-76; ptnr., prin. Brooks & Larson, P.S., Yakima, Wash., 1976-87; ptnr. Bogle & Gates, Yakima, 1987-93, Larson & Perkins, 1994—. Author: (with others) Commercial Law Deskbook, 1981. Pres. Cardio & Pulmonary Inst., Yakima, 1981; bd. dirs. Yakima YMCA, 1981—, Yakima Youth Commn., 1989-93, Yakima Valley chpt. ARC, 1990-93; bd. dirs. Sisters of Providence Med. Ctr.-Yakima Found., 1986—, pres., 1992-93. Mem. ABA (standing com. lawyer's responsibility for client protection 1984-89), Wash. State Bar Assn. (spl. dist. counsel, 1985—, pres. corp. bus. and banking sect. 1987-88), Yakima Estate Planning Coun. (pres. 1981), Rotary. Republican. Office: Larson & Perkins 2311 W Chestnut Ave Yakima WA 98902-3746

LARSON, PAUL ROMAN, state agency administrator; b. Worcester, Mass., May 7, 1943; s. Roy Carl and Mary c. (Klemsieski) L.; m. Phyllis Hayes Nunn, Aug. 17, 1968; children: Paul R. Jr., Alexandra G. AA in Liberal Arts, Worcester (Mass.) Jr. Coll., 1963; BS in Wildlife Biology, U. Alaska, 1973, MS in Environ. Scis., 1974. Rsch. biologist Alaska Dept. Fish and Game, Ketchikan, 1974-76; rsch. biologist Alaska Dept. Fish and Game, Juneau, 1976-79, regional mgmt. biologist, 1979-89, dep. dir. for fisheries, 1989—. Mem. Elks, Moose. Home: 8935 Trio St Juneau AK 99801 Office: PO Box 25526 Juneau AK 99802

LARSON, PEGGY LOUISE See TILLMAN, PEGGY LOUISE

LARSON, RONALD ALLEN, information specialist and programmer, analyst; b. Bakersfield, Calif., Aug. 22, 1950; s. Roger Keith and Frances Ann (Appel) L. BS in BA, Calif. Poly. State U., 1979, MS in Computer Sci., 1981. With Hewlett-Packard, Mountain View, Calif., 1980—. Home: 148 S Lake Merced Hls San Francisco CA 94132-2935

LARSON, SWEN, mayor. Mayor City of Redlands, Calif., 1996—; steering com. Inland Empire Legislative Caucus; chmn. bd. dirs. Home Again; bd. dirs. Youth Accountability, Omni, Sanbag. Bd. dirs. Congrl. Ch.; past v.p. League Calif. Cities, Redlands C. of C.; past pres. House Neighborly Svc., Redlands Optimist Club, San Bernardino Internat. Airport Authority; past chmn. Redlands Planning Commn., Redlands Cmty. Hosp. Bd. Named Man of Yr. Redlands Svc. Orgn. and C. of C., 1994, Disting. Citizen award Boy Scouts by Inland Empire Coun., 1994; recipient Civic Achievement award LWV. Mem. Automobile Club (adv. bd. So. Calif.). Home: 30 Cajon St Redlands CA 92373

LARSON, WANDA Z(ACKOVICH), writer, poet; b. Cle Elum, Wash., Aug. 27, 1926; d. Stanley Aloysius and Anele (Valente) Zackovich; m. Glen B. Larson, Nov. 18, 1950 (div. Mar. 1967); children: Karen Holk, Margot Huffman, Lisa Larson Landrey. BA, U. Wash., 1949. Columnist North Bend Herald, Snoqualmie, Wash., 1955-61, Goldendale (Wash.) Sentinel, 1962-67; news editor West Seattle Herald, 1950-51; editor employee newsletter Alaska Steamship Co., Seattle, 1951; editl. asst. AP, Portland, Oreg., 1970-72; staff writer Associated Publs., Portland, Oreg., 1974-78; pub., editor Blue Unicorn Press Inc., Portland, 1990—; poet, host program Sta. KOPB, Portland, 1991—. Author: Portlandia, 1991, Miracle at Blowing Rock, 1992, Elisabeth: A Biography, 1997. Co-recipient 2nd pl. award Poetry Forum Quar., 1990; hon. mention Still Water Press, 1990, Internat. Mss, 1990. Baptist. Office: Blue Unicorn Press Inc Ste 9 1935 SE Main Portland OR 97214

LASAROW, WILLIAM JULIUS, retired federal judge; b. Jacksonville, Fla., June 30, 1922; s. David Herman and Mary (Hollins) L.; m. Marilyn Doris Powell, Feb. 4, 1951; children: Richard M., Elisabeth H. BA, U. Fla., 1943; JD, Stanford U., 1950. Bar: Calif. 1951. Counsel judiciary com. Calif. Assembly, Sacramento, 1951-52; dep. dist. atty. Stanislaus County, Modesto, Calif., 1952-53; pvt. practice law L.A., 1953-73; bankruptcy judge U.S. Cts., L.A., 1973-94; chief judge U.S. Bankruptcy Ct., Central dist., Calif., 1978-90; judge Bankruptcy Appellate Panel 9th Fed. Cir., 1980-82; fed. judge U.S. Bankruptcy Ct., L.A., 1973; faculty Fed. Jud. Ctr. Bankruptcy Seminars, Washington, 1977-82. Contbg. author, editor legal publs.; staff: Stanford U. Law Review, 1949. Mem. ABA, Am. Coll. Bankruptcy, Am. Bankruptcy Inst., L.A. County Bar Assn., Wilshire Bar Assn., Blue Key, Phi Beta Kappa, Phi Kappa Phi. Home: 11623 Canton Pl Studio City CA 91604-4164

LASCH, ROBERT, former journalist; b. Lincoln, Neb., Mar. 26, 1907; s. Theodore Walter and Myrtle (Nelson) L.; m. Zora Schaupp, Aug. 22, 1931 (dec. 1982); children: Christopher (dec. 1994), Catherine; m. Iris C. Anderson, Sept. 14, 1986. A.B., U. Nebr., 1928; postgrad. (Rhodes scholar), Oxford, 1928-31; Nieman fellow, Harvard, 1941-42. Reporter, state editor, editorial writer Omaha World-Herald, 1931-41; editorial writer, then chief editorial writer Chgo. Sun and Sun-Times, 1942-50; editorial writer St. Louis Post-Dispatch, 1950-57, editor editorial page, 1957-71, ret. Contbr. to: Newsmen's Holiday, 1942; Author: For a Free Press, 1944 (Atlantic Monthly prize), Breaking The Building Blockade, 1946. Recipient; St. Louis Civil Liberties award, 1966; Pulitzer prize for distinguished editorial writing, 1966. Home: 685 S La Posada Cir # 703 Green Valley AZ 85614-5118

LASHLEY, LENORE CLARISSE, lawyer; b. N.Y.C., June 3, 1934; d. Leonard Livingston and Una Ophelia (Laurie) L.; children: Donna Bee-Gates, Michele Bee, Maria Bee. BA, CUNY, 1956; MSW, U. Calif., Berkeley, 1970, MPH, 1975; JD, U. Calif., San Francisco, 1981. Bar: Calif. 1981. Atty. W.O.M.A.N., Inc., San Francisco, 1982-84; pvt. practice San Francisco Law Office, 1984-87; dep. dist. atty. Monterey Dist. Atty., Salinas, Calif., 1987-89; trial atty. State Bar of Calif., L.A., 1989; dep. dist. atty. L.A. Dist. Atty., 1989; city atty., dep. City Atty. L.A., 1989—; chair, bd. dirs. St. Anthony's Dining Room, San Francisco, 1986-87; sec., bd. dirs. NAAC, Monterey, 1987-88; bd. dirs. Childrens Home Soc., Oakland, Calif., 1966-68. Recipient Cert. of Merit, Nat. Assn. Naval Officers, 1987. Mem. L.A. County Bar Assn. (del. to state bar 1992, 93). Roman Catholic. Office: City Atty LA 200 N Main St # 1700 Che Los Angeles CA 90012-4110

LASIC, DANILO DUSAN, physicist; b. Ljubljana, Slovenia, Aug. 7, 1952; came to U.S., 1988; s. Dusan H. and Vida (Tom) L.; m. Alenka Dvorzak, Jan. 7, 1988; 1 child, Eva. BS in Chemistry, U. Ljubljana, 1975, MS in Chemistry, 1977, PhD in Physics, 1979. Rsch. assoc. Inst. J. Stefan, Ljubljana, 1977-81; postdoctoral fellow Duke U., Durham, N.C., 1981-82; vis. scientist Eidgenossische Technische Hochschule, Zurich, Switzerland, 1982-84; prof. Biophysics U. Ljubljana, 1984-86; vis. prof. U. Waterloo (Ont., Can.), 1986-88; sr. scientist Liposome Tech. Inc., Menlo Park, Calif., 1988-94, Mega Bios Corp., San Carlos, Calif., 1994-96; ind. cons. liposomes, drug and gene delivery, 1996—; dir. Nuclear Magnetic Resonance Inst. U. Waterloo, Ont., 1986-88; cons. Immunotherapeutics, Fargo, N.D., 1987-88, Liposome Tech. Inc., Menlo Park, 1994—. Author: Liposomes: From Physics to Applications, 1993, Liposomes in Gene Delivery, 1997; co-editor: Nuclear Magnetic Resonance in Physics, Chemistry and Biology, 1989, Stealth Liposomes, 1994, Nonmedical Applications of Liposomes, Vols. I, II, III, and IV, Medical Applications of Liposomes, 1997; contbr. numerous articles to profl. jours. Home: 7512 Birkdale Dr Newark CA 94560-1512

LASKIN, BARBARA VIRGINIA, legal association administrator; b. Chgo., July 2, 1939; d. Cyril Krieps and Gertrude Katherine (Kujawa) Szymanski; children: Dawn Katherine Doherty, Amy Lynn Anderson. BA, U. Ill., Chgo., 1967; MA, Am. U. Beirut, 1978, Georgetown U., 1985. Asst. buyer Carson, Pirie, Scott & Co., Chgo., 1967-69; fgn. svc. officer Dept. State, Washington, 1969-79; mgr. gift shops Marriott Hotels, Washington, 1979-81; office mgr. Robt Schwinn & Assoc., Bethesda, Md., 1983-85; exec. dir. Internat. Acad. Trial Lawyers, San Jose, Calif., 1985—. Fellow Rotary Club San Jose; mem. AAUW (v.p. 1987), Am. Soc. Assn. Execs., Meeting Planners Internat., Internat. Spl. Events Soc. (v.p. membership 1996), Internat. Spl. Events Found. (dir.), Profl. Conservation Mgrs. Assn. Roman Catholic. Office: Internat Acad Trial Lawyers 4 N 2nd St Ste 175 San Jose CA 95113-1306

LASKO, ALLEN HOWARD, pharmacist; b. Chgo., Oct. 27, 1941; s. Sidney P. and Sara (Hoffman) L.; BS (James scholar), U. Ill., 1964; m. Janice Marilynn Chess, Dec. 24, 1968 (div. Aug. 1993); children: Stephanie Paige, Michael Benjamin. Staff pharmacist Michael Reese Hosp. and Med. Center, Chgo., 1964-68; clin. pharmacist City of Hope Med. Center, Duarte, Calif., 1968-73; chief pharmacist Monrovia (Calif.) Cmty. Hosp., 1973-74, Santa Fe Meml. Hosp., L.A., 1974-77; pvt. investor, 1977-93; clin. pharmacist Foothill Presbyn. Hosp., Glendora, Calif., 1993—. Recipient Roche Hosp. Pharmacy Rsch. award, 1972-73. Mem. Magic Castle, Flying Samaritans, Mensa, Rho Pi Phi. Jewish. Author: Diabetes Study Guide, 1972, A Clinical Approach to Lipid Abnormalities Study Guide, 1973, Jet Injection Tested As An Aid in Physiologic Delivery of Insulin, 1973. Home: 376 Hill St Monrovia CA 91016-2340 Office: Foothill Presbyn Hosp 250 S Grand Ave Glendora CA 91741-4218

LASLETT, LAWRENCE J., physician, educator; b. Boston, Apr. 17, 1942. BS, Iowa State U., Ames, 1964; MD, U. Iowa, Iowa City, 1969. Diplomate Am. Bd. Internal Medicine, sub-bd. Cardiology. Intern Hennepin County Gen. Hosp., Mpls., 1969-70; resident in internal medicine U. Calif., Davis, 1973-76, fellow in cardiology, 1976-78, asst. prof. clin. medicine, 1978-85, assoc. prof. clin medicine, 1985-96, dir. fellowship tng. in cardiology, 1994—; dir. cardiac catheterization lab. U. Calif. Davis Med. Ctr., Sacramento, 1984-94; prof. clin. medicine U. Calif., Davis, 1996—. Contbr. articles to med. jours. Mem. tech. adv. com. on free-standing catheterization labs. Calif. Dept. Health Svcs., Sacramento, 1990-94. Served to lt. comdr. USPHS, 1979-81. Fellow Am. Coll. Cardiology (chair Calif. chpt. govt. rels. com.); mem. ACP, Am. Heart Assn. Office: U Calif Divsn Cardiology 4150 V St Sacramento CA 95817

LASLEY, MONA CAROL, elementary education educator, consultant; b. Oroville, Calif., Aug. 17, 1944; d. Harvey Dean and Helen Margaret (Post) Northcutt; m. Victor LeRoy Lasley, June 10, 1967; 1 child, Robert. BA, Chico (Calif.) State Coll., 1966. Cert. tchr., Calif. Tchr. Thermalito Sch. Dist., Oroville, 1967-68, Pierce Joint Unified Sch. Dist., Arbuckle, Calif., 1969-88, Natomas Unified Sch. Dist., Sacramento, 1988—; math. cons. No. Calif. Math. Project, Davis, 1986—, tchr., rschr., 1989—, mentor tchr., 1987-90, 91-92, also co-dir. and coord. for profl. devel.; math. coach demonstration Bay Area Math. Project, Berkeley, Calif., 1990-91; cons. D-Q U. Math. and Sci. Acad. Tchrs. and Am. Indian Students, 1992-94; del. U.S.-Russia 1st Joint Conf. Math. Edn., 1993. Grantee Calif. Math. Projects, 1990—, Calif. Math. Tech., 1992. Mem. ASCD, Nat. Coun. Tchrs. of Math., No. Calif. Math. Project, Calif. Math. Coun., Calif. Tchr.'s Assn. Home: 1732 W Miramonte Dr Woodland CA 95695-5267 Office: Bannon Creek Elem Sch 2775 Millcreek Sacramento CA 95833

LASORDA, THOMAS CHARLES (TOMMY LASORDA), professional baseball team manager; b. Norristown, Pa., Sept. 22, 1927; s. Sam and Carmella (Covatto) L.; m. Joan Miller, Apr. 14, 1950; children: Laura, Tom Charles. Student pub. schs., Norristown. Pitcher Bklyn. Dodgers, 1954-55, Kansas City A's, 1956; with L.A. Dodgers, 1956—; mgr. minor league clubs L.A. Dodgers, Pocatello, Idaho, Ogden, Utah, Spokane, Albuquerque, 1965-73; coach L.A. Dodgers, 1973-76, mgr., 1976-96, v.p. fin., 1997—. Author: (with David Fisher) autobiography The Artful Dodger, 1985. Served with U.S. Army, 1945-47. Named Pitcher of Yr. Internat. League, 1958; L.A. Dodgers winner Nat. League pennant, 1977, 78, 81, 88, winner World Championship, 1981, 88; 2d Nat. League mgr. to win pennant first two yrs. as mgr.; named Nat. League Mgr. Yr. UPI, 1977, AP, 1977, 81, Baseball Writers' Assn. Am., 1983, 1988, Sporting News, 1988, Baseball Writers Assn. Am., 1983, 88; recipient Milton Richman Meml. award Assn. Profl. Baseball Players Am.; coach Nat. League All-Star team, 1977, 83-84, 86, 93. Mem. Profl. Baseball Players Am. Roman Catholic. Club: Variety of Calif. (v.p.). Office: care Los Angeles Dodgers 1000 Elysian Park Ave Los Angeles CA 90012-1112*

LASSEN, BETTY JANE, educator; b. Topeka, Kans., Apr. 19, 1923; d. Harvey Leroy and Anna Elizabeth (Day) Rose; m. Emil Lassen Jr., June 5, 1944 (dec. Sept. 1989); 1 child, Emil III. Instr., guide YMCA-YWCA, Albuquerque, 1975-84, U. N.Mex. Continuing Edn., Albuquerque, 1979—, Ft. Lewis Coll. Continuing Edn., Durango, Colo., 1992-93; liaison, asst. coord. San Juan Coll. Elder Hostel, Farmington, N.Mex., 1993-94; owner, pres. Outdoor Adventure Tours, Inc., Albuquerque, 1982—; mem. curriculum com., human svcs. tng. coun. gerontology divsn. continuing edn. U. N.Mex., 1979-82; spkr. in field. Designer ski equipment; contbr. articles, poetry to profl. publs. Vol. instr., guide for disabled Easter Seals Soc., Albuquerque, 1983; vol. campground host Nat. Park Svc., Chaco Canyon Ruins, N.Mex., 1990; campaign vol. Dem. Party, Albuquerque, 1976. Recipient Appreciation award Easter Seals Soc., 1983. Mem. Puerto Del Sol Ladies Golf Assn. (pres. 1976-77), N.Mex. Outfitters/Guides, N.Mex. Cross-Country Ski Club (sec. 1973-76), N.Mex. Mountain Club. Home: 2916 Santa Clara SE Albuquerque NM 87106-2947

LASSESEN, CATHERINE AVERY CLAY, small business owner, manager, trainer; b. Corte Madera, CA, Nov. 8, 1961; d. Ralph Kindel Boyland Clay and Susan Avery (Kendall) Clay; m. B. Rune Lassesen, Mar. 2, 1991. BA in Hotel Adminstrn., U. Nev., 1985. Promotions asst. Tropicana Hotel, Las Vegas, Nev., 1985; front desk mgr. Marriott Corp., various locations, 1986-88; mgr. Six Ravens Ranch, Boonville, Calif., 1988-96, CEO, 1988-92; owner/mgr. Custom Engraving by Catherine, Boonville, Calif., 1989-96; co-owner, trainer Bridgegate Stables & Tack Barn One, Boonville, 1991-93; owner, instr. Flying Colors An Equine Edn. Svc. Six Ravens Ranch, Boonville, Calif., 1994-96; mgr. Hestehaven, 1996—; coach Mendocino County vaulting team, 1994-96; horse show mgr. Skandifest, Turlock, Calif., 1997. Publicity dir. Mendocino County Fair and Apple Show, 1992-94. Named one of the Women of Yr., Clark County, Las Vegas, Nev., 1986. Mem. Ind. Career Women (historian 1991-92, v.p. 1992-93), U. Nev. Las Vegas Alumni Assn., Delta Zeta (province alumnae dir. 1991-93, nat. alumnae/collegiate rels. chmn. 1995-96, area alumnae dir. great western states 1996—), Am. Vaulting Assn., Am. Quarter Horse Assn., Am. Paint Horse Assn., N.Am. Horseman Assn., Am. Horse Show Assn., Calif. Gymkhana Assn. (judge 1992—, dist. 37 pres. 1992-93, co-chmn. 1993-94), N.Am. Riding for the Handicapped Assn., Inc., Norwegian Fjord Horse Registry. Office: Hestehaven PO Box 160 Days Creek OR 97429

LAST, DIANNA LINN SCHNEIDER, marketing company executive; b. Canton, Ohio, Dec. 29, 1944; d. Ld Mervyn and Veronica Lee Schneider; m. David D. Last, Nov. 29, 1969; 1 child, Jason Holden. BA in German, Ohio State U., 1966. Rsch. asst., programmer trainee high-energy physics dept. Ohio State U., Columbus, 1964-66; mfg. programmer RANCO, Inc., Columbus, 1966-68; sr. edn. rep. Honeywell Info. Systems, Cleve., 1968-72; dist. mgr. Honeywell Info. Systems, Orlando, Fla., 1972-78, telecommunications cons., 1978-79; mgr. networking edn. Honeywell Info. Systems, Phoenix, 1979-81; mgr. distributed systems, 1981-84; account and tech. mgr. Honeywell Info. Systems, Beijing, People's Republic of China, 1985; resident dir., chief rep. Honeywell Bull (formerly Honeywell Info. Systems), Beijing, People's Republic of China, 1985-87; dir. Integrated Info. Architecture Honeywell Bull, Phoenix, 1987-88; dir. info. mgmt. U.S. mktg. Bull (formerly Honeywell Bull), Phoenix, 1988-90; pres. Last Concepts Internat. Mktg. & Export Mgmt. Co., Phoenix, 1990—; bd. advisors Internat. Bus. Orgn., Am. Grad. Sch. Internat. Mgmt., 1981-84, 90—; cons., speaker in field; co-founder, co-chair Ariz. Internat. Trade Orgn., 1992—; co-founder, chmn. Am. High-Tech Forum, Beijing, 1985-87; co-chair mktg. com. Enterprise Network, 1990—; adj. faculty internat. bus. Maricopa Colls., 1994—; mem. governing bd. Internat. Studies Acad. 7-12 Charter Sch.; bd. dirs. Digital Network Access, 1995—. Chalice bearer, lay reader St. John Baptist Episcopal Ch., Phoenix, 1983—, mem. bishop's com., 1980-83, mem. vestry, 1991-92; adv. bd. Ariz. Assn. Children and Adults with Learning Disabilities, 1983-84; design task force Maricopa C.Cs., 1984; active World Trade Ctr. Ariz., 1992—; mem. internat. adv. coun. Paradise Valley Coll., 1994—; bd. dirs. Ctr. for New Dirs., Phoenix, 1987-90. Mem. IEEE (past vice chmn. programs), Coun. Fgn. Rels. (mem. Phoenix com. 1994—), Ariz. Software Assn. (internat. com. 1990-92). Home: 1274 E Marconi Ave Phoenix AZ 85022-3232

LASTER, MARTIN, school superintendent; b. Jersey City, Nov. 19, 1952; s. Sidney Edward and Annette (Weinstein) L.; m. Jonna Johnson, June 27, 1976; children: Ian Arthur, Katlyn Eva. BA, Ohio U., 1976; MA, U. Denver, 1982, MPA, 1983, PhD, 1984. Tchr. Fed Hocking Schs., Stewart, Ohio, 1976-78, Anchorage/Mat-Su Sch., Alaska, 1978-81; with ctrl. office N.W. Arctic Schs., Kotzebue, Alaska, 1984-87; prin. Mat-Su Schs., Palmer, Alaska, 1987-90, asst. supt., 1990-93; supt. Craig (Alaska) Schs., 1993-96, Darrington (Wash.) Schs., 1996—; mem. steering com. Alaska Dept. of Edn. Stds. and Assessment, Juneau, Alaska, 1991-95, exec. com. S.E. Regional Resource Ctr., Juneau, 1993-96; bd. mem. Mt. Edgecombe H.S. Adv. Bd., Sitka, Alaska, 1994-96; spkr. confs. Co-author: (instrnl. materials) ANCSA Video Series, 1985; supr.: (lang. text) Inupiat Language Series, 1985. Bd. mem. Very Spl. Arts Alaska, Anchorage, 1990-93; bd. dirs. Palmer Rotary, 1991-93; mem. Mat-Su Econ. Devel. Commn., Palmer, 1993. Named Supt of Yr. Am. Assn. Sch. Adminstr., Alaska, 1996. Mem. C. of C. (chair quality of life 1993), Moose. Office: Darrington Sch Dist Box 27 Darrington WA 98241

LATHAM, JAMES RICHARD, research scientist; b. Pomona, Calif., July 1, 1946; s. James Richard and Norma Elizabeth (Mills) L.; m. Pamela June Staley Latham, Aug. 31, 1968, 1 child, Joan Elizabeth Latham. Student, U. Calif., Berkeley, 1964-65, Chabot Coll., Hayward, Calif., 1965-72. Technician Coast Mfg./Hexel Co., Livermore, Calif., 1966-69, Crown Zellerbach Co., San Leandro, Calif., 1969-70; sr. rsch. technician Kaiser Aluminum & Chem. Corp., Pleasanton, Calif., 1970-82; sr. technician Clorox Tech. Ctr., Pleasanton, Calif., 1982—. Patentee in field. Named Merit Scholarship Finalist; recipient NROTC scholarship. Mem. Am. Chemical Soc., Div. Chemical Technicians (treas. 1993-94), Livermore Amateur Radio Klub (sec.). Mem. LDS Ch.

LATHI, BHAGAWANDAS PANNALAL, electrical engineering educator; b. Bhokar, Maharashtr, India, Dec. 3, 1933; came to U.S., 1956; s. Pannalal Rupchand and Tapi Pannalal (Indani) L.; m. Rajani Damodardas Mundada, July 27, 1962; children: Anjali, Shishir. BEEE, Poona U., 1955; MSEE, U. Ill., 1957; PhD in Elec. Engring., Stanford U., 1961. Research asst. U. Ill., Urbana, 1956-57, Stanford (Calif.) U., 1957-60; research engr. Gen. Electric Co., Syracuse, N.Y., 1960-61; cons. to semicondr. industry India, 1961-62; assoc. prof. elec. engring. Bradley U., Peoria, Ill., 1962-69, U.S. Naval Acad., Annapolis, Md., 1969-72; prof. elec. engring. Campinas (Brazil) State U., 1972-78, Calif. State U., Sacramento, 1979—; vis. prof. U. Iowa, Owa City, 1979. Author: Signals, Systems and Communication, 1965, Communication Systems, 1968 (transl. into Japanese 1977), Random Signals and Communication Theory, 1968, Teoria Signalow I Ukladow Telekomunikacyjnych, 1970, Sistemy Telekomunikacyjne, 1972, Signals, Systems and Controls, 1974, Sistemas de Comunicacion, 1974, 86, Sistemas de Comunicacao, 1978, Modern Digital and Analog Communication Systems, 1983, 89 (transl. into Japanese 1986, 90), Signals and Systems, 1987, Linear Systems and Signals, 1992, Signal Processing and Linear Systems, 1997; contbr. articles to profl. jours. Fellow IEEE. Office: Calif State U 6000 J St Sacramento CA 95819-2605

LATHROP, ANN, librarian, educator; b. L.A., Nov. 30, 1935; d. Paul Ray and Margaret (Redfield) W.; divorced; children: Richard Harold, John Randolph, Rodney Grant. BA in History summa cum laude, Ea. N.Mex. U., 1957; MLS, Rutgers U., 1964; PhD, U. Oreg., 1988. Cert. elem. tchr., Calif.; cert. libr., Calif; adminstrv. credential, Calif. Elem. sch. tchr. Chalfont (Pa.) Boro Sch., 1960-61, Livingston Elem. Sch., New Brunswick, N.J., 1961-63, Rosedale Elem. Sch., Chico, Calif., 1964-65; libr. Chico (Calif.) H.S., 1965-72, Princeton (Calif.) H.S., 1972-73, Santa Maria (Calif.) H.S., 1973-77; libr. coord. San Mateo County Office Edn., Redwood City, Calif., 1977-89; assoc. prof. Calif. State U., Long Beach, 1989-92, prof., 1993—; dir. Calif. Software Clearinghouse, Calif. State U., Long Beach. Author: Online Information Retrieval as a Research Tool in Secondary School Libraries, 1988; co-author: Courseware in the Classroom, 1983; editor: Online and CD-ROM Databases in School Libraries, 1989, The 1988-89 Educational Software Preview Guide, 1988, Technology in the Curriculum Resource Guides, 1988; editor, founder: (jours.) The Digest of Software Reviews: Education, 1983-86, Software Reviews on File, 1985-86; editor: (database) California Online Resources in Education, 1989-94, Technology in the Curriculum Online, 1995—; contbr. chpts. to books, articles to profl. jours. Mem. ALA, NEA, Am. Assn. Sch. Librs., Assn. State Tech. Using Tchr. Educators, Calif. Faculty Assn., Calif. Sch. Libr. Assn., Computer Using Educators, Internat. Soc. for Tech. in Edn. Office: Calif State U 1250 N Bellflower Blvd Long Beach CA 90840-0006

LATHROP, MITCHELL LEE, lawyer; b. L.A., Dec. 15, 1937; s. Alfred Lee and Barbara (Mitchell) L.; m. Denice Annette Davis; children: Christin Lorraine Newlon, Alexander Mitchell, Timothy Trewin Mitchell. B.Sc., U.S. Naval Acad., 1959; J.D., U. So. Calif., 1966. Bar: D.C. 1966, Calif. 1966, U.S. Supreme Ct. 1969, N.Y. 1981; registered environ. assessor, Calif. Dep. counsel Los Angeles County, Calif., 1966-68; with firm Brill, Hunt, DeBuys and Burby, L.A., 1968-71; ptnr. Macdonald, Halsted & Laybourne, L.A. and San Diego, 1971-80; sr. ptnr. Rogers & Wells, N.Y.C., San Diego, 1980-86; sr. ptnr. Adams, Duque & Hazeltine, L.A., San Francisco, N.Y.C., San Diego, 1986-94, exec. com., 1986-94, firm chmn., 1992-94; sr. ptnr. Luce, Forward, Hamilton & Scripps, San Diego, N.Y.C., San Francisco, L.A., Chgo., 1994—; presiding referee Calif. Bar Ct., 1984-86, mem. exec. com., 1981-88; lectr. law Calif. Judges Assn., Practicing Law Inst. N.Y., Continuing Edn. of Bar, State Bar Calif., ABA, others. Author: State Hazardous Waste Regulation, 1991, Environmental Insurance Coverage, 1991, Insurance Coverage for Environmental Claims, 1992. Western Regional chmn. Met. Opera Nat. Coun., 1971-81, v.p., mem. exec. com., 1971—, now chmn.; trustee Honnold Libr. at Claremont Colls., 1972-80; bd. dirs. Music Ctr. Opera Assn., L.A., sec., 1974-80; bd. dirs. San Diego Opera Assn., 1980—, v.p., 1985-89, pres.-elect, 1993, pres., 1994-96; bd. dirs. Met. Opera Assn., N.Y.C.; mem. nat. steering coun. Nat. Actors Theatre, N.Y. Mem. ABA, N.Y. Bar Assn., Fed. Bar Assn., Fed. Bar Council, Calif. Bar Assn., D.C. Bar Assn., San Diego County Bar Assn. (chmn. ethics com. 1980-82, bd. dirs. 1982-85, v.p. 1985), Assn. Bus. Trial Lawyers, Assn. So. Calif. Def. Counsel, Los Angeles Opera Assos. (pres. 1970-72), Soc. Colonial Wars in Calif. (gov. 1970-72), Order St. Lazarus of Jerusalem, Friends of Claremont Coll. (dir. 1975-81, pres. 1978-79), Am. Bd. Trial Advocates, Judge Advocates Assn. (dir. Los Angeles chpt. 1974-80, pres. So. Calif. chpt. 1977-78), Internat. Assn. Def. Counsel, Brit. United Services Club (dir. Los Angeles 1973-75), Mensa Internat., Calif. Soc., S.R. (pres. 1977-79), Calif. Club (Los Angeles), Valley Hunt Club (Pasadena, Calif.), Met. Club (N.Y.C.), The Naval Club (London), Phi Delta Phi. Republican. Home: 455 Silvergate Ave San Diego CA 92106-3327 Office: Luce Forward Hamilton and Scripps 600 W Broadway Fl 26 San Diego CA 92101-3311 also: Citicorp Ctr 153 E 53rd St Frnt 26 New York NY 10022-4611

LATIMER, HEATHER, writer; b. Essex, England; d. Robin and Jessie (Rose) L.; m. Walther B. Neubauer, Aug. 24, 1957 (dec. Apr. 1976). Student, Pitmans Coll., 1943-46. Photographers model Head & Shoulders, London, 1946-53; asst. to pres. W.H. Schneider Advt., N.Y.C., 1965-67; patron rels. Met. Opera, N.Y.C., 1968-70; asst. to dir. Bide-A-Wee Animal Protection Assn., N.Y.C., 1970-72; contbg. editor Dogs Mag., N.Y.C., 1972-77; freelance writer N.Y.C., 1971-94, Las Vegas, 1994—. Author: How to Make Money as a Professional Party Organizer in the Great Leisuretime Market, 1971, Tidypet: How to Make Your Dog an Indoor Toilet and Train Your Puppy or Grown Dog to Use It, 1972, Dogs: Everything You Need to Know to Care for Your Pet, 1979, Cats: Everything You Need to Know to Care for Your Pet, 1982, Louis Wain - King of the Cat Artists, 1860-1939, 1987, 2nd edit., 1990, One is Fun: Guide to a Happy and Rewarding Single Lifestyle, 1996, Is Forever Too Long?, 1996, In the Eyes of the Cats, 1997, (audio books) The Artist, 1992, Curse of the Painted Cats, 1994. Vol. docent N.Y. Botanical Garden, N.Y.C., 1989-94; pres. Internat. League N.Y., N.Y.C., 1957-67. Mem. Princeton Club (N.Y.C.), English Speaking Union, Las Vegas Art Mus. Mem. Ch. of England. Office: PO Box 27383 Las Vegas NV 89126

LATINI, HENRY PETER, real estate management executive; b. Portland, Maine; s. Joseph and Mary Rose (Di Santo) L.; m. Betty Shevock, Oct. 20, 1951; children: Mary Celeste, Lisa Ann Kirkendall, Monica Louise King. AB, U. Miami, Coral Gables, Fla., 1951; postgrad., U. Maine, 1980-81, U. Hawaii, 1984. Spl. agt. FBI, Washington, 1951-79; owner, pres. Nat. Bur. Spl. Investigations, Portland, 1979-84; owner, v.p. Data Base Inc., Reston, Va., 1980-84; v.p. Cert. Mgmt. Inc., Honolulu, 1985-94, Latini-Kirkendall: Architecture, Seattle and Honolulu, 1992—; owner Residential

Mgmt. Cons., Seattle, Wash., 1992—; mng. ptnr. Latini-Kirkendall Architecture, Seattle and Honolulu, 1992—; co-owner Koapaka Ctr Inc., Honolulu, 1992-95; chmn. bd. dirs. A.R. Corp., Honolulu, 1987-92, CMI, 1992-95; mem. Cmty. Assns. Inst., Honolulu; pres. Common Area Maintenance Co., 1991-95; co-owner Koapaka Ctr., Inc. Membership chair Portland Club, 1980-84; mem. Civil Svc. Commn., Cape Elizabeth, Maine, 1981-83; dir. security Mus. of Art, Portland, Maine, 1982-83; vol. Hawaiian Open and Ko'Olina Sr. Invitational Tournament. Mem. Soc. Former Spl. Agts. of the FBI Inc. (Hawaii chpt., sec. 1987-88, v.p. 1988-89, chmn. 1989-90), Inst. Real Estate Mgmt. Am. Soc. for Indsl. Security (Maine chpt., founder 1980, pres. 1980-82), Elks. Republican. Roman Catholic.

LATTANZIO, STEPHEN PAUL, astronomy educator; b. Yonkers, N.Y., June 29, 1949; s. Anthony Raymond and Anella Lattanzio; m. Barbara Regina Knisely, Aug. 14, 1976; children: Gregory Paul, Timothy Paul. BA in Astronomy, U. Calif., Berkeley, 1971; MA in Astronomy, UCLA, 1973, postgrad., 1973-75. Planetarium lectr. Griffith Obs., Los Angeles, 1973-75; instr. astronomy El Camino Coll., Torrance, Calif., 1974-75; planetarium lectr. Valley Coll., Los Angeles, 1975; prof. astronomy Orange Coast Coll., Costa Mesa, Calif., 1975—, planetarium dir., 1975—; mem. adv. commn. Natural History Found. Orange County, Calif., 1988-91; scientific advisor instructional TV series Universe: The Infinite Frontier, 1992—. Co-author: Study Guide for Project: Universe, 1978, 2d rev. edition 1981; textbook reviewer, 1978—; co-screenwriter Project: Universe instructional TV series episode, 1979; contbr. articles to profl. jours. Mem. Astron. Soc. Pacific, The Planetary Soc., Sigma Xi (assoc.), Phi Beta Kappa. Office: Orange Coast Coll 2701 Fairview Rd Costa Mesa CA 92626-5563

LATTMAN, LAURENCE HAROLD, retired academic administrator; b. N.Y.C., Nov. 30, 1923; s. Jacob and Yetta (Schwartz) L.; m. Hanna Renate Cohn, Apr. 12, 1946; children—Martin Jacob, Barbara Diane. BSChemE, Coll. City N.Y., 1948; MS in Geology, U. Cin., 1951, PhD, 1953. Instr. U. Mich., 1952-53; asst. head photogeology sect. Gulf Oil Corp., Pitts., 1953-57; asst. prof. to prof. geomorphology Pa. State U., 1957-70; prof., head dept. geology U. Cin., 1970-75; dean Coll. of Mines U. Utah, 1975-83, dean Coll. Engring., 1978-83; pres. N.Mex. Tech., Socorro, 1983-93, pres. emeritus, 1993—; bd. dirs. Pub. Svc. Co. of N.Mex.; cons. U.S. Army Engrs., Vicksburg, Miss., 1965-69, also major oil cos. Author: (with R.G. Ray) Aerial Photographs in Field Geology, 1965, (with D. Zillman) Energy Law; Contbr. articles to profl. jours. Environ. improvement bd. NMex., 1996—. Served with AUS, 1943-46. Fenneman fellow U. Cin., 1953. Fellow Geol. Soc. Am.; mem. Am. Assn. Petroleum Geologists, Am. Soc. Photogrammetry (Ford Bartlett award 1968), Soc. Econ. Paleontologists and Mineralogists, AIME (Disting. mem. 1981, Mineral Industries Edn., award 1986—), Assn. Western Univs. (chmn. bd. dirs. 1986-87), Sigma Xi. Home: 11509 Penfield Ln NE Albuquerque NM 87111-6506

LAU, BETH, English language educator; b. Milw., Dec. 16, 1951; d. Milford H. and Janet (Towse) L.; m. Martin J. Camargo, Dec. 27, 1974 (div. 1982). BA in English, U. Ill., 1974, MA, 1976, PhD, 1980. Teaching asst. U. Ill., Urbana, 1974-78; adj. prof. various colls. and univs., Ala., Mo., 1979-82; asst. prof. N.Mex. State U., 1982-85, Ripon Coll., 1985-90; assoc. prof. Calif. State U., Long Beach, 1990-95, prof., 1995—. Author: Keats's Reading of the Romantic Poets, 1991; co-editor Approaches to Teaching Brontë's Jane Eyre, 1993; contbr. articles and revs. to profl. jours. Travel grantee Am. Coun. Learned Socs., 1986. Mem. MLA, Keats-Shelley Assn., Wordsworth-Coleridge Assn., Interdisciplinary 19th Century Studies, Philological Assn. Pacific Coast, N.Am. Soc. for Study of Romanticism. Home: 2621 E 20th St Unit 17 Signal Hill CA 90804-1004 Office: Calif State U Dept English 1250 N Bellflower Blvd Long Beach CA 90840-0006

LAU, FRED H., protective services official. Chief of police San Francisco. Office: 850 Bryant St Ste 525 San Francisco CA 94103

LAU, HENRY, mechanical engineer, consultant; b. Hong Kong, Feb. 4, 1941; s. Mo Ngok and Julia (Seto) L.; m. Bing Sin, June 6, 1970; 1 child, Ryan. BS, U. Tenn., 1966; MS, Duke U., Durham, N.C., 1969, PhD, 1973. Rsch. assoc. Duke U., Durham, 1973-74; mech. engr. Ayres & Hayakawa Energy Mgrs., L.A., 1974-77; tech. dir. Ayres Assocs., L.A., 1977-85; prin. and tech. dir. Ayres, Ezer, Lau Inc., L.A., 1985-92; sr. engr. So. Calif. Edison, San Dimas, 1992—; cons. Lawrence Berkeley (Calif.) Lab., 1978-84, Calif. Energy Commn., Sacramento, 1978-82, Martin Marietta, L.A., 1981. Contbr. articles to profl. jours. Grantee Dow Chem., 1965, ASHRAE, 1974, U.S. Army Rsch., 1969. Mem. ASHRAE, ASME, Sigma Xi. Roman Catholic. Home: PO Box 67641 Los Angeles CA 90067-0641 Office: Southern Calif Edison Co 300 N Lone Hill Ave San Dimas CA 91773-1741

LAU, KAM YUNG, physician, educator; b. Hong Kong, Oct. 7, 1951; came to U.S., 1974; s. Hong Wai and Wong Yee Lau; m. Sylvia Ho, June 30, 1979; 1 child, Jason. MB, Nat. Def. Med. Coll., Taipei, Taiwan, 1973. Diplomate Am. Bd. Internal Medicine, sub-splty. Bd. Critical Care Medicine, sub-splty. Bd. Pulmonary Disease, Am. Bd. Pediats.; lic. physician, Calif., Tex., Va., Wash.; cert. advanced cardiac life support instr. Intern in pediats. Misericordia Hosp., Bronx, N.Y., 1974-75, resident in pediats., 1975-76; resident in pediats. Meml. U. Nfld., St. John's, Can., 1976-77; hosp. privileges Bon Secours Hosp., Lawrence (Mass.) Gen. Hosp., Methuen, 1977-78; pvt. practice specializing in pediats. Kadlec Hosp., Richland, Wash., 1978-80; resident in internal medicine Tex. Tech. U. Health Scis. Ctr., El Paso, 1980-82; pvt. practice specializing in emergency medicine Sierra Med. Ctr., El Paso, 1982-83; fellow in pulmonary medicine of internal medicine UCLA, 1983-85; attending physician, chief pulmonary svcs. dept. medicine, med. dir. dept. of respiratory therapy R. E. Thomason Gen. Hosp., El Paso, 1985-88; attending physician dept. medicine Riverside (Calif.) Comty. Hosp., 1988—, 1988—; co-dir. critical care unit R. E. Thomason Gen. Hosp., El Paso, 1987-88; asst. prof. medicine, chief pulmonary divsn. Tex. Tech. U. Health Scis. Ctr., El Paso, 1985-88; asst. clin. prof. medicine Loma Linda (Calif.) U. Med. Ctr., 1989—; presenter in field. Contbr. articles to profl. jours. Recipient Outstanding Overseas Student award Overseas Affairs Commn., Govt. of Republic of China, 1973. Fellow ACP, Am. Acad. Pediats., Am. Coll. Chest Physicians; mem. Am. Thoracic Soc., Tex. Soc. for Respiratory Care (med. dir. S.W. region 1986-88). Office: Riverside Med Clinic 3660 Arlington Ave Riverside CA 92506-3912

LAUBE, ROGER GUSTAV, retired trust officer, financial consultant; b. Chgo., Aug. 11, 1921; s. William C. and Elsie (Drews) L.; m. Irene Mary Chadbourne, Mar. 30, 1946; children: David Roger, Philip Russell, Steven Richard. BA, Roosevelt U., 1942; postgrad., John Marshall Law Sch., 1942, 48-50; LLB, Northwestern U., 1960; postgrad., U. Wash., 1962-64. Cert. fin. cons. With Chgo. Title & Trust Co., Chgo., 1938-42, 48-50, Nat. Bank Alaska, Anchorage, 1950-72; mgr. mortgage dept. Nat. Bank Alaska, 1950-56, v.p., trust officer, mgr. trust dept., 1956-72; v.p., trust officer, mktg. dir., mgr. estate and fin. planning div. Bishop Trust Co., Ltd., Honolulu, 1972-82; instr. estate planning U. Hawaii, Honolulu, 1978-82; exec. v.p. Design Capital Planning Group, Inc., Tucson, 1982-83; pres., sr. trust officer, registered investment adviser Advanced Capital Advisory, Inc. of Ariz., Tucson, 1983-89; registered rep., pres. Advanced Capital Investments, Inc. of Ariz., Prescott, 1983-89; pres., chief exec. officer Advanced Capital Devel., Inc. of Ariz., Prescott, 1983-89; mng. exec. Integrated Resources Equity Corp., Prescott, 1983-89; pres. Anchorage Estate Planning Coun., 1960-62, Charter mem., 1960-72, Hawaii Estate Planning Coun., 1972-82, v.p., 1979, pres., 1980, bd. dirs., 1981-82; charter mem. Prescott Estate Planning Coun., 1986-90, pres. 1988. Charter mem. Anchorage Community Chorus, 1946, pres., 1950-53, bd. dirs., 1953-72, Alaska Festival of Music, 1960-72; mem. Anchorage camp Gideons Internat., 1946-72, Honolulu camp, 1972-82, mem. Cen. camp, Tucson, 1982-85, Prescott, 1985-90, Port Angeles-Sequim Camp, 1990—; mem. adv. bd. Faith Hosp., Glenallen, Alaska, 1960—, Cen. Alaska Mission of Far Ea. Gospel Crusade, 1960—; sec., treas. Alaska Bapt. Found., 1955-72; bd. dirs. Anchorage Symphony, 1965-72; bd. dirs. Bapt. Found. of Ariz., 1985-90; bd. dirs., mem. investment com. N.W. Bapt. Found., 1991—; mem. mainland adv. coun. Hawaii Bapt. Acad., Honolulu, 1982—; pres. Sabinovista Townhouse Assn., 1983-85; bd. advisers Salvation Army, Alaska , 1961-72, chmn., Anchorage, 1969-72, bd. advisers, Honolulu, 1972-82, chmn. bd. advisers, 1976-78; asst. staff judge adv. Alaskan Command, 1946-48; exec. com. Alaska Conv., 1959-61, dir. music Chgo., 1938-42, 48-50, Alaska, 1950-72, Hawaii, 1972-82, Tucson, 1982-85, 1st So. Bapt. Ch., Prescott Valley, Ariz., 1985-90; 1st Bapt. of Sequim, Wash., 1990—; chmn. bd. trustees Hawaii, 1972-81, Prescott Valley, 1986-89, Sequim, Wash., 1991—; worship leader Waikiki Ch., 1979-82. 1st lt., JAGD, U.S. Army, 1942-48. Recipient Others award Salvation Army, 1972. Mem. Am. Inst. Banking (instr. trust div. 1961-72), Am. Bankers Assn. (legis. com., trust div. 1960-72), Nat. Assn. Life Underwriters (nat. com. for Ariz.), Yavapai County-Prescott Life Underwriters Assn. (charter), Anchorage C. of C. (awards com. 1969-71), Internat. Assn. Fin. Planners (treas. Anchorage chpt. 1969-72, exec. com. Honolulu chpt. 1972-82, Ariz. chpt. 1982-90, del. to World Congress Australia and New Zealand 1987), Am. Assn. Handbell Ringers. Baptist. Home: Sunland Country Club 212 Sunset Pl Sequim WA 98382-8515

LAUBER, MIGNON DIANE, food processing company executive; b. Detroit, Dec. 21; d. Charles Edmond and Maud Lillian (Foster) Donaker. Student Kelsey Jenny U., 1958, Brigham Young U., 1959; m. Richard Brian Lauber, Sept. 13, 1963; 1 child, Leslie Viane (dec.). Owner, operator Alaska World Travel, Ketchikan, 1964-67; founder, owner, pres. Oosick Soup Co., Juneau, Alaska, 1969—. Treas., Pioneer Alaska Lobbyists Soc., Juneau, 1977—. Mem. Bus. and Profl. Women, Alaska C. of C. Libertarian, Washington Athletic Club. Author: Down at the Water Works with Jesus, 1982; Failure Through Prayer, 1983, We All Want to Go to Heaven But Nobody Wants to Die, 1988. Home: 321 Highland Dr Juneau AK 99801-1442 Office: PO Box 1625 Juneau AK 99802-0078

LAUBSCHER, RODERICK, engineering company executive; b. San Francisco; s. Fred and Myrtle Louise (Bazzini) L. BA in History, U. Calif., Santa Cruz, 1970; MS in Journalism, Columbia U., 1972. News reporter KSFO Radio, San Francisco, 1970-74, KGTV (NBC), San Diego, 1975-77, KRON-TV (NBC), San Francisco, 1977-80; pvt. practice polit. cons. San Francisco, 1980-81; mgr. corp. comm. Becntel Group, Inc., San Francisco, 1981—. Dir. San Francisco (Calif.) C. of C., 1986-87, San Francisco (Calif.) Beautiful, 1990-93; mem. Citizen's Adv. Com. on Transp., San Francisco, 1991-95, San Francisco Planning and Urban Rsch., 1995—. Pulitzer fellow Columbia U., N.Y.C., 1972; recipient Emmy award Acad. TV Arts and Sci., San Francisco, 1978. Mem. City Club San Francisco (founding chmn., gov. 1988—). Office: Bechtel Group Inc 50 Beale St San Francisco CA 94105-1813

LAUCHENGCO, JOSE YUJUICO, JR., lawyer; b. Manila, Philippines, Dec. 6, 1936; came to U.S., 1962; s. José Celis Sr. Lauchengco and Angeles (Yujuico) Sapota; m. Elisabeth Schindler, Feb. 22, 1968; children: Birthe, Martina, Duane, Lance. AB, U. Philippines, Quezon City, 1959; MBA, U. So. Calif., 1964; JD, Loyola U., L.A., 1971. Bar: Calif. 1972, U.S. Dist. Ct. (cen. dist.) Calif. 1972, U.S. Ct. Appeals (9th cir.) 1972, U.S. Supreme Ct. 1975. Banker First Western Bank/United Calif. Bank, L.A., 1964-71; assoc. Demler, Perona, Langer & Bergkvist, Long Beach, Calif., 1972-73; ptnr. Demler, Perona, Langer, Bergkvist, Lauchengco & Manzella, Long Beach, 1973-77; sole practice Long Beach and L.A., 1977-83; ptnr. Lauchengco & Mendoza, L.A., 1983-92; pvt. practice L.A., 1993—; mem. commn. on jud. procedures County of L.A., 1979; tchr. Confraternity of Christian Doctrine, 1972-79; counsel Philippine Presdl. Commn. on Good Govt., L.A., 1986. Chmn. Filipino-Am. Bi-Partisan Polit. Action Group, L.A., 1978. Recipient Degree of Distinction, Nat. Forensic League, 1955. Mem. Nat. Assn. Criminal Def. Lawyers, Criminal Cts. Bar Assn., Calif. Attys. Criminal Justice, Calif. Pub. Defenders Assn., Philippine-Am. Bar Assn. (bd. dirs.), U. Philippines Vanguard Assn. (life), Beta Sigma. Roman Catholic. Lodge: K.C. Office: 3545 Wilshire Blvd Ste 247 Los Angeles CA 90010-2305

LAUER, GEORGE, environmental consultant; b. Vienna, Austria, Feb. 18, 1936; came to U.S., 1943; s. Otto and Alice (Denton) L.; m. Sandra Joy Comp, Oct. 1, 1983; children by previous marriage: Julie Anne, Robert L. BS, UCLA, 1961; PhD, Calif. Inst. Tech., 1967. Mem. tech. staff N.Am. Aviation, Canoga Park, Calif., 1966-69; mgr. Rockwell Internat., Thousand Oaks, Calif., 1969-75; div. mgr. ERT, Inc., Westlake Village, Calif., 1975-78; dir. Rockwell Internat., Newbury Park, Calif., 1978-85; dir. Tetra-Tech Inc., Pasadena, Calif., 1985-86; pres. Environ. Monitoring and Services, Inc., 1986-88; sr. cons. Atlantic Richfield, Inc., Los Angeles, 1988—. Contbr. articles to profl. jours.; patentee in field. Mem. adv. bd. Environment Rsch. and Tech.; mem. adv. coun. Scaqmo, 1996—. Served with U.S. Army, 1957-59. Fellow Assn. for Computing Machinery; mem. Am. Chem. Soc., Am. Statistical Soc., Air Pollution Control Assn. Republican. Jewish. Home: 6009 Maury Ave Woodland Hills CA 91367-1052 Office: Atlantic Richfield Inc 515 S Flower St Los Angeles CA 90071-2201

LAUER, STEFANIE DOROTHEA, painter, writer; b. Berlin, Apr. 28, 1928; came to U.S., 1945; d. Max and Margaret Minna (Stöckel) Blank; m. James Lothar Lauer, Sept. 4, 1955; children: Michael Solon, Ruth Lauer Manenti. Diploma in Theatre, Dramatic Workshop of New Sch., N.Y.C., 1947; BA in English with honors, Smith Coll., 1950; MA in English with distinction, Harvard U., 1952; postgrad. in art, SUNY, Albany, 1981. Cert. tchr. English Pa., N.Y., art, N.Y. Instr. Mitchell Coll., New London, Conn., 1952-54; asst. prof. SUNY, Cortland, 1954-55; asst. editor Curtis Publishing Co., Phila., 1955-56; asst. prof. Brandywine Coll., Wilmington, Del., 1974-77; copy editor United Ch. of Christ, N.Y.C., 1978-80; artist pvt. practice, Burnt Hills,, N.Y., 1980-93, San Diego, 1994—. Author: Home is the Place, 1959; contbr. reviews art mags.; editor (newsletter) DASH, 1980-90; artist: solo exhibitions: (paintings and photography) Penn Wynne (Pa.) Libr., 1976, Schenectady, N.Y. C. of C., 1982, Smith Coll., Northampton, Mass., 1984, Galeria Grupo Arte, Albany, N.Y., 1993, KEX Copy Source Corp. Hdqs., Albany, 1993; group shows include: SUNY Fine Arts Bldg., Albany, 1981, U. Tex., Tyler, 1988, Ariel Gallery, N.Y.C., 1988, 89, Stuyvesant Plaza Invitational, 1989 (award), San Diego Art Inst. Art Prospect, La Jolla, 1995, others. Program chmn., pres., chmn. nominating com. Penn Wynne Sch. Parents Assn., 1970-80; Braille Inst. reader Temple Beth Hillel, Wynwood, Pa., 1978; writer, editor, bd. mem., officer Congregation Ohav Shalom, Albany, N.Y., 1983-89; interviewer Harvard Club Ea. N.Y., Albany, 1980-92; interviewer Harvard Club of San Diego, 1994—. Named fellow Breadloaf Writers Conf., 1955, finalist Artists' Mag. Still-life Competition, 1988; recipient 1st prize Montgomery County Arts Coun., Amsterdam, N.Y., 1987, RCCA landscape competition 1st, 1990, gallery exhibit 2nd, 1990, photography exhibit 1 of 5 awards, 1993, Juror's Choice award SDAI. Mem. Phi Beta Kappa. Democrat. Home: 7622 Palmilla Dr # 78 San Diego CA 92122

LAUFER, NATHAN, cardiologist; b. Montreal, Mar. 12, 1953; came to U.S., 1981; s. Jack and Pearl (Brachfeld) L.; m. Judy Franceska Egett, Sept. 2, 1986; 1 child, Andrew. DCS, McGill U., 1972, MD, 1977. Diplomate Nat. Bd. Med. Examiners, Am. Bd. Internal Medicine; cert. Profl. Corp. Physicians Que. Intern, resident U. Toronto, Can., 1977-81; fellow cardiology U. Mich., Ann Arbor, 1981-83, faculty dept. cardiology, 1983-84; cardiologist Affiliated Cardiologists, Phoenix, 1984—; dir. coronary care Good Samaritan Hosp., Phoenix, 1986-92; clin. asst. prof. medicine, U. Ariz., Tucson, 1986—; pres. Cardiovascular Soc., Phoenix, 1986—; vis. prof. Chigasaki Tokushu-kai Med. Ctr., Kanagawa-ken, Japan, 1988, Leningrad Postgrad. Med. Inst., St. Petersburg, Russia, 1991; mem. dirs. Integrated Cardiovasc. Group, 1996—. Contbr. articles to profl. jours. Fellow ACP, Am. Coll. Cardiology, Am. Coll. Chest Physicians, Royal Coll. Physicians and Surgeons Can.; mem. AMA, N.Am. Soc. Pacing and Electrophysiology, Soc. Cardiac Angiography and Intervention, Am. Assn. Nuclear Cardiology, Am. Heart Assn. (pres.-elect Ariz. affiliate), Ariz. Med. Assn., Can. Cardiovascular Soc., Maricopa County Med. Assn., Cardiovascular Soc. Ariz. (founder, pres.). Home: 9100 N 55th St Paradise Valley AZ 85253 Office: Affiliated Cardiologists 3710 E Virginia Phoenix AZ 85004

LAURANCE, MARK RODNEY, applications engineer, entrepreneur; b. Seattle, Nov. 27, 1959; s. Sidney Laurance and Patricia Louise Sadlier; m. Brendalynn Legarda. BS in Astronomy, U. Wash., 1984, BS in Physics, 1984, MS in Astronomy, 1992. Computer ops. programmer Seattle Police Dept., Seattle, 1980-85; researcher U. Wash., Seattle, 1984-90; lighting engr. Korry Electronics Co., Seattle, 1990-92; optical engr. Can.-France-Hawaii Telescope Corp., Kamuela, Hawaii, 1992-96; pres. Digitek Hawai'i, Inc., Kamuela, Hawaii, 1995-96; applications engr. Tech. Instrument Co., Sunnyvale, Calif., 1996—; owner Laurance Design Group, San Francisco, 1996—. Contbr. articles to profl. jours. Mem. chpt. mgmt. program mgr., exec. bd. dirs. Hawaii State Jaycees, 1995; exec. v.p. Kona Jaycees, 1994, comty. fundraising dir., 1993; cert. prime trainer Jr. Chamber Internat., 1994; mem. nat. nominations com. Outstanding Young Men of Am., 1997, Outstanding Young Women of Am., 1997. Recipient C. William Brownfield Meml. award for outstanding first yr. jaycee Kona Jaycees, 1994, Presdl. Excellence award Hawaii State Jaycees, 1995, First Place Speak-Up Competition award Hawaii State Jaycees, 1995; named to Outstanding Young Men of Am., 1989, Outstanding Exec. V.P. of Quar., Hawaii Jaycees, 1995, Finalist Three Outstanding Young Persons of Hawaii Jaycees, 1995, Outstanding Young Men of Am., 1997, Outstanding Young Ams. Nat. Nominating Com., 1997. Mem. SPIE Internat. Soc. Optical Engring. Office: 650 N Mary Ave Sunnyvale CA 94086

LAUREN, PAUL GORDON, history educator; b. Seattle, Feb. 17, 1946. BA with highest honors, Wash. State U., 1968; MA, Stanford U., 1969, PhD, 1973. Prof. history U. Mont., Missoula, 1974-86, Mansfield prof. of ethics and pub. affairs, 1986-91, regents prof., 1992—; vis. prof. history Stanford U., Calif., 1973, 79, 82; bd. dirs. Mansfield Found. Author: Diplomats and Bureaucrats, 1976, Power and Prejudice, 1988, 96, Kokka to Jinshuhenkeu, 1995; editor: Diplomacy: New Approaches, 1979, The China Hands' Legacy, 1989, Destinies Shared, 1989; contbr. articles to profl. jours. and chpts. to books. Named Disting. Speaker UN, Geneva, 1990; Woodrow Wilson fellow, Nat. Peace fellow, Rockefeller Found. fellow, 1980, Paul Harris fellow, 1994; sr Fulbright scholar, 1994. Office: U Mont Dept History Missoula MT 59812

LAUTER, JAMES DONALD, retired stockbroker; b. L.A., Sept. 3, 1931; s. Richard Leo and Helen M. (Stern) L.; BS, UCLA, 1956; m. Neima Zwieli, Feb. 24, 1973; children: Walter James (dec.), Gary. Market rsch. mgr. Germain's Inc., L.A., 61; sr. v.p. investments, former branch mgr. Dean Witter Reynolds, Inc., Pasadena, Calif., 1961-96, ret., 1996. With Armed Forces, 1954-56. Recipient Sammy award L.A. Sales Execs. Club, 1961. Mem. AARP, UCLA Alumni Assn., UCLA Chancellors Assocs., Pasadena Bond Club (pres. 1995-96), Bruin Athletic Club. Home: 17237 Sunburst St Northridge CA 91325-2922

LAUTZENHEISER, MARVIN WENDELL, computer software engineer; b. Maximo, Ohio, Feb. 19, 1929; s. Milton Leander and Mary Lucetta (Keim) L.; m. Jean Bethene Baker, Oct. 26, 1946 (div. Nov. 1986); children: Constance Kay, Thomas Edward, Jan Stephen; m. Paula Ann Keane, Mar. 10, 1990. BS in Math., Mt. Union Coll., 1953. Spl. agt. FBI, Washington, 1953-59; computer analyst Tech. Ops., Washington, 1959-64; pres. Anagram Corp., Springfield, Va., 1964-83; computer analyst Onyx Corp., McLean, Va., 1983, Inmark, Springfield, 1983-84, Memory Scis., McLean, 1984-85; software scientist Zitel Corp., San Jose, Calif., 1985—. Inventor, designer in field. Mem. Mensa, Am. Iris Soc. Home: 7216 Neuman St Springfield VA 22150-4421 Office: Zitel Corp 47211 Bayside Pky Fremont CA 94538-6517

LAUVER, EDITH BARBOUR, nonprofit organization administrator; b. Tarrytown, N.Y., Mar. 2, 1933; d. John Alan and Adelaide Cora (Marden) Barbour; m. Robert Mitchell Lauver, Dec. 16, 1961; children: Alan Jackson, Donald Marden, Robert Barbour. BSN, Skidmore Coll., 1954; MA, Columbia U., 1957; postgrad., U. Ariz., 1980-95. Sch. nurse, tchr. Pub. Schs. of Tarrytowns, North Tarrytown, N.Y., 1956-60; instr. St. Mary's Hosp. Sch. Nursing, Tucson, 1960-62; asst. prof. Coll. Nursing U. Ariz., Tucson, 1969-73, grad. teaching, rsch. assoc., 1980-85; asst. dir. nursing for pediatrics U. Ariz. Med. Ctr., Tucson, 1973-74; asst. adminstr. patient care Pima County/Kino Community Hosp., Tucson, 1974-77; asst. dir. nursing for staff devel. U. Ariz. Health Scis. Ctr., Tucson, 1978-80; dir. Interfaith Coalition for Homeless, Tucson, 1987—; mem. staff Thomas-Davis Clinic, Tucson, 1963-64; staff nurse surg. unit St. Joseph's Hosp., Tucson, 1964-65; adminstrv. asst. Tucson Ecumenical Coun., 1987; weekend relief staff nurse Handmaker Jewish Geriatric Ctr., Tucson, 1988-89. Active Accord Interfaith Soc. Action Group, 1983-94, St. Mark's Prebyn. Presch. and Kindergarten, 1965-87, St. Mark's Presbyn. Ch., 1986—, elder, 1986-92; bd. dirs. Ariz. Coalition for Human Svcs., 1987—; Mobile Meals Tucson, Inc., 1976-87, sec. 1981-83; bd. dirs. Interfaith Coalition for Homeless 1987—; participant Ariz. Women's Town Hall, 1986, 87; mem. adv. bd. Tucson Met. Ministry's Cmty. Closet, 1988-92; bd. dirs. Tucson Met. Ministry, 1989-92; active various other civic activities. Mem. ANA, Ariz. Nurses' Assn. (fin. com. 1985-87, ANA del. 1986-87, dist. bd. dirs. 1982-84, pres.-elect, pres. dist. 1985-87, various coms.), Soc. Southwestern Authors, Skidmore Coll. Alumni Assn., Sigma Theta Tau (mem. nat. fin. com. 1981-83, treas. local chpt. 1978-81, fin. com. 1974-88, pres.-elect 1990—, pres. 1988-92), Pi Lambda Theta, Phi Delta Kappa, Kappa delta Pi. Home and Office: 445 S Craycroft Rd Tucson AZ 85711-4549

LAUZZANA, RAYMOND GUIDO, computer graphics technology educator; b. Detroit, Aug. 22, 1941; arrived in The Netherlands, 1989; s. Guido Giovanni and Clara Anne (Bronowski) L.; m. Gail Peterson, 1966 (div. 1972); children: Emile, Julian; m. Denise Elaine Penrose, Jan. 1991. MArch, U. Mich., Ann Arbor, 1965; MS, U. Mass., Amherst, 1975. Ptnr. Berline Assoc. Architects, San Francisco, 1970-71; staff architect Kaiser Permanente, Oakland, Calif., 1971-73; rsch. assoc. USAF Astronomy Rsch. Lab., Lexington, Mass., 1973-77; sr. scientist Calma Corp., Sunnyvale, Calif., 1977-79; editor Computer Graphics World, San Francisco, 1979-82; dir. new products Horizon-Latticorp, San Francisco, 1983-85; assoc. prof. U. Mass., 1985-89; prof. media tech. Hogeschool Voor Kunst, Utrech, The Netherlands, 1989-93; pub. Penrose Press, San Francisco, 1993—; rsch. asoc. Ctr. Knowlede Tech., Utrech, 1989-93; v.p. Art, Sci. & Tech. Network, Paris, 1988—. Editor Jour. Formal Langs. for Word, Image and Sound, 1990—, Internat. Dir. of Design, 1994—; contbr. articles to profl. jours.; developer in field. Recipient Print Coun. Purchase prize Phila., 1970, 22nd Nat. Print Show Purchase prize U.S. Congress, 1971, Art Commn. prize San Francisco, 1972, Bicentenial Purchase prize Nat. Gallery, 1976; Oakland Mus. Founder's trophy, 1973; grantee Intel Corp., 1984, Digital Equipment Corp., 1985, Systems Rsch. Found., Fed. Republic of Germany, 1986, AT&T Bell Labs., 1987, Canon, Kodak, Sony, 1988-89, Apple Computer, 1988-90. Mem. IEEE, AAAS, AAUP, Optical Soc. Am., European Soc. Computer Graphics, Mass. Tchrs. Assn., N.Y. Acad. Scis., Assn. Computing Machines, Inter-Soc. Color Coun., Internat. Soc. Artists and Scientists, Soc. Info. Display, Soc. Photographic Scientist and Engrs., Nat. Computer Graphics Assn., N.Am. Pattern Classification Soc., Internat. Soc. Electronic Art, Art, Sci. and Tech. Network. Buddhist. Home: 1167 Pacific Ave San Francisco CA 94133-4231 Office: PO Box 470925 San Francisco CA 94133 Office: Penrose Press PO 470925 San Francisco CA 94147

LAVENTHOL, DAVID ABRAM, newspaper editor; b. Phila., July 15, 1933; s. Jesse and Clare (Horwald) L.; m. Esther Coons, Mar. 8, 1958; children: Peter, Sarah. BA, Yale U., 1957; MA, U. Minn., 1960; LittD (hon.), Dowling Coll., 1979; LLD (hon.), Hofstra U., 1986. Reporter, news editor St. Petersburg (Fla.) Times, 1957-62; asst. editor, city editor N.Y. Herald-Tribune, 1963-66; asst. mng. editor Washington Post, 1966-69; assoc. editor Newsday, L.I., N.Y., 1969, exec. editor, 1969, editor, 1970-78, pub., chief exec. officer, 1978-86; group v.p. newspapers Times Mirror Co., L.A., 1981-86, sr. v.p., 1987-93, pres., 1987-93; pub., chief exec. officer L.A. Times, 1989-93; editor-at-large Times Mirror Co., L.A., 1994—; mem. Pulitzer Prize Bd., 1982-91, chmn., 1988-89; vice chmn. Internat. Press Inst., 1985-93, chmn., 1993-95; dir. Am. Press Inst., 1988—. Bd. dirs. United Negro Coll. Fund, 1988, Mus. Contemporary Art, L.A., 1989—, chmn., 1993—; bd. dirs. Associated Press, 1993-96, Columbia Journalism Sch., 1995—, Nat. Parkinson Found., 1995—, Saratoga Performing Arts Ctr., 1993-96. With Signal Corps AUS, 1953-55. Recipient Columbia Journalism award for Disting. Svc., 1994. Mem. Am. Soc. Newspaper Editors (chmn. writing awards bd. 1980-83), Council Fgn. Relations. Clubs: Century (N.Y.C.), Regency (L.A.). Office: LA Times Times Mirror Sq Los Angeles CA 90053-3816

LAVIGNE, PETER MARSHALL, environmentalist, lawyer, consultant; b. Laconia, N.H., Mar. 25, 1957; s. Richard Byrd and D. Jacquiline (Cobleigh) L.; m. Nancy Gaile Parent, Sept. 20, 1979. BA, Oberlin Coll., 1980; MSL cum laude, Vt. Law Sch., 1983, JD, 1985. Bar: Mass. 1987. History tchr. Cushing Acad., Ashburnham, Mass., 1983-84; rsch. writer Environ. Law Ctr., Vt., 1985; lobbyist Vt. Natural Resources Coun., Montpelier, 1985; exec. dir. Westport (Mass.) River Watershed Alliance, 1986-88, Merrimack River Watershed Coun., West Newbury, 1988-89; environ. cons. Mass., N.H., Vt., and Oreg., 1990—; N.E. coord. Am. Rivers, Washington, 1990-92; dir. river leadership program River Network, Portland, Oreg., 1992-95;

dir. spl. programs River Network, Portland, 1995-96; dep. dir. For the Sake of the Salmon, Portland, 1996—; adj. prof. Antioch New Eng. Grad. Sch., Keene, N.H., 1991-92, Portland State U., 1997—; chair adv. bd. Cascadia Times, Portland, 1995—, Amigos Bravos, Taos, N.Mex., 1993—; trustee Rivers Coun. Washington, Seattle, 1993—; bd. mem. Alaska Clean Water Alliance, 1995—, Watershed adv. group Natural Resources Law Ctr. U. Colo., 1995—; coastal resources adv. bd. Commonwealth of Mass., Boston, 1987-91; adj. assoc. prof. Portland State U., 1997—. Co-author: Vermont Townscape, 1987; contbr. articles to profl. jours. Dir. Mass. League of Environ. Voters, Boston, 1988-92; mem. steering com. N.H. Rivers Campaign, 1988-92; co-founder, co-chair New England Coastal Campaign, 1988-92; EMT South Royalton (Vt.) Vol. Rescue Squad, 1982-86; dir., chairperson Vt. Emergency Med. Svcs. Dist. 8, Randolph, 1984-86; co-founder, v.p. Coalition for Buzzards Bay, Bourne, Mass., 1987; housing renewal commn. City of Oberlin, Ohio, 1980-81; mem. properties com. First Unitarian Ch., 1995. Recipient Environ. Achievement award Coalition for Buzzards Bay, 1988; land use rsch. fellow Environ. Law Ctr., Vt. Law Sch., 1984-85; Mellon found. rsch. grantee Oberlin Coll., 1980. Mem. Natural Resources Def. Coun., Oreg. Natural Resources Coun., Pacific Rivers Coun., League of Conservation Voters, Sierra Club. Democrat. Unitarian-Universalist. Home: 3714 SE 11th Ave Portland OR 97202-3724 Office: For the Sake of the Salmon 45 82nd Dr Ste 100 Gladstone OR 97027-2522

LAVIN, LAURENCE MICHAEL, lawyer; b. Upper Darby, Pa., Apr. 27, 1940; s. Michael Joseph and Helen Clair (McGonigle) L. BS, St. Joseph's U., Phila., 1962; JD, Villanova (Pa.) U., 1965. Bar: Pa., S.C. Vol. U.S. Peace Corps, Thika, Kenya, 1966-67; atty. Community Legal Svcs., Phila., 1968-70, exec. dir., 1971-79; exec. dir. Palmetto Legal Svcs., Columbia, S.C., 1981-85; dir. Law Coordination Ctr., Harrisburg, Pa., 1985-88, Nat. Health Law Program, L.A., 1988—; chmn. Orgn. Legal Svc. Backup Ctrs., 1991—; bd. dirs., chmn. civil com. Nat. Legal Aid and Defender, Washington, 1976-78. Editor Health Advocate, 1988—. Founding mem. Pa. Coun. to Abolish Death Penalty, Harrisburg, 1986; bd. dirs. L.A. Poverty Dept., 1996—. Mem. ABA, Pa. Bar Assn. (chmn. legal svcs. to pub. com. 1985-88), Legal Assistance Assn. Calif. (bd. dirs.). Democrat. Home: 1133 22nd St Santa Monica CA 90403-5721 Office: Nat Health Law Program 2639 S La Cienega Blvd Los Angeles CA 90034-2603

LAVIN, MATTHEW T., horticultural educator. Assoc. prof. biology dept. Mont. State U., Bozeman. Recipient N.Y. Botanical Garden award Botanical Soc. Am., 1993. Office: Montana State U Dept Biology 310 Lewis Hall Bozeman MT 59717-0002

LAVINE, JOEL EDWARD, physician, medical educator; b. Cleve., Oct. 16, 1953; s. Morton Elmer and Yvette (Miller) L.; m. Deborah Lynn Andrews, Mar. 26, 1983; children: Mallory, Danielle, Spencer. AB, U. Calif., Berkeley, 1975; PhD, U. Calif., Santa Barbara, 1980; MD, U. Calif., San Diego, 1984. Intern in pediatrics U. Calif., San Francisco, 1984-85, resident in pediatrics, 1985-86, postdoctoral fellow in pediatric gastroenterology, 1986-89, asst. prof., 1989-91; asst. prof. Harvard Med. Sch., Boston, 1991-95; dir. liver rsch., attending physician Children's Hosp., Boston, 1991-95; assoc. prof. pediats. U. Calif., San Diego, 1995—; chief pediat. gastroenterology and nutrition U. Calif. San Diego Med. Ctr., Children's Hosp., San Diego, 1995—. Guest editor, author: Seminars in Liver Disease, 1994; mem. editl. bd.: (jour.) Hepatology, 1994—; contbr. chpt. to book; patentee in field. Recipient Pediatric Rsch. prize Am. Liver Found., 1989, Rsch. Scholar award, 1991-94. Fellow Am. Acad. Pediatrics, Am. Gastroenterol. Assn. (Rsch. Scholar award 1991-94); mem. Am. Assn. for Study Liver Diseases, N.Am. Soc. for Pediatric Gastroenterology, Western Soc. for Pediatric Rsch., Harvard Digestive Disease Ctr. Office: U Calif Med Ctr Dept Pediatrics San Diego CA 92103-8450

LA VINE, MARK LESLIE, financial advisor; b. Chgo., Feb. 24, 1932; s. Herman H. and Sarah (Davis) LaV.; m. Mona Moster, Aug. 23, 1953 (div. Feb. 1971); children: Terise Parnes, Ronald, Elyse; m. June Lee Bennett, Feb. 9, 1975. CLU; ChFC; enrolled actuary. Vice chmn. Integrated Fin., Encino, 1982-90; pres. Profl. Planning Corp., Woodland Hills, Calif., 1982—; mem. adv. bd. Sun Life Can., Boston, 1993-95. Author: Idea Book, 1993. Bd. dirs. Million Dollar Round Table Found., Chgo., 1994—, Jewish Home for Aging, L.A., 1996—. With USAF, 1951-52. Mem. L.A. Exec. Club (pres. 1985). Office: Profl Planning Corp 21800 Oxnard St Ste 400 Woodland Hills CA 91367

LAVINE, STEVEN DAVID, academic administrator; b. Sparta, Wis., June 7, 1947; s. Israel Harry and Harriet Hauda (Rosen) L.; m. Janet M. Sternburg, May 29, 1988. BA, Stanford U., 1969; MA, Harvard U., 1970, PhD, 1976. Asst. prof. U. Mich., Ann Arbor, 1974-81; asst. dir. arts and humanities Rockefeller Found., N.Y.C., 1983-86, assoc. dir. arts and humanities, 1986-88; pres. Calif. Inst. Arts, Valencia, 1988—; adj. assoc. prof. NYU Grad. Sch. Bus., 1984-85; cons. Wexner Found., Columbus, Ohio, 1986-87; selection panelist Input TV Screening Conf., Montreal, Can., and Granda, Spain, 1985-86; cons., panelist Nat. Endowment for Humanities, Washington, 1981-85; faculty chair Salzburg Seminar on Mus., 1989; co-dir. Arts and Govt. Program, The Am. Assembly, 1991; mem. arch. selection jury L.A. Cathedral. Editor: The Hopwood Anthology, 1981, Exhibiting Cultures, 1991, Museums and Communities, 1992; editor spl. issue Prooftexts jour., 1984. Bd. dirs. Sta. KCRW-FM (NPR), 1989—, J. Paul Getty Mus., 1990—, L.A. Philharm. Assn., 1994—, Endowments, Inc., Bond Portfolio for Endowments, Inc., 1994—. Recipient Class of 1923 award, 1979, Faculty Recognition award, 1980 U. Mich.; Charles Dexter traveling fellow Harvard U., 1972, Ford fellow, 1969-74, vis. rsch. fellow Rockefeller Found., N.Y.C., 1981-83. Jewish. Office: Calif Inst Arts Office Pres 24700 Mcbean Pky Santa Clarita CA 91355-2340

LAVOIE, STEVEN PAUL, writer, librarian; b. Madison, Minn., Oct. 9, 1953; s. Clarence Donald and Lovetta (Gearhart) L.; m. Teresa Pei-Shiung Shen. BA, U. Calif., Berkeley, 1975, M of Libr. and Info. Studies, 1986. Head libr., writer Marin Ind. Jour., Novato, Calif., 1986-89; columnist, dir. of librs. Oakland (Calif.) Tribune, 1989-96; info. specialist MRW and Assocs., Oakland, Calif., 1996—; founder Black Bart Poetry Soc., Oakland, 1982; pres. Pacific Ctr. for Book Arts, San Francisco, 1990-92, treas., 1994—; bd. dirs. Oakland Heritage Alliance, 1995—, Macarthur Metro, 1996—. Author: On The Way, 1982, Erosion Surface, 1984, Nine Further Plastics, 1984; conbg. author: The Mus. of Calif. Recipient Doris Green award, 1982, Mark Twain prize, 1984, Oakland Ptnr.'s in Preservation award, 1995. Mem. Spl. Librs. Assn., Soc. Am. Baseball Rsch. Home: PO Box 9779 Oakland CA 94613

LAVRETSKY, HELEN, geriatric psychiatrist, researcher; b. Zaporghie, Ukraine, Mar. 8, 1962; d. Ilya G. and Eleonor P. (Shmarian) L.; m. Eugene Gleizer, Oct. 3, 1984; 1 child, Philip. MD, Moscow, 1985. Tng. in psychiatry Moscow State Ctr. Mental Health, 1985-88; resident in psychiatry UCLA, 1991-94, fellow in geriatric psychiatry, 1994-96, fellow in neurosci., 1996—. VA Neurosci. fellow, 1996. Home: 1401 S Bentley Ave Los Angeles CA 90025

LAW, FLORA ELIZABETH (LIBBY LAW), retired community health and pediatrics nurse; b. Biddeford, Maine, Sept. 11, 1935; d. Arthur Parker and Flora Alma (Knutti) Butt; m. Robert F. Law, 1961; children : Susan E., Sarah F., Christian A., Martha F.; m. John F. Brown, Jr., 1982. BA, Davis and Elkins (W.Va.) Coll., 1957; postgrad., Cornell U.-N.Y. Hosp., N.Y.C., 1960; BSN, U. Nev., Las Vegas, 1976, MS in Counseling Edn., 1981. RN, Nev.; cert. sch. nurse. Staff nurse So. Nev. Community Hosp. (now Univ. Med. Ctr.), Las Vegas, 1975-76; relief charge nurse Valley Psychiat. Inst., Las Vegas, 1976; pub. health nurse Clark County Dist. Health Dept., Las Vegas, 1977-78; sch. nurse Clark County Sch. Dist., Las Vegas, 1978-94; ret., 1994. Chair task force on sch. nursing Nev.'s Commn. for Profl. Standards in Edn.; mem. nurse practice act revision com. Nev. State Bd. Nursing. Mem. Nat. Assn. Sch. Nurses (past state dir., sch. nurse liaison Clark County Tchrs. Assn.), NEA, Clark County Assn. Sch. Nurses (past pres.), Sigma Theta Tau. Home: 3420 Clandara Ave Las Vegas NV 89121-3701

LAWES, PATRICIA JEAN, art educator; b. Mathis, Tex., June 28, 1940; d. Thomas Ethan and Alma Dena (Pape) Allen; m. Elmer Thomas Lawes, Apr. 9, 1960; children: Linda Lee, Tracy Dena. BA in Art Edn., U. Wyo., 1976; MA in Curriculum and Instruction, Leslie Coll., 1988. Cert. tchr., Wyo. Elem. art tchr. Laramie County Sch. Dist. # 1, Cheyenne, Wyo., 1977—, facilitator elem. art. and gifted edn., 1979-87; ret. Laramie County Sch. Dist. #1, 1994, storyteller, 1995; owner, sec. Dundele Ltd. Liability Co., Mesa, Ariz., 1994-95; artist in the sch. Mesa, Ariz., 1994-95; ednl. cons. gifted edn. Bozman, Mont., 1995-96; judge F.W. Warren AFB Artist Craftsman Show, Cheyenne, 1988-92; adjudicator for music festival for Assn. Christian Schs. Internat., Tempe, Ariz., 1995-97; storyteller Laramie County Sch. Dist. 1, 1995-96; presenter in field; artist in the sch., Tempe; instr. Smith Driving Sys. Salt River Project, Phoenix, 1996—; ednl. cons. Assn. Christian Schs. Internat., Phoenix, 1995. Author, mem. visual arts task force various curricula; Author, dir: The Apron Caper, 1989 (recognition 1990), Oh Where Oh Were Have Those Little Dawgs Gone, 1989 (recognition 1990); exhibitions include Wyoming Artists Assn., Wyo., 1977, Washington Congressional Exhibit, 1977-78. Mem. state bd. dirs. Very Spl. Arts Wyo., 1995—. Recipient Cert. of Appreciation Mayor Erickson, Cheyenne, 1986, MWR Vol. Recognition F.E. Warren Moral, Welfare, Recreation Dept., Cheyenne, 1988-93; grantee Coun. on Arts, Cheyenne, 1987-91. Mem. NEA, Am. Fedn. Tchrs., Nat. art Edn. Assn., Wyo. Assn. Gifted Edn. (bd. dirs., W.E. rep. 1986—, presenter, chmn. state ass. award 1992—), Wyo. Arts Alliance for Edn. (presenter, bd. dirs. 1987—, sec. 1988-91, visual arts task force, chmn. state arts award 1990-92), Wyo. Coun. Arts (slide bank 1986—), Wyo. Odessey of Mind (bd. dirs. 1991-92), Wyo. Women's Fedn. Club (chmn. state safety 1972-75), Order of Eastern Star (presiding officer, worthy matron 1984-85, grand officer 1990-91), Daughters of Nile, Assn. of Christian Schs. Internat. Music Festival (adjudicator 1995). Address: 4410 E Kiva Phoenix AZ 85044-2403

LAWLESS, JOHN HOWARD, minister; b. Colorado Springs, Colo., Jan. 23, 1948; s. Howard Rae and Mildred (Mercer) L.; m. Dana Lynn Rae, Sept. 29, 1968; children: Hiedi Witcher, Jenny McDermott, John. Cert., Inst. Counseling, Akron, Ohio, 1993; AA with honors, Fresno City Coll., 1996. Ordained min. Ch. of Christ. Min. Ch. of Christ, Boulder, Colo., 1978-85, Fresno, Calif., 1985—; vol. Help In Emotional Trouble, Fresno, 1992-93; marriage seminar dir. Anchor Ministries, Fresno, 1993-96, dir., 1994-96; adv. bd. mem. South Houston Bible Inst., 1994-96. Contbr. articles to profl. jours. Officer, v.p. Free Bible Distbn. to Needy, 1992-96. Mem. Phi Theta Kappa. Republican. Home: 4641 N Woodson Ave Fresno CA 93705-0748

LAWRENCE, GARY SHELDON, academic administrator; b. Portland, Oreg., Aug. 31, 1946; s. Harry Sheldon and Nellie Maude (Mackey) L.; m. Maya Tsuji, Sept. 22, 1974; children: Katherine, Matthew. BA cum laude, Claremont Men's Coll., 1968; MLS, U. Calif., Berkeley, 1973, M in Pub. Policy, 1975, D in Libr. and Info. Studies, 1980. Lab. asst. Inst. Libr. Rsch. U. Calif., Berkeley, 1973, cons. to Office of Asst. Chancellor-Budget and Planning, 1974-75, rsch. asst. Inst. Libr. Rsch., 1976, tchg. assoc. Sch. Libr. and Info. Sci., 1976, project mgr. online catalog evaluation project, 1981-83, statis. cons. mgmt. affirmative action working group, 1981-83, sr. adminstrv. analyst Libr. Studies and Rsch. Divsn., 1976-80, assoc. mgr. rsch. and analysis Office of Pres., 1980-82, dir. Libr. Studies and Rsch. Divsn. Office of Pres., 1982-87, coord. libr. affairs Office Assoc. V.P. Acad. Affairs, 1987-93, coord. librs. & academic computing Office Vice Provost Rsch.; cons. Manifest Sys., Inc., Coun. on Libr. Resources, Inc., J. Matthews and Assocs., Inc., Grass Valley, Calif., Libr. and Info. Svcs. for the N.W., Fred Meyer Charitable Trust, Portland, Oreg., Assn. Coll. and Rsch. Librs., ALA, Chgo., Ohio Bd. Regents, Columbus, U. Ariz., Capital Facilities Planning Office; prin. investigator costs and features of online catalogs Coun. on Libr. Resources, Inc., 1982-83; U. Calif. del. Document Delivery Com. of Calif. Libr. Authority for Sys. and Svcs., 1983-84. Author: (with others) Advances in Library Organization and Administration, 1984; rsch. notes editor Coll. and Rsch. Librs., 1984-90; contbr. articles to profl. jours. 1st lt. U.S. Army, 1969-71. Mem. ALA (mem. editl. bd. Assn. Coll. and Rsch. Librs. 1984-90; chair rsch. com. Libr. and Info. Tech. Assn. 1993-94, Gaylord award com. 1993-94, chair libr. rsch. task force 1992-93, rep. to ALA rsch. and statistics assembly 1992-94, chair fuzzy match interest group 1986-89; co-chair machine-assisted ref. sect. ann. conf. program com. Ref. and Adult Svcs. Divsn. 1987, Libr. Rsch. Round Table 1977-89, Libr. Rsch. Roundtable 1977-78), Am. Soc. for Info. Sci. (treas. Bay Area chpt. 1979). Office: U Calif Office Libr Affairs 300 Lakeside Dr Fl 18 Oakland CA 94612-3524

LAWRENCE, JEROME, playwright, director, educator; b. Cleve., July 14, 1915; s. Samuel and Sarah (Rogen) L. BA, Ohio State U., 1937, LHD (hon.), 1963; DLitt, Fairleigh Dickinson U., 1968; DFA (hon.), Villanova U., 1969; LittD, Coll. Wooster, 1983. Dir. various summer theaters Pa. and Mass., 1934-37; reporter, telegraph editor Wilmington (Ohio) News Jour., 1937; editor Lexington Daily News, Ohio, 1937; continuity editor radio Sta. KMPC, Beverly Hills, Calif., 1938-39; sr. staff writer CBS, Hollywood, Calif. and N.Y.C., 1939-42; pres., writer, dir. Lawrence & Lee, Hollywood, N.Y.C. and London, 1945—; vis. prof. Ohio State Univ., 1969, Salzburg Seminar in Am. Studies, 1972, Baylor Univ., 1978; prof. playwriting Univ. So. Calif. Grad. Sch., 1984—; co-founder, judge Margo Jones award, N.Y.C., 1958—; co-founder, pres. Am. Playwrights Theatre, Columbus, Ohio, 1970-85; bd. dirs. Am. Conservatory Theatre, San Francisco, 1970-80, Stella Adler Theatre, L.A., 1987—, Plumstead Playhouse, 1986—; keynote speaker Bicentennial of Bill of Rights, Congress Hall, Phila., 1991; hon. mem. Nat. Theatre Conf., 1993; adv. bd. Am. Theatre in Lit. Contemporary Arts Ednl. Project, 1993—. Scenario writer Paramount Studios, 1941; master playwright NYU Inst. Performing Arts, 1967-69; author-dir. for: radio and television UN Broadcasts; Army-Navy programs D-Day, VE-Day, VJ-Day; author: Railroad Hour, Hallmark Playhouse, Columbia Workshop; author: Off Mike, 1944, (biography, later made into PBS-TV spl.) Actor: Life and Times of Paul Muni, 1978 (libretto and lyrics by Lawrence and Lee, music by Billy Goldenberg); co-author, dir.: (album) One God; playwright: Live Spelled Backwards, 1969, Off Mike, (mus. with Robert E. Lee) Look, Ma, I'm Dancin', 1948 (music by Hugh Martin), Shangri-La, 1956 (music by Harry Warren, lyrics by James Hilton, Lawrence and Lee), Mame, 1966 (score by Jerry Herman), Dear World, 1969 (score by Jerry Herman), (non-mus.) Inherit the Wind (translated and performed in 34 langs., named best fgn. play of year London Critics Poll 1960), Auntie Mame, 1956, The Gang's All Here, 1959, Only in America, 1959, A Call on Kuprin, 1961, Diamond Orchid (revised as Sparks Fly Upward, 1966), 1965, The Incomparable Max, 1969, The Crocodile Smile, 1970, The Night Thoreau Spent in Jail, 1970, (play and screenplay) First Monday in October, 1978, (written for opening of Thurber Theatre, Columbus) Jabberwock: Improbablilities Lived and Imagined by James Thurber in the Fictional City of Columbus, Ohio, 1974, (with Robert E. Lee) Whisper in the Mind, 1994, The Angels Weep, 1992, (novel) A Golden Circle: A Tale of the Stage and the Screen and Music of Yesterday and Now and Tomorrow and Maybe the Day After Tomorrow, 1993; Decca Dramatic Albums, Musi-Plays., Selected Plays of Lawrence and Lee, 1996; contbg. editor Dramatics mag., mem. adv. bd., contbr. Writer's Digest; Lawrence and Lee collections at Libr. and Mus. of the Performing Arts, Lincoln Ctr., N.Y., Harvard's Widener Libr., Cambridge, Mass., Jerome Lawrence & Robert E. Lee Theatre Rsch. Inst. at Ohio State U., Columbus, est. 1986. A founder, overseas corr. Armed Forces Radio Service; mem. Am. Theatre Planning Bd.; bd. dirs. Nat. Repertory Theatre, Plumstead Playhouse; mem. adv. bd. USDAN Center for Creative and Performing Arts, East-West Players, Performing Arts Theatre of Handicapped., Inst. Outdoor Drama; mem. State Dept. Cultural Exchange Drama Panel, 1961-69; del. Chinese-Am. Writers Conf., 1982, 86, Soviet-Am. Writers Conf., 1984, 85; Am. Writers rep. to Hiroshima 40th Anniversary Commemorative, Japan, 1985; mem. U.S. Cultural Exchange visit to theatre communities of Beijing and Shanghai, 1985; adv. coun. Calif. Ednl. Theatre Assn., Calif. State U., Calif. Repertory Co., Long Beach, 1984—. Recipient N.Y. Press Club award, 1942, CCNY award, 1948, Radio-TV Life award, 1948, Mirror awards, 1952, 53, Peabody award, 1949, 52, Variety Showmanship award 1954, Variety Critics poll 1955, Outer-Circle Critics award 1955, Donaldson award, 1955, Ohioana award, 1955, Ohio Press Club award, 1959, Brit. Drama Critics award, 1960, Moss Hart Meml. award, 1967, State Dept. medal, 1968, Pegasus award, 1970, Lifetime Achievement award Am. Theatre Assn., 1979, Nat. Thespian Soc. award, 1980, Pioneer Broadcasters award, 1981, 95, Diamond Circle award Pacific Pioneer Broadcasters, 1995, Ohioana Library career medal, Master of Arts award Rocky Mountain Writers Guild, 1982, Centennial Award medal Ohio State U., 1970, William Inge award and lectureship Independence Community Coll., 1983, 86—, Disting. Contbr. award Psychologists for Social Responsibility, 1985, ann. awards San Francisco State U., Pepperdine U., Career award Southeastern Theatre Conf., 1990; named Playwright of Yr. Baldwin-Wallace Coll., 1960; named to Honorable Order of Ky. Colonels, 1965, Tenn. Colonels, 1988; named to Theater Hall of Fame, 1990. Fellow Coll. Am. Theatre, Kennedy Ctr.; mem. Nat. Theatre Conf. (hon.), Acad. Motion Picture Arts and Scis. (nominating com. best fgn. films 1997), Acad. TV Arts and Scis. (2 Emmy award 1988), Authors League (coun.), ANTA (dir., v.p.), Ohio State U. Assn. (dir.), Radio Writers' Guild (founder, pres.), Writers Guild Am. (dir., founding mem. Valentine Davies award), Dramatists Guild (coun.), ASCAP, Calif. Ednl. Theatre Assn. (Profl. Artist award 1992), Century Club N.Y., Phi Beta Kappa, Sigma Delta Chi. *I want people to leave the theatre after seeing a play I have written feeling as if they were taller human beings, as if their souls had been sandpapered. A work must have meanings many layers deep so that it illumines our lives and our times.*

LAWRENCE, JOYCE L., mayor; m. Roger Lawrence; 1 child, Steven. BSN, Calif. State U., Long Beach. Office: PO Box 7061 Downey CA 90241

LAWRENCE, PAUL FREDERIC, educational consultant; b. Paterson, N.J., Mar. 20, 1912; s. Joshua Emanuel and Louise (Hill) L.; m. Vivian Ann Hall, Sept. 21, 1941; children: Katherine Louise, Robin Ann. BS in Edn., Kean Coll., 1935; MA in Edn., Stanford U., 1945, EdD, 1947; LHD, Kean Coll., 1965. Teaching and adminstrn. credentials, N.J., Calif. Tchr., art supr. Princeton (N.J.) Pub. Schs., 1935-41; assoc. prof., asst. dir. Howard U., Washington, 1948-56; supt. of schs. Willowbrook Sch. Dist., L.A., 1956-60; prof. edn., dean counseling State Coll. Alameda County, Hayward, Calif., 1960-63; assoc. state supt. pub. instrn., chief Divsn. Higher Edn. State Calif., 1963-67; regional commr. edn. Region IX Federal Govt., 1967-73; dep. assoc. commr. U.S. Office Edn., Washington, 1973-77; dir. postsecondary liaison U.S. Office of Edn., Washington, 1978-83; owner, dir. Cons. in Edn. Policy and Adminstrn., Sacramento, 1983—; bd. dirs. Scholastic Mag., N.Y.C.; com. mem. Nat. Acad. Sci., Washington, Nat. Conf. Christians and Jews, L.A.; desegregation monitor 9th Dist. Fed. Ct., San Francisco, spl. monitor desegregation case, 1984—. Co-author: Negro American Heritage, 1965, Opportunities in Interracial Colleges, 1947; contbr. articles to profl. jours. With USAF, 1942-46, Lt. col. USAFR, 1946-70. Recipient Disting. Svc. award NABSE, New Orleans, Outstanding Svc. awards City of San Bernardino, Calif., U.S. Dept. HEW, Washington, Calif. Senate and Assembly, Sacramento; named to Educators Hall of Fame Multi-Cultural Educators Hall of Fame, 1996. Mem. Nat. Conf. Parents and Tchrs., USAF Acad. (liason advisor), Calif. State Commn. on Edn., Exploratory Commn. on Edn., Select Com. Study Higher Edn., Phi Delta Kappa. Home: 4837 Crestwood Way Sacramento CA 95822-1660 Office: Cons in Ednl Policy 615 J St Sacramento CA 95814-2405

LAWRENCE, PAULA DENISE, physical therapist; b. Ft. Worth, May 21, 1959; d. Roddy Paul and Kay Frances (Spivey) Gillis; m. Mark Jayson Lawrence, Apr. 20, 1985. BS, Tex. Women's U., 1982. Lic. phys. therapist, Tex., Calif. Sales mgr. R. and K Camping Ctr., Garland, Tex., 1977-82; staff physical therapist Longview (Tex.) Regional Hosp., 1982-83, dir. phys. therapy, 1983-87, dir. rehab. svcs., 1987-88; staff phys. therapist MPH Home Health, Longview, Tex., 1983-84; owner, pres. Phys. Rehabil. Ctr., Hemet, Calif., 1988—; mem. adv. com. div. health occupations Kilgore (Tex.) Coll., 1985-88; mem. profl. adv. bd. Hospice Longview, 1985-88. Bd. dirs. V.I.P. Tots. Mem. NAFE, Am. Phys. Therapy Assn., Calif. Phys. Therapy Assn., Am. Bus. Women's Assn. (v.p. 1987, 89, pres. 1990, Woman of Yr. 1988, 91), Assistance League Aux., Soroptomist (corr. sec. 1992, dir. 1993-95, sec. 1995-97), Hemet C. of C. (bd. dirs.), Psi Chi, Omega Rho Alpha. Home: 43725 Mandarin Dr Hemet CA 92544-8529 Office: 901 S State St Ste 500 Hemet CA 92543-7127

LAWRENCE, SALLY CLARK, academic administrator; b. San Francisco, Dec. 29, 1930; d. George Dickson and Martha Marie Alice (Smith) Clark; m. Henry Clay Judd, July 1, 1950 (div. Dec. 1972); children: Rebecca, David, Nancy; m. John I. Lawrence, Aug. 12, 1976; stepchildren: Maia, Dylan. Docent Portland Art Mus., Oreg., 1958-68; gallery owner, dir., Sally Judd Gallery, Portland, 1968-75; art ins. appraiser, cons. Portland, 1975-81; interim dir. Mus. Art. Sch., Pacific Northwest Coll. Art, Portland, 1981, asst. dir., 1981-82, acting dir., 1982-84, dir., 1984-94, pres., 1994—; bd. dirs. Art Coll. Exch. Nat. Consortium, 1982-91, pres., 1983-84. Bd. dirs. Portland Arts Alliance, 1987—, Assn. Ind. Colls. of Art and Design, 1991—, pres., 1995-96, sec. 1996—. Mem. Nat. Assn. Schs. Art and Design (bd. dirs. 1984-91, treas. bd. dirs. 1994-96, pres. 1996—), Oreg. Ind. Coll. Assn. (bd. dirs. 1981—, exec. com. 1989-94, pres. 1992-93). Office: Pacific NW Coll of Art 1219 SW Park Ave Portland OR 97205-2430

LAWRENCE, SANFORD HULL, physician, immunochemist; b. Kokomo, Ind., July 10, 1919; s. Walter Scott and Florence Elizabeth (Hull) L. AB, Ind. U., 1941, MD, 1944. Fellow in biochemistry George Washington U., 1941; intern Rochester (N.Y.) Gen. Hosp., 1944-45; resident Halloran Hosp., Staten Island, N.Y., 1946-49; chief med. svce. Ft. Ord Regl. Hosp., 1945-46; dir. biochemistry rsch. lab. San Fernando (Calif.) VA Hosp.; asst. prof. UCLA, 1950—; cons. internal medicine and cardiology U.S. Govt., Los Angeles County; lectr. Faculte de Medicine, Paris, various colls. Eng., France, Belgium, Sweden, USSR, India, Japan; chief med. svc. Ft. Ord Regional Hosp.; chmn. Titus, Inc., 1982—. Author: Zymogram in Clinical Medicine, 1965; contbr. articles to sci. jours.; author: Threshold of Valhalla, Another Way to Fly, My Last Satyr, and other short stories; traveling editor: Relax Mag. Mem. Whitley Heights Civic Assn., 1952—; pres. Halloran Hosp. Employees Assn., 1947-48. Served to maj. U.S. Army, 1945-46. Recipient Rsch. award TB and Health Assn., 1955-58, Los Angeles County Heart Assn., 1957-59, Pres. award, Queen's Blue Book award, Am. Men of Sci. award; named one of 2000 Men of Achievement, Leaders of Am. Sci., Ky. Col., named Hon. Mayor of West Point, Ky. Mem. AAAS, AMA, N.Y. Acad. Scis., Am. Fedn. Clin. Research, Am. Assn. Clin. Investigation, Am. Assn. Clin. Pathology, Am. Assn. Clin. Chemistry, Los Angeles County Med. Assn. Republican. Methodist. Home: 2014 Whitley Ave Los Angeles CA 90068-3235 also: 160 rue St Martin, 75003 Paris France

LAWRENCE, STEPHEN LEE, elementary school principal, mechanic; b. Salt Lake City, Mar. 11, 1946; s. Don and Helen Lawrence; m. Geraldine Lawrence, July 25, 1969; children: Neil, Nathan, Mark, Miles, Drew. BS, Weber State U., 1971; MEd, Utah State U., 1990; EdD, U. Utah, 1995. Cert. in adminstrn.; cert. master mechanic. Prin. Tooele (Utah) County Schs., 1987—. Author: Cooperative Learning, 1990; contbr. articles to profl. jours. Founder, dir. Tooele Cmty. Theatre, 1995; mem. Deseret Peak coun. Boy Scouts Am., 1990-92. Recipient Centennial Sch. award Utah State Office Edn., 1995, 96, Svc./Learning award Utah State Office Edn., 1996, Grand Champion Chile award Tooele County Commn., 1996. Mem. Utah Assn. Elem. Sch. Prins. (Region 13 dir. 1996-97). Office: West Elem Sch 451 West 300 South Tooele UT 84074

LAWRENCE, WILLIAM, JR., elementary education educator; b. L.A., Mar. 2, 1930; s. Willie and Nellie (January) L.; m. Elizabeth Johnson, Jan. 13, 1951; children: William III, Timothy Dwight, Walter Fitzgerald. BA in Psychology, Columbia Coll., Mo., 1981; LLB, LaSalle U., 1982; MA in Edn., Claremont Coll., 1992; postgrad., Calif. Coast U., 1992—. Enlisted U.S. Army, 1947, advanced through grades to lt., 1957, commd. sgt. maj., 1965; served U.S. Army, Vietnam, 1965-70; instr. U.S. Military Acad., West Point, N.Y., 1970-73; with Berlin Brigade, U.S. Army, Berlin, Germany, 1973-76; dep. sheriff L.A., 1958-65; probation officer San Bernardino County, Calif., 1985-89; own recognizance investigator L.A. County, 1989; tchr. Pomona Unified Sch. Dist., Pomona, Calif., 1989—; sch. site technician, 1996. Decorated U.S. Army Dist. Svc. Cross for Extraordinary Heroism in Combat, Silver Star, 7 Purple Hearts. Mem. Legion of Valor, 555Th Parachute Battalion (pres.). Democrat. Roman Catholic. Home: 1456 S Lilac Ave Bloomington CA 92316-2130 Office: Pomona Unified Sch Dist 800 N Garey Ave Pomona CA 91767-4616

LAWRENCE-FORREST, LORI LOUISE, restaurateur; b. Brockton, Mass., Oct. 12, 1950; d. Hallett Thompson and Dorothy Mae (McElroy) L.; m. David John Forrest, 1994; 1 child, Cameron Stuart Forrest. AA, Canada Coll., Redwood City, Calif., 1970; postgrad., Chapman Coll., 1971-72, Foothill Coll., 1973-74. Owner, operator The Natural Gourmet, Palo Alto, Calif., 1974-76, Quiche Lori, Palo Alto, 1976-81, Lori's Kitchens, Palo Alto, 1982-91, The Rose & Crown, Palo Alto, 1991—; Contbr. articles to pubs. Recipient award dessert category Cook Your Way to France Profl. Chef's

Contest, 1990. Mem. San Francisco Profl. Food Soc. Office: The Rose & Crown 547 Emerson St Palo Alto CA 94301-1608

LAWSON, JONATHAN NEVIN, academic administrator; b. Latrobe, Pa., Mar. 27, 1941; s. Lawrence Winters and Mary Eleanor (Rhea) L.; m. Leigh Farley (div.); children: Paul, Joshua, Jacob; m. Pamela Cross. AA, York Coll. Pa., 1962; BFA, Tex. Christian U., 1964, MA, 1966, PhD, 1970. Dir. composition St. Cloud (Minn.) State U., 1971-77, assoc. dean, 1977-81; asst. vice chancellor Minn. State U. System, St. Paul, 1980-81; dean liberal arts Winona (Minn.) State U., 1981-84; dean arts and scis. U. Hartford, West Hartford, Conn., 1984-86; sr. v.p., dean of faculty U. Hartford, 1986-95; v.p. acad. affairs Idaho State U., Pocatello, 1995—. Author: Robert Bloomfield, 1980; editor: Collected Works: Robert Bloomfield, 1971; contbr. articles and papers to scholarly publs; assoc. editor Rhetoric Soc. Quar., St. Cloud, 1974-79. Mem. regional adv. bd. Greater Hartford C.C., 1992-94; mem. bd. trustees Hartford Coll. for Women, 1992-94; mem. ID State bd. for edn. acad. affairs com., 1995—. Mem. Am. Coun. Edn., Coun. Fellows Alumni, Coun. Liberal Learning, Assn. Gen. and Liberal Studies, Assn. Am. Colls., N.E. Assn. Schs. and Colls. (chmn. commn. on instns. higher edn. 1992-95), Asian Studies Consortium (chmn. bd. 1991-94), Lambda Iota Tau (hon.), Alpha Chi (hon.). Episcopalian. Home: 1401 Juniper Hill Dr Pocatello ID 83204 Office: Idaho State U Campus Box 8063 Pocatello ID 83209

LAWSON, MICHAEL LEE, educator; b. Livingston, Mont.; s. Don Clifford and Doris Louise (Robert) Taylor; m.Donna Marie Thiel, June 7, 1970 (div. Nov. 1985); children: Debra Ann, Elizabeth Marie, Babe Alaine, Molly Jane; m. Annette Gail Torgerson. BS in Secondary Edn., Western Mont. Coll. Edn., 1989; MEd, Lesley Coll., 1996. Oper. engr. Mont., 1971-74, constrn. boiler maker, 1974-84; tchr. high sch. welding Butte (Mont.) Sch. Dist. #1, 1991—. Sgt. USMC, 1965-69. Decorated Bronze Star with combat v, Purple Heart. Mem. Am. Welding Soc., Disabled Am. Vets., Am. Legion, Lions (pres. Mile High chpt. 1996—, Lion of Yr. 1995). Lutheran. Home: 3103 Sanders St Butte MT 59701-3636 Office: Butte High Sch 401 S Wyoming St Butte MT 59701-2655

LAWSON, THOMAS, artist; b. Glasgow, Scotland, July 16, 1951; came to U.S., 1975; s. Edward and Margaret Lawson; m. Susan Morgan. MA (hons), U. St. Andrews, Scotland, 1973; MA, U. Edinburgh, Scotland, 1975; MPhil, CUNY, 1979. Artist various cities worldwide, 1975—; founding editor Real Life Mag., N.Y.C., 1979-94; instr. Sch. Visual Arts, N.Y.C., 1981-90; dean Calif. Inst. of the Arts, Valencia, 1990—; N.Y. advisor Alba Mag., Edinburgh, 1984-89; vis. instr. Rhode Island Sch. Design, Providence, N.Y., 1988-89; vis. faculty Calif. Inst. of the Arts, Valencia, 1986-89; selector Brit. Art Show 4, 1995-96. Executed mural Manhattan Mcpl. Bldg., 1989-92; contbr. articles to profl. jours. Artist advisor Rotunda Gallery, Bklyn., 1985-90. Nat. Endowment for the Arts artists fellow, 1982-83, 85-86, 89-90; Real Life Mag. publ. grantee Nat. Endowment for the Arts, 1979-94, N.Y. State Coun. Arts, 1980-89. Mem. Coll. Art Assn. Office: Calif Inst of the Arts 24700 Mcbean Pky Valencia CA 91355-2340

LAWSON, THOMAS CHENEY, fraud examiner; b. Pasadena, Calif., Sept. 21, 1955; s. William McDonald and Joan Bell (Jaffee) L.; children: Christopher, Brittany. Student, Calif. State U., Sacramento, 1973-77. Cert. internat. investigator, fraud examiner. Pres. Tomatron Co., Pasadena, 1970-88, Tom's Tune Up & Detail, Pasadena, 1971-88, Tom's Pool Svc., Sacramento, 1975-78, Tom Supply Co., 1975—; mgmt. trainee Permoid Process Co., L.A., 1970-75; prof. automechanics Calif. State U., Sacramento, 1973-75; regional sales cons. Hoover Co., Burlingame, 1974-76; mktg. exec. River City Prodns., Sacramento, 1977-78; territorial rep. Globe div. Burlington House Furniture Co., 1978; So. Calif. territorial rep. Marge Carson Furniture, Inc., 1978-80; pres. Ted L. Gunderson & Assos., Inc., Westwood, Calif., 1980-81; pres., CEO Apscreen, Newport Beach, Calif., 1980—; founder Crditbase Co., Newport Beach, Calif., 1980-89, Worldata Corp., Newport Beach, 1980-89, Trademark Enforcement Corp., L.A., 1985-86; pres. Carecheck, Inc., Newport Beach, 1990—, CEO Badchex, Inc., Newport Beach, 1992—. Editl. rev. bd.: The White Paper. Calif. Rehab. scholar, 1974-77. Mem. Christian Businessmen's Com. Internat., Coun. Internat. Investigators, Am. Soc. Indsl. Security (cert., chmn. Orange County chpt. 1990), Nat. Pub. Records Rsch. Assn., Pers. and Indsl. Rels. Assn., World Assn. Detectives, Assn. Cert. Fraud Examiners (editl. rev. bd. 1995—), Soc. Human Resource Mgmt. Office: 2043 Westcliff Dr Ste 300 Newport Beach CA 92660-5511

LAWSON, WILLIAM HAROLD, college dean, labor economist; b. San Jose, Calif., Nov. 2, 1934; s. Minter Bryan and Ruth Josephine (Hill) L.; m. Patricia Marguerette O'Carroll, Aug. 15, 1958 (div. Apr. 1979); children: Ronald W., Brian T., Thomas W.; m. Patricia Jeanne Prevedello, Feb. 6, 1982; children: Kathleen Ann Clark, George T., Tim J. BS in Civil Engring., San Jose State U., 1958, MBA, 1961; PhD in Labor Econs., Claremont Grad. Sch., 1969. Engr. Pacific Telephone, San Francisco, 1957-60; mgmt. intern U.S. Dept. Labor, Washington, 1961, pers. officer, 1962-64; instr. bus. San Bernardino (Calif.) Valley Coll., 1964-67, chmn. bus. dept., 1965-67; from tech. div. chmn. to asst. dean instrn. Moorpark (Calif.) Coll., 1967-72; dist. asst. supt. Ventura (Calif.) County Community Coll., 1972-83; dean vocat. edn. & econ. devel. Oxnard (Calif.) Coll., 1983-95, ret., 1995, tchr. credentialling mentor, 1995—; cons. Evaluation Tech. Corp. and Lawson Cons. Group, Ventura, Calif., 1968—, Chancellor's office Calif. Cmty. Colls., Sacramento, 1977-83, with spl. assignments Calif. State Dept. Edn., Sacramento, 1977-80. Producer TV shows U.S. Dept. Edn., San Bernardino Valley Coll., 1975. Legis. cons. Calif. Adv. Com. Vocat. Edn., Sacramento, 1974-76; joint com. chmn. Joint Community Coll. Dept. Edn. Plan for Vocat. Edn., Sacramento, 1977-78; chmn. community adv. bd. Calif. Conservation Corps, Camarillo, 1987-94. Mem. Am. Vocat. Assn., Calif. C.C. Adminstrn. Occupational Edn. (v.p. 1991-94), Oxnard Coll. Ctr. Internat. Trade Devel. (dir. 1989-95), Oxnard Coll. Workplace Learning Ctr. (dir. 1992-94), Econ. Devel. Network (co-founder 1987-94), Econ. Devel. Network Internat. (trade devel. com. chmn. 1988-91, chair resource devel. com. Calif. State U. Northridge-Ventura Campus 1993-95). Republican. Roman Catholic. Home: 4496 Pomona St Ventura CA 93003-1920

LAWTON, LARRY DAVID, lawyer; b. Cheyenne, Wyo., June 12, 1942; s. David Dwight and June Creole (Estes) L.; m. Ida Beth Aullman, June 8, 1966; children: Lynn David, Lowell Dale, Lance Donald, Lorin Michael. BS in Polit. Sci., U. Wyo., 1969; JD, Duke U., 1970. Bar: Calif. 1971, Wyo. 1973, U.S. Dist. Ct. Wyo., U.S. Dist. Ct. (no. dist.) Calif., U.S. Supreme Ct., U.S. Cir. Ct. (10th cir.). Law clk. Arter & Hadden, Cleve., 1969; law clk. L.A. County Dist. Atty., 1970-71, dep. dist. atty., 1971-73; assoc. Guy, Williams & White, Cheyenne, 1973-78; trial atty., founder Lawton, Edwards & Johnson, Cheyenne, 1978-86; sole practice Oakland, Calif., 1986-90; Superfund atty., advisor Office of Regional Counsel, USAF, San Francisco, 1990—. Rep. nominee for dist. atty. Laramie County, Cheyenne, 1982; pres. Larmaie County Young Reps., 1980. Mem. LDS Ch. Home: 1271 New Hampshire Dr Concord CA 94521-3820 Office: HQ USAF Office Regional Counsel 333 Market St S 625 San Francisco CA 94105-2196

LAWTON, MICHAEL JAMES, entomologist, pest management specialist; b. Balt., Aug. 6, 1953; s. James William and Mary Eileen (O'Connor) L.; m. Barbara Ann Byron, Dec. 19, 1983. BS, U. Md., 1975. Cert. entomologist. Technician, tech. dir. Atlas Exterminating Co., Towson, Md., 1975-78; asst. tech. dir. Western Exterminator Co., Irvine, Calif., 1978-83, tng. and tech. dir., 1984-95, dir. sales and mktg., 1996, v.p. sales and mktg., 1997—. Democrat. Office: Western Exterminator Co 1732 Kaiser Ave Irvine CA 92614-5739

LAX, KATHLEEN THOMPSON, federal judge. BA, U. Kans., 1967; JD, U. Calif., L.A., 1980. Law clk. U.S. Bankruptcy Ct., L.A., 1980-82; assoc. Gibson, Dunn & Crutcher, L.A., 1982-88; judge ctrl. dist. U.S. Bankruptcy Ct., L.A., 1988—; bd. dirs. L.A. Bankruptcy Forum, 1988—; bd. govs. Fin. Lawyers Conf., L.A., 1991-92, 94—. Bd. editors: Calif. Bankruptcy Jour., 1988—. Office: US Bankruptcy Court 21041 Burbank Boulevard Woodland Hills CA 91367

LAYCOCK, MARY CHAPPELL, gifted and talented education educator, consultant; b. Jefferson City, Mo., Jan. 11, 1915; d. Alvin E. and Ollie (Harris) Chappell; m. James Charles Laycock, June 22, 1937; children: Charles, Ann, Donald E., Jane. AB, Judson Coll., 1937; MA in Math. Edn., U. Tenn., 1961. Math. tchr. various, 1938-41; math. tchr. Kingsport (Tenn.) Jr. High Sch., 1942; math. coord. Oak Ridge (Tenn.) City Schs., 1956-68, high sch. math. tchr., 1945-68; math. specialist Nueva Ctr. for Learning, Hillsborough, Calif., 1968—; cons. Hayward, Calif., 1990—. Author many books including Mathematics for Meaning, The Fabric of Mathematics, Algebra in Concrete, Focus on Geometry, Hands On Mathematics for Secondary Teachers, Weaving Your Way from Arithmetic to Mathematics, 1993, The Magician's Castle Fantasy, 1995; developed documentary Don't Bother Me, I'm Learning, 12 videotapes on teaching manipulatives; contbr. articles to profl. jours. Recipient Calif. Educator award, 1989, Elem. Math. Tchr. award Calif. Math. Coun. and State of Calif., 1989, Award of Recognition Calif. Assn. for the Gifted. 1984. Mem. NEA, Nat. Coun. Tchrs. Math., Oreg. Math. Coun., Calif. Math. Coun. (life), Fla. Math. Coun., Greater San Diego Math. Coun., San Mateo County Math. Coun., Calif. Assn. for the Gifted. Home and Office: 20655 Hathaway Ave Hayward CA 94541-3740

LAYDEN, FRANCIS PATRICK (FRANK LAYDEN), professional basketball team executive, former coach; b. Bklyn., Jan. 5, 1932; m. Barbara Layden; children: Scott, Michael, Katie. Student, Niagara U. High sch. basketball coach L.I., N.Y.; head coach, athletic dir. Adelphi-Suffolk Coll. (now Dowling Coll.); head basketball coach, athletic dir. Niagara U., Niagara Falls, N.Y., 1968-76; asst. coach Atlanta Hawks, 1976-79; gen. mgr. Utah Jazz, Salt Lake City, 1979-88, head coach, 1981-88, v.p. basketball ops., until 1988, pres., 1989—. Bd. dirs. Utah Soc. Prevention Blindness; bd. dirs. Utah chpt. Multiple Sclerosis Soc., Utah Spl. Olympics. Served to 1st lt. Signal Corps, AUS. Office: Utah Jazz Delta Ctr 301 W South Temple Salt Lake City UT 84101-1216*

LAYE, JOHN E(DWARD), contingency planning and business continuity consulting executive; b. Santa Monica, Calif., May 26, 1933; s. Theodore Martin and Evelyn Rosalie (Young) L.; m. Jeanne Tutt Curry, Dec. 23, 1955; children: John Russell, Linda Helen. A.A., Los Angeles Community Coll., 1952; B.A., Naval Postgrad. Sch., 1967; M.S., U. So. Calif., 1975. Cert. mgmt. cons. Inst. Mgmt. Cons. Enlisted U.S. Navy, 1951, advanced through grades to lt. comdr., 1965; naval aviator, project mgr., worldwide, 1955-75; ret., 1975; emergency services exec. Marin County, Calif., 1975-76, Solano County, Calif., 1976-82; cons., pres. Contingency Mgmt. Cons. (formerly Applied Protection Systems), Moraga, Calif., 1982—; mem. faculty Emergency Mgmt. Inst., Nat. Emergency Tng. Ctr., Emmitsburg, Md., 1982—; mem. faculty U. Calif. Bus. and Mgmt. extenstion, 1993—; dir. Emergency Preparedness Mgrs. Cert. Program, 1993—; pres. Calif. Emergency Services Assn., 1988; chpt. bd. dirs., lectr. internat. contingency planning and disaster recovery, 1976—. Decorated Air medal, Navy Commendation medal, Navy Achievement medal, Viet Nam cross of Gallantry; recipient commendation Gov.'s Office Emergency Svcs., State Fire Marshal, Calif. Emergency Svcs. Assn., City Orinda. Mem. Nat. Coordinating Council Emergency Mgmt. (chmn. bus. and industry com. 1992-95), Orinda Assn. (bd. dirs. 1988-90, pres. 1989, Vol. Yr. award 1991), U. So. Calif. Alumni (bd. dirs. 1980-87, pres. east bay club 1984), U. So. Calif. Inst. Safety and Systems Mgmt. Triumvirate (founding bd. mem.). Presbyterian. Office: Contingency Mgnt Cons 346 Rheem Blvd Ste 202 Moraga CA 94556-1588

LAYMAN, CHARLES DONALD, plastic surgeon; b. Portland, Mar. 20, 1949. MD, U Oreg. Health Scis. U., 1975. Plastic surgeon St. Vincent Med. Ctr., Portland; clin. assoc. prof. plastic surgery U. Oreg. Health Sci. Ctr. Office: 9155 SW Barnes Rd Ste 220 Portland OR 97225-6629

LAYMAN, RICHARD DEAN, historian, editor; b. Des Moines, Apr. 16, 1928; s. Charles Raymond and Elva Mabel (Jennings) L.; m. Marget Murray Irrgang, Mar. 19, 1954 (dec. Jan. 1992); m. Patricia Foster Kulp, May 29, 1993 (dec.); stepchildren: Jacqueline Jeske, Claire Irizarry. News editor Midvale (Utah) Sentinel, 1948-49; copy editor Salt Lake Tribune, Salt Lake City, 1949-51; news editor Sebastopol (Calif.) Times, 1951, Hemet (Calif.) News, 1951-53, Siskiyou Daily News, Yreka, Calif., 1953-54; asst. news editor San Rafael (Calif.) Ind.-Jour., 1954-62; asst. chief copy editor San Francisco Chronicle, 1962-91; copy editor Relevance (Jour. of The Great War Soc.), Palo Alto, Calif., 1992—; issue editor Over the Front, 1992—. Author: To Ascend From a Floating Base: Shipboard Aeronautics and Aviation, 1783-1914, 1979, The Cuxhaven Raid: The World's First Carrier Air Strike, 1985, Before the Aircraft Carrier: The Development of Aviation Vessels 1849-1922, 1989, Naval Aviation in the First World War: Its Impact and Influence, 1996; co-author: (with Stephen McLaughlin) The Hybrid Warship: The Amalgamation of Big Guns and Aircraft, 1991; contbr. numerous articles to profl. jours. Mem. Am. Aviation Hist. Soc., Air Force Hist. Found., Airship Hist. Trust, Gallipoli Assn., Great War Soc., Internat. Naval Rsch. Orgn., Lighter-Than-Air Soc., League of World War I Aviation Historians (Thornton D. Hooper award for excellence in aviation history 1995), Soc. for Mil. History, Soc. of Friends of the Fleet Air Arm Mus., Soc. of First World War Aviation Historians, Seaplane Spl. Interest Group, Internat. Plastic Modelers' Soc., Small Air Forces Clearing House, U.S. Naval Inst., Western Front Assn. Home and Office: 50 Mohawk Ave Corte Madera CA 94925

LAYTON, DONALD MERRILL, aeronautics educator; b. Cuyahoga Falls, Ohio, Sept. 23, 1922; s. Clifton Merrill and Flossie Belle (Payne) L.; m. Kathleen Gingras, Sept. 3, 1948; children: Mary, Patricia, Jane, Susan (dec.), Carol, James, Robert (dec.). BS in Sci., U.S. Naval Acad., 1945; MS in Aeros., Princeton U., 1954; MS in Mgmt., Naval Postgrad. Sch., 1968. Registered profl. safety engr., Calif. Commd. ensign USN, 1945, advanced through grades to comdr., 1960, ret., 1968; from faculty to prof., chmn. dept. Naval Postgrad. Sch., Monterey, Calif., 1968-88; vis. prof. Stellenbosch U., South Africa, 1985-89; lectr., pilot Nat. Test Pilot Sch., 1985-95; pres. Per Safe, Salinas, Calif., 1985—. Author: System Safety, 1981, Helicopter Performance, 1984, Performance for Flight test, 1985, Aircraft Performance, 1986, Handling Qualities for Flight Test, 1987, Helicopter Conceptual Design, 1991. Fellow AIAA (assoc., chpt. pres. 1976-78, mem. tech. com. 1975—); mem. Am. Soc. Safety Engrs., System Safety Soc. (sr., bd. dirs. 1974-77, Safety Educator of Yr. 1985), Navy League of U.S. (bd. dirs. 1978-81, past pres.), Sigma Xi (Rsch. award 1976), Masons. Republican. Episcopalian. Home and Office: 44 Seca Pl Salinas CA 93908-8817

LAYTON, MARILYN SMITH, English language educator; b. Des Moines, Nov. 29, 1941; d. Sam Solomon and Mollie (Leiserowitz) Hockenberg; m. Charles Kent Smith, July 1, 1962 (div. Nov. 1974); children: Laurence Joseph, Eleanor Gwen; m. Richard Howard Layton, Dec. 14, 1975. BA, Northwestern U., 1963; MA, U. Mich., 1964; postgrad., U. Wash., 1972-74. Instr. part time English and humanities North Seattle Community Coll., 1969-74, tenured instr., 1975—; lectr., cons. on pedagogy. Author: (with others) Let Me Hear Your Voice, 1983 (Gov.'s Writers' award 1984), (with H. Collins) Intercultural Journeys Through Reading and Writing, 1991, Choosing to Emerge As Readers and Writers, 1993; mem. editorial bd. Jour. Basic Writing, 1986-89, Teaching English in the Two-Yr. Coll., 1987-90; contbr. articles to profl. jours. Mem. Conf. on Coll. Composition and Communication (mem. exec. com. 1983-86, editorial bd. 1987-90), Nat. Coun. Tchrs. English (chmn. nat. two-yr. coll. coun. 1985-86), Pacific N.W. Conf. on English in the Two-Yr. Coll. (chmn., 1982-83), Wash. C.C. Humanities Assn. Office: North Seattle Community Coll Dept Humanities 9600 College Way N Seattle WA 98103-3514

LAYTON, TERRY WAYNE, college basketball coach; b. Oakland, Calif., Aug. 29, 1947; s. Charles Wayne and Doris Marie (Cronk) L.; m. Nancy D. Sonnenberg, Sept. 6, 1969; children: Teralynn, Jamie. BA in Phys. Edn., Social Sci., Pasadena Coll., 1970; MS in Phys. Edn., Mankato State U., 1971; Spanish Intermediate, Inst. de Lenguas Espanola. Asst. basketball coach Mankato State U., 1971-72, various H.S., 1972-75; head basketball, tennis coach N.W. Nazarene Coll., Nampa, Idaho, 1975-82; head basketball coach Panhandle State U., Goodwell, Okla., 1982-83, Nebr. Western Coll., Scottsbluff, 1983-85, Azusa Pacific U., Azusa, Calif., 1985-87; asst. basketball coach Azusa Pacific U., 1988-91; Mexican nat. coach, 1991-92; head basketball coach Adams State Coll., Alamosa, Col., 1992—; coached Guatemalan, Mexican nat. teams, pro teams in Costa Rica, P.R. and Venezuela; coached in L.A. pro summer league; toured teams in Asia, Ctrl. Am., Europe and S.Am.; traveled or coached in 40 countries; conducted internat. clinics, 1969—, camps, 1982-95; coached Olympic teams in Guatemala and Mexico. Author 2 books; contbr. 12 articles to profl. jours.; Lifetime coll. record of 248-204, jr. coll. record of 32-32, internat. record of 230-32; total record 510-268; team at Panhandle State U. had 35-5 record, ranked 6th in nation in class, most wins of any team in nation. Named Outstanding Young Men Am.; N.W. Coach of Yr., 1977-78, Dist. IX Coach of Yr., 1982. Mem. Nat. Assn. Basketball Coaches (internat. com. 1988—, membership com. 1979-80, conv. com. 1979-83), Nat. Assn. Intercollegiate Athletics (nat. tournament com. 1989-91, GSAC basketball chmn. 1989-91, Dist. II chmn. 1989-91, Dist. 3 chmn. 1980-82, nat. rater 1989-90, Dist. II Hall of Fame, 1991). Home: 707 Murphy Dr Alamosa CO 81101-2040

LAZARUS, GERALD SYLVAN, physician, university dean; b. N.Y.C., Feb. 16, 1939; s. Joseph W. and Marion (Goldstein) L.; m. Sandra Jacob, Sept. 3, 1961 (dec. 1985); children: Mark, Elyse, Lynne, Laura; m. Audrey Fedyszyn Jakubowski, Apr. 7, 1990. B.A., Colby Coll., 1959; M.D., George Washington U., 1963. Intern, then resident U. Mich., Ann Arbor, 1963-64; resident in medicine U. Mich., 1964-65; NIH research asso. NIH, Bethesda, Md., 1965-68; resident in dermatology Harvard U., Cambridge, Mass., 1968-70; research fellow Strangeways Labs., Cambridge, Eng., 1970-72; assoc. prof. medicine, co-dir. dermatology tng. program Albert Einstein Med. Coll., N.Y.C., 1972-75; J. Lamar Callaway prof. Duke U., Durham, N.C., 1977-82; chief dermatology Duke U., 1975-82; Milton B. Hartzell prof. U. Pa. Sch. Medicine, Phila., 1982—, chmn. dept. dermatology, 1982-93; dean Sch. Medicine U. Calif., Davis, 1993—; mem. study sect. NIH, 1976-80. Author: (with L. Goldsmith) Diagnosis of Skin Disease, 1980, (with Herman Beerman) Tradition of Excellance: History of Dermatology at Univ. Pa. Sch. of Medicine; asso. editor: Jour. Investigative Dermatology, 1977-82; contbr. numerous articles to profl. jours. Served with USPHS, 1965-68. Carl Herzog fellow Am. Dermatology Assn., 1970-72; John Simon Guggenheim fellow U. Geneva, 1986; sr. investigator Arthritis Found., 1972-77; grantee NIH. Fellow ACP, Assn. Am. Physicians, Am. Soc. Clin. Investigation; mem. Am. Dermatol. Assn., Soc. Investigative Dermatology (dir., pres. 1996-97, Disting. alumnus award George Washington U. 1996), Biochem. Soc., Am. Acad. Dermatology (Sultzberger award 1986). Republican. Jewish. Office: U Calif Sch Medicine Office of Dean Davis CA 95616

LAZARUS, RICHARD STANLEY, psychology educator; b. N.Y.C., Mar. 3, 1922; s. Abe and Matilda (Marks) L.; m. Bernice H. Newman, Sept. 2, 1945; children—David Alan, Nancy Eve. A.B., City Coll. N.Y., 1942; M.S., U. Pitts., 1947, Ph.D., 1948; Dr. honoris causa, Johannes Gutenberg U., Mainz, Fed. Republic Germany, 1988, U. Haifa, Israel, 1995. Diplomate in clin. psychology Am. Bd. Examiners in Profl. Psychology. Asst. prof. Johns Hopkins, 1948-53; psychol. cons. VA, 1952—; assoc. prof. psychology, dir. clin. tng. program Clark U., Worcester, Mass., 1953-57; assoc. prof. psychology U. Calif. at Berkeley, 1957-59, prof. psychology, 1959-91, prof. emeritus, 1991—; prin. investigator Air Force contracts dealing with psychol. stress, 1951-53, USPHS grant on personality psychol. stress, 1953-70; NIA, NIDA, and NCI grantee on stress, coping and health, 1977-81, MacArthur Found. research grantee, 1981-84; USPHS spl. fellow Waseda U., Japan, 1963-64. Author 18 books, numerous publs. in profl. jours. Served to 1st lt. AUS, 1943-46. Recipient Disting. Sci. Achievement award Calif. State Psychol. Assn., 1984, Div. 38 Health Psychology, 1989; Guggenheim fellow, 1969-70; Army Rsch. Inst. rsch. grantee, 1973-75. Fellow AAAS, APA (Disting. Sci. Contbn. award 1989); mem. Western Psychol. Assn., Argentina Med. Assn. (hon.). Home: 1824 Stanley Dollar Dr Apt 3B Walnut Creek CA 94595-2833 Office: Univ Calif Dept Psychology Berkeley CA 94720

LE, DIANA LYNN, county worker; b. Leon, Iowa, Mar. 21, 1956; d. Charles Edward Sr. and Nora Eunice (Dickerson) W. BSW, Graceland Coll., 1980; student, U. Kans., 1981-83. Social work intern St. Michael's (Ariz.) Sch., 1979, Father Benedict Justice Sch. and Seton Ctr., Kansas City, Mo., 1980, Mattie Rhodes Ctr., Kansas City, Mo., 1982-83; child care worker Gillis Home for Boys, Kansas City, 1980-84; community work experience program worker Social and Rehab. Svcs. State of Kans., Kansas City, 1983-84; contractual assignee Reorganized Ch. of Jesus Christ of Latter-day Saints, San Jose, Calif., 1984-87; counselor II summer youth NOVA/Summer Youth Employment Program, 1987; ESL instr. Wilson Adult Edn. Ctr., 1987-88, Overfelt Adult Edn. Ctr., 1987—; eligibility worker II East Valley Social Svcs., Santa Clara County, Calif., 1992-94; family support officer Dist. Atty.'s Office Santa Clara County, 1994—. Counselor in tng. for camps and Bible schs. Reorganized Ch. Jesus Christ Latter-day Saints, Iowa, 1969-73, counselor children's camp, San Jose, 1985, mem. ethnic community program com., East San Jose, 1984-87. Honored for Community Outreach in Ethnic Ministries, Reorganized Ch. Jesus Christ Latter-day Saints, 1985-87. Club: Intercultural (Lamoni, Iowa) (activity chmn. 1977-79).

LE, KHANH TUONG, utility executive; b. Saigon, Vietnam, Feb. 25, 1936; parents Huy Bich and Thi Hop; m. Thi Thi Nguyen, Apr. 22, 1961; children: Tuong-Khanh, Tuong-Vi, Khang, Tuong-Van. BS in Mech. Engring., U. Montreal, 1960, MS in Mech. Engring., 1961. Cert. profl. engr. Project mgr. Saigon Met. Water Project Ministry Pub. Works, Saigon, 1961-66; dep. dir. gen. Cen. Logistics Agy. Prime Min. Office, Saigon, 1966-70; asst. dir., chief auditor Nat. Water Supply Agy. Min. Pub. Works, Saigon, 1970-75; mgr. Willows Water Dist., Englewood, Colo., 1975—; dean sch. mgmt. scis., asst. chancellor acad. affairs Hoa-Hao U., Long-Xuyen, Vietnam, 1973-75; chmn. bd. dirs. Asian Pacific Devel. Ctr., 1994-96. Treas. Met. Denver Water Authority, 1989-92; mem. Arapahoe County Adv. Bd., Douglas County Water Authority, 1993—; mem. Front Range Water Forum presided over by Gov. Roy Romer, Colo., 1993—; vol. Water for People, 1994—; mem. bus. adv. com. C.C. of Denver. Recipient Merit medal Pres. Republic Vietnam, 1966, Pub. Health Svc. medal, 1972, Edn. Svc. 1st class medal, 1974, Pub. Works 1st class medal, 1972, Rural Reconstrn. 1st class medal, 1973, Svc. award Asian Edn. Adv. Coun., 1989; co-recipient Engring. Excellence award Am. Cons. Engrs Coun., 1994; named to Top Ten Pub. Works Leaders in Colo., Am. Pub. Works Assn., 1990. Mem. Am. Water Works Assn., Water Environ. Fedn., Colo. Water Congress, Asian C. of C. (bd. dirs. 1993—), Vietnamese Profl. Engrs. Soc. (founder), Amnesty Internat., Friendship Bridge. Buddhist. Office: Willows Water Dist 6970 S Holly Cir Ste 200 Englewood CO 80112-1066

LE, NGUYEN MINH, computer company executive; b. Dong Thap, Vietnam, Mar. 22, 1952; came to U.S., 1975; s. Vinh Phat Le and Banh Thi Nguyen; m. Nuong Thi Liet Huynh, 1973; children: Dan, Long. MS in Tech. Mgmt., Pepperdine U., Malibu, Calif., 1996. Painter Dallas Apartments, 1976-77; machinist N.W. Industries, Oklahoma City, 1978-79; auto mechanic Harbor Auto Sales, Long Beach, Calif., 1980-81; operator L.A. County Sanitation Dist., Carson, 1981-84; pres. Dan Long Landscape, Long Beach, 1982-85, Dolphin Microcomputer Corp., Long Beach, 1985—; chmn. Tinvi Computers, Vietnam, 1991—. Mem. Rep. Senatorial Trust, Washington, 1992—, Bus. Execs. for Nat. Security, 1997—, Progressive Nat. Movement, Saigon, 1969-75, Tan Dai Viet Party, Vietnam, 1969—; pres. Nguyen Ngoc Huy Found., Long Beach, 1991—. Buddhist. Home: 6466 E Bixby Hill Rd Long Beach CA 90815-4709 Office: Dolphin Microcomputer Corp 1234 E South St Long Beach CA 90805-4321

LE, YVONNE DIEMVAN, chemist; b. Vietnam, Nov. 21, 1961; d. Hien Trung and Thanh-Hoa Thi (Luu) L. BA in Chemistry, Math., San Jose State U., 1984. Chem. technician Hewlett Packard Co., Palo Alto, Calif., 1983; assoc. chemist Ampex Corp., Sunnyvale, Calif., 1984-86; chemist II Info. Memory Corp., Santa Clara, Calif., 1986-88; R&D project engr. Komag, Inc., Milpitas, Calif., 1988—. Mem. Am. Chem. Soc. Roman Catholic. Office: Komag Inc 275 S Hillview Dr Milpitas CA 95035-5417

LEABHART, THOMAS GLENN, art educator, performer; b. Charleroi, Pa., Oct. 23, 1944; s. Thomas G. and Tresa Rose (Lacher) L.; m. Sally Diane Garfield, Apr. 29, 1972. BA, Rollins Coll., Winter Park, Fla., 1966; MA, U. Ark., 1968; postgrad., Ecole de Mime Decroux, Paris, France, 1968-72. Instr. U. Ark., Fayetteville, 1972-76; artistic dir. Wis. Sch. of Mime, Spring Green, 1976-78; resident artist Grand Valley State Coll., Allendale, Mich., 1978-81; asst. prof. Ohio State U., Columbus, 1981-82; assoc. prof., resident artist Pomona Coll., Claremont, Calif., 1982—; mem. artistic staff Internat. Sch. Theatrical Anthropology, Holstobro, Denmark. Author: Modern and Post Modern Mime, 1989; editor: Mime Jour., 1974—; performances yearly in U.S., Can., S.Am. and Europe. Fulbright fellow, 1968-69, Ohio Arts Coun. Choreography fellow, 1982, NEA fellow, 1980, 84, 85; grantee Calif. Arts Coun. for Mime Jour., 1985, 87, 88, Internat. Rsch. Exchs. Bd, 1975.

Mem. (founder, pres. 1986, 87) Nat. Movement Theatre Assn., Assn. Theatre in Higher Edn. Office: Pomona Coll Theatre Dept Claremont CA 91711

LEACH, GARY EDWARD, urologist, educator; b. Detroit, Nov. 20, 1950; s. John and Antoinette (Isca) L.; m. Barbara Jean Williams; children: Andrew, Jody, Cory. BS in Biology, U. Mich., 1972; MD, Wayne State U., 1976. Diplomate Am. Bd. Urology. Intern and resident Kaiser Permanente, L.A., 1976-81; fellow in female urology UCLA, 1981-82; chief urology Kaiser Permanente, L.A., 1988-96; assoc. clin. prof. urology UCLA, 1990—; dir. Tower Urology Inst. for Continence, L.A., 1996—. Author: chpts. in urology texts; contbr. articles to profl. jours. Patentee in field. Mem. Am. Urol. Assn. (chmn. guidelines panel 1993—), Calif. Urologic Assn. (Western sect.), Soc. Internat. de Urologie, L.A. Urologic Soc., Urodynamics Soc. (pres. 1996—). Office: Cedars-Sinai Med Office Tower 8631 W 3d St Ste 915 East Los Angeles CA 90048

LEACH, JOHN F., newspaper editor, journalism educator; b. Montrose, Colo., Aug. 6, 1952; s. Darrell Willis and Marian Ruth (Hester) L.; m. Deborah C. Ross, Jan. 2, 1982; children: Allison, Jason. BS in Journalism, U. Colo., 1974, MA in Journalism, 1979; MA in Am. Studies, U. Sussex, Falmer, Brighton, Eng., 1983. News reporter Boulder (Colo.) Daily Camera, 1974-79; news reporter Ariz. Republic, Phoenix, 1979-85, asst. city editor, 1985-93; news editor The Phoenix Gazette, 1993-94; asst. mng. editor Phoenix Gazette, 1994-95; asst. mng. editor, news ops. The Ariz. Republic and The Phoenix Gazette, 1995-97; sr. editor The Ariz. Republic, Phoenix, 1997—; faculty assoc. Ariz. State U., Tempe, 1990—; pres., dir. First Amendment Funding Inc., Phoenix. Bd. Regents scholar U. Colo., 1970, Rotary Found. scholar, 1982. Mem. Ariz. Press Club (treas. 1984-86, pres. 1986-87), Soc. Profl. Journalists, Reporter's Com. for Freedom of Press, Soc. Newspaper Design, Investigative Reporters and Editors. Home: 4313 E Calle Redonda Phoenix AZ 85018-3733 Office: The Ariz Republic 200 E Van Buren St Phoenix AZ 85004-2238

LEACH, RICHARD MAXWELL, JR. (MAX LEACH, JR.), corporate professional; b. Chillicothe, Tex., June 14, 1934; s. Richard Maxwell and Lelia Booth (Page) L.; m. Wanda Gail Groves, Feb. 4, 1956; children: Richard Clifton, John Christopher, Sandra Gail, Kathy Lynn. BS in Acctg. magna cum laude, Abilene Christian U., 1955. Registered Fin. Planner., CLU. Asst. dir. agys. Am. Founders Ins. Co., Austin, Tex., 1960-62; owner A.F. Ins. Planning Assocs., Temple, Tex., 1962-65; v.p. sales Christian Fidelity Life Ins. Co., Waxahachie, Tex., 1966-67; exec. v.p. Acad. Computer Tech., Inc., Dallas, 1968-69; pres., chief exec. officer Inta-Search Internat., Inc., Dallas, 1969-71; prin., chief exec. officer, fin. cons. Leach and Assocs., Albuquerque, 1971—; pres. The Wright Edge, Inc., 1988-90; pres., CEO Action Mktg. Programs, Inc., 1989-92; CEO Vacation Premiums Internat., Inc., 1990-92; pres., CEO ITM Corp., Albuquerque, 1993—; chmn. bd. United Quest Inc., Albuquerque, Hosanna Inc., Albuquerque; real estate broker; commodity futures broker; exec. dir., bd. dirs. New Heart, Inc., Albuquerque, 1975-85; owner Insta-Copy, Albuquerque, 1973-76, Radio Sta. KYLE-FM, Temple, 1963-64. Editor, author Hosanna newspaper, 1973-74. Gen. dir. Here's Life, New Mexico, Albuquerque, 1976; exec. dir. Christians for Cambodia, Albuquerque, 1979-80. Served with U.S. Army, 1955-57. Home: 3308 June St NE Albuquerque NM 87111-5029 Office: 9920 Bell Ave SE # B Albuquerque NM 87123-3313 *Personal philosophy: Success is doing what God wants you to do and being where God wants you to be.*

LEADBETTER, MARK RENTON, JR., orthopedic surgeon; b. Phila., Nov. 7, 1944; s. Mark Renton and Ruth (Protzeller) L.; m. Alethia Ashby, July 28, 1973 (div. June 1990); m. Jan Saker, 1991. BA, Gettysburg Coll., 1967; MSc in Hygiene, U. Pitts., 1970; MD, Temple U., 1974. Surg. intern Univ. Hosps., Boston, 1974-75, resident in surgery, 1975-76; emergency room physician Sturdy Meml. Hosp., Attleboro, Mass., 1976-78; resident in orthopaedics U. Pitts., 1978-81; orthopaedic physician Rockingham Meml. Hosp., Harrisonburg, Va., 1981-82, courtesy staff, 1982—; pvt. practice, Staunton, Va., 1982—; mem. active staff King's Daus. Hosp., Staunton, 1982—; active staff Samaritan Hosp., Moses Lake, Wash.; courtesy staff Columbia Basin Hosp., Ephrata, Wash. Contbr. articles to med. jours.; patentee safety syringes, safety cannulas, designer of medecal equipment. Mem. Am. Coll. Sports Medicine, So. Med. Assn., So. Orthopaedic Assn., County Med. Soc., Nat. Futures Assn. (assoc.). Republican. Home: 246 Rainier View Ln Moses Lake WA 98837

LEADER, JEFFERY JAMES, mathematics educator; b. Elmira, N.Y., Oct. 27, 1963; s. Dennis Thomas and Jeanne Diane (Smith) L.; m. Margaret Ellen Nieburg, Aug. 26, 1989; children: Derek James, Corrinne Janet. BS, Syracuse U., 1985, BSEE, 1985; ScM, Brown U., 1987, PhD, 1989. Vis. asst. prof. math. Harvey Mudd Coll., Claremont, Calif., 1989-90; asst. prof. Naval Postgrad. Sch., Monterey, Calif., 1990-93, U.S. Mil. Acad., West Point, N.Y., 1993-95; asst. prof. applied math. Santa Clara (Calif.) U., 1995—. Mem. Am. Math. Soc., Math. Assn. Am., Soc. for Indsl. and Applied Math., Phi Beta Kappa, Tau Beta Pi, Sigma Xi.

LEAHY, T. LIAM, marketing and management consultant; b. Camp Legeunne, N.C., Apr. 15, 1952; s. Thomas James and Margaret May (Munnelly) L.; m. Shannon Kelly Brooks, Apr. 21, 1990. BS, St. Louis U., 1974, MA, 1975; postgrad., Hubbard Coll. of Adminstrn., L.A., 1989. V.p. sales Cablecom Inc., Chgo., 1978-81, Kaye Advt., N.Y.C., 1981-83; group pubr. Jour. Graphics Pub., N.Y.C., 1983-85; gen. mgr. Generation Dynamics, N.Y.C., 1985-86; pres. Leahy & Assocs., N.Y.C., 1982-86, Tarzana, Calif., 1982—; assoc. Am Coun. of Execs. Assoc., Glendale, 1991—; bd. dirs. Cons. Assn., Dental Am., Midland, Tex., Comprotech Svcs. Contbr. articles to profl. jours. Fellow Success Mgmt. Ctrs. (sr.); mem. Am. Coun. Execs. (bd. dirs. 1993-95), Turnaround Mgmt. Assn., L.A. C. of C. Office: Leahy & Assocs 19131 Enadia Way Reseda CA 91335-3828

LEAKE, BRENDA GAIL, enterostomal therapist nurse practitioner; b. Harriman, Tenn., Aug. 5, 1950; d. James Frank and Pauline Ruby (McGuffey) Judd; m. Lee Leake, Aug. 1, 1970 (div. Apr. 1974). AS in Nursing, U. Nev., Las Vegas, 1971, BN, 1986; cert. enterostomal therapist, U. Calif., San Diego, 1975. RN, Nev.; cert. enterostomal therapist, urol. nurse. Staff nurse Humana Hosp. Sunrise, Las Vegas, 1971-73, relief charge nurse, 1973-76, enterostomal therapist, 1976—; speaker Hospice Vol. program, Las Vegas, 1982—, I Can Cope program, Las Vegas, 1984—. Author instructional guide. Vol. Am. Cancer Soc., 1983—, mem. program devel. nurse edn. com. Mem. Intenat. Assn. Enterostomal Therapists (cert.), Nat. Assn. Pediatric Pseudobstructure Soc., Am. Nurses Assn., So. Nev. Nurses Assn., World Council Enterostomal Therapists, Am. Urol. Assn. (cert.), So. Nev. Ostomy Assn. (med. advisor 1976—), Crohns & Colitis Assn., Advanced Practitioners Nursing (cert., program chmn. 1986—), Wound Healing Soc. Republican. Presbyterian. Office: Sunrise Hosp 3186 S Maryland Pkwy Las Vegas NV 89109-2317

LEAKE, ROSEMARY DOBSON, physician; b. Columbus, Ohio, July 14, 1937; d. Joseph Lawrence and Rosemary Elizabeth (Brockmeyer) Dobson; m. Donald Leake, Aug. 20, 1964; children: John, Elizabeth, Catherine. BA, Ohio State U., 1959, MD, 1962. Diplomate Am. Bd. Neonatal-Perinatal Medicine. Intern, pediatrics Mass. Gen. Hosp., Boston, 1962-63, resident, pediatrics, 1963-64; rsch. fellow Maternal Infant Health Collaborative Study The Boston Lying-In Hosp., Boston, 1965-67; neonatal fellow Stanford U. Hosp., Palo Alto, Calif., 1968-69; co-dir. NIH sponsored perinatal tng. program Harbor-UCLA Med. Ctr., Torrance, 1979, program dir. NIH sponsored perinatal rsch. ctr., 1980—; prof. pediatrics UCLA Sch. of Medicine, L.A., 1982—; dir. regionalized fellowship Harbor-UCLA/King-Drew Med. Ctr., Torrance, 1986-92; chair pediatrics Harbor-UCLA Med. Ctr., Torrance, 1992—; dir. perinatal crisis care program Harbor-UCLA Med. Ctr., Torrance, 1972-76, dir. neonatal ICU, 1974-81, assoc. prof. pediatrics, 1976-82, assoc. chief div. neonatology, 1976-77. Named UCLA Woman of Sci., 1985, Outstanding Woman Academician of Yr. Nat. Bd. Award of the Med. Coll. of Pa., 1989; recipient Alumni Achievement award Ohio State U. Sch. Medicine, 1987. Mem. Am. Pediatric Soc., Soc. for Pediatric Rsch. Home: 2 Crest Rd W Rolling Hills CA 90274-5003 Office: Harbor-UCLA Med Ctr 1000 W Carson St Torrance CA 90502-2004

LEAL, GEORGE D., engineering company executive; b. 1934. B in Civil Engrng., MA, Santa Clara U., 1959. With Dames & Moore, Inc., L.A., 1959—, CEO, 1981—, now CEO, pres.; bd. dirs. BW/IP Internat. Inc. Office: Dames & Moore Inc 911 Wilshire Blvd Ste 700 Los Angeles CA 90017-3436*

LEAL, STEVE, city council; married. BA in Polit. Sci., U. Calif. Property mgmt. and devel., 1985—; adminstrv. specialist Pima County, 1993—; city coun., 1989—; cmty. svc. Salvation Army Hospitality House, Tucson-Pima County Hist. Commn., Citizens Adv. Commn. Democrat. Office: 4300 S Park Ave Tucson AZ 85714

LEALE, OLIVIA MASON, import marketing company executive; b. Boston, May 5, 1944; d. William Mason and Jane Chapin (Prouty) Smith; m. Euan Harvie-Watt, Mar. ll, 1967 (div. Aug. 1979); children: Katrina, Jennifer; m. Douglas Marshall Leale, Aug. 29, 1980. BA, Vassar Coll., 1966. Cert. paralegal. Sec. to dir. Met. Opera Guild, N.Y.C., 1966; sec. to pres. Friesons Printers, London, 1974-75; guide, trainer Autoguide, London, 1977-79; ptnr. Inmark Internat. Mktg. Inc., Seattle, 1980—. Social case worker Inner London Ednl. Authority, 1975-76. Democrat. Presbyterian. Home and Office: 5427 NE Penrith Rd Seattle WA 98105-2842

LEAPHART, W. WILLIAM, judge; b. Butte, Mont., Dec. 3, 1946; s. Charles William and Cornelia (Murphy) L.; m. Barbara Berg, Dec. 30, 1977; children: Rebecca, Retta, Ada. Student, Whitman Coll., 1965-66; BA, U. Mont., 1969, JD, 1972. Bar: Mont. 1972, U.S. Dist. Ct., U.S. Ct. Appeals (9th cir.) 1975, U.S. Supreme Ct. Law clk. to Hon. W.D. Murray U.S. Dist. Ct., Butte, 1972-74; ptnr. Leaphart Law Firm, Helena, Mont., 1974-94; justice Mont. Supreme Ct., Helena, 1995—. Home: 510 Dearborn Ave Helena MT 59601-2761 Office: Mont Supreme Ct Justice Bldg 215 N Sanders St Helena MT 59601-4522*

LEARY, G. EDWARD, state finance commisioner; m. Betty Chamberlain; 5 children. BS in Polit. Sci., U. Utah, 1971, MBA, 1981. Cert. Internat. Rels. With collections and lending dept. Draper Bank and Trust, 1974-77; examiner Utah Dept. Fin. Instns., Salt Lake City, 1977-82, industry supr., 1982-87, chief examiner, 1987-92, commr., 1992—; chmn. Bd. Fin. Instns.; mem. Utah Housing Fin. Agy. Bd., Utah Appraiser Registration and Cert. Bd. With USN, 1971-73. Capt. USNR, ret. 1995. Mem. Conf. State Bank Supr. (chmn.-elect). Office: Utah Dept Fin Instns PO Box 89 324 South State Ste 201 Salt Lake City UT 84110-0089

LEARY, LORY DIANE MARY B., publishing executive; b. New Haven, June 20, 1936; d. James Vincent and Eileen Marie (Kennedy) Bica; m. Robert Arthur Leary (dec. Oct. 1991). Dir., owner Alaskan Art Gallery, Seward, 1976-86; owner, pub. Alaskan Viewpoint Pub., Seward, 1986—. Author: Dreamwish, 1991, An Alaskan Child's Garden of Verse, 1990, (reference) Who's Who in Alaskan Art, 1990; author, pub. (collection) Jour. of Alaskan Women, 1994. Bd. dirs., grant officer Moose Pass Sportsmen Club; chmn. Moose Pass Rep. Com., 1990—; adv. planning commn. mem. Kenai Borough, Alaska; mem. Moose Pass Vol. Fire Co., past v.p. Mem. Nat. Fedn. Ind. Bus., Nat. Press Women, Alaska Press Women, United Alaska Artists, Moose Pass C. of C. (founder, pres. 1994), Rebekah Lodge 6A (vice grand 1994). Roman Catholic. Office: Alaskan Viewpoint Pub HC 64 Box 453 Seward AK 99664-9707

LEASE, JANE ETTA, environmental science consultant, retired librarian; b. Kansas City, Kans., Apr. 10, 1924; d. Joy Alva and Emma (Jaggard) Omer; B.S. in Home Econs., U. Ariz., 1957; M.S. in Edn., Ind. U., 1962; M.S. in L.S., U. Denver, 1967; m. Richard J. Lease, Jan. 16, 1960; children—Janet (Mrs. Jacky B. Radifera), Joyce (Mrs. Robert J. Carson), Julia (Mrs. Earle D. Marvin), Cathy (Mrs. Edward F. Warren); stepchildren—Richard Jay II, William Harley. Newspaper reporter Ariz. Daily Star, Tucson, 1937-39; asst. home agt. Dept. Agr., 1957; homemaking tchr., Ft. Huachuca, Ariz., 1957-60; head tchr. Stonebelt Council Retarded Children, Bloomington, Ind., 1960-61; reference clk. Ariz. State U. Library, 1964-66; edn. and psychology librarian N.Mex. State U., 1967-71; Amway distbr., 1973—; cons. solid wastes, distressed land problems reference remedies, 1967; ecology lit. research and cons., 1966—. Ind. observer 1st World Conf. Human Environment, 1972; mem. Las Cruces Community Devel. Priorities Adv. Bd. Mem. ALA, Regional Environ. Edn. Research Info. Orgn., NAFE, P.E.O., D.A.R., Internat. Platform Assn., Las Cruces Antique Car Club, Las Cruces Story League, N.Mex. Library Assn. Methodist (lay leader). Address: 2145 Boise Dr Las Cruces NM 88001-5149

LEASE, RICHARD JAY, police science educator, former police officer; b. Cherokee, Ohio, Dec. 10, 1914; s. Harold and Mabelle (Fullerton) L.; m. Marjorie Faye Stoughton, Sept. 2, 1939 (div. Apr. 1957); children: Richard Jay II, William Harley; m. Jane Etta Omer, Jan. 16, 1960; stepchildren: Janet Radifera, Joyce Carson, Julia Marvin, Catherine Warren; adopted children: Alan Fudge, Stephen V. Graham. Student, Wittenberg U., 1932-33; BA, U. Ariz., 1937, MA, 1961; postgrad., Ind. U., 1950, 60, Ariz. State U., 1956, 63-65, 67—; grad., U. Louisville So. Police Inst., 1955. Grad. asst . U. Ariz., Tucson, 1937-38; with Tucson Police Dept., from 1938; advanced from patrolman to sgt., also served as safety officer Pima County Sheriff's Dept., Tucson, 1953, patrol supr., 1953-55, investigator, 1955-56; tchr. sci. pub. schs. Tucson, 1957-59; lectr. dept. police adminstrn. Ind. U., Bloomington, 1960-65; asst. prof. dept. police sci. N.Mex. State U., Las Cruces, 1965—; cons. law enforcement problems HEW, 1960, Indpls. Police Dept., 1962, Harrisburg Community Coll. Police Sci. Dept., 1967, Phoenix Police Dept., 1968—; advisor police tng. programs several small city police depts., Ind., 1960-63, Indpls., 1962; mem. oral bd. for selection chief in Bateville, Ind., 1962, oral bd. for selection sgts. and lts., Las Cruces Police Dept., 1966—. Author: (with Robert F. Borkenstein) Alcohol and Road Traffic: Problems of Enforcement and Prosecution, 1963, The Dreams, Hopes, Recollections and Thoughts of a Professional Good Samaritan; cons. editor Police, various rsch. publs. on chem. intoxification tests, psychol. errors of witnesses, reading disabilities, delinquency. Participant numerous FBI seminars; active youth work, philanthropy, among Am. Indians in Southwest; founder awards outstanding ROTC cadets N.Mex. State U., 1967—; founder Wiltberger ann. awards Nat. Police Combat Pistol Matches; scoutmaster Yucca council Boy Scouts Am., 1966—. Served to 1st lt. USMCR, 1942-45, PTO. Fellow Am. Acad. Forensic Scis. (sec. gen. sect.); mem. Internat. Assn. Chiefs of Police, Internat. Assn. Police Profs., Brit. Acad. Forensic Scis., Can. Soc. Forensic Sci., Am. Soc. Criminology, Ret. Officers Assn., Assn. U.S. Army (2d v.p. 1969—), NEA, N.Mex. Edn. Assn., N.Mex. Police and Sheriffs Assn., Internat. Crossroads, NRA (benefactor mem.), Marine Corps League (life), Sigma Chi. Lodges: Masons, Elks. Home and Office: 2145 Boise Dr Las Cruces NM 88001-5149

LEASURE, ROBERT ELLIS, writer, photographer; b. Lamar, Colo., Oct. 20, 1921; s. Henry Naley and Pansy Margaret (Leatherman) L.; m. Betty Jean Stulck, July 4, 1945; twins: Mary Margaret and David Lee. Grad. high sch., Lamar, Colo. Cryptographer 15th Air Force Air Def. Command, Colorado Springs, Colo., 1946; staff Colorado Springs (Colo.) Post Office, 1946-76; freelancer photographer, writer, 1976—. Author: Black Mountain, 1975; exhibited at Tex. Fine Art Assn. Mem. Colorado Springs Fine Arts Guild.Sgt. U.S. Army, 1942-45. Mem. VFW. Presbyterian. Home: 1210 Milky Way Colorado Springs CO 80906-1715

LEAVER, BETTY LOU, educational administrator, writer; b. Rochester, N.H., Feb. 16, 1950; d. Herman Nathan and Mary Elizabeth (Germon) Ham; m. Carl Don Leaver, Mar. 20, 1970; children: Echo Elizabeth, Fawn Noelle, Shawn Thomas, Shenan Carl. BA, Pa. State U., 1971, MA, 1978. Officer U.S. Army, 1974-82; tchg. fellow U. Pitts., 1978-82; instr. Allegheny County (Pa.) C.C., Monroeville, 1982-83; lang. tng. supr. Fgn. Svc. Inst. U.S. Dept. State, Arlington, Va., 1983-89; dean Sch. Ctrl. European Langs. Def. Lang. Inst., 1992-93; dean Sch. Slavic Langs. Def. Lang. Inst., Monterey, Calif., 1989-92; pres. Am. Global Studies Inst., Salinas, Calif., 1993—; vis. prof. Middlebury (Vt.) Coll., 1994, Bryn Mawr (Pa.) Coll., 1995, 96, Monterey Inst. Internat. Studies, 1996, U. Helsinki, 1989; cons. Portland (Oreg.) Pub. Schs., Accels and Uzbekistan Ministry of Justice, 1995, Ctr. for Advancement of Lang. Learning, Washington, 1994, 95, pub. schs., Krasnoyarsk, Siberia, 1993—, joint U.S./Russian Space Agy. projects, 1996, Soros Founds., Belarus, 1993, Russia, 1993-94, Ukraine, 1994, Ohio State U., 1988-91, 93, numerous others; external evaluator Hot Line & White House Communicators, 1984-89; interpreter in U.S. and Russia; mem. fgn. lang. adv. com. Arlington County (Va.) Pub. Schs., 1985-88, chmn. 1988; founder consortia CIFLI Georgetown U., Am. Global Studies Inst., Columbia U., UCLA, Harvard U., Middlebury Coll., Bryn Mawr Coll., U. Md., 1994—, U.S. Nval Acad., West Point, N.Y., CIA, NSA, Def. Lang. Inst., Fgn. Svc. Inst., U.S. Air Force Acad., others. 1st lt. U.S. Army, 1974-78. Mem. Am. Assn. for Advancement of Slavic Studies (coord. open house 1985 World Congress), Am. Coun. Tchrs. of Russian (bd. dirs. 1988—, editor newsletter 1987-92), Am. Coun. Tchg. Fgn. Langs., Prunedale Grange, Profl. Women's Network. Home: 747 Saint Regis Way Salinas CA 93905-1624 Office: Am Global Studies Inst 14 Spreckels Ln Salinas CA 93908-8941

LEAVITT, JEROME EDWARD, childhood educator; b. Verona, N.J., Aug. 1, 1916; s. Thomas Edward and Clara Marie (Sonn) L.; m. Florence Elizabeth Wilkins, Aug. 23, 1963. B.S., Newark State Coll., 1938; M.A., N.Y. U., 1942; Ed.D., Northwestern U., 1952. Tchr. pub. schs. Roslyn Heights, N.Y., 1938-42; instr. Sperry Gyroscope, Bklyn., 1942-45; prin., supr. pub. schs. Los Alamos, N.Mex., 1945-49; prof. edn., exec. asst. to dean Portland (Oreg.) State U., 1952-66; prof. edn. U. Ariz., Tucson, 1966-69; prof. elem. edn., coordinator Child Abuse Project, Calif. State U., Fresno, 1969-81; pres. Jerome Leavitt, Inc., 1981—. Author: Nursery-Kindergarten Edn., 1958, Carpentry for Children, 1959, By Land, By Sea, By Air, 1969, The Beginning Kindergarten Teacher, 1971, America and Its Indians, 1971, The Battered Child, 1974, Herbert Sonn: Yosemite's Birdman, 1975, Child Abuse and Neglect: Research and Innovation, 1983, others; contbr. articles to profl. jours. Mem. ASCD (life), NEA (life), Assn. Childhood Edn. Internat. (life), Soc.Profs. Edn., Calif. Tchrs. Assn., Profs. Curriculum, Phi Delta Kappa, Kappa Delta Pi, Epsilon Pi Tau. Home and Office: Villa Campana 6653 E Carondelet Dr Apt 124 Tucson AZ 85710-2138

LEAVITT, MAIMON, psychiatrist; b. Bklyn., Jan. 26, 1921; s. William and Leah (Wolson) L.; m. Peggy Berne, May 19, 1943; children: Richard M., Andrew M., Susan J., Jane E. BS, Harvard Coll., 1940; MD, NYU Coll. Medicine, 1943. Intern Michael Reese Hosp., Chgo., 1944; resident in neurology Goldwater Meml. Hosp., N.Y., 1945; resident in psychology Menninger Fedn., Topeka, 1945-47, staff psychiatrist, 1945-50; psychiatrist pvt. practice, L.A., 1950—; dir. L.A. Psychoanalytic Inst., 1970-73; prof. UCLA, 1960—; pres. Stoller Found., L.A., 1992—. contbr. articles to profl. jours. Com. chmn. Boy Scouts Am., L.A., 1955-58. Maj. U.S. Army, 1950-53. Mem. L.A. Psychoanalytical Soc. & Inst. (dir. 1970-73, pres. 1965-68). Office: 1800 Fairburn Ave Los Angeles CA 90025-4968

LEAVITT, MICHAEL OKERLUND, governor, insurance executive; b. Cedar City, Utah, Feb. 11, 1951; s. Dixie and Anne (Okerlund) L.; m. Jacalyn Smith; children: Michael Smith, Taylor Smith, Anne Marie Smith, Chase Smith, Weston Smith. BA, So. Utah U., 1978. CPCU. Sales rep. Leavitt Group, Cedar City, 1972-74, account exec., 1974-76; mgr. underwriting Salt Lake City, 1976-82; chief operating officer, 1982-84, pres., chief exec. officer, 1984—, gov., state of Utah, 1993—; bd. dirs. Pacificorp, Portland, Oreg., Utah Power and Light Co., Salt Lake City, Great Western Thrift and Loan, Salt Lake City. Utah Bd. Regents, chmn. instl. coun. So. Utah State U., Cedar City, 1985-89; campaign chmn. U.S. Sen. Orrin Hatch, 1982, 88, U.S. Sen. Jake Garn, 1980, 86; cons. campaign Gov. Norman Angerter, 1984; mem. staff Reagan-Bush '84. 2d lt. USNG, 1969-77. Named Disting. Alumni So. Utah State Coll. Sch. Bus., 1986. Mem. Chartered Property Casualty Underwriters. Republican. Mormon. Office: Office of the Governor 210 State Capitol Building Salt Lake City UT 84114-1202*

LEAVY, EDWARD, judge; m. Eileen Leavy; children: Thomas, Patrick, Mary Kay, Paul. AB, U. Portland, 1950, LLB, U. Notre Dame, 1953. Dist. judge Lane County, Eugene, Oreg., 1957-61, cir. judge, 1961-76; magistrate U.S. Dist. Ct. Oreg., Portland, 1976-84, judge, 1984-87, cir. judge U.S. Ct. Appeals (9th cir.), 1987—. Office: US Ct Appeals Pioneer Courthouse 555 SW Yamhill St Ste 216 Portland OR 97204-1323

LEBADANG, artist; b. Vietnam, 1922. Student, Sch. Fine Arts, Toulouse, France. Exhibited in group shows Cin. Art Mus., Newman Contemporary Art Gallery, Phila., Galerie Fontaine, Paris, Frost and Reed Gallery, London, Wonderbank Gallery, Frankfurt, Germany; represented in permanent collections Univ. Art Gallery, Lund, Sweden, Phoenix Art Mus., also pvt. and corp. collections. Address: care Circle Gallery 2501 San Diego Ave San Diego CA 92110-2841*

LEBEJOARA, OVIDIU, artist; b. Ciupa, Romania, Dec. 14, 1952; came to U.S., 1986; s. Petre and Ileana (Telegaru) L. BFA, N. Tonitza Sch., Bucharest, Romania, 1973; BA, Otis Parsons Sch., L.A., 1988; MA in Illustration, Syracuse U., 1997. Graphic artist Recom, Bucharest, 1975-79, Siderma, Bucharest, 1979-86, L.A. Signs & Graphics, 1987-94; artist Arts & Signs, L.A., 1994—. Exhibited in group shows in Romania, 1975-86, Anca Colbert Gallery, L.A., 1987, 88, Julleux Gallery, Kansas City, Mo., 1989, Main Street Gallery, Visalia, Calif., 1990, 91, L.A. Modern Art Gallery, 1990, Calif. Expn. and State Fair, 1991, United Pastelists Am., N.Y., 1991, Cedar-Lily Gallery, Murfreesboro, Tenn., 1991-92, Barakat Gallery, Beverly Hills, Calif., 1992, Modern Art Mus. Unet, France, 1993, New Eng. Fine Art Inst., Boston, 1993, City Hall Paris, May Mus. Modern Art, 1994, Romfest, Downey, Calif., 1994, Napoleon Found., 1995, City Hall Paris, 1995, Agora Gallery, Soho, N.Y., 1995, Abney Gallery, N.Y., 1996, L.A. Mcpl. Art Gallery, 1996, Internat. Art Gallery, Stockholm, 1996, Ucci Gallery, N.Y., 1996, numerous others. Founder Romanian Am. Ctr., L.A., 1989. Recipient award of merit Calif. Expn. and State Fair, 1991, Discovery award Art of Calif. mag., 1993, 94. Mem. Knickerbocker Artists, Am. Pastelists, Graphic Artists Guild. Orthodox. Home and Studio: 3115 Montrose Ave Apt 12 Glendale CA 91214-3690

LE BERTHON, ADAM, lawyer; b. L.A., June 12, 1962; s. Edward Lynch and Veronica Rose (Franks) Le B; m. Kelly Elizabeth McKee, Mar. 23, 1996. BA cum laude with dept. honors, U. San Diego, 1985; JD, U. So. Calif., L.A., 1989. Bar: Calif. 1989, U.S. Dist. Ct. (ctrl. dist.) Calif. 1989, U.S. Ct. Appeals (9th cir.) 1989, U.S. Dist. Ct. (so. dist.) Calif. 1990, (no. dist.) Calif. 1990, (ea. dist.) Calif. 1990. Assoc. White & Case, L.A., 1989-91, Straw & Gilmartin, Santa Monica, Calif., 1991—. Editor So. Calif. Law Rev., 1988-89; contbr. articles to profl. jours. Recipient Am. Jurisprudence award U. So. Calif., 1987. Mem. Calif. State Bar Assn., L.A. County Bar Assn., Order of the Coif, Phi Alpha Delta, Omicron Delta Epsilon, Kappa Gamma Pi. Home: 125 Montana Ave Apt 207 Santa Monica CA 90403-1054 Office: Straw & Gilmartin 100 Wilshire Blvd Ste 1325 Santa Monica CA 90401-1114

LEBL, MICHAL, peptide chemist; b. Prague, Czechoslovakia, Aug. 21, 1951; came to U.S., 1991; s. Bedrich and Olga (Krystofova) Leblova; m. Zuzana Bucinova, June 9, 1973; children: Martin, George. MS, Inst. Chem. Tech., Prague, 1974; PhD, Inst. Organic Chemistry and Biochemistry, Prague, 1978, DSc, 1992. Scientist Inst. Organic Chemistry and Biochemistry, Prague, 1978-87, group leader, 1987-89, dept. head, 1989-91; dir., owner CSPS, Prague, Tucson, San Diego, 1990—; dir. chemistry Selectide Corp., Tucson, 1991-96; pres. Spyder Instruments Inc., 1993—; dir. robotics, synthetic automation Trega Bioscis., Inc., San Diego, 1996—; vis. prof. McMaster U., Hamilton, Can., 1982, U. Ariz., Tucson, 1983, 86, cons., 1989; mem. bd. chemistry Czechoslovak Acad. Sci., Prague, 1988-91; mem. program com. European Peptide Symposium, Interlaken, Switzerland, 1992. Author, editor: Handbook of Neurohypophysial Hormone Analogs, 1987, numerous sci. publs.; author: (software) Peptide Companion, 1994; editor-in-chief: (jour.) Collection of Czechoslovak Chem. Commn., 1987-91; editor: Molecular Diversity, 1995—; edtl. bd. Internat. Jour. Peptide and Protein Rsch., 1989—, Peptide Rsch. jour., 1988—; contbr. articles to profl. jours.; patentee in field. Sci. grantee NIH, 1992-95, Czechoslovak Acad. Scis., 1991-93; recipient prize Czech Republic. Govt., 1990, Czechoslovak Acad. Scis., 1980, 86, 89. Mem. Am. Chem. Soc., Am. Peptide Soc., European Peptide Soc. (Zervas prize 1990), Czechoslovak Chem. Soc. Office: Trega Bioscis Inc 6550 Gen Atomics Ct San Diego CA 92121

LEBLON, JEAN MARCEL, retired French language educator, consultant; b. Chimay, Hainaut, Belgium, June 7, 1928; came to U.S., 1947; s. Alfred and Marcelle (Lefèvre) L.; m. Mary Lorraine Hovorka, June 3, 1952; children: Mitzi, Simone. BS in Edn., Emporia State U., 1951; PhD, Yale U., 1960. Instr. Conn. Coll., New London, 1953-59, CCNY, 1959-62; assoc. prof. Hollins (Va.) Coll., 1962-65; prof. French Vanderbilt U., Nashville, 1966-87; chmn., 1976-85; tchg. assoc. U. Wash., Seattle, 1988-90; vis. prof.

U. Maine, Orono, 1962, Emporia (Kans.) State U., 1965, Fairfield (Conn.) U., 1966; cons. Ednl. Testing Svc., Princeton, N.J., 1963-87, Oxford U. Press, London, 1985-86, Champs-Elysees, Inc., Nashville, 1985-90, Wash. Acad. Lang., Seattle, 1987—. Co-author: Précis de Civilisation Française, 1966; translator: Zola (Marc Bernard), 1960; editor Les Choses (Georges Perec), 1969; editor, terminologist Microsoft Corp., 1990-95. Mem. MLA (regional del. 1974-76), Am. Assn. Tchrs. French, N.W. Translators and Interpreters Soc. (pres. 1991-93), Am. Translators Assn., Seattle-Nantes Sister City Assn. (v.p. 1990—), Alliance Française (v.p. 1990—). Home: 1130 5th Ave S Apt 104 Edmonds WA 98020-4666

LE BON, DOUGLAS KENT, investment manager; b. Rapid City, S.D., Oct. 27, 1953; s. Stanley and Elodis (Holm) Le B.; m. Eva Marie Dyer; 1 child, Shauna. BSBA, Calif. State U., Dominguez Hills, 1976, MBA, 1979. Valuation cons. Houlihan, Lokey, Howard & Zukin, L.A., 1979-83; v.p., prin. Wilshire Assocs., Inc., Santa Monica, Calif., 1983-90; founder, mng. dir. Pathway Capital Mgmt., L.A., 1990—. Vice chmn., chmn. fin. com. L.A. area coun. Boy Scouts Am., 1991-96; mem. corp. bd. Sch. Mgmt., Calif. State U., Dominguez Hills, 1994-96. Office: Pathway Capital Mgmt 18101 Von Karman Ave Ste 1860 Irvine CA 92612-1047

LEBOW, BENNETT S., communications executive; b. Phila., 1938; 1 child, Geri. BEE, Drexel U.; postgrad., Princeton U. Prin. DSI Systems Inc., Rockville, Md., from 1961, B.S. LeBow Inc.; chmn. Western Union Corp., Upper Saddle River, N.J., New Valley Corp. (formerly Western Union Corp.), Upper Saddle River, 1993—, New Valley Corp., Miami, FL, 1995—. Office: Mai Basic Four Inc 14101 Myford Rd Tustin CA 92780-7020 also: New Valley Corp 100 SE 2nd St # 32 Miami FL 33131-2100*

LEBRATO, MARY THERESA, lawyer, psychologist; b. Ft. Wayne, Ind., June 13, 1950; d. Joseph James and Veronica (Adamonis) L. BA, U. Dayton, 1971; MA, U. Ala., Tuscaloosa, 1973, PhD, 1975; JD, Lincoln Law Sch., 1986. Bar: Calif. 1986; lic. psychologist, Calif. Psychologist Ala. Dept. Mental Hygiene, Tuscaloosa, 1975, Calif. Dept. Health, Eldridge, Calif., 1975-77; chief statewide evaluation devel. svcs. Calif. Dept. Health, Eldridge, 1977-79; dir. evaluation Oakland Perinatal Health Project, Calif. Dept. Health, Sacramento, 1979-81; coord. Maternal, Child and Adolescent Health, Sacramento, 1981-82; dir. sexual harassment in employment project Calif. Commn. on Status of Women, Sacramento, 1982-85; chief long range planning Calif. Dept. Devel. Svcs., Sacramento, 1985-88; staff counsel Calif. State Lottery, Sacramento, 1988-91. Co-author (with Marilyn Pearman) Sexual Harassment Investigators Guidebook, 1984; author, editor: Help Yourself: A Manual for Dealing with Sexual Harassment, 1986. Adv. bd. mem. Calif. State Pers. Bd., Appeals Div. Adv. Com., 1987-91; bd. mem. Sacramento Rape Crisis Ctr., 1988. Recipient fellowships in psychology NIMH, U. Ala., Tuscaloosa, 1971, 72, 73, teaching asst. in psychology U. Ala., Tuscaloosa, 1974-75. Mem. APA, ABA, Am. Assn. on Mental Deficiency, Calif. State Bar Assn., Calif. State Psychol. Assn., Calif. Women Lawyers, Sacramento County Bar Assn., Women Laywers Sacramento (bd. mem., chair del. com. 1989, chair scholarship 1990). Home: 335 Del Wes Ln Rio Linda CA 95673-2031

LECHNYR, RONALD JOSEPH, psychologist; b. Mpls., July 21, 1942; s. Joseph Albert and Leila (Lilijedahl) L.; m. Celia Ann Filter, Aug. 15, 1964; children: David R., Michelle, Terri A., Sandra M. BA in Clin. Social Work, Wartburg Coll., 1964; MSW in Clin. Social Work, Smith Coll., 1967; DSW in Clin. Social Work, U. Utah, 1973; PhD in Psychology, U. Oreg., 1982. Diplomate Internat. Acad. of Behavioral Medicine & Psychotherapy & Counseling, Am. Acad. Pain Mgmt., Am. Bd. Med. Psychotherapists, Am. Bd. Examiners in Clin. Social Work. Intern Family Svc. Assn. Greater Boston, Boston, 1965-66; intern dept. psychiatry Mass. Gen. Hosp., Boston, 1966-67; commd. helath svc. officer USPHS, 1967; intern Marriage & Family Counseling Clinic U. Utah, Salt Lake City, 1972-73; advanced through grades to chief dept. psychiatry USPHS Med. Ctr., Gallup, N.Mex., 1974-76; post-doctoral resident in psychology Pain Therapy Clinic, Eugene, 1980-83; dir. psychotherapy clinic The Eugene (Oreg.) Hosp. & Clinic, 1976-81; clin. psychologist in pvt. practice Eugene, 1981—; clin. dir., co-founder Oreg. Pain Ctr., Springfield, 1985-91; clin. dir., co-owner Oreg. Health Rehab., Springfield, 1991-96; clin. assoc. dept. psychiatry U. N.Mex., 1973-76; faculty advisor univ. without walls program Loretto Heights Coll., Denver, 1973-76; clin. instr. U. Utah, Salt Lake City, 1972-73; field instr. Portland (Oreg.) State U. 1989-90. Columnist (newspaper) Blackberry Ink, Eugene, 1990-94; contbr. articles to profl. jours. Fellow Am. Orthopsychiat. Assn., Am. Assn. for Marriage and Family Therapy, Biofeedback Cert. Inst. Am.; mem. Oreg. Psychol. Assn., Lane County Psychol. Assn., Am. Pain Soc., Western U.S.A. Pain Soc., Internat. Soc. for Study of Pain, Prescribing Psychologists' Register Inc. (charter mem.), Phi Kappa Phi. Democrat. Lutheran. Home: 1955 Mclean Blvd Eugene OR 97405-1720 Office: Dr Ron Lechnyr & Assocs 2440 Willamette St Ste 102 Eugene OR 97405-3170

LECKART, BRUCE, psychologist; b. N.Y.C., Mar. 8, 1940; s. Samuel and Adele (Chesler) L.; m. Karen Iris Leckart, Mar. 30, 1969; 1 child, Steven. BA, Mich. State U., 1962, MA, 1963, PhD, 1965. Lic. psychologist, Calif. Asst. prof. Ohio U., Athens, 1965-68; assoc. prof. psychology San Diego State U., 1968-72, prof. psychology, 1972-93, prof. emeritus, 1994—; psychologist Westwood Evaluation and Treatment Ctr, L.A., 1986—; postdoctoral clin. intern L.A. Cmty. Mental Health Ctr., Long Beach, Calif., 1971-73, supr. clin. psychologist Family Svcs., Cerritos, Calif., 1985-86; vis. prof. Calif. State U., L.A., 1974-75; Qualified med. evaluator State of Calif., 1990—; pvt. practice L.A., San Diego, Oxnard, Santa Ana, Ontario and Ventura, Calif., 1977—. Author: Up From Boredom, Down From Fear, 1979; editl. cons. psychol. jours.; contbr. articles to profl. jours. USPHS fellow, 1963-65. Mem. APA, Psi Chi. Office: Westwood Evaluation Ctr & Treatment 11340 W Olympic Blvd Los Angeles CA 90064

LE CLAIR, DOUGLAS MARVIN, lawyer, educator; b. Montreal, Nov. 13, 1955; s. Lawrence M. and Joan B. Le Clair; m. Debra L. Garland, Oct. 12, 1985. BA, Loyola U., 1977; JD, Southwestern U., 1980; peace officer cert., Mesa C.C. Law Enforcement Acad., 1985. Bar: Ariz. 1982, U.S. Dist. Ct. Ariz. 1983, U.S. Ct. Appeals (9th cir.) 1983, U.S. Tax. Ct. 1987, U.S. Ct. Claims 1987, U.S. Supreme Ct. 1987; ordained deacon Roman Cath. Ch., 1995. Pvt. practice Mesa, Ariz., 1983—; mem. faculty law & acctg. Sterling Sch., Phoenix, Ariz., 1992-96. Author: Le Clair/Morgan Income Tax Organizer, 1982-83; prodn. editor Computer Law Jour., 1979-80. Res. officer Mesa Police Dept., 1984-92. Named One of Outstanding Young Men Of Am., 1979. Mem. ABA, Ariz. Bar Assn., Maricopa County Bar Assn., Internat. Platform Assn., Southwestern Student Bar Assn. (exec. bd. 1978-79), Southwestern U. Tax Law Soc., Mesa C. of C., Delta Theta Phi, Phi Alpha Theta. Office: 141 N MacDonald St Mesa AZ 85201

LECOCQ, KAREN ELIZABETH, artist; b. Santa Rosa, Calif., Nov. 4, 1949; d. Maynard Rodney and Lois May (Lessard) LeC.; m. David Lawrence Medley, Sept. 7, 1995. BA, Calif. State U., Fresno, 1971, MA, 1975; postgrad., Calif. Inst. of the Arts, L.A., 1971-72. Founding mem. Feminist Art Program, Fresno, Calif., 1971, Calif. Inst. of the Arts, L.A., 1972; One woman shows include Calif. State U. Art Gallery, Fresno, 1970, 76, Merced (Calif.) Coll., 1969, 77, 91, Calif. Inst. of the Arts, L.A., 1972, Recent Sculptures, Fresno, 1977, 78, Womanart Gallery, N.Y.C., 1980, Merced, 1987, Arts Coun. Gallery, Merced, 1989, Amos Eno Gallery, N.Y.C., 1994, 750 Gallery, Sacramento, 1995, Meridian Gallery, San Francisco, 1996, others; commissions include Absolut Vodka, 1993; vis. artist Merced County Schs., 1977-78, 79-82, 88-91; grad. instr. Calif. State U., Fresno, 1976-78, Merced Coll., 1973-76. Group shows include Womanhouse, L.A., 1972, Off Centre Centre, Calgary, Alta., Can., 1985, 86, Ryosuke Gallery, Osaka, Japan, 1986, Gallery Six Oh One, San Francisco, 1989, Fresno Art Mus., 1989, Ann Saunders Gallery, Jamestown, Calif., 1991, Pro arts Gallery, Oakland, Calif., 1991, Calif. Mus. Art, Santa Rosa, 1991, Harbs Gallery, Lexington, Va., 1992, Russell Sage Gallery, Troy, N.Y., 1992, Amos Eno Gallery, 1992-96, ARC Gallery, Chgo., 1993, 96, Lengyel Gallery, San Francisco, 1995, 750 Gallery, Sacramento, 1994-96, L.A. Mus. Contemporary Art, 1995, Armand Hammer Mus., L.A., 1996, many others. Docent Gallery Guide Art Train, Merced, 1983; artistic dir. Black and White Ball, Merced Regional Arts Coun., 1989-96. Cora T. McCord scholar; CETA grantee, Merced, 1978, Fresno, 1977; Calif. Inst. Arts scholar, 1972. Mem. Internat. Sculpture Source, No. Calif. Women's Caucus for Art, Pro Arts of Oakland, San Francisco Mus. Art. Democrat. Home and Office: PO Box 2204 Merced CA 95344-0204

LECRON, MARY FRAZER See **FOSTER, MARY FRAZER**

LEDBETTER, LOGAN SCOTT, management consultant; b. Phila., Oct. 2, 1958; s. Thomas Velt and Elizabeth Kinloch (Logan) L. BA in Polit. Sci., U. Ga., 1982; MS in Strategic Intelligence, Def. Intelligence Coll., 1991. Commd. ensign USN, 1983, advanced through grades to lt. comdr., 1993; naval intelligence officer USS Dwight D. Eisenhower, Norfolk, Va., 1984-86, Def. Intelligence Agy., Washington, 1986-89, USS Am., Norfolk, 1989-91; resigned USN, 1991; mgmt. cons. Booz, Allen and Hamilton, Inc., Mountain View, Calif., 1992-93, Colorado Springs, 1993—. With USNR. mem. U.S. Naval Inst., The Woodrow Wilson Ctr., The Naval Res. Assn. Episcopalian. Office: Booz Allen & Hamilton Inc 1050 S Academy Blvd Ste 148 Colorado Springs CO 80910

LEDBURY, DIANA GRETCHEN, adult education educator; b. Denver, Mar. 7, 1931; d. Francis Kenneth and Gretchen (Harry) Van Ausdall; m. Chander Parkash Lall, Dec. 26, 1953 (div. Aug. 1973); children: Anne, Neil, Kris; m. Eugene Augustus Ledbury, Sept. 13, 1976; stepchildren: Mark, Cindy, Rob. BA in Sociology, Colo. U., 1953. Instr. Home, and Family Life Seattle Pub. Schs. Adult Edn., 1957-62, Seattle C.C., Seattle, 1962-69, Green River C.C., 1969-71; asst. tchr. Renton Sch. Dist., Wash., 1974-83; adult edn. instr. Mental Health Network, Renton, 1984-85; coord. Inter-Study, Renton, 1985-86, program dir. Crossroads Child Care, 1985-86, family svcs. coord. , 1986-87, program supr. Candyland Too Child Care Ctr., 1987—, Candyland Also, 1987-90; coord. child care staff Washington Fitness Ctr., 1991-93. Mem. Renton Area Youth Svcs. Bd., Sch. and Community Drug Prevention Program, Renton dist. coun. PTA, Renton Citizen's Com. on Recreation; vol. Griffin Home for Boys; coord. Modern Dance Prodn., Carco Theater; adult leader Camp Fire Girls' Horizon Club; mem. bd. Allied Arts of Renton; mem. Bicentennial Com. for a Cultural Arts, Edn. and Recreation Ctr.; PTA rep. Dimmit Jr. High Sch.; mem. Sch. and Community Recreation Com.; founder Handicapped Helping Themselves, Mental Health Network; precinct committeeperson 11th dist. Republican party, Wash., 1976-85. Recipient Golden Acorn award Wash. State Congress PTA, Renton, 1972. Mem. AAUW (legis. chair 1983-87, mem. com. on strategic sch. policy safety in schs. 1993-94, com. on getting parents involved. 1994-95, pub. policy chair AAUW 1994-96), Assn. Social and Health Services (mem. com. 1984-85). Episcopalian. Avocations: arts; culture; recreation; child and family advocate.

LEDERER, MARION IRVINE, cultural administrator; b. Brampton, Ont., Can., Feb. 10, 1920; d. Oliver Bateman and Eva Jane (MacMurdo) L.; m. Francis Lederer, July 10, 1941. Student, U. Toronto, 1938, UCLA, 1942-45. Owner Canoga Mission Gallery, Canoga Park, Calif., 1967—; cultural heritage monument Canoga Mission Gallery, 1974—; Vice pres. Screen Smart Set women's aux. Motion Picture and TV Fund, 1973—; founder sister city program Canoga Park-Taxco, Mexico, 1963; Mem. mayor's cultural task force San Fernando Valley, 1973—; mem. Los Angeles Cultural Affairs Commn., 1980-85. Mem. Los Angeles Cultural Affairs Commn., 1980-85. Recipient numerous pub. service awards from mayor, city council, C. of C. Mem. Canoga Park C. of C. (cultural chmn. 1973-75, dir. 1973-75). Presbyn. Home: PO Box 32 Canoga Park CA 91305-0032 Office: Canoga Mission Gallery 23130 Sherman Way Canoga Park CA 91307-1402

LEDFORD, GARY ALAN, real estate developer; b. San Diego, Dec. 30, 1946; s. Loren Oscar and Madge Francis (Condon) L.; m. Winifred Jess Ledford, Nov. 19, 1994; children: Kelly, Jeanne, Robert. BSCE, U.S. Army Engring. Coll., 1967. Pres. Mastercraft Contractors/Mastercraft Diversified Svcs., Inc./Masterplan, Inc., Colo. Springs, 1969-73; v.p. K.L. Redfern, Inc., Orange, Calif., 1973-75; pres. Ledford Industries, Inc./G.A. Ledford & Assocs., 1975-82, Watt Jess Ranch, Inc., Apple Valley, Calif., 1985-94; chmn. Jess Ranch, Apple Valley, 1994—, Jess Ranch Water Co., Apple Valley, 1986—; pres., ceo Jess Ranch Devel. Co., Inc., 1996—; pres. Jess Ranch Security Co., Inc., 1996—; v.p., gen. mgr. Jess Ranch Realty, 1996—; gen. ptnr. GLBT Assocs., 1978-79; chmn. Watt-Jess/Ledford, Apple Valley, 1992-94; pres. LJ&J Investments, Inc., Apple Valley, Ledford-Schaffer/Rogers, Apple Valley. Designer computer software, 1979. Past pres. Cultural Arts Found., 1991-92, Victorville, Calif; bd. trustees Apple Valley Christian Care Ctr., High Desert Questors, Victorville; past pres. Victor Valley Mus. Assn., Baldy View B.I.A. Capt. C.E., U.S. Army, 1967-69, Vietnam. Mem. Internat. Coun. Shopping Ctrs., Nat. Assn. Home Builders', Nat. Planning Assn., NRA (life), High Desert Constrn. Indsutry Assn. (past v.p.), Bldg. Industry Assn., VFW, Sr. Housing Coun. Republican. Home: 11401 Apple Valley Rd Apple Valley CA 92308-7503 Office: Jess Ranch 11401 Apple Valley Rd Apple Valley CA 92308-7503

LEDFORD, JAMES C., JR., mayor. Mayor Palmdale, Calif. Address: 38300 N Sierra Hwy Palmdale CA 93550

LEDVOROWSKI, THOMAS EDMUND, secondary education educator; b. Milw., Feb. 11, 1960; s. Richard Joseph and Dorthy (Dymerski) L. BS in Math., Mercy Coll., Detroit, 1982; MS in Math. Edn., Purdue U., West Lafayette, Ind., 1985; postgrad., Cath. Theol. Union, Chgo., 1987-89, U. So. Calif. Grad. asst. Purdue U., West Lafayette, 1983-85; tchr. math. Roger Bacon High Sch., Cin., 1986-87; student mem. Franciscan Friars, Cin., 1987-89; tchr. math. Chino (Calif.) Unified Sch. Dist., 1985-86, 89-96, dept. chmn., 1993-96, swimming coach, 1991-93; secondary sch. math. mentor tchr., 1994-96; tchr. math. Roosevelt High Sch. N.E. Ind. Sch. Dist., San Antonio, 1996—; reader Advanced Placement Calculus Exam., 1995, 96, 97. Mem. Nat. Coun. Tchrs. Math., Am. Math. Assn. Roman Catholic. Home: 5539 Timber Canyon San Antonio TX 78250 Office: T Roosevelt High Sch 5110 Walzem San Antonio TX 78218

LEE, ADAM SIDNEY, lawyer; b. San Francisco, Nov. 20, 1968; s. Walter Sidney and Patricia Joan (Stethem) L. BA, San Francisco State U., 1991; JD, John F. Kennedy U., Walnut Creek, Calif., 1995; reader cert., Oxford (Eng.) U., 1994. Bar: Calif. 1995. Senate fellow Senator Bill Leonard, Calif. Senate, 1995—; cons. Calif. State Allocation Bd., 1996—; lectr. criminal justice San Francisco State U., 1996—; cons. in criminal procedure, edn., trade and fin., banking, vets. affairs State Senator Bill Leonard, Calif., 1996—. Vol. Make-A-Wish Found., Sacramento, 1995. Recipient Am. Jurisprudence award torts, N.Y.C., 1993, Am. Jurisprudence award legal writing, N.Y.C., 1994, award for outstanding legal scholarship West Pub., 1995; fellow Calif. State Senate. Mem. ABA, Calif. State Bar, Sacramento Bar Assn. Presbyterian. Home: 15 Manzanita Ave San Rafael CA 94901 Office: Office Senator Bill Leonard State Capitol Rm 3074 Sacramento CA 95814-4906

LEE, ALDORA G., social psychologist; b. Schenectady, N.Y.; d. Alois W. and M. Dorothy (Swigert) Graf. AB, Ind. U.; MA, Stanford U.; PhD, U. Colo. Dir. women studies Wash. State U., Pullman, 1976-78, dir. unit on aging, 1976-81; cons. in market research Syva, Palo Alto, Calif., 1982; staff market rsch. analyst Allstate Rsch. and Planning Ctr., Menlo Park, Calif., 1983—; rep. Wash. Assn. Gerontol. Edn., N.W. region rep. Nat. Women's Studies Assn., 1978-81. Contbr. articles to profl. jours. Mem. Menlo Park Libr. Commn., 1984-92, chmn., 1985-87; instr. Career Action Ctr., Palo Alto, 1984-87; Menlo Park rep. system adv. bd. Peninsula Libr. System, 1992—; mem. Allstate Found. Com., San Francisco Bay area, 1993-94, No. Calif., 1995—, mem. regional com., 1993—. Recipient Allstate Good Hands award for Cmty. Svc., 1994, 96. Mem. Am. Mktg. Assn., Am. Psychol. Soc., Am. Sociol. Assn., Western Psychol. Assn., SRI Organon Toastmasters (Toastmaster of Yr. 1989, Able Toastmaster, Competent Toastmaster, mentor GeoSpeakers 1994), Phi Beta Kappa, Sigma Xi.

LEE, BELLAVANCE, writer, publishing executive; b. Passaic, N.J.. BA in History and Social Studies, Boston U., 1971; MA in English, U. Utah, 1988. Copywriter The Tilo Co., Stratford, Conn., 1974-75; cmty. projects coord. Milford (Conn.) C. of C., 1975-76; advtsg. rep. Wood River Jour., Hailey, Idaho, 1977-79; tv corr. KMVT-Channel 11, Twin Falls, Idaho, 1979-81; newspaper corr. The Idaho Statesman, Boise, 1979-84; news dir. Channel 13, Sun Valley, Idaho, 1981-83; reporter, editor AP Wire Svc., Salt Lake City, 1984; mgr., writer, marketing professional, 1985-89; publicist Pioneer Theatre Co. U. Utah, Salt Lake City, 1989-92, writer, prodr. Reaching Out publ., 1992—; literary mag. aide Quarterly West, 1986-88; conf. asst. Writers at Work, 1987-88; instr. not for credit Lifelong Learning program U. Utah, 1996; invited reader City Arts Series Mount Tabor Ch., Nunmaker Place Westminster Coll., Salt Lake City, 1995. Contbr. short stories to The Event, Ellipsis, poems to Folio, Ellipsis, Private Eye, Wasatch Canyon Reporter. Vol. Sundance Film Festival, 1992—. Hon. mention Boston U. Alumni Poetry comptetion, 1989; winner Utah Poetry on the Bus competition, 1995. Home: 130 13th E # 803 Salt Lake City UT 84102

LEE, BLAINE NELSON, executive consultant, educator, author; b. Olympia, Wash., Apr. 3, 1946; s. Elwyn Earl and Thelma Marie (Woods) Reeder; m. Shawny Christian Lee; children: Blaine, Benjamin, Adam, Michal, Joseph, Joshua, Casey, Abraham, Eliza, Gabriel, Celeste. BS in Psychology, Brigham Young U., Provo, Utah, 1969, MS in Ednl. Psychology, 1972; PhD in Ednl. Psychology, U. Tex., 1982. Cert. ednl. specialist, secondary edn., ednl. adminstrn. Dir. instrnl. sys. USAF, San Antonio, 1972-75; assoc. prof. USAF Acad., Colorado Springs, Colo., 1975-78; edn. dir. Heritage Sch., Provo, Utah, 1978-81; asst. prof. Utah Valley State Coll., Orem, Utah, 1981-84; pres. Skills for Living, Salem, Utah, 1984-86; v.p. Covey Leadership Ctr., Provo, Utah, 1986—; ednl. cons. in field. Author: Affective Objectives, 1972, Personal Change, 1982, Stress Strategist, 1986, Principle Centered Leadership, 1990, Power Principle: Influence with Honor, 1997; contbr. articles to profl. jours. High councilman LDS Ch., mem. gen. bd., 1970-72; pres. Provo PTO. Named Outstanding Young Man of Am., U.S. C. of C., 1976, 84. Mem. APA, ASTD, Am. Mgmt. Assn., Nat. Spkrs. Assn., Phi Delta Kappa. Home: 10435 S 600 E Salem UT 84653-9389 Office: Covey Leadership Ctr 360 W 4800 N Provo UT 84604

LEE, CANDIE CHING WAH, retail executive; b. Hong Kong, British Crown Colony, June 17, 1950; came to U.S., 1973:; d. Willard W. and Yuk Ching (Yau) L. Student, Hong Kong Tech. Coll., Kowloon, 1968-70. Office mgr. Crown Enterprises, Ltd., Hong Kong, 1970-73; buyer, mgr. Hawaii Resort Industries, Inc., Honolulu, 1973-76, v.p., 1976-82; pres. Hawaii Resort Shops, Inc., Honolulu, 1983—. Mem. Am. Mgmt. Assn., Oahu Country Club. Republican. Office: Hawaii Resort Shops Inc 468 Ena Rd Honolulu HI 96815-1734

LEE, DAVID DEWITT, industrial hygienist; b. Detroit, Feb. 16, 1948; s. Floyd Herbert and Anne Theresa (Damask) L.; m. Lorraine Angeline Wozniak, Sept. 6, 1969; children: Jennifer, Mary, Brian, Jonathan, Sarah. BS Psychology, No. Mich. U., 1975; M Indsl Safety, U. Minn., 1988. Cert. indsl. hygienist, safety profl. Ops. foreman Nat. Steel Pellet Co., Keewatin, Minn., 1976-78, 84-86; safety engr. Hanna Mining Co. Agts., Hibbing, Minn., 1978-81, Butler Tacconite, Nashwauk, Minn., 1981-84; indsl. hygienist Sonora (Calif.) Mining Co., 1988-89, State Indsl. Ins. System, Reno, Nev., 1990-92; indsl. hygienist, safety specialist Univ./C.C. System Nev., Reno, 1992—. Accredited vis., vis. chmn. Mended Hearts, Inc., Reno, 1993-95. With USN, 1967-70, Vietnam. Recipient scholarship Semi-Conductor Safety Assn. Mem. Am. Indsl. Hygiene Assn., Am. Conf. of Govt. Indsl. Hygienist, Am. Acad. Indsl. Hygiene, Am. Bd. Indsl. Hygiene, Am. Soc. Safety Engrs. (chpt. sec. 1994—, chpt. pres.-elect 1995, pres. 1996), Bd. Cert. Indsl. Hygienist and Safety Profls. Republican. Roman Catholic. Office: U Nev Environ Health & Safety MS 328 Reno NV 89557

LEE, DOROTHY WONG, secondary art educator; b. L.A., Aug. 17, 1948; d. Leonard G.Y. and Ginger (Hom) Wong; m. Kenny Lee, Nov. 24, 1973; children: Brandon Joel, Brittany Jene. BA, UCLA, 1971; std. secondary tchg. credential, Calif. State U., L.A., 1973. Secondary art tchr., chmn. dept. art L.A. (Calif.) Unified Sch. Dist., 1973—; buyer, retailer Imperial Dragon Gifts, Inc., L.A., 1978-94. Recipient Tchg. award Otis Art Inst., L.A., 1992, Bravo award L.A. (Calif.) County Music Ctr., 1994. Mem. United Tchrs. L.A., Art Educators L.A., L.A. County Art Mus. Home: PO Box 29893 Los Angeles CA 90029-0893

LEE, EDMUND, photojournalist; b. San Francisco, Mar. 2, 1968; s. Jeffrey Kuenka and Maria Lai Ping (Chan) L. AS in Photography, City Coll. San Francisco, 1992; BA in Journalism, San Francisco State U., 1992-97. Photo editor/staff photographer The Guardsman, San Francisco, 1989-90; stringer photographer San Mateo (Calif.) Times, 1992-93, Petaluma (Calif.) Argus-Courier, 1992-94, Marin Ind. Jour., Novato, Calif., 1992-94, AP, San Francisco, 1992-94; photography intern Metro Newspaper Group, San Jose, Calif., 1994, staff photographer, 1994-95; staff photographer The Golden Gater, San Francisco, 1995-96; summer photography intern Austin Am.-Statesman, 1996. Recipient awards for photography. Mem. Asian Am. Journalists Assn., Soc. Profl. Journalists, Nat. Press Photographers Assn., Calif. Press Photographers Assn., San Francisco Bay Area Press Photographers Assn. Home: 7 Crestview Ave Daly City CA 94015-4502 Office: Metro Newspaper Group 245 Almendra Ave Los Gatos CA 95030-7210

LEE, ELIZABETH ANNE, marketing executive; b. Carbondale, Ill., Sept. 5, 1952; d. Kenneth O. and Velma Marquerite (Mizner) McGee; m. Steven Robin Lee, Mar. 27,1987; 1 child, Kelsey Erin. BS in Applied Sci., Miami U., 1974; MBA, St. Louis U., 1978. Staff supr. Southwestern Bell, St. Louis, 1978-80; mgr. market rsch. Angelica Uniform Group, St. Louis, 1980-83; sr. analyst consumer rsch. May Dept. Stores Co., St. Louis, 1983-84; v.p. Data Support Svcs., Inc., St. Louis, 1984-87; pres. Concours Rsch., Inc., St. Louis, 1987-89, also bd. dirs.; ptnr. Steve Lee & Assocs., 1994—; cons. Project Bus., St. Louis, 1983-84; mem. adj. faculty U. Mo., 1987—, Webster U., 1988—, Menlo Coll., 1995. Editor: Quantitative Models for Bus. Decisions (Kwak), 1978. Bd. dirs. The St. Louis Ballet, 1989-90. Fellow St. Louis U., 1977-78. Mem. BBB, Am. Mktg. Assn. Republican. Congregationalist. Office: 21550 Oxnard St Ste 300 Woodland Hills CA 91367

LEE, ELIZABETH TAN, mathematics educator; b. Singapore, July 7, 1944; came to U.S., 1962; d. Keng Huat and Siok Eng (Chan) Tan; m. David Oi Lee, Aug. 7, 1966 (div. Dec. 1994); 1 child, Andrea K.E. Lee-Wolf. BA, North Ctrl. Coll., Naperville, Ill., 1966; MA, U. N.Mex., 1981. Cert. tchr., N.Mex. Computer programmer Continental Casualty Co., Chgo., 1966; computer programmer, substitute tchr., math. tchr. Albuquerque Pub. Schs., 1967-72; tchr. math. Los Lunas (N.Mex.) H.S., 1977-78; tchr. math. and computer sci. Albuquerque Pub. Schs., 1978—. Republican. Methodist. Office: Cibola HS 1510 Ellison Dr NW Albuquerque NM 87114-5101

LEE, GEORGIA, archaeologist, editor, publisher; b. Alameda, Calif., Jan. 12, 1926. BA, Calif. Coll. Arts and Crafts, 1948; MA, U. Calif., 1978; PhD in Archaeology, UCLA, 1986. Cert. tchr., Calif. Editor, publisher Rapa Nui Jour., Los Osos, Calif., 1986—; rsch. assoc. UCLA, L.A., 1987-97; v.p. Easter Island Found., Houston, Tex., 1989—; rsch. assoc. Santa Barbara (Calif.) Mus. Natural History, 1990—; dir. U. Calif. Rsch. Expedition, Berkeley, Calif., 1981—; cons. BBC-Nova Film, Easter Island, Chile, 1987, World Monuments Fund, N.Y.C., 1988; lectr. Getty Conservation Inst. Author: (books) An Uncommon Guide to Easter Island, 1990, The Rock Art of Easter Island, 1992, Rapa Nui, 1995; editor Rapa Nui Jour., 1986—. Mem. Soc. for Am. Archaeology, Am. Rock Art Rsch. Assn., (v.p. 1980-82, nat. chmn. com. for conservation and preservation 1991-93, Wellmann award 1996). Office: Rapa Nui Jour PO Box 6774 Los Osos CA 93412

LEE, GILBERT BROOKS, retired ophthalmology engineer; b. Cohasset, Mass., Sept. 10, 1913; s. John Alden and Charlotte Louise (Brooks) L.; m. Marion Corinne Rapp, Mar. 7, 1943 (div. Jan. 1969); children: Thomas Stearns, Jane Stanton, Frederick Cabot, Gilbert Eliot Frazar. BA, Reed Coll., 1937; MA, New Sch. for Social Rsch., 1949. Asst. psychologist U.S. Naval Submarine Base Civil Svc., Psychophysics of Vision, New London, Conn., 1950-53; rsch. assoc. Project Mich., Vision Rsch. Labs., Willow Run, 1954-57; rsch. assoc. dept. ophthalmology U. Mich., Ann Arbor, 1958-72, sr. rsch. assoc., 1972-75, sr. engring. rsch. assoc. ophthalmology, 1975-82, part-time sr. engr. ophthalmology, 1982—; sec. internat. dept., 23d St. YMCA, N.Y.C.; cons. W.K. Kellogg Eye Ctr., Ann Arbor, 1968—. Local organizer, moderator (TV program) Union of Concerned Scientists' Internat. Satellite Symposium on Nuclear Arms Issues, 1986; producer (TV show) Steps for Peace, 1987; designer, builder portable tristimulus Colorimeter; (videotape) Pomerance Awards, UN.; broken lake ice rescue procedure rsch., by one person in a dry suit, all weather conditions, 1966, 89-93 (videotape). Precinct del. Dem. County Conv., Washtenaw County, 1970, 74; treas. Dem.

Club, Ann Arbor, Mich., 1971-72, 74-79; vice chmn. nuclear arms control com., 1979; chmn. Precinct Election Inspectors, 1968-75; scoutmaster Portland (Oreg.) area coun. Boy Scouts Am., 1932-39. Capt. AUS, 1942-46, 61-62. Mem. AAAS, Nat. Resources Def. Coun., Fedn. Am. Scientists, N.Y. Acad. Sci., Nation Assocs., ACLU, Sierra Club, Amnesty Internat. Home: 4131 E Pinchot Ave Phoenix AZ 85018-7115

LEE, GLENN RICHARD, medical administrator, educator; b. Ogden, Utah, May 18, 1932; s. Glenn Edwin and Thelma (Jensen) L.; m. Pamela Marjorie Ridd, July 18, 1969; children—Jennifer, Cynthia. B.S., U. Utah, 1953, M.D., 1956. Intern Boston City Hosp.-Harvard U., 1956-57, resident, 1957-58; clin. asso. Nat. Cancer Inst., NIH, 1958-60; postdoctoral fellow U. Utah, 1960-63; instr. U. Utah Coll. Medicine, 1963-64, asst. prof. internal medicine, 1964-68, assoc. prof., 1968-73, prof., 1973-96, assoc. dean for acad. affairs, 1973-76, dean, 1978-83, prof. emeritus, 1996—; chief of staff Salt Lake VA Med. Ctr., 1985-95. Author: (with others) Clinical Hematology, 9th edit, 1993; Contbr. (with others) numerous articles to profl. jours.; editorial bd.: (with others) Am. Jour. Hematology, 1976-79. Served with USPHS, 1958-60. Markle Found. scholar, 1965-70; Nat. Inst. Arthritis, Metabolic and Digestive Disease grantee, 1977-82. Mem. A.C.P., Am. Soc. Hematology, Am. Soc. Clin. Investigation, Western Assn. Physicians, Am. Inst. Nutrition. Mem. LDS Ch. Home and Office: 3781 Ruth Dr Salt Lake City UT 84124-2331

LEE, GRACE TZE, controller; b. Taipei, Republic of China, Aug. 11, 1953; came to U.S., 1974; d. Tang Chi and Ming (Shu) L. BA, Nat. Taipei U., 1974; BS, U. Nev., 1977; postgrad., UCLA, 1988. Fgn. currency specialist Deak-Perera Co., L.A., 1977-80; asst. mgr. Universal Supply Co., L.A., 1980; contr. AJR Electronics Inc., L.A., 1981-84; western zone asst. mgr. Samsung Electronics Co., L.A., 1984; contr. Gideon Nol Inc., L.A., 1985-87, James G. Wiley Co., L.A., 1987-91, Jetset Tours Inc. (N.Am.), L.A., 1991-95, DER Travel Inc., L.A., 1995-96, The Virtual Office, L.A., 1996—; with G.L. Fin. Svc., 1988—, Real Estate Investment Svc., 1988—, The Virtual Office, L.A., 1996—. Home: 23442 Batey Ave Harbor City CA 90710-1204

LEE, HO JOHN, electrical engineer; b. Boston, Nov. 4, 1962; s. Kwan Young and Kum Hwa (Yoo) L.; m. Insook Amy Jeon, May 8, 1993; 1 child, Emily Soohyun. BSEE, MSEE, MIT, 1985. Mem. tech. staff Hewlett Packard Labs., Palo Alto, Calif., 1983—, project leader, 1988-89; project mgr. Hewlett Packard Labs, Palo Alto, Calif., 1994-97; founder, pres. Tetra Systems Inc., Palo Alto, 1989-93; project mgr. HP Labs., Palo Alto, Calif., 1994-96; mgr. Internet imaging architectures HP Internet Tech. Group, Cupertino, Calif., 1997—; mem. faculty dept. elec. engring. Northwestern Poly. U., 1985-88. Author NewView image processing system, 1986; co-author FlashPix image format, 1996; Webmaster; patentee in field. Mem. IEEE, Assn. Computing Machinery, Internet Soc. (webmaster image hp com, 1996), Korean Am. Profl. Soc. (bd. dirs. 1992-95). Office: HP Internet Tech Group 11000 Wolfe Rd Cupertino CA 95014

LEE, JAMES GORDON, air force officer; b. Willimantic, Conn., Nov. 7, 1956; s. Jesse Richard and Mary Francis (Kelley) L.; m. Debevon Deneice Duncan, Aug. 15, 1980; 1 child, Shaun Duncan. BS in Computer Sci., N.Mex. State U., 1978; MA in Computer Resources, Webster U., 1985; MA in Airpower Studies, Air U., Maxwell AFB, Ala., 1993. Commd. 2d lt. USAF, advanced through grades to lt. col., 1994; space computer plans officer Hdqs. USAF Space Command, Colorado Springs, Colo., 1982-85; space weapons officer Hdqs. USAF, Washington, 1985-86; exch. officer Hdqs. U.S. Army, Washington, 1986-87; space and strategic def. analyst Hdqs. USAF, Washington, 1987-89; dir. systems and logistics 5 Def. Space Comm. Squadron, Woomera, South Australia, 1989-91; dep. chief space policy, doctrine and strategy Hdqs. Air Force Space Command, Colorado Springs, 1993-94, comdr. 4th space surveillance squadron, 1994-96, comdr. 614 space ops. squadron, 1996—. Author: Counter-Space Operations for Information Dominance, 1993. City councilman Woomera (South Australia) Bd., 1989-91; mem. com. Boy Scouts Am., 1992-96. Mem. Air Force Assn.

LEE, JAMES GYEONG-JIN, health facility administrator; b. Seoul, South Korea, Apr. 11, 1966; arrived in Brazil, 1969; came to U.S., 1988; s. Kiung and Deokye (Kim) L. BA, Sch. Bus. Adminstrn., Brazil, 1987; MPH, Loma Linda U., 1989, M Health Adminstrn., 1991. Adminstrv. resident Castle Med. Ctr., Kailua, Hawaii, 1990-91, dir. quality mgmt., 1993-94, adminstr. dir. quality and info. svcs., 1994-95, adminstrv. dir. mgmt. svcs., 1996—; asst. dir. for operational improvement Hinsdale (Ill.) Hosp., 1991-93; asst. to comml. dir. Pemalex Textile Mfrs., Sao Paulo, 1984-88; cons. Loma Linda (Calif.) U., 1989-90; presenter at confs. in field. Contbr. articles to profl. jours. Treas., sec. Internat. Assn. Temperance, Sao Paulo, 1986-88; mem. exec. com., pers. com. Ill. Conf. Seventh-day Adventists, Brookfield, Ill., 1992-93. Mem. Am. Coll. Healthcare Execs. (diplomate), Am. Soc. Quality Control, Healthcare Fin. Mgmt. Assn. Office: Castle Med Ctr 640 Ulukahiki St Kailua HI 96734-4454

LEE, JAMES JUI-CHANG, public relations executive; b. Taipei, Taiwan, Dec. 19, 1963; came to U.S., 1965; s. John C. and Nancy H. Lee. BS in Bus., U. So. Calif., 1987, BA in Journalism, 1987. Dep. campaign mgr. Calif. for Pete Wilson, San Diego, 1988; state press sec. U.S. Senator Pete Wilson, L.A., 1988-90; dep. press sec. Pete Wilson for Gov., L.A., 1990, Gov. Pete Wilson, Sacramento, Calif., 1990-92; Calif. press sec. Bush-Quayle '92, Sacramento, 1992; comms. dir. Calif. EPA, Sacramento, 1992-94; dir. Burson-Marsteller, L.A., 1994—. Mem. Young Execs. of Am., L.A. Jr. Chamber, Jr. Statesman Found. (bd. trustees 1996). Republican. Unitarian. Office: Burson-Marsteller 1800 Century Park E # 200 Los Angeles CA 90067

LEE, JAMES KING, technology corporation executive; b. Nashville, July 31, 1940; s. James Fitzhugh Lee and Lucille (Charlton) McGivney; m. Victoria Marie Marani, Sept. 4, 1971; children: Gina Victoria, Patrick Fitzhugh. BS, Calif. State U., Pomona, 1964; MBA, U. So. Calif., 1966. Prodn. and methods engring. foreman GM Corp., 1963-65; engring. adminstr. Douglas MSSD, Santa Monica, Calif., 1965-67; gen. mgr. mgmt. systems, computer tech. TRW Systems, Redondo Beach, Calif., 1967-68; v.p. corp. devel. DataStation Corp., L.A., 1968-69; v.p., gen. mgr. Aved Systems Group, L.A., 1969-70; mng. ptnr. Corp. Growth Cons., L.A., 1970-81; chmn., pres., CEO Fail-Safe Tech. Corp., L.A., 1981-93; pres., COO The Flood Group Inc., Torrance, Calif., 1994-96, pres., CEO, CyberSense Sys. Corp., 1996—. Author industry studies, 1973-79. Mem. L.A. Mayor's Cmty. Adv. Com., 1962-72, aerospace conversion task force L.A. County Econ. Devel. Commn., 1990-92; bd. dirs. USO Greater L.A., 1990—, v.p. personnel 1990-92, exec. v.p., 1992-93, pres. 1993-96; asst. adminstr. SBA, Washington, 1974; vice chmn. Traffic Commn., Rancho Palos Verdes, Calif., 1975-78; chmn. Citizens for Property Tax Relief, Palos Verdes, 1976-80; mem. Town Hall Calif. Recipient Golden Scissors award Calif. Taxpayers' Congress, 1978. Mem. So. Calif. Tech. Execs. Network, Am. Electronics Assn. (chmn. L.A. coun. 1987-88, vice chmn. 1986-87, nat. bd. dirs. 1986-89), Nat. Security Industries Assn. Republican. Baptist. Home: 28874 Crestridge Rd Palos Verdes Estates CA 90275-5063 Office: CyberSense Sys Corp 3521 Lomita Blvd Ste 201 Torrance CA 90505-5016

LEE, JAMES NORMAN, bioengineering researcher, educator; b. Santa Monica, Calif., Dec. 20, 1956; s. Robert Martin and Nila (Stubbs) L.; m. Carolyn Kim Bailey, Aug. 23, 1957; children: Bethany, Jessica, Christina. BA in Applied Physics, U. Utah, 1980, MS in Physics Instrumentation, 1982; PhD in Biomed. Engring., Duke U., 1986. Postdoc. fellow Duke U., Durham, N.C., 1986-88; rsch. asst. prof. Dept. Radiology U. Utah, Salt Lake City, 1988-93; adj. asst. prof. Dept. Bioengring. U. Utah, Salt Lake City, 1993—; reviewer small bus. innovation rsch. grants Dept. HHS, Washington, 1993—; prin. investigator The Whitaker Found., 1990-93, GE Med. Systems, 1993, NIH, 1993-94. Patentee in field of biomed. engring. instrumentation; contbr. articles to profl. jours. Mem. Soc. Magnetic Resonance Imaging, Soc. Magnetic Resonance in Medicine. Republican. Mem. Ch. Latter Day Sts. Office: U Utah Med Imaging Rsch Labs AC 213 Sch Medicine Salt Lake City UT 84108

LEE, JERRY CARLTON, university administrator; b. Roanoke, Va., Nov. 21, 1941; m. Joan Marie Leo; 1 child, Zan. BA, W.Va. Wesleyan Coll., 1963; postgrad., W.Va. U. Grad. Sch. Indsl. Relations, 1963-64, U. Balt. Sch. Law, 1967-69; MA, Va. Poly. Inst., 1975, EdD, 1977; LLD (hon.), Gallaudet U., 1986. Mgmt. trainee Gen. Motors Corp., 1964-65; v.p. adminstrn. Comml. Credit Indsl. Corp., Washington, 1965-71; dir. gen. services Gallaudet Coll., Washington, 1971-77, asst. v.p. bus. affairs, 1978-82, v.p. adminstrn. and bus., 1982-84; pres. Gallaudet U. (formerly Gallaudet Coll.), Washington, 1984-88, Nat. U., San Diego, 1989—. Hon. bd. dirs. D.C. Spl. Olympics; commn. in adminstrn. org. Rehab. Internat.; bd. dirs. People to People, Deafness Research Found., Am. Assn. Univ. Adminstrs., Am. Coun. on Edn. Commn. on Women in Higher Edn.; hon. advocacy bd. Nat. Capital Assn. Coop. Edn.; mem. Personnel Policies Forum Bur. Nat. Affairs. Served with USAR, 1966-72. Recipient Nat. Service award, Hon. Pres. award Council for Better Hearing and Speech, 1986, One-of-a-Kind award People-to-People, 1987, Advancement Human Rights & Fundamental Freedoms award UN, U.S.A., Disting. Alumni award Va. Poly. Inst., 1985, Pres.' award Gallaudet Coll. Alumni Assn., Gallaudet Community Relations award, U.S. Steel Found. Cost Reduction Incentive award Nat. Assn. Coll. and Univ. Bus. Officers, award Am. Athletic Assn. Deaf, 1987. Mem. Am. Assn. Univ. Adminstrs. (Eileen Tosney award 1987), Consortium of Univs. Washington Met. Area (exec. com.), Nat. Collegiate Athletic Assn. (pres.' commn.), Nat. Assn. Coll. Aux. Services (jour. adv. bd., journalism award), Alpha Sigma Pi (Man of Yr. award 1983-84). Lodge: Sertoma (life, found. nat. adv. com.). Office: Nat Univ 11255 N Torrey Pines Rd La Jolla CA 92037-1011

LEE, JOHN JIN, lawyer; b. Chgo., Oct. 20, 1948; s. Jim Soon and Fay Yown (Young) L.; m. Jamie Pearl Eng, Apr. 30, 1983. BA magna cum laude, Rice U., 1971; JD, Stanford U., 1975; MBA, 1975. Bar: Calif. 1976. Assoc. atty. Manatt Phelps & Rothenberg, L.A., 1976-77; asst. counsel Wells Fargo Bank N.A., San Francisco, 1977-79, counsel, 1979-80, v.p., sr. counsel, 1980, v.p., mng. sr. counsel, 1981—; mem. governing com. Conf. on Consumer Fin. Law, 1989-93. Bd. dirs. Asian Bus. League of San Francisco, 1981—, gen. counsel, 1981. Fellow Am. Coll. Consumer Fin. Svcs. Attys., Inc., (bd. regents 1995—), mem. ABA (chmn. subcom. on housing fin., com. on consumer fin. svcs., bus. law sect. 1983-90, vice chmn. on subcom. securities products, com. on consumer fin. svcs. bus. law sect. 1993-95, chmn. subcom. on securities products, com. on consumer fin. svcs., bus. law sect. 1995-96, chmn. subcom. on electronic banking, com. on consumer fin. svcs., bus. law sect. 1996—), Consumer Bankers Assn. (lawyers com.), Soc. Physics Students, Stanford Asian-Pacific Am. Alumni/ae Club (bd. dirs. 1989-93, v.p. 1989-91). Democrat. Baptist. Office: Wells Fargo Bank NA Legal Dept 111 Sutter St San Francisco CA 94104-4504

LEE, JOLI FAY EATON, elementary education educator; b. Holdredge, Nebr., Sept. 24, 1951; d. Ray Lee and Lois Ileen (Willoughby) Larkins; m. James Edward Eaton, Aug. 16, 1969 (div. Jan. 1979); children: Threva, James, Beth; m. Chris Lee, Aug. 13, 1991; stepchildren: Michael Lee, Robyn Lee. BS in Elem. Edn., N.Mex. State U., Las Cruces, 1980, MA in Curriculum and Instruction, 1984. Cert. elem. tchr., N.Mex. Tchr. elem. Alamogordo (N.Mex.) Pub. Schs., 1980—; co-chmn. City Elem. Sci. Fair, Alamogordo, 1989-90, chmn., 1990-92; with Summer Sci. Pilot Program, 1992-94. Contbr. articles to profl. jours. Nat. conv. co-chmn. Nat. Speleological Soc., Tularosa, N.Mex., 1986; joint venturer Cave Rsch. Found., 1983—; person. dir., Guadalupe Area Cave Rsch. Found., N.Mex., 1987-90; del. Cave Exploration Del. to People's Republic of China, 1993. Crimson scholar N.Mex. State U., 1980. Mem. NEA, Nat. Speleological Soc. (sec. Southwestern region 1984, 91-92, 93, Southwestern regional chmn. 1985-86). Republican. Episcopalian. Home: 1405 4th St Tularosa NM 88352-2003 Office: North Elem Sch 1300 Florida Alamogordo NM 88310-6331

LEE, JONG HYUK, accountant; b. Seoul, Korea, May 6, 1941; s. Jung Bo and Wol Sun L. BS Han Yang U., Seoul, Korea, 1964, BA, Sonoma State U. Rohnert Park, Calif., 1971; MBA in Taxation, Golden Gate U., San Francisco, 1976. CPA Calif. m. Easter Kim Jan. 24, 1970. Cost Acct., internal auditor Foremost-McKesson Co., San Francisco, 1971-74, sr. acct. clerk, Wong, Foulkes & Barbieri, CPAs. Oakland , Calif., 1974-77, pres. J.H. Lee Accountancy Corp., Oakland, 1977-89, 95—, Bay Cities Restaurants, Inc., Wendy 's Franchise, 1989-94; Instr., Armstrong Coll., Berkeley, Calif., 1977-78; lectr. acctg., dir. sch. of bus., The U.S. Korea Bus. Inst., San Francisco State U.; adv. bd. mem. Ctr. or Korean Studies, Insts. of East Asian Studies U. Calif.,Berkely; dir. United Labor Bank, Oakland bd. dirs. Korean residents Assn., 1974, Multi-svc. Ctr. for Koreans, 1979, BetterBus. Bur., 1984-87; chmn. cacus Calif.-Nev. ann. conf. United Meth Ch., 1977; commr. Calif. State Office Econ. Opportunity, 1982-86; pres. Korean Am. Dem. Network; mem. Dem. Nat. Fin. Coun.; regional chmn. Adv. Coun. on Peaceful Unification Policy, Republic of Korea; Commr. Asian Art Mus. San Francisco, 1988-91, Commr. Oakland Cmty. and Econ. Devel. 1997; bd., dir., East Bay Asian Local Devel. Corp with Korean Marine Corps, 1961-64; 1st lt. Calif. State Mil. Res. Mem. Am. Inst. CPAs. Nat. Assn. Asian Am. CPAs (bd. dir.), Am. Acctg. Assn., Nat. Assn. Accts., Internat Found. Employee Benifit Plans, Calif. Soc. CPAs, Oakland C. of C., Korean Am. C. of C. (pres. Pacific North Coast Rotary. Democrat. Author tax and bus. column Korea Times, 1980. Home: 180 Firestone Dr Walnut Creek CA 94598-3645 Office: 369 13th St Oakland CA 94612-2636

LEE, JOYCE ANN, administrative assistant; b. Safford, Ariz., Sept. 18, 1942; d. Roy and Minnie R. (Mobley) Brewer; m. Eugene W. Gaddy Jr., Mar. 16, 1970 (div. 1985); children: Carol, Kevin, Aaron; m. Glenn A. Lee, Oct. 16, 1992. AA, Ea. Ariz. Coll., 1980, AAS, 1993; BA in Mgmt., U. Phoenix, 1995. Dispatcher Mohave County Sheriff's Office, Kingman, Ariz., 1969-74; sec. Globe (Ariz.) Mobile Home Sales, 1975-83; data entry supr. SMC & Assocs., Globe, 1985-88; tax preparer H&R Block Co., Globe, 1992; adminstrv. asst. Am. Pub. Co., Globe, 1994—; instr. computer, bus. classes Ea. Ariz. Coll. Gila Pueblo campus, Globe, 1996—. Girls camp dir. LDS Ch., Globe, 1985-90; mem. com. Boy Scouts Am., Globe. Mem. NAFE, Phi Theta Kappa. Democrat. Home: Rt 1 CC 179 Globe AZ 85501 Office: Ea Ariz Coll Gila Pueblo Campus Globe AZ 85501-1416

LEE, KAI-FU, computer company executive; b. Taipei, Taiwan, Dec. 3, 1961; came to the U.S., 1973; s. Tien-Min and Yah-Ching (Wong) L.; m. Shen-Ling Hsieh, Aug. 6, 1983; 1 child, Jennifer Lee. BA in Computer Sci. summa cum laude, Columbia U., 1983; PhD in Computer Sci., Carnegie Mellon U., Pitts., 1988. Rsch. scientist, asst. prof. Sch. Computer Sci. Carnegie Mellon U., Pitts., 1988-90; prin. speech scientist spl. projects Apple Computer, Inc., Cupertino, Calif., 1990-91, mgr. speech and lang. lab., advanced tech. group, 1991-93, dir. interactive media lab., advanced tech. group, 1993-94, v.p. interactive media group, 1995-96; v.p., gen. mgr. Web Products divsn. Silicon Graphics, Inc., 1996—; adj. prof. Carnegie Mellon U. Sch. Computer Sci., 1990—; keynote spkr. Eurospeech Conf., Paris, 1989, Berlin, 1993, AVIOS Mtg., San Jose, Calif., 1993; lectr. in field; cons. to major corps. Reviewer, numerous profl. jours., book proposals and grant proposals in field; author: Automatic Speech Recognition: The Development of the SPHINX System, 1989, (with A.H. Waibel) Readings in Speech Recognition, 1990; contbr. chpt. to Recent Progress in Speech Signal Processing, 1990, Recent Advances in Speech Understanding and Dialog Systems, 1987; contbr. numerous articles, conf. papers and tech. reports to profl. publs. NSF grad. fellow, 1983-86; recipient paper award IEEE Signal Processing Soc., 1991, Most Innovative Sci. Innovation award Bus. Week, 1988; named Othello champion N.Am. Computer, 1989. Mem. IEEE (reviewer procs. and transactions, mem. speech tech. com. 1991-95, IEEE ICASSP Conf. organizing com. 1992, organizing com. workshop on speech recognition 1991), Acoustical Soc. Am. (reviewer jour.), DARPA (coord. com. spoken lang. 1989=90, lang. and speech workshop com. 1991, chair speech session workshop on speech and lang. 1989), Chinese Software Profl. Assn. (adv. com. 1993—); Sigma Xi, Phi Beta Kappa.

LEE, KANG S., artist, educator; b. Seoul, Korea, June 5, 1937; came to U.S., 1967; d. Kee Young and Young Sook (Choy) L.; m. Frank James Sheppard (dec. 1990). BFA, Univ. Hong Ik, Seoul, 1963; postgrad., Univ. Colo., 1968-70; MA, Univ. Phoenix, 1989. Cert. tchr. Mgr. advt., presentation J.C. Penney, Colorado Springs, 1970-79; dist. merchandise presentation mgr. J.C. Penney, Denver, 1980-85; prof. Pikes Peak C.C., Colorado Springs, 1991—; prof. Univ. Colo., Colorado Springs, 1992—. Exhibited in group shows Nat. Art Exhibition, Seoul, 1962-66 (Creative Excellence awards); also one-woman shows. Judge mktg. and distributive edn. Colo. and Nat., 1975-86; v.p. Friendship Force Internat., 1990—; coord. Internat. Cultural Celebration, Colorado Springs, 1993-95; mem. Common Ground Arts and Cultural, Colorado Springs, 1994—, sr. adv. com. Colorado Springs, 1995—; deacon First Presbyn. Ch., Colorado Springs. Recipient 6 Corporation awards, 1974-79. Republican. Home: 525 Quebec Circle Colorado Springs CO 80911

LEE, KENNETH, secondary education educator. Elem. tchr. Highlands Intermediate Sch., Pearl City, Hawaii. Recipient Tchr. Excellence award Internat. Tech. Edn. Assn., Hawaii, 1992. Office: Highlands Intermediate Sch 1460 Hoolaulea St Pearl City HI 96782-2139

LEE, KERRY YOUNGAE, school program director; b. Seoul, Korea, Sept. 15, 1957; came to U.S., 1976; d. Yong Sun and Seung Ok (Park) Kim; m. Jonathan Jonghon Lee, July 9, 1989; children: Christopher, Benjamin. BA, U. Calif., Irvine, 1981; MA, U. So. Calif., 1986, EdD, 1991. Substitute tchr. Montebello (Calif.) Unified Sch. Dist., 1981-82; bilingual tchr. L.A. Unified Sch. Dist., 1982-91; dir. Torrance (Calif.) Unified Sch. Dist., 1991—. Grantee L.A. Partnership, 1985. Mem. Calif. Assn. Bilingual Educators. Presbyterian. Home: 10009 Karmont Ave South Gate CA 90280

LEE, LILA JUNE, historical society officer, library director; b. Ukiah, Calif., July 12, 1923; d. Arthur L. and Leila Edna (Rose) Romer; m. Dale R. Laney, May 1, 1944 (div. Sept. 1952); m. Robert James Lee, Apr. 16, 1955; children: Arthur John, Margarett June. Officer Mendocino County Hist. Soc., Ukiah, 1960-95; libr. dir. Held Poage Libr., Ukiah, 1970—. Mem. conf. of Calif. Hist. Soc. (regional v.p. 1980—), Mendocino County Hist. Soc. (v.p., treas., fin. sec.). Republican. Presbyterian. Office: Mendocino County Hist Soc 603 W Perkins St Ukiah CA 95482-4726

LEE, LILY KIANG, scientific research company executive; b. Shanghai, China, Nov. 23, 1946; came to U.S., 1967, naturalized, 1974; d. Chi-Wu and An-Teh (Shih) Kiang; m. Robert Edward Lee; children: Jeffrey Anthony, Michelle Adrienne, Stephanie Amanda, Christina Alison. BS, Nat. Cheng-Chi U., 1967; MBA, Golden Gate U., San Francisco, 1969. Acct., then acctg. supr. Am. Data Systems, Inc., Canoga Park, Calif., 1969-73; sr. acct. Pertec Peripheral Equipment div. Pertec Corp., Chatsworth, Calif., 1973-76; mgr. fin. planning and acctg., then mgr. fin. planning, program and internal control Sci. Ctr. div. Rockwell Internat., Thousand Oaks, Calif., 1976—. Mem. NAFE, Am. Mgmt. Assn., Nat. Mgmt. Assn., Nat. Property Mgrs. Assn. Republican. Baptist. Office: Rockwell Sci Ctr PO Box 1085 1049 Camino Dos Rios Thousand Oaks CA 91358

LEE, LILY SHINY, medical consultant; b. Taipei, Taiwan, July 4, 1960; came to U.S., 1978; d. Duke Dar-Jin and Dorra Ping-Juan (Chang) L.; m. Li Chen, Jan. 5, 1984; children: Solomon L., Annabelle Clair. MPH in Health Edn. Adminstrn., Loma Linda U., 1981; PhD in Hosp. Adminstrn., Keingston U., 1983; D of Clin. Hypnotherapy, Am. Inst. Hypnotherapy, 1996. RN; cert. clin. hypnotherapist, nursing adminstr., nursing instr. Health educator Taiwan Adventist Hosp., Taipei, 1977-78; health edn. specialist Sickle Cell Orgn., Riverside, Calif., 1981-83; staff nurse Gen. Med. Ctr., Orange, Calif., 1983-89; hosp. auditor FHP, Long Beach, Calif., 1984-89; instr. nursing Concorde Career Inst., Anaheim, Calif., 1994—; svc. specialist MetraHealth, Long Beach, 1989—. Author: Nclex Review, 1996. Mem. Med. Auditor Assn. (bd. dirs. 1987-96). Office: Shiny Transformation Ctr PO Box 1993 West Covina CA 91793

LEE, LONG CHI, electrical engineering and chemistry educator; b. Kaohsiung, Taiwan, Oct. 19, 1940; came to U.S., 1965; s. Chin Lai Lee and Wen Wang; m. Laura Meichau Cheng, Dec. 1, 1967 (dec. Dec. 1988); children: Gloria, Thomas; m. Masako Suto, Jan. 6, 1990 (dec. July 1996); m. Linda L. Chang, Apr. 8, 1997. BS in Physics, Taiwan Normal U., Taiwan, 1964; MA in Physics, U. So. Calif., L.A., 1967, PhD in Physics, 1971. Rsch. staff U. So. Calif., L.A., 1971-77; physicist SRI Internat., Menlo Park, Calif., 1977-79, sr. physicist, 1979-81; prof. elec. engring. San Diego State U., 1982—, adj. prof. chemistry, 1986—; adj. asst. prof. U. So. Calif., L.A., 1977; chmn. bd. Fiber Does, Inc., 1994—, Superior Evaporants, Inc., 1994—; bd. dirs. Genix, Biotech, Inc. Contbr. papers to profl. jours. Pres. Taiwanese Cultural Assn. in San Diego, 1983, 93. Rsch. grantee NSF, 1980-94, NASA, 1979-94, Air Force Office Sci. Rsch., 1980-89, Naval Rsch. Office, 1986-89. Mem. IEEE, Am. Phys. Soc., Am. Geophys. Union, Inter-Am. Photochem. Soc., Formesan Assn. for Pub. Affairs (pres. San Diego chpt. 1990-91), Taiwanese-Am. Investment Club (pres. 1995-96). Office: San Diego State U Dept Elec & Computer Engring San Diego CA 92182

LEE, LORRIN L., marketing executive, architect, designer, author, speaker; b. Honolulu, July 22, 1941; s. Bernard Chong and Betty (Lum) L.; m. Nina Christine Fedoroscko, June 10, 1981. BArch, U. Mich., 1970; MBA, Columbia Pacific U., 1981, PhD in Psychology, 1981. Registered arch., Hawaii. Arch. Clifford Young AIA, Honolulu, 1971-72, Aotani & Oka AIA, Honolulu, 1972-74, Geoffrey Fairfax FAIA, Honolulu, 1974-76; seminar leader Lorrin Lee Program, Honolulu, 1976-81; star grand master coord. Enhance Corp., 1981-83; 5-diamond supr. Herbalife Internat., L.A., 1984-85, mem. global expansion team, 1993—; presdl. dir. Uni-Vite Internat., San Diego, 1989-92; rep. Internat. Pen Friends, 1995—; mgr. Cyber Media Sales, 1996 . Author: Here is Genius, 1980. Editor Honolulu Chinese Jaycees, Honolulu, 1972, v.p., 1983; active Makiki Cmty. Ctr., Honolulu, 1974. 1st lt. U.S. Army, 1967-70, Okinawa. Recipient Braun-Knect-Heimann award, 1959, 1st prize in design Kidjel Cali-Pro Internat., 1975, Kitchen Design award Sub-zero Contest, 1994; named Honolulu Chinese Jaycee of Yr., Honolulu Chinese Jaycees, 1973. Mem. Nature Conservancy, Sierra Club. Office: 2357 S Beretania St # 750 Honolulu HI 96826-1413

LEE, LOUIS, II, security services company executive; b. Phila., Jan. 18, 1956; s. Louis I and Lucille (Bell) L.; m. Kare Jones, Nov. 23, 1978 (dec. June 1984); children: Louis III, Aaron, Akeem Ngozi, Akeem Ngozi. AD, L.A. City Coll., 1982; BA, U. So. Claif., 1986. Sch. counselor La Canada (Calif.) Sch. Dist., 1986-87; instr. Barclay Adult Coll., L.A., 1987-90; ops. mgr. Falcon Internat. Security, L.A., 1990-93; co-owner N.G.L. Security Svcs., Inglewood, Calif., 1993—; mem. adv. bd. L.A. City Coll., 1989—. Scoutmaster Boy Scouts Am., L.A., 1985-86. Ernie Freeman scholar, 1982. Mem. NRA, Calif. Alliance of Lic. Security and Guard Svcs., Guard Svc. Assn., Epsilon Alpha Gamma. Republican. Christian. Home: 2621 Pauline St West Covina CA 91792-2617 Office: NGL Security Svc 111 N La Brea Ave Ste 408 Inglewood CA 90301-4604

LEE, MARGARET ANNE, social worker, psychotherapist; b. Scribner, Nebr., Nov. 23, 1930; d. William Christian and Caroline Bertha (Benner) Joens; m. Robert Kelly Lee, May 21, 1950 (div. 1972); children: Lawrence Robert, James Kelly, Daniel Richard. AA, Napa Coll., 1949; student, U. Calif., Berkeley, 1949-50; BA, Calif. State Coll., Sonoma, 1975; MSW, Calif. State U., Sacramento, 1977. Diplomate clin. social worker; lic. clin. social worker, Calif.; lic. marriage and family counselor, Calif.; tchr. Columnist, stringer Napa (Calif.) Register, 1946-50; eligibility worker, supr. Napa County Dept. Social Services, 1968-75; instr. Napa Valley Community Coll., 1978-83; practice psychotherapy Napa, 1977—; oral commr. Calif. Dept. Consumer Affairs, Bd. Behavioral Sci., 1984—; bd. dirs. Project Access, 1978-79. Trustee Napa Valley C.C., 1983—, v.p. bd., 1984-85, pres. bd., 1986, 90, 95, clk., 1988-89; bd. dirs. Napa County Coun. Econ. Opportunity, 1984-85, Napa chpt. March of Dimes, 1957-71, Mental Health Assn. Napa County, 1983-87; vice chmn. edn. com. Calif. C.C. Trustees, 1987-88, chmn. edn. com., 1988-89, legis. com., 1985-87, bd. dirs., 1989—, 2d v.p., 1991, 1st v.p., 1992, pres., 1993; mem. student equity rev. group Calif. C.C. Chancellors, 1992; bd. dirs. C.C. League Calif., 1992-95, 1st v.p., 1992. Recipient Fresh Start award Self mag., award Congl. Caucus on Women's Issues, 1984; named Woman of distinction, soroptimist Internat., 1997. Mem. NASW, Calif. Elected Women's Assn. Edn. and Rsch. Democrat. Lutheran. Office: 1100 Trancas St Napa CA 94558-2908 *Personal philosophy: I believe in treating people as I would like to be treated - with dignity and respect. My attitude toward life has been "Of course you can."*

LEE, MARTHA, artist, writer; b. Chehalis, Wash., Aug. 23, 1946; d. William Robert and Phyllis Ann (Herzog) L.; m. Peter Reynolds Lockwood, Jan. 25, 1974 (div. 1982). BA in English Lit., U. Wash., 1968; student, Factory of Visual Art, 1980-82. Reporter Seattle Post-Intelligencer, 1970; personnel counselor Theresa Snow Employment, 1971-72; receptionist Northwest Kidney Ctr., 1972-73; proprietress The Reliquary, 1974-77; travel agt. Cathay Express, 1977-79; artist, 1980—; represented by Ricciardi Gallery, Astoria, Oreg., WhiteBird Gallery, Cannon Beach, Oreg., Campiche Studios, Seaview, Wash. Painter various oil paintings; exhibitor group and one-person shows. Home and Studio: 24309 Pacific Way Ocean Park WA 98640-3839

LEE, MICHAEL ANTHONY, cardiologist, electrophysiologist; b. Tucson, Jan. 6, 1954; s. Tony S.B. and Bella (Wong) L.; m. Mei-Gee Chang, June 1, 1980; children: Michael Jr., Andrew. BS in Biology, MIT, 1976; MD, U. Calif., San Francisco, 1980. Diplomate Am. Bd. Internal Medicine, Nat. Bd. Med. Examiners; bd. cert. cardiology and electrophysiology. Intern V.A. Wadsworth Med. Ctr., L.A., 1980-81; resident U. Calif., San Francisco, 1981-83; clin. instr. Georgetown U., Washington, 1984-86; cardiology fellow U. Ariz. Med. Ctr., Tucson, 1986-88; cardiac electrophysiology fellow U. Calif., San Francisco, 1988-90, asst. clin. prof. medicine, 1990-91; co-dir. East Bay Electrophysiology and Arrhythmia Ctr., Oakland, 1991—. Contbr. articles to profl. jours. Fellow Lincoln Found., 1975, NIH, 1983-86; grantee Am. Heart Assn., 1987-88. Mem. AMA, Am. Heart Assn., Alameda/Contra Costa Med. Assn., N.Am. Soc. Pacing and Electrophysiology, Cardiac Electrophysiology Soc., N.Am. Soc. Pacing and Electrophysiology. Republican. Office: E Bay Arrhythmia & Electrophys Ctr 365 Hawthorne Ave Ste 201 Oakland CA 94609-3114

LEE, MICHAEL ERIC, editor, designer; b. Eugene, Ore., Apr. 28, 1959; s. M. James and Aileen May (Kronquist) L. BA in Journalism, U. Ore., 1981, MA in Philosophy, 1991. News editor News Register, McMinnville, Ore., 1981-83; from morning music host to devel. dir. KWAX-FM, Eugene, 1985-90; from assoc. editor to editor Ore. Quarterly, Eugene, 1990-95; editor, designer Emergency Horse Creative Svcs., Eugene, 1995—; pub. Intangible Pubs., Eugene, 1993—. Office: Emergency Horse Creative Svcs Ste 200 1430 Willamette Eugene OR 97401

LEE, MURLIN E., program manager; b. Crescent City, Calif., Jan. 4, 1957; s. George Lee and Ida Burl (Wilson) M.; m. Jeanine Marie Metcalfe, Apr. 13, 1985; children: Kimberly, Kristen, Gina. BS in Bus. Adminstrn., Calif. Poly. U., Pomona, 1981; MS in Software Engring., Nat. U., San Jose, Calif., 1988. Mgr. George M. Lee Enterprises Inc., Crescent City, Calif., 1979-80, Wells Aviation, Ontario, Calif., 1980-81, Bard Software, San Jose, Calif., 1982-84; software engr. Litton Applied Techology, San Jose, 1984-89; program mgr. Condor Systems, Inc., San Jose, 1989-95; tech. mktg. staff Aspect Devel. Inc., Mountain View, Calif., 1995—. Republican. Home: 4081 Will Rogers Dr San Jose CA 95117-2730 Office: Aspect Development Inc 1300 Charleston St Mountain View CA 94043

LEE, NANCY JANE MCCLEARY, American studies educator; b. Indpls., Jan. 21, 1951; d. John Albert and Sue Jane (Lapping) McCleary; m. Thomas Eugene Lee, Dec. 30, 1971; children: Bryan Thomas Stephen, Dustin David Adam, Travis Scott James. Student, U. Calif., Santa Barbara, 1969-70, L.A. Pierce Coll., 1970, 71; BA in History, English and Edn., Adams State Coll., 1974; MA in History, Calif. State U., Northridge, 1979; postgrad., Calif. Luth. U., U. Calif., Santa Barbara, LaVerne Coll. Cert. secondary edn. tchr. Substitute tchr. Conejo Unified Sch., 1975-78; home tchr., 1977; tchr. Simi Valley H.S., 1978-90, Apollo H.S., 1990—; tchr./trainer curriculum program Simi Valley Unified Sch. Dist., 1990—, facilitator student support groups, 1984—, faculty senate, acad. standards com., sch. site coun.; sch. site coun. Apollo H.S., rep. dist. curriculum coun., 1990—. Mem. adv. bd. Scholastic Search mag., 1993-95. Active polit. elections and campaigns. Mem. NEA, Calif. Tchrs. Assn., Calif. Edn. Assn., Calif. Assn. Dirs. Activities, Nat. Coun. for Social Studies, Nat. Coun. for Tchrs. English, Calif. Continuing Edn. Assn., Simi Educators Assn. (rep. coun., exec. bd. dirs.). Democrat. Home: 3093 Cobb Cir Simi Valley CA 93065-5261 Office: Apollo H S 3150 School St Simi Valley CA 93065-3967

LEE, OLIVER MINSEEM, political science educator; b. Shanghai, Dec. 7, 1927; came to U.S., 1946; s. Ginffa and Gerta (Scheuermann) L.; m. May Yee Lee, July 9, 1950; children: Vivien, Steven, Anthony. AB, Harvard Coll., 1951; MA, U. Chgo., 1955, PhD, 1962. Intelligence analyst U.S. Army Res., Chgo., 1957-58; instr. govt. and politics U. Md., College Park, 1958-62; Far Eastern analyst Legis. Reference Svc., Libr. Congress, Washington, 1962-63; asst. prof. U. Hawaii, Honolulu, 1963-73, assoc. prof. polit. sci., 1973—. Candidate for U.S. Senate, Peace and Freedom party, Hawaii, 1968. Mem. Harvard Club Hawaii, U. Chgo. Club Honolulu. Home: 690 Hao St Honolulu HI 96821-1647 Office: U Hawaii at Manoa Dept Polit Sci 2424 Maile Way Honolulu HI 96822-2223

LEE, PALI JAE (POLLY JAE STEAD LEE), retired librarian, writer; b. Nov. 26, 1929; d. Jonathan Everett Wheeler and Ona Katherine (Grunder) Stead; m. Richard H.W. Lee, Apr. 7, 1945 (div. 1978); children: Catherine Lani Kain, Karin Lee Robinson, Ona G., Laurie Brett, Robin Louise Lee Halbert; m. John K. Willis, 1979 (dec. 1994). Student, U. Hawaii, 1944-46, Mich. State, 1961-64. Cataloguer and processor U.S. Army Air Force, 1945-46; with U.S. Weather Bur. Film Library, New Orleans, 1948-50, FBI, Wright-Patterson AFB, Dayton, Ohio, 1952, Ohio Wholesale Winedealers, Columbus, Ohio, 1956-58, Coll. Engring., Ohio State U., Columbus, 1959; writer tech. manual Annie Whittenmeyer Home, Davenport, Iowa, 1960; with Grand Rapids (Mich.) Pub. Library, 1961-62; dir. Waterford (Mich.) Twp. Libraries, 1962-64; acquisition librarian Pontiac (Mich.) Pub. Libraries, 1965-71, dir. East Side br., 1971-73; librarian Bishop Mus., Honolulu, 1975-83; pub. Night Rainbow Pub., Honolulu, 1984—. Author: Mary Dyer, Child of Light, 1973, Giant: Pictorial History of the Human Colossus, 1973, History of Change: Kaneohe Bay Area, 1976, English edit., 1983, Na Po Makole-Tales of the Night Rainbow, 1981, rev. edit., 1988, Mo'olelo O Na Pohukaina, 1983, Ka Ipu Kukui, 1994; contbr. articles to profl. jours. Chmn. Oakland County br. Multiple Sclerosis Soc., 1972-73, co-chmn. Pontiac com. of Mich. area bd., 1972-73; sec. Ohana o Kokua, 1979-83, Paia-Willis Ohana, 1982-91, Ohana Kame'ekua, 1988-91; bd. dirs. Detroit Multiple Sclerosis Soc., 1971; mem. Mich. area bd. Am. Friends Svc. com., 1961-69; mem. consumer adv. bd. Libr. for Blind and Physically Handicapped, Honolulu, 1991-96; pres. consumer 55 plus bd. Honolulu Ctr. for Ind. Living, 1990-94, pres., 1995-96; pres. Honolulu chpt. Nat. Fedn. of Blind, 1991-94, 1st v.p. #93 state affiliate, 1991-94, editor Na Na Maka Aloha newsletter, 1990-94; 1st v.p. Hawaii chpt. Talking Book Readers Club, 1994-95, pres., 1996. Recipient Mother of the Yr. award Quad City Bus. Men, 1960, Bowl of Light award Hawaiian Community of Hawaii, 1989. Mem. Internat. Platform Assn., Soc. Friends. Office: PO Box 10706 Honolulu HI 96816-0706

LEE, PAMELA ANNE, accountant, business analyst; b. San Francisco, May 30, 1960; d. Larry D. and Alice Mary (Reece) L. BBA, San Francisco State U., 1981. CPA, Calif. Typist, bookkeeper, tax acct. James G. Woo, CPA, San Francisco, 1979-85; tutor bus. math. and statistics San Francisco State U., 1979-80; teller to ops. officer Gibraltar Savs. and Loan, San Francisco, 1978-81; sr. acct. Price Waterhouse, San Francisco, 1981-86; corp. acctg. mgr. First Nationwide Bank, Daly City, Calif., 1986-89, v.p., 1989-91, v.p., project mgr., 1991-92, sr. conversion and bus. analyst, 1992-93; sr. bus. analyst, asst. v.p. Bank of Am., 1993-96, sr. bus. analyst, v.p. Bank of Am., 1996—; acctg. cons. New Performance Gallery, San Francisco, 1985, San Francisco Chamber Orch., 1986. Founding mem., chair bd. trustees Asian Acctg. Students Career Day, 1988-89. Mem. NAFE, Am. Inst. CPA's, Calif. Soc. CPA's, Nat. Assn. Asian-Am. CPA's (bd. dirs. 1986, news editor 1987, pres. 1988). Republican. Avocations: reading, music, travel, personal computing, needlework. Office: 50 California St Fl 11 San Francisco CA 94111-4624 *Personal philosophy: You make your own future.*

LEE, PAUL PAK-HING, artist, educator; b. Hong Kong, July 2, 1962; came to U.S., 1982; BA, Hamilton Coll., 1985; MFA, Cranbrook Acad. Art, Bloomfield Hills, Mich., 1987. Vis. instr. Cleve. Inst. Art, 1987-88; asst. prof. San Antonio Art Inst., 1988-89; asst. prof. Wash. State U., Pullman, 1989-95, assoc. prof., 1995—. Solo exhbns. include San Antonio Art Inst., 1988, Hartung Theatre, U. Idaho, Moscow, 1990, Columbia Arts Ctr., Vancouver, Wash., 1991, Greg Kucera Gallery, Seattle, 1994; two-person exhbns. include Johnson Bldg., Clinton, N.Y., 1984, Pontiac (Mich.) Art Ctr., 1987, S p a c e s Gallery, Cleve., 1989; group exhbns. include Munson Williams Proctor Inst., Utica, N.Y., 1985, Muhlenberg Coll., Pa., 1986, Emerson Gallery, Clinton, 1986, Detroit Inst. Art, 1986, Kingswood Gallery, Bloomfield Hills, 1986, Cleve. Inst. Art, 1987, Indpls. Art League, 1987, 88, N.A.M.E. Gallery, Chgo., 1988, Cleve. Mus. Art, 1988, U. Tex. San Antonio, 1989, Blue Star, San Antonio, 1989, Mus. Art, Washington State U., 1989, 90, Ridenbaugh Art Gallery, U. Idaho, 1989, Evanston (Ill.) Art Ctr., 1991, Prichard Gallery, Moscow, Idaho, 1992, Cheney Cowles Mus., Spokane, Wash., 1992, Cranbrook Acad. Art Mus., Bloomfield Hills, 1992, Bumbershoot 93, Seattle, 1993, Bellevue (Wash.) Art Mus., 1993, Cyberspace Gallery, L.A., 1993, N.Mex. State U. Art Mus., Las Cruces, Evergreen State Coll., Olympia, Wash., 1993, Artetage Gallery, Vladivostok, Russia, 1994, Seafirst Gallery, Seattle, 1995, COLA Brandywine Workshop, 1996. NEH fellow 1994; grantee Rockefeller Found., 1993, 94, Wash. State China Rels. coun. Project, 1994, Phila., 1997, others. Home and Studio: SW 220 Blaine St Pullman WA 99163

LEE, QWIHEE PARK, plant physiologist; b. Republic of Korea, Mar. 1, 1941; came to U.S., 1965; d. Yong-sik and Soon-duk (Paik) Park; m. Ick-whan Lee, May 20, 1965; children: Tina, Amy, Benjamin. MS, Seoul Nat. U., Republic of Korea, 1965; PhD, U. Minn., 1973. Head dept. plant physiology Korea Ginseng and Tobacco Inst., Seoul, 1980-82; instr. Sogang U., Seoul, 1981, Seoul Women's U., 1981; research assoc. U. Wash., Seattle, 1975-79. Exec. dir. Korean Community Counseling Ctr., Seattle, 1983-86. Named one of 20 Prominent Asian Women in Wash. State, Chinese Post Seattle, 1986. Mem. AAAS. Buddhist. Home: 13025 42nd Ave NE Seattle WA 98125-4624 Office: U Wash Dept Pharm SJ-30 1959 NE Pacific St Seattle WA 98195-0004

LEE, RICHARD CARL, government official; b. Chgo., July 19, 1950; s. Carl Lee and Helen Louise (Webster) L. BSME, Calif. State Poly. U., Pomona, 1973; BFA in Printmaking, U. Oreg., 1980; postgrad., U. Mo., 1982-83, Calif. State U., L.A., 1984-85. Pipeline engr. pipeline div. Bechtel Corp., San Francisco, 1973-74; test engr. power sys. div. United Techs., South Windsor, Conn., 1974-76; salesman Ea. Mountain Sports, hartford, Conn., 1976-77; grad. teaching asst. visual arts resources U. Oreg. Art Mus., 1977-80; iron worker Eugen, Oreg., 1980-81; energy auditor Student Conservation Assn., Vashon Island, Wash., 1981-82; house painter Fontana, Calif., 1982-83; printing procurement specialist U.S. Govt. Printing Office, San Francisco, 1986—. Mem. Sierra Club, Tau Beta Pi, Pi Tau Sigma. Office: US Govt Printing Office 536 Stone Rd Ste I Benicia CA 94510-1170

LEE, RICHARD FRANCIS JAMES, evangelical clergyman, media consultant; b. Yakima, Wash., Sept. 13, 1967; s. Richard Francis and Dorothy Aldean (Blackwell). Diploma, Berean Coll., Springfield, Mo., 1989; BA, U. Wash., Seattle, 1990; postgrad., Gonzaga Sch. Law, 1994-97, Fuller Theol. Seminary, 1997—. Lic. clergyman Gen. Coun. of the Assemblies of God, Seattle, 1989—. Author: Tell Me the Story, 1982, The Crimson Detective Motion Picture, 1996. Named Most Likely to be President, Franklin High Sch., Seattle, 1986. Pentecostal. Home: 2604 E Boone Ave Spokane WA 99202-3718 Office: Evangel Outreach Ministries 2604 E Boone Ave Spokane WA 99202-3718

LEE, ROBERT EDWARD, medical educator, researcher; b. Worcester, Mass., Sept. 15, 1942; s. Robert Edward and Helen Carol (Thomas) L.; m. Patricia Ann Grasso, July 6, 1968; children: Nicole Regina, Alana May, Christian Robert. BSc, Cornell U., 1964; PhD, U. Mass., 1971. Lectr. U. Witwatersrand, Johannesburg, South Africa, 1971-76; assoc. prof. Shiraz (Iran) U., 1977-79; staff fellow Schepens Eye Rsch. Inst., Boston, 1979-81; mem. affiliate faculty Med. Sch. Harvard U., Cambridge, Mass., 1979-81; prof. anatomy, mgr. Colo. State U., Ft. Collins, 1981—. Author: Phycology, 1st edit., 1981, 2d edit., 1989, Scanning Electron Microscopy, 1992. 1st lt. U.S. Army, 1964-66, Vietnam. Mem. Phi Kappa Phi. Home: 1925 Kingsborough Dr Fort Collins CO 80526-1511 Office: Colo State U Dept Anatomy and Neurobiol Fort Collins CO 80523

LEE, ROBERT ERICH, information technology consultant; b. Spokane, Wash., Dec. 26, 1955; s. Robert Edward Lee and Edith Freida (Klasen) Moore; m. Vicky Ann Rowland, Jan. 31, 1981 (div.); children: Erich Rowland, Christopher Michael. Student, Vanderbilt U., 1973-77, Corpus Christi (Tex.) State U., 1977, U. Tex., El Paso, 1980. Mgr., instr. Neptune Equipment Co., Nashville, 1976-77; customer engr. Hewlett-Packard Co., Los Angeles, 1977-82, dist. service mgr., 1982-85; region service adminstrn. mgr. Hewlett-Packard Co., North Hollywood, Calif., 1985-86; dir. mgmt. info. Tova Corp., Beverly Hills, Calif., 1986-87; dir. info. tech. PrimeSource/Sequoia Supply, Inc., Irvine, Calif., 1987-92; pres. Results From Tech.!, 1992—; spkr. in field. Author: The ISDN Consultant, 1996, Serving the Internet, 1997; columnist Interex Press, 1995—; writer Interact, 1995—, Sun World Online, Microsfot Certified Professional. Mem. Town Hall Calif., Eagle Scout, Cub Scout Woodbadge. Mem. IEEE, Assn. for Computing Machinery, Interex. Republican. Home and Office: Results From Tech! 404 Santa Barbara Irvine CA 92606

LEE, ROBERT W(ILLIAM), journalist, researcher; b. Salt Lake City, June 19, 1937; s. William Orme Jr. and Golda Alice (Anderson) L.; m. Karen Brinkerhoff, Nov. 24, 1958; children: Michael Don, Gary Dean, William Reed, Robert Bruce, Lawrence Alan. BS, U. Utah, 1960. Pres. Thermotech, Inc., Salt Lake City, 1960-65; adminstrv. asst. John Birch Soc., Washington, 1965-72, Washington rep., 1972-77; adminstrv. asst. Salt Lake County Commn., 1979-81; contbg. editor Am. Opinion Mag., Belmont, Mass., 1981-85, Rev. of the News Mag., Belmont, 1969-85, Conservative Digest Mg., Ft. Collins, Colo., 1985-89; talk-show host Radio Sta. KTKK, Salt Lake City, 1989-94; contbr. The New Am. Mag., Appleton, Wis., 1985—. Author: The United Nations Conspiracy, 1981; co-author: A Taxpayer Survey of the Grace Commission Report, 1984, Flight 007: Were There Survivors?, 1986; editor/pub. newsletter Comments and Corrections, 1981—. Mormon.

LEE, RUBY BEI-LOH, multimedia and computer systems architect; b. Singapore; came to the U.S., 1970, naturalized, 1996; m. Howard F. Lee, July 27, 1974; children: Patrick, Josephine. AB in Computer Sci. and Comparative Lit. with distinction, Cornell U., 1973; MS in Computer Sci., Stanford U., 1975, PhDEE, 1980. Asst. prof. elec. engring. Stanford (Calif.) U., 1980-81; lead architect Hewlett Packard Co., Palo Alto, Calif., 1982-84, lead designer microprocessors, 1984-86; project mgr. Hewlett Packard Co., Cupertino, Calif., 1987-90, chief architect computer sys. architecture, multimedia, 1991—; cons. assoc. prof. elec. engring. Stanford U., 1990-95, cons. prof., 1995—. Designer PA-RISC (Precision Architecture-Reduced Instrn. Set Computer) architecture, Multimedia Acceleration EXtensions (MAX) architecture; contbr. articles to profl. jours.; inventor, patentee in field, including 12 U.S. patents and several foreign ones. Mem. IEEE (mem. exec. com., mem. tech. com. on microprocessors, mem. program com. Compcon conf. San Francisco 1991—, program chairperson Hot-Chips Symposium, Stanford 1992-93, mem. editl. bd. IEEE Micro and Spectrum, guest editor spl. issue IEEE MICRO 1996), Assn. for Computing Machinery, Phi Beta Kappa, Alpha Lambda Delta. Methodist. Office: Hewlett-Packard Co 19410 Homestead Rd Cupertino CA 95014-0606

LEE, W. BRUCE, management consultant; b. Sacramento, Calif., Jan. 23, 1953; s. Wade Bruce and Marguerite (Stogner) L.; m. Nell Jeanette Alford, Aug. 13, 1977; children: Jessica, Amanda. BA in Adminstrn., U. Calif., Davis, 1971-75; MPA in Adminstrn., Calif. State U., 1977, MA in Internat. Affairs, 1977. Cert. in bus. and industry mgmt., mktg. and distbn., govt., pub. adminstrn. Adminstr./cons. State of Calif., Sacramento, 1973-76; mng. dir. Horizon Rsch. and Managerial Cons., Sacramento, 1978-87; exec. dir. Calif. Bus. League, Sacramento, 1987-90, Calif. Refuse Removal Coun., Sacramento, 1990-94; pres. Horizon Mgmt. and Assn. Svcs., Roseville, Calif., 1995—; commentator internat. affairs KXPR Pub. Radio, Sacramento, 1977-78; newspaper columnist Sacramento Union, 1990-94. Author: Beyond Accounting, 1985; contbr. articles to profl. jours. Mayor, City of Loomis, Calif., 1991-96; chmn. Placer County Flood Control Dist., Auburn, Calif., 1993-96; treas. Sierra Econ. Devel. Dist., Auburn, 1994; founder South Placer Cmty. Prayer Breakfast, Rocklin, 1993—; mem. Local Agy. Formation Commn., Auburn, 1991-92; mem. Placer County Water Agy., Auburn, 1996—; co-chmn. fin. com. Billy Graham Crusade, Sacramento, 1995-96. Recipient Calif. Senate Rules Com. Resolution of Commendation, Calif. Assembly Resolution of Commendation. Mem. Calif. Soc. Assn. Execs., Am. Soc. Assn. Execs., Sacramento Jaycees (state dir. 1978, Outstanding Lt. Gov. 1971), Calif. Jaycees (Presdl. Award of Merit, mem. legis. coun. 1977).

LEE, WAYLAND SHERROD, otolaryngologist; b. Spur, Tex., Apr. 23, 1939; s. Wayland Alfred and Lucye Marie (Blair) L.; m. Joyce Shaeffer, June 12, 1960; children: Amy (dec.), Christopher S., Paul W. BA, Stanford U., 1963, MD, 1965. Diplomate Am. Bd. Otolaryngology, Head and Neck Surgery. Commd. lt. USN, 1966; pvt. practice otolaryngology Hobbs, N.Mex.; intern in surg Palo Alto-Stanford Hosp, 1965-66; active duty USN, 1966-74; resident in OTO-HNS Naval Regional Med. Ctr., San Diego, Calif., 1968-72; advanced through grades to capt. USN, 1988; ret., 1993. Mem. ACS, Rotary. Republican. Mem. Ch. of Christ. Office: 5419 N Lovington Hwy # 24 Hobbs NM 88240

LEE, YEU-TSU MARGARET, surgeon, educator; b. Xian, Shensi, China, Mar. 18, 1936; m. Thomas V. Lee, Dec. 29, 1962 (div. 1987); 1 child, Maxwell M. AB in Microbiology, U. S.D., 1957; MD, Harvard U., 1961. Cert. Am. Bd. Surgery. Assoc. prof. surgery Med. Sch., U. So. Calif., L.A., 1973-83; commd. lt. col. U.S. Army Med. Corps, 1983, advanced through grades to col., 1989; chief surg. oncology Tripler Army Med. Ctr., Honolulu, 1983—; assoc. clin. prof. surgery Med. Sch., U. Hawaii, Honolulu, 1984-92, clin. prof. surgery, 1992—. Author: Malignant Lymphoma, 1974; author chpts to books; contbr. articles to profl. jours. Pres. Orgn. Chinese-Am. Women, L.A., 1981; active U.S.-China Friendship Assn., 1991—. Recipient Chinese-Am. Engrs. and Scis. Assn., 1987; named Sci. Woman Warrior, Asian-Pacific Womens Network, 1983. Mem. ACS, Soc. Surg. Oncology, Assn. Women Surgeons. Office: Tripler Army Med Ctr Dept Surgery Honolulu HI 96859

LEE, YOUNG HO (JINWOL), Buddhist monk, educator; b. Uiwang, Kyonggi, Korea, Apr. 28, 1950; came to U.S., 1986; s. Chong Taek and Kyong Bok (Kim) L. BA, Dongguk U., Seoul, 1984, Sogang U., Seoul, Korea, 1986; MA, U. Hawaii, 1990; postgrad., U. Calif., Berkeley, 1996—; Diploma, Haein Sangha Coll., Korea. Buddhist monk. Pres. Soc. Zen Studies, Seoul, 1982-83; Dharma tchr. Kiwonjong-sa Temple, Seoul, 1984-86; Dharma and Zen tchr. Daewonsa Temple, Honolulu, 1986-92; v.p. Hawaii Assn. Internat. Buddhists, Honolulu, 1992-94; internat. advisor Soc. Buddhist Christian Studies, Pitts., 1994-96; Zen and Dharma tchr. Group in Buddhist Studies U. Calif., Berkeley, 1996—; cons. United Religion, San Francisco, 1996. Contbr. articles to profl. jours. Mem. Am. Acad. Religion, Soc. Buddhist-Christian Studies, Calif. buddhist Assn. (founder, pres., advisor 1992-96). Home: 2452 Parker St Berkeley CA 94704 Office: Univ of Calif-Berkeley Group in Buddhist Studies Berkeley CA 94704

LEED, JEAN ANN, religious organization administrator; b. Akron, Ohio, Feb. 8, 1942; d. Clifford John and Laura Rosetta (Drescher) Burg; m. Roger Melvin Leed, Apr. 1, 1967; children: Craig, Maren, Jennifer. BA magna cum laude, Radcliffe Coll., 1964; MA, U. Mich., 1965, candidate in philosophy, 1967. Dir. devel. A Contemporary Theatre, Seattle, 1979-82; dir. devel. Arts and Scis. U. Wash., Seattle, 1982-90; dir. major gifts Sta. KCTS, Seattle, 1991-92; v.p. for devel. Sta. KTCA, St. Paul, 1992-93; dir. stewardship and devel. Episcopal Diocese of Olympia, Seattle, 1993—; instr. cert. program in fundraising, U. Wash., Seattle, 1986-89. Editor: Part-Time Careers in Seattle, 1976. Bd. dirs. YWCA, Seattle, 1978-81. Woodrow Wilson fellow, 1964. Mem. Nat. Soc. Fund Raising Execs. (pres. Wash. chpt. 1988-89, bd. dirs. 1986-90, 93-95), City Club (bd. dirs. 1986-90), Phi Beta Kappa. Democrat. Episcopalian. Office: Episcopal Diocese Olympia PO Box 12126 Seattle WA 98102-0126

LEEDS-HORWITZ, SUSAN BETH, school system administrator, speech-language pathology educator; b. L.A., Mar. 14, 1950; d. Henry Herbert and Lee (Weiss) Leeds; m. Stanley Martin Horwitz, Nov. 28, 1975; 1 child, Brian David. BA, Calif. State U., Northridge, 1971; MEd, U. S.C., 1973; adminstrv. credential, U. LaVerne, 1984. Itinerant speech pathologist L.A. City Schs., 1973-74; severe lang. disorders tchr. L.A. County Bd. Edn., Downey, Calif., 1974-88; tchr. on spl. assignment Santa Clarita Valley Spl. Edn. Local Plan Area, Newhall, Calif., 1986-88; coord. spl. programs, testing, evaluation and migrant edn. Castaic (Calif.) Union Sch. Dist., 1988-94, adminstr., 1988-1994; ednl. cons. Richmond, Calif., 1994-95; coord. grants & project devel. Glendale (Calif.) Unified Sch. Dist., 1995—. Author: Project Próspero: A Traditional Bilingual Education Program for Grades 2-8, 1991, Project TEAM: Together Everyone Achieves More Comprehensive School Program, 1995, Hoover-Keppel-Keppel Healthy Start Family Resource Center, 1996, Volunteers for Youth: From the Community for the Community, 1996, FRANKLIN: Focusing on Educational Restructuring and Needs of Kids and Their Families Through Upgraded Learning and Instruction with a Neighborhood Learning Center, 1996, SB1510 School-Based Educational Technology Program, Daily High School, 1996. Grantee student enhancement program Kaiser-Permanente Community Svcs., 1992. Mem. ASCD, Am. Speech Lang and Hearing Assn. (cert.), So. Calif. Assn. Alumnae Panhellenic (pres. 1993-94), Down Syndrome Congress, Assn. Calif. Sch. Adminstrs., San Fernando Valley Panhellenic Assn. (rep. 1976-96, pres. 1993-95), Glendale Schs. Mgmt. Assn., Santa Clarita Valley C. of C. (edn. com., anti-gang com., tchr. tribute com.), Delta Kappa Gamma, Alpha Xi Delta (Edna Epperson Brinkman award 1985), Phi Delta Kappa, Delta Rho Bldg. Corp. of Alpha Xi Delta (pres. 1996—). Office: 223 N Jackson St Glendale CA 91206-4334

LEELAND, STEVEN BRIAN, electronics engineer; b. Tampa, Fla., Dec. 27, 1951; s. N. Stanford and Shirley Mae (Bahner) L.; m. Karen Frances Hayes, Dec. 20, 1980; children: Crystal Mary, April Marie. BSEE, MSEE magna cum laude, U. South Fla., 1976. Registered profl. engr., Ariz. Engr. Bendix Avionics, Ft. Lauderdale, Fla., 1976-77; prin. engr., instr. Sperry Avionics, Phoenix, 1977-84; prin. staff engr. Motorola Govt. Electronics Group, Scottsdale, Ariz., 1984-88; engring. fellow, mgr. dept. software engring. Fairchild Data Corp., Scottsdale, 1988—; cons. Motorola Govt. Electronics Group, 1991. Patentee systolic array, 1990; contbr. articles to profl. jours. Mem. IEEE (Phoenix chpt. Computer Soc. treas. 1978-79, sec. 1979-80, chmn. 1980-81, 81-82), Tau Beta Pi, Pi Mu Epsilon, Phi Kappa Phi, Omicron Delta Kappa, Themis. Republican. Adventist. Home: 10351 E Sharon Dr Scottsdale AZ 85260-9000 Office: Fairchild Data Corp 350 N Hayden Rd Scottsdale AZ 85257-4601

LEERABHANDH, MARJORIE BRAVO, chemist, educator; b. Negros Occidental, Philippines; came to U.S., 1982; d. Rustico Ginese and Monica Tolosa (Tolosa) Bravo; m. Sunai Leerabhandh, Oct. 2, 1986. BS in chemistry cum laude, U. Santo Tomas, 1979; PhD in chemistry, U. So. Calif., 1990. Rsch. teaching asst. chem. dept. U. So. Calif., L.A., 1984-89; faculty mem. chem. dept. Moorpark (Calif.) Coll., 1992—; project mgr. Med. Analysis Sys., Inc., Camarillo, Calif., 1989-93, rsch. team leader, 1993-94, mgr. rsch. and devel., 1994—. Author: Nitrogen Tixation Research Progress, 1985, Nitrogen Fixation: 100 Years After, 1988; contbr. articles to profl. jours. Mem. Am. Chem. Soc., Am. Assn. for Clinical Chem., Chem. Soc. U. Santo Tomas Manila (pres., 1979). Office: Med Analysis Sys Inc 542 Flynn Rd Camarillo CA 93012

LEES, FRED ARTHUR, middle school educator, retired; b. Wahoo, Nebr., Apr. 29, 1940; s. Fred A. and Mary E. (Brabec) L.; m. Marilyn Maxine Nichols, Aug. 20, 1966; children: Stephanie Lynne, Robert Arthur. BS in Edn., U. Nebr., Kearney, 1962. Math.-sci. tchr., coach Polk (Nebr.) Pub. Schs., 1962-63, Cook (Nebr.) Pub. Schs., 1963-65; math. tchr. Lincoln (Nebr.) Pub. Schs., 1965-68; math. tchr. Jefferson County (Colo.) R-I Schs., 1968-97, ret., 1997. Ch. usher, bd. trustees, adminstrv. bd., staff parish bd. Lakewood (Colo.) United Meth. Ch. Colo. recipient Presdl. award NSF, 1985. Mem. Nat. Coun. Tchrs. Math., Coun. Presdl. Awardees in Math., Phi Delta Kappa. Home: 1666 S Hoyt St Denver CO 80232-6434 Office: Carmody Mid Sch 2050 S Kipling St Denver CO 80227-2122

LEESON, THOMAS AUBERT, painter; b. Chgo., Mar. 16, 1945; s. Cecil Burton and Louise Larose (Gamble) L.; m. Lee Ann Carroll, June 3, 1967 (div. Mar. 1992). BS, Ball State U., 1968; MA, UCLA, 1971. instr. UCLA, 1977-79, 83-94, U. Calif., Santa Barbara, 1982. One-man shows include Kenmore Galleries, Phila., 1973, Dobrick Gallery, Chgo., 1976, OK Harris, N.Y.C., 1979, Peperdine U., Malibu, Calif., 1980, L.A. County Mus. Art, 1985-86, Ovsey Gallery, L.A., 1986, 89, 95; exhibited in group shows at James Yu Gallery, N.Y.C., 1974, John Gunn Gallery, L.A., 1976, L.A. Inst. Contemporary Art, 1977, L.A. Mcpl. Art Gallery, 1978, 82, Western Assn. Art Mus., 1983, Loyalo Law Sch., L.A., 1984, Riverside (Calif.) Art Mus.,

1989, and others. Home and Office: 4748 W Washington Blvd Los Angeles CA 90016-1526

LE FAVE, GENE MARION, polymer amd chemical company executive; b. Green Bay, Wis., May 18, 1924; s. Thomas Paul and Marie Agnes (Young) Le F.; m. Rosemary Beatrice Sackinger, Aug. 28, 1948; children: Laura, Deborah, Michele, Mark, Camille, Jacques, Louis. BS, U. Notre Dame, 1948; MS, Butler U., 1950. Staff engr. P.R. Mallory & Co., Indpls., 1953-54; sr. staff engr. Lear, Inc., Santa Monica, Calif., 1954-56; chief engr. G.M. Giannini & Co., Pasadena, Calif., 1956; v.p., dir. Coast Pro Seal & Mfg. Co., Compton, Calif., 1956-64; cons. Input/Output, Whittier, Calif., 1964-67, Diamond Shamrock, Painesville, Ohio, 1967-71; mem. bd. cons. U.S. Army Corps of Engrs., Mariemont, Ohio, 1964-71; cons. Joslyn Mfg. & Supply Co., Chgo., 1964-72, Arco Chem. Co., Phila., 1969-75; pres. Fluid Polymers, Inc., Las Vegas, Nev., 1970-96; cons. polymer chemistry Las Vegas, 1995—; bd. dirs. Polimeros Flexibles de Monterrey (Mexico), SA, Desert Industries, Inc., Las Vegas. Contbr. articles to profl. jours. Bd. dirs. adv. com. Nat. Bus., Las Vegas, 1990—; mem. regents com. on sci. and tech. U. Nev., Las Vegas, 1990-96; mem., chmn. Rep. Party, Whittier, 1965-67. Mem. Am. Inst. Chem. Engrs., Am. Inst. Chemists, Am. Concrete Inst. Byzantine Catholic. Home: 1568 Leatherleaf Dr Las Vegas NV 89123-1942

LEFEVER, ERIC BRUCE, anesthesiologist; b. La Mesa, Calif., Mar. 22, 1960; s. David Welty Jr. and Cecelia Anne (Jenks) L.; m. Kathleen Anne Howlett, Aug. 20, 1983; children: Kevin, Craig, Scott. BS in Biochemistry, U. Calif., Davis, 1983; MD, Med. Coll. Wis., 1987. Diplomate Am. Bd. Anesthesiology. Intern physician Naval Hosp., Oakland, Calif., 1987-88, staff anesthesiologist, 1991-93; resident in anesthesiology Brooke Army Med. Ctr., San Antonio, 1988-91; staff anesthesiologist Fremont-Rideout Health Group, Yuba City, Calif., 1993—, chair anesthesiology dept., 1996—, dir. pain mgmt. anesthesiology dept., 1996—. Contbr. chpts. to book. Youth soccer coach Yuba Sutter Youth Soccer League, Yuba City, 1994—; vestry mem. St. John's Episcopal Ch., Marysville, Calif., 1996—. Lt. comdr. USNR. Mem. Am. Soc. Anesthesiology, Calif. Soc. Anesthesiology. Office: Fremont Rideout Health Group 970 Plumas St Yuba City CA 95991

LEFEVRE, GREG, bureau chief; b. Los Angeles, Jan. 28, 1947; s. Robert Bazille and Anna Marie (Violé) L.; m. Mary Deborah Bottoms, July 10, 1971. AA, Valley Coll., 1970; BS, San Diego State U., 1972, postgrad. Asst. news dir. Sta. KDEO, San Diego, 1971-73; reporter Sta. KFMB-TV, San Diego, 1973-75; sr. reporter Sta. KDFW-TV, Dallas, 1976-81; news dir. Sta. KSEE-TV, Fresno, Calif., 1981-83; corr. Cable News Network, San Francisco, 1983-89, bur. chief, 1989—. Mem. AP Broadcasters, Soc. Profl. Journalists, Radio and TV News Dirs. Assn. Club: Dallas Press (v.p. 1978-81). Office: CNN Am Inc 50 California St Ste 950 San Francisco CA 94111-4606

LEFLY, DIANNE LOUISE, research psychologist; b. Denver, July 17, 1946; d. Gordon Eugene Boen and Elizabeth (Welsh) Tuveson. AB, U. No. Colo., 1968; MA, U. Colo., 1980; PhD, U. Denver, 1994. Classroom tchr. Adam County Sch. Dist. #12, Thornton, Colo., 1968-77; rschr. John F. Kennedy Child Devel. Ctr., Denver, 1979-81, U. Colo. Health Scis. Ctr., 1981-89, U. Denver, 1989—; statis. cons. Colo. Dept. Pub. Health and Environment, Colo. Dept. Edn., 1997. Contbr. articles to profl. jours. Mem. Colo. Rep. Party, Denver, 1968—. Scholarship U. No. Colo., 1964-68; fellowship U. Denver, 1989. Mem. Mensa. Republican. Home: 8650 W 79th Ave Arvada CO 80005-4321 Office: U Denver 2155 S Race St Denver CO 80210-4638

LEFRANC, MARGARET (MARGARET SCHOONOVER), artist, illustrator, editor, writer; b. N.Y.C., Mar. 15, 1907; d. Abraham and Sophie (Teplitz) Frankel; m. Raymond Schoonover, 1942 (div. 1945). Student, Art Students League, N.Y.C., Kunstschule des Westerns, Berlin, NYU Grad. Sch., Andre L'Hote, Paris, Acad. Grande Chaumiere, Paris. Tchr. art Adult Edn., Los Alamos, 1946, Miami (Fla.) Mus. Modern Art, 1975-76. Exhibited in one-person shows at Mus. N.Mex., Santa Fe, 1948, 51, 53, Phlbrook Art Ctr., Tulsa, 1949, 51,, Okla. Art Ctr., 1950, Recorder Workshop, Miami, 1958, St. John's Coll., Santa Fe, 1993, 97, A Lifetime of Imaging (works on paper), 1921-95, Figurative Works, 1920-30, Cline Fine Art Gallery, 1997; group shows include Salon de Tuileries, Paris, 1928, 29, 30, Art Inst. Chgo., 1936, El Paso Mus. Art, 1964, Mus. Modern Art, 1974, North Miami Mus. Contemporary Art, 1984, Miami Collects, 1989, Women's Caucus Invitational, 1990, Gov.'s Gallery, Santa Fe, 1992, Gene Autry Western Heritage Mus, 1995, Gilcrease Mus., Tulsa, 1996, Mus. N.Mex. Santa Fe, 1996, Brigham Young U., Provo, Utah, 1996; in collections at Beiles Artes, Mexico City, Mus. Fine Arts, Santa Fe. Bd. dirs., pres. Artist Equity of Fla., 1964-68; v.p. Miami Art Assn., 1958-60; founder, bd. dirs. Guild Art Gallery, N.Y.C., 1935-37. Recipient Illustration award Fifty Best Books of Yr., Libr. of Congress, Hon. Mention award Rodeo Santa Fe, Mus. N.Mex., others, Gov.'s award for Excellence and Achievement in the Arts, 1996.

LEFTWICH, JAMES STEPHEN, management consultant; b. Stevenage, Eng., Nov. 30, 1956; came to U.S., 1957; s. James Wright and Del Maureen (Thomson) L.; m. Carol Petersen, Nov. 7, 1980 (div. Jan. 1982). AA in Criminal Justice, Butte Coll., Oroville, Calif., 1981; BA, S.W. U., 1993. Lic. internat. accredited safety auditor; cert. hazardous material specialist. Prodn. mgr. Artistic Dyers Inc., El Monte, Calif., 1976-80; mgr. loss control and risk mgmt. Mervyn's Dept. Stores, Hayward, Calif., 1982-91; dir. risk mgmt. Save Mart Corp., Modesto, Calif., 1991-93; v.p. ops. I.C.S. Corp., San Ramon, Calif., 1993-94; pres. I.C.S. Corp., Irvine, Calif., 1994-95; v.p. Health Systems of Am. Internat., 1995-96; COO CHSI Ins. Svcs., Walnut Creek, Calif., 1996—; bd. dirs. Am. Real Eatate Bur., 1996—; cons. R.I.M. Assocs., Walnut Creek, Calif., 1989-96; instr. Claims Mgmt. Inst., 1993. Scriptwriter, tech. advisor 12 safety videos; contbr. articles on safety and risk mgmt. to profl. publs. Res. police officer Cotati (Calif.) Police Dept., 1983-85; fundraiser United Way, Hayward, 1986, Am. Found. for AIDS Rsch., L.A., 1990; bd. dirs. Bay Area Safety Coun., Oakland, Calif., 1987-88; trustee Calif. Safety Ctr., Sacramento, 1990-91, dir., 1991—. Mem. Am. Soc. for Safety Engrs., Nat. Safety Mgmt. Soc., Nat. Fire Protection Assn., Risk and Ins. Mgmt. Soc., Nat. Assn. Chiefs Police, Nat. Environ. Tng. Assn. Office: CHSI Insurance Svcs Ste 290 2121 N California Blvd Walnut Creek CA 94596

LÉGARÉ, HENRI FRANCIS, archbishop; b. Willow-Bunch, Sask., Can., Feb. 20, 1918; s. Phillippe and Amanda (Douville) L. B.A., U. Ottawa, 1940; theol. student, Lebret, Sask., 1940-44; M.A., Laval U., 1946; Dr. Social Sci., Cath. U. Lille, France, 1950; LL.D. (hon.), Carleton U., Ottawa, 1959, Windsor (Ont.) U., 1960, Queens U., Kingston, Ont., 1961, U. Sask., 1963, Waterloo (Ont.) Luth. U., 1965, U. Ottawa, Can., 1984; Doctor of Univ., U. of Ottawa. Ordained priest Roman Cath. Ch., 1943; prof. sociology Laval U., 1947, U. Ottawa, 1951; exec. dir. Cath. Hosp. Assn. Can., 1952-57; dean faculty social scis. U. Ottawa, 1954-58, pres., 1958-64; provincial Oblate Fathers, Winnipeg, Man., 1966-67; bishop of Labrador, 1967-72; archbishop Grouard-McLennan, Alta., 1972-96. Contbr. articles to profl. jours. Chmn. Canadian Univs. Found., 1960- 62. Decorated grand cross merit Order Malta, 1964; order merit French Lang. Assn. Ont., 1965. Mem. Assn. Canadian Univs. (pres. 1960-62), Can. Conf. Cath. Bishops (pres. 1981-83), Internat. Assn. Polit. Sci. Office: Archbishop's House, CP 388, McLennan, AB Canada T0H 2L0

LEGER, RICHARD ROUBINE, public relations executive, writer; b. Schenectady, N.Y., Oct. 27, 1935; s. Roubine Joseph and Catherine Bernice (Waikas) L.; m. Lawrence Lowell Putnam, Sept. 14, 1957 (div. 1971); children: Philip Augustus, William Richard, Catherine Lowell; m. Dianne Lee Williams, May 14, 1978. BA, U. Rochester, 1957. Reporter Wall St. Jour., N.Y.C., 1960-63, 69-70, Atlanta, 1963-69, San Francisco, 1972-76; fgn. corr. Wall St. Jour., London, 1976-78; bur. chief Wall St. Jour., Nairobi, Kenya, 1978-80; econ. editor San Francisco Chronicle, San Francisco, 1982-84; owner/pub. Sebastopol Times, Sebastopol, Calif., 1985-86; pres. Leger Networks, Inc., San Francisco, 1988—.

LEGG, DAVID E., entomologist, educator; b. Kansas City, Mo., Sept. 25, 1955; s. William J. and Ruth Ann (Thompson) L.; m. Cynthia Sue Volden, July 20, 1985; children: Sarah Kristen, Taylor Marie. BS in Agr., U. Mo., 1978, MS in Entomology, 1980; PhD in Entomology, U. Minn., 1983. Postdoctoral fellow U. Ky., Lexington, 1983-84; prin. investigator Ky. State U., Frankfort, 1984-88; assoc. prof. entomology U. Wyo., Laramie, 1988—; cons. FAO, Bangkok, 1986, 87. Contbr. articles to refereed sci. jours. Grantee USDA, 1985, 86, 87, 90, 91, 92, 93, 94-96. Mem. Ky. Acad. Sci. (bd. govs. 1987-88), Entomol. Soc. Am., S.C. Entomol. Soc., Sigma Xi, Gamma Sigma Delta. Office: Univ Wyo PO Box 3354 Laramie WY 82071-3354

LEGGE, CHARLES ALEXANDER, federal judge; b. San Francisco, Aug. 24, 1930; s. Roy Alexander and Wilda (Rampton) L.; m. Janice Meredith Sleeper, June 27, 1952; children: Jeffrey, Nancy, Laura. AB with distinction, Stanford U., 1952, JD, 1954. Bar: Calif. 1955. Assoc. Bronson, Bronson & McKinnin, San Francisco, 1956-64, ptnr., 1964-84, chmn., 1978-84; judge U.S. Dist. Ct. (no. dist.) Calif., San Francisco, 1984—. Served with U.S. Army, 1954-56. Fellow Am. Coll. Trial Lawyers; mem. Calif. Bar Assn. (past chmn. adminstrn. justice com.). Republican. Clubs: Bohemian, World Trade (San Francisco); Orinda (Calif.) Country. Office: US Dist Ct PO Box 36060 Rm 19-5424 450 Golden Gate Ave San Francisco CA 94102*

LEGINGTON, GLORIA R., middle school educator. BS, Tex. So. U, Houston, 1967; MS, U. So. Calif., L.A., 1973. Cert. adminstr. (life). Tchr., mentor L.A. Unified Sch. Dist., 1991-93; grade level chair L.A. Unified Schs., 1975-78, faculty chairperson, 1978, 80, 84, Black history/Martin Luther King program chair, 1978, 80, 83, 86, 88, 90-92, social chair, bus. coord., svc. club sponsor, 1978-80, Indian edn. chair, 1980-84, opportunity chair, 1976-78, grade level chair, 1984; Black edn. commn. liaison, 1989-90, impact tchr., 1991-92, human rels. sponsor, 1991-92, coun. Black adminstrs.-student conf. facilitator, 1992, tchr. inservice classes for area colloqium, parents, tchrs., faculty shared decision making coun., 1993-94, mem. faculty senate, 1992-93, mem. sch. improvement, 1993-94, mem. discipline com., 1993-94; del. U.S.-Spain Joint. Conf. on Edn., Barcelona, 1995. Chair United Way, 1988, 90; sponsor, 8th Grade, 1994—; del. US/Spain Joint Conf. on Edn., Barcelona, 1995. Mem. NEA, Internat. Reading Assn., Calif. Reading Assn., United Tchrs. L.A., Calif. League of Mid. Schs.

LEGRAND, SHAWN PIERRE, computer systems programmer; b. San Diego, Nov. 27, 1960; s. Roger and Violet Louise (Howe) L. Grad. high sch., El Cajon, Calif.; student, U. Calif., San Diego, 1992—. Cert. computer programmer; cert. in neural networks. Computer operator Grossmont CCD, El Cajon, 1978-79; computer systems programmer ICW, San Diego, 1979—. Recipient Math. Achievement award Bank of Am., 1978. Mem. IEEE Computer Soc., Astron. Soc. Pacific, Assn. Computing Machinery. Republican. Office: ICW 11455 El Camino Real San Diego CA 92130

LEHANE, ANDREW DESMOND, civil engineer; b. San Francisco, June 23, 1964; s. Thomas Jeremiah and Evelyn Marie (Desmond) L.; m. Nena Duran, May 27, 1989; 1 child, Christopher Joseph. BS, U. Santa Clara, 1986. Registered profl. engr., Calif. Project mgr. Interstate Constrn., Inc., South San Francisco, Calif., 1986-87, T.I. Systems, Inc., Los Altos, Calif., 1987-89; project engr. Pacific Environ. Group, Inc., San Jose, Calif., 1989—. Mem. Am. Soc. Civil Engrs., NSPE, U. Santa Clara Alumni Assn. Democrat. Roman Catholic. Office: Pacific Environ Group Inc 2025 Gateway Pl Ste 440 San Jose CA 95110-1006

LEHINGER, SUSAN ELIZABETH, school psychologist; b. Grannis, Ark., Dec. 3, 1934; d. Richard Erskine and Rhoda Jane (Barton) Thames; m. Alfred Lee Lehinger, Feb. 3, 1950; children: Debra Lynne, Scott Keith, Sheila Helen, Valerie Jane, Cass Theodore, Katje Jill. BA Sociology, B Social Work with honors, Ea. Wash. U., 1970, MS in Psychology with honors, 1975, BA in Anthropology with honors, 1980, MPA with honors, 1982; PhD with honors, Gonzaga U., 1983. Cert. sch. psychologist, Wash. Social worker Cmty. Action Coun., Spokane, Wash., 1970-71; social worker, counselor Booth Meml. Hosp., Spokane, 1971-72; caseworker II and III Wash. Dept. Social and Health Svcs., Spokane, 1972-75; psychologist III, Lakeland Village Sch. for Devel. Disabled, Medical Lake, Wash., 1975-84; prof., dir. human svcs. dept. Flathead Valley C.C., Kalispell, Mont., 1984-92, faculty rep. to bd., 1990-92; sch. psychologist, behavior specialist Wenatchee (Wash.) Sch. Dist. 246, 1992—. Contbr. articles to profl. jours. and various publs. Vice chmn. Spokane County Dem. Ctrl. Com., 1963-66; dist. office mgr. Congressman Thomas S. Foley, Spokane, 1965-66; mem. fin. com. Booth Gardiner for Gov. Com., Spokane, 1984; bd. rep. United Way Kalispell, 1985-87; v.p. bd. Columbia Valley Cmty. Health, Wenatchee, 1994-96, pres. bd., 1996—. Mem. NASP, AAUW, Pi Gamma Mu, Alpha Kappa Delta, Phi Delta Kappa. Roman Catholic. Home: 491 7th St NE East Wenatchee WA 98802 Office: Wenatchee Sch Dist 246 112 S Elliott Wenatchee WA 98801

LEHMAN, GARY DOUGLAS, real estate broker; b. Abington, Pa., Feb. 7, 1951; s. Robert Ralston Sr. and Jane Anna (Springer) L. BA in Social Sci., Mich. State U., 1971; postgrad., Calif. Culinary Acad., San Francisco, 1976-77. Exec. chef Holiday Inn, Honolulu, 1979-80; domestic chef Allan Carr, Honolulu, Beverly Hills, Calif., 1980-81, Clare Boothe Luce, Honolulu, 1981-83, Mr. and Mrs. Bernard Cantor, Beverly Hills, 1984-85, Mr. Joseph Ridder, Honolulu, 1985-86, Mr. and Mrs. Sid Bass, Ft. Worth, 1986-87, Mr. and Mrs. John Devine, Tuxedo Park, N.Y., 1987, Mr. and Mrs. Frank Pearl, Washington, 1989; realtor Wiser Realty, Lompoc, Calif., 1990-96, Prudential Hunter Realty, Lompoc, 1996—; state dir. Calif. Assn. Realtors, 1993—; pres. Lompoc Valley Bd. Realtors, 1994. Named Realtor of Yr., Lompoc Valley Bd. Realtors, 1994. Democrat. Home: 517 Venus Ave Lompoc CA 93436-1935 Office: Prudential Hunter Realty 531 N H St Lompoc CA 93436

LEHMAN, LARRY L., judge. Judge Wyo. County Ct., 1985-88, Wyo. Dist. Ct. (2nd dist.), 1988-94; justice Wyo. Supreme Ct., Cheyenne, 1994—. Office: Supreme Court Bldg Cheyenne WY 82002*

LEHMAN, (ISRAEL) ROBERT, biochemistry educator, consultant; b. Tauroggen, Lithuania, Oct. 5, 1924; came to U.S., 1927; s. Herman Bernard and Anne (Kahn) L.; m. Sandra Lee Teper, July 5, 1959; children: Ellen, Deborah, Samuel. AB, Johns Hopkins U., 1950, PhD, 1954; MD (hon.), U. Gothenberg, Sweden, 1987; DSc (hon.), U. Pierre et Marie Curie, Paris, 1992. Instr. biochemistry Washington U., St. Louis, 1957-59; asst. prof. Stanford (Calif.) U., 1959-61, assoc. prof., 1961-66, prof., 1966—; sci. adv. bd., dirs. U.S. Biochem. Corp., Cleve., 1984—; sci. adv. RPI, Boulder. Author: Principles of Biochemistry, 6th edit., 1978, 7th edit., 1984. Sgt. U.S. Army, 1943-46, ETO. Recipient ASBMB-Merk award Am. Soc. for Biochemistry, 1995. Mem. NAS, Am. Acad. Arts and Scis., Am. Soc. Biol. Chemistry and Molecular Biology (Merck award 1995). Democrat. Jewish. Home: 895 Cedro Way Palo Alto CA 94305-1002 Office: Stanford U Dept Biochemistry Beckman Ctr Stanford CA 94305

LEHMANN, ERICH LEO, statistics educator; b. Strasbourg, France, Nov. 20, 1917; came to U.S., 1940, naturalized, 1945; s. Julius and Alma Rosa (Schuster) L.; m. Juliet Popper Shaffer; children: Stephen, Barbara, Fi-a. M.A., U. Calif. at Berkeley, 1943, Ph.D., 1946; D.Sc. (hon.), U. Leiden, 1985, U. Chgo., 1991. Asst. dept. math. U. Calif. at Berkeley, 1942-43, asso., 1943-46, instr., 1946-47, asst. prof., 1947-51, asso. prof., 1951-54, prof., 1954-55, prof. dept. stats., 1955-88, emeritus, 1988—, chmn. dept. stats., 1973-76; vis. assoc. prof. Columbia, 1950-51, Stanford, 1951-52; vis. lectr. Princeton, 1951. Author: Testing Statistical Hypotheses, 1959, 2d edit., 1986, (with J.L. Hodges, Jr.) Basic Concepts of Probability and Statistics, 1964, 2d edit, 1970, Nonparametrics: Statistical Methods Based on Ranks, 1975, Theory of Point Estimation, 1983. Recipient Fisher award Coms. of Pres. Stats. Socs. in N.Am., 1988; Guggenheim fellow, 1955, 66, 79; Miller research prof., 1962-63, 72-73; recipient Samuel S. Wilks Meml. medal Am. Statis. Assn., 1996. Fellow Inst. Math. Stats., Am. Statis. Assn., Royal Statis. Soc. (hon.); mem. Internat. Statis. Inst., Am. Acad. Arts and Scis., Nat. Acad. Scis. Office: Educational Testing Service Mail Stop 15-T Princeton NJ 08541

LEHNER, GREGORY MICHAEL, federal agency administrator; b. Buffalo, Sept. 29, 1948; s. Albert M. and Dorothy J. (Nawrocki) L.; m. Karen A. Boeheim, July 25, 1970; children: Beth M., Kelly M., Michael G. BA in Psychology, St. Bonaventure U., 1970, postgrad., 1972-74; postgrad., U. Ariz., 1976-78. Therapist N.Y. State Dept. Mental Hygiene, Buffalo, 1970, 72-74; intelligence officer U.S. Army Intelligence Ctr., Fort Huachuca, Ariz., 1971-72; mktg. mgr. Master Distbrs., Tucson, Ariz., 1974-75; mgr. Circle K Corp., Tucson, 1975-76; gen. mgr. McDonald's Corp., Tucson, 1976-80; letter carrier U.S. Postal Svc., Tucson, 1980, EEO counselor, 1981-82, supr., 1982-85, mgr., 1985-94, postmaster, 1995-96, mgr. customer svc. ops., 1993, 94, 96—; co-owner, operator K&G Enterprises, Tucson, 1992—; treas. M.D.U. Cable, Phoenix, 1995—; mng. dir. Cambridge Comms., 1996—. Cubmaster Cub Scouts Am., Tucson, 1985-87; mem. planning com. Cmty. Food Bank, Tucson, 1992-95, Juvenile Diabetes Assn. Walkathon; active PTO, 1975—. Maj. USAR, 1970-89. Recipient Leadership award Niagara Mohawk Power Corp., 1970. Mem. DAV, Res. Officers Assn., Am. Legion, Nat. Assn. Postal Suprs., Nat. Assn. Postmasters of the U.S., League of Postmasters. Home: 3035 N Tomas Rd Tucson AZ 85745-9370 Office: US Postal Svc 1501 S Cherrybell Stra Tucson AZ 85726-9901

LEHR, JEFFREY MARVIN, immunologist, allergist; b. N.Y.C., Apr. 29, 1942; s. Arthur and Stella (Smellow) L.; m. Suzanne Kozak, June 10, 1946; children: Elisa, Alexandra, Vanessa, Ryan. BS, City Coll., Bklyn., 1963; MD, NYU, 1967. Intern, resident Beth Israel Hosp., N.Y.C., 1967-69; resident in allergy/immunology, internal medicine Roosevelt Hosp., N.Y.C., 1969-72; chief of allergy/immunology USAF, Wright Patterson AFB, Ohio, 1972-74; allergist, immunologist Monterey, Calif., 1974—. Chmn. Monterey Bay Ari Pollution Hearing Bd., 1982-95; v.p. Lyceum of Monterey, 1977-83. Fellow Am. Acad. Allergy/Immunology, Am. Coll. Allergy/Immunology, Am. Assn. Cert. Allergists; mem. Am. Lung Assn. (v.p. 1989-91), Monterey County Med. Soc. (pres. 1988-89). Office: 798 Cass St Monterey CA 93940-2918 also: 262 San Jose St Salinas CA 93901-3901

LEHRER, WILLIAM PETER, JR., animal scientist; b. Bklyn., Feb. 6, 1916; s. William Peter and Frances Reif (Muser) L.; m. Lois Lee Meister, Sept. 13, 1945; 1 child, Sharon Elizabeth. BS, Pa. State U., 1941; MS in Agr., MS in Range Mgmt., U. Idaho, 1946, 55; PhD in Nutrition and Biochemistry, Wash. State U., 1951; LLB, U. Chgo., 1972, JD, 1974; MBA, Pepperdine U., 1975. Mgmt. trainee Swift & Co., Charleston, W.Va., 1941-42; farm mgr. Maple Springs Farm, Middletown, N.Y., 1944-45; rsch. fellow U. Idaho, Moscow, 1945; asst. prof. to prof. U. Idaho, 1945-60; dir. nutrition Albers Milling Co., L.A., 1960-62; dir. nutrition and rsch. Albers Milling Co., 1962-74, Albers Milling Co. & John W. Eshelman & Sons, L.A., 1974-76, Carnation Co., L.A., 1976-81; ret.; cons. in field; speaker, lectr. more than 40 univs. in U.S. and abroad. Contbr. 115 articles to profl. jours.; co-author: The Livestock Industry, 1950, Dog Nutrition, 1972; author weekly column Desseret News, Salt Lake City. Mem. rsch. adv. co. U.S. Brewers Assn., 1969-81; mem. com. on dog nutrition, com. animal nutrition Nat. Rsch. Coun. NAS, 1970-76. With U.S. Army Air Corps, 1942-43. Named Disting. Alumnus, Pa. State U., 1963, 83, Key Alumnus, 1985; named to U. Idaho Alumni Hall of Fame, 1985; recipient Alumni Achievement award Wash. State U., 1993. Fellow AAAS, Am. Soc. Animal Sci.; mem. Am. Inst. Nutrition, Coun. for Agrl. Sci. & Tech., Am. Registry of Profl. Animal Scientists, Am. Inst. Food Technologists, Animal Nutrition Rsch. Coun., Am. Dairy Sci. Assn., Am. Soc. Agrl. Engrs., Am. Feed Mfrs. Assn. (life, nutrition coun. 1962-81, chmn. 1969-70), Calif. State Poly. U. (adv. coun. 1965-81, Meritorious Svc. award), The Nutrition Today Soc., Am. Soc. Animal Sci., Poultry Sci. Assn., Nat. Block & Bridle Club, Hayden Lake Country Club, Alpha Zeta, Sigma Xi, Gamma Sigma Delta (Alumni Award of Merit), Xi Sigma Pi. Republican. Home: Rocking L Ranch 12180 Rimrock Rd Hayden Lake ID 83835

LEHRMAN, LEWIS BARRETT, artist, writer; b. N.Y.C., May 18, 1933; s. Joseph D. and Minna (Agranoff) L.; m. Lola Glanzberg, Aug. 26, 1961; children: Matthew Robert, Jo Ann Lehrman Tierney. BS in Printing Mgmt., Carnegie Inst. Tech., 1954; postgrad., Pratt Inst., Bklyn., 1958-61. Prodn. asst. United Catalog Pubs., Hempstead, N.Y., 1957-58; pres. Design Unltd./Culinary Concepts, Hempstead, N.Y., 1958-84; profl. artist Mill River, Mass., 1985-92, Scottsdale, Ariz., 1992—; watercolor instr. Scottsdale Artists' Sch., 1992—, Sun Lakes, Ariz., 1995—; producer, moderator panel discussion series Insight: Art, 1993—; rep. by Long Gallery, Scottsdale. Author: Becoming a Successful Artist, 1995, Energize Your Paintings with Color, 1993, Freshen Your Paintings with New Ideas, 1994, (with Ted Goerschner) Oil Painting Fresh and Bright, 1995, (with Marilyn Simandle) Capturing Light in Watercolor, 1996. With U.S. Army, 1954-56. Home: 9123 N 115th Pl Scottsdale AZ 85259-5922 Office: Lewis B Lehrman Studio Studio E 4240 N Brown Ave Scottsdale AZ 85251

LEHTIHALME, LARRY (LAURI) K., financial planner; b. Montreal, Que., Can., Feb. 26, 1937; came to U.S., 1964; s. Lauri Johann and Selma Maire (Piispanen) L.; m. Elizabeth Speed Smith, Sept. 9, 1961; children: Tina Beth, Shauna Lyn. Student, Sir George Williams U., Montreal, 1960-64, Mission Coll., San Fernando, Calif., 1978-80, Pierce Coll., Woodland Hills, Calif., 1990-92. Lic. in variable annuity, life and disability ins., Calif.; lic. securities series 7 SEC, series 63. Acct., customer svc. cons. No. Electric, Montreal, 1957-64; salesman Remington Rand Systems, Wilmington, Del., 1964-67; account exec., comm. cons. Pacific Tel. & Telegraph Co., L.A., 1968-84; tech. customer support specialist AT&T, L.A., 1984-85; fin. adv., registered rep. Am. Express Fin. Advisors, L.A., 1987—. Mem. ctrl. com. Calif. 39th Assembly Dist. Rep. Com., 1976-81, City of L.A., 12th dist.; pres. North Hills Jaycees, 1969-70; sec.-treas. Com. Ind. Valley City and County Govt., 1978-82; subchmn. allocations United Way, Van Nuys, Calif., 1990; fundraiser North Valley YMCA, 1986—, Kids Safe Edn. Found.; formerly active numerous comty. and polit. orgns. in San Fernando Valley. Named Jaycee of Yr., Newark (Del.) Jaycees, 1966, Granada Hills Jaycees, 1971; recipient cert. of merit U.S. Ho. of Reps., 1973, cert. appreciation City of L.A., 1980, 84, State of Calif., 20th senate dist., 1983, Comty. Spirit award, 1990. Mem. L.A. Olympic Organizing Com. Alumni Assn., Jr. Chamber Internat. (life, senator 1973), U.S. Jaycees (life, Jaycee of Yr. 1965, Outstanding Local Jaycee 1965-66, Presdl. award Honor 1967, Jaycee of Month 1966-67, asst. gen. chmn. 1970-71, state dir. N. Hollywood chpt. 1970-71, Cert. Merit 1971, state gen. chmn., 1971-72, 72-73, Outstanding State Chmn. Calif. dist. 22 1973-74), Granada Hills C. of C. (bd. dirs. 1976-83, Man of Yr. award 1973), Granada Hills Jr. C. of C. Episcopalian. Home: 11408 Haskell Ave Granada Hills CA 91344-3959 Office: Am Express Fin Advisors 11145 Tampa Ave Ste 20A Northridge CA 91326-2264

LEIBERT, RICHARD WILLIAM, special events producer; b. N.Y.C., Nov. 11, 1948; s. Richard William and Rosemarie Martha (Bruns) L. BS, Boston U., 1966-70; student, Northwestern U., 1971. Producer Sta. WBZ AM/FM, Boston, 1968-70; prodn. dir. Sta. WMMR-FM, Phila., 1970; exec. producer Sta. WIND-AM, Chgo., 1970-72; program dir. Sta. KGB AM-FM, San Diego, 1972-80; pres. Events Mktg., Inc., L.A., 1980—; dir. Nat. Fireworks Ensemble, Los Angeles, Calif., 1985—. Creator (mascot, publicity stunts) Sta. KGB Chicken, 1974; creator, producer (radio fireworks show) Sta. KGB Sky Show, 1976; writer, producer (network radio show) New Music News, 1983; creator, dir. (touring co.) Nat. Fireworks Ensemble, 1985. Recipient Emmy award, 1978; named Program Dir. of Yr. Billboard Mag., 1976, Radio Program of Yr. Billboard Mag., 1976. Office: Events Mktg Inc PO Box 65694 Los Angeles CA 90065-0694

LEIBOVIT, ARNOLD L., film producer, director; b. Miami Beach, Fla., June 18, 1950; s. Meyer and Geraldine L.; m. Barbara Schimpf. AA, U. Fla., 1971; BA cum laude, UCLA, 1973. dir. Sedona (Ariz.) Spirit Theatre, 1989-92; pres., dir. Talking Rings Entertainment, Beverly Hills Calif., 1988-96. Dir., editor (shorts) The Fatherland, 1973, Judgement: An Essay on War, 1974, Penny Lane, 1975; assoc. dir., editor: Rascal Dazzle, 1980; prodr., dir., writer (film/documentary) The Fantasy Film Worlds of George Pal, 1986; prodr., writer (motion picture) The Puppetoon Movie, 1987; prodr. (record, CD) The Time Machine, 1987. Recipient Saturn award Acad. Sci. Fiction & Fantasy, 1986, Golden Eagle award CINE, 1974, 86. Office: Arnold Leibovit Prodns PO Box 80141 Las Vegas NV 89180

LEIBOWITZ, ARLEEN A., economist; b. Binghamton, N.Y., June 11, 1942; d. Albert E. and Mae Smigel; m. Robert D. Leibowitz, Aug. 22, 1965; children: Nora, Karen. BA, Smith Coll., 1964; PhD, Columbia U., 1972. Economic analyst Arthur D. Little, Cambridge, Mass., 1965-67; rsch. assoc. Nat. Bureau of Econ. Rsch., N.Y.C., 1971-74; vis. asst. prof. econs. Brown U., Providence, R.I., 1972-75; adj. asst. prof. U. Miami, 1975-76; rsch. prof. law U. Miami (Fla.), 1976-77; economist Rand Corp., Santa Monica, Calif., 1977—; prof. UCLA Sch. Pub. Policy and Social Rsch., 1996—. Mem. L.A. Task Force on Access to Health Care, 1992-94. Office: UCLA Sch Pub

Policy & Social Rsch Dept Policy Studies 3250 Public Policy Bldg Los Angeles CA 90095-1656

LEIDL, PETER JANOS, internist; b. Budapest, Hungary, Mar. 4, 1942; came to U.S., 1959; s. Erno T. and Klara (Mellinger) L.; m. Rose Dumlao, July 26, 1991. BA in Chemistry, Lehigh U., 1965; MS in Chemistry, Fairleigh Dickinson U., 1975; MD, Autonomous U., Guadalajara, Mex., 1981. Diplomate Am. Bd. Internal Medicine, Am. Bd. Geriatric Medicine. Rsch. chemist Schering Plough Corp., Bloomfield, N.J., 1965-77; intern St. Barnabas Med. Ctr., Livingston, N.J., 1981-82; resident Chgo. Med. Sch., North Chicago, Ill., 1982-85; staff physician Talbert Med. Group, Long Beach, Calif., 1986—. Mem. AMA, ACP. Home: 424 N Bellflower Blvd Unit 307 Long Beach CA 90814-2006 Office: 500 Alamitos Ave Long Beach CA 90802-1513

LEIGH, VINCENTA M., health administrator; b. N.Y.C., June 27, 1947; d. Emanuel and Ines Masciandara; m. Hoyle Leigh, Sept. 16, 1967; 1 child, Alexander. BA, Lehman Coll., 1968; MSN, Yale U., 1973. Psychiat. clinician Jacobi Hosp., Bronx, N.Y., 1971; pediatric nurse Conn. Mental Health Ctr., New Haven, 1971-73; instr. in psychiat. nursing Yale U., New Haven, 1973-77; asst. dir. mental health nursing edn. Conn. Valley Hosp., Middletown, 1980-81; nurse coord. Inst. of Living, Hartford, Conn., 1981-85, asst. dir. nursing, 1985-89; asst. clin. profl. psychiatry U. Calif., San Francisco, 1989—; coord. Intensive outpatient program Kaiser Permanente, Fresno, Calif., 1996—. Contbr. articles to profl. jours. Mem. ANA, Am. Psychosomatic Soc., Internat. Coll. Psychosomatic Medicine, Am. Orthopedic Assn., Jr. League.

LEIGHNINGER, DAVID SCOTT, cardiovascular surgeon; b. Youngstown, Ohio, Jan. 16, 1920; s. Jesse Harrison and Marjorie (Lightner) L.; m. Margaret Jane Malony, May 24, 1942; children: David Allan, Jenny. BA, Oberlin Coll., 1942; MD, Case Western Res. U., 1945. Intern Univ. Hosps. of Cleve., 1945-46, resident, 1949-51, asst. surgeon, 1951-68; rsch. fellow in cardiovascular surgery rsch. lab. Case Western Res. U. Sch. Medicine, Cleve., 1948-49, 51-55, 57-67, instr. surgery, 1951-55, sr. instr., 1957-64, asst. prof., 1964-68, asst. clin. prof., 1968-70; resident Cin. Gen. Hosp., 1955-57; practice medicine specializing in cardiovascular surgery, Cleve., 1957-70; pvt. practice medicine specializing in cardiovascular and gen. surgery Edgewater Hosp., Chgo., 1970-82, staff surgeon, also dir. emergency surg. services, 1970-82; staff surgeon, also dir. emergency surg. svcs. Mazel Med. Ctr., Chgo., 1970-82; emergency physician, Raton, N.Mex. and Trinidad, Colo., 1982-85; assoc., courtesy, or cons. staff Marymount Hosp., Cleve., Mt. Sinai Hosp., Cleve., Geauga Community Hosp., Chardon, Ohio, Bedford Community Hosp (Ohio), 1957-70. Tchr. tng. courses in CPR for med. personnel, police, fire and vol. rescue workers, numerous cities, 1950-70. Served to capt., M.C., AUS, 1946-48. Recipient Chris award Columbus Internat. Film Festival, 1964, numerous other award for sci. exhibits from various nat. and state med. socs., 1953-70; USPHS grantee, 1949-68. Fellow Am. Coll. Cardiology, Am. Coll. Chest Physicians; mem. AMA, N.Mex. Med. Assn., Colfax County Med. Assn., Ill. Med. Assn., Chgo. Med. Assn., Mont Reid Surg. Soc. (Cinn.). Contbr. numerous articles to med. jours., chpts. to med. texts; spl. pioneer research (with Claude S. Beck) in physiopathology of coronary artery disease and CPR; developed surg. treatment of coronary artery disease; achieved 1st successful defibrillation of human heart, 1st successful reversal of fatal heart attack; provided 1st intensive care of coronary patients. Home: HC 68 Box 77 Fort Garland CO 81133-9708

LEIGHTON, HENRY ALEXANDER, physician, consultant; b. Manila, Nov. 12, 1929; (parents U.S. citizens).; s. Raymond Harry and Theola Marie (Alexander) L.; m. Helga Maria Hell, Jan. 17, 1970; children: Alan Raymond, Henry Alexander, Michael Ballinger, John, Marni, Tammy Ballinger. BA in History, U. Calif., Berkeley, 1952, MPH, 1971; MD, U. Calif., San Francisco, 1956. Diplomate Am. Bd. Preventive Medicine. Intern So. Pacific Gen. Hosp., San Francisco, 1956-57; resident in surgery Brooke Gen. Hosp., Ft. Sam Houston, Tex., 1960-62; commd. 2d. lt. U.S. Army, 1957, advanced through grades to col., 1971; div. surgeon 8th Inf. div. U.S. Army, Germany, 1964-66; comdr. 15th Med. Bn. U.S. Army, Vietnam, 1966-67; instr. Med. Field Service Sch. U.S. Army, San Antonio, 1968-70; resident preventive medicine U.S. Army, Ft. Ord, Calif., 1971-72, chief preventive medicine, 1973-76; chief preventive medicine U.S. Army-Europe, 1976-79, ret., 1979; chief occupational health MEDDAC U.S. Army, Ft. Ord, 1981-89; pvt. practice Salinas, Calif., 1990—. Neighborhood commr. Boy Scouts Am., 1964-66; bd. dirs. Am. Lung Assn. of Calif., 1982-84, and of affiliate, 1980-86, The Calif. Acad. Preventive Medicine, 1994-96; pres. The Bluffs Homeowners Assn., 1986. Decorated Air medal with oak leaf cluster, Bronze Star, Legion of Merit, Meritorious Service medal. Fellow Am. Coll. Preventive Medicine; mem. Am. Pub. Health Assn., Am. Coll. Occupational Medicine, Assn. Mil. Surgeons, Ret. Officers Assn., Assn. U.S. Army, Theta Xi. Lodges: Masons, Shriners. Office: 14096 Reservation Rd Salinas CA 93908-9208

LEIGHTON, JACK RICHARD, small business owner, former educator; b. Boise, Idaho, May 10, 1918; s. Ralph Waldo and Lucia Marie (Strub) L.; m. Helen Louise Wirtenberger, July 24, 1942; 1 child, James Carl. Student, U. Wash., 1938-39; BS, U. Oreg., 1941, MS, 1942, PhD, 1954; postgrad., U. Iowa, 1950. Dir. phys. edn. and athletics Montpelier (Idaho) H.S., 1941-42; exec. asst. phys. medicine rehab. svc. Vancouver (Wash.) VA Hosp., 1946-50; assoc. prof. phys. edn. Pa. State U., State College, 1952-53; assoc. prof. Ea. Wash. U., Cheney, 1953-56, prof., 1956-81, dir. divsn. health, phys. edn., recreation and athletics, 1953-81; pres. Leighton Flexometer Co., Spokane, Wash., 1985—; Mem. com. on secondary sch. health and phys. edn. Idaho Dept. Edn., Boise, 1942; cons. state adv. com. on sch. activity and phys. edn. Wash. Dept. Pub. Instrn., Olympia, 1954-55, mem. com. on phys. edn. curriculum guide, 1957-58. Author: Physical Education for Boys, 1942, Objective Physical Education, 1946, Progressive Weight Training, 1961, Fitness, Body Development & Sports Conditioning Through Weight Training, 1983; assoc. editor Rsch. Quar. AAHPERD, 1960-63, Jour. Health, Phys. Edn. and Recreation, 1967-68; editor Jour. Assn. for Phys. and Mental Rehab., 1963-67; mem. editl. bd. Am. Corrective Therapy Jour., 1972-79; contbr. articles to profl. jours., chpts. to books; patentee instrument to measure range of joint motion. With AUS, 1942-46. Fellow Am. Coll. Sports Medicine; mem. AAHPERD (necrology com. 1955-58, chmn. fitness sect. 1960-61, mem. rsch. coun., com. to study purpose and propose revisions of structure and procedures gen. divsn. 1960-61; mem. N.W. dist. honor awards com. 1955-57, 76-79, chmn. 1976-77, mem. constn. com. 1957-60, chmn. rsch. sect. 1957-58, v.p. phys. edn. 1957-58, chmn. fitness sect. 1963-64, pres. 1971-72), Wash. Assn. Health, Phys. Edn. and Recreation (phys. fitness steering com. 1955-57, constn. com. 1957-58, chmn. tchr. tng. sect. 1956-57, phys. fitness steering com. 1957-59, v.p. ea. dist. 1957-58, pres. 1959-60), Spokane United Sch. Groups (Ea. Wash. U. rep. 1957-60), Phi Delta Kappa, Phi Epsilon Kappa. Home and Office: E 1321 55th St Spokane WA 99223

LEIGHTON, PETER ELLIOTT, marketing executive; b. Millbrae, Calif., Jan. 31, 1962; s. Elliott Leighton and Barbara (Reines) Lazear; m. Joy Robin Brown, Mar. 22, 1987; children: Sarah R., Allison J. Student, U. Fla., 1980-84, New Sch. for Social Rsch., 1984. Account exec. G/D Advt., Miami, Fla., 1984; sr. account exec. Goldcoast Advt., Miami, 1985; exec. v.p. Advisors, Ft. Lauderdale, Fla., 1985-89; pres. Leighton/Brydger/Gottron, Ft. Lauderdale, 1989-91; account dir. Gauger & Silva Assocs., San Francisco, 1991-96; dir. mktg. InterHealth Nutritionals, Concord, Calif., 1996—; pres., contbg. editor Bus. Builders, San Francisco, 1992-93. Contbg. writer Health Foods Bus., Frozen Food Age, Gourmet Retailer. Recipient Price Waterhouse's Up & Comer Achievement awards, 1988, 91. Democrat. Jewish. Office: InterHealth Nutritionals 1320 Galaxy Way Concord CA 94520

LEINEWEBER, PETER ANTHONY, forest products company executive; b. Portland, Oreg., Sept. 28, 1944; s. Peter Cornelius and Isabel (Brown) L.; m. Heidi Milly Baxter, July 14, 1978; children: John James, Joseph Stephen, Thomas Gregory. BS, Portland State U., 1968; MBA, U. Wash., 1970. Loan officer U.S. Nat. Bank Oreg., Portland, 1962-69; mgr. Pacific N.W. Bell, Portland, 1970-76; sr. v.p. Market Transport, Ltd., Portland, 1976-90; v.p. Crown Pacific, Portland, 1990—; dir. Market Transport, Ltd., Portland, Oreg. Forest Resources Inst., Portland, Timber Operators Coun., Tigard, Oreg. Dir. Portland State U. Found. Mem. Oreg. Trucking Assns. (Mem. of Yr. 1990), Multnomah Athletic Club. Democrat. Roman Catholic. Office: Crown Pacific 121 SW Morrison St Ste 1500 Portland OR 97204-3145

LEININGER, CHRIS J., physician; b. Chgo., Oct. 27, 1947; s. Philip W. and Lorie (Dodge) L.; m. Jyl P. Jacobowitz, Sept. 8, 1979; 1 child, Alex Carl. BA, Amherst Coll., 1969; MS, U. Pa., 1971; MD, NYU, 1975. Diplomate Am. Bd. Family Practice. Resident, chief resident in family practice Doctors Hosp., Seattle, 1975-78; physician Greenlake Med. Ctr., Seattle, 1979-85; physician Greenwood Family Medicine, Seattle, 1985-94, med. mgmt. cons., 1992—; dir. profl. svcs. Swedish Med. Svcs., Seattle, 1994—; asst. clin. prof. Sch. Medicine, U. Wash., Seattle, 1978—; attending faculty Swedish Family Practice Program, Seattle, 1980—. Fellow Am. Acad. Family Practice. Home: 7606 E Green Lake Dr N Seattle WA 98103-4911 Office: Swedish Medical Services 747 Broadway PO Box 14999 Seattle WA 98114-0999

LEINO, DEANNA ROSE, business educator; b. Leadville, Colo., Dec. 15, 1937; d. Arvo Ensio Leino and Edith Mary (Bonan) Leino Malenck; adopted child, Michael Charles Bonan. BSBA, U. Denver, 1959, MS in Bus. Adminstrn., 1967; postgrad. Community Coll. Denver, U. No. Colo., Colo. State U., U. Colo., Met. State Coll. Cert. tchr., vocat. tchr., Colo. Tchr. Jefferson County Adult Edn., Lakewood, Colo., 1963-67; retired tchr. bus., coordinator coop. office edn., Jefferson High Sch., Edgewater, Colo., 1959-93, ret., 1993; sales assoc. Joslins Dept. Store, Denver, 1978—; mem. ea. team, clk. office automation Denver Svc. Ctr. Nat. Park Svc, 1993-94, U.S. Dept. Labor, 1994—, wage hour asst.; instr. Community Coll. Denver, Red Rocks, 1967-81, U. Colo. Denver, 1976-79, Parks Coll. Bus. (name now Parks Jr. Coll.), 1983—; dist. adviser Future Bus. Leaders Am. Active City of Edgewater Sister City Project Student Exchange Com.; pres. Career Women's Symphony Guild; treas. Phantoms of Opera, 1982—; active Opera Colo. Assocs. & Guild, I Pagliacci; ex-officio trustee Denver Symphony Assn., 1980-82. Recipient Disting. Svc. award Jefferson County Sch. Bd. 1980, Tchr. Who Makes A Difference award Sta. KCNC/Rocky Mountain News, 1990, Youth Leader award Lakewood Optimist Club, 1993; inducted into Jefferson High Sch. Wall of Fame 1981 Mem. NEA (life), Colo. Edn. Assn., Jefferson County Edn. Assn., Colo. Vocat. Assn., Am. Vocat. Assn., Colo. Educators for and about Bus., Profl. Secs. Internat., Career Women's Symphony Guild, Profl. Panhellenic Assn., Colo. Congress Fgn. Lang. Tchrs., Wheat Ridge C. of C. (edn. and scholarship com.), Federally Employed Women, Delta Pi Epsilon, Phi Chi Theta, Beta Gamma Sigma, Alpha Lambda Delta. Republican. Roman Catholic. Club: Tyrolean Soc. Denver. Avocations: decorating wedding cakes, crocheting, sewing, music, world travel. Home: 3712 Allison St Wheat Ridge CO 80033-6124

LEIPPER, DIANE LOUISE, association administrator; b. San Diego, Nov. 6, 1946; d. Dale F. and Virginia A. (Harrison) L. Student, Tex. A&M U., 1966-67; BA in Social Work, U. Nev., 1982. Lic. social worker, Nev. Program dir. Sierra Nevada Girl Scout Coun., Reno, 1984-88; disaster/comty. svc. dir. Sierra Nevada chpt. ARC, Reno, 1989-90; vol. supr. Washoe Med. Ctr., Reno, 1990-95; ptnr., cons. Leipper Mgmt. Group, Reno, 1995—; mem. legis. subcom. Am. Soc. Dirs. of Vol. Svc.; mem. dir.'s coord. coun. Calif. Assn. Hosps. and Health Care Sys., Sacramento, 1993-95; co-creator vol. program Critical Care Family Support Program, 1994; presenter in field. Co-author, prodr.: (booklet) Legislative Advocacy, 1993; creator: (manual) Vendor Management, 1994. Mem. adv. bd. No. Nev. Career Coll., Sparks, 1993-95; coun. mem. St. Mary's Hospice No. Nev., Reno, 1994—; vol., trainer, bd. dirs. Crisis Call Ctr., Reno, 1978-83. Recipient Sertoma Svc. to Mankind award Comstock Sertoma, 1995, Thanks badge Sierra Nevada Girl Scout Coun., 1990. Mem. Internat. Assn. Vol. Effort, Assn. Vol. Adminstrs. (presenter), Am. Soc. Assn. Execs., No. Calif. Assn. Dirs. Vol. Svcs. (legis. chair edn. com. 1991-94, pres.-elect 1995), Sparks Optimist. Office: Leipper Mgmt Group 714 Terra Ct Reno NV 89506

LEIS, MARIETTA PATRICIA, artist; b. Newark; d. George Francis and Marietta Roma (Napoliello) L. BA, Antioch Coll. West, 1975; MA in Painting/Drawing, U. N.Mex., 1985, MFA in Painting/Drawing, 1988. Art instr. Coll. Fine Arts, Albuquerque, 1985-88; art instr. cmty. coll. divsn. continuing edn. U. N.Mex., Albuquerque, 1988—; artist-tchr. MFA program Vt. Coll. of Norwich U., Montpelier, 1991—. One-person shows include St. John's Coll., Santa Fe, N.Mex., 1990, Pacific Internat. Art Gallery, Palo Alto, Calif., 1991, U. N.Mex. Continuing Edn. Conf. Ctr., Albuquerque, 1993, Jonson Gallery, U. N.Mex., Albuquerque, 1996; exhibited in group shows at Oakland C.C., Farmington Hills, Mich., 1993, Gallery Per Tutti, Boston, 1993, Merrill Chase Galleries, Buffalo Grove, Ill., 1993, Cooperstown (N.Y.) Art Assn., 1993, Allentown (Pa.) Art Mus., 1993, also pub. collections; contbr. articles to profl. jours. Artist grantee Artist Space, N.Y.C., E.D. Found., 1994, 95, 96; recipient Hon. Distinction award Internat. Art Biennial, Mus. Hisico, Capranica, Italy, 4th Ann. Faber Birren Color award Stanford (Conn.) Art Assn., Art-in-Opera Merit award Met. Opera Guild, Inc. Mem. Nat. Assn. Women Artists. Home and Office: PO Drawer D Corrales NM 87048-0159

LEISEY, DONALD EUGENE, educational materials company executive, educator; b. Pa., Sept. 23, 1937; s. Alvin L. and E. Marie L.; BS in Edn., West Chester (Pa.) State U., 1959; MA in Adminstrn., Villanova U., 1962; EdD in Adminstrn., U. So. Calif., 1973; m. Patricia M. Leisey; children: Kristen, Kendra. Tchr., Coatesville, Pa., 1959-62; prin., Downingtown, Pa., 1962-64; prin. Dept. Def. Dependent Schs., Japan, 1964-67; asst. supt. Lennox Schs., Inglewood, Calif., 1967-71; dir. adminstrv. services San Rafael (Calif.) City Sch. Dist., 1971-73, supt. schs., 1973-79; v.p., regional mgr. Am. Learning Corp., Huntington Beach, Calif., 1979-80; v.p., treas. Kittredge Sch. Corp., San Francisco, 1980-83; instr. Calif. State U. at Hayward, 1981; pres., chmn. bd. Merryhill Schs. Inc., Sacramento, 1981-89; pres., chmn. bd. The Report Card, Citrus Heights, Calif., 1990—. Apptd. to Gov.'s Child Care Task Force, Calif., 1984, Gov.'s Child Devel. Programs Adv. Com., Calif., 1985—. Recipient Disting. Alumnus award West Chester State U., 1983, Disting. Service award L.A. County Sheriff, 1969, Hon. Svc. award PTA, 1970. Mem. Delta Epsilon, Phi Delta Kappa. Certifications: gen. adminstrv., gen. secondary, gen. elementary, Calif. Home: 21 Silk Oak Cir San Rafael CA 94901-8301 Office: 6366 Tupelo Dr Citrus Heights CA 95621-1700

LEISSRING, JOHN COTHER, pathologist; b. Milw., Mar. 29, 1935; s. William Frederick and Alice Jane (Webb) Leissring; m. Judith Lee Lentz, June 1959 (div. 1981); children: Matthew William, Malcolm Arthur. BS, U. Wis., 1957, MS in Anatomy, 1961, MD, 1961. Diplomate Bd. Med. Examiners, Wis., Calif., Am. Bd. Pathology, Am. Bd. Dermatology. Rsch. asst. dept. endocrinology U. Wis., 1955-57, rsch. asst. dept. anatomy, 1957-59; intern U.S. Naval Hosp., Oakland, Calif., 1961-62; resident in pathology Stanford U. Med. Ctr., 1965-69; instr. pathology Stanford (Calif.) Med. Sch., 1968-69; asst. clin. prof. U. Calif. Med. Sch., San Francisco, 1969-74; pathologist Santa Rosa (Calif.) Meml. Hosp., 1969—. Author: Life and Work of Michael Brenner, 1991, Songs My Father Never Sang, 1996; contbr. articles to profl. jours. Lt. comdr. USN, 1959-65. Recipient Borden award in rsch. Borden Inst., Madison, Wis., 1961. Fellow Coll. Am. Pathologists, Am. Soc. Clin. Pathologists; mem. Pacific Derm. Soc., Calif. Soc. Pathologists, Pacific Dermatologic Soc., Press Club of San Francisco, Musicians Union, AFL/CIO, Pho Kappa Phi, Alpha Omega Alpha. Home: 1015 Mcdonald Ave Santa Rosa CA 95404-3524 Office: Drs Leissring and DeMeo 1144 Montgomery Dr Santa Rosa CA 95405-4802

LEISTER-CAMPBELL, BETTY ANN, special education educator; b. Chicoteague, Va., Aug. 29, 1955; d. Joesph William and Sallie Kay (Hollingshead) Leister; 1 child from previous marriage, Beau Mullins; m. Gregory Leo Campbell, Oct. 13, 1989. BA, UCLA, 1978; MA, Calif. State U., Carson, 1991. Cert. tchr. elem. and spl. edn. K-12, Calif. Aerobics instr., supr. Manhattan Club for Women, Manhattan Beach, Calif., 1982-85; bookkeeper Manhattan Club for Men, Manhattan Beach, 1983-85; 4th grade tchr. South Bay Christian Sch., Redondo Beach, Calif., 1985-87; latchkey coord., tchr. Inglewood (Calif.) Unified Sch. Dist., 1987-89; spl. edn. tchr. L.A. Sch. Dist., Lomita, Calif., 1989, Palos Verdes (Calif.) Unified Sch. Dist., 1990, Lawndale (Calif.) Unified Sch. Dist., 1990-92; resource specialist Paramount (Calif.) Unified Sch. Dist., 1992-93; evaluation asst. Humboldt Unified Sch. Dist., Prescott Valley, Ariz., 1993-95, intinerant spl. edn. tchr., 1995—; court apptd. spl. advocate Yavapai County, Prescott, 1994—. Mem. Citizens Quality Edn., Prescott, 1996, Coun. Exceptional Children, 1990-93, 96; mem. edn. com. co-chair Assn. Retarded Children, Phoenix, 1994—. Mem. Coun. for Exceptional Children, Calif. Div. Learning Disabilities (sec. 1990, treas. 1991, pres. elect 1992). Republican.

LEIWEKE, TIMOTHY, sales executive, marketing professional; b. St. Louis, Apr. 21, 1957; s. John Robert and Helen (Caicuey) L.; m. Pamela Leiweke, Nov. 1, 1984. Grad. high sch., St. Louis. Salesperson New Eng. Mut. Life Ins. Co., St. Louis, 1976-79; asst. gen. mgr. St. Louis Steamers/MISL, 1979-80; gen. mgr. Balt. Blast/MISL, 1980-81; v.p., gen. mgr. Kansas City (Mo.) Comets/MISL, 1981-84; v.p. Leiweke and Co., Kansas City, 1984-85; pres. Kansas City Comets/MISL, 1986-88; v.p. sales and mktg. div. Minn. Timberwolves, Mpls., 1988-91; sr. v.p. of bus. ops. Denver Nuggets, Denver, 1991-92; pres. Denver Nuggets, Denver, CO, 1992-96; pres., CEO LA Kings, Los Angeles, 1996—. Bd. dirs. Kidney Found., Minn., 1989—, Spl. Olympics, Minn., 1989—, Timberwolves Community Found., Minn., 1989—. Named Rookie of the Yr., Mo. Life Underwriters, 1976, Kansas Citian of the Yr., Kansas City Press Club, 1983; recipient William Brownfield award U.S. Jaycees, 1978, William Brownfield award Mo. Jaycees, 1978, Excalibur award Am. Cancer Soc., 1987. Mem. Kansas City Mktg. and Sales Execs., Mpls. Club. Home: 1635 Clay St Denver CO 80204-1799 Office: LA Kings NHL 3900 W Manchester Blvd Inglewood CA 90305-2200*

LEM, RICHARD DOUGLAS, painter; b. L.A., Nov. 24, 1933; s. Walter Wing and Betty (Wong) L.; B.A., UCLA, 1958; M.A., Calif. State U.-Los Angeles, 1963; m. Patricia Ann Soohoo, May 10, 1958; 1 son, Stephen Vincent. Exhibited in one-man shows at Gallery 818, Los Angeles, 1965; group shows at Lynn Kottler Galleries, N.Y.C., 1973, Palos Verdes Art Gallery, 1968, Galerie Mouffe, Paris, France, 1976, Le Salon des Nations, Paris, 1984, numerous others; represented in permanent collections; writer, illustrator: Mile's Journey, 1983, 2nd edit., 1995; cover illustrator: The Hermit, 1990, The Hermit's Journey, 1993. Served with AUS, 1958-60. Mem. UCLA Alumni Assn. Address: 1861 Webster Ave Los Angeles CA 90026-1229 *Personal philosophy: It requires a great deal of inner strength to pursue your personal vision with single mindedness - it's a challenge that justifies my existence.*

LEMASTER, SUSAN M., marketing consultant, writer; b. Cody, Wyo., May 9, 1953; d. Floyd Morris and Virginia Kristena (Renner) LeM.; B.A., U. Wyo., Casper, 1979; A.A., Casper Coll., 1977. Reporter, night editor Casper Star Tribune, 1972-76; copy editor, editor In Wyo. mag., Casper, 1979; info. dir. Wyo. Rural Electric Assn., Casper, 1980-81; story editor Wyo. Horizons mag., Casper, 1981-82; asst., instr. English lab. Casper Coll., 1982-84; mktg. mgr. Chen & Assocs., Inc., 1984-87; mktg. cons., 1987-90; dir. mktg. KaWES and Assocs., Inc., 1990-91, pub. rels./mktg. cons., 1992-95; comm. mgr. Arthur Andersen, 1995—; freelance writer and editor, 1982—; night sch. instr. Casper Coll., 1983-84, summer sch. instr., 1984. Editor Casper Jour., 1983-84. Recipient First Place News Story, Wyo. Press Assn., 1973; first pl. Editing award Wyo. Press Women, 1980. Mem. L.A. Press Club, Phi Theta Kappa, Phi Kappa Phi, Alpha Mu Gamma. Democrat. Home: 1820 N Bel Aire Burbank CA 91504 Office: Arthur Andersen 633 W 5th St Los Angeles CA 90071

LEMBECK, JAMES PETER, nutritionist, consultant; b. Huntington, N.Y., Nov. 21, 1955; s. Gustav William and Eileen Mary (McEnery) L. BS, Buffalo State U., 1980; MS, Westbrook U., 1992; D, Lafayette U., 1994. Cert. herbalist, N.Mex. Nutrition/fitness dir. Apple Health and Fitness, N.Y.C., 1978-79; nutrition cons. J.L. Consulting, Watertown, N.Y.C., Mass., 1982-89, Silerhawk Inc., Parker, Colo., 1994-95; pres. Advanced Nutrient Sci., Parker, 1995-97; cons. Nutrition Industry, 1977—, Parker, 1991—, Perkins Sch. for Blind, Watertown, 1982-84. Mem. adv. bd. Nat. Body Bldg. Mag., 1986—; contbr. articles to profl. trade & consumer mags. With USAR, 1984-88. Mem. Nat. Nutritional Foods Assn., Herbal Rsch. Found. Roman Catholic. Home: 11587 N Hot Springs Dr Parker CO 80134 Office: PO Box 668 Parker CO 80134

LEMERT, JAMES BOLTON, journalist, educator; b. Sangerfield, N.Y., Nov. 5, 1935; s. Jesse Raymond and Caroline Elizabeth (Brown) L.; m. Rosalie Martha Bassett, Mar. 23, 1972. AB, U. Calif., Berkeley, 1957, M in Journalism, 1959; PhD, Mich. State U., 1964. Newspaper reporter Oakland (Calif.) Tribune, 1955-56, Chico (Calif.) Enterprise-Record, 1957, 58-60; asst. prof. journalism So. Ill. U., Carbondale, 1964-67; asst. prof. U. Oreg., Eugene, 1967-69, assoc. prof., 1969-76, prof. sch. journalism/comm., 1976—, dir. divsn. comm. rsch., 1967-94, dir. grad. program Sch. Journalism, 1983-86, 88-93; chairperson task force to revise faculty governance U. Oreg., 1983-84, mem. senate, 1981-83, 86-88, 93-94, mem. pres.'s adv. coun., 1990-91, chairperson pres.'s adv. coun., 1991-92, mem. grad. coun., 1984-86, 89-90, 94-96, chairperson grad. coun., 1993-94, chairperson task force on rsch. and grad. edn., 1990-91. Prodr., on-air host Old Grooves show Sta. KWAX-FM, 1977-80, 82-84; author: Does Mass Communication Change Public Opinion After All? A New Approach to Effects Analysis, 1981, Criticizing the Media: Empirical Approaches, 1989, News Verdicts, The Debates and Presidential Campaigns, 1991, Politics of Disenchantment: Bush, Clinton, Perot and the Press, 1996; editor Daily Californian, 1957; contbr. articles to profl. jours., newspapers and mags. Mem. Oreg. Alcohol and Drug Edn. Adv. Com., 1968-69; pres. South Hills Neighborhood Assn., 1976-77, bd. dirs., 1982-84, 86-88; bd. dirs. Traditional Jazz Soc. Oreg., 1981-83, 87; v.p. Met. Cable Access Corp., 1983-84; mem. exec. bd. AAUP, 1975-76, 91-94; mem. state exec. com., head chpt. Assn. Oreg. Faculties, 1981-83, 85-87, state v.p., 1987-89, del. to Oreg. Faculties Polit. Action Com., 1986-89. Recipient Outstanding Journalist award Sigma Delta Chi, 1957, Donald M. McGammon Communication Rsch. Ctr. critical rsch. grantee, 1988-89, Allen Family Found. grantee; NSF fellow, 1963, 64; Calif. Newspaper Pubs. fellow, 1957; Butte County Alumni scholar, 1953-54. Mem. Assn. Edn. in Journalism and Mass Comm. (vice chairperson civic journalism interest group 1995-96), Am. Assn. Pub. Opinion Rsch., Am. Polit. Sci. Assn., Phi Beta Kappa (membership chmn. 1985-86, v.p., pres. 1989-91). Home: 10 E 40th Ave Eugene OR 97405-3487 *Journalism is one of the more tradition-bound crafts. A constant underlying theme in the research and writing I do is that the research might help journalism redefine itself. There certainly is much need for change in long-held journalistic practices. Habit and "we've always done it this way" are no longer good enough reasons— if they ever were.*

LEMIRE, DAVID STEPHEN, school psychologist, educator; b. Roswell, N.Mex., May 23, 1949; s. Joseph Armon and Jeanne (Longwill) L.; BA, Linfield Coll., 1972, MEd, 1974; EdS, Idaho State U., 1978; postgrad. U. Wyo.; EdS in Ednl. Adminstrn. and Instructional Leadership, U. Wyo., 1988; postgrad. U. Wyo. Cert. sch. counselor, student pers. worker, psychology instr., Calif. Sch. counselor, psychol. technician and tchr. Goshen County Sch. Dist. 1, Torrington, Wyo., counselor Aspen High Sch., Aspen, Colo.; sch. counselor Unita County Sch. Dist., Evanston, Wyo., coord. R&D Lifelong Learning Ctr. 1986-87; dir. spl. svcs. and sch. psychologist Bighorn County Sch. Dist. #4, Basin, Wyo., 1989-90; sch. psychologist Sweetwater County Sch. Dist. #2, Green River, Wyo., 1990-91; dir. housing, residence supr. Pratt (Kans.) Community Coll., 1991-92; pres. David Lemire Software Enterprises, Evanston; dir. Inst. for Advanced Study of Thinkology. Mem. ASCD, Nat. Assn. Sch. Psychologists (cert.), Am. Psychol. Assn. Former editor WACD Jour.; former mng. editor Jour. Humanistic Edn.; contbr. articles to profl. jours. Address: PO Box 6266 Kansas City KS 66106-0266 also: Creative Therapeutics Adminstrv Offices 2390 Riviera St Reno NV 89509-1144 *Personal philosophy: Teaching is the most important function of higher education. All education should focus on what students are successful at, then help students (young or old) to shape their own skills and learn more effectively. In general, my concern is with the quality of instruction more than with the quantity of instruction.*

LEMKE, HERMAN ERNEST FREDERICK, JR., retired elementary education educator, consultant; b. Argo, Ill., July 13, 1919; s. Herman and Augusta Victoria (Stahl) L.; m. Geneva Octavane, Sept. 5, 1942; children: Patricia, Herman E.F. III, Gloria, John, Elizabeth. BA, George Peabody Coll., 1949, MA, 1952. Cert. social sci. tchr., Tenn., elem. tchr., Calif. Tchr. Cadd Parish Sch., Shreveport, La., 1950-55, Pacific Sch. Dist., Sacramento, 1956-58, Sacramento Sch. Dist., 1958-89; part-time tchr. Sacramento County Sch., 1974-84. Co-author: Natural History Guide, 1963, (field guide) Outdoor World of Sacramento Region, 1975; contbr. articles to profl. jours. Asst. dist. Commn. Boys Scouts Am., Shreveport, 1954, cubmaster, 1954;

leader 4-H Club, Shreveport, 1950-54; elder Faith Luth. Ch., Fair Oaks, Calif., 1981-88. Recipient Scouter award, Boy Scouts Am., Shreveport, 1954, Honorary Svc. award Am. Winn Sch. PTA, 1982, Calif. Life Diploma Elem. Schs., 1961. Mem. Calif. Congress Parents Tchrs. Inc. (life). Democrat. Home: 7720 Magnolia Ave Fair Oaks CA 95628-7316

LEMKHIN, MIKHAIL, photographer, journalist; b. Leningrad, USSR, Feb. 11, 1949; came to U.S., 1983, naturalized, 1990; s. Abram and Anna (Denkevich) L.; m. Irina Margolin, July 18, 1969; children: Nathan, Marina. MA in Journalism and Photo-journalism, Leningrad State U., 1973. Freelance and staff journalist, photographer various newspapers and publs., Leningrad; freelance photographer San Francisco, 1983—. Numerous photographic portraits, including Joan Baez, Joseph Mankeiwicz, Allen Ginsberg, Dizzy Gillespie, Richard Avedon, Peter Gabriel, Julian Lennon, Randy Newman, Joyce Carol Oats, Sting, Pete Seeger, Paul Simon, Joseph Brodsky, Andrey Sakharov, Michalangelo Antonioni, Czeslaw Milosh, and many others; one-man shows include Viborgsky Cultural Ctr., Leningrad, Russia, 1965, 66, Leningrad State U., 1968, Koret Gallery, Palo Alto, Calif., 1987, Stanford (Calif.) U., 1989, St. John's Coll., Santa Fe, 1989, Montgomery Gallery, San Francisco, 1990, Peter and Paul Fortress, Leningrad, 1991, Lenin Cultural and Hist. Ctr. Ukraine, Kiev, 1991, Concourse Pavilion, San Francisco, 1991, 3287 Folsom, San Francisco, 1992, Park Lane's Parc Fifty Five Hotel, San Francisco, 1993, San Francisco Internat. Airport, 1993, Eighth St. Gallery, Berkeley, Calif., 1993, Cafe Les Croissants, San Francisco, 1993, Owl and Monkey Cafe, San Francisco, 1994, Belcher Gallery, San Francisco, 1995, Hollywood Palladium, L.A., 1995, Koret Gallery, Palo Alto, 1996, Stanford U., 1996; represented in pub. and pvt. collections such as U. Calif. Pacific Film Archive, Stanford U. Green Libr., San Jose U., San Francisco Film Soc. Contbd. photographs to The Christian Science Monitor, San Francisco Chronicle, Nikon News, Moscow News, Ogonyok Mag.; author: Missing Frames, 1995. Mem. Internat. PEN Club, Fedn. Internat. de L'Art Photographique, Nat. Press Photographers Assn. Home: 1811 38th Ave San Francisco CA 94122-4147

LEMKIN, PAMELA AYLEEN, health facility administrator, oncological nurse, consultant; b. Torrance, Calif., Aug. 10, 1953; d. John Andrew and Jane Angela (Seymour) Renke; m. Stephen Richard Lemkin, July 16, 1986; 1 child, Victoria Jane. AA, El Camino Coll., Torrance, 1974; BSN, Calif. State U., Dominguez Hills, 1989. Staff nurse Harbor and UCLA Med. Ctr., Carson, Calif., 1974, Ann Arundel Gen. Hosp., Annapolis, Md., 1975-76; head nurse, oncology specialist Torrance Meml. Med. Ctr., 1976-83, clin. educator, 1979-83; dir. edn. Active Care, Torrance, 1983; v.p. Doctors Home Tech, Inc., Torrance, 1984-93; pres. DHT and Torrance Meml. Home Health and Hospice, 1993—; chmn. adv. bd. DHT and Torrance Meml. Home Health and Hospice, 1983—; mem. adv. bd. Cambrian Home Health, Torrance, 1993—. Author: (with others) Everyone's Guide to Cancer Therapy, 2d ed., 1994, 3d ed., 1997; contbr. articles to various profl. periodicals; host (TV ednl. program) Health Quest, 1993—. Recipient PRO award Pub. Communicators L.A., 1996, PRISM award Pub. Rels. Soc. Am., 1996. Mem. Nat. Assn. Home Care, Nat. Hospice Orgn., Calif. Assn. Health Svc. at Home. Office: DHT Torrance Meml Home Health and Hospice 3440 Lomita Blvd # 320 Torrance CA 90505

LEMLEY, DIANE CLAIRE BEERS, principal; b. Hollywood, Calif., Sept. 24; d. LaVerne and Claire Beers; married, 1966; children: Tina Slangas,Lea Devine, Chad Lemley. BA, U. Ariz., 1965, MEd, 1972; EdD, U. San Francisco, 1988. Tchr. Lagune Beach (Calif.) Pub. Schs., 1965-68, Territory Guam Schs., Dededo, Guam, 1969-71; counselor Window Rock high Sch., Ft. Defiance, Ariz., 1976; counselor, instr. Cochise Coll., Sierra Vista, Ariz., 1981-84; tchr. gifted Sierra Vista Pub. Schs., 1989-94; instr. Chapman U., Sierra Vista, 1990-93; prin. Mammoth (Ariz.) Elem. Sch., 1994—. cons. Advanced Tech. Systems, McLean, Va., 1985-87; pres. Student NEA, Tucson, 1960-61; speaker and presenter in field. Chmn., vice chmn. Sci. & Tech. Commn., Sierra Vista, 1990-94. Named Toastmaster of Yr., San Francisco, 1987. Mem. ASCD, Nat. Assn. Elem. Prins., Ariz. Sch. Adminstrs., Ariz. Educators fot. Gifted & Talented (pres. 1990-94), Rotary (nominee Tchr. of Yr. 1993), Phi Delta Kappa. Home: PO Box 791 San Manuel AZ 85631 Office: Mammoth Elem Sch PO Box 406 San Manuel AZ 85631

LEMMONS, GREGORY BERTRAM, SR., accountant; b. Oakland, Calif., July 19, 1950; s. Toy Sr. and Lela (Witt) L.; m. Sandra G. Wesley, Aug. 17, 1974; children: Gregory, Rashanya, Jacobian. BS, U. Calif., Berkeley, 1974; MBA, John F. Kennedy U., 1995. Cost engr. Kaiser Engrs., Oakland, 1968-76; acct. Safeway Stores, Walnut Creek, Calif., 1978-80; gen. acct. Hunt Wesson Foods, Fullerton, Calif., 1980-81; acct. Kaiser Health Plan, Oakland, 1981—. Asst. program dir. Eastlake YMCA, Oakland, 1968; athletic coach's asst. St. Augustine Sch., Oakland, 1985-93; fundraiser Cate Sch., Carpinteria, Calif., 1992-96; basketball coach Castilleja Sch., Palo Alto, Calif., 1993-94; adv. bd. mem. A Better Chance Program, Boston, 1993—; bus. libr. asst. John F. Kennedy U., Orinda, Calif., 1995—. Democrat. Baptist. Home: 4543 Fieldcrest Way Antioch CA 94509-7136 Office: Kaiser Permanente Med Program 1950 Franklin St Oakland CA 94612

LEMON, LESLIE GENE, consumer services company executive; b. Davenport, Iowa, June 14, 1940. BS, U. Ill., 1962, LLB, 1964. Bar: Ill. 1964, Ariz. 1972. Asst. gen. counsel Am. Farm Bur. Fedn., Chgo., 1964-69; sr. atty. Armour and Co., Chgo., 1969-71; with Viad Corp (formerly The Dial Corp and The Greyhound Corp.), Phoenix, 1971—; gen. counsel The Dial Corp (formerly Greyhound Corp.), Phoenix, 1977-96, v.p., 1979—; bd. dirs. FINOVA Group, 1992—. Vestryman All Saints Episcopal Ch., Phoenix, 1975-81; trustee Phoenix Art Mus., 1985—; bd. dirs. Phoenix Children's Hosp., 1985—; bd. visitors U. Calif. Med. Sch., Davis, 1983—. Mem. ABA, Assn. Gen. Counsel, Maricopa County Bar Assn., State Bar Ariz., Phoenix C. of C. (bd. dirs. 1989-95), Am. Arbitration Assn. (bd. dirs. 1996—), Food the Drug Law Inst. (bd. dirs. 1995-97). Home: 1136 W Butler Dr Phoenix AZ 85021-4428 Office: Viad Corp 1850 N Central Ave Phoenix AZ 85077

LEMONDS, JAMES EDWARD, JR., English language educator; b. Longview, Wash., Aug. 21, 1950; s. James Edward Sr. and Evelyn (Berndt) LeM.; m. Sherry Marie Carter, July 24, 1971; children: Kimberly Jill, Kami Deleice. BA in Edn., Western Wash. U., 1972; MA in Edn., Lewis & Clark Coll., 1976. Cert. secondary tchr. Tchr. social studies and lang. arts Cascade Jr. H.S., Longview, 1972-80; tchr. English Robert A. Long H.S., Longview, 1980—; chmn. English dept. Robert A. Long H.S., Longview, 1984—, sr. project coord., 1988—; football coach Longview Sch. Dist., 1972-89; cons. workshops and seminars, Seattle, Portland, Las Vegas, Vancouver, 1994—. Author: South of Seattle, 1997. Mem. NEA, Nat. Coun. Tchrs. English, Wash. Edn. Assn., Longview Edn. Assn. Home: 465 Growlers Gulch Castle Rock WA 98611 Office: 2903 Nichols Blvd Longview WA 98632

LEMPERT, PHILIP, advertising executive, author, syndicated columnist, TV correspondent; b. East Orange, N.J., Apr. 17, 1953; s. Sol and Lillian E. L.; married Laura Gray; 1 son. BS in Mktg., Drexel U., 1974; degree in Package Design, Pratt Inst., 1978. With Lempert Co., Belleville, N.J., 1974-89; pres. Consumer Insight, Inc., 1990-96; sr. v.p., sr. ptnr. AGE Wave Inc., 1991-93; columnist Chgo. Tribune, 1993—, Knight-Ridder/Tribune Syndicate; correspondent Today Show, WGN-TV, KTLA-TV, WGNX-TV, Tribune TV; Columnist, Supermarket News, founder, CEO Supermarket Alliance, 1993—; adj. prof. Fairleigh Dickinson U., Seton Hall U. Pub., editor newsletter The Lempert Report; also TV corr., lectr. Author: Phil Lempert's Supermarket Shopping and Value Guide, 1996, Top Ten Trends for Baby Boomers for Business, 1997. Chmn. Tribune Food Task Force, 1996—. Mem. Am. Assn. Advt. Agencies (bd. govs. 1986-88, legis. liason 1988-90, legis. coord. 1987-90), Nat. Food Brokers Assn. (chmn. food svcs. com.). Office: Tribune Broadcasting 5800 Sunset Blvd Hollywood CA 90028

LENARD, LISA H., writer, educator; b. Buffalo, June 23, 1952; d. Baryl Lenard and Donna Joyce Krohn Lenard Goldman; m. Michael E. Kushner, Apr. 8, 1978 (div. Apr. 1984); 1 child, Kaitlin Baryl. BA with honors, U. Buffalo, 1981; MFA in Writing, Vt. Coll., Montpelier, 1993. Adminstrv. asst. Mgmt. Scis., Inc., Albuquerque, 1982-84; asst. to pres. KNC, Inc., Albuquerque, 1984-86; instr. Antelope Valley Coll., Lancaster, Calif., 1990, Pueblo C.C., Mancos, Colo., 1992; fiction editor New Am. Zeen, Montpelier, 1996—; co-editor San Juan Almanac, Durango, Colo., 1996—; vis. prof. Ft. Lewis Coll., Durango, 1992—; co-host Voices of the S.W., KDUR-FM, Durango, 1996—; judge ann. fiction/poetry contest Images Mag., Durango, 1995; vis.writer Turkey Buzzard Hill Writers' Retreat, Cortez, Colo., 1994, 95. Author: (novels) Best Girl, 1993, Dissonance, 1995; editor: (anthology) From the Mountains to the Prairies, 1996; author short stories. Head Start artist in schs. So. Ute Tribe, Ignacio, Colo., 1996; mem. cmty. adv. bd.KSUT Pub. Radio, Ignacio, 1994—; artist in the schs. Mancos Valley Sch. Dist., 1994, 95; mem. Women's Resource Ctr., Durango, 1995—. Colo. Visions lit. grantee Colo. Coun. on the Arts, 1995; Regents scholar, 1970. Mem. Assoc. Writing Programs, Nat. Coll. Tchrs. of English, Cortez U. Ctr., Mancos Valley Arts Coun., Pinon Arts Coun., Cedar Song S.W. Writers (bd. dirs.).

LENDERMAN, JOANIE, elementary education educator; b. Medford, Oreg., Jan. 20, 1946; d. Jay Lenderman and Vivian Spencer. BS in Edn., So. Oreg. Coll., Ashland, 1969; MS in Edn., Portland State U., 1972; postgrad., U. Va., 1985. Elem. tchr. Beaverton (Oreg.) Schs., 1972-76, Internat. Sch. Svcs., Isfahan, Iran, 1976-78; ESL instr. Lang. Svcs., Tucker, Ga., 1983-84; tchr. Fairfax (Va.) Schs., 1985-86; elem. tchr. Beaverton (Oreg.) Schs., 1990-96. Mem. Nat. Trust for Hist. Preservation, Hist. Preservation League of Oreg., Portland. Mem. AAAS, AAUW, U.S. Hist. Soc., Platform Soc., Smithsonian Instn., Am. Mus. Natural History, Nat. Mus. Women in Arts, U.S. Hist. Soc., The UN, The Colonial Williamsburg Found., Wilson Ctr., N.Y. Acad. Sci., Nat. Trust for Hist. Preservation, Hist. Preservation League of Oreg. Home: 4920 NW Salishan Dr Portland OR 97229

LENEAU, THOMAS ERVIN, gas company executive; b. Mpls., Aug. 3, 1950; s. Thomas J. and Evelyn F. (Schwantees) LeN. BS in Math., St. Cloud State U., 1972; MEd, U. Minn., 1977; B in Acctg., U. Minn., Duluth, 1979; MBA, Ariz. State U., 1985. CPA, Ariz., Minn. Math. instr. Duluth Pub. Schs., 1972-78; acctg. instr. U. Minn., Duluth, 1978-79; auditor Deloitte, Haskins & Sells, Mpls., 1979-81; v.p. fin. Rio Verde Devel., Scottsdale, Ariz., 1981-86; pres., CEO Black Mountain Gas Co., Cave Creek, Ariz., 1986—, also bd. dirs. Treas. Foothills Community Found., Carefree, Ariz., 1989-94; mem. adv. bd. Desert Foothills Land Trust, Cave Creek, Ariz., 1995—, treas. 1997—; treas. Desert Foothills Land Trust, 1996. Mem. AICPA. Office: Black Mountain Gas Co PO Box 427 Cave Creek AZ 85331-0427

LENGYEL, CORNEL ADAM (CORNEL ADAM), author; b. Fairfield, Conn., Jan. 1, 1915; s. Elmer Alexander and Mary Elizabeth (Bismarck) L.; m. Teresa Delaney Murphy, July 10, 1933; children: Jerome Benedict, Paul Joel, Michael Sebastian, Cornelia (Mrs. Charles Burke). LittD (hon.), World Acad. of Arts and Culture, Taiwan, 1991. Editor, supr. Fed. Research Project, San Francisco, 1938-41; music critic The Coast, San Francisco, 1937-41; shipwright, personnel officer Kaiser Shipyard, Richmond, Calif., 1942-44; mgr. Forty-Nine Theatre, Georgetown, Calif., 1946-50; editor W.H. Freeman Co., San Francisco, 1952-54; founder, exec. editor Dragon's Teeth Press, Georgetown, 1969—; vis. prof., lectr. English lit. Calif. State U., 1962-63; writer-in-residence Hamline U., St. Paul, 1968-69; guest lectr. MIT, 1969; transl. from Hungarian; editorial cons. HEW; ednl. dir. ILGWU. Author: (history) American Testament: The Story of the Promised Land, 1956, Four Days in July, 1958, I, Benedict Arnold: The Anatomy of Treason, 1960, Presidents of the U.S.A., 1961, Ethan Allen and the Green Mountain Boys, 1961, Jesus the Galileean, 1966, The Declaration of Independence, 1969; (poetry) Thirty Pieces, 1933, First Psalms, 1950, Fifty Poems, 1965, Four Dozen Songs, 1970, The Lookout's Letter, 1971, Late News from Adam's Acres, 1983, El Dorado Forest: Selected Poems, 1986, Advice to a Future Poet: Poems Early and Late, 1996; (plays) The World's My Village, 1935, Jonah Fugitive, 1936, The Giant's Trap, 1938, The Atom Clock, 1951, Eden, Inc., 1954, rev. edit. The Master Plan, 1963, Will of Stratford, 1964, Three Plays, 1964, The Case of Benedict Arnold, 1975, Doctor Franklin, 1976, The Shadow Trap, 1977, The Second Coming, 1985, Mengele's Passover, 1987, A Clockmaker's Boy: Part One, 1987; (novel) Malunkyaputta: His Quest for Edification, 1996; (essay) The Creative Self, 1971, contbr. to anthologies, The Golden Year, 1960, Interpretation for Our Time, 1966, The Britannica Library of Great American Writing, 1961, The Menorah Treasury, 1964, The Courage to Grow Old, 1988, From These Hills, 1990, Blood to Remember, 1991, Anthology of Contemporary Poets, 1992, World Poetry, 1993, We Speak for Peace, 1993, also Poet Lore, The Coast, The Argonaut, Saturday Rev., Menorah Jour., Kayak, Old Crow, Mandrake Rev. Served with U.S. Merchant Marine, 1944-45. Recipient Albert M. Bender award in lit., 1945; recipient 1st prize Maritime Poetry Awards, 1945, 1st prize Poetry Soc. Va., 1951, Maxwell Anderson award drama, 1950, Di Castagnola award Poetry Soc. Am., 1971, Internat. Who's Who in Poetry award, 1972; Huntington Hartford Found. resident fellow, 1951, 64; MacDowell Colony resident fellow, 1967; Ossabaw Island Found. fellow, 1968; Nat. Endowment for Arts fellow, 1976-77. Mem. MLA, AAUP, PEN, Poetry Soc. Am., Poetry Soc. Eng., Authors Guild. Address: Adam's Acres Georgetown CA 95634 *What would a writer convey through his work? His vision of life, his response to the oddity, terror, humor, beauty, pathos, or grandeur of experience. He would renew our original sense of wonder at the mystery of things and speak in a human voice fittingly of man's mortal adventures amid the immortal dance of the elements . . . To endure, a book must stir a variety of men in any generation. Though all that we do may prove perishable, we must proceed as if . . . Do one thing well enough to endure, we tell ourselves. A thing done well is well done for all time.*

LENHART, JAMES ROBERT, sales manager, food service administrator; b. Detroit, Apr. 29, 1952; s. Robert Bernard and Harriett Frances (Ebert) L.; m. Lauren Michi Fujimoto, Oct. 1, 1983; children: Amanda Mariko, Samuel James Kai. Student, Naval Schs. of Photography, Pensacola, Fla., 1973, U. Hawaii, 1977-79. Beverage mgr. Bobby McGee's, Honolulu, 1978-79, Marriott Hotels, Maui, Hawaii, 1979-81; bartender various restaurants, Maui, 1981-82; owner Plantation Prime Rib Restaurant, Kauai, Hawaii, 1982-85; account exec. Inter Island Distributors, Kauai, 1985-86; sales mgr. Superior Coffee and Foods, Honolulu, 1986—. With USN, 1973-77, PTO. Mem. VFW, Am. Culinary Assn., Internat. Food Svc. Execs., Hawaii Mfrs. Assn., Chefs de Cuisine/Hawaii, Hawaii Restaurant Assn., Hawaii Hotel Assn. Republican. Methodist. Home: 7007 Hawaii Kai Dr Honolulu HI 96825-3134 Office: Superior Coffee and Foods 99-910 Iwaena St Aiea HI 96701-3248

LENING, JANICE ALLEN, physical education educator; b. Topeka, Mar. 10, 1946; d. John Otis and Bertha May (Simon) Allen; m. Jay Ridley Lening, Dec. 26, 1976; children: Brooke Michelle, Chad Allen. BA in Phys. Edn., U. Denver, 1968; MA in Elem. Edn., U. No. Colo., 1980. Lic. tchr. phys. edn., elem. edn., Colo. Tchr. Denver Pub. Schs., 1968-69; phys. edn. tchr. Jefferson County Schs., Lakewood, Colo., 1969—, gymnastics coach, 1969, 76-79, gymnastics judge, 1970-75; mem. budget com. Shaffer Elem. Sch., Littleton, 1985-86, accountability com., 1985-86; wellnes rep. Shaffer, Colorow, Gov. Racn Elem., Littleton, 1985-97; mem. social com. Lasley, Green Gables, Shaffer, Gov. Ranch Elem. Lakewood and Littleton, 1970-97; student coun. supr. Green Gables Elem., Lakewood, 1978-85, credit union rep., 1980-85. Leader Girl Scouts, Littleton, 1986-87; coach Columbine Soccer Assn., Littleton, 1986-91; judge Odyssey of the Mind, Littleton, 1986-97. Recipient Gold medal Am. Heart Assn., Denver, 1991, Bronze award, 1994-95 State Champion award sch. Pres. Coun. on Phys. Fitness, 1990-96; chairperson Precedures Com., 1994-97. Mem. AAPHERD, NEA, PAC, Colo. Edn. Assn., JCEA. Republican. Home: 6546 W Hoover Pl Littleton CO 80123-3632 Office: Govs Ranch Elem Sch 5354 S Field St Littleton CO 80123-7800

LENNOX, GLORIA (GLORIA DEMEREE), real estate executive; b. Baden, Pa., Feb. 14, 1931; d. Gilbert and Marion (Slosson) Whetson; m; William Lennox, June 19, 1954 (div. 1985); children: Cheryl Lennox Watson, Lynda Lennox Huerta, Jim; m. Philip Demeree, July 4, 1985. BS in Edn., Kent State U., 1954; MA in Spl. Edn., Ariz. State U., 1968; grad., Realtor's Inst. Grad. Realtor Inst.; cert. residential specialist, cert. residential broker state and nat. Tchr. Maple Leaf Sch., Garfield Heights, Ohio, 1954-55, Madison (Ind.) Dist. Elem. Sch., 1958, Scottsdale (Ariz.) Schs., 1961-68, Devereux Sch., 1968-70, Tri-City Mental Health Sch., Mesa, Ariz., 1970-71; br. mgr. M. Leslie Hansen, Scottsdale, 1972-74; v.p., gen. mgr. John D. Noble and Assocs., Scottsdale, 1974-83; pres., broker Gloria Lennox & Assocs., Inc., Scottsdale, 1983-96; sales mgr., v.p. Coldwell Banker Success, Scottsdale, 1996—. Chmn. bd. Interfaith Counseling Svc., 1988, 89; trustee Scottsdale Congl. United Ch. of Christ, 1986-88, 92, 96. Kent State U. scholar, 1950-54. Mem. Nat. Assn. Realtors, Ariz. Assn. Realtors (Realtor Assoc. of Yr. 1975), Scottsdale Assn. Realtors (life, Hall of Fame award 1992, Disting. Career award 1994), Women's Coun. Realtors, Realtor Nat. Mktg. Inst., Scottsdale Bd. Realtors (pres. 1981-82, Realtor of Yr. 1982), Ariz. Town Halls, Ariz. Country Club. Republican. Home: 7561 N Via Camello Del Sur Scottsdale AZ 85258-3005 Office: Coldwell Banker Success Office VP 8201 N Hayden Rd Scottsdale AZ 85258-2453

LENTES, DAVID EUGENE, corporate executive; b. Spokane, Wash., Dec. 14, 1951; s. William Eugene and Ellen Elsie L.; m. Debra Kay White, May 19, 1973 (div. 1984); children: Janette Adele, Damon Arthur; m. Marlene J. Livingston, Sept. 15, 1990. AA, Spokane Falls C.C., 1972; BBA, Gonzaga U., 1975. V.p. Dellen Wood Products, Inc., Spokane, 1972-95, also bd. dirs.; v.p. Custom Computer Services, Inc., Spokane, 1980-87, also bd. dirs.; mng. ptnr. Com-Lease, 1980-87, Len-Lease, 1980-95; v.p., bd. dirs. DWP Trucking, Inc., 1982-85, Sentel Corp., 1983-88, BDR Investment Corp., 1983-95; pres., bd. dirs. ASA Mgmt. Corp., 1984—, also Lenmark Corp., Inc., 1985—. Treas. Dishman Hills Natural Area Assn., 1970-96; elder Bethany Presbyn. Ch., 1980-83. Mem. Spokane C. of C., Coeur D'Alene C. of C., Post Falls C. of C., Timber Products Mfrs. (mem. bd. dirs.), Hoo-Hoo Internat. Republican.

LENTHALL, JUDITH FAITH, non-profit corporation administrator; b. L.A., Mar. 17, 1949; d. Byron Freland and Betty Faith (Bostrom) L.; m. David Wheeler Johnson, Sept. 2, 1980; children: Jeremy Wheeler Lenthall-Johnson, Jamison David Lenthall-Johnson. BA in Sociology and Psychology, U. Hawaii, 1970, MA in Sociology, 1972; cert. in demography, East-West Ctr., 1972. Asst. v.p. Bank of Am., L.A., 1981-83; sr. housing planner City of San Diego Planning Dept., 1984-89; pres. Home Aid, Diamond Bar, Calif., 1990-91; family self-sufficiency counselor Kauai County Housing Agy., Lihue, Hawaii, 1992-94; exec. dir. Kauai Food Bank, Lihue, 1995—; cons. in field. Contbr. articles to profl. jours. Affialiate, sec. bd. Kalawai Youth Little League, 1992-94; affiliate Cub Scouts Pack 143, 1993-95; hula dancer Haawi Hemolele O Keakawaiole, Poipu, Kauai, 1995-96. Recipient innovations award Ford Found. and Harvard U. Kennedy Sch. Govt., 1988; Weinberg fellow Hawaii Pacific U., 1996. Democrat. Office: Kauai Food Bank 3285 Waapa Rd Lihue HI 96766-9566

LENZ, PHILIP JOSEPH, municipal administrator; b. Monterey Park, Calif., Sept. 15, 1940; s. Philip George and Irene Mary (Bowers) L.; m. Mary Lou Antista, July 16, 1966; children: Brian Joseph, Jonathan Thomas. BA, Calif. State U., L.A., 1966; MS, Pepperdine U., 1974; cert. instr. total quality mgmt., Calif. State U., San Bernardino, 1993. Dir. West Valley div. San Bernardino County (Calif.) Probation Dept., 1977-79, dir. juvenile div., 1979-82, dir. adminstrv. services, 1982-88, dir. dist. services, 1988-90; dep. chief probation officer, 1990—; instr. dept. bus. Calif. State U., San Bernardino; instr. dept. social rels. Loma Linda U., 1988. Sec. bd. trustees Upland (Calif.) Sch. Dist., 1986—, pres. sch. bd., 1989-90, 94-96; mgr., coach Upland Am. Little League, 1981-90, bd. dirs., 1982-90; pres. Fontana (Calif.) Family Svc. Agy., 1972-74; mem. adv. com. corrections Chaffey Coll., Alta Loma, Calif., 1977-97; mem. Upland Parks and Recreation Com., 1986—, chmn., 1989-91; bd. dirs. Highlander Ednl. Found., v.p., 1991-96; mem. Calif. Youth Authority CADRE of Cons. Recipient Tim Fitzharris award Chief Probation Officers of Calif., 1987. Mem. Calif. Probation, Parole and Correctional Assn. (liaison, regional v.p. 1981-83, 2d v.p. 1985-86, 1st v.p. 1986—, pres. 1987—), Probation Bus. Mgr.'s Assn. (regional chmn. 1984-86, v.p. 1987), Western Correctional Assn., Assn. for Criminal Justice Rsch. (bd. dirs.), Probation Adminstrs. Assn. (regional chair 1992-93). Democrat. Roman Catholic. Home: 1375 Stanford Ave Upland CA 91786-3147 Office: San Bernardino County Dept Probation 175 W 5th St San Bernardino CA 92401-1401

LENZI, JERRY C., state official; b. Pocahantas, Ark., Oct. 21, 1944. BSCE, St. Martin's Coll., 1970; MPA, Evergreen State Coll., 1982; postgrad., U. Ind., 1992. Registered profl. engr., Wash., profl. land surveyor, Wash.; cert. value engrng. facilitator. Journeyman retail clk. Seamart Grocery, 1967-69; engrng. technician I, 2 and 3, dist. 3 Wash. State Dept. Transp., Tumwater, 1966-67, 69-70; hwy. engr. I Wash. State Dept. Transp., Trimwater, 1970-72, project inspector, hwy. engr. 2, 1972-76, field/design engr., hwy. engr. 3, 1976-78, asst. project engr., 1978-80, project engr., 1980-85, mgr. multimodal br. planning, rsch. and pub. transp. divsn., 1985-87, mgr. transp. planning office, 1987-90; region adminstr. Wash. State Dept. Transp., Spokane, 1990—; mem. subcom. on rail issues, subcom. on multimodal investment optimization, subcom. on characteristics and changes in freight transp. demand Transp. Rsch. Bd.; mem. Wash. State Rail Devel. Commn.; mem. acad. adv. com. St. Martin's Coll.; mem. engrng. adv. coun. Gonzaga U.; mem. Rd. Jurisdiction Com.; mem. exec. com. Wash. State Transp. Rsch. Coun.; mem. Disappearing Task Force for Curriculum Devel., South Puget Sound C.C., Upper Gt. Plains Transp. Inst., S.E. Wash. Transp. Needs. Contbr. articles to profl. jours. Mem. Spokane Regional Transp. Coun. Mem. ASCE (student chpt. advisor), Order of Engr., Nat. Conf. State Rwy. Ofcls. (vice chair), Am. Assn. State Hwy. Transp. Ofcls. (standing subcom., mem. policy rev. com., domestic freight policy devel. and intermodal issues com., Pres. Intermodal award), Rotary of Spokane. Office: Wash State Dept Transp Eastern Region 2714 N Mayfair St Spokane WA 99207-2090

LENZO, THOMAS JOHN, training and development consultant; b. Waterbury, Conn., Nov. 19, 1949; s. John Anthony (dec.) and Mary Louise (Perezella) L. BA, Fairfield U., 1971; MEd, Calif. State U., L.A., 1980. Media coord. Valley Vocat. Ctr., Industry, Calif., 1977-78; libr. Washington Sch., Pasadena, Calif., 1978-79; tng. specialist Data Electronics Inc., Pasadena, 1979-82; engrng. instr. Litton Data Systems, Van Nuys, Calif., 1982-83; cons. B.P.W. Inc., Costa Mesa, Calif., 1983-86; pvt. practice Pasadena, 1986—. Contbr. articles to profl. jours. Mem. Towards 2000 mayoral com., Pasadena, 1984-85; speaker advisor All Sts. Ch., Pasadena, 1989—; with USAF, 1972-76. Mem. Am. Soc. Tng. & Devel., Internat. Soc. Performance & Instrn., Soc. Tech. Communications (bd. dirs.), Pasadena IBM PC User Group (bd. dirs.). Roman Catholic. Home: 2473 Oswego St Apt 10 Pasadena CA 91107-4239

LEO, LOUIS JOSEPH, university administrator; b. Chgo.; m. Karen Ann Leo. BA, U. Mich., 1966, JD, 1969. Dean for adminstrn., dean of students Calif. State U., Stanislaus, 1969-77; vice chancellor student svcs. U. Calif., Riverside, 1977-96. Home: 15665 Rancho Viejo Riverside CA 92506

LEO, MARY GAYE, school administrator; b. Colorado Springs, Colo., Oct. 19, 1951; d. Bernard Johnston and Mary Ellen (Hardy) Lamar; m. Dominick Louis Leo; children: Dominick Christopher, Rachel Gabreilla. BA, U. Colo., 1973, MA, 1978; PhD in Ednl. Adminstrn. Denver U., 1985. Cert. bicultural/bilingual instr. Communications & group dynamics instr., Denver area, 1972-73; with Denver Pub. Sch. Sys., 1973-94, arts mgmt./theater dir., 1973-87; asst. prin. Lake Mid. Sch., 1987-89, Martin Luther King Mid. Sch., Denver Pub. Schs., 1989-91; asst. prin. West H.S., Denver, 1991-94; prin. Skyview H.S., Denver, 1994-96; with Mapleton Pub. Sch. Sys., 1994-96; prin. Rifle (Colo.) Middle Sch., 1996—; adj. faculty U. Colo., Boulder, Colo.; adj. edn. faculty Met. State Coll., Denver; prof. edn. adminstrn. U. Phoenix. Author: (musical) Celebration, 1979, (children's fantasy) Bob, The Magical Unicorn, 1981, (book) The Raven and I-E Locus of Control as Measures of High Ability; developer Authentic School Project for Drop Out Prevention, Academy Model for Middle Level Education. Lectr., workshop coord. Colo. Arts and Humanities Coun., 1974-75. Gov.'s Creativity grantee, 1990-91, Recipient Colo. Hispanic Bar Assn. Cmty. Svc. award, 1994. Mem. ASCD, NAFE, Nat. Council Tchrs. English, Colo. Assn. Sch. Execs., Colo. Partnership. Home: 4554 S Alton St Englewood CO 80111-1207

LEON, BRUNO, architect, educator; b. Van Houten, N.Mex., Feb. 18, 1924; s. Giovanni and Rose (Cunico) L.; m. Louise Dal-Bo, Sept. 4, 1948 (dec. 1974); m. Bonnie Bertram, Sept. 12, 1976; children: Mark Jon, John Anthony, Lisa Rose. Student, Wayne State U., 1942, U. Detroit, 1945-48; LHD (hon.), U. Detroit, 1984; BArch, N.C. State Univ., 1953. Registered architect, Mich., N.C., Mass., N.Y., N.Mex., Fla. Head design staff Fuller Research Found., Raleigh, N.C., 1954-55; archtl. designer I.M. Pei & Assos., N.Y.C., 1955-56; instr. Mass. Inst. Tech., 1956-59; designer Catalano & Belluschi (architects), Cambridge, Mass., 1958-59; asst. prof. U. Ill. at

Urbana, 1959-61; dean Sch. Architecture, U. Detroit, 1961-93, dean emeritus, 1993; pvt. practice architecture, 1956—. Served with USAAF, 1942-45. Fellow AIA (dir. Detroit 1963-64); mem. Alpha Sigma Nu (hon.), Phi Kappa Phi. Home: 9 Redonda Ct Santa Fe NM 87505-8308 *I believe the integral quality of the human spirit to be the ability to dream rather than to rationalize.*

LEONARD, DAVID KING, political science educator; b. Orange, N.J., Nov. 11, 1941; s. Rowland K. and Mary Jane (Kerr) L.; m. Leslie Leggett Leonard, Aug. 23, 1965; children: Kenneth L., Joanna E., Christopher K., James K. BA with honors, Haverford Coll., 1963; MA, U. Chgo., 1967, PhD, 1974. Programme sec. YMCA, Harare, Zimbabwe, 1963-64; dist. sec. YMCA, Kitwe, Zambia, 1965; lectr. U. Nairobi, Kenya, 1969-73; sr. lectr. U. Dar es Salaam, Tanzania, 1974-76; prof. U. Calif., Berkeley, 1976—; vis. lectr. U. Calif., Berkeley, 1973-74; prin. investigator U.S. Agy. for Internat. Devel. Project on Mng. Decentralization, 1979-81; mgmt. advisor Ministries of Agr. and Livestock Devel., Nairobi, 1980-82; mem. adv. panel Office of Tech. Assessment, U.S. Congress, Washington, 1985-86; chair African Studies Ctr., Berkeley, 1986-92, chair Peace and Conflict Studies, Berkeley, 1996—. Author: Reaching the Peasant Farmer, 1977, African Successes, 1991; author, editor: Institutions of Rural Development for the Poor, 1982. pres. Coun. of U. Calif. Faculty Assns., Grenada Hills, 1995-97; chair Berkeley Faculty Assn., 1994-96. Fellow Danforth Found., 1965-68, Fulbright fellow U.S. Dept. Edn., Kenya, 1985-86; recipient 1st prize Rsch. for 3d World award Govt. Netherlands, 1992. Democrat. Quaker. Home: 1309 Ordway St Berkeley CA 94702-1123 Office: Univ Calif Dept Polit Sci Berkeley CA 94720-1950

LEONARD, GEORGE EDMUND, real estate, bank, and consulting executive; b. Phoenix, Nov. 20, 1940; s. George Edmund and Marion Elizabeth (Fink) L.; m. Gloria Jean Henry, Mar. 26, 1965 (div. Feb. 1981); children: Tracy Lynn, Amy Theresa, Kristin Jean; m. Mary C. Short, Sept. 22, 1990. Student, Ariz. State U., 1958-60; BS, U.S. Naval Acad., 1964; postgrad., Pa. State U., 1969-70; MBA, U. Chgo., 1973. Commd. ensign, USN, 1964, advanced through grades to lt. comdr., 1975; v.p. 1st Nat. Bank Chgo., 1970-75; exec. v.p., chief banking, chief fin. and chief lending officer Mera Bank, Phoenix, 1975-90, also bd. dirs., 1982-90; pres., chief exec. officer Cen. Savs., San Diego, 1985-87; chmn., CEO AmBank Holding Co. of Colo., Scottsdale, Ariz., 1990-91, Consumer Guarantee Corp., Phoenix, 1996; pres., CEO Diversified Mgmt. Svcs., Inc., Phoenix, 1991—, GEL Mgmt. Inc., Phoenix, 1991—; CFO Western Pacific Airlines, Colorado Springs, 1996—, bd. dirs., 1996—; bd. dirs. Beverly Hills (Calif.) Savs., , Am. Nat. Bank of Scottsdale, Bank of Santa Fe, 1990-91, Bank of Colo. Springs. Active Phoenix Thunderbirds, 1979—; bd. dirs. Maricopa C.C.s Found., treas., 2d v.p., 1991-93, 1st v.p., 1993-94, pres., 1994-95, past pres., 1995-96, Camelback Charitable Trust, 1991-92, The Samaritan Found., 1993-96, chmn. fin. com., 1994-96, vice chmn., 1996. Mem. Phoenix Met. C. of C. (bd. dirs. 1975-82), Inst. Fin. Edn. (bd. dirs. 1980-87, nat. chmn. 1985-86), Ariz. State U. Coll. of Bus. Deans Coun. of 100, Paradise Valley Country Club (bd. dirs. 1991—, treas. 1992-95, pres. 1995-97), Univ. Club (San Diego), Kiwanis. Republican. Roman Catholic. Home: 60A Watch Hill Dr Colorado Springs CO 80906 Office: Western Pacific Airlines Inc 2864 S Circle Rd Ste 1100 Colorado Springs CO 80906

LEONARD, GLEN M., museum administrator; b. Salt Lake City, Nov. 12, 1938; s. Burnham J. and Allene (Green) L.; m. Karen Wright, Mar. 15, 1968; children: Cory, Kyle, Keith. BA, U. Utah, 1964, MA, 1966, PhD, 1970. Mng. editor Utah State Hist. Soc., Salt Lake City, 1970-73; sr. rsch. assoc. history divsn. Ch. of Jesus Christ of Latter-day Saints, Salt Lake City, 1973-78; dir. Mus. Ch. History and Art, Salt Lake City, 1979—; mem. adv. bd. editors Utah Hist. Quarterly, Salt Lake City, 1973-88; assoc. editor Jour. Mormon History, Provo, Utah, 1974-80; bd. dirs. Western Studies Ctr., Brigham Young U., Provo. Co-author: The Story of the Latter-day Saints, 1976; contbr. articles to profl. publs. Mem. Hist. Preservation Commn., Farmington, Utah, 1986-92; mem. adv. coun. Mormon Pioneer Nat. Hist. Trail, Nat. Pk. Svc., 1980-86; mem. Utah Pioneer Sesquicentennial Celebration Coordinating Coun., 1995-97. Recipient Dale Morgan Article award Utah State Hist. Soc., 1973, Mormon History Assn. Article awards, 1990, 96. Mem. Orgn. Am. Historians, Western History Assn., Am. Assn. Mus. (mus. assessment program cons.), Western Mus. Assn., Utah Mus. Assn. (bd. dirs. 1980-83), Am. Assn. State and Local History. Office: Mus Ch History and Art 45 N West Temple Salt Lake City UT 84150-1003

LEONARD, HUBERT ARNOLD, neurologist; b. Astoria, Oreg., Mar. 18, 1945; s. Hubert F. and June (Groth) L. AB, Brown U., 1967; PhD in Biochemistry, U. Oreg., 1971, MD, 1973. Diplomate Am. Bd. Neurology, Am. Bd. Psychiatry. Med. resident UCLA, 1973-74; neurology resident U. Oreg., 1974-77; dir. neurology resident program Good Samaritan Hosp., Portland, 1977-79; neurologist pvt. practice, Portland, 1979—; tchr. nursing biochemistry Oreg. Health Scis. U., 1969, 70, 71, tchr. med. neuroanatomy, 1975, 76; lectr. and presenter in field. Contbr. articles to profl. jours. Bd. dirs. Ballet Oreg., Portland, 1981-88. Grantee Sandoz Pharm., 1979-82, 95, Eli Lilly Labs., 1982-90, Glaxo Pharms., 1989-90, 90-91, 93-94, 94-95, 95; Biochemistry fellow NIH, 1967-70. Mem. Am. Assn. for Study of Headaches, Am. Acad. Neurology, North Pacific Soc. Neurology and Psychiatry, Oreg. Med. Assn., Med. Soc. of Greater Portland. Office: Neurological Clinic 1040 NW 22nd Ave Portland OR 97210-3057

LEONARD, JEFFREY S., lawyer; b. Bklyn., Sept. 14, 1945; m. Maxine L. Bortnick, Dec. 28, 1967; children: Deborah, Jennifer. AB in History, U. Rochester, 1967; JD, U. Ariz., 1974. Bar: Ariz. 1974; U.S. Dist. Ct. Ariz. 1974, U.S. Ct. Appeals (9th cir.) 1974, U.S. Supreme Ct. 1985. Law clk. to judge U.S. Dist. Ct. Ariz., 1974-75. Mem. editorial bd. Ariz. Law Rev., 1973-74. Mem. Order of Coif. Office: Leonard Collins & Kelly PC Two Renaissance Sq 40 N Central Ave Ste 2500 Phoenix AZ 85004-4405

LEONARDI, ROSARIUS ROY, special education educator; b. Bklyn., July 19, 1942; s. Benedict T. and Victoria (Ciulla) L.; m. Bonnie Rae, Mar. 18, 1967; children: Ben, Frank. BS, SUNY, New Paltz, 1964; MEd, Univ. Vt., 1973, EdD, 1994. Cert. tchr. severely handicapped, resource specialist spl. edn., social studies tchr., adminstr., Calif. Tchr. N.Y.C. Schs., 1969-71, Burlington (Vt.) Sch. Dept., 1971-80; human resources mgr. Digital Equipment Corp., Maynard, Mass., 1980-90; tchr. severely handicapped Santa Clara County Office Edn., San Jose, Calif., 1991—; sr. human resources rep. Akashic Memories, Milpitas, Calif., 1995—; mentor tchr. Santa Clara County Office Edn., San Jose, 1996. Author: Fire on the Beach, 1996; poet. Coach Burlington Internat. Games, 1975-87. Mem. NEA, Assn. Calif. Sch. Adminstrs., Parents Helping Parents, Amnesty internat., Acad. Am. Poets. Democrat. Home: 2479 Twyla Ct Campbell CA 95008-3718 Office: Akashic Memories Corp 690 Gibraltar Dr Milpitas CA 95035-6317

LEONG, CAROL JEAN, electrologist; b. Sacramento, Jan. 9, 1942; d. Walter Richard and Edith (Bond) Bloss; m. Oliver Arthur Fisk III, Apr. 12, 1964 (div. 1973); 1 child, Victoria Kay. BA in Sociology, San Jose (Calif.) State Coll., 1963; degree, Western Bus. Coll., 1964; cert. in electrolysis, Bay Area Coll. Electrolysis, 1978. Registered and cert. clin. profl. electrologist, Calif. Model various orgns., Calif., 1951-64; employment counselor Businessmen's Clearinghouse, Cin., 1966-67; dir. personnel Kroger Food Corp., Cin., 1967-68; prin. Carol Leong Electrolysis, San Mateo, Calif., 1978—; prin. Designs by Carol, San Mateo, 1987—; mem. Profl. Women's Forum, 1988—. Contbr. articles to profl. publs. Pres. Peninsula Aux. Lighthouse for the Blind, 1984-85, 95, 96, 1st v.p., 1993, 94, 95; mem. Civic Garden Club, 1995—, Best Friends Animal Orgn., 1992—, The Nature Conservancy, 1995—, Nat. Fedn. Rep. Women, 1996; vol. Nat. Kidney Found. No. Calif., 1995—. Recipient Cert. of Appreciation San Francisco Lighthouse for the Blind, 1981-82, 83. Mem. Internat. Guild Profl. Electrologists (mem. continuing edn. com.), NAFE, Profl. Women's Forum, Peninsula Humane Soc., San Francisco Zool. Soc., Friends of Filoli, Am. Electrologists Assn., Electrologists Assn. Calif., Internat. Platform Assn, Chi Omega. Republican. Presbyterian. Home: 1447 Woodberry Ave San Mateo CA 94403-3712 Office: Carol Leong Electrolysis 359 N San Mateo Dr Ste 4 San Mateo CA 94401-2513

LEONG, LAM-PO (LANBO LIANG), artist, educator; b. Canton, Guangdong, China, July 3, 1961; came to U.S., 1983; BFA in Chinese Brush Painting, Canton Fine Arts Inst., 1983; MFA in Painting with high distinction, Calif. Coll. Arts & Crafts, 1988. Instr. art Calif. Coll. Arts and Crafts, Oakland, 1986-87, U. Calif. Ext. and ASUC, Berkeley, 1989, 90—, San Jose (Calif.) State U. Ext., 1989-91, Chabot Coll., Hayward, Calif., 1989-94; lectr. San Francisco State U., 1988-95, asst. prof., 1996—; instr. Laney Coll., Oakland, Calif., 1997—; artistic dir. Oakland Asian Cultural Ctr., Calif., 1990-92; lectr. and spkr. in field, including TV appearances, Asian Art Mus. San Francisco, Chinese Cultural Ctr., San Francisco, 1985, 90, 92, 93, 95, 96. One-man shows include Markings Gallery, Berkeley, 1984, Sumitomo Bank, Albany, Calif., 1985, Calif. Coll. Arts & Crafts, 1985, Rosicrucian Egyptian Mus., San Jose, 1986, U. Utah, Salt Lake City, 1986, Patrick Gallery, Regina, Sask., Can., 1986, Mus. Macao Luis De Camoes, Macao, 1986, Kai Ping County Mus., Guangdong, 1987, Chinatown Gallery, San Francisco, 1987, Guangzhou Fine Arts Mus., Canton, 1988, The Arlington Gallery, Oakland, 1989, Moy Ying Ming Gallery, Chgo., 1990, Chinese Culture Ctr., San Francisco, 1991, Stanwood Gallery, San Francisco, 1992, Sanuk Fine Asian Collectables, San Francisco, 1992, The Univ. Gallery, San Francisco, 1994, Michael Thompson Gallery, San Francisco, 1995, 97, China Art Expo '95, Guangzhou, China, 1995, Chinese Art Gallery, San Leandro, Calif., 1997, MTC Gallery, Oakland, Calif., 1996, Galerie du Monde, Hong Kong, 1997; exhibited in group shows at Hong Kong Arts Ctr., 1980, Chinese Painting Exhibit Guangdong Province, 1981 (3d Prize award 1981), Macao Artists Assn. Exhbn., 1982, 96, Mus. Canton Fine Arts Inst., 1983, Nat. Mus. Art, Beijing, 1985, Macao Young Artist Exhbn. (Excellence award, 1st prize 1985), Pacific Art Ctr., Seattle, 1985, Chinese Culture Ctr., 1986, Faculty & MFA Show Calif. Coll. Arts & Crafts, San Francisco Campus, 1986, Chinese-Am. Artist Exhbn., Taipei, Taizhong, Taiwan, 1986, Sullivan Galleries, Salt Lake City, 1987, Oriental Gallery, N.Y., 1987, Santa Cruz Art League (Spl. award 1988, 1st prize 1990), Asian Resource Gallery, Oakland, 1988, Nat. Mus. Fine Arts, Beijing, 1988, 90, Chinese Art Gallery, San Leandro, Calif., 1989, Stanwood Gallery, 1989, Gallery Imago, San Francisco, 1990, Sun Gallery, Hayward, 1990, N.Y. Art Expo, N.Y.C., 1991, Gallery 5, Santa Monica, Calif., 1991, Butterfield & Butterfield Auction, San Francisco, 1992, 95-96, Asian Art Mus., San Francisco, 1992, Ke Shan Art Gallery, Taipei, 1993, Wan Fung Art Gallery, Hong Kong, 1993, Gallery On The Rim, San Francisco, 1994, Resource for Art, 1995, Ginsberg Collection, 1995, Macao Art Expo, 1988-96, Acad. Art Coll., San Francisco, 1996, Shanghai Arts Mus., 1997; work represented in various mus., corp. and pvt. collections including Guangzhou Arts Mus., Macao Camoes Mus., Mus. Canton Fine Arts Inst., Asian Art Mus. San Francisco, United Savs. Bank, Calif., Hotel East 21, Tokyo, The Tokyo Westin Hotel, Comml. Bank, San Francisco, Westin Surabaya, Indonesia; author: Brush Paintings of Lam-Po Leong, 1986, Journey of the Heart, 1994; illustrator: Brushstrokes-Styles and Techniques of Chinese Painting, 1993, The Tao of Power, 1986; designer (granite courtyard) New Chinatown Pk., San Francisco, 1993; (multi-image projection) Ctr. Arts Yerba Buena Gardens, San Francisco, 1996. Recipient Outstanding Merit award Young Art Now Competition, 1980, Decade of Achievement award Asian/Pacific Heritage Week, 1988, 2d prize Zunyi Internat. Brush Painting Competition, 1989; inductee Pan-Pacific Asian Hall of Fame at San Francisco Internat. Expo., 1987; grantee City of Oakland Cultural Arts Divsn., 1994-96. Mem. Asian Artists Assn. Am., Oriental Art Assn., U.S.A. (v.p.), Macao Soc. Social Scis., Hai-Ri Artists Assn. (China), Nat. Modern Meticulous Painting Soc. (China), Chinese Am. Culture Exch. Assn. (co-founder, dir. 1992—). Office: Brushwork Gallery 166 Palisades Dr Daly City CA 94015-4517

LEONTE, DINU IOAN, software engineer; b. Ploiesti, Romania, July 16, 1941; came to U.S., 1990; s. Dumitru and Filotea (Dinescu) L.; m. Oana Mariana Vetrici, July 11, 1964; 1 child, Laura Daria Leonte Lawson. MS in Math., U. Bucharest, Romania, 1965; MSEE, Poly. Inst., Bucharest, 1972, PhD, 1983. Programmer analyst Nat. Electric Power Dispatch, Bucharest, 1969-82, sr. software engr., 1984-90; software engr. EMS and SCADA systems/Siemens, Erlangen, Germany, 1982-84; CAD software engr. Popa Kihlthau S.e.C., Campbell, Calif., 1990-92; software engr. A.D. Costas Projects, Pleasanton, Calif., 1992; sr. software engr. First Pacific Networks, Inc., San Jose, Calif., 1992-95, Automatic Data Processing, San Ramon, Calif., 1995—. Democrat. Roman Catholic. Home: 1137 Walpert St Apt 69 Hayward CA 94541-6724 Office: Automatic Data Processing 2010 Crow Canyon Pl San Ramon CA 94583-1344

LEOUNG, GIFFORD S., physician; b. N.Y.C., July 8, 1953; s. Will and Judy (Yuen) L.; m. Mee Mee Kiong, May 21, 1989; children: Jasmine, Mitchell. BS, Columbia U., 1975; MD, Cornell U., 1979. Resident in internal medicine Washington Hosp. Ctr., 1979-82; fellow in infectious diseases U. Calif./San Francisco Gen. Hosp., 1983-85; fellow in pulmonary medicine U. Calif. Davis/VA Hosp., Martinez, 1985-86; asst. clin. prof. medicine U. Calif., San Francisco, 1988—; pvt. practice specializing in infectious diseases San Francisco, 1989—; med. dir. HIV care St. Francis Meml. Hosp., San Francisco, 1994—. Contbr. articles to profl. jours. Recipient CIBA award for cmty. svc., 1977; numerous awards and commendations for work in AIDS. Mem. ACP, Calif. Med. Assn., Am. Soc. Microbiology, Am. Thoracic Soc., Am. Coll. Chest Physicians, Bay Area Infectious Disease Soc., Infectious Disease Soc. Am. Office: 1199 Bush St # 400 San Francisco CA 94109-5999

LEPIE, ALBERT HELMUT, chemist, reseacher; b. Malapane, Silesia, Germany, Aug. 6, 1923; came to U.S., 1963; s. Albert and Emilia (Zachlod) L.; m. Claire Kortz, 1956 (div. 1964); 1 child, Karin. Degree in chem. engring., Staatliche Ing. Schule, Essen, Germany, 1953; diploma in chemistry, Tech. Hochschule, Aachen, Germany, 1959; D in Natural Scis., Tech. Hochschule, Munich, Germany, 1961. Chem. engr. Pahl'sche Gummi & Asbest, Düsseldorf, 1953-59; chemist Deutsche Versuchanstalt für Luftfahrt, Munich, 1961-63; rsch. chemist U.S. Naval Propellant Plant, Indian Head, Md., 1963-64; rsch. chemist Naval Weapons Ctr., China Lake, Calif., 1964-95, ret., 1995; chmn. mech. properties panel Joint Army, Navy, NASA, and Air Force Interagy. Rocket Propulsion, 1977-84. Inventor air curtain incinerator for energetic materials and fiber peal force measurement device, flywheel high rate tensile tester for viscoelastic materials. Recipient Joint Army, Navy, NASA, and Air Force award, 1984, William B. McLean award Naval Weapons Ctr. Mem. Am. Chem. Soc. (sec. China Lake chpt. 1968, 69), China Lake Astron. Soc., Sigma Xi. Roman Catholic. Home: 121 S Desert Candles St Ridgecrest CA 93555-4218

LEPORE, VINCENT DONALD, JR., plastic surgeon; b. Rome, Mar. 30, 1955; came to U.S., 1957; s. Vincent Donald and Mary Louise Lepore; m. Margaret Mary Scura; 1 child, Nicholas. AB, Dartmouth Coll., 1977; MD, U. Cin., 1981. Diplomate Am. Bd. Plastic Surgery. Resident in plastic surgery Stanford (Calif.) U., 1981-87; founder, owner Plastic & Reconstructive Surgery Assocs., Inc., Palo Alto, Calif., 1987—. Rufus Choate scholar Dartmouth Coll., 1977. Mem. Am. Soc. Plastic and Reconstructive Surgeons, Calif. Med. Assn., Calif. Soc. Plastic Surgeons, Alpha Omega Alpha. Office: Plastic & Reconstructive Surgery Assocs Inc 900 Welch Rd Ste 110 Palo Alto CA 94304-1802

LEPORIERE, RALPH DENNIS, quality engineer; b. Elizabeth, N.J., Nov. 8, 1932; s. Maximo and Christian (Lello) L.; m. Judith Louise Crowhurst, Nov. 19, 1960; children: Bonnie Ann, David Anthony. BS in Chemistry, Rutgers U., 1954. Registered profl. engr., Calif. Chemist N.Y. Quinine & Chemical Works, Newark, 1954-55; asst. to chief quality control C.D. Smith Pharmacal Co., New Brunswick, N.J., 1955-56; asst. supr. quality control White Labs., Kenilworth, N.J., 1958-60; statistician Calif. and Hawaiian Sugar Co., Crockett, Calif., 1960—; instr., chmn. quality control dept. Laney C.C., Oakland, Calif., 1967-87; asst. prof., chmn. quality control dept. John F. Kennedy U., Martinez, Calif., 1967-72; instr., mem. adv. com. ann. statis. short course U. Calif., Davis, 1969-94. Pres. PTA Napa Junction Elem. Sch., Napa County, Calif., 1971-73; mem. early childhood com., program adv. com. Napa Valley Unified Sch. Dist., Napa County, 1972-76; v.p. Am. Canyon County Water Dist., American Canyon, Calif., 1971-73, pres., 1973-83, gen. mgr., 1981. Recipient Hon. Service award Calif. State PTA, 1973. Fellow Am. Soc. Quality Control (cert. quality engr., chmn. San Francisco sect., founder East Bay Subsect. 1970-71); mem. Soc. Mfg. Engrs. (sr.), Am. Statis. Soc., Am. Chem. Soc. Republican. Roman Catholic. Home: 618 Kilpatrick St Vallejo CA 94589-1305 Office: Calif & Hawaiian Sugar Co 830 Loring Ave Crockett CA 94525-1104

LEPORT, PETER CARY, surgeon; b. N.Y.C., Jan. 15, 1949; s. Hyman Bert Leport; m. Christina Rizza, Dec. 1984; children: Franciso, Aurora, Christopher. BA, SUNY, Binghamton, 1970; MD, SUNY, Bklyn., 1975. Diplomate Am. Bd. Surgery. Intern Kings County Hosp., Bklyn., 1974-75, resident, 1975-78; Bd. dirs. Ayn Rand Inst. Mem. ACS, Am. Free Choice in Medicine. Office: 11180 Warner Ave Ste 461 Fountain Valley CA 92708-7505

LEPOWSKY, WILLIAM LEONARD, mathematics and statistics educator. BA summa cum laude, Harvard U., 1967; MA, U. Calif., Berkeley, 1968, 76, postgrad., 1981. Instr. Laney Coll., Oakland, Calif., 1969—; chair dept. math. Laney Coll., Oakland, 1979-80, supr. math. lab., 1987—; statis. cons. Panel on Skin Cancer, NAS, Washington, 1976-77; curriculum cons. Vista Coll., Berkeley, 1989; statis. cons. and expert witness, Berkeley, 1989—. Author: (textbook) Statistics in Action, 1994; contbr. articles to profl. jours. Scholar Nat. Honor Soc., Harvard Coll., Cambridge, 1963; Nat. Merit scholar, Harvard Coll., 1963-67; Harvard Coll. scholar, 1964-67; NSF grad. fellow U. Calif., Berkeley, 1967-68; Profl. Devel. grantee Laney Coll., Oakland, Calif., 1989. Mem. Am. Statis. Assn., Calif. Math. Coun. for C.C. (bd. dirs. 1974-75), Phi Beta Kappa. Office: Laney Coll 900 Fallon St Oakland CA 94607-4808

LEPP, STEPHEN HENRY, physicist, educator; b. Duluth, Minn., June 7, 1956; s. Henry and Maxine (Foster) L. BS in Physics, U. Minn., Duluth, 1978; PhD in Physics, U Colo., 1984. Postdoctoral fellow Harvard U., Cambridge, Mass., 1984-87, rsch. assoc., 1987-91; asst. prof. physics U. Nev., Las Vegas, 1991-95, assoc. prof., 1995—. Contbr. articles to profl. jours. Mem. Am. Astron. Soc., Internat. Astron. Union (Young Astronomer grant 1991). Office: U Nev Physics Dept 4505 S Maryland Pky Las Vegas NV 89154-9900

LERAAEN, ALLEN KEITH, financial executive; b. Mason City, Iowa, Dec. 4, 1951; s. Myron O. and Clarice A. (Handeland) L.; m. Mary Elena Partheymuller, Apr. 14, 1978. BBA in Data Processing and Acctg., No. Ariz. U., 1975. CFA. Data processing supr. Stephenson & Co., Denver, 1978-81, contr., 1981-85, arbitrageur, trader, 1985-88, v.p., 1985-90, exec. v.p., 1990—; v.p., sec. bd. dirs. Circle Corp., Denver, 1985—. Mem. Assn. Investment Mgmt. and Rsch., Denver Soc. Security Analysts. Home: 5692 S Robb St Littleton CO 80127-1942 Office: 100 Garfield St Fl 4 Denver CO 80206-5550

LERIT, DELIA TUMULAK, school nurse; b. Lapulapu City, The Philippines, July 16, 1954; d. Nephtali and Presentacion (Tubongbanua) Tumulak; m. Felix Lerit, Jr., Apr. 9, 1983; children: Vanessa Joy, Chloe Mae. BSN, Velez Coll. Nursing, Cebu City, The Philippines, 1975; health svc. credential, Calif. State U., L.A., 1990, MSN, 1995. RN, Calif., B.C., Can. Staff nurse White Meml. Med. Ctr., L.A., Vancouver (B.C.) Gen. Hosp., Shaughnessy Hosp., Vancouver; sch. nurse L.A. Unified Sch. Dist. Named Employee of Month, 1986. Mem. Philippine Nurses Assn., L.A. Coun. Sch. Nurses, Sigma Theta Tau.

LERMAN, EILEEN R., lawyer; b. N.Y.C., May 6, 1947; d. Alex and Beatrice (Kline) L. BA, Syracuse U., 1969; JD, Rutgers U., 1972; MBA, U. Denver, 1983. Bar: N.Y. 1973, Colo. 1976. atty. FTC, N.Y.C., 1972-74; corp. atty. RCA, N.Y.C., 1974-76; corp. atty. Samsonite Corp. and consumer products div. Beatrice Foods Co., Denver, 1976-78, assoc. gen. counsel, 1978-85, asst. sec., 1979-85; ptnr. Davis, Lerman, & Weinstein, Denver, 1985-92, Eileen R. Lerman & Assocs., 1993—; bd. dir. Legal Aid Soc. of Met. Denver, 1979-80. Bd. dirs., vice chmn. Colo. Postsecondary Ednl. Facilities Authority, 1981-89; bd. dirs., pres. Am. Jewish Com., 1989-92; mem. Leadership Denver, 1983. Mem. ABA, Colo. Women's Bar Assn. (bd. dir. 1980-81), Colo. Bar Assn. (bd. govs.), Denver Bar Assn. (trustee), N.Y. State Bar Assn., Rhone Brackett Inn (pres.-elect 1996), Denver Law Club, Rutgers U. Alumni Assn., University Club. Home: 1018 Fillmore St Denver CO 80206-3332 Office: Lerman & Assocs LLC 50 S Steele St Ste 420 Denver CO 80209-2809

LERNER, ALEXANDRIA SANDRA, artist; b. Phila., Jan. 1, 1946. Student, Pa. Acad. Fine Arts, 1970-75; BFA, Phila. Coll. Art, 1978. founding mem., trustee Found. for Toaday's Art, 1975—; co-dir. Synapse: A Visual Art Press, 1980-85. Exhibited works in shows at Nexus Gallery, Phila., 1976, 77, 78, 80, 94, Marion Locks Gallery, Phila., 1976, 82, Phila. Coll. Art, 1977, 1977, A.C.T. Gallery, Toronto, 1978, N.A.M.E. Gallery, Chgo., 1979, Phila. Art Alliance, 1979, 80, 89, So. Alleghenies, Mus., Loretteo, Pa., 1979, 80, 82, Phila. Acad. Fine Arts, 1980, A.I.R. Gallery, N.Y.C., 1980, A.B.F. Gallery, Hamburg, Germany, 1980, Art Inst. Chgo., 1980, Washington Sq. Gallery, N.Y.C., 1980, Tweed Mus., Duluth, Minn., 1981, Mus. Found. for Visual Arts, Phila., 1981, For Art's Sake Gallery, Martha's Vineyard, Mass., 1981, Kathryn Markel Gallery, N.Y.C., 1983, Port of History Mus., Phila., 1989, Phila. Mus. Art, 1990, Mangel Gallery, Phila., 1991, Harwood Found. Mus., Taos, N.Mex., 1991, Spirit Gallery, Santa Fe, 1993; permanent collections include Phila. Mus. Art, So. Alleghenies Mus., Art Inst. Chgo., Jean Brown Archives, Shaker Seed House, Maine, Franklin Furnace Archive, N.Y.C., Tweed Mus., Nat. Inst. Design, Ahmedabad, New Delhi, India, Phila. Sci. Ctr., others. Home: Box 5304 Taos NM 87571

LERNER, VLADIMIR SEMION, computer scientist, educator; b. Odessa, Ukraine, Sept. 12, 1931; came to U.S., 1990; s. Semion N. and Manya G. (Grosman) L.; m. Sanna K. Gleyzer, Sept. 28, 1954; children: Alex, Tatyana, Olga. BSEE, Odessa Poly. Inst., 1954; MEE, Inst. Problem's Controls, Moscow, 1959; PhD in Elec. Engring., Moscow Power Inst., 1961; D Sci. in Systems Analysis, Leningrad State U., 1974. Prof. elec. engring. Kishinev (Moldova) State U., 1962-64; prof. elec. engring. and control systems Kishinev Poly. Inst., 1964-79; sr. scientist in applied math. Acad. Sci., Kishinev, 1964-79; dir. math. modeling and computer sci. lab. Rsch. Inst., Odessa, 1979-89; sr. lectr. UCLA, 1991-93, rschr., 1993-; chmn. computer sci. dept. West Coast U., L.A., 1993—; mem. adv. bds. Acad. Sci., Kishinev, 1964-79, Poly. Inst., Kishinev, 1964-79; vis. prof. Leningrad State U., 1971-73; cons., mem. adv. bd. Poly. Inst., Odessa, 1979-89; mem. hon. editl. adv. bd. Encyclopedia of Life Support Syss., Informational Macrodynamics. Author: Physical Approach to Control Systems, 1969, Superimposing Processes in Control Problems, 1973, Dynamic Models in Decision Making, 1974, Special Course in Optimal and Self Control Systems, 1977, Lectures in Mathematical Modelling and Optimization, 1995, Mathematical Foundations of Informational Macrodynamics, 1996, Lectures in Informational Macrodynamics, 1996, Informational Macrodynamics: Theory, Numerical Insights and Applications, 1997; contbr. numerous articles to sci. jours.; holder 23 patents; founder new sci. discipline informational Macrodynamics. Recipient Silver medal for rsch. achievements, Moscow, 1961, outstanding achievements in edn., Kishinev, 1975. Office: West Coast U 440 Shatto Pl Los Angeles CA 90020-1704

LEROY, NORBERT GHISLAIN, management and financial consultant; b. Boitsfort, Belgium; came to U.S., 1940; s. Julian J. and Marie (Huygens) L.; m. Janet E. Dishington, Feb. 11, 1967 (div. Mar. 1974). BA, Iona Coll., 1947; BS, Columbia U., 1949; BA, MA, Cambridge U., Eng., 1951. Various to v.p. J.P. Morgan & Co., N.Y.C., 1951-66; dir., pres., treas. Polyroy, Inc., Montroy Properties, Ltd., N.Y./Mont., 1968-79; dir., v.p. The Pilot Corp. (merged with Polyroy, Inc.), Billing, Mont., 1988—. With Royal Air Force, 1941-45. Mem. The Brook Club (N.Y.), Racquet and Tennis Club (N.Y.), Coun. on Fgn. Rels., The Travellers (Paris), Billings Area C. of C., others. Roman Catholic. Office: Polyroy Inc Ste 321 769 Fallow Ln Billings MT 59102-7051

LE SAGE, BERNARD E., lawyer; b. Pasadena, CAlif., Mar. 29, 1949. BA, U. Notre Dame, 1971; JD, Loyola U., L.A., 1974. Bar: Calif. 1974. Extern clk. to Hon. William P. Clark Calif. Supreme Ct., 1974; with Buchalter, Nemer, Fields & Younger, L.A. Mem. ABA, State Bar Calif., Los Angeles County Bar Assn. (trustee 1982-84), Los Angeles County Bar Barristers (pres. 1983-84), Chancery Club. Office: Buchalter Nemer Fields & Younger 601 S Figueroa St Fl 25 Los Angeles CA 90017-5704

LESCH, BARRY M., lawyer; b. N.Y.C., Apr. 26, 1945. BA, U. Pa., 1965; MA, Ind. U., 1971; JD, U. Calif., Berkeley, 1975. Bar: Calif. 1975, U.S. Supreme Ct. 1980. With Laughlin, Falbo, Levy & Moresi, Sacramento.

Mem. State Bar Calif. (cert. specialist workers compensation law). Office: Laughlin Falbo Levy & Moresi 106 K St Fl 2 Sacramento CA 95814-3213

LESKO, RONALD MICHAEL, osteopathic physician; b. Homestead, Pa., Mar. 25, 1948; s. Andrew Paul and Elizabeth Ann (Tarasovic) L.; m. Helena Alexandra Shalayeva, July 29, 1990. BS, U. Pitts., 1970; DO, Coll. Osteo. Medicine & Surgery, Des Moines, 1973; MPH, Loma Linda U., 1985. Diplomate Am. Osteo. Bd. Family Physicians, Am. Osteo. Bd. Preventive Medicine (bd. dirs., chmn. pub. health rep., chmn. bd. exam. com. 1991-97). Family physician pvt. practice Port Richey, Fla., 1974-80; flight surgeon USN, NAS Chase Field Beeville, Tex., 1981-83; resident gen. preventive medicine Loma Linda (Calif.) U. Med. Ctr., 1983-85; pvt. practice family and preventive medicine, pvt. practice, Del Mar, Calif., 1988—; flight surgeon, capt. USNR, NAS Miramar, San Diego, 1988-95; ret. USNR, Loma Linda, Calif., 1996; attending physician ambulatory care svc. J.L. Pettis Meml. VA Hosp., Loma Linda, Calif., 1986-88; staff physician Scripps Meml. Hosp., La Jolla, Calif., 1990—; lectr., 1985—; cons. Jour. Am. Osteo. Assn., Chgo., 1987, phys. rediness div. USN, Washington, 1988; med. advisor blue ribbon adv. com. Nutrition Screening Initiative, Washington, 1991. Contbr. articles to med. jours.; rschr. in nutrition and metabolism in human physiology. Med. adviser March of Dimes Suncoast chpt., New Port Richey, 1977-79; bd. dirs. Fla. Gulf Health Systems Agy., Region IV, 1977-79, Price-Pottenger Nutrition Found., San Diego, 1988—. Fellow Am. Osteo. Coll. Occupational and Preventive Medicine (trustee 1989-91, chmn. pub. health divisional com. 1989-91), Am. Coll. Preventive Medicine; mem. APHA, Am. Osteo. Assn., San Diego Osteo. Med. Assn., Osteo. Physicians and Surgeons Calif., Am. Coll. Family Physicians-Osteo., U.S. Naval Flight Surgeons. Office: 13983 Mango Dr Ste 103 Del Mar CA 92014-3146

LESLIE, JACQUES ROBERT, JR., journalist; b. L.A., Mar. 12, 1947; s. Jacques Robert and Aleen (Wetstein) L.; m. Leslie Wernick, June 21, 1980; 1 child, Sarah Alexandra. BA, Yale U., 1968. Tchr. New Asia Coll., Chinese U., Hong Kong, 1968-70; free-lance journalist Washington, 1970-71; fgn. corr. L.A. Times, Saigon, 1972-73, Phnom Penh, 1973, Washington, 1974; chief New Delhi (India) bur. L.A. Times, 1974-75, Madrid, 1975-76; chief Hong Kong bur. L.A. Times, 1976-77; freelance journalist, 1977—; contbg. writer Wired Mag., 1993—. Author: The Mark: A War Correspondent's Memoir of Vietnam and Cambodia. Recipient Best Fgn. Corr. award Sigma Delta Chi, 1973, citation reporting Overseas Press Club, 1973. Home: 124 Reed St Mill Valley CA 94941-3448

LESLIE, ROBERT ANDREW, physician; b. Eldorado, Kansas, June 19, 1931; s. Robert Wilson and Eleanor Bertha (Cumming) L.; m. Lynette Leslie. MD, Duke Univ., 1955. Dispensary SAC, USAF, APO 147, N.Y., 1956-58; medical officer U.S. Naval Repair Facility, San Diego, 1958-61; physician Seaview Medical, Long Beach, Calif., 1961-63, Carl G. Johnson, Long Beach, Calif., 1963-75; physician, medical dir. ACACIA Medical, Anaheim, Calif., 1975-80; physician Health Affilites, Long Beach, 1980-86; intra medical group L.A., 1986-92; physician Reservoir Medical Group, Pomona, Calif., 1992—; utilization com., Long Beach Hosp., 1984-85, medical com., 1984-85. With USAF, 1956-58. Mem. Soc. Contemporary Medicine and Surgery, Rotary Club, Am. Legion. Home: 243 Berkeley Irvine CA 92612-4606 Office: Reservoir Med Group 945 E Holt Ave Pomona CA 91767-5729

LESLIE, ROBERT LORNE, lawyer; b. Adak, Alaska, Feb. 24, 1947; s. J. Lornie and L. Jean (Conelly) L.; children—Lorna Jean, Elizabeth Allen. B.S., U.S. Mil. Acad., 1969; J.D., Hastings Coll. Law, U. Calif.-San Francisco, 1974. Bar: Calif. 1974, D.C. 1979, U.S. Dist. Ct. (no. dist.) Calif. 1974, U.S. Ct. Claims 1975, U.S. Tax Ct. 1975, U.S. Ct. Appeals (9th and D.C. cirs.), U.S. Ct. Mil. Appeals 1980, U.S. Supreme Ct. 1980. Commd. 2d lt. U.S. Army, 1969, advanced through grades to maj., 1980; govt. trial atty. West Coast Field Office, Contract Appeals, Litigation Div. and Regulatory Law Div., Office JAG, Dept. Army, San Francisco, 1974-77; sr. trial atty. and team chief Office of Chief Trial Atty., Dept. Army, Washington, 1977-80; ptnr. McInerney & Dillon, Oakland, Calif., 1980—; lectr. on govt. contracts CSC, Continuing Legal Edn. Program; lectr. in govt. procurement U.S. Army Materiel Command. Col. USAR. Decorated Silver Star, Purple Heart. Mem. ABA, Fed. Bar Assn., Associated Gen. Contractors, The Beavers. Office: Ordway Building Fl 18 Oakland CA 94612-3610

LESLY, CRAIG EDWARDS, marketing professional; b. Evanston, Ill., Sept. 14, 1942; s. Philip and Ruth (Edwards) L.; m. Carole McLaughlin, July 31, 1964 (div.); children: Elizabeth Lesly Stevens, Melissa Lesly Cooper; m. Penni McRoberts, Aug. 16, 1986; 1 child, Alexander McRoberts. BA, DePauw U., 1964; MBA, Stanford U., 1966. Group mgr. new products Libby, McNeill and Libby, Chgo., 1966-70; sr. acct. exec. N. W. Ayer, Chgo., 1970-73; v.p. McCann-Erickson, San Francisco and L.A., 1973-81; v.p. mktg. and sales Chef America, Sylmar, Calif., 1981-84; v.p., dir. acct. mgmt. Hakuhodo Advt., L.A., 1984-86; gen. mgr. Four 'N Twenty, Tustin, Calif., 1986-91; mktg. cons. Santa Ana, Calif., 1991-97. Named Outstanding Young Men, Jr. C. of C., 1976. Republican. Home: 2007 E Fruit St Santa Ana CA 92701-4409

LESNICK, STEPHEN WILLIAM, artist. BA, Silvermine Coll. of Art, Art Career Sch., N.Y.; studied with Revington Arthur, Jon McClelland, Gail Symon, Herb Olson. Tchr. comml. and fine arts various locations; owner Lesnick Art Studio, Inc., Las Vegas, Nev., 1965—; art dir. Kelly-Reber Advt. Agy.; comml. artist, illustrator E.G. & G.; art editor, columnist Las Vegas Sun, 1971-90; art instr. Clark County C.C.; advisor on art tax fraud to FBI and IRS. Contbr. illustrations to numerous mags., including Readers Digest, Bus. Week, Newseek; exhibited in 31 one man shows; represented in pvt. and pub. permanent collections, including Burndy Libr. Arts and Scis., Norwalk, Conn.; designer Helldorado Medallions to commemorate Boulder Dam, 1971-80 series, Commerative Medallions Nev. State Mus., 50th Anniversary Gambling Medallion for State of Nev.; author (books) How to Draw, Figure Drawing; inventer Funny Brush, The Leaning Bridge, The Pen-Save, the Artist's Palette, The Artist Brush Holder. Recipient 1st and 2d ann. prize Conn. Religious Show, 1st Place award All New Eng. Show, purchase prize Barnum Festival, 1st place award Internat. Art Competition, Tokyo, 1st place and purchase prize Helldorado Western Art Show, 1st place prize designer Nev. Medallion for Franklin Mint Bicentennial Yr., 1987, The Lincoln Meml. Region I Painting award Nat. Arts for Parks, Purchase prize 10th Ann. Arts for the Parks Nat. Show, Kitty Hawk, N.C., 1996. Office: Lesnick Art Studio Inc PO Box 71945 Las Vegas NV 89170-1945

LESSER, WENDY, literary magazine editor, writer, consultant; b. Santa Monica, Calif., Mar. 20, 1952; d. Murray Leon Lesser and Millicent (Gerson) Dillon; m. Richard Rizzo, Jan. 18, 1985; 1 stepchild, Dov Antonio; 1 child, Nicholas. BA, Harvard U., 1973; MA, Cambridge (Eng.) U., 1975; PhD, U. Calif., Berkeley, 1982. Founding ptnr. Lesser & Ogden Assocs., Berkeley, 1977-81; founding editor The Threepenny Rev., Berkeley, 1980—; Bellagio resident Rockefeller Found, Italy, 1984. Author: The Life Below the Ground, 1987, His Other Half, 1991, Pictures at an Execution, 1994, A Director Calls, 1997; editor: Hiding in Plain Sight, 1993. Fellow NEH, 1983, 92, Guggenheim fellow, 1988, ACLS, 1996. Democrat. Office: The Threepenny Rev PO Box 9131 Berkeley CA 94709-0131

LESTER, JOHN JAMES NATHANIEL, II (SEAN LESTER), engineer, environmental analyst, human rights activist; b. Houston, May 7, 1952; s. John James Nathaniel Lester and Margaret Louise (Tisdale) Sharp; m. Elisabeth Bluml., Dec. 31, 1995. Student, U. Tex., 1970, Lee Coll., 1971; AS, Grossmont Coll., 1979; BA in Behavioral Sci., Nat. U., 1987; y. Registered profl. stationary engr., Tex. Nuclear power specialist USN, various, 1971-77; microbiology lab. technician VA, San Diego, 1978; prin. engring. asst. San Diego Gas & Electric, 1979-85, engring. environ. analyst, 1985-88; owner Calif. Triad Gem & Mineral Co.; founder Ctr. for Creative Healing. Dir. logistics, mem. regional bd. Gary Hart Presdl. Campaign, San Diego, 1984; founding mem. Inlet Drug Crisis Ctr., Houston, 1970; vol. dir. Aid for Guatemalan Refugees and Orphans, 1988; vol. for Dali Lama, Tibetan Refugee Rights and Ceremonies, 1989; mem. bldg. com. Tibetan Sch. Medicine, Crestone, Colo.; mem. San Luis Valley Tibetan Project, Crestone; active Clinton Presdl. Campaign, 1992; founder Pema Tashi Ling Found. for Tibetan Studies, 1992—. Mem. ASME, IEEE (interim pres., founding mem. San Diego region Ocean Engring. Soc. 1984-85), Mensa, Assn. Humanistic Psychology, Amnesty Internat., Hunger Project, Earth Stewards, Human Rights Watch, Tibet Watch, Sierra Club. Buddhist. Home and Office: PO Box 710 Makawao HI 96768-0710

LETA, DAVID EDWARD, lawyer; b. Rochester, N.Y., June 9, 1951; married; 2 children. BA, SUNY, Binghamton, 1973; JD, U. Utah, 1976. Bar: Utah, U.S. Ct. Appeals (9th and 10th cir.), U.S. Tax Ct., U.S. Supreme Ct. Assoc. Roe & Fowler, 1976-80, ptnr., 1980-82; ptnr. Hansen, Jones, & Leta and predecessor firms Hansen, Jones, Maycock & Leta, Hansen & Anderson, 1982-92, Snell & Wilmer, Salt Lake City, 1992; adj. prof. U. Utah. 1978-80; presenter, lectr. numerous seminars and legal edn. seminars. Contbr. articles to profl. jours. Trustee, chmn. fin. com. Children's Dance Theatre, U. Utah. Mem. ABA (bankruptcy cts., rules and legislation subcoms. bus. bankruptcy section), Utah State Bar (first chmn. bankruptcy sec.), Utah Bankruptcy Lawyers Forum (initial trustee). Office: Snell & Wilmer 111 E Broadway Ste 900 Salt Lake City UT 84111-1004

LETTS, J. SPENCER, federal judge; b. 1934. BA, Yale U., 1956; LLB, Harvard U., 1960. Commd. U.S. Army, 1956, advanced through grades to capt., resigned, 1965; pvt. practice law Fulbright & Jaworski, Houston, 1960-66, Troy, Malin, Loveland & Letts, L.A., 1973-74, Hedlund, Hunter & Lynch, L.A., 1978-82, Latham & Watkins, L.A., 1982-85; gen. counsel Teledyne, Inc., 1966-73, 75-78, legal cons., 1978-82; judge U.S. Dist. Ct. (cen. dist.) Calif., L.A., 1986—. Contbr. articles to profl. jours. Mem. ABA, Calif. State Bar, Tex. State Bar, L.A. Bar Assn., Houston Bar Assn. Office: US Dist Ct 312 N Spring St Rm 243J Los Angeles CA 90012-4701*

LEUNG, ALEXANDER KWOK-CHU, pediatrician educator; b. Hong Kong, Oct. 1, 1948; s. Ping and Wai (Tai) L.; m. Miriam M.L. Leung, Apr. 13, 1975 (div. May 1982); children: Albert, Alex Jr.; m. Rita S.W. Ho, Mar. 4, 1987; children: Amy, Alan, Andrew. MB BS, U. Hong Kong, 1973; DCH, Royal Coll. Physicians London, 1977, Royal Coll. Physicians Ireland, 1979. Intern U. Hong Kong, 1973-74; pediatric resident U. Calgary, Alberta, Can., 1974-77; lectr. in child health U. Queensland, Brisbane, Australia, 1977; pediatric endocrine fellow U. Calgary, Alberta, Can., 1978-80; pediatric cons. Foothills Provincial Hosp., Calgary, 1980-92, Alberta Children's Hosp., Calgary, 1980—; clin. asst. prof. pediatrics U. Calgary, 1980-90, cons. Univ. Med. Info. Svc.., 1988—, clin. assoc. prof. pediatrics, 1990—; med. dir. Asian Med. Ctr., U. Calgary Med. Clin., 1994—; hon. advisor Am. Biog. Inst. of Rsch., Raleigh, N.C., 1987—, Internat. Biog. Ctr., Cambridge, Eng., 1988—. Mem. editl. bd. Advances in Therapy, 1995—, Can.'s Clin. Jour. Medicine, 1995, Med. Scope Monthly, 1996—; contbr. numerous sci. articles to profl. publs., 7 chpts. to books. Recipient Physician Recognition award AMA, 1985, 88, 90, 93, 96, Gold Medal award Am. Biog. Inst., 1987, Golden Acad. award Am. Biog. Inst., 1992. Fellow Royal Coll. Physicians of Can., Royal Coll. Physicians of Edinburgh, Royal Coll. Physicians of Ireland, Royal Acad. Medicine, Royal Coll. Physicians and Surgeons Glasgow, Royal Soc. Health (Eng.), Royal soc. Medicine, Royal Acad. Medicine, Am. Acad. Pediats. (PREP Fellowship award 1987, 90, 96), Can. Pediat. Soc. Office: Alberta Children's Hosp, 1820 Richmond Rd SW, Calgary, AB Canada T2T 5C7

LEUNG, DAVID WAI-HUNG, molecular biologist; b. Hong Kong, Aug. 2, 1951; came to U.S., 1969; BA, Whittier Coll., 1973; PhD, U. Ill., 1978. Post-doctoral fellow U. B.C., Vancouver, Can., 1978-80; sr. scientist Genentech, Inc., South San Francisco, Calif., 1980-92; dir. molecular biology Cell Therapeutics, Inc., Seattle, 1992—. Office: Cell Therapeutics Inc 201 Elliott Ave W Seattle WA 98119-4230

LEUNG, KASON KAI CHING, computer specialist; b. Hong Kong, July 2, 1962; came to U.S., 1963; s. Patrick Kin Man and Esther Mo Chee (Shum) L. BA in Computer Sci., U. Calif., 1984. Microcomputer specialist Coopers & Lybrand, San Francisco, 1985-87; freelance computer specialist San Francisco, 1988-90; computer applications specialist T.Y. Lin Internat., San Francisco, 1990-92; tech. specialist Ziff-Davis Labs., Foster City, Calif., 1993-94; tech. analyst PC Mag., Foster City, Calif., 1995; sr. tech. specialist Ziff-Davis Labs., Foster City, Calif., 1996; sr. tech. analyst Ziff-David Labs., Foster City, Calif., 1997—. Mem. Assn. for Computing Machinery. Home: 90 Stanford Heights Ave San Francisco CA 94127-2318

LEUNG, PUI-TAK (PETER LEUNG), physicist, educator, researcher; b. Macau, China, Aug. 23, 1953; s. Chin-Pang and Han-Yin (Luk) L.; m. Pei-Yi Feng, Apr. 19, 1985; children: Jonathan Li-Chung, Rosalyn Roh-Shi. BSc, Chinese U. Hong Kong, 1976; MEd, MA, SUNY, Buffalo, 1979, PhD, 1982. Assoc. prof. physics Tamkang U., Tamsui, Taiwan, 1982-85; rsch. assoc. SUNY, Buffalo, 1985-88; asst. prof. physics Portland (Oreg.) State U., 1988-91, assoc. prof. physics, 1991-96, prof. physics, 1996—; affiliate staff scientist Pacific Northwest Labs., Richland, Wash., 1994—; cons. in biosensor rsch. Amersham Internat. plc, Buckinghamshire, Eng., 1989-92; vis. scientist in laser rsch. IBM Almaden Rsch. Ctr., San Jose, Calif., 1991-92; invited speaker Soc. Photo-Optical Instrumentation Engrs. conf., 1989; invited visitor Pollards Wood Labs., Eng., 1989. Contbr. over 50 articles to profl. jours.; presenter in field. Equipment grantee Amersham Internat. plc, 1989, IBM, 1992; recipient Outstanding Jr. Faculty award Portland State U., 1992; Faculty fellow U.S. Dept. of Energy, 1995. Mem. Am. Phys. Soc. Home: 3342 NW Brandt Pl Portland OR 97229-8508 Office: Portland State University Dept of Physics PO Box 751 Portland OR 97207-0751

LEUPP, EDYTHE PETERSON, retired education educator, administrator; b. Mpls., Nov. 27, 1921; d. Reynold H. and Lillian (Aldridge) Peterson; m. Thomas A. Leupp, Jan. 29, 1944 (dec.); children: DeEtte (dec.), Patrice, Stacia, Roderick, Braden. BS, U. Oreg., 1947, MS, 1951, EdD, 1972. Tchr. various pub. schs. Idaho, 1941-45, Portland, Oreg., 1945-55; dir. tchr. edn. Northwest Nazarene Coll., Nampa, Idaho, 1955-61; sch. adminstr. Portland Pub. Schs., 1963-84; dir. tchr. edn. George Fox Coll., Newberg, Oreg., 1984-87; ret., 1987; s; vis. prof. So. Nazarene U., Bethany, Okla., 1988-95; adj. prof. Warner Pacific Coll., Portland, 1996—; pres. Portland Assn. Pub. Sch. Adminstrs., 1973-75; dir.-at-large Nat. Coun. Adminstrv. Women in Edn., Washington, 1973-76; state chmn. Oreg. Sch. Prins. Spl. Project, 1978-79; chair Confdn. Oreg. Sch. Adminstrs. Ann. Conf.; rschr. 40 tchr. edn. programs in colls. and univs.; designer tchr. edn. program George Fox Coll. Author tchr. edn. materials. Pres. Idaho State Aux. Mcpl. League, 1957, Nampa PTA, 1958, Nampa unit AAUW, 1956; bd. dirs. Portland Fedn. Women's Clubs, 1963. Recipient Golden Gift award, 1982; named Honored Tchr. of Okla., 1993, Hazel Fishwood scholar, 1970; Idea fellow Charles Kettering Found., 1978, 80, 87, 91, 92, 93, 94. Mem. ASCD, Am. Assn. Colls. Tchr. Edn., Delta Kappa Gamma (pres. Alpha Rho 1986-88), Phi Delta Kappa, Pi Lambda Theta. Republican. Nazarene. Home: 8100 SW 2nd Ave Portland OR 97219-4602

LEUS MCFARLEN, PATRICIA CHERYL, water chemist; b. San Antonio, Mar. 12, 1954; d. Norman W. and Jacqueline S. (Deason) Leus; (div.); 1 child, Kevin Bryant. AA, Highline Community Coll., 1974; BS in Chemistry, Eastern Wash. U., 1980. Cert. operator grade II water treatment and distbn., grade I wastewater and collection operator Ariz. Dept. Environ. Quality; cert. in asbestos identification through microscopy; cert. CPR and first aid. Lab. technician, oil analyst D.A. Lubricant, Vancouver, Wash., 1982-83; plant chemist Navajo Generating Sta., Page, Ariz., 1983-92, chemist, 1992—. Sci. judge Page Schs. Sci. Project Fair, 1985, 91; chemist Navajo Generating Sta./Page Sch. Career Day, 1986, 89, 90; life mem. Girl Scouts Am.; vol., leader AWANA Clubs Internat., 1992—. Mem. Am. Chem. Soc., Cousteau Soc., Menninger Soc., Sigma Kappa (life mem., treas. 1976-78). Methodist. Office: Navajo Generating Sta Lab Svcs Dept PO Box 850 Page AZ 86040-1949 *Personal philosophy: I strive to do the best I can at all tasks, whether they are pleasant or not. The sense of accomplishment is rewarding to me.*

LEUTY, GERALD JOHNSTON, osteopathic physician and surgeon; b. Knoxville, Iowa, July 23, 1919; s. John William and Mable Reichard (Johnston) L.; m. Martha L. Weymouth, Jan. 24, 1940 (div. 1957); children: Maxine Joanne, Robert James, Gerald Johnston Jr., Karl Joseph; m. Norma Jean Hindman, Dec. 30, 1969; children: Barbara Jayne, Patrick Jack. AB, Kemper Mil. Sch., Boonville, Mo., 1939; postgrad., Drake U., Des Moines, 1944-45; DO, Des Moines Coll. Osteopathy, 1949; embalmer, Coll. Mortuary Sci., St. Louis, 1941. Mortician/embalmer Cauldwell-McJihon Funeral Home, Des Moines, 1939-40; aero. engr. Boeing Aircraft Co., Wichita, Kans., 1941-42; osteopathic physician and surgeon Knoxville (Iowa) Osteopathic Clinic, 1949-56; dir. Leuty Osteopathic Clinic, Earlham, Iowa, 1957-77; osteopathic physician and surgeon in pvt. practice Santa Rosa, Calif., 1977—; prof. clin. med. Coll. Osteopathic Medicine of the Pacific, Pomona, Calif., 1985—. With U.S. Army, 1942-46. Named Physician of the Yr., 6th Dist. Iowa Ostepathic Soc., 1975, Disting. Leadership award, Am. Biog. Inst., 1988, others. Fellow Internat. Co.. Angiologists; mem. Am. Osteopathic Assn. (ho. of dels., life mem. 1989), Iowa Osteopathic Soc. (pres. 6th dist. 1974), Soc. Osteopathic Physicians, No. Calif. Osteopathic Med. Soc. (pres. 1981), Osteopathic Physicians and Surgeons of Calif. (pres. 1982), Am. Acad. Osteopathy (chmn. component socs. com. 1988, pres. Calif. divsn. 1987, pres. No. Calif. divsn. 1989, 91-93, 95), North Coast Osteopathic Med. Assn. (pres. 1992), Am. Med. Soc. Vienna (life mem.), Am. Legion (6th dist. comdr. 1974-75), Lions (pres. 1946). Republican. Presbyterian. Home: 5835 La Cuesta Dr Santa Rosa CA 95409-3914

LEV, LEORA, cinema educator, arts journalist; b. N.Y.C.; d. Robert Lev and Varda Hadassah Sherman. BA, Brandeis U., 1982; AM, Harvard U., 1984, PhD, 1992. Tchg. fellow Harvard U., Cambridge, Mass., 1984-87, 90; instr. Harvard Ext. Sch., Cambridge, 1987-93; lectr. Brandeis U., Waltham, Mass., 1991-94; asst. prof. No. Ariz. U., Flagstaff, 1994—. Contbg. author: Post-Franco, Postmodern: The Films of Pedro Almodóvar, 1995; contbr. articles to profl. jours. Mem. MLA, Feministas Unidas, Soc. for Cinema Studies Assn., Lit. and Film Assn., Assn. Internat. de Valleinclanistas. Jewish. Office: No Ariz U PO Box 6004 MODL Flagstaff AZ 86011

LEVADA, WILLIAM JOSEPH, archbishop; b. Long Beach, Calif., June 15, 1936; s. Joseph and Lorraine (Nunez) L. B.A., St. John's Coll., Camarillo, Calif., 1958; S.T.L., Gregorian U., Rome, 1962, S.T.D., 1971. Ordained priest Roman Cath. Ch., 1961, consecrated bishop, 1983. Assoc. pastor Archdiocese of L.A., 1962-67; prof. theology St. John's Sem., Camarillo, Calif., 1970-76; ofcl. Doctrinal Congregation, Vatican City, Italy, 1976-82; exec. dir. Calif. Cath. Conf., Sacramento, 1982-84; aux. bishop Archdiocese of L.A., 1983-86; archbishop Archdiocese of Portland, Oreg., 1986-95; Archbishop of San Francisco, 1995—. Trustee Cath. U. Am.; chmn. bd. dirs. Pope John XXIII Med.-Moral Rsch. and Edn. Ctr. Mem. Nat. Conf. Cath. Bishops (com. on doctrine), U.S. Cath. Conf., Cath. Theol. Soc. Am., Canon Law Soc. Am. Office: Archbishop of San Francisco 445 Church St San Francisco CA 94114-1720*

LEVENDOSKY, CHARLES LEONARD, journalist, poet; b. Bronx, N.Y., July 4, 1936; s. Charles Leonard and Laura (Gregorio) L.; m. Charlotte Ann Jaeger, July 15, 1962; children: Alytia, Ixchel. BS in Physics, U. Okla., 1958, BA in Math., 1960; MA in Edn., NYU, 1963. Tchr. Christiansted H.S., V.I., 1963-65; tutor Kyoto (Japan) U., 1965-66, Elizabeth Irwin H.S., N.Y.C., 1966-67; asst. prof. English NYU, N.Y.C., 1967-71; poet in schs. arts couns. of N.Y., Ga., N.J., 1967-71; poet-in-residence Wyo. Arts Coun., Cheyenne, 1972-82; editl. page editor Casper (Wyo.) Star-Tribune, 1982—; columnist The New York Times, 1995—; co-dir. Bill of Rights seminar, Casper, 1991; chmn. Ad Hoc Com. for Judicial Fellowship, Casper, 1991-94. Author: Hands and Other Poems, 1986, Circle of Light, 1995; editor: Ucross: The First Ten Years, 1992; contbr. articles to profl. jours.; creator, editor Casper Star-Tribune's First Amendment Web site-FACT (Editor and Pub. award for best original feature for newspaper's online svcs. 1996), First Freedom Op-Ed Svc., ALA, 1995. Panelist First Amendment Congress, Williamsburg, Va., 1986, del., 1991, 97; adv. bd. Wyo. St. Hist. Records, Cheyenne, 1992. Appointed Poet Laureate of Wyo., Cheyenne, 1988-96, Humanities scholar Humanities Coun. in Pub. TV series, Wyo., 1991; recipient Intellectual Freedom award ALA, 1987, First Amendment award Hugh M. Hefner Found., 1987, H.L. Mencken award Free Press Assn., 1988, Print Media award Wyo. chpt. Am. Bd. Trial Advocates, 1992, Silver Gavel award ABA, 1994, H.L. Mencken award Balt. Sun, 1994. Mem. ACLU, PEN, Ams. United for Separation of Ch. and State, Freedom to Read Found., Nat. Coalition Against Censorship, Nat. Press Found. Office: Casper Star-Tribune 170 Star Ln Casper WY 82601

LEVENTHAL-STERN, BARBARA LYNN, artist, marriage and family counselor; b. Springfield, Ohio, Feb. 16, 1948; d. Harry Edwin and Shirley (Ungar) Leventhal; m. Michael David Stern, Sept. 12, 1970; children: Joshua Meyer, Nathaniel Benjamin. BFA, Boston Mus. Sch.-Tufts U., 1972; MA in Art, San Jose State U., 1985; MA in Counseling and Ednl. Psychology, U. San Francisco, 1989. Lic. marriage and family counselor, Calif. instr. Morris Stulsaft Found., Pacific Art League, Palo Alto, Calif., 1986, project coord. traveling art project, 1987-89. Illustrator: The Adventures of Judah and Yona, 1975; one-woman show Springfield (Ohio) Art Ctr., 1988; exhibited in group shows Fresno (Calif.) Art Mus., 1987, Mus. Modern Art, Ljubljana, Yugoslavia, 1987, U. Wis., Milwaukee, 1987, Hard Times Gallery, Bristol, England, 1988, Barbicon Ctr., London, 1989, Taipei Fine Arts Mus., Taiwan, 1990, Fitchburg (Mass.) Art Mus., 1990, Banner Spangenberg Gallery, Palo Alto, 1991, Banska Bystrica, Czech Republic, Davis (Calif.) Art Ctr., 1991, Euphrat Gallery De Anza Coll., Cupertino, Calif., 1991, Prieto Gallery Mills Coll., Oakland, Calif., 1992, Palo Alto Cultural Ctr., 1993, Triton Mus., Santa Clara, Calif., 1993, Bade Mus. Pacific Sch. Religion, Berkeley, Calif., 1994, Michael Himovitz Gallery, Sacramento, 1995. Rep. human rels. com. Palo Verde Sch., Palo Alto Unified Sch. Dist., 1994-95; mem. planning com. Project Dialogue, Jewish Ccmty. Ctr., Palo Alto, 1996; bd. dirs. Women's Alliance, Jewish Cmty. Fedn., Palo Alto, 1996-97; com. mem. disability task force Jewish Family Svcs., San Francisco, 1996-97. Recipient 1st place award for woodcut No. Calif. Print Competition, 1984, purchase award Purdue U., 1984, Rank-Xerox Corp., Eng., 1985, young leadership award Albert L. Schultz Jewish Cmty. Ctr., Palo Alto, 1984; grantee Conn. Com. on Arts, 1975-76, Pensinsula Cmty. Found., 1986, Santa Clara Arts Coun., 1996; Ann Flanagan fellow Kala Inst., 1985. Mem. Womens Caucus for Art, Am. Print Alliance, Calif. Soc. Printmakers (publicity coord. 1987-88), Calif. Assn. Marriage and Family Counselors, Arts and Healing Network, Jewish Art Cmty. of Bay. Democrat.

LE VEQUE, MATTHEW KURT, public affairs and marketing consultant; b. Los Angeles, May 24, 1958; s. Edward Albert and Vera Eleanora (Behne) LeV. BA in Polit. Sci., UCLA, 1981. Reapportionment cons. Calif. State Legislature, Sacramento, 1981; cons. Berman and D'Agostino Campaigns, Inc., L.A., 1982-91; coord. L.A. Olympic com., 1984; spl. asst. Congressmen H. Waxman and H. Berman, Calif., 1982-85; cons. The Helin Orgn., Newport Beach, Calif., 1984-86; sr. cons. Calif. State Senate, L.A. and Sacramento, 1985-92; campaign fin. coord Levine for U.S. Senate, L.A., 1991; sr. assoc. Pacific West Comms. Group, L.A., 1992-93; chief staff L.A. State Assemblyman Terry Friedman, 1993-94; pub. affairs and mktg. exec. Rogers & Assocs., L.A., 1995—. Active numerous local and nat. Dem. polit. campaigns. Office: 531 24th St Hermosa Beach CA 90254-2618

LEVEQUE, THOMAS JOSEPH, elementary school educator, writer; b. Burbank, Calif., July 25, 1951; s. Francois Dazincourt and Marquerite June (Brodie) L.; m. Carolyn Jean Bauer, Aug. 26, 1978 (div. Dec., 1991); children: Julie Elaine, Holly Nicole. BA, Loyola U., L.A., 1973; MA, Calif. State U., L.A., 1994; postgrad studies in Edn., UCLA, 1994—. Dir. comedy devel. Comsky/Kander Prodns., L.A., 1974-76; dir. creative affairs Avco Embassy Pictures, L.A., 1976-82, Internat. Cinema Corp., L.A., 1982-85; v.p. creative affairs Frank Capra Prodns., L.A., 1985-87; v.p. acquisitons Trans World Entertainment, L.A., 1987-89; tchr. Nevin Ave. Elem. Sch., L.A., 1989—; rep. instrnl. cabinet L.A. Unified Sch. Dist., 1994; chair Leadership Team Nevin Ave. Elem. Sch., L.A., 1995, mem. sch. mgmt. team, 1996—. Mem. choir St. Jerome's Ch., L.A., 1981, liturgy com. 1991-94. Mem. Computer Use in Edn. Group, United Tchrs. L.A. Democrat. Roman Catholic. Office: Nevin Ave Elem Sch 1569 E 32nd St Los Angeles CA 90011-2213

LEVI, DAVID F., federal judge; b. 1951. BA, Harvard U., MA, 1973; JD, Stanford U. Bar: Calif. 1983. U.S. atty. ea. dist. State of Calif., Sacramento, 1986-90; judge U.S. Dist. Ct. (ea. dist.) Calif., 1990—; chmn. task force on race, religious and ethnic fairness U.S. Ct. Appeals (9th cir.), 1994—, mem. jury com., 1993-95. Adv. com. on Civil Rules, 1994—; vis. com. U. Chgo. Law Sch., 1995—. Mem. Am. Law Inst., Milton L. Schwartz Inn of Ct. (pres. 1992-95). Office: 2504 Fed Bldg 650 Capitol Mall Sacramento CA 95814-4708

LEVI, HERBERT A., deputy city manager, consultant; b. Dunkirk, Ind., May 31, 1931; s. Lawrence Warren and Virginia Roselyn (Avery) L.; m.

Virginia Elizabeth Webster, Dec. 7, 1950; children: Victor Herbert, Michael David, Demetrius Titus. BA, Ball State U., Muncie, Ind., 1952; MPA, Calif. State U., Long Beach, 1978. Cert. tchr., Calif. Debit mgr. Mammoth Life Ins. Co., Muncie, 1951-53; chemist City of L.A. Pub. Works, 1954-55, sr. indsl. waste inspector, 1959-66, safety engring. asst., 1967-69, sr. personnel analyst, 1969-71, contract compliance officer, 1971-75; adminstrv. analyst III City of Long Beach (Calif.) City Mgr., 1975-78; personnel analyst III City of Long Beach Personnel, 1978-82; adminstrv. officer Long Beach Pub. Libr., 1982-90; dep. city mgr., exec. dir. police complaint commn. City of Long Beach, 1990-91; ret., 1991—, cons. to bus. and govt., 1993—; mem. policy bd. Ctr. for Pub. Policy and Adminstrn., Calif. State U., 1986-90. Author: Equal Opportunity Compliance for Cities, 1978; co-author: Contract Compliance Manual, 1976. Founder Vet. Stadium Citizen's Com., Long Beach, Calif., 1983; mem. Lakewood (Calif.) High Sch. Community Adv. Coun., 1974; chair Hamilton High Sch. Community Adv. Coun., L.A., 1969; mem. KLON-FM 88 Community Adv. Bd., Long Beach, 1985. Recipient Excellence in Performance award City of L.A. Bd. Pub. Works, 1977, Employee of Yr. award City of Long Beach, Personnel, 1981. Mem. Am. Soc. Pub. Adminstrn., Internat. Personnel Mgmt. Assn., Equal Opportunity Compliance Officers Assn. (pres., co-founder 1971-77), So. Calif. Personnel Mgmt. Assn. (v.p. programs 1983-84), Long Beach Mgmt. Club, Pi Alpha Alpha (v.p. 1989-91). Home and Office: 5153 E Hanbury St Long Beach CA 90808-1845

LEVIN, ALAN SCOTT, pathologist, allergist, immunologist, lawyer; b. Chgo., Jan. 12, 1938; s. John Bernhard and Betty Ruth (Margulis) L.; m. Vera S. Byers, June 15, 1971. BS in Chemistry, U. Ill., Champaign-Urbana, 1960; MS in Biochemistry, U. Ill., Chgo., 1963, MD, 1964; JD, Golden Gate U., 1995. Diplomate Am. Bd. Allergy and Immunology, Am. Bd. Pathology; bar: Calif. 1995. Intern Children's Hosp. Med. Ctr., Boston, 1964-65; adj. instr. pediatrics U. Calif., San Francisco, 1971-72, asst. prof. immunology dept. dermatology, 1972-78, adj. assoc. prof., 1978-88; dir. lab. immunology U. Calif. & Kaiser Found. Rsch. Inst. Joint Program Project, San Francisco, 1971-74; attending physician dept. medicine Mt. Zion/U. Calif. San Francisco Hosps., 1971—; dir. div. immunology Western Labs., Oakland, Calif., 1974-77; med. dir. MML/Solano Labs. Div. Chemed-W.R. Grace, Inc., Berkeley, Calif., 1977-79; med. dir. Levin Clin. Labs., Inc., San Francisco, 1979-81; pvt. practice San Francisco, 1981—. Contbr. articles to profl. jours., chpts. to books. Lt. USN, 1966-69, Vietnam. Decorated Bronze Star, Silver Star, 4 Air medals; Harvard Med. Sch. traineeship grantee, 1964, USPHS hematology tng. grantee U. Calif., San Francisco Med. Ctr., 1969-71; recipient Faculty Rsch. award Am. Cancer Soc., 1970-74. Fellow Coll. Am. Pathologists, Am. Coll. Emergency Physicians, Am. Soc. Clin. Pathologists; mem. AMA, Am. Acad. Allergy and Immunology, Am. Coll. Allergy and Immunology, Am. Assn. Clin. Chemists, Am. Acad. Environ. Medicine, Calif. Med. Assn., San Francisco Med. Soc. Jewish. Office: Immunology Inc 500 Sutter St Ste 512 San Francisco CA 94102-1114

LEVIN, ALVIN IRVING, composer, educator; b. N.Y.C., Dec. 22, 1921; s. David and Frances (Schloss) L.; m. Beatrice Van Loon, June 5, 1976 (div. 1981). BMus in Edn., U. Miami (Fla.), 1941; MA, Calif. State U., L.A., 1955; EdD with honors, UCLA, 1968. Composer, arranger for movies, TV, theater Allied Artists, Eagle-Lion Studios, Los Angeles, 1945-65; tng. and supervising tchr. Los Angeles City Schs., 1957-65, adult edn. instr., 1962-63; research specialist Los Angeles Office Supt. edn., 1965-67; asst. prof. ednl. research Calif. State U., Los Angeles, 1968; asst. prof. elem. edn. Calif. State U., Northridge, 1969-73; self-employed, Northridge, 1973—; founder, pres. Alvin Irving Levin Philanthropic Found., 1973—, ordained to ministry Ch. of Mind Sci., 1975; founder, pres. Divine Love Ch. An Internat. Metaphys. Ch., 1977—, Meet Your New Personality, A Mind Expansion Program, 1975-77. Bd. overseers Calif. Sch. Profl. Psychology, 1974—; gen. chmn., producer Fiftieth Anniversity Pageant of North Hollywood Park, 1977. Author: My Ivory Tower, 1950, Symposium: Values in Kaleidoscope, 1973, (TV series) America, America!, 1978-79, (docudrama) One World, 1980; composer: Symphony for Strings, 1984, Tone Poem for MaleChorus and Brass, 1984, Hymn to the United Nations for chorus and Male Chorus and Brass, 1984, Hymn to the United Nations for chorus and symphonyorch., 1991, Hiawatha Suite for Chorus and Symphony Orch., 1994, We Are Not Alone, Chorus and Symphony Orchestra, 1996, North Hollywood: Metamorphosis, A Symphonic Suite, 1996-97, Introspection for Symphony Orchestra, 1997 (music-drama) Happy Land, 1971, (musical plays) A Tale of Two Planets, 1988, Blueprint for a New World Model, 1991; prodr. UN Festival Calif. State U., Northridge, 1991; compiler, contbr. U.S. Dept. Edn. reports Adult Counseling and Guidance, 1967, Parent Child Preschool Program, 1967, English Classes for Foreign Speaking Adult Professionals, 1967, Blueprint for New World Order, 1991. Recipient plaque State of Calif., 1977, Golden Merit medal. Rep. Presdl. Task Force, 1985.Named to Rep Task Force Presdl. Commn., 1986. Mem. Nat. Soc. for Study Edn., AAUP, Am. Statis Assn., Internat. Coun. Edn. for Tchg., L.A. World Affairs Coun., Internat. Platform Assn., World Federalist Assn. (pres. San Fernando Valley chpt. 1991—), North Hollywood C. of C. (dir. 1976—), Phi Delta Kappa. Home and Office: 5407 Colfax Ave Apt 223 North Hollywood CA 91601-5209 *Personal philosophy: Always dream the impossible dream; then make it come true, with every possible action!.*

LEVIN, BARRY RAYMOND, rare book dealer; b. Phila., June 11, 1946; s. Sidney and Bertha (Zwerman) L.; m. Sally Ann Fudge, Aug. 19, 1983. Student, Santa Monica City Coll., 1964-65. Various aerospace positions McDonnell Douglas, AstroPeen, 1967-72; owner Barry R. Levin Sci. Fiction & Fantasy Lit., 1973—; cons. sci. fiction, fantasy and horror films, 1976—. Author: (rare book catalogs) Titles from the Back Room, 1981, Great Works and Rarities of Science Fiction and Fantasy, 1982, One Small Step, 1983, Newsletters, 1980—, others; contbr. articles to profl. jours. With U.S. Army, 1965-67. Mem. Antiquarian Booksellers Assn. Am., Am. Booksellers Assn., Bibliog. Soc. Am., Bibliog. Soc. Great Britain, New Eng. Sci. Fiction Assn., So. Calif. Booksellers Assn., Internat. League Antiquarian Booksellers, Internat. Assn. of the Fantastic in the Arts, Internat. Platform Assn., Sci. Fiction Writers Am., Horror Writers Am., Manuscript Soc., Sci. Fiction Rsch. Assn., Assn. Sci. Fiction and Fantasy Artists, Lewis Carroll Soc., others. Jewish. Office: Barry R Levin Sci Fiction & Fantasy Lit 720 Santa Monica Blvd Santa Monica CA 90401-2602

LEVIN, BARRY SHERWIN, physician; b. Dec. 17, 1940. BS in Hisotry, U. Wis., 1962; MD, U. Ill., 1966. Diplomate Am. Bd. Internal Medicine, Am. Bd. Nephrology. Intern then resident U. Ill. Rsch. and Edn. Hosp., Chgo., 1966-68; resident U. Calif., San Francisco, 1967-68, asst. clin. prof. medicine, 1975-82; fellow Peter Brent Brigham Hosp., Boston, 1969-71; asst. prof. medicine U. Chgo., 1974-75; med. dir. transplantation program Calif. Pacific Med. Ctr., San Francisco, 1979—; med. dir. Calif. Transplant Donor Network, 1987-88; staff physician Andrews AFB, Md., 1971-73, Washingotn Hosp., Calif. Pacific Med. Ctr., San Francisco, 1975—; assoc. attending physician, dir. Michael Reese Hosp., Chgo., 1974-75. Contbr. articles to profl. jours. Fellow NIH, 1969-71. Mem. Am. Soc. Nephrology, Am. Soc. Transplant Physicians (pres. 1988-89), Internat. Soc. Nephrology, Transplantation Soc., Alpha Omega Alpha. Office: Calif Pacific Med Ctr 2340 Clay St San Francisco CA 94115-1932

LEVIN, HAL ALAN, psychiatrist; b. Bklyn., Feb. 13, 1935; s. David and Rose M. (Rosen) L.; children of former marriage: Julie Levin Keith, Susan Levin Davis, Mark D. Levin; m. Sharon Greenleaf, Feb. 9, 1973; children: Anne Levin Warrick, Julie Elizabeth, Alisa M., Kimberly L. Grimes, Christopher Lenk. BS, Roosevelt U., 1958; MD, Tulane Med. Sch., New Orleans, 1967. Diplomate Am. Bd. Psychiatry and Neurology, Am. Bd. Forensic Examiners, Am. Bd. Forensic Medicine. Intern Norfolk (Va.) Gen. Hosp., 1967-68; resident in psychiatry Sheppard & Enoch Pratt Hosp., Towson, Md., 1968-70, Crownsville (Md.) Hosp., 1970-71; fellow in forensic psychiatry U. So. Calif., L.A., 1983-84; staff psychiatrist Atascadero (Calif.) State Hosp., 1971-72; pvt. practice psychiatry San Bernardino, Calif., 1972-85; asst. prof. clin. psychiatry Mich. State U., East Lansing, 1985-86; asst. dir. mental health State of Mich., Lansing, 1985-86; dir. mental health State of Ariz., Phoenix, 1986-87; pvt. practice psychiatry Tempe, Ariz., 1987—; cons. psychiatrist San Bernardino County Hosp., 1972-85, San Bernardino Superior Ct., 1972-85; dir. Desert Valley Clinic, Apple Valley, Calif., 1973-80; med. dir. Big Bear (Calif.) Psychiat. Clinic, 1980-84; med. dir. Ctr. for Behavioral Health, Tempe, 1989—. cons. Jewish Family Svcs., Tempe, 1990—, Interfaith Counseling, Mesa, Ariz., 1991—. Mem. AMA, Am. Psychiat. Assn., Ariz. Med. Assn., Am. Acad. Psychiatry & the Law, Am. Bd. Forensic Examiners, Friends of Phoenix Symphony. Democrat. Office: 5410 S Lakeshore Dr # 103 Tempe AZ 85283-2171

LEVIN, JACK, physician, educator, biomedical investigator; b. Newark, Oct. 11, 1932; s. Joseph and Anna (Greengold) L.; m. Francine Corthesy, Apr. 13, 1975. B.A. magna cum laude, Yale U., 1953, M.D. cum laude, 1957. Diplomate: Am. Bd. Internal Medicine. Intern in medicine Grace-New Haven Hosp., 1957-58, asst. resident in medicine, 1960-62; chief resident in medicine Yale-New Haven Med. Ctr., 1964-65; clin. assoc. Nat. Cancer Inst., Bethesda, Md., 1958-60; fellow in hematology Johns Hopkins U. Sch. Medicine and Hosp., Balt., 1962-64, mem. faculty, 1965-82, prof. medicine, 1978-82; prof. lab. medicine, prof. medicine U. Calif. Sch. Medicine, San Francisco, 1982—; dir. hematology lab. and blood bank San Francisco VA Med. Ctr., 1982-93, dir. flow cytometry facility, 1987-90; cons. in field. Author: (with P.D. Zieve) Disorders of Hemostasis, 1976; editor: (with E. Cohen and F.B. Bang) Biomedical Applications of the Horseshoe Crab (Limulidae), 1979, (with S.W. Watson and T.J. Novitsky) Endotoxins and Their Detection with the Limulus Amebocyte Lysate Test, 1982, Detection of Bacterial Endotoxins with The Limulus Amebocyte Lysate Test, 1987, (with others) Bacterial Endotoxins. Structure, Biomedical Significance, and Detection with the Limulus Amebocyte Lysate Test, 1985, Megakaryocyte Development and Function, 1986, Bacterial Endotoxins. Pathophysiological Effects, Clinical Significance, and Pharmacological Control, 1988, Molecular Biology and Differentiation of Megakaryocytes, 1990, Bacterial Endotoxins: Cytokine Mediators and New Therapies for Sepsis, 1991, Bacterial Endotoxin: Recognition and Effector Mechanisms, 1993, Bacterial Endotoxins: Basic Science to Anti-Sepsis Strategies, 1994, Bacterial Endotoxins: Lipopolysaccharides from Genes to Therapy, 1995; mem. editorial bd. Blood, Jour. Endotoxin Rsch.; contbr. numerous articles to profl. jours; developer (with F.B. Bang) Limulus test for bacterial endotoxins. Mem. Yale Alumni Schs. Com. for Md., 1967-82, for San Francisco, 1986—; mem. sci. adv. bd. Nat. Aquarium, Balt., 1978-82; mem. corp. Marine Biol. Lab., 1965—; trustee Marine Biol. Lab., 1988-93; mem. panel ind. assessors for rsch. project grants awards Nat. Health and Med. Rsch. Coun. Australia, 1982—. Served with USPHS, 1958-60. Markle scholar, 1968-73; recipient USPHS Rsch. Career Devel. award, 1970-75; Royal Soc. Medicine fellow Oxford (Eng.) U., 1972; Josiah Macy Jr. Found. faculty scholar, 1978-79; Frederik B. Bang award for rsch. in bacterial endotoxins, 1986. Fellow ACP; mem. Am. Soc. Hematology, Am. Soc. Clin. Investigation, Internat. Soc. Hematology, Internat. Soc. Explt. Hematology, Am. Soc. Investigative Pathology, Am. Fedn. Clin. Rsch., Soc. Exptl. Biology and Medicine, Internat. Endotoxin Soc., So. Soc. Clin. Investigation, Western Assn. Physicians, Soc. Invertebrate Pathology, Soc. Analytical Cytology, Cell Kinetics Soc., Internat. Soc. Artificial Cells, Blood Substitutes and Immobilization Biotech., Calif. Acad. Medicine, Phi Beta Kappa, Sigma Xi. Clubs: 14 W Hamilton St, Tudor and Stuart; Yale (San Francisco).

LEVIN, JOHN STEWART, education educator; b. Orange, N.J., Dec. 29, 1946; s. Norman Levin and Sonia Matoff Nagler; m. Lee Stewart, July 25, 1978; children: Tracy, D'Arcy, Simon, Jeremy. BA with honors, U. B.C., Vancouver, Can., 1968, EdD, 1989; MA, York U., Toronto, 1969. Lectr. U. B.C., 1969-70; instr. Douglas Coll., New Westminster, B.C., 1970-81; dir. acad. programs Kwantlen Coll., Surrey, B.C., 1981-91; campus dir. North Island Coll., Port Alberni, B.C., 1991-93; prof. U. Ariz., Tucson, 1993—; higher edn. cons., 1989—; lectr. U. B.C., 1989-90; dir. Cmty. Coll. Inst., Tucson, 1993—, Coun. Univs. and Colls., 1996—. Author: Renewal and Responsiveness, 1989; also articles. Trustee West Coast Gen. Hosp., Port Alberni, 1992-93. Can. Study grantee, 1995; Social Sci. and Humanities Rsch. Coun. grantee, 1996—. Mem. Can. Soc. for Study of Higher Edn. (dir. 1990-92), Assn. for Study of Higher Edn., Am. Assn. C.C.s. Office: U Ariz Ctr for Study Higher Edn Tucson AZ 85721

LEVIN, MARC ALAN, librarian; b. Balt., Apr. 21, 1955; s. Hyman and Pauline (Glatt) L. BA in History, Gettysburg Coll., 1977; MLS, U. Hawaii, 1979; MPA, Calif. State U., Hayward, 1987. Archivist Nat. Archives, Washington, 1976-77; libr. U. Hawaii, Honolulu, 1979-80; head libr. U. Calif., Berkeley, 1980—. Mem. editl. bd. Index to Current Urban Documents, 1991—; contbr. articles to profl. jours. Grand juror San Franciso Civil Grand Jury, 1995-96. Mem. ASPA (bd. dirs. 1992-93), Spl. Librs. Assn. (bd. dirs. San Francisco chpt. 1990-92), Western Govtl. Rsch. Assn. (editl. bd. 1990-96). Democrat. Roman Catholic. Home: 348 Church St # 203 San Francisco CA 94114 Office: U Calif Inst Govtl Studies Libr 109 Moses Hall Rm 2370 Berkeley CA 94720-2370

LEVINE, ARNOLD MILTON, retired electrical engineer, documentary filmmaker; b. Preston, Conn., Aug. 15, 1916; s. Samuel and Florence May (Clark) L.; m. Bernice Eleanor Levich, Aug. 31, 1941; children: Mark Jeffrey, Michael Norman, Kevin Lawrence. BS in Radio Engring., Tri-State U., Angola, Ind., 1939, DSc, 1960; MS, U. Iowa, 1940. Head sound lab. CBS, N.Y.C., 1940-42; asst. engr., div. head ITT, N.Y.C. and Nutley, N.J., 1942-65; lab. head, lab. dir. ITT, San Fernando, Calif., 1965-71; v.p. aerospace, gen. mgr., sr. scientist ITT, Van Nuys, Calif., 1971-86; ret., 1986. Patentee fiber optics, radar, motion picture digital sound, communications and TV fields. Past mem. bd. dirs., v.p., pres. Am. Jewish Congress, L.A. Recipient San Fernando Valley Engr. of Yr. award, 1968; Profl. designation Motion Picture Art & Scis., UCLA, 1983. Fellow IEEE (life), Soc. Motion Picture and TV Engrs., USCG Aux. (vice comdr. 1990-91, flotilla cmdr. 1992-94). Home: 10828 Fullbright Ave Chatsworth CA 91311-1737

LEVINE, BENJAMIN JACOB, secondary education educator; b. L.A., Jan. 14, 1940; s. Leo Harry and Rebecca (Haim) L. BA, U. Calif., L.A., 1962; MS, Calif. State U., Northridge, 1971. Calif. standard tchg. credential; Calif. C.C. instr. credential. Tchr. Hillel Acad., Beverly Hills, Calif., 1965-67, Mary Star of the Sea H.S., San Pedro, Calif., 1967-68, Alemany H.S., Mission Hills, Calif., 1968-70; part-time instr. Los Angeles Harbor Coll., Wilmington, Calif., 1971-79, Santa Monica (Calif.) Coll., 1974-79; programmer Gen. Motors-Hughes Electronics, El Segundo, Calif., 1979-88; tutor Colin McEwen H.S., Malibu, Calif., 1992-93; tchr. grades 8-12 Noonnoppi, La Crescenta, Calif., 1994—; grievance com. chair Santa Monica (Calif.) Coll. United Faculty Assn., 1976-78. Contbr. articles to profl. jours. Mem. Chamber Pot Soc. Home: 6261 Condon Ave Los Angeles CA 90056-1905 Office: Noonnoppi 1521 W Glenoaks Blvd Glendale CA 91201-1912

LEVINE, C. BRUCE, lawyer; b. Liberty, N.Y., Aug. 20, 1945. Student, Stanford U.; BA magna cum laude, UCLA, 1967; JD cum laude, Harvard U., 1971. Bar: Calif. 1971. Mem. Greenberg, Glusker, Fields, Claman & Machtinger, L.A. Editor Harvard Law Rev., 1970-71. Mem. State Bar Calif., L.A. County Bar Assn. (chmn. income tax com. tax sect. 1979-80), Beverly Hills Bar Assn. (chmn. taxation com. 1977-78), Phi Beta Kappa, Pi Gamma Mu. Office: Greenberg Glusker Fields Claman & Machtinger 20th Flr 1900 Avenue Of The Stars Fl 20 Los Angeles CA 90067-4301

LEVINE, MARILYN ANNE, artist; b. Medicine Hat, Alta., Can., Dec. 22, 1935; came to the U.S., 1973; d. Herman Rutherford and Annie Louise (Waldo) Hayes; m. Sidney Levine, Sept. 30, 1959 (div. 1977). BSc, U. Alta., Edmonton, 1957; MSc, U. Alta., 1959; MA, U. Calif., Berkeley, 1970, MFA, 1971. Tchg. fellow dept. chemistry U. Alta., Edmonton, 1957-59; chemist I Geology Survey Can., Ottawa, 1959-61; chemistry instr. Campion Coll., U. Sask., Regina, Can., 1962-64; ceramics instr. dept. ext. U. Regina, Sask., 1966-69; ceramics instr. U. Regina, 1971-73; vis. art instr. U. Calgary, Alta., summers 1968, 71; lectr. in art U. Calif., Davis, 1972; visual arts lectr. U. Regina, 1972-73; asst. prof. art U. Utah, Salt Lake City, 1973-76; vis. asst. prof. art-sculpture U. Calif., Berkeley, 1975-80; vis. art lectr. Calif. State Coll., Hayward, 1981. One-woman shows include Hansen Fuller Gallery, San Francisco, 1971, 75, 80, 83, Norman Mackenzie Art Gallery, Regina, 1974, O.K. Harris Works of Art, N.Y.C., 1974, 76, 79, 81, 84, 85, 91, Inst. Contemporary Art, Boston, 1981, Galerie Alain Blondel, Paris, 1981, Rena Bransten Gallery, San Francisco, 1990; group exhibits include Nat. Mus. Modern Art, Kyoto, 1971, Sidney Janis Gallery, N.Y., 1972, Musee d'Art de la Ville de Paris, 1973, Whitney Mus. Am. Art Downtown Br., N.Y., 1974, Mus. Contemporary Crafts, N.Y., 1975, Australian Nat. Gallery, Canberra, 1977, Everson Mus. Art, Syracuse, N.Y., 1979, Denver Art Mus., 1979, Pa. Acad. Fine Arts, Phila., 1981-83, Mackenzie Art Gallery, U. Regina, 1980, Abbaye Saint-Andre, Meymac, Correze, France, 1983, Am. Craft Mus., N.Y., 1986-92, Philbrook Mus. Art, Tulsa, 1987-89, Scripps Coll., Claremont, Calif., 1994-96; represented in permanent collections U. Art Mus., Berkeley, Can. Coun. Art Bank, Australian Nat. Gallery, Canberra, Mus. Contemporary Art, Chgo., Nelson-Atkins Mus. Art, Kansas City, Mo., Nat. Mus. Modern Art, Kyoto, Montreal Mus. Fine Art, Va. Mus. Fine Arts, Richmond, San Francisco Mus. Modern Art, Everson Mus. Art, Syracuse, Philbrook Mus. Art, Tulsa. Recipient David P. Gardner Faculty Rsch. grantee U. Utah, Salt Lake City, 1975, Sr. Arts Grant award Can. Coun., Ottawa, Ont., Can., 1976; Visual Artists Fellowship grantee Nat. Endowment for the Arts, Washington, 1976, 80. Home: 950 Sixty First St Oakland CA 94608

LEVINE, MICHAEL, public relations executive, author; b. N.Y.C., Apr. 17, 1954; s. Arthur and Virginia (Gaylor) L. Student, Rutgers U., 1978. Owner, operator TV News Mag., Los Angeles, 1977-83; owner Levine/Schnieder Pub. Rels., now Levine Comms. Office, Inc., Los Angeles, 1982—; mem. Gov.'s adv. bd. State Calif., Sacramento, 1980-82; pres., owner Aurora Pub., L.A., 1986—; moderator Thought Forum; lectr. in field; founder, moderator L.A. Media Roundtable. Author: The Address Book: How to Reach Anyone Who's Anyone, 1984, The New Address Book, 1986, The Corporate Address Book, 1987, The Music Address Book, 1989, Environmental Address Book, 1991, Kid's Address Book, 1991, Guerrilla P.R., Lessons at Halfway Point, Take It From Me; pub., writer For Consideration newsletter. Mem. Ronald Reagan Pres.'s Libr.; founder The Actor's Conf., Aurora Charity, 1987; bd. dirs. Felice Found., Micah Ctr.; adv. bd. Dare America. Mem. TV Acad. Arts and Scis., Entertainment Industries Coun., Musician's Assistance Program, West Hollywood C. of C. (bd. dirs. 1980-82). Jewish. Office: 433 N Camden Dr Fl 4 Beverly Hills CA 90210-4426

LEVINE, MICHAEL JOSEPH, insurance company executive; b. Boston, Mar. 23, 1945; s. Sam and Helen Alice (Michelman) L.; m. Margaret Mary Gutierrez, Aug. 6, 1983; children: Samuel Jacob, Rebecca Lynn. BA, Boston U., 1967; MBA, N.Mex. State U., 1991. Supr. underwriting Comml. Union. Ins., Boston, 1969-73; mgr. Harris-Murtagh Ins., Boston, 1973-75, Cohen-Goldenberg Ins. Agy., Boston, 1975-77; v.p. Southwest Underwriters Ins., Deming, N.Mex., 1977-83, pres., 1983-86; pres. Consol. Ins. Cons., Deming, N.Mex., 1985—; instr. fin. and ins., N.Mex. State U., Las Cruces. V.p. Border Area Mental Health Svcs., So. N.Mex., 1978—; pres. Deming Arts Council, 1979-81; treas. Luna County (N.Mex.) Crimestoppers, Inc., 1979—. Mem. Mensa, Soc. CPCU's (cert.), Soc. Cert. Ins. Counselors (cert.), Ins. Mktg. Assocs., Luna County C. of C. (v.p. 1981-84), Ind. Ins. Agts. N.Mex. (state dir. 1985—), Southwest N.Mex. Ind. Ins. Agts. (treas. 1981-83, pres. 1983-85). Home: PO Box 6028 Alpine TX 79832-0001 Office: Consol Ins Cons Inc 318 S Columbus Rd Deming NM 88030-3867

LEVINE, PHILIP, poet, educator; b. Detroit, Jan. 10, 1928; s. A. Harry and Esther Gertrude (Priscol) L.; m. Frances Artley, July 12, 1954; children: Mark, John, Teddy. B.A., Wayne State U., 1950, A.M., 1955; M.F.A., U. Iowa, 1957, studied with John Berryman, 1954. Instr. U. Iowa, 1955-57; instr. Calif. State U., Fresno, 1958—; prof. English Calif. State U., 1969-92, Tufts U.; tchr. Princeton U., Columbia U., U. Calif., Berkeley.; Elliston lectr. poetry U. Cin.; poet-in-residence Vassar Coll., Nat. U. Australia; chmn. lit. panel Nat. Endowment Arts, 1985; adj. prof. NYU, Spring, 1984; Univ. prof. Brown U., spring 1985; tchr. NYU, U. Iowa, Vanderbilt U. Author: On the Edge, 1961, Silent in America: Vivas for Those Who Failed, 1965, Not This Pig, 1968, 5 Detroits, 1970, Thistles, 1970, Pili's Wall, 1971, Red Dust, 1971, They Feed They Lion, 1972, 1933, 1974, On The Edge & Over, 1976, The Names of the Lost, 1976 (Lenore Marshall award Best Am. Book Poems 1976), 7 Years from Somewhere, 1979 (Nat. Book Critics Circle prize 1979, Notable Book award Am. Libr. Assn. 1979), Ashes, 1979 (Nat. Book Critics Circle prize 1979, Nat. Book award 1979), Don't Ask, 1979, One for the Rose, 1981, Selected Poems, 1984, Sweet Will, 1985, A Walk with Tom Jefferson, 1988 (Bay Area Book Reviewers award), What Work Is, 1991 (L.A. Times Book Prize 1991, Nat. Book award for poetry, 1991), New Selected Poems, 1991, Earth, Stars, and Writers, 1992, The Bread of Time: Toward an Autobiography, 1994, Simple Truth, 1994 (Pulitzer Prize for poetry 1995); editor: (with Henri Coulette) Character and Crisis, 1966, (with E. Trejo) The Selected Poems of Jaime Sabines, (with Ada Long) Off the Map, The Selected Poems of Gloria Fuertes, 1984, (with D. Wojahn and B. Henderson) The Pushcart Prize XI, 1986, The Essential Keats, 1987. Active anti-Vietnam war movement. Recipient Joseph Henry Jackson award San Francisco Found., 1961, The Chaplebrook Found. award, 1968, Frank O'Hara Meml. prize, 1973; Amer. Academy of Arts and Letters Award of Merit, 1974; Levinson Prize, 1974; Harriet Monroe Meml. prize for poetry, 1976; Golden Rose award New Eng. Poetry Soc., 1985, Ruth Lilly Poetry Prize, Modern Poetry Assn. and Am. Council Arts, 1987, Elmer Bobst award NYU, 1990, Lit. Lion New York Public Library 1993; named outstanding lectr. Calif. State U., Fresno, 1971, outstanding prof. Calif. State U. System, 1972; Stanford U. poetry fellow, 1957, Nat. Inst. Arts and Letters grantee, 1973, Guggenheim fellow, 1973-74, 80; Nat. Endowment for Arts grantee, 1969, 70 (refused), 76, 81, 87. *My hope is to write poetry for people for whom there are no poems.**

LEVINSON, DAVID W., engineering educator, consultant; b. Chgo., Feb. 24, 1925; s. Louis E. and Ethel (Paul) L.; m. Betty L. Sachnoff Levinson, Aug. 28, 1949; children: Louis E., Joseph P., Jeanne L. BSChemE, Ill. Inst. Tech., Chgo., 1948; MS in Metall. Engring., 1949, PhD, 1953. Instr. Ill. Inst. Tech., Chgo., 1949-53; rsch. metallurgist Armour Rsch. Found., Chgo., 1953-56, supr. non-ferrous met., 1956-60; asst. dir. met. rsch. IIT Rsch. Inst., Chgo., 1960-62, scientific advisor met. & ceramics, 1962-64; prof. Dept. Engring. U. Ill., Chgo., 1964-87, dean of engring., 1968-70; dir. forensic sci. Triodyne Taussig Inc., Niles, Ill., 1987-89; adjunct prof. metallurgy U. Ariz., Tucson, 1990—; pres. David W. Levinson Cons., Inc., Northbrook, Ill., 1966-87; panel mem. U.S. Natl. Adv. Bd., Washington, 1963-64; v.p. engring. Fotofabrication Corp., Chgo., 1970-87. Contbr. over 40 articles to profl. jours. Dir. Northbrook Civil Def., 1960-64. Mem. Am. Soc. for Materials, Am. Inst. Mining, Metallurgical and Petroleum Engrs. Home: 990 W Placita De La Cotonia Green Valley AZ 85614-1305 Office: Univ Arizona Dept MSE Tucson AZ 85721

LEVINSON, KENNETH LEE, lawyer; b. Denver, Jan. 18, 1953; s. Julian Charles and Dorothy (Milzer) L.; m. Shauna Titus, Dec. 21, 1986. BA cum laude, U. Colo.-Boulder, 1974; JD, U. Denver, 1978. Bar: Colo. 1978, U.S. Ct. Appeals (10th cir.) 1978. Assoc. atty. Balaban & Lutz, Denver, 1979-83; shareholder Balaban & Levinson, P.C., 1984—, pres., 94—. Contbr. articles to profl. jours. Pres. Dahlia House Condominium Assn., 1983-85, bd. dirs., 1991-94; intern Reporters Com. For Freedom of the Press, Washington, 1977; atty. grievance hearing bd., 1988—. J.V. volleyball coach Good Shephard Catholic Sch., 1992-95. Recipient Am. Jurisprudence award Lawyers Co-op., 1977; 3rd Place award Rocky Mt. Fiction Writers Mystery Novel Contest, 1994. Mem. Denver Bar Assn., Colo. Bar Assn. (profl. liability com. 1991-94), Am. Arbitration Assn. (arbitrator). Club: Denver Law.

LEVINSON, MARK, retired engineering educator; b. Bklyn., June 12, 1929; s. Samuel Eleazer and Rose (Tartakow) L.; m. Suzanne Josephson, Dec. 27, 1953; children: Robert Matthias, Madeline Jane. B Aero. Engring. summa cum laude, Poly. Inst. Bklyn., 1951, MS, 1960; PhD, Calif. Inst. Tech., 1964. Registered profl. engr., Ont., Can. Stress and vibration analyst Foster Wheeler Corp., N.Y.C., 1957-59; asst. prof. mech. engring. Oreg. State U., Corvallis, 1960-61; assoc. prof. mech. engring. Clarkson Coll. Tech., Potsdam, N.Y., 1964-66; assoc. prof. theo. and applied mech. W.Va. U., Morgantown, 1966-67; prof. engring. mech. McMaster U., Hamilton, Ont., Can., 1967-80; A.O. Willey prof. mech. engring., dir. tech./soc. project U. Maine, Orono, 1980-90; engring. educator, rschr. U. Wash., Seattle, 1989—; cons. in field, 1963-94. Contbr. over 50 articles to profl. jours. V.p. Heritage Hamilton Ltd., 1973-78. With U.S. Army, 1952-54. Fellow Ford Found., 1961-62, Woodrow Wilson Found., 1964, A. W. Mellon Found., 1984-85, NSF, 1988-89. Fellow AAAS, AIAA (assoc.); mem. ASME, Soc. for History of Tech., Soc. for Indsl. and Applied Math., Am. Aviation Hist. Soc. Home: 630 Giltner Ln Edmonds WA 98020-3001 Office: U Wash Dept Aero and Astronautics FS-10 Seattle WA 98195

LEVINSON, SHAUNA T., financial services executive; b. Denver, Aug. 1, 1954; d. Charles and Geraldine D. Titus; m. Kenneth L. Levinson, Dec. 21, 1986. BA cum laude, U. Puget Sound, 1976; M Bank Mktg. with honors, U. Colo., 1986. Cert. fin. planner. Fin. planning analyst Swift and Co., Chgo., 1977-79; from credit analyst to asst. v.p. Ctrl. Bank of Denver, 1979-84; v.p.

fin. svcs. First Nat. Bank S.E. Denver, 1984-94; dir. mktg. First Nat. Banks, 1991-94; pres., CEO Fin. Directions, Inc., Denver, 1994—; mem. bankers edn. com. Colo. Bankers Assn., Denver, 1992-94. Contbr. articles to profl. jours. Chmn. human resources com., mem. adminstrv. coun. Jr. League of Denver, 1983—; mem. cmty. assistance fund, placement adv. com.; fundraiser Women's Libr. Assn. U. Denver, 1990-94, 96—, Good Shepherd Cath. Sch., 1986-95, Jewish Cmty. Ctr., Denver, 1990-95, St. Mary's Acad., 1995—, Theodore Herzl Day Sch., 1996—. Recipient Gold Peak award Am. Bankers Assn.-Bank Mktg. Assn., 1987; named Businessperson of Week Denver Bus. Jour., 1995. Mem. AAUW, Am. Inst. Banking, Jr. League Denver, U. Denver Pioneer Hockey Club, Kappa Alpha Theta (Chgo. NW alumnae 1977-79, program chair 1979), Phi Kappa Phi. Office: 1624 Market St Ste 475 Denver CO 80202-1518

LEVINSON, STEVEN H., judge; b. Cin., June 8, 1946. BA with distinction, Stanford U., 1968; JD, U. Mich., 1971. Bar: Hawaii 1972, U.S. Dist. Ct. Hawaii 1972, U.S. Ct. Appeals (9th cir.) 1972. Law clk. to Hon. Bernard H. Levinson Hawaii Supreme Ct., 1971-72; pvt. practice Honolulu, 1972-89; judge Hawaii Cir. Ct. (1st cir.), 1989-92; assoc. justice Hawaii Supreme Ct., Honolulu, 1992—. Staff mem. U. Mich. Jour. of Law Reform, 1970-71. Active Temple Emanu-El. Mem. ABA (jud. adminstrn. divsn. 1989—), Hawaii State Bar Assn. (dir. young lawyers divsn. 1975-76, dir. 1982-84), Nat. Jud. Coll. (state jud. leader 1991—). Jewish. Address: Ali'iolani Hale 417 S King St Honolulu HI 96813

LEVISTER, ERNEST CLAYTON, JR., physician; b. N.Y.C., Feb. 4, 1936; s. Ernest Clayton and Ruth D. Levister; m. Sandra P. Levister (div.); children: Michelle N., E. Clay; m. Christine M. Miller, May 18, 1991. AB in Chemistry, Lincoln U., Pa., 1958; BS in Chem. Engring., Lafayette Coll., 1958; MD, Howard U., 1964. Diplomate Am. Bd. Internal Medicine. Maj., physician internal medicine & cardiology U.S. Army European Command, Fed. Republic Germany, 1969-72; pvt. practice internal medicine & cardiology Houston, 1972-73, Group Health Assn., Washington, 1973-74, Norfolk, Va., 1974-78; med. attaché Embassy of the U.S., 1978-79; internal med. & cardiology Occupational Med. & Toxicology, San Bernardino, Calif., 1979—; ind. med. examiner Dept. Indsl. Rels., Divsn. Ind. Accidents, San Bernardino, 1979—, qualified med. examiner, 1991—. Columnist (newspaper) Voice News. Mem. environ. protection commn. City of Riverside, Calif., 1989-92. Recipient Alumni award Lincoln U., 1988, Award Nat. Assn. for Equal Opportunity in High Edn., 1995, NAFTA award, 1995, Media award, 1995. Fellow ACP, Am. Coll. Preventive Medicine. Office: 1738 N Waterman Ave Ste 1 San Bernardino CA 92404-5131

LEVITAN, ROGER STANLEY, lawyer; b. Washington, Jan. 31, 1933; s. Simon Wolfe and Bessie (Abramson) L.; m. Maria Anneli Stennius, May 27, 1975 (div. 1980); 1 child, Mark Howard; m. Laurel Lynn Allen, July 9, 1982; 1 child, Brandon Wolfe. BS in Econs., U. Pa., 1954; JD, Columbia U., 1957. Bar: D.C. 1957, U.S. Ct. Appeals (D.C. cir.) 1957, Ariz. 1976. Tax specialist, reorgn. br. IRS, Washington, 1957-62; atty. McClure & Trotter, Washington, 1962-65; assoc. ptnr. Main Lafrentz, Washington and N.Y.C., 1970-72; dir. taxes U.S. Industries, Inc., N.Y.C., 1972-73; asst. tax counsel Am. Home Products Co., N.Y.C., 1973-75; ptnr., Bilby & Shoenhair, P.C., Tucson, 1976-89; ptnr. Snell & Wilmer, Tucson, 1989-90; ptnr. Molloy, Jones & Donohue P.C., Tucson, 1991-92; counsel Hecker, Phillips & Zeeb, 1992—; lectr. Am. Law Inst., State Bar Ariz. Legal counsel Tucson Community Found., 1981—. Contbr. articles to profl. jours. Mem. ABA (chmn. ann. report com. 1965-67, continuing legal edn. com. 1969-70), Ariz. Bar Found., State Bar Ariz. (chmn. sect. taxation 1987-88, mem. tax specialization adv. bd., 1991-93). Home: 727 E Chula Vista Rd Tucson AZ 85718-1028 Office: 405 W Franklin St Tucson AZ 85701-8209

LEVITT, IRENE HANSEN, sales associate, writer, artist; b. Berkeley, Calif., Aug. 18, 1953; d. Alvin Kenneth and Bertha (Schiff) Hansen; m. Kim De Wayne, Oct. 22, 1983. BA in Art, Calif. Luth. U., 1976. Bookkeeper, data processor, sec. pvt. contractor, 1984-95; sales assoc. Dayton Hudson Corp., 1995—. Photographer with exhibits of greeting card and prints in numerous art galleries in the Seattle area; exhibited in art show, Oakland, Calif., 1972, L.A., 1986, Seattle, 1994; author: (plays) A Cancer of Proximity, 1987, The Price of the Retreat, 1987, Sacrifices to the Compromise, 1987, In Order to Bury Our Dead, 1987, Foxtrot, 1993, The Loom, 1993, (novel) The Renaisance of the Poppy, 1991, (anthology) Diaries of the Affluent, 1993. Vol., alumni rep. Calif. Luth. U., Thousand Oaks, Calif., 1987; vol. Am. Cancer Soc., Modesto, Calif., 1991-92; vol. Remond Cmty. Celebration of the Arts, 1995. Recipient award in art Alameda County Art Com., 1972, Mark Van Doren Meml. Poetry prize Calif. Luth. U., 1976; Undergrad. scholar VA, 1972-76, U.S. Civil Svc. Commn., 1972-75.

LEVY, ALAN DAVID, real estate executive; b. St. Louis, July 19, 1938; s. I. Jack and Natalie (Yawitz) L.; grad. Sch. Real Estate, Washington U., 1960; m. Abby Jane Markowitz, May 12, 1968; children: Jennifer Lynn, Jacqueline Claire. Property mgr. Solon Gershman Inc., Realtors, Clayton, Mo., 1958-61; gen. mgr. Kodner Constrn. Co., St. Louis, 1961-63; regional mgr. Tishman Realty & Constrn. Co., Inc., N.Y.C., 1963-69, v.p., Los Angeles, 1969-77; exec. v.p., dir. Tishman West Mgmt. Corp., 1977-88; pres. Tishman West Cos., 1988-92, chmn. Tishman Internat. Cos., 1993—; guest lectr. on real estate mgmt. to various forums. Mem. L.A. County Mus. Art; former chmn. Am. Art Coun.; trustee Archives Am. Art, Harvard-Westlake Sch.; bd. govs. W.L.A. coun. Boy Scouts Am. Mem. Bldg. Owners and Mgrs. Assn. L.A. (dir.), N.J. (co-founder, hon. dir.), Inst. Real Estate Mgmt. (cert. property mgr.), Urban Land Inst., Internat. Council Shopping Centers. Contbr. articles on property mgmt. to trade jours. Office: 10900 Wilshire Blvd Ste 510 Los Angeles CA 90024-6528

LEVY, DAVID, lawyer, insurance company executive; b. Bridgeport, Conn., Aug. 3, 1932; s. Aaron and Rachel (Goldman) L. BS in Econs., U. Pa., 1954; JD, Yale U., 1957. Bar: Conn. 1958, U.S. Supreme Ct. 1963, D.C. 1964, Mass. 1965, N.Y. 1971, Pa. 1972; CPA, Conn. Acct. Arthur Andersen & Co., N.Y.C., 1957-59; sole practice Bridgeport, 1959-60; specialist tax law IRS, Washington, 1960-64; counsel State Mut. Life Ins. Co., Worcester, Mass., 1964-70; assoc. gen. counsel taxation Penn Mut. Life Ins. Co., Phila., 1971-81; sole practice Washington, 1982-87; v.p., tax counsel Pacific Mut. Life Ins. Co., Newport Beach, Calif., 1987—. Author: (with others) Life Insurance Company Tax Series, Bureau National Affairs Tax Management Income Tax, 1970-71. Mem. adv. bd. Tax Mgmt., Washington, 1975-90, Hartford Inst. on Ins. Taxation, 1990—; bd. dirs. Citizens Plan E Orgn., Worcester, 1966-70. With AUS, 1957. Mem. ABA (vice-chmn. employee benefits com. 1980-86, ins. cos. com. 1984-86, torts and ins. practice sect., subcom. chair ins. cos. com. tax sect. 1994—), Assn. Life Ins. Counsel, AICPA, Beta Alpha Psi. Jewish.

LEVY, DAVID, broadcasting executive; b. Phila.; s. Benjamin and Lillian (Potash) L.; m. Lucile Alva Wilds, July 25, 1941 (div. 1970); children: Lance, Linda; m. Victoria Robertson, Apr. 23, 1987; 1 stepchild, Kate Jolson. BS in Econs., U. Pa., 1934, MBA, 1935. With Young & Rubicam, Inc., N.Y.C., 1938-59, v.p., assoc. dir. radio-TV dept., mem. agy. plans bd.; v.p. charge network programs and talent NBC, N.Y.C., 1959-61; exec. producer Filmways, L.A., 1964-68, Goodson-Todman Prodns., West Coast, 1968-69; exec. v.p., dir. Golden Orange Broadcasting Co., Anaheim, Calif., 1969-88, bd. dirs.; exec. v.p. charge TV activities Four Star Internat., Inc., Beverly Hills, Calif., 1970-72; pres. Wilshire Prodns. Inc., Beverly Hills, 1972—; mem. faculty Calif. State U., Northridge, 1973-77; TV advisor Citizens for Eisenhower, 1952, 56, Haig for Pres., 1988; dir. radio and TV for Citizens for Eisenhower-Nixon, 1956; prodr., writer 3-network program for closing Rep. campaign broadcast Four More Years, 1956; writer, co-prodr. closing program election eve behalf of Wendell Willkie, 1940; cons. Sec. Treasury, 1944-46; chief radio sect. war fin. divsn. Treasury Dept. Exec. prodr. Double Life of Henry Phyffe, 1965; exec. prodr., creator TV series Addams Family, 1964-66, The Pruitts of Southampton ABC-TV, 1966-67; prodr. world premier Sarge, also exec. prodr., creator TV series Universal Studios NBC, 1971-72; creator Hollywood Screen Test, Bat Masterson, Appointment with Adventure, Outlaws, The Americans, Real West, The Kate Smith Daytime Hour, others; launched Maverick, Shirley Temple, National Velvet, Father Knows Best, Godfrey's Talent Scouts, People's Choice, I Married Joan, Life of Riley, Dr. Kildare, Bonanza, Hitchcock Presents, Thriller, Saturday Night at the Movies, Walt Disney's Wonderful World of Color, Robert Taylor and the Detectives, The Deputy, Car 54, 1st Bob Newhart Show, 1st Phil Silvers Show, Goodyear TV Playhouse, Peter Pan (starring Mary Martin), What's My Line, Make the Connection, Say When, others; prodr. Paramount TV, 1972-73, Hanna Barbera Prodns. NBC, 1973-74; creative cons. Name That Tune, Ralph Edwards Prodns. and Sandy Frank Prodns., 1974-81; creative cons. You Asked For It, Battle of the Planets; TV cons. Mark Goodson Prodns., 1989—; co-creator, exec. prodr. Face the Music TV series, 1980-81; author: (novels) The Chameleons, 1964, The Network Jungle, 1976, The Gods of Foxcroft, 1970, Potomac Jungle, 1990; contbr. short stories to popular mags. Lt. USNR, 1944-46. Recipient Treasury medal and disting. svc. citation U.S. Treasury Dept., 1946. Mem. ASCAP, TV Acad., Writers Guild Am., Prodrs. Guild Am. (past sec., bd. dirs.), Hollywood Radio-TV Soc. (pres. 1969-70, award 1970), Caucus for Prodrs., Writers and Dirs. (sec., steering com., exec. dir. 1974—, Disting. Svc. award 1985, Spl. award of merit for 20 yrs. svc. 1994). Republican. Jewish. Office: 210 S Spalding Dr Beverly Hills CA 90212-3608

LEVY, DAVID STEVEN, college administrator; b. L.A., Mar. 9, 1955; s. Henry and Gloria Grace (Barouh) L. BA, Occidental Coll., 1977; MA, 1979. Asst. dir. fin. aid Calif. State Coll., San Bernardino, 1978-79; fin. aid counselor Calif. State U.-Northridge, 1979-80; assoc. dir. student fin. aid Calif. State U.-Dominguez Hills, 1980-82; dir. fin. aid Occidental Coll., L.A., 1982-88; dir. fin. aid Calif. Inst. Tech., Pasadena, Calif., 1988—, assoc. dean of students, 1991—; mem. Title IA Adv. Com. Calif., 1977-80; negotiator U.S. Dept Edn. Mem. life-long learning com. Calif. Postsecondary Edn. Commn., 1980—, mem. student fin. aid issues com., 1984—; mem. Sallie Mae Fin. Aid Adv. Bd., 1994—. Richter fellow Princeton U., 1976; Calif. State U. adminstrv. fellow, 1981—. Mem. Nat. Assn. Student Fin. Aid. Adminstrs. (Meritorious Achievement award 1988, bd. dirs. 1991—, commn. dir. 1994-95), Mortar Board Alumni Assn. (pres. 1977—), Calif. Assn. Student Fin. Aid Adminstrs. (ind. segmental rep. 1984, sec. 1985, treas. 1986-88, lifetime mem. 1996, Pres.'s award 1986, 93, Meritorious Svc. award 1994, Segmental Leadership award 1992, Creative Leadership award 1990), Western Assn. Student Fin. Aid Adminstrs. (Disting. Svc. award 1990, Pres. Disting. Svc. award 1992), Nat. Assn. Student Fin. Aid Adminstrs., Phi Beta Kappa, Delta Phi Epsilon, Psi Chi, Phi Alpha Theta, Sigma Alpha Epsilon. Jewish. Co-editor Calif. Student Aid Commn. Student Aid Workbook, 1977—; co-author, contbr. Playing the Selective College Admissions Game, 1994; contbr. Paying Less for College, Top Colleges for Science. Home: 2704 Franklin St La Crescenta CA 91214 Office: CalTech 515 S Wilson Ave Pasadena CA 91106-3212

LEVY, DENA CHRISTINE, television producer, director; b. Woodland Hills, Calif., Sept. 28, 1965; d. Stanley Gerald and Deanna Marie (Coury) L.; children: Lonna Weber, Dena Levy. BA in Journalism, U. So. Calif., 1986. Profl. tennis player Women's Tennis Assn., USTA, 1986-88; prodr., dir. Two-D Prodns., Hollywood, Calif., 1989—. Recipient Best Documercial award Nat. Infomercial Mktg. Assn., 1994. Office: Two-D Prodns 584 N Larchmont Blvd Hollywood CA 90004

LEVY, EZRA CESAR, aerospace scientist, real estate broker; b. Habana, Cuba, Sept. 22, 1924; s. Mayer D. and Rachel Levy; m. Gaynor D. Popejoy, 1980; children from previous marriage: Daniel M., Diana M. Levy Friedman, Linda R. Levy Brenden. MS, UCLA, 1951. Sect. head Douglas Aircraft Co., Santa Monica, Calif., 1951-54; dept. head Lockheed Aircraft Co., Van Nuys, Calif., 1954-56, Librascope, Glendale, Calif., 1956-57, Radioplane, Van Nuys, 1957-58; asst. dept. mgr. Space Tech. Labs., Redondo Beach, Calif., 1958-60; asst. divsn. dir. TRW, Redondo Beach, Calif., 1960-74; now real estate broker Regency Realty Corp., Temple City, Calif. Author: Laplace Transform Tables, 1958; contbr. articles to profl. jours. Cpl. U.S. Army, 1944-46. Mem. Temple City C. of C. (bd. dirs. 1992-97), Masons (past master and sec.). Democrat. Jewish.

LEVY, JEROME, dermatologist; retired naval officer; b. Bklyn., Aug. 17, 1926; s. Alexander and Pauline (Wollkof) L.; m. Leona Elsie Eligator, June 6, 1948; children—Andrew B., Eric J., Peter C., David J. Student, Wesleyan U., 1944-45; postgrad., 1952-54; A.B., Yale U., 1947; M.D., Albany Med. Coll., 1958. Diplomate Am. Bd. Dermatology. Commd. ensign M.C., U.S. Navy, 1957, advanced through grades to capt., 1972; intern U.S. Naval Hosp., Newport, R.I., 1958-59; resident U.S. Naval Hosp., Phila., 1960-62, U. Pa. Grad. Sch. Medicine, Phila., 1962-63; chief dept. dermatology U.S. Naval Hosp., Memphis, 1963-67, Yokosuka, Japan, 1967-70, Long Beach, Calif., 1974-75; head outpatient dermatology clinic San Diego Naval Hosp., 1970-72; sr. med. officer Keflavik, Iceland, 1972-74; ret., 1975; med. dir. dermatology Westwood Pharm Co., Buffalo, 1975-82; acting chief dermatology dept. Buffalo Gen. Hosp., 1981-82; cons. Erie County Health Dept., 1979-82; clin. assoc. prof. SUNY, Buffalo Med. Sch., 1980-82; practice medicine specializing in dermatology, Coronado, Calif., 1982-90. Contbr. articles to med. jours. Decorated Navy Commendation medal, Joint Service Commendation medal; Knight's Cross of the Order of Falcon (Iceland). Fellow Am. Acad. Dermatology, ACP; mem. AMA, So. Med. Assn., Assn. Mil. Surgeons, U.S., Navy League, Alpha Omega Alpha. Republican. Jewish. Home: 3352 Lucinda St San Diego CA 92106-2932

LEVY, LEONARD ALVIN, podiatric medicine educator, college president; b. N.Y.C., Aug. 19, 1935; s. David and Jessie (Frankel) L.; m. Eleanore Auerbach, Dec. 18, 1960; children: Andrew Lincoln, Sarilyn Joan. BA, NYU, 1956; MPH, Columbia U., 1967; D Podiatric Medicine, N.Y. Coll. Podiatric Medicine, 1961. Diplomate Am. Bd. Podiatric Pub. Health, Am. Bd. Primary Podiatric Medicine. Dean, v.p. Calif. Coll. Podiatric Medicine, San Francisco, 1967-74; dean, prof. SUNY Health Sci. Ctr., Stony Brook, 1974-76; cons. to pres. U. Tex. Health Sci. Ctr., Houston, 1976-81; prof. podiat. medicine, dean Coll. Podiat. Medicine/Surgery U. Osteo. Medicine and Health Scis., Des Moines, 1981—, v.p. planning and rsch., 1996—; cons. USPHS, Rockville, Md., 1967; mem. sec.'s med. adv. group VA, Washington, 1990-94; mem. dean's com., Yale U. Sch. of Medicine, VA Med. Ctr., West Haven, 1993—. Author, editor: (monograph) Clinics in Podiatry/Systemic Diseases, 1985, Principles and Practice of Podiatric Medicine, 1990; contbr. to Podiatric Med. Assisting, 1992—, also over 70 articles to podiatric med. jours. Bd. dirs. Iowa Jewish Sr. Life Ctr., Des Moines, 1983-89, Elsie Mason/Liguitti Towers Sr. Housing, Des Moines, 1988-90, Des Moines Birthing Place-Woman Care, 1990-92. USPHS grantee, 1984—. Fellow APHA, Am. Coll. Podopediatrics (pres. 1987-88); mem. Am. Podiatric Med. Assn. (fellow 1966), Am. Acad. Dermatology (affiliate), Am. Assn. Colls. Podiatric Medicine (chmn. bd. dirs. 1989-90), Gerontol. Soc. Am., Iowa Podiatric Med. Assn. Office: Calif Coll Podiatric Medicine 1210 Scott St San Francisco CA 94115-4009

LEVY, LOUIS, chess master; b. N.Y.C., Feb. 10, 1921; s. Victor and Sarah (Caffina) L.; m. Gloria Alice Cressy, Jan. 21, 1972. B.S., N.Y. U., 1941. Engaged in car washing business, 1947-66, chess and bridge player, 1939—; Bd. dirs. N.J. Bridge League, 1969-73. Served with USAAF, 1942-46. Named U.S. Internat. Master Am. Contract Bridge League, 1972. Mem. Marshall, Manhattan chess clubs, Am. Contract Bridge League. Address: 12317 Ridge Cir Bellaire CA 90049*

LEVY, RICARDO BENJAMIN, chemical company executive; b. Quito, Ecuador, Jan. 11, 1945; came to U.S., 1962; s. Leopoldo and Kate (Bamberg) L.; m. Noella Luke, June 15, 1967; children: Tamara, Brian. BS, Stanford U., 1966, PhDChemE, 1972; MS, Princeton U., 1967. Gen. mgr. Sudamericana, Quito, 1967-70; research engr. Exxon Research & Engring. Corp. subs. Exxon Corp., Florham Park, N.J., 1972-74; v.p., co-founder Catalytica Inc., Mountain View, Calif., 1974—, exec. v.p., chief operating officer, 1982—, pres., CEO, 1991—; bd. dirs. Catalytica, Inc., Catalytica Combustion Sys., Inc., Catalytica Fine Chems., Inc., GENXON Power Sys. Co-Author: Catalysis in Coal Conversion; patentee in field. Mem. Am. Inst. Chem. Engrs., Comml. Devel. Assn., Phi Beta Kappa. Office: Catalytica Inc 430 Ferguson Dr Bldg 3 Mountain View CA 94043

LEVY, WAYNE DAVID, psychiatrist; b. Balt., Sept. 18, 1958; s. Alfred and Gertrude (Levinson) L.; m. Ann Fay-Ling, Sept. 4, 1992. BS in Chemistry summa cum laude, Loyola Coll., Balt., 1980; MD, Emory U., 1984. Diplomate Am. Bd. Psychiatry and Neurology. Commd. officer U.S. Army, 1984-90, advanced through grades to maj., 90-93; res. maj., 1993—; intern, then resident in psychiatry Walter Reed Army Med. Ctr., Washington, 1984-88; div. psychiatrist 2d Inf. Div., Korea, 1988-89; staff psychiatrist Tripler Army Med. Ctr., Honolulu, 1989-93; resigned, 1993; psychiatrist Kaiser Permanente Med. Group, 1993—. Maj. USAR, 1981-84, 93—. Presdl. scholar Loyola Coll., 1976. Mem. Am. Psychiat. Assn.

LEW, ALAN AUGUST, geography and urban planning educator, consultant; b. Sacramento, Calif., Apr. 13, 1955; s. Gimpock P. and Inger Ida (Berg) L.; m. Mable Wong, Dec. 26, 1987; children: Lauren Asia, Skylan Sunjong, Chynna Kymberlee. BA in Geography, U. Hawaii, Hilo, 1981; MA in Geography, U. Oreg., 1983, M in Urban Planning, 1983, PhD in Geography, 1986. Rsch. asst. pub. works and planning divsn. U. Oreg., Eugene, 1981-82, grad. tchg. fellow in geography, 1981-86; asst. prof. geography and pub. planning No. Ariz. U., Flagstaff, 1986-92, assoc. prof. geography and urban planning, 1992—; prin. ptnr. Lew Assocs., Flagstaff, 1991—; vis. asst. prof. geography U. Oreg., summer 1986; vis. prof. geography U. Tubingen, Germany, spring 1989; cons. Willamette Pass Ski Corp., 1982, Grand Canyon Mgmt. Inc., 1986, Yavapai-Apache Nation, 1986-87, Tohonto O'odham Nation, 1987-89, Hopi Tribe, 1990-91, 94-95, Coconino County Recorders Office, 1991, Bur. Land Mgmt., 1992, City of Williams, 1993, Ariz. State Parks Dept., 1993, U. Ariz., 1994, Ea. Ariz. Counties Orgn., 1994-95, Yavapai County, 1995-96, Navajo Nation, 1996; organizer and chair numerous confs. and workshops in field. Author: (with others) Politics and Public Policy in Arizona, 1993, Travel, Tourism and Hospitality Research: A Handbook for Managers and Researchers, 1994; editor, author: (with others) Tourism in China: Geographical, Political and Economic Perspectives, 1995; contbr. articles to profl. jours. Grantee Environ. Sys. Rsch. Inst., 1992; Fulbright award Nat. U. Singapore, 1983-84. Mem. Assn. Am. Geographers (bd. dirs. recreation, tourism and sport specialty group 1987-89, 93-95, chmn. 1995—), Assn. Pacific Coast Geographers (sec.-treas. 1993—), Am. Planning Assn. (info. sys. divsn., univ. liaison Ariz. chpt. 1989-90), Am. Inst. Cert. Planners, Nat. Coun. Geog. Edn., Assn. Collegiate Schs. Planning, Assn. for Asian Studies, Nat. Recreation and Parks Assn. (soc. park and recreation edn., comml. recreation and tourism sect.), Travel and Tourism Assn., Internat. Geog. Union (U.S. rep., Sustainable Tourism Study Group 1995—). Democrat. Home: 716 W Aspen Ave Flagstaff AZ 86001-5312 Office: No Ariz U Dept Geog/Urban Planning Flagstaff AZ 86011-5016

LEW, DONALD EVAN, accountant; b. Sacramento, Calif., Jan. 13, 1948; s. Sam Gene and Mamie (Quon) L.; m. Linda Elkins, July 8, 1972; children: Brian Danforth, Karissa Lynae. BS, Oreg. State U., 1975. CPA, Oreg. Prodn. planner, shipper GE Co., Portland, Oreg., 1969-72; acctg. clk. Oreg. Dept. of Commerce, Salem, 1972-73; acct. Oreg. System of Higher Edn., Corvallis, 1974; audit mgr., sr. auditor Audits divsn. Oreg. Sec. of State, Salem, 1974-94; acctg. analyst Oreg. State Contr.'s Divsn., Salem, 1994—; staff acct. Morgan, Holland & Connelly, CPA's, Salem, 1975; prin. Donald E Lew, CPA, Salem, 1978—. Bd. chair, trustee 1st Congl. Ch., Salem, 1986-88, moderator, pres., 1985-90; mgr., coach Battlecreek Little League, Salem, 1989-93; equipment chair Sprague High sch. Band Boosters, Salem, 1993-95, v.p. Mem. AICPA. Home: 155 Kevin Way SE Salem OR 97306-1928 Office: Oregon State Contrs Divsn Dept Adminstrv Svcs 155 Cottage St NE Salem OR 97310-1324

LEW, JOYCELYNE MAE, actress; b. Santa Monica, Calif., Feb. 25, 1962; d. George and Mabel Florence (Lum) L. BA in Theatre Arts, UCLA, 1981, teaching credential, 1982; MA in Urban Edn., Pepperdine U., 1984; bilingual cert., U. So. Calif., 1983; postgrad., Stella Adler Acad., 1988; studied with, The Groundlings Improv Group, 1987. Appeared in films Tai-Pan, 1987, Fatal Beauty, 1989, The Royal Affair, 1993, Shattered Image, 1993, Dr. Boris and Mrs. Duluth, 1994, Hindsight, 1996, Fire in My Heart, 1996; TV programs The Young and the Restless, 1990, Phil Donahue Show, 1993, Hard Copy, 1994, Current Affair, 1995, Gordon Elliott, 1995, Married With Children, 1997, True Hollywood Stores, E Entertainment; voice over artist, mag. model, body double, dancer; appeared in comml. Good Seasons, 1996, Pillsbury Doughboy, 1996, Pacific Bell, 1996; co-writer film script They Still Call Me Bruce, 1986 (award); song lyricist Nighttime Blues. Mem. judging com. for film grants Nat. Endowment for Arts, 1986; mem. L.A. Beautiful, 1993. Mem. AFTRA, SAG, AEA, NATAS (blue ribbon com. for Emmy awards 1986-96), Assn. Asian Pacific Am. Artists (treas. 1983-89), Nat. Asian Am. Telecomms. Assn., Am. Film Inst. Conservatory Workshop, Calif. PTA (life). Home and Office: 1958 N Van Ness Ave Los Angeles CA 90068-3625

LEW, RONALD S. W., federal judge; b. L.A., 1941; m. Mamie Wong; 4 children. BA in Polit. Sci., Loyola U., L.A., 1964; JD, Southwestern U., 1971. Bar: Calif. 1972. Dep. city atty. L.A. City Atty's. Office, 1972-74; ptnr. Avans & Lew, L.A., 1974-82; commr. fire and police pension City of L.A., 1976-82; mcpl. ct. judge County of L.A., 1982-84, superior ct. judge, 1984-87; judge U.S. Dist. Ct. (cen. dist.) Calif., L.A., 1987—; Bar: Calif. 1971. Mem. World Affairs Council of L.A., 1976—, Christian Businessmen's Com. of L.A., 1982—. 1st lt. U.S. Army, 1967-69. Recipient Vol. award United Way of L.A., 1979, cert. of merit L.A. Human Relations Commn., 1977, 82. Mem. Am. Judicature Soc., Calif. Assn. of Judges, So. Calif. Chinese Lawyer's Assn. (charter mem. 1976, pres. 1979), Chinese Am. Citizens Alliance, San Fernando Valley Chinese Cultural Assn., Delta Theta Phi. Office: US Dist Ct 312 N Spring St Los Angeles CA 90012-4701

LEW, WEYMAN, artist; b. San Francisco, Feb. 17, 1935; s. Jee and Him Jeung (Ng) L. BS, U. Calif., Berkeley, 1957. Guest instr. M.H. De Young Meml. Mus., San Francisco, 1970-72. One-man shows include Kelley Galleries, San Francisco, 1967, 68, John Bolles Gallery, San Francisco, 1969, 73, M.H. de Young Meml. Mus., San Francisco, 1970, Instituto de Arte Contemporaneo, Lima, Peru, 1970, Shaw Rimmington Gallery, Toronto, 1970, 72, 75, Santa Barbara (Calif.) Mus. Art, 1971, Galeria Lirolay, Buenos Aires, 1971, Jodi Scully Gallery, L.A., Galerie Smith Andersen, Palo Alto, Calif., Ames Gallery, Berkeley, Calif., 1972, 75, Husstege Gallery, Amsterdam, Wallnuts Gallery, Phila., 1972, 74, 77, 80, Bonython Art Gallery, Sydney, Australia, 1972, 75, Galerie Unicorn, Copenhagen, 1972, Art Gallery Greater Victoria, Can., 1972, Linda Farris Gallery, Seattle, 1973, Rubicon Gallery, Los Altos, Calif., 1974, 76, Muirhead Galleries, Costa Mesa, Calif., 1977, 78, Gryphon Galleries, Denver, 1980, Marshall-Myers Gallery, San Francisco, 1983, Sande Webster Gallery, Phila., 1984, Hank Baum Gallery, San Francisco, 1987, Internat. Art Exhbn. Ctr., Beijing, 1991, Chinese Culture Ctr., San Francisco, 1991, Acad. Art Gallery, San Francisco, 1994; selected pub. collections include M.H. de Young Meml. Mus., San Francisco Mus. Modern Art, Oakland (Calif.) Mus., Bklyn. Mus., Instituto de Arte Contemporaneo, Lima, Chinese Artists Assn., Beijing; author, artist: Weyman Lew Sketches Away, 1981; illustrator: Echoes of Oxford, 1991. Mem. art adv. bd. Chinese Cultural Found., San Francisco; adv. bd. Asian Am. Arts Found., San Francisco. Recipient Disting. award for culture and svc. Chinese Cultural Found., 1991. Mem. Calif. Soc. Printmakers, Phi Beta Kappa, Beta Gamma Sigma. Home: 2810 Pacific Ave San Francisco CA 94115-1107

LEWALLEN, WILLIAM M., JR., ophthalmologist; b. McGregor, Tex., Aug. 31, 1927; s. William M. and Lois Pauline (Sherrill) L.; m. Katherine Louise Mosley, June 12, 1947 (div. Nov. 1985); children: Margaret Anne, William Michael, Susan, Cynthia. BS, Southern Meth. Univ., 1944; MD, Southwestern Med. Coll. Tex., 1947. Diplomate Am. Bd. Otolaryngology, Am. Bd. Ophthalmology. Internship Baylor Univ., Dallas, 1947-48; residency otolaryngology Southwestern Medical Coll., Dallas, 1948-50; residency ophthalmology Jefferson Davis Hosp., Houston, 1953-54; pvt. practice Pueblo, Colo., 1955—; asst. clin. prof. Univ. Colo. Medical Sch., Denver, 1956—; cons. Colo. State Hosp., Pueblo, 1956—, U.S. VA Hosp., Ft. Lyon, Colo., 1956—; chief ophthalmology St. Mary-Corwin Hosp., 1970-72, exec. com., 1970-74. Contbr. articles to profl. jours. Bd. dirs. YMCA, Pueblo, 1958-60; pres. bd. dirs. Rocky Mountain Coun. Boy Scout Am., 1960-72; mem. sch. bd. Pueblo Sch. Bd. Dist. 60, 1959-71, pres. sch. bd., 1967-69; pres., chmn. bd. dirs. Pueblo Blvd. Bank, 1979-93; pres. Rotary Club, 1975-76, dir., 1974-77. Lt. comdr. U.S. Navy, 1950-52. Fellow Am. Acad. Ophthalmology. Republican. Protestant. Home and Office: William Lewallen MD 205 Dunsmere Ave Pueblo CO 81004

LEWANDOSKI, ROBERT HENRY, editor, publisher; b. N.Y.C., Jan. 21, 1951. BA, Pace U., N.Y.C., 1972. Editor, pub. The Former Presidents Quar., RHL Enterprises, Fullerton, Calif., 1993—; freelance author Model Ship Builder, Cedarburg, Wis., 1981-92. Office: RHL Enterprises PO Box 6443 Fullerton CA 92834

LEWEY, SCOT MICHAEL, gastroenterologist, army officer; b. Kansas City, Mo., Sept. 10, 1958; s. Hugh Gene and Janice Vivian (Arnold) L.; divorced; children: Joshua Michael, Aaron Scot, Rachel Anne; m. Jennifer L. Hill. BA in Chemistry, William Jewell Coll., 1980; DO, U. Health Scis., 1984. Diplomate Am. Bd. Internal Medicine, Am. Bd. Gastroenterology, Am. Bd. Hepatology, Am. Bd. Pediat. Commd. 2d lt. U.S. Army, 1980, advanced through grades to lt. col., 1994; resident internal medicine and pediatrics William Beaumont Army Med. Ctr., El Paso, Tex., 1985-89; asst. chief pediatric svc. Irwin Army Hosp., Ft. Riley, Kans., 1989-90; asst. chief dept. medicine Irwin Army Hosp., Ft. Riley, 1990, chief emergency med. svcs., 1990; comdr. F co. 701st support bn. 1st inf. Operation Desert Shield Operation Desert Storm U.S. Army, Saudi Arabia, 1990-91; chief dept. pediatrics Munson Army Hosp., Ft. Leavenworth, Kans., 1991-92, chief dept. medicine, 1992-93; fellow in gastroenterology Fitzsimons Army Med. Ctr., Aurora, Colo., 1993-95, staff gastroenterology svc., 1995-96; chief gastroenterology svc. Evans Army Hosp., Ft. Crason, Colo., 1996—; clin. instr. medicine U. Colo. Health Scis. Ctr. Sch. Medicine. Decorated Bronze STar; named Outstanding Young Man of Am.; recipient Jr. Scientist Rsch. award William Baumont Soc. of Army Gastroenterologists, 1994. Fellow ACP, Am. Acad. Pediatrics; mem. AMA (physician recognition award), Am. Coll. Gastroenterology, Am. Osteo. Assn., Am. Gastroenterol. Assn., Am. Soc. Gastrointestinal Endoscopy, Assn. Mil. Osteo. Physicians and Surgeons. Republican. Mem. Christian Ch. Office: Evans Army Hosp Gastroenterology Svc Fort Carson CO 80913

LEWIN, RALPH ARNOLD, biologist; b. London, Apr. 30, 1921; came to U.S., 1947; s. Maurice and Ethel Lewin; m. Joyce Mary Chismore, June, 1950 (div. 1965); m. Cheng Lanna, June 3, 1969. BA, Cambridge U., Eng., 1942, MA, 1946; PhD, Yale U., 1950; ScD, Cambridge U., Eng., 1973. Instr. Yale U., New Haven, Conn., 1951-52; sci. officer Nat. Research Council, Halifax, N.S., Can., 1952-55; ind. investigator NIH, Woods Hole, Mass., 1956-59; assoc. prof., now prof. U. Calif., La Jolla, 1960—. Editor: Physiology and Biochemistry of Algae, 1962, Genetics of Algae, 1976, Biology of Algae, 1979, Biology of Women, 1981, Origins of Plastids, 1993, Internacia Vortaro de Mikroba Genetiko, 1994; co-editor: Prochloron, a microbial enigma, 1989; transl. Winnie-La-Pu (Esperanto), 1972, La Dektri Horlogoj, 1993. Served with British Army, 1943-46. Mem. Phycological Soc. Am. (pres. 1970-71, Darbaker prize 1963). Home: 8481 Paseo Del Ocaso La Jolla CA 92037-3024 Office: U Calif San Diego Scripps Inst Oceanogra # 0202 La Jolla CA 92093

LE WINN, LAURENCE RYNES, plastic & reconstructive surgeon; b. Phila., Nov. 12, 1940; s. Claire Le Winn; married; children: Kaja Z., Laurence Jr. BS, Trinity Coll., 1962; MD, Jefferson Med. Coll., 1966. Diplomate Am. Bd. Plastic & Reconstructive Surgery. Intern N.Y. Hosp./Cornell U. Med. Ctr., 1966-67, resident gen. surgery, 1967-68, 70-72, resident plastic surgery, 1972-74; asst. prof. plastic surgery, 1974-80; dir. dept. plastic surgery Geisinger Med. Ctr., Danville, Pa., 1980-86; founder, dir. The Plastic Surgery Inst., Palm Springs, Calif., 1986—; dir. divsn. plastic surgery, active staff Eisenhower Med. Ctr., Rancho Mirage, Calif., 1986—; com. mem. Am. Soc. Plastic and Reconstructive Surgery Edn. Found., 1976-77; co-chmn. awards program Robert Ivy Soc., 1993-96; spokesman Am. Soc. Aesthetic Surgery (mem. pub. edn. com.). Inventor of Le Winn Needleholder, Aesculap Instrument Co. Chmn. Palm Valley High Campaign Com., Palm Springs, Calif.; vol. surgeon Barbara Sinatra Ctr., Rancho Mirage, Calif. Lt. Commdr. U.S. Navy Res. Mem. Am. Bd. Plastic and Reconstructive Surgeons. Office: Plastic Surgery Inst 71874 Sahara Rd Rancho Mirage CA 92270

LEWIS, ANDREA ELEN, editor; b. Detroit, June 4, 1957; d. Frank Joe and Mae (Shaw) L. BS, Ea. Mich. U., 1982. Arts and entertainment editor Plexus: West Coast Women's Press, Oakland, Calif., 1984-88; rsch. editor Mother Jones mag., San Francisco, 1990-92; editl. asst. Harper Collins Pubs., San Francisco, 1992-94; sr. editor Third Force mag., Oakland, 1992—; assoc. editor Pacific News Svc., San Francisco, 1996—; mem. adv. bd. Nat. Radio Project, 1996—; bd. dirs. Media Alliance, San Francisco, 1996—. Contbg. writer: The Black Women's Health Book, 1990, Beyond Identity Politics, 1996; contbg. artist (CD rec. project) Bob Ostertag's Fear No Love, 1995; commentator (radio broadcasting) Pacifica Radio, 1995, 96, 97. chorus mem. San Francisco Symphony Chorus, 1987—, sect. leader, alto, 1991, 92, 93, 95, mem. artistic adv. com., 1995, 96; facilitator Cmty. Journalism Cross-Tng., San Francisco, 1995; mem. planning com., panelist, spkr. Media and Democracy Congress, San Francisco, 1996. Mem. NARAS (Grammy awards for best choral recording 1992, 95). Office: Pacific News Svc 450 Mission St # 204 San Francisco CA 94105-2505

LEWIS, CARSON MCLAUGHL, retired plastic surgeon; b. Dallas, 1931. MD, U. Tex., Galveston, 1956. Plastic surgeon Scripps Meml. Hosp., Calif.; dir. Total Body Wellness Inc., La Jolla, Calif.; mem. tchg. staff U. Hosp., San Diego. Mem. Internat. Soc. Aesehetre Plastic Surgeons (dir. ednl. found.). Office: 8236 Caminito Lacauo La Jolla CA 92037-1210

LEWIS, CHARLES S., III, lawyer; b. Baker, Oreg., Aug. 19, 1953. Student, U. So. Calif.; BS magna cum laude, Lewis and Clark Coll., 1975; JD magna cum laude, Willamette U., 1978. Bar: Oreg. 1978, U.S. Tax Ct. 1978. Mem. Stoel Rives, LLP, Portland, Oreg., 1978—. Co-author: The Tax Reform Act of 1986: Analysis and Commentary, 1987. Mem. ABA (taxation and bus. law sects.), Delta Mu Delta. Office: Stoel Rives LLP 900 SW 5th Ave Ste 2300 Portland OR 97204-1232

LEWIS, EDWARD B., biology educator; b. Wilkes-Barre, Pa., May 20, 1918; s. Edward B. and Laura (Histed) L.; m. Pamela Harrah, Sept. 26, 1946; children: Hugh, Glenn (dec.), Keith. B.A., U. Minn., 1939; Ph.D., Calif. Inst. Tech., 1942; Phil.D., U. Umea, Sweden, 1982; DSc, U. Minn., 1993. Instr. biology Calif. Inst. Tech., Pasadena, 1946-48, asst. prof., 1949-56, prof., 1956-66, Thomas Hunt Morgan prof., 1966-88, prof. emeritus, 1988—; Rockefeller Found. fellow Sch. Botany, Cambridge U., Eng., 1948-49; mem. Nat. Adv. Com. Radiation, 1958-61; vis. prof. U. Copenhagen, 1975-76, 82; researcher in developmental genetics, somatic effects of radiation. Editor: Genetics and Evolution, 1961. Served to capt. USAAF, 1942-46. Recipient Gairdner Found. Internat. award, 1987, Wolf Found. prize in medicine, 1989, Rosenstiel award, 1990, Nat. Medal of Sci. NSF, 1990, Albert Lasker Basic Med. Rsch. award, 1991, Louisa Gross Horowitz prize Columbia U., 1992, Nobel Prize in Medicine, 1995. Fellow AAAS; mem. NAS, Genetics Soc. Am. (sec. 1962-64, pres. 1967-69, Thomas Hunt Morgan medal), Am. Acad. Arts and Scis., Royal Soc. (London) (fgn. mem.), Am. Philos. Soc., Genetical Soc. Great Britian (hon.). Home: 805 Winthrop Rd San Marino CA 91108-1709 Office: Calif Inst Tech Div Biology 1201 E California Blvd Pasadena CA 91125-0001

LEWIS, EDWARD C., plastic surgeon; b. L.A., May 7, 1925. MD, U. Pitts., 1949. Plastic surgeon VA Med. Ctr., St. Mark's Hosp., Salt Lake City; clin. assoc. prof. surgery U. Utah Sch. Medicine, Salt Lake City. Office: Saint Marks Med Office Bldg 1220 E 3900 S Ste 2-h Salt Lake City UT 84124-1304

LEWIS, EDWIN REYNOLDS, biomedical engineering educator; b. Los Angeles, July 14, 1934; s. Edwin McMurtry and Sally Newman (Reynolds) L.; m. Elizabeth Louise McLean, June 11, 1960; children: Edwin McLean, Sarah Elizabeth. AB in Biol. Sci., Stanford U., 1956, MSEE, 1957, Engr., 1959, PhD in Elec. Engring., 1962. With research staff Librascope div. Gen. Precision Inc., Glendale, Calif., 1961-67; mem. faculty dept. elec. engring. and computer sci. U. Calif., Berkeley, 1967—, dir. bioengring. tng. program, 1969-77, prof. elec. engring. and computer sci., 1971-94, prof. grad. sch., 1994—, assoc. dean grad. div., 1977-82, assoc. dean interdisciplinary studies coll. engring., 1988-96, prof. Grad. Sch., 1996—; chair joint program bioengring. U. Calif., Berkeley and San Francisco, 1988-91. Author: Network Models in Population Biology, 1977, (with others) Neural Modeling, 1977, The Vertebrate Inner Ear, 1985, Introduction to Bioengineering, 1996; contbr. articles to profl. jours. Grantee NSF, NASA, 1984, 87, Office Naval Rsch., 1990-93, NIH, 1975—; Neurosci. Rsch. Program fellow, 1966, 69; recipient Disting. Teaching Citation U. Calif., 1972; Jacob Javits neurosci. investigator NIH, 1984-91. Fellow IEEE, Acoustical Soc. Am.; mem. AAAS, Assn. Rsch. in Otolaryngology, Soc. Neurosci., Toastmasters (area lt. gov. 1966-67), Sigma Xi. Office: Dept Elec Engring & Computer Scis U Calif Berkeley CA 94720

LEWIS, FRANCES MARCUS, nursing educator. BSN summa cum laude, Loretto Heights Coll., 1967; MN, U. Wash., 1968; MA, Stanford U., 1974, PhD, 1977; postdoctoral, Johns Hopkins U., 1978. Instr. Sch. Nursing, U. Wash., Seattle, 1968-70; nurse clinician Cedar-Riverside Clinic, Mpls., 1970-71; asst. prof. nursing U. Minn., Mpls., 1970-71; asst. prof. nursing U. Md., 1976-77, assoc. prof., 1977-78; assoc. prof. nursing U. Wash., Seattle, 1978-84, prof., 1984—, Am. Cancer Soc. Oncology Nursing prof., 1988-92; invited panelist Inst. Medicine, NAS, 1986; mem. cancer control rev. com. Nat. Cancer Inst., 1987-90, mem. planning bd. cancer commn., 1990-93, mem. cancer clin. investigation rev. com., 1992-94, invited mem. pres. cancer panel, 1993, mem. rev. com. E, 1994—. Co-author: Evaluation and Measurement in Health Education and Health Promotion; co-editor, co-author: Health Behavior and Health Education: Theory, Research, and Practice, 1997; mem. editl. bd. Nursing Rsch., Western Jour. Nursing Rsch., Pub. Health Nursing, Health Edn. Quar., 1986-92; contbr. articles to profl. jours. Posdoctoral Nursing fellow Pub. Health Svc., 1974-77; recipient Mayhew Derryberry award APHA, 1992. Fellow Japanese Soc. for Promotion of Sci. Office: U Wash Family and Child Nursing Box 357262 Seattle WA 98195

LEWIS, FREDERICK THOMAS, insurance company executive; b. Tacoma, Apr. 1, 1941; s. Arthur Thomas and June Louise (Levenhagen) L.; m. Sarah Carolyn Boyette, Apr. 18, 1971; adopted children: Johanna, Elizabeth, Sarah, Jonathan, Matthew. Student, Concordia Coll., Portland, Oreg., 1959-61, Dominican Coll., San Rafael, Calif., 1967-71. Registered health underwriter. Enroute coord. Trans World Airlines, N.Y.C., 1961-62, 64-66; customer svc. rep. Trans World Airlines, Oakland, Calif., 1966-75; dist. rep. Aid Assn. for Luths., Twin Falls, Idaho, 1975-96, dist. mgr., 1984-88. Vocalist Oakland Symphony Chorus, 1972-75; soloist Magic Valley Chorale, Twin Falls, 1979-83. Cantor Immanuel Luth. Ch., Twin Falls, 1984—; organizer Theos of Magic Valley, Filer, Idaho, 1984. Served with U.S. Army, 1962-64. Mem. Nat. Assn. Life Underwriters (tng. coun. fellow 1984, nat. quality award, nat. sales achievement ward, health ins. quality award 1978—), So. Idaho Life Underwriters (pres. 1980-81, edn. chmn. 1984-86, nat. local com. mem. 1986-89), So. Idaho Health Underwriters (bd. dirs. 1986-88), Idaho State Assn. Life Underwriters (area v.p. 1988-89, sec. 1989-90, pres.-elect 1990-91, pres. 1991-92, state conv. exhibitor chmn. 1992-94, Bill Rankin Life Underwriter of Yr. award 1993), Idaho Fraternal Congress (ins. counselor 1976, bd. dirs. 1976-85, pres. 1981-82), Lions (local v.p. 1979-81, pres. 1982-83, organizer women's aux. 1983, sec. 1986-87, 92-93, treas. 1993-94, sec./treas. multiple dist. 31 1994-95, vice dist. gov. 39W 1995-96, dist. gov. 39W 1996-97). Republican. Home and Office: 1612 Targhee Dr Twin Falls ID 83301-3546

LEWIS, GERALD JORGENSEN, judge; b. Perth Amboy, N.J., Sept. 9, 1933; s. Norman Francis and Blanche M. (Jorgensen) L.; m. Laura Susan McDonald, Dec. 15, 1973; children by previous marriage: Michael, Marc. AB magna cum laude, Tufts Coll., 1954; JD, Harvard U., 1957. Bar: D.C. 1957, N.J. 1961, Calif. 1962, U.S. Supreme Ct. 1968. Atty. Gen. Atomic, LaJolla, Calif., 1961-63; ptnr. Haskins, Lewis, Nugent & Newnham, San Diego, 1963-77; judge Mcpl. Ct., El Cajon, Calif., 1977-79; judge Superior Ct., San Diego, 1979-84; assoc. justice, Calif. Ct. of Appeal, San Diego, 1984-87; dir. Fisher Scientific Group, Inc., 1987—, Bolsa Chica Corp., 1991-93, Gen. Chemical Group, Inc., 1996—; of counsel Latham & Watkins, 1987—; dir. Wheelabrator Techs., Inc., 1987-93, Henley Mfg., Inc., 1987-89; adj. prof. evidence Western State U. Sch. Law, San Diego, 1977-85, exec. bd., 1977-89; faculty San Diego Inn of Ct., 1979—, Am. Inn of Ct., 1984—. Cons. editor: California Civil Jury Instructions, 1984. City atty. Del Mar, Calif., 1963-74, Coronado, Calif., 1972-77; counsel Comprehensive Planning Orgn., San Diego, 1972-73; trustee San Diego Mus. Art., 1986-89; bd. dirs. Air Pollution Control Dist., San Diego County, 1972-76. Served to lt. comdr. USNR, 1957-61. Named Trial Judge of Yr., San Diego Trial Lawyers Assn., 1984. Mem. Am. Judicature Soc., Soc. Inns of Ct. in Calif., La Jolla Wine and Food Soc., Confrerie des Chevaliers du Tastevin, Order of St. Hubert (Knight Commdr.), Friendly Sons of St. Patrick. Republican. Episcopalian. Clubs: Bohemian; LaJolla Country (dir. 1980-83); Venice Island Hunt Club; Prophets. Home: 6505 Caminito Blythefield La Jolla CA 92037-5806 Office: Latham & Watkins 701 B St Ste 2100 San Diego CA 92101-8116

LEWIS, GREGORY ALLEN, computer programmer and analyst, consultant; b. Ft. Morgan, Colo., Nov. 24, 1961; s. John Marion and Mary Loretta (Dorsey) L.; m. Tina Helena Hofer, Aug. 13, 1983; children: Daniel Gregory, Cynthia Grace, Sarah Ashley, Maria Bethany, Amanda Naomi. BS, Regis Coll., Colorado Springs, Colo., 1989. Operator, jr. programmer Cen. Electric Co., Denver, 1983; tech. leader Logical Systems, Colorado Springs, 1983-86; sr. programmer, analyst Fed. Express Corp., Colorado Springs, 1986-94; lead software engr. Optika Imaging Sys., Inc., Colorado Springs, 1994—; founder Au Courant Consulting, 1997—; cons. Colorado Springs. Neurol. Assocs., 1986-88, Rose Rehab., Colorado Springs, 1987; founder Au Courant Cons., 1997. Tchr. World Bible Sch., 1989—. Home: 13630 Bucknell Cir Elbert CO 80106

LEWIS, IAN DAVID, special education educator; b. London, Dec. 10, 1955; s. Louis Sol and Rebecca Katherine (Moses) L.; m. Terrie Reiss Spritzer, July 8, 1984 (div. 1987); 1 child, Charles Laurence. BA honors, U. York, Eng., 1978; MA, Calif. State U., Northridge, 1986; postgrad. cert. in edn., U. Cambridge, Eng. Tchr. music and spl. edn. Cambridgeshire County Coun., Eng., 1979-81, L.A. Unified Sch. Dist., 1982-87; asst. prof. spl. edn. L.A. Mission Coll., 1992-96, learning disability specialist, 1993—; assoc. prof. spl. edn., learning disability specialist L.A. Valley Coll., 1992—; ednl. cons. entertainment industry, Hollywood, Calif., 1989-94. Mem. Calif. Assn. Post-Secondary Educators (jour. editor 1994), Assn. Ednl. Therapists (profl. mem.). Home: 939 Palm Ave West Hollywood CA 90069-6403

LEWIS, JAN PATRICIA, education educator; b. Seattle, Mar. 6, 1954; d. James Alfred and Jean Louise (Hamilton) L. BA in Edn., Oreg. State U., 1976; MA in Tchg., Lewis & Clark Coll., 1979; PhD in Curriculum and Instrn., U. Oreg., 1989. Cert. tchr. K-8 elem., 4-12 English, K-12 reading, Wash. Elem. tchr. Boring (Oreg.) Sch. Dist., 1976-86; grad. tchg. fellow U. Oreg., Eugene, 1986-89; asst. prof. Pacific Luth. U., Tacoma, Wash., 1989-95; assoc. prof. Pacific Luth. U., 1995—; mem. adj. faculty Lewis and Clark Coll., Portland, Oreg., 1984-89; literacy cons., 1984-96. Co-editor N.W. Reading Jour., 1993-96. Mem. Internat. Reading Assn., Nat. Coun. Tchrs. of English, Wash. Orgn. Reading Devel. Office: Pacific Luth U Sch Edn Tacoma WA 98447

LEWIS, JANIE CAROL, tax preparer, accounting consultant; b. Hollandale, Miss., Mar. 20, 1957; d. Elijah Elbert and Josephine (Clay) Lewis. BBA, Delta State U., 1978. Data entry supr. II Hughes Aircraft Co., El Segundo, Calif., 1980-89; pvt. practice tax preparer Inglewood, Calif., 1989—; beauty cons. Aloette Cosmetics of Long Beach, Calif. Mem. Alpha Kappa Alpha (charter). Democrat. Mem. Pentecostal Ch. Home: 536 Evergreen St Apt 4 Inglewood CA 90302-1959

LEWIS, JASON ALVERT, JR., communications executive; b. Clarksville, Tex., Aug. 17, 1941; s. Jason Allen and Mary (Dinwiddie) L. Student, Stockton Coll., 1959-60, San Jose Jr. Coll., 1962-63. Field engr. telephone tech. Pacific Bell, San Francisco, 1983-84; systems technician AT&T, San Francisco, 1984—. Patentee in field. With U.S. Army, 1964-66. Mem. Internat. Platform Assn., Cousteau Soc., Astron. Soc. Pacific, San Francisco Zool. Soc., Planetary Soc., U.S. Naval Inst. Democrat. Home: 139 Pecks Ln South San Francisco CA 94080-1744

LEWIS, JERRY, congressman; b. Oct. 21, 1934. BA, UCLA, 1956. Former underwriter life ins. underwriter; field rep. for former U.S. Rep. Jerry Pettis; mem. Calif. State Assembly, 1968-78; vice chmn. rules com., chmn. subcom. on air quality; mem. 96th-103rd Congresses from 35th (now 40th) Calif. dist., 1979—; chmn. appropriation com. Va.-HUD subscom., mem. defense subcom., select com. on intelligence, chmn. subcom. on human intelligence; co-chair Calif. Congl. Delegation. Presbyterian. Office: 2112 Rayburn Bldg Washington DC 20515

LEWIS, JOHN CHRISTOPHER, allergist; b. Boston, Oct. 15, 1950. MD, Loyola U., Maywood, 1982. Asst. prof. medicine Mayo Med. Sch., Scottsdale, Ariz., Scottsdale Meml. Hosp. North. Office: Mayo Clinic Scottsdale 13400 E Shea Blvd Scottsdale AZ 85259-5404

LEWIS, JOHN CLARK, JR., manufacturing company executive; b. Livingston, Mont., Oct. 15, 1935; s. John Clark and Louise A. (Anderson) L.; m. Carolyn Jean Keesling, Sept. 4, 1960; children: Robert, Anne, James. BS, Fresno (Calif.) State U., 1957. With Service Bur. Corp., El Segundo, Calif., 1960-70, Computer Scis. Corp., 1970; with Xerox Corp., El Segundo, 1970-77, pres. bus. systems div., 1977; pres. Amdahl Corp., Sunnyvale, Calif., 1983-87, chief exec. officer, 1983—, chmn., 1987—. Served with USNR, 1957-60. Roman Catholic. Office: Amdahl Corp 1250 E Arques Ave Sunnyvale CA 94088-4730*

LEWIS, JOHN WILSON, political science educator; b. King County, Wash., Nov. 16, 1930; s. Albert Lloyd and Clara (Lewis) Seeman; m. Jacquelyn Clark, June 19, 1954; children: Cynthia, Stephen, Amy. Student, Deep Springs Coll., 1947-49; AB with highest honors, UCLA, 1953, MA, 1958, PhD, 1962; hon. degree, Morningside Coll., 1969, Lawrence U., 1986, Russian Acad. Sci., 1996. Asst. prof. govt. Cornell U., 1961-64, assoc. prof., 1964-68; prof. polit. sci. Stanford U., 1968—, William Haas prof. Chinese politics, 1972—, co-dir. arms control and disarmament program, 1971-83, co-dir. NE Asia U.S. Forum on Internat. Policy, 1980-90, co-dir. Ctr. for Internat. Security and Arms Control, 1983-91, sr. fellow, 1991—, dir. Project on Peace and Cooperation in the Asian-Pacific Region; chmn. Internat. Strategic Inst., 1983-89; chmn. joint com. on contemporary China Social Sci. Rsch. Coun.-Am. Coun. Learned Socs., 1976-79; mng. dir. Generation Ventures, 1994—; former vice chmn., bd. dirs. Nat. Com. on U.S.-China Rels.; cons. Senate Select Com. on Intelligence, 1977-81, Los Alamos Nat. Lab., Lawrence Livermore Nat. Lab., Dept. of Def., 1994-96; mem. Def. Policy Bd., 1994-96; chmn. com. advanced study in China Com. Scholarly Comm. with People's Republic of China, 1979-82; mem. com. on internat. security and arms control Nat. acad. Scis., 1980-83; organizer first univ. discussion arms control and internat. security matters Chinese People's Inst. Fgn. Affairs, 1978, first academic exch. agreement Dem. People's Repb. of Korea, 1988; negotiator first univ. tng. and exch. agreement People's Rep. of China, 1978. Author: Leadership in Communist China, 1963, Major Doctrines of Communist China, 1964, Policy Networks and the Chinese Policy Process, 1986; co-author: The United States in Vietnam, 1967, Modernization by Design, 1969, China Builds the Bomb, 1988, Uncertain Partners: Stalin, Mao, and the Korean War, 1993, China's Strategic Seapower: The Politics of Force Modernization in the Nuclear Era, 1994; editor: The City in Communist China, 1971, Party Leadership and Revolutionary Power in China, 1970, Peasant Rebellion and Communist Revolution in Asia, 1974; contbr.: Congress and Arms Control, 1978, China's Quest for Independence, 1979, others; mem. editl. bd. Chinese Law and Govt., China Quar., The Pacific Rev. Served with USN, 1954-57. Mem. Assn. Asian Studies, Am. Polit. Sci. Assn., Coun. Fgn. Rels. Home: 541 San Juan St Stanford CA 94305-8432 Office: Stanford U 320 Galvez St Stanford CA 94305-6105

LEWIS, LOUISE MILLER, gallery director, art history educator; b. St. Louis, Dec. 4, 1940; d. Hugh Milton and Jeanne (Vical) Miller; m. Guy R. Lewis, Nov. 26, 1966; 1 child, Kevin. BA with distinction, 1963; cert. practique de la langue Francaise, U. Paris, 1963; MA in French, U. N.Mex., 1966, MA in Art History, 1972. Curator Art Mus. U. N.Mex., Albuquerque, 1966-70, asst. dir., 1970-72, acctg. dir., 1970, 71-72; assoc. dir. Art Gallery Calif. State U., Northridge, 1972-80, dir., 1980—; asst. prof. art history/recent art of internat. origins Calif. State U., 1972-79, assoc. prof., 1979-83, prof., 1983—, v.p. faculty, 1990-92, pres. faculty, 1992-94. Mem. Phi Beta Kappa. Office: Calif State U 18111 Nordhoff St Northridge CA 91330-0001

LEWIS, MARION ELIZABETH, social worker; b. Los Alamos, Calif., Dec. 7, 1920; d. James Henry and Carolina Sophia (Niemann) Eddy; m. William Ernest Lewis, May 30, 1943 (dec. Oct. 1954); children: Doris Lenita Lewis Terrill, Paul William. Student, Jr. Coll., Santa Maria, Calif., 1939-40, Bus. Coll., Santa Barbara, Calif., 1940-41, Alan Hancock Coll., 1958-61; BA in Sociology cum laude, Westminster Coll., Salt Lake City, 1964. Office clk. Met. Life Ins. Co., Santa Barbara, 1942-43; sales clk. Sprouse Reitz Co., Laguna Beach, Calif., 1943-44; office clk. U.S. Army, Santa Maria AFB, 1944-45; sch. crossing guard Calif. Hwy. Patrol, Los Alamos, 1956-58; office clk. Holaday Children's Ctr., Salt Lake City, 1964; social worker Sonoma County Social Svc., Santa Rosa, Calif., 1964-78, ret., 1978; sales rep. Avon Products, Los Alamos, 1957-61; sales clk. Gen. Store, Los Alamos, 1957-59; office clk. Sonoma County Pub. Health Dept., 1979-80. Deacon Presbyn. Ch., 1956—, moderator Presbyn. Women, First Presbyn. Ch., Santa Rosa, Calif., 1990-91, vice moderator, 1989-90, sem. rep., 1978-80, 92-94. Mem. AAUW, R.I. Geneal. Soc., Sonoma County Geneal. Soc., Calif. Automobile Assn., Nat. Geographic Soc., Sonoma County Assn. Ret. Employees, Sequoia Club, Westminster Coll. Alumni Assn., Alpha Chi (alumni chpt.). Republican. Home: 61 Sequoia Cir Santa Rosa CA 95401-4992

LEWIS, MARK EARLDON, city manager; b. Boston, June 27, 1951; s Frederick Cole Lewis and Barbara (Forsyth) Corrigan; m. Kristine Mietzner, May 1, 1983; children: Anna Kristine, Benjamin Mark. BA, Washington State U., 1975; BS, We. State U., 1993, JD, 1995. Bar: Calif. 1996. Adminstrv. asst. City and Borough of Juneau, Alaska, 1975-77; city mgr. City of Valdez, Alaska, 1978-82; commr. State of Alaska Dept. of Community and REgional Affairs, Juneau, 1982-83; dep. city mgr. City of South San Francisco, Calif., 1984-87, city mgr., 1987-88; city mgr. City of Monterey Park, Calif., 1988-91, City of Colton, Calif., 1991-93, Union City, 1995—. Dir. Monterey Park Boys' and Girls' Club, 1990; vice chmn. allocation team United Way, 1990, area group chmn. 1989-90; exec. com. mem. Calif., colo., Ariz. and Nev. Innovation Group, 1987. Mem. State Bar Calif., Calif. City. Mgrs. Assn. (exec. com. 1996). Home: 4350 Coventry Ct Union City CA 94587 Office: 34009 Alvarado Niles Rd Union City CA 94587-4452

LEWIS, NANCY PATRICIA, speech and language pathologist; b. Miami, Fla., Sept. 23, 1956; d. James and Sara (Gilman) L. BS, U. Fla., 1978; MS, U. Ariz., 1980. Postgrad. fellow U. Tex. Med. Br., Galveston, 1979-80, speech lang. pathologist, 1980-81; speech lang. pathologist Albuquerque Pub. Schs., 1982-84; child devel. specialist Albuquerque Spl. Presch., 1984—; pvt. practice speech-lang. pathology Albuquerque, 1985—; coord. Project Ta-kos, 1987—; artist Trash Warrior wearable art; instr. Express Ability in movement, 1992—; speaker in field. Author (diagnostic procedure) Khan-Lewis Phonological Analysis, 1986; (therapeutic materials) Familiar Objects and Actions, 1985. Labor coord. Lama Found., San Cristobal, 1988, fundraiser, 1988-91, speech pathology cons., 1990—, bd. dirs., 1990—; bd. dirs. Vol. for Outdoors, Albuquerque, 1984—; cmty. vol. mediator N.Mex. Ctr. for Dispute Resolution, 1993—; cons. Robert Wood Johnson Found. City of Santa Fe Carino Children's Project, 1993—; developer, instr. Conflict Resolution Curriculum, 1993—. Fellow U. Tex. Med. Br., Galveston, 1981. Mem. Am. Speech Lang. and Hearing Assn., N.Mex. Speech Lang. and Hearing Assn. Democrat. *Personal philosophy: I see the beauty and the suffering of everyday life as vital elements of the human experience. I ask for guidance in staying present in the moment.*

LEWIS, NORMAN, English language educator, writer; b. N.Y.C., Dec. 30, 1912; s. Herman and Deborah (Nevins) L.; m. Mary Goldstein, July 28, 1934; children—Margery, Debra. B.A., CUNY, 1939; M.A., Columbia U., 1941. Instr., lectr CUNY, N.Y.C., 1943-52; assoc. prof. English NYU, N.Y.C., 1955-64; instr. Compton Coll., Calif., summers 1962-64, UCLA, 1962-69; prof. English Rio Hondo Coll., Whittier, Calif., 1964-91, chmn. communications dept., 1964-75. Author: (with others) Journeys Through Wordland, 1941, Lessons in Vocabulary and Spelling, 1941, (with Wilfred Funk) Thirty Days to a More Powerful Vocabulary, 1942, rev. edit., 1970, Power with Words, 1943, How to Read Better and Faster, 1944, rev. edit., 1978, The Lewis English Refresher and Vocabulary Builder, 1945, How to Speak Better English, 1948, Word Power Made Easy, 1949, rev. edit., 1978, The Rapid Vocabulary Builder, 1951, rev. edit., 1980, 3d edit., 1988, How to Get More Out of Your Reading, 1951, Twenty Days to Better Spelling, 1953, The Comprehensive Word Guide, 1958, Dictionary of Correct Spelling, 1962, Correct Spelling Made Easy, 1963, rev. edit. 1987, Dictionary of Modern Pronunciation, 1963, New Guide to Word Power, 1963, The New Power with Words, 1964, Thirty Days to Better English, 1964, The Modern Thesaurus of Synonyms, 1965, RSVP-Reading, Spelling, Vocabulary, Pronunciation (books I-III), 1966, 77, See, Say, and Write! (books I and II), 1973, Instant Spelling Power, 1976, R.S.V.P. for College English Power (books I-III), 1977-79, R.S.V.P. with Etymology (books I and II), 1980-81, Instant Word Power, 1980, New American Dictionary of Good English,

1987; editor: New Roget's Thesaurus of the English Language in Dictionary Form, 1961; also numerous articles in nat. mags.

LEWIS, OLI PAREPA, curator; b. Cleve., Dec. 14, 1958; d. Raymond Joseph and Yarmila Manlet; m. Fred Lewis. BA, U. Las Vegas. Gen. mgr., curator Guinness World Records Mus., Las Vegas, Nev., 1990—; pres. Mus. and Attractions in Nev. Recipient Voluntourism award Nev. Commn. Tourism, 1994. Office: Guinness World Records Mus 2780 Las Vegas Blvd S Las Vegas NV 89109

LEWIS, PHILIP CHRISTIE, psychiatrist; b. Lincoln, Nebr., July 19, 1942; s. Norman R. and Annabeth (Kurtzweil) L.; m. Rosa E. Dragone, Sept. 17, 1965; children: Diana Patricia, Miriam Elizabeth, Susana Graciela. MD, U. Nat. Cordoba, Argentina, 1969; MA, Western Sem., Portland, Oreg., 1993. Diplomate Am. Bd. Psychiatry and Neurology. Commd. capt. U.S. Army, 1971, advanced through grades to col., 1984; intern Madigan Gen. Hosp., Tacoma, Wash., 1971-72; resident Letterman Army Med. Ctr., San Francisco, 1972-75; chief cmty. mental health svc. U.S. Army Meddac, Ft. Clayton, Canal Zone, 1975-79; pvt. practice Cordoba, 1979-88; chief dept. psychiatry SB Hays Army Cmty. Hosp., Fort Ord, Calif., 1988-93, dep. comdr. clin. svcs., 1993-94; chief dept. psychiatry Tripler Army Med. Ctr., Honolulu, 1994—; clin. asst. prof. psychiatry Uniformed Svcs. U. of Health Scis. Decorated Meritorious Svc. medal; named to Order of Mil. Med. Merit, U.S. Army. Mem. Am. Psychiatric Assn., Christian Med. and Dental Soc. Evangelical. Office: US Army Dept Psychiatry Tripler Army Med Ctr Honolulu HI 96859

LEWIS, RALPH JAY, III, management and human resources educator; b. Balt., Sept. 25, 1942; s. Ralph Jay and Ruth Elizabeth (Schmeltz) L. BS in Engring., Northwestern U., 1966; MS in Adminstrn., U. Calif., Irvine, 1968; PhD in Mgmt., UCLA, 1974. Rsch. analyst Chgo. Area Expressway Surveillance Project, 1963-64, Gen. Am. Transp. Co., Chgo., 1965-66; assoc. prof. mgmt. and human resources mgmt. Calif. State U., Long Beach, 1972—; cons. Rand Corp., Santa Monica, Calif., 1966-74, Air Can., Montreal, Que., 1972-73, Los Angeles Times, 1973;. Co-author: Studies in the Quality of LIfe, 1972; author instructional programs, monographs; co-designer freeway traffic control system. Bd. dirs. Project Quest, Los Angeles, 1969-71. Mem. AAAS, APA, The World Future Soc., Soc. of Mayflower Descendants, SAR (Ill. Soc.), Beta Gamma Sigma. Democrat. Office: Calif State U Dept Human Resources Mgmt Long Beach CA 90840

LEWIS, ROBERT TURNER, retired psychologist; b. Taft, Calif., June 17, 1923; s. D. Arthur and Amy Belle (Turner) L.; m. Jane Badham, Mar. 23, 1946; children: Jane, William, Richard. BA, U. So. Calif., 1947, MA, 1950; PhD, U. Denver, 1952. Diplomate Am. Bd. Profl. Disability Cons.; lic. psychologist, Calif. Chief psychologist Hollywood Presbyn. Hosp., L.A., 1953-58; dir. psychol. svcs. Salvation Army, Pasadena, Calif., 1958-68; dir. Pasadena Psychol. Ctr., 1964-74; successively asst. prof., assoc. prof. and prof., Calif. State U., L.A., 1952-83, prof. emeritus, 1984—; assoc. dir. Cortical Function Lab., L.A., 1972-84; clin. dir. Diagnostic Clinic, West Covina, Calif., 1983-85; dir. Job Stress Clinic, Santa Ana, Calif., 1985-95. Author: Taking Chances, 1979, A New Look at Growing Older, 1995, Money Hangups, 1995; co-author: Money Madness, 1978; Human Behavior, 1974; The Psychology of Abnormal Behavior, 1961. Served to lt. (j.g.) USNR, 1943-46, PTO. Mem. APA, Calif. State Psychol. Assn. Republican.

LEWIS, ROSE, plastic surgeon; b. New Orleans, 1942. MD, U. Calif., San Francisco, 1974. Plastic surgeon Mt. Zion Hosp., San Francisco. Office: 203 Willow St Ste 303 San Francisco CA 94109-7731

LEWIS, ROY ROOSEVELT, physicist; b. Richmond, Va., Mar. 4, 1935; s. Jesse NMN and Elizabeth (Lewis) L.; m. Debra Blondell, Sept. 21, 1968 (div. Aug. 1974); 1 child, Roy Jr.; m. Linda Eleanor, Dec. 19, 1985. BS, Va. Union U., Richmond, 1958; MS, Howard U., 1962, UCLA, 1969; PhD, UCLA, 1972. Mem. tech. staff Hughes Rsch. Lab., Malibu, Calif., 1972-75, Aerospace Corp., El Segundo, Calif., 1977-81, TRW, Redondo Beach, Calif., 1981-82; dir. minority engring. Calif. State U., Long Beach, 1982-83; assoc. prof. Calif. State U., 1982-86, Calif. State Polytech. U., Pomona, Calif., 1986-89; faculty fellow Jet Propulsion Lab. Cal. Inst. Tech., Pasadena, Calif., 1987-89; mem. tech. staff Jet Propulsion Lab. Cal. Inst. Tech., 1989-93; pres. Roy Lewis & Assocs., a sci. cons. firm, Inglewood, Calif., 1993—. Author: LewLearns, Science Lessons For Children, 1977; contbr. articles to profl. jours. Mem. Am. Soc. Engring. Edn., Nat. Soc. Black Physicists, L.A. Coun. Black Engrs., IEEE, Inglewood Dem. Club, Sigma Xi, Alpha Phi Alpha, Sigma Phi Sigma. Episcopalian. Home: 1401 Overhill Dr Inglewood CA 90302-1346

LEWIS, SANDRA JEAN, cardiologist; b. Portland, Oreg., Apr. 11, 1949; d. Stanley Bernard and Susanne Laurel (White) L.; m. James Todd Rosenbaum, June 27, 1970; children: Lisa Rosenbaum, Jennifer Rosenbaum. BA, Stanford U., 1971, MD, 1977. Diplomate Am. Bd. Cardiology. Intern Stanford (Calif.) Univ. Hosp., 1977-78, resident, 1978-80, fellow cardiology, 1980-83; cardiologist Kaiser Permanente, San Francisco, 1983-85, The Heart Clinic, Portland, 1985-94; clin. asst. prof. medicine Oreg. Health Scis. U., 1986-89; cardiologist Portland Cardiovascular Inst., 1995—; Oreg. Health Scis. U., 1986—; chief cardiology Good Samaritan Hosp., Portland, 1990-93. Fellow Am. Coll. Cardiology; mem. AMA, Am. Med. Womens Assn., Am. Heart Assn.

LEWIS, SHEILA MURIEL O'NEIL, retired communications management specialist; b. Glendive, Mont., Sept. 23, 1937; d. John Edward and Muriel Christine (Johnson) O'Neil; m. Lyndell W. Lewis, Dec. 14, 1957 (div. 1973); children: Sheri Lynne, Debra Lynne, Linda Marie, Valerie Jean. AA, Colo. Women's Coll., 1957; BS, U. No. Colo., 1976; postgrad., Stanford U. Adminstrv. asst. DAFC/Dept. Defense DOT/FAA, Denver, 1956-64; substitute tchr. Portland (Oreg.) Public Schs., 1964-72; communications operator Denver Air Rt. Traffic Control Ctr., 1972-78, communications specialist, 1978-80, computer programmer, 1980-82, air traffic controller, 1982-86; communications specialist Air Force Space Command, Falcon AFB, Colo., 1986-95, retired, 1995. Troop leader Campfire Girls, Las Vagas, 1964-72, pres. PTA, Las Vagas, 1964-72. Mem. AAUW, Armed Forces Communications and Electronics Assn., Aviation Space Edn. Assn., Civil Air Patrol, Univ. Aviation Assn., Order of Eastern Star, Order of White Shrine Jerusalem, Chi Omega. Democrat. Lutheran. Home: 4934 Daybreak Cir Colorado Springs CO 80917-2657

LEWIS, SHIRLEY JEANE, psychology educator; b. Phoenix, Aug. 23; d. Herman and Leavy (Hutchinson) Smith; AA, Phoenix C.C., 1957; BA, Ariz. State U., 1960; MS, San Diego State U., 1975, MA, 1986; MA, Azusa Pacific U., 1982; PhD, U. So. Calif., 1983. Cert. Tchr., Calif.; m. Edgar Anthony Lewis (div.); children: Edgar Anthony, Roshaun, Lucy Ann Jonathan. Recreation leader Phoenix Parks and Recreation Dept., 1957-62; columnist Ariz. Tribune, Phoenix, 1958-59; tchr. phys. edn. San Diego Unified Schs., 1962—; adult educator San Diego C.Cs., 1973—, instr. psychology, health, Black studies, 1977—, counselor, 1981—; cmty. counselor S.E. Counseling and Cons. Svcs. and Narcotics Prevention and Edn. Systems, Inc., San Diego, 1973-77; counselor educator, counselor edn. dept. San Diego State U., 1974-77; marriage, family, child counselor Counseling and Cons. Ctr., San Diego, 1977—; inservice educator San Diego Unified and San Diego County Sch. Dists., 1973-77; Fulbright Exch. counselor, London, 1994-96; lectr. in field. Girl Scout phys. fitness cons., Phoenix, 1960-62; vol. cmty. tutor for high sch. students, San Diego, 1963; sponsor Tennis Club for Youth, San Diego, 1964-65; troop leader Girl Scouts U.S., Lemon Grove, Calif., 1972-74; vol. counselor USN Alcohol Rehab. Center, San Diego, 1978; mem. sch. coun.'s adv. bd. San Diego State U. Named Woman of Year, Phoenix, 1957, One of Outstanding Women of San Diego, 1980; recipient Phys. Fitness Sch. award and Demonstration Sch. award Pres.'s Coun. on Phys. Fitness, Taft Jr. High Sch., 1975, Excel award Corp. Excellence Edn., 1989; Delta Sigma Theta scholar, 1957-60; Alan Korrick scholar, 1956. Mem. NEA, Calif. Tchrs. Assn., San Diego Tchrs. Assn., Assn. Marriage and Family Counselors, Am. Personnel and Guidance Assn., Calif. Assn. Health, Phys. Edn. and Recreation (v.p. health), Am. Alliance of Health, Phys. Edn. and Recreation, Assn. Black Psychologists (corr. sec. 1993), Assn. African-Am. Educators, Delta Sigma Theta (Delta of Yr. 1987). Democrat. Baptist. Contbr. articles to profl. jours. Home: 1226 Armacost Rd San Diego CA 92114-3307 Office: 2630 B St San Diego CA 92102-1022 *Personal philosophy: High self-esteem, responsibility, self-discipline and striving to achieve personal goals are necessary for a healthful lifestyle regardless of one's personal, historical circumstances. The initial access to such characteristics, in reality, may only be in one's invention of fantasy.*

LEWIS, TONY LLOYD, pastor; b. Lake Charles, La., Sept. 4, 1951; s. Gloria Mae Lewis-Smith; m. Esther Ann Craven, Oct. 1, 1988; 1 child, Kimberly Josephine. Bachelors, Bishop Coll., 1979; Masters, Pitts. Theol. Sem., 1981; DD (hon.), Bethany Theol. Sem., 1987; D of Ministry, Triune Bible Coll. and Sem., 1990. Ordained to ministry, Bapt. Ch., 1980. Youth minister Prosperity Bapt. Ch., L.A., 1975-76; minister of evangelism Concord Bapt. Ch., Dallas, 1977-79; assoc. minister Ctrl. Bapt. Ch., Pitts., 1979-81; sr. pastor Morning Star Bapt. Ch., Portland, Oreg., 1982-91, Macedonia Bapt. Ch., Pomona, Calif., 1991—. Author: (tract) Whatever Happened to that Family Who Joined Our Church Last Month, 1993, From Bootcamp to the Battlefield, Read to Serve, 1996. Exec. bd. dirs. NAACP, Pomona, 1994; invitee White House Inauguration, 1988. Recipient Outstanding Leadership award Bapt. Ministers Fellowship of Portland, 1991, Cert. of Appreciation, Census Complete County Com., 1990. Mem. Nat. Bapt. Conv. Am. (bd. dirs. 1982—), San Gabriel Valley Bapt. Assn. of Pomona Calif. and Vicinity, Inc. (founder, exec. dir. 1991—). Office: 710 S Hamilton Blvd Pomona CA 91766-2823

LEWIS MILL, BARBARA JEAN, psychologist; b. Sacramento, Sept. 12, 1959; d. William Vasse and Mary Allene (Bridges) Lewis; m. Thomas Steven Mill, Oct. 17, 1981; 1 child, Thomas William. BA, U. Calif., Davis, 1981; MA, U. Calif., Santa Barbara, 1984. Pupil pers. svcs. credentials; cert. basic and sch. psychologist. Pub. rels. asst. Coll. Agrl. and Environ. Scis., U. Calif., Davis, 1979-81; adminstrv. asst. libr. U. Calif., Santa Barbara, 1981-84; sch. psychologist intern Ventura (Calif.) County Supt. of Schs. Office, 1984-85, sch. psychologist, 1985-91; sch. psychologist Rio Sch. Dist., Oxnard, Calif., 1985, Ojai (Calif.) Sch. Dist., 1991-92, Santa Paula (Calif.) Sch. Dist., 1991—; coord. Primary Intervention Program, Santa Paula (Calif.) Sch. Dist., 1992-94; mem. planning com. Dropout Prevention/Outreach Program, Grace Thille Sch., Santa Paula, 1994. Mem. adv. bd. Pleasant Valley Rainbow Girls, Camarillo, Calif., 1986-89; bd. dirs. Strawberry Patch Presch., Oxnard, 1995-96. Apptd. state officer Grand Scribe, Internat. Order Rainbow for Girls, Calif., 1979. Mem. ASCD, Nat. Assn. Sch. Psychologists (nat. cert. sch. psychologist), Internat. Reading Assn., Calif. Assn. Sch. Psychologists, Ventura County Assn. Sch. Psychologists (exec. bd. 1987-91, 93-94, dir. pub. rels. 1991-93, 94-96, pres. elect 1997—, Outstanding Sch. Psychologist 1989, Meritorious Svc. award 1993), Internat. Order of the Ea. Star, Kappa Delta Pi.

LEWITZKY, BELLA, choreographer; b. Los Angeles, Jan. 13, 1916; d. Joseph and Nina (Ossman) L.; m. Newell Taylor Reynolds, June 22, 1940; 1 child, Nora Elizabeth. Student, San Bernardino Valley (Calif.) Jr. Coll., 1933-34; hon. doctorate, Calif. Inst. Arts, 1981; PhD (hon.), Occidental Coll., 1984, Otis Parsons Coll., 1989, Juilliard Sch., 1993; DFA, Santa Clara U., 1995. Chmn. dance dept., chmn. adv. panel U. So. Calif., Idyllwild, 1956-74; founder Sch. Dance, Calif. Inst. Arts, 1969, dean, 1969-74; vice chmn. dance adv. panel Nat. Endowment Arts, 1974-77, mem. artists-in-schs. adv. panel, 1974-75; mem. Nat. Adv. Bd. Young Audiences, 1974—, Joint Commn. Dance and Theater Accreditation, 1979; com. mem. Am. chpt. Internat. Dance Coun. of UNESCO, 1974—; trustee Calif. Assn. Dance Cos., 1976—, Idyllwild Sch. Music and Arts, 1986-95, Dance/USA, 1988-95, Calif. State Summer Sch. of Arts, 1988—; cons. the dance project WNET, 1987—. Co-founder, co-dir. Dance Dance Assocs., L.A., 1951-55; founder, 1966; artistic dir. Lewitzky Dance Co., L.A.; choreographer, 1948—; founder, former artistic dir. The Dance Gallery, L.A.; contbr. articles in field; choreographed works include Trio for Saki, 1967, Orrenda, 1969, Kinaesonata, 1971, Pietas, 1971, Ceremony for Three, 1972, Game Plan, 1973, Five, 1974, Spaces Between, 1975, Jigsaw, 1975, Inscape, 1976, Pas de Bach, 1977, Suite Satie, 1980, Changes and Choices, 1981, Confines, 1982, Continuum, 1982, The Song of the Woman, 1983, Nos Duraturi, 1984, 8 Dancers/8 Lights, 1985, Facets, 1986, Impressions #1, 1987, Impressions #3, 1988, Agitime, 1989, Impressions #3, 1989, Episode #1, 1990, Glass Canyons, 1991, Episode #2, 1992, Episode #3, 1992, Episode #4, 1993, Meta 4, 1994, Four Women in Time, 1996. Mem. adv. com. Actors' Fund of Am., 1986—, Women's Bldg. Adv. Council, 1985-91, Calif. Arts Council, 1983-86, City of Los Angeles Task Force on the Arts, 1986—; mem. artistic adv. bd. Interlochen Ctr. for Arts, 1988—. Recipient Mayoral Proclamation, City of L.A., 1976, 1982, ann. award Dance mag., 1978, Dir.'s award Calif. Dance Educators Assn., 1978, Plaudit Award, Nat. Dance Assn., 1979, Labor's Award of Honor for Community Svc., L.A. County AFL-CIO, 1979, L.A. Area Dance Alliance and L.A. Junior C. of C. Honoree, 1980, City of L.A. Resolution, 1980, Distguished Artist Award, City of L.A. and Music Ctr., 1982, Silver Achievement award YWCA, 1982, California State Senate Resolution, 1982, 1984, Award of Recognition, Olympic Black Dance Festival, 1984, Distinguished Women's Award, Northwood Inst., 1984, California State U. Distinguished Artist, 1984, Vesta Award, Woman's Bldg, L.A., 1985, L.A. City Council Honors for Outstanding Contributions, 1985, Woman of the Year, Palm Springs Desert Museum, Women's Committee, 1986, Disting. Svc. award Western Alliance Arts Adminstrs., 1987, Woman of Achievement award, 1988, Am. Dance Guild Ann. award, 1989, So. Calif. Libr. for Social Studies & Rsch. award, 1990, Am. Soc. Journalists & Authors Open Book award, 1990, Internat. Soc. Performing Arts Adminstrs. Tiffany award, 1990, Burning Bush award U. of Judaism, 1991, 1st recipient Calif. Gov.'s award in arts for individual lifetime achievement, 1989; honoree L.A. Arts Coun., 1989, Heritage honoree, Nat. Dance Assn., 1991, Vaslav Nijinsky award, 1991, Hugh M. Hefner First Amendment award, 1991, Artistic Excellence award Ctr. Performing Arts U. Calif., 1992, Lester Horton Lifetime Achievement award Dance Resource Ctr. of L.A., 1992, Occidental Coll. Founders' award, 1992, Dance/USA honor, 1992, Visual Arts Freedom of Expression award Andy Warhol Found., 1993, Artist of Yr. award L.A. County High Sch. Arts, 1993, Freedom of Expression honor Andy Warhol Found. Visual Arts, 1993, Calif. Alliance Edn. award, 1994, Lester Horton Sustained Achievement award, 1995 Danie Resource Ctr. of L.A., Lester Horton award for Restaging and Revival, Dance Resource Ctr. of L.A., 1996, Disting. Artists of 1996, High Sch. of Performing Arts, Houston Tex., Bill of Rights award, Am. Civil Liberties Union of So. Calif., Nat. Medal of Arts, 1996, Gypsy award Profl. Dancers Soc., 1997, Nat. Medal Arts, 1997; grantee Mellon Found., 1975, 81, 86, Guggenheim Found., 1977-78, NEA, 1969-94; honoree Women's Internat. League Peace and Freedom, 1995; presented with Key to the City, Cin., 1997. Mem. Am. Arts Alliance (bd. dirs. 1977), Internat. Dance Alliance (adv. council 1984—), Dance/USA (bd. dirs. 1988), Phi Beta (hon.). Office: Lewitzky Dance Co 1055 Wilshire Blvd Ste 1140 Los Angeles CA 90017-2498 *Dance is communicative of personal, emotive knowledge-- of sensory information common to all. The feel of the wind, the exhilaration of clear space, the headiness of an enormous height, the marvel of human power, one's personal worth-- can take shape and be illuminated in dance. How wonderful to work at something you love! How remarkable to be given the opportunity to utilize one's whole being, one's physical knowledge, intellectual capacity, imagination and creativity in a single persuit. How good to practice dance and know that it will not engage you in mass murders of warfare; it will not destroy our environment. It is capable of healing, celebrating, and sharing human resources. My philosophy is predicated on the belief that choreography is the taskmaster of us all. In each work, I attempt to discover again the truth of that statement.*

LEY, DAVID CHANPANNHA, secondary education educator; b. Phnom Penh, Cambodia, May 23, 1966; came to U.S., 1988; s. Ley Savun Dom and Samonn Khieu Mao; m. Nancy Panida Thy, Mar. 11, 1992 (div. Jan. 1996); 1 child, Kevin Vitou. Cert. in econs., Phnom Penh City Coll., 1987; AA in Math., Lang. Arts, Laney Coll., Oakland, Calif., 1991; BA in Social Welfare, U. Calif., Berkeley, 1993; MA in Edn., Calif. State U., Dominguez Hills Carson, Calif., 1996; postgrad., U. So. Calif. Cert. tchr., Calif. Study group facilitator Laney Coll. Transfer Ctr., Oakland, 1989-93; tchr. Whittier Sch., Long Beach Unified Sch. Dist., Calif., 1993—; student advisor Laney Coll. Info. Dept., Oakland, 1990; counselor, tutor Nat. Hispanic U., Oakland, 1990. Vol. interpreter Phillippines Refugee Ctr., Bataan, The Phillippines, 1987; vol. tutor Roosevelt Jr. High Sch., Oakland, 1993. Odell Wilson scholar U. Calif., Berkeley, 1991-92, E. Armstrong scholar, 1992-93, L. Wrasse scholar, 1992-93, Title VII scholar Calif. STate U., Dominguez Hills, 1994—. Mem. Nat. Assn. Edn. Achievement Cambodian, Loation, Vietnames Ams., Calif. Assn. Asian and Pacific Am. Edn., Khmer Educators Orgn., Univ. Calif. Berkeley Alumni Assn. (life, scholarship, cert.), Phi Kappa Phi (life, cert.), Golden Key Nat. Honor Soc. (life, cert.). Office: Whittier Sch Long Beach Unified Sch Dist 1761 Walnut Ave Long Beach CA 90813

LEYDEN, NORMAN, conductor; m. Alice Leyden; children: Robert, Constance. Grad., Yale U., 1938; MA, Columbia U., EdD, 1968. Bass clarinetist New Haven Symphony; arranger Glenn Miller Air Force Band, Eng., France; chief arranger Glenn Miller Orch., 1946-49; freelance arranger N.Y.C.; mus. dir. RCA Victor Records, Arthur Godfrey, 1956-59; with Oreg. Symphony, 1970—, assoc. conductor, 1974—; music dir. Seattle Symphony Pops, 1975-93; tchr. Columbia U.; guest condr. over 40 Am. symphony orchs. including Boston Pops, Minn. Orch., Pitts. Symphony, St. Louis Symphony, San Diego Symphony, San Francisco Symphony, Nat. Symphony, Utah Symphony; condr. Army Air Force. Office: Oreg Symphony Orch 711 SW Alder St Ste 200 Portland OR 97205

LEYDET, FRANÇOIS GUILLAUME, writer; b. Neuilly-sur-Seine, France, Aug. 26, 1927; came to U.S., 1940, naturalized, 1956; s. Bruno and Dorothy (Lindsey) L. AB, Harvard, 1947, postgrad. Bus. Sch., 1952; postgrad. Johns Hopkins Sch. Advanced Internat. Studies, 1952-53; Bachelier-es-lettres-philosophie, U. Paris (France), 1945; m. Patience Abbe, June 17, 1955 (div.); step-children: Catherine Abbe Geissler, Lisa Amanda O'Mahony; m. Roslyn Carney, June 14, 1970; step-children: Walter E. Robb IV, Rachel R. Avery, Holly H. Prunty, Mary-Peck Peters. Past dir. Marin County Planned Parenthood Assn., Planned Parenthood Center Tucson; docent Ariz.-Sonora Desert Mus. 1st lt. French Army, 1947-48. Mem. Nat. Parks Assn., Wilderness Soc., Sierra Club, Nat. Audubon Soc., World Wildlife Fund, Am. Mus. Natural History, Environ. Def. Fund, Ariz.-Sonora Desert Mus., Ariz. Hist. Soc., LWV, Ariz. Opera League, Commonwealth Club. Author: The Last Redwoods, 1963, Time and the River Flowing: Grand Canyon, 1964, The Coyote: Defiant Songdog of the West, 1977; editor: Tomorrow's Wilderness, 1963; editor Noticias; contbr. to Nat. Geog. mag. Died Mar. 4, 1997. Home: 5165 N Camino Real Tucson AZ 85718-5026

LHOTKA, SIDNEY BRUNO, tax accountant; b. Sevetin, Bohemia, Czechsolvakia, Apr. 4, 1926; came to U.S., 1956; s. Vaclav Vojtech and Helena (Valkova) L.; m. Jana M. Lhotka, Mar. 29, 1958. A in Acctg., U. Queensland, Australia, 1958, B in Comm., 1959. Acct., acctg. mgr. Bechtel Corp., San Francisco, 1956-61, product svcs. mgr., 1964-66, 68-83; asst. svcs. mgr. Transport Co. of Tex., Kwajalein, Mich., 1962-64; office mgr. systems and procedures RMK-BRJ Vietnam, Saigon, 1966-68; prin. Fin. and Tax Svcs., Concord, Calif., 1983—. Fellow Australian Soc. of Cert. Practicing Accts.; mem. Nat. Soc. of Pub. Accts., Nat. Assn. of Enrolled Agts., Internat. Assn. of Fin. Planning. Home: 1314 Corte De Los Vecinos Walnut Creek CA 94598-2902 Office: Fin and Tax Svcs Concord CA 94520

LI, CINDY, scientist; b. Shanghai, People Republic China, Mar. 30, 1962; came to U.S., 1990; s. Mao-Shen Li and Wang-Ying (Mo) Mo; m. Xiang Y. Yao, Dec. 18, 1986; 1 child, Jamie L. Yao. MD, Shanghai Medical U., 1985. Rsch. assoc. Osaka (Japan) Univ. Sch. Medicine, 1987-90; rsch. fellow Hosp. of the Good Samaritan, L.A., 1990-94; staff scientist Allymax Rsch. Inst., Santa Clara, Calif., 1994—. Contbr. articles to profl. jours. Recipient rsch. scholarship Osaka U., 1988-89. Home: 1043 Ridgemont Dr Milpitas CA 95035-7838 Office: Affymax Rsch Inst Santa Clara CA 95051

LI, DAVID LEIWEI, English and Asian American studies educator; b. Shanghai, Nov. 23, 1959; came to U.S., 1985; s. Zhen Ting Li and Min Zhi Tao; m. Cherry Wenying, May 26, 1985; 1 child, Art Ling. BA in English, Shanghai Fgn. Langs. Inst., 1982; MA in English/ESL, Indiana U. of Pa., 1986; PhD in English, U. Tex., 1991. Lectr. English dept. Shanhhai Internat. Studies U., 1982-85; asst. prof. English U. So. Calif., L.A., 1991—. Zumberg fellow U. So. Calif., 1994. Mem. MLA (chair Asian Am. discussion group, 1995, mem. exec. com. 1991-95). Office: U So Calif Dept English University Park Los Angeles CA 90089-0354

LI, FU, electrical engineering educator, editor; b. Chengdu, Sichuan, China, Sept. 12, 1958; came to U.S., 1985; s. Zhi and Xiu-Juan (Ding) L.; m. Grace Hui Fang, Mar. 18, 1984; children: Susan J., Karen M. BS in Physics, Sichuan U., 1982, MS in Physics, 1985; PhD in Elec. Engring., U. R.I., 1990. Profl. engr., Oreg. Rsch./teaching asst. U. R.I., Kingston, 1986-89; rsch. staff Philips Labs., Briarcliff Manor, N.Y., summer 1987; tech. staff Prime Computer, Inc., Bedford, Mass., 1989-90; asst. prof. elec. engring. Portland (Oreg.) State U., 1990-94, assoc. prof. elec. engring., 1994—. Author chpts. to 4 books, 1991-94; contbr. articles to profl. jours. Recipient Faculty Devel. award Portland State U., 1991, Pew Teaching Leadership award 2d Nat. Conf. on Teaching Assts., 1989, Excellent Paper award Chinese Assn. Sci. and Tech., 1986. Mem. NSPE, IEEE (sr., assoc. editor Transactions on Signal Processing 1993—, organizer Oreg. chpt. 1993, chair 1993-95, exec. com. 1993—, session chair internat. conf. on acoustice, speech and signal processing 1993-96, session chair statis. signals and array processing workshop 1992, 94, tech. com. on statis. signals and array processing 1992—, chair tech. subcom. power spectrum estimation 1992—, chair 1994—, recognition award 1993, chpt. chmn. award 1994, outstanding counselor award 1995), Eta Kappa Nu. Office: Portland State Univ Dept Elec Engring 1800 SW 6th Ave Portland OR 97201-5204

LI, SHENGQIANG, virologist; b. Ziyang, Sichuan, China, Feb. 28, 1964; came to U.S., 1990; s. Guojun and Suzhen (Zhu) L.; m. Ou He, Dec. 27, 1989; 1 child, Helen. MS, BS, Justus-Liebig U., Giessen, Germany, 1987, DVM, 1990. Grad. rsch. asst. Sch. Vet. Medicine, Giessen, 1987-89; postdoctoral fellow Mt. Sinai Sch. Medicine, N.Y.C., 1990-93; staff scientist Aviron, Mountain View, Calif., 1993—. Contbr. articles to profl. jours.; patentee in field. Recipient Karl-Pfizer prize, 1990; SBIR grantee NIH, 1995; Alexander von Humbolt Found. fellow, 1987-89, Fritz-Thyssen Found. fellow, 1989-90. Office: Aviron 297 Bernardo Ave Mountain View CA 94043-5205

LI, SHUGUANG, research scientist; b. Taiyuan, China, June 22, 1953; came to U.S., 1991; s. Yu Li and Yu Wu; m. Suyu Liu, July 25, 1979; 1 child, Lei Li. MD, Nanjing Railway Med. U., China, 1978; MS, Hunan Med. U., China, 1981; PhD, Leiden U., The Netherlands, 1989. Lectr. Dept. Immunology Hunan Med. U., China, 1981-85; vis. scholar, PhD Rsch. Dept. Immunohematology and Rsch. Blood Bank Leiden U., The Netherlands, 1986-89; post doctoral rsch. fellow Inst. Immunology and Rheumatology Oslo U., Norway, 1990-91; dir. spl. chemistry dept., sr. rsch. scientist Specialty Labs., Inc., Santa Monica, Calif., 1991—; reviewer Scandanavian Jour. Immunology, Oslo, Norway, 1990-92. Mem. AAAS, Assn. Immunologists, Clin. Immunology Soc., Internat. Union Immunological Soc., Norwegian Soc. for Immunology, Chinese Soc. for Immunology, Chinese Soc. for Microbiology. Office: Specialty Labs Inc 2211 Michigan Ave Santa Monica CA 90404

LI, VICTOR ON-KWOK, electrical engineering educator; b. Hong Kong, Oct. 11, 1954; came to the U.S., 1973; s. Chia-Nan and Wai-Ying (Chan) L.; m. Regina Yui-Kwan Wai, Aug. 14, 1977; children: Ronald, Nathan. SB in Elec. Engring. and Computer Sci., MIT, 1977, SM in Elec. Engring. and Computer Sci., 1979, ScD in Elec. Engring. and Computer Sci., 1981. Asst. prof. dept. elec. engring. U. So. Calif., L.A., 1981-87, assoc. prof. dept. elec. engring., 1987-92, prof. dept. elec. engring., 1992—, comm. group leader dept. elec. engring., 1988-91, co-dir. dept. elec. engring. Comm. Scis. Inst., 1991-93, dir., 1993-94, 95—; Disting. lectr. Nat. Sci. coun., Taiwan, 1993; hon. speaker IEE, 1995; lectr. and cons. in field. Editor: IEEE Networks, 1986-92, ACM/BaltzerWireless Networks, 1993—, Telecom.Sys., 1991-95; guest editor spl. issue IEEE Jour. on Selected Areas in Comm., 1987; contbr. articles to profl. jours. Named Disting. lectr. Calif. Poly. Inst., Pomona, 1990. Fellow IEEE (Svc. award 1984, 85, gen. chmn., tech. program chmn. 4th Annual Computer Comm. Workshop, Dana Point, Calif., Oct. 1989, Comm. Soc. tech. com. on computer comm. 1987-89, chmn. L.A. chpt. IEEE Info. Theory Soc. 1983-85, steering com. chair Internat. Conf. on Computer Comm. and Networking, 1992—, tech. program chair symposium on personal comm. svcs., 1995, keynote spkr. internat. conf. 1996), Inst. for Advancement Engring. Office: Univ So Calif Dept Elec Engring Los Angeles CA 90089-2565

LI, ZHI, process engineer; b. Bazhong, Sichuan, People's Republic of China, Apr. 2, 1961; s. Qingxiang Li and Kamin Zhou; m. Fan Yang, Dec. 20, 1987; 1 child, Rosa Jane. BSEE, Sichuan U., Chengdu, People's Republic of China, 1982; MSEE, U. Wash., 1987, PhD in Elec. Engring., 1993. Electronics engr. Sichuan U., 1982-85; process engr. Lattice Semiconductor Co., Hillsboro, Oreg., 1991—. Mem. Tau Beta Pi, Eta Kappa Mu. Office: Lattice Semiconductor Corp 5555 NE Moore Ct Hillsboro OR 97124-6421

LIANG, JEFFREY DER-SHING, retired electrical engineer, civil worker, diplomat; b. Chungking, China, Oct. 25, 1915; came to U.S., 1944, naturalized, 1971; s. Tze-hsiang and Sou-yi (Wang) L.; m. Eva Yin Hwa Tang, Jan. 2, 1940; 1 child, Shouyu. BA, Nat. Chengchih U., Chungking, 1940; BAS, U. B.C., Vancouver, 1960. Office asst. Ministry of Fgn. Affairs, Chungking, 1940-43; vice consul, Chinese consulate Ministry of Fgn. Affairs, Seattle, 1944-50; consulate-gen. Ministry of Fgn. Affairs, San Francisco, 1950-53; consul, Chinese consulate-gen. Ministry of Fgn. Affairs, Vancouver, 1953-56; engr.-in-tng. Can. Broadcasting Corp., Vancouver, 1960-65; assoc. engr. Boeing Co., Seattle, 1965-67, rsch. engr., 1967-70, engr., 1970-73, sr. engr., 1973-75, specialist engr., 1975-78; cons. Seattle, 1979-81. Mem. chancelor's cir. Wesbrook Soc. U. B.C., Vancouver, 1986—, Seattle-King County Adv. Coun. on Aging, 1984-88, Gov.'s State Coun. on Aging, Olympia, 1986-88, Pres. Coun., Rep. Nat. Com.; permanent mem. Rep. Nat. Senatorial Com., Washington State Rep. Party, Seattle Art Mus.; life mem. Am. Assn. Individual Investors, Rep. Presdl. Task Force; sustaining mem. Rep. Nat. Congl. Com., Rep. Presdl. Adv. Com.,. Mem. IEEE (life), Heritage Found., Nat. Trust Hist. Preservation, Hwa Sheng Chinese Music Club (v.p. 1978-79, chmn. nomination com. 1981-88, 90-94). Republican. Mem. Christian Ch. Home: 1750 152d Ave NE Apt 302 Bellevue WA 98007-4270 *Always try to do one's best since that is a sure way to go through life without regrets.*

LIANG, JUNXIANG, aeronautics and astronautics engineer, educator; b. Hangzhou, Zhejiang, China, Aug. 17, 1932; s. Yigao and Yunruo (Yu) L.; m. Junxian Sun, Jan. 27, 1960; 1 child, Song Liang. Grad., Harbin Inst. Tech., 1960. Head control dept. Shenyang (Liaoning, China) Jet Engine R&D Inst., 1960-70, China Gas Turbine Establishment, Jiangyou, Sichuan, China, 1970-78; assoc. chief engr. China Gas Turbine Establishment, Jiangyou, 1978-83; vis. scientist MIT, Cambridge, Mass., 1984-86; prof. China Aerospace Inst. Systems Engring., Beijing, China, 1986—; grads. supr. Beijing U. Aero-Astronautics, Beijing, 1986—; chief engr. Full Authority Digital Elec. Engine Control China Aerospace Industry Ministry, Beijing, 1986-93; mem. China Aerospace Sci. and Tech. Com., Beijing, 1983-94, Aero-engine R&D Adv. Bd., Beijing, 1991-95; bd. dirs. China Aviation Ency. Editl. Bd., Beijing, 1991-95; tech. support supr., mgmt. info. svc. mgr. Am. PC, Inc., Union City, Calif., 1993—. Author: Nonlinear Control System Oscillation, 1964; contbr. articles to Jour. Aeronautics and Astronautics, Jour. Propulsion Tech., Internat. Aviation, Acta Aeronautica et Astronautica Sinica. Recipient Nat. Sci. and Tech. 2d award, China Nat. Sci. and Tech. Com., Beijing, 1965, Sic. and Tech. Progress award, China Aerospace Industry Ministry, 1991, Nat. Outstanding Sci. and Tech. Contbn. award, 1992. Mem. AIAA, Chinese Soc. of Aeronautical, Astronautical Engine Control (mem. commn. 1987—). Home: 2973 Carmel St Oakland CA 94602-3410

LIANG, LOUISE LINDA, medical group executive, pediatrician. MD, Georgetown U., 1972. Diplomate Am. Bd. Med. Mgmt., Am. Acad. Pediatrics. Resident in pediatrics Tufts U., Boston, 1972-75; divsn. head pediatrics and adolescent medicine Henry Ford Hosp., Dearborn, Mich., 1975-77; White House fellow, spl. asst. to sec. Dept. Health, Edn. and Welfare, Washington, 1977-78; program mgr. Nat. Childhood Immunization Initiative Dept. Health and Human Svcs., 1978-79; dir. divsn. of health svc. del. USPHS, Boston, 1979-81; asst. to assoc. med. dir. Harvard Cmty. Health Plan, Boston, 1981-83; health ctr. dir. Harvard Cmty. Health Plan, Peabody, Mass., 1983-85; assoc. med. dir., corp. officer Harvard Cmty. Health Plan, Boston, 1985-92; v.p. clin.ops. and chief operating officer Straub Clinic and Hosp., Inc., Honolulu, 1992-97; med. dir. Group Health Coop of Puget Sound, Seattle, 1997—; instr. pediatrics Harvard Med. Sch., Boston, 1983-92; clin. instr. pediatrics U. Mich., Ann Arbor, 1976-77; asst. pediatrician Mass. Gen. Hosp., Boston, 1983-92; program co-chair Nat. Forum on Quality Improvement in Healthcare, 1990-91; bd. dirs. Inst. for Healthcare Improvement, 1995—. Alpha Omega Alpha. Office: Group Health Coop Puget Sound 521 Wall St Seattle WA 08121-1536

LIBERTY, JOHN JOSEPH, librarian; b. Sacramento, Dec. 14, 1927; s. John and Josephine (Zobac) L.; m. Irma Elizabeth Madsen, Aug. 25, 1951 (div. Oct. 1979); children: Kristine Elizabeth (dec. Aug. 1970), Marya Liberty. BA, Calif. State U., 1953; MA, U. Denver, 1963. Sr. law clk. Calif. State Libr., Sacramento, 1953-62, acquisitions libr., 1963-64, social sci. libr., 1964-92; faculty Calif. State U. Libr., 1963—; libr. emeritus, adj. faculty, dissent and social change collection Calif. State U. Libr., Sacramento, 1992—. Author: Currents on the Left, 1974, Facing Right, 1977, Journals of Dissent and Social Change, 7th edit., 1993. Mem. ACLU. Home: 5231 Carrington St Sacramento CA 95819-1609 Office: Calif State Univ Libr 2000 Jed Smith Dr Sacramento CA 95819-6039

LICENS, LILA LOUISE, administrative assistant; b. Puyallup, Wash., Feb. 18, 1949; d. C.L. and Joan L. (Rubert) Vormestrand. Cert., Knapp Bus. Coll., 1968. Cert. profl. sec. Adminstrv. asst. Weyerhaeuser Co., Tacoma, 1968-93, adminstrv. asst. bleached paperboard, 1993—. Mem. adv. bd. Bates Tech. Coll., 1994—. Mem. Profl. Sec. Internat. (pres. Mt. Rainier chpt. 1994—, pres. Wash.-Alaska divsn. 1990-91, pres.-elect 1989-90, sec. 1987-89, pres. Sea-Tac chpt. 1985-87), Fed. Way Women's Network (treas. 1988, sec. 1989, pes. 1995, 96). Home: 771 108th St S Tacoma WA 98444-5666

LICHTENBERG, LARRY RAY, chemist, consultant, researcher; b. Marceline, Mo., July 25, 1938; s. Kenneth Ray and Evelyn (Lauck) L.; m. Clarice Elaine Dameron, Dec. 23, 1961; children: Julia-Isabel Dameron. BS in Chemistry, Northeast Mo. State U., 1962. Chemist Bell & Howell, Chgo., 1962-62; jr. chem. engr. Magnavox Corp., Urbana, Ill., 1963-64; process engr. Gen. Electric Co., Bloomington, Ill., 1964-70; mfg. engr. Burr-Brown, Tucson, 1970-72; sr. staff engr. Motorola, Scottsdale, Ariz., 1972—; mem. corp. tech. council Motorola, Scottsdale, 1982—. Contbr. articles to profl. jours. Mem. Am. Chem. Soc., Internat. Soc. Hybrid Microelectronics (pres. Phoenix chpt. 1981-82). Republican. Baptist. Home: 13018 N 32nd Ave Phoenix AZ 85029-1206 Office: Motorola 5005 E Mcdowell Rd # SP5 Phoenix AZ 85008-4229

LIDDELL, BARBARA ANNE, school administrator; b. Chgo., Jan. 4, 1938; d. Harold and Margaret (Schutte) Fly; m. Wingham John Hunter Liddell, Jr., Apr. 6, 1961 (div. Dec. 1982); 1 child, Letitia. BA, Stanford U., 1959; MA, San Francisco State U., 1970; MEd, St. Mary's Coll., Moraga, Calif., 1980. Tchr. Orinda (Calif.) Schs., 1964-78; prin. Hillsborough (Calif.) City Schs., 1978-81, dir. adminstrv. svcs., 1981-84; asst. supt. Piedmont (Calif.) City Schs., 1984-87; assoc. supt. Palo Alto (Calif.) Schs., 1987—. Bd. dirs. Consortium of Calif. Edn. Founds., San Francisco, 1984-88, Bay Area Global Edn. Project, San Francisco, 1985-88. Fulbright-Hays fellow, 1993, Japan Found. fellow, 1990. Mem. ASCD, Am. Assn. Sch. Adminstrs., Calif. Sch. Adminstrs. Assn. Office: Palo Alto Sch Dist 25 Churchill Ave Palo Alto CA 94306-1005

LIDDICOAT, RICHARD THOMAS, JR., professional society administrator; b. Kearsarge, Mich., Mar. 2, 1918; s. Richard Thomas and Carmen (Williams) L.; m. Mary Imogene Hibbard, Sept. 21, 1939. BS in Geology, U. Mich., 1939, MS in Mineralogy, 1940; grad. gemologist, Gemological Inst. Am., 1941; MS in Meteorology, Calif. Inst. Tech., 1944. Cert. gemologist (hon.) Am. Gem Soc. With Gemological Inst. Am., L.A., 1940-42, 46-76, Santa Monica, Calif., 1976—; dir. edn. Gemological Inst. Am., 1942, 46-49, asst. dir., 1950-52, exec. dir., 1952-83, pres., 1970-83, chmn. bd., 1983—, also author courses; editor Gem and Gemology, 1952—; hon. mem. rsch. staff L.A. Mus. Natural History, 1968—; U.S. dep. to Internat. Gem Conf., 1960, 64, 66, 68, 70, 72, 75, 77, 79, 81, 83, 85, 89; del. Pres.'d Conf. on Small Bus., 1957. Author: Handbook of Gem Identification, 12th edit, 1987, (with others) The Diamond Dictionary, 1960, 2d edit., 1977, (with Copeland) Jewelers Manual, 2d edit, 1967; numerous articles.; contbr. to Ency. Britannica Jr., Ency. Americana, McGraw-Hill Ency. of Sci. and Tech. Trustee Nat. Home Study Coun., 1983-88. Recipient Lifetime Achievement award Modern Jeweler's mag., 1985, award Internat. Soc. Appraisers, 1985, Spl. award Internat. Colored Stone Assn., 1984, Lifetime Achievement award Morris B. Zale, 1987; named Man of Yr., Consol. Jewelers Assn. Greater N.Y., 1984; named to Nat. Home Study Coun. Hall of Fame, 1991; Liddicoatite species of tourmaline group named for him. Fellow Mineral. Soc. Am., Geol. Soc. Am., Gem Assn. Gt. Britain (hon.); mem. AAAS, Am. Gem Soc. (supr. ednl. sessions ann. conclaves 1948-83, Shipley award 1976), Am. Gem Trade Assn. (hon.), Gem Assn. Australia (hon. v.p.), Gem Testing Lab. Gt. Britain (1st hon. life mem.), Bel Air Country Club (bd. dirs. 1980-83, Twenty-Four Karat Club (N.Y.C. and So. Calif.), Sigma Xi, Sigma Gamma Epsilon. Home: 1484 Allenford Ave Los Angeles CA 90049-3614 Office: Gemological Inst Am 5345 Armada Dr Carlsbad CA 92008

LIDDLE, JACQUELINE S., secondary education educator; b. Whittier, Calif., Mar. 4, 1954; d. Alma Ballantyne and Patricia (Hatch) Sonne; m. Gordon Allen Liddle, Apr. 13, 1979; 1 child, Colin Sonne. BA, Brigham Young U., 1978. Cert. secondary sch. tchr., Utah. English tchr. Brockbank Jr. H.S., Magna, Utah, 1981-88; tchr. English, Latin, broadcast journalism Cottonwood H.S., Salt Lake City, 1988—. Pres. Am. Fedn. Tchrs., Magna, 1985-86. Mem. Am. Classical League. Mormon. Home: 11573 Oakshire Lane Sandy UT 84092

LI DESSAU, KATHRYN DAIROH, product manager; b. Red Bank, N.J., Oct. 4, 1965; d. Tingye and Edith (Wu) Li; m. Daniel Stephen Dessau, Sept. 9, 1990. AB, Princeton U., 1987; MA, Stanford U., 1989, PhD, 1992. Product mgr. New Focus, Inc., Sunnyvale, Calif., 1992—. Contbr. articles to profl. jours. Recipient Fannie and John Hertz fellow Hertz Found., 1987-92, Grad. Rsch. Program for Women grant AT&T, 1987-92, Achievement award Coll. Scientists Found. scholarship, 1992. Mem. IEEE, Optical Soc. Am. Office: 1450 Oakleaf Cir Boulder CO 80304

LIDMAN, ROGER WAYNE, museum director; b. June 8, 1956; s. Arthur Arvid and Elna G. (Bernson) L.; m. Cynthia Louise Platt, May 26, 1988. BA in Anthropology, Ariz. State U., 1987, postgrad. studies, 1987-91. Mus. aide Pueblo Grande Mus., Phoenix, 1976-84, exhibit preparator, 1984-86, ops. coord., 1986-89, acting dir., 1989-90, dir., 1990—; vice chair Ariz. Archaeol. Adv. Commn., 1996. Mem. Am. Assn. Mus. (officer small mus. adminstr. com. 1993-94, treas. 1994-96), Mus. Assn. Ariz. (v.p. 1994-95, pres. 1995-96), Ctrl. Ariz. Mus. Assn. (v.p. 1992, pres. 1993-94, 95-96). Office: Pueblo Grande Mus 4619 E Washington St Phoenix AZ 85034-1909

LIDOFSKY, STEVEN DAVID, medical educator; b. Bklyn., Jan. 19, 1954; s. Leon Julian and Eleanor Helen (Liebman) L.; m. Elisabeth Tang Barfod, May 3, 1982; children: Benjamin Barfod, Anna Barfod. BA, Columbia U., 1975, PhD, 1980, MD, 1982. Bd. cert. in gastroenterology and internal medicine Am. Bd. Internal Medicine. Intern U. Colo., Denver, 1982-83, resident, 1983-85, chief med. resident, 1985-86; fellow in gastroenterology U. Calif., San Francisco, 1986-90, asst. prof. medicine, 1990—. Contbr. articles to profl. jours. Recipient Liver Scholar award Am. Liver Found., 1990-93, Rsch. award Am. Diabetes Assn., 1996. Mem. Am. Assn. for Study of Liver Diseases, Am. Fedn. for Clin. Rsch., Am. Gastroenterol. Assn. (Fiterman Found. Rsch. award 1994), Calif. Acad. Medicine, Western Soc. Clin. Investigation. Office: Univ Calif San Francisco GI Unit S357 San Francisco CA 94143-0538

LIEBAU, FREDERIC JACK, JR., investment manager; b. Palo Alto, Calif., Sept. 30, 1963; s. Frederic Jack and Charlene (Conrad) L. BA, Stanford U., 1985. Press aide Office of V.P., Washington, 1982; intern L.A. Times, 1983; analyst Capital Rsch. Co., L.A., 1984-86; ptnr., portfolio mgr. Primecap Mgmt. Co., Pasadena, Calif., 1986—; owner Liebau Farms, Bakersfeld, Calif. Home: 1014 Fairview Ave Apt 5 Arcadia CA 91007-7163 Office: Primecap Mgmt Co 225 S Lake Ave Pasadena CA 91101

LIEBERMAN, ANNE MARIE, financial executive; b. Jersey City, Aug. 28, 1946; d. Ralph Norman and Kathleen Celestine (Dooris) L.; m. Stephen Bruce Oshry, Sept. 21, 1986. BA, Sonoma State U., 1968; MLS, U. Calif., 1970, MBA, 1977. Cert. fin. planner; cert. fund specialist. V.p. Bank of Am., San Francisco, 1977-81, Lawrence A. Krause & Assocs., San Francisco, 1982-86; pres. Lieberman Assocs., San Rafael, Calif., 1986—. Author: Marketing Your Financial Planning Practice, 1986, Mastering Money, 1987; contbg. author: Financial Planning Can Make You Rich, 1987, The Expert's Guide to Managing a Successful Financial Planning Practice, 1988, About Your Future, 1988; columnist The Bus. Jour. Bd. dirs. Marin Gen. Found. Hosp., 1995. Mem. Inst. Cert. Fin. Planners (Fin. Writer's award 1986), Nat. Endowment for Fin. Edn. (bd. dirs.), Nat. Ctr. for Fin. Edn. (trustee 1994). Office: Lieberman Assocs Ste 116 100 Smith Ranch Rd San Rafael CA 94903-1900

LIEBERMAN, CAROLE ILENE, media psychiatrist, commentator, consultant. BA in Psychology with honors, SUNY, Stony Brook; MD, U. de Louvain, Belgium. Diplomate Am. Bd. Psychiatry and Neurology. Intern Mt. Sinai Hosp., Hartford, Conn., N.Y. Infirmary, N.Y.C.; resident in psychiatry NYU/Bellevue Psychiatry Hosp., N.Y.C.; ednl. cons. Met. State Hosp., L.A.; mem. assoc. staff Cedars Sinai Hosp./Thalians Mental Health Ctr., L.A.; pvt. practice Beverly Hills; asst. clin. prof. psychiatry UCLA/Neuropsychiat. Inst.; med. advisor/med. editor (cable TV programs) Your Mental Health-Informathon, Depression Informathon, The Nephronauts; lectr. in field; media psychiatrist; media personality/commentator; testified before Congress: House Judiciary Subcom. on Crime and Criminal Justice, 1992, House Subcom. on Nat. Security, Internat. Affairs and Criminal Justice, 1996. Author: Love Transplant: A High Risk Affairs of the Heart, 1990, Bad Boys: Why We Love Them, How to Live with Them, and When to Leave Them, 1997; columnist Show Biz Shrink Nat. Examiner, 1994-95; columnist, contbr. The Malibu Times, Malibu Surfside News, Ency. Britannica, 1990, Michael Jackson, The Magic and the Madness, Your View, 1991, Health Net News, 1992, Doctors Book of Home Remedies for Children, Glam Scam, Abuse of Discretion: The Rodney King Story; (TV scripts) Stranger Dangers, My House to Yours, Seeds of Success, What If It Were Real?, Feeling Female and Fine, Feelings Behind the Masks, America's Unwanted; contbr. articles to profl. jours., mags., and newspapers; host/prodr. (cable TV series) Real Talk about Reel Life, 1992, What You Always Wanted to Know about Psychiatry...But Were Afraid to Ask, The Seven Warning Signals of Mental Illness, (dramatic therapy) Psycho-Theatre; host Understanding Asthma, Lifetime TV, (weekly radio series) Life Perspectives with Dr. Carole Lieberman, 1990, Real Talk about Reel Life with Dr. Carole Lieberman, Sta. KWNK, 1991-92, Sta. KGIL, 1992, Media on Your Mind, Sta. KYPA, 1996-97; host (radio shows) Psychiatry and the Media, 1990-92, Hollywood Correspondent, 1993—; numerous TV, radio appearances and psychology call-in shows. Recipient Film Adv. Bd. Excellence award, 1990, Mayor Bradley commendation for script consulting, City of L.A., Emmy award, 1992, 93, Writers Guild of Am. West Outstanding Achievement for TV Children's Script, O'Henry prize for lit. N.Y. Mem. Am. Psychiat. Assn., So. Calif. Psychiat. Soc. (pub. info. com., co-chair), Malibu Med. Soc. (chair pub. info. com.), NYU/Bellevue Psychiat. Soc., Nat. Coalition on TV Violence (chair 1992-93, bd. dirs. 1990-93, spokesperson), AFTRA, Motion Picture Assn. Am. (press credentials), Acad. TV Arts and Scis., SAG.

LIEBERMAN, FREDRIC, ethnomusicologist, educator; b. N.Y.C., Mar. 1, 1940; s. Stanley and Bryna (Mason L.). MusB, U. Rochester, 1962; MA in Ethnomusicology, U. Hawaii, 1965; PhD in Music, UCLA, 1977; diploma in Electronics, Cleve. Inst. Electronics, 1973; cert. Inst. for Ednl. Mgmt., Harvard U., 1984. Asst. prof. music Brown U., Providence, 1968-75; assoc. prof. U. Wash., Seattle, 1975-83, chmn. dir. ethnomusicology, 1977-80, dir. sch. music, 1981-83; prof. U. Calif., Santa Cruz, 1983—, dir. divsn. arts, 1983-85, provost Porter Coll., 1983-85, chmn. dept. music, 1988-92; expert witness and forensic musicology cons. Virgin Records and others, 1991—; fieldworker, Taiwan and Japan, 1963-64, Sikkim, winter 1970, Madras, India, winters 1977, 78, 82, 83; mem. folk arts panel Nat. Endowment for Arts, 1977-80, internat. panel, 1979-80; panelist basic rsch. divsn. NEH, 1982-84, Calif. Arts Coun., 1993, Mass. Cultural Coun., 1995; fieldworker, presenter Smithsonian Instn. Festival Am. Folklife, 1978-82; reviewer Ctr. for Scholarly Comm. with China, 1979-91; exch. lectr. U. Warsaw, Poland, spring 1980; co-dir. summer seminar for coll. tchrs. NEH, 1977; dir. Am. Mus. Heritage Found., 1991-96. Author: Chinese Music: An Annotated Bibliography, 1970, 2d edit, 1979, A Chinese Zither Tutor: The Mei-An Ch-in-P'u, 1983, (with Mickey Hart) Drumming at the Edge of Magic, 1990, Planet Drum: A Celebration of Percussion and Rhythm, 1991, Lou Harrison: Composing a World, 1997, (with Leta Miller) Composing a Life: The World of Lou Morrison, 1997; editor: (with Fritz A Kuttner) Perspectives on Asian Music: Essays in Honor of Lawrence Picken, 1975; gen. editor Garland Bibliographies in Ethnomusicology, 1980-86; mem. editl. bd. Musica Asiatica, 1984—; contbr. numerous articles and revs. to profl. publs.; composer: Suite for Piano, 1964, Sonatina for Piano, 1964, Two Short String Quartets, 1966, Leaves of Brass (for brass quartet), 1967, Psalm 136: By the Rivers of Babylon (for chorus), 1971; records include China I: String Instruments, 1969, China II: Amoy Music, 1971, Music of Sikkim, 1975; ethnomusicology cons. 360 Degrees Prodns., 1988—; filmer, editor (with Michael Moore) Traditional Music and Dance of Sikkim, Parts I and II, 1976; prodr., dir., editor videotape Documenting Traditional Performance, 1978, South Indian Classical Music House Concert, 1994. Mem. exec. bd. Pub. Radio Sta. KRAB-FM, Seattle, 1977-78; mem. King County Arts Commn., Seattle, 1977-80. Grantee Nat. Endowment for the Arts, 1978, NEH, 1978, 80, 95-97, N.Y. State Regents fellow, 1958-62, East-West Ctr. fellow and travel grantee, 1962-65, UCLA Chancellor's tchg. fellow, 1965-69, John D. Rockefeller 3d Fund rsch. fellow, 1970-71. Mem. NARAS, Soc. for Ethnomusicology (editor Ethnomusicology 1977-81, nat. coun. 1970-72, 74-76, 78-81, 83-86), Soc. for Asian Music (editorial bd. Asian Music 1968-77, editor publs. series 1968-83), Assn. Rsch. Chinese Music (mem. adv. bd. 1987—), Coll. Music Soc. (nat. coun. 1973-75, exec. bd. 1974-75, 76-77), Conf. on Chinese Oral and Performing Lit. (exec. bd. 1971-74, 78-80), ASCAP, Internat. Coun. Traditional Music, Am. Musical Heritage Found. (treas. 1991-96), Phi Mu Alpha Sinfonia. Office: U Calif Porter Coll Santa Cruz CA 95064

LIEBHABER, MYRON I., allergist; b. Dec. 28, 1943. MD, U. Ariz., 1972. Allergist College Hosp., Santa Barbara, Calif.; asst. vis. clin. prof. UCLA. Office: Santa Barbara Med Found Clinic 215 Pesetas Ln Santa Barbara CA 93110-1416

LIEGEL, LEON HERMAN, soil scientist, research forester; b. Richland Center, Wis., Sept. 30, 1947; s. Luke Alois and Elizabeth Theresa (Dischler) L.; m. Beth Appleton, Mar. 26, 1978; children: Lea Noel, Lora Hope. BS, U. Wis., 1970; MS, SUNY, Syracuse, 1973; D, N.C. State U., 1981. Forester Soil Conservation Svc. USDA, Bayamon, P.R., 1970; rsch. forester Forest Svc. USDA, Rio Piedras, P.R., 1974-79, soil scientist, 1979-85; soil scientist Forest Svc. USDA, Corvallis, Oreg., 1985-91; rsch. forester Forest Svc. USDA, Corvallis, 1991—; natural resources specialist P.R. Dept. Natural Resources, San Juan, 1971-73; cons. U.S. Agy. for Internat. Devel., Haiti, 1982, Forest Svc., USDA, Venezuela, 1993; forest soils scientist EPA, Corvallis, 1985-91. Author: (with others) Forest Nursery Management in the Caribbean, 1987. Grantee NSF, 1970-71, Forest Svc. USDA, Raleigh, N.C., 1976-78, Man and the Biosphere Program, 1980, 93, U.S. Agy. for Internat. Devel., 1983-87, Oreg. State U., 1996, Sustainable Forestry Partnership, 1996. Mem. Soil Sci. Soc. Am., Soc. Am. Foresters (Mary's Peak chpt.), Am. Soc. Photogrammetry and Remote Sensing, Internat. Soc. Tropical Foresters. Office: Pacific NW Rsch Sta 3200 SW Jefferson Way Corvallis OR 97331-8550

LIEHR, ROBERT JOSEPH, private school educator; b. N.Y.C., Oct. 5, 1947; s. Arthur and Gloria Margaret (Sadlier) Carcanis. AA, Alpena (Mich.) C.C., 1967; BA, San Jose State U., 1969; postgrad., U. Calif., Santa Cruz, 1973, U. Santa Clara, 1974. Standard scondary edn. credential, Calif. Tchr. history Woodrow Wilson Jr. H.S., San Jose, Calif., 1970, Bret Harte Jr. H.S., San Jose, 1971-75, John Steinbeck Jr. H.S., San Jose, 1975-82; tchr. history, head dept. Gunderson H.S., San Jose, 1982-92; tchr., internat. baccalaureate instr. San Jose High Acad., 1992—; mem. Ctr. for Rsch. on Context Secondary Sch. Teaching, Stanford U., Palo Alto, Calif., 1988-92. With U.S. Army, 1970-76. Named Educator of Yr., Calif. League of H.S. Region 5, 1995-96. Mem. NEA, Calif. Tchrs. Assn., San Jose Tchrs. Assn., San Jose State U. Alumni Assn. Office: San Jose High Acad 275 N 24th St San Jose CA 95116-1109

LIGGINS, GEORGE LAWSON, microbiologist, diagnostic company executive; b. Roanoke, Va., June 19, 1937; m. Joyce Preston Liggins, Sept. 3, 1966; 1 child, George Lawson Jr. BA, Hampton U., 1962; cert. med. technician, Meharry Med. Sch., 1963; MPH, U. N.C., 1969; PhD, U. Va., Charlottesville, 1975. Med. technician Vets. Hosp., Hampton, Va., 1963-66; rsch. technician U. N.C. Med. Sch., Chapel Hill, 1966-69; postdoctoral fellow Scripps Clinic, La Jolla, Calif., 1975-76, Salk Inst., La Jolla, 1976-77; rsch. mgr. Hyland div. Baxter, Costa Mesa, Calif., 1977-78; R & D dir. diagnostics div. Baxter, Roundlake, Ill., 1978-83; pres., COO Internat. Immunology, Murrieta, Calif., 1983-86; chmn., CEO Bacton Assay Systems, Inc., San Marcos, Calif., 1986—; cons. Beckman Instruments, Inc., Brea, Calif., 1987-90, Paramax divsn. Baxter, Irvine, Calif., 1988-90, Scantibodies Lab., Santee, Calif., 1990-92; presenter in field; mem. virology study Cold Spring Harbor Lab., L.I., N.Y., 1974. Contbr. articles to profl. jours. Fellow NIH, 1975, Am. Cancer Soc., 1976. Mem. Am. Soc. Microbiology, Am. Assn. Clin. Chemistry, Van Slyke Soc. of Am. Assn. Clin. Chemistry (chmn. elect 1997. program chmn. San Diego Conf. Nucleic Acids 1996), Am. Heart Assn., Nat. Hampton Alumni Assn. (v.p. 1996—), Omega Psi Phi. Republican. Methodist. Office: Bacton Assay Systems Inc 772 N Twin Oaks Valley Rd San Marcos CA 92069-1773

LIGHT, IVAN HUBERT, sociology educator; b. Chgo., Nov. 3, 1941; s. Ivan Huber and Lily Ann (Schulz) L.; m. Leah Lazarovitz, June 15, 1966; children: Matthew, Nathaniel. BA, Havard, 1963; MA, PhD, U. Calif., 1969. Prof. U. Calif., L.A., 1969—. Author: Ethnic Enterprise in America, 1972, Immigrant Entrepreneurs, 1988, Cities in World Perspective, 1983, Immigration & Entrepreneurship, 1993, Race, Ethnicity and Entrepreneurship in Urban America, 1995. Pres. Claremont Dem. Club, 1993-97. Rsch. fellowship Nat. Sci. Found., Washington, 1976-79, 85-86, 88-89. Mem. Am. Assn. Univ. Profs. (pres. UCLA chpt. 1994-95), Am. Sociological Assn. (pres. 1969), Sierra Club (pres. 1971). Democrat. Episcopalian. Office: UCLA Dept Sociology 405 Hilgard Ave Los Angeles CA 90095

LIGHTELL, KENNETH RAY, education educator; b. Oak Park, Ill., Nov. 13, 1944; s. Ray and Mildred (Miller) L.; m. Charlotte Hawkins, Aug. 3, 1989. BA, North Ctrl. Coll., Naperville, Ill., 1966; grad. studies in edn., U. Mo., 1969; grad. studies in computers, Depaul U., 1983; MLA, Houston Bapt. U., 1995. Tchr., coach Roycemore Sch., Evanston, Ill., 1966-68; dir. middle sch. Bklyn. Friends Sch., 1969-81; dir. Olympia (Wash.) Ind. Sch., 1982-83; tchr., coach The Lexington (Ky.) Sch., 1984-88; prin. Charles Wright Acad., Tacoma, 1988-89; dir. of mid. sch. John Cooper Sch., Woodlands, Tex., 1989-92; headmaster St. James Episcopal Sch., Houston, 1993-94, The McClelland Sch., Pueblo, Colo., 1995—; owner, dir. Washinee Woods Camp, Taconic, Conn., 1975-81, Wilderness Adventures, Bklyn., 1970-75; pres., CEO S.L.K. Inc., N.Y.C., 1975-83. Editor: N.C.C. Spectrum, 1966; dir. Festival of the Arts, 1986. Pres. NCC Young Rep., Naperville, Ill., 1964-65; trustee Assn. Colo. Ind. Schs., Pueblo Day Nursery Found. Mem. B.P.O.E. Elks, Nat. Mid. Sch. Assn., Alpha Sigma Lambda. Home: 415 S Pin High Dr Pueblo West CO 81007

LIGHTSTONE, RONALD, lawyer; b. N.Y.C., Oct. 4, 1938; s. Charles and Pearl (Weisberg) L.; m. Nancy Lehrer, May 17, 1973; 1 child, Dana. AB, Columbia U., 1959; JD, NYU, 1962. Atty. CBS, N.Y.C., 1967-69; assoc. dir. bus. affairs CBS News, N.Y.C., 1969-70; atty. NBC, N.Y.C., 1970; assoc. gen. counsel Viacom Internat. Inc., N.Y.C., 1970-75; v.p., gen. counsel, sec. Viacom Internat. Inc., 1976-80; v.p. bus. affairs Viacom Entertainment Group Viacom Internat., Inc., 1980-82, v.p. corp. affairs, 1982-84, sr. v.p. corp. and legal affairs, 1984-87; exec. v.p. Spelling Entertainment Inc., L.A., 1988-91, CEO, 1991-93; chmn. Multimedia Labs. Inc., 1994—; bd. dirs. Starsight Telecast, Inc. Served to lt. USN, 1962-66. Mem. ABA (chmn. TV, cable and radio com.), Assn. Bar City N.Y., Fed. Communications Bar Assn.

LIGHTWOOD, CAROL WILSON, writer; b. Tacoma, Wash., Oct. 2, 1941; d. Harry Edward and Cora H. Wilson; m. Keith G. Lightwood (div. Dec. 1968); children: Miles Francis, Clive Harry. BA, Smith Coll., 1963. Writer various advt. agencies, 1968-82; v.p. Wakeman & DeForrest, Newport Beach, Calif., 1985-86; owner Lightwood & Ptnrs., Santa Barbara, Calif., 1986—. Author: Malibu, 1984; contbr. articles to profl. jours. Chair mus. coun. Long Beach Mus. Art, 1989; docent William O. Douglas Outdoor Classroom. Mem. Sierra Club, Sisters in Crime. Episcopalian.

LIKENS, JAMES DEAN, economics educator; b. Bakersfield, Calif., Sept. 12, 1937; s. Ernest LeRoy and Monnie Jewel (Thomas) L.; m. Janet Sue Pelton, Dec. 18, 1965 (div.); m. Karel Carnohan, June 4, 1988 (div.); children: John David, Janet Elizabeth. BA in Econs., U. Calif., Berkeley, 1960, MBA, 1961; PhD in Econs., U. Minn., 1970. Analyst Del Monte Corp., San Francisco, 1963; economist 3M Co., Mpls., 1968-71; asst. prof. econs. Pomona Coll., 1969-75, assoc. prof. econs., 1975-83, prof. econs., 1983-85, Morris B. Pendleton prof. econs., 1989—; vis. asst. prof. econs. U. Minn., 1970, 71, vis. assoc. prof., 1976-77; pres., dean Western CUNA Mgmt. Sch., Pomona Coll., 1975—; chmn. bd. 1st City Savs. Fed. Credit Union, 1978—; coord. So. Calif. Rsch. Coun., L.A., 1980-81, 84-85; mem. adv. coun. Western Corp. Fed. Credit Union, 1993—; cons. in field. Author: (with Joseph LaDou) Medicine and Money, 1976, Mexico and Southern California: Toward A New Partnership, 1981, Financing Quality Education in Southern California, 1985; contbr. articles to profl. jours. Served with USCG, 1961-67. Rsch. grantee HUD-DOT, Haynes Found., Filene Rsch. Inst. Mem. ABA, Am. Econ. Assn., Western Econ. Assn. Home: 725 W 10th St Claremont CA 91711-3719 Office: Pomona Coll Dept Econs Claremont CA 91711

LILLA, JAMES A., plastic surgeon; b. Comfrey, Minn., June 12, 1943. MD, Stanford U., 1969. Plastic surgeon Sutter Cmty. Hosp., Calif. Office: Hand Surg Assocs 1201 Alhambra Blvd Ste 410 Sacramento CA 95816-5243

LILLEGRAVEN, JASON ARTHUR, paleontologist, educator; b. Mankato, Minn., Oct. 11, 1938; s. Arthur Oscar and Agnes Mae (Eaton) L.; m. Bernice Ann Hines, Sept. 5, 1964 (div. Feb. 1983); children: Brita Anna, Ture Andrew; m. Linda Elizabeth Thompson, June 5, 1983. BA, Long Beach State Coll., 1962; MS, S.D. Sch. Mines and Tech., 1964; PhD, U. Kans., 1968. Professional geologist, Wyo. Postdoctoral fellow Dept. Paleontology U. Calif., Berkeley, 1968-69; from asst. prof. to prof. zoology San Diego State U., 1969-75; from assoc. prof. to prof. geology and zoology U. Wyo., Laramie, 1975—, assoc. dean Coll. Arts and Scis., 1984-85, temp. joint appointment dept. geography, 1986-87; program dir. NSF Systematic Biology, Washington, 1977-78; assoc. dean U. Wyo. Coll. Arts and Scis., 1984-85, temporary joint appointment Dept. Geography, 1986-87; U.S. sr. scientist Inst. for Paleontology Free U., Berlin, 1988-89; mem. adv. panel geology and paleontology program NSF, 1997—. Author, editor: Mesozoic Mammals the First Two Thirds of Mammalian History, 1979, Vertebrates, Phylogeny and Philosophy, 1986; mem. editl. bds. of Research and Exploration (Nat. Geographic Soc.), Jour. of Mammalian Evolution, Jour. of Vertebrate Paleontology; co-editor, contbr. Geology, Rocky Mountain Geology; contbr. articles to profl. jours. Recipient numerous rsch. grants NSF, 1970-97, George Duke Humphrey Disting. Faculty award, Humboldt prize. Mem. Am. Soc. Mammalogists, Am. Assn. Petroleum Geologists, Paleontol. Soc., Soc. Vertebrate Paleontology (pres. 1985-86), Linnean Soc. London, Soc. Mammalian Evolution, Sigma Xi.

LILLY, LUELLA JEAN, academic administrator; b. Newberg, Oreg., Aug. 23, 1937; d. David Hardy and Edith (Coleman) L. BS, Lewis and Clark Coll., 1959; postgrad., Portland State U., 1959-61; MS, U. Oreg., 1961; PhD, Tex. Woman's U., 1971; postgrad., various univs., 1959-72. Tchr. phys. edn. and health, dean girls Cen. Linn Jr.-Sr. High Sch., Halsey, Oreg., 1959-60; tchr. phys. edn. and health, swimming, tennis, golf coach Lake Oswego (Oreg.) High Sch., 1960-63; instr., intramural dir., coach Oreg. State U., Corvallis, 1963-64; instr., intercollegiate coach Am. River Coll., Sacramento, 1964-69; dir. women's phys. edn., athletics U. Nev., Reno, 1969-73, assoc. prof. phys. edn., 1971-76, dir. women's athletics, 1973-75, assoc. dir. athletics, 1975-76; dir. women's intercollegiate athletics U. Calif., Berkeley, 1976—; organizer, coach Lue's Aquatic Club, 1962-64; v.p. PAC -10 Conf., 1990-91. Author: An Overview of Body Mechanics, 1966, 3d rev. edit., 1969. Vol. instr. ARC, 1951; vol. Heart Fund and Easter Seal, 1974-76, Am. Heart Assn., 1991-95, ofcl. Spl. Olympics, 1975; mem. L.A. Citizens Olympic Com., 1984. Recipient Mayor Anne Rudin award Nat. Girls' and Women's Sports, 1993, Lifetime Sports award Bay Area Women's Sports Found., 1994, Golden Bear award Vol. of Yr., 1995; inducted Lewis and Clark Coll. Athletic Hall of Fame, 1988; named to U. Calif. First 125 Yrs. Women of Honor. Mem. AAHPER (life), AAUW, Nat. Soc. Profs., Nat. Assn. Coll. Women Athletic Adminstrs. (divsn. I-A women's steering com. 1991-92), Women's Athletic Caucus, Coun. Collegiate Women Athletics Adminstrs. (membership com. 1989-92), Western Soc. Phys. Edn. Coll. Women (membership com. 1971-74, program adv. com. 1972, exec. bd. 1972-75), Western Assn. Intercollegiate Athletics for Women (exec. bd. dirs. 1973-75, 79-82), Oreg. Girls' Swimming Coaches Assn. (pres. 1960, 63), Ctrl. Calif. Bd. Women Ofcls. (basketball chmn. 1968-69), Calif. Assn. Health, Phys. Edn. and Recreation (chmn.-elect jr. coll. sect. 1970), Nev. Bd. Women Ofcls. (chmn. bd., chmn. volleyball sect., chmn. basketball sect. 1969), No. Calif. Women's Intercollegiate Conf. (sec. 1970-71, basketball coord. 1970-71), No. Calif. Intercollegiate Athletic Conf. (volleyball coord. 1971-72), Nev. Assn. Health Phys. Edn. and Recreation (state chmn. 1974), No. Calif. Athletic Conf. (pres. 1979-82, sec. 1984—), Soroptimists Club (bd. dirs. 1988-95, v.p. 1989, 92-93, sec. 1993-95), Phi Kappa Phi, Theta Kappa. Home: 60 Margrave Ct Walnut Creek CA 94596-2511 Office: U Calif 177 Hearst Gym Berkeley CA 94720-4425

LILLY, MICHAEL ALEXANDER, lawyer, author; b. Honolulu, May 21, 1946; s. Percy Anthony Jr. and Virginia (Craig) L.; m. Kathryn I. Collins, Aug. 10, 1991; children: Michael Jr., Cary J., Laura B., Claire F., Winston W. AA, Menlo Coll., Menlo Park, Calif., 1966; BA, U. Calif., Santa Cruz, 1968; JD with honors, U. of Pacific, 1974. Bar: Calif. 1974, U.S. Dist. Ct. (no., so. and ea. dists.) Calif. 1974, U.S. Ct. Appeals (9th cir.) 1974, Hawaii 1975, U.S. Dist. Ct. Hawaii 1975, U.S. Ct. Appeals (D.C. cir.) 1975, U.S. Supreme Ct. 1978, U.S. Ct. Appeals (7th cir.) 1979. Atty. Pacific Legal Found., Sacramento, 1974-75; dep. atty. gen. State of Hawaii, Honolulu, 1975-79, 1st dep. atty. gen., 1981-84, atty. gen., 1984-85; ptnr. Feeley & Lilly, San Jose, Calif., 1979-81, Ning, Lilly & Jones, Honolulu, 1985—. Author: If You Die Tomorrow-A Layman's Guide to Estate Planning. Pres., dir. Diamond Head Theatre; Lt. USN, 1968-71, Vietnam; capt. USNR. Named hon. Ky. col. Mem. Nat. Assn. Attys. Gen., Hawaii Law Enforcement Ofcls. Assn., Navy Res. Assn. (pres. 14th dist. 1986-89), Navy League (nat. dir., contbg. editor Fore 'N Aft mag., dept. judge adv. to bd. Honolulu coun.), Outrigger Canoe Club. Home: 2769 Laniloa Rd Honolulu HI 96813-1041 Office: Ning Lilly & Jones 707 Richards St Ste 700 Honolulu HI 96813-4623 *Personal philosophy: Always do what you are afraid to do. Never give up. Forgive your enemies.*

LILLY-HERSLEY, JANE ANNE FEELEY, nursing researcher; b. Palo Alto, Calif., May 31, 1947; d. Daniel Morris Sr. and Suzanne (Agnew) Feeley; children: Cary Jane, Laura Blachree, Claire Foale; m. Dennis C. Hersley, Jan. 16, 1993. BS, U. Oreg., 1968; student, U. Hawaii, 1970; BSN, RN, Sacramento City Coll., 1975. Cert. ACLS, BCLS. Staff and charge nurse, acute rehab. Santa Clara Valley Med. Ctr., San Jose, Calif., staff nurse, surg. ICU and trauma unit; clin. project leader mycophenolate mofetil program team Syntex Rsch., Palo Alto; pres. Clin. Rsch. Consultation, Santa Cruz, Calif. Co-founder, CFO and dir. scientific rsch. Citizens United Responsible Environmentalism, Inc., CURE (internat. non-profit edn./rsch. orgn.). Mem. AACN.

LIM, ALAN YOUNG, plastic surgeon; b. St. Louis, Apr. 11, 1953. MD, U. Calif., San Diego, 1979. Plastic surgeon Kaiser-Permanente, Sacramento, Calif.; asst. clin. prof. U. Calif. Davis. Office: Plastic Surg 2025 Morse Ave Sacramento CA 95825-2115

LIM, KENNETH TING, interactive multimedia analyst; b. Tucson, Mar. 29, 1958; m. Nancy Ann Wong, Aug. 10, 1985; children: Brian Christopher, Jordan Kendall, Steven Marshall. BS in Bus. Mgmt. and Mktg., San Jose State U., 1980, MS in cybernetic systems, 1980. Rsch. assoc. Search for Extra-Terrestrial Intelligence NASA Ames Rsch. Ctr., Mountain View, Calif., 1975-77; industry analyst personal computers Dataquest, Inc., San Jose, Calif., 1981-86; mgr. market intelligence Apple Computer, Inc., Cupertino, Calif., 1986-90, mgr. corp. tech. devel., chief futurist, 1991-93; chmn., chief futurist The CyberMedia Group, Cupertino, 1994—; chmn. U.S. Microcomputer Statistics Consortium, Washington, 1992-93, mem. exec. com., 1990-93; mem. Computer Market Analysis Group, 1991-93. Author: (with others) Demistifying Multimedia, 1993, New Media Industry: Report from Hakone Forum, 1993, Digital Money: The New Era of Internet Commerce, 1996. Mem. Internat. Interactive Comm. Soc., Computer Game Devels.' Assn., Multimedia Devels.' Group. Home and Office: The CyberMedia Group 10410 San Fernando Ave Cupertino CA 95014-2867

LIM, LARRY KAY, university official; b. Santa Maria, Calif., July 4, 1948; s. Koonwah and Nancy (Yao) L.; m. Louise A. Simon, Aug. 15, 1988. BA, UCLA, 1970, teaching cert., 1971. Asst. engr. Force Ltd., L.A., 1969; teaching asst. UCLA, 1970-71; tchr. L.A. Sch. Dist., 1971-82; dir. minority programs Sch. Engring., U. So. Calif., L.A., 1979—; presenter minority math.-based intervention symposium U. D.C., Washington, 1988. Newsletter editor, 1981-92. Bd. dirs. Developing Ednl. Studies for Hispanics, L.A., 1983-88. Named Dir. of Yr., Math., Engring., Sci. Achievement Ctr. Adv. Bd., 1986, 91, 92. Mem. Nat. Assn. Pre-Coll. Dirs., Nat. Assn. Minority Engring. Program Adminstr., Lotus/West Club (pres. 1977-83). Office: U So Calif Sch Engring OHE 104 Los Angeles CA 90089-1455

LIM, SALLY-JANE, insurance consultant; b. Manila; came to U.S., 1990; d. Teddy and Sonia (Yii) L.; children: Robin Michael, Rodney Jovin, Romelle Gavin Lim Velasco. BA, BS in Commerce magna cum laude, Coll. of Holy Spirit, Manila. CPA, The Philippines. Treas. contr. Ky. Fried Chicken, Makati, Philippines, 1968-73; ins. rep. Insular Life Assurance Co., Makati, 1972-82; project analyst Pvt. Devel. Corp. of Philippines, Makati, 1972-78; account exec. Genbancor Devel. Corp., Makati, 1978-80; risk mgr. Filcapital Devel. Corp., Makati, 1978-82; pres., gen. mgr., ins. broker Sally-Jane Multiline Insce., Inc., Makati, 1978-90; real estate broker Sally-Jane Realty, Inc., Manila, 1980-90; ins. rep. Sun Life of Can./AIU (Philippines) AFIA/CIGNA, Makati, 1982-91; rep. Prudential Ins. & Fin. Svcs., Prudential Property & Casualty/Ins., Co. PruCare of Calif.; registered rep. Pruco Securities Corp. L.A. Dist., South Pasadena, Calif., 1990-92; Asian Pacific Dist. Pruco Securities Corp., South Pasadena, Calif., 1992—. Recipient Young Achiever award Young Achiever Found., Quezon City, Philippines, 1988, Golden Scroll award Philippine Ednl. Youth Devel., Inc., Quezon City, 1988, Young Famous Celebrity Mother's award Golden Mother/Father Found., Quezon City, 1990, Recognition of Excellence cert. San Gabriel Valley YWCA, 1992, Most Outstanding Ins. Exec. of The Philippines bronze trophy Consumers' Union of the Philippines, Manila, 1983, 88, Ten Outstanding Profl. Svc. award Achievement Rsch. Soc., Manila, 1988, numerous others. Fellow, Life Underwriters Tng. Coun.; mem. Million Dollar Round Table (Life mem.) Nat. Assn. Life Underwriters, Calif. Assn. Life Underwriters, Arcadia C. of C., Asian Bus. Assn., Filipino-Am. C. of C., Greater Pasadena Assn. Life Underwriters, Chinese C. of C. (bd. dirs. L.A. 1992—). Home: 1006 Royal Oaks Dr # A Monrovia CA 91016-3737 Office: Prudential of Am Penthouse 1255 Corporate Center Dr Monterey Park CA 91754-7609

LIM, SHIRLEY GEOK LIN, English language educator, author; b. Malacca, Malaysia, Dec. 27, 1944; came to U.S., 1969; d. Chin Som and Chye Neo; m. Charles Bazerman, Nov. 1972; 1 child, Gershom Kean. BA with 1st class honors, U. Malaya, 1967, postgrad., 1967-69; MA, Brandeis U., 1971, PhD, 1973. Tchg. fellow Queens Coll. CUNY, Flushing, 1972-73; asst. prof. Hostos C.C. CUNY, Bronx, 1973-76; assoc. prof. Westchester C.C. SUNY, Valhalla, 1976-90; prof. Asian Am. studies U. Calif., Santa Barbara, 1990-93, prof. women's studies and English, 1990—; part-time lectr. U. Malaya, Kuala Lumpur, 1967-69, U. Sains, 1974; vis. fellow Nat. U. of Singapore, 1982, writer in residence, 1985; Asia Found. fellow Ctr. for Advanced Studies, 1989; Mellon fellow Grad. Ctr. CUNY, 1983, 87; minority discourses fellow Interdisciplinary Rsch. Ctr. U. Calif., Irvine, 1993; writer in residence East-West Ctr., Honolulu, 1988; Fulbright Disting. Lectureship, Singapore, 1996; presenter workshops in field. Author: Crossing the Peninsula and Other Poems, 1980 (Commonwealth Poetry prize 1980), Another Country and Other Stories, 1982, No Man's Grove, 1985, Modern Secrets: New and Selected Poems, 1989, Nationalism and Literature: English-Language Writers from the Philippines and Singapore, 1993, Monsoon History, 1994, Writing South/East Asia in English, 1994, Life's Mysteries, 1995, Among the White Moon Faces: An Asian American Memoir of Homelands, 1996, Two Dreams, 1997; editor: Approaches to Teaching Kingston's "The Woman Warrior", 1991; co-editor: Reading Asian-American Literatures, 1992, One World of Literature, 1992; co-editor, author: Introduction: The Forbidden Stitch: An Asian American Women's Anthology, 1989 (Am. Book award 1989). Mem. N.Y. Gov.'s Commn. on Librs., 1990. Wein internat. fellow, 1969-72; Fulbright scholar, 1969-72; grantee NEH, 1978, 87, Westchester Found., 1987. Mem. MLA (exec. com. divsn. Lit. in English Other Than Brit. and Am. 1986-90, founder discussion group on Asian Am. lit. 1985, chair exec. com. 1989, exec. com. divsn. ethnic lit. 1993—, chair com. langs. and lit. of the U.S. 1995), Internat. PEN, Am. Studies Assn. (programs com. 1994, chair minority scholars com. 1995—), Assn. Asian Am. Studies, Nat. Women's Studies Assn., Multi-Ethnic Lit. of U.S., Coord. Coun. Lit. Mags. (bd. dirs. 1983-88, chair 1986-87, exec. coun. 1987-88), Assn. Commonwealth Langs. and Lits. Office: U Calif Dept of English Santa Barbara CA 93106

LIMA, SAMUEL MENDONCA, probation officer, martial arts instructor; b. Rio de Janeiro, Mar. 12, 1956; s. Leonel Costa and Ruth Mendonca Lima; m. Sharon Kunkel, Jan. 1, 1981; children: Celina K., Cherylyn K. BA, Patten Coll., 1985; postgrad., Calif. State U., Hayward, 1986-90. Patrol officer Mills Coll., Oakland, Calif., 1984-87; dir. student activities Patten Coll., Oakland, 1985-87; martial arts instr., owner Jun Fan Muay Thai USA, Dublin, Calif., 1986-96; probation officer San Mateo County, San Mateo, Calif., 1990—; pvt. investigator, 1996—; pres. Intelnet Security and Detective Agy. Inc., Daly City, Calif., 1997—; cons., advisor Muay Thay USA, Springfield, Mo., 1993-96; instr. Internat. Inst. Exec. Protection, San Jose, 1993-96; firearms instr. NRA, 1997—. Author: Improvised Weapons, 1992; author, demonstrator: (video) Explosive Muay Thay, 1995; maker martial arts dummy, 1996. Student advisor Upward Bound, Oakland, 1986-88. Recipient Tao of Fist, Shorinryu Karate, Oakland, 1994. Mem. Police Martial Arts Assn., Livermore Rod/Gun Club. Republican. Office: San Mateo County Probation 2415 University Ave East Palo Alto CA 94303-1148

LIN, DORIS BISHYNG, optometrist; b. Tainan, Taiwan, Apr. 23, 1947; came to U.S., 1971; d. Chung-Lee and Shou-Ching Shieh; m. Wunan Lin, July 10, 1971. BS in Physics, U. Calif., Berkely, 1965; MS, U. Calif. Berkeley, 1974, OD, 1976, PhD, 1993. Cert. tchr., Calif. Optometrist specializing in contact lens, low vision and visual tng., Castro Valley, Calif., 1976—; pub. health adv. bd. mem. Alameda County, Calif., 1993—. Co-chair Pacific Rim Internat. com. U. Calif., Berkeley, 1994—; bd. dirs. Asian Am. Together, Castro Valley, Calif. Mem. Am. Optometrists Assn., Calif. Optometrists Assn., Alameda/Contra Costa Counties Optometry Soc., Rotary Internat. Office: 3550 Castro Valley Blvd Castro Valley CA 94546-4402

LIN, HENRY C., gastroenterologist, researcher; b. Taiwan, China, Mar. 10, 1958; came to U.S., 1969; s. Titus S.M. and Helen J.Y. (Jin) L.; m. Susan Kao, Nov. 18, 1989; children: Jessica Yoon-en, Jaimie Yoon-Xin. BS magna cum laude, CCNY, 1980; MD cum laude, SUNY, Syracuse, 1982. Diplomate Am. Bd. Internal Medicine, Am. Bd. Gastroenterology. Intern Harbor-UCLA Med. Ctr., Torrance, 1982-83, resident, 1983-85; fellow integrated tng. program UCLA, 1985-87; assoc. investigator Sepulveda (Calif.) VA Med. Ctr., 1987-90; dir. sect. nutrition Cedars-Sinai Med. Ctr., L.A., 1990—, dir. GI motility program, 1991—. Fellow ACP, Am. Coll. Nutrition; mem. Am. Gastroenterology Assn., Am. Soc. Parenteral & Enteral Nutrition, Am. Fedn. Clin. Rsch., Am. Motility Soc. Office: Cedars Sinai Med Ctr 7511/GI Unit 8700 Beverly Blvd Los Angeles CA 90048-1804

LIN, HUN-CHI, molecular biologist; b. Yun-Lin, Taiwan, Republic of China, Nov. 8, 1953; came to U.S., 1980; s. Shun-Tau and Yu-Hwa (Tsai) L.; m. Shau-Ping Lei, July 6, 1980; children: Victoria, Benita. BS, Nat. Taiwan U., Taipei, 1976, MS, 1978; PhD, UCLA, 1984. Teaching asst. UCLA, 1983; rsch. scientist Ingene, Santa Monica, Calif., 1984-85, project dir., 1985-87, prin. investigator, 1985-87; rsch. dir. Sinogen, L.A., 1987; pres., dir. rsch. Trigen, Inc./Splty. Lab., Inc., Santa Monica, 1987—, assoc. rsch. dir., 1991-96, dir. clin. trials, 1995—. Contbr. articles to profl. jours. Lt. Chinese Army, 1978-80. Mem. Am. Soc. Microbiology, Drug Info. Assn. Office: Splty Lab Inc 2211 Michigan Ave Santa Monica CA 90404-3905

LIN, LAWRENCE SHUH LIANG, accountant; b. China, July 5, 1938; s. Wan Chow and Inn Chi Lin; came to U.S., 1967, naturalized, 1979; LLB, Soochow U., 1963; MBA, Pepperdine U., 1970; m. Grace Yu, July 31, 1966; children: Ray, Lester. Spl. project acctg. supr. Motown Records, Hollywood, Calif., 1975; chief acct. Elektra/Asylum/Nonesuch Records, Beverly Hills, Calif., 1976-77, United Artists Music Pub. Group, Hollywood, 1977-80; contr.-adminstr. Pasadena (Calif.) Guidance Clinics (name now Pacific Clinics, 1980-86; v.p. Stew Kettle Corp., L.A., 1986-87; pres. LKL Corp., L.A., 1987-89; internat. fin. cons. Pacific Capital Mgmt., Alhambra, Calif., 1989—. Mem. Inst. Mgmt. Accts., Nat. Assn. Security Dealers. Baptist. Office: Pacific Capital Mgmt 670 Monterey Pass Rd Monterey Park CA 91754-2419

LIN, TAO, software engineer; b. Shanghai, Aug. 6, 1958; came to U.S., 1986; s. Zheng-hui Lin and Wei-jing Wu; m. Ping Kuo, Aug. 18, 1989; children: Jason, Jessie. BS, East China Normal U., Shanghai, 1982; MS, Tohoku U., Sendai, Japan, 1985; PhD, Tohoku U., 1990. Technician Dongtong Electronics Inc., Shanghai, 1977-78; rsch. asst. Electronics Rsch. Lab U. Calif., Berkeley, 1986-87, postgrad. researcher, 1987-88; applications engr. Integrated Device Technology Inc., Santa Clara, Calif., 1988-90; sr. applications engr. Sierra Semiconductor Corp., San Jose, Calif., 1990-91; applications mgr. Sierra Semicondr. Corp., San Jose, Calif., 1991-92, software engring. mgr., 1992-94; strategic planning and applications engring. mgr. IC Works Inc., San Jose, 1994-95; sr. mem. tech. staff NeoMagic Corp., Santa Clara, 1995—. Contbr. articles to profl. jours. Mem. IEEE. Home: 3552 Rockett Dr Fremont CA 94538-3425 Office: NeoMagic Corp 3260 Jay St Santa Clara CA 95054

LIN, THOMAS WEN-SHYOUNG, accounting educator, researcher, consultant; b. Taichung, Republic of China, June 3, 1944; came to U.S., 1970; s. Ju-chin and Shao-chin (Tseng) L.; m. Angela Kuei-fong Hou, May 19, 1969; children: William Margaret. BA in Bus. Adminstrn., Nat. Taiwan U., Taipei, 1966; MBA, Nat. Chengchi U., Taipei, 1970; MS in Acctg. and Info. Systems, UCLA, 1971; PhD in Acctg., Ohio State U., 1975. Cert. mgmt. acct., Calif. Internal auditor Formosa Plastics Group, Taipei, 1967-69, spl. asst. to the pres., 1969-70; asst. prof. U. So. Calif., L.A., 1975-80, assoc. prof., 1980-86, prof. acctg., 1986-90, acctg. cir. prof., 1990—, dir. doctoral studies acctg., 1982-86; cons. Intex Plastics, Inc., Long Beach, Calif., 1979-81, Peat, Marwick, Mitchell, L.A., 1982, City of Chino, Calif., 1982. Author: Planning and Control for Data Processing, 1984, Use of Mathematical Models, 1986, Advanced Auditing, 1988, Using Accounting Information in Business Planning, Product Costing, and Auditing, 1991; mem. editl. bd. Internat. Jour. Bus., Jour. Acctg. Edn., Quarterly Jour. Bus. and Econs., Am. Jour. Math. and Mgmt. Scis., Chinese Acctg. Rev., Hong Kong Jour. Bus. Mgmt., 1988—; contbr. articles to profl. jours. Bd. dirs. U. So. Calif. Acctg. Circle, L.A., Taiwan Benevolent Assn. Am., Washington, 1986; pres. Taiwan Benevolent Assn. Calif., L.A., 1986-88. 2d lt. China Army, 1966-67. Recipient cert. appreciation L.A. City Mayor Tom Bradley, 1988, Congressman Martinez award for outstanding community svc., 1988; Faculty Rsch. scholar U. So. Calif. Bus. Sch., L.A., 1984-87. Mem. Am. Acctg. Assn. (bd. dirs. 1986-88), Chinese Acctg. Profs. N.Am. (founding pres. 1976-80), Inst. Cert. Mgmt. Accts. (cert. of disting. performance 1978), Inst. Mgmt. Accts. (coord. 1984—, Author's trophy 1978, 79, 81, 87), EDP Auditor Assn., Inst. Mgmt. Scis. Republican. Baptist. Home: PO Box 8023 Rowland Heights CA 91748-0023 Office: U So Calif Leventhal Sch Acctg Univ Park ACC 109 Los Angeles CA 90089-1421

LINAHON, JAMES JOSEPH, music educator, musician; b. Mason City, Iowa, Sept. 6, 1951; s. Robert Eugene and Teresa Darlene (Mulaney) L.; m. Kathryn Anne Tull, Apr. 12, 1987; children: Michael, Katie, Joseph. BA in Music, U. No. Iowa, 1973; M in Music Edn., North Tex. State U., 1975. Assoc. dir. jazz studies Chaffey Coll., Rancho Cucamonga, Calif., 1975-80; prof. music, dir. jazz studies Fullerton (Calif.) Coll., 1980—; cons. U. No. Colo., U. Alaska, U. Calif., U. Ariz., U. Hawaii, DePaul U., Chgo., U. So. Calif., Wash. State U., S.D. State U., 1978—; cons., artist Playboy Jazz Festival, Reno Internat. Jazz Festival, Queen Mary Jazz Festival, Disneyland, All That Jazz; record producer MCA, Warner Bros, ABC, Columbia; performer for Frank Sinatra, Henry Mancini, Beverly Sills, Ella Fitzgerald, Sarah Vaughan, Tony Bennett, Merv Griffin; U.S. Jazz amb., worldwide, 1996. Artist, producer: (jazz compact disc) Time Tripping, 1984 (Album of Yr. Downbeat Mag., 1987), (classical compact disc) Gradus Ad Parnassum, 1990, (compact disk) Season of Our Lives, 1994; composer: (musical composition) Snow Wisp, 1986 (finalist Columbia Artists search). Performer, producer Theatre Palisades, Pacific Palisades, Calif., 1986, Claremont (Calif.) Community Found., 1992; guest soloist Claremont (Calif.) Symphony Orch., 1991. Recipient Major Landers scholarship Iowa Band Master's Assn., Iowa, 1969; named Dee Bee Album of Yr. (5 awards) Downbeat Mag., 1978-87. Mem. NARAS (Oustanding Recordings 1989), Internat. Assn. Jazz Educators (higher edn. rep. 1992-93), Internat. Trumpet Guild, Internat. Assn. Jazz Edn., Am. Soc. Composers, Authors and Publishers, Nat. Assn. Coll. Wind and Percussion Instrs., Am. Fedn. Musicians. Roman Catholic. Home: 560 W 10th St Claremont CA 91711-3714 Office: Fullerton College 321 E Chapman Ave Fullerton CA 92832-2011

LINAWEAVER, WALTER ELLSWORTH, JR., physician; b. San Pedro, Calif., Oct. 16, 1928; s. Walter Ellsworth and Catherine Breathed (Bridges) L.; m. Lydia Anne Whitlock, Oct. 6, 1957; children: Catherine Ann, Nancy Alyn, Walter E. III. BA cum laude, Pomona Coll., 1952; MD, U. Rochester, 1956. Diplomate Am. Bd. Allergy and Immunology, Am. Bd. Pediatrics, Am. Bd. Pediatric Allergy. Intern pediatrics Med. Ctr. U. Rochester, N.Y., 1956-57, resident pediatrics Med. Ctr., 1958-59; asst. resident pediatrics Med. Ctr. UCLA, 1957-58; fellow allergy and immunology Med. Ctr. U. Colo., Denver, 1959-61, instr. pediatrics Sch. Medicine, 1961; pvt. practice Riverside (Calif.) Med. Clinic, 1962—; asst. clin. prof. pediatrics Loma Lida U. Med. Sch., 1965—. Elder Presbyn. Ch. Staff sgt. U.S. Army, 1946-48. Inducted into Athletic Hall of Fame Pomona Coll., Claremont, Calif., 1979. Fellow Am. Acad. Allergy, Asthma & Immunology, Am. Acad. Pediat., Southwestern Pediat. Soc. (emeritus, v.p. 1978), L.A. Acad. Medicine; mem. Riverside County Med. Soc. (councillor), Riverside County Heart Assn. Republican. Home: 1296 Tiger Tail Dr Riverside CA 92506-5475 Office: Riverside Med Clinic 3660 Arlington Ave Riverside CA 92506-3912

LINCOLN, ALEXANDER, III, financier, lawyer, private investor; b. Boston, Dec. 1, 1943; s. Alexander Jr. and Elizabeth (Kitchel) L.; m. Isabel Fawcett Ross, Dec. 27, 1969. BA, Denver U., 1967; JD, Boston U., 1971. Bar: Colo. 1972, U.S. Ct. Appeals (10th cir.) 1972, U.S. Supreme Ct. 1979. Atty. Dist. Ct. Denver, 1973-78, Colo. Ct. Appeals, Denver, 1978-80; mng. ptnr. Alexander Lincoln & Co., Denver, 1980—. Mem. Colo. Bar Assn. (fin. com. 1975-76), Colo. Soc. Mayflower Descendants (life, bd. dirs. 1975—), Order of Founders and Patriots (life). Republican. Home and Office: 121 S Dexter St Denver CO 80222-1052

LINCOLN, SANDRA ELEANOR, chemistry educator; b. Holyoke, Mass., Mar. 11, 1939; d. Edwin Stanley and Evelyn Ida (Mackie) L. BA magna cum laude, Smith Coll., 1960; MSChem, Marquette U., 1970; PhD in Inorganic Chemistry, SUNY, Stony Brook, 1982. Tchr., prin. Oak Knoll Sch., Summit, N.J., 1964-74; tchr. Holy Child High Sch., Waukegan, Ill., 1974-76; lectr. chemistry, dir. fin. aid Rosemont (Pa.) Coll., 1976-78; teaching asst. SUNY, Stony Brook, 1978-82; assoc. prof. chemistry U. Portland, Oreg., 1982-96; prof. chemistry U. Portland, 1997—. Contbr. articles to profl. jours. Cath. sister Soc. Holy Child Jesus, 1963—. Recipient Pres.'s award for Teaching, SUNY, Stony Brook, 1981; Burlington No. Outstanding scholar, 1987. Mem. Am. Chem. Soc., Phi Beta Kappa, Sigma Xi. Democrat. Home: 5431 N Strong St Portland OR 97203-5711 Office: U Portland 5000 N Willamette Blvd Portland OR 97203-5743

LIND, LEVI ROBERT, classics educator, author; b. Trenton, N.J., July 29, 1906; s. John Edward and Lydia (Nieminen) L.; m. Elena Marchant y Riquelme, Aug. 25, 1929; 1 dau., Rosa Elena (Mrs. D.C. Fuchs). B.A., U. Ill., 1929, M.A., 1932, Ph.D., 1936. Asst. prof., assoc. prof. classics Wabash Coll., Crawfordsville, Ind., 1929-40; successively asst. prof., assoc. prof., prof., Univ. Disting. prof. classics U. Kans., Lawrence, 1940—; chmn. dept. U. Kans., 1940-64; vis. research prof. history medicine UCLA, summer 1959, U. Ill., summer 1937, 45; sec. Am. Com. on Medieval Latin Dictionary, UAI, 1937-41; U. Kans. rep. to adv. council Am. Acad. in Rome; pres.

Central Labor Union, AFL, Lawrence, 1948-49. Author: Medieval Latin Studies: Their Nature and Possibilities, 1941, The Vita Sancti Malchi of Reginald of Canterbury: a critical edition, 1942, The Epitome of Andreas Vesalius, 1949, Lyric Poetry of the Italian Renaissance: an Anthology With Verse Translations, 1954, Ten Greek Plays in Contemporary Translations, 1957, Latin Poetry in Verse Translation, 1957, Ecclesiale by Alexander of Villa Dei, 1958, Berengario da Carpi, A Short Introduction to Anatomy, 1959, Vergil's Aeneid, 1963, Aldrovandi on Chickens: The Ornithology of Ulisse Aldrovandi (1600), 1963, Epitaph for Poets and Other Poems, 1966, Twentieth Century Italian Poetry: a Bilingual Anthology, 1974, Johann Wolfgang von Goethe, Roman Elegies and Venetian Epigrams, 1974, Studies in Pre-Vesalian Anatomy, 1975, Ovid, Tristia, 1975, André Chénier, Elegies and Camille, 1978, Gabriele Zerbi, Gerontocomia: On the Care of the Aged and Maximianus, Elegies on Old Age and Love, 1988, The Letters of Giovanni Garzoni: Bolognese Humanist and Physician (1419-1505), 1992, Berengario da Carpi, On Fracture of the Skull or Cranium, 1990, An Epitaph Years After, 1990; editor: Problemata Varia Anatomica, 1968. Fulbright research grantee Rome, Italy, 1954-55; NIH grantee in history of medicine, 1960-63; Am. Council Learned Socs. fellow, 1940. Mem. Am. Philol. Assn., Classical Assn. Middle West and South, Medieval Acad. Am., Soc. Ancient Medicine, Phi Beta Kappa (com. qualifications united chpts. 1955-61). Club: Discussion. Home: 4817 Baja Court NE Albuquerque NM 87111

LIND, LYNN HUNTER, reporter; b. Artesia, N.Mex., Mar. 4, 1950; d. William Samuel and Betty (Angle) H. BS in Journalism, Ea. N.Mex. U., 1972. Reporter Roswell (N.Mex.) Daily Record, 1972-75; reporter, news editor Clovis (N.Mex.) News-Jour., 1978-80; mng. editor The Pampa (Tex.) News, 1980-82; reporter, news editor Artesia Daily Press, 1983-96; reporter Deming (N.Mex.) Headlight, 1996—. Contbr. articles to profl. jours. Founder Teensafe, Inc. Recipient Nat. Citation, AP Mng. Editors Assn., 1978, 1st pl. AP Mng. Editors N.Mex., 1987, E.H. Shaffer award N.Mex. Press Assn., 1st pl. news writing, 1996. Home: RR 2 Box 117A Deming NM 88030 Office: Deming Headlight PO Box 881 Deming NM 88030

LIND, TERRIE LEE, social services administrator; b. Spokane, Wash., June 5, 1948; d. Clifford and Edna Mae (Allenbach) Presnell; m. Stephen George Lind, Aug. 29, 1970 (div. Mar. 1981); children: Erica Rachel, Reid Christopher. BA cum laude, Wash. State U., 1970, MA, 1971. Cert. tchr., Wash., Ariz.; cert. in Porch Index Communicative Ability. Specialist communication disorders U. Tex., Houston, 1971-73; clin. supr. The Battin Clinic, Houston, 1973-76; specialist communication disorders Spokane Guilds Sch., 1980-82; program coord. Fresno (Calif.) Community Hosp., 1982-87; program adminstr. Advantage 65* sr. access program Health Dimensions, Inc., San Jose, Calif., 1987-90; dir. patient svcs. San Jose Med. Ctr., 1990-92; v.p. comty. svcs. Planned Parenthood Mar Monte, San Jose, 1992—; cons. Adolescent Chem. Dependency Unit, Fresno, 1984-87. Mem. AAUW (officer 1976-82), Am. Speech and Hearing Assn. (cert., Continuing Edn. award 1985-86), Wash. Speech and Hearing Assn. (co-chmn. state conv. program com. 1981-82), Soc. Consumer Affairs Profls. in Bus., Wash. State U. Alumni Assn. Home: 1717 Don Ave San Jose CA 95124-1905 Office: Planned Parenthood 1691 The Alameda San Jose CA 95126-2203

LINDAUER, JOHN HOWARD, II, newspaper publisher; b. Montclair, N.J., Nov. 20, 1937; s. John Howard and Louise (Platts) L.; m. Jacqueline Shelly, Sept. 2, 1960 (dec. 1992); children: Susan, John Howard; m. Dorothy Oremus, Sept. 1995. BS, Ariz. State U., 1960; PhD in Econs., Okla. State U., 1964. Asst. prof. econs. Occidental Coll., L.A., 1964-66; assoc. prof. Claremont (Calif.) Men's Coll. and Grad Sch., 1966-70, prof., chmn. econs., 1970-74; dean Coll. Bus. Murray (Ky.) State U., 1974-76; chancellor U. Alaska, Anchorage, 1976-78; commr. Alaska Pipeline, Anchorage, 1978; pres., chief exec. officer Alaska Industry and Energy Corp., Anchorage, 1978—; mem. Alaska Ho. of Reps., 1983-84; Rep. candidate for gov., 1990; bd. dirs. various cos.; owner various newspapers and radio sta.; cons. econ. policy and devel. U.S. Congress; cons. econs. U.S. corps; mem. AF Adv. Bd. Author: Macroeconomics, 1968, 71, 76, Economics: The Modern View, 1977, Land Taxation and the Indian Economic Development, 1979; editor Macroeconomic Readings; contbr. articles to profl. jours. Co-founder, vice chmn. Group against Smog Pollution, 1968; pres. So. Calif. Econ. Assn., 1974. With Army U.S., 1955-57. Fulbright prof., India, 1972; vis. prof. U. Sussex, Eng., 1972-73. Home: 3933 Geneva Pl Anchorage AK 99508-5055

LINDBECK, STEPHEN EMANUEL, state agency administrator; b. Tacoma, Wash., Jan. 14, 1955; s. Edwin Emanuel and Mary Ann (Persson) L.; m. Martha Jane Ginsburg, July 18, 1992. BA in Polit. Sci., Stanford U., 1980. News editor Anchorage Daily News, 1979-81, editorial page editor, 1981-85, contbg. editor, 1987-88; John S. Knight profl. journalism fellow Stanford (Calif.) U., 1985-86; copy editor Boston Globe, 1986-87; editorial page editor Everett (Wash.) Herald, 1988-89; freelance reporter, 1989; chief writer and editor Alaska Oil Spill Commn., 1989-90; issues dir., ofcl. spokesman Knowles for Alaska Campaign, 1990; exec. dir. Alaska Humanities Forum, Anchorage, 1991—. Home: 2600 Redwood St Anchorage AK 99508-3973 Office: Alaska Humanities Forum 421 W 1st Ave Ste 210 Anchorage AK 99501-1661

LINDE, GARY J., goldsmith; b. Rolla, Mo., Sept. 9, 1950; s. Kenneth P. and Willowe J. (Palmer) L.; m. Karen M. Anderson, May 22, 1979. Grad Goldsmith and Gemologist, U. Kans., 1972; degree in diamond & diamond grinding, Gemological Inst. Am., 1989, 90; student, Carlyle Smith at U. Kans. Owner, master goldsmith Del Oro-Goldsmith, Alamogordo, N.Mex., 1972—. Bd. dirs., treas. City Zoo; bd. dirs., founding pres., treas., v.p. Alamogordo Friends of Zoo. Recipient numerous trophies for antique cars. Home: PO Box 1242 Alamogordo NM 88311-1242 Office: Del Oro-Goldsmith 800 New York Ave Alamogordo NM 88310-7108

LINDE, HANS ARTHUR, state supreme court justice; b. Berlin, Germany, Apr. 15, 1924; came to U.S., 1939, naturalized, 1943; s. Bruno C. and Luise (Rosenhain) L.; m. Helen Tucker, Aug. 13, 1945; children: Lisa, David Tucker. BA, Reed Coll., 1947; JD, U. Calif., Berkeley, 1950. Bar: Oreg. 1951. Law clk. U.S. Supreme Ct. Justice William O. Douglas, 1950-51; atty. Office of Legal Adviser, Dept. State, 1951-53; pvt. practice Portland, Oreg., 1953-54; legis. asst. U.S. Sen. Richard L. Neuberger, 1955-58; from assoc. prof. to prof. U. Oreg. Law Sch., 1959-76; justice Oreg. Supreme Ct., Salem, 1977-90, sr. judge, 1990—; Fulbright lectr. Freiburg U., 1967-68, Hamburg U., 1975-76; cons. U.S. ACDA, Dept. Def., 1962-76; mem. Adminstrv. Conf. U.S., 1978-82. Author: (with George Bunn) Legislative and Administrative Processes, 1976. Mem. Oreg. Constl. Revision Commn., 1961-62, Oreg. Commn. on Pub. Broadcasting, 1990-93; bd. dirs. Oreg. Pub. Broadcasting, 1993—. With U.S. Army, 1943-46. Fellow Am. Acad. Arts and Scis.; mem. Am. Law Inst. (council), Order of Coif, Phi Beta Kappa.

LINDE, LUCILLE MAE (JACOBSON), motor-perceptual specialist; b. Greeley, Colo., May 5, 1919; d. John Alfred and Anna Julia (Anderson) Jacobson; m. Ernest Emil Linde, July 5, 1946 (dec. Jan. 27, 1959). BA, U. No. Colo., 1941, MA, 1947, EdD, 1974. Cert. tchr. Calif., Colo., Iowa, N.Y.; cert. ednl. psychologist; guidance counselor. Dean of women, dir. residence C.W. Post Coll. of L.I. Univ., 1965-66; asst. dean of students SUNY, Farmingdale, 1966-67; counselor, tchr. West High Sch., Davenport, Iowa, 1967-68; instr. grad. tchrs. and counselors, univ. counselor, researcher No. Ariz. U., Flagstaff, 1968-69; vocat. edn. and counseling coord. Fed. Exemplary Project, Council Bluffs, Iowa, 1970-71; sch. psychologist, counselor Oakdale Sch. Dist., Calif., 1971-73; sch. psychologist, intern Learning and Counseling Ctr., Stockton, Calif., 1972-74; pvt. practice rsch. in motor-perceptual tng. Greeley, 1975—; rschr. ocumeter survey Lincoln Unified Sch. Dist., Stockton, 1980, 81, 82, Manteca (Calif.) H.S., 1981; spkr. Social Sci. Edn. Consortium, U. Colo., Boulder, 1993; presenter seminars in field. Author: Psychological Services and Motor Perceptual Training, 1974, Guidebook for Psychological Services and Motor Perceptual Training (How One May Improve in Ten Easy Lessons!), 1992, Manual for the Lucille Linde Ocumeter: Ocular Pursuit Measuring Instrument, 1992, Motor-Perceptual Training and Visual Perceptual Research (How Students Improved in Seven Lessons!), 1992, Effects of Motor Perceptual Training on Academic Achievement and Ocular Pursuit Ability, 1992; inventor ocumeter, instrument for measuring ocular tracking ability, 1989, target for use, 1991; patentee in field. Mem. Rep. Presdl. Task Force, 1989-96, trustee, 1991-92, charter mem., 1994—, life mem., 1994-95; mem. Rep. Nat. Com., 1990, 93-96, 97, Rep. Nat. Com. on Am. Agenda, 1993, Nat. Rep. Congl. Com., 1990, 92, 93, 95, 96, Nat. Fedn. Rep. Women, Greeley Rep. Women, 1996; advisor Senator Bob Dole for Pres.; charter mem. Rep. Newt Gingrich's Speaker's Task Force, Senator Phil Gramm's Presdl. Steering Com.; at-large-del. Rep. Platform Planning Com.; team leader Nat. Rep. Rapid Response Network, Campaign America, 1996; active Heritage Found., Attention Deficit Disorder Adv. Group, Christian Bus. Men's Assn., Friends U. N.C. Librs., Citizens Against Govt. Waste, 1996, Concerns of Police Survivors, 1996, Nat. Assn. of Police Org. Recipient Presdl. medal of merit and lapel insignia, 1990, Nat. Rep. Senatorial Com., 1991-96, cert. of appreciation Nat. Rep. Congl. Com., 1992, 95, lapel pin Rep. Senatorial Inner Circle, 1990-96, Rep. Presdl. commemorative honor roll, 1993, Rep. Senatorial Freedom medal, 1994, Rep. Legion of Merit award, 1994, 96, Rep. Congl. Order of Freedom award, 1995, Convention medallion Rep. Senatiroial Inner Cir., 1996, Lapel Pin award RNC, 1996, Leadership citation Rep. Senatorial Inner Cir./ Rep. Nat. Conv., 1996, Legion of Merit Rep. Presdl. exec. com., 1996, Honor cert. House Spkr. Newt Gingrich, 1996; named to Rep. Nat. Hall of Honor, 1992. Mem. AAUP, NAFE, Nat. Assn. Sch. Psychologists and Psychometrists (spkr. at conf. 1976), Rep. Senatorial Inner Cir. (name engraved on Ronald Wilson Reagan Eternal Flame of Freedom, 1995, on the Nat. Rep. Victory Monument, Washington, 1996, Rep. Sen. Inner Cir. Conv. Medallion 1996, RNG Mems. Only pin 1996), The Smithsonian Assocs., Nat. Trust for Hist. Preservation, Am. Pers. and Guidance Assn., Nat. Assn. Student Pers. Adminstrs., Nat. Assn. Women Deans and Counselors, Calif. Tchrs. Assn., Internat. Platform Assn., Independence Inst., Assn. Children Learning Disabilities (conf. spkr. 1976), Learning Disabilities Assn. (spkr. internat. conv. 1976), Greeley Rep. Women's Club, Pi Omega Pi, Pi Lambda Theta. Home: 1954 18th Ave Greeley CO 80631-5208

LINDEGREN, JACK KENNETH, elementary and secondary education educator; b. Fresno, Calif., Feb. 9, 1931; s. Henry Jack and Katherine (Metzler) L.; m. Betty Jo Rowland, Dec. 1960 (div. Apr. 1963); m. Elaine Finnegan, Apr. 27, 1963; children: Susan Carol, Karen Ann. BA, Fresno State Coll., 1954; MA, Calif. State U., Fresno, 1976. Educator, adminstr. Fresno County, Firebaugh, Calif., 1954-5; educator Calaveras County Schs., San Andreas, Calif., 1964-66, Kings County Schs., Corcoran, Calif., 1966-80, Kern County Schs., Bakersfield, Calif., 1985-87, L.A. Unified Schs., 1985—; educator L.A. Unified Schs., 1977-92; instr. ARC, Hanford, Calif., 1974-79.; instr. County Sci. Insvc., 1985. Inventor electroanalysis device Chrysler award., 1965. Participant Desert Opera, Palmdale, Calif., 1986-88; bd. mem., chmn. ARC, Hanford, 1973-78. Sgt. U.S. Army, 1955-57. Mem. NAS, AAAS, NEA, Nat. Assn. Legions of Honor, Nat. Space Soc., Tehran Shrine, Fresno East/West Game Corcoran Band Club, Santa Clara U. Alumni Assn., Internat. DeMolay Alumni Assn. (life), Assn. Calif. Sch. Adminstrs., Calif. State U. of Fresno Alumni Assn. (life), Scottish Rite (life), Corcoran/Tulare Masons (life, Bethel guardian 1978-80, Pin 1980), Odd Fellows (30 Yr. Mem. award 1991), Mensa (elder, deacon bushop, 10 v.p. Membership award). Presbyterian.

LINDEMAN, ROBERT DEAN, medical educator, researcher, consultant; b. Ft. Dodge, Iowa, July 19, 1930; s. Verlus F. and Dorothy L. (Cawelti) L.; m. Janet Ruth Lyman, Apr. 12, 1954 (div. June 1982); children: William Douglas, Ann Denise Hendrix, James Lawrence, Peter Verlus, David Matthew; m. Edith Lynn Lind, Aug. 14, 1982; stepchildren: Lauren Lind Lisinski, Lisa Lind Ringhoff, Kristine Lind Cannaday, Robert Mathew Lind. BS, SUNY, Syracuse, 1952, MD, 1956. Diplomate Am. Bd. Internal Medicine. Intern in internal medicine Blodgett Meml. Hosp., Grand Rapids, Mich., 1956-57; resident in internal medicine Upstate Med. Ctr., Syracuse, 1957-60; chief renal sect. Dept. Medicine U. Okla., Oklahoma City, 1966-77; assoc. chief of staff in rsch. Oklahoma City VA Med. Ctr., 1966-76; chief of staff Louisville VA Med. Ctr., 1977-83; assoc. dean VA affairs Sch. Medicine U. Louisville, 1977-83; chief of staff VA Med. Ctr., Washington, 1983-88; assoc. dean VA affairs, prof. medicine Sch. Medicine George Washington U., Washington, 1983-88; prof. medicine, chief divsn. gerontology U. N.Mex., Albuquerque, 1988—; mem. panel chair nutrition U. S. Pharmacopeia, Rockville, Md., 1975—; mem. adv. bd. Am. Assn. Ret. Persons, Washington, 1990—. Contbr. more than 140 articles to profl. jours. Pres. Nat. Kidney Found. (Okla. chpt.), Oklahoma City, 1970-71, pres.-elect and pres., Ky. chpt., Louisville, 1978-81. Recipient Ralph C. Williams Rsch. award U. N.Mex., 1992, Gerontology Assoc. award, 1992. Fellow ACP, Am. Geriat. Soc., Am. Coll. Nutrition (pres., pres.-elect, v.p. 1981-87); mem. Nat. Assn. VA Chiefs of Staff (pres., pres.-elect 1984-86), Gerontol. Soc. Am., Am. Soc. Nephrology, Internat. Soc. Nephrology, So. Soc. for Clin. Investigation, Ctrl. Soc. for Clin. Rsch., Western Assn. Physicians. Democrat. Home: 2513 Myra Pl NE Albuquerque NM 87112 Office: U NMex Sch Medicine 2121 Lomas Blvd NE Albuquerque NM 87106

LINDEN, MOLLY KATHLEEN, nursing administrator, educator; b. Spokane, Wash., Dec. 30, 1952; d. Robert Michael and Agnes Patricia (Gill) L. Student, Wash. State U., 1971-73; BSN magna cum laude, Seattle U., 1976; MS in Nursing, U. Wash., 1983. RN, Wash.; cert. case mgr. Staff nurse Univ. Hosp. Med. Ctr., Seattle, 1976-83; clin. nurse specialist Pacific Med. Ctr., Seattle, 1983-87, supr. adminstrv. nursing; supr. clin. nursing Swedish Med Ctr., Seattle, nursing adminstr., 1987-94, coord. care specialist, case mgr., 1994—; adj./part-time faculty Seattle U. Contbr. articles to profl. jours. Mem. ANA, King County Nurses Assn. (Nurse of Day award), Wash. State Nurses Assn., Seattle U. Alumni Assn. (bd. dirs., pres. 1991-93), Sigma Theta Tau (Outstanding Leader award 1992, pres. 1994-96).

LINDENBAUER, LEO KENNITH, chiropractor; b. Yakima, Wash., Mar. 28, 1921; s. Lester Kennith Lindenbauer and Josephine Angeline (Lyons) Rowe; m. (dec. May 1978); 1 child, Donna Lee Flick. Pers. Farrogot (Idaho) Naval Base; head acct. Baxter Gen. Hosp., Spokane, Wash.; elect layout leadman Associated Shipyards, Seattle; circulation supr. Spokesman Rev., Spokane; pvt. practice chiropractor Wash.; spkr. alternative heatlh care. Inventor solar trailer; contbr. articles to profl. jours. Candidate for Mayor, Spokane, 1950. Mem. C. of C., Jr. C. of C., Elks (founding mem.), Eagles. Republican. Office: Chiropractice Nerve Rsch Found 6221 N Cannon St Spokane WA 99205-6955

LINDERMAN, WILLIAM EARL, elementary school educator, writer; b. San Francisco, Mar. 22, 1955; s. Earl William and Marlene (Melamed) L.; m. Marilyn Monica Spitz, June 28, 1980; children: David William, Eva Alicia. BA in Elem. Edn., Ariz. State U., 1978, MA in Elem. Edn. Elem. sch. tchr., Ariz. Tchr. grade 6 Paradise Valley Sch. Dist., Phoenix, 1979—. Author: Calculator Fun, Hands on Math, One Minute Motivators, numerous others; featured in ABC Radio Nat. News. Asst. youth ch. Phoenix Assembly of God; lay min. homeless mission Ch. on the St., Phoenix; song leader at svcs. Towers Jail, Phoenix. Recipient Golden Bell award Ariz. Sch. Bd. Assn., Thanks to Tchrs. award Nat. Found. Improvement Edn./Nat. Alliance of Bus./Apple Computer. Republican. Home: 18021 N 50th Pl Scottsdale AZ 85254-7567 Office: Village Vista Elem Sch 4215 E Andora DR Phoenix AZ 85254-7667

LINDHOLM, DONALD WAYNE, lawyer; b. Des Moines, Dec. 12, 1937; s. Rudolf William and Hazel Marie (Yoder) L.; m. E. DeAnne Wilson, Feb. 4, 1962; children: Dawn DeRae, Dow William. LLB, U. Ariz., 1966. Bar: Ariz. 1966, U.S. Dist. Ct. Ariz. 1966, U.S. Claims Ct. 1975, U.S. Ct. Appeals (9th cir.) 1988. Asst. city atty. City of Phoenix, 1966-74; ptnr. Flynn, Kimerer, Thinnes, Derrick & Lindholm, Phoenix, 1974-78; shareholder Donald W. Lindholm, P.C., Phoenix, 1978-81; counsel Treon, Warnicke & Roush, Phoenix, 1981; owner Capt. Jack's Landing Channel Island Harbor, Oxnard, Calif., 1982-85; shareholder Burch & Cracchiolo, P.A., Phoenix, 1985—. Fellow Ariz. Bar Found.; mem. ABA (family law section), Assn. Trial Lawyers Am., Nat. Inst. Mcpl. Law Officers (zoning and planning com.), State Bar of Ariz. (family law section, cert. specialist in domestic relations bd. of legal specialization), Ariz. Trial Lawyers Assn., Maricopa County Bar Assn. (family law sect.). Office: Burch and Cracchiolo PA 702 E Osborn Rd # 200 Phoenix AZ 85014-5215

LINDHOLM, RICHARD THEODORE, economics and finance educator; b. Eugene, Oreg., Oct. 5, 1960; s. Richard Wadsworth and Mary Marjorie (Trunko) L. m. Valaya Nivasananda, May 8, 1987. BA, U. Chgo., 1982, MA, 1983, PhD, 1993. Ptnr. Lindholm and Osanka, Eugene, 1986-89, Lindholm Rsch., Eugene, 1989—; guest lectr. Nat. Inst. Devel. Adminstrn., Bangkok, Thailand, 1989; pres. Rubicon Inst., Eugene, 1988—; adj. asst. prof. U. Oreg., Eugene, 1988—. Campaign co-chmn. Lane C.C. Advocates, Eugene, 1988; coord., planner numerous state Rep. Campaigns, Oreg., 1988—; campaign mgr. Jack Roberts for Oreg. State Labor Commn., 1994; mem. staff Oreg. Senate Rep. Office, 1989-90; precinct committeeperson Oreg. Rep. Party, 1987-92, 94—; bd. dirs. Rubicon Soc., Eugene, 1987—, pres., 1993—. Republican. Lutheran. Home: 3335 Bardell Ave Eugene OR 97401-8021

LINDLEY, F(RANCIS) HAYNES, JR., foundation president, lawyer; b. L.A., Oct. 15, 1945; s. Francis Haynes and Grace Nelson (McCanne) L.; m. Hollinger McCloud Lindley, Apr. 1, 1977; 1 child, Anne Hollinger Lindley. BA, Claremont (Calif.) Men's Coll., 1967; MFA, Claremont (Calif.) Grad. Sch., 1972; JD, Southwestern U., L.A., 1976. Bar: Calif. 1976, U.S. Supreme Ct. 1980. Deputy pub. defender Office of Pub. Defender, L.A., 1977-79; staff atty., Dept. Trial Counsel The State Bar of Calif., L.A., 1979-81; pvt. practice, 1981-90; pres. John Randolph Haynes and Dora Haynes Found., L.A., 1987—; trustee John Randolph Haynes and Dora Haynes Found., L.A., 1978—. Mem. bd. dirs. TreePeople, L.A., 1985-87, So. Calif. Assn. Philanthropy, L.A., 1985-89; mem. bd. fellows Claremont (Calif.) U. Ctr. and Grad. Sch., 1987—; mem. bd. dirs. Marin Agrl. Land Trust, 1995—. Recipient Disting. Svc. award The Claremont (Calif.) Grad. Sch., 1994. Mem. The Calif. Club. Home: PO Box 1404 Ross CA 94957-1404 Office: John Randolph Haynes and Dora Haynes Found 888 W 6th St Ste 1150 Los Angeles CA 90017-2737

LINDLEY, JUDITH MORLAND, cat registry administrator; b. Burbank, Calif., Mar. 25, 1948; d. Howard Paxson Conrow and Hazel Mary (Morland) Conrow-Caesar; m. William Ames (div. 1972); m. J. Lindley (div. 1983); widowed, 1990; children: Pamela Ames-Ortega, Jimmy J. Lindley, Joseph Bettoni, Patricia Bettoni. Grad in Animal Sci., Internat. Correspondence Sch., 1995. Pres., founder Calico Cat Registry, Morongo Valley, Calif., 1978—; pres., owner Animal Helpline, Morongo Valley, 1979—. Author: Calico Cat Registry Handbook, 1978; contbr. articles to mags. Home and Office: 48981 Oregon Trail PO Box 944 Morongo Valley CA 92256

LINDLEY, NORMAN DALE, physician; b. Henrietta, Tex., July 18, 1937; s. Hardie Lindley and Hope (Clement) Mourant; m. Luise Ann Moser, May 29, 1964; children: Norman Dale Jr., Roger Paul. BS, N.Mex. Highlands U., 1960; MD, U. Colo., 1964. Diplomate Am. Bd. Ob-Gyn. Rotating intern Kans. City (Mo.) Gen. Hosp., 1964-65; resident in ob-gyn. St. Joseph Hosp., Denver, 1965-68; med. officer USAF, Cheyenne, Wyo., 1968-70; pvt. practice physician Alamogordo, N.M., 1970—; dir. N.Mex. Found. for Med. Care, Albuquerque, 1985-88, N.Mex. Med. Rev. Assn., Albuquerque, 1985-88; physician liaison Am. Assn. Med. Assts., Chgo., 1987-93; physician advisor N.Mex. Soc. Med. Assts., 1984—. Bd. dirs. Otero County Boys and Girls Club, Alamogordo, 1977—, pres., 1979-81; bd. dirs. Otero County Assn. for Retarded Citizens, 1985-91, pres., 1989-90; bd. dirs. Otero County chpt. Am. Cancer Soc., 1970-72. Capt. USAF, 1968-70. Rsch. grantee NSF, 1959, 60. Fellow Am. Coll. Ob-Gyn.; mem. AMA, Am. Fertility Soc., Am. Inst. Ultrasound in Medicine, Am. Soc. Colposcopists and Cervical Pathologists, N.Mex. Med. Soc. (councilor 1985-88), Otero County Med. Soc. (pres. 1972-73, 83-84), Rotary (pres. White Sands chpt. 1981-82, bd. dirs. 1988-89, Svc. Above Self award 1979, Paul Harris fellow 1987). Home: 2323 Union Ave Alamogordo NM 88310-3849 Office: Thunderbird Ob-Gyn 1212 9th St Alamogordo NM 88310-5842

LINDLY, DOUGLAS DEAN, elementary school educator, administrator; b. San Diego, Aug. 22, 1941; s. George A. and Jessie V. L.; m. Brenda J., Oct. 22, 1971; children: Elizabeth, David. MA in Curriculum, Pepperdine U., 1967, student, 1975; credential edn., USC, 1971; student, U. Oreg., 1981-85, Oreg. State U., 1981-85; credential adminstrn., Calif. State U., Fullerton, 1991; cert. in spl. edn., Calif. State U., L.A., 1994. Cert. in profl. adminstrv. svcs., Calif., gen. teaching, Calif., standard designated adult edn., Calif., standard elem. teaching, Oreg., standard adminstrv., Oreg.; cert. lang. devel. specialist, Calif., Learning Handicapped and Resource Specialist credential. Supervising tchr. Imperial Schs., Pasadena, Calif., 1965-70; tchr. Charter Oak Unified Sch. Dist., Covina, Calif., 1970-78, Sweet Home (Oreg.) Unified Sch. Dist., 1978-81, Rialto (Calif.) Unified Sch. Dist., 1989-90; prin. Lewis and Clark Sch. Dist., Astoria, Oreg., 1981-86, Barstow (Calif.) Unified Sch. Dist., 1986-88; spl. edn. dir. River Delta Unified Sch. Dist., Walnut Grove, Calif., 1988-89; resource specialist Los Angeles Unified Sch. Dist., 1990—; tchr. motivational program Great Kids Club, 1982—. Author: A Handbook for Parents, 1967, Summer Education Handbook, 1970; contbr. numerous articles on ednl. programs to newspapers and mags., 1970-89. Vol. ARC, Pasadena/Covina, 1970-78; cubmaster Boy Scouts Am., Astoria and Barstow, 1982-88 (Outstanding Svc. award 1988); coach Little League, Astoria, 1985; leader youth group Ch. of God, 1975-81. Grantee Adventures in Success, 1976-78; scholar Future Tchrs. Am. and Eugene Tchrs. Assn., 1959; named San Gabriel Valley Outstanding Educator, San Gabriel Valley Endl. Consortium, 1977; recipient Outstanding Speaker award Toastmasters Internat., 1986, Outstanding Svc. award PTA, 1988. Mem. NEA, ASCD, Assn. Am. Educators, Calif. Assn. Gifted, Calif. Tchrs. Assn., Assn. Calif. Sch. Adminstrs. (assoc.), Kappa Delta Pi. Home: PO Box 1058 962 E Mountain View Ave Glendora CA 91741-2871

LINDQUIST, LOUIS WILLIAM, artist, writer; b. Boise, Idaho, June 26, 1944; s. Louis William and Bessie (Newman) L.; divorced; children: Jessica Ann Alexandra, Jason Ryan Louis. BS in Anthropology, U. Oreg., 1968; postgrad., Portland State U., 1974-78. Researcher, co-writer with Asher Lee, Portland, Oreg., 1977-80; freelance artist, painter, sculptor Oreg., 1980-91, 97—. Sgt. U.S. Army, 1968-71, Vietnam. Mem. AAAS, Internat. Platform Assn., N.Y. Acad. Scis. Democrat. Home and Office: PO Box 991 Bandon OR 97411-0991

LINDSAY, CAROL FRANCES STOCKTON, art specialist; b. Haileyville, Okla., Dec. 25, 1940; d. Buel Benjamin and Natalie Frances (Bailey) Stockton; m. Robert Carr Lindsay, Oct. 15, 1961; children: Matthew Robert, Mark Stockton, Michael George. AA, Stockton Coll., 1960; BA, Calif. State U., Sacramento, 1970; MEd, U. Nev., 1982, EdS, 1990. Cert. tchr., adminstr., Calif. Tchr. 2d grade Taft Elem. Sch., Stockton, Calif., 1966-67; tchr. 2d and 3rd grades Dry Creek Joint Elem. Sch., Roseville, Calif., 1967-69; tchr. 1st-5th grades Chartville Elem. Sch., Linden, Calif., 1970-77; tchr. 1st grade Northside Elem. sch., Fallon, Nev., 1977-80; tchr. 3rd grade West End Elem. Sch., Fallon, 1980-83; tchr. 5th-8th grades Roosevelt Roads Midd./High Sch., Ceiba, P.R., 1983-85, fine arts dept. coord., 1984-85; student svcs. coord., tchr. Stead Elem. Sch., Reno, 1986-89; student svcs. coord. Silver Lake Elem. Sch., Reno, 1989-93, dean students, 1993-94; art specialist Clark County Sch. Dist., 1994-95; sch. rep. Antilles Consolidated Sch. System Curriculum Coun., Ceiba, P.R., 1983-85. Co-author: Art Goals and Objectives, 1989; author: Site Based Management, 1990. Co-chairperson Muscular Dystrophy Telethon, Fallon, 1980-82; neighborhood supr. Am. Heart Assn., Reno, 1985-86; mem. PTA. Named one of Outstanding Tchr. of Am., 1972. Mem. AAUW, ASCD, Linden Edn. Assn. (bldg. rep., exec. bd. dirs. 1970-77), Churchill County Edn. Assn. (bldg. rep., exec. bd. dirs. 1980-83), Nev. Assn. Sch. Adminstrs., Internat. Reading Assn., Washoe County Tchrs. Assn. (Disting. Svc. award 1988, Dedicated Svc. award 1992, bldg. rep. 1989-92), Clark County Classroom Tchrs. Assn., Nat. Art Edn. Assn.

LINDSAY, DONALD GENE, retired dermatologist, educator, writer; b. Kokomo, Ind., Mar. 27, 1922; s. Clifford George and Velma L.; m. Mary Katharine Smith, June 20, 1945 (div. 1972); children: Jan Corwin, Diane Kay, James Christopher; m. Donann Sisler, July 10, 1986. BS, U. Ill., 1943, MD, 1947; postgrad., UCLA, 1955-58, U. So. Calif., 1972-74. Diplomate Am. Bd. Dermatology, Am. Bd. Dermal Pathology, Am. Bd. Endocrinology. Intern Calif. Hosp., Los Angeles, 1947-48; resident in gen. practice San Luis Obispo County Hosp., San Luis Obispo, Calif., 1948-49; pvt. practice specializing in gen. practice Dinuba, Calif., 1949-52; resident in internal medicine Good Samaritan Hosp., L.A., 1954-55; resident in dermatology U. So. Calif., Long Beach Vets. Hosp., L.A. and Long Beach, 1955-58; dermatologist, clin. prof. U. So. Calif., Ventura and L.A., 1958-90; postdoctoral fellow in endocrinology Harbor Hosp., Torrance and L.A., 1972-74; tng. in psychiatry U.S. Army Hosp., Fort Sam Houston, Tex., 1951-52; pres. Found. for Research in Aging, Ventura, Calif., 1965—; rsch. cons. Pickard, Lowe & Garrick Inc., Newport Beach, Calif., Washington, 1987-88; genetic engrng. rsch. tng. Univ. Colorado, Boulder, 1989. Author:

Medical Cost Crisis! A Solution, 1993 (Best Seller 1994). Active various govt. orgns., 1992—. Capt. U.S. Army M.C., Korea, 1952-54. Mem. AMA, Am. Acad. Dermatology, Pacific Dermatol. Soc., Am. Geronotol. Soc., Calif. Med. Assn., Ventura County Med. Soc., Alpha Omega Alpha. Republican. Home: 5300 Cliffside Cir Ventura CA 93003-1125

LINDSAY, ELENA MARGARET, nurse; b. Evansville, Ind., Oct. 6, 1941; d. Gordon Graham and Irma Louise (Berkemeier) Kuhn; m. Robert Dean Lindsay Jr., Dec. 29, 1988; children: Maria, Robert. BS in Nursing, U. Evansville, 1963. RN, Utah; cert. BCLS, ACLS. Evening coord., head nurse Welborn Meml. Bapt. Hosp., Evansville, 1969-74; dir. nurses Warrick Hosp., Boonville, Ind., 1975-76; head nurse St. Mary's Med. Ctr., Evansville, 1976-87; staff nurse, HIV counselor VA Med. Ctr., Salt Lake City, 1987—. Mem. Epilepsy Found. 2d lt. U.S. Army, 1961-64. Mem. DAV (life aux. mem.), AACN, Soc. Orthopedic Nurses (past pres.), Am. Heart Assn. Republican. Mem. United Ch. of Christ. Home: 5064 South Heath Ave Kearns UT 84118-6972 Office: 500 Foothill Dr Salt Lake City UT 84148-0001

LINDSAY, NORMAN ROY, systems consultant; b. Pitts., May 17, 1936; s. Norman Ward and Beverly Mae (Norris) L.; m. Camille Kaye Biddinger, Nov. 29, 1969. BA, Oberlin Coll., 1958; tech. degree, Control Data Inst., San Francisco, 1977. Budget analyst First Ch. Christ Scientist, Boston, 1965-68; office mgr. Christian Sci. Benevolent Assn., San Francisco, 1968-70; instr. Turner Enterprises, Orlando, Fla., 1970-73; various, 1973-77; computer specialist Lawrence Livermore Nat. Lab., Livermore, Calif., 1977-84; assoc. systems analyst Pacific Bell, San Ramon, Calif., 1984-90; cons. Solution Software, Inc., Livermore, Calif., 1990-92; owner RCL Enterprises, Livermore, 1993—; mng. ptnr. S.E. PCS Ptnrs. Contbr. articles to profl. jours. Capt. USAF, 1958-65. Mem. USE (com. chair 1987-90, treas. 1991-93, plaque 1990, 91), UNITE (v.p. 1993-96, Star award 1994). Republican. Christian Scientist. Home: 130 El Caminito Livermore CA 94550-4004 also: 977 E Stanley Blvd Ste 262 Livermore CA 94550-4009

LINDSEY, D. RUTH, physical education educator; b. Kingfisher, Okla., Oct. 26, 1926; d. Lewis Howard and Kenyon (King) L. BS, Okla. State U., 1948; MS, U. Wis., 1954; PEd, Ind. U., 1965. Registered kinesiotherapist, 1970. Instr. Okla. State U., Stillwater, 1948-50, Monticello Coll., Alton, Ill., 1951-54, DePauw U., Greencastle, Ind., 1954-56; prof. Okla. State U., Stillwater, 1956-75; vis. prof. U. Utah, Salt Lake City, 1975-76; prof. phys. edn. Calif. State U., Long Beach, 1976-88; prof. emeritus phys. edn. Calif. State U., 1988—; freelance author, cons. Westminster, Calif. Co-author: Fitness for the Health of It, 6th edit., 1989, Concepts of Physical Fitness, 9th edit., 1997, Fitness for Life, 4th edit., 1997, Concepts of Physical Fitness and Wellness, 2d edit., 1997, The Ultimate Fitness Book, 1984, Survival Kit for Those Who Sit, 1989, A Menu of Concepts: Physical Fitness Concepts, Toward Active Lifestyles and Fitness and Wellness Concepts, Toward Health Lifestyles, 1996; editor, pub.: Why Don't You Salt the Beans, 1997; editor: Perspectives: Jour. of Western Soc. for Phys. Edn. Coll. Women, 1988-95. Amy Morris Homans scholar, 1964; recipient Disting. and Meritorious Svc. Honor award Okla. Assn. Health, Phys. Edn. and Recreation, 1970, Meritorious Performance award Calif. State U., 1987, Julian Vogel Meml. award Am. Kinesiotherapy Assn., 1988. Fellow AAHPERD, Am. Kinesiotherapy Assn., Calif. Assn. Health, Phys. Edn., Recreation and Dance, Nat. Coun. Against Health Fraud, Orange County Nutrition Coun., Tex. and Acad. Authors Assn., Western Soc. for Phys. Edn. of Coll. Women (Hon. Mem. award 1995), Phi Kappa Phi. Republican. Baptist.

LINDSKOOG, KATHRYN ANN, writer, educator; b. Petaluma, Calif., Dec. 27, 1934; d. John Welby and Margarete Marie (Zimmerman) Stillwell; m. John Samuel Lindskoog, Aug. 15, 1959; children: Jonathan Cooper, Peter Christopher. BA magna cum laude, U. Redlands, 1956; MA magna cum laude, Calif. State U., Long Beach, 1957. Cert. secondary and cmty. coll. tchr., Calif. Tchr. English, lit. Orange (Calif.) H.S., 1957-64; adj. instr. Fuller Theol. Sem., Pasadena, Calif., 1975, 80, 87, Chapman U., Orange, 1976, New Orleans Bapt. Sem., 1979, New Coll. Berkeley, Calif., 1979, Seattle Pacific U., 1981, Rancho Santiago Coll., Santa Ana, Calif., 1982-87, Biola U., La Mirada, Calif., 1983, 87-88, Simon Greenleaf Sch. of Law, Anaheim, Calif., 1989. Author: C.S. Lewis: Mere Christian, 1973, rev., 1981, 2d rev. edit, 1987, 3d rev. edit., 1997, The Lion of Judah in Never-Never Land, 1973, Up from Eden, 1976, Spanish translation, 1977, Loving Touches, 1977, How To Grow A Young Reader, 1978, rev., 1989, The Gift of Dreams, 1979, A Child's Garden of Christian Verses, 1983, Around the Year with C.S. Lewis and His Friends, 1986, The C.S. Lewis Hoax, 1988, Creative Writing, for People Who Can't Not Write, 1989, Over the Counter, 1989, Fakes, Frauds and Other Malarkey, 1993, Light in the Shadowlands: Protecting the Real C.S. Lewis, 1994, Finding the Landlord: A Guidebook to C.S. Lewis's Pilgrim's Regress, 1995, Light Showers, 1996, Dante's Inferno, 1997, Journey into Narnia, 1997, Dante's Purgatory, 1997; pub., editor The Lewis Legacy, 1989—; editor The Young Readers Libr. Series, 1990-93; contbg. editor Reformed Jour., The Wittenburg Door, 1974-90; contbr. over 250 articles to mags. and jours. including Books and Religion, Can. C.S. Lewis Jour., Christian Century, Christianity and Lit., Christianity Today, English Jour., Eternity, Inside English, Jour. of Psychology and Theology, Mark Twain Jour., Mythlore, Wittenburg Door, The World and I. Recipient scholarship Mythopoeic Soc., 1974, Gold medal Christian Booksellers Assn., 1993. Home: 1344 E Mayfair Ave Orange CA 92667

LINDSTROM, KRIS PETER, environmental consultant; b. Dumont, N.J., Oct. 18, 1948; s. Sven Rune and Moyra Hilda (Coughlan) L.; m. Annette Gail Chaplin, June 25, 1978; 1 child, Karl Pierce. MPH, U. Calif., Berkeley, 1973; MS in Ecology, U. Calif., Davis, 1983. Registered environ. health specialist, Calif. Sr. lab. analyst County Sanitation Dists. Orange County, Fountain Valley, Calif., 1970-72, environ. specialist, 1973-74; environ. specialist J.B. Gilbert and Assocs., Sacramento, 1974-78; prin. K.P. Lindstrom, Inc., Sacramento, 1978-84; pres. K.P. Lindstrom, Inc., Pacific Grove, Calif., 1985—; mem. rsch. adv. bd. Nat. Water Rsch. Inst., Fountain Valley, 1991—. Author: Design of Municipal Wastewater Treatment Plants, 1992; editor publs., 1989, 90. Chmn. City of Pacific Grove (Calif.) Mus. Bd., 1992-96, City of Seal Beach (Calif.) Environ. Bd., 1970. Mem. Water Environ. Fedn. (chmn. marine water quality com. 1987-90), Calif. Water Pollution Control Assn., Pacific Grove Residents Assn. (bd. dirs., pres., v.p. 1992—). Office: KP Lindstrom Inc PO Box 51008 Pacific Grove CA 93950-6008

LINEBAUGH, DAVID EUGENE, fire marshal; b. Colorado Springs, Colo., Aug. 26, 1955; s. Gary Eugene and Doris Irene (Llewellyn) Finch; m. Beverly Joan Good, Feb. 14, 1985; children: Christopher Aaron, Quinlan Scott. AAS, Pikes Peak C.C., Colorado Springs, 1992; BS, Colo. Christian U., 1994, MS, 1997. Dispatcher/patrolman Manitou Springs (Colo.) Police Dept., 1975-76, Colo. State Patrol, Colorado Springs, 1976-77; v.p. High Country Heat Pumps and Air Conditioning, Colorado Springs, 1978-84; combination inspector Regional Bldg. Dept., Colorado Springs, 1984-87; chief inspector Colorado Springs Fire Dept., 1987-90, dep. fire marshal, 1990-94, fire marshal, 1994—; prof. fire sci. Pikes Peak C.C., 1994—. Contbr. articles to profl. jours. Mem. Regional Bldg. Commn., Pikes Peak Regional Bldg. Dept., Colorado Springs, 1983-84; mem. Pikes Peak leadership com. Citizens Goals, Colorado Springs, 1995-96; mem. cmty. action com. City of Colorado Springs, 1996; bd. dirs. Wagon Wheel Coun.-Girl Scouts Am., 1997. Recipient Achievement award Colorado Springs C. of C., 1993, Disting. Achievement award Colo. Christian U., 1994, Pikes Peak Leadership Grad. award Citizens Goals, 1995. Mem. Internat. Fire Code Inst. (chmn. edn. and cert. com. 1995—), Nat. Fire Protection Assn. (inspector qualification com. 1991—), Fire Marshals Assn. N.Am., Internat. Conf. Bldg. Ofcls., Fire Marshals Assn. Colo. (sec. 1993), Colo. Christian Univ. Alumni Assn. (bd. dirs. 1997). Republican. Methodist. Home: 3440 Rio Vista Dr Colorado Springs CO 80917-2783 Office: Colorado Springs Fire Dept Arson Divsn 705 S Nevada Ave Colorado Springs CO 80903-1231

LINEHAN, ALLAN DOUGLAS, prosthodontist; b. L.A., Dec. 30, 1954; s. Charles K. and P. Alene (Rohrbaugh) L.; m. Anita J. Peterson, Aug. 1, 1981; children: Chelsea L., Keegan H. BA, Lewis and Clark Coll., 1978; D in Dental Medicine, Oreg. Health Scis. U., 1983; MS in Prosthodontics, U. Tex., 1993. Diplomate Am. Bd. Prosthodontics. Gen. dental officer USAF Clinic Kadena, Okinawa, Japan, 1983-86, USAF Clinic Bitburg, Bitburg, Germany, 1986-90; prosthodontic resident Wilford Hall USAF Medical Ctr. Lackland Air Force Base, San Antonio, 1990-93; chief of prosthodontics 10th Dental Squadron USAF Acad., Colorado Springs, Colo., 1993—. Contbr. articles to profl. jours. Dir. for fundraising Explorer Elem. Sch., Colo. Springs, 1995—. Recipient John J. Sharry Prosthodontic Rsch. competition award Am. Coll. Prosthodontics, 1993, Tylman Rsch. grant Am. Acad. Fixed Prosthodontics, 1992. Fellow Am. Coll. Prosthodontics; mem. Acad. Gen. Dentistry, Psi Omega (v.p. 1979-83). Home: 3337 Birnamwood Dr Colorado Springs CO 80920 Office: 10th Medical Group SGD 2348 Sijan Dr Ste 2a41 U S A F Academy CO 80840-8200

LINENBRINK, CECILIA, educator; b. Callaway, Nebr., Dec. 3, 1924; d. Henry and Margaret Helen (Brosius) L. BA, Regis U., 1959; MA, St. Louis U., 1961; PhD, U. Colo., 1968. Joined Sisters of St. Francis, Roman Cath. Ch., 1942. Tchr. elem. & secondary schs. St. Francis (S.D.) Indian Mission, 1949-58, St. Elizabeths Sch., Denver, 1945-59; founder, exec. dir. Adult Learning Source Literacy Program, Denver, 1964-91; provincial min. Sisters of St. Francis, Denver, 1991-95; exec. dir. Marycrest Devel. Office, Denver, 1996—; prof. Regis U., Denver, 1996—. Mem. Marycrest Health Sys., Denver, 1991—, Adult Learning Source, Denver, 1991—. Recipient Alumni Achievement award Regis U., Centenary award, 1977, award of merit Mountain Plains Adult Edn. Assn., Denver, 1985, Friend of Literacy award U.S. Dept. Labor, Denver, 1989. Democrat. Roman Catholic. Home: 3227 Bryant St Denver CO 80211 Office: 2851 W 52d Ave Denver CO 80221

LING, DAVID CHANG, international book dealer; b. Shanghai, Feb. 17, 1939; s. H.C. and Katherine (Chang) L.; m. Janine Peters, June 20, 1970 (div. Feb. 1975). BA, U. Ore., 1962; MA, U. Wis., 1964, PhD, 1971. Vis. instr. U. of the South, Sewanee, Tenn., 1964-65; asst. prof. U. Wis., Kenosha, 1969-73; owner Ling's Internat. Books, San Diego, 1974—. Mem. Phi Beta Kappa. Democrat. Home: 5012 Westminster Ter San Diego CA 92116-2103 Office: Ling's Internat Books 7531 Convoy Ct San Diego CA 92111-1113

LINGENFELTER, ANDREA D., translator, writer; b. Walnut Creek, Calif., Nov. 1959; m. David Salesin; 1 child. BA, U. Calif., San Diego, 1981; MA, Yale U., 1984; postgrad., U. Wash. Translator Miramax Films, N.Y.C., 1996—; tour dir. Inter Pacific Tours, N.Y.C., 1982-83; freelance writer Seattle Weekly, 1992-93; translator William Harrar & Co., N.Y.C., 1990-93. Translator: The Last Princess of Manchuria, 1992, Farewell to My Concubine, 1993, (subtitles for film) Temptress Moon, 1996; author restaurant revs. and essays.

LINGLE, CRAIG STANLEY, glaciologist, educator; b. Carlsbad, N.Mex., Sept. 11, 1945; s. Stanley Orland and Margaret Pearl (Ewart) L.; m. Diana Lynn Duncan, Aug. 21, 1972; 1 child, Eric Glenn. BS, U. Wash., 1967; MS, U. Maine, 1978; PhD, U. Wis., 1983. Nat. rsch. coun. resident rsch. assoc. Coop. Inst. for Rsch. in Environ. Scis., U. Colo., Boulder, 1983-84, rsch. assoc., 1984-86; program mgr. polar glaciology divsn. polar programs NSF, Washington, 1986-87; cons. Jet Propulsion Lab., Pasadena, Calif., 1987-88; nat. rsch. coun. resident rsch. assoc. NASA Goddard Space Flight Ctr., Oceans and Ice Branch, Greenbelt, Md., 1988-90; rsch. assoc. prof. Geophys. Inst., U. Alaska, Fairbanks, 1990—. Contbr. articles to profl. jours. Recipient Antarctic Svc. medal of U.S., NSF, 1987, Rsch. Project of Month award Office of Health and Environ. Rsch., U.S. Dept. Energy, 1990, Group Achievement award NASA, 1992. Mem. AAAS, Internat. Glaciological Soc., Am. Geophys. Union, Sigma Xi. Office: Geophys Inst Univ Alaska PO Box 757320 Fairbanks AK 99775-7320

LINGLE, LINDA CROCKETT, mayor. Mayor City of Wailuku, Hawaii. Office: City of Wailuku 200 S High St Wailuku HI 96793

LININGER, SCHUYLER WHITE, hotelier; b. Evanston, Ill., Oct. 29, 1923; s. Homer D. and Cornelia (Bosch) L.; m. Helen Wicker, May 28, 1963; children: Schuyler White Jr., Christopher W., Mitchell H., Gretchen L. Barbatelli. BA in Bus. Adminstrn., 1947. Owner, operator The Lodge on the Desert, Tucson, 1947-97 . Vice chmn. Tucson Civil Service Commn., 1970-75, chmn. 1978-83; mem. Tucson City Council, 1977; chmn. adv. council Ariz. Office Tourism, 1978-84. Served to 1st lt. U.S. Army, 1943-46, PTO, col. Res. ret. Recipient Disting. Alumni Service award U. Ariz. Coll. Med., 1981, named confrere Order of St. John Jerusalem, 1979. Mem. Am. Hotel-Motel Assn. (chmn. resort hotels com. 1972-73), Nat. SKAL Clubs U.S.A. (pres. 1985-86), SKAL of Tucson, N.Am. Area SKAL Com. (pres. 1986-87). Republican. Episcopalian. Clubs: Bohemian, Rotary (pres. 1975-76).

LINK, JULIA ANNE, urban horticulture educator; b. San Diego, June 8, 1955; d. Charles Dickenson and Alice Mary (Maben) L. AS in Dental Assisting, Pacific Coll., 1973; BA in Fine Arts, San Diego Art Inst., 1978; postgrad., Solano Coll., 1990. Registered dental asst., Calif. Dental asst. Office of Robert Prario, DMD, San Diego, 1981-86; ind. sign designer Fairfield, Calif., 1986-89; greenhouse mgr. Solano Coll., Suisun, Calif., 1986-90; biol. aide U.S. Forest Svc., Berkeley, Calif., 1987-89, pub. rels. specialist, 1988-89; educator, program coord. U. Calif. Coop. Extension, Fairfield, Calif., 1990—; cons. in field; chair adv. com. agr./horticulture Solano Coll., 1996—. Author: Prisms, 1991, Moments & Memories, 1993; contbr. 28 poems to profl. publs. Poetry reading, spkr. in field. Recipient Editor's Choice award Nat. Libr. Poetry, 1993, 94, Pres. award, 1994; Calif. Assn. Nurseryman scholar, 1988. Mem. Internat. Soc. Poets, Am. Forests, Lit. Book Rev. Guild. Office: U Calif Coop Extension 2000 W Texas St Fairfield CA 94533

LINK, MATTHEW RICHARD, video producer; b. Monte Nido, Calif., Nov. 22, 1969; s. Richard George and Leslie Jonquil (Schubel) L. AA, City Coll. San Francisco, 1991. Assoc. prodr. City TV Santa Monica, Calif., 1988-89; script evaluator Jerry Seigel & Assocs., L.A., 1989; owner, mgr. Corp. Video Prodns., Hayward, Calif., 1990-92, Missing Link Prodns., San Francisco, 1992—; presentation dir. Star TV, Hong Kong, 1992-93; freelance journalist Frontiers Mag., San Francisco, 1993-95, Metro Lifestyle Mag., San Francisco, 1993-96; writer Ferrari Guides, San Francisco, 1996-97, Gay Access Hawaii Guide, 1997. Video prodr. (documentaries) Male Escorts of San Francisco, 1992, Battle Mountain, 1994, Positive Faith, 1994 (award 1994); video artist (film and video) Origin of Her Virus, 1995. Activist Equal Rights Marriage Project, Kona, Hawaii, 1996. Mem. Film Arts Found., MacDowell Arts Colony (artist). Democrat. Home: 87-3202 Guava Rd Captain Cook HI 96704

LINK, MICHAEL PAUL, pediatrics educator; b. Cleve., Jan. 3, 1949; s. J. Alexander and Betty Irene (Lewis) L.; m. Vicki L. Rumpff, May 30, 1985; 1 child, Alexis Arielle. AB, Columbia Coll., 1970; MD, Stanford U., 1974. Diplomate Am. Bd. Pediatrics, subbd. Pediatric Hematology/Oncology. Prof. pediatrics Stanford (Calif.) U., 1991—. Mem. Phi Beta Kappa, Alpha Omega Alpha. Office: Stanford U Children's Hosp 725 Welch Rd Palo Alto CA 94304-1601

LINKER, DAVID THOR, cardiologist; b. Reykjavik, Iceland, July 27, 1951. BS in Biology, Stanford (Calif.) U., 1972, MD, 1976. Diplomate Am. Bd. Internal Medicine, Am. Bd. Pediatrics, Am. Bd. Pediatric Cardiology, Am. Bd. Cardiology. Intern in internal medicine U. Calif. Davis/Sacramento Med. Ctr., 1976-77; resident in internal medicine U. Wash. Hosp., 1977-79, resident in pediatrics, 1979-81, fellowship adult cardiology, 1981-83; fellowship pediatric cardiology Stanford U. Med. Ctr., 1983-84; asst. prof. biomed. engring. U. Trondheim, 1985-91, chmn. dept. of biomed. engring., 1990-91; assoc. prof. divsn. of cardiology Dept. of Medicine, U. Wash., 1993—; acting attending physician, divsn. of cardiology Regional Hosp., Trondheim, 1985-86, attending physician divsn. of cardiology, 1987-91; head divsn. of echocardiography, dept. of cardiology, Thorax Ctr. Acad. Hosp. of Rotterdam, 1991-93; attending physician divsn. cardiology, dept. medicine, U. Wash., 1993—. Contbr. articles to profl. jours. Grantee Fulbright-Hays, 1985-86; recipient Nedron award for Rsch., 1988. Fellow Am. Coll. Cardiology (echocardiography com.), European Soc. Cardiology (organizer subgroup on intravascular ultrasound 1991-93); mem. Am. Soc. Echocardiography (physics and instrumentation com.), Soc. Pediat. Echocardiography, IEEE, IEEE Computer Soc., Seattle Seafair Clowns (Charlie Choate award 1983), Norwegian Soc. for Diagnostic Ultrasound, Norwegian Soc. for Pattern Analysis and Image Processing (exec. com. 1987-88), Norwegian Med. Assn., Internat. Cardiac Doppler Soc. (sec. Euro-African sect. 1993), Am. Heart Assn. Office: U Wash Divsn Cardiology PO Box 356422 Seattle WA 98195-6422

LINK-JOBE, JANNICE LOUISE, education educator; b. Oregon City, Oreg., Apr. 8, 1947; d. Wilford Martin and Helen Louise (Hart) Link; m. Harvey Richard Jobe, May 31, 1973; 1 child, Tiffany Danielle-Louise. BS in Natural Scis., Oreg. Coll. Edn., Monmouth, Oreg., 1975, MS in Natural Scis. and Edn., 1977; EdD in Secondary Edn., Oreg. State U., Corvallis, 1996. Chemistry tchr. Ctrl. H.S., Independence, Oreg., 1977-89; asst. prin. Central High, 1989-91; prin. Talmadge Mid. Sch., Monmouth, 1991-96; prof. edn. Western Oreg. State U., Monmouth, 1996—; writer chemistry questions Am. Coll. Testing, Chgo., 1984-88. Contbr. articles to Oreg. Sci. Jour., 1983-86. Bd. mem. Gang Task Force, Monmouth, 1991—; bd. dirs. YMCA, Salem, Oreg., 1995—. U.S. Presdl. finalist for sci. tchg. State of Oreg., 1985, 86, Tchr. of the yr., 1983-84. Fellow NAESP, Am. Soc. Curriculum Devel., Nat. Assn. Secondary Sch. Prins., Confederation of Sch. Adminstrn, Oregon Mid Level Assn., Phi Delta Kapa (v.p. Willamette Valley chpt., 1996—), Oreg. Counselors Assn. (hon., Adminstr. of Yr. State of Oreg., 1994), Oreg. Sci. Tchrs. (pres. 1984-85). Home: 414 Stadium Dr S Monmouth OR 97361 Office: Western Oreg State Coll Dept Education Monmouth OR 97361

LINKLETTER, ARTHUR GORDON, radio and television broadcaster; b. Moose Jaw, Sask., Can., July 17, 1912; s. Fulton John and Mary (Metzler) L.; m. Lois Foerster, Nov. 25, 1935; children: Jack, Dawn, Robert (dec.), Sharon, Diane (dec.). A.B., San Diego State Coll., 1934. Program dir. Sta. KGB, San Diego, 1934; program dir. Calif. Internat. Expn., San Diego, 1935; radio dir. Tex. Centennial Expn., Dallas, 1936; San Francisco World's Fair, 1937-39; pres. Linkletter Prodns.; ptnr., co-owner John Guedel Radio Prodns.; chmn. bd. Linkletter Enterprises; owner Art Linkletter Oil Enterprises. Author: theme spectacle Cavalcade of Golden West, 1940; author and co-producer: theme spectacle Cavalcade of Am, 1941; writer, producer, star in West Coast radio shows, 1940-55; former star, writer: People Are Funny, NBC-TV and radio, Art Linkletter's House Party, CBS-TV and radio; Author: People Are Funny, 1953, Kids Say The Darndest Things, 1957, The Secret World of Kids, 1959, Confessions of a Happy Man, 1961, Kids Still Say The Darndest Things, 1961, A Child's Garden of Misinformation, 1965, I Wish I'd Said That, 1968, Linkletter Down Under, 1969, Oops, 1969, Drugs at My Door Step, 1973, Women Are My Favorite People, 1974, How to be a Super Salesman, 1974, Yes, You Can!, 1979, I Didn't Do It Alone, 1979, Public Speaking for Private People, 1980, Linkletter on Dynamic Selling, 1982, Old Age is not for Sissies, 1988; lectr. convs. and univs. Nat. bd. dirs. Goodwill Industries; commr. gen. to U.S. Exhibit at Brisbane Expo 88, Australia, 1987; amb. to The 200th Anniversary Celebration, Australia, 1987—; bd. regents Pepperdine U.; pres. bd. advisors Ctr. on Aging, UCLA; chmn. bd. French Found. for Alzheimers Rsch. Recipient numerous awards. Address: 8484 Wilshire Blvd Ste 205 Beverly Hills CA 90211-3220

LINN, BRIAN JAMES, lawyer; b. Seattle, July 8, 1947; s. Bruce Hugh and Jeanne De V. (Weidman) L.; m. Renee Diane Mousley; children: Kelly, Kareem, Kari. BA in Econs., U. Wash., 1972; JD, Gonzaga Sch. Law, 1975. Bar: Wash. 1975, U.S. Supreme Ct. 1979. Mng. atty. Legal Svcs. for Northwestern Pa., Franklin, 1975-76; staff atty. The Nat. Ctr. for Law and the Handicapped, 1976-78, U. Notre Dame Law Sch., South Bend, Ind., 1976-78; pvt. practice, Seattle, 1978—; lectr. Seattle U., 1980-85. Chmn. civil and legal rights subcom. Gov.'s Com. on Employment of the Handicapped, 1981-87; arbitrator King County Superior Ct., 1981—, judge pro tem, 1989—. Editor Gonzaga Law Rev., 1974-75. Mem. Wash. State Devel. Disabilities Planning Council, 1980-83; trustee Community Service Ctr. for the Deaf and Hard of Hearing, Seattle, 1982-84; chmn. legal rights task force Epilepsy Found. Am., 1979-81; mem. Witness for Peace Delegation, Nicaraqua, 1993. Served with U.S. Army, 1967-69; Vietnam. Mem. Wash. State Bar Assn. (chair world peace through law sect. 1990-91, spl. dist. counsel 1991-95), Omicron Delta Epsilon. Democrat. Methodist. Hon. editor DePaul Law Rev., 1978; contbr. articles to profl. jours. Home: 9716 S 204th Ct Kent WA 98031-1400 Office: 245 SW 152nd St Seattle WA 98166-2307

LINN, CAROLE ANNE, dietitian; b. Portland, Oreg., Mar. 3, 1945; d. James Leslie and Alice Mae (Thorburn) L. Intern, U. Minn., 1967-68; BS, Oreg. State U., 1963-67. Nutrition cons. licensing and cert. sect. Oreg. State Bd. Health, Portland, 1968-70; chief clin. dietitian Rogue Valley Med. Ctr., Medford, Oreg., 1970—; cons. Hillhaven Health Care Ctr., Medford, 1971-83; lectr. Local Speakers Bur., Medford. Mem. ASPEN, Am. Dietetic Assn., Am. Diabetic Assn., Oreg. Dietetic Assn. (sec. 1973-75, nominating com. 1974-75, Young Dietitian of Yr. 1976), So. Oreg. Dietetic Assn., Alpha Lambda Delta, Omicron Nu. Democrat. Mem. Christ Unity Ch. Office: Rogue Valley Med Ctr 2825 E Barnett Rd Medford OR 97504-8332

LINN, DAVID EDWARD, artist; b. Palo Alto, Calif., Sept. 2, 1959; s. Charles William and Dixie Joyce (Rawlins) L. BFA, Brigham Young U., 1986, MFA, 1997. Selected exhbns. include Am. Inst. Graphic Artists Invitational Exhbn., San Francisco 1987 (Purchase award 1987), Soc. of Illustrators, N.Y.C., 1988 (award of merit 1988), Commn. Arts, Palo Alto, Calif., LDS Internat. Art Exhbn, Salt Lake City, 1992 (award of Merit, Peoples Choice award 1992), 1994 (award of Merit 1997, Purchase award 1997, Visitors Choice award), Springville Mus. Art, 1994 (Dirs. award 1994), Utah Arts Coun. (Traveling Exhibit award 1996). Missionary LDS Ch., Buenos Aires, 1980-82. Named Outstanding Young Men of Am., 1988. Home: 629 W 800 N Provo UT 84601

LINN, TODD ALEXANDER, lawyer; b. Denver, Jan. 17, 1962; s. Theodore A. and Arlene A. (Engleman) L.; m. Annette C. Weiman. BA cum laude, The Colo. Coll., Colorado Springs, 1985; JD, U. Denver, 1990, LLM in Tax, 1992. Bar: Colo. 1990, U.S. Tax Ct. 1990. Atty. Wesborn, Dufford, Baron & Tooley, Denver, 1991-92; pvt. practice Denver, 1992—. Res. police officer Englewood (Colo.) Police Dept., 1992—. Mem. Phi Beta Kappa. Republican. Office: 657 Gilpin St Denver CO 80218-3631

LINSTONE, HAROLD ADRIAN, management and systems science educator; b. Hamburg, Fed. Republic Germany, June 15, 1924; came to U.S., 1936; s. Frederic and Ellen (Seligmann) L.; m. Hedy Schubach, June 16, 1946; children: Fred A., Clark R. BS, CCNY, 1944; MA, Columbia U., 1947; PhD, U. So. Calif., 1954. Sr. scientist Hughes Aircraft Co., Culver City, Calif., 1949-61, The Rand Corp., Santa Monica, Calif., 1961-63; assoc. dir. planning Lockheed Corp., Burbank, Calif., 1963-71; prof. Portland (Oreg.) State U., 1970—; pres. Systems Forecasting, Inc., Santa Monica, 1971—; cons. 1973—. Author: Multiple Perspectives for Decision Making, 1984; co-author: The Unbounded Mind, 1993, The Challenge of the 21st Century, 1994; co-editor The Delphi Method, 1975, Technological Substitution, 1976, Futures Research, 1977; editor-in-chief Technol. Forecasting Social Change, 1969—. NSF grantee, Washington, 1976, 79, 85. Mem. Inst. Mgmt. Scis., Ops. Rsch. Soc., Internat. Soc. Systems Scis. (pres. 1993-94). Office: Portland State U PO Box 751 Portland OR 97207-0751

LINTON, MARIGOLD L., psychology educator; b. Morongo Reservation, Banning, Calif.; d. Walter Alexander and Wistaria (Hartmann) L.; m. Robert Ellis Barnhill, Feb. 12, 1983; children: John, Margaret. BA, U. Calif.-Riverside, 1958; postgrad., U. Iowa, 1960; PhD, UCLA, 1964. Lectr., prof. San Diego State U., 1964-74; prof. U. Utah, Salt Lake City, 1974-86; dir. edn. svcs. Coll. Edn. Ariz. State U., Tempe, 1986-94; dir. Am. Ind. Program SUMMS Inst. Ariz. State U., Tempe, 1994-96; dir. Am. Indian Programs Ariz. State U. East, Mesa, 1996—; vis. prof. U. Calif.-San Diego, 1971-72; vis. scholar Learning Research and Devel. Ctr. U. Pitts., 1980-81; mem. nat. adv. research resources council NIH, 1982-86. Co-author: (with Gallo) The Practical Statistician, 1975. Contbr. articles to profl. jours., chpts. to books. Bd. dirs. Malki Mus., 1971-78; bd. dirs. Soc. Adv. Chicanos Native Am. Sci., 1989-95, treas., 1994-95; trustee Carnegie Found. Advancement Teaching, 1977-85. NIH research grant, 1980, Edn. grant NASA, 1994—, Edn. grant NSF, 1994—; recipient Founders medal Soc. Adv. Chicanos Native Am. Sci., 1993; recipient U. Calif.-Riverside Alumni award, 1994, Svc. award Soc. Adv. Chicanos Native Am. Sci., 1995. Fellow APA (bd. advancement psychol. pub. interest 1993-96), Am. Psychol. Soc.; mem. Am. Ednl. Rsch. Assn., Nat. Indian Edn. Assn. (founder, Cert. Honor award 1976), Phi Beta Kappa, Phi Kappa Phi. Office: Ariz State U-E Office of Provost Mesa AZ 85206

LINXWILER, JAMES DAVID, lawyer; b. Fresno, Calif., Apr. 9, 1949; s. George Edwin and Stella Ruth (Schmidt) L.; m. Robyn Kenning, July 12, 1986; children: Elizabeth Ann, John Edwin, Jeffrey David. BA, U. Calif.-Berkeley, 1971; JD, UCLA, 1974. Bar: D.C. 1976, Alaska 1977, U.S. Ct. Appeals (9th and D.C. cirs.), U.S. Dist. Ct. Alaska, U.S. Supreme Ct. Lawyer, Dept. Interior, Washington, 1974-76; lawyer, Cook Inlet Region Inc., Anchorage, 1976-78; lawyer Sohio Petroleum Co., Anchorage, 1978-81; shareholder Guess & Rudd, Anchorage, 1981—; spkr. seminars on environ. and natural resources law. Contbr. chpts. to book, articles to profl. jours. Chmn. Alaska Coalition Am. Energy Security, 1986-87, Alliance Arctic Nat. Wildlife Refuge Com., 1986-97; bd. dirs., Commonwealth North, 1993-97. Mem. ABA, FBA, Alaska Bar Assn. (chmn., exec. com. nat. resources sect. 1988-93), D.C. Bar Assn. Democrat. Home: 2407 Loussac Dr Anchorage AK 99517-1272 Office: Guess & Rudd 510 L St Ste 700 Anchorage AK 99501-1959

LINXWILER, LOUIS MAJOR, JR., retired finance company executive; b. Blackwell, Okla., Mar. 7, 1931; s. Louis Major and Flora Mae (Horton) L.; m. Susan Buchanan, July 27, 1963; children: Louis Major III, Robert William. BS, Okla. State U., 1953. Mgr. credit dept. Valley Nat. Bank, Tucson, 1957-60; sales rep. Vega Industries, Syracuse, N.Y., 1960-62; program dir. Am. Cancer Soc., Phoenix, 1962-67; v.p., mgr. credit dept. United Bank Ariz., Phoenix, 1967-76; dean edn. Am. Inst. Banking, Phoenix, 1976-80; cons. Phoenix, 1980-81, United Student Aid Funds Inc., Phoenix, 1981-82; founder, pres., chief exec. officer Ariz. Student Loan Fin. Corp., Phoenix, 1982-88, also bd. dirs.; founder, chmn., chief exec. officer Western Loan Mktg. Assn., Phoenix, 1984-90, also bd. dirs.; pres. Precision Design and Engrng., Inc., Escondido, Calif., 1993—, Circulator Motor Co., Phoenix, 1996—. Editor: Money and Banking, 1978. Pres. City Commn. Sister Cities, Phoenix, 1986-87, Am. Inst. Banking, Phoenix, 1973-74, Phoenix YMCA Bd. Dirs., 1974-75; v.p. North Mountain Behavioral Inst., Phoenix, 1975-77. Served to 1st lt. U.S. Army, 1954-56. Mem. Shriners, Hiram Club, Rotary (bd. dirs. 1982-83, 93-94, 96-97), Beta Theta Pi. Republican. Presbyterian. Home: 3311 E Georgia Ave Phoenix AZ 85018-1424

LIONAKIS, GEORGE, architect; b. West Hiawatha, Utah, Sept. 5, 1924; s. Pete and Andriani (Protopapadakis) L.; student Carbon Jr. Coll., 1942-43, 46-47; BArch., U. Oreg., 1951; m. Iva Oree Braddock, Dec. 30, 1951; 1 dau., Deborah Jo. With Corps Engrs., Walla Walla, Wash., 1951-54; architect Liske, Lionakis, Beaumont & Engberg, Sacramento, 1954-86, Lionakis-Beaumont Design Group, 1986—. Mem. Sacramento County Bd. Appeals, 1967—, chmn., 1969, 75, 76; pres. Sacramento Builders Exchange, 1976. Served with USAAF, 1943-46. Mem. AIA (pres. Central Valley chpt., 1972—), Constrn. Specifications Inst. (pres. Sacramento chpt., 1962; nat. awards, 1962, 63, 65), Sacramento C. of C. (code com., 1970—). Club: North Ridge Country (pres. 1987). Lodge: Rotarian (pres. East Sacramento 1978-79). Prin. works include Stockton (Calif.) Telephone Bldg., 1968, Chico (Calif.) Main Telephone Bldg., 1970, Mather AFB Exchange Complex Sacramento, 1970, Base Chapel Mather AFB, Sacramento, 1970, Woodridge Elementary Sch., Sacramento, 1970, Pacific Telephone Co. Operating Center Modesto, Calif., 1968, Sacramento, 1969, Marysville, Calif., 1970, Red Bluff, Calif., 1971, Wells Fargo Banks, Sacramento, 1968, Corning, Calif., 1969, Anderson, 1970, Beale AFB Exchange Complex, Marysville, 1971, Cosumnes River Coll., Sacramento, 1971, base exchanges at Bergstrom AFB, Austin, Tex., Sheppard AFB, Wichita Falls, Tex., Chanute AFB, Rantoul, Ill., McChord AFB, Tacoma, Wash., health center Chico State U., Sacramento County Adminstrn. Center, Sacramento Bee Newspaper Plant. Home: 160 Breckenwood Way Sacramento CA 95864-6968 Office: Lionakis Beaumont Design Group 1919 19th St Sacramento CA 95814-6714

LIOU, KUO-NAN, atmospheric science educator, researcher; b. Taipei, Taiwan, Republic of China, Nov. 16, 1944; m. Agnes L.Y. Hung, Aug. 3, 1968; children: Julia C.C., Clifford T.C. BS, Taiwan U., 1965; MS, NYU, 1968, PhD, 1970. Rsch. assoc. Goddard Inst. for Space Studies, N.Y.C., 1970-72; asst. prof. atmospheric sci. U. Wash., Seattle, 1972-74; assoc. prof. U. Utah, Salt Lake City, 1975-80, prof., 1980—, dir. grad. studies in meteorology, 1981-84, dir. Ctr. for Atmospheric and Remote Sounding Studies, 1987—, rsch. prof. physics, 1992—; adj. prof. geophysics, 1992—; vis. prof. UCLA, 1981, U. Ariz., Tucson, 1995; affiliated prof. Peking U., Beijing, China, 1991—; vis. scholar Harvard U., 1985; cons. NASA Ames Rsch. Ctr., Moffett Field, Calif., 1984-94, Los Alamos (N.Mex.) Nat. Lab., 1984-88. Author: An Introduction to Atmospheric Radiation, 1980, Radiation and Cloud Processes in the Atmosphere, 1992; editor: Atmospheric Radiation Progress and Prospects, 1987; contbr. articles to profl. jours. Fellow NRC, Washington, 1970, David Gardner fellow U. Utah, Salt Lake City, 1978; recipient Founders Day award NYU, 1971, NSF grant, 1974—. Fellow Optical Soc. Am., Am. Meterol. Soc. (chmn. atmospheric radiation com. 1982-84), Am. Geophys. Union; mem. AAAS. Home: 4480 Adonis Dr Salt Lake City UT 84124-3923 Office: U Utah Dept Meteorology Salt Lake City UT 84112

LIPCHIK, HAROLD, company executive; b. N.Y.C., Apr. 17, 1928; s. Samuel and Ida (Gutterman) L.; m. Elaine Greenberg, Mar. 23, 1952; children: Alan Scott, Debra Anne. BS in Mech. Engrng., Carnegie Mellon U., 1948; postgrad., NYU, 1948-49. Project engr. Pub. Svc. Commn. N.Y. State, N.Y.C., 1949-50, Bendix Aviation, South Bend, Ind., 1950-51, Hamilton Standard div. United Aircraft, Windsor Locks, Conn., 1951-52; v.p. AMF Inc., N.Y.C., 1952-66, Chromalloy Am. Corp., Clayton, Mo., 1966-71; pres. Halco Industries, Glendale, Calif., 1971-82, Halco Assocs., Tarzana, Calif., 1982—; v.p. Nat. Tech. Systems, Calabasas, Calif., 1984—; pres. Water Treatment Corp., City of Industry, Calif., 1968-71; dir. Halco Assocs., Tarzana. Pres. United Synagogue Am., L.A., 1976-78, L.A. Hebrew High Sch., L.A., 1978-84. Jewish. Home: 4429 Trancas Pl Tarzana CA 91356-5302 Office: Nat Tech Systems 24007 Ventura Blvd Calabasas CA 91302-1458

LIPINSKI, BARBARA JANINA, psychotherapist, psychology educator; b. Chgo., Feb. 29, 1956; d. Janek and Alicja (Brzozkiewicz) L.; m. Bernard Joseph Burns, Feb. 14, 1976 (div. 1985). B of Social Work, U. Ill., Chgo., 1978; MFCC, MA, U. Calif., Santa Barbara, 1982; PhD, U. So. Calif., 1992. Diplomate Am. Bd. Forensic Medicine; cert. tchr., Calif., psychology tchr., Calif.; cert. adminstr., non-pub. agent; lic. marriage, family and child therapist; bd. cert. forensic examiner. Police svc. officer Santa Barbara (Calif.) Police Dept., 1978-79; peace officer Airport Police, Santa Barbara, 1979-80; emergency comms. Univ. Police, Santa Barbara, 1980-82; facilitator, instr. Nat. Traffic Safety Inst., San Jose, Calif., 1981-87; assoc. dir. Community Health Task Force on Alcohol and Drug Abuse, Santa Barbara, 1982-86; instr. Santa Barbara C.C., 1987-88; patients' rights adv. Santa Barbara County Calif. Mental Health Adminstrn., 1986-89; pvt. practice psychotherapist Santa Barbara, 1985—; faculty mem., clin. coord. Pacifica Grad. Inst., Carpinteria, Calif., 1989—; intern clin. psychology L.A. County Sheriff's Dept., 1991-92, cons. Devereaux Found., Santa Barbara, 1993-95, Ctr. for Law Related Edn., Santa Barbara, 1986; cons., trainer Univ. Police Dept., Santa Barbara, 1982, 89. Vol. crisis work Nat. Assn. Children of Alcoholics, L.A., 1987; crisis intervention worker Women in Crisis Can Act, Chgo., 1975-76; vol. counselor Santa Barbara Child Sexual Assault Treatment Ctr.-PACT, Santa Barbara, 1981-82. Recipient Grad. Teaching assistanship U. So. Calif., 1990-92. Mem. APA, Am. Profl. Soc. on Abuse of Children, Am. Coll. Forensic Examiners, Internat. Critical Incident Stress Found., Calif. Assn. Marriage and Family Therapists, Internat. Soc. for Traumatic Stress Studies. Home: 301 Los Cabos Ln Ventura CA 93001-1183 Office: Pacifica Grad Inst 249 Lambert Rd Carpinteria CA 93013-3019

LIPKE, JAMES SCOTT, municipal official; b. Lakewood, Ohio, Sept. 17, 1947. BA in Biology, U. Calif. San Diego, La Jolla, 1975. Cert. tchr. cmty. coll., Calif. Tchr. computer info. scis. San Diego Mesa Coll., 1984-96; coord. data sys. City of San Diego, 1979-96; spkr. Computer Fair, San Diego, 1991-96. With USN, 1966-70. Mem. AFIO, Internat. Spl. Interest Group, Assn. Former Intelligence Officers (pres. 1990), San Diego Computer Soc. Office: City of San Diego 202 C St # 2A San Diego CA 92101-4806

LIPKIN, MARY CASTLEMAN DAVIS (MRS. ARTHUR BENNETT LIPKIN), retired psychiatric social worker; b. Germantown, Pa., Mar. 4, 1907; d. Henry L. and Willie (Webb) Davis; m. William F. Cavenaugh, Nov. 8, 1930 (div.); children: Molly C. (Mrs. Gary Oberbillig), William A.; m. Arthur Bennett Lipkin, Sept. 15, 1961 (dec. June 1974). Student, Pa. Acad. Fine Arts, 1924-28; postgrad., U. Wash., 1946-48, Seattle Psychonalytic Assn., 1959-61. Nursery sch. tchr. Miquon (Pa.) Sch., 1940-45; caseworker Family Soc. Seattle, 1948-49, Jewish Family and Child Service, Seattle, 1951-56; psychiat. social worker Stockton (Calif.) State Hosp., 1957-58; supr. social service Mental Health Research Inst., Fort Steilacoom, Wash., 1958-59; engaged in pvt. practice, Bellevue, Wash., 1959-61. Former mem. Phila. Com. on City Policy. Former diplomate and bd. mem. Conf. Advancement of Pvt. Practice in Social Work; former mem. Chestnut Hill women's com. Phila. Orch; mem. Bellevue Art Mus., Assoc. Am. Assn. of U. Women, Wing Luke Mus. Mem. ACLU, LWV, Linus Pauling Inst. Sci. and Medicine, Inst. Noetic Scis., Menninger Found., Smithsonian Instn., Union Concerned Scientists, Physicians for Social Responsibility, Center for Sci. in Pub. Interest, Asian Art Council, Seattle Art Mus., Nature Conservancy, Wilderness Soc., Sierra Club. Home: 10022 Meydenbauer Way SE Bellevue WA 98004-6041

LIPOMI, MICHAEL JOSEPH, health facility administrator; b. Buffalo, Mar. 9, 1953; s. Dominic Joseph and Betty (Angelo) L.; m. Monica Lipomi; children: Jennifer, Barrett, Ryan. BA, U. Ottawa, 1976; MS in Health Adminstrn., U. Colo., 1994. Mktg. dir. Am. Med. Internat. El Cajon Valley Hosp., Calif., 1980-83; dir. corp. devel. Med. Surg. Ctrs. Am., Calif., 1983-85; exec. dir. Stanislaus Surgery Ctr., Modesto, Calif., 1985—. Author: Complete Anatomy of Health Care Marketing, 1988; co-host med. TV talk show Health Talk Modesto. Bd. dirs. Am. Heart Assn., Modesto, 1988-89; pres. Modesto Community Hospice, 1987-88; active local govt.; sec.-treas. Modesto Industry and Edn. Council, 1989. Mem. Calif. Ambulatory Surgery Assn. (pres. 1988-89, mem. legis. com. 1994, mem. rsch. and edn. found. bd. 1994—), No. Calif. Assn. Surgery Ctrs. (pres. 1986-88), Federated Ambulatory Surgery Assn. (mem. govt. rels. com. 1988, bd. dirs. 1989—, chmn. govt. rels. com. 1990), Modesto C. of C. (bd. dirs. 1989-92), Rotary. Office: Stanislaus Surgery Ctr 1421 Oakdale Rd Modesto CA 95355-3359

LIPPE, PHILIPP MARIA, physician, surgeon, neurosurgeon, educator, administrator; b. Vienna, Austria, May 17, 1929; s. Philipp and Maria (Goth) L.; came to U.S., 1938, naturalized, 1945; m. Virginia M. Wiltgen, 1953 (div. 1977); children: Patricia Ann Marie, Philip Eric Andrew, Laura Lynne Elizabeth, Kenneth Anthony Ernst; m. Gail B. Busch, Nov. 26, 1977. Student Loyola U., Chgo., 1947-50; BS in Medicine, U. Ill. Coll. Medicine, 1952, MD with high honors, 1954. Rotating intern St. Francis Hosp., Evanston, Ill., 1954-55; asst. resident gen. surgery VA Hosp., Hines, Ill., 1955, 58-59; asst. resident neurology and neurol. surgery Neuropsychiat. Inst., U. Ill. Rsch. and Ednl. Hosps., Chgo., 1959-60, chief resident, 1962-63, resident neuropathology, 1962, postgrad. trainee in electroencephalography, 1963; resident neurology and neurol. surgery Presbyn.-St. Luke's Hosp., Chgo., 1960-61; practice medicine, specializing in neurol. surgery, San Jose, Calif., 1963—; instr. neurology and neurol. surgery U. Ill., 1962-63; clin. instr. surgery and neurosurgery Stanford U., 1965-69, clin. asst. prof., 1969-74, clin. assoc. prof., 1974-96, clin. prof. 1996—; staff cons. in neurosurgery O'Connor Hosp., Santa Clara Valley Med. Ctr., San Jose Hosp., Los Gatos Cmty. Hosp., El Camino Hosp. (all San Jose area); chmn. divsn. neurosugery Good Samaritan Hosp, 1989—; founder, exec. dir. Bay Area Pain Rehab. Center, San Jose, 1979—; clin. adviser to Joint Commn. on Accreditation of Hosps.; mem. dist. med. quality rev. com. Calif. Bd. Med. Quality Assurance, 1976-87, chmn., 1976-77. Served to capt. USAF, 1956-58. Diplomate Am. Bd. Neurol. Surgery, Nat. Bd. Med. Examiners, Am. Bd. Pain Medicine. Fellow ACS, Am. Coll. Pain Medicine (bd. dirs. 1991-94, v.p. 1991-92, pres. 1992-93); mem. AMA (Ho. of Dels. 1981—), Am. Coll. Physician Execs., Calif. Med. Assn. (Ho. of Dels. 1976-80, sci. bd., council 1979-87, sec. 1981-87, Outstanding Svc. award 1987), Santa Clara County Med. Soc. (coun. 1974-81, pres. 1978-79, Outstanding Contbn. award 1984, Benjamin J. Cory award 1987), Chgo. Med. Soc., Congress Neurol. Surgeons, Calif. Assn. Neurol. Surgeons (dir. 1974-82, v.p. 1975-76, pres. 1977-79, Pevehouse disting. svc. award 1997), San Jose Surg. Soc., Am. Assn. Neurol. Surgeons (chm. sect. on pain 1987-90, dir. 1983-86, 87-90, Disting. Svc. award 1986, 90), Western Neurol. Soc., San Francisco Neurol. Soc., Santa Clara Valley Profl. Standards Rev. Orgn. (dir., v.p., dir. quality assurance 1975-83), Fedn. Western Socs. Neurol. Sci., Internat. Assn. for Study Pain, Am. Pain Soc. (founding mem.), Am. Acad. Pain Medicine (sec. 1983-86, pres. 1987-88, Philipp M. Lippe Disting. Svc. award 1995, exec. med. dir. 1996—), Am. Bd. Pain Medicine (pres. 1992-93, exec. v.p., 1994—), Alpha Omega Alpha, Phi Kappa Phi. Assoc. editor Clin. Jour. of Pain; contbr. articles to profl. jours. Pioneered med. application centrifugal force using flight simulator. Office: 2100 Forest Ave Ste 106 San Jose CA 95128-1422

LIPPITT, LOUIS, physical science educator, aerospace engineer; b. N.Y.C., Mar. 19, 1924; s. Louis Sr. and Susan Davie (Anderson) L.; m. Adele Dorothy Wissmann, June 27, 1948; children: Laurie, Craig, Bonnie, Nancie. BS, CUNY, 1947; MA, Columbia U., 1953, PhD, 1959. Registered geologist, geophysicist, Calif. Physicist Columbia U., N.Y.C., 1947-51, NYU, N.Y.C., 1951-53; geophysicist Chevron, Calif., 1954-58; staff engr. Lockheed Missiles and Space Co., Vandenberg AFB, Calif., 1958-87; tchr. part time Hancock Coll., Santa Maria, Calif., 1967—, Chapman Coll., Vandenberg AFB, 1985-86. Project leader, 4-H, Calif., 1960-77. Served with U.S. Army, 1943-46. Recipient Honorarium, State of N.Y., 1952. Fellow Geol. Soc. Am. (sr.); mem. Am. Geophys. Union. Lutheran. Home: 696 Raymond Ave Santa Maria CA 93455-2760

LIPPMANN, BRUCE ALLAN, rehabilitative services professional; b. Balt., Aug. 29, 1950; s. Allan L. and Phyllis Marie (Bunyea) L.; m. Barbara Jean Wood, May 26, 1973 (div. Aug. 1979); m. Susan K. Shampanier, Feb. 1, 1981 (div. Nov. 1990); m. Frances G. Scruggs, Dec. 31, 1991; children: Joshua Rae Holt, Stuart Holt, Joshua Lippmann, Grant Lippmann. BA, U. Md., Catonsville, 1972; MS, Loyola U., 1979; cert., San Diego Inst., 1989; postgrad., Calif. Sch. Profl. Psychology, 1992-93, Nat. U., 1996—. Cert. rehab. counselor, ins. rehab. specialist. Social worker Md. Children's Ctr., Catonsville, 1970-72; vocat. cons. St. Md. Workers Compensation Commn., Balt., 1975-79; sr. counselor McGuinness Assocs., Fresno, Calif., 1980-84; pres., CEO Sierra Rehab. Svcs. Inc., Fresno, 1984-91; vocat. counselor Fresno, 1991-94; health care mgr. GAB Robins N.Am. Inc., Fresno, 1994-96; cons. Healthcare and Workplace Mgmt., Fresno, 1996—; resource specialist Rowell Elem. Sch., Fresno, 1996—; cons. Doctors Med. Ctr., Modesto, Calif., 1989-92, Calif. Ctr. Rehab. Svcs., Fresno, 1986-89, U.S Dept. Labor, San Francisco, 1984—; curriculum cons. Microcomputer Tng. Inst., Fresno, 1986-91. Mem. Metro Circle-Fresno Metro Mus., 1986—, Fresno Zool. Soc., 1985—, Fresno Arts Mus., 1984—, Bulldog Found., Fresno State U., 1985-91. With U.S. Army, 1972-75. Mem. APA, Central Calif. Rehab. Assn. (pres. 1984-85), Nat. Assn. Rehab. Profls. (Counselor of Yr. 1987, Pvt. Sector Rehab. Counselor or Yr. 1988), Calif. Nat. Assn.Rehab. Profls. Pvt. Sector (membership com. 1984-85, Meritorious Svc. 1985, Cert. of Recognition 1986), Calif. Assn. Rehab. Profls., Nat. Rehab. Assn., Nat. Rehab Counseling Assn. Democrat. Jewish. Office: 3331 W Bullard Ave Fresno CA 93711 also: Rowell Elem Sch 3460 E McKenzie Fresno CA 93702

LIPPOLD, ROLAND WILL, surgeon; b. Staunton, Ill., May 1, 1916; s. Frank Carl and Ella (Immenroth) L.; m. Margaret Cookson, June 1, 1947; children: Mary Ellen Lippold Elvick, Catherine Anne Lippold Rolf, Carol Sue Lippold Webber. BS, U. Ill., 1940, MD, 1941. Diplomate Am. Bd. Surgery. Intern Grant Hosp., Chgo., 1941-42, resident in surgery, 1942-43, 47-48; resident in surgery St. Francis Hosp., Evanston, Ill., 1946-47; fellow in pathology Cook County Hosp., Chgo., 1947-48, resident in surgery, 1949-50; practice medicine specializing in surgery Chgo., 1950-53; also asst. in anatomy U. Ill., Chgo., 1950-53; practice medicine specializing in surgery Sacramento, 1953-68; chief med. officer No. Reception Ctr.-Clinic, Calif. Youth Authority, Sacramento, 1954-68, chief med. services, 1968-79; cons. in med. care in correctional instns.; cons. Calif. State Personnel Bd. Contbr. articles to med. publs. Chmn. Calif. Expn. Hall of Health, 1971-72. Comdr. M.C., USNR, 1943-73, PTO. Mem. Sacramento Surg. Soc., Sacramento County Med. Soc., Calif. Med. Assn., AMA, Sacramento Hist. Soc. (life). Republican. Lutheran. Home: 1811 Eastern Ave Sacramento CA 95864-1724

LIPSCHUTZ, MARIAN SHAW, secondary education educator, writer; b. Bklyn., Apr. 1, 1940; d. Melville Austin Shaw and Marguerite Frances (Van Dyke) Morgan; m. Ernst Lipschutz, Oct. 16, 1967 (dec. Sept. 1995); children: David Alexander, Sirene Rose Alexandra. BA, U. Mich., 1961; MA, Calif. State U., L.A., 1967; MFA, U. Calif., Irvine, 1977. Tchr. English, Westridge Sch., Pasadena, Calif., 1964—. Author: (novel) Land of Hunchbacks, 1988.

LIPSCOMB, ANNA ROSE FEENY, entrepreneur, arts organizer, fundraiser b. Greensboro, N.C., Oct. 29, 1945; d. Nathan and Matilda (Carotenuto) L. Student langs., Alliance Francaise, Paris, 1967-68; BA in English and French summa cum laude, Queens Coll., 1977; diploma advanced Spanish, Forester Instituto Internacional, San Jose, Costa Rica, 1990; postgrad. Inst. Allende San Miguel de Allende, Mex., 1991. Reservations agt. Am. Airlines, St. Louis, 1968-69, ticket agt., 1969-71; coll. rep. CBS, Holt Rinehart Winston, Providence, 1977-79, sr. acquisitions editor Dryden Press, Chgo., 1979-81; owner, mgr. Historic Taos (N.Mex.) Inn, 1981-89, Southwest Moccasin and Drum, Taos; pres., co-owner Southwest Products, Ltd., 1991—; owner, pres. All One Tribe, Inc., 1996—; fundraiser Taos Arts Celebrations, 1989—; bd. dirs. N.Mex. Hotel and Motel Assn., 1986—; sem. leader Taos Women Together, 1989; founder All One Tribe Found., 1994, All One Tribe Drumming Festival, 1991—; mem. adv. bd. Drum Bus. Mag., 1996—. Editor: Intermediate Accounting, 1980; Business Law, 1981. Contbr. articles to profl. jours.; patentee in field. Bd. dirs., 1st v.p. Taos Arts Assn., 1982-85; founder, bd. dirs. Taos Spring Arts Celebration, 1983—; founder, dir. Meet-the-Artist Series, 1983—; bd. dirs. and co-founder Spring Arts N.Mex., 1986; founder Yuletide in Taos, 1988, A Taste of Taos, 1988; bd. dirs. Music from Angel Fire, 1988—; founding mem. Assn. Hist. Hotels, Boulder, 1983—; organizer Internat. Symposium on Arts, 1985; bd. dirs. Arts in Taos, 1983, Taoschool, Inc., 1985—; mem. adv. bd. Chamisa Mesa Ednl. Ctr., Taos, 1990—; founder All One Tribe Found., 1994; bd. dirs. Roadrunner Recyclers, 1995—. Recipient Outstanding English Student of Yr. award Queens Coll., 1977; named Single Outstanding Contbr. to the Arts in Taos, 1986. Mem. Millicent Rogers Mus. Assn., Taos Lodgers Assn. (mktg. task force 1989), Taos County C. of C. (1st v.p. 1988-89, bd. dirs. 1987-89, advt. com. 1986-89, chmn. nominating com. 1989), Internat. Platform Assn., Taos Women Bus. Owners, Phi Beta Kappa. Home: Talpa Rte Taos NM 87571 Office: PO Drawer N Taos NM 87571

LIPSCOMB, JEFFREY JON, fund specialist, insurance agent; b. San Diego, May 8, 1946; s. Willis L. and Marjorie (Jones) L.; m. Jo Ann Elaine Nielsen, Oct. 1, 1983; 1 child, Amanda Nielsen. Student, Occidental Coll., 1964-68, Harvard U., 1971, New England Conservatory Music, 1972. Chief cash flow analyst St. Johnsbury Co., Cambridge, Mass., 1970-81; pvt. investor San Diego, 1981-88; registered rep. New England Securities, Sacramento, 1988—; registered investment specialist Bankamerican Investment Svcs., West Sacramento, Calif., 1997—; registered investment specialist Bankam. Investment Svcs., 1997—. Columnist (fin. commentary) The Bus. Jour. Sacramento, 1990-91. Mem. East Sacramento (Calif.) Improvement Assn., 1988-97; pianist celebrity benefit concerts Stanford Children's Home, Sacramento, 1989. Mem. Inst. Cert. Fund Specialists, Internat. Assn. Fin. Planning (practitioner divsn. 1993—), Nat. Assn. Life Underwriters, Sacramento Assn. Life Underwriters, New Eng. Leaders Assn., Sutter Lawn Tennis Club (pres. 1992-93), The Sutter Club, Investment Trust Boston Cornerstone Club. Republican. Presbyterian. Office: 1551 W Capitol Ave West Sacramento CA 95691

LIPSICK, JOSEPH STEVEN, research scientist, medical educator; b. Sharon, Pa., Jan. 6, 1955; m. Laurel Most, June 30, 1978; children: Samuel, Leslie. BA, Oberlin Coll., 1974; PhD, U. Calif., San Diego, 1981; MD, U. Calif., 1982. Resident pathology, postdoctoral UCLA, 1983-85; asst. prof. U. Calif., San Diego, 1986-89; assoc. prof. SUNY, Stony Brook, 1989-93, Stanford (Calif.) U., 1993—. Recipient Career Devel. award VA, 1986-89, Rsch. Career Devel. award Nat. Cancer Inst., 1989-94, Scholar award Leukemia Soc. Am., 1989-94. Office: Stanford U Dept Pathology 300 Pasteur Dr Palo Alto CA 94304-2203

LIPSKY, IAN DAVID, contracting executive; b. Bklyn., May 26, 1957; s. Eugene Herman and Janet Dorothy (Heller) L; m. Cheryl Joy Weinberg. BS in Marine Engrng., Maine Maritime Acad., 1979. Third asst. engr. Interlake Steamship Co., Cleve., 1979-81; port engr. Exxon Internat. Co., Florham Park, N.J., 1981-84; prodn. supr. Alfred Conhagen Inc. Calif., Hercules, 1984-87, gen. mgr., 1987-89, v.p., 1989—. Mem. Soc. Naval Architects & Marine Engrs., Marine Port Engrs. N.Y., Inst. Marine Engrs. (London), Port Engrs. San Francisco, Nat. Soc. Profl. Engrs. Democrat. Jewish. Home: 153 Koch Rd Corte Madera CA 94925-1263 Office: Alfred Conhagen Inc Calif 3900 Oregon St Benicia CA 94510-1102

LIPTON, JUDITH EVE, psychiatrist; b. Chgo., Mar. 7, 1951; d. Morris Abraham and Barbara (Steiner) L.; m. Peter Sisk, June, 1969 (div. Dec., 1974); m. David Philip Barash, Mar. 10, 1977; children: Jacob Sisk, Ilona Anne, Nanelle Rose. BA, Reed Coll., 1974; MD, U. N.C., 1974. Diplomate Am. Bd. Psychiatry & Neurology. Resident in psychiatry U. Wash., Seattle, 1975-77; clin. instr. dept. psychiatry and behavioral scis. U. Wash., 1979-80; resident in psychiatry Stanford U., 1978-79; consulting psychiatrist Family Counseling Ctr., Lynnwood, Wash., 1980-82; med. staff mem. Overlake Hosp., Bellevue, Wash., 1981-91; med. staff Evergreen Hosp., Kirkland, Wash., 1985-87; pvt. practice Meydenbauer Psychiat. Group, Bellevue, 1980-85, Redmond (Wash.) Med. Ctr., 1985-92, Woodinville, Wash., 1992—. Contbr. articles to profl. jours. Leadership Redmond, Class of 1991; libr. Sammamish String Orch., 1992-93; camp dr. Chaspen Summer Music Festival, 1993; founder Emerald Hills Pony Club, 1985-89. Recipient Merck award for Excellence in Med. Studies, 1972, Ralph Bunche award Wash. State Bar Assn., 1983, Woman of Distinction Matrix Table award Women in Comm. AAUW, 1987; scholar in residence Bellagio Study and Conf. Ctr., Rockefeller Found., Como, Italy, 1984; guest govt. USSR Forum on Nuclear Disarmament, Moscow, 1987. Fellow Am. Psychiat. Assn. (chmn. Com. on Nuclear Issues, 1987-89); mem. Wash. State Med. Soc., King County Med. Soc., Physicians for Social Responsibility (pres., founder Wash. Physicians for Social Responsibility 1979-83, rsch. and writing award 1983, Paul Beeson award 1986), nat. bd. dirs. 1980-86, spkr. fellowship 1983), Assn. Women Psychiatrists, Am. Soc. Clin. Psychopharmacology. Office: Woodinville Med Ctr Ste 204 17000 140th Pl NE Woodinville WA 98072-6928

LISA, ISABELLE O'NEILL, law firm administrator, mergers and acquisitions executive; b. Phila., Mar. 12, 1934; d. Thomas Daniel and Margaret Marie (Hayes) O'Neill; m. Donald Julius Lisa, June 15, 1957; children: Richard Allan, Steven Gregory. Student, Harper Community Coll., Rolling Meadows, Ill., 1976, Scottsdale Community Coll., 1980, Ariz. State U., 1981-82. Cost control clk. Curtis Pub. Co., Phila., 1952-56; sec. United Ins. Co., Annapolis, Md., 1956-57; firm adminstr., legal sec. Law Offices Donald J. Lisa, Bloomingdale, Ill., 1987; legal sec. Lisa & Kubida, P.C., Phoenix, 1987-88, firm adminstr., 1987-89; firm adminstr. Lisa & Assocs., Phoenix, 1989-90, Lisa & Lisa, Phoenix, 1990-91, Lisa & Assocs., Scottsdale, Ariz., 1991-95, Law Offices of Donald J. Lisa, Scottsdale, 1995-96; v.p. adminstrn. Lisa & Co., Scottsdale, 1987-97; pres. IAWYA, Ltd., Scottsdale, 1996—; pres. IAWYA, Ltd., Scottsdale, 1996. Den mother Cub Scouts Am., Millburn, N.J., 1965; founder, pres. Pro-Tem Rutgers U. Law Wives Assn., 1962-63; bd. advisors Am. Inst., Phoenix, 1991—. Mem. NAFE, Maricopa County Bar Assn. (legal adminstrs. sect. 1992-95), Internat. Platform Assn., Rotary. Republican. Roman Catholic. Home and Office: 8661 E Carol Way Scottsdale AZ 85260

LISALDA, SYLVIA ANN, primary education educator; b. San Diego, Oct. 14, 1949; d. Joseph and Irene (Valdez) Lisalda; m. Robert Holguin Marquez, Sept. 1, 1979 (div. 1986). AA, Valley Coll., Van Nuys, Calif., 1964; BA in English, Calif. State U., Northridge, 1971. Tchr. kindergarten L.A. Unified Schs., 1965—. Democrat. Roman Catholic. Office: Sylmar Elem Sch 13291 Phillippi Ave Sylmar CA 91342-2810

LISNEK, MARGARET DEBBELER, artist, educator; b. Covington, Ky., Sept. 26, 1940; d. Aloysius Frank and Mary Elizabeth (Haubold) Debbeler; m. Schiller William Lisnek, June 26, 1966 (dec. May 1995); 1 child, Kimberly Anne. AA with honors, Mt. San Antonio Coll., 1985; BA in Art with honors, Calif. State U., Fullerton, 1991. Cert. substitute tchr. Freelance artist, 1985—; tchr. art Rorimer Elem. Sch., La Puente, Calif., 1992-93, City of Walnut (Calif.) Recreation Svcs., 1992—, Christ Luth. Sch., West Covina, Calif., 1993—, Los Molinos Elem. Sch., Hacienda Heights, Calif., 1993—, Los Altos Elem. Sch., Hacienda Heights, 1993—; mem. Getty Inst. Insvc. Resource Team. One-woman shows include Calif. State U., Fullerton, 1990;

exhibited in group shows. Sec., treas., social chair PTA, Los Altos Elem. Sch., Hacienda Heights, 1972-73; membership and social chair Friends of Libr., Hacienda Heights, 1974-75; active Nat. Mus. Women in the Arts, L.A. County Art Mus., Norton Simon Mus., Pasadena, Calif. Mem. Calif. Art Edn. Assn.

LISTON, ALBERT MORRIS, administrator, educator, investor; b. Carlinville, Ill., Aug. 6, 1940; s. Joseph Bostick and Hazel Marie (Smalley) L.; AB in Econs., U. Calif., Davis, 1963; MA in Govt., Calif. State U., Sacramento, 1970; postgrad., U. Calif., Santa Barbara, 1980—; m. Phyllis Clayton, Feb. 27, 1967 (div. July 1970). Rsch. analyst Ombudsman Activities Project polit. sci. dept. U. Calif., Santa Barbara, 1970-72; asst. prof. polit. sci. dept. Calif. State U., Fullerton, 1973-79; investor, 1980—. Lt. Supply Corps, USNR, 1963-66. Mem. Am. Polit. Sci. Assn., Commonwealth Club Calif., Kappa Sigma, Phi Kappa Phi. Democrat. Office: PO Box 8027 Missoula MT 59807-8027

LITINSKY, VADIM ARPADOVICH, geophysicist, geologist; b. Petrozavodsk, Russia, Oct. 9, 1929; came to U.S., 1980; s. Arpad Szabados and Nina Nikolaevna Litinsky; m. Mina E. Ratner, Oct. 29, 1964 (div. Sept. 1990); children: E. Eugene, Alla V.; m. Elena Davidovna Sirochinsky, Oct. 29, 1991; 1 child, Tanya N. MS, Sch. Mines, Leningrad, USSR, 1953; PhD, State U., Moscow, 1972. Sr. engr., sr. geophysicist, chief engr. Polar expdn. NIIGA-Sci. Rsch. Inst. for the Geology of the Arctic, Leningrad, 1953-79; sr. geophysicist EDCON-Exploration Data Cons., Inc., Denver, 1980-86; cons. geophysicist Denver, 1986-88, Vadim Litinsky, Geocons. on Russia and Former Soviet Union, Denver, 1989—; Contbr. numerous articles to profl. jours. Mem. Am. Geophys. Union, Soc. Exploration Geophysicist, Am. Assn. Petroleum Geologists. Republican. Home and Office: 1075 Dawson St Aurora CO 80011-6914

LITMAN, ROBERT BARRY, physician, author, television and radio commentator; b. Phila., Nov. 17, 1947; s. Benjamin Norman and Bette Etta (Saunders) L.; m. Niki Thomas, Apr. 21, 1985; children: Riva Belle, Nadya Beth, Caila Tess, Benjamin David. BS, Yale U., 1967, MD, 1970, MS in Chemistry, 1972, MPhil in Anatomy, 1972, postgrad. (Life Ins. Med. Rsch. Fund fellow) Yale U., Univ. Coll. Hosp., U. London, 1969-70; Am. Cancer Soc. postdoctoral rsch. fellow Yale U., 1970-73. Diplomate Am. Bd. Family Practice. Resident in gen. surgery Bryn Mawr (Pa.) Hosp., 1973-74; USPHS fellow Yale U. Sch. Medicine, 1974-75; pvt. practice medicine and surgery, Ogdensburg, N.Y., 1977-93, San Ramon, Calif., 1993—; mem. med. staff A. Barton Hepburn Hosp., 1977-93, John Muir Med. Ctr., 1993—, San Ramon (Calif.) Regional Med. Ctr., 1993—, also chmn. med. edn.; commentator Family Medicine Stas. WWNY-TV and WTNY-Radio, TCI Cablevision, Contra Costa T.V.; clin. preceptor dept. family medicine State Univ. Health Sci. Ctr., Syracuse, 1978—. Author: Wynnefield and Limer, 1983, The Treblinka Virus, 1991, Allergy Shots, 1993; contbr. articles to numerous sci. publs. Pres. Am. Heart Assn. No. N.Y. chpt., 1980-84. Fellow Am. Coll. Allergy, Asthma, and Immunology, Am. Acad. Family Physicians; mem. AMA (Physicians Recognition award 1970—), Calif. State Med. Assn., Alameda-Contra Costa County Med. Assn., Joint Coun. Allergy and Immunology, Nat. Assn. Physician Broadcasters (charter), Acad. Radio and TV Health Communicators, Book and Snake Soc., Gibbs Soc. of Yale U. (founder), Sigma Xi, Nu Sigma Nu, Alpha Chi Sigma. Home and Office: PO Box 1857 San Ramon CA 94583-6857

LITTLE, CHARLES GORDON, geophysicist; b. Liuyang, Hunan, China, Nov. 4, 1924; s. Charles Deane and Caroline Joan (Crawford) L.; m. Mary Zughaib, Aug. 21, 1954; children: Deane, Joan, Katherine, Margaret, Patricia. BSc with honors in Physics, U. Manchester, Eng., 1948; PhD in Radio Astronomy, U. Manchester, 1952. Jr. engr. Cosmos Mfg. Co. Ltd., Enfield, Middlesex, Eng., 1944-46; jr. physicist Ferranti Ltd., Manchester, Lancashire, Eng., 1946-47; asst. lectr. U. Manchester, 1952-53; prof. dept. geophysics U. Alaska, 1954-58, dep. dir. Geophys. Inst., 1954-58; cons. Ionosphere Radio Propagation Lab. U.S. Dept. Commerce Nat. Bur. Standards, Boulder, Colo., 1958-60, chief Upper Atmosphere and Space Physics divsn., 1960-62, dir. Central Radio Propagation Lab., 1962-65; dir. Inst. Telecommunication Sci. and Aeronomy, Environ. Sci. Services Adminstrn., Boulder, Colo., 1965-67; dir. Wave Propagation Lab. NOAA (formerly Environ. Sci. Services Adminstr.), Boulder, Colo., 1967-86; sr. UCAR fellow Naval Environ. Prediction Research Facility, Monterey, Calif., 1987-89; George J. Haltiner rsch. prof. Naval Postgrad. Sch., Monterey, 1989-90. Author numerous sci. articles. Recipient U.S. Dept. Commerce Gold medal, 1964, mgmt. and sci. research awards NOAA, 1969, 77, Presdl. Meritorious Exec. award, 1980. Fellow IEEE, Am. Meteorol. Soc. (Cleveland Abbe award 1984); mem. NAE, AIAA (R.M. Losey Atmos. Sci. award 1992). Address: 4907 Country Club Way Boulder CO 80301

LITTLE, LAWRENCE ALAN, health facility administrator; b. Downey, Calif., Jan. 23, 1947; s. Eugene R. and Naomia Little. Student, Long Beach City Coll., 1964-66; PharmD, U. Calif., San Francisco, 1970. Registered pharmacist, Calif., Nev. Pharmacist French Hosp., San Francisco, 1970-76, asst. dir. pharmacy, 1976-80, dir. pharmacy, 1980-81; assoc. dir. pharmacy Herrick Hosp., Berkeley, Calif., 1981-82; dir. pharmacy Herrick Hosp., Berkeley, 1982-86; dir. pharmacy Alta Bates Med. Ctr., Berkeley, 1986-96, dir. pharmacy respiratory svcs., 1996—; mem. nat. adv. com. Purchase Connection Pharmacy, L.A., 1980-88; mem. nat. pharmacy coun. Vol. Hosps. Am., Dallas, 1994—; asst. clin. prof. U. Calif. Sch. Pharmacy, San Francisco, 1981—. Pres. bd. dirs. Herrick Credit Union, Berkeley, 1985-87. Mem. Am. Soc. Health Sys. Pharmacists. Office: Alta Bates Med Ctr 2450 Ashby Ave Berkeley CA 94705-2067

LITTLE, LOREN EVERTON, musician, ophthalmologist; b. Sioux Falls, S.D., Oct. 28, 1941; s. Everton A. and Maxine V. (Alcorn) L.; m. Christy Gyles; 1 child, Nicole Moses; children from previous marriage: Laurie, Richard. BA, Macalester Coll., 1963; BS, U. S.D., 1965; MD, U. Wash., 1967. Prin. trumpeter Sioux Falls Mcpl. Band, 1956-65; trumpeter St. Paul Civic Orch., 1960-62; leader, owner Swinging Scots Band, St. Paul, 1960-63; trumpeter Edgewater Inn Show Room, Seattle, 1966-67, Jazztet-Arts Council, Sioux Falls, 1970-71, Lee Maxwell Shows, Washington, 1971-74; residency in ophthalmology Walter Reed Med. Ctr., Washington, 1974; co-leader, trumpeter El Paso (Tex.) All Stars, 1975; freelance trumpeter, soloist various casinos and hotels, Las Vegas, Nev., 1977—. Trumpeter (album) Journey by R. Romero Band, 1983; soloist for numerous entertainers including Tony Bennett, Burt Bacharach, Jack Jones, Sammy Davis Jr., Henry Mancini, Jerry Lewis Telethon, for video Star Salute to Live Music, 1989; with Stan Mark Band Nat. Pub. Radio Broadcast, 1994, 95; soloist on video Stan Mark Live at the 4 Queens Hotel, Las Vegas; prodr. Carl Saunders Solo Album Out Of the Blue, 1996. Trustee Nev. Sch. of the Arts, Las Vegas, 1983—; pres. S&L Music SNL Rec. Served to lt. col. U.S. Army, 1968-76, Vietnam. Decorated Silver Star, Purple Heart, Bronze Star, Air medal; fellow Internat. Eye Found., 1974; Dewitt Wallace scholar Readers Digest, 1963-65. Fellow ACS, Am. Acad. Ophthalmology; mem. Am. Fedn. Musicians, Nat. Bd. Med. Examiners. Presbyterian.

LITTLE, MARK DOUGLAS, secondary school educator; b. Boulder, Colo., Feb. 11, 1961; s. John Russell and Joanne Jean (Bartelma) L. BS, Colo. State U., 1986; MA, U. Denver, 1994. Lic. tchr., Colo. Part-time tchr. Boulder Valley RE2 Schs., Broomfield, Colo., 1987-88, substitute tchr., 1988-90; tchr. sci. Broomfield H.S., 1990—; alt. sta. mgr., cons. Cmty. Radiation Monitoring Program, Broomfield, 1994—. Named Tchr. of the Yr., Mosaic Lodge 184, 1990, 97; Woodrow Wilson fellow, 1996, 97. Mem. NEA, Nat. Sci. Tchrs. Assn., Nat. Assn. Biology Tchrs. Presbyterian. Home: 9488 W 89th Cir Westminster CO 80021 Office: Broomfield High School 1 Eagle Way Broomfield CO 80020-3532

LITTLE, PAUL EDWARD, communications executive, city official; b. Westerly, R.I., June 29, 1955; s. John Edmund and Gloria (Capalbo) L.; m. Laurie Lee Bollman, May 24, 1980; children: Cameron, Courtney. BS, Loyola U., 1979; MA, U. Tex., 1982. Steelworker, shipfitter Electric Boat, Groton, Conn., 1974-75; various positions Fries Entertainment, L.A., 1982-85; dir. devel. Fries Entertainment, Hollywood, Calif., 1985-88; assoc. prodr. devel. Spanish Trail Prodns., Universal City, Calif., 1989-92; freelance journalist; dir. of comms. Pacific Asia Mus., Pasadena, Calif., 1993—; chair of bd. Project Day, Pasadena, 1995—; bd. dirs. San Gabriel Valley Coun. Govs., Azusa, Calif.; co-chair electricity com. SGVOG, Azusa, 1996—; mem. fin. com. City of Pasadena, 1996—, mem. bus. enterprise com., 1995—. Mem. City Coun., City of Pasadena, 1995—; bd. dirs. Bungalow Heaven Neighborhood Assn., Pasadena, 1985-95; treas. Pasadena Comm. Access Corp., 1992-95; co-chair Celebrating a Family Comty., Pasadena, 1996; chair Linking for Econ. Opportunities Com., Pasadena, 1996—. Mem. NATAS, Nat. League Cities. Office: City of Pasadena 100 N Garfield Ave Pasadena CA 91109

LITTLEFIELD, EDMUND WATTIS, mining company executive; b. Ogden, Utah, Apr. 16, 1914; s. Edmond Arthur and Marguerite (Wattis) L.; m. Jeannik Mequet, June 14, 1945; children: Edmund Wattis, Jacques Mequet, Denise Renee. BA with great distinction, Stanford U., 1936, MBA, 1938. With Standard Oil Co. of Calif., 1938-41, Golden State Co., Ltd., 1946-50; v.p., treas. Utah Internat. Inc. (formerly Utah Constrn. & Mining Co.), San Francisco, 1951-56; exec. com., dir. Utah Internat. Inc. (formerly Utah Constrn. & Mining Co.), 1951—, exec. v.p., 1956, gen. mgr., 1958—, pres., 1961—, chmn. bd., 1971—, chief exec. officer, 1971-78, chmn. exec. com., dir., 1978-86; bd. dirs. SRI Internat., FMC Gold. Served as lt. (j.g.) USNR, 1941-43; spl. asst. to dep. adminstr. Petroleum Adminstrn. for War 1943-45. Recipient Ernest C. Arbuckle award Stanford Bus. Sch. Assn., 1970, Golden Beaver award, 1970, Bldg. Industry Achievement award, 1972, Harvard Bus. Statesman award, 1974, Internat. Achievement award World Trade Club, 1986, Lone Sailor award U.S. Naval Found., 1997; named to Nat. Mining Hall of Fame. Mem. San Francisco C. of C. (pres. 1956), Bus. Council (hon. mem., past chmn.), Conf. Bd., Phi Beta Kappa, Chi Psi. Clubs: Burlingame (Calif.) Country; Pacific Union, San Francisco Golf (San Francisco); Augusta National Golf, Eldorado Country; Bohemian, Cypress Point (Pebble Beach, Calif.); Vintage. Office: 550 California St San Francisco CA 94104-1006

LITTLETON, C(OVINGTON) SCOTT, anthropology educator, consultant; b. L.A., July 1, 1933; s. Scott and Adeline (Hotchkiss) L.; m. Mary Ann Wuest, Aug. 26, 1961; children: Leslie Ann Littleton Rodriguez, Cynthia. AB, UCLA, 1957, MA, 1962, PhD, 1965. Prof. anthropology Occidental Coll., L.A., 1962—; Fulbright prof. Waseda U., Tokyo, 1980-81, sr. Fulbright rschr., 1994. Author: The New Comparative Mythology, 3d edit., 1982; co-author: From Scythia to Camelot, 1994; editor: Eastern Wisdom, 1996; mem. adv. bd. The World Book Encyclopedia, 1972—; mem. editl. adv. bd. Jour. Indo-European Studies, 1971—; contbr. articles to profl. jours. With U.S. Army, 1950-52, Korea. ACLS grantee, 1972, 78; Wenner-Gren Found. grantee, 1983. Fellow Am. Anthrop. Assn.; Mem. Am. Ethnol. Assn., Soc. Cultural Anthropology, Am. Philos. Soc., Phi Beta Kappa. Democrat. Home: 1600 La Loma Rd Pasadena CA 91105 Office: Occidental Coll 1600 Campus Rd Los Angeles CA 90041

LITTLETON, GAYE DARLENE, nonprofit executive director; b. Parma, Idaho, Nov. 1, 1938; d. Donald Lyle and June E. (Shelton) Graham; m. Jerry M. Littleton, June 11, 1960; children: Leslie, Clark, Laura, Stacey. BS in Edn., U. Idaho, 1960; MS in Ednl. Adminstrn., Utah State U., 1980. Tchr. Seattle, 1960-62; tchr. jr. high sch. Ogden (Utah) Sch. Dist., 1975-76; tchr. Utah State Sch. for the Blind, Ogden, 1976-80; ednl. equity program coord. Weber State Coll., Ogden, 1979-81; councilwoman Ogden City Coun., 1983—; exec. dir. Your Cmty. Connection, 1981—; bd. dirs. Zion's State Bank, First Security Bank Housing Com.; rschr. in field. Contbr. articles to profl. jours. Commr. Ogden Redevel. Agy., Ogden Housing Agy., 1993; mem. human devel. com. Nat. League of Cities; bd. dirs. Weber County Dept. Aging, City Parks and Recreation, Nature Ctr., Arts Commn., Equal Employment Opportunity; mem. Weber County Social Svcs. Coordinating Coun.; past chair Weber County Title XX Coun.; mem. Weber County Resource Coalition, Weber County Human Rights Coalition, Weber County Homeless Coordinating Com.; mem. ethics com. McKay Dee Hosp., 1990—. Recipient Acad. scholarship for Cmty. Svc., 1956, Thesian award U. Idaho, 1959, LWV Cmty. Svc. award Weber County Mental Health, 1974, Cmty. Svc. award, VIP award Hill AFB, Utah, 1977, Liberty Bell award Utah Bar Assn., 1977, Leadership award Nat. YWCA, 1979, Susa Young Gates award Utah Women's Polit. Caucus for Outstanding Contbn. to Women and Minorities, 1980, Jane Addams award, 1982, Women Helpin Women award, 1983, Utah Women of Achievement award, 1984, Golden Deeds award, 1988, Athena award, Disting. Alumni award WSU, 1994, Outstanding Rotarian Housing Commr., 1990. Mem. LWV, AAUW (Woman of Yr. 1988), Ogden Rotary Club (First Woman Rotarian 1992), Ogden C. of C. (Athenia award 1992). Home: 1708 Hislop Dr Ogden UT 84404-5320 Office: Your Cmty Connection 2261 Adams Ave Ogden UT 84401-1510

LITVACK, SANFORD MARTIN, lawyer; b. Bklyn., Apr. 29, 1936; s. Murray and Lee M. (Korman) L.; m. Judith E. Goldenson, Dec. 30, 1956; children—Mark, Jonathan, Sharon, Daniel. BA, U. Conn., 1956; LLB, Georgetown U., 1959. Bar: N.Y. 1964, D.C. 1979. Trial atty. antitrust div. Dept. Justice, Washington, 1959-61; asst. atty. gen. Dept. Justice, 1980-81; asso. firm Donovan, Leisure, Newton & Irvine, N.Y.C., 1961-69; ptnr. Donovan, Leisure, Newton & Irvine, 1969-80, 81-86, Dewey, Ballantine, Bushby, Palmer & Wood, N.Y.C., 1987-91; sr. exec. v.p., chief of corp. ops., gen. counsel The Walt Disney Co., Burbank, Calif., 1991—, also bd. dirs. Bd. dirs. Bet Tzedek. Fellow Am. Coll. Trial Lawyers; mem. ABA, Fed. Bar Coun., N.Y. State Bar Assn. (sec. antitrust sect. 1974-77, chmn. antitrust sect. 1985-86), Va. Bar Assn. Office: The Walt Disney Co 500 S Buena Vista St Burbank CA 91521-0001

LITVAK, JOHN, neurosurgeon; b. Denver, Oct. 5, 1927; s. Isadore and Celia (Luper) L.; m. Adrienne Kirshenbaum, Dec. 7, 1947; children: Stacy Michael, David Lee, Jacqueline Beth, Jeffrey Scott. BA, U. Denver, 1952; MD, U. Colo., 1954; MS, McGill U., 1959. Diplomate Am. Bd. Neurol. Surgery. Resident in surgery Montreal Children's Hosp./Gen. Hosp., 1955-56; fellow in exptl. surgery McGill U., Montreal, 1956; resident in neurology Montreal Neurol. Inst., 1956-57, fellow in neuropathology, 1957; resident in neurol. surgery The Neurol. Inst., N.Y.C., 1957-60; asst. prof. neurosurgery U. Colo. Med. Ctr., Denver, 1974—; pvt. practice neurosurgery, 1960—; chief of surgery St. Anthony Hosp., 1978-79, chair neurosurg. divsn., 1970-72, 76-77, 94-96. Served in U.S. Navy, 1945-46. Fellow ACS; mem. AMA, Colo. State Med. Soc., Am. Assn. Neurol. Surgeons, Rocky Mountain Neurol. Soc., Congress Neurol. Surgeons, Colo. Neurol. Soc. Office: 1471 Stuart St Denver CO 80204-1244

LIU, DON, ophthalmologist, medical researcher; b. Nanjing, China, July 17, 1947; came to the U.S., 1964; s. Robert Ching Ming and I. Tu Liu; m. Helen Cheng, June 21, 1975; children: David, Grace, Glory, Daniel. BS in Physics, Purdue U., 1969; MS in Physics, U. Mass., 1971; MD, SUNY, Buffalo, 1977. Dir. oculoplastics/orbit. Ford Hosp., Detroit, 1982-90; dir. oculoplastics/orbit. svc. U. So. Calif.-L.A. County Hosp., L.A., 1990—; assoc. dir. tech. transfer U. So. Calif., 1995—; organizer Internat. Conf. U.S.A., China and Hong Kong, Taiwan, 1985, 87, 89, 92, 93, 95; cons. to med. industries, state govt. and the Chinese govt. on health care; sci. referee Ophthalmology, 1990—, Am. Jour. Ophthalmology, 1991—, Ophthalmalic, Plastic and Recontructive Surgery, 1991—, Ophthalmic Surgery and Lasers, 1994—; mem. adv. bd. Med. Books for China, Internat., 1985—; vis. prof., lectr. various institutions in U.S., China, Taiwan, Indonesia, England, and Holland. Contbr. numerous book chpts. and articles to textbooks and profl. jours.; mem. editl. bd. numerous jours. Campaign fundraiser Mike Woo for Mayor, L.A., 1993; So. Calif. coord. Bush/Quayle, 1992, L.A.; sponsor San Marino (Calif.) Sch. Dist., 1990—; active Boy Scouts Am., Amnesty Internat., ch. activities. Recipient numerous tchg. awards, hon. degrees and titles from Chinese med. instns. Fellow ACS, Am. Acad. Facial Plastic and Reconstructive Surgery (com. mem. 1992-96), Am. Soc. Ophthalmic, Plastic and Reconstructive Surgery (fellowship dir. 1994—, Outstanding fellow 1981), Am. Acad. Ophthalmology (hon. award 1994), Am. BdOphthalmology (assoc. examiner 1991—); mem. AMA, Chinese Am. Ophthalmologic Soc.(sec.-treas. 1988-92), Internat. Soc. Oculplastic Surgeons (bd. dirs.), Com. of 100. Office: 1975 Zonal Ave KAM 516 Los Angeles CA 90033

LIU, FU-TONG, allergist, biomedical researcher, dermatologist; b. Taipei, Taiwan, July 16, 1948; came to the U.S., 1971; s. Yung-Piao and Chu-Yeh (Muira) L.; m. Sheimei Rose Chen, July 29, 1972; children: Jane May, Ray Chung. BS in Chemistry, Nat. Taiwan U., 1970; PhD, U. Chgo., 1976; MD, U. Miami, 1987. Diplomate Am. Bd. Dermatology. Asst. mem. Scripps Rsch. Inst., La Jolla, Calif., 1979-82, assoc. mem., head allergy rsch. sect., 1990-96; assoc. mem. Med. Biology Inst., La Jolla, 1982-87, mem., 1987-90; mem. divsn. dermatology Scripps Clinic Med. Group, La Jolla, 1993—; mem., head divsn. allegy La Jolla Inst. for Allergy and Immunology, 1996—; mem. adv. com. allergy & immunology NIH, Bethesda, Md., 1985-89, allergy, immunology and transplantation, 1993—. Assoc. editor: Jour. Clin. Investigation, 1993—. Scholar Leukemia Soc. Am., 1982. Mem. Am. Chem. Soc., Am. Assn. Immunologists, Am. Soc. for Investigative Pathology, Am. Soc. for Clin. Investigation, Soc. Investigative Dermatology, Am. Acad. Dermatology. Home: 4351 Mensha Pl San Diego CA 92130-2448 Office: LaJolla Inst for Allergy and Immunology 10355 Science Center Dr San Diego CA 92121

LIU, KATHERINE CHANG, artist, art educator; b. Kiang-si, China; came to U.S., 1963; d. Ming-fan and Ying (Yuan) Chang; m. Yet-zen Liu; children: Alan S., Laura Y. MS, U. Calif., Berkeley, 1965. Instr. U. Va. Ext., Longwood Coll.; mem. tchg. staff master class Hill Country Arts Found., Tex., 1995, 96, 97; invited mem. L.A. Artcore Reviewing and Curatorial Bd., 1993; invited juror, lectr. over 75 exhbns. and orgns., Alaska, Ga., Tex. and Okla. Watercolor Soc. Anns., 1997; juror, lectr. Ala. Watercolor Soc. Ann., 1996, Midwest Watercolor Soc. Nat. Exhibit, 1996, Watercolor West Nat. Open, 1996. One-woman shows include Harrison Mus., Utah State U., Riverside (Calif.) Art Mus., Ventura (Calif.) Coll., Fla. A&M U., Louis Newman Galleries, L.A., L.A. Artcore, Lung-Men Gallery, Taipei, Republic of China, State of the Arts International Biennial, Parkland Coll. Ill., 1989, 91, 97, Inaugural Exhibit, The Union Ctr. for the Arts, L.A., 1997, Treasures for the Community: The Chrysler Mus. Collects, 1989-96, 97, Watercolor U.S.A. Hon. Soc. Invitational, 1989, 91, 93, 95, Hunter Mus. Art, Tenn., 1993, Bakersfield Art Mus., 1994, Sandra Walters Gallery, Hong Kong, 1994, Horwitch-Newman Gallery, Scottsdale, Ariz., 1995, Hong Kong U. Sci. and Tech. Libr. Art Gallery, 1996, J.J. Brookings Gallery, San Francisco, 1996, John N Joe Gallery, L.A., 1996, Bill Armstrong Gallery, Springfield, Mo., 1996, Chrysler Mus. Fine Art, Norfolk, Va., 1997; Invitational, U. B.C. Art Gallery, 1992, U. Sydney Art Mus., 1992, Ruhr-West Art Mus., Wise, 1992, Macau Art Mus., 1992, Rosenfeld Gallery, Phila., 1994, Mandarin Oriental Fine Arts, Hong Kong, 1994; contbr. works to 21 books and 33 periodicals. Co-curator Taiwan-USA-Australia Watermedia Survey Exhbn., Nat. Taiwan Art Inst., 1994; sole juror San Diego Watermedia Internat., 1993, Triton Mus. Open Competition, 1994, Northern Nat. Art Competition, 1994, Watercolor West Nat., 1993, Tenn., Utah, Hawaii, N.C. Watercolor Socs., North Am. Open, Midwest Southwest and over 30 statewide competitions in watermedia or all-media; co-juror Rocky Mountain Nat., San Diego Internat. and West Fedn. Exhibits. Recipient Rex Brandt award San Diego Watercolor Internat., 1985, Purchase Selection award Watercolor USA and Springfield (Mo.) Art Mus., 1981, Gold medal, 1986, Mary Lou Fitzgerald meml. award Allied Arts Am. Nat. Arts Club, N.Y.C., 1987, Achievement award of Artists Painting in Acrylic Am. Artists Mag., 1993; NEA grantee, 1979-80. Mem. Nat. Watercolor Soc. (life, chmn. jury 1985, pres. 1983, Top award 1984, cash awards 1979, 87), Watercolor U.S.A. Honor Soc., Nat. Soc. Painters in Casein and Acrylic (2nd award 1985), Rocky Mountain Nat. Watermedia Soc. (juror 1984, awards 1978, 80, 86).

LIU, YOSEN, nuclear engineer; b. Wuchang, Hupei, China, Oct. 31, 1935; came to U.S., 1977; s. Henry C. and Chin-Feen (Chou) L.; m. Johanna S. Lui, Sept. 2, 1967; children: Sieglinde, Siegrid, Steve. BS, Naval Coll. Tech., 1958; dipl. engr., Tech. Hochschule, Germany, 1966, D of Engring., 1970. Rsch. scientist Kernforschungsanlage, Juelich, Germany, 1968-70; assoc. prof. Nat. Tsing Hua U., Hsinchu, Taiwan, 1970-75; nuclear engr. Kraftwerk Union, Erlangen, Germany, 1975-77; prin. engr. Combustion Engring. Inc., Windsor, Conn., 1977-80; mgr. bus. devel. Combustion Engring. Inc., Taipei, Taiwan, 1980-87; sr. cons. physicist ABB Combustion Engring. Inc., Windsor, 1987-90; staff engr. Battelle Pacific Northwest Lab., Richland, Wash., 1990—. Mem. Am. Nuclear Soc., Rotary Internat. Roman Catholic. Home: 218 Sitka Ct Richland WA 99352-8730 Office: Battelle Pacific NW Lab Battelle Blvd Richland WA 99352

LIU, YOUNG KING, biomedical engineering educator; b. Nanjing, China, May 3, 1934; came to U.S., 1952; s. Yih Ling and Man Fun (Teng) L.; m. Nina Pauline Liu, Sept. 4, 1964 (July, 1986); children—Erik, Tania; m. Anita Beeth, Aug. 14, 1994. BSME, Bradley U., 1955; MSME, U. Wis.-Madison, 1959; PhD, Wayne State U., 1963. Cert. acupuncturist, Calif. Asst. prof. Milw. Sch. of Engring., 1956-59; instr. Wayne State U., Detroit, 1960-63; lectr. then asst. prof. U. Mich., Ann Arbor, 1963-69; assoc. prof. then prof. Tulane U., New Orleans, 1969-78; prof. biomed. engring., dir. dept. U. Iowa, Iowa City, 1978-93; pres. U. No. Calif., Petaluma, 1993—. Contbr. articles to profl. jours., chpts. to books. NIH spl. research fellow, 1968-69; recipient Research Career Devel. award NIH, 1971-76. Mem. Internat. Soc. Lumbar Spine (exec. com., central U.S. rep.), Orthopedic Research Soc., Am. Soc. Engring. Edn., Sigma Xi. Democrat.

LIVDAHL, ROGER C., wine appraiser; b. Bismark, N.D., Mar. 26, 1938; s. Norman Thurstan and Viola Helen Livdahl. Student, U. Mont., 1956-60, U. Kans., 1961-62. Cert. sr. appraiser Am. Soc. Appraisers. Territory mgr. Union Bag Camp Paper, Chgo., 1963-65; regoinal sales coord. Sunbeam Corp., various locations, 1965-69; founder, pres. Lindahl Enterprise, St. Louis, 1969-83, Livdahl Wine Appraisals, L.A., 1983—; mem. Am. Arbitration assn. Panel, 1985; disting. expert Nat. Forensic Ctr., 1984. Contbr. articles to profl. jours. With U.S. Army, 1961-63. Office: 2157 N Vine St #8 Los Angeles CA 90068

LIVERMORE, DONALD RAYMOND, elementary/secondary education educator, library media specialist, educational/technology consultant; b. Stockton, Calif., May 14, 1947; s. Harry Guy and Cora Edith (Ambrose) L. AA, Delta Jr. Coll., Stockton, Calif., 1967; BS, BA, Chico State U., 1971; MLS, San Jose State U., 1995. Cert. elem., secondary tchr. libr. media, Calif. Salesman/mgr. Magor's Mens Wear, Tracy, Calif., 1961-75; tchr., K-6 Monterey (Calif.) Peninsula Unified Sch. Dist., 1971—, mentor tchr., cons., trainer and presenter multimedia presentations, 1984—, trainer and presenter multimedia presentations, 1995, 96; instr. Chapman Coll., Monterey, 1982—, Calif. State U., Monterey Bay, 1982—; aquarium guide Monterey Bay Aquarium, 1985-93, mentor guide, trainer, 1986-97, VVIP tour guide, 1988—; program quality reviewer State of Calif., Monterey County Office Edn., Salinas, 1982-92; mem. IMEP history and social sci. textbook adoption com. Calif. Bd. Edn., 1990, 93; libr. media specialist Manzanita Elem. Sch., 1990-95, Los Arboles Mid. Sch., 1995—. Author: (resource workbook) Hands on History; collaborator (with Randy Reinstedt): More Than Memories, 1985; coord. history project curriculum Memories Shared, 1984-94. Pres. bd. dirs. PTA, Olson, 1976-78, Hayes, 1986-88. Apple Computers Ptnrs. in Edn. grantee, 1994-97, NSF grantee for virtual canyon electronic field trips project Monterey Bay Aquarium and Rsch. Inst.; recipient Kern County Hist. award, Social Sci. Consortium award, Fresno, Calif., 1985; named Tchr. in Marine Rsch., Monterey County Office Edn., Salinas, 1988, Vol. of Yr., Monterey Peninsula Hospitality Industry, 1993. Mem. Monterey Bay Tchrs. Assn. (faculty rep. 1975-77). Democrat. Lutheran. Office: Los Arboles Mid Sch 294 Hillcrest Ave Marina CA 93933

LIVESAY, THOMAS ANDREW, museum administrator, lecturer; b. Dallas, Feb. 1, 1945; s. Melvin Ewing Clay and Madge Almeda (Hall) L.; m. Jennifer Clark, June 15, 1985 (div.); 1 child, Russell; m. Amanda Haralson, Nov. 12, 1994; children: Heather Marie, Seth Stover. BFA, U. Tex., Austin, 1968, MFA, 1972; postgrad., Harvard U. Inst. Arts Adminstrn., 1978. Curator Elisabet Ney Mus., Austin, 1971-73; dir. Longview (Tex.) Mus. and Arts Center, 1973-75; curator Amarillo (Tex.) Art Center, 1975-77, dir., 1977-80; asst. dir. for adminstrn. Dallas Mus. Fine Arts, 1980-85; dir. Mus. of N.Mex., Santa Fe, 1985—; mem. touring panel Tex. Commn. Arts; mem. panel Nat. Endowment Arts, Inst. Mus. Svcs.; adj. prof. U. Okla., Coll. Liberal Studies, 1992—, U. N.Mex., 1992—; chmn. N.Mex. State Records and Archives Commn., 1986—. Author: Young Texas Artists Series, 1978, Made in Texas, 1979; editor: video tape American Images, 1979, Ruth Abrams, Paintings, 1940-85, NYU Press. Served with U.S. Army, 1969-71. Mem. Am. Assn. Mus. (coun. 1986-89, commn. on ethics 1992—, accreditation commn. 1994—, chmn. accreditation commn. 1997—), Tex. Assn. Mus. (v.p. 1981, pres. 1983), Rotary. Methodist. Office: Mus of New Mexico 113 Lincoln PO Box 2087 Santa Fe NM 87504-2087

LIVESAY, VALORIE ANN, security analyst; b. Greeley, Colo., Sept. 9, 1959; d. John Albert and Mary Magdalene Yurchak. BA in Edn., U. No.

Colo., 1981; M in Computer Info. Sys., U. Denver, 1991; AAS in Fashion Mktg., Colo. Inst. Art, 1996. Drafter Computer Graphics, Denver, 1981, Advanced Cable Sys., Inc., Denver, 1981-82, Am. TV Comm. Corp., Englewood, Colo., 1982-83; janitor Rockwell Internat., Golden, Colo., 1983-84, analytical lab tech., 1984-86, metall. operator, 1986-88; nuclear material coord. EG&G Rocky Flats Inc., Golden, 1988-92, lead security analyst, 1992-95. Active Channel 6, Denver, 1985, World Wildlife Fund, Westminster, Colo., 1987, Denver Dumb Friends League, 1987, The Nature Conservancy, Boulder, Colo., 1989. Mem. NAFE, Am. Soc. Insdl. Security. Home: 6344 W 115th Ave Broomfield CO 80020-3034

LIVINGSTON, LOUIS BAYER, lawyer; b. N.Y.C., Dec. 12, 1941; s. Norman and Helen (Bayer) L.; m. Mari Livingston, Apr. 6, 1968; children: Diana, Alex, Ann. BA, Yale U., 1963; LLB, Harvard U., 1966. Bar: N.Y. 1967, Oreg. 1971. Atty. NLRB, Memphis, 1967-68, Poletti, Freidin et al., N.Y.C., 1968-71; ptnr. Miller, Nash, Wiener, Hager & Carlsen, Portland, Oreg., 1971—. Office: Miller Nash Wiener Hager & Carlsen 111 SW 5th Ave Portland OR 97204-3604

LIVINGSTON, MYRAN JAY, film writer, film director, film producer; b. N.Y.C., Mar. 19, 1934; s. Myran Jabez and Anne Josephine (White) L.; m. Elizabeth Rasmussen, July 28, 1956 (div. May 1971); 1 child, Lisa Browning; m. Bernice Helen Beck, Nov. 8, 1971; children: Simon Jabez, Sarah Gustine. Student, Kenyon Coll., 1952-56, U.C.L.A., 1957-58. Writer/dir. CBS TV Network, L.A., 1956-64, McCann-Erickson, San Francisco, 1965-71, Eastman Kodak, Rochester, N.Y., 1980-83; owner, operator Promethean Prodns., L.A., 1983—; guest lectr. Coll. of Marin, San Franciso, 1972-73, Loyola Marymount U., L.A., 1979, Rochester Inst. of Tech., 1982. Author: (novels) The Prodigy, 1979, The Synapse Function, 1985,. Tchr. in comml. prodn. San Francisco Women in Advertising, 1976, The Del Monte Corp., San Francisco, 1970, Van Nuys (Calif.) H.S., 1980, Mira Catalina Sch., Palos Verdes, Calif., 1986. Recipient 7 Golden Eagle awards Coun. on Internat. Theatrical Events, 1982-84, 1st place Gold Camera award U.S. Indsl. Film Festival, 1984, CLIO for "Most Beautiful Spot" award Bullocks, 1978, 4 Telly Silver and Bronze awards 14th and 17th Ann. Competition, 1993,96. Mem. Writer's Guild of Am., The Author's Guild. Episcopalian. Home and Office: Promethean Prodns 841 Corbett Ave San Francisco CA 94131

LIVO, NORMA JOAN, writer; b. Tarentum, Pa., July 31, 1929; d. David John and Della Mae (Kline) Jackson; m. George Oliver Livo, Jan. 26, 1951; children: Lauren J., Keith Eric, Kim Bruce, Robert Craig. BS, U. Pitts., 1962, MEd, 1963, EdD, 1969. Geophys. asst. Gulf Rsch. Lab., Harmarville, Pa., 1950-51; demonstration tchr. Talk Lab. Sch.-U. Pitts., 1962-66; prof. U. Colo., Denver, 1968-92. Author: Who's Afraid? Facing Ch's Fears, 1994 (Storytelling World award 1995); co-author: Storytelling Folklore Sourcebook, 1991 (Storytelling World award 1995), Of Bugs & Beasts, 1995 (Best Book 1995); editor: Troubadour's Storybag, 1996. Pres. Colo. Coun. Internat. Reading Assn., 1976-77. Recipient Gov.'s award for Excellence in the Arts, 1995. Mem. Nat. Storytellers Assn. (bd. dirs. 1991-93, Leadership award 1996), Colo. League Authors, Denver Womens Press Club.

LIVSEY, HERBERT C., lawyer; b. Salt Lake City, Aug. 20, 1941. BS, U. Utah, 1967, JD, 1969; LLM in Taxation, NYU, 1971. Bar: Utah 1969. Shareholder, fin. dir. Ray, Quinney & Nebeker P.C., Salt Lake City. Assoc. editor: Utah Law Review, 1968-69; graduate editor: Tax Law Review, 1970-71. Fellow Am. Coll. Trust and Estate Counsel; mem. Utah State Bar Assn. (chmn. tax sect. 1978-79), Order of the Coif, Phi Kappa Phi, Delta Theta Phi. Office: Ray Quinney & Nebeker PC PO Box 45385 Salt Lake City UT 84145-0385

LIVZIEY, JAMES GERALD, secondary school educator; b. Buffalo, July 30, 1927; s. James Ephlyn and Helena Charlote (Kiener) L.; m. June Ellen Andersen, July 25, 1955; children: Naomi Lynn, Patricia Ellen. AA, Southwestern Jr. Coll., 1970; BA, San Diego State U., 1972. Enlisted U.S. Navy, 1945, advanced through grades to lt. comdr., 1967, ret., 1969; high sch. instr. SWHS Dist., Chula Vista, Calif., 1972—. Recipient award Freedoms Found., 1991; fellow Taft Inst., 1977, Pacific Acad. Advanced Studies, 1978. Fellow Alpha Gamma Sigma; mem. Naval Inst. USN, Masons, Knight Comdr. Ct. Honor (32d degree). Home: 675 Mariposa Cir Chula Vista CA 91911-2510

LJUBICIC DROZDOWSKI, MILADIN PETER, consulting engineer; b. Zajecar, Yugoslavia, Sept. 28, 1921; came to U.S., 1959; s. Peter Miladin and Martha Jovan (Viktorovic) Ljubicic; m. Dusica Cile Pavic, Sept. 9, 1948. Diploma in engring., U. Belgrade, Yugoslavia, 1951, 52; ancien éleve, Ecole Nationale Superieure de l'Armement, Paris, 1956; MSME, UCLA, 1964, PhD in Mec. Engring., 1971. Design and test engr. Fed. Mogul Bower, El Monte, Calif., 1959-62; chief advanced armament analytical support Hughes Helicopters, Culver City, Calif., 1962-78; engring. supr. Bechtel Power Corp., Norwalk, Calif., 1978-80; engring. adviser Bechtel Espana, Madrid, 1980-87; v.p. Koach Engring., Sun Valley, Calif., 1987; engring. cons. Mission Viejo, Calif., 1987—; asst. to chmn. continuum mechanics, Belgrade, 1955-56; guest lectr. Sch. Engring. and Applied Sci., UCLA, 1971; prof., Loyola Marymount U., L.A., 1978-80. Contbr. to profl. publs. Mem. Am. Soc. Mech. Engrs., Am. Def. Preparedness Assn., Spanish Nuclear Soc. Home and Office: 26426 Lope De Vega Dr Mission Viejo CA 92691-3316

LLAURADO, JOSEP G., nuclear medicine physician, scientist; b. Barcelona, Catalonia, Spain, Feb. 6, 1927; s. José and Rosa (Llaurado) García; m. Deirdre Mooney, Nov. 9, 1966; children—Raymund, Wilfred, Mireya; m. Catherine D. Entwistle, June 28, 1958 (dec.); children—Thadd, Oleg, Montserrat. B.S., B.A., Balmes Inst., Barcelona, 1944; M.D., Barcelona U., 1950; Ph.D. in Pharmacology, 1960; M.Sc. Biomed. Engring., Drexel U., 1963. Diplomate: Am. Bd. Nuclear Medicine. Resident Royal Postgrad. Sch. Medicine, Hammersmith Hosp., London, 1952-54; fellow M.D. Anderson Hosp. and Tumor Inst., Houston, 1957-58, U. Utah Med. Coll., Salt Lake City, 1958-59; asst. prof. U. Otago Dunedin, N.Z., 1954-57; sr. endocrinologist Pfizer Med. Research Lab., Groton, Conn., 1959-60; assoc. prof. U. Pa., 1963-67; prof. Med. Coll. Wis., Milw., 1970-82, Marquette U., 1967-82; clin. dir. nuclear medicine service VA Med. Ctr., Milw., 1977-82; chief nuclear medicine service VA Hosp., Loma Linda, Calif., 1983—; prof. dept. radiation scis. Loma Linda U. Sch. Medicine, 1983—; U.S. rep. symposium on dynamic studies with radioisotypes in clin. medicine and research IAEA, Rotterdam, 1970, Knoxville, 1974. Editor: Internat. Jour. Biomed. Computing; dep. editor Environ. Mgmt. and Health; contbr. numerous articles to profl. jours. Merit badge counselor Boy Scouts Am., 1972—; pres. Hales Corners (Wis.) Hist. Soc., 1981-83. Recipient Commendation cert. Boy Scouts Am., 1980. Fellow Am. Coll. Nutrition; mem. Soc. Nuclear Medicine (computer and acad. councils), IEEE (sr.), IEEE in Medicine and Biology Soc. (nat. adminstrv. Com. 1986-89), Biomed. Engring. Soc. (charter), Am. Physiol. Soc., Am. Soc. Pharmacology and Exptl. Therapeutics, Soc. Math. Biology (founding), Endocrine Soc., Royal Soc. Health, Societat Catalana de Biologia, Casal dels Catalans de Calif. (pres. 1989-91), Calif. Med. Assn. (sci. adv. panel nuclear medicine 1983—). Office: VA Hosp Nuclear Med Svc Rm 115 11201 Benton St Loma Linda CA 92357-0001

LLOYD, DAVID NIGEL, song writer, poet, performer; b. Mombasa, Kenya Protectorate, Mar. 16, 1954; came to U.S., 1962; s. Gerald Lloyd and Madeline Jean (Cooke) Steinberg; m. Elizabeth Shannon Meehan, July 31, 1976 (div. 1979); m. Gita Freimann, June 21, 1982; 1 child, Ursula Jane. Student, Seneca Coll., Willowdale, Ont., Can., 1971-73. Social worker Met. Toronto Assn. for Mentally Retarded, 1975; sales clk. Montgomery Ward, Canoga Park, Calif., 1976-79; prodn. asst. Spungbuggy Works, Hollywood, Calif., 1979-81; composer/performer Hollywood, 1980-83; shift mgr. Bodhi Tree Books, Hollywood, 1983-89; West Coast tour mgr. Robin Williamson Prodns., Hollywood, also Cardiff, Wales, 1991-93; song poet/pergormer California Hot Springs, 1990—; film composer Low End Prodns., L.A., 1983, 95; film composer, poet, Spike Stewart Films, L.A., 1991-95. Author: (chap book/poetry) Death in Los Fumos, 1994; composer/performer: (music recordings) Dark Ages, 1984, An Age of Fable, 1987, Death in Los Fumos, 1994. Vol. folk music tchr. Hot Springs Elem. Sch., California Hot Springs, 1991-96; folk music fundraising concert dir. Hot Springs Parent Group, 1994-95. Mem. N.Am. Folk and Dance Alliance.

LLOYD, JOSEPH WESLEY, physicist, researcher; b. N.Mex., Jan. 31, 1914; s. William Washington and Mattie May (Barber) L.; m. Lenora Lucille Hopkins, Jan. 24, 1944 (dec. June 1969); 3 children (dec.); m. Ruth Kathryn Newberry, Nov. 19, 1988; children: Kathryn Ruth Jordan, Mary Evelyn Jordan. Student, Pan Am. Coll., 1942. Plumber Pomona, Calif., 1951-57; plumber, pipefitter Marysville, Calif., 1957-79; ret., 1979; ind. researcher in physics and magnetism, Calif., 1944—. With CAP, 1944-45. Mem. AAAS, N.Y. Acad. Scis. Mem. Ch. of Christ.

LLOYD, WILLIAM JUDD, JR., obstetrician, gynecoloist; b. Sacramento, Calif., Feb. 22, 1948; s. William Judd Lloyd Sr. and Dorothea Theresa (Munz) Jones; m. Cheri Beatrice Jacobsen, May 3, 1969; children: William III, Alaina, Tricia, Natalie. BS, U. Nev., 1971, postgrad., 1973; MD, U. Iowa, 1975. Diplomate Am. Bd. Ob-Gyn. Rotating intern Akron Gen. Med. Ctr., 1975-76; ob-gyn. resident Kaiser Found. Hosp., Sacramento, Calif., 1976-79; ob-gyn. staff physician Darnall Army Hosp., Ft. Hood, Tex., 1979-81; pvt. practice Carson City, Nev., 1981-87, Reno, Nev., 1987—. Maj. U.S. Army, 1979-81. Fellow Am. Coll. Ob-Gyn.; mem. AMA, Nev. State Med. Assn., Am. Assn. Gyn. Laparoscopists, No. Nev. Ob-Gyn. Soc., Am. Fertility Soc., Washoe County Med. Soc. Republican. Office: 601 Ralston St # 200 Reno NV 89503-4436

LO, SHUI-YIN, physicist; b. Canton, Oct. 20, 1941; came to the U.S., 1959; s. Long tin and Ty-Fong (Chow) L.; m. Angela Kwok-Kie Lau, Dec. 18, 1969; children: Alpha Wei-min, Fiona Ai-ming, Hao-min. BS, U. Ill., 1962; PhD, U. Chgo., 1966. Rsch. assoc. Rutherford High Energy Lab., Chilton, United Kingdom, 1966-69, Glasgow (United Kingdom) U., 1969-72; sr. lectr. U. Melbourne, Australia, 1972-89; pres. Inst. for Boson Studies, Pasadena, Calif., 1986-92; dir. Sinotronic Co., Hong Kong, 1980—; exec. v.p., dir. rsch. Am. Environ. Tech. Group, Monrovia, Calif., 1993—; vis. assoc. Calif. Inst. Tech.; prof. physics Zhong Shan U. Author: Scientific Studies of Chinese Character, 1986; author, editor: Geometrical Picture of Hadron Scattering, 1986; contbr. over 100 articles to profl. jours. Prin. Chinese Sch. of Chinese Fellowship Victoria, Australia, 1977-84. Fellow Australian Inst. Physics; mem. Am. Phys. Soc.

LO, WAITUCK, artist; b. Honolulu, June 9, 1919; s. Wai Tong and Kam T. Lo; m. Agnes Ching, Jan. 4, 1958; children: Edwina, Felix, Lisa Ann. BS, Utopia U., Shanghai, China, 1942; postgrad., Yen Yu Inst. Fine Art, Shanghai, Ind. U. Exhibited in group shows at Assn. Honolulu Artist Jury Art Show, 1956, 57 (Most Decorative award 1956, 57), Assn. Honolulu Artists non-jury show, 1957 (Popular award 1957), Narcissus Festival Art Exhbn., 1960 (Kaiser award 1960, Most Popular award 1960), Maul County Fair Art Exhbn., 1963 (2d prize 1963); commd. silk painting Pepsi-Cola U.S.A., 1987; paintings reproduced by Regency Card Co. Recipient 1st Place Water Color award Assn. Honolulu Artists, 1965, 68, Hayward award Assn. Honolulu Artists, 1968, 1st Place Water Color award Home Builders Assn. Art Show, 1966; Honorable Mention in Oil and Water Color, Assn. Honolulu Artists, 1966, Internat. Assn. Artists, 1979. Club: Toastmasters (Honolulu) (pres. 1986).

LOARIE, JOHN ADAMS, engineer; b. Evanston, Ill., Jan. 15, 1942; s. Willard John and Lucille V. (Finnegan) L.; divorced; children: Michael, Julie, Christopher, Jennifer, Amy, Carrie; m. Barbara Fitzpatrick, Apr. 24, 1993. BSME, U. Notre Dame, 1964; MBA, Long Beach State U., 1977. Engr. Am. Can Co., Vernon, Calif., 1970-73; engring. mgr. Pharmaseal divsn. Am. Hosp. Supply, Duarte, Calif., 1973-78; prodn. mgr. Dupaco divsn. Pharmaseal, San Marcos, Calif., 1977-78; v.p. tech. and regulatory affairs GST Labs., La Jolla, Calif., 1978-79; v.p. ops. KIMCO, San Marcos, Calif., 1979-85; prodn. mgr. Astromec, Carson City, Nev., 1986-88; v.p. engring. Shurflo, Santa Ana, Calif., 1988-92, v.p. recreation vehicle marine, 1992-96; v.p. motor products Shurflo, 1996—. Lt. USN, 1964-70; Vietnam. Recipient Achievement award Sec. of Navy, 1968. Home: 22 Via Perico Rancho Santa Margarita CA 92688-3429 Office: Shurflo 12650 Westminster Ave Santa Ana CA 92706-2139

LOARIE, THOMAS MERRITT, healthcare executive; b. Deerfield, Ill., June 12, 1946; s. Willard John and Lucile Veronica (Finnegan) L.; m. Stephanie Lane Fitts, Aug. 11, 1968 (div. Nov. 1987); children: Thomas M., Kristin Leigh Soule. BSME, U. Notre Dame, 1968; Student, U. Minn., 1969-70, U. Chgo., 1970-71, Columbia U., 1978. Registered profl. engr., Calif. Prodn. engr. Honeywell, Inc., Evanston, Ill., 1968-70; various positions Am. Hosp. Supply Co., Evanston, Ill., 1970-83, pres. Heyer-Schulte divsn., 1979-83; pres. COO Novacor Med. Corp., Oakland, Calif., 1984-85, also bd. dirs.; pres. ABA Bio Mgmt., Danville, Calif., 1985-87; chmn., CEO Keravision, Inc., Fremont, Calif., 1987—; founder, chmn., med. device CEO Roundtable, 1993—; asst. prof. surgery Creighton U. Med. Sch., Omaha, 1986-94; speaker in field. Contbr. articles on med. tech. and pub. policy to Wall St. Jour., others. Bd. dirs. Marymount Sch. Bd., 1981-84; bd. dirs. United Way Santa Barbara, 1981-84, assoc. chairperson, 1982-83, treas., 1983. Named One of 50 Rising Stars: Exec. Leaders for the 80's Industry Week mag., 1983. Mem. Assn. for Rsch. in Vision and Ophthalmology, Contact Lens Assn. Ophthalmology, Health Industry Mfrs. Assn. (spl. rep. bd. dirs. 1993-96, bd. dirs. 1997—), Am. Entrepreneurs for Econ. Growth. Roman Catholic. Office: KeraVision Inc 48630 Milmont Dr Fremont CA 94538-7353

LOBACH, MELISSA RENEE, English language educator; b. San Diego, Nov. 28, 1965; d. James Edward Lobach and Dyahna Rose (Brittain) Riall; children: Corinthea Procopis, Beau Williams. BA, Met. State Coll., Denver, 1994. Cert. secondary tchr., Colo. Security officer Laird Internat. Studios, Culver City, Calif., 1984; sr. staff asst. Met. State Coll., Denver, 1989-94; instr. Aurora (Colo.) C.C., 1996—; asst. dir. Hollywood for Kids, Denver, 1992; tchr.-participant Westridge Young Writers Workshop, Lakewood, Colo., 1993, 95. Contbr. articles to profl. jours. Tchg. asst. Cherry Creek (Colo.) Schs. Spl. Needs Summer Program, 1992. Recipient Colo. Scholars scholarship Met. State Coll., Denver, 1991-94. Mem. NEA, Internat. Reading Assn. (Colo. coun.), Writers Anonymous (co-founder, bd. dirs. 1991—), Golden Key Honor Soc.

LOBANOV-ROSTOVSKY, OLEG, arts association executive; b. San Francisco, July 12, 1934; s. Andrei and Grace S. (Pope) L-R.; m. Susan Waters, Sept. 8, 1979; 1 child, Alexandra; children by previous marriage: Christopher, Nicholas. BA, U. Mich., 1956. Community concert rep. Columbia Artists Mgmt. Inc., 1958-59; mgr. Columbus (Ohio) Symphony Orch., 1959-62, Hartford (Conn.) Symphony Orch., 1962-65, Balt. Symphony, 1965-69; program officer div. humanities and arts Ford Found., 1969-75; exec. dir. Denver Symphony Orch., 1975-76; mng. dir. Nat. Symphony Orch., Washington, 1977-80; cons. Fed. Coun. on Arts, 1980-81; exec. dir. Del. Ctr. for Performing Arts, 1981-82; exec. v.p., mng. dir. Detroit Symphony Orch., 1982-83, pres., 1983-89; ind. cons., 1989-90; mng. ptnr. Middle Am. div. Jerold Panas, Young & Ptnrs. Inc., Chgo., 1990-91; pres. Calif. Ctr. for the Arts, Escondio, Calif., 1991—.

LOBAUGH, LESLIE E., JR., holding company executive, corporate lawyer. AB, Santa Clara U., 1967; JD, Georgetown U., 1970. Bar: Calif. Assoc. Holdberg, Finger, Brown & Abramson, 1971-75; staff atty. Pacific Lighting, 1975-77, sr. counsel, 1977-82, asst. gen. counsel, 1982-85, assoc. gen. counsel, 1985-86; v.p., gen. counsel Pacific Enterprises, 1986—, So. Calif. Gas Co., 1986—. Office: Pacific Enterprises 633 W 5th St Ste 5200 Los Angeles CA 90071-2015*

LOBEL, CHARLES IRVING, physician; b. Phila., Nov. 9, 1921; s. Maurice and Dora (Barnett) L.; m. Julia Valentine Skellchock, June 12, 1955; children: Meredith Anne Lobel-Angel. AA, San Jose State U., 1948; student, Stanford U., 1948-49; MD, U. So. Calif., 1953. Physician Permanente Med. Group, Inc., South San Francisco, 1954-65; physician, courtesy staff Chope Community Hosp., San Mateo, Calif., 1965-89, Sequoia Hosp., Redwood City, Calif., 1965-94; physician Permanente Med. Group, Inc., Redwood City, Calif., 1965-95; clin. prof. medicine div. rheumatology Stanford U. Sch. Medicine, 1965—; chief profl. edn. Kaiser Found. Hosp., Redwood City, 1968-80, rehab. coord, 1968-80, pres med. staff, 1968-70; mem. Calif. Med. Assn. Staff Survey Com., San Francisco, 1970-90; mem. 4th dist. Bd. Med. Quality Assurance State Calif., 1979-84. 1st Lt. U.S. Army, 1942-46. Decorated Combat Infantry Badge, Bronze Star, Presdl. Unit citation, 3 Battle Stars. Fellow Am. Acad. Family Physicians, Am. Coll. Rheumatology; mem. AMA, AAAS, San Mateo County Med. Soc. (bd. dirs. 1975-78), Calif. Med. Soc. (alt. del. 1979-83), N.Y. Acad. of Sci., Am. Heart Assn., Royal Soc. of Med., Med. Friends of Wine, Arthritis Found. No. Calif., Phi Delta Epsilon. Office: Stanford U Clinic Dept Rheumatology 900 Blake Wilbur Dr Palo Alto CA 94304-2205

LOBSINGER, THOMAS, bishop; b. Ayton, Ont., Can., Nov. 17, 1927. Ordained priest Roman Cath. Ch., 1954, bishop, 1987. Bishop Whitehorse, Y.T., Can., 1987—. Home: 5119 5th Ave, Whitehorse, YK Canada Y1A 1L5*

LOBUE, ANGE JOSEPH, psychiatrist, author; b. Hammond, La., Aug. 12, 1937; s. Joseph Vincent and Augustine (Palmintier) L.; m. Elizabeth Tallent; 1 child, Gabriel Smoots. BS in Pharmacy, U. Miss., 1960; MD, La. State U., 1964; MPH, UCLA, 1968. Diplomate Am. Bd. Psychiatry and Neurology. Med.-surg. intern So. Pacific Meml. Hosp., San Francisco, 1964-65; resident in psychiatry Dept. Preventive and Social Medicine UCLA Sch. Medicine, 1968-71, resident in psychiatry Dept. Psychiatry, 1969-72, asst. clin. prof., 1972-92; instr. Sch. Cinema-TV U. So. Calif., L.A., 1987-92; pvt. practice Santa Rosa, Calif., 1988—, Mendocino and Palo Alto, Calif.; vis. fellow U. Belgrade (Yugoslavia) and the Fed. Inst. Pub. Health, U. Edinburgh (Scotland) and the Ministry of Health, 1969, St. Thomas' Hosp. and the Ministry of Health, London, 1969; vis. scholar, spl. asst. to adminstr. Health Svcs. and Mental Health Adminstrn., HEW, Washington, 1970; vis. scholar, asst. to pres. N.Y.C. Health and Hosps. Corp., 1970-71; registered pharmacist, mgr. Briargrove Pharmacy, Houston, Tex., 1960; writer, spkr., lectr., program presenter numerous workshops, hosps., colls., univs., TV, assns.; apptd. staff Meml. Hosp. Med. Ctr., Long Beach, Calif., Santa Rosa Meml. Hosp., UCLA Ctr. Health Scis., Warrack Hosp., Santa Rosa. Editor: Psychiatry and the Media, 1983; contbr. articles to profl. jours. Sr. pub. health physician Venice Youth Clinic, L.A., 1969. Capt. U.S. Army Med. Corps, 1965-67. Fellow Acad. Psychosomatic Medicine, Am. Coll. Preventive Medicine (assoc.), Am. Geriatrics Soc. (founding), Royal Soc. Health; mem. NATAS, Am. Film Inst. Alumni Assn., Am. Med. Writers Assn., Biofeedback Cert. Inst. Am., Mendocino-Lake County Med. Soc., Nat. Thespian Soc., Physicians Coun. on Drug Dependence, Sonoma County Med. Assn., UCLA Alumni Assn., Delta Omega. Office: PO Box 2390 45121 Ukiah St Mendocino CA 95460-2390 also: 66 Pearce Mitchell Pl Stanford CA 94305

LOCATELLI, PAUL LEO, university president; b. Santa Cruz, Calif., Sept. 16, 1938; s. Vincent Dino and Marie Josephine (Piccone) L. B.S. in Acctg., Santa Clara U., 1961; MDiv, Jesuit Sch. Theology, 1974; DBA, U. So. Calif., 1971. CPA, Calif. Ordained priest Roman Cath. Ch., 1974. Acct., Lautze & Lautze, San Jose, Calif., 1960-61, 1973-74; prof. acctg. Santa Clara (Calif.) U., 1974-86, assoc. dean Bus. Sch. and acad. v.p., 1978-86, pres., 1988—. bd. dirs. Silicon Valley, Tech. Mus.; bd. trustee Inst. of European & Asian Studies; mem. Nat. Cath. Bishops and Pres.' Com.; mem. adv. couns. Parents Helping Parents and Community Found.; past rector Jesuit Community at Loyola Marymount U. Past trustee U. San Francisco, Seattle U., St. Louis U. and Loyola Marymount U., Regis U.; past mem. Sr. Commn. of Western Assn. Schs. and Colls., Acctg. Edn. Change Commn. Mem. AICPA, Calif. Soc. CPAs (Disting. Prof. of the Yr award, 1994), Am. Acctg. Assn., NCCJ (bd. dirs.), Assn. Jesuit Colls. and Univs. (chair), Ind. Colls. Calif., Am. Leadership Forum (bd. dirs.). Democrat. Office: Santa Clara U 500 El Camino Real Santa Clara CA 95053-0015

LOCH, PATRICIA ANN, software company executive, consultant; b. Omaha, May 2, 1944; d. Frank and Elizabeth (Duffield) Barrick; m. Charles Joseph Loch, Nov. 25, 1967; children: Michelle Kathleen, Justin Randall. BS in Math., Wake Forest U., 1966. Programmer IBM, Raleigh, N.C., 1966-68, Almay Cosmetics, Raleigh, N.C., 1968; contract programmer Kelly Assocs., Mpls., 1969-70, Bre-Mar Systems, N.Y.C., 1971; systems analyst Met. Life Ins. Co., N.Y.C., 1970-71; cons. Bd. Coop. Edn. Svcs., Yorktown, N.Y., 1972-75; pres., cons. P. Loch Assocs., Danville, Calif., 1975—; cons. Target Pub., Pleasanton, Calif., 1976-88. Mem. Assn. Small System Users (dir. membership 1981-82, dir. facilities 1985-87), NAFE, AAUW, Round Hill Country (Alamo, Calif.), Amador Athletic Club (Pleasanton). Home: 8071 E Del Trigo Scottsdale AZ 85258-1751

LOCHER, MARIANNE, marketing professional; b. Washington, Oct. 27, 1959; d. Paul R. and Anne (Farrelly) L. BA cum laude, Rosemont Coll., 1981; Cert., N.Y. Sch. Interior Design, 1986; MFA, Columbia U., 1989. Asst. to dir. of mktg. Sotheby's, N.Y.C., 1983-85; spl. asst. to pres. Asprey, N.Y.C., 1985-88; asst. to exec. dir. Assoc. Art Mus. Dirs., N.Y.C., 1988-89; spl. projects staff Paul Segal Assocs., Architects, N.Y.C., 1989; mktg. coord. Archtl. Interiors, Washington, 1991-92; spl. projects mktg. mgr. Hornberger & Worstell, Inc., San Francisco, 1992-94; mktg. mgr. Hellmuth, Obata & Kassabaum, San Francisco, 1994-96, Holey Assocs., San Francisco, 1996—. Mem. Delta Epsilon Sigma.

LOCHER, WALTER, agricultural products company; b. 1943. With Volcom (formerly Volkart Holding AG), Winterhur, Switzerland, 1966—; pres. Volkart Am. Inc., Phoenix, 1988—; CEO Anderson Clayton Corp., Phoenix, 1990—. Office: Anderson Clayton Corp 615 S 51st Ave Phoenix AZ 85043-4706*

LOCKART, BARBETTA, counselor, jeweler, artwear designer, artist; b. Sacramento, Calif., Feb. 28, 1947; d. Bernard Elwood and Naomi Joyce (Wilson) L.; m. Michael Stanley Ray, Dec. 29, 1982 (div). AA in English, Southwestern Coll., Chula Vista, Calif., 1974; BA, San Diego State U., 1975; MA in Edn. Adminstrn., N.Mex. State U., Las Cruces, 1979, MA in Counseling and Guidance, 1981. Sec., interim coord., tchr. Indian Edn. Project, Palm Springs (Calif.) Unified Sch. Dist., 1976-79; outreach counselor Tecumseh House/Boston Indian Coun., 1980-81, asst. dir., 1981; acad. counselor, coord. native Am. affairs Ea. N.Mex. U., Portales, 1981-82; ind. researcher in field of counseling, Albuquerque, 1982-89, Sacramento, Calif., 1989—; pres., Sacramento, 1989—; owner Dearwater Designs, Albuquerque, 1985-88, Sacramento, 1988-90, Barbetta's Beds & Art, Sacramento, 1990-97, ITSA, 1997—; speaker in field of community ed n., alcoholism, urban native Am. women. Rockefeller Found. fellow, 1978-79; Nat. Inst. Edn. fellow, 1979-80. Author: Resolving Discipline Problems for Indian Students: A Preventative Approach, 1981, Auctions and Auction-Going: Make Them Pay Off for You; contbr. articles to profl. jours. *Personal philosophy: Respect - to be respectful of people, animals, plants etc. and of the rhythm of things and to enjoy and learn from the myriad of cultural philosophical and spiritual variations that make life and living such an adventure.*

LOCKE, FRANCIS PHILBRICK, retired editorial writer; b. Lincoln, Nebr., May 1, 1912; s. Walter Leonard and Annette Elizabeth (Philbrick) L.; m. Carroll Day, Dec. 31, 1936; children: Margaret Locke Newhouse, Alice Locke Carey, Walter Day. BA, Harvard Coll., 1933; posgrad., Harvard U., 1946-47. Reporter Miami (Fla.) Daily News, 1934-36, editorial writer, 1936-41; editorial writer St. Louis Post-Dispatch, 1941; editor of editorial page Miami Daily News, 1941-46; Nieman fellow Harvard U., Cambridge, Mass., 1946-47; assoc. editor Dayton (Ohio) Daily News, 1947-63; editorial writer Riverside (Calif.) Press-Enterprise, 1963-72. Author: (chpt.) Public Men In & Out of Office, 1943; contbr. articles to profl. jours. Bd. dirs. Mission Inn Found., Riverside, 1987-95; mem. adv. bd. YWCA, Riverside; trustee Miami U., Oxford, Ohio, 1954-63; divsn. chmn. United Way, Dayton, 1956-57. Recipient aviation writing award TWA, 1956. Mem. Nat. Conf. Editorial Writers, Soc. Profl. Journalists (nat. editorial writing prize 1946), Harvard U. Alumni Assn. (S.W. and Pacific regional dir. 1980-86, Harvard medal 1983), Harvard-Radcliffe Club So. Calif. (bd. dirs. 1975-92), Harvard Club Dayton (pres. 1961-63). Democrat. Congregationalist. Home: 7368 Westwood Dr Riverside CA 92504-2729

LOCKE, GARY, governor; b. Jan. 21, 1950; s. James and Julie L.; m. Mona Lee Locke, Oct. 15, 1994. BA in Polit. Sci., Yale U., 1972; JD, Boston U., 1975. Dep. prosecuting atty. State of Wash., King County; with Ho. of Reps., Wash., 1982-93; cmty. rels. mgr. U.S. West; chief exec. King County, 1993. Named First in effectiveness among Puget Sound area lawmakers Seattle Times, 1990. Office: Office of the Gov PO Box 40002 Olympia WA 98504

LOCKRIDGE, ALICE ANN, secondary education educator; b. Gread Bend, Kans., Mar. 27, 1951; d. Richard Lee and Madeleine McMillan; m. Patrick

Henry Lockridge, Jan. 1, 1988. AS, Pratt (Kans.) Community Coll., 1971; BS, U. Kans., 1973; MS in Phys. Edn., U. Wash., 1977. Cert. fitness instr., phys. fitness specialist/trainer; accredited exam preparation trainer Am. Coun. on Exercise. Tchr. Kansas City (Kans.) Pub. Schs., 1973-74, Highline Pub. Sch. Dist., Seattle, 1974-76; fitness instr. Seattle Fire Dept., 1977-79; insvc. trainer various sch. dists., 1984—; prog. instr./health fitness technologist Renton (Wash.) Vocat. Tech. Inst., 1985-87; fitness instr. Apprenticeship and Non-Traditional Employment for Women, Renton, 1981-87; exercise physiologist Seattle City Light and Snohomish, 1988—; owner PRO-FIT, Renton, 1983—, Exercise Express, Renton, Wash., 1995—; fitness cons. police dept., Seattle, 1991; testing cons. police, fire, electric and water depts., various cities, 1991; tchr. tng. lectr., various sch. dists., 1984—. Author: (book/study cards) PRO-FACTS, 1986, (edn. chart) Training Heart Rate Chart, 1983, (slide show series) Do It Right...Teach It Safe, 1985, (consumer edn. series) Never Exercise with a Jerk, 1990. Recipient Presdl. Sports awards, Presdl. Coun. on Phys. Fitness, 1978-86, Outstanding Support award Apprenticeship and Non-Traditional Employement for Women, 1988. Mem. IDEA, AAHPERD, Assn. for Fitness Profls. (com. mem.), Am. Coun. on Exercise (cert. com. 1986, cert. trainer of fitness instrs., accredited exam prep. trainer, 1989—), Wash. Alliance of Health, Physical Edn., Recreation and Dance, Nat. Speakers Assn. (Pacific N.W. chpt. bd. dirs. 1992-93), Nat. Dance Assn. (advocacy com.). Office: PRO-FIT 12012 156th Ave SE Renton WA 98059-6317

LOCKYER, KATHLEEN LOIS, high school principal; b. Washington, Nov. 20, 1949; d. Lester R. and Florence (Ward) Ferriss; m. Thomas Don, Nov. 8, 1948; 1 child, David. BA, U. Calif., Sacramento, 1971; MA, St. Mary's Coll., Moraga, Calif., 1981; supt. endorsement, U. Mont., Missoula, 1991. Tchr. Mt. Diablo Dist., Concord, Calif., 1971-80; tchr., vice prin. Dept. Def. Dependant Schs., Germany, 1980-90; prin. St. Regis (Mont.) Dist., 1990-91; tchr. DoDDS, Nurnberg, Germany, 1991-92; supt. Power/Dutton, Mont., 1992-94; prin. Helena (Mont.) Sch. Dist., 1994—. Home: 3730 Wildfire St East Helena MT 59635-3384 Office: Capital HS 100 Valley Dr Helena MT 59601-0163

LODEN, D. JOHN, advertising executive. Pres., CEO FCB Healthcare, San Francisco, Calif. Office: One Lombard St San Francisco CA 94111*

LODGE, EDWARD JAMES, federal judge; b. 1933. BS cum laude, Coll. Idaho, 1957; JD, U. Idaho, 1969. Mem. firm Smith & Miller, 1962-63; probate judge Canyon County, Idaho, 1963-65; judge Idaho State Dist. Ct., 1965-88; U.S. bankruptcy judge State of Idaho, 1988; dist. judge, now chief judge U.S. Dist. Ct. Idaho, 1989—. Recipient Kramer award for excellence in jud. adminstrn.; named three time All-Am., disting. alumnus Coll. Idaho, Boise State U.; named to Hall of Fame Boise State U., Coll. Idaho. Mem. ABA, Idaho Trial Lawyer Assn., Idaho State Bar Assn., U.S. Fed. Judges Assn., Boise State Athletic Assn., Elks Club. Office: US Dist Ct MSC 040 550 W Fort St 6th Flr Boise ID 83724-0101

LOEB, PAUL ROGAT, writer, lecturer; b. Berkeley, Calif., July 4, 1952; s. Yosal Rogat and Magd (Kosches) Rogat Loeb Waingrow. Student, Stanford U., 1970-72; BA in Social Scis., New Sch. for Social Rsch., 1972. Writer, critic, 1977—, lectr., 1982—; vis. lectr. numerous colls. and univs. including Harvard U., MIT, Cath. U., Brandeis U., Emory U., Trinity U., U. Calif., U. Wis.; scholar-in-residence Dartmouth U., Mercer U., Hobart and William Smith Coll., La. State U., U. Wash., SUNY, Plattsburgh, others. Author: Nuclear Culture: Living and Working at The World's Largest Atomic Complex, 1982, 86, Hope in Hard Times: America's Peace Movement and the Reagan Era, 1987, Generation at The Crossroads: From Apathy to Action in American College Students, 1994; editor: Liberation mag., 1974-76; cons. editor: Nuclear X-Change, 1983-86; assoc. editor: Clinton St. Quar., 1985-91; contbr. to numerous publs. including N.Y. Times, Washington Post, L.A. Times, Psychology Today, Mother Jones, Utne Reader, Village Voice, Internat. Herald Tribune. Mem. Inst. for Global Security Studies. Home: 3232 41st Ave SW Seattle WA 98116-3445

LOEHWING, RUDI CHARLES, JR., publicist, marketing, advertising, internet, commerce, radio broadcasting executive, journalist; b. Newark, July 26, 1957; s. Rudy Charles Sr. and Joan Marie (Bell) L.; m. Claire Popham, Sept. 4, 1987; children: Aspasia Joyce, Tesia Victoria, Rudi Douglas, Anna Marie, Samantha Diane, Ian Ryan. Student, Biscayne U., 1975, Seton Hall U., 1977, Hubbard Acad., 1980. Announcer radio sta. WHBI FM, N.Y.C., 1970-72; producer Am. Culture Entertainment, Belleville, N.J., 1973-74; exec. producer Am. Culture Entertainment, Hollywood, Calif., 1988-94; CEO Broadcaster's Network Internat., Hollywood, U.K., also U.K., 1989—, Broadcaster's Network Internat., Ltd., Hollywood, also U.K.; v.p. pub. rels. The Dohring Co.; bd. dirs. First Break, Hollywood, also U.K., 1988—. Author: Growing Pains, 1970; exec. producer TV documentaries and comml. advertisements, 1983; patentee in field. Devel. dir. Tricentennial Found., Washington, 1989-90; bd. dirs. Civic Ligh Opera of South Bay Cities, Just Say No to Drugs, L.A., 1989, Hands Across the Atlantic, Internat. Country Top 10, The Rock of Russia, Job Search, Hollywood, U.K. and Russia. Named Youngest Comml. Radio Producer and Announcer for State of N.Y., Broadcaster's Network Internat., 1972. Mem. Broadcasters Network Assn. (bd. dirs. 1977—), Profl. Bus. Comms. Assn. (founder 1989), BNI News Bur. (chmn. 1991—), Civic Light Opera of South Bay Cities (bd. dirs. 1996—). Office: Broadcasters Network Internat Ltd 2624 Medlow Ave Ste B Los Angeles CA 90065-4617

LOETE, STEVEN DONALD, pilot; b. Tacoma, Aug. 21, 1959; s. Donald Kenneth and Ida Lorraine (Buck) L.; 1 child, Samantha. BA, Pacific Luth. U., 1984. Pilot contracting office USAF, Williams AFB, Ariz., 1985; flight instr. Clover Park Tech. Coll., Tacoma, 1986; charter pilot Stellar Exec., Chandler, Ariz., 1986-87; pilot, airline capt. Maui Airlines, Guam, 1987; airline capt., checkairman Westair Airlines, Fresno, Calif., 1987—. Contbr. Save the Children, 1988-90; mem. Angel Flight, U. Puget Sound, 1981-83; bd. dirs. aviation adv. com. Clover Park Tech. Coll., 1991—. 1st lt. USAF, 1983-93. Mem. Airline Pilots Assn. (chmn. organizing com. 1989, chmn. coun. 1989-91). Republican. Methodist. Home and Office: PO Box 57 Spanaway WA 98387

LOEUP, KONG, cultural organization administrator; b. Battambang, Cambodia, May 26, 1944; s. Kong Niem and Chhit Roeun; m. Ly Keo Thim, Aug. 1968; children: Kong Bandaul, Kong Panlauk. Diploma in edn., U. Phnom Penh, 1965; BA, Antioch U., 1983; MA, U. Colo., Denver, 1987; PhD, Columbia Pacific U., 1987. Tchr. Ministry Edn., Phnom Penh, 1964; counselor, community case worker Internat. Refugee Ctr., Denver, 1983; refugee program coord./counselor Refugee Camps, Thailand; cons. Cambodian Buddhist Soc. of Colo., Denver; counselor Cambodian Community Colo., Denver; pres. Cambodian Cultural Ctr., Denver, 1992—. Pres. Cambodian Fine Arts Preservation Group Colo.; mem. Asian Edn. Adv. Coun., Rep. Presdl. Task Force, 1986. Mem. ASCD. Home and Office: 1804 S Eliot St Denver CO 80219-4904

LOEWENHARDT, JOSEPH H., museum director. Pres. Hawaii Bottle Mus., Honokaa. Office: Hawaii Bottle Mus Inc 27 Kalopa Mawka Rd Honokaa HI 96727-1635

LOEWY, DANA, English educator, translator; b. Děčín, Czech Republic, July 15, 1960; came to U.S., 1988; d. Georg Jakob L. MA in English and Comm., Rheinische Friedrich-Wilhelms U, Bonn, Germany, 1987; MA in English, U. So. Calif., L.A., 1989, PhD in English, 1995. Lectr. Marymount Coll., Palos Verdes, Calif., 1991-93, Glendale (Calif.) C.C., 1995-96; asst. lectr. U. So. Calif., L.A., 1989-96; lectr. Calif. State U., Fullerton, 1996—; linguistic cons. I.D. Entity-Brand Naming, Brea, Calif., 1995—; prin., proprietor Fine Lines Language Svc., L.A., 1993—. Author/translator: The Early Poetry of Jaroslav Seifert, 1997, Das verhängnisvolle Bündnis, 1984; author/translator excerpts from novel: Two Lines, 1996. Am. Lit. Translation Assn. Found. fellow and Witter Bynner fellow, 1994, 95; Quadrille Ball grantee Germanistic Soc. Am., 1992. Mem. MLA, Am. Lit. Translators Assn., Am. Translators Assn. (accredited, Student translation prize 1992), Assn. of Lit. Scholars and Critics, Mensa, Phi Beta Delta. Home: 11857 Nebraska Ave Los Angeles CA 90025 Office: Calif State Univ 800 N State College Fullerton CA 92834-6848

LOEWY, ERICH HANS, bioethicist, educator; b. Vienna, Austria, Dec. 31, 1927; s. Oskar W. and Gertrude A. (Commenda) L.; m. Roberta A. Springer, Mar. 8, 1974; children: Oliver, Tom, David. BA, NYU, 1950; MD, SUNY, Syracuse, 1954. Sr. instr. Case Western Res. U., Cleve., 1960-77; asst. prof. Albany (N.Y.) Med. Coll., 1977-81, U. Conn., Harford, 1981-84; assoc. prof. bioethics U. Ill., Peoria and Chgo., Ill., 1984-93, prof., 1991—; prof. and endowed alumni assn. chair of bioethnics assoc. dept philosophy U. Calif., Davis, 1996—; cons. in field. Author: Moral Dilemmas in Medicine, 1987, Textbook of Medical Ethics, 1989, Suffering and the Beneficent Community: Beyond Libertarianism, 1991, Freedom and Community: the Ethics of Interdependence, 1992, Ethische Fragen in der Medizin, 1995, Textbook of Health Care Ethics, 1996, Moral Strangers, Moral Acquintance and Moral Friends: connectedness and its conditions, 1996; contbr. numerous articles to profl. jours. Capt. AUS, 1955-57. Mem. Soc. Health and Human Values (faculty assoc. chair), European Soc. Philos. Medicine and Health Care, Am. Coll. Physicians, Phys. Soc. Responsibility. Home: 2701 Corabel Ln Apt 10 Sacramento CA 95821-5230 Office: U Calif Davis PCC 3107 2221 Stockton Blvd Sacramento CA 95817

LOFGREN, ZOE, congresswoman; b. San Mateo, Calif., Dec. 21, 1947; d. Milton R. and Mary Violet L.; m. John Marshall Collins, Oct. 22, 1978; children: Sheila Zoe Lofgren Collins, John Charles Lofgren Collins. BA in Polit. Sci., Stanford U., 1970; JD cum laude, U. Santa Clara, 1975. Bar: Calif., 1975. D.C. Adminstrv. asst. to Congressman Don Edwards, San Jose, Calif., 1970-79; ptnr. Webber and Lofgren, San Jose, 1979-81; mem. Santa Clara County Bd. Suprs., 1981-94; congresswoman 104th U.S. Congress, Calif. 16th Dist., 1995—; part-time prof. Law, U. Santa Clara, 1978-80; jud. com., judiciary subcom. on comml. and adminstrv. law, subcom. on crime, sci. com. subcoms. on basic rsch. & tech.; house com. on sci., subcommittee on tech., basic rsch. Exec. dir. Community Housing Developers, Inc., 1979-80; trustee San Jose Community Coll. Dist., 1979-81; bd. dirs. Community Legal Svcs., 1978-81, San Jose Housing Svc. Ctr., 1978-79; mem. steering com. sr. citizens housing referendum, 1978; del. Calif. State Bar Conv., 1979-82, Dem. Nat. Conv., 1976; active Assn. Immigration and Nationality Lawyers, 1976-82, Calif. State Dem. Cen. Com., 1975-78, Santa Clara County Dem. Cen. Com., 1974-78, Notre Dame High Sch. Blue Ribbon Com., 1981-84, Victim-Witness Adv. Bd., 1981-94. Recipient Bancroft-Whitney award for Excellence in Criminal Procedure, 1973. Mem. Santa Clara County Bar Assn. (trustee 1979—), Santa Clara County Women Lawyers Com. (exec. bd. 1979-80), Sanata Clara Law Sch. Alumni Assn. (v.p. 1977, pres. 1978), Nat. Women's Polit. Caucus, Assn. of Bay Area Govts. (exec. bd. 1981-86). Office: US House Reps 318 Cannon House Office Bldg Washington DC 20515-0516 also: 635 N 1st St Ste B San Jose CA 95112-5110

LOFLAND, JOHN FRANKLIN, sociologist, educator; b. Milford, Del., Mar. 4, 1936; s. John Purnell and Juanita (Jobe) L.; m. Lyn Hebert, Jan. 2, 1965. B.A., Swarthmore Coll., 1958; M.A., Columbia U., 1960; Ph.D., U. Calif., Berkeley, 1964. Asst. prof. sociology U. Mich., 1964-68; assoc. prof. sociology Calif. State U., Sonoma, 1968-70; asso. prof. sociology U. Calif., Davis, 1970-74; prof. U. Calif., 1974-94; prof. emeritus U. Calif., Davis, 1994—. Author: Doomsday Cult, 1966, 77, Analyzing Social Settings, 1971, 3d edit., (with L. H. Lofland) 1995, Protest, 1985, Polite Protestors, 1993, Social Movement Organizations, 1996, 6 other books; founding editor Jour. Contemporary Ethnography, 1970-74; contbr. articles and revs. to profl. lit. Mem. Am. Sociol. Assn. (chair sect. on collective behavior and social movements 1980-81, chair sect. on sociology of peace and war 1989-90, Outstanding Scholarship award 1987), Pacific Sociol. Assn. (pres. 1980-81), Soc. Study Symbolic Interaction (pres. 1986-87, G.H. Mead award for outstanding career contbns. 1995). Home: 523 E St Davis CA 95616-3816 Office: U Calif Sociology Dept Davis CA 95616

LOFTHOUSE, RUSS WILBERT, school administrator; b. Chgo., Jan. 21, 1945; s. Russell Wilber and Anne Marie (Daker) L.; m. Pamlin I. Axelson, Aug. 7, 1976; one child, James. BA in Elem. Edn., U. Denver, 1971; MA in Elem. Edn., U. Colo., Denver, 1978, PhD in Edn., 1991. Cert. elem tchr., Colo., elem. prin., Colo. Tchr. Cherry Creek Schs., Englewood, Colo., 1971-86, prin., 1986—; mem. adv. bd. Teaching and Computers, N.Y.C., 1986—. Recipient Disting. Tchr. award Cherry Creek Schs., 1985; named Colo. Tchr. of Yr., Colo. Dept. Edn., 1986; runner-up Nat. Tchr. of Yr., 1986. Mem. Assn. Supervision and Curriculum Devel., Am. Acad. and Inst. Human Reason (dir. community leaders and succesful schs.), Fulbrite Tchrs. Alumni Assn., NEA, Nat. State Tchs. of Yr., Phi Delta Kappa. Home and Office: 8505 E Temple Dr Apt 502 Denver CO 80237-2545

LOFTIN, ORRIN KEITH, retired officer, poet, actor; b. Fayetteville, N.C., Mar. 16, 1960; s. Leonza and Willie Elizabeth (Adams) L.; m. Sandra Denise Chisholm, Apr. 3, 1985; 1 child, Jauté Desireé, Procasius Darnell. BS in Math., Fayetteville State U., 1984; MA in Space Sys. and Computer Sys., Webster U., 1992. Enlisted USAF, 1985, advanced through grades to capt., 1985—; pres., founder Loftin, Algorithms, Inc., 1993-94. Author: (poetry) Infinity of Blue, The Rent, Am. Poetry Assn. award, 1990. Republican. Presbyterian. Home: 3805 7th St NE Trlr 114 Great Falls MT 59404-1155

LOFTUS, THOMAS DANIEL, lawyer; b. Seattle, Nov. 8, 1930; s. Glendon Francis and Martha Helen (Wall) L. BA, U. Wash., 1952, JD, 1957. Bar: Wash. 1958, U.S. Ct. Appeals (9th cir.) 1958, U.S. Dist. Ct. Wash. 1958, U.S. Ct. Mil. Appeals 1964, U.S. Supreme Ct. 1964. Trial atty. Northwestern Mut. Ins. Co., Seattle, 1958-62; sr. trial atty. Unigard Security Ins. Co., Seattle, 1962-68, asst. gen. counsel, 1969-83, govt. rels. counsel, 1983-89; of counsel Groshong, LeHet & Thornton, 1990—; mem. Wash. Commn. on Jud. Conduct (formerly Jud. Qualifications Commn.), 1982-88, vice-chmn., 1987-88; judge pro tem Seattle Mcpl. Ct., 1973-81; mem. nat. panel of mediators Arbitration Forums, Inc., 1990—. Sec., treas. Seattle Opera Assn., 1980-91; pres., bd. dirs. Vis. Nurse Svcs., 1979-88; pres., v.p. Salvation Army Adult Rehab. Ctr., 1979-86; nat. committeeman Wash. Young Rep. Fedn., 1961-63, vice chmn., 1963-65; pres. Young Reps. King County, 1962-63; bd. dirs. Seattle Seafair, Inc., 1975; bd. dirs., gen. counsel Wash. Ins. Coun., 1984-86, sec., 1986-88, v.p., 1988-90, Am. Mediation Panel of Mediators, 1990-96; bd. dirs. Arson Alarm Found., 1987-90; bd. visitors law sch. U. Wash., 1993—. 1st lt. U.S. Army, 1952-54, col. Res., 1954-85. Fellow Am. Bar Found.; mem. Am. Arbitration Assn. (nat. panel arbitrators 1965—), Am. Arbitration Forums, Inc. (nat. panel arbitrators 1992), Nat. Assn. Security Dealers (bd. arbitrators 1997—), Am. Mediation Panel, Wash. Bar Assn. (gov. 1981-84), Seattle King County Bar Assn. (sec., trustee 1977-82), ABA (ho. of dels. 1984-90), Internat. Assn. Ins. Counsel, U.S. People to People (del. Moscow internat. law-econ. conf. 1990), Def. Rsch. Inst., Wash. Def. Trial Lawyers Assn., Wash. State Trial Lawyers Assn., Am. Judicature Soc., Res. Officers Assn., Judge Advocate General's Assn., Assn. Wash. Gens., U. Wash. Alumni Assn., Coll. Club Seattle, Wash. Athletic Club, Masons, Shriners, Ranier Club, Pi Sigma Alpha, Delta Sigma Rho, Phi Delta Phi, Theta Delta Chi. Republican. Presbyterian. Home: 3515 Magnolia Blvd W Seattle WA 98199-1841 Office: 2133 3rd Ave Seattle WA 98121-2321

LOGAN, GLENN RAYMOND, mental health professional, counselor; b. Indio, Calif., Mar. 23, 1937; s. Raymond Nelson Logan and Ardis Lenore (McComb) Mangold; m. Rosalie Theresa Gallegos, Oct. 5, 1956; children: Glenn M., Benjamin N., Leonard F., James R., Patricia L., Karen M. BS in Mil. Sci., U. Md., 1969; MA in Counseling, U. Colo., 1989. Lic. prof. counselor, Colo.; cert. sr. chem. addictions counselor, Colo. Enlisted U.S. Army, 1953, advanced through grades to 1st lt., 1960, intelligence analyst, 1961-72, sr. intelligence ops. supr., 1972-74, ret., 1974; CEO Techtran Corp., Glen Burnie, Md., 1974-77, GlenRo Inc., Colorado Springs, Colo., 1977-87; counselor The Ark, Green Mountain Falls, Colo., 1991-92, Vet. Ctr., Colorado Springs, 1993-95; psychiat. evaluator Penrose/St. Francis Hosp., Colorado Springs, 1995—; counselor Genesis, Colorado Springs, 1995—; adj. prof. psychology Pikes Peak C.C., 1996—. Contbr. articles to profl. jours. Mgr. Little League, Odenton, Md., 1966-76; comdg. officer U.S. Naval Sea Cadets, Colorado Springs, 1986. Maj. USAR. Decorated twelve air medals. Mem. Assn. Former Intelligence Officers (life), Disabled Am. Vets. (life), Ret. Officers Assn. (life), Vietnam Vets. Am. (life, chpt. sec. 1989-90), Vets. of Underage Mil. Svc. (charter), Clin. Mental Health Counselors Assn. Republican. Roman Catholic.

LOGAN, JAMES SCOTT, SR., emergency analyst; b. Stanford, Ky., June 18, 1948; s. James M.H. and Lillian Elizabeth (Givens) L.; m. Rose Marie Helm, Aug. 31, 1968; children: James Matthew, Tasha Marie. AA, Columbia (Mo.) Coll., 1990, BS/BA cum laude, 1992; postgrad., U. Colo., 1992—. Unit adminstr. USAR, Lakewood, Colo., 1972-82; continuity of govt. planner Fed. Emergency Mgmt. Agy. Region VIII, Lakewood, 1983-90, tech. hazards program specialist, 1991-92, sr. tech. hazards program specialist, 1992-95; team leader state and local programs Fed. Emergency Mgmt. Agy. Region VIII, Lakewood, Colo., 1995—; emergency analyst Office of Regional Dir., Denver, 1995—; bd. dirs. Rocky Mountain Human Svcs. Coalition, 1995—. Mem. NAACP, Denver, 1992; mem. NCOA NCO Assn., Denver, 1979—; mem. citizen's adv. com. polit. sci. dept. U. Colo., Denver. With U.S. Army, 1968-71, Vietnam, USAR, 1972. Decorated Legion of Merit. Mem. VFW, Am. Legion, Pi Sigma Alpha. Democrat. Baptist. Home: 16952 E Bates Ave Aurora CO 80013-2243 Office: FEMA Region VIII PO Box 25267 Bldg 710 Denver CO 80225-0267

LOGAN, JOHN LANDISS, physician; b. Shelbyville, Ill., Apr. 19, 1945; s. Manford Alexander and Drusilla Ruth (Rumrill) L.; m. Rita Janet Starriett, Aug. 27, 1984 (div. Feb. 1993); 1 child, Ryan Alexander. BS, U. Ill., 1967, MD, 1971. Diplomate Am. Bd. Urology. Surgery resident Torrance, Calif., 1971-73; urology resident Kaiser Permanente, L.A., 1973-76; attending urologist Kaiser Permanente, Harbor City, Calif., 1976-79; urologist, pvt. practice Camarillo, Calif., 1979-92, Durango, Colo., 1992—. Bd. dirs. United Way, La Plata, Colo., 1995, Am. Cancer Soc., Ventura, Calif., 1984-86. Mem. Am. Urology Assn., Rotary. Office: Edward A Rhodes & John L Logan PC 2005 E 18th Ave Denver CO 80206

LOGAN, LEE ROBERT, orthodontist; b. L.A., June 24, 1923; s. Melvin Duncan and Margaret (Seltzer) L.; m. Maxine Nadler, June 20, 1975; children: Fritz, Dean, Scott, Gigi, Chad, Casey. BS, UCLA, 1952; DDS, Northwestern U., 1956, MS, 1961. Diplomate Am. Bd. Orthodontics. Gen. practice dentistry, Reseda, Calif., 1958-59; practice dentistry specializing in orthodontics, Northridge, Calif., 1961—; pres. Lee R. Logan DDS Profl. Corp.; mem. med. staff Northridge Hosp., Tarzana Hosp.; owner Maxine's Prodn. Co.; owner Maxine's Talent Agy.; guest lectr. UCLA, U. So. Calif., dir dental edn. Northridge Med. Ctr. Contbr. articles to profl. jours. Served to lt. USNR, 1956-58. Named (with wife) Couple of Yr. Autistic Children Assn., 1986; recipient Nat. Philanthropy award, 1987, 1st Pl. winner Autistic Jogathon, 1981-95, 1st Pl. Mem. Am., San Fernando Valley Dental Assn. (pres.-elect), Am. Assn. Orthodontists, Pacific Coast Soc. Orthodontists (dir., pres. so. sect. 1974-75, chmn. membership 1981-83), Found. Orthodontic Research (charter mem.), Calif. Soc. Orthodontists (chmn. peer rev. 1982-93), G.V. Black Soc. (charter mem.), Angle Soc. Orthodontists (pres. 1981-82, bd. dirs. 1982-96, nat. pres. 1985-87, dir. 1985-96), U. S.C. Century Club Fraternity, Xi Psi Phi, Chi Phi. Home: 4830 Encino Ave Encino CA 91316-3813 Office: 18250 Roscoe Blvd Northridge CA 91325-4226

LOGAN, LYNDA DIANNE, elementary education educator; b. Detroit, June 22, 1952; d. Horatio Bernard and Ruby (Newsom) Graham; m. Keith L. Logan, Aug. 16, 1980; 1 child, Lauren Nicole. BS, Ea. Mich. U., 1974, MA, 1980. Cert. tng. program quality rev., Calif.; cert. tchr., Calif., Miss., Mich.; cert. Lang. Devel. Specialist (CLAD), 1996; lic. guidance counselor basic related edn., Miss.; cert. counselor pupil pers. svc. credential, Mich., Calif. Substitute tchr. Detroit Pub. Schs., 1974-76; mid. sch. tchr. Inkster (Mich.) Pub. Schs., 1976-80; CETA vocat. counselor Golden Triangle Vocat.-Tech. Ctr., Mayhew, Miss., 1980-82, basic related educator, 1980-82; elem. tchr. Inglewood (Calif.) Unified Sch. Dist., 1982-93, resource tchr., 1993-96; tchr. Crozier Mid. Sch., Inglewood, Calif., 1996—; mem. forecast adv. bd. COED Mag., N.Y.C., 1979-80; advisor/founder Newspaper Club Fellrath Mid. Sch., Inkster, 1979-80; mem. interviewing com. Golden Triangle Vocat.-Tech. Ctr., Mayhew, 1980-82, evaluation and follow-up com., 1980-82; pronouncer spelling bee Inglewood Unified Sch. Dist., 1991, 94; organizer student body team meetings Worthington Sch., Inglewood, 1993-96, coord. reading program, 1993-96; mem. interviewing com., 1987-95; co-chair yearbook com., 1993-94, prin. adv. bd., 1987-92, ct.-liaison and child welfare attendance rep. L.A. County Edn., 1995-96, supt. adv. coun., 1995-96, reading is fundamental coord., 1993-96, mem. team earthquake preparedness com., 1994-96. youth co-chairperson March of Dimes, Detroit, 1976-80; com. mem. Nat. Coun. Negro Women, L.A. chpt., 1982-84; com. mem. Cmty. Action Program, Eternal Promise Bapt. Ch., L.A., 1991, pres. choir, 1991, v.p. hospitality com., 1987-88; co-chmn. women's com., 1990; mem. parent adv. com. Knox Presbyn. Ch. Nursery Sch., L.A., 1988-89. Mem. ASCD, AAUW, NAFE, Black Women's Forum, Ladies Aux. Knights of St. Peter Claver, Ea. Mich. U. Alumni Assn., Phi Gamma Nu. Office: Crozier Middle School 151 N Grevillea Ave Inglewood CA 90301-1705

LOGAN, PETER B., lawyer; b. Boston, Apr. 23, 1953; s. William Donald and Nancy L.; m. Beth Gerken, Aug. 28, 1982; children: Christopher, Andrew, Caroline. BA magna cum laude, Bowdoin Coll., 1975; JD, Georgetown U., 1978. Bar: Calif. 1978. Assoc. Bronson, Bronson & McKinnon, San Francisco, 1978—, ptnr., 1984-87; prin. Wright, Robinson, Osthimer & Tatum, San Francisco, 1987—. Notes editor American Criminal Law Review, 1977-78. Councilman, Town of Tiburon, Calif., 1988-92, mayor, 1989-91. Mem. ABA, Def. Rsch. Inst., Assn. Def. Counsel No. Calif., San Francisco Bar Assn. Office: Wright Robinson Osthimer & Tatum 44 Montgomery St Ste 1800 San Francisco CA 94104-4705

LOGE, GARY WAYNE, scientist; b. Evansville, Ind., June 23, 1951; s. Howard Ellis and Doris Elizabeth (Elmendorf) L. BS in Chemistry, Purdue U., 1973; MS in Chemistry, U. Cin., 1976; PhD in Chem. Physics, Ind. U., 1979. Postdoctoral rsch. assoc. Cornell U., Ithaca, N.Y., 1980-81; postdoctoral staff photochemistry and photophysics group Los Alamos (N.Mex.) Nat. Lab., 1981-84, staff mem. photochemistry and photophysics group, 1984-90, guest scientist isotope geochemistry group, 1991-93, subcontractor to Ewing Tech. Design, Inc., 1993-94; exec. officer Laser Diagnostics LLC, Los Alamos, 1993—. Contbr. articles to tech. jours. Mem. Soc. Applied Spectroscopy, Optical Soc. Am. Office: Laser Diagnostics LLC PO Box 4627 35 Bonnieview Dr Ste B Los Alamos NM 87544

LOGGINS, WILLIAM CONLEY, industrial engineer; b. Springfield, Ohio, July 15, 1953; s. Harvey Quinn and Madelyn Mary (Conley) Licklider. BS in Psychology, Wright State U., 1977; MEd in Counseling and Guidance, U. Ariz., 1981, MS in Indsl. Engring., 1989. Social worker Head Start, Dayton, Ohio, 1976-78; collective mem. Small Planet Bakery, Tucson, 1978-81; human rels. trainer Prescott, Ariz., 1982-83; domestic violence counselor Tucson Ctr. for Women and Children, Tucson, 1983-84; info. engr. Tucson Med. Ctr., 1987; indsl. engr. Allied Signal Aerospace Co., 1987; ops. analyst Tucson Pub. Libr., 1987-88; tech. analyst Pima (Ariz.) Assn. of Govts., 1988-89; info. analyst Evans and Sutherland Computer Corp., 1989-91; data analyst and info. engr. Execusoft, Inc., 1992-94; indsl. engr. Merit Decision Tech., Inc., Salt Lake City, 1993—. Youth leader and career night organizer St. Francis in the Foothills Meth. Ch., Tucson, 1986-89; tennis instr. and youth leader Parks and Recreation Dept./YMCA, Springfield, 1970-73. Mem. ACM Spl. Interest Groups on Human Computer Interaction and Simulation, No. Utah Computer-Human Interaction Spl. Interest Group of ACM, Toastmasters (Award for best table topic and humor speeches 1993), Wasatch Mountain Club (bd. dirs. 1991-92, Outstanding Leader 1991, 93). Office: Merit Decision Techs Inc 1422 E 7380 S Salt Lake City UT 84121-4739

LOH, EDITH KWOK-YUEN, oncology nurse, health education specialist; b. Hong Kong, May 1, 1948; came to U.S., 1972; d. Chun Wing and Pui King (Chan) Lee; m. Kevin Kai-Tsu Loh, Mar. 30, 1972; children: Elizabeth, Jennifer, Jeffrey. RN, Hong Kong Govt. Nursing Sch., 1971, Tex. Woman's U., 1976; BSN magna cum laude, Hawaii Loa Coll., 1989; MPH, U. Hawaii, 1990, postgrad., 1994—. Cert. health edn. specialist; RN, Hawaii, Tex., Hong Kong, Eng. Student gen. nurse Hong Kong Govt. Hosps., 1968-70; pediatric nurse Queen Elizabeth Hosp., Hong Kong, 1971-72; head nurse oncology Ctr. Pavillion Hosp., Houston, 1972-75; oncology nurse Dr. Kevin Loh, Inc., Honolulu, 1978-90; nurse coord., health instr. Hawaii Hematology, Oncology, Inc., Honolulu, 1991-92; vol. rschr. immunol. studies U. Hawaii, 1990, guest lectr. Sch. Pub. Health, chmn. edn. for continuation credits for CHES Sch. Pub. Health; health educator Baby S.A.F.E., Adminstrv. Office Dept. Health, Honolulu, 1993-94; presenter Am. Indian and Alaska Native Caucus 123d ann. meeting APHA, San Diego, 1995. Vol. recruitor Hawaii Bone Marrow Donor Registry, Honolulu, 1992; chmn.

cmty. svc. com., Honolulu, 1992—; dir. Health Svcs. for Sr. Citizens, 1993; bd. dirs. Hawaii Cancer Children Found., 1992-94. Recipient Award of Merit, Nat. Dean's List, Nat. Collegiate Nursing award, 1989; named All American Scholar, 1989. Mem. AMA, APHA, Hawaii Pacific U. Nursing Honor Soc., Am. Cancer Soc., Soc. for Pub. Health Edn.-Hawaii (bd. dirs., sec., life), Assoc. Chinese Univ. Women Inc. (chmn. welfare com. 1992, chmn. comty. svc. com. 1991-95, mem. in parliamentary procedure legis. com. 1992, v.p. 1996, pres.-elect 1997), Soc. Pub. Health Edn. (bd. dirs. 1992-97, sec. 1992-93), Hawaii Soc. for Health Care Edn. and Tng. (planner, fundraiser and subcom. chmn. 1996, chmn. edn. and v.p. 1997), Navy League of U.S. (life mem. Honolulu coun.), Sigma Theta Tau. Home: 1815 Kumakani Pl Honolulu HI 96821-1327

LOHMAN, ARTHUR GROVER, civilian military employee; b. Barksdale AFB, La., Dec. 6, 1950; s. Paul Oswald and Julia Alice (Rider) L.; m. Julie Rae Bohn, July 25, 1975 (div. Dec. 5, 1986); children: Arthur G. Jr., Timothy E.; m. Terry Ann Hess, Jan. 10, 1988 (div. Nov. 19, 1990). Student logistics, C.C. of the Air Force, Maxwell AFB, 1974, 77-78; student, Weber State U., 1969, 74, 83-85. Enlisted USAF, 1970, advanced through the grades to sgt., ret., 1982; electronics tech. LN-12 navigation sect. USAF, Hill AFB, Utah, 1984-88, electronics tech. cir. bd. mfg. sect., 1988-92, electronics tech. aim 9 sidewinder missile sect., 1992-95, electronics tech. F16/B1 aircraft microwave sect., 1995—; mail clk., date transcriber IRS, Ogden, Utah, 1983-84; mem. hazardous waste process action team, safety monitor working group Air Craft Avionics Divsn., Hill AFB, Utah, 1989-90; hazardous waste site mgr. Cir. Card Mfg., Hill AFB, Utah, 1988-90, mem. quality com., 1989-90. Creator: Cartoon Bug, 1982. Pub. affairs cmty. escort Ogden Air Logistics Ctr., Hill AFB, Utah, 1988-90; judge sci. fair Bonneville H.S., Weber State Univ., Ogden, Utah, 1989, speech contest judge, 12th Annual Health Occupation Students Am. Nat. Leadership Conf., Utah, 1989; master of ceremonies Hill AFB Talent Competition, 1993; jr. olympic bowling coach Young Am. Bowling Alliance, Layton, 1996—. Mem. Utah State Poetry Soc. (affil. Acad. Am. Poets and Nat. Fedn. State Poetry Socs.), Learning Disabilities Assn. Utah, Toastmasters Internat. (gov.'s award 1990). Office: OO-ALC/LARPJ 7274 Wardleigh Rd Hill Air Force Base UT 84056-5137

LOHMAN, LORETTA CECELIA, social scientist, consultant; b. Joliet, Ill., Sept. 25, 1944; d. John Thomas and Marjorie Mary (Brennan) L. BA in Polit. Sci., U. Denver, 1966, PhD in Am. History, 1996; MA in Social Sci., U. No. Colo., 1975. Lectr. Ariz. State U., Tempe, 1966-67; survey researcher Merrill-Werthlin Co., Tempe, 1967-68; edn. asst. Am. Humane Assn., Denver, 1969-70; econ. cons. Lohman & Assocs., Littleton, Colo., 1971-75; rsch. assoc. Denver Rsch. Inst., 1976-86; rsch. scientist Milliken Chapman Rsch. Group, Littleton, 1986-89; owner Lohman & Assocs., Littleton, 1989—; affiliate Colo. Water Resources Rsch. Inst., Ft. Collins, Colo., 1989-91; tech. adv. com. Denver Potable Wastewater Demo Plant, 1986-90; cons. Constrn. Engrng. Rsch. Lab., 1984—; peer reviewer NSF, 1985-86, Univs. Coun. Water Resources, 1989—; WERC consortium reviewer N.Mex. Univs.-U.S. Dept. Energy, 1989—; course cons. Regis Coll., Denver, 1992—. Contbr. articles to profl. jours. Vol. Metro Water Conservation Projects, Denver, 1986-90; vol. handicapped fitness So. Suburban Parks and Recreation. Recipient Huffsmith award Denver Rsch. Inst., 1983; Nat. Ctr. for Edn. in Politics grantee, 1964-65. Mem. ASCE (social and environ. objectives com.), Am. Water Works Assn., Am. Water Resources Assn., Orgn. Am. Historians, Pub. Hist. Assn., Colo. Water Congress, Water Environ. Fedn., Sigma Xi, Pi Gamma Mu, Phi Alpha Theta. Home and Office: 3375 W Aqueduct Ave Littleton CO 80123-2903 *Personal philosophy: Recognition of biological, social, and cultural interdependence leads to a cooperative spirit emphasizing sharing and open-mindedness. This allows one to be true to oneself.*

LOHNES, WALTER F. W., German language and literature educator; b. Frankfurt, Germany, Feb. 8, 1925; came to U.S., 1948, naturalized, 1954; s. Hans and Dina (Koch) L.; m. Claire Shane, 1950; children: Kristen, Peter, Claudia. Student, U. Frankfurt, 1945-48, Ohio Wesleyan U., 1948-49, U. Mo., 1949-50; PhD, Harvard U., 1961. Asst., Inst. German Folklore, U. Frankfurt, 1947-48; instr. German U. Mo., 1949-50; head dept. German, Phillips Acad., Andover, Mass., 1951-61; asst. prof. Stanford (Calif.) U., 1961-65, assoc. prof., 1965-68, prof., 1969-95, prof. emeritus, 1995—, dir. NDEA Inst. Advanced Study, 1961-68, chmn. dept. German studies, 1973-79, dir. Inst. Basic German, 1975-95, prin. investigator NEH grant, 1978-80; vis. prof. Woehler-Gymnasium, Frankfurt, 1956-57, Middlebury Coll., 1959, U. N.Mex., 1980, 81, 86, U. Vienna, 1990, Coll. de France, Paris, 1992; mem., chmn. various coms. of examiners Ednl. Testing Svc. and Coll. Bd.; chmn. German Grad. Record Exam. Author: (with V. Nollendorfs) German Studies in the United States, 1976, (with F. W. Strothmann) German: A Structural Approach, 1968, 4th rev. edit., 1988; (with E.A. Hopkins) Contrastive Grammar of English and German, 1982, (with Martha Woodmansee) Erkennen und Deuten, 1983, (with J.A. Pfeffer) Grunddeutsch, Texte zur gesprochenen deutschen Gegenwartssprache, 3 vols., 1984, (with D. Benseler and V. Nollendorfs) Teaching German in America: Prolegomena to a History, 1988; contbr. numerous articles to profl. jours.; editor: Unterrichtspraxis, 1971-74. Bd. dirs. Calif. Youth Symphony, 1977-78, Oakland (Calif.) Symphony Youth Orch., 1978-80. Decorated Fed. Order of Merit (Germany); Medal of Honor in Gold (Austria); German Govt. grantee, 1975, 76, 78. Mem. MLA, Am. Assn. Tchrs. German (v.p. 1961-62, 70-71, Outstanding Educator award; hon. 1995), Am. Assn. Applied Linguistics, Am. Coun. on Teaching Fgn. Langs., German Studies Assn., Internat. Vereinigung Germanische Sprach und Literaturwissenschaft. Home: 733 Covington Rd Los Altos CA 94024-4903 Office: Stanford U Dept German Studies Stanford CA 94305-2030

LOHR, GEORGE E., state supreme court justice; b. 1931. BS, S.D. State U.; JD, U. Mich. Bar: Colo. 1958, Calif. 1969. Former judge Colo. 9th Dist. Ct., Aspen; assoc. justice Colo. Supreme Ct., Denver, 1979—. Office: Supreme Ct Colo State Judicial Bldg 2 E 14th Ave Denver CO 80203-2115

LOHRLI, ANNE, retired English educator, author; b. Bake Oven, Oreg., Feb. 9, 1906; d. Gottfried and Anna (Hüsser) L. BA, Occidental Coll., L.A., 1927, MA, 1928; MA, Columbia U., 1932; PhD, U. So. Calif., L.A., 1937. Tchr. L.A. city schs., 1937-45; prof. English N.Mex. Highlands U., Las Vegas, 1945-65; vis. prof. U. Trieste, 1954. Compiler: Household Words, List of Contributors, etc., 1973; contbr. some 40 articles in Dickensian, Princeton U. Rev., Victorian Studies, Pacific Historian, others, 1963-94. Home: 901 Marlene St Apt 3 Ukiah CA 95482

LOKEY, FRANK MARION, JR., broadcast executive, consultant; b. Ft. Worth, Oct. 15, 1924; s. Frank Marion Sr. and Corinne (Whaley) L. Student, Smith-Hughes Evening Coll., 1955-59. Announcer, newscaster, disc jockey, morning personality Radio Stas. WAPI, WBRC and WSGN, Birmingham, Ala., 1941-52; pres. WRDW-TV, Augusta, Ga., 1952-55; asst. gen. mgr., mgr. sales, news anchor Sta. WLW-A TV (now named WXIA-TV), Atlanta, 1955-66; co-owner, gen. mgr. Sta. WAIA, Atlanta, 1960-62; S.E. news corr., talk show host CBS News N.Y., N.Y.C., 1960-66; asst. to owner, gen. mgr. Sta. WBIE-AM-FM, Atlanta, 1962-64; asst. to pres., gen. mgr. Stas. KXAB-TV, KXJB-TV, KXMB-TV, Aberdeen, Fargo, Bismarck, S.D., N.D., 1966-67; exec. v.p., gen. mgr. St. WEMT-TV, Bangor, Maine, 1967-70; pres., gen. mgr. Stas. KMOM-TV, KWAB-TV, Odessa-Midland, Big Spring, Tex., 1970-75; exec. v.p., gen. mgr. Sta. KMUV-TV (now named KRBK-TV), Sacramento, Calif., 1975-77; CEO Lokey Enterprises, Inc., Sacramento, L.A., El Centro, Calif., 1977—, also chmn. bd. dirs.; cons., troubleshooter 16 TV stas. nationwide, 1977—; cons., actor 5 movie prodn. cos., Hollywood, Calif., 1980—; cons., outside dir. Anderson Cons., Manhattan, L.I., N.Y., 1981—; network talk show host/news corr. for 7 news orgns. worldwide, 1984—; bd. dirs. Broadcast Audience Behavior Rsch., Manhattan, 1986—, mem. inner circle, 1986—; owner/franchiser The Party Place. Creator, originator approach to real estate mktg. Hon. mem. Imperial County Bd. Suprs., El Centro, 1986—, El Centro City Coun., 1987—. Mem. Am. Legion. Baptist. Home: 2709 Hwy 111 Imperial CA 92251-9772 Office: Lokey Enterprises Inc 626 W Main St El Centro CA 92243-2920

LOLLAR, KATHERINE LOUISE, social worker, therapist; b. Cin., Nov. 1, 1944; d. Robert Miller and Dorothy Marie L.; div.; 2 children. BA, U. Kans., 1966; MSW, Loyola U., 1971. Lic. clin. social worker, Oreg.; cert. social worker, Wash.; bd. cert. diplomate clin. social work. Head activity therapy dept. Fox Children's Ctr., Dwight, Ill., 1966-68; child care worker Madden Mental Health Ctr., Hines, Ill., 1968-69, social worker, 1971-74; pvt. practice therapy Wheaton and Oakbrook, Ill., 1977-82; intern Monticello Care Unit alcohol and drug treatment program, 1983; cons. Residential Facility for Developmentally Disabled Adults, Battle Ground, Wash., 1983-85; therapist Cath. Community Svcs., Vancouver, Wash., 1983-88; outsta. mgr. Wash. Div. Devel. Disabilities, Vancouver, 1987—; pvt. practice therapy Vancouver, 1988—. Troop cons. Columbia River coun. Girl Scouts Am., 1984-86, internat. trip leader, 1993, 96-97, alt. leader, 1995-96, life mem.; mem. Friends of Sangam INternat. Com., 1994-97; mem. Internat. Field Selection Team, 1994-96; mem. Unity of Vancouver. Mem. NASW (sec. Vancouver chpt. 1982-84, co-chair 1985-87, unit rep. Wash. state unit 1990-92), Singles on Sat. Sq. Dance Club, Recycles Sq. Dance Club (pres. 1995-97). Office: 650 Officers Row Vancouver WA 98661-3836

LOLLI, ANDREW RALPH, industrial engineer, former army officer; b. Seatonville, Ill., Oct. 15, 1907; s. Joseph Fredrick and Adolfa (Fiocchi) L. Student Armed Forces Staff Coll., 1950, Nat. War Coll., 1957, N.Y. Inst. Fin., 1971; BS, Dickinson Coll., 1952; postgrad. Fordham U., 1952. Enlisted in U.S. Army, 1940, advanced through grades to maj. gen., 1960; chief plans and priorities Allied Forces So. Europe, 1952-56; comdr. Air Def. units, N.Y. and San Francisco, 1957-60; comdr. XX U.S.A. Corps, 1961-62, XV, 1962-63, comdr. Western NORD Region, Hamilton AFB, Calif., 1963-66; ret., 1966; exec. asst. Hughes Aircraft Co., Fullerton, Calif., 1967; dir. gen. services State of Calif., Sacramento, 1967-70; v.p. Sigmatics, Newport Beach, Calif., 1970-73, Intercoast Investments Co., Sacramento, 1975-76; pres. Andrew R. Lolli Assocs. Inc., San Francisco, 1973—, Lolman Inc., San Francisco, 1976—; commr. Small Bus. Adv. Commn., San Francisco, 1989-93; pres. bd. trustees Commonwealth Equity Trust, 1974-80; vice chmn. Calif. Pub. Works bd., 1967-69; mem. adv. panel Nat. Acad. Scis. and Engrng. in Research, Washington, 1968-70; mem. fed., state and local govt. adv. panel Fed. Gen. Services, Washington, 1968-69. Bd. dirs. Columbia Boys Park Club, San Francisco, Lab. for Survival, San Francisco; mem. Presido of San Francisco Restoration Adv. Bd., 1994. Decorated D.S.M., Legion of Merit with oak leaf cluster, Bronze Star with oak leaf cluster; named Man of Year, Italian Sons of Am., 1964. Mem. Nat. Assn. Uniformed Services, Assn. U.S. Army, Ret. Officers Assn. Roman Catholic. Developed short notice inspection system for army air def. missiles, 1960. Home: 1050 N Point St San Francisco CA 94109-8302 Office: 286 Jefferson St San Francisco CA 94133-1126

LOLLICH, LESLIE NORLENE, journalist, educator; b. Nevada City, Calif., June 14, 1959; d. James Frazier L. and Melanie Anne (LeGate) Kuhnel; m. Paul Leslie Allen, June 5, 1982; children: Nicholas Charles L. Allen, Nathan James L. Allen. BA in Journalism, Humboldt State U., 1981. Clk. Ukonom Ranger Dist., Somes Bar, Calif., 1977-78; bookkeeper Willis & Daus. Auto Parts, Eureka, Calif., 1978-82; reporter KINS Radio, Eureka, Calif., 1983-86; bur. chief KRCR/KAEF TV, Eureka and Redding, Calif., 1986-95; lectr. Humboldt State U., Arcata, Calif., 1990-96; news dir., asst. gen. mgr. KAEF TV, Eureka, Calif., 1995—; co-owner Paul's Auto Repair, Arcata, Calif., 1986—. Mem. Mad River commn. Hosp. Adv. Bd., Arcata, Calif., 1996—; bd. dirs. United Way, Eureka, Calif., 1992-94; pres. Marshall Sch. PTA, Eureka, 1995-97; mem. Humboldt Bot. Gardens, Eureka, 1995—. Mem. Soc. Profl. Journalists (chpt. pres. 1980-81), Soroptimist Internat. (pres. Humboldt Bay 1992-94), W. End Indsl. Park Assn. (sec. 1996—), Humboldt Press Club (pres. 1989-94). Office: KAEF TV 540 E Eureka Eureka CA 95501

LOMBARDI, DENNIS M., lawyer; b. L.A., May 15, 1951; s. Peter Joseph and Jean (Nelson) L.; m. Suan Choo Lim, Jan. 9, 1993; children: Alexis Jeanne, Erin Kalani. BA, U. Hawaii, 1974; JD summa cum laude, U. Santa Clara, 1977. Bar: Calif. 1977, U.S. Dist. Ct. Hawaii, 1981. Assoc. Frandzel & Share, Beverly Hills, Calif., 1977-79; pvt. practice Capistrano Beach, Calif., 1979-81; ptnr. Case, Bigelow & Lombardi, Honolulu, 1982—. Office: Case Bigelow & Lombardi 737 Bishop St Fl 26 Honolulu HI 96813-3201

LOMBARDI, EUGENE PATSY, orchestra conductor, violinist, educator, recording artist; b. North Braddock, Pa., July 7, 1923; s. Nunzio C. and Mary (Roberto) L.; m. Jacqueline Sue Davis, Mar. 1955; children: Robert, Genanne. BA, Westminster Coll., 1948; MA, Columbia U., 1948; Edn. Specialist, George Peabody Coll., 1972; MusD, Westminster Coll., 1981. Band dir. Lincoln High Sch., Midland, Pa., 1948-49; orch. dir. Male High Sch., Louisville, 1949-50, Phoenix Union High Sch., 1950-57; orch. dir., prof. Ariz. State U., Tempe, 1957-89. Condr. Phoenix Symphonette, 1954-61, 70-73, Phoenix Symphony Youth Orch., 1956-66, Phoenix Pops Orch., 1971-83, Fine Arts String Orch., 1995—; asst. concertmaster Phoenix Symphony Orch., 1950-62, concermaster, 1962-69, asst. condr., 1968-69; mem. Newart String Quartet, 1965-89; concertmaster Flagstaff Festival Symphony, 1967-81, Flagstaff Festival Chamber Orch., 1967-81, Phoenix Chamber Orch., 1970-83; condr., music dir. Sun City (Ariz.) Symphony Orch., 1983-87. Condr. fine arts strings, Phoenix, 1995—. With USAAF, 1943-46. Decorated Bronze Star; named Outstanding Grad. Westminster Coll., 1948; recipient Alumni Achievement award, 1976, gold medal Nat. Soc. Arts and Letters, 1973, Disting. Tchr. award Ariz. State U. Alumni, 1974, Phoenix Appreciation award, 1983. Mem. Music Educators Nat. Conf., Am. String Tchrs. Assn. (pres. Ariz. unit 1965-67), Am. Fedn. Musicians, Ariz. Music Educators Assn. (pres. higher edn. sect. 1973-75, Excellence in Teaching Music award 1989), Ind. Order Foresters, Phi Delta Kappa, Phi Mu Alpha, Alpha Sigma Phi. Republican. Presbyterian. Home: 920 E Manhatton Dr Tempe AZ 85282-5520

LOMBARDI, PHILLIP ERNEST, banker; b. Pocatello, Idaho, Aug. 2, 1956; s. Richard Elmer and Eva May (Woolley) L. BA in Bus. and French, U. Puget Sound, 1977; MBA in Fin., U. Chgo., 1984. Commercial lender Wash. Mut. Savs. Bank, Seattle, 1977-81; project mgr. 666 Venture, Inc., Chgo., 1981-85; v.p. commercial asset mgmt. Citicorp Savs. of Ill., Chgo., 1985-90; v.p. fin. Citicorp Real Estate Inc., L.A., 1990—. Treas. adv. coun. Salvation Army Family Svc. Div., Chgo., 1985-88. Republican. Office: Citicorp Real Estate Inc 725 S Figueroa Los Angeles CA 90017-2301

LOMELI, MARTA, elementary education educator; b. Tijuana, Baja Calif, Mex., Oct. 28, 1952; came to U.S. 1954; d. Jesus and Guadalupe (Ascencio) Lomeli; m. Rudolph Benitez, 1978 (div. 1982); children: Pascual Lomeli Benitez; m. David E. Miller, Aug. 16, 1991. BA, San Diego State U., 1977. With M & N Tree Nursery, Vista, Calif., 1957-70; libr. Vista Boys Club, 1969-70; vol. tutor MECHA U. Calif. San Diego, La Jolla, 1971-73; tchr. aide San Diego City Schs., 1976-77; bilingual educator National City (Calif.) Schs., 1978—; mem. restructuring com. Lincoln Acres Sch., 1991. Author numerous poems. Mem. Lincoln Acres Com. to Advise the Prin., National City, 1986-88, Com. to Advise the Supt., National City, 1986-88; art editor Lincoln Jr. H.S., Vista, Calif., 1964-65, Third World U. Calif., San Diego, 1970-73; mem. Lincoln Acres Sch. Site Coun., 1988-89; mem. high tech. com. Nat. Sch. Dist., 1993-94; vol. tchr. St. Vincent de Paul's Ctr. for Homeless, San Diego, 1991-93, Shaolin Kempo Karate (black belt 2d degree); mem. Paradise Hills Citizens Patrol, 1994—. Mem. Calif. Tchrs. Assn. (site rep. Nat. City 1985), Calif. Assn. Bilingual Edn. (sec. 1986), Nat. Assn. Bilingual Edn., La Raza Club (pres., co-founder 1970). Democrat. Home: Box 113 2939 Alta View Ste O San Diego CA 92139

LOMELÍ, REFUGIO (JESSE LOMELÍ), athletics educator; b. Aguascalientes, Mex., July 23, 1941; came to U.S., 1954, naturalized, 1965; s. J. Jesus and Maria Guadalupe (Ascencio) L.; m. Barbara L. McMinn, Aug. 24, 1968; children: Lorena, Maya, Marc. Assoc., Palomar Coll., 1962; Bachelors degree, U. of the Americas, Mexico City, 1965; Masters degree, San Diego State U., 1972; postgrad., U. Pitts., 1972-74. Firefighter U.S. Forest Service, So. Calif. region, 1962-66; tchr. Santana H.S., Santee, Calif., 1967-73; counselor, tchr., soccer coach Mira Costa Coll., Oceanside, Calif., 1973—. Named Community Coll. Soccer Coach of Yr., Pacific Coast Conf., 1985. Mem. Nat. Assn. Fgn. Student Advisors, Am. G.I. Forum. Lodge: KC. Home: 1250 Vista Colina Dr San Marcos CA 92069-4956 Office: Mira Costa Coll PO Box 586312 Oceanside CA 92056

LOMET, DAVID BRUCE, computer scientist; b. Neptune, N.J., Aug. 2, 1939; s. Pierre and Helen (Foster) L.; m. Charlotte Jean Vandermark, Aug. 15, 1964; children: Bruce, Kevin. BS in Physics, Lafayette Coll., Easton, Pa., 1961; MS in Math., George Washington U., Washington, 1966; PhD in Computer Sci., U. Pa., Phila., 1969. Vis. researcher U. Newcastle (U.K.)-upon-Tyne, 1975-76; mem. rsch. staff IBM Corp., Yorktown Heights, N.Y., 1969-85; prof. computer sci. Wang Inst. Grad. Studies, Tyngsboro, Mass., 1985-87; sr. info. cons. Digital Equipment Corp., Nashua, N.H., 1987-89; sr. cons. engr. and mem. rsch. staff Digital Equipment Corp., Cambridge, Mass., 1989-94; sr. rschr. Microsoft Corp., Redmond, Wash., 1995—; grant reviewer NSF, NASA, NRC (Can.); chair program com. FODO93, vice chair program com. 1995, Data Engrng. Conf. Editor Data Engrng. Bull., VLDB Jour., Parallel and Distributed Database Systems Jour.; contbr. articles to profl. jours. Mem., v.p. Bd. Edn., Yorktown Heights, N.Y., 1980-85. IBM resident grad. fellow, 1966. Mem. IEEE, AAAS, Assn. Computer Machinery, Phi Beta Kappa. Democrat. Office: Microsoft Corp One Microsoft Way Redmond WA 98052

LOND, HARLEY WELDON, editor, publisher; b. Chgo., Feb. 5, 1946; s. Henry Sidney and Dorothy (Shaps) L.; m. Marilyn Moss, Aug. 20, 1981; 1 child Elizabeth. BA in Journalism, Calif. State U., L.A., 1972. Adminstrv. dir. Century City Ednl. Arts Project, L.A., 1972-76, hon. dir., 1982—; founder, editor Intermedia mag., L.A., 1974-80; prodn. mgr. FilmRow Publs., L.A., 1981; assoc. editor Box Office mag., Hollywood, Calif., 1981-84, editor, assoc. pub., 1984-94; dir. publs. Entertainment Data, Inc., 1994-95; pres. CyberPod Prodns., 1995—; chief copy editor The Hollywood Reporter, 1995—; syndicated columnist Continental Features, Washington, Tel-Aire Publs., Dallas, 1986—; hon dir. Monterey (Calif.) Film Festival, 1987; mem. media adv. bd. Cinetex Internat. Film Festival, 1988; cons. Take 3 Info. Svc.; web architect-master, OnVideo website, 1995—. Editor: Entertainment Media Electronic Info. Svc.; contbr. articles to profl. publs. Calif. Arts Council grantee, 1975, Nat. Endowment for Arts grantee, 1976-77. Mem. MLA, Soc. Profl. Journalists, Assn. for Edn. in Journalism and Mass Communication, Speech Communication Assn., Soc. for Cinema Studies. Home and Office: PO Box 17377 Beverly Hills CA 90209-3377

LONDON, ADELE, poet; b. Brussels, Aug. 25, 1930; came to U.S., 1952; d. Charles and Helen (Hecht) Lubin; m. Ed F. London, Sept. 17, 1960; 1 child, Alan Lewis. Student, U. Belgium. Underwriter Ins. Co., L.A., 1952-60; writer of short stories in English and French, 1960—, French poet, 1950—; provider readings for French groups in Calif. and Can., 1952. Author: Maintenant et Jadis, 1992, Sentiments, 1994; poems written in French publs., translated into English, 1993-94. Pres. L.A. PTA, 1972-74; other sch. offices. Mem. Alliance Francaise, 1939 Club.

LONDON, ANDREW BARRY, film editor; b. Bronx, N.Y., Jan. 1, 1949; s. Max Edward and Nellie (Steiner) L. BA in Cinema magna cum laude, U. So. Calif., 1970. Represented by Mont. Artists, Santa Monica, Calif. Prin. works include: (features) The Meteor Man, 1993, F/X 2, 1991, Rambo III, 1988, Planes, Trains and Automobiles, 1987, Link, 1986, Cloak & Dagger, 1984, Psycho II, 1983, The True Story of Eskimo Nell, 1975, (TV shows) Before He Wakes, 1997, Perfect Crime, 1997, Divided By Hate, 1997, The Crying Child, 1996, Evil Has a Face, 1996, Don't Talk to Strangers, 1994, Day of Reckoning, 1993, Mortal Sins, 1992, Running Delilah, 1992, True Tales, 1992, Sweet Poison, 1991, Tales from the Crypt, 1989-90, Beauty and the Beast pilot, 1987, The Christmas Star, 1986; sound editor: Wolfen (MPSE Golden Reel award 1982), Hammett, Roadgames, Psycho II, I'm Dancing As Fast As I Can, Perfect, Protocol, Coal Miner's Daughter, The Long Riders, others. Mem. Acad. Motion Picture Arts and Scis., Motion Picture Sound Editors (Golden Reel award 1982), Phi Beta Kappa. Office: 2622 Armstrong Ave Los Angeles CA 90039-2613

LONEGAN, THOMAS LEE, retired restaurant corporation executive; b. Kansas City, Mo., July 4, 1932; s. Thomas F. and Edna L. (Payton) L.; m. Donna F. Ednie, Apr. 11, 1958; children: Timothy L., John M. BSME, Gen. Motors Inst., 1955; MS in Mgmt., USN Post Grad Sch., 1963; grad., Indsl. Coll. Armed Forces, Washington, 1970; postgrad., Calif. State U., Long Beach, 1979-83; grad., Coll. for Fin. Planning, Denver, 1984. Registered profl. engr.; CFP. Commd. ensign USN, 1956, advanced through grades to comdr., 1978; dir. pub. works Naval Weapons Sta., Seal Beach, Calif., 1974-78; ret., 1978; dir. cen. staff McAthco Enterprises, Inc., Camarillo, Calif., 1985, exec. v.p., CFO, 1986-90, pres., CEO,, 1991-93, exec. v.p., CFO, 1994-95; ret. Author: Analysis and Attenuation of Air Borne Noise in Industrial Plants, 1955, Formalized Training of Maintenance Personnel, 1963. Vol. various couns. Boy Scouts Am., 1968-74. Decorated Bronze Star with combat device, Meritorious Svc. medal, Jt. Svcs. Commendation medal, Navy Achievement medal; recipient Order of Chamoro Govt.of Guam; named Sr. Engr./Arch. Yr. Naval Facilities Engr. Command, 1972. Fellow Soc. Am. Mil. Engrs., Ret. Officers Assn., GM Inst. Robots Honor Soc.; mem. Beta Gamma Sigma. Home: 8578 Amazon River Cir Fountain Valley CA 92708-5510

LONERGAN, MICHAEL HENRY, development administrator, journalist; b. Richland, Wash., Sept. 19, 1949; s. Joseph Thornberg and Gertrude (Foxen) L.; m. Cyndi Lou Kniffin, Jan. 8, 1971 (div. 1981); m. Paula Elizabeth Wallace, Jan. 8, 1983; children: Joseph, Ricardo. Student, U. Chgo., 1967-69; BA in History, U. Wash., 1979. News reporter Sta. WTRC Radio, Sta. WSJV-TV, Elkhart, Ind., 1968-71; gen. mgr. Sta. KURB, Mountlake Terrace, Wash., 1972-73; advt. rep. Enterprise Newspaper, Lynnwood, Wash., 1974-77; news dir. Sta. KBRO-AM-FM, Bremerton, Wash., 1977-78; communications rep. Motorola, Inc., Bellevue, Wash., 1980-81; radio announcer Sta. KTNT/KPMA, Tacoma, 1981-84; dir. mktg. TACCOMM, Tacoma, 1984-85; dir. community rels. The Salvation Army, Tacoma, 1985-92; exec. dir. Tacoma Rescue Mission, 1993—. Host Cityline TV program, 1992—. Rep. candidate 6th dist. U.S. Congress, Wash., 1984. Mem. NAACP, Tacoma N.W. Gideons (pres. 1990-94), Tacoma Downtown Kiwanis, Phi Beta Kappa. Mem. Christian Ch. Home: 3715 N 27th St Tacoma WA 98407-5810 Office: Tacoma Rescue Mission PO Box 1912 702 Pacific Ave Tacoma WA 98402-5208

LONERGAN, THOMAS FRANCIS, III, criminal justice consultant; b. Bklyn., July 28, 1941; s. Thomas Francis and Katherine Josephine (Roth) L.; m. Irene L. Kaucher, Dec. 14, 1963; 1 son, Thomas F. BA, Calif. State U., Long Beach, 1966, MA, 1973; MPA, Pepperdine U., L.A., 1976; postgrad., U. So. Calif., L.A., 1973-76. Dep. sheriff Los Angeles County Sheriff's Dept., 1963-70; U.S. Govt. program analyst, 1968—; fgn. service officer USIA, Lima, Peru, 1970-71; dep. sheriff to lt. Los Angeles Sheriff's Office, 1971-76, aide lt. to div. chief, 1976-80; dir. Criminal Justice Cons., Downey, Calif., 1977—; cons. Public Adminstrv. Service, Chgo., 1972-75, Nat. Sheriff's Assn., 1978, 79; cons. Nat. Inst. Corrections, Washington, 1977-89, coordinator jail ctr., 1981-82 ; tchr. N. Calif. Regional Criminal Justice Acad., 1977-79; lectr. Nat. Corrections Acad., 1980-83; spl. master Chancery Ct. Davidson County, Tenn., 1980-82, U.S. Dist. Ct. (no. dist.) Ohio, 1984-85, Santa Clara Superior Ct. (Calif.), 1983-89, Calif. Supreme Ct., 1984-87; U.S. Dist. Ct. Ga., Atlanta, 1986-87, U.S. Dist. Ct. (no. dist.) Calif., 1982-93—, U.S. Dist. Ct. (no. dist.) Idaho, 1986, U.S. Dist. Ct. Oreg. 1986, U.S. Dist. Ct. Portland 1987, U.S. Dist. (no. dist.) Calif. 1984-89, 95—. Author: California-Past, Present & Future, 1968; Training-A Corrections Perspective, 1979; AIMS-Correctional Officer; Liability-A Correctional Perspective; Liability Law for Probation Administrators; Liability Reporter; Probation Liability Reporter; Study Guides by Aims Media. Mem. Am. Correctional Assn., Nat. Sheriff's Assn. Roman Catholic.

LONERGAN, WALLACE GUNN, economics educator, management consultant; b. Potlatch, Idaho, Mar. 18, 1928; s. Willis Gerald and Lois (Gunn) L.; m. Joan Laurie Penoyer, June 1, 1952; children: Steven Mark, Kevin James. BA, Coll. Idaho, 1950; MBA, U. Chgo., 1955, PhD, 1960. Asst. dir., asst. prof. bus. Indsl. Relations Ctr. U. Chgo., 1960-70, assoc. dir., assoc. prof., 1970-74, dir., prof., 1974-84; vis. prof. Rikkyo U., Tokyo, 1985; vis. fellow Merton Coll. Oxford (Eng.) U., 1986; chair, prof. bus., econs. divsn. Albertson Coll. Idaho, Caldwell, 1987—; v.p. Human Resources Research Cons., Chgo., 1980-87. Author: Leadership and Morale, 1960, Group Leadership, 1974, Performance Appriasal, 1978, Leadership and Management, 1979. Chmn. Episcopal Commn. on Higher Edn., Chgo., 1970-80, mgmt. com. United Way Chgo., 1982-85. 1st lt. U.S. Army, 1950-53, Korea. Named Disting. Alumni Coll. Idaho, 1962; vis. scholar Internat. Anglican Exchange, N.Y.C., 1976, Tokyo, 1986. Mem. Internat. House Japan, Internat. Indsl. Relations Research Assn., Acad. Mgmt., Rotary. Home: 812 E Linden St Caldwell ID 83605-5335 Office: Albertson Coll Idaho Bus Econs Divsn 2112 Cleveland Blvd Caldwell ID 83605-4432

LONG, BETTY JEAN, library director; b. Olton, Tex., Aug. 30, 1951; d. Fred D. and Thelma Bennnie (Cowart) L. BA, Tex. Woman's U., 1972, MLS, 1973. Br. libr. east br. Amarillo (Tex.) Pub. Libr., 1976-80; youth libr. southwest branch Amarilla (Tex.) Pub. Libr., 1973-74, youth libr. east branch, 1974-76; asst. coord. Tex. Panhandlw Libr. System, Amarillo, 1980-85; dir. Roswell (N.Mex.) Pub. Libr., 1985—; del. second N.Mex. Conf. on Librs. and Info. Svcs., 1991, White House Conf. on Librs. and Info. Svcs., 1993; chair adult basic edn. adv. coun. Eastern N.Mex. U., 1991-92, 92-93. Bd. dirs. N.Mex. Coalition for Literacy, 1989-91, co-chair pub. rels. com. 1990-91; sec. Roswell Literacy Coun., 1986, v.p. 1987, pres. 1988-89; sec. Altrusa Club of Roswell, 1987, dir. 1988-89, v.p. 1989-90, pres. 1990-91; v.p. Altrusa Found., 1992-93, pres. 1993-94; com. mem. Chaves County Courthouse Restoration and Preservation; K-6 com. mem. Reach 2000, 1990-91; steering com. Roswell Indep. Sch. Dist. Master Plan; active Friends of Roswell Pub. Libr., Chaves County Literacy Action Coalition; bd. dirs. Amigos, 1996—. Mem. ALA, N.Mex. Libr. Assn. (chair conf. arrangements com. 1987, membership com. 1987-88, chair libr. devel. com. 1988-89, 93-94, co-chair conf. arrangements com. 1991, 2d v.p. 1995-96, 1st v.p. 1996, pres. 1997-98), Mcpl. Librs. Assn. N.Mex. (mcpl. league vice-chair 1987-88, chair 1988-89), Los Pocos Locos (pres. 1990-91, 93-94), Roswell Rotary. Office: Roswell Pub Libr 301 N Pennsylvania Ave Roswell NM 88201-4663

LONG, CONNIE SUE, church youth worker; b. Warrensburg, Mo., Sept. 4, 1954; d. Raymond Barnes and Charlene (Frampton) L. MusB, Cen. Mo. State U., Warrensburg, 1976, MS, 1982. Choir dir. Slater (Mo.) Christian Ch., 1983-87; youth worker, choir dir. United Meth. Ch., Ft. Morgan, Colo., 1987—; guidance counselor Ft. Morgan KE-3 Schs., 1986-91; guidance and placement specialist Morgan C.C., Ft. Morgan, 1991—; counselor Up With Youth, Estes Park, Colo., 1988, 90. Contbr. articles to newspapers. Bd. dirs. United Way, Ft. Morgan, 1990-93. Mem. United Meth. Women, Clarinet Soc., Music Educators N.C., P.E.O. (treas.). Office: Sch to Career Region 1 Resource Center Fort Morgan CO 80701-4324

LONG, JEANINE HUNDLEY, state legislator; b. Provo, Utah, Sept. 21, 1928; d. Ralph Conrad and Hazel Laurine (Snow) Hundley; m. McKay W. Christensen, Oct. 28, 1949 (div. 1967); children: Cathy Schuyler, Julie Schulleri, Kelly M. Christensen, C. Brett Christensen, Harold A. Christensen; m. Kenneth D. Long, Sept. 6, 1968. AA, Shoreline C.C., Seattle, 1975; BA in Psychology, U. Wash., 1977. Mem. Wash. Ho. of Reps., 1983-87, 93-94, mem. bd. joint com. pension policy, Inst. Pub. Policy; mem. Wash. Senate, 1995—; chair Human Svcs. and Corr. com., Wash. Senate, vice chair Sen. Rep. Caucus. Mayor protem, mem. city coun. City of Brier, Wash., 1977-80. Republican. Office: PO Box 40482 Olympia WA 98504-0482

LONG, MARK CHISTOPHER, English educator; b. LaJolla, Calif., Nov. 30, 1959; s. Wendell Oliver and Mary Ellen (Ricketts) L.; m. Rebecca Elizabeth Todd, Sept. 10, 1994; 1 child:Nathaniel Carroll Todd Long. BA, Ithaca (N.Y.) Coll., 1990; MA, U. Wash., 1992, PhD, 1996. Profl. ski instr., back-country guide Profl. Ski Instrs. of Am., Calif., 1980-86; tchg. asst. U. Wash., Seattle, 1991-96, asst. dir. writing ctr., 1992-93, asst. dir. expository writing program, 1993-95, acting instr. dept. English, 1996—. Author: U.S. Marine Corps Ski Instruction Manual, 1994; contbr. articles to profl. jours. Mem. MLA, Nat. Coun. Tchrs. English, Assn. for Study of Lit. and the Environment, Phi Alpha Tehta, Phi Kappa Phi. Democrat. Unitarian. Home: 4115 Francis Ave N Seattle WA 98103 Office: U Wash Dept English Box 354330 Seattle WA 98195

LONG, ROBERT MERRILL, retail drug company executive; b. Oakland, Calif., May 19, 1938; s. Joseph Milton and Vera Mai (Skaggs) L.; m. Eliane Quilloux, Dec. 13, 1969. Student, Brown U., 1956-58; BA, Claremont Men's Coll., 1960. With Longs Drug Stores Inc., Walnut Creek, Calif., 1960—, dist. mgr., 1970-72, exec. v.p., 1972-75, pres., 1975-77, pres., chief exec. officer, 1977-91; chmn., chief exec. officer Longs Drug Stores, Walnut Creek, Calif., 1991—. Mem. Nat. Assn. Chain Drug Stores (dir.). Office: Longs Drug Stores Corp PO Box 5222 141 N Civic Dr Walnut Creek CA 94596-3858

LONG, THEODORE DIXON, writer, investor; b. Youngstown, Ohio, June 26, 1933; s. Theodore Samuel and Gertrude (Drew) L.; m. Ellen Corning, Aug. 18, 1962 (dec. July 1989); children: Samuel Dixon, Maudalison; m. Ruthanne Betlach, June 21, 1994. BA, Amherst Coll., 1955; MA, Tufts U., 1958; PhD, Columbia U., 1968. Cons. OECD, Paris, 1964-67; asst. prof. Case Western Res. U., Cleve., 1967-74; assoc. prof. Case Western Res. U., 1974-81, prof., 1981-94, dean Western Res. Coll., 1977-85, prof., dean emeritus, 1994—; chmn. Springcreek Corp., Corte Madera, Calif., 1994—. Author: Science Policy-Japan, 1967; author, editor: Science Policies of Industrial Nations, 1972, Markets of Provence, 1996. Trustee, past pres. Holden Arboretum, Kirtland, Ohio, 1971—; trustee Western Res. Acad., Hudson, Ohio, 1974—, Strybing Arboretum Soc., San Francisco, 1994—. With U.S. Army, 1955-57, Korea. NAS fellow, Washington, 1973-74. Mem. Internat. House of Japan. Home: 123 Sturdivant Ave San Anselmo CA 94960-2528 Office: Springcreek Corp 770 Tamalpais Ave Ste 210 Corte Madera CA 94925

LONG, WILLIAM JOSEPH, software engineer; b. Kokomo, Ind., Feb. 1, 1956; s. George Alexander and Rebecca Bethina (Burgan) L. BA, Harvard U., 1979; cert. in project mgmt., U. Calif., Berkeley, 1994. Cons. Bechtel Corp., San Francisco, 1982-85; assoc. prof. Dalian (Liaoning, China) Inst. Tech., 1985-86; software engr. Bechtel Corp., San Francisco, 1986-92; EDI project mgr. Pacific Gas & Electric Co., San Francisco, 1992-94; software engr. Am. Pres. Lines, Oakland, Calif., 1994-95; mem. adv. bd. Synetics, Inc., San Francisco, 1987—; owner William J. Long and Assocs., Oakland, Calif., 1990—. Vol. English tutor, Oakland, Calif., 1983 . Rsch. grantee Smithsonian Astrophys. Obs., Cambridge, Mass., 1976. Mem. IEEE, Assn. Computing Machinery, Am. Assn. Artificial Intelligence, Math. Assn. Am. Home and Office: William J Long and Assocs 2225 7th Ave #33 Oakland CA 94606-1969

LONG, ZELMA REED, winery administrator, winemaker; b. The Dalles, Oreg., Dec. 1, 1943; d. Leo Casper and Lulu Jean Reed; m. Phillip Freese, Dec. 1, 1990. BS, Oreg. State U., 1965. Lic. dietician. Dietetic intern U. Calif. Med. Ctr., San Francisco, 1965; dietitian Highland Alameda Hosp., Oakland, Calif., 1967-68; asst. enologist Robert Mondavi Winery, Napa, Calif., 1970-71, chief enologist, 1972-79; sr. v.p., winemaker Simi Winery, Healdsburg, Calif., 1979-88, pres., 1988-90, pres., CEO, 1990-96; exec. v.p. Moët Hennessey Calif. Wineries, 1996—; cons. Ruffino Chianti, 1983-84, Bodegas Chandon, 1992—; mem. Vitis Corp. adv. com. Adv. Group to Nat. Plant Germplasm Sys. U.S. Dept. Agr., 1987-89; mem. indsl. adv. com. Found. Plant Material Sci., U. Calif., Davis, 1987-89, policy adv. com. Sch. Agr., 1987-89, mem. dept. viticulture and enology, industry adv. com., 1989—; co-owner, Long Vineyards, Napa Valley, Calif., 1977—; lectr. panel discussions. Contbr. articles to profl. jours. Mem. Calif. Regional Water Quality Control Bd., North Coast Region, 1985-90; mem. Internat. Womens Forum, Bay Area chpt., Calif., 1990—, dir., 1994-96; bd. trustees UC Davis Found., Calif. Agrl. Found., U. Calif., Davis, 1991-93, exec. bd., 1994—. Recipient Wine and Food Achievement award No. Calif. chpt. Am. Soc. Wine and Food, 1989, MASI award, Verona, Italy, 1991, Tete de Cuvee award Cote de Coeur, 1996, Alumni Achievement award Kappa Kappa Gamma, 1996; named Calif. Wine Pioneer, 1993, Woman of Yr. Roundtable for Women in Food Svc., 1994, Woman of the Yr. Women for WineSense, 1995; named to James Beard Found. Hall of Fame, 1996. Mem. Napa Valley Wine Tech. Group (past pres.), Sonoma County Wine Tech. Group (past dir.), Am. Soc. Enology and Viticulture (dir. 1982-83), Am. Vineyard Found. (founding pres.), Women for Wine Sense (dir. 1990-93, adv. bd. 1990-94), North Coast Viticultural Rsch. Group (founder), United Winegrowers (dir. 1990-96), Alexander Valley Winegrowers (founder, pres. 1992-96), Am. Vinters Assn. (bd. dir. 1994—). Office: Simi Winery 16275 Healdsburg Ave Healdsburg CA 95448-9618

LONGAN, GEORGE BAKER, III, real estate executive; b. Kansas City, Mo., Apr. 20, 1934; s. Benjamin Hyde and Georgette Longan O'Brien; divorced; 1 child, Nancy Ann Longan LaPoff. BSBA, U. Ariz., 1956; postgrad., U. Kans., 1956-57. Cert. real estate broker. Sr. v.p., gen. mgr. Paul Hamilton Co., Kansas City, 1963-84; pres. Eugene D. Brown Co., Kansas City, 1984-93; v.p. J.C. Nichols Real Estate, 1993-94; bd. dirs. Genesis Relocation Network, N.J. Served to staff sgt. USAF, 1958-62. Mem. Nat. Real Estate Assn. (bd. dirs. 1991-94), Mo. Real Estate Assn. (bd. dirs. 1987-90), Real Estate Bd. Kansas City (bd. dirs. 1987-90), Met. Kansas City Real Estate Bd. (pres. 1992), Beta Sigma Psi, Sigma Chi. Episcopal. Home: 2701 E Camino Pablo Tucson AZ 85718-6625 Office: Long Realty Co 5683 N Swan Rd Tucson AZ 85718-4565

LONGENECKER, MARTHA W., museum director. BA in Art, UCLA; MFA, Claremont Grad. Sch.; studied with Millard Sheets, Shoji Hamada, Tatsuzo Shimaoka. Owner ceramics studio Claremont, Calif.; prof. art, now prof. emeritus San Diego State U.; founder, dir. Mingei Internat. Mus. Folk Art, San Diego; coord. editing, design and prodn. of exhbn. documentary publs. Mingei Internat. Mus. World Folk Art.; condr. tours. Contbr. chpts. to books; developer videotapes; exhibited at Dalzell Hatfield Galleries. San Diego State U. Found. grantee, 1967, Calif. State U. Rsch. grantee, 1978; recipient Disting. Alumna award Claremont Grad. Sch., 1980, Essence of Life award ElderHelp of San Diego, 1993, Living Legacy award Women's Internat. Ctr., 1994, Women of Distinction award Soroptimist Internat. of La Jolla, 1994. Office: Mingei Internat Mus Folk Art Balboa Park Plaza de Panama 1439 El Prado San Diego CA 92101 Address: PO Box 553 La Jolla CA 92038

LONGMAN, ANNE STRICKLAND, special education educator, consultant; b. Metuchen, N.J., Sept. 17, 1924; d. Charles Hodges and Grace Anna (Moss) Eldridge; m. Henry Richard Strickland, June 22, 1946 (dec. 1960); m. Donald Rufus Longman, Jan. 20, 1979 (dec. 1987); children: James C., Robert H. BA in Bus. Adminstrn., Mich. State U., 1945; teaching credentials, U. Calif., Berkeley, 1959; postgrad., Stanford U., 1959-60; MA in Learning Hand, Santa Clara U., 1974. Lic. educator. Exptl. test engr. Pratt & Whitney Aircraft, East Hartford, Conn., 1945-47; indsl. engr. Marchant Calculators, Emeryville, Calif., 1957-58; with pub. rels. Homesmith, Palo Alto, Calif., 1959-62; cons. Right to Read Program, Calif., 1978-79; monitor, reviewer State of Calif., Sacramento, 1976-79; tchr. diagnosis edn. Cabrillo Coll., Aptos, Calif., 1970-79; lectr. edn. U. Calif., Santa Cruz, 1970-79; cons. Santa Cruz Bd. Edn., 1970-79; reading rschr. Gorilla Found., Woodside, Calif., 1982—; bd. mem. Western Inst. Alcoholic Studies, L.A., 1972-73; chmn. Evaluation Com., Tri-County, Calif., 1974; speaker Internat. Congress Learning Disabilities, Seattle, 1974; ednl. cons. rsch. on allergies, 1993—. Author: Word Patterns in English, 1974-92, Cramming 3D Kids, 1975—, 50 books for migrant students, 1970-79; contbr. articles on stress and alcoholism and TV crime prevention for police, 1960-79. Founder Literacy Ctr., Santa Cruz, 1968-092; leader Girl Scouts U.S.A., San Francisco, 1947-50; vol. Thursday's Child, Santa Cruz, 1976-79, Golden Gate Kindergarten, San Francisco, 1947-57. Recipient Fellowships Pratt & Whitney Aircraft, 1944, Stanford U., 1959. Mem. Internat. Reading Assn. (pres. Santa Cruz 1975), Santa Clara Valley Watercolor Soc., Los Altos Art Club (v.p. 1992), Eichler Swim and Tennis Club. Republican. Episcopalian. Home and Office: 153 Del Mesa Carmel Carmel CA 93923-7950

LONGO, LAWRENCE DANIEL, physiologist, obstetrician-gynecologist; b. Los Angeles, Oct. 11, 1926; s. Frank Albert and Florine Azelia (Hall) L.; m. Betty Jeanne Mundall, Sept. 9, 1948; children: April Celeste, Lawrence Anthony, Elisabeth Lynn, Camilla Giselle. BA, Pacific Union Coll., 1949; MD, Coll. Med. Evangelists, Loma Linda, Calif., 1954. Diplomate: Am. Bd. Ob-Gyn. Intern Los Angeles County Gen. Hosp., 1954-55, resident, 1955-58; asst. prof. ob-gyn UCLA, 1962-64; asst. prof. physiology and ob-gyn U. Pa., 1964-68; prof. physiology and ob-gyn Loma Linda U., 1968—; dir. ctr. for perinatal biology Loma Linda U. Sch. Medicine, 1974—; mem. perinatal biology com. Nat. Inst. Child Health, NIH, 1973-77; co-chmn. reprodn. scientist devel. program NIH; NATO prof. Consiglio Nat. delle Richerche, Italian Govt. Editor: Respiratory Gas Exchange and Blood Flow in the Placenta, 1972, Fetal and Newborn Cardiovascular Physiology, 1978, Charles White and A Treatise on the Management of Pregnant and Lying-in Women, 1987; co-editor: Landmarks in Perinatology, 1975-76, Classics in Obstetrics Gynecology, 1993; editor classic pages in ob-gyn. Am. Jour. Ob-Gyn.; contbr. articles to profl. jours. Served with AUS, 1945-47. Founder Frank A. and Florine A. Longo lectureship in faith, knowledge, and human values Pacific Union Coll., 1993. Fellow Royal Coll. Ob-Gyns., Am. Coll. Ob-Gyns.; mem. Am. Assn. History Medicine (coun.), Am. Osler Soc. (bd. govs., sec.-treas.), Am. Physiol. Soc., Assn. Profs. Ob-Gyn., Perinatal Rsch. Soc., Soc. Gynecologic Investigation (past pres.), Neurosci. Soc., Royal Soc. Medicine. Adventist. Office: Loma Linda U Sch Medicine Ctr Perinatal Biology Loma Linda CA 92350

LONGO, PATRIZIA, political science educator; b. Vicenza, Italy, May 29, 1957; d. Domenico and Maria Grazia (Tramma) L.; 1 child, David. BA in Langs., Scuola Superiore per Interpret, Traduttori, Florence, Italy, 1980; BA in Polit. Sci., U. Pa., 1983; MA in Polit. Sci., U. Calif., Berkeley, 1984, PhD in Polit. Sci., 1989. Part-time instr. Italian, translator and interpreter The Berlitz Sch. of Langs., Jenkintown, Pa., 1981-83; rsch. asst. Dept. English U. Pa., 1982-83; translator/interpreter Am. Translators Internat., Stanford, Calif., 1984—; tchng. asst. in polit. theory U. Calif., Berkeley, 1984-87, instr. of Italian, 1987-89; instr. dept. polit. sci. Calif. State U., Hayward, 1991; instr. St. Mary's Coll., Moraga, Calif., 1991—. Contbr. articles to profl. publs. Grantee NEH, 1993, Irvine Grant Workshop, 1992, 93. Mem. Soc. Utopian Studies, Am. Polit. Sci. Assn., Western Polit. Sci. Assn., So. Soc. Philosophy and Psychology, Bay Area Women in Polit. Sci. Office: St Marys Coll Dept of Govt Moraga CA 94575

LONGVILLE, JOHN, mayor; b. St. Paul, Sept. 21, 1949; m. Victoria Brookins, Jan. 1975 (dec. 1991); 1 child, Regan Brookins-Longville. Student, U. Minn., 1968. From polit. aide to press sec. U.S. Rep. George Brown, Calif., 1968-79; councilman City of Rialto, Calif., 1980-84, 86-88, mayor, 1988—; bd. dirs. Omnitrans, So. Calif. Regional Rail Authority. Vol. United Farm Workers, 1969; project dir. Viewer sponsored TV Found., L.A., 1970-71; past pres. Am. Cancer Soc., Rialto. Jr. Achievement scholar. Mem. NAACP (life), MADD, So. Calif. Assn. Govts. (pres. 1996—), Jaycees, Kiwanis. Address: 150 S Palm Rialto CA 92376

LOO, THOMAS S., lawyer; b. 1943. BS, U. So. Calif., JD. Bar: Calif. 1969. Ptnr. Bryan Cave LLP, Santa Monica, Calif. Office: Bryan Cave LLP 120 Broadway Ste 500 Santa Monica CA 90401-2386

LOOK, JANET K., psychologist; b. Bklyn., Mar. 11, 1944; d. Harry and Isabelle (Chernoff) Kaplan; divorced; children: Howard, Erika (dec.). AB, NYU, 1964; EdM, Rutgers U., 1967, EdD, 1976. Lic. psychologist; cert. sch. psychologist. Asst. examiner Ednl. Testing Svc., Princeton, N.J., 1964-66; instr. Rutgers U., New Brunswick, N.J., 1968-69; psychologist Seattle Pub. Schs., 1991—; pvt. practice Kirkland, Wash., 1993—; adj. instr. U. Conn., Waterbury, 1973-91; appearances on various TV and radio shows including the Today Show; interviews include Litchfield County Times, 1987, Waterbury Rep.-Am., 1983-87, Manchester Jour. Inquirer, 1986, Danbury News-Times, 1985; presenter APA, San Francisco, 1991, Nation's Concern and Its Response, U. Wis., Milw., 1991, Nat. Assn. Sch. Psychologists, Dallas, 1991, Divorce Issues Inst., So. Conn. State U., New Haven, 1989. Author: (with others) The Troubled Adolescent, 1991; contbr. articles to newspapers, including N.Y. Times. Mem. APA, Wash. State Psychol. Assn., Nat. Assn. Sch. Psychologists, Wash. State Assn. Sch. Psychologists (area rep., bd. dirs. 1991-93). Office: 1104 Market St Kirkland WA 98033-5441

LOOMIS, CHRISTOPHER KNAPP, metallurgical engineer; b. San Francisco, May 6, 1947; s. Richard and Evaline Elsie (Crandal) L.; m. Merril Ellen Purdy, Dec. 8, 1968; 1 child, Nicole Lee; m. Sandra Lee Marsh, Feb. 14, 1993. Profl. Engring. degree, Colo. Sch. Mines, 1969. Process engr. Alcan Aluminum Corp., Riverside, Calif., 1969-73, prodn. supt., 1973-76; process engr. Alcan Aluminum Corp., Oswego, N.Y., 1976-78, maintenance engr., 1978-80; metall. engr. Hazelett Strip-Casting Corp., Colchester, Vt., 1980-81; chief engr. ARCO Metals Co., Chgo., 1981-84; maintenance supt. Cerro Metal Products, Paramount, Calif., 1984-85, mgr. engring. and maintenance, 1985-86; supt. tech. svcs. Golden Aluminum Co., Ft. Lupton, Colo., 1987-88; process devel. engr. Golden Aluminum Co., Lakewood, Colo., 1988-91, corp. environ. and process engr., 1991; engr. IV Coors Brewing Co., Golden, Colo., 1991-93, material engr. V, 1993-96; owner Loomis Engring. and Design, Arvada, Colo., 1996—. Mem. Am. Soc. for Metals, Metall. Soc., Colo. Sch. Mines Alumni Assn., Am. Soc. for Quality Control, Fedn. Fly Fishers (life), Trout Unltd. (life). Episcopalian. Home: 6572 Owens Ct Arvada CO 80004-2765 Office: Loomis Engring and Design 6572 Owens Ct Arvada CO 80004

LOOMIS, JAMES ARTHUR, broadcast technician, newsletter editor; b. Portland, Oreg., June 10, 1953; s. Frank Clark Jr. and Jacqulyn Hope (Shade) L. AA in Electronics Tech., Shasta Coll., Redding, Calif., 1976. Cert. Microcomputer Tech., Nat. Radio Inst., Washington, 1987, HVAC/refrigeration, 1990. Computer technician Redding, 1975; electronics technician various TV repair shops, Redding, 1975-77; broadcast maintenance engr. KGO-ABC TV, San Francisco, 1977-79, KATU-Fisher Broadcasting, Portland, Oreg., 1979—. Editor newsletter The Trainmaster, 1995 (Jack Holst award 1996). Mem. Nat. Railway Hist. Soc., Refrigeration Svc. Engrs. Soc. Home: 12440 SE Stephens St Portland OR 97233-1336

LOONEY, GERALD LEE, medical educator, administrator; b. Bradshaw, W.Va., Nov. 22, 1937; s. Noah Webster and Anna Belle (Burris) L.; m. Linda Louise Pluebell, Oct. 19, 1962 (div. Apr. 1975); children: Deborah Lynn, Catherine Ann, Karen Marie, Kelli Rachelle; m. Patricia Marie Terrazas, Dec. 22, 1987. AB, Johns Hopkins U., 1959, MD, 1963; MPH, Harvard U., 1968. Diplomate Am. Bd. Preventive Medicine, Am. Bd. Pediatrics. Resident pediatrics Tufts-New Eng. Med. Ctr., Boston, 1965-67; physician-in-chief Kennedy Meml. Hosp., Boston, 1969-71; asst. prof. family and cmty. medicine U. Ariz. Coll. Medicine, Tucson, 1971-72; asst. prof. emergency medicine U. So. Calif. Sch. Medicine, L.A., 1972-77; assoc. clin. prof. medicine U. Calif., Irvine, 1991—; emergency dept. dir. Glendale (Calif.) Adventist Med. Ctr., 1978-84; edn. dir. Orthopaedic Hosp., L.A., 1985-88; urgent care dir. Bay Shore Med. Group, Torrance, Calif., 1988-93; med. dir. Surecare and LAX Clinics Centinela Hosp., Inglewood, Calif., 1993-95; dir. med. svc. McDonnell Douglas Aerospace, Long Beach, Calif., 1996—; bd. dirs. Beach Cities Health Dist., Redondo Beach, Calif., 1992-93. Office: McDonnell Douglas MTA C-17 Program PAC 174-11 2401 E Wardlow Rd Long Beach CA 90807-4418

LOONEY, RALPH EDWIN, newspaper editor, author, photographer; b. Lexington, Ky., June 22, 1924; s. Arville Zone and Connie Elizabeth (Boyd) L.; m. Clarabel Richards, Dec. 7, 1944. BA, U. Ky., 1948. Various positions including proof reader, photographer, chief photographer, sports writer, reporter Lexington Leader, 1943-52; reporter Albuquerque Tribune, 1953-54; reporter, copy editor, chief copy editor St. Louis Globe-Democrat, 1955-56; city editor Albuquerque Tribune, 1956-68, asst. mng. editor, 1968-73, editor, 1973-80; editor Rocky Mountain News, Denver, 1980-89; columnist Scripps Howard News Svc., 1989-93, Tribune, Albuquerque, 1989-93. Author: Haunted Highways, The Ghost Towns of New Mexico, 1969, O'Keeffe and Me, 1995; contbr. articles to mags. including Nat. Observer, others; photographs to mags. Founder, N.Mex. Motion Picture Commn., 1967-76; v.p., bd. dirs. Albuquerque C. of C., 1971-75; bd. dirs. Albuquerque Indsl. Devel. Svc., 1971-80, Newspaper Features Coun., 1984-89; bd. advisors Lovelace Med. Ctr., Albuquerque, 1976-80, UPI, 1983-86; exec. coun. St. Joseph Hosp., 1986-89. Recipient N.Mex. medal of Merit, 1968, Robert F. Kennedy Journalism award, 1970, George Washington Honor medal Freedoms Found., 1969, 19 E.H. Shaffer awards N.Mex. Press Assn., 1965-80; named Colo. Newspaper Person of the Yr., 1988, Newspaper Features Coun. Jester award, 1989. Mem. N.Mex. Press Assn. (state pres. 1976), Colo. Press Assn. (bd. dirs. 1982-85), Sigma Delta Chi (N. Mex. pres. 1960). Methodist. Home: 6101 Casa De Vida Dr NE Albuquerque NM 87111

LOPATA, MARTIN BARRY, executive; b. Bronx, N.Y., Apr. 6, 1939; s. Julius A. and Rose (Silverman) L.; m. Sarah G. Lopata, July 4, 1965 (div. 1978; children: Warren A., Lawrence M.; m. Lynette Wyrick, May 6, 1989 (div. 1991). Grad., High Sch. of Art and Design, N.Y.C.; attended N.Y.C. Community Coll., Bklyn. Sales mgr. H. Natoway Co., Los Angeles, 1961-62; contract mgr. A.S. Aloe Co., Los Angeles, 1962-64; merchandise mgr. S.E. Rykoff Co., Los Angeles, 1964-70; v.p. Kirby Sales, Los Angeles, 1970-71; pres. MBL Industries Inc., Santa Ana, Calif., 1971-87, Unicorn Seminars Inc., Huntington Beach, Calif., 1987-88, Unicorn Investments Internat., Huntington Beach, 1988-91; chair Yes Educational Systems, Reno, Nev., 1995-97; chmn. Soviet Am. Internat. Co., 1988-92; joint venture Sovaminco Soviet Am. Internat. Co. #104, Moscow; pres. Coastal-West Industries, 1991-92. Patron Am. Mus. Nat. History, N.Y.C., 1984-91; bus. chmn. Ctr. for Soviet-Am. Dialogue, Washington, 1987-91; chmn. Com. on Bus.-A New Way of Thinking in a New Age, Moscow, 1987; bd. dirs. Three Mountain Found., Lone Pine, Calif., 1987-88, Inside Edge, Irvine, Calif., 1987-94, found. pres., 1993-94; vice chmn. United Ch. Religious Science, Los Angeles, 1986-87, pres. Huntington Beach Ch. Religious Sci., 1985. Mem. Masons (32d degree), Shriners. Home: 16391 Wimbledon Ln Huntington Beach CA 92649-2188

LOPER, D. ROGER, retired oil company executive; b. Mpls., Dec. 14, 1920; s. Donald Rust and Agnes (Yerxa) L.; m. Sylvia Lee Brainard, Aug. 16, 1946 (dec. Apr. 1973); children: Ann Kathleen, Michael Brainard, Joyce Elizabeth, Nancy Jean Loper Woods; m. Genevieve Jean Kusles, May 4, 1974. BSMetE, Carnegie Tech. Inst., 1947. Registered chem. engr., Calif. Div. supr. Standard Oil of Calif., San Francisco, 1958-64, asst. chief engr., 1964-74; gen. mgr. Chevron Petroleum, London, 1974-80; pres. Chevron Shale Oil Co., Denver, 1980-82; v.p. Chevron Overseas Petroleum, San Francisco, 1982-85; cons. Loper Assocs., Carmel, Calif., 1985—. Inventor hydrocracking reactor, remote inspection device. Pres. Our Saviour Luth. Ch., Lafayette, Calif., 1971-72. Maj. U.S. Army, 1942-46. Republican. Home and Office: 2804 Pradera Rd Carmel CA 93923-9717

LOPER, JAMES LEADERS, broadcasting executive; b. Phoenix, Sept. 4, 1931; s. John D. and Ellen Helen (Leaders) L.; m. Mary Louise Brion, Sept. 1, 1955; children: Elizabeth Margaret Sehran (Mrs. Michael K. Sehran), James Leaders Jr. BA, Ariz. State U., 1953; MA, U. Denver, 1957; PhD, U. So. Calif., 1967; DHL (hon.), Columbia Coll., 1973; LLD (hon.), Pepperdine U., 1978. Asst. dir. bur. broadcasting Ariz. State U., Tempe, 1953-59; news editor, announcer Sta. KTAR, Phoenix, 1955-56; dir. ednl. TV, Calif. State U., Los Angeles, 1960-64; v.p. Community TV So. Calif., Los Angeles, 1962-63; asst. to pres. Sta. KCET-Pub. TV, Los Angeles, 1963-65, sec., 1965-66, dir. ednl. services, 1964-65, asst. gen. mgr., 1965-66, v.p., gen. mgr., 1966-69, exec. v.p., gen. mgr., 1969-71, pres., gen. mgr., 1971-76, pres., CEO, 1976-82; exec. dir. Acad. TV Arts and Scis., 1983—; bd. dirs., chmn. audit com. Western Fed. Savs. and Loan Assn., L.A., 1979-93; bd. dirs. Global View, Washington; bd. dirs. Tennessee Ernie Ford Enterprises, 1994—; chmn. bd. Pub. Broadcasting Service, Washington, 1969-72; dir. Calif. Arts Coun., 1991—; adj. prof. Sch. Cinema and TV U. So. Calif., 1984—; sr. lectr. U. So. Calif., Los Angeles, 1969-70; pres. Western Ednl. Network, 1968-70; mem. Gov.'s Ednl. TV and Radio Adv. Com., Calif., 1968-74; U.S. rep. CENTO Conf. Radio and TV, Turkey, 1978, trustee Internat. Council Nat. Acad. TV Arts and Scis., 1988—. Contbr. articles to profl. jours; contbr. to ETV: The Farther Vision, 1967, Broadcasting and Bargaining: Labor Relations in Radio and Television, 1970. Mem. adv. bd. Jr. League of Los Angeles, 1970-76, Jr. League of Pasadena, 1972-75, Los Angeles Jr. Arts Ctr., 1968-72; exec. v.p. Assocs. of Otis Art Inst., 1971-77, pres., 1975-77; chmn., dir. The Performing Tree, Los Angeles; bd. dirs. Sears-Roebuck Found., 1976-79; chmn. bd. visitors Annenburg Sch. Communications, U. So. Calif., 1975-80; trustee Poly. Sch., Pasadena; mem. Calif. State Arts Commn., 1991. Recipient Disting. Alumnus award Ariz. State U., 1972; Alumni award of Merit, U. So. Calif., 1975; Gov's. award Hollywood chpt. Nat. Acad. TV Arts and Scis., 1975; Alumni Achievement award Phi Sigma Kappa, 1975; named Centennial Alumnus Nat. Assn. of State Univs. and Land Grant Colls., 1988. Named to Hall of Fame Walter Cronkite Sch. Comms., Ariz. State U., 1994 Mem. Acad. TV Arts and Scis. (past gov., v.p. Hollywood chpt., trustee nat. acad.), TV Acad. Found., Hollywood Radio and TV Soc. (treas., dir.), Western Ednl. Soc. Telecommunications (past pres.), Assn. Calif. Pub. TV Stas. (past pres.), Young Pres.'s Orgn., Phi Sigma Kappa, Pi Delta Epsilon, Alpha Delta Sigma, Sigma Delta Chi. Presbyterian (chmn. Mass Media Task Force So. Calif. synod 1969-75). Clubs: Valley Hunt (Pasadena), Bel-Air Bay, California, Los Angeles, 100 of Los Angeles, Calif. (Los Angeles), Twilight Pasadena, Lincoln Club, L.A. Office: Acad TV Arts and Scis PO Box 7344 North Hollywood CA 91603

LOPES, JAMES LOUIS, lawyer; b. Watsonville, Calif., Feb. 1, 1947; s. Allen M. and Norma Maxine (McElroy) L.; m. Gail R. Lopes, Mar. 24, 1979; children: Elizabeth, Jane. BS, U.Calif., Davis, 1969; JD, U. Pacific, 1974; LLM, Harvard U., 1975. Bar: Calif. 1974, U.S. Ct. Appeals (9th cir.), U.S. Dist. Ct. (no., ea., ctrl. dists.) Calif. Assoc. Gendel, Raskoff, Shapiro &

Quittner, L.A., 1975-78; ptnr. Gordon, Peitzman & Lopes, San Francisco, 1978-81, Howard, Rice & Nemerovski, San Francisco, 1982—; adv. com. bankruptcy/creditors' rights Practicing Law Inst., 1992—. Co-author: Law and Business of Computer Software, 1989; contbr. articles to profl. jours. Mem. ABA (bankruptcy com., 1980—), Calif. Bankruptcy Forum (bd. dirs. 1990-93), Calif. State Bar Assn., Turnaround Mgmt. Assn. (bd. dirs. 1996—). Office: Howard Rice & Nemerovski 7th Fl 3 Embarcadero Ctr Ste 7 San Francisco CA 94111-4003

LOPEZ, ANA MARIA, medical educator, physician; b. Bolivia, Apr. 23, 1960. AB, Bryn Mawr (Pa.) Coll., 1982; MD, Jefferson Med. Coll., 1988; MPH, U. Ariz., 1994. Diplomate Am. Bd. Internal Medicine, Nat. Bd. Med. Examiners. Resident in internal medicine U. Ariz. Health Ctr., Tucson, 1988-91, fellow in gen. internal medicine, 1991-92, chief med. resident, 1991-92, fellow hematology/oncology, 1992-95, postdoctoral NIH rsch. fellow cancer prevention, 1993-95, instr. Coll. of Pharmacy, 1992—, instr. Coll. of Medicine, 1991—; rsch. asst. prof. medicine, 1995—; presenter in field. Contbr. numerous articles to profl. jours. Mem. ACP (assoc., health and pub. policy com. Ariz. chpt. 1991—, chair coun. of assocs. Ariz. chpt. 1992-94, coun. of assoc. 1991-93, ACP house staff rep. to the Assn. of Program Dirs. in Internal Medicine, 1992-94, health and pub. policy com. 1993-94, mem. enhancement com. 1994—), Soc. Gen. Internal Medicine (mem. devel. com. 1994—), Ariz. Women's Cancer Netowrk (legis. policy and advocacy com. 1993—), Am. Med. Women's Assn. (faculty advisor to student chpt. 1992—, Scholarship award 1986, 87, 88), Am. Cancer Soc. (profl. edn. com. 1990—, Vol. award So. Ariz. chpt. 1990), Ariz. Pub. Health Soc. (mem. legis. com. 1990-92), Physicians Social Responsibility (mem. spkrs. bur. 1983). Office: Ariz Cancer Ctr Sect Hematology/Oncology 1501 N Campbell Ave Tucson AZ 85724-0001

LOPEZ, ANDY, university athletic coach. Head coach Pepperdine U. Waves, 1989-94, U. Florida, 1994—. NCAA Divsn. 1A Champions, 1992. Office: U Florida P O Box 14485 Gainesville FL 32604*

LOPEZ, ANGELO CAYAS, freelance illustrator; b. Norfolk, Va., Mar. 29, 1967; s. Felizardo Pardo and Teresita (Cayas) L. BS in Graphic Design, San Jose State U., 1992. Cashier Marriott's Great Am., Santa Clara, Calif., 1985; page tech. svc. dept. Sunnyvale (Calif.) Pub. Libr., 1985-90, tech. svc. clk., 1993—; intern Palo Alto (Calif.) Fast Stats, 1990-91; framer Aaron Bros., Sunnyvale, 1991-92; cashier Linden Tree Children's Bookstore, Los Altos, Calif., 1992-94; Executed mural Beryessa br. San Jose Pub. Libr.; contbr. illustrations to books including Two Moms A Zark and Me, 1993, Night Travelers, 1994; contbr. illustrations and cartoons to mags. Contbr. illustrations to books including Two Moms A Zark and Me, 1993, Night Travelers, 1994; contbr. illustrations and cartoons to mags. Vol. Arts Project, Santa Clara, 1990; tutor San Jose (Calif.) Chinese Alliance Ch., 1993-95; active Santa Clara U. Mission Ch., 1992-95. Democrat. Home: 4430 Albany Dr Apt 87 San Jose CA 95129-1627

LOPEZ, CARL A. TAYLOR, lawyer; b. Chgo., Oct. 23, 1948; s. Abraham Nieves and Faye Ellen (Taylor) L.; m. Diana Callahan, May 31, 1980; children: Taylor, Derek, Carlyn. BA, Willamette U., 1972; JD, Georgetown U., 1975. Bar: Wash. 1975, U.S. Dist. Ct. (we. dist.) Wash. 1978, U.S. Ct. Appeals (9th cir.) 1978, U.S. Ct. of Claims 1994. Prin. Francis, Lopez & LePley, Seattle, 1977-84, Lopez & Fantel, Seattle, 1985—. Mem. ATLA, Wash. State Trial Lawyers Assn. Office: Lopez & Fantel 1510 14th Ave Seattle WA 98122-4024

LOPEZ, DANIEL HERALDO, academic administrator; b. Puerto de Luna, N.Mex., Feb. 14, 1946; s. Julian and Tiofila (Ocaña) L.; m. Linda Vigil, July 12, 1975. BA in Polit. Sci., U. N.Mex., 1970, MA in Polit. Sci., 1972, PhD in Polit. Sci., 1982. Cabinet sec. N.Mex. Dept. Fin. and Adminstrn., Santa Fe, 1984-86; chief of staff for senate fin. and sr. staff analyst House Appropriations and Fin. Com., Santa Fe, 1987-89; assoc. and dep. dir. terminal effects rsch. and analysis N.Mex. Inst. Mining and Tech., Socorro, 1987-89, adj. prof., 1994—; v.p. institutional devel. N.Mex. Inst. Mining and Technology, Socorro, 1989-93, pres., 1993—; exec. dir. N.Mex. Adv. Coun. on Vocat.-Tech. Edn., 1973-82; adj. prof. U. N.Mex., Albuquerque, 1975-82, N.Mex. Inst. Mining and Tech., Socorro, 1994—; cabinet sec. N.Mex. Employment Security Dept., Albuquerque, 1983-84. Mem. League of United Latin Am. Citizens, Albuquerque; mem., past pres. Albuquerque Hispano C. of C. Staff Sgt. USAF, 1968-69, Korea. Mem. N.Mex. Tech. Rsch. Found. (v.p. 1994), N.Mex. First Exec. Com. (v.p. 1994), N.Mex. Children's Found., N.Mex. Industry Network Corp. (exec. com. 1994), N.Mex. Amigos, Rio Grande Tech. Found. Home: One Olive Ln Socorro NM 87801 Office: NMex Inst Mining and Tech Office of the Pres Socorro NM 87801

LOPEZ, MANUEL M., mayor. Mayor Oxnard, Calif. Address: 305 W 3d St Oxnard CA 93030

LOPEZ, STEVEN RICHARD, small business owner, consultant; b. Flagstaff, Ariz., Dec. 14, 1944; s. John and Trinidad (Rodriquez) L.; (div. 1983); children: David Allen, Laura Marie, Jonel Christina, Steven Christopher. BFA, U. Ariz., 1968; MBA, U. Phoenix, 1992. Art dir. Curran-Morton Advt., Phoenix, 1968-70; owner Steve Lopez Graphic Design, Phoenix, 1970-73; asst. art dir. Ulrich Studios, Phoenix, 1973-78; artist, illustrator Goodyear (Ariz.) Aerospace/Loral Def. Systems, 1978-90; pres. Z-Boz, Inc., Glendale, Ariz., 1990-92; owner L&A Janitorial/Clean Room Specialists, 1994—; pres. Exigency Alert, Inc., Glendale, 1988-90; owner Lopez & Assocs., Glendale, 1989—, pres., 1991; v.p. South Paw, Inc., Peoria, Ariz., 1990-91; cons. Teddy Bear Factory, Inc., Peoria, 1990-91, Beanies Soft Toy Factory, Phoenix, 1990, Maquiladoras, Mex.; exec. advisor Jr. Achievement, Phoenix, 1979-80; amb. to Mex., U.S. JCI Senate, Tulsa, 1987-88. Patentee eyeglass floatation apparatus. Mem. adv. com. City of Glendale, 1985, City of Glendale Cable TV Task Force, 1987; bd. dirs. All Am. Cities Com., Glendale; bd. trustees Valley of the Sun United Way, Phoenix. Mem. Glendale C. of C., U.S. Jaycees (Excellence award 1977, Upson award 1982), Ariz. Jaycees (life, pres. 1985-86, Excellence award 1986), Glendale Jaycees (pres. 1978-81, Chmn. of the Yr. 1977). Democrat. Roman Catholic. Home: 4927 W Mclellan Rd Glendale AZ 85301-4010

LOPEZ-NAVARRO, EDUARDO LUIS, family therapist; b. Santiago de Cuba, Oriente, Cuba, June 29, 1959; came to U.S. 1970; s. Eduardo Regino and Alicia Del Pilar (Navarro) Lopez. BA, UCLA, 1982; MS in Psychology with honors, Calif. State U., L.A., 1991. Counselor L.A. Unified Sch. Dist., 1982-90; family therapist Family Counseling Svcs., San Gabriel, Calif., 1990-93; program coord. El Centro del Pueblo, L.A., 1993—; family therapist Hillsides Home for Children, Pasadena, Calif., 1992—, El Centro Del Pueblo, L.A., 1993—; dir. North Ctrl. L.A. Family Preservation Project; cons. (counselor) UCLA/Valley Alternative Magnet Sch., Ban Nuys, 1990; rsch. asst. UCLA/Fernald Sch., 1981; lectr. in field; expert presenter and cons. various TV programs including Univision and Telemundo Networks, L.A., 1993—. Author: Voces: Aprendiendo a escuchar mas alla de las palabras, 1997; contbr. articles to profl. jours.; author video: The World of Perpetual Night: Insights into the Psychology of Street Prostitution, 1990. Counselor Hollywood Sunset Cmty. Clinic, L.A., 1986-89; family counselor St. Matthias Ch.; mem. san Gabriel Valley Child Abuse Coun.; educator/trainer Latino Family Preservation, L.A., 1994. Am. Assn. for Marriage and Family Therapy Minority fellow, 1981; recipient Counseling Dept. Spl. Recognition award Hollywood Sunset Cmty. Clinic, 1988, Exito Internat. award. Mem. Calif. Assn. Marriage and Family Therapists, Am. Assn. Marriage and Family Therapists. Roman Catholic. Office: El Centro Del Pueblo 1157 Lemoyne St Los Angeles CA 90026-3206

LOPICCOLO, JOHN, conductor, music director; m. Mary Lopiccolo; children: Sabrina, John Michael. MusB in Music Edn., San Francisco State U.; MusM in Orchestral Conducting, Ea. Washington U. Music dir., conductor Idaho Falls (Idaho) Symphony Soc., Inc.; founder, music dir., conductor Idaho Falls Symphony Chorale; concert programmer ann. POPS concerts, Idaho; guest condr. Charlotte, Dubuque, Spokane, S.D., Bremerton, Great Falls, Lethbridge, Walla Walla, Fla. Festival Symphonies, Mont. All-State Orch.; cover-condr. Boise Philharm., 1995-96. Guest condr. (play) Porgy and Bess, Vancouver, B.C. Judge Idaho State Civic Symphony, Idaho Falls Symphony Young Artist Competition, Idaho Falls Music Club Scholarship Awards. Recipient Outstanding Svc. award Greater Idaho Falls C. of C. Office: Idaho Symphony Soc Inc 545 Shoop Ave Ste 101 Idaho Falls ID 83402*

LOPINA, LOUISE CAROL, artist; b. Chgo., Nov. 24, 1936; d. Don and Eva Bernice (Rice) Petersen; m. Robert Ferguson Lopina, June 21, 1958; children: Kimberly, Sandra, Amy. BS, Purdue U., 1958. One-woman shows include Norwood Galleries Ltd., Denver, 1970, Garden of the Gods Gallery, Colorado Springs, Colo., 1972, Air Univ. Libr., Montgomery, Ala., 1977, Christ Ch. Little Gallery, Kettering, Ohio, 1980, 81, Cin. Club, 1981, Nissequoque Golf Club, L.I., N.Y., 1986, Nat. Mgmt. Assn., Newport Beach, Calif., 1991; exhibited in group shows at Ill. Woman's Fedn., Internat. Red Cross Round the World Tour, Colorado Springs (Colo.) Fine Arts Ctr., 1974, Nat. Scholastic Art Awards, Nat. Nature Art Exhn. (Best Painting in Show 1978, 79, 82, Salmagundi Club, N.Y.C., 1979, Clayton Bruckner Meml. award), Cin. Mus. Natural History, 1980, Adler Gallery, N.Y.C., 1981, Game Coin Internat., San Antonio, Tex., Wondrous Wildlife, Cin., 1983, G&R Gallery, 1983, Nora Gallery, Great Neck, N.Y., 1985, Country Gallery, Locust Valley, N.Y., Outdoor Expo, Albany, N.Y., 1985, So. Alleghenies Mus. Art, 1986, Calif. Acad. Scis., San Francisco, 1986, Cumming Nature Ctr.-Rochester Mus. and Sci. Ctr., 1988, St. Hubert's Giralda, Madison, N.J., Prestige Gallery Ltd., 1989, 90, Mus. Sci., Boston, 1989-90, Wichita (Kans.) Kennel Club, Dog Mus., St. Louis, 1992, 94, 96, San Bernardino County Mus., Redlands, Calif., 1992, 93, 94, East African Wild Life Soc., Nairobi, 1991-92, So. Vt. Fine Arts Ctr., Columbus Ohio Fine Arts Ctr., Grand Ctrl. Galleries, N.Y.C., Owen Gallery, Oklahoma City, Denver Mus. Natural History, Cleve. Mus. Natural History, Exhbn. Hall Crown Ctr., Kansas City, and numerous other gallery exhbns.; represented in permanent collections Cin. Club, Miami Bank Ohio, G and R Tackle Co., Nissequoque Golf Club, Hartwood Club, San Bernardino County Mus., The Dog Mus., Cin. Natural History Mus., Bronx Zoo, Cin. Zoo, Bank Smithtown; commissioned poster for 8th Annual Snow Leopard Symposium, Islamabad, Pakistan. Chmn. landscape com. Sea Pointe Estates, 1993-96. Mem. Soc. Animal Artists (chmn. exhbns. 1985-88). Home and Office: Wild Brook Studio 7 Calle Agua San Clemente CA 92673-2749

LORANCE, ELMER DONALD, organic chemistry educator; b. Tupelo, Okla., Jan. 18, 1940; s. Elmer Dewey and Imogene (Triplett) L.; m. Phyllis Ilene Miller, Aug. 20, 1969; children: Edward Donald, Jonathan Andrew. BA, Okla. State U., 1962; MS, Kansas State U., 1967; PhD, U. Okla., 1977. NIH research trainee Okla. U., Norman, 1966-70; asst. prof. organic chemistry So. Calif. Coll., Costa Mesa, 1970-73, assoc. prof., 1973-80, prof., 1980—, chmn. div. natural scis. and math., 1985-89, chmn. chemistry dept., 1990-93, chmn. divsn. natural scis. and math., 1993—. Contbr. articles to profl. jours. Mem. AAAS, Am. Chem. Soc., Internat. Union Pure and Applied Chemistry (assoc.), Am. Inst. Chemists, Am. Sci. Affiliation, Phi Lambda Upsilon. Republican. Mem. Ch. Assembly of God. Office: So Calif Coll 55 Fair Dr Costa Mesa CA 92626-6520

LORBEER, GEORGE COE, retired science educator; b. Cedarville, Calif., May 4, 1920; s. George Coe Sr. and Jeannette (Reeves) L.; m. Dorothea Margaret Weber, July 17, 1943; children: Kathleen, Mary, George, Rebecca. BA, San Francisco State U., 1942; MA, Stanford U., 1946; EdM, U. Ill., 1950, EdD, 1953. Cert. tchr., Calif. Tchr. Jordan Jr. H.S., Palo Alto, Calif., 1946-50; rsch. asst. U. Ill., Urbana, 1950-53; asst. prof. edn. L.A. State Coll., 1953-56; assoc. prof. edn. San Fernando Valley State Coll., Northridge, Calif., 1956-58; prof. edn. Calif. State U., Northridge, Calif., 1958-89; retired Calif. State U., Northridge, 1989; secondary dept. chmn. Calif. State U., Northridge, 1956-62, 68-72, 78-82; coord. program instrn. L.A. Unified Sch. Dist., 1968-79, rep. edn. forum, 1958-75; cmty. adv. bd. Chatsworth (Calif.) H.S., 1962-66; adj. prof. Lawrence U., Santa Barbara, Calif., 1972-74. Author: Science Activities for Elementary Children, 1952—, Science Activities for Children, vol. II, 1992—; editor: Circle of the World, 1971, Readings in Educational Leadership, 1969. pres. Chatsworth Cmty. Coord. Coun., 1968-72; chmn. fund drive ARC, Chatsworth, 1969, water safety instr., 1958; active PTA, 1962—. Lt. comdr. USN, 1942-47. Mem. AAAS, NEA, Nat. Sci. Tchrs. Assn., Calif. Coll. and U. Assn., B Sharp Square Dancers, Rotary (pres. 1962, 68, 72). Democrat. Roman Catholic. Home: 16439 Knollwood Dr Granada Hills CA 91344-1805

LORD, CAROLYN MARIE, artist; b. L.A., Oct. 6, 1956; m. Robert Bryce Anglin, Nov. 1, 1980; 1 child, Devin Lord Anglin. BA, Principia Coll., 1978. Artist, 1978—; juror of award Ariz. Aqueous Tubac Ctr. of Arts, 1992; juror of slide Adirondack Nat. Exhbn. Am. Watercolor, Arts Ctr. Old Forge, N.Y., 1993; workshop instr. La Romita Sch. Art, Terni, Italy, 1991, Santa Cruz (Calif.) Art League, 1990-95. One-woman shows include Maybeck Gallery, Elsah, Ill., 1978-83, Fireside Gallery, Carmel, Calif., 1978-92, Northeastern Nev. Mus., Elko, 1985, 90, Art e Espaco, Aracatuba, Brazil, 1988, Ojai (Calif.) Gallery and Design Studio, 1990, Stary-Sheets Fine Art Galleries, Laguna Beach, Calif., 1983—, Banaker Gallery, San Francisco, 1993-96; exhibited in group shows at Valley Art Ctr., Walnut Creek, Calif., 1987-94, Winfield Gallery, Carmel, Calif., 1995—; artist art reproduction notecards. Recipient Rouse medallion Adirondack Nat. Exhbn. Am. Watercolor, 1987, Exhbn. award Watercolor U.S.A., 1988, 96, Exhbn. award San Diego Art Inst., 1992, Hon. Mention award Triton Mus. Watercolor Biennial, 1994. Mem. Nat. Watercolor Soc., Watercolor U.S.A. Honor Soc., Calif. Lawyers for Arts. Christian Scientist.

LORD, HAROLD WILBUR, electrical engineer, electronics consultant; b. Eureka, Calif., Aug. 20, 1905; s. Charles Wilbur and Rossina Camilla (Hansen) L.; B.S., Calif. Inst. Tech., 1926; m. Doris Shirley Huff, July 25, 1928; children—Joann Shirley (Mrs. Carl Cook Disbrow), Alan Wilbur, Nancy Louise (Mrs. Leslie Crandall), Harold Wayne. With Gen. Electric Co., Schenectady, 1926-66, electronics engr., 1960-66; pvt. cons. engr., Mill Valley, Calif., 1966—. Coffin Found. award Gen. Electric Co., 1933, GE Inventors award, 1966. Fellow IEEE (life, tech. v.p. 1962, Centennial medal 1984, IEEE Magnetics Soc. 1984 Achievement award). Contbr. articles to profl. jours. Patentee in field. Home and Office: 1565 Golf Course Dr Rohnert Park CA 94928-5638

LORD, JACKLYNN JEAN, student services representative; b. Sacramento, Feb. 2, 1940; d. Jasper Jackson and Celia (Moreno) Opdyke; m. Roger O'Dell Large Sr., Sept. 30, 1958 (div.); 1 child, Roger O'Dell Jr.; m. Brent Andrew Nielsen, Aug. 6, 1966 (dec. Sept. 1974); 1 child, Taumie Celia; m. Mark William Lord, Mar. 5, 1983; 1 child, Jacklynn Michelle. Student, Sacramento State U., 1958-60, Cabrillo Coll., 1962-66, Sacred Coll. of Jamilian Theology and Div. Sch., Reno, 1976—. Ordained Ch. Internat. Community Christ. Communications cons. Pacific Telephone Co., San Jose, Calif., 1966-74, Nev. Bell Co., Reno, 1974-76; student services rep. for extension program Jamilian U. of Ordained, Reno, 1976—; asst. music dir. Internat. Community Christ, Reno, 1980—; choral instr. Jamilian Parochial Sch., Reno, 1976—; sexton Jamilian Handbell Choir, Reno, 1981—; organist Symphonietta, Reno, 1983—. Composer/performer (albums) Children Love Trumpet, 1993, Lovers Love Trumpet, 1994, Five Suites for Piano and Trumpet, 1995, Sonata for Piano & Flugelhorn, 1997. Mem. Nat. League Concerned Clergywomen. Republican. Home: 1990 Humboldt St Reno NV 89509-3645 Office: Internat Community Christ 643 Ralston St Reno NV 89503-4436

LORD, JOHN WILLIAM, educational materials developer, writer; b. Pitts., Dec. 13, 1938; s. John William and Helen Scott (Hardie) L.; m. Carol Diane Bodey, 1970; children: Jennifer K., Benjamin Alexander. BA, Harvard U., 1961; MA, UCLA, 1965. Dir. product devel. Film Assocs. Calif., L.A., 1964-69; pres. Paideia, Santa Monica, Calif., 1970-79, 89—; editor-in-chief Enterprise for Edn., Santa Monica, 1979-89. Author: Sizes, 1995; curriculum materials. Office: PO Box 1583 Santa Monica CA 90406-1583

LORD, MIA W., world peace and disarmament activist; b. N.Y.C., Dec. 2, 1920; m. Robert P. Lord (dec. Nov. 1977); children: Marcia Louise, Alison Jane. BA in Liberal Arts cum laude, Bklyn. Coll., 1940; postgrad., San Francisco State U., 1984—. Hon. sec. Commonwealth of World Citizens, London; membership sec. Brit. Assn. for World Govt., London; sec. Ams. in Brit. for U.S. Withdrawal from S.E. Asia, Eng.; organizer Vietnam Vigil to End the War, London; pres. Let's Abolish War chpt. World Federalist Assn., San Francisco State U.; appointed hon. sec. Commonwealth of World Citizens, London; officially invited to Vietnam, 1973; organizer Vietnam Vigil to End the War, London. Author: The Practical Way to End Wars and Other World Crises: the case for World Federal Government: listed in World Peace through World Law, 1984, and in Strengthening the United Nations, 1987, War: The Biggest Con Game in the World, 1980. Hon. sec., nat. exec. mem. Assn. of World Federalists-U.K.; founder, bd. dirs. Crusade to Abolish War and Armaments by World Law. Nominated for the Nobel Peace Prize, 1975, 92, 93; recipient four Merit awards Pres. San Francisco State U. Mem. Secretariat of World Citizens USA (life), Assn. of World Federalists USA, Brit. Assn. for World Govt. (membership sec.), Crusade to Abolish War and Armaments by World Law (founder, dir.), World Govt. Orgn. Coord. Com., World Fed. Authority Com., Campaign for UN Reform, Citizens Global Action, World Constitution and Parliament Assn., World Pub. Forum, Internat. Registry of World Citizens. Home: 174 Majestic Ave San Francisco CA 94112-3022

LORENZ, BRIAN, lawyer; b. Bombay, India, 1939. Grad., Williams Coll., 1960; JD, Harvard U., 1963. Ptnr. Bleakley Platt & Schmidt; sec. Franklin Custodian Funds, San Mateo, Calif. Home: One Pine Ter Bronxville NY 10708 Office: Franklin Calif Tax Free Inc 777 Mariners Island Blvd San Mateo CA 94404-1584

LORENZ, TIMOTHY CARL, real estate agent; b. Glendale, Calif., June 9, 1947; s. Raymond Jerome and Majorie Nadine (Bevis) L.; m. Jeanann Carrington, Apr. 16, 1966 (div. 1982); children: Julianne, Todd; m. Nadyne Claire Buck, Sept. 11, 1982; stepchildren: Ron, Eve, SeAnn, Dray. BA in Psychology, Calif. State U., Los Angeles, 1969, MA in Psychology, 1972. Lic. real estate agt., Calif. Chief investigator L.A. County Dept. Consumer Affairs, 1976-81; co-owner Newport Holistic Health Clinic, Newport Beach, Calif., 1981-83; chief investigator Orange County Office Consumer Affairs, Santa Ana, Calif., 1983-86; agt. Century 21 Niguel, Laguna Niguel, Calif., 1986-94, mgr.; owner The Carousel, San Juan Capistrano, Calif., 1987-93, Depot...Pourri Gift Shop, San Juan Capistrano, 1991-93; v.p. Landingham Composites, Inc., San Clemente, 1994-96; sec. MTD, Inc., Overland, Kans., 1995—; instr. psychology Mt. San Antonio, Walnut, Calif., 1976-83; chmn. bd. dirs. Real Reasons, Laguna Niguel, 1982-90; distbr. Amway, Dana Point, Calif., 1983—; instr. Saddleback Coll., 1992-93; dir., treas.-sec. Landingham Composites, 1994-96. Co-author Renter Rights and Responsibilities, 1978; producer T.V. talk show Coping in Today's World, 1982 (Best of Pub. Access award 1982). Pres. Bur. Electronic and Appliance Repair Bd., Sacramento, Calif., 1980, 86, legis. com., 1979; founding mem. Nat. Automobile Dealers Consumer Action Panel, L.A., 1978-81. Recipient Letter Commendation Atty. Gen., L.A., 1980. Mem. Nat. Assn. Realtors, Assn. Foster Parents North Cen. South Orange County (pres. 1986-88), State Calif. Foster Parent Assn., Nat. Assn. Foster Parents, Dana Point C. of C., Newport Beach C. of C. Republican. Home: 32802 Pointe Stirling Apt F Dana Point CA 92629-3144

LORENZEN, ROBERT FREDERICK, ophthalmologist; b. Toledo, Ohio, Mar. 20, 1924; s. Martin Robert and Pearl Adeline (Bush) L.; m. Lucy Logsdon, Feb. 14, 1970; children: Roberta Jo, Richard Martin, Elizabeth Anne. BS, Duke, 1948, MD, 1948; MS, Tulane U., 1953. Intern, Presbyn. Hosp., Chgo., 1948-49; resident Duke Med. Center, 1949-51, Tulane U. Grad. Sch., 1951-53; practice medicine specializing in ophthalmology, Phoenix, 1953—; mem. staff St. Joseph's Hosp., St. Luke's Hosp., Good Samaritan Hosp., Surg. Eye Ctr. of Ariz. Pres. Ophthalmic Scis. Found., 1970-73; chmn. bd. trustees Rockefeller and Abbe Prentice Eye Inst. of St. Luke's Hosp., 1975—. Recipient Gold Headed Cane award, 1974; named to Honorable Order of Ky. Cols. Fellow ACS, Internat. Coll. Surgeons, Am. Acad. Ophthalmology and Otolaryngology, Pan Am. Assn. Ophthalmology, Soc. Eye Surgeons; mem. Am. Assn. Ophthalmology (sec. of ho. of dels. 1972-73, trustee 1973-76), Ariz. Ophthal. Soc. (pres. 1966-67), Ariz. Med. Assn. (bd. dirs. 1963-66, 69-70), Royal Soc. Medicine, Rotary (pres. Phoenix 1984-85). Republican. Editor in chief Ariz. Medicine, 1963-66, 69-70. Office: 367 E Virginia Ave Phoenix AZ 85004-1202

LORING, THOMAS JOSEPH, forest ecologist; b. Haileybury, Ont., Can., May 27, 1921; s. Ernest Moore and Margaret Evangeline (Bacheller) L.; m. Beth Rogers McLaughlin, Oct. 29, 1966; children: John Francis, Christopher Thomas. BSc in Forestry, Mich. Tech. U., 1946; M Forestry, N.Y. State Coll. Forestry, 1951. Forester McCormick Estates, Champion, Mich., 1947; cons. Porteous and Co., Seattle, 1948-49; forester Penokee Veneer Co., Mellon, Wis., 1951-53; cons. E.M. Loring Consulting, Noranda, Que., Can., 1954-55; forester USDA Forest Svc., Albuquerque, 1956-81; cons. Tom Loring, Cons., Victoria, B.C., Can., 1986—; mem. Parks and Recreation Commn., Victoria, 1988-92, mem. environment adv. com., 1993-97. Editor: Directory of the Timber Industry in Arizona and New Mexico,1 972; co-editor: Ecology, Uses and Management of Pinyon-Juniper Woodlands, 1977. Pres. Shawnigan Lake Residents and Rate Payers Assn., B.C., 1985-86. Mem. Soc. Am. Foresters (sect. chair 1960-62), Ecol. Soc. Am., Forest Products Soc. (regional rep. 1980-81), Can. Inst. Forestry, Soc. Ecol. Restoration, Forest Products Soc. Home: 59 Moss St, Victoria, BC Canada V8V 4M1

LOSH, CHARLES LAWRENCE, vocational education administrator; b. North Platte, Nebr., May 15, 1939. BS in Edn., U. Nebr., 1969; MS in Edn., Ind. U., 1972, EdS, 1976; PhD, Ga. State U., 1983. Dep. assoc. supr. Ariz. Dept. of Edn., Phoenix, 1988-95, state dir. of vocat. edn., 1995—; pres. Intructional Sys. Ltd., Phoenix, 1985—. Editor Am. Tech. Edn. Assn. Jour., 1987—. Office: Ariz Dept Edn 1535 W Jefferson St Phoenix AZ 85007-3209

LOTHROP, GLORIA RICCI, educator; b. L.A., Dec. 30, 1934; d. Leo N. and Maria (Angeli) R. AB in English (with honors), Immaculate Heart Coll., 1956, MA in Edn., 1963; student, U. of Pisa, Italy, 1960, U. Mysore, India, 1963; postgrad., U. Calif., L.A., 1964-65; PhD in History, U. So. Calif., 1970. Tchr. English, History Sacred Heart High School, 1956-60; tng. tchr., teaching internship program UCLA, 1964; tchr. History Beverly Hills High School, 1962-64; part time supr. of teaching interns Las Virgenes Unified Sch. Dist., 1964-65, Univ. Calif., Riverside, 1965; coord. of tchr. tng., summer internship program Univ. Calif., L.A., 1965; part time instr., U.S. History L.A. Valley C.C., 1966-67; archivist Southwest Regional Lab. for Ednl. Rsch. and Devel., 1967; lecture series coord., Current Affairs Loyola Marymount Univ, 1969-72; vis. lectr., Western Am. History Univ. Calif., 1969-70; supr. student tchrs., asst. prof., History Calif. State Polytechnic Univ., Pomona, 1970-74, supr. student tchrs., assoc. prof., History, 1974-79; vis. prof. Art Ctr. Coll. of Design, 1978-80; acting chair, Dept. of Liberal Studies Calif. State Polytechnic Univ., 1974, 77; adj. prof., Master in Liberal Arts Program Univ. So. Calif., 1980-86; CSU adminstrv. fellow, Office of the Dean of Sch. of Letters and Sci. Calif. State Univ., L.A., 1981-82; prof. history State Polytechnic U., 1979-94; Whitsett chair Calif. history Calif. State U., Northridge, 1994—; cons. Ontario Mus. of History and Art, 1992, Rancho Los Cerritos, 1991, Constitutional Rights Found., 1988, USC Sch. of Cinema, 1988-89, CSU Inst. for Teaching and Learning, 1989—, Calif. Heritage Quilt Project, 1987-88, L.A. History Project, Public T.V. Sta. KCET, 1986-88, Calif. Project, 1987-89, Afro-Am. Mus., 1985-88, El Pueblo State Historic Park, 1986—, Cattlekate Productions, 1987, So. Calif. Gas Co. and Radio Sta. KFAC-AM-FM, 1980-88, Ontario Centennial Celebration, 1980, CBS T.V. "Bicentennial Minutes", 1979-80, and participation in numerous other profl. activities. Author: Recollections of the Flathead Mission: The Memorie of Fr. Gregory Mengarini, S.J., 1977, Chi Siamo: The Italians of L.A., 1981, California Woman, A Historic Profile, 1986, Guide to the Historic Resources of the State of Calif., 1989, Rancho San Jose, A Sesquacentennial Tribute, 1987, Pomona Valley: A Centennial History, 1988, A Guide to Historic Outings in Southern Calif., 1991, Quality of Life at California State Polytechnic University, Pomona, 1991, Los Angeles Ethnic Profile, 1994; contbr. articles to numerous profl. jours. bd. govs. Calif. Maritime Acad., 1980-82, 82-85, bd. dirs. Photo Friends, L.A. Public Libr., 1990—, pres. Com. to Save Italian Hall, 1990—, mem. State and Local Hist. Day Coms., 1987-89, pres. bd. dirs. El Pueblo Park Assn., 1984-85, bd. dirs., 1986-87, pres. emeritus 1988, mem. L.A. 200 Exec. Com. and acting chair edn. com., 1979-91, mem. citizens Adv. Com. for the 1984 Olympics, 1981-84, bd. dirs. L.A. Internat. Visitors Coun., 1981-87, sec. to the exec. com. L.A. Archdiocesan Archival Ctr., 1982-89, chair publications com. and bd. mem. Calif. Hist. Soc., 1987-88. Recipient Community Enrichment award Hist. Soc. of Southern Calif., 1993, Carl Wheat award, 1990, Woman of Distinction award Today's Women's Forum Citrus Coll., 1987, Outstanding Achievement award Southern Calif. Social Sci. Assn., 1987, Calif. Polytechnic Authors Golden Leaves award, 1986, 87, 89, 90, tchr. award

Daughters of Colonial Wars award, 1983, Outstanding Italian Am. award Targhe d'Oro, Regione Puglia, Italia, 1982, Dist. Alumnae award, Immaculate Heart Coll. Alumnae Assn., 1981, George Danielson Historical Writing Excellence award Westerners Internat., 1978, Outstanding Feminist of the Pomona Valley award NOW, 1974, Outstanding Tchr. award DAR; Haynes Huntington Rsch. fellow Huntington Library, 1986, 91, Fulbright fellow, 1963, Calif. Hist. Soc. fellow, 1995, So. Calif. Hist. Soc. fellow, 1996; Daniel Murphy Found. grantee, 1987. Mem. Am. Hist. Assn., Am. Italian Hist. Assn., Orgn. of Am. Historians, Nat. Women's Studies Assn., Western Hist. Assn., Southwest Labor Studies Assn., West Coast Assn. for Women Historians, Hist. Soc. of So. Calif., Friends of the Huntingt. Democrat. Roman Catholic. Home: 1480 Poppy Peak Dr Pasadena CA 91105 Office: Calif State Univ Northridge CA 91330

LOTRICK, JOSEPH, aeronautical engineer; b. Plymouth, Pa.; s. Stephen and Catherine (Turpak) L.; m. Barbara Sue Vining; 1 child, Pegge Jo. Student, U. Pa., 1943; BS in Aero. Engring., Northrop U., 1962. Sr. engr. flight test N.Am. Aviation, L.A., 1952-86; project engr. Rockwell Internat., L.A., 1986—. With USN, 1943-46. Mem. AAAS, AIAA (mem. nat. tech. com. flight test 1984-86), Assn. Naval Aviation, Aircraft Owners and Pilots Assn., Elks. Republican. Home: 2531 Highcliff Dr Torrance CA 90505-7305 Office: Rockwell Internat 201 N Douglas St # 21 El Segundo CA 90245-4637

LOTT, DAVIS NEWTON, advertising agency executive, publisher; b. San Antonio, May 8, 1913; s. James and Sissilla (Davis) L.; m. Arlene Marion Peterson, Nov. 1, 1942; children: Vicki Arlene, Christy Sue, Laurie Ann. B.S., Northwestern U., 1935; post-grad. UCLA. With Better Homes and Gardens and Successful Farming, Des Moines, Iowa, 1935-36; with Abbott, Labs., North Chicago, Ill., 1936-37; copywriter J. Walter Thompson, Chgo., 1938-39; owner and pres. Lott Advt. Agy., L.A., 1939-41, 46—; pres. USA Corp., Marina Del Rey, Calif.; pres. Lott Publs., Santa Monica, Calif.; pub. Am. Carwash Rev., Am. Personal Protection Rev., Candy WORLD, Tobacco and Sundries WORLD, Specialty/Fancifoods WORLD, Chocolate and Nut WORLD, SugarFree WORLD, New Inventions WORLD, Organic WORLD, Teen Scene, Bubble 'n' ChewinGum WORLD, Cracker/Snack WORLD, Surfing Illustrated, Smoker's Digest, Books and Authors WORLD, New Products and Mail Order WORLD, The Cosa News; dir. spl. projects Microlert Systems Internat. Past bd. dirs. Los Angeles Library Assn. Comdr. USNR, 1941-46, 1951-52, World War II, Korea. Named Assoc. Dean of Candy Industry, Nat. Candy Wholesalers Assn., 1974. Author: Rules of the Road, 1942, Handbook of the Nautical Road; Emergency Shiphandling Manual, 1943, Collision Prevention, 1947, Treasure Trail, 1944, Star Spangled Broadcast, 1950, Mystery of Midnight Springs, 1954, Dodge City Justice, 1957, The Inaugural Addresses of the American Presidents, 1964, The Presidents Speak, 1965, See How They Ran 1972, The Presidents Illustrated, 1976, Jimmy Carter-And How He Won, 1976; co-author: (with Bruce Greenland) musical comedy The Music Room, 1982, The Presidents Speak-The Inaugural Addresses from Washington to Clinton, 1995, 3d edit., 1997. Recipient George Washington medal for lit. excellence Freedoms Found., 1995, Home: 13222 Admiral Ave Unit B Marina Dl Rey CA 90292-7042 Office: Lott Pub Co Candy World PO Box 9669 Marina Del Rey CA 90295

LOTZ, ALBERT FRANK, III (TREY LOTZ), religious organization auditor; b. Buffalo, N.Y., Apr. 13, 1945; s. Albert Frank and Carolyn Kathleen (Rouse) L.; m. Delores Ismay Simons Pierson, Oct. 25, 1968 (div. June 1978); m. Barbara Sager, Aug. 26, 1989. BA, Hamilton Coll., 1967. Cert. class 8 Scientology auditor. Minister Trey Lotz Field Ministry, L.A., 1970, pastoral counselor, 1970-94. Named Field Auditor of Yr., Ch. of Scientology, L.A., 1976.

LOTZ, LINDA ANN, religious organizer; b. Phila., May 12, 1949; d. Joseph S. and Charlotte (Stanbaugh) Lotz; m. Imad A. Alduri, Oct. 1, 1993. BA in Polit. Sci., Univ. Shippensberg, Pa., 1971. Dir., editor Legis. Info. Ctr., Harrisburg, Pa., 1973-74; field organizer Campaign for Polit. Rights, Washington, 1976-81; dir. Three Mile Island Pub Interest Resource Ctr., Harrisburg, Pa., 1981-82; lobbyist Senate of Pa., Harrisburg, 1982-84; dir. of programs regional office Am. Friends Svc. Com., Pasadena, Calif., 1985-96; interfaith organizer Clergy and Laity United for Econ. Justice, L.A., 1996—. Photographer: photos exhibited at Am. Friends Svc. Corps and Publs., 1991—; also contbr. articles to jours. Mem. Nat. Organizers Alliance.

LOUCKS, NANCY J., association executive; b. Lansing, Mich., Mar. 21, 1957; d. John Robert and Marian Elizabeth (Lemmon) L. BS in Edn., Cen. Mich. U., 1980. Therapeutic counselor Hope Ctr. for Youth, Houston, 1981-82; recreation therapist Mental Health/Mental Retardation Assn., Houston, 1983-86; case mgr. Mental Health/Mental Retardation Assn., 1986-87; area dir. Tex. Spl. Olympics, Houston, 1988-91; program dir. Tex. Spl. Olympics, Austin, Tex., 1991-95; dir. sr. sports Wash. Spl. Olympics, Seattle, 1995—; cons. YMCA, Houston, 1985-87; event dir. Internat. Spl. Olympic Games, Baton Rouge, 1983. Vol. Mental health/Mental Retardation Assn. of Houston, 1988—; spl. friend Tex. Spl. Olympics, 1988. Mem. Assn. Retarded Citizens, Lambda Chi Alpha.

LOUD, OLIVER SCHULE, physical sciences educator, retired; b. Vernal, Utah, Jan. 16, 1911; s. Oliver Blanchard and Julia Sophia (Schule) L.; m. Goldie Frances Dworken, Apr. 28, 1935; children: Julia Frances Loud Albertin, David Oliver. AB summa cum laude, Harvard U., 1929; MA, Columbia U., 1940, EdD, 1943. Master Nichols Sch. for Boys, Buffalo, N.Y., 1929-32; counselor Medomak Camp for Boys, Washington, Maine, 1927-34, 52-57; instr. Ohio State U. Lab. High Sch., Columbus, 1932-36; tchr. Bryn Mawr (Pa.) Summer Sch. for Women in Industry, 1934-38, Sarah Lawrence Coll., Bronxville, N.Y., 1936-40; rsch. assoc. Bur. of Ednl. Rsch. in Sci. Columbia U., N.Y.C., N.Y., 1939-43; tech. supr. Tenn. Eastman Corp., Oak Ridge, 1944-45; prof. Antioch Coll., Yellow Springs, Ohio, 1943-44, 45-76, Disting. prof., 1976-81; adj. prof. Antioch U., 1982-94; staff, summer workshop for coll. tchrs., Great Lakes Colls. Assn., Ann Arbor, Mich., 1977-89. Author: The Challenge of the Human Future, 1991, A Utopian Fragment, 1991. Mem. nat. com. Progressive Party, 1947-52, state chmn. Ohio, 1947-52, platform com. 1947-52. Mem. Reform Judaism. Home: 815 18th Ave Seattle WA 98122-4705

LOUDERBACK, TRUMAN EUGENE, environmental project manager; b. Sterling, Colo., Jan. 17, 1946; s. George DeWayne and Lillian Louise (Harrach) L.; m. Dena Marie Chambers, June 1, 1985; children: Nicole Marie, Kyle Eugene, Matthew Joseph. BS, Colo. State U., 1968; postgrad., U. Colo., 1974-75. Project investigator and biologist, research inst. Colo. Sch. Mines, Golden, 1972-78; adminstr. quality assurance Cleveland-Cliffs Iron Co., Casper, Wyo., 1979, dir. environ. affairs, 1980-83; dir. environ. affairs Cleveland-Cliffs Iron Co., Rifle, Colo., 1984-88, Cliffs Engring., Inc., Rifle, Colo., 1984-88; pvt. practice cons. Lakewood, Colo., 1978-79, 96-97, Rifle, 1988-89; sr. project mgr., quality asurance mgr. Roy F. Weston, Inc., Lakewood, Colo., 1989-96; sr. project mgr., assoc. Burns & McDonnell, Kansas City, Mo., 1997—; chmn. environ. com. Pacific Shale Project, Rifle, 1983-87, also mgr. environ. impact statement, 1983-84. Contbr. articles to profl. jours. Industry rep. Colo. Joint Rev. Process Team, Colo. Dept. Nat. Resources, 1983; organizer Denver Environ. Forum, 1995. Republican. Methodist. Lodge: Rotary (bd. dirs. Rifle chpt. 1984), Masons. Home: 1037 SW Sunflower Dr Lees Summit MO 64081

LOUGANIS, GREG E., former Olympic athlete, actor; b. San Diego, Jan. 29, 1960; s. Peter E. and Frances I. (Scott) L. Student, U. Miami, Fla., 1978-80; B.A. in Drama, U. Calif., Irvine, 1983. Mem. U.S. Nat. Diving Team, 1976—. Author: Breaking The Surface, 1995. Recipient Silver medal Olympic Games, 1976, 2 Olympic Gold medals, 1984, 2 Olympic Gold medals, 1988; James E. Sullivan award, Olympic Games, 1984; inducted into Olympic Hall of Fame, 1985; winner 48 U.S. nat. diving titles; World Diving Champion (platform and springboard) 1986, Jesse Owens award, 1987, Pan Am Gold medal, 1979, 83, 87; Gold medalist (platform and springboard) Seoul Olympics, 1988. Home: PO Box 4130 Malibu CA 90264-4130*

LOUGHEED, PETER, lawyer, former Canadian official; b. Calgary, Alta., Can., July 26, 1928; s. Edgar Donald and Edna (Bauld) L.; m. Jeanne Estelle Rogers, June 21, 1952; children—Stephen, Andrea, Pamela, Joseph. B.A., U. Alta., 1950, LL.B., 1952; M.B.A., Harvard U., 1954. Bar: Alta 1955. With firm Fenerty, Fenerty, McGillivray & Robertson, Calgary, 1955-56; sec. Mannix Co., Ltd., 1956-58, gen. counsel, 1958-62, v.p., 1959-62, dir., 1960-62; individual practice law, from 1962; formerly mem. Alta. Legislature for Calgary West; formerly leader Progressive Conservative Party of Alta., 1965-85; premier of Alta., 1971-85; ptnr. Bennett Jones Verchere, Calgary, 1986—. Office: Bennett Jones Verchere, 4500 Bankers Hall E 855 2d St SW, Calgary, AB Canada T2P 4K7

LOUGHMAN, WILLIAM DOSTER, retired lab director; b. Oklahoma City, July 10, 1932; s. William Noland and Mary Vyola (Bubb) Loughman; m. Linnet Neale Goodrich, 1956 (div. 1966); children: Paul Owen, Elizabeth Leigh, Donald Ewan; m. Katharine Jean Hershey, Feb. 11, 1967. BS, U. Calif., Berkeley, 1960, MS, 1964, PhD, 1973. Diplomate Am. Bd. Med. Genetics. Biophysicist U. Calif., Berkeley, 1965-74; dir. cytogenetics lab. U. Calif., San Francisco, 1975-82; spl. cytogeneticist Children's Hosp., Oakland, Calif., 1982-89, dir. cytogenetics lab., 1989-96; adj. assoc. prof. pediatrics U. Calif., San Francisco, 1980-82; cons. CDC, Atlanta, 1980, Pacific States Regional Genetics Network, Berkeley, 1987—, Sutter Meml. Hosp., Sacramento, 1993-94, Stanford (Calif.) U. Med. Ctr., 1994-95. Contbr. over 60 articles to profl. jours. Active, office holder various mountain rescue groups, Calif., 1960-90. Fellow Am. Coll. Med. Genetics (founding); mem. AAAS, Am. Soc. Human Genetics, Sigma Xi.

LOUIE, DAVID A., television journalist; b. Lakewood, Ohio, June 19, 1950; s. Troy and May (Chan) L. BS in Journalism, Northwestern U., 1972. Reporter KGO-TV, San Francisco, 1972-77, reporter, bur. chief, 1979-95, bus. editor and anchor, 1995—; asst. news dir. WXYZ-TV, Detroit, 1977-79. Contbr. articles to profl. jours. Bd. dirs. United Way of Bay Area, San Francisco, 1980-82, Peninsula Humane Soc., San Mateo, Calif., 1981. Mem. NATAS (exec. com., vice chmn. bd. dirs. 1990-94, chmn. bd. dirs. 1994-96, trustee 1986-90, Emmy award 1980, 88, Silver Circle award 1995), Asian Am. Journalists Assn. (nat. pres. 1990-92, Lifetime Achievement award 1996), Radio TV News Dirs. Assn. (ex-officio bd. dirs.). Office: KGO-TV 900 Front St San Francisco CA 94111

LOUIE, RONALD RICHARD, pediatric hematologist, oncologist, educator; b. Columbus, Ohio, Nov. 11, 1954. BA, Case Western Reserve U., 1976; MD, Med. Coll. Ohio, 1980. Diplomate in pediatrics and pediatric hematology-oncology Am. Bd. Pediatrics. Pediatric hematologist and oncologist Group Health Coop., Redmond, Wash., 1988—; clin. asst. prof. pediatrics U. Wash., Seattle, 1988—. Vol. pediatrician and hematologist Internat. Dist. Cmty. Health Ctr., Seattle. Fellow Am Acad. Pediatrics: mem. Am. Soc. Clin. Oncology, Am. Soc. Hematology, Children's Cancer Group (affiliate investigator). Office: Group Health Cooperative 2700 152d NE Redmond WA 98052

LOUK, DONNA PAT, elementary education educator, music educator; b. Phoenix, Mar. 26, 1954; d. Donald Duane and Patsy Lea Louk. BA in Christian Edn. and Church Music, Pacific Christian Coll., Fullerton, Calif., 1978; MusM, Ariz. State U., 1985; postgrad. in music edn., U. Ariz., Tucson, 1993—. Elem. edn. cert. with music endorsement, Grand Canyon U., Phoenix, 1982; Kodaly Cert., Holy Names Coll., Oakland, Calif., 1987-89; Dalcroze cert. Ariz. State U., 1986; Orff Level I, No. Ariz. U., Flagstaff, 1985, Orff Level II, U. Ariz., 1994. Elem. music tchr. Alhambra Elem. Sch. Dist. #68, Phoenix, 1983-93; music coord. Alhambra Elem. Dist., 1989-91; 5th grade tchr. Alhambra Elem. Sch. Dist. #68, 1994—; grad. tchg. asst. U. Ariz., 1993-94; presenter in field of music edn., various confs. and workshops in Ariz.; children's choir dir., h.s. choir pianist, Sunnyslope Christian Ch., Phoenix, 1972-74; pvt. piano tchr. Fullerton, 1977-78, Phoenix, 1984-86; pianist Santa Ana (Calif.) Christian Ch., 1978; ;ch. musician, Peoria (Ariz.) Christian Ch., 1995. Newsletter editor Alhambra Dist. Assn. Classroom Tchrs., 1989-90 (Sch. Bell award for outstanding publ.). Adjudicator All-State Solo & Ensemble, Choral Dirs. Assn., 1992-95. Mem. Orgn. Am. Kodaly Educators (hospitality chair/steering com. nat. conf. Provo, Utah 1996), Am. Orff Schulwerk Assn., Music Educators Nat. Conf., Ariz. Music Educators Assn., Ariz. Soc. Gen. Music (regional rep. 1987-93), Ariz. Kodaly Tchrs. Soc. (pres. 1991, 94, newsletter editor 1990—). Republican. Home: 4617 W Solano Dr S Glendale AZ 85301

LOUNSBERRY, JOYCE BEVERLY, occupational health consultant; b. Cloquet, Minn., Jan. 31; d. Eino Harold and Lempi Maria (Maijala) Halmet-Sohn; m. Richard Harrington Lounsberry, Mar. 17; children: Teresa, Mark, Kenneth. BA, U. Redlands, 1981; MA, U. Phoenix, 1992, Inst. Transpersonal Psychology, 1995; postgrad., Inst. Transpersonal Psychology, 1996. RN, Minn.; cert. occupl. health nurse, creative expression. Instr. Lawton Sch. Med. Assts., 1968-73; occupational health nurse, pers. generalist Teledyne Semiconductor, 1973-78; corp. dir., occupl. health cons. Calif. Indsl. Med. Clinic, Inc., 1978-84; pres. Lounsberry Cons. Svcs., Cupertino, Calif., 1984—; occupational health cons. Digital Equipment Corp., 1988-92. Sec. Santa Clara (Calif.) Vanguard, 1979-81; bd. dirs. Prince of Peace Ch., Saratoga, Calif., 1993-94; ambassador People to People, China and Mongolia, 1994. Recipient Occupl. Health Nurse award Schering Corp., 1989. Mem. AAOHN (past chmn. coms., bd. dirs.), Am. Holistic Nurses Assn., Calif. Assn. Occupl. Health Nurses (2d v.p., chmn. coms.), Western Assn. Occupl. Health Nurses (pres., v.p., bd. dirs. mem. coms.), El Camino Real Assn. Occupl. Health Nurses (bd. dirs., v.p. chmn. com.), Assn. Transpersonal Psychology. Home: 1598 Jamestown Dr Cupertino CA 95014-5313 Office: Lounsberry Cons Svcs 1598 Jamestown Dr Cupertino CA 95014-5313

LOUNSBURY, JOHN FREDERICK, geographer, educator; b. Perham, Minn., Oct. 26, 1918; s. Charles Edwin and Maude (Knight) L.; m. Dorothea Frances Eggers, Oct. 3, 1943; children—John Frederick, Craig Lawrence, James Gordon. B.S., U. Ill., 1942, M.S., 1946; Ph.D., Northwestern U., 1951. Asst. dir. rural land classification program Insular Govt., P.R., 1949-52; cons., research analyst Dayton Met. Studies, Inc., Ohio, 1957-60; chmn. dept. earth scis., prof. geography Antioch Coll., 1951-61; prof. geography, head dept. geography and geology Eastern Mich. U., 1961-69; chmn. dept. geography Ariz. State U., 1969-77; dir. Ctr. for Environ. Studies, 1977-80; prof. emeritus Ariz. State U., 1987—; project dir. Geography in Liberal Edn. Project, Assn. Am. Geographers, NSF, 1963-65, project dir. commn. on coll. geography, 1965-74; dir. environment based edn. project US. Office Edn., 1974-75; dir. spatial analysis of land use project NSF, 1975-85. Author articles, workbooks, textbooks. Mem. Yellow Springs Planning Commn., Ohio, dir. research, 1957-60; mem. Ypsilanti Planning Commn., 1961-66; research com. Washtenaw County Planning Commn., 1961-69; mem. cons. Ypsilanti Indsl. Devel. Corp., 1961-63. Served with AUS, 1942-46, ETO. Named Man of Yr., Yellow Springs C. of C., 1956-57. Fellow Ariz.-Nev. Acad. Sci.; mem. Assn. Am. Geographers (chmn. East Lakes div. 1959-61, mem. nat. exec. council 1961-64, chmn. liberal edn. com. 1961-65), Nat. Council Geog. Edn. (chmn. earth sci. com. 1961-68, regional coord. 1961-63, mem. exec. bd. 1968-71, 77-83, v.p. 1977-78, pres. 1978-80, Disting. Svc. award 1988, Disting. Mentor award 1990), Mich. Acad. Sci. Arts and Letters (chmn. pub. relations com. 1964-69, past chmn. geography sect.), Ohio Acad. Sci. (past exec. v.p.), Mich. Acad. Sci., Ariz. Acad. Sci., Am. Geog. Soc., AAAS, Sigma Xi, Delta Kappa Epsilon, Gamma Theta Upsilon. Home: 7850 E Vista Dr Scottsdale AZ 85250-7641 Office: Ariz State U Dept Geography Tempe AZ 85281

LOUNSBURY, STEVEN RICHARD, lawyer; b. Evanston, Ill., July 26, 1950; s. James Richard and Reba Janette (Smith) L.; m. Dianne Louise Daley, Apr. 16, 1983; children: Jimson, Cody, Richard. BA, U. Calif., Santa Barbara, 1973; JD, U. West L.A., 1977. Bar: Calif. 1979, U.S. Dist. Ct. (cen. dist.) Calif. 1979, Oreg. 1997. Pvt. practice L.A., 1979-83; contract atty. FAA, L.A., 1981; trial atty. Hertz Corp., L.A., 1983-86; mng. counsel 20th Century Ins. Co., Woodland Hills, Calif., 1986-94; mng. atty. Lounsbury and Assocs., Brea, Calif., 1986-94; sr. trial atty. Bollington, Lounsbury and Chase, Brea, 1994—; arbitrator Orange County Superior Ct., Santa Ana, Calif., 1992—. Dir. internat. rels. Rotary Internat., Venice-Marina Club, Calif., 1980-81; dir. L.A. Jr. C. of C., 1981-82. Mem. Calif. Bar Assn., Oreg. Bar Assn., So. Calif. Def. Counsel, Assn. Calif. House Counsel (bd. dirs., chmn. membership 1993-94). Office: Bollington Lounsbury and Chase 1800 E Imperial Hwy Ste 101 Brea CA 92821-6012

LOUVAU, GORDON ERNEST, management consultant, educator; b. Oakland, Calif., May 29, 1928; s. Ernest and Ella Meta (Meins) L.; m. Lois Louvau Peterson, June 9, 1984; children: John Pierre, Tanya Lissette, Charles Frederic. Student U. Calif., 1946-49; postgrad. Calif. State U., Hayward, 1975-77; MBA, John F. Kennedy U., 1980. Cert. mgmt. acct., 1975. Accountant, Oakland, 1950-59; asst. controller U.S. Leasing, Inc., San Francisco, 1960-61; pres. Louvau Systems Co., Oakland, 1962-66; v.p., gen. mgr. Prescolite div. U.S. Industries Co., San Leandro, Calif., 1966-68; cons. acctg. systems, 1969—; vis. prof. acctg. U. S.Africa, 1970-71; dir. Inst. Research and Bus. Devel., asst. prof. acctg. Calif. State U. at Hayward, 1972-80; asst. dean., asso. prof. mgmt., dir. acctg. programs J.F. Kennedy U., 1969-85; adj. prof. Golden Gate U., San Francisco, 1985—; instr. U. Calif. Ctr. Media and Independent Learning, 1973—; lectr. Naval Postgrad. Sch., Monterey, 1990—. Mem. Inst. Mgmt. Accts. (dir. 1972-74), Am. Acctg. Assn. Author: Financial Management of the Clinical Laboratory, 1974; Management and Cost Control Techniques for the Clinical Laboratory, 1977; Computers in Accountant's Offices, 1981. Office: PO Box 5808 Carmel CA 93921-5808

LOUX, GORDON DALE, organization executive; b. Souderton, Pa., June 21, 1938; s. Curtis L. and Ruth (Derstine) L.; m. Elizabeth Ann Nordland, June 18, 1960; children: Mark, Alan, Jonathan. Diploma, Moody Bible Inst., Chgo., 1960; BA, Gordon Coll., Wenham, Mass., 1962; BD, No. Bapt. Sem., Oak Brook, Ill., 1965, MDiv, 1971; MS, Nat. Coll. Edn., Evanston,Ill., 1984; LHD (hon.), Sioux Falls Coll., 1985. Ordained to ministry, Bapt. Ch., 1965. Assoc. pastor Forest Park (Ill.) Bapt. Ch., 1962-65; alumni field dir. Moody Bible Inst., Chgo., 1965-66, dir. pub. rels., 1972-76; dir. devel. Phila. Coll. Bible, 1966-69; pres. Stewardship Svcs., Wheaton, Ill., 1969-72; exec. v.p. Prison Fellowship Ministries, Washington, 1976-84, pres., CEO, 1984-88; pres., CEO Prison Fellowship Internat., Washington, 1979-87; pres. Internat. Students, Inc., Colorado Springs, Colo., 1988-93, Stewardship Svcs. Group, Colorado Springs, 1994—, Trinity Cmty. Found., 1996—. Author: Uncommon Courage, 1987, You Can Be a Point of Light, 1991; contbg. author: Money for Ministries, 1989, Dictionary of Christianity in America, 1989. Bd. dirs. Evang. Coun. for Fin. Accountability, Washington, 1979-92, vice chmn., 1981-84, 86-87, chmn., 1987-89; vice chmn. Billy Graham Greater Washington Crusade, 1985-85; bd. dirs. Evang. Fellowship of Mission Agys., 1991-94. Named Alumnus of Yr., Gordon Coll., 1986. Mem. Broadmoor Golf Club (Colo. Springs). Republican. Home: 740 Bear Paw Ln Colorado Springs CO 80906-3215 Office: PO Box 38898 Colorado Springs CO 80937-8898

LOUX, JONATHAN DALE, business development consultant; b. Oak Park, Ill., Mar. 23, 1966; s. Gordon Dale and Elizabeth (Nordland) L.; m. Jan Mary Peters, July 22, 1989; children: Kara Leigh, Kurtis Dale. BS, Eastern Coll., St. Davids, Pa., 1988. CPA, Ill. Acctg. supr. Capin, Crouse, LLP, Wheaton, Ill., 1989-93; supr. internal audit Select Beverages, Ind., Darien, Ill., 1993-94; exec. v.p. Gordon D. Loux & Co., LLC, Colorado Springs, Colo., 1994—; pres. Loux Group, LLC, Colorado Springs, 1996—. Mem. AICPA, Ill. CPA Soc. Republican. Presbyterian. Home and Office: 6335 Moccasin Pass Ct Colorado Springs CO 80919

LOVE, LAURIE MILLER, science editor; b. Fed. Republic Germany, May 7, 1960; came to U.S., 1961; d. Thomas Walter and Jacquelyn (Jolley) Miller; m. Raymond Lee Love. Student, U. Minn., 1979-80; BA in Psychology, Scripps Coll., 1983; postgrad., UCLA. Programmer specialist Control Data Corp., San Diego, 1982, asst. mgr. software retail store, 1983-84; support technician Ashton-Tate, Torrance, Calif., 1984, editor-in-chief, 1985-87; mgr. tech. pub. Ashton-Tate, Torrance, 1986-87; product mgr. Apple Products, Nantucket Corp., Los Angeles, 1987-88; sr. mktg. cons. Macintosh Market Launch Systems, Rancho Palos Verdes, Calif., 1988; pres. Miller Tech. Pub., Santa Cruz, 1987—; contractor, writer, editor Claris Corp., Santa Clara, Calif., Apple Computer, Cupertino, Calif., Live Picture, Inc., Soquel, Calif., Aladdin Sys., Watsonville, Calif.; dir. Live Picture, Inc., 1996—. Tech. and devel. editor Addison-Wesley, Osborne/McGraw Hill, TAB books; author Using ClarisWorks, 1992, Using ClarisWorks for Windows, 1993; contbr. feature articles to monthly mag., 1985—, computer product manuals, 1987—. Recipient Live Picture User Guide Excellence awards (3) The Soc. for Tech. Comm., 1996. Mem. Soc. Tech. Comm. (sr., Silicon Valley chpt., Excellence awards 1996), Women in Tech. Internat., Phi Beta Phi (asst. treas. 1980). Democrat. Methodist. *Personal philosophy: Each new day brings an opportunity for me to be the best person, professional, and student of life that I can be.*

LOVE, SANDRA RAE, information specialist; b. San Francisco, Feb. 20, 1947; d. Benjamin Raymond and Charlotte C. Martin; B.A. in English, Calif. State U., Hayward, 1968; M.S. in L.S., U. So. Calif., 1969; m. Michael D. Love, Feb. 14, 1971. Tech. info. specialist Lawrence Livermore (Calif.) Nat. Lab., 1969—. Mem. Spl. Libraries Assn. (sec. nuclear sci. div. 1980-82, chmn. 1983-84, bull. editor 1987-89), Soc. of Competitive Intelligence Profls., Beta Sigma Phi. Democrat. Episcopalian. Office: Lawrence Livermore Nat Lab PO Box 808 # L387 Livermore CA 94551-0808

LOVE, SUSAN MARGARET, surgeon, educator, medical administrator; b. N.J., Feb. 9, 1948; d. James Arthur and Margaret Connick (Schwab) L.; life ptnr. Helen Sperry Cooksey, Sept. 8, 1982; 1 child, Katherine Mary Love-Cooksey. BS, Fordham U., 1970; MD, SUNY, N.Y.C., 1974; DSc (hon.), Northeastern U., 1991; D of Humane Sci. (hon.), Simmons Coll., 1992. Clin. fellow in surgery Harvard Med. Sch., Boston, 1977-78, clin. instr. in surgery, 1980-87; dir. breast clinic Beth Israel Hosp., Boston, 1980-88; clin. assoc. in surg. oncology Dana Farber Cancer Inst., Boston, 1981-92; dir. Faulkner Breast Ctr. Faulkner Hosp., Boston, 1988-92; asst. clin. prof. surgery Harvard Med. Sch., Cambridge, 1987-92; assoc. prof. clin. surgery UCLA Sch. Medicine, 1992-96; dir. UCLA Breast Ctr., 1992-96; adj. prof. surgery UCLA, 1996—; mem. adv. coun. Breast and Cervical Cancer Coun., State of Calif. Dept. Human Svcs., 1994—; mem. NSABP Oversight Com., Pitts., 1994; mem. adv. com. Women's Health Initiative Program, Washington, 1993-95; prin. investigator Nat. Surg. Adjuvant Breast and Bowel Project, 1985-96; mem. Pres.'s Nat. Action Plan on Breast Cancer, DHHS, 1994—; co-chair Biol. Resources Working Group, 1994—, mem. exec. and steering coms., 1995—. Author: Dr. Susan Love's Breast Book, 1990, 95, Dr. Susan Love's Hormone Book, 1997; (book chpts.) Breast Disease, 1987, Clinics in Oncology: Breast Cancer, 1989, The Woman's Guide to Good Health, 1991; contbr. articles to profl. jours. Founder, bd. dirs. Nat. Breast Cancer Coalition, 1991—; mem. breast cancer subcom. divsn. cancer treatment Bd. Sci. Counselors, Nat. Cancer Inst., 1992-95; conf. com. co-chair Sec.'s Conf. to Establish Nat. Action Plan on Breast Cancer, 1993. Recipient Rose Kushner award Am. Med. Writers Assn., 1991, Achievement award Am. Assn. Physicians for Human Rights, 1992, Women Making History award U.S. Senator Barbara Boxer, 1993, Woman of Yr. award YWCA, 1994, Frontrunner award Sara Lee Corp., 1994, Spirit of Achievement award Albert Einstein Coll. of Yeshiva U., 1995, Abram L. Sachar medallion Brandeis U., 1996; prin. investigator grantee Dept. of Def., 1994, 96. Mem. Am. Med. Women's Assn. (pres. br. 39 1987), Soc. for Study of Breast Disease, Am. Soc. Preventive Oncology, Southwestern Oncology Group (women's health and breast com. 1992-96, surg. rep. 1992-96), L.A. Med. Soc., Boston Surg. Soc., N.Am. Menopause Soc. Office: Box 846 Pacific Palisades CA 90272

LOVELACE, SUSAN ELLEN, professional society administrator; b. Lafayette, Ind., Dec. 31, 1953; d. Frederic William and Ellen Lorraine (Brady) Kingdon; m. Mark Robert Lovelace, May 21, 1977. BA, Washington State U., 1976. Pub. rels. rep. Nev. Soc. CPAs, Reno, 1984-87; info. officer S.I.M., Monrovia, Liberia, 1987-88; mng. editor Calif. Dental Assn., Sacramento, 1989-95; exec. dir. San Diego County Dental Soc., 1995—; bd. mem. Internat. Assn. Bus. Communicators, Sacramento, 1994-95. Mng. editor, contbr. Jour. Calif. Dental Assn., 1989-95 (Maggie award 1991, 94), CDA Update, 1989-95 (numerous awards). Recipient Crystal writing award Internat. Assn. Bus. Communicators, Sacramento, 1991, 92, 93, Golden Publ. of Yr. award Internat. Coll. Dentists, 1992. Mem. Am. Soc. Assn. Execs., Am. Assn. Dental Editors (membership chair 1995-96), Assn. Calif. Soc. Execs., San Diego Soc. Assn. Execs. Office: San Diego County Dental Soc 1275 W Morena Blvd # B San Diego CA 92110-3837

LOVELAND, WALTER DAVID, chemist, chemistry educator; b. Chgo., Dec. 23, 1939; s. Walter Hubert and Anna Emelia (Reese) L.; m. Patricia Marie Rice, Sept. 7, 1962. SB, MIT, 1961; PhD, U. Wash., Seattle, 1965. Postdoctoral fellow Argonne (Ill.) Nat. Lab., 1966-67; rsch. asst. prof. Oreg. State U., Corvallis, 1967-68, from asst. to prof., 1968—; vis. scientist

Argonne (Ill.) Nat. Lab., 1968, 76, Lawrence Berkeley (Calif.) Lab., 1976-77, 83-84. Author: Radiotracer Methods, 1975, Nuclear Chemistry, 1982, Elements Beyond Uranium, 1990; contbr. numerous articles to profl. jours. NSF fellow, 1962, Tartar fellow Oreg. State U., 1977. Mem. Am. Chem. Soc., Am. Phys. Soc., AAAS, MIT Alumni Assn., Sigma Xi. Democrat. Office: Oreg State U Radiation Ctr Corvallis OR 97331

LOVELESS, EDNA MAYE, English language educator; b. Keene, Tex., Jan. 15, 1929; d. Luther Ray and May (Willhelm) Alexander; m. William Alfred Loveless, Aug. 17, 1952; children: Marti Sue Loveless Olson, Marilynn Kaye Loveless Stepniak. BA, Walla Walla Coll., 1950; PhD, U. Md., 1969. Instr. English Walla Walla Coll., College Place, Wash., 1950-52, Columbia Union Coll., Takoma Park, Md., 1952-53; prof. English Columbia Union Coll., Takoma Park, 1980-90; textbook writer, editor Review Publishers, Hagerstown, Md., 1970-80; prof. English La Sierra U., Riverside, Calif., 1990—; advisor student newspaper Columbia Union Coll., Takoma Park, 1980-90, dir. writers' conf., 1988, 89; advisor student newspaper LaSierra U., 1994—; lectr. Profl. Writers' Conf., Review Publs. Hagerstown, 1989; dir. freshman English program La Sierra U., Riverside, 1991—; participant and presenter Internat. Conf. on Critical Thinking, 1991, 94, 95, 96; presenter Nat. Conf. on Critical Thinking, 1992, Pa. State Conf. in Rhetoric, 1994, Calif. Assn. English Tchrs. Conf., 1996, 97, Nat. Coun. Tchrs. English, 1997, No. Tex. Lang. Linguistics Conf., 1997. Author: (book and tchr.'s manual) What Shall I Live For?, 1976, What Is of Most Worth?, 1978; author: (with others) Penn's Example to the Nations, 1987, Masterplots II, Juvenile and Adult Fiction, 1991, Critical Thinking, 1994. Recipient NDEA fellowship U. Md., 1964-68, 2nd prize Scholastic Mag. Writing Contest for High Sch. Tchrs., 1967. Office: La Sierra U 4700 Pierce St Riverside CA 92505-3331

LOVELL, CAROL, museum director. Dir. Kauai Mus., Lihue, Hawaii. Office: Kauai Mus 4428 Rice St Lihue HI 96766

LOVELL, CHARLES C., federal judge; b. 1929; m. Ariliah Carter. BS, U. Mont., 1952, JD, 1959. Assoc. Church, Harris, Johnson & Williams, Great Falls, Mont., 1959-85; judge U.S. Dist. Ct. Mont., Helena, 1985—; chief counsel Mont. Atty Gen.'s Office, Helena, 1969-72. Served to capt. USAF, 1952-54. Mem. ABA, Am. Judicature Soc., Assn. Trial Lawyers Am. Office: US Dist Ct PO Drawer 10112 301 S Park Ave Rm 504 Helena MT 59626

LOVELL, HOWELL, JR., non profit organization executive; b. San Jose, Calif., Oct. 12, 1938; s. Howell and Rebecca (Oser) L.; m. Donna Lovell, Apr. 21, 1965 (div. Apr. 1994); children: Howell III, Eric, Kathleen. BA, Stanford U., 1960, JD, 1963. Pvt. practice lawyer San Francisco, 1965-92; exec. dir. Pets in Need, Redwood City, Calif., 1992-93, Recording for The Blind & Dyslexic, Palo Alto, Calif., 1995-96. Dir. Palo Alto YMCA, sec., 1990-91, 93-94. Mem. Nat. Soc. Fund Raising Execs., Palo Alto C. of C., Ferne Ave. Home Owners Assn. (pres. 1996), Internat. Domino Assn. (bd. dirs., treas. 1994—), San Francisco Down Town Garden Club (pres. 1994), Kiwanis (bd. dirs. Palo Alto chpt.). Home: 124 Ferne Ave Palo Alto CA 94306-4644 Office: Recording for The Blind & Dyslexic 488 West Charleston Rd Palo Alto CA 94306

LOVELL, TIM P., orthopedic surgeon; b. Hammond, Ind., Dec. 5, 1958; s. Lewis L. and Alice M. Lovell. BS in Chemistry magna cum laude, Univ. Wash., 1981; MD, UCLA, 1985. Intern in gen. surgery Va. Mason Hosp., Seattle, 1985-86; resident in orthopedic surgery Univ. Wash., Seattle, 1986-91; fellow in surgery of arthritis Hosp. Spl. Surgery, N.Y.C., 1991-92; orthopedic surgeon Rockwood Clinic, Spokane, Wash., 1992—; rsch. asst. dept. orthop. Orthop. Rsch. Labs., Univ. Wash., 1986-87; presenter in field. Contbr. articles to profl. jours. Grantee Orthop. Rsch. Edn. Found., 1987-88. Mem. Am. Acad. Orthop. Surgeons, Wash. State Med. Assn., Wash. State Orthop. Assn., Spokane County Med. Soc., Phi Beta Kappa, Alpha Omega Alpha (2nd prize rsch. award 1985). Office: Rockwood Clinic 400 E Fifth Ave Spokane WA 99223

LOVEN, CHARLES JOHN, human resource executive; b. N.Y.C., Feb. 17, 1937; s. John and June Emma (Custer) Azzaro. BA, Occidental Coll., 1962; MA, Calif. State U., L.A., 1967. Group scheduler Douglas Space Systems, Huntington Beach, Calif., 1963-65; personnel rep. Shell Oil Co., L.A., 1965-71; dir. indsl. rels. Calif. Computer Products, Anaheim, 1971-80; sr. v.p., dir. personnel dept. Thompson Recruitment Advt., L.A., 1980-92; dir. pers. dept. UAW/Labor Employment and Tng. Corp., Bell, Calif., 1994-95; cons., 1995—. With USCG, 1954-58. Mem. Employment Mgrs. Assn., Exec. Human Resources Round Table, PIHRA, SHRM.

LOVENTHAL, MILTON, writer, playwright, lyricist; b. Atlantic City; s. Harry and Clara (Feldman) L.; m. Jennifer McDowell, July 2, 1973. BA, U. Calif., Berkeley, 1950, MLS, 1958; MA in Sociology, San Jose State U., 1969. Researcher Hoover Instn., Stanford, Calif., 1952-53, spl. asst. to Slavic Curator, 1955-57; librarian San Diego Pub. Library, 1957-59; librarian, bibliographer San Jose (Calif.) State U., 1959-92; tchr. writing workshops, poetry readings, 1969-73; co-producer lit. and culture radio show Sta. KALX, Berkeley, 1971-72; editor, pub. Merlin Press, San Jose, 1973—. Author: Books on the USSR, 1951-57, 57, Black Politics, 1971 (featured at Smithsonian Inst. Special Event, 1992), A Bibliography of Material Relating to the Chicano, 1971, Autobiographies of Women, 1946-70, 72, Blacks in America, 1972, The Survivors, 1972, Contemporary Women Poets an Anthology, 1977, Ronnie Goose Rhymes for Grown-Ups, 1984; co-author: (Off-Off-Broadway plays) The Estrogen Party to End War, 1986, Mack the Knife, Your Friendly Dentist, 1986, Betsy & Phyllis, 1986, The Oatmeal Party Comes to Order, 1986, (plays) Betsy Meets the Wacky Iraqi, 1991, Bella and Phyllis, 1994; co-writer (mus. comedy) Russia's Secret Plot to Take Back Alaska, 1988. Recipient Bill Casey Award in Letters, 1980; grantee San Jose State U., 1962-63, 84. Mem. Assn. Calif. State Profs., Calif. Alumni Assn., Calif. Theatre Coun. Office: PO Box 5602 San Jose CA 95150-5602

LOVERIDGE, RONALD O., mayor; b. Antioch, Calif., 1938; m. Marsha Jean Loveridge, 1964; 2 children. BA in Polit. Sci., U. Pacific, 1960; MA Polit. Sci., Stanford U., 1961, PhD in Polit. Sci., 1965. Assoc. prof. polit. sci. U. Calif., Riverside, 1965—, assoc. dean coll. social scis., 1970-72, chair acad. ednl. policy com., 1990-92; mem. Riverside City Coun., 1979-94; mayor City of Riverside, 1994—; chair land use com. Riverside City Coun., 1980-94; exec. com. Western Riverside Coun. of Govts., 1994—. Contbr. articles to profl. jours. Chair Earth Day City of Riverside, 1990; co-chair Citrus Heritage Tourism Task Force, 1991; mem. Californians Against Waste. Mem. Greater Riverside C. of C., Northside Improvement Assn., Urban League, So. Calif. Assn. Govts. (exec. com. 1994—). Office: 3900 Main St Riverside CA 92522

LOVIN, HUGH TAYLOR, history educator; b. Pocatello, Idaho, Dec. 10, 1928; s. Robert Scott and Hazel Viora (Gleim) L.; m. Ida Carolyn Edwards, June 3, 1956; 1 child, Jeffrey Douglas. BA, Idaho State Coll., 1950; MA, Wash. State U., 1956; PhD, U. Wash., 1963. Instr. history U. Alaska Mil. Br., Elmendorf AFB, 1957-61; asst. prof. history Southwestern Oreg. Coll., North Bend, 1963-64, Kearney (Nebr.) State Coll., 1964-65; assoc. prof. history Boise (Idaho) State U., 1965-68, prof. history, 1968-93, emeritus prof. history, 1993—; abstracter pub. hist. materials Am. Bibiog. Ctr., CLIO Press, Santa Barbara, Calif., 1970—; book reviewer in profl. history jours., 1969—. Editor: Labor in the West, 1986; contbr. numerous articles to profl. jours. including Pacific N.W. Quarterly, Jour. of the West, The Old Northwest. Fellow Nat. Endowment for Humanities, 1982. Home: 1310 Gourley St Boise ID 83705-6042 Office: Boise State U Dept History Boise ID 83725

LOVINS, L. HUNTER, public policy institute executive; b. Middlebury, Vt., Feb. 26, 1950; d. Paul Millard and Farley (Hunter) Sheldon; m. Amory Bloch Lovins, Sept. 6, 1979; 1 child, Nanuq. BA in Sociology, Pitzer Coll., 1972, BA in Polit. Sci., 1972; JD, Loyola U., L.A., 1975; LHD, U. Maine, 1982. Bar: Calif. 1975. Asst. dir. Calif. Conservation Project, L.A., 1973-79; exec. dir., co-founder Rocky Mountain Inst., Snowmass, Colo., 1982—; vis. prof. U. Colo., Boulder, 1982; Henry R. Luce vis. prof. Dartmouth Coll., Hanover, N.H., 1982; pres. Nighthawk Horse Co., 1993, Lovins Group, 1994. Co-author: Brittle Power, 1982, Energy Unbound, 1986, Least-Cost Energy Solving the CO2 Problem, 2d edit., 1989. Bd. dirs. Renew Am., Basalt and Rural Fire Protection Dist., E Source, Roaring Fork Polocrosse Assn.; vol. EMT and firefighter. Recipient Mitchell prize Woodlands Inst., 1982, Right Livelihood Found. award, 1983, Best of the New Generation award Esquire Mag., 1984. Mem. Calif. Bar Assn., Am. Quarter Horse Assn., Am. Polocrosse Assn. Office: Rocky Mountain Inst 1739 Snowmass Creek Rd Snowmass CO 81654-9115

LOVVIK, DARYL VAUGHN, consulting geologist; b. Eau Claire, Wis., July 26, 1941; s. Oscar W. and Pearl B. (Johnson) L.; m. Sherly Berog; children: Liezel Bayo, Lenie Bayo, Welanie Bayo. B.S. in Geology, W. Tex. State U., 1975; MBA, U. of Phoenix. Cert. profl. geologist; registered profl. geologist, Alaska, Ariz., Ark. Cons. geologist, Golden, Colo., 1975-77; exploration geologist Cotter Corp., Moab, Utah, 1977-79; pres. Southwestern Geol. Survey, Mesa, Ariz., 1979-86; water resource dir. Tohono O'Odham Nation, Sells, Ariz., 1986-89, Ariz. Dept. Water Resources, 1990-96; pres. Southwestern Geol., Tempe, Ariz., 1986—, Pac-Isle Enterprises, Tacloban, Philippines, 1994—, Philippine Connection, Tempe, 1993—. Contbr. articles to profl. jours. With USAF, 1960-64. Mem. Am. Inst. Profl. Geologists, Geol. Soc. Am., Am. Assn. Petroleum Geologists, Am. C. of C. (The Philippines), Soc. Mining Engrs. Republican. Episcopalian. Home: 410 E Beatrice St Tempe AZ 85281-1004

LOW, MARY LOUISE (MOLLY LOW), documentary photographer; b. Quakertown, Pa., Jan. 3, 1926; d. James Harry and Dorothy Collyer (Krewson) Thomas; m. Antoine Francois Gagné, Nov. 3, 1945 (div.); children: James L., David W., Stephen J., Jeannie Wolff-Gagné; m. Paul Low, July 11, 1969 (dec. July 1991). Student, Oberlin Conservatory of Music, 1943-44, Oberlin Coll., 1944; cert., Katharine Gibbs Sec. Sch., 1945; degree in psychiat. rehab. work, Einstein Coll. Medicine, 1968-70. Sec. Dept. Store, N.Y.C., 1945; sec., treas. Gagné Assocs., Consulting Engrs., Binghamton, N.Y., 1951-66; psychiat. rsch. asst. Jacobi Hosp., Bronx, 1969-70; asst. to head of sch. Brearley Sch., N.Y.C., 1976-78; pvt. practice documentary photographer San Diego, 1984—. Contbr. articles to profl. jours. Pres., bd. trustees Unitarian-Universalist Ch. Recipient Dir.'s award for excellence Area Agy. on Aging, San Diego, 1993, Citizen Recognition award County of San Diego, Calif., 1993. Office: Molly Low Photography 5576 Caminito Herminia La Jolla CA 92037-7222

LOW, MERRY COOK, civic worker; b. Uniontown, Pa., Sept. 3, 1925; d. Howard Vance and Eleanora (Lynch) Mullan; m. William R. Cook, 1947 (div. 1979); m. John Wayland Low, July 8, 1979; children: Karen, Cindy, Bob, Jan. Diploma in nursing, Allegheny Gen. Hosp., Pitts., 1946; BS summa cum laude, Colo. Women's Coll., 1976. RN, Colo. Dir. patient edn. Med. Care and Rsch. Found., Denver, 1976-78. Contbr. chpt. to Pattern for Distribution of Patient Education, 1981. Bd. dirs. women's libr. assn. U. Denver, 1982—, vice chmn., 1985-86, chmn., 1986-87, co-chmn. spl. event, 1992; bd. dirs. Humanities Inst., 1993—, co-chair Founder's Day, 1994, chair Culturefest, 1995, 96; mem. adv. com. U. Denver Women's Coll., 1995—; docent Denver Art Mus., 1979—, mem. vol. exec. bd., 1988-94, mem. nat. docent symposium com., 1991, chmn. collectors' choice benefits, 1988, pres. vols., trustee 1988-90; mem. alumni assn. bd. U. Denver, 1994—, sec., 1996—; bd. dirs. Lamont Sch. Music Assocs., 1990-96; mem. search com. for dir. Penrose Libr., 1991-92; trustee ch. coun., chmn. invitational art show 1st Plymouth Congl. Ch., Englewood, Colo., 1981-84; co-chmn. art auction Colo. Alliance Bus., 1992, 93, com., 1994—. Recipient Disting. Svc. award U. Denver Coll. Law, 1988, King Soopers Vol. of Week award, 1989, Citizen of Arts award Fine Arts Found., 1993, Outstanding Vol. Colo. Alliance of Bus., 1994, U. Denver Cmty. Svc. award, 1996. Mem. Am. Assn. Mus. (vol. meeting coord. 1990-91), P.E.O. (pres. Colo. chpt. DX 1982-84), U. Denver Alumni Assn. (bd. dirs., sec. 1996—). Republican. Congregationalist. Home: 2552 E Alameda Ave Apt 11 Denver CO 80209-3324

LOWE, BARBARA ANNETTE, elementary education educator; b. Klamath Falls, Oreg., Mar. 5, 1938; d. Wayne Randall and Evelyn Emaline (Burg) Maxson; m. Robert Eugene Lowe, Mar. 28, 1958; children: Sharon, Larry, Judy, Kathy, David. BS in Elem. Edn., So. Oreg. Coll., 1971. Tchr. Eagle Point (Oreg.) Sch. Dist., 1970—; bd. dirs. People for the Improvement of Edn., Tigard, Oreg., 1977-86, Oreg. Edn. Assn., Tigard, 1980-86; pres. Choice Welfare Benefits Trust, Tigard, 1993-96. Chairperson Jackson County Ctrl. Com., Medford, Oreg., 1984, 86; bd. dirs. Jackson County Fair, Ctrl. Point, Oreg., 1987-96; pres. Rogue Valley Women's Polit. Caucus, Medford, Oreg., 1995-96. Mem. NEA, Eleanor Rossevelt League, Wednesday Night Discussions, Delta Kappa Gamma. Democrat. Home: 2234 Cady Rd Jacksonville OR 97530

LOWE, CLAUDIA MARIE, childbirth assistant; b. Cleve., Mar. 7, 1955; m. Michael Lowe, Feb. 23, 1980; children: Alexander, Adam, Aaron. Cert. perinatal educator. Childbirth educator Am. Acad. Husband-Coached Childbirth, San Jose, Calif., 1983-89, Cert. Perinatal Educators Assn., 1983—; dir. Nat. Assn. Childbirth Assts., 1985-95, Women's Resources (formerly Health Awareness Ctr.), 1991—, Birth Support Providers Internat., 1992—; guided self-hypnosis practitioner, 1990—; clin. hypnotherapist Nat. Guild of Hypnotists, 1991—; breast feeding counselor Breastfeeding Support Cons., 1992—; birth ball trainer and cons., 1995—. Editor, pub. The Childbirth Asst. Jour., 1987—, Birth Support Providers Internat., (newsletters) You and Me, 1989, The Childbirth Assistant Journal Information Exchange, 1992; author: (manual) Becoming a Childbirth Assistant, 1990, (guidebook) Planning for a Positive Pregnancy, 1990; Guided Self-Hypnosis for Childbirth and Beyond, 1994, Critical Concepts of Obstetric and Maternity Care for the 21st Century, Marketing Tips for Birth Support Providers, 1994, Perinatal Fitness with the Birth Ball, 1995. Com. mem. Calif. State Assembly Cesarean Info. Bill, Sacramento, 1990-91. Mem. Nat. Assn. Childbirth Assts. (founder 1985—), Internat. Childbirth Edn. Assn., Hypnosis Info. Network, La Leche League Internat. (reserve), Internat. Cesarean Awareness Network, ASPO Lamaze. Office: 3941 Park Dr # 20-114 El Dorado Hills CA 95762-4549

LOWE, JAMES ALLEN, lawyer; b. L.A., Apr. 23, 1946; s. Fitzhugh Lee and Dorothy Helen (Van Kirk) L.; m. Francis Elaine Pirnat, June 6, 1967 (div. Aug. 1979); children: David T., Michael D.; m. Sandra Sue Larson, May 31, 1984 (dec. June 1988); children: Tammy Krieger, Robert, Krueger; m. Caroline Margaret Gellrick, June 6, 1992; children: Bryce Otsuka, Cardene Otsuka, Brent Otsuka. BA, U. Colo., 1968, JD, 1970. Bar: Colo. 1971, Ct. Mil. Appeals 1971, U.S. Dist. Ct. (10th cir.) 1988, U.S. Dist. Ct. (fed. cir.) 1989, U.S. Supreme Ct. 1993. Judge adv. USAF, 1971-75; chief deputy dist. atty. Dist. Attys. Office, Pueblo, Colo., 1975-80; atty. Sobol & Sobol, Denver, 1980-82, pvt. practice, Denver, 1982-95; ptnr. Lowe, Meyer & Seth, Denver, 1996—. Lt. col. USAF, 1971-95. Republican.

LOWE, OARIONA, dentist; b. San Francisco, June 17, 1948; d. Van Lowe and Jenny Lowe-Silva; m. Evangelos Rossopoulos, Dec. 18, 1985; 1 child, Thanos G. BS, U. Nev., Las Vegas, 1971; MA, George Washington U., 1977; DDS, Howard U., 1981; pediatric dental cert., UCLA, 1984. Instr. Coll. Allied Health Scis. Howard U., Washington, 1974-76, asst. prof., 1976-77; research asst. Howard U. Dental Sch., Washington, 1977-81; resident gen. practice Eastman Dental Ctr., Rochester, N.Y., 1981-82; dir. dental services City of Hope Med. Ctr., Duarte, Calif., 1984-86; dental staff Whittier (Calif.) Presbyn. Hosp., 1987—, chief dental staff, 1992-94; asst. prof. Loma Linda (Calif.) U., 1991—; vis. lectr. pediatric dentistry UCLA; mem. oral cancer task force Am. Cancer Soc., Pasadena, Calif., 1985—. Contbr. articles to profl. jours. Del. People to People Internat. Mem. ADA, Am. Soc. Dentistry for Children (v.p.), Nat. Soc. Autistic Children, Calif. Dental Assn., Am. Acad. Pediatric Dentistry, San Gabriel Valley Dental Soc. (chmn. 1991—), Sigma Xi, Alpha Omega. Republican. Presbyterian. Office: 8135 Painter Ave Ste 202 Whittier CA 90602-3154 *Personal philosophy: If you tell yourself that you can succeed and really believe you can, you will.*

LOWE, RICHARD GERALD, JR., computer programming manager; b. Travis AFB, Calif., Nov. 8, 1960; s. Richard Gerald and Valerie Jean (Hoefer) L.; m. Claudia Maria Arevalo, 1993; 1 child, Alvaro Arevalo. Student, San Bernardino Valley Coll., 1978-80. Tech. specialist Software Techniques Inc., Los Alamitos, Calif., 1980-82, sr. tech. specialist, 1982-84, mgr. tech. services, 1984-85; mgr. cons. services Software Techniques Inc., Cypress, Calif., 1985-86; sr. programmer BIF Accutel, Camarillo, Calif., 1986-87; systems analyst BIF Accutel, Camarillo, 1987-88; mgr. project Beck Computer Systems, Long Beach, Calif., 1986-91, v.p. devel., 1991-93; dir. tech. svcs. Trader Joe's Co., S. Pasadena, Calif., 1994—. Author: The Autobiography of Richard G. Lowe, Jr., 1991, The Lowe Family and Their Relatives, 1992; contbr. articles to profl. jours. Vol. min., field staff mem. L.A. Found. Ch. of Scientology, 1993—; active Concerned Citizens for Human Rights. Mem. Assn. Computing Machinery, Digital Equipment Corp. Users Group, UniData Users Group, Internat. Assn. Scientologists. Office: Trader Joe's Co 538 Mission St South Pasadena CA 91030-3036

LOWE, ROBERT STANLEY, lawyer; b. Herman, Nebr., Apr. 23, 1923; s. Stanley Robert and Ann Marguerite (Feese) L.; m. Anne Kirtland Selden, Dec. 19, 1959; children: Robert James, Margaret Anne. AB, U. Nebr., 1947, JD, 1949. Bar: Wyo. 1949. Ptnr. McAvoy & Lowe, Newcastle, 1949-51, Hickey & Lowe, Rawlins, 1951-55; county and pros. atty. Rawlins, 1955-59, pvt. practice, 1959-67; assoc. dir. Am. Judicature Soc., Chgo., 1967-74; counsel True Oil Co. and affiliates, 1974—; bd. dirs., sec. Hilltop Nat. Bank, Casper; legal adv. divsn. Nat. Ski Patrol Sys., 1975-88; city atty. City of Rawlins, 1963-65; atty., asst. sec. Casper Mountain Ski Patrol, 1988—. Mem. Wyo. Ho. of Reps., 1952-54; bd. dirs. Vols. in Probation, 1969-82; leader lawyer del. to China, People to People, 1986; mem. Wyo. Vets Affairs Coun., 1994—, chmn., 1996—; mem. legis. com. United Vets. Coun. Wyo., 1993—; trustee Troopers Found., Inc., 1994—, pres., 1994-96; pres. Casper WW II Commemorative Assn., 1995-96. Recipient Dedicated Community Worker award Rawlins Jr. C. of C., 1967, Yellow merit star award Nat. Ski Patrol System, 1982, 85, 87, 88. Fellow Am. Bar Found. (life); mem. VFW (post adv. 1991-96, nat. aide-de-camp 1993-94, judge adv. dist. 3 Dept. Wyo., 1994—, mil. order of cootie grand judge adv. 1994—), ABA (sec. jud. adminstrn. divsn. lawyers conf., exec. com. 1975-76, chmn. 1977-78, chmn. judicial qualification and selection com. 1986-93, coun. jud. adminstrn. divsn. 1977-78, mem. com to implement jud. adminstrn. stds. 1978-83, Ho. of Dels. state bar del. 1978-80, 86-87, state del. 1987-93, Assembly del. 1980-83), Am Judicature Soc. (dir. 1961-67, 85-89, bd. editors 1975-77, Herbert Harley award 1974), Wyo. St. Bar (chmn. com. on cts. 1961-67, 77-87), Nebr. St. Bar Assn., Ill. St. Bar Assn., D.C. Bar, Inter-Am. Bar Assn., Selden Soc., Inst. Jud. Adminstrn., Rocky Mountain Oil and Gas Assn. (legal com. 1976—, chmn. 1979-82, 90-91), Rocky Mountain Mineral Law Found. (trustee 1980-94), Am. Law Inst., Order of Coif, Delta Theta Phi (dist. chancellor 1982-83, chief justice 1983-93, assoc. justice 1993—; Percy J. Power Meml. award 1983, Gold Medallion award 1990), Casper Rotary Club (pres. 1985-86), Casper Rotary Found. (dir., sec. 1990—). Mem. Ch. of Christ, Scientist. Home: 97 Primrose Casper WY 82604-4018 Office: 895 River Cross Rd Casper WY 82601-1758

LOWE, ROLLAND CHOY, surgeon; b. San Francisco, Sept. 29, 1932; s. Laurence and Eva (Chan) L.; m. Kathryn Lew, Jan. 7, 1957; children: Larry, Randall, Yvonne. AB, U. Calif., Berkeley, 1952; MD, U. Calif., San Francisco, 1955. Diplomate Am. Bd. Surgeons. Intern San Francisco Gen. Hosp., 1956; resident in surgery U. Calif., San Francisco, 1958-63, assoc. clin. prof., 1964-92; pvt. practice San Francisco, 1992—; commr. bd. med. examiners State of Calif., 1979-80; chmn. bd. Chinese Hosp., 1984-85, 91, vice chmn., 1979-81, 83, 90, 92, chief of staff, 1971, 73-74, chief of surgery, 1977-78, bd. dirs., 1979-93. Trustee San Francisco Found., Asian Am. Health Forum, mem. exec. com.; trustee U.S.-China Edn. Inst.; mem. exec. com. San Francisco Comprehensive Health Planning Coun., 1974-76, bd. dirs., 1972-76; mem. bd. overseers U. Calif., San Francisco, 1990-91; chair Lawrence Choy Lowe Meml. Fund, Found. for Chinese Democracy; vice chair San Francisco 2000, 1990-92; chair Mayor's Citizen Adv. Com. on I-Hotel Block Devel., 1980-92; civil svc. comr. City and County of San Francisco, 1979-80. Capt. USAR, 1956-58. Mem. ACS, Howard Naffziger Surg. Soc., San Francisco Surg. Soc., San Francisco Med. Soc. (treas. 1979-80, pres.-elect 1981, pres. 1982), Calif. Med. Assn. (trustee 1987-94, chmn. bd. trustees 1994-95, pres.-elect 1996, pres. 1997). Office: 929 Clay St # 401 San Francisco CA 94108-1556

LOWELL, JAMES DILLER, geologist; b. Lincoln, Nebr., Aug. 17, 1933; s. James Russell and Pearl Evelyn (Diller) L.; m. Suzanne Hewitt, Nov. 1, 1957; children: Jennifer, Carey, Elizabeth, Alexandra. BS, U. Nebr., 1955; MA, Columbia U., 1957, PhD, 1958. Sr. geologist Am. Overseas Petroleum Ltd., Tripoli, Libya and The Hague, The Netherlands, 1958-65; asst. prof. geology Washington and Lee U., Lexington, Va., 1965-66; sr. rsch. specialist Esso Prodn. Rsch., Houston, 1966-73; exploration geologist Exxon Co., USA, Englewood, Colo., 1973-74; mgr. geology N.W. Exploration Co., Denver, 1974-76; pres. Colexcon Inc., Littleton, Colo., 1976—; mem. adv. bd. U. Nebr., Lincoln, 1984-87, 89—, Schramm prof., 1987; Crosby vis. prof. MIT, Cambridge, 1987. Author: Structural Styles in Petroleum Exploration, 1985; editor: Foreland Basins and Uplifts, 1983; contbr. articles to profl. jours. Recipient Disting. Alumni award U. Nebr., 1994, Esso Disting. Lectr., Esso Australia/U. Sydney, 1989. Fellow Geol. Soc. Am.; mem. Am. Assn. Petroleum Geologists (adv. bd. 1985-94, assoc. editor 1992-94, Disitng. lectr. 1994-95), Rocky Mountain Assn. Geologists (pres., 1st v.p., Scientist of Yr. 1979; hon. mem.), Wyo. Geol. Assn., Explorers Club. Home: 5836 Colorow Dr Morrison CO 80465-2210 Office: Colexcon Inc 2200 W Berry Ave Littleton CO 80120-1100

LOWELL, WAVERLY B., archivist; b. N.Y.C., Mar. 2, 1951; d. Allan and Evelyn S. Lowell. BA in History, U. R.I., 1972; MA, Rutgers U., 1976; MLS, U. Calif., Berkeley, 1979. Grad. student instr. women's studies Rutgers U., New Brunswick, N.J., 1975-76; asst. photography curator San Francisco Maritime Mus., 1977-78; libr. San Francisco Mus. Art, 1978-79; curator of manuscripts, archivist Calif. Hist. Soc., 1980-84; acting curator historic documents Nat. Maritime Mus., 1985; archives ad rsch. cons., 1984—; dir. Calif. Coop. Preservation of Archtl. Records, 1985-87, Nat. Archives-Pacific Sierra Region, 1987—; cons. to Carey & Co. Architects, Calif. Acad. Scis., Sequoia Kings Canyon Nat. Parks, Chevron Corp., numerous others; instr. Calif. State U., San Jose, John F. Kennedy Univ. Ctr. for Mus. Studies; mem. faculty Soc. Calif. Archivists, Western Archives Inst.; presenter in field. Author: Architectural Records in the San Francisco Bay Area: A Guide to Research, 1988; editor Friends of Terra Cotta newsletter, 1980-86; contbr. articles to profl. jours. Recipient Archivist award of excellence Calif. Heritage Preservation Commn., 1993. Mem. Soc. Am. Archivists (coun. 1991-94), Nat. Assn. Govt. Archives and Records Adminstrs. (bd. dirs. 1989-91), AIA, Soc. Calif. Archivists (pres. 1989-90), Friends of Terra Cotta (bd. dirs. 1980-88).

LÖWEN, PETRA ELISABETH, social worker; b. Düsseldorf, Germany, July 31, 1951; came to U.S., 1976; d. Matthias and Elisabeth (Bauernfeind) L.; m. David D. Diaz, Dec. 7, 1983 (div. June 1995); children: Quicheeta K. Löwen-Diaz, Aquivo I. Löwen-Diaz, Tuhri K. Löwen-Diaz. MSW, Eberhard Karls U., Tübingen, Germany, 1978. Outpatient and discharge asst. Rehab. Inst., Santa Barbara, Calif., 1980-83; attendent referral specialist III, Ind. Living Resource Ctr., Santa Barbara, 1983-91; tel. solicitor RAD Thrift Store, Santa Barbara, 1991-92; field supr. Nat. Homecare Sys., Santa Barbara, 1992-95; resident svcs. and activity dir. Pilgrim Terrace Coop. Homes, Santa Barbara, 1995—; chmn. cmty. adv. bd. Health Initiative, Santa Barbara, 1984-95; chmn. svc. com. South Coast Transiition Adv. Coun., Santa Barbvara, 1993-96. Roman Catholic. Home: 1733 Gillespie St Santa Barbara CA 93101 Office: Pilgrim Terrace Coop Homes 649 Pilgrim Terrace Dr Santa Barbara CA 93101

LOWEN, ROBERT MARSHALL, plastic surgeon; b. Detroit. MD, U. Mich. Med. Sch., 1971. Diplomate Am. Bd. Plastic Surgery, cert. surgery of the hand. Internship Pacific Presbyn., San Francisco, 1971-72; resident general surgery Stanford U. Med. Ctr., 1983-85; resident plastic surgery U. Okla. HSC, Okla. City, 1985-86; fellow hand surgery U. Colo. HSC, Denver, 1986-87, resident plastic surgery, 1987-88; pvt. practice Mountain View, Calif., 1988—; mem. staff El Camino Hosp., Mountain View, Calif., 1988—. Mem. Am. Soc. Plastic and Reconstructive Surgeons, Am. Soc. Lasers in Medicine aSurgery, Calif. Med. Soc., Lipoplasty Soc. North Am., Santa Clara County Med. Assn. Home and Office: 305 South Dr Ste 2 Mountain View CA 94040-4207

LOWI, ALVIN, JR., mechanical engineer, consultant; b. Gadsden, Ala., July 21, 1929; s. Alvin R. and Janice (Haas) L.; m. Guillermina Gerardo Alverez, May 9, 1953; children: David Arthur, Rosamina, Edna Vivian, Alvin III. BME, Ga. Inst. Tech., 1951, MSME, 1955; PhD in Engring.,

UCLA, 1956-61. Registered prof. engr., Calif. Design engr. Garrett Corp., Los Angeles, 1956-58; mem. tech. staff TRW, El Segundo, Calif., 1958-60, Aerospace Corp., El Segundo, 1960-66; prin. Alvin Lowi and Assocs., San Pedro, 1966—; pres. Terraqua Inc., San Pedro, Calif., 1968-76; v.p. Daeco Fuels and Engring. Co., Wilmington, Calif., 1978—; also bd. dirs. Daeco Fuels and Engring. Co.; pres. Lion Engring., Inc.; vis. research prof. U. Pa., Phila., 1972-74; sr. lectr. Free Enterprise Inst., Monterey Park, Calif., 1961-71; bd. dirs. So. Calif. Tissue Bank; research fellow Heather Found., San Pedro, 1966-. Contbr. articles to profl. jours.; patentee in field. Served to lt. USN, 1951-54, Korea. Fellow Inst. Humane Studies; mem. ASME, NSPE, Soc. Automotive Engrs., Soc. Am. Inventors, So. Bay Chamber Music Soc., Scabbard and Blade, Pi Tau Sigma. Jewish. Home and Office: 2146 W Toscanini Dr Palos Verdes Peninsula CA 90275-1420

LOWMAN, MARY BETHENA HEMPHILL (MRS. ZELVIN D. LOWMAN), civic worker, realtor; b. Lewis, Kans., Feb. 10, 1922; d. Frederick William and Gladys (Follin) Hemphill. A.B., Western State Coll., Colo., 1945; m. Zelvin D. Lowman, Oct. 24, 1943; children: Freda Ruth, James Fredrick, William Martin, Elizabeth June (Mrs. Joseph Herbst) (dec.). Tchr. Stout Creek Sch., Colo., 1942-43, San Diego City Sch. Dist., 1944-45, L.A. City Sch. Dist., 1948-50; pvt. sch. tchr. So. Inst. Music, 1956-57. Troop leader Frontier coun. Girl Scouts U.S., 1957-70, mem. exec. bd., 1961-73, 2d v.p., 1962-63, pres., 1968-71, chmn. established camp com., 1963-67, dir. Camp Foxtail, 1965, 67, chmn. Gold award com., 1986-87; mem. Calico Task Group, 1986-89, chmn., 1988-89; mem. Girl Scouts U.S. Region VI Com., 1973-75, chmn. Region VI Com., mem. nat. bd., mem. exec. com. and couns. com., 1975-78; mem. Am. Field Svc. Exchange Student Bd. So. Nev., 1961. Parliamentarian, West Charleston PTA, 1957-59, Nev. Congress, 1960-61; elder, trustee Presbyn. Ch., 1964-67, 89—; chmn. Christian Edn. Commn., 1964-65; chmn. Commn. on Mission of Ch., 1966; chmn. exec. com. Clark County Bicentennial Commn., 1974-76; chmn. bd. First Presbyn Pre-Sch. Day Care Ctr., 1982-85; chmn. stewardship fin. com. 1st Presbyn. Ch., 1990-92; chmn. bd. dirs. 1st Presbyn. Acad. and Preschool, 1990-96; elder nominating com. 1st Presbyn. Ch., 1997—. Family chosen as Nev. All-Am. Family, 1960. Recipient Thanks Badge U.S. Girl Scouts U.S., 1963, Thanks Badge II, 1989; Mary and Zel Lowman Sch. named in honor, 1992. Mem. Gen. Fedn. Women's Clubs (dir. 1958-60, 62-64, 72-78, chmn. scholarships and student aid 1974-76, chmn. family living div., 1976-78; treas. Western States Conf. 1968-70, sec. 1970-72, pres. 1972-74), Nev. Fedn. Women's Clubs, (past pres.), Md. fedn. women's Clubs (past jr. dir.), Clark County Pan-Hellenic Assn., So. Nev. Alumni Club (pres. 1961-62), Internat. Platform Assn. Presbyn. (elder, dir. capital stewarship canvas program, 1987-88), Las Vegas Bd. Realtors (chmn. membership com. 1988-90, chmn. by-laws com. 1990-91), Las Vegas Mesquite Club (past pres.), Jr. Women's Club (past pres., College Park, Md.), Newcomers Club (past pres.), Nat. Presbyn. Mariners Club (past pres.), Nevada-Sierra District Mariners Club, Las Vegas Nautilus Mariners Club. Home: 1713 Rambla Ct Las Vegas NV 89102-6103

LOWNDES, DAVID ALAN, programmer analyst; b. Schenectady, N.Y., Oct. 28, 1947; s. John and Iris Anne (Hepburn) L.; m. Peggy Welco, May 3, 1970; children: Diana Justine, Julie Suzanne. AB, U. Calif., Berkeley, 1969, postgrad., 1972-73. Acct., credit mgr. The Daily Californian, Berkeley, 1973-75; bus. mgr. The Daily Californian, 1975-76; acct. Pacific Union Assurance Co., San Francisco, 1976-77, acctg. mgr., 1977-78; sr. acct. U. Calif., San Francisco, 1978-88, programmer analyst, 1988—. Home: 1829 Gaspar Dr Oakland CA 94611-2350 Office: U Calif 250 Executive Park Blvd San Francisco CA 94134-3306

LOWRY, LARRY LORN, management consulting company executive; b. Lima, Ohio, Apr. 12, 1947; s. Frank William and Viola Marie L.; m. Jean Carroll Greenbaum, June 23, 1973; 1 child, Alexandra Kristin. BSEE, MIT, 1969, MSEE, 1970; MBA, Harvard U., 1972. Mgr. Boston Consulting Group, Menlo Park, Calif., 1972-80; sr. v.p., mng. ptnr. Booz, Allen & Hamilton Inc, San Francisco, 1980—. Western Electric fellow, 1969, NASA fellow, 1970. Mem. Sigma Xi, Tau Beta Pi, Eta Kappa Nu. Presbyterian. Home: 137 Stockbridge Ave Atherton CA 94027-3942

LOWRY, MIKE, former governor, former congressman; b. St. John, Wash., Mar. 8, 1939; s. Robert M. and Helen (White) L.; m. Mary Carlson, Apr. 6, 1968; 1 child, Diane. B.A., Wash. State U., Pullman, 1962. Chief fiscal analyst, staff dir. ways and means com. Wash. State Senate, 1969-73; govtl. affairs dir. Group Health Coop. Puget Sound, 1974-75; mem. council King County Govt., 1975-78, chmn., 1977; mem. 96th-100th congresses from 7th dist. Wash., 1979-1989; governor State of Wash., 1993-96. Chmn. King County Housing and Community Devel. Block Grant Program, 1977; pres. Wash. Assn. Counties, 1978. Democrat. Address: 3326 Park Ave Renton WA 98056*

LOYA, RANALDO, senior physician assistant; b. Whittier, Calif., July 1, 1954; s. Bernard Romero and Nora (Valverde) L. AA in Gen. Edn., Rio Hondo Coll., Whittier, Calif., 1980; BS in Health Sci., Calif. State U., Dominguez Hills, 1982; postgrad., U. LaVerne, 1989—. Cert. primary care physician asst., L.A., 1981. Emergency med. technician, ambulance driver, attendant Adams Ambulance Co., South Gate, Calif., 1974-75; emergency room technician, clerk Maywood-Bell Cmty. Hosp., Bell, Calif., 1975; sr. physician asst. Physician Asst. Svcs., L.A., 1981-94; physician asst. urgent care Ball-Taft Med. Clinic Ctr., Anaheim, Calif., 1984-85; sr. physician asst., corp. v.p., admin. Signal Med. Mgmt., Long Beach, Calif., 1985-88; sr. physician asst. U. Calif. Irvine Med. Ctr., Orange, Calif., 1988-90, U. So. Calif. Emergency Med. Assoc., L.A., 1989-90, U. Calif. Mt. Zion Med. Ctr., San Francisco, 1990-94, La Clinica Esperanza Mission Neighborhood Health Ctr., San Francisco, 1991-94; fellow: Am. Acad. Physician Assts., Washington, 1982—; Calif. Acad. Physician Assts., Anaheim, 1982 ; past mem. instl. review bd., Project Inform, San Francisco, 1991-92. Contbr. New England Journal of Medicine, 1990; mem. editl. bd. Clinician Reviews. Human rights commr., City of Palm Springs, Calif., 1996—; mem. Long Beach Pride, Inc., 1987-90, past v.p.; mem. Human Rights Campaign Fund, Washington, 1996—; mem Orange County Gay and Lesbian Comm. Svcs. Ctr., Garden Grove, Calif., 1987-88. With USN, 1975-79, Hawaii. Recipient Meritorious Mast, USN, 1978. Mem. Internat. AIDS Soc., Drew U. Med. Sch. Alumni Assn. Republican. Mem. Unity Ch. Home: 1179 N Calle Rolph Palm Springs CA 92262-4938

LU, GUIYANG, electrical engineer; b. Guiyang, China, May 10, 1946; came to U.S., 1982; s. Wen and Yunqiu Deng; m. Jing Du; 1 child, Jia. Degree in elec. engring., Tsing Hua U., Beijing, 1970; postgrad., South China U. Tech., Guangzhou, 1980-81; MA in Math., Calif. State U., Fresno, 1984; MSEE, Poly. U., N.Y.C., 1986. Instr. in elec. engring. South China U. Tech., Guangzhou, 1973-80; v.p. engring. Kawahara Corp., N.Y.C., 1986-88; H.S. math. tchr. N.Y.C. Bd. Edn., 1988-90; sr. R&D engr. Avid Inc., Norco, Calif., 1991—. Mem. IEEE. Home: 1718 Eastgate Ave Upland CA 91784-9210 Office: Avid Inc 3179 Hamner Ave Norco CA 91760-1983

LU, PAUL HAIHSING, mining engineer, geotechnical consultant; b. Hsinchu, Taiwan, Apr. 6, 1921; came to U.S., 1962; m. Sylvia Chin-Pi Liu, May 5, 1951; children: Emily, Flora. BS in Mining Engring., Hokkaido U., Sapporo, Japan, 1945; PhD in Mining Engring., U. Ill., 1967. Sr. mining engr., br. chief Mining Dept. Taiwan Provincial Govt., Taipei, 1946-56; sr. indsl. specialist mining and geology U.S. State Dept./Agy. for Internat. Devel., Taipei, 1956-62; rsch. mining engr. Denver Rsch. Ctr. Bur. of Mines, U.S. Dept. Interior, 1967-90; geotech. cons. Lakewood, Colo., 1991—. Contbr. over 60 articles to profl. jours. Rsch. fellow Hokkaido U., 1945-46, Ill. Mining Inst., 1966-67. Mem. Internat. Soc. for Rock Mechanics, Am. Rock Mechanics Assn., Mining and Materials Processing Inst. Japan, Chinese Inst. of Mining and Metall. Engrs. (dir., mining com. chair 1960-62, Tech. Achievement award 1962, merit award 1996). Home and Office: 1001 S Foothill Dr Lakewood CO 80228-3404

LUBECK, MARVIN JAY, ophthalmologist; b. Cleve., Mar. 20, 1929; s. Charles D. and Lillian (Jay) L. A.B., U. Mich., 1951, M.D., 1955, M.S., 1959. Diplomate Am. Bd. Opthamology; m. Arlene Sue Bitman, Dec. 28, 1955; children: David Mark, Daniel Jay, Robert Charles. Intern, U. Mich. Med. Ctr., 1955-56, resident ophthalmology, 1956-58, jr. clin. instr. ophthalmology, 1958-59; pvt. practice medicine, specializing in ophthalmology, Denver, 1961—; mem. staff Rose Hosp., Porter Hosp., Presbyn. Hosp., St. Luke's Hosp.; assoc. clin. prof. U. Colo. Med. Ctr. With U.S. Army, 1959-61. Fellow ACS; mem. Am. Acad. Ophthalmology, Denver Med. Soc., Colo. Ophthalmol. Soc. Home: 590 S Harrison Ln Denver CO 80209-3517 Office: 3600 E Alameda Ave Denver CO 80209-3111

LUBENOW, GERALD CHARLES, journalist; b. Sheboygan, Wis., Nov. 14, 1939; s. Vincent Ewald and Cecelia Virgin (King) L.; m. Joan Marie Gerza, June 20, 1965; children: Michael Hugh, Kristin Britt. A.B., Harvard U., 1961, postgrad. Bus. Sch., 1963; postgrad., U. Wis. Sch. Journalism, 1964-65. Corr. Newsweek mag., Detroit, 1965, Atlanta, 1966-69; San Francisco bur. chief Newsweek mag., 1969-83, 84-87, London bureau chief, 1987-89; asst. to exec. editor San Francisco Chronicle, 1983-84; dir. publs. Inst. Govtl. Studies, U. Calif., Berkeley, 1990—; sr. adviser pub. affairs U. Calif., Berkeley, 1996—; lectr. colls. and univs. Bd. dirs. Telegraph Hill Neighborhood Assn., San Francisco, 1970-73, chmn., 1971-73; bd. dirs. Telegraph Hill Dwellers, San Francisco; chmn. Garfield Sch. Bldg. Com., 1976-78; co-chmn. Mayor's Adv. Com. to Remove the Embarcadero Freeway, 1979; adv. bd. San Francisco State U. Sch. Bus.; media adv. com. Calif. State Bar Assn. Recipient Page One award (2) N.Y. Newspaper Guild, 1977, Gavel award Am. Bar Assn., 1978. Roman Catholic. Clubs: Harvard. Office: U Calif Berkeley 109 Moses Hall Berkeley CA 94720-2371

LUBLINER, IRVING, mathematics educator, consultant; b. Oakland, Calif., Aug. 29, 1952; s. Abram and Felicia (Bornstein) L.; m. Joanne C. May Kliejunas. BA, U. Calif., Berkeley, 1974; MA in Teaching, U. Calif., Davis, 1988. Cert. tchr., Calif. Tchr. math. and computer programming, chmn. math. dept. Novato (Calif.) Unified Sch. Dist., 1976-85; program dir., math. specialist Black Pine Circle Sch., Berkeley, 1985-90; tchr., coord. math. and sci. Bentley Sch., Oakland, 1990-95, math. tchr. and coord. grades 6-8, 1995—; instr. U. calif., Davis, 1975-76; dir. Kindercamp, Oakland, 1972-76, Camp Kee Tov, Berkeley, 1980-83; tchr. Marin County Office Edn., San Rafael, Calif., 1982-83; speaker Bur. of Edn. and Rsch., 1992—; speaker, cons., Oakland, 1974—. Contbr. articles to profl. jours. Recipient Hon. Svc. award Calif. Congress Parents and Tchrs., 1985, Spl. Honors award for contbn. to tchg. highly talented youth Johns Hopkins U.—Calif. Tchr. Recognition Program, 1991, 94, 97; Sarah D. Barton—S. Mark Taper Found. fellow Johns Hopkins U.'s Ctr. for Talented Youth, 1994. Mem. Nat. Coun. Tchrs. Math., Calif. Math. Coun., Alameda and Contra Costa Counties Math. Educators. Home: 878 Longridge Rd Oakland CA 94610-2445 Office: Bentley Sch 1 Hiller Dr Oakland CA 94618-2301

LUBMAN, RICHARD LEVI, physician, educator, research scientist; b. Bklyn., Dec. 10, 1956; m. Sue Ann Feinberg, Dec. 14, 1986; children: Rachel, Louisa. BA, Cornell U., 1977; MD, SUNY, Bklyn., 1981. Diplomate Am. Bd. Internal Medicine, Am. Bd. Pulmonary Diseases; cert. in critical care medicine. Intern, then resident in internal medicine SUNY Downstate Med. Ctr., 1981-84; chief resident SUNY-Bklyn. VA Hosp., 1984-85; fellow in pulmonary and critical care medicine N.Y. Hosp.-Cornell U. Med. Ctr., N.Y.C., 1985-88, instr. medicine, 1988-91; asst. prof. U. So. Calif., L.A., 1991—; expert reviewer Med. Bd. Calif., 1996—. Parker B. Francis fellow Francis Families Found., 1986-88. Fellow ACP, Am. Coll. Chest Physicians; mem. Am. Thoracic Soc., Am. Heart Assn. (initial investigator Greater L.A. affiliate 1993-95), Am. Physiol. Soc., Internat. Union Against Tb and Lung Disease. Office: U So Calif HMR 900 2011 Zonal Ave Los Angeles CA 90033

LUBY, CHARLES STRONG, company executive; b. Pitts., Dec. 8, 1937; s. Charles Leopold and Helen Marie (Adams) L.; m. Robin Dorothy Briscoe, Aug. 10, 1963. BA in Chemistry, San Diego State U., 1959, MS in Chemistry, 1964. Materials engr. Gen. Atomics, San Diego, 1960-68, mgr. nuclear fuel testing, 1968-71, mgr. fuel planning, 1971-73, exec. asst., 1973-76, mgr. internat. programs, 1977-82, mgr. proposals, 1982—. Patentee in field. Mem. Am. Nuclear Soc. (sect. chmn. 1978), Univ.Club. Office: Gen Atomics 3550 General Atomics Ct San Diego CA 92121

LUCAS, BETH ANNE, television producer; b. Grand Rapids, Mich., Sept. 15, 1960; d. Gordon Patrick and Phyllis (Sablack) Galka; m. Mark Fordham, Mar. 19, 1982 (div. 1985); m. Gus Lucas, June 3, 1991. BA in Psychology, Antioch U., 1995. Segment producer Breakaway, Metromedia TV, Hollywood, Calif., 1983; asst. dir. Anything for Money, Paramount TV, Hollywood, 1984; post prodn. supr. Heathcliff DIC, Hollywood, 1984; post prodn. supr. Beauty and the Beast, Witt-Thomas Prodns., Hollywood, 1986-88; assoc. producer Anything But Love, 20th Century Fox, Hollywood, 1989; assoc. producer Easy Street Viacom Prodns., Hollywood, 1984-85; mgr. post prodn. Matlock, Perry Mason, Father Dowling, Jack and the Fatman, Hollywood, 1990-91; project coord. Teen Dating Violence Prevention Team, Haven Hills, Inc. Vol. Children Are Our Future, Haven Hills Battered Woman's Shelter; mem. AIDS Project, L.A., L.A. Mission, Children Def. Fund. Mem. NASW, APA, NOW, Amnesty Internat., Am. Profl. Soc. on the Abuse of Children, Calif. Profl. Soc. on the Abuse of Children, Nature Conservancy, Nat. Parks and Conservation Assn., Feminist Majority, Nat. Abortion Rights Action League, Greenpeace, Smithsonian Assocs., Mus. Contemporary Art, Los Angeles County Mus., Sta. KCET, UCLA Alumni Assn., Child Help USA, Childreach, Mus. of Tolerance.

LUCAS, DONALD LEO, private investor; b. Upland, Calif., Mar. 18, 1930; s. Leo J. and Mary G. (Schwamm) L.; BA, Stanford U., 1951, MBA, 1953; m. Lygia de Soto Harrison, July 15, 1961; children: Nancy Maria Lucas Thibodeau, Alexandra Maria Lucas Ertola, Donald Alexander Lucas. Assoc. corp. fin. dept. Smith, Barney & Co., N.Y.C., 1956-59; gen., ltd. ptnr. Draper, Gaither & Anderson, Palo Alto, Calif., 1959-66; pvt. investor, Menlo Park, Calif., 1966—; bd. dirs. Cadence Design Systems, San Jose, Calif., Coulter Pharm., Inc., Palo Alto, Amati Comm., Corp., San Jose, Oracle Corp., Redwood Shores, Calif., Racotek, Inc., Mpls., Macromedia, San Francisco, TriCord Systems, Inc., Plymouth, Minn., Transcend Svcs., Inc., Atlanta, Coulter Pharms., Palo Alto, Calif.; Mem. bd. regents Bellarmine Coll. Prep., 1977—; regent emeritus U. Santa Clara, 1980—. 1st lt. AUS, 1953-55. Mem. Am. Coun. Capital Formation (dir.), Stanford U. Alumni Assn., Stanford Grad. Sch. Bus. Alumni Assn., Order of Malta, Stanford Buck Club, Vintage Club (Indian Wells, Calif.), Menlo Country Club (Woodside, Calif.), Menlo Circus Club (Atherton, Calif.), Jackson Hole Golf and Tennis Club, Teton Pines Club, Zeta Psi. Home: 224 Park Ln Atherton CA 94027-5411 Office: 3000 Sand Hill Rd # 3-210 Menlo Park CA 94025-7116

LUCAS, GEORGE W., JR., film director, producer, screenwriter; b. Modesto, Calif., May 14, 1944. Student, Modesto Jr. Coll.; BA, U. So. Calif., 1966. Chmn. Lucasfilm Ltd., San Rafael, Calif. Creator short film THX-1138 (Grand prize Nat. Student Film Festival, 1967); asst. to Francis Ford Coppola on The Rain People; dir. Filmmaker (documentary on making of The Rain People); dir., co-writer THX-1138, 1970, American Graffiti, 1973; dir., author screenplay Star Wars, 1977; exec. producer More American Graffiti, 1979, The Empire Strikes Back, 1980, Raiders of the Lost Ark, 1981, Indiana Jones and the Temple of Doom, 1984, Labyrinth, 1986, Howard the Duck, 1986, Willow, 1988, Tucker, 1988, Radioland Murders, 1994; exec. producer, co-author screenplay Return of the Jedi, 1983; co-exec. producer Mishima, 1985; co-author, co-exec. producer Indiana Jones and the Last Crusade, 1989; exec. producer (TV series) The Young Indiana Jones Chronicles, 1992-93. Office: Lucasfilm Ltd PO Box 2009 San Rafael CA 94912-2009

LUCAS, JAMES BRUNO, public relations consultant; b. Berkeley, Calif., Nov. 15, 1950; s. James M. and Elizabeth A. (Pilorz) L.; m. Liesel C. Friedrich, Dec. 21, 1985; children: Charles M., Benjamin A. BA, Kenyon Coll., 1973; MA, Duke U., 1980. Accredited Pub. Rels. Soc. Am. Staff writer The Raleigh (N.C.) Times, 1978-80; sr. pub. info. rep. Met. Water Dist. So. Calif., L.A., 1981-84; copywriter Corp. Comm. Group, Marina del Rey, Calif., 1984-87; sr. account exec. Burson-Marsteller, L.A., 1987-89; cons. Lucas Corp. PR and Investor Rels., Santa Monica, Calif., 1989-90, 94—; dir. Pub. Rels. Health Net, Woodland Hills, Calif., 1990-94. Recipient 1st place investigative reporting N.C. Press Assn., 1979, Annual Report awards Fin. World Mag., N.Y., 1992, 93. Home and Office: PO Box 1305 Santa Monica CA 90406-1305

LUCAS, LINDA LUCILLE, dean; b. Stockton, Calif., Apr. 22, 1940; d. Leslie Harold Lucas and Amy Elizabeth (Callow) Farnsworth. BA, San Jose State Coll., 1961, MA, 1969; EdD, U. San Francisco, 1982. Dist. libr. Livermore (Calif.) Elem. Schs., 1962-64; libr. Mission San Jose High Sch., Fremont, Calif., 1964-69; media reference libr. Chabot Coll., Hayward, Calif., 1969-75; asst. dean instrn. Chabot-Las Positas Coll., Livermore, 1975-91; assoc. dean instrn. Las Positas Coll., Livermore, 1991-94, dean acad. svcs., 1994—; participant Nat. Inst. for Leadership Devel., 1991. Bd. dirs. Tri-Valley Community TV, Livermore, 1991—, Valley Choral Soc., 1993—, Chabot-Las Positas Colls. Found., Pleasanton, Calif., 1991-94; mem. needs assessment com Performing Arts Coun., Pleasanton. Mem. ALA, Coun. Chief Librs., Assn. Calif. Community Coll. Adminstrs., Calif. Libr. Assn. Office: Las Positas Coll 3033 Collier Canyon Rd Livermore CA 94550-9797

LUCAS, STEPHANIE HEUNE, elementary education educator; b. Santa Rosa, Calif., Jan. 28, 1963; d. William K. and Patricia A. Ruehmann; m. Rick A. Lucas, July 18, 1993; 1 child, Sarah Nichole Heune Lucas. AA, Santa Rosa (Calif.) Jr. Coll., 1983; BA, U. Calif., Davis, 1986. Cert. elem. tchr., Calif. Camp dir. YMCA, Sebastopol, Calif., 1987-88; tchr. Delano (Calif.) Schs., 1988-95, Math Matters Cluster leader, 1995—. Office: Math Matters DUES 1405 12th Ave Delano CA 93215-2416

LUCAS, SUZANNE, statistician, entrepreneur; b. Baxter Springs, Kans., Jan. 16, 1939; d. Ralph Beaver and Marguerite (Sansocie) L.; children: Patricia Sue Jennings, Neil Patric Jennings. BA in Math., Calif. State U., Fresno, 1967, MA in Ednl. Theory, 1969; MS in Stats., U. So. Calif., 1979. Asst. to dir. NSF Inst., Calif. State U., Fresno, 1968; Tchr. secondary math. Fresno city schs., 1968-78; statistician corp. indsl. relations Hughes Aircraft Co., Los Angeles, 1979-80; personnel adminstr. Hughes Aircraft Co. Space and Communications Group, Los Angeles, 1981-82, mem. tech. staff in math., 1982-85, staff engr., 1986-87; mem. tech. staff cost analysis The Aerospace Corp., 1987-90; sr. staff engr. Hughes Aircraft Co. Electro Optical Systems, 1990-93, scientist, engr., 1993—; owner, math. cons. Lucas Ednl. Consultants, Manhattan Beach, Calif., 1989—; owner Lucas Enterprises, Manhattan Beach, 1993-96; lectr. in biostats. U. So. Calif., 1979. Kiwanis scholar, 1958. Mem. Internat. Soc. Parametric Analysts (pres. So. Calif. chpt. 1991-92), Soc. Cost Estimating and Analysis (cert.), Am. Psychol. Assn., Am. Statis. Assn., U. So. Calif. Alumni Assn. (life), Kappa Mu Epsilon. Office: Hughes Electronics Corp EOS PO Box 902 EO/E1/A118 El Segundo CA 90245-0902 also: Lucas Ednl Cons PO Box 3868 Manhattan Beach CA 90266

LUCENTE, ROSEMARY DOLORES, educational administrator; b. Renton, Wash., Jan. 11, 1935; d. Joseph Anthony and Erminia Antoinette (Argano) Lucente; BA, Mt. St. Mary's Coll., 1956, MS, 1963. Tchr. pub. schs., Los Angeles, 1956-65, supr. tchr., 1958-65, asst. prin., 1965-69, prin. elem. sch., 1969-85, 86—, dir. instrn., 1985-86, 1986—; nat. cons., lectr. Dr. William Glasser's Educator Tng. Ctr., 1968—; nat. workshop leader Nat. Acad. for Sch. Execs.-Am. Assn. Sch. Adminstrs., 1980; L.A. Unified Sch. Dist. rep. for nat. pilot of Getty Inst. for Visual Arts, 1983-85, 92—, site coord., 1983-86, team leader, mem. supt.'s adv. cabinet, 1987—. Recipient Golden Apple award Stanford Ave. Sch. PTA, Faculty and Community Adv. Council, 1976, resolution for outstanding service South Gate City Council, 1976, named Woman of Yr., Calif. State Senate, 1997. Mem. Nat. Assn. Elem. Sch. Prins., L.A. Elem. Prins. Orgn. (v.p. 1979-80), Assn. Calif. Sch. Adminstrs. (charter mem.), Assn. Elem. Sch. Adminstrs. (vice-chmn. chpt. 1972-75, city-wide exec. bd., steering com. 1972-75, 79-80). Assn. Adminstrs. Los Angeles (charter), Pi Theta Mu, Kappa Delta Pi (v.p. 1982-84), Delta Kappa Gamma. Democrat. Roman Catholic. Home: 6501 Lindenhurst Ave Los Angeles CA 90048-4733 Office: Figueroa St Sch 510 W 111th St Los Angeles CA 90044-4231

LUCHTERHAND, RALPH EDWARD, financial advisor; b. Portland, Oreg., Feb. 9, 1952; s. Otto Charles II and Evelyn Alice (Isaac) L.; children: Anne Michelle, Eric Alexander, Nicholas Andrew. BS, Portland State U., 1974, MBA, 1986. Registered profl. engr., Oreg.; gen. securities broker NYSE/NASD, CFP. Mech. engr. Hyster Co., Portland, 1971-75, svc. engr., 1975-76; project engr. Lumber Systems Inc., Portland, 1976-79; prin. engr. Moore Internat., Portland, 1979-81, chief product engr., 1981-83; project engr. Irvington-Moore, Portland, 1983, chief engr., 1983-86; ind. cons. engr., 1986; engring. program mgr. Precision Castparts Corp., Portland, 1986-87; personal fin. adv., Am. Express Fin. Advs., Clackamas, Oreg., 1987-94, sr. fin. adv., 1994—; ptnr. Bacon, Luchterhand Wilmot & Assocs. Divsn. of Am. Express Fin. Advisors, Clackamas, Oreg., 1996—; apptd. to Silver Team, 1991, Gold Team, 1994. Treas. Village Bapt. Ch., Beaverton, Oreg., 1988-91; bd. dirs. Carus Community Planning Orgn., Oregon City, Oreg., 1993—; active Rolling Hills Cmty. Ch., Tualatin, Oreg., 1995—. Republican. Home: 24440 S Eldorado Rd Mulino OR 97042-9629 Office: Bacon Luchterhand Wilmot & Assocs Am Express Fin Advisors 8800 SE Sunnyside Rd Ste 300 Clackamas OR 97015-9786

LUCK, KENNETH LEVERETT, healthcare executive, author; b. Oxnard, Calif., Oct. 3, 1964; s. William Emsley and Delfina (Carbulido) L.; m. Christine Ellen Watson; children: Cara Marie, Ryan Kenneth. BA in Polit. Sci., UCLA, 1986; postgrad., Fuller Sem., Pasadena, Calif., 1996—. Missionary Campus Crusade for Christ, Spain, Russia, U.S., 1984-85; comms. dir. Josh McDowell Ministry, Richardson, Tex., 1986-89; exec. dir. Athletes Serving Bus., Rancho Santa Margarita, Calif., 1989-91; west region dir. ops. New Life Clinics, Laguna Beach, Calif., 1991—; sr. assoc. Corp. for Standards and Outcomes, Pitts., 1997—. Author: 52 Ways to Stretch a Buck, 1992, 52 Ways to Nurture Your Child's Natural Abilities, 1994. Baptist. Home: 25 Via Zapador Rancho Sta Margarita CA 92688 Office: New Life Clinics 570 Glenneyre Laguna Beach CA 92651

LUCKETT, BYRON EDWARD, JR., air force chaplain; b. Mineral Wells, Tex., Feb. 2, 1951; s. Byron Edward and Helen Alma (Hart) L.; m. Kathryn Louise Lambertson, Dec. 30, 1979; children: Florence Louise, Byron Edward III, Barbara Elizabeth, Stephanie Hart. BS, U.S. Mil. Acad., 1973; MDiv, Princeton Theol. Sem., 1982; MA, Claremont Grad. Sch., 1987. Commd. 2d lt. U.S. Army, 1973, advanced through grades to maj.; stationed at Camp Edwards, Korea, 1974-75; bn. supply officer 563rd Engr. Bn., Kornwestheim, Germany, 1975-76; platoon leader, exec. officer 275th Engr. Co., Ludwigsburg, Germany, 1976-77; boy scout project officer Hdqrs., VII Corps, Stuttgart, Germany, 1977-78; student intern Moshannon Valley Larger Parish, Winburne, Penn., 1980-81; Protestant chaplain Philmont Scout Ranch, Cimarron, N.Mex., 1982; asst. pastor Immanuel Presbyn. Ch., Albuquerque, 1982-83, assoc. pastor, 1983-84; tchr. Claremont High Sch., 1985-86; Protestant chaplain 92nd Combat Support Group, Fairchild AFB, Wash., 1986-90; installation staff chaplain Pirinclik Air Station, Turkey, 1990-91; protestant chaplain Davis-Monthan AFB, Ariz., 1991-95; dir. readiness ministries Offutt AFB, Nebr., 1995, sr. protestant chaplain, 1996; mem. intern program coun. Claremont (Calif.) Grad. Sch. Contbr. articles to profl. jours. Bd. dirs. Parentcraft, Inc., Albuquerque, 1984, United Campus Ministries, Albuquerque, 1984, Proclaim Liberty, Inc., Spokane, 1987-90; bd. dirs. western region Nat. Assn. Presbyn. Scouters, Irving, Tex., 1986-89, chaplain, 1991-93; mem. N.Mex. Employer Co, in Support of the Guard and Reserve, Albuquerque, 1984, Old Baldy coun. Boy Scouts Am., 1986; chmn. Fairchild Parent Coop., Fairchild AFB, 1986-87; pres. Co. Grade Officers Coun., Fairchild AFB, 1987-88. Capt. U.S. Army Reserve; chaplain USAF Reserve 1983-86, maj. 1990—. Recipient Dist. Award of Merit for Disting. Svc. Boy Scouts Am., 1977. Mem. Soc. Cin. Md., Mil. Order Fgn. Wars U.S., Civil Affairs Assn. Presbyterian. Home: 12909 S 29th Ave Bellevue NE 68123-1929 Office: 55 WG/HC 301 Lincoln Hwy Offutt AFB NE 68113

LUCKMAN, CHARLES, architect; b. Kansas City, Mo., May 16, 1909; m. Harriet McElroy, 1931; children: Charles, James M., Stephen A. Grad. magna cum laude, U. Ill., 1931; LLD, U. Miami, Fla., 1950; AFD (hon.), Calif. Coll. Arts and Crafts, 1958; DFA (hon.), Adelphi U., 1986; LLD (hon.), Pepperdine U., 1989. Lic. architect, 1931 Registered architect, 48 states and D.C. sr. registration Nat. Archtl. Registration Bds. Employed in architect's office for license qualifications, 2 years; joined Colgate- Palmolive-Peet Co. as retail salesman, 1931, Chgo. sales supr., 1933; mgr. Colgate-Palmolive-Peet Co. as retail salesman (Wis. dist.), 1934; divisional mgr. Colgate- Palmolive-Peet Co. as retail salesman (Cin. hdqrs.), 1935; with Pepsodent Co. (later Pepsodent Div. of Lever Bros. Co.), 1935-50, sales promotion mgr., sales mgr., 1935-36, v.p. in charge sales, 1936, in charge sales and advt., 1937, v.p., gen. mgr., 1938, exec. v.p., 1942-43, pres., 1943-46; exec. v.p. Lever Bros., Jan.-July 1946, pres., 1946-50; pres., partner Pereira & Luckman, Los Angeles, 1950-58; founder, ptnr. The Luckman Partnership,

Inc., 1958—; chmn. bd., chief exec. officer Ogden Devel. Corp., 1968-74, Luckman Mgmt. Co., 1973—; dir. Hollywood Bowl. Maj. projects include Madison Sq. Garden, N.Y.C., Conv. and Exhbn. Center, Los Angeles, U.S. World's Fair Pavilion, N.Y.C., Los Angeles World Zoo, U. Calif. at Santa Barbara, Civic Plaza, Phoenix, Prudential Center, Boston, State Office Bldg, Madison, Wis., Phoenix Civic Plaza, Los Angeles Internat. Airport, First Nat. Bank of Ariz, Phoenix, Broadway Plaza, Los Angeles, United Calif. Bank, Los Angeles, U. Del. Student Living Center, La Jolla VA Hosp, Aloha Stadium, Honolulu, 9200 Sunset Tower, Los Angeles, Manned Space Craft Center, Houston, VA Hosp, West Los Angeles, Calif., Hoover Library and Linear Accelerator Center, Stanford U., 1st Natl Bank of Oreg, Portland, Forum, Inglewood, Calif., Ralph M. Parsons Co. hdqrs, Pasadena, Calif., Nat. Security and Resources Study Center, Los Alamos, Hyatt Regency Hotels, Dearborn, Mich., The Harriet & Charles Luckman Fine Arts Complex, L.A., The Harriet & Charles Luckman Child Guidance Clin., L.A., Phoenix, City Hall and Police Bldg., Inglewood, Xerox Corp. hdqrs., Stamford, Conn., Warner Bros. Office Bldg., Burbank, Calif., Orange County Conv./Civic Ctr., Orlando, Fla.; also numerous other pub. bldgs; author: (autobiography) Twice in a Lifetime, 1988. Pres., chmn. bd. Los Angeles Orchestral Soc., 1962; v.p., dir. So. Calif. Symphony Assn.; mem. bd. assocs., pres. council George Pepperdine Found., Los Angeles; trustee Calif. State Colls.; chmn. bd. trustees, 1963-65; bd. govs. Library Presdl. Papers; trustee Nat. Art Mus. Sport; mem. U. Ill. Found.; Calif. mem. Ednl. Commn. of States; mem. bd. Am. Nat. Red Cross, YMCA; bd. dirs., past pres. AID-United Givers.; Mem. Pres.'s Commn. on Equality of Treatment and Opportunity in Armed Services and Civil Rights, Gov.'s Commn. Met. Area Problems; dir. Advt. Council; trustee Adelphi U.; chmn. Citizens Food Com., 1947; mem. Commerce and Industry Assn. N.Y.C., Los Angeles World Affairs Council, Com. Econ. Devel., Council U.S. Assocs. of Internat. C. of C.; bd. dirs. Nat. Adv. Council Community Chest, Am. Heritage Found.; bd. assocs. Northwestern U., Calif. Inst. Tech.; chmn. Nat. Council Trustees of Freedoms Found. at Valley Forge, 1986. Decorated Star of Solidarity Republic of Italy; chevalier Nat. Order Legion of Honor France; Order of St. John; recipient Horatio Alger award Am. Schs. and Colls. Assn., George Washington Honor medal Freedom's Found., 1964, 67, 68, Make Am. Beautiful award Nat. Assn. Realty Bds.; named Outstanding Mgmt. Exec. N.Y. Mgmt. Club, Man of Year Constrn. Industries, 1974; Disting. Achievement award U. Ill., 1970; Henry Laurence Gantt medal Am. Mgmt. Assn. and ASMF, 1981. Mem. AIA (Fellowship award 1963), Ill. Soc. Architects, U.S. Jr. C. of C. (One of Outstanding Young Men 1945, dir.), Tau Beta Pi, Theta Tau, Gargoyle. Home and Office: The Luckman Management Co 9220 W Sunset Blvd West Hollywood CA 90069-3501

LUDLOW, JAMES ALDEN, physicist; b. Salt Lake City, July 19, 1967; s. Walter Wilson Ludlow and Dawn Louise Horne. BS in Physics, U. Utah, 1991. Rsch. physicist Ceramatec, Salt Lake City, 1990—; ski instr. Park City (Utah) Ski Area, 1986-95. Mem. Electrochem. Soc., Profl. Ski Instrs. of Am. (level III instr. 1986—), U.S. Ski Coaches Assn. (level II coach 1993—). Office: Ceramatec 900 W 2425 S Salt Lake City UT 84119

LUEBTOW, JOHN GILBERT, artist; b. Milw., Apr. 2, 1944; s. Gilbert and Evelyn Luebtow; m. Goldi Luebtow; 1 child, Matthew John. BA, Calif. Luth. Coll., 1967; MA, UCLA, 1969, MFA, 1976. Dir. archtl. and exptl. ceramics depts. De Porcelyne Fles Co., Delft, The Netherlands, 1969-71; instr. Harvard Sch., North Hollywood, Calif., 1971—, chairperson arts dept., 1980; part time instr. painting Calif. Luth. Coll., Thousand Oaks, 1972-73. Exhibited in numerous group and one-man shows including Patricia Correia Gallery, Venice, Calif., 1994, 96, 98, Glass Now '94, Tokyo, 1994, Mus. Collectors Coun. Santa Barbara Mus. Art, 1993, Finegood Art Gallery, West Hills, Calif., 1993, L.A. County Mus. of Art, 1995, Detroit Inst. of the Arts, 1996, Tucson Mus. Art, 1997, many others; works commd. by numerous orgns. including Kawamura Haneda Hotel, Japan, Sheraton Hotel, Bal Harbor, Fla., The Scripps Rsch. Inst., La Jolla, Calif., Nestles Corp., Glendale, Calif., Supreme Ct. Nev., Am. Airlines, N.Y.C., Atlantic Richfield Corp., L.A., MCI, Atlanta, and numerous pvt. collections. Active art com. L.A. Bicentennial, 1980-81, Mus. Contemporary Art, L.A., L.A. County Mus. Art, Craft and Folk Art Mus., L.A. Mem. Nat. Coun. on Edn. Ceramics, Glass Arts Soc., Am. Crafts Coun., Calif. Art Edn. Assn., Nat. Art Edn. Assn., L.A. Inst. Contemporary Art, Calif. Assn. Ind. Schs. Home and Studio: 10954 Independence Ave Chatsworth CA 91311-1560

LUEDTKE, ROGER A., lawyer; b. Wausau, Wis., Apr. 10, 1942. BS, U. Wis., 1964, MA, 1968, JD, 1974. Bar: Wis. 1974, Oreg. 1974. Atty. Schwabe, Williamson & Wyatt, Portland, Oreg. Mem. Oreg. State Bar, Phi Eta Sigma. Address: Schwabe Williamson & Wyatt Stes 1600-1950 Pacwest Ctr 1211 SW 5th Ave Portland OR 97204-3713

LUEGGE, WILLARD ARTHUR, chemist, consultant; b. Oak Park, Ill., Mar. 19, 1931; s. Theodore Wilhelm and Irma Minnie (Schoepfer) L.; m. Joanna Carleen Wechter, Sept. 1, 1951; children: Sherylene, Lynette. BA, Ind. U., 1953; postgrad., Ind. U., U. Louisville, UCLA, 1954-64. Rsch. chemist Louisville Cement Co., Speed, Ind., 1956-60; quality control chemist Cal Portland Cement Co., Mojave, Calif., 1960-61; chemistry tchr. Palmdale (Calif.) High Sch., 1961-90; owner-dir. PM Labs, Lancaster, Calif., 1968-89; cons. extractive metallurgical chemistry Lancaster, 1989—; sci. dept. chmn. Palmdale High Sch., 1964-79; mem. Calif. Assn. Chemistry Tchrs., 1963-89; rsch. chemist USAF Rocket Propulsion Lab., Edwards AFB, summers, 1966, '67, '68; bd. dirs. Bryman Refining Co., Inc. Inventor assay kit, 1970. Recipient Tchr. of the Yr. award Am. Chem. Soc., 1967; NSF grantee, 1963, 64. Mem. Western Mining Coun., Western States Pub. Lands Coalition. Presbyterian. Home and Office: 560 E Avenue J1 Lancaster CA 93535-3828

LUEPKE, GRETCHEN, geologist; b. Tucson, Nov. 10, 1943; d. Gordon Maas and Janice (Campbell) Luepke; B.S., U. Ariz., 1965, M.S., 1967; U. Colo., summer, 1962. Geol. field asst. U.S. Geol. Survey, Flagstaff, Ariz., 1964; with U.S. Geol. Survey, Menlo Park, Calif., 1967—, geologist, Pacific Br. of Marine Geology, 1976—. Registered geologist, Ore. Mem. U.S. Congress Office Tech. Assessment Workshop, Mining and Processing Placers of EEZ, 1986. Fellow Geol. Soc. Am. (Interdisciplinary Perspectives on the Hist. Earth Scis., Penrose Conf. 1994); mem. Soc. Econ. Paleontologists and Mineralogists (chmn. com. libraries in developing countries 1988-91), Ariz. Geol. Soc., Peninsula Geol. Soc., Bay Area Mineralogists (chmn. 1979-80), History of the Earth Scis. Soc., Internat. Assn. Sedimentologists, Internat. Marine Minerals Soc. (charter), Geospeakers Toastmasters Club (charter, Competent Toastmaster 1995), Sigma Xi. Editor: Stability of Heavy Minerals in Sediments; Econ. Analysis of Heavy Minerals in Sediments; editor book rev. Earth Scis. History, 1989—. Contbr. articles on heavy-mineral analysis to profl. jours. Office: 345 Middlefield Rd Menlo Park CA 94025-3561

LUEVANO, FRED, JR., computer systems executive; b. Alamogordo, N.Mex., June 21, 1943; s. Fred Macias and Margaret (Baca) L.; m. Lupe Olmos, July 11, 1964; children: Michael, James Paul. AA in bus., Fullerton Coll., 1975; BA in Mgmt., U. Redlands, 1979, MA in Mgmt., 1985. Cert. data processing mgr., disaster recovery planner. Mgr. computer ops. Hoffman Electronics, El Monte, Calif., 1971-76; mgr. computer ops. and tech. services City of Anaheim, Calif., 1976-79; mgr. data processing Wyle Data Services, Huntington Beach, Calif., 1979-83; mgr. corp. computer ops. Northrop Grumman Corp., Pico Rivera, Calif., 1983, mgr. corp. computing, 1985—, dir. disaster revovery program, 1983—, dir. disaster recovery and security, 1988-90; Northrop Grumman Corp. Pico Rivera, Calif., 1990-92; mgr. data processing Northrop Grumman Corp., Pico Rivera, Calif., 1992—; cons. on info. sys., La Habra, Calif., 1971—; chmn. cert. bd. dirs. Disaster Recovery Inst., spkr., 1991-95. Cub master Boy Scouts Am., La Habra, 1979-84, chmn. com. 1975-79; councilman candidate City of La Habra Heights, Calif., 1982; pres. Red Coach Club, 1979-80, 86-88; pres. La Habra Parents for Swimming Inc., 1986-88. Served with USN, 1961-65. Mem. Am. Mgmt. Assn., Telecom. Assn., Assn. Computer Ops. Mgrs. (speaker 1983-94), Northrop Mgmt. Club. Republican. Roman Catholic. Office: Northrop Grumman Corp MS 770/XC 8900 Washington Blvd Pico Rivera CA 90660-3765

LUFT, HERBERT, history educator, former dean; b. Frankfurt, Germany, Aug. 17, 1942; came to U.S., 1961; s. Theodor and Hedwig (Theismann) L.; married; children: Sebastian, Rebecca. BA, Pepperdine U., 1965, MA, 1966; PhD, U. So. Calif., 1976. Mem. faculty Pepperdine U., Malibu, Calif., 1967—, prof. history, 1982—, exec. v.p., 1981-83; dean European programs Pepperdine U., Malibu, London, Heidelberg (Germany) and Florence (Italy), 1983-93. Mem. Kiwanis, Phi Alpha Theta. Mem. Ch. of Christ. Home: 24255 PCH Malibu CA 90263-4225

LUFT, RENE WILFRED, civil engineer; b. Santiago, Chile, Sept. 21, 1943; came to U.S., 1968; s. David and Malwina (Kelmy) L.; m. Monica Acevedo, Aug. 24, 1970; children: Deborah Elaine, Daniel Eduardo. CE, U. Chile, 1967; MS, MIT, 1969, DSc, 1971. Registered profl. engr., Alaska, Calif., Wash., Mass., N.H., R.I., Republic of Chile; registered structural engr., Vt. Asst. prof. civil engring. U. Chile, 1967-68; research asst. MIT, Cambridge, Mass., 1969-71, vis. lectr., 1983-84; staff engr. Simpson, Gumpertz & Heger Inc., Arlington, Mass., 1971-74, sr. staff engr., 1975-78, assoc., 1978-83, sr. assoc., 1984-90; prin. Simpson, Gumpertz & Heger Inc., San Francisco, 1990-91; head design div. Simpson, Gumpertz & Heger Inc., 1991-95; sec. seismic adv. com. Mass. Bldg. Code Commn., 1978-80, chmn., 1981-82; mem. Boston seismic instrumentation com. U.S. Geol. Survey; mem. slabs on ground com. Post-Tensioning Inst., 1994—. Contbr. articles to profl. jours. Mem. design overview com., bldg. seismic safety coun. Earthquake Hazards Reduction Program, 1983-91, chmn. rsch. com. 1987-88. Mem. ASCE, Boston Soc. Civil Engrs. (chmn. seismic design adv. com. 1981-86, Clemens Herschel award for tech. paper 1980, pres.'s award for leadership in earthquake engring. 1984), Am. Concrete Inst., Earthquake Engring. Research Inst., Structural Engrs. Assn. Calif., NSPE (Young Engr. of Yr., 1979), Sigma Xi, Chi Epsilon. Home: 107 Glendon Way Petaluma CA 94952 Office: 221 Main St Ste 1500 San Francisco CA 94105-1934

LUGG, JAMES R., agricultural products executive; b. 1934. Agrl. agent U. Calif., Salinas, 1956-63; rsch. Bruce Church, Inc., Salinas, Calif., 1963-66; with Transfresh Corp., 1996—. Office: Transfresh Corp 607 Brunken Ave Salinas CA 93901-4362*

LUGG, MARLENE MARTHA, health information systems specialist, health planner; b. Wauwatosa, Wis., Mar. 6, 1938; d. Armand Werner and Elise (Kuehni) Heinrich; m. Richard S.W. Lugg, June 11, 1966 (div. Dec. 1976); children: Jennifer Elsie, William Thomas Armand. BS, U. Wis., 1960; MPH, U. Pitts., 1966, DrPH, 1981. Dep. chairperson Nat. Com. on Health and Vital Stats., Canberra, Australia, 1973-83; dir. State Ctr. for Health Stats. and Planning Health Dept. Western Australia, Perth, 1966-83; dir. health info. systems program UCLA, 1983-88; vis. prof. pub. health Calif. State U., Northridge, 1987—; health info. systems specialist Kaiser-Permanente-So. Calif., Pasadena, 1988—; cons. software applications, L.A., 1987—; examiner L.A. Civil Svc. Commn., 1986-88; vis. prof. Pasadena City Coll., 1992—; mem. Calif. State Health Info. Policy Interagy. Com., 1992-94; mem. Calif. Health Data Coordinating Coun., 1995—; bd. dirs. Pub. Health Found. Enterprises, L.A., 1990—, sec., 1995—. Author: Medical Manpower in Western Australia, 1978; contbr. articles on injury, health data systems, immunization, air quality and illness, injury control and Pub. Health Conf. stats./records to profl. jours. Leader, trainer Girl Scouts U.S.A., Milw., Pitts., L.A., 1956—, Australian Girl Guides, Perth, Australia, 1966-82; explorer leader, trainer Boy Scouts Am., Western L.A. and Verdugo Hills, 1983—; del. Girl Scouts Nat. Coun., 1996—. Recipient Broughton award Izaak Walton League Am., Wis., 1966, Fisher award Am. Med. Technologists, 1971, Outstanding Young Person award Jaycees, Perth, Australia, 1977, Take Pride in Am. award U.S. Govt., Washington, 1990, Wm. T. Hornaday Gold medal Boy Scouts Am., 1991, Thanks Badge Girl Scouts U.S.A., 1990, Outstanding Family award, 1992, UN Environ. Conservation award, 1992, Wm. Spurgeon award, 1995, Nat. Vohs Quality award Kaiser Permanente, 1995; named Career Woman of Yr., Daily News, 1983, Woman of the Year San Fernando Valley Girl Scouts, 1995; Nat. Health and Med. Rsch. Coun. pub. health fellow, Australia, 1978. Fellow APHA, Australian Coll. Health Execs. (state bd. dirs. 1977-82), Royal Soc. Health, London; mem. Internat. Epidmiological Assn., So. Calif. Pub. Health Assn. (bd. dirs. 1987-95), N.Y. Acad. Scis., Pub. Health Found. (bd. dirs. 1992—, sec. 1995—). Lutheran. Office: Kaiser-Permanente So Calif 393 E Walnut St # 991 Pasadena CA 91188-0001

LUHN, ROBERT KENT, writer, magazine editor; b. Oakland, Calif., Nov. 23, 1953; s. Joel Adrian and Norma Jeanne (Arnold) L.; m. Marla Mieko Miyashiro, Sept. 14, 1992; 1 child, Pudge. Student, U. Calif., Davis, 1972-76. Freelance writer, 1968—; broadcaster, 1979-82; sr. editor PC World mag., San Francisco, 1983-90, contbg. editor, 1990-94; contbg. editor Calif. Republic mag., San Francisco, 1990-94, editor in chief Computer Currents Mag., 1994—. Author: The Swedish Catfish & Other Tales, 1979, Collected Works, Vol. 3, 1985, Going West, 1988, The Wit is Out, 1993; contbr. fiction, features and poetry to numerous publs., including Harper's, Mother Jones, Omni, Am. Film, Hudson Rev., Nantucket Rev., Christian Sci. Monitor, San Francisco Chronicle, Chgo. Tribune, Phila. Inquirer, PC mag., Computerworld, The Oregonian, Exec. Update, Grapevine Weekly; columnist Computer Currents, 1993—. Adv. bd. mem. Baykeeper, San Francisco, 1994-96. Mem. ACLU, Amnesty Internat., Greenpeace, Environ. Defense Fund.

LUHRMANN, TANIA MARIE, social anthropologist; b. Dayton, Ohio, Feb. 24, 1959; arrived in Eng., 1981; d. George William and Winifred Myrtle (Bruce) L. BA, Harvard U., 1981; MPhil, Cambridge U., 1982, PhD, 1986. Research fellow Christ's Coll. U. Cambridge, 1985-89; asst. prof. dept. anthropology U. Calif., San Diego, 1989-92, assoc. prof. dept anthropology, 1992—. Author: Persuasions of the Witch's Craft, 1989, The Good Parsi, 1996; contbr. articles to jours. Recipient Partington prize, Soc. History of Alchemy and Chemistry, 1984. Mem. Am. Anthrop. Assn. (Stirling prize 1986), Royal Anthrop. Inst. Office: U Calif San Diego Dept Anthropology 9500 Gilman Dr La Jolla CA 92093

LUIZZI, RONALD, wholesale distribution executive; b. Neptune, N.J., Apr. 7, 1953; s. Alfredo Luizzi and Mary Kay (Mumford) Figart; m. Kim T. Richardson, May 14, 1994. BA in Psychology, Trenton State Coll., 1975. Pres., chief exec. officer Profl. Divers, Inc., Neptune, 1975-78; nat. dir. projects Nat. Assn. Scuba Diving Schs., Long Beach, Calif., 1978-81; sales mgr. TW Systems, Inc., Honolulu, 1981-85; gen. mgr. TW Systems, Ltd.-Kona, Kailua-Kona, Hawaii, 1985—; East coast regional dir. Nat. Assn. Scuba Diving Schs., Neptune, 1977-78. Contbg. author: (trng. manual) Gold Book, 1977, Safe Scuba, 1977. Scuba advisor YMCA-Kona, Kailua-Kona, 1985—. Mem. Nat. Assn. Instnl. Laundry Mgrs. (cert.), Hawaii Assn. Instnl. Laundry Mgrs. (allied), Nat. Exec. House Keepers Assn. (allied), Hawaii Hotel Assn. (allied), Rotary (sec. 1988-89, v.p. 1989-90, pres. 1990-91), Kona-Kohala C. of C. Home: 76-6303 Kaheiau St Kailua Kona HI 96740-2275 Office: TW Systems Ltd-Kona 74-5622 Alapa St Kailua Kona HI 96740-3108

LUJAN, HERMAN D., academic administrator; m. Carla Lujan; 3 children. B in Polit. Sci., St. Mary's Coll. Calif.; M in Polit. Sci., U. Calif., Berkeley; PhD in Polit. Sci., U. Idaho. Faculty mem., adminstr. U. Kans., dir. inst. social and environ. studies, 1972-78; dir. divsn. state planning and rsch. Gov. of Kans., 1974-75; prof. polit. sci. dept. U. Wash., lectr. Japanese exec. mgmt. program, sch. bus., v.p. minority affairs, 1978-88, vice provost, 1988-91; pres. U. No. Colo., 1991—; bd. dirs. Bank One, Greeley, Colo. Author several books; contbr. articles to profl. jours. Bd. dirs. Boy Scouts Am., Latin Am. Ednl. Found. Mem. Rotary (Greeley). Office: U No Colo Office of Pres Greeley CO 80639

LUKE, DAVID KEVIN, investment company executive; b. Las Vegas, Nev., Dec. 14, 1960; s. Freddie Allen and Janet Anne (Shelton) L.; Lee-Ann Marie Petryshyn, Apr. 22, 1983; children: Krista Lee-Ann, David Nathan, Spencer Matthew, Ruth Alyssa, Zane Louis-Allan. BA, Brigham Young U., 1984; M of Internat. Mgmt., Am. Grad. Sch. of Internat. Mgmt., 1986. cert. investment broker. Cons. Internat. Small Bus. Inst., Denver, 1985; mgmt. trainee GM Can., Oshawa, Ont., 1986-87; supr. GMAC Can., Toronto, Ont., 1987-89; investment broker A.G. Edwards & Sons, Scottsdale, Ariz., 1989-96; assoc. v.p. investments Everen Securities, Inc., Scottsdale, 1996—; incorporator Protip, Inc., 1991-93. Instr. Ariz. Coun. on Econ. Edn., Tucson, Ariz., 1990-93; treas. Kyrene Schs. Cmty. Found., Tempe, Ariz., 1993-94, appointee Supt. Fin. Com., Advancement Chmn. 1994-95, Troop 375, Phoenix. Mem. Ch. Jesus Christ Latter Day Saints. Home: 6135 E Gold Dust Ave Paradise Valley AZ 85253 Office: Everen Securities Inc 7150 E Camelback Rd Ste 444 Scottsdale AZ 85251-1257

LUKER, KRISTIN, sociology educator; b. San Francisco, Aug. 5, 1946; d. James Wester and Bess (Littlefield) L. BA, U. Calif., Berkeley, 1968; PhD, Yale U., 1974. Postdoctoral fellow U. Calif., Berkeley, 1974-75, asst. prof. sociology, San Diego, 1975-81, assoc. prof., 1981-85, prof., 1985-86, co-dir. women's studies program, 1984-85, prof. jurisprudence and social policy, sociology, Berkeley, 1986—; Doris Stevens prof. women's studies, prof. sociology Princeton (N.J.) U., 1993-95. Author: Taking Chances: Abortion and the Decision Not to Contracept, 1976 (hon. mention Jessie Bernard award), Abortion and the Politics of Motherhood, 1984 (Charles Horton Cooley award 1985). Bd. dirs. Ctr. for Women's Studies and Services, San Diego, Ctr. for Population Options, Washington. Recipient Disting. Teaching award U. Calif., San Diego, 1984; Guggenheim Found. grantee, 1985. Mem. Am. Sociol. Assn., Sociologists for Women in Soc. Office: U Calif Berkeley Jurisprudence & Social Policy 2240 Piedmont Ave Berkeley CA 94720-2151

LUM, HERMAN TSUI FAI, retired state supreme court chief justice; b. Honolulu, Nov. 5, 1926; s. K.P. and Helen (Tom) L.; m. Almira Ahn, June 17, 1949; children: Forrest K.K., Jonathan K.K. Student, U. Hawaii, 1945-46; LL.B., U. Mo., 1950. Bar: Hawaii 1950. Asst. public prosecutor City and County Honolulu, 1950-52; chief atty. Hawaii Ho. of Reps., 1955, chief clk., 1956-61; partner Suyenaga, Sakamoto & Lum, Honolulu, from 1956; atty. U.S Dist. Ct. Hawaii, 1961-67; judge Cir. Ct. Honolulu, 1967-76, sr. judge Family Ct., 1977-80; assoc. justice Supreme Ct. Hawaii, 1980-83, chief justice, 1983-93; Pres. Jr. Bar Assn. Hawaii, 1957. Mem. ABA, Bar Assn. Hawaii, Fed. Bar Assn. Hawaii (pres. 1963), Phi Delta Phi, Lambda Chi Alpha. Home: 2508 Makiki Heights Dr Honolulu HI 96822-2548 Office: Hawaii Supreme Ct 417 S King St Honolulu HI 96813-2560*

LUM, JEAN LOUI JIN, nurse educator; b. Honolulu, Sept. 5, 1938; d. Yee Nung and Pui Ki (Young) L. BS, U. Hawaii, Manoa, 1960; MS in Nursing, U. Calif., San Francisco, 1961; MA, U. Wash., 1969, PhD in Sociology, 1972. Registered nurse, Hawaii. From instr. to prof. Sch. Nursing U. Hawaii Manoa, Honolulu, 1961-95, acting dean, 1982, dean, 1982-89, prof. emeritus, 1995—; project coordinator Analysis and Planning Personnel Svcs., Western Interstate Commn. Higher Edn., 1977; extramural assoc. div. Rsch. Grants NIH, 1978-79; mem. mgmt. adv. com. Honolulu County Hosp., 1982-96; mem. exec. bd. Pacific Health Rsch. Inst., 1980-88; mem. health planning com. East Honolulu, 1978-81; mem. rsch. grants adv. coun. Hawaii Med. Svcs. Assn. Found., Nat. Adv. Coun. for Nursing Rsch., 1990-93. Contbr. articles to profl. jours. Trustee Straub Pacific Health Found., Honolulu; bd. dirs. Friends of the Nat. Inst. of Nursing Rsch., 1994—. Recipient Nurse of Yr. award Hawaii Nurses Assn., 1982; named Disting. Practitioner in Nursing, Nat. Acads. of Practice, 1986; USPHS grantee, 1967-72. Fellow Am. Acad. Nursing; mem. Am. Nurses Assn., Am. Pacific Nursing Leaders Conf. (pres. 1983-87), Council Nurse Researchers, Nat. League for Nursing (bd. rev. 1981-87), Western Council Higher Edn. for Nurses (chmn. 1984-85), Western Soc. for Research in Nursing, Am. Sociol. Assn., Pacific Sociol. Assn., Assn. for Women in Sci., Hawaii Pub. Health Assn., Hawaii Med. Services Assn. (bd. dirs. 1985-92), Western Inst. Nursing, Mortar Bd., Phi Kappa Phi, Sigma Theta Tau, Alpha Kappa Delta, Delta Kappa Gamma. Episcopalian. Office: U Hawaii-Manoa Sch Nursing Webster 409 2528 The Mall Honolulu HI 96822

LUM, JODY MAE KAM QUON, real property appraiser; b. Honolulu, Sept. 15, 1961; d. Joseph Tai and Alice Moi (Lau) L. BA, U. Hawaii, 1983. Cert. residential appraiser. Asst. appraiser Hanamura Appraisal Co., Honolulu, 1986-87; real estate staff appraiser Am. Savs. Bank, Honolulu, 1987-89; real property appraiser III City and County of Honolulu, Hawaii, 1989-90; real property appraiser IV City and County of Honolulu, 1990—. Active, profl. yound adult co-leader Kalihi Union Ch., 1993—. Named Outstanding Woman of Yr., 1991. Mem. Honolulu Chinese Jaycees (rec. sec. 1989-90, mem. devel. v.p. 1990-91, community devel. v.p. 1991-92, Woman of Yr. 1989-90, Outstanding Community Devel. v.p. 1991-92). Office: City and County Honolulu 842 Bethel St Honolulu HI 96813-4320

LUMAN, ROBERT M., protective services official; m. Annette Luman; 2 children. MPA, U. So. Calif.; grad., FBI Nat. Acad., 1991. From patrol officer to dep. chief Long Beach (Calif.) Police Dept., 1968-96, chief of police, 1996—. Bd. dirs. Am. Heart Assn., Long Beach, ARC, Long Beach; active Long Beach Cmty. Partnership, Nat. Conf., St. Marys Bd. Trustees. Mem. Internat. Assn. Chiefs Police, L.A. County Police Chiefs Assn., Calif. Peace Officers Assn. (Law Enforcement Profl. Achievement award 1992), Long Beach Area C. of C. (bd. dirs.), Rotary. Office: Long Beach Police Dept 400 W Broadway Long Beach CA 90802

LUNA, B. MARTIN, lawyer; b. Waimea, Kauai, Hawaii, July 25, 1938. BA, Emory U., 1960, MA, 1962; LLB, George Washington U., 1967. Bar: Hawaii 1968, U.S. Dist. Ct. Hawaii, U.S. Ct. Appeals (9th cir.), U.S .Supreme Ct. Office: Carlsmith Ball Wichman Case Mukai & Ichiki PO Box 1086 2200 Main St Ste 400 Wailuku HI 96793-1691

LUNA, BARBARA CAROLE, expert witness, accountant, appraiser; b. N.Y.C., July 23, 1950; d. Edwin A. and Irma S. (Schub) Schlang; m. Dennis Rex Luna, Sept. 1, 1974; children: John S., Katherine E. BA, Wellesley Coll., 1971; MS in Applied Math. and Fin. Analysis, Harvard U., 1973, PhD in Applied Math. and Fin. Analysis, 1975. Cert. gen. real estate appraiser. Investment banker Warburg Paribas Becker, L.A., 1975-77; cons./mgr. Price Waterhouse, L.A., 1977-83; sr. mgr. litgation Pannell Kerr Forster, L.A., 1983-86; nat. dir. litigation cons. Kenneth Leventhal & Co., L.A., 1986-88; ptnr. litigation svcs. Coopers & Lybrand, L.A., 1988-93; sr. ptnr. litigation svcs. White, Zuckerman, Warsavsky & Luna, Sherman Oaks, Calif., 1993—. Wellesley scholar, 1971. Mem. AICPA, Assn. Bus. Trial Lawyers (com. on experts), Am. Soc. Appraisers, Assn. Cert. Real Estate Appraisers, Assn. Cert. Fraud Examiners, Assn. Insolvency Accts., Inst. Mgmt. Cons., Calif. Soc. CPAs (steering com. L.A. litigation svcs. com. econ. damages Common Interest Mem. Svcs. com., fraud Common Interest Mem. Svcs. com., bus. valuation Common Interest Mem. Svcs. com.), Am. Bd. Forensic Examiners. Home: 18026 Rodarte Way Encino CA 91316-4370 Office: White Zuckerman Warsavsky & Luna 14455 Ventura Blvd Ste 300 Sherman Oaks CA 91423

LUNA, GREGORY KEVIN, surgeon; b. Oakridge, Oreg., Sept. 26, 1953. AS cum laude, North Idaho Coll., Coeur d'Alene,, 1972; BS summa cum laude, U. Idaho, 1974; MD, U. Colo., 1978; MPH, U. Wash., 1987. Diplomate Am. Bd. Surgery, qualifications insurg. critical care and vascular surgery; lic. physician, Wash., Ont.; cert. ATLS, ATLS instr. Surg. resident U. Wash. Allifiated Hosps., Seattle, 1978-80, 81-84; preventive medicine resident U. Wash., Seattle, 1987, acting instr. dept. surgery, 1984-87, asst. prof., 1987-89, clin. asst. prof., 1991—; vascular fellow U. Ottawa, Ont., Can., 1988-89, asst. prof. dept. surgery, 1989-90; emergency rm. physician Valley Gen. Hosp., Renton, Wash., 1980-81; dir. emergency rm. surg. svcs. Harborview Med. Ctr., Seattle, 1984-89; dir. ICU Valley Med. Ctr., Renton, Wash., 1991—, blood svcs. com., emergency svcs. com., ICU com., 1990—; mem. organ procurement adv. com. N.W. Kidney Ctr., 1988-89; epidemiological cons. Mont. Critical Illness and Trauma Found., 1988—; presenter various orgns., meetings, confs. Contbr. articles to profl. jours., chpts. to books. Fellow ACS (state com. on trauma, vice chmn. edn. 1988—); mem. AAAS, Am. Trauma Soc., King County Med. Soc., Assn. Acad. Surgery, Henry M. Harkins Surg. Soc., Seattle Surg. Soc., North Pacific Surg. Assn., North Pacific Vascular Soc., Pacifice Coast Surg. Assn., Phi Kappa Phi. Home: 104 W 5th Ave Ste 320E Spokane WA 99204-2480 Office: 5th & Browne 350 East Spokane WA 99204

LUND, VICTOR L., retail food company executive; b. Salt Lake City, 1947; married. BA, U. Utah, 1969, MBA, 1972. Audit mgr. Ernst and Whinney, Salt Lake City, 1972-77; sr. v.p. Skaggs Cos. Inc., from 1977; v.p., contr. Am. Stores Co., 1980-83, sr. v.p., contr., from 1983, exec. v.p., co-chief exec. officer, vice-chmn., chief fin. and adminstrv. officer, pres., CEO, dir., 1992-95, now chmn., CEO, dir., 1995—. Office: Am Stores Co PO Box 27447 Salt Lake City UT 84127-0447 also: Am Stores Co 709 E South Temple Salt Lake City UT 84102-1205

LUNDBERG, LARRY THOMAS, business executive; b. Pleasanton, Kans., Mar. 19, 1938; s. William Rex and Lucille Maxine (Rosebrook) L.; m. Sharon Colleen Kirksey, Jan. 26, 1957; children: Julie, John, William. BA,

U. Wash., 1965; postgrad., Wash. State U., 1974-80. Cert. secondary tchr. Clerk G.N.Ry., Wenatchee/Seattle, 1957-65; tchr. Grandview (Wash.) Sch. Dist., 1965-66, South Kitsap Sch. Dist., Port Orchard, Wash., 1966-67; acctg. supr. Weyerheauser Co., Tacoma, 1967-69; pres., chief exec. officer Commander Bd. Wash., Seattle, 1969-70; asst. exec. dir. Wash. State Sch. Dirs., Olympia, 1970-80; gen. mgr., CEO Trout, Inc., Chelan, Wash., 1980—. Author: Negotiations, 1978. Bd. dirs. Traffic Assn., Wenatchee, Wash., 1987—. With U.S. Army, 1957-60. Mem. Internat. Apple Inst. (bd. dirs. 1988—), Chelan, Wash. C. of C. (bd. dirs. 1989—). Office: Trout Inc PO Box 669 Chelan WA 98816-0669*

LUNDBLAD, ROGER LAUREN, research director; b. San Francisco, Oct. 31, 1939; s. Lauren Alfred and Doris Ruth (Peterson) L.; m. Susan Hawly Taylor, Oct. 15, 1966 (div. 1985); children: Christina Susan, Cynthia Karin. BSc, Pacific Luth. U., 1961; PhD, U. Wash., 1965. Rsch. assoc. U. Wash., Seattle, 1965-66, Rockefeller U., N.Y.C., 1966-68; asst. prof. U. N.C., Chapel Hill, 1968-71, assoc. prof., 1971-77, prof. pathology and biochemistry, 1977-91; adj. prof., 1991—; dir. sci. tech. devel. Baxter-Biotech, Duarte, Calif., 1991—; vis. scientist Hyland div. Baxter Healthcare, Glendale, Calif., 1988-89. Author: Chemical Reagents for Protein Modification, 1984, 2d edit., 1990; editor: Chemistry and Biology of Thrombin, 1977, Chemistry and Biology of Heparin, 1980, Techniques in Protein Modification, 1994; editor-in-chief: Biotechnology and Applied Biochemistry, 1996—; contbr. articles to profl. jours. Recipient Career Achievement award U. N.C., 1986. Mem. Am. Soc. Biochem. Molecular Biology, Am. Soc. Microbiology, Am. Heart Assn., Sigma Xi. Office: Baxter Biotech Hyland Divsn 1720 Flower Ave Duarte CA 91010-2923

LUNDE, DOLORES BENITEZ, retired secondary education educator; b. Honolulu, Apr. 12, 1929; d. Frank Molero and Matilda (Francisco) Benitez; m. Nuell Carlton Lunde, July 6, 1957; 1 child, Laurelle. BA, U. Oreg., 1951, postgrad., 1951-52; postgrad., U. So. Calif., L.A., 1953-54, Colo. State U., 1957-58, Calif. State U., Fullerton, 1967-68. Cert. gen. secondary tchr., Calif.; cert. lang. devel. specialist. Tchr. Brawley (Calif.) Union High Sch., 1952-55; tchr. Fullerton (Calif.) Union High Sch. Dist., 1955-73; tchrs. aide Placentia (Calif.) Unified Sch. Dist., 1983-85; tchr. continuing edn. Fullerton Union High Sch. Dist., 1985-91; tchr. Fullerton Sch. Dist., 1988, Fullerton Union H.S. Dist., 1989-94; presenter regional and state convs., so. Calif., 1986-88. Innovator tests, teaching tools, audio-visual aids. Vol. Luth. Social Svcs., Fullerton, 1981-82, Messiah Luth., Yorba Linda, Calif., 1981-88, 91—. Recipient Tchr. of Yr. award Fullerton Union High Sch. Dist., 1989. Mem. NEA, AAUW (life, bull. editor 1979-80, corr. sec. 1981-83, program v.p. 1983-84, gift honoree Fullerton br. 1985), Calif. State Tchrs. Assn., Fullerton Secondary Tchrs. Assn., Internat. Club/Spanish Club (advisor La Habra, Calif. 1965-72), Tchrs. English to Speakers Other Langs., Calif. Assn. Tchrs. English to Speakers Other Langs. Home: 4872 Ohio St Yorba Linda CA 92886-2713

LUNDE, DONALD THEODORE, physician; b. Milw., Mar. 2, 1937; m. Marilynn Krick; children: Montgomery, Christopher, Glenn, Evan, Bret. BA with distinction, Stanford U., 1958, MA in Psychology, 1964, MD, 1966. Diplomate Nat. Bd. Med. Examiners. Ward psychologist Palo Alto (Calif.) VA Hosp., 1965-66, chief resident in psychiatry, 1969-70, assoc. chief tng. and research sect., 1970-72, acting chief tng. and research sect., 1971-72; intern in internal medicine Palo Alto/Stanford Hosp., 1966-67; resident in psychiatry Stanford (Calif.) U. Sch. Medicine, 1967-69, instr. psychiatry, 1969-70, asst. prof. psychiatry, 1970-75, dir. med. sch. edn. in psychiatry, 1971-74, clin. assoc. prof. psychiatry, 1978-89, clin. prof. psychiatry, 1989—; lectr. Law Sch. Stanford U., 1971-81; staff physician Atascadero (Calif.) State Hosp., 1968. Author books and articles in field. Served with USN, 1958-61. Fellow Am. Psychiat. Assn., Am. Coll. Forensic Psychiatry; mem. No. Calif. Psychiat. Soc., Phi Beta Kappa, Alpha Omega Alpha. Office: Stanford U 900 Welch Rd Ste 400 Palo Alto CA 94304-1804

LUNDEEN, RONALD ARTHUR, theology educator; b. St. Paul, Sept. 17, 1943; s. Arthur Olaf and Marilynn Barbara Lundeen; m. Linda Kalmoe; children: Aaron, Nathan, Joel, Rachel, Margo, Karissa. BA, Luther Coll., Decorah, Iowa, 1965; MDiv, Luther Theol. Sem., St. Paul, 1969; DMin, San Francisco Theol. Sem., 1979. Cert. fund raising exec. ACFRE. Pastor Grace Luth. Ch., Duluth, Minn., 1969-71, Messiah Luth. Ch., Mankato, Minn., 1971-74; dir. planned giving Luther Coll., 1974-77; pastor Advent Luther Ch., Des Moines, 1977-80; dir. devel. Luther Sem., 1980-83; pastor Messiah Luth. Ch., Fargo, N.D., 1983-85; dir. of major gifts L.C.A., N.Y.C., 1983-87; pres. N.W. Devel., St. Paul, 1986-91; v.p. Luth. Social Svcs. of New Eng., Natick, Mass., 1991-96; v.p. for advancement San Francisco Theol. Sem., San Anselmo, Calif., 1996—; Pres. Northwest Devel. Counselors, Inc., St. Paul, 1985-91. Author: Stewardship and Fiscal Responsibility, 1979. Bd. dirs. Planned Parenthood, Minn., 1970-75, Luth. Youth Found., Mpls., 1985—, Fellowship, Inc., Phoenix, 1990-93. Mem. Rotary. Home: 54 Aaron Dr Novato CA 94949-5497 Office: SFTS 2 Kensington San Anselmo CA 94960

LUNDEEN, SAMUEL EDWARD, elementary education educator; b. Crookston, Minn., Feb. 16, 1944; s. Arthur Gehard and Agatha Margit (Hamre) L.; m. Angela F. Fitzhugh, Jan. 11, 1968; children: Gairdt, Bjorn. BA, Humboldt State U., 1968, postgrad., 1971, 80. Cert. elem. tchr., Calif. Tchr. mid. sch. Escambia County Pub. Schs., Pensacola, Fla., 1969-70; tchr. elem. sch. Arcata (Calif.) Elem. Sch. Dist., 1971—; house painter, Arcata, 1970-71; mem. sch. site coun., Arcata, 1989-93. With USN, 1967-69. Mem. Sierra Club, Greenpeace, Nature Conservancy, Beau Pre Golf Club. Democrat. Lutheran/Unity. Home: PO Box 2055 Trinidad CA 95570-2055

LUNDERVILLE, GERALD PAUL, bilingual education educator; b. Springfield, Mass., Feb. 22, 1941; s. Leon Albert and Florence Marion (Jolivette) L.; m. Martha Ann Sumner, Mar. 26, 1966 (div. Aug. 1971); m. Bony Lek, June 30, 1984. BA cum laude, U. N.H., 1963; MA, Middlebury Coll., 1969, U. Rochester, 1973, Calif. State U., Long Beach, 1994. Instr. Spanish Berwick Acad., South Berwick, Maine, 1963-64; tchr. French, Spanish Barnstable High Sch., Hyannis, Mass., 1967-68; instr. Spanish Cape Cod Community Coll., West Barnstable, Mass., 1968-71; tchr. French, Spanish Stevens High Sch. Annex, Claremont, N.H., 1973-74; tchr. English Centro de Estudios Norteamericanos, Valencia, Spain, 1974-75; dept. head fgn. langs. Merrimack (N.H.) High Sch., 1975-80; tchr. Spanish El Camino Coll., Torrance, Calif., 1980-85; tchr. ESL Wilson High Sch., Long Beach, Calif., 1980—, dept. head ESL, 1987-88, tchr. bilingual social studies/Spanish, 1992—. Author: 20th Century Baseball Trivia, 1992; contbr. articles to Am. Atheist Mag. Active Long Beach Area Citizens Peace, 1982—, Animal Protection Inst. Am., Sacramento., 1983—. Served with U.S. Army, 1964-67, Vietnam. Mem. NEA, ACLU, NOW, Modern and Classical Lang. Assn. So. Calif., Tchrs. of English as a 2d Lang., Soc. for Preservation of English Lang. and Lit., VERBATIM, Nat. Humane Edn. Soc., Merrimack Tchrs. Assn. (sec. 1977-80), Lambda Pi. Home: 1740 E Washington St Long Beach CA 90805-5535

LUNDGREN, LEONARD, III, retired secondary education educator; b. San Francisco, June 22, 1933; s. Leonard II and Betty (Bosold) L.; m. Jane Gates, June 12, 1976. AA, City Coll. San Francisco, 1952; AB, San Francisco State U., 1954, MA, 1958, postgrad., 1958-71. Cert. tchr., Calif. Phys. edn. tchr., athletic coach Pelton Jr. High Sch., San Francisco, 1958-59; social studies tchr., dept. chair, phys. edn. tchr., athletic coach Luther Burbank Jr. High Sch., San Francisco, 1959-78; history, govt. econs., geography tchr. George Washington High Sch., San Francisco, 1978-93; water safety instr. ARC, San Francisco, 1946-61; mem. Calif. Quality Teaching Ctr. Conf. Bd., 1965-67. Author: Guide for Films and Filmstrips, 1966, Teacher's Handbook for Social Studies, 1966, Guide for Minority Studies, 1968. V.p. Lakeside Property Owners Assn., San Francisco, 1986-88, legis. advocate, 1988-95; v.p. West of Twin Peaks Coun., San Francisco, 1986-87; pub. affairs polit. econ. cons., Calif., 1993—. With USN, 1954-56. Fulbright scholar, Greece, 1963; recipient Svc. Pin, ARC, 1961. Mem. NEA (life, del. 1970, 72-76), Calif. Tchrs. Assn. (state coun. rep. 1963-74), Nat. Coun. Social Studies, Calif. Coun. Social Studies (v.p. San Francisco chpt. 1969-70), San Francisco Classroom Tchrs. Assn. (pres. 1972-73, Gavel award 1973), PTA (sch. v.p. 1980-81), Calif. Ret. Tchrs. Assn. (life, legislation chmn. San Francisco divsn. 1995—), Am. Assn. Ret. Persons (cmty. coord. San Francisco 1996—), San Francisco State U. Alumni Assn. (life, treas. 1959), Calif. Assn. Health, Phys. Edn., Recreation and Dance (life, treas. San Francisco chpt. 1959-60), Nat. Geog. Soc. (life), Phi Delta Kappa (life, pres. chpt. 1965-66). *A career in education for me is my life from learning to teaching over and over again. History, government, geography and economics are my major subjects. World travel gives me the chance to see the places I studied and taught.*

LUNDGREN, SUSAN ELAINE, counselor, educator; b. Martinez, Calif., May 31, 1949; d. Elmer Alfred and Shirley (Bright) L.; 1 child, Alicia Hadiya. AA, Diablo Valley Coll., 1969; BA in English, San Francisco State U., 1971, MA in Counseling, 1975; EdD, U. San Francisco, 1983; cert. in gen. mgmt., John F. Kennedy U., 1988. Instr., counselor Diablo Valley Coll., Pleasant Hill, Calif., 1976—, coordinator, 1986-90, women's ctr. faculty dir., 1983-85; adj. prof. grad. career devel. John f. Kennedy U., Orinda, Calif., 1982—. Sec., bd. dirs. Rape Crisis Ctr., Concord, Calif., 1985. Named participant in leadership devel. inst. AAUW and Nat. Assn. Community Colls., 1985. Mem. Eureka Consortium (conf. speaker 1984, 86). Home: 3738 Victor Ave Oakland CA 94619-1533 Office: Diablo Valley Coll 321 Golf Club Rd Pleasant Hill CA 94523-1529

LUNDGREN, SUSAN ELIZABETH, information technology consultant, musician; b. Tacoma, June 21, 1964; d. Lawrence L. and Diane E. Lundgren. BS in Math., U. Wash., 1988; postgrad., U. Alaska, 1995—. Software tester Logicon/RDA, Tacoma, 1988, software engr., 1989, project mgr., 1990-92; software engr. ctg-Alaska, Anchorage, 1992-93, sr. software engr., 1993—, project leader, 1993—, instr., 1994, systems analyst, 1996—. Mem. IEEE, Assn. for Computing Machinery.

LUNDIN, JOHN E., lawyer; b. Mpls., May 9, 1940. BA, U. Ariz., 1962, JD with distinction, 1967. Bar: Ariz. 1967, U.S. Supreme Ct. 1977. Mem. Gallagher & Kennedy, Phoenix, Ariz.; judge pro tem Ariz. Ct. Appeals, 1984-85, 91. With U.S. Army, 1963-65. Fellow Ariz. Bar Found. (dir. ex officio 1989—); mem. State Bar Ariz. (bd. govs. 1985—, v.p. 1991-92), Maricopa County Bar Assn. (bd. dirs. 1977-85, pres. 1984-85), Ariz. Commn. on Judicial Performance Rev. (chair 1995—), Phi Delta Phi. Office: Gallagher & Kennedy 2600 N Central Ave Phoenix AZ 85004-3050

LUNDSTROM, MARJIE, newspaper editor. Grad., U. Nebr. Columnist, editor, nat. corr. The Denver Post, 1981-89; with The Sacramento Bee, 1989-90, 91—; nat. corr. Gannett News Svc., Washington, 1990-91. Recipient Pulitzer Prize for nat. reporting, 1991. Office: The Sacramento Bee 2100 Q St PO Box 15779 Sacramento CA 95852

LUNDSTROM, MARY MEYER, naval contracts technician, educator; b. Hollywood, Calif., June 23, 1948; d. Archibald deNorville and Ivy Kate (Whitworth) Meyer; 1 child, Tara Carina. BA in Art, San Diego State U., 1971. Lic. real estate salesperson, Calif. Draftsman Genge Industries, Ridgecrest, Calif., 1967-68; draftsman Naval Weapons Ctr., China Lake, Calif., 1969, illustrator, 1970; substitute tchr. Albuquerque Pub. Schs., 1971-72, Kern County High Sch. Dist., China Lake, 1972-74; real estate salesperson Coldwell Banker Best Realty, Ridgecrest, 1974-86; art instr. Cerro Coso C.C., Ridgecrest, 1986-91; art curator Maturango Mus., Ridgecrest, 1987-95; mus. store mgr. Matruango Mus., Ridgecrest, 1993-95; in contracts Naval Air Warfare Ctr., China Lake, Calif., 1995—; freelance artist, 1970—. Juror Lancaster Art Mus. Mixed Media Show, 1990, Millie Funk Western Art Show, 1991, Bakersfield Coll. Mixed Media Open Art Show. Mem. AAUW (past pres., name grant award 1987), Enamel Guild West, Enamelist Soc., Inst. Mus. Svcs. (grant reviewer), Nat. Contract Mgrs. Assn., Rotary, Sister City Assn. Home: 731 W Howell Ave Ridgecrest CA 93555-3445 Office: Naval Air Warfare Ctr China Lake Nwc CA 93555

LUNDY, GILBERT MOULTON, JR., computer science educator; b. New Orleans, Sept. 29, 1954; s. Gilbert Moulton and Loretta Maureen (Taylor) L.; m. Yong Ae Yi, Feb. 18, 1978 (div. 1988); children: Benjamin Lee, Miriam Yong. BA in Math., Tex. A&M U., 1976; MS in Computer Sci., U. Tex., Dallas, 1983; PhD in Computer Sci., Ga. Inst. Tech., 1988. Software engr. E-Systems, Inc., Dallas, 1981-84; rsch. asst. Ga. Inst. Tech., Atlanta, 1984-88; assoc. prof. computer sci. U.S. Naval Postgrad. Sch., Monterey, Calif., 1988—. Contbr. articles on computer and telecom. networks to sci. jours. 1st lt. U.S. Army, 1977-81. Mem. IEEE, Assn. for Computing Machinery. Office: US Naval Postgrad Sch Dept Computer Sci Code CS Monterey CA 93943

LUNGREN, DANIEL EDWARD, state attorney general; b. Long Beach, Calif., Sept. 22, 1946; s. John Charles and Lorain Kathleen (Youngberg) L.; m. Barbara Kolls, Aug. 2, 1969; children: Jeffrey Edward, Kelly Christine, Kathleen Marie. A.B. cum laude, Notre Dame U., 1968; postgrad., U. So. Calif. Law Sch., 1968-69; J.D., Georgetown U., 1971. Bar: Calif. 1972. Staff asst. Sen. George Murphy, Sen. William Brock, 1969-71; spl. asst. to co-chmn. Rep. Nat. Com., dir. spl. programs, 1971-72; assoc., selected as ptnr. Ball, Hunt, Hart, Brown & Baerwitz, Long Beach, 1973-78; mem. 96th-97th Congresses from 34th, 98th-100th Congresses from 42d Calif. Dist., 1979-1989, Rep. State Cen. Com. Calif., 1974-89; ptnr. Diepenbrock, Wulff, Plant & Hannegan, Sacramento, 1989-90; atty. gen. State of Calif., Sacramento, 1991—. Bd. dirs. Long Beach chpt. ARC, Boy's Club, 1976-88; committeeman Rep. Nat. Com., Calif., 1988-96. Recipient Good Samaritan award Los Angeles Council Mormon Chs., 1976. Republican. Roman Catholic. Office: Office of the Atty Gen 1300 I St Sacramento CA 95814-2913

LUNINE, JONATHAN IRVING, planetary scientist, educator; b. N.Y.C., June 26, 1959. BS magna cum laude, U. Rochester, 1980; MS, Calif. Inst. Tech., 1983, PhD, 1985. Rsch. assoc. U. Ariz., Tucson, 1984-86, asst. prof. planetary scis., 1986-90; vis. asst. prof. UCLA, 1986, assoc. prof., 1990-95, prof., 1995—, faculty mem. program in applied math., 1992—; interdisciplinary scientist on joint U.S.-European Cassini mission to Saturn; mem. com. planetary and lunar exploration space sci. bd. NAS, 1986-90; chmn. NASA Solar Sys. Exploration subcom., 1990-95; chmn. Pluto Express Sci. Definition Team, 1995. Contbr. articles to profl. jours.; co-editor: Protostars and Planets III, 1993. Mem. Internat. Mars Exploration Adv. Panel NASA, 1993-94, space sci. adv. com., 1990-95. Recipient Cospar Zeldovich prize Soviet Intercosmos and Inst. for Space Rsch., 1990. 1 of the 50 emerging leaders Time Mag., 1994; Co-Recipient James B. Macelwane Young Investigator medal Am. Geophysical Union, 1995. Fellow Am. Geophys. Union (Macelwane medal 1995); mem. Am. Astron. Soc. (Harold C. Urey prize 1988), Internat. Acad. Astronautics (corr. mem.), Internat. Coun. Sci. Unions, Sigma Xi. Office: U Ariz Dept Planetary Scis PO Box 210092 Lunar & Planetary Lab Tucson AZ 85721-0092

LUNSFORD, JACK WILLIAM, government relations director; b. Phoenix, Oct. 13, 1950; s. Kenneth William and Barbara Jean (Wiggett) L.; m. Sandra Faye Johnson Noyes, June 7, 1975 (div. Mar. 1984); 1 child, Amber Dyan Lunsford; m. Anna Denise Villa, Apr. 20, 1985; children: Kelsey Lynn, Erin Michelle. BFA, So. Meth. U., 1972. Asst. mgr. First Nat. Bank Ariz., Phoenix, Flagstaff, Williams, 1972-77; sports announcer Sta. KCLS-AM-FM, Flagstaff, 1977-80; gen. mgr. Sta. KBWA-AM, Williams, 1977-80; asst. mgr. First Interstate Bank, Phoenix, 1980-81; account exec. Mountain Bell and AT&T, Phoenix, 1981-84; dir. gov. rels. Maricopa Cmty. Colls., Phoenix, 1984—; legis. consulting Ariz. Assn. Clks. Superior Ct., Phoenix, 1993. County Assessor Coconino County, Flagstaff, 1977-80; chmn. Ariz. Tax Conf., 1978; mem. Ariz. State Coun. Vocat. Edn., Phoenix, 1986-96; congl. fellow Office U.S. Senator Dennis DeConcini, Washington, 1986; founding pres. Western Maricopa Coalition, Phoenix, Glendale, Ariz., 1988-91; Chair Ariz. Commn. Postsecondary Edn., Phoenix, 1989—; bd. dirs. Kids Voting Ariz., Phoenix, 1993-96, Ariz. Cultural Devel., Phoenix, 1996—; mem. state rels. taskforce Coun. Advancement Support Edn., 1996—. Mem. Pub. Affairs Profls. Ariz. (bd. dirs. 1990—, pres.). Office: Maricope Cmty Colls 2411 W 14th St Tempe AZ 85281

LUPPER, EDWARD, artist; b. Trenton, N.J., Jan. 4, 1936; s. Julius Lupper and Irene Rich. Studied with, Wesley Lea, Frenchtown, N.J., 1952-54; student, Trenton Jr. Coll., 1953, Parsons Sch. Design, 1958, San Francisco Art Inst., 1959-60, San Francisco State Coll., 1960-61. One man shows include Naples (Fla.) Art Gallery, 1986-97; exhibited in group shows at Balt. Mus. Art, 1955, Tucson Art Ctr., San Francisco Mus. of Art, Am. Embassy, Belgium, 1977-78, Ft. Worth Art Ctr.; artist Sunrise Pub. Co., 1988—, Gt. Am. Puzzle co., 1994—; represented in collections Teddy Bear Mus., Naples, L.A. Maritime Mus.; represented in pvt. and corp. collections in U.S., Europe, Asia, Australia, U.K. and Can. With USN, 1954-57. Huntington Hartford fellow, 1964. Mem. San Francisco Pub. Health Found., San Francisco Nat. Wildlife Fedn. (donor 1993-94). Democrat. Studio: 1255 Pacific Ave San Francisco CA 94109-2715

LURVEY, IRA HAROLD, lawyer; b. Chgo., Apr. 6, 1935; s. Louis and Faye (Grey) L.; m. Barbara Ann Sirvint, June 24, 1962; children: Nathana, Lawrence, Jennifer, Jonathan, David, Robert. BS, U. Ill., 1956; MS, Northwestern U., 1961; JD, U. Calif., Berkeley, 1965. Bar: Calif. 1965, Nev. 1966, U.S. Dist. Ct. (cen. dist.) Calif. 1966, U.S. Tax Ct. 1966, U.S. Ct. Appeals (9th cir.) 1966, U.S. Supreme Ct. 1975. Law clk. to hon. justices Nev. Supreme Ct., Carson City, 1965-66; from assoc. to ptnr. Pacht, Ross, Warne, Bernhard & Sears, Inc., 1966-84; predecessor firm Shea & Gould, Los Angeles; founding ptnr. Lurvey & Shapiro, Los Angeles, 1984—; lectr. legal edn. programs; mem. Chief Justice's Commns. on Ct. Reform, Weighted Caseloads; mediator family law L.A. Supreior Ct. Editor Community Property Jour., 1979-80, Primary Consultant CFL 2d, 1994; columnist Calif. Family Law Monthly; contbr. articles to profl. jours. Former chmn. L.A. Jr. Arts Ctr.; past pres. Cheviot Hills Homeowners Assn.; exec. v.p., counsel Hillel Acad. Sch., Beverly Hills, Calif., 1977—. With U.S. Army, 1957-58. Fellow Am. Acad. Matrimonial Lawyers (pres. So. Calif. chpt. 1991-92, mem. nat. bd. govs. 1992-94), Internat. Acad. Matrimonial Lawyers; mem. ABA (sec. 1993-94, vice-chair 1994-95, chair family law sect. 1996— governing coun. 1986—, fin. officer 1991-92, chmn. support com., chmn. CLE, chmn. policy and issues com., vice chmn. com. arbitration and mediation, bd. of editors Family Adv. mag.), Calif. Bar Assn. (editor jour. 1982-85, chmn. family law sect. 1986-87, exec. com. family law sect. 1982-88, specialization adv. bd. family law 1979-82), L.A. County Bar Assn. (chmn. family law sect. 1981-82, exec. com. family law 1989-92), Beverly Hills Bar Assn. (chmn. family law sect. 1976-77). Home: 2729 Motor Ave Los Angeles CA 90064-3441 Office: Lurvey & Shapiro Ste 1550 2121 Avenue Of The Stars Los Angeles CA 90067-5010

LUSBY, GRACE IRENE, infection control nurse practitioner; b. Huntington Park, Calif., Aug. 20, 1935; d. Fletcher Homer and Charlotte Ione (Hayden) L. BS in Nursing, U. Calif., San Francisco, 1964, MS, 1968; cert. program in epidemiology, U. Calif., San Diego, 1981. RN, pub. health nurse, psychiat. nurse. Staff nurse, head nurse cancer rsch. unit U. Calif., San Francisco, 1964-66; pvt. duty nurse open heart surgery Profl. Registry, San Francisco, 1966-68; infection control coord. San Francisco Gen. Hosp., 1969-92; infection control cons. Oakland, Calif., 1992—; infection control rep. Calif. Task Force on AIDS, Sacramento, 1983-87, U.S. AIDS Task Force, San Francisco, 1983-92; co-establisher 1st infection control program for AIDS, San Francisco Gen. Hosp., 1983; mem. infection control-adv. coms. Svc. Employees Internat. Union, Calif. Nurses Assn., Mayor's Homeless Com., CAL-OSHA, also others, San Francisco, 1985—; infection control cons. emergency, home care, skill nursing, psychiatry, San Francisco, 1985—. Contbr. chpts. to books. Recipient Founder's award U. Calif.-San Francisco AIDS/ARC Update, 1988. Mem. Assn. Practitioners Infection Control (past treas., rec. sec., chmn. AIDS resource group), Women's AIDS Network (charter), PEO (rec. sec., corr. sec.), Sigma Theta Tau. Home and Office: 5966 Chabolyn Ter Oakland CA 94618-1914

LUSH, PAMELA GRACE MEINE, international publishing company executive; b. Wellsboro, Pa., Apr. 1, 1961; d. Stanley Gale and Karen (Kohler) L. BA, Colo. State U., 1983. Traffic coord. Leo Burnett Advt., Chgo., 1983-85; sr. account exec. Cardiff Pub., Englewood, Colo., 1985-88; pres. PGL Assocs., Denver, 1988-90; v.p. Interfax-US, Denver, 1991-92; pres. DGL Internat. Pub., Denver, 1990-93, DGL Publs., Denver, 1990-93. Editor, pub.: The Child Care Directory, 1991; pub.: The Family Resource Guide, 1992, The Petroleum Tech. Resource Guide, 1992, The Agricultural Technical Resource Guide, 1992, The Mining/Environmental Technical Resource Guide, 1992. Mem. Soviet Task Force Under Gov. Roy Romer, Denver, 1990-92, Internat. Gateway Com., Denver, 1990-92. Named nominee for Pulitzer Prize for Internat. Reporting, 1991, Pulitzer Prize for Meritorious Pub. Svc., 1991. Presbyterian.

LUSKY, JOHN A., lawyer; b. Louisville, Oct. 30, 1951. BA, Harvard U., 1973; JD, Stanford U., 1977. Bar: Oreg. 1977. Ptnr. Miller, Nash, Wiener, Hager & Carlsen, Portland, Oreg. Mem. Oreg. State Bar. Office: Miller Nash Wiener Hager & Carlsen 111 SW 5th Ave Portland OR 97204-3699

LUSSER, CAROLE ANNE, nurse; b. Amarillo, Tex., Oct. 12, 1952; d. James Carroll and Alma Doris Loretta (Henderson) Killman; m. Michael Kevin O'Meara, July 31, 1976 (div. Apr. 1981); 1 child, Jennifer beth; m. René Joseph Lusser, July 27, 1996. Student, Okla. State U., 1971-72, 73-75; Diploma in Nursing, St. Anthony Hosp. Sch. Nursing, Oklahoma City, 1977. RN, Okla.; CCRN, AACN. Staff nurse San Juan County Hosp., Monticello, Utah, 1986-87, St. Anthony Hosp., Oklahoma City, 1977-89; staff nurse ICU St. John's Hosp., Jackson, Wyo., 1989-96; staff nurse Teton Valley Hosp. Home Health Care, Driggs, Idaho, 1996—; ACLS instr. Am. Heart Assn., Jackson, 1992-96. Vol. Teton Valley C. of C., 1996, Teton Valley Hosp. Health Fair, 1996. Mem. ACCN. Home: 111 Teton Ave Driggs ID 83422

LUST, PETER, JR., microwave engineer, consultant; b. Montreal, Que., Can., Apr. 21, 1960; came to U.S., 1975, naturalized, 1987; s. Peter Clark and Evelyn (Heymanson) L.; Gloria Ruth Bingle, Apr. 5, 1985; children: Peter Alexander III, Elizabeth Ann, Matthew Eric. Student, Lowry Tech. Tng. Ctr., Community Coll. A.F., Albuquerque, USAF Acad.; BSEE, Pacific Western U., 1990. Computer meterologist Electro Rent, Burbank, Calif., 1982-84; microwave engr., program mgr. satellite and space shuttle communications systems Transco Products, Camarillo, Calif., 1984-90, internat. tech. mktg. mgr., 1990-93; prin. Electronic Note Co., Port Hueneme, Calif., 1984—; rep. ANT, Teledix, Germany, Spar Space Sys., Can., Bosch Telecom. With USAF, 1979-82. Recipient Technol. award USAF, 1980, Discovery award NASA, 1987, Internat. Leaders in Achievement award, Cambridge. Mem. Assn. Old Crows, Channel Islands Health Club. Office: Electronic Note Co 300 E Esplanade Dr Ste 900 Oxnard CA 93030-1251

LUSTGARTEN, CELIA SOPHIE, freelance consultant, writer; b. N.Y.C., Oct. 24, 1941; d. Benjamin and Sarah Goldie (Marcus) L. Contbr. short stories and poetry to lit. publs., including Shameless Hussy Rev., Cow in Road, Egad!, Cacanadada Rev., Grasslands Rev., New Can. Rev., Herspectives, Rhythm-and-Rhyme, Spokes, T.O.P.S. 10 Poetry mag. Recipient 1st prize for short story Alt. Realities Soc. and Imaginative Fiction Soc., Victoria, B.C., Can., 1986. Mem. Poets and Writers. Home: 317 3d Ave San Francisco CA 94118

LUSTICA, KATHERINE GRACE, publisher, artist, marketing consultant; b. Bristol, Pa., Nov. 20, 1958; d. Thomas Lustica and Elizabeth Delores (Moyer) De Groat. Student, Hussian Sch. Art, Phila., 1976-78, Rider Coll., 1980-82, U. Utah, 1993—. Comml. artist, illustrator Bucks County Courier Times Newspapers, Levittown, Pa., 1978-82; account exec. Trenton (N.J.) Times Newspapers, 1982-84; promotions and account exec. Diversified Suburban Newspapers, Murray (Utah) Printing, 1984-88; pub. Barclays Ltd. Salt Lake City, 1988—; cover artists, illustrator Accent mag., Bristol, 1978-82; freelance artist, 1978—; advt. and creative cons. Everett & Winthrop Products Group, Salt Lake City, 1988-90, Multi Techs. Internat., Salt Lake City, 1990-91. Newcombe scholar, 1981-82. Mem. Golden Key. Presbyterian. Office: 4638 S Stratton Dr Salt Lake City UT 84117-5558

LUTALI, A. P., governor of American Samoa; b. Aunu'u, American Samoa, Dec. 24, 1919; married. Gov. Am. Samoa, 1985-89, 93—; spkr. of the House Senate, Am. Samoa, 1956-57, pres., 1965-67, v.p., 1988—; chair Constnl. Conv., 1966. Mem. Am. Samoa Bar Assn. (founder 1972). Office: Governor's Office Pago Pago AS 96799

LUTHER, AMANDA LISA, producer; b. La Mesa, Calif., Apr. 27, 1959; d. Edward Earl Jr. and Hilda (Bender) Marsh; m. Jeffrey Henry Luther, June 18, 1994; 1 child, April Wilhelmina. Student, UCLA, 1977-79; BA in Fine Arts, Columbia Coll., 1981. Freelance prodn. mgr. L.A., 1980-90; Coordinating prodr. Telepictures, Burbank, Calif., 1991-94, Saban Entertainment,

Valencia, Calif., 1995—. Mem. Earth Comms. Office. Home: 37402 Harrow Ct Palmdale CA 93550

LUTHER, ROBERT CHESTER, psychiatrist, consultant; b. Palo Alto, Calif., July 9, 1934; s. Chester Francis and Helen Eva (Yeomans) L.; m. Norma Gene Juenemann, June 18, 1960; children: Douglas Robert, Andrew Donald, David Allen. BS, Whitman Coll., 1955; MD, U. Oreg. Med. Sch., 1959. Psychiat. resident, fellow Menninger Sch. Psychiatry, Topeka, Kans., 1960-62, 64-65; pvt. practice psychiatry Psychiat. Assocs., Medford, Oreg., 1965-94; mem. psychiat. dept. staff Rogue Valley Med. Ctr., Medford, 1965-97, bd. dirs., 1986-93; bd. dirs. So. Oreg. Leadershp Coun., Medford, 1992—, Prime Care IPA, Medford, 1993-97; lectr. in psychiatry Kans. U. Med. Ctr., 1961-65; clin. instr. psychiatry U. Oreg. Med. Sch., 1967-77, clin. asst. prof. psychiatry, 1977—; psychiat. cons. Ft. Vannoy Job Corps Ctr., 1965-68, Josephine County Mental Health Clinic, 1965-74; med. dir. methadone program Jackson County Mental Health Svcs., 1970-82, med. svcs. cons., 1995—. Mem. adv. com. Medford Sch. Dist., 1970-79; mem. So. Oreg. steering com. Re-Elect Mark Hatfield Com., 1990; bd. dirs. Medford Babe Ruth Baseball, 1976-78; pres. So. Oreg. Tennis Club, Medford, 1981-82; v.p. U. Oreg. Med. Sch. Alumni Assn., 1973-74; mem. citizen adv. bd. So. Oreg. State Coll., 1990—, pres., 1995-96; chmn. Jackson County Bd. Health, 1974-76, 80-82; treas. Jackson County Rep. Ctrl. Com., 1994—. Capt. U.S. Army, 1962-64. Mem. Am. Psychiat. Assn., Oreg. Med. Assn. (bd. med. examiners liaison com. 1991—), ho. dels. 1970-72, Oreg. Psychiat. Assn. (mem. legis. com. 1991—, exec. coun. 1990-93), Jackson County Med. Soc. (pres. 1974), Medford Rotary Club (pres. 1976-77), Rogue Valley Country Club. Congregationalist. Home: 2241 Dellwood Ave Medford OR 97504-8012

LUTHY, JOHN FREDERICK, management consultant; b. Kansas City, Mo., Dec. 12, 1947; s. Walter Frederick Luthy and Loraine Florence Tramill; children: Roslyn, Bryan, John Paul. BA, Baker U., 1969; MS, U. Mo., 1973; MPA, Boise State U., 1978; EdD, U. Idaho, 1991. Mgr. State Com. Disease Edn., Topeka, 1973; dir. Divsn. Health Edn., Johnson County, Kans., 1973-75; state dir. Bur. Health Edn., Boise, Idaho, 1975-80; dir. Gen. Svcs. Adminstrn., Boise, 1980-84; dir. bus. devel. Morrison Knudsen Tech. Inc., Boise, 1984-86; pres. The Futures Corp., Boise, 1986—; pres. Exec. Mgmt. Devel. Inst., Boise, 1991—; del. to China People to People, 1994. Author: (manual) Grantsmanship--A Time of Plenty, 1988; contbr. articles to profl. jours. Staff sgt. USAR, 1969-75. Recipient Nat. Early Career award APHA, 1978; named one of Outstanding Young Men of Am., U.S. Jaycees, 1977. Mem. ASTD, Am. Mgmt. Assn., U.S. Powerlifting Fedn. (exec. bd. dirs., regional chmn. 1981-86), Phi Delta Kappa. Office: The Futures Corp 1109 Main St Ste 299A Boise ID 83702-5642

LUTIN, DAVID LOUIS, real estate development and finance consultant; b. East Hartford, Conn., Apr. 18, 1919; s. Solomon and Esther (Newman) L.; A.B., Ohio No. U., 1946; M.B.A., Syracuse U., 1949; m. Dorothy Marmor, Dec. 3, 1944; children—Gary, Marnie (Mrs. George Wittig). Housing economist and field rep. HHFA, Washington, 1950-57; dir. urban renewal City of Brookline, Mass., 1957-58; cons. on urban renewal and housing Com. for Econ. Devel., N.Y.C., 1958-59; propr. David L. Lutin Assocs., real estate devel. and fin. cons., Rye, N.Y., 1959-73, Phoenix, 75—; v.p. real estate and mortgages Am. Bank and Trust Co., N.Y.C., 1973-75. Research assoc. Albert Farwell Bemis Found., M.I.T., 1951-52. Served to capt. AUS, 1942-46. Decorated Purple Heart. Mem. Am. Econ. Assn., Nat. Planning Assn., Mortgage Bankers Assn., Urban Land Inst., Am. Planning Assn., Am. Statis. Assn., Nat. Assn. Home Builders. Contbr. articles and reports on econs., housing and urban devel. to profl. jours. Home and Office: 11419 N Century Ln Scottsdale AZ 85254-4827

LUTRIN, CARL EDWARD, political science educator; b. Far Rockaway, N.Y., June 11, 1940; s. Louis and Mildred S. (Fertel) L.; m. Patricia Lutrin, Aug. 24, 1982; 1 child, Lawren. BA, Adelphi U., 1962; MS, U. Wis., 1965; PhD, U. Mo., 1971. Prof. polit. sci. Calif. Poly. Inst., San Luis Obispo, Calif., 1970—. Author: American Public Administration, 1976, 4th edit., 1995. Mem. Am. Polit. Sci. Assn., Am. Soc. Pub. Adminstrn., Western Polit. Sci. Assn. Democrat. Jewish. Home: 74 Rafael Way San Luis Obispo CA 93405-1524 Office: Calif Poly State U Dept Polit Sci San Luis Obispo CA 93407

LUTTRELL, ERIC MARTIN, oil company executive; b. Wheeling, W.Va., May 12, 1941; s. Lauren Robert and Gertrude Dorothy (Olson) L.; m. Janet Marie Quigg, June 8, 1963; children: Dawn Alexandra, Brooke Catherine. BS in Geology, U. Wis., 1963, MS in Geology, 1965; PhD in Geology, Princeton U., 1968. Geologist Texaco Inc., New Orleans, 1968-70; rsch. geologist Texaco Inc., Bellaire, Tex., 1970-75, rsch. supr., 1975-79; exploration mgr. Texaco Inc., New Orleans, 1979-80; divsn. geologist Sohio Petroleum Co., Dallas, 1980-82, exploration mgr., 1986-86; exploration mgr. onshore U.S. BP Exploration, Houston, 1986-89; exploration mgr. L.Am. BP Exploration, London, 1989-91; v.p. exploration BP Exploration, Anchorage, 1991—. Bd. dirs., v.p. United Way of Anchorage, 1992-94; bd. dirs. Performing Arts Ctr., Anchorage, 1994. Mem. Am. Assn. Petroleum Geologists, Geol. Soc. Am. Office: BP Exploration Alaska 900 E Benson Blvd Anchorage AK 99508-4254

LUTZ, JOHN SHAFROTH, lawyer; b. San Francisco, Sept. 10, 1943; s. Frederick Henry and Helena Morrison (Shafroth) L.; m. Elizabeth Boschen, Dec. 14, 1968; children: John Shafroth, Victoria. BA, Brown U., 1965; JD, U. Denver, 1971. Bar: Colo. 1971, U.S. Dist. Ct. Colo. 1971, U.S. Ct. Appeals (2d cir.) 1975, D.C. 1976, U.S. Supreme Ct. 1976, U.S. Dist. Ct. (so. dist.) N.Y. 1977, U.S. Tax Ct. 1977, U.S. Ct. Appeals (10th cir.) 1979, N.Y. 1984, U.S. Ct. Appeals (9th cir.) 1990, U.S. Dist. Ct. (no. dist.) Calif. 1993. Trial atty. Denver regional office U.S. SEC, 1971-74; spl. atty. organized crime, racketeering sect. U.S. Dept. Justice, So. Dist. N.Y., 1974-77; atty. Kelly, Stansfield and O'Donnell, Denver, 1977-78; gen. counsel Boettcher & Co., Denver, 1978-87, Kelly, Stansfield and O'Donnel, Denver, 1987; spl. counsel, 1987-88, ptnr., 1988-93; of counsel LeBoeuf, Lamb, Greene and Mac Rae, L.L.P., 1993-94, ptnr. 1995—; spkr. on broker, dealer, securities law and arbitration issues to various profl. orgns. Contbr. articles to profl. jours. Bd. dirs. Cherry Creek Improvement Assn., 1980-84, Spalding Rehab. Hosp., 1986-89; chmn., vice-chmn. securities sub sect. Bus. Law Sect. of Colo. Bar, 1990, chmn., 1990-91. Lt. (j.g.), USNR, 1965-67. Mem. ABA, Colo. Bar Assn., Denver Bar Assn., Am. Law Inst., Securities Industry Assn. (state regulations com. 1982-86), Nat. Assn. Securities Dealers, Inc. (nat. arbitration com. 1987-91), St. Nicholas Soc. N.Y.C., Denver Law Club, Denver Country Club, Denver Athletic Club (dir. 1990-93), Rocky Mountain Brown Club (founder, past pres.), Racquet and Tennis Club. Republican. Episcopalian. Office: LeBoeuf Lamb Greene & MacRae LLP 633 17th St Ste 2800 Denver CO 80202-3660

LUTZ, REINHART, English language educator, writer; b. Taipei, Taiwan, Feb. 28, 1960. BA, Free U. Berlin, 1983; MA, U. Calif., Santa Barbara, 1985, PhD, 1991. Asst. prof. U. of the Pacific, Stockton, Calif., 1991-96, assoc. prof. dept. english and film studies, 1996—. Pvt. 1st class German Army, 1979-81, NATO. Mem. MLA, Soc. for Cinema Studies. Office: U Pacific Dept English Stockton CA 95211

LUTZ, WILLIAM LAN, lawyer; b. Chgo., May 18, 1944; s. Raymond Price and Sibyl (McCright) L.; m. Jeanne M. McAlister, Dec. 27, 1969; children: William Lan, David Price. BS, U. Tex., 1965, JD, 1969. Bar: Tex. 1969, N.Mex. 1970. Assoc. Martin, Lutz, Cresswell & Hubert and predecessor firms, Las Cruces, N.Mex., 1969-82; former U.S. atty. dist. N.Mex. U.S. Dept. Justice, Albuquerque, 1982-91; ptnr. Martin, Lutz & Brower, P.C., Las Cruces, 1991—. Mem. ABA, N.Mex. Bar Assn. (mem. bd. bar commrs. 1995—); Aggie Sports Assn. (bd.dirs.) N.Mex. State U. Methodist. Office: Martin Lutz & Brower PO Drawer 1837 2100 N Main St Ste 3 Las Cruces NM 88004-1837

LUTZE, ROBERT STEPHEN, engineering director; b. Sheboygan, Wis., Apr. 3, 1954; s. Ernest A. and Elva E. (Lund) L.; m. Mary E. Hoel, Oct. 1, 1983; children: Kyle S., Alexandra E. BS in Applied Math. and Physics, U. Wis., 1976, BSEE, 1977, MSEE, 1978. Engr. Hewlett Packard, Ft. Collins, Colo., 1979-82; engring. mgr. Honeywell Solid State, Mpls., 1982-88, Brooktree Corp., San Diego, 1988-96; engring. dir. Avanti Corp., 1996—. Contbr. numerous papers to tech. jours. and confs. Mem. IEEE.

LUTZKY, FRANK JOSEPH, JR., science educator, project management consultant; b. Flagtown, N.J., Feb. 4, 1934; s. Frank J. and Esther (Buckshaw) L.; m. Donna Wyglendowski, June 17, 1943; children: Angela, Robert, Albert, David, Kristen, Scott. BS in Engring., Rutgers U., 1955. Lic. real estate broker. Instr. sci. Ctrl. Oreg. C.C., N.Y.C., 1955-61; supr. svc. ops. Bell Labs., Murray Hill, N.J., 1961-69; dep. head ops. svc. ops. Bell Labs., Holmdel, N.J., 1969-72; dept. head engring. svc. ops. Bell Labs., Murray Hill, N.J., 1972-75, dept. head space planning plant engring., 1975-79; dir. svc. ops. Bell Labs., Holmdel, 1979-84, dir. facilities mgmt. adminstrn. systems, 1984-86; v.p. Weichert Comml. Realtors, Princeton, N.J., 1986-89; pres. Weichert Comml. Realtors, Morris Plains, N.J., 1989-90; sci. instr. Cen. Oreg. Community Coll., Bend, 1991—; cons., 1988—. Mgr. Little League, Hillsborough, 1980-83; sponsor dir. Jr. Achievement, Holmdel, 1976-86. 2d lt. U.S. Army, 1957-58. Mem. Nat. Assn. Corp. Real Estate Execs., Morris County Bd. Realtors, Princeton Area C. of C. Roman Catholic. Home: 60612 Brasada Way Bend OR 97702-9655 Office: Ctrl Oreg CC Bend OR 97701

LUXENBERG, JAY S., medical facility administrator; b. Newark, N.J.; s. Allen and Marilyn (Juman) L.; m. Jan Uhley, July 11, 1982; children: Adam, Evan. BS, Rensselaer Polytechnic Inst., 1979; MD, Albany Med. Coll., 1979. Diplomate Am. Bd. Internal Medicine, Am. Bd. Geriatric Medicine. Intern Mt. Zion Hosp. and Med. Ctr., San Francisco, 1979-80, resident in internal medicine, 1980-82; fellow in geriatric medicine Mt. Zion/U. Calif., San Francisco, 1982-84; med. staff fellow Nat. Inst. on Aging/NIH, Bethesda, Md., 1984-87; pvt. practice geriatrics and internal medicine San Francisco, until 1996; MD Jewish Home for Aged, San Francisco, 1996—; assoc. clin. prof. U. Calif., San Francisco, 1992—, asst. clin. prof., 1987-92, clin. assoc., 1982-84, dir. fellowship program in geriatric medicine, 1991-95. Contbr. articles to profl. jours. Mem. physician's adv. com. UCSF/Mt. Zion Ctr. on Aging, San Francisco, 1987—, others. Office: Jewish Home for Aged 302 Silver Ave San Francisco CA 94112

LYASHENKO, NIKOLAI NIKOLAEVICH, mathematician, educator; b. Leningrad, Russia, Jan. 19, 1946; came to U.S., 1990; s. Nikolai Makarovich and Rufina Stepanovna (Poshekhonova) L.; m. Tatiana Vasilievna Giga, June 21, 1969; 1 child, Anna Nikolaevna. BS, Leningrad U., 1966, MS, 1969, PhD in Physics and Math. Scis., 1974, D in Phys. Math. Scis., 1986. Assoc. prof. Leningrad Elec. Engring. Inst., 1975-85; prof. Leningrad Poly. Inst., 1986-88; dir. info. processing lab. Leningrad Inst. Informatics and Automation, 1988-90; vis. prof. George Mason U., Fairfax, Va., 1991—; pres. Knowledge Extraction Tools, Inc., L.A. Contbr. numerous articles to profl. jours.; patentee in field. Home: 4614 W 131st St Hawthorne CA 90250-5107 Office: 801 S Grand Ave Fl 10 Los Angeles CA 90017-4613

LYBARGER, JOHN STEVEN, business development consultant, trainer; b. Yuba City, Calif., June 13, 1956; s. Rodger Lee and Phyllis Ruth (Roseman) L.; m. Marjorie Kathryn Den Uyl, Aug. 22, 1981; children: Ashley Ann, Ryan Christopher. AA, Yuba Community Coll., 1977; BS in Christian Edn., Biola U., La Mirada, Calif., 1980; MS in Counseling, Calif. State U., Fullerton, 1984; PhD in Psychology, Calif. Coast U., 1985. Lic. marriage family and child counselor; cert. alternative dispute resolution educator/practitioner. Assoc. dir. Concept 7 Family Svcs., Tustin, Calif., 1981-85; exec. dir. Family Life Ctr., Tustin, 1984-86; pres. Marriage & Family Counseling, La Habra, Calif., 1985-89; clin. dir. New Life Treatment Ctrs., Inc., Laguna Beach, Calif., 1988-89; faculty Loma Linda (Calif.) U. Sch. Medicine, 1990—; dir. partial hospitalization programs CPC Brea Canyon Hosp., 1991-93; clin. dir. Oasis Counseling Ctr., Denver, 1993-95; dir. Oasis Counseling Ctr., Denver; tng. cons. Dale Carnegie Tng., Denver; pres., CEO Nat. Coun. on Sexual Addiction, Atlanta, 1990-94. Mem. Am. Assn. for Marriage and Family Therapy (clin.). Republican. Home: 8489 W 95th Dr Westminster CO 80021 Office: Ste 300 4949 S Syracuse Pky Ste 300 Denver CO 80237

LYBARGER, MARJORIE KATHRYN, nurse; b. Holland, Mich., Apr. 23, 1956; d. Richard Simon and Mary Kathryn (Homan) Denuyl; m. John Steven Lybarger, Aug. 22, 1981; children: Ashley Ann, Ryan Christopher. BA in Psychology, Biola U., Calif., 1979, BS in Nursing, 1984. RN, Calif. Staff nurse Presbyn. Intercommunity Hosp., Whittier, Calif, 1985-86, Healthcare Med. Ctr., Tustin, Calif., 1986-88; staff nurse med.-telemetry unit Friendly Hills Regional Med. Ctr., La Habra, Calif., 1988-90; staff nurse telemetry unit Riverside (Calif.) Community Hosp., 1990-93; staff nurse med. telemetry unit St. Anthony's Ctrl. Hosp., Denver, 1993-94; clin. RN 1 cardiovascular intermediate care unit St. Anthony's Ctr., Denver, 1994—. Mem. Acad. Med.-Surg. Nurses (Rocky Mountain chpt.), Gamma Phi Beta. Republican. Home: 8489 W 95th Dr Broomfield CO 80021-5330

LYE, WILLIAM FRANK, history educator; b. Kimberley, B.C., Can., Feb. 19, 1930; came to U.S., 1955, naturalized, 1981; s. Arthur Percy and Jessie Loretta (Prince) L.; m. Velda Campbell, Oct. 16, 1953; children: William Mark, Matthew Campbell, David Arthur, Victoria, Regina. Student Ricks Coll., 1953-55, Duke U., 1963; BS, Utah State U., 1959; MA, U. Calif.-Berkeley, 1959; PhD, UCLA, 1969. Instr. polit. sci. Ricks Coll., Rexburg, Idaho, 1959-63, 67-68, head dept. polit. sci., 1959-63; teaching asst. dept. history UCLA, 1964-65; asst. prof. Utah State U., Logan, 1968-69, acting head dept. history and geography, 1969-70, assoc. prof., head dept. history and geography, 1970-73, prof., head dept. history and geography, 1973-76, dean Coll. Humanities, Arts and Social Scis., 1976-83, v.p. for univ. relations, prof. dept. history and geography, 1983-91, prof. history, 1991-95, emeritus, 1996—; vis. lectr. dept. history Brigham Young U., Provo, Utah, 1970; temporary lectr. dept. history U. Cape Town, Republic of South Africa, 1974; social cons. for project design teams in land conservation, U.S. Agy. for Internat. Devel. Khartoum, Sudan, 1978, Maseru, Lesotho, 1979; mem. higher edn. taskforce on telecommunications, Utah, 1977-82; chmn. State of Utah Telecommunications Coop., 1987, Regents' Com. on Credit by Exam., Utah, 1976; mem. adv. com. Sta. KULC-TV, State Ednl. Telecommunications Operating Ctr., 1986-90; bd. dirs., exec. com. Children's Aid Soc. Utah, 1985-89, pres., 1990-91; mem. Utah Statehood Centennial Commn., 1989-96, Utah Christopher Columbus Quincentenary Commn., 1990-91. Author: (with Colin Murray) Transformations on the Highveld: The Tswana and Southern Sotho, 1980, paperback edit., 1985; editor: Andrew Smith's Journal of His Expedition into the Interior of South Africa, 1834-36, 1975. Producer (TV series) Out of Africa, 1977, The God Seekers, 1978; contbr. articles and book revs. to profl. publs. Chmn. State Day celebration, Logan, Utah, 1973, univ. drive for new Logan Regional Hosp; bishop LDS Ch., 1993-96; chair bd. Nora Eccles Harrison Mus. of Art, 1996—; Recipient Leadership award Standard of Calif., 1957, Idea of Yr. award Utah State U., 1971, Faculty Service award Associated Students, Utah State U., 1977-78, Nicholas and Mary Kay Leone Leadership award, 1991; Woodrow Wilson Nat. fellow 1958, Foreign Area fellow Social Sci. Research Council, Republic of South Africa, England, 1966-67, 67-68; faculty devel. grantee Utah State U., 1972, Human Sci. Research Council of South Africa publ. grantee, 1975, Mauerberger Trust grantee, 1976. Mem. African Studies Assn., Royal African Soc., Western Assn. Africanists (program chmn. 1972-74, pres. 1974-76), Am. Soc. Landscape Architects (accreditation bd. 1967-93), Phi Kappa Phi, Phi Alpha Theta. Home: 60 Raymond Ct Logan UT 84321-4259 Office: Utah State U Dept History 650 N 1100 E Logan UT 84322-0710 *Personal philosophy: I support education for everyone as the means by which we make our fullest contribution to society, and it is by service to others that we earn our place on earth.*

LYKINS, JAY ARNOLD, economic development director; b. Shattuck, Okla., Feb. 13, 1947; s. George Eldridge and Lucy Lee (Croom) L.; m. (Mary) Lynn Turner, Jan. 3, 1970; children: Mary Lee and Amy Lynn (twins), Jason. BA, Covenant Coll., 1973; MBA in 3rd World Econ. Devel., Kennedy-Western U., 1987, PhD in Internat. Bus., 1988. Credit specialist Gen. Electric Supply Co., Nashville, 1974-75; owner, mgr. Environment Control Co., Nashville, 1975-78; bus. adminstr. Youth for Christ, Atlanta, 1978-81; controller Young Life, Colorado Springs, Colo., 1981-82, internat. adminstr., 1982-86; exec. dir. Global Reach, Pleasanton, Calif., 1982—; cons. Royal Donuts, Lima, Peru, Barnabas Group, Vancouver, B.C., Manna Corp., Bulawayo, Zimbabwe, Denver Bridge Corp.; started more than 110 businesses in 30 countries, serving over 50 chs., missions. Author: Values in the Marketplace, 1985, Development and Technology: Economics for the Third World, 1987, Islamic Business: Philosophy and Methods, 1988. Served with USN, 1966-68. Mem. Internat. Council for Small Bus., Am. Cons. League, Assn. MBA Execs., Ctr. Enterpreneurial Mgmt. Club: Nob Hill Country (Snellville, Ga.) (pres. 1980). Office: Global Reach 39 California Ave Ste 203 Pleasanton CA 94566-6281

LYLE, JOHN TILLMAN, landscape architecture educator; b. Houston, Aug. 10, 1934; s. Leo Tillman and Martha Ellen (Rawlins) L.; m. Harriett Laverna Fancher, Dec. 28, 1967; children: Alexander Tillman, Cybele Katsura. BArch, Tulane U., 1957; postgrad., Royal Acad. of Fine Arts, Copenhagen, 1965-67; M of Landscape Architecture, U. Calif., Berkeley, 1966. Registered architect, Calif. Architect Stanford (Calif.) U., 1959-62; urban designer John Carl Warnecke & Assocs., San Francisco, 1963-65; prof. Calif. State Poly. U., Pomona, 1968—; vis. prof. Liubliana (Yugoslavia) U., 1982, Instituto Universitario Di Architectura, Venice, Italy, 1988, U. Sao Paulo, Brazil, 1989, Kyushu Inst. Design, Fukuoka, Japan, 1990; dir. design bldg. and landscape Ctr. for Regenerative Studies, 1984—. Author: Design for Human Ecosystems, 1985 (award Assn. Am. Pubs. 1985, Am. Soc. Landscape Architects 1986), Regenerative Design for Sustainable Development, 1994; contbr. articles to profl. jours. Mem. bd. govs. Desert Studies Consortium, Mojave Desert, 1984-88. Recipient Honor award Calif. Coun. Landscape Architects, 1988, Disting. Educator award Coun. Educators in Landscape Architecture, 1989; named Fulbright Disting. prof. U.S. Dept. State, 1982. Fellow Am. Soc. Landscape Archs. (Regenerative Design for Sustainable Devel. award 1994, ASLA medal 1996). Democrat. Home: 580 N Hermosa Ave Sierra Madre CA 91024-1117 Office: Calif State Poly U 3801 W Temple Ave Pomona CA 91768-2557

LYNCH, CHARLES ALLEN, investment executive, corporate director; b. Denver, Sept. 7, 1927; s. Laurence J. and Louanna (Robertson) L.; divorced; children: Charles A., Tara O'Hara, Casey Alexander; m. Justine Bailey, Dec. 27, 1992. BS, Yale U., 1950. With E.I. duPont de Nemours & Co., Inc., Wilmington, Del., 1950-69, dir. mktg., 1965-69; corp. v.p. SCOA Industries, Columbus, Ohio, 1969-72; corp. exec. v.p., also mem. rotating bd. W.R. Grace & Co., N.Y.C., 1972-78; chmn. bd., chief exec. officer Saga Corp., Menlo Park, Calif., 1978-86, also dir.; chmn., chief exec. officer DHL Airways, Inc., Redwood City, Calif., 1986-88; also dir.; pres., chief exec. officer Levolor Corp., 1988-89, also bd. dir., chmn. exec. com. of bd., 1989-90; chmn. Market Value Ptnrs. Co., Menlo Park, Calif., 1990-95; chmn., dir. Fresh Choice, Inc., Santa Clara, Calif., 1995—, chmn., 1995—; also bd. dirs.; bd. dirs. Pacific Mut. Life Inst. Co., Nordstrom, Inc., PST Vans, Inc., SRI Internat., Palo Alto Med. Found., Age Wave, Inc.; chmn. BJ Holdings, Inc., La Salsa Franchise, Inc. Bd. dirs. United Way, 1990-92, past chmn. Bay Area campaign, 1987; chmn., dir. Bay Area Coun.; past chmn. Calif. Bus. Roundtable; mem. adv. bd. U. Calif.-Berkeley Bus. Sch., Governance Bd. Mem. Yale Club (N.Y.C.), Internat. Lawn Tennis Club, Menlo Country Club (Calif.), Pacific Union Club (San Francisco), Coral Beach and Tennis Club (Bermuda), Vintage Club (Indian Wells, Calif.), Menlo Circus Club. Republican. Home: 96 Ridge View Dr Atherton CA 94027-6464 Office: 2901 Tasman Dr Ste 109 Santa Clara CA 95054-1137

LYNCH, EUGENE F., federal judge; b. 1931. B.S., U. Santa Clara, 1953; LL.B., U. Calif., 1958. Assoc. O'Connor, Moran, Cohn & Lynch, San Francisco, 1959-64, ptnr., 1964-71; judge Mcpl. Ct., San Francisco, 1971-74; justice Superior Ct. City and County San Francisco, 1974-82; judge U.S. Dist. Ct. (no. dist.) Calif., San Francisco, 1982—. Office: US Dist Ct PO Box 36060 450 Golden Gate Ave San Francisco CA 94102*

LYNCH, MARTIN ANDREW, retail company executive; b. Chgo., Oct. 5, 1937; s. George Irwin and Cecilia Veronica (Corley) L.; children: Kathleen Marie, Kevin Michael, Karen Ann, Daniel Patrick, Michelle Eileen. BSc, DePaul U., 1962. CPA, Ill., Calif. Audit mgr. Price Waterhouse & Co., Chgo., 1962-69; asst. to pres. Scot Lad Foods, Chgo., 1969-70; v.p. fin. N.Am. Car Corp., Chgo., 1970-76; sr. v.p. fin. Tiger Internat. Inc., L.A., 1976-83; exec. v.p., chief fin. officer Duty Free Shoppers Group Ltd., San Francisco, 1983-89, Casino USA Inc., Santa Barbara, Calif., 1989—, Smart & Final Inc., Santa Barbara, 1989—. Mem. AICPA, Calif. CPA Soc., Fin. Execs. Inst., Nat. Assn. Whole Grogery, Inst. Food Distbn. Assn., Bel Air Country Club (L.A.). Roman Catholic. Office: Smart & Final Inc 4700 S Boyle Vernon CA 90058

LYNCH, ROBERT BERGER, lawyer; b. LaCrosse, Wis., June 10, 1931; s. Jan P. and Eve (Berger) L.; B.S., U.S. Merchant Marine Acad., 1955; J.D., U. of the Pacific, 1967; m. Ann Godfrey, May 30, 1980; children: Jan Fredrick Lynch, Jerry Wayne Coggins. Engr. Aerojet Gen. Corp., Sacramento, Calif., 1955-61, proposal mgr., 1961-63, asst. contract adminstrn. mgr., 1963-66, contract adminstrn. mgr., 1967-70; admitted to Calif. bar, 1969, U.S. Supreme Ct. bar, 1972; individual practice law. Rancho Cordova, Calif., 1969—; instr. bus. law Solano Community Coll., 1977-79, San Joaquin Delta Coll., 1978-79; mediator family law panel Sacramento Superior Ct. Active various charity fund-raising campaigns in Sacramento Calif., 1966-68; mem. mission com. St. Clements Episcopal Ch., Rancho Cordova, Calif., 1967-68; trustee Los Rios Community Coll. Dist., Calif., 1971-79. With USCG, 1949-51, USNR 1951-80, Nat. Guard 1988-91, Maj. AUS, ret. Mem. IEEE, Calif. Wildlife Fedn., Internat. Turtle Club, Marines Meml. Assn., Am. Legion, Mensa. Home: 93 Lexington Dr Chico CA 95973-8341 Office: 10615 Coloma Rd Rancho Cordova CA 95670-3939

LYNCH, ROBERT MICHAEL, university administrator; b. N.Y.C., May 30, 1944; s. John Patrick and Emily Maria (Matson) L.; m. Terry Lynn Bell, Dec. 13, 1969; children: Christopher, Cary. BS, SUNY, Brockport, 1966; postgrad., U. Rochester, 1967-68; PhD, U. No. Colo., 1971. Prof. Coll. of Bus. U. No. Colo., Greeley, 1973—, dean, 1994—; Fulbright prof. Thammasat U., Bangkok, Thailand, 1978-79, cons., researcher Oakridge (Tenn.) Assoc. U., 1982-83; vis. prof. U. Virgin Islands, St. Thomas, 1982-83, Edith Cowen U., Perth, Australia, 1986-87; asst. to v.p. U. No. Colo.. 1987 (summer); researcher cons., State of Wyo. Health Dept., Cheyenne, 1990—. Editor of books on research methods and information systems; contbr. articles to profl. jours.; editor Internat. Bus. Sch. Computing Quarterly. Fellow Royal Stats. Soc.; mem. Internat. Assn. for Computer Info. Systems (sec. 1988-90, v.p. 1990-92, pres. 1992-94), Internat. Bus. Schs. Computing Assn. (bd. dirs.). Office: U No Colo Coll Bus Keper 2053 Greeley CO 80639

LYNCH, ROBERT MONTGOMERY, newspaper publisher; b. San Francisco, Aug. 9, 1920; s. Ernest Glenn and Alice Ramona (Granice) L.; m. Jean Helen Allen, Nov. 9, 1941; children: William, James, John. AA, Santa Rosa Jr. Coll., 1940; postgrad., Cornell U., 1945. Petty officer 1st class U. S. Naval Intelligence, San Francisco, 1942-45; ensign instr. U.S. Naval Acad. Prep Sch., Port Deposit, Md., 1945-46; reporter and ad salesman The Sonoma (Calif.) Index-Tribune, 1946-49, editor and publ., 1949-90, publ., owner, 1990—. Author (history book) The Sonoma Valley Story: Pages Through the Ages, 1997. Recipient Svc. to Media award Sonoma Co. Sch. Bd. Assn., 1989. Mem. Calif. Newspaper Publ. Assn. (pres. 1980), Calif. Press Assn. (pres. 1981, 92, bd. dirs. 1978-96, Calif. Newspaper Exec. of Yr. 1989), Sonoma Men's Golf Assn., Sonoma Kiwanis Club (pres. 1965). Home: P O Box C Sonoma CA 95476 Office: The Sonoma Index-Tribune 117 W Napa St Sonoma CA 95476-6639

LYNCH, TIMOTHY BRUCE, city adminstrator; b. Lewistown, Pa., Dec. 30, 1949; s. James F. and Elsie Lynch; m. Cecilia P. Resendez; children: Dennis, Kelly, Johnny, Michael. BS in Biology, U. Calif., Riverside, 1971; MPA, Harvard U., 1984. Cert. govt. fin. mgr. Rsch. asst. U. Calif., Riverside, 1971-72, spl. asst., 1985; campaign mgr. Brown for Congress, Riverside, 1972; legis. asst. Congressman George Brown, Washington, 1973-80, adminstrv. asst., 1980-84; exec. asst. Memel, Jacobs, Pierno, Gersh & Ellsworth, L.A., 1985-87; membership and devel. dir. The Planetary Soc., Pasadena, Calif., 1987-91; dep. contr. City of L.A., 1991—. Active Riverside Press Coun., 1973-74, Environ. Protection Com., Riverside, 1973-74; bd. dir. Return Brown to Cong. campaign, San Bernardino, 1984; mem. Calif. Dem. State Ctrl. Com. Recipient Internat. Achievement award Am. Soc. Assn. Execs. for internat. mktg. for the planetary soc., 1989. Mem. AAAS, U. Calif.-Riverside Alumni Assn., U. Calif. Advocates, Common Cause. Assn. Govt. Accts., Govt. Fin. Officers Assn. Democrat. Home: 12753 Emelita St North Hollywood CA 91607-1018 Office: City Hall Rm 220 Los Angeles CA 90012

LYNCH, WANDA FOLGERT, secondary education educator; b. Phillips, Wis., Dec. 29, 1939; m. Donald James Lynch, Sept. 6, 1986. BA, U. Wis., Eau Claire, 1962; MA, Ariz. State U., 1971; postgrad., Cambridge (Eng.) U.,

1983, Ariz. State U., 1972-89, 90-95. Cert. tchr., Wis., Ariz. Tchr. English Menasha (Wis.) H.S., 1962-63, Oconomowoc (Wis.) H.S., 1963-65, Menomonee Falls (Wis.) H.S., 1965-70, Saguaro H.S., Scottsdale, Ariz., 1970-87, 90-95; tchr. ESL Can. Internat. Sch., New Territories, Hong Kong, 1988; tchr. specialist Career Ladder Profl. Devel., Scottsdale, 1995—; tchr. on sabatical, New Zealand and Australia, 1985-86; exchange tchr., Latvian Tchr. Exchange, Riga, 1992. Mem. NEA, Ariz. Edn. Assn., Nat. Coun. Tchrs. of English, Nat. Staff Devel. Coun., Scottsdale Edn. Assn., Delta Kappa Gamma Soc. Internat. Office: Career Ladder Profl Devel 8505 E Valley View Rd Scottsdale AZ 85250-6768

LYNN, JONATHAN ADAM, director, writer, actor; b. Bath, England, Apr. 3, 1943; s. Robin and Ruth (Eban) L.; m. Rita Merkelis, Aug. 1, 1967; 1 child. MA, Pembroke Coll., 1964; MA (hon.), Sheffield U. Actor Cambridge Circus, N.Y.C., 1964, The Ed Sullivan Show, 1964; repertory actor Leicester, Edinburgh, Bristol Old Vic, London; artistic dir. Cambridge Theatre Co., 1977-81. Author: (novels) A Proper Man, 1976, Mayday, 1993; co-author: (with Anthony Jay) The Complete Yes Minister, 1984, Yes, Prime Minister, the Diaries of the Rt. Hon. James Hacker, vol. I, 1986, vol. II, 1987; performed in: (plays) Green Julia, 1965, Fiddler on the Roof, 1967-68, Blue Comedy, 1968, The Comedy of the Changing Years, 1969, When We are Married, 1970, (TV movies) Barmitzvah Boy, 1975, The Knowledge, 1979, Outside Edge, 1982, Diana, 1984; dir.: (London) The Plotters of Cabbage Patch Corner, 1970, The Glass Managerie, 1977, The Gingerbread Man, 1977, 78, The Unvarnished Truth, 1978, The Matchmaker, 1978, Songbook, 1979 (SWET award 1979), Tonight at 8:30, 1981, Arms and the Man, 1981, Pass the Butler, 1982, Loot'nt, 1984, A Little Hotel on the Side, 1984, Jacobowski and the Colonel, 1986, Three Men on a Horse, 1987 (Olivier award), RSC: Anna Christie, 1980, (Broadway) The Moony Shapiro Songbook, 1981, (short film) Mick's People, 1982; TV scriptwriter situation comedies, including: My Brother's Keeper, 1974, 75 (also co-starred), Yes, Minister (also radio scripts), 1980, 81, 82, (Broadcasting Press Guild award 1980, Pye TV Writers award 1981), Yes, Prime Minister, 1986, 87 (Pye TV Writers award 1986, Broadcasting Press Guild award 1986, ACE award 1988); film scriptwriter: The Internecine Proect, 1974; film scriptwriter and dir.: Clue, 1986, Nuns on the Run, 1990, My Cousin Vinny, 1991; film dir. The Distinguished Gentleman, 1992, Greedy, 1995, Sgt. Bilko, 1996, Trial and Error, 1997. Recipient Writer's award BAFTA, 1987,. Office: ICM 8942 Wilshire Blvd Beverly Hills CA 90211-1934 also: Peters Fraser & Dunlop, The Chambers Lots Rd 5th fl, London SW10 0XF, England

LYNN, KATHERINE LYN, quality engineer, chemist; b. Nagoya, Japan, June 25, 1954; (parents Am. citizens); d. Jimmie Frank and Barbara Sue (Whiteside) Sutton; m. Richard Shelly Lynn, Feb. 28, 1981. BS in Chemistry cum laude, Calif. State U., Fullerton, 1979. Cert. quality engr.; cert. quality auditor. Technician U.S. Borax Corp., Anaheim, Calif., 1974-79; chemist Armstrong World Industries, Southgate, Calif., 1979-82; project engr. Hydril Co., Whittier, Calif., 1982-84; sr. quality engr. So. Calif. Gas Co., L.A., 1984—. Patentee fluorspar flotation. Bd. dirs. East Side Christian Ch., 1987-89. Mem. So. Calif. Thermal Analysis Group (chair 1988, sec. 1985-87), Soc. Plastic Engrs., Am. Soc. for Quality Control (cert. quality engr., cert. quality auditor), Am. Chem. Soc., Sierra Club. Mem. Christian Ch. Home: 5120 Faust Ave Lakewood CA 90713-1924 Office: So Calif Gas Co Box 3249 3249 Terminal Annex ML 2782 Los Angeles CA 90051

LYNN, NANNE JOYCE, educator; b. Muncie, Ind., Sept. 27, 1938; d. Hal Paul and Rose Mary (Femyer) Duffey; divorced;children: Joel Robert, Michael Charles, Lorry Rose. BA, Ball State U., 1960, MA, 1974. Cert. secondary tchr. Dir. child welfare Del. County Dept. of Welfare, Muncie, 1958-63; tchr. Coachella Valley Unified Sch. Dist., Thermal, Calif., 1978—, chmn. dept. English, 1995-97; student travel coord., guide Europe and Soviet Union tours, 1987, 88, Italy, 1989; freelance reporter Desert Sun, Palm Springs, Calif., Palm Desert (Calif.) Post, 1978-80. Vol. Birch Bayh for Pres. campaign, Ind., 1970-71. Recipient Soroptimist award Women Who Make A Difference, 1996, Andrew Mellon grant, 1996. Mem. Palm Desert C. of C. (pub. relations 1980-83), Bus. Profls. Women (ednl. chmn. 1973-74), Phi Delta Kappa, Alpha Phi Gamma. Office: Coachella Valley High Sch 83-800 Airport Blvd Thermal CA 92274-9367

LYNN, RICHARD JOHN, Chinese language and literature educator; b. Binghamton, N.Y., June 28, 1940; s. Joseph Richard Lynn and Margaret Krutulis; m. Rosie Lucia Chu, Apr. 25, 1964 (div. Sept. 1979); children: Anne Margaret, Joseph Paul. BA in Art and Archaeology magna cum laude, Princeton U., 1962, postgrad., 1962-63; MA in Chinese Lit. and History, U. Wash., 1966; postgrad., U. Chgo., 1966-67; PhD in Asian Langs., Stanford U., 1971. Lectr. dept. Asian langs. and lits. U. Auckland, New Zealand, 1970-72; asst. prof. Chinese and comparative lit. U. Mass., Amherst, 1972-75, Ind. U., Bloomington, 1975-77; sr. lectr., head dept. Chinese Macquarie U., Sydney, Australia, 1977-80; dir. Corp. Asian Lang. Tng., Palo Alto, Calif., 1983—; prof., chair Dept. East Asian Studies U. Alberta, Edmonton, Can., 1993—; vis. scholar dept. Asian langs. Stanford (Calif.) U., 1980-81, 86-92; vis. asst. prof. U. B.C., Vancouver, 1981-82; vis. lectr. Chinese lang. and lit. U. Calif., Santa Barbara, 1983; cons., data base editor Rsch. Librs. Group, Stanford, 1983, 84, 87, 88; vis. prof. Chinese lang. and lit. U. Calif., Berkeley, 1987-88, 1988-89; program officer, humanities adminstr. NEH, Washington, 1992-93. Author: Chinese Literature: A Draft Bibliography in Western European Languages, 1980, Kuan Yun-shih, 1980, Guide to Chinese Poetry and Drama, 1984, The Classic of Changes: A New Translation of the I Ching as Interpreted by Wang Bi, 1994; editor: Language-Paradox-Poetics: A Chinese Perspective, 1988; contbr. articles and revs. to profl. jours., chpts. to books. Nat. Def. Fgn. Langs. fellow, 1962-63, 63-64, 66-67, 71; Rsch. Tng. fellow Kyoto U., Humanistic Scis. Rsch. Ctr., 1969; Fgn. Area fellow Ford Found., 1969; Am. Coun. Learned Socs. fellow, 1980-81; NEH fellow, 1986; Princeton Alumni scholar, 1958-62. Mem. Assn. Asian Studies. Democrat. Home: 9239-118 St, Edmonton, AB Canada T6G 1T8 Office: U Alberta Dept East Asian Studies, 400 Arts Bldg, Edmonton, AB Canada T6G 2E6

LYON, BRUCE ARNOLD, lawyer, educator; b. Sacramento, Sept. 24, 1951; s. Arnold E. and Arlene R. (Cox) L.; m. Patricia J. Gibson, Dec. 14, 1974; children: Barrett, Andrew. AB with honors, U. Pacific, 1974; JD, U. Calif.-Hastings Coll. Law, 1977. Bar: Calif. 1977, U.S. Dist. Ct. (ea. and no. dists.) Calif. 1977. Ptnr. Ingoglia, Marskey, Kearney & Lyon, Sacramento, 1977-84; sole practice, Auburn, Calif., 1984-91; ptnr. Robinson, Robinson & Lyon, Auburn, Calif., 1991—; counsel Placer Savs. Bank, Auburn, 1987—; instr. in law Sierra Coll., Rocklin, Calif., 1983—. Mng. editor Comment, A Jour. of Communications and Entertainment Law, 1974. Contbr. articles to trade publs. Dir. Auburn Cmty. Found. Mem. State Bar Calif., ABA (liaison student div. 1974), Calif. Trial Lawyers Assn., Placer County Bar Assn., Sacramento County Bar Assn., Thurston Soc., Mensa, Internat. Platform Assn., Order of Coif., Calif. League of Savings Inst. (atty's. com.), Native Sons of the Golden West. Office: Robinson Robinson & Lyon One California St Auburn CA 95603

LYON, JAMES KARL, German language educator; b. Rotterdam, Holland, Feb. 17, 1934; came to U.S., 1937; s. T. Edgar and Hermana (Forsberg) L.; m. Dorothy Ann Burton, Dec. 22, 1959; children: James, John, Elizabeth, Sarah, Christina, Rebecca, Matthew, Melissa. BA, U. Utah, 1958, MA, 1959; PhD, Harvard U., 1963. Instr. German Harvard U., Cambridge, Mass., 1962-63, asst. prof., 1966-71; assoc. prof. U. Fla., Gainesville, 1971-74; prof. U. Calif. San Diego, La Jolla, 1974-94, provost Fifth Coll., 1987-94; prof. dept. Germanic and Slavic langs. Brigham Young U., Provo, Utah, 1994—; vis. prof. U. Augsburg, Germany, 1993. Author: Konkordanz zur Lyrik Gottfried Benns, 1971, Bertolt Brecht and Rudyard Kipling, 1975, Brecht's American Cicerone, 1978, Bertolt Brecht in America, 1980, Brecht in den USA, 1994. Capt. M.I., U.S. Army, 1963-66. NEH fellow, 1970, Guggenheim Found. fellow, 1974; Ford Found. grantee, 1988, 91. Mem. MLA, Am. Assn. Tchrs. German, Internat. Brecht. Soc., Phi Beta Kappa. Democrat. Mormon. Office: BYU Dept Germanic & Slavic Lang 4094 Jesse Knight Human Bld Provo UT 84602-6120

LYON, RICHARD, mayor, retired naval officer; b. Pasadena, Calif., July 14, 1923; s. Norman Morais and Ruth (Hollis) L.; m. Cynthia Gisslin, Aug. 8, 1975; children: Patricia, Michael, Sean; children by previous marriage: Mary, Edward, Sally, Kathryn, Patrick (dec.), Susan. B.E., Yale U., 1944; M.B.A., Stanford U., 1953. Commd. ensign USN, 1944; advanced through grades to rear adm. SEAL, 1974; served in Pacific and China, World War II; with Underwater Demolition Team Korea; recalled to active duty as dep. chief Naval Res. New Orleans, 1978-81; mayor City of Oceanside, Calif., 1992; mem. Chief Naval Ops. Res. Affairs Adv. Bd., 1978-81; exec. v.p. Nat. Assn. Employee Benefits, Newport Beach, Calif., 1981-90; mem. Bd. Control, U.S. Naval Inst., 1978-81; pres. Civil Svc. Commn., San Diego County, 1990, Oceanside Unified Sch. Bd., 1991. Pres. bd. trustees Children's Hosp. Orange County, 1965, 72. Decorated Legion of Merit. Mem. Nat. Assn. Securities Dealers (registered prin.), Newport Harbor Yacht Club, Rotary Club (Anaheim, Calif. pres. 1966), Oceanside Yacht Club. Republican. Episcopalian. Home: 4464 Inverness Dr Oceanside CA 92057-5052

LYON, WILLIAM JAMES, psychotherapist, sociologist; b. El Paso, Tex., Feb. 22, 1957; s. James William and Ana (Mendez) L.; m. Brandi A. Ferrari; children: Kim, Aaron. BA, U. Tex., El Paso, 1982, MA, 1984. Therapist Cath. Soc. Svc., Phoenix, 1989—; pvt. practice Phoenix, 1993—; mem. adj. faculty Lewis-Clark State Coll., Lewiston, Idaho, 1989, Paradise Valley C.C., Phoenix, 1992—. Nat. Hispanic Fund scholar Wash. State, 1985-86, 87-88. Mem. AAUP. Office: 1825 W Northern Ave Phoenix AZ 85021

LYONS, STEPHEN H., medical educator; b. Rochester, Minn., June 15, 1951; s. Henry R. and Margaret (Mumway) L. AS in EMT, Santa Fe C.C., 1985. Cert. EMT-Paramedic, Colo.; cert. instr. ACLS, BTLS, EMT. EMS coord Crested Butte First Protection Dist.; flight paramedic, program cons. Shands Teaching Hosp., U. Fla., Gainesville; trauma technologist dept. emergency medicine George Washington U., Washington; surg. asst. pvt. practice gen. surgery Gainesville; dir., CEO EMSED; pres., owner Wilderness Profl. Tng., Crested Butte, Colo.; instr. Wilderness Med. Assocs., Bryant Pond, Maine, Wilderness Medicine Inst., SOLO West, Pitkin, Colo.; cons. Wilderness Med. Assocs., NASAR Wilderness Med. Programs; faculty instr. NASAR Ednl. Programs, Fairfax, Va.; instr. emergency care courses Georgetown U. Sch. of Medicine, Washington. Past instr. trainer Aquatics, First Aid & CPR, Small Craft Safety, ARC; past program coord. EMS Assoc./Tech. Degree Programs, Santa Fe C.C., Gainesville, Fla.; mem. State of Colo. EMS Task Force; guide Wildwater, Ltd., Section IV, Chattooga River. Mem. Nat. Assn. EMTs, Nat. Assn. Search and Rescue, EMT Assn. of Colo., Nat. Assn. EMS Physicians, Wilderness Med. Soc. Office: Wilderness Profl Tng PO Box 759 602 Butte Ave #1 Crested Butte CO 81224

LYONS, TERRENCE ALLAN, merchant banking, investment company executive; b. Grande Prairie, Alta., Can., Aug. 1, 1949; s. Allan Lynnwood and Mildred Helen (Smith) L. B.Applied Sci., U. B.C., 1972; MBA, U. Western Ont., 1974. Registered profl. engr., B.C. Gen. mgr. Southwestern Drug Co., Vancouver, B.C., Can., 1975-76; mgr. planning Versatile Corp., Vancouver, 1976-83, asst. v.p., 1983-86, v.p., dir., 1986-88; pres., mng. ptnr. B.C. Pacific Capital Corp., 1988—; bd. dir. BRL Enterprises, Inc., 1987—, Morgan Fin. Corp., Ariz. Goldfields Inc.; pres., chief exec. officer FT Capital Ltd., 1990—; pres., dir. Westfield Minerals Ltd., 1993—, Northgate Exploration Ltd., 1995—; vice chmn. Westmin Resources Ltd. Author articles on mfg. tech. Office: BC Pacific Capital Corp Royal Ctr, PO Box 11179, 1632-1055 W Georgia St, Vancouver, BC Canada V6E 3R5

LYOU, JOHN CHRISTIAN, corrections services administrator; b. L.A., Jan. 9, 1952; s. John Jones and Nobuko (Watanabe) L. BA, U. Calif., Berkeley, 1974. Cmty. developer North Pacific Rim Native Corp., Anchorage, 1975-76; gen. mgr. English Bay (Alaska) Corp., 1976-77; dir. planning and bus. enterprises Cook Inlet Native Assn., Anchorage, 1977-84; cons. bus. devel. and planning Cook Inlet Devel. Housing Corp., Anchorage, 1984-85; resource reallocation project coord. Alaska Native Health Bd. Inc., Anchorage, 1985-87; grievance and compliance adminstr. Alaska Dept. Corrections, Anchorage, 1988—. Chmn. bd. dirs. Anchorage Neighborhood Health Ctr., 1977-82; chmn. bd. commrs. Anchorage Econ. Devel. Commn., 1982-87; chmn. Sand Lakes Cmty. Sch. Bd., 1983-86; loan com. Anchorage Neighborhood Housing Svcs. Inc., 1986-87; active Anchorage Port Commn., 1995—. Named Outstanding Young Man of Am., Alaska Dem. Party, 1985; recipient Ommie award Office of Ombudsman, 1994, 95. Mem. Pacific Asian Com. (founder), Japanese Heritage Club (founder). Office: Dept Corrections Office Commr 4500 Diplomacy Dr Ste 340 Anchorage AK 99508

LYTHGOE, DENNIS LEO, newspaper columnist; b. Salt Lake City, Jan. 23, 1939; s. Leo Thomas and Lavinia (Mitchell) L.; m. Marti Lynn Sorensen, Aug. 27, 1965; children: Darrin James, Kelly, David Alan, Charles Edward, Spencer Brent. BA in History, U. Utah, 1964, MA in History, 1966, PhD in History, 1969. Cert. secondary sch. tchr., Utah. Asst. prof. history Bridgewater (Mass.) State Coll., 1969-72, assoc. prof., 1972-76, prof., 1976-89, chair dept. history, 1985-89; adj. prof. U. Utah, Salt Lake City, 1989—; columnist Deseret News, Salt Lake City, 1989—; mem. adv. bd. John F. Kennedy Presdl. Libr., Boston, 1983-89. Author: Let 'Em Holler: Biography of J. Bracken Lee, 1982, Marriage of Equals, 1985, The Sensitive Leader, 1986; mem. editl. bd. Jour. Mormon History, 1977-83, Dialogue Jour., 1976-82; contbr. articles to profl. jours., numerous articles to Mass. and Utah newspapers. Bishop Hingham (Mass.) ward LDS Ch., 1977-82, West Bridgewater (Mass.) ward, 1986-89. Recipient Gov.'s Media award for reporting on women State of Utah, 1991. Mem. Nat. Soc. Newspaper Columnists, Org. Am. Historians, Am. Hist. Assn. Democrat. Office: Deseret News PO Box 1257 30 E 1st St S Salt Lake City UT 84110

LYTTLE, MATTHEW HALDEMAN, chemist; b. Santa Barbara, Calif., July 8, 1953; s. Richard Bard and Jean May (Haldeman) L.; m. Vana Gates Smith, June 25, 1988; children: Lonicera Geneva Lyttle, Poppy Chanel Lyttle. BS in Chemistry, U. Calif., Berkeley, 1979, PhD in Chemistry, 1983. Rsch. chemist Biosearch, San Rafael, Calif., 1982-91; sr. scientist Terrapin Techs., South San Francisco, Calif., 1991-93; dir. organic chemistry Terrapin Techs., South San Francisco, 1993-95; dir. chemistry BTI, Inc., San Rafael, Calif., 1995—; cons. Millipore Corp., Bedford, Mass., 1991-92. Contbr. articles to profl. jours. Patentee in field. Mem. Am. Chem. Soc. Democrat. Home: 251 B St PO Box 1166 Point Reyes Station CA 94956

MA, ALAN WAI-CHUEN, lawyer; b. Hong Kong, Apr. 20, 1951; s. Pak Ping and Oi Quon (Hung) M.; m. Carrie Pak, Mar. 17, 1993. BBA, U. Hawaii, 1975; MBA, Chaminade U., 1981; JD, Golden Gate U., 1983. Bar: Hawaii 1984, U.S. Dist. Ct. Hawaii 1984, U.S. Ct. Appeals (9th cir.) 1986, U.S. Supreme Ct. 1989. Ptnr. Oldenberg & Ma, Honolulu, 1984-90; prin. Law Offices Alan W.C. Ma, Honolulu, 1990-95; counsel Goodsill Anderson Quinn & Stifel, Honolulu, 1995—; adj. prof. law U. Hawaii, Honolulu, 1988—. Co-editor: New Waves for Foreign Investors, 1990. Recipient Outstanding Vol. award Hawaii Cmty. Svc. Coun., 1990. Mem. ABA, Am. Immigration Lawyers Assn. (chpt. chair 1993-94), Internat. Bar Assn., Inter-Pacific Bar Assn., U.S. Japan Vols. Assn. (bd. dirs. 1989—), Overseas Chinese Am. Assn. (bd. dirs. 1993-94). Office: Goodsill Anderson et al 1800 Alii Pl 1099 Alakea St Honolulu HI 96813-4500

MA, FENGCHOW CLARENCE, agricultural engineering consultant; b. Kaifeng, Honan, China, Sept. 4, 1919; came to U.S., 1972; s. Chao-Hsiang and Wen-Chieh (Yang) Ma; m. Fanny Luisa Corvera-Achá, Jan. 20, 1963; 1 child, Fernando. BS in Agr., Nat. Chekiang U., Maytan, Kweichow, China, 1942; postgrad., Iowa State U., 1945-46. Cert. profl. agronomist, Republic of China, 1944; registered profl. agrl. engr., Calif. Chief dept. ops. Agrl. Machinery Operation and Mgmt. Office, Shanghai, China, 1946-49; sr. farm machinery specialist Sino-Am. Joint Commn. on Rural Reconstrn., Taipei, Taiwan, Republic of China, 1950-62; agrl. engrng. adviser in Bolivia, Peru, Chile, Ecuador, Liberia, Honduras, Grenada, Bangladesh FAO, Rome, 1962-80; consulting agrl. engr. to USAID projects in Guyana & Peru IRI Rsch. Inst., Inc., Stamford, Conn., 1981-82, 83, 85; chief adviser Com. Internat. Tech. Coop., Taipei, 1984-85; pres. FCM Assocs., Inc., 1962—; short consulting missions to Paraguay, Saudi Arabia, Indonesia, Malawi, Swaziland, Barbados, Dominica, Ivory Coast, Vietnam, Philippines, Nicaragua and others. Author papers, studies; contbr. articles to profl. publs. Mem. Am. Soc. Agrl. Engrs. Home: 1004 Azalea Dr Sunnyvale CA 94086-6747 Office: PO Box 70096 Sunnyvale CA 94086-0096

MA, L. EVE ARMENTROUT, lawyer, non profit administrator, historical consultant; b. Greenville, S.C., Dec. 28, 1943; d. Edward Goodwin and Lucy McIver (Watson) Ballard; m. David Parker Armentrout, 1966 (div. 1969); 1 child, Lucy Ann; m. Jeong-Huei Ma, Jan. 1970 (div. 1986); children—William Marshall, Edward Benjamin. Student Middlebury Coll., 1961-63; B.A., San Francisco State Coll., 1968; postgrad. in Chinese, Stanford U., 1971; M.A., Calif. State U.-Hayward, 1972; Ph.D. in Chinese History, U. Calif.-Davis, 1977, J.D. U. Calif., San Francisco, 1993. Bar Calif., 1994. Teaching asst. history dept. U. Calif., Davis, 1973-76, research assoc. anthropology dept., 1977-79, asst. prof. history dept., 1980, research assoc. applied behavioral scis. dept., 1982-83; cons. Golden Gate Nat. Rec. Area, San Francisco, 1979-80, Oakland (Calif.) Mus., 1981, 84, ARC Assocs., Inc., Oakland, 1981-82, James R. Moore Atty. at Law, San Francisco, 1982, Pacific Ocean div. U.S. Army Corps Engrs. Hawaii, 1983-85, Tapau Engr. dist. U.S. Army Corps Engrs. Camp Zama, Japan, 1985-87; lectr. Calif. State U., Hayward, 1987-89; asst. prof. Mills. Coll., Calif., 1988-90; pvt. practice law, 1993—. Author: (with others) Chinese of Oakland, 1982, Revolutionaries, Monarchists and Chinatowns, 1990; editor: One Day, One Dollar, 1984, Chung-Hsi Liao-way T'ai (newsletter), 1986; contbr. articles to scholarly volumes and jours. Mem. hist. and interpretive rev. com. Calif. Dept. Parks and Recreation Multicultural Ctr., 1982-84; mem. design rev. com. Calif. State Railroad Mus., 1982-83; vol. tchr. pub. and pvt. schs., San Francisco Bay Area, 1973-86; local Girl Scout leader, 1976-79; local Cub Scout leader, 1985—; officer neighborhood assn., Richmond, Calif., 1974-78; bd. dirs. Chinese/Chinese Am. History Assn., El Cerrito, Calif., 1979-86, Chinese Hist. Soc. Am., 1983-90, Oakland Asian Culture Ctr., 1993—, Celebrating Culture & Cmty., 1996—. Nat. Def. Fgn. Lang. fellow Stanford U., 1971, Am.-East Asian Relations fellow U. Calif., Davis, 1972-73, Kellogg Found. grantee 1977-79; Calif. Council for Humanities grantee, 1981, 83-84. Mem. Chinese Hist. Soc. Am. (bd. dirs. 1983—), Assn. for Asian Studies, Am. Hist. Assn., Inst. for Hist. Study, Ind. Scholars Asia, U. Calif.-Berkeley Ctr. for Chinese Studies. Democrat. Address: 1355 Arlington Blvd El Cerrito CA 94530-2514

MAAS, DONALD KENNETH, education educator, consultant; b. Orange, Calif., Jan. 14, 1944; s. Richard Kenneth and Mary McClelland (Goodner) M.; m. Cheryl Lynn Corley, Aug. 18, 1967; children: Nathaniel William, Erika Nicole, Lee Kenneth. BA, UCLA, 1966; MEd, SUNY, Buffalo, 1969, EdD, 1971. Cert. secondary and elem. tchr. Demonstration tchr. Fernald Sch., Westwood, Calif., 1966-67; substitute tchr. Buffalo City Schs., 1967-70; coord. EPIS SUNY, Buffalo, 1970-71; from asst. prof. to assoc. prof. U. Guam, Agana, 1971-76; from asst. prof. to prof. Calif. Polytech. U., San Luis Obispo, Calif., 1976—; coord. TRI-Tchr. Edn. and Computers, San Luis Obispo, 1982-85; chmn. Print Media award Internat. Reading Assn., 1980-82. Author: Guamerican Heritage, 1976, Teaching in the Secondary School, 1992, Maintaining Instructional Effectiveness, 1993; author video tape series: Maintaining Teacher Effectiveness, 1990. Pres. San Luis Obispo County Reading Assn., 1978-79; mem. U.S. legis. com. Internat. Reading Assn., Newark, Del., 1982-85. Recipient Margaret Lynch Exemplary Svc. award Calif. Reading Assn., 1985. Mem. Phi Delta Kappa (life, Outstanding Educator 1986), Alpha Gamma Omega (pres. 1965-66). Home: 3158 Spring Ct San Luis Obispo CA 93401-6014 Office: Calif Polytech U Univ Ctr for Tchr Edn San Luis Obispo CA 93407

MAAS, JOAN LOUISE, training and development consultant; b. San Jose, Calif., Apr. 26, 1961; d. Elmer Alvin Maas and Betty Lu Rowe. BA, Whitman Coll., 1983; MA in Psychology, U.S. Internat. U.; postgrad., U. So. Calif., 1996—. Asst. mgr. New Times Clothing Co., Costa Mesa, Calif., 1984-85; bus. analyst Dun and Bradstreet, Long Beach, Calif., 1985-86; intern McDonnell Douglas, Huntington Beach, Calif., 1986; training and personnel asst. Western Digital, Irvine, Calif., 1986-88; instrl. designer Toastmasters Internat., Rancho Santa Margarita, Calif., 1988-91; prin. Maas Tng. and Devel., Mission Viejo, Calif., 1991-92; staff cons. Richard Chang Assocs., Irvine, 1992; orgnl. devel. specialist Anaheim Meml. Hosp., 1992-95. Author Orangespiel newsletter, 1991. Mem. Orange County (Calif.) Young Reps., 1986—, South Orange County Young Reps., 1991. Mem. ASTD (sec. 1992, dir. spl. interest groups 1993, Orange County Merit award 1994), Orange County Nat. Soc. for Performance and Instrn., Toastmasters (v.p. edn. 1991). Home and Office: 20 E Main St Apt 20 Los Gatos CA 95032

MABEE, JOHN RICHARD, physician assistant, educator; b. San Francisco, Sept. 18, 1956; s. Robert John and Mary Sachiko (Nose) M.; m. Cheryl Ann Saxton, June 24, 1978 (div. Aug. 1995); children: Jonathan, Alan. BS, Regents Coll., 1981; MS, Calif. State U., L.A., 1991; postgrad., Union Inst., Cin., 1994—. Cert. physician asst., Nat. Commn. Cert. Physician Assts. Physician asst. resident dept. emergency medicine LA County/U. So. Calif. Med. Ctr., 1984-85, emergency medicine physician asst., 1985—; rsch. asst. dept. biology Calif. State U., L.A., 1987-88, lectr., 1988-91, physician asst., 1992; rsch. physician asst. U. So. Calif. Emergency Medicine Assocs., L.A., 1993-95, clin. instr. dept. emergency medicine, 1994—, conscious sedation adv. com., 1995—, lectr. sch. medicine, 1995—. Contbr. articles to profl. jours. Named Alumnus of Yr., Emergency Medicine Physician Asst. Residency, 1994. Fellow Am. Acad. Physician Assts.; mem. Soc. Emergency Medicine Physician Assts. (founding, election com., 1988—). Democrat. Home: 717 S Almansor St # A Alhambra CA 91801-4508 Office: LAC-USC Med Ctr Unit I Rm 1060 1200 N State St Los Angeles CA 90033

MABRY, MONTE DEL, geophysicist; b. Dunlap, Tenn., Apr. 18, 1958; s. John D. and Marjorie A. (Metz) M.; m. Jennifer Head, July 15, 1984; children: Laurel, Heather, Sarah, Solomon. BS in Geophysics, Kans. State U., Manhattan, 1980. Geophysicist ARCO Oil & Gas Co., Houston, 1981-85; sr. geophysicist ARCO Alaska, Anchorage, 1986-91, staff geophysicist, 1992—. Mem. Geophys. Soc. Alaska (pres. 1994-95), Am. Assn. Petroleum Geologists, Soc. Exploration Geophysicists, Aircraft Owners and Pilots Assn. Home: 11741 Pinto Cir Anchorage AK 99516-2316 Office: ARCO Alaska 700 G St Anchorage AK 99501-3439

MACALISTER, ROBERT STUART, oil company executive; b. L.A., May 22, 1924; s. Robert Stuart and Iris Grace (Doman) MacA.; m. Catherine Vera Willby, Nov. 15, 1947 (dec. 1994); children: Rodney James, Sara Marjorie Pfirrmann; m. Grace V. LeClerc, Dec. 2, 1995. Student, Brighton Coll., Sussex, Eng., 1945; BSME, Calif. Inst. Tech., 1947. Registered profl. engr., Tex. Petroleum engr. Shell Oil Co., 1947-56; mgmt. trainee Royal Dutch Shell, The Hague, Netherlands, 1956-57; with exec. staff, mgr. Shell Oil Co., U.S.A., 1957-68; v.p., ops. mgr. Occidental Petroleum Corp., Tripoli, Libya, 1968-71; mng. dir.various subs. London, 1971-76; mng. dir., pres. Occidental Internat. Oil, Inc., London, 1976-78; pres., chmn. bd. Can. Occidental Petroleum Ltd., Calgary Alberta, 1978-81; mng. dir. Australian Occidental Petroleum Ltd., Sydney, 1982-83, Hamilton Bros. Oil & Gas Ltd., London, 1983-86; petroleum cons. Camarillo, Calif., 1986—; exec. U.K. Offshore Operators, London, 1972-78, 83-86. Cubmaster Boy Scouts Am., Larchmont, N.Y., 1964-65, scoutmaster, Houston, 1965-68. Sgt. U.S. Army, 1944-45, ETO. Mem. Am. Assn. Petroleum Geologists, Soc. Petroleum Engrs., Can. Petroleum Assn. (bd. govs. 1978-81), Las Posas Country Club, Gold Coast Srs. Republican. Episcopalian. Home and Office: 78 Lopaco Ct Camarillo CA 93010-8846

MACALUSO, FRANK AUGUSTUS, oil company executive; b. Cheyenne, Wyo., May 27, 1931; s. Frank R. and Thelma Elizabeth (Speight) M.; m. Margaret Ann Lynch, Oct. 14, 1950; children: Anne Marie Macaluso Foust, Elizabeth Mary Macaluso Nance, Margaret Mary Macaluso Walters, Teresa Marie Macaluso Fleming, Frank A. Jr. ABBA, Regis Coll., 1950. Asst. cashier Merchants Bank, Gallup, N.Mex., 1950-52, Citizens Bank, Aztec, N.Mex., 1952-56; v.p. 1st Nat. Bank, Farmington, N.Mex., 1957-59; founder, chmn., CEO Macaluso Oil Co., Farmington, 1959—; dir. Four Corners Savings Bank, Farmington, 1969-85; organizer, chmn. bd. dirs. Sunwest Bank, Farmington, 1974—; dir. Sunwest Fin. Svcs., Albuquerque, 1988-92; pres., chmn. bd. dirs. Amigo Petroleum Co., Albuquerque, 1988—; chmn. Texaco Wholesale Coun., 1994; pres., dir. Star Mktg. Acceptance Corp., Starmac Acceptance Corp., Star Merketers Acct. Corp., Houston, 1994-97. Mem. Gov's. Bus. Adv. Coun., N.Mex. State Bd. Fin., Santa Fe, 1970-82, 91-95, N.Mex. Engery Conversation Comm., N.Mex. 1st, Albuquerque, 1986—; bd. dirs. U. N.Mex. Found., Albuquerque, 1988—. Named Boss of Yr. by Jaycees, 1971. Mem. N.Mex. Petroleum Marketers Assn. (pres. 1974-75), N.Mex. Amigos, San Juan County Club (pres. 1980-82), Farmington C. of C., KC, Elks. Democrat. Roman Catholic. Office: PO Box 90 2501 E Main St Farmington NM 87499-0090

MACARAY, LAWRENCE RICHARD, art educator; b. Elsinore, Calif., May 8, 1921; s. Frank and Bessie Juliana (Cooper) M.; m. Kathleen Louise Vincent, 1943; children: David Lawrence, Peggy Lyn. AA, Santa Ana (Calif.) Jr. Coll., 1941; BA, Whittier Coll., 1951; MA, Calif. State U., Long Beach, 1955. Cert. tchr., Calif. Tchr. art Torrance (Calif.) Sch. Dist., 1954-62; prof. art El Camino Coll., Via Torrance, Calif., 1962-87; art cons. Fullerton, Calif., 1988—; art and travel editor Torrance Press-Herald, Torrance, 1963-70. Author, illustrator: Sketches/Irish Detour, 1976, The De Sombre House, 1994; illustrator: Yarns/Tales Great Smokies, 1978; painting exhibns. L.A. Mus. of Art, 1971-72, Joslyn Ctr. for the Arts, Torrance, 1982, Bertrand Russell Centenary, Nottingham, Eng., 1973, Carte Blanche, 1996. Sgt. U.S. Army, 1942-45, PTO. Mem. Am. Fedn. Tchrs. Democrat. Home: 780 N Malden Ave Fullerton CA 92832-1233

MACARTHUR, CAROL JEANNE, pediatric otolaryngology educator; b. Glendale, Calif., Aug. 23, 1957; d. Seth Gerald and Barbara Jeanne (Shaw) MacA.; m. Geoffery Buncke, Dec. 14, 1990; children: Keith Davis, Michelle Jeanne. BS, Occidental Coll., 1979; MD, UCLA, 1984. Diplomate Am. Bd. Otolaryngology. Intern U. Calif., Davis, 1984-85, resident in otolaryngology, 1985-90; fellow in pediatric otolaryngology Boston Children's Hosp., 1990-91; instr. dept. otolaryngology U. Calif.-Davis, Sacramemto, 1989-90; clin. fellow in otology and laryngology Harvard U. Med. Sch., Boston, 1990-91; asst. prof. U. Calif., Irvine, 1991—, asst. prof. dept. pediatrics, 1993—, program dir. dept. otolaryngology-head and neck surgery, 1992-95. Recipient investigator devel. award Am. Acad. Facial Plastic and Reconstructive Surgery, 1993. Fellow ACS, Am. Acad. Pediatrics; mem. Am. Soc. Pediat. Otolaryngology, Soc. for Ear, Nose and Throat Advances in Children, Am. Cleft Palate Craniofacial Assn., Am. Acad. Otorhinolaryngology-Head and Neck Surgery, Alpha Omega Alpha. Office: 302 W La Veta #201 Orange CA 99266-6000

MACARTHUR, JOHN REED, physician; b. Santa Barbara, Calif., Nov. 20, 1961; s. Allison Tainter and Virginia Lee (Reed) MacA; m. Yuzana Hmwe Khin, Dec. 22, 1995. BA in Chemistry with distinction, U. Calif., Santa Barbara, 1984; MD, Georgetown U., 1991; MPH, Johns Hopkins U., 1996. Diplomate Am. Bd. Family Practice. Intern and resident family and community medicine U. Calif.-San Francisco/San Francisco Gen. Hosp., 1991-94; fellow health and human rights Harvard U., Cambridge, Mass., 1994-96; resident in preventive medicine Johns Hopkins U., Balt., 1996—. Human rights rschr.; clin. health mgr. Internat. Rescue Com., Thailand-Burma Border, 1994-96; adv. com. Doctors for Global Health. Mem. APHA, Am. Coll. Preventive Medicine, Am. Acad. Family Practice, Physicians for Human Rights, Physicians for Social Responsibility. Home: 3036 Paseo Del Refugio Santa Barbara CA 93105-2809

MACCALLUM, (EDYTHE) LORENE, pharmacist; b. Monte Vista, Colo., Nov. 29, 1928; d. Francis Whittier and Berniece Viola (Martin) Scott; m. David Robertson MacCallum, June 12, 1952; children: Suzanne Rae MacCallum Barslund and Roxanne Kay MacCallum Batezel (twins), Tracy Scott, Tamara Lee MacCallum Johnson, Shauna Marie MacCallum Bost. BS in Pharmacy U. Colo., 1950. Registered pharmacist, Colo. Pharmacist Presbyn. Hosp., Denver, 1950, Corner Pharmacy, Lamar, Colo., 1950-53; rsch. pharmacist Nat. Chlorophyll Co., Lamar, 1953; relief pharmacist, various stores, Delta, Colo., 1957-59, Farmington, N.Mex., 1960-62, 71-79, Aztec, N.Mex., 1971-79; mgr. Med. Arts Pharmacy, Farmington, 1966-67; cons. pharmacist Navajo Hosp., Brethren in Christ Mission, Farmington, 1967-77; sales agt. Norris Realty, Farmington, 1977-78; pharmacist, owner, mgr. Lorene's Pharmacy, Farmington, 1979-88; tax cons. H&R Block, Farmington, 1968; cons. Pub. Svc. Co., N.Mex. Intermediate Clinic, Planned Parenthood, Farmington; first woman registered pharmacist apptd. N.Mex. Bd. Pharm., 1982-92. Author numerous poems for mag. Advisor Order Rainbow for Girls, Farmington, 1975-78. Mem. Nat. Assn. Bds. Pharmacy (com. on internship tng., com. edn., sec., treas. dist. 8, mem. impaired pharmacists adv. com., chmn. impaired pharmacists program N.Mex., 1987—, mem. law enforcement legis. com., chmn. nominating com. 1992), Nat. Assn. Retail Druggists, N.Mex. Pharm. Assn. (mem. exec. coun. 1977-81), Order Eastern Star (Farmington). Methodist. Home and Office: 1301 Camino Sol Farmington NM 87401-8075 *Personal philosophy: Live life to the fullest, make every minute count. Enjoy yourself--it's later than you think.*

MACCAULEY, HUGH BOURNONVILLE, banker; b. Mt. Vernon, N.Y., Mar. 12, 1922; s. Morris Baker and Alma (Gardiner) MacC.; m. Rachael Gleaton, Aug. 30, 1943 (div. May 1980); m. Felice Cooper, Dec. 2, 1980. Student, Rutgers U., 1939-41, Tex. Christian U., 1948-50, U. Omaha, 1957-59. With 102nd Cavalry, Essex Troop N.J. Nat. Guard, 1940-42; commd. 2d lt. U.S. Army, 1943; advanced through grades to col. U.S. Army, USAF, Washington, 1943-73; v.p. Great Am. Securities, San Bernardino, Calif., 1979-94; founder., chmn. bd. Desert Cmty. Bank, Victorville, Calif., 1980-95, chmn. emeritus, 1995; account exec. Gorian Thornes, Inc., San Bernardino, Calif., 1995-96. bd. dirs. Air Force Village West, 1986-88; chmn. bd. and CEO Gen. and Mrs. Curtis E. Lemay Found., 1987—. Decorated Air medal, Legion of Merit. Mem. Daedalian Soc., Rotary, Internat. Platform Soc., Balboa Bay Club. Republican. Presbyterian. Home: 214 Golden West St Huntington Beach CA 92648 *Personal philosophy: Whatever the game play by the rules.*

MACCLEAN, WALTER LEE, dentist; b. Sheridan, Wyo., July 10, 1935; s. Edward Satterlee and Eleanor Elizabeth (Weir) Mac.; m. Nancy Lee Strale, Sept. 4, 1965 (div. 1975); children: David Satterlee, Carrie Lynn. BS with honors, U. Wyo., 1957, postgrad., 1958; DMD, U. Oreg., Portland, 1962. Mil. dental adv. Korean Mil. Adv. Group, Wonju, 1962-63; chief dental svc. Dugway Chem. Testing Ctr., Utah, 1965-68; pvt. dental practice Cheyenne, Wyo., 1968-70; assoc. prof. Sheridan Coll., Wyo., 1970-76; staff dentist VA Hosp. Med. Ctr., Ft. Meade, S.D., 1976-93; ret., 1993; cons., lectr. Health Edn. Program Svc., Ft. Meade, 1984-93. With U.S. Army 1962-68. Mem. ADA. Episcopalian. Home: PO Box 450 Hardin MT 59034-0450 also: Highbourne House, 13-15 Marylebone High St, London W1M 3PE, England

MACCORKLE, EMMETT WALLACE, III, insurance agent; b. Portsmouth, Va., Feb. 10, 1942; s. Emmett Wallace and Nelda (Reymann) MacC.; m. Carol Britton, Dec. 27, 1964; children: Jeffrey W., Steven M. BA, Cornell U., 1964. CLU. Agt. Northwestern Mut. Life, San Francisco, 1967-72; dist. agt. Northwestern Mut. Life, San Mateo, 1972-80; pres. MacCorkle Ins. Svcs., San Mateo, 1980—. Mem. Cornell U. Coun., Ithaca, N.Y., 1986-89; mem. Bellarmine Coll. Prep. Bd. Regents, San Jose, Calif., 1988-91; mem. devel. com. Cartoon Art Mus., San Francisco, 1989-90. With USMC, 1964-67, Vietnam. Named Man of Yr., Peninsula Assn. Life Underwriters, San Mateo, 1980. Mem. Bohemian Club (San Francisco), Menlo Circus Club (Menlo Park, Calif.), Cornell Club No. Calif. (pres. 1974). Democrat. Home: 1060 Continental Dr Menlo Park CA 94025-6652 Office: MacCorkle Ins Svcs 1650 Borel Pl Ste 100 San Mateo CA 94402-3507

MACCRACKEN, GORDON STUART, columnist, wire editor; b. Roseburg, Oreg., July 28, 1954; s. Charles Gordon and Aileen Mary (Chamberlain) MacC.; m. Carol Sue Cutting, Aug. 23, 1975; children: Mark Andrew, Julia Anne. BS, U. Oreg., 1976. Reporter The Chronicle, Centralia, Wash., 1976-80; copy editor The Chronicle, Centralia, 1980-81, city editor, 1981-84, news editor, 1984-94, wire editor, 1994—, columnist, 1990—. Coach Centralia (Wash.) Youth Soccer, 1989-90, Centralia (Wash.) Little League Baseball, 1989-92. Recipient various journalism awards Soc. Profl. Journalists, 1983-93. Home: 502 S Oak St Centralia WA 98531-3928 Office: The Chronicle PO Box 580 321 N Pearl St Centralia WA 98531

MACCRACKEN, PETER JAMES, marketing executive, communications executive; b. Trieste, Italy, Dec. 27, 1952; came to U.S., 1956; s. James and Kirsten (Koch) MacC.; divorced. BA summa cum laude, Albion Coll., 1975; MA, U. Calif., Santa Barbara, 1978. Asst. mgr. GranTree Furniture Rental, San Leandro, Calif., 1979-81; freelance writer San Diego, 1981-82; corp. editor Scripps Meml. Hosps., La Jolla, Calif., 1982-84; sr. v.p. Berkman & Daniels Mktg., San Diego, 1984-89; v.p. Stoorza Ziegaus & Metzger, Inc., San Diego, 1989-90; pres. MacCracken & McGaugh, San Diego, 1990—. Contbr. over 500 articles, photographs to numerous publs. Bd. dirs. Downtown San Diego Partnershpi, 1997—. Recipient 30 bus. comm. awards. Mem. Pub. Rels. Soc. Am. (bd. dirs. 1992-96, pres. San Diego chpt. 1996), Internat. Assn. Bus. Communicators (pres. San Diego chpt. 1985), Am. Inst. Wine and Food (bd. dirs. 1990-95, sec. San Diego chpt. 1995), Phi Beta Kappa. Democrat. Office: 750 B St Ste 1950 San Diego CA 92101

MACDONALD, ANDREW STEPHEN, management consulting firm executive; b. Fairbanks, Alaska, July 15, 1953; s. Bernard L. and Rosemary (Unger) MacD.; m. Josephine A. Joanne, Aug. 4, 1972; children: Peter, Stephen, Charles. BA in Acctg., Seattle U., 1974. CPA, cert. mgmt. cons. Acct. Boeing Aerospace, Seattle, 1976-79; owner, pres. Triak Corp., Seattle, 1977—; pres. Exec. Cons. Group, Inc., Seattle, 1979—. Mem. AICPA, Inst. Mgmt. Cons., Wash. Soc. CPAs, Columbia Tower Club. Home: 10030 Lake Shore Blvd NE Seattle WA 98125-8158 Office: Exec Cons Group Inc 1111 3rd Ave Ste 2700 Seattle WA 98101-3207

MACDONALD, ANGUS, writer, editor; b. San Francisco, 1959; m. K.A. Callahan, 1986. BA, U. Calif., Berkeley, 1980's. Writer Blue Cross of Calif., Oakland, 1984-85, The Training Co., San Francisco, 1985-87, ACC, Inc., Oakland, 1987-88; mgr. publs. Innovative Data Design, Inc., Concord, Calif., 1989-95; writer, editor Teradyne, Inc., Walnut Creek, Calif., 1995—. Editor, publisher: (jour.) Calif. Entertainment Rev.; reviewer: Whole Earth Rev., 1992-93. Mem. Sci. Fiction Writers Am. Buddhist. Office: Calif Entertainment Rev Box 577 Concord CA 94522-0577

MACDONALD, DON, psychotherapist, educator; b. Dowagiac, Mich., Mar. 24, 1950. BA, U. Tex., 1972; MS, Ind. U., 1973; PhD, Mich. State U., 1984. cert. mental health counselor, Wash. Tchr. aide Migrant Edn. Program, Sister Lakes, Mich., 1971-72; resident asst. Ind. U., Bloomington, Ind., 1973; resident dir. Seattle Pacific U., 1973-76; elem. tchr. Northshore Sch. Dist., Kenmore, Wash., 1975-76; grad. asst. Mich. State U., East Lansing, 1976-79; staff psychologist House of Commons, Lansing, Mich., 1977-79; psychology intern Psychological Evaluation & Treatment Ctr., East Lansing, 1977-79; prof. Seattle Pacific U., 1980—; mem. sch. counselor cert. bd. Supt. Pub. Instrn., Olympia, Wash., 1980-87; mem. bd. adv. two pvt. practices, Seattle, 1981-86; editl. cons. Brooks/Cole, Longman, Prentice-Hall, Zondorvan, 1985-96; mem. mental health cert. bd. Dept. Health, Olympia, 1988-93. Coauthor: (book) Social and Psychological Foundations of Education, 1986; contbr. articles to profl. jours. Serving elder North Seattle Alliance Ch., 1992-94. Recipient Mental Health Counselors award Wash. Assoc. Mental Health Counselors, 1988; Weter Award ectr., 1996; Faculty Rsch. grantee Seattle Pacific U., 1986, 89, Academic Renewal grantee, 1984. Mem. APA, Wash. Counseling Assn., Wash. State Assn. Counselor Educators and Suprs. (pres. 1985-86). Office: Family Psychology Seattle Pacific Univ Seattle WA 98119

MACDONALD, DONALD WILLIAM, architect; b. Calgary, Alta., Can., May 7, 1935; came to U.S., 1957; s. Wallace Harold and Dorothy Louise (DeFaye) MacD.; m. Kerstin Maria Lindberg, July 22, 1965 (div. 1979); children: Pia, Ian, Denise. BArch, U. Okla., 1962; MS, Columbia U., 1963. Registered architect, Calif., Nev., N.Mex., Colo. Archtl. draftsman Bell and McCulloch Architects, Edmonton, Alta., 1955-57; archtl. designer Anshen and Allen Architects, San Francisco, 1965-67; prin. Donald MacDonald Architects, San Francisco, 1967—; assoc. prof. U. Calif.-Berkeley, 1965-66; prof. advisor Cogswell Coll., San Francisco, 1979-81, U. Okla., Norman, 1982—; lectr. archtl. sch. Idaho State U., Pocatello, 1974, Posnan (Poland) Inst. Art and Architecture, 1974, Portsmouth Inst. Tech., Eng., 1974, U. Okla., Norman, 1982, Tex. Tech U., Lubbock, 1984, Auburn (Ala.) U., 1986, Tulane U., New Orleans, 1987, Moscow Inst. Architecture, 1987, U. Calif. Berkeley, 1987, Mich. State U., Lansing, 1988, Ga. Inst. Tech., 1993, San Francisco Inst. Architecture, 1992—, U. Okla. Coll. Architecture, 1992, Archtl. Inst. B.C. Vancouver, 1991, McGill U., 1991, U. Cin., 1991, Woodbury U., Burbank, 1993, Boston Archtl. Sch., 1993, San Jose State U., 1994, San Francisco Inst. Architecture, 1994, 95, U. Wis., 1995, U. Calif., Berkeley, 1995, 96, U. N.C., 1996, N.C. State U., 1996, U. N.Mex., 1997; lectr. in field; jury mem. Nat. Competition of Plywood Structures, Seattle, 1972, La. AIA Archtl. Design Competition, 1988, Miss. AIA Archtl. Competition, 1988, McGill U., 1991, Northern Calif. Home and Garden, 1991, City Boston Pub. Facilities Dept., 1992, San Diego Housing Commn., 1992, Meccano Erector Contest, 1993, Internat. Making Cities Livable Conf. Urban Spaces Competition, 1995, San Francisco Planning and Urban Rsch. Assn., 1997; mem. juror panel in field; mem. San Francisco Civil Service Archtl. Selection Com., 1974; examiner Calif. Archtl. Registration Bd., 1979; prof. Calif. Coll. Arts and Crafts, San Francisco, 1988; faculty design studio San Francisco Inst. Architecture, fall 1990, Alberta Assn. Architects, 1994; jury chmn. N.C. AIA Archtl. Design Competition, 1988, Alta. Assn. Archs. U. Calgary, 1994, panel mem. 1994; East-West advisor energy conservation in housing Greenpeace, U.S.A.; presenter 9th Ann. Monterey Design Conf., 1989. Author: Democratic Architecture, 1996; co-author: Bruce Goff: Toward Absolute Architecture, 1988; guest editor: Architecture and Urbanism, 1978; contbr. articles to profl. and consumer jours., U.S., Eng., Germany, Can., Poland, Russia, China, Italy, Japan. Received recognition through the media ABC, CNN, NBC, Time, People, Internat. Herald Tribune, Der Spiegel, London Observer, etc. for the invention of the City Sleeper, an exptl. environment for the homeless, studio house, and earthquake bed, 1987-91; exhbns. of architectural designs include Royal Inst. British Architects, London, 1985, 92, Contract Design Ctr., San Francisco, 1989, Calif. Coll. Arts and Crafts, San Francisco, 1989, Contemporary Realist Gallery, San Francisco, 1989, San Francisco chpt. AIA, 1989, Calif. Sch. Bd. Assn., San Jose, Calif., 1989, Philippe Bonnafont Archtl. Drawings, San Francisco, 1990, Columbia U., N.Y.C., 1991, Mill Valley (Calif.) City Hall, 1991, San Mateo (Calif.) County Fair, 1991, Randolph Street Gallery, Chgo., 1991, Portland (Oreg.) chpt. AIA, 1993, San Francisco Examiner Home Buyers and Sellers Fair, 1993, San Francisco Embarcadero Waterfront Competition Exhibit, 1993. Recipient Regolo d'Or award Domas Milan, Italy, 1966, Okla. U. Regent's Disting. Alumni award, 1988, Honor award Calif. Coun. AIA, 1987, Commendation award for Golden Gate Toll Plaza in San Francisco Calif. Counc. AIA, 1987, also for toll booth award of excellence in archtl. conservation Found. for San Francisco Archtl. Heritage, 1989, Community Assistance award for innovative housing Calif. Coun. AIA, 1989, selected projects award Rolex Awards for Excellence, 1990, Fed. Design Achievement award, Presdl. Design awards, Nat. Endowment for Arts, 1991, World Habitat awards, grand prize Bldg. and Social Housing Foundation World Habitat awards, 1990, Gold Nugget awards, Grand award, Merit award Pacific Coast Builders and Sun/Coast ArchitectBuilder mag., 1991, SF mag. and Showplace Sq. Group Designers on Parade award, 1991, Maxwell award of excellence Fannie Mae, 1992, Oakland Orchids award AIA and Oakland Design Advocates, 1992, WorldDesign 92 award City and County of San Francisco, 1992, Cert. of Spl. Congressional Recognition for Outstanding Creative Leadership, 1996, HUD award for Building Innovation in Home Ownership, 1996, 97; Internat. Making Cities Livable, City of Vision award, 1997; winner Hon. Mention Am. Plywood Assn., 1986, first place Housing Cost Reduction Co., Mich. State Housing Authority, 1987, No. Calif. Home and Garden mag. DIFFA Design Competition, 1990. Fellow AIA (honor awards San Francisco chpt. 1983, jury mem. San Mateo (Calif.) design awards program 1990, Colo. ann. design awards 1995, Oakland Design awards 1995, Archtl. Photography Spl. Commendation award 1993); mem. Constrn. Specification Inst., McIntosh Archtl. Soc. Scotland, Columbia Archtl. League N.Y., Archtl. Assn. London. Clubs: St. Andrews Soc. (San Francisco); Chelsea Art (London); Columbia N.Y. Home: 743 Northpoint St San Francisco CA 94109-1316 Office: 91 S Van Ness Ave San Francisco CA 94103-1226

MACDONALD, KIRK STEWART, lawyer; b. Glendale, Calif., Oct. 24, 1948; s. Bruce Mace and Phyllis Jeanne MacDonald. BSCE, U. So. Calif., 1970; JD, Western State U., 1982. Bar: Calif. 1982, U.S. Dist. Ct. (cen. dist.) Calif. 1982, U.S. Ct. Appeals (9th cir.) 1982, U.S. Dist. Ct. (no. dist.) Calif. 1984, U.S. Dist. Ct. (so. dist.) Calif. 1985, U.S. Dist. Ct. (ea. dist.) Calif. 1987. Dist. engr. Pacific Clay Products, Corona, Calif., 1971-76, Nat. Clay Pipe Inst., La Mirada, Calif., 1976-82; ptnr. Gill and Baldwin, Glendale, Calif., 1982—. Mem. ABA, L.A. County Bar Assn., Water Environ. Assn., Calif. Water Environ. Assn. Office: Gill and Baldwin 130 N Brand Blvd Fl 4 Glendale CA 91203-2617

MACDONALD, NORVAL (WOODROW), safety engineer; b. Medford, Oreg., Dec. 8, 1913; s. Orion and Edith (Anderson) MacD.; m. Elizabeth Ann Clifford, Dec. 8, 1937; children: Linda (Mrs. Bob Comings), Peggy (Mrs. Don Lake), Kathleen (Mrs. Michael Nissenberg). Student, U. So. Calif., 1932-34. Registered profl. safety engr., Calif. Safety engr. Todd Shipyards, San Pedro, Calif., 1942-44, Pacific Indemnity Ins. Co., San Francisco, 1944-50; area safety engring. chief safety engr. Indsl. Ind., San Francisco, 1950-76; supervising safety engr. Beaver Ins. Co., 1976-82, v.p. loss control, 1982-88; tchr. adult evening classes U. San Francisco, 1960-63, Golden Gate U., 1969-76. Contbr. articles to profl. jours.; producer safety training films. Mem. ASME, Am. Soc. Safety Engrs. (pres. 1958, 59), Las Posas Country Club, Masons, Shriners. Methodist. Home: 1710 Shoreline Dr Camarillo CA 93010-6018

MACDONALD, ROBBIN RIECK, clergyman; b. Martins Ferry, Ohio, Oct. 14, 1944; s. Robert Peebles and Wilma Pearl (Henry) MacD.; 1 child, Robbin, Jr. BA, Muskingum Coll., 1966; MDiv, San Francisco Theol. Sem., 1970, DMin, 1972. Asst. pastor First Presbyn. Ch., Modesto, Calif., 1970-72; pastor United Presbyn. Ch., Terra Bella, Calif., 1972-78; sr. pastor Bethany Presbyn. Ch., Grandview, Wash., 1978-82, First Presbyn. Ch., Pomona, Calif., 1982-89; interim pastor N.Mex. and Ariz., 1989-91; pastor Shepherd of the Valley Presbyn. Ch., Safford, Ariz., 1991—; adj. instr. Northland Pioneer Coll., Ariz., 1992—, No. Ariz. U., 1992—, Ea. Ariz. Coll., 1992—. Mem. Gila Valley Ministerial Assn. (pres. 1993-94), Safford Lions Club (v.p. 1993-94, pres. 1994—), de Cristo Presbytery. Home: 3433 S Robinson Ave Thatcher AZ 85552 Office: Shepherd of the Valley Presbyn Ch PO Box 827 Safford AZ 85552

MACDONNELL, PHILIP J., lawyer; b. Boston, Apr. 22, 1948. BA magna cum laude, Harvard U., 1971, JD cum laude, 1974. Bar: Ariz. 1974, U.S. Dist. Ct. Ariz. 1975, U.S. Ct. Appeals (9th cir.) 1976, U.S. Supreme Ct. 1978. Asst. atty. gen. Ariz. Atty. Gen.'s Office, 1975-77, chief counsel special prosecutions divsn., 1977-81; asst. U.S. atty. Dist. Ariz., 1981-85; supt. Ariz. Dept. Liquor Licenses and Control, 1985-87; atty. Jennings, Strouss and Salmon, Phoenix. Editor Harvard Law Rev., 1972-73, sr. editor, 1973-74. Office: Jennings Strouss and Salmon 1 Renaissance Sq 2 N Central Ave Phoenix AZ 85004-2322

MACDONOUGH, ROBERT HOWARD, retired consulting engineer; b. Chgo., Jan. 24, 1941; s. John Haaf and Helen Margaret (McWilliams) MacD.; m. Joan Carol Rosecrants, Dec. 28, 1963 (div. Nov. 1975); children: John Haaf, Thomas William, Mark Peter. BS in Engring. Ops., Iowa State U., 1962; MA in Econ., Drake U., 1966. Registered profl. engr., Iowa; enrolled agent. Assoc. Mgmt. Sci. Am., Palo Alto, Calif., 1969; mng. assoc. Theo. Barry & Assoc., Los Angeles, 1970-72; mgr. indsl. engring. Advanced Memory Systems, Sunnyvale, Calif., 1972-73; mgr. planning and engring. Signetics, Sunnyvale, 1973-75; pres. Facilities Cons., Mountain View, Calif., 1976—; instr. H&R Block. Mem. Inst. Indsl. Engrs. (sr.), Phi Gamma Delta. Republican.

MACE, SUSAN LIDGATE, comparative literature educator, researcher; b. San Francisco, Apr. 24, 1945; d. Anthony William and Pauline Kathryn (Quirk) Lidgate; m. Gerald Norman Mace, Aug. 14, 1970. AB in Comparative Lit., U. Calif., Berkeley, 1967, PhD in Comparative Lit., 1991; MA in Comparative Lit., San Francisco State U., 1970. Tchg. asst. in comparative Lit. San Francisco State U., 1968-70, vis. asst. prof., 1992-93; lectr. lit. U. Calif., Santa Cruz, 1986-87; lectr. European lit. Ea. Mich. U., Europe, 1988-89; sr. lectr. lit. Maria Curie-Sklodowska U., Lublin, Poland, 1991-92, Internat. Rsch. and Exch. Bd. lectr., 1996; Fulbright prof. Am. studies and lit. U. Zagreb, Croatia, 1993-95; assoc. in comparative lit. U. Calif., Berkeley, 1973-75, 78-79, acting instr., 1980-83, 85-86, vis. scholar, 1995—; dir. Florence Howe award for Feminist Literary Criticism (MLA), 1980; panel chmn. 20th Century Lit. Conf., U. Louisville, 1986, 89, 91, 93, 96, 97; performance cons. Theatre Neu, Barcelona, Spain, 1995; judge Nat. Jr. Classical League Essay Contest, Am. Classical League, 1985-87; conf. presenter and participant in field, including Internat. Conf. on English-Am. Culture and Lang., Opatija, Croatia, 1994, 20th Century Lit. Conf., Louisville, 1997; various TV, radio and press interviews. Assoc. editor, prin. writer Polish lit. Ency. of Women's Lit., 1997; contbr. articles to profl. jours. Grantee U. Calif., Berkeley, 1973-82, humanities rsch. grantee, 1981-83; rsch. grantee Newhouse Found., 1981-82, Heller Fund, 1987, 89, 90, Internat. Rsch. and Exch. Bd., 1996; Fulbright sr. scholar U. Zagreb, 1993-95. Fellow Calif. Scholarship Fedn. (life); mem. MLA, AAUP, Am. Soc. for Theatre Rsch., Women's Caucus for Modern Langs. (western regional dir. 1980-82), Pacific Ancient and MLA (presiding officer slavic and East European lit. sect. 1987), Am. Studies Assn., Am. Comparative Lit. Assn., Internat. Comparative Assn., MELUS: Soc. for Study Multi-Ethnic Lit. U.S., N.Am. Conf. on Brit. Studies, Fulbright Assn. Democrat. Home: 1698 San Lorenzo Ave Berkeley CA 94707 Ofice: U Calif Dept Comparative Lit Dwinelle Hall Berkeley CA 94720

MACELVAINE, WILLIAM STEPHEN, rancher, consultant; b. Topeka, Sept. 27, 1944; s. Robert Capps and Gretchen (Swatszel) MacE.; m. Susan Lynn Allison, June 14, 1968; children: Dianna, LeeAnn, Steve Jr., Brian. BS in Farm Mgmt., Calif. Poly. State Coll., San Luis Obispo, 1969. Water treatment plant operator I, II; comml. pilot. Owner, operator Souza Ranch, Morro Bay, Calif., 1965—, Rancho Colina Mobile Home Cmty., Morro Bay, Calif., 1971—; owner MacElvaine Consulting, Morro Bay, 1992—; dir. Mid State Fair Bd., Paso Robles, Calif., 1996—. County supr. dist. 2, Bd. Suprs. San Luis Obispo County, 1979-83; regional commr. So. Ctrl. Region Coastal Commn., San Luis Obispo, Santa Barbara and Ventura Counties, Calif., 1979-81; mem. Calif. Coastal Commn., 1983-92; Rep. nominee from dist. 18, Calif. Sentate, 1994. With Calif. N.G., 1963-69. Mem. San Luis Obispo County Farm Bur., Flying Samaritans (pilot 1990—), Calif. C. of C. Republican. Evangelical. Home: 1325 Atascadero Rd Morro Bay CA 93442-1803 Office: Rancho Colina Mobile Home Cmty 1045 Atascadero Rd Morro Bay CA 93442-1800

MACER, GEORGE ARMEN, JR., orthopedic hand surgeon; b. Pasadena, Calif., Oct. 17, 1948; s. George A. and Nevart Akullian M.; m. Celeste Angelle Lyons, Mar. 26, 1983; children: Christiana Marilu, Marina Lynn, Emily Sue. BA, U. So. Calif., 1971, MD, 1976. Diplomate Am. Bd. Med. Examiners, Am. Bd. Orthop. Surgery; cert. in surgery of hand. Intern Meml. Hosp. Med. Ctr., Long Beach, Calif., 1976; resident Orthop. Hosp./U. So. Calif., 1977-81; pvt. practice hand surgery Long Beach, 1983—; asst. clin. prof. orthops. U. So. Calif., Long Beach, 1983-89, 90—; cons. hand surgery svc. Rancho Los Amigos Hosp. Downey, 1990—; cons. Harbor UCLA Med. Ctr., Torrance, 1983—. Joseph Boyes Hand fellow, 1982; mem. AMA, Calif. Med. Assn., Los Angeles County Med. Assn., Western Orthop. Assn., Am. Soc. for Surgery of Hand, Am. Acad. Orthop. Surgery. Republican. Office: 3550 Linden Ave Ste 2 Long Beach CA 90807-4577

MACFARLAND, CHRISTOPHER JOHN, military officer; b. Albany, N.Y., Oct. 12, 1962; s. F. Garth and Nancy E. (Manning) MacF.; m. Elizabeth A. Santos, July 31, 1982; children: C. Matthew, Bridget M. BS, U. Miami, Coral Gables, Fla., 1985. Hdqs. troop exec. officer HST 3-6 CAV, Ft. Hood, Tex., 1985-86; leader scout platoon C Troop 3-6 CAV, Ft. Hood, 1987-88; leader attack platoon B Troop 3-6 CAV, Ft. Hood, 1989-90; comdr. attack co. B Troop 6-6 CAV, Illesheim, Germany, 1991-92; hdqs. troop comdr. HST 6-6 CAV, Illesheim, 1992-93; asst. S-3 11th Aviation Rgt., Illesheim, 1993-94; observer contr. A Co. Ops. Group, Ft. Irwin, Calif., 1994—. TAFT team leader, Abu Dhabi, United Arab Emirates, 1996. Major U.S. Army, 1985—. Decorated Bronze Star, 1992; recipient Army Commendation medal, 1990, Air medal, 1992, Meritorious Svc. medal, 1992. Mem. VFW, Army Aviation Assn. Am. Republican. Roman Catholic. Home: 73 Barclay St Canajoharie NY 13317

MACGILLIVRAY, MARYANN LEVERONE, marketing professional; b. Mpls., Oct. 18, 1947; d. Joseph Paul and Genevieve Gertrude (Ozark) Leverone; B.S., Coll. of St. Catherine, St. Paul, 1969; Med. Technologist, Hennepin County Gen. Hosp., 1970; M.B.A., Pepperdine U., 1976; m. Duncan MacGillivray, Apr. 28, 1973; children: Duncan Michael, Catherine Mary and Monica Mary (twins), Andrew John. Med. technologist Mercy Hosp., San Diego, 1970-72; with Diagnostics div. Abbott Labs., South Pasadena, Calif., 1972-79, tech. service rep., 1972-74, sr. tech. service rep., 1974-75, product coordinator, mktg., 1975-77, mktg. product mgr., 1977-79; clin. diagnostic mktg. cons., Sierra Madre, Calif., 1979-88; founder, mktg. dir. Health Craft Internat., Pasadena, Calif., 1988—; elected council woman City of Sierra Madre, 1990-94, mayor, 1994-95, re-elected council woman, 1994—. Recipient Pres.'s award Abbott Diagnostics Div., 1975. Mem. Biomed. Mktg. Assn., Am. Assn. Clin. Chemistry, Am. Assn. Clin. Pathologists, Am. Soc. Med. Tech., Calif. Assn. Med. Lab. Technologists, Pasadena Symphony Assn. Roman Catholic. Home: 608 Elm Ave Sierra Madre CA 91024-1245

MACGINITIE, WALTER HAROLD, psychologist; b. Carmel, Calif., Aug. 14, 1928; s. George Eber and Nettie Lorene (Murray) MacG.; m. Ruth Olive Kilpatrick, Sept. 2, 1950; children: Mary Catherine, Laura Anne. B.A., UCLA, 1949; A.M., Stanford U., 1950; Ph.D., Columbia U., 1960. Tchr. Long Beach (Calif.) Unified Sch. Dist., 1950, 1955-56; mem. faculty Columbia U. Tchrs. Coll., 1959-80, prof. psychology and edn., 1970-80; Lansdowne scholar, prof. edn. U. Victoria, B.C., Can., 1980-84; research assoc. Lexington Sch. Deaf, N.Y.C., 1963-69; mem. sci. adv. bd. Ctr. for Study of Reading, 1977-80, chmn. 1979-80. Co-author: Gates-MacGinitie Reading Tests, 1965, 78, 89, Psychological Foundations of Education, 1968; Editor: Assessment Problems in Reading, 1972; co-editor: Verbal Behavior of the Deaf Child, 1969. Life mem. Calif. PTA. Served with USAF, 1950-54. Fellow APA, AAAS, Am. Psychol. Soc., Nat. Conf. Research English, N.Y. Acad. Scis.; mem. Internat. Reading Assn. (pres. 1976-77, Spl. Svc. award 1981), Reading Hall of Fame (pres. 1989-90). Home and Office: PO Box 1789 Friday Harbor WA 98250-1789

MACHLEDER, HERBERT IVAN, surgeon, educator; b. N.Y.C., May 10, 1937; m. Karin Machleder; children: Dietrich, Anton. AB, Columbia Coll., 1958; MD, U. Rochester, 1961. Diplomate Am. Bd. Surgery. Intern UCLA, 1962-64, resident in surgery, 1964-65; fellow Mayo Clinic, Rochester, Minn., 1965-68; chief resident in surgery UCLA, 1968-70; prof. Stanford U., Calif., 1970, UCLA, 1988-90; attending surgeon, chief staff UCLA Med. Ctr. Author: Vascular Disorders of the Upper Extremity, 1990. Lt. comdr. USPHS, 1965. Fogarty internat. fellow U.S. Nat. Inst. Health, Bristol, Eng., 1981. Mem. Am. Surg. Assn., Soc. Vascular Surgery. Office: UCLA Sch Medicine Divsn Gen Surgery PO Box 956904 Los Angeles CA 90095-6904

MACK, BRENDA LEE, sociologist, public relations consulting company executive; b. Peoria, Ill., Mar. 24; d. William James and Virginia Julia (Pickett) Palmer; m. Rozene Mack, Jan. 13 (div.); 1 child, Kevin Anthony. AA, L.A. City Coll.; BA in Sociology, Calif. State U., L.A., 1980. Ct. clk. City of Blythe, Calif.; ptnr. Mack Trucking Co., Blythe; owner Brenda Mack Enterprises, L.A., 1981—; conflict mediator, cultural sensitivity cons.; lectr., writer, radio and TV personality; cons. European cmty.; co-originator advt. concept View/Door Project; pub. News from the United States newsletter through U.S. and Europe; Cultural Sensitivity Cons.; Conflict Mediator. Past bd. dirs. Narcotic Symposium, L.A. With WAC, U.S. Army. Mem. Women For, Calif. State U. L.A. Alumni Assn., World Affairs Coun., German-Am. C. of C., European Cmty. Studies Assn. Home: 8749 Cattaraugus Ave Los Angeles CA 90034-2558 Office: Brenda Mack Enterprises/Mack Media Presents PO Box 5942 Los Angeles CA 90055-0942

MACK, CHARLES DANIEL, III, labor union executive; b. Oakland, Calif., Apr. 16, 1942; m. Marlene Helen Fagundes, Oct. 15, 1960; children: Tammy, Kelly, Kerry, Shannon. B.A., San Francisco State Coll., 1964. Truck driver Garrett Freight Lines, Emeryville, Calif., 1962-66; bus. agt. Teamsters Local No. 70, Oakland, 1966-70, sec.-treas., 1972—; legis. rep. Calif. Teamsters Pub. Affairs Council, Sacramento, 1970-71; trustee Western Conf. Teamsters Pension Trust Fund, 1980—, pres. Teamsters' Joint Council 7, San Francisco, 1982—; mem. Calif. Inst. for Fed. Policy Rsch., 1993—. Bd. dirs. Econ. Devel. Corp. of Oakland, 1980-90, Calif. Compensation Ins. Fund, San Francisco, 1980-86, Calif. Coun. Econ. and Environ. Balance, The Calif. Found. on Environ. and the Economy.

MACK, DONALD, publisher; b. St. Louis, June 23, 1931; s. Herman and Mary (Schvack) M.; divorced; 5 children. BA, U. Mo., 1967. Constrn. co. owner Ho. of Tomorrow, St. Louis, 1955-60; pres., editor Towerhigh Pub. Inc., L.A., 1960—. Pub. Today's Policeman, 1960—, Today's Fireman, 1960—. Bd. dirs Greater Kansas City Shelter for Mentally Handicapped, 1969-74. With U.S. Army, 1951-54. Office: Towerhigh Pub Inc PO Box 875108 Los Angeles CA 90087-0208

MACK, J. CURTIS, II, civic organization administrator; b. Los Angeles, Dec. 22, 1944; s. James Curtis and Ahli Christina (Youngren) M.; m. Tamara Jo Kriner, Jan. 23, 1988; children: James Curtis III, Robert Lee. BA cum laude, U. So. Calif., 1967, M in Pub. Adminstrn., 1969, MA, 1976. Asst. to regional dir. VA, Los Angeles, 1973-79; exec. dir. Citizens for the Republic, Santa Monica, Calif., 1979-85; asst. sec. oceans and atmosphere U.S. Dept. Commerce, Washington, 1985-88; pres. Los Angeles World Affairs Coun., 1988—; bd. dirs. Brentwood Bank of Calif. Mem. Pres.'s Commn. on White House Fellowships, 1984-85. Col. USAFR, 1969—. Mem. Nat. Space Club (bd. dirs. 1987-88). Republican. Episcopalian. Office: Los Angeles World Affairs Coun 911 Wilshire Blvd Ste 1730 Los Angeles CA 90017-3409

MACKAY, DEWEY CALDER, health facility executive, retired physician; b. Granger, Utah, June 2, 1920; s. Dewey C. and Agnes (Reynolds) MacK.; m. Lorraine Nordberg, Sept. 1, 1945; children: Dewey C. III, Calvin R., Connie Lyn MacKay Johansen, Lorin C. BA, U. Utah, 1944, MD, 1947. Diplomate Am. Bd. Family Physicians. Intern Milwaukee County Hosp., 1948-49; resident VA Hosp., Salt Lake City, 1949-50; ptnr. South Davis Med. Ctr., Bountiful, Utah, 1950-88; ret., 1988; dir. South Davis Cmty. Hosp., Bountiful, 1961-63, 76-95, chief of staff, 1961-62, chmn., bd. dirs., 1994—; dir. Utah Bank and Trust, Bountiful, 1963-93. Precinct chair Rep. Dist., Bountiful, 1994-95. Surgon USPHS, 1954-56. Mem. LDS Ch. Home: 1022 Oakridge Ln Bountiful UT 84010-2029

MACKAY, NANCY, librarian, archivist; b. Boston, May 7, 1945; m. Feb. 14, 1970 (div. July, 1982); children: Michael Siano, Christiaan Siano. BA, U. Calif., 1967, MLIS, 1983; postgrad., Oakland Calif., 1994—. Libr. Hispanex, Oakland, Calif., 1983-86; catalogue libr. U. Calif., Berkeley, 1986-87; libr. tech. svcs. Mills Coll., Oakland, Calif., 1989—; mem. adv. bd. Legacy Oral History Project, San Francisco, 1996—. Co-author: Swimming Across the West, 1985, Swim Bay Area, 1988; contbr. articles to book. Dancer, performer Slavonijo Dance Ensemble, San Francisco, 1985-91, costume dir., 1986-90. Mem. MLA, Dance Librs. Discussion Group, Dance Heritage Coalition, Coll. and Rsch. Librs. Assn. Office: Mills Coll 5000 MacArthur Blvd Oakland CA 94613

MACKELLAR, KEITH ROBERT, hospital administrator; b. Chgo., Dec. 26, 1943; s. Duncan Harvey and Julie Marie MacK.; m. Deborah Marie Boone, Aug. 26, 1967; children: Andrea Kathleen, Bethany Kristine. AA, Morton Coll., 1969; B in Orgnl. Behavior, Northwestern U., 1978; M in Human Resources, Loyola U. Chgo., 1987. Dir. Ill. Masonic Med. Ctr., Chgo., 1967-74, Northwestern Meml. Hosp., Chgo., 1974-80; div. dir. AMA, Chgo., 1980-89; dir. human resources Physicians & Surgeons Hosp., Shreveport, La., 1989-91; v.p. resource mgmt. Eastern N.Mex. Med. Ctr., Roswell, 1991—; past chmn. N.Mex. Hosp. Workers Compensation Bd. Sec. Sch. Bd. Dist. #88, Bellwood, Ill., 1980-83. Sgt. USMC, 1962-66, Vietnam. Mem. Am. Coll. Healthcare Execs., Am. Soc. Healthcare Human Resources Assn., Am. Mgmt. Assn., Soc. Human Resources Mgmt., N.Mex. Healthcare Human Resources Assn. (pres. 1996-97), Rotary Internat., Leadership Roswell Alumni Assn. (past pres.). Baptist. Home: 808 La Paloma Roswell NM 88201 Office: Eastern NMex Med Ctr 405 W Country Club Rd Roswell NM 88201-5209

MACKENZIE, DONALD MATTHEW, JR., minister; b. Chgo., Mar. 25, 1944; s. Donald Matthew Sr. and Ruth Vicory (Yoakum) M.; m. Judith Joy Petterson, May 31, 1966; children: Mary Hye Won, Alice Eun Ah. AB, Macalester Coll., 1966; MDiv, Princeton (N.J.) Sem., 1970, ThM, 1971; PhD, NYU, 1978. Assoc. dir. field edn. Princeton Sem., 1971-80; assoc. pastor Nassau Presbyn. Ch., Princeton, 1980-83; pastor The Ch. of Christ at Dartmouth Coll., Hanover, N.H., 1983-95; examiner D in Ministry program Princeton Sem., 1980—; min. and head of staff U. Congl. United Ch. of Christ, Seattle, 1995—; adj. prof. practical theology Bangor (Maine) Theol. Sem., 1991-95. Contbr. articles to profl. jours. Bd. dirs. Trenton (N.J.) Ecumenical Area Ministry, 1977-83, Wesley-Westminster Found., Princeton U., 1981-83. Mem. Assn. Profs. and Researchers in Religious Edn., United Ch. of Christ, Washington, North Idaho, Conf. United Ch. of Christ (trustee 1990-92), Phi Delta Kappa. Democrat. Home: 16011 36th Ave NE Seattle WA 98155-6623 Office: U. Congl. United Ch. of Christ 16th Ave NE Seattle WA 98105 *I think the biggest challenge facing us in the near future is to accept the essential uncertainty of human experience and to look for guidance to the Gospel, which I believe is a guide to living with uncertainty.*

MACKENZIE, PETER SEAN, instructional designer; b. L.A., Aug. 25, 1954; s. William Duncan and Patricia Ann (Kronschnabel) Mack; m. Carin Willette, Dec. 28, 1983; 1 child, Liam Reynolds. BA, Western Wash. U., 1976. Bus. editor Skagit Valley Herald, Mount Vernon, Wash., 1976-79; mng. editor Stanwood (Wash.)-Camano News, 1979-84; graphic artist Pacific Media Group, Seattle, 1985-90, editor, 1990-94; instnl. designer Mosaix, Inc. (formerly Digital Systems Internat.), Redmond, Wash., 1994—; instr. U. Wash. Exptl. Coll., Seattle, 1990-91, 96—. Author: Jumper, 1989; rec. artist LP KEZX Album Project, 1987, Victory Music Vol. # 2, 1988; speaker Viacom Cable Pub. Access TV, Seattle, 1990. V.p. Stanwood, Wash. C. of C., 1983. Recipient 1st place newswriting award Wash. Newspaper Pubs. Assn., 1981, 82, 2d place award for comprehensive coverage, 1982, 3d place awards in newswriting, features and spot news, 1983. Mem. Soc. Profl. Journalists (2d place award for investigative reporting 1982, 3d place award for editls. 1983). Home: 316 NW 86th St Seattle WA 98117-3125 Office: Mosaix Inc 6464 185th Ave NE Redmond WA 98052-5032

MACKEY, MAUREEN ELISE, rehabilitation medicine physician; b. Teaneck, N.J., Oct. 10, 1943; d. Thomas D. Jr. and Regina (Morley) M. BA with honors, U. Dallas, Irving, 1969; MD, U. Tex., Houston, 1974. Diplomate Am. Bd. Phys. Medicine and Rehab.; cert. expert in diagnosis of drug and alcohol abuse, cert. as examiner for permanent partial disability, cert. as expert witness; lic. physician, Tex., Nev., Mo. Intern USPHS Hosp., New Orleans, 1974-75; resident in phys. medicine and rehab. Parkland Meml. Hosp., Dallas, 1978-80; attending staff Jean Hanna Clark Rehab. Ctr., Las Vegas, 1981-88, 90—; cons. staff Humana Sunrise Hosp., Las Vegas, 1984-88, Valley Hosp., Las Vegas, 1983-88, Univ. Med. Ctr., Las Vegas, 1982-87, 91—; cons. VA Outpatient Clinic, Las Vegas, 1992—. Precinct chair Dem. Party, Dallas, 1978-80, committeewoman, 1978-80, del. to State Conv., 1978-80, committeewoman, Las Vegas, 1981-83; vol. med. cons. Salvation Army, Las Vegas, 1983-87, We Care Women's Alcohol Recovery House, Las Vegas, 1983-93; bd. dirs. Sunrise Home Health Svcs., Las Vegas, 1984-87. Surgeon USPHS, 1973-78. Fellow Am. Acd. Phys. Medicine and Rehab., Am. Acad. Disability Evaluating Physicians; mem. AMA, Nev. State Soc. Phys. Medicine and Rehab. (past pres.), Am. Soc. for Addiction Medicine, Nev. State Med. Soc., Clark County Med. Soc. Democrat. Office: Ste 201 1120 Almond Tree Ln Las Vegas NV 89104

MACKEY, WAYNE ALLISON, electrical engineer; b. Pitts., Sept. 22, 1955; s. George Allison and Dorothy Jayne (Ross) M.; m. Mary Lou Herbers, Nov. 16, 1984; children: Benjamin Paul, Craig Thomas. BSEE and Econs., Carnegie Mellon U., 1977; MS in Engring., Loyola Marymount U., L.A., 1982. Engr. space and info. systems Raytheon Co., Sudbury, Mass., 1977-78; mem. tech. staff Hughes Aircraft Co., El Segundo, Calif., 1978-84, head tech. sect., 1984-87, sr. scientist, engr., 1987-90, div. sr. scientist, 1990—, team leader event based concurrent engring., 1991—, team leader estimating process improvement, 1992, team leader customer focused quality and orgn. metrics system, 1993, team leader 6 Sigma quality, 1994, team leader RCS supplier devel., 1995; team leader 6 Sigma quality, 1994; exec. advisor to Mgmt. Roundtable Inc., 1995; conf. chmn., spkr. Metrics for Product Devel. and Project Mgmt., 1996; team leader Nat. Metrics Task Force, 1997. Inventor automated environ. tester, universal FLIR tester, automatic bid/spread sheet, four steps metric process. Fellow Hughes Corp. Edn. Coun., 1980. Mem. Am. Soc. Quality Control, Assn. Proposal Mgmt. Profls., Tau Beta Pi. Home: 1315 10th St Manhattan Beach CA 90266-6035 Office: Hughes Aircraft Co PO Box 902 E180 El Segundo CA 90245

MACKIE, RICHARD ALLEN, small business owner, publishing company executive; b. L.A., July 8, 1933; s. Stanley Warren and Marjorie Eugenia (Stewart) M.; m. Patricia Ann Bentz, July 14, 1956 (div. Nov. 1978); children: Wendy Kay Mackie Baird, Gerald Bruce, Kenneth Edward; m. Jean Hicks McNeill, Apr. 24, 1983; stepchildren: Mike McNeill, Jane Moses. BS, San Diego State U., 1955; MS, U. Idaho, 1957. C.C. teaching credential, Calif. Agr. insp. San Diego County Dept. Agr., San Diego, 1957-59, pub. health entomologist, 1959-71; chief pub. health officer Guam Dept. Pub. Health, Magnilao, 1971-79; med. mgmt. cons. Health Mgmt. Internat., Calabasas, Calif., 1979-81; mgr. Olsten Corp., San Jose, Calif., 1981-83; v.p. Newton Assocs., Walnut Creek, Calif., 1983-91; owner, pres. R. Mackie Assocs., Concord, Calif., 1991—, Solution Pub., Concord, 1994—; country rep. to WHO, The Philippines, 1972-79; chmn. Guam Health Coordinating Coun., Agana, 1976-79; coord. Operation New Life, Guam, 1975; chmn. Gov.'s White Paper on Health Care, Guam, 1977. Author, pub. Beat the Devil, 1994; author: Take This Job and Sell It, 1994, Publishing on the Internet, Operation New Life; contbg. author: We Pulled Together and Won, 1993; contbr. articles to profl. jours. French horn player San Diego Youth Symphony, 1948-54, San Diego Symphony, 1954-55. Home and Office: 1790 Ellis St Apt 8 Concord CA 94520-2743

MACKIN, GLENN ALEXANDER, neurologist; b. Phila., Nov. 2, 1954; s. Alexander and Evelyn Jean (Manbeck) M.; m. Lynn Marie Posbergh, Aug. 13, 1994. BA in Polit. Sci., Haverford Coll., 1976; MD, Jefferson Med. Coll., 1983. Bd. cert. internal med., 1986, neurology, 1991, electrodiagnostic med., 1993, spl. qualifications in clin. neurphysiology, 1996; med. lic. State Colo. Intern internal med. Evanston (Ill.) Hosp., 1983-84, resident internal med., 1984-86; resident neurology U. Wash. Hosp., Seattle, 1986-87, Boston City Hosp., 1987-89; fellow multiple sclerosis Brigham Women's Hosp., Boston, 1989-91; fellow electromyography and neuromuscular U. Pa. Med. Ctr., Phila., 1991-93; asst. prof. of Neurology, dir. Electromyography U. Colo. Health Sci. Ctr., Denver, 1993—; reviewer Neurology Expert Drug Multum Info. Svcs., Denver, 1994—. Mem. ACP, Am. Acad. Neurology (chmn. neuro socs. congress comm. com. 1996, ethics and humanities subcom. 1997—), U. Colo. Health Sci. Ctr. (ethics com. 1996—), Peripheral Nerve Soc., Boston Soc. Neurology, Colo. Soc. Clin. Neurologists (pres. 1995-97), Pen and Pencil Club Phila. Soc. of Friends. Office: U Colo Health Sci Ctr 4200 E 9th Ave Box B 150 Denver CO 80262

MACKIN, TERRENCE CHRISTIAN, infosystems consultant; b. St. Paul, Minn., July 21, 1947; s. Donald and Laura Ann (Mumm) M.; m. Leah Adrian Amilaner, June 11, 1972 (div. Sept. 1984); children: Aaron Jacob, Sasha Esther; m. Judith Kaye Applen, Sept. 17, 1989; 1 child, Katherine Applen. BS, Hamline U., 1969; postgrad., Syracuse U., 1969-70, U. Minn., 1975-76. Systems mgr. Infinite Graphics, Mpls., 1972-75; computer ops. B. Dalton Bookseller, Mpls., 1975-77, mgr. store systems, 1977-87; computer security analyst N.W. Bank Corp., Mpls., 1977; sr. cons. Peter R. Johnson & Assoc., Richmond, Calif., 1987-91; bus. cons. No. States Power Co., Mpls., 1991-93; mgr. stove systems Mervyn's, Hayward, Calif., 1993—. Mem. Planning Dist. 10 St. Paul, Minn., 1979-81. With U.S. Army, 1970-72. Recipient Summer Rsch. Grant Nat. Sci. Found. Macalester Coll., 1968, Grad. Fellowship Nat. Sci Found. Syracuse U., 1969-70. Mem. Res. Officers Assn., IBM POS User Group (bd. dirs. 1985), DTS POS User Group (pres. Minn. 1983). Office: Mervyn's MS M4AY 22301 Foothill Blvd Hayward CA 94541-2709

MACKINTOSH, FREDERICK ROY, oncologist; b. Miami, Fla., Oct. 4, 1943; s. John Harris and Mary Carlotta (King) MacK.; m. Judith Jane Parnell, Oct. 2, 1961 (div. Aug. 1977); children: Lisa Lynn, Wendy Sue; m. Claudia Lizanne Flournoy, Jan. 7, 1984; 1 child, Gregory Warren. BS, MIT, 1964, PhD, 1968; MD, U. Miami, 1976. Intern then resident in gen. medicine Stanford (Calif.) U., 1976-78, fellow in oncology, 1978-81; asst. prof. med. U. Nev., Reno, 1981-85, assoc. prof., 1985-92, prof. medicine, 1992—. Contbr. articles to profl. jours. Fellow ACP; mem. Am. Soc. Clin. Oncology, Am. Cancer Soc. (pres. Nev. chpt. 1987-89, Washoe chpt. 1988-90), No. Nev. Cancer Coun. (bd. dirs. 1981-92), No. Calif. Cancer Program (bd. dirs. alt. 1983-87, bd. dirs. 1987-91). Office: Nev Med Group 781 Mill St Reno NV 89502-1320

MACKO, NANCY, artist, educator; b. Oceanside, N.Y., Apr. 29, 1950; d. Emil E.M. and Arline (Walker) Kelly; m. Jan Blair, Dec. 24, 1985. BS in Liberal Arts, U. Wis., River Falls, 1977; MA, U. Calif., Berkeley, 1980, MFA in Painting and Printmaking, 1981, Ma in Edn. Psychology, 1989. Assoc. registrar Asian Art Mus., San Francisco, 1985-86; asst. prof. art Scripps Coll., Claremont, Calif., 1986-92, assoc. prof. art, 1992—; vis. lectr. U. Calif., Davis, 1983-84; vis. artist, prof. La Corte della Miniera, Urbino, Italy, 1990; adj. prof. Claremont Grad. Sch., 1986-91; dir. Scripps Computer Art Program, 1990—; cons. in field. Mem. exhbn. com. L.A. Ctr. Photographic Studies, 1994, 96, Barnsdall Mcpl. Art Gallery, L.A., 1996—. Faculty rsch. grantee, 1986-95; rsch. fellow Scripps Coll., 1989, 96. Mem. Calif. Soc. Printmakers (pres. 1984-85), Coll. Art Assn. N.Y. (bd. dirs. 1994—, exec. bd. 1995—, sec. 1996—). Democrat. Home: 810 Kodak Dr Los Angeles CA 90026-2708 Office: Scripps Coll 1030 Columbia Ave Claremont CA 91711-3905

MACLAUCHLIN, ROBERT KERWIN, communications artist, educator; b. Framingham, Mass., Oct. 8, 1931; s. Charles Lewis and Elinor Frances (Kerwin) MacL.; m. Elizabeth D'Ann Willson, June 13, 1964. BA in Sociology, U. Mass., Amherst, 1954; MEd, Bridgewater State Coll., 1958; MS in Radio and TV, Syracuse U., 1959; PhD in Speech, Radio, TV, Mich. State U., 1969. Personnel trainee Nat. Security Agy., Washington, 1954-55; elem. sch. tchr. Mattapoisett (Mass.) Pub. Schs., 1957-58; asst. prof., dir. programming Maine Ednl. TV Network, Orono, 1959-66; assoc. prof. speech communications, dir. TV-Radio instrn. Colo. State U., Ft. Collins, 1969-76, prof., dir. TV-Radio instrn., 1976—; cons. U. Maine, Orono, 1968, Ft. Collins Presbyn. Ch., 1976-78, Sta. KCOL-AM-FM, Ft. Collins, 1978, Pub. Health Assn., Ft. Collins, 1985; archives program guest Maine Pub. Broadcast, Orono, 1983. Served with inf. U.S. Army, 1955-57. Recipient Excellence in Teaching award Mich. State U., 1969, Friend of Broadcasting award Colo. Broadcasters Assn., 1985; named Disting. Vis. Prof. U. Vt., Burlington, 1983, A Teacher Who Makes A Difference Denver's Rocky Mountain News, KCNC-TV, 1987. Mem. NATA (panel Colo. chpt. 1989—), Broadcast Edn. Assn. (Industry State chmn. 1981-86, panel 1991—, chmn. faculty internship com. 1991—), Colo. Broadcasters Assn. (edn. com. 1972—, Hall of Fame com. 1980—, human resources com. 1991, Friends of Broadcast award 1985, panelist summer conv. 1994, panelist summer conv. 1995), Speech Comm. Assn., Kiwanis (Disting. past pres. 1979-80). Republican. Home: 1407 Country Club Rd Fort Collins CO 80524-1907 Office: Colo State U Dept Speech Communicat Fort Collins CO 80523 *Personal philosophy: Set high goals, enjoy people and laughter, and always seek to give back more to society than you take from it.*

MACLEAN, EDNA AHGEAK, language educator, researcher; b. Barrow, Alaska, Nov. 5, 1944; d. Joseph A. and Maria (Brower) Ahgeak; m. Stephen F. MacLean, July 11, 1967 (div. June 1992); children: Stephen, Andrew. BA, Colo. Women's Coll., 1967; cert. in tchg., U. Calif., Berkeley, 1969; MEd, U. Wash., 1991; PhD, Stanford U., 1995. Rsch. asst. Naval Arctic Rsch. Lab., Barrow, Alaska, summer 1971; Inupiaq lang. specialist U. Alaska, Fairbanks, 1973-75, asst. prof. Inupiaq-Eskimo, 1976-87; Alaska Native edn. coord. Alaska Dept. Edn., Juneau, 1987-90; Inupiaq curriculum developer North Slope Borough Sch. Dist., Barrow, 1992; pres. Ilisagvik Coll., 1995—; mem. steering com. Internat. Cross-Cultural Edn. Seminar Series in the Circumpolar North, 1983—; mem. Inuit Circumpolar Conf. Com. on Edn., 1978-83; mem. com. on arctic social scis., Polar Rsch. Bd., NRC, 1987-91; v.p. for Alaska Inuit Circumpolar Exec. Coun., 1989-92. Author: (with others) Genealogical Record of Barrow Eskimo Families, 1973, Eskimo Languages, Their Present-Day Conditions, 1979; contbr. articles to profl. jours. Mem., pres. North Slope Borough Commn. on History, Lang., and Culture, Barrow, 1973-83. Recipient Shareholder of Yr. award, Ukpeagvik Inupiat Corp., 1982, Cert. of Spl. Recognition, City of Barrow, 1982. Fellow Arctic Inst. N.Am. Home: PO Box 261 Barrow AK 99723-0261 Office: PO Box 1277 Barrow AK 99723-1277

MACLEOD, ALEX, newspaper editor; b. Seattle. Student, Whitman Coll. Night reporter to city editor to asst. mng. editor-news Seattle Times, 1976-84, assoc. mng. editor, 1984-86, mng. editor, 1986—. Office: Seattle Times Fairview Ave Seattle WA 98111

MACLEOD, RICHARD PATRICK, foundation administrator; b. Boston, Apr. 2, 1937; s. Thomas Everett and Margaret Gertrude (Fahey) MacL.; children: Kimberly Margaret Hamelin, Richard Alexander MacLeod. BA in Govt., U. Mass., 1960; MA in Internat. Rels., U. So. Calif., 1968. Instr. polit. sci. USAF Acad., 1968-71; Commd. 2d lt. USAF, 1960, advanced through grades to col., 1981; sr. rsch. fellow The Nat. Def. U., Washington, 1978-79; chief Space Policy Br., dep. chief Plans USAF Aerospace Def. Command, 1979-80; exec. officer to the comdr. in chief USAF Aerospace Def. Command, NORAD, 1980-81; chief of staff NORAD, 1981-84, USAF Space Command, 1982-84; ret. U.S. Space Found., 1985; exec. dir. U.S. Space Found., Colorado Springs, Colo., 1985-88; pres. U.S. Space Found., Colorado Springs, 1988-97; bd. dirs. Analytical Surveys, Inc., Colorado Springs, 1985—, U.S. Space Found., 1997—; space edn. advisor Coll. Engring. Adv. Coun., U. Colo., Colorado Springs. Author: Peoples War in Thailand, Insurgency in the Modern World, 1980. Mem. White House Space Policy Adv. Bd.; bd. dirs. Pike's Peak Coun. Boy Scouts Am., Colorado Springs; past pres. Colorado Springs Symphony Coun.; past dir. World Affairs Coun., Colorado Springs. Fellow Brit. Interplanetary Soc.; mem. AIA, Air Force Acad. Found. (bd. dirs., trustee), U.S. Space Found. (founding), Aviation Space Writers Assn., Air Force Space Ops. Assn., GPS Internat. Assn., Am. Legion, The Co. of Fifers and Drummers. Office: US Space Found 2860 S Circle Dr Ste 2301 Colorado Springs CO 80906-4107

MACMILLAN, KIP VAN METRE, foundation executive; b. Evanston, Ill., Dec. 18, 1937; s. Charles Daniel and Janet Marvia (Van Metre) M.; m. Linda Jean Griesbach, Dec. 22, 1962; children: Christopher, Julia. Sgt., lt., div. comdr. Evanston Police Dept., 1961-88; supr. Polio Plus campaign Rotary Found., Evanston, 1988-90, ret., 1990. Bd. dirs. Youth Orgn. Umbrella, Evanston, 1974, McGaw YMCA, Evanston, 1976-89, Shore Cmty. Svcs. for Retarded Citizens, Evanston, 1986-90, Teton County Crime Stoppers; pres. Teton Youth & Family Svcs.; chmn. Evanston March of Dimes, 1987, Teton County Congl. Awards Com., Browse and Buy Bd. St. John's Ch., Wildcat dist. com. Boy Scouts Am.; mem. adv. com. Cook County Dept. Children and Family Svcs., Chgo., 1987-90; mem. Ill. Coord. System Response Project-Mass Abuse of Children, Springfield, 1987-89; dir., treas. Evanston Sister City Found., 1989-90; vol. Grand Teton Music Festival; vestryman St. John's Episcopal Ch.; bd. dirs. Wyo. Spl. Olympics. Recipient Top Vol. of Yr. award North Shore mag., 1987, Jay Moore award Youth Orgn. Umbrella, 1988, William Harper award McGaw YMCA, 1975. Mem. Nat. Soc. Fundraising Execs., Rotary (bd. dirs. Evanston club 1986-89, bd. dirs. Jackson Hole club, pres. Jackson Hole club 1994-95, Outstanding Rotarian Evanston club 1988), Am. Soc. Indsl. Security, Teton County Peace Officers Assn. Republican. Episcopalian.

MACMILLEN, RICHARD EDWARD, biological sciences educator, researcher; b. Upland, Calif., Apr. 19, 1932; s. Hesper Nichols and Ruth Henrietta (Golder) MacM.; m. Ann Gray, June 12, 1953 (div. 1975); children: Jennifer Kathleen, Douglas Michael; m. Barbara Jean Morgan, Oct. 23, 1980; 1 child, Ian Richard. BA, Pomona Coll., 1954; MS, U. Mich., 1956; PhD, UCLA, 1961. From instr. to assoc. prof. Pomona Coll., Claremont, Calif., 1960-68, Wig Disting. prof., 1965; assoc. prof., then prof. U. Calif., Irvine, 1968—, chair dept. population and environ. biology, 1972-74, chair dept. ecology and evolutionary biology, 1984-90; prof. emeritus, 1993—; adj. prof. biology So. Oreg. State U., Ashland, 1996—; mem. award panel NSF, Washington, 1976-80; coord. U. Calif. Multi-Campus Supercourse in Environ. Biology, White Mountain Rsch. Sta., spring 1996, 97. Contbr. numerous articles to profl. jours. Chair sci. adv. bd. Endangered Habitats League, 1991-93. Recipient rsch. awards NSF, 1961-83; Fulbright-Hays advanced rsch. fellow Monash U., Australia, 1966-67. Fellow AAAS; mem. Am. Soc. Mammalogists (life), Ecol. Soc. Am. (cert. sr. ecologist), Am. Ornithologists Union, Cooper Ornithol. Soc. (life, bd. dirs. 1982-84). Democrat. Home: 705 Foss Rd Talent OR 97540 Office: So Oreg State U Dept Biology Ashland OR 97520 *As world human populations continue to increase, our natural world continues to degrade. It is incumbent upon all of us to accept the responsibility of stewarding our land and its biota as precious and renewable resources.*

MACMULLEN, DOUGLAS BURGOYNE, writer, editor, retired army officer, publisher; b. Berkeley, Calif., Dec. 26, 1919; s. T. Douglas and Florence (Burgoyne) MacM.; ed. San Francisco State U., 1937-41, Stanford U., U. Calif., Fgn. Svc. Inst., Strategic Intelligence Sch., Indsl. Coll. of the Armed

Forces, Air War Coll., Army Mgmt. Sch.; m. Sherry Bernice Auerbach, Mar. 11, 1942; 1 child, Douglas Burgoyne Jr. Commd. 2d lt. F.A. Res. U.S. Army, 1941; advanced through grades to col. M.I., 1967; Army gen. staff Psychol. Ops. Fgn. Svc., PTO; ret., 1972; exec. editor Am. Rsch. Assoc., Sherman Oaks, Calif.; cons. in communication; accredited corr. Def. Dept. Bd. govs. Monte Vista Grove Homes, Pasadena, Calif., Shriners Hosps. for Crippled Children, L.A.; pres. Clan MacMillan Soc. N.Am., 1973-77, trustee, 1975—; mem. L.A. Olympics Citizens Adv. Commn., 1982-84; mem. L.A. Philanthropic Found.; bd. dirs. Masonic Press Club, L.A., 1975, 84-88; mem. steering com. Mayor L.A. Coun. Internat. Visitors and Sister Cities, 1969; hon. dep. sheriff San Bernardino County, Calif., 1996—; chmn. Los Angeles-Glasgow Sister Cities Ad Hoc Com.; former mem. San Francisco Mayor's Mil. and Naval Affairs Com.; mem. wills and gifts com. Shriners Hosp. Crippled Children, Al Malaikah Temple, L.A., 1974-80; cons. com. on pub. info. Masons Grand Lodge of Calif., 1985-86. Decorated Legion of Merit, Army Commendation medal (U.S.), Knight Comdr. Order of Polonia Restituta (Free Poland), Red Cross of Constantine; Royal Order Scotland. Mem. Internat. Inst. Strategic Studies, Nat. Mil. Intelligence Assn., Assn. Former Intelligence Officers (pres. L.A. County chpt.), U.S. Naval Inst., Assn. U.S. Army, Company Mil. Historians, Am. Def. Preparedness Assn., St. Andrew's Soc. Los Angeles (past pres., trustee), Air Force Assn., Stanford U. Alumni Assn., Calif. Newspaper Pubs. Assn., Nat. Def. Exec. Res., Sigma Delta Chi. Republican. Presbyterian. Clubs: Press, Caledonian (London); Army & Navy Club (Washington), San Francisco Press. Lodges: Masons (32 deg.), K.T., Shriners (editor, pub. The Al Malaikahan, former imperial news editor Shrine of N.Am.), Quatuor Coronati C.C. Co-author: Psychological Profile of Cambodia, 1971; author-editor: A Sentimental Journey--The History of the First Hundred Years, 1988; numerous other publs. and articles; radio commentator and newspaper columnist on mil., polit. and internat. affairs. Address: PO Box 5201 Sherman Oaks CA 91413-5201

MACNAUGHTON, ANGUS ATHOLE, finance company executive; b. Montreal, July 15, 1931; s. Athole Austin and Emily Kidder (MacLean) MacN.; children: Gillian Heather, Angus Andrew. Student, Lakefield Coll. Sch., 1941-47, McGill U., 1949-54. Auditor Coopers & Lybrand, Montreal, 1949-55; acct. Genstar Ltd., Montreal, 1955; asst. treas. Genstar Ltd., 1956-61, treas., 1961-64, v.p., 1964-70, exec. v.p., 1970-73, pres., 1973-76, vice chmn., chief exec. officer, 1976-81, chmn. or pres., chief exec. officer, 1981-86; pres. Genstar Investment Corp., 1987—; bd. dirs. Can. Pacific Ltd., Sun Life Assurance Co., Can., Ltd., Barrick Gold Corp., Diversified Collection Svcs., Inc., Varian Assocs., Inc.; past pres. Montreal chpt. Tax Execs. Inst. Bd. govs. Lakefield Coll. Sch.; past chmn. San Francisco Bay Area coun. Boy Scouts Am.; bd. dirs. San Francisco Opera; trustee World Affairs Coun. of No. Calif. Mem. Pacific Union Club, World Trade Club, Villa Taverna (San Francisco), Mt. Royal Club (Montreal), Toronto Club. Office: Genstar Investment Corp 950 Tower Ln Ste 1170 Foster City CA 94404-2127 also: Barrick Gold Corp, 200 Bay St Ste 2700, Toronto, ON Canada M5J 2J3

MAC NEIL, JOSEPH NEIL, archbishop; b. Sydney, N.S., Can., Apr. 15, 1924; s. John Martin and Kate (Mac Lean) Mac N. BA, St. Francis Xavier U., Antigonish, N.S., 1944; postgrad., Holy Heart Sem., Halifax, N.S., 1944-48, U. Perugia, 1956, U. Chgo., 1964; JCD, U. St. Thomas, Rome, 1958. Ordained priest Roman Cath. Ch., 1948. Pastor parishes in N.S., 1948-55; officialis Chancery Office, Antigonish, 1958-59; adminstrn. Diocese of Antigonish, 1959-60; rector Cathedral Antigonish, 1961; dir. extension dept. St. Francis Xavier U., Antigonish, 1961-69, v.p., 1962-69; bishop St. John, N.B., Can., 1969-73; chancellor U. St. Thomas, Fredericton, N.B., 1969-73; archbishop of Edmonton, Alta., 1973—; chmn. Alta Bishops' Conf., 1973—; chmn. bd. Newman Theol. Coll., Edmonton, 1973—, St. Joseph's Coll. U. Alta., Edmonton, 1973—. Vice chmn. N.S. Voluntary Econ. Planning Bd., 1965-69; bd. dirs. Program and Planning Agy., Govt. of N.S., 1969; exec. Atlantic Provinces Econ. Coun., 1968-73, Can. Coun. Rural Devel., 1965-75; bd. dirs. Futures Secretariat, 1981, Ctr. for Human Devel., Toronto, Ont., Can., 1985—; mem. bd. mgmt. Edmonton Gen. Hosp., 1983-92, Edmonton Caritas Health Group, 1992—; mem. Nat. Com. for Can. Participation in Habitat, 1976. Mem. Can. Assn. Adult Edn. (past pres. N.S.), Can. Assn. Dirs. Univ. Extension and Summer Schs. (past pres.), Inst. Rsch. on Pub. Policy (founding mem.), Can. Conf. Cath. Bishops (pres. 1979-81, mem. com. on ecumenism 1985-91, com. on missions 1991-96, mem. permanent coun. 1993-95). Address: Archbishop of Edmonton, 8421 101st Ave, Edmonton, AB Canada T6A 0L1

MACNEILL, BRIAN F., oil and natural gas company executive; b. 1939; married; 4 children. B in Comms., Mont. State U., 1965. CPA. Acct. Haskins & Sells, San Francisco, 1967; v.p., treas. Hiram Walker Resources Ltd., 1980-82; v.p. fin., CFO Home Oil Co., Ltd.; also bd. dirs.; pres., CEO Interprovincial Pipe Line, Inc., Edmonton, Alta., Can., 1990-94; pres. & CEO IPL Energy, Inc., Calgary, 1994—; bd. dirs. IDC Energy, TD, Bank, Pelo Canada, Veritas, others. Mem. Fin. Execs. Inst., CICA, Calgary Petroleum Club, Canyon Meadows Golf & Country. Office: IPL Energy Inc, 2900 421 7th Ave SW, Calgary, AB Canada T5J 2J9

MACON, CAROL ANN GLOECKLER, micro-computer data base management company executive; b. Milw., Mar. 25, 1942; d. William Theodore and Gwendolyn Martha (Rice) Gloeckler; m. Jerry Lyn Macon, Aug. 28, 1981; children: Christian, Marie. BS in Edn. cum laude, U. Wis., Milw., 1969; postgrad., Midwestern State U., Wichita Falls, Tex., 1977, U. Tex., San Antonio, 1978, U. Colo., Colorado Springs. Tchr. Lubbock, Tex.; patient affairs coord. Cardiac Assocs., Colorado Springs; founder, CFO Macon Systems, Inc., Colorado Springs. Artist, Australia, Tex., Colo. Founding mem., bd. dirs. Pikes Peak Botanic Gardens. Mem. Software Pubs. Assn., Colorado Springs BBB, Colorado Springs Fine Arts Ctr., Pikes Peak Rose Soc. (v.p.), Glen Eyrie Garden Soc., Pikes Peak Botanic Garden (founding mem., bd. dirs.), Colo. Mountain Club, Phi Kappa Phi, Kappa Delta Pi, Sigma Tau Delta, Psi Chi.

MACON, JERRY LYN, software company owner, software publisher; b. Okla., Jan. 10, 1941; s. James Westwood and Mary Isabelle (Hankins) M.; m. Carol Ann Gloeckler, Aug. 28, 1981; children: Heather, Scott, Karla. BS in Physics magna cum laude, Colo. Coll., 1963; MS in Physics, MIT, 1966; MBA in Fin., U. Colo., 1980. Physics instr. U.S. Naval Acad., Annapolis, Md., 1966-69; stockbroker Merrill Lynch, Colorado Springs, 1969-71; dir. systems analysis and programming Colorado Springs Pub. Schs., 1971-80; co-founder, pres. Alpine Software, Inc., Colorado Springs, 1980-82, Macon Systems Inc., Colorado Springs, 1981—. Author: (software) DB Master, 1980, Advanced DB Master, 1981, Advanced DB Master for Windows Version 6.0, 1995. Mem. Colorado Springs Fine Arts Ctr., 1982—, Colorado Springs Better Bus. Bur., 1990—. Cmdr. U&SN, 1966-69. Boettcher Found. scholar, 1959; Woodrow Wilson fellow, 1963; MIT rsch. assistantship, 1964. Mem. Nat. Fedn. Ind. Bus., Software Pubs. Assn., Pikes Peak Rose Soc., Colo. Mountain Club, Phi Beta Kappa. Office: Macon Systems Inc 724 S Tejon St Colorado Springs CO 80903-4042

MACPHERSON, KEVIN DAN, artist; b. Orange, N.J., Apr. 9, 1956; s. James F. and May Rose (McCrink) M.; m. Wanda Lynn Robbins, Oct. 21, 1979. BFA, No. Ariz. U., 1978; student, Scottsdale Artists Sch., 1986-93. Illustrator graphic studio, Phoenix, 1978-80; freelance illustrator, artist, Taos, N.Mex., 1980-90; fine artist Taos, 1987—; tchr. various art guilds country-wide, 1990—. One man show Trailside Americana Galleries, 1996; group shows at Plein Air Painters Am. Show, Avalon, Calif., 1987—, O'Brien's Art Emporium, Scottsdale, Ariz., 1989, 92, 94, Oil Painters of Am., 1992-94, Redfern Gallery, Laguna, Calif., 1994-95; represented in numerous permanent collections. Stacey scholar Nat. Acad. Western Art, 1990. Mem. Oil Painters Am. (hon. signature mem.), Plein Aire Painters Am. (pres. 1996—). Home and Studio: 12 Clint Rd Taos NM 87571

MACUMBER, JOHN PAUL, insurance company executive; b. Macon, Mo., Jan. 21, 1940; s. Rolland Deardorf and Althea Villa (Cason) M.; BA, Cen. Meth. Coll., Fayette, Mo., 1962; Asso. in Risk Mgmt., Ins. Inst. Am., 1978; m. Marilyn Sue Ashe, Nov. 10, 1962; children—Leanne, Cheryl. Casualty underwriter U.S. Fidelity & Guaranty Co., St. Louis, 1962-66; automobile underwriter Am. Indemnity Co., Galveston, Tex., 1966-69; auto casualty underwriter St. Paul Cos., New Orleans, 1969-73; sr. comml. casualty underwriter Chubb/Pacific Indemnity, Portland, Oreg., 1973-75; casualty underwriter Interstate Nat. Corp., L.A., 1975-76, underwriting supr., 1976-78, v.p., br. mgr., Mpls., 1978-82, also v.p. subs. Chgo. Ins. Co.; umbrella/spl. risk supr. Guaranty Nat. Ins. Co., Englewood, Colo., 1982-85; br. mgr. Burns & Wilcox, Ltd.-West, Salt Lake City, 1985-96; v.p. M.J. Kelly Ins. Brokers of Utah, Sandy, 1997—. With USAF, 1962-68. Nat. Methodist scholar, 1958; named Co. Person of Yr. Profl. Ins. Agts Utah, 1991, Ind. Ins. Agts. of Utah, 1996. Mem. Ins. Assn. Utah (sec.-treas. 1992-93, v.p. 1993-94, pres. 1994-95), Profl. Ins. Agts. Utah, Ind. Ins. Agts. Utah, Surplus Line Assn. Utah (bd. dirs. 1994—), Nat. Assn. Profl. Surplus Lines Offices. Republican. Mem. Unity Ch. of Salt Lake City (v.p., bd. dirs. 1988). Lodges: Optimists (charter pres. 1968) (Friendswood, Tex.); Kiwanis (charter pres. 1979) (Bloomington, Minn.). Clubs: Insurance, Blue Goose (Salt Lake City). Home: 9683 Buttonwood Dr Sandy UT 84092-3245 Office: 9683 S Buttonwwod Dr Sandy UT 84092-3245

MACY, RICHARD J., state judge; b. Saranac Lake, N.Y., June 2, 1930; m. Emily Ann Macy; children: Anne, Patty, Mark. BS in Bus., U. Wyo., 1955, JD, 1958. Pvt. practice Sundance, Wyo., 1958-85; justice Wyo. Supreme Ct., Cheyenne, 1985—; Crook County atty., 1970-85; mem. Nat. Conf. Commrs. on Uniform State Laws, 1982—. Mem. Sigma Chi (Nat. Outstanding Sig award 1986). Office: Wyo Supreme Ct Supreme Ct Bldg 2301 Capitol Ave Cheyenne WY 82002*

MADARA, THOMAS ALBERT, retired federal agency administrator; b. Spring Township, Pa., Apr. 18, 1940; s. John Albert and Anna Susan (Krezdorn) M.; m. Kathryn Wieland Skjod, June 24, 1969. BA in Philosophy, UCLA, 1970. Bond sales promotional rep. U.S. Dept. Treasury Savings Bond Divsn., L.A., 1972-78; L.A. dist. dir. U.S. Dept. Treasury Savings Bond Divsn., 1978-92; western regional dir. U.S. Dept. Treasury Savings Bond Divsn., L.A., 1992-95; ret., 1995. With USAF, 1957-61. Home: 1620 Oak St Santa Monica CA 90405

MADDEN, EDWARD P., protective services official. Chief police Flagstaff (Ariz.) Police Dept. Office: Flagstaff Police Dept 120 N Beaver St Flagstaff AZ 86001

MADDEN, PAUL ROBERT, lawyer; b. St. Paul, Nov. 13, 1926; s. Ray Joseph and Margaret (Meyer) M.; m. Rosemary R. Sorel, Aug. 7, 1974; children: Margaret Jane, William, James Patrick, Derek R. Sorel, Lisa T. Sorel. Student, St. Thomas Coll., 1944; AB, U. Minn., 1948; JD, Georgetown U., 1951. Bar: Ariz. 1957, Minn. 1951, D.C. 1951. Assoc. Hamilton & Hamilton, Washington, 1951-55; legal asst. to commr. SEC, Washington, 1955-56; assoc. Lewis and Roca, Phoenix, Ariz., 1957-59, ptnr., 1959-90; ptnr. Beus, Gilbert & Morrill, Phoenix, 1991-94; ptnr. Chapman and Cutler, Phoenix, 1994—. Sec. Minn. Fedn. Repl. Clubs, 1947-48; chmn. 4th dist. Minn. Young Rep. Club, 1948; nat. co-chmn. Youth for Eisenhower, 1951-52; mem. Ariz. Rep. Com., 1960-62; bd. dirs. Found. Jr. Achievement Ctrl. Ariz., Cath. Community Found., Phoenix, Heritage Hills Homeowners Assn., St. Joseph the Worker; past bd. dirs. Camelback Charitable Trust, The Samaritan Found., Phoenix; past bd. dirs., past. pres. Ariz. Club, Phoenix, 1990-93; past bd. dirs., past chmn. Found. for Sr. Living; past bd. dirs., vice chmn., Cen. Ariz. chpt. ARC; past bd. dirs., vice chmn., Cen. Ariz. chpt. ARC; past bd. dirs., past pres. Jr. Achievement Cen. Ariz., Inc.; mem. nat. bd. vis. U. Ariz. Law Sch. With USNR, 1946-48. Mem. ABA, Ariz. Bar Assn., Maricopa County Bar Assn., Fed. Bar Assn., Fedn. Ins. Counsel, Nat. Health Lawyers Assn., Am. Soc. Hosp. Attys., Phi Delta Phi. Clubs: The Barristers (Washington), Arizona. Home: 5847 N 46th St Phoenix AZ 85018-1234 Office: Chapman & Cutler Two N Central Ave Ste 1100 Phoenix AZ 85004

MADDEN, RICHARD BLAINE, forest products executive; b. Short Hills, N.J., Apr. 27, 1929; s. James L. and Irma (Twining) M.; m. Joan Fairbairn, May 24, 1958; children: John Richard, Lynne Marie, Kathryn Ann, Andrew Twining. B.S., Princeton U., 1951; J.D., U. Mich., 1956; M.B.A., NYU, 1959; PhD (hon.), St. Scholastica Coll., 1994. Bar: Mich. 1956, N.Y. 1958. Gen. asst. treas.'s dept. Socony Mobil Oil Corp., N.Y.C., 1956-57; spl. asst. Socony Mobil Oil Corp., 1958-59, fin. rep., 1960; asst. to pres. Mobil Chem. Co.; also dir. Mobil Chems. Ltd. of Eng., 1960-63; exec. v.p., gen. mgr. Kordite Corp.; also v.p. Mobil Plastics, 1963-66; v.p. Mobil Chem. Co., N.Y.C., 1966-68; group v.p. Mobil Chem. Co., 1968-70; asst. treas. Mobil Oil Corp., 1970-71; chmn. Mobil Oil Estates Ltd., 1970-71; pres., chief exec. to chmn., chief exec. officer Potlatch Corp., San Francisco, 1971-94; ret., 1994; bd. dirs. Potlatch Corp., PG&E Corp., CNF Transp. Inc., URS Corp.; former bd. dirs. Del Monte Corp., AMFAC Inc., Bank Calif. N.A. and BankCal Tri-State Corp.; from lectr. to adj. assoc. prof. fin. NYU, 1960-63. Bd. dirs. Smith-Kettlewell Eye Rsch. Inst., Nat. Park Found., mem. fin. com., devel. com.; trustee emeritus, former chmn. Am. Enterprise Inst.; bd. govs., mem. adminstrv. compensation, audit & labor rels. com. San Francisco Symphony; hon. trustee Com. for Econ. Devel. Lt. (j.g.) USNR, 1951-54. Mem. N.Y. Bar Assn., Mich. Bar Assn. Roman Catholic. Clubs: Bohemian (San Francisco); Lagunitas (Ross, Calif.); Metropolitan (Washington).

MADDOX, DAVID DANIEL, military officer; b. Guam, Mar. 12, 1962; s. Raymond G. and Helen Fern (Sanders) M.; m. Robin Elise Lickers, Apr. 15; children: Erica Elena, Forrest David, Archer Robin. BA in Social Sci., U. No. Colo., 1984; MS in Internat. Rels., Troy State U., Geilenkirchen, Germany, 1994. Commd. 2d. lt. USAF, 1985, advanced through grades to capt.; tchr. history Grand Junction (Colo.) H.S., 1985; weapons assignment officer 729 Tactical Control Squadron, Hill AFB, Utah, 1990-92; chief current ops. NATO Airborne Warning and Control Squadron, Geilenkirchen, 1992-95; comdr. air def. ops. ctr. crew Cheyenne Mountain Ops. Ctr., Colorado Springs, 1995—. Decorated Def. Meritorious Svc. medal, Aerial Achievement medal (6).

MADDUX, PARKER AHRENS, lawyer; b. San Francisco, May 23, 1939; s. Jackson Walker and Jeanette Ahrens M.; m. Mathilde G.M. Landman, Mar. 20, 1966; 1 child, Jackson Wilhelmus Quentin. AB, U. Calif., 1961; JD, Harvard U., 1964. Bar: Calif. 1965, U.S. Dist. Ct. (no. so., ea., ctrl. dist.) Calif. 1965, U.S. Ct. Appeals (9th cir.) 1972, U.S. Ct. Claims, 1974, N.Y. 1981, U.S. Supreme Ct. 1982, Assoc., Pillsbury Madison & Sutro, San Francisco, 1965-72, ptnr., 1973-97; dir. litigation Tandem Computers Inc., Cupertino, Calif., 1997—; lectr. in field. Fulbright fellow, 1964-65. Mem. ABA, Calif. Bar Assn., San Francisco Bar Assn., Harvard Club (N.Y.C.), Pacific Union Club. Republican. Unitarian. Contbr. articles to profl. jours. Office: Tandem Computers Inc 10435 N Tantau Loc 200-16 Cupertino CA 95014

MADDY, DONALD LEE, computer company executive, software developer; b. Whittier, Calif., Aug. 27, 1949; s. Keith Thomas and Colleen Joanne (Barlow) M.; m. Lynne Louise Juhnke, June 29, 1985; children: Crystal Lynne, Michael Donald. Nuclear weapons, electronics student, Sandia AFB, 1970; BS in Computer Sci., Calif. State U., Sacramento, 1976; cert. in Data Processing, Stanford U., 1982, cert. in Internet Security, 1996. Lic. realtor. Nuclear weapons electronics specialist U.S. Army, Istanbul, Turkey, 1970-71; programmer Water Resources Control Bd. Div. Water Quality, Sacramento, 1974-75, Calif. State Coll., Bakersfield, 1976-78; programmer, analyst Sierra Pacific Power Co., Reno, Nev., 1979-80; sr. programmer, analyst State of Idaho Transp. Dept., Boise, 1980-81, United Grocers Warehouse, Oakland, Calif., 1981-84; sr. programming cons. Farmers Savings & Loan, Davis, Calif., 1984-87, Pacific Gas & Electric Co., Avila Beach, Calif., 1987—; pres. Maddy Corp., 1984—. Co-author: Computer Software Security System for Plant Info. Mgmt. System, 1992. With U.S. Army, 1969-72. Mem. Assn. Sys. Mgrs., Data Processing Mgmt. Assn., Assn. Computing Machinery, Am. Nuclear Soc. Republican. Office: The Maddy Corp 1220 16th St Ste D Los Osos CA 93402-1422

MADDY, JANET MARIE, retired educator, dean of students; b. Crestline, Ohio, Feb. 20, 1939; d. Hubert Franklin and Mabel May (Hotelling) M. AA, Pasadena City Coll, 1959; BA, Calif. State U., L.A., 1965, MA, 1972. Instr. Calif. State Coll., L.A., fall 1965; tchr. phys. edn. Irving Jr. High, L.A. Unified Sch. Dist., spring 1966, Bret Harte Jr. High Sch., L.A. Unified Sch. Dist., 1966-67; tchr., phys. edn. tchr., dept. chair Walton Jr. High Sch.-Compton (Calif.) Unified Sch. Dist., 1967-72; tchr. phys. edn./ coach Dominguez H.S., Compton, 1972-78; prin. Westchester Luth. Schs., L.A., 1978-84; tchr. phys. edn., dept. chair Nimitz Middle Sch., L.A. Unified Sch. Dist., Huntington Park, Calif., 1985-94, dean of students-C Track, 1994-97; mem. shared decision making coun. Nimitz Middle Sch., Huntington Park, 1992-96; mentor tchr. selection com. L.A. Unified Sch. Dist., 1993-94; women in sports delegation to China, Citizen Amb. Program, Spokane, Wash., 1994, U.S. China Joint Conf. on Women's Issues, China, 1995, Internat. Conf. on Domestic Violence, Delhi, India, 1998. Synod womens orgn. bd. ELCA Women, L.A., 1990-93, 94-96, chair references and counsel com. triennial nat. conf., Washington, 1993, del. triennial conv., Mpls., 1996; chair cmty. com. Police Activity League, Ingelwood, Calif., 1990-93; co-chair Neighborhood Watch, Ingelwood, 1988-97. Comdr. USNR, ret., 1960-83. Mem. CAHPER, AAHPER, CTA, UTLA. Democrat. Lutheran. Home: 501 E Bucyrus St Crestline OH 44827

MADER, DOUGLAS PAUL, quality engineering manager; b. Brookings, S.D., May 16, 1963; s. Lawrence Harold Mader Jr. and Susan Margaret (Littleton) Burk; m. Darla Sue Hower, Dec. 30, 1991; children: Alyssa, Megan, Matthew. BS in Engring. Physics, S.D. State U., 1985; MS in Math., Colo. Sch. of Mines, 1990; PhD in Mech. Engring., Colo. State U., 1994. Cert. quality engr. Am. Soc. Quality Control, 1990-93. Quality control engr. Govt. Electronics Group, Motorola, Scottsdale, Ariz., 1985-87; integrated circuit test engr. Semiconductor Products sector, Motorola, Mesa, Ariz., 1987-88; sr. staff engr. Six Sigma Rsch. Inst., Motorola, Schaumburg, Ill., 1990-92, prin. staff scientist, 1992; cons. Rockwell Internat., Cedar Rapids, Iowa, 1992-93; quality engring. mgr. Advanced Energy Industries, Ft. Collins, Colo., 1993-95; instr. stats. and mech. engring. Colo. State U., 1993-94; statistician Hewlett-Packard Co., Greeley, Colo., 1995-96, sr. quality cons., 1996-97, quality engring. mgr., 1997—. Author: Process Control Methods, 1993 (videotapes) Concurrent Engineering - The Foundation of Six Sigma Quality, 1992; mem. editorial bd. Internat. Jour. of Ops. and Quantitative Mgmt., 1994—. Mem. Am. Statis. Assn., Inst. Indsl. Engrs., Am. Soc. Quality Control (mem. standing rev. and mix media rev. bd. 1992—, mem. editl. bd. for quality engring. 1994—), Inst. Ops. Rsch. and Mgmt. Sci., Decision Scis. Inc. Office: Hewlett-Packard Co 700 71st Ave Greeley CO 80634

MADERA, MARIE LOUISE, magazine publishing executive; b. Los Angeles, June 11, 1955; d. Leroy James and Helen Jean (Clark) M. BA, Calif. State U., Long Beach, 1978. Art dir. Keyboard World mag., Downey, Calif., 1978-79, Popular Ceramics mag., Glendale, Calif., 1980; mgr. prodn. Creative Age Pubs., Van Nuys, Calif., 1980-86; dir. prodn. High Tech Pubs., Torrance, Calif., 1986; dir. pubs. Family Living Mag., Buena Park, Calif., 1986-93; prodn. mgr. Fancy Publs., Irvine, Calif., 1993-96; ops. dir. World Trade Mag., Irvine, Calif., 1996—; host Theatre Scene local cable TV show. Choreographer community theatres, 1981—. Mem. NAFE, Western Pubs. Assn., Advt. Prodn. Assn. So. Calif., Pubs. Prodn. Mgr. Club So. Calif. NOW. Roman Catholic. Home: 2502 E Willow St Unit 201 Long Beach CA 90806-2231 Office: 17702 Cowan Ste 100 Irvine CA 92614-6035

MADIX, ROBERT JAMES, chemical engineer, educator; b. Beach Grove, Ind., June 22, 1938; s. James L. and Marjorie A. (Strohl) M.; children: Bradley Alan, David Eric, Micella Lynn, Evan Scott. BS, U. Ill., 1961; PhD, U. Calif., 1964. NSF postdoctoral fellow Max Planck Inst., Göttingen, Fed. Republic of Germany, 1964-65; asst. prof. chem. engr. Stanford (Calif.) U., 1965-72, assoc. prof., chem. engr., 1972-77; prof. chem. engring. Stanford U., 1977—, chmn., chem. engr., 1983-87, prof. chemistry, 1981—; cons. Monsanto Chem., St. Louis, 1975-84, Shell Oil Co., Houston, 1985-86; Peter Debye lectureship Cornell U., 1985; Eyring lectr. chemistry Ariz. State U., 1990; Barnett Dodge lectr. Yale U., 1996; disting. prof. lectr. U. Tex., Austin, 1980; chmn. Gordon Rsch. Conf. on Reactions on Surfaces, 1995. Assoc. editor Catalysis Rev., 1986—, Catalysis Letters, 1992—, Rsch. on Chem. Intermediates, 1994—; contbr. numerous articles to profl. jours. Recipient Alpha Chi Sigma award AIChemE, 1990, Paul Emmett award Catalysis Soc. N.Am., 1984, Humboldt U.S. Sr. Scientist prize, 1978, Henry J. Albert award Internat. Precious Metals Inst., 1997; Ford Found. fellow, 1969-72. Mem. Am. Chem. Soc. (Irving Langmuir Disting. Lectr. award 1981, Arthur Adamson award 1997), Am. Phys. Soc., Am. Vacuum Soc., AIChE, Calif. Catalysis Soc. Office: Stanford Univ Dept Chemical Engring Stanford CA 94305

MADLANG, RODOLFO MOJICA, urologic surgeon; b. Indang, Cavite, The Philippines, Apr. 9, 1918; came to U.S., 1953; s. Simeon Fajardo and Eugenia R. (Mojica) Madlangsacay; m. Lourdes Recto Gregorio, Dec. 8, 1946; children: Cesar, Rodolfo G., Mercy Lynn. AA, U. Philippines, Manila, 1939, MD, 1945. Diplomate Am. Bd. Urology. Resident in gen. surgery Philippine Gen. Hosp., Manila, 1946-49; resident in urology St. Francis Hosp., Peoria, Ill., 1953-55; asst. prof. physiology Far Ea. U. Inst. Medicine, Manila, 1956-58, cons. in urology, 1956-58; attending urologist St. Catherine Hosp., East Chicago, Ind., 1958-81, chief surgery, 1977-79; attending urologist St. Margaret Hosp., Hammond, Ind., 1960-81; chief urology U.S. VA Outpatient Clinic, L.A., 1982—. Fellow ACS; mem. AMA, Am. Urol. Assn., Pan Pacific Surg. Assn., Assn. Mil. Surgeons of the U.S., Ind. State Med. Assn., N.Y. Acad. Scis. Republican. Roman Catholic. Office: VA Outpatient Clinic 351 E Temple St Los Angeles CA 90012-3328

MADNI, ASAD MOHAMED, engineering executive; b. Bombay, Sept. 8, 1947; came to U.S., 1966; s. Mohamed Taher and Sara Taher (Wadiwalla) M.; Gowhartaj Shahnawaz, Nov. 11, 1976; 1 child, Jamal Asad. Gen. cert. edn., U. Cambridge, Eng., 1964; AAS in Electronics, RCA Insts., Inc., 1968; BS in Engring., UCLA, 1969, MS in Engring., 1972; postgrad. exec. inst., Stanford U., 1984; cert. in engring. mgmt., Calif. Inst. Tech., 1987; PhD in Engring., Calif. Coast U., 1987; sr. exec. program, MIT, 1990. Sr. instr. Pacific States U., L.A., 1969-71; sr. electronics auditor Pertec Corp., Chatsworth, Calif., 1973-75; project engr., sr. engr., prog. mgr., dir. advanced programs Microwave div. Systron Donner, Van Nuys, Calif., 1975-82, dir. engring., 1982-92; gen. mgr. Microwave and Instrument div. Systron Donner, Van Nuys, Calif., 1985-90; chmn., pres., chief exec. officer Systron Donner Corp., 1990-92; pres., CEO Sensors and Controls Group BEI Electronics, Inc., 1992-93, BEI Motion Sys. Co., 1993-94, BEI Sensors & Sys. Co., 1994—; vice-chmn. IEEE-MTTS, San Fernando Valley chpt., 1991-92, chmn., 1992-94; tech. advisor Test and Measurement World, Boston, 1982-90; adv. Calif. State U. Northridge. Mem. editorial rev. bd., West coast chmn. Microwave Systems News and Communications Tech., 1982-90; contbr. more than 60 articles to numerous tech. publs.; patentee in field. Mem. AAAS, IEEE (sr.), NRA (life), Soc. Automotive Engrs., N.Y. Acad. Scis., Assn. Old Crows (life, gold cert. of merit 1992), Calif. Rifle and Pistol Assn. (life), MIT Soc. Sr. Execs. (life), UCLA Alumni Assn. (life), MIT Alumni Assn. (life). Home: 3281 Woodbine St Los Angeles CA 90064-4836 Office: BEI Sensors & Systems Co 13100 Telfair Ave Sylmar CA 91342-3573 *Personal philosophy: There is no substitute for talent and vision complemented by perseverance, dedication and integrity.*

MADRIL, LEE ANN, writer; b. Burbank, Calif., Sept. 16, 1944; d. George Mathew McDougall; 1 child, Francis Michael. Student, Granada Hills (Calif.) Coll., 1962. Freelance writer, 1986-90; shoot out artist, life mem. Bad Co., Auburn, Calif., 1990—; writer Idaho State Newspaper, Just Horses, Indian Valley, 1994—; cons. in authenticity, Calif. State Horsemen, Santa Rosea, 1988-90, Bad Co., 1990. Writer Idaho State Newspaper Just Horses; contbr. articles to profl. jours. Vol. Red Cross, Soques, Calif., 1982, Salinas (Calif.) Valley Meml. Hosp., 1979, Greenpeace, Humane Soc. U.S. Recipient Kodak KINSA award, 1989, winner County and State photo awards, 1993. jem. Calif. State Horseman's Assn. (state champion 1989-90), Silver Spurs, Moose. Republican. Roman Catholic. Home and Office: PO Box 121 Newcastle CA 95658

MADSEN, BARBARA A., judge. Justice Washington Supreme Ct., Olympia.

MADSEN, FRANCIS ARMSTRONG, JR., investor, lawyer, consultant; b. Salt Lake City, Jan. 6, 1931; s. Francis Armstrong and Elen Louise (Wallace) M.; m. Constance Clayton, Feb. 3, 1954; children: Michelle Madsen Ahlgren, Susan Madsen Moore, Karen Madsen Densford, Kathleen Madsen Morrill. BS, U. Utah, 1954, MBA, JD, 1956. Bar: Utah 1955, U.S. Dist. Ct. Utah 1955, U.S. Ct. Mil. Appeals 1959, U.S. Supreme Ct. 1959. Asst. mgr. Madsen Furniture Co., Salt Lake City, 1954-56, mgr., 1959-76, v.p., bd. dirs., 1954-91; pvt. practice, Salt Lake City, 1959-76; adminstr. asst. to Senator Orrin G. Hatch, U.S. Senate, Washington, 1976-85, legis. dir., chief counsel, 1985-88, gen. counsel, minority gen. counsel labor-human resources com., 1984-88; pres. Mass. Boston Mission LDS Ch., Cambridge, 1988-91; investor, cons., Salt Lake City, 1995—. Capt. USAF, 1956-59. Mem. Phi Kappa Phi, Beta Gamma Sigma, Phi Eta Sigma, Sigma Chi. Republican. Home and Office: 2493 E Field Rose Dr Salt Lake City UT 84121-1571

MADSEN, SUSAN ARRINGTON, writer; b. Logan, Utah, Aug. 25, 1954; d. Leonard J. and Grace F. Arrington; m. Dean Madsen, Aug. 20, 1974; children: Emily, Rebecca, Sarah, Rachel. BS in Journalism, Utah State U., 1975. Mem. adj. faculty Logan Latter-day Saints Inst. Religion, 1991-95. Author: Christmas: A Joyful Heritage, 1984, The Lord Needs a Prophet, 1990, I Walked to Zion: True Stories of Young Pioneers on the Mormon Trail, 1994, Growing Up in Zion: True Stories of Young Pioneers Building the Kingdom, 1996; co-author: (with Leonard J. Arrington) Sunbonnet Sisters: True Stories of Mormon Women and Frontier Life, 1984, Mothers of the Prophets, 1987; contbr. numerous articles to Collier's Ency. Yearbooks. Chair Hyde Pk. (Utah) Bd. Adjustments, 1985-94. Honoree Utah State U. Nat. Women's History Week, 1985; recipient Cmty. Svc. award Nat. Daus. Utah Pioneers, 1990. Mem. LDS Ch.

MADSEN, WILLIAM MARSHALL, media specialist; b. L.A., Aug. 15, 1939; s. William Felix Madsen and May Francis (Beattie) Atkins; m. Bettie Wanda Berkes, July 17, 1965 (div. sept. 1974); m. Charleen Joy Kelly, July 18, 1976; children: Cynthia, Lesovsky. AA in Mktg., Fresno City Coll., 1963; BA in Radio, TV and Film, Fresno State Coll., 1971. Dir. med. and dental bldg. J. H. Hedrick Co., San Gabriel, Calif., 1977-78; v.p. constrn. sales and mktg. Jud Perkins Co., L.A., 1978-79; account exec. various automotive aftermarket cos., L.A., 1980-85; advt. dir. mag., TV acct. exec. Argus Pubs. Corp., L.A., 1985-93; media dir. Torco Internat. Corp., Santa Fe Springs, Calif., 1994; advt. dir. Main Stream Pub., Upland, Calif., 1995-96; advt. dir. Offshore Racing Mag. Keenan Sports Mgmt. & Pub., Dana Point, Calif., 1996-97; regional sls. mgr. S.E. Leonard's Guide, Arcadia, Calif., 1997—. Republican. Mem. Ch. of Abundant Life.

MADSON, DAVID JOHN, fundraising executive; b. Mpls., Sept. 29, 1955; s. John Richard and Kleda Rae (Thompson) M.; m. Helen M. DeMichiel, Oct. 5, 1986; 1 child, Antonia Kleda Madson. BS magna cum laude in Visual Comm., U. Minn., Mpls., 1979; postgrad., U. Minn., 1986-87. Advanced cert. fund raiser exec. Media arts instr. ACTION Cmty. Outreach Program, 1976-77; photography instr. Inver Hills C.C. Program, 1978-84; assoc. dir. devel. Film in the Cities, St. Paul, 1981-84; exec. dir. Boston Film/Video Found., 1984-85; assoc. devel. officer propsect rsch. U. Minn. Found., 1985-86; chief devel. officer Coll. Edn. U. Minn., Mpls., 1987-93, chief devel. officer Cancer Ctr., 1993-95; chief devel. officer Sch. Nursing U. Calif., San Francisco, 1995—; mem. adv. panels Minn. State Arts Bd., St. Paul, 1993-95, Nat. Endowment Arts, Washington, 1991, 93, 94; cons. Jerome Hill Theatre Devel., 1985; prodr. Cable Arts TV Project, 1985; panelist photography fellowships Minn. State Arts Bd., 1985; cons. Media Arts Ctr. Project, Artspace, Mpls., 1985-86; cons. nat. satellite distbn. project Deep Dish Pub. Access TV, N.Y.C., 1985-87; panelist McKnight Found./Mpls. Arts Commn., 1986-88; devel. cons. Mgmt. Assistance Project, 1991; media grants rev. panelist Minn. Humanities Commn., 1991; program com. Minn. Coun. on Planned Giving Conf., 1992; co-founder Midwest/Big Ten Edn. Advancement Network, 1991-93. Exhibited in group photography shows at St. Paul Sci. and Art Ctr., 1974, Kennedy Ctr. for Arts, Washington, 1975, Nash Gallery, 1976, 81, Coffman Union Gallery, 1977, 78, Film in the Cities, 1977, Hunt Gallery. Treas. Univ. Film Soc., Mpls., 1981-84, 89-95, KFAI Cmty. Radio, Mpls., 1989-92; pres. Seward Cmty. Coop., Mpls., 1993-95; bd. dirs. United Cerebral Palsy, San Francisco, 1996—; bd. dirs. Minn. Span Assn., 1988-93; pres. Red Eye Collaboration Theater, Mpls., 1986-91; bd. dirs. Lowertown Cmty. Coun., 1981-83, Palace Theater Co., 1982-84, So. Theater, 1986-89; arts adv. com. City of St. Paul Planning Dept., 1982-84; com. mem. childhood devel. study Citizens League, 1987-88; mem. Chain of Lakes planning com. City of Mpls. Park Bd., 1989; bd. dirs. Powderhorn Cmty. Coun., 1985-90, treas., 1986-88; bd. dirs., co-founder Lowertown Lofts Artist Housing Coop., 1982-90, treas., 1983-88; facilities com. Minn. chpt. Am. Youth Hostels, 1990-93; mem. devel. com. Headwaters Fund, 1990-93; bd. dirs. Prevention Alliance, 1988-93; bd. dirs. Film in the Cities, 1992-95, sec., 1993-95; mem. fin. com. Berkeley Montessori Sch., 1995—. Mem. Nat. Assn. Fund Raising Execs. (v.p. edn. Golden Gate chpt. 1996—, bd. dirs. Minn. chpt. 1993-95), U. Minn. Alumni Assn. (nat. bd. 1996—, pres. San Francisco charter 1995—. Office: U Calif Box 0248 San Francisco CA 94143

MAEDA, J. A., data processing executive; b. Mansfield, Ohio, Aug. 24, 1940; d. James Shunso and Doris Lucille Maeda; m. Robert Lee Hayes; 1 child, Brian Sentaro Hayes. BS in Math., Purdue U., 1962, postgrad., 1962-63; postgrad., Calif. State U., Northridge, 1968-75; cert. profl. designation in tech. of computer operating systems and tech. of info. processing, UCLA, 1971. Cons., rsch. asst. computer ctr. Purdue U., West Lafayette, Ind., 1962-63; computer operator, sr. tab operator, mem. faculty Calif. State U., Northridge, 1969, programmer cons., tech. asst. II, 1969-70, supr. acad. applications, EDP supr. II, 1970-72, project tech. support coord. programmer II, office of the chancellor, 1972-73, tech. support coord. statewide timesharing tech. support, programmer II, 1973-74, acad. coord., tech. support coord. instrn., computer cons. III, 1974-83; coord. user svcs. info. ctr., mem. tech. staff IV CADAM INC subs. Lockheed Corp., Burbank, Calif., 1983-86, coord. user svcs., tech. specialist computing dept., 1986-87; v.p., bd. dirs. Rainbow Computing, Inc., Northridge, 1976-85; dir. Aki Tech/Design, Northridge, 1976—; mktg. mgr. thaumaturge Taro Quipu Cons., Northridge, 1987—; tech. cons. Digital Computer Cons., Chatsworth, Calif., 1988; computer tech., fin. and bus. mgmt., sys. integration, 1988-90; tech. customer software support Collection Data Sys., Westlake, Calif., 1991; sr. tech. writer Sterling Software Info. Mgmt. Divsn., 1992—. Author, editor more than 300 user publs., tutorials, reference manuals, user guides; contbr. articles and photos to profl. jours. Mem. IEEE, SHARE, DECUS (ednl. spl. interest group 1977-83, ednl. steering com. RSTS/E 1979-82), Soc. for Tech. Communicators. Office: Sterling Software Info Mgmt Divsn 5900 Canoga Ave Woodland Hills CA 93167

MAEHL, WILLIAM HARVEY, historian, educator; b. Bklyn., May 28, 1915; s. William Henry and Antoinette Rose (Salamone) M.; m. Josephine Scholl McAllister, Dec. 29, 1941; children: Madeleine, Kathleen. BSc, Northwestern U., 1937, MA, 1939; PhD, U. Chgo., 1946. Asst. prof. history St. Louis U., 1941-42, Tex. A&M U., College Sta., 1943, De Paul U., Chgo., 1944-49; historian Dept. of Def., Karlsruhe, Stuttgart, Fed. Rep. Germany, 1950-52; chief briefing office U.S. hdqrs. U.S. Hdqs. European Command, Frankfurt, Germany, 1952-53; chief historian Arty. Sch., Okla., 1954; with War Plans Office, Hdqs. No. Air Materiel Area for Europe, Burtonwood, Eng., 1954-55; assoc. prof. European history Nebr. Wesleyan U., Lincoln, 1955-57, prof., 1958-62, 65-68; prof. German history Auburn (Ala.) U., 1968-81, prof. emeritus, 1981—; vis. prof. U. Nebr., 1962, U. Auckland, New Zealand, 1963-64, Midwestern U., Wichita Falls, Tex., 1965. Author: German Militarism and Socialism, 1968, History of Germany in Western Civilization, 1979, A World History Syllabus, 3 vols., 1980, August Bebel, Shadow Emperor of the German Workers, 1980, The German Socialist Party: Champion of the First Republic, 1918-33, 1986; author monographs for U.S. Army in Europe, chpts. in books, atomic, biol. and emergency war plans for No. Air Materiel Area for Europe; contbr. poetry to Question of Balance, Tears of Fire, Disting. Poets Am., Best Poems of 1995, Journey of Mind; contbr. articles to profl. jours. Grantee Nebr. Wesleyan U., 1959, Auburn U., 1969-73, 79-80, Am. Philosophical Soc., 1973-74, Deutscher Akademischer Austauschdienst, 1978. Mem. Am. Hist. Assn., Phi Kappa Phi, Phi Alpha Theta.

MAEHL, WILLIAM HENRY, historian, university administrator, educational consultant; b. Chicago Heights, Ill., June 13, 1930; s. William Henry and Marvel Lillian (Carlson) M.; m. Audrey Mae Ellsworth, Aug. 25, 1962; 1 child, Christine Amanda. B.A., U. Minn., 1950, M.A., 1951; postgrad (Fulbright fellow), King's Coll., U. Durham, Eng., 1955-56; Ph.D., U. Chgo., 1957; LHD (hon.), Fielding Inst., 1993. Asst. prof. Montclair (N.J.) State Coll., 1957-58; asst. prof. Washington Coll., Chestertown, Md., 1958-59, U. Okla., Norman, 1959-64; asso. prof. U. Okla., 1964-70, prof. English history, 1970-86; dean Coll. Liberal Studies, 1976-86, vice provost for continuing edn. and public service, 1979-86; pres. The Fielding Inst., Santa Barbara, Calif., 1987-93, pres. emeritus, 1993—; prin. investigator Project for a Nation of Lifelong Learners, Regents Coll., Albany, N.Y., 1994-97; vis. prof. U. Nebr., summer 1965; vis. fellow Wolfson Coll. Oxford (Eng.) U., spring 1975; fellow Salzburg Seminar in Am. Studies, 1976. Author: The Reform Bill of 1832, 1967; editor: R.G. Gammage, Chartist Reminiscences, 1981, Continuum: Jour. of the Nat. Continuing Edn. Assn., 1980-83, also articles. Bd. dirs. Alliance for Alternative Degree Programs, 1988-90; trustee Coun. for Adult and Exptl. Learning, 1990-94; mem. coun. Nat. Ctr. for Adult Learning, 1990—. Leverhulme Research fellow, 1961-62; grantee Am. Philos. Soc., 1961-62, 67-68, 71, 76. Fellow Royal Hist. Soc., Assn. of Grad. Liberal Studies Programs; mem. Am. Hist. Assn., Conf. on Brit. Studies, Soc. for Study Labour History. Office: PO Box 6580 Santa Fe NM 87502

MAES, PAT JULIAN, secondary education educator; b. Clayton, N.M., Dec. 12, 1950; s. Celestino and Amalia (Gonzales) M.; m. Rose Ann Arguello, June 20, 1980; 1 child, Julie Ann. BA, Ea. N.M. Univ., 1972, MA, 1983. Cert. tchr., N.M. Tchr. Vaughn (N.M.) Mcpl. Sch., 1972—; counselor Vaughn Mcpl. Sch., 1980—. Recipient Advocate of Edn. award N.M. Highlands U., 1991, Friend in Edn. award N.M. State U., 1992, Svc. award N.M. Dept. Game and Fish, 1995. Mem. NEA (pres. 1974—, Svc. award), Rotary (sec. 1974, v.p. 1976). Home: PO Box 147 Vaughn NM 88353 Office: Vaughn Mcpl Schs Box 158 Vaughn NM 88353

MAESTAS, ALEX WALTER, state agency clerk; b. Espanola, N. Mex., Jan. 18, 1954; s. Mariano E. and Stella Dora M.; m. Carol Paulette Pino, June 26, 1976; children: Andrew Arthur, Pamela Marie, Nicholas Alex. BS, U. N. Mex., 1976; Diploma, Victory Bible Sch. of Ministry, 1993. Ins. cert., 1990-94; cert. elem. tchr., N.Mex. Elem. sch. tchr. Annunciation Sch., Albuquerque, 1979-84, Albuquerque Pub. Schs., 1984-86; statistical analyst Workers' Compensation Adminstrn., Albuquerque, 1986-88, record mgr., 1988-96, clk. of ct. bur. chief, 1996—. Mem. exec. bd. Albuquerque Parochial League, 1980-84; pres. Zia Little League, Albuquerque, 1995-96. Mem. Worker's Compensation Assn. N. Mex., Nat. Assn. Ct. Mgmt. Home: 240 Parsifal NE Albuquerque NM 87123 Office: N Mex Workers Compensation Adminstrn PO Box 27198 Albuquerque NM 87125

MAESTAS, AMY, journalist; b. Salt Lake City, Jan. 26, 1968; d. Levay J. and Cynthia (Corless) M. BA, U. Utah, 1994. Investigator ASCAP, Denver, 1994-96; mng. editor The Event Newspaper, Salt Lake City, 1993-96; asst. editor Bank Investment Rep., Salt Lake City, 1994-95; city and bus. editor Durango (Colo.) Herald, 1996—. Mem. Soc. Profl. Journalists, Utah Headliners.

MAGALNICK, ELLIOTT BEN, retail medical supply company executive; b. Cleve., Aug. 19, 1945; s. Joseph Hyman and Ann (Resnick) M.; m. Diane Kerner, May 26, 1968 (div. Feb. 1988); children: Joel A., David A.; m. Judy Banjavic, June 9, 1991; stepchildren: Daniel Banjavic, David Banjavic. BS in Bus. Mgmt., Temple U., 1968. Cert. orthopedic fitter Health Industries Dealer Assn. Retail mgr. Milner Surg. Supply Co., Phila., 1970-72, Colo. Surg. Supply Co., Denver, 1972-73; mgr. non wheelchair retail Wheelchairs, Inc., Englewood, Colo., 1973-77; asst. mgr. ops. Denver Surg. Supply Co., 1977-78; owner, founder The Get Well Shop, Inc., Aurora, Colo., 1978—. Mem. chorus Shir Ami Singers, Denver, 1978-95, Colo. Symphony Orch., Denver, 1986-96; vol. Allied Fedn. Denver, 1984-87; mem. Legion of Merit, Rep. Party, Denver, 1992; donor Belle Bonfils Blood Ctr., 1976—; cantor Temple Micah, Denver, 1991-95, Temple Shalom, Colorado Springs, Colo., 1996-97. Named Disting. Pres., Optimist Internat., 1987. Mem. Colo. Assn. Med. Equipment Suppliers (dealer mem., mem. state bd.), Health Industries Dealer Assn. (cert. orthopedic fitter, bd. dirs. 1986-87), Luncheon Optimist Club Windsor Gardens (pres. 1986), Masons (master mason Columbian lodge), Colo. Consistory, El Jebel Temple, Rocky Mtn. Cantors Assn. Jewish. Office: The Get Well Shop Inc 12028 E Mississippi Aurora CO 80012

MAGGAY, ISIDORE, III, engineering executive, food processing engineer; b. San Diego, Calif., Sept. 12, 1952; s. Isidore Jr. and Dolores (Ambay) M.; m. Karen Elizabeth, Dec. 25, 1981; children: Adrienne Leigh, Brittany Elizabeth. BSME, Calif. Maritime Acad., 1973; MBA, Nat. U., 1980. Registered environ. assessor, Calif.; cert. hazardous material contractor, Calif. Project engr. Ralston Purina, San Diego, 1976-78; dist. engr. Carnation Co., L.A., 1978-81; dir. engring. Sara Lee Corp., San Francisco, 1981-85; v.p. engring. Alex Foods Inc., Anaheim, Calif., 1986-89; pres. Acad. Engring., Vista, Calif., 1989—; gen. engring. contractor, Contractors State Lic. Bd., Calif., 1989—. Commr. Environ. Quality Commn., Vista, 1991-92. Lt. Commdr. USNR, 1973—. Mem. Am. Inst. Plant Engrs., Environ. Assessment Assn., Nat. Soc. Profl. Engrs. Roman Catholic. Office: 1045 Linda Vista Dr Ste 107 San Marcos CA 92069-2622

MAGGI, GAYLE J.B., secondary school educator; b. Artesia, Calif., Feb. 18, 1951; d. Frank Eugene and Margarethe (Vogel) Brumley; divorced; 1 child, Dante. BA in Psychology, Calif. State U., Fullerton, 1973, postgrad., 1977; postgrad., Calif. State U., San Diego, 1983. Cert. tchr., bilingual tchr., standard elem. credential, bilingual cert. competency, Calif. Substitute tchr. Eureka (Calif.) City Schs., 1974-76; bilingual metric coord. ABC Unified Sch. Dist., 1976-79, metric resource tchr., 1977-79, elem. tchr., 1980-81; bilingual math. and math. resource tchr., chmn. math. dept. Sweetwater Union H.S. Dist., Chula Vista, Calif., 1981—, math. demonstration coach, math. Renaissance Cluster leader, 1981—; RD. Mem. Nat. Coun. Tchrs. Math., Calif. Math. Coun., Calif. Fedn. Tchrs. (membership chmn. 1977-78). Scientologist. Office: Castle Park Middle Sch 160 Quintard St Chula Vista CA 91911-4414

MAGID, GAIL AVRUM, neurosurgeon, neurosurgery educator; b. Chgo., Oct. 15, 1934; s. Harry M. and Henrietta (Busch) M.; m. Janet Louise Reinhardt, June 15, 1962 (div.); children: Allison Magid London, Jonathan Alward; m. Roseanne Cipra Muirhead, Sept. 4, 1982. BSc, U. Ill., 1954; MD, Chgo. Med. Sch., 1958. Diplomate Am. Bd. Neurol. Surgery. Intern Cook County Hosp., Chgo., 1958-59; resident, then fellow neurol. surgery Mayo Clinic, Rochester, Minn., 1959-61, 63-65; clin. instr. neurosurgery U. Calif., San Francisco, 1965-70, asst. clin. prof., 1970-79, assoc. prof., 1979—; chmn. Dominican Neurol. Inst., Santa Cruz, Calif., 1975—; bd. dirs. Dominican Found.; cons. neurosurgery U.S. Army, San Francisco Gen. Hosp. Assoc. editor: Clinical Neurosurgery, 1974. Bd. dirs. Santa Cruz Symphony Assn., 1983-85, U. Calif. Friends of Arts, Santa Cruz, 1985-86. Served to lt. comdr. USN, 1961-63. Fellow ACS, Internat. Coll. Surgeons; mem. AMA, Calif. Med. Assn., Internat. Soc. Pediatric Neurosurgeons, Am. Assn. Neurol. Surgeons, We. Neurosurg. Soc. (v.p. 1996—), Cong. Neurol. Surgeons, San Francisco Neurol. Soc. (pres.-elect 1991, pres. 1992), St. Francis Yacht Club (San Francisco). Republican. Home: 241 4th Ave Santa Cruz CA 95062-3815 Office: 1661 Soquel Dr Santa Cruz CA 95065-1709

MAGINN, STEPHEN ARTHUR, financial company executive; b. Orange, N.J., Mar. 5, 1952; s. Wallace Alton and La Verne (Chappell) M.; m. Linda Marie Stewart, Oct. 7, 1989; children: Brett Marshall, Todd Randall, Ryan Michael, Sean Christopher. BS in Commerce, U. Va., 1974. Cert. gen. securities prin. Nat. Assn. Securities Dealers. Securities broker Merrill Lynch, Newark, 1974-77, A.G. Becker, Inc., N.Y.C., 1977-79; regional v.p. Petro-Lewis Securities Corp., Denver, 1979-85; sr. v.p., co-founder Greystone Securities, Evergreen, Colo., 1985-86; regional v.p. NTS Securities, Louisville, 1986-87; sr. v.p., regional mgr. G.T. Global Fin. Svcs. (now GT Global, Inc.), San Francisco, 1987—. Mem. Internat. Assn. for Fin. Planning (nat. bd. dirs.). Home: 519 S Juanita Ave Redondo Beach CA 90277-3827 Office: GT Global Inc 50 California St 27th Fl San Francisco CA 94111

MAGINNIS, TARA MICHELE, costume designer, educator; b. San Francisco, Jan. 30, 1959; d. Charles Leo Patrick and Marion Ruth (Simon) M. BA in History, San Francisco State U., 1981; MA in Theatre, Calif. State U., Fresno, 1985; PhD in Theatre, U.Ga., 1991. Costume designer Producer's Assocs., Oakland, Calif., 1983; cutter Santa Barbara (Calif.) Repertory Theatre, 1984; grad. teaching asst. Calif. State U., Fresno, 1983-85; costume crafts supr. Houston Shakespeare Festival, Houston, 1985; grad. teaching asst. U. Ga., Athens, 1985-87; vis. asst. prof. U. Alaska, Fairbanks, 1988-89, asst. prof., 1990—; webmistress/designer UA-AAUP/AFT, Info. Site & The Costumer's Manifesto, Alaska, 1996; guest artist Theatre Terra Mobile, St. Petersburg, Russia, 1994-95, Interstudio Theatre, Tzarkoe Selo, Russia, 1994, Fairbanks Light Opera Theatre, 1995. Costume designer for 20 shows for U. Alaska Fairbanks including Much Ado About Nothing, 1991, Comedy of Errors, 1995, Marat Sade, 1989, The Island, 1996; contbr. articles to Costume, Theatre Design and Tech., Theatre Crafts, others; web author and costume designer numerous other prodns. Recipient Spl. Achievement award in costume design, 1992. Mem. United Academics-AAUP/AFT, U.S. Inst. for Theatre Tech., Costume Soc. Am., Costume Soc. U.K. Democrat. Office: Theatre U Alaska Fairbanks PO Box 755700 Fairbanks AK 99775-5700

MAGLIOCCO, PETER ANTHONY, editor, writer; b. Glendale, Calif., Oct. 26, 1948; s. George Peter and Viola Julia (Pazzelli) M. BA in Fine Arts, Calif. State U., Northridge, 1975. Artist Northridge, Calif., 1975-82; editor, writer Limited Editions Press, Northridge, 1982-85, Las Vegas, 1985—. Author: Among a Godly Few, 1982, Poetica Rex., 1994, In a Land of Techno-Rave, 1994, Non-Parables, 1996, Kiss of Space, 1997; editor Art mag., 1984—. With U.S. Army, 1967-70. Office: Limited Editions Press PO Box 70896 Las Vegas NV 89170

MAGNABOSCO, LOUIS MARIO, chemical engineer, researcher, consultant; b. Glarus, Switzerland, Nov. 29, 1938; s. Josef and Maria (Schlittler) M.; m. Vreni S. Zentner, Mar. 18, 1966 (div. Sept. 1985); 1 child, Henry Louis; m. D'Ella P. Phelon, Apr. 25, 1990; 1 child, Deon M. BSChemE, Swiss Fed. Inst. Tech., Zurich, 1961, MSChemE, 1963, ScD, 1967. Sr. scientist FMC Corp., Santa Clara, Calif., 1967-68; from engr. to project engr. Shell Devel. Co., Emeryville, Calif., 1968-72; sr. engr. Shell Devel. Co., Houston, 1972-74, staff engr., 1974-76; processing specialist ARCO, Harvey, Ill., 1976-79; mgr. process devel. ARCO, Harvey, 1979-85; cons. Magna Assocs., Olympia Fields, Ill., 1985-87; mgr. processes and catalysis Enimont, Zurich, 1987-90; pres. Chem. Engring. Ptnrs., Newport Beach, Calif., 1990-93; v.p. R&D Intercat, Sea Girt, N.J., 1993-94; cons. Magna Assocs., 1994—. Contbr. articles to internat. profl. jours.; conducted seminars and gave lectures on hydroprocessing internationally in petroleum field. Mem. AIChE, AAAS, Am. Chem. Soc. Catalysis Club.

MAGNESS, RHONDA ANN, microbiologist; b. Stockton, Calif., Jan. 30, 1946; d. John Pershing and Dorothy Waneta (Kelley) Wetter; m. Barney LeRoy Bender, Aug. 26, 1965 (div. 1977); m. Gary D. Magness, Mar. 5, 1977; children: Jay D. (dec.), Troy D. BS, Calif. State U., 1977. Lic. clin. lab. scientist, Calif., med. technologist; cert. clin. lab. scientist. Med. asst. C. Fred Wilcox, MD, Stockton, 1965-66; clk. typist Dept. of U.S. Army, Ft. Eustis, Va., 1967, Def. Supply Agy., New Orleans, 1967-68; med. asst. James G. Cross, MD, Lodi, Calif., 1969, Arthur A. Kemalyan, MD, Lodi, 1969-71, 72-77; med. sec. Lodi Meml. Hosp., 1972; lab. aide Calif. State U., Sacramento, 1977; phlebotomist St. Joseph's Hosp., Stockton, 1978-79; supr. microbiology Dameron Hosp. Assn., Stockton, 1980—. Active Concerned Women Am., Washington, 1987—. Mem. AAUW, Calif. Assn. Clin. Lab. Technologists, San Joaquin County Med. Assts. Assn., Nat. Geog. Soc., Nat. Audubon Soc. Baptist. Lodge: Jobs Daus. (chaplain 1962-63). Home: 9627 Knight Ln Stockton CA 95209-1961 Office: Dameron Hosp Lab 525 W Acacia St Stockton CA 95203-2405

MAGNUSSEN, MAX GENE, psychologist; b. Roland, Iowa, Sept. 12, 1927; s. Arthur Christian and Mary E. (Rakard) M.; m. Margaret Anne Hahn, Feb. 2, 1952 (div. Apr. 1985); 1 child, Anne H. BA, U. Iowa, 1952, MA, 1953; PhD, U. Ky., 1958. Lic. psychologist, Pa., N.Mex.; registered health svc. provider in psychology. Staff psychologist VA Hosp., Cin., 1958-59; clin. psychologist, asst. dir., psychol. cons. aircraft nuclear propulsion dept. GE Co., Cin., 1959-60; chief psychologist to dir. Lincoln-Lancaster Child Guidance Ctr., Lincoln, Nebr., 1960-68; chief psychologist to acting dir. Pitts. Child Guidance Ctr., 1968-80; dir. to attending sr. psychologist Programs for Children/U. N.Mex. Med. Ctr., Albuquerque, 1980—; pvt. practice 1995—; instr. to asst. prof. U. Cin., 1958-60; asst. prof. U. Nebr., 1961-68; assoc. to full prof. U. Pitts., 1968-80; prof. of psychiatry and psychology U. N.Mex., 1980-95, prof. emeritus, 1995—; vis. prof. Inst. of Psychiatry, London, 1988-89; site vis. APA, Washington, 1972—; field specialist site vis. HEW, 1977—; cons. PHS/Indian Health Svc., Gallup (N.Mex.) Indian Med. Ctr., 1996—; manuscript reviewer Psychiat. Svcs., 1996—. Contbg. author various books including Individual Versus Family Therapy, 1982, Multiple Impact Therapy, 1982, Development of a Minimal Clinical Data System, 1982, others; author: Pittsburgh Child Guidance Center Data System, 1974, others; contbr. articles to profl. jours. Mem. Health Systems Agy., Southwest Pa., Pitts., 1977-80, monitor, 1977-80. Sgt. U.S. Army, 1946-48. Recipient commendation Calif. Psychol. Assn., 1986—. Fellow APA (divsn. clin. psychology 1996—, fellow divsn. children, youth and families 1997, grantee 1973, vis. psychologist 1974), Am. Psychiat. Assn. (site visitor), Am. Orthopsychiat. Assn., Pa. Psychol. Assn. (ins. chmn. 1979), Soc. Personality Assessment; mem. Can. Psychol. Assn. (site visitor, accreditation panel), Nebr. Psychol. Assn. (sec./treas. 1963-66, pres. 1966-67), Internat. Assn. Applied Psychology. Office: U NMex Sch Medicine 1020 Quincy Ave NE Albuquerque NM 87110

MAGOWAN, PETER ALDEN, professional baseball team executive, grocery chain executive; b. N.Y.C., Apr. 5, 1942; s. Robert Anderson and Doris (Merrill) M.; m. Jill Tarlau (div. July 1982); children: Kimberley, Margot, Hilary; m. Deborah Johnston, Aug. 14, 1982. BA, Stanford U.; MA, Oxford U., Eng.; postgrad., Johns Hopkins U. Store mgr. Safeway Stores Inc., Washington, 1968-70; dist. mgr. Safeway Stores Inc., Houston, 1970-71; retail ops. mgr. Safeway Stores Inc., Phoenix, 1971-72; divsn. mgr. Safeway Stores Inc., Tulsa, 1973-76; mgr. internat. divsn. Safeway Stores Inc., Toronto, Ont., Can., 1976-78; mgr. western region Safeway Stores Inc., San Francisco, 1978-79; CEO Safeway Stores Inc., Oakland, Calif., 1980-93, chmn. bd. dirs., 1980—; pres., mng. gen. ptnr. San Francisco Giants, 1993—; bd. dirs. Chrysler Corp., Caterpillar. Office: San Francisco Giants 3Com Pk at Candlestick Pt San Francisco CA 94124

MAGUEN, EZRA, ophthalmologist, researcher; b. USSR, Mar. 5, 1945; came to U.S., 1974; m. Talma Greenhouse, Sept. 23, 1971; children: Shira, Barak, Jonathan. Grad., Faculte de Medecine, Nancy, France, 1968; MD, Tel Aviv U., 1971. Diplomate Am. Bd. Ophthalmology. Rotating internship Beilinson Hosp., Petah Tikva, Israel, 1971-72, internal medicine resident, 1972-73; ophthalmology resident Case Western Res. U., Mt. Sinai Hosp., Cleve., 1974-77; corneal and external disease fellow Estelle Doheny Eye Found., U. So. Calif. Sch. Medicine, L.A., 1977-79, tchr., 1977-85; attending surgeon Cedars-Sinai Med. Ctr., L.A., 1980—; assoc. clin. prof. Jules Stein Eye Inst., L.A., 1985—; prin. Am. Eye Inst., L.A., 1981—; prin. investigator NIH, 1979; clin. instr. U. So. Calif., Sch. Medicine, L.A., 1979-81, asst. clin. prof. ophthalmology, 1981-85; assoc. clin. prof. ophthalmology UCLA Sch. Medicine, 1985—; rsch. assoc. Discovery Fund for Eye Rsch., L.A., 1985—; mem. sci. adv. bd. Lions Dohey Eye Bank, 1988—; lectr. in field. Contbr. articles to profl. jours. Recipient The Factor Found. award, 1986. Mem. ACS, Am. Acad. Ophthalmology, AAm. Soc. Cataract and Refractive Surgery, Internat. Coll. Surgeons, Internat. Soc. Optical Engring. (mem. program com. 1994), Internat. Soc. Refractive Keratoplasty (bd. dirs. 1988), Calif. Med. Assn. (sec. sci. adv. panel sect. ophthalmology 1987-89, sect. chmn. sci. adv. panel on ophthalmology 1989-90), L.A. County Med. Assn., L.A. Soc. Ophthalmology, Assn. Rsch. in Vision and Ophthalmology, Max Fine Corneal Assn., Rsch. Study Club in Ophthalmology L.A., Contact Lens Assn. Ophthalmology. Office: Am Eye Inst 8635 W 3rd St Ste 390W Los Angeles CA 90048-6101

MAGUIRE, JAMES HENRY, English language educator; b. Denver, Apr. 2, 1944; s. Joseph Cornelius Jr. and Margaret Louise (Monson) M.; m. Betty Joan Keller, Sept. 8, 1967; children: Emily Ann, Stephen Joseph. BA, U. Colo., 1966; AM, Ind. U., 1969, PhD, 1970. Teaching assoc. Ind. U., Bloomington, 1967-69; asst. prof. Boise (Idaho) State U., 1970-75, assoc. prof., 1975-87, prof. English, 1987—. Author: (booklet) Mary Hallock Foote, 1972; author, editor: (anthology) Literature of Idaho, 1986 (Idaho Libr. Assn. award 1987); sect. editor: A Literary History of the American West, 1987; contbr. chpt. to The Columbia History of the American Novel, 1991; co-editor: Boise State U. Western Writer Series, 1971—, Into the Wilderness Dream: Exploration Narratives of the American West, 1500-1805, 1994. Mem. Zero Population Growth, Washington, 1970—, ACLU, Snake River Alliance, Boise, 1979—. Mem. Western Lit. Assn. (pres. 1981), MLA, Am. Studies Assn., Mark Twain Cir., Hemingway Soc., Henry James Soc., Melville Soc., Emily Dickinson INternat. Soc., Sierra Club. Democrat. Home: 933 Pierce Ct Boise ID 83712-7448 Office: Boise State U English Dept 1910 University Dr Boise ID 83725-0001

MAGUIRE, JOHN DAVID, academic administrator, educator, writer; b. Montgomery, Ala., Aug. 7, 1932; s. John Henry and Clyde (Merrill) M.; m. Lillian Louise Parrish, Aug. 29, 1953; children: Catherine Merrill, Mary Elizabeth, Anne King. A.B. magna cum laude, Washington and Lee U., 1953, Litt.D. (hon.), 1979; Fulbright scholar, Edinburgh (Scotland) U., 1953-54; B.D. summa cum laude, Yale, 1956, Ph.D., 1960; postdoctoral research, Yale U. and U. Tübingen, Germany, 1964-65, U. Calif., Berkeley, 1968-69, Silliman U., Philippines, 1976-77; HLD (hon.), Transylvania U., 1990. Dir. Internat. Student Ctr., New Haven, 1956-58; mem. faculty Wesleyan U., Middletown, Conn., 1960-70; asso. provost Wesleyan U., 1967-68; vis. lectr. Pacific Sch. Religion and Grad. Theol. Union, Berkeley, 1968-69; pres. SUNY Coll. at Old Westbury, 1970-81, Claremont (Calif.) U. Ctr. and Grad. Sch., 1981—. Author: The Dance of the Pilgrim: A Christian Style of Life for Today, 1967; also numerous articles. Mem. Conn. adv. com. U.S. Commn. Civil Rights, 1961-70; participant White House Conf. on Civil Rights, 1966; advisor, permanent trustee and 1st chmn. bd. dirs. Martin Luther King Ctr. for Social Change, Atlanta, 1968—; bd. dirs. Nassau County Health and Welfare Coun., 1971-81, pres., 1974-76; trustee United Bd. Christian Higher Edn. in Asia, 1975-81, Inst. Internat. Edn., 1980-86; charter trustee Tomás Rivera Policy Inst., Claremont, Calif., 1984—, vice chmn., 1987-94, treas., 1995—, Assn. Ind. Calif. Colls. and Univs., 1985—, chmn. 1990-92, mem. exec. com., 1992—, The Calif. Achievement Coun., 1985-94, chmn. 1990-94, Transylvania U. Bingham Trust, 1987—, Lincoln Found. and Lincoln Inst. of Land Policy, Inc., 1987-94, The JL Found., 1988—, The Bus. Enterprise Trust, 1989—, Ednl. Found. for African Ams., 1991—; bd. dirs. Assn. Am. Colls. and Univs., 1981-86, chmn., 1984-85; bd. dirs. Legal Def. and Edn. Fund. NAACP, 1991—, west coast div., 1981—, Thacher Sch., Ojai, Calif., 1982-94, vice chmn., 1986-90, Salzburg Seminar, 1992-96; charter mem. Pacific Coun. Internat. Policy, 1995—; mem. Am. Com. on U.S.-Soviet Rels., 1981-92, Blue Ribbon Calif. Commn. on Teaching Profession, 1984-86; mem. governing coun. Aspen Inst. Wye Faculty Seminar, 1984-94; mem. Coun. on Fgn. Rels., 1983—; adv. bd. RAND Ctr. Rsch. Immigration Policy, 1994—; mem. Pres.'s Adv. Coun. to Commn. on Calif. Master Plan for Higher Edn., 1986-87, L.A. Ednl. Alliance for Restructuring Now, 1992—, Calif. Bus. Higher Edn. Forum, 1992—. Recipient Julia A. Archibald High Scholarship award Yale Div. Sch., 1956; Day fellow Yale Grad. Sch., 1956-57; Kent fellow, 1957-60; Howard Found. postdoctoral fellow Brown U. Grad. Sch., 1964-65; Fenn lectr., 7 Asian countries, 1976-77; recipient Conn. Prince Hall Masons' award outstanding contbns. human rights in Conn., 1965; E. Harris Harbison Gt. Tchr. prize Danforth Found., 1968. Fellow Soc. Values Higher Edn. (pres. 1974-81, bd. dirs. 1972-88); mem. Phi Beta Kappa, Omicron Delta Kappa. Democrat. Office: Claremont U Ctr & Grad Sch Office of Pres 160 E 10th St Claremont CA 91711-5909

MAGUIRE, YU PING, cell biologist, medical scientist; b. Hanon, China, May 27, 1947; came to U.S., 1962.; d. Shao Wen and Charlin (Yu) Yen; m. Russell Gene Maguire, June 13, 1968; 1 child, Jennifer Wei-Shing. MS, Rutgers U., 1976, PhD in Food Sci. and Tech., 1978. Pathology fellow U. Wash. Med. Sch., Seattle, 1979-80, hematology, oncology fellow, 1981-84; sr. scientist Tumor Inst. Swedish Hosp., Seattle, 1984-88; dir. tumor diagnostic Baxter Diagnostics, Bartels Div., Issaquah, Wash., 1988-93; dir. clin. oncology Bartels Prognostics, Inc., Issaquah, 1993—; vis. scientist dept. med. pathology U. Naples (Italy) Med. Sch., 1980-81; immunology cons. Oncogene Bristol Meyers, Seattle, 1985-88; biotech. cons. JWM, Inc., Bellevue, Wash., 1993—. Patentee in field. Mem. AAAS, Am. Assn. Cancer Rsch., Am. Acad. Sci., N.Y. Acad. Scis., Wash. State Biotech. Assn., Women in Cancer Rsch., Orgn. Regulatory and Clin. Assn. Home: 500 W Lake Sammamish Pkwy NE Bellevue WA 98008-4256 Office: Bartels Prognostics Inc 2005 NW Sammamish Rd Issaquah WA 98027-5364

MAHADEV, RAJESH, strategic marketing professional; b. Madras, India, Apr. 17, 1966; came to U.S., 1988; s. R.K. and Padma (Alwa) M.; m. Ana Elisa Mendes De Oliveira, Jan. 23, 1992. B. Commerce in Acctg., U. Bangalore (India), 1987; MBA in Mktg. and Fin., U. Denver, 1990. Sr. account exec. Communication Workshop, Bangalore, 1987-88; turnaround specialist Corriere & Assocs., Inc., Englewood, Colo., 1992-94; assoc. dir. U.S. West, Inc., Englewood, Colo., 1994-95; dir. mktg. BPL U.S. West Cellular, Ltd. India, 1996—. Educator Jr. Achievement of Denver, 1992; amb. Greater Denver Chamber, 1992—. Mem. Am. Mensa Ltd. Office: US West Inc # 310 9785 S Maroon Cir # 420 Englewood CO 80112-5919

MAHAN, BRAD HAVER, mental health services professional, artist; b. Tucson, July 8, 1959; s. Dale Orville and Sylvia Sue (Stewart) M.; m. Rebecca Lee Soggs, Sept. 14, 1991. BA in Photocommunications, Pepperdine U., 1982; MS in Psychology, Mt. St. Mary's Coll., L.A., 1994. Freelance photographer, artist Pacific Palisades, Calif., 1982—; art therapist Ea. N.C. Sch. for the Deaf, Wilson, spring 1995; prin., diagnostician Children's Psychosocial Svcs., Pacific Palisades, 1995—; coord. children's program 1st Presbyn. Ch. Santa Monica, Calif., 1995—. Author, photographer: Shutters: Writings & Photographs of Brad Haver Mahan, 1989; exhibited in show at M.O.P.A., 1990. Vol. pediat. U. Calif. San Diego Med. Ctr., 1993-94. Mem. Calif. Assn. Marriage and Family Therapists. Office: Childrens Psychosocial Svc 2955 Ocean St # 6 Carlsbad CA 92008

MAHARIDGE, DALE DIMITRO, journalist, educator; b. Cleve., Oct. 24, 1956; s. Steve and Joan (Kopfstein) M. Student, Cleve. State U., 1974-75. Free-lance reporter various publs., Cleve., 1976; reporter The Gazette, Medina, Ohio, 1977-78; free-lance reporter Cleve. Plain Dealer, 1978-80; reporter The Sacramento Bee, 1980-91; lectr. Stanford U., Palo Alto, Calif., 1992—. Author: Journey to Nowhere: The Saga of the New Underclass, 1985, repub. with introduction by Bruce Springsteen, 1996, And Their Children After Them, 1989 (Pulitzer Prize for gen. nonfiction 1990), The Last Great American Hobo, 1993, The Coming White Minority: California's Eruptions and the Nation's Future, 1996; contbr. articles to profl. jours. Nieman fellow Harvard U., 1988; grantee Pope Found., 1994, Freedom Forum, 1995. Democrat. Office: Stanford U Dept Comm Bldg 120 Stanford CA 94305

MAHER, CHRISTINE RITA, emergency room nurse, sexual assault specialist; b. Great Lakes, Ill., Jan. 21, 1952; d. Medard and Rita (Kobus) Schronski; m. William J. Maher, Aug. 23, 1986. BS, U. Ill., Chgo., 1973; AS, Los Medanos Coll., Pittsburg, Calif., 1980. RN, Calif.; cert. emergency nurse, trauma nurse, sexual assault nurse examiner; cert. emergency pediatric nurse; cert. BLS, ACLS. Nursing asst. Contra Costa County Hosp., Martinez, Calif., 1974-78, surg. technician, 1978-80, RN, 1980-84; emergency room nurse, educator, com. mem. North Bay Med. Ctr., Fairfield, Calif., 1984-91; co-founder ind. nursing group practice, co-dir. William J. Maher RN, Fairfield, Calif., 1991—; educator, forensic nurse coord. West Contra Costa County Sexual Assault Response Team, 1995—. Day camp dir. Benicia (Calif.) Recreation Dept., 1980; mobile ICU nurse, Solano County, 1985-92. Mem. AACN, Emergency Nurses Assn. (cert. TNCC), Nat. Nurses in Bus. Assn. Office: William J Maher RN 906 Hidden Cove Way Suisun City CA 94585-3511

MAHER, DAVID L., drug store company executive; b. Iowa City, 1939. Grad., U. Iowa, 1964. Pres., COO Am. Stores Co., Salt Lake City. Office: American Stores Co 709 E South Temple Salt Lake City UT 84102

MAHER, JAN, artist, educator; b. Huntington, Ind., Feb. 10, 1946. BA, New Sch. Social Rsch., N.Y.C., 1969; MA in English Lit., Millersville (Pa.) U., 1988. Cert. 4-12 tchr. Artist in residence Seattle Arts Commn., Seattle Pub. Schs., 1980—; pres., project dir. Local Access, Seattle, 1990—; guest lectr. Seattle U., 1991—, Western Wash. U., Seattle, 1993—. Author (plays) Intruders, 1992 (Best of Festival), Ismene, 1992, Solitaire, 1993, Widow's Walk, 1995; co-author: Southeast Asian Americans, African Americans, Irish Americans, Mexican Americans, Japanese Americans, Inhabiting History, 1990. Mem. bd. dirs. New City Theater, Seattle, 1988-91; mem. adv. bd. Seattle Fringe Theater Festival, 1993-95. mem. Nat. Writers Union, N.W. Playwrights Guild, Dramatists Guild.

MAHER, JOHN FRANCIS, financial executive; b. Berkeley, Calif., Apr. 25, 1943; s. Edward John and Emilia A. (Radovan) M.; m. Ann Elizabeth Breeden (div. 1975); children: Edward John II, Elizabeth Ann; m. Helen Lee Stillman, Mar. 20, 1976; children: Michael Stillman, Helen Cathline. BS, Menlo Coll., 1965; MBA, U. Pa., 1967. Gen. ptnr. Eastman Dillon, N.Y., 1971; 1st v.p. Blyth Eastman Dillon, N.Y., 1972; exec. v.p. Blyth Eastman Dillon, L.A., 1976-79; exec. v.p., chief fin. officer Gt. Western Fin., Chatsworth, Calif., 1973-76; also bd. dirs. Gt. Western Fin., Beverly Hills, Calif.; mng. dir. Lehman Bros. Kuhn Loeb, L.A., 1979-86; CEO, pres. Great Western Fin. Corp., Chatsworth, 1986—; bd. dirs. Gt. Western Fin. Corp., Chatsworth, Baker Hughes Inc.; chmn., chief exec. officer Gt. Western Bank. Bd. dirs. Big Bros. L.A., Inc.; nat. bd. trustees Boys and Girls Clubs Am.; overseer art collections and gardens Huntington Libr.; trustee Cate Sch.; bd. trustees Trout Unlimited. Joseph Wharton fellow U. Pa., 1965-67. Mem. Calif. Bus. Roundtable Group, The L.A. World Affairs Coun. (dir.). Office: Gt Western Fin Corp N 11 02 9200 Oakdale Ave Chatsworth CA 91311-6519

MAHIN, GLENDA GORDON, product development specialist, hydrologist; b. Merced, Calif., Dec. 3, 1950; d. Alvin L. and Velma (Boyer) Gordon; m. Edward Milton Froeliger, Dec. 18, 1970 (dec. Aug. 1975); children: Edward Glen Froeliger, Frances Glen Froeliger Meyer; m. Donald Alan Mahin, Feb. 6, 1988. BS, Calif. State Poly. U., 1973; MS, U. Nev., Reno, 1991. Lic. tchr., Nev. Nutrition cons. Stockton and Martinez, Calif., 1973-82; elem. sch. tchr. Reno, 1982-86; rsch. asst. U. Nev., Reno, 1987-91; rsch. hydrologist Desert Rsch. Inst., Reno, 1990-93; hydrologist, product devel. specialist Vector Environ. Techs., Inc., Sparks, Nev., 1994—; hydrologist Mahin & Assocs., Reno, Nev., 1994—. Contbr. articles to profl. jours. Del. Sierra Nevada coun. Girl Scouts U.S., 1989—; treas., editor Golden Valley Homeowners Assn., Reno, 1984-87. Named Girl Scout Leader of Yr., Sierra Nev. coun. Girl Scouts, 1993; Exxon grantee, 1970, U.S. Agrl. Rsch. grantee U. Nev., Reno, 1988, U.S. Geol. Rsch. grantee, 1988. Mem. ASCE, AAUW, Assn. Gen. Contractors, Am. Meteorol. Soc., Assn. Groundwater Scientists and Engrs., Air and Waste Mgmt. Soc. Home: 2300 Sagittarius Dr Reno NV 89509-8900 Office: Mahin & Assocs 4790 Caughlin Pkwy # 217 Reno NV 89509-0907

MAHMOOD, AAMER, computer system architect; b. Lahore, Pakistan, Jan. 27, 1956; came to U.S., 1979; s. Muhammad Iftikhar Quereshi and Farakh (Sultana) Iftikhar; m. Samira Aftab, June 28, 1985; children: Muhammad Bilal, Umer Ali. BSEE with honors, U. Engring. & Tech., Lahore, 1979; MSEE, Stanford U., 1980, PhD in Elec. Engring., 1986. Lectr. U. Egnring. & Tech., 1979; teaching asst. Stanford (Calif.) U., 1980-82, rsch. asst., 1983-85; mem. tech. staff Rolm Milspec Computers, San Jose, Calif., 1986-88; mgr., tech. leader CPU and memory systems Amdahl/Advanced Systems, Sunnyvale, Calif., 1988-93; mgr. architect network hardware Cisco Systems, San Jose, 1994—. Contbr. articles to profl. jours. Bd. of Secondary Edn. merit scholar, Lahore, 1971, Bd. of Intermediate Edn. talent scholar, Lahore, 1973. Mem. IEEE (sr.), Assn. Computing Machinery, Stanford Alumni Assn. (life). Home: 1098 Cardinal Way Palo Alto CA 94303-3540

MAHON, TOM, novelist, insurance analyst; b. N.Y.C., Jan. 8, 1943; s. Edward J. and Kathleen (Boyle) M.; m. Sheila Seitz, Nov. 30, 1985. AA with honors, City Coll. San Francisco, 1967. Assoc. in Risk Mgmt., Internat. Inst. Am. Claims examiner Met. Life, San Francisco, 1967-68, Equitable Life Ins. Co., N.Y.C., 1968-70; sr. claims examiner U.S. Life Ins. Co., N.Y.C., 1970-74, Guardian Life Ins. Co., N.Y.C., 1975-76; benefits mgr. Harry M. Stevens, Inc., N.Y.C., 1976-82; claims mgr. Calif. Healthplan, San Diego, 1983-84; ins. analyst U.S. Dept. of Def., L.A., 1984-95. Author: (play) Secrets, 1983, (novel) The Sanction Primeval, 1986, (novel) The Special People. Chmn. Com. for Release of Polit. Prisoners (to assist Chinese dissidents), 1994. Recipient Spl. Achievement award Def. Logistics Agy., L.A., 1988. Home: 15050 Sherman Way Apt 106 Van Nuys CA 91405

MAHONEY, ANN DICKINSON, fundraiser; b. Topeka, Sept. 12, 1961; d. Jacob Alan II and Ruth (Curd) Dickinson; m. Michael James Mahoney, May 29, 1993; 1 child, James Junius Castle Mahoney. AB in History, Grinnell Coll., 1983; postgrad., McGill U., Montreal, Quebec, Can., 1985. Analyst, corp. fin. dept. E.F. Hutton & Co., Inc., N.Y.C., 1983-85; pres., owner The Dark Side, N.Y.C., 1985-87; asst. dir. individual giving Meml. Sloan-Kettering Cancer Ctr., N.Y.C., 1987-88, dir. spl. gifts, 1988-91; assoc. dir. devel. Sch. Humanities and Scis. Stanford (Calif.) U., 1991—; devel. asst. regional office Brandeis U., N.Y.C., 1987. Vol. interviewer Grinnell Coll., N.Y.C., San Francisco, 1983—; vol. Tom Huening for Congress, Palo Alto, Calif., 1992. Mem. Nat. Soc. Fund Raising Execs., Jr. League San Francisco (com. chmn. 1996—), Pacific Rsch. Inst. for Pub. Policy, Hist. Topeka (Kans.) Assn., Friends of Filoli (Woodside, Calif.), Peninsula Assn. Retarded Children & Adults Aux., Spokane Club (Wash.). Republican. Episcopalian. Office: Stanford U Bldg One Stanford CA 94305

MAHONY, ROGER M. CARDINAL, archbishop; b. Hollywood, Calif., Feb. 27, 1936; s. Victor James and Loretta Marie (Baron) M. A.A., Our Lady Queen of Angels Sem., 1956; B.A., St. John's Sem. Coll., 1958, B.S.T., 1962; M.S.W., Catholic U. Am., 1964. Ordained priest Roman Cath. Ch., 1962, ordained bishop, 1975, created cardinal priest, 1991. Asst. pastor St. John's Cathedral, Fresno, Calif., 1962, 68-73, rector, 1973-80; residence St. Genevieve's Parish, Fresno, Calif., 1964—, adminstr., 1964-67, pastor, 1967-68; titular bishop of Tamascani, aux. bishop of Fresno, 1975-80; chancellor Diocese of Fresno, 1970-77, vicar gen., 1975-80; bishop Diocese of Stockton (Calif.), 1980-85; archbishop Archdiocese of L.A., 1985-91, cardinal priest, 1991—; diocesan dir. Cath. Charities and Social Svc. Fresno, 1964-70, exec. dir. Cath. Welfare Bur., 1964-70; exec. dir. Cath. Welfare Bur. Infant of Prague Adoption Service, 1964-70; chaplain St. Vincent de Paul Soc., Fresno, 1964-70; named chaplain to Pope Paul VI, 1967; mem. faculty extension div. Fresno State U., 1965-67; sec. U.S. Cath. bishops ad hoc com. on farm labor Nat. Conf. Bishops, 1970-75; chmn. com. on pub. welfare and income maintenance Nat. Conf. Cath. Charities, 1969-70; bd. dirs. West Coast Regional Office Bishops Com. for Spanish-Speaking, 1967-70; chmn. Calif. Assn. Cath. Charities Dirs., 1965-69; trustee St. Patrick's Sem., Archdiocese of San Francisco, 1974-75; mem. adminstrv. com. Nat. conf. Cath. Bishops, 1976-79, 82-85, 87-90, com. migration and refugees, 1976—, chmn. com. farm labor, 1981—, com. moral evaluation of deterrence, 1986-88; cons. com., chmn. for ProLife Activities, 1990—; mem. com. social devel. and world peace U.S. Cath. Conf., 1985, chmn. internat. policy sect., 1987-90; com. justice and peace, Pontifical Couns., 1984-89, 90—, pastoral care of migrants and itinerant peace, 1986—, social communications, 1989—. Mem. Urban Coalition of Fresno, 1968-72, Fresno County Econ. Opportunities Commn., 1964-65, Fresno County Alcoholic Rehab. Com., 1966-67, Fresno City Charter Rev. Com., 1968-70, Mexican-Am. Council for Better Housing, 1968-72, Fresno Redevel. Agy., 1970-75, L.A. 2000 Com., 1985-88, Fed. Commn. Agrl. Workers, 1987—, Blue Ribbon Com. Affordable Housing City of L.A., 1988; mem. commn. to Draft an Ethics Code for L.A. City Govt., 1989-90; bd. dirs. Fresno Community Workshop, 1965-67; trustee St. Agnes Hosp., Fresno. Named Young Man of Yr. Fresno Jr. C. of C., 1967. Mem. Canon Law Soc. Am., Nat. Assn. Social Workers. Home: 114 E 2nd St Los Angeles CA 90012-3711 Office: Archdiocese of LA 3424 Wilshire Blvd Los Angeles CA 90010-2241*

MAHOUR, GHOLAM HOSSEIN, pediatric surgeon, educator; b. Shiraz, Iran, Aug. 3, 1935; came to U.S., 1963; s. Alie and Shariat (Meshkin) M.; m. Barbara Lee Younggren, June 26, 1966; children: Michelle Marie, Elizabeth Victoria. BS, U. Shiraz, 1955, MD, 1959; MS in Surgery, Mayo Grad. Sch. Medicine, 1968. Diplomate Am. Bd. Surgery in gen. surgery, pediat. surgery and surg. critical care. Assoc. in surgery Harvard U. Sch. Medicine, Boston, 1970-71; from asst. prof. surgery to assoc. prof. surgery U. So. Calif., L.A., 1972-84, prof. surgery, 1984—; chief divsn. pediat. surgery Children's Hosp. L.A., 1978-93, dir. trauma program, 1983—, sr. coord. surg. edn., 1993—. Contbr. numerous sci. papers to med. jours. Grantee March of Dimes, 1973-75, 79-80. Fellow ACS, Am. Acad. Pediatrics, Royal Coll. Surgeons Can.; mem. AAUP, Am. Pediat. Surg. Assn. (grantee 1981-90), Am. Assn. for Surgery of Trauma, Soc. Critical Care Medicine, Am. Trauma Soc. (founding mem.), Brit. Assn. Pediat. Surgeons, Pacific Assn. Pediat. Surgeons, Western Surg. Assn., James T. Priestly Surg. Soc. Office: Childrens Hosp LA 4650 W Sunset Blvd Los Angeles CA 90027-6062

MAHRENHOLTZ, DAYLA DIANNE, elementary school principal; b. Glendale, Calif., Apr. 12, 1957; d. Preston Paul Buby and Evangeline Ruth (Sickler) B.; m. Laurence J. Mahrenholtz, Nov. 21, 1987 (div. Feb. 1993). AA, El Camino Jr. Coll., Torrance, Calif., 1975-77; BA, Calif. State U., Carson, 1979; MA, Calif. State U., L.A., 1990; EdD, U. LaVerne, Calif., 1996. Cert. edn. adminstr., Calif. Teller Ban of Am., Lawndale, Calif., 1977-79; tchr. Whittier (Calif.) City Sch. Dist., 1980-88, tchr., mentor, 1988-92; prin. Los Nietos Sch. Dist., Whittier, Calif., 1992—. Mem. AAUW, Calif. Assn. Bilingual Edn., Assn. Calif. Adminstrs., Computer Users in Edn., Whittier Area Sch. Adminstrs. (program chair 1993—). Democrat. Office: Aeolian Sch 700 Esplanade Ste 21 Redondo Beach CA 90606-3306

MAIER, ANTHONY ALVIN, pastor, counselor; b. Bellingham, Wash., Feb. 23, 1947; s. Alvin E. and Ethal (Ator) M.; m. Sondra Kay Sents, Aug. 20, 1971; children: Jennifer Kay, Mindy Nicole. MDiv, Western Evang. Sem., 1976; MA in Counseling Psychology, George Fox U., 1996. Pastor, counselor Free Meth. Ch. N.Am., various locations; pastor, mental health counselor Harbor Free Meth., Hoquiam, Wash., 1991—. Contbr. to newspapers. With U.S. Army, 1970-72. Mem. ACA, Am. Assn. Christian Counselors, Grays Harbor C. of C. Republican. Office: Harbor Free Meth 2740 Simpson Ave Hoquiam WA 98550-2931

MAIER, EDWARD KARL, foreign language educator; b. Toledo, Ohio, Feb. 28, 1954; s. Edward and Martha May (Winners) M.; m. Virginia Elizabeth Heym, Oct. 6, 1986 (div. Nov. 1994); children: Catherine Heym, Nathaniel. BA, No. Ariz. U., 1977; MA, U. Colo., 1987; PhD, U. Calif., Davis, 1994. Instr. U. Colo., Denver, 1988; assoc. instr. U. Calif., Davis, 1993-94; adj. faculty Monterey (Calif.) Inst. Internat. Studies, 1993; vis. prof. Ohio U., Athens, 1994-96; adj. prof. U. Colo., Boulder, 1997—. Recipient U. Colo. Boulder Grad. Tchg. Excellence award, 1989, Humanities Grad. Rsch. award U. Calif.-Davis, 1992-93; U. Colo. Doctoral fellow, 1987-89, U. Calif.-Davis Doctoral fellow, 1990-91, 92-93. Mem. MLA, Am. Assn. Tchrs. German. Democrat. Buddhist. Home: 4473 51st St Boulder CO 80301

MAIER, GERALD JAMES, natural gas transmission and marketing company executive; b. Regina, Sask., Can., Sept. 22, 1928; s. John Joseph and Mary (Passler) M. Student, Notre Dame Coll. (Wilcox), U. Man., U. Alta., U. Western Ont. With petroleum and mining industries Can., U.S., Australia, U.K.; responsible for petroleum ops. Africa, United Arab Emirates, S.E. Asia; chmn. TransCan. PipeLines, Calgary, 1985—, also bd. dirs.; chmn., bd. dirs. Epic Energy, Inc., 1996—; bd. dirs. BCE Inc., Bank of N.S., Petro-Can., XPronet Inc.; immediate past chmn. Can. Nat. Com. for World Petroleum Congresses; chmn. Van Horne Inst. for Internat. Transp.; dep. chmn. Coun. Can. Unity. Bd. dirs. Notre Dame Coll. Named Hon. Col. King's Own Calgary Rgt., Resource Man of Yr. Alta. Chamber of Resources, 1990; recipient Can. Engr.'s Gold medal Can. Coun. Profl. Engrs., 1990, Disting. Alumni award U. Alta., 1992, Mgmt. award McGill U., 1993, Centennial award Alta Assn. Engrs., Geologists and Geophysicists. Fellow Can. Acad. Engring.; mem. Assn. Profl. Engrs., Geologists and Geophysicists Alta. (past pres.), Can. Inst. Mining and Metallurgy (Past Pres.'s Meml. medal 1971). Office: TransCan PipeLines Ltd, 2900 240-4 Ave SW, Calgary, AB Canada T2P 4L7

MAIER, JOHN MARK, organizational leadership educator; b. Leonardtown, Md., May 27, 1954; s. Hanns John and Jacqueline Roper (Capps) M.; m. Lori Zucchino, Aug. 29, 1982; children: Dana Maier-Zucchino, Evan Maier-Zucchino. BA in Environ. Studies, Rollins Coll., 1976; MA in Sociology, Cornell U., 1978, PhD in Sociology, 1986. Instr. mgmt. Ithaca (N.Y.) Coll., 1983-86; asst. prof. human devel. and leadership studies SUNY, Binghampton, 1986-94; assoc. prof. orgnl. leadership Chapman U., Orange, Calif., 1994—; cons. in field, Ithaca and Orange, 1980—. Prodr., dir.: (video) A Major Malfunction...The Story Behind the Space Shuttle Challenger Disaster, 1992; contbr. articles to profl. jours. Co-founder Pro-Feminist Men's Network, Ithaca, 1984-94. Recipient Fritz Roethlisberger prize Orgnl. Behavior Tchg. Soc., 1994; GTE lectr. in tech. and ethics, 1991; Woodrow Wilson fellow, 1978. Mem. Acad. Mgmt. (mem. exec. com. Women in Mgmt. divsn. 1995-98, Dorothy Harlow Disting. Paper 1996). Unitarian-Universalist. Office: Chapman U 333 N Glassell St Orange CA 92866

MAIER, PETER KLAUS, law educator, investment adviser; b. Wurzburg, Germany, Nov. 20, 1929; came to U.S., 1939, naturalized, 1945; s. Bernard and Joan (Sonder) M.; m. Melanie L. Stoff, Dec. 15, 1963; children: Michele Margaret, Diana Lynn. BA cum laude, Claremont McKenna Coll., 1949; JD, U. Calif., Berkeley, 1952; LLM in Taxation, NYU, 1953. Bar: Calif. 1953, U.S. Supreme Ct. 1957; cert. specialist in taxation law, Calif. Atty. tax div. U.S. Dept Justice, Washington, 1956-59; mem. firm Bacigalupi, Elkus, Salinger & Rosenberg, San Francisco, 1959-69, Brookes & Maier, San Francisco, 1970-73, Winokur, Maier & Zang, San Francisco, 1974-81; of counsel Crosby, Heafy, Roach & May, Oakland, Calif., 1986—; prof. law Hastings Coll. Law, U. Calif., San Francisco, 1967-95; vis. prof. U. Calif. Boalt Sch. Law, Berkeley, 1988-89, Stanford U. Sch. Law, 1996—; pres. Maier & Siebel, Inc., Larkspur, Calif., 1981—; prin. Wood Island Investment Counsel, Inc., Larkspur, 1981—. Author books on taxation; contbr. articles to profl. jours. Chmn. Property Resources Inc., San Jose, Calif., 1968-77; pres. Calif. Property Devel. Corp., San Francisco, 1974-81. Capt. USAF, 1953-56. Mem. San Francisco Bar Assn. (chmn. sect. taxation 1970-71), Order of Coif. Home: PO Box 836 Belvedere CA 94920 Office: Maier & Siebel Inc 80 E Sir Francis Drake Blvd Larkspur CA 94939-1709

MAIERHAUSER, JOSEPH GEORGE, entrepreneur; b. Yankton, S.D., Mar. 23, 1927; s. Joseph and Angela M. (Jung) M.; m. Reta Mae Brockelsby, Nov. 25, 1948 (div. 1965); 1 child, Joe; m. Martha Helen Kuehn, Dec. 10, 1965. Student, U. S.D., Vermillion, 1946, S.D. Sch. Mines and Tech., Rapid City, 1947. Sales mgr. Black Hills Reptile Gardens, Rapid City, S.D., 1949-54; operator Colossal Cave Park, Vail, Ariz., 1956—; ptnr. Sta. KRNR, Roseburg, Oreg., 1961—. Mem. adv. bd. Salvation Army, Tucson, 1979-86; govs. appointee San Pedro Rparian Nat. Cons. Area Adv. Com., 1989—; past pres. So. Ariz. Internat. Livestock Assn., 1987-88; bd. dirs. Friends of Western Art., Tucson; co-founder Pima County Parklands Found.. With U.S. Navy Air Corps., 1944-45. Mem. Mountain Oyster Club (pres. 1989-91, bd. dirs. 1980-83). Republican. Home: Bear Paw Vail AZ 85641 Office: Colossal Cave Mountain Park PO Box D70 Vail AZ 85641-0070

MAILER, KATHLEEN, university dean; b. Boston, June 1, 1942; d. Thomas Vincent and Martha Louise (O'Hagan) O'Sullivan; m. Colin Mailer, Oct. 4, 1969. BS in Chemistry, U. Toronto, 1964; MS in Inorganic Chemistry, St. Francis Xavier U., Antigonish, N.S., Can., 1966; PhD, U. B.C., 1970. Biochemistry specialist U. Wis., Milw., 1974-75; lectr. U. N.B., Fredericton, Can., 1976; hon. rsch. assoc. U. N.B., Fredericton, 1975-90; asst. dir. chemistry Chalmers Hosp., Fredericton, 1977-81; from asst. prof. to prof. St. Mary's U., Halifax, N.S., Can., 1981-90; dean of sci. Athabasca U., Antigonish, 1990-92; dean sci. and engring. Seattle U., 1992—; vis. scientist Oncogen (now Bristol Myers), Seattle, 1989-90; cons. Bristol Myers, Syracuse, N.Y., 1984-86; rsch. chair Alta. Oil Sands Tech. and Rsch. Authority, 1992; co-dir. Regional Adv. Tech. Consortium, Bellevue, Wash., 1995—; found. assoc. Pacific Sci. Ctr., Seattle, 1994—. Author textbooks; contbr. chpts. to books, articles to profl. jours. Mem. bd. govs. St. Mary's U., Halifax, 1986-89; vol. Telephone Crisis Line, Halifax, 1986-89; organizer ann. meeting Sr. Women Acad. Adminstrs. Can., Banff, Alta., 1992; convenor meetings. Recipient Edn. award Can. Internat. Devel. Agy., 1992—; grantee NRC of Can., 1980-87, Med. Rsch. Coun. Can., 1981-84, Heart Found., Can., 1978-85. Mem. AAUW, Rainier Club, Engring. Deans Inst. Roman Catholic. Office: Seattle U 900 Broadway Seattle WA 98122-4338

MAIMON, ELAINE PLASKOW, English educator, university provost; b. Phila., July 28, 1944; d. Louis J. and Gertrude (Canter) Plaskow; m. Morton A. Maimon, Sept. 30, 1967; children: Gillian Blanche, Alan Marcus. AB, U. Pa., 1966, MA, 1967, PhD, 1970. Asst. prof. Haverford (Pa.) Coll., 1971-73; lectr. Beaver Coll., Glenside, Pa., 1973-75, asst. prof., dir. writing, 1975-77, assoc. prof., 1977-83, assoc. dean, 1980-84, assoc. v.p., prof. English, 1984-86; adj. assoc. prof. U. Pa., Phila., 1982-83; assoc. dean of coll. Brown U., Providence, 1986-88; dean, prof. English Queens Coll. CUNY, Flushing, N.Y., 1988-96; provost, v.p. Ariz. State U. West, Phoenix, 1996—; nat. bd. cons. NEH, 1977-81; mem. adv. bd. Cox Comms. Co-author: Writing in the Arts and Sciences, 1981; co-editor: Readings in the Arts and Sciences, 1984, Thinking, Reasoning and Writing, 1989. Mem. exec. bd. Sch. to Work, Western Maricopa County. Elaine Maimon award for Excellence in Writing named in her honor Beaver Coll., 1994. Mem. MLA (exec. com., teaching of writing divsn., 1991), Nat. Coun. Tchrs. English (nominating com. 1986-87), Conf. on Coll. Composition Comm. (exec. com. 1985-87), Assn. Am. Colls.,

Phi Beta Kappa. Home: 20726 N 55th Ave Glendale AZ 85308 Office: Ariz State U W PO Box 37100 4701 W Thunderbird Rd Phoenix AZ 85069-7100

MAIN, BETTY JO, management analyst; b. Hatch, N.Mex., May 22, 1939; d. Truman Oliver and Madeline Kate (Bennett) Hickerson; m. Andrew Allan Burich, June 21, 1958 (div. Sept. 1977); children: Cari Lynn, Andrew Allan Jr.; m. Ralph Monroe Main, Apr. 21, 1979; stepchildren: Michael, Randall, Kelly. AA in Liberal Arts, Marymount Coll., 1988; BS in Bus. & Mgmt., U. Redlands, 1993, MBA, 1996. Escrow officer Palos Verdes Escrow, San Pedro, Calif., 1975-80; sec. City of L.A., San Pedro, 1980-85, wharfinger, 1985-87, mgmt. aide, 1987-89, mgmt. analyst II, 1989—. Mem. City of L.A. Tutoring Program, City of L.A. Spkrs. Bur. Mem. AAUW, Marymount Coll. Alumni, U. Redland Alumni, Alfred North Whitehead Leadership Soc., Emblem Club (L.A.). Episcopalian. Home: 2238 W Paseo Del Mar San Pedro CA 90732-4521 Office: City of LA 425 S Palos Verdes St San Pedro CA 90731-3309

MAIN, GLORIA LUND, history educator; b. San Francisco, June 1, 1933; d. Howard Gates and Eifiona May (Llewelyn) Lund; m. Jackson Turner Main, June 16, 1956; children: Jackson, Eifiona, Judson. BA, San Jose State U., 1955; MA, SUNY, Stony Brook, 1969; PhD, Columbia U., 1972. Asst. prof. U. Colo., Boulder, 1983-88, assoc. prof., 1988—. Author: Tobacco Colony, 1983. Mem. Am. Antiquarian Soc., Am. Hist. Assn., Social Sci. History Assn., Orgn. Am. Historians, Econ. History Assn. (trustee 1989-92), Inst. Early Am. History and Culture (assoc. mem., coun. 1993-95). Home: 2305 Dartmouth Ave Boulder CO 80303 Office: U ColoCampus Dept History PO Box 234 Boulder CO 80309

MAIN, ROBERT GAIL, communications educator, training consultant, television and film producer, former army officer; b. Bucklin, Mo., Sept. 30, 1932; s. Raymond M. and Inez L. (Olinger) M.; m. Anita Sue Thoroughman, Jan. 31, 1955; children: Robert Bruce, David Keith, Leslie Lorraine. BS magna cum laude, U. Mo., 1954; grad. with honors, Army Command and Gen. Staff Coll., 1967; MA magna cum laude in Communications, Stanford U., 1968; PhD, U. Md., 1978. Commd. 2d lt. U.S. Army, 1954, advanced through grades to lt. col., 1968; mem. faculty Army Command and Gen. Staff Coll., 1968-70; chief speechwriting and info. materials div. U.S. Army Info. Office, 1971, chief broadcast and film div., 1972-73; dir. def. audiovisual activities Office of Info. for Armed Forces, 1973-76, ret., 1976; chmn. dept. comml. design, prof. instructional technology Calif. State U., Chino, 1976—; dir. Inst. Digital Electronic Art; tng. cons. Author: Rogues, Saints and Ordinary People, 1988; contbr. articles on computer based tng. and telecoms. to scientific and profl. jours.; producer: Walking Wounded, TV documentary, 1983; producer Army Info. Films, Army Radio Series, 1972-73. Decorated Legion of Merit, Meritorious Service medal, Commendation medal with oak leaf cluster, combat Inf. Badge; Vietnamese Cross of Gallantry; recipient Freedom Found. awards, 1972, 73, 74; Bronze medal Atlanta Film Festival, 1972; Best of Show award Balt. Film Festival, 1973; Creativity award Chgo. Indsl. Film Festival, 1973; Cine gold award Internat. Film Producers Assn., 1974; named an Outstanding Prof. Calif State U., 1987-88. Mem. Phi Eta Sigma, Alpha Zeta, Phi Delta Gamma, Omicron Delta Kappa, Alpha Gamma Rho.

MAINWARING, WILLIAM LEWIS, publishing company executive, author; b. Portland, Oreg., Jan. 17, 1935; s. Bernard and Jennie (Lewis) M.; m. Mary E. Bell, Aug. 18, 1962; children: Anne Marie, Julia Kathleen, Douglas Bernard. B.S., U. Oreg., 1957; postgrad., Stanford U., 1957-58. With Salem (Oreg.) Capital Jour., 1958-76, editor, pub., 1962-76; pub. Oreg. Statesman, 1974-76; pres. Statesman-Jour. Co., Inc., Salem, 1974-76, Westridge Press, Ltd., 1977—; pres. MediAmerica, Inc., Portland, 1981-96, CEO, 1988-96; bd. dirs. MediAmerica, Inc. Author: Exploring the Oregon Coast, 1977, Exploring Oregon's Central and Southern Cascades, 1979, Exploring the Mount Hood Loop, 1992, Government, Oregon-Style, 1996. Pres. Salem Beautification Coun., 1968, Marion-Polk County United Good Neighbors, 1970, Salem Social Svcs. Commn., 1978-79, Salem Hosp. Found., 1978-81. 2d lt. AUS, 1958; capt. Res. Ret. Mem. Salem Area C. of C. (pres. 1972-73), Oreg. Symphony Soc. Salem (pres. 1973-75), Salem City Club (pres. 1977-78), Sigma Chi. Republican. Presbyterian (ruling elder). Home and Office: 1090 Southridge Pl S Salem OR 97302-5947

MAIO, SAMUEL JOSEPH, English language and literature educator; b. Raton, N.Mex., May 16, 1955; s. Ernest James and Norma Sara (Giardino) M.; m. Kathryn Todd, May 29, 1978; children: Arnesti Giacomo, Cristina Mary, Tiara Sara, Nicolina Gina. BA, U. Utah, 1977, MA, 1979; PhD, U. So. Calif., 1986. Tchg. asst. U. Utah, 1978-79; instr. Trinidad (Colo.) State Jr. Coll., 1979-81; asst. lectr. U. So. Calif., 1981-85; lectr. U. Calif., Davis, 1985-90; asst. prof. San Jose State U., 1990-93, assoc. prof., 1993—, coord. creative writing program, 1992-95; poetry judge Pacific Internat. Contest, 1992, Robert Francis Meml. Prize, 1994, T.S. Eliot Prize, 1997. Author: Creating Another Self: Voice in Modern American Personal Poetry, 1995, The Burning of Los Angeles, 1997; author numerous poems, essays and revs. Recipient prize Acad. Am. Poets, 1984, rsch. award Calif. State U., 1992; dean's grantee San Jose State U. Coll. Humanities and Arts, 1996. Mem. Phi Kappa Phi. Office: San Jose State U Dept English One Washington Sq San Jose CA 95192-0090

MAIROSE, PAUL TIMOTHY, mechanical engineer, consultant; b. Mitchell, S.D., Aug. 4, 1956; s. Joseph E. and Phyllis R. (Glissendorf) M.; m. Connie L. Nickell, Apr. 1, 1989 (dec. June 8, 1992); m. Donna M. Ward, Sept. 10, 1993; 1 child, Carly J. BSME, S.D. Sch. Mines and Tech., 1978; postgrad., Tulane U., 1986. Registered profl. engr., Wash. Mech. engr. UNC Nuclear Industries, Richland, Wash., 1979-80, Wash. Pub. Power Supply System, Richland, 1980-85, 89; cons. La. Power & Light Co., New Orleans, 1985-86, Erin Engring. & Rsch. Inc., Walnut Creek, Calif., 1986-87, Sacramento Mcpl. Utility Dist., 1987-89; mech. engr. GE, Portland, Oreg., 1989-90; sr. cons. Rocky Flats Project Cygna Energy Svcs., 1990-91; v.p. mktg. Data Max, 1991—; pvt. practice cons. engr. Vancouver, Wash., 1991—; project engr. Mactec, Inc., Richland, Wash., 1990-91; pres. Project Tech. Mgmt., 1990—; chief engr. S.W. Air Pollution Control Authority, Vancouver, Wash., 1992—; mem. Wash. State Title V Permit Writers Subcom., 1994—, Wash. State New Source Rev. Subcom., 1994—. Co-author: Topical Report on Extreme Erosion at Yucca Mountain, Nevada, 1993. Mem. polit. action com. Sacramento Mcpl. Utility Dist., 1988. Mem. ASME (assoc.), ASHRAE (assoc.), Aircraft Owners and Pilots Assn., Profl. Assn. Diving Instrs., Air & Waste Mgmt. Assn., Sierra Club, Bards of Bohemia. Republican. Roman Catholic. Home: 4606 NW 387th St Woodland WA 98674-3423

MAIS, DALE EUGENE, chemist, pharmacologist; b. South Bend, Ind., Mar. 24, 1952; s. Rollin Charles and Violet Maybel (Paine) M.; m. Ellen Maria Barrell, May 9, 1976; children: James Charles, Maryellen Clare. BS in Chemistry, Ind. U., 1974, MS in Organic Chemistry, 1977, PhD in Pharmacology, 1983. Undergrad. rsch. asst. Ind. U., Bloomington, Ind., 1972-74, teaching asst. in chemistry, grad. rsch. asst., 1973-77, 74-77; mgr. organic synthesis Lafayette (Ind.) Pharmacal Inc., 1977-79; teaching asst. anatomy, grad. rsch. asst. Ind. U., Bloomington, 1979-80, 79-83; postdoctoral fellow, asst. prof. Med. U. of S.C., Charleston, 1983-86, 86-89; sr. pharmacologist dept. cardiovascular pharmacology Eli Lilly and Co., Indpls., 1989-92; adj. assoc. prof. Ind. U. Sch. of Medicine, Indpls., 1990-92; sr. rsch. scientist Ligand Pharm., Inc., San Diego, 1992—; expert analyst Organic Chemistry Edition of Chemtracts, 1990—. Editor: Eicosanoids in the Cardiovascular and Renal Systems, 1988; patentee in field; contbr. numerous articles to profl. jours. and chpts. to books. Named Ira E. scholar Ind. U., 1974, Drug Sci. Found. scholar, 1983-86; recipient Grad. Grant-in-Aid, Ind. U., 1982, 83, Nat. Rsch. Svc. award, 1983-86, First Pl. in Postdoctoral Divsn. of Student Rsch. Day Competition, 1984, 85, Louis N. Katz Basic Rsch. award-Finalist, 1985. Mem. Am. Socs. of Pharmacology and Exptl. Therapeutics, Am. Chem. Soc., S.C. Acad. Sic., Sigma Xi. Office: Ligand Pharms 9393 Towne Centre Dr Ste 100 San Diego CA 92121-3093

MAJKUT, PAUL THEODORE, newspaper editor; b. East St. Louis, Calif., Mar. 14, 1942; s. Paul John and Katherine Ann (Pavlich) M.; m. Denise Ronay Sheppard, June 12, 1968 (div. Apr. 18, 1975); 1 child, Paul Ezra; m. Gabriela Romani Hopfenblatt, July 24, 1978; 1 child, Natale Han. BA in English and Philosophy, U. San Diego, 1964; MA in Am. Lit., Scranton U., 1966; PhD in Am. Lit., Ind. U., 1986. Instr. Spring Hill Coll., Mobile, Ala., 1967-68, Brock U., St. Catherines, Ont., Can., 1968-69; cmty. organizer Adelante Cmty. Project, Berkeley, Calif., 1975-79; fgn. expert Dalian (China) Fgn. Lang. Inst., 1981-83; prof. King Saud U., Riyadh, Saudi Arabia, 1984-88; columnist Al-Yamama Riyadh Daily, 1986-88; editor The San Diego Rev., 1990—; editor Utility Consumers Action Network jour., Environ. Health Coalition jour., San Diego, 1995—. Author: Sandstorm, 1988, Asterion, The Mintaur, 1993. Bd. dirs. African Cmty. Svcs., San Diego, 1993—; mem. San Diego Dem. Coun. of Clubs, 1995—; pres. Green Dems. of San Diego, 1996, newsletter editor, 1993—. Coast Cmty. Coll. faculty fellow, 1981; Tiananmen Sq. Found. human rights grantee, 1995. Mem. San Diego Press Club, United Faculty, Environ. Health Coalition, San Diego Econ. Conversion Coun., Utility Consumers Action Network. Democrat. Home: 5932 Trojan Ave San Diego CA 92115-5406 Office: The San Diego Rev PO Box 15668 San Diego CA 92175

MAJOR, CAROL ANN, perinatologist, obstetrician/gynecologist; b. Berkeley, Calif., Oct. 30, 1959. BA, Stanford U., 1981; MD, Case Western Res. U., 1981-85. Diplomate Am. Bd. Ob-Gyn., Am. Bd. Maternal-Fetal Medicine. Intern U. Calif., San Francisco, 1985-86, resident, 1986-89; fellow U. Calif., Irvine, 1989-91; asst. prof. U. Calif. Irvine Med. Ctr., Orange, 1991—; bd. dirs. Orange County (Calif.) Perinatal Coun. Contbr. articles to profl. jours. Mem. Am. Women's Med. Assn., Orange County Ob-Gyn. Soc.

MAJOR, KARL BURCE, air force officer; b. Kansas City, Mo., Feb. 13, 1960; s. Schwab Samuel and Wilma Jean (Briscoe) M.; m. Sari Lane, Dec. 9, 1989; 1 child, McKayla Kristen. BSME, Okla. State U., 1982; MSME, Calif. State U., Fresno, 1993. Comd. 2d lt. USAF, 1982, advanced through grades to maj., 1995; pilot 41st Aero. Rescue & Recovery, McClellan AFB, Calif., 1984-87; instr. pilot 1550th Combat Crew Tng. Wing, Kirtland AFB, Calif., 1989-90; experiment test pilot 412th Test Wing, Edwards AFB, Calif., 1990-94; instr. USAF Test Pilot Sch., 1994—. Recipient Comendation for Exemplary Svc. in USAF, City of Kansas City, 1990. Mem. AIAA, Soc. Experimental Test Pilots, Phi Kappa Phi. Home: 44910 13th St E Lancaster CA 93535-1104 Office: USAF Test Pilot Sch 220 S Wolfe Ave Edwards CA 93524-6402

MAJURE, JOYCE ARLENE, surgeon; b. Kansas City, Mo., May 30, 1951; d. Oliver Davis and Betty Lou (Tucker) M.; m. Christopher Al Moreno, Apr. 14, 1984; children: Thomas Daniel, James Luis, Alana Joy. BA, Yale U., 1973; MD, U. Kans., 1976. Diplomate Am. Bd. Surgery. Resident in surgery U. Colo. Health Scis., Denver, 1976=80, 81-82; rsch. fellow Beth Israel Hosp., Boston, 1980-81; pvt. practice Rifle, Colo., 1982-84; surgeon Ctr. for Plastic and Reconstructive Surgery, Denver, 1984-86; pvt. practice Moscow, Idaho, 1986-87, Lewiston, Idaho, 1987—; cancer liaison physician St. Joseph Regional Med. Ctr., Lewiston, 1988—. Author and editor The Pocket Mentor: A Manual for Surgical Interns and Residents, 1993. Fellow ACS (pres. Idaho chpt. 1994, exec. com. of com. on oper. rm. environment); mem. Idaho Med. Assn., Assn. Women Surgeons (chmn. comm. com. 1989-94, editor newsletter 1989-94, v.p., program chair 1995, pres. 1996). Office: 307 Saint Johns Way Ste 11 Lewiston ID 83501-2435

MAK, STANLEY MING, radio broadcasting management executive; b. Chengdu, People's Republic of China, Feb. 17, 1949; came to U.S., 1969; s. Fung and Sui-Fun (Yil) M.; m. Suzanne Debra Phelps, June 9, 1971; children: Justin, Kristin, Kathryn. BA in Radio/TV Mgmt., Ea. Washington State U., 1972. Account exec. KREM AM/FM/TV, Spokane, Wash., 1973-77, KING TV, Seattle, 1977-79; local sales mgr. KINK Radio, Portland, Oreg., 1979-80, gen. sales mgr., 1980-81, gen. mgr., 1981-83, v.p., gen. mgr., 1983-87; sr. v.p. King Broadcasting Co., Seattle, 1987-92; pres. Mak Pacific, Inc., Bellevue, Wash., 1993-95; gen. mgr. KUPL & KKJZ Radio, Portland, Oreg., 1995—; sec. Portland Area Radio Coun., 1985-87. Mem. exec. bd. ARC, Oreg. Trail chpt., Portland, 1986-87; mem. exec. bd. Seattle Youth Symphony, 1990-92, bd. dirs., 1988-90. Republican. Home: 9604 NW Fleischner Portland OR 97229

MAKOWSKI, HEIDI MICHELLE, academic program director; b. Orem, Utah, Nov. 6, 1958; d. Bert William and Betty Gay (Callahan) Wagstaff; m. Edward Dennis Makowski, July 21, 1989. BS, U. Utah, 1983. Asst. to dean Coll. Fine Arts U. Utah, Salt Lake City, 1984-90, dir. of devel. Coll. Fine Arts, 1990—. Mem. Utah Soc. of Fund Raisers, Coun. for Advancement and Support of Edn., Jr. League of Salt Lake, Alumni Assn. Bd. Democrat. Office: U Utah 250 AAC Coll Fine Arts Salt Lake City UT 84112

MALA, THEODORE ANTHONY, physician, consultant; b. Santa Monica, Calif., Feb. 3, 1946; s. Ray and Galina (Liss) M.; children: Theodore S., Galina T.; m. Cynthia A. Mala, 1996; 1 stepchild, Rebecca Smith. BA in Philosophy, DePaul U., 1972; MD, Autonomous U., Guadalajara, Mex., 1976; MPH, Harvard U., 1980. Spl. asst. for health affairs Alaska Fedn. Natives, Anchorage, 1977-78; chief health svcs. Alaska State Div. of Corrections, Anchorage, 1978-79; assoc. prof., founder, dir. Inst. for Circumpolar Health Studies, U. Alaska, Anchorage, 1982-90; founder Siberian med. rsch. program U. Alaska, Anchorage, 1982, founder Magadan (USSR) med. rsch. program, 1988; commr. Health and Social Svcs. State of Alaska, Juneau, 1990-93; pres. chief exec. officer Ted Mala, Inc., Anchorage, 1993—; pres., ptnr. Mexican-Siberian Trading Co., Monterrey, Mex., 1994—; mem. Alaska rsch. and publs. com. Indian Health Svc., USPHS, 1987-90; advisor Nordic Coun. Meeting, WHO, Greenland, 1985; mem. Internat. Organizing Com., Circumpolar Health Congress, Iceland, 1992-93; chmn. bd. govs. Alaska Psychiat. Inst., Anchorage, 1990-93; cabinet mem. Gov. Walter J. Hickel, Juneau, 1990-93; advisor humanitarian aid to Russian Far East U.S. Dept. State, 1992—; cons. USAID on U.S.-Russian Health Programs, 1994. Former columnist Tundra Times; contbr. articles to profl. jours. Trustee United Way Anchorage, 1978-79; chmn. bd. trustees Alaska Native Coll., 1993—. Recipient Gov.'s award, 1988, Outstanding Svc. award Alaska Commr. Health, 1979, Ministry of Health citation USSR Govt., 1989, Citation award Alaska State Legislature, 1989, 90, 94, Commendation award State of Alaska, 1990, Alaska State Legislature, 1994, Honor Kempton Svc. to Humanity award, 1989, citation Med. Comty. of Magadan region, USSR, 1989; Nat. Indian fellow U.S. Dept. Edn., 1979. Mem. Assn. Am. Indian Physicians, N.Y. Acad. Scis., Internat. Union for Circumpolar Health (permanent sec.-gen. 1987-90, organizing com. 8th Internat. Congress on Circumpolar Health 1987-90). Office: 205 E Dimond Blvd Ste 544 Anchorage AK 99515-1909 *Personal philosophy: Progress in the North will come only when circumpolar countries put aside their geopolitical thinking and work together as one northern family.*

MALCOLM, ANDREW HOGARTH, journalist, writer; b. Cleve., June 22, 1943; s. Ralph Monteith and Beatrice Florence (Bowles) M.; m. Connie D'Amelio, Nov. 28, 1981; children: Christopher, Spencer, Emily, Keddy. BJ, Northwestern U., 1966, MJ, 1967. Clk. The N.Y. Times, N.Y.C., 1967-68, met. reporter, 1969-70; nat. corr. The N.Y. Times, Chgo., 1971-73, San Francisco, 1974-75; fgn. corr. The N.Y. Times, Vietnam, Thailand, Guam, 1975, Tokyo, 1975-78, Republic of Korea, 1975-78; bur. chief The N.Y. Times, Toronto, Ont., Can., 1978-82, Chgo., 1982-87; asst. nat. editor The N.Y. Times, N.Y.C., 1987-88, nat. affairs corr., columnist, 1988-93; exec. asst., dir. comm. Govs. Office, Helena, Mont., 1993—. Author: Unknown America, 1975, The Canadians, 1985, Final Harvest, 1986, This Far and No More, 1987, Someday, 1991, U.S. 1: America's Original Main Street, 1991, The Land and People of Canada, 1991, Huddle: Fathers, Sons, and Football, 1992, Mississippi Currents: A Journey Through Time and A Valley, 1996, Fury, 1997. Recipient George Polk award L.I. U., 1975, Page One award N.Y. Newspaper Guild, 1975, 83. Office: Governor's Office State Capitol Helena MT 59620-0801

MALCOLM, JOAN EDWARDS, principal, elementary education educator; b. Tampa, Fla., Nov. 25, 1947; d. David Jonathan and Eleanor (Edwards); m. Denis M. Malcolm, Feb. 4, 1967; children: Andrea, Jonathan. BA, Calif. Bapt. Coll., 1969; MA, Calif. State U., San Bernardino, 1984. Life tchg. credential, Calif.; adminstrv. svcs. credential, Calif. Tchr. Riverside (Calif.) Unified Sch. Dist., 1969-94, mentor tchr., 1989-94, spl. assignment vice principal, 1994—; dist. rep. Calif. Tchr. Credential Commn., 1993-96. Author, editor: (textbook) Riverside's History from Indian's to the Present, 1994. Named Alumnus of Yr., Calif. Bapt. Coll., 1994, Outstanding Alumni in Edn., 1992, Leader in Edn., Calif. State U., 1992. Mem. Kappa Kappa Iota (state pres. 1986-88, various offices 1973—). Home: 3068 Saratoga St Riverside CA 92503-5435

MALCOLM, RICHARD DOUGLAS, JR., resort administrator; b. San Francisco; s. Richard Douglas and Elisabeth (Elmiger) M.; m. Rebecca L. Muir; 1 child, Morel Muir. Student, U. Ariz., 1979-82. Mgr. Evergreen Restaurant, Ketchum, Idaho, 1984-89; owner X's on Main Restaurant-Pub, Ketchum, 1989-95; food and beverage dir. Schweitzer Mountain Resort, Sandpoint, Idaho, 1995—. Home: 322 Saint Clair Ave Sandpoint ID 83864 Office: Schweitzer Mountain Resort PO Box 815 Sandpoint ID 83864

MALCOLM, RICHARD WARD, academic administrator, consultant; b. Columbus, Ohio, July 27, 1933; s. Ralph James and Beatrice (Ward) M.; 1 child, Gwynn Malcolm Socolich. BS, U. Findlay (Ohio), 1956; MA, Ariz. State U., 1960; MEd, U. So. Calif., 1965, EdD, 1966. Acad. dean Martin Coll., Pulaski, Tenn., 1965-67; dean instrn. Arapahoe C.C., Littleton, Colo., 1967-71; chair edn. divsn. Chapman U., Orange, Calif., 1971-80; assoc. prof. U. So. Calif., 1976-77; dean instrn. Mesa (Ariz.) C.C., 1980-91; asst. to provost Chandler (Ariz.)/Gilbert C.C., 1991-92, chair divsn. social and behavioral scis., 1993-96; dir. R & D Williams campus Maricopa C.C., 1996—. Author: Mental Measurement Yearbook, 1972. Pres. Ariz. Rail Pasenger Assn., Phoenix, 1984-93. Mem. Am. Assn. Higher Edn., Ariz. Acad. Adminstrv. Assn. (treas. 1991—), Rotary. Methodist. Office: Williams Edn Ctr 6001 S Power Rd Bldg 410 Mesa AZ 85206

MALCOLM-CALLIS, KATHRYN JANETTE, animal scientist; b. Livingston, Mont., May 29, 1958; d. Orlin Rae and Dorothy Helen (Anderson) Malcolm; m. Quint F. Callis (div.); 1 child, Kaitlyn Sarah. BS in Animal Sci., Mont. State U., 1980; MS, N.Mex. State U., 1986, PhD, 1990. With Pub. Auction Yards, Billings, Mont., 1978-79; intern Colmey Vet. Clinic, Livingston, 1980; rsch. tech. Mont. State U., 1980-84; grad. rsch. and teaching asst. N.Mex. State U., 1985-86, 1987-89; rsch. specialist Clayton (N.Mex.) Livestock Rsch. Ctr., 1990—. Contbr. articles and abstracts to profl. jours. Sunday sch. tchr. Paradise Valley Community Ch. Mem. Am. Soc. Animal Sci., Lariet Cowbelles. Office: Clayton Livestock Rsch Ctr RR 1 Box 109 Clayton NM 88415-9501

MALCOR, LINDA A., writer, researcher; b. Pasadena, Calif., Feb. 3, 1962; d. Victor Carl and Gloria Gail (Russ) Peterson; m. Daniel Roy Malcor, Dec. 19, 1987; 1 child, Joseph Victor. AB in English cum laude, Occidental Coll., 1984; MA, UCLA, 1986, PhD in Folklore and Mythology, 1991. Writing adviser Occidental Coll., L.A., 1982-83; rsch. asst., teaching asst. UCLA, 1985-86, 2d bibliographer, 1987-89; course instr. Learning Tree U., Chatsworth, Calif., 1990-93; freelance rschr., 1985—, freelance writer, 1987—; adj. faculty Antioch U., Marina Del Rey, Calif., 1992-94. Author: the Chalice at the Cross, 1991; co-author: From Scythia to Camelot, 1994; freelance screenwriter Morris, Inc., Torrance, Calif., 1992-96; option feature script to High Velocity Entertainment, Simi Valley, Calif., 1994, 95; freelance writer for Ency. of Am. Popular Beliefs and Superstitions, L.A., 1989; author articles, poetry, fan fiction. Deacon Prsbyn. Ch., Pasadena, 1987-89, Presbyn. Ch., Inglewood, Calif., 1992-94, mem. nursery sch. bd., 1995-96; judge Election Bd., L.A., 1990-91, insp., 1992-97. Recipient Victor Gruen award, 1978; UCLA Grad. Div. travel grantee, 1985-87. Mem. Am. Folklore Soc.,Calif. Folklore Soc., So. Calif. Acad. Scis. (Best Paper award 1984, 86, 87), Tugs (skipper 1992-93), Phi Alpha Theta. Republican. Home and Office: 3223 Bagley Ave Apt 101 Los Angeles CA 90034-2971

MALDONADO, ABEL, mayor; b. Santa Maria, Calif.; m. Laurie Maldonado; 2 children. Student, Calif. Poly. Owner Agro-Jal, Santa Maria, 1988—; from councilman to mayor City of Santa Maria; bd. dirs. Calif. Strawberry Commn., Santa Barbara County Air Pollution Control Dist.; state rep. Calif. Rep. Party State Ctrl. Com. Mem. convention com. League of Calif. Cities, 1996. Mem. Econ. Devel. Assn., Santa Maria Valley C. of C., Kiwanis. Office: 110 E Cook St Rm 1 Santa Maria CA 93454 also: PO Box 1862 Santa Maria CA 93456

MALDONADO, GREGORY MATTHEW, music director, educator; b. Merced, Calif., June 8, 1958; s. Daniel Robert and Elaine Louise (Turrey) M. MusB, UCLA, 1990. Music dir., founder L.A. Baroque Orch.; mem. faculty U. So. Calif., 1988—; instr. in Baroque violin UCLA, 1989—; founder, music dir. La Stravaganza, L.A., Eroica String Quar., L.A., L.A. Fortepiano Trio, L.A. Supporter Greenpeace Internat., San Francisco, 1989, Pesticide Watch, L.A., 1990—. Mem. So. Calif. Early Music Soc. Home: 2844 Avenel St Los Angeles CA 90039-2071

MALDONADO, JENNIFER ANN, special events and marketing executive; b. Portland, Oreg., May 10, 1968; d. Sergio and Julie Ann (Rigotti) Cettina; m. Dirk Silvester Maldonado, May 4, 1991. BS in Comm. Mgmt. magna cum laude, U. Portland, 1990. Asst. editor Progressive Woman and Women's Yellow Pages Directory Svcs. Inc., Portland, 1989-90; media rels. asst. Whitman Advt. and Pub. Rels., Portland, 1990; pub. rels. specialist Oreg. State Bar, Lake Oswego, 1991-94, ann. meeting coord., community svcs. specialist, 1994—. Sr. editor: Senior Law Handbook: A Oregon Legal Inforamtion and Reference Guide for Older Adults, 1992 (Spotlight award Pub. Rels. Soc. Am. 1992, Pub. Svc. Achievement award Nat. Assn. Bar Execs. 1993). Mem. vol. recognition program com. Internat. Assn. Bus. Communicators, 1994—; mem. law day com. Classroom Law Project, 1994—. Recipient Pub. Svc. award ABA, 1992. Mem. Meeting Profls. Internat. Office: Oreg State Bar 5200 Meadows Rd Lake Oswego OR 97035-3255

MALIK, SOHAIL, chemistry educator, researcher, consultant; b. Karachi, Pakistan, Nov. 7, 1958; came to U.S., 1986; s. Bakhtiar Malik and Amna Begum; m. Rubina Sial, Jan. 1, 1990; 1 child, Shahbaz. BSc with honors, U. Karachi, 1980, MS, 1982, PhD, 1986; postgrad., Stanford U., 1986-88. Instr. div. chemistry and nephrology, depts. lab. medicine and medicine U. Wash., Seattle, 1988-89, asst. prof. depts. lab. medicine and medicine, 1989-96; head natural products lab. dept. lab. medicine, 1990-96; co-dir. div. chemistry, dept. lab. medicine U. Wash., Seattle, 1991-96; pres., dir. R&D BioFrontiers, Inc., Redmond, Wash., 1996—; postdoctoral rsch. assoc. dept. chemistry Stanford (Calif.) U., 1986-88; peer rev. cons. NIH/Alcohol Drug Abuse and Mental Health Adminstrn. Mem. editorial bd. Current Medicinal Chemistry; contbr. articles to profl. jours.; patentee in field. Fellow Am. Inst. Chemists, Stanford U. scholar, 1986-88. Mem. Am. Assn. Advancement Sci., Am. Chem. Soc., Am. Soc. Pharmacognosy, Internat. Isotope Soc., Acad. Clin. and Lab. Physicians and Scientists. Office: BioFrontiers Inc 14712 NE 87th St Redmond WA 98052-3400

MALINOWSKI, WALTER WILLIAM, manufacturing engineer; b. Perth Amboy, N.J., Dec. 6, 1924; s. Walter Thom Malinofsky and Gisella Mahnofsky; m. Liane Claire Malinofsky, May 9, 1959 (div. Jan. 1981); children: Gisele Liane, William Walter. BS in Physics, Rutgers U., 1951; MS in Physics, Poly. U., Bklyn., 1967. Supervisory engr. U.S. Army Electronics Command, Ft. Monmouth, N.J., 1951-70; sr. technician Kaiser Aluminum & Chemicals Co., Pleasanton, Calif., 1971-75; acting mfg. engr. Memorex Corp., Sunnyvale, Calif., 1976-78; ceramic engr. GTE Wesgo, Belmont, Calif., 1978-81; mfg. engr. Datatape-Consolidated Magnetics Corp., Santa Clara, Calif., 1981-85; sr. specialist engr. Boeing Aerospace Co., Kent, Wash., 1985-88; gen. engr. USAF Satellite and Missile Sys. Ctr., El Segundo, Calif., 1988-95; cons. on magnetic materials U.S. Army Electronics Command, Ft. Monmouth, 1959-70; spkr. in field. Author: (with others) Crystal Structures, 1956; contbr. articles to profl. jours.; inventor in field. Staff sgt. U.S. Army, 1943-46, ETO. Decorated Bronze Star; named Person of the Month, Civic Bus. Group, 1967. Mem. IEEE, Am. Vacuum Soc., Am. Ceramic Soc., Soc. Mfg. Engrs., Internat. Soc. Photo-Optical Instrumentation Engrs., Air Force Assn., 99th Inf. Divsn. Assn., Assn. Advancement of Ret. People, Alpha Phi Alpha. Democrat. Methodist. Home: 1681 Gramercy Ave Torrance CA 90501 Office: Malinowski Co Ste 179 1659 Gramercy Ave Torrance CA 90501

MALINS, DONALD CLIVE, biochemistry, researcher; b. Lima, Peru, May 19, 1931; came to U.S., 1947; s. Richard Henry and Mabel (Madeline) M.; m. Mary Louise Leiren, 1962; children: Christopher W., Gregory S., Timothy J. BA, U. Washington, 1953; BS in chem., Seattle U., 1956; PhD in biochemistry, U. Aberdeen, 1967, DSc, 1976. Dir. environ. conservation div. Nat. Marine Fisheries Svc., Seattle, 1974-87; sr. scientific cons. U.S. Dept. Justice, Washington, 1989-91; scientific cons. Nat. Ocean & Atmosphere Adminstrn., 1990-92; head molecular epidemiology program Pacific Northwest Rsch. Found., Seattle, 1992—; rsch. prof. dept. chem. Seattle U.,

1972-95; affiliate prof. dept. environ. health U. Washington, 1984—, Coll. Ocean & Fishery Scis. U. Washington, 1974-91; editor-in-chief Aquatic Toxicology, 1980-95; lectr., speaker in field. Contbr. articles to profl. jours.; inventor in field. Bd. dirs. Am. Oceans Campaign, 1989-91; adv. bd. Internat. Jt. Commn., 1990-91. Recipient U.S. Dept. Commerce Golf medal, 1982. Mem. NAS, Am. Soc. Biochemistry and Molecular Biology, Am. Chem. Soc., Am. Assn. for Cancer Rsch. Office: Pacific Northwest Rsch Found 720 Broadway Seattle WA 98122-4327

MALISH, DAVID MARC, physician; b. Phila., Dec. 29, 1947; s. Irvin and Esther (Divor) M.; (div. 1990); children: Jennifer, Scott; m. Shari Boxer, Sept. 26, 1992; 1 child, Jack. BS, Knox Coll., 1969; MD, Hahnemann U., 1973. Diplomate Am. Bd. Internal Medicine, Am. Bd. Allergy and Immunology. Intern Hahnemann Hosp., Phila., 1973-74; internal medicine resident Monmouth Med. Ctr., Long Branch, N.J., 1974-76; fellow in allergy and immunology Kaiser Found. Hosp.-Sunset facility, UCLA Immunodeficiency Clinic, Children's Hosp., L.A., 1976-78; locum tenems Drs. Cenci and Krall, West Hartford and Hartford, Conn., 1978-79; pvt. practice San Jose, Calif., 1979—; staff internist Monte Villa Hosp., Morgan Hill, Calif., 1979-81; med. dir., staff internist Good Samaritan Recovery Ctr., Good Samaritan Hosp., San Jose, 1991-94, med. cons. Samaritan Pain Ctr., San Jose. Bd. dirs. Am. Lung Soc., Santa Clara, 1980—; med. dir. Camp Superstuff-Asthmatic Camp for Children, 1985—; head pediat. asthma sect. Am. Lung Assn., Santa Clara County, 1994—; mem. fin. bd. for physicians Com. to Reelect Congressman Norm Mineta. Fellow Am. Acad. Allergy and Immunology, Am. Coll. Allergy; mem. Am. Acad. Physicians, Calif. Soc. Addiction Medicine (cert.), Santa Clara Med. Assn. Office: 2505 Samaritan Dr Ste 606 San Jose CA 95124-4016

MALLEN, MARY A., secondary school science educator; b. Chgo., July 4, 1961; d. James Robert and Marguerite C. (McDouough) M. BS, Calif. Poly. Tech. U., Pomona, 1981; MEd, Loyola Marymont U., L.A., 1991. Tchr. Ramona Convent Secondary Sch., Alhambra, Calif., 1981-90, Los Altos H.S., Hacienda Hghts., Calif., 1990—; Leadership team, Los Altos H.S., Hacienda Heights, Calif., 1992—, sch. site coun., 1992—. Recipient Burns Found. scholarship, Loyola Marymount U., 1989-91. Democrat. Roman Catholic. Office: Los Altos H S 15325 Los Robles Ave Hacienda Heights CA 91745-2717

MALLEN, MICHAEL PAUL, telephone company executive; b. N.Y.C., Feb. 20, 1947; s. Charles and Mildred Mallen; m. Lisabeth Anne Hays, Sept. 12, 1970; 1 child, David Howard. BS in Chemistry, San Francisco State U., 1968; MBA, U. So. Calif., L.A., 1980; Advanced Cert. Mgmt., Duke U., 1994. Police officer San Francisco Police Dept., 1969-76; asst. budget dir. City and County of San Francisco, 1977-79; maintenance mgr. Pacific Telephone, San Mateo, Calif., 1980, San Francisco, 1981-84; regional sales mgr. Pacific Bell, San Francisco, 1984-90, dir. sales, 1990-94, sales v.p., 1994-95, v.p. industry mkts., 1995—. Scoutmaster Boy Scouts Am., San Ramon, Calif., 1988-89, dist. chmn., Walnut Creek, 1989-90. 1st lt. U.S. Army, 1969-70. Republican. Office: Pacific Bell 370 3d St Rm 704D San Francisco CA 94107

MALLISON, ROBERT ANDREW, neurologist; b. St. Mary's, Pa., Apr. 16, 1939; s. Bernard M. and Florence (Geeck) M.; m. Lois Mallison, May 29, 1965; children: Christine, Karen, Denise, Kevin, Brian, Stacey. BA, St. Vincent Coll., 1961; MD, Loyola U., Chgo., 1965. Intern St. Mary's Hosp., San Francisco, 1965-66; resident U. Calif., San Francisco, 1966-69; pvt. practice neurology San Jose, Calif., 1971—; mem. faculty U. Tenn., 1969-71, U. Calif., 1971-76, Stanford U., 1972-90. Chmn. stroke divsn. Santa Clara County Heart Assn., 1971-76. Comdr. USN, 1969-71. Mem. AMA, Calif. Med. Assn., Am. Acad. Neurology, Nat. Headache Found., Am. Acad. Clin. Neurophysiology, Am. Assn. Electrodiagnostic Medicine, Am. Assn. Study Headache, Santa Clara County Med. Assn., Peripheral Neuropathy Inst. Office: 2505 Samaritan Dr Ste 309 San Jose CA 95124-4011

MALLO, ANNMARIE, elementary educator; b. Eglin Field, Fla., Sept. 18, 1949; d. Jack Donald and Carmela (Trassari) Cradduck; m. Arthur Ray Mallo, Mar. 19, 1977; children: Chad Arthur, Alicia Marie; 1 stepson, Greg R. AA, Solano Jr. Coll., Vallejo, Claif., 1969; BA in Internat. Rels., Calif. State U., Sacramento, 1971, student, 1989-90. Cert. tchr., Calif., Nat. Tchg. Certification Program. From mgt. trainee to dept. mgr. Sears Roebuck & Co., Sacramento, 1971-74; sales rep. Clairol Inc., N.Y.C., 1974-76; sales rep. profl. svcs. divsn. Procter & Gamble, Cin., 1976-85; interior decorator Interiors By Design, Sacramento, 1987-90; tchr. Eureka Union Sch. Dist., Granite Bay, Calif., 1990—; bd. dirs. Touch of Understanding, Granite Bay, 1996. Eureka Union Sch. Dist., Granite Bay, 1985-90. Mem. ASCD, Internat. Reading Assn., Calif. Reading Assn., Eureka Union Sch. Dist. Tchrs. Orgn. Home: 5603 Carlile Ct Granite Bay CA 95746-9016

MALLON, PETER, archbishop; b. Prince Rupert, Can., Dec. 5, 1929; s. Joseph P. and Sheila M. (Keenan) D. Grad., Seminary Christ the King, Burnaby and Mission, B.C. ordained to ministry Roman Cath. Ch., 1956;. Asst. Holy Rosary Cath., Vancouver, B.C., 1956-64, rector, 1966-82; chancellor Archdiocese Vancouver, 1964-65, dir. religious edn., 1971-73; adminstr. Guardian Angels Parish, Vancouver, 1964-65; pastor St. Anthony's, West Vancouver, 1982-89; bishop Nelson, B.C., 1989-95; archbishop of Regina Sask., Can., 1995—. Address: 445 Broad St N, Regina, SK Canada S4R 2X8

MALLORY, STEVEN REECE, software engineering executive; b. Lynwood, Calif., Nov. 23, 1947; s. Joseph William and Edith Pauline (Robertson) M.; m. Kelly Kay Walsh, Jan. 2, 1977 (div. June 1980); m. Elizabeth Margaret Kuntz, Sept. 1, 1990; 1 child, Lauren Beth. BS in Applied Math., Calif. State Poly. Coll., 1971, MS in Computer Sci., 1976. Mem. tech. staff Hi-Shear Corp., Torrance, Calif., 1971, 73-74, Sci. Applications, Inc., San Diego, 1971-72, Planning Rsch. Corp., San Diego, 1972-73, Universal Analytics, Inc., Westchester, Calif., 1976-77; mgr. tng. applications divsn. Sci. Applications Inc., San Diego, 1977-84; mgr. computer and sys. applications group Photon Rsch. Inc., San Diego, 1984-86; dep. v.p., mgr. engring. ops. Titan Sys. Inc., San Diego, 1986-88; mgr. software devel. engring. IVAC Corp., San Diego, 1988-95; sys. verification mgr. Cardiac Pathways Corp., Sunnyvale, Calif., 1996—; cons. and presenter in field. Author: Software Development and Quality Assurance for the Healthcare Manufacturing Industries, 2d edit., 1996, Software Quality Assurance SOPs for Healthcare Manufacturers, 1997; mem. editl. bd. Med. Device and Diagnostic Industry; contbr. articles to profl. jours. Mem. IEEE, Nat. Assn. Watch and Clock Collectors, Assn. for Advancement of Med. Instrumentation, Assn. for Computer Machinery, Soc. for Computer Simulation, Soc. Indsl. and Applied Math., Am. Soc. Quality Control. Republican. Home: 833 Intrepid Ln Redwood City CA 94065-1748 Office: 995 Benecia Ave Sunnyvale CA 94086

MALLOTT, BYRON IVAR, holding corporation executive; b. Yakutat, Alaska, Apr. 6, 1943; s. Jay B. and Emma M. (Brown) M.; m. Evelyn Anderson Converse, 1964 (div. 1971); children: Byron, Meredith; m. Antoinette Mary Evans, May 7, 1972; children: Anthony, Joseph, Benjamin Lee. Student, Eastern Wash. State Coll., 1961-62, Western Wash. State Coll., 1962-64; HHD (hon.), U. Alaska, 1984. Spl. asst. U.S. Senator Mike Gravel, 1969; exec. dir. Rural Alaska Action Program, Anchorage, 1970; dir. State of Alaska Local Affairs Agy., Juneau, 1971-72, commr. State Dept. Community and Regional Affairs, 1972-74; chmn. Sealaska Corp., Juneau, 1976-84, chief exec. officer, 1982-92, pres., 1990-92; co-owner Alaska Native Resources, Inc., Yakutat, 1974-78; bd. dirs. Alaska Air Group (parent co. of Alaska Airlines), Security Pacific Bank Washington, Security Pacific Bancorp. N.W.; bd. dirs. Alaska Permenent Fund Corp., chmn., 1985-86, 87-88. Mayor City of Yakutat, 1965; mem. Alaska Reapportionment Bd., Juneau, 1979—, chmn., 1980; mem. U. Alaska Found., Fairbanks, 1980-85. Recipient Gov.'s award Alaskan of Year Com., 1982. Mem. Alaska Fedn. Natives (pres. 1977-78, Citizen of Year 1982), Young Pres.' Orgn. Democrat. Roman Catholic. Club: Alaska Native Brotherhood (v.p. 1968-69). Office: Sealaska Corp 1 Sealaska Plz Juneau AK 99801-1249*

MALM, RONALD LEE, physician; b. Cheyenne, Wyo., June 29, 1966; s. Kendrick E. and Linda K. (Conger) M. BS, U. Wyo., 1988; DO, U. Health Scis., 1992. Diplomate Am. Bd. Family Medicine. Intern Granview Hosp. and Med. Ctr., Dayton, Ohio, 1992-93; resident Smoky Hill Family Practice, Salina, Kans., 1993-95; physician A.L. Gruber & P.J. Schiel, M.D., P.C., Cheyenne, Wyo., 1995—. MEm. Wyo. Med. Soc., Laramie County Med. Soc., Am. Acad. Family Physicians, Wyo. Acad. Family Physicians, Soc. Tchrs. Family Medicine (Resident Tchrs. award 1995). Office: 5416 Education Dr Cheyenne WY 82009-4094

MALM, ROYCE ELLIOTT, musician; b. Los Angeles, Nov. 22, 1929; s. Albin Nils and Mildred Elizabeth (Aden) M.; Mus.B., U. So. Calif., 1952, M.Mus. in Composition, 1954; m. Enid Elliott Malm; children: Jaime Louise, Lorraine Elise. Tchr. public schs. in Calif., 1957-89; tchr. secondary choral music and music appreciation Burbank (Calif.) Unified Sch. Dist., 1964-89; ret. 1989; mem. Burbank Symphony Assn., 1971-91, pres., 1975-78, exec. dir., 1979—; dir. ch. choirs, 1953—; v.p. Burbank Community Concerts Assn., 1973-75, Symphony League Los Angeles County, 1975-78, Performing Arts Fedn. Burbank, 1977-78; music cons., estate and radio music archivist, recording restoration Cambria Records, 1992—. Composer: Reflections, 1980; others. Served with AUS, 1954-56. Mem. Music Educators Nat. Conf., NEA, Burbank Tchrs. Assn., Calif. Tchrs. Assn., Choral Conductors Guild Calif., So. Calif. Vocal Assn., Pro Musica Sana, Sir Thomas Beecham Soc., Pi Kappa Lambda, Phi Mu Alpha. Democrat. Presbyterian. Home: 5905 Ironwood St Palos Verdes Peninsula CA 90275-1762 Office: Cambria Master Recordings PO Box 374 Lomita CA 90717-0374

MALMGREN, DICK, retired school principal, educator; b. Leadville, Colo., Oct. 27, 1940; s. Walter Gustav and Antonia (Peltin) M.; m. Connie Lee Montoya, June 11, 1964 (div. Dec. 1975); children: James, Danielle Malmgren Swenson; m. JoAnne Wright, July 2, 1977. BS in Phys. Edn. & History, U. Colo., 1962; MA in Secondary Adminstrn., Western State Coll., 1967; EdD in Adminstrn./Supervision/Curriculum, U. Colo., 1981. Tchr., coach Leavenworth (Wash.) High Sch., 1962-63, Battle Mountain Jr. Sr. High Sch., 1963-66; prin. Soroco High Sch., 1967-68, Battle Mountain Jr. Sr. High Sch., 1968-75, Nederland Jr. Sr. High Sch., 1975-85; dir., prin. Boulder Valley Community Schs./Dist. Summer Sch., 1985-86; tchr., prin. Fairview High Sch./Dist. Summer Sch., Boulder, Colo., 1986-1996; ret., 1996. Past. pres. Orange Orchard Homeowners; past officer West Vail (Colo.) Water Bd.; pres. Mountain Side Condo Assn., Frisco, Colo. Mem. NEA, Nat. Assn. Secondary Sch. Prins. (pres. 1980-81), Colo. Assn. Sch. Execs., Colo. Assn. Secondary Sch. Prins. (pres. 1978-79), North Ctrl. Assn. (exec. bd. 1979-82), Colo. Assn. Cmty. Educators, Boulder Valley Prins. Assn., Colo. High Sch. Activities Assn., Colo. Edn. Assn., Wash. Edn. Assn., Nederland C. of C., Rotary, Ski Club Vail, U.S. Ski Assn., Colo. Ski Race Ofcls. (internat. cert.). Home: 4271 Peach Way Boulder CO 80301-1736

MALMGREN, RENÉ LOUISE, educational theater administrator; b. Mpls., Nov. 14, 1938; d. Albert William (dec.) and Hildegarde Ann (Topel) Erickson; m. Donald Elwin Malmgren, Dec. 27, 1958; children: D. Gustaf, Ericka Susan, Beret Kristina. BA in Theatre, Speech and English, Colo. Women's Coll., 1966; MA in Edn. Adminstrn and Curriculum Devel., U. Colo., 1981. Cert. supt., adminstr., ESL cert., Ariz. Cons. creative drama cultural arts program Denver Pub. Schs., 1970-72; tchr. APS Crawford Elem. Sch., Aurora, Colo., 1972-78; instr. Colo. Women's Coll., Denver, 1974-75; ednl. dir. Colo. Children's Theatre Co., Denver, 1977-86; coord. curriculum Aurora Pub. Schs., 1982-85; asst. dir. instrn. fine arts Tucson Unified Sch. Dist., 1985-90; mng. dir. Ariz. Children's Theatre Co., Tucson, 1990-96; adminstr. svcs. Tucson Ctr. for Performing Arts, 1992-94; editor dramatic arts curriculum Ariz. Dept. Edn., Phoenix, 1989; rev. panelist Ariz. Commn. on Arts, Phoenix, 1986-87. Co-author satellite TV curriculum, 1987; appeared in premier of play The Only Woman Awake, 1984. Del. Colo. Dem. Conv., Denver, 1980; peacekeeper Take Back the Night March-Rape Assistance and Awareness Program, Denver, 1982-84; mem. policy. com. Tucson Cable Arts Channel, 1986-87; mem. edn. com. Tucson Symphony Orch., 1988-92; bd. dirs. Arts and Creativity Early Childhood, 1990-93, Arts Genesis, 1990-92. Mem. ASCD, Nat. Art Edn. Assn., Ariz. Arts Supervisory Coalition, Ariz. Theatre Educators Assn. (bd. dirs. 1985-89, pres. 1988-89), Phi Delta Kappa. Home: 2612 E La Cienega Dr Tucson AZ 85716-1546

MALOFF, STEPHEN MARTIN, plastic surgeon; b. Phila., Dec. 21, 1941; s. Abraham and Ruth (Skolkin) M.; m. Joan Fayette Baker; children: Erin, Kerstin. BA, Emory U., 1963; MD, U. Tenn., Knoxville, 1967; degree, U. N.Mex., 1976; student, Grady Meml. Hosp., Atlanta, 1967-68, U. Louisville, 1973-74. Diplomate Am. Bd. Plastic Surgery. Intern Grady Meml. Hosp., Atlanta, 1967-68; resident gen. surgery U. N.Mex. Sch. Medicine, Albuquerque, 1971-72, resident plastic surgery, 1974-76; fellow hand surgery U. Louisville, 1973-74; pvt. practice Pocatello, Idaho, 1976—; adj. staff mem. Idaho State U., Pocatello, 1990—. Maj. USAF, 1969-71, Vietnam. Mem. Am. Soc. Plastic and Reconstructive Surgeons, Rocky Mountain Assn. Plastic Surgeons, Skyline Med. Assn. Office: PO Box 4948 Pocatello ID 83205-4948*

MALOHN, DONALD A., manufacturing executive, retired; b. South Bend, Ind., Mar. 26, 1928; s. Harry A. and Opal (Baker) M.; m Myla Claire Lockwood, Feb. 9, 1948; 1 child, Chris. BSEE, Tri-State U., Angola, Ind., 1952. Engr. jet engine div. Studebaker Corp., South Bend, Ind., 1952-54; prodn. rsch. engr. Ford Motor Co., Dearborn, Mich., 1954-61; sr. analytical engr. Solar, San Diego, 1961-62; dept. mgr. Sundstrand Aviation, Denver, 1962-66; asst. dir. engring. Ai Rsch. Mfg. Co., Phoenix, 1966-78; exec. v.p. Tiernay Turbines, Phoenix, 1978-94. Inventor: five patents, 1963; contbr. tech. jours. Mem. ASME, Am.Soc. Metals, Soc. Automotive Engrs., Life Mem. Soc. Republican. Home: 7848 E Sage Dr Scottsdale AZ 85250-7648

MALONE, JOHN C., telecommunications executive; b. 1941; m. Leslie. Attended Yale U., Johns Hopkins U. Formerly pres. Jerrold Electronics Corp.; pres., chief exec. officer Tele-Communications, Inc., Denver, chmn. and CEO, 1996—. Office: Tele-Comm Inc 5619 Dtc Pkwy Englewood CO 80111-3017*

MALONE, KARL, professional basketball player; b. Summerfield, La., July 24, 1963. Student, La. Tech. U., 1981-85. Basketball player Utah Jazz, 1985—; mem. U.S. Olympic Basketball Team (received Gold medal), 1992. Mem. NBA All-Star team, 1988-94; recipient NBA All-Star Game MVP award, 1989, co-recipient, 1993; mem. All-NBA first team, 1989-94; mem. All-NBA second team, 1988; mem. NBA All-Defensive second team, 1988; mem. NBA All-Rookie Team, 1986; co-leader most seasons (8) with 2000 points, 1987-95. Office: Utah Jazz Delta Ctr 301 W South Temple Salt Lake City UT 84101-1216*

MALONE, MICHAEL PETER, academic administrator, historian; b. Pomeroy, Wash., Apr. 18, 1940; s. John Albert and Dolores Frances (Cheyne) M.; m. Kathleen Malone, Apr. 17, 1983; children: John Thomas, Molly Christine. BA in History, Gonzaga U., 1962; PhD in Am. Studies, Wash. State U., Pullman, 1966. Asst. prof. history Tex. A&M U., College Station, 1966-67; asst. prof., prof. history Mont. State U., Bozeman, 1967—, dean grad. studies, 1979-89, v.p. acad. affairs, 1989-90; pres. Mont. State U., 1991—; bd. dirs. Buttrey Food and Drug, Commn. on Colls. of N.W. Assn. of Schs. and Colls. Author: The Battle for Butte, 1981 (Sick award 1981), Historians and The American West, 1983, (with others) Montana: A History of Two Centuries, 1976, 2d edit., 1991, The American West: A 20th Century History, 1989, James J. Hill, Empire Builder of the Northwest, 1995. Mem. Western History Assn., Nat. Assn. State Univs. and Land-Grant Colls. (exec. bd. dirs.). Home: 2310 Springcreek Dr Bozeman MT 59715-6035 Office: Mont State U Bozeman MT 59717

MALONE, MICHAEL WILLIAM, electronics executive, software engineer; b. Belmore L.I., N.Y., Mar. 31, 1956; s. Daniel Joseph Malone and Frances Ann (Reilly) Coppersmith; m. Jane Pauline Raese, Aug. 20, 1988. BS in Elec. Engring. and Computer Sci., U. Colo., 1986. Test engr. Catalina Controls, Longmont, Colo., 1984-86; design engr. Inlab, Inc., Broomfield, Colo., 1986-87, mgr. engring., 1987-89; software engr. UMG, Inc., Golden, Colo., 1989-90, sr. software engr., 1990-91, v.p., 1991-94; sr. software engr. RELA, Boulder, Colo., 1994—. Developer software. With USN, 1975-79. Office: Rela Inc 6175 Longbow Dr Boulder CO 80301-3205

MALONEY, JOHN WILLIAM, lawyer; b. Santa Barbara, Calif., Dec. 6, 1930; s. John Joseph and Mildred (Brunenmeyer); m. Jean Anderson, Nov. 18, 1966; children: Patrick Maloney, Cynthia Maloney. BA in Econs., U. Calif., Santa Barbara, 1953; JD, UCLA, 1958. Bar: Calif. 1959, U.S. Dist. Ct. (no., ctrl., ea., so. dists.) Calif. 1959. Assoc. Fogel McInery, Santa Monica, Calif., 1959-62; ptnr. Rhodes Barnard & Maloney, Santa Monica, 1963-82, Rhodes, Maloney et al., Santa Monica, 1983-88; prin. Maloney & Mullen, Santa Monica, 1989-96; ptnr. Real Estate Investors, 1970—. Pres. Santa Monica Legal Aid Soc., 1960-63. Capt. U.S. Army, 1953-55. Mem. Lions. Republican. Roman Catholic.

MALONEY, PATSY LORETTA, university official, nursing educator; b. Murfreesboro, Tenn., Feb. 19, 1952; d. Buford Leon Browning and Ina (Bush) Dubose; m. Richard J. Maloney, July 26, 1975; children: Katherine Nalani, Nathaniel Allen, Elizabeth Maureen. BS in Nursing, U. Md., 1974; MA, Cath. U., 1984, MS in Nursing, 1984; EdD, U. So. Calif., 1994. Commd. 1st lt. U.S. Army, 1974, advanced through grades to lt. col., 1989; asst. chief nurse evenings and nights DeWitt Army Hosp., Ft. Belvoir, Va.; chief nurse, tng. officer 85th EVAC Hosp., Ft. Lee, Va.; clin. head nurse emergency rm./PCU Tripler Army Med. Ctr., Honolulu, chief nursing edn.; chief surg. nursing sect. and acute care nursing sect. Madigan Army Med. Ctr., Tacoma, 1991-94; ret., 1994; dir. Ctr. for Continued Nursing Learning Pacific Luth. U., Tacoma, Wash., 1994—; asst. prof., dir. ctr. for continued nursing learning Pacific Luth. U., Tacoma, 1994—. Mem. Emergency Nurses Assn., Nat. Nursing Staff Devel. Orgn., Assn. Mil. Surgeons, Acad. Med. Surg. Nurses, Sigma Theta Tau, Phi Kappa Phi. Home: 7002 53rd St W University Place WA 98467-2214 Office: Pacific Luth U Ctr Cont Nursing Learning Tacoma WA 98467

MALONEY, ROBERT KELLER, ophthalmologist, medical educator. AB in Mathematics summa cum laude, Harvard U., 1979; MA in Philosophy, Politics and Econs., Oxford (Eng.) U., 1981; MD, U. Calif., San Francisco, 1985. Diplomate Am. Bd. Ophthalmology. Rsch fellow dept. physiology Cambridge (Eng.) U., 1985; intern U. Calif., L.A., 1985-86; resident Wilmer Ophthalmol. Inst. Johns Hopkins Hosp., Balt., 1986-89; head fellow cornea and refractive surgery Emory U., Dept. Ophthalmology, Atlanta, 1989-91; asst. prof. ophthalmology UCLA Sch. Medicine, Jules Stein Eye Inst., 1991—; cons. Premier Laser Systems, for devel. of Erbium-YAG sys. for corneal refractive surgery. Contbr. numerous articles to profl. jours.; presenter and spkr. in field; assoc. editor (N.Am.) Jour. Refractive and Corneal Surgery, 1991-95; internat. editl. bd. European Jour. Implant and Refractive Surgery, 1995; reviewer Am. Jour. Ophthalmology, Ophthalmology, Archives of Ophthalmology, Jour. Cataract and Refractive Surgery, Ophthalmic Surgery and Lasers. Rhodes scholar, 1979, Heed Found. fellow, 1989-90, Heed/Knapp fellow, 1990-91, John Harvard scholar, 1978; recipient Detur and Edward Whitaker prizes, Harvard U., Rsch. to Prevent Blindness Career Devel. award, 1992. Mem. Am. Acad. Ophthalmology (long-range planning com. 1989-92, quality of care com. 1987-91, retina preferred practice pattern subcom., refractive errors preferred practice pattern subcom.; chmn. ann. meeting program com. for young ophthalmologists, 1990-92; adv. group to ad hoc com. on orgnl. design 1991, young ophthalmologists' com. 1992-94; Honor award 1993), Assn. Rsch. in Vision and Ophthalmology, Internat. Soc. Refractive Surgery, Calif. Assn. Ophthalmology, Max Fine Corneal Soc., Phi Beta Kappa. Office: UCLA Sch Medicine Jules Stein Eye Inst 100 Stein Plaza Los Angeles CA 90024-7003

MALONEY, THOMAS J., anthropologist, educator, writer; b. Arlington, Mass., Nov. 16, 1922; s. Thomas Joseph and Doris Eleanor (Edwards) M.; m. Elizabeth Gartner, Feb. 7, 1948; children: Susan, Margaretha, Elizabeth, Thomas Jefferson. BSChemE, Northeastern U., 1948; STB, Harvard U., 1952; AM in Sociology, Wash. U., St. Louis, 1956; PhD in Anthropology, Wash. U., 1966. Chem. engr. Gen. Aniline & Film Corp., Easton, Pa., 1948, U. Colo. Experiment Sta., Boulder, Colo., 1948-49, Aircraft Gas Turbine divsn. GE, Boston, 1950-52; min. Unitarian Ch., Davenport, Iowa, 1952-53, Quincy, Ill., 1953-56; tech. pers. assoc. Bettis Atomic Power divsn. Westinghouse Electric Corp., Pitts., 1956-57; part-time instr. dept. anthropology U. Colo., Boulder, 1957-59; min. Unitarian Ch., Boulder, 1957-62; asst. prof. N.Mex. Highlands U., Las Vegas, 1962-67; assoc. prof. anthropology and sociology Ripon (Wis.) Coll., 1967-69; prof. anthropology So. Ill. U., Edwardsville, 1969-87, prof. emeritus, 1987—. With U.S. Army, 1942-44, with USMC, 1944-46; 1st lt. USAR, 1949-52. Fellow AAAS, Am. Anthrop. Assn. Address: 1309 City Park Ave Fort Collins CO 80521-4442

MALOOF, GILES WILSON, academic administrator, educator, author; b. San Bernardino, Calif., Jan. 4, 1932; s. Joseph Peters and Georgia (Wilson) M.; m. Mary Anne Ziniker, Sept. 5, 1958 (dec. Oct. 1976); children: Mary Jane, Margery Jo. BA, U. Calif. at Berkeley, 1953; MA, U. Oreg., 1958; PhD, Oreg. State U., 1962. Petroleum reservoir engr. Creole Petroleum Corp., Venezuela, 1953-54; mathematician electronics div. research dept. U.S. Naval Ordnance Rsch. Lab., Corona, Calif., 1958-59; asst. prof. math. Oreg. State U., Corvallis, 1962-68, rsch. assoc. dept. oceanography, 1963-68, vis. prof. math., 1977-78; prof. math. Boise (Idaho) State U., 1968—, head dept., 1968-75, dean grad. sch., 1970-75; project dir. Dept. Energy Citizens' Workshop Energy Environment Simulator for Eastern Oreg., No. Nev. and Idaho, 1976—. Served with Ordnance Corps, AUS, 1950, 54-56. Author, reviewer of coll. textbooks; contbr. to profl. jours. Recipient Carter award, 1963, Mosser prize, 1966, Oreg. State U. Mem. Math. Assn. Am., Am. Math. Soc., Soc. Indsl. and Applied Math., Northwest Coll. and Univ. Assn. for Sci. (dir. 1973—, pres. 1990-92), Northwest Sci. Assn. (trustee 1977-80), Assoc. Western Univs. (mem. edn. and rsch. com. 1993—), Sigma Xi, Pi Mu Epsilon, Phi Kappa Phi. Home: 1400 Longmont Ave Boise ID 83706-3730

MALPHURS, ROGER EDWARD, biomedical marketing executive; b. Lake Worth, Fla., Dec. 15, 1933; s. Cecil Edward and Muriel Thelma (Ward) M.; m. Carolyn Sue Calapp, Feb. 2, 1963(div. 1993); children: Steven, Brian, Darren, Regina, Victoria. *The generations preceding the name Malphurs, had their origins in Switzerland (Malpas), Italy (Malpaso), France (Malphrus), England (Malpass), and maybe even as far back as 711 AD when a Malpass led a military contingent against the Moors during the invasion of Spain in that year.* BS, U. Utah, 1961; D of Chiropractic, Palmer Coll. Chiropractic West, 1990. Cert. med. technologist; lic. chiropractor, Calif., Ariz. Supr. spl. chemistry Cen. Pathology Lab., Santa Rosa, Calif., 1968-73; mgr. lab. Cmty. Hosp., Santa Rosa, 1973-76; supr. chem., staff asst. Meml. Hosp., Santa Rosa, 1976-85; pres., CEO R.E. Malphurs Co., Sunnyvale, Calif., 1972Ô; owner, developer REMCO Mktg. Assocs., Santa Rosa, 1970-71; pvt. commodity trader, 1974Ô; owner Better Bus. Forms and Typeset, Santa Rosa, 1977-81, commodity pool operator, 1979-80; dept. mgr. immunochemistry Spectra Labs., Fremont, Calif., 1990-95; clin. trials cons. hematology Abbott Diagnostics, Santa Clara, Calif., 1995-97. Author: A New, Simple Way to Win at Blackjack, 1972. Served as squadron commdr. CAP USAF Aux., 1982-84. Mem. APHA, Am. Chiropractic Assn., Calif. Chiropractic Assn., Optimists Internat. (youth awards chmn. 1969-74), Toastmasters (sec./treas. 1988-89), Rep. Senatorial Inner Circle. Republican.

MALSON, REX RICHARD, drug and health care corporation executive; b. Stanberry, Mo., Nov. 26, 1931; s. Albert J. Curtis and Nellie E. Coburn (Bussey) M.; m. Jimmie S., May 25, 1956 (dec. 1980); children: Richard Gary, Gregory Neil; m. Vicki L., Feb. 10, 1983 (div. Aug. 1984). B.B.A., Ga. State U., 1961; postgrad. grad. exec. program, U. Chgo., 1967; postgrad. exec. program hon., Stanford U., 1983; LHD (hon.), L.I. U., 1989. Gen. transp. mgr. John Sexton & Co., Chgo., 1964-68; dir. distbn. system Keebler Co., Chgo., 1968-73; with drug and health care group McKesson Corp., San Francisco, 1973-92, vice pres., 1984-86, exec. v.p. ops., 1986-89, pres. & chief operating officer, 1989-92, also vice chmn.,bd. dirs.; ret., 1992; bd. dirs. Sunbelt Beverage Co., Balt., Stationers Distbg. Co., Ft. Worth; chmn. bd. dirs. Armor All Products Corp. Served with U.S. Navy, 1951-55, Korea. Mem. Am. Soc. Traffic and Transp. Republican.

MALTIN, FREDA, retired university administrator; b. Calgary, Alta., Can., June 4, 1923; came to the U.S., 1958; d. Meyers Wolfe and Ida (Kohn) Rosen; m. Manny Maltin, Aug. 25, 1950; 1 child, Richard Allan. Diploma Garbutt's Bus. Coll., Calgary, 1942. Various secretarial and bookkeeping positions, 1951; mem. adminstrv. staff U. So. Calif., 1960-92, asst. to exec. dir. Davidson Conf. Ctr., 1987-92, Grad. Sch. Bus. Adminstrn., 1981-92. Recipient staff achievement award U. So. Calif., 1991. Mem. U. So. Calif.

Staff Club (charter), U. So. Calif. Skull and Dagger (hon.), U. So. Calif. Town and Gown.

MALTIN, LEONARD, television commentator, writer; b. N.Y.C., Dec. 18, 1950; s. Aaron Isaac and Jacqueline (Gould) M.; m. Alice Tlusty, Mar. 15, 1975; 1 child, Jessica Bennett. BA, NYU, 1972. Mem. faculty New Sch. for Social Rsch., N.Y.C., 1973-81; curator Am. Acad. Humor, N.Y.C., 1975-76; guest curator dept. film Mus. Modern Art, N.Y.C., 1976; film critic and corr. Entertainment Tonight, Hollywood, Calif., 1982—; columnist Microsoft Cinemania Online, 1996. Author: Movie Comedy Teams, 1970, rev. edit., 1985, Behind the Camera (reprinted as The Art of the Cinematographer), 1971, The Great Movie Shorts (reprinted as Selected Short Subjects), 1971, The Disney Films, 1973, rev. edit., 1995, The Great Movie Comedians, 1978, Of Mice and Magic: A History of American Animated Cartoons, 1980, rev. edit., 1987; co-author: Our Gang: The Life and Times of the Little Rascals, 1977, reprinted as The Little Rascals: The Life and Times of Our Gang, 1992; editor: Leonard Maltin's Movie & Video Guide, 1969, rev. annually, Leonard Maltin's Movie Encyclopedia, 1994; producer, writer, host (video) Cartoons for Big Kids, 1989; writer (TV spl.) Fantasia: The Making of a Disney Classic, 1990; writer, host (video) The Making of The Quiet Man, 1992, The Making of High Noon, 1992, Cartoon Madness: The Fantastic Max Fleischer Cartoons, 1993, Cliffhanger!, 1993. Mem. steering com. Hollywood Entertainment Mus., 1989—. Mem. Authors Guild, Soc. for Cinephiles (pres. 1990-91, Man of Yr. 1973), L.A. Film Critics Assn. (pres. 1995-96). Office: care Entertainment Tonight Paramount TV 5555 Melrose Ave Los Angeles CA 90038-3112

MALTZAN, MICHAEL THOMAS, architect; b. Roslyn Heights, N.Y., Oct. 10, 1959; s. William George and Jacqualine (Cain) M.; m. Amy Louise Murphy, Sept. 25, 1988. Student, Wentworth Inst. Tech., 1977-79; BFA, RISD, 1984, BArch, 1985; MArch with letter of distinction, Harvard U., 1988. Lic. architect, Calif. Architect The Architects, Glastonbury, Conn., 1978-80, Williamd D. Warner Assocs., Exeter, R.I., 1980-83, Steven Lerner Assocs., Providence, 1983-84, Schwartz/Silver Assocs., Boston, 1984-86, Machado-Silvetti Assocs., Boston, 1986-88, Frank O. Gehry Assocs., L.A., 1988-95; pvt. practice architecture L.A., 1995—; instr. RISD, Providence, 1987, Harvard U., Cambridge, Mass., 1988; co-instr. UCLA, 1989; invited jury critic Harvard U., RISD, So. Calif. Inst. Architecture, L.A., Ariz. State U., tempe, Calif. Coll. Arts and Crafts, San Francisco, U. SO. Calif., L.A., UCLA, Iowa State U., Ames, Miami (Ohio) U. Prin. works include Unitarian-Universalist Ch., Vernon, Conn., 1979, Providence Riverfront Study, 1982, Harvard Law Sch. Alumni Bldg. Addition, Cambridge, 1984, 330 Congress St. Renovation, Boston, 1985, 280 Summer St. Renovation, Boston, 1986, City of Leonforte, Italy Master Plan, 1987 (Progressive Arch. award), North Park Apt. Complex Renovation, Chevy Chase, Md., 1988, Walt Disney Concert Hall, 1988— (Progressive Arch. award), Culver City (Calif.) Retail Complex Master Plan, 1990, Villa Olympica Retail and Entertainment Complex, Barcelona, Spain, 1992, U. Toledo Art Sch., 1992 (AIA award), Inner-City Arts Sch., L.A., 1994, Harvard West Lake Art Ctr., 1997, Getty Culture Lab., 1997. Recipient Gold medal AIA. Office: 2801 Hyperion Ave # 107 Los Angeles CA 90027*

MAMALIS, NICK, ophthalmologist, researcher; b. Wyo., Sept. 22, 1955. BA in Biochemistry, Harvard U., 1978; MD, U. Utah, 1982. Diplomate Am. Bd. Ophthalmology. Intern in internal medicine Loyola U. Med. Ctr., Ill., 1983; fellow in opthalmic pathology U. Utah, 1984; lectr. in ophthalmic pathology Loyola U., Maywood, Ill., 1984-87; resident in opthalmology Loyola U. Med. Ctr., 1987; asst. prof. ophthalmology U. Utah, Salt Lake City, 1987-91, dir. ophthalmic pathology, 1988—, dir. Intermountain Ocular Rsch. Ctr., 1988—, assoc. prof. ophthalmology, 1991-95, prof. ophthalmology, 1995—; chief ophthalmology divsn. VA Hosp., Salt Lake City, 1989—; manuscript cons. Jour. Pediat. Ophthalmology and Strabismus, Ophthalmology, Survey of Ophthalmology. Author: Intraocular Lenses: Evolution Design, Complications and Pathology, 1989; author: (with others) Current Therapy in Ophthalmic Surgery, 1988, Management and Care of the Cataract Patient, 1992; assoc. editor Jour. Cataract and Refractive Surgery, 1990—. Ophthalmologic assoc. Rsch. to Prevent Blindness; bd. dirs. Nat. Soc. to Prevent Blindness. Rsch. grantee Am. Intraocular Implant Soc., 1983, U. Utah, 1989, 90. Mem. AMA, Am. Acad. Ophthalmology, Am. Assn. Ophthalmic Pathologists, Am. Soc. of Cataract and Refractive Surgery (grantee 1988), Assn. for Rsch. in Vision and Ophthalmology, Michael Hogan Ophthalmic Pathology Soc. Office: U Utah John Moran Eye Ctr Dept Ophthalmology 50 N Medical Dr Salt Lake City UT 84132-0001

MAN, LAWRENCE KONG, architect; b. Kowloon, Hong Kong, July 4, 1953; s. Hon-Kwong Man and Sau-Ching Luk. Student, U. Redlands, 1971-72; BArch, U. Oreg., 1977; MArch, Harvard U., 1978. Registered architect, Mass. Designer, project architect Shepley Bulfinch Richardson & Abbott, Boston, 1978-86; project designer, project architect E. Verner Johnson & Assoc., Boston, 1987-91; owner Lawrence Man Architect, Cambridge, Mass., 1992-95, L.A., 1994-95. Prin. works include LCP Studio, Somerville, Mass., New Asia Restaurants, Danvers and Arlington, Mass., Tai Pan Restaurant, Cambridge, Mass. (Honor award AIA 1993, New Eng. award Excellence in Architecture 1993, Design Excellence award Nat. Orgn. Minority Architects 1993), Ti-Sales Office, Sudbury, Mass. (Design Excellence award Nat. Orgn. Minority Architects 1993), Dental Clinic, Reading, Mass (AIA Interior Architecture award 1992, Interior Design Project award Am. Soc. Interior Designers 1991, Boston Exports citation AIA 1990, Boston Soc. of Architects/New Eng. Healthcare Assembly honor award, 1994), Mus. Ctr. Union Terminal, Cin. (Reconstrn. award 1991), Ramesses Pavilion Boston Mus. Sci. (Double Vision award/Double Silver Soc. Environ. Graphics 1990), Smithsonian South Quadrangle Mus., Washington (Boston Exports award/citation AIA 1990, Honor award AIA 1989), Pub. Mus. Grand Rapids (Mich.) River Front Devel., U. Vt. Student Ctr., Burlington, Campus Ctr. Study and Libr. addition Franklin & Marshall Coll., Andover (Mass.) Co. Corp. Hdqs., Emerson Hosp., Concord, Mass., pvt. residences, others. Mem. AIA, Am. Assn. Mus., Boston Soc. Architects, Nat. Orgn. Minority Architects. Home: 2158 Valentine Pl San Marino CA 91108-2343 *There are ups and downs in life. It is more rewarding to experience them all, nomatter how hard it may get sometimes. It allows you to become a more complete person. That is, in my view, a ture achievement.*

MANARY, RICHARD DEANE, manufacturing executive; b. Des Moines, Nov. 11, 1944; s. Robert Claude and Veronica (Cornwell) M.; m. Eileen Cecile, Aug. 16, 1986; children: Erica (dec.), Matthew, Stephen, Lauren. AA in Indsl. Engring., Southwestern Coll., 1976; BA in History, Calif. State U., San Diego, 1967, BS in Edn., 1973; grad., Stanford U. Bus. Ext., 1991; MBA, Nat. U., 1993. Registered profl. engr., Calif.; cert. elem. tchr., Calif. Mfg. engr. Rohr Industries, San Diego, 1967-78; chief R&D div. Rohr Industries, Riverside, Calif., 1978-80, project mfg. mgr., 1980-84; dep. program mgr. Rohr Industries, Wichita, Kans., 1984-87; mgr. Titan 3d, Titan IV missile programs Rohr Industries, Riverside, 1987-89; program mgr. MD-11 Rohr Industries, 1989-91; gen. program mgr. Boing mil. programs Rohr Industries, Chula Vista, Calif., 1991-95; gen. mgr. Space Products Divsn., 1995—. Contbr. articles to profl. jours. Chmn. employee and community assistance program Rohr Industries, Riverside, 1981-85; adv. Riverside chpt. Jr. Achievement, 1978-79. Mem. Soc. Mfg. Engrs. (sr., assoc., chmn. 1978-79), Soc. Automotive Engrs., Soc. Material and Process Engrs., Am. Soc. Metals, Nat. Mgmt. Assn. (chmn. 1980-81), Aerospace Industries Assn. (space com.), Air Force Assn., KC. Democrat. Roman Catholic. Home: 4098 Martin Canyon Ct Bonita CA 91902-2562 Office: 850 Lagoon Blvd Chula Vista CA 91912-0878

MANASC, VIVIAN, architect, consultant; b. Bucharest, Romania, May 19, 1956; d. Bercu and Bianca (Smetterling) M.; m. William A. Dushenski, Feb. 25, 1984; children: Peter Gabriel, Lawrence Alexander. BS in Architecture, McGill U., Montreal, Que., Can., 1977, BArch, 1979; MBA, U. Alta., Edmonton, 1982. Architectural insp. Transport Can., Edmonton, 1977-79; project architect Bell Spotowski Architects, Edmonton, 1980-82; asst. dir. design constrn. Edmonton Pub. Schs., 1982-84; mgr., prin. Ferguson, Simek, Clark Architects Ltd., Edmonton, 1985-88; mng. dir. FSC Groves Hodgson Manasc Architects Ltd., Edmonton, 1988—; adj. asst. prof. of architecture, U. Calgary. Contbr. articles to profl. jours. and confs. Sect. chair, co-chair innovative practice group in arch. United Way Edmonton; advisor YWCA, Edmonton, 1980-82; mentor RAIC Syllabus Program, Edmonton, 1982-88; bd. dirs. Design Workshop, Edmonton, 1983. Scholar McGill U., 1974. Mem. Royal Archtl. Inst. Can. (past chmn. architecture for healthcare com., assoc. regional dir.), Alta. Assn. Archs., Manitoba Assn. Archs., B.C. Assn. Archs., Saskatchewan Assn. Archs., Coun. Edn. Facility Planners, Nat. Coun. Jewish Women (past pres. Edmonton sect.), Jewish Fedn. Edmonton (v.p. planning). Office: FSC Groves Hodgson Manasc, 10417 Saskatchewan Dr, Edmonton, AB Canada T6E 4R8

MANASSERO, WILLIAM JOSEPH, software executive, consultant; b. San Diego, May 26, 1955; s. Albert Joseph and Kathleen Veronica M.; m. Susette Rodriguez, June 1990; children: Ariana Kathleen, Vienna Grace; step children: Jasmine Brooke Jakubowski, Jordan Christopher Jakubowski. AA, Columbia Coll., 1975; BA, Calif. State U., 1981; profl. designation in Pub. Rels., UCLA, 1986. V.p., advt. mgr. US Life Savings and Loan, L.A., 1979-81; pres., CEO Manassero & Assocs., L.A., 1981-88; v.p. Kalman Comm., Santa Monica, 1988-90; v.p., acct. dir. Bob Thomas & Assocs., L.A., 1990-93; sr. v.p. The Spindler Orgn., L.A., 1993-94; exec. dir. Software Coun. of So. Calif., Torrance, 1994—; comm. com. chmn. L.A. Bus. Coun., 1989-90. Contbr. articles to profl. jours. Elected mem. Dem. Ctrl. Com. Tuolomne County, Calif., 1975. Recipient Golden Mirror award Fin. Mktg. Assn., 1985-86. Mem. Pub. Rels. Soc. Am., Christian Businessmen's Com. Republican. Baptist. Office: Software Council So Calif 21041 S Western Ave Ste 160 Torrance CA 90501-1727

MANASSON, VLADIMIR ALEXANDROVICH, physicist; b. Chernovtsy, Ukraine, Mar. 4, 1952; came to U.S., 1991; s. Alexander and Chaya (Finkelsteyn) M.; m. Katrine Kokhanovskaya, Aug. 2, 1975; children: Alexander, Julia. BSEE, Moscow Inst. Electronic Mfg., 1973, MSEE, 1974; PhD in Physics, Chernovtsy U., 1984. Entr. Acad. of Scis. of the Ukraine Material Sci. Inst., 1975-78, sr. engr., 1978-80, jr. rsch. assoc., 1980-85, sr. rsch. assoc., 1985-90; rsch. scientist Phys. Optics Corp., Torrance, Calif., 1991-94, sr. scientist, 1994-95; leader antenna devel. WaveBand Corp., Torrance, Calif., 1996—. Patentee several photosensitive devices and antennae. Grantee: NSF, 1993-94, 97, Dept. Def., 1994-97, Dept. Transp., 1994, 95, 96, 97. Mem. IEEE, Optical Soc. Am., Assn. of Old Crows. Office: WaveBand Corp Ste 1105 375 Van Ness Ave Torrance CA 90501

MANATT, CHARLES TAYLOR, lawyer; b. Chgo., June 9, 1936. BS, Iowa State U., 1958; JD, George Washington U., 1962. Bar: Calif. 1962, U.S. Supreme Ct. 1967, D.C. 1985. Ptnr. Manatt, Phelps & Phillips, Washington. Bd. editors George WAshington Law Rev., 1960-62. Mem. ABA, Calif. State Bar, L.A. County Bar Assn., San Fernando Valley Bar Assn. (pres. 1971-72), Century City Bar Assn., Phi Delta Phi, Delta Sigma Rho. also: Manatt Phelps & Phillips Trident Ctr E Tower 11355 W Olympic Blvd Los Angeles CA 90064-1614

MANAYAN, HENRY C., corporate executive, mayor; b. N.Y.C., Nov. 3, 1955; s. Henry A. and Lorraine M. BA, Syracuse U., 1979; Reader-in-Law, Oxford U., 1980; JD, Santa Clara U., 1983. Assoc. Hartsell & Caselli, San Jose, Calif., 1983; real estate advisor Park Cen. Investments, Alameda, Calif., 1984; dir. real estate Brugger Corp., Redwood City, Calif., 1985; pres. Advance Data, Inc., San Francisco, Calif., 1986; pres., CEO Transpacific Cos., San Jose, 1990—; chmn. of the bd. Commonwealth Ctrl. Credit Union, San Jose; chmn. polit. action com. San Jose Real Estate Bd. Bd. dirs. Arts Coun., San Jose, 1991—, Milpitas (Calif.) C. of C., 1990—; transp. commr. Santa Clara County Transp. Agy., San Jose, 1991-93; planning commr. Milpitas Planning Commr., 1993-94; commr. Community Adv. Com., Milpitas, 1990-93; elected city councilman, Milpitas, Calif., 1994, elected mayor, 1996—; chmn., dir. San Jose Performing Arts Consortium, 1988-93. Recipient Bus. Leadership award Arts Coun. Santa Clara County, 1991, named Outstanding Businessman of Yr., Chamber of Commerce, San Jose, 1992. Mem. Toastmasters (v.p.), Rotary (bd. dirs.), ABA, Hawaii Bar Assn., Silicon Valley Capital Club, Met. C. of C., Milpitas C. of C., Calif. Assn. Realtors (dir. 1994—, chair reg. govt. rels. com.). Office: Transpacific Capital Corp 1150 N 1st St Ste 120 San Jose CA 95112-4925

MANCHESTER, ARTHUR HERSCHELL, English and foreign language educator; b. Aberdeen, Wash., July 25, 1933; s. Forrest E. and Annie (Nuttall) M.; m. Barbara Jane Sanford, Aug. 10, 1962; children: Vance Arthur, Eric Andrew. AB, N.W. Nazarene Coll., Nampa, Idaho, 1955; MA, U. Colo., 1958. Cert. in secondary edn., Oreg. Teaching asst. U. Colo., Boulder, 1957-58; prof. N.W. Nazarene Coll., 1958-60; tchr. R.E. Bennett Jr. H.S., Chehalis, Wash., 1960-62, Gresham (Oreg.) Union H.S., 1962-91; home instr. Multnomah County (Oreg.) Pub. Schs., 1996; home and hosp. tchr. Portland (Oreg.) Pub. Schs., 1991—; tchr. Gresham (Oreg.) Sam Barlow H.S., 1996-97; analytical writing scorer Multnomah County and State of Oreg. Schs., 1987—. Author: Math Puzzles and Games, 1977, 2d edit., 1994. Recipient Dankstipendium, Deutscher Akademischer Austauschdienst, 1956-57, summer stipend NDEA, 1963, Honorarium, NEH, 1978. Mem. NEA, Oreg. Edn. Assn., Confedn. Oreg. Fgn. Lang. Tchrs. (pres. 1981-82, bd. dirs. 1978-80, 82-83). Republican. Nazarene. Home: 3039 SE 174th Ave Portland OR 97236-1011

MANCINI, ROBERT KARL, computer analyst, consultant; b. Burbank, Calif., May 13, 1954; s. Alfred Robert and Phyllis Elaine (Pflugel) M.; m. Barbara Diane Bacon, Aug. 4, 1979; children: Benjamin Robert, Bonnie Kathryn, Brandon Peter, Bailey Andrew. BA in Econs., UCLA, 1976; cert. in bibl. studies, Multonmah Sch. of the Bible, 1981; MBA, Santa Clara (Calif.) U., 1987. Process clk. Am. Funds Svc. Co., L.A., 1976-77; exec. asst. Sierra Thrift & Loan Co., San Mateo, Calif., 1977-78; sci. programming specialist Lockheed Missiles & Space Co., Sunnyvale, Calif., 1978-90; mgr. tech. publs. Diversified Software Systems Inc., Morgan Hill, Calif., 1990—; cons. Mancini Computer Svcs., San Jose and Morgan Hill, 1985—; instr. Heald Coll., San Jose, Calif., 1990. Mem. fin. coun. Hillside Ch., 1990-91; mem. blue ribbon budget rev. com. City of Morgan Hill, 1992. Mem. Phi Kappa Sigma (expansion com. 1976-78). Republican. Home: PO Box 1602 Morgan Hill CA 95038-1602

MANCLARK, CHARLES ROBERT, microbiologist, researcher; b. Rochester, N.Y., June 22, 1928; s. Charles and Mary (Powell) M.; m. Doloras Jolly, Dec. 19, 1953; children: Charles Scott, Timothy Brooks. BS in Biology, Calif. Poly. State U., 1953; PhD in Bacteriology, UCLA, 1963. Rsch. and teaching asst. UCLA, 1956-61; asst. prof. Calif. State U., Long Beach, 1961-64; rsch. bacteriologist UCLA, 1963-65; asst. prof. U. Calif., Irvine, 1965-67; chief lab. of pertussis Ctr. for Biologics Evaluation and Rsch., Bethesda, Md., 1967-93; dir. WHO Collaborating Ctr., Bethesda, 1978-93; cons. WHO, UN, Pan. Am. Health Orgn., UNICEF and many fgn. countries worldwide, 1971—. Author of 2 lab. manuals for bacteriology; editor of 9 books on pertussis and pertussis vaccine; contbr. over 100 articles to profl. jours. Patentee in field. Cpl. U.S. Army, 1953-55. Recipient Merit award FDA, 1985, Group Recognition award 1989, medal Institutos de Salud, Lima, Peru, 1980, Disting. Svc. award for biomed. rsch. Dept. HHS, 1992; named Honored Alumnus in Sci. and Math., Calif. Poly. State U., 1992; Univ. fellow in microbiology UCLA, 1960. Fellow Am. Acad. Microbiology; mem. Am. Soc. for Microbiology, Internat. Assn. Biol. Standardization, Sigma Xi, Beta Beta Beta (pres. Epsilon Pi chpt. 1952-53). Home and Office: 3236 Braemar Dr Santa Barbara CA 93109-1067

MANCUSI, TIMOTHY JOHN, artist, illustrator; b. Levittown, N.Y., Nov. 19, 1950; s. Ettore Giavanni and Jean Catherine (Hogan) M. Mail clk. U.S. Post Office, San Francisco, 1969-70; traffic mgr. Esprit, San Francisco, 1970-76; artist Technokron, Berkeley, Calif., 1976-78, Nepenthe Prodns., San Francisco, 1978-80, Personal Stamp Exch., Santa Rosa, Calif., 1980—. Editor Weekly Breeder, 1972-74; artist (illustration) El Perfecto, 1973, Smokefree Travel Guide, 1988, Clearing the Air, 1996, Heat Wave, 1996; one-man shows include Heindesign, Hagan, Germany, 1994. Contbr. Whitney Mus., N.Y.C., 1970; artist and illustrator Am. Non-Smokers Rights, Berkeley, 1987-97. Democrat. Home: 153 Verde Cir Rohnert Park CA 94928 Office: Personal Stamp Exch 360 Sutton Pl Santa Rosa CA 95407

MANDAC, BENJAMIN REYES, pediatric rehabilitation physician; b. Philippines, Jan. 8, 1956. BS, UCLA, 1979; MD, U. Calif. Davis, 1984. Diplomate Am. Bd. Pediat.; bd. cert. Am. Bd. Phys. Medicine and Rehab. Staff pediatrician Catherine McAuley Health Ctr., Ann Arbor, Mich., 1987-90; asst. prof. Loma Linda (Calif.) U. Med. Ctr., 1990-92; dir. pediat. rehab. Santa Clara Valley Med. Ctr., San Jose, Calif., 1992—; med. dir. spina bifida clinic Lucile Salter Packard Children's Hosp., Palo Alto, Calif., 1993—; med. cons. Calif. Children's Svcs., Monterey, Calif., 1994—.

MANDEL, MARTIN LOUIS, lawyer; b. L.A., May 17, 1944; s. Maurice S. and Florence (Byer) M.; m. Duree Dunn, Oct. 16, 1982; 1 child, Max Andrew. BA, U. So. Calif., 1965, JD, 1968; LLM, George Washington U., 1971. Bar: Calif. 1969, U.S. Dist. Ct. (cen. dist.) Calif. 1972, U.S. Ct. Claims, 1971, U.S. Tax Ct. 1971, U.S. Supreme Ct. 1972. With office of gen. csl. IRS, Washington, 1968-72; ptnr. Stephens, Jones, LaFever & Smith, L.A., 1972-77, Stephens, Martin & Mandel, 1977-79, Fields, Fehn, Feinstein & Mandel, 1979-83; sr. v.p., gen. counsel Investment Mortgage Internat., Inc., 1983-84; ptnr. Feinstein, Gourley & Mandel, 1984-85, Mandel & Handin, San Francisco, 1985—; pres. The Mandel Group, 1988—; gen. counsel L.A. Express Football Club, 1983-85; instr. corps. U. West L.A., 1973-83. Mem. ABA, L.A. County Bar Assn., L.A. Athletic Club, Phi Delta Phi. Office: 131 Steuart St Ste 700 San Francisco CA 94105-1230

MANDEL, ROBERT MICHAEL, social sciences educator; b. Washington, Oct. 30, 1949; s. Philip and Alice Grace Mandel; m. Annette Colleen Kelley, Aug. 1, 1981; children: Travis Scott, Laura Diane. AB, Brown U., 1972; MA, Yale U., 1974, MPhil, 1975, PhD, 1976. Intern CIA, Washington, 1974-75; asst. prof. internat. affairs Lewis and Clark Coll., Portland, Oreg., 1976-82; assoc. prof. internat. affairs Lewis and Clark Coll., Portland, 1982-88, prof. internat. affairs, 1988—, dean social sci. divsn., 1990-92, chair internat. affairs, 1994—; acad. assoc. Atlantic Coun., Washington, 1985—; vis. scholar Def. Intelligence Coll., Washington, 1989; adv. bd. mem. Microsoft, Redmond, Wash., 1993—. Author: Perception, Decision Making and Conflict, 1979, Irrationality in International Confrontation, 1987, Conflict Over the World's Resources, 1988, The Changing Face of National Security, 1994; assoc. editor: (jour.) Armed Forces and Society, 1993—. Mem. Am. Polit. Sci. Assn., Internat. Studies Assn., Phi Beta Kappa. Office: Lewis and Clark Coll 0615 SW Palatine Hill Rd Portland OR 97219-7879

MANDELSTEIN, PAUL STANLEY, book publishing executive; b. Bklyn., May 18, 1946; s. Max and Esther (Friedman) M.; m. Cornelia S. Pratt, Feb. 21, 1973 (div. June 1993); children: Zachary, Naomi, Nicolas. Student, Bklyn. Coll., 1965. Pres. Quantum Pub., Mill Valley, Calif., 1984—, The Book Pub. Co., Summertown, Tenn.; mktg. cons. Farm Foods, Summertown, Tenn., 1975—, Solar Electronics, Summertown, 1976—, Shambhala Pubs., 1994—; bus. cons. Audio Scholar, Mendocino, Calif., 1991. Author: The Nightingale and the Wind, 1993, The Lute Player, 1994, The Divorced Father's Survival Guide, 1996. Home: 1204 El Cide Ct Mill Valley CA 94941-3401 Office: 65 Main St Saint Johnsbury VT 05819-2204

MANDERS, SUSAN KAY, artist; b. Burbank, Calif., Dec. 29, 1948; d. Gus H. and Erika (Stadelbauer) M.; m. Allan D. Yasnyi, Dec. 18, 1992; children: Brian Mallut. Attended, U. Guadalajara, 1969; BA, Calif. State U., 1971; postgrad., Otis Parsons, L.A., 1985, Royal Coll. of the Arts, London, 1987; grad., Silicon Digital Arts. Owner, dir., tchr. The Art Experience Sch. and Gallery, Studio City, Calif., 1978—; cons. in field. One-woman shows include La Logia, Studio City, Calif., 1991, Il Mito, Studio City, 1991, Bamboo, Sherman Oaks, Calif., 1991—, L.A. Art Installations, 1990, 92, Fed. Bldg., L.A., 1993, Art Experience, Studio City, 1993, Emerson's Gallery, Sherman Oaks, 1994, Raphael's, Beverly Hills, Calif., 1994; group shows include Beverly Hills Affair in the Gardens, 1984, 94, Otis Parsons, L.A., 1987, Hilderbrand Galleries, New Orleans, 1993, Studio City Art Festival, 1994, Parents Found., New Haven, Conn., 1994, Project Studio 8, San Francisco, 1994, Bistango Studio-Gallery, Irvine, Calif., 1994—, Montserrat Gallery, N.Y.C., 1995, Annenberg Ctr., U. So. Calif., 1997—; creator, publ. prints Iron Jane Collections, 1994, Children's Hosp. Docent UCLA; active Tuesday's Child, Pillars of Hope Project San Fernando Valley County Fair, 1995. Mem. L.A. Art Assn., Beverley Hills Art Assn., Nat. Mus. Women in the Arts, L.A. County Mus. of Art, Dada, L.A., Mus. Contemporary Art Coun., Women in Animation. Office: The Art Experience 11830 Ventura Blvd Studio City CA 91604-2617

MANDLER, GEORGE, psychologist; b. Vienna, Austria, June 11, 1924; came to U.S., 1940, naturalized, 1943; s. Richard and Hede (Goldschmied) M.; m. Jean Matter, Jan. 19, 1957; children: Peter Clark, Michael Allen. B.A., NYU, 1949; M.S., Yale U., 1950, Ph.D., 1953; postgrad., U. Basel, Switzerland, 1947-48. Asst. prof. Harvard U., 1953-57, lectr., 1957-60; prof. U. Toronto, Ont., Can., 1960-65; prof. psychology U. Calif., San Diego, 1965-94, chmn. dept. psychology, 1965-70, prof. emeritus, 1994—; dir. Ctr. Human Info. Processing, U. Calif., San Diego, 1965-90; hon. rsch. fellow Univ. Coll. London., 1977-78, 82-90, vis. prof., 1990—. Author: Mind and Emotion, 1975, (German edit.), 1980, Mind and Body, 1984, (Japanese edit.), 1987, Cognitive Psychology, 1985, Japanese edit., 1991; contbr. articles and revs. to profl. jours.; editor: Psychol. Rev., 1970-76. Served with U.S. Army, 1943-46. Fellow Ctr. for Advanced Study in Behavioral Scis., 1959-60; vis. fellow Oxford U., Eng., 1971-72, 78; Guggenheim fellow, 1971-72. Fellow AAAS, Am. Acad. Arts and Scis.; mem. AAUP, Am. Assn. Advancement Psychology (1974-82); Psychonomic Soc. (governing bd., chmn. 1983), Am. Psychol. Soc., Am. Psychol. Assn. (pres. div. exptl. psychology 1978-79, pres. div. gen psychology 1982-83, mem. coun. reps. 1978-82, William James prize 1986), Internat. Union Psychol. Scis. (U.S. com. 1985-90), Soc. Exptl. Psychologists, Fedn. Behavioral Psychol. and Cognitive Scis. (pres. 1981). Home: 1406 La Jolla Knoll La Jolla CA 92037-5236 Office: U Calif San Diego Dept Psychology La Jolla CA 92093-0109 also: 3 Perrins Lane, London NW3 1QY, England

MANDOLF, JUDY, artist; b. Logansport, Ind., Jan. 10, 1937; d. Albert Harold and Lillian (Rothermel) Arnold; m. Norbert E. Mandolf, Nov. 9, 1928. Student, U. Calif., San Diego, 1996. Cert. court reporter. Pers. mgr. Hydro Products, San Diego, 1966-73; freelance artist, photographer, 1980—; freelance ct. reporter, San Diego, 1971—. Exhibited in shows at Del Mar, Calif., 1995, 96 (Best of Show), Art Photography Competition, Fallbrook, Calif., 1996 (Best of Show). Named Photographer of Yr. Internat. Photographer Mag., 1988; recipient Gold Medal Discovery award Art of Calif. mag., 1992. Mem. San Diego Women in Creative Photography. Roman Catholic. Home: 2945 Denver St San Diego CA 92117

MANEATIS, GEORGE A., retired utility company executive; b. 1926. BSEE, Stanford U., 1949, MSEE, 1950. With GE, 1950-53; with Pacific Gas & Elec. Co., San Francisco, 1953-91, v.p., 1979-81, sr. v.p., 1981-82, exec. v.p., 1982-86, pres., 1986-91, also bd. dirs. Office: Pacific Gas & Electric Co PO Box 770000 123 Mission St H17F San Francisco CA 94177

MANELLA, NORA M., prosecutor. BA in Italian with highest honors, Wellesley Coll., 1972; JD, U. So. Calif., 1975. Bar: Calif. 1976, U.S. Ct. Appeals (5th cir.) 1976, D.C. Ct. Appeals 1978, U.S. Dist. Ct. (ctrl., so., no. and ea. dists.) 1980-81, U.S. Ct. Appeals (9th cir.) 1982. Law clk. to Hon. John Minor Wisdom U.S. Ct. Appeals (5th cir.), New Orleans, 1975-76; legal counsel Subcom. on Constn., Senate Com. on Judiciary, Washington, 1976-78; assoc. O'Melveny & Myers, Washington and L.A., 1978-82; trial asst. with asst. dist. atty. U.S. Dept. Justice, L.A., 1982-85, dep. chief, criminal complaints, 1986-87, chief criminal appeals, 1988-90; judge L.A. Mcpl. Ct., 1990-92; justice pro tem Calif. Ct. Appeals (2nd dist.), 1992; judge L.A. Superior Ct., 1992-93; U.S. atty. for ctrl. dist. Calif. U.S. Dept. Justice, L.A., 1994—; instr. U.S. Atty. Gen. Advocacy Inst., 1984-86, Calif. Jud. Coll., 1992-93. Mem. editl. bd. State Bar Criminal Law Newsletter, 1991-92. Mem. adv. bd. Monroe H.S. and Govt. Magnet, 1991-94; acad. specialist USAID Delegation, 1993; judge L.A. Times Cmty. Partnership Awards, 1993. Mem. Am. Law Inst., Calif. Judges Assn., Nat. Assn. Women Judges, Calif. Women Lawyers, Women Lawyers of L.A. Office: US Atty Ctrl Dist Calif 1200 US Courthouse 312 N Spring St Los Angeles CA 90012-4701*

MANETTA, ALBERTO, gynecologic oncologist; b. Buenos Aires, Feb. 17, 1944; came to U.S., 1968; s. Guido and Raquel Manetta; m. Nancy Mosard, Nov. 14, 1969; children: Edward, Katy. BS in Biol. Sci., Liceo San Martin, Buenos Aires, 1962; MD, U. Buenos Aires, 1968. Diplomate Am. Bd. Ob-Gyn. Resident Winthrop U. Hosp., SUNY, Stony Brook, 1968-72; dir. Blair County Prenatal Ctr., 1974-77; attending physician pvt. practice Altoona (Pa.) Hosp. Ob-Gyn, 1972-82; clin. asst. prof. family and cmty. medicine Coll. Medicine Pa. State U., Hershey, 1976-82; fellow in gynecologic oncology Georgetown U. Med. Ctr., Washington, 1982-84; asst. prof. ob-gyn divsn. gynecol. oncology Coll. Medicine Pa. State U., Hershey, 1984-88;

attending physician Univ. Hosp., Milton S. Hershey Med. Ctr., Hershey, 1984-88, U. Calif.-Irvine Med. Ctr., Orange, Calif., 1988—; asst. prof. ob-gyn divsn. gynecol. oncology U. Calif., Irvine, 1988-90, assoc. prof., 1990, assoc. prof. ob-gyn., 1992-94, sr. assoc. dean ednl. affairs, 1993—, prof. dept. ob-gyn. divsn. gynecologic oncology, 1995—; cons. staff dept. ob-gyn U. Nev. Sch. Medicine, 1988—; cons. staff dept. surgery City of Hope Nat. Med. Ctr., Duarte, Calif., 1988—; exec. chief proctor Nat. Bd. Med. Examiners, 1992—; presenter in field. Assoc. editor Am. Jour. Ob-Gyn; reviewer jours. in field; contbr. articles to profl. jours., chpts. to books; patentee in field. Recipient rsch. award Am. Cancer Soc., 1986, 1st Excellence in Teaching award Assn. Profs. Gynecology and Obstetrics, 1992; grantee Am. Cancer Soc., 1987-88, 1992, 93, U.S. Biosci., Phila., 1989, Cetus Corp., 1989, UCI, 1989-90, Wyeth-Ayerst Labs., 1991, Meml. Health Svcs. Grant Com., 1991-92, 93, 94, Nat. Cancer Inst., 1994. Fellow ACS, Am. Coll. Obestricians and Gynecologists (Physicians Recognition award 1986, Continuing Med. Edn. award 1989-92, 92—); mem. AMA (Physicians Recognition award 1993-96), Assn. Profs. Gynecologic Oncology, Assn., Assn. Am. Med. Colls. (dean's del. group on ednl. affairs com. 1993—), Soc. Gynecologic Oncologists (found. award 1986), Gynecologic Urology Soc. (charter), Mid-Atlantic Gynecologic Oncology Soc., Am. Soc. Clin. Oncology, Orange County Med. Assn., Western Assn. Gynecologic Oncologists (pres.-elect 1995-96, pres. 1996—), Am. Assn. Cancer Rsch., Gynecologic Oncology Group (mem. coms.). Office: UCI Med Ctr Divsn Gyn/Oncology 101 The City Dr S Bldg 23 Orange CA 92868-3201

MANEVICH, LEONARD A., cultural organization administrator, composer; b. Novosibirsk, Russia, Mar. 18, 1966; came to U.S., 1992; s. Liliya I. Manevich; m. Irina Y. Levitskaya, Aug. 20, 1988; 1 child, Berta. Grad. in composition, music tchg., Musical Coll., Novosibirsk, 1987; grad. in TV and radio prodn., State Theater Artistic Inst., Alma-Ata, Kazakhstan, 1990; grad. in journalism, State Ural Univ., Ekaterinsburg, Russia, 1991. Cert. Russian-English interpreter, Wash. Journalist, broadcaster, editor Regional TV and Radio Co., Novosibirsk, 1982-92; music tchr. Children's Musical Sch., Novosibirsk, 1987-89; founder, pres. Kolobok Arts' Inspiration, Woodinville, Wash., 1982—. Composer, poet over 50 songs and musical pieces, including children's music; contbr. articles and photos to various Russian and Kazakhstanian newspapers and mags. Mem. Am. Musician's Union. Home: 14110 NE 179th St Apt 27 Woodinville WA 98072 Office: Kolobok Arts Inspiration Ste 107 14136 NE Woodinville-Duvall Rd Woodinville WA 98072

MANGAN, TERENCE JOSEPH, police chief; b. Utica, N.Y., Feb. 17, 1938; s. Lawrence and Eloise (Roth) M.; m. Charlotte Mauss, June 19, 1971; children: Sean, Megan. B.A., St. Mary's Coll., Norwalk, Conn., 1961; M.A., St. Albert's Coll., 1965; postgrad. in Pub. Adminstrn., Adminstrn. Justice, U. So. Calif., 1972-76; Grad. FBI Nat. Acad. Cert. Wash. State Criminal Justice Tng. Commn., Calif. Peace Officers Standards and Tng. Commn.; grad. Northwest Law Enforcement Exec. Command Coll., 1986; cert. Gov.'s Rev. Team Child Abuse Services, 1986. With Seaside (Calif.) Police Dept., 1967-72; with Lakewood (Calif.) Police Dept., 1972-76, chief, dir. community safety, to 1976; chief Bellingham (Wash.) Police Dept., 1976-87; chief Spokane (Wash.) Police Dept., 1987—; past chair Wash. State Criminal Justice Tng. Commn.; mem. Mgmt. Adv. Group Organized Crime and Narcotics Enforcement; appointed to Death Investigations Coun., Spl. Task Force on Child Abuse, Gov's Criminal Justice Adv. Bd.; master mentor Waspc's Exec. Leadership Inst., coord. Northwest Law Enforcement Exec. Command Coll. Program; mem. Wash. Law Enforcement Exec. Forum, past chair; mem. Wash. State Inst. Cmty. Oriented Policing; lectr. FBI Acad. Mem. archdiocesan steering com. Ann. Catholic Appeal, 1982; chair fund-raising drives Am. Cancer Soc., Am. Heart Assn., Salvation Army, Easter Seal Soc., Assn. for Retarded Citizens; bd. advs. Holy Names Ctr.; exec. bd. Boy Scouts of Am., Inland Empire Coun.; bd. dirs. Spokane Goodwill Industries, United Way, Whatcom County, Calif. Recipient citation U.S. Secret Service, 1969, Congressional Com. Internal Security, 1971, Svc. award City of Seaside, 1972, Disting. Svc. award City of Lakewood, also Wash. Assn. Sheriffs and Police Chiefs, 1978-81, Police Officer of Yr. award Nat. Exchange Club, 1979, Lawman of Yr. award Vets. of Foreign Wars, 1980, Law Enforcement Officer of Yr. award Wash. VFW, 1980, Community Service award Wash. Toastmasters Internat., 1980, Pres. award Pacific Lutheran U., 1981, Paul Harris fellow Rotary Internat., 1986. Mem. Internat. Assn. Chiefs Police (com. terrorism), Nat. Council Crime and Delinquency, Wash. Assn. Sheriffs and Police Chiefs (past pres.), Internat. Peace Arch Law Enforcement Council. Roman Catholic. Office: Spokane Police Dept Office of the Chief 1100 W Mallon Ave Spokane WA 99260-2043

MANGHAM, CHARLES ADLEY, SR., psychiatrist, psychoanalyst; b. San Antonio, Jan. 17, 1919; s. Arthur Decatur and Emma Evelyna (Flanagan) M.; m. Aileen Muriel Ramberg, Apr. 15, 1944; children: Charles A. Jr., A. Deborah, Joel R. BS, U. Va., 1939, MD, 1942. Diplomate Am. Bd. Psychiatry and Neurology; cert. child and adult psychoanalysis. Intern Virginia Mason Hosp., Seattle, 1942-43; med. officer U.S. Army Med. Corps, 1943-46; resident in medicine Emergency Hosp., Washington, 1946-47; resident in psychiatry Cin. Gen. Hosp., 1947-50; instr. psychiatry U. Wash., Seattle, 1950-51; pvt. practice child psychoanalysis Seattle, 1951—; clin. prof. dept. behavioral scis. U. Wash., 1968—; tng. analyst Seattle Inst. Psychoanalysis. Mem. Assn. Child Psychoanalysis (pres. 1990-92), Am. Psychoanalytic Assn., Wash. State Med. Assn., King County Med. Assn. Office: 4033 E Madison St Seattle WA 98112-3117

MANGIN, RENÉ-MARC, management consultant, systems scientist; b. Paris, July 11, 1956; came to U.S., 1961; s. Melvyn B. and Jeanne Marie (Bradin) M.; m. Susan Beth Burger; children: Alexandre Marceau, Genevieve Marie. BS in Cell Biology, BS in Environ. Sci., Wash. State U., 1979, MS in Environ. Toxicology, 1982; postgrad., U. Wash., 1984-85; PhD, Wash. State U., 1989. Writer, editor USDA Coop. Ext., Pullman, Wash., 1977-79; instr. environ. sci. Wash. State U., Pullman, 1980-81, soil scientist, 1981-82, toxicologist, 1983; ecologist, consulting toxicologist U.S. Forest Svc., Missoula, Mont., 1982-83, regional pest control mgr., 1982-87; environ. program mgr. U.S. Dept. Energy, Richland, Wash., 1987-88, spl. cons. to Tri-Party Agreement, 1987-88; ext. prof. polit. sci. Wash. State U., Pullman, 1989-91; conflict resolution cons. Nat. Ctr. Assocs., Tacoma, Wash., 1990-94; mgmt. cons. Bonneville Power Adminstrn., Portland, Oreg., 1993—; interim chief regulatory analysis Bonneville Power Adminstrn., Portland, 1992-93, interim chief environ. policy & strategy, 1992-93; adj. prof. Maryhurst Coll., 1995—. Author: Culture Clash: Natural Resource Conflicts in the West, 1996; contbr. articles to profl. jours., chpt. to book. Vol. Habitat for Humanity, Portland, 1992. Boeing Acad. scholar, 1977; recipient Lake Roosevelt Mgmt. Planning grant award N.W. Area Found., 1990; named Ark. Traveler by Gov. Bill Clinton, 1991. Mem. Soc. Profls. in Dispute Resolution (pres. N.W. chpt.), Am. Soc. Pub. Adminstrn., Speech Communication Assn. Home: 1547 NE 51st Ave Portland OR 97213-2701

MANGINI, RICHARD ALAN, religious organization executive; b. Concord, Calif., Oct. 23, 1940; s. Raymond A. and Margaret E. (Levada) M. MDiv, St. Patrick's Sem., 1967; MJ, U. Calif., Berkeley, 1972; MA in Sprituality, U. San Francisco, 1982. Editor The Cath. Voice, Oakland, Calif., 1973-80; adminstr. St. Charles Ch., Livermore, Calif., 1976; pastor St. Leander Ch., San Leandro, Calif., 1976-90; dir. strategic planning Diocese of Oakland, 1990-95; pastor St. Bonaventure Ch., Concord, Calif., 1996—, Concord Hispanic Cmty., 1996—. Mem., chair Human Rels. Commn., City of San Leandro, 1980-87, Ecumenical Assn., 1980-87. Recipient Medal of Merit, Govt. of Portugal, 1992. Democrat. Roman Catholic.

MANGUM, WILLIAM, management consulting company executive; b. Memphis, Dec. 7, 1931; s. Cary P. and Jennie Elizabeth (Matthews) M.; m. Maria Elena Smith, Apr. 2, 1978 (div.); children: Christopher, Stacy. BS, U. So. Calif., 1954. With Fairchild Camera & Instruments Corp., L.A., 1954-59; pres. Thomas Mangum Co., L.A., 1960—. Author: 99 Minutes to Your Ideal Job, 1995, The Job Search Workbook, 1995. Pres. Save Our Rural Environ., L.A., 1976-82, La Habra Heights Improvement Assn., L.A., 1982; bd. dirs., pres. La Habra Heights Planning Com., 1978-84. Recipient President's award La Habra Heights Improvement Assn., 1984; named One of Top 250 Exec. Recruiters in U.S.A. Industry/Peer Survey, 1991, 94. Mem. AIAA, IEEE, Am. Soc. Quality Control, Soc. Photo-Optical Instrument Engrs., Am. Mgmt. Assn., Calif. Exec. Recruiters Assn., Internat. Assn. Corp. Profl. Recruiters. Office: 1655 Hasting Ranch Dr Pasadena CA 91107 Office: 2469 Cahuilla Hills Dr Palm Springs CA 92264-8901

MANHEIM, THOMAS L., public affairs officer; b. L.A., May 19, 1949; s. Henry L. and Carolyn Adele (Fox) M.; m. Nancy Ellen Shanfeld, Sept. 4, 1952. BA in Journalism, Ariz. State U., 1971, M.Counseling, 1976. Cert. Tng. and Human Resource Devel. Marriage and family counselor Santa Cruz, Calif., 1976-79; reporter KSBW-TV, Salinas, Calif., 1979-81, prodr., 1981-83, bur. chief, 1983-86; dep. bur. chief CNN, L.A., 1987-89; news writer/assoc. prodr. KCBS-TV, L.A., 1986-87, 89-90; cmty. info. coord. City of West Covina, Calif., 1990-92; pub. affairs officer Monterey Bay (Calif.) Unified Air Pollution Control Dist., 1992-96; sole proprietor Manheim Media & Comm., Monterey, 1995—; mgr. pub. edn. and cmty. outreach City of San Jose (Calif.), 1996—. Bd. dirs. Meals on Wheels of the Monterey Peninsula, 1994-96; founding mem. Monterey Lang. Capitol Advocates, 1994—; mem. Monterey Cable Adv. Com., 1994-96. Recipient award for best small mkt. newscast UPI-Calif., Nev. and Hawaii, 1980, for best videotape editing No. Calif. Radio and TV News Dirs. Assn., 1983, for best news story, 1983, Emmy nomination for field producing live coverage unscheduled news event L.A. Area Emmys, 1986. Mem. Soc. Profl. Journalists (best feature writing award 1971), Radio and TV News Dirs. Assn., Pub. Rels. Soc. Am., Calif. Assn. Pub. Info. Ofcls. (pres. 1996—).

MANK, EDWARD WARREN, marketing professional; b. Boothbay Harbor, Maine, Oct. 2, 1962; s. Edward Raymond Jr. and Sandra Gail (Strahan) M. Assoc. in Liberal Arts, C.C. Vt., 1985; cert. ophthalmic technician, Nat. Edn. Ctr., San Francisco, 1992; cert. real estate broker, Am. Sch. Mortgage Banking, Walnut Creek, Calif., 1994. Lic. real estate salesman, Calif.; cert. Am. Bd. Optometry Dispensing. Tng. coord. Burger King Corp., South Burlington, Vt., 1985-87, San Francisco, 1988-89; asst. mgr. Bonanza Family Restaurant, South Burlington, 1987-88; supr. U.S. Census Bur., San Francisco, 1990; sales rep. Viacom Cablevision, San Francisco, 1991; programming researcher NBC, San Francisco, 1992; mktg. cons. Calyx & Corolla, San Francisco, 1993; mktg. rep. Alliance Bancorp, Millbrae, Calif., 1993—. Sustaining mem. Rep. Nat. Com., Washington, 1989—; sponsor Heritage Found., Washington, Cato Inst., Washington. Mem. Acad. Polit. Sci., Coun. Fgn. Rels., World Affairs Coun., Nat. Rifle Assn. (life), Reason Found. Republican. Episcopalian. Home: 3401 E 18th St Apt 3 Oakland CA 94601-3003 Office: Alliance Bancorp 800 El Camino Real Millbrae CA 94030-2010

MANLEY, RICHARD WALTER, insurance executive; b. Malone, N.Y., Dec. 26, 1934; s. Walter E. and Ruth (St. Mary) M.; m. Linda Kimberlin, Dec. 18, 1965; children: Stephanie, Christopher. BS in Bus., U. So. Miss., 1960. Cert. real estate broker. Account exec. Colonial Life and Accident, Hattiesburg, Miss., 1960-63; dist. mgr. Colonial Life and Accident, Oklahoma City, 1963-66; regional dir. Colonial Life and Accident, Denver, 1966-76, zone dir., 1976-82; pres. Commonwealth Gen. Group, Denver, 1982-96, Manley Properties Inc., Denver, 1982-90, Richard W. Manley Commonwealth Gen. Grps., Inc., Denver, 1982—; cons. Capitol Am. Life Ins. Co., Cleve., 1987-96; bd. dirs. (merco) Mercy Hosp., Denver, 1982-87. With USAF, 1956-59. Mem. Cherry Hills C. of C., Rotary, Alpha Tau Omega. Roman Catholic. Home: 6510 E Lake Pl Englewood CO 80111-4411

MANN, CLARENCE CHARLES, real estate company official; b. Oradell, N.J., Oct. 15, 1929; s. Clarence Theodore and Martha Barbara (Koster) M.; m. Joan Elizabeth Schnoor, Nov. 25, 1951 (div. Jan. 1985); 1 child, Gary John. BA, NYU, 1951; MA, U. Pa., 1958, Am. U., Beirut, Lebanon, 1963. Grad. Realtors Inst.; accredited buyers rep. grad. Commd. 2d. lt. U.S. Army, 1951, advanced through grades to col., ret., 1977; def. attache to Jordan, 1973-77; mktg. mgr. Litton Industries, Jordan, Saudi Arabia, 1977-81; mktg. mgr. Mid-East Hughes Aircraft Co., Fullerton, Calif., 1981-91; dir. relocation ERA Gem Realty, Tucson, 1992—. Author: Abu Dhabi: Birth of an Oil Shaikhdom, 1964. Decorated Legion of Merit. Mem. Met. Tucson Conv. and Visitors Bureau, Chamber Mil. Affairs Com., Tucson C. of C.

MANN, CLAUD PRENTISS, JR., retired television journalist, real estate agent; b. Galveston, Tex., June 30, 1925; s. Claud Prentiss and Henrietta Anno (Cline) M.; m. Loris Lea Padgett, Sept. 18, 1948; children: Beatrice Anno, Claudea Padgett, Claud Prentiss III. BS, U. Houston, 1949. Cert. tchr., Calif.; lic. real estate agt., Wash. Fellow Fund for Adult Edn. Mass Media U. Calif., Berkeley, 1958-59; anchor, reporter, writer, prodr., commentator Sta. KTVU-TV, San Francisco, Oakland, Calif., 1962-87; news dir., anchor, prodr. Sta. KTIE-TV, Oxnard, Santa Barbara, Calif., 1987-88; freelance writer, producer, pub. info. specialist, 1988—; journalism instr. Highline and South Seattle Community Colls., 1990-92. Bd. dirs. Vashon-Maury Sr. Ctr. Recipient No. Calif. Emmy awards for reporting and anchor work, 1975, 76, 77, 79, 81, John Swett award for Edn. Reporting; commendations U.S. State Dept., City of Oakland, City of San Francisco, Calif. State Legis. Mem. AFTRA, NATAS (Silver Circle), Vashon Allied Arts (bd. dirs. 1989-91), Soc. Profl. Journalists. Home: 25115 122nd Ave SW Vashon WA 98070-7820

MANN, EVERETT EDWARD, retired social sciences educator; b. New London, Conn., June 23, 1930; s. Everett Edward and Mary Evelyn (Woods) M.; m. Pamela Ruth Hicks, Oct. 7, 1953 (div. 1982); children: Charles Edward, Evelyn Ruth, Brian Everett; m. Jennifer Marian Bittel, Aug. 26, 1984. BA in Psychology, UCLA, 1953; MEd in Psychology, Oreg. State U., 1965; MA in Govt., Claremont (Calif.) Grad. Sch., 1982, PhD, 1984. Commd. 2d lt. U.S. Army, advanced through grades to lt. col., 1969, ret., 1975; adj. prof. Ctr. Adminstrn. of Justice, dir. Nat. Inst. Info. and Privacy, Nat. Inst. Profl. Edn. for Investigators Am. U., Washington Sch. Govt. and Pub. Affairs, 1975-79; mem. faculty Sch. Bus. and Pub. Adminstrn. Calif. State U., Bakersfield, 1984-92, prof. emeritus pub. policy and adminstrn., 1992—; assoc. dir. Applied Rsch. Ctr., Calif. State U., Bakersfield, 1992—. Office: Calif State U Applied Rsch Ctr Bakersfield CA 93311

MANN, MICHAEL MARTIN, electronics company executive; b. N.Y.C., Nov. 28, 1939; s. Herbert and Rosalind (Kaplan) M.; m. Mariel Joy Steinberg, Apr. 25, 1965. BSEE, Calif. Inst. Tech., 1960, MSEE, 1961; PhD in Elec. Engring. and Physics, U. So. Calif., 1969; MBA, UCLA, 1984. Cert. bus. appraiser, profl. cons., mgmt. cons., lic. real estate broker, Calif. Mgr. high power laser programs office Northrop Corp., Hawthorne, Calif., 1969-76; mgr. high energy laser systems lab. Hughes Aircraft Co., El Segundo, Calif., 1976-78; mgr. E-0 control systems lab. Hughes Aircraft Co., El Segundo, 1978-83, asst. to v.p., space & strategic, 1983-84; exec. v.p. Helionetics Inc., Irvine, Calif., 1984-85, pres., chief exec. officer, 1985-86, also bd. dirs.; ptnr. Mann Kavanaugh Chernove, 1986-87; sr. cons. Arthur D. Little, Inc., 1987-88; chmn. bd., pres., CEO, Blue Marble Devel. Group, Inc., 1988—; exec. assoc. Ctr. Internat. Cooperation and Trade, 1989—; sr. assoc. Corp. Fin. Assocs., 1990—; exec. assoc. Reece and Assocs., 1991—; dir. Reece & Assocs., 1991—; mng. dir. Blue Marble Ptnrs. Ltd, 1991—; chmn. bd. dirs., CEO Blue Marble Ptnrs., 1992—; chmn., CEO, En Compass Techs., Inc., Torrance, Calif., 1994—; mem. Army Sci. Bd., Dept. Army, Washington, 1986-91; chmn. Ballistic Missile Def. Panel, Directed Energy Weapon Panel, Rsch. and New Initiatives Panel; cons. Office of Sec. of Army, Washington, 1986—, Inst. of Def. Analysis, Washington, 1978—, Dept. Energy, 1988—, Nat. Riverside Rsch. Inst., 1990—; bd. dirs. Datum, Inc.,1988—, Fail-Safe Tech., Corp., 1989-90, Safeguard Health Enterprises, Inc., 1988—, Am. Video Communications, Inc., Meck Industries, Inc., 1987-88, Decade Optical Systems, Inc., 1990—, Forum Mil. Application Directed Energy, 1992—, Am. Bus. Consultants, Inc., 1993—; chmn. bd. Mgmt. Tech., Inc. 1991—, Encompass Tech., Inc., 1994—; bd. dirs., mem. adv. bd. Micro-Frame, Inc., 1988-91; chmn. bd. HLX Laser, Inc., 1984-86; bd. dirs. Cons's. Roundtable, 1992—, Am. Bus. Cons., Inc., 1993—; rsch. assoc., mem. extension teaching staff U. So. Calif., L.A., 1964-70; chmn. Ballistic Missile Def. Subgroup, 1989-90, Tactical Directed Energy Weapons Subgroup, 1988-90; chmn., chief exec. officer Mgmt. Tech., Inc., 1991—; dir. Am. Bus. Cons., Inc., 1993—. Contbg. editor, mem. adv. bd. Calif. High-Tech Funding Jour., 1989-90; contbr. over 50 tech. articles to profl. jours.; patentee in field. Mem. adv. com. to Engring. Sch., Calif. State U., Long Beach, 1985—; chmn. polit. affairs Am. Electronics Assn., Orange County Coun., 1986-87, mem. exec. com., 1986-88; adv. com. several Calif. congressmen, 1985—; mem. dean's coun. UCLA Grad. Sch. Mgmt., 1984-85; bd. dirs. Archimedes Circle U. Soc. Calif., 1983-85, Ctr. for Innovation and Entrepreneurship, 1986-90, Caltech/MIT Venture Forum, 1987-91; chmn. adv. coun. and adj. prof., indsl. and sys. engring. U. So. Calif., 1996—. Hicks fellow in Indsl. Rels. Calif. Inst. Tech., 1961, Hewlett Packard fellow. Mem. IEEE (sr.), So. Calif. Tech. Execs. Network, Orange County CEO's Network, Orange County CEO's Roundtable, Pres. Roundtable, Nat. Assn. Corp. Dirs., Aerospace-Def. CEO's Roundtable, Am. Def. Preparedness Assn., Security Affairs Support Assn., Acad. Profl. Cons. and Advisors, Internat. Platform Assn., Inst. Mgmt. Cons. (bd. dirs. So. Calif. chpt.), Pres. Assn., Cons. Roundtable, King Harbor Yacht Club. Republican. Home: 4248 Via Alondra Palos Verdes Peninsula CA 90274-1545 Office: Blue Marble Partners 406 Amapola Ave Ste 200 Torrance CA 90501-6229

MANN, NANCY LOUISE (NANCY LOUISE ROBBINS), entrepreneur; b. Chillicothe, Ohio, May 6, 1925; d. Everett Chaney and Pauline Elizabeth R.; m. Kenneth Douglas Mann, June 19, 1949 (div. June 1979); children: Bryan Wilkinson, Laura Elizabeth. BA in Math., UCLA, 1948, MA in Math., 1949, PhD in Biostatistics, 1965. Sr. scientist Rocketdyne Div. of Rockwell Internat., Canoga Park, Calif., 1962-75; mem. tech. staff Rockwell Sci. Ctr., Thousand Oaks, Calif., 1975-78; rsch. prof. UCLA Biomath., L.A., 1978-87; pres., CEO, owner Quality Enhancement Seminars, Inc., L.A., 1982—; pres., CEO Quality and Productivity, Inc., L.A., 1987—; curriculum adv. UCLA Ext. Dept. of Bus. and Mgmt., L.A., 1991—; mem. com. on Nat. Statistics, Nat. Acad. Scis., Washington, 1978-82; mem adv. bd. to supt. U.S. Naval Posgrad. Sch., Monterey, Calif., 1979-82. Co-author: Methods for Analysis of Reliability and Life Data, 1974; author: Keys to Excellence, 1985, The Story of the Deming Philosophy, 2d edit., 1987, 3d edit., 1989; contbr. articles to profl. jours. Recipient award IEEE Reliability Soc., 1982, ASQC Reliability Divsn., 1986. Fellow Am. Statis. Assn. (v.p. 1982-84); mem. Internat. Statis. Inst. Office: Quality and Productivity Inc 1081 Westwood Blvd # 213 Los Angeles CA 90024-2911

MANN, STEPHEN J., councilman; b. Modesto, Calif., July 14, 1951; s. Jerry and Nancy M.; m. Jill Davis, July 1, 1978; children: Katy, Kelly. AABA, Delta Coll. Sales Lodi Cable TV, Radio Sta. KCVR-FM, Lodi; owner Delta Publ. Co., 1996—; councilman City of Lodi, Calif., 1996—; founder Lodi Life and Times, 1975. With USNG, 1971-77. Baptist. Office: PO Box 3006 Lodi CA 95241

MANN, WESLEY F., newspaper editor. Editor Investor's Business Daily, L.A. Office: Investor's Business Daily 12655 Beatrice St Los Angeles CA 90066*

MANN, ZANE BOYD, editor, publisher; b. St. Paul, Jan. 28, 1924; s. Michael M. and Rose Lee (Reuben) M.; m. Esther Zeesman, Mar. 25, 1945; children: Michael L., Eric F. Personal Fin. Planning, U. Calif., Riverside, 1986. Registered investment advisor Securities and Exch. Commn. Mcpl. fin. cons. Ehlers Mann & Assoc., Mpls., 1956-64; v.p. mcpl. bond underwriter Ebin Robertson, Mpls., 1964-70; v.p. mcpl. dept. Piper Jaffrey & Co., Mpls., 1970-72; ret., 1972; editor, pub. monthly investment newsletter Calif. Mcpl. Bond Advisor, Palm Springs, Calif., 1984—. Author: Fair Winds and Far Places, 1978; contbr. articles to profl. jours. Mem. Twin City Met. Planning Commn., St. Paul, 1958-70; bd. dirs. CORAL, Riverside County, Calif., 1984-91. Staff sgt. U.S. Army, 1942-45. Decorated DFC with cluster, Air medal with cluster, Soldier's medal, Purple Heart U.S. Army Air Corp. Mem. Nat. Fedn. Mcpl. Analysts, Calif. Soc. Mcpl. Analysts, Internat. Combat Camera Assn., Writers Guild Am. (ret.), Com. for the Sci. Investigation of Claims of the Paranormal (assoc.), Royal Corinthian Yacht Club (life, Cowles, Eng.), Mensa., Sports Car Club Am. Home: 1300 E Verbena Dr Palm Springs CA 92262-5873 Office: Calif Mcpl Bond Advisor 1037 S Palm Canyon Dr Palm Springs CA 92264-8378

MANNERS, NANCY, retired mayor; b. Catania, Sicily, Italy; d. Gioacchino Jack and Maria Providenza (Virzi) Marasa; m. George Manners, Dec. 20, 1941; children: Gene David, Nancy Ellen Manners Sieh, Joan Alice. BA in Pub. Adminstrn., U. La Verne, 1979. Asst. city mgr. City of Covina, 1963-74; mcpl. mgmt. cons., 1975-85; mem. city coun. City of West Covina, Calif., 1984-97; pres. Ind. Cities Risk Mgmt. Authority, West Covina, 1988; mayor City of West Covina, 1988-89, 92-93; pres. Ind. Cities Assn., 1989-90. Pres. Covina Coord. Coun., 1970-71, Altrusa Club of Covina-West, 1971-72, Ea. San Gabriel Valley Regional Occupation Program, 1974-76, San Gabriel Valley Planning Com., 1986-87, Mid-Valley Mental Health Coun., 1988-89; regional chmn. San Gabriel Valley Lung Assn., 1971-73; trustee Covina-Valley Unified Sch. Dist., 1973-77; foreman pro tem L.A. County Grand Jury, 1980-81; chmn. L.A. County Solid Waste Mgmt. Com., 1986-89; treas., bd. dirs. San Gabriel Valley Commerce and Cities Consortium, 1991, policy and steering com. Nat. League Cities, 1991-96; chmn. employee rels. policy com. League Calif. Cities; bd. dirs. L.A. County Sanitation Dist., 1992-94, San Gabriel Valley Coun. of Govts., San Gabriel Valley Mosquito Abatement Dist., 1994-97. Named Covina Citizen Yr., 1977, West Covina Citizen Yr., 1983, Woman Yr., Calif. State Legislature, 1990; recipient Woman of Distinction award Today's Woman Forum, 1988, Woman of Achievement award YWCA, 1987, 88, Community Svc. award West Covina C. of C., 1989, Meritorious Pub. Svc. award Rsch. Inst. Claremont McKenna Coll., 1990, Disting. Leader award San Gabriel Valley Boy Scouts of Am., 1997, others. Mem. LWV (pres. San Gabriel Valley 1978-79), Am. Heart Assn. (mem. bd. dirs.), Mcpl. Mgmt. Assocs. of So. Calif. (v.p. 1972-73), Queen of the Valley Hosp. 2100 (pres. 1996-97), Ind. Cities Assn. (v.p. 1988, pres. 1989), West Covina Hist. Soc. (v.p. 1995—), West Covina Rotary (bd. dirs.). Home: 734 N Eileen Ave West Covina CA 91791-1042

MANNIK, MART, medical educator; b. Tallinn, Estonia, Jan. 21, 1932; came to U.S., 1950; s. Paul and Martha (Partelpoeg) M.; Zita A. Lundell, Nov. 15, 1976. AB, Ohio No. U., 1955; MD, Western Res. U., 1959. Diplomate Am. Bd. Internal Medicine, subspecialty rheumatology. Med. intern Mass. Gen. Hosp., Boston, 1959-60, asst. resident medicine, 1960-61; guest investigator, asst. physician to hosp. Rockefeller U., N.Y.C., 1961-63; asst. prof. Rockefeller Univ., N.Y.C., 1965-67; clin. assoc. rheumatology br. Nat. Inst. Arthritis and Metabolic Diseases, Bethesda, Md., 1963-65; assoc. prof. medicine U. Wash., Seattle, 1967-73, prof. medicine, 1973—, head divsn. rheumatology, 1967—; cons. Children's Orthopaedic Hosp. and Med. Ctr., Seattle, 1968-75; attending staff Harborview Med. Ctr., Seattle, 1967—; attending physician Univ. Hosp., U. Wash., Seattle, 1967—; assoc. resident physician Rockefeller U. Hosp., N.Y.C., 1965-67; mem. arthritis tng. grants com. Nat. Inst. Arthritis and Metabolic Diseases, 1969-72; co-chmn. rsch. work group Nat. Arthritis Commn., 1975-76; cons. subspecialty com. rheumatology Am. Bd. Internal Medicine, 1975-76, mem. com. on rheumatology, 1976-80; mem. arthritis ctrs. ad hoc study sect. Nat. Inst. Arthritis, Diabetes, Digestive and Kidney Diseases, 1978, 79-80, cons. spl. projects rev. group A, 1981-84; mem. med. adv. bd. Lupus Found. Am., 1983-87; mem. Nat. Arthritis and Musculoskeletal and Skin Diseases adv. coun. NIH, 1987-90, mem. nat. rsch. plan task force, 1991. Mem. editorial bd. Arthritis and Rheumatism, 1970-82, 85-89, Kidney, 1971-74, Inflammation, 1979—, Clin. Aspects of Autoimmunity, 1988-92, Jour. Clin. Immunology, 1989-92, Scandinavian Jour. Immunology, 1991—; adv. editor Immunochemistry, 1976-78, Molecular Immunology, 1979-80; contbr. articles to profl. publs. Bd. dirs., bd. govs. Arthritis Found., 1969-75, rsch. com., 1989-91, trustee, 1985-86, mem. evaluation rsch. in rheumatic diseases com., 1972. Recipient Lee Howley prize for rsch. in arthritis Arthritis Found., 1988, Disting. Alumnus award Case Western Res. U. Sch. Medicine, 1989. Fellow AAAS; mem. Am. Coll. Rheumatology (chmn. com. on postgrad. tng. in rheumatology 1967-70, chmn. membership com. 1969-76, chmn. gen. publs. com. 1972-75, mem. various coms.), Harvey Soc., Am. Assn. Immunologists (chmn. adv. bd. Manual on Clin. Immunology 1974-76), Am. Soc. Clin. Investigation (v.p. 1977-78), Western Soc. Clin. Investigation, N.W. Rheumatism Soc. (exec. com. 1969—), Western Assn. Physicians, Assn. Am. Physicians, Alpha Omega Alpha. Office: U Wash Dept Medicine Box 356428 Seattle WA 98195-6428

MANNING, CHRISTOPHER ASHLEY, finance educator, consultant; b. L.A., June 26, 1945; s. Ashley and Vivian LaVerne (Wagner) M.; m. Cathy Ann Nichols, July 30, 1977 (div. Sept. 1993). BS, San Diego State U., 1967; MBA, Northwestern U., 1971; PhD, UCLA, 1983. Corp. loan officer Security Pacific Nat. Bank, L.A., 1971-75; v.p. fin. Solitude Ski Resort, Bravo Ski Corp., Salt Lake City, 1975-78; pres. Sequoia Spa Co., L.A., 1976-79; pres. Manning and Co. L.A., 1971-86, Manning's Little Red Piano Shop, L.A., 1971-86; instr. corp. fin. Pepperdine U., L.A., 1979-83; instr.

corp. fin. and real estate Long Beach State U. (Calif.), 1983-86; assoc. prof. fin. Loyola Marymount U., L.A., 1986-92, prof. fin., 1992—; mng. prin. Denver office Houlihan Valuation Advisors, 1993-94; founder, mng. prin. Manning Advisors. Mem. editl. bd. Jour. of Real Estate Rsch., 1988-90, 91-93, 94—; contbr. articles to profl. jours. 1st lt. U.S. Army, 1967-70. Decorated Bronze Star. Mem. Am. Real Estate Soc. (bd. dirs. 1994-96, 97—), Beta Gamma Sigma, Phi Eta Sigma. Republican. Episcopalian. Home: 29438 Quailwood Dr Rancho Palos Verdes CA 90275 Office: Manning Advisors 29438 Quailwood Dr Rancho Palos Verdes CA 90275

MANNING, DONNA, banker; b. Cavite, The Philippines, Dec. 8, 1953; d. Donald F. DiRienzo and LuDean (Dover) Hagge; m. Dee T. Manning, Sept. 29, 1971; children: Natalie Dawn, Jeremy Dee. Closing officer Wells fargo Mortgage, Layton, Utah, 1979-81; br. mgr. Crossland Mortgage Corp., Roy, Utah, 1981-88; asst. v.p., area mgr. First Fed. Am. Bank, Salt Lake and Ogden, Utah, 1988-90; regional v.p. mortgage divsn. First Security Bank, Ogden, 1990—. Bd. dirs., treas. Your Cmty. Connection, Ogden, 1992—. Mem. No. Wasatch Homebuilders Assn. (bd. dirs., assoc. v.p. 1990-95, Parade of Homes chair 1996, Assoc. of the Yr. 1996), Ogden Assn. Profl. Mortgage Women (past pres., treas., bd. dirs.), Ogden Bd. realtors (past affiliate chair, affiliate com. 1990-92). Office: First Security Bank NA 2404 Washington Blvd 2d Fl Ogden UT 84401

MANNING, JOHN JOSEPH, physician, healthcare administrator; b. N.Y.C., Nov. 13, 1938; s. John Joseph and Maryon (Ives) M.; m. Elizabeth Ann Coonan (div.); m. Ruby Elizabeth Boykin, Nov. 24, 1990; stepchildren: Shawn, Ryan. BS, U. Dayton, 1960; MD, Marquette U., 1964; MSc, U. Wis., 1994. Diplomate Am. Bd. Otolaryngology, Am. Bd. Plastic Surgery. Intern U. Miami, Fla., 1964-65; resident in gen. surgery Walter Reed Hosp., Washington D.C., 1967-68; resident in gen. surgery Kaiser Found. Hosp., Oakland, Calif., 1969-70, resident in otolaryngology, 1970-73; resident in reconstructive surgery George Washington (D.C.) U., 1977-79; pvt. practice medicine specializing in otolaryngology and plastic surgery, Lancaster, Calif., 1973—; mem. med. rev. bd. State of Calif., 1987-89. Bd. dirs. Antelope Valley Hosp., Lancaster, 1996—; parks commr. City of Lancaster, 1986-89. Maj. U.S. Army, 1965-68. Republican. Roman Catholic. Office: 44404 16th St W Lancaster CA 93534

MANNING-WEBER, CLAUDIA JOY, medical radiography administrator, consultant; b. Oak Park, Ill., Mar. 17, 1950; d. Charles Lawrence and Carrie Joy (Lund) Manning. AAS, Coll. of DuPage, 1980; BA with honors, Nat. Coll. of Edn., 1986, MS, 1989. Registered med. radiography technologist, Am. Registry of Radiologic Technologists; cert. med. radiography technologist, Ariz.; cert. adult and continuing edn. tchr., Ariz. State Cmty. Coll. Bd. Faculty Coll. of DuPage, Glen Ellyn, Ill., 1987-90, South Suburban Coll., South Holland, Ill., 1989-91; mentor tchr. Prescott (Ariz.) Coll., 1992—; dir. Ariz. Continuing Edn. Svcs., Avondale, 1992—; clin. instr. Phoenix Bapt. Hosp., 1992-93; program dir. PTR Bryman Sch., 1993-95; program dir. med. radiography Apollo Coll., 1995—; contbr., cons. EDUMED Co., Lakeville, Minn., 1995—; treas. ASSRT, Mesa, Ariz., 1993-94; cons. Coll. of DuPage, 1988-91. Author: Distance Delivered Education in Nuclear Medicine Technology, 1989. Mem. ASCD, AAUW, Internat. Soc. Radiographers and Radiologic Technicians, Assn. for Educators in Radiologic Sci., Am. Soc. Radiologic Technologists, Ariz. State Soc. Radiologic Technologists (ednl. dir. 1992-93, treas. 1993-94, seminar presenter 1991, 92), Delta Kappa Gamma. Home: 10938 W Bermuda Dr Avondale AZ 85323 Office: Apollo Coll 2701 W Bethany Home Rd Phoenix AZ 85017-1705

MANNINO, J. DAVIS, psychotherapist; b. Patchoque, N.Y., Sept. 27, 1949; s. Joseph I. and Adrienne Adele (Davis) M. BA magna cum laude, SUNY, Stony Brook, 1971; MSW summa cum laude, San Francisco State U., 1974; EdD in Counseling and Ednl. Psychology, U. San Francisco, 1989. Lic. psychotherapist, Calif.; lic. clin. social worker, Calif., marriage, family and child counselor. Instr. U. Malaysia, 1974-76; dir. refugee programs City San Francisco, 1979-82; instr. U. San Francisco, 1979-85; pvt. practice specializing in psychology San Francisco, Sonoma Counties, 1979—; cons. foster care Calif. State Legis., 1980, community rels., San Francisco Police Dept., 1982-87, Hospice Sonoma County, 1990, Sonoma County Mental Health, 1990; forensic task force on AIDS, San Francisco Pub. Health Dept., 1984-85; child abuse investigation supr. City of San Francisco, 1985-88; supr. Reasonable Efforts to Families Unit; project coord. Edna McConnell Clark Found. Family Mediation Demonstration Grant, 1987-88; prof. child growth and devel., death and dying, Intro. to Psychology Santa Rosa Jr. Coll., 1990—; commr. Calif. Bd. Behavioral Sci. Examiners, 1990. Author: Grieving Days, Healing Days, 1997; contbr. articles to profl. jours.; local psychology columnist Art of Caregiving, 1986—. Mem. Am. Psychol. Assn., Nat. Assn. Social Workers (diplomate clin. social work), Orthopsychiat. Assn., Am. Assn. Counseling and Devel., Calif. Assn. Marriage Family and Child Therapists, Golden Gate Bus. Assn. (ethics com. 1986, Disting. Svc. award, 1985), Am. Assn. Marriage and Family Therapists, Nat. Register Clin. Social Workers, Lions (bd. dirs. San Francisco chpt. 1986). Office: 4597 18th St San Francisco CA 94114-1831 also: PO Box 14031 San Francisco CA 94114-0031 *Personal philosophy. A life is to be enjoyed not endured. How people get through life is a piece of art not a piece of cake. Everyday is a canvas and our actions brushstrokes, let our brushstrokes be bold each day.*

MANOLAKAS, STANTON PETER, watercolor artist; b. Detroit, July 25, 1946; s. Constantine Stamatios and Angela (Kaloyerpolous) M.; m. Barbara Soldathos, July 25, 1971. Student, Eastman Sch. of Music, 1964-65; BA in Psychology, U. So. Calif., L.A., 1969; postgrad., Calif. State U., Long Beach, 1969-70. Represented by Art Angle's Gallery, Orange, Calif., 1985-94, Gallery Tatewari, Sedona, Ariz., Wild Wings, Lake City, Minn.; represented Wild Wings Gallery, Lake City, Minn., 1995—. Exhibited in group show at Zantman Galleries, Carmel, Calif., 1989, Dossin Great Lakes Mus., 1994; demonstration artist City Art exhibit Millard Sheets Gallery, L.A. County Fair, Pomona, Calif., 1994, L.A. Heritage Sq. Mus., 1994; represented in permanent collections Bechtel Industries, San Francisco, Marriott Hotel Corp., Newton, Mass., Gallagher & Heffernan Inc., San Francisco, The Borovay Group, L.A., Datum Inc., Anaheim, Calif., Tarbell Realty Inc., Costa Mesa, Calif. Active AFL-CIO County Fedn. of Labor, L.A., 1982-92; mem. Saint Sophia Cathedral Choir, L.A., 1970-82, Burbank Symphony Orch., 1973-76, Glendale (Calif.) Symphony Orch., 1975-77. Mem. Am. Fedn. of Musicians (local 47). Republican. Eastern Orthodox. Home: 2500 Las Flores Dr Los Angeles CA 90041-1021

MANOLIU-MANEA, MARIA, linguist; b. Galatz, Romania, Mar. 12, 1934; came to U.S., 1978, naturalized, 1987; d. Ion T. and Ana S. (Codescu) Manoliu; m. Ion S. Manea, Nov. 26, 1968. BA, French Coll., Galatz, 1951; MA, U. Bucharest, Romania, 1955, PhD, 1966. Asst. prof. Romance linguistics U. Bucharest, 1957-61, assoc. prof., 1961-68, prof., 1968-77; prof. linguistics U. Calif., Davis, 1978—; vis. prof. U. Chgo., 1972-74, H. Heine Universitat, Dusseldorf, 1994; cons. NEH, 1980—; mem. adv. bd. Revue Romane, Copenhagen, 1972—, Romance Philology, Berkeley, Calif., 1984—, Philologica Canariensia, Spain, 1992—. Author: Sistematica Substitutelor, 1968 (Ministry of Edn. award 1968), Gramatica Comparata a limbilor romanice, 1971, El Estructuralismo Lingüistico, 1979, Tipología e Historia, 1985, Gramatica, Pragmasemantica si Discurs, 1993, Discourse and Pragmatic Constraints on Grammatical Choices. A Grammar of Surprises, 1994; editor-in-chief Bull. de la S.R.L.R., Bucharest, 1975-78; contbr. articles to profl. jours. Recipient Evenimentul award for Outstanding Contbn. to Romanian Culture, 1991; grantee Internat. Com. Linguists, 1972, Fulbright Found., 1972-74, 91, 92, IREX, 1993, U. Calif., 1970—. Mem. MLA, Am. Romanian Acad. (pres. 1982-95, hon. pres. 1995—), Academia Română (hon.), Soc. de Linguistique Romane, Soc. Roumaine de Linguistique Romane (v.p. 1974—), Internat. Assn. Hist. Linguistics, Linguistics Soc. Am., Internat. Assn. Pragmatics, Romanian Studies Assn. Am. (pres. 1986-88). Office: U Calif Dept French and Italian 509 Sproul Hall Davis CA 95616

MANSELL, CATHERINE, writer, editor, economist; b. El Paso, Tex., Mar. 22, 1961; d. Roger and Carolyn (Mayo) M.; m. Agustín Guillermo Carstens, July 19, 1986. BA in Econs., U. Chgo., 1982, MA in Econs., 1985. Economist CBI Casa de Bolsa, Mexico City, 1987; mgr. futures and options analysis EuroAm. Capital Corp., Ltd., Mexico City, 1988-89, chief economist, 1989; prof. econs. Inst. Tecnológico Autónomo de Méx., Mexico City, 1990-95; editor, writer Tameme, Mexico City and Los Altos, Calif., 1995—. Author: (as Catherine Mansell Carstens) Las Nuevas Finanzas en México, 1992, Las Finanzas Populares en México, 1995, (as C.M. Mayo) Sky Over El Nido, 1995 (Flannery O'Connor award for Short Fiction 1994); editor: Liberalizacíócion e innovación financiera, 1995. Fellow MacDowell Colony, 1993, 95, Yaddo, 1995, Sewanee Writers Conf., 1996, Bread Loaf Writers Conf., 1996; recipient Flannery O'Connor award U. Ga. Press. Mem. The Authors Guild. Office: Tameme, Callejón de Torresqui 12, Mexico City Mexico

MANSFIELD, ELAINE SCHULTZ, molecular geneticist, automation specialist; b. Boulder, Colo., Apr. 20, 1954; d. William Varley and Juanita M. (Zingg) M.; m. Gary G. Schultz, Nov. 24, 1983; children: Matthew, Greggory Mark. BA in Molecular Biology, San Jose State U., 1975; MS in Genetics, U. Calif., Berkeley, 1978, PhD in Genetics, 1983. Diplomate Am. Bd. Med. Genetics (fellow), Am. Bd. Clin. Molecular Genetics. Customer cons. IntelliGenetics, Mountain View, Calif., 1980-81; staff scientist Applied Biosys., Foster City, Calif., 1978-80; sr. staff scientist Molecular Dynamics, Sunnyvale, Calif., 1993—; lectr. in the field. Author (with others) Mutations in the Human Genome, 1993; contb. to profl. jours.; patentee in field. U. Calif. grant, Chancellors Patent Fund grant U. Calif. Mem. AAAS, Am. Soc. Human Genetics, Am. Soc. Histocompatibility and Immunogenetics, Women in Sci., Black Masque (pres. 1975). Office: Molecular Dynamics 928 E Arques Ave Sunnyvale CA 94086-4520

MANSFIELD, ROGER LEO, astronomy and space publisher; b. Boston, Feb. 18, 1944; s. Roy D. Sr. and Nellie E. (Venzlowski) M.; m. Alice Lee Waring, Nov. 1, 1969 (div. Mar. 1983); 1 child, Jason Benjamin; m. Karen June Sprout, June 27, 1987. BS in Chemistry with high honors, U. Cin., 1965; MA in Math., U. Nebr., 1972. Chemist Lockheed Missiles & Space Co., Palo Alto, Calif., 1967; orbital analyst USAF, Offutt AFB, Nebr., 1967-73; instr. Dept. of Math. USAF Acad., Colorado Springs, Colo., 1973-74; aerospace engr. Philco-Ford Corp., Palo Alto, 1974-75, Data Dynamics Inc., Mountain View, Calif., 1975-76, Ford Aerospace & Communications Corp., Colorado Springs, 1976-90; prin. engr. Loral Aerospace Corp., Colorado Springs, 1990-95; owner Astron. Data Svc., 1976—. Pub. Skywatcher's Almanac, Local Planet Visibility Report, Photographer's Almanac, Comparative Ephemeris, Space Birds, WeatherBirds Utilities; contbr. articles to profl. jours. Mem. Am. Astron. Soc., Math. Assn. Am., Internat. Planetarium Soc., Rocky Mountain Planetarium Assn., Phi Beta Kappa, Phi Eta Sigma. Home and Office: 3922 Leisure Ln Colorado Springs CO 80917-3502

MANSOURI, LOTFOLLAH (LOTFI MANSOURI), opera stage director, administrator; b. Tehran, June 15, 1929; arrived in Can., 1976; s. Hassan and Mehri (Jalili) M.; m. Marjorie Anne Thompson, Sept. 18, 1954; 1 child, Shireen Melinda. AB, UCLA, 1953. Asst. prof. UCLA, 1957-60; resident stage dir. Zurich Opera, 1960-65; chief stage dir. Geneva Opera, 1965-75; gen. dir. Can. Opera Co., Toronto, Ont., 1976-88, San Francisco Opera, 1988—; dramatic coach Music Acad. West, Santa Barbara, Calif., 1959; dir. dramatics Zurich Internat. Opera Studio, 1961-65, Centre Lyrique, Geneva, 1967-72; artistic adviser Tehran Opera, 1973-75; opera adviser Nat. Arts Centre, Ottawa, Ont., 1977; v.p. Opera America, 1979—; operatic cons. dir. Yes, Giorgio, MGM, 1981; dir. opera sequence for film Moonstruck (Norman Jewison), 1987. Guest dir. opera cos. including Met. Opera, San Francisco Opera (60 prodns.), N.Y.C. Opera, Lyric Opera of Chgo., Canadian Opera Co. (30 new prodns.), Houston Grand Opera, La Scala, Covent Garden, Verona Opera, Kirov Opera, Australian Opera, Vienna Staatsoper, Vienna Volksoper, Salzburg Festival, Amsterdam Opera, Holland Festival, Nice (France) Opera, Festival D'Orange, France, Verona Arena Festival; co-author: An Operatic Life, 1982. Decorated chevalier Order Arts and Letters (France), 1992. Mem. Am. Guild Mus. Artists, Can. Actors Equity Assn.

MANTES, GEORGE, state senator; b. Tooele, Utah; m. Mary Ann Ballard, Aug. 25, 1963. BS in Mktg., U. Utah, 1959. Auto dealer Mantes Chevrolet Co., Tooele, 1968—; mem. Utah State Senate, 1990—, minority whip, 1995-96; mem. Exec. Appropriations com., Nat. Conf. State Legislatures, Tooele County Econ. Devel. Coun. Bd. dirs. Blue Cross/Blue Shield Utah. Mem. Tooele C. of C., Tooele Jaycees (past pres.), Utah Auto Dealers Assn. (past pres.). Democrat. Home: 327 Upland Dr Tooele UT 84074 Office: 185 N Main St Ste 201 Tooele UT 84074

MANWILLER, DEBI, casting director. BFA, Calif. Inst. of the Arts, 1983. Ptnr., owner Pagano/Manwiller Casting, L.A. Recipient Emmy award for best episodic casting of Chgo. Hope, 1996. Mem. Casting Soc. Am. Office: Pagano/Manwiller Casting care 20th Century Fox 10201 W Pico Blvd Los Angeles CA 90035

MANZ, BRUNO JULIUS, retired government agency executive; b. Dortmund, Germany, June 26, 1921; came to U.S., 1957; s. Albrecht and Erna (Müller) M.; m. Renate Boerner, Sept. 19, 1953; children: Matthias, Bettina, Susanne, Julius. Diploma in physics, U. Mainz, Germany, 1952; PhD, Tech. U., Aachen, Germany, 1957. Rsch. scientist Siemens A.G., Mühlheim, Germany, 1955-57, Army Ballistic Missile Agy., Ala., 1957-59; ops. analyst USAF, Albuquerque, 1959-88; ret., 1988.; adj. prof. U. N.Mex., Albuquerque, 1960-71, Chapman Coll., Albuquerque, 1972-74, Highlands U., Albuquerque, 1974-80. Author: West Deutsch. Verl, Theory Irreversible Pr., 1958; contbr. to book: Mathematicus Umbraticola, 1962; contbr. articles to profl. jours. Recipient Johannes Gutemberg award City of Mainz, 1949. Home: 1004 Casa Grande Ct Albuquerque NM 87112

MANZANARES, DENNIS, lawyer; b. Santa Fe, N.Mex., Sept. 20, 1950; s. Ercilia E. Martinez. BA, Coll. Santa Fe, 1973; JD, Georgetown U., 1976. Bar: N.Mex. 1976, U.S. Dist. Ct. N.Mex. 1976, U.S. Ct. Appeals (10th cir.) 1979, U.S. Supreme Ct. 1981. Asst. pub. defender State of N.Mex., Albuquerque, 1976-79; gen. counsel to state auditor State of N.Mex., Santa Fe, 1979-82; sole practice Santa Fe, 1983-90; town atty. Taos, N.Mex., 1990-94; sole practice, 1994-95; atty. Taos County, 1995—; instr. U. N.Mex., Taos; accident prevention counselor FAA; adj. instr. FEMA, N.Mex. Dept. Pub. Safety; instr. Grad. and Undergrad. Programs U. Phoenix. V.p. N.Mex. Young Dems., 1979-82; judge Marriage Tribunal Archdiocese Santa Fe, 1978-85; air and field search and rescue coordinator N.Mex. State Police Search and Rescue, 1985-95; mem. jud. coun. N.Mex. Dem. Party, 1981-85, Santa Fe Airport Adv. Bd., 1985-88. Mem. ABA, N.Mex. Bar Assn. (chmn. pub. advocacy sect. 1983-84, S.W. regional v.p.), Lawyer Pilot Bar Assn., Nat. Transp. Bd. Bar Assn., Nat. Dist. Attys. Assn., N.Mex. Civil Air Patrol (comdr., legal officer S.W. region 1983-91, comdr. Santa Fe squadron 1985-87, comdr. N.Mex. wing 1995—, Outstanding Sr. Mem. award 1983-84, Gill Robb Wilson award 1985, Search & Rescue Find award 1984-85), Taos County Bar Assn. (pres. 1993-96), N.Mex. Mcpl. Attys. (pres. 1993-94), N.Mex. Pilots Assn. (v.p. 1986-92, Leadership and Safety awards 1985—), N.Mex. Woodworkers Guild (v.p. 1983-85), Young Astronaut Program (chpt. sponsor). Home: 80 Los Alamitos Rd Taos NM 87571 Office: PO Box 7401 Taos NM 87571-7401

MANZITTO, ARTHUR SEBASTIAN, nursing and hospital administrator; b. Omaha, Jan. 30, 1943; s. Sebastian John and Lela Mae (Hike) M.; m. Sara Esther Rovetto, Dec. 31, 1962 (div. July 1969); 1 child, Kevin Dale. BSN, U. N.Mex., 1973; M of Healthcare Adminstrn., Chapman U., 1989. Cert. profl. in healthcare quality., C.P.H.Q. Commd. ensign USN, 1962, advanced through grades to lt. comdr., 1983; nurse educator St. Joseph Hosp., Albuquerque, 1983-85; asst. adminstr. West Mesa Healthcare Ctr., Albuquerque, 1985-86; night nursing supr. Carrie Tingley Hosp., Albuquerque, 1986-89; adminstr. Ft. Bayard (N.Mex.) Healthcare Ctr., 1989-91; owner, CEO Ivory Healthcare Mgmt. Sys., Albuquerque, 1991-93; coord. quality programs U. N.Mex./Carrie Tingley Hosp., Albuquerque, 1993—; creator edn. programs physician orientation to navy medicine, 1983. Mem. N.Mex. Healthcare Quality Assn. (v.p. 1996—). Democrat. Roman Catholic. Home: 4307 Marquette Ave NE Albuquerque NM 87108-1119 Office: U NMex Carrie Tingley Hosp 1127 University Blvd NE Albuquerque NM 87102-1740

MAPES, JEFFREY ROBERT, journalist; b. San Francisco, Nov. 21, 1954; s. James Robert and Phyllis June (Bloemker) M.; m. Karen Jane Minkel, Aug. 20, 1978; children: Katharine, James. BA, San Jose State U., 1976. Reporter Napa (Calif.) Register, 1976-79; Washington corr. Scripps League Newspapers, 1979-83; reporter The Oregonian, Portland, 1984-87, chief polit. reporter, 1987—. Office: The Oregonian 1320 SW Broadway Portland OR 97201-3411

MARAK, LOUIS BERNARD, JR., art educator; b. Shawnee, Okla., Sept. 9, 1942; s. Louis Bernard and Ann Elizabeth (Sakach) M.; m. Noelle Stephanie Cusumano, Dec. 10, 1966; children: Jason Matthew, Ethan Andrew. Assoc. in Bus. Adminstrn., St. Gregory's Jr. Coll., 1962; BFA in Crafts, U. Ill., Champaign, 1965; MFA in Ceramics, Alfred U., 1967. Instr. of art Keuka Coll., Keuka Park, N.Y., 1967-69; prof. art Humboldt State U., Arcata, Calif., 1969—. Nat. Endowment for the Arts Craftsmen's fellowship grantee, 1975; Calif. Arts Coun. artist fellowship grantee, 1994. Home: 1110 Freshwater Rd Eureka CA 95503-9558

MARANGI, VITO ANTHONY, SR., claim administrator; b. Utica, N.Y., Jan. 1, 1932; s. Mary Margaret Lokey, Apr. 10, 1960 (div. July 1973); children: Vito Anthony Jr., Vanetta Gayle, Gregory Alan; m. Diann Louise Bunch, Apr. 11, 1987. BS, SUNY, Potsdam, 1958. Asst. regional claims mgr. Hartford Ins. Group, Fresno, Calif., 1958-67; supervising adjuster Underwriters Adjusting Co., Fresno, 1967-70; home office claim supr. Meritplan Ins. Co., Newport Beach, Calif., 1970-71; appeals referee State of Nev., Reno and Carson City, 1971-73, 76-79; br. mgr. Brown Bros. Adjusters, Reno, 1974-87; ind. ins. adjuster Tony Marangi, Adjuster, Carson City, 1987—; vice chmn., bd. trustees Carson-Tahoe Hosp., 1991-96. Scout master Boy Scouts Am., Utica, N.Y., Fresno, Calif., Carson City, 1953-85. With USN, 1949-53. Mem. Nev. State Claims Assn. (pres., v.p., treas., sec.), No. Nev. Claims Assn. (pres., v.p., treas., sec.), Nat. Assn. of Adminstrv. Law Judges, Internat. Assn. of Arson Investigators (Nev. chpt.), Carson City Elks Lodge, VFW, Carson City C. of C. (bus. edn. com. 1987—, transp. com. 1987—). Home: PO Box 843 Carson City NV 89702-0843 Office: Carson Tahoe Hosp PO Box 2168 Carson City NV 89702-2168

MARAVICH, MARY LOUISE, realtor; b. Fort Knox, Ky., Jan. 4, 1951; d. John and Bonnie (Balandzic) M. AA in Office Adminstrn., U. Nev., Las Vegas, 1970; BA in Sociology and Psychology, U. So. Calif., 1972; grad. Realtors Inst. Cert. residential specialist. Adminstrv. asst. dept. history U. So. Calif., L.A., 1972-73; asst. pers. supr. Corral Coin Co., Las Vegas, 1973-80; realtor, Americana Group div. Better Homes and Gardens, Las Vegas, 1980-85, Jack Matthews and Co., 1985-93, Realty Execs., Las Vegas, 1993— . Mem. Nev. Assn. Realtors (cert. realtors inst.), Las Vegas Bd. Realtors, Nat. Assn. Realtors, Women's Council of Realtors, Am. Bus. Women's Assn., NAFE, Million Dollar Club, Pres.'s Club. Office: Realty Execs 1903 S Jones Blvd Ste 100 Las Vegas NV 89102-0900

MARCANT, CHRISTOPHE, company executive; b. Lyon, France, Apr. 22, 1960; came to U.S., 1984; s. Pierre and Odile (Galons) M.; m. Evelyn Santos, Dec. 15, 1988; children: Anthony, Emmanuel, Matthew. DEA in Artificial Intelligence, U. Paris VI, 1982; Engr., Sch. Mines, Paris, 1982. Region mgr. Gensym, Redwood City, Calif., 1989-94; CEO Objectwise, San Francisco, 1994-96; program mgr. TCSI Software Co. Tele Mktg. Industry, Berkeley, Calif., 1996—. One mans show: Karl Bornstein, Los Angeles, 1987, 85, 84, 82, Arco Ctr., for Visual Arts, with James Turrell, Los Angeles, Calif., 1976; Group Shows, LA Co. Mus. Arts, 1982, CSUN, CSU, Domingues, Hills, U. Hawaii, 1979, Saskatoon, Canada, 1979, Collections Capital Group Los Angeles, Standard of New Jersey, Smithonian Archives of Am. Art, Loyola Law Sch., Los Angeles Libr. of Congress, Cedars Sinai Hospital, Los Angeles, Calif., Chase Manhattan Bank, N.Y.C. Office: TCSI 2121 Allston Way Berkeley CA 94704-1301

MARCELYNAS, RICHARD CHADWICK, management consultant; b. New London, Conn., Aug. 21, 1937; s. Anthony F. and Elizabeth A. (Chadwick) M.; m. Betty A. Forray, July 1, 1961; children: Michael R., Thomas R. BA in Bus. Adminstrn., U. Wash., 1961; postgrad. Seattle U., 1971-72. Mgmt. trainee, installation foreman Pacific Bell, Fullerton, Calif., 1964-65; cost acct. Scott Paper Co., Everett, Wash., 1965-68; asst. v.p. pers. and adminstrn. Nat. Pub. Svc. Ins. Co., Seattle, 1968-77; mgr. indsl. rels. Heath Tecna Precision Structures Inc., Kent, Wash., 1978-85; mgmt. con. Pilon Mgmt. Co., Seattle, 1985-90; pers. adminstr. Peninsula Group Olympia, Wash., 1990-94; mgmt. cons., Olympia, 1994—; pres. Chadwick & Assocs., Olympia, 1994—; cons., lectr. Served to maj. USMCR, 1961-77. Decorated commendations for bravery and tech. expertise, 1962-64; recipient Seattle chpt. Pacific N.W. Personnel Mgrs. Assn. Bd. Dirs. award, 1975. Mem. Am. Soc. Personnel Adminstrs., Pacific N.W. Personnel Mgrs. Assn. (past pres. Tacoma chpt.). Office: 623 Sherman St SW Olympia WA 98502-5454

MARCEY, JEAN LAVERNE, educational association administrator; b. Tillamook, Oreg., May 1, 1962; d. Myron LaVerne and Helen Louise (Rose) M.; m. Frank A. Shaffer, July 17, 1994. BS, U. Alaska, 1985; EdD, Oreg. State U., 1992. Dist. program asst. U. Alaska, Anchorage, 1988-90, state program asst., 1990-91, program assoc., 1995, asst. prof. extension 4-H youth devel., 1995—; cons. Anchorage, 1993-94; vocat. counselor State Alaska Youth Corps., Anchorage, 1994-95; mem. task force sch. to work implementation Dept. Edn., Juneau, Alaska, 1996—. Contbr. articles to profl. publs. Grantee Nat. 4-H Coun., 1996. Mem. Nat. Assn. Extension 4-H Agents, Alaska State Vocat. Assn., Am. Vocat. Assn. Anchorage Assn. Vol. Adminstrs., Nat. Future Farmers Am. Alumni (Am. Farmer Degree 1981), C. of C. (edn. com., rsch. sub-com 1996—). Office: U Alaska Ste 118 2221 E Northern Lights Anchorage AK 99508

MARCH, GEORGE PATRICK, retired naval officer; b. Corvallis, Oreg., Jan. 16, 1924; s. George Clayton and Margaret Isobel (Motley) M.; m. Betty Eileen Saum, Dec. 20, 1946; children: Maureen, Terese, Margaret. B.S., U.S. Naval Acad., 1946; M.A., Georgetown U., 1952, Ph.D., 1965. Commd. ensign U.S. Navy, 1946, advanced through grades to rear adm., 1973; staff and command assignments (Atlantic and Pacific fleets); shore duty in Morocco, Cyprus, Germany, Eng. and Japan, 1946-73; asst. dir. (Nat. Security Agy.), Washington, 1973-74; comdr. (Naval Security Group Command), dir. electronic warfare and cryptology div. on staff of chief of naval ops., 1974-78, ret. 1978. Author: Cossacks of the Brotherhood, 1990, Eastern Destiny: Russia in Asia and the North Pacific, 1996. Decorated Legion of Merit (2). Mem. U.S. Naval Inst., Am. Hist. Assn., Am. Assn. for the Advancement of Slavic Studies, Phi Gamma Delta, Phi Alpha Theta. Address: 3043 Old Port Ln NW Olympia WA 98502-3963 *The key to human survival and progress is discipline—not a harsh one imposed from above, but rather one based on mutual understanding and acceptance of that very basic Christian precept—the Golden Rule. Whatever success I have achieved in command and management of people is owed to the effective application of this simple, fundamental idea.*

MARCH, JAMES GARDNER, social scientist, educator; b. Cleve., Jan. 15, 1928; s. James Herbert and Mildred (MacCorkle) M.; m. Jayne Mary Dohr, Sept. 23, 1947; children: Kathryn Sue, Gary Clifton, James Christopher, Roderic Gunn. BA, U. Wis., 1949; MA, Yale U., 1950, PhD, 1953; hon. doctorate, Copenhagen Sch. Econs., 1978, Swedish Sch. Econs., 1979, U. Wis., Milw., 1980, U. Bergen, 1980, Uppsala U., 1987, Helsinki Sch. Econs., 1991, Dublin City U., 1994. From asst. prof. to prof. Carnegie Inst. Tech., 1953-64; prof., dean Sch. Social Scis. U. Calif., Irvine, 1964-70; prof. mgmt., higher edn., polit. sci. and sociology Stanford (Calif.) U., 1970-95, prof. emeritus, 1995—; cons. in field, 1954—; Mem. Nat. Council Ednl. Research, 1975-78; mem. Nat. Sci. Bd., 1968-74; mem. sociol.-social psychology panel NSF, 1964-66; social sci. tng. com. NIMH, 1967-68; mem. math. social sci. com. Social Sci. Research Council, 1958-60; mem. Assembly Behavioral and Social Sci., NRC, 1973-79, chmn. com. on aging, 1977-82, chmn. com. on math., sci., tech. edn., 1984-86. Author: (with H.A. Simon) Organizations, 1958, 2nd edit., 1993, (with R.M. Cyert) A Behavioral Theory of the Firm, 1963, 2nd edit., 1992, Handbook of Organizations, 1965, (with B.R. Gelbaum) Mathematics for the Social and Behavioral Sciences, 1969, (with M.D. Cohen) Leadership and Ambiguity, 1974, 2nd edit., 1986, Academic Notes, 1974, (with C.E. Lave) An Introduction to Models in the Social Sciences, 1975, (with J.P. Olsen) Ambiguity and Choice in Organizations, 1976, Aged Wisconsin, 1977, Autonomy as a Factor in Group Organization, 1980, Pleasures of the Process, 1980, Slow Learner, 1985, (with R. Weissinger-Baylon) Ambiguity and Command, 1986, Decisions and Organizations, 1988, (with J.P. Olsen) Rediscovering Institutions, 1989, Minor Memos, 1990, A Primer on Decision Making, 1994, Fornuft og Forandring,

1995, (with J.P. Olsen) Democratic Governance, 1995; contbr. articles to profl. jour. Fellow Ctr. Advanced Study in Behavioral Scis., 1955-56, 73-74; recipient Wilbur Lucius Cross medal Yale U., 1968; named knight 1st class Royal Norwegian Order of Merit, 1995. Mem. NAS, Nat. Acad. Edn., Accademia Italiana di Economia Aziendale, Royal Swedish Acad. Scis., Norwegian Acad. of Sci. and Letters, Am. Acad. Arts and Scis., Am. Econ. Assn., Am. Polit. Sci. Assn. (v.p. 1983-84, John Gaus award 1997), Am. Psychol. Assn., Am. Sociol. Assn., Acad. Mgmt., Russell Sage Found. (trustee 1985-94, chmn. 1990-93), Finnish Soc. Scis. and Letters, Phi Beta Kappa, Sigma Xi. Home: 837 Tolman Dr Stanford CA 94305-1025 Office: Stanford U Scancor 509 Ceras Stanford CA 94305-3084

MARCH, MARION D., writer, astrologer, consultant; b. Nürnberg, Germany, Feb. 10, 1923; came to the U.S., 1941; d. Franz and Grete Dispeker; m. Nico D. March, Sept. 1, 1948; children: Michele, Nico F. Diploma, Ecole de Commerce, Lausanne; attended, Columbia U. Cons. astrologer L.A., 1970—; founder, pres., tchr. Aquarius Workshops, L.A., 1975—; internat. lectr. in field, 1976—; chmn. bd. dirs., convention dir. United Astrology Congress, 1986, 89, 92; co-founder, mem. bd. dirs. Assn. for Astrological Networking; cons. in astrology to psychology profls. Author: (books) (with Joan McEvers) The Only Way To... Learn Astrology, 1981-94 (6 vol. series), Astrology: Old Theme, New Thoughts, 1984; editor (mag.) ASPECTS, 1976-93; contbr. numerous articles to jours. in field. Recipient Regulus award for edn. United Astology Congress, 1989, for community svc., 1992, PAI Annual award Profl. Astrologers, Inc., 1990, Syotisha Ratna award Syotish Samsthan of Bombay, India, 1986, Robert Carl Jansky Astrology Leadership award, 1994. Mem. Nat. Coun. for Geocosmic Rsch. (mem. adv. bd.), Internat. Soc. Astrological Rsch., Profl. Astrologers Inc., Astrological Assn. Great Britain. Office: care Publisher ACS PO Box 34487 San Diego CA 92163-4487

MARCHETTI, KAREN J., advertising executive; b. Coronado, Calif., Mar. 2, 1958; d. Salvatore and Frances R. (Piscotty) M. BBA, San Diego State U., 1981, MS in Bus. Adminstrn., 1986. Mktg. intern Am. Airlines, San Diego, 1981-83; mktg. specialist Point Loma FCU, San Diego, 1983-84; asst. product mgr. Home Fed. Bank, San Diego, 1984-86; new product mgr. Security Pacific Fin. Svcs., San Diego, 1986-89; account supr. Rosenfield/Vinson, Inc., San Diego, 1989-90, dir. client svcs., 1990-91; v.p., dir. client svcs. Strategic Mktg. and Advt., Inc., San Diego, 1991—; cons. U.S. Olympic Tng. Ctr., San Diego, 1991, Planning Forum, San Diego, 1992, Annabooks, 1994-96, Gen. Instrument, 1995-96, Qualcomm Eudora Divsn., 1996, Autosplice, 1996, Pulse Engring., 1996; instr. U. San Diego, U. San Francisco, Calif. State U.-Long Beach, U. Calif.-San Diego. Contbr. articles to profl. jours. and mags. Mem. Am. Mktg. Assn. (pres. 1994-95), Bank Mktg. Assn. (v.p. membership, bd. dirs.), San Diego Direct Mktg. Assn. (pres. 1995-96), Direct Mktg. Club of So. Calif., Computer Electronics Mktg. Assn. Office: Strategic Mktg and Advt Inc 11758 Caminito Missiones San Diego CA 92128

MARCHI, JON, cattle rancher, exporter, former investment brokerage executive; b. Ann Arbor, Mich., Aug. 6, 1946; s. John Robert and Joan Trimble (Toole) M.; m. Mary Stewart Sale, Aug. 12, 1972; children: Aphia Jessica, Jon Jacob. Student Claremont Men's Coll., 1964-65; BS, U. Mont., 1968, MS, 1972. Sec., treas. Marchi, Marchi & Marchi, Inc., Morris, Ill., 1968-69; account exec. D. A. Davidson & Co., Billings, Mont., 1972-75, asst. v.p., office mgr., 1976-77, v.p. mktg. and adminstrn., Great Falls, Mont., 1977—; sec., dir., v.p. fin. svcs. and exec. devel., D. A. Davidson Realty Corp., Great Falls, 1978-85, chmn. rsch. com., 1980; cattle rancher, Polson, Mont., 1985—; bd. dirs. Big Sky Airlines, Billings, Mont., chmn. bd. dirs., 1995; bd. dirs. Energy Overthrust Found., Mansfield Found., Mont. Beverages, Mont. Venture Capital Network, Direct Advantage, Inc., Hamilton, Mont., Mont. Naturals Internat., Inc., Eclipse Techs., Inc., Mont. Small Bus. Investment Corp.; chmn., dir. Devel. Corp. Mont., Helena, 1995. Chmn. Mont. Gov.'s Subcom. for Venture Capital Devel., Mont. Cmty. Fin. Corp., Helena; chmn. investment com., State of Mont. Sci. and Tech. Alliance, 1985—; chmn. seed capital com. State of Mont., bd. dirs. job svc. com. Mem. Mont. Peoples Action; sec.-treas. Valley View Assn., 1987—; trustee sch. dist. # 35, Polson, Mont., 1990—, chmn., 1991—; bd. dirs. Mont. Entrepreneurship Ctr., Missoula, Mont., 1990—; pres., dir., sec./treas. Mont. Pvt. Capital Network, Bozeman, Mont., 1990—, pres., 1992—; chmn., dir. Mont. Naturals Internat., Inc., 1991; dir. Mont. State Rural Devel. Coun., 1992, Mont. SBA Adv. Coun., 1992; dir. Ctr. Econ. Renewal and Tech. Transfer Mont. State U., Bozeman, 1994—; del. to White House Conf. on Small Bus., Washington, 1994-95; chmn. Glacier Venture Fund, Helena, Mont., 1996—. With U.S. Army, 1969-71. Mem. Nat. Cattlemen's Assn. (fgn. trade com.), Am. Wagyu Assn., Can. Wagyu Assn., Polson C. of C. (bd. dirs.), Valley View Assn. (bd. dirs.), Mont. Cattle Feeders Assn., Montana Angus Assn., Am. Angus Assn., Western Mont. Stockgrowers Assn., Securities Industry Assn., Mont. Stock Growers Assn., Mont. Ambassadors (dir. 1995), Polson C. of C. (dir.), Leadership Great Falls Club, Ski Club, Mont. Club, Helena Wilderness Riders Club, Rotary. Episcopalian. Home: 7783 Valley View Rd Polson MT 59860-9302 Office: Marchi Angus Ranches 7783 Valley View Rd Polson MT 59860-9302

MARCINKO, RANDALL WAYNE, information industry executive, organic chemist; b. Edmonton, Alta., Can., Feb. 21, 1956; s. James Wilfred and Jeanne Theresa (Meunier) M. BSc, U. Alta., 1978; postgrad., Stanford U. Lab. rschr. U. Alta., Edmonton, 1977-78; pres., owenr Dynamic Info. Corp., Burlingame, Calif., 1978-94; v.p. EBSCOdoc, Burlingame, 1994-96; pres., owner Info. Can., Edmonton, 1988—; dir. Culinarius, San Francisco, 1996—; bd. dirs. SEEK Info. Svcs., Glendale, Calif., Documentation Abstracts Inc. Contbr. articles to profl. jours. Mem. Assn. Info. Dissemination Ctrs. (pres. 1982—), European Assn. Info. Svcs., So. Calif. Online Users Group, Spl. Librs. Assn., Am. Soc. Info. Sci. Home: 785 Golden Gate # 403 San Francisco CA 94102 Office: Marcinko Enterprises Inc 785 Golden Gate # 403 San Francisco CA 94102

MARCKWARDT, HAROLD THOMAS, association executive; b. Chgo., May 4, 1920; s. Herman and Carrie (Polachek) M.; AB, U. So. Calif., 1949, AM, 1953; MS, U. Calif., 1970, postgrad., 1970—; m. Patricia Ann Hoffman, Apr. 7, 1945; children: Craig, Diana, Brad, Glenn. Tool and machinery designer Douglas Aircraft, Santa Monica, Cal., 1939-43; playground leader County L.A., 1946-47; cmty. program dir. Hollywood (Calif.) YMCA, 1947-51, dir. cmty. program and bldg., 1952-55; exec. dir. Westchester YMCA, L.A., 1955-63; area dir. Nat. Coun. YMCA, 1963-66, pres. Western Center Assocs., L.A., 1966-89; internat. mgmt. cons., Indonesia, 1985-91, Sri Lanka, 1989; field assoc. Internat. Exec. Service Corps, 1987—. Exec. dir. Calif. Youth and Govt. Statewide Com., 1965, del. seminar UN, 1959. Colliver lectr. U. Pacific, 1965. Trainer, Leadership Devel. Camp, L.A., 1959; mem. Mayor's Steering Com., 1973-75, chmn. Mayor's Facilitators com. Conf. Children, Youth and Sr. Citizens, 1974; mem. employment and tng. subcom. L.A. County Task Force, 1977; mem. Task Force on Equity for Women in Employment, 1976-77. Served to 1st lt., USAAF, 1943-46, USAF (SAC), 1950-52. Recipient One of Hollywood's Top Ten Young Men award, 1954. Mem. Am. Soc. Tool Engrs. (charter mem.), Pacific S.W. Area YMCA Assn. Profl. Dirs. (pres. 1963-66), Orgn. Devel. Network, Airplane Owner's and Pilots Assn., Am. Soc. Tng. and Devel. (v.p. 1979, pres. 1980), Internat. Fedn. Tng. and Devel. Orgns., Pacific Asia Travel Assn. (exec. bd. 1994—), Indonesian Bus. Soc., Am. Soc. Travel Agts., Indonesian Trade Mission, World Span-One Club (pres. 1993-94, v.p. 1991-93). Democrat. Author: The Leader Makes The Difference, 1968; Leading Discussion Groups, 1972; How to Make Executive Decisions About Training, 1976; 16 Steps to the Job You Want, 1979; The Quality Circles Kit, 1982. Home: 4216 Colbath Ave Sherman Oaks CA 91423-4210 Office: 4716 Woodman Ave Sherman Oaks CA 91423-2498

MARCUS, AARON, graphic artist; b. Omaha, May 22, 1943; s. Nathan and Libbie (Burstein) M.; m. Susan Wightman Douglas, Sept. 9, 1968; children: Joshua, Elisheva; m. Leslie Becker, Dec. 15, 1985. BA, Princeton U., 1965; BFA, MFA, Yale U., 1968. Asst. prof. Princeton (N.J.) U., 1969-76; lectr. Hebrew, Jerusalem and Bezalel Acad., 1976-77; research fellow East-West Ctr., Honolulu, 1978; lectr. U. Calif., Berkeley, 1979-80; staff scientist Lawrence Berkeley Lab., 1980-82; pres. Aaron Marcus and Assocs., Inc., Berkeley, 1983—. Author: (monograph) Soft Where, Inc., Volume 1, 1976, Volume 2, 1981; co-author: (with Greenberg et al) The Computer Image, 1982, (with Ronald Baecker) Human Factors and Typography for More Readable Computer Programs, 1990, (with Smilonich and Thompson) The Cross-GUI Handbook for Multiplatform User Interface Design, 1995; author: Graphic Design for Electronic Documents and User Interfaces, 1992. Recipient Design awards Soc. Typographic Arts, Art Dirs. Club of N.Y., Soc. Publ. Designers, 1974-76, Industry Achievement award Nat. Computer Graphics Assn., 1992. Mem. Human Factors and Ergonomics Soc., Spl. Interest Group on Computer Graphics and Interactive Techniques of Assn. Computing Machinery, Spl. Interest Group on Computer and Human Interaction of Assn. Computing Machinery, Soc. Tech. Communicators, IEEE. Democrat. Jewish. Office: Aaron Marcus and Assocs Inc 1144 65th St Ste F Emeryville CA 94608-1053

MARCUS, DONALD MORTON, psychoanalyst; b. Bklyn., Aug. 29, 1924; s. Phineas and Claire (Ingleson) M.; m. Sylvia Roslyn Kinberg, May 22, 1949; children: Andrea Gayle, Donna Joy, Leslie Rochelle. BS, Ind. U., 1945, MD, 1948; PhD, So. Calif. Psychoanalytic Inst, 1962. Diplomate in psychiatry Am. Bd. Psychiatry and Neurology. Cons. L.A. (Calif.) County Probation Dept., 1955-59; assoc. clin. prof. psychiatry U. So. Calif., L.A. (Calif.) County Med. Ctr., 1959-82; faculty So. Calif. Psychoanalytic Inst., Beverly Hills, 1962-85; cons. VA Hosp., Sepulveda, Calif., 1970-73; tng. and supervising analyst Psychoanalytic Ctr. of Calif., L.A., 1985—; pvt. practice psychiatry and psychoanalysis Beverly Hills, 1955—. Contbr. articles to profl. jours. Lt. USNR, 1943-52. Mem. Alpha Omega Alpha, Sigma Xi. Office: 9735 Wilshire Blvd Ste 445 Beverly Hills CA 90212-2103

MARCUS, HUBERT C., ophthalmologist; b. San Francisco, Mar. 27, 1931; s. Herman and Rose B. (Steinberg) M.; m. Diane F. Libby, Apr. 12, 1959; children: Deborah L., David S., Anne L. BA, U. Calif., Berkeley, 1952; MD, U. Calif., San Francisco, 1955. Diplomate Am. Bd. Ophthalmology. Resident in ophthalmology U. Calif. Sch. Medicine, San Francisco, 1958-61; pvt. practice Peninsula Eye Physicians Med. Group, Inc., San Mateo, Calif., 1961—; assoc. clin. prof. ophthalmology U. Calif., San Francisco, 1961—. Capt. U.S. Army, 1956-58. Mem. Frederick C. Cordes Eye Soc. (pres. 1993-94). Home: 801 Parrott Dr San Mateo CA 94402-3225 Office: Peninsula Eye Physicians 101 S San Mateo Dr San Mateo CA 94401-3819

MARCUS, JANET, city council; married; 3 children. MEd in Counseling and Guidance, U. Ariz.; MA, Radcliffe U.; BA in English, Wellesley Coll. Nat. bd. mem. Common Cause, 1976-79; pres. Planned Parenthood of Southern Ariz., 1985-87; mem. Energy & Environ. Policy Com. Nat. League Cities, 1989—; city coun., 1987-91, 1991—. Office: 7575 E Speedway Tucson AZ 85710

MARCUS, JEFFREY HOWARD, electronic security system company executive; b. Albany, N.Y., June 4, 1950; s. Paul and Phyllis (Zippert) M.; m. Carol Ellen Marcus, Aug. 28, 1994. BS in Elec. Engring. and Computer Sci., U. Colo., Denver, 1977; MBA, U. Phoenix, Denver, 1985. Specialist counter intelligence U.S. Army, Washington, 1971-73; v.p. engring. Securus, Inc. (formerly Photo-Scan of Colo.), Denver, 1977-81, pres., 1981—; also bd. dirs. Securus (formerly Photo-Scan of Colo.), Denver; bd. dirs. PSA Fin. Svcs., Inc., Westminster; chmn. bd., tech. com. PSA Security NEtwork, Westminster. Democrat. Office: Securus Inc 12411 E 37th Ave Denver CO 80239-3404

MARCUS, KAREN MELISSA, foreign language educator; b. Vancouver, B.C., Can., Feb. 28, 1956; came to the U.S., 1962; d. Marvin Marcus and Arlen Ingrid (Sahlman) Bishop; m. Jorge Esteban Mezei, Jan. 7, 1984 (div. Mar. 1987). BA in French, BA in Polit. Sci., U. Calif., Santa Barbara, 1978, MA in Polit. Sci., 1981; MA in French, Stanford U., 1984, PhD in French, 1990. Lectr. in French Stanford (Calif.) U., 1989-90; asst. prof. French No. Ariz. U., Flagstaff, 1990-96, assoc. prof. French, 1996—; cons. Houghton Mifflin, 1993, Grand Canyon (Ariz.) Natural History Soc., 1994. Vol., letter writer Amnesty Internat. Urgent Action Network, 1991-95; vol. No. Ariz. Aids Outreach Orgn., Flagstaff, 1994-95. Recipient medal for outstanding achievement in French, Alliance Francaise, Santa Barbara, 1978; named Scholarship Exch. Student, U. Geneva, Switzerland, 1979-80; doctoral fellow Stanford (Calif.) U., 1981-85. Mem. MLA, Am. Assn. Tchrs. French, Am. Coun. on the Tchg. Fgn. Langs., Am. Literary Translators Assn., Women in French, Coordination Internat. des Chercheurs Sur Les Litteratures Maghrebines, Phi Beta Kappa, Pi Delta Phi, Alpha Lambda Delta. Democrat. Jewish. Office: No Ariz Univ Modern Lang Dept Box 6004 Flagstaff AZ 86011

MARCUS, RUDOLPH ARTHUR, chemist, educator; b. Montreal, Que., Can., July 21, 1923; came to U.S., 1949, naturalized, 1958; s. Myer and Esther (Cohen) M.; m. Laura Hearne, Aug. 27, 1949; children: Alan Rudolph, Kenneth Hearne, Raymond Arthur. BS in Chemistry, McGill U., 1943, PhD in Chemistry, 1946, DSc (hon.), 1988; DSc (hon.), U. Chgo., 1983, Poly. U., 1986, U. Göteborg, Sweden, 1987, U. N.B., Can., 1993, Queens U., Can., 1993, U. Oxford, Eng., 1995, Yokohama Nat. U., 1996, U. N.C., 1996, U. Ill., 1997. Rsch. staff mem. RDX Project, Montreal, 1944-46; postdoctoral rsch. assoc. NRC of Can., Ottawa, Ont., 1946-49, U. N.C., 1949-51; asst. prof. Poly. Inst. Bklyn., 1951-54, assoc. prof., 1954-58, prof., 1958-64; prof. U. Ill., Urbana, 1964-78; Arthur Amos Noyes prof. chemistry Calif. Inst. Tech., Pasadena, 1978—; vis. prof. theoretical chemistry U. Oxford, 1975-76; Baker lectr. Cornell U., Ithaca, N.Y., 1991; Linnett vis. prof. chemistry Cambridge (Eng.) U., 1996; hon. prof. Fudan U., Shanghai, 1994—; hon prof. Inst. Chemistry Chinese Acad. Scis., Beijing, 1995—; professorial fellow Univ. Coll., Oxford, hon. fellow, 1995—; mem. Courant Inst. Math. Scis., NYU, 1960-61; trustee Gordon Rsch. Confs., 1966-69, chmn. bd. dirs., 1968-69, mem. coun., 1965-68; mem. rev. panel Argonne Nat. Lab., 1966-72, chmn., 1967-68; mem. rev. panel Brookhaven Nat. Lab., 1971-74; mem. rev. com. Radiation Lab., U. Notre Dame, 1975-80; mem. panel on atmospheric chemistry climatic impact com. NAS-NRC, 1975-78, mem. com. kinetics of chem. reactions, 1973-77, chmn., 1975-77, mem. com. chem. scis., 1977-79, mem. com. to survey opportunities in chem. scis., 1982-86; mem. math. panel Internat. Benchmarking of U.S. Rsch. Fields, 1996—; adv. com. for chemistry NSF, 1977-80, external adv. bd. NSF ctr. Photoinduced Charge Transfer, 1990—, mem. presdl. chairs com., Chile, 1994-96; advisor Ctr. for Molecular Scis., Chinese Acad. Scis. and State Key Lab. for Structural Chemistry of Unstable and Stable Species, Beijing, 1995—. Former mem. editl. bd. Jour. Chem. Physics, Ann. Rev. Phys. Chemistry, Jour. Phys. Chemistry, Accounts Chem. Rsch., Internat. Jour. Chem. Kinetics Molecular Physics, Theoretica Chimica Acta, Chem. Physics Letters, Faraday Trans., Jour. Chem. Soc.; mem. editl. bd. Laser Chemistry, 1982—, Advances in Chem. Physics, 1984—, World Sci. Pub., 1987—, Internat. Revs. in Phys. Chemistry, 1988—, Progress in Physics, Chemistry and Mechanics (China), 1989—, Perkins Transactions 2, Jour. Chem. Soc., 1992—, Chem. Physics Rsch. (India), 1992—, Trends in Chem. Physics Rsch. (India), 1992—; hon. editor Internat. Jour. Quantum Chemistry, 1996—. Treas. L.A. Cen. City Assn., 1995. Alfred P. Sloan fellow, 1960-61, sr. postdoctoral fellow NSF, 1960-61; sr. Fulbright-Hays scholar, 1972; recipient Sr. U.S. Scientist award Alexander von Humboldt-Stiftung, 1976, Electrochem. Soc. Lecture award Electrochem. Soc., 1979, 96, Robinson medal Faraday divsn. Royal Soc. Chemistry, 1982, Centenary medal Faraday divsn., 1988, Chandler medal, Columbia U., 1983, Wolf prize in Chemistry, 1985, Nat. Medal of Sci., 1989, Evans award Ohio State U., 1990, Nobel prize in Chemistry, 1992, Hirshfelder prize in Theoretical Chemistry, U. Wis., 1993, Golden Plate award Am. Acad. Achievement, 1993, Lavoisier medal French Chem. Soc., 1994; named Hon. Citizen, City of Winnipeg, 1994, Treasure of L.A., Ctrl. City Assn., 1995. Fellow AAAS, Am. Acad. Arts and Scis. (hon., exec. com. western sect., co-chmn. 1981-84, rsch. and planning com. 1989-91), Am. Phys. Soc., Internat. Soc. Electrochemistry (hon.), Royal Soc. Chemistry (hon.), Royal Soc. London (hon.), Internat. Acad. Quantum Molecular Sci. (hon.), Royal Soc. Can. (hon.); mem. NAS (hon.), Am. Philos. Soc. (hon.), Korean Chem. Soc. (hon.), Am. Chem. Soc. (past divsn. chmn., mem. exec. com., mem. adv. bd. petroleum rsch. fund, Irving Langmuir award in chem. physics 1978, Pter Debye award in phys. chemistry 1988, Willard Gibbs medal Chgo. sect. 1988, S.C. Lind Lecture, East Tenn. sect. 1988, Theodore William Richards medal Northwestern sect. 1990, Edgar Fahs Smith award Phila. sect. 1991, Ira Remsen Meml. award Md. sect. 1991, Pauling medal Portland, Oreg., and Puget Sound sect. 1991, Auburn-Kosolapoff award 1996, Theoretical Chemistry award 1997), Internat. Acad. Quantum Molecular Sci. (hon.), Korean Chem. Soc. (hon.). Home: 331 S Hill Ave Pasadena CA 91106-3405

MARCUS, STEPHEN HOWARD, lawyer; b. N.Y.C., June 30, 1945; s. Jacob and Mildren (Cohen) M.; m. Carol Sylvia Beatrice, June 11, 1967; children: Joshua David, Rebecca Lynn, Daniel Benjamin. BME, MIT, 1967; JD, Harvard U., 1970. Bar: Calif. 1971, U.S. Dist. Ct. (cen. dist.) Calif. 1971, U.S. Dist. Ct. (so. dist.) Calif. 1974, U.S. Dist. Ct. (so. dist.) Calif. 1975, U.S. Ct. Appeals (9th cir.) 1980. Assoc. Mitchell, Silberberg & Knupp, L.A., 1971-72, Greenberg, Bernhard, Weis & Karma, L.A., 1972-76; ptnr. Greenberg, Bernhard, Weiss & Rosin, L.A., 1976-85; assoc. Frandzel & Share, L.A., 1985-87, ptnr., 1987—; judge pro tem L.A. Mcpl. Ct., 1976-83. Editor Harvard Law Rev., 1970. Mem. Los Angeles County Bar Assn. (client rels. com. arbitrator 1982—, vice chair, 1996—), Century City Bar Assn. (bd. govs. 1984-90), MIT Club So. Calif. (pres. 1978-79, bd. govs. 1979—), Sigma Xi, Tau Beta Pi. Democrat. Jewish. Office: Frandzel & Share 6500 Wilshire Blvd Los Angeles CA 90048-4920

MARDIAN, DANIEL, construction company director; b. Pasadena, Calif., Apr. 10, 1917; s. Samuel and Akabe (Lekerian) M.; m. Katherine Evkhanian, Jan. 30, 1942; children: Daniel Jr., Tom, John, Paul, Scott. Student, Pasadena City Coll., 1937; diploma, U.S. Army Engring. Sch., Ft. Belvoir, Va., 1944, U.S. Army Command and Gen. Staff Coll., 1961. Commd. U.S. Army, 1942, advances through grades to lt. col., 1962, ret., 1970; ptnr. Mardian Constrn. Co., Phoenix, 1945-47, exec. v.p., 1947-66, pres., 1966-78, also bd. dirs.; past chmn., mem. Nat. Joint Apprenticeship/Tng. commn. Oper. Engrs., Washington, 1975-78; mem. adv. bd. constrn. programs Ariz. State U., Tempe, 1957—, mem. adv. bd. Coll. Engring., 1957—; mem. adv. bd. constrn. program No. Ariz. U., Flagstaff; bd. dirs. Citibank, Phoenix, 1962-87. Pres. Am. Coun. Constrn. Edn., Monroe, La., 1991-93; past pres., bd. dirs. Fiesta Bowl, Tempe, 1986-92; gen. campaign chmn. United Way, Phoenix, 1967; pres. Met. Phoenix C. of C., 1967-68. Capt. C.E., U.S. Army, 1942-46, PTO, 1970—. Recipient Hall of Fame award Ariz. State U., 1990, medallion of merit, 1984, Excellence in Constrn. award Am. Subcontractors Assn., 1988, Hall of Fame award Nat. Football Found., 1987, Brotherhood award Ariz. chpt. NCCJ, 1981, Fellow award Am. Inst. Constructors, 1996. Mem. Associated Gen. Contractors Am. (life bd. dirs., chmn. yr. award 1970, mem. workforce devel. com., trustee, chmn. laborers tng. com., 1969—), Sun Angel Found. (chmn. 1989-91), Ariz. Acad., Phoenix Country Club (bd. dirs., pres. 1985-86), Phoenix Kiwanis Club (past dir.). Republican. Mem. United Ch. Christ. Home: 7215 N 3rd St Phoenix AZ 85020-4904 Office: Perini Building Co 360 E Coronado Rd Phoenix AZ 85004-1524

MARDIAN, ROBERT CHARLES, JR., restauranteur; b. Orange, Calif., Feb. 1, 1947; s. Robert Charles Sr. and Dorothy Driscilla (Denniss) M.; m. Jayne Marie Garvin, June 21, 1970 (div. 1977); 1 child, Robert Charles III; m. Kathleen Frances Dixon, Oct. 13, 1984 (div. 1991); children: Alexandra Quinn, Ashley Michele. BA, Stanford U., 1969; MBA, Pepperdine U., 1986. Gen. mgr. Loft Restaurant, San Jose, Calif., 1969-71; chief exec. officer/chmn. bd. Wind & Sea Restaurants, Inc., Dana Point, Calif., 1971—; bd. dirs. Dana Niguel Bank, cons. U.S. Olympic Com., Colorado Springs, 1984-88. Commr. Dana Point Econ. Devel. Mem. Young Pres. Orgn. Republican. Home: 34699 Golden Lantern St Dana Point CA 92629-2908 Office: Wind & Sea Restaurants Inc 34699 Golden Lantern St Dana Point CA 92629-2908

MAREE, WENDY, painter, sculptor; b. Windsor, Eng., Feb. 10, 1938. Student, Windsor & Maidenhead Coll., 1959; studied with Vasco Lazzlo, London, 1959-62. Exhibited in group shows at Windsor Arts Festival, San Bernardino (Calif.) Mus.; one-woman shows include Lake Arrowhead (Calif.) Libr., 1989, Amnesty Internat., Washington, 1990, Phyllis Morris Gallery, Many Horses Gallery, L.A., 1990, Nelson Rockefeller, Palm Springs, Calif., 1992, 94, Stewart Gallery, Rancho Palos Verdes, Calif., Petropavlovsk (Russia) Cultural Mus., Kamchatka, Russia, 1993, Coyle-Coyle Gallery, Blue Jay, Calif., 1995, La Quinta Sculpture Park, Calif., 1995, Avante-Garde Gallery, Palm Springs, 1996, Avante-Garden Gallery, La Jolla, Calif., 1996, Avante Garde Gallery, La Jolla, 1996, Carmichael Gallery, Rancho Mirage, Calif., 1997, others; represented in pvt. collections His Royal Highness Prince Faisal, Saudi Arabia, Gena Rowlands, L.A., John Cassavetes, L.A., Nicky Blairs, L.A., Guilford Glazer, Beverly Hills, Calif., June Allyson, Ojai, Calif., Amnesty Internat., Washington; commd. Ingleside Inn, Palm Springs. Recipient award San Bernardino County Mus., 1988, Gov. Kamchatka of Russia, 1993. Mem. Artist Guild of Lake Arrowhead.

MAREFAT, MICHAEL M., electrical and computer engineering educator; b. Sept. 21, 1963; came to U.S., 1980; s. Abdolhossein and Akram (Mosavat) M.; m. Ai-Nhi Tran, June 23, 1990. BA in Math. Scis., Rice U., 1986, BS in Elec. and Computer Engring., 1986; MSEE, Purdue U., 1988, PhD in EE, 1991. Registered profl. engr., Tex. Computer programmer Baylor Coll. of Medicine, Houston, 1986; rsch. asst. Purdue Engring. Rsch. Ctr. for Intelligent Mfg., 1987-91; rsch. scientist Schlumberger Lab. for Computer Sci., Austin, Tex., 1990; asst. prof. elec. and computer engring. U. Ariz., Tucson, 1992—, dir. intelligent systems lab., 1992—; proposal referee, panel mem. NSF, Arlington, Va., 1992, 1995; mem. exec. com. Ctr. for Advanced Integration Mfg. Scis. and Techs., Tucson, 1993—. Author: (with others) Handbook of Expert Systems Applications in Manufacturing, 1994; contbr. articles to profl. jours. Mem. IEEE, Am. Assn. for Artificial Intelligence, Assn. for Computing Machinery, Tau Beta Pi, Eta Kappa Nu. Office: U Ariz Dept Elec and Computer Engring 1230 E Speedway Blvd Tucson AZ 85719

MAREI, IBRAHIM, medical technologist; b. Marowe, Sudan, Dec. 6, 1939; s. Hassan and Shafika (Mohamed) M. BS in Chemistry, U. Cairo, 1966; MS in Med. Tech., Calif. State U., 1980. Lic. clinical chemist tech., Calif., clinical lab. tech., Calif. Clinical chemist SmithKline-Beecham, Van Nuys, Calif., 1969-71; supr. ctr. critically ill lab. Hollywood Presbyn. Med. Ctr., L.A., 1971-75; sr. toxicologist, clin. chemist spl. chemistry dept., instr. on the job tng. and edn. new students, tech. staff Reference Labs., Newbury Park, Calif., 1975-88; clin. chemist endochronology dept., med. technologist Smith Kline Biosci. Labs., Van Nuys, Calif., 1988—, gen. supr., 1996—. Mem. Am. Soc. Clinical Pathologists (cert.), Am. Chem. Soc., Am. Assn. Clinical Chemists (cert.), Am. Pub. Health Assn. Calif. Assn. for Med. Lab. Tech. Home: 7441 Hazeltine Ave Apt 107 Van Nuys CA 91405-1486 Office: Smith Kline Biosci Labs 7600 Tyrone Ave Van Nuys CA 91405-1449

MARESH, NANCY MAE, educational entrepreneur; b. Iowa City, June 27, 1946; d. Gerald Stanley and Ethel (Nelson) M. Grad. high sch., Denver. Chmn. bd. Ednl. Discoveries, Inc. (formerly Quantum Ednl. Discoveries), 1983—; founder, CEO Creative Learning Internat., Boulder, 1994—. Patentee The Acctg. Game, 1982. Grantee State of Vt., 1978. Home: 3505 23rd St Boulder CO 80304-2508 Office: Creative Learning Internat 3505 23d St Boulder CO 80304-2508

MARGESON, DOUGLAS WILLIAM, reporter; b. Seattle, Aug. 23, 1946; m. Apr. 12, 1969; 2 children. BA in Comms., Editorial Journalism, U. Wash., 1968. Pubs. dir. Seattle Pacific U., 1971-73; speech writer Pacific N.W. Bell, Seattle, 1973-75; reporter, editor Lynnwood (Wash.) Enterprise, 1975-78; reporter, feature writer Fournier Newspapers, Renton, Wash., 1978-82; feature writer, investigative reporter Bellevue (Wash.) Jour. Am., 1982—; lectr. at profl. meetings, ednl. instns., 1983-86. With USMC, 1968-70. Recipient 183 Journalism awards for his work from Nat. Press Women Assn., Suburban Newspapers of Am., Wash. Press Assn., Sigma Delta Chi, N.W. Region Soc. Profl. Journalists, Wash. Newspaper Pubs. Assn. Mem. ACLU, Soc. Profl. Journalists, Wash. Press Assn., N.W. Screenwriters Alliance, Pacific N.W. Writers Conf., Sigma Delta Chi. Home: 18131 NE 191st St Woodinville WA 98072-8239

MARGO, KENNETH CRAIG, counselor; b. Oklahoma City, Apr. 22, 1953; s. Marvin Kenneth and Bobbie June (Cravens) M.; m. Laura Leslie Brooks, June 19, 1980. BA in Psychology, Centenary Coll., Shreveport, La., 1975; MEd in Counseling Psychology, Ctrl. State U., Edmond, Okla., 1978. Lic. profl. counselor, Okla., Wyo. Staff psychologist Okla. Children's Meml. Hosp., Oklahoma City, 1978-82; psychologist, clinic dir. Lincoln County Guidance Ctr., Chandler, Okla., 1982-84; pvt. practice Oklahoma City, 1984-86, 89-90; staff psychologist Mental Health Svcs. So. Okla., Ardmore, 1986-88; therapist, staff devel. coord. St. Joseph's Childrens Home, Oklahoma City, 1988-89; supr. outpatient substance abuse program Ctrl. Wyo. Counseling Ctr., Casper, 1990—; exec. dir. Sublette Cmty. Counseling Svcs., Pinedale, Wyo., 1990—. Mem. Okla. Youth and Suicide Task Force,

Oklahoma City, Health Planning Commn., Chandler. Mem. ACA, Am. Mental Health Counselors Assn., Wyo. Mental Health Counselors Assn., Wyo. Counseling Assn., Okla. Assn. Counseling & Devel. (pres. 1989). Office: Sublette Cmty Counseling Svcs PO Box 856 41 1/2 S Franklin Pinedale WY 82941

MARGOLIS, BERNARD ALLEN, library administrator; b. Greenwich, Conn., Oct. 2, 1948; s. Sidney S. and Rose (Birkenfeld) M.; m. Amanda Batey, Nov. 2, 1973. BA in Polit. Sci., U. Denver, 1970, MLS, 1973. Cert. libr., Mich. Libr. asst. Denver Pub. Libr., 1970-72; br. head Virginia Village Libr., Denver Pub. Libr., 1972-73; dep. dir. Monroe County Libr. Sys., Mich., 1973-75; dir. Raisin Valley Libr. Sys., Monroe, 1976-78, S.E. Mich. Regional Film Libr., Monroe, 1976-88, Monroe County Libr. Sys., 1976-88, Pikes Peak Libr. Dist., Colorado Springs, Colo., 1988-97; pres. Colo. Ctr. for Books, 1989-92, Colo. Ctr. for the Book, 1993-97; pres. Boston Pub. Libr., 1997—; cons. in libr. pub. rels., 1976—; founding trustee United Colo. Investment Trust, 1993-95; chmn. Colo. Gov.'s Conf. on Libr. and Info. Svcs., 1990; lectr. Western Mich. U., Kalamazoo, 1978-81; appraiser rare books, Monroe, Colorado Springs, 1970—. Contbr. articles to profl. jours; mem. editl. bd. Bottom Line Mag. Fin. Mgmt. for Librs., 1986—. Bd. dirs. Monroe Sen. Citizens Ctr., 1976-80, Monroe Fine Arts Coun., 1978-81, Am. the Beautiful Centennial Celebration, Inc., 1993, The Libr. Consortium, 1993-97, Downtown Colo. Springs, Inc., 1994-97, Care & Share, Inc., sec., 1994—, vice chmn., 1995, chmn., 1995-97; chmn. Blue Cross-Blue Shield Consumer Coun., Detroit, 1984-88; mem. adv. bd. Access Colo. Libr. and Info. Network (ACLIN), 1991—, Mercy Meml. Hosp., Monroe, 1984-86, 5th Congl. Art Competition Com., 1992-97; Dem. candidate for Mich. Senate, 1986; mem. allocations com. Pikes Peak United Way, 1988-91, chmn., 1990-91, bd. dirs., 1990-91, 94—; chmn. Great Pikes Peak Cowboy Poetry Gathering, 1990, 91, 92, 94, 95, 96; del. White House Conf. on Libr. and Info. Scis.; mem. El Paso County, Colo. Retirement Bd., 1995—, sec. 1996-97. Recipient Mayoral Cert. Commendation award Denver, 1972, 73; named Mich. Libr. of Yr., 1985, Colo. Libr. of Yr., 1990; commendation John F. Kennedy Ctr. for Performing Arts, 1993, Frank Waters award Pikes Peak Writer's Conf., 1996; Mem. ALA (governing coun. 1986—, endowment trustee 1989-93, sr. endowment trustee 1993—, chmn. resolutions com. 1991-92, cons. ann. swap and shop 1979-84, John Cotton Dana award 1977, 91, Libr. Awareness Idea Search award Washington 1982), Colo. Libr. Assn. (mem. legis. com., Intellectual Freedom award 1993), Libr. Adminstrv. Mgmt. Assn., Pub. Libr. Assn. Democrat. Jewish. Home: 99 Grayfield Ave Boston MA 02132 Office: Boston Pub Libr Copley Sq Boston MA 02116

MARGULEAS, HOWARD P., agricultural products executive; b. 1934. U. Calif., Berkeley, 1957. With Heggblade-Marguleas-Tenneco, Bakersfield, Calif., 1957-74, Sun World, Inc., Bakersfield, Calif., 1974—; with Sun World Internat. Corp., 1980—, chmn. bd., CEO; now mng. account-owner Ag Accounting LLC, Incline Village, Nev. Office: Ag Accounting LLC PO Box 7800 Incline Village NV 89452*

MARGULIES, LEE, newspaper editor. Television editor Los Angeles Times, Calif. Office: Los Angeles Times Times Mirror Sq Los Angeles CA 90053

MARIANI, MARK A., food products executive; b. 1952. With Mariani Packaging Co., Inc., 1973—, now pres. Office: Mariani Packing Co Inc 3800 Black Hawk Rd Danville CA 94506-3206*

MARIGOLD, LAWRENCE LEE, international energy consultant; b. Tecachapi, Calif., Oct. 14, 1940; s. George Austin and Pauline M. (Vukich) M.; m. Julie Ann Chohon, Sept. 9, 1978; 1 child, Michelle. AA, Contra Costa Coll., 1961; BS, U. San Francisco, 1964; MBA, Golden Gate U., 1967. Mgr. Chevron, San Francisco, 1965-70; group mgr. Unical, Palatine, Ill., 1970-74; dir., corp. rep. Anheuer Busch Inc., St. Louis, 1974-84; pres., CEO Marigold Ventures, Fair Oaks, Calif., 1984-93, 94-95; dir. methanol mktg. MG Refining & Mktg., Forest Hill, Md., 1993-94; cons. to Internat. Metallgeshellschaft, Frankfort, Germany, 1984—, ICI, State of Calif., others; prof. Golden Gate U., 1996—. Contbr. articles to profl. jours. Spkr. various civic and polit. groups, Calif., 1984—. Roman Catholic. Home and Office: Marigold Ventures 4925 Saint Thomas Dr Fair Oaks CA 95628-5312

MARINACCI, TERESA DENISE, theater director; b. Exeter, Calif., Jan. 31, 1964; d. Elmer Dean Longest and Billie Rae (Hunter) Butler; m. Christopher Marinacci, July 20, 1985. BA in Psychology/BA in Theater Arts with honors, U. Calif., Santa Cruz, 1989; MFA, U. Calif., Davis, 1992. Br. sales mgr. Thrifty Bus. Systems, 1983-85; pvt. instr. in Drama various cities, Calif., 1982—; dir., playwright various theaters, various cities, Calif., 1984—; instr. U. Calif., Davis, 1989-91; artistic dir. King's Ct. Players, San Francisco, 1992-94, 94-96; artistic dir., pres. bd. TheatreMakers, San Francisco, 1993—; creator, adminstr. arts and culture re-grant program Solano County Arts Coun., 1994—; quality assurance engr., computer graphic artist, designer Cosmi Corp., 1994—; bd. dirs., pres., membership chair Solano County Arts Coun., Fairfield, Calif.; credentials analyst NCOE, 1996-97. Asst. dir. (play) Redwood Trilogy, 1991, The Queen's Garden, 1992-93 (4 Dramalogue awards), on tour, 1994—, Dell Arte Player's Slapstick, 1994; collaborator Brenda Wong Aoki's Random Acts of Kindness, 1994-96; playwright, dir.: Legend of the 5th World, 1992, Tellin' Tall Tales, 1993; playwright, dir., producer: Starving Actors Perform-A Showcase of Music, Dance, Sorrow & Laughter, 1993; dir. co-author (K. Carner's) Wisdom While on my Back (Part I-Fiat Lux), 1994-95; author for the Oakland Lyric Opera, dir. Love, Romance & Passion, 1995-96, Romantic Notions, 1996., mixed media artwork maj. pieces Goddess of the Night, Goddess of the Night II, 1996, Motherhood Eternal, 1996; editor-in-chief Expressions, NCOE Newsladder, Interagy Link, Esprit du Soleil. Mem. We the People, 1992. Mem. NAFE, AAUW, Nat. Mus. Women in Arts, Theatre Bay Area, Theatre Comm. Group, Oreg. Shakespeare Festival, Solano County Arts Coun., Alumni Assn. U. Calif. Santa Cruz, Calif. Aggie Alumni Assn. Office: TheatreMakers PO Box 421708 San Francisco CA 94142-1708

MARINELLY, RALPH, retired secondary education educator; b. Akron, Ohio, Dec. 28, 1931; s. Ralph and Ruth (Biggie) M.; m. Lori Stanaley, Oct. 13, 1935; children: Michael, Mark, Steven, Jennifer. BA, Calif. State U., 1954, MA, 1960; postgrad., U. Calif., Berkeley, 1960-63. Cert. tchr., adminstr., Calif. Tchr., counselor Oakland (Calif.) Pub. Schs., 1956-64, dir. student activities, adminstrv. asst.; tchr., coord. instrnl. improvement program San Mateo Union H.S. Sch. Dist., 1964—; prin. Am. program U. Stranieri, Perugia, Italy, 1965; coord. gifted program Crestmoor H.S., faculty pres., 1972, 73, mem. faculty senate, 1976, legis. rep., 1974, 75; dept. head social sci. Burlingame H.S., San Mateo H.S. Commr., chmn. Piedmont (Calif.) Park Commn., 1984-90, vice chmn. recycling com., 1991—; pres. Piedmont High Sch. Dad's Club, 1977-79; dir. Piedmont Hist. Soc., 1992—. Recipient Commendation Piedmont City Coun., 1989. Mem. Calif. Tchrs. Assn. (legis. rep. 1956—), NEA. Republican. Roman Catholic. Home: 312 Jerome Ave Piedmont CA 94610-1024

MARINER, WILLIAM MARTIN, chiropractor; b. Balt., Jan. 2, 1949; s. William Joseph and Ellen (Dexter) M. AA, Phoenix Coll., 1976; BS in Biology, L.A. Coll. of Chiropractic, 1980, D Chiropractic summa cum laude, 1980; DD (hon.), Universal Life Ch., Modesto, Calif., 1986. Health food restaurant mgr. Golden Temple of Conscious Cookery, Tempe, Ariz., 1974-75; health food store mgr. Guru's Grainery, Phoenix, 1975; physical therapist A.R.E. Clinic, Phoenix, 1975-76; research dir., founder G.R.D. Healing Arts Ctr., Phoenix, 1974-77; aminstrv. asst., acad. dean L.A. Coll. Chiropractic, Whittier, Calif., 1977-80; faculty Calif. Acupuncture Coll., L.A., 1978-80; ednl. cons. Avanti Inst., San Francisco, 1985-91; found, dir., head clinician Pacific Healing Arts Ctr., Del Mar, Calif., 1980-93, Mt. Shasta, Calif., 1993—; ednl. cons. John Panama Cons., San Francisco, 1991—. Patentee in field. Co-dir. "We Care We Share" Charitable Orgn., San Diego, 1985-86. Named Outstanding Sr., L.A. Coll. Chiropractic, 1980. Mem. Calif. Chiropractic Assn., Am. Chiropractic Assn., Internat. Coll. Applied Kinesiology, Holistic Dental Assn., Brit. Homopathic Assn. Office: Pacific Healing Arts Ctr PO Box 192 Mount Shasta CA 96067-0192

MARINO, MIKE, newspaper editor. Editor Standard-Examiner, Ogden, Utah. Office: Standard-Examiner 455 23d St Ogden UT 84401

MARIO, ERNEST, pharmaceutical company executive; b. Clifton, N.J., June 12, 1938; s. Jerry and Edith (Meijer) M.; m. Mildred Martha Daume, Dec. 10, 1961; children: Christopher Bradley, Gregory Gerald, Jeremy Konrad. B.S. in Pharmacy, Rutgers U., 1961; M.S. in Phys. Scis., U. RI., 1963, Ph.D. in Phys. Scis., 1965. Registered pharmacist, R.I., N.Y. Vice pres. mfg. Smith Kline Corp., Phila., 1975-77; v.p. mfg. ops. U.S. Pharm. Co. (divsn. E. R. Squibb), New Brunswick, N.J., 1977-79; v.p., gen. mgr. chem. div. E. R. Squibb, Princeton, N.J., 1979-81; pres. chem. and engring. div., sr. v.p. Squibb Corp., Princeton, 1981-84; v.p. Squibb Corp., 1984-86; pres., COO Glaxo Inc., 1986-88, chmn., CEO, 1988, chmn., 1989-91; CEO Glaxo Holdings plc, 1989-93, dep. chmn., 1991-93; co-chmn., CEO, Alza Corp., Palo Alto, Calif., 1993—; grad. asst., instr. U. R.I., Kingston, 1961-66; research fellow Inst. Neurol. Diseases, Bethesda, Md., 1963-65. Contbr. articles to profl. jours. Trustee Duke U., Rockefeller U., U. R.I. Found.; mem. pres.'s coun. U. R.I.; chmn. Am. Found. for Pharm. Edn.; bd. dirs. Nat. Found. Infectious Diseases, Antigenics, Pharm. Product Devel., Stanford Health Svcs., Tech. Mus. Innovation; mem. Calif. gov.'s coun. on biotech. Office: Alza Corp 950 Page Mill Rd Palo Alto CA 94304-1012

MARIUCCI, STEVE, coach professional and college football; b. Iron Mountain, Mich., Nov. 4, 1955; m. Gayle Mariucci; 4 children. Football coach No. Mich. U., 1978-79, Calif. State U., Fullerton, 1980-82; asst. head coach U. Louisville, 1983-84; receivers coach Orlando Renegades U.S. Football League, 1985; quality control coach L.A. Rams, 1985; receivers/spl. teams coach U. So. Calif., L.A., 1986, wide receivers/spl. teams coach, 1987-89, quarterbacks coach, offensive coord., 1990-91; quarterbacks coach Green Bay (Wis.) Packers, 1992-95; head coach Golden Bears U. Calif., 1996—; head coach San Francisco 49ers, 1996—. Office: San Francisco 49ers 4949 Centennial Blvd Santa Clara CA 95054-1225

MARK, ARTHUR, information systems specialist; b. San Francisco, Aug. 1, 1948; s. Bo You and Chew Lin (Oyoung) M.; m. Alice Look, Sept. 1, 1973 (div. Oct. 1987); children: Jennifer, Brandon. BS, Calif. State U., 1971, MS, 1977. Cert. data processing, info. systems auditor, internal auditor. Instr. info. systems Calif. State U., Sacramento, 1978—, Am. River Coll., Sacramento City Coll.; with State of Calif., Sacramento, 1977-85, 88—. Active United Way. Maj. USMC, 1985-88. Mem. MENSA, Inst. Internal Auditors. Republican. Home: 8985 Laguna Place Way Elk Grove CA 95758-5366

MARK, MAXINE CATHERINE SCHLIEKER, writer; b. Lisco, Nebr., Dec. 13, 1932; d. Arnold H. and Irene M. (Kummer) Schlieker; m. Thomas R. Mark, July 9, 1953; children: Gregory A., Brian M. BA, Colo. State U., 1954, MA, 1966. Math. and English tchr. Berea (Ohio) Sch. Dist., 1956-57; part-time English prof. Colo. State U., Ft. Collins, 1957-69, 91-92; honors tchr. Blevins Jr. H.S., Ft. Collins, 1969-79; AP coord., tchr. Rocky Mountain H.S., Ft. Collins, 1979-90; tchr. U. Budapest, Hungary, 1990-91, 96; writer, editor MM Writer/Communications, Ft. Collins, 1991—; ednl. test reader Ednl. Testing Svc., Princeton, N.J., 1985-96; conductor advanced placement seminars Colo. State U., Ft. Collins, summers 1988—; vis. prof. U. Budapest, 1996. Devel. and copy editor: Colorado and Budapest, Hungary. Newsletter editor Phi Delta Kappa, Ft. Collins, 1991-92; active Alzheimers Assn., Ft. Collins, 1994. Mem. MLA. Home and Office: MM/Writer Communications 1309 Parkwood Dr Fort Collins CO 80525

MARK, RUFUS JAMES, physician, educator; b. Castro Valley, Calif., Dec. 28, 1957; s. Hans Michael and Marion Genevieve (Thorpe) M.; m. Katherine Ann Johnson, Jan. 30, 1988; children: Phillip, Nicholas, Juliette. BS summa cum laude, Yale U., 1981; MD, UCLA, 1986. Diplomate Am. Bd. Radiology. Intern Presbyn. Hosp., Pacific Med. Ctr., 1986-87; resident in radiation oncology UCLA Med. Ctr., 1987-90, asst. clin. prof., 1990—; asst. clin. prof. U. Calif. San Diego Med. Ctr., 1991—; physician radiation oncology Radiation Med. Group, San Diego, 1991-95, Good Samaritan Hosp., L.A., 1995—; med. dir. dept. radiation oncology Good Samaritan Hosp., L.A. Contbr. more than 30 articles to med. jours. Mem. AMA, Am. Cancer Soc., Am. Soc. Therapeutic Radiation Oncology, Calif. med. Assn., N.Y. Acad. Scis., Phi Beta Kappa. Home: 2405 Abadejo La Verne CA 91750 Office: Good Samaritan Hosp Dept Radiation Oncology 1225 Wilshire Blvd Los Angeles CA 90017-1901

MARKARIAN, ALEXIA MITRUS, artist; b. Binghamton, N.Y.; m. Raymond Markarian. Studied with Robert Beverly Hale, Art Students League, N.Y.C. Artist, 1985—; juror 10th Ann. Congressional Arts Caucus, 41st Dist., 1991, Scott Watson Meml. Salon, Soc. Calif. Assn. Camera Clubs, 1991, North County Artist's Coop., Escondido, Calif., 1993, San Diego Art Inst., 1992, lectr. isomata master class, Idyllwild, Calif., 1992; originator Photopolis 95 Internat. Photo/Art Exhbn., San Diego, 1995. Solo shows include Fla. So. State Coll. Melvin Art Gallery, Lakeland, 1988, U. Mo. Gallery 210, St. Louis, 1988, Witter Gallery, Storm Lake, Iowa, 1988, Mira Costa Coll. James Crumley Gallery, Oceanside, Calif., 1988, Dietrich Jenny Gallery, San Diego, 1989, Cazenovia (N.Y.) Coll. Chapman Cultural Ctr., 1989, Rogue C.C. Wiseman Gallery, Grants Pass, Oreg., 1989, U. No. Colo. Miriani Gallery, Greeley, Colo., 1989, Memphis State U., 1989, Butte Coll. Coyote Gallery, Oroville, Calif., 1990, Oneiros Gallery, San Diego, 1991, Visual Arts Ctr. Alaska, Ancorage, 1991, Wichita Falls Mus. and Art Ctr., 1991, Edmonton Art Gallery, Alta., Can., 1992, Robertson Ctr. Arts and Scis., Binghamton, N.Y., 1992, Washington and Jefferson Coll., Washington, Pa., 1992, Art Gallery Greater Victoria, B.C., Can., 1993, Kelowna (Can.) Mus., 1993, Red Venus Gallery, San Diego, 1994; exhibited in group shows at Orange County Art Assn. Nat., Brea, Calif., 1985, Internat. Soc. for Airbrush Arts, 1985, Pitts. Ctr. for Arts, 1985, Chautauqua Nat. Exhibit of Am. Art, N.Y., 1985, Touring Group Exhibit "Five Women Artists, 1986, Small Works Nat., N.Y., 1986, San Diego Art Inst. Ann. Nat., 1986, San Diego Mus. Art, 1986, Riverside Art Mus., Calif., 1986, Butler Inst. Am. Art, Youngstown, Ohio, 1985, Calif. Watercolor and Drawing Survery, 1986, Butler Inst. Am. Art, Youngstown, Ohio, 1987, San Diego Art Inst., 1987 (Mid Winter award), Fresno Arts Ctr., 1987, Mus. No. B.C., Prince Rupert, Can., 1987. Elvehjem Mus. Art, Madison, Wis., 1987, Minot (N.D.) Art Gallery, 1987, Coll. Ea. Utah, Price, 1987, Mt. Mercy Coll., Cedar Rapids, Iowa, 1987, Masur Mus. Art, Monroe, La., 1988, Fla. Nat./Fla. State U., Tallahassee, 1988, LaGrange (Ga.) Nat. XIII, 1988 (Purchase award), Tex. A&M U., College Station, 1988, John Thomas Gallery, Fullerton, Calif., 1989, Dietrich Jenny Gallery, San Diego, 1989, San Diego Art Inst., 1990 (award), Artists Union Gallery, Moscow, 1990, San Diego Mus. Art, 1991, Calif. Ctr. for Arts, Escondido, 1993, Centro Cultural, X Festival Internacional, Tijuana, Mex., 1994, Mcpl. Art Gallery, L.A., 1995, Galeria Dos Damas, San Diego, 1996, Miracosta Coll., Oceanside, Calif., 1996, Oakland Mus. of Art, Calif., 1997, Facere Jewelry Art Gallery, Seattle, 1997, others; represented in pvt. and public collections. Recipient Visual Arts fellowship Calif. Arts Coun., 1989-90, Pub. Art grant Calif. Transp./City Heights Community Devel. Corp., 1993. Home: 4411 Alamo Way San Diego CA 92115-5909

MARKELL, EDWARD KINGSMILL, medical parasitologist, educator; b. N.Y.C., Apr. 14, 1918; s. Edward Louis and Genevieve Janet (Williams) M.; m. Nancy Jean Hiler, Mar. 14, 1953; children: Edward Christopher, Anne Elizabeth. BA in Zoology with high honors, Pomona Coll., 1938; PhD in Zoology, U. Calif., Berkeley, 1942; MD, Stanford U., 1951. Diplomate Am. Bd. Med. Microbiology. Teaching asst. zoology, head teaching asst. parasitology U. Calif., Berkeley, 1938-41, rsch. fellow zoology, 1946; intern medicine Stanford U. Hosps., 1950-51; asst. prof. infectious diseases UCLA, 1951-58, Markle fellow med. sci., 1952-57; mem. dept. internal medicine Permanente Med. Group, Oakland, Calif., 1958-84; clin. assoc. prof. community and preventive medicine Stanford U., 1962-70, clin. prof. family, community and preventive medicine, 1970-84, prof. emeritus, 1984—; clin. prof. medicine and tropical medicine U. Calif., San Francisco, 1985—; cons. parasitology Calif. State Dept. Pub. Health, 1952-58; mem. standards and examination com. Am. Bd. Microbiology, 1960-67; mem. parasitology adv. bd. U.S. Pharmacopeia, 1988—. Author: Diagnostic Medical Parasitology, 1958, Medical Parasitology, 1965, 7th edit., 1992, Parasitologia: Diagnostico, Prevencion y Tratamiento, 1984; author: (with others) Hunter's Tropical Medicine, 1984, 91, Current Therapy of Pediatric Infectious Diseases, 1986, 3d edit., 1993, Parasitic Infections in Pregnancy and the Newborn, 1988, Tropical Medicine/Medical Parasitology, 1989; editorial cons. Dorland's Illustrated Medical Dictionary, 1969-74. Vestry All Souls Episcopal Ch., Berkeley, 1960-63, 76-79, 87-90, sr. warden, 1963, 79. With USNR, 1942-46. Mem. Am. Soc. Tropical Medicine and Hygiene (delegation to China 1978), Am. Soc. Parasitologists (chmn. edn. com. 1976-79, chmn. clin. lab. com. 1980-83, del. clin. lab. standards 1981-83), Calif. Med. Assn., Alameda-Contra Costa County Med. Assn. (mediation com. 1970-91), Royal Soc. Tropical Medicine and Hygiene, Phi Beta Kappa, Sigma Xi, Alpha Omega Alpha. Home and Office: 28 Senior Ave Berkeley CA 94708-2212

MARKER, MARC LINTHACUM, lawyer, investor; b. Los Angeles, July 19, 1941; s. Clifford Harry and Voris (Linthacum) M.; m. Sandra Yocom, Aug. 29, 1965; children: Victor, Gwendolyn. BA in Econs. and Geography, U. Calif.-Riverside, 1964; JD, U. So. Calif., 1967. Asst. v.p., asst. sec. Security Pacific Nat. Bank, L.A., 1970-73; sr. v.p., chief counsel, sec. Security Pacific Leasing Corp., San Francisco, 1973-92; pres. Security Pacific Leasing Svcs. Corp., San Francisco, 1977-85, dir., 1977-92; bd. dirs., sec. Voris, Inc., 1973-86; bd. dirs. Refiners Petroleum Corp., 1977-81, Security Pacific Leasing Singapore Ltd., 1983-85, Security Pacific Leasing Can. Ltd., 1989-92; lectr. in field. Served to comdr. USCGR. Mem. ABA, Calif. Bar Assn., D.C. Bar Assn., Am. Assn. Equipment Lessors. Republican. Lutheran. Club: Univ. (L.A.). Office: 471 Magnolia Ave # B Larkspur CA 94939-2034

MARKEY, THOMAS ADAM, financial officer; b. Dayton, Ohio, June 12, 1956; s. Paul Robert Markey and Cathleen Wilgus. BA, Ariz. State U., 1980, MBA, 1992. CPA. Fin. analyst Maricopa County Sch. Supt., Phoenix, 1982-84; EDP acct. Maricopa County Fin. Dept., Phoenix, 1984-88, sr. fin. acct., 1988-90, sr. budget analyst, 1990-92; dir. bus. and human resources East Valley Inst. Tech., Mesa, Ariz., 1992—. Sustaining mem. SW Assn. Indian Affairs, Santa Fe, N.Mex., 1990—; active mem. Intertribal Indian Ceremonial Assn., Gallup, N.Mex., 1990—. Mem. AICPA, Ariz. Soc. CPAs, Ariz. Assn. Sch. Bus. Ofcls., Western Govtl. Rsch. Assn., Gov. Fin. Officers Assn., Beta Gamma Sigma. Democrat. Home: 200 S Center St Mesa AZ 85210-1502 Office: East Valley Inst Tech 200 S Center St Mesa AZ 85210-1502

MARKHAM, REED B., education educator, consultant; b. Alhambra, Calif., Feb. 14, 1957; s. John F. and Reeda (Bjarason) M. BA, Brigham Young U., 1982, MA, 1982; BS, Regents Coll., 1981, MA, 1982; MPA, U. So. Calif., 1983; MA, UCLA, 1989; PhD, Columbia Pacific U., 1991. Mem. faculty Brigham Young U., Provo, Utah, 1984; mem. faculty Calif. State U., Fullerton and Long Beach, 1984, Northridge, 1985; mem. faculty El Camino Coll., Torrance, Calif., 1986, Orange Coast Coll., Costa Mesa, Calif., 1986, Pasadena (Calif.) Coll., 1986, Fullerton (Calif.) Community Coll., 1986; instr., mem. pub. rels. com. Chaffey (Calif.) Coll., 1986-87; prof., CARES dir. Calif. State Poly. U., Pomona, 1987—; adj. prof. Calif. State U., L.A., 1992-93, dir. Ctr. for Student Retention, 1995—; rsch. asst. to pres. Ctr. for the Study of Cmty. Coll., 1985; mem. faculty Riverside (Calif.) Coll., 1989-90, Rio Hondo (Calif.) Coll., 1989-90, English Lang. Inst., 1994, Calif. Poly Summer Bridge, 1989-95, East L.A. Coll.; speechwriter U.S. Supreme Ct., Washington, 1980; cons. gifted children program Johns Hopkins U./Scripps Coll., Claremont, Calif., 1987-88; mem. faculty PACE Program East L.A., 1995-96; faculty East L.A. Coll., 1996-97. Author: Power Speechwriting, 1983, Power Speaking, 1990, Public Opinion, 1990, Advances in Public Speaking, 1991, Leadership 2000: Success Skills for University Students, 1995; co-author: Student Retention: Success Models in Higher Education, 1996, Upward Bound Program Grant Proposal, 1996, editor Trojan in Govt., U. So. Calif., 1983; editl. bd. mem. Edn. Digest, Speaker and Gavel, Innovative Higher End., Pub. Rels. Rev., Nat. Forensic Jour., The Forensic Educator, Clearinghouse for the Contemporary Educator, Hispanic Am. Family Mag.; writer N.Y. times, Christian Sci. Monitor; ednl. columnist San Bernardino (Calif.) Sun., 1992-97. Pres. bd. trustees Regents Coll., 1986. Mem. Doctorate Assn. N.Y. Scholars, Nat. Assn. Pvt. Nontraditional Colls. (accrediting com. 1989—), Pub. Rels. Soc. Am. (dir.-at-large inland empire 1992-93, faculty advisor). LDS. Home: 801 E Alosta Ave # T-307 Azusa CA 91702-2744 Office: Calif Polytech U Communications Dept 3801 W Temple Ave Pomona CA 91768-2557

MARKHAM, RICHARD GLOVER, research executive; b. Pasadena, Calif., June 18, 1925; s. Fred Smith and Maziebelle (Glover) M.; m. Jonne Louise Pearson, Apr. 29, 1950; children: Janet B., Fred S., Charles R., Richard G., Marilyn A. Student, Stanford U., 1943; BS, Calif. Inst. Tech., Pasadena, 1945; MS, Stanford U., 1947. Pres., owner Aquarium Pump Supply, Prescott, Ariz., 1957-78; 1st v.p., dir. Bank of Prescott, 1981-87; also v.p., bd. dirs. Oxycal Labs., Prescott, 1981—. Patentee in field. Mem. Ariz. Dept. Econ. Planning and Devel., 1967-72; treas. Ariz. State Rep. Com., 1970-72; active Ariz. Acad., 1974—; trustee Orme Sch., Mayer, Ariz., 1970-83, Prescott Coll., 1979-83. Office: Oxycal Labs 533 Madison Ave Prescott AZ 86301-2432

MARKKULA, A. C., JR., entrepreneur, computer company executive. Cofounder, former pres., chief exec. officer Apple Computer Inc., now chmn. bd. dirs.; founder, chmn. Echelon, Los Gatos, Calif. Office: Apple Computer Inc 20525 Mariani Ave Cupertino CA 95014-6201

MARKOVICH, PATRICIA, economist; b. Oakland, Calif.; d. Patrick Joseph and Helen Emily (Prydz) Markovich; BA in Econs., MS in Econs., U. Calif.-Berkeley; postgrad. (Lilly Found. grantee) Stanford U., (NSF grantee) Oreg. Grad. Rsch. Ctr.; children: Michael Sean Treece, Bryan Jeffry Treece, Tiffany Helene Treece. Cert. Emergency Mgmt. Planner. Pub. rels. Pettler Advt., Inc.; pvt. practice polit. and econs. cons.; aide to majority whip Oreg. Ho. of Reps.; lectr., instr., various Calif. instns., Chemeketa (Oreg.) Coll., Portland (Oreg.) State U.; commr. City of Oakland (Calif.), 1970-74; chairperson, bd. dirs. Cable Sta. KCOM; mem. gen. plan commn. City of Piedmont, Calif.; with Oakland Mus. Archives of Calif. Artists. Mem. Internat. Assn. Feminist Economists, Mensa (officer San Francisco region), Bay Area Artists Assn. (coord., founding mem.), Berkeley Art Ctr. Assn., San Francisco Arts Commn. File, Calif. Index for Contemporary Arts, Pro Arts, YLEM: Artists Using Sci. and Tech., NAFE, No. Calif. Pub. Ednl. and Govt. Access Cable TV Com. (founding), Triple Nine Soc., Nat. Coord. Coun. Emergency Mgmt., Am. Econ. Assn., Allied Social Scis. Assn., N.Y. Acad. Scis.

MARKOVITS, ANDREI STEVEN, political science educator; b. Timisoara, Romania, Oct. 6, 1948; came to U.S., 1960, naturalized, 1971; s. Ludwig and Ida (Ritter) M. B.A., Columbia U., 1969, M.B.A., 1971, M.A., 1973, M.Phil., 1974, Ph.D., 1976. Mem. faculty N.Y.U., 1974, John Jay Coll. Criminal Justice, CUNY, 1974, Columbia U., 1975; rsch. assoc. Inst. Advanced Studies, Vienna, Austria, 1973-74, Wirtschafts und Sozialwissenschaftliches Inst., German Trade U. Fedn., Duesseldorf, Fed. Republic Germany, 1979, Internat. Inst. Comparative Social Rsch., Sci. Ctr. Berlin, 1980; asst. prof. govt. Wesleyan U., Middletown, Conn., 1977-83; assoc. prof. polit. sci. Boston U., 1983-92; prof., chair dept. politics U. Calif., Santa Cruz, 1992—; Fulbright prof. U. Innsbruck, Austria, 1996; vis. prof. Tel Aviv U., 1986, Osnabruck U., 1987, Bochum U., 1991; sr. rsch. assoc. Ctr. for European Studies, Harvard U., 1975—. Author, editor books and papers in field; TV and radio commentator. Univ. Pres.'s fellow Columbia U., 1969, B'nai B'rith Found. fellow, 1976-77, Kalmus Found. fellow, 1976-77, Ford Found. fellow, 1979, Hans Boeckler Found. fellow, 1982; N.Y. State scholar Columbia U., 1969. Mem. N.Y. Acad. Scis., Am. Polit. Sci. Assn., Internat. Polit. Sci. Assn., AAUP. Home: 287 Harvard St Cambridge MA 02139-2383 Office: U Calif Merrill Coll Bd Studies in Politics Santa Cruz CA 95064 also: Harvard U Ctr European Studies 27 Kirkland St Cambridge MA 02138-2043

MARKS, ARNOLD, journalist; b. Phila., Aug. 4, 1912; s. Morris M. and Esther (Joel) M.; m. Isabelle Ruppert, Oct. 3, 1942 (dec.); 1 son, Rupert William Joel (dec.); m. Emi Seligman Simon. B.A., U. Wash., 1935; M.S., Columbia U., 1939. Editor Pasco (Wash.) Herald, 1946; with Oreg. Jour., Portland, 1946-78; drama, TV, entertainment editor Oreg. Jour., 1948-58, entertainment editor, 1958-78, ret., 1978, freelance writer. Served with AUS, 1942-46. Mem. Sigma Delta Chi, Sigma Alpha Mu. Club: University (Portland). Home: PO Box 590 Gleneden Beach OR 97388-0590 also: 2393 SW Park Pl Portland OR 97205-1056 *In retrospect, there is great satisfaction in the thought that the years seem more loaded with heartwarming memories than with disappointments.*

MARKS, GREGORY TODD, mathematics educator; b. Hollywood, Calif., Oct. 5, 1970; s. Richard Earl Marks and Judith Eden (Gelfand)

Howard. SB, MIT, 1992. Grad. student instr. U. Calif., Berkeley, 1992—. Home: 3116 38th Ave Apt 312 Oakland CA 94619-1256 Office: U Calif Dept Math Berkeley CA 94720

MARKS, LEONARD, JR., retired corporate executive; b. N.Y.C., May 22, 1921; s. Leonard M. and Laura (Colegrove) Rose; m. Antonia Saldaña Riley, July 19, 1986; children from previous marriage: Linda, Patricia Anne, Peter K. A.B. in Econs., Drew U., 1942; M.B.A., Harvard U., 1948, D.B.A., 1961. Asst. prof. bus. adminstrn. Harvard U., 1949-55; prof. fin. Stanford U., 1955-64; asst. sec. USAF, Washington, 1964-68; v.p. corp. devel. Times Mirror Co., Los Angeles, 1968-69; sr. v.p. Wells Fargo Bank, San Francisco, 1969-72; exec. v.p. Castle & Cooke Inc., San Francisco, 1972-85; gen. ptnr. Marks-Hoffman Assocs., Venture Capital, 1985-92; ind. corp. dir., 1992—; bd. dirs. Airlease Mgmt. Svcs., Alexion Pharm. Inc., No. Trust Bank of Ariz. Co-author: Case Problems in Commercial Bank Management, 1962; contbg.: Credit Management Handbook, 1958. Capt. AUS, 1942-46, ret. brig. gen. USAFR.

MARKS, MERTON ELEAZER, lawyer; b. Chgo., Oct. 16, 1932; s. Alfred Tobias and Helene Fannie (Rosner) M.; m. Radee Maiden Feiler, May 20, 1966; children: Sheldon, Elise Marks Vazelakis, Alan, Elaine Marks Ianchiou. BS, Northwestern U., 1954, JD, 1956. Bar: Ill. 1956, U.S. Ct. Mil. Appeals 1957, Ariz. 1958, U.S. Dist. Ct. Ariz. 1960, U.S. Ct. Appeals (9th cir.) 1962, U.S. Supreme Ct. 1970. Assoc. Moser, Compere & Emerson, Chgo., 1956-57; ptnr. Morgan, Marks & Rogers, Tucson, 1960-62; asst. atty. gen. State of Ariz., Phoenix, 1962-64, counsel indsl. commn., 1964-65; assoc., then ptnr. Shimmel, Hill, Bishop & Greunder, Phoenix, 1965-74; ptnr. Lewis & Roca, Phoenix, 1974—; lectr. on pharm., health care, product liability, ins. and employers' liability subjects; Judge Pro Tempore Ariz. Ct. Appeals, 1994. Contbr. more than 35 articles to profl. jours. Capt. JAGC, USAR, 1957-64. Mem. ABA (tort and ins. practice sect., chmn. spl. com. on fed. asbestos legis. 1987-89, chmn. workers compensation and employers liability law com. 1983-84), Am. Bd. Trial Advocates, Am. Coll. Legal Medicine, Internat. Bar Assn., Drug Info. Assn., Am. Soc. Pharmacy Law, State Bar Ariz. (chmn. workers compensation sect. 1969-73), Nat. Coun. Self Insurers, Ariz. Self Insurers Assn., Fedn. Ins. and Corp. Counsel (chmn. pharm. litig. sect. 1989-91, chmn. workers compensation sect. 1977-79, v.p. 1978-79, 81, bd. dirs. 1981-89), Internat. Assn. Def. Counsel, Ariz. Assn. Def. Counsel (pres. 1976-77), Maricopa County Bar Assn., Def. Rsch. Inst. (drug and device com., chmn. workers compensation com. 1977-78), Assn. Internat. Droit Assurances, Union Internat. des Avocats. Office: Lewis & Roca 40 N Central Ave Phoenix AZ 85004-4424

MARKS, PETER AMASA, technical consulting company administrator; b. Passaic, N.J., Dec. 5, 1948; s. Amasa A. and Eunice L. (Irwin) M.; BS in Design Engring., U. Cin., 1972, MA in Media Communications, 1973, postgrad. in human factors engring. Rsch. asst. dept. mech. engring. U. Cin., 1972; sr. engr. Ford Motor Co., Sharonville, Ohio, 1972-75; prin. Design Insight Cin., 1976—; mng. dir. SDRC TEC Services, Milford, Ohio, 1978-84, dir. product planning and devel., SDRC, Inc., Milford, 1981-84; sr. v.p. ops. Automation Tech., Campbell, Calif., 1985-88; CEO, Design Insight, 1988—. lectr., cons. on product design tech. implementation, U.S., Asia, Europe, also for Am. Mgmt. Assns.; co-founder, head bd of judges Am. Product Excellence (APEX) Awards. Grad. fellow; Gen. Motors grantee in design, 1970; winner nat., internat. competitions for tech. programs. Mem. ASME, IEEE, Soc. Mfg. Engrs. Author books, articles and films in field. Office: Design Insight 3760 Old Pilkington Rd Santa Cruz CA 95065-2120

MARKS, ROBERT ARTHUR, lawyer, attorney general; b. Dayton, Ohio, Oct. 9, 1952; s. Arthur Kenneth and Patricia Marks; m. Victoria Scurlock, Oct. 21, 1978; two sons. BA, U. Wis., 1974; JD, U. Cin., 1977. Bar: Ohio 1977, Hawaii 1978, U.S. Ct. Appeals (6th cir.) Ohio 1977, U.S. Ct. Appeals (9th cir.) Hawaii 1978, U.S. Supreme Ct. 1992. Pvt. practice Honolulu, 1978-84; dep. atty. gen. State of Hawaii, Honolulu, 1984-87, supr. dep. atty. gen., 1987-92, 1st dep. atty. gen., 1992, atty. gen., 1992—; counsel Alston, Hunt, Floyd & Ing, Honolulu, 1995-97, Price, Okamoto Himeno & Lum, Honolulu, 1997—. Office: Price Okamoto Himeno Lum Ste 728 707 Richards St Honolulu HI 96813

MARKS, SHARON LEA, primary school educator, nurse; b. Arroyo Grande, Calif., June 12, 1942; d. Donald Elmore and Gertrude (Grieb) Shaffer; m. George Conrad Schmidt, June 23, 1963 (div. 1975); children: Kerrilynn, Robert, Marianne; m. Keith Dalton Marks, June 4, 1978; children: Joseph, Erik, Alice. Diploma, Sch. Nursing Samuel Merritt Hosp., 1963; BS in Nursing, Lewis and Clark State Coll., 1984, BS in Mgmt., 1986. RN, Calif.; cert. tchr., Calif. Staff nurse Vesper Meml. Hosp., San Leandro, Calif., 1968-74; night nurse supr. Tuolumne Gen. Hosp., Sonora, Calif., 1975; nurse Orleans (Calif.) Search and Rescue Team, 1975-78; instr. nursing Pasadena (Calif.) City Coll., 1978-79; resource coord. learning ctr. div. health sci. Spokane (Wash.) Community Coll., 1979-84; staff nurse Kootenai Med. Ctr., 1979-85; instr. North Idaho Coll., Coeur d'Alene, 1984-85; staff nurse North Idaho Home Health, Coeur d'Alene, 1985-86; coord. br. office Family Home Care, Spokane, 1986-87; devel., dir. Good Samaritan Home Health Plummer, Idaho and Fairfield, Washington, 1987-88; mgr. patient svcs. VNS Seattle-King County, Tukwila, Wash., 1988-89; co-owner, v.p. The Wooden Boat Shop, Seattle, 1989—; primary sch. tchr. Marisposa Sch., 1994-95, Corona Sch., 1995-96, West Randall Sch., Yucaipa, Calif., 1996—; owner Marks and Assocs., 1994—; instr. in emergency med. tech. Orleans campus Coll. Redwoods, Eureka, Calif., 1977-78; book reviewer Brady Co., Besterfield and Assocs., 1994; film reviewer Olympia Media Info. Mem. Nat. Head Injury Found., Wash. State Head Injury Found. Office: 11884 4th St Yucaipa CA 92399-2718

MARKS, STANLEY JACOB, lawyer, historian, lecturer, author; b. Chgo., Apr. 26, 1914; s. Samuel and Sarah Marks; m. Ethel Milgrom, Aug. 1, 1936; 1 child, Roberta E. AB, U. Ill., 1934; LLB, JD, John Marshall Law Sch., Chgo., 1937. Bar: Ill. 1939. Pres., chmn. bd. Beauti-Dor, Inc., Chgo., 1939—, Glamour Glass Door, Inc., Chgo., 1939—; pvt. practice Calif., 1964—; internat. and nat. legal and bus. cons. L.A., 1964—; lectr. on polit. and social/econ. events worldwide. Author: (with Ethel Marks) The Bear That Walks Like a Man, 1943, Murder Most Foul, 1967, Two Days of Infamy, 1969, Coup d'Etat!, 1970, Through Distorted Mirrors, 1974, Judaism Looks at Christianity, 1986, A Year in the Lives of the Damned, Reagn, Reaganism, 1986, The 1991 U.S. Consumer Market, 1991, Yes, Americans, A Conspiracy Murdered JFK!, 1992, Jews, Judaism and the U.S., 1992, Justice For Whom?, 1996, others; playwright: Judgement Day, 1997, Judaism - Civilization's Las Hope, 1997; pub. weekly polit. newsletter Diogenes, 1984, 88. Writer Dem. Nat. Com., 1936, 40, 48, 52, 60, 91, 96. With AUS, 1944-46. Recipient various Army decorations. Mem. Am. Acad. Polit. and Social Scis., Soc. Am. Mil. Engrs., Authors League Am., Libr. of Congress Assn., Anti-Defamation League, Dramatists Guild (life), Masons, Shriners, Anti Discrimination League, World Jewish Congress, Dramatist Guild.

MARKS, WILLIAM H., organ transplant program director, pharmacologist, pharmacognosist, and director for laboratory transplantation biology; b. Chgo., Aug. 16, 1948; s. Louis M. and Bertha M. (Michaelson) M.; m. Christine M. Marks, Nov. 1971; children: Annika, Daniel, Susie, Julia. BS, Loyola U., Chgo., 1970; MS, U. Ill., Chgo., 1973; MD, Loyola U., 1977; PhD, Lund U., 1983. Instr. U. Mich., Ann Arbor, 1983-85; asst. prof. surgery and biochemistry Loyola U., Maywood, Ill., 1985-87; assoc. prof. surgery Yale U., New Haven, Conn., 1987-93; adj. assoc. prof. pharmacology Nat. Products Chemistry U. Ill., Chgo., 1987—; dir. organ transplantation Swedish Med. Ctr., Seattle, 1994—; dir. lab. for transplant biology; surg. adv. bd. Smith Kline Beecham, Phila., 1992—; USMLE surg. step II Nat. Bd. Med. Examiners, Phila., 1992-95. Editor Resident Surgery, 1992—, Phytomedicine, 1994; editl. bd. Resident Surgery, 1992—; contbr. articles to profl. jours.; patentee in field. Mem. exec. com. N.W. Kidney Ctrs., Seattle, 1993; sec. bd. dirs. Life Ctr. NW, 1996—; bd. dirs. CenterSpan, Inc., 1996—. Fellow ACS (SK&F fellowship 1985, 86); mem. Am. Soc. Transplant Surgeons, Am. Soc. Transplant Physicians, Soc. Univ. Surgeons, The Transplant Soc., Soc. Surgery of the Alimentary Tract. Office: Organ Transplant Program 1120 Cherry St # 400 Seattle WA 98104-2023

MARLATT, DOROTHY BARBARA, university dean; b. Tarrytown, N.Y., Dec. 1; d. Joseph S. and Evelyn M. (McGinnis) Porcano; m. Gene R. Marlatt, Aug. 20, 1960; children: David D., Julia Jeanne Marlatt Kelley. BA, Wheaton (Ill.) Coll., 1960; MA, U. Colo., 1966; EdD, Internat. Grad. Sch., St. Louis, 1987. Tchr. Alexandria (Va.) Pub. Schs., 1961-62, Westminster (Colo.) Pub. Schs., 1962-66, Jeffco Pub. Schs., Lakewood, Colo., 1966-69; elem. prin. Denver Pub. Schs., 1970-94; assoc. prof. edn. Rockmont Coll., Lakewood, 1976-93; prof. edn. Colo. Christian U., Lakewood, 1993-96, dean edn., 1994-96; adj. prof. Union Grad. Sch., Cin., 1995—. Recipient Svc. to Youth award YMCA, 1960, Svc. award Big Bros., 1970, Pub. Rels. Recognition award Denver Pub. Schs., 1972. Fellow Acad. Nat. Staff Devel., Inst. for Devel. of Ednl. Activities, Nat. Elem. Sch. Prins. Assn.; mem. Optimists, Kappa Delta Pi. Republican. Presbyterian. Office: Colo Christian U 180 S Garrison St Lakewood CO 80226-1053

MARLATT, MICHAEL JAMES, lawyer; b. L.A., Jan. 15, 1957; s. James Raymond and Norma Jean (Greenfield) M.; m. Donna Marie Healey, Apr. 13, 1985. BA, Calif. Poly. U., 1981; JD, Pepperdine U., 1984. Bar: Calif. 1984, U.S. Dist. Ct. (ctrl. dist.) Calif. 1985, U.S. Supreme Ct. 1990. Project liaison U. So. Calif., Sch. Medicine, L.A., 1975-78; documentation rschr. NASA-Jet Propulsion Lab., Pasadena, Calif., 1978-81; ptnr. Thompson & Colegate, Riverside, Calif., 1984—; bd. dirs. Assn. So. Calif. Def. Counsel, L.A., U. Calif., Riverside; lectr. Princeton U., 1993, U. Amsterdam Law Sch., 1994, Loma Linda (Calif.) U. Sch. Medicine, 1991-94; lectr., spkr. to ins. cos. on health care, 1988—; bd. dirs. Mission Inn Found., v.p.; radio commentator Stas. KCKC, KCAL, and KMEN. Mem. ctr. com. Calif. Rep. Party, Sacramento, 1990-93; bd. dirs. U. Calif., Riverside, pres., 1996-97; bd. dirs. Mission Inn Found., v.p., 1996-97. Mem. So. Calif. Assn. Hosp. Risk Mgrs., Victoria Country Club, Phi Alpha Delta. Roman Catholic. Office: Thompson & Colegate PO Box 1299 3610 14th St Riverside CA 92501-3847

MARLER, LARRY JOHN, private investor; b. Chgo., Sept. 22, 1940; s. Walter William and Lena Inez (Killen) M.; m. Katy Jo Hibbits, Oct. 17, 1962 (div. Apr. 1971); 1 child, Preston Scott; m. Linda Lee Sorg, Sept. 2, 1982. BA, Christian Coll. Am., 1987; MA, Houston Grad. Sch. Theology, 1988; PhD, U.S. Internat. U., San Diego, 1992. Acct. Shell Oil Co., New Orleans and Houston, 1964-73; acctg. supr. We. Geophys. Co. Am., Houston, 1974; payroll supr. Olsen Inc., Houston, 1975-77; corp. credit mgr. Grant Corps., Houston, 1977-82; rschr., student contractor Navy Pers. R&D Ctr., San Diego, 1990-92; entrepreneur Denver, 1992—. Served with USCG, 1959-62. Mem. Am. Psychol. Soc., Am. Soc. Quality Control, Toastmasters Internat. Republican. Protestant.

MARLETT, DE OTIS LORING, retired management consultant; b. Indpls., Apr. 19, 1911; s. Peter Loring and Edna Grace (Lombard) M.; m. Ruth Irene Pillar, Apr. 10, 1932 (dec. Feb., 1969); children: De Otis Neal, Marilynn Ruth; m. Marie Manning Ostrander, May 1, 1970 (dec. Apr. 1982); m. Peggie P. Whittlesey, Jan. 15, 1983 (dec. Oct., 1993); m. Estelle B. Brewer, Sept. 23, 1994. B.A., M.A., U. Wis., 1934; postgrad., Northwestern U., (part time), 1934-39, Harvard U.; postgrad. (Littauer fellow in econs. and govt.), 1946-47. CPA, Wis., 1935. Staff mem. Ill. Commerce Commn., 1934-39; lectr. in econs. and pub. utilities Northwestern U., (part time), 1936-39; staff mem. Bonneville Power Adminstrn., U.S. Dept. Interior, 1939-45, asst. adminstr., 1945-52; acting adminstr. Def. Electric Power Adminstrn., 1950-51; asst. to v.p., gen. mgr. Dicalite and Perlite divs. Great Lakes Carbon Corp., 1952-53; v.p., also gen. mgr. Dicalite, Perlite, Mining and Minerals divs. Gt. Lakes Carbon Corp., 1953-62, v.p. property investment dept., 1962-81; pres., chief exec. officer Great Lakes Properties, Inc., 1981-83, ret., 1983; past pres., dir. Rancho Palos Verdes Corp., G.L.C. Bldg. Corp., Del Amo Energy Co., Torrance Energy Co.; former mem. L.A. arbitration panel N.Y. Stock Exch. Contbr. articles and reports on public utility regulation, operation and mgmt. to profl. jours. Past bd. dirs. United Cerebral Palsy Assn. Los Angeles County; bd. dirs., past co-chmn. So. Calif. region NCCJ, mem. nat. trustee, mem. nat. exec. bd., nat. protestant co-chmn., 1987-90; past mem. Orthopaedic Hosp. Adv. Coun.; past trustee City of Hope; past pres., dir. Los Angeles area coun., past chmn. relationships com., past pres. Sunshine area, pres. Western region Boy Scouts Am., 1978-81, nat. exec. bd., 1978-88, past mem. nat. exec. com., past chmn. properties com., chmn. logistics for world jamboree delegation to Australia, 1987-88; past trustee Nat. Scouting Mus.; mem. internat. com. Baden Powell fellow World Scouting Found., 1984; past mem. Western Govs. Mining Adv. Coun., Calif. State Mining Bd.; bd. govs. Western div. Am. Mining Congress, chmn., 1962-63; incorporator, past pres., bd. dirs. Torrance Meml. Med. Center Health Care Found.; region III dir., past mem. corp. adminstrn. and fin. com., Los Angeles United Way. Recipient Disting. Service medal U.S. Dept. Interior, 1952; named knight Order of Crown Belgium; commd. Ky. Col.; recipient Silver Beaver, Silver Antelope, Silver Buffalo awards Boy Scouts Am., 1984. Mem. AIME, AICPA, Fin. Execs. Inst., L.A. World Affairs Coun., Wis. Alumni Assn., Perlit Inst. (past pres., dir.), L.A. C. of C. (past dir., chmn. mining com.), Mining Assn. So. Calif. (past pres., dir.), Calif. Mine Operators Assn. (past dir.), Bldg. Industry Assn. So. Calif., Calif. Club, Portuguese Bend Club (past pres.), Palos Verdes Bay Club (past v.p.), Phi Kappa Phi, Beta Gamma Sigma, Phi Beta Kappa, Beta Alpha Psi, Lambda Alpha Internat. Democrat. Home: 32759 Seagate Dr Unit 204 Palos Verdes Peninsula CA 90275

MARLIN, ROBERT MATTHEW, secondary school educator; b. Buffalo, N.Y., June 11, 1940; s. Clarence Lewis and LaVerna (Haentgus) M.; m. Margaret Mary Steve, July, 1962 (div. July 1970); 1 child, Wendy. BEd, U. Alaska, 1967; student, Alaska Pacific U., 1967-71, U. Ga., 1970, U. Salamanca, Spain, 1987, Calif State U., 1984-87. Cert. tchr., Calif. Radio traffic analyst USAF Security Svc., Anchorage, 1958-63; copywriter Anchorage Daily Times, 1963-67; tchr. Anchorage Sch. Dist., 1967-72; mgr. Transamerica Corp., L.A., 1972-84; tchr. L.A. Unified Sch. Dist., 1984—; participant sci. seminar on quality of edn., Pinar de Rio, Cuba, 1995, Matanzas, Cuba, 1996. Bd. dirs. Upward Bound, Alaska Meth. Univ., Anchorage, 1969; vol. counselor Gay and Lesbian Cmty. Svcs. Ctr., L.A., 1975-76; cons. Constl. Rights Found., L.A., 1994—. With USAF, 1958-63. Grantee U.S. Dept. Commerce, 1969, NSF, 1970, 71, L.A. Unified Sch. Dist., 1988. Mem. NEA, Gay, Lesbian, Straight Tchrs. Alliance, Calif. Tchrs. Assn., United Tchrs. L.A. (gay lesbian issues com.). Democrat. Home: 531 W Avenue 46 Los Angeles CA 90065-5007 Office: Berendo Middle Sch 1157 S Berendo St Los Angeles CA 90006-3301

MARLOW, EDWARD A., career officer; b. Cleve., Nov. 22, 1946. AA, Long Beach City Coll., 1971; cert., Officer Candidate Sch., Ft. Benning, 1974, Basic Infantry Officer Course, Ft. Benning, 1976; student, Am. Law Inst., N.Y., 1979-80; cert., Advance Armor Officer Course, Ft. Knox, 1982, U.S. Army Command and Gen. Staff Coll., 1986; BS in Bus. Mgmt. and Polit. Sci., SUNY, 1987; MPA, U. So. Calif., 1990; cert., Advance Intelligence Officer Course, Ft. Huachuca, 1991. Registered investment adv. 1978-90 SEC. Commd. 2nd lt. infantry U.S. Army, 1974, advanced through grades to maj., 1988; chief real property branch Mil. Dept., Sacramento, 1968—; pres. and dir. TEAM Mgmt. Corp., 1978—. Mng. sr. ptnr. Caribbean Basin Latin Am. Devel. Orgn., Sacramento, 1988—; trustee Hosp. Relief Fund Caribbean, Inc., Washington, 1989-92; mem. Caribbean Pvt. Sector Disaster Coord. Subcommittee White House Internat. Disaster Adv. Com., 1991-92; sr. ptnr. Caribbean Basin Latin Am. Devel. Orgn. Endowment Group, Sacramento, 1992—; chair bd. trustees Cabalado Relief Fund, Inc., 1993—. Mem. Latin Am. Pacific Trade Assn. (dir. 1994—).

MARMADUKE, ARTHUR SANDFORD, educational administrator; b. Long Beach, Calif., May 29, 1926; s. William Sandford and Nina Belle (Romberger) M.; m. Carolyn Ann Tilden, Aug. 21, 1949; children: Jennifer, Stephen, Scott. AB, Occidental Coll., 1950; MPA, U. Mich., 1952; DPA (hon.), U. Pacific, 1970. Adminstrv. analyst Office Legis. Analyst Calif. State Legis., Sacramento, 1951-55; dir. admissions Occidental Coll., L.A., 1955-60; dir. Calif. Student Aid Commn., Sacramento, 1960-85; exec. dir. Eureka Project, Sacramento, 1986-90; dir. Independent Solution Project, 1989-91; cons. Weingart Found., 1987, Bush Found., 1985, Marin Ednl. Fund.; vice chmn. nat. task force on student aid programs KEppel Com., 1974-75; chmn. Coll. Scholarship Svc., Coll. Entrance Examination Bd., 1967-69; mem. planning com., dir. Calif. Higher Edn. Policy Ctr., 1991-93. Contbr. author several student aid books. Trustee Sacramento Country Day Sch. Recipient Disting. Service award Calif. Student Fin. Aid Adminstrs., 1982, Raol Wallenberg New Traditional High Sch., San Francisco, 1985, Coll. Bd. Scholarship Service, N.Y.C., 1985. Home: 1516 Del Dayo Dr Carmichael CA 95608-6011

MARMANN, SIGRID, software development company executive; b. Voelklingen, Saarland, Fed. Republic Germany, Feb. 8, 1938; s. Leo and Karoline Anna (Weidenhof) M. Postgrad., Norwood Coll., London, 1962; BS in Acctg., Ind. & Handelskammer, Saarbruecken, Fed. Republic Germany, 1956; postgrad., Golden Gate U., 1970-85; BA in Mgmt., St. Mary's Coll., Moraga, Calif., 1984. Controller M.O.M., Paris, 1965-69; bookkeeper Chrissa Imports, Brisbane, Calif., 1970-78; acctg. mgr. Highcity Internat., San Anselmo, Calif., 1978-80; acctg. mgr., system analyst Kukje Korean Trading Co., Rutherford, N.J., 1980-81; asst. treas. Am. Mercantile Co., Brisbane, 1981-84; controller Provident Credit Union, Burlingame, Calif., 1984; owner Datatech EDI Systems, San Rafael, Calif., 1984—; pres., chief owner Datatech EDI Systems, San Rafael, 1989—; pres. Telepay Express, Inc., 1989. Founder No. Calif. Electronic Data Interchange Users Group, San Francisco, 1990. Mem. ANSI ASC X12 Electronic Data Interchange (fin. subcom. Alexandria, Va. chpt., nominee Membership award 1990) Great Plains Software (qualified installer), Computer Assocs. Internat. (installer). Home: 30 Newport Way San Rafael CA 94901-4411

MARMARELIS, VASILIS ZISSIS, engineering educator, author, consultant; b. Mytilini, Greece, Nov. 16, 1949; came to U.S., 1972; s. Zissis P. and Elpis V. (Galinos) M.; m. Melissa Emily Orme, Mar. 12, 1989; children: Zissis Eugene and Myrl Galinos. Diploma in elec. and mech. engring., Nat. Tech. U. of Athens, Greece, 1972; MS in Info. Sci., Calif. Inst. Tech., 1973, PhD in Engring. Sci., 1976. Rsch. fellow Calif. Inst. Tech., Pasadena, 1976-78; asst. prof. U. So. Calif., L.A., 1978-83, assoc. prof., 1983-88, prof., 1988—, also dir. biomed. simulations resource, 1985—, chmn. dept. biomed. engring., 1990-96; pres. Multispec Corp., L.A., 1986—. Author: Analysis of Physiological Systems, 1978, translated in Russian 1981, translated in Chinese 1990; Advanced Methods of Physiological Systems Modeling, vol. I, 1987, vol. II, 1989, vol. III, 1994; contbr. numerous articles to profl. jours. Fellow IEEE; mem. AAAS, Internat. Fedn. Automatic Control, N.Y. Acad. Scis., Biomed. Engring. Soc., Neural Networks Soc. Office: U So Calif OHE 500 Los Angeles CA 90089-1451

MARMYSZ, JOHN ALEXANDER, philosophy educator, consultant; b. San Rafael, Calif., Dec. 9, 1964. BA in Sociology, San Francisco State U., 1987, MA in Philosophy, 1994, cert. tchg. critical thinking, 1994. Asst. mgr. Landmark Corp., San Francico, 1991-94; tchg. asst. San Francisco State U., 1992-93; instr. in philosophy Melo Coll., Atherton, Calif., 1994—, Santa Rosa Jr. Coll., 1994—; cons. Santa Rosa (Calif.) City Schs., 1996. Editor (jour.) Twilight of the Idols, 1991-93 (editor's choice Factsheet 5 1993); also articles. With US Army Reserve, 1989-93. Mem. N. Am. Nietzche Soc., Am. Philos. Assn., Soc. for Philos. Study of Contemporary Visual Arts. Home: 3739 Balboa St Apt 142 San Francisco CA 94121-2605

MAROON, MICKEY, clinical social worker; b. Flint, Mich., July 20, 1948; d. Harold Clifford and Dorothy Ruth (Fuller) McDaniel; m. Michael Martin Maroon, Aug. 22, 1970. BA, Bradley U., 1970; MSW, Denver U., 1975. Lic. clin. social worker, Colo.; bd. cert. diplomate. Social worker Ill. Dept. Children and Family Svcs., Peoria, Ill., 1970-73; clin. social worker Adams County Social Svcs., Westminster, Colo., 1975-77, Bethesda Hosp., Denver, 1977-84; pvt. practice Denver, 1979—; clin. cons. Human Svcs., Inc., Denver, 1988-91; vol. faculty Health Sci. Ctr. U. Colo., Denver, 1987—; chair attending social work staff West Pines Hosp., Wheat Ridge, Colo., 1988-89. Mem. NASW (pres. Colo. chpt. 1994-96, chair clin. social work com. 1996, Social Worker of Yr. Colo. chpt. 1997), Colo. Soc. Clin. Social Work (Denver chpt. pres. 1992, state pres. 1993, Cmty. Svc. award 1996).

MAROTTA, GEORGE RAYMOND, money manager, research institute fellow; b. Scotia, N.Y., Oct. 6, 1926; s. Giuseppe and Rosa (Fasulo) M.; m. June Alison Mortlock, Aug. 29, 1948; children: Raymond, Paul, David. AB, Syracuse U., 1950, MPA, 1951; cert. fin. planner. Mgmt. officer Dept. State, Washington, 1951-53; planner, coordinator Nat. Security Council, Washington, 1953-61; Univ. relations officer Peace Corps, Washington, 1961-62; internat. security planner Dept. Defense, Washington, 1962-67; foreign service reserve officer Agency Internat. Devel., Washington, 1967-75; pub. affairs coordinator Hoover Instn., Stanford, Calif., 1975-84, research fellow, 1977—; lectr. Stanford U., 1995—; investment portfolio mgr. Marotta Asset Mgmt. Recipient Meritorious Honor award Agency Internat. Devel., 1968, Honorable Achievement award Pub. Relations Soc. Am., 1980. Mem. Internat. Assn. Fin. Planners, Inst. Cert. Fin. Planners, Nat. Assn. Personal Fin. Advisors, Pub. Relations Soc. Am. (accredited mem.). Office: Stanford U Hoover Instn Stanford CA 94305

MARQUAND, IAN MACDONALD, television producer; b. Denver, June 2, 1956; s. Kenneth Earl and Betty Harlina (Farley) M.; m. Susan Carol MacDonald, July 4, 1982; children: Adrienne Coral, Ashley Elizabeth. BA in Radio/TV with high honors, U. Mont., 1979. News reporter, anchor KPAX-TV, Missoula, Mont., 1978-81, news dir., 1982-84; interim sports dir. Mont. TV Network, Billings, 1984; state capitol bur. chief Mont. TV Network, Helena, 1984-85; news dir. KTVH-TV, Helena, 1986-89, KPAX-TV, Missoula, 1989-92; spl. projects. coord. KPAX/KRTV/KXLF, Missoula, 1992—; v.p. Mont. Freedom of Info. Hotline, Helena, 1988—. V.p. Missoula Advocacy Program for the Disabled, 1980-84; adv. mem. Helena AIDS Task Force, 1988-89, Missoula Habitat for Humanity, 1993—, Mont. Tobacco Control Coalition, Helena, 1994. Named Mont. TV Broadcaster of Yr., Mont. Broadcasters Assn., 1989, 90, 92, Mont. TV Program of the Yr., Mont. Broadcasters Assn., 1987, 89, 90, 92, 94, 96, Mont. News Enterprise of the Yr., 1988, 89; recipient Silver Gavel award Mont. Bar Assn., 1992. Mem. Soc. Profl. Journalists (state pres. 1988, pres. 1994—), Japan Kumamoto club of Western Mt., (pres. 1994—). Office: KPAX-TV 2204 Regent St Missoula MT 59801-7941

MARQUESS, LAWRENCE WADE, lawyer; b. Bloomington, Ind., Mar. 2, 1950; s. Earl Lawrence and Mary Louise (Coberly) M.; m. Barbara Ann Bailey, June 17, 1978; children: Alexander Lawrence, Michael Wade. BSEE, Purdue U., 1973; JD, W.Va. U., 1977. Bar: W.Va. 1977, Tex. 1977, U.S. Dist. Ct. (so. dist.) W.Va. 1977, U.S. Dist. Ct. (no. dist.) Tex. 1977, Colo. 1980, U.S. Dist. Ct. Colo. 1980, U.S. Ct. Appeals (10th cir.) 1980, U.S. Supreme Ct. 1984, U.S. Dist. Ct. (no. dist.) Ohio 1988, U.S. Ct. Appeals (DC cir.) 1997. Assoc. Johnson, Bromberg, Leeds & Riggs, Dallas, 1977-79, Bradley, Campbell & Carney, Golden, Colo., 1979-82, ptnr., 1983-84; assoc. Stettner, Miller & Cohn P.C., Denver, 1984-85, ptnr., 1985-87; of counsel Nelson & Harding, Denver, 1987-88, Heron, Burchette, Ruckert & Rothwell, 1989-90, Harding & Ogborn, 1990-94, Otten, Johnson, Robinson, Neff & Ragonetti, Denver, 1994—. Mem. faculty Am. Law Inst.-ABA Advanced Labor and Employment Law Course, 1986, 87. Mem. ABA (labor, antitrust and litigation sects.), Colo. Bar Assn. (co-chmn. labor law com. 1989-92), Denver Bar Assn., 1st Jud. Dist. Bar Assn., Sierra Club, Nat. Ry. Hist. Soc., ACLU. Democrat. Methodist. Home: 11883 W 27th Dr Lakewood CO 80215-7000 Office: Otten Johnson Robinson Neff & Raginetti 950 17th St Ste 1600 Denver CO 80202-2828

MARQUEZ, MARTINA ZENAIDA, elementary education educator; b. Santa Rosa, N.Mex., Nov. 5, 1935; d. Jose Zenon and Adelina (Romero) Sanchez; m. George J. Marquez, June 17, 1972. Student, Mt. St. Scholastica Coll., 1954-56, Regis Coll., 1956-59; BA, Coll. Santa Fe, 1963; MA, U. N.Mex., 1968. Cert. tchr., N.Mex. Elem. tchr. St. Rose Lima Sch., Santa Rosa, 1959-67, Cristo Rey Sch., Santa Fe, 1967-68, Los Lunas (N.Mex.) Consol. Schs., 1975-78, head tchr. adults operation; SER Manpower Devel. Tng. Act, Albuquerque, 1968-71, 73-75; tchr., cons. Regional Resource Ctr., N.Mex. State U., Las Cruces, 1971-72; counselor, coord. Taos (N.Mex.) Career Edn. Program, 1972-73; chpt. I reading tchr. Grants (N.Mex.) & Cibola County Schs., 1978—; chmn. ethics com. Profl. Standards Commn., N.Mex. Dept. Edn., 1986-88. Dir. choir St. Vivian's Ch., Milan, N.Mex., 1978—; del. Dem. Women's Club, Grants, N.Mex., 1981—; v.p. Literacy Vols. Am. of Cibola County. Named 1991 Cibola County Woman of Achievement 3d Ann. Women's Resource Conf., N.Mex. Tchr. of Yr., 1996; recipient Nat. Educator award Milken Family Found., 1996. Mem. AAUW (bylaws chmn. 1984, Grants Woman of Yr. award 1988), Internat. Reading Assn. (1st v.p. Malpais coun. 1988-89, pres. 1989-90, state pres. 1992-93, dist. 3 facilitator, Local Literacy award 1986, State Literacy award 1987, state pres. N.Mex. 1992-93, N.Mex. State coord. 1997), Delta Kappa Gamma (pres. Psi chpt. 1986-88). Democrat. Roman Catholic. Home: PO Box 11 Bluewater NM 87005-0011 Office: Grants-Cibola County Schs Jemez and Del Norte St Grants NM 87020

MARQUIS, MATTHEW ELLIOT, lawyer; b. San Rafael, Calif., Aug. 7, 1965; s. Harold Holliday and Nancy Josephine (Heinz) M. BA in Polit. Sci., U. Calif., Berkeley, 1987; JD, Am. U., 1991. Atty. Graham & James, Washington, 1991-94, San Francisco, 1994-96; atty. Cooley, Godward, Castro, Huddleson & Tatum, Palo Alto, Calif., 1996—; clk. U.S. Attys. Office for D.C., Washington, 1989-90. Contbr. articles to profl. jours. Vetter of cabinet and sub-cabinet presdl. nominees Office of Pres.-elect, Presdl. Transition Team, Washington, 1992-93. Mem. Calif. Coun. Internat. Trade (pub. policy com. 1994—), Calif. Commonwealth Club, World Affairs Coun., German-Am. Bus. Coun., U.S.-China Bus. coun. Home: 114 Douglass St San Francisco CA 94114-1921 Office: Cooley Godward Castro Huddleson & Tatum 5 Palo Alto 3000 El Camino Real Palo Alto CA 94306-2120

MARRA, THOMAS, psychologist, health facility administrator; b. Oakland, Calif., Apr. 13, 1955; s. Angelo and Iwana Minchew M.; m. Judith Irene Lies; children: Daniel, Steven. BA, U. of the Pacific, 1977; PhD, Calif. Sch. Profl. Psychology, 1981. Pvt. practice Monterey, Calif., 1983—; CEO, clin. dir. Monterey Psychiat. Health Facility, 1995—. Capt. U.S. Army, 1981-83. Mem. Calif. Psychol. Assn. (bd. dirs. 1987-91, chmn. long range healthcare planning com. 1989-90, govtl. affairs com. 1991-92, Silver Psi award 1990, Jacquline Bohotsos Media award 1992, Disting. Svc. award 1993), Mid-Coast Psychol. Assn. (pres. 1986). Office: Monterey Psychiat Health Facility 5 Via Joaquin Monterey CA 93940

MARRE, DIANA KATHERINE, author, theater educator; b. Fort Smith, Ark., June 5, 1953; d. Raymond Anthony and Rowena Frances (White) M. BA, Washington U., 1974, MFA, MA, 1982; PhD, U. Calif., Berkeley, 1987. Instr. Washington U., St. Louis, 1979-82, U. Calif., Berkeley, 1982-87; asst. prof. U. Puget Sound, Tacoma, 1987-93; assoc. faculty Tacoma C.C., 1994—; dir. stage prodns. Ghetto Pad Prodns., St. Louis, 1979-82, U. Calif., Berkeley, 1982-87, U. Puget Sound, Tacoma, 1988-93, New City Theater, Seattle, 1991. Author: (play) Hired Hands, 1983 (A.E. Hotchner award 1984), (novel) A Dyke Like Me, 1996; author, performer (one woman musical) A Really Big Shoe, 1990-93. Sustaining mem. Puget Sound Area Task Force for Human Rights, Seattle, 1988-93; mem., fundraiser South Sound Alliance for Gay Rights, Seattle and Tacoma, 1993-96; participating faculty Cultural Diversity Initiative, Tacoma C.C., 1995—. Mem. Assn. for Theatre in Higher Edn. (forum rep. 1988-94), West Coast Women in Theater, Black Theater Assn. (conf. planner 1990-92, chair 1992-94), Literary Mgrs. and Dramaturgs USA (v.p. for N.W. region 1989-92). Democrat. Roman Catholic. Home: 8814 35th St W Tacoma WA 98466-2106

MARRINGTON, BERNARD HARVEY, retired automotive company executive; b. Vancouver, B.C., Can., Nov. 9, 1928; s. Fredrick George and Constance Marie (hall) M.; m. Patricia Grace Hall, Sept. 3, 1953 (div. 1993); children: Jodie Lynn, Stacey Lee. Student, U. Pitts., 1982, Bethany Coll., W.Va., 1983; BS in Mktg. Mgmt., Pacific Western U., 1985. V.p., sales mgr. W & L of La Mesa, Calif., 1960-66; pres., gen. mgr. W & L of La Mesa, 1966-68; regional mgr. PPG Industries, Inc., L.A., 1977-88, regional mgr. profit ctr., 1988-91; cons. L.A. Unified Sch. Dist., 1972, South Coast Air Quality Mgmt. Dist., El Monte, Calif., 1987-91; adv. com. So. Calif. Regional Occupational Ctr., Torrance, 1978-91; mem. Ford Arbitration bd. U. Wis., 1997. Contbr. articles to profl. jours. Sustaining sponsor Ronald Reagan Presdl. Found., Simi, 1987—; sustaining mem. Rep. Nat. Com., L.A., 1985-92, Rep. Presdl. Legion of Merit, 1986-94; del. Rep. Platform Planning com., L.A., 1992; charter mem. Nat. Tax Limitation Com., Washington, 1988, Jarvis Gann Taxpayers Assn., L.A., 1979-94; sponsor Reagan Presdl. Libr., 1986; mem. Fotd Arbitration Bd., U. Wis., 1997. Recipient Award for Outstanding Community Support, So. Calif. Regional Occupational Ctr., 1986. Episcopalian.

MARROW, DEBORAH, foundation executive, art historian; b. N.Y.C., Oct. 18, 1948; d. Seymour Arthur and Adele (Wolin) M.; m. Michael J. McGuire, June 19, 1971; children: David Marrow McGuire, Anna Marrow McGuire. BA cum laude, U. Pa., 1970, PhD, 1978; MA, Johns Hopkins U., 1972. Resch. asst. Phila. Mus. of Art, 1974-75; mng. editor Chrysalis Mag., L.A., 1978-80; asst. prof. Occidental Coll., L.A., 1979, 81-82; pubs. coord. The J. Paul Getty Trust, L.A., 1983-84; program officer The Getty Grant Program, L.A., 1984-86, asst. dir., 1987-89, dir., 1989—; mem. internat. com. Coun. on Founds., Washington, 1992-96; mem. internat. adv. Group Nat. Endowment for the Arts, 1992; mem. adv. com. Calif. Cmty. Found., L.A., 1991—; mem. Excellence and Equity task force Am. Assn. of Mus., Washington, 1989-91. Author: The Art Patronage of Maria de Medici, 1982; contbr. articles to profl. jours. Chair cultural diversity com. The J. Paul Getty Trust, L.A., 1995—. Samuel H. Kress Found. fellow, N.Y.C., 1975-77. Mem. Coll. Art Assn. of Am., So. Calif. Assn. for Philanthropy (program com., 1988-89, 97), Grantmakers in the Arts, Art Table, Internat. Coun. of Mus., Penn Women (trustee coun.). Office: The Getty Grant Program 1200 Getty Center Dr Ste 800 Los Angeles CA 90049-1685

MARROW, MARVA JAN, photographer, writer, video and multimedia producer; b. Denver, Apr. 22, 1948; d. Sydney and Helen Berniece (Garber) M. Student, Carnegie-Mellon U., 1965-67. Singer, songwriter RCA Records, Italy, 1972-77; pvt. practice photography Italy and U.S., 1976—; dir. acquisitions RAI TV, L.A., 1990-91; mng. agt. Thomas Angel Prodns., L.A., 1991-94; represented by Shooting Star Photo Agy., Agenzia Marka, Agenzia Masi, Italy, Uniphoto Press Internat., Japan; corr., photographer Italian TV Guide, Milan, 1979—; collaborator, photographer for other U.S. and European publs., radio and TV; TV news and documentary prodr. RAI TV, 1990—. Composer numerous songs for Italian pop artists, including Lucio Battisti, Battiato, Premiata Forneria Marconi (PFM), Patty Pravo, 1972—; author: (photobook) Inside the L.A. Artist, 1988; project dir. (CD-ROM) Digital Art Mus., 1994—; prodr. (CD-ROM) The Kat's Meow, 1996, The Top Dog, 1996, The World of Makeup, 1996; prodr., designer: (website) allpets.com; desogmer Bev's Beautyrama for Am. online; contbr. photographs for covers and articles to nat. and internat. mags. Mem. Motion Picture Assn. of Am., Fgn. Press Assn. Democrat. Home and Studio: 2080 N Garfield Ave Altadena CA 91001-2959 Office: Ayzenberg Group 39 E Walnut St Pasadena CA 91103

MARRS, LINDA DIANE, manufacturing executive; b. Portland, Oreg., May 4, 1964; d. David Gilbert and Diane (Sause) A. BA in Econs., U. Wash., 1991. Office mgr. Hawaii Wood Preserving Co., Kahului, 1984-85, v.p., 1987-94, pres., 1994—; with inventory contrl dept. Monarch Bldg. Supply, Kahului, 1986-87. Adminstrv. asst. I Have A Dream Program, Kahului, 1990-91; mem. area com. Spl. Olympics Maui County, 1993—; unified softball coach Spl. Olympics, 1994. Mem. Am. Wood Preservers Assn., Maui Contrs. Women's Aux. (pres. 1996—), Chi Omega (pres. Phi chpt. 1985). Republican. Mem. Christian Ch. Home: 125-A Akea Pl Kula HI 96790 Office: Hawaii Wood Preserving Co 356 Hanakai St Kahului HI 96732-2407

MARRS, ROY ALONZO, magazine editor, educator; b. Dale, Okla., Nov. 28, 1924; s. Mitchell Siler Marrs and Vida Emily Kerns Marrs Christenson; m. Claudia Ruth Whitford, Feb. 1946 (dec. July 1957); m. Alvina Miller; children: Lucille, Lawrence, Loren, John, Jim. BA, Phillips U., Enid, Okla., 1952; MA, Long Beach (Calif.) State U., 1970. Ordained minister Ch. of God, 7th Day, 1954; cert. h.s. tchr., elem. tchr., Calif. Min., pastor Ch. of God, 7th Day, Okla., Wis., Mo., Oreg., Colo., 1948-56, 83-94; coll. dir. Midwest Bible Coll., Stanberry, Mo., 1953-56; linotype operator Springfield (Oreg.) Daily News, 1958, Bible Advocate Press, Stanberry, 1957-58; elem. sch. tchr. Hawthorne (Calif.) Elem. Sch. Dist., 1958-86; editor-in-chief Bible Advocate Mag., Denver, 1992—; pres. ministerial coun. Gen. Conf. Ch. of God, 7th Day, Denver, 1990-92, v.p. gen. conf., 1991-92. Served with U.S. Army, 1943-46, ETO. Decorated 3 Bronze Stars. Republican. Home: 102 Mokelumne River Dr Lodi CA 95240-7612 Office: Bible Advocare 330 W 152nd Ave Broomfield CO 80020-9100

MARSDEN, EUGENE DENNIS, SR., bleacher seating manufacturing executive; b. Madison, Wis., June 5, 1930; s. Glenn R. and Frieda Marsden; m. Margot Boice, Apr. 29, 1950; children: Eugene D. Jr., David B. Jeffrey. BS, UCLA, 1954. Pres. Marsden Bros. Inc., Santa Monica, Calif., 1960—. 1st lt. U.S. Army, 1954-56. Republican. Roman Catholic. Office: Marsden Bros Inc 127 Esparta Way Santa Monica CA 90402-2138

MARSH, DENNIS CHARLES, state agency official; b. York, Nebr., Aug. 17, 1949; s. Gyle Melvin and Shirley Lyone (Rogers) M.; m. Lila Charlene Sales, Aug. 5, 1972 (div. 1983); children: Zachary Aaron, Erin Lila. BA in Edn., Western Wash. U., 1971; MA, Pacific Lutheran U., 1980. Secondary sch. tchr. Tacoma (Wash.) Sch. Dist., 1974-78; labor rels. adminstr. Boeing, Seattle, 1978-82; asst. pers. dir. Pierce County, Tacoma, 1982-87; exec. officer Indeterminate Sentence Rev. Bd., Olympia, Wash., 1987—. Mem. Assn. Paroling Authorities Internat., Am. Correctional Assn., Wash. Correctional Assn. Office: Indeterminate Sentence Rev Bd PO Box 40907 Olympia WA 98504

MARSH, FRANK RAYMOND, engineering technical writer, artist; b. Waterville, Maine, Aug. 5, 1938; s. Gerald Raymond and Dorothy Marion (Haines) M. B of Gen. Studies, Chaminade U., Honolulu, 1968; BFA, Otis Art Inst., 1971, MFA, 1973; BS in Computer Sci., West Coast U., 1984, MS in Computer Sci., 1986, MIBA, 1987, MMIS, 1988, MSMIS, 1990, BS in Elec. Engring., 1993. Editor, cartographer Thomas Bros. Maps, L.A., 1974-80; engring. writer Singer Co., Glendale, Calif., 1983-87; sr. tech. writer Amperpif Corp., Chatsworth, Calif., 1987-89; prin. engring. writer Litton Data Systems, Agoura Hills, Calif., 1990-96. One-man shows include Westwood (Calif.) Art Assn., 1973, Westwood Ctr. of the Arts, 1975, Villa Montalvo, Saratoga, Calif., 1975, Sr. Eye Gallery, Long Beach, Calif., 1979, 81, Studio 1617 Gallery, L.A., 1984; numerous group exhbns. and juried invitationals; permanent collections include Detroit Mortgage Co., Gulf and Western, Homes Savs. and Loan Bank, Otis Art Inst., Palmcrest Ho., United Calif. Bank. Mem. L.A. Art Mus. Graphics Coun., 1976—. With USAF, 1961-69. Mem. IEEE, Artists Equity, L.A. Printmaking Soc., Soc. for Tech. Comm. Home: 2800 Lambert Dr Los Angeles CA 90068-2323

MARSH, JOHN HARRISON, environmental planner, lawyer; b. Auburn, Wash., June 25, 1954; s. F. A. Buzz and Margery Ann (Greene) M.; m. Debra Rose Raniere, June 18, 1977; children: Jenna Rose, Christian John. BS in Fisheries Scis., Oreg. State U., 1977; JD, Lewis & Clark Coll., 1985, cert. natural resources and environ. law, 1985. Bar: Oreg. 1986. Rsch. asst. EPA, Corvallis, Oreg., 1975-77; fisheries biologist Nat. Marine Fisheries Svc., Portland, Oreg., 1977-78, Oreg. Dept. Fish and Wildlife, Astoria, 1978; pub. info. officer Columbia River Inter-Tribal Fish Commn., Portland, 1978-79, fisheries ecologist, 1979-85; system planning coord. N.W. Power Planning Coun., Portland, 1985-96, mgr. habitat and prodn., 1996—; speaker, expert witness in field; guest lectr. Lewis and Clark Coll., 1984, 95. Contbr. articles to profl. publs. Organizer food drive Friends of Seasonal Workers, 1987; chair ann. NPPC food drive Sunshine Divsn., 1987-96; bd. dirs. Panavista Park Homeowners Assn., 1991-93, mem. archtl. rev. com., 1990—, chair, 1991—; Riverwest Ch. lead Sunday sch. instr. grades 5-6, 1992-96, adult Bible study instr., 1995—, Kinship leader, 1994—, Mex. Youth Mission team, 1994, 95, libr. coord., 1995—; asst. scoutmaster Boy Scouts Am., 1972-73. Mem. Am. Fisheries Soc. (cert. profl. fisheries scientist, exec. com. Portland chpt. 1981-84, v.p. 1981-82, pres. 1982-83, chair legis. com. Oreg. chpt. 1988-89, program com. 1980-81, riparian com. Western div. 1982-83, convenor various sessions, mem. native peoples fisheries com. 1982-88, chair 1984-86, resolutions com. 1985-86, strategic plan devel com., 1993-95, other coms.), Oreg. State Bar Assn., Native Am. Fish and Wildlife Assn., Oreg. Wine Brotherhood (chair Benefit Auction and Barrel Tasting 1995), Great Lovers of Wine Soc. (pres. 1988). Office: NW Power Planning Coun 851 SW 6th Ave Ste 1100 Portland OR 97204-1348

MARSH, KATHERINE CYNTHIA, writer, journalist, poet; b. Salem, Oreg., Apr. 23, 1956; d. Emanuel Louis and Mary Elizabeth (Dooper) M. Student, Chemeketa C.C., Salem, 1976, 86, U. Oreg., 1977-78; AA, Linn-Benton C.C., Albany, Oreg., 1986. Freelance writer Salem, 1976—; freelance corr. The Oreg. Herald, Albany, 1979; reporter The Willamette Valley Examiner, Salem, 1984-85, The Commuter, Albany, 1985-86; corr. Sr. News, Salem, 1988-90, Keizer(Oreg.)/South Salem Times, 1989-90; freelancer, corr. The West Side, Salem, 1989-90; reviewer bus. publs.; collaborator various books, 1994—. Contbr. essays, poetry to jours., revs. Recipient Poetry award Nashville Newsletter, 1979, 81, Soc. Am. Poets, 1994. Mem. Poets Guild, Internat. Women's Writing Guild. Office: PO Box 613 Salem OR 97308

MARSH, MALCOLM F., federal judge; b. 1928. BS, U. Oreg., 1952, LLB, 1954, JD, 1971. Ptnr. Clark & Marsh, Lindauer & McClinton (and predecessors), Salem, Oreg., 1958-87; judge U.S. Dist. Ct. Oreg., Portland, 1987—. With U.S. Army, 1946-47. Fellow Am. Coll. Trial Lawyers; mem. ABA. Office: US Dist Ct 114 US Courthouse 620 SW Main St Portland OR 97205-3037*

MARSH, RICHARD ALAN, lawyer; b. Grand Island, Nebr., Nov. 27, 1952; s. M. Robert and A. Yvonne (Nitzel) M.; m. Kay Palmer, Aug. 21, 1982; children: Alexa K., Madelyn B. BA, Northwestern U., 1975; JD with honors, Ill. Inst. Tech.-Chgo. Kent, 1979. Bar: Ill. 1979, Colo. 1985. Assoc. law Schumacher Jones Kelly Olson & Pusch, Chgo., 1979-84; ptnr. Grant McHendrie Haines & Crouse, Denver, 1984-90, Marsh & Kolko, Denver, 1990-91, Massey Showalter & Marsh, Denver, 1991-95; pvt. practice Eads, Colo., 1995—. Bd. dirs. Keep the Lites Found., Denver, 1989-95; precinct chair Jefferson County Republican Party, Littleton, Colo.; dir. South Metro Denver Bus. Polit. Action Com., Littleton. Mem. ABA, Colo. Bar Assn., Denver Bar Assn., South Metro Denver C. of C. (bd. dirs. 1988-92). Methodist. Office: 1103 Luther St Box 374 Eads CO 81036

MARSH, ROBERTA REYNOLDS, elementary education educator, consultant; b. Kokomo, Ind., June 2, 1939; d. Elwood Bert and Mildred Bell Reynolds; m. Ronald Dean Marsh Sr., Apr. 5, 1958; children: Ronald Jr., Bryan William, Joel Allen. BEd, Ind. U., Kokomo, 1970; MEd, Ind. U., Bloomington, 1971. Cert. tchr., spl. edn. tchr., Ind., Ariz. Tchr. spl. edn. Kokomo Ctr. Schs., 1970-77; tchr. spl. edn. Tempe (Ariz.) Elem. Dist. #3, 1978-86, tchr. civics, geography, English/lit., 1986—. Local dir. Spl. Olympics, Kokomo, 1974-77, Tempe Assn. Retarded Citizens, 1978-88; den mother Boy Scouts Am., Kokomo, 1967-73; leader 4-H Club, Kokomo, 1974-77. Recipient Excellence in Edn. award Tempe Diablo, 1991. Mem. Coun. for Exceptional Children (state pres. 1986-87, Tempe chpt. pres. 1994-95, outstanding leader award 1985, outstanding regular tchr., 1996, Tempe coun. 1995-96), Internat. Reading Assn., Assn. for Children with Learning Disabilities, Ind. U. Alumni Assn., Alpha Delta Kappa (corr. sec. 1986-88, Theta pres. 1990-92). Democrat. Home: 4113 E Emelita Cir Mesa AZ 85206-5109 Office: Hudson Sch 1325 E Malibu Dr Tempe AZ 85282-5742

MARSH, WILLIAM DAVID, government operations executive; b. Hot Springs, Ark., July 6, 1948; s. Robert W. G. and DeMaris (Graham) M.; m. Linda K. Adams, June 23, 1996. BSBA, Henderson State U., 1970; MS in Psychol. Counseling, Wayne State U., 1973; MS in Contract and Acquisition Mgmt., Fla. Inst. Tech., 1990. Commd. 2d. lt. U.S. Army, 1970, advanced through grades to maj., 1987, ret.; owner Stinson Aviation Corp., San Antonio, 1980-83; officer, contracting officer, divsn. chief Walter Reed Army Med. Ctr., 1987-90; officer, chief contracting office Health Svcs. Command Acquisition Activity, El Paso, Tex., 1990-93; contracts adminstr., dir. contracts Omni Corp., Albuquerque, 1994-96, v.p. ops., 1996—; cons. in field, Albuquerque, 1994—. Decorated Order Mil. Med. Merit, 1993. Mem. Nat. Contract Mgmt. Assn. (cert. profl. contract mgr. 1991). Home: 7504 Laster Ave NE Albuquerque NM 87109-6058 Office: Omni Corp 4100 Montgomery Blvd NE Albuquerque NM 87109

MARSHAK, HARRY, physician, plastic surgeon; b. L.A., Oct. 1, 1961; s. Herbert and Pearl (Engelson) M. BS, U. Calif., Riverside, 1981; MD, UCLA, 1984. Diplomate Am. Bd. Surgery, Am. Bd. Plastic Surgery. Pvt. practice Beverly Hills, Calif., 1991-97. Fellow ACS (hon.), Internat. Coll. Surgeons; mem. Am. Soc. Plastic and Reconstructive Surgeons, Calif. Soc. Plastic Surgery. Republican. Office: 150 N Robertson Blvd Ste 140 Beverly Hills CA 90211-2143

MARSHALL, ARTHUR K., lawyer, judge, arbitrator, educator, writer; b. N.Y.C., Oct. 7, 1911. BS, CUNY, 1933; LLB, St. John's U., N.Y.C., 1936; LL.M., U. So. Calif., 1952. Bar: N.Y. State 1937, Calif. 1947. Practice law N.Y.C., 1937-43, Los Angeles, 1947-50; atty. VA, Los Angeles, 1947-50; tax counsel Calif. Bd. Equalization, Sacramento, 1950-51; inheritance tax atty. State Controller, Los Angeles, 1951-53; commr. Superior Ct. Los Angeles County, 1953-62; judge Municipal Ct., Los Angeles jud. dist., 1962-63, Superior Ct., Los Angeles, 1963-81; supervising judge probate dept. Superior Ct., 1968-69, appellate dept., 1973-77; presiding judge Appellate Dept., 1976-77; pvt. practice arbitrator, mediator, judge pro tem, 1981—; acting asst. prof. law UCLA, 1954-59; grad. faculty U. So. Calif., 1955-75; lectr. Continuing Edn. of the Bar; mem. Calif. Law Revision Commn., 1984—, chmn., 1986-87, 92-93; chmn. com. on efficiency and econs. Conf. Calif. Judges, past chmn. spl. action com. on ct. improvement; past chmn. probate law cons. group Calif. Bd. Legal Specialization. Author: Joint Tenancy Taxwise and Otherwise, 1953, Branch Courts, 1959, California State and Local Taxation Text, 2 vols., 1962, rev. edit., 1969, supplement, 1979, 2d editn., 1981, Triple Choice Method, 1964, California State and Local Taxation Forms, 2 vols., 1961-75, rev. edit., 1979, California Probate Procedure, 1961, 5th rev. edit., 1994, Guide to Procedure Before Trial, 1975; contbr. articles to profl. jours. Mem. Town Hall. With AUS, 1943-46; lt. col. JAGC, USAR ret. Named Judge of Yr. Lawyers Club L.A. County, 1975; first recipient Arthur K. Marshall award established by estate planning, trust and probate sect. L.A. Bar Assn., 1981, Disting. Jud. Career award L.A. Lawyers Club, award L.A. County Bd. Suprs., 1981. Fellow Am. Bar Found.; mem. ABA (probate litigation com. real property, probate and trust sect.), Am. Arbitration Assn. (mem. nat. panel of arbitrators), Internat. Acad. Estate and Trust Law (academician, founder, 1st pres., now chancellor), Calif. State Bar (advisor to exec. com. real property, probate and trust sect. 1970-83), Santa Monica Bar Assn. (pres. 1960), Westwood Bar Assn. (pres. 1959), L.A. Bar Assn., Am. Legion (comdr. 1971-72), U. So. Calif. Law Alumni Assn. (pres. 1969-70), Phi Alpha Delta (1st justice alumni chpt.). Office: 300 S Grand Ave Fl 28 Los Angeles CA 90071-3109

MARSHALL, CONRAD JOSEPH, entrepreneur; b. Detroit, Dec. 23, 1934; s. Edward Louis Fedak and Maria Magdalena Berzsenyi; m. Dorothy Genieve Karnafil, Dec. 1, 1956 (div. 1963); children: Conrad Joseph Jr., Kevin Conrad, Lisa Marie; m. Beryle Elizabeth Callahan, June 15, 1965 (div. 1972); children: Brent Jasmer, Farah Elizabeth. Diploma, Naval Air Tech. Tng. Ctr., Norman, Okla., 1952; student, Wayne State U., 1956-59; Diploma, L.A. Police Acad., 1961. Dir. mktg. Gulf Devel., Torrance, Calif., 1980-83; sales mgr. Baldwin Piano Co., Santa Monica, Calif., 1977-80; dir. mktg., v.p. Western Hose, Inc., L.A., 1971-76; city letter carrier U.S. Post Office, L.A., 1969-71; writer freelance L.A., 1966—; police officer L.A. Police Dept., 1961-66; asst. sales mgr. Wesson Oil Co., Detroit, 1958-60; agt. Life Ins. Co. of Va., Wayne, Mich., 1956-58; pres. Am. Vision Mktg., L.A., 1990—, Con-Mar Prodns., L.A., 1983—; sr. v.p. Pacific Acquisition Group, 1992—, Invest. Admin. HealthCom., Int., 1993—; pres. Midway TV Co., 1994—; tech. advisor Lion's Gate Films, Westwood, Calif., 1970-74, Medicine Wheel Prodns., Hollywood, Calif., 1965-75; mng. gen. ptnr. Encino Wireless #1, 1994—; CEO Midway TV Inc., 1995; v.p. nat. bus. affairs MMA Internat., 1997. Author: (series) "Dial Hot Line", 1967, (screenplay) "Heads Across the Border", 1968, "The Fool Card", 1970, "Probable Cause", 1972; co-author: The Fedak File, 1995; albums include Song Shark, 1992, Conrad Marshall Quintet, 1991. Campaign vol. Dem. Ctrl. Com., L.A., 1976, Rep. Ctrl. Com., 1994. Mem. Screen Actors Guild, Internat. Platform Assn. Home: 11853 Kling St Apt 17 Valley Village CA 91607-4048 Office: Con-Mar Prodns 2026 Holly Hill Ter Hollywood CA 90068-3812

MARSHALL, CONSUELO BLAND, federal judge; b. Knoxville, Tenn., Sept. 28, 1936; d. Clyde Theodore and Annie (Brown) Arnold; m. George Edward Marshall, Aug. 30, 1959; children: Michael Edward, Laurie Ann. A.A., Los Angeles City Coll., 1956; B.A., Howard U., 1958, LL.B., 1961. Bar: Calif. 1962. Dep. atty. City of L.A., 1962-67; assoc. Cochran & Atkins, L.A., 1968-70; commr. L.A. Superior Ct., 1971-76; judge Inglewood Mcpl. Ct., 1976-77, L.A. Superior Ct., 1977-80, U.S. Dist. Ct. Central Dist. Calif., L.A., 1980—; lectr. U.S. Information Agy. in Yugoslavia, Greece and Italy, 1984, in Nigera and Ghana, 1991, in Ghana, 1992. Contbr. articles to profl. jours.; notes editor Law Jour. Howard U. Mem. adv. bd. Richstone Child Abuse Center. Recipient Judicial Excellence award Criminal Cts. Bar Assn., 1992; research fellow Howard U. Law Sch., 1959-60. Mem. State Bar Calif., Calif. Women Lawyers Assn., Calif. Assn. Black Lawyers, Calif. Judges Assn., Black Women Lawyers Assn., Los Angeles County Bar Assn., Nat. Assn. Women Judges, NAACP, Urban League, Beta Phi Sigma. Office: US Dist Ct 312 N Spring St Rm 155 Los Angeles CA 90012-4701

MARSHALL, DAVID BROWNELL, biologist, consultant; b. Portland, Oreg., Mar. 7, 1926; s. Earl Andrew and Dorothy Southwick (Brownell) M.; m. Betty Irene Jones, Aug. 13, 1949 (div. Jan. 15, 1990); children: Janet Carolyn, John Frederick. BS in Fish and Game Mgmt., Oreg. State Coll., 1950. Cert. wildlife biologist. Resident biologist Stillwater Wildlife Mgmt. Area, Fallon, Nev., 1950-53; resident biologist Sacramento Nat. Wildlife Refuges, Willows, Calif., 1953-55, Malheur Nat. Wildlife Refuge, Burns, Oreg., 1955-60; regional refuge biologist U.S. Fish & Wildlife Svc., Portland, 1960-72; wildlife biologist U.S. Fish & Wildlife Svc., Washington, 1972-76; sr. staff biologist U.S. Fish & Wildlife Svc., Portland, 1976-81; consulting wildlife biologist Portland, 1981—; lectr. Humboldt State Coll., Arcata, Calif., 1971, Portland State U., 1982, 83. Author: Birds of Northwest Fields, Forests and Gardens, 1973; contbr. articles to nature mags. and sci. jours. Apptd. by gov. Natural Heritage Adv. Coun., Salem, Oreg., 1980-83, chair, 1982; v.p. Portland Audubon Soc., 1961-65, 90-95; apptd. by mayor Portland Zoo Commn., 1971-72, Harney County Sch. Bd., 1957-60; Oreg. chair The Nature Conservancy, 1972. Staff Sgt. U.S. Army, 1944-46, ETO. Recipient Disting. Grad. award Oreg. State U., 1995. Mem. Am. Ornithologists Union (chmn. conservation com. 1968-70), The Wildlife Soc. (pres. Oreg. chpt. 1967, Oreg. Wildlife Soc. award 1993, Past Pres.'s award 1966, pres. N.W. Sect. 1979, Wildlife Diversity award 1997), Pacific N.W. Bird and Mammal Soc. (v.p. Oreg. 1966, 72), Cooper Ornithol. Soc., Soc. for Conservation Biology. Home and Office: 4265 Chesapeake Ave Portland OR 97201-1344

MARSHALL, DAVID STANLEY, lawyer; b. Seneca Falls, N.Y., Aug. 23, 1950; s. James Stanley and Ruth Catherine (Cratty) M.; m. Jo Ann Breuninger, Mar. 20, 1993; 1 child, Matthew Stanley. BA, Cornell U., 1970; JD, U. Calif., Berkeley, 1974. Bar: Wash. 1981, Calif. 1975. Dep. pros. atty. Pierce County, Tacoma, Wash., 1981-84; assoc. atty. Williams Kastner & Gibbs, Seattle, 1984-85; shareholder Prince, Kelley, Marshall & Coombs, Seattle, 1985-96; pvt. practice Seattle, 1997—. Chair fellowship bd. Univ. Congl. Ch., 1985-85; chair adv. com. Metro Citizen's Transit, Seattle, 1988-90; vol. Big Brothers King County, Seattle, 1992—; bd. dirs. Transit Discussion Group, 1995-96. Democrat. United Church of Christ. Home: 153 Hayes St Seattle WA 98109 Office: 900 4th Ave # 3250 Seattle WA 98164-1005

MARSHALL, DONALD THOMAS, medical technologist; b. Omaha, June 9, 1955; s. William A. and Alma J. (Jorgensen) M.; m. Beverly Ann Everett, Sept. 22, 1990. Med. tech., Pikes Peak Inst. Med. Tech., 1977; EMT, Pikes Peak C.C., Colorado Springs, 1979; PhD of Religion, Universal Life Ch., 1995, D of Metaphysics (hon.), 1995. Registered med. technologist; cert. clin. lab. technologist. Technician x-ray/med. St. Joseph Hosp. of Plains, Cheyenne Wells, Colo., 1977-79; technician med. lab. Conejos County Hosp., La Jara, Colo., 1979-84; med. technologist Nat. Health Lab., Englewood, Colo., 1984-91; lab. tech. cons. neighborhood health program Denver Dept. Health and Hosps., 1996—. EMT, fireman La Jara Vol. Fire Dept., 1979-84, Meritorious Svc. Citation, 1983. Mem. Internat. Soc. Clin. Lab. Tech., Am. Med. Technologists, East Denver Masonic Lodge Ancient, Free and Accepted Masons (Master 1994). Republican.

MARSHALL, JAMES KENNETH, academic administrator; b. Providence, Dec. 25, 1952; s. James William and Eileen Frances (O'Connell) M.; m. Mary H. Jackson, Mar. 17, 1987. BA in Chemistry, SUNY, Plattsburgh, 1974; MBA in Fin., U. R.I., 1977; postgrad., U. Wash., 1978-79. Fin. instr. U. R.I., Kingston, 1978; teaching assoc. U. Wash., Seattle, 1978-79; asst. dir. facilities mgmt. U. Colo., Boulder, 1979-86, dir. buying and contracting, 1986-90; transp. mgr. Town of Vail, Colo., 1991-92; v.p. Women at the Wheel Automotive Cons. and Consumer Edn. Svc., Bozeman, Mont., 1990-96; assoc. dir. computing and network svcs. U. Colo., Boulder, 1996—; honorarium instr. U. Colo., Denver, 1981-85; bd. dirs. Minority Enterprises, Inc., 1988-90. Contbr. chpt. to book on plant administration. Recipient Job Well Done award U. Colo. Boulder Dept. Facilities Mgmt., 1983. Mem. Beta Gamma Sigma, Phi Kappa Phi. Office: U Colo Campus Box 379 Boulder CO 80309

MARSHALL, ROBERT HERMAN, economics educator; b. Harrisburg, Pa., Dec. 6, 1929; s. Mathias and Mary (Bubich) M.; m. Billie Marie Sullivan, May 31, 1958; children: Mellisa Frances, Howard Hylton, Robert Charles. A.B. magna cum laude, Franklin and Marshall Coll., 1951; M.A., Ohio State U., 1952, Ph.D., 1957. Teaching asst. Ohio State U., 1952-57; mem. faculty, then prof. econs. U. Ariz., Tucson, 1957-95, prof. emeritus, 1995; dir. Internat. Bus. Studies Project, 1969-71; research observer Sci.-Industry Program, Hughes Aircraft Co., Tucson, summer 1959. Author: Commercial Banking in Arizona: Structure and Performance Since World War II, 1966, (with others) The Monetary Process, 2d edit, 1980. Bd. dirs. Com. for Econ. Opportunity, Tucson, 1968-69. Faculty fellow Pacific Coast Banking Sch., summer 1974. Mem. Am. Econ. Assn., Phi Beta Kappa, Beta Gamma Sigma, Pi Gamma Mu, Phi Kappa Phi, Delta Sigma Pi. Democrat. Roman Catholic. Home: 6700 N Abington Rd Tucson AZ 85743-9795

MARSHALL, RONALD E., media and communications educator; b. Fargo, N.D., Aug. 12, 1947; s. Kenneth and Ruth Marshall; m. Mary A. Olson, Aug. 12, 1970 (div. Mar. 16, 1984); children: Ava, Sharla; m. Jane Landgren, Aug. 5, 1991; children: Matthew Prentice, Robert Prentice. BS, U. N.D., 1969; Master's, Lesley Coll., 1987. Media and comm. educator El Paso County Schs., Colorado Springs, 1969; publ. Photoflash, 1980; comml. artist The Western Horseman mag., 1980; aerial photographer Colo. Space Ops./U.S. Corps of Engrs., 1983; film/TV prodn. coord. TV commls., catalog photo shoots Gatorade, Colo., 1995, Spiegel, Colo., 1994, Gen. TV Arts, Colo., 1992; ghostwriter, media cons., Colo., 1990; real estate broker, Colo., 1983; TV reporter, videographer Grass Roots TV, Aspen, Colo., 1979; media dir. Colo. Legislator, 1976; photo agt. New World Prodns., Colo., 1976; newspaper reporter The Forum, Fargo, 1967.

MARSHALL, SCOTT, advertising agency executive. V.p. Ogilvy & Mather, N.Y.C., sr. v.p., 1986-88; pres. Cole & Weber, Inc., Seattle, 1988—; pres Hal Riney & Ptnrs., Inc., San Francisco. Office: Hal Riney & Ptnrs 735 Battery St San Francisco CA 94111*

MARSTON, MICHAEL, urban economist, asset management executive; b. Oakland, Calif., Dec. 4, 1936; s. Lester Woodbury and Josephine (Janovic) M.; m. Alexandra Lynn Geyer, Apr. 30, 1966; children: John, Elizabeth. BA, U. Calif., Berkeley, 1959; postgrad. London Sch. Econs., 1961-63. V.p. Larry Smith & Co., San Francisco, 1969-72, exec. v.p. urban econ. divsn., 1969-72; chmn. bd. Keyser Marston Assocs., Inc., San Francisco, 1973-87; gen. ptnr. The Sequoia Partnership, 1979-91; pres. Marston Vineyard and Winery, 1982—, Marston Assocs., Inc., 1982—, The Ctr. for Individual and Instnl. Renewal, 1996—. Cert. rev. appraiser Nat. Assn. Rev. Appraisers and Mortgage Underwriters, 1984—. Chmn., San Francisco Waterfront Com., 1969-86; chmn. fin. com., bd. dirs., mem. exec. com., treas. San Francisco Planning and Urban Rsch. Assn., 1976-87, Napa Valley Vintners, 1986—, mem. gov. affairs com.; trustee Cathedral Sch. for Boys, 1981-82, Marin Country Day Sch., 1984-90; v.p. St. Luke's Sch., 1986-91; pres. Presidio Heights Assn. of Neighbors, 1983-84; chmn. Presidio Com. 1991—; v.p., bd. dirs., mem. exec. com. People for Open Space, 1972-87; mem. Gov.'s Issue Analysis Com. and Speakers Bur., 1966; mem. speakers bur. Am. Embassy, London, 1961-63; v.p., bd. dirs. Dem. Forum, 1968-72; v.p., trustee Youth for Service. Served to lt. USNR. Mem. Napa Valley Vintners, Urban Land Inst., World Congress Land Policy (paper in field), Order of Golden Bear, Chevalier du Tastevin, Bohemian Club, Pacific Union Club, Lambda Alpha. Contbr. articles to profl. jours. Home: 3375 Jackson St San Francisco CA 94118-2018 *Personal philosophy: Success is what you do with what you have not what others think or what is in vogue.*

MARSTON, RICHARD ALAN, geography educator, consultant; b. Bethesda, Md., Apr. 6, 1952; s. Alan Douglas and Nancy (Burdick) M.; m. Linda Mary Crowe, July 16, 1977. BA, UCLA, 1974; MS, Oreg. State U., 1976, PhD, 1980. Environ. sci. V.T.N.-Colo., Denver, 1974-76, EPA, Corvallis, Oreg., 1976-77; hydrologist U.S. Forest Service, Waldport, Oreg., 1978-79; asst. prof. geography U. Tex., El Paso, 1980-86; asst. prof. geography U. Wyo., Laramie, 1986-88, assoc. prof., 1988-94, prof., 1994—; vis. prof. U. Alaska S.E., 1996-97; participant Found. for Glacier and Environ. Rsch. and Juneau Icefield Rsch. Program, 1996-97; cons. environ. geoscis., 1980—. Contbr. articles to profl. jours. Grantee Ft. Bliss Mil. Reservation, 1981, Horizon Cmtys. Improvement Assn., 1983, Assn. Western Univs., 1984, U.S. Forest Svc., 1988, 93, U.S. Geol. Survey, 1987, Wyo. Water Rsch. Ctr., 1988, Nat. Pk. Svc., 1989-93, NSF, 1995-98, Fulbright Rsch. Commn., France, 1993. Mem. Assn. Am. Geographers (Warren Nystrom award 1981), Am. Geophys. Union, Geol. Soc. Am., Am. Water Resources Assn., Assn. Geoscientists for Internat. Devel., Royal Geographical Soc., Explorers Club, Internat. Glaciol. Soc., Sigma Xi. Office: U Alaska Southeast 1108 F St Juneau AK 99801

MARTIN, AGNES, artist; b. Maklin, Sask., Can., 1912; came to U.S., 1932, naturalized, 1950; Student, Western Wash. State Coll., 1935-38; BS, Columbia U., 1942, MFA, 1952. One-woman shows include Betty Parsons Gallery, N.Y.C., 1958, 59, 61, Robert Elkon Gallery, N.Y.C., 1961, 63, 72, 76, Nicolas Wilder Gallery, Los Angeles, 1963-66, 67, Visual Arts Ctr., N.Y.C., 1971, Kunstraum, Munich, 1973, Inst. Contemporary Art U. Pa., Phila., 1973, Pace Gallery, N.Y.C., 1975, 76, 77, 78, 79, 80-81, 81, 83, 84, 85, 86, 89, 91, 92, 94, 95, Mayor Gallery, London, 1978, 84, Galerie Rudolf Zwirner, Cologne, Fed. Republic Germany, 1978, Harcus/Krakow Gallery, Boston, 1978, Margo Leavin Gallery, Los Angeles, 1979, 85, Mus. N.Mex., Santa Fe, 1979, Richard Gray Gallery, Chgo., 1981, Garry Anderson Gallery, Sydney, Australia, 1986, Waddington Galleries Ltd., London, 1986, Stedelijk Mus., Amsterdam, 1991, Whitney Mus. Am. Art, N.Y.C., 1992; exhibited in group shows at Carnegie Inst., Pitts., 1961, Whitney Mus. Am. Art, N.Y.C., 1962, 66, 67, 74, 77, 92, Tooth Gallery, London, 1962, Gallery Modern Art, Washington, 1963, Wadsworth Atheneum, Hartford, Conn., 1963, Solomon R. Guggenheim Mus., N.Y.C., 1965, 66, 76, Mead Corp., 1965-67, Mus. Modern Art, N.Y.C., 1967, 76, 85, Inst. Contemporary Art, Phila., 1967, Detroit Inst. Art, 1967, Corcoran Gallery Art, Washington, 1967, 81, Finch Mus., N.Y., 1968, Phila. Mus., 1968, Zurich Art Mus., Switzerland, 1969, Ill. Bell Telephone Co., Chgo., 1970, Mus. Contemporary Art, Chgo., 1971, Inst. Contemporary Art U. Pa., Phila., 1972, Randolph-Macon Coll., N.C., 1972, Kassel, Fed. Republic Germany, 1972, Stedelijk Mus., Amsterdam, 1975, U. Mass., Amherst, 1976, Venice Biennale, Italy, 1976, 80, Cleve. Mus. Art, 1978, Albright-Knox Gallery, Buffalo, 1978, Inst. Contemporary Art, Boston, 1979, Art Inst. Chgo., 1979, San Francisco Mus. Modern Art, 1980, ROSC Internat. Art Exhbn., Dublin, Ireland, 1980, Marilyn Pearl Gallery, N.Y.C., 1983, Kemper Gallery, Kansas City Art Inst., 1985, Am. Acad. and Inst. Arts and Letters, N.Y.C., 1985, Charles Cowles Gallery, N.Y.C., 1986, Moody Gallery Art U. Ala., Birmingham, 1986, Butler Inst. Am. Art, 1986, Art Gallery Western Australia, Perth, 1986, Mus. Contemporary Art, Los Angeles, 1986, Boston Fine Arts Mus., 1989; represented in permanent collections Mus. of Modern Art, N.Y.C., Albright-Knox Gallery, Aldrich Mus., Ridgefield, Conn., Art Gallery Ont., Can., Australian Nat. Gallery, Canberra, Grey Art Gallery and Study Ctr., N.Y.C., Solomon R. Guggenheim Mus., High Mus. Art, Atlanta, Hirshhorn Mus. and Sculpture Garden, Washington, Israel Mus., Jerusalem, La Jolla (Calif.) Mus. Contemporary Art, Los Angeles County Mus. Art, Mus. Art R.I. Sch. Design, Providence, Mus. Modern Art, Neuegalerie der Stadt, Aachen, Fed. Republic Germany, Norton Simon Mus. Art at Pasadena, Calif., Stedelijk Mus., Amsterdam, The Netherlands, 1992, Mus. Modern Art, paris, 1992, Tate Gallery, London, Wadsworth Atheneum, Walker Art Ctr., Mpls., Whitney Mus. Am. Art, 1993, Sofia, Madrid, 1993, Huosten, 1993, Worcester (Mass.) Art Mus., Yale U. Art Gallery, New Haven; subject of various articles. Office: 414 Placitas Rd # 37 Taos NM 97571-2513

MARTIN, BOYD ARCHER, political science educator emeritus; b. Cottonwood, Idaho, Mar. 3, 1911; s. Archer Olmstead and Norah Claudine (Imbler) M.; m. Grace Charlotte Swingler, Dec. 29, 1933; children: Michael Archer, William Archer. Student, U. Idaho, 1929-30, 35-36, B.S., 1936; student, Pasadena Jr. Coll., 1931-32, U. Calif. at Los Angeles, summer 1934; A.M., Stanford, 1937, Ph.D., 1943. Rsch. asst. Stanford U., 1936-37, teaching asst., 1937-38; instr. polit. sci. U. Idaho, 1938-39; acting instr. polit. sci. Stanford U., 1939-40; John M. Switzer fellow, summer 1939-40; chief personnel officer Walter Butler Constrn. Co., Farragut Naval Tng. Center, summer 1942; instr. polit. sci. U. Idaho, 1940-43, asst. prof. polit. sci., 1943-44, asso. prof. polit. sci., 1944-47; prof., head dept. social sci., asst. dean coll. letters and sci. U. Idaho, 1947-55, dean, 1955-70, Borah Distinguished prof. polit. sci., 1970-73, prof., dean emeritus, 1973—; vis. prof. Stanford U., summer 1946, spring 1952, U. Calif., 1962-63; affiliate Center for Study Higher Edn., Berkeley, 1962-63; mem. steering com. N.W. Conf. on Higher Edn., 1960-67, pres. conf., 1966-67; mem. bd. Am. Assn. of Partners of Alliance for Progress; chmn. Idaho Adv. Coun. on Higher Edn.; del. Gt. Plains UNESCO Conf., Denver, 1947; chmn. bd. William E. Borah Found. on Causes of War and Conditions of Peace, 1947-55; mem. Commn. to Study Orgn. Peace; dir. Bur. Pub. Affair Rsch., 1959-73, dir. emeritus, 1973—; dir. Martin Peace Inst., 1970—. Author: The Direct Primary in Idaho, 1947, (with others) Introduction to Political Science, 1950, (with other) Western Politics, 1968, Politics in the American West, 1969, (with Sydney Duncombe) Recent Elections in Idaho (1964-70), 1972, Idaho Voting Trends: Party Realignment and Percentage of Voters for Candidates, Parties and Elections, 1890-1974, 1975, In Search of Peace: Starting From October 19, 1980, 1980, Why the Democrats Lost in 1980, 1980, On Understanding the Soviet Union, 1987; editor: The Responsibilities of Colleges and Universities, 1967; contbr. to: Ency. Britannica, 1990, 91; also articles. Mem. Am. Polit. Sci. Assn. (exec. council 1952-53), Nat. Municipal League, Am. Soc. Pub. Adminstrn., Fgn. Policy Assn., UN Assn., AAUP, Western Polit. Sci. Assn. (pres. 1950), Phi Beta Kappa, Pi Gamma Mu, Kappa Delta Pi, Pi Sigma Alpha. Home: 516 N Eisenhower St Moscow ID 83843-9596 *Attempt to contribute to society to the maximum of your ability. Assume responsibility in positions commensurate with the obligations and accountability of the position. In making decisions, first gather all factual data, interpret it fairly, make the decision, and assume responsibility for the decision. In dealing with people, whether family, friends, professionals, or adversaries, try to remember the sensitivity of personal feelings and personal pride. Commend people who achieve and contribute. Be completely honest; when you don't know, admit it.*

MARTIN, CATHERINE ELIZABETH, anthropology educator; b. N.Y.C., Feb. 14, 1943; d. Walter Charles and Ruth (Crucet) Strodt; children: Kai Stuart, Armin Wade. BA, Reed Coll., 1965; MA, UCLA, 1967, PhD, 1971. Cert. C.C. tchr., Ariz., Calif. From asst. to full prof. anthropology Calif. State U., L.A., 1970-96; prof. emeritus —, —, 1996; coord. women's studies Calif. State U., L.A., 1979-88, acting dir. acad. advisement, 1992-93, dir. Can. studies, 1991, advisement coord., 1996, prof. emeritus, 1996; assoc. faculty Mohave C.C., Kingman, Ariz., 1996—; adj. prof. No. Ariz. U., 1997—. Contbr. chpts. to books and poetry to profl. publs. Cubmaster, den mother Boy Scouts Am., L.A. and Pasadena, 1982-85; leader Tiger Cubs, Boy Scouts Am., 1983. Recipient Outstanding Tiger Cub Leader award Boy Scouts Am., L.A., 1983, Cub Scout Growth award Boy Scouts Am., L.A., 1984. Fellow Soc. Applied Anthropology; mem. Am. Anthropol. Assn., Southwestern Anthropol. Assn.

MARTIN, CLYDE VERNE, psychiatrist; b. Coffeyville, Kans., Apr. 7, 1933; s. Howard Verne and Elfrieda Louise (Moehn) M.; m. Barbara Jean McNeilly, June 24, 1956; children: Kent Clyde, Kristin Claire, Kerry Constance, Kyle Curtis. Student Coffeyville Coll., 1951-52; AB, U. Kans., 1955; MD, 1958; MA, Webster Coll., St. Louis, 1977; JD, Thomas Jefferson Coll. Law, Los Angeles, 1985. Diplomate Am. Bd. Psychiatry and Neurology. Intern, Lewis Gale Hosp., Roanoke, Va., 1958-59; resident in psychiatry U. Kans. Med. Ctr., Kansas City, 1959-62, Fresno br. U. Calif.-San Francisco, 1978; staff psychiatrist Neurol. Hosp., Kansas City, 1962; practice medicine specializing in psychiatry, Kansas City, Mo., 1964-84; founder, med. dir., pres. bd. dirs. Mid-Continent Psychiat. Hosp., Olathe, Kans., 1972-84; adj. prof. psychology Baker U., Baldwin City, Kans., 1969-84; staff psychiatrist Atascadero State Hosp., Calif., 1984-85; clin. prof. psychiatry U. Calif., San Francisco, 1985—; chief psychiatrist Calif. Med. Facility, Vacaville, 1985-87; pres., editor Corrective and Social Psychiatry, Olathe, 1970-84, Atascadero, 1984-85, Fairfield, 1985—. Contbr. articles to profl. jours. Bd. dirs. Meth. Youthville, Newton, Kans. 1965-75, Spofford Home, Kansas City, 1974-78. Served to capt. USAF, 1962-64, ret. col. USAFR. Oxford Law & Soc. scholar, 1993. Fellow Am. Psychiat. Assn., Royal Soc. Health, Am. Assn. Mental Health Profls. in Corrections, World Assn. Social Psychiatry, Am. Orthopsychiat. Assn.; mem. AMA, Assn. for Advancement Psychotherapy, Am. Assn. Sex Educators, Counselors and Therapists (cert.), Assn. Mental Health Adminstrs. (cert.), Kansas City Club, Masons, Phi Beta Pi, Pi Kappa Alpha. Methodist (del. Kans. East Conf. 1972-80, bd. global ministries 1974-80). Office: PO Box 3365 Fairfield CA 94533-0587

MARTIN, DAVID ARTHUR, magazine editor, writer; b. Champaign, Ill., Sept. 30, 1938; s. Wilbert Arthur and Martha Lucile (Spickerman) M.; m. Lois Elizabeth Overton, Mar. 18, 1962; children: Laura Beth Martin Barnes, Arthur B., Daniel D. BJ, U. Mo., 1960. Cert. comml. pilot. News dir. KNCM Radio, Moberly, Mo., 1960; reporter Rocky Mountain News, Denver, 1960; tech. editor Canon and Sullivan Pubs., Denver, 1961; commd. ensign USN, 1961, advanced through grades to comdr., 1982; West Coast editor Glider Rider mag., Chattanooga, 1983-84; editor, group editor Fancy Publs., Irvine, Calif., 1984—. Editor-in-chief Kitplanes mag., 1987—; contbr. articles to mags. including RCM, Air Progress, Plane and Pilot, Pvt. Pilot, Aero, Horse Illustrated, 73, Ultralight Planes, Glider Rider, Kitplanes, Coastal Cruising. Active San Diego Presbytery, 1986-95; trumpet player Kearney Mesa Concert Band, San Diego, 1983—. Decorated Air medals (6), Navy Commendation medals (2); recipient Amb. award Fancy Publs., 1993. Mem. Exptl. Aircraft Assn. (chpt. 14 bd. dirs. 1983-86, v.p. 1984-85, Best Low and Slow Airplane 1985), Pt. Mugu Flying Club (flight instr., pres. 1979-82), Armed Forces Flying Club (flight instr.). Home: 6261 Dorothy Dr San Diego CA 92115-2418 Office: Kitplanesls 8755 Aero Dr 309 San Diego CA 92123

MARTIN, DAVID LEE, computer scientist; b. Hickory, N.C., Apr. 4, 1953; s. Boyce Neil and Juanita Rose (Warren) M.; m. Barbara Ann Deines, Oct. 5, 1991; 1 child, Douglas Lee. BS in Computer Sci., Calif. State U., Northridge, 1987; MS in Computer Sci., UCLA, 1992. Sr. software engr. Mark V Systems, Encino, Calif., 1986-94; computer scientist SRI Internat., Menlo Park, Calif., 1994—. Calif. Grad. fellow State of Calif., 1988, 89; Ocean Tech. Corp. undergrad. scholar, L.A., 1985, Litton Data Systems Mgmt. Club scholar, L.A., 1986. Mem. IEEE, Assn. Computing Machinery, Am. Assn. Artificial Intelligence, Computer Profls. for Social Responsibility, Behavioral and Brain Scis. (assoc.). Office: SRI Internat 333 Ravenswood Ave Menlo Park CA 94025-3453

MARTIN, DERIC KRISTON, securities broker; b. Abilene, Tex., June 30, 1959; s. Hollis Deon and Patsy Janelle (Morrow) M.; married. BSBA in Fin. summa cum laude, U. Denver, 1981. Account exec. Dean Witter, Denver, 1981-96, v.p., 1994, assoc. v.p., 1986—, 1st v.p., 1996; retirement planning specialist Dean Witter, 1991; mut. fund coord. Dean Witter, Denver, 1984—, investment lectr., 1984—; pre-retirement planning cons. Allstate Pre-Retirees, Rocky Mountain Region, 1988—. Charter mem. Second Century Found., Denver, 1985—, Citizens Against Govt. Waste, 1986—. Recipient Wall Street Jour. award, 1981. Mem. Lakewood Bus. Network, U. Denver 1864 Club, South Met. Denver C. of C., Nat. Bus. Execs. (v.p. Rocky Mountain chpt. 1996, pres. Rocky Mountain chpt. 1997), Aurora Rotary Club, Beta Gamma Sigma. Republican. Methodist. Office: Dean Witter 4582 S Ulster St Ste 300 Denver CO 80237-2634

MARTIN, DONALD WALTER, author, publisher; b. Grants Pass, Oreg., Apr. 22, 1934; s. George E. and Irma Ann (Dallas) M.; m. Kathleen Elizabeth Murphy, July, 1970 (div. May 1979); children: Daniel Clayton, Kimberly Ann; m. Betty Woo, Mar. 18, 1985. Enlisted USMC, 1952; advanced through grades to staff sgt. USMC, Japan, Republic of Korea, Republic of China, 1956-61; reporter Blade-Tribune, Oceanside, Calif., 1961-65; entertainment editor Press-Courier, Oxnard, Calif., 1965-69; mng. editor Argus-Courier, Petaluma, Calif., 1969-70; assoc. editor Motorland mag., San Francisco, 1970-88; founder, prin., CEO Pine Cone Press, Inc., Columbia, Calif., 1988—. Author: Best of San Francisco, 1986, 90, 94, Best of the Gold Country, 1987, 92, San Francisco's Ultimate Dining Guide, 1988, Inside Francisco, 1991, Best of the Wine Country, 1991, 95, Oregon Discovery Guide, 1993, 95, 96, Northern California Discovery Guide, 1993, The Ultimate Wine Book, 1993, Washington Discovery Guide, 1994, Utah Discovery Guide, 1995, Adventure Cruising, 1996, Arizona Discovery Guide, 1996, Arizona in Your Future, 1991, 93, 97, The Toll-Free Traveler, 1997, The Best of Las Vegas, 1997. Recipient Diane Seely award Ventura County Theatre Council, 1968. Mem. Soc. Am. Travel Writers. Republican. Home: 1649 Justin Cir Henderson NV 89015 Office: Ste 138 631 N Stephanie St Henderson NV 89014

MARTIN, DORIS ELLEN, publisher, management consultant; b. Chgo., Oct. 26, 1927; d. John L. and Marie (Miller) Martin; m. Morton Rosenberg, Dec. 15, 1963 (div. 1964). BS, NYU, 1952; MS, Boston U., 1958; EdD, Columbia U., 1964. Instr. Colby Coll., Waterville, Maine, 1952-54; dir. edn. dept. YWCA, Honolulu, 1954-59; dir. The Conf. Ctr., U. Hawaii, Honolulu, 1960-65; dir. spl. projects and assoc. prof. NYU, N.Y.C., 1965-66; dir. of spl. project state plan Dept. Planning/Econ. Devel., State of Hawaii, Honolulu, 1966-69; spl. asst. George Washington U., Washington, 1970; mgmt. cons. Dr. D. Martin Assocs., Wailuku, Hawaii, 1980—. Editor, pub. Martin Mgmt. Books, Wailuku, Hawaii, 1985—; author 13 books. Mem. Rep. Nat. Com., 1975—. Mem. Pubrs. Mktg. Assn. Home and Office: 2108 Kahekili Hwy Wailuku HI 96793-9207

MARTIN, FRANCIS F., retired computer consultant; b. Hughson, Calif., July 26, 1923; s. Frank C. and Olga Augusta (Fernandes) M.; m. Peggy Jane Milnor, June 15, 1951; children: Gary, Bruce. BA, U. Calif., Berkeley, 1947, MA, 1951. Music tchr. Willits (Calif.) H.S., 1947-49, Lassen (Calif.) H.S., 1950-52, Fremont Jr. H.S., Anaheim, Calif., 1953-54; sys. analyst Hughes Aircraft, Fullerton, Calif., 1956-65, 70-75; cons. Francis Martin Cons., Calif. and Ariz., 1968-78; security analyst Calif. Fed. Bank, L.A., 1978-88; ret., 1988. Author: Computer Modeling, 1968 (Sci. book of Yr. award 1970). Lt. (j.g.) USN, 1941-46, ETO, PTO. Democrat. Home: 4275 Maryland St San Diego CA 92103

MARTIN, FRED, artist, college administrator; b. San Francisco, June 13, 1927; s. Ernest Thomas and Leona (Richey) M.; m. Genevieve Catherine Fisette, Jan. 29, 1950 (dec.); children: T. Demian, Fredericka C., Anthony J.; m. Stephanie Zuperko Dudek, 1992. B.A., U. Calif.-Berkeley, 1949, M.A., 1954; postgrad. Calif. Sch. Fine Arts, 1949-50. Registrar Oakland (Calif.) Art Mus., 1955-58; dir. exhbns. San Francisco Art Inst., 1958-65, dir. coll., 1965-75, dean acad. affairs, 1983-92; dean acad. affairs emeritus; represented by Frederick Spratt Gallery, San Jose, Calif., Ebert Gallery, San Francisco. Exhibited one man shows, Zoe Dusanne Gallery, Seattle, 1952, M.H. deYoung Meml. Mus., San Francisco, 1954, 64, Oakland Art Mus., 1958, San Francisco Mus. Modern Art, 1958, 73, Dilexi Gallery, San Francisco, 1961, Minami Gallery, Tokyo, 1963, Royal Marks Gallery, N.Y.C., 1965-70, Hansen Fuller Gallery, San Francisco, 1974, 75, 76, Quay Gallery, San Francisco, 1979, 81, 84, Natsoulas Gallery, Davis, Calif., 1991, Belcher Studios Gallery, San Francisco, 1994, Frederick Spratt Gallery, San Jose, 1996, Ebert Gallery, San Francisco, 1997, Art and Consciousness Gallery/John F. Kennedy U., Berkeley, 1997; represented in permanent collections, Mus. Modern Art, N.Y.C., San Francisco Mus. Modern Art, Oakland Art Mus., Whitney Mus., Fogg Mus.; author: Beulah Land, 1966, Log of the Sun Ship, 1969, Liber Studiorum, 1973, A Travel Book, 1976, From an Antique Land, 1979; Bay area corr.: Art Internat.; contbg. editor Art Week, 1976-93. Recipient prizes Oakland Art Mus., 1951, 58, prizes San Francisco Mus. Art, 1957, 58, prizes Richmond (Calif.) Art Center, 1962, prizes Nat. Found. for Arts, 1970. Home: 232 Monte Vista Ave Oakland CA 94611-4922 Office: San Francisco Art Inst 800 Chestnut St San Francisco CA 94133-2206

MARTIN, GEORGE, psychologist, educator; b. L.A., May 8, 1940; s. George Leonard and Margaret (Padigamus) M.; m. Penny Harrell, June 22, 1963 (div. 1986); children: Jeni, Kimberle. BA, UCLA, 1965; MA, Calif. State U., L.A., 1967; MS, Calif. State U., Fullerton, 1994. Systems analyst L.A. Dept. Water & Power, 1965-67; project coord. L.A. Police Dept., 1967-70, edn. cons., 1980-83; alcohol researcher Pomona (Calif.) Coll., 1970-73; tng. systems researcher Lanterman State Hosp., Pomona, 1973-77; prof. psychology Mt. San Antonio Coll., Walnut, Calif., 1970—, dir. rsch., 1986-94. Contbr. articles to profl. jours. Rsch. dir. Orange County Dem. Party, 1985-86. With U.S. Army, 1959-61. Grantee Nat. Inst. Law Enforcement, 1967-70, Nat. Inst. Alcohol, 1970-74. Mem. APA, NSA. Home: 1313 N Grand Ave Ste 326 Walnut CA 91789-1317 Office: Mt San Antonio Coll 1100 N Grand Ave Walnut CA 91789-1341

MARTIN, GEORGE FRANCIS, lawyer; b. Yuba City, Calif., July 7, 1944; s. John Severd and Albina Marie M.; m. Linda Louise D'Aoust, Mar. 17, 1968; children: Brandon, Bry. BA in Govt., Calif. State U., Sacramento, 1968; JD, U. Calif., Davis, 1971. Bar: Calif. Adminstr. asst. Assemblyman E. Richard Barnes, Sacramento, 1967-68; with Borton, Petrini & Conron, Bakersfield, Calif., 1971—; mng. gen. ptnr. Borton, Petrini & Conron, Bakersfield, 1977—; dean Calif. Pacific Sch. Law, Bakersfield, 1993-95; holdings numerous ventures, partnerships; lectr. in field; founder, owner theatrical bus. Mgmt. by Martin, Inc., Shower of Stars, Frantic Records, 1962-67. Editor-in-chief Verdict Jour. of Law, 1984-85, Calif. Def. Mag.; newspaper reporter Appeal Democrat, Marysville, Calif., 1959-62. Former vice chmn. Kern County Rep. Ctrl. Com.; past pres. So. Calif. Def. Counsel; past chmn. Ctrl. Calif. Heart Inst.; bd. dirs. Calif. State U. at Bakersfield Found., Kern County Food Bank, Calif. Coun. Partnerships, Kern Hospice, Kern Econ. Devel. Corp. Mem. Greater Bakersfield C. of C. (bd. dirs., past pres.). Office: Borton Petrini & Conron 1600 Truxtun Ave Bakersfield CA 93301-5104

MARTIN, GWENDOLYN ELAINE, school librarian; b. Warrensburg, Wash., Sept. 16, 1949; d. Glenn C. and Lose Rose (Winfrey) M. BEd, Ctrl. Wash. State U., Ellensburg, 1971; MEd, City U., Seattle, 1996. Cert. continuing tchg., Wash, supt. pub. instrn.; gen. radio/telephone lic. Tchr. Sch. Dist. 57, Prince George, B.C., Can., 1974-76, Palo Verde Unified Schs., Blythe, Calif., 1971-72, 77-80, Cape Flattery Schs., Neah Bay, Wash., 1980-83; broadcast engr. KBCI TV, Boise, Idaho, 1985-87; tchr. Quilayute Valley Schs., Forks, Wash., 1989-91, Colegio Neuva Granada, Bogota, Colombia, 1991-93; tchr. libr. Federal Way (Wash.) Pub. Schs., 1994—; cons. Eclectic Internat., Federal Way, 1996—. Mem. Cmty. Players, Blythe, Calif., 1977-80, PTA, Federal Way, 1994—. Mem. Wash. Edn. Assn., Wash. Libr.-Media Assn., Cape Flattery Edn. Assn. (pres. 1980-83). Office: Silver Lake Elem 1310 SW 325th Pl Federal Way WA 98023-4930

MARTIN, JAMAL, public health scientist, researcher; b. Norfolk, Va., Apr. 15, 1954; s. James Edward and Susie (Woodley) M.; m. Jahaan Peterson, June 18, 1977; children: Kamaal, Fatimah, Ismail, Na'iyma. BA, Hawaii Pacific U., 1985; MPH, U. Hawaii, 1987. Cert. in respiratory care. Rsch. asst. Rsch. Corp. U. Hawaii, Honolulu, 1980; respiratory therapist Queen's Med. Ctr., Honolulu, 1983-87; asst. sec.- gen. Asia Pacific Acad. Consortium Pub. Health, Bangkok, 1987-88; epidemiologist Hawaii State Dept. Health, Honolulu, 1989-91; project coord. Kadiolani Med. Ctr. for Women & Children, Honolulu, 1991-95; rsch. assoc. Straub Clinic & Hosp., Honolulu, 1995-96; project coord. Pacific Health Rsch. Inst., Honolulu, 1996—; cons. Faculty of Pub. Health, Mahidol U., Bangkok, 1988, Faculty of Medicine, U. Malaysia, Kuala Lumpur, 1988, Coll. of Edn., U. Hawaii, Honolulu, 1990, Dept. of Pediatrics, 1993—. Active PTA, Honolulu, 1982—; vol. Hawaii Pub. TV Fund Drives, Honolulu, 1995—. Hawaii Pacific U. scholar, 1987; recipient Trainee award USPHS, 1987. Mem. N.Y. Acad. Sci., Hawaii Soc. History Medicine and Pub. Health. Office: Pacific Health Rsch Inst 846 S Hotel St Honolulu HI 96813

MARTIN, JIM, copy editor, writer; b. Eugene, Oreg., Apr. 18, 1949; s. James Doud and Julia M. (Danilowicz) M. Student, U. Portland, Oreg., 1967-69; BA in History, U. Santa Clara, Calif., 1971. Proofreader The Oreg. Statesman, Salem, 1971-72; news editor Mt. Angel (Oreg.) News, 1973-75; copy editor Legis. Counsel Com., Salem, 1976—. Author: A Bit of a Blue, 1992. Mem. Oreg. Hist. Soc., Portland, 1977—, Oreg. Cultural Heritage Commn., 1995—, Marion County Hist. Soc., 1993—, Friends of the Salem Pub. Libr., 1993—. Recipient Cert. Merit Marion County Hist. Soc., Salem, 1992. Mem. Pacific N.W. Booksellers Assn. Republican. Roman Catholic. Home: 1371 Peace St SE Apt 12 Salem OR 97302-2572

MARTIN, JOHN STEWART, software engineer; b. Tacoma, June 20, 1965; s. Richard and Catherine Jesse (Stewart) M.; m. Tami Renee Ewing, Feb. 25, 1992; 1 child, Devon Irene. Grad. high sch., Portland, Oreg. Rsch. asst. Inst. Neurosci. U. Oreg., Eugene, 1990-93; asst. dir. software devel. Covox, Inc., Eugene, 1993-95; pres. EIJA, Inc., Eugene, 1995—. Creator: (Internet virtual world) Singlenesia, 1991. Mem. Eugene Area C. of C. Office: Singlenesia Software 2852 Willamette St Ste 502 Eugene OR 97405

MARTIN, JOSEPH, JR., retired lawyer, former ambassador; b. San Francisco, May 21, 1915; m. Ellen Chamberlain Martin, July 5, 1946; children: Luther Greene, Ellen Myers. AB, Yale U., 1936, LLB, 1939. Assoc. Cadwalader, Wickersham & Taft, N.Y.C., 1939-41; ptnr. Wallace, Garrison, Norton & Ray, San Francisco, 1946-55, Pettit & Martin, San Francisco, 1955-70, 73-95; gen. counsel FTC, Washington, 1970-71; ambassador, U.S. rep. Disarmament Conf., Geneva, 1971-76; ret.; mem. Pres.'s Adv. Com. for Arms Control and Disarmament, 1974-78; bd. dirs. Astec Industries, Inc. Pres. Pub. Utilities Commn., San Francisco, 1956-60; Rep. nat. committeeman for Calif., 1960-64; treas. Rep. Party Calif., 1956-58; bd. dirs. Patrons of Art and Music, Calif. Palace of Legion of Honor, 1958-70, pres., 1963-68; bd. dirs. Arms Control Assn., 1977-84; pres. Friends of Legal Assistance to Elderly, 1983-87. Lt. comdr. USNR, 1941-46. Recipient Ofcl. commendation for Outstanding Service as Gen. Counsel FTC, 1973, Distinguished Honor award U.S. ACDA, 1973, Lifetime Achievement award Legal Assistance to the Elderly, 1981. Fellow Am. Bar Found. Clubs: Burlingame Country, Pacific Union. Home: 2879 Woodside Rd Woodside CA 94062-2441

MARTIN, JOSEPH BOYD, neurologist, educator; b. Bassano, Alta., Can., Oct. 20, 1938; s. Joseph Bruce and Ruth Elizabeth (Ramer) M.; m. Rachel Ann Wenger, June 18, 1960; children: Bradley, Melanie, Douglas, Neil. BSc, Eastern Mennonite Coll., Harrisonburg, Va., 1959; MD, U. Alta., 1962; PhD, U. Rochester, N.Y., 1971; MA (hon.), Harvard U., 1978; ScD (hon.), McGill U., 1994, U. Rochester, 1996. Resident in internal medicine Univ. Hosp., Edmonton, Alta., 1962-64; resident in neurology Case-Western Res. U. Hosps., 1964-67; rsch. fellow U. Rochester, N.Y., 1967-70; mem. faculty McGill U. Faculty Medicine, Montreal, Que., Can., 1970-78; prof. medicine and neurology, neurologist-in-chief Montreal Neurol. Inst., 1976-78; chmn. dept. neurology Mass. Gen. Hosp., Boston, also Dorn prof. neurology Harvard U. Med. Sch., 1978-89; dean Sch. Medicine U. Calif., San Francisco, 1989-93; chancellor U. Calif., San Francisco, 1993-97; dean faculty medicine Harvard U., Boston, 1997—; mem. med. adv. bd. Gairdner Found., Toronto, 1978-83; adv. council neurol. disorders program Nat. Inst. Neurol., Communicative Disorders and Stroke, 1979-82. Co-author: Clinical Neuroendocrinology, 1977, The Hypothalmamus, 1978, Clinical Neuroendocrinology: A Pathophysiological Approach, 1979, Neurosecretion and Brain Peptides: Implications for Brain Functions and Neurological Disease, 1981, Brain Peptides, 1983; editor Harrison's Principles of Internal Medicine, 1980—, Clin. Neuroendocrinology 2d edit., 1987. Recipient Moshier Meml. gold medal U. Alta. Faculty Medicine, 1962, John W. Scott gold med. award, 1962; Med. Research Council Can. scholar, 1970-75. Mem. NAS, Am. Neurol. Assn. (pres. 1990), Am. Physiol. Soc. (Bowditch lectr. 1978), Royal Coll. Phys. and Surg. Can., Endocrine Soc., Soc. Neurosci., Am. Soc. Clin. Investigation, Assn. Am. Physicians, Am. Acad. Arts and Scis., Inst. of Medicine, Nat. Adv. Coun., Nat. Inst. Aging. Office: U Calif 513 Parnassus Ave Ste 126 San Francisco CA 94122-2722

MARTIN, JOY ANNE, clinical psychologist, consultant; b. Andover, Mass.; d. Edward and Ethel Mae (McGonigle) Fengya. BS, Boston U., 1966, EdM, 1976; PhD, Calif. Sch. Profl. Psychology, 1988; cert. in Adv. Tng. Program in Psychoanalytic Psychotherapy, San Diego Psychoanalytic Soc. and Inst., 1997. Lic. psychologist, Calif. Tchr. Dept. Def. Dependent Schs., Japan, Fed. Republic Germany, 1972-83; grad. asst. Old Dominion U., Norfolk, Va., 1983-84; clin. practitioner inpatient substance abuse program U.S. Naval Air Sta., Mirimar, Calif., 1985-86; pvt. practice, La Jolla, Calif., 1986—; postdoctoral fellow Mercy Hosp. and Med. Ctr., San Diego, 1988-89; clin. psychologist Balboa Naval Hosp. HIV Evaluation Unit, San Diego, 1990—, Psychiat. Ctrs. San Diego, 1988—; researcher Juvenile Crisis Ctr., YMCA, San Diego. Mem. APA (western regional trainer HIV office for psychology edn., mem. mil. task force HIV office for psychology edn.), Am. Coll. Forensic Examiners, Assn. for the Advancement of Psychology, Nat. Register Health Svc. Providers in Psychology, Calif. Psychol. Assn., San Diego Acad. Psychologists, Calif. Sch. Profl. Psychology Alumni Assn. (bd. dirs.), Sierra Club. Home: 8613 Via Mallorca Apt C La Jolla CA 92037-2596

MARTIN, JUNE JOHNSON CALDWELL, journalist; b. Toledo, Oct. 6; d. John Franklin and Eunice Imogene (Fish) Johnson; m. Erskine Caldwell, Dec. 21, 1942 (div. Dec. 1955); 1 child, Jay Erskine; m. Keith Martin, May 5, 1966. AA, Phoenix Jr. Coll., 1939-41; BA, U. Ariz., 1941-43, 53-59; student Ariz. State U., 1939, 40. Free-lance writer, 1944—; columnist Ariz. Daily Star, 1956-59; editor Ariz. Alumnus mag., Tucson, 1959-70; book reviewer, columnist Ariz. Daily Star, Tucson, 1970-94; ind. book reviewer and audio tape columnist, Tucson, 1994—; panelist, co-producer TV news show Tucson Press Club, 1954-55, pres., 1958; co-founder Ariz. Daily Star Ann. Book & Author Event. Contbg. author: Rocky Mountain Cities, 1949; contbr. articles to World Book Ency., and various mags. Mem. Tucson CD Com., 1961; vol. campaigns of Samuel Goddard, U.S. Rep. Morris Udall, U.S. ambassador and Ariz. gov. Raul Castro. Recipient award Nat. Headliners Club, 1959, Ariz. Press Club award, 1957-59, 96, Am. Alumni Council, 1966, 70. Mem. Nat. Book Critics Circle, Jr. League of Tucson, Tucson Urban League, PEN U.S.A. West, Planned Parenthood of So. Ariz., Pi Beta Phi. Democrat. Methodist. Club: Tucson Press. Home: Desert Foothills Sta PO Box 65388 Tucson AZ 85728

MARTIN, KENA SUE, educator; b. Las Vegas, N.Mex., Sept. 20, 1943; d. Billie Martin and Jewel B. McGlothlin; m. Gilbert John Archuleta, Apr. 28, 1977; 1 child, Jonathan Blake. BA in Polit. Sci., Ea. N.Mex. U., 1966, MA in Ednl. Adminstrn., 1988. Cert. tchr., N.Mex. Tchr. Clovis (N.Mex.) Mcpl. Schs., 1966-67, Las Cruces (N.Mex) Pub. Schs., 1967-68, Lubbock (Tex.) Ind. Schs., 1968-69; tchr., dept. chair Taos (N.Mex.) Mcpl. Schs., 1973-78; tchr. Floyd (N.Mex.) Pub. Schs., 1979-80, Menaul Sch., Albuquerque, 1980-82; tchr., adminstr. curriculum devel., dir. activities Taos Mcpl. Schs., 1983—; cons. in field; mem. com. for rev. social studies competencies N.Mex. Dept. Edn., 1990. Mem. Taos Community Chorus, 1988. GRantee NSF, 1975, NEH, 1988. Mem. ASCD, N.Mex. Coun. Social Studies. Office: Taos Mcpl Schs Taos NM 87571

MARTIN, LINDE BENISON, artist, interior designer; b. Erlangen, Germany, Jan. 2, 1930; came to U.S., 1953; d. Michael and Thea (Jetzelsberger) Kuchenreuther; m. James Bruce Martin, Nov. 16, 1966 (div.); 1 child, Cornelia Johnson. Student, Sorbonne, Paris, 1947-50, Cabrillo Coll., Aptos, Calif., 1961-65, San Jose (Calif.) State U., 1965. Tchr. Creativity Workshop, Zurich, 1988-90. Exhibited works in solo shows at Redding Gallery, Carmel, Calif., 1963, Jungain Ctr., San Francisco, 1973, Stanford U., 1975, Carmel Gallery Fine Arts, 1985, Kunsthalle, Nuremberg, Germany, 1991, U. Calif. Santa Cruz Women's Ctr., 1993, Christ Luth. Ch., Tiberon, Calif., U. Phoenix, Santa Cruz, 1994, others; group shows include Vorpal Gallery, San Francisco, Open Studios Art Tour, Santa Cruz, O Gallery, Westport, Conn., Syntex Corp., San Jose, Met. Art Care, Los Altos, Calif., Mus. Modern Art, Miami, Fla., Montreal Internat. Competition, San Jose, Wax Lander Galleries, Santa Fe, 1997; represented in collections at U. Phoenix,, U. Calif. at Santa Cruz, First Congl. Ch., Santa Cruz, also pvt. collections including that of Itzac Perlman, N.Y.C.; commns. include watercolor illustration for children's books, art glass windows and paintings. Named Best Artist of 1996 Spectra Art Mag. Home: 244 Seaborg Pl Santa Cruz CA 95060

MARTIN, LOREN WINSTON, physician; b. Albertsville, Ala., Apr. 20, 1938; s. Loren d. and Byrda G. (Crotwell) M.; m. Vivian Elizabeth Sanger Martin, Dec. 29, 1960; children: Lori Ann, Karen Lynn, James Winston. BA in Chemistry, Duke U., 1959; MD, U. Tenn., 1962. Lic. physician, Ariz. Rotating internship Fitzsimons Army Hosp., Denver, 1963; med. residency Honolulu, 1964-67; med. officer U.S. Army, 1962-70; fellowship allergy U. Colo., Denver, 1970-71; pvt. practice Tucson, 1971—. Decorated Bronze Star. Fellow Am. Acad. Allergy & Immunology, Am. Coll. Allergy & Immunology; mem. Pima County Med. Soc. Republican. Office: 5300 E Erickson Dr Ste 120 Tucson AZ 85712-2809

MARTIN, LUCY Z., public relations executive; b. Alton, Ill., July 8, 1941; d. Fred and Lucille J. M. BA, Northwestern U., 1963. Adminstrv. asst., copywriter Batz-Hodgson-Neuwoehner, Inc., St. Louis, 1963-64; news reporter, Midwest fashion editor Fairchild Publs., St. Louis, 1964-66; account exec. Milici Advt. Agy., Honolulu, 1967; publs. dir. Barnes Med. Ctr., St. Louis, 1968-69; comms. cons. Fleishman-Hillard, St. Louis, 1970-74; comms. cons., CEO, pres. Lucy Z. Martin & Assocs., Portland, Oreg., 1974—; spkr. Marylhurst Coll., 1991, 92, 93, Concordia Coll., 1992, Women Entrepreneurs of Oreg., 1992, Oreg. Assn. Hosps. and Health Sys. Trustees, 1992, Healthcare Assn. Hawaii, Honolulu, 1993, USBancorp for Not-for-Profits, 1993, Multnomah County Ret. Srs. Vol. Program, 1993, Healthcare Fin. Mgmt. Assn., N.W., 1993, Healthcare Comms. Oreg., 1994, Area Health Edn. Ctrs., OHSU/statewide, 1994, Columbia River chpt. Pub. Rels. Soc. Am., 1994, 96; spkr., workshop conducter Healthcare Assn. Hawaii, 1993, USBancorp Not-for-Profit, 1993, Healthcare Communicators Oreg., 1994, Pathways to Career Transition, 1995, among others; bd. dirs. Ctrs. Airway Sci. Featured in Entrepreneurial Woman mag.; contbr. articles to profl. jours. Chmn. women's adv. com. Reed Coll., Portland, 1977-79; mem. Oreg. Commn. for Women, 1984-87; bd. dirs. Ronald McDonald House Oreg., 1986, Oreg. Sch. Arts and Crafts, 1989—, Northwestern U. Alumni Coun., 1992—; bd. dirs. Good Samaritan Hosp. Assocs., 1991-94, chair 1993-94; mem. pub. policy com. YMCA, 1993-95; mem. adv. bd. Jr. League, 1994-97. Recipient MacEachern Citation Acad. Hosp. Pub. Relations, 1978, Rosey awards Portland Advt. Fedn., 1979, Achievement award Soc. Tech. Comms., 1982, Disting. Tech. Comm. award, 1982, Exceptional Achievement award Coun. for Advancement and Support Edn., 1983, Monsoon award Internat. Graphics, Inc., 1984; named Woman of Achievement Daily Jour. Commerce, 1980. Mem. Pub. Rels. Soc. Am. (pres. Columbia River chpt. 1984, chmn. bd. 1980-84, Oreg. del. 1984-86, jud. panel N. Pacific dist 1985-86, exec. bd. health care sect. 1986-87, mem. Counselors Acad., Spotlight awards 1985, 86, 87, 88, nat. exec. com. 1987-91), Portland Pub. Rels. Roundtable (chmn. 1985, bd. dirs. 1983-85), Assn. Western Hosps. (editl. adv. bd. 1984-85), Best of West awards 1978, 80, 83, 87), Oreg. Hosp. Pub. Rels. Orgn. (pres. 1981, chmn. bd. 1982, bd. dirs. 1992-93), Acad. Health Service Mktg., Am. Hosp. Assn., Am. Mktg. Assn. (Oreg. chpt. bd. dirs. 1992-93), Am. Soc. Hosp. Mktg. & Pub. Rels., Healthcare Communicators Oreg. (conf. keynote speaker 1994), Internat. Assn. Bus. Communicators (18 awards 1981-87), Oreg. Assn. Hosps. (keynote speaker for trustee, 1991, speaker, 1993, bd. dirs. 1992-93), Oreg. Press Women, Nat. and Oreg. Soc. Healthcare Planning and Mktg., Women in Comms. (Matrix award 1977), Bus. Social Responsibility, Inst. for Managerial and Profl. Women (bd. dirs. 1992-94). Office: 1881 SW Edgewood Rd Portland OR 97201-2235

MARTIN, MICHAEL, publisher; b. Fort Lauderdale, Fla., Aug. 30, 1960; s. Earl Perkinson and Patricia Veronica Martin. BA in Journalism, San Francisco State U., 1993. Reporter Ind. Newspaper Group, Burlingame, Calif., 1993-94; pub. We. Edit., San Francisco, 1995—. Big Bros. Glide Meml. Ch., San Francisco, 1990—. Mem. Soc. Profl. Journalists (Mark of Excellence award 1992), Assn. Free Cmty. Newspapers, First Amendment Coalition Calif. Office: Western Edition 400A Haight St San Francisco CA 94117

MARTIN, MICHAEL ALBERT, protective services official, poet; b. Akron, Ohio, Feb. 29, 1940; s. Albert Leo and Beatrice Marie (Flasck) M.; m. Jeanine E. Johnson, June 10, 1972 (div. Dec. 1976). Hotel Sch. diploma, Universal Schs., Miami, Fla., 1969. Security officer Boyd Group, Las Vegas, Nev., 1991—. Author: Atlantis Secrets Revealed, 1994, Hilltop Country Songbook, 1997, (poetry) Noet You Poet, 1995; author (songs) To Eva My Love, Western Song, Your Song of Love, Reaching Out; contbr. to The Best Poems of 1995, The Best Poems of 1997, The Best Poems of the 90s. Staff sgt. USAF, 1964-68. Recipient Ednl. awards USAF, 1964-65, others; named to the Internat. Poetry Hall of Fame, 1996. Mem. Internat. Soc. Poets (hon., 12 Editors Choice award for poetry), Am. Legion, Masons (Scottish Rite pres. 1973—), Shriners. Democrat. Roman Catholic. Home: Duck Creek Village 5330 Duralite St # 103 Las Vegas NV 89122

MARTIN, MICHAEL LEE, orthotist; b. Long Beach, Calif., May 30, 1947; s. Troy Lee and Ruth Elizabeth (Hummer) M.; m. Sharon Lee Johnson, Aug. 23, 1969; 1 child, Tanya Lee. Student, Northwestern U., 1973; AA, Cerritos (Calif.) Coll., 1976; student, UCLA, 1976. Diplomate Am. Bd. Orthotists and Prosthetist. Cable splicer Gen. Telephone, Dairy Valley, Calif., 1965-66; orthotic technician Johnson's Orthopedic, Santa Ana, Calif., 1969-73, orthotist, 1974—; pres. Johnson's Orthopedic, Orange, Calif., 1989—; rsch. orthotist Rancho Los Amigos Hosp., Downey, 1973; mem. rsch. adv. bd. Rancho Los Amigos Hosp. Mem. rsch. adv. com. on tech. for children Rancho Los Amigos Hosp., Downey. With U.S. Army, 1966-68, Vietnam. Mem. Am. Acad. Orthotists and Prosthetists (sec., pres. So. Calif. chpt. 1976-79, sec., pres. Region IX 1979-87, bd. dirs. 1994—, Practitioner of Yr. award 1992), Orthotic and Prosthetic Provider Network (pres. Calif. chpt. 1988—), Internat. Soc. for Prosthetics and Orthotics. Democrat. Home: 19 Fontaire Coto De Caza CA 92679-4904 Office: Johnson's Orthopedic 1920 E Katella Ave Ste G Orange CA 92867-5146

MARTIN, MYRON GREGORY, foundation administrator; b. Houston, Jan. 14, 1958; s. Monty Gene and Vera Mae (Saurage) M. MusB, U. North Tex., 1980; MBA, Golden Gate U., 1989. Various sales and mktg. positions Baldwin Piano Co., N.Y.C., 1980-1990, dir. concert and artists, 1990-95; exec. dir. Liberace Found., Las Vegas, Nev., 1995—. Mem. adv. bd. Thelonious Monk Inst., Washington, D.C., 1994-95; bd. dirs. Cystic Fibrosis Found., Chgo., 1990, Liberace Found., 1993-95, Museums and Attractions, Las Vegas, 1996—. Recipient Special award Cystic Fibrosis Found., 1990. Home: 5121 Breakers Ln Las Vegas NV 89113 Office: Liberace Found 1775 E Tropicana Ave Las Vegas NV 89119

MARTIN, NEIL ALFRED, neurosurgeon; b. Phila., June 5, 1951; s. Alfred Nicholas and Mary (Ziegler) M.; m. Colleen Patricia Cudahy, Sept. 22, 1991; children: Neil Alfred Jr., Nicholas Alexander. BS, Yale U., 1973; MD, Med. Coll. of Va., 1978. Intern U. Calif., San Francisco, 1978-79, resident in neurosurgery, 1979-84; neurovascular fellowship Barrow Neurol. Inst., Phoenix, 1984-85; asst. prof. UCLA Med. Sch., 1985-90, assoc. prof., 1990-95, prof., 1995—, dir. vascular neurosurgery, 1986—, dir. cerebral blood flow lab., 1989—. Contbr. more than 100 articles to profl. jours., chpts. in books in field. Rsch. grantee NIH, 1991-96. Mem. Am. Assn. Neurol. Surgeons, Congress of Neurol. Surgeons, Neurosurgical Soc. Am., Western Neurosurgical Soc. Office: UCLA Sch Medicine 74-140 CHS 10833 Le Conte Ave Los Angeles CA 90024-1602

MARTIN, PAUL, hepatologist, medical educator; b. Dublin, Ireland, July 13, 1954; came to the U.S., 1987; s. Nicholas Colman and Maura Josephine (Bugler) M.; m. Maria Teresa Abreu, Apr. 9, 1994; 1 child, Brian Carlos Martin. MD, U. Coll., Dublin, 1978. Cert. Am. Bd. Internal Medicine; cert. gastroenterology. Intern and resident St. Vincent Hosp., Dublin, 1978-82; resident U. Alt., Edmonton, Can., 1982-84; gastroenterology fellow Queen's U., Ont., 1984-86; hepatology fellow U. Toronto, Ont., 1986-87; med. staff fellow NIH, Bethesda, Md., 1987-89; asst. prof. medicine Jefferson Med. Coll., Phila., 1989-92; dir. hepatology UCLA, 1992-95, assoc. prof. medicine, 1995—. Editor: Viral Hepatitis, 1994; contbr. articles to profl. jours. Fellow ACP, Royal Coll. Physicians Can. and Ireland; mem. Am. Assn. for the Study Liver Disease. Democrat. Roman Catholic. Office: UCLA Sch Medicine 77-123 DCHS 10833 Le Conte Ave Los Angeles CA 90095-1749

MARTIN, PRESTON, financial services executive; b. L.A., Dec. 5, 1923; s. Oscar and Gaynell (Horne) M.; 1 child, Pier Preston. BS in Fin., U. So. Calif., 1947, MBA, 1948; PhD in Monetary Econs., U. Ind., 1952. Prof. fin. Grad. Sch. Bus. Adminstrn. U. So. Calif., 1950-60; prin. in housebldg. firm, 1952-56; with mortgage fin. and consumer fin. instns., 1954-57; commr. savs. and loan State of Calif., 1967-69; chmn. Fed. Home Loan Bank Bd., Washington, 1969-72; founder, CEO PMI Mortgage Ins. Co., 1972-80; chmn., CEO Seraco Group subs. Sears, Roebuck & Co., 1980-81, also bd. dirs. parent co.; chmn., CEO WestFed Holdings Inc., L.A., 1986-92, SoCal Holdings, Inc., L.A., 1987-93, H.F. Holdings, Inc., San Francisco, 1986-92; vice-chmn. Fed. Res. Bd., Washington, 1982-86; founder Fed. Home Loan Mortgage Corp.; prof. bus. econ. and fin. Inst. per lo Studio Organizitzatione Aziendale, Italy. Author: Principles and Practices of Real Estate, 1959. Mem. President's Commn. on Housing, 1980-81; prin. Coun. Excellence in Govt., Washington. Recipient House and Home award, 1969, award Engring. News Record, 1971, Turntable award Nat. Assn. Home Builders, 1973. Mem. Lambda Chi Alpha. Presbyterian.

MARTIN, RALPH MICHAEL (RICK MARTIN), patent lawyer, marketing consultant; b. Bklyn., Aug. 18, 1944; s. William James and Muriel (MInard) M.; div.; children: William, Michael, Alex. BS in Physics, Bucknell U., 1966; JD, Nova Law Sch., 1985. Bar: Fla., Colo., U.S. Patent Bar; registered patent atty. U.S. Dept. Commerce. Computer salesman IBM, N.Y.C., 1969-75; software divsn. mgr. Adtech, N.Y.C., 1976-81; program mgr. NCR, Dayton, Ohio, 1982; lawyer Oltman & Flynn, Ft. Lauderdale, Fla., 1984-87; patent atty. Ft. Lauderdale, 1987-88, Longmont, Colo., 1992—; contract adminstr. Vactec, Boulder, Colo., 1989-90; Spkr. nat. innovation workshops, U.S. Dept. Commerce, 1994—; bd. dirs. Lightning Eliminators, Boulder; mem. Rocky Mountain Inventors Congress, Denver. With USMC, 1966-67. Mem. Rockies Venture Club (corp. sponsor), Rotary. Republican. Presbyterian. Home and Office: 609 Terry St Longmont CO 80501

MARTIN, ROBERT BURTON, management and marketing consultant; b. Takoma Park, Md., Mar. 17, 1935; s. Herbert Lester and Lenora Marie (Sponseller) M.; m. Mary Lou Rushworth, Sept. 7, 1959 (div. Dec. 1982); children: Laurajean, Kenneth, Donna Beth. BEE, Cornell U., 1958; MS, Northwestern U., 1966, PhD, 1967. Dir. mgmt. systems Denver and Rio Grande Western R.R., 1967-71; v.p. Mgmt. Design Assoc., Denver, 1971-79; owner Martin & Assoc., Denver, 1979—; founder Martin Aquatics, LLC, Denver, 1993—; treas. Rocky Mountain chpt. Inst. of Mgmt. Sci., Denver, 1968-70; opening speaker AICPAs, Las Vegas, Nev., 1988. Author, pub.: (newsletter) Martin Reports, 1981-90, Bob Martin-Chris Frederiksen Marketing and Management Report for CPAs, 1990-94. Served to lt. USN, 1958-63. Mem. Inst. Mgmt. Cons., Alpha Pi Mu, Sigma Xi. Home and Office: PO Box 6886 Denver CO 80206-0886

MARTIN, ROBERT JOSEPH, dermatologist; b. Williston, N.D., Feb. 1, 1943; s. Joseph Bramblee and Louise Ruby (Herbeth) M.; m. Gayle Rae Kircher, June 23, 1943 (div. July 1984); children: Joseph Scott, Jeffrey Thomas, Jennifer Ruby; m. Janice Irene Atkinson, Mar. 29, 1997. BA, U. Oreg., 1964, MD, 1968. Diplomate Am. Bd. Dermatology (fellow Am. Acad. Dermatology 1973). Intern Tripler Army Med. Ctr., Honolulu, 1968-69; med. resident Fitsimons Army Med. Ctr., Denver, 1969-70, dermatology resident, 1970-73; asst. chief dermatology Madigan Army Med. Ctr., Tacoma, Wash., 1973-74, chief dermatology, 1974-76; pvt. practice Tacoma, 1976—. Contbr. articles to profl. jours. Lt. U.S. Army, 1968-76. Mem. AMA, Pacific Dermatology Assn., Pacific N.W. Dermatology Assn., Washington State Med. Assn. Presbyterian. Home: 5918 78th Ave NW Gig Harbor WA 98335 Office: 1033 Regents Blvd Fircrest WA 98466

MARTIN, ROBERT MICHAEL, lawyer; b. N.Y.C., Nov. 28, 1922; s. Charles Augustus and Mary Corcoran (Shannon) M.; m. Monica Maria Schmid, Jan. 22, 1951; children: Tara J., C. Brian, Stacy D. BA, Amherst Coll., 1949; grad. cert., Trinity Coll., Dublin, Ireland, 1950; JD, U. So. Calif., 1965; diploma in law, Nat. D.A. Coll., 1973. Bar: Calif. 1966. Mem. faculty Chadwick Sch., Rolling Hills, Calif., 1952-56; mgmt. Servo-Mechanisms, Torrance, Calif., 1956-58, Systems Devel.Corp., Santa Monica, Calif., 1958-62, Douglas Missile & Space, Santa Monica, Calif., 1962-63; v.p. Automation Svc. Co., Beverly Hills, 1963-65; dep. pub. defender L.A. County, 1965-67, spl. asst. dist. atty., dept. dist atty., 1971-93; chief counsel, exec. officer Calif. Alcohol Beverage Control Bd., 1967-69; state dir. Calif. Dept. of Social Welfare, Sacramento, 1969-71; ptnr. Donahue, Donahue and Martin, Redondo Beach, Calif., 1995—; instr. travel law West L.A. Coll. Author: Automation in Medicine. Sgt. U.S. Army Air Corp., 1942-45. Mem. Calif. Bar Assn., Calif. Dist. Atty. Assn., Irish-Am. Bar Assn., Asia-Pacific Lawyers Assn., Internat. Forum of Travel and Tourism Advocates, Air Force Assn., 454th Bombardment Group Assn., Amherst Coll. Alumni Assn., U. So. Calif. Alumni Assn. Republican. Office: Donahue Donahue and Martin 116 Avenue I Fl 2 Redondo Beach CA 90277-5401

MARTIN, RONALD GENE, logistics program manager; b. San Bernardino, Calif., Apr. 24, 1954; s. Donald Arthur Sr. and Beverly Jean (Willis) M.; m. Mary Alice Acosta, Oct. 14, 1978 (div. Mar. 1990); 1 child, Natalie Rebecca; m. Desiree Pietzsch, Jan. 9, 1991; 1 stepchild, Tara Brianna. AS, C.C. Air Force, 1981; AA, San Bernardino Valley Coll., 1977; BA, Calif. State U., San Bernardino, 1981, MA, 1989. Cert. acquistion profl. Quality assurance rep. Western Space & Missile Ctr., Vandenberg AFB, Calif., 1984-85; logistics program mgr. Ballistic Missile Office, Norton AFB, Calif., 1985-88; integrated logistics support mgr. Ballistic Systems Divsn., Norton AFB, Calif., 1988-91; dep. dir. logistics Pacific Air Forces, Hickam AFB, Hawaii, 1991-93; sr. acquisitions mgr. Space & Missile Systems Ctr., L.A. AFB, 1993—; instr. Air Force Inst. Tech., Hickam AFB, Hawaii, 1991-93. With USAF, 1972-75, USAFR, 1975-84. Democrat. Home: PO Box 2286 Redlands CA 92373-0761 Office: Space & Missile Systems Ctr (AXD) 155 Discoverer Blvd # 2208A Los Angeles AFB CA 90245-4692

MARTIN, SALLY S. KEES, family studies educator; b. Lovelock, Nev., Aug. 9, 1943; d. Clarence Emil and Marjorie (Simpson) Sommer; m. Patrick James Martin, Dec. 28, 1974; 1 child, Kenneth Alexander Kees. BS, U. Nev., Reno, 1967, MS, 1971; PhD, Oreg. State U., 1992. Cert. family life educator. Instr. U. Nev., Reno, 1967-69, rsch. asst., 1970-71, asst. prof., 1972-78, state extension specialist, 1978—, assoc. prof. family studies, 1987—; cons. region IX Head Start, 1960-72. Contbr. articles to profl. publs. Recipient Excellence in Teen Programming award Nat. Assn. Extension 4H Agts., 1994, Nat. CAreer Achievement award State Family Life Specialists, 1995, Strengthening Our Capacity to Care, DeWitt Wallace-Reader's Digest, 1986, Outstanding Educator in Nev. award Gamma Sigma Delta, 1996. Mem. Nat. Coun. on Family Rels. (chair edn. and enrichment sect. 1996—, bd. dirs. 1996—), Nat. Assn. for Edn. of Young Children, Internat. Soc. for Prevention of Child Abuse and Neglect, Am. Profl. Soc. on Abuse of Children, Am. Assn. Family and Consumer Scis., PEO.

MARTIN, THOMAS HENRY, JR., water resource engineer, software writer; b. Plainfield, N.J., Aug. 3, 1957; s. Thomas Henry Sr. and Audrey May (Goldhammer) M.; m. Lisa Marie Burley, July 1, 1995. BS in Civil Engring., U. Vt., 1981; cert. advanced studies in applied electronics, Harvard U., 1988. Registered profl. engr., Maine, Wash.; cert. water distbn. mgr., Wash. Hydropower engr. ind. cons., Fanwood, N.J., 1981; geotech. engr. Geotech Assocs., Fanwood, 1981; water resource engr. Camp Dresser & McKee Inc., Boston, 1982-86, systems engr., 1986-88; software engr. WSI Corp., Billerica, Mass., 1988-90; civil engr. EA Engring., Redmond, Wash., 1991-92; water resource engr. Foster Wheeler Environ. Corp. (formerly Ebasco), Bellevue, Wash., 1992—. Co-author: Vermont Hydro-Logic: Small-Scale Licensing and Governing Issues, 1981, (computer automated weather info. system) WxWindows: Touchscreen System, 1989; engr. removal of dam from East Fork Salmon River, Idaho, 1991; engr. water quality computer model Columbia River System Operation Rev. EIS, 1994; mem. ecology water reuse adv. com. Washington Dept. Health, 1996. Andrew Mellon Environ. and Natural Resources grantee, Burlington, Vt., 1979. Mem. ASCE, IEEE, Am. Water Works Assn. Home: 7550 Roosevelt Way NE Seattle WA 98115-4221

MARTIN, WILFRED WESLEY FINNY, psychologist, property owner and manager; b. Rock Lake, N.D., Dec. 3, 1917; s. William Isaac and Anna Liisa (Hendrickson-Juntunen) M.; m. Stella Helland, Sept. 25, 1943; children: Sydney Wayne, William Allan. BA, Jamestown Coll., 1940; army specialized tng. program, Hamilton Coll., 1944; MS, EdD, U. So. Calif., 1956. Highsch. prin., coach pub. sch., Nekoma, N.D., 1940-42; contact rep., psychologist VA, L.A., 1946-49, psychologist, chief rehab., 1972-77; guidance dir. Moorehead (Minn.) Pub. Schs., 1951-53; instr. Concordia Coll., Moorhead, 1951-53; from intern to resident Fargo (N.D.) VA Hosp., Moorhead, Minn., 1953-58; psychologist VA, Fargo, N.D., 1953-57; assoc. Sci. Rsch. Assoc./IBM, Boulder, Colo., 1957-65; regional dir. Sci. Rsch. Assoc./IBM, L.A., 1966-72; owner, mgr. Martin Investments, Huntington Beach, Calif., 1977—; adjutant U. Miss., Oxford, 1942; trustee Wilfred W. and Stella Martin Trust, Huntington Beach, 1991. Author: Veterans Administration Work Simplification, 1948, 57. Charter mem. Rep. Presdl. Task Force, 1980; adv. sr. ptnrs. bd. dirs. U. Calif. Med. Sch., Irvine, 1990; donor Dr. and Mrs. W.W. Martin Endowment, Jamestown Coll., N.D., 1985; mem. Assocs. of James Ford Bell Libr., U. Minn. With U.S. Army, 1942-45. Mem. Am. Psychol. Assn., Cardinal & Gold U. So. Calif., Jamestown Coll. Heritage Circle (charter), Suomi Coll. Second Century Soc., Elks. Republican. Lutheran. Home: PO Box 5445 Huntington Beach CA 92615-5445 *The dominant force in my life is described by the Finnish word SISU, which means perseverence, determination, competitiveness, and tenacity toward goal-oriented achievements. Due to SISU, faith, and hard work I enjoy an active successful life.*

MARTIN, WILLIAM BAXTER, business owner; b. Polson, Mont., June 11, 1930; s. John W. Martin and Lottie Broadhead; m. Joan Rasmussen, June 6, 1953; children: John W., Lori, Carla. Grad. h.s., Ronan, Mont. Owner City Electric, Concord, Calif., 1970—, Elec. Specialties Mfg., Lodi, Calif., 1988—, Am. Boxing Inc., Las Vegas, Nev., 1995—. Inventor plastic parts for elec. industry. With USAF, 1947-48. Mem. Masons, Shriners. Office: Elec Specialties Mfg 1341F Galaxy Way Concord CA 94520

MARTIN, WILLIAM CHARLES, lawyer; b. Shenandoah, Iowa, May 25, 1923; s. J. Stuart and Chloe Irene (Anderson) M.; m. Marilyn Forbes, Oct. 18, 1947 (div. 1979); children: Ann, James; m. 2d, Kathryn Ann Fehr, Sept. 17, 1979. BA, U. Iowa, 1946, JD, 1947. Bar: Iowa 1947, Oreg. 1948. Sr. ptnr. Martin Bischoff, Templeton, Biggs & Ericsson, Portland, Oreg., 1951-86; mem. Oreg. Bd. Bar Examiners, 1966-69; instr. Lewis and Clark Coll. Law, 1973-75, U. Hawaii-Hilo, West Hawaii, 1989—. Bd. dirs. Eastmoreland Gen. Hosp., Portland, 1960-84, chmn., 1978-81; mem. Lawyers Com. for Civil Rights Under Law, Jackson, Miss., 1965; bd. dirs. Lake Oswego (Oreg.) Pub. Libr., 1981-84, chmn., 1982-84; mem. Kona bd. Am. Cancer Soc. 1st lt. USAAF, WWII. Mem. ABA, Oreg. State Bar, Kona Heavens Assn. (pres. 1994-95), Univ. Club, Kona Outdoor Cir. (Kailua Kona), Keauhou Yacht Club (dir. 1996—), Phi Delta Phi, Sigma Nu. Democrat. Episcopalian. Home: 73-4825 Anini St Kailua Kona HI 96740-9202

MARTINEAU, HOLLY LOW, dietitian; b. Mesa, Ariz., May 22, 1971; d. Gordon Jesse and Stephanie (Phillips) Low; m. Michael Reed Martineau, Feb. 12, 1993; children: Joshua, Michael. BS cum laude, Brigham Young U., 1994. Nutritionist Spl. Supplemental Foods for Women, Infants and Children, Salt Lake City, 1994-95; clin. dietician Pioneer Valley Hosp., 1995-96. Vol. Primary Children's Med. Ctr. Festival of Trees, Salt Lake City, 1993, store coord. Am. Heart Assn.'s Fest, Salt Lake City, 1994. Trustees scholar Brigham Young U., 1989-93. Mem. Am. Dietetic Assn. (registered dietitian), Phi Kappa Phi. Republican. Mem. LDS Ch. Home: 4677 Quail Park Dr Apt B Salt Lake City UT 84117

MARTINES, KAREN LOUISE, hospital administrator, nurse; b. Paris, Ont., Can., July 24, 1952; d. Norman Walter and Shirley Lorraine (Ford) Watts; m. Lawrence James Martines, Feb. 23, 1980; 1 child, Maria Nicole. BSN, U. Western Ont., London, Can., 1976; MS, Chapman U., 1983. Cert. healthcare quality profl. RN Centinela Hosp., Inglewood, Calif., 1976-77, gastroenterology RN III, 1977-83; med./surg. mgr. Flagstaff (Ariz.) Med. Ctr., 1983-87, cluster mgr. med./surg., 1987-89; dir. managed care McKenzie-Willamette Hosp., Springfield, Oreg., 1989-94; dir. quality resource svcs. St. Mary-Corwin Regional Med. Ctr., Pueblo, Colo., 1994-96; mgr. integrated care St. mary's Regional Med. Ctr., Reno, 1996—. Mem. NAFE, Profl. Women's Network, Calif. Soc. Gastrointestinal Assts. (v.p. 1981-82, pres. 1982-83), Soc. Gastrointestinal Assts. (by-laws com. 1982-83), Nat. Assn. Quality Assurance Profls., Am. Soc. Health Risk Mgmt. Office: St Mary Regional Med Ctr 235 West Sixth St Reno NV 89520

MARTINETTI, RONALD ANTHONY, lawyer; b. N.Y.C., Aug. 13, 1945; s. Alfred Joseph and Frances Ann (Battipaglia) M. Student, U. Chgo., 1981-82; JD, U. So. Calif., 1982. Bar: Calif. 1982, U.S. Dist. Ct. (cen. and no. dists.) Calif. 1982, U.S. Dist. Ct. Ariz., 1992; U.S. Ct. Appeals (9th cir.) 1982. Ptnr. Kazanjian & Martinetti, Glendale, Calif., 1986—; co-founder Am. Legends Website, 1996, Am. Legends Pub., 1996. Author: James Dean Story, 1995. Vol. trial lawyer Bet Tzedek Legal Svcs., 1987—; judge pro tem L.A. Superior Ct., 1994—. Mem. Calif. Bar Assn. Roman Catholic. Office: Kazanjian & Martinetti 520 E Wilson Ave Glendale CA 91206-4374

MARTINEZ, ANTHONY JOSEPH, real estate appraiser; b. San Pedro, Calif., Nov. 2, 1947; s. Antonio Jose and Frances (Gonzales) M.; m. Judith Lyn Miller, July 24, 1971; children: Ronda Adrienne, Amanda Elizabeth, Melanie Melissa. AA, Cerritos Coll., 1968; BA, U. Americas, Mexico City, 1970. Cert. secondary tchr., Calif.; cert. gen. real estate appraiser, Ariz. Corp. officer Canyon Savs. & Loan, Prescott, Ariz., 1976-80; Ariz. dir. Nat. Assn. Ind. Fee Appraisers, Phoenix, 1989-91; with bd. dirs. Ariz. State Bd. Appraisal, Phoenix, 1990-96, chmn., 1990-94; owner RAM Enterprises, Prescott, 1980-86, A.J. Martinez & Assocs., Prescott, 1986—; instr. Yavapai Coll., Prescott, 1973—; chmn. Bus. Adv. Coun. Yavapai Coll., 1988-89; with accredited residential sq. footage stds. com. Am. Nat. Stds. Instn., 1995-96. Tech. editor: Principios De La De Bienes Raices Residenciales, 1983. Charter mem. Prescott Town Hall. Mem. Nat. Assn. Ind. Fee Appraisers (sr., cert. instr. 1984—), Assn. Regulatory Ofcls. (nat. pres. 1994-95), Outward Bound-Prescott (bd. dirs. 1976-80), West Yavapai Guidance Clinic (bd. dirs. 1978-84), Prescott Sister Cities Assn. (pres. 1975-78), Lions (pres. Prescott Sunrise club 1979-80). Republican. Lutheran. Office: Anthony J Martinez & Assocs PO Box 4195 Prescott AZ 86302-4195

MARTINEZ, AUGUSTINE P., academic administrator; b. Durango, Colo., Oct. 25, 1948; m. Gladys S. Herrera, Sept. 5, 1994. BA in Psychology/Phys. Edn., Ft. Lewis Coll., 1971; MA in Phys. and Recreational Sources, Adams State Coll., 1973; PhD in Edn./Adminstrn., U. N.Mex., 1983. Dir. housing, coord. campus life, asst. prof. Colo. Mountain Coll., Glenwood Springs, Colo., 1971-73; registrar, instr. freshman composition Ft. Lewis Coll., Durango, 1973-88; dir. S.W. Ctr. Pueblo C.C., Cortez, Durango, 1989-92; pres. Navajo C.C., Tsaile, Ariz., 1992-93; campus dir. U. N.Mex., Taos, 1993—; cons., pub. spkr., nationwide. Trustee Millicent Rogers Mus.; bd. dirs. Taos Arts Assn., U. N.Mex. Dean's Coun. Mem. Am. Assn. C.C. (mem. pres.'s acad.), N.Mex. Cont. Educators Assn., N.Mex. C.C. Pres.'s Assn., Colo. Commn. on Higher Edn., Mountain Plains Adult Edn. Assn., colo. Assn. Cont. Edn., Nat. Assn. of Title III Adminstrs., Nat. Assn. for Bilingual/Bicultural Edn., Am. Assn. of Collegiate Registrars and Admissions Officers, Coll. Placement Coun., Rocky Mountain Placement Assn., Kiwanis Internat., Toastmasters Internat., Nat. Spkrs. Assn., Phi Delta Kappa. Office: U NMex Taos 115 Civic Plz Dr Taos NM 87571

MARTINEZ, EDGAR, professional baseball player; b. N.Y.C., Jan. 2, 1963. Student, American Coll., Puerto Rico. Baseball player Seattle Mariners, 1982—. Named. to Am. League All-Star Team, 1992, 95, 96, Am. League Silver Slugger Team, 1992, 95. Office: Seattle Mariners PO Box 4100 411 1st Ave S Seattle WA 98104

MARTINEZ, ELIZABETH COONROD, Spanish language educator; b. Austin, Tex., June 3, 1954; d. Holmes Thomas Coonrod and Phyllis D (Berry) Gaxiola. BA in English, Portland State U., 1983; MA in Hispanic Civilization, NYU, 1991; PhD in Latin Am. Lit., U. N.Mex., 1995. Pub. info. reporter Portland (Oreg.) State U. Pub. Info., 1981-83; reporter, photographer Woodburn (Oreg.) Ind., 1983-84; reporter The Oregonian, Portland, 1984-86; reporter, asst. editor The New Haven Ind., 1986-89; mng. editor Albuquerque Monthly mag., 1989; anchor, news dir. Sta. KLUZ-TV, Albuquerque, 1989-91; instr. Spanish U. N.Mex., Albuquerque, 1991-95, instr. journalism, 1992-94; asst. prof. Spanish Sonoma State U., Rohnert Park, Calif., 1995—; host Sta. KNME Pub. TV, Albuquerque, 1990, 93; dir., instr. Mex. Summer Abroad Program, U. N.Mex., Albuquerque, 1993, minority H.S. students summer workshop in journalism, 1994. Author: (biographies) Sor Juana, A Trailblazing Thinker, 1993, Henry Cisneros, Mexican-American Leader, 1993, Edward James Olmos, Mexican-American Actor, 1994, (history) Coming to America: The Mexican-American Experience, 1995; contbr. to Christian Sci. Monitor, N.Y. Times, 1989-90; contbr. articles to profl. jours. Speaker Cuba (N.Mex.) H.S. Commencement Address, 1990; chair HIV prevention comty. awareness task force, U. N.Mex. Hosp., Albuquerque, 1990-91; mem. centennial pub. rels. com. U. N.Mex., Albuquerque, 1991, panelist comty. and regional planning com., 1993, mem. Grad. Student Assn., 1993-95. Recipient Ednl. Travel award Univision TV, 1990, 1st pl. Opinion Column award Conn. Sigma Delta Chi Press Assn., 1988, Sammy award, 1986, News Feature award Sigma Delta Chi, 1986, Best Editl. Column award, 1986, Investigative Journalism award New Eng. Press Assn., 1987; Challenge Assistantship fellow U. N.Mex., 1993-94; Latin Am. travel rsch. grantee Latin Am. Inst., U. N.Mex., 1993; Teaching fellow Poynter Inst., 1995. Mem. AAUW, MLA, Latin Am. Studies Assn., Rocky Mountain Modern Lang. Assn., S.W. Writers Workshop. Office: Sonoma State U Dept Fgn Languages Rohnert Park CA 94928

MARTINEZ, JOHN STANLEY, entrepreneur; b. Phila., Apr. 14, 1930; s. Joseph Vincent and Helen Leeds (Simpson) M.; m. Britta K. Ponder, Dec. 29, 1987; children: John Jr., Joseph G., Mary Lynn. BChemE, Rensselaer Poly. Inst., 1951; diploma, Oak Ridge Sch. Reactor Tech., 1957; PhD, U. Calif., Berkeley, 1962. Rsch. engr. N.Am. Aviation Co., Santa Susanna, Calif., 1954-55, Jet Propulsion Lab., Calif. Inst. Tech., Pasadena, Calif., 1955-61; rsch. assoc. Livermore (Calif.) Nat. Lab., 1959-61; with TRW Systems Group, Redondo Beach, Calif., 1961-76, mgr. high energy laser bus. area, 1970-76; pres. Physics Internat. Co., San Leandro, Calif., 1976-84, Jamar Enterprises, Moraga, Calif., 1970—, HLX Laser Inc., San Diego, 1986-87, Air-Sea Comm. Corp., San Diego, 1988-89; pres., CEO Jamar Tech. Co., San Diego, 1987-89, Calif. Jamar, Inc., 1989-92; chmn. Surgilase, Inc., Warwick, R.I., 1991-94; CEO and chmn. JMAR Industries, San Diego, 1993—; chmn. Pacific Precision Labs., Inc., Chatsworth, Calif., 1993—, Calif. ASIC, Inc., 1996—; supervisory dir. Pisces Internat., Netherlands, 1982-84; pres., chmn. Hermosa Entertainment Corp., Hermosa Beach, Calif., 1969-72. Contbr. articles to profl. publs.; patentee in field. Chmn. Hermosa Beach City Improvement Commn., 1968-70. Capt. USMC, 1951-54, Korea. AEC fellow, 1958, Ford Found. fellow, 1960. Mem. IEEE, Sigma Xi, Tau Beta Pi. Home: PO Box 1030 Del Mar CA 92014-1030 Office: 3956 Sorrento Valley Blvd San Diego CA 92121-1403

MARTINEZ, JOSE RAFAEL, writer, educator; b. Monte Vista, Colo., Aug. 16, 1943; s. Jose Delfino Martinez and Rose Madril Fennell; m. Fredrika Audrey McGraw, Dec. 24, 1975; children: Ashley Rose, Brian Thomas. BS in Journalism, U. Colo., 1972. News reporter KMGH-TV, Denver, 1971-73; freelance journalist La Voz de Colo., Focus, others, Denver, 1974-77; info. officer City and County of Denver, 1977-86; instr. U. Colo., Boulder, 1986-95; freelance writer Boulder, 1995—; dir. writing workshop The Frank Waters Found., Arroyo Seco, N.Mex., 1995—; lit. judge The Peter and Madeleine Martin Found., Taos, N.Mex., 1996-97; lit. presentations/workshops The Millicent Rogers Mus., Taos, 1996-97. Author short fiction, acad. criticism, lit. journalism. Sgt. USAF, 1964-68. Recipient The Frank Waters Writing award for lit. achievement Peter and Madeleine Martin Found., 1994. Home: 1834 Marine St Boulder CO 80302-6420

MARTINEZ, MATTHEW GILBERT, congressman; b. Walsenburg, Colo., Feb. 14, 1929; children: Matthew, Diane, Susan, Michael, Carol Ann. Cert of competence, Los Angeles Trade Tech. Sch., 1959. Small businessman and bldg. contractor; mem. 97th-103rd Congresses from 30th (now 31st) Calif. dist., 1982—; mem. edn. and labor com., fgn. affairs com. Mem. Monterey Park Planning Commn., 1971-74; mayor City of Monterey Park, 1974-75; mem. Monterey Park City Council, 1974-80, Calif. State Assembly, 1980-82; bd. dirs. San Gabriel Valley YMCA. Served with USMC, 1947-50. Mem. Congl. Hispanic Caucus, Hispanic Am. Democrats, Nat. Assn. Latino Elected and Apptd. Ofcls., Communications Workers Am., VFW, Am. Legion, Latin Bus. Assn., Monterey Park C. of C., Navy League (dir.). Democrat. Lodge: Rotary. Office: US Ho of Reps 2239 Rayburn Bldg Ofc Washington DC 20515-0005*

MARTINEZ, MIGUEL ACEVEDO, urologist, consultant, lecturer; b. Chihuahua, Mex., Aug. 18, 1953; came to U.S., 1956; s. Miguel Nuñez and Velia (Acevedo) M. AB, Stanford U., 1976; MD, Yale U., 1983. Diplomate Am. Bd. Urology. Intern U. S.C. Med. Ctr., 1983-84; resident in urology White Meml. Med. Ctr., L.A., 1984-89, urologist, 1989—; cons., lectr. physician asst. program U. So. Calif., L.A., 1990—, clin. instr.; patient edn. cons. ICI Pharm., Del., 1991—, Zeneca's Speaker Forum; patient edn. and med. cons., lectr. Abbott Labs., 1991—; mem. edn.cons. several radio/TV stas., 1991—; mem. subcom. for diseases on kidney and transplantation NIH, Washington, 1991. Author: Intercellular Pathways, 1981. Polit. cons. Xavier Becerra, U.S. Congress, 1992, Luis Caldera, State Assembly, Calif., 1992, Martha Escutia, Calif. State Assembly, 1993, others; bd. dirs. Latino Ctr. for Prevention and Action in Health, Orange County, calif.; bd. govs., sec., rep. Zeneca Urology Econ. Summit, Washington, 1993. Named one of Outstanding Young Men of Am., 1981. Mem. AMA, Am. Urological Assn., Calif. Med. Assn. (polit. action com. bd. dirs. 1997—, del.), L.A. Med. Assn. (polit. action com. 1992—), L.A. County Med. Assn., Yale Alumni Assn., Stanford Alumni Assn., L.A. Athletic Club. Office: White Meml Med Ctr 1701 Cesar Chavez Ave # 500 Los Angeles CA 90033-2438

MARTINEZ, OSCAR JAQUEZ, educator, author; b. Mex., Mar. 4, 1943; s. Bernardo and Magdalena (Jaquez) M.; children: Jamie, Gabriel, Daniel, David, Andres. BA, Calif. State U., L.A., 1969; MA, Stanford (Calif.) U., 1970; PhD, UCLA, 1975. Prof. of history U. Tex., El Paso, 1975-88, dir. inst. of oral history, 1975-82, dir. ctr. for Inter-Am. and border studies, 1982-87; prof. history U. Ariz., Tucson, 1988—, dir. Latin Am. area ctr., 1994—; vis. prof. Yale U., 1995. Author: Border People, 1994, Troublesome Border, 1988, Border Boom Town, 1978, author, editor: Fragments of the Mexican Revolution, 1983; editor: Across Boundaries, 1986, The U.S.-Mexico Borderlands, 1995. With U.S. Army, 1963-65. Fellowship Ctr. for Advanced Study in the Behavioral Scis., 1981-82. Mem. Assn. for Borderlands Scholars (pres. 1985-87, Achievement award 1992), Latin Am. Studies Assn. (bd. dirs. 1980-82). Office: U Ariz History Dept Tucson AZ 85721

MARTINEZ, RAY, museum director. Dir. Ghost Ranch Living Mus., Albuquerque. Office: Ghost Ranch Living Mus HCR 77 Box 15 Albuquerque NM 87510

MARTINEZ, STEPHANIE ROBERTA, state agency administrator; b. Albuquerque, June 24, 1963; d. Robert A. and Trinidad L. (CHavez) M.; Todd R. Berenger, Aug. 24, 1991. BA in Sociology, U. N.Mex., 1988; MPA in Personnel, Troy State Univ., Bitburg, Germany, 1993. Registrar City Coll. Chgo., Bitburg, 1992-93; ednl. asst. State N.Mex., Albuquerque, 1994, adminstrv. health planner, 1994—. Juvenile probation officer, vol., Second Judicial Children's Ct., Albuquerque, 1996—; adminstrv. support vol. Habitat for Humanity, Albuquerque, 1996—; mem. Dept. Health Violence Task Force. Air Force Spouse Tuition scholar, Bitburg, 1992-93. Mem. Am. Soc. Pub. Adminstrs., Hispanic Women's Coun., Interagy. Com. Violence, Rio Ranch C. of C. (Leadership Sandoval Adv. Bd. scholar 1995-96). Home: 1804 Golf Course Rd NW Rio Rancho NM 87124 Office: Ste 325 2500 Louisiana Blvd NE Albuquerque NM 87110

MARTINEZ, VIRGINIA MARCELINA, dietitian; b. Denver, June 2, 1942; d. Maximo and Maria R. (Salas) M.; m. Jimmy Allen Tanhoff, Nov. 15, 1967 (div. Dec. 1989). MS, Mont. State U., 1990, BS, 1987. Lic. nutritionist Mont. Bd. Med. Examiners; registered dietitian. Sr. acctg. clk. 1st Bank Bozeman, Mont., 1974-80; rsch. asst. Mont. State U., Bozeman, 1984-90; nutritionist County of Big Horn, Hardin, 1992-95, Indian Health Svc./Crow Agy., 1995—; dietitian Yellowstone, Billings, Mont., 1996—; part-time instr. Little Big Horn Coll., Crow Agency, Mont., 1991—; part-time women, infants and children program dir. No. Cheyenne Bd. of Health, Lame Deer, Mont., 1992—; with Deering Cmty. Health Ctr., Billings. With USN, 1960-63. Recipient Outstanding Presentation award U. Minn., 1986; scholar Mont. Pub. health Assn., Am. Dietetic Assn., Mont. State U. Coll. Edn., Mex.-Am. Nat. Women's Assn. Mem. Am. Dietetic Assn., Pub. Health Nutrition Practice Group. Roman Catholic. Home: RR 1 Box 1187 Hardin MT 59034-9719 Office: Deering Clinic 123 S 27th Billings MT 59101

MARTINI, ROBERT EDWARD, wholesale pharmaceutical and medical supplies company executive; b. Hackensack, N.J., 1932. BS, Ohio State U., 1954. With Bergen Brunswig Corp., Orange, Calif., 1956-92, v.p., 1962-69, exec. v.p., 1969-81, pres., 1981-92, CEO, 1990—; chmn. Bergen Brunswig Corp., Orange, 1992—; chmn. exec. com. Bergen Brunswig Corp. Capt. USAF, 1954. *

MARTINS-GREEN, MANUELA, cell biologist; b. Luso, Moxico, Angola, Dec. 30, 1947; came to U.S., 1973; d. Joaquim P. and Maria Alice (Marques) Martins; m. Harry W. Green, II, May 15, 1975; children: Alice, Harry, Maria Green. BS, U. Lisbon, 1970; MS, U. Calif., Riverside, 1975; PhD, U. Calif., Davis, 1987. Chief scientist EM lab Agronomical Sta., Oeiras, Portugal, 1970-73; electron microscopist, dept. ophthalmology U. Calif., Davis, 1975-82; postdoctoral researcher Lawrence Berkeley Lab., U. Calif., 1987-88, rsch. scientist, 1992-93; adj. asst. prof. Rockefeller U., 1991-92; asst. prof. biology U. Calif., Riverside, 1993—; vis. lectr. U. Wuhan, China, 1988. Contbr. articles to profl. jours., books. Recipient Nat. Rsch. Svc. award, 1988-91, NIH traineeship, 1986-87; Fulbright Travel grantee Internat. Exch. Scholars, Riverside, 1973, NIH grantee, 1992—; dept. fellow U. Calif., Riverside, 1973-75, Regents fellow U. Calif., Davis, 1985, Regents Faculty fellow U. Calif.-Riverside, 1995-96. Mem. Am. Cancer Soc., Am. Soc. for Cell Biology, Am. Soc. Devel. Biology, Elec. Microscopy Soc. of Am., Women for Cell Biology, Wound Healing Soc., Phi Kappa Phi. Office: U Calif Dept Biology Riverside CA 92521

MARTINSON, CONSTANCE FRYE, television program hostess, producer; b. Boston, Apr. 11, 1932; d. Edward and Rosalind Helen (Sperber) Frye; m. Leslie Herbert Martinson, Sept. 24, 1955; 1 child, Julianna Martinson Carner. BA in English Lit., Wellesley Coll., 1953. Dir. pub. relations Coro Found., Los Angeles, 1974-79; producer/host KHJ Dimensions, Los Angeles, 1979-81, Connie Martinson Talks Books, Los Angeles, 1981—; instr. dept. humanities UCLA, 1981—; moderator, instr. Univ. Judaism; celebrity advisor Book Fair-Music Ctr., L.A., 1986; advisor, moderator L.A. Times Festival of Books, 1996; bd. dirs. Friends of English UCLA; TV rep. L.A. Pub. Libr. L.A. Cityview, Sta. WNYE, Channel Am. Author Dramatization of Wellesley After Images, 1974; book editor, columnist Calif. Press Bur. Syndicate, 1986—. Pres. Mayor's adv. council on volunteerism, Los Angeles, 1981-82; chmn. community affairs dept. Town Hall of Calif., Los Angeles, 1981-85; bd. dirs. legal def. fund NAACP, Los Angeles, 1981-84. Mem. Women in Cable, Am. Film Inst., Jewish TV Network (bd. dirs. 1985-87), PEN, Nat. Book Critics Assn., Wellesley Coll. Club (pres. 1979-81), Mulholland Tennis Club. Democrat. Jewish. Home and Office: 2288 Coldwater Canyon Dr Beverly Hills CA 90210-1756

MARTONE, FREDERICK J., judge; b. Fall River, Mass., Nov. 8, 1943. BS, Coll. Holy Cross, 1965; JD, U. Notre Dame, 1972; LLM, Harvard U., 1975. Bar: Mass. 1972, Ariz. 1974, U.S. Dist. Ct. Mass. 1973, U.S. Dist. Ct. Ariz. 1974, U.S. Ct. Appeals (1st cir.) 1973, U.S. Ct. Appeals (9th cir.) 1974, U.S. Supreme Ct. 1977. Law clk. to Hon. Edward F. Hennessey Mass. Supreme Judicial Ct., 1972-73; pvt. practice Phoenix, 1973-85; assoc. presiding judge Superior Ct. Ariz., Maricopa County; judge Superior Ct. Ariz., Maricopa County, Phoenix, 1985-92; justice Supreme Ct. Ariz., Phoenix, 1992—. Editor notes and comments Notre Dame Lawyer, 1970-72; contbr. articles to profl. jours. Capt. USAF, 1965-69. Mem. ABA, Ariz. Judges Assn., Maricopa County Bar Assn. Office: Supreme Ct Arizona 1501 W Washington St Phoenix AZ 85007-3231*

MARTY, LAWRENCE A., magistrate; b. Leigh, Nebr., June 17, 1926. Student Wayne State U., 1944-46, Creighton Sch. Law, 1946-48; J.D., U.Wyo., 1954. Bar: Wyo. 1954. Sole practice, Green River, Wyo., 1954-67; ptnr. Mart & Clark, Green River, 1967-74; ptnr. Marty & Ragsdale, Green River, 1975—; judge Green River Mcpl. Ct., 1956-58; U.S. Magistrate Dist. Wyo., 1958—. Alt. del. Rep. Nat. Conv., 1964. Mem. ABA, Wyo. Bar Assn., Sweetwater County Bar Assn. Office: 20 E Flaming Gorge Way Green River WY 82935-4210

MARTZ, CAROL ANN, career and organization development specialist; b. Ft. Benning, Ga., Dec. 28, 1938; d. Charles Harlow and Annetta Mae (Moore) Miles; m. Richard Woods, Aug. 6, 1960; children: Janet Foster, Brian, Roger; m. Harry Franklin Martz, Nov. 27, 1982. Student, U. Md., Munich, Germany, 1955-57; BA in Spanish/Edn., Douglass Coll., New Brunswick, N.J., 1959; MA in Counseling, U. N.Mex., 1993. Registered mental health counselor. Jr. high tchr. Spanish/French Bloomfield (N.J.) Schs., 1959-60, Hamden (Conn.) Schs., 1960-61; sec. Los Alamos (N.Mex.) Nat. Lab., 1981-88, tech. writer, editor, 1988-93, tng. specialist, 1993—. Mem. ACA, Nat. Career Devel. Assn., N.Mex. Counseling Assn., N.Mex. Career Devel. Assn., P.E.O. Republican. Methodist. Home: 29 Los Arboles Dr Los Alamos NM 87544-3089 Office: Los Alamos Nat Lab Tng and Devel MS M589 PO Box 1663 Los Alamos NM 87545

MARTZEN, BARBARA AILEEN, retired teacher; b. Couquille, Oreg., Sept. 22, 1930; d. Dwight Lyman and Ruth Heath (Benson) Hackett; m. Joseph George Martzen, Dec. 28, 1951; children: Rebecca Jo, John Gerald, Pamela Aileen. BA, Fresno State U., 1952; postgrad., U. Calif., 1970-80. Tchr. Grand View Sch., Dimuba, Calif., 1952-53, Wilson Sch., Dinuba, Calif., 1953-54; substitute tchr. Selma (Calif.) Schs., 1963-86, ret., 1986; ind. produce salesperson, Calif., 1983—. Contbr. poems to Poets of the West, Poetalk, Slugfest, Ltd., Nat. Libr. Poetry. Supporter Congressman Richard Lehman campaign, Calif., 1994. Republican.

MARTZEN, PHILIP D., physicist, software developer; b. Dinuba, Calif., Oct. 23, 1948; s. Dave and Vivian M.; m. Eloise Thompson, Jan. 29, 1972 (div. May 1988); Children: Natashya, Kinarii; m. Cynthia Stapp Landriz, July 1, 1995. BS, U. Calif., Santa Barbara, 1973, PhD, 1979. Staff mem. Geodynamics Corp., Santa Barbara, Calif., 1979-95; cons. Frontier Tech. Inc., Santa Barbara, Calif., 1996; cons. speech tech. lab. Panasonic, Santa Barbara, 1997; sr. mem. tech. staff Aerospace Corp., El Segundo, Calif., 1997—. Contbr. to profl. jours. V.p. REACTS, Santa Barbara, 1995-96; mem. Sci. and Engering. Coun. Santa Barbara, 1995—. Republican. Episcopalian. Home: 4166 San Martin Way Santa Barbara CA 93110

MARUOKA, JO ANN ELIZABETH, information systems manager; b. Monrovia, Calif., Jan. 1, 1945; d. John Constantine and Pearl (Macovei) Gotsinas; m. Lester Hideo Maruoka, Nov. 8, 1973 (div. Aug. 1992); stepchildren: Les Scott Kaleohano, Lee Stuart Keola. BA with honors, UCLA, 1966; MBA, U. Hawaii, 1971. Office mgr. and asst. R. Wenkam, Photographer, Honolulu, 1966-69; computer mgmt. intern and sys. analyst Army Computer Sys. Command, Honolulu, 1969-78; reservations mgr. Hale Koa Hotel, Honolulu, 1978-79; equal employment opportunity specialist U.S. Army Pacific Hdqs., Honolulu, 1979-80, computer specialist, 1980-87, supervisory info. sys. mgr., chief plans and programs, 1987—; bd. dirs. High Performance Computing and Comm. Coun., Tiverton, R.I.; pacific v.p. Fedn. Govt. Info. Processing Couns., Washington, 1992-95. Mem. Nat. and Hawaii Women's Polit. Caucus, Honolulu, 1987—; advisor Fed. Women's Coun. Hawaii, Honolulu, 1977—. Recipient EEO Excellence award Sec. of Army, 1989, Pacific Fed. Mgr. award Honolulu-Pacific Fed. Exec. Bd., 1990, Info. Resources Mgmt. award Interagy. Com. on Info. Resources Mgmt., 1991, Lead Dog Leadership award Fedn. Govt. Info. Processing Couns., 1993; named One of Fed. 100 (Execs.) of Yr., Fed. Computer Week, 1996. Mem. NAFE, Nat. Women's Polit. Caucus, AAUW, LWV, Armed Forces Comm.-Electronics Assn. (Hawaii chpt., Internat. award for Info. Resources Mgmt. Excellence 1992), Assn. U.S. Army (Pacific Fed. Mgr. award 1990), Federally Employed Women (advisor Aloha and Rainbow chpts. 1977—), Army Signal Corps Regimental Assn., Hawaii Intergovt. Info. Processing Coun. (pres. 1988-89, svc. award 1989). Democrat. Office: US Army Pacific Hdqrs APIM-PR Fort Shafter HI 96858

MARVIN, GRACE MARIA, sociology, educator; b. Athens, Greece, Mar. 25, 1950; d. Donald M. and Rickel Barbara (Kehr) M. BA in Philosophy, Coll. of William and Mary, 1972; MS in Sociology, Va. Commonwealth U., 1975; PhD in Sociology, U. Va., 1983. Teaching asst. U. Va., Charlottesville, 1975-76; lectr. Sweet Briar Coll., Va., 1976; instr. sociology U. Va., Charlottesville, 1977-78, U. S.C., Spartanburg, 1979-82; asst. prof. sociology Southwestern U., Memphis, 1982-84; asst. prof. Calif. State U., Chico, 1984-88, assoc. prof. sociology, 1988-94, prof., 1994—. Contbr. articles to profl. jours. Am. Sociol. Assn. scholar, 1979, NEH scholar, 1984, Ctr. Middletown Studies scholar, 1988, U. Tubingen (Germany) scholar, 1991-92, Humboldt U. scholar, 1994. Mem. Am. Sociol. Assn., Pacific Sociol. Assn., Internat. Sociol. Assn., Assn. Humanist Sociology. Office: Calif State U Dept Sociology Chico CA 95929-0445

MARX, WESLEY, writer, environmental educator; b. L.A., Nov. 2, 1934; s. Edward Howard and Kathleen (Woods) M.; m. Judith Ann Mell, Aug. 26, 1962; children: Christopher, Heather, Tyler. BA in Polit. Sci., Stanford U., 1956. Reporter Pasadena (Calif.) Star News, 1960-61; contbg. editor L.A. Magazine, Beverly Hills, Calif., 1961-64; author, lectr. Irvine, Calif., 1966—; mem. NRC coastal sci. and policy panel, 1992, marine monitoring, 1987-88; lectr. social ecology, U. Calif., Irvine; cons. Calif. Coastal Commn., San Francisco. Author: The Pacific Shore, 1974, The Protected Ocean, 1972, Oilspill, 1971, Man and His Environment: Waste, 1971, The Frail Ocean, 1967, Acts of God, Acts of Man, 1977, The Oceans: Our Last Resource, 1981, Pacific Coast, 1988, The Frail Ocean, 1991; contbr. articles to profl. jours. Mem. Calif. Tahoe Reg. Planning Agy., Lake Tahoe, 1981-83, Calif. Atty. Gen.'s Environ. Task Force, 1972-78, Irvine Planning Commn., 1972-73. Mem. Ctr. for Law in Pub. Interest (trustee 1979—), Water Environ. Fedn., Nat. Marine Edn. Assn., Friends of Newport Bay. Home: 3 Butler St Irvine CA 92612-2724

MASAGATANI, ERNESTA, retired school superintendent; b. Sept. 24, 1937; d. Louis Keahiuaokalani Sr. and Lei Lincoln Collins; children: Jason T.K., Jesse L.K., Jobie M.K. BE, U. Hawaii, 1960, M of Ednl. Adminstrn., 1983. Cert. tchr., Hawaii. Tchr. Aiea High Sch., Kailua High Sch., 1962-66; beginning tchr. supr. Windward Dist. Office, 1966-69, dist. resource tchr., 1971-75; tchr. Kainalu Elem. Sch., 1969-71; vice prin. Kalaheo High Sch., Kailua High Sch., Palisades Elem. Sch., 1975-79; prin. Robert Louis Stevenson Intermediate Sch., 1979-87; dep. dist. supt. Honolulu Dist., 1987-93, dist. supt., 1993—; pers. specialist Pers. Indsl. Rels. Bd., Office Pers. Svcs. Dept. Edn. State of Hawaii, 1995, ret., 1995. Mem. Liliuokalani Trust Adv. Coun., Pihana Na Mano Adv. Coun., Alii Pauahi Civic Club; ednl. cons. ARC, 1995-96, chair, 1996; ch. officer Kawaiahao Ch.; vol. ednl. and comty. projects Pihana Na Mano, Milotii Project; group facilitator. Mem. Daus. Hawaii. Mem. Kawaiahao Ch. Home: 249 Aikane Street Kailua HI 96734-1604

MASAYKO, RAY, mayor. Mayor City of Carson City, Nev. Office: City of Carson City 2621 Northgate Ln Ste 2 Carson City NV 89701

MASCHEK, ROGER ALAN, counselor; b. Chgo., Mar. 31, 1945. AA in Psychology, Coll. So. Idaho, 1988; BS in Psychology, Idaho State U., 1991; MEd in Counseling, Albertson Coll. Idaho, 1994. Pvt. practice counselor Twin Falls, Idaho, 1994—. Vol. Region V Mental Health, Twin Falls, 1996. Mem. ACA, Am. Mental Health Counselors Assn., Idaho Counseling Assn., Idaho Mental Health Counselors Assn., Am. Legion. Home: 357 N Ostrander Twin Falls ID 83301 Office: PO Box 949 Kimberly ID 83341

MASI, EDWARD A., computer company executive; b. Medford, Mass., May 7, 1947; s. Joseph Carl and Rita Olivine (Metras) M.; m. Kristine Ann Lauderbach Masi, Jan. 24, 1970. BSME, Tufts U., 1969. Mktg. sales IBM, Boston, 1969-76; commercial analysis IBM, Westchester, N.Y., 1976-78; mktg. mgr. IBM, Bethesda, Md., 1978-80; region mgr. mktg. sales Cray Rsch., Calverton, Md., 1980-87; exec. v.p. mktg. Mpls., 1988-92; corp. v.p., gen. mgr. Intel Corp., Beaverton, Oreg., 1992. Mem. Am. Electronics Assn. (vice chair 1991-92). Office: Intel Enterprise Servers Group Server Sys Product Divsn 5200 NE Elam Young Pkwy Hillsboro OR 97124-6463

MASI, ROBIN, artist, humanities educator; b. Palo Alto, Calif., July 29, 1960; d. Joseph Louis and Dale (Avella) M.; m. Steven Wayne Kuettel; 1 child, Benjamin Westmont. BFA, Tufts U. Sch. of Mus. of Fine Arts, 1983, 1994; MFA graduation with appreciation, Acad. of Art Coll., San Francisco, 1994. Vis. faculty Sch. Mus. Fine Arts, 1996—; faculty women's art history Sonoma State U., 1992-94; with Coll. of Marin, Greenbrae, Calif., 1994-95; instr. women's art history Acad. of Art Coll., 1995—; artist, 1980—. Producer (CD-ROM) Women Artists: A Multimedia History, 1996. Project Mgr., Dir., The Women's Artist Database Project, 1992. Treas., bd. dirs. No. Calif. Women's Caucus for Art, Berkeley, 1991-95; co-founder The Varo Registry of Women Artists, 1995—; moderator Feminist Art History and Women Artist Listserves, Cotati, 1996—. Mem. College Art Assn., Visual Resources Assn. Democrat. Roman Catholic. Office: 21 Pine St Concord MA 01742

MASKUS, KEITH EUGENE, economist; b. Dodge City, Kans., Sept. 16, 1954; s. Jack Lawrence and Dorothy Louise (Leighty) M.; m. Susan Emily Rehak, Dec. 30, 1978; 1 child, Carol Lillian. BA, Knox Coll., 1976; PhD, U. Mich., 1981. Asst. prof. econs. U. Colo., Boulder, 1981-88, assoc. prof., 1988-95, prof., 1995—; vis. scholar Fed. Res. Bank, Kansas City, Mo., 1983-84; sr. economist U.S. Dept. of State, Washington, 1986-87; cons. UN, Geneva, 1995, The World Bank, Washington, 1995-96. Author: International Trade Theory, 1995; contbr. articles to profl. jours. Mem. Am. Econ. Assn., Internat. Econs. and Fin. Assn. (jour. editor 1995—). Office: Univ Colo Dept Econs Campus Box 256 Boulder CO 80309

MASLACH, CHRISTINA, psychology educator; b. San Francisco, Jan. 21, 1946; d. George James and Doris Ann (Cuneo) M.; m. Philip George Zimbardo, Aug. 10, 1972; children: Zara, Tanya. B.A., Harvard-Radcliffe Coll., 1967; Ph.D., Stanford U., 1971. Prof. psychology U. Calif.-Berkeley, 1971—. Author: Burnout: The Cost of Caring, 1982; co-author: Influencing Attitudes and Changing Behavior, 1977, Maslach Burnout Inventory (rsch. scale), 1981, 2d edit., 1986, 3d edit., 1996, Experiencing Social Psychology, 1979, 2d edit., 1984, 3d edit., 1993, Professional Burnout, 1993, The Truth About Burnout, 1997. Recipient Disting. Teaching award, 1987, Best Paper award Jour. Orgnl. Behavior, 1994. Fellow AAAS, APA, Am. Psychol. Soc., Soc. Clin. and Exptl. Hypnosis (Henry Guze rsch. award 1980), We. Psychol. Assn. (pres. 1989); mem. Soc. Exptl. Social Psychology. Democrat. Office: U Calif Tolman Hall #1650 Dept Psychology Berkeley CA 94720-1650

MASLANSKY, CAROL JEANNE, toxicologist; b. N.Y.C., Mar. 3, 1949; d. Paul Jeremiah and Jeanne Marie (Filiatrault) Lane; m. Steven Paul Maslansky, May 28, 1973. BA, SUNY, 1971; PhD, N.Y. Med. Coll., 1983. Diplomate Am. Bd. Toxicology; cert. gen. toxicology. Asst. entomologist N.Y. State Dept. Health, White Plains, 1973-74; sr. biologist Am. Health Found., Valhalla, N.Y., 1974-76; rsch. fellow N.Y. Med. Coll., Valhalla, 1977-83, Albert Einstein Coll. Medicine, Bronx, N.Y., 1983; copr. toxicologist Texaco, Inc., Beacon, N.Y., 1984-85; prin. GeoEnviron. Cons., Inc., White Plains, N.Y., 1982-97, Maslansky GeoEnviron. Inc., Prescott, Ariz., 1997—; lectr. in entomology Westchester County Parks and Preserves, 1973-96, lectr. toxicology and hazardous materials, 1985—. Author: Air Monitoring Instrumentation, 1993, Health and Safety at Hazardous Waste Sites, 1997, (with others) Training for Hazardous Materials Team Members, 1991 (manual, video) The Poison Control Response to Chemical Emergencies, 1993. Mem. Harrison (N.Y.) Vol. Ambulance Corps., 1986-91, Westchester County (N.Y.) Hazardous Materials Response Team, 1987-96. Monsanto Fund Fellowship in Toxicology, 1988-90; grad. fellowship N.Y. Med. Coll., 1977-83. Mem. AAAS, Nat. Environ. Health Assn., N.Y. Acad. Sci., Am. Coll. Toxicology, Am. Indsl. Hygiene Assn., Environ. Mutagen Soc.

MASLIN, HARRY, recording industry executive, producer; b. Phila., Apr. 4, 1948; s. Philip and Sarah (Jacobs) M. Rec. engr. Regent Sound, N.Y.C., 1969-71; chief engr. Hit Factory Studios, N.Y.C., 1971-73, 74-75; rec. engr. Record Plant Studios, N.Y.C., 1973-74; record producer HRM Prodns., Hollywood, Calif., 1975—; co-owner, pres. Image Rec. Studios, Hollywood, 1983—. Recipient 20 gold and platinum records Rec. Industry Assn. of Am. Mem. Nat. Acad. Rec. Arts and Scis., ASCAP, Audio Engring. Soc. Office: Image Rec Studios 1020 N Sycamore Ave Los Angeles CA 90038-2308

MASLIN, HARVEY LAWRENCE, staffing service company executive; b. Chgo., Oct. 22, 1939; s. Jack and Shirley Maslin; m. Marcia Silberman, Aug. 21, 1960; children: Elaine, Shelley, Bonnie. BS, U. Ariz., 1961, JD, 1964. Bar: Ariz., 1964, Calif., 1966, U.S. Dist. Ct., 1964, 66. Ptnr. Maslin, Rotundo & Maslin, Sherman Oaks, Calif., 1966-67; gen. counsel Western Temporary Svcs., Inc., San Francisco, 1967-71, v.p., 1972-78, sr. v.p., sec., 1979-84; pres., chief oper. officer Western Staff Svcs., Inc., Walnut Creek, Calif., 1985-95, vice chmn. bd. dirs., chief adminstrv. officer, 1996—; dir. Western Staff Svcs., USA, Western Staff Svcs., U.K. Ltd., London, Western Staff Svcs. Pty Ltd., Melbourne, Australia, Western Staff Svcs. (N.Z.) Ltd., Auckland, Western Svc. A/S, Copenhagen, Denmark, Western Svc./Kontorsvc. A/S Oslo, Western Svc., Inc., Zurich, Western Video Images, Inc., San Francisco. Mem. Rep. Presidential Task Force, Washington, 1981. Mem. Nat. Assn. Temporary and Staffing Svcs. (bd. dirs.), Calif. Bar Assn., Ariz. Bar Assn., Phi Alpha Delta. Office: Western Staff Svcs Inc Exec Offices 301 Lennon Ln Walnut Creek CA 94598-2418

MASLINE, RICHARD CHARLES, financial executive; b. N.Y.C., July 12, 1942; s. Charles Andrew and Annabelle Masline; m. Mary Elizabeth Davis, Mar. 19, 1966; 1 child, Kathryn Ann. AB, Davidson Coll., 1965; MBA, Pepperdine U., 1980; MSCS, West Coast U., 1991. Exec. asst. Anvil Brand, High Point, N.C., 1965-67; programmer Duke Power, Charlotte, N.C., 1967-69; sys. analyst J.P. Stevens, Charlotte, 1969-71; project mgr., DB cons. Burroughs Corp., Detroit, 1971-78; sr. staff, group mgr. Transaction Tech. City Corp., Santa Monica, Calif., 1978-84; mem. tech. staff Jet Propulsion Lab., Pasadena, Calif., 1984-93; exec. v.p. Geo-Capital, Glendale, Calif., 1994; founder The Geo Group, Valencia, Calif., 1994; engring. mgr. Calif. Microwave, Woodland Hills, Calif., 1996—; sr. lectr. West Coast U., L.A., 1981-93. Author: Data Handling Options for Space Station Freedom, 1989. Active Habitat for Humanity, San Fernando, Calif., 1993-94, Homeless Shelter Com., Valencia, 1993-96; area coord. Episcopal Marriage Encounter, L.A. County, 1994; vol. ARC, Santa Clarita, Calif., 1994. Mem. IEEE (L.A. area cons. network), AIAA (Calif. synergistic acquisition transfer), Assn. for Computing Machinery, Orange County IEEE Cons. Network. Republican. Office: Calif Microwave 6022 Variel Ave Woodland Hills CA 91354

MASLOW, RICHARD EMANUEL, psychology consultant; b. Bklyn., Dec. 20, 1929; s. Louis William and Helen Lillian (Danziger) M.; m. Karen Mae Olson, May 11, 1956; children: Troy Mae, Darcy Sue. BS, Western N.Mex. U., 1952, MS, 1957. Tchr., coach Eddyville High Sch., Nebr., 1955-57; tchr., coach, counselor Quincy High Sch., Calif., 1957-62; psychology instr. San Joaquin Delta Coll., Stockton, Calif., 1963-91; student tchr. supr. Calif. State U., Stanislaus, 1993; stress mgmt. cons.; text book cons. Harper & Row, McGraw Hill, Houghton-Mifflin; basketball ofcl. No. Calif. Coll. Basketball Ofcls., 1979-90. Contbr. articles to profl. jours. Mem. sch. bd. Lincoln Unified Sch. Dist., Stockton, Calif., 1978-96, pres. bd., 1980, 85, 88, 91, 95, 96. Served with U.S. Army, 1952-55. Mem. APA, Am. Psychol. Soc., Western Psychol. Assn., San Joaquin County Psychol. Assn. (pres. 1977-78), Calif. Sch. Bd. Assn., Nat. Sch. Bd. Assn. Home and Office: 3788 W Benjamin Holt Dr Stockton CA 95219-3324

MASOLO, GAY ANN, state legislator; b. Townsend, Mont., June 24, 1942; d. Lawrence Daniel and Marie Emma (Meyer) Sullivan; m. Charles Robert Masolo, Nov. 30, 1963; 1 child, David Charles. BA in Edn., Carroll Coll., 1964; MA in Edn., U. No. Mont., 1991. Tchr. Cecelia Hazelton Sch., Townsend, 1964-69, Main St. and Eastgate Sch., East Helena, Mont., 1970-92; mem. Mont. State Ho. of Reps., Helena, 1995—, mem. agr., bus. and labor and edn. coms.; pub. mem. Mt. Brd. Pvt. Security and Pvt. Investigation, Helena. Sec.-treas. Broadwater Rep. Com., Townsend, 1978—; mem. Broadwater County Centennial, Townsend, 1996—; chair Broadwater County Fair, Townsend, 1996—; mem. adv. com. Carroll Coll., Helena. Named to NASA Honors Program, 1993; recipient Girls State Alumna award, 1995. Mem. East Helena Edn. Assn. (pres.), Delta Kappa Gamma. Roman Catholic. Home: 20 Buck Dr Townsend MT 59644 Office: Mont State Ho Reps Capitol Bldg Helena MT 59620-0400

MASON, CAROLYN S., career coordinator; b. Spokane, Wash., July 23, 1944; d. Garvin A. and Dorothy L. (Kaiser) Pierce; m. Gary L. Mason, Feb. 19, 1972; children: Ryan Lee, Megan Sue. BE, Colo. State U., 1969, MEd, 1994. Cert. Type D adminstr. Tchr. vocat. sch. Poudre Sch. Dist., Ft. Collins, Colo., 1970-94, sch.-to-career coord., 1994—; pres. spl. needs divsn. Colo. Vocat. Assn., 1989-90; lead tchr. futuring steering com. Poudre Sch. Dist., 1989-94; rep. career edn. Pvt. Industry Coun., Ft. Collins, 1993—. Chair Partnership F.C. Ft. Collins C. of C., 1990-91; Vol. Larimer County 4-H, Ft. Collins, 1991—; mem. sch.-to-career focus group Colo. Gov. Romer, Denver, 1994; adv. mem. Larimer County Ednl. Consortium, 1994—; mem. K-15 coordinating coun., 1995—, Colo. Tech Prep focus group, 1996—. Named Outstanding Spl. Coop Program, Colo. Vocat. Assn., 1988, recipient Tchr. Yr. award, 1991; Sch.-to-Career grantee Colo. Lt. Gov. office, 1995-97. Mem. Job Developers Network, 1994—. Home: 6419 E County Rd 44 Fort Collins CO 80524 Office: Poudre Sch Dist 2407 Laporte Ave Fort Collins CO 80521

MASON, DEAN TOWLE, cardiologist; b. Berkeley, Calif., Sept. 20, 1932; s. Ira Jenckes and Florence Mabel (Towle) M.; m. Maureen O'Brien, June 22, 1957; children: Kathleen, Alison. BA in Chemistry, Duke U., 1954, MD, 1958. Diplomate Am. Bd. Internal Medicine, Am. Bd. Cardiovasc. Diseases, Nat. Bd. Med. Examiners. Intern, then resident in medicine Johns Hopkins Hosp., 1958-61; clin. assoc. cardiology br., sr. asst. surgeon USPHS, Nat. Heart Inst., NIH, 1961-63, asst. sect. dir. cardiovascular diagnosis, attending physician, sr. investigator cardiology br., 1963-68; prof. medicine, prof. physiology, chief cardiovascular medicine U. Calif. Med. Sch., Davis-Sacramento Med. Center, 1968-82; dir. cardiac ctr. Cedars Med. Ctr., Miami, Fla., 1982-83; physician-in chief Western Heart Inst., San Francisco, 1983—; chmn. dept. cardiovascular medicine St. Mary's Med. Ctr., San Francisco, 1986—; co-chmn. cardiovasuclar-renal drugs U.S. Pharmacopeia Com. Revision, 1970-75; mem. life scis. com. NASA; med. rsch. rev. bd. VA, NIH; vis. prof. numerous univs., cons. in field; mem. Am. Cardiovascular Splty. Cert. Bd., 1970-78. Editor-in-chief Am. Heart Jour., 1980—; contbr. numerous articles to med. jours. Recipient Research award Am. Therapeutic Soc., 1965; Theodore and Susan B. Cummings Humanitarian award State Dept.-Am. Coll. Cardiology, 1972, 73, 75, 78; Skylab Achievement award NASA, 1974; U. Calif. Faculty Research award, 1978; named Outstanding Prof. U. Calif. Med. Sch., Davis, 1972. Fellow Am. Coll. Cardiology (pres. 1977-78), A.C.P., Am. Heart Assn., Am. Coll. Chest Physicians, Royal Soc. Medicine; mem. Am. Soc. Clin. Investigation, Am. Physiol. Soc., Am. Soc. Pharmacology and Exptl. Therapeutics (Exptl. Therapeutics award 1973), Am. Fedn. Clin. Research, N.Y. Acad. Scis., Am. Assn. U. Cardiologists, Am. Soc. Clin. Pharmacology and Therapeutics, Western Assn. Physicians, AAUP, Western Soc. Clin. Research (past pres.), Phi Beta Kappa, Alpha Omega Alpha. Republican. Methodist. Club: El Macero Country. Home: 44725 Country Club Dr El Macero CA 95618-1047 Office: Western Heart Inst St Mary's Med Ctr 450 Stanyan St San Francisco CA 94117-1079

MASON, FRANK HENRY, III, automobile company executive, leasing company executive; b. Paris, Tenn., Nov. 16, 1936; s. Frank H. and Dorothy (Carter) M.; children—Robert C., William C. B.E.E., Vanderbilt U., 1958; M.S. in Indsl. Mgmt., MIT, 1965. With Ford Motor Co., 1965-71, asst. controller Ford Brazil, Sao Paulo, Brazil, 1971-74, mgr. overseas financing dept., Dearborn, Mich., 1974 76, asst. controller engine div., 1976-78, mgr. facilities and mgmt. services, 1978-81; controller Ford Motor Credit Co., Dearborn, 1981-87; dir. finance Ford Fin. Services Group, Dearborn, 1987-89; exec. v.p., chief fin. officer U.S. Leasing, Internat., San Francisco, 1989-92; ret. 1992. Served to lt. USN, 1958-63.

MASON, JAMES ALBERT, museum director, university dean; b. Eureka, Utah, 1929; married, 1956; 3 children. BA, Brigham Young U., 1955, MA, 1957; EdD, Ariz. State U., 1970. Cons., clinician in fine arts, 1955—; former chmn. dept. music Brigham Young U., Provo, dean Coll. Fine Arts and Communications, 1982-93; dir. Mus. of Art Brigham Young U., 1993-96; retired, 1996; vis. prof., lectr. Ind. U., Northwestern U., Cin. Coll.-Conservatory, U. Tex., Central Conservatory, Beijing, Internat. Soc. Music Edn., Warsaw; chmn. nat. symposium Applications of Psychology to the Teaching and Learning of Music; chmn., bd. dirs. The Barlow Endowment for Music Composition; co-founder, 1st pres. Utah Valley Symphony Orch.; past condr. Utah Valley Youth Orch.; bd. trustees Utah Opera Co.; commr. Utah Centennial of Statehood. Editor: The Instrumentalist, Orch. News, Utah Music Educator, Research News column, Jour. Research in Music Edn. Bd. dirs. Presser Found. Mem. Music Educators Nat. Conf. (past nat. pres., council), Nat. Music Council (past bd. dirs.), Am. Music Conf. (past bd. dirs.).

MASON, JEFFREY DANIEL, theater educator; b. San Francisco, Aug. 30, 1952; s. Lawrence Albert and Nancy Lavinia (Griffitts) M.; m. Susan Sefton, Aug. 4, 1979; 1 child, Ashley Siobhan. AB in English and Music, Stanford U., 1974, MA in Edn., 1975; MA in Drama, Calif. State U., Sacramento, 1980; PhD in Dramatic Art, U. Calif., Berkeley, 1983. Cert. stage combatant in armed and unarmed techniques, 1983. Assoc. instr. dramatic art U. Calif., Berkeley, 1980-82; instr. performing arts Diablo Valley Coll., 1982; lectr. theatre arts, artistic dir. Madrigal Dinner San Francisco State U., 1983-84; lectr. theatre Calif. State U., Bakersfield, 1984-85, asst. prof., 1985-87, assoc. prof., 1987-92, prof., 1992—, chair fine arts dept., 1991—; artistic dir. Kern Art Theatre, Bakersfield, 1985—. Author: Wisecracks: The Farces of George S. Kaufman, 1988, Melodrama and the Myth of America, 1993, (plays) Sherlock Holmes: The Legend, 1988, Camille, 1989, (novel under name Daniel Mason) Cousin Jack, 1996; contbr. articles and revs. to profl. jours.; dir. plays Encore Dinner Theatre, 1985, Musica da Camera, 1985, Kern Art Theatre, 1985-90, Walnut Creek Civic Arts Repertory, 1982, Los Altos Conservatory Theatre, 1982, Foothill Theatre Co., Nevada City, Calif., 1992, Calif. State U., Bakersfield, 1984—; also others; actor various plays. Mem. bd. Foothill Theatre Co., Nevada City. Pearl Hickman fellow, U. Calif., Berkeley, 1979-80, 82-83, Calif. state fellow in edn., 1974-75; grantee Com. on Teaching, U. Calif., Berkeley, 1981, Calif. State U., Bakersfield Univ. Rsch. Coun., 1988-89. Mem. Am. Studies Assn., Am. Theatre and Drama Soc. (mem. bd. 1991-95), Am. Soc. Theatre Rsch., Assn. Theatre in Higher Edn. Office: Calif State U Fine Arts Dept 9001 Stockdale Hwy Bakersfield CA 93311-1022

MASON, MARSHALL W., theater director; b. Amarillo, Tex., Feb. 24, 1940; s. Marvin Marshall and Lorine (Chrisman) M. B.S. in Speech, Northwestern U., 1961. Prof. Ariz. State U., 1994—; chief drama critic New Times, Phoenix, 1994-96. Founder, artistic dir. Circle Repertory Co., 1969-87, guest artistic dir., Ctr. Theater Group, 1988; dir. Broadway prodns. Redwood Curtain, 1993, The Seagull, 1992, Solitary Confinement, 1992, Burn This, 1987, As Is, 1985 (Drama Desk award, Tony nomination), Passion, 1983, Angels Fall, 1983 (Tony nomination), Fifth of July, 1981 (Tony nomination), Talley's Folly, 1980, (Pulitzer Prize, N.Y. Drama Critics Circle award, Tony nomination), Murder at the Howard Johnsons, 1979, Gemini, 1977, Knock Knock, 1976 (Tony nomination); Off-Broadway prodns. Sympathetic Magic, 1997, Robbers, 1997, Cakewalk, 1996, A Poster of the Cosmos/The Moonshot Tape, 1994, The Destiny of Me, 1992, Sunshine, 1989, Talley and Son, 1985, Childe Byron, 1980, Hamlet, 1979, Serenading Louie, 1976 (Obie award), Knock Knock, 1976 (Obie award), The Mound Builders, 1975 (Obie award), Battle of Angeles, 1974 (Obie award), The Sea Hourse, 1974, The Hot L Baltimore, 1973 (Obie award); dir. numerous prodns. including Who's Afraid of Virginia Woolf?, Tokyo, 1985, Talley's Folly, 1982, London, Home Free! and The Madness of Lady Bright, 1968, London, Nat. Tour Sleuth, 1988, Summer and Smoke, 1988, Whisper in the Mind, 1990; dir. numerous TV prodns. including Picnic, 1986, Kennedy's Children, 1982, The Fifth of July, 1983. Recipient Vernon Rice award, 1975, Drama Desk award, 1977, Margo Jones award, 1977, Outer Critics Circle award, 1978, Theatre World award, 1979, Shubert's Vaughan award, 1980, Obie award for Sustained Achievement, 1983, Inge Festival award for lifetime achievement, 1990, Last Frontier award, 1994, Erwin Piscator award, 1996. Mem. Soc. Stage Dirs. and Choreographers (pres. 1983-85), Dirs. Guild Am., Actors Equity Assn. Address: 1948 E Ellis Circle Mesa AZ 85203

MASON, NAOMI ANN, interior designer; b. Kansas City, Mo., Mar. 11, 1934; d. Hugh Fredrick and Lottie Elizabeth (Granstrom) Guilford; m. Ronald A. Mason, May 28, 1954; children: Teresa Elizabeth, Sheryl Lynn, Christina Marie, Ronald Anthony Jr. AA, Kansas City (Mo.) Jr. Coll., 1954; BA, Calif. State U., Long Beach, 1980. Cert. interior designer, Calif. Owner Design Ctr. Interiors, Orange, Calif., 1985—. Co-host (TV show) A Slice of Orange. Mem. Orange Planning Commn., 1982-86; bd. dirs., 2d v.p. Orange C. of C., 1987-92; bd. dirs. Orange Elderly Svcs., 1987-91, Red Ribbon 100, 1987-95; pres., 1st v.p., 2d v.p. Orange Rep. Women Fedn., 1991-95; bd. dirs. Pacific S.W. dist. Mo. Synod Luth. Ch., 1994—. Named Citizen of Yr. City and Chamber, Orange, 1992, Women of Distinction Soroptimist, 1993. Mem. Am. Soc. Interior Designers (bd. dirs. 1986-90), Rotary. Republican. Lutheran. Home and Office: 525 S Arlington Rd Orange CA 92869-5127

MASON, ROGER DEEN, archaeologist; b. Seattle, Aug. 10, 1949; s. Alden C. and Donna M. (Young) M. BA, U. Wash., 1971; PhD, U. Tex., 1980. Hist. archaeologist Cannon Reservoir human ecology project U. Nebr., Perry, Mo., 1978-80; vis. asst. prof. Cen. Mich. U., Mt. Pleasant, 1981-82; sr. archaeologist Sci. Resource Surveys, Huntington Beach, Calif., 1983-87, Tetra Tech, Inc., San Bernardino, Calif., 1987-88; mng. archaeologist The Keith Cos., Costa Mesa, Calif., 1988-90, dir. archaeology, 1990-93; dir. cultural resources Chambers Group, Inc., Irvine, Calif., 1993—; prin. author guidelines for archaeol. reports Orange County (Calif.) Archaeology Forum, 1990; lectr. cultural resources mgmt. U. Calif., Irvine, Pacific Coast Archaeol. Soc., 1990-96. Author: A Late Fomrative Irrigation Community Below Monte Alban, 1982, Euro-American Pioneer Settlement Systems...Northeast Missouri, 1984; contbr. articles to profl. publs. Title IV fellow NSF, U. Tex., 1971-73; dissertation improvement grantee, 1975-76, rsch. grantee U. Tex., 1975, 78. Mem. Soc. Profl. Archaeologists (cert.), Soc. Am. Archaeology, Am. Anthropol. Assn., Soc. Calif. Archaeology. Office: Chambers Group Inc 16700 Aston St Irvine CA 92606

MASON, TERENCE K., critical care nurse; b. Elgin, Ill., June 10, 1953; s. LeRoy B. and Doris M. (Kelly) M.; m. Cheryl S., Apr. 23, 1989. AA, Phoenix Coll., 1977; BSN, Ariz. State U., 1981, postgrad. RN, Ariz.; cert. critical care nurse, ACLS, BCLS provider and instr. Staff nurse SCU Valley Luth. Hosp., Mesa, Ariz., 1985-86; freelance nurse, Tempe (Ariz.) St. Luke's Hosp., Phoenix, 1989-90; charge nurse coronary ICU, Tempe (Ariz.) St. Luke's Hosp., 1981-85, 86-88; asst. clin. dir. coronary ICU, Tempe (Ariz.) St. Luke's Hosp., Phoenix area, Ariz., 1988-89, 91-95, staff nurse emergency rm., 1995—. Sgt. U.S. Army, 1971-74. Mem. AACN. Office: Tempe St Luke's Hosp 1500 S Mill Ave Tempe AZ 85281-6630

MASOUREDIS, SERAFEIM PANAGIOTIS, pathologist, educator; b. Detroit, Nov. 14, 1922; s. Panagiotis and Lemonia (Moniodis) M.; m. Marion Helen Mykytew, Oct. 1943; children: Claudia, Linus. AB, U. Mich., 1944, MD, 1948; PhD in Med. Physics, U. Calif., Berkeley, 1952. Diplomate Am. Bd. Pathology. Intern U. Calif. Svc./San Francisco Gen. Hosp., 1952-53, asst. resident in medicine, 1954-55; fellow Clinic Hematology/Donner Lab./Univ. Calif., Berkeley, 1953-54; asst. prof., then assoc. prof. pathology U. Pitts. Med. Sch., 1955-59; asst. dir. Cen. Blood Bank Pitts., 1955-59; assoc. prof. preventive medicine U. Calif., San Francisco, 1959-62, assoc. prof. medicine, 1962-67, assoc. prof. clin. pathology, 1966-67; prof. medicine Marquette U., Milw., 1967-69; exec. dir. Milw. Blood Ctr., 1967-69; prof. pathology U. Calif., San Diego, 1969-90, prof. emeritus, 1990—; cons. WHO, Geneva, 1965-67; bd. dirs. Am. Assn. Blood Banks, Washington,1 981-83. Assoc. editor Jour. Transfusion, Washington, 1981-90; contbr. sci. articles and rsch. papers to various publs. Emily Cooley Meml. lectr. Am. Assn. Blood Banks, 1973, recipient Karl Landsteiner Meml. award, 1979. Mem. Am. Assn. Immunologists, Am. Soc. Clin. Investigation, Am. Soc. Hematology, Brit. Soc. Immunology, Am. Assn. Cancer Rsch., Internat. Soc. Blood Transfusion, Western Assn. Physicians. Office: U Calif San Diego Dept Pathology Sch Medicine La Jolla CA 92093-0612

MASRI, MERLE SID, biochemist, consultant; b. Jerusalem, Palestine, Sept. 12, 1927; came to U.S., 1947; s. Said Rajab and Fatima (Muneimné) M.; m. Maryjean Loretta Anderson, June 28, 1952 (div. 1974); children: Kristin Corinne, Allan Eric, Wendy Joan, Heather Anderson. BA in Physiology, U. Calif., Berkeley, 1950; PhD in Mammalian Physiology and Biochemistry, U. Calif. Berkeley, 1953. Rsch. asst. Dept. Physiology, Univ. Calif., Berkeley, 1950-53; predoctoral fellow Baxter Labs., Berkeley, 1952-53; rsch. assoc. hematology Med. Rsch. Inst., Michael Reese Hosp., Chgo., 1954-56; sr. rsch. biochemist Agrl. Rsch. Svc., USDA, Berkeley, 1956-87; supervisory rsch. scientist Agrl. Rsch. Svc., USDA, N.D. State U. Sta., Fargo, N.D., 1987-89; pvt. practice as cons. Emeryville, Calif., 1989—; lectr. numerous confs. Contbr. articles to profl. jours. and books. Recipient Spl. Svc. and Merit awards USDA, 1966, 76, 77, Superior Svc. award USDA, 1977. Mem. AAAS, Am. Chem. Soc., Am. Oil Chemists Soc., Am. Assn. Cereal Chemists, N.Y. Acad. Scis., Inst. Food Technologists, Commonwealth Club Calif., Internat. Platform Assn., Sigma Xi. Home: 9 Commodore Dr Emeryville CA 94608-1652

MASSARO, ANTHONY SCOTT, environmental consultant; b. Denver, June 23, 1957; s. Nicholas Ross and Barbara E. (Peila) M.; 1 child, Patrick. BS in Polit. Sci. and Econs., Colo. State U., 1979. Exec. dir. Coloradoans for Recycling, 1981-82; dir. environ. affairs Office of Mayor, Denver, 1983-91; pub. affairs mgr. Eric Group, Inc., 1991-92; sr. ptnr. Rocky Mountain Environ. Strategies, Inc., Denver, 1992—; guest lectr. U. Colo., Denver, U. Denver, Regis Coll., Va. Poly. Inst. and State U. Contbr. articles and papers to profl. jours. Mem. exec. com. Gov.'s Alternative Fuels Task Force, 1990-91, mem. regional air quality coun., 1989-91; chmn. Brown Cloud com. Metro Air Quality Coun., 1985-89; mem. nat. nuclear waste transp. planning com. U.S. Dept. Energy, 1989-91; bd. dirs. Am. Lung Assn. Colo., 1985-87; participant 1st Internat. Conf. for Protection of Mountain Gorilla, Kigali, Rwanda, 1990; founding sponsor Women's Polit. Tng. Inst., 1984; active Vols. for Outdoor Colo., 1992—. Recipient Pub. Svc. award Mayor Federico Peña, 1991, Cert. of Appreciation for Environ. Action, City of Denver, 1991, Environ. Achievement cert. Friends of UN and Renew America, 1991; McCloy fellow, 1990. Mem. Air and Waste Mgmt. Assn.,

Nat. Assn. Environ. Profls. Democrat. Office: Rocky Mountain Environ Strategies Inc 3047 W 26th Ave Denver CO 80211-4059

MASSARO, KAREN THUESEN, artist; b. Copenhagen, Oct. 23, 1944; came to U.S., 1946; d. Jens and Amalie (Andersen) Thuesen; m. Dominic William. BS in Art Edn., SUNY, Buffalo, 1966; MFA in Ceramics, U. Wis., 1972. Tchr. art elem. schs., Warwick, N.Y., 1966-67; vis. asst. prof. art Beloit (Wis.) Coll., 1972-77; lectr. dept. art U. Wis., Madison, 1976, 78; vis. artist Artist in Industry Program Kohler Co., 1976, 79; vis. artist Ohio State U., Columbus, 1977; mem. vis. faculty Scripps Coll., Claremont, Calif., 1980; artist Kohler Co., Wis., 1984; studio artist Santa Cruz, Calif., 1980—; lectr. U. Calif., Santa Cruz Ext., 1995; guest curator The Art Mus. of Santa Cruz County, 1996-97; leader workshops, spkr. Mendocino (Calif.) Arts Ctr., 1992, Butte Coll., Oroville, Calif., 1994, U. Wis., Madison and Eau Claire, 1996. One-woman shows include Porter Coll., U. Calif. Santa Cruz, 1995; exhibited in group shows at Helen Drutt Gallery, Phila., 1993, San Diego Mus. Art, 1993-95, Monterey (Calif.) Peninsula Mus. Art, 1993, Nancy Margolis Gallery, Portland, Maine, 1993, Craft Alliance, St. Louis, 1993, Texas Tech U., Lubbock, 1994, Butte Coll., Oroville, Calif., 1994, U. Wis., Eau Claire, 1996. NEA fellow, grantee, 1976, Wis. Arts Bd. grantee, 1977; recipient Merit award The Guild Am. Crafts, N.Y.C., 1987. Mem. Nat. Coun. on Edn. for Ceramic Arts (dir.-at-large 1977, chair exhbns. 1978-80), Am. Crafts Coun. Home: 617 Arroyo Seco Santa Cruz CA 95060-3147

MASSARO, MIKE, advertising executive. COO, exec. v.p. Goldberg, Moser & O'Neill, San Francisco, Calif. Office: 77 Maiden Ln San Francisco CA 94108*

MASSEY, HENRY P., JR., lawyer; b. Montclair, N.J., Sept. 2, 1939. AB, Cornell U., 1961, JD with distinction, 1968. Bar: Calif. 1969. Assoc. Jackson, Tufts, Cole & Black, San Francisco, 1968-72, ptnr., 1973-82; ptnr. Wilson, Sonsini, Goodrich & Rosati, Palo Alto, Calif. Bd. editors Cornell Law Rev., 1967-68. Mem. ABA (sects. on corp., banking and bus. law, taxation law), State Bar Calif. (mem. corps. com. bus. law sect. 1979-82), Order of Coif, Phi Kappa Phi. Office: Wilson Sonsini Ste 900 Two Palo Alto Sq Palo Alto CA 94306

MASSEY, LAWRENCE MARTIN, manufacturing executive; b. Jersey City, N.J., Dec. 14, 1949; s. Dominic Raymond and Mary Adrian (O'Hagan) M. Student, San Diego State U., 1969, 72-75, U. Md., 1970-71, King's Coll., Cambridge, England, 1971. V.p. internat. ops. Garden Am. Inc., Carson City, Nev., 1977-90; v.p. internat. ops. James Hardie Industries, Sydney, Australia, 1990-91, Laguna Niguel, Calif., 1990-91; exec. v.p. Stone Products Corp., Napa, Calif., 1991—; dir., vice chmn. Perdura Stone Sade C.V., Zapopan, Mex., 1993—; dir. Mathios Refractories, Piracus, Greece, 1994—. Contbr. articles to profl. jours. Mem. P.G. Wodehouse Soc. Roman Catholic. Home: 1 Dickerson Ln Napa CA 94558

MASSEY, PAUL J., newspaper publisher; m. Jane Massey; children: Paul Jr., Mark, Jennifer, Moira. BS in Printing Mgmt., Carnegie Mellon U., 1956; MS in Acctg., Bentley Coll. Acctg. and Fin., 1978. Publisher various newspapers, Boston, Cleve., elsewhere, 1972-92, Fairbanks (Alaska) Daily News-Miner, 1992—; adv. bd. Alaska Airlines, Fairbanks Internat. Airport. Bd. dirs. Fairbanks Cmty. Food Bank, Festival Fairbanks, Fairbanks Mus. Expansion Com., Fairbanks Shakespeare Theater; mem. bd. visitors, U. Alaska Fairbanks; mem. leadership adv. coun. UAF; co-chair United Way Drive, Fairbanks, 1997. Mem. Fairbanks Rotary Club, Fairbanks C. of C. (bd. dirs.). Office: Fairbanks Daily News-Miner 200 N Cushman St Fairbanks AK 99707-0710

MASSIE, BARRY MICHAEL, cardiologist; b. St. Louis, May 23, 1944; s. Edward and Felice (Ozerovich) M.; m. Ellen Sue Weisberg, May 29, 1970; children: Jennifer Nicole, Rebecca Elizabeth. BA, Harvard Coll., 1966; MD, Columbia U., 1970. Resident Bellevue Hosp., N.Y.C., 1970-74; prof. medicine U. Calif., San Francisco, 1978-83, assoc. prof., 1983-89, prof., 1989—; dir. coronary care unit, chief hypertension unit VA Med. Ctr., San Francisco, 1978—; staff mem. Cardiovascular Rsch. Inst., San Francisco, 1981—; chmn., adv. panel Food & Drug Adminstrn., Rockville, Md., 1992-96. Fellow Am. Coll. Cardiology, Am. Heart Assn. (coun. clin. cardiology); mem. Am. Fedn. Clin. Rsch., Western Soc. Clin. Rsch., Western Assn. Physicians. Office: VA Hosp Cadiology 111C 4150 Clement St San Francisco CA 94121-1545

MASSIER, PAUL FERDINAND, mechanical engineer; b. Pocatello, Idaho, July 22, 1923; s. John and Kathryn (Arki) M.; m. Miriam Parks, May 1, 1948 (dec. Aug. 1975); children: Marilyn Massier Schwegler, Paulette Massier Holden; m. Dorothy Hedlund Wright, Sept. 12, 1978. Cert. engring., U. Idaho (so. br.), 1943; BSME, U. Colo., 1948; MSME, MIT, 1949. Engr. Pan-Am. Refining Corp., Texas City, Tex., 1948; design engr. Maytag Co., Newton, Iowa, 1949-50; research engr. Boeing Co., Seattle, 1951-55; sr. research engr. and supr. dep. sect. mgr. Jet Propulsion Lab. Calif. Inst. Tech., Pasadena, 1955-84, task mgr., 1984-88, mem. tech. staff, 1989-94. Contbr. articles to profl. jours. Mem. Arcadia High Sch. Music Club, 1966-71. Served with U.S. Army, 1943-46. Recipient Apollo Achievement award NASA, 1969, Basic Noise Rsch. award NASA, 1980, Life Mem. Svc. award Calif. PTA, 1970, Layman of Yr. award Arcadia Congl. Ch., 1971, Mil. Unit Citation award, 1946. Fellow AIAA (assoc., Sustained Svc. award 1980-81), Am. Biog. Inst. Rsch. Assn., Internat. Biographical Assn.; mem. N.Y. Acad. Scis., Planetary Soc., Sigma Xi, Tau Beta Pi, Pi Tau Sigma, Sigma Tau. Congregationalist. Home: 1000 N 1st Ave Arcadia CA 91006-2533

MASSON, JEFFREY MOUSSAIEFF, writer; b. Chgo., Mar. 28, 1941; s. Jacques Victor Masson and Diana Zeiger; m. Thérèse Claire Alter, Aug. 21, 1971 (div. Aug. 1982); 1 child, Simone; m. Leila Rubina Siller, 1996; 1 child, Ilan. BA magna cum laude, Harvard U., 1964, PhD, 1971. Instr. religious studies Brown U., Providence, 1967-69; from asst. prof. Sanskrit to assoc. prof. Sanskrit U. Toronto, Ont., Can., 1971-76, prof., 1976-80; dir. Freud Archives Libr. of Congress, Washington, 1981-82; rsch. assoc. U. Berkeley, Calif., 1979—. Author: Against Therapy, 1988, Assault on Truth, 1984, When Elephants Weep, 1994, Lost Prince, 1995. Home: 1841 Addison St Berkeley CA 94703

MASTANDREA, EVA, museum education educator. Prof. Western Mont. Coll. Gallery Mus., Dillion. Office: Western Mont Coll Mus 710 S Atlantic Dillon MT 59725

MASTERS, ELAINE, educator, writer; b. Kansas City, Kans., Oct. 6, 1932; d. David Shepherd and Stella Frances (Ragan) M.; m. Donald Ramon Masters, Apr. 27, 1951; children: David, Vicki, Jennifer, Kevin. BS in Edn. with honors, U. Mo., Kansas City, 1968. Cert. tchr., Mo., Va. Tchr. grade 4 Am. Sch., Manila, 1956-57; tchr. grade 5 Escuela Gloria Felix, Caracas, Venezuela, Venezuela, 1960-62; tchr. grade 6 Okinawa Christian Sch., Urasoe, 1968-70; tchr. grade 5 Flint Hill Elem. Sch., Vienna, Va., 1970-73; tchr. Bible Inst. Hawaii, Honolulu, 1991-92; dir. Christian edn. St. Thomas United Meth. Ch., 1983-84; tchr. children's ministries Salvation Army, Kaneohe, Hawaii, 1991-94; evangelist, Hong Kong, Malaysia, Nigeria, Thailand, Russia; seminar leader on Bible and Christian living, Hong Kong, Malaysia, Nigeria, Thailand; advisor Pentecostal Assemblies of Tribes, Chiang Mai, Thailand, 1991—; lectr. Christian Writers Workshop, 1993—. Author: Ali and the Ghost Tiger, 1967, Teach Us To Pray, 1970, Day Camp and Day Care Handbook, 1989; contbr. articles to mags. and newspapers; inventor cricket transposer tool for musicians. Mem. spkrs. bur. Alzheimer's Assn., Honolulu, 1991—. Mem. Women's Aglow Fellowship Internat., Nat. Writers Club, Soc. Children's Book Writers and Illustrators (regional advisor State of Hawaii 1996—). Home: 2355 Ala Wai Blvd Apt 502 Honolulu HI 96815-1809

MASTERS, LORRAINE SUSANNE, religious organization administrator; b. Humboldt, S.D., July 13, 1923; d. Claude Bartine and Susan (Menth) M. BA, Ursuline/Bellerman, 1966; M of Religious Edn., St. Thomas U., 1975. Tchr. Our Lady of Victory Missionary Sisters, Huntington, Ind., 1945—; dir. ethnic ministry Cath. Diocese of Salt Lake City, 1983—; clk. fingerprints FBI, Washington, 1942-45; mem. Bishop's Cabinet, Salt Lake City, 1991—. Rep. sister's coun. Women's State Legis. C., Salt Lake City, 1987-92, 95, 97; mem. Utah/Bolivia Ptnrs., Salt Lake City, 1991—, Citizens Positive Comty. Values, Salt Lake City, 1993; bd. dirs. Indian Walk-In Ctr., Salt Lake City, 1988-93; mem. So. Poverty Ctr., Tekakwitha Nat. Conf., 1981-97. Mem. FBI (alumni mem.), Nat. Mus. Am. Indian (charter mem.), Amnesty Internat. Roman Catholic. Office: Cath Diocese of Salt Lake City 27 C St Salt Lake City UT 84103

MASTRINI, JANE REED, social worker, consultant; b. Lincoln, Nebr., July 23, 1948; d. William Scott and Ellen (Daly) Cromwell; m. Charles James Mastrini, July 19, 1969. BA, Western State Coll., Gunnison, Colo., 1970; MSW, U. Denver, 1980. Lic. social worker Colo.; cert. alcohol counselor Colo. and nat. Tchr. Flandreau (S.D.) Indian Sch., 1970; social worker S.D. Dept. Welfare, Pierre, 1970-75; child care worker Sacred Heart Home, Pueblo, Colo., 1975-76; counselor Fisher Peak Alcohol Treatment Ctr., Trinidad, Colo., 1976-77; family therapist West Nebr. Gen. Hosp., Scottsbluff, 1980-81; adolescent coord. St. Luke's Hosp., Denver, 1981-86; exec. dir. New Beginnings At Denver, Lakewood, Colo., 1986-90; pres. Counseling Dimensions of Colo., Denver, 1990-92; trainer Mile High Inst., 1987-93; outpatient mgr. Arapahoe House, 1992-94; therapist Kaiser Permanente, Denver, 1994—; cons. Colo. Counseling Consortium, Denver, 1984-90; field work supr. U. Denver, 1983—. Lectr., group leader Colo. Teen Inst., Denver, 1984-85. Mem. NASW (cert.), P.E.O. (pres. 1984-87, 94-95), Colo. Counseling Consortium, Colo. Assn. Addiction Treatment Programs (v.p. 1991-92). Democrat. Episcopalian. Home: 11785 W 66th Pl # D Arvada CO 80004-2473 Office: Kaiser Permanente CDTP 10230 E Dakota Ave Denver CO 80231-1312

MASUCHIKA, GLENN NORIO, librarian, university official, book reviewer; b. Hilo, Hawaii, Dec. 25, 1954; s. Toshito and Asako (Nakano) M.; m. Gail Boldt, Feb. 8, 1962; 1 child, Kai Dylan. BA with distinction, U. Hawaii, 1976, MA in Urban and Regional Planning, 1983; MA in Theological Studies, Harvard U., 1986; M Libr. Info. Svcs., U. Calif., Berkeley, 1990. Libr. asst. Harvard U. Librs., Cambridge, Mass., 1984-87; head serials processing Bio Scis. Libr. U. Calif., 1987-90; libr., sys. adminstr. Chaminade U. Libr., Honolulu, 1990—; book reviewer Libr. Jour., 1992—. Mem. AAUP, Nat. Book Critics Cir., Hawaii Libr. Assn. Office: Chaminade U Sullivan Libr 3140 Waialae Ave Honolulu HI 96816

MASUDA, YOSHINORI, systems analyst; b. Kasai, Hyogo, Japan, Apr. 6, 1953; came to U.S., 1977, naturalized, 1993; s. Saburo and Mitsuyo (Masuda) M. BL, Kobe U., Japan, 1977; MBA, U. San Francisco, 1980. Gen. mgr. Kotobuki Trading Co., San Francisco, 1980-85; distbn. analyst Kikkoman Internat. Inc., San Francisco, 1986-87, mgr. mgmt. info. system, 1987-88, mgr. electronic data interchange, 1988-93, mgr. distbn./customer svc./electronic data interchange, 1993—. Mem. Japanese C. of C. No. Calif. Govt. Rels., Beta Gamma Sigma. Home: 480 Wellesley Ave Mill Valley CA 94941-3540 Office: Kikkoman Internat Inc 50 California St Ste 3600 San Francisco CA 94111-4760

MATA, MICHAEL ANTHONY, religion educator; b. Houston, Aug. 5, 1953; s. Jose G. and Josephine (Arias) M.; m. Kristina Jean Craig, Aug. 18, 1984; 1 child, Diane; foster children: Mary, Jerry. BA in Biblical Lit., Pt. Loma Nazarene Coll., 1975, MA in Religion, 1977; MDiv in Theology, Nazarene Theol. Sem., 1980; M City Planning, U. Calif., Berkeley, 1987. Ordained elder Ch. of the Nazarene, 1984. Instr. in theology Mex. Nazarene Sem., Mexico City, 1983; lectr. in urban studies Bresee Inst., L.A., 1983-93; teaching asst. dept. city and regional planning U. Calif., Berkeley, 1987; minister to youth L.A. First Ch. of Nazarene, 1980-85; assoc. pastor L.A. First Ch. of Nazarene, L.Z., 1983-85, 87—; Mildred M. Hutchinson prof. urban ministry Sch. of Theology at Claremont, Calif., 1993—, dir. Urban Leadership Inst., 1993—; cons. to various non-profit community orgns., L.A., 1989—; adj. faculty mem. in urban ministry Nazarene Theol. Sem., Kansas City, Mo., Mid-Am. Nazarene Coll., Olathe, Mo., Azusa (Calif.) Pacific U. Grad. Sch. Theology, So. Nazarene U., Bethany, Okla., N.W. Nazarene Coll., Nampa, Idaho; program planner Golden Gate Ministries, San Francisco, 1986-87; dir. Bresee Inst., L.A., 1987-93; ch.-based cmty. devel. coord. L.A. World Vision, U.S. Programs, Monrovia, Calif., 1990-93. Mem. ctrl. com. Calif. State Dem. Party, L.A., 1990-93; vice chair 46th Assembly Dist. Com., 1993-94; bd. dirs. West Angeles Cmty. Devel. Corp., 1994-96, Affordable Housing Svcs., 1993—, Wilshire Stakeholders, Inc., 1988-93, So. Calif. Adv. Coun. for World Vision, 1992-93, Wilshire Ctr. Cmty. Involvement Assn., Inc., 1981-85, 87-90, P.F. Bresee Found., 1987-90, 93—, John M. Perkins Found. for Reconcillation and Devel., 1991—, Sports Outreach of L.A., 1994-96; mem. City of Berkeley Planning Commn., 1986; sec. bd. dirs. So. Calif. Coalition of Ethnic Religious Leaders, 1992-93; mem. adv. bd. Jimmy Carter L.A. Work Proejct, 1993-95; mem. cabinet Interfaith Coalition to Heal L.A., mem. subcom. econ. devel., 1992—; mem. steering com. Consortium of Urban Leadership Devel. Programs, 1991—; mem. New Ethnic Majority Econ. Task Force, 1990—; mem. steering com. Native Am. Gathering Table, 1988—; mem. adv. bd. Fransican Health Ctr., 1990-92; exec. mem. bd. dirs. Hope-Net, 1988-92; mem. steering com. So. Calif. Interfaith Hunger Coalition, 1988-89, 91-93; mem. regional adv. coun. Hispanic Assn. (Bilingual/Bicultural Ministries, 1993—; treas. bd. dirs. L.A. Coun. of Chs., 1994. Recipient Cert. of Commendation, L.A. City Coun., 1983, Cert. of Appreciation, L.A. City Coun., 1984, 89, 94, Cert. of Recognition for Cmty. Svc., Calif. State Assembly, 1989, Acad. Excellence award Calif. Planning Found., 1987; named Urban Role Model, Urban Family Mag., 1993, Point Loma alumni award, 1994; Oakley fellow, 1996. Mem. Am. Planning Assn., So. Calif. Assn. Non-Profit Housing, Hispanic Assn. Theol. Edn., Nat. Soc. Internships and Exptl. Edn., Am. Planning Assn., Internat. Urban Assocs., Christian Cmty. Devel. Assn., Calif. Cmty. Econ. Devel. Assn. Office: Sch Theology 1325 N College Ave Claremont CA 91711-3154

MATAN, LILLIAN KATHLEEN, educator, designer; b. Boston, Aug. 18, 1937; d. George Francis and Lillian May (Herbert) Archambault; m. Joseph A. Matan, Aug. 6, 1960; children: Maria, Meg, Tony, Elizabeth, Joan, Molly. BS, Seton Hall Coll., 1960; MA, San Francisco State U., 1984; postgrad. studies, U. San Francisco. Tchr. St. Jone de Chantal, Bethesda, Md., 1956-60; tchr. home econs. Surrottsville (Md.) H.S., 1960-61; tchr., head home econs. dept. Bruswick (Md.) H.S., 1972-73; designer Dudley Kelley and Assocs., San Francisco, Calif., 1976-84; designer (prin.) K. Matan Antiques and Interiors, Ross, Calif., 1985-87; designer Charles Lester Assocs., San Francisco, 1987-88; dean of students St. Rose Acad., San Francisco, 1988-90; dir., asst. devel. The Branson Sch., Ross, Calif., 1990-92; prin. St. Anselm Sch., San Anselmo, Calif., 1993-94; adminstrv. head Ring Mt. Day Sch., Tiburon, Calif., 1995-96; ednl. cons. Head Start, Frederick County, Md., 1972-73. Pres. Cath. Charities, Marin County, Calif.; mem. Ecumenical Assn. for Housing, Marin County. Mem. KM (dame), ASCD, Am. Assn. Interior Design (cert. interior designer Calif.), Am. Assn. Family and Consumer Scis., Serra Club, Phi Delta Kappa. Democrat. Roman Catholic. Home: PO Box 1140 Ross CA 94957-1140

MATARAZZO, HARRIS STARR, lawyer; b. Portland, Oreg., July 24, 1957; s. Joseph Dominic and Ruth Wood (Gadbois) M.; m. Judith Grace Hudson, Jan. 2, 1988. AB in Polit. Sci., Brown U., 1979; JD, Northwestern Sch. Law, Portland, 1983. Bar: Oreg. 1986, U.S. Dist. Ct. Oreg. 1986, U.S. Ct. Appeals (9th cir.) 1986, U.S. Supreme Ct. 1992. With Aitchison, Imperati, Paull, Barnett and Sherwood, Portland, 1986; assoc. Parks & Bauer, Salem, Oreg., 1987-88; pvt. practice Portland, 1988—; sprk. Mental Health and the Law conf. Med. Ednl. Svcs., Inc., 1995, 96. Contbr. to Criminal Law Handbook, 1994. Mem. Hist. Preservation League Oreg., Portland, 1984—, Oreg. State Pub. Interest Rsch. Group, Portland, 1985—, The Old Ch. Soc., Portland, 1986; bd. dirs. Bosco Milligan Found., 1992—, Rape Survivors Inc., 1994, Morrison Ctr., 1996—, Lincoln H.S. Alumni Assn., 1995—; mem. vestry Trinity Epsicopal Ch., 1992-95; mem. Oreg. Advocacy Ctr. Mental Health Adv. Coun., 1996—. Mem. ABA, Fed. Bar Assn., Oreg. State Bar Assn., Oreg. Criminal Def. Lawyers Assn. (spkr. State of Mind. conf. 1990), Multnomah County Bar Assn. Office: Bank Am Fin Ctr 121 SW Morrison St Ste 1020 Portland OR 97204-3140

MATARÉ, HERBERT F., physicist, consultant; b. Aachen, Germany, Sept. 22, 1912; came to U.S., 1953; s. Josef P. and Paula (Broicher) M.; m. Ursula Krenzien, Dec. 1939; children: Felicitas, Vitus; m. Elise Walbert, Dec. 1983; 1 child, Victor B. BS in Physics, Chemistry and Math., Aachen U. Geneva, 1933; MS in Tech. Physics, U. Aachen, 1939; PhD in Electronics, Tech. U. Berlin, 1942; PhD in Solid State Physics summa cum laude, Ecole Normale Supérieure, Paris, 1950. Asst. prof. physics & electronics Tech. U. Aachen, 1936-45; head of microwave receiver lab. Telefunken, A.G., Berlin, 1939-46; mgr. semicondr. lab. Westinghouse, Paris, 1946-52; founder, pres. Intermetall Corp., Düsseldorf, Fed. Republic Germany, 1952-56; head semincondr. R & D, corp. rsch. labs. Gen. Telephone & Electronics Co., N.Y.C., 1956-59; dir. rsch. semicondr. dept. Tekade, Nürnberg, Fed. Republic Germany, 1959-61; head quantum physics dept. rsch. labs. Bendix Corp., Southfield, Mich., 1961-64; tech. dir., acting mgr. hybrid microelectronics rsch. labs. Lear Siegler, Santa Monica, Calif., 1963-64; asst. chief engr. advance electronics dept. Douglas Aircraft Co., Santa Monica, 1964-66; tech. dir. McDonnell Douglas Missile Div., 1964-69; sci. advisor to solid state electronics group Autonetics (Rockwell Internat.), Anaheim, Calif., 1966-69; pres. Internat. Solid State Electronics Cons., L.A., 1973—; prof. electronics U. Buenos Aires, 1953-54; vis. prof. UCLA, 1968-69, Calif. State U., Fullerton, 1969-70; dir. Compound Crystals Ltd., London, 1989—; cons. UN Indsl. Devel. Orgn. to 15 Indian insts. and semiconductor cos. with conf. talks at India Inst. Tech., New Delhi and Bombay, 1978. Author: Receiver Sensitivity in the UHF, 1951, Defect Electronics in Semiconductors, 1971, Conscientious Evolution, 1978, Energy, Facts and Future, 1989, (with P. Faber) Renewable Energies, 1993; patentee first European transistor, first vacuum growth of silicon crystals with levitation, growth of bicrystals, first low temperature transistor with bicrystals, optical heterodyning with bicrystals, first crystal TV transmission link, first color TV transmission over fiber with LEDs and bicrystals, liquid phase epitaxy for LEDs and batch process for III-V-solar cells; contbr. over 100 articles to profl. jours. Fellow IEEE (life); mem. AAAS, IEEE Nuclear Plasma Scis. Soc., IEEE Power Engring. Soc., Inst. for Advancement of Man (hon.), Am. Phys. Soc. (solid state div.), Electrochem. Soc., Am. Vacuum Soc. (thin film div.), Materials Rsch. Soc., N.Y. Acad. Scis. (emeritus). Home: 23901 Civic Center Way Apt 130 Malibu CA 90265-4881 Office: ISSEC PO Box 2661 Malibu CA 90265-7661

MATAS, MYRA DOROTHEA, interior architect and designer, kitchen and bath designer; b. San Francisco, Mar. 21, 1938; d. Arthur Joseph and Marjorie Dorothy (Johnson) Anderson; m. Michael Richard Matas Jr., Mar. 15, 1958; children: Michael Richard III, Kenneth Scott. Cert. interior design, Canada Coll.; cert. interior design, Calif. Owner, operator Miquel's Antiques Co., Millbrae, Calif., 1969-70, Miguel's Antiques & Interiors Co., Burlingame, Calif., 1970-79, Country Elegance Antiques & Interiors Co., Menlo Park, Calif., 1979-84, La France Boutique Co., 1979-84, Myra D. Matas Interior Design, San Francisco, 1984—, Lafayette, La., 1994—; mgr. La France Imports, Inc., 1982-92; pres., gen. contractor Artisans 3 Inc., Burlingame, 1988-92; gen. contractor Matas Constr., Millbrae, 1993—; instr. interior design dept. Canada Coll. Mem. Calif. Coun. Interior Design. Contbr. articles in field to profl. jours. Office: 101 Henry Adams St Ste 348 San Francisco CA 94103-5213 also: 324 rue Jefferson Lafayette LA 70501

MATASEJE, VERONICA JULIA, sales executive; b. St. Ann's, Ontario, Can., Apr. 5, 1949; came to U.S., 1985; d. John and Anna Veronica M. Grad. H.S., Smithville, Can. Clk. typist, typesetter Crown Life Ins. Co., Toronto, Can., 1966-70; typesetter Toronto Life/Calendar Mag., 1970-71; typesetter, exec. sec. Cerebrus Prodns. Ltd., Toronto, 1971-74; pres. Veron Prodns. Ltd., Toronto, 1975-81, Acclaim Records Inc., Toronto, 1981-88; pvt. health care provider Las Vegas, Nev., 1989-94; retail sales mgr. Top Cats, Las Vegas, Nev., 1994—. Campaign vol. Dist. Atty., Las Vegas, 1994; vol. pilot Angel Planes, Las Vegas, 1989. Home: 4326 Caliente St Las Vegas NV 89119-5801 Office: Top Cats PO Box 61173 Las Vegas NV 89160-1173

MATELIC, CANDACE TANGORRA, museum studies educator, consultant, museum director; b. Detroit, Aug. 21, 1952; d. Paul Eugene and Madeline Marie (Tangora) M.; m. Steven Joseph Mrozek, Sept. 17, 1983 (div. Sept. 1987); 1 child, Madeline Rose. BA, U. Mich., 1974; MA, SUNY, Oneonta, 1977; postgrad., SUNY, Albany. Interpretive specialist Living History Farms, Des Moines, 1978-80; mgr. adult edn. Henry Ford Mus./Greenfield Village, Dearborn, Mich., 1981-82, mgr. interpretive tng., 1982-84; dir., prof. mus. studies Cooperstown grad. program SUNY, Oneonta, 1986-94; exec. dir. Mission Houses Mus., Honolulu, 1994-96, Historic St. Mary's City, Md., 1997—; faculty mem. St. Mary's Coll., 1997—; cons. history mus., 1979—; lectr., tchr. nat. and regional confs., workshops, seminars, 1979—; grant reviewer Nat. Endowment for the Humanities and Inst. for Mus. Svc., Washington, 1982—. Author: (with others) Exhibition Reader, 1992; co-author: A Pictorical History of Food in Iowa, 1980, Survey of 1200-Plus Museum Studies Graduates, 1988; contbr. articles and videos on mus. interpretation and tng., 1979—; author conf. proceedings. Trustee Motown Hist. Mus., 1989—; bd. dirs. Hawaii Youth Opera Chorus, 1996. Mem. Am. Assn. State and Local History (sec., bd. dirs. 1988-93, program chmn. ann meeting 1988, mem. edn. com. 1996—, co-chair task force on edn. and tng. 1994-96), Assn. Living Hist. Farms and Agrl. Mus. (bd. dirs. 1980-88, pres. 1985, John T. Schlebecker award Lifetime Disting. Svc. 1996), Midwest Open Air Mus. Coordinating Coun. (founder, bd. dirs., pres. 1978-80), Am. Assn. Museums (mus. studies com. 1986-94), Internat. Coun. Museums, Nat. Trust for Hist. Preservation, Hawaii Museums Assn. (bd. dirs.), Honolulu Rotary. Democrat. Roman Catholic. Office: Historic St Mary's City PO Box 39 Saint Marys City MD 20686

MATERA, FRANCES LORINE, elementary educator; b. Eustis, Nebr., June 28, 1926; d. Frank Daniel and Marie Mathilda (Hess) Daiss; m. Daniel Matera, Dec. 27, 1973; children: Richard William Post, Mary Jane Post Craig. BS in Edn., Concordia Tchrs. Coll., Seward, Nebr., 1956; MEd, U. Oreg., 1963; Luth. tchrs. diploma, Concordia Tchrs. Coll., Seward, 1947. Elementary tchr. Our Savior's Luth. Ch., Colorado Springs, Colo., 1954-57; tchr. 5th grade Monterey (Calif.) Pub. Schs., 1957-59; tchr. 1st grade Roseburg (Oreg.) Schs., 1959-60; tchr. several schs. Palm Springs (Calif.) Unified Sch. Dist., 1960-73; tchr. 3rd grade Vista del Monte Sch., Palm Springs, Calif., 1973-93; ret., 1993. Named Tchr. of the Yr., Palm Springs Unified Schs. Mem. Kappa Kappa Iota (chpt. and state pres.).

MATHAUDHU, SUKHDEV SINGH, mechanical engineer; b. Dhamtan Sahib, Haryana, India, Sept. 11, 1946; came to U.S., 1965; s. Kesho Ram and Channo Devi (Dhiman) M.; m. Veena Chand, Aug. 20, 1972; children: Suveen Nigel, Suneel Adrian. BSME, Walla Walla (Wash.) Coll., 1970. Registered profl. engr., Calif., Pa. Mech. engr. McGinnis Engring., Inc., Portland, Oreg., 1970-71, Can. Union Coll., LaCombe, Alta., Can., 1971-72, H.D. Nottingham & Assocs., McLean, Va., 1972; project engr. Shefferman & Bigelson Co., Silver Spring, Md., 1973-77; mech. engr. Buchart Assocs., York, Pa., 1977-78; sr. mech. engr. Gannett Fleming, Harrisburg, Pa., 1978-80; chief mech. engr. Popov Engrs., Newport Beach, Calif., 1981-83; pres. Mathaudhu Engring., Inc., Riverside, Calif., 1983—. Vice chmn. LaSierra Acad. of SDA, Riverside, 1988-92; law adv. counselor SE Conf. SDA, 1987-92. Mem. ASHRAE (chpt. pres. 1988-90, regional vice-chmn. 1990-92, jour. com. 1992-93, bd. dirs., region chmn. 1993-96), NSPE, Am. Soc. Plumbing Engrs., Soc. Am. Mil. Engrs., Am. Cons. Engrs. Coun. Calif. Soc. Profl. Egnrs. (pres. 1985-86, state dir. 1986-87), Cons. Engrs. Assn. Calif. Republican. Seventh-Day Adventist. Home: 5394 College Ave Riverside CA 92505-3123 Office: 3833 Jurupa Ave Riverside CA 92506-2221

MATHEIS, LAWRENCE PAUL, association executive, public health consultant; b. St. Louis, Apr. 11, 1948; s. Lawrence Paul and Theresa (Lady) M.; m. Mary Francis Manning, Apr. 2, 1947; 1 child, Michelle Marie Whitaker. AB, Washington U., St. Louis, 1976, MSW, 1978. Sr. cmty. assoc. Greater St. Louis Health Sys. Agy., 1976-79; dir. planning and implementation Cardinal Health Agy., Lumberton, N.C., 1979-81; exec. dir. Clark County Health Sys. Agy., Las Vegas, 1981-86; instr. health policy U. Nev., Las Vegas, 1982—; exec. dir. Nev. State Med. Assn., Reno, 1982—; instr. health policy Coll. St. Francis, Las Vegas, 1986; instr. stats. C.C. of So. Nev., Las Vegas, 1983-86; state health adminstr. State of Nev., Carson City, 1986-88; chair Nev. Health Issues Coalition, 1988—. Newspaper columnist Las Vegas Rev., 1984-86; contbr. chpt. to book. Bd. dirs. Nev. Tobacco Prevention Coalition, Las Vegas. Sgt. U.S. Army, 1970-73. Mem. Am. Soc. Assn. Execs., Am., Assn. Med. Soc. Execs. Unitarian-Universalist. Home: 5276 Rambling Rd Las Vegas NV 89120 Office: Nev State Med Assn 2590 E Russell Rd Las Vegas NV 89120-2417

MATHENY, SUSAN KAY, news editor; b. Sleepyeye, Minn., Nov. 21, 1950; d. Harvey B. and Elisabeth Dallmann; m. Ronald Edward Matheny, Sept. 16, 1973; children: Lisa, Marty. BA in English, Oreg. State U., 1975. Sec., receptionist C. Robert Hall, M.D., Corvallis, Oreg., 1975-79; transcriptionist Howard Korn, M.D., Corvallis, Oreg., 1979-80; sec. Ctrl. Oreg.

Cmty. Edn. Ctr., Madras, Oreg., 1987-89; news editor Madras Pioneer, 1989—. Contbr. articles to profl. publs. Mem. adv. bd. Ctrl. Oreg. C.C., Madras, 1987—; mem. Oreg. Peaceworks, Madras, 1987-94; jr. H.S. youth group leader United Meth. Ch., Madras, 1992-94, sr. H.S. youth group asst., 1994—. Home: 3010 NE Elm Ln Madras OR 97741-8971 Office: Madras Pioneer Newspaper 241 SE 6th St Madras OR 97741-1635

MATHER, E. COTTON, geography educator; b. West Branch, IA, Jan. 3, 1918; s. Anders Vetti and Alleda (Zwickey) M.; m. Julia Marie Eiler, Dec. 23, 1944; children: Cotton Vetti, J'Lee Alleda. AB, U. Ill., Champaign, 1940, MS, 1941; PhD, U. Wis., Madison, 1950. Geographer Army Map Svc., Washington, 1941; rsch. analyst Office of Strategic Svcs., Washington, 1942-44; instr. U. Wis., Madison, Wis., 1945-46; assoc. to full prof., dept. chmn. U. Minn., Mpls., 1957-85; pres. N.Mex. Geog. Soc., Mesilla, N.Mex., 1985-94; vis. prof. numerous univs. U.S., Can., overseas, 1959-88. Co-editor: Atlas of Kentucky, 1977, (14) International Geographical Guidebooks of North America, 1992; co-author: India, Cultural Patterns and Processes, 1982, Prairie Border Country, 1980, Upper Coulee Country, 1975, St. Croix Border Country, 1968, Beyond the Great Divide, 1992, Registered Places of New Mexico, 1994. Recipient research award, Assn. of Am. Geographers, 1954, Ford Found., 1964, 65. Fellow Royal Geog. Soc.; mem. Assn. Am. Geographers, Pierce County Geog. Soc., Internat. Geog. Union, N.Mex. Geog. Soc., Ctr. Am. Places (dir.), Explorers Club. Home: PO Box 1184 Mesilla NM 88046-1184 Office: NMex Geograph Soc PO Box 1201 Mesilla NM 88046-1201

MATHERS, MARGARET, charitable agency consultant, political activist, newspaper copy editor, proofreader; b. Ada, Okla., Feb. 16, 1929; d. Robert Lee and Josiephine Margaret (Reed) Erwin; m. Coleman F. Moss, Sept. 1956 (div. 1966); children: Carol Lee Doria, Marilyn Frances; m. Boyd Leroy Mathers, Apr. 10, 1967. BS in Music, Tex. U., 1950. Svc. rep. Gen. Tel. Co., Santa Monica, Calif., 1955-58; tchr. pvt. sch., Santa Monica, 1958-60; computer program and data analyst System Devel. Corp., Santa Monica, 1961-66; computer programmer Inst. Def. Analyses, Arlington, Va., 1966-70; typist, transcriber, Edgewater, Md., 1971-80; sec. People Assisting the Homeless, 1992-94, bd. dirs., 1985-95; asst. dir. San Juan Cath. Charities, Farmington, N.Mex., 1993—; proofreader, copy editor, Farmington Daily Times, 1993—; sec. Cmty. Network Coun., 1992-94, treas. 1994—; pres. San Juan Coun. Cmty. Agys., 1986-87, treas., 1987-89, 92—, sec., 1989-90; pres. Davidsonville-Mayo Health Assn., Edgewater, 1973-76, 77-80; cons. in field, 1983—. Chmn. county Libertarian Party of N.Mex., San Juan County, 1985, sec. ctrl. com., 1988-92, mem. ctrl. com., 1988—; asst. sec. Our Lady of Perpetual Help, Parish Coun., Edgewater, 1979-82, Parish Coun. Sacred Heart, Farmington, 1987, sec., 1988-90, mem. social justice com., 1992; mem. adv. bd. San Juan County DNA Legal Aid, 1992, sec., 1993; sec. River Club Community Assn., Edgewater, 1975-82; mem. selection com. Habitat for Humanity, 1990; mem. San Juan County Task Force on Housing, 1991, Task Force on Transp., 1991; sec. Com. Preserve 2d Amendment Rights, 1994. Mem. Informed Citizens Alliance, Secular Franciscan Order. Roman Catholic. Avocations: nature study, birdwatching, reading, music, Indian studies. Office: The Daily Times PO Box 450 Farmington NM 87499

MATHESON, DONNA JANE, communications executive, editor; b. Tacoma, Nov. 20, 1956; d. Donald McPherson Matheson and Pauline Eloise (Campbell) Camille; m. Darnell Curtis Sr., Apr. 16, 1983 (div. Feb. 1995); children: David Curtis, Cecilia Curtis, Tamara Curtis, Darnell "Buddy" Curtis Jr. Cert. multicultural mgmt., U. Mo., 1994; student, U. Idaho, 1995, 96, 97—, North Idaho Coll. Editor Tacoma Indians News, 1978-79; ct. adminstr. Coeur D'Alene Tribal Ct., Plummer, Idaho, 1980-84; pub. info. officer Coeur D'Alene Head Start, Desmet, Idaho, 1984-86; comm. dir. Coeur D'Alene Tribe, Plummer, 1986—. Contbr. articles to local periodicals. Mem. higher edn. com. Coeur D'Alene Tribe, Desmet, 1992-95; warrior, scholar, and nurturer N.A.I.T.I.V.E. Project, Spokane, Wash., 1992; vol. Clinton-Gore '96, Boise, Idaho. Fellow Howard Simons Found.; mem. Nat. Newspapers Assn. (mem. gov. affairs com. 1995—), Native Am. Journalists Assn. (chairperson election bd. 1997—), Soc. Profl. Journalists, Investigative Reporters and Editors. Native Am. Ch. Office: Coeur D Alene Tribe Indians PO Box 408 Plummer ID 83851

MATHEWS, ANNE JONES, consultant, library educator and administrator; b. Phila.; d. Edmond Fulton and Anne Ruth (Reichner) Jones; m. Frank Samuel Mathews, June 16, 1951; children: Lisa Anne Mathews-Bingham, David Morgan, Lynne Elizabeth Bietenhader-Mathews, Alison Fulton Sawyer. AB, Wheaton Coll., 1949; MA, U. Denver, 1965, PhD, 1977. Mem. field staff Intervarsity Christian Fellowship, Chgo., 1949-51; interviewer supr. Colo. Market Rsch. Svcs., Denver, 1952-64; reference libr. Oreg. State U., Corvallis, 1965-67; program dir. Ctrl. Colo. Libr. Sys., Denver, 1969-70; inst. dir. U.S. Office of Edn., Inst. Grant, 1979; dir. pub. rels. Grad. Sch. Librarianship and Info. Mgmt. U. Denver, 1970-76, dir. continuing edn., 1977-80, assoc. prof., 1977-79, prof., 1979-85; dir. Office Libr. Programs, Office Ednl. Rsch., Improvement U.S. Dept. Edn., Washington, 1986-91; dir. Nat. Libr. Edn., Washington, 1992-94; cons. Acad. Ednl. Devel., Washington, 1994—; vis. lectr. Simmons Coll. Sch. Libr. Sci., Boston, 1977; cons. USIA, 1984-85, mem. book and libr. adv. com., 1981-91; faculty assoc. Danforth Found., 1974-84; speaker in field; mem. secondary sch. curriculum com. Jefferson County Pub. Schs., Colo., 1976-78; mem. adv. com. Golden H.S., 1973-77; mem. adv. coun. White House Conf. on Librs. and Info. Svcs., 1991; del. Internat. Fedn. Libr. Assn., 1984-93. Author, editor 6 books; contbr. articles to profl. jours., numerous chpts. to books. Mem. rural librs. and humanities program Colo. planning and resource bd. NEH, 1982-83; bd. mgrs. Friends Found. of Denver Pub. Libr., 1976-82; pres. Faculty Women's Club, Colo. Sch. Mines, 1963-64. Mem. ALA (visionary leaders com. 1987-89, coun. mem. 1979-83, com on accreditation 1984-85, orientation com. 1974-77, 83-84, pub. rels. com.), Am. Soc. Info. Sci. (pub. rels. chmn. 1971), Mountain Plains Libr. Assn. (profl. devel. com. 1979-80, pub. rels. and publs. com. 1973-75, continuing edn. com. 1973-76), Colo. Libr. Assn. (pres. 1974, bd. dirs. 1973-75, continuing edn. com. 1976-80), Assn. Libr. & Info. Sci. Edn. (communication com. 1978-80, program com. 1977-78), Cosmos Club (Washington). Home: 492 Mount Evans Rd Golden CO 80401-9626

MATHEWS, BARBARA EDITH, gynecologist; b. Santa Barbara, Calif., Oct. 5, 1946; d. Joseph Chesley and Pearl (Cieri) Mathews; AB, U. Calif., 1969; MD, Tufts U., 1972. Diplomate Am. Bd. Ob-Gyn. Intern, Cottage Hosp., Santa Barbara, 1972-73, Santa Barbara Gen. Hosp., 1972-73; resident in ob-gyn Beth Israel Hosp., Boston, 1973-77; clin. fellow in ob-gyn Harvard U., 1973-76, instr., 1976-77; gynecologist Sansum Med. Clinic, Santa Barbara, 1977—; faculty mem. ann. postgrad. course Harvard Med. Sch.; bd. dirs. Sansum Med. Clinic, vice chmn. bd. dirs., 1994-96; dir. ann. postgrad course UCLA Med. Sch. Bd. dirs. Meml. Rehab. Found., Santa Barbara, Channel City Club, Santa Barbara, Music Acad. of the West, Santa Barbara, St. Francis Med. Ctr., Santa Barbara; mem. citizen's continuing edn. adv. council Santa Barbara C.C.; moderator Santa Barbara Cottage Hosp. Cmty. Health Forum. Fellow ACS, Am. Coll. Ob-gyn.; mem. AMA, Am. Soc. Colposcopy and Cervical Pathology (dir. 1982-84), Harvard U. Alumni Assn., Tri-counties Obstet. and Gynecol. Soc. (pres. 1981-82), Phi Beta Kappa. Clubs: Birnam Wood Golf (Santa Barbara). Author: (with L. Burke) Colposcopy in Clinical Practice, 1977; contbg. author Manual of Ambulatory Surgery, 1982. Home: 2105 Anacapa St Santa Barbara CA 93105-3503 Office: 317 W Pueblo St Santa Barbara CA 93105-4355

MATHEWS, ELDEN CLAIR, art instructor, sculptor, painter; b. Beloit, Wisc.; s. Clair Baldwin and Leona Beatrice (Hoadley); m. Darlene Dora Lowthers Dec. 30, 1961; children: Anne Elma, Craig Richard, Moira Lynn. B.S. in Art Edn., U. Wisc., 1950, M.S. in Applied Arts, 1951; grad. student, U. Denver, 1957-58. Art supr., tchr. Mount Morris (Mich.) Pub. Sch., 1951-52, Winneconne (Wisc.) Pub. Sch., 1952-55; art tchr. Oshkosh (Wisc.) Pub. Sch., 1955-56; art supr. tchr. Gallup (N.Mex.) Pub. Sch., 1956-57; art supr. Moab (Utah) Pub. Sch., 1958-59; art instr. Tucson (Ariz.) Dist #1 Schs., 1959-87; mem. faculty coun., Tucson High Sch., 1969-73, (pres. 1970-71), Tucson Arts Coalition, 1987—. Artist Painting (Encaustic) Clouds Fields & Shadows, 1952 (Life Mag.); art show, First Internat. Science Art Symposium, Hong Kong, 1994, Second Internat. Science Art Symposium, Berlin, 1997, Ariz. Art Archives, Phoenix Art Com., 1993; contbr. articles to profl. jours. Mem. church coun., Unitarian Univ. Church, Tucson, 1969-70; cpl., Infantry, 1943-46. Democrat. Zen. Home: 4337 E Burns St Tucson AZ 85711

MATHEWS, KENNETH PINE, physician, educator; b. Schenectady, N.Y., Apr. 1, 1921; s. Raymond and Marguerite Elizabeth (Pine) M.; m. Alice Jean Elliott, Jan. 26, 1952 (dec.); children: Susan Kay, Ronald Elliott, Robert Pine; m. Winona Beatrice Rosenburg, Nov. 8, 1975. AB, U. Mich., 1941, MD, 1943. Diplomate Am. Bd. Internal Medicine, Am. Bd. Allergy and Immunology (past. sec.). Intern, asst. resident, resident in medicine Univ. Hosp., Ann Arbor, Mich., 1943-45, 48-50; mem. faculty dept. medicine med. sch. U. Mich., 1950—, assoc. prof. internal medicine, 1956-61, prof., 1961-86, prof. emeritus, 1986—, head div. allergy, 1967-83; adj. mem. Scripps Clinic and Research Found., La Jolla, Calif., 1986—; past chmn. residency rev. com. for allergy and immunology, past chmn. allergy and immunology rsch. com. NIH. Co-author: A Manual of Clinical Allergy, 2d edit, 1967; editor: Jour. Allergy and Clin. Immunology, 1968-72; contbr. numerous articles in field to profl. jours. Served to capt. M.C. AUS, 1946-48. Recipient Disting. Service award Am. Acad. Allergy, 1976; Faculty Disting. Achievement award U. Mich., 1984. Fellow Am. Acad. Allergy (past pres.), A.C.P. (emeritus); mem. Am. Assn. Immunologists (emeritus), Ctrl. Soc. Clin. Rsch. (emeritus), Am. Fedn. Clin. Rsch., Alpha Omega Alpha, Phi Beta Kappa. Home: 7080 Caminito Estrada La Jolla CA 92037-5714

MATHIAS, BETTY JANE, communications and community affairs consultant, writer, editor, lecturer; b. East Ely, Nev., Oct. 22, 1923; d. Royal F. and Dollie B. (Bowman) M.; student Merritt Bus. Sch., 1941, 42, San Francisco State U., 1941-42; 1 child, Dena. Asst. publicity dir. Oakland (Calif.) Area War Chest and Community Chest, 1943-46; pub. rels. Am. Legion, Oakland, 1946-47; asst. to pub. rels. dir. Cen. Bank of Oakland, 1947-49; pub. rels. dir. East Bay chpt. of Nat. Safety Council, 1949-51; propr., mgr. Mathias Pub. Rels. Agy., Oakland, 1951-60; gen. assignment reporter and teen news editor Daily Rev., Hayward, Calif., 1960-62; freelance pub. rels. and writing, Oakland, 1962-66, 67-69; dir. corp. communications Systech Fin. Corp., Walnut Creek, Calif., 1969-71; v.p. corp. communications Consol. Capital companies, Oakland, 1972-79, v.p. community affairs, Emeryville, Calif., 1981-84, v.p. spl. projects, 1984-85; v.p., dir. Consol. Capital Realty Svcs., Inc., Oakland, 1973-77; v.p., dir. Centennial Adv. Corp., Oakland, 1976-77; communications cons., 1979—; cons. Mountainair Realty, Cameron Park, Calif., 1986-87; pub. rels. coord. Tuolumne County Visitors Bur., 1989-90; lectr. in field; bd. dirs. Oakland YWCA, 1944-45, ARC, Oakland, So. Alameda County chpt., 1967-69, Family Ctr., Children's Hosp. Med. Ctr. No. Calif., 1982-85, March of Dimes, 1983-85, Equestrian Ctr. of Walnut Creek, Calif., 1983-84, also sec.; adult and publs. adv. Internat. Order of the Rainbow for Girls, 1953-78; communications arts adv. com. Ohlone (Calif.) Coll., 1979-85, chmn., 1982-84; mem. adv. bd. dept. mass communications Calif. State U.-Hayward, 1985; pres. San Francisco Bay Area chpt. Nat. Reyes Syndrome Found., 1981-86; vol. staff Columbia Actors' Repertory, Columbia, Calif., 1986-87, 89; mem. exec. bd., editor newsletter Tuolumne County Dem. Club, 1987; publicity chmn. 4th of July celebration Tuolumne County C. of C., 1988; vol. children's dept. Tuolumne County Pub. Libr., 1993—; vol. Annual Cmty. Christmas Eve Dinner, Sonora, Calif., 1988—; mem. adv. com. Ride Away Ctr. for Therapeutic Riding for the Handicapped, 1995-96, vol., Hold Your Horses Therapeutic Riding Acad. Recipient Grand Cross of Color award Internat. Order of Rainbow for Girls, 1955. Order Eastern Star (life, worthy matron 1952, publicity chmn. Calif. state 1955), Northeastern Nev. Hist. Soc. Editor East Bay Mag., 1966-67, TIA Traveler, 1969, Concepts, 1979-83. Home: 20575 Gopher Dr Sonora CA 95370-9034

MATHIAS, LESLIE MICHAEL, electronic manufacturing company executive; b. Bombay, Dec. 17, 1935; came to U.S., 1957; s. Paschal Lawrence and Dulcine (D'Souza) M.; m. Vivian Mae Doolittle, Dec. 16, 1962. BSc, U. Bombay, 1957; BS, San Jose (Calif.) State U., 1961. Elec. engr. Indian Standard Metal, Bombay, 1957; sales engr. Bleisch Engring. and Tool, Mt. View, Calif., 1958-60; gen. mgr. Meadows Terminal Bds., Cupertino, Calif., 1961-63; prodn. mgr. Sharidon Corp., Menlo Park, Calif., 1963-67, Videx Corp., Sunnyvale, Calif., 1967-68, Data Tech. Corp., Mt. View, 1968-69; pres. L.G.M. Mfg., Inc., Mt. View, 1969-83; pvt. practice plating cons. Los Altos, Calif., 1983-87; materials mgr. Excel Cirs., Santa Clara, Calif., 1987-91, 93—, acct. mgr., 1991-93, materials mgr., 1993—. Social chmn. Internat. Students, San Jose, 1958-59. Mem. Nat. Fedn. Ind. Bus., Calif. Cirs. Assn., Better Bus. Bur., Purchasing Assn., U.S. C. of C. Roman Catholic. Home: 20664 Mapletree Pl Cupertino CA 95014-0449

MATHIS, TERESA GALE, association executive; b. Tacoma, Wash., July 18, 1952; d. Charles Edward and Shirley Grace (Konrad) M. BA in English, Carleton Coll., Northfield, Minn., 1974. Exec. dir. Wash. Assn. Criminal Def. Lawyers, Seattle, 1988—. Editor Wash. Criminal Def., 1988—; contbr. articles to profl. jours. Treas., mem. exec. com. Am. Friends Svc. Com., Seattle, 1986-92, mem. nat. cmty. rls. com., 1992—; vice chair Murder Victims Families for Reconciliation, Atlantic, Va., 1991-96, chair, 1996—; mem. steering com. Wash. Coalition to Abolish the Death Penalty, Seattle, 1984—, chair, 1988-91; mem. Nat. Criminal Justice Task Force, Phila., 1992—; mem. Am. Friends Svc. Com. Mem. Am. Soc. Assn. Execs. Quaker. Office: Wash Assn Criminal Def Lawyers 810 3rd Ave Ste 421 Seattle WA 98104-1614

MATHIS-GAMBER, KATHLEEN ANNE, special education educator; b. Atlantic City, N.J., Mar. 14, 1948; d. William E. and Ella K. (Clark) Mathis; m. Charles Allen Gamber, Jan. 22, 1983. AA, Atlantic C.C., Mays Landing, N.J., 1969; BA, Glassboro (N.J.) State U., 1971. Cert. spl. edn. and elem. edn. Spl. edn. tchr. Little Egg Harbor (N.J.) Twp. Elem. Sch., 1971-75, dir. spl. svcs., 1975-77; florist Hyatt Regency Hotel, Honolulu, 1977-78; tchr. 3rd grade Conservative Bapt. Mission Bd., Morrison Acad., Taiwan, 1978-79; tchr. pre-1st grade Atlantic Christian Sch., Ocean City, N.J., 1979-80; critic casino shows, prodr. local commercials WOND/WMGM Radio Sta., Linwood, N.J., 1982-83; resource rm. spl. edn. tchr. kindergarten - 8th Pleasantville (N.J.) Sch. Dist., 1983-85; tchr. severely handicapped teens Wahiawa (Hawaii) Intermediate Sch., 1985-89; tchr. spl. edn. Pahoa (Hawaii) High and Intermediate Sch., 1989—, dir. spl. edn., 1991—; sch. bd. based mgmt. bd. Pahoa High and Elem. Sch., 1989-91; spkr. workshops sch. violence and crack babies, 1995, 96. Author: (short story) Pahoa School Litary, 1996. Mem. NEA, NRA, Hawaii State Tchrs. Assn. (local chpt. pres. 1990-92, bd. dirs. 1992-96, polit. action com. 1986-96), Parent, Student, Tchr. Assn., Pu'ula Ohana Hula Troop (dancer 1989-92). Office: Pahoa High and Intermediate Puna Rd Pahoa HI 96778

MATHUR, ASHOK, telecommunications engineer, educator, researcher; b. Gorakhpur, Uttar Pradesh, India; came to U.S., 1979; s. Raj Swarup and Savitri Mathur; m. Jayanti Srivastava, May 31, 1978; children: Menka, Puja. BS, U. Agra, India, 1963, MS, 1965; PhD, U. Southampton, Hampshire, Eng., 1974. Cert. telecommunications engr., Calif.; teaching credential, Calif. Lectr. upper atmospheric physics Kanpur, India, 1965-68; doctoral researcher U. Southampton, 1968-73; postdoctoral research fellow U. Poitiers, Vienne, France, 1973-74; assoc. prof., research supr U. Kanpur, 1974-79; mem. tech. staff telecomms. sci. and engring. divsn. Jet Propulsion Lab. Calif. Inst. Tech., Pasadena, 1979-92; prin. systems engr. applied tech. divsn. Computer Scis. Corp., Pasadena, 1992—. Contbr. numerous publs. to profl. jours.; mem. editorial bd. Acta Ciencia Indica Jour., 1975-78. Recipient 10-Yr. Svc. award Jet Propulsion Lab. Calif. Inst. Tech., 1990, Overseas Students award Brit. Coun., London, 1968, Délégation Générale a la Recherche Scientifique et Technique award, Paris, 1973, cert. of merit for disting. svcs. Internat. Biographical Ctr., Cambridge, Eng., 1988, Group Achievement award NASA, 1991. Mem. IEEE (sr.), AIAA (vice chmn. pub. policy San Gabriel Valley, sec. L.A. 1987-92), The European Phys. Soc., Calif. Inst. Tech. Mgmt. Club, Armed Forces Comms. and Electronics Assn. Home: 1923B Huntington Dr Duarte CA 91010-2637 Office: DIRECTV Hughes Electronics MS RE/R8/N353 2230 E Imperial Hwy El Segundo CA 90245 *Personal philosophy: To achieve in any field of endeavor choose a goal and work towards it with full dedication. Remember that initial failures are part of the success story. The laws of nature apply to every aspect of life and the natural sequence of happenings (the logic) directs the course of action for a goal.*

MATICH, MATTHEW P., secondary school English educator; b. San Pedro, Calif., June 30, 1962. B Fine and Comm. Arts, Loyola Marymount U., 1985; MEd, Nat. U., 1995; grad., Am. Sch. X-Ray, L.A., 1992. Cert. secondary sch. English tchr., Calif. Records retention clk. Starkist Foods, Terminal Island, Calif., 1979-83; producer, newswriter KMET Radio, Hollywood, Calif., 1981-83, 85-86; news dir., broadcaster KXLU Radio, L.A., 1983-87; instr., counselor Columbia Sch. Broadcasting, Hollywood, 1985-88; radio reporter KRTH Radio, L.A., 1987-88; radio producer Transtar Radio Network, Hollywood, 1987-88; deck crew/customer svc. Catalina Island (Calif.) Express, Avalon, 1989-91; substitute tchr. L.A. Unified Sch. Dist., 1989-92; English tchr., head coach football and track San Pedro (Calif.) H.S., 1992—, head coach freshman/sophomore football and track coach, 1993—; founder, mem. adv. bd. Acad. Athletes (now Extracurricular Academics), San Pedro, 1994—; founder local ethnic tribute/holiday Burrito Day in L.A., 1983—; instr. ESL San Pedro/Narbonne Adult Sch., 1996—. Writer, prodr. radio program The Bluez Shift, 1983-87, poetry: It Can't Be, 1996. Mem. San Pedro Pirate Boosters, 1987. Mem. United Tchrs. L.A., Am. Fedn. Tchrs., Nat. Coun. Tchrs. English, Calif. Assn. Tchrs. English, Dalmation Am. Club, Elks Club (scholarship com. 1990). Home: 2731 S Averill Ave San Pedro CA 90731-5632 Office: San Pedro HS 2731 Averillain San Pedro CA 90731

MATIN, A., microbiology educator, consultant; b. Delhi, India, May 8, 1941; came to U.S., 1964, naturalized, 1983; s. Mohammed and Zohra (Begum) Said; m. Mimi Keyhan, June 21, 1968. BS, U. Karachi, Pakistan, 1960, MS, 1962; PhD, UCLA, 1969. Lectr. St. Joseph's Coll., Karachi, 1962-64; research assoc. UCLA, 1964-71; sci. officer U. Groningen, Kerklaan, The Netherlands, 1971-75; from asst. prof. to full prof. microbiology and immunology Stanford U., Calif., 1975—; prof. Western Hazardous Substances Rsch. Ctr. Stanford U., 1981—; cons. Engenics, 1982-84, Monsanto, 1984-86, Chlorox, 1992-93; chmn. Stanford Recombinant DNA panel; mem. Accreditation Bd. for Engring. and Tech.; mem. internat. adv. com., Internat. Workshop on Molecular Biology of Stress Response: Meml. Found., Banaras U. and German Min. of Rsch., mem. panel Yucca Mountain Microbial Activity, Dept. of Energy, mem. study sect.; participant DOE, NABIR program draft panel; convenor of microbiol. workshop and confs.; rev. panel DOE environ. mgmt. program; mem. rev. panel DOE NABIR program, mem. Stanford Biosafety Panel. Mem. editl. bd. Jour. Bacteriology, Ann. Rev. Microbiol.; reviewer NSF and other grants; contbr. numerous publs. to sci. jours. Fulbright fellow, 1964-71; recipient rsch. awards NSF, 1981-92, Ctr. for Biotech. Rsch., 1981-85, EPA, 1981—, NIH, 1989-92, U.N. Tokten, 1987, DOE, 1993—, Dept. Agrl., 1995—. Mem. AAAS, AAUP, Am Soc. for Microbiology (Found. lectr. 1991-93), Soc. Gen. Microbiology, Soc. Indsl. Microbiology, No. Soc. Indsl. Microbiology (bd. dirs.), Biophys. Soc., Am. Chem. Soc. Home: 690 Coronado Ave Stanford CA 94305-1039 Office: Stanford U Fairchild Sci Bldg Dept Microbiology & Immunology Stanford CA 94305-5402

MATLEY, BENVENUTO GILBERT (BEN MATLEY), computer engineer, educator, consultant; b. Monroe, La., Sept. 8, 1930; s. Welcome Gilbert and Lucette Marie (Renaud) M.; m. Patricia Jean McWilliams, June 21, 1959; children: Elizabeth, Katherine, John, Stephen, Richard, David. AB, San Diego State U., 1960; MBA, U. So. Calif., 1964; EdD, Nova U., 1980. Cert. data processor. Mathematician, engr. various data processing and computing firms, San Diego and L.A., 1956-64; sr. computer systems engr. Nortronics div. Northrop Corp., Hawthorne, Calif., 1964-69; prof. data processing and math. Ventura (Calif.) Coll., 1969—; lectr. in mgmt. and computer sci. West Coast U., L.A., 1982—; software cons, ednl. cons., Ventura, 1972—. Author: Principles of Elementary Algebra: A Language and Equations Approach, 1991; sr. author: National Computer Policies, 1988; contbr. chpts. to books, articles to profl. jours. Active Ventura County coun. Boy Scouts Am., 1979-82; cons. Calif. Luth. U., Thousand Oaks, Calif., 1989. Lt. (j.g.) USNR, 1952-55, Europe. Mem. IEEE Computer Soc. (Disting Visitor 1988-91), Assn. for Computing Machinery, Math. Assn. Am. Office: Ventura Coll 4667 Telegraph Rd Ventura CA 93003-3872

MATORY, W(ILLIAM) EARLE, JR., plastic surgeon, educator; b. Richmond, Va., Nov. 20, 1950; s. William Earle Sr. and Deborah L. (Love) M.; m. Yvonne Marie, Nov. 17, 1948; 1 child, William Earle III. BS, Yale U., 1972; MD, Howard U., 1976. Fellow Lahey Clinic, Boston, U. Calif., San Francisco; fellow U. Calif., San Francisco; from. asst. to assoc. prof. U. Mass. Med. Ctr. Author: Evolving Strategies in the Management of Breast Disease, 1995, Ethnic Considerations in Facial Aesthetic Surgery, 1997, Aesthetic Contouring of the Lips, 1997. Bd. dirs. Youth at Risk Breakthrough Found., San Francisco, 1993. Recipient Distinction award Nat. Med. Assn., 1991, Surg. Sect. award, Arthur L. Gaines award Columbia U., Edw. J. Mason award. Mem. ACS, Am. Soc. Plastic and Reconstructive Surgeons, Am. Soc. Aesthetic Plastic Surgeons, Am. Assn. Plastic Surgery. Office: A New You Plastic Surgery Med Group 250 E Yale Loop Ste A Irvine CA 92604-4697

MATOSSIAN, JESSE NERSES, physicist; b. L.A., Feb. 2, 1952; s. Hagop Sarkis and Alice Elizabeth (Barsoomian) M. BS in Physics, U. So. Calif., L.A., 1975; MS in Physics, Stevens Inst. Tech., Hoboken, N.J., 1976; PhD in Physics, Stevens Inst. Tech., 1983. Mem. tech. staff Hughes Rsch. Labs., Plasma Physics Lab., Malibu, Calif., 1983-91, sr. mem. tech. staff, sr. rsch. staff physicist, 1992—. Reviewer Jour. Propulsion and Power, 1987-91; contbr. over 45 articles to profl. jours. and tech. publs.; 10 patents, 10 patents pending in field. Patron mem. L.A. County Mus. of Art; bd. dirs. Graphic Arts Coun. Mem. AIAA, IEEE, Am. Phys. Soc. (life), N.Y. Acad. Scis., Sigma Xi.

MATOVICH, MITCHEL JOSEPH, JR., motion picture producer, executive; b. Watsonville, Calif., Dec. 16, 1927; s. Mitchel Joseph and Mildred Florence (Ingrom) M.; widowed, 1968; divorced, 1983; children: Wayne, Mark, Laura; m. Patte Dee Matovich, 1989. Student, San Jose State U., 1946-49. Mechanical designer Stanford Rsch. Inst., Menlo Park, Calif., 1955-59; rsch. specialist Lockheed Missiles & Space Co., Sunnyvale, Calif., 1959-70; mgr. NASA and Dept. of Def. bus. sect. Engineered Systems Div. FMC Corp., San Jose, Calif., 1970-77; pres. and chief exec. officer Morton Co. Div. of Haycor Corp., Hayward, Calif., 1977-82; pres. Concept Devel. Co., Newark, Calif., 1982-89, Matovich Prodns., Hollywood, Calif., 1987—, Stereotronics Inc., Beverly Hills, Calif., 1988—; co-owner Vagabond Theatre, L.A., 1990-91. Author: The Image Machine, feature length screenplays, stories for screenplays, short stories; producer (feature films) Lightning in a Bottle, 1993 (Gold award Houston Film Festival, Award of Excellence Film Adv. Bd.), I Don't Buy Kisses Anymore, 1992 (named Best Ind. Feature Houston Internat. Film Festival, Award of Excellence Film Adv. Bd., Angel award Excellence in Media, Top Applause award Santa Clarita Valley Internat. Film Festival 1994); co-producer: Social Suicide; co-inventor: Stereotronics 3-D Video System; patentee in field. Chmn. bd. Santa Clarita Internat. Film Festival, 1995. With USN, 1945-46, 51-52, Korea. Mem. Acad. TV Arts and Scis., Soc. Motion Picture and TV Engrs., Producers' Guild, Mensa, Intertel. Home: 26313 Green Terrace Dr Newhall CA 91321-1324 Office: Matovich Prodns Inc PO Box 5744 Beverly Hills CA 90209-5744

MATRAY, JAMES IRVING, history educator; b. Evergreen Park, Ill., Dec. 6, 1948; s. Theodore John and Caroline Kathryn (Werstler) M.; m. Mary Karin Heine, Aug. 14, 1971; children: Benjamin Robert, Amanda Jane. BA in European and Am. History, Lake Forest Coll., 1970; MA in Am. History, U. Va., 1973, PhD, 1977. Vis. asst. prof. History N.Mex. State U., Las Cruces, 1980-82, asst. prof. History, 1982-87, assoc. prof. History, 1987-92, prof. History, 1992—; vis. assoc. prof. History U. So. Calif., L.A., 1988-89; disting. vis. scholar grad. inst. peace studies Kyung Hee U., Seoul, Korea, 1990. Author: The Reluctant Crusade: American Foreign Policy in Korea, 1941-1950, 1985, Historical Dictionary of the Korean War, 1991, Korea and the Cold War: Division, Destruction, and Disarmament, 1993; contbr. chpts. to various books, articles to profl. jours., entries in various dictionaries; bd. editors Pacific Historical Review, 1989-92. With Ill. Nat. Guard, 1970-71, USAR, 1971-80. N.Mex. State U. rsch. grantee, 1982, 83, 84, 86, 90, Harry S Truman Found. rsch. grantee, 1975, 82, MacArthur Meml. Libr. rsch. grantee, 1984, NEH grantee, 1985, 90. Mem. Am. Hist. Assn. (Pacific Coast br.), Assn. for Asian Studies, Orgn. of Am. Historians, Soc. for Historians of Am. Fgn. Rels. Democrat. Home: 4426 Echo Canyon Rd Las Cruces NM 88011-7530 Office: NMex State Univ Dept History Box 3H Las Cruces NM 88003

MATSCH, RICHARD P., judge; b. Burlington, Iowa, June 8, 1930. A.B., U. Mich., 1951, J.D., 1953. Bar: Colo. Asst. U.S. atty. Colo., 1959-61; dep. city atty. City and County of Denver, 1961-63; judge U.S. Bankruptcy Ct., Colo., 1965-74; judge U.S. Dist. Ct. for Colo., 1974-94, chief judge, 1994—; mem. Judicial Conf. of the U.S., 1991-94, mem. com. on criminal law, 1988-94; mem. bd. dirs. Fed. Judicial Ctr., 1995—. Served with U.S. Army, 1953-55. Mem. ABA, Am. Judicature Soc. Office: Byron White Court House 1823 Stout St Denver CO 80257-1823*

MATSEN, BRYNN MARIE, elementary school educator, consultant; b. Seattle, Nov. 14, 1952; d. William Jacob and Mary Elizabeth (Schrick) Dreyer; m. Stephen Nels Matsen, Nov. 11, 1978; children: Mary-Averill, Anthony Neal, Justin Corey. BA, U. Wash., 1974; MSW, Eastern Wash. U., 1981; cert., St. Louis U., 1980; cert. in cooperative learning, Cen. Wash. U., 1990. Cert. elem. tchr., English, psychology, sociology and anthropology, Wash. Tchr. Population Dynamics, Seattle, 1973-76; counselor, rsch. asst. Planned Parenthood, Seattle, 1976-78; dir. fin., devel. Lower Valley Hospice, Sunnyside, Wash., 1979-81; mgr., cons. Planned Parenthood, Yakima, Wash., 1982-83; ind. adminstrv. cons. Bickleton, Wash., 1982—; primary tchr. Bickleton Sch. Dist. #203, 1988—; cons. ESD 123, Walla Walla, Wash., 1991, ESD 105, Yakima Wash., 1994—, Sunnyside (Wash.) Sch. Dist., 1994—. Educator United Way, Yakima, 1981; mem. Bickleton Presbyn. Ch., Goodwill Soc. Presbyn. Ch., 1978—, nominating com., 1987-90. Recipient Svc. award Lower Valley Hospice, Sunnyside, 1981, Cal. Luth. Sch., Sunnyside, 1985, United Way, Yakima, 1986; named one of Outstanding Young Women of Am., 1985. Mem. NASW, ASCD, Nat. Aerospace Educators (svc. award 1991), NASA Space Orientation for Educators (participation award 1990), Yakima County Extension Homemakers (treas. 1985-87), Alpha Delta Mu (Gamma Theta chpt.). Democrat. Presbyn. Home: 50 Crider Valley Rd Bickleton WA 99322-9703 Office: Bickleton Sch Dist 203 10 Mkt St Bickleton WA 99322

MATSEN, JOHN MARTIN, academic administrator, pathologist; b. Salt Lake City, Feb. 7, 1933; s. John M. and Bessie (Jackson) M.; m. Joneen Johnson, June 6, 1959; children: Marilee, Sharon, Coleen, Sally, John H., Martin K., Maureen, Catherine, Carl, Jeri. BA, Brigham Young U., 1958; MD, UCLA, 1963. Diplomate Am. Bd. Pediatrics, Am. Bd. Pathology, Spl. Competence in Med. Microbiology. Intern UCLA, 1963-65; resident L.A. County Harbor/UCLA, Torrance, Calif., 1965-66; USPHS fellow U. Minn., Mpls., 1966-68, asst. prof., 1968-70, assoc. prof., 1971-74, prof., 1974; prof. U. Utah, Salt Lake City, 1974—, assoc. dean, 1979-81, chmn. Dept. of Pathology, 1981-93, univ. v.p. health scis., 1993—; pres. Associated Regional and Univ. Pathologists, Inc., Salt Lake City, 1983-93, chmn. bd. dirs., 1993—. Author over 200 publs. in field. Recipient Sonnenwirth Meml. award Am. Soc. Microbiology, 1993. Mem. Acad. Clin. Lab. Physicians and Scientists (pres. 1978-79), Assn. of Pathology Chmn. (pres. 1990-92). Mem. LDS Church. Home: 410 South 10 West Farmington UT 84025-2203 Office: U Utah Health Scis Ctr 50 N Medical Dr Salt Lake City UT 84132-0001

MATSUDA, STANLEY KAZUHIRO, secondary education educator; b. Glendale, Calif., Oct. 10, 1963; s. Shindo and Naoe (Nomura) M.; m. Marjorie Denine Paige, Dec. 17, 1989; 1 child, Keiko Paige. BS, Loma Linda U., 1986; MS, U. So. Calif., L.A., 1993. Cert. tchr. math., elementary and sr. math. Tchr. Glendale Adventist Elem. Sch., 1988-93; tchr. math. Glendale Adventist Acad., 1993-96, sch. bd. rep., 1991-92, tutorial svc. dir., 1993-95, chair math. dept., 1996—. Contr. Sansei Day Camp, L.A., 1991—; treas. L.A. Ctrl. Japanese-Am. Seventh-day Adventist ch., 1994—. Loma Linda U. scholar, 1982, Hughes scholar, 1985. Republican. Home: 4825 Agnes Ave Temple City CA 91780-3959

MATSUI, DOROTHY NOBUKO, elementary education educator; b. Honolulu, Jan. 9, 1954; d. Katsura and Tamiko (Sakai) M. Student, U. Hawaii, Honolulu, 1972-76, postgrad., 1982; BEd, U. Alaska, Anchorage, 1979, MEd in Spl. Edn., 1986. Clerical asst. U. Hawaii Manoa Disbursing Office, Anchorage, 1974-76; passenger service agt. Japan Air Lines, Anchorage, 1980; bilingual tutor Anchorage Sch. Dist., 1980, elem. sch. tchr., 1980—; facilitator for juvenile justice courses Anchorage Sch. Dist., Anchorage Police Dept., Alaska Pacific U., 1992-93; mem. adv. bd. Anchorage Law-Related Edn. Advancement Project. Vol. Providence Hosp., Anchorage, 1986, Humana Hosp., Anchorage, 1984, Spl. Olympics, Anchorage, 1981, Municipality Anchorage, 1978, Easter Seal Soc. Hawaii, 1975. Mem. NAFE, NEA, Alaska Edn. Assn., Smithsonian Nat. Assoc. Program, Nat. Space Soc., Smithsonian Air and Space Assn., World Aerospace Edn. Orgn., Internat. Platform Assn., Nat. Trust for Hist. Preservation, Nat. Audubon Soc., Planetary Soc., Cousteau Soc., Alaska Coun. for the Social Studies, Alaska Coun. Tchrs. Math., World Inst. Achievment, U.S. Olympic Soc., Women's Inner Circle Achievement, U. Alaska Alumni Assn., World Wildlife Fund, Japanese-Am. Nat. Mus., Alpha Delta Kappa (treas. Alpha chpt. 1988-92, corr. sec. 1993-96, sgt. at arms 1996—). Office: Anchorage Sch Dist 7001 Cranberry St Anchorage AK 99502-7145

MATSUI, JIRO, importer, wholesaler, small business owner; b. Honolulu, Hawaii, Apr. 5, 1919; s. Juro and Tsuta (Murai) M.; m. Barbara Toshiko Tanji; children: Kenneth Jiro, Alan Kiyoshi, Carol Ritsu. BA, U. Hawaii, 1949. Owner Honolulu Aquarium and Pet Supply, Honolulu, 1946-77, Bird House, Honolulu, 1957-61; owner, pres., chmn. Petland, Inc., Honolulu, 1961—, Pets Pacifica, Inc., Honolulu, 1977—, Global Pet Industries, Honolulu, 1975—; organizer, coord. first Pet Consumer Show in U.S., 1979, pres. 1979-82; first Internat. Pet Show; cons. Japan Pet Product Mfr. Assn. Fair, Japan, 1981—. Pres. Waikiki Vets. Club, Kapahulu, Oahu, Hawaii, 1948-66, Waiawa (Oahu) Farmers, 1948-88; sr. adv. com. plants and animals State of Hawaii, 1974—. Sgt. U.S. Army, 1941-46. Decorated Bronze Star; named retailer of yr. Retail Merchants of Hawaii, 1993. Mem. Am. Pet Soc. (pres. 1979-82, chmn. 1989-92), World Wide Pet Supply Assn. (bd. dirs. 1974-93, pres. 1989-90, Edward B. Price award 1982), Honolulu C. of C. (bd. dirs. 1974—), Merchants of Hawaii. Office: Pets Pacifica Inc 94-486 Ukee St Waipahu HI 96797-4211

MATSUI, ROBERT TAKEO, congressman; b. Sacramento, Sept. 17, 1941; s. Yasuji and Alice (Nagata) M.; m. Doris Kazue Okada, Sept. 17, 1966; 1 child, Brian Robert. AB in Polit. Sci, U. Calif., Berkeley, 1963; JD, U. Calif., San Francisco, 1966. Bar: Calif. 1967. Practiced law Sacramento, 1967-78; mem. Sacramento City Council, 1971-78, vice mayor, 1977; mem. 96th-104d Congresses from 5th Calif. dist., 1979—; ranking minority mem., mem. ways and means subcom. on oversight; dep. chair Dem. Nat. Com., 1995—; chmn. profl. bus. forum Dem. Congl. Campaign Com.; congl. liaison nat. fin. council Dem. Nat. Com.; mem. adv. council on fiscal policy Am. Enterprise Inst. chmn. Profl. Bus. Forum of the Dem. Congl. Co. and Com.; congl. liaison Nat. Fin. Council, Dem. Nat. Com.; mem. Am. Enterprise Inst. Adv. Council on Fiscal Policy. Named Young Man of Yr. Jr. C. of C., 1973; recipient Disting. Service award, 1973. Mem. Sacramento Japanese Am. Citizens League (pres. 1969), Sacramento Met. C. of C. (dir. 1976). Democrat. Clubs: 20-30 (Sacramento) (pres. 1972), Rotary (Sacramento). Office: US Ho of Reps 2311 Rayburn HOB Washington DC 20515-0505*

MATSUMORI, DOUGLAS, lawyer; b. Salt Lake City, Oct. 22, 1947. BS, U. Utah, 1973; JD, Harvard U., 1976. With Ray, Quinney & Nebeker P.C., Salt Lake City. Mem. Utah State Bar, Phi Beta Kappa. Office: Ray Quinney & Nebeker Ste 400 PO Box 45385 79 S Main St Salt Lake City UT 84111-0385

MATSUMURA, MASAZUMI, research scientist, biochemist; b. Osaka, Japan, Oct. 3, 1952; came to U.S., 1986; s. Masayuki and Sadako (Noda) M.; m. Masako Izuka, Apr. 11, 1982 (div. June 1993); children: Yosuke, Maki; m. Mayumi Fujita, Feb. 14, 1996; 1 stepchild, Junichi Fujita. BSc, Osaka U., 1974, MSc, 1976, PhD, 1984. Rsch. assoc. Osaka U., 1979-86; postdoctoral fellow U. Oreg., Eugene, 1986-89; asst. prof. The Scripps Rsch. Inst., La Jolla, Calif., 1989-93; sr. scientist Supragen, Inc., Lakewood, Colo., 1993—. Contbr. articles to profl. jours. Grantee NIH, 1993-94. Mem. AAAS, Am. Soc. Soc., Am. Soc. for Biochemistry and Molecular Biology, Japanese Soc. of Molecular Biology. Home: 5609 S Lansing Way Englewood CO 80111-4105

MATSUNAGA, GEOFFREY DEAN, lawyer; b. L.A., Sept. 30, 1949; s. Hideo Arthur and Yuri (Yamazaki) M.; m. Masako Inoue, Aug. 20, 1981; children: Ayako, Hideko, Lisa Fumi. BS, USAF Acad., 1971; MBA, UCLA, 1972; postgrad., Inter U. Ctr. Japanese Lang. Studies, 1979-80; JD, U. Calif., Berkeley, 1982. Bar: Calif. 1982, U.S. Dist. Ct. (cen. dist.) Calif. 1982, N.Y. 1983, U.S. Dist. Ct. (so. dist.) N.Y. 1983. Jud. extern U.S. Dist. Ct. (cen. dist.), L.A., 1981; assoc. Milbank, Tweed, Hadley & McCloy, N.Y.C., 1982-84, Tokyo, 1984-87; assoc. Sidley & Austin, Tokyo, 1987-88, L.A., 1988-91; counsel Sheppard, Mullin, Richter & Hampton, L.A., 1991-94; ptnr. Kagei & Matsunaga, L.A., 1995—. Founding bd. dirs. Futures Industry Assn., Japan, 1987; counsel East West Players, 1992-95. Lt. USN, 1972-78. Japan Found. fellow, Tokyo, 1979-80. Mem. Japan Bus. Assn. Southern Calif., Japan Am. Soc. So. Calif. (adv. bd. South Bay 1992-95). Episcopalian. Office: Kagei & Matsunaga Ste 420 19191 S Vermont Ave Los Angeles CA 90502

MATSUOKA, ERIC TAKAO, mathematics educator; b. Honolulu, May 9, 1967; s. Kenneth Tamotsu and Hilda Sumie (Hino) M. BA in Math. with distinction, U. Hawaii, 1987, MA in Math., 1994. Acctg. clk. Wayne Choo, CPA, Honolulu, 1987-88; lab. instr. in math. Leeward Community Coll., Pearl City, Hawaii, 1988-91, lectr. in math., 1989-94; contr. Computronics, Honolulu, 1989-93; instr. math., 1994—. Mem. Math. Assn. Am. (Instnl. award 1987). Office: Leeward CC 96-045 Ala Ike St Pearl City HI 96782-3366

MATSUURA, KENNETH RAY, counselor, articulation officer; b. Urbana, Ill., July 17, 1954; s. George Shigeo and Sally Sueko (Kawasaki) M.; m. Peggy Ai Iwata, May 27, 1995. BA, U. Calif., Santa Barbara, 1976; MA, UCLA, 1978, PhD, 1996. Career counselor Calif. State U. Dominguez Hills, Carson, 1984-85; grad. recruitment coord. U. Calif., Irvine, 1985-90; counselor/articulation officer Cerritos Coll., Norwalk, Calif., 1990—; mem. accreditation team Western Assn. Schs. and Colls., L.A., 1994; program reviewer Am. Coll. Pers. Assn. Ann. conf., Washington, 1988; presenter to confs. UCLA Grad. Advancement Program fellow, 1977-78. Home: 1066 Rocton Dr Pasadena CA 91107-5917 Office: Cerritos College 11110 Alondra Blvd Norwalk CA 90650-6203

MATTATHIL, GEORGE PAUL, communications specialist, consultant; b. Kottayam, India, May 12, 1957; came to U.S., 1985; s. Paul and Annamma M. Bs, U. Kerala (India), 1973-78; MS, Indian Inst. Tech., 1978-82. Project engr. Tekelec, Calabasas, Calif., 1986-89; sr. systems analyst Security Pacific Automation, L.A., 1989-90; sr. design. engr. Telenova, Camarillo, Calif., 1990-91; cons. Raynet, Menlo Park, Calif., 1991, Larse, Santa Clara, Calif., 1991—, NEC, 1992—, Level One Comm., Sacramento, 1994—, DigitalLink, 1994—, Verilink, San Jose, 1994—, Telebit, Sunnyvale, 1995—, Hitachi, San Jose, 1995—, C-Cor Electronics, Fremont, 1996, Xylan, Calabasas, Calif., 1996—, GoDigital Telecomm., Fremont, 1996—. Nat. Sci. Talent scholar, India, 1975-80. Mem. IEEE, Profl. and Tech. Cons. Assn., Assn. Computing Machinery, Software Forum, Soc. Telecom. Cons. Office: Silicom Inc PO Box 2264 Cupertino CA 95015-2264

MATTERN, DOUGLAS JAMES, electronics reliability engineer; b. Creede, Colo., May 19, 1933; s. John A. and Ethel (Franklin) M.; student San Jose (Calif.) City Coll., San Jose State U., 1956-58; m. Noemi E. Del Cippo, May 4, 1963. Reliability engr. Intersil, Sunnyvale, Calif., 1973-80; sr. engr. Data Gen. Corp., Sunnyvale, 1981-87; staff engr. Apple Computer, 1987—. Sec. Gen. World Citizens Assembly, San Francisco, 1975-86; dir. World Citizens Internat. Registry, U.S. Ctr., San Francisco, 1976—, World Citizen Diplomats, Palo Alto, Calif., 1988—; del. Peoples Congress, Paris, 1980—; pres. Assn. World Citizens, San Francisco, 1989—; pres. World Citizens Found., 1991—; chmn. World Citizens Assembly, San Francisco, 1995. Served with USN, 1951-55. Author resolution To End the Arms Race; contbg. author: Building a More Democratic United Nations, 1991; editor World Citizen Newsmag., 1973—; contbr. 45 articles to profl. jours. Mem. Nat. Electron Microscopy Assn., Union of Concerned Scientists Promoting Enduring Peace. Home: 2671 South Court St Palo Alto CA 94306-2462 Office: 55 New Montgomery St Ste 224 San Francisco CA 94105

MATTES, MARTIN ANTHONY, lawyer; b. San Francisco, June 18, 1946; s. Hans Adam and Marion Jane (Burge) M.; m. Catherine Elvira Garzio, May 26, 1984; children: Nicholas Anthony, Daniel Joseph, Thomas George. BA, Stanford U., 1968; postgrad., U. Chgo., 1968-69, U. Bonn, Fed. Republic Germany, 1971; JD, U. Calif., Berkeley, 1974. Bar: Calif. 1974, U.S. Ct. Appeals (D.C., 5th and 9th cirs.) 1978, U.S. Dist. Ct. (no. dist.) Calif. 1979, U.S. Dist. Ct. (ea. dist.) Calif. 1991. Asst. legal officer Internat. Union Conservation of Nature and Natural Resources, Bonn, 1974-76; staff counsel Calif. Pub. Utilities Commn., San Francisco, 1976-79, legal advisor to pres., 1979-82, adminstrv. law judge, 1983, asst. chief adminstrv. law judge, 1983-86; ptnr. Graham & James, San Francisco, 1986—; mem. adv. group. to Calif. Senate Subcom. on Pub. Utilities Commn. Procedural Reform, 1994. Mng. editor Ecology Law Quar., 1973-74; contbr. articles to profl. publs. Mem. Conf. Calif. Pub. Utility Counsel (treas. 1988-90, v.p. 1990-91, pres. 1991-92), Internat. Coun. Environ. Law, San Francisco Bar Assn. Office: Graham & James 1 Maritime Plz Ste 300 San Francisco CA 94111-3406

MATTEUCCI, DOMINICK VINCENT, real estate developer; b. Trenton, N.J., Oct. 19, 1924; s. Vincent Joseph and Anna Marie (Zoda) M.; BS, Coll. of William and Mary, 1948; BS, Mass. Inst. Tech., 1950. Registered profl. engr., Calif.; lic. gen. bldg. contractor, real estate broker; m. Emma Irene DeGuia, Mar. 2, 1968; children: Felisa Anna, Vincent Eriberto. Owner, Matteucci Devel. Co., Newport Beach, Calif.; pres. Nat. Investment Brokerage Co., Newport Beach. Home: 2104 Felipe Newport Beach CA 92660-4040 Office: PO Box 10474 Newport Beach CA 92658-0474

MATTEUCCI, SHERRY SCHEEL, lawyer; b. Columbus, Mont., Aug. 17, 1947; d. Gerald F. and Shirley Scheel; m. William L. Matteucci, Dec. 26, 1969 (div. June 1976); children: Cory, Cody. Student, Kinman Bus. U., 1965-66, Mont. State U., 1967-69, Gonzaga U., 1971-72; BS, Eastern Wash. State U., 1973; JD, U. Mont., 1979. Bar: Mont., U.S. Dist. Ct. Mont., U.S. Ct. Appeals (9th cir.), U.S. Supreme Ct. Mont. Spl. asst. Commr. Higher Edn., 1974-76; assoc. Crowley, Haughey, Hanson, Toole & Dietrich, Billings, Mont., 1979-83, ptnr., 1984-93; U.S. atty. Dist. of Mont., Billings, 1993—; bd. visitors U. Mont. Law Sch., 1988—. Mem. editorial bd. U. Mont. Law Rev., 1977-78, contbg. editor, 1978-79. Bd. dirs. Big Bros. & Sisters, Billings, 1982-85, City/County Library Bd., Billings, 1983—, Billings Community Cable Corp., 1986, chmn., 1987; vice chmn., bd. dirs. Parmley Billings Library Found. Named one of Outstanding Young Women in Am., 1983. Mem. ABA, State Bar Mont. (chmn. jud. polling com. 1985-87, chmn. women's law sect. 1985-86, trustee, sec., treas. 1988—), Yellowstone County Bar Assn. (dir. 1984-87, pres.-elect 1986-87, pres. 1987-88), Billings C. of C. (leadership com. 1986, legis. affairs com. 1984), Mont. Assn. for Female Execs, Mont. Lawyers for Peace. Democrat. Mem. Unitarian Ch. Home: 1804 Virginia Ln Billings MT 59102-3626 Office: PO Box 1478 Billings MT 59103-1478

MATTEY, ANGELA MARIE, author, psychic, educator; b. Springfield, Ohio, Dec. 4, 1941; d. William Joseph and Cecelia Agnes (Duggan) Mayer; m. Thomas John Mattey. BA, U. Urbana, 1961; BS, U. Dayton, 1965. Cert. elem. tchr., Ohio; cert. hypnotherapist, Ariz. Tchr. St. Mary's Cath. Sch., Springfield, Ohio, 1960-61, St. Anthony's Cath. Sch., Dayton, Ohio, 1964-65, Montgomery Co. Pub. Schs., Dayton, 1966-67, Dayton Pub. Schs., 1967-72; co-owner Sun Suzuki, Phoenix, 1973-78; artist Ariz. China Painting Schs., Phoenix, Mesa, 1978-84; psychic Tam Enterprises, Phoenix, 1983-96; practice psychic Tam Enterprises, Ignacio, Colo., 1996—. Author and editor: The Key to Spiritual and Psychic Development, 1993; author: (audio tapes) How to be an Awakened Human, 1996; contbr. on line newsletter. Mem. Ignacio Arts Force, 1997—, Ignacio Artist On Line, 1997—; website coord. and architect Ignacio Cmty. Network, 1996—. Recipient Peggy award Ariz. State Ceramic Assn., 1980. Mem. Internat. New Thought Alliance, Pub. Mktg. Assn., Am. Table Tipping Assn. (dir. 1996). Office: Tam Enterprises PO Box 276 Ignacio CO 81137

MATTHAU, CHARLES MARCUS, film director; b. N.Y.C., Dec. 10, 1964; s. Walter and Carol M. BA, U. So. Calif., 1986. Pres. The Matthau Co., L.A., 1986—. Dir. motion picture; Doin' Time on Planet Earth, 1990 (Saturn award Coun. Film Orgns., Silver Scroll award Acad. Sci. Fiction); dir., producer TV show Mrs. Lambert Remembers Love, 1993 (Golden Angel award Best TV spl. 1993, Golden Medal award Best Drama Prodn. 1993, Grand award The Houston Internat. Film Festival); dir., producer motion picture The Grass Harp, 1996 (recipient Best Dir. Family film awards 1996); dir. over 50 feature shorts. Nat. spokesperson Am. Lung Assn., L.A., 1989—; active Action on Smoking and Health, Washington, 1986—. Recipient Cine award, Coun. Non-Theatrical Events, Washington, 1985, Golden Seal award, London Amateur Film Festival, 1986. Mem. Dirs. Guild Am., Am. Film Inst., Acad. Sci.-Fiction, Fantasy and Horror Films.

MATTHEW, LYN, sales and marketing executive consultant, educator; b. Long Beach, Calif., Dec. 15, 1936; d. Harold G. and Beatrice (Hunt) M.; m. Wayne Thomas Castleberry, Aug. 12, 1961 (div. Jan. 1976); children: Melanie, Cheryl, Nicole, Matthew. BS, U. Calif.-Davis, 1958; MA, Ariz. State U., 1979. Cert. hotel sales exec., 1988, meeting profl. Pres., Davlyn Cons. Found., Scottsdale, Ariz., 1979-82; cons., vis. prof. The Art Bus., Scottsdale, 1982—; pres., dir. sales and mktg. Embassy Stes., Scottsdale, 1987—, bd. trustees Hotel Sales and Mktg. Assn. Internat. Found., 1988—, chmn., 1991-93, mem. exec. com., 1993—; vis. prof. Maricopa C.C., Phoenix, 1979—, Ariz. State U., Tempe, 1980-83; cons. Women's Caucus for Art, Phoenix, 1983-88. Bd. dirs. Rossom House and Heritage Square Found., Phoenix, 1987-88. Author: The Business Aspects of Art, Book I, 1979, Book II, 1979; Marketing Strategies for the Creative Artist, 1985. Mem. Women Image Now (Achievement and Contbn. in Visual Arts award 1983), Women in Higher Edn., Nat. Women's Caucus for Art (v.p. 1981-83), Ariz. Women's Caucus for Art (pres. 1980-82, hon. advisor 1986-87), Ariz. Vocat. Edn. Assn. (sec. 1978-80), Ariz. Visionary Artists (treas. 1987-89), Hotel Sales and Mktg. Assn. Internat. (pres. Great Phoenix chpt. 1988-89, regional dir. 1989-90, bd. dirs. 1985-90), CHSE (profl. designation tng. chair), Meeting Planners Internat. (v.p. Ariz. Sunbelt chpt. 1989-91, pres. 1991-92, Supplier of Yr. award 1988, CMP certification trainer), Soc. Govt. Meeting Planners (charter bd. dirs. 1987, Sam Gilmer award 1992, nat. conf. co-chmn. 1993-94), Ariz. Visionary Artists (treas. 1987-88), Ariz. Acad. Performing Arts (v.p. bd. dirs. 1987-88, pres. 1988-89).

MATTHEWS, DAVID FORT, military weapon system acquisition specialist; b. Lancaster, N.H., Sept. 25, 1944; s. Clinton Fort and Mabel Sawin (Oaks) M.; m. Eva Mae Horton, Nov. 10, 1990. BA, Vanderbilt U., 1966; MA, Mid. Tenn. U., 1973. Cert. acquisition mgr. Rsch. and devel. officer U.S. Army Rsch. Inst., Washington, 1974-77; exec. officer 194th Maintenence Battalion-Camp Humphreys, Korea, 1978-79; career program mgr. U.S. Army Mil. Pers. Ctr., Washington, 1979-82; logistics staff officer Dep. Chief of Staff Logistics, Washington, 1982-83; team chief Chief of Staff Army Study Group, Washington, 1983-85; logistics div. chief Multiple Launch Rocket System Project Office, Huntsville, Ala., 1985-88; comdr. Ordanance Program Div., Riyadh, Saudi Arabia, 1988-90; project mgr. Army Tactical Missile System, Huntsville, 1990-94; sr. lectr. weapon systems acquisition Naval Postgrad. Sch., Monterey, Calif., 1994—. Decorated Legion of Merit, Bronze Star; recipient award as project mgr. of yr. Sec. of Army, 1991. Mem. Am. Ordinance Assn., Am. Def. Prepardness Assn., Assn. U.S. Army. Home: 83 High Meadow Ln Carmel CA 93923 Office: Naval Postgrad Sch Monterey CA 93943

MATTHEWS, EUGENE EDWARD, artist; b. Davenport, Iowa, Mar. 22, 1931; s. Nickolas Arthur and Velma (Schroeder) M.; m. Wanda Lee Miller, Sept. 14, 1952; children: Anthony Lee, Daniel Nickolas. Student, Bradley U., 1948-51; BFA, U. Iowa, 1953, MFA, 1957. Prof. fine arts grad. faculty U. Colo., Boulder, 1961-96, prof. fine arts emeritus, 1996—, dir. vis. artists program, 1985-96; vis. artist Am. Acad. Rome, 1989. One-man shows include U. Wis., Milw., 1960, Brena Gallery, Denver, 1963, 65, 67, 70, 74, 76, 78, 80, 83, 88, Colorado Springs Fine Arts Ctr., 1967, Sheldon Art Gallery, U. Nebr., 1968, Denver Art Mus., 1972, James Yu Gallery, N.Y.C., 1973, 77, Dubins Gallery, L.A., 1981, Galeria Rysunku, Poznan, 1983, CU. Art Galleries, U. Colo., Boulder, 1996; exhibited in numerous group shows U.S., Europe, Africa, Asia; internat. watercolor exhbn. New Orleans, 1983, Louvre, Paris, Met. Mus. of Art, N.Y.C., Internat. Art Ctr., Kyoto, Japan, Mus. of Modern Art, Rijeka, Yugoslavia, Taipei Fine Arts Mus., Taiwan, Republic of China, Internat. Watercolor Biennial-East/West, Champaign, Ill., 1997; represented in permanent collections Nat. Mus. Am. Art, Washington, Denver Art Mus., Butler Inst. Am. Art, Chrysler Art Mus., others. Recipient Penello d'Argento award Acitrezza Internazionale, 1958, S.P.Q.R. Cup of Rome, Roma Olimpionica Internazionale, 1959, Gold medal of honor Nat. Arts Club, N.Y.C., 1969, Bicentennial award Rocky Mountain Nat. Watercolor Exhbn., 1976, Am. Drawings IV Purchase award, 1982, others; fellow in painting Am. Acad. Rome, 1957-60, U. Colo. Creative Rsch. fellow, 1966-67. Mem. Watercolor U.S.A. Honor Soc. (charter). Home: 720 Hawthorn Ave Boulder CO 80304-2140

MATTHEWS, GLENNA CHRISTINE, historian; b. L.A., Nov. 7, 1938; d. Glen Leslie and Alberta Marie (Nicolais) Ingles; m. James Duncan Matthews (div. Jan. 1978); children: Karen, David. BA, San Jose State U., 1969; MA, Stanford U., 1971, PhD, 1977. Assoc. prof. history Okla. State U., 1978-85. Author: Just a Housewife, 1987, The Rise of Public Woman, 1992; co-author: Running as a Woman, 1993. Recipient The Sierra prize Western Assn. Women Historians. Mem. Am. Hist. Assn., Orgn. Am. Historians.

MATTHEWS, KEVIN MICHAEL, architecture educator, researcher; b. Eugene, Oreg., Jan. 5, 1959; s. Herbert Maurice and Jennifer (Saunders) M.; m. Donna Marie Meredith. BA, U.Calif., 1982; MArch, U. Calif., 1988. Intern Esherick, Homsey, Dodge, Davis, San Francisco, 1987; lectr. U. Calif., Berkeley, 1988-89; prin. Matthews Assoc., Berkeley, 1985-90; CAD coord. Superconducting Super Collider, Dallas, 1989; asst. prof. dept. arch. U. Oreg., Eugene, Oreg., 1990—; dir. Design Integration Lab., Eugene, Oreg., 1992—; pres. Artifice, Inc., Eugene, Oreg., 1993—; CAD cons. SSC Central Design Group, Berkeley, 1987-88. Author: The Great Buildings Collection, 1994, DesignWorkshop, 1993. Recipient Rsch. grant Apple Computer Inc., 1991, 92, Curriculum Devel. grant., 1992. Mem. Am. Inst. Arch. (assoc.), Assn. Computing Machinery, Soc. Arch. Historians, Assn. Collegiate Schs. Arch. Office: Design Integration Lab 204 Pacific Hall Eugene OR 97403-1206

MATTHEWS, MARILYN ANN, college development director; b. Anderson, Ind., Dec. 28, 1931; d. Fred and Doris Newbert (Denney) Betz; m. Russell T. Matthews, Jan. 13, 1951 (div. June 1992); children: Linda Ann Morgan, Susan Louise Rae. BS in Art Edn., Minot State U., 1968; MA, U. No. Colo., 1974; MEd, Colo. State U., 1983. Cert. tchr. N.D., Colo. Tchr. R2-J Sch. Dist., Loveland, Colo., 1968-78; slide librarian Colo. State U., Ft. Collins, 1978-80; coord. adult edn. Cen. Wyo. Coll., Riverton, 1984-87; dir. higher edn. Ctr. Carbon County Bd. Higher Edn., Rawlins, Wyo., 1987-90; dir. devel. projects San Juan Coll., Farmington, N.Mex., 1991—; adv. bd. mem. Project Read, Farmington, 1991—, ABE Program, Farmington, 1993-94. Exhibited in shows in N.D., Colo., N.Mex., Wyo., S.D., 1968—; contbr. article to profl. jours. Bd. dirs. N.W. N.Mex. Fine Arts, Farmington, 1992-93, San Juan Coll. Fine Arts, Farmington, 1994—. Recipient Kellogg award U. Ga., 1989-90, Women Helping Women award Soroptimist Internat., 1990, Partnerships award N.Mex. Orton Dyslexia Assn., 1994; Quota Club art scholar, 1965, Mott fellow, 1981. Mem. Am. Assn. Adult Continuing Edn., N.Mex. Adult Edn. Assn., N.Mex. Vocat. Edn. Assn., Nat. Vocat. Edn. Assn., Orton Dyslexia Assn., Mountain Plains Adult Edn. Assn. (bd. dirs.). Republican. Episcopalian. Home: 1603 E 21st St Farmington NM 87401-4337 Office: San Juan Coll 4601 College Blvd Farmington NM 87402-4609

MATTHEWS, NORMAN SHERWOOD, JR., insurance company executive; b. San Antonio, Tex., Apr. 23, 1944; s. Norman Sherwood and Alice Ann (Hathaway) M.; student Middle Tenn. State U., 1962-64, Ventura Coll., 1965, Calif. State U., 1965-66, U. Md., 1968-70; BBA, U. Tex., 1972; postgrad. U. Hawaii, 1977-79; m. Masayo Nakamura, Sept. 1, 1970; children: Debbie Ann, Scott Tsuyoshi. Research asst. State Farm Ins. Co., Murfreesboro, Tenn., 1963-64; inventory control analyst Minn. Mining & Mfg. Co., Camarillo, Calif., 1964-65; sr. acct. Peat, Marwick, Mitchell & Co., Honolulu, 1973-75; dir. mgmt. analysis Hawaii Med. Service Assn., Honolulu, 1975-89; asst. v.p. mgmt. analysis and security Hawaii Med. Svc. Assn., 1989—. With USAF, 1966-70. Decorated Air medal with 8 oak leaf clusters. CPA, Hawaii; cert. internal auditor. Mem. AICPA, Hawaii Soc. CPAs, Am. Mgmt. Assn., Inst. Mgmt. Accts., Inst. Internal Auditors, Info. Sys. Audit and Control Assn. Home: 2724 Kahoaloha Ln Apt 1903 Honolulu HI 96826-3338 Office: Hawaii Med Svc Assn 818 Keeaumoku St Honolulu HI 96814-2365

MATTHEWS, PATRICIA DENEISE, special education educator; b. Salt Lake City, Apr. 25, 1957; d. Eli R. and Dora Santistevan; m. Jed H. Matthews, Apr. 11, 1979; children: Melisa, Tracey, Jennifer, Christine. BS in Edn., U. Utah, 1979, MEd, 1987. Resource tchr. Granite Sch. Dist., Salt Lake City, 1982-90, prevention specialist, 1990—; demonstration tchr., Granite Sch. Dist., Salt Lake City, 1983-85, tchr. mentor spl. edn., 1991-92; aux. faculty dept. edn. U. Utah, Salt Lake City, 1986-90; mem. adv. com. hispanite edn. Utah State Office Edn., Salt Lake City, 1987-88; self contained Learning Disabities and Commn. Disordered educator Taylorsville High School, Salt Lake City, 1995—. Contbr. articles to profl. publs. mem. NEA, Utah Edn. Assn. Office: Granite Sch Dist 340 E 3545 S Salt Lake City UT 84115

MATTHEWS, SHAW HALL, III, reliability engineer; b. Washington, May 29, 1942; s. Shaw Hall Matthews Jr. and Helen Louise (Evans) Floyd; m. Judith Arlene Jones, Aug. 2, 1976; children: Louise Anna, Alyson Ross. BS in Math., U. Ill., Chgo., 1972; MS in Ops. Rsch., Ill. Inst. Tech., 1979. Reliability engr. Zenith Corp., Chgo., 1967-73, reliability engring. mgr., 1973-76; component engring. mgr. Zenith Corp., Glenview, Ill., 1976-79; reliability and quality assurance mgr. Burr-Brown Corp., Tucson, 1979-82; systms reliability mgr. Storage Tech. Corp., Louisville, 1982-93, sys. test mgr., 1994-96; reliability and quality mgr. Tut Syss., Inc., Pleasant Hill, Calif., 1996—; mem. Joint Electron Devices Engring. Coun., 1980-82; chmn., mem. Electronics Adv. Group, State Bd. Community Colls. and Occupational Edn., Colo., 1984-86. Contbr. articles to profl. jours. Mem. Longmont (Colo.) Symphony Orch., 1988—, Mahler Fest Orch., Boulder, Colo., 1988—. Sgt. USAF, 1963-67. Mem. Soc. Applied and Indsl. Math., IEEE (treas. 1974-75).

MATTHEWS, WARREN WAYNE, state supreme court justice; b. Santa Cruz, Calif., Apr. 5, 1939; s. Warren Wayne and Ruth Ann (Maginnis) M.; m. Donna Stearns, Aug. 17, 1963; children: Holly Maginnis, Meredith Sample. A.B., Stanford U., 1961; LL.B., Harvard U., 1964. Bar: Alaska 1965. Assoc. firm Burr, Boney & Pease, Anchorage, 1964-69, Matthews & Dunn, Matthews, Dunn and Baily, Anchorage, 1969-77; assoc. justice Alaska Supreme Ct., Anchorage, 1977—, justice. Bd. dirs. Alaska Legal Services Corp., 1969-70. Mem. Alaska Bar Assn. (bd. govs. 1974-77), ABA, Anchorage Bar Assn. *

MATTHIESEN, DAVID KARL, netware engineer; b. Seattle, May 21, 1967; s. Hal Bruce and Patricia Ann (Stilwell) M. BBA in Mgmt. Info. Sys., Wash. State U., 1989. Cert. netware engr., sys. engr. Analyst Chevron Info. Tech. Co., San Ramon, Calif., 1990-95; cons. Matthiesen Integration Svcs., Danville, Calif., 1995—; franchise developer Internat. Leadership Devel., Danville, 1992—; dir. integration svcs. Master Design & Devel., Inc., San Ramon, 1996—. Contbr. articles to profl. publs. Campaign vol. Dan Evans for Wash. State Senate, 1984; vol. recruiter Pitch, Hit & Run Contest, Dublin, Calif., 1994. Mem. Network Profls. Assn.

MATTICE, JACK SHAFER, electric power research manager; b. Hobart, N.Y., Aug. 25, 1941. BS, SUNY, Stony Brook, 1963; PhD, Syracuse U., 1971. Teaching asst. Syracuse U., 1965-67, rsch. asst., 1967-68, predoctoral fellow, 1968-70; postdoctoral rsch. fellow dept. hydrobiology Inst. Ecology, Warsaw, Poland, 1970-71; rsch. staff mem. Environ. Scis. div. Oak Ridge (Tenn.) Nat. Lab., 1972-81; sr. project mgr. ecol. studies program Elec. Power Rsch. Inst., Palo Alto, Calif., 1981—; adj. asst. prof. Tenn. Technol. U., Cookeville, 1980-81. Author: (with others) Water Chlorination: Environmental Impact and Health Effects, Vol. 1, 1978, Vol. 2, 1978, Vol. 3, 1980, Vol. 5, 1985, Hydropower Engineering Handbook, 1991; editor, author: (with others) Water Chlorination: Environmental Impact and Health Effects, Vol. 4, 1983, Vol. 6, 1990. Mem. AAAS, ASTM, Am. Fisheries Soc., Ecol. Soc. Am., N.Am. Benthological Soc., Soc. Environ. Toxicology and Contamination, Sigma Xi. Office: Elec Power Rsch Inst 3412 Hillview Ave Palo Alto CA 94304-1395

MATTISON, ROSE ELAINE BACOTE, elementary and secondary education educator; b. Kingstree, S.C., Aug. 20; d. Samuel Sheldon and Fannie LaMaude (Wright) B.; m. Willie Williford, Apr. 2, 1967 (div. Nov. 1990); children: Stacey Willette, Sonja Elaine. BA, U. Md., Eastern Shore, 1965. High sch. music tchr. Dorchester County Sch. Dist., Summerville, S.C., 1965-67; 6th grade tchr. Greenville (S.C.) County Schs., 1967-69; math. tchr. Dallas Ind. Sch. Dist., 1971-72; music specialist Aurora (Colo.) Pub. Schs., 1978—. Author: The Journey to Nevis, 1994, One Sided Love Story, 1995. Mem. Delta Sigma Theta.

MATULEF, GIZELLE TERESE, secondary education educator; b. Budapest, Jan. 17, 1945; came to the U.S., 1948; d. Louis and Gizelle Beke; m. Gary Matulef, Mar. 21, 1975; 1 child, Margaret. AA in Bus., Phoenix (Ariz.) Coll., 1964; BS in Edn., No. Ariz. U., 1966; MA, Ind. U., 1970, PhD in Comparative Lit., 1983. Cert. secondary teaching credential, Calif., C.C. instr. credential, Calif. Bus. instr. Drake Bus. Coll., N.Y.C., 1973, Cerro Coso Coll., Ridgecrest, Calif., 1973-74; English and bus. instr. Sawyer Bus. Coll., Westwood, Calif., 1974-75; bus. instr. Sierra Sands Adult Sch., Ridgecrest, 1975-82; Indian edn. dir. Sierra Sands Unifed Sch. Dist., Ridgecrest, 1980-82; sch. improvement program dir. Murray Jr. High Sch., Ridgecrest, 1982-89; English and econs. instr. Trona (Calif.) High Sch., 1989-92; tng. dir. High Desert Experience Unlimited Career Counseling, Ridgecrest, 1991-92; substitute tchr. Sierra Sands Unified Sch. Dist., Ridgecrest, 1993-96; archives asst. Albert Michelson Mus., Naval Weapons Ctr., China Lake, Calif., 1976-77, editorial asst. Tech. Info. Dept., 1977-78. Contbr. articles to profl. jours. Active PTA, Ridgecrest Schs., 1983-93, Music Parents Assn., Ridgecrest, 1985-93. Recipient fellowship Ind. U., Bloomington, 1966-69. Mem. AAUW (pres. China Lake/Ridgecrest br. 1992-96), NEA. Home: 1028 Las Flores Ave Ridgecrest CA 93555

MATUS, NANCY LOUISE, artist; b. Wichita, Kans., Jan. 22, 1955; d. Joseph John and Josephine Emily (Kulina) M.; m. Kenneth Lee Walker, Feb. 14, 1990. AA, Phoenix Coll., 1980; student, U. Ariz., 1978, 79, Ariz. State U., 1984, 85. Exhibited in group shows Ariz. Sate Capitol, Phoenix, 1985, Movimento Artistico del Rio Salado Gallery, Phoenix, 1986, 87, 89, 91, 92, Tempe (Ariz.) Arts Ctr., 1987, U. Ariz., Phoenix, 1987, Nat. Acrylic Painters Assn., Long Beach, Calif., 1996; represented in numerous pvt. collections; represented in Best of Acyrlic Painting, 1996. Mem. Nat. Acrylic Painters Assn. (signature), Knickerbocker Artists (assoc.), Western Acad. Women Artists (assoc.), Cottonwood Country Club. Address: 25802 S Cloverland Dr Chandler AZ 85248

MATZDORFF, JAMES ARTHUR, investment banker, financier; b. Kansas City, Mo., Jan. 3, 1956. BS, U. So. Calif., 1978; MBA, Loyola U., Los Angeles, 1980. Comml. loan officer Bank of Am., Los Angeles, 1976-78; mng. dir. James A. Matzdorff & Co., Beverly Hills, Calif., 1978—. Mem. Rep. Nat. Com., 1980—. Mem. NRA, Am. Fin. Assn., Mercedes Benz Car Club, Harley Davidson Club, Phi Delta Theta. Office: 9903 Santa Monica Blvd Ste 374 Beverly Hills CA 90212-1671

MAUER, CHARLES M., elementary school educator; b. Milw., June 14, 1946; s. Wilbert C. and Idabelle J. (Butterfield) M.; m. Karen L. Mauer, Mar. 25, 1972; children: Paul R., Mark W. BA, St. Martin's Coll., 1968, cert., 1972. Cert. elem. tchr., Wash. Adj. faculty mem. St. Martin's Coll., Lacey, Wash.; elem. sch. specialist in gifted edn. North Thurston Sch. Dist., Lacey, 1979-87; elem. tchr. N. Thurston Sch. Dist., Lacey, 1968—, tchr. elem. gifted program, 1990—; mem. cert. guidelines com. State of Wash., 1986-87; computer instr. Community Enrichment Program, 1990—. Mem. NEA (life). Home: 3916 18th Ave NE Olympia WA 98506-3604

MAUL, TERRY LEE, psychologist, educator; b. San Francisco, May 6, 1946; s. Chester Lloyd and Clella Lucille (Hobbs) M.; AB, U. Calif., Berkeley, 1967, MA, 1968, PhD, 1970; student Coll. San Mateo, 1964-65; m. Gail Ann Retallick, June 27, 1970 (div. Dec. 1986); 1 son, Andrew Eliot. Prof. psychology San Bernardino Valley Coll., San Bernardino, Calif., 1970—, chmn. dept., 1979-82, 96-97; researcher self-actualization. Mem. AAUP (chpt. pres. 1971-73), Am. Psychol. Assn., Audubon Soc., Mensa, Nature Conservancy, Rachel Carson Council, Wilderness Soc., Sierra Club. Democrat. Author: (with Eva Conrad) Introduction to Experimental Psychology, 1981; (with Gail Maul) Beyond Limit: Ways to Growth and Freedom, 1983; contbg. author other psychol. texts. Home: 6155 Bluffwood Dr Riverside CA 92506-4605 Office: San Bernardino Valley Coll 701 S Mount Vernon Ave San Bernardino CA 92410-2705

MAUPIN, BILL, associate justice; children: Allison, Michael. BA, U. Nev., 1968; JD, U. Ariz. Law Sch., 1971. Atty., ptnr. Thorndal, Backus, Maupin and Armstrong, Las Vegas, 1976-93; judge 8th Jud. Dist. Clark County, 1993-97; assoc. justice Supreme Ct. Nev., 1997—; bd. govs. Nev. State Bar, 1991-95. Recipient highest rating for Retention as Dist. Ct. Judge, 1994, 96, Highest Qualitative Ratings, 1996, Las Vegas Review Jour., Clark County Bar Assn. Mem. Nev. Supreme Ct. (study com. to review jud. elections, chair 1995, alternate dispute resolution implementation com. chairperson, 1992-96). Office: Supreme Ct Bldg Carson City NV 89710

MAURER, JOHN IRVING, psychiatrist; b. Madison, Wis., Sept. 10, 1934; s. Irving John and Kathryn (Fischer) M.; m. Linda Collins, Sept. 17, 1961 (div. Jan. 1982); children: Kathryn, Karen Walker, Paul. Student, U. Wis., 1952-53; BS, Stanford U., 1956, MD, 1960. Cert. Am. Bd. Psychiatry. Intern Hartford (Conn.) Hosp., 1960-61; psychiatric resident Stanford Med. Sch., 1961-62, 64-66; staff psychiatrist Stanford Student Health Svcs., 1966-70; ptnr. Palo Alto Med. Clinic, 1966-70; founding dir. Emanuel Cmty. Health Ctr., Turlock, Calif., 1970-73; program dir., psychiatrist Tuolumne County Mental Health Svcs., 1973-74; staff psychiatrist, cons. Stanislaus County Mental Health Svcs., 1974-76; pvt. practice psychiatrist, 1976—; clin. instr. Stanford Med. Ctr., 1966-70; tchg. faculty in psychiatry Scenic Gen. Hosp., 1978-83; cons. Turlock (Calif.) Sch. Sys, 1979-81-86, Tuum Est Drug Treatment Program, 1981; founding med. dir. Crossroads In-Patient Unit, Meml. South Hosp., Ceres, Calif., 1986-87; founding dir. Eating Disorders In-Patient Unit, Modesto (Calif.) Psychiat. Ctr., 1987-88. Contbr. articles to profl. jours. Bd. dirs. Medic Alert Found. Internat., 1961-85, chmn. bd. 1977-78; mem. steering com. Turlock (Calif.) Counseling Ctr., 1977-81; pres., bd. dirs. Turlock Golf and Country Club, 1977-78; co-founding dir. Alcoholism Coun. Stanislaus County/ Nat. Coun. Alcoholism, 1980-81; mem. Stanislaus County Mental Health Adv. Bd., 1980-82. Capt. USAF, 1962-64. Fellow Acad. Psychosomatic Medicine, Am. Psychiat. Assn.; mem. AMA, Calif. Med. Assn., Stanislaus Med. Soc., Internat. Soc. for Study Multiple Personality Disorders, Ctrl. Calif. Psychiat. Soc. (pres. Modesto/Stockton chpt. 1981, 90, nominating com. 1981, 87, exec. coun. 1982). Office: Therapy Offices of Turlock 600 E Main St Ste 220 Turlock CA 95380-4547

MAURER, LAWRENCE MICHAEL, acting school administrator, educator; b. Bklyn., Oct. 2, 1935; s. Charles and Ethel (Ryan) M.; married Mar. 20, 1970 (div. 1971); 1 child, Lalaine; m. Carol Schneider, July 27, 1971. B of Vocat. Edn., San Diego State U., 1976; MS in Sch. Adminstrn., Nat. U., 1981. Cert. sch. adminstr., tchr., c.c. educator, Calif. Commd. ensign USN, 1953; advanced through grades to chief, 1969, ret., 1972; tchr. San Diego County Office Edn., 1972—, acting vice prin., 1989—; bd. dirs. Multi-cultural Affairs Comn., San Diego, 1991—, Self Esteem Devel. C.C., San Diego, 1990—, Vocat. Edn. Commn., San Diego, 1986—; cons. Vocat. Edn. in Ct. Schs., San Diego, 1986—; adj. prof. U. Calif., San Diego; mentor tchrs. in technology San Diego Office Edn., 1996—. Organizer Dem. party. Named Excellent Tchr. of Yr. Corp. for Excellence in Pub. Edn., 1992, mentor Tchr.-Tech., 1996; vocat. grantee, 1988. Mem. ASCD (bd. dirs.), Nat. Vocat. Educators, Calif. Reading Assn., Calif. Ct. Sch. Adminstrs. Home: 98-80 Magnolia Ave Santee CA 92071 Office: San Diego County Office Edn 6401 Linda Vista Rd San Diego CA 92111-7319

MAURICE, ALFRED PAUL, educator, artist; b. Nashua, N.H., Mar. 11, 1921; s. Paul and Gertrude (Martel) M.; m. J. Dolores Robson, Feb. 23, 1946. Student, U. N.H., 1940-42; BA, Mich. State U., 1947, MA, 1950. Muralist Nat. Youth Adminstrn., 1939-40; instr. Macalester Coll., 1947-49; teaching asst. Mich. State U., 1949-50; asst., then assoc. prof. SUNY at New Paltz, 1950-57; exec. dir. Md. Inst., 1957-59; dir. Kalamazoo Inst. Arts, 1959-65; prof. art U. Ill. at Chgo. Circle Campus, 1965-86, prof. emeritus, 1987—, chmn. dept., 1965-67, assoc. dean faculties, 1969-72; acting dean U. Ill. Chgo. Coll. of Architecture and Art, 1975-77; typographer-calligrapher, painter-printmaker, 1947—; art and mus. cons., lectr., 1957—. One-man shows Central Mich. U., 1964, Kalamazoo Inst. Arts, 1976, U. Ill., Chgo., 1982, Bradley U., 1982, Mich. State U., 1983, Chgo. Pub. Library Cultural Ctr., 1983, Joy Horwich Gallery, Chgo., 1984, R.H. Love Gallery, 1988, 89; pub. collection in Libr. of Congress, Washington, So. Ill. U., Edwardsville, Anderson Art Ctr., Ind., Mus. of Contemporary Art, Chgo., Kalamazoo Coll., Kalamazoo Inst. Arts, Portland (Oreg) Art Mus. Bd. dirs. Stuart Town Homes Corp., 1970; mem. Gov. Mich. Council Arts, 1964-65; mem. research bd. Mercy Hosp., Chgo., 1979—; mem. Exec. Service Corps of Chgo., 1989—. Served with AUS, 1942-46. Recipient medal of Honor Audubon Artists, 1984, Flora Merit award Chgo. Hort. Soc., 1986, Reginald Dellow award Union League Club of Chgo. Annual Art Exhbn., 1989. Mem. Nat. Soc. Painters in Casein and Acrylic (Dr. David Soletsky award 1983, Marion de Sola Mendes Meml. award 1985), Pastel Soc. Am. Studio: 104 W 9th St Vancouver WA 98660-3190

MAURICE, DON, personal care industry executive; b. Peoria, Ill., Aug. 29, 1932; s. Imajean (Webster) Crayton; m. Cindalu Jackson, Aug 31, 1990. Student, Loma Linda U., 1984-86; cert. paralegal studies, Calif. State U., San Bernardino, 1994. Lic. hair stylist, skin therapist; cert. paralegal, notary pub. Owner 2 schs. in advanced hair designs, San Diego, 1962-64, D & M Enterprises, Advt. Agy., 1964-78; now cons. D&M Enterprises Advt. Agy.; dist. mgr. AqRo Matic Co. Water Purification Systems, San Diego, 1972-75; profl. sales educator Staypower Industries, San Diego, 1972-76, 3d v.p., 1975-76; regional bus. cons. Estheticians Pharmacology Rsch., Garden Grove, Calif., 1975-81; owner, operator Don Maurice Hair Designs, Hemet, Calif., 1980-83; dir., operator Hair Sytles by Maurice, Loma Linda, Calif., 1984-88; owner, pres. Grooming Dynamics, Redlands, Calif., 1988—; bus cons. Yogurt Place, Paradise Valley, Ariz., 1978-79, others; regular guest Channel 6/Channel 8, San Diego, 1968-78; cons. infomercial Pre-Paid Legal Svcs., Inc., 1994—. Author: The New Look For Men, 1967, The Art of Men's Hair Styling, 1968 (accepted by Library of Congress), Baldness, To Be or Not To Be, 1989. Promoter Spl. Olympics, Hemet, 1981. Sgt. U.S. Army, 1950-53, Korea. Decorated Purple Heart, 1952; named Leading Businessman in His Profession, Union and Evening Tribune, 1969. Mem. Internat. Platform Assn., Christian Businessmen's Assn. Office: Grooming Dynamics PO Box 1279 Loma Linda CA 92354-1279

MAURO, RICHARD FRANK, lawyer, investment manager; b. Hawthorne, Nev., July 21, 1945; s. Frank Joseph and Dolores D. (Kreimeyer) M.; m. LaVonne M. Madden, Aug. 28, 1965; 1 child, Lindsay Anne. AB, Brown U., 1967; JD summa cum laude, U. Denver, 1970. Bar: Colo. 1970. Assoc. Dawson, Nagel, Sherman & Howard, Denver, 1970-72; assoc. Van Cise, Freeman, Tooley & McClearn, Denver, 1972-73, ptnr., 1973-74; ptnr. Hall & Evans, Denver, 1974-81, Morrison & Forester, Denver, 1981-84; of counsel Parcel, Mauro, Hultin & Spaanstra, P.C., Denver, 1984—, pres., 1988-90, of counsel, 1992—; pres. Sundance Oil Exploration Co., 1985-88; exec. v.p. Castle Group, Inc., 1992—; adj. prof. U. Denver Coll. Law, 1981-84. Symposium editor: Denver Law Jour., 1969-70; editor: Colorado Corporation Manual; contbr. articles to legal jours. Pres. Colo. Open Space Coun., 1974; mem. law alumni coun. U. Denver Coll. Law, 1988-91. Francis Wayland scholar, 1967; recipient various Am. jurisprudence awards. Mem. ABA, Colo. Bar Assn., Denver Bar Assn., Colo. Assn. Corp. Counsel. (pres. 1974-75), Am. Arbitration Assn. (comml. arbitrator), Order St. Ives, Denver Athletic Club (bd. dirs. 1986-89). Home: 2552 E Alameda Ave No 128 Denver CO 80209-3320 Office: 475 17th St Ste 750 Denver CO 80202-4017

MAURO, RICHARD JOSEPH, JR., government official; b. Denver, Aug. 12, 1955. BA, U. Colo., 1977, MA, 1981. Rsch. assoc. Colo. Legis. Coun. Staff, Denver, 1981-87; policy analyst Denver Regional Coun. Govts., 1987-93, dir. legis. and membership svc., 1993—. Mem. Internat. City Mgmt. Assn., Am. Soc. Pub. Adminstrn. Office: Denver Regional Coun Govts 2480 W 26th Ave Ste 200B Denver CO 80211-5304

MAUS, JOHN ANDREW, computer systems engineer; b. Whittier, Calif., July 13, 1945; s. Kenneth Waring and Bertha Estella (Eckman) M.; M. Diana Barba, April 16, 1977 (div. May 1, 1983); m. Colette An Moschelle, Nov. 23, 1985; stepchildren: BreAnn, Adam; children: Steven Andrew, Terra An. BA in Physics, U. Calif., Riverside, 1963-67; MS in Physics, San Diego State U., 1967-70. Cert. data processor, 1983. Programmer, analyst San Diego State Found., 1970-72; instr. bus. San Diego State U., 1971-73; systems programmer San Diego State U., San Diego, 1971-74; data processing mgr. M.H. Golden Co., San Diego, 1974-79; computer systems engr. Hewlett-Packard Co., Spokane, Wash., 1979-84, sr. systems engr., 1984-86, network systems engr., 1986-89, sr. tech. cons., 1989—; physics lab. asst. USDA Salinity Lab., Riverside, 1965-67; underwater acoustics programmer Naval Undersea Ctr., San Diego, 1967-70; programmer San Diego Inst. Pathology, 1972-76; adv. com. Computer Sci. Bus. Applications North Idaho Coll., 1989—; mem. career network U. Calif., Riverside, 1990—; dist. tech. com. Nine Mile Falls (Wash.) Sch., 1994—. Author: INTEREX Conference Proceedings, 1989; co-author: Chemical Physics Letters, 1971, Electronic and Atomic Collisions, 1971. Merit badge counselor Spokane chpt. Boy Scouts Am., 1983—. Mem. Assn. Computing Machinery (founder Spokane chpt., chpt. chmn. 1980-82, service award 1981). Home: 12417 W Sunridge Dr Nine Mile Falls WA 99026-9311 Office: Hewlett-Packard Co 1121 N Argonne Rd Ste 121 Spokane WA 99212-2686

MAU-SHIMIZU, PATRICIA ANN, lawyer; b. Honolulu, Jan. 17, 1953; d. Herbert G.K. and Leilani (Yuen) Mau; 1 child, Melissa Rose. B.S., U. San Francisco, 1975; J.D., Golden Gate U., 1979. Bar: Hawaii 1979. Law clk. State Supreme Ct., Honolulu, 1979-80; atty. Bendet, Fidell & Sakai, Honolulu, 1980-81; legis. atty. Honolulu City Council, 1981-83; legi. atty. House Majority Staff Office, Honolulu, 1983-84, dir., 1984-93, chief clk. Hawaii Ho. of Reps., 1993—. Mem. Hawaii Bar Assn., Hawaii Women Lawyers, Jr. League Hawaii. Democrat. Roman Catholic. Home: 7187 Hawaii Kai Dr Honolulu HI 96825-3115 Office: State House Reps 415 S Beretania St Rm 027 Honolulu HI 96813-2407

MAUTER, WARREN EUGENE, chemist, business development manager; b. Denver, Aug. 27, 1953; s. Jacob Martin and Harriette June (Kaiser) M.; m. Deborah Lee Long, Jan. 22, 1983 (div. 1987). BS in Chemistry, Met. State Coll., 1976; MS in Engring., U. Colo., 1980, MBA, 1986. Cert. rsch. technician, rsch. chemist. Rsch. chemist Manville Corp., Denver, 1973-80, group leader, 1980-83; applications mgr. Cardinal Chem., Columbia, S.C., 1983-84; prin. Alpine Cons., Denver, 1984-88; corp. mgr. COBE Labs., Inc., Lakewood, Colo., 1988—; instr. econs. and fin. U. Colo. Coll. Engring, 1987-89; mem. bd. advisors. Shuck Found., 1986-88. Bd. reviewers Jour. Vinyl Tech., 1981-83; contbr. articles to profl. jours. Sci. and Tech. Colo. scholar Met. State Coll., 1971-74. Mem. ASTM, Soc. Plastics Engrs. (bd. dirs. vinyl div. 1982-86), Nat. Sanitation Found. (industry adv. bd. 1980-84), Am. Chem. Soc., Am. Mgmt. Assn., Colo. Mountain Club, U. Colo. Execs. Club (Denver, v.p. 1987, pres. 1988). Republican. Home: 1649 S Marion St Denver CO 80210-2752 Office: COBE Labs Inc 1185 Oak St Lakewood CO 80215-4407

MAUZY, MICHAEL PHILIP, environmental consultant, chemical engineer; b. Keyser, W.Va., Nov. 14, 1928; s. Frank and Margery Ola (Nelson) M.; m. Nancy Shepherd Watson, Mar. 27, 1949; children: Michael P. Jr., Jeffrey A., Rebecca A. BSChemE, Va. Poly. Inst., 1950; MSChemE, U. Tenn., 1951. Registered profl. engr., Va., Ill. With Monsanto Co., St. Louis, 1951-71, dir. engring. and mfg., 1968-71; mgr. comml. devel. Kummer Corp., Creve Coeur, Mo., 1971-72; mgr. labs. Ill. EPA, Springfield, 1972-73, mgr. water pollution control, 1973-74, mgr. environ. programs, 1974-77, dir., 1977-81; v.p. Roy F. Weston, Inc., West Chester, Pa., 1981-88, Vernon Hills, Ill., 1988-93, Albuquerque, 1993—; also bd. dirs. Roy F. Weston, Inc., West Chester, Pa.; bd. dirs. DeTox Internat. Corp., St. Charles, Ill.; provider Congl. testimony, 1974-81; presenter various workshops, symposia and seminars, 1974—. Contbr. articles on environ. mgmt. to profl. publs., 1974—. Mem. Ohio River Valley Water Sanitary Commn., Cin., 1976-81. 1st lt. U.S. Army, 1951-53. Recipient Environ. Quality award Region V, U.S. EPA, Chgo., 1976, Disting. Svc. award Cons. Engrs. Coun. of Ill., 1978, Ill. award Ill. Assn. Sanitary Dists., 1979, Clarence W. Klassen award Ill. Assn. Water Pollution Control Ops., 1984. Mem. Am. Pub. Works Assn., Am. Inst. Chem. Engring., Water Pollution Control Assn., Am. Mgmt. Assn.

MAVADY, KAYKHAM, electrical engineer, drafting; b. Savannakhet, Laos, Sept. 15, 1970; came to U.S., 1979; s. Phom and Keo M. Cert., Area Tech. Trade Ctr., 1988; BS, U. the Pacific, 1993. Head tech. asst. U. the Pacific, Stockton, Calif., 1990-93; drafting tech., WAN/LAN adminstr. Honeywell, Las Vegas, Nev., 1993—; project mgr. Centurion Integrated Systems, Las Vegas, 1997—. Mem. IEEE (v.p. 1992), Order of the Engr. Republican. Office: Centurion Integrated Sys 3147 W Post Las Vegas NV 89118

MAVROS, GLENN SCOTT, insurance agency executive; b. Chgo., Feb. 18, 1948; s. Andrew John and Dorothy Jane (Fechtman) M.; m. Lucy Jane Ludlow, July 12, 1976 (div. 1980); children: Christopher Glenn, Laura Jane; m. Ellen Mary Torrence, Nov. 12, 1988; 1 child, Alyssa Jane. Student, Monmouth (Ill.) Coll., 1970. Underwriter Chubb & Sons, Inc., Chgo., 1970-74; account exec. Heil & Heil, Inc., Evanston, Ill., 1974-78; v.p. Jardine Ins., L.A., 1978-83; pres. Glenn S. Mavros Ins. Svcs., Inc., Torrance, Calif., 1983—. Mem. Profl. Ins. Agents Assn. Lutheran. Office: Glenn S Mavros Ins Svcs Inc 23720 Arlington Ave Ste 5 Torrance CA 90501-6124

MAWHINNEY, CHARLES HENRY, III, computer science educator; b. Washington, Pa., Apr. 14, 1943; s. Charles Henry Jr. and Margaret Rose (Trembour) M.; m. Mary Lou Bloom, Apr. 3, 1964 (div. Apr. 1974); children: Margaret Lucille Barta, Charles Henry IV; m. Annette M. Lege, Aug. 27, 1982; 1 child, Michael David. Student, U.S. Naval Acad., Annapolis, 1961-64; BS in Math., Carnegie Inst. Tech., 1967; MBA, U. Pitts., 1970, PhD in Bus., 1986. Rsch. asst. B.F. Drakenfeld (Hercules, Inc.), Washington, Pa., 1964-69; lectr. Ahmadu Bello U., Zaria, Nigeria, 1972-73; assoc. prof. Ind. U. of Pa., 1974-86; asst. prof. Bentley Coll., Waltham, Mass., 1986-91; assoc. prof. Met. State Coll. Denver, 1991-95, prof., 1995—; part-time lectr. Robert Morris Coll., Pitts., 1974, U. Pitts., 1971, 74; ptnr. Bear Enterprises, Indiana, Pa., 1983-86, Littleton, Colo., 91—; book reviewer CBS Coll. Pub., N.Y.C., 1986, Wm. C. Brown Pubs., Dubuque, Iowa, 1990, Bus. Media Resources, Corte Madera, Calif., 1991; grant reviewer Yankee Ingenuity Initiative, Conn. Innovations, Inc., Dept. Econ. Devel., 1992, 93; jour. reviewer Jour. of MIS, Comms. of the Assn. of Computing Machinery, Jour. Mgmt. Sys., Jour. of End User Computing. Author: A Modular Approach to dBASE III Plus, 1989, A Modular Approach to dBASE IV-MS DOS Version, 1992; author: (with G. Miller) The Boston SIM Information Management Careers Prototype Videotape, 1990, (with D.R. Callaghan, D.R. Chand and C. Whitcomb) A Modular Approach to DOS, Wordstar 5.5, Lotus 1-2-3 Version 2.2, and dBASE IV, 1992; mem. editl. bd. Jour. Computer Pers. Rsch.; contbr. articles to profl. jours. Bd. dirs. Ken-Caryl Fond., 1993—; mem. hogback fundraising com., 1992—. Mem. Inst. Mgmt. Sci., Assn. for Computing Machinery, Decision Scis. Inst., Soc. for Info. Mgmt., Info Resources Mgmt. Assn., Assn. Computing Educators, Internat. Bus. Schs. Computer Assn., Am. Prodn. and Inventory Control Soc. (v.p. advanced planning PIts. chpt. 1982-83), Beta Gamma Sigma. Office: Met State Coll Denver PO Box 193362 Campus Box 45 Denver CO 80217

MAXCY, LAWRENCE STAHL, education administrator; b. Rochester, N.Y., May 28, 1935; s. William Frank and Gertrude (Stahl) M.; m. Carol Marie Silvernail, June 1, 1957; children: Ann, Lee, Frank, Paul, Mark. AB, Syracuse U., 1958, MPA, 1960. Administr. NIH, Bethesda, Md., 1960-62; administrv. officer NIH Latin Am. Office, Rio de Janeiro, 1962-66; administr. NIH, Bethesda, Md., 1966-68; asst. to dean U. Calif. Div. Natural Scis., Santa Cruz, Calif., 1968-91. Contbr. articles to popular mags. Pres. Santa Cruz Schs. Pers. Commn., 1975-81; active Santa Cruz Vol. Ctr., 1981-91 (pres. 1987-89), Santa Cruz County (Oreg.) Grand Jury, 1988-89; mktg. specialist, dist. coord. So. Oreg. Assn. Retired Persons Tax-Aide program, 1995-97, Oreg. state coord. AARP Tax-Aide program, 1997—. Democrat. Home: 221 Dick George Rd Cave Junction OR 97523-9619

MAXEY, DIANE MEADOWS, artist; b. Lufkin, Tex., Feb. 26, 1943; d. Warren Gaston and Jackie Meadows; m. William Brant Maxey, Sept. 5, 1964; children: Dananne, Robert Warren. BA in Art and Edn., U. North Tex., 1965; postgrad., U. Tex., Arlington, Tex. Tech U., Lubbock; studied with Al Brouilette, Bud Biggs, Edgar Whitney, Dick Phillips, Robert E. Wood, Rex. Brandt, Milford Zornes. Art tchr. Dallas Pub. Schs., 1965-66; substitute tchr. Arlington Pub. Schs., 1969-72; pvt. classes San Angelo, Tex., 1973-77, Scottsdale, Ariz., 1978-92; owner Maxi Watercolor Studio, Paradise Valley, 1978—, Bandanna Tours, Scottsdale, 1988-91; mem. staff Scottsdale

Artist Sch., The Sherman Art Ctr., North Coast Art Ctr., Dillman's Art Found. Exhibited at Gold Nuggett Art Gallery, Wickenburg, Ariz.; featured artist in Freshening Your Paintings with New Techniques, Fresh Flowers—The Best of Flower Painting. Dir. visual ministry First So. Bapt. Ch., Scottsdale, 1988-95. Recipient numerous awards. Mem. Western Fedn. Watercolor Soc. (gen. chmn. 1981-82), Southwestern Watercolor Assn. (signature), Ariz. Artist Guild (hon. life; pres. 1982-83), Ariz. Watercolor Assn., Tex. Watercolor Assn. (signature), 22 x 30 Profl. Critique Group. Home and Office: Maxi Watercolor Studio 7540 N Lakeside Ln Paradise Valley AZ 85253-2857

MAXIM, DAVID NICHOLAS, artist; b. L.A., May 11, 1945; s. Ernest and Lorraine Mary (Bley) M.; life ptnr. Walter Henry Gorman. BA, UCLA, 1966, MA, 1968; postgrad., U. Calif., Santa Barbara, 1970-71. Exhibited in group shows, including Deutschen Architectur Mus., Frankfurt, Germany, 1985, Carnegie Inst. Art, Pitts., 1988, Kunstverein, Heidenheim, Germany, 1993, U. Calif.-Berkeley Mus., Danville, 1994; represented in permanent collections Mus. for Modern Art, Frankfurt, Brit. Mus., London, Graphische Sammlung Albertina, Vienna, Austria, Carnegie Inst. Art, Sam Francisco Mus. Modern Art, Fine Arts Mus. San Francisco, Sunrise Mus., Charleston, W.Va., Oakland (Calif.) Mus., San Jose (Calif.) Mus., Long Beach (Calif.) Mus. Art. Home: 224 Guerrero St San Francisco CA 94103-2313

MAXSON, ROBERT C., university president. Former sr. v.p. acad. affairs U. Houston Systems, Houston; pres. U. Nev., Las Vegas, 1984-94, Calif. State U., Long Beach, 1994—. Office: Calif St Univ Long Beach 1250 N Bellflower Blvd Long Beach CA 90840-0006*

MAXWELL, DONALD STANLEY, publishing executive; b. L.A., May 30, 1930; s. Harold Stanley and Margaret (Trenam) M.; m. Martha Helen Winn, Dec. 5, 1952; children: Sylvia Louise, Cynthia Lynn, Bruce Stanley, Bradley Erl, Walter James, Wesley Richard, Amy Bernice. Student, Long Beach City Coll., 1948-50; BBA, Woodbury Coll., 1956; D of Bus. Adminstrn. (hon.), Woodbury U., 1991. CPA. Ptnr. Robert McDavid & Co. (CPAs), L.A., 1955-61; controller Petersen Pub. Co., L.A., 1961-68; v.p. fin. Petersen Pub. Co., 1969; controller L.A. Times, 1969-79; v.p. Los Angeles Times, 1977-79, v.p. fin., 1979-81; asst. treas. Times Mirror Co., 1971-82, v.p., controller, 1982-87, v.p., chief acctg. officer, 1987-93, v.p., 1993, exec. dir. fin. program, 1993-95; ret., 1995. Trustee Woodbury U., 1981—, chmn. bd. trustees, 1984-87. Served with AUS, 1950-52. Mem. Fin. Execs. Inst. (dir. 1979-82, pres. L.A. chpt. 1973-74), Internat. Newspaper Fin. Execs. (dir. 1978-82, pres. 1980-81), Am. Inst. CPAs, Calif. Soc. CPAs, Am. Horse Council, Internat. Arabian Horse Assn., Arabian Horse Assn. So. Calif., Friendly Hills Country Club. Republican. Baptist. Home: 2160 Le Flore Dr La Habra CA 90631-8020

MAXWELL, MARILYN JULIA, elementary education educator; b. Flint, Mich., Apr. 3, 1933; d. Clement Daniel and Gwendoline Mae (Evans) Rushlow; m. Dewey Theodore Maxwell, Apr. 22, 1965; 1 child, Bruce Dewey. Student, Baldwin-Wallace Coll., 1951-53; BS, U. Tenn., 1954-56, MEd, 1962. Cert. elem. edn. tchr.; lang. devel. specialist. Elem. tchr. Guy Selby Sch., Flint, Mich., 1956-58, Henry L. Barger Sch., Chattanooga, Tenn., 1958-63, Dept. of Def. Sch., Seville, Spain, 1963-65, Loma Vista Elem. Sch., Lompoc, Calif., 1965-66, Crestview Elem. Sch., Lompoc, 1966-68, LaHonda Elem. Sch., Lompoc, 1969—; lang. arts mentor tchr. Lompoc Unified Schs., 1985-86. Mem. Internat. Reading Assn., Nat. Coun. Tchrs. of Math., Calif. Tchrs. of English to Speakers of Other Langs., Nat. Trust for Hist. Preservation, Am. Fedn. Tchrs. Home: 4219 Centaur St Lompoc CA 93436-1229 Office: LaHonda Elem Sch 1213 N A St Lompoc CA 93436-3514

MAXWELL, MARY SUSANNA, psychology educator; b. Dallas, Mar. 28, 1948; d. Otis Allen and Emma Vee (Dunlap) M.; m. Barry Lafean Lutz, July 25, 1981. BA, U. Tex., 1970, PhD, 1978. Lic. psychologist, Ariz. Asst. prof. psychology No. Ariz. U., Flagstaff, 1978-85, dir. sch. psychology programs, 1979-85, assoc. prof., 1985-89, cons. personnel dept., 1984-86, prof., 1989—; coord. grad. programs Ctr. Excellence in Edn., Flagstaff, 1987-89; assoc. dean Coll. Social and Behavioral Scis. No. Ariz. U., Flagstaff, 1991-93; dean Coll. Social and Behavioral Scis., 1993—; editorial cons. Holt, Rinehart & Winston, 1980-81, MacMillan, 1984. Mem. editorial bd. Sch. Psychology Rev., 1983-87. Recipient Pres.'s award for Outstanding Faculty, 1986. Mem. Am. Psychol. Assn., Nat. Assn. Sch. Psychologists, Ariz. Assn. Sch. Psychologists (exec. bd. 1983, 87-89, No. regional dir. Pres. award 1983), Ariz. State Psychol. Assn. (exec. bd. 1992-94), Coun. Dirs. Sch. Psychology Programs (exec. bd. 1984-87, 88-91). Democrat. Home: 3340 S Skye Way Flagstaff AZ 86001-9115

MAXWELL, RAYMOND ROGER, accountant; b. Parmer County, Tex., Jan. 7, 1918; s. Frederick W. and Hazel Belle (Rogers) M.; m. Jeanne Hollarn, June 16, 1945 (dec. Dec. 1987); children: Donald R., Bruce Edward, Sabrina G. Ed.B., Western Ill. State Tchrs Coll., 1941; MBA in Acctg., U. Fla., 1949; postgrad., UCLA, 1965-68. CPA, Fla., Calif. Asst. to bus. mgr. Western Ill. State Tchrs. Coll., Macomb, 1939-41; apprentice acct. Charles H. Lindfors, CPA, Ft. Lauderdale, Fla., 1946-48; acct./auditor Frederic Dunn-Rankin & Co. CPA, Miami, Fla., 1948-49; CPA staff Charles Costar, CPA, Miami, 1951; resident auditor/CPA prin. Raymond R. Maxwell CPA, Ft. Lauderdale, 1951-56; supt. pub. instrn. Broward County, Ft. Lauderdale, 1956-61; staff asst. in fin. North Am. Aviation, Inc., El Segundo, Calif., 1961-65; tchr. Calif. Polytechnic, 1967; acctg. prin. Raymond R. Maxwell, CPA, Whittier, Calif., 1968—; tchr. Calif. State U., Fullerton, 1989; part-time rsch. asst. UCLA, 1965, teaching asst., 1966, 67; instr. Calif. Poly., 1967. Active precinct election bds., Whittier, L.A. County, 1989; 1st reader First Ch. of Christ, Scientist, Whittier, 1990-92, 96—, exec. bd., 1989, exec. bd. chmn., 1993, participant Bible Explorations, 1991-92. 1st lt. USAAF, 1942-46. Named Eagle Scout. Republican. Office: 8235 Painter Ave Whittier CA 90602-3108 *One, with God, is a majority.*

MAXWELL-BROGDON, FLORENCE MORENCY, school administrator, educational adviser; b. Spring Park, Minn., Nov. 11, 1929; d. William Frederick and Florence Ruth (LaBrie) Maxwell; m. John Carl Brogdon, Mar. 13, 1957; children: Carole Alexandra, Cecily Ann, Daphne Diana. B.A., Calif. State U., L.A., 1955; MS, U. So. Calif., 1957; postgrad. Columbia Pacific U., San Rafael, Calif., 1982-86. Cert. tchr., Calif. Dir. Rodeo Sch., L.A., 1961-64; lectr. Media Features, Culver City, Calif., 1964—; dir. La Playa Sch., Culver City, 1968-75; founding dir. Venture Sch., Culver City, 1974—, also chmn. bd.; bd. dirs., v.p. Parent Coop. Preschools, Baie d'Urfe Que., Can., 1964—; del. to Ednl. Symposium, Moscow-St. Petersburg, 1992, U.S./China Joint Conf. on Edn., Beijing, 1992, Internat. Confedn. of Prins., Geneva, 1993, Internat. Conf., Berlin, 1994. Author: Let Me Tell You, 1973; Wet'n Squishy, 1973; Balancing Act, 1977; (as Morency Maxwell) Framed in Silver, 1985; (column) What Parents Want to Know, 1961—; editor: Calif. Preschooler, 1961-74; contbr. articles to profl. jours. Treas. Democrat Congl. Primary, Culver City, 1972. Mem. Calif. Council Parent Schs. (bd. dirs. 1961-74), Parent Coop. Preschools Internat. (advisor 1975—), Pen Ctr. USA West, Mystery Writers of Am. (affiliate), Internat. Platform Assn., Nat. Assn. Secondary Sch. Prins., Libertarian. Home: 10814 Molony Rd Culver City CA 90230-5451 Office: Venture Sch 5333 Sepulveda Blvd Culver City CA 90230-5215

MAY, CLIFFORD DANIEL, newspaper editor, journalist; m. Lou Ann Brunwasser; children: Miranda Rose, Evan Phillip Barr. Cert. in Russian lang. and lit., U. Leningrad, 1972; BA, Sarah Lawrence Coll., 1973; M Journalism, Columbia U., 1975, M Internat. Affairs, 1975. Assoc. editor Newsweek, 1975-78; roving fgn. corr. Hearst Newpapers, 1978-79; sr. editor Am. edit. Geo mag., 1979-80; gen. editor Sunday Mag., Washington corr. N.Y. Times, 1980-89; chief West Africa bur. N.Y. Times, Abidjan, Ivory Coast, 1984; assoc. editor Rocky Mountain News, Denver, 1989—; spl. corr. CBS Radio News, Bill Moyers' Jour./Internat. Report-PBS-TV, 1970's; host, prodr. Roundtable, Sta. KRMA, Colo.; freelance writer, 1979-89. Contbg. editor World Press Rev. Mag.; host, prodr. roundtable Sta. KRMA, Denver, 1994—; host Race for the Presidency TCI News, 1995-96. Office: Rocky Mountain News 400 W Colfax Ave Denver CO 80204-2607

MAY, EUGENE FRANK, neuro-ophthalmologist; b. New Orleans, Jan. 28, 1961; s. Martin M. and Renate A. (Teichman) M.; m. Patricia A. Shuster, Aug. 26, 1990; children: Allan J., Nathan S., Emma S. BS in Engring., Tulane U., 1982; MD, U. Chgo., 1987. Diplomate Am. Bd. Psychiatry and Neurology, 1992, Nat. Bd. Med. Examiners. Commd. 2nd lt. U.S. Army, 1987, advanced through grades to maj., 1993; intern Walter Reed Army Med. Ctr., Washington, 1987-88, resident in neurology, 1988-91; neuro-ophthalmologist Madigan Army Med. Ctr., Tacoma, 1992—. Mem. AMA, Am. Acad. Neurology, Am. Acad. Ophthalmology, N.Am. Neuro-Ophthalmology (assoc.). Office: Polyclinic 1145 Broadway Seattle WA 98122

MAY, LAWRENCE EDWARD, lawyer; b. N.Y.C., Aug. 7, 1947; s. Jack and Ann Marie (Schnell) M.; m. Rosalind Marsha Israel, Feb. 3, 1979; children: Jeremy, Lindsey. BA, UCLA, 1969, JD, 1972. Bar: Calif. 1972, N.Y. 1973. Assoc. Paul, Weiss, Rifkind, Wharton & Garrison, N.Y.C., 1972-76, Levine, Krom & Unger, Beverly Hills, Calif., 1976-79, Weissburg & Aronson, L.A., 1979-81, Valensi & Rose, L.A., 1981-83; ptnr. Pollet & May, L.A., 1983-84; prin. Lawrence E. May, P. C., L.A., 1984—; bd. dirs. Pub. Counsel, 1989—, pres., 1995-96. Mem. editorial adv. bd. L.A. Jewish Jour., 1985-91, adv. bd. L.A. Area Coun. Boy Scouts Am., 1985—, exec. com. Pacific S.W. Region Anti-Defamation League, 1985—. Mem. State Bar Calif., Los Angeles County Bar Assn. (trustee 1987-88, pro bono coun. 1995—), Beverly Hills Bar Assn. (bd. govs. 1981-90, pres. 1988-89, chmn. bus. law sect. 1984-85). Democrat. Office: Ste 800 10100 Santa Monica Blvd Los Angeles CA 90067-6037

MAY, MICHAEL WAYNE, technical school executive; b. Springhill, La., Mar. 31, 1949; s. Willie Wilmer and Ethel Florene (Sigler) M. Student So. Ark. U., 1968-70, La. Tech. U., 1970-71. Prodn. dir. Sta. KKAM, Pueblo, Colo., 1973-75; quality control dir. Sta. KBOZ, Bozeman, Mont., 1975-78; music dir., dir. rsch., disk jockey Sta. KOOK, Billings, Mont., 1978-80; founder, operator May Tech. Coll., Billings, Great Falls, 1980—; owner Sta. KMAY, Billings, Mont. Mem. Career Coll. Assn. (state capt. for Mont.). Author: Building with the Basics: Radio Personality Development, 1979, Radio Personality Basics, 1992. Home: 80 Skyline Dr Billings MT 59105-3038 Office: PO Box 127 Billings MT 59103-0127

MAY, PHILIP ALAN, sociology educator; b. Bethesda, Md., Nov. 6, 1947; s. Everette Lee and Marie (Lee) M.; m. Doreen Ann Garcia, Sept. 5, 1972; children: Katrina Ruth, Marie Ann. BA in Sociology, Catawba Coll., 1969; MA in Sociology, Wake Forest U., 1971; PhD in Sociology, U. Mont., 1976. NIMH predoctoral fellow U. Mont., Missoula, 1973-76; dir. health stats. and rsch. Navajo Health Authority, Window Rock, Ariz., 1976-78; asst. prof. U. N.Mex., Albuquerque, 1978-82, assoc. prof., 1982-89, prof., 1989—, dir. Ctr. on Alcoholism, Substance Abuse and Addictions, 1990—; mem. fetal alcohol syndrome study com., Inst. of Medicine/Nat. Acad. Scis., 1994-95; cons. various govt. agys., 1976—; dir. Nat. Indian Fetal Alcohol Syndrome Prevention Program, Albuquerque, 1979-85; mem. adv. bd. Nat. Orgn. on Fetal Alcohol Syndrome, Washignton, 1990—; rsch. assoc. Nat. Ctr. for Am. Indian and Alaska Native Mental Health Rsch., 1986—. Contbr. chpts. to books and articles to profl. jours. Mem. Ctrl. United Meth. Ch., Albuquerque, 1980-90, First United Meth. Ch., Albuquerque, 1990—. Lt. USPHS, 1970-73. Recipient Spl. Recognition award U.S. Indian Health Svc., 1992, award Navajo Tribe and U.S. Indian Health Svc., 1992, Human Rights Promotion award UN Assn., 1994, Program award for Contbns. to Mental Health of Am. Indians, U.S. Indian Health Svc., 1996. Mem. APHA, Am. Sociol. Assn., Population Ref. Bur., Coll. on Problems of Drug Dependence. Home: 4610 Idlewilde Ln SE Albuquerque NM 87108-3422 Office: U NMex CASAA 2350 Alamo Ave SE Albuquerque NM 87106-3202

MAYBAY, DUANE CHARLES, recycling systems executive; b. Ft. Dodge, Iowa, Oct. 5, 1922; s. John H. and Florabel (Hibbard) Lungren; m. Mary Tribble Parrish, Dec. 18, 1947 (div. Oct. 1972); children: Tina Biggs, Karen Woodward. BA in Mktg., U. Wis., 1948. Product engr. Gates Rubber Co., Denver, 1948-50; asst. dir. sales & mktg. Hi-C divsn. Hi-C and Snow Crop Divsn. Minute Maid Corp., N.Y.C., 1951-63; mktg. dir. Knudsen Foods, L.A., 1963-70; owner Mountain Foods, Altadena, Calif., 1970-76, Maybay Recycling Sys., Irvine, Calif., 1976-84; ptnr. Resource Recovery Sys., Irvine, 1984—. Served to lt. col. U.S. Army Air Corps, 1943-45, Italy. Home: 104 Pergola Irvine CA 92612-1704 Office: Resource Recovery Sys PO Box 17426 Irvine CA 92623

MAYBERG, STEPHEN W., state agency administrator. Dir. Calif. Mental Health Svcs. Office: Dept Mental Health Health & Welfare Agy 1600 9th St Rm 151 Sacramento CA 95814

MAYBERRY, HERBERT SYLVESTER, lawyer; b. Enid, Okla., Jan. 20, 1927; s. Herbert Sylvester and Pearl Wilma (Bridal) M.; m. Gladys Anne Cody, Nov. 21, 1951 (div. Feb. 1974); children: Martha Rebecca, Molly Nanette; m. Joan Wilma Burnette, Dec. 28, 1974. BS in Geology, U. Okla., 1949; JD, U. Denver, 1959. Bar: Colo. 1959, Tex. 1979. Geologist Shell Oil Co., Denver, 1949-58; mgr. Ball Assocs. Ltd., Denver, 1958-65; exec. asst. Western Geophys. Co., Shreveport, La., 1965-66; v.p., gen. counsel, sec. McAlester (Okla.) Fuel Co., 1966-81; assoc. gen. counsel Enstar Corp., Houston, 1977-84; v.p., gen. counsel, sec. Ultramar Oil and Gas Co., Houston, 1985-89; pvt. practice Grand Junction, Colo., 1989—. With USNR, 1945-46. Mem. ABA, Am. Assn. Petroleum Geologists, Am. Inst. Profl. Geologists. Home: 1701 Cortland Ct Grand Junction CO 81506

MAYER, GEORGE ROY, educator; b. National City, Calif., Aug. 28, 1940; s. George Eberly and Helen Janet (Knight) M.; m. Barbara Ann Fife, Sept. 9, 1964 (div. June 1986); children: Kevin Roy, Debbie Rae Ann; m. Jocelyn Volk Finn, Aug. 3, 1986. BA, San Diego State U., 1962; MA, Ind. U., 1965, EdD, 1966. Cert. sch. psychologist; registered behavior analyst. Sch. counselor, psychologist Ind. U., Bloomington, 1964-66; asst. prof. guidance and ednl. psychology So. Ill. U., Carbondale, 1966-69; prof. edn. Calif. State U., L.A., 1966—; cons. in field; mem. adv. bd. Dept. Spl. Edn., L.A., 1986—, Alamansor Edn. Ctr., Alhambra, Calif., 1986-90, Jay Nolan Ctr. for Autism, Newhall, Calif., 1975-86; lectr. in field. Co-author: Behavior Analysis for Lasting Change, 1991; contbr. articles to profl. jours. Recipient Outstanding Prof. award Calif. State U.-L.A., 1988; U.S. Dept. Edn. grantee, 1996—. Mem. ACA (elem. conf. coord.), Assn. for Behavior Analysis, Nat. Assn. Sch. Psychologists, Calif. Assn. Behavior Analysis (pres., treas.), Calif. Assn. Sch. Psychologists (chmn. practitioners conf. 1994—). Home: 10600 Pinyon Tujunga CA 91042

MAYER, HERBERT CARLETON, JR., computer consultant; b. Newton, Mass., Aug. 2, 1922; s. Herbert Carleton and Elsie Marie (Hauser) M.; m. Maryetta Brodkord, Aug. 21, 1948; children: Judith Marie, Christine Louise. BS, Parsons Coll., 1943; MS, U. Iowa, 1947; PhD, U. So. Calif., 1975. Instr. math. U. Idaho, Moscow, 1947-48, U. Utah, Salt Lake City, 1949-51; edn. adminstr. Gen. Electric co., Richland, Wash., 1951-59; systems engr., univ. industry specialist IBM, Chgo., 1959-81; assoc. prof. mgmt. info. systems Wash. State U., Pullman, 1980-82; assoc. prof. U. Wis.-Parkside, Kenosha, 1982-85, Eastern Wash. U., Cheney, 1985-90; adj. prof. mgmt. U. Tex., El Paso, 1976-78. Pres. Tri-City Heights Assn., Kennewick, Wash., 1956-58, PTA, Kennewick, 1957-58; v.p. Kennewick Sch. Bd., 1958-59, pres., 1959. Mem. Math. Assn. Am., Internat. Assn. Computing in Edn., Am. Soc. Engring. Edn., Data Processing Mgmt. Assn. (bd. dirs., sec. Spokane chpt. 1988, v.p. edn. Spokane chpt. 1989, v.p. student chpt. 1990), Manito Lions Spokane (membership chmn. 1991-92, program chmn. 1992-93, v.p. 1993—), Phi Delta Kappa (found. chmn. Spokane chpt. 1992-94). Home: 3334 S Bernard St Spokane WA 99203-1636

MAYER, NEIL STEPHEN, economist, consultant; b. Milw., May 13, 1947; s. Arnold M. and Edith I. (Franks) M.; m. Loduskia R. Pierce, Mar. 27, 1983; 1 child, Jeremy Pierce. BA, Harvard U., 1968; PhD, U. Calif., Berkeley, 1978. Analyst Congl. Budget Office, Washington, 1975-77; sr. rsch. assoc. Urban Inst., Washington, 1977-85; cons. Neil S. Mayer and Assocs., Berkeley, 1980-85; dir. econ. devel. City of Berkeley, 1985-91, dir. cmty. devel., 1991-95; pres. Neil Mayer and Assocs., 1995—. Author: Keys to the Growth of Neighborhood Development Organizations, 1981, Neighborhood Organizations and Community Development, 1984; contbr. articles to profl. jours. Mem. Berkeley Planning Commn., 1972-75; chair Bay Area Housing Support Collaborative, San Francisco, 1991—; mem. no. Calif. adv. bd. Local Initiatives Support Group, San Francisco, 1985—. NSF resident scientist, Berkeley, 1980-82; Nat. Merit scholar, 1964-68. Mem. Am. Econ. Assn., Am. Planning Assn., Nat. Cmty. Devel. Assn. Democrat. Jewish. Home: 1039 Sierra St Berkeley CA 94707-2526 Office: Neil Mayer & Assocs 160 Sansome St Ste 700 San Francisco CA 94104-3713

MAYER, PATRICIA JAYNE, financial officer, management accountant; b. Chgo., Apr. 27, 1950; d. Arthur and Ruth (Greenberger) Hersh; m. William A. Mayer Jr., Apr. 30, 1971. AA, Diablo Valley Coll., 1970; BSBA, Calif. State U., Hayward, 1975. Cert. mgmt. acct. Staff acct., auditor Elmer Fox Westheimer and Co., Oakland, Calif., 1976; supervising auditor Auditor's Office County of Alameda, Oakland, 1976-78; asst. acctg. mgr. CBS Retail Stores doing bus. as Pacific Stereo, Emeryville, Calif., 1978-79; contr. Oakland Unified Sch. Dist., 1979-84; v.p. fin., CFO YMCA, San Francisco, 1984-96; v.p. fin. customer segments Charles Schwab & Co., San Francisco, 1996—; instr. acctg. to staff YMCA, San Francisco, 1984-96, CBS Retail Stores, 1978-79. Draft counselor Mt. Diablo Peace Ctr., Walnut Creek, Calif., 1970-72; dep. registrar of voters Contra Costa County Registrar's Office, Martinez, Calif., 1972-77. Mem. Fin. Execs. Inst. (bd. dirs. San Francisco chpt.), Inst. Mgmt. Accts. (pres.-elect Diablo Valley chpt. 1995—, pres. 1995-96), Dalmatian Club No. Calif., Dalmation Club Am. Democrat. Jewish. Office: Charles Schwab & Co 101 Montgomery St San Francisco CA 94104

MAYER, PATRICIA LYNN SORCI, mental health nurse, educator; b. Chgo., July 22, 1942; d. Ben and Adonia (Grenier) Sorci; 1 child, Christopher David Mayer. AGS with high honors, Pima Community Coll., Tucson, 1983; BSN with honors, U. Ariz., 1986, MS in Nursing, 1987. RN, Ariz.; cert. addictions counselor, chem. dependency therapist; lic. pvt. pilot. Nurse educator Tucson. Contbr. articles to profl. jours. Mem. Nat. Nurses Soc. on Addictions, Phi Kappa Phi, Sigma Theta Tau, Pi Lambda Theta, Golden Key.

MAYER, THOMAS, economics educator; b. Vienna, Austria, Jan. 18, 1927; s. Felix and Helen (Pollatschek) M.; m. Dorothy JoAnne Harmison, Apr. 7, 1963. BA, Queens Coll., 1948; MA, Columbia U., 1949, PhD, 1953. Economist Treasury Dept., 1951-52, Office of Price Stabilization, 1952, Bur. of Mines, 1953; asst. prof. U. Notre Dame, 1954-56; from asst. to assoc. prof. Mich. State U., 1956-61; vis. assoc. prof. U. Calif., Berkeley, 1961-62; prof. U. Calif., Davis, 1962-93, prof. emeritus, 1993—; vis. ast. prof. W.Va. U., 1953-54. Author: Monetary Policy in the United States, 1968, Permanent Income, Wealth and Consumption, 1972; (with D.C. Rowan) Intermediate Macroeconomics, 1972; (with others) The Structure of Monetarism, 1978; (with others) Money, Banking and the Economy, 1981, 6th edit., 1996, Chinese edit., 1988, Portuguese edit., 1995; Revealing Monetary Policy, 1987, Monetarism and Macroeconomic Policy, 1990, Truth Versus Precision in Economics, 1993, Polish edit., 1996, Doing Economics: Essays on the Applied Methodology of Economics, 1995; editor: The Political Economy of American Monetary Policy, 1990, Monetary Theory, 1990, (with F. Spinelli) Studies in Macroeconomics and Monetary Policy Issues, 1991; mem. editorial bd. Jour. of Econ. Lit., 1985-97, others. Mem. Am. Econ. Assn., Am. fin. Assn., Internat. Network Econ. Method (chmn. 1993—), Western Econ. Assn. (v.p. 1976-77, pres. 1978-79), Royal Econ. Soc. Home: 3054 Buena Vista Way Berkeley CA 94708-2020

MAYERSON, PETER, psychiatrist, educator; b. New Orleans, Apr. 1, 1933; m. Lois Bain, July 23, 1960; children: Michele L., Keith B. BA cum laude, Brown U., 1955; MD, Tulane U., 1962; cert. psychoanalysis, Denver Inst. Psychoanalysis, 1975. Bd. cert. psychiatry and psychoanalysis. Intern in medicine U. Calif., H.C. Moffit Hosp., San Francisco, 1962-63; resident in psychiatry U. Cin., Cin. Gen. Hosp., 1963-66; instr., asst. dir. emergency psychiat. svc. U. Colo. Health Scis. Ctr., 1966-68, asst. prof., dir. emergency psychiat. svc., 1968-69, asst. clin. prof., 1969-90, assoc. clin. prof., 1990—; guest lectr. U. Denver, 1975-77; asst. tchr. Denver Inst. for Psychoanalysis, 1975-77, 81-82, assoc. faculty, 1982-84, faculty, 1984—; tng. and supervising analyst, 1987—; faculty, tng. and supervising analyst Colo. Ctr. for Psychoanalytic Studies, 1985—; faculty postgrad. psychotherapy program Menninger Found., 1985-88; exec. bd. mem. Colo. Ctr. for Psychoanalytic Studies, 1985-89; mem. planning com. Western Clin. Psychoanalytic Meetings, 1990—; cons. Byerly & Co., 1990—, med. dir., 1991—; courtesy staff U. Hosp., Denver, Bethesda PsycHealth, Denver, Rose Med. Ctr., Denver; presenter in field. Contbr. articles to profl. jours. Line officer USN, 1955-58. Fellow Am. Psychiat. Assn. (rep. area VII coun. 1984, rep. bd. dels. 1984-85), Colo. Psychiat. Soc. (mem. continuing edn. com. 1969-78, chmn. continuing edn. com. 1978-81, trustee exec. com. 1980-82, sec. 1983-84, pres. 1984-85); mem. Am. Psychoanalytic Assn. (del. to supervision workshop 1976, del. to exec. coun. 1989-91, del. to cert. com. 1991, del. to bd. of profl. stds. 1992-95), Am. Group Psychotherapy Assn., Colo. Soc. for Psychology and Psychoanalysis, Colo. Group Cons. (founder), Denver Psychoanalytic Soc. (mem. cmty. ext. com. 1974-79, tchr. in continuing edn. program 1975—, chmn. local arrangements com. 1981-85, chmn. program com. 1987-89, pres. 1989-91), Denver Inst. Psychoanalysis (mem. various coms. 1975—, treas. 1992-95, exec. com. 1992-95), Phi Beta Kappa, Alpha Omega Alpha, Sigma Xi. Home: 9 Red Fox Ln Greenwood Village CO 80111 Office: 3955 E Exposition Ave Ste 402C Denver CO 80209-5033

MAYES, SHARON SUZETTE, sculptor, educator; b. Sparta, Ind., Apr. 18, 1948; d. Herbert Franklin and Alma Sue (Keller) M.; m. David Allenberg Katzenstein, Dec. 25, 1983; 1 child, Melissa Sanders-Self. BA, Mich. State U., 1969; MPh, Yale U., 1972, PhD, 1974; MA in Clin. Psychology, Wright Inst., Berkeley, Calif., 1982. Asst. prof. U. Md., College Park, 1974-80; assoc. prof. U. Calif., San Diego, 1981-82; writer, sculptor pvt. practice, Berkeley, Calif., 1982-84; assoc. prof. Macalester Coll., St. Paul, Minn., 1984-86; dir., curator Modern Africa Gallery, Menlo Park, Calif., 1989—. Author: Immune, 1988; contbr. numerous articles and short stories to various publs.; sculptor: works included in juried shows, 1994—. Phi Beta Kappa. Home: 435 San Mateo Dr Menlo Park CA 94025-5348

MAYFIELD, SIGNE, curator of exhibitions; b. Woodbury, N.J., Mar. 14, 1942; d. James P. and Helen (Curtis) Shambaugh; m. William B. Mayfield, Jan. 24, 1946; children: Ross D., Kendra. BA, U. Calif., Berkeley, 1965; postgrad., George Washington U. Curator The Art Corridor, Menlo Park, Calif., 1984-87; gallery dir. Miller-Brown Gallery, San Francisco, 1988-89; curator of exhbns. Palo Alto (Calif.) Cultural Ctr., 1989—; bd. dirs. Art Table, 1994—; mem. adv. coun. Am. Art Study Ctr., M.H. de Young Mus., Fine Arts Mus. San Francisco. Revs., articles and featured exhbns. in Art of Perception (Australia), Artweek, Am. Craft Mag., Fiberworks, Design, Woodturning (Eng.), San Francisco Chronicle, Washington Post, Art News, Wall St. Jour.; author exhbn. catalogs Directions in Bay Area Printmaking, Christopher Brown: Works on Paper, Marriage in Form: Kay Sekimachi and Bob Stocksdale, Dominic Di Mare.

MAYHUE, RICHARD LEE, dean, pastor, writer; b. Takoma Park, Md., Aug. 31, 1944; s. J. Richard Mayhue and Myrtle Lorraine (Hartsell) Lee; m. Lois Elaine Nettleingham, June 18, 1966; children: Lee, Wade. BS, Ohio State U., 1966; MDiv, Grace Theol. Seminary, Winona Lake, Ind., 1974, ThM, 1977, ThD, 1981. Ordained pastor. Asst. pastor Grace Brethren Ch. of Columbus (Ohio), 1975-77; asst. prof. New Testament and Greek, Grace Theol. Seminary, Winona Lake, 1977-80; assoc. pastor Grace Cmty. Ch., Sun Valley, Calif., 1980-84, 89—; sr. pastor Grace Brethren Ch., Long Beach, Calif., 1984-89; sr. v.p., dean, prof. systematic theology and pastoral mins. The Master's Seminary, Sun Valley, 1989—; bd. dirs. Grace Theol. Sem., 1987-89. Author: (booklets) The Biblical Pattern for Divine Healing, 1979, Snatched Before the Storm, 1980, (books) Divine Healing Today, 1983, How to Interpret the Bible for Yourself, 1986, A Christian's Survival Guide, 1987, Unmasking Satan, 1988, Spiritual Intimacy, 1990, Spiritual Maturity, 1992, The Healing Promise, 1994, What Would Jesus Say About Your Church?, 1995; contbr., editor: Rediscovering Expository Preaching, 1992, Rediscovering Pastoral Ministry, 1994; contbr. New Am. Std. Study Bible, 1997; contbr., assoc. editor MacArthur Study Bible, 1997; contbr. articles to profl. jours. Lt. USN, 1966-71, Vietnam. Recipient Bronze Star with Combat V USN, 1969. Mem. Evang. Theol. Soc., Nat. Fellowship Grace Brethren Ministers (pres. 1988), Far West Region Evang. Theol. Soc. (pres. 1995), Slavic Gospel Assn. (bd. dirs. 1993—). Office: The Master's Seminary 13248 Roscoe Blvd Sun Valley CA 91352-3739

MAYNARD, E. ROSE, retired school health services coordinator; b. Mosquero, N.Mex., Feb. 7, 1934; d. E.H. and Eudora M. (Freeland) McGlothlin; m. Bob Maynard, Aug. 2, 1952; children: Michael, Michele, Mark. BSN with hons., Calif. State U., L.A., 1971, MA, 1974. CPNP, RN, Calif. Sch. nurse ABC Unified Sch. Dist., Cerritos, Calif., 1970-86, pediatric nurse practitioner, 1977-86; dept. chmn. health svcs. Lancaster (Calif.) Sch. Dist., 1986-92, pediatric nurse practitioner, 1986-96, DATE coord., 1990-96, coord. health svcs., 1992-96; ret., 1996; presenter Ednl. Conf., Hawaii, 1982; PASS Project Replicator, CSNO and NASN, Calif., 1987-91; presenter Calif. Sch. Bd. Ann. State Conf., San Jose, 1994. Coord. Calif. State Contest, 1985. CPR/FA instr. ARC, Quartz Hill, Calif., 1986—; mem. Tobacco Task Force, Am. CA Soc., Palmdale, Calif., 1989—. Fellow Nat. Assn. Pediat. Nurses; mem. Calif. Sch. Nurses Assn. (bd. dirs. so. sect. 1991-93), Nat. Assn. Sch. Nurses, Assn. Calif. Sch. Adminstrs., Alpha Gamma Sigma. Republican.

MAYNARD, GLENN C., healthcare administrator, counselor; b. Longview, Wash., May 28, 1949; s. Glenn Colan and Anne Therese (Gramlick) M.; m. Jill E. Miller, Aug. 29, 1970; children: Meegan, Katy, Molly. BS in Sociology, Portland State U., 1971; MEd in Counseling, Lewis and Clark Coll., 1977. Lic. profl. counselor, Oreg.; nat. cert. counselor. Caseworker Pub. Welfare/Adult & Family Svcs., Portland, 1972-76; casework supr. Adults & Family Svcs., Portland, 1976-78; mental health specialist Washington County Mental Health, Hillsboro, Oreg., 1978-79; dir. LINC/adult day Clackamas County Mental Health, Gladstone, Oreg., 1979-87; clin. supr., dir. dual diagnosis svcs. Providence Med. Ctr., Portland, 1987-91, dir. addictions/svcs., 1991-94, dir. chem. dependency svc., 1994—; pvt. practice counseling Portland, 1980—; dir. access/age svcs. Providence Health Sys., 1995—; chmn. mental health/chem. dependency com. Providence Health Plans, 1989-96. Mem. citizen adv. com. David Douglas Sch. Bd., Portland, 1989-93, chair, 1990. Recipient Meritorious Svc. award Oreg. Mental Health Assn. Mem. Am. Counseling Assn., Am. mental Health Counselor Assn. Office: Providence Mental Health Chem Dependency Svcs 5228 NE Hoyt St Portland OR 97213-3055

MAYNARD, JOHN HERBERT, electronics engineer; b. Glendale, Calif., Mar. 17, 1935; s. Herbert Walter and Marjorie Edna (Orson) M.; m. Diane Parker, Feb. 2, 1957 (div. 1972); childrne: Laurie Loder, Debra Leebolt, John Herbert Jr.; m. Rosalie Ann Kostanzer, Aug. 12, 1977 (div. 1992); m. Norma Jean Sheahan, June 6, 1992. BS, San Diego State U., 1957; MS, U.S. Internat. U., San Diego, 1972; postgrad., UCLA, 1957-66, U. Hawaii, 1972. Electronics engr. Navy Electronics Lab., San Diego, 1957-64, radar br. head, 1967-68, microwave div. head, 1968-76; exchange scientist Admirality Surface Weapons, Portsmouth, Eng., 1965-66; dept. head Naval Ocean Systems Ctr., San Diego, 1977-84, tech. mgr., 1985-92; tech. mgr. Office Naval Rsch., Arlington, Va., 1993; dept. dir. ops. Naval Command Control Ocean Surveillance Ctr., San Diego, 1993—; owner Norjon Enterprises, San Diego, 1980—; lectr. U.S. Naval War Coll., Newport, R.I., 1988-92. Contbr. articles to profl. jours. Mem. San Diego Opera Assn., 1985—, San Diego Mus. Art, 1986—, La Jolla Mus. Contemporary Art, 1986—. Recipient Achievement in Mgmt. award Dept. of Navy, 1975. Mem. IEEE (sr.), Aerospace and Electronic Systems Soc. of IEEE (chmn. 1971-72), San Diego State U. Alumni Assn., San Diego Apt. Assn. Republican. Presbyterian. Home: 5473 Drover Dr San Diego CA 92115-1129 Office: Naval Command Control and Ocean Surveillance Ctr 53570 Silvergate Ave San Diego CA 92152-5008

MAYNARD, KENNETH DOUGLAS, architect; b. Hackensack, N.J., Aug. 16, 1931; s. Douglas Harry and Eva (Whiting) M.; m. Myrna Myrtle James, Feb. 4, 1956; children: Colin, Vivien Regan. Cert. in Architecture, U. Natal, Durban, Republic of South Africa, 1958. Registered architect Alaska. Draftsman Morross & Graff, Johannesburg, Republic of South Africa, 1950-51, Anglo-Am. Corp., Johannesburg, Republic of South Africa, 1951-54, Moir & Llewellyn, Empangeni, Zululand, Republic of South Africa, 1955-57; architect Pearse Aneck-Hahn & Bristol, Johannesburg, 1957-60, Manley & Mayer, Anchorage, 1960-61, FAA, Anchorage, 1961-62, Crittenden Cassetta Wirum & Jacobs, Anchorage, 1962-65; prin. Schultz & Maynard, Anchorage, 1965-68, Kenneth Maynard Assocs., Anchorage, 1968-78; pres. Maynard & Partch, Anchorage, 1978-96; prin. USKH, Inc., Anchorage, 1996—. Active Western Alaska Coun. Boy Scouts. Am., Anchorage, 1965-84; bd. dirs. Salvation Army Adv. Bd., Anchorage, 1981-87, Anchorage Mus. Assn., 1969-86, Anchorage Opera Co., 1983-90; chmn. Mayor's Comprehensive Homeless Program Strategy Group, 1992-94. Fellow AIA (pres. Alaska chpt. 1969, N.W. regional rep. for nat. com. on design 1976-89); mem. Constrn. Specification Inst. (pres. Cook Inlet chpt. 1993-94), Soc. Am. Mil. Engrs. Republican. Home: 2237 Forest Park Dr Anchorage AK 99517-1324 Office: USKH 2515 A St Anchorage AK 99503

MAYNARD, MICHAEL, librarian; b. Yuma, Ariz., July 8, 1955; s. Ernest Ray and Refugio (Guerrero) M. AAS in Electronic Tech., Phoenix Coll., 1986; BA in German, Ariz. State U., 1989; postgrad., U. Leipzig, 1990, Eberhard-Karls U., Tubingen, Germany, 1990-91; MLS, U. Ariz., 1992. Asst. libr. Chapel Libr., Venice, Fla., 1983-84; security officer Anderson Agy., Phoenix, 1984-89; grad. asst. U. Ariz., Tuscon, 1989-90, libr. asst. main libr. acquisitions dept., 1992; asst. libr. Internat. Bapt. Coll., Tempe, Ariz., 1992-94; head libr. Fitch Libr., Mesa, Ariz., 1994—. Author: History of the Debate Over I John 5:7-8, 1995. Scholar U. Ariz., 1989-90, Herman Weinel scholar, 1990. Mem. ALA, Assn. Christian Librs., Ch. and Synagogue Libr. Assn. Baptist. Home: 1008 W Laird St Tempe AZ 85281-5310 Office: Comma Publs PO Box 1625 Tempe AZ 85281-1625

MAYO, CESAR M., neurologist; b. Lipa City, Batangas, Philippines, Feb. 23, 1939; came to the U.S., 1961; s. Bartolome Lantin and Concepcion Reyes Mayo; m. Corazon Ordoveza Gomez, Feb. 17, 1962; children: Bernadette, Maria Christina, Martin. AA in Pre-Medicine, U. Santo Tomas, Manila, 1955, MD, 1960. Diplomate Am. Bd. Psychiatry and Neurology, Am. Bd. Electrodiagnostic Medicine. Intern USAF Hosp. Clark AFB, Pampanga, Philippines, 1959-60; adj. resident internal medicine and neurology Santo Tomas U., Manila, 1960-61; resident neurology U. Louisville (Ky.) Hosps., 1961-62, chief resident neurology, 1963-64; resident neurology Detroit (Mich.) Receiving Hosp., 1962-63; fellow neuropathology Northwestern U. Med. Sch., Chgo., 1964-66, clin. asst. in neurology and psychiatry, 1964-65, instr. neurology, 1965-67, assoc. neurology, 1967-68, asst. prof. neurology, 1968-69; asst. prof. neurology Albany (N.Y.) Med. Coll., 1969-70, assoc. prof. neurology, 1970-71; asst. attending neurologist Albany Med. Ctr. Hosp., 1969-70, attending neurologist, 1970-71; chief neurology svc. VA Hosp., Martinez, Calif., 1971-72; pvt. practice neurology San Jose, Calif., 1972—; pres. Pacific Imaging Svcs., Inc., San Jose; resident coord. neurology svc. VA Hosp., Hines, Ill., 1965-66, sect. chief neurology svc., 1966-69, asst. chief-acting chief neurology svc., 1969; cons. in neurology Elgin (Ill.) State Hosp., 1967-69; attending physician Neurology Clinics, Northwestern U. Med. Sch., Chgo., 1966-69; attending neurologist Hinsdale (Ill.) Hosp. and Sanatorium, 1968-69; chief neurology svc. VA Hosp., Martinez, Calif., 1971-72; ind. med. examiner Ct. of Indsl. Rels., State of Calif., 1980—. Contbr. articles to profl. jours. Fellow ACP, Am. Acad. Neurology, Am. Geriatric Soc.; mem. AMA, Calif. Med. Assn., Am. Assn. Electromyography and Electrodiagnosis, Am. EEG Soc. (assoc.), Am. Acad. Clin. Neurophysiology, Am. Soc. Neuroimaging, Am. Imaging Assn., Am. Fedn. Clinic Rsch., Western Electroencephalography Soc., N.Y. Acad. Scis., Royal Soc. Medicine (London; affiliate), Santa Clara County Med. Soc. Office: Pacific Imaging Svcs 361 S Monroe St San Jose CA 95128-5107

MAYO, ROBERT N., software engineer; b. Washington, Aug. 23, 1959; s. Robert P. and Marian A. Mayo. BS in Computer Sci., Washington U., St. Louis, 1981; MS in Computer Sci., U. Calif., Berkeley, 1983, PhD of Computer Sci., 1987. Asst. prof. U. Wis., Madison, 1988; software engr. Digital Equipment Corp., Palo Alto, Calif., 1989—. Mem. Assn. Computer Machinery. Office: Digital Equipment Corp 250 University Ave Palo Alto CA 94301-1713

MAYOL, RICHARD THOMAS, advertising executive, political consultant; b. Springfield, Ill., Oct. 30, 1949; s. Richard McFaren and Marjorie (Maddex) M. AA, Springfield Coll., 1969; BS, U. Tulsa, 1972. Co-owner First Tuesday Inc., Phoenix, 1976-85; pres. Mayol and Assocs., Phoenix, 1985—; CEO New West Policy Group, Prescott, Ariz., 1993—; cons. Dem. candidates, Dem. candidates ballot issues, corp. pub. policy Western U.S., Nev. Dem. Party, Ariz. Dem. Party, Del Webb Corp., Prop. 102, McDowell Mt. Preserve Initiative. Mem. Phoenix Film Commn., 1985—. Mem. Am. Assn. Polit. Cons., Phoenix Grand Prix Commn. Home and Office: 348 Moreland Cir Prescott AZ 86303-4035 also: 223 Union St Prescott AZ 86303-3813

MAYS, WILLIE HOWARD, JR. (SAY HEY KID), former professional baseball player; b. Westfield, Ala., May 6, 1931; s. William Howard and Ann M.; m. Mae Louise Allen, Nov. 27, 1971; 1 adopted son, Michael. Baseball player Birmingham Black Barons, 1948-50, Trenton Inter-State League, 1950-51, Mpls. Millers, Am. Assn., 1951, N.Y. Giants, 1951-57, San Francisco Giants, 1958-72, N.Y. Mets, 1972-73; with Bally's Park Place, Atlantic City, 1980—; pub. rels. exec. San Francisco Giants, 1986—. Author: Willie Mays: My Life In and Out of Baseball, 1966, Say Hey: The Autobiography of Willie Mays, 1988. Served with AUS, 1952-54. Named Most Valuable Player Nat. League, 1954, 65; named Player of Yr. Sporting News, 1954, Baseball Player of Decade Sporting News, 1970, Male Athlete of Yr. AP, 1954, Rookie of the Yr., 1951, Most Exciting Playin Sport Sporting News, 1954, All-Star Game, 1954-73; recipient Hickok belt, 1954, Golden Bat award to commemorate 600 home runs, Gold Glove award (12 times), 1st Commissioner's award, 1970, Golden Plate awarded to America's Captains of Achievement by Am. Acad. Achievement, 1976, Spirit of Life award City of Hope, 1988, Sportsman of Decade, Cong. Racial Equality, 1991, Legendary Star award HBO Video; inducted into Ala. Sports Hall of Fame, Baseball Hall of Fame, 1979, Black Hall of Fame, 1973, Calif. Sports Hall of Fame. Office: care San Francisco Giants Candlestick Park San Francisco CA 94124*

MAYTHAM, THOMAS NORTHRUP, art and museum consultant; b. Buffalo, July 30, 1931; s. Thomas Edward and Margaret (Northrup) M.; m. Daphne Chace, Dec. 30, 1960 (div.); 1 child, T.F. Gifford; m. Gloria Maytham, June 11, 1994. BA in Art History, Williams Coll., Williamstown, Mass., 1954; MA in Art History, Yale U., 1956; cert. in German, Colby Coll., 1954. Intern Wadsworth Atheneum, 1955; rsch. asst. Yale U., 1956; head dept. paintings Boston Mus. Fine Arts, 1957-67; assoc. dir., acting dir. Seattle Art Mus., 1967-74; dir. Denver Art Mus., 1974-83; art cons., pub. Artadvisors LLC, Denver, 1983—; mus. accreditation program evaluator Am. Assn. Museums; past trustee, mem. exhbns. adv. com. Am. Fedn. Arts, N.Y.; past mem. mus. program panel, grants reviewer Nat. Endowment for Arts, Washington; grants reviewer Nat. Endowment for Humanities, Washington; mem. adv. panel, grants reviewer Nat. Mus. Act, Smithsonian Instn.; past mem. policy panel and adv. com., econ. impact of arts study Colo. Coun. Arts and Humanities; co-founder Consortium of Rocky Mountain Regional Conservation Ctr., U. Denver; founder dirs. assn. Denver cultural agys.; del. Inter-Am. Museums Conf., Oaxaca, Mexico; co-founder United Arts Fund, Seattle; mem. art adv. com. Airport Art Program, Port of Seattle; vis. faculty Leadership Denver program, Pres.'s Leadership class U. Colo.; cons. Aspen Ctr. Visual Arts, Sangre de Cristo Arts Ctr., Pueblo, Western States Arts Found., Santa Fe, BBHC, Cody, Wyo.; lectr. museums, colls., corporate groups and art assns. Exhbns. organized include Ernst Ludwig Kirchner Retrospective, Seattle, Pasadena and Boston museums, 1968-69, Am. Painting from the Boston and Met. Museums, Nat. Gallery, St. Louis and Seattle museums, 1970-71; contbr. articles to profl. jours.; presenter TV programs on collections and exhbns. Boston Pub. TV, WGBH-TV. Trustee Internat. Exhbns. Found., Washington. Recipient Gov.'s Arts award Seattle Airport Art Program, 1972, Denver Art mus., award Downtown Denver Inc., 1978. Mem. Assn Art Mus. Dirs. (officer, trustee, ops. com. sec., future directions. com. chmn.). Office: Artadvisors LLC 3882 S Newport Way Denver CO 80237-1246

MAYTUM, HARRY RODELL, retired physician; b. Alexandria, S.D., Jan. 25, 1913; s. Wellington James and Lillian May (Syferd) M.; m. Louetta Susanna Stoltz, Apr. 27, 1937; children: James, Nancy, Joan. BS magna cum laude, U. Wis., 1936, MD, 1938. Intern Alameda County Hosp., Oakland, Calif., 1938-39, resident in surgery, 1946-47; resident in surgery Merced County Hosp., Merced, Calif., 1939-41; pvt. practice, Merced, 1947-95; ret., 1995; chief staff Mercy Hosp., Merced, Merced County Hosp. Bd. dirs. Merced County Mosquito Abatement Dist., 1954-64. Lt col. M.C., USAAF, 1941-47, ETO. Fellow Am. Geriatric Soc., Am. Acad. Family Practice (charter); mem. AMA, Calif. Med. Assn. (Plessner Meml. award 1992), Merced-Mariposa County Med. Soc. (pres. 1955), Merced C. of C. (bd. dirs. 1973-77, former chmn. health affairs com., Merced Citizen of Yr. award 1989), Kiwanis (pres. Merced 1953), Elks, Phi Beta Kappa, Alpha Omega Alpha. Republican. Home: 2887 Forist Ln Merced CA 95340-2553

MAZELIS, MENDEL, plant biochemist, educator, researcher; b. Chgo., Aug. 31, 1922; s. Jacob and Anna (Brvarnick) M.; m. Noreen Beimer, Mar. 24, 1969; 1 son, Jacob Russell. B.S., U. Calif.-Berkeley, 1943, Ph.D., 1954. Jr. research biochemist U. Calif.-Berkeley, 1954-55; research assoc., instr. U. Chgo., 1955-57; assoc. chemist Western Regional Research Lab., Albany, Calif., 1957-61; asst. prof. U. Calif.-Davis, 1961-64, assoc. prof., 1964-73, prof., 1973-91, prof. emeritus, 1991—. Served to lt. (j.g.) USN, 1943-46. Mem. Am. Soc. Plant Physiologists, Am. Soc. Biochemists and Molecular Biologists, Biochem. Soc. London, Phytochem. Soc. N.Am., Phytochem. Soc. Europe, Inst. Food Technologists. Office: U Calif Dept Food Sci/Tech Davis CA 95616

MAZID, MOHAMMED ABDUL, chemist; b. Mymensingh, Bangladesh, Mar. 16, 1950; s. Shafdur Rahman and Jamila Khatoon; m. Sanjida Shahnaz, July 22, 1978; 1 child, Imrul. BS with hons., U. Dhaka, Bangladesh, 1971, MS, 1973; MS, Lakehead U., Thunder Bay, Can., 1978; PhD, U. Ottawa, Can., 1981. Various to rsch. assoc. scientist Export Packers Co., Ltd., Winnipeg, Manitoba, Can., 1983-85; with Inrad Indsl. Rsch. and Devel., Ltd., Winnipeg, 1985-86; rsch. assoc. dept. chemistry U. Alberta, Edmonton, Can., 1986-87; sr. scientist, group leader biochem. devel. Chembiomed Ltd., Edmonton, 1987-91; sr. devel. scientist, mfg. technologies Alberta Rsch. Coun., Edmonton, 1991-92; prin. R & D scientist Glyko Inc., Novato, Calif., 1992-94; project mgr. Sepragen Corp., Hayward, Calif., 1994-96; vis. fellow Nat. Sci. and Engring. Rsch. Coun. Can., 1981-83. Patentee in field; contbr. to profl. publs. Univ. rsch. fellow Lakeheed U., 1976-77, grad. rsch. fellow U. Ottawa, 1978-79. Mem. Am. Chem. Soc., Soc. Biomaterials. Office: Sepragen Corp 30689 Huntwood Ave Hayward CA 94544

MAZUR, MEREDITH MARGIE HANDLEY, reading educator; b. Tulsa, Mar. 27, 1941; d. Joyce Samuel and MaryPaul (Ellsworth) Handley; m. Don Leroy Mazur, Aug. 31, 1962 (div. Nov. 1974); children: Susan Diane, Michael. BA in Art, U. Tulsa, 1962, M of Teaching Arts in Spl. Edn., 1967; postgrad., Calif. State U., L.A., UCLA, Purdue U., Calumet, Ind., San Jose State U. Accredited tchr., reading specialist, adminstr., Calif. Classroom tchr. Tulsa Pub. Schs., 1963-65; fellow, clinician, diagnostician, instr. Mabee Reading Clinic, U. Tulsa, 1965-67; instr. So. Meth. U. Reading Clinic, Dallas, fall 1969; classroom tchr. L.A. Unified Sch. Dist., 1975-76; reading specialist Sierramont Middle Sch., Berryessa Union Sch. Dist., San Jose, Calif., 1976-87; tchr. Laneview Elem. Sch., 1989-92; tchr., Calif. Tchrs. Assn. Berryessa site rep. Majestic Way Elem., 1993—, exec. bd. Calif. Tchrs. Assn. Berryessa, 1996; pvt. tutor, San Jose, 1976—; owner, operator Eastside Learning Ctr. and Reading Clinic, San Jose, 1978-82; Calif. lang. devel. tng. specialist, 1991. Cons., activist in women's and children's rights in child-support enforcement; chmn. child-support enforcement task force San Jose-South Bay chpt. NOW, 1984-85; mem. child support div. rev. ad-hoc. com. Santa Clara County Bd. Suprs. Entrance Exam. scholar U. Tulsa, 1959; John Mabee grad. fellow, 1966; recipient 1st place Bronze award Am. Waltz, Palo Alto, Calif., 1987, 1st Place Silver award Am. Fox Trot and Silver Viennese Waltz, Palo Alto, 1989. Mem. Women Leaders in Edn., Mortar Bd., Alpha Delta Kappa, Kappa Alpha Theta (chpt. pres. 1961-62). Mem. Bahai Faith Ch. Avocations: ballroom dancing, sailing, reading. Home: PO Box 32744 San Jose CA 95152-2744

MAZUREK, JOSEPH P., state attorney general, former state legislator; b. San Diego, July 27, 1948; B.A., U. Mont., 1970, J.D., 1975; m. Patty Mazurek; 3 children. Bar: Mont. 1975; atty. Gough, Shanahan, Johnson, and Waterman, Helena, Mont.; mem. Mont. Senate from 23d Dist., 1981-92; Senate pres., 1991-92; atty. gen., State of Mont., 1993—; mem. Revenue Oversight Com., 1983-92; chmn. Senate Judiciary Com.; assoc. editor Mont. Law Rev., 1974-75. Served with U.S. Army, 1970-72. Mem. ABA, Beta Gamma Sigma, Phi Delta Phi, Phi Delta Theta. Office: Justice Bldg PO Box 201401 215 N Sanders 3rd Fl Helena MT 59620*

MAZUREK, STEPHEN JEROME, foreign language educator; b. Natrona Heights, Pa., Mar. 5, 1951; s. Edward Thaddeus and Hedwig Anne (Nowakowski) M. AB, U. Pitts., 1973; MA, NYU, 1975, U. Calif., Berkeley, 1978; PhD, U. Calif., Berkeley, 1986. Calif. C.C. instr.'s credential for Russian. Tchg. asst. U. Calif., Berkeley, 1976-78, tchg. assoc., 1978-80; various positions Berkeley (Calif.) Unified Sch. Dist., 1983—; instr. Piedmont (Calif.) Adult Edn., 1989-91, Cabrillo Coll., Aptos, Calif., 1991—, Columbia Pacific U., San Rafael, Calif.; presenter in field. Internat. Rsch. and Exch. Bd. grantee, 1992. Mem. MLA, Am. Assn. for the Advancement Slavic Studies, Am. Assn. Tchrs. Slavic and East European Langs., Linguistic Soc. Am., Fgn. Lang. Assn. No. Calif., Oakland-Nakhodka Sister City Assn. Home: 1207A University Ave Berkeley CA 94702-1708

MAZZOLINI, JAMES WILLIAM, engineering administrator. MSEE, Loyola Marymount, L.A., 1985; MBA, Peperdine U., 1995. Mem. tech. staff Hughes Aircraft Co., 1983-87; pres. Trendware Software Co., 1988; engr. mgr. Casio-Phonemate, Torrance, Calif., 1989-94; mgr. engring. Casio Phonemate, Inc., Torrance, Calif., 1995—. Republican. Roman Catholic. Home: 5101 W 133rd St Hawthorne CA 90250-5054 Office: Casio Phonemate Inc 20665 Manhattan Pl Torrance CA 90501-1827

MCADAMS, CHARLES MICHAEL, academic administrator; b. Camp Pendleton, Calif., May 8, 1947; s. John and Trudy Mae (Fleming) McA.; m. Barbara M. Austin, Feb. 27, 1995. BA in History, U. The Pacific, 1976; MA in History, John Carroll U., 1978; postgrad. in Edn., U. San Francsico, 1978-82. Regional dir. U. San Francisco, 1978—; cons. in field. Author monographs. Advisor Calif. State Assembly, 1974-78; founder, chair Com. on Higher Edn., Sacramento, 1982-88; foreman U.S. Grand Jury, ea. dist. Calif., 1988-91; bd. dirs. Croatian Scholarship Found., Calif., 1990—. ABA fellow, 1976-77, Sourissea Acad. fellow, 1978-80. Mem. Am. Assn. Advancement Slavic Studies, Croatian Acad. Am., Croatian Studies Found. Australia and New Zealand, Assn. Croatian Studies, El Inst. Croata Latin Am. de Cultura, Phi Alpha Theta.

MCAFEE, SUSAN JACQUELINE, educator; b. L.A., June 3, 1944; d. Nat and Lillian Dorothy (Taylor) Louis; m. Robert Richard McAfee, Apr. 27, 1965; children: Robert Jack, Lani Laurelle. BA in English, Mont. state U., 1969; M.Ednl. Adminstrn., No. Ariz. U., 1991. Cert. tchr., adminstr., Ariz. Tchr. Lake Havasu (Ariz.) Jr. H.S., 1981-92; vice prin. Bigfork (Mont.) Elem. sch., 1992-93; instr. English Mohave C.C., Lake Havasu City, 1993-96; master tchr. Telesis Ctr. for Learning, Lake Havasu City, 1994-95; basic edn./GED tchr. Mohave County Career Ctr., Lake Havasu City, 1995—. Mem. ASCD. Office: Mohave County Career Ctr PO Box 711 Kingman AZ 86402

MCALISTER, MICHAEL HILLIS, architect; b. Bakersfield, Calif., May 22, 1945; s. Doyle R. and Mary E. McAlister. AA, Bakersfield Coll., 1967; BArch, Calif. Polytech. U., 1971. Planning technition Bakersfield City Hall, 1963; carpenter Del Webb Corp., Kern City, Calif., 1964; architectural draftsman Goss & Choy Architects, Bakersfield, 1965-67; architect, v.p. D.G.C. & Assocs., Bakersfield, 1971-80; dir. architecture, v.p. N.B.A. & Assocs., Architects, Bakersfield, 1980-83; architect, pres. Michael H. McAlister, A.I.A., Bakersfield, 1983—; nepthrology design cons. for various treatment groups and hosps., 1987—. Commr., architectural advisor Historic Preservation Commn., Bakersfield, 1986-87; bd. dirs. Camp Fire Coun., Kern County, Calif., 1980-84. Recipient Architectural Pub. Bldg. Hist. award Beautiful Bakersfield Com., City of Bakersfield's City Coun. and Hist. Preservation Commn., 1985, 87, Exterior Environ. Design Excellence Bakersfield C. of C., 1988, Comml. Design Excellence award, 1984, Design Excellence and Beautification award City of Taft, Calif., 1989, Design Excellence award State of Nev., 1992. Mem. AIA (Calif. Coun., Golden Empire chpt.). Office: 5030 Office Park Dr Ste B Bakersfield CA 93309-0612

MCALLISTER, (RONALD) ERIC, pharmaceutical executive, physician; b. Halifax, N.S., Can., Apr. 15, 1942; s. (James) Ronald and Barbara Hope (Curry) McA.; m. Carol M. Browne, Feb. 8, 1967 (div. July 1981); children: Natasha Naomi, Neil Eric; m. Suzanne Yee, Apr. 8, 1989; 1 child, Petra Camille Mei-Fong. BSc with honors, Dalhousie U., Halifax, 1962, MSc, 1963, MD, 1976; DPhil, Oxford (Eng.) U., 1967. Asst. prof. Dalhousie U., 1968-76; intern Sunnybrook Med. Ctr. U. Toronto, Can., 1976-77; med. practitioner Murakami Clinic, Hope, B.C., Can., 1977-78; physician in pvt. practice San Leandro, Calif., 1978-84; assoc. med. dir. Syntex Corp., Palo Alto, Calif., 1984-87; med. dir. G.D. Searle & Co., Skokie, Ill., 1987-89; exec. med. dir. Bristol-Myers Squibb Co., Princeton, N.J., 1989-90; v.p. clin. affairs Cholestech Corp., Hayward, Calif., 1990-92; pvt. practice medicine, prin. investigator Ukiah, Calif., 1992—; clin. assoc. divsn. family practice U. Calif., San Francisco, 1986-87. Contbr. articles to profl. jours. Rhodes scholar, 1963-65. Home: 1225 Vista Verde Rd Ukiah CA 95482-7554 Office: 1165 S Dora St E-1 Ukiah CA 95482-6353

MCALLISTER, PETER MICHAEL, real estate broker; b. Glendale, Calif., Mar. 27, 1938; s. Paul Blanchard and Blanche Isabell (Kirkpatrick) McA.; m. Diane Marie Williams, Feb. 4, 1961; children: Kevin Michael, Paul Scott, Kim Marie, Jeannie Isabella. BS in Indsl. Mgmt., U. So. Calif., 1961. Asst. plant dir. Krasne div. Royal Industries, L.A., 1968-69; dir. mgmt. engring. Am. Medicorp, Inc., L.A., 1970-73; chief oper. officer Sunrise Hosp., Las Vegas, Nev., 1973-82; adminstr. Huntington Park Community Hosp., L.A., 1982-83; cons. McAllister & Assocs., Las Vegas, 1983-84; salesman Americana Group Realtors, Las Vegas, 1984-85, Real Corp., Las Vegas, 1985-86; cons. Adelman & Assocs., Las Vegas, 1986-88; dir. mgmt. svcs. U. Med. Ctr., Las Vegas, 1988-95; broker, salesman Las Vegas Bus. Brokers, 1995—. Capt. USMC, 1961-66, Vietnam. Decorated Air medal, Purple Heart. Mem. Nev. Hosp. Assn. (chmn. so. coun. 1975-76, pres. 1981-82). Home: 7435 Rogers St Las Vegas NV 89139-5750 Office: Las Vegas Bus Brokers 1555 E Flamingo Rd Ste 326 Las Vegas NV 89119

MCANINCH, JACK WELDON, urological surgeon, educator; b. Merkel, Tex., Mar. 17, 1936; s. Weldon Thomas and Margaret (Canon) McA.; m. Barbara B. Buchanan, Dec. 29, 1960 (div. Aug. 1972); m. Burnet B. Sumner, Dec. 29, 1987; children: David A., Todd G., Brendan J. BS, Tex. Tech U., 1958; MS, U. Idaho, 1960; MD, U. Tex., 1964. Diplomate Am. Bd. Urology (trustee 1991-97, pres. 1996-97). Commd. capt. U.S. Army, 1964-66, advanced through grades to col., 1977, ret., 1977; col. USAR; intern then resident Letterman Army Med. Ctr., San Francisco, 1964-69; chief urol. surgery San Francisco Gen. Hosp., 1977—; prof. urol. surgery U. Calif., San Francisco, 1977—. Editor: Urogenital Trauma, 1985, Urologic Clinics of North America, 1989, Smith's General Urology, 1995; section editor: Early Care of the Injured Patient, 1990, Traumatic and Reconstructive Urology, 1996. Col. US Army, 1964-72. Recipient Disting. Alumnus award Tex. Tech U., 1994; named Disting. Alumnus U. Idaho, 1997. Fellow ACS (gov. 1992-97); mem. Am. Urol. Assn. (pres. we. sect. 1992-93, bd. dirs. 1990—, pres. 1996-97), Genitourinary Reconstructive Surgeons (pres.), Am. Assn. Surgery Trauma (v.p.), Soc. Univ. Urologists, Am. Bd. Urology (pres. 1996-97). Office: San Francisco Gen Hosp Dept Urology 1001 Potrero Ave San Francisco CA 94110-3518

MCARTHUR, ELDON DURANT, geneticist, researcher; b. Hurricane, Utah, Mar. 12, 1941; s. Eldon and Denise (Dalton) McA.; m. Virginia Johnson, Dec. 20, 1963; children: Curtis D., Monica McArthur Bennion, Denise, Ted O. AS with high honors, Dixie Coll., 1963; BS cum laude, U. Utah, 1965, MS, 1967, PhD, 1970. Postdoctoral rsch. fellow, dept. demonstrator Agrl. Rsch. Coun. Gt. Britain, Leeds, Eng., 1970-71; rsch. geneticist Intermountain Rsch. Sta. USDA Forest Svc., Ephraim, Utah, 1972-75; rsch. geneticist Shrub Scis. Lab., Intermountain Rsch. Sta. USDA Forest Svc., Provo, Utah, 1975-83, project leader, chief rsch. geneticist, 1983-97; project leader, chief rsch. geneticist Rocky Mountain Rsch. Sta., USDA Forest Svc., Provo, Utah, 1997—; adj. prof. dept. botany and range sci. Brigham Young U., Provo, 1976—. Author more than 270 rsch. papers; contbr. chpts. to books; editor symposium procs. Named USDA Forest Svc. Superior Scientist, 1990, Disting. Scientist, 1996; Sigma Xi grantee, 1970, NSF grantee, 1981, 85, 96, Coop. State Rsch., Svc. grantee, 1986, 91. Mem. Soc. Range Mgmt. (pres. Utah sect. 1987, Outstanding Achievement award 1992), Botan. Soc. Am., Soc. Study Evolution, Am. Genetic Assn., Shrub Rsch. Consortium (chmn. 1983—), Intermountain Consortium for Aridlands Rsch. (pres. 1991—). Mormon. Home: 555 N 1200 E Orem UT 84097-4350 Office: USDA Forest Svc Shrub Scis Lab 735 N 500 E Provo UT 84606-1856

MCARTHUR, JOHN D., communications executive; b. San Diego, Jan. 3, 1942; s. Arthur Paine and Marjorie (Moore) McA.; m. Carole Jayne Golob, Sept. 27, 1969; 1 child, Mary K. BA in Mktg. and Econs., San Diego State U., 1966. Contract mgr. Bell Helicopter, Ft. Worth and, Iran, 1973-79; comml. mgr. Cubic Corp., San Diego, 1979-81, Arabian Am. Oil Co., Saudi Arabia, 1981-82; internat. comml. mgr. Hughes Aircraft Co., Fullerton, Calif., 1982-95; dir. internat. comml. bus. Hughes Space and Comms., L.A., 1995—; guest lectr. Calif. State U., Fullerton, 1990—; mem. U.S. Mil. Acad. selection bd. 39th Congl. Dist., Calif., 1984—; mem. adv. bd. internat. bus. Nat. Contract Mgmt. Assn., Washington, 1990—; instr. U. Calif. Internat. Bus., Irvine, 1992—. Developer curriculum materials in field. Mem. various coms. Arthritis Found., 1974—. Capt. U.S. Army, 1966-72, helicopter pilot. Decorated Bronze Star, 23 Air medals. Mem. Am. Legion, Am. Legion Yacht Club (various coms.). Republican. Roman Catholic. Office: Hughes Space and Comms PO Box 92919 B/S41 A374 M/S Los Angeles CA 90009

MCATEE, RICHARD EVERETT, retired chemist, consultant; b. Springfield, Mo., Dec. 14, 1929; s. Eslie Howard and Esther Marie (Rippey) McA.; m. Wande Joyce Houston, Jan. 20, 1952; children: Peggy Jo, Diana Gay, Nancy Beth. BS, Ft. Hayes Kans. State Coll., 1962; MS, U. Idaho, 1964. Spectrochemist Phillips Petroleum Co., Idaho Falls, 1964-68; chemist Idaho Nuclear Corp., Idaho Falls, 1968-71; sr. chemist Allied Chem. Co., Idaho Falls, 1971-78; sci. specialist EG&G, Idaho Inc., Idaho Falls, 1978—; cons. in chem. processing, 1990-94; mem. EPA adv. com. for geothermal sampling, Las Vegas, Nev., 1981. Contbr. articles to profl. jours.; inventor chemical logging of geothermal wells, polyphosphozene membranes and spray forming membranes. Bd. dirs. Atomic Workers Credit Union, Idaho Falls, 1973-82; pres. Idaho Falls Figure Skating Club, 1989. With U.S. Army, 1948-50. Mem. Am. Nuclear Soc., Am. Chem. Soc. (health and safety divsn.), VFW. Republican. Methodist. Home: 646 E 16th St Idaho Falls ID 83404-5950 Office: LITCO PO Box 1625 Idaho Falls ID 83415-0001

MCAULEY, MILTON KENNETH, author, book publisher; b. Dunsmuir, Calif., Apr. 23, 1919; s. William Clear and Grace (Frentress) McA.; m. Maxine E. Laurenson, Mar. 16, 1942; children: Patricia L., Barbara A., William K. BS, U. Ill., 1956; postgrad., Calif. State U., Northridge, Calif. Luth. U., 1970-71. Commd. USAF, 1941-61, advanced through grades to maj., ret., 1961; engr. Navigation & Control divsn. Bendix, L.A., 1961-70; pub./editor Canyon Pub. Co., Canoga Park, Calif., 1980—. Author: Hiking Trails of the Santa Monica Mountains, 1980, Hiking Topanga State Park, 1981, Hiking trails Point Mugu State Park, 1982, Hiking Trails Malibu Creek State Park, 1982, Wildflowers of the Santa Monica Mountains, 1985, Wildflower Walks of the Santa Monica Mountains, 1987, Guide to the Backbone trail, 1990. Mem. Ventura County Archaeol. Soc., Santa Monical Mountains Trails Coun., Sierra Club (Environ. award on S.C. 100th birthday 1994). Home and office: 8561 Eatough Ave Canoga Park CA 91304

MCAULEY, SKEET, artist; b. Monahans, Tex., Mar. 7, 1951; s. George Clifford and Thelma Lee (Martin) McA.; m. Karen Suzanne Gee, June 25, 1994. BA, Sam Houston State U., 1976; MFA, Ohio U., 1978. Instr. photography Spring Hill Coll., Mobile, Ala., 1978-79, Tyler (Tex.) Jr. Coll., 1979-81; assoc. prof. photography U. N.Tex., Denton, 1981-93; featured in numerous articles and publs. One-person exhibits include Christopher Grimes Gallery, Santa Monica, Calif., 1995, Lowinsky Gallery, N.Y.C., 1993, U.S. Golf Assn. Mus., Far Hills, N.J., 1993, Dallas Mus. Art, 1992, Moody Gallery, Houston, 1992, Tyler Mus. of Art, 1992, The Heard Mus., Amherst, Mass., 1991, Calif. Mus. Photography, Riverside, 1991, Etherton/Stern Gallery, Tucson, Ariz., 1991, The Albuquerque Mus., 1990; group exhibits include Cleve. Mus. Art, 1994, Virginia Beach Ctr. for Arts, 1994, others, San Francisco Mus. Modern Art, 1996, Whitney Mus. Am. Art, N.Y.C., 1996; author: Sign Language: Contemporary Southwest Native America, 1989. Grantee Polaroid Copr., 1988, Nat. Endowment for the Arts Individual Artist fellowship, 1984, 86. Mem. Soc. Photographic Education (bd. dirs. 1990-93). Democrat. Office: 3516 Madera Ave Los Angeles CA 90039-1930

MCBEAN, SHARON ELIZABETH, church administrator; b. Chgo., July 15, 1937; d. Archibald Lewis Jr. and Mary Elizabeth (Rees) McBean; children: Debra Sue Sanders, Catherine Leigh Sanders Ferguson. BA cum laude, La Roche Coll., 1977; MS in Edn., Duquesne U., 1978. Cert. ch. bus. adminstr. Adminstrv. asst. 1st Presbyn. Ch., Santa Barbara, Calif., 1988-89, bus. mgr., 1989—; deacon 1st Presbyn. Ch., Santa Barbara, 1987-89. Mem. adv. bd. Valle Verde Retirement Comty., chair health svcs. com. Mem. AAUW, Presbyn. Ch. Bus. Adminstrn. Assn., Nat. Assn. Ch. Bus. Adminstrs.

MCBEATH, GERALD ALAN, political science educator, researcher; b. Mpls., Sept. 13, 1942; s. Gordon Stanley and Astrid Elvira (Hjelmeir) McB.; m. Jenifer Huang, June 7, 1970; children: Bowen, Rowena. BA, U. Chgo., 1963, MA, 1964; PhD, U. Calif., Berkeley, 1970. Vis. asst. prof. polit. sci. Rutgers Coll., New Brunswick, N.J., 1970-72; asst. prof. John Jay Coll., CUNY, N.Y.C., 1972-74, 75-76; assoc. prof. Nat. Chengchi U., Mucha, Taipei, Taiwan, 1974-75; prof. U. Alaska, Fairbanks, 1976—, acting dean coll. liberal arts, 1991-93, dir. faculty devel., 1990-92; cons. Inst. Social and Econ. Rsch., Anchorage, 1976-77; contract rschr. Alaska Dept. Natural Resources, Alaska Dept. Edn., Nat. Inst. Edn., others; staff dir. task force on internat. trade policy Rep. Conf., U.S. Senate. Sr. author: Dynamics of Alaska Native Self-Government, 1980; author monograph: North Slope Borough Government and Policymaking, 1981; jr. author: Alaska's Urban and Rural Governments, 1984; sr. editor Alaska State Government and Politics, 1987; co-author: Alaska Politics and Government, 1994 (Am. Assn. State & Local History Commendation cert. 1995); author: The Alaska State Constitution, 1997; editor: Alaska's Rural Development, 1982. Mem. bd. edn. Fairbanks North Star Borough, 1986-95, pres. 1989-90, 93-94, treas., 1991-93. Recipient Emil Usibelli Disting. Svc. award 1993; Chiang Ching-Kuo Found. fellow, 1995—; named Outstanding Faculty Mem., Assn. Students U. Alaska, Fairbanks, 1979, Alumni Assn. U. Alaska, Fairbanks, 1981; grantee Nat. Inst. Edn., 1980-83, Alaska Coun. on Sci. and Tech., 1982-84, Spencer Found., 1987-88, Chiang Ching-Kuo Found., 1995—. Mem. Asian Studies on Pacific Coast (program chmn. 1983, bd. dirs. 1982-83), Assn. Asian Studies, Western Polit. Sci. Assn. (mem. editl. bd. Western Govtl. Rschr.), Am. Polit. Sci. Assn., Fairbanks N. Star Borough Bd. Edn. Democrat. Home: 1777 Red Fox Dr Fairbanks AK 99709-6625 Office: U Ala Dept Polit Sci Fairbanks AK 99775

MCBRIDE, CAROL ANN, visual arts educator; b. Pt. Chester, N.Y., July 14, 1947; d. Alexander Joseph and Rose Alice (Tedesco) Mainero; m. James William McBride, Aug. 17, 1969; children: J. Garrett, Lindsay E. BS, Skidmore Coll., 1969; MA in Edn., U. Denver, 1970; MA in Visual Arts, U. No. Colo., 1989. Cert. in elem. edn. Elem. tchr. Aurora (Colo.) Pub. Schs., 1970-75, visual arts tchr., 1975—; mentor induction program Aurora Pub. Schs., 1995—, mem. curriculum devel. task force, 1994—, arts and humanities content com., 1994—, specialists' task force, 1995—, mem. essential programs, 1996—, implementation task force, 1997—; coord.-artist-in-residence program Century Sch., Aurora, 1985—. Vol. Boy Scouts of Am., 1988-94. Recipient Unique Tchr. award PTA, 1996. Mem. NEA, ASCD, Nat. Art Edn. Assn., Artsource Colo. (charter mem. leadership team), Delta Kappa Gamma. Office: Aurora Pub Schs 1085 Peoria St Aurora CO 80011-6203

MCBRIDE, JOHN P., state insurance commissioner; b. Buffalo, Wyo., Mar. 23, 1951. Grad., U. Wyo., 1973, law school grad., 1976. Lawyer Jones, Vines and Hunkins, Wheatland, Wyo., 1981-89; staff atty. to dep. commr. State of Wyo. Ins. Dept., Cheyenne, 1989-92, ins. commr., 1992—. U.S. Army Judge Advocate Gen. Corps, 1977-81. Office: State of Wyoming Insurance Dept Herschler Bl 122 W 25th St Cheyenne WY 82002

MCBRIDE, LINDA CARROLL, psychologist; b. Pensacola, Fla., Nov. 12, 1943; d. Carroll James and Helen Katherine (Berchtold) McBride; m. William Marion Gurka, June 4, 1966 (div. Nov. 1980); children: Valerie Lynn, Elaine Melanie. BA in French and German, Purdue U., 1965; MA in French Lit., U. Mo., 1967, MEd in Counseling Psychology, 1987, PhD in Counseling Psychology, 1994. French instr. U. Mo., Columbia, 1966-79, rsch. asst., 1989-93; French instr. Stephens Coll., Columbia, 1967-68; French/German tchr. Columbia Pub. Schs., 1980-88; profl. psychology intern U. Calif. Davis Counseling Ctr., 1993-94; psychol. asst., 1994-97; outreach presenter stress mgmt., eating disorders, multicultural issues U. Calif., Davis, 1993-94. Soprano Columbia Choral Ensemble, 1980-87, 92-93, Winifred Baker Chorale, San Francisco, 1994-95, Winifred Baker Chamber Chorus, 1994-95, Davis Chorale, 1995—, Sacramento Area Bach Festival, 1995. NEH grantee, 1983. Mem. APA, Sierra Club. Home: 1330 Antelope Ave # 16 Davis CA 95616-2836 Office: 433 F St Davis CA 95616-2836

MCBURNEY, CONSTANCE C., foreign language educator; b. St. Paul, June 17, 1957; d. Tom Henning and Carol Francis (Waggoner) Hill; children: Ivan Joseph, Jonas Lee; m. Charles Edward McBurney, Dec. 24, 1996. ESL tchr. Centro de Estudios N.Am., Valencia, Spain, 1978-79; Spanish tchr. Blackfoot (Idaho) H.S., 1981—, French tchr., 1994—, mem. acad. coun., 1982—. Author: (textbook) El eslabon perdido, 1995. Mem. Idaho Assn. Tchr. of Langs. and Cultures (pres. 1995-97). Home: 741 W 150 N Blackfoot ID 83221

MCBURNEY, LINDA LEE, health facility administrator; b. Denver, June 10, 1942; d. Maurice J. and Dorothy Mae (Whitman) Mooney; m. Kenneth Robert McBurney, June 16, 1962 (div. 1980); children: Scott Robert (dec.), Laura Lynn, Brenda Sue, Valerie Kaye. BSBA, Regis Coll., 1985. Office mgr. elec. co., Lakewood, Colo., 1980; sec. Safeco Ins. Co., Lakewood, 1980-82; office mgr. oil co., Golden, Colo., 1982; from clerical specialist to exec. sec. Cobe Labs., Lakewood, 1982-86; beauty cons. Mary Kay Cosmetics, Lakewood, 1986-87; adminstrv. mgr. Cobe Labs., Lakewood, 1986-89, med. systems mfr., adminstrn. & fin. mgr. worldwide svc. orgn., 1989-90, mgr. customer engring. response ctr., 1990-91; admissions coord. Hospice of Met. Denver, 1992—. Mem. Golden Area Sch. Adv. Com., 1974-80, Jefferson County Sr. High Curriculum Coun., 1980; room mother Kyffin Elem. Sch., Golden, numerous years; vol. Luth. Hosp. Med. Ctr., Wheatridge, Colo., 1973-92; pres. Women's Assn. Arvada (Colo.) Presbyn. Ch., 1979. Mem. AAUW (v.p. programs), Assn. Field Svc. Mgrs., Hospice of Metro Denver/Colo. Assn. of Home Health Agys., Gamma Phi Beta. Republican. Home: 11280 W 20th Ave # 36 Lakewood CO 80215-9999 Office: Hospice Metro Denver 425 S Cherry St Ste 700 Denver CO 80222-1234

MCCABE, MONICA JANE, oncological nurse; b. Anaheim, Calif.; d. Thurman Huston and Marcia Diane (Gandy) Walker; m. Roger Alan McCabe, July 27, 1985; children: Justin Robert, Sarah Jane. Assoc. Nursing, N.Mex. State U., Alamogordo, 1993. RN, N.Mex., Ariz. Med.-surg. nurse Meml. Med. Ctr., Las Cruces, N.Mex., 1993-94; oncology nurse Dr. Bishnu Rauth, Las Cruces, 1994-95; oncology and bone marrow transplant nurse Univ. Med. Ctr., Tucson, 1995—, mem. reengring. core team, 1996; nurse clinician Nat. Med. Care Homecare, Tucson, 1995-96; computer cons. Meml. Med. Ctr., Las Cruces, 1994; mem. Caring Environ. Patient Edn. Team. Mem. ANA, Ariz. Nursing Assn., N.Mex. Nurses Assn., Oncology Nursing Soc. (cert. Oncology Nursing Cert. Corp. subs.), So. Ariz. Oncology Nursing Soc. Home: PO Box 91198 Tucson AZ 85752

MCCAFFERTY, STEVEN GARTH, English educator; b. Montrose, Colo., May 7, 1951; s. Walter Doan and Audrey Jane McCafferty; m. Reiko McCafferty, Apr. 26, 1985. BA, Calif. State U., Northridge, 1973-75; MA, U. Hawaii, Manoa, 1984; PhD, U. N.Mex., 1995. Lectr. Inst. Internat. Studies and Tng., Shizuoka, Japan, 1984-85, Kanazawa (Japan) Inst. Tech., 1985-87, Cornell U., Ithaca, N.Y., 1992-95; asst. prof. U. Nev., Las Vegas, 1995—; contbr. Lang. Arts Framework, State of Nev., 1995—. Contbr. articles to profl. jours. Office: University of Nevada PO Box 4505 Las Vegas NV 89154

MCCAIG, JEFFREY JAMES, transportation company executive; b. Moose Jaw, Sask., July 5, 1951; s. John Robert and Anne Shorrocks (Glass) McC.; m. Marilyn Graves, July 7, 1983; children: Robbert Angus, Scott Thomas, Christa Mae. Student, Can. Jr. Coll. Lausanne, Switzerland, 1970; AB, Harvard Coll., 1973; LLB, Osgoode Hall Law Sch., Can., 1976; MSc in Mgmt., Leland Stanford Jr. U., 1984. Assoc. MacKimmie Matthews, 1976-81; owner, sr. officer Jeffery J. McCaig Profl. Corp., 1981-83; v.p. planning and corp. devel. Trimac Corp., Calgary, Alta., Can., 1983-87; exec. v.p. Trimac Ltd., Calgary, Alta., Can., 1987-90, pres., 1990-94, pres., CEO, 1994—; chmn. Bovar, Inc., Calgary, 1994—; bd. dirs. Bovar, Inc., chmn. bd. dirs. Trimac Corp., Greyhound Can. Transp. Corp., Richland Petroleum Corp., Conf. Bd. Can., ATA Found., Parks Found. Mem. Law Soc. Alta., Young Pres.'s Orgn., Calgary Golf and Country Club, Calgary Petroleum Club, Glencoe Club, 400 Club. Home: 708 Riverdale Ave SW, Calgary, AB Canada T2S OY3 Office: Trimac Corp, 800 5 Ave SW Ste 2100, Calgary, AB Canada T2P 3T6

MCCAIN, BUCK, artist; b. San Diego, Feb. 17, 1943; children: Jessica, Anthony Smith. Student, U. Guadalajara, Mex., U. San Diego, Imperial Valley Coll. represented by Joe Wade Fine Arts, Santa Fe, Troy's Western Heritage Gallery, Scottsdale. Prin. works include bronze monuments at Southgate Bank, Kansas City, Kans., City of Tucson, Albuquerque 1% for Arts Program, Western Devcor, Inc. and Bixby Ranch Co., Scottsdale, Ariz., Fleischer Mus. Am. Expressionism, Scottsdale, Pinnacle of Scottsdale retail ctr., Rex Allen Ariz. Cowboy Mus., Willcox, St. Thomas the Apostle Cath. Ch., Tucson, Mus. of the Southwest, Midland, Tex., Colossal Cave Mountain Park, Tucson.; represented in pvt. collections Valley Nat. Bank, Phoenix, Tucson Mus. Art, S.W. Savs. & Loan, Phoenix, Nita Stewart Haley Meml. Libr., Midland, Mus. of the Southwest, Midland, K Mart Corp., Troy, Mich., Interwest Bank Ariz., Tucson, Harmsen Found., Denver, Giant Industries, Inc., Scottsdale, Franklin Mint, Phila., Franchise Fin. Corp. Am., Scottsdale, Eiteljorg Collection, Indpls., others; contbr. to various mags. Recipient Gold medal for oil painting Franklin Mint, 1974. Mem. Nat. Sculpture Soc., Mountain Oyster Club. Home: PO Box 970 Eagar AZ 85925-0970 Office: McCain Studios Inc 1094 W Central Ave PO Box 970 Eagar AZ 85925

MCCAIN, JOHN SIDNEY, III, senator; b. Panama Canal Zone, Aug. 29, 1936; s. John Sidney and Roberta (Wright) McC.; m. Cindy Hensley, May 17, 1980; children: Doug, Andy, Sidney, Meghan, Jack, Bridget. Grad. U.S. Naval Acad., 1958; grad., Nat. War Coll., 1973-74. Commd. ensign U.S. Navy, 1958, capt., navy pilot, 1977; prisoner of war Hanoi, Vietnam, 1967-73; dir. Navy Senate Liaison Office, Washington, 1977-81; mem. 98th-99th Congress from 1st Ariz. Dist.; U.S. senator from Ariz., 1987—. Bd. dirs. Community Assistance League, Phoenix, 1981-82. Decorated Legion of Merit; decorated Silver Star, Bronze Star, Purple Heart, D.F.C., Vietnamese Legion of Honor. Mem. Soc. of the Cin., Am. Legion, VFW. Republican. Episcopalian. Office: US Senate 241 Russell Senate Office Washington DC 20510*

MCCAIN, NANCY SCHLOERKE, library director; b. Highland Park, Mich., Feb. 25, 1950; d. Wallace C. and Janice E. (Fletcher) Schloerke; m. Jeffrey W. McCain; children: Zebulon S., Starr D., Ewan S. BFA, U. Iowa, 1972; MLS, Emporia State U., 1993. Bookmobile driver Park County Libr. Sys., Hartsel, Colo., 1982-86; br. mgr. Park County Libr. Sys., Fairplay, Colo., 1986-93; dir. Lake County Pub. Libr., Leadville, Colo., 1993—. Mem. ALA, Colo. Libr. Assn. Office: Lake County Pub Libr 1115 Harrison Ave Leadville CO 80461-3398

MCCAIN, WARREN EARL, retired supermarket company executive; b. Logan, Kans., Dec. 17, 1925. A.A., Oreg. State U., 1948; postgrad., U. Ill. Supr. sales Mountain States Wholesale Co., 1951-59; with Albertson's Inc., Boise, Idaho, owner, operator supermarkets, 1959—, became mgr. non-foods, 1959, mgr. store, 1962-65, supr. merchandise, 1965-67, dir. intermountain region, 1967-68, v.p. ops., 1968-72, exec. v.p., 1972-74, pres., 1974-84, chmn. bd., chief exec. officer, 1976-94, also dir.; dir. Idaho 1st Nat. Bank. Office: Albertson's Inc PO Box 20 250 E Parkcenter Blvd Boise ID 83726*

MCCALL, ELIZABETH KAYE, columnist, consultant; b. Columbus, Ohio, Mar. 18, 1951; d. Frank and Patricia J. McCall. BA in Sociology, Miami U., Oxford, Ohio, 1973; MBA, Ryokan Coll., 1985. Writer horse industry, travel and various spiritual publs., Malibu, Calif., 1981—; cons. Elizabeth Kaye McCall & Assocs., Malibu, 1989—; pres. Magic Horse Prodns., Malibu, 1991—; pub. rels. advisor Equestrian Edn. Ctr. Pepperdine U., Malibu, 1986—; mktg. and pub. rels. cons. Author: Rapid Ride, 1987; prodr. holiday program Main Street Magic, 1990; contbr. to various profl. publs. Mem. Am. Horse Coun. Office: PO Box 6894 Malibu CA 90264

MCCALL, FRANCEEN KAY, social services administrator; b. Scottsbluff, Nebr., Aug. 10, 1950; d. Francis Leroy and Waunetа Mae (Unzicker) Pecht; m. Donald Gene Kelley, Nov. 22, 1970 (div. 1983); children: Jodi Kay, Jill Allison. AA, Nebr. Western Coll., 1970; BS, Chadron State Coll., 1972, MA, 1988. Social worker Nebr. State Dept. Social Svcs., Gering, 1978-82; elem. tchr. St. Agnes Elem. Sch., Scottsbluff, 1982-87; counseling/advising specialist Western Nebr. C.C., Scottsbluff, 1987-89; exec. dir. House of Neighborly Svc., Loveland, Colo., 1990—; bd. dirs. Friends Inc., Scottsbluff; mem. State Foster Care Rev. Bd., Scottsbluff, 1985; mem. FEMA bd. County of Larimer, Fort Collins, Colo., 1990—. Author: A Handbook for Disenfranchised Women, 1989, The Searing Desert, 1990, (newsletter) The Neighbor, 1990—. Mem. Chi Sigma Iota, Phi Theta Kappa.

MCCALL, LAURA, education educator, writer; b. Ill., Nov. 8, 1951; d. Richard Joseph and Corinne (Durava) McC. Cert. in French Lang. and Lit., U. Geneva, 1971; BA in History, Northwestern U., Evanston, Ill., 1973; MA in History, U. Mich., 1980, PhD, 1988. History tchr., womens basketball coach Shattuck Prep. Sch., Faribault, Minn., 1976-78; tchr. Gunnison (Colo.) H.S., 1979-86; history teaching fellow U. Mich., Ann Arbor, 1980-82; history instr. U. Mich., Dearborn, 1980-82; from instr. to asst. prof. history Western State Coll., Gunnison, 1982-90, asst. chair dept. history, politics and econs., 1987-90, chair dept., 1990; assoc. prof. history Met. State Coll., Denver, 1990—; chair athletic coun. Met. State Coll., Denver, 1991—, promotion and tenure com. history dept., 1990—, com. on internat. edn., 1991—; chair dept. history, politics and econ. Western State Coll., Colo., 1990, asst. chair, 1987-90, chair Livermore Scholarship, 1988-90, student adv. corps., gen. edn. com., 1989-90; faculty athletic rep. NCAA, Denver, 1993—; adj. prof. liberal arts and internat studies Colo. Sch. Mines, Golden, spring 1992. Mem. editorial bd. Jour. of the Early Republic, 1988-95; contbr. articles to profl. jours. Host, lectr. for advanced placement history students Adams County H.S., 1991; Arbor Day participant Lake Elem. Sch., 1990; pub. sch. vol. Blackstocks Elem. Sch., 1989-90; Colo. Knowledge Bowl sponsor Gunnison H.S., 1985-86. Namaed Tchr. of Yr., Golden Key Nat. Honor Soc., 1995-96; Teaching fellow U. Mich., 1980-82, John D. Pierce fellow, 1982, Program in Am. Instn. fellow, 1986-87, Newberry Libr. Chgo. fellow, 1986-87; NEH grantee, 1989. Mem. Soc. for Historians the Early Republic, Orgn. Am. Historians, Rocky Mountain MLA, Colo. History Group, Northwestern Alumni Assn., Sierra Club, World Wildlife Fund, Nature Conservancy, Phi Beta Kappa, Phi Alpha Theta (host, organizer Regional Conf. 1988, faculty sponsor 1987-90, Best Chpt. award 1991, Best Sponsor award 1995), Alpha Lambda Delta, Delta Kappa Gamma. Office: Met State Coll PO Box 173362 Denver CO 80217-3362

MCCALL, STEPHEN SHAWN, philanthropist; b. Balt., July 29, 1950; s. Henry David and Olivia Genevieve (Gunkel) McC.; m. Irene Takeko Kitagawa, Feb. 24, 1985; children: Emily Teiko, Stephen Hideo. BS, Towson State U., 1972. Educator Balt. City Pub. Sch. System, 1972-79; trainer, tech. writer Hawaii Med. Svcs. Assn., Honolulu, 1990—; founder, pres. Johanna Hawkins Meml. Inst. for the Humanities, Inc., Honolulu, 1984—. Mem. Am. Mensa Ltd. Democrat. Home: 3249 Hoolulu St Honolulu HI 96815-3840 Office: Johanna Hawkins Meml Inst Humanities Inc 3249 Hoolulu St Honolulu HI 96815-3840

MCCALL, SUSAN ELIZABETH, small business owner; b. Ogden, Utah, Nov. 21, 1945; d. Edward George and Virginia Alene (Davis) Mester; children: Melissa M., Ian E. Spencer. BFA, Utah State U., 1975. Office mgr. Sewing Dist., Phoenix, Ariz., 1969-70; art tchr. North Ogden City Schs., 1970-71; graphic arts Permaloy Corp., Ogden, 1972-74; regional purchasing agt. USDA Forest Service, Ogden, 1976; owner, mgr. The Flower Co., Albuquerque, 1976-89; dir. dist. 8-J Florists Transworld Delivery Assn., 1988-89; mgr. Spring Flowers, Sydney, 1990-91; owner, mgr. Floral Arts Design Sch. N. Mex., 1994-96. Recipient First Place award Utah Soc. Art, 1964. Mem. West Tex. Florist Assn., N.Mex. Floral Assn., Albuquerque Vis.' Conv. (mktg. com. 1986-90), Fla. Transworld Delivery Assn. (dir. Dist. 8-J, 1988), Profl. Women in Bus.

MCCALL, WILLIAM CALDER, oil and chemical company executive; b. Hoquiam, Wash., Feb. 1, 1906; s. Dougall Hugh and Hughena (Calder) McC.; m. Marian Hall, Mar. 22, 1946; children—Ernest, Robert. Student U. Oreg., 1924-28; LHD Lewis & Clark Coll., 1992. Asst. sales mgr. Anaconda Sales Co., Chgo., 1932-39; chmn. McCall Oil & Chem. Corp., Portland, Oreg., 1939—, Gt. Western Chem. Co., Portland, 1975—; dir. Oreg. Bank, Portland, King Broadcasting Co., Seattle. Pres. Oreg. Art Mus., Portland; trustee Lewis and Clark Coll., Portland; exec. v.p. Oreg. Symphony Soc.; dir. Oreg. Health Scis. Found., Good Samaritan Hosp. Found., Portland. Republican. Episcopalian. Clubs: Eldorado Country (Indian Wells, Calif.) (pres. 1978-79); Arlington (Portland); Pacific-Union (San Francisco); Los Angeles Country, Vintage (Palm Desert, Calif.), Waverley Country, Rainier (Seattle). Office: McCall Oil and Chem Corp 808 SW 15th Ave Portland OR 97205-1907

MCCAMBRIDGE, DENNIS, marshal. Chief dep. U.S. marshal U.S. Dist. Ct., Boise. Office: Fed Bldg and US Courthouse 550 W Fort St MSC 010 Boise ID 83724

MCCANN, JACK ARLAND, former construction and mining equipment company executive, consultant; b. Chestnut, Ill., Apr. 16, 1926; s. Keith Ogden and Miriam Imogene McC.; m. Marian Adele Gordon, Mar. 31, 1956; 1 child, Christopher John. A.B., Bradley U., 1950. Mgr. Washington Office, R.G. LeTourneau Inc., 1950-58; mgr. def. and spl. products Westinghouse Air Brake Co., 1958-64, mgr. nat. accounts, 1964-67, mng. dir. Belgian plant and European mktg., 1967-70; gen. sales mgr. WABCO div. Am. Standard Inc., Peoria, Ill., 1970-73, v.p. mktg., 1973-80, v.p. staff, 1980-82, ret., 1982; now cons. Vestryman St. Francis-in-Valley Episcopal Ch., Green Valley Ariz.

MCCANN, RICHARD JAMES, economist, consultant; b. Grand Rapids, Mich., Apr. 30, 1958; s. John J. McCann and Helen Jane Matekel; m. Ellen Moratti, Feb. 23, 1992. BS Polit. Economy of Natural Resources, U. Calif., Berkeley, 1981; M of Pub. Policy, U. Mich., 1985; MS in Agrl. & Resource Econs., U. Calif., Berkeley, 1990; postgrad., U. Calif., 1990—. Staff economist Dames & Moore, San Francisco, 1985-86; sr. rsch. assoc. QED Rsch. Inc., Palo Alto, Calif., 1986-88; grad. student researcher, teaching asst. U. Calif., Berkeley, 1989-92; sr. economist Foster Assocs./Spectrum Econs., San Francisco, 1989-92; econ. and policy cons., ptnr. M. Cubed, West Sacramento, Calif., 1993—. Contbr. articles to profl. jours. Mem. Housing and Cmty. Devel. Adv. Commn., Yolo County, Calif., 1993—; mem. Overall Econ. Devel. Plan Task Force, Yolo County, West Sacramento, 1994. Mem. Am. Agrl. Econs. Assn., Assn. Environ. and Resource Economists, Am. Econs. Assn., Western Econs. Assn. Internat., Assn. Environ.Profls., Track and Field Writers Assn., Phi Beta Kappa. Home: M Cubed 2516 Bombadil Ln Davis CA 95616

MC CARDLE, RANDALL RAYMOND, real estate developer; b. Phila., Sept. 2, 1931; s. Russell Henry and Ruth Hertha (Snyder) McC.; m. Yong Suk Yi; 1 child, Mark. AA, Orange Coast Coll., 1956; BA, Chapman Coll., 1958, MA, 1966; PhD, Colo. U., 1974; Real estate broker, Newport Beach, Calif., 1953-95; founder, pres. The Real Estaters, Orange County, Calif., 1961—, Treeco Escrow Co., Inc., Costa Mesa, Calif., 1971—; founder Bank of Costa Mesa, 1972, dir. bus. devel., 1973—; also newspaper columnist, lectr., investment counselor. Fund-raising chmn. Boys' Club of Am., Harbor area, 1979-80; bd. dirs. Boys Club Harbor Area; mem. adv. com. Orange Coast Coll., 1964—, Golden West Coll., 1969—; dir. Harbor Ridge Masters, 1990-95; mem. St. Andrews Presbyn. Ch. With USN, 1950-53. Decorated Nat. Def. Svc. medal, UN Svc. medal, Korean Svc. ribbon with 2 stars; recipient Appreciation award Bd. Realtors, 1967, 68, 70, 76, 80, UN citation; inducted into Orange Coast Coll. Hall of Fame, 1983; named Realtor of Yr., 1989. Mem. Calif. Assn. Realtors (state dir. 1963-67), Calif. Assn. Real Estate Tchrs. (state dir. 1966-80), Orange County Coast Assn. (dir. 1974—), C. of C., Nat. Assn. Real Estate Appraisers, Bd. Realtors (pres. 1966-67 long-range planning com. 1981), U. So. Calif. Bd. Faculty Assn., Red Baron Flying Club, Big Canyon Country Club, Mason, Shriner. Contbr. articles to profl. jours. Office: 1000 Quail St Ste 260 Newport Beach CA 92660-2721

MCCARTHY, CHARLOTTE MARIE, microbiologist, educator; b. Watford City, N.D., Sept. 7, 1937; d. Walter James and Mildred Christine (Johnson) McC. BS, Idaho State U., 1958; MS, Oreg. State U., 1961; PhD, U. Wash., 1967. Microbiologist Park-Davis & Co., Detroit, 1958-59, Nat. Jewish Hosp., Denver, 1968-71; microbiologist, instr. U. Oreg. Dental Sch., Portland, 1961-63; asst. prof. microbiology N.Mex. State U., Las Cruces, 1972-75, assoc. prof. microbiology, 1975-83, prof. microbiology, 1983—; reviewer NIH, Bethesda, Md., 1985—, Ford Found., Washington, 1993-95, USDA, Washington, 1990—. NIH grantee, 1970-87, 87-90, 89-93. Mem. AAAS, Am. Soc. Microbiology (chair elect. divsn. U 1986, chair 1987), N.Mex. Network of Women in Sci. and Engring. (sec. 1984), Sigma Xi. Office: NMex State U Biology Dept 3 AF Las Cruces NM 88003-0001

MCCARTHY, COLLEEN, mayor; b. 1957. Resource allocation specialist U.S. West Comm., Helena, Mont., 1977—; commr. City of Helena, 1991-95, mayor, 1995—. Office: Office of Mayor 316 N Park Ave Rm 321 Helena MT 59623

MCCARTHY, LAURENCE JAMES, physician, pathologist; b. Boston, Aug. 11, 1934; s. Theodore Clifford and Mary Barrett (Moran) McC.; m. Cynthia Marion DeRoch, Aug. 28, 1978; children: Laurence J. Jr., Jeffrey A., Karen E., Patrick K., Ryan N. BA, Yale U., 1956; student, Georgetown U. Sch. Med., 1956-58; MD, Harvard U., 1960; MS, U. Minn., 1965. Cert. Am. Bd. Pathology, 1965. Intern Boston City Hosp., 1960-61; resident in pathology Mayo Clinic, Rochester, Minn., 1961-65; pathologist Honolulu Heart Program, 1965-67; chief pathology Kelsey-Seybold Clinic, Houston, 1967-68; clin. asst. pathologist M.D. Anderson Hosp., Houston, 1967-68; chief pathology Straub Clinic, Honolulu, 1968-72; assoc. pathologist Wilcox Hosp., Lihue, Hawaii, 1972-74; chief pathology A.R. Gould Hosp., Presque Isle, Maine, 1975-78; assoc. pathologist Kuakini Med. Ctr., Honolulu, 1978—. Med. dir. USPHS, 1965-67. Fellow Coll. Am. Pathologists, Am. Soc. Clin. Pathologists; mem. AMA, Hawaii Soc. Pathologists (pres. 1970), Am. Acad. Forensic Sci., Hawaii Med. Assn., Honolulu County Med. Soc. (del. 1982-83). Roman Catholic. Home: 249 Kaelepulu Dr Kailua HI 96734-3311 Office: Kuakini Med Ctr 347 N Kuakini St Honolulu HI 96817-2306

MCCARTHY, MARY FRANCES, hospital foundation administrator; b. Washington, Apr. 16, 1937; d. Joseph Francis and Frances (Oddi) McGowan; m. Charles M. Sappenfield, Dec. 14, 1963 (div. June 1990); children: Charles Ross, Sarah Kathleen; m. Daniel Fendrich McCarthy, Jr., Aug. 25, 1990. BA, Trinity Coll., Washington, 1958; cert. in bus. adminstrn., Harvard U.-Radcliffe Coll., 1959; MA, Ball State U., Muncie, Ind., 1984. Systems engr. IBM, Cambridge, Mass., 1959-61; editl. asst. Kiplinger Washington Editors, 1961-63; feature writer pub. info. dept. Ball State U., 1984-85, coll. editor Coll. Bus., 1985-86, coord. alumni and devel., 1986-88, dir. major gift clubs and donor rels., 1988-90; dir. devel. Sweet Briar (Va.) Coll., 1990-91; adminstr. St. Mary's Hosp. and Med. Ctr. Found., Grand Junction, Colo., 1991—. Editor: A History of Maxon Corporation, 1986, Managing Change, 1986, Indiana's Investment Banker, 1987; assoc. editor Mid-Am. Jour. Bus., 1985-86. Participant Leadership Lynchburg, 1990, Jr. League; mem. Sr. Companions Bd., Grand Junction, 1992—; mem. Mesa County Healthy Cmtys. Steering Com., 1992—; mem. Mesa County Health Assessment, 1994—; regional dir. IX, Assn. for Healthcare Philanthropy, 1996—. Recipient Golden Broom award Muncie Clean City, 1989; svc. of distinction award Ball State U. Coll. Bus., 1990. Mem. Coun. for Advancement and Support of Edn., Assn. of Healthcare Philanthropy (regional 9 cabinet 1992—), Nat. Soc. Fundraising Execs. (cert., Colo. chpt. bd. dirs. 1994—). Republican. Office: St Marys Hosp/Med Ctr Found 2635 N 7th St Grand Junction CO 81501-8209

MCCARTHY, STEVEN M., lawyer; b. Morristown, N.J., May 2, 1949; s. George Doane and Frances (Jones) McC. BA in Philosophy, U. Va., 1971; MA in Philosophy, Calif. State U., San Francisco, 1975; JD, Golden Gate U., 1978. Diplomate Nat. Inst. for Trial Advocacy; bar: Calif. 1979, U.S. Dist. Ct. (no. dist.) Calif. 1979; cert. tchr. secondary school law, philosophy, religion, Calif.; cert. diver rescue specialist, instr. Law clk. United Farm Workers Union, 1973, San Francisco Lawyers' Com. on Urban Affairs, 1975, San Francisco Pub. Defender, 1975, Bayview Hunters' Point Cmty. Defender, 1976-77; pvt. practice, 1979-88; ptnr. McCarthy & Wakeley, Oakland, Calif., 1988—; judge pro tempore Contra Costa Superior Ct. Judge Pro Tem Panel and EASE program evaluator, 1993—; domestic violence emergency protective order judge Solano County Superior Ct., 1994—; arbitrator Solano County Mcpl. Ct., 1994—, Alameda County Bar Assn. Fee Arbitration Panel, 1989—, sml. claims and traffic, Alameda County Mcpl. Jud. Dist., 1981—, others. Assoc. editor The Rapier. Bd. dirs. Mental Health Assn. of Alameda County, 1994-97; pres. bd. dirs. Elms Homeowners Assn., 1992-94; treas. bd. dirs. Oaks Homeowners Assn., 1989-90; lectr. Alameda H.S. Spkrs. Program. Mem. NRA, Calif. State Bar Assn. (spl. master), Alameda County Bar Assn., Solano County Bar Assn., N.Am. Horsemen's Assn., Back Country Horsemen of Calif., Calif. Rifle and Pistol Assn., San Leandro C. of C., Alameda Divers, Ctrl. Calif. Coun. Dive Clubs, Chabot Gun Club. Home: 591 Blue Jay Dr Hayward CA 94544-6701 Office: 2100 Embarcadero #100 Oakland CA 94606

MCCARTHY, WILLIAM JAMES, research psychologist, consultant, psychology educator; b. Paris, May 20, 1951; came to U.S. 1969; s. John Robert and Helen Ruth (House) McC.; m. Angela Wong, Mar. 23, 1974 (div. 1984); m. Bambi Batts Young, Aug. 7, 1988; 1 child, Jordan Robert. BA, Columbia U., 1973; MA, U. Ill., 1976; PhD, Yale U., 1980. Vis. asst. prof. Hampshire Coll., Amherst, Mass., 1978-79; instr. Pepperdine U., Los Angeles and Malibu, Calif., 1979; asst. research psychologist UCLA, 1980—, adj. asst. prof., 1987—; dir. sci. Pritikin Systems, Inc. (subs. Quaker Oats Co.), 1992-94, Pritikin Longevity Ctr., 1994—; cons. Am. Heart Assn. of Los Angeles, 1982-83; cons., bd. dirs. Am. Cancer Soc. Coastal, Los Angeles, 1982—, v.p. pub. issues, 1989-93, pres. 1993-95; bd. dirs. Calif. divsn., Am. Lung Assn. of Los Angeles, 1983-90, Internat. Chem. Workers' Union, Akron, Ohio, 1984-85, Nat. Cancer Inst., Bethesda, Md., 1986-92, Calif. Dept. Health, Sacramento, 1986, Karl Lorimar Video Prodns., 1986-87, Los Angeles County Dept. Health Services, 1986-88. Editor: So. Calif. Language and Gender Interest Group Newsletter, 1980-88, Psychology of Women Quarterly, 1986-89; consulting editor: Health Psychology, 1992-93. Bd. dirs. So. Calif. Skeptics, Pasadena, 1986-88; mem. L.A. Year 2000 Program; mem. grants review bd. Am. Lung Assn. Los Angeles County, 1984-89, Healthy Mothers Healthy Babies Coalition Los Angeles, 1985-88. Mem. Coalition for Clean Air, Santa Monica, Calif. Consulting editor Health Psychology. Grantee NIH, 1980-84, Am. Lung Assn., 1982, Nat. Cancer Inst., 1985, 86, 87-92, 96—, tobacco-related disease program U. Calif., 1990-93; recipient Fitness Leadership award L.A. County, Calif., 1994, Capitol Dome Pub. Svc. award Am. Cancer Soc., 1994. Mem. AAAS, APHA, Am. Psychol. Soc., Am. Cancer Soc. (mem. smoking cessation subcom. 1984-89, nutrition subcom., 1990—), Soc. Behavioral Medicine. Democrat. Home: 2050 Newell Rd Malibu CA 90265-2938 Office: UCLA Psychology Dept 1282 Franz Hall Los Angeles CA 90024 also: Pritikin Longevity Ctr 1910 Ocean Front Walk Santa Monica CA 90405-1014

MCCARTHY-TUCKER, SHERRI NEVADA, psychology educator, consultant, researcher, writer; b. Topeka, June 2, 1958; d. Wallace Gene and Lois Elaine (McDyson) McCarthy; m. Scott Newlin Tucker, Feb. 14, 1983; children: Colin Apollo, Chrysallis Altair. AA in Liberal Arts, Phoenix Coll., 1981; BA in Psychology, BEd in English, Ariz. State U., 1984, MA in Spl. Edn., 1987, PhD in Ednl. Psychology, 1995. Cert. kindergarten -12 spl. edn., ESL tchr., Ariz. Mng. editor Scottsdale (Ariz.) Free Press, 1977-78; instr. English Skills Ctr. Phoenix C.C., 1978-80; spl. instr. Title I Creighton Sch. Dist., Phoenix, 1980-81; lit. instr. CTY program Johns Hopkins U., 1985; gifted specialist Fountain Hills (Ariz.) Schs., 1985-87; writing instr. Ariz. State U. Ctr. Acad. Precocity, 1986; tchr. ESL Chandler-Gilbert C.C., Chandler, Ariz., 1986-87; tchr. of gifted Chandler (Ariz.) Unified Schs., 1987-90; psychology tchr., cons. Maricopa County C.C., Tempe, Ariz., 1988—; asst. prof. ednl. psychology No. Ariz. U., Yuma, 1993—; freelance writer, 1974—; spl. edn. tchr. Hawaii Dept. Edn., 1990-91; mem. faculty assoc. ednl. psychology Ariz. State U., Phoenix, 1992-96; tchr. English Mesa (Ariz.) C.C., 1993-96; advisor, asst. honors coord. Phi Theta Kappa, 1994-96; gifted ednl. specialist Kyrene Pub. Schs., Chandler, Ariz., 1995-96. Author: Metamorphosis-A Collection of Poems, 1975, Speed Communication, 1979, A Matter of Time, 1980, A Death in the Family, 1988, Coping with Special Needs Classmates, 1993; staff writer Ariz. Hwy. Patrolman mag., Phoenix, 1979-82; newsletter editor Ednl. Opportunity Ctr., Tempe, Ariz., 1982-83; contbr. articles to profl. jours. Bd. dirs. Young Astronauts, Fountain Hills, 1985-87. Mem. Odyssey of the Mind (mem. bd. govs. 1987-89, Creativity award 1986, 87). Home: 698 S 10th Ave Yuma AZ 85364 Office: Northern Ariz Univ at Yuma PO Box 6236 Yuma AZ 85366

MCCAW, BRUCE R., insurance executive, airline and communications executive; b. Washington, June 26, 1946; s. J. Elroy and Marion O. (Oliver) McC. Student Colo. Coll., 1964-66, U. Wash., 1967-68. Lic. ins. broker, comml. pilot. Pres. Jet Air Corp., Everett, Wash., 1968-72, Delta Aviation Ins. Brokers Inc., Bellevue, Wash., 1972-80; v.p. and dir. McCaw Communications Cos. Inc., Bellevue, 1969—, Horizon Air Industries Inc., Seattle, 1981-87; chmn. Westar Ins. Group Inc., Bellevue, 1979—; vice chmn. Forbes Westar Inc., 1986—; barnstormer Mus. of Flight, Seattle, 1983—; exec. dir. Assn. Am. Air Travel Clubs, Bellevue, 1974-79. Bd. trustees Poncho, Seattle, 1983-84; dir. Lynnwood Rotary Air Show, Everett, 1968-77; aviation chmn. Everett C. of C. Recipient Disting. Alumnus Achievement award Lakeside Sch., Seattle, 1984. Mem. Nat. Bus. Aircraft Assn., Aviation Ins. Assn., Regional Airline Assn. Republican. Episcopalian. Lodge: Rotary. Office: Forbes Westar Inc PO Box 1607 Bellevue WA 98009-1607

MCCAW, CRAIG O., communications executive; b. Centralia, Wash., 1949. Grad., Stanford U., 1971. Pilot; chmn., CEO McCaw Cellular Comm., Inc., 1968-88; chmn. bd. dirs., CEO McCaw Cellular Comm., Inc., Kirkland, Wash., 1982—; chmn., CEO Lin Broadcasting Co., 1990—. Office: McCaw Cellular Comm Inc 2300 Carillon Pt Kirkland WA 98033-7353

MCCAWLEY, WILLIAM DALE, II, ethnohistorian, author, corporate accountant; b. Long Beach, Calif., Nov. 26, 1952; s. William Dale and Antoinette Gertrude (Wolke) McC.; children: Michael Breier, Jonathan William. BA in Psychology with honors, Calif. State U., Long Beach, 1974, cert. tchg. CFO, dir. fin. and adminstrn. McDonnell Douglas Physician Systems Co., Gardena, Calif., 1981-88; dir. adminstrn. U. Phoenix, Fountain Valley, Calif., 1988-89; sr. acct., sys. mgr. Robert-John Industries, Inc., Huntington Beach, Calif., 1989-91; asst. contr. Tallon Termite and Pest Control, Inc., Long Beach, Calif., 1991-95; cons., project acct. LSA Assocs., Inc., Irvine, Calif., 1995-96; acctg. mgr. MicroAge Computer Ctr., Fountain Valley, Calif., 1997—; cons. Rancho Los Alamitos Hist. Ranch and Gardens, Long Beach, 1993—, Channel Islands Nat. Pk., Ventura, Calif., 1991—. Author: The First Angelinos: The Gabrielino Indians of Los Angeles, 1996; mem. edtl. bd. Ballena Press, 1995—; contbr. articles to profl. and edtl. jours. Recipient Hon. Mention Nat. Writer's Club, 1992. Home and Office: 14672 Monroe St Midway City CA 92655

MCCLAFFERTY, WILLIAM MARK, film company executive; b. Wilmington, Del., Jan. 4, 1949; s. William Thomas and Margaret (Rash) McC.; m. Pamela Edwards, Dec. 22, 1988; 1 child, Kate. BA, U. Del., 1972; postgrad., Rutgers U., 1974. Dir. mktg. and rsch. ABC Network, L.A., 1978-82; dir. creative affairs Paramount Pictures, L.A., 1982-84; v.p. dramatic programming ABC Network, L.A., 1984-86; exec. v.p. Glen Larson Prodn. Fox Studios, L.A., 1986-88; pres. Eddie Murphy Prodn. Paramount Studios, L.A., 1988-94; chmn. Spellbound Pictures, Beverly Hills, Calif., 1994—. Campaign dir. U.S. Senator Joseph R. Biden (D), Del., 1972. Recipient scholar U. Del. Mem. Writers Guild Am., Prodrs. Guild Am., Omicron Delta Kappa. Roman Catholic. Home: 13400 Mulholland Dr Beverly Hills CA 90210 Office: Spellbound Pictures 301 N Canon Dr Beverly Hills CA 90210

MCCLAIN, RICHARD STAN, cinematographer; b. Los Angeles, Oct. 7, 1951; m. Kim Girard, Nov. 7, 1987. Founder Pasadena Camera Sys., Inc. Aerial cameraman: (feature films) The Client, I Love Trouble, Lightning Jack, Tombstone, Falling Down, Heart and Soul, So, I Married an Axe Murderer, The Good Son, Made in America, This Boy's Life, Fearless, Passenger 57, Wind, At Play in the Fields of the Lord, The Right Stuff, The Iceman, Rambo, Firebirds, Wind, Basic Instinct, Innerspace, Buster, U2 Rattle and Hum, Crazy People, The Hunt for Red October, The Doors, Flatliners, Nell, Murder in the First, Drop Zone, Get Shorty, The Money Train; (TV shows) Magnum P.I., Airwolf. Recipient Best Cinematography award London Internat. Advt. Awards, 1993, Telly award (2), 1993, (1), 1994. N.Y. Festival Silver award, 1993, Telly award (2) 1994, (4) 1995, (2), 1996. Mem. Internat. Photographers, Screen Actors Guild, Dirs. Guild Am.

MCCLAIN, SAMUEL ALBERT, marketing professional; b. Pitts., June 4, 1962; s. Samuel and Leila May McC. BS in Bus. Adminstrn., Pa. State U., 1984. Asst. buyer Kaufmann's Dept. Store, Pitts., 1984-86; product specialist Ohio Valley Audio, Columbus, 1986-87, sales rep., 1987-88; dist. sales mgr. Hamburg Brothers, Pitts., 1988-89; asst. brand mgr. Pioneer Electronics, Long Beach, Calif., 1989-92; brand mgr. Pioneer Electronics, Long Beach, 1992-96, sr. br. mgr., 1996—. Home: 2304 N Poinsettia Ave Manhattan Beach CA 90266-2662 Office: Pioneer Electronics 2265 E 220th St Long Beach CA 90810-1639

MCCLANAHAN, CLARENCE EDWARD, university official. BA in English, William Paterson Coll., 1973; MA in English, NYU, 1977, PhD in Comparative Lit., 1981. Prof. City Coll. San Francisco, 1980-84, Armstrong U., Berkeley, Calif., 1988-90; cons. San Francisco Corps., 1985-87; adminstr. U.S.-Japan Tech. Mgmt. Ctr., Stanford (Calif.) U., 1991—. Author: European Romanticism, 1990; contbr. articles, essays to profl. publs. Recipient cert. Goethe Inst., 1979. Mem. Elks. Home: 360 Hyde St Apt 202 San Francisco CA 94109-8020 Office: Stanford U US Japan Ctr 322 McCullough Bldg Stanford CA 94305

MCCLANE, ANGELA DAWN, marriage, family and child counselor; b. Fort Benning, Ga., Mar. 7, 1961; d. Victor Lee and Lucerne Cordelia (Parks) Weber; m. George Eddington McClane, May 14, 1994. BS, Ill. State U., Normal, 1983; MA, Trinity Divinity Sch., Deerfield, Ill., 1989. Recreation therapist F. Edward Herbert Hosp., New Orleans, 1984-86; rsch. asst. Alex Masterson, M.D., Loma Linda, Calif., 1989-90; marriage, family & child counseling intern Loma Linda Behavioral Med. Ctr., 1990-91, Riverside (Calif.) Psychiat. Med. Group, 1991-94; psychiat. emergency team Knollwood Hosp., Riverside, 1992-94. Mem. Am. Counseling Assn., Calif. Assn. Marriage & Family Therapists.

MCCLATCHY, JAMES B., editor, newspaper publisher; b. Sacramento; s. Carlos K. and Phebe (Briggs) McC.; m. Susan Brewster; children: Carlos F., William B. B.A., Stanford U.; M.S., Columbia U. Reporter Sacramento Bee; reporter, editor Fresno Bee, Calif.; pub. McClatchy Newspapers, Sacramento.; past pres., dir. InterAm. Press Assn. Trustee Nat. Ctr. Internat. Schs. Mem. Am. Press Inst. (bd. dirs.). Office: McClatchy Newspapers 21st & Q Sts Sacramento CA 95813

MCCLATCHY, KATE, political candidate. Candidate for v.p. U.S., 1996. Home: 1801 A Cedar St Berkeley CA 94707

MCCLELLAN, CRAIG RENE, lawyer; b. Portland, Oreg., June 28, 1947; s. Charles Russell and Annette Irene (Benedict) McC.; m. Susan Armistead Nash, June 7, 1975; children: Ryan Alexander, Shannon Lea. BS in Econs., U. Oreg., 1969; JD magna cum laude, Calif. We. U., 1976. Bar: Calif. 1976, U.S. Dist. Ct. (so. dist.) Calif. 1976, U.S. Dist. Ct. (ea., ctrl., no. dists.) Calif. 1991, U.S. Supreme Ct. 1991. Compliance specialist Cost of Living Coun. and Price Commn., Washington, 1972-73, dir. Oil Policy subcom., 1973; ptnr. Luce, Forward, Hamilton & Scripps, San Diego, 1976-87; owner McClellan & Brown, San Diego, 1987—. Chmn. annual fundraising auction KPBS, 1984. Capt. USMC, 1969-72. Mem. Assn. Trial Lawyers Am., Am. Bd. Trial Advocates, Am. Inns of Ct. (master), Calif. State Bar Assn., San Diego County Bar Assn., Calif. Trial Lawyers Assn. (bd. govs. 1985-87), San Diego Trial Lawyers Assn. (bd. dirs. 1983-90), Nat. Forensics League, Phi Gamma Delta, Phi Alpha Delta. Presbyterian. Office: McClellan & Brown 1144 State St San Diego CA 92101-3529

MCCLELLAN, GLORIA, mayor. Owner, mgr. ladies apparel shop Vista, Calif.; matron Sheriff's Dept. City of Vista; mayor City of Vista, 1980-81, 86-98. Mem. coun. City of Vista, 1972-80, 81-86, past mayor pro tem, chairperson mobile home task force, 1986-94, chairperson redevel. commn., 1986-97, chairperson airport commn., 1992-97, sr. citizen's advisor to city coun., 1990-97, chairperson subcom. on crime, 1988, past mem. water reclamation bd., crime commn. advisor; mem. various city and county coms., commns.; mem. Vista coun. Argis bd. for evaluation of criminal status and sheriff svcs. in San Diego County, 1986-88, 88-97; chmn. budget com. SANDAG, bd. dirs., 1982-84, 96-97, chmn. bd. dirs., 1992-96; chmn. Buena Sanitation Dist., 1987-91, 94-97; vice chairperson San Diego divsn. League of Calif. Cities, 1986-87, pres., 1986-88; vice chairperson State of Calif. Clean Air Com.; past vice chmn. LAFCO, chairperson cities adv. com., 1975, 77-79; assoc. mem. women's aux. Boys Club; active Sr. Citizen's Aux., 60-Plus Aux., Friends of Libr., Vista Emblem Club, Vista Hist. Soc., Vista Women's Club; mem. adv. bd. ARC, 1987-88; pres. North County Cmty. Theatre, 1985-86; past sponsor Girl's softball Fast Pitch Ball. Mem. Am. Legion Aux., VFW Aux., Beta Sigma Phi. Office: City of Vista PO Box 1988 Vista CA 92085

MCCLELLAN, ROBERT EDWARD, civil engineer; b. Atlanta, Feb. 27, 1922; s. Robert Edward and Maria Elizabeth (Ameln) McC.; m. Mary Margaret Billetter, Oct. 21, 1944; children: Kathleen Mary, Mary Elizabeth, Patricia Maura, Eileen Mary, Robert Edward III, Mary Margaret, Thomas Francis. BCE, U. So. Calif., 1947, MSCE, 1956, PhD in Engring., 1970. Registered profl. civil and structural engr., Calif. Gen. supr. design Rocketdyne, Canoga Park, Calif., 1959-62; mem. tech. staff The Aerospace Corp., El Segundo, Calif., 1962-69, mgr. strategic studies, 1980-85; chief tech. staff The Ralph M. Parsons Co., Pasadena, Calif., 1969-80; v.p. research and devel. Apollo Systems Tech., Canyon Country, Calif., 1985-88, also bd. dirs. Served to lt. (j.g.) USN, 1943-46, PTO. Recipient Outstanding Civil Engring. Grad. award U. So. Calif., 1977. Mem. AIAA, Am. Def. Preparedness Assn., AAAS, N.Y. Acad. Scis., L.A. Athletic Club, Sigma Xi, Tau Beta Pi, Chi Epsilon. Republican. Roman Catholic.

MCCLELLAND, KAMILLA KURODA, news reporter, proofreader, book agent; b. Bozeman, Mont., June 16, 1964; d. Yasumasa and Alice (Kassis) Kuroda; m. Craig Alexander McClelland, June 25, 1989. BA in Asian Studies, U. Calif., Berkeley, 1987; MS in Print News, U. Ill., Champaign-Urbana, 1989. Legis. aide Hawaii State Ho. of Reps., Honolulu, 1987; grad. asst. U. Ill. Dept. Journalism, Champaign, 1987-89; asst. op-ed editor The Daily Illini, Champaign, 1988-89; reporter AP, Seattle, 1989, Tacoma News Tribune, 1989-90; bus. news reporter The Olympian, Olympia, Wash., 1990-97; editor-in-chief N.W. Nikkei, Seattle, 1997—; proofreader Minerva Rsch., Inc., Honolulu, 1982—. Vol. Am.-Arab Anti Disc Com., Berkeley, Calif., 1984-87, Capital City Marathon, Olympia, 1993-95, Olympia Symphony, 1996, Black Hills Triathalon, 1993—, Olympia Chamber Orch., 1996; active Japanese Am. Citizens League, Honolulu, also Berkeley, 1983-89. Recipient Recognition awards for newswriting Gannett, 1991, 92, 95, 1st Pl., Best of Gannett award for bus. and consumer reporting, 1994, Well Done Bus. Reporting Gannett award, 1995, 2nd place bus. and consumer reporting Best of Gannett award, 1995. Mem. Asian Am. Journalists Assn. Office: The Olympian PO Box 407 Olympia WA 98507-0407

MCCLENDON, IRVIN LEE, SR., company executive, computer consultant, writer and editor; b. Waco, Tex., June 12, 1945; s. Irvin Nicholas and Evelyn Lucile (Maycumber) McC.; divorced; children: Michael Boyd, Irvin Lee Jr., Laura Ann, Paul Nicholas, Richard Lester. Student El Camino Coll., 1961-63, U. So. Calif., 1962-66; BA in Math., Calif. State U.-Fullerton, 1970, postgrad. in bus. adminstrn., 1971-76; cert. nat. security mgmt. Indsl. Coll. Armed Forces, 1974; postgrad. in religion Summit Sch. Theology, 1982-84. Engring. lab. asst. Rockwell Internat. Corp., Anaheim, Calif., 1967-68, test data analyst, 1968, assoc. computer programmer, 1968-70, mem. tech. staff, 1970-82; systems programmer A-Auto-trol Tech. Corp., Denver, 1982-84, sr. tech. writer, 1984-86; sr. tech. writer, editor Colo. Data Systems, Inc., Englewood, Colo., 1986-87; engring. writer III CalComp subs. Lockheed Co., Hudson, N.H., 1987; sr. tech. writer CDI Corp., Arvada, Colo., 1987-88; staff cons. CAP GEMINI AM., Englewood, 1989; sr. tech./instrnl. writer & editor TTS Inc., Aurora, Colo., 1990-96, sr. multimedia developer, 1996-97; gen. mgr., chief editor The Berkeley Group, LLC, Denver, 1997—. Sec. of governing bd. Yorba Linda Libr. Dist., 1972-77; mem. St. Paul's United Meth. Ch., Denver, 1997—, mem. The Colorado Chorale, 1988, 97—; trustee Ch. of God (Seventh Day), Bloomington, Calif., 1979-81, treas., 1980-81, mem. Calif. State U. and Coll. Statewide Alumni Coun., 1976-77; 2d v.p. Orange County chpt. Calif. Spl. Dists. Assn., 1976, pres., 1977; mem. Adams County Rep. Cen. Com., 1984-90, Republican Ctrl. Com., 1992-95; tech. support adviser to chmn. Colo. Rep. Com.; chmn. Denver County Rep. Ctrl. Com. Dist. 2 Subcom. for Precinct Devel. and Support. With USAFR, 1967-71. USAF Nat. Merit scholar, 1963-67. Mem. Calif. Assn. Libr. Trustees and Commrs. (exec. bd., So. Calif. rep. 1976-77), Nat. Eagle Scout Assn. (life), Bible Sabbath Assn. (life), Calif. State U.-Fullerton Alumni Assn. (dir. 1975-77). Republican. Office: PO Box 12615 Alcott Sta Aurora CO 80212-0615

MCCLENNEN, MIRIAM J., former state official; b. Seattle, Sept. 16, 1923; d. Phillip and Frieda (Golub) Jacobs; m. Louis McClennen, Apr. 25, 1969; stepchildren: Peter Adams, James C.A., Helen, Persis, Crane, Emery. BA, U. Wash., 1945; MBA, Northwestern U., 1947. Exec. trainee Marshall Field & Co., Chgo., 1945-47; asst. buyer Frederick & Nelson (subs. of Marshall Field), Seattle, 1947-49; buyer Frederick & Nelson (subs. of Marshall Field), 1949-57; fashion coordinator, buyer Levy Bros., Burlingame/San Mateo, Calif., 1957-63; buyer Goldwaters, Phoenix, 1963-67; adminstrv. asst. to pres. Ariz. State Senate, Phoenix, 1973-76; dir. publs. Office of Sec. of State, Phoenix, 1976-87; chairwoman legis. subcom. adminstrv. procedure Ariz. State Legislature, Phoenix, 1984-85. Original compiler, codifier, editor publ. Ariz. Adminstrv. Code, 1973-87, Ariz. Adminstrv. Register, 1976-87. Bd. dirs., mem. Phoenix Art Mus. League, 1972-90; mem. exec. bd. Phoenix Symphony Guild, 1969-88; bd. dirs., sec. Combined Met. Phoenix Arts and Scis., 1974-90, mem. adv. bd., 1990-95; bd. dirs. Phoenix Art Coun., 1973-78, Master Apprentice Programs, 1980-83; bd. dirs., mem. exec. com. Heard Mus., 1982-88, 90—, chmn. publs. com., 1982-88, chmn. exhibit and edn. com., 1990-93; mem. adv. bd. Ariz. State Hist. Records, 1987-90, Ariz. Commn. on Arts, 1989-96, Phoenix Art Mus., 1966—, dir.'s circle, 1988—; bd. dirs. Arizonans for Cultural Devel., 1996—; mem. Cape Cod Mus. of Fine Arts, 1996—. Recipient Disting. Svc. award Atty. Gen. Ariz., 1987, Outstanding Svc. to People, Ariz. State Senate, 1987, Nat. Assn. Secs. of State award, 1987. Mem. English Speaking Union, Nat. Soc. Arts and Letters, Charter 100 (bd. dirs. 1981-85), Phoenix Country Club, Ariz. Club, Eastward Ho! Country Club (Chatham, Mass.). Home: 5311 N La Plaza Cir Phoenix AZ 85012-1415 also (summer): 2267 Orleans Rd Chatham MA 02633

MCCLOUD, PAUL DUANE, chemical engineer; b. Akron, Ohio, Feb. 19, 1959; s. Paul Richard and Martha Lee (Mayberry) McC.; m. Mary Elizabeth Wojcik, July 6, 1985. BS in Chem. Engring., U. Akron, Ohio, 1982. Registered profl. engr., Ohio. Engr. II mech. engring. divsn. Am. Electric Power, Columbus, Ohio, 1982-90; plant engr. Del. Ranch plant Magma Power Co., Calipatria, Calif., 1990-91, asst. plant supt. Vulcan/Hoch, 1991-94; sr. project engr. Cal Energy Co.I, Pasadena, Calif., 1995—. Mem. ASTM (com. D-5 1988-90), AIChE. Home: 2611 Willowglen Dr Duarte CA 91010-3622 Office: The C E Holt Co 201 S Lake Ave Ste 300 Pasadena CA 91101-3017

MCCLUNE, MICHAEL MARLYN, real estate asset management company executive; b. Denver, July 12, 1950; s. Raymond Earl and Lorraine Elva (Bohm) McC.; m. Elizabeth Ann Butler, Sept. 18, 1982; children: Kristin Elizabeth, Michael Ryan. BSCE magna cum laude, U. So. Calif., 1972, MBA, 1974. Lic. real estate broker, Calif. Real estate investment broker Vistar Fin., Marina del Rey, Calif., 1979-81; program bus. mgr. Hughes Aircraft Co., El Segundo, Calif., 1981-85; v.p. LaSalle Ptnrs. Ltd., L.A., 1985-93; pres., CEO, New Am. Asset Mgmt. Svcs., Long Beach, Calif., 1993—; pres. New Am. Cons. Svcs., Long Beach, 1994—; pres., bd. dirs. Indsl. Complex Camarillo, Calif., 1988-93; founder, ptnr. CyberLease, Costa Mesa, Calif., 1990-92. Capt. USAF, 1974-79. Mem. Bldg. Owners and Mgrs. Assn. Greater L.A. (bd. dirs. 1994—, chmn. bd. dirs. 1995-96, President's award 1993), Long Beach Mgrs. Assn. (v.p. 1988-90), Long Beach C. of C., Rotary, Tau Beta Pi. Office: New Am Asset Mgmt Svcs 400 Oceangate Ste 210 Long Beach CA 90802

MCCLUNG, MICHAEL ROY, physician, medical educator, researcher; b. Louisville, June 19, 1943; s. Roy C. and Juyne Genelle (Bucklew) McC.; 1

child, Daniel ;m. Betsy Claire Willims, June 5, 1993. BA in Biology, Rice U., 1965; MD, U. Tex. S.W. Med. Sch., 1969. Diplomate Am. Bd. Internal Medicine, Am. Bd. Endocrinology and Metabolism. Intern Parkland Meml. Hosp., Dallas, 1969-70, resident, 1970-72; fellow in endocrinology NIH, Bethesda, Md., 1972-75; asst. prof. medicine Oreg. Health Scis. U., Portland, 1976-80, assoc. prof. medicine, 1980—; chief sect. endocrinology VA Med. Ctr., Portland, 1980-86; asst. dir. dept. med. edn. Providence Med. Ctr., Portland, 1987—, dir. osteoporosis ctr., 1987—; dir. dept. diabetes, metabolism and endocrinology Chiles Rsch. Inst., Portland, 1988—; cons. endocrinology VA Med. Ctr., Portland, 1977-81, staff physician, 1980-87; dir. Endocrinology Clinic, Univ. Hosp., Portland, 1977-81, dir. Bone and Mineral Clinic, 1981-87, dir. Osteoporosis Ctr., 1985-87. Editor-in-chief Nat. Osteoporosis Found. Clin. newsletter, 1995—; contbr. numerous articles, abstracts to profl. jours., chpts. to books. Recipient Chief Residents Tchg. award, 1981. Mem. Am. Soc. Bone and Mineral Rsch., The Endocrine Soc. (program com. 1977, clin. day program com. 1989-90, chmn. program com. 1991), Soc. for Clin. Deusitometry, Oreg. Med. Assn., Multnomah County Med. Soc., Alpha Omega Alpha. Office: Oreg Osteoporosis Ctr 5050 NE Hoyt St Ste 651 Portland OR 97213-2990

MCCLURE, JAMES A., lawyer, retired senator; b. Payette, Idaho, Dec. 27, 1924; s. W. R. and Marie McC.; m. Louise Miller; children: Marilyn, Kenneth, David. JD, U. Idaho, 1950; DL (hon.), Coll. Idaho, 1986. Mem. Idaho State Senate, 1961-66; asst. majority leader, 1965-66; city atty. City of Payette, Idaho; pros. atty. Payette County, Idaho; mem. 90th-92nd Congresses 1st Idaho Dist., 1967-73; senator Idaho, 1973-90; chmn. Energy and Natural Resources Com., 1981-86; mem. Com. on Rules and Adminstrn., Com. on Appropriations; pres. McClure, Gerard & Neuenschwander, Inc., Washington, 1990—; ptnr. Givens, Pursley, & Huntley, Boise, Idaho, 1990—. Trustee Kennedy Ctr., Meth. Ch. Mem. Elks, Masons, Kiwanis, Phi Alpha Delta. Methodist. Office: McClure Gerard & Neuenschwander Inc 201 Maryland Ave NE Washington DC 20002 also: Givens Pursley & Huntley Ste 200 Park Pl 277 N 6th St Boise ID 83701

MCCLURE, WILLIAM OWEN, biologist; b. Yakima, Wash., Sept. 29, 1937; s. Rexford Delmont and Ruth Josephine (Owen) McC.; m. Pamela Preston Harris, Mar. 9, 1968 (div. 1979); children: Heather Harris, Rexford Owen; m. Sara Joan Rorke, July 27, 1980. BSc, Calif. Inst. Tech., 1959; PhD, U. Wash., 1964. Postdoctoral fellow Rockefeller U., N.Y.C., 1964-65; rsch. assoc. Rockefeller U., 1965-68; asst. prof. U. Ill., Urbana, 1968-75; assoc. prof. U. So. Calif., L.A., 1975-79; prof. biology, prof. neurology U. So. Calif., 1979—; v.p. sci. affairs Nelson Rsch. & Devel. Co., Irvine, Calif., 1981-82; acting v.p. rsch. & devel. Nelson Rsch. & Devel. Co., 1985-86; dir. program. neurol. info. sci. U. So. Calif., 1982-92, dir. program in psychobiology, 1991—; dir. cellular biology U. So. Calif., 1979-81, dir. neurobiology, 1982-88, dir. prog. psychobiology, 1991—; cons. in field; dir. Marine & Freshwater Biomed. Ctr., U. So. Calif., 1982-83; co-dir. Baja Calif. Expedition of the R/V Alpha Helix, 1974, others; chmn. Winter Conf. on Brain Rsch., 1979, 80, others; lectr. in field; sci. adv. bd. Nelson R & D, 1972-91; mem. bd. commentators Brain and Behavioral Scis., 1978—. Editor or author 3 books; co-editor: Wednesday Night at the Lab; patentee in field; mem. editorial bd. Neurochem. Rsch., 1975-81, Jour. Neurochemistry, 1977-84, Jour. Neurosci. Rsch., 1980-86; contbr. over 100 articles to profl. jours. Bd. dirs. San Pedro and Peninsula Hosp. Found., 1989—, Faculty Ctr., U. So. Calif., 1991-95, San Pedro Health Svcs., 1992—. Scripps Inst. fellow, 1958, NIH fellow, 1959-64, 64-65, Alfred P. Sloan fellow, 1972-76, others; recipient rsch. grants, various sources, 1968—; Intersci. Rsch. Inst. fellow, 1989. Mem. AAAS, Am. Soc. Neurochemistry, Soc. for Neurosci., Am. Soc. Biol. Chemistry and Molecular Biology, Internat. Soc. Neurochemistry, Assn. Neurosci. Depts. and Programs, Univ. Park Investment Group, Bay Surgical Soc., N.Y. Acad. Scis. Republican. Presbyterian. Home: 30533 Rhone Dr Palos Verdes Peninsula CA 90275-5742 Office: U So Calif Dept Biol Scis Los Angeles CA 90089

MCCLUSKEY, LOIS THORNHILL, photographer; b. Boston, Apr. 7, 1945; d. Fred S. and Mary (Evans) T.; BA, Middlebury Coll., 1966; postgrad. U. St. Thomas, Houston, 1967-69; MA, NYU, 1971; cert. in graphic design U. Calif.-Santa Cruz, 1983; m. Edward J. McCluskey, Feb. 14, 1981. Research technician dept. virology Baylor Sch. Medicine, Houston, 1966-68; with Kelly Girls, Palo Alto, 1971-72; slide curator dept. art Stanford (Calif.) U., 1972-80; founder, pres. Stanford Design Assocs., Palo Alto, 1981—; cons. copy and museum photography; designer, producer custom lecture slides. Mem. Smithsonian Assos. Home: 895 Northampton Dr Palo Alto CA 94303-3434 Office: PO Box 60451 Palo Alto CA 94306-0451

MCCOLL, CAROL ANN, financial executive, educator; b. Arlington Heights, Ill., June 10, 1953; d. Charles Richard and Jean (Gore) Barton; m. Donald Bruce McColl, Dec. 6, 1975 (div. July 1984); 1 child, Donald Daniel. BA, Colo. Coll., 1974; MBA, U. Colo., 1987. Office mgr. Worksafe, Inc., Denver, 1979-83; divsn. adminstr. Dysan Corp., Colorado Springs, 1984-86; exec. dir. Tech. Assistance Ctr., Denver, 1987-90; v.p. fin. and adminstrn. McRel, Aurora, Colo., 1990—; adj. instr. Regis U., Denver, 1992—. Mem. fin. com. Archdiocese of Denver, 1993—; vice chair, bd. dirs. Metro Denver Gives, 1989-90; sec., bd. dirs. Colo. Lawyers for the Arts, Denver, 1991; vol. Tech. Assistance Ctr., Denver, 1990—. Mem. Beta Gamma Sigma. Roman Catholic. Office: McRel 2550 S Parker Rd Ste 500 Aurora CO 80014-1678

MCCOLLUM, ALVIN AUGUST, real estate company executive; b. L.A., Jan. 20, 1920; s. Nile Clarkson and Ida Martha (Kuhlman) McC.; m. Maxine Eleanor Seeberg, July 29, 1944; children: Robert Michael, James Alan, Patricia Kathleen. BA, UCLA, 1941; postgrad., U.S. Naval Acad., 1946, Southwestern U., 1949-50. Exec. v.p., dir. Strout Realty, N.Y.C., 1948-61, Del E. Webb Corp., Phoenix, 1961-67; pres., dir. Sahara Nev. Corp., Las Vegas, 1964-67, Devel. Svcs., Inc., Scottsdale, Ariz., 1967-69; pres., chmn. Recreation Leisure Land, Inc., Scottsdale, 1969-71; asst. pres., dir. A.J. Industries, Inc., L.A., 1971-74; pres., dir. Carefree (Ariz.) Ranch, Inc., 1974-76; pres., bd. dir. Cons. Internat., Scottsdale, 1976—; chmn. CEO Greenway Environ. Svs., Inc., Gilbert, Ariz., 1992—; pres., bd. dirs. Combined Assets, Inc., Westlake Village, Calif., First Realty Fin., Inc., L.A., Corp. Capital Resources, Inc., Westlake Village. Bd. dirs. Admiral Nimitz Found., Fredericksburg, Tex., 1970—, Boys Club Las Vegas, 1964-68, United Fund, Las Vegas, 1966; co-chmn. NCCJ, Las Vegas, 1966; elder Presbyn. Ch. USA, 1954—. Lt. USN, 1943-48, PTO. Mem. Masons, Shriners, Am. Legion, Mt. Shadows Country Club (bd. dirs. 1962-64). Republican. Home: 215 N Power Rd # 180 Mesa AZ 85205 Office: Greenway Environ Svcs Inc 644 E Southern Ave Ste 204 Mesa AZ 85204-4934

MCCOLM, GEORGE LESTER, international agricultural consultant, journalist; b. Colby, Kans., Aug. 2, 1911; s. Theodore Harrison and Jane (Speirs) McC.; m. Emma Victoria Davis, Aug. 9, 1936 (dec. Sept. 1959); children: Carol Ann, Patricia Alice; m. Elizabeth Jane Gunder Funderburg, May 1, 1975. BS in Agr., Kans. State U., 1935; postgrad., U. Ariz., 1961-64. Cert. profl. agronomist. Various soil conservation and agrl. positions, 1935-41; dir. crop. prodn. War Relocation Authority, Topaz, Utah, 1942-43; soil conservationist Bur. Indian Affairs, Shiprock and Window Rock, Ariz., 1947-52; soil conservationist Bur. Indian Affairs, Shiprock, 1949-52, dir. nursery, 1953-57; dir. B Square Ranch Expt. Sta., Farmington, N.Mex., 1958-61; educator U. Ariz., 1961-66; with U.S. Dept. State, India, 1964-66; tech. rep. internat. Mekong River devel. com. U.S. Dept. State, Vietnam, 1966-72; rancher Lewiston, Calif., 1973-87; owner Lewiston Nursery, 1987—; part-time agrl. advisor Mex. Govt., 1976-81; with Office Strategic Svcs. in WWII conf., Washington, D.C., 1991. Contbr. articles to sci. jours. Bd. dirs. Trinity County Fair Assn. Lt. USNR, 1944-46, PTO. Mem. NRA, CAST, Am. Soc. Agronomy and Soil Sci., Calif. Soc. Agronomy and Soil Sci., Am. Asst. Ret. Persons, Lewiston C. of C., Am. Legion, Alpha Gamma Rho, 4-H Club (Edison medal). Republican. Methodist. Home: Box 330 Lewiston CA 96052 Office: Lewiston Nursery Deadwood Rd Lewiston CA 96052

MCCOMB, KARLA JOANN, educational curriculum and instruction administrator, consultant; b. Tacoma, July 23, 1937; d. John Frank and Lorraine Beatrice (Winters) Bohac; m. Russell Marshall McComb, Nov. 27, 1959 (div.); children: Marsha McComb Hayes, Kathleen McComb Bridge. Cert. instr. French, U. Paris, 1958; BA, Calif. State U.-Sacramento, 1960; MS, Nova U., 1984. Cert. secondary tchr., Nev. Tchr. French and music Sacramento Waldorf Sch., 1960-62; tchr. French, Red Bluff High Sch., 1967-68; tchr. French and music Pocatello (Idaho) Schs., 1969-71; tchr., chairperson dept. Clark County Sch. Dist., 1971-76; curriculum cons. social sci., fgn. lang., profl. growth, Las Vegas, 1976-84; cons. staff devel. and profl. growth, 1984-91, dir. staff devel., multicultural edn. and substance abuse edn., 1991-93, dir. multicultural edn., substance abuse edn., 1993—; cons. Taft Inst. Govt., Salt Lake City, 1977—, Tchr. Inservice, Follett Pub. Co., 1980-81; author: A Cultural Celebration, 1980, Project MCE: Multicultural Education in the Clark County School District, 1992; editor The Nevada Holocaust Curriculum, 1987. Coordinator Nev. Close-Up Program, 1980-88. Mem. Sacramento Symphony Orch., 1954-66, Nev. Humanities Com., Nev. commn. Holocaust; pres., bd. dirs. Ctr. Ind. Living, 1995—; v.p. Nev. Assn. Handicapped, 1994—, pres., 1996—; bd. dirs. Love All People Youth Group, supt. Love All People Sch., 1983—, producer staff devel. films, 1986—; v.p., bd. dirs. Nev. Assn. Handicapped, pres., bd. dirs. Ctr. Ind. Living. Mem. Clark County Fgn. Lang. Tchrs. Assn. (pres.), Nat. Council Social Studies, Social Studies Suprs. Assn., Nev. Fgn. Lang. Tchrs. Assn. (pres., Outstanding Humanities Nevadan 1994), Gov. Workforce adv. bd., 1996—. AAUW, Phi Theta Kappa, Mu Phi Epsilon, Alpha Delta Kappa, Phi Delta Kappa. Democrat. Clubs: Vegas Valley Dog Obedience (pres.), Jackpot Obedience Assn. (pres.). Home: 409 N Lamb Blvd # A Las Vegas NV 89110-3370 Office: 601 N 9th St Las Vegas NV 89101-2536

MCCOMB, RONALD GRAEME, rolfer; b. Burns, Oreg., Jan. 6, 1938; s. Oliver Graham and Melba Viettia (Oard) McC.; m. Annie Bernice Duggan, Nov. 1968 (div.); 1 child, Siobhan Ariel Duggan. Student, Portland Art Mus. Sch., 1957-61; Cert., Rolf Inst., Boulder, Colo., 1971. Cert. rolfer. Artist, 1961-66; film maker Union Light Co., N.Y.C., 1966-70, Am. Film Inst., Hollywood, Calif., 1970; rolfer pvt. practice Portland, Seattle, 1971—. Contbr. articles to profl. jours. Mem. Rolf Inst.

MCCONKEY, MAX, association executive; b. Altoona, Pa., Mar. 14, 1945; s. Robert Paul and Ruth Lenora (Moyer) McC.; m. Judith Elizabeth Colvin, Mar. 28, 1965 (div. 1980); children: Lisa Christine, Aaron Thoreau; m. Anne Maley, Aug. 29, 1987. BA, Pa. State U., 1967; postgrad., U. Mass., 1976. Tchr., dept. chair William Penn Sr. High Sch., York, Pa., 1967-69; cartoonist Lancaster (Pa.) Ind. Press, Liberation News Svc., 1968-72; reporter, desk editor The Gazette & Daily, York, 1968-69; tchr., dept. chair Mt. Anthony Union High Sch., Bennington, Vt., 1969-72; reporter, columnist The Bennington Banner, 1970-71; dir. The Network, Inc., Andover, Mass., 1972-92; exec. dir. Nat. Dissemination Assn., Tucson, Ariz., 1981—; dir. Ariz. office WestEd, San Francisco, 1992—; cons., pub. speaker in field. Editor, writer, pub. (newsletter) The Update, 1982-96; pub. Dissemination Perspective, 1996—; editorial cartoonist Lawrence Eagle newspaper, 1979-85; collage artist. Del. Dem. Nat. Conv., 1968. Mem. Am. Ednl. Rsch. Assn. (chair nat. outreach com. 1993-96, mem. strategic planning task force 1996—). Office: WestEd 4732 N Oracle Rd Ste 217 Tucson AZ 85705

MCCONNEL, RICHARD APPLETON, aerospace company official; b. Rochester, Pa., May 29, 1933; s. Richard Appleton Sr. and Dorothy (Merriman) McC.; m. Mary Francis McInnis, 1964 (div. 1984); children: Amy Ellen, Sarah Catherine; m. Penny Kendzie, 1993. BS in Naval Engring., U.S. Naval Acad., 1957; MS in Aerospace Engring., USN Postgrad. Sch., 1966. Commd. ensign USN, 1957; naval aviator Operation ASW, 1959-63, 68-71, 75-79; asst. prof. math. U.S. Naval Acad., 1966-68; program mgr. P3C update Naval Air Devel. Ctr., 1971-75; range program mgr. Pacific Missile Test Ctr., 1979-82; ret. USN, 1982; program mgr. Electromagnetic Systems div. Raytheon Co., Goleta, Calif., 1982-87; sr. engr. SRS Techs., Inc., Camarillo, Calif., 1987-92, High Tech. Solutions, Inc., Camarillo, Calif., 1992—. Mem. Internat. Test and Evaluation Assn., Assn. Old Crows. Republican. Office: High Tech Solutions 1000 Paseo Camarillo # S120 Camarillo CA 93010-6021

MCCONNELL, CALVIN DALE, clergyman; b. Monte Vista, Colo., Dec. 3, 1928; s. Roy and Leota Fern (Taylor) McC.; m. Mary Caroline Bamberg, Sept. 2, 1952 (dec. Apr. 1986); children: David William, Mark Andrew; m. Velma Duell, Dec. 17, 1988. B.A., U. Denver, 1951; M.Div., Iliff Sch. Theology, 1954; S.T.M., Andover Newton Theol. Sem., 1967. Ordained to ministry United Meth. Ch.; pastor Meth. Ch., Williams, Calif., 1955-58, 1st United Meth. Ch., Palo Alto, Calif. and Stanford U. Wesley Found., 1958-61; chaplain and asst. prof. religion Willamette U., Salem, Oreg., 1961-67; pastor Christ United Meth. Ch., Denver, 1968-72; pastor 1st United Meth. Ch., Boulder, Colo., 1972-79, Colorado Springs, Colo., 1979-80; bishop United Meth. Ch., Portland Area, 1980-88, Seattle Area, 1988-96; retired, 1996.

MCCORD, THOMAS B., geophysicist, educator; b. Elverson, Pa., Jan. 18, 1939; s. Thomas M. and Hazel Violet (Bard) M.; m. Carol S. Bansner, Dec. 20, 1962. BS, Pa. State U., 1962; MS, Calif. Inst. Tech., 1964, PhD, 1968. From asst. to assoc. prof. (tenured) MIT, Boston, 1969-77; sr. research scientist Ctr. for Space Research, MIT, Boston, 1977-86; tenured prof. planetary scis., depts. geology and geophysics, and physics and astronomy U. Hawaii, Honolulu, 1976—; vis. assoc. Planetary Sci., Calif. Inst. Tech., 1969-72; dir. George R. Wallace Jr. Astrophys. Obs., MIT, Boston, 1970-77; asst. dir. Inst. for Astronomy, U. Hawaii, Honolulu 1976-79; chmn. div. planetary sci. Hawaii Inst. Geophysics U. Hawaii, 1979-90; co-founder, chmn. chief sci. SETS Inc., Honolulu, 1978-96; mem. NASA teams on 8 past and current space missions, positions included team leader Comet Rendezvous Asteroid Flyby Project and team mem. Galileo, Cassini, Rosetta, and Mars 96 mission. Pres. Pacific Space Ctr., 1988-90. With USAF 1958-62. Named Research Fellow in Planetary Sci., Calif. Inst. Tech., 1968; recipient numerous research grants from various govt. and private agencies including NASA, Jet Propulsion Lab., Nat. Oceans and Atmospheres Adminstrn., and NSF, 1968—, W.M. Keck Found. grant, 1986, Honolulu City and County award; asteroid discovered in 1985 named for him. Fellow Am. Geophys. Union (pres. planetology sect. 1986-90), AAAS; mem. Am. Astron. Soc. (pres. divsn. planetary sect. 1980-82), Internat. Astron. Union, European Geophys. Soc., Explorers Club. Office: U Hawaii Hawaii Inst Geophysics and Planetology Honolulu HI 96821 also: SETS Tech Inc Mililani Tech Pk 300 Kahelu Ave Mililani HI 96789-3911

MCCORKLE, ROBERT ELLSWORTH, agribusiness educator; b. Salinas, Calif., Apr. 3, 1938; s. Stanley Harold and Muriel Eugenia (Vosti) McC.; m. Mary E. McCorkle, June 26, 1965; children: Bonnie Kathleen, Robyn Krystyna. BSc in Farm Mgmt., Calif. Poly. State U., San Luis Obispo, 1960; MSc in Agrl. Econs., U. Calif., Davis, 1962; postgrad., U. Wis., 1969, Oreg. State U., 1966. Rsch. statistician U. Calif., Davis, 1960-62; asst. prof. agrl. bus. Calif. Poly. State U., San Luis Obispo, 1962-66, dir. internat. edn., 1970-74, asst. prof. agrl. mgmt., 1969-76, prof. agribus., 1976—; chief farm mgmt. officer Ministry Agr., Lusaka, Zambia, 1967-69; dir., owner McCorkle Farms, Inc., Willows, Calif., 1970—; vis. prof. Mich. State U., U.S. AID, Washington, 1984-85; dir., owner McCorkle Trucking, Glenn, Calif., 1988—; agrl. economist U.S. AID-Redso ESA, Nairobi, Kenya, 1984-85. Author: Guide for Farming in Zambia, 1968. Pres. Cabrillo Property Owners Assn., Los Osos, Calif., 1976-78; vol. Atty. Gen.'s Adv. Com., Calif., 1972-74; bd. dirs. Nat. Alpha Zeta Found. U.S. Peace Corps strategy grantee, Washington, 1976—. Mem. Am. Agrl. Econs. Assn., Am. Soc. Farm Mgrs. and Rural Appraisers, Western Agrl. Econs. Assn., Calif. Poly. Farm Mgmt. Club, Calif. Poly. Alumni Assn., Blue Key, Alpha Zeta (founding mem., sr. advisor Delta chpt., nat. high coun. chronicler, treas., bd. dirs.), Nat. Alpha Zeta Found. (bd. dirs.). Republican. Episcopalian. Office: Calif Poly State U San Luis Obispo CA 93407

MC CORMAC, WESTON ARTHUR, retired educator and army officer; b. Tacoma, Mar. 5, 1911; s. Jesse Carney and Jessie (Myron) McC.; B.A., Golden Gate U., M.B.A., 1968; diploma Nat. War Coll., 1956; M.P.A., U. So. Calif., 1972; M.A., Calif. Poly. State U., 1975. m. Mary Jeanne Rapinac, Sept. 5, 1940. Account exec. Merrill, Lynch, Pierce, Fenner & Beane, Tacoma, Seattle, 1929-40; commd. lt. U.S. Army, 1940, advanced through grades to col., 1946; asst. chief of staff 7th Army G 1, 1952-54; comdg. officer 35th F.A. Group, Germany, 1956-58; dep. chief of staff V Corps, 1958-60, asst. chief of staff G 1, Pacific, 1962-65; ret., 1966; prof. bus., dept. chmn. Calif. Poly. State U., San Luis Obispo, 1968-80, ret., 1980. Decorated Legion of Merit with 2 oak leaf clusters, Silver Star, Bronze Star medal, Commendation medal with oak leaf cluster. Fellow Fin. Analysts Fedn.; mem. Los Angeles Soc. Fin. Analysts. Home: 16732 Lew Allen Cir Riverside CA 92518-2909

MCCORMACK, DENNIS K., clinical psychologist; m. Nancy K. McCormack; children: Kelly, Karen. BA in Math., Calif. Western U., 1969; MA, U.S. Internat. U., 1971, PhD in Leadership and Human Behavior, PhD in Psychology, 1974, 78. Diplomate Internat. Council Profl. Counseling and Psychotherapy, Am. Inst. Counseling and Psychotherapy, Internat. Acad. Health Care Profls. Pvt. practice family therapist Coronado, Calif.; chief psychologist, Trauma Svc. Group Winn Army Cmty. Hosp., supervisory clin. psychologist, 1994—; chief Family Therapy Winn Army Hosp., 1994—, acting chief Psychology and Psychiatry svcs., 1994—; guest spkr. at numerous clubs, lodges and local orgns. Contbr. articles to profl. jours. Mem. Sr. Citizen Adv. Com., 1982—, Land Use Adv. Com., Coronado, 1979-80; chmn. Coronado Planning Commn., 1978-83, St. Paul's United Meth. Ch., 1978-81, personnel com., 1978-81, mem. adminstrv. bd., 1983—; pres. Coronado Coordinating Council, 1983—; mem. adv. bd. Mil. Affairs Com., 1984—; bd. dirs. Vietnam Vets. Leadership Program, 1984—, Coronado Hosp. Found., 1988—; mem. Southbay Chember Exec. Com., 1986—, Coronado Visitor Promotion Bd., 1986—. Fellow Internat. Council of Sex Edn. and Parenthood of Am. U., Am. Bd. Med. Psychotherapists (clin. assoc.), S.D. Acad. Psychologists (chmn. membership com. 1988—), Coronado C. of C. (pres. 1986—). Office: PO Box 577 Richmond Hill GA 31324-0577

MCCORMICK, BETTY LEONORA, accountant; b. Missoula, Mont., July 18, 1961; d. George Oliver and Betty June (Dolton) Welch; m. 1993. BBA, U. Mont., 1983. CPA, Mont. Staff acct. Ellis & Assocs., Boise, Idaho, 1984; acct. Glacier Electric Coop., Cut Bank, Mont., 1984-86, office mgr., 1986—; income tax cons. Mem. AICPA, Beta Gamma Sigma. Democrat. Roman Catholic. Avocations: skiing, sewing, reading, hunting. Office: Glacier Electric Coop Inc 410 E Main St Cut Bank MT 59427-3012

MCCORMICK, FLOYD GUY, JR., agricultural educator, college administrator; b. Center, Colo., July 3, 1927; s. Floyd Guy and Gladys (Weir) McC.; m. Constance P. Slane; children: Angela Lynn, Craig Alan, Kim Ann, Robert Guy. BS, Colo. State U., 1950, MEd, 1959; PhD, Ohio State U., 1964. Tchr. vocat. agr. State of Colo., 1956-62; asst. prof. agrl. edn. Ohio State U., 1964-67; mem. com. agr. edn. com. edn. in agr. and natural resources Nat. Acad. Scis., 1967-69; prof. agrl. edn., head dept. U. Ariz., 1967-89, prof. emeritus, dept. head emeritus, 1990—; cons. in-svc. edn., div. vocat. edn. Ohio Dept. Edn., 1963-64; vis. prof. Colo. State U., 1973, U. Sierra Leone, Njala Univ. Coll., 1989; external examiner U. Sierra Leone, 1984, 85, 87; adv. trustee Am. Inst. Cooperatives, Washington, 1985-88; mem. Nat. Coun. Vocat. and Tech. Edn. in Agr., Washington, 1985-88. Co-author: Teacher Education in Agriculture, 1982, Supervised Occupational Experience Handbook, 1982; author: The Power of Positive Teaching, 1994, also instrl. units, tech. bulls., articles in profl. jours.; spl. editor: Agrl. Edn. mag., 1970-74. Trustee Nat. FFA Found. Served with USNR, 1945-46. Named hon. state farmer Colo., 1958, Ariz., 1968, Am. farmer, 1972; recipient Centennial award Ohio State U., 1970, E.B. Knight award NACTA Jour., 1980, Regional Outstanding Tchr. award Nat. Assn. Coll. Tchrs. Agr., 1989, also fellow, 1988, VIP citation Nat. FFA Assn., 1990, Diamond Anniversary award Ohio State U., 1992. Mem. Am. Vocat Assn. (mem. policy com. agrl. edn. divsn. 1976-79. v.p. divsn. 1985-88, chmn. membership com. 1980-83, sec. agrl. edn. divsn. 1983-86, pres. 1985-88, outstanding svc. awrd 1989), Nat. Vocat. Agr. Tchrs. Assn. (life, Outstanding Svc. award Region I 1974, 83, 96), Am. Assn. Tchr. Educators in Agr. (disting. lectr. 1984, editor newsletter 1975-76, pres. 1976-77, Disting. Svc. award 1978, 88, Rsch. award western region rsch. 1988), Alpha Zeta, Alpha Tau Alpha (hon.), Gamma Sigma Delta, Phi Delta Kappa, Epsilon Pi Tau. Home: 6933 E Paseo San Andres Tucson AZ 85710-2203

MCCORMICK, FRANK EDWARD, economist; b. Elmira, N.Y., Oct. 3, 1939; s. John Michael and Sara Theresa (Sweeney) McC.; m. Judith Mary Klink, July 2, 1966; children: Erin Marie, Daniel Francis. BS in Physics, Villanova U., 1961; PhD in Econs., U. Calif., Berkeley, 1971. Qualified to operate nuclear reactor AEC. Asst. prof. econs. U. Calif., Riverside, 1971-75; economist Fed. Res. Bd., Washington, 1975-79; v.p., sr. economist Bank of Am., San Francisco, 1979—. Contbr. articles to sci. jours. Lt. USN, 1961-66. Mem. Am. Econs. Assn., Nat. Assn. Bus. Economists, Western Econs. Assn. Home: 506 Monarch Ridge Dr Walnut Creek CA 94596-2935 Office: Bank of Am Econs Dept # 13015 Box 37000 San Francisco CA 94137

MCCORMICK, RICHARD, telecommunications company executive; b. Fort Dodge, Iowa, July 4, 1940; s. Elmo Eugene and Virgilla (Lawler) McC.; m. Mary Patricia Smola, June 29, 1963; children: John Richard, Matthew David, Megan Ann, Katherine Maura. B.S. in Elec. Engring., Iowa State U., 1961. With Bell Telephone Co., 1961-85; N.D. v.p., CEO Northwestern Bell Telephone Co., Fargo, 1974-77; asst. v.p. human resources AT&T, Basking Ridge, N.J., 1977-78; sr. v.p. Northwestern Bell, Omaha, 1978-82, pres., CEO, 1982-85; exec. v.p. U S West Inc., Englewood, Colo., 1985-86, pres., COO, 1986-90, pres., CEO, 1990-91, chmn., pres., CEO, 1992—; bd. dirs. Norwest Corp., United Airlines Corp. Mem. Phi Gamma Delta. Office: U S West Inc 7800 E Orchard Rd Ste 200 Englewood CO 80111-2526

MCCOWN, LINDA JEAN, medical technology educator; b. Pitts., Mar. 18, 1953; d. William Earnest and Mary Elizabeth McC. BS, Pa. State U., 1975; MS, U. Pitts., 1979. Cert. med. technologist, clin. lab. scientist. Microbiology aide Pa. State U., University Park, 1973-74; med. technologist, asst. supr., rsch. technologist Children's Hosp. of Pitts., 1975-80; asst. prof. med. tech., assoc. program dir. Ctrl. Wash. U., Ellensburg, 1980—; critiquer, insp. Nat. Accreditation Agy. for Clin. Lab. Scis., Chgo., 1984—; test item writer Nat. Cert. Agy., Washington, 1989—; recruiter Am. Soc. Clin. Pathologists, Chgo., 1988—; guest lectr. physician asst. program U. Wash., Seattle, 1996—. Contbr. articles to profl. jours. Stephen ministry, deacon First Presbyn. Ch., Yakima, Wash., 1992—; bd. dirs. The Campbell Farm, Wapato, Wash., 1990-95; rally chmn. Heifer Project Internat., Wapato, 1991-94. Mem. Am. Soc. for Med. Tech. (mem. commn. on accreditation 1988-91), Wash. State Soc. for Clin. Lab. Sci. (conv. chair 1992, edn. chair 1986-94, 95—, Pres.'s award 1992), Columbia Basin Soc. Clin. Lab. Sci. (pres.-elect 1993, pres. 1994-95), Omicron Sigma. Home: 1305 Jefferson Ave Yakima WA 98902-2528 Office: Ctrl Wash U Ctr Med Tech 1120 W Spruce Yakima WA 98902

MCCOY, DOUGLAS MICHAEL, social services administrator, clergyman; b. Altadena, Calif., Jan. 29, 1945; s. Burton Douglas and Margaret Ellen (Ledbetter) McC.; m. Edna Catherine DeChambeau, Mar. 23, 1968; children: Douglas Arthur, Robert Carl, Lewis Aaron. AA, Sacramento City Coll., 1964; BA in Am. History, Literature, Univ. Calif., 1966; MDiv., Pacific Sch. Religion, 1969. Ordained elder Meth. Ch. Youth dir. First United Meth. Ch., Redwood City, Calif., 1967-68; assoc. pastor 1st United Meth. Ch., Redwood City, 1968-69; pastor Cmty. United Meth. Ch., Georgetown, Calif., 1969-71, Christ United Meth. Ch., Sacramento, 1971-73; assoc. pastor 1st United Meth. Ch., Reno, 1973-82; exec. dir. Kairos Outreach, Inc., Reno, 1982-88, Nome (Alaska) Cmty. Ctr., Inc., 1988—; founder, spiritual dir. Nev. Kairos Prison Ministry, Reno, 1981-87. Pres. No. Nev. Sponsoring Com., Reno, 1975-78; mem. Planned Parenthood, Reno, 1981-85, Mental Health Adv. Com., Nome, 1988-91, Nome Visitor's Assn., 1990-94; chmn. Interagy. Child Advocates, Nome, 1988-91; mem. Action for Alaska Children, 1990—; mem. exec. com., Alaska Food Coalition, 1996—. Democrat. Office: Nome Cmty Ctr Inc PO Box 98 Nome AK 99762

MCCOY, EUGENE LYNN, civil engineer; b. Ridgefield, Wash., Apr. 9, 1926; s. Eugene Victor McCoy and Thelma Lucinda (Ayres) Martin; m. Marcia Helen Schear, Sept. 14, 1955 (div. 1974); children: Thomas Edwin, Susan Lynn, Molly Kay (dec.). AS, Lower Columbia Coll., 1948; BS, Wash. State U., 1950; MS, U. Wash., 1955. Registered profl. engr., Wash. Successively civil engr. soils, chief soils engr. sect., chief geotech. br. Portland (Oreg.) dist., chief geotech. br. North Pacific div. U.S. Army Corps. Engrs., 1955-85; staff cons. Shannon and Wilson, Portland, 1985-88, Cornforth Cons. Inc., Tigard, Oreg., 1988—; tech. specialist delegation for design of Longtan Dam, U.S. Army Corps. Engrs., Beijing, 1981, People to People's delegation Dams and Tunnels, 1987. Contbr. articles to profl jours. Active camp com. Campfire Girls, 4-H Clubs, Oregon City; vol. Loaves and Fishes,

Oreg. State U. Ext., AARP Tax Aid. Radio officer U.S. Merchant Marine, 1944-46; with U.S. Army, 1950-52. Mem. ASCE, U.S. Com. Large Dams, Oreg. Master Gardener. Democrat. Unitarian. Home: 20551 S Fischers Mill Rd Oregon City OR 97045-9646 Office: Cornforth Cons Inc 10250 SW Greenburg Rd Ste 111 Portland OR 97223-5460 *Personal philosophy: To be an honest, caring, gentle person dedicated to caring for family, community and country.*

MC COY, FRANK MILTON, concert pianist, educator, lecturer; b. El Centro, Calif., s. Henderson C. and Annie (Lee) McC.; A.B. (Rotary scholar), San Francisco State Coll., 1949, MA, 1960; postgrad. U. Wash., 1952-53, U. Calif. at Santa Barbara, 1957-58, U. So. Calif., 1961-65, U. Valencia (Spain), summer 1967; PhD Walden U., 1980; studied piano under Jean Le Duc, 1947-49, Madame Berthe Poncy-Jacobsen, 1952-53, Amparo Iturbi, 1960-62, Oria Kenah, Gladys Fawcette, Charles Shatto. Grad. asst. Sch. Music, U. Wash., Seattle, 1952-53; tchr. music edn. San Diego City Schs., 1953-54, El Centro Pub. Schs., 1954-57; counselor Social Service Center, Calexico, Calif., 1955-59; prof. piano and English Compton Coll., 1971-73; chmn. dept. music Portola Jr. H.S., L.A., 1985; personal rep. Odyssey Internat. Attractions. Piano, soloist All Am. Chorus tour 1956; 1st Am. to concertize on islands of St. Pierre and Miguelon, 1960; made concert tours Europe, Can., Latin Am., U.S., North Africa, Carribean, Middle East, USSR, China, Hong Kong; TV appearance CBC, 1965; appeared in Ebony mag., Sepia mag.; music critic Gilmore Piano Festival, Kalamazoo, Mich., 1994; adjudicator piano div. Southwestern Youth Music Festival, 1964; mem. bd. adjudicators Nat. Piano Playing Auditions, 1965; music-drama critic Post-Press Newspapers; founder, chmn. Annie Lee McCoy-Chopin Meml. Piano Award, 1975—; Mem. Founders Ch. of Religious Sci.; master tchr. in music L.A. City Schs., 1983-84. Bd. dirs. El Centro Cmty. Concert Assn. Recipient Leona M. Hickman award U. Wash., 1953, Mayor Tom Bradley commendation, 1991. Mem. Music Educators Nat. Conf., Nat. Guild Piano Tchrs., Am. Guild Mus. Artists, Music Critics Assn. North Am., Southeast Symphony Assn. (bd. dirs.), Internat. Platform Assn., Greater L.A. Press Club, Kiwanis (Angelus Mesa chpt. L.A.). Author: Black Tomorrow: A Portrait of Afro-American Culture, 1976 (children's book) Fruits and Vegetables A.B.C. Book; Playlet: Music Masters, Old and New, 1966, We, Too, Are Americans, 1977; music critic L.A. Sentinel, 1988—. Home: 234 S Figueroa St Apt 431 Los Angeles CA 90012-2509

MCCOY, HARRY E., II, lawyer; b. Parkersburg, W.Va., June 27, 1938. BA, U. Utah, 1967, JD, 1970. Bar: Utah 1970, Tex. 1974. Ptnr., dir. Jones, Waldo, Holbrook & McDonough, P.C., Salt Lake City; founding dir., v.p., Internat. Timeshare Found., 1983—; bd. dirs. and chair of mem. svcs. coun. Am. Resort Devel. Assn. Mem. Utah State Bar. Office: Jones Waldo Holbrook & McDonough 1500 First Interstate Pla 170 S Main St Salt Lake City UT 84101-1605

MC COY, LOIS CLARK, emergency services professional, retired county official, magazine editor; b. New Haven, Oct. 1, 1920; d. William Patrick and Lois Rosilla (Dailey) Clark; m. Herbert Irving McCoy, Oct. 17, 1943; children: Whitney, Kevin, Marianne, Tori, Debra, Sally, Daniel. BS, Skidmore Coll., 1942; student Nat. Search and Rescue Sch., 1974. Asst. buyer R.H. Macy & Co., N.Y.C., 1942-44, assoc. buyer, 1944-48; instr. Mountain Medicine & Survival, U. Calif. at San Diego, 1973-74; cons. editor Search & Rescue Mag., 1975; cons. editor, Rescue Mag., 1988-97; editor Press On Newsletter, 1992—. coord. San Diego Mountain Rescue Team, La Jolla, Calif., 1973-75; exec. sec. Nat. Assn. for Search and Rescue, Inc., Nashville and La Jolla, 1975-80, comptr., 1980-82; disaster officer San Diego County, 1980-86, Santa Barbara County, 1986-91, ret. Contbr. editor Rescue Mag., 1989-97, editor-in-chief Response! mag., 1982-86; editor Press On! Electronic mag., 1994—; mem. adv. bd. Hazard Montly, 1991—; cons. law enforcement div.; Calif. Office Emergency Svcs., 1976-77; pres. San Diego Com. for Los Angeles Philharmonic Orch., 1957-58. Bd. dirs. Search and Rescue of the Californias, 1976-77, Nat. Assn. for Search and Rescue, Inc., 1980-87, pres., 1985-87, trustee, 1987-90, mem. Calif. OES strategic com., 1992-96; CEO Nat. Inst. For Urban Search, 1989—; mem. Gov.'s Task Force on Earthquakes, 1981-82, Earthquake Preparedness Task Force, Seismic Safety Commn., 1982-85. Recipient Hal Foss award for outstanding service to search and rescue, 1982, Diamond Safety award for outstanding work in emergency services, 1996. Mem. IEEE, Armed Forces Comm. and Electronics Assoc., Nat. Assn. for Search & Rescue (life, Svc. award 1985), San Diego Mountain Rescue Team (hon. life), Santa Barbara Amateur Radio Club. Episcopalian. Author: Search and Rescue Glossary, 1974; contbr. to profl. jours. Office: PO Box 91648 Santa Barbara CA 93190-1648

MCCRACKEN, JOHN HARVEY, painter, sculptor; b. Berkeley, Calif., Dec. 9, 1934; s. John H. and Marjorie McC.; m. Gail Barringer, May 4, 1991; children: David Gordon, Patrick Daniel. BFA, Calif. Coll. Arts & Crafts, 1962, postgrad., 1962-65. Tchr., U. Calif., Irvine, 1965-66, L.A., 1966-68, Santa Barbara, 1974-85, Sch. Visual Arts, N.Y.C., 1968-69, Hunter Coll., N.Y.C., 1970-71, U. Nev., Reno, 1971-72, Las Vegas, 1972-75. One man shows include: Robert Elkon Gallery, N.Y.C., 1966, 67, 68, 72, 73, Galerie Ileana Sonnabend, Paris, 1969, Sonnabend Gallery, N.Y.C., 1970, Ace Gallery, L.A., 1985, PS 1, Long Island City, N.Y., 1986, Newport Harbor Art Mus., Calif., 1987, Contemporary Arts Mus., Houston, 1989, Hoffman Borman Gallery, Santa Monica, Calif., 1988, Konrad Fischer Gallery, Düsseldorf, Germany, 1989, Lisson Gallery, London, 1990, 97, Galerie Nordenhake, Stockholm, 1990, Fred Hoffman Gallery, L.A., 1990, Galerie Froment & Putman, Paris, 1991, 96, Sonnabend Gallery, N.Y.C., 1992, Louver Gallery, L.A., 1993-95, 97, Galerie Xavier Hufkens, Brussels, 1993, Galerie Art & Public, Geneva, 1994, Galerie Tanit, Munich, 1995, Hochshule Fur Angwandte Kunst, Vienna, 1995, Kunsthalle Basel, Switzerland, 1995, David Zwirner Gallery, N.Y., 1997; exhibited in group shows at Solomon R. Guggenheim Mus., N.Y.C., 1967, Saatchi Gallery, London, 1985, Venice (Italy) Biennale, 1986, Centro de Arte Reina Sofia, Madrid, 1987, Musee St. Pierre Art Contemporain, Lyon, France, 1988, Solomon R. Guggenheim Mus., N.Y.C., 1989-90, Carnegie Internat., Carnegie Mus. Art, Pitts., 1991, Corcoran Biennal, Washington, 1995; represented in permanent collections at Art Inst. Chgo., Solomon R. Guggenheim Mus., N.Y.C., Mus. Modern Art, N.Y.C., San Francisco Mus. Art, Whitney Mus. Art, N.Y.C., Mus. Contemporary Art, L.A., L.A. County Mus. Art. Grantee, NEA, 1968.

MC CRACKEN, PHILIP TRAFTON, sculptor; b. Bellingham, Wash., Nov. 14, 1928; s. William Franklin and Maude (Trafton) McC.; m. Anne MacFetridge, Aug. 14, 1954; children—Timothy, Robert, Daniel. B.A. in Sculpture, U. Wash., 1954. Asst. to Henry Moore Eng., 1954. One-man shows: Willard Gallery, N.Y.C., 1960, 65, 68, 70, Seattle Art Mus., 1961, Wash. State Capitol Mus., Olympia, 1964, Art Gallery of Greater Victoria, B.C., 1964, LaJolla (Calif.) Mus. Art, 1970, Anchorage Hist. and Fine Arts Mus., 1970, Tacoma Art Mus., 1980, Kennedy Galleries, N.Y.C., 1985, Lynn McAllister Gallery, Seattle, 1986, 89, Valley Mus. N.W. Art, La Conner, Wash., 1993, Whatcom Mus., Bellingham, Wash., 1994, Schneider Mus. Art, 1994, So. Oreg. State Coll., 1994, others; group shows include: Mus. Art, Ogunquit, Maine, 1957, Chgo. Art Inst., 1958, Detroit Inst. Arts, 1958, Pa. Acad. Fine Arts, 1958, Contemporary Art Gallery, Houston, 1958, DeYoung Meml. Mus., San Francisco, 1960, Los Angeles Mcpl. Art Mus., 1960, Galerie Claude Bernard, Paris, 1960, Phillips Gallery, Washington, 1966, Corcoran Gallery, 1966, Mus. Art, Akron, 1967, Finch Coll., N.Y.C., 1968, Rutgers U., 1968, Whitney Mus. Art, 1978, Portland Art Mus., 1976, Mont. State U., Bozeman, 1979, Brigham Young U., 1980, Bellvue (Wash.) Art Mus., 1986, Lynn McAllister Gallery, 1986, Am. Acad. Arts and Letters, N.Y.C., 1986, Schmidt Bingham Gallery, N.Y.C., 1987, Wash. State Capital Mus., 1987, 89, Cheney-Cowles Mus., Spokane, Wash., 1988, Smithsonian Instn., 1991—, Nat. Mus., Ottawa, Can., 1991-92, Gallery Three-Zero, N.Y.C., 1993, Seattle Art Mus., 1994, SA Gallery Christ Ch., New Zealand, 1996, others; sculptures represented: Norton Bldg., Seattle, Kankakee (Ill.) State Hosp., Swinomish Indian Tribal Center, LaConner, UN Assn., N.Y.C., King County King Dome, Seattle, City Hall, Everett, Wash., others. (Recipient numerous prizes, awards). Address: 401 Guemes Island Rd # B Anacortes WA 98221-9534

MCCRAVEN, EVA STEWART MAPES, health service administrator; b. L.A., Sept. 26, 1936; d. Paul Melvin and Wilma Zech (Ziegler) Stewart; m. Carl Clarke McCraven, Mar. 18, 1978; children: David Anthony, Lawrence James, Maria Lynn Mapes. ABS magna cum laude, Calif. State U., Northridge, 1974, MS, Cambridge Grad. Sch. Psychology, 1987; PhD, 1991. Dir. spl. projects Pacoima Meml. Hosp., 1969-71, dir. health edn., 1971-74; asst. exec. dir., v.p., Hillview Community Mental Health Center, Lakeview Terrace, Calif., 1974—, supr. for all clin. depts; past dir. dept. consultation and edn. Hillview Ctr., developer, mgr. long-term residential program, 1986-90; former program mgr. Crisis Residential Program, Transitional Residential Program and Day Treatment Program for mentally ill offenders, dir. mentally ill offenders svcs.; former program dir. Valley Homeless Shelter Mental Health Counseling Program; dir. Integrated Services Agy., Hillview Mental Health Ctr., Inc., 1993—; Former pres. San Fernando Valley Coordinating Coun. Area Assn., Sunland-Jujunga Coordinating Coun.; bd. dirs. N.E. Valley Health Corp., 1970-73, Golden State Community Mental Health Ctr., 1970-73. Recipient Resolution of Commendation award State of Calif., 1988, Commendation award, 1988, Spl. Mayor's plaque, 1988, Commendation awards for community svcs. City of L.A., 1989, County of L.A., 1989, Calif. State Assembly, 1989, Calif. State Senate, 1989, award Sunland-Tujunga Police Support Coun., 1989, Woman of Achievement award Sunland-Tujunga BPW, 1990. Mem. Assn. Mental Health Adminstrs., Am. Pub. Health Assn., Valley Univ. Women, Health Services Adminstrn. Alumni Assn. (former v.p.), Sunland-Jujunga Bus. and Profl. Women, LWV. Office: Hillview Community Mental Health Ctr 11500 Eldridge Ave San Fernando CA 91342-6523

MCCRAW, LESLIE G., engineering and construction company executive; b. Sandy Springs, S.C., Nov. 3, 1934; s. Leslie Gladstone and Cornelia (Milam) McC.; m. Mary Earle Brown; children: Leslie Gladstone III, James B., John. BSCE, Clemson U., 1956. Registered profl. engr., Del. Design engr. Gulf Oil Corp., Phila., 1956-57; various engring. and constrn. positions E.I. DuPont Co., Wilmington, Del., 1960-75; v.p., mgr. div. Daniel Constrn. Co., Greenville, S.C., 1975-82, pres., 1982-84; pres., chief exec. officer Daniel Internat., Greenville, 1984-86, Fluor Daniel, Greenville and Irvine, Calif., 1986-88; pres. Fluor Corp., Irvine, 1988-90, vice chmn., chief exec. officer, 1990-91, chief exec. officer, chmn. bd. dirs., 1991—. Bd. dirs. Allergan, N.Y. Life Ins. Co., U.S.-China Bus. Coun.; trustee Hampden-Sydney Coll., Va.; adv. bd. rsch. found., pres.'s adv. coun. Clemson U.; bd. visitors U. Calif. Grad. Sch. Mgmt.; internat. adv. bd. Br.-Am. Bus. Coun. Mem. NAM (bd. dirs.), Bus. Roundtable, Constrn. Industy's Presidents' Forum, Calif. Bus. Roundtable, Palmetto Bus. Forum, Pres.'s Export Coun. Republican. Presbyterian. Office: Fluor Corp Inc 3333 Michelson Dr Irvine CA 92730*

MCCREADY, KENNETH FRANK, past electric utility executive; b. Edmonton, Alta., Can., Oct. 9, 1939; s. Ralph and Lilian McCready; m. Margaret E. Randall, Sept. 2, 1961; children: John, Janet, Brian. BSc, U. Alta., 1963. Supr. data processing and systems Calgary (Alta.) Power Ltd., 1965-67, supr. rates and contracts, 1967-68, adminstrv. asst. to exec. v.p., 1968-72, asst. mgr. mgmt. cons. div., 1972-75; mgr. mgmt. systems dept., gen. mgr. Montreal Engring. Co., Calgary, 1975-76; v.p. adminstrn. Calgary (Alta.) Power Ltd., 1976-80; sr. v.p. ops. TransAlta Utilities, Calgary, 1980-85, pres., COO, 1985-89, also bd. dirs., 1988-96; pres., CEO TransAlta Corp., 1989-96; CEO TransAlta Energy Corp., 1989-96; pres. K. F. McCready & Assocs. Ltd., Calgary; bd. dirs. PanCan. Petroleum Ltd., Hewlett Packard (Can.) Ltd., ABB Asea Brown Boveri Environment adv. bd., Aurich, Marigold Found. Ltd., Exergy, Inc., San Francisco, Tech. Devel. Corp., Toronto, Computer Modelling Group, Calgary, Internat. Inst. Sustainable Devel., Winnipeg; past chmn. Conf. Bd. Can.; past chmn. bd. Advanced Computing Techs., Inc.; mem. Dow Chem. Corp. Adv. Coun., Midland, Tata Energy Rsch. Inst. adv. bd., Washington. Past dep. chmn. bd. govs. So. Alta. Inst. Tech.; past chair Alta. Round Table on Environment and Econ.; past mem. com. on trade and environment Govt. Can. Internat. Trade Adv.; past pres. Western Electric Power and Light Assn. Mem. Assn. Profl. Engrs., Geologists and Geophysicists of Alta., Ranchmen's Club.

MCCREARY, LORI L., entertainment business executive; b. Antioch, Calif., Feb. 14, 1961; d. Ronald Royce and Sharon A. (Rich) McC. BS in Computer Sci., UCLA, 1984. V.p. tech. svcs. CompuLaw Inc., Culver City, Calif., 1982-85; owner McCreary and Assocs., Santa Monica, Calif., 1985-95; CEO, pres. Revelations Entertainment, Santa Monica, 1996—. Office: Revelations Entertainment 301 Arizona Ave # 303 Santa Monica CA 90401

MCCRONE, ALISTAIR WILLIAM, university president; b. Regina, Can., Oct. 7, 1931. BA, U. Sask., 1953; MSc, U. Nebr., 1955; PhD, U. Kans., 1961. Instr. geology NYU, 1959-61, asst. prof., 1961-64, assoc. prof., 1964-69, prof., 1969-70, supr. Rsch. Ship Sea Owl on L.I. Sound, 1959-64; asst. dir. univ. program NYU, Sterling Forest, 1965-66; resident master Rubin Internat. Residence Hall NYU, 1966-69, chmn. dept. geology, 1966-69, assoc. dean Grad. Sch. Arts and Scis., 1969-70; prof. geology, acad. v.p. U. Pacific, 1970-74, acting pres., 1971; prof. geology, pres. Calif. State U. Sys. Humboldt State U., Arcata, 1974—; mem. sys. exec. coun. Calif. State U. Sys., 1974—, acad. senate Humboldt State U., 1974—, mem. chancellor's com. on innovative programs, 1974-76, trustees' task force on off-campus instrn., 1975-76, presdl. search com. Sonoma State U., 1976-77, exec. com. Chancellor's Coun. of Pres., 1976-79, Presdl. search com. Calif. State U., Chico, 1979-80, adv. group. exec. coun., 1980-81; Calif. state del. Am. Assn. State Colls. and Univs., 1977-80; mem. Commn. on Ednl. Telecomm., 1983-86; chair Calif. State U. Statewide Task Force on Earthquake and Emergency preparedness, 1985-88, 95; chmn., mem. accreditation teams Western Assn. Schs. and Colls.; mem. western sect. Am. Coun. Edn. Adminstrv. Intern Selection Panel, 1973; chair com. on energy and environ. Am. Assn. State Colls. and Univs., 1980-84; chair program com. Western Coll.Assn., 1983-84, panelist, 1983; mem. bd. dirs. Assn. Am. Colls., 1989-93, chair, 1992-93. Contbr. articles to profl. jours.; lectr. on geology Sunrise Semester program CBS Nat. Network, 1969-70; various appearances on local TV stas. Bd. trustees Presbyn. Hosp.-Pacific Med. Ctr., San Francisco, 1971-74; mem. Calif. Coun. for Humanities, 1977-82; mem. local campaign bd. United Way, 1977-83; mem. Am. Friends Wilton Park, 1980—; bd. dirs. Humboldt Convention and Visitors Bur., 1980-87, Redwood Empire Assn., 1983-87; bd. dirs. Calif. State Automobile Assn., 1988—, Am. Automobile Assn., 1990-93; bd. trustees Calif. State Parks Found., 1994—. Shell fellow in geology U. Nebr., 1954-55; Danforth assoc. NYU, 1964. Fellow Calif. Acad. Scis.; mem. AAAS, Geol. Soc. Am., Am. Assn. U. Adminstrs. (nat. bd. 1986-89, 96—), Rotary, St. Andrews Soc. N.Y. (life), Sigma Xi (pres. NYU chpt. 1967-69), Phi Kappa Phi. Office: Humboldt State U Univ Campus Arcata CA 95521

MCCUAIG, IAN CARRUTHERS, fundraising consultant; b. Orillia, Ont., Can., Mar. 5, 1962; came to U.S., 1992; s. Alan Hayes and Elizabeth Louise (Bonnell) McC.; m. Sarah Elizabeth Robertson, July 2, 1994. Student, Royal Conservatory of Music, Toronto, Ont., 1983; BA in Internat. Rels., U. Toronto, 1990; CSPG, Calif. State U., 1997. Devel. cons. UN Assn., Toronto, 1988-89; account exec. Gordon L. Goldie Co., Ltd., Toronto, 1989-92; cons. Marts & Lundy, Inc., San Francisco, 1992-96; sr. dir. Devel. Goodwill, San Francisco, 1996—. Contbr. articles to profl. publs. Nat. sec. Amnesty Internat. Can., Ottawa, Ont., 1986-88; chair human rights com. UN Assn., Toronto, 1988-89; elder Timothy Eaton Meml. Ch., Toronto, 1984-92; deacon Calvary Presbyn. Ch., San Francisco, 1992-96; mem. Dem. Nat. Com. Mem. World Affairs Coun., Nat. Soc. Fundraising Execs. (cert., v.p. Golden Gate chpt.), Internat. Diplomacy Coun., Nat. Com. on Planned Giving Can.-Am. C. of C., St. Francis Yacht Club, Commonwealth Club of Calif. Office: Goodwill 1500 Mission St San Francisco CA 94103-2513

MCCUE, DENNIS MICHAEL, management consultant; b. Pitts., July 28, 1952; s. Stephen J. and Mary (Maddalon) McC.; m. Cynthia Anne Roberts, Oct. 22, 1988. BA, U. Dayton, 1974. Dist. exec. Allegheny Trails Coun., Boy Scouts Am., Pitts., 1974-77; area mgr. The Nestle Co., Pitts., 1977-79; account mgr. So. Pacific Communications, Pitts., 1979-82; dir. sales and mktg. Amertel Co., Pitts., 1982-84, ITT Bu. Communications, Newport Beach, Calif., 1985-86; dir. mktg. Damac Products, Santa Fe Springs, Calif., 1986-87; ptnr. Hunter-McCue Mgmt. Cons., Newport Beach, Calif., 1987-89; pres. McCue Assocs., Costa Mesa, Calif., 1989—; instr. computer info. sys. Cerritos Coll., Norwalk, Calif., 1996—. Contbr. articles to profl. jours. Grad. Leadership Tomorrow, 1988, program chmn., bd. dirs., 1993-95. Mem. Nat. Assn. Corp. Dirs., Nat. Bur. Profl. Mgmt. Cons. (cert. profl. mgmt. cons.), Inst. Mgmt. Cons. (cert. mgmt. cons.), Lew Epstein Men's Club (mgr. 1986-90). Office: 4570 Campus Dr # 60 Newport Beach CA 92660-8809

MCCULLOCH, FRANK WALTER, JR., editor; b. Fernley, Nev., Jan. 26, 1920; s. Frank Walter and Frieda (Sieke) McC.; m. Jakie Caldwell, Mar. 1, 1942; children—Michaele Lee McCulloch Parman, Candace Sue, David Caldwell. B.A. in Journalism, U. Nev., 1941. With UP, San Francisco, 1941-42; with San Francisco Chronicle, 1945-46; gen. assignment reporter, legis. reporter, sports editor Reno Evening Gazette, 1946-53, Time Inc., 1953-60, 63-72; bur. chief Time Life News Service, Dallas, 1954-56, Los Angeles, 1957-60; mng. editor Los Angeles Times, 1960-64; bur. chief Time Life, Hong Kong and Saigon, 1964-68, Life, Washington, 1968-69, Time-Life, N.Y.C., 1969-72; v.p., editor Learning Mag., Palo Alto, Calif., 1972-75; mng. editor Sacramento Bee, 1975-80; dir. McClatchy Newspapers, Sacramento, 1978-85, exec. editor, 1980-85; mng. editor San Francisco Examiner, 1985-91. Served with USMCR, 1942-45. Mem. Sigma Delta Chi, Phi Kappa Phi, Kappa Tau Alpha, Sigma Nu.

MCCULLOH, REGINA THERESA, elementary school educator, writer; b. Norfolk, Nebr., Nov. 16, 1937; d. James Leslie and Elizabeth Eileen (O'Brien) Markey; m. Douglas Kenneth McCulloh, Sept. 20, 1975; children: Ann Elizabeth, Maureen Clare. BA in Elem. Edn., Loretto Heights Coll., 1959. Cert. elem. sch. tchr., Colo. Tchr. grade 1 Fairview Elem. Denver Pub. Schs., 1959-62; tchr. grade 1 Ben Gerir (Morocco) Elem. Dept. Def., 1962-63, tchr. grade 1 Wiesbaden (Germany) Air Base Elem., 1963-66; tchr. grade 1 Yukai (Japan) Elem. Dept. Def., Johnson AFB, 1966-67; tchr. grade 1 Westview Elem. Adams County Dist. 12, Northglenn, Colo., 1967-75, tchr. grade 1 Leroy Dr. Elem., 1977-78; tchr. grade 1, pre-sch. vol. Notre Dame Elem., Denver, 1984-92. Author: Alzheimer's Day by Day (A Cup of Tea), 1995. Democrat. Roman Catholic.

MCCULLOUGH, EDWARD EUGENE, patent agent, inventor; b. Baldwin, N.D., June 4, 1923; s. Elmer Ellsworth and Emma Izelda (Nixon) McC. BA, U. Minn., 1957; postgrad., Utah State U., 1965. Machine designer Sperry Rand Corp., Mpls., 1952-58; patent adminstr. Thiokol Corp., Brigham City, Utah, 1958-86; patent cons. Thiokol Corp., Brigham City, 1986; pvt. practice, 1986—. Inventor 33 patents including instruments for making perspective drawings, apparatus for forming ignition surfaces in solid propellant motors, passive communications satellite or similar article, flexible bearings and process for their manufacture, rocket nozzel support and pivoting system, cavity-shaping machine, among others; patents in field. Pianist Aldersgate Meth. Ch., Brigham City, 1959—. Staff Sgt. U.S. Army, 1949-52. Decorated two battle stars. Home: PO Box 46 784 Highland Blvd Brigham City UT 84302

MCCULLOUGH, GAYLE JEAN, graphic artist, publisher; b. Mare Island, Calif., Feb. 7, 1943; d. Earl Martin and Dorothy Clare (Vincent) Hoos; m. Norris Henry Hill; m. James Arthur McCullough, Feb. 19, 1979; children: Kareena Jean, Michael Earl, Michelle Lin. AA in Graphic Arts, Sacramento City Coll., 1970. Composing operator Cal-West Life Ins., Sacramento, 1972-75; sr. graphic artist Dept. Social Svcs. State of Calif., Sacramento, 1975—; mem. AOA implementation team State COSS, Sacramento, 1993—, mem. equal employment opportunity disabled adv. bd., 1986-87. Author, illustrator: Feud for Thought, 1993; author: Everything Hearing People Know About Deafness, 1994, What's Next?, 1994; author, illustrator, pub. (mag.) Life After Deafness, 1993-94. V.p. cmty. coun. NorCal Ctr. on Deafness, Sacramento, 1993-94. Recipient Swimming and Diving Champion award Sacramento City and County, 1957-59, Gold Keys for Art award Brueners & Hallmark Cards, 1959, 60; grantee Bank of Am., 1970. Mem. Calif. Assn. Late Deafened Adults (bd. dirs. 1993-94), Assn. Late Deafened Adults Sacramento (pres., founder 1990—). Home: 6773 Starboard Way Sacramento CA 95831-2413 Office: COSS MS 7-182 744 P St Sacramento CA 95814-6413

MCCULLOUGH, WILLIAM EDWARD, metrologist; b. Anacortes, Wash., Apr. 25, 1941; s. Ray Edward and Florence Sadie (Torpey) McC.; m. Sharon Lea Lenhart, Dec. 21, 1968; children: Shaunna, Debra. AGS, Western Nev. C.C., Carson City, 1991; BS in Mgmt., Calif. Coast U., 1994. Calibration technician Philco Tech., Vanderberg AFB, Calif., 1963-65; field svc. engr. Lockheed, Sunnyvale/Vanderberg AFB, and Kodiak, Alaska, 1965-68; metrology engr. Ford Aerospace (Philco Ford), Palo Alto, Calif., 1968-75; metrology mgr. Bently Nevada, Minden, Nev., 1975—; del. Nat. Conf. Standards Labs., Boulder, Colo., 1975—;. Founding mem. United We Stand Am., Dallas, 1993-94. With USN, 1959-63. Home: 1936 June Cir Carson City NV 89706-2625 Office: Bently Nevada Corp PO Box 157 Minden NV 89423

MCCUNE, ELLIS E., retired university system chief administrator, higher education consultant; b. Houston, July 17, 1921; s. Ellis E. and Ruth (Mason) McC.; m. Hilda May Whiteman, Feb. 8, 1946; 1 son, James Donald. Student, Sam Houston State U., 1940-42; B.A., UCLA, 1948, Ph.D., 1957; LHD, Golden Gate U., 1994. Teaching asst. UCLA, 1949-51; from instr. to assoc. prof. polit. sci. Occidental Coll., Los Angeles, 1951-59; chmn. applied politics and econs. curriculum Occidental Coll., 1951-56; asst. prof. Calif. State U., Northridge, 1959-61, assoc. prof., chmn. dept. polit. sci., 1961-63, prof., 1963, dean letters and sci., 1963; dean acad. planning Calif. State Univs. and Colls., 1963-67; pres. Calif. State U., Hayward, 1967-90, pres. emeritus, 1991—; acting chancellor The Calif. State U. System, 1990-91, ret., 1991; cons. govtl. units and agys.; lectr., panelist; mem. Calif. State Scholarship and Loan Commn., 1964-68, chmn., 1967-68; pres. Govtl. Adminstrn. Group Los Angeles, 1959; chair planning com., mem. exec. com., bd. dirs. Eden Med. Ctr. Found., 1994—, pres.-elect, 1995-97, pres., 1997—. Chmn. univs. and colls. div. United Bay Area Crusade, 1969-70, 73-74; bd. dirs. Oakland (Calif.) Museum Assn., 1974-77, 86-88; vice chmn. higher edn. div., East Bay United Way, 1989-90; mem. arts adv. council, 1986-87, devel. com., 1988-89, Bay Area Urban League, bd. trust Calif. Coun. Econ. Edn. No. sect., Emergency Shelter Program Adv. Coun., Hayward Area Hist. Assn., NAACP Hayward chpt.; trustee Calif. Council Econ. Edn.; sec. bd. dirs. Eden Community Found., 1978-79; rsch. fellow Haynes Found, 1957. With USAAF, 1942-46. Mem. Am. Coun. Edn. (adv. com. 1970-72, inst. coll. & univ. adminstrs. 1973-74, bd. dirs. 1985-86), Western Assn. Schs. and Colls. (accrediting commn. sr. colls. and univs. 1974-78, chmn., 1978-82, pres. 1979-81), N.W. Assn. Schs. and Colls. (commn. colls. 1974-80), Assn. Am. Colls. (bd. dirs. 1972-75, vice chmn. 1975-76), Assn. Western Univs. (bd. dirs.), Coun. Postsecondary Accreditation (bd. dirs. 1977-88, exec. com. 1979-88, chmn. 1985-87, immediate past chmn., 1988-89, chmn. com. recognition 1982-84), Am. Assn. State Colls. and Univs. (chmn. accreditation com. 1983-86, com. acad. pers. and acad. freedom 1987-88, com. on acad. affairs 1988-91), Calif. Coun. Edn. (trustee), Western Polit. Sci. Assn. (exec. coun. 1958-61), Hayward C. of C. (dir. 1968-71, 73-76, 77-80, 82-85, 86-90), Regional Assn. East Bay Colls. and Univs. (exec. com. 1974-90, sec. 1975-76, 87-88, vice chmn. 1976-77, 84-85, chmn. 1977-79, 85-86), Rotary, Phi Beta Kappa, Pi Gamma Mu, Pi Sigma Alpha. Club: Bohemian (San Francisco). Home: 17577 Parker Rd Castro Valley CA 94546-1227 Office: Calif State U Pres Emeritus LI 3167 Hayward CA 94542-3053

MCDADE, DONNA MARIE, writer; b. Cleve., Apr. 29, 1949; d. Daniel and Frieda (Dresp) Forkapa; 1 child, Jason C. Gorman. Student, Bowling Green U., 1967-68. LPN, Ariz. Oper. rm. technician Parma (Ohio) Hosp., 1969-71; with ER staff Providence Gen. Hosp., 1971; with ICU-CCU staff St. Josephs Hosp., Reading, Pa., 1972; operating room technician Reading Hosp., 1973-75; with CCU staff Parma Cmty. Hosp., 1975-76; with ICU, CCU, MICU and ER staffs U. Med. Ctr., 1977-79, with ER staff, 1983; with ICU, CCU, MICU and ER staffs Tucson Med. Ctr., 1977-79, with radiation oncology staff Ariz. Health Scis. Ctr., 1989-94; with ER staff Meml. Hosp., Colorado Springs, Colo., 1981-83; mgr. patient rels., triage nurse Cigna Healthplan, Tucson, 1984-89; lectr. in field. Writer poetry; contbr. articles to profl. jours. Recipient Nurse of Yr. award U.M.C. Tucson Achievements, 1991, Achievement awards 1992, 93, 94, 95.

MCDADE, J. MICHAEL, port commissioner. BS in Internat. Affairs, Georgetown U., 1963; JD, U. San Diego, 1968. Tchr., adminstr. St. Augustine H.S., San Diego, 1964-70; ptnr. Sullivan Wertz McDade & Wallace, San Diego, 1970—; commr. Port of San Diego, 1993—, chmn. bd. port commrs., 1997—; polit. cons. various politicians, Calif., 1976—; chief of staff County Supr. Roger Hedgecock, 1978-79; chief of staff San Diego mayor Roger Hedgecock, 1983-85; mem. mayor's tidelands adv. coun. City of San Diego, 1993-95. Mem. San Diego Bar Assn. Office: Sullivan Wertz McDade & Wallace 945 Fourth Ave San Diego CA 92101

MCDANIEL, BRUCE ALAN, economist, educator; b. Warsaw, Ind., June 12, 1946; s. Maurice M. and Hattie M. (Stidham) McD.; m. Darcy L. Stouder, Dec. 29, 1972; children: Rachel L., Nathan A., Jordan J. BS, Manchester Coll., 1968; MA, Ball State U., 1972; PhD, Colo. State U., 1979. Instr. Colo. State U., Fort Collins, 1975-79; asst. prof. Ind. U., Indpls., 1979-82. Marquette U., Milw., 1982-85; pres., owner Prarieland, Atwood, Ind., 1985—; asst. prof. U. No. Colo., Greeley, 1992—; owner Prairieland, Inc., Loveland, Colo. Contbr. articles to profl. jours. Mem. Assn. for Social Econs. (midwest regional dir. 1986-92, exec. coun. 1983-92, Helen Potter award 1983), Phi Kappa Phi, Omicron Delta Epsilon. Office: U No Colo Dept Econs Greeley CO 80639

MCDANIEL, GARY ALLAN, geologist; b. Enid, Okla., Oct. 14, 1931; s. William Taylor and Golda Mae (Bell) McD.; m. Elizabeth Marie Vacin, June 15, 1951 (div. 1980); children: Mark, Gari Lynn, Dana, Lance, Lisa; m. Linda R. LaMascus, Mar. 4, 1987. BSc in Geology, U. Okla., 1953, MSc in Geology, 1959. Geologist, Shell Oil Co., 1959-62; advanced geologist Skelly Oil Co., 1962-66; geologist Midwest Oil Co., Oklahoma City, Okla., 1966-68; dist. geologist Champlin Petroleum Co., Oklahoma City, 1968-70; div. geologist Clarcan Petroleum Corp., Oklahoma City, 1970-74; v.p. May Petroleum Co., Dallas, 1974-75; cons., Oklahoma City, 1975-89; chief geologist Bradmar Petroleum Corp, Oklahoma City, 1990-92; cons., 1992—. Contbr. articles to profl. publs. Served to 1st lt. USMC, 1953-56. Mem. Am. Assn. Petroleum Geologists (chmn. publicity com. 1974-75, award of Merit 1975), Oklahoma City Geol. Soc. (pres. 1972-73, award of Recognition 1969, 73, 78, award of Appreciation 1971), Am Inst. Profl. Geologists (pres. Okla. sect. 1980, award of Recognition 1980), Sigma Xi, Sigma Gamma Epsilon (E.L. McCullough award 1959), Phi Kappa Psi. Home: 4057 Lupine Dr Vail CO 81657-4816

MCDANIEL, JOSEPH CHANDLER, lawyer; b. Covington, Va., Mar. 24, 1950; s. Everts Hardin and Betty (Chandler) McD.; m. Sandra Lee Bonds, Dec. 27, 1976; children: Sean Kenneth, Caitlin Bonds. BA in Philosophy, Ariz. State U., 1974, JD, 1980. Bar: Ariz. 1980, U.S. Dist. Ct. Ariz. 1981; cert. specialist bankruptcy law Ariz. Bd. Legal Specialization, cert. specialist consumer bankruptcy law Am. Bankruptcy Bd. Specialization, cert. specialist bus. bankruptcy law. Law clk. U.S. Bankruptcy Ct., Phoenix, 1980-82; pvt. practice Phoenix, 1982-84; ptnr. McDaniel and Jaburg, P.C., Phoenix, 1984-89, McDaniel and Lee, Phoenix, 1989-91, McDaniel & Gan, P.C., 1991-93, McDaniel & Kaup, P.C., 1993-94, Lerch, McDaniel & Kaup, P.L.C., 1994-96, Lerch, McDaniel, DePrimn & Kaup, P.L.C., 1996—; lectr. in field; mem. Scriveners Com. Local Rules of Ct. for Dist. of Ariz. Bankruptcy Cts., Phoenix, 1980. Author: A Guide to Researching Bankruptcy Law, 1980; editor: (with others) Arizona Civil Remedies, 1982; lectr. in field. Bd. dirs. St. Patrick's Day Parade, 1988-89, Irish Cultural Assn. Phoenix, 1988-89. Mem. ABA (gen. practice sect. bankruptcy com., chmn., sr. vice chmn. membership com. pubs. bd.), Ariz. Bar Assn. (lectr., co-chmn. continuing legal edn. com., bankruptcy sect. 1987-88, chmn. 1988-89, co-chmn. jud. rels. com. 1990-92), Maricopa County Bankruptcy Practitioners (chmn.), Ariz. Bankruptcy Coalition (bd. dirs. 1986—, chair speakers com. 1994-96), Maricopa County Bar Assn., Am. Bankruptcy Inst. Democrat. Roman Catholic. Office: Lerch McDaniel et al 2700 N Central Ave Ste 1500 Phoenix AZ 85004-1112

MCDANIEL, RICKEY DAVID, senior living executive; b. Rochester, Minn., Apr. 10, 1946; s. Malcolm David and Elaine (Lee) McD.; m. Shelley Ann Sorensen, May 10, 1980; children: Michael, Mathew, Joseph. AA, Rochester Jr. Coll., 1966; BA, Winona State U., 1969. Clin. mgr. St. Mary's Hosp., Rochester, Minn., 1971-74; long term care adminstr. Roderick Enterprises, Inc., Portland, Oreg., 1974-78; regional dir. Roderick Enterprises, Inc., Portland, 1978-80, v.p. ops., 1980-84; pres. Health Sys. Mgmt. and Devel., L.A., 1984-86; ops. dir. Brim Enterprises, Inc., Portland, 1987-88, v.p., 1988-92, sr. v.p., 1992-93; pres. Brim Sr. Living, Inc., Portland, 1993-97; sr. v.p. Encore Sr. Living, LLC, 1997—; bd. dirs. Brim Homestead, Inc., Portland, Dominican Life Care Svcs., Portland, Belmar, Inc., Portland, also v.p. 1989—; pres. Care Mgmt., Inc., A Fla. Employee Leasing Corp., 1991—; developer alzheimer patients care and housing program, 1993. Cpl. USMC, 1969-71. Republican. Lutheran. Home: 16492 S Arrowhead Dr Oregon City OR 97045-9287 Office: Brim Inc 305 NE 102nd Ave Portland OR 97220-4170

MCDANIEL, SUSAN ROBERTA, academic administrator; b. Austin, Tex., Apr. 29, 1947; d. Frederick Cecil and Sybil Vermont (Catterall) McD.; m. Andrew Wear Elting, Mar. 22, 1980 (dec. Dec. 1992); m. Stuart Wesley Conner, June 14, 1996. BA, Smith Coll., 1969; MA, Middlebury Coll., 1970; PhD, Yale U., 1976. Owner, mgr. Cloverleaf Vet. Svcs., Columbus, Mont., 1982-87; cons. hist. arch. Nat. Park Svc./Mont. Hist. Preservation Office, Miles City, Mont., 1988-89; exec. dir. Custer County Art Ctr., Miles City, 1989-94; dir. grants Rocky Mountain Coll., Billings, Mont., 1994-96, acad. v.p., 1996—; mem. Town-Gown Steering, Billings, 1996—. Co-author: Miles City: Historic Architecture, 1988, Beautiful City of Miles, 1989. Trustee Mont. Hist. Soc., Helena, Mont., 1989-2000, pres., 1995-97; precinctwoman, state committeewoman Mont. Rep. Party, Custer County, 1988-94; precinctwoman, treas. Mont. Rep. Party, Stillwater County, 1983-87; mem. Econ. Devel. Com., Miles City, 1991-93, Miles City Arts/Preservation Commn., Miles City, 1990-94; panelist local arts agys. NEA, Washington, 1993-94. Home: 3030 Smokey Ln Billings MT 59102 Office: Rocky Mountain Coll 1511 Poly Dr Billings MT 59102

MCDAVID, DOUGLAS WARREN, systems consultant; b. San Francisco, Feb. 25, 1947; s. James Etheridge and Elizabeth Rae (Warren) McD.; m. Nancy Kathleen Somers, June 1968 (div. 1980); 1 child, Amy Kemp; m. Carleen Ann Richmond, Feb. 14, 1987; 1 child, Amanda Claire. BA in Sociology, U. Calif., Santa Cruz, 1969; MA in Libr. Sci., San Jose State U., 1972. Libr. Palo Alto (Calif.) City Libr., 1969-81; systems analyst Tymnet (Tymshare), Cupertino, Calif., 1981-84; mgr. systems architecture Tymnet McDonnell Douglas, San Jose, Calif., 1984-86; data modeling cons. Fireman's Fund Ins., Terra Linda, Calif., 1986-87, Bank of Calif., San Francisco, 1988; systems cons. Pacific Bell, San Ramon, Calif., 1989-93; prin. Integrated Info., 1994—; dir. Computer Resources Group, San Francisco; spkr. Entity/Relationship Conf. Internat., Burlingame, Calif., 1991, DAMA Internat. Conf., 1994—; sr. cons. in bus. semantic modeling for object oriented applications IBM Corp., 1994—; 1996 spkr. Bus. Rules Conf. OOPSLA, IBM Object Technology Conf., Ind. Labor & Mgmt. Coun. Assoc. editor: Handbook of Object Technology. Mem. IEEE, Assn. for Computing Machinery, Data Adminstrn. Mgmt. Assn. (San Francisco bd. dirs. 1987-91, Sacramento bd. dirs. 1992, speaker 1991, 92), Data Processing Mgmt. Assn. (speaker 1992), Am. Assn. Artificial Intelligence (speaker 1993). Home and Office: 8611 Kingslynn Ct Elk Grove CA 95624-3135

MCDERMOTT, DAVID (JOHN), artist, writer, photographer; b. Wrangell, Alaska, Apr. 8, 1958; s. A.W. and Margaret (Price) McD.; m. Rebeca Reyna, Dec. 29, 1978; children: Amy, Rachel, Kelly. Student, Seattle Pacific Coll., 1976-77. Nat. registered and cert. emergency med. technician; cert. instr. NRA. Pres., owner Mut. Devel. Co., Ketchikan, 1980—; fireman, emergency med. technician Ketchikan Vol. Fire Dept., 1989-91; contbg. cons. bodybldg. books and mags., 1986—; feature article Musclemag Internat. mag., 1990. Artist ltd. edit. art print series, 1977—. Recipient Expert Rifleman award U.S. Govt., 1973, 1st, 2d & 3d Profl. Painting prizes Arts Guild Show, 1995. Mem. NEA (del. state/nat. governing assemblies), Ketchikan Edn. Assn. (exec. bd. 1992—, pres. 1994—), Nat. Assn. EMTs, Nat. Soc. EMT-Paramedics, Nat. Soc. EMS Adminstrs., Soc. EMT Tech. Instr./Coords. Home: 626 Anderson Dr Ketchikan AK 99901-5404 Office: Mut Devel Co 627 Carlanna Ketchikan AK 99901-5620

MCDERMOTT, DIRK WADE, geophysicist; b. Denver, Aug. 23, 1956; s. Willard Henry and Joyce Ellen (Wade) McD.; m. Carol Elizabeth Fitzgerald, Aug. 13, 1988. MS in Geophysics, Stanford U., 1981, MBA, 1991. Cert. profl. geophysicist, Alta., Can. Spl. projects geophysicist LL&E, New Orleans, 1981-84; sr. geophysicist LL&E, Denver, 1984-85; chief geophysicist LL&E Can., Calgary, Alta., 1985-89, Louisiana Land & Exploration, Denver, 1989—. Mem. Am. Assoc. Petroleum Geologists, Soc. Exploration Geophysicist. Republican. Lutheran. Home: 2212 Birch St Denver CO 80207-3736 Office: Altira Group 370 17th St #4250 Denver CO 80207

MCDERMOTT, JAMES A., congressman, psychiatrist; b. Chicago, Ill., Dec. 28, 1936; children: Katherine, James. BS, Wheaton Coll., 1958; MD, U. Ill., 1963. Intern Buffalo Gen. Hosp., 1963-64; resident in adult psychiatry U. Ill. Hosps., Chgo., 1964-66; resident in child psychiatry U. Wash. Hosps., Seattle, 1966-68; asst. clin. prof. dept. psychiatry U. Wash., Seattle, 1970-83; mem. Wash. Ho. of Reps., 1971-72, Wash. Senate, 1975-87; regional med. officer U.S. Fgn. Svc., 1987-88; mem. 101st-105th Congresses from 7th Wash. dist., 1989—; former chmn. stds. of ofcl. conduct com., mem. ways and means com., ranking minority mem., mem. stds. of ofcl. conduct com.; mem. exec. and edn. com. Nat. Conf. State Legislatures, chair ethics com. Mem. Wash. State Arts Commn., Wash. Coun. for Prevention Child Abuse and Neglect; Dem. nominee for gov., 1980. Lt. comdr. M.C., USN, 1968-70, . Mem. Am. Psychiat. Assn., Wash. State Med. Assn., King County Med. Soc. Democrat. Episcopalian. Office: US Ho of Reps 2349 Rayburn HOB Washington DC 20515*

MCDEVITT, CHARLES FRANCIS, state supreme court justice; b. Pocatello, Idaho, Jan. 5, 1932; s. Bernard A. and Margaret (Hermann) McD.; m. Virginia L. Heller, Aug. 14, 1954; children: Eileen A., Kathryn A., Brian A., Sheila A., Terrence A., Neil A., Kendal A. LLB, U. Idaho, 1956. Bar: 1956. Ptnr. Richards, Haga & Eberle, Boise, 1956-62; gen. counsel, asst. sec. Boise Cascade Corp., 1962-65; mem. Idaho State Legislature, 1963-66; sec., gen. counsel Boise Cascade Corp., 1965-67, v.p. sec., 1967-68; pres. Beck Industries, 1968-70; group v.p. Singer Co., N.Y.C., 1970-72, exec. v.p., 1973-76; pub. defender Ada County, Boise, 1976-78; co-founder Givens, McDevitt, Pursley & Webb, Boise, 1978-89; justice Idaho Supreme Ct., Boise, 1987-97, chief justice, 1993-97; served on Gov.'s Select Com. on Taxation, Boise, 1988-89. Home: 4940 Boise River Ln Boise ID 83706-5706 Office: Idaho Supreme Ct 451 W State St Boise ID 83702-6006

MCDEVITT, JOHN ALFRED, program manager, military officer, retired; b. Woburn, Mass., Dec. 16, 1951; s. William Richard and Inez Demetrie (Ireland) McD.; m. Patricia Ann Walsh, June 23, 1973; children: Jennifer Kristen, Michelle Christine, Sean Patrick. BS, USAF Acad., 1973; MBA in Mgmt., Rensselaer Poly. Inst., 1980. Commd. 2d lt. USAF, 1973, advanced through grades to lt. col., 1982; radar navigator, wing staff officer Griffiss AFB, N.Y. and Pease, N.H., 1973-82; program mgr. Combat Identification System Program Office, Wright-Patterson AFB, Ohio, 1982-85, Office of Asst. Sec. of Air Force for Acquisition, 1985-89; sr. project lead Hqrs. Air Force Space Command, 1989-93; ret. USAF, 1996; mgr. TASC, Colorado Springs, Colo., 1993-96; mgr. comml. engring. svcs. divsn. STA, Inc., Colorado Springs, 1996—. Mem. Assn. Grads. Office: STA Inc Ste 116 1250 Academy Park Loop Colorado Springs CO 80910

MCDONALD, ALAN ANGUS, federal judge; b. Harrah, Wash., Dec. 13, 1927; s. Angus and Nell (Britt) McD.; m. Ruby K., Aug. 22, 1949; children: Janelle Jo, Saralee Sue, Stacy. BS, U. Wash., 1950, LLB, 1952. Dep. pros. atty. Yakima County, Wash., 1952-54; assoc. Halverson & Applegate, Yakima, 1954-56; ptnr. Halverson, Applegate & McDonald, Yakima, 1956-85; judge U.S. Dist. Ct. (ea. dist.) Wash., Yakima, 1985-95, sr. judge, 1995—. Fellow Am. Coll. Trial Lawyers; Yakima C. of C. (bd. dirs.). Clubs: Yakima Country, Royal Duck (Yakima). Office: US Dist Ct PO Box 2706 Yakima WA 98907-2706

MC DONALD, BARBARA ANN, psychotherapist; b. Mpls., July 15, 1932; d. John and Georgia Elizabeth (Baker) Rubenzer; B.A., U. Minn., 1954; M.S.W., U. Denver, 1977; m. Lawrence R. McDonald, July 27, 1957 (dec. Sept. 1993); children—John, Mary Elizabeth. Diplomate Am. Bd. Social Work; lic. psychotherapist. Day care cons. Minn. Dept. Public Welfare, St. Paul, 1954-59; social worker Community Info. Center, Mpls., 1959-60; exec. dir. Social Synergistics Co., Littleton, Colo., 1970—; cons. to community orgns., Indian tribes. Family therapist , 1979—. Bd. dirs. Vol. Bur. Sun Cities, Ariz., 1988, 89, 90. Named 1 of 8 Women of Yr. and featured on TV spl. Ladies Home Jour., 1974; Clairol scholar, 1974; Am. Bus. Women's Assn. scholar, 1974; Alpha Gamma Delta scholar, 1974. Mem. Minn. Pre-Sch. Edn. Assn. (hon. life), AAUW(Sun City West chpt.), Nat. Assn. Social Workers, Ariz. Assn. Social Workers, Assn. Clin. Social Workers, Am. Bus. Women's Assn., U. Minn. Alumni Club (sun cities chpt.), Alpha Gamma Delta (Disting. Citizen award 1975). Club: Altrusa (hon.). Author: Selected References on the Group Day Care of Pre-School Children, 1956; Helping Families Grow: Specialized Psychotherapy with Hearing Impaired Children and Their Families, 1984. Office: 13720 W Franciscan Dr Sun City West AZ 85375-5219

MCDONALD, JOHN PETER, management and technology consultant; b. Boston, June 23, 1940; s. Peter A. and Monica A. McDonald; m. Barbara G. McDonald, Nov. 7, 1959; children: Peter, Ian, Kevin, Christine. AA, Santa Ana (Calif.) Coll., 1966; JD, Pepperdine U., 1970. Bar: Calif. 1973, U.S. Supreme Ct. 1973. Sys. analyst O.C. Orange County Supreme Ct., Santa Ana, 1968-71; trial atty. Cohen, Stokke, Owen & Davis, Santa Ana, 1971-73; exec. dir. Legal Aid Soc. Orange County, Santa Ana, 1973-79; dir. mgmt. devel. and tng. Legal Svcs. Corp., Washington, 1979-82, dir., 1979-82; owner McDonald Assocs., Laguna Beach, Calif., 1982-87; v.p. Orion, San Diego, 1987-89; pres. Profl. Advisers, Inc., Carlsbad, Calif., 1989—, X'iT Group Creative Inc., Carlsbad, Calif., 1996—. Recipient Franklin C. West award, Orange County Bar Assn., 1973. Mem. Assn. for Psychol. Type. Home: 1552 Madrid Dr Vista CA 92083 Office: X'iT Group Creative Inc 3915 Mission Ave # 7620 Oceanside CA 92054-7801

MCDONALD, JOSEPH LEE, insurance broker; b. Bremerton, Wash., Aug. 15, 1931; s. Joseph Okane and Ida Elizabeth (Finholm) McD.; m. Glorietta Maness, Jan. 22, 1954 (dec. 1984); children: Holly Ann Chaffin, Andrew Lee McDonald; m. Beverly Mae Falkner, June 22, 1986. BS, U. Wash., 1954. Various mgmt. positions AT&T, 1956-62; broker, ptnr. McDonald & McGarry Co., Seattle, 1962-84; ptnr., exec. McDonald Ins. Group, Kirkland, Wash., 1984—; v.p., bd. dirs. Chimayo Inc., Seattle, 1990—, Santa Fe Food Corp., Seattle, 1991—. City councilman City of Bellevue, 1971-75; commr. Water Dist. #97, Bellevue, 1967-71, Lake Hills Sewer Dist., Bellevue, 1965-71; pres. Wash. State Assn. of Sewer Dists., Seattle, 1969. With U.S. Army, 1954-56. Mem. Coll. Club of Seattle, Overlake Golf and Country Club, Western Assn. of Ins. Brokers, Ind. Ins. Agts. Assn., Seattle Master Builders Assn., Nat. Wildlife Fedn., Natures Conservancy, Apt. Assn. of Seattle and King County, Roche Harbor Yacht Club. Home: 7235 91st Pl SE Mercer Island WA 98040-5803 Office: McDonald Ins Group 416-6th St South Kirkland WA 98033

MC DONALD, LEE CAMERON, political science educator; b. Salem, Oreg., Feb. 22, 1925; s. O. Lyman and Mabel (Duncan) McD.; m. Claire Elizabeth Kingman, Aug. 17, 1946; children: Mary, Alison, Julia (dec.), Devon (dec.), Thomas, Paul. Student, U. Oreg., 1942-43; B.A., Pomona Coll., 1948; M.A., UCLA, 1949; Ph.D., Harvard U., 1952. Teaching asst. UCLA, 1948-49; teaching fellow Harvard U., 1950-52; mem. faculty Pomona Coll., Claremont, Calif., 1952—; prof. govt. Pomona Coll., 1962—, Thompson prof. govt., 1980—, emeritus, 1990—, dean coll., 1970-75; Chmn. com. faculty interests, dept. higher edn. Nat. Council Chs., 1966-69; mem. adv. council Danforth Found. Assocs. Program, 1964-67; mem. Commn. on Liberal Learning Assn. Am. Colls., 1974-76; adj. prof. The Claremont Grad. Sch., 1991—. Author: Western Political Theory: The Modern Age, 1962, Western Political Theory: Origins to the Present, 1968; editor: Human Rights and Educational Responsibility, 1979; editorial bd.: Western Polit. Quar, 1963-66, 68-70, Claremont Quar, 1960-64; contbr.: Reformed Faith and Economics, 1989, Three Beginnings: Revolution, Rights and the Liberal State, 1994. Elder Presbyn. Ch., 1958—, chair Peacemaking Com. of San Gabriel Presbytery, 1995-97, steering com. mobilization for the human family, 1996—. Served with USAAF, 1943-45. Recipient Harbison Distinguished Teaching award Danforth Found., 1963; NEH fellow, 1982-83. Mem. Am. Polit. Sci. Assn., Western Polit. Sci. Assn. (exec. council 1972-74), So. Calif. Polit. Sci. Assn. (pres. 1969-70), Am. Soc. Polit. and Legal Philosophy, Am. Conf. Acad. Deans (dir. 1973-76), Phi Beta Kappa, Pi Sigma Alpha. Democrat. Home: 239 W 11th St Claremont CA 91711-3804

MCDONALD, MARIANNE, classicist; b. Chgo., Jan. 2, 1937; d. Eugene Francis and Inez (Riddle) McD.; children: Eugene, Conrad, Bryan, Bridget, Kirstie (dec.), Hiroshi. BA magna cum laude, Bryn Mawr Coll., 1958; MA, U. Chgo., 1960; PhD, U. Calif., Irvine, 1975, doctorate (hon.) Am. Coll. Greece, 1988, hon. diploma Am. Archaeological Assn. Teaching asst. classics U. Calif., Irvine, 1974, D Litt (hon.) U. Athens, Greece, 1994, U. Dublin, 1994. instr. Greek, Latin and English, mythology, modern cinema, 1975-79, founder, rsch. fellow Thesaurus Linguae Graecae Project, 1975—; bd. dir. Centrum. Bd. dirs. Am. Coll. of Greece, 1981-90, Scripps Hosp., 1981; Am. Sch. Classical Studies, 1986—; mem. bd. overseers U. Calif. San Diego, 1985—; nat. bd. advisors Am. Biog. Inst., 1982—; pres. Soc. for the Preservation of the Greek Heritage, 1990—; founder Hajime Mori Chair for Japanese Studies, U. Calif., San Diego, 1985, McDonald Ctr. for Alcohol and Substance Abuse, 1984, Thesaurus Linguarum Hiberniae, 1991—; vis. prof. U. Dublin, 1990—; adj. prof. theatre U. Calif., San Diego, 1990, prof. theatre and classics, 1994. Recipient Ellen Browning Scripps Humanitarian award, 1975; Disting. Svc. award U. Calif.-Irvine, 1982, Irvine medal, 1987, 3rd Prize Midwest Poetry Ctr. Contest, 1987; named one of the Community Leaders Am., 1979-80, Philanthropist of Yr., 1985, Headliner San Diego Press Club, 1985, Philanthropist of Yr. Honorary Nat. Conf. Christians and Jews, 1986, Woman of Distinction Salvation Army, 1986, Eleventh Woman Living Legacy, 1986, Woman of Yr. AHEPA, 1988, San Diego Woman of Distinction, 1990, Woman of Yr. AXIOS, 1991; recipient Bravissimo gold medal San Diego Opera, 1990, Gold Medal Soc. Internationalization of Greek Lang., 1990, Athens medal, 1991, Piraeus medal, 1991, award Desmoi, 1992, award Hellenic Assn of Univ. Women, 1992, Academy of Achievement award AHEPA, 1992, Woman of Delphi award European Cultural Ctr. Delphi, 1992, Civis Universitatis award U. Calif. San Diego, 1993, Hypatia award Hellenic U. Women, 1993, Am.-Ireland Fund Heritage award, 1994, Contribution to Greek Letters award Aristotle U. Thessaloniki, 1994, Mirabella Mag. Readers Choice One of 1000 Women for the Nineties, 1994, Order of the Phoenix, Greece, 1994, citations from U.S. Congress and Calif. Senate, Alexander the Gt. award Hellenic Cultural Soc., 1995, made hon. citizen of Delphi and gold medal of the Amphiktuonon, Delphi, Greece, 1995, award European Cultural Ctr. of Delphi, 1995, Women Who Mean Bus. award for Fine Arts San Diego Bus. Jour., 1995. Vol. of Decade Women's International Ctr., 1994, 96. Mem. MLA, AAUP, Am. Philol. Assn., Soc. for the Preservation of the Greek Heritage (pres.), Libr. of Am., Am. Classical League, Philol. Assn. Pacific Coast, Am. Comparative Lit. Assn., Modern and Classical Lang. Assn. So. Calif., Hellenic Soc., Calif. Fgn. Lang. Tchrs. Assn., Internat. Platform Assn., Greek Language Found., Royal Irish Acad., Greece's Order of the Phoenix (commdr. 1994), KPBS Producers Club, Hellenic Univ. Club (bd. dir.). Author: Terms for Happiness in Euripides, 1978, Semilemmatized Concordances to Euripides' Alcestis, 1977, Cyclops, Andromache, Medea, 1978, Heraclidae, Hippolytus, 1979, Hecuba, 1984, Hercules Furens, 1984, Electra, 1984, Ion, 1985, Trojan Women, 1988, Iphigenia in Taurus, 1988, Euripides in Cinema: The Heart Made Visible, 1983; translator: The Cost of Kindness and Other Fabulous Tales (Shinichi Hoshi), 1986, (chpt.) Views of Clytemnestra, Ancient and Modern, 1990, Classics and Cinema, 1990, Modern Critical Theory and Classical Literature, 1994, A Challenge to Democracy, 1994, Ancient Sun/Modern Light: Greek Drama on the Modern Stage, 1990, Star Myths: Tales of the Constellations, 1996; contbr. numerous articles to profl. jours. Avocations: karate, harp (medieval), skiing, diving. Home: PO Box 929 Rancho Santa Fe CA 92067-0929 Office: U Calif at San Diego Dept Theatre La Jolla CA 92093

MCDONALD, MARK DOUGLAS, electrical engineer; b. Princeton, N.J., Aug. 3, 1958; s. James Douglas and Jacquelyn (Milligan) McD.; m. Patricia Joann Watson, Sept. 12, 1980. BSE, Duke U.; MS, N.C. State U. Product engr. Exide Electronics, Raleigh, N.C., 1981-84; rsch. asst. N.C. State U., Raleigh, 1985-86; mem. tech. staff Avantek (Hewlett Packard), Newark, Calif., 1987-90; prin. engr. Nat. Semiconductor, Santa Clara, Calif., 1990-92, engring. project mgr., 1992-95; design engring. mgr. Linear Tech. corp., Milpitas, Calif., 1995—; session chmn. Wireless Symposium, Santa Clara, 1993—, RF and Microwave Applications Conf., Santa Clara, 1992; mem. com. Symposium on VLSI Circuits Program, 1995—. Contbr. articles to profl. jours. Precinct capt. various polit. campaigns, Fremont, Calif., 1988. Mem. IEEE (sr.), Cairn Terrier Club of No. Calif. (asst. chairperson 1995, specialty show chairperson 1996—, bd. govs. 1996—). Office: Linear Tech Corp 1630 Mccarthy Blvd Milpitas CA 95035-7417

MCDONALD, PENNY S(UE), educational administrator; b. Portland, Oreg., May 1, 1946; d. Norman James and Edna (Kaufmann) McD. BA, Oreg. State U., 1968, MEd, 1974; EdD, Portland State U./U. Oreg., 1981, Harvard U., summer 1987. Tchr. English, Fleming Jr. High Sch., Los Angeles, 1968-69; tchr. lang. arts and social studies Highland View Jr. High Sch., Corvallis, Oreg., 1970-72; tchr. English, dir. student activities Crescent Valley High Sch., Corvallis, 1973-78; grad. asst. Portland State U., Oreg., 1978-80; evaluation intern N.W. Regional Edn. Lab., Portland, 1980; Nat. Inst. Edn. assoc., edn. policy fellow Nat. Commn. on Excellence in Edn., Washington, 1981-83; prin. Inza R. Wood Middle Sch., West Linn Sch. Dist., Wilsonville, Oreg., 1983-88; adminstr. in residence for ednl. adminstrn. Lewis & Clark Coll., Portland, 1988-91; prin. Adams Hillside Alternative Elem., Eugene (Oreg.) Sch. Dist., 1991—; cons. Oreg. Dept. Edn., 1980-81; sr. counselor Oreg. Assn. Student Councils Camps, 1976-78, 80; adj. prof. ednl. adminstrn. Lewis & Clark Coll., 1987-88, 95-96. Coord., com., adminstr. Oreg. Mentorship Program, 1986-87. Named to Outstanding Young Woman Am., U.S. Jaycees; AFL-CIO scholar Oreg. State U., Corvallis, 1964; Univ. scholar Oreg. State U., 1965-68; nat. Alpha Delta Pi scholar Oreg. State U., 1967-68; Delta Kappa Gamma scholar Portland State U./U. Oreg. 1979-81. Mem. Nat. Assn. Student Councils, Oreg. Assn. Activities Advisors (chmn. 1976-77, bd. dirs. 1977-78), Oreg. Assn. Student Councils, Confedn. Oreg. Sch. Adminstrs. (curriculum commn. 1985-86, asst. chmn., sec. 1986-87, chmn. 1987-88, ex-officio mem. exec. bd. 1987-88), Nat. Assn. Secondary Sch. Prins., N.W. Women in Ednl. Adminstrn. (Oreg. bd. dirs., chairperson 1993-94), Delta Kappa Gamma (chpt. rec. sec.), Phi Delta Kappa. Democrat. Office: Adams Traditional Hillside Elem Sch 950 W 22nd Ave Eugene OR 97405-2119

MCDONALD, ROBERT WAYNE, cardiac sonographer; b. Butte, Mont., Dec. 16, 1958; s. Clyde Wayne and Stella Mary (Radonich) McD.; m. Mary Jo Rice, Aug. 9, 1986. AAS, Spokane C.C., 1983. Registered cardiovascular technologist. Staff cardiac sonographer Oreg. Health Scis. U., Portland, 1983-88, supr., cardiac sonographer, 1988-91, sr. cardiac sonographer, 1991—; cons. Oreg. Regional Primate Rsch. Ctr., Beaverton, 1991—; cons., adj. faculty, clin. preceptor, Spokane C.C., 1984—; instr., clin. preceptor Seattle U., 1984-95. Editor-in-chief Pediat. Ultrasound Today, 1995—; editl. bd./reviewer Jour. Am. Soc. Echocardiography, 1994—. Mem. dist. coun. Boy Scouts Am., Portland, 1991—, advancement chmn. Pioneer dist., 1994—, process and rev. vice chmn. Cascade Pacific coun., 1995—. With U.S. Army, 1978-81. Decorated Army Commendation medal with oak leaf cluster; recipient Dist. Award of Merit, Boy Scouts Am., 1993. Mem. Am. Soc. Echocardiography (bd. dirs. 1996—), Am. Registry of Diagnostic Med. Sonographers (registered, pediat. echo exam rep. 1996—), Willamette Valley Soc. Echocardiography (pres. 1991-95). Office: Oregon Health Scis Univ 3181 SW Sam Jackson Pk Rd Portland OR 97201

MCDONALD, THOMAS EDWIN, JR., electrical engineer; b. Wapanucka, Okla., June 19, 1939; s. Thomas Edwin and Rosamond Bell (Enoch) McD.; m. Myrna Kay Booth, Sept. 10, 1961; children: Stephen Thomas, Jennifer Kay, Sarah Lynn. BSEE, U. Okla., 1962, MSEE, 1963; PhDEE, U. Colo., 1969. Registered profl. engr., N.Mex. Asst. prof. elec. engring. U. Okla., Norman, 1969-70; planning engr. Okla. Gas and Electric Co., Oklahoma City, 1970-72; staff mem. Los Alamos (N.Mex.) Nat. Lab., 1972—, group leader, 1974-80, program mgr., 1980-92; program mgr. Centurion program Los Alamos (N.Mex.) Nat. Lab., Los Alamos, 1986-90; dep. program dir. inertial confinement fusion program Los Alamos (N.Mex.) Nat. Lab., 1990-92, program coord. mine detection and laser tech., 1992-93; project mgr. Nat. Ctr. for Advanced Mfg. Tech., 1993-96, project leader high-speed electronic imaging tech. devel., 1996—; adj. prof. elec. engring. U. Okla., 1970-72; cons. Los Alamos Tech. Assocs., 1980—, mgr. design sect., 1980-81. Rschr. in inertial confinement fusion, high-speed electronic imaging and neutron radiography; contbr. articles to profl. jours. Bd. dirs., mem. United Ch. Los Alamos, 1987—, chmn. bd. elders, 1992. Served to capt. U.S. Army, 1963-67. Mem. IEEE (chmn. Los Alamos sect.), AASE, Soc. for Info. Display, Soc. Photo-Optical Instrumentation Engrs., Los Alamos Gymnastics Club (treas., bd. dirs. 1980-88), Rotary (sec. Los Alamos, v.p.), Sigma Xi, Eta Kappa Nu. Republican. Home: 4200 Ridgeway Dr Los Alamos NM 87544-1956 Office: Los Alamos Nat Lab PO Box 1663 MS 0406 Los Alamos NM 87544-0600

MCDONALD, THOMAS ROBERT, materials technologist, consultant, business owner; b. Denver, Dec. 2, 1945; s. Phillip John and Anne Winslow (Jewell) McD.; m. Mary Kathleen Pfannenstiel, Mar. 6, 1970; children: Michael T., Patrick R. BS in Bus. Fin., U. Colo., 1974. Project materials technician Colo. Dept. Hwys., Denver, 1964-71; pub. works inspector, project mgr. City of Lakewood, Colo., 1971-76; quality control supr., construct materials lab. mgr. Brannan Sand & Gravel Co., Denver, 1976-82; area mgr. Soiltest, Inc., Evanston, Ill., 1982-84; pavement maintenance specialist Western Technologies, Phoenix, 1984-87, Brewer Cote of Ariz., Glendale, 1987-88; sales mgr., estimator Driveway Maintenance of Ariz., Phoenix, 1988-92; owner Pavement Maintenance Info. Source, Mesa, Ariz., 1992—; materials quality control cons. Colo. Dept. Hwys., Denver, 1964-71, Brannan Sand & Gravel, Denver, 1976-82; pavement maintenance cons. Western Technologies, Phoenix, 1984-87, Brewer Cote of Ariz., Glendale, 1987-88, Pavement Maintenance Inf. Source, Mesa, 1992—. Author: (software) Ecopave, 1986, (book) Property Managers Guide to Pavement Maintenance, 1992, Asphalt Estimating, 1995; contbr. articles to property mgmt. and pavement maintenance mags. Mem. Leadership Mesa, 1986. With USN, 1965-68. Recipient Most Innovative Pavement Maintenance Program award FAA, 1986. Mem. ASCE, Bldg. Owners and Mgrs. Assn. (bd. dirs. 1984-93), Multihousing Assn. Ariz. (instr. 1987, 89, 91), Am. Assn. Asphalt Paving Technologists, Internat. Platform Assn., Nat. Assn. Aviation Ofcls., Calif. Assn. Aero. Execs. Office: Pavement Maintenance Info Source PO Box 30567 Mesa AZ 85275-0567

MCDONALD, TIM, professional football player; b. Fresno, Calif., Jan. 6, 1965. Student, U. So. Calif. With St. Louis Cardinals, 1987; safety Phoenix Cardinals (formerly St. Louis Cardinals), 1988-92; with S.F. 49ers, 1993—. Named defense back The Sporting News All-America team, 1985. Office: San Francisco 49ers 4949 Centennial Blvd Santa Clara CA 95054-1229*

MCDONNEL, WILLIAM GEORGE, chemical instrumentation executive; b. Rabat, French Morocco, May 10, 1952; came to U.S., 1953; s. Harold Albert and Anna (Yoos) McD.; BS in Chemistry/Biochemistry, Calif. State U., Fullerton, 1974, MBA Pepperdine U., 1987; m. Nancy Ann Hopwood, Aug. 27, 1977; children: Melissa, Allison Roe. Product specialist Process Instruments div. Beckman Instruments, Inc., Fullerton, 1974; sr. tech. specialist ion selective electrodes Lab. Products div. Orion Research Inc., Cambridge, Mass., 1975-87; region mgr. Milton Roy Inc., 1988-91; gen. mgr. Southwest Sci., Inc., 1991—; speaker in field. Mem. Am. Chem. Soc., Am. Electroplaters Spc., Phi Kappa Tau. Republican. Home: 27412 Cenajo Mission Viejo CA 92691-1418

MCDONNELL, JEANNE FARR, museum director; b. Akron, Ohio, Mar. 26, 1931; d. Ernest and Marie (Koerber) Farr; m. Eugene Edward McDonnell, Oct. 18, 1926; children: Julia, Luke, Peter, Albert, James. AA, Stephens Coll., 1950; BA, Ohio State U., 1952; MA, Columbia U., 1956. Adminstrv. asst. Houghton Mifflin Publs., Palo Alto, Calif., 1981-83; exec. dir. Nature Explorations, Palo Alto, Calif., 1979-84, Womens Heritage Mus., Palo Alto, Calif., 1985—. Editor: (newsletter) Women's Heritage Mus., 1985—. Bd. dirs. Youth Advocates, Media, Pa., 1972-74, LWV, Yorktown Heights, N.Y., 1969-70, Assn. Performing Arts, Yorktown Heights, 1965-70. Fulbright scholar, U. Brussels, 1952-53; Rsch. grantee Sourisseau Acad., San Jose, Calif., 1981, Inst. Hist. Study, San Francisco, 1982. Mem. Western Assn. Women Historians, Orgn. Am. Historians, Women's Club Palo Alto (1st v.p. 1983-84). *

MCDONNELL, JOHN FINNEY, aerospace and aircraft manufacturing executive; b. Mar. 18, 1938; s. James Smith and Mary Elizabeth (Finney) McD.; m. Anne Marbury, June 16, 1961. BS in Aero. Engring., Princeton U., 1960, MS in Aero. Engring., 1962; postgrad. in bus. adminstrn., Washington U., St. Louis, 1962-66. Strength engr. McDonnell Aircraft Co. (subs. McDonnell Douglas Corp.), St. Louis, 1962, corp. analyst, 1963-65, contract coord., adminstr., 1965-68; asst. to v.p. fin. Douglas Aircraft Co. (subs. McDonnell Douglas Corp.), 1968; v.p. McDonnell Douglas Fin. Corp. (subs. McDonnell Douglas Corp.), 1968-71; staff v.p. fiscal McDonnell Douglas Corp., 1971-75, corp. v.p. fin. and devel., 1975-77, corp. exec. v.p., 1977-80, pres., 1980—, mem. exec. com., 1975—, chmn., 1988—, past CEO, also bd. dirs.; bd. dirs. Ralston Purina Co. Bd. commrs. St. Louis Sci. Ctr.; trustee KETC, Washington U., also chmn. nat. coun. faculty arts and scis. com. Office: McDonnell Douglas Corp PO Box 516 Saint Louis MO 63166-0516*

MCDONOUGH, KAREL JOY, secondary education educator, musician; b. Rupert, Idaho, Dec. 19, 1944; d. Earl M. and Lorna D. (Thompson) Doop; m. Kenneth E. Moller, June 16, 1962 (dec. May 1966); 1 child, Kelly B.; m. Gregory M. Smith McDonough, Sept. 9, 1967; children: Shea K., Darby, Casey O., Tye F., Evan P., Quinn C. BS in Psychology, U. Utah, 1970, MEd in Edn. Adminstrn., 1991. Cert. secondary tchr., Utah; cert. adminstrv. ednl. supr., Utah. Substitute tchr. Salt Lake City Pub. Schs., 1982-88; supr. Snowbird (Utah) Resort, 1989-90; testing asst. U. Utah, Salt Lake City, 1991-92; tchr. Brockbank Jr. H.S., Magna, Utah, 1992—; percussionist Mormon Symphony Orch., Salt Lake City, 1968-72, 93—, Triad Theatre, Salt Lake City, 1986, Jay Welch Orch., Salt Lake City, 1984-95. Treas., incorporator NHS, Salt Lake City, 1973-75; candidate Utah Ho. of Reps., 1976, 1980; Rep. legis. dist. chmn., Salt Lake City, 1981-83; bd. dirs. Tracy Aviary, Salt Lake City, 1989-94; vol. coord. Emerson Elem. Sch., Salt Lake City, 1982-84. Mem. Assn. Supervisory and Curricular Devel., Music Educators Nat. Conf., PTSA. Republican. Mormon. Office: Brockbank Jr High Sch 2935 S 8560 W Magna UT 84044-1252

MCDONOUGH, PATRICIA MARIE, education educator; b. Boston, Sept. 24, 1952; d. William Francis and Winifred Elizabeth (Donovan) McD. BA, U. Mass., 1974; MA, George Washington U., 1980, Stanford (Calif.) U., 1991; PhD, Stanford (Calif.) U., 1992. Co-founder edn. dir. Washington Ctr., 1975-80; policy analyst Nat. Manpower Inst., Washington, 1980-81; edn. dir. Bus. and Profl. Women's Fedn., Washington, 1981-82; faculty coord. Stanford (Calif.) Linear Accelerator Ctr., 1983-85; dir. upward bound Stanford U., 1986-87, rsch. asst., 1987-91; asst. prof. Grad. Sch. of Edn., UCLA, 1991-96, assoc. prof., 1996—; cons. Office of the Pres., U. Calif., 1991, Far West Labs., San Francisco, 1991. Predoctoral fellowship Nat. Inst. Mental Health/Stanford Ctr. for Orgns. Rsch., 1987-89; recipient Nat. Acad. of Edn. Spencer Postdoctoral fellowship, 1995-97. Mem. Am. Ednl. Rsch. Assn., Assn. for Study of Higher Edn., Am. Sociol. Assn. Office: UCLA Grad Sch Edn 405 Hilgard Ave Los Angeles CA 90024-1301

MCDONOUGH, RUSSELL CHARLES, retired state supreme court justice; b. Glendive, Mont., Dec. 7, 1924; s. Roy James and Elsie Marie (Johnson) McD.; m. Dora Jean Bidwell, Mar. 17, 1946; children: Ann Remmich, Michael, Kay Jensen, Kevin, Daniel, Mary Garfield. JD, George Washington U., 1949. Bar: Mont. 1950. Pvt. practice Glendive, Mont., 1950-83; judge Gen. Jurisdiction State of Montana, Glendive, 1983-87; justice Mont. Supreme Ct., Helena, 1987-93, ret., 1993. City atty. City of Glendive, 1953-57; county atty. Dawson County, Mon., 1957-63; del. Mont. Constl. Conv., Helena, 1972. 1st lt. AC, U.S. Army, 1943-45, ETO. Decorated DFC. Mem. Mont. Bar Assn. Roman Catholic. Home: 1805 Joslyn St Trlr 131 Helena MT 59601-0113

MCDOUGALL, DONALD BLAKE, retired government official, librarian; b. Moose Jaw, Sask., Can., Mar. 6, 1938; s. Daniel Albert and Donela (McRae) McD.; m. Norma Rose Peacock, May 19, 1962. BA, U. Sask., 1966, BEd, 1966; BLS, U. Toronto, 1969, MLS, U. Alta., 1983, cert. pub. adminstrn. U. Alta., 1990. Classroom tchr., Regina Bd. Edn., Sask., 1960-63, vice prin., 1963-68; asst. chief libr. Stratford Pub. Libr., Ont., Can., 1969, chief. libr., 1970-72; supr. info. svcs. Edmonton Pub. Libr., Alta., Can., 1972, head pub. svcs., 1973-74; legislature libr. Province of Alta., Edmonton, 1974-87; asst. dep. min., legis. libr. Legis. Assembly Alta., 1987-93, ret., 1993. Editor microfilm: Alberta Scrapbook Hansard, 1906-1964, 1976, editor Book: A History of the Legislature Library, 1979, Princess Louise Caroline Alberta, 1988, Canada's Parliamentary Libraries, 1989, Lieutenant-Governors of the Northwest Territories and Alberta, 1876-1991, 1991, Premiers of the Northwest Territories and Alberta, 1897-1991, 1991. Govt. Sask. scholar, 1965; recipient Queen's Silver Jubilee medal Govt. Can., 1977; named Hon. Clk.-At-The-Table, Legis. Assembly Alberta, 1987-93. Mem. Alta. Govt. Libraries Coun. (chmn. 1975), Assn. Parliamentary Librarians in Can. (pres. 1980-82), Edmonton Libr. Assn., Hist. Soc. Alta. (v.p. Edmonton chpt. 1987), Libr. Assn. Alta., Can. Libr. Assn., Beta Phi Mu. Presbyterian. Clubs: Edmonton Jaguar Drivers, Edmonton Scottish Soc. Home: 209 Rhatigan Rd W NW, Edmonton, AB Canada T6R 1A2

MCDOUGALL, JACQUELYN MARIE HORAN, therapist; b. Wenatchee, Wash., Sept. 24, 1924; d. John Rankin and Helen Frampton (Vandivort) Horan; m. Robert Duncan McDougall, Jan. 24, 1947 (div. July 1976); children: Douglas, Stuart, Scott. BA, Wash. State U., 1946. Lic. therapist, Wash.; cert. nat. addiction counselor II. Pres. oper. bd. Ctr. for Alcohol/Drug Treatment, Wenatchee, 1983-85; sec. Wash. State Coun. on Alcoholism, 1988-89, supr. out-patient svcs., 1989-90; case mgmt. counselor Lakeside Treatment Ctr., East Wenatchee, Wash., 1991-92; ret., 1994. Treas. Allied Arts, Wenatchee, 1984; pres. Rep. Women, Wash., 1969-70.

MCDOWELL, JENNIFER, sociologist, composer, playwright, publisher; b. Albuquerque; d. Willard A. and Margaret Frances (Garrison) McD.; m. Milton Loventhal, July 2, 1973. BA, U. Calif., 1957; MA, San Diego State U., 1958; postgrad., Sorbonne, Paris, 1959; MLS, U. Calif., 1963; PhD, U. Oreg., 1973. Tchr. English Abraham Lincoln High Sch., San Jose, Calif., 1960-61; free-lance editor Soviet field, Berkeley, Calif., 1961-63; rsch. asst. sociology U. Oreg., Eugene, 1964-66; editor, pub. Merlin Papers, San Jose, 1969—, Merlin Press, San Jose, 1973—; rsch. cons. sociology San Jose, 1973—; music pub. Lipstick and Toy Balloons Pub. Co., San Jose, 1978—; composer Paramount Pictures, 1982-88; tchr. writing workshops; poetry readings, 1969-73; co-producer radio show lit. and culture Sta. KALX, Berkeley, 1971-72. Author: (with Milton Loventhal) Black Politics: A Study and Annotated Bibliography of the Mississippi Freedom Democratic Party, 1971 (featured at Smithsonian Inst. Spl. Event 1992), Contemporary Women Poets, 1977, Ronnie Goose Rhymes for Grown-Ups, 1984; co-author: (plays off-off Broadway) Betsy and Phyllis, 1986, Mack the Knife Your Friendly Dentist, 1986, The Estrogen Party To End War, 1986, The Oatmeal Party Comes To Order, 1986, (plays) Betsy Meets the Wacky Iraqui, 1991, Bella and Phyllis, 1994; contbr. poems, plays, essays, articles, short stories, and book revs. to lit. mags., news mags. and anthologies; rschr. women's autobiog. writings, contemporary writing in poetry, Soviet studies, civil rights movement, and George Orwell, 1962—; writer: (songs) Money Makes a Woman Free, 1976, 3 songs featured in Parade of Am. Music; co-creator mus. comedy Russia's Secret Plot To Take Back Alaska, 1988. Recipient 8 awards Am. Song Festival, 1976-79, Bill Casey Award in Letters, 1980; doctoral fellow AAUW, 1971-73; grantee Calif. Arts Coun., 1976-77. Mem. Am. Sociol. Assn., Soc. Sci. Study of Religion, Poetry Orgn. for Women, Dramatists Guild, Phi Beta Kappa, Sigma Alpha Iota, Beta Phi Mu, Kappa Kappa Gamma. Democrat. Office: care Merlin Press PO Box 5602 San Jose CA 95150-5602

MCDOWELL, MARCIA ANN, security professional; b. Toronto, Ont., Can., May 14, 1956; came to U.S., 1956; d. William James and Thelma Rose (Smith) McD. BS, Thomas A. Edison State Coll., 1993; postgrad., U. Phoenix, 1996—. Provincial constable Ont. (Can.) Provincial Police; spl. svcs. officer Ann Arbor (Mich.) City Police; profl. dealer Bicycle Club Casino, Bell Gardens, Calif.; owner, instr. Gold Coast Sch. Dealing, Downey, Calif.; instr. C.C. South Nev., Las Vegas; surveillance specialist Sahara Hotel & Casino, Las Vegas; lectr. in field. Author: Techniques of Casino Surveillance, 1995, Signature Bets-A Guide to Recognizing Roulette Advantage Play, 1996. Recipient Arnold Fletcher award Thomas A. Edison State Coll., Trenton, N.J., 1993. Mem. Am. Mgmt. Assn.

MCDOWELL, MARION, state agency director. BA in Sociology, U. Ariz.; MA in Pub. Personnel Adminstrn., George Washington U. Mem. grad. faculty for pub. personnel mgmt. Coll. Notre Dame, Belmont, Calif.; dep. supt. personnel svcs. Sequoia Union High Sch. Dist., 1988-95; pres. Calif. State Bd. of Edn., 1995—. Mem. Civil Svc. Commn. for San Mateo County, 1987—. Mem. Am. Soc. Personnel Adminstrn., Am. Assn. for Sch. Personnel Adminstrn., Calif. Ednl. Placement Assn., Assn. Calif. Sch. Adminstrs., No. Calif. Human Resources Coun. Office: State Bd of Edn 721 Capitol Mall Rm 532 Sacramento CA 95814-4702*

MCDOWELL, SHERRIE LORRAINE, secondary education educator; b. Manchester, Ky., Apr. 20, 1948; d. Alonzo and Madge Loudean (Christensen) Garrison; m. Gary Lynn McDowell, July 11, 1970; 1 child, Marc Ryan. BA, U. No. Colo., 1970; MA, Lesley Coll., 1989; postgrad., U. Wyo. Cert. tchr., Wyo. Tchr. English St. Mary's Cath. Sch., Cheyenne, Wyo., 1971-72; instr. homebound program Laramie County Sch. Dist., Cheyenne, 1978-84; English instr. Cen. High Sch., Cheyenne, 1984—; Wyo. coach Nat. Tournament of Acad. Excellence, 1988-90; recorder NCTE Conv., Boston, 1996. Mem. NEA (Assembly rep. 1993-96, cadre trainer state level women's leadership tng. program 1995-96), AAUW (sec. 1975-77), Wyo. Edn. Assn. (co-chair profl. standards and practices commn. 1995—, chair summer Inst. 1996-97), Nat. Coun. Tchrs. English, Cheyenne Tchrs. Edn. Assn. (edn. assn. del. 1992—, chair instrnl. issues 1995, co-chair pub. rels. 1988-90, editor ACCENTS 1988-90, sec. 1995—), Wyo. Assn. Tchrs. English (presenter), Wyo. Chautauqua Soc. (pres. 1985-86, bd. dirs. 1984-85), Delta Kappa Gamma (state scholarship chair 1989-90, pres. chpt. 1988-90). Home: 100 Grandview Ct Cheyenne WY 82009-4912 Office: Ctrl High Sch 5500 Education Dr Cheyenne WY 82009-4008

MCELDOWNEY, ROLAND CONANT, gold mining company executive; b. Newton, Mass., Nov. 14, 1940; s. Richard Lancaster and Virginia Davis (Conant) McE.; m. Barbara Lynn Read, Mar. 26, 1966; children: Richard Read, Scott Roland, Kathryn Ramsay. BA in Geology, Franklin & Marshall Coll., 1963; MS in Geology, San Diego State U., 1971. Cert. geologist, Maine. Vol. geologist U.S. Peace Corps, Ghana, 1963-66; geologist U.S. Army C.E., San Francisco, 1966-68; sr. geologist Geodata Systems Inc., Orange, Calif., 1969-71; assoc. sr. geologist Dames & Moore, Denver, 1972-79; v.p. Apache Energy and Minerals Co., Lakewood, Colo., 1979-84; pres., owner Wolf Creek Exploration Co., Evergreen Colo., 1984—; sr. v.p. Internat. Gold Resources Corp., Houston, Tex., 1985-96; mng. dir. Internat. Gold Resources, Inc., Bibani, Ghana, 1990-96 (discovered Bibani Open Pit Gold Deposit). Artist, producer silver proof coin World Cup Skiing, Breckenridge, Colo., 1991-92; contbr. numerous articles to profl. geol. and engring. jours. Mem. Soc. Econ. Geologists, Soc. for Mining, Metallurgy and Exploration, Geol. Soc. Am., Kiwanis (past mem. bd. dirs. Blue Spruce). Republican. Home: 29434 Greenwood Ln Evergreen CO 80439

MCELROY, LEO FRANCIS, communications consultant, journalist; b. Los Angeles, Oct. 12, 1932; s. Leo Francis and Helen Evelyn (Silliman) McE.; m. Dorothy Frances Montgomery, Nov. 3, 1956 (div. 1981); children: James, Maureen, Michael, Kathleen; m. Judith Marie Lewis, May 30, 1992. BS in English, Loyola U., L.A. 1953. News dir. KFI, KRLA, KABC Radio, L.A., 1964-72; pub. affairs host Sta. KCET, Pub. TV, L.A., 1967-74; v.p. Sta. KROQ AM/FM, L.A., 1972-74; polit. editor Sta. KABC-TV, L.A., 1974-81; pres. McElroy Communications, L.A. and Sacramento, 1981—; pres. sec. Lt. Gov.'s Office, Sacramento, 1983-84; chmn. Calif. AP Broadcasters, 1972-74; cons. State Office Migrant Edn., Sacramento, 1974, Californians for Water, L.A. , 1982, Calif. Water Protection Coun., Sacramento, 1982, Planning and Conservation League, Sacramento, 1984—, Common Cause, Sacramento, 1988—. Author: Uneasy Partners, 1984; author plays: Mermaid Tavern, 1956, To Bury Caesar (Christopher award 1952), 1952, Rocket to Olympus, 1960, The Code of Whiskey King, 1995. State del. Western Am. Assembly on Prison Reform, Berkeley, Calif., 1973; chmn. State Disaster Info. Task Force; Calif., 1973-74; campaign media cons. statewide issues, various candidates, Sacramento, L.A., 1981—; bd. dirs. Vols. in Victim Assistance, Sacramento, 1984, Rescue Alliance, Sacramento, 1987—, Mental Health Assn., Sacramento, 1985-89, Leukemia Soc., 1992—. Recipient Gabriel award Cath. Archdiocese, L.A., 1972, Golden Mike award Radio-TV News Assn., L.A., 1973; Hon. Resolution, Calif. State Assembly, Sacramento, 1981. Mem. ASCAP, AFTRA, Screen Actors Guild, Am. Assn. Polit. Cons. Mem. Reform Party. Roman Catholic. Home: 8217 Oakenshaw Way Orangevale CA 95662-2953 Office: McElroy Comm 2410 K St Ste C Sacramento CA 95816-5002 *No gift is greater than the gift of oneself - honestly given, honestly received.*

MCELWEE, JEANETTE GAYE, management and philanthropic consultant; b. New Castle, Pa., Sept. 23, 1950; d. George Thomas McElwee and Bernice Elaine (Welker) Haines. BS in Music Edn., Ea. Nazarene Coll., 1972; MusM, Kent State U., 1976; postgrad., UCLA, 1980. Tchr. New Kensington (Pa.) Pub. Schs., 1972-74; asst. prof. Edinboro (Pa.) State U., 1976-77, Oberlin (Ohio) Coll. Conservatory of Music, 1977-79; dir. external and cmty. affairs Carter Hawley Hale Stores, 1981-92; prin. The McElwee Group, Burbank, Calif., 1993—; vis. lectr. S.N.D.T. U., Bombay, India, 1978, pres., co-founder Arts, Inc.; pres. Aman Internat. Music & Dance Co. Mem. Mayor's Task Force on Volunteerism, L.A.; commn. on arts edn. Calif. Dept. Edn.; mem. strategic planning com. L.A. United Way; mem. Getty Fund for Visual Arts, Calif. Cmty. Found. Mem. So. Calif. Assn. for Philanthropy (chair), Asia Soc./So. Calif. Ctr., Am. Women for Internat. Understanding, Cmty. Ptnrs. Office: McElwee Group 724 S Victory Blvd Ste 203 Burbank CA 91502

MCELYEA, ULYSSES, JR., veterinarian; b. Ft. Collins, Colo., Oct. 29, 1941; s. Ulysses and Hazel (Hall) McE.; m. Rexanna Bell, Dec. 29, 1975 (div. 1980). BS in Pharmacy, U. N.Mex., 1963; DVM, Colorado State U., 1967, MS, 1968. Diplomate Am. Bd. Vet. Practicioners; cert. in companion animals. Owner Alta Vista Animal Clinic, Las Cruces, N.Mex., 1970—; bd. dirs. N.Mex. Acad. Vet. Practice, Albuquerque, bd. dirs. state of N.Mex. Bd. Vet. Examiners, v.p., 1989-92, vice chair, 1992, chair, 1992—, Bank of the Rio Grande. Pres. Las Cruces Community Theater, 1974; founder, bd. dirs. Dona Ann Arts Coun., Las Cruces, 1976-80. Capt. U.S. Army, 1968-70. Mem. AVMA, Am. Pharm. Assn., Am. Assn. Feline Practitioners, Am. Soc. Vet. Ophthalmologists, N.Mex. Vet. Med. Assn. (bd. dirs. 1976-82), So. N.Mex. Vet. Assn. (pres. 1974, 84), N.Mex. State U. Athletic Assn. 9bd. dirs. 1976—, pres.-elect 1992-93, pres. 1993-94), N.Mex. State U. Pres.'s Assn. 9bd. dirs. 1988-91), U. N.Mex. Alumni Assn. (bd. dirs. 1976-80). Democrat. Home: 2635 Fairway Dr Las Cruces NM 88011-5044 Office: Alta Vista Animal Clinic 725 S Soiano Dr Las Cruces NM 88001-3244

MCENTEE, JAMES PATRICK, SR., human relations executive; b. Oakland, Calif., Apr. 9, 1931; s. James and Mary (Kelly) McE.; m. Ann J. Mainland, Aug. 18, 1973; children: Mona, Jesse, Maria Elena, Dianne, James, Chinecy, Amy K., Peter M. BA, St. Joseph's Coll., 1957; MDiv., St. Patrick's Sem., 1973; AA, San Jose City Coll., 1979. Pastoral assoc. Roman Catholic Archdiocese of San Francisco, 1957-73; exec. dir. Vol. Action Ctr., San Jose, Calif., 1973-76; dir. human rels. County of Santa Clara, San Jose, Calif., 1976—; counselor A&J Assoc., San Jose, 1974-94. Pres. Calif. Assn. Human Rights Orgn., 1986-90; chairperson Mexican Am. United for Progress, Morgan Hill, Calif., 1969-73. Recipient Commendation award NAACP, 1990, Commendation award Asian Law Alliance, 1984, Commendation award Am. Indian Ctr., 1989; named Family of Yr. B'Hai Cmty., San Jose, 1994. Democrat. Roman Catholic. Office: Office Human Rels County Santa Clara 70 W Hedding St San Jose CA 95110-1705

MCEVOY-JAMIL, PATRICIA ANN, English language educator; b. Butler, Pa., June 26, 1955; d. Joseph Lawrence McEvoy and Janet Ann (McConnell) Beier; m. M. Jamal Jamil, Nov. 23, 1977; 1 child, Amirah M. *Husband M. Jamal Jamil is an assistant professor in the Middle Eastern School at the Defense Language Institute. After a post-doctoral fellowship at Harvard University in 1978, he served as Deputy Minister of Foreign Affairs at the Yemeni President's Office until his appointment as Director General of Public Relations at the Yemen Oil and Mineral Resources Corporation. He has been employed with the federal government of the United States since 1981.* MA in TESOL, Monterey Inst. Internat. Studies, 1984; MA in English, Coll. Notre Dame, 1995; EdD, U. San Francisco, 1996. Calif. C.C. credential for life. Instr. ESL City Coll. San Francisco, 1989—, Canada Coll., Redwood City, Calif., 1989—; lectr. ESL Stanford (Calif.) U., 1989—, Coll. Notre Dame, Belmont, Calif., 1991—; presenter in field. Recipient ELITE Patron of Honor award ELITE Stanford (Calif.) Hosp., 1989, 90. Mem. Nat. Coun. Tchrs. English, Calif. Tchrs. English to Speakers of Other Langs., Phi Delta Kappa. *Patricia McEvoy-Jamil's academic research has primarily focused on the qualitative investigation of the second language acquisition issues associated with the education of international college students. The findings of some of this qualitative research resulted in the integration of community-based projects in the English as a Second Language classrooms at the College of Notre Dame and at the City College of San Francisco.*

MCEWAN, GORDON FRANCIS, archaeologist, museum curator; b. Bremerhaven, Germany, Apr. 2, 1951; s. Donald Hall and Kathryn Helen (Peterson) McE.; m. Nancy Jean Van Andel, Aug. 23, 1975; children: Andrew, Alexander. BA, Tex. A&M U., 1977; MA, U. Tex., 1979, PhD, 1984. Asst. curator Dumbarton Oaks, Harvard U., Washington, 1984-91; assoc. curator Denver Art Mus., 1991-95, curator, 1995—; cons. Time-Life Books, Alexandria, Va., 1986-94, Nat. Geog. Soc., Washington, 1986—. Author: Middle Horizon in the Valley of Cuzco, 1987; co-editor: Huari Political Organization, 1991. Grantee NSF, 1989, 96, NEH, 1992; Fulbright Hays fellow, 1981. Fellow The Explorers Club; mem. Soc. for Am. Archaeology, Inst. Andean Studies. Office: Denver Art Mus New World Dept 100 W 14th Ave Pkwy Denver CO 80204

MCFADDEN, MICHAEL J., utilities industry consultant; b. Chgo., Mar. 30, 1950; s. Edward P. and Joan M. (Mulcahy) McF.; divorced; children: Michael J. Jr., Joseph W., Brian P. BSBA, Regis U., 1972; MBA, U. Denver, 1973. Dir. rate regulatory svcs. dept. Pub. Svc. Co. Colo., 1974-86, staff asst. to sr. v.p. fin. and CFO, 1986-89; mgr. fin. svcs. & adminstrn., asst. treas., asst. sec. Western Gas Supply Co., 1989-93; v.p., treas., sec. WestGas Trans Colo Inc., Gathering, Inc., WestGas InterState, Inc., 1989-93; bd. dirs. WestGas Gathering, Inc., WestGas InterState, Inc.; prin. Hagler Bailly Consulting, Inc., Boulder, Colo., 1993-95; sr. advisor Hagler Bailly Consulting, Inc., Boulder, 1995—; pres. McFadden Consulting Group, Inc., Arvada, Colo., 1995—; mem. adj. faculty Regis U., 1981-82, Met. State Coll., 1989-94; mem. faculty Colo. divsn. U. Phoenix, 1992—, chair fin. area, 1992-93; expert witness, presenter in field. Mem. Interstate Natural Gas Assn. Am. (former mem. rate and policy com.), Colo. Assn. Commerce and Industry (50 for Colo.), Rocky Mountain Natural Gas Assn., Regis U. Alumni Assn., U. Denver Alumni Assn. Office: McFadden Consulting Group 6158 W 84th Ave Arvada CO 80003

MCFADIN, HELEN LOZETTA, retired elementary education educator; b. Tucumcari, N.Mex., Sept. 7, 1923; d. Henry J. and LaRue Altha (Ford) Stockton; m. John Reece McFadin, July 3, 1946; 1 child, Janice Lynn McFadin Koenig. AB in Edn./Psychology, Highlands U., Las Vegas, N.Mex., 1956; MA in Teaching, N.Mex. State U., 1968; postgrad., U. N.D., 1965, St. Leo's Coll., St. Leo, Fla., 1970. Cert. tchr., K-12 reading/psychology specialist, N.Mex. Tchr. 1st and 2d grades Grant County Schs., Bayard, N.Mex., 1943-44; tchr. 4th grade Durango (Colo.) Pub. Schs., 1946-48; tchr. 2d grade Artesia Pub. Schs., Loco Hills, N.Mex., 1955; tchr. 3d grade Alamogordo (N.Mex.) Pub. Schs., 1957-66, h.s. reading specialist, 1966-72, elem. reading specialist, 1972-77, tchr. 4th grade, 1977-82, reading tchr. 7th grade, dept. chair, 1982-87; ret. N.Mex. State U., Alamogordo, 1987, instr. edn., 1987-90; organizer reading labs. h.s., elem. schs., Alamogordo, 1966-77, designer programs and curriculum, 1957-89; presenter/cons. in field; cons. Mary Kay Cosmetics; advanced rep. Excel Telecomm., Inc. Contbr. articles to profl. jours. Local and dist. judge spelling bees and sci. fairs Alamogordo Pub. Schs., 1987—. Recipient Literacy award Otero County Reading Coun., 1986; inducted in Women's Hall of Fame, Alamogordo Women's Clubs, 1989. Mem. Am. Bus. Women's Assn. (pres. 1986-87, Woman of the Yr. 1988), C. of C., NEA (del. 1957-87, Dedicated Svc. award 1987), N.Mex. Edn. Assn., Internat. Reading Assn. (mem. Spl. League of the Honored 1985, pres. 1975-76), N.Mex. Reading Assn. (bd. dirs. 1988-94, del. to 1st Russian reading conf. 1992, Dedicated Svc. award 1994), Beta Sigma Phi, Kappa Kappa Iota (Disting. Educator Emeritus Cert. of Merit 1988). Republican. Baptist. Home: 2364 Union Ave Alamogordo NM 88310-3848

MCFARLAND, JON WELDON, retired county commissioner; b. Wenatchee, Wash., Aug. 23, 1938; s. Charles Edward and Maud Elizabeth (Brennan) McF.; m. Kay Annette Erbes, Apr. 5, 1956; children: Colleen, Michael, Heather. BS in Edn., Eastern Wash. State U., 1961; MS in Personnel Adminstrn., George Washington U., 1966; Grad., Command and Gen. Staff Coll., Fort Leavenworth, Kans., 1970, U.S. Army War Coll., Carlisle Barracks, Pa., 1980. Commd. U.S. Army, 1961, advanced through grades to col., 1981, retired, 1988; ops. officer European Hdqtrs. U.S. Army, Heidelberg, Fed. Republic Germany, 1980-83; commdr. 16th mil. police brigade U.S. Army, Fort Bragg, N.C., 1983-85; asst. commandant, commdr. of troops U.S. Army

Mil. Police Sch., Fort McClellan, Ala., 1985-88; county commr. Columbia County, Wash., 1989-96; dir., owner Mr. Mc's Direct Mktg. Svcs., 1992—; owner, dir. Spectro-Optics of Ea. Wash., Dayton, 1994—; Wash. staff for courthouse security, 1995-96; vice chmn. Southeastern Emergency Med. and Trauma Coun., Wash., 1990-94, chmn., 1995-97; chmn. Columbia County Bd. Commrs., 1990, 96; bd. dirs. Emergency Mgmt. Svcs., Columbia County. Author: History of Civil Disturbance 1960-68, 1969. Bd. dirs. Columbia County Pub. Health Dist., Dayton, 1989-96, chmn., 1995-96; bd. dirs. Project Timothy Pub. Svcs., bd. dirs., Columbia County Health Found., 1989—; vice chmn. Palouse Econ. Devel. Corp., 1990-92, chmn., 1993-95. Decorated Legion of Merit, Bronze Star, numerous others. Mem. Assn. U.S. Army, Wash. State Assn. Counties, U.S. Army War Coll. Found., Kiwanis (bd. dirs. Dayton 1990—). Democrat. Roman Catholic. Home: RR 3 Box 248 Dayton WA 99328-9792 Office: Columbia County 205 S 4th St Dayton WA 99328-9792

MC FARLAND, NORMAN FRANCIS, bishop; b. Martinez, Calif., Feb. 21, 1922; student St. Patrick's Sem., Menlo Park, Calif.; J.C.D., Cath. U. Am. Ordained priest Roman Catholic Ch., 1946, consecrated bishop, 1970; titular bishop of Bida and aux. bishop of San Francisco, 1970-74; apostolic adminstr. Diocese of Reno, 1974-76; bishop Diocese of Reno-Las Vegas, 1976-87, Diocese of Orange, Calif., 1987—. Office: Marywood Ctr 2811 E Villa Real Dr Orange CA 92867-1932

MCFARLANE, RICHARD ALAN, lawyer; b. Salt Lake City, July 6, 1962; s. Richard Stevens and Kathleen Irene (Rice) McF; m. LeAnne Skyles, Mar. 20, 1987; children: Adam, Aubreelyn. BA, Calif. State Univ., Fullerton, 1987; JD, Southwestern U., L.A., 1991. Law clerk L.A. City Atty., 1989-92; prin. Law Office Richard McFarlane, Anaheim, Calif., 1992—. Mem. State Bar Calif., Utah State Bar, D.C. Bar, Internat. Bar Assn., Orange County Bar Assn., L.A. Bar Assn. Office: 2323 W Lincoln Ave Ste 127 Anaheim CA 92801-5100

MCFARLANE, WILLIAM JOHN, software development company executive; b. Edinburgh, Scotland, Nov. 27, 1949; came to U.S., 1985; s. David Duncan and Doreen (Penney) McF.; m. TamaraLee Taylor, Nov. 4, 1979 (div. 1996); children: Robert William, Aran James. Grad., Dundee Coll. Tech., 1980; MBA, U. Edinburgh, 1984. V.p. Associated Travel Network, Chgo., 1985-86; gen. mgr. Corp-Net Internat., Libertyville, Ill., 1986-88; v.p. Galileo N.Am., Rosemont, Ill., 1988-90; prin. Bill McFarlane & Assocs., Norcross, Ga., 1990-93; pres., CEO AGUA Software Products, Inc., Santa Ana, Calif., 1993—. Contbr. articles to trade mags. Republican. Home: 3601 Marin Dr Irvine CA 92606-1713 Office: AGUA Software Products Inc 1241 E Dyer Rd Ste 210 Santa Ana CA 92705-5611

MCFARLANE, WILLIS MCKEE, buffalo company executive; b. Cleve., May 27, 1933. BA in Econs. cum laude, Amherst Coll., 1955. Exec. Nowthwestern Mut. Life Ins., 1955-60; ptnr. life ins. co. Files, Cristal, and McFarlane, 1956—; founder AIRCOA, Cleve., 1968-79, Denver, 1979-90; co-owner Denver Buffalo Mktg. Co., 1990—, Buffalo Bar, Colorado Springs & Idaho, 1995—. Chmn. bd. dirs. Colo. Symphony Orch.; bd. dirs. Colo. Wildlife Heritage Found. Mem. Cherry Hills Country Club. Office: Denver Buffalo Co 1120 Lincoln St Ste 905 Denver CO 80203

MCGANN, JOHN MILTON, real estate executive; b. Omaha, Mar. 18, 1948; s. John Byron and Donna M. (Rehnquist) McG.; m. Barbara June Scott, June 2, 1978. BSBA, cert. real estate, U. Nebr., Omaha, 1971. Property mgr. Boetel & Co., Omaha, 1971-73; asst. office bldg. mgr. The Irvine Co., Newport Beach, Calif., 1973-74; property mgr. Harbor Investment Co., Corona Del Mar, Calif., 1974-76, Robert A. McNeil Corp., Santa Ana, Calif., 1976-78; gen. mgr. Daon Mgmt., Newport Beach, 1978-80; v.p. August Mgmt. Inc., Long Beach, Calif., 1980-82, Calif. Fed. Asst. Mgmt., L.A., 1982-83; pres. Wespac Mgmt. Realty Corp., Newport Beach, 1983-87; v.p., dir. asset mgmt., pres. CalFed Asset Mgmt. Co., L.A., 1987-90; v.p. com. ops. Pinnacle Realty (formerly Sovereign/Ring), Santa Monica, 1990-95; pres., ptnr. Churchill McGann, Inc., L.A., 1995—. Mem. Inst. Real Estate Mgmt. (L.A. chpt., cert. property mgr.), Internat. Coun. Shopping Ctrs. (cert. shopping ctr. mgr.), Lambda Chi Alpha, Delta Sigma Pi, Rho Epsilon (pres.). Republican. Mem. Christian Sci. Ch. Home: 1009 4th St Hermosa Beach CA 90254-4802 Office: Churchill McGann Inc 10351 Santa Monica Blvd Ste 410 Los Angeles CA 90025-6937

MCGAVIN, JOCK CAMPBELL, airframe design engineer; b. L.A., Sept. 14, 1917; s. Campbell and Irene (LeMarr) McG.; m. Catherine Marcelle Glew, Jan. 12, 1952; 1 child, James Campbell. AA, L.A. City Coll., 1950; AB, U. So. Calif., 1970, MS, 1975; PhD, Calif. Coast U., 1989. Airframe design engr. Rockwell Internat. Corp., L.A., 1946-82; ret., 1982; sr. design engr. X-15 airplane, Apollo Command Module, space shuttle, others. Vol. mem. pub. involvement subcom. Puget Sound Water Quality Authority, Seattle, 1987-89; commd. Ky. Col., ETO svc., 1994. Capt. C.E. U.S. Army, 1940-46, ETO. Recipient Apollo Achievement award NASA, 1969; named to Honorable Order of Ky. Colonels. Mem. Soc. for History Astronomy, Izaak Walton League Am. (pres. Greater Seattle chpt. 1991-93, vol. worker environ. projects 1985—), U. So. Calif. N.W. Alumni Club (pres. 1987-89). Home: 12939 NE 146th Pl Woodinville WA 98072-4632

MCGEE, ANASTASIA GUINIVIERE, visual effects coordinator; b. Riverside, Calif., May 19, 1964; d. Gordon Edward Pflug and Delores Anne (Bell) Stromberg; married; 1 child. Comm/VA, U. Calif., San Diego, 1985; BFA in Film, Art Ctr. Coll., 1988. Personal asst. Peloria Corp., L.A., 1988-89; temp. asst. Right Connections, L.A., 1989-90; park films coord. Buena Vista Visual Efx, Burbank, Calif., 1990-92, coord. park films and libr. restoration, 1992-94, visual effects coord., 1994-96; dept. coord. Buena Vista Imaging, Burbank, 1996—; mem. adv. bd. Disney U., Burbank, 1994—; mem. steering com. Disney Vols., Burbank, 1995—. Recipient 5-Yrs. Continuous Svc. award Walt Disney Co., 1995. Office: Buena Vista Imaging 500 S Buena Vista St Burbank CA 91521-5070

MCGEE, LINDA JEANNE DANNER, school counselor; b. St. Louis, Sept. 21, 1948; d. George Julues and Vera Margaret (Purnell) Danner; m. Kenneth Allen McGee, Sept. 7, 1968; children: Jennifer Lyn and Stephanie Jeanne (twins). BS in Elem. Edn., U. Mo., 1970, MEd in Counseling and Student Pers. Svc., 1973; postgrad., Va. Poly. Inst., 1977-84, Seattle Pacific U., 1986-88. Cert. tchr., Mo., Wash., counselor, prin., Wash. Rsch. asst. agrl. chemistry dept. U. Mo., Columbia, 1968-70; elem. sci. tchr. Jefferson City (Mo.) Pub. Schs., 1970-72; counselor, tchr. Congl. Schs. Va., Falls Church, 1972-81, headmistress elem. div., 1981-84; counselor McLoughlin Middle Sch., Vancouver, Wash., 1984—; dist. testing com. mem. Vancouver Sch. Dist., 1984-87, guidance/counseling steering com. mem., 1984-88, bldg. leader team guidance/counseling com. McLoughlin Middle Sch., 1986—, parent edn. workshop, 1986-90, parent workshop transitions, 1990—, adv. planning com., 1989-90, adv. coord. McLoughlin, 1988-90; com. mem. Commn. on Student Learning, Olympia, Wash., 1994; presenter in field. Contbr. articles to profl. jours. Pres. No. Va. Counselor Assn., 1982-83, exec. bd. dirs., 1978-84, treas., 1979-80; active PTA. Named Chpt. Member of Yr. No. Va. Counselors Assn., 1983. Mem. NEA, Am. Sch. Counselor Assn. (middle/jr. high v.p. 1991-93, named Middle Sch. Counselor of Yr. 1994), Am. Counseling Assn., Nat. Middle Sch. Assn., Wash. Edn. Assn., Vancouver Edn. Assn., Washington Sch. Counselor Assn. (pres. 1989-91, conf. chair 1989-91, nominations/elections chair 1990-91, bylaws chair 1992-93, named Middle Sch. Counselor of Yr. 1994), Washington Counseling Assn. (pres. 1994—, exec. bd. dirs. 1989-90), Kappa Delta Kappa, Phi Delta Kappa, Phi Lambda Theta. Home: 13210 NE 6th Ct Vancouver WA 98685-2664 Office: McLoughlin Mid Sch 5802 Macarthur Blvd Vancouver WA 98661-7462

MCGEE, MICHAEL JAY, fire marshal, educator; b. Ft. Worth, June 9, 1952; s. Cecil Carl McGee and Helen Ruth (Peeples) McGee-Furrh; m. Carol Lee Garbarino, Sept. 18, 1982; children: Megan Rose, John Michael, Molly Caitlin. Student, U. Tex., 1970-73, Western Oreg. State U., 1983; AAS in Fire Protection Tech., Colo. Mountain Coll., 1990. Lic. fire suppression systems insp., Colo., vocat. educator, Colo.; cert. hazardous materials technician, Colo., 1992, EMT, Colo.; cert. fire safety hazardous materials instr., evaluator. Driver Massengale Co., Austin, Tex., 1970-73; gen. mgr. Sundae Palace, Austin, 1973-74; staff mem. Young Life, Colorado Springs, Colo., 1970-75; mgr. Broadmoor Mgmt. Co., Vail, Colo., 1974-76; technician Vail Cable Communications, 1976-77; fire marshal Vail Fire Dept., 1977—, fire sci. coord., 1995—, emergency med. program coord., 1996—; v.p. HAZPRO (Hazardous Materials and Fire Safety Consulting Firm), 1996—; dist. rep. Joint Coun. Fire Dist. Colo., 1983-85; co-chmn. Eagle County Hazardous Materials, 1984-85, mem. planning com., 1987-90; mem. accountability com. Eagle County Sch. Dist., 1991-96, mem. budget rev. com., 1991-93, vice chair accountability com. 1992-93, chmn. accountability com., 1993-96; mem. policy rev. com., 1993-96, bldg. coord., team coach Odyssey of the Mind at Eaglevalle Elem. Sch., 1995; invited dir. workshops Colo. Dept. Edn. Dist. Accountability Convention, Colo. Springs, 1995. Chmn. Eagle County chpt. ARC, 1980-83, disaster chmn., 1977-80; tng. officer Eagle Vol. Fire Dept., 1988-90; mem. parish coun. St. Mary's Parish, Eagle County, 1989-90; mem. citizen's adv. com. Colo. Mountain Coll., 1990-91, bd. dirs. 1990; bldg. coord., team coach Odessey of the Mind, Eagle Valley Elem. Sch., 1994-95; mem. facilities master planning com. Engle County Sch. Dist., 1996-97. Mem. Internat. Assn. Arson Investigators (Colo. chpt.), Internat. Platform Assn., Nat. Fire Protection Assn., Colo. State Fire Marshals Assn., Colo. State Fire Chiefs Assn. Office: Vail Fire Dept 42 W Meadow Dr Vail CO 81657-5705

MCGEE, MIKE JAMES, gallery director, writer; b. Ft. Lee, Va., Mar. 2, 1955; s. Lloyd James and Sylvia L. (Mounts) McG. BA, Calif. State U., Fullerton, 1978; MFA, U. Calif.-Irvine, 1980. Dir. The Edge Gallery, Fullerton, 1982-85; programs coord. Laguna Art Mus., Laguna Beach, Calif., 1986-88; writer, educator various instns., 1988—; art gallery dir. Orange Coast Coll., Costa Mesa, Calif., 1989-91; art forum lecture series head Rancho Santiago Jr. Coll., Santa Ana, 1991—; art gallery dir., asst. prof. Calif. State U., Fullerton, 1992—. Pres. bd. trustees Orange County Ctr. for Contemporary Art, Santa Ana, 1990-96; arts com. chair Orange County Arts Alliance, Santa Ana, 1982; bd. dirs. Arts Orange County, 1995—. Mem. Am. Assn. Museums. Home: PO Box 3154 Fullerton CA 92634-3154 Office: Calif State U Fullerton CA 92634-9480

MCGEE, REX ALAN, motion picture screenwriter; b. Cleburne, Tex., Nov. 22, 1951; s. Theo Rex and Ella Lucille (Clark) McG.; m. Sandra Marie Pace, Dec. 31, 1992. BBA, U. So. Calif., 1975. Personal asst. to film dir. Billy Wilder L.A. and Munich, 1974, 77; journalist Am. Film, Playboy, L.A. and TV Guide, 1979-82; motion picture story analyst United Artists/The Ladd Co., L.A., 1977-80; screenwriter, 1981—; Intern for dir. Am. Film Inst., L.A., 1974. Author: (motion picture) "Pure Country", 1992. Mem. Leadership Cleburne, Tex., 1992; advisor Main Street Project, Cleburne, 1993-95; trustee Johnson County Com. on Aging, Cleburne, 1994-96; bd. dirs. Carnegie Players, 1996—. Mem. Writers Guild of Am. West, Dramatists Guild. Home: 305 N Pendell St Cleburne TX 76031-3529 Office: 9507 Santa Monica Blvd Ste 206 Beverly Hills CA 90210-4542

MCGEE, WILLIAM DEAN (WILLIE MCGEE), professional baseball player; b. San Francisco, Nov. 2, 1958. Student, Diablo Valley Coll., Pleasant Hill, Calif. Baseball player N.Y. Yankees, 1977-81, St. Louis Cardinals, 1981-90, 95—, Oakland Athletics, 1990, San Francisco Giants, 1990-95. Mem. Nat. League All-Star Team, 1983, 85, 87-88; recipient Gold Glove Award, 1983, 85-86; named Nat. League Most Valuable Player, Baseball Writers Assoc. of Am., 1985; Sporting News Nat. League Player of the Year, 1985; recipient Silver Slugger award, 1985; Nat. League Batting Champion, 1985, 90. Office: San Francisco Giants Candlestick Park San Francisco CA 94124-3998*

MCGEORGE, DAVID, mayor. Mayor City of Redding, Calif. Office: City of Redding 760 Parkview Ave Redding CA 96001

MCGHAY, JON DAVIES, engineer; b. Enid, Okla., June 7, 1959; s. Donald L. and E. Marie (Davies) McG. BS in Geology, Okla. State U., 1982, MBA, 1988. Owner Lightning Lectr. Notes Inc., Stillwater, Okla., 1984-86; mgr., bd. dirs. TLT Inc., Stillwater, Okla., 1981-88; fin. analyst Lomas Mortgage USA, Dallas, 1988-89; account mgr. Texaco Refining and Mktg. Inc., Dallas, 1989-90; lubrication engr. Texaco Refining and Mktg. Inc., Phoenix, 1990—. Mem. Am. Assn. Petroleum Geologists, Soc. of Tribiologists and Lubrication Engrs., Okla. State U. Alumni Assn. (bd. dirs. Ariz. chpt. 1993—, pres. 1996—). Home: 1901 E Osborn Rd Apt 136 Phoenix AZ 85016-7263 Office: Texaco Lubricants Co 3333 E Camelback Rd Ste 170 Phoenix AZ 85018-2323

MCGIHON, MICHAEL EDWIN, sheet metal manufacturing executive; b. Long Beach, Calif., July 31, 1949; s. Alvin Frances and Edna Lona (Windes) McG.; m. Phyllis Rachel Tiner, Aug. 15, 1970; 1 child, Scott Del. Student, Long Beach C.C., 1971. Apprentice McGihon Sheet Metal, Long Beach, 1967-71, journeyman, foreman, 1971-91, pres., 1991—, cons. R&D, 1985—. Mem. Aircraft Owners and Pilots Assn., Long Beach Ski Club (asst. v.p. 1992-93). Democrat. Lutheran. Home: 2901 N Heather Rd Long Beach CA 90815-1052

MCGILL, LAMONT EDMOND, fire and explosion investigator, educator; b. L.A., May 8, 1940; s. Oliver E. and Georgia W. (Landers) McG.; m. Vicki McMillin, Feb. 21, 1948; children: Linda Weaver, Melanie Cooke. BS in Pub. Adminstrn., Pepperdine U., 1974; AA in Police Sci., Valley Coll., 1974. Patrolman LaHabra (Calif.) Police Dept., 1963-67; detective San Bernardino (Calif.) County Sheriff, 1967-77; bomb tech., fire investigator, instr. Calif. State Fire Marshal Office, Willits, 1977-95; fire/explosion investigator, instr. McGill Cons. & Investigation, Willits, 1995—. Mem. Internat. Assn. Arson Investigators, Internat. Assn. Bomb Techs. and Investigators, No. Calif. Fraud Investigators Assn., Calif. Conf. Arson Investigators. Republican. Office: McGill Cons & Investigation PO Box 1433 Willits CA 95490

MCGILLICUDDY, JOAN MARIE, psychotherapist, consultant; b. Chgo., June 23, 1952; d. James Neal and Muriel (Joy) McG. BA, U. Ariz., 1974, MS, 1976; PhD, Walden U., 1996. Cert. nat. counselor. Counselor ACTION, Tucson, 1976; counselor, clin. supr. Behavioral Health Agy. Cen. Ariz., Casa Grande, 1976-81; instr. psychology Cen. Ariz. Coll., Casa Grande, 1978-83; therapist, co-dir. Helping Assocs., Inc., Casa Grande, 1982—, v.p., sec., 1982—; cert. instr. Silva Method Mind Devel., Tucson, 1986—. Mem. Mayor's Com. for Handicapped, Casa Grande, 1989-90, Human Svcs. Planning, Casa Grande, 1985-95. Named Outstanding Am. Lectr. Silva Midn Internat., 1988-96. Mem. ACA. Office: Helping Assocs Inc 1901 N Trekell Rd Casa Grande AZ 85222-1706

MCGILVERY, LAURENCE, book publisher, dealer; b. L.A., May 21, 1932; s. Neil Lee and Joan (Girard) McG.; m. Geraldine Malloy, July 5, 1955; children: Lynette, Lise, Erin, Justin. BA, Pomona Coll., 1954. Engr. Walter Dorwin Teague Assocs., Pomona, Sunnyvale, Calif., 1954-60; owner, bookseller Nexus, La Jolla, Calif., 1960-66; antiquarian book dealer La Jolla, 1966—. Mem. ACLU, Antiquarian Booksellers Assn. Am. (pres. So. Calif. chpt. 1987), Art Librs. Soc. N.Am., San Diego Booksellers Assn. (bd. dirs.). Democrat. Office: PO Box 852 La Jolla CA 92038-0852

MCGINNES, JAMES MARC, lawyer, lecturer; b. Murray, Utah, Sept. 27, 1941; s. Alfred James and Fern (Furner) McG.; m. Seyburn Zorthian, Sept. 4, 1982; children: Skye McGinnes, Zachary McGinnes. BA in History, Stanford U., 1963; JD, U. Calif., Berkeley, 1966. Bar: Calif. 1967. Lawyer Thelen, Marrin, Johnson and Bridges, San Francisco, 1967-69, Westwick, Collison and Talaga, Santa Barbara, Calif., 1969-71; pvt. practice Santa Barbara, 1971-77; founder, exec. dir., counsel Environ. Def. Ctr., Santa Barbara, 1977—; lectr. in environ. studies U. Calif., Santa Barbara, 1971—; founding pres. Cmty. Environ. Coun., Inc., Santa Barbara, 1970-74. Author: Principles of Environmental Law, 1980. Dir. Congress on Optimum Population and Environment, Chgo., 1970-72, Earth Island Inst., San Francisco, 1986-88; founder, dir. Peaceful Resolutions Inst., Santa Barbara, 1986—. Found. fellow Rotary Internat., France, 1966-67. Mem. Calif. Bar Assn., Santa Barbara County Bar Assn. Office: U Calif Environ Studies Santa Barbara CA 93106

MCGINNIS, DEBORAH CHERYL, county official; b. Oak Park, Ill., Feb. 2, 1955; d. Victor and Wanda Ann (Konieczny) Kaminski; m. Danny Allyn McGinnis, Feb. 14, 1973 (div. Sept. 1986); children: Brandy Lyn, Jonathan Dylan. Grad., high sch., 1972. Cert. document examiner. Title searcher Safeco Title Ins., San Bernardino, Calif., 1978-79, title examiner, 1979-80; dep. examiner San Bernardino Recorder, 1980-90, rec. supr., 1990—; guest speaker to various orgns.; liaison between local real estate orgns. Active in local politics. Mem. Nat. Ptnrs. in Homeownership.

MCGINNIS, MICHAEL PATRICK, psychotherapist; b. Madison, Wis., Oct. 4, 1950; s. James and Patricia Jane (Cole) McG.; m. Carol Ann Bailey, Aug. 8, 1982; children: Arielle Dominque, Chandra Eden. Student, U. Wis., 1968-69, U. Maine, 1971-73; BA, Sonoma State U., 1980, MA, 1984. Cert. marriage, family and child counselor, Calif. Offset printer Portland (Maine) Printing Co., 1970-71, Pronto Prints, Madison, 1972-74; mental health specialist Sheltered Workshop, Madison, 1975-77; mental health worker social svc. dept. Treatment Alternatives to Street Crimes, Santa Rosa, Calif., 1977-79; counselor Nat. Coun. on Alcoholism, Santa Rosa, 1978-79, exec. dir. Sonoma County, 1979-81; counselor, trainer Sonoma County Family Svc. Agy., Santa Rosa, 1981-86; pvt. practice, Healdsburg, Calif., 1985—; trainer, cons. domestic violence treatment Calif. Dept. Mental Health, 1979-84, YWCA Women's Emergency Shelter, Santa Rosa, 1980-86. Mem. Calif. Assn. Marriage and Family Therapists (clin.), Am. Profl. Soc. on Abuse on Children (clin.), Calif. Profl. Soc. on Abuse of Children (clin.). Democrat. Home and Office: 610 Alta Vista Dr Healdsburg CA 95448-4651

MCGLAUGHLIN, THOMAS HOWARD, publisher, retired naval officer; b. Cin., Jan. 12, 1928; s. George Godden and Cordelia (Herrlinger) McG.; m. Moana Maharam-Stone, Jan. 4, 1984. BS in Elec. Engring., U.S. Naval Acad., 1950. Lic. master mariner. Commd. ensign U.S. Navy, 1950, advanced through grades to capt., 1970; White House aide to Pres. John F. Kennedy, Washington, 1960-63; exec. officer USS Prichett, Long Beach, Calif., 1963-65; comdg. officer USS Maddox, Long Beach, 1965-67; exec. officer USS Boston, Boston, 1967-70; chief naval ops. Comdr.-in-Chief, Pacific, Honolulu, 1970-74; chief of staff Mil. Sealift Command, N.Y.C., 1974-79; ret. U.S. Navy, 1979; pres. Falmouth Press, Honolulu, 1983—; marine surveyor R.W. Dickieson Internat., Inc., Honolulu, 1982—; master M.V. Rella Mae, Honolulu, 1981-90, Royal Taipan, Cebu, Philippines, 1990. Hon. police chief Boston Police Dept., 1969. Decorated Bronze Star; recipient medal for Outstanding Svc., Am. Legion, Pitts., 1942. Mem. Nat. Def. Transp. Assn., VFW (life), U.S. Naval Acad. Alumni Assn. (life), The Retired Officers Assn. Republican. Presbyterian. Home: The Royal Iolani #1702 581 Kamoku St Honolulu HI 96826-5250 Office: RW Dickieson Internat Inc 46-208 Kahuhipa St Kaneohe HI 96744-3905

MCGLONE, DAVID ANTHONY JOSEPH, publishing executive; b. Castle AFB, Calif., Feb. 28, 1952; s. Willard Estel and Joan Marianne (Legrande) M.; m. Carolyn Frances Illig, July 30, 1973 (div. 1976); m. Deborah Snavely, May 1, 1977 (div. 1996). Student, San Diego State U., 1970-72. Cook various restaurants, San Diego, Riverside, Calif., 1972-77; keypunch operator Mrs. Keypunch, San Francisco, 1977-78; messenger, dispatcher Bradford Security Trust Co., San Francisco, 1978-81; with customer support dept. Tymshare, Sunnyvale, Calif., 1983; tech., software developer Tandem Computers, Cupertino, Calif., 1984-92; pres. Lambda Software Pub., Eugene, Oreg., 1988-96, McGlone, Huovinen & Assocs., Eugene, 1997—. Editor, pub. The Z-Letter, 1988-96, Eagle Computer User Group NL, 1987-90, Kirjasto, 1982-84; author: (software) LPascal, 1992-93, Lambda Access, 1996, Spellbinder CD-ROM, 1997. Contbr. So. Poverty Law Ctr., 1985—. SSG. USAR, 1976-82. Mem. Hist. Computer Soc., Amnesty Internat., ACLU, Soc. for Creative Anachronism (Order of Laurel 1976, Order of Pelican 1979). Democrat. Home and Office: 149 W Hilliard Ln Eugene OR 97404-3057

MCGLYNN, BETTY HOAG, art historian; b. Deer Lodge, Mont., Apr. 28, 1914; d. Arthur James and Elizabeth Tangye (Davey) Lochrie; m. Paul Sterling Hoag, Dec. 28, 1936 (div. 1967); children: Peter Lochrie Hoag, Jane Hoag Brown, Robert Doane Hoag; m. Thomas Arnold McGlynn, July 28, 1973. BA, Stanford U., 1936; MA, U. So. Calif., 1967. Cert. secondary tchr., Calif. Rsch. dir. So. Calif. Archives of Am. Art, L.A., 1964-67, Carmel (Calif.) Mus. Art, 1967-69; dir. Triton Mus. Art, Santa Clara, Calif., 1970; archivist, libr. San Mateo County (Calif.) Hist. Soc. Mus., 1972-74; cons. Monterey Peninsula Mus. Art, Calif., 1964—; tchr. art extension Monterey Peninsula Coll., Calif., 1970, San Jose City Coll., 1971; lectr. in field. Author: The World of Mary DeNeale Morgan, 1970, Carmel Art Association: A History, 1987; contbg. author: Plein Air Painters of California, The North, 1986, Orchid Art and The Orchid Isle, 1982, Hawaiian Island Artists and Friends of the Arts, 1989; editor, author of jours. La Peninsula (San Mateo County Hist. Soc.), 1971-75, Noticias (Monterey History and Art Assn.), 1983-88, 95; author of booklets; contbr. articles to profl. jours. Appraiser art work City of Carmel, 1967, City of Monterey, 1981; mem. Friends of Harrison Meml. Libr., Carmel, Friends of Sunset Found., Carmel, Pacific Grove Art Ctr., Monterey Bay Aquarium. Mem. Butte (Mont.) Arts Chateau, Carmel Art Assn. (hon.), Carmel Heritage Soc., Carmel Found., Carmel Residents Assn., Chinese Hist. Soc., Monterey History and Art Assn. (art cons.), Monterey Peninsula Mus. Art (acquisitions bd.), Gallatin County Hist. Soc. (Mont.), Stanford Alumni Assn., Robinson Jeffers Tor House Found. (art cons.), Hawaiian Hist. Soc., Mont. Hist. Soc., Nat. Mus. of Women in Arts, The Westerners, P.E.O., Book Club of Calif. Republican. Home and Office: PO Box 7189 Carmel CA 93921-7189

MC GOVERN, WALTER T., federal judge; b. Seattle, May 24, 1922; s. C. Arthur and Anne Marie (Thies) McG.; m. Rita Marie Olsen, June 29, 1946; children: Katrina M., Shawn E., A. Renee. B.A., U. Wash., 1949, LL.B., 1950. Bar: Wash. 1950. Practiced law in Seattle, 1950-59; mem. firm Kerr, McCord, Greenleaf & Moen; judge Municipal Ct., Seattle, 1959-65, Superior Ct., Wash., 1965-68, Wash. Supreme Ct., 1968-71, U.S. Dist. Ct. (we. dist.) Wash., 1971—; chief judge, 1975-87; mem. subcom. on supporting personnel Jud. Conf. U.S., 1981-87, chmn. subcom., 1983, mem. adminstrn. com., 1983-87, chmn. jud. resources com., 1987-91. Mem. Am. Judicature Soc., Wash. State Superior Ct. Judges Assn., Seattle King County Bar Assn. (treas.), Phi Delta Phi. Club: Seattle Tennis (pres. 1968). Office: US Dist Ct US Courthouse 5th Fl 1010 5th Ave Seattle WA 98104-1183

MCGOWAN, JOSEPH ANTHONY, JR., news executive; b. Sheridan, Wyo., May 16, 1931; s. Joseph Anthony and Eda B. (Harris) McG.; m. Patricia Donnette Mitchell, June 7, 1958 (div. 1980); children: Joseph Howard, Colleen Diane; m. Catherine Doris Netick, June 12, 1982; stepchildren: Nancy Malick, Diane Malick, Laura Malick. B.S., U. Wyo. Newsman AP, Miami, Fla., 1960-64; bur. chief AP, New Delhi, India, 1965-68, Lima, Peru, 1968-70, Indpls., 1970-75, Boston, 1975-78, Denver, 1978—; lectr. U. Denver, 1978—, Colo. U., Boulder, 1978—, Northeastern U., Boston, 1975-78. Scoutmaster Boy Scouts Am., Sudbury, Mass., 1977-78. Served with USNR, 1953-55. Named Disting. Alumnus, U. Wyo., 1992; Knight Internat. Press fellow to Pakistan, 1995. Mem. Denver Press Club (bd. dirs. 1989-92), Press Club Boston, Colo. Assn. Commerce and Industry (communications council 1986-89), Sigma Delta Chi (Big Hat award 1983). Republican. Office: AP 1444 Wazee St Ste 130 Denver CO 80202-1326

MCGOWAN, MITCHELL JOSEPH, director, actor, stage manager; b. Nebraska City, Nebr., Aug. 20, 1964; s. Ward Allan and Karen Rae McG.; m. Cynthia Lynne Cox, Sept. 6, 1987. BFA, U. Victoria, B.C., Can., 1987. Dir. Tall Tales, No More Beets, The Purple Testament, The Lion In Winter, Empire Builder, My Cup Ranneth Over, Grey Matters, Drought, Passion, Poison and Petrifaction, My Daughter, My Son; asst. dir. Hamlet, Dramaturg. Assassins; prodn. stage mgr. Twelfth Night; stage mgr. Medea, Once in a Lifetime, No, No, Nanette, Age of Wonders, Shenandoah, A Little Night Music, And The Soul Shall Dance, The Tempest, As You Like It, Machinal, Kitty-Kitty/Last Supper, Rodgers & Hart; appeared in Tall Tales Moby Dick—Rehearsed, The Grapes of Wrath, A Midsummer Night's Dream, Man of La Mancha, Tintypes, The Eunuch, Sweet Charity, Philadelphia, Here I Come, Sleeping Beauty, The Good Doctor, The Rainmaker, The Boyfriend. Home: 14058 NE 181st St Ste F-304 Woodinville WA 98072-6853

MCGOWAN, THOMAS RANDOLPH, religious organization executive; b. Balt., Apr. 19, 1926; s. Robert and Mary (Miller) McG.; m. Bernice A. Bernard, May 20, 1967 (dec. Nov. 1981); children: Howard, James, Terry; m. Roedean Olivia Oden, Feb. 9, 1985; children: Karen White, Kevin, Kurt. AA, Oakland Jr. Coll., 1964; postgrad., San Francisco State Coll., 1964-68; BS, U. Md., 1978. Lt. security police Oakland (Calif.) Army Base,

1955-60; chief motor pool San Francisco Procurement Agy., Oakland, 1960-64, contract specialist, 1964-68; contract specialist Harry Diamond Labs., Washington, 1968-79, br. chief procurement divsn., 1972-79; chief procurement directorate Yuma (Ariz.) Proving Ground, 1979-82; dir. ecumenism Roman Cath. Diocese of Oakland, 1983—; dir. African Am. Cath. Pastoral Ctr., Diocese of Oakland, 1991—. Convenor Interreligious Coun. of Oakland, 1988—; trustee Greater Oakland Interfaith Network, 1989-92; mem. East Oakland Renewal Task Force, 1990—; bd. dir. Columbia (Md.) Found., 1972-74, chmn., 1975-79; div. Bd. Cons., Graymoor, N.Y., 1990—; bd. dirs. Thea Bowman Manor, Oakland, 1989—. With U.S. Army, 1944-46. Mem. Knights of Peter Claver, Rotary. Democrat. Home: 139 Pinto Dr Vallejo CA 94591-8451

MCGOWN, JOHN, JR., lawyer; b. Bowling Green, Ky., June 15, 1949; s. John Stanley and Margaret (Deatherage) McG.; m. Mary Grunewald, Apr. 20, 1978; children: Erin Margaret, Brenna Kathryn. BS, U. Ky., 1971; JD, U. Colo., 1974; LLM in Taxation, U. Denver, 1981. Bar: Colo. 1975, U.S. Tax Ct. 1981, Idaho 1982; CPA, Idaho, Colo. Dep. dist. atty. Weld County, Colo., 1974-78; assoc. Montgomery, Little, Young, Campbell, & McGrew, Denver, 1979-80; rschr. appellate divsn. IRS, Denver, 1980-81; mem. staff tax dept. Price Waterhouse, Denver, 1981-82; ptnr. Hawley, Troxell, Ennis & Hawley, Boise, Idaho, 1982—; adj. prof. Boise State U., 1983; guest lecturer U. Idaho Coll. Law, Moscow, 1990; guest speaker various tax seminars, 1983—. Contbr. over 40 articles to profl. jours. Bd. dirs. Assn. for Retarded Citizens Ada County, Inc., 1987-93, pres. 1991-92, Assoc. Taxpayers Idaho, Inc., 1993—, exec. com., 1995—; audit review panel United Way Ada County, 1986-91; IRS vol. tax asst. program 1982, 87. Fellow Am. Coll. of Trust and Estate Counsel; mem. ABA (taxation sect.), Idaho State Bar Assn. (founding mem., taxation probate and trust law sect.), Idaho Soc. CPAs (fed. and state taxation com. 1984-89, bus. legis. com. 1989-91), Boise Bar Assn., Toastmasters (pres. 1991), Beta Gamma Sigma, Sigma Chi. Home: 1824 N 19th St Boise ID 83702-0707 Office: Hawley Troxell Ennis & Hawley 877 Main St Boise ID 83702-5858

MCGRATH, ERIKA WEIS, economics educator, management consultant; b. Laufenselden, Hessen, Federal Republic of Germany, Nov. 17, 1937; d. Wilhelm A. and Auguste Louise (Vogt) Weis; m. Thomas J. McGrath, Oct. 1, 1963 (dec. Sept. 1984). BA, U. Calif., Santa Cruz, 1982; MA, Calif. State U., San Jose, 1984; PhD, U. Calif., Santa Barbara, 1989. Adj. assoc. prof. Golden Gate U., Monterey, Calif., 1990—; adj. asst. prof. Monterey Inst. Internat. Studies, 1992—; mgmt. cons. Weis Consulting, Monterey, 1992—. Mem., 1st chair Monterey County Commn. on Status of Women, Monterey, 1990-93; mem. LWV, Monterey, 1994—, Dem. Women's Club, Monterey, 1994—, Profl. Women's Network, Monterey, 1991—. Mem. ASTD, Profl. Orgn. Women in Edn., Kappa Delta Pi. Democrat. Home: 625 Filmore St Monterey CA 93940-1614

MCGRATH, J. NICHOLAS, lawyer; b. Hollywood, Calif., Feb. 12, 1940; m. Margaret Crowley, Oct. 4, 1980; children: Nicholas Gerald, Molly Inez. BA with honors, Lehigh U., 1962; LLB magna cum laude, Columbia U., 1965. Bar: D.C. 1966, Calif. 1969, U.S. Supreme Ct. 1970, Colo. 1971. Law clk. to presiding justice U.S. Ct. Appeals (D.C. cir.), 1965-66; law clk. to assoc. justice Thurgood Marshall U.S. Supreme Ct., Washington, 1967-68; assoc. Pillsbury, Madison & Sutro, San Francisco, 1968-70; from assoc. to ptnr. Oates, Austin, McGrath, Aspen, Colo., 1970-80; ptnr. Austin, McGrath & Jordan, Aspen, 1980-82; sole practice Aspen, 1982—; chmn. grievance com. Colo. Supreme Ct., 1989, mem. 1984-89. Mem. bd. editors Columbia Law Review, 1964-65. Vice chair Pitkin Co. Home Rule Charter Com., 1976-78; mem. Planning Commn., Town of Basalt, Colo., 1992-93, town trustee, 1993-94; bd. dirs. CLE in Colo., Inc., 1995-96, lectr. nat. and state CLE programs on ethics, litigation and land use subjects; pres. Basalt Children's Recreation Fund, Inc., 1994—; chair Basalt Hwy. 82 Citizens Task Force, 1996—; mem. Aspen-Pitkin Co. Alt. H Hwy 82 Task Force, 1996-97, cmty. forum task force on Pitkin Co. charter, 1997—; bd. dirs. Club 20. Mem. Colo. Bar Assn. (v.p. 1991-92), Assn. Trial Lawyers Am., Pitkin County Bar Assn. (pres. 1977). Democrat. Office: 600 E Hopkins Ave Ste 203 Aspen CO 81611-2933

MCGRATH, PATRICK JOSEPH, bishop; b. Dublin, Ireland, July 11, 1945; came to U.S., 1970; Grad., St. John's Coll. Sem., Waterford, Ireland; student, Lateran U., Rome. Ordained priest Roman Cath. Ch., 1970, titular bishop of Allegheny. Aux. bishop Archdiocese San Francisco, 1989—. Office: Archdiocese San Francisco Chancery Office 445 Church St San Francisco CA 94114-1720*

MCGRAW, DONALD JESSE, biologist, historian of science, writer; b. Altadena, Calif., Oct. 27, 1943; s. Jesse E. and Mary L. (Hajostek) McG.; m. Laura Lee Hansen, July 13, 1968; children: Adrienne, Holly, Rachel. BS in Biol. Scis., Calif. State Poly. Coll., 1965; MS, Utah State U., 1967; PhD, Oreg. State U., 1976. Registered microbiologist Am. Acad. Microbiology. Research asst. microbiology Utah State U., 1965-66, teaching asst. food and aquatic microbiology, 1966-67; grad. teaching asst. gen. biology Oreg. State U., 1970-72, instr., 1972-73; tchr. phys. and biol. scis. U.S. Bur. Indian Affairs Boarding Sch., Shonto, Ariz., 1974-75; asst. prof. biology Franklin Coll., Ind., 1975-78; adj. asst. prof. biology Ind. Central U., Indpls., 1977-78; adj. asst. prof. Ind. U.-Purdue U., Columbus, 1978; mem. faculty Yavapai Community Coll., Prescott, Ariz., 1978-79; assoc. dir. Ute Research Lab., Ft. Duchesne, Utah, 1980-81, dir., 1981-82; vis. prof. biology Bard Coll., N.Y., Spring 1984, Coll. St. Thomas, Minn., 1985-87; adj. asst. prof. biology, assoc. provost U. San Diego, 1988—; ranger-naturalist U.S. Nat. Park Svc., summers, 1970-79, 83-86; writer, 1968—; adj. faculty Southwestern Coll., 1989-92. Contbr. numerous articles on history of microbiology and history of antibiotics to sci. publs. Commr. San Diego County Columbian Quincentenary Commn., 1990-93, chmn. edn. com., 1990-93; mem. pres.'s adv. com. San Diego Zool. Soc., 1995—; trustee Quail Bot. Gardens Found., 1995—. Recipient Disting. Alumnus award, Calif. State Poly. U., 1991, Monrovia High Sch., 1991; Eli Lilly doctoral grantee Oreg. State U., 1973-74. Mem. AAAS, History of Sci. Soc., Soc. for Econ. Botany, Cabrillo Hist. Assn. (bd. dirs. 1989-94, vice chair 1992, chair 1993, 94), Alpha Scholastic Honor Soc. of Franklin Coll. (pres. 1976-78), Sigma Xi (sec. San Diego chpt. 1996-97), Beta Beta Beta. Office: U San Diego Office of Provost 5998 Alcala Park San Diego CA 92110-2429

MCGRAW, SUSAN CATHERINE, interior designer; b. Long Beach, Calif., Apr. 16, 1945; d. Thomas Printis and Mary Ruth (Reese) Gregg; m. Don George McGraw, Nov. 21, 1964; children: DeAnna Coulombe, Katrina Daymude. Dental assistant diploma, Career Tng. Inst., 1964. Cert. interior designer, 1993. Ptnr., buyer The Corner, Garden Grove, Calif., 1971-79; interior designer Kris Noel & Assoc., Huntington Beach, Calif., 1980-85; owner, designer A.I. Designs, Huntington Beach, Calif., 1986-94; ptnr., designer Ross-McGraw Studio, Huntington Beach, Calif., 1994—. Bd. dirs. Parent Help USA, Huntington Beach, 1992; sec. Seacliff Home Owners Assn., Huntington Beach, 1992-93; v.p. way and means Huntington Youth Shelter Guild, Huntington Beach, 1994-96, pres., 1996-97. Mem. Am. Soc. Interior Design (profl. mem.).

MCGREGOR, DARREN JAMES, counselor, researcher; b. Pensecola, Fla., Feb. 22, 1961; s. Elwood Ralph McGregor and Regina June (Dolan) Thiele; m. Cordelia T. Grimm, Sept. 10, 1994. BA in Humanities cum laude, U. So. Calif., 1991; MS, Calif. State U., Northridge, 1996. Cert. mediator, Dispute Resolution Svcs. Rsch. coord. VA Hosp., Sepulveda, Calif., 1993-94, psychology technician, 1994; intern in counseling Beverlywood Mental Health Ctr., L.A., 1995-96; counselor, course coord., instr. Independence Ctr., L.A., 1993—, dir. job devel., 1994-96; airport marina counseling svc., 1996—. Mem. ACA, Am. Acad. on Physician and Patient, Southern Calif. Med. Assoc., Assn of Family Physician, Sierra Club, Gold Key Honor Soc.

MCGREGOR, JAMES ALLAN, obstetrician, gynecologist; b. Hawkesbury, Ont., Can., Aug. 2, 1944; came to U.S., 1947; s. James Duncan and Margaret Eleanor (Moyle) McG.; children: Alison, Andrew, Margaret. AB, Dartmouth Coll., 1966; MDCM, McGill U., 1970. Diplomate Am. Coll. Obstetricians and Gynecologists. Prof. obstetrics and gynecology U. Colo. Sch. Medicine, Denver, 1977—. Bd. dirs. Planned Parenthood, Denver, 1985-88. Office: U Colo Health Scis Inst Obstetrics and Gynecology 4200 E 9th Ave Denver CO 80220-3706

MCGROGAN, MICHAEL PATRICK, molecular and cell biologist; b. San Francisco, Apr. 4, 1947; s. John Thomas and Veneta Almeta (Wideman) McG.; m. Sharol Kay Hudson, Sept. 13, 1969; 1 child, Melissa Catherine. Student, U. Mo., St. Louis, 1965-67; BA in Microbiology, U. Mo., Columbia, 1969; student, St. Louis U., 1971-73; PhD in Molecular and Cell Biology, Washington U., St. Louis, 1977. Postdoctoral rschr. Wash. U. Med. Sch., St. Louis, 1977-78; NCI postdoctoral fellow dept. bio. scis. Stanford (Calif.) U., 1978-81; scientist, rsch. group leader molecular biology dept. Cetus Corp., Emeryville, Calif., 1981-85; sr. scientist, rsch. group leader molecular biology dept. InVitron Corp., Redwood City, Calif., 1985-90; dir., sr. staff scientist Dept. of Gene Expression, Berlex Biosci., Alameda, Calif., 1990-93; chief scientific officer Sierra BioSource, Gilroy, Calif., 1993-96; dir. R&D Layton BioSci., Gilroy, Calif., 1996—; project leader Interleukin 2 (IL-2) Cetus Corp., 1982-84; primary investigator Protease Nexin, InVitron Corp., Redwood City, 1986-88; rsch. leader for granulocyte proteins project, 1988-90; developer human hNT-Neuron products. Contbr. articles to profl. jours.; patentee in field. Fellow NDEA, St. Louis U., 1971; rsch. grantee NIH, Wash. U., 1973. Mem. AAAS, Am. Soc. of Microbiology. Office: Layton BioSci 1180 Day Rd # C Gilroy CA 95020-9308

MCGUIGAN, FRANK JOSEPH, psychologist, educator; b. Oklahoma City, Dec. 7, 1924. BA, UCLA, 1945, MA, 1949; PhD, U. So. Calif., 1950. Instr. Pepperdine Coll., 1949-50; asst. prof. U. Nev., 1950-51; rsch. assoc. Psychol. Corp., 1950-51; rsch. scientist, sr. rsch. scientist, acting dir. rsch. Human Resources Rsch. Office, George Washington U., 1951-55; prof. psychology (Hollins Coll.), Roanoke, Va., 1955-76; chmn. dept. (Hollins Coll.), 1955-76; rsch. prof. (Grad. Sch.); prof. dept. psychology, dep. psychiatry and behavioral scis. (Sch. Medicine); dir. Performance Rsch. Lab., Inst. Advanced Study, U. Louisville, 1976-83; disting. rsch. prof., dir. Inst. Stress Mgmt. U.S. Internat. U., San Diego, 1983—; adj. prof. psychiatry and behavioral scis. U. Louisville Sch. Medicine, 1986—; adj. rsch. prof. N.C. State U., 1970-72; vis. prof. U. Hawaii, summer 1965, U. Calif., Santa Barbara, 1966, Hiroshima Shudo U., 1984; Nat. Acad. Scis. vis. scientist, Hungary, 1975, Bulgaria, 1987; sr. rsch. fellow Naval Health Rsch. Ctr., summer 1991. Author: numerous books in field including The Biological Basis of Behavior, 1963, Contemporary Studies in Psychology, 1972, Cognitive Psychophysiology - Principles of Covert Behavior, 1978, Experimental Psychology: Methods of Research, 6th edit., 1993, Psychophysiological Measurement of Covert Behavior—A Guide for the Laboratory, 1979, Calm Down—A Guide for Stress and Tension Control, 2d edit., 1992, Stress and Tension Control: Procs. of Internat., Interdisciplinary Conf. on Stress and Tension Control, 1980, vol. 2, 1984, vol. 3, 1989; (with Edmund Jacobson) cassettes Self-Directed Progressive Relaxation Training Instructions, 1981, Critical Issues in Psychology, Psychiatry and Physiology, 1986, Biological Psychology--A Cybernetic Science, 1994; editor numerous works in field.; editor, Internat. Jour. Stress Mgmt.; contbr. articles to profl. jours.; mem. editorial bd. Archiv fur Arzneitherapie, Biofeedback and Self-regulation, Activitas Nervosae Superioris. Served with USNR, 1942-46. Recipient award for outstanding contbns. to edn. in psychology Am. Psychol. Found., 1973, Blue medal of honor Union Scientists Bulgaria, 1980, medal of Sechenov USSR Acad. Med. Scis., 1983, medal of Anohkin, 1984, Pres.'s medal U. Hiroshima-Shudo, 1982, medal Okayama U., 1987, medal Tbilisi (USSR) Inst. Physiology, 1989, Edmund Jacobson award for stress mgmt., 1995, Gold medal award for lifetime achievement in application of psychology Am. Psychol. Found., 1995. Fellow APA, Internat. Soc. Rsch. on Aggression; mem. Am. Assn. Advancement of Tension Control (now Internat. Stress Mgmt. Assn.) (exec. dir. 1973-82, pres. 1985-89, exec. dir. 1992—, chmn. bd. dirs.), Pavlovian Soc. (mem. exec. bd. 1973—, pres. 1975-86, editor, chmn. publ. bd. Pavlovian Jour. Biol. Sci.), Am. Physiol. Soc., Biofeedback Soc. Am., Internam. Soc. Psychology, Internat. Congress of Applied Psychology, Psychonomic Soc., Soc. Psychophysiol. Rsch., Bulgarian Soc. for Psychiatry (hon.), Sigma Xi. Office: US Internat U Inst for Stress Mgmt 10455 Pomerado Rd San Diego CA 92131-1717

MCGUIRE, GERARD JOSEPH, engineering executive; b. Enniscorthy, Ireland, Dec. 8, 1952; came to U.S., 1991; s. Daniel and Maureen (Buckley) McG.; m. Joan Marie Kavanagh, July 10, 1982; children: Tristan Patrick, Barry Colm, Clara Megan, Conor Damian. B of Engring. with honors, U. Coll. Dublin, Ireland, 1975. Registered profl. engr. Sales engr. ITTUP Hollowcore Ltd., Vancouver, B.C., Can., 1980-81; project engr. Con-Force (Precast) Ltd., Vancouver, 1981-87; sales mgr. Con-Force P/T Divsn., Ajax, Ont., Can., 1987-88; tech. dir. CPCI P/T Divsn., Toronto, Ont., Can., 1988-91; exec. dir. Post Tensioning Inst., Phoenix, 1991—. Bd. dirs. Arcadia Water Co., Scottsdale, Ariz., 1995—. Mem. Am. Water Works Assn. (com. mem. 1992—), Am. Concrete Inst. (various coms. 1991—), Can. Standards Coun. (com. mem. 1987—). Office: Post Tensioning Inst 1717 W Northern Ave # 114 Phoenix AZ 85021

MCGUIRE, JAMES CHARLES, aircraft company executive; b. St. Louis, Aug. 8, 1917; s. John Patrick and Anna Beulah (Erbar) McG.; AB, Washington U., St. Louis, 1949, MA (Univ. fellow), 1953, PhD, 1954; m. Eunice Leota Sloop, Mar. 21, 1942 (div. June 1948); 1 child: Judith Lynn; m. Ingrid Elisabeth Getreu, Sept. 16, 1954. Research assoc. Ohio State U., 1953-56; rsch. psychologist Aeromed. Lab., Wright Patterson AFB, Ohio, 1956-59; group supr. Boeing Airplane Co., Seattle, 1959-61; dept. mgr. Internat. Electric Corp., Paramus, N.J., 1961-62; sr. human factors scientist System Devel. Corp., Santa Monica, Calif., 1962-67; v.p. Booz-Allen Applied Rsch., Saigon, Vietnam, 1967-72; v.p. Assoc. Cons. Internat., Saigon, 1972-75, Bethesda, Md., 1975-78; br. chief Human Factors, System Tech. Devel., 1978-82; prin. staff engr. tech. modernization methodology Douglas Aircraft Co., Long Beach, Calif., 1982-85; program mgr. cockpit automation tech. program, Northrop Aircraft div., Hawthorne, Calif., 1985-87; sect. mgr. aircraft programs human factors engring. dept. Douglas Aircraft Co., Long Beach, 1987-90, sr. staff engr. Crew Systems Tech., 1990-93; prin. engr. tech. McDonnell Douglas Aerospace Transport Aircraft, 1993-94; prin. engr.-scientist, crew sys. tech., advanced transport aircraft devel., McDonnell Douglas Aerospace, 1995—; lectr. Nat. Def. Coll., Vietnamese Armed Forces, Saigon, 1971. Served with AUS, 1940-46. Decorated Bronze Star medal with oak leaf cluster; recipient Tech. Svc. First Class medal Republic South Vietnam Armed Forces, 1968. Mem. Am. Psychol. Assn., IEEE, Computer Soc. of IEEE, Human Factors and Ergonomics Soc., Am. Assn. Artificial Intelligence, Phi Beta Kappa, Sigma Xi. Republican. Home: 23201 Mindanao Cir Dana Point CA 92629-3625 Office: McDonnell Douglas Aerospace Mail code C0071-0011 2401 E Wardlow Rd Long Beach CA 90807-5309

MCGUIRE, JOSEPH SMITH, physician; b. Logan, W.Va., Apr. 19, 1931; s. Joseph Smith and Ruby Kellogg (Rose) McG.; m. Margaret Michael, June 5, 1954 (div. 1966); children: Mary Elizabeth, Joseph Smith III, Alison Litz, D. Thompson; m. Mary Lake Polan, 1979, Joshua Lake, Lindsay Kellogg, Scott Hunter. AB, W.Va. U., 1952; MD, Yale U., 1955. Clin. assoc. NIH, Bethesda, Md., 1956-59; asst. prof. dermatology Yale U., New Haven, 1961-64, assoc. prof., 1964-72; prof., 1972-90; Carl Herzog prof. dermatology, pediatrics Stanford (Calif.) U., 1990—. Sr. asst. surgeon USPHS, 1956-59. Mem. Am Soc. Clin. Investigation, Am. Soc. Cell Biology, Soc. Investigative Dermatology (pres. 1988-89), Am. Dermatol. Assn., Am. Acad. Dermatology, Pacific Dermatology Assn. Office: Stanford U Dept Dermatology MSLS P-204 Stanford CA 94305-5486

MCGUIRE, MARTIN CYRIL, economics educator; b. Shanghai, People's Republic of China, Dec. 12, 1933; came to U.S., 1939; s. Martin Cyril and Margaret (Walsh) M. BS, U.S. Mil. Acad., 1955; BA, Oxford U., England, 1958; PhD, Harvard U., 1964. Commd. 2nd lt. U.S. Army, 1955, advanced through grades to capt., 1961, ret., 1961; analyst Office Sec. Defense, 1964-65; dir. program analysis U.S. Commerce Dept., 1965-67; prof. econs. U. Md., College Park, 1967-92; Clifford S. Heinz prof. econs. of global peace and security U. Calif., Irvine, 1992—. Author: Secrecy and the Arms Race, 1965; contbr. articles to profl. jours. Rhodes scholar, 1955, Fulbright scholar, 1988. Mem. Cosmos Club. Office: U Calif Dept Econs Irvine CA 92717

MCGUIRE, MICHAEL FRANCIS, plastic and reconstructive surgeon; b. St. Louis, Oct. 4, 1946; s. Arthur Patrick and Virginia Claribel (Gannon) McG. BA, Columbia U., 1968, MD, 1972. Diplomate Am. Bd. Surgery, Am. Bd. Plastic Surgery. Intern UCLA, 1972-73, resident in gen. surgery, 1973-77, resident in plastic surgery, 1978-80; fellow in plastic surgery rsch. Stanford (Calif.) U., 1977-78; traveling fellow in plastic surgery Gt. Britain, 1980; chief plastic surgery L.A. County-Olive View Med. Ctr., Sylmar, Calif., 1980-85; pvt. practice Santa Monica, Calif., 1980—; chief plastic surgery St. John's Health Ctr., 1990—, chair surg. rev., 1996—; bd. dirs. Calif. Med. Rev., Inc., sec.-treas., 1997—. Charter patron L.A. Music Ctr. Opera, 1983—; sponsoring patron Los Angeles County Art Mus., 1986—; patron Colleague Helpers in Philanthropic Svc., Bel Air, Calif., 1987, 93, 95; pres. Found. for Surg. Reconstrn., 1996—. Fellow ACS, Royal Soc. Medicine; mem. Am. Soc. Plastic and Reconstructive Surgeons (membership chmn. 1997—), Am. Soc. Aesthetic Plastic Surgery, Los Angeles County Med. Assn. (v.p. 1995—), Calif. Med. Assn. (del., exec. com., splty. delegation 1994—), Calif. Soc. Plastic Surgery (exec. com., auditor 1988-89, program chmn. 1990, exec. coun. 1991-94, treas. 1994-97, v.p. 1997—), Am. Assn. Accreditation of Ambulatory Surgery (facilities ops. com. 1995-96, bd. dirs. 1996, treas. 1996—), Alpha Omega Alpha. Democrat. Episcopalian. Office: 1301 20th St Ste 460 Santa Monica CA 90404-2054

MC GUIRE, MICHAEL JOHN, environmental engineer; b. San Antonio, June 29, 1947; s. James Brendan and Opal Mary (Brady) McG.; BS in Civil Engring., U. Pa., 1969; MS in Environ Engring., Drexel U., 1972, PhD in Environ. Engring., 1977; diplomate Am. Acad. Environ. Engring.; m. Deborah Marrow, June 19, 1971; children: David, Anna. San. engr. Phila. Water Dept., 1969-73; rsch. assoc. Drexel U., Phila., 1976-77; prin. engr. Brown & Caldwell Cons. Engrs., Pasadena, Calif., 1977-79; water quality engr. Met. Water Dist. of So. Calif., L.A., 1979-84, water quality mgr., 1984-86, dir. water quality, 1986-90, asst. gen. mgr., 1990-92; pres. McGuire Environ. Cons., Inc., Santa Monica, Calif., 1992—; cons. to subcom. on adsorbents, safe drinking water com. Nat. Acad. Scis., 1978-79; cons. mem. Techs. Workgroup USEPA, DBP Reg Neg, 1992-93. Registered profl. engr., Pa., N.J., Calif. Mem. Am. Water Works Assn. (Acad. Achievement award 1978, edn. div. chmn. 1982-83, chair taste and odor com. 1993—, Calif.-Nev. sect., chmn. water quality and resources div. 1982-83, governing bd. 1984-87, 89-96, exec. com. 1989-96, chmn. 1991-92, nat. dir. 1993-96, trustee Research Found. 1983-86, nat. v.p. 1994-96, nat. exec. com. 1994-96, Fuller award 1994), Am. Chem. Soc., ASCE, Internat. Water Supply Assn., Internat. Assn. on Water Quality (specialist group on taste and odor control 1982—, chmn. organizing com. 1991, off-flavor symposium 1987-91), Internat. Ozone Assn. (internat. bd. dirs. 1992-95), Sigma Xi, Sigma Nu, Sigma Tau. Editor: (with I.H. Suffet) Activated Carbon Adsorption of Organics From the Aqueous Phase, 2 vols., 1980; Treatment of Water by Granular Activated Carbon, 1983; contbr. articles to profl. jours. Office: McGuire Environ Cons Inc 469 25th St Santa Monica CA 90402-3103

MCGULPIN, ELIZABETH JANE, nurse; b. Toledo, Oct. 18, 1932; d. James Orville and Leah Fayne (Helton) Welden; m. David Nelson Buster, Apr. 9, 1956 (div. Nov. 1960); children: David Hugh, James Ray, Mark Stephen; m. Fredrick Gordon McGulpin, Oct. 7, 1973. AA in Nursing, Pasadena City Coll., 1968. RN, Wash. Lic. nurse Las Encinas Hosp., Pasadena, Calif.; nurse Hopi Indian Reservation HEW, Keams Canyon, Ariz., 1969-70; nurse, enterostomal therapist Pasadena Vis. Nurse Assn., 1972-74; nurse Seattle King County Pub. Health, 1977-81; home care nurse Victorville, Calif., 1983-85; nurse Adult Family Home, Woodinville, Wash., 1986—; vol. nurse, counselor Child Protective Svcs., Victorville, 1984; realtor Century 21, Lynden, Wash., 1993—. Vol. nurse Am. Cancer Soc., Pasadena, 1973-75, United Ostomy Assn., Los Angeles, Victorville, 1973-84; RN, ARC, 1996—. Am. Cancer Soc. grantee. Mem. Nat. Assn. Realtors, Wash. Assn. Realtors, Whatcom County Assn. Realtors, Vis. Nurse Assn. (Enterostomal Therpay grantee 1973). Home: 106 Kale St Everson WA 98247-9660 *Personal philosophy: Life is very fragile; it goes so fast! We must all strive to be compassionate; supportive and yet strong enough to meet adversary with strength and positiveness. It isn't easy but it is possible with God's help.*

MCGWIRE, MARK DAVID, professional baseball player; b. Pomona, Calif., Oct. 1, 1963; s. John and Ginger McGwire; m. Kathy McGwire; 1 child, Matthew. Student, U. So. Calif. With Oakland Athletics, 1984—; player World Series, 1988, 89, 90. Named Am. League Rookie of Yr. Baseball Writers' Assn. Am., 1987, Sporting News, 1987; recipient Gold Glove award, 1990; named to All-Star team, 1987-92, 95-96; recipient Silver Slugger Award, 1992; Am. League Home Run Leader, 1987; mem. U.S. Olympic Baseball Team, 1984. Office: Oakland Athletics Oakland-Alameda County Coliseum 7000 Coliseum Way Oakland CA 94621-1945*

MCHARDY, JOHN ALEXANDER, lawyer; b. Mpls., Apr. 17, 1933; s. John Alexander and Marjorie Jean (Kehr) McH.; m. Gail Frances Gustafson, Mar. 27, 1955; children: Heather, Scott, Stuart, Gregor, Fiona, Megan. BSL, U. Minn., 1955, JD, 1957. Bar: Minn. 1957, Colo. 1987. Atty. Burkhardt & Dunlap, Plainview, Minn., 1957-67; commd. 2d lt. U.S. Army, 1967, advanced through grades to lt. col.; judge advocate U.S. Army, worldwide, 1967-87; ret. U.S. Army, 1987; legal access atty. Colo. Dept. Corrections, Canon City, 1992-96; mem. Mission to Nigeria Ch. of Jesus Christ of Latter-day Saints, 1996—; bd. dirs. Pueblo West Met. Dist., 1991-96. County atty. Wabasha County, Wabasha, Minn., 1964-67. Decorated Bronze Star. Mem. Assn. U.S. Army, Ret. Officers Assn., Am. Legion, VFW. Republican. Mormon. Home: 382 S Escalante Plz Pueblo West CO 81007-2212

MCHENRY, PATRICIA ROSE, state agency administrator; b. Burbank, Calif., Mar. 24, 1950; d. Clarence U. and Neota Etta (Common) Benton. BA with distinction, U. N.Mex., 1977. Office mgr. S.W. Cable TV, Espanola, N.Mex., 1978-79; exec. asst. Baha'i' Internat. Ctr., Haifa, Israel, 1980-83; exec. mgmt. analyst N.Mex. Dept. Fin. and Adminstrn., Santa Fe, 1979, exec. budget analyst, 1983-85; sr. fiscal analyst N.Mex. Legis. Fin. Com., Santa Fe, 1985-88; dep. dir. adminstrv. svcs. divsn. N.Mex. Dept. Corrections, Santa Fe, 1988-89; adminstr. data processing N.Mex. Human Svc. Dept., Santa Fe, 1990-92; dep. dir. property control divsn. N.Mex. Gen. Svc. Dept., Santa Fe, 1992—. V.p. Mil. Hist. Found. N.Mex. Mem. Baha'i' Faith. Office: NMex Gen Svc Dept Property Control Divsn 1100 S Saint Francis Dr Santa Fe NM 87505-4147

MC HUGH, MARGARET ANN GLOE, psychologist; b. Salt Lake City, Nov. 8, 1920; d. Harold Henry and Olive (Warenski) Gloe; m. William T. McHugh, Oct. 1, 1943; children: Mary Margaret McHugh-Shuford, William Michael, Michelle McHugh Sprague. BA, U. Utah, 1942; MA in Counseling and Guidance, Idaho State U., 1964; PhD in Counseling Psychology, U. Oreg., 1970. Lic. psychologist; nat. cert. counselor . Tchr. kindergarten, Idaho Falls, Idaho, 1951-62, tchr. high sch. English, 1962-63; counselor Counseling Center, Idaho State U., Pocatello, 1964-67; instr. U. Oreg., Eugene, 1967-70; asst. prof. U. Victoria, B.C., Can., 1970-76; therapist Peninsula Counseling Center, Port Angeles and Sequim, Wash., 1976-81, McHugh & Assocs. Counseling Center, 1981—, ret. 1995. Served with WAVES, 1943-44. Mem. APA, ACA, Am. Assn. Marriage and Family Therapy, Wash. Psychol. Assn. (rsch. women issues, rels's., depression and women, sexual abuse, adults with childhood and abuse trauma). Home: 1175 Cameron Rd Sequim WA 98382-9437

MCHUGH, PETER, mayor; b. Boston; m. Gail Marie Parnagian; children: Sean Michael, Tatia Marie. Student, Boston U. Sch. Bus. Adminstrn., 1963; BS in Bus. Adminstrn., UCLA, 1969. With IBM, 1964; mem. city coun. Milpitas, Calif., 1976-78, 82-90; mayor Milpitas, 1978-82, 90-96; bd. suprs. dist. 3 County of Santa Clara, 1996—. Recipient numerous honors and acknowledgments for cmty. svc. including Calif. State Assembly, Calif. State Senate, U.S. Congress. Office: 70 West Heading St 10th Flr San Jose CA 95110

MCILVAINE, WILLIAM BROWN, JR., pediatric anesthesiologist; b. Lake Forest, Ill., Apr. 8, 1952; s. William Brown McIlvaine Sr. and Adele Ellis (Arrowsmith) Douglas; m. Stephan Barnes Parsons, Oct. 30, 1946; children: Julia Margaret Fenno, William Brown III. BA with honors, Stanford U., 1974; MD, CM, McGill U., Montreal, Can., 1978. Diplomate Am. Bd. Anesthesiology, Nat. Bd. Med. Examiners. Intern Queen Elizabeth Hosp., Montreal, 1978-79; resident in anaesthesia McGill U., Montreal, 1979-82; fellow in pediat. anesthesia Children's Meml. Hosp. & Northwestern U., Chgo., 1982-83; asst. prof. anesthesiology Health Scis. Ctr. U. Colo., Denver, 1983-85, asst. clin. prof. anesthesiology, 1985—, dir. pediat. anesthesia Univ. Hosp., 1983-85, med. dir. operating rms. Univ. Hosp., 1983-85; mem. staff

Children's Hosp., Denver, 1985—, Littleton (Colo.) Hosp., 1989—; mem. courtesy staff Aurora (Colo.) Regional Med. Ctr., 1990—, Rose Med. Ctr., Denver, 1990—, Porter Meml. Hosp., Englewood, Colo., 1993—, Swedish Med. Ctr., Englewood, 1993—; mem. active staff Presbyn.-St. Luke's Med. Ctr., Denver, 1990—, St. Joseph's Hosp., Denver, 1990—; assoc. examiner Am. Bd. Anesthesiology, 1988—; vis. prof. pediat. anesthesia Richland Meml. Hosp. and U. S.C., Columbia, 1989; presenter Hosp. for Sick Children, Toronto, 1983, Children's Hosp., Denver, 1983; presenter numerous confs. Author: (with others) Ocular Therapeutics and Pharmacology, 1985, Textbook of Paediatric Anesthetic Practice, 1989, Clinical Practice of Regional Anesthesia, 1991, Acute Pain: Mechanisms and Management, 1992; contbr. articles to profl. jours. Fellow Royal Coll. Physicians and Surgeons (Can.), Am. Acad. Pediat.; mem. Am. Soc. Anesthesiologists, Can. Anesthetists' Soc., Colo. Med. Soc., Denver Med. Soc., Internat. Anesthesia Rsch. Soc., Soc. for Pediat. Anesthesia. Home: 191 University Blvd Ste 314 Denver CO 80206-4613 Office: Pediat Anesthesia Cons PO Box 18248 Denver CO 80218-0248

MCINNIS, SCOTT STEVE, congressman, lawyer; b. Glenwood Springs, Colo., May 9, 1953; s. Kohler McInnis and Carol Kreir; m. Lori McInnis; children: Daxon, Tessa, Andrea. BA, Ft. Lewis Coll., 1975; JD, St. Mary's Law Sch., 1980. Atty. Delaney & Balcomb P.C., Glenwood Springs, Colo., 1981—; mem. Colo. Ho. of Reps., 1984-93; majority leader, 1990-93; mem. 103d-105th Congresses from 3d Colo. Dist., 1993—; chmn. agrl. livestock and natural resources com., 1986-90, mem. rules com. Recipient Florence Sabin award, 1984, Guardian of Small Bus. award Nat. Fed. Ind. Bus., 1990, Lee Atwater Leadership award, 1991, and various awards from United Vets. Commn.; named Legislator of Decade and Legislator of Yr by Colo. Ski Country and Colo. Wildlife Found. Mem. Elks, Rotary, Phi Delta Phi. Republican. Roman Catholic. Office: US Ho of Reps 215 Cannon HOB Washington DC 20515-0603*

MCINNIS, SUSAN MUSÉ, corporate communications specialist; b. Seattle, July 22, 1955; d. Emmett Emory Jr. and Florence Howardine (McAteer) McI. BSBA, U. Denver, 1977; cert. in environ. design, UCLA, 1985; MA in Journalism, Calif. State U., Fullerton, 1992. Researcher Denver Gen. Hosp., summer 1973; mktg. coord. 3M Bus. Products, Emeryville, Calif., 1978-79; spl. libr. Reel Grobman & Assocs., L.A., 1981-83; tchr. Mayfield Sr. Sch., Pasadena, Calif., 1985-87; advt. coord. Reynolds Advt., 1987; cmty. and employee rels. mgr. Calif.-Am. Water Co. (oper. co. Am. Water Works), San Marino, Calif., 1988—. Mem. Am. Water Works Assn. (cert. water distbn.), Pub. Rels. Soc. Am., Kiwanis (pres. Duarte, Calif. chpt. 1994-95).

MCINTOSH, GARY LYNN, theology educator, consultant, writer; b. Colorado Springs, Colo., Feb. 9, 1947; s. William Vance and Billie Colleen (Thompson) McI.; m. Carol Ann Kurylow, June 21, 1968; children: Gary Lynn II, Aaron James. BA, Rockmont Coll., 1970; MDiv, Western Bapt. Sem., 1975; DMin, Fuller Sch. Theology, 1982. Sr. pastor Grace Bapt. Ch., San Bernardino, Calif., 1976-83; v.p. consulting svcs. Ch. Growth Inc., Pasadena, Calif., 1983-86; dir. DMin program, prof. practical theology Talbot Sch. Theology, La Mirada, Calif., 1986—. Co-author: Finding Them; Keeping Them, 1992, The Issachar Factor, 1994; author: (with others) Handbook of Practical Theology, Vol. 2, 1994; author: Three Generations, 1995, The Exodus Principle, 1995; editor (newsletter) Church Growth Network, 1989—; editor Jour. Am. Soc. Ch. Growth, 1996—. Mem., bd. dirs. Conservative Bapts. Assn., Anaheim, Calif., 1980-83; founder, dir. The Ch. Growth Network, San Bernardino, 1989—; chmn., bd. dirs. Christian H.S., San Bernardino, 1991-94. Mem. Am. Soc. Ch. Growth (pres. 1995, 96), Assn. Doctor Min. Dirs. (pres. 1995—). Office: Talbot Sch Theology 13800 Biola Ave La Mirada CA 90639-0002

MCINTOSH, GREGORY STEPHEN, artist; b. Ojai, Calif., May 7, 1946; s. Donald Frederick James and Hedwig Marie (Berend) McI. BA, Santa Clara U., 1968, MA, 1971. Cert. secondary tchr. history and fine arts, Calif. Teaching asst. fine arts Santa Clara (Calif.) U., 1967-70; instr. fine arts, asst. prof. history St. Patrick's Coll., Mountain View, Calif., 1971-72; profl. artist Ojai, Calif., 1973—. Exhibited works at shows in Ventura County Hist. Mus., 1982-84, Ojai Art Ctr., 1985—, Long Beach Mus. Art, 1987, Vizcaya Mus., Miami, 1988, Tampa (Fla.) Mus. Art, 1988, Ft. Lauderdale (Fla.) Mus. Art, 1988, Crocker Ctr., Boca Raton, Fla., 1988, Walt Disney Corp., Orlando, Fla., 1989, Alliance for the Arts, Guilford, Conn., 1990, Artist-in-Residency, Paris, 1991, City of Miami Beach, 1992, Lipsett Gallery NIH, Washington, 1993, New Eng. Fine Arts Inst., Boston, 1993; represented in permanent collections at Library of Congress, Washington, Calif. Palace of Legion of Honor, San Francisco, San Francisco Mus. of Modern Art, L.A. County Mus. of Art, The Oakland Mus., Muskegon (Mich.) Mus. of Art. Maestro grantee Calif. Arts Coun., 1983; recipient Martin Sudars Meml. Painting award of excellence Deerpath Art League, 1996, Painting award Kenosha (Wis.) Pub. Mus., 1996, Ft. Lauderdale Mus. Art, 1996. Mem. Pastel Soc. Am. Office: PO Box 961 Ojai CA 93024-0961

MCINTURFF, KIM, design engineer, mathematician; b. Spokane, Wash., June 13, 1948; s. Don R. and Mae (Lancaster) McI.; m. Denise E. Lockhart, July 17, 1976; children: Ian, Margo. BS in Math., Stanford U., 1971; MA in Math., U. Calif., Santa Barbara, 1976, MSEE, 1986. Software engr. Raytheon ESD, Goleta, Calif., 1978-82; design engr. E Systems, Goleta, Calif., 1983—. Contbr. articles on antenna design and analysis to profl. jours.; co-patentee multibeam antenna system. Mem. Math. Assn. Am. Home: 5433 Thames Ct Santa Barbara CA 93111-1074 Office: E Systems 1 South Los Carneros Goleta CA 93117

MCINTYRE, GUY MAURICE, professional football player; b. Thomasville, Ga., Feb. 17, 1961. Student, U. Ga. Offensive guard San Francisco 49ers, 1984-94; played in Super Bowl XIX, 1984, XXIII, 1988, XXIV, 1989. *

MCINTYRE, JERILYN SUE, academic administrator; m. W. David Smith. Student, Stanford U., Italy, 1962; AB in History with distinction, Stanford U., 1964, MA in Journalism, 1965, cert. Summer Radio-TV Inst., 1965, tchrs. cert., 1968; PhD in Comms., U. Washington, 1973; postgrad. Inst. Ednl. Mgmt., Harvard U., 1993. Corr. World News Bureau McGraw-Hill Pub. Co., L.A.; asst. prof. dept. mass comm. Chico (Calif.) State Coll., 1968-70; asst. prof. Sch. Journalism U. Iowa, Iowa City, 1973-77; acting dir. divsn. journalism and mass comm. U. Utah, Salt Lake City, 1978-79, assoc. prof., prof. dept. comm., 1977—, assoc. dean Coll. Humanities, 1984-88, assoc. v.p. acad. affairs, 1988-90, interium pres., 1991, v.p. acad. affairs, 1990—; dir. Wall St. Jour. Publs. workshop Chico State Coll., 1968; mem. ednl. adv. bd. NFL, 1996—; mem. exec. com. coun. acad. affairs Nat. Assn. State Univs. and Land Grant Colls., 1995—, chair-elect, 1996-97; mem. steering com. Utah Edn. Network, 1995—. Editl. asst. Chemical Week Mag., 1965-66, World News Bureau, 1966-67; mem. editl. bd. Journalism History; past mem. editl. bd. Comms. Peports, Critical Studies in Mass Comm., Journalism Monographs, Jour. Comm. Inquiry, Journalism Quarterly, Western Jour. Speech Comm.; contbr. articles to profl. jours., chpts. to books. Mem. Utah Women's Forum, pub. awareness and comm. com. Utah Partnership Edn. and Econ. Devel., others. Pub. Rels. Soc. Am. fellow, 1968, U. Washington grantee, 1972, 73, U. Iowa grantee, 1976, U. Utah grantee, 1981, 82, David P. Gardner fellow, 1984; recipient Yesterday's Girl Scout Today's Successful Woman award Utah Girl Scout Coun., 1996. Mem. AAUW (Dist. Woman Utah Salt Lake City chpt. 1994), Assn. Fedn in Journalism and Mass Comm. (mem. com. on status women 1979-80, sec. and editor CLIO 1979-80, vice head hist. divsn. office 1980-91, head 1981-82, mem. publs. com. 1981-84, mem. adv. com. 1981-82, mem. standing com. on rsch. 1989-95), Rotary (Salt Lake City chpt., chmn. sch. and edn. com.), Kappa Tau Alpha (pres. U. Utah chpt.). Office: U Utah Salt Lake City UT 84112*

MCINTYRE, NORMAN F., petroleum industry executive; b. Pangman, Sask., Can., Oct. 21, 1945; s. Donald and Jean (Cruickshank) McI.; m. Lana Jean, June 10, 1967; children: Jason Lee, Spencer James. BSc in Petroleum Engring., U. Wyo., 1971; MS in Mgmt., MIT, 1991. Various positions with Mobil Oil, U.S., Can., to 1982; group mgr. engring. offshore divsn. Petro-Can., 1982-83, gen. mgr. frontier devel. offshore divsn., 1983, v.p. frontier devel., 1983-86, v.p. prodn. devel., 1986-89; sr. v.p. western region Petro-Can. Products, 1989-90; pres. Petro-Can. Resources, Calgary, Alta., Can., 1990-95, exec. v.p., 1995—; chmn., dir. Panarctic Oils Ltd.; dir. Petroleum Transmission Co.. Office: Petro-Canada, 150-6th Ave SW PO Box 2844, Calgary, AB Canada T2P 3E3

MCINTYRE, ROBERT MALCOLM, utility company executive; b. Portland, Oreg., Dec. 18, 1923; s. Daniel A. and Bessie W. (Earsley) McI.; m. Marilyn Westcott, Aug. 27, 1949; 1 child, Julie. BA, UCLA, 1950; postgrad., UCLA, U. Soc. Calif., Columbia U. With So. Calif. Gas Co. (subs. Pacific Enterprises), L.A., 1952-67, gen. sales mgr., 1967-70, v.p., 1970-74, sr. v.p., 1974-80, pres., 1980-85, chmn., chief exec. officer, 1985-88; also bd. dirs. So. Calif. Gas Co. (subs. Pacific Enterprises); regent's prof. U. Calif., Irvine. Mem. Korean Am. Centennial Commn., Huntington Libr. Soc. Fellows, L.A. Olympic Citizens Adv. Commn.; mem. bus. coun. Newport Harbor Art Mus.; mem. steering com. Orange County Bus. Com. for Arts; mem. ad hoc com. on city fin,., L.A.; bd. dirs. NCCJ, Calif. Coun. Environ. and Econ. Balance, Calif. Found. Environment and Economy, L.A. United Way, Hoag Meml. Hosp.; trustee UCLA Found., L.A. Orthopaedic Hosp., mem. exec. com.; pres. Hoag Hosp. Found., L.A. Chamber Assocs. Lt. USN, 1942-46. Decorated Order of the Rising Sun with Gold Rays and Ribbon (Japan); recipient Outstanding Svc. award Mex. Am. Legal Def. Fund, 1981, Humanitarian award NCCJ, Roy Wilkins award L.A. chpt. NAACP, others. Mem. Pacific Coast Gas Assn. (past dir., 49er Club award 1979), Am. Gas Assn., Inst. Gas Tech. (trustee), U.S.-Mex. C. of C., L.A. C. of C. (past chmn. Medici award), Calif. Club, 100 Club, Big Canyon Country Club, Center Club, Pacific Club, The Lakes Country Club, Phi Kappa Psi. Republican. Presbyterian. Office: So Calif Gas Co 555 W 5th St Los Angeles CA 90013-1010*

MCINTYRE, ROBERT WHEELER, conservation organization executive; b. Chgo., Aug. 26, 1936; s. Henry Langenberg and Winifred (Wheeler) McI.; m. Emily Beardsley Taylor, Oct. 12, 1961 (div. 1985); children: W. Burley, Nancy T., Oliver W., Shanna L., Amanda K.; m. Miriam de Jesus Zarate, June 23, 1990. AB in Sociology, Stanford U., 1959; MBA, Harvard U., 1964. Loan analyst Wells Fargo Bank, San Francisco, 1964-65; supr. budget analysis Ford Aerospace, Palo Alto, Calif., 1965-69; controller Allied Life Scis., San Leandro, Calif., 1969-70; ptnr. Diplomat Mfg. Co., Palo Alto, 1970-71; staff cons. Opportunity Through Ownership, San Francisco, 1971-72; gen. mgr. Quality Metal Finishers, San Francisco, 1972-73; sr. v.p., chief fin. officer The Trust for Pub. Land, San Francisco, 1973—. Adv. bd. Peninsula Open Space Trust, Menlo Park, 1978—, Resource Renewal Inst., Sausalito, 1988—, Wter Heritage Trust, Sausalito, 1988—, Dorothy Erskine Open Space Fund, San Francisco, 1978—; bd. dirs. Environ. Vols., Palo Alto, 1980—; bd. dirs., treas. Robert C. Wheeler Found., Palo Alto, 1965—. Lt. (j.g.) USNR, 1959-62. Recipient Presdl. Citation award, The Trust for Pub. Land, 1988, Spl. Svc. award, Environ. Vols., 1989. Mem. Harvard Club N.Y., Harvard Club Boston, Sundown Tennis Club (San Mateo), San Francisco Tennis Club. Office: The Trust for Public Land 116 New Montgomery St Fl 4 San Francisco CA 94105-3607

MCINTYRE-RAGUSA, MARY MAUREEN, social services consultant; b. Decatur, Ill.; d. Leo M. and Madge Eleanor (Daniels) McInroe; m. David McIntyre (dec. Sept. 1978); children: Laura, Kathy, Michael, Ellen, Paul; m. John Ragusa. AA in Journalism/Comm., Cosumnes River Coll., 1994. Founder, dir. Sheltering Wings, Elk Grove, Calif., 1984—; dir. Sheltering Wings, Washougal, Wash., 1996—. Author: 8 Steps to Successful Living, 1987, (puppet prodn. script) Rochester Betsy, 1989, songs; contbr. articles to newspapers. Bd. dirs. Calvary Chapel, Camas, Wash., sec.-treas., 1996. Office: Sheltering Wings PO Box 777 Washougal WA 98671

MCJONES, PAUL ROBERT, computer scientist, software engineer; b. Inglewood, Calif., July 6, 1949; s. Robert Wayne and Norma Jeane (Prater) McJ.; m. Raquel Atkinson, Feb. 20, 1970. BS in Engring. Math., U. Calif., Berkeley, 1971. Computer programmer Athena Programming, Redondo Beach, Calif., 1967, U. Calif., Berkeley, 1967-72, Virtual Memory Sys., Orinda, Calif., 1973-74; rsch. staff mem. IBM San Jose (Calif.) Rsch. Lab., 1974-76; cons. mem. programming staff Xerox Corp., Palo Alto, Calif., 1976-81; software designer Tandem Computers Inc., Cupertino and Austin, 1981-85; cons. software engr. Digital Equipment Corp./Sys. Rsch. Ctr., Palo Alto, 1985—. Contbr. articles to profl. jours. Fellow Assn. for Computing Machinery. Home: 710 View St Mountain View CA 94041-2151 Office: DEC Sys Rsch Ctr 130 Lytton Ave Palo Alto CA 94301-1044

MCKASSON, MOLLY ELIZABETH, city council; m. Richard Morgan, 1976; children: Lily, Clay. BS in Speech, Northwestern U. Free lance journalist various mags. including Tucson Weekly, Guide, City Mag.; actor, dir., playwright; city coun. Tucson, 1989—; mem. Mayor and Coun. sub-coms. Comty. Svcs., Pub. Safety, Defense Restructuring Adv. Com. of Greater Tucson Econ. Coun., Exec. Air Quality Com. Pima Assn. Govts., Small Bus. Task Force Pima County Econ. Devel. Coun., Santon Domingo Sister City Project, Campus Comty. Rels. Com., City of Tucson, U. Ariz. Jt. Planning Com. Office: PO Box 27210 255 W Alameda St Tucson AZ 85714

MC KAUGHAN, HOWARD PAUL, linguistics educator; b. Canoga Park, Calif., July 5, 1922; s. Paul and Edith (Barton) McK.; m. Barbara Jean Budroe, Dec. 25, 1943; children: Edith (Mrs. Daniel Skene Santoro), Charlotte (Ms. Charlotte Barnhart), Patricia (Mrs. Stephen B. Pike), Barbara (Mrs. Ronald Chester Bell), Judith (Ms. Judith B. Achilles). AB, UCLA, 1945, MTh, Dallas Theol. Sem., 1946; MA, Cornell U., 1952, PhD, 1957. Mem. linguistic rsch. team Summer Inst. Linguistics, Mexico, 1946-52; asso. dir. Summer Inst. Linguistics, Philippines, also assoc. dir. summer sessions U. N.D., 1952-57, dir. Philippine br., 1957-61; rsch. asst. prof. anthropology U. Wash., 1961-62; rsch. assoc. prof., 1962-63; assoc. prof. linguistics U. Hawaii, 1963-64, prof. linguistics, 1964-88, prof. emeritus, 1988—, chmn. dept., 1963-66, dir. Pacific and Asian Linguistics Inst., 1964, 1966-69, assoc. dean grad. div., 1965-72, dean grad. div., dir. rsch., 1972-79, acting chancellor, 1979, interim vice chancellor acad. affairs, 1981-82, acting dir rsch., 1982-84, acting dean grad. div., 1982-83, dean, 1984-87, dir. rsch. rels., 1987-88; lectr. linguistics U. Philippines, summers, 1954, 60; Fulbright vis. prof. Philippine Normal Coll.-Ateneo-De La Salle Consortium, Philippines, 1977, De La Salle U., Philippines, 1992; vis. prof. lingustics Bukidnon State Coll., Malaybalay, Philippines, 1993, 94; linguistic cons. Summer Inst. Linguistics, Malaysia branch, 1995—; prin. Wycliffe Sch. Linguistics, summers 1953, 61; vis. prof. Australian Nat. U., Canberra, 1970; adj. prof. linguistics U. Okla., summers 1984, 85, 86; vis. prof., head dept. linguistics Payap U., Chiang Mai, Thailand, 1989-90. Sr. scholar East-West Ctr., Honolulu, 1964; NDEA Maranao-Philippines research grantee, 1963-65; Office of Edn. Hawaii English grantee, 1965-66; NSF Jeh Language of South Vietnam grantee, 1969-70, Maranao Linguistic Studies, 1971-72, numerous other research grants. Mem. linguistic socs. Am., Philippines, Western Assn. Grad. Schs. (pres. 1978), Hawaii, Linguistic Circle N.Y., Philippine Assn. Lang. Tchrs., Hawaii Govt. Employees Assn., Phi Beta Kappa, Phi Kappa Phi. Author (with B. McKaughan): Chatino Dictionary, 1951; (with J. Forster) Ilocano: An Intensive Language Course, 1952; The Inflection and Syntax of Maranao Verbs, 1959; (with B. Macaraya): A Maranao Dictionary, 1967, rev. edit., 1996. Editor: Pali Language Texts: Philippines, 21 vols., 1971; The Languages of the Eastern Family of the East New Guinea Highlands Stock, 1973; Maranao Stories, 1995; Stories from the Darangen, 1995; contbr. articles, chpts. to books, sci. jours. Home: 420 S Hill Rd Mcminnville OR 97128-9105

MCKAY, ALICE VITALICH, academic administrator; b. Seattle, Sept. 6, 1947; d. Jack S. and Phyllis (Bourne) Vitalich; m. Larry W. McKay, Aug. 14, 1973 (div. Jan. 1983). BA, Wash. State U., 1969; MEd, U. Nev., Las Vegas, 1975; EdD, U. Nev., Reno, 1986. High sch. tchr. Clark County Sch. Dist., Las Vegas, 1972-77, specialist women's sports, 1977-80, high sch. counselor, 1980-84, high sch. asst. prin., 1984-95; dir. Project Lead U. Nev., Reno, 1995—; pres. Lotus Profit, Inc., Las Vegas, 1985-86; dir. Nev. Project Lead. Sec. exec. bd. Gang Alternatives Partnership, 1993—. Mem. Am. Assn. Counseling and Devel. (committee on women 1985—), Nev. State Counseling and Devel. (pres. 1985-86), Nat. Assn. Female Execs., AAUW, Phi Delta Kappa (exec. bd. 1980-82). Office: U Nev Coll Edn Reno NV 89557-0217

MCKAY, JOHN, lawyer; b. Seattle, June 19, 1956; s. John Larkin and Kathleen (Tierney) M. BA, U. Wash., 1978; JD, Creighton U., 1982. Bar: Wash. 1982, U.S. Dist. Ct. (we. dist.) Wash. 1982, U.S. Supreme Ct. 1990, U.S. Ct. Appeals (9th cir.) 1990. Ptnr. Lane Powell Spears Lubersky, Seattle, 1982-92, Cairncross & Hempelmann, Seattle, 1992-97; pres. Legal Svcs. Corp., Washington, 1997—. White House fellow, Washington, 1989-90. Mem. ABA (bd. govs. 1991-94), Wash. State Bar Assn. (pres. young lawyers divsn. 1988-89). Republican. Roman Catholic. Office: Cairncross & Hempelmann 701 5th Ave Ste 7000 Seattle WA 98104-7009 also: Legal Svcs Corp 750 First St NW Washington DC 20002

MCKAY, KATHRYN LEE, historian; b. N.Y.C., May 3, 1958; d. Robert Budge and Sara Kate (Warmack) McK.; m. Bryan Wane Nichols, July 7, 1990. BA in Classics, Williams Coll., 1980; MA in Am. History, U. Del., 1985. Archeol. technician Flathead Nat. Forest, Kalispell, Mont., 1988-91; owner Tracks of the Past, Hist. and Archaeol. Svcs., Columbia Falls, Mont., 1991—. Adv. bd. Cultural and Aesthetics Projects, Helena, Mont., 1991—; long-range planning com. Flathead County Libr., Kalispell, 1995—. Eleutherian Mills-Hagley fellow, 1983-85. Mem. Mont. Wilderness Assn., Mont. Preservation Alliance, Mont. Hist. Soc., Soc. Indsl. Archaelogy, Save Old Main Assn. (founder). Address: 491 Eckelberry Dr Columbia Falls MT 59912-9224

MCKAY, MICHAEL JOSEPH, religious educational products developer, theologian; b. Chgo., Aug. 6, 1949; s. Joseph Patrick and Shirley Fredricka (Haas) McK.; m. Mary Alicia Powers, Jan. 15, 1994; children: Sean Michael, Kevin Patrick. BA in Philosophy, Pontifical Coll. Josephinum, Worthington, Ohio, 1971; B of Sacred Theology, Pontifical Gregorian U., Rome, 1975; D of Sacred Theology, Cath. U. Am., Washington, 1991. Ordained priest Roman Cath. Ch., 1976. Assoc. pastor Diocese of San Diego, 1976-81, master catechist, 1978-81; adj. faculty U. San Diego, 1984-92, dir. campus ministry, 1984-92; v.p. Divinity Religious Products, Carlsbad, Calif., 1993—; bd. dirs. San Diego Ecumenical Conf., 1988-91; mem. Interfaith Coun., San Diego, 1991. Author (religious ednl. games) Divinity, The Cath. Catechism Learning Sys., 1994, Cath. Quiz, 1995. Mem. Cath. Theol. Soc. Am. Office: Divinity Religious Products Inc 5115 Avenida Encinas Ste B Carlsbad CA 92008-4387

MCKAY, MONROE GUNN, federal judge; b. Huntsville, Utah, May 30, 1928; s. James Gunn and Elizabeth (Peterson) McK.; m. Lucile A. Kinnison, Aug. 6, 1954; children: Michele, Valanne, Margaret, James, Melanie, Nathan, Bruce, Lisa, Monroe. B.S., Brigham Young U., 1957; J.D., U. Chgo., 1960. Bar: Ariz. 1961. Law clk. Ariz. Supreme Ct., 1960-61; assoc. firm Lewis & Roca, Phoenix, 1961-66; ptnr. Lewis & Roca, 1968-74; assoc. prof. Brigham Young U., 1974-76, prof., 1976-77; judge U.S. Ct. Appeals for 10th Cir., Denver, 1977-91, chief judge, 1991-94, sr. judge, 1994—. Mem. Phoenix Community Council Juvenile Problems, 1968-74; pres. Ariz. Assn. for Health and Welfare, 1970-72; dir. Peace Corps, Malawi, Africa, 1966-68; bd. dirs., pres. Maricopa county Legal Aid Soc., 1972-74. Served with USMCR, 1946-48. Mem. ABA, Ariz. Bar Assn., Maricopa County Bar Assn., Am. Law Inst., Am. Judicature Soc., Order of Coif, Blue Key, Phi Kappa Phi. Mem. LDS Ch. Office: US Ct Appeals for 10th Cir Rm 6012 Fed Bldg 125 S State St Salt Lake City UT 84138-1102*

MC KEE, ALLEN PAGE, investment company executive; b. L.A., July 26, 1941; s. Norman C. and Eleanor (Page) McK.; BA in Econs., U. Mich., 1964; MBA, U. Calif.-Berkeley, 1971. Area relations officer internat. div. Bank of Am., San Francisco, 1967-70; investment officer BankAm. Internat. Fin. Corp., San Francisco, 1971-73; v.p. and dir. internat. investments Union Bank, San Francisco, 1973-74; pres. Montgomery Assocs., Inc., San Francisco, 1975—, dir., 1977—; mng. dir. Fal N.V., 1979-87, Willhurst Co., 1980—; dir., CFO Advanced Combustion Techs., Inc., 1995—; v.p., CFO, dir. Procyon Power Sys., Inc., 1996—; bd. dirs. Hawaiian Plantations, Inc., 1981-83, Dynodata, Inc., 1983—, Analytical Products, Inc., 1984-92. Served to lt. USN, 1964-67, Vietnam. Mem. World Affairs Coun. No. Calif., Soc. Calif. Pioneers, Calif. Bus. Alumni Assn., Delta Kappa Epsilon. Republican. Club: Commonwealth of Calif. Home: 23 Turtle Rock Ct Belvedere Tiburon CA 94920-1301 Office: PO Box 2230 50 California St Ste 1400 San Francisco CA 94126

MCKEE, BYRON DUNCAN, livestock broker; b. Denver, June 24, 1935; s. B. Duncan and Adeline Janet (O'Neal) McK.; children: B. Duncan III, James John, Carole Anne. Laborer Nat. Commn. Co., 1955-56; laborer, bookkeeper John O'Dea Livestock Commn. Co., 1956-57; advt. profl. Denver Dry Goods, 1954-55; clk. and asst. store mgr. Safeway Stores, 1957-59; fat and feeder cattle buyer Armour & Co., 1959-61; feedlot mgr. Wilhelm/Mancini Feedlots, 1961-62; dir. livestock purchase and sales McKee Cattle Co., 1962-67; mgr. feedlots, purchase and sales of livestock Farr Farms Co., 1967-80; pres., founder Front Range Cattle Co., Livestock Corp. and Consulting, Greeley, Colo., 1980—. Home: 1832 26th Ave Greeley CO 80631-4915 Office: Front Range Livestock Corp 1832 26th Ave Greeley CO 80631-4915

MC KEE, JOHN ANGUS, oil company executive; b. Toronto, Ont., Can., Aug. 31, 1935; s. John William and Margaret Enid (Phippen) McK.; m. Susan Elizabeth Harley, May 30, 1970; children: John Andrew, Mary Susan. Student, U. Toronto, 1954-58, Upper Can. Coll., Port Hope, Ont., Trinity Coll. Sch., Port Hope, Ont. With Dominion Securities Corp. Ltd., Toronto, 1958-60; mng. dir. Patino Mining Group, Toronto and London, Eng., 1960-71; with Consolidated Tin Smelters, Brit. Tin Investment Corp., Amalagamated Metal Corp., 1964-71; pres. J. Angus McKee & Assoc., 1971-83; pres., chief exec. officer Can. Occidental Petroleum Ltd., 1983-93; bd. dirs., chmn. Gulfstream Resources, Ltd., Calgary, Alta., 1993—; dir. Conor Pacific Environ. Techs. Inc., Big Rock Brewery Ltd., Gerling Global Ins. Group, Hankin Atlas Industries Ltd., Stone & Webster Can. Ltd., Stone & Webster, Inc. Bd. govs. Trinity Coll. Sch.. Mem. Toronto Club, York Club, Badminton and Racquet Club, Ranchmen's Club, Calgary Petroleum Club, Knickerbocker Club (N.Y.C.), Craigleith Ski Club, Internat. Order of St. Hubert, Goodwood Club, Alpha Delta Phi (bd. govs. and dir.). Office: Gulfstream Resources Ltd, 855 2d St SW 34th Fl, Calgary, AB Canada T2P 4J8

MCKEE, ROGER CURTIS, federal magistrate judge; b. Waterloo, Iowa, Feb. 11, 1931; s. James A. and Leonace (Burrell) McK.; m. Roberta Jeanne Orvis, Sept. 3, 1954; children: Andrea Jane, Brian Curtis, Paul Robert. BA, State Coll. of Iowa, 1955; MA, U. Ill., 1960; JD, U. San Diego, 1968. Bar: Calif. 1970, U.S. Dist. Ct. (so. dist.) Calif. 1969, U.S. Ct. Appeals (9th cir.) 1971. Telegrapher, agt. Ill. Cen. R.R., 1950-55; tng. asst. No. Ill. Gas Co., Aurora, 1959-60; with indsl. rels. dept. Convair div. Gen. Dynamics Corp., San Diego, 1960-68; contract adminstr. and supr. Datagraphix div. Gen. Dynamics Corp., San Diego, 1968-69, asst. counsel, 1969-70; ptnr. Powell & McKee, San Diego, 1970-75, Millsberg, Dickstein & McKee, San Diego, 1975-83; magistrate judge U.S. Dist. Ct. for So. Dist. Calif., San Diego, 1983—; presiding magistrate judge, 1993—. Bd. trustees So. Calif. Presbyn. Homes, L.A., 1979-81; moderator Presbytery of San Diego, 1980. Capt. USNR, 1949-85. Mem. Calif. Bar Assn., Fed. Magistrate Judges Assn., Navy League U.S., Naval Res. Officers Assn., Res. Officers Assn., Dixieland Jazz Soc. (bd. dirs. San Diego chpt. 1984—). Republican. Office: US Cts Bldg 940 Front St San Diego CA 92101-8994

MCKEE, SUZANNE PESHETTE, vision scientist; b. Vallejo, Calif., May 19, 1941; d. Eugene Wilfred and Margaret Helen (Lundblad) Peshette; m. Christopher Fulton McKee, June 20, 1965; children: William Arthur, Christopher Eugene, Maria Helene. AB, Vassar Coll., 1963; PhD, U. Calif., Berkeley, 1970. Instr. St. Mary's Coll., Moraga, Calif., 1969-70, Calif. State U./Calif. Poly. Inst., L.A./Riverside, 1970-71; scientist Polaroid Corp., Cambridge, Mass., 1971-74; asst. rsch. physiologist U. Calif., Berkeley, 1974-81; sr. scientist Smith-Kettlewell Eye Rsch. Inst., San Francisco, 1981-90, assoc. dir., 1990—; chair com. on vision NRC, Washington, 1989-91. Assoc. editor Perception, London, 1985—; author numerous rsch. reports, articles and book chpts. NSF fellow, 1963-68. Mem. Assn. for Rsch. in Vision and Ophthalmology (trustee 1994—), Optical Soc. Am. (fellow, 1994), Psychonomic Soc., Phi Beta Kappa. Democrat. Roman Catholic. Office: Smith-Kettlewell Eye Rsch 2232 Webster St San Francisco CA 94115-1821

MCKEEN, EDWIN CLIFFORD, psychologist; b. Bend, Oreg., Jan. 31, 1939; s. Edwin Owen and Margaret Carla (Eckelman) McK.; m. Patti M. Ooley, Jan. 3, 1992; children: Rachel, Lindsey, Alexandria. BA, Portland (Oreg.) State U., 1964, MA, 1969; PhD, U. Oreg., 1973. Lic. psychologist, Oreg.; cert. sch. psychologist Tchrs. Stds. and Practices Commn. Psychol.

examiner Portland Pub. Schs., 1966-69; rsch. asst. U. Oreg., Eugene, 1970-72; psychologist Josephine County Mental Health, Grants Pass, Oreg., 1972-76; dir. spl. svcs. Grants Pass Pub. Schs., 1976-78, psychologist, 1978-81; pvt. practice, Astoria, Oreg., 1981-84, Tigard, Oreg., 1986—; counselor Am. Sch. in Japan, Tokyo, 1984-86; sch. psychologist Beaverton (Oreg.) Sch. Dist., 1986-95; advisor to adminstrv. bd. Stepping Stone House, Grants Pass, 1974-76; del. behavior therapist Person to Person Program, China, 1982; psychologist, ednl. cons. Tokyo Cmty. Counseling Svcs., 1984-86; adj. instr. Lewis and Clark Coll., Portland, 1994; guest lectr. Portland State U., 1991-94; presenter in field. Chmn. Juvenile Svcs. Commn., Grants Pass, 1980-82; mem. biomed. ethics com. Columbia Meml. Hosp., Astoria, 1983-84; vol. Head Start programs Washington County (Oreg.) Cmty. Action, 1992-94; mem. Washington County Commn. on Children and Families, 1996—. Grantee Law Enforcement Assistance Agy., Jackson and Josephine Counties, Oreg., 1972-75. Mem. APA, NASP, Assn. for Advancement Behavior Therapy, Oreg. Psychol. Assn., Oreg. Sch. Psychologists Assn. (charter, 1st co-chmn. 1971-72). Office: 15350 SW Sequoia Pkwy Ste 195 Tigard OR 97224-7172

MCKEEVER, MIKE PIERCE, economics and business educator; b. Glendale, Calif., Mar. 3, 1941; s. Samuel Pierce and Martha Frances (Darby) McK.; m. Jeanetta Ross, Oct. 20, 1964 (div. June 1970); 1 child, Nancy; m. Marjorie Alice McKean, Dec. 17, 1970; children: Michael P. Jr., Johnathan Brooks. BA with honors, Whittier (Calif.) Coll., 1963; MS in Econs., London Sch. Econs., 1966. Life credential bus., econs., social sci. Calif. C.C. Owner Counseling Brokerage Group, Santa Rosa, Calif., 1980-84, Bus. Plan Workshop, Santa Rosa, 1980-95; asst. prof. econs. and bus. Armstrong U., Berkeley, Calif., 1994—; founder McKeever Inst. Econ. Policy Analysis, Berkeley, 1995—. Author: How to Write a Business Plan, 1981, Conceptual Economics, 1993. Dir. Inst. Small Bus. Dept. Sonoma State U., 1981; pres. We Care, Santa Rosa, 1984; chmn. adv. com. Suppression of Drug Abuse in Schs. Sonoma County, Santa Rosa, 1985. Recipient award Role Recognition-Downtown Devel., Santa Rosa City Coun., 1983; named Vol. of Yr. Santa Rosa City Schs., 1984. Home: 2719 Acton St Berkeley CA 94702-2302 Office: Armstrong U 3254 Pierce St Richmond CA 94804

MCKELVEY, TANYA HOPE, histocompatibility technologist; b. Bethesda, Md., Aug. 10, 1966; d. Gregory Ellis and Sally Jo (Addicott) McK. BA, Whitman Coll., Walla Walla, Wash., 1988; MA, Ariz. State U., Tempe, 1993. Histocompatibility technologist Blood Systems Inc., Scottsdale, Ariz., 1994-95, blood sys. quality assurance specialist, 1995-96, design asst., 1997—. Mem. AAUW, Nat. Endometriosis Assn. Office: Judis 7722 E Gray Rd Scottsdale AZ 85260

MCKENDREE, JOHN W., lawyer; b. Taft, Calif., Aug. 8, 1936. BA, U. Calif., Berkeley, 1955; JD, U. Denver, 1963. Mcpl. judge City of Sheridan, Colo., 1966-86; gen. counsel Oil Chemical Workers Nat. Union, Denver, 1986-91; pvt. practice Denver, 1991—. Office: 1244 Grant St Denver CO 80203-2306

MCKENNA, JEANETTE ANN, archaeologist; b. N.Y.C., Aug. 6, 1953; d. Edward Patrick and Ann Jeanette (O'Brien) McKenna; children: Stephanie Jane, Daniel Glen Edward. AA in Phys. Edn., Mount San Antonio Jr. Coll., 1974; BA in Anthropology, Calif. State U., Fullerton, 1977, MA in Anthropology, 1982; postgrad., Ariz. State U., 1981-84, U. Calif., Riverside, 1991-92. Field archaeologist Archaeol. Rsch., Inc., Costa Mesa, Calif., 1976-79; rsch. asst. Calif. State U., 1979; lab. dir. Environ. Rsch. Archaeologists, L.A., 1978-79; staff archaeologist Ariz. State U., Tempe, 1979-82; rsch. archaeologist Soil Systems, Inc., Phoenix, 1982-84, Sci. Resource Surveys, Huntington Beach, Calif., 1984-87; co-owner, prin. Hatheway & McKenna, Mission Viejo, Calif., 1987-89; owner, prin. McKenna et al., Whittier, Calif., 1989—; dir. Divsn. Cultural Resource Mgmt. Svcs. EIP Assocs., Chino, Calif., 1996—. Contbr. numerous articles to profl. jours. and reports. Bd. dirs. Whittier Conservancy, 1987—, interim treas., 1994, pres., 1994-95. Recipient Gov.'s award for Hist. Preservation/Calif., The Whittier Conservancy, 1995. Mem. Soc. Profl. Archaeologists (bd. dirs. 1993—), Archaeol. Inst. Am., Am. Soc. Conservation Archaeology, Am. Mus. Natural History, Soc. Am. Anthropology, Ariz. Archaeol. Coun., Ariz. Hist. Found., Calif. Hist. Soc., Nat. Arbor Day Found., Nat. Parks and Conservation Assn., Nat. Trust for Historic Preservation, Soc. Calif. Archaeology, Soc. Hist. Archaeology, S.W. Mus. Assn., Wilderness Soc., Whittier Conservancy, Southwestern Anthrop. Assn., Gene Autry Western Heritage Mus. Assn., Nature Conservancy, Smithsonian Assocs., Sierra Club, otehrs. Democrat. Roman Catholic. Home: 6008 Friends Ave Whittier CA 90601-3724 Office: McKenna et al 6008 Friends Ave Whittier CA 90601-3724

MC KENNA, MARIAN CECILIA, historian; b. Scarsdale, N.Y., July 3, 1926; d. John Francis and Marguerite (Hanfling) McK. BS, Columbia U., 1949, MA, 1950, PHD in History (Am. Philos. Soc. Penrose award 1952-53, Erb fellow), 1953. Instr. Hunter Coll., CUNY, 1953-59; assoc. prof. Manhattanville Coll., Purchase, N.Y., 1959-66; prof. Am . history U. Calgary, Alta., Can., 1966-93; prof. emeritus U. Calgary, 1993—; cons. Nat. Endowment for Humanities. Author: Borah, 1960, Pictorial History of Catholicism, 1961, Myra Hess: a Portrait, 1976, Tapping Reeve and the Litchfield Law School, 1986, Canadian and American Constitutions in Comparative Perspective, 1993. Danforth fellow, 1965; recipient Can. Coun. award, 1967, 68, 69, 72, 76, Social Scis. and Humanities Rsch. Coun. Can. award, 1989, 90, Faculty of Social Sci. Disting. Tchr. award U. Calgary, 1993. Mem. Orgn. Am. Historians, Am. Hist. Assn., Am. Soc. Legal History. Roman Catholic. Home: 3343 Upton Pl NW, Calgary, AB Canada T2N 4G9 Office: U Calgary History Dept, 2500 University Dr NW, Calgary, AB Canada T2N 1N4

MCKENZIE, RICHARD ELVIN, aerospace engineer; b. San Rafael, Calif., Sept. 27, 1951; s. Cecil L. and Estelle B. McKenzie; m. Iris Y. Cavazos, Apr. 28, 1972; children: Jacqueline Nicole, Alexander Scott. BS, U. Tex., 1975, MS, 1976. Consulting engr. Pollak & Skan, Dallas, 1981-85; sr. staff scientist Merit Tech., Inc., Dallas, 1985-89; sr. staff engr. Geodynamics Corp., Denver, 1989—; co-founder The Computer Coll., Dallas, 1982-85; cons. System Specialists, Dallas, 1981-85. Patentee for A Terrain Avoidance Algorithm. Pres. Ramshorn Coop., Austin, 1969-70. Sr. mem. AIAA; mem. Assn. Old Crows, Sigma Gamma Tau. Home: 165 Wuthering Heights Dr Colorado Springs CO 80921-2571

MCKEON, ELAINE, museum administrator. Chmn. San Francisco Mus. of Modern Art, Calif. Office: San Francisco Mus Modern Art 151 Third St San Francisco CA 94103*

MCKEON, HOWARD P. (BUCK MCKEON), congressman, former mayor; b. Los Angeles; m. Patricia; 6 children. BS, Brigham Young U. Mem. Coun. City of Santa Clarita, Calif., 1987-92, mayor, 1987-88; mem. 103rd Congress from 25th Calif. dist., 1993—; founding dir., chmn. Valencia Nat. Bank; co-owner Howard & Phil's Western Wear, Inc. Hon. chmn. Leukemia Soc. Celebrity program, 1990, Red Cross Community Support Campaign, 1992; active Dist. Com. Boy Scouts Am.; chmn., trustee William S. Hart Sch. dist., 1979-87; chmn., dir. Henry Mayo Newhall Meml. Hosp., 1983-88; mem. Calif. Rep. State Ctrl. Com., 1988-92; bd. dirs. Santa Clarita Valley Sml. Bus. Devel. Ctr., 1990-92, Canyon Country C. of C., 1988-92. Office: US Ho of Reps 307 Cannon Ho Ofc Bldg Washington DC 20515*

MCKIBBEN, HOWARD D., federal judge; b. Apr. 1, 1940; s. James D. and Bernice McKibben; m. Mary Ann McKibben, July 2, 1966; children: Mark, Susan. B.S., Bradley U., 1962; M.P.A., U. Pitts., 1964; J.D., U. Mich., 1967. Assoc. George W. Abbott Law Office, 1967-71; dep. dist. atty. Douglas County, Nev., 1969-71, dist. atty., 1971-77; dist. ct. judge State of Nev., 1977-84; judge U.S. Dist. Ct. Nev., Reno, 1984—. Mem. ABA, Nev. Bar Assn., Am. Inns of Ct. (pres. Nev. chpt. 1986-88). Methodist. Home: PO Box 588 Verdi NV 89439-0588 Office: US Dist Ct 400 Virginia St # 804 Reno NV 89501

MCKIBBEN, RYAN TIMOTHY, newspaper executive; b. Watertown, S.D., June 25, 1958; s. Bernard Dean and Patricia Martha (Loehr) McK.; m. Mary Elizabeth O'Donnell, Oct. 3, 1981; children: Sean Robert, Michael Patrick. Grad. high sch., Janesville, Wis. Classified advt. exec. Green Bay (Wis.) Press Gazette, 1977-79; display advt. exec. Racine (Wis.) Jour. Times, 1979-80; advt. dir. Oshkosh (Wis.) Northwestern, 1980-82, dir. sales/mktg., 1982-84; advt. dir. Reno Gazette-Jour., 1984-85, Madison (Wis.) Newspapers Inc., 1985-88; v.p., advt. dir., sr. v.p. advt. and mktg. Denver Post, 1988-90, exec. v.p., gen. mgr., 1990-93, pub., 1993—; bd. dirs. Newspapers First, N.Y.C. Mem. mktg. com. Metro Area Boys Clubs, Denver, 1988—; bd. dirs. Nat. Jewish Ctr. for Immunology and Respiratory Medicine, Denver, Denver Metro Conv. Bur., Denver Ctr. for Performing Arts, Colo. Symphony, Colo. Forum, Colo. Concer, Castle Pines Golf Club. Mem. Am. Press Inst., Newspaper Advt. Coop. Network (bd. dirs. 1989—), Internat. Newspaper Advt./Mktg. Execs., (com. mem. 1989—), Denver Advt. Fedn., Boys and Girls Club, Columbine Country Club. Republican. Roman Catholic. Home: 5350 S Race Ct Littleton CO 80121-1430 Office: Denver Post 1560 Broadway Denver CO 80202-6000

MCKIM, HARRIET MEGCHELSEN, education educator; b. Keokuk, Iowa, Oct. 17, 1919; d. Herbert John and Florence Josephine (Ottowa) Megchelsen; m. Lanier McClure, Nov. 1, 1944 (div. 1948); 1 child, Janet Gray; m. L.A. McKim, July 28, 1950 (div. 1968). BA, Calif. State U., Sacramento, 1952; MA, U. So. Calif., 1963, EdD, 1979. Tchr., prin. Cumberland County Schs., Crossville, Tenn., 1939-42; sec. Tenn. Valley Authority, Oak Ridge Def. Plant, Mare Island Naval Shipyard and Cal-West Ins., 1942-52; tchr., vice-prin., reading specialist, dir. ESEA I various pub. schs., Oxnard, Orcutt, Sacramento, Edwards AFB, Calif. and Spokane, Wash., 1950-64; coord. Yuba City and Yuba County Schs., 1964-70; cons. Calif. Dept. Edn., 1970-83; part-time instr. Alan Hancock Community Coll., Santa Maria, Calif., Sacramento City Coll., Polytech. U., San Luis Obispo, Calif., U. Calif., Davis, Santa Barbara, 1964-84; supr. student tchrs. Calif. State U., Sacramento, 1984; adj. prof. edn. Nat. U., Sacramento, 1986-88; rep. Child Devel. Assocs., 1992—. Vol. tchr. ARC parenting classes, Sacramento, 1984-85; docent, spkr. Crocker Art Mus.; vol. Loaves and Fishes; bd. dirs. Elderhostel Calif. State U.; docent Sacramento History Ctr.; deacon Fremont Presbyn. Ch.; bd. mem. Sacramento World Affairs Coun., Friendship Inspiration Recreation and Svc. Group. Mem. AAUW, Nat. Assn. Edn. Young Children, Calif. Ret. Tchrs., Am. Assn. Ret. Persons, Profs. of Early Childhood Edn., Sacramento Affiliates, Amnesty Internat., Sierra Club, Delta Kappa Gamma, Phi Delta Kappa. Address: 5332 State Ave Sacramento CA 95819-1738

MCKINLEY, JOSEPH WARNER, health science facility executive; b. Champaign, Ill., Jan. 9, 1943; s. Lyle Warner and Eloise M. (Coleman) McK. BS, Georgetown U., 1968; MBA, George Washington U., 1973. Asst. adminstr. Weiss Meml. Hosp., Chgo., 1973-75; assoc. v.p. Rockford (Ill.) Meml. Hosp., 1975-78; v.p. ops. Phoenix Meml. Hosp., 1978-84, exec. v.p., CEO, 1984-88; exec. v.p. St. Francis Med. Ctr., Lynwood, Calif., 1988-90; CEO Meridian Point Rehab. Hosp., Scottsdale, Ariz., 1990-95, St. Agnes Med. Ctr./Nazareth Hosp., Phila., 1995-96; prin./owner Lawrenz Cons., Phoenix, 1996—. Capt. U.S. Army, 1968-71, Vietnam. Mem. Am. Coll. of Healthcare Execs., Ariz. Club. Republican. Episcopalian. Home: 6 Colonia Miramonte Paradise Valley AZ 85253

MCKINLEY, PATRICK, protective services official. Chief of police Fullerton, Calif. Office: 237 W Commonwealth Ave Fullerton CA 92632

MCKINNEY, JOHN GAGE, purchasing agent, writer; b. Oceanside, Calif., Apr. 21, 1951; s. Verlon David and Jacqueline Yvonne (Hughes) McK.; m. Linda Christine Brown, Dec. 29, 1974 (div. June 1979); m. Ilka Maria Weber, Aug. 1, 1986. BA in English, U. Calif., Berkeley, 1973; MA in English, U. Calif., Irvine, 1975. Gen. mgr., v.p. MacBeth Hardwood Co., L.A., 1975-81; pres. McKinney Hardwood Co., Mountain View, Calif., 1981-83; purchasing agt. Lockheed Missiles and Space Co., Sunnyvale, Calif., 1983-95, Recognition Sys., Inc., Campbell, Calif., 1995—. Author: Hardwood People, 1981, A High and Holy Place: A Mining Camp Church at New Alamader, 1997; editor: Four Mining Engineers, 1996. Recipient Lit. Arts award Montalvo Found., Saratoga, Calif., 1987, Calif. Essay award Calif. Pioneers, San Jose, 1991. Mem. Phi Beta Kappa. Episcopalian.

MC KINNEY, ROBERT MOODY, newspaper editor and publisher; b. Shattuck, Okla., Aug. 28, 1910; s. Edwin S. and Eva (Moody) McK.; married, 1943; 1 child, Mrs. Meade Martin; m. Marie-Louise de Montmollin, May 7, 1970. AB, U. Okla., 1932; LLD, U. N.Mex., 1964. Investment analyst Standard Stats. Co., Inc. (now Standard and Poor's Co.), 1932-34; ptnr. Young-Kolbe & Co., 1934-38, Robert R. Young & Co., 1938-42; exec. v.p., treas. Pathe Film Co., 1934-39, Allegheny Corp., 1936-42, Pittston Corp. and subs., 1936-42; v.p. Fremkir Corp., 1937-50, Allan Corp., 1937-50; exec. v.p., treas. Mo. Pacific R.R., 1938-42; ptnr. Scheffmeyer, McKinney & Co., 1945-50; editor, pub. Santa Fe New Mexican, 1949—; chmn. bd. The New Mexican, Inc., 1949—; profl. corp. dir. 10 N.Y.S.E. cos., 1934-86; chmn. Robert Moody Found.; chmn. N.Mex. Econ. Devel. Commn. and Water Resources Devel. Bd., 1949-51; asst. sec. U.S. Dept. Interior, 1951-52; chmn. panel to report to Congress on impact of Peaceful Uses of Atomic Energy, 1955-56; permanent U.S. rep. to Internat. Atomic Energy Agy., Vienna, 1957-58; U.S. rep. Internat. Conf. Peaceful Uses Atomic Energy, Geneva, 1958; U.S. ambassador to, Switzerland, 1961-63; exec. officer Presdl. Task Force on Internat. Investments, 1963-64; chmn. Presdl. Commn. on Travel, 1968; chmn. bd. visitors U. Okla., 1968-72; U.S. rep. Internat. Centre Settlement Investment Disputes, Washington, 1967-74. Author: Hymn to Wreckage: A Picaresque Interpretation of History, 1947, The Scientific Foundation for European Integration, 1959, On Increasing Effectiveness of Western Science and Technology, 1959, The Red Challenge to Technological Renewal, 1960, Review of the International Atomic Policies and Programs of the United States, 1960, The Toad and the Water Witch, 1985, Variations on a Marxist Interpretation of Culture, 1986. Served from lt. (j.g.) to lt. USNR, 1942-45. Recipient Disting. Service medal U.S. Dept. Treasury, 1968, Disting. Service medal U. Okla., 1972. Mem. Am. Soc. Newspaper Editors, Coun. Fgn. Rels., Coun. of Am. Ambs., Newspaper Assn. of Am., Phi Beta Kappa, Phi Gamma Delta. Democrat. Episcopalian. Clubs: Chevy Chase (Md.); Metropolitan (Washington); University, Brook, Century, Links, Knickerbocker, River (N.Y.C.). Home: Wind Fields 39850 Snickersville Tpke Middleburg VA 20117-3002 Office: PO Box 1705 Santa Fe NM 87504-1705

MC KINNON, CLINTON D., editor, former congressman; b. Dallas, Feb. 5, 1906; s. John C. and Tennie Clifdell (Hawkins) McK.; m. Lucille Virginia McVey, Oct. 15, 1932; children—Clinton Dan, Michael, Connie. A.B., U. Redlands, Calif., 1930, L.H.D. (hon.), 1967; postgrad., U. Geneva, Switzerland, 1930. Reporter, editor, advt. mgr. on various So. Calif. newspapers, 1931-35; pres., gen. mgr. Valley News Corp., North Hollywood, Calif., 1935-43; established San Fernando Valley Times, 1935, Los Angeles Aircraft Times, 1940, Long Beach Shipyard Times, 1941; established San Diego Daily Jour., 1944, editor, pub. and owner, 1944-48; co-owner Coronado Jour., 1953-72; owner Radio Sta. KSDJ (Columbia affiliate), San Diego, 1945-48; pres., editor and pub. Los Angeles Daily News, 1954; pres., gen. mgr. Alvarado Television Co., Inc., KVOA-TV, Tucson and KOAT-TV, Albuquerque, 1955-63; chmn. San Diego North Shores Pub. Co., San Diego, 1953-72, Sentinel Savs. and Loan Assn., 1963-69, San Diego Transit Co., 1966-71; sec. South Tex. Telecasting Co. Inc., 1963-79; Chmn. Indsl. Devel. Commn., San Diego, 1964-66, Econ. Devel. Corp., San Diego County, 1966-67, San Diego Urban Coalition, 1967-69; mem. Gov.'s Bus. Adv. Council, Calif. Bd. dirs. U. Calif., San Diego Sch. Medicine, 1979—; bd. dirs. Cancer Center Research Bd., U. Calif., San Diego, 1981—; Mem. 81st-82d Congresses from Calif.; vice chmn. Democratic State Central Com. of Calif., 1952-54. Recipient San Diego Golden Man and Boy award, 1968; San Diego Mayor's award of merit, 1971; named to San Diego Transit Hall Fame, 1987. Clubs: Rotarian, San Diego Yacht. Home: 1125 Pacific Beach Dr Apt 401 San Diego CA 92109-5155 Office: 945 Hornblend St San Diego CA 92109-4057*

MCKINNON, JAMES BUCKNER, real estate sales executive, writer, researcher; b. Tacoma, Dec. 5, 1916; s. James Mitchell and Rochelle Lenore (Buckner) McK.; m. Mary C. Corbitt, Dec. 1961 (div. June 1963); 1 child, James H.C.; m. Marylyn Adelle Coote, Mar. 12, 1967 (div. May 1977); 1 child, Michelyn; m. Martha Sackmann, June 12, 1977. BA in Internat. Studies, U. Wash., 1983, H.M. Jackson Sch. Police detective Los Angeles Police Dept., 1946-50; bn. security officer 1st med. bn. 1st Marine div. Fleet Marine Force, 1950-53; owner, operator, mgr., dir. promotional sales The Saucy Dog Drive-In, Venice, Calif., 1953-63; salesman new car sales and leasing Burien Mercury, Seattle, 1963-66; real estate salesman and appraiser various firms Seattle, 1966—; instr., lectr. U.S. Naval Support Activity, Sandpoint, Wash., 1964-74; mem., lectr. NRC 11-8, Naval Postgrad. Sch., Monterey, Calif., 1975-76; Burien Mercury announcer KOMO TV. Author: (poetry) On the Threshold of a Dream, Vol. III, 1992, Best Poems of the 90's, 1992; contbr. to anthologies: Where Words Haven't Spoken, 1993, Fire From Within, 1994; contbr. articles to various newspapers and mil. jours. Mem. br. adv. com. Wash. State YMCA, Seattle, 1994—, treas., 1986-94, 95, mem. so. dist. fin. bd., 1989-93, 94, 95-96. With USN, 1939-53, PTO, Korea. Recipient Wilmer Culver Meml. award Culver Alumni Fictioneers, Seattle, 1979, Silver Poet award World of Poetry Press, 1986, Golden Poet award, 1987-92, Best Poet of the 90's Nat. Libr. of Poetry, 1992, First Place with Editor's Preference award Creative Arts and Scis. Enterprises, 1996; Occidental Coll. scholar, 1935; named to Honorable Order Ky. Cols., 1976; named One of Best New Poets, Am. Poetry Assn. Anthology, 1988; inducted into the Internat. Poetry Hall of Fame, 1996. Mem. Internat. Soc. Authors and Artists (1st place award for 1997 poem), Internat. Platform Assn., U.S. Naval Inst. (life), Internat. Soc. Poets (life), N.W. Writers Conf., Ret. Officers Assn. (life), Mensa, Acad. Am. Poets, KP, Masons. Republican. Home: 2312 41st Ave SW Seattle WA 98116-2060 *Personal philosophy: To realize one's greatest potential pursue goals that hold the greatest potential meaning in life.*

MCKINNON, ROBERT SCOTT, swimming educator; b. Portland, Oreg., Oct. 27, 1937; s. Angus and Vivian Pearl (Moggey) McK.; m. Suzanne Reavely Cook, May 5, 1960; children: Christopher, Wendy. BE, U. Mont., 1961. Cert. H.S. English tchr., Mont. English tchr. Poplar (Mont.) Schs., 1961, Great Falls (Mont.) Pub. Schs., 1962-93; Amateur Athletic Union age group coach Great Falls (Mont.) Swim Team, 1962-71; swim instr. McKinnon Swim Sch., 1971-96; U.S. Swimming age group coach Gus' Guppies, Great Falls, 1979-86; swim coach Charles Marion Russell & Great Falls High Sch. Swim Teams, 1980-90. Author: Moose, Bruce and The Goose, 1969, reprint 1996, To Yellowstone: A Journey Home, 1975, Jesse's Hound, 1995, (play) Sport of Kings, 1960 (U. Mont. Playwriting award 1960), (movie) The River Busters, 1960, (musical) The Kissin River, 1961, (children's play) The Tooth Fairy Came to Gopher Gulch, 1996. Home: 1608 7th St S Great Falls MT 59405-4332

MCKINSTRY, LYDIA, chemistry educator; b. Albuquerque, May 7, 1966; d. William Weaver and Katherine (Angevine) McK. BS, Ft. Lewis Coll., Durango, Colo., 1989; PhD, Mont. State U., 1994. Postdoctoral rsch. fellow in chemistry Calif. Inst. Tech., Pasadena, 1994—; supr. nuclear magnetic resonance facility Mont. State U., Bozeman, 1992-93. Contbr. articles to Tetrahedron, Tetrahedron Letters, Jour. Organic Chemistry. Recipient Patricia Roberts Harris Chemistry Achievement award, 1991, others. Mem. Am. Chem. Soc., Beta Beta Beta, Kappa Mu Epsilon. Republican. Christian.

MCKNIGHT, GARY LEE, biochemist, researcher; b. Grants Pass, Oreg., Aug. 30, 1954; s. Raymond Leroy and Betty Louise (Sparks) McK.; m. Therese Anne Tutino, July 29, 1984 (div. Feb. 1990); m. Claire Joan Laush, Apr. 24, 1994. BS, Oreg. State U., 1976; MS, U. Rochester, 1979, PhD, 1981. Postdoctoral fellow U. Wash., Seattle, 1981-83, rsch. assoc., 1983-84; assoc. dir. ZymoGenetics, Inc., Seattle, 1984—. Contbr. articles to profl. jours. Mem. Am. Diabetes Assn. Office: ZymoGenetics Inc 1201 Eastlake Ave E Seattle WA 98102-3702

MCKNIGHT, LENORE RAVIN, child psychiatrist; b. Denver, May 15, 1943; d. Abe and Rose (Steed) Ravin; m. Robert Lee McKnight, July 22, 1967; children: Richard Rex, Janet Rose. Student, Occidental Coll., 1961-63; BA, U. Colo., 1965, postgrad. in medicine, 1965-67; MD, U. Calif., San Francisco, 1969. Diplomate Am. Bd. Psychiatry and Neurology. Cert. adult and child psychiatrist Am. Bd. Psychiatry. Intern pediatrics Children's Hosp., San Francisco, 1969-70; resident in gen. psychiatry Langley Porter Neuropsychiat. Inst., 1970-73, fellow child psychiatry, 1972-74; child psychiatrist Youth Guidance Center, San Francisco, 1974-74; pvt. practice medicine specializing in child psychiatry, Walnut Creek, Calif., 1974-93; asst. clin. prof. Langley Porter Neuropsychiat. Inst., 1974—; asst. clin. prof. psychiatry U. Calif. San Francisco Med. Ctr. Internat.; med. dir. CPC Walnut Creek (Calif.) Hosp., 1990-93. Insts. Edn. fellow U. Edinburgh, 1964; NIH grantee to study childhood nutrition, 1966. Fellow Am. Acad. Child and Adolescent Psychiatry; mem. Am. Coll. Physician Execs., Internat. Arabian Horse Assn., Diablo Arabian Horse Assn. Avocation: breeding Arabian Horses. Office: Kaiser Martinez Inpat Psych 200 Muir Rd Martinez CA 94553-4614

MCKNIGHT, STEVEN LANIER, molecular biologist; b. El Paso, Tex., Aug. 27, 1949; s. Frank Gillespie and Sara Elise (Stevens) McK.; m. Jacquelynn Ann Zimmer, Sept. 16, 1978; children: Nell, Grace, Frances, John Stevens. BA, U. Tex., 1974; PhD, U.Va., 1977. Postdoctoral fellow Carnegie Instn. Washington, Balt., 1977-79, staff assoc., 1979-81, mem. staff, 1984-92; co-founder, dir., dir. rsch. Tularik Inc., 1991—; prof., chmn. dept. biochemistry U. Tex. Southwestern Med. Ctr., 1995—; hon. prof. Johns Hopkins U. Contbr. articles to jours. in field. With U.S. Army, 1969-71, Vietnam. Decorated ARCOM medal; recipient Eli Lilly prize Am. Soc. Microbiology, 1987, Newcomb-Cleveland prize Sci. mag., 1989, NAS Molecular Biology award Nat. Acad. Sci., 1991. Fellow Carnegie Inst. Washington (hon.), Am. Soc. Microbiology (hon.); mem. NAS, Am. Acad. Arts and Scis., Am. Soc. for Biochemistry and Molecular Biology, Am. Soc. for Clel Biology, Japanese Biochem. Soc. (hon.). Home: 3717 Euclid Ave Dallas TX 75205 Office: U Tex Southwestern Med Ctr Dept Biochemistry 5323 Harry Hines Blvd Dallas TX 75235 Office: Tularik Inc Two Corp Dr South San Francisco CA 94080

MC KNIGHT, WILLIAM WARREN, JR., publisher; b. Normal, Ill., June 9, 1913; s. William Warren and Isabel Alida (Travis) McK.; m. Alice McGuire, Oct. 30, 1937; children: William Warren, III, Michael Joe, John James. B.S. in Bus. Adminstrn., Northwestern U., 1938. With McKnight Pub. Co., Bloomington, Ill., 1938-83; sec.-treas. McKnight Pub. Co., 1949-56, pres., 1956-67, chmn. bd., 1968-79; bd. dirs. Gen. Telephone Co. Ill., Champion Fed. Savs. & Loan Assn., chmn. bd. Pres. Bloomington Rotary Club, 1952, Bloomington C. of C., 1954; mem. Ill. Commn. Higher Edn., 1956-60; chmn. Bloomington-Normal Airport Authority, 1965-70, CETA Pvt. Industry Council Ill. Balance of State, 1979-81. Served with USNR, 1942-46. Recipient Disting. Service award Bloomington Kiwanis Club, 1963, Disting. Service award Normal C. of C., 1973; Good Govt. award Bloomington Jaycees, 1970; Edn. Constrn. award Edn. Council Graphic Arts Industry, 1974; Disting. Alumni award Ill. State U., 1978; Disting. Service award Spirit of McLean County, 1982; Disting. Service citation Epsilon Pi Tau, 1983; award of Merit Am. Vocat. Assn., 1990; disting. assoc. award Coun. on Tech. Tchr. Edn., 1995. Mem. Graphic Arts Edn. Assn., Internat. Tech. Edn. Assn., Nat. Assn. Indsl. and Tech. Tchrs. Educators, Ill. C. of C. (dir. 1964-69), Ill. Mfrs. Assn. (dir. 1954-62). Republican. Presbyterian. Clubs: Coll. Alumni, Bloomington Country. Home: 401 W Vernon Ave Normal IL 61761-3542 Home (winter): 7788 E Stallion Rd Scottsdale AZ 85258-3485

MCKUSICK, MARSHALL KIRK, computer scientist; b. Wilmington, Del., Jan. 19, 1954; s. Blaine Chase and Marjorie Jane (Kirk) McK.; domestic ptnr. Eric P. Allman. BSEE with distinction, Cornell U., 1976; MS in Bus. Adminstrn., U. Calif., Berkeley, 1979, MS in Computer Sci., 1980, PhD in Computer Sci., 1984. System designer Hughes Aircraft Co., 1977-79; software cons., 1982—; rsch. computer scientist U. Calif., Berkeley, 1984-93. Author: The Design and Implementation of the 4.4BSD Operating System, 1996 (trans. into German, 1997, Japanese, 1997, French, 1997); contbr. articles to profl. publs. Mem. IEEE, Usenix Assn. (Lifetime Achievement award 1992, pres. 1990-92, bd. dirs. 1986-92), Assn. Computing Machinery. Democrat. Office: 1614 Oxford St Berkeley CA 94709-1608

MCLAIN, WILLIAM ALLEN, lawyer; b. Chgo., Oct. 19, 1942; s. William Rex and Wilma L. (Raschka) McL.; divorced; children: William A., David M., Heather A.; m. Kristine R. Zierk. BS, So. Ill. U., 1966; JD, Loyola U., Chgo., 1971. Bar: Ill. 1971, U.S. Dist. Ct. (no. dist.) Ill. 1971, U.S. Ct. Appeals (7th cir.) 1971, Colo. 1975, U.S. Dist. Ct. Colo. 1975, U.S. Ct. Appeals (10th cir.) 1975. Law clk. U.S. Dist. Ct. (no. dist.) Ill., Chgo., 1971-

72; assoc. Sidley & Austin, Chgo., 1972-75; ptnr. Welborn, Dufford, Brown & Tooley, Denver, 1975-86; pres. William A. McLain PC, 1986—; ptnr. McLain & Singer, 1990—. Mem. Dist. 10 Legis. Vacancy Commn., Denver, 1984-86. Served with U.S. Army, 1966-68. Recipient Leadership and Scholastic Achievement award Loyola U. Alumni Assn., 1971. Mem. ABA, Colo. Bar Assn. (lobbyist 1983-85), Denver Bar Assn., Colo. Assn. Commerce and Industry (legis. policy coun. 1983-88), Colo. Mining Assn. (state and local affairs com. 1978-88), Inst. Property Taxation. Republican. Clubs: Mount Vernon Country Club, Roundup Riders of the Rockies. Lodges: Masons, Shriners, Scottish Rite, York Rite. Home and Office: 3962 S Olive St Denver CO 80237-2038

MCLAREN, ARCHIE CAMPBELL, JR., marketing executive; b. Atlanta, Sept. 25, 1942; s. Archie Campbell and Virginia Lynn (Sides) McL.; m. Georgia Mae Blunt, 1969 (div. 1971); 1 child, Leslie Michelle; m. Yvette Rubio, June 17, 1995. BA, Vanderbilt U., 1964; JD, Memphis State U., 1968. Clk. FBI, Memphis, 1965-66; tchr., tennis coach Memphis U. Sch., 1966-68; tchr. Hunt High Sch., Columbus, Miss., 1968-69; tennis coach Miss. State U., Starkville, Miss., 1968-69; concierge The Roosevelt Hotel, New Orleans, 1969-70; sales rep. West Pub. Co., St. Paul, 1970-84, adminstr. internat. mktg. The Orient, 1985-90; freelance wine cons., 1985—; cons. Calif. Ctrl. Coast Wine Growers Assn., Santa MAria, 1987-91; lectr. advanced wine appreciation Calif. Poly. U. Extended Edn., San Luis Obispo, 1986-90; dir. KCBX Ctrl. Coast Wine Classic, San Luis Obispo, 1985—, KHPR Wine Classic, Honolulu, 1987-91, Winesong, Ft. Bragg, Calif., 1987—. WETA Washington Wine Classic, 1989-90, KCRW Summerday, 1991; auction cons. Am. Inst. of Wine and Food, 1994—. Host talk show Pub. Radio Sta. KCBX, San Luis Obispo, 1984—; columnist (newspaper) San Luis Obispo Telegram-Tribune, 1992-95, New Times San Luis Obispo, 1995-96; contbg. writer: Adventures in Dining, 1994-95. Bd. dirs. Avila Beach County Water Dist., 1992-95, pres., 1992-94; bd. dirs. San Luis Obispo (Calif.) Mozart Festival, 1988-92, pres., 1991-92; dir. Internat. Festival Champagne and Sparkling Wine, 1992—, Santa Barbara Wine Auction, 1992-94, 97; mem. Avila Valley Adv. Coun., 1993-95; bd. dirs. Guild South County Ctr. for Performing Arts, 1993-94. Mem. Calif. Cen. Coast Wine Soc. (pres. 1985), Am. Soc. Wine Educators, German Wine Soc. Honolulu, Vintners Club San Francisco, Avila Bay Wine Soc., Cen. Coast Chaine des Rotisseurs (chpt. pres. 1987, 88, 89), Marin County Food and Wine Soc., Internat. Food, Wine & Travel Writers' Assn., Austrian Wine Brotherhood, Avila Bay Club, Pismo Beach Athletic Club. Office: PO Box 790 Avila Beach CA 93424-0790

MCLAREN, M(ALCOM) BRUCE, library director; b. Detroit, Nov. 17, 1940; s. Cameron G. and Pearl M. (Baker) McL.; m. Karlene M. Lamberton, Jan. 29, 1965; children: Cameron B., Kathleen M., Sean M. BA, Western Mich. U., 1963; MEd, Wayne State U., 1968. Libr., tchr. history Holly (Mich.) High Sch., 1963-65; resource ctr. coord. Waterford (Mich.) Mason Jr. High Sch., 1965-67; libr./media specialist Oakland County Ind. Sch. Dist., Mich., 1967-68; curriculum resource ctr. developer, asst. prof. edn. L.I. (N.Y.) U., 1968-71; dist. dir. media svcs. Wayne-Westland Schs., Mich., 1971-76; dir. Toles Learning Ctr. N.Mex. Mil. Inst., 1976—; vis. prof. Eastern Mich. U., 1975-76; vis. lectr. Eastern N.Mex. U., 1977-80; ednl. cons. U.S. Merchant Marine Acad., N.Y., 1980-81, Doyle & Assoc., Mich., 1973-76, The Baker & Taylor Co., N.Y., 1969-76, Lamar U., Tex., 1977-78, N.Mex. Ednl. Stds. Com., 1976-77, N.Mex. Commn. on Pub. Broadcasting, 1979-83. Contbr. articles to profl. jours. Chmn. Roswell Parks and Recreation Commn.; bd. dirs. Eastern N.Mex. Med. Ctr. Found., Am. Cancer Soc.; comdr. N.Mex. State Def. Force; host family Fgn. Exch. Student, 1992. Recipient Commendation award, 1985, 90, Meritorious Svc. award, 1985, Sch. Media Specialist Teamwork award, 1985, CLSI Online recognition, 1985, Seven Seals award U.S. Dept. Def., 1989, Svc. award, 1991, Centennial Commn. recognition, 1991; named Outstanding Mem. of Roswell Cmty. by RISD Bilingual Program, 1989. Mem. Assn. for Ednl. Comm. and Tech., Cmty. Coll. Assn. for Instrn. and Tech. (pres.), Broadcast Edn. Assn., Am. Assn. Cmty. Colls., Nat. Coun. Learning Resources and Instrnl. Telecomm. Consortium, Internat. TV Assn. Office: N Mex Mil Inst 101 W College Blvd Roswell NM 88201-5174

MCLARNAN, DONALD EDWARD, banker, corporation executive; b. Nashua, Iowa, Dec. 19, 1906; s. Samuel and Grace (Prudhon) McL.; m. Virginia Rickard, May 5, 1939; children: Marilyn, Marcia, Roxane. A.B., U. So. Calif., 1930; grad., Southwestern U. Law Sch., 1933; postgrad., Cambridge U. Trust appraiser, property mgr. Security-Pacific Nat. Bank, Los Angeles, 1935-54; regional dir. SBA for, So. Calif., Ariz., Nev., 1954-61; area adminstr. SBA for, Alaska, Western U.S., Hawaii, Guam, Samoa, U.S. Trust Terr., 1969-73; pres. Am. MARC, Inc. (offshore oil drillers and mfr. diesel engines), 1961-63, Terminal Drilling & Prodn. Co., Haney & Williams Drilling Co., Western Offshore, 1961-63; v.p., dir. Edgemar Dairy, Santa Monica Dairy Co., 1954-70; founder, pres., chmn. bd. Mission Nat. Bank, 1963-67; pres. Demco Trading Co., Mut. Trading Co.; dir. Coast Fed. Savs. & Loan; cons. numerous corps.; guest lectr. various univs. Contbr. articles on mgmt. and fin. to profl. jours. Chmn. fed. agys. div. Community Chest, 1956; nat. pres. Teachers Day, 1956; bd. councillors U. So. Calif.; founder, chmn., pres. Soc. Care and Protection Injured Innocent; adv. bd. Los Angeles City Coll.; bd. dirs. Calif. Easter Seal Soc.; nat. chmn. U. So. Calif. Drug Abuse Program. Recipient Los Angeles City and County Civic Leadership award, 1959. Mem. Nat. Assn. People with Disabilities (pres.); Mem. Skull and Dagger, Delta Chi. Clubs: Mason (Los Angeles) (K.T., Shriner), Los Angeles (Los Angeles), Jonathan (Los Angeles). Home: 135 S Norton Ave Los Angeles CA 90004-3916 Office: 1111 Crenshaw Blvd Los Angeles CA 90019-3112

MCLAUGHLIN, DIXIE GOERES, medical humanities administrator; b. Missoula, Mont., Feb. 9, 1962; d. Lee M. and Colette Y. (Manning) Goeres; m. Gary E. McLaughlin, Aug. 18, 1984. BA, U. Mont., 1985. Lic. ins. agt. Siegel Goeres & Assocs., Missoula, 1982-89; adminstrv. asst. Red Lion Hotels & Inns, Missoula, 1989-91; project coord. Inst. Medicine and Humanities, Missoula, 1991—; program dir. Mont. Com. for Humanities Grant, Missoula, 1994-96; mem. employee recommendation com. St. Patrick Hosp., Missoula, 1994—; mem. Ridge Libr. Com., Missoula, 1991—. Parking commr. Missoula Parking Commn., 1995-98; basketball coach YMCA. Grantee for program Mont. Com. for Humanities, 1994, 96. Mem. Soc. for Health and Human Values (presenter poster session 1992). Home: 203 Pattee Canyon Dr Missoula MT 59803 Office: Inst Medicine and Humanities Ste 242 500 W Broadway Missoula MT 59802

MCLAUGHLIN, JAMES DANIEL, architect; b. Spokane, Wash., Oct. 2, 1947; s. Robert Francis and Patricia (O'Connel) McL.; B.Arch., U. Idaho, 1971; m. Willa Kay Pace, Aug. 19, 1972; children: Jamie Marie, Robert James. Project architect Neil M. Wright, Architect, AIA, Sun Valley, Idaho, 1971-74, McMillan & Hayes, Architects, Sun Valley, 1974-75; now pres., prin. McLaughlin Architects Chartered, Sun Valley. Prin. works include Oakridge Apts., Moscow, Idaho (Excellence in Design award AIA), Walnut Ave. Mall, Ketchum, Idaho (Excellence in Design award AIA, 1987), McMahan Residence, Sun Valley (Excellence in Design award AIA, 1987). Chmn., Ketchum Planning and Zoning Commn., Ketchum Planning Commn., Ketchum Zoning Commn.; chmn. Sun Valley Planning and Zoning Commn.; vice-chmn. Idaho Archtl. Licensing Bd. Served to 1st lt. U.S. Army. Registered architect, 10 states including Idaho. Mem. AIA, Nat. Coun. Archtl. Registration Bds., Nat. Home Builders Assn., Ketchum-Sun Valley C. of C. (dir.). Roman Catholic. Club: Rotary. Prin. archtl. works include James West Residence, First Fed. Savs., Fox Bldg. Rehab., Walnut Ave. Mall, First St. Office Bldg. Home: PO Box 6 Lot # 5 Red Cliffs Subdivsn Ketchum ID 83340-0006 Office: McLaughlin Architects Chartered PO Box 479 Sun Valley ID 83353-0479

MCLAUGHLIN, JOSEPH MAILEY, lawyer; b. L.A., July 10, 1928; s. James Aloysius and Cecilia Ann (Mailey) McL.; m. Beverly Jane Walker, July 24, 1949; children: Stephen Joseph, Lawrence James, Suzanne Carol, Eileen Louise. JD, Loyola U., L.A., 1955. Bar: Calif. 1955, U.S. Supreme Ct. 1959. Mem. firm McLaughlin and Irvin, L.A., 1955—, San Francisco, 1969—; lectr. labor relations Loyola U., L.A., 1958-60, mem. bd. visitors law sch., 1987—; pres. Food Employers Coun., Inc., 1984-89; pres. L.A. Stock Exch., 1972. Contbg. author: Labor Law for General Practitioners, 1960. Served to 1st lt. USAF, 1951-53. Mem. San Francisco, Long Beach, Los Angeles County, Fed., Am., Internat., Inter-Am. bar assns., State Bar Calif., Am. Judicature Soc., Assn. Bus. Trial Lawyers, Am. Soc. Internat. Law, Calif. Club. Office: 818 W 7th St Ste 920 Los Angeles CA 90017-3432

MCLAUGHLIN, LINDA LEE HODGE, federal judge; b. 1942. BA, Stanford U., 1963; LLB, U. Calif., Berkeley, 1966. With Keatinge & Sterling, L.A., 1966-70, Richards, Martin & McLaughlin, Beverly Hills and Newport Beach, Calif., 1970-73, Bergland, Martin & McLaughlin, Newport Beach, 1973-76, Bergland & McLaughlin, Costa Mesa, Calif., 1976-80; judge North Orange County Mcpl. Ct., Fullerton, Calif., 1980-82, Orange County Superior Ct., Santa Ana, Calif., 1982-92, U.S. Dist. Ct. (ctrl. dist.) Calif., Santa Ana, 1992—; mem. adv. com. jud. forms Jud. Coun., 1978—, mem. adv. com. gender bias in cts., 1987-90. Active Edgewood Sch. Parents Assn., Cate Sch. Parents Aux.; mem. governing bd. Victim-Witness Assistance Program Orange County. Mem. Nat. Assn. Women Judges, Calif. State Bar Assn. (mem. com. profl. ethics 1976-80, disciplinary referee dist. 8 1978-80), Calif. Women Lawyers (gov. dist. 8 1978-80), Calif. Judges Assn. (chair civil law and procedure com. 1985-86), Orange County Bar Assn. (mem. com. adminstrn. justice 1975-78, client rels. com. 1978-80, com. jud. appointments 1979-80), Orange County Women Lawyers, Boalt Hall Alumni Assn., Stanford U. Alumni Assn., Cap and Gown Hon. Soc. Office: US District Court Rm 713 751 W Santa Ana Blvd Santa Ana CA 92701-4599*

MCLAUGHLIN, MARGUERITE P., state senator, logging company executive; b. Matchwood, Mich., Oct. 15, 1928; d. Harvey Martin and Luella Margaret (Livingston) Miller; m. George Bruce McLaughlin, 1947; children: Pamela, Bruce Jr., Cynthia. Owner, operator contract logging firm, Orofino, Idaho; mem. Idaho Ho. of Reps., 1978-80; mem. Idaho Senate, 6th term., asst. Dem. leader, 1990, 91, 92, 93; chair Democrat Caucus, 1995—. mem. Senate Fin. Com., 1987—, Gov.'s Adv. Coun. Workers Compensation, 1990—, State of Idaho Endowment Fund Investment Bd., 1991—, legis. coun., 1989-94, State of Idaho Job Tng. Coun., 1989—. Trustee Joint Sch. Dist. 171, 1976-80; pres. Orofino Celebration, Inc. Democrat. Roman Catholic. Office: Idaho State Senate State Capital Boise ID 83720*

MCLAUGHLIN, PETER DONALD, research scientist; b. Greenville, S.C., Sept. 17, 1946; s. Raymond Gerard and Marguerite (Prosser) McL.; m. Jacquelyn Kenna Cox, Oct. 27, 1967; 1 child, Michelle Dawn. BS in Aviation Mgmt., Embry-Riddle Aero. Univ., Dayton Beach, Fla., 1974; MS in Indsl. Engring., Kans. State Univ., 1980. Commd. 2d lt. U.S. Army, 1967; advanced through grades to lt. col. U.S. Army, 1983; tech. group mgr. Battelle-Seattle Rsch. Ctr., 1989—; ops. rsch. analyst TRADOC Sys. Analysis Agy., White Sands Missile Range, N.M., 1980-83; chief ops. rsch. office Army Devel. and Employment Agy., Fort Lewis, Wash., 1983-89. Office: Battelle 4000 NE 41st St Seattle WA 98105-5428

MCLEAN, AMY C., secondary school educator; b. Phoenix, Sept. 17, 1971; d. Charles Ross and Mary S. W. BA, Azusa (Calif.) Pacific U., 1993. Tchr. aid, lab asst. Azusa Pacific U., 1993-94; tchr. Faith Christian Acad., Arvada, Colo., 1994—; athletic trainer Faith Christian Acad., Arvada, 1994. Mem. Jour. Physical Edn. Recreation Dance, Alpha Chi.

MCLEAN, HUGH ANGUS, management consultant; b. Salt Lake City, Feb. 19, 1925; s. George Mark and Rose (Powell) McL.; m. Martha Lane Green, Nov. 23, 1949; children: Michael Hugh, Merrie Smithson. Student, U. Kans., 1943-44; BSME, Iowa State U., 1946; postgrad., U. Utah, 1946, 61-66. Registered profl. engr., Utah. With Utah Oil Refining Co., Boise, Idaho, Twin Falls, Idaho and Salt Lake City, 1953-61, Am. Oil Co., Salt Lake City and 11 western states, 1961-66; cons. Standard Oil (Ind.), Chgo., 1966-69; v.p. Mahler Assocs., Midland Park, N.J., 1969-76; pres. McLean Mgmt. Systems, Wyckoff, N.J., 1976-84, Heber City, Utah, 1984—. Author: There Is a Better Way to Manage, 1982, Developmental Dialogues, 1972, Career Planning Program, 1975; creator, host (TV) live shows and commls., 1956-57; creator stewardship mgmt. system, 1987. Rep. election judge, Salt Lake City, 1964, Operation Eagle Eye, Chgo., 1968; pub. communications dir. Ch. Jesus Christ Latter-Day Saints, N.Y. metro area, 1981-84; introduced SAFE HOMES in county and state, 1987; chmn. bd. dirs. Town Hall Playhouse, 1990-96; elected Daniel Twp. Planning and Zoning Bd., 1996—. Served to lt. (j.g.) USNR, 1943-46. Recipient Silver award Am. Petroleum Inst., 1957. Mem. Am. Soc. Tng. Devel. (chmn. N.Y. metro chpt. field trips 1972-74). Home: PO Box 251 Heber City UT 84032-0251 Office: McLean Mgmt Systems PO Box 251 Heber City UT 84032-0251 *Personal philosophy: How the critical decision-points are handled by the decision-makers in a business is the key to managing productivity, innovation, and leadership.*

MCLEAN, IAN SMALL, astronomer, physics educator; b. Johnstone, Scotland, Aug. 21, 1949; s. Ian and Mary (Small) McL.; (div.); 1 child, Jennifer Ann; m. Janet Wheelans Yourston, Mar. 4, 1983; children: Joanna, David Richard, Graham Robert. BS with hons., U. Glasgow, Scotland, 1971, PhD, 1974. Rsch. fellow dept. astronomy U. Glasgow, 1974-78; rsch. assoc. Steward Obs. U. Ariz., Tucson, 1978-80; sr. rsch. fellow Royal Obs. U. Edinburgh, Scotland, 1980-81, sr. sci. officer Royal Obs., 1981-86; prin. sci. officer Joint Astronomy Ctr., Hilo, Hawaii, 1986-89; prof. dept. physics and astronomy UCLA, 1989—, dir. Infrared Imaging Detector Lab., 1989—. Author: Electronic and Computer-Aided Astronomy: From Eyes To Electronic Sensors, 1989, Infrared Astronomy with Arrays: The Next Generation, 1994, Electronic Imaging in Astronomy: Detectors and Instrumentation, 1997; contbr. articles to profl. jours. Recipient Exceptional Merit award U.K. Serc, Edinburgh, 1989; NSF grantee, 1991, 93. Fellow Royal Astron. Soc.; mem. Internat. Astron. Union (pres. com. Paris chpt. 1988-91, v.p. 1985-88), Inst. Physics, Am. Astron. Soc. Office: UCLA Dept Physics & Astronomy 405 Hilgard Ave Los Angeles CA 90095-1562

MCLEAN, ROBIN JENNIFER, marketing, advertising professional; b. Denver, Dec. 15, 1960; d. Robert Earl and Marjorie Lee (Worland) McL. BA, U. Denver, 1983, postgrad., 1986—. Prodn. asst. Sta. KOA, Denver; advt. intern Colle & McVoy, Englewood, Colo.; advt. sales rep. Dow Jones & Co., Inc., Englewood, 1983-85; acct. exec. Univ. Graphics, Inc., Englewood, 1985-86; v.p. Columbine Mktg., Denver, 1986-90; acct. exec. Century Media, 1990-91; dir. advertising, mktg. Cherry Creek Locale, Denver, 1992-95; owner, investigator Alpine Investigations, 1995—; advisor U. Denver, 1985—; mktg. and pub. rels. cons. U.S. West, Inc. Mem. Denver Mus. of Natural History, Denver Botantical Gardens. Republican. Roman Catholic. Home: 270 Glencoe St Denver CO 80220-5716

MCLENDON, ROBERT, state legislator. Asst. minority leader dist. 5 Ariz. Ho. of Reps., Yuma, 1983—; mem. appropriations, edn., and rules coms. Democrat. Office: Ariz Ho Reps 777 N 14th St Yuma AZ 85364

MCLENNAN, GEOFFREY THOMAS, state agency real estate executive; b. Montreal, June 22, 1953; came to U.S., 1954; s. William Thomas and Mary V. (Fennessey) McL.; m. Constance Kendall, June 2, 1986; 1 child, Thomas. BA in Polit. Sci., U. Calif., Berkeley, 1971; student, Sacramento City Coll., 1981; MPA, Calif. State U., Sacramento, 1986. Cons. labor econs. Calif. Legislature, Sacramento, 1976-80; dep. commr. Dept. Real Estate, Sacramento, 1980-88; planning commr. City of Rocklin, Calif., 1988-93; exec. City of Rocklin Centennial, 1992-93; real estate officer State of Calif., Sacramento, 1988—; Judge of the Jubilee, City of Rocklin, 1993. Active Soc. for the Blind, Sacramento, 1986. Recipient Pub. Svc. award City of Rocklin, 1993, Svc. award Bldg. Industry Assn., 1988, Svc. award Safety Employees, 1988. Mem. Am. Soc. Pub. Adminstrn. (coun. 1986—, pres.-elect 1996—), Bldg. Owners and Mgrs. Assn. Roman Catholic. Office: Real Estate and Design Svcs 400 R St Ste 5000 Sacramento CA 95814-6200

MCLEOD, BRUCE ROYAL, electrical engineering educator, consultant; b. Greeley, Colo., Jan. 17, 1939; s. Royal and Alma McLeod; m. Peggy Sue Hubbard, Sept. 30, 1961; children: Robert Royal, Cathryn Elaine McLeod. BSEE, Colo. State U., 1961; MSEE, U. Colo., 1965, PhD in Elec. Engring., 1968. Elec. engr. light mil. electronics dept. GE Co., Utica, N.Y., 1961-64; rsch. engr. Boeing Aerospace Group, Seattle, 1968-70; asst. prof. elec. engring. Mont. State U., Bozeman, 1970-74, assoc. prof., 1974-79; owner, operator Spear Lazy U Ranch, Wilsall, Mont., 1974—; prof. Mont. State U., Bozeman, 1979-89, 90-96; head dept. elec. engring. Mont. State U., Bozeman, Mont., 1996—; pres. Life Resonances Inc., Bozeman, 1987—, cons., 1990—; vis. rsch. scientist Columbia Presbyn. Hosp., N.Y.C., VA Hosp., U. Ky. Med. Ctr., 1981-82; cons. Devel. Tech. Corp., Bozeman, 1972, Infosystems, Bozeman, 1972, La Jolla (Calif.) Tech. Inc., 1983-85, Finnegan, Henderson, Farabow, Garret & Dunner, Washington, 1983, 85-86, IatroMed Inc., Phoenix, 1989-90. Contbr. over 30 articles to profl. jours. and books; presenter over 35 abstracts at nat. & internat. meetings; invited spkr. in field; holder of 27 U.S. patents, 8 Australian patent, 2 Can. patent, 1 Japanese patent. Pres. Park County Legis. Assn., Livingston, Mont., 1988-90. Mem. IEEE (sr., chmn. Mont. sect. 1983-84), AAAS, Bioelectromagnetics Soc. (program com.), Bioelec. Repair and Growth Soc. (program com. 1985-86, chmn. program com. 1988-90, coun. 1986-88, pres.-elect 1990, pres. 1991), Nat. Cattleman's Assn., Park County Stockgrowers Assn., Masons, Shriners, Sigma Xi (v.p. Mont. State U. chpt. 1979-80, pres. 1980-81), Sigma Tau, Eta Kappa Nu, Kappa Mu Epsilon, Sigma Xi. Office: Montana State University Electrical Engring Dept Bozeman MT 59717-3780

MCLEOD, JOHN HUGH, JR., mechanical and electrical engineer; b. Hattiesburg, Miss., Feb. 27, 1911; s. John Hugh and Martha (Caldwell) McL.; m. Suzette Boutell, 1951; children: John Hugh III, Robert Boutell. BS, Tulane U., 1933. Registered profl. engr., Calif. Engr. various firms, 1933-39; field engr. Taylor Instrument Co., Rochester, N.Y., 1940-42; rsch. and devel. engr. Leeds & Northrup Co., Phila., 1943-47; sect. head guidance systems and guided missiles U.S. Naval Air Missile Test Ctr., Point Mugu, Calif., 1947-56; design specialist Gen. Dynamics/Astronautics, San Diego, 1956-63, cons., 1963-64; pvt. practice mech. and elec. engring. cons., La Jolla, Calif., 1964—; disting. vis. prof. Calif. State U. Chico, 1975; mem. exec. com. Fall Joint Computer Conf. Am. Fedn. Info. Processing Socs., 1965. Co-founder San Diego Symposium for Biomed. Engring., 1961. Author: Simulation: The Dynamic Modeling of Ideas and Systems with Computers, 1968, Computer Modeling and Simulation: Principles of Good Practice, 1982; editor, pub.: Simulation Council Newsletter, 1952-55; editor: Simulation, 1963-74; assoc. editor Instruments & Control Systems, 1955-63, Behavioral Sci., 1973—; tech. editor Simulation in the Service of Soc., 1971—; co-author: Large-Scale Models for Policy Evaluation, 1977. With USN, 1942-43. Recipient Sr. Sci. Simulation award Electronic Assocs., Inc., 1965, TIMS award Inst. Mgmt. Scis., 1986; NEH, NSF grantee, 1983; McLeod Inst. Simulation Sci. named in his honor at 18 acad. instns. including Calif. State U., Chico, 1991, U. Calgary, Can., U. Ottawa, Can., U. Ghent, Belgium, Istituto per la Recerca, Naples, Italy, Polish Acad. Scis., Warsaw, U. Edinburgh, Scotland, Beijing U. Aeronautics and Astronautics, Riga Tech. U., Latvia, Hungarian Acad. Scis., Budapest. Mem. IEEE, AAAS, Soc. Computer Simulation (chmn. com. on profl. ethics, publs. advisor, John McLeod award 1987). Home: 8484 La Jolla Shores Dr La Jolla CA 92037-3019 Office: Soc Computer Simulation PO Box 17900 San Diego CA 92177-7900

MCLEOD, SUSAN MARGARET, English language educator; b. Shreveport, La., Nov. 27, 1942; d. Milton Frederick and Margaret Ellis Herminghaus; m. Douglas B. McLeod, Dec. 28, 1965; children: Alison Marie, Jonathan Mark. BA, Principia Coll., 1964; MA, U. Wis., 1965, PhD, 1972. Lectr. Haile Selassie I U., Addis Ababa, Ethiopia, 1966-68; instr. San Diego State U., 1974-79, 81-86; assoc. prof. Wash. State U., Pullman, 1986-92, prof. English, assoc. dean, 1992-96, chair English dept., 1996—; mem. exec. com. Conf. on Coll. Composition and Comm., 1990-92, Coun. of Writing Program Adminstrs.; bd. cons. Nat. Network Writing Across the Curriculum Programs. Author: Notes on the Heart, 1997; editor: Strenghthening Programs for WAC, 1988, Writing About the World, 1991, 2d edit., 1994, WAC: A Guide to Developing Programs, 1992. Recipient Tchg. Excellence award Burlington No., 1989. Mem. MLA, Conf. Coll. Composition and Comm., Nat. Coun. Tchrs. English, Rocky Mountain MLA (pres. 1989-90). Office: Wash State U Dept English Pullman WA 99164-5020

MCLURKIN, THOMAS CORNELIUS, JR., lawyer; b. L.A., July 28, 1954; s. Thomas Cornelius and Willie Mae (O'Connor) McL.; m. Charmaine Bobo. BA, U. So. Calif., 1976, MPA, 1980, PhD in Pub. Adminstrn., 1997; JD, U. LaVerne, 1982. Bar: Calif. 1984, U.S. Dist. Ct. (ctrl. dist.) Calif. 1984, U.S. Dist. Ct. Hawaii 1984, U.S. Ct. Appeals (9th cir.) 1984, U.S. Dist. Ct. (ea., no. and so. dists.) Calif. 1985, U.S. Tax Ct. 1988, U.S. Ct. Mil. Appeals 1989, U.S. Army Ct. Mil. Rev. 1993, U.S. Supreme Ct., 1995. Law clk. Dept. Water and Power City of L.A., 1979-82; jud. clk. U.S. Dist. Ct. (cen. dist.) Calif., L.A., 1982-83; law clk. Office City Atty., L.A., 1983-84, Dep. City Atty., 1984—. Author (with others): Facts in American History, 1968, 2nd edit. 1989, Eagle Scout, 1970. Mem. L.A. World Affairs Coun., 1980—, Smithsonian Assocs.; bd. dirs. L.A. Area coun. Boy Scouts Am., Hillsides Homes for Children; provisional patron Tournament of Roses Assn., Pasadena, 1994—; mem. Verdugo Hills Area coun. Boy Scouts Am. Mem. ABA, ALA, L.A. County Bar Assn., Assn. Trial Lawyers Am., Langston Law Assn. L.A., Am. Soc. Pub. Adminstrs., U. So. Calif. Gen. Alumni Assn. (bd. govs. exec. bd. 1986-90), U. So. Calif. Black Alumni Assn.-Ebonics (pres. 1988-89), U. So. Calif. Pres.'s Cir., Elks, Am. Legion, Phi Alpha Delta, Kappa Alpha Psi. Republican. United Methodist. Office: LA City Atty Office Ste 340 111 N Hope St Los Angeles CA 90012-5701

MCMAHAN, LOIS GRACE, state representative; b. Culdesac, Idaho, May 14, 1942; d. Hugh Edwin Juliann and Martha Trimble (Crane) Norbo; m. Jerry Carl McMahan, Apr. 22, 1963; children: Rick Allan, William Titus, Juliana Crystal, Jeremy Carl, Ladeva Grace Martha. Diploma, Prairie Coll., Alberta, Can., 1963. Tchr. elem. sch. C.D. Somes Pub. Sch., Batchawana, Ont., Can., 1963-68, Morningside Christian Sch., Sioux City, Iowa, 1979; mem. Wash. Ho. of Reps., Olympia, 1995—. Precinct com. officer Kitsap County Rep. Party, Olalla, Wash., 1984-92; state committeewoman Wash. State Rep. Party, Bellevue, 1992-94. Named Woman of Yr., South Kitsap Rep. Party, 1996. Office: Ho of Reps PO Box 422 Gig Harbor WA 98335

MCMANIS, JAMES, lawyer; b. Haverhill, Mass., May 28, 1943; s. Charles and Yvonne (Zinn) McM.; m. Sara Wigh, Mar. 30, 1968. BA, Stanford U., Palo Alto, Calif., 1964; JD, U. Calif., Berkeley, 1967. Bar: Calif. 1967, U.S. Dist. Ct. (no. dist.) Calif. 1967, U.S. Ct. Appeals (9th cir.) 1967, U.S. Supreme Ct. 1971. Dep. dist. atty. Santa Clara County Dist. Atty., 1968-71; mem. McManis, Faulkner & Morgan, San Jose, Calif., 1971—; spl. master tech. equities litigation, 1987—; spl. examiner State Bar Calif., 1995—; prof. law Lincoln U. Law Sch., San Jose, 1972-82; lectr. Calif. Continuing Edn. of Bar, 1989-90; instr. U. Calif. Law Sch., 1992-96, Stanford U. Sch. Law, 1994-96. Pres. Santa Clara County Bar Assn. Law Found., 1996, dir., 1987—. Mem. ABA, State Bar Calif., Calif. Trial Lawyers Assn., Santa Clara County Bar Assn., Boalt Hall Alumni Assn. Office: McManis Faulkner & Morgan Inc 10th Fl 160 W Santa Clara St San Jose CA 95113

MCMILLAN, JOAN, poet; b. Burbank, Calif., June 7, 1959; d. David Gordon and Kathleen Joan (Indrisano) McM.; m. Dan Robert Barnett, Sept. 28, 1984 (div. Jan. 1997); children: Christopher, Stephanie, Emily, Matthew. BA, U. San Diego, 1981. Poet-in-schs. Spectra Arts-in-Edn., Santa Cruz, Calif., 1984-94; poet Santa Cruz, 1994—; ednl. rschr. Child Devel. Project, Salinas, Calif., 1993-94. Contbr. poems to profl. jours. Grantee Women's Assistance Fund, 1994-95. Democrat. Roman Catholic. Home: 11822 Lakeshore Dr Felton CA 95018

MCMILLAN, JOHN A., retail executive; b. 1931. BA, U. Wash., 1957. With Nordstrom Inc., Seattle, 1957—, exec. v.p., 1975—, pres., 1989—, co-chmn., 1991—, dir., 1995—. Office: Nordstrom Inc 1501 5th Ave Seattle WA 98101-1603*

MCMILLAN, LEONARD DAVID, family life specialist, consultant, lecturer; b. Harvard, Ill., Dec. 7, 1938; s. Pearly and Jean (Carter) McM.; m. Karen R. Meyer, Dec. 8, 1956; 1 child, Mitchel D. BA, Andrews U., Berrien Springs, Mich., 1972, MDiv, 1975; PhD, Ephraim-Moore U.-Theol. Sem., Holden, Mo., 1984. Dir. family life and youth Wis. Conf., 7th-day Adventist Ch., Madison, 1974-76; mem. Wash. Conf. 7th-day Adventist Ch., Bothell, 1976-83; mem. South African Union 7th-day Adventist Ch., Bloemfontein, 1983-84; pastor Upper Columbia Conf. 7th-day Adventist Ch., Spokane, Wash., 1984-86; dir. family life Potomac Conf. 7th-day Adventist Ch., Staunton, Va., 1986-95; dir. family life Pacific Health Edn. Ctr. Author: Why Can't My Mate Be More Like Me?, 1986, An Owner's Guide to Male Midlife Crisis, 1986, Person to Person, 1987, The Family of God and How to Live with Them, 1988, Slaying Your Dragons, 1989, Parentwise, 1993, ParentTeen, 1993, First Class Male, 1994, Putting Up with Mr. Right, 1996. With USAF, 1956-60. Mem. Am. Assn. Pastoral Counselors, Nat. Coun. on

Family Rels. (cert. family life educator), Assn. Adventist Family Life Profls. (pres. 1991-95), Am. Assn. Christian Conf. Office: Pacific Health Edn Ctr 5300 California Ave Ste 200 Bakersfield CA 93309 *In my opinion, all of life now and hereafter can be summed up in a single word: Relationships!.*

MCMILLAN, STEPHEN WALKER, artist; b. Berkeley, Calif., Dec. 21, 1949; s. Edwin Mattison and Elsie Walford (Blumer) McM.; m. Susan Irene Sanford, Mar. 25, 1989. BA in Art, U. Calif., Santa Cruz, 1972, BFA in Art, 1975. Artist Graphic Arts Workshop, San Francisco, 1975-79, Kala Inst., Berkeley, Calif., 1989-84, 87-92, Petaluma, Calif., 1993—; instr. aquatint etching Kala Inst., 1980-92. Artist, sculptor; creator over 225 aquatint etchings and 25 lithographs; exhibited work in over 40 galleries across the U.S. Recipient James D. Phelan Art Award in Printmaking, The San Francisco Found., 1995, 4th prize 3d Kochi (Japan) Internat. Triennial Exhbn. of Prints, 1996. Mem. Calif. Soc. Printmakers.

MCMILLAN, TERRY L., writer, educator; b. Port Huron, Mich., Oct. 18, 1951; d. Edward McMillan and Madeline Washington Tillman; 1 child, Solomon Welch. BA in Journalism, U. Calif., Berkeley, 1979; MFA, Columbia Univ., N.Y.C., 1979. Instr. U. Wyoming, Laramie, 1987-90; prof. U. Ariz., Tucson, 1990-92. Author: Mama, 1987, Disappearing Acts, 1989, Waiting to Exhale, 1992, How Stella Got Her Groove Back, 1996; editor: Breaking Ice: An Anthology of Contemporary African-American Fiction, 1990; screenwriter (with Ron Bass) (movie) Waiting to Exhale, 1995. Recipient National Endowment for the Arts fellowship, 1988.

MC MILLION, JOHN MACON, retired newspaper publisher; b. Coffeyville, Kans., Dec. 25, 1929; s. John Dibrell and Mattie Anna (Macon) McM.; m. Melanie Ann McMillion; children: John Thomas, Johanna, Jennifer, Amanda. Student, Vanderbilt U., 1947-49; B.S. in Journalism, U. Kans., 1956. Police reporter Amarillo (Tex.) Globe-News, 1956; sports editor, telegraph editor Grand Junction (Colo.) Daily Sentinel, 1956-58; mng. editor Alliance (Nebr.) Times-Herald, 1958-59, Clovis (N.Mex.) Jour., 1959-62; gen. mgr. Pasadena (Tex.) Citizen, 1962; bur. mgr. UPI, 1962-66; exec. editor Albuquerque Jour., 1966-69; bus. mgr. Albuquerque Pub. Co., 1971-75; pub. Herald and News-Tribune, Duluth, Minn., 1975-86, Akron (Ohio) Beacon Jour., 1986-90, ret.; campaign mgr. gubernatorial campaign, 1969-71. Served with USN, 1950-54. Address: 12404 Royal Oak Ct NE Albuquerque NM 87111-6237

MCMURDO, C(HARLES) GREGORY, state official, lawyer; b. Klamath Falls, Oreg., Apr. 30, 1946; s. Charles Andrew and Juanita Berniece (Bell) McM.; B.A., Oreg. State U., 1968; J.D., Lewis and Clark Coll., 1972. Bar: Oreg. 1972, U.S. Dist. Ct. Oreg. 1975, U.S. Ct. Appeals (9th cir.) 1980, U.S. Supreme Ct. 1984. Legal counsel Oreg. Ho. of Reps., Salem, 1972-76; asst. sect. state State of Oreg., Salem, 1976-81, dep. sec. state, 1981-85; mem. Workers Compensation Bd., 1985-88; dir of govt. rels, Metro, Portland, 1988-90; dep. supt. of pub. instrn., State of Oreg., 1990—. Mem. Oreg. State Bar. Republican. Episcopalian. Office: Oreg Dept of Edn Pub Svc Bldg 255 Capitol St NE Salem OR 97310-1341

MCMURTY, JUDY JEAN, school counselor; b. Denver, Apr. 5, 1939; d. Lonnie G. and Veva H. (Corlett) Pippin; m. Ray McMurty, Dec. 21, 1958; children: Jerry, Patricia, Michael, Suzan. BA, Adams State Coll., 1963; MA, Calif. State U., 1991. Cert. counselor, Calif. Tchr. Colo. Christian Schs., Denver, 1975-78; libr. media ctr. dir. Melodyland Schs., Anaheim, Calif., 1979-80, adminstrv. asst., 1980-85; counselor So. Calif. Christian Schs., Orange, 1985-88; tchr. Val Verde Unified Sch. Dist., Perris, Calif., 1988-91, counselor, 1991—, mem. crisis intervention team, 1993-94; adj. prof. Azusa (Calif.) Pacific U., summers 1992, 93; counseling dept. chair Vista Verde Mid. Sch., Moreno Valley, Calif., 1991-97; mem. grad. com. Rancho Verde H.S., Moreno Valley, 1991. Worship team instrumentalist Mission Cmty. Ch., Riverside, Calif., 1993-97, Christian Life Ctr., Riverside, 1991-93. Mem. Am. Counseling Assn., Calif. Sch. Counselors Assn., Riverside/San Bernardino County Counselors Assn., Am. Assn. Christian Counselors (charter). Republican. Office: Vista Verde Mid Sch 25777 Krameria St Moreno Valley CA 92551-2093

MCNALL, SCOTT GRANT, sociology educator; b. New Ulm, Minn., Jan. 16, 1941; s. Everett Herman and Dorothy Grant (Brown) McN.; m. Sally Anne Allen, Oct. 31, 1960; children—Miles Allen, Amy Ellen. BA, Portland State U., 1962; PhD, U. Oreg., 1965. Instr. sociology U. Oreg., Eugene, 1964-65; asst. prof. U. Minn., Mpls., 1965-70; from assoc. prof. to prof. Ariz. State U., Tempe, 1970-76; prof., chmn. dept. sociology U. Kans., Lawrence, 1976-89, prof, chmn. dept. Am. studies, 1989-90; dean coll. arts and scis. U. Toledo, 1990-94; provost, v.p. acad. affairs Calif. State U., Chico, 1994—. Author: The Sociological Experience, 1969, 3d edit., 1974, The Greek Peasant, 1974, Social Problems Today, 1975, Career of a Radical Rightist, 1975, (with Sally A. McNall) Plains Families: Exploring Sociology Through Social History, 1983, The Road to Rebellion, 1988; editor: The Sociological Perspective, 1968, 4th edit., 1977, Theoretical Perspectives in Sociology, 1979, Current Perspectives in Social Theory, 1980, 6th edit., 1985, Political Economy: A Critique of American Society, 1981, (jour.) Current Perspectives in Social Theory, 1980-87, (with others) Studies in Historical Social Change, 1986—, The Road to Rebellion: Class Formation and Kansas Populism, 1865-1900, 1988, (with Rhonda Levine) Bringing Class Back In, 1991, (with Sally A. McNall) Sociology, 1992; assoc. editor: The Am. Sociologist, 1975-78, Jour. Polit. and Mil. Sociology, 1982—; adv. editor: Sociol. Quar., 1969-72; contbr. articles to profl. jours. Fulbright lectr., Greece, 1968-69; East-West Center vis. fellow, 1978; Mid-Am. State U. Assn. vis. lectr., 1982-83; Fulbright grantee, 1983. Mem. Midwest Sociol. Soc. (pres. 1982-83), Am. Sociol. Assn. (chair Marxist sect. 1989-90), Pacific Sociol. Soc. Democrat. Congregationalist. Home: 520 Crestwood Dr Paradise CA 95969-3825 Office: Calif State Univ VPAA Office Chico CA 95929

MCNALLY, CONNIE BENSON, editor, publisher, antiques dealer; b. Chgo., May 8, 1936; d. Peter D. and Joanna (Savas) Agriostathes; m. m. Dick Benson Nov. 19, 1955 (div. Mar. 1961); 1 child, Douglas W.; William C. McNally, July 27, 1975. Student, Univ. Wis., 1954-55; BA, Baylor, 1962. Midwest supr. Slenderella Internat., Chgo., 1955-59; dir. John Roberts Powers Sch., Dallas, 1960-62; backgammon tchr., profl. Racquet Club, Palm Springs, Calif., 1969-75, La Costa (Calif.) Resort, 1973-75; antique dealer Palm Springs, 1975—; ptnr. Carriage Trade Antiques, 1975-78; owner, mgr. McNally Co. Antiques, 1978—; editor, pub. Silver Mag., Inc., Rancho Santa Fe, Calif., 1993—. Mem. Country Friends (vol. chair 1985-87, area dir. 1988-89, publicity chair 1990-91, program chair 1992-93, corr. sec. 1994-95, bd. dirs.), Social Svc. League la Jolla, Soc. Am. Silversmiths, Nat. Assn. Antique Dealers, Rancho Santa Fe Rep. Women's Club. Office: Silver Mag Inc PO Box 9690 6033L Paseo Delicias Rancho Santa Fe CA 92067

MCNALLY, JAMES HENRY, physicist, defense consultant; b. Orange, N.J., Dec. 18, 1936; s. James Osborne and Edith Maude (Jones) McN.; m. Nancy Lee Eudaley, July 4, 1976. B. in Engring. Physics, Cornell U., 1959; PhD in Physics, Calif. Inst. Tech., 1966. Staff mem. program mgr. Los Alamos (N.Mex.) Nat. Lab., 1965-74; asst. dir for laser and isotope separation tech. AEC/ERDA, Washington, 1974-75; assoc. div. leader, dep. for inertial fusion, asst. for nat. sec. issues Los Alamos Nat. Lab., 1975-86; dep. asst. dir. Arms Control and Disarmament Agy., Washington, 1986-88; dir. office staff Los Alamos Nat. Lab., 1988-90, Washington Inst., 1990-94; cons., 1990—; U.S. del. Geneva Conf. on Disarmament, 1969, 73, 74, Threshold Test Ban Treaty, Moscow, 1974, Nuclear Testing Talks, Geneva, 1986-88. Bd. dirs. Wilson Mesa Met. Water Dist., 1976-88; mem., v.p., pres. Mountain Canine Corps, 1994—. Recipient Meritorious Honor award Arms Control and Disarmament Agy., 1988. Mem. AAAS, Am. Phys. Soc., Internat. Inst. Strategic Studies. Home and Office: 550 Rim Rd Los Alamos NM 87544-2931

MCNAMARA, JOHN STEPHEN, artist, educator; b. Cambridge, Mass., Feb. 16, 1950; s. John Stephen and Mary (Adams) McN. BFA in Painting, Mass. Coll. Art, Boston, 1971, MFA in Painting, 1977. Tchr. Mus. Fine Arts Sch., Boston, 1983, 90-92; undergrad. and grad. painting tchr. Mass. Coll. Art, Boston, 1988; undergrad. painting tchr. Boston Archtl. Ctr., Boston, 1977; color fundamentals tchr. Mass. Coll. Art, Boston, 1987, undergrad. drawing, 1975-88; vis. lectr. San Francisco Art Inst., 1992, 93, U. Calif., Berkeley, 1993—. One-man shows include The Exhbn. Space at 112 Greene St., N.Y.C., 1982, Stavaridis Gallery, Boston, 1983-85, 86-89, Bess Cutler Gallery, N.Y.C., 1984, 85, 86, 88, Mass. Coll. Art, 1986, Honolulu Acad. Fine Art, 1987, Nielson Gallery, 1990, 92, Miller Block Gallery, Boston, 1995, others; exhibited in group shows at Boston Collects, Mus. Fine Arts, Stavaridis Gallery, 1986, Bess Cutler Gallery, N.Y.C., 1987, Am. Painters and Sculptors, Met. Mus. Art, N.Y.C., 1988, Resonant Abstraciton, Fuller Mus. Art, Brockton, Mass., 1989-90. Mass. Art and Humanities grantee, 1980, 83, 86, 89, Award in the Visual Arts grantee, 1982, Nat. Endowment Arts grantee, 1981; McDowell Colony fellow, 1985. Home: 2127 California St Berkeley CA 94703

MCNAMARA, KAY COPELAND, publishing executive; b. San Antonio, July 4, 1946; d. Joseph Bryson and Gladys (Ware) Copeland; m. Landon Schultz, Oct. 1, 1973 (div. Apr. 1975); m. Stephen McNamara, June 10, 1978; children: Christopher, Morgan. BA in Math. and Psychology, U. Tex., 1970; MPH, U. Tex., Houston, 1971. Alcohol and drug abuse adminstr. Tex. Dept. Mental Health and Mental Retardation, Austin, 1971-75; v.p. Marin Sun Printing, Inc., Mill Valley, Calif., 1978-93, Marin Solar Village Corp., Mill Valley, Calif., 1978—; gen. ptnr. Sunrise Investment Co., Mill Valley, Calif., 1980—; circ. mgr., prodn. mgr., advt. mgr., assoc. pub., pub. cons. Pacific Sun Pub., Mill Valley, 1990—. Treas. parent bd. Marin Country Day Sch., Corte Madera, Calif., 1989; mem. parent bd. San Francisco U. H.S., 1994—. Mem. Chi Omega. Democrat. Home: 2 Bradford Way Mill Valley CA 94941 Office: Pacific Sun Pub 21 Corte Madera Ave Mill Valley CA 94941-1800

MCNAMARA, STEPHEN, newspaper executive; b. Chgo., July 9, 1934; s. Robert Charles McNamara Jr. and Susan (Deuel) Shattuck; m. Hanne Morgensen Petterson, Feb. 21, 1960 (div. Aug. 1968); children: Lise, Natalie, Kevin; m. Kay Copeland, June 10, 1978; children: Christopher, Morgan. AB in Am. History, Princeton U., 1955. Reporter Winston-Salem (N.C.) Jour., 1955-57; sports writer Miami Herald, 1957-59; contbg. European editor Car & Driver, N.Y.C., 1960; asst. news editor, exec. sports editor, Sunday editor San Francisco Examiner, 1961-67; CEO, editor, pub. Pacific Sun, Mill Valley, Calif., 1967—; co-pub. The Ark, Tiburon, Calif., 1987—; pres. Marin Sun Printing Co., Mill Valley, 1967-93; mng. gen. ptnr. Sunrise Investment Co., Mill Valley, 1980—; vis. lectr. San Francisco State U., 1967; mem. innovation and planning commn. Calif. Dept. Edn., Sacramento, 1980; co-founder, pres. Marin Solar Village Corp., Mill Valley, 1976—, Marin Cmty. Video, Mill Valley, 1973-78. Mem. Soc. Profl. Journalists, Nat. Assn. Alternative Newsweeklies (pres. 1978-81), Calif. Assn. Alternative Newsweeklies (pres. 1990-92), Calif. Soc. Newspaper Editors (pres. 1985-86, bd. dirs. 1983-93), Calif. Newspaper Pubs. Assn. (bd. dirs. 1989-93), San Francisco Press Club (1st place newspaper writing award 1967, 3-2d place awards), Cap and Gown Club (Princeton U.). Democrat. Home: 2 Bradford Way Mill Valley CA 94941 Office: Pacific Sun Pub 21 Corte Madera Ave Mill Valley CA 94941-1800

MCNAMEE, STEPHEN M., federal judge; b. 1942. B.A., U. Cinn., 1964; M.A., J.D., U. Ariz., 1969. U.S. atty. Dist. of Ariz., Phoenix, 1985-90; judge U.S. Dist. Ct. Ariz., Phoenix, 1990—. Office: City of Phoenix US Court Hse & Fed Bldg 230 N 1st Ave Phoenix AZ 85025-3386*

MC NEALY, SCOTT, computer company executive; b. 1954. BA, Harvard U., 1976; MBA, Stanford U., 1980. Chmn., pres., chief exec. officer Sun Microsystems Inc., Mountain View, Calif.; with Rockwell Internat. Corp., Troy, Mich., 1976-78, sales engr.; staff engr. FMC Corp., Chgo., 1980-81; dir. ops. Onyx Systems, San Jose, Calif., 1981-82; chmn. bd., pres., CEO Sun Microsystems Inc., Mountain View, Calif., 1982—, now chmn. bd., pres., chief exec. officer, 1982, also dir., 1985. Office: Sun Microsystems Inc 2550 Garcia Ave Mountain View CA 94043-1109*

MCNEIL, DAVID JAMES, communications executive, marketing consultant; b. Torrance, Calif., Jan. 20, 1958; s. James Eugene and Nancy Anne (Williams) McN.; m. Sheryl Lillian Stark, Aug. 31, 1980. BA in Bus. Adminstrn. and Mktg., Calif. State U., Northridge, 1982. Pres. McNeil Glass Co., Westlake, Calif., 1978-81; coordinator mktg., pay-per-view devel. Group W Cable, Torrance, 1982-86; mgr. mktg., programming Daniels Cablevision, Arcadia, Calif., 1986, bus. mgr. pay-per-view, 1986; mgr. prodn. and devel. pay-per-view United Artists Entertainment, Inc., Glendora, Calif., 1986-89; asst. v.p. Calif. Casualty Mgmt. Co., Orange, Calif., 1989—; mktg. cons. Cornucopia Mktg. Co., Torrance, 1986-88, Golden Rule Mktg. Co., Torrance, 1986-88. Mem. Am. Mktg. Assn. (life), So. Calif. Mktg. Coun., Mensa, Torrance C. of C., Simi Valley Jaycees, Torrance Sister City Assn., Delta Sigma Pi (life). Home: 28879 Modjeska Canyon Rd Silverado CA 92676-9748 Office: Calif Casualty Mgmt Co 600 City Pkwy W Ste 500 Orange CA 92868-2946

MCNEIL, DEE DEE, singer, songwriter; b. Detroit; d. Frank Lawton and Mary V. (Graham) Elkins; children: Maricea, Harry IV, William Chappell. Owner, adminstr. Double Dee Pub. & Prodn. Co., Encinitas, Calif.; owner Dee Square Record Co., Studio City, Calif. Author: (children's poetry) Dee Dee Doodles, 1972, Griot's Works, 1972; contbr. revs., articles, poetry to numerous anthologies, mags.; songwriter for various rec. artists, including Discover Me (And You'll Discover Love) for Diana Ross & The Supremes, Feel Free for the Four Tops, Flower Child for David Ruffin, There'll Always Be Forever for Nancy Wilson, What Is a Man? for The Four Tops, Why Girl for Precisions, numerous others; songwriter, artist (CD) Where Can Our Leaders Be?, 1994. Recipient Cert. of Merit, Am. Song Festival, 1977, Hon. Mention award Iliad Lit. Awards Program, 1992. Fellow Internat. Acad. Poets (founder); mem. Internat. Assn. Jazz Educators, Jazz Heritage Found. (life), 88 Club of KLON Jazz Sta. Office: Double Dee Pub & Prodn Co 132 El Camino Real # 154 Encinitas CA 92024

MCNEIL, JOHN STUART, publisher; b. L.A., Oct. 17, 1935; s. Murray Charles and Helen Katherine (Curtis) McN.; divorced; children: Elizabeth Ann, Kenneth John, Karen Lynn. BS, San Jose State U., 1962. Asst. dean for fiscal affairs U. Hawaii Sch. Medicine, Honolulu, 1968-72; fiscal officer Postgrad. Med. Edn. Program for Ryukyus, Honolulu, 1968-72; bus. mgr. Ann. Revs., Inc., Palo Alto, Calif., 1962-68, chief exec. officer, 1973-81; sec.-treas. Ann. Revs., Inc., Palo Alto, 1973—, pub., 1981—; lectr. on econs. sci. book pub., 1973—; mem. adv. coun. Astron. Soc. Pacific, 1991—; trustee Soc. for Promotion Sci. and Scholarship, 1982—. Vol. United Way Santa Clara County, San Jose, 1988—. With USN, 1954-56. Mem. Internat. Group Sci., Tech. and Med. Pubs., Bookbuilders West. Democrat. Office: Ann Revs Inc PO Box 10139 Palo Alto CA 94303-0139

MCNICHOLS, ROBERT RAY, forester; b. Columbus, Ohio, Oct. 16, 1950; s. Ralph Curtis and Martha Elizabeth (Payne) McN.; m. Paula Marie Thompson, Nov. 9, 1968; children: Kevin Matthew, Melissa Marie. A in Applied Sci., Hocking Tech. Coll., Ohio, 1970; B in Gen. Studies, Ohio Univ., 1977. Cert. economic developer. Forestry technician U.S. Forest Svc., Delaware, Ohio, 1969-78; natural resources mgr. Bur. Indian Affairs, Peach Springs, Ariz., 1978—; owner, pres., cons., contractor Native Am. Resources Network, Kingman, Ariz., 1995—. mem. Am. Econ. Devel. Coun., Soc. Am. Foresters, Soc. Range Conservation. Republican. Baptist. Home & Office: Native Am Resources Network 2175 Seneca St Kingman AZ 86401

MCNULTY, FRANCIS ROBERT, writer, graphic artist; b. Chgo., Apr. 5, 1938; s. Frank and Evelyn (Brown) McN.; m. Mary Loretta Farris, Dec. 28, 1963; children: Patricia, Margaret, Elizabeth. Student, Loyola U., 1958-60, Am. Acad. Art, Chgo., 1968-73. Graphic artist various cos., Chgo., 1970-91, art dir., 1975-91; co-owner, v.p. TLA, Omega Studios, Chgo., 1972-82; writer Chgo. and Ariz., 1982—. Author: Black Cats and Blue Birds, 1995. With U.S. Army, 1963-65. Republican. Roman Catholic. Home: 15233 S 15th Ave Phoenix AZ 85045

MCNUTT, STEPHEN RUSSELL, volcanologist, geophysical scientist; b. Hartford, Conn., Dec. 21, 1954; s. Elmer Ellsworth and Leona (LaPointe) McN. BA, Wesleyan U., Middletown, Conn., 1977; MA, Columbia U., 1982, MPhil, 1984, PhD, 1985. Sr. seismologist Calif. Div. Mines and Geology, Sacramento, 1984-91; rsch. prof. U. Alaska, Fairbanks, 1991—; cons. U. Costa Rica, San José, 1982—, U. Nat. Automata de Mexico, 1994—. Contbr. articles to profl. jours. Mem. Seismol. Soc. Am., Am. Geophys. Union, Internat. Assn. Volcanology and Chemistry of Earth's Interior (U.S. nat. com. chmn. 1996—), Buffalo Chips Running Club (Sacramento, bd. dirs. 1986-90). Democrat. Roman Catholic. Office: U Alaska Geophys Inst Alaska Volcano Obs PO Box 757320 Fairbanks AK 99775-7320

MCPEAK, WILLIAM JOHN, science and technical author, consultant; b. Glendale, Calif., Dec. 8, 1948; s. John Joseph and Grace Marie (Mosley) McP.; m. Yvette Sheree Richardson, Mar. 17, 1979; 1 child, Logan William. BA in Atmospheric Sci., U. Calif., L.A., 1971; MA in History of Sci., Pepperdine U., 1977. Cert. Calif. coll. instrnl.-engring. and history. Meteorologist USAF Air Weather Svc., Omaha, 1972-76; mem. tech. staff Hughes Aerospace, El Segundo, Calif., 1978—; grant reviewer sci., soc. and tech. program NSF, Washington, 1992—. Contbg. author encys. and periodicals. With USAF, 1972-76. Mem. Am. Geophys. Union (atmospheric sect., assoc. history of geophysics com. 1997), Inst. for Hist. Study, History of Sci. Soc. (book reviewer 1990—). Home: 25215 Miles Ave Lake Forest CA 92630-4122

MCPHADEN, MICHAEL JAMES, oceanographer, educator; b. Buffalo, N.Y., Oct. 22, 1950; s. William Francis and Irene (Scholl) McP.; m. Elisabeth Boice, Aug. 14, 1982; 1 child, Megan Boice. BS magna cum laude, SUNY, Buffalo, 1974; PhD in Phys. Oceanography, U. Calif., San Diego, 1980. Postdoctoral fellow Nat. Ctr. for Atmospheric Rsch., Boulder, Colo., 1980-82; rsch. asst. prof. Sch. Oceanography U. Wash., Seattle, 1984-86, from affiliate asst. prof. to affiliate assoc. prof., 1988-93, affiliate prof., 1993—; oceanographer NOAA-Pacific Marine Environ. Lab., Seattle, 1986—; dir. Tropical Atmosphere Ocean Array project office, Seattle, 1992—; vis. rsch. scientist Joint Inst. Study of Atmosphere and Ocean U. Wash., 1982-84; mem./chmn. various nat. and internat. sci. coms. overseeing ocean climate rsch. Contbr. numerous sci. articles to profl. publs. Mem. Am. Geophys. Union, Am. Meteorol. Soc., The Oceanography Soc., Phi Beta Kappa. Office: Pacific Marine Environ Lab 7600 Sand Point Way NE Seattle WA 98115-6349

MC PHERSON, ROLF KENNEDY, clergyman, church official; b. Providence, Mar. 23, 1913; s. Harold S. and Aimee (Semple) McP.; m. Lorna De Smith, July 21, 1931 (dec.); children—Marlene (dec.), Kay; m. Evangeline Carmichael, Jan. 31, 1997. Grad., So. Cal. Radio Inst., 1933; D.D. (hon.), L.I.F.E. Bible Coll., 1944; LLD (hon.), L.I.F.E. Bible Coll., Los Angeles, 1988. Ordained to ministry Internat. Ch. Foursquare Gospel, 1940. Pres. Internat. Ch. Foursquare Gospel, L.A., 1944-88, dir., 1944-92; pres. emeritus, 1988—; pres., dir. L.I.F.E. Bible Coll., Inc., L.A., 1944-88. Mem. Echo Park Evangelistic Assn. (pres. 1944—). Office: Internat Ch Foursquare Gospel 1910 W Sunset Blvd Ste 200 Los Angeles CA 90026-0176

MCQUERN, MARCIA ALICE, newspaper publishing executive; b. Riverside, Calif., Sept. 3, 1942; d. Arthur Carlyle and Dorothy Louise (Krupke) Knopf; m. Lynn Morris McQuern, June 7, 1969. BA in Polit. Sci., U. Calif., Santa Barbara, 1964; MS in Journalism, Northwestern U., 1966. Reporter The Press-Enterprise, Riverside, 1966-72, city editor, 1972-74, capitol corrs., 1975-78, dep. mng. editor news, 1984-85, mng. editor news, 1985-87, exec. editor, 1988-94, pres., 1992—; editor, publisher, 1994—; asst. metro editor The Sacramento Bee, 1974-75; editor state and polit. news The San Diego Union, 1978-79, city editor, 1979-84; juror Pulitzer Prize in Journalism, 1982, 83, 92, 93. Mem. editorial bd. Calif. Lawyer mag., San Francisco, 1983-88. Bd. advisors U. Calif.-Berkeley Grad. Sch. Journalism, 1991-96, U. Calif.-Riverside Grad. Sch. Mgmt., 1994—; pres. Riverside Cmty. Coll. Found., 1996; bd. trustees U. Calif. Riverside, 1996—. Recipient Journalism award Calif. State Bar Assn., 1967, Sweepstakes award Twin Counties Press Club, Riverside and San Bernardino, 1972, Athena award YWCA, 1994. Mem. Am. Soc. Newspaper Editors (bd. dirs. 1992—), Calif. Soc. Newspaper Editors (bd. 1988-95), Calif. Newspaper Pubs. Assn. (bd. dirs. 1992—), Calif. Press Assn. (bd. dirs. 1996—), Soc. Profl. Journalists, U. Calif.-Santa Barbara Alumni Assn. (bd. dirs. 1983-89). Home: 5717 Bedford Dr Riverside CA 92506-3404 Office: Press-Enterprise Co 3512 14th St Riverside CA 92501-3814

MCQUILKIN, GEOFFREY JAMES, communications director; b. Pasadena, Calif., Mar. 21, 1969; s. George H. McQuilkin and Sally Barngrove. BA magna cum laude, Harvard U., 1991. Program coord. Mono Lake Com., Lee Vining, Calif., 1992-94; comm. dir. Mono Lake Com., Lee Vining, 1994—. Editor: (book series) Mono Lake Field Guide Series, 1994—; editor Mono Lake Newsletter, 1994—. Firefighter Lee Vining (Calif.) Vol. Fire Dept., 1994—. Mem. Am. Soc. Environ. History. Home: PO Box 451 Lee Vining CA 93541-0451 Office: Mono Lake Com PO Box 29 Lee Vining CA 93541

MCQUILLIN, RICHARD ROSS, management consultant; b. Elyria, Ohio, Oct. 15, 1956; s. Wayne Rupp and Frana Rose (Romp) McQ.; m. Riko K. McQuillin; 1 child, Richard K. BS, Ohio State U., 1979; MS, U. So. Calif., L.A., 1983; MBA, UCLA, 1990. Sr. staff mem. TRW Inc., Redondo Beach, Calif., 1979-88; sr. cons. Deloitte & Touche, L.A., 1990-91; cons. mgr. NetBase Computing, Torrance, Calif., 1993—. Treas., controller Patio Creek Homeowners Assn., Torrance, Calif., 1986-91, pres. 1991—; pres. TRW Investment Club, Redondo Beach, 1984-87. UCLA fellow, 1989. Mem. IEEE, Beta Gamma Sigma. Home: 19028 Entradero Ave Torrance CA 90503-1360 Office: NetBase Computing Inc 3625 Del Amo Blvd Ste 220 Torrance CA 90503-1691

MCRAE, HAMILTON EUGENE, III, lawyer; b. Midland, Tex., Oct. 29, 1937; s. Hamilton Eugene and Adrian (Hagaman) McR.; m. Betty Hawkins, Aug. 27, 1960; children: Elizabeth Ann, Stephanie Adrian, Scott Hawkins. BSEE, U. Ariz., 1961; student, USAF Electronics Sch., 1961-62; postgrad., U. Redlands, Calif., 1962-63; JD with honors and distinction, U. Ariz., 1967; LHD (hon.), Sterling Coll., 1992; vis. fellow, Darwin Coll. and Martin Ctr., Cambridge (Eng.) U. Bar: Ariz. 1967, U.S. Supreme Ct. 1979; cert. real estate specialist, Ariz. Elec. engr. Salt River Project, Phoenix, 1961; assoc. Jennings, Strouss & Salmon, Phoenix, 1967-71, ptnr., 1971-85, chmn. real estate dept., 1980-85, mem. policy com., 1982-85, mem. fin. com., 1981-85, chmn. bus. devel. com., 1982-85; ptnr. and co-founder Stuckey & McRae, Phoenix, 1985—; co-founder, chmn. bd. Republic Cos., Phoenix, 1985—; magistrate Paradise Valley, Ariz., 1983-85; juvenile referee Superior Ct., 1983-85; pres., dir. Phoenix Realty & Trust Co., 1970—; officer Indsl. Devel. Corp. Maricopa County, 1972-86; instr. and lectr. in real estate; officer, bd. dirs. other corps.; adj. prof. Frank Lloyd Wright Sch. Architecture, Scottsdale, Ariz., 1989—; instr. Ariz. State U. Coll. Architecture and Environ. Design; lead instr. ten-state-bar seminar on Advanced Real Estate Transactions, 1992; evaluation com. for cert. real estate specialist Ariz. Bar, 1994-96; mem. real estate adv. commn. Ariz. Bar, 1996—. Exec. prodr. film documentary on relief and devel. in Africa, 1990; contbr. articles to profl. jours. Elder Valley Presbyn. Ch., Scottsdale, Ariz., 1973-75, 82-85, 96—, chair evangelism com. 1973-74, corp. pres., 1974-75, 84-85, trustee, 1973-75, 82-85, chmn. exec. com., 1984, mem. mission com. 1993—; trustee Upward Found., Phoenix, 1977-80, Valley Presbyn. Found., 1982-83, Ariz. Acad., 1971—; trustee, mem. exec. com. Phi Gamma Delta Ednl. Found., Washington, 1974-84; trustee Phi Gamma Delta Internat., 1984-86; bd. dirs. Archon, 1986-87; founder, trustee, pres. McRae Found., 1980—; bd. dirs. Food for Hungry Inc. (Internat. Relief), 1985-95, exec. com., 1986—, chmn. bd. dirs., 1987-92; chmn. bd. dirs. Food for Hungry Internat., 1993-95, pres. adv. coun., 1995—; trustee, mem. exec. com. Ariz. Mus. Sci. and Tech., 1984—, 1st v.p., 1985-86, pres., 1986-88, chmn. bd. dirs., 1988-90; Lambda Alpha Internat. Hon. Land Econs. Soc, 1988—; sec.-treas. Ariz. State U. Coun. for Design Excellence, 1989-90, bd. dirs. 1988—, pres. 1990-91; mem. Crisis Nursery Office of the Chair, 1988-89, Maricopa Community Colls. Found., 1988—, sec. 1990-91, 2d v.p. 1993-94, 1st v.p. and pres. elect 1994-95, pres. 1995—, capital campaign cabinet, 1995-96, mem. nominating com., 1997, Phoenix Cmty. Alliance, 1988-90, Interchurch Ctr. Corp., 1987-90, Western Art Assocs., bd. dirs., 1989-91, Phoenix Com. on Fgn. Rels., 1988—, U. Ariz. Pres.'s Club, 1984—, chmn., 1991-92; bd. dirs. Econ. Club of Phoenix, 1987— , sec.-treas., 1991-92, v.p., 1992-93, pres. 1993-94; bd. dirs. Ctrl. Ariz. Shelter Svcs., 1995—, Ariz. Community Found., 1996—, investing com., 1996—; founding mem. Alliance to Abolish Homelessness, 1996—, bd. dirs., 1996—, mem. exec. com., 1996—; mem. adv. bd. Help Wanted USA, 1990-92; vol. fund raiser YMCA, Salvation Army, others; bd. dirs. Frank Lloyd Wright Found., 1992—; mem. Taliesin Coun., 1985—; bd. dirs. Taliesin Arch., 1992—, Taliesin Conservation Com. (Wis.); founding mem. Frank Lloyd Wright Soc., 1993—; mem. fin. com. Kyl for Congress, 1985-92, bd. dir. campaign bd. Kyl for U.S. Senate, 1993-94; Senator Kyl Coun., 1995—; campaign com. Symington for Gov. '90, 1989—, mem. gubernatorial adv. bd., 1990-91; mem. Gov.'s Selection Com. for State Revenue Dir., 1993; mem. bond com. City of Phoenix, 1987-88; mem. Ariz. State U. Coun. of 100, 1985-89, investment com., 1985-89; bd. govs. Twelve Who Care Hon Kachina, 1991; mem. adv. coun. Maricopa County Sports Authority, 1989-93; mem. Ariz. Coalition for Tomorrow, 1990-92; founding mem., bd. dite Not Inc., 1992-96, pres., 1990-92, chmn., 1992-94, adv. bd. 1996—; bd. dirs. Garden Homes at Teton Pines Home Owners Assn., 1996—; selected as bearer for the Olympic Torch Relay Team, 1996. 1st lt. USAF, 1961-64,. Recipient various mil. award. Mem. ABA, AIEE, AIME, Ariz. Bar Assn., Maricopa County Bar Assn., U. Ariz. Alumni Assn., Nat. Soc. Fund Raising Execs., Clan McRae Soc. N.Am. Phoenix Exec. Club, Internat. Platform Assn., Am. Friends of the U. Cambridge (Eng.), Jackson Hole Racquet Club, Teton Pines Country Club, Tau Beta Pi. Republican. Home: 8101 N 47th St Paradise Valley AZ 85253-2907 Office: Republic Cos 2425 E Camelback Rd Ste 900 Phoenix AZ 85016-4215

MCRAE, MARION ELEANOR, critical care nurse; b. Kingston, Ont., Can., Sept. 19, 1960; d. James Malcolm and Madeline Eleanor (MacNamara) McR. BSN, Queen's U., Kingston, 1982; MSN, U. Toronto, 1989. RN, Calif., CCRN; cert. BCLS, ACLS, PALS. Staff nurse thoracic surgery Toronto (Can.) Gen. Hosp., 1982-83, staff nurse cardiovascular ICU, 1983-85; nurse clinician critical care St. Michael's Hosp., Toronto, 1985-87; external critical care clin. tchr. Ryerson Poly. Inst., Toronto, 1986-87; staff nurse cardiovascular ICU The Toronto Hosp.-Toronto Gen. Divsn., 1987-89; clin. nurse specialist cardiac surgery The Toronto Hosp., 1989-90; clin. nurse II cardiothoracic ICU UCLA Med. Ctr., 1990-92, clin. nurse III cardiothoracic ICU, 1992—; mem. critical care nursing adv. bd. George Brown Coll., Toronto, 1987-88. Contbr. articles to profl. nursing jours. Recipient Open Master's fellowship U. Toronto, 1987-88, M. Keyes bursary Toronto Gen. Hosp., 1988-89, Nursing fellowship Heart and Stroke Found. Ont., 1988-89, Outstanding Svc. award UCLA Med. Ctr., 1994, Cardiothoracic ICU Nurse of Yr. award UCLA, 1995. Mem. AACN, Am. Heart Assn. Coun. on Cardiovascular Nursing. Home: 1400 Midvale Ave Apt 210 Los Angeles CA 90024-5498 Office: UCLA Med Ctr Cardiothoracic ICU 10833 Le Conte Ave Los Angeles CA 90095

MCREE, DUNCAN EVERETT, molecular biologist, researcher; b. San Francisco, Feb. 5, 1957; s. John Everett and Joan Marie (Kilburn) McR.; m. Janice Anne Yuwiler, May 15, 1983; children: Alexander Marc, Kevin Lawrence. BS, U. Calif., Davis, 1978; PhD in Biochemistry, Duke U., 1984. Helen Hay Whitney fellow The Scripps Rsch. Inst., La Jolla, Calif., 1985-89, asst. mem., 1989—. Author: Practical Protein Crystallography, 1993, (software) Xtal View, 1992. Calif. State scholar, 1975-77; NIH grantee, 1990-96. Office: The Scripps Rsch Inst MB4 10666 N Torrey Pines Rd La Jolla CA 92037-1027

MCVAY, JOHN EDWARD, professional football club executive; b. Bellaire, Ohio, Jan. 5, 1931; s. John A. and Helen (Andrews) McV.; m. Eva Lee; children: John R., James P., Timothy G. B.S. in Edn., Miami U., Oxford, Ohio, 1953; M.A. in Sch. Adminstrn., Kent (Ohio) State U., 1963. Asst. football coach, instr. phys. edn. Mich. State U., 1962-65; head coach, dir. athletics U. Dayton, Ohio, 1965-74; head coach, gen. mgr. Memphis in World Football League, 1974-76; head football coach N.Y. Giants, NFL, 1976-78; dir. player pers. San Francisco 49ers, NFL, 1979-80, dir. football ops., 1980-81, v.p. adminstrn., 1981-83, gen. mgr., v.p., 1983-89, v.p. football ops., 1990-96; prin. McVay Sports Cons. Inc., Sanibel, Fla., 1996—. Exec. dir. Catholic Youth Council, Canton, Ohio, 1959-62. Recipient Disting. Citizen award Massillon H.S., 1996; named to Miami U. Athletic Hall of Fame; named NFL Exec. of Yr., 1989. Mem. Sigma Chi (Significant Sig award), Phi Epsilon Kappa, Phi Delta Kappa. •

MCVEIGH-PETTIGREW, SHARON CHRISTINE, communications consultant; b. San Francisco, Feb. 6, 1949; d. Martin Allen and Frances (Roddy) McVeigh; m. John Wallace Pettigrew, Mar. 27, 1971; children: Benjamin Thomas, Margaret Mary. B.A. with honors, U. Calif.-Berkeley, 1971; diploma of edn. Monash U., Australia, 1975; M.B.A., Golden Gate U., 1985. Tchr., adminstr. Victorian Edn. Dept., Victoria, Australia, 1972-79; supr. Network Control Ctr., GTE Sprint Communications, Burlingame, Calif., 1979-81, mgr. customer assistance, 1981-84, mgr. state legis. ops., 1984-85, dir. revenue programs, 1986-87; communications cons. Flores, Pettigrew & Co., San Mateo, Calif., 1987-89; mgr. telemarketing Apple Computer, Inc., Cupertino, Calif., 1989-94; prin. The Call Ctr. Group, San Mateo, Calif., 1995—; telecomm. cons. PPG Svcs., 1994—; telecomm. spkr. Dept. Consumer Affairs, Sacramento, 1984. Panelist Wash. Gov.'s Citizens Council, 1984; founding mem. Maroondah Women's Shelter, Victoria, 1978; organizer nat. conf. Bus. Women and the Polit. Process, New Orleans, 1986; mem. sch. bd. Boronia Tech. Sch., Victoria, 1979. Recipient Tchr. Spl. Responsibilities award Victoria Edn. Dept., 1979. Mem. Women in Telecommunications (panel moderator San Francisco 1984), Am. Mgmt. Assn., Peninsula Profl. Women's Network, Am. Telemktg. Assn. (bd. dirs. 1992), Women's Econ. Action League. Democrat. Roman Catholic.

MCVICAR, HEATHER LYN, actress; b. Taipei, Taiwan, Nov. 26, 1967; d. James Paul and Sally Jane (Hill) Bishop; m. Michael Craig McVicar, July 4, 1995. BS in Theatre, Communication, Eastern Mich. U., 1989. Free-lance prodn. asst. film & video Detroit, 1989-90, Miami, Fla., 1989-90; area dir. Mktg. and Mgmt. Corp. Am., Denver, 1990—; cmty. coord. Program Acad. Exch., Castle Rock, Colo., 1996—; instr. dance Joamme's Dance Studio, Castle Rock, 1996—; speaker in field. Author: Romantic Recipes, 1995. Vol. Big Sisters Colo., Denver, 1993—, Philip S. MillerLibr., Castle Rock, 1996—; mem. Douglas County Cmty. Theatre Players, 1996—. Mem. Castle Rock C. of C. (adopt-a-sch. liaison 1996—). Home: 5991 S Rock Creek Dr Castle Rock CO 80104

MCWHORTER, RUTH ALICE, counselor, marriage and family therapist; b. Norfolk, Va., May 14, 1946; d. Lester Arthur and Mabel Winifred (Hopwood) Gorman; m. Dean Gundersen, Dec. 27, 1967 (div. Oct. 1971); m. R. Dale Lawhorn, Jan. 6, 1972 (div. Nov. 1979); m. Brent Wilson McWhorter, Aug. 16, 1986; stepchildren: Daniel Chastin, Kenley Reid, Scott Jason. BA in Edn., Ariz. State U., 1970, M of Counseling Psychology, 1979. Cert. profl. counselor, Ariz., cert. marriage and family therapist, Ariz. Tchr. lang. arts Globe (Ariz.) Mid. Sch., 1969-72; tchr. English Isaac Jr. High Sch., Phoenix, Ariz., 1973-74; real estate salesperson Ben Brooks & Assocs., Phoenix, 1975-76, Century 21 Metro, Phoenix, 1976-77; overnight counselor The New Found., Phoenix, 1978-80; family therapist Youth Svc. Bur., Phoenix, 1980-81; owner, corp. officer, profl. counselor/marriage & family Family Devel. Resources (now Family Psychology Assocs.), Phoenix, 1981—; cons., vol. counselor Deseret Industries, Phoenix, 1992-96. Bd. dirs. Westside Mental Health Svcs., Phoenix, 1982-87; vol. facilitator Ariz. Multiple Sclerosis Soc., Phoenix, 1988. Mem. ACA, Internat. Assn. Marriage and Family Therapists, Am. Assn. Marriage and Family Therapists, Am. Mental Health Counselors Assn., Ariz. Counselors Assn., Ariz. Mental Health Counselors Assn. (sec.-treas. ctrl. chpt. 1982, sec. ctrl. chpt. 1995), Am. Assn. Christian Counselors, Assn. Mormon Counselors and Psychotherapists (sec.-treas. 1990—). Office: Family Devel Resources PC PO Box 55291 Phoenix AZ 85078-5291

MCWILLIAMS, MARGARET ANN, home economics educator, author; b. Osage, Iowa, May 26, 1929; d. Alvin Randall and Mildred Irene (Lane) Edgar; children: Roger, Kathleen. BS, Iowa State U., 1951, MS, 1953; PhD, Oreg. State U., 1968. Registered dietitian. Asst. prof. home econs. Calif. State U., L.A., 1961-66, assoc. prof., 1966-68, prof., 1968-92, prof. emeritus, 1992—, chmn. dept., 1968-76; pres. Plycon Press, 1978—. Author: Food Fundamentals, 1966, 6th edit., 1995, Nutrition for the Growing Years, 1967, 5th edit., 1993, Experimental Foods Laboratory Manual, 1977, 4th edit., 1994, (with L. Kotschevar) Understanding Food, 1969, Illustrated Guide to Food Preparation, 1970, 7th edit., 1995, (with L. Davis) Food for You, 1971, 2d edit., 1976, The Meatless Cookbook, 1973, (with F. Stare) Living Nutrition, 1973, 4th edit., 1984, Nutrition for Good Health, 1974, 2d edit., 1982, (with H. Paine) Modern Food Preservation, Fundamentals of Meal Management, 1978, 2d edit., 1993, 3d edit., 1997, (with H. Heller) World of Nutrition, 1984, Foods: Experimental Perspectives, 1989, 3d edit., 1997. Chmn. bd. Beach Cities Symphony, 1991-94. Recipient Alumni Centennial award Iowa State U., 1971, Profl. Achievement award, 1977; Phi Upsilon Omicron Nat. Founders fellow, 1964; Home Economist in Bus. Nat. Found. fellow, 1967; Outstanding Prof. award Calif. State U., 1976. Mem. Am. Dietetic Assn., Inst. Food Technologists, Phi Kappa Phi, Phi Upsilon Omicron, Omicron Nu, Iota Sigma Pi, Sigma Delta Epsilon, Sigma Alpha Iota. Home: PO Box 220 Redondo Beach CA 90277-0220

MCWILLIAMS, SPENCER ALBERT, academic administrator; b. Oakland, Calif., Apr. 4, 1944; s. Russell Allen and Adeleen Emma McW. AA, Otero Jr. Coll., 1964; BA, Calif. State U., Long Beach, 1966; PhD, U. Rochester, 1971. Lic. psychologist, Ariz. Pub. health rep. USPHS, Balt., 1966-67; asst. prof. psychology U. Ariz., Tucson, 1971-77, assoc. prof. psychology, 1977-85; prof., chmn. dept. psychology Winthrop U., Rock Hill, S.C., 1985-88; acting dean Winthrop U. Coll. Arts & Sci., Rock Hill, 1988-89; v.p. for acad. affairs Warren Wilson Coll., Asheville, N.C., 1989-94; v.p. acad. affairs Naropa Inst., Boulder, Colo., 1994—. Contbr. over 50 articles to profl. jours. Mem. Am. Assn. for Higher Edn., Polyani Soc. Home: 2850 Darley Ave Boulder CO 80303-6308 Office: The Naropa Inst 2130 Avapolne Ave Boulder CO 80302

MEAD, BEVERLY MIRIUM ANDERSON, author, educator; b. St. Paul, May 29, 1925; d. Martin and Anna Mae (Oshanyk) Anderson; m. Jerome Morton Nemiro, Feb. 10, 1951 (div. May 1975); children: Guy Samuel, Lee Anna, Dee Martin; m. William Isaac Mead, Aug. 8, 1992. Student Reed Coll., 1943-44; BA, U. Colo., 1947; postgrad., U. Denver. Tchr., Seattle Pub. Schs., 1945-46; fashion coord., dir. Denver Dry Goods Co., 1948-51; fashion dir. Denver Market Week Assn., 1952-53; free-lance writer, Denver, 1958—; moderator TV program Your Preschool Child, Denver, 1955-56; instr. writing and communications U. Colo. Denver Ctr., 1970—, U. Calif., San Diego, 1976-78, Met. State Coll., 1985; dir. pub. relations Fairmont Hotel, Denver, 1979-80; free lance fashion and TV model; author, co-author: The Complete Book of High Altitude Baking, 1961, Colorado a la Carte, 1963, Colorado a la Carte, Series II, 1966, (with Donna Hamilton) The High Altitude Cookbook, 1969, The Busy People's Cookbook, 1971 (Better Homes and Gardens Book Club selection 1971), Where to Eat in Colorado, 1967, Lunch Box Cookbook, 1965, Complete Book of High Altitude Baking, 1961, (under name Beverly Anderson) Single After 50, 1978, The New High Altitude Cookbook, 1980. Co-founder, pres. Jr. Symphony Guild, Denver, 1959-60; active Friends of Denver Libr., Opera Colo. Recipient Top Hand award Colo. Authors' League, 1969, 72, 79-82, 100 Best Best Books of Yr. award N.Y. Times, 1969, 71; named one of Colo.'s Women of Yr., Denver Post, 1964. Mem. Am. Soc. Journalists and Authors, Colo. Authors League (dir. 1969-79), Authors Guild, Authors League Am., Friends Denver Library, Rotary, Kappa Alpha Theta. Address: 23 Polo Club Dr Denver CO 80209-3309

MEAD, KATHRYN NADIA, astrophysicist, educator; b. Jacksonville, Fla., Aug. 6, 1959; d. Charles A. Mead and Nadia L. Mead. BS in Physics, Rensselaer Poly. Inst., 1981, MS in Physics, 1983, PhD in Physics, 1986. Cooperative rsch. assoc. Naval Rsch. Lab., Washington, 1986-88; adj. asst. prof. Union Coll., Schenectady, N.Y., 1988-90, vis. asst. prof., 1990-93; vis. sci. Nat. Radio Astronomy Obs., 1994—; adj. prof. Pima County C.C., 1997. Mem. bd. visitors Bolles Sch., Jacksonville Fla. Recipient Career Devel. award Dudley Observatory, 1990, Faculty Rsch. Fund award Union Coll., 1990, 92, award Fund for Astrophysical Rsch., 1992. Mem. AAUW, Am. Astron. Soc. (editor Status 1995—, Gaposchkins Rsch. Fund award 1991), Assn. for Women in Sci. (pres.-elect southern Ariz. chpt.), Sigma Xi, Sigma Pi Sigma. Office: NRAO Campus Bldg 65 949 N Cherry Ave Tucson AZ 85719

MEAD, LINDA MCCULLOUGH, secondary education educator; b. Lubbock, Tex., May 15, 1946; d. Hugh Davenport and Maxine (Fry) McCullough; children: Richards Mead III, Erin Kate Mead. BS, U. Tex., 1968; postgrad., UCLA, Pepperdine U., 1970-84, No. Ariz. U., 1996—. Cert. secondary tchr., Tex., Calif., Ariz.; cert. trainer Nat. Ctr. for Family Literacy. Tchr. L.A. Unified Sch. Dist., 1968-84; tchr., coord., specialist Mesa (Ariz.) Pub. Schs., 1987—; tchr. Rio Salado Coll., Phoenix, 1988-92. Torchbearer U.S. Olympics, Phoenix, 1996. Mem. ASCD, Kappa Kappa Gamma. Democrat. Methodist. Office: Mesa Pub Schs 549 N Stapley Dr Mesa AZ 85203-7203

MEAD, TERRY EILEEN, clinic administrator, consultant; b. Portland, Oreg., Mar. 14, 1950; d. Everett L. and Jean (Nonken) Richardson; divorced; 1 child, Sean Knute Wade Adcock. AA summa cum laude, Seattle U., 1972; postgrad., U. Wash., 1971. Project mgr. Assoc. Univ. Physician, Seattle, 1971-74; pathology supr. Swedish Hosp., Seattle, 1974-77; svcs. supr. Transamerica, Seattle, 1977-78; various mgmt. positions Providence Hosp., Seattle, 1978-83; CEO Mead's Med. Mgmt. Cons. Firm, Chiloquin, Oreg., 1980—; adminstr. Evergreen Surg. Ctr., Kirkland, Wash., 1983-86; bus. mgr. Ketchikan (Alaska) Gen. Hosp., 1986—; instr. U. Alaska, Ketchikan, 1990; adminstr. Bethel (Alaska) Family Clinic, 1994—; CEO Southeast Oreg. Rural Health Network, 1996—, Mead's Med. Mgmt., 1980—; sec. S.E. adv. bd. U. Alaska, Ketchikan, 1987-94; cons. to hosps. and physicians, Wash., Alaska, 1980—; mgr. Practice Mgmt. Cons., Seattle, 1982-83. Mem. City Charter Rev. Com., Ketchikan, 1990-94; High Sch. Facilities Com. Ketchikan, 1990; S.E. dir. search com. U. Alaska, Ketchikan, 1990; treas. Calvary Bible Ch., Ketchikan, 1989-91; bd. dirs. S.E. Alaska Symphony, 1992-94, Jr. Achievement, 1992-93; chmn. fin. com. City of Bethel, 1994-96. Mem. Rotary Internat. Home: PO Box 1287 Chiloquin OR 97624-1287 Office: PO Box 379 Chiloquin OR 97624-0379

MEAD, TRAY C., museum director; b. Mesa, Ariz., Apr. 1, 1950; s. Norman Wesley and Peggy Lee (Barrows) M.; Barbara Celaya, Feb. 9, 1981; children: Michael Adam, Kristiana Nicole. BA in Edn., Ariz. State U., 1973. Cert. tchr., Ariz. Publisher Ariz. Northland Mag., Flagstaff, 1973-77; mus. dir. Mesa Southwest Mus., 1977—; founding dir. Ariz. Fed. Credit Union, Phoenix, 1980-85. Author: Mesa, Beneath the Superstitions, 1988, Sirrine House Story, 1992; editor: Mesa Grande, 1979, Capturing the Canyon, 1987; field editor Ariz. White Mountain Mag., 1965—; contbg. editor Tonto Trails Mag., 1970—. Founding dir. Mesa Conv. and Tourism Bureau, 1989—; founding chmn. S.W. Svc. Corp., Phoenix, 1981-85; bd. dirs., founding pres. Arts in Mesa, 1980—. Recipient Excellence award Centennial Com., 1978, Golden Quill award Caligraphic Soc. Ariz., 1987, Native Am. Heritage award U.S.M.C. Netherlands, 1991; named Hon. Medicine Man, Ft. Apache Tribe, 1973, Hon. Chmn. Mesa Parade, Mayor City of Mesa, 1980. Mem. Nat. Trust Hist. Preservation, Am. Assn. State and Local Histories, Am. Assn. Mus., Mus. Assn. Ariz. (founding mem., v.p. 1982—), Ctrl. Ariz. Mus. Assn. (founding pres. 1978—), Mesa C. of C. (com. chmn. 1979-89). Home: 370 E Pinon Way Gilbert AZ 85234-4573 Office: Mesa Southwest Museum 53 N Macdonald Mesa AZ 85201-7325

MEADE, KENNETH JOHN, realty company owner, broker; b. N.Y.C., Nov. 25, 1925; s. John Joseph and Blanche (Woodworth) M.; m. Alice Elizabeth (Steinmann), Nov. 8, 1952; children: Steven, Janet, Patricia. Student, N.Y. Inst. Fin., 1960-62. Cert. real estate residential broker. Sales broker Del Webb Devel., Sun City, Ariz., 1974-82; mgr. Mull Realty Inc., Sun City, Ariz., 1982-83; broker, owner 6 offices Ken Meade Realty Inc., Sun City, Ariz., 1983—; dir., treas. Sun City Bd. Realtors, 1988—. Bd. dirs., v.p. Sun City Ambs., 1988—. With USN, 1942-45. Mem. Nat. Assn. Realtors, Ariz. Assn. Realtors, Dale Carnegie Club (past instr. sales course, Outstanding Achievment 1964). Republican. Lutheran. Home: 13306 W Meeker Blvd Sun City West AZ 85375-3815 Office: Ken Meade Realty Inc 17001 N Del Webb Blvd Sun City AZ 85373-1804

MEADER, JONATHAN GRANT (KYTHE ASCIAN), artist; b. Orange, N.J., Aug. 29, 1943; s. William Granville and Audrey Meader. One-man shows Corcoran Dupont Center, 1969, Lunn Gallery, Washington, 1972, Pyramid Gallery, Washington, 1973, 74, Plum Gallery, Md., 1976, 78, 78, Klein-Vogel Gallery, Mich., 1976, Harlan Gallery, Tucson, 1977, Swearingen Gallery, Ky., 1977, Schoolhouse Gallery, Fla., 1978, 83, Ethel Putterman Gallery, Mass., 1978, Washington Project for Arts, 1981, Galerie Grüner Panther, Frankfurt, W. Ger., 1982, Illuminarium Gallery, Los Angeles, 1985, Illuminarium Gallery, Larkspur, Calif., 1985; Illuminarium, Mill Valley, Calif., 1982, 83, Gallery Show, Tokyo, 1985, Kraskin Gallery, Potomac, Md., 1986, Midtown Gallery, Washington, 1986, Kunst-Utmsyknig Gallery, Norway, 1987, House of Artists, Moscow, 1989; group shows include Corcoran Gallery Art, Washington, 1972, Balt. Mus. Traveling Show, 1972, Phillips Collection, Washington, 1972, Iowa U. Mus., 1975, Plum Gallery, 1975, Hall of Artists, Moscow, 1989, ARI Gallery, Mill Valley, Calif., 1991; represented in permanent collections, Whitney Mus. Am. Art, N.Y.C., Met. Mus. Art, N.Y.C., Nat. Gallery, Washington, Hirshhorn Mus., Washington, Zenith Gallery, Washington, 1987; author: The Wordless Travel Book, 1995. Wurlitzer Found. grantee, 1967; Stern Family grantee, 1970; Nat. Endowment Arts grantee, 1974. Address: PO Box 97 Mill Valley CA 94942-0097 *Help uncover life's mysteries, care for everyone (especially the less fortunate) and be positive.*

MEADOR, JAMES PARNELL, toxicologist; b. Long Beach, Calif., June 23, 1952; s. James Gene and Alice M.; m. Susan Jean Picquelle, Sept. 19, 1981. BA in Zoology, Humboldt State U., 1975; MS in Biology and Physiology, San Diego State U., 1981; PhD in Aquatic Toxicology, U. Wash., 1988. Staff rsch. assoc. Scripps Inst. Oceanography U. Calif., San Diego, 1975-81; sr. rsch. biologist Computer Sci. Corp., San Diego, 1982; analyst Computer Scis. Corp., San Diego, 1983; predoctoral rsch. asst. U. Wash., Seattle, 1983-88; sr. assoc. scientist Envirosphere Co., Seattle, 1988-89; rsch. assoc. Nat. Rsch. Coun., 1989-90; rsch. fisheries biologist Nat. Marine Fisheries, NOAA, 1990—; instr. Centro de Investigacion Cientifica y de Educacion Superior de Ensenada, Baja Calif., Mex., 1982. Contbr. articles to profl. jours. Geil Meml. scholar, 1986, Egtvedt scholar, 1985, summer rsch. scholar U. Wash. Sch. Fisheries, U. Wash., 1986, 88. Mem. Soc. of Environ. Toxicology and Chemistry (bd. mem. Pacific Northwest chpt.), Pacific Estuarine Rsch. Soc.

MEAGHER, MICHAEL, radiologist; b. New Rochelle, N.Y., Oct. 24, 1942; s. Joseph Aloysius and Elizabeth (Ahern) M.; m. Martha Batten Mitchell, 1968; children: Kelly, Courtney. Student, Rensselaer Poly. Inst., 1960-62; AB with distinction, U. Rochester, 1964; MD, Stanford U., 1969. Diplomate Am. Bd. Radiology, Nat. Bd. Med. Examiners. Intern in medicine Cornell U., N.Y. Hosp., 1969-70; jr. asst. resident in diagnostic radiology U. Wash., Seattle, 1970-71, sr. asst. resident diagnostic radiology, 1973-74, resident diagnostic radiology, 1974-75; active staff mem. dept. radiology Queen's Med. Ctr., Honolulu, 1975—, Leahi Hosp., Honolulu, 1981—, Kahuku (Hawaii) Hosp., 1988—; pres. Radiology Assocs., Inc., 1978, 81-84, 90-94; chmn. dept. radiology Queen's Med. Ctr., 1979-80, 82-86, 88-90, dir. dept. radiology, 1985-91, dir. magnetic resonance imaging, 1991—, chmn. cancer com., 1980-82; mem. med. staff Hawaii Health Tech. Magnetic Resonance Imaging Facility, Honolulu, 1986—, chief of staff, 1978; clin. instr. dept. radiology U. Hawaii Sch. Medicine, 1983-89, clin. assoc. prof., 1989-93, clin. prof., 1993—, asst. rsch. prof. Cancer Rsch. Ctr. Hawaii, 1989—; clin. asst. prof. dept. radiology U. Wash. Sch. Medicine, 1980-88; presenter in fld. Contbr. articles to profl. publs. Chmn. high tech. adv. com. State Health Planning and Devel. Agy., 1983—; bd. dirs. Friends of Hawaii Pub. TV, 1979-81; pres., CEO Queen's Health Care Plan, Honolulu, 1985-89, chmn. bd. dirs., 1989-91; bd. dirs. Managed Care Mgmt., Inc., Honolulu, 1990; v.p. bd. dirs. Hawaii Opera Theatre, 1990-91, treas., 1991—. Lt. comdr. USN, 1971-73. NIH fellow, 1966; Kaiser Found. grantee, 1967. Fellow Am. Coll. Radiology; mem. AMA, Hawaii State Radiol. Soc. (sec.-treas. 1978-79, v.p. 1979-80, pres. 1980-81), Radiol. Soc. N.Am., Soc. Computer Applications in Radiology (charter), Am. Roentgen Ray Soc. Home: 1234 Maunawili Rd Kailua HI 96734-4642 Office: Queen's Med Ctr Dept Radiology Honolulu HI 96813

MEALS, PAMELA F., publishing executive; 1 child, Laura. Student, We. Oreg. State Coll. With advtsg. The Oreg. Statesman and Capital Jour., Salem; advtsg. mgr. The Idaho Statesman, Boise, 1979, pres., publ., 1994—; publ. Coffeyville (Kans.) Jour., 1979-82, The Palladium-Item, Richmond, Ind., 1982-85, The Olympian, Olympia, Wash., 1985-94. Bd. dirs. Boise Pub. Schs. Edn. Found., Idaho Shakespeare Festival, Albertson Coll. Annual Fund, FUNDSY, William Allen White Found. Mem. Boise Area C. of C. (bd. dirs.), Rotary Club, Idaho Bus. Coun., Pacific N.W. Newspaper Assn. (bd. dirs.), Newspaper Assn. Am. Office: The Idaho Statesman 1200 N Curtis Rd Boise ID 83707

MEANS, JAMES ANDREW, engineer; b. Heavener, Okla., Oct. 11, 1937; s. Edward Andrew and Lorena (Nobles) M.; Therese Louise Zimmermann, Feb. 21, 1959; children: James A. Jr., William R., Charles E., Vicky M. Locken. BSEE, U. Ariz., 1962, MSEE, 1966; PhD, U. Calif., Santa Barbara, 1972; MS in Computer Sci., Chapman U., Orange, Calif., 1988. Engr. Pacific Missile Test Ctr., Pt Mugu, Calif., 1962-72; engr. mgr. Pacific Missile Test Ctr., 1972-79; tech. dir. Space and Missile Test Orgn., Vandenberg AFB, Calif., 1979-89; sr. tech. advisor SRI Internat., Menlo Park, Calif., 1990—; cons. Agri-Craft, Camarillo, Calif., 1968-70, Astro-Geo-Marine, Ventura, Calif., 1972-74. Patentee in field. Mem. Internat. Found. for Telemetering (pres. 1989-95), Internat. Test and Evaluation Assn. (Allen R. Mattews Award, 1991). Democrat. Baptist. Home: 284 St Andrews Way Lompoc CA 93436-1355

MEANY, DAVID WILLIAM, civil engineer; b. Sydney, Australia, Oct. 26, 1937; m. Maire Meany; m. Jan. 1967. BSc in Civil Engring., U. NSW, 1964; MSc in Civil Engring., World Open U., 1979; MBA in Fin., Golden Gate U., 1980; MA in Internat. Econs., U. San Francisco, 1981; MBA in Info. Systems, Golden Gate U., 1983; diploma in Fin. Mgmt., U. New England, 1989; BS in Acctg., SUNY, Albany, 1994; BA in Psychology, Thomas Edison State Coll., 1997. Project mgr. Foster Engring., San Francisco, 1989-90; resident engr. City of Tracy, Calif., 1990-92; project mgr. Zone 7 Water Agy., Pleasanton, Calif., 1992—. Mem. ASCE, ASME, Grad. Mgmt. Assn. (Australia), Instn. Civil Engring. (U.K.), Instn. Profl. Engrs. New Zealand. Home: 7744 Creekside Dr Pleasanton CA 94588-3687 Office: Zone 7 Water Agy 5997 Parkside Dr Pleasanton CA 94588-5127

MEAUX, ALAN DOUGLAS, facilities technician, sculptor; b. Joliet, Ill., Sept. 10, 1951; s. Berry Lee and Luella Ann (Ferguson) M.; m. Letta Sue Nygaard, Sept. 15, 1984; children: Ashley Nicole, Lacey Marie. Student, Joliet Jr. Coll., 1969-71, Bradley U., 1971-72, U.S. Dept. Agr. Grad. Sch., 1972, Skagit Valley Coll., 1983-85. Photographer J.J.C. Blazer, Joliet Herald News, Joliet, 1969-71; auto mechanic Pohanka Olds and Fiat, Hillcrest Heights, Md., 1972-74, Hoffman Olds and Rolls Royce, Hartford, Conn., 1974-75; carpenter Klappenbach Constrn. Co., Moscow, Idaho, 1975-79; property mgr. Olympic Builders, Oak Harbor, Wash., 1979-86; maintenance technician Troubleshooters Inc., Oak Harbor, 1986-87; facilities technician Island County Govt., Coupeville, Wash., 1987—; bronze sculptor Ronin Art Prodns., Oak Harbor, 1979—; appraiser class A Mid-Am. Appraisers Assn., Springfield, Mo., 1986—; bd. dirs. North West Token Kai, U. Wash., Seattle, 1989—, lectr., 1985; contbr. Nanka Token Kai, L.A., 1985—. Author: Japanese Samurai Weapons, 1989; prin. works exhibited at Mini Guild Children's Orthopedic Show, Ballard, Wash., 1986, Worldfest/Ethnic Heritage Coun., Seattle, 1988, 89, 90, Stanwood (Wash.) Invitational Art Show, 1988. Mem. NRA (life), Law Enforcement Alliance Am. (life), Japanese Sword Soc. U.S. (life), N.W. Token Kai (charter, bd. dirs. 1989-91), Western Mus. Conf., Wash. Mus. Assn., Ethnic Heritage Coun., Nanka Token Kai, Japan Soc., Wash. Arms Collectors Assn., North Whidbey Sportmen's Assn. (chmn. range com., trustee), Ctrl. Whidbey Sportmen's Club. Office: Ronin Art Prodns PO Box 1271 Oak Harbor WA 98277-1271

MEBRAHTU, YEMANE BERHAN, medical microbiologist, entomologist, researcher; b. Men-Defera, Seraye, Eritrea, July 12, 1950; came to U.S., 1993; s. Mebrahtu Hagos and Leteberhan G. Michael; m. Lula A. Asmelash, May 14, 1978; children: Jonathan Yemane, Fanuel Yemane. BS in Biology, Chemistry, Haile Sellaisie I U., Addis Ababa, Ethiopia, 1972; MS in Med. Entomology, Nairobi U., Kenya, 1984, PhD in Med. Microbiology, 1991. Assoc. rsch. scientist Ctrl. Lab. and Rsch. Inst., Addis Ababa, 1972-77; lectr. (part-time) Addis Ababa U., 1977-79; head vector control div. Ctrl. Lab. and Rsch. Inst., Addis Ababa, 1977-80; sr. rsch. officer U.S. Army Med. Rsch. Unit, Nairobi, 1983-93, Biomed. Scis. Rsch. Ctr., Kenya Med. Rsch. Inst., Nairobi, 1983-93; vis. asst. rsch. scientist U. Ariz., Tucson, 1993—. Reviewer Sinet, Ethiopian Jour. of Sci., 1976-80; contbr. articles to profl. jours. Recipient grant WHO, Kenya, 1980-83, grant Walter Reed Army Inst. Rsch., 1988-91, grant Commn. of European Community, The Netherlands, 1989. Mem. Am. Soc. Tropical Medicine and Hygiene, Am. Assn. Advancement of Sci., Haile Sellasie I U. Biology Assn. (sec. 1970-71, pres. 1971-72). Home: 555 E Limberlost Dr Apt 1077 Tucson AZ 85705-

2883 Office: Univ Ariz Dept Entomology Forbes Bldg # 410 Tucson AZ 85721

MECHAM, GLENN JEFFERSON, lawyer, mayor; b. Logan, Utah, Dec. 11, 1935; s. Everett H. and Lillie (Dunford) M.; m. Mae Parson, June 5, 1957; children: Jeff B., Scott R., Marcia, Suzanne. BS, Utah State U., 1957; JD, U. Utah, 1961; grad. Air Command and Staff Coll., Air War Coll., 1984. Bar: Utah 1961, Supreme Ct. U.S., U.S. Ct. Appeals (10th Cir.), U.S. Dist. Ct. Utah, U.S. Ct. Claims. Gen. practice law, 1961-65; atty. Duchesne County, Utah, 1962, City of Duchesne, 1962; city judge Roy City, Utah, 1963-66; judge City of Ogden, Utah, 1966-69, mayor, 1992—; lectr. law and govt. Stevens-Henager Coll., Ogden, 1963-75; asst. U.S. atty., 1969-72; ptnr. Mecham & Richards, Ogden, Utah, 1972-82; pres. Penn Mountain Mining Co., South Pacific Internat. Bank, Ltd.; mem. Bur. Justice Stats. Adv. Bd., U.S. Dept. Justice, U.S. Conf. Mayors. Chmn. Ogden City Housing Authority; chmn. bd. trustees Utah State U., Space Dynamics Lab. Utah State U.; mem. adv. coun. Fed. Home Loan Bank; pres. Utah League Cities and Towns, 1981-82. Col. USAF, 1957. Mem. ABA, Weber County Bar Assn. (pres. 1966-68), Utah Bar Assn., Am. Judicature Soc., Weber County Bar Legal Svcs. (chmn. bd. trustees 1966-69), Utah Assn. Mcpl. Judges (sec.), Sigma Chi, Phi Alpha Delta. Home: 1715 Darling St Ogden UT 84403-0556 Office: City of Ogden 2484 Washington Blvd Ste 300 Ogden UT 84401-2319

MECOY, LAURA HOPE, reporter; b. Beaumont, Tex., Apr. 4, 1956; d. Donald Lee Mecoy and Alice Mae Musser; m. Cary Christopher Walker, Sept. 2, 1989; 1 child, Ryan Walker. BA, U. Okla., 1978. Wash. corr. Tulsa Tribune, 1979-83; with capitol bur. Sacramento Bee, 1983-88, with Washington bur., 1988-93, L.A. bur. chief, 1993—; L.A. corr. Money Mag., N.Y., 1993—. Contbg. writer Los Angeles Mag., 1996—. Recipient St. Francis award Archdiocese of San Francisco, 1989; Paul Miller fellow Freedom Forum, 1989-90, Knight fellow U. Md., 1992. Mem. Phi Beta Kappa. Office: Ste 188 1601 Sepulveda Blvd Manhattan Beach CA 90266-5133

MEDAVOY, MIKE, motion picture company executive; b. Shanghai, China, Jan. 21, 1941; came to U.S., 1957, naturalized, 1962; s. Michael and Dora Medavoy; m. Irena Medavoy; 1 child, Brian. B.A., UCLA, 1963. With Casting dept. Universal Studios, 1963; agt. Bill Robinson Assos., Los Angeles, 1963-64; v.p. motion picture dept. GAC/CMA Co., 1965-71, IFA Co., 1971-74; sr. v.p. United Artists Corp., 1974-78; one of founders, exec. v.p. Orion Pictures Co., Burbank, Calif., 1978-82; exec. v.p. Orion Pictures Corp. (formerly Orion Pictures Co.), Burbank, 1982-90; chmn. Tri-Star Pictures, Inc., Burbank, 1990—, Phoenix Picture Corp., 1995—; bd. dirs. Sony Pictures Corp., co-chmn. Am. Cinematech.; jury chmn. Tokyo Film Festival 1994; hon. co-chair St. Petersburg Film Festival, 1992; adv. bd. Swawghai Film Conf. Mem. vis. com. Boston Museum Fine Arts.; chmn. Ctr. Internat. Strategic Affairs, UCLA, Com. to Cure Cancer through Immunization UCLA; co-chmn. Olympic Sports Fedn. Com., Music Ctr. Unified Fund Campaign; co-founder Sundance Film Inst.; bd. govs. Sundance Inst., 1980-86; bd. dirs. Calif. Mus. Sci. and Industry, 1984-87. Recipient Academy award for One Flew Over the Cuckoo's Nest, Rocky, Annie Hall, Amadeus, Platoon, Dances With Wolves, Silence of the Lamb. Mem. Acad. Motion Picture Arts and Scis. (gov. 1977-81), UCLA Found., UCLA Chancellors Assocs.

MEDDLES, SHARON DIANE GUNSTREAM, school counselor; b. Pasadena, Calif., Feb. 9, 1947; d. Jarrell William and Vivian Irene (Heffner) Gunstream; m. Larry Wayne Meddles, June 16, 1973; children: Brittany Dawn, Brooke Reneé. BA in English, Pasadena Coll., 1968; MEd in Counseling, U. Phoenix, 1996. Cert. tchr., Ariz. Jr. high tchr. Adams County Dist. 12, Northglenn, Colo., 1969-72; jr. high tchr. Washington Elem. Sch. Dist. 6, Phoenix, 1972-76, homebound tchr., 1985-86, 88-90; sr. high tchr. N.W. Christian Acad., Glendale, Ariz., 1986-87; jr. high tchr. Washington Sch. Dist., Phoenix, 1990-96, elem. sch. counselor, 1996—. Core group leader Cmty. Bible Study, Phoenix, 1988-90; bd. dirs. Orangewood Ch. of the Nazarene, Phoenix, 1982-84, 93; local pres. Nazarene World Missionary Soc., 1982-84; dist. dir. Point Loma Alumni Bd., San Diego, 1990-93, sec., 1993-96; mem. Valley Cathedral. Republican. Home: 1115 W Le Marche Ave Phoenix AZ 85023-4429

MEDEL, REBECCA ROSALIE, artist; b. Denver, Mar. 26, 1947; d. Natividad and Josefa (Apodaca) M. BFA, Ariz. State U., 1970; MFA, UCLA, 1982. Art instr. 9-12 Tucson Sch. Dist., Santa Rita H.S., 1973-78; substitute tchr. Alameda and Richmond Sch. Dists., Calif., 1978-79; weaving asst. to Yoshiko Wada Berkeley, 1979; asst. Tomasello Fabric Showroom, L.A., 1979-81; rsch. ast. Hunter Coll., N.Y. and Pasadena, 1981-83; asst. prof. fibers dept. head Tenn. Technol. U., Smithville, 1983-88; lectr. Dept. of Design, UCLA, 1989-91; studio artist, 1991—; lectr. N.C. State U., Raleigh, San Diego State U., SUNY, Purchase, 1992, Penland Sch. Asheville, N.C., Textile Study Group, N.Y.C., Calif. Coll. of Arts & Crafts, Oakland, Calif., San Jose State U., Am. Ctr., Kyoto, Japan, City Ctr., Sapporo, Japan, 1986; vis. artist U. N.D., 1985. One-woman shows include Neuberger Mus. of Art, Purchase, N.Y., 1992-93, Bellas Artes Gallery, N.Y.C., 1991, N.D. Mus. Art, Grand Forks, 1985, Maya Behn Galerie, Zurich, 1984, UCLA, 1982; two-person exhbns. include Heath Gallery, Atlanta, 1987, Maya Behn Gallerie, 1986; group shows include Bellas Artes Gallery, Santa Fe, N.Mex., 1992, N.C. State U. Gallery, 1992, Portland Art Mus., 1995, Madison (Wis.) Art Ctr., 1995, Santa Monica (Calif.) Art Gallery, 1995, Maya Behn Gallerie, 1991, Mus. Van Bommel-Van Dam, Venlo, Netherlands, 1990, Palo Alto Cultural Ctr., 1990, many others. Fellowship Nat. Endowment for the Arts Visual Artist, 1986, 88, fellowship for emerging visual artists So. Arts Fedn. NEA, 1985; scholarship to Arcosanti Nat. Endowment for the Arts, 1976; recipient Bronze medal Triennial of Tapestry, 1985. Home & Office: 7134 Potomac St Riverside CA 92504-3936

MEDINA, DANIEL ANDREW, corporate development executive; b. Monterey Park, Calif., Nov. 23, 1957; s. Andrew and Maria (Barboa) M.; m. Laura Martin, July 16, 1983; children: Andrew Martin, Laura Maria. AB, Harvard Coll., 1979, MBA, 1983. Assoc. Salomon Bros. Inc., N.Y.C. and L.A., 1983-86; v.p. Bear, Stearns & Co. Inc., L.A., 1986-90; mng. dir. mcht. banking Union Bank, L.A., 1992-96; v.p. acquisitions Avco Fin. Svcs., Inc., L.A., 1996—. Bd. dirs. Broadway Fed. Savs. and Loan Assn., 1993—. Home: 1825 W Haven Rd San Marino CA 91108-2567 Office: Avco Fin Svcs Inc 600 Anton Blvd Costa Mesa CA 92628-5011

MEDINA, JAVIER MICHAEL, musician, entertainer; b. El Paso, Tex., Sept. 19, 1958; s. FElipe and Ramona (Saavedra) M. Student, U. Tex., El Paso, 1984-87. Free lance musician, entertainer L.A.; mgr. customer svc. dept. Golden Screen Infomercials, Culver City, Calif., 1996—; asst. prodr. Latin Market Albums, El Paso, 1988; owner Javier Medina Entertainment, El Paso, 1991-93; CEO Flying Eagle Prodns., El Paso, 1991—. Author: Anthology of Poetry, 1988; composer: (music score classical) Mi Gueli, 1987, (music score jazz) Barrio, 1986, over 100 compositions. Winner Concierto Competition, U. Tex., El Paso, 1987.

MEDINA, RAMON M., housing professional, consultant. BS in Urban and Regional Planning, Calif. State Poly. U., Pomona, 1997. Draftsman Keith French Group, San Clemente, Calif., 1987-91; cons. Urban Design Group, San Clemente, 1992; intern planning, econ. devel. and adminstrn. City of San Juan Capistrano, Calif., 1995—; cons. Blas Aguilar Adobe Found., 1996—; assoc. Affordable Housing Profls., Huntington Beach, Calif., 1996—. Recipient Team Player award City of San Juan Capistrano, 1996; recipient various scholarships. Mem. Am. Planning Assn., Nat. Contract Mgmt. Assn. Home: 3630 Raven Dr Lake Elsinore CA 92530

MEDINA-PUERTA, ANTONIO, scientist; b. Almeria, Spain, Jan. 20, 1956; s. Antonio and Maria Mar (Puerta) Medina; m. Mary Medina-Puerta, Sept. 20, 1986. MS, U. Politecnica, Madrid, 1979, MIT, 1982; OD, U. Complutense, Madrid, 1979; diploma in elec. engring., MIT, 1981; PhD, U. Politecnica, Madrid, 1983. Optometrist Centro de Vision Luz, Almeria, 1978-79; engr. Philips, Eindhoven, The Netherlands, 1979-80; rsch. asst. MIT, Cambridge, 1981-83; sci. assoc. Eye Rsch. Inst., Boston, 1983-88; task mgr. Calif. Inst. Tech., Pasadena, 1988-91; adviser NASA, Washington, 1988—, USN, 1989—. Contbr. articles to profl. publs.; patentee in field. Fellow Christ's Coll., Cambridge Univ., Eng. Fellow Acad. Applied Sci.; mem. IEEE, Optical Soc. Am., Soc. Photo-optical Instrumentation Engrs., Biomed. Soc. Roman Catholic. Home and Office: 281 E Colorado Blvd # 1002 Pasadena CA 91101-1903

MEDLEY, NANCY MAY, nurse; b. Knoxville, Oct. 8, 1948; d. Donald Raymond and Josephine Ruth (Blakley) M. AA, Riverside City Coll., 1970. RN, Calif. Staff nurse in medicine Riverside Gen. Hosp., Calif., 1970-71; staff nurse neonatal unit Kaiser Permanente Hosp., Hollywood, Calif., 1971-72; critical care nurse neuro unit Harbor-UCLA Hosp., Torrance, 1972-78, head nurse CCU, 1978—, temp. head nurse Neurosurg. ICU, 1988-90; head nurse surg. ICU and cardiothoracic units Harbor UCLA Med. Ctr., Torrance, 1992-94, nurse mgr. cardiology svcs. med.-surg. unit, 1994—. Mem. AACN, Am. Heart Assn. Republican. Presbyterian. Home: 636 Manhattan Ave Apt C Hermosa Beach CA 90254-4529 Office: Harbor-UCLA Hosp 1000 W Carson St Torrance CA 90502-2004

MEDOFF, MARK HOWARD, playwright, screenwriter, novelist; b. Mt. Carmel, Ill., Mar. 18, 1940; s. Lawrence Ray and Thelma Irene (Butt) M.; m. Stephanie Thorne, June 24, 1972; children: Debra, Rachel, Jessica. B.A., U. Miami, Fla., 1962; M.A., Stanford U., 1966; D.H.L., Gallaudet Coll., 1981. Instr. English and drama N.Mex. State U., 1966-79, dramatist in residence, 1974—, head dept. drama, 1978-87, prof. drama, 1979-93, artistic dir., 1982-87; artistic dir. Am. S.W. Theatre Co., 1984-87. Author: (plays) When You Comin' Back, Red Ryder?, 1974, The Wager, 1975, The Kramer, 1975, The Halloween Bandit, 1978, The Conversion of Aaron Weiss, 1978, Firekeeper, 1978, The Last Chance Saloon, 1979, Children of a Lesser God, 1980 (Soc. West Theatres best play award 1982), The Majestic Kid, 1981, The Hands of Its Enemy, 1984, Kringle's Window, 1985, The Heart Outright, 1986 (novel) Dreams of Long Lasting: (films) When You Comin' Back, Red Ryder?, 1979, Off Beat, 1986, Apology, 1986, Children of a Lesser God, 1986, Good Guys Wear Black, 1978, Clara's Heart, 1988, The Majestic Kid, 1988, City of Joy, 1992, Homage, 1995, Santa Fe, 1997; works appear in Best Plays, 1973-74, 75-75, 79-80, Best Short Plays, 1975, The Homage that Follows, 1987; plays Stumps, 1989, Stefanie Hero, 1990, Showdown On Rio Road, 1995, Gila, 1995, A Christmas Carousel, 1996. Guggenheim fellow, 1974-75; recipient Obie award, Drama Desk award, Outer Critics Circle award, Media award Pres.'s Com. Employment Handicapped, Tony award; Oscar award nominee for Best Screenplay for Children of A Lesser God, 1987. Mem. Dramatists Guild, Writers Guild Am., Actors Equity Assn., Screen Actors Guild Pen. Office: PO Box 3072 Las Cruces NM 88003-3072

MEDUSKI, JERZY WINCENTY, nutritionist, biochemist; b. Kalusz, Poland, Oct. 29, 1918; s. Dobieslaw Antoni and Katarzyna (Barbowska) M.; came to U.S., 1962, naturalized, 1969; M.D., Warsaw (Poland) Med. Sch., 1946; Ph.D. in Biochemistry, U. Lodz (Poland), 1951; 1 child, Jerzy Dobieslaw. Organizer, chief pharmacology labs. Polish Nat. Inst. Hygiene, Warsaw, 1945-52, organizer, head lab. of intermediary metabolism, 1952-59; asso. prof. biochemistry Warsaw Med. Sch., 1955-59; asst. prof. neurology U. So. Calif. Sch. Medicine, Los Angeles, 1973—; pres. Nutritional Cons. Group, Inc. Mem. Los Angeles County Bd. Suprs. Task Force on Nutrition. WHO fellow, Holland, Scotland, 1948-49; research grantee, USSR, 1956. Mem. Polish Acad. Sci. (sci. sec. biochem. com. 1952-59), Polish Med. Assn. (sci. sec. nat. bd. 1958-59), Polish Biochem. Soc. (founding mem.), Biochem. Soc. London, Royal Soc. Chem. London, Internat. Soc. on Toxinology, AMA, Am. Soc. Microbiology, Internat. Soc. on Oxygen Transport to Tissues, Sigma Xi. Author 3 books on biochemistry; contbr. more than 80 articles to internat. jours.; author textbook on nutritional biochemistry, 1977. Home: 1922 12th St Santa Monica CA 90404-4604 Office: U So Calif Sch Medicine 2025 Zonal Ave Los Angeles CA 90033-4526

MEE, JOY ANNE, city planning executive; b. Verona, N.J., Sept. 30, 1946; d. Irving Jones and Lorene Ada (Weissenborn) Greenslade; m. William Robert Mee, Jr., Oct. 9, 1970; children: Christopher Stanton, Nathan Frederick. BA, Principia Coll., Elsah, Ill., 1968; M of Urban Planning, U. Ill., 1970. Planner City of Phoenix, 1971-79, prin. planner, 1979-84, asst. planning dir., 1984—; mem. planning adv. cou., dept. urban and regional planning U. Ill., Urbana, 1985—. Author: (govt. document) Phoenix Housing Element, 1975. Mem. citizens adv. coun. Madison Sch. Dist., Phoenix, 1985-95, mem. fin. oversight com., 1990-95. Mem. Am. Inst. Cert. Planners (cert.; mem. accreditation team 1990—), Ariz. Planning Assn., Soroptimist Internat. (chair Ariz. Women's Townhall 1995, pres.-elect Phoenix chpt.). Home: 2550 E Denton Ln Phoenix AZ 85016-3641 Office: City of Phoenix Planning Dept 200 W Washington St Phoenix AZ 85003-1611

MEECHAM, WILLIAM CORYELL, engineering educator; b. Detroit; s. William Edward and Mabel Catherine (Wilcox) M.; m. Barbara Jane Brown, Sept. 4, 1948 (dec.); children: Janice Lynn, William James; m. Della Fern Carson,. BS, U. Mich., 1948, MS, 1948, PhD in Physics, 1954. Head acoustics lab. Willow Run Labs., Ann Arbor, Mich., 1959-60; asst. prof. U. Mich., Ann Arbor, 1958-60; prof. U. Minn., Mpls., 1960-67; prof. fluid mechanics and acoustics UCLA, 1967—, chmn. dept. mechanics and structures, 1972-73; cons. Aerospace Corp., El Segundo, Calif., 1975-80, Rand Corp., Santa Monica, Calif., 1964-74, Bolt, Beranek and Newman, Cambridge, Mass., 1968-73, Arete Assocs., Encino, Calif., 1976—, CRT Corp., Chatsworth, Calif., 1985—. Author: (with R. Lutomirski) Lasar Systems, 1973; author 140 papers on fluid mechanics and acoustics. Treas. Unitarian Ch., Ann Arbor, Mich., 1958-60; advisor U.S. Congress Com. on Pub. Works, Congl. Record Report N.J., 1972; mem. Calif. Space and Def. Council, U.S. Congress, 1982—. Served with U.S. Army, 1944-46. Mich. Alumni scholar 1942-44, Donovan scholar U. Mich., 1944-45; UCLA senate rsch. grantee, 1968—, NASA rsch. grantee, 1971—, Office Naval Rsch. grantee, 1977-85; recipient Disting. Svc. award U.S. Army. Fellow Acoustical Soc. Am. (gen. chmn. meeting 1973), AIAA (assoc. fellow); mem. Internat. Inst. Acoustics and Vibration, Am. Phys. Soc. (fluid dynamics div.), Inst. Noise Control Engring., Sigma Xi, Tau Beta Pi. Home: 927 Glenhaven Dr Pacific Palisades CA 90272-2202 Office: UCLA Sch Engring & Applied Sci Los Angeles CA 90024

MEECHAM, WILLIAM JAMES, ophthalmologist; b. Ann Arbor, Mich., Nov. 30, 1958; s. William Coryell and Barbara (Brown) M.; m. Amanda Roberts. AB in Zoology, U. Calif., Berkeley, 1980, MA in Biophysics, 1983; MD, U. Calif., San Francisco, 1987. Diplomate Nat. Bd. Med. Examiners, Am. Bd. Ophthalmology. Med. intern Cabrini Med. Ctr., N.Y.C., 1987-88; resident in ophthalmology U. Calif., San Francisco, 1988-91, ocular oncology fellow, 1991-92, clin. asst. prof., 1991—, ocular plastics fellow, 1992-93; sr. physician depts. ophthalmology and mohs surgery Kaiser Permanente, San Rafael, 1993—. Contbr. articles to profl. publs.; editor-in-chief U. Calif.-San Francisco Synapse, 1984-85. Mem. Am. Acad. Ophthalmology, Am. Soc. Ophthalmic Plastic and Reconstructive Surgeons. Office: 99 Montecillo Rd San Rafael CA 94903-3300

MEECHAN, RICK JAMES, lawyer; b. Rochester, July 17, 1955; s. James A. and Kathyrn (Devereaux) M.; m. Susan Marie Fisher, Aug. 16, 1982; children: Alexandria, Jacob. BA in Mgmt., Sonoma State U., 1979; JD, Empire Coll., 1987. Bar: Calif. 1987. Asst. mgr. Chicago Pizza, Petaluma, Calif., 1980-81; solar energy salesman Native Sun, Petaluma, Calif., 1982; new accounts rep. Northbay Savings & Loan, Rohnert Park, Calif., 1983-85; assoc. Richens L. Wootton, Santa Rosa, Calif., 1985-90; pvt. practice Santa Rosa, Calif., 1990—; Mem. adv. bd. Compensation Alert, Santa Rosa, 1992-96. Editor: Basic Stuff, 1991, (newsletter) Donkey Tail, 1986. Bd. dirs. Ctrl. Soccer, Santa Rosa, 1993-96, Sant Rosa Youth Soccer League, 1996, Christ Meth. Ch., 1991-93. With USN, 1973-79; Capt. USNG, 1982-89. Mem. Northbay Applicants Attorneys, Empire Soccer Club. Democrat. Office: 50 Santa Rosa Ave Fl 4 Santa Rosa CA 95404-4901

MEEHAN, EILEEN R., communications educator; b. San Francisco, Aug. 3, 1951; d. James Anthony and K. (McGroary) M.; m. Alfred J. Babbitt, Aug. 15, 1978. BA in Social Sci., San Francisco State Coll., 1973; MA, U. Pa., 1975; PhD, U. Ill., 1982. From lectr. to asst. prof. dept. comm. U. Iowa, Iowa City, 1982-89; asst. prof. dept. media arts U. Ariz., Tucson, 1989-93, assoc. prof. dept. media arts, 1993—; assoc. prof. comparative culture & lit.; vis. asst. prof. dept. comm. arts U. Wis., Madison, 1992; spkr. Univ. Bus. and Profl. Womens Assn., Tucson, 1991, Ariz. Bus. & Profl. Womens Assn., 1992, Tucson Cmty. Cable Corp., 1994. Mem. editl. bd. Comm. Perspectives, 1978-85; contbr. articles to profl. jours. Panelist LWV, Tucson, 1993. Grantee U. Ariz., 1992, 94, U. Wis., 1992. Mem. Union for Dem. Comm. (consultative group mem. 1990-94, chair steering com. 1984-89), Internat. Assn. for Comm. Rsch., Speech Comm. Assn. (newsletter editor 1985-86). Democrat. Office: Univ Ariz Dept Media Arts Harvill Bldg Tucson AZ 85721

MEEHAN, MICHAEL JOSEPH, lawyer; b. St. Louis, Aug. 28, 1942; s. Joseph Michael and Frances (Taylor) M.; m. Sharon Kay McHenry (div. 1988); m. Patricia Ann Shive, July 8, 1989. BS in Engring., U.S. Coast Guard Acad., 1964; JD with high distinction, U. Ariz., 1971. Bar: Ariz. 1971, U.S. Ct. Appeals (6th, 8th, 9th and 10th cirs.), U.S. Supreme Ct. 1975. Law clk. Assoc. Justice William H. Rehnquist, U.S. Supreme Ct., 1972; assoc. Molloy, Jones & Donahue, P.C., Tucson, 1971-75, shareholder, 1975-93; chmn. exec. com., head trial dept., 1986-93; founder Meehan & Assocs., Tucson, 1993—; mem. fed. appellate rules adv. com. Jud. Conf. U.S., 1994—. Author chpt. on appellate advocacy: State Bar of Arizona Appellate Practice Handbook. Fellow Am. Acad. Appellate Lawyers; mem. ABA (sect. on litigation), Ariz. Bar Assn. (mem. exec. coun. appellate advocacy sect. 1995—). Republican. Lutheran. Office: Meehan & Assocs PO Box 1671 Tucson AZ 85702-1671

MEEK, GERRY, library director. Dir. Calgary (Alta.) Pub. Libr., Can. Office: Calgary Pub Libr, 616 Macleod Trail SE, Calgary, AB Canada T2G 2M2*

MEEKER, ARLENE DOROTHY HALLIN (MRS. WILLIAM MAURICE MEEKER), manufacturing company executive; b. Glendale, Calif., June 13, 1935; d. Haddon Eric and Martha (Randow) Hallin. Grad. John Muir Jr. Coll., 1953; Student, L.A. Valley Coll., 1956-58, BA, Whittier Coll., 1973, MBA, 1980; m. William Maurice Meeker, Aug. 19, 66; 1 child, William Michael. Statewide sec. pub. rels. United Reps. Calif., L.A., 1964; pers. specialist Sanford Mgmt. Svcs., Inc., L.A., 1964-66; v.p. pers. Grover Mfg. Corp., Montebello, Calif., 1966-75, pres., 1975—, bd. dir., 1969—, chmn. of bd. 1975—; bd. dir. Brit. Marine Industries, Montebello, 1969-86, chmn. bd. 1986—, Grover Ltd., Clonakilty, County Cork, Ireland, 1986—, Grover Internat., 1969—. Author: Stress Differences Between Male and Female Executives, 1980. Mem. City of Whittier Transp. and Parking Commn., 1976-84, chmn. commn., 1977-79, vice-chmn., 1982-84; coun. mem. L.A. County Art Mus., 1969-80; chmn. fine arts bd. Hillcrest Congl. Ch., mem. ch. coun., 1977-79; trustee Oxford Prep. Sch., Whittier, Calif., 1981-86; visitors bd. Whittier Coll., 1983-89; press chmn. Whittier Rep. Women Federated, 1977-78, 1st v.p., 1981-83; Rep. precinct capt., 1964; active L.A. World Affairs Coun.; pres. Friendly Hills Property Owners Assn, 1982-84. Mem. Docian Soc. (pub. rels. chmn. 1967-68), AAUW, Conglist., Ocean Club Homeowners Assn. (treas., pres. 1996—), Newport Harbor Yacht Club (Newport Beach, Calif.), Friendly Hills Country Club (Whittier, Calif.), Whitter Lincoln Club (pres. 1982-84). Home: 9710 Portada Dr Whittier CA 90603-1326 Office: 620 S Vail Ave Montebello CA 90640-4952

MEEKER, MILTON SHY, manufacturing company executive; b. Knob Noster, Mo., Nov. 9, 1933; s. David and Helen Elizabeth (Kendrick) M.; m. Nancy Orbison, Nov. 27, 1976 (dec.); 1 child, Sherwin Kendrick. BA, U. Calif., Berkeley, 1955, BS, 1959; MBA, U. Mich., 1963. With Ford Motor Co., 1959-68; dir. purchasing, mktg., rsch. mgr. Paccar, Inc., Seattle, also Newark, Calif., 1968-71; commr. fed. supply svc., commr. automated data and telecommunications, assoc. dep. adminstr. GSA, Washington, 1972-75; dir. purchasing chem. group FMC Corp., Phila., 1975-77, dir. purchasing planning and adminstrn., Chgo., 1977-79; gen. sales mgr. Peterbilt Motors Co. div. Paccar, Newark, Calif., 1979-80, mktg. mgr., 1980-89, dir. dealer devel., Bellevue, Wash., 1989-91, exec. asst. to vice chmn., 1991—. Chmn., Pres.'s Com. for Purchase of Products from Blind, 1973-74; bd. dirs. Nat. Industries for the Blind, 1976-86. With U.S. Army, 1957-58. Republican. Home: 7900 NE 32nd St Medina WA 98039 Office: PO Box 1518 Bellevue WA 98009-1518

MEEKS, CHRISTOPHER NELSON, writer; b. Mpls., Sept. 13, 1953; s. George Nelson Meeks and Sidney (Young) Wear; m. Carol Anne Fuchs, May 26, 1985; 1 child, Zachary Edward Meeks. BA in Mass Comm./Psychology, U. Denver, 1976; MFA in Profl. Writing, U. So. Calif., L.A., 1983. Freelance writer various publs. including N.Y. Times, Writer's Digest, others, 1982—; book reviewer The L.A. Herald-Examiner, 1985-86; writing cons. The Annenberg Sch. of Comms., U. So. Calif., 1986-87; sr. editor Prelude Press, 1983-87; nationally syndicated columnist Personal Computers jour., 1985-96; theatre critic Daily Variety, 1989-96; inst. writer, editor-in-chief CalArts/Current jour. The Calif. Inst. of the Arts, 1987—, faculty mem., 1994—; owner Inherit the Earth Technologies, 1990-95. Author: Roald Dahl/Reaching Your Goal Series, 1993, Arnold Schwarzenegger/Reaching Your Goal Series, 1993, Skydiving, 1991, Japan: World Partner, 1990, The Personal Computer Book (with Peter McWilliams), 1990, On Being A Writer, 1989, others; playwright: Suburban Anger, 1993, Who Lives?, 1997. Recipient 1st place U. So. Calif.'s Playwright's Festival/Fiveplay, 1983, Donald Davis Dramatic Writing award/Henry's Room, 1982; grantee Pilgrim's Project, 1997. Mem. Dramatists Guild, PEN Ctr. USA West. Office: Calif Inst of the Arts 24700 McBean Pky Valencia CA 91355-2397

MEEKS, CRAWFORD RUSSELL, JR., mechanical engineer; b. Winston-Salem, N.C., Oct. 17, 1931; s. Crawford Russell and Grace Alice (Sheppard) M.; m. Rebecca Ann Weavil, May 12, 1954 (div. Aug. 1972); 1 child, Clark Eugene; m. Shirlyne Myrtle Parsons, Jan. 31, 1988. BSME with high honors, N.C. State U., 1959. Design engr. Marquardt Aircraft, Van Nuys, Calif., 1959-61; rsch. engr. Atomics Internat., Canoga Park, Calif., 1961-66; chief scientist Hughes Aircraft Co., El Segundo, Calif., 1966-88; pres. AVCON, Inc., Agoura Hills, Calif., 1988—. Contbr. over 30 articles to profl. jours. Vol. psychol. counselor to area low-income patients, 1973-79. With U.S. Army, 1953-55. Mem. AIAA, ASME (mem. wear com.), Soc Tribologists and Lubrication Engrs., Phi Kappa Phi. Home: 3924 Coral Pl Calabasas CA 91302 Office: AVCON Inc 21050 Erwin St Woodland Hills CA 91367

MEGALOS, BILL, film director; b. N.Y.C., Oct. 30, 1953; s. Arthur Christopher and Malamo (Corniotes) M.; m. Judie Lee Hammond, Sept. 25, 1983; children: Elena, Sultana. BA, Columbia Coll., 1977; MFA, Columbia U., 1981. Tech. dir. Nikolais Dance Theatre, N.Y.C., 1974-75; prodn. stage mgr. Eliot Feld Ballet Co., N.Y.C., 1975-76; lighting designer various rock groups, 1976-80; freelance dir. cameraman, 1980—; v.p., dir. programming The Recovery Network; adj. prof. Sch. Visual Arts, N.Y.C., 1984-88. Dir./producer: (TV features) Jack Benny: Comedy in Bloom, Ultimate Challenge, Moving Pictures, Springsteen, Take Back American/Jerry Brown for President 1992, Leadership '92, Strange Turf; dir./cameraman: (music videos) D.R.I., Kate and Anna McGarrigle, Dianne Reeves, A.C. Black, Rebel Pebbles, others. (commls.) Alpo, Broadway Bound, Bide-A-Wee Home, Yes on Six, Red Cross Water Safety PSA, Family Planning in Bangladesh, (others) Into the Woods, The Secret Garden, Showscan 'Space Race', more. Recipient Canon Cinematography award 1976, Best Cinematography, WHO, Beijing, 1984, Acad. award 1987, Acad. award nomination 1993, Emmy award 1990.

MEHDIZADEH, PARVIZ, insurance company executive; b. Tehran, Iran, Sept. 15, 1934; came to U.S., 1981; s. Alexander and Sedigheh (Siavooshy) M.; m. Manijeh Sadri, Sept. 12, 1961; children: Sheida, Peyman, Pejman. BS, Forestry Sch., Tehran, 1958; MS, N.C. State U., 1963, PhD, 1966. Pres. Research Inst. Natural Resources, Tehran, 1968-73; assoc. prof. U. Tehran, 1973-74; prof. environ. sci. U. Tabriz, Iran, 1974-76; chmn. resolution com. FAO, Rome, 1976-77; chmn. natural resources Cen. Treaty Orgn., Ankars, Turkey, 1977-78; spl. adviser to sec. Ministry of Agr., Tehran, 1978-79; dist. mgr. Am. Family Life Assurance Co., Beverly Hills, Calif., 1981—; v.p. Point Internat. Corp. Inc., Los Angeles, 1986—; pres. ZMS Fin. Network Corp. Inc., Beverly Hills, Calif., 1995—; cons. Ministry of Sci., Tehran, 1972-75, UN U., Tokyo, 1975-76; chmn. bd. dirs. Active Universal Corp., Inc.; gen. agent AFLAC, 1995. Author: Flowering Plants of Semi-Arid Regions, 1976, Economizing of Water Use in Agriculture, 1977; editor Khandamhayeh Hafteh, 1979. Mem. U.S. Senatorial Club, Washington, 1984; charter mem. Rep. Presdl. Task Force, Washington, 1984. Mem. Life Underwriters Assn. (L.A. chpt., Health Ins. Quality award 1985, 88, 89), Rotary (chmn. dist. 5280 1992, Paul Harris Fellow award 1989). Office: Am Family Life Assurance 9301 Wilshire Blvd Ste 508 Beverly Hills

CA 90210-5411 *Personal philosophy: The future belongs to those with vision and understanding of their environment. Nature conservancy and the wise use of renewable natural resources are the keys to a prosperous future for man kind.*

MEHLMAN, BENJAMIN, psychologist, educator; b. Bklyn., Feb. 29, 1924; s. Harry and Minnie (Breitman) M.; m. Mary Robinson, Sept. 5, 1947; children: Marc, Rick, Barbara. BA, Bklyn. Coll., 1944; PhD, Syracuse U., 1951. Lic. psychologist, Calif. Clin. psychologist Toledo (Ohio) State Hosp., 1950-51; assoc. prof. psychology Kent (Ohio) State U., 1951-60; scientist/adminstr., psychologist NIH, Bethesda, Md., 1960-62; prof. psychology Calif. State U., Northridge, 1962-92, chmn. dept., 1962-65; pvt. practice clin. psychology Northridge, 1979—. Contbr. articles to profl. jours. Sgt. U.S. Army, 1943-46.

MEHLMAN, LON DOUGLAS, information systems specialist; b. Los Angeles, Apr. 29, 1959; s. Anton and Diane Mehlman. BA, UCLA, 1981; MBA, Pepperdine U., 1983. Systems programmer Ticom Systems Inc., Century City, Calif., 1978-81; systems analyst NCR Corp., Century City, 1981-83; sr. systems analyst Tandem Computers Inc., L.A., 1983-91; sr. computer scientist Computer Scis. Corp., El Segundo, Calif., 1991—. Author: Establishing an Enterprise Information Systems Infrastructure, 1995, Implimenting TQM, 1995, Lessons Learned from the Navstar GPS Engineering Management System Project, 1997. Mem. Am. Mgmt. Assn., Assn. for Info. and Image Mgmt., Armed Forces Communications and Electronics Assn., Sierra Club, Phi Delta Theta. Office: Computer Scis Corp 2100 E Grand Ave El Segundo CA 90245-5024

MEHLUM, DAVID L., otolaryngologist; b. Phoenix, Sept. 10, 1950; s. Charles J. and Jessaline (V.) M.; m. Mary Jo Mills, June 17, 1972; children: N. Eric, Kristen M. AA, Phoenix Coll., 1970; BS, U. Ariz., 1972; MD, U. Tex., Dallas, 1976. Diplomate Am. Bd. Otolaryngology. Intern U. Tex. Southwestern Affiliated Hosp., Dallas, 1976-77, resident, 1977-80; med. staff mem. Group Health Coop., Seattle, 1983—; cons. Indian Health Svc., Ariz., Nev., 1981-83; clin. asst. prof. otolaryngology U. Calif., San Francisco, 1981-83; clin. instr. otolaryngology U. Wash. Med. Sch., Seattle, 1984—; chief of otolaryngology Group Health-Cen., Seattle, 1987-90. Contbr. articles to profl. jours. Lt. comdr. USNR, 1980-83. Recipient Medallion of Merit, Ariz. State U., 1970. Mem. ACS, Am. Acad. Otolaryngology, Am. Assn. Facial Plastic and Reconstructive Surgery, Nat. Ski Patrol (bd. dirs. ski acres patrol 1989—, nat. appointment 1992, asst. patrol dir. 1992-96, patrol dir. 1996—). Lutheran. Office: Group Health Coop Dept Otolaryngolgy 125 16th Ave Seattle WA 98122-5610

MEHNER, WILLIAM MICHEL, real estate executive; b. Ada, Okla., Aug. 5, 1943; s. Dors Jenkins and Minnie (Brooks) Snyder; m. Bonnie Lee Hackett, May 31, 1965; children: Bethany Anne, Whitney Alison. BA, Alaska Meth. U., 1965; postgrad., Stanford U., 1983, U. Nebr., 1995; grad., Real Estate Inst., 1997. Mgr. Alaska divsn. Equitable, Anchorage, 1969-89, Mut. of Omaha, Anchorage, 1989-93; agent Jack White Real Estate, Anchorage, 1993—; commr. Mcpl. Light and Power Anchorage Elec. Utility, 1996—. Bd. dirs. Western coun. Boy Scouts Am., Anchorage, 1980-87, Glacier Creek Acad., Girdwood, Alaska, 1985-94, Chugach Elec. Assn., 1994-95; chmn. Humana Hosp., 1990-91, Alaska Conservatory Music, Anchorage, 1985-87; del. Anchorage Rep. Com., 1988; pres. Columbia Alaska Regional Hosp., 1994-97. 1st lt. U.S. Army, 1965-69. Mem. Alaska Assn. Life Underwriters (pres. 1983-84, bd. dirs.), So. Alaska Life Underwriters (bd. dirs. 1972-85), Gen. Agts. and Mgrs. Assn. (pres. 1986-87, life qualified mgmt. award), Equitable Regional Mgrs. Assn. (pres. 1985), Rotary. Home: 2923 McCollie Ave Anchorage AK 99517-1341 Office: Jack White Co 3201 C St Ste 200 Anchorage AK 99503-3934

MEHRING, CLINTON WARREN, engineering executive; b. New Haven, Ind., Feb. 14, 1924; s. Fred Emmett and Florence Edith (Hutson) M.; m. Carol Jane Adams, Mar. 9, 1946; children—James Warren, Charles David, John Steven (dec.), Martha Jane. B.S., Case Inst. Tech., 1950; M.S., U. Colo., 1956. Registered profl. engr., Wyo., Colo., Nev. Design engr. U. S. Bur Reclamation, Denver, 1950-56; design engr. Tipton & Kalmbach, Denver, 1956-58; asst. resident engr. Tipton & Kalmbach, Quito, Equador, 1959-61; asst. chief design engr. Tipton & Kalmbach, Lahore, Pakistan, 1962-65; v.p. Tipton & Kalmbach, Denver, 1966-73, exec. v.p., 1973-79, pres., 1979—, also bd. dirs. Served with AUS, 1943-45. Recipient Theta Tau award as outstanding grad. Case Inst. Tech., 1950. Fellow ASCE (life); mem. Am. Cons. Engrs. Coun., U.S. Com. on Large Dams, Am. Concrete Inst., U.S. Com. Irrigation and Drainage (life), Sigma Xi, Tau Beta Pi, Theta Tau, Sigma Chi, Blue Key. Methodist. Club: Denver Athletic. Home: 1821 Mount Zion Dr Golden CO 80401-1733 Office: 1331 17th St Denver CO 80202-1566

MEHTA, ZUBIN, conductor, musician; b. Bombay, India, Apr. 29, 1936; came to U.S., 1961; s. Mehli Nowrowji and Tehmina (Daruvala) M.; m. Nancy Diane Kovack; children: Zarina, Merwan. Student, St. Xavier's Coll., Bombay, 1951-53, State Acad. Music, Vienna, Austria, 1954-60; LL.D., Sir George Williams U., Montreal, 1965; D.Mus. (hon.), Occidental Coll.; hon. doctorate, Colgate U., Brooklyn Coll., Westminster Choir Coll., Juilliard Sch., Weizmann Inst. Sci. (Israel). Music dir., Montreal (Can.) Symphony Orch., 1961-67, Los Angeles Philharmonic Orch., 1962-78; mus. dir.: Israel Philharmonic, from 1969, appointed dir. for life, 1981; music dir., N.Y. Philharmonic, 1978-91, guest condr., Met. Opera, Salzburg (Austria) Festival, Vienna Philharmonic, Berlin Philharmonic, La Scala, Milan, Italy, music dir., Maggio Musicale Florence, Italy, rec. artist for, Decca, CBS, RCA, New World Records, (recipient 1st prize Liverpool (Eng.) Condrs. Competition 1958). Decorated Padma Bhushan India, 1967, commendatore of Italy. Office: Israel Philharm Orch, 1 Huberman St Box 11292, 61112 Tel Aviv Israel also: Orch Maggio Musicale, Teatro, Comunale Via Solferino 15, I-50123 Florence Italy

MEI, TOM Y. K., lawyer; b. Kuantan, Malaysia, July 24, 1940; came to U.S., 1958; s. Hung Po and Hannah (Chung) M.; m. Margene Suzuki Mei, Sept. 1964; children: Rodney, Todd. BA in econ., Calif. State U. at L.A., 1963; JD, Western State U. Coll. Law, 1975. Bar: Calif. 1976. Claim rep. CNA Ins., L.A., 1964-66; claim supr. CNA Ins., San Diego, 1966-76; assoc. attorney Murchison & Cumming, Santa Ana, 1976-88, ptnr., 1988—; pres. San Diego Claims Mgr. Council, 1973. Mem. Am. Bd. Trial Advocates (bd. dirs.), Defense Rsch. Inst., Orange County Bar Assoc. Office: Murchison & Cumming 200 W Santa Ana Blvd Ste 801 Santa Ana CA 92701-4134

MEIER, ROBERT JOHN, secondary education educator; b. Glendale, Calif., July 8, 1956; s. Robert Walter and Mary Jane (Pellizzer) M. AA, Glendale C.C., 1975; BA, Calif. State U., Northridge, 1978; MS, U. La Verne, 1989. Educator, counselor Rogers High Sch., Van Nuys, Calif., 1983—. Mem. AFTRA, Nat. Assn. Biology Tchrs., Nat. Sci. Tchrs. Assn., Calif. Continuation Edn. Assn. (treas. 1992-95, pres. 1995—), United Tchrs. L.A., Actors Equity Assn., Screen Actors Guild. Office: Will Rogers High School 15141 Lemay St Van Nuys CA 91405-4529

MEIER, THOMAS JOSEPH, museum director, author; b. Denver, June 23, 1939; s. Henry Joseph and Helen Miriam (Croke) M.; m. Beverly Joyce Loeffler, June 8, 1963; children: Thomas, John. BS in Edn., U. Colo., 1964. Cert. Tchr. Space mgmt. dir. U. Colo., Boulder, 1966-69; owner Stürtz & Copeland, Boulder, 1969-77; historian and writer Mesa Press, Boulder, 1977-90; dir. Boulder Mus. History, Boulder, 1990—; instr. Boulder History, U. Colo continuing. Edn., 1996—, Judge State History Fair,1993-94. Author: (Book) The Pictureman, 1994, (Booklet) The Early History of Boulder 1993, contbr. articles to profl. jours. Mass Transit Com. Mem., City of Boulder, 1973, U. City Rels. Com., U. Colo., 1967-69, USMC, 1957-60. Mem. Boulder Historical Soc. (pres. 1985), Colo. Historical Soc., Colo. Chautaugua Assn., mem. bd. City Boulder, Colo., Landmark, mem. bd., 1974-75. Home: 2850 Vassar Dr Boulder CO 80303 Office: Boulder Mus of History 1206 Euclid Ave Boulder CO 80302

MEIERAN, EUGENE STUART, material scientist; b. Cleve., Dec. 23, 1937; s. Elias and Rae (Linetsky) M.; m. Rosalind Berson, Mar. 25, 1962; children—Sharon Elizabeth, Andrew Marc. B.S. in Metallurgy, Purdue U., 1959; M.S. in Metallurgy, MIT, 1961, Sc.D. in Material Sci., 1963. Sr. mem. tech. staff Fairchild R & D., Palo Alto, Calif., 1963-73; engring. mgr. Intel Corp., Santa Clara, Calif., 1973-77, sr. mgr. quality assurance, 1977-84, Intel fellow, 1984—, mgr. Applications Lab., 1989—; dir. rsch. LFM program MIT, 1993—; vis. lectr. Technion, Haifa, Israel, 1970-71, H.H. Wills Physics Lab., Bristol, Eng., 1970-71. Contbr. articles to profl. jours. Mem. adv. bd. Lawrence Berkeley Lab., 1984—. AEC fellow, 1960; recipient Internat. Reliability awards, 1970, 79, 85.; appt. Disting. Engring. Alumnus Purdue U., 1988. Mem. AIME (chmn. electronic material symposium 1973—), Electron Microscope Soc. U.S.A., Tau Beta Pi, Phi Lambda Upsilon. Democrat. Jewish. Home: 5421 E Camello Rd Phoenix AZ 85018-1910 Office: Intel Corp 5000 W Chandler Blvd Chandler AZ 85226-3601

MEIGEL, DAVID WALTER, military officer, retired musician; b. Chgo., Feb. 27, 1957; s. Thomas Arent and Annie Elizabeth (Thomas) M. Diploma, USAF NCO Leadership Sch., Chanute AFB, Ill., 1981, USAF/CAP SQD Officer Sch., 1987, USAF NCO Acad., Norton AFB, Calif., 1991. Enlisted USAF, 1976; commd. staff sgt. to 2d lt. CAP, Travis AFB, Calif., 1986; advanced through grades to tech. sgt. USAF, 1989; percussionist 724th USAF Band, McChord AFB, Wash., 1976-78, 752d USAF Band, Elmendorf AFB, Alaska, 1978-80, 505th USAF Band, Chanute AFB, Ill., 1980-84, 504th USAF Band, Travis AFB, 1984-90; prin. percussionist, chief of adminstrn. Am.'s Band in Blue, USAF, Travis AFB, 1990-92. Prin. percussionist San Diego (Calif.) Civic Orch., 1973-76, Poway (Calif.) High Sch. Band, 1974-75; percussionist Anchorage (Alaska) Civic Opera, 1979-80, Anchorage (Alaska) Scottish Soc., 1979-80, Fairfield Civic Theatre, Fairfield, Calif., 1984—; communications officer USAF Civil Air Patrol, Travis AFB, 1986—. Recipient Gov.'s medal Youkon Internat. Invitational Scottish Games, Whitehorse City Coun., B.C., 1980; decorated USAF Achievement medal 1989, 93, USAF Commendation medal 1986, Comdrs. Commendation medal; named one of Outstanding Young Men Am., 1988, 92. Mem. CAP, USAF Aux. Home: 3600 Data Dr # 544 Rancho Cordova CA 95670 Office: Intel Corp 1900 Prairie City Rd Folsom CA 95630

MEIGHAN, STUART SPENCE, hospital consultant, internist, writer; b. Glasgow, Scotland, Jan. 30, 1923; came to U.S., 1962; s. Stuart Spence and Annie Louise (Brown) M; m. Anne Stewart Henderson, Nov. 4, 1952 (div. 1968); children: Jane Spence, Stuart Spence; m. Louise Rhys McGregor, July 7, 1985. MB, U. Glasgow, 1945. Registrar, sr. registrar Nat. Health Svc., U.K., 1948-57; sr. staff mem. Allan Blair Meml. Clinic, Regina, Sask., Can., 1957-62; internist Cleland Clinic, Oregon City, Oreg., 1962-64; dir. med. affairs Good Samaritan Hosp., Portland, Oreg., 1964-78; pres. Spence Meighan and Assocs., Portland, 1978—; cons. several hosps. and orgns. Contbr. over 100 articles to profl. jours. Lt. Royal Navy, 1946-48. Recipient Disting. Svc. award Am. Soc. Internal Medicine. Fellow Am. Coll. Physicians, Royal Coll. Physicians. Home and Office: 408 NW Rainier Ter Portland OR 97210-3347

MEIGS, JOHN LIGGET, artist; b. Chgo., May 10, 1916; s. James L. and Mary Margaret (Cookly) M.; 1 adopted son, Clinton Taylor (dec.). Student, U. Redlands, 1933-34, Gand Chaumier Acad., Paris. 50 one-man shows in U.S., France; author: Peter Hurd The Lithographs, Peter Hurd Sketch Book, Cowboy in American Graphics; contbr. numerous articles to profl. jours. With USN, 1951, PTO. Home and Office: Box 107 San Patricio NM 88384

MEIKLEJOHN, ALVIN J., JR., state senator, lawyer, accountant.; b. Omaha, June 18, 1923; B.S., J.D., U. Denver, 1951; m. Lorraine J. Meiklejohn; children: Pamela Ann, Shelley Lou, Bruce Ian, Scott Alvin. Mem. Colo. Senate from 19th dist., 1976-96, chmn. com. edn.; mem. Edn. Commn. of States, 1981-96, chmn. Colo. Commn. on Ach. in Edn., 1995; chmn., 1993-96. Mem. Jefferson Sch. Dist. No. R-1 Bd. Edn., 1971-77, pres., 1973-77; commr. Commn. on Uniform State Laws, 1988-96. Served to capt. U.S. Army, 1940-46; to maj. USAF, 1947-51. Mem. Colo. Soc. CPA's, Arvada C. of C. Republican. Clubs: Masons, Shriners. Home: 7540 Kline Dr Arvada CO 80005-3732 Office: Jones & Keller PC 1625 Broadway Ste 1600 Denver CO 80202-4725

MEILLEUR, CYNTHIA CLARK, school system administrator; b. Seattle, Sept. 3, 1947; d. James Elliot and Jan Marie (Williams) Clark; m. Raoul Joseph Meilleur, June 27, 1970; 1 child, Elise Catherine. BA, Stanford U., 1969, MA, 1970; Doctorate, U. Wash., 1989. Cert. tchr. grades K-12, prin., supt. Tchr. Sunnyvale H.S., Fremont, Calif., 1969-70, Nickerson Sch., Paris, 1970-72, Bellevue (Wash.) Pub. Schs., 1972-74; tchr. Am. Sch., Mexico City, 1974-77, adminstr., 1977-79; tchr. Newburyport (Mass.) H.S., 1980-81; tchr., adminstr. Seattle Pub. Schs., 1982-84; adminstr. Lake Washington Sch. Dist., Kirkland, Wash., 1984-88; dir. employee rels./spl. svcs. Lake Washington Sch. Dist., Kirkland, 1988-91, asst. supt., 1991—. Mem. ASCD, Assn. Sch. Adminstrs., Nat. Soc. for the Study of Edn., Kirkland C. of C. (edn. com. 1996—). Home: 238- 171st Pl NE Bellevue WA 98008

MEINDL, ROBERT JAMES, English language educator; b. Wausau, Wis., Sept. 17, 1936; s. George Martin and Adeline Emilie (Goetsch) M.; m. Victoria Lynn Chavez; children: Karin Rose, George Andrew, Damian Kurt, Erika Wittmer, Christopher Smith, Gabrielle Remelia. BS, U. Wis., 1958; MA, U. Conn., 1960; PhD, Tulane U., 1965; postdoctoral studies, U. Calif., Berkeley, 1967-68, Goethe Inst., Liblar, Germany, 1879, U. Cologne, Germany, 1970. Teaching asst. U. Conn., Storrs, 1958-60; teaching fellow Tulane U., 1960-62; lectr. U. Wis., Green Bay, 1963-65; from asst. to full prof. English Calif. State U., Sacramento, 1965—. Translator: Studies in John Gower, 1981; book rev. editor Studia Mystica Jour., 1984-89; contbr. numerous articles to profl. jours. With USNR, 1953-61, 79-96. Nat. Endowment for the Humanities fellow Stanford U., 1982. Mem. MLA, Medieval Acad. Am., Medieval Assn. of Pacific, Early English Text Soc., John Gower Soc., New Chaucer Soc. Home: 2301 Pennland Dr Sacramento CA 95825-0329 Office: Calif State U 6000 J St Sacramento CA 95819-2605

MEINEL, MARJORIE PETTIT, optical engineer; b. Pasadena, Calif., May 13, 1922; d. Edison and Hannah (Steele) Pettit; m. Aden Baker Meinel, Sept. 5, 1944; children: Carolyn, Walter, Barbara, Elaine, Edward, Mary, David. BA, Pomona Coll., Claremont, Calif., 1943; MA, Claremont Coll., 1944. Rsch. assoc. Calif. Inst. Tech., Pasadena, 1944-45, U. Ariz., Tucson, 1974-85; mem. tech. staff Jet Propulsion Lab., Pasadena, 1985—; vis. faculty Nat. Cen. U., Chung-Li, Taiwan, 1978-80; commr. Ariz. Solar Energy Commn., Phoenix, 1975-81; mem. office tech. assessment U.S. Congress, Washington, 1974-79. Author: Applied Solar Energy, 1977, Sunsets, Twilights and Evening Skies, 1983; patentee in field. Recipient Exceptional Svc. medal Nat. Aeronautics and Space Adminstrn., Kingslake medal. Fellow Internat. Soc. Optical Engring. (Gold medal). Lutheran.

MEISTER, GERRY, social studies educator; b. North Bend, Oreg., Dec. 7, 1935; d. Allen C. and Julia A. (Eakin) Smith; m. Richard A. Meister, Dec. 15, 1956. BA, Stanford U., 1957. Cert. secondary educator. Tchr. Sacramento (Calif.) Unified Sch. Dist., 1959-61, San Francisco Unified Sch. Dist., 1962—. Democrat. Home: 666 28th St San Francisco CA 94131 Office: UESF 655 14th St San Francisco CA 94114

MEISTER, JOHN EDWARD, JR., consultant, technical educator, systems analyst; b. Elgin, Ill., Nov. 17, 1956; s. John Edward and Marilyn Barbara (Futter) M.; m. Rebecca Marie Buehner, Nov. 15, 1975; children: Christine Marie, Mark Christopher. AA, Cen. Tex. Coll., 1979, U. Md., 1980; BS cum laude, U. Md., 1981; postgrad., Western Conservative Baptist Sem., 1982-83. Enlisted U.S. Army, 1974, advance through grades to staff sgt., 1980; electronics technician Frankfurt, Fed. Republic of Germany, 1974-77; maintenance supr. Darmstadt, Fed. Republic of Germany, 1978-81; transferred from 232d Signal Co. Telecommunications, 1981; instr. U.S. Army Signal Sch., Ft. Gordon, Ga., 1981-82; resigned U.S. Army, 1982; sr. electronics instr. ITT Tech. Inst., Portland, Oreg., 1982-83; equipment engring. and engring. svcs. technician Intel Corp., Aloha, Oreg., 1983-85; ind. lifetime AMSOIL Dealer, Snohomish, Wash., 1983—; electronic designer Boeing Electronics Co., Everett, Wash., 1985-89; systems analyst Boeing Comml. Airplanes, Everett, 1989-95; telecomm. designer UNIX Network Boeing Info. and Support Svcs., 1995; UNIX instr. Boeing Info. & Support Svcs., Delivery Sys. Cert. and Tng., Bellevue, Wash., 1995-96; cons. Clearview Cons., Snohomish, Wash., 1996—; instr. computing Boeing Off-Hour Tng., 1994-96; electronics engr. Innovative Designs and Electronic Sys. Techs., Portland, 1982-85. Bd. dirs. Machias Ridge East Homeowner's Assn., 1988-91; fin. advisor Jr. Achievement, Everett High Sch., 1988-89. Mem. NRA, Pacific N.W. 4-Wheel Dr. Assn. Republican. Baptist. Home and Office: 14809 SR9 SE Snohomish WA 98296 *Personal philosophy: I always try to see the big picture while keeping an eye on the bottom line, I believe the Bible teaches such a balance. My primary objective is to be a good steward and to get the job done, success comes from knowing I did the best I could with what I had.*

MEITZLER, LELAND KEITH, executive editor; b. Enumclaw, Wash., Apr. 13, 1950; s. Theodore Canfield and Virginia Francis (Cornett-Feller) M.; m. Patty Sue Daffern, Sept. 1, 1968; children: Leland Neal, Dale Ralph. AA with honors, Green River C.C., Auburn, Wash., 1983. Mgr. Meitzler's Greenhouse & Nursery, Puyallup, Wash., 1970-72; sales mgr. Meitzler's Wholesale Greenhouses, Orting, Wash., 1972-75; terminal mgr. Green Thumb Products Corp., Apopka, Fla., 1975-76; owner, mgr. Northwest Tropicals, South Prairie, Wash., 1976-82; pres. Meico Assocs., South Prairie, Wash., 1982-84; co-founder, pres. Heritage Quest Mag., Orting, 1985-92; mng. editor Heritage Quest Mag., Bountiful, Utah, 1992-95, exec. editor, 1996—; touring editor Am. Geneal. Lending Libr., Bountiful, 1993—. Mem. Assn. Profl. Genealogists, Tacoma-Pierce County Geneal. Soc. (corr. sec. 1982-83, pres. 1983-85), South Prairie Hist. Soc. (pres. 1982-85). Republican. Office: Am Genealogy Lending Libr PO Box 329 Bountiful UT 84011

MEITZLER, NEIL, artist; b. Pueblo, Colo., Sept. 14, 1930; s. Herbert Claussen and Virginia (Fellar) M.; m. Darlene Dinwiddie, Oct. 1, 1951 (div. 1965); children: Kenneth Neil Palmore, Charlotte Meitzler Engelhart, Carrie Meitzler Leonard. MFA, U. Wash., 1957. Exhbns. include Bellevue (Wash.) Art Mus., 1986, Washington County Art Mus., Hagerstown, Md., 1986, Walla Walla (Wash.) Coll., 1989, others; represented in permanent collections Seattle Art Mus., County Mus. Art, Hagerstown, Md., Memphis Acad. Art, Emperor of Japan, Tokyo. Recipient Kathrine Baker award Seattle Art Mus., 1958; grantee Nat. Endowment for Arts, 1967. Home and Studio: 637 Pleasant St Walla Walla WA 99362-3367

MELENDEZ, JAMES PATRICK, editor; b. Albuquerque, Oct. 2, 1966; s. James Patrick and M.C. (Roybal) M. BA, U. N.Mex., 1992; postgrad., St. Mary's U. of Minn., 1996. Coord. comms. ctr. U. N.Mex. Cancer Ctr., Albuquerque, 1988-93; assoc. editor dept. English U. N.Mex., Albuquerque, 1993-94; mng. editor Am. Literary Realism, Albuquerque, 1993-94, Blue Mesa Rev., Albuquerque, 1993-94; asst. to exec. vice chair Dept. Psychiatry, U. N.Mex., 1996—. Mem. Am. Polit. Sci. Assn., Am. Sociol. Assn., SIG-Graph, Nat. Soc. Fundraising Execs. Democrat.

MELENDY, HOWARD BRETT, historian, educator; b. Eureka, Calif., May 3, 1924; s. Howard Burton and Pearl Marjorie (Brett) M.; m. Marian Ethel Robinson, Mar. 29, 1952; children: Brenda Dale, Darcie Brett, Lisa Marie. AB in English, Stanford U., 1946, MA in Edn., 1948, PhD in History, 1952. V.p. cmty. colls., prof. history U. Hawaii, Honolulu, 1970-79; prof. history San Jose (Calif.) State U., 1955-70, 79-93; historian Cupertino, Calif., 1993—. Author: Governors of California, 1965, Asian Americans, 1981, Chinese and Japanese Americans, 1984, Walter Dillingham of Hawaii, 1996. Fellow Am. Coun. Edn., 1967-68; grantee NEH, 1974, 76-77, 70-82. Mem. Humboldt Lodge #79. Democrat. Presbyterian. Home and Office: 23500 Cristo Rey Dr # 309E Cupertino CA 95014

MELESE-D'HOSPITAL, PATRICK YVES, veterinarian, ethologist; b. Versailles, France, Mar. 3, 1957; came to U.S., 1958; s. Gilbert Bernard Melese and Yolande d'Hospital; m. Betsy Noelle Stroll, Dec. 23, 1996; 1 child, Andrew Jacques-Yves. BS, U. Calif., Davis, 1979, MA, 1980, DVM, 1986. Veterinarian Academy Animal Hosp., Solana Beach, Calif., 1987-90, Center Vet. Clinic, San Diego, 1990-91, Animal Hosp. of La Jolla, Calif., 1991-92; vet. dir., owner Vet. Behavior Cons., San Diego, 1988—, Tierrasanta Vet. Hosp., San Diego, 1994—. Mem. AVMA, Calif. Vet. Med. Assn., San Diego County Vet. Med. Assn., Am. Vet. Soc. Animal Behavior, Animal Behavior Soc., Delta Soc. (pres. San Diego chpt. 1987-89), Internat. Soc. of Applied Ethology. Roman Catholic. Office: 10799 Tierrasanta Blvd San Diego CA 92124

MELICH, MITCHELL, retired lawyer; b. Bingham Canyon, Utah, Feb. 1, 1912; s. Joseph and Mary (Kalembar) M.; m. Doris M. Snyder, June 3, 1935; children: Tanya (Mrs. Noel L. Silverman), Michael, Nancy, Robert A. LL.B., U. Utah, 1934. Bar: Utah 1934. Pvt. practice Moab, 1934-63, city atty., 1934-55; county atty. Grand County, 1940-42; sec., dir. Utex Exploration Co., Moab, 1953-62; pres., dir. Uranium Reduction Co., Moab, 1954-62; cons. to pres. Atlas Minerals, div. Atlas Corp., 1962-67; dir., treas. New Park Mining Co., 1962-65; assoc. Ray, Quinney & Nebeker, 1973-96; ret., 1996; solicitor Dept. Interior, Washington, 1969-73;. Mem. of Colorado River Com. of Utah, 1945-47; mem. Utah Water and Power Bd., 1947; chmn. Citizens Adv. Com. on Higher Edn., 1968; mem. nat. adv. council U. Utah, 1976—; Mem. Utah Senate, 1942-50, minority leader, 1949-50; mem. Utah Legislative Council, 1949-54; del. Republican Nat. Conv., 1952-72; mem. Rep. Nat. Com. for Utah, 1961-64; Rep. candidate for gov., 1964; cons. on staff Congressman Sherman P. Lloyd, Utah, 1967-68; bd. dirs. St. Marks Hosp., 1973-87; bd. regents U. Utah, 1961-65, also mem. devel. fund com., mem. nat. adv. council, 1968-73, 76—; mem. Utah Statewide Health Coordinating Coun., 1985; mem. Utah Fusion Energy Coun., 1989—. Recipient Disting. Alumni award U. Utah, 1969, Man of Yr. award, Arthritis Found., 1991. Mem. Am. Bar Assn., Utah State Bar, Utah Mining Assn. (pres. 1962-63), Kappa Sigma. Republican. Club: Alta Salt Lake Country (Salt Lake City). Lodges: Masons; Shriners. Home: 900 Donner Way Apt 708 Salt Lake City UT 84108-2112

MELING, ERIC M., food executive; b. 1953. Grad., Calif. State U., Fresno, 1975. With Wilshire & Doss, CPA, Hanford, Calif., 1975-77, County of Tulare, Visalia, Calif., 1977-79, M. Green & Co. Accountancy Corp., Visalia, 1979-87, Westbrook Bastrire Accountancy Corp., Visalia, 1987-91; CFO, treas. Klink Citrus Assn., Ivanhoe, Calif., 1991—. Office: Klink Citrus Assoc 32921 Road 159 Ivanhoe CA 93235-1455*

MELLOR, RONALD JOHN, history educator; b. Bklyn., Sept. 30, 1940; s. Ronald Green and Eleanor Teresa (Walsh) M.; m. Anne Tidaback Kostelanetz, June 7, 1969; 1 child, Ronald Blake. AB, Fordham Coll., 1962; cert., U. Louvain, Belgium, 1961; AM, Princeton U., 1964, PhD in Classics, 1968. Acting asst. prof. Classics Stanford (Calif.) U., 1965-68, asst. prof. Classics, 1968-75; assoc. prof. history UCLA, 1976-82, prof. history, 1982—, vice chair history, 1991-92, chair history, 1992-97; visitor Princeton Inst. Advanced Studies, 1997-98. Author: Thea Rhome, 1975, From Augustus to Nero: The First Dynasty of Imperial Rome, 1990, Tacitus, 1993, Tacitus and the Classical Tradition, 1995, The Historians of Ancient Rome, 1997. Fellow NEH, 1969, Am. Coun. Learned Socs., 1972, Humanities Rsch. Ctr. Australian Nat. U., Canberra, Australia, 1990; hon. fellow U. Coll. London, Eng., 1969, 72, 83-85. Mem. Am. Hist. Assn., Am. Philol. Assn., Am. Inst. Archaeology, Assn. Ancient Historians, Soc. for the Promotion of Roman Studies. Democrat. Home: 2620 Mandeville Canyon Rd Los Angeles CA 90049-1004 Office: UCLA Dept History 405 Hilgard Ave Los Angeles CA 90024-1301

MELLOW, JUDITH ELIZABETH, lawyer; b. South Bend, Ind., Aug. 29, 1935; d. Joseph and Mary (Dechter) M.; m. Gerald S. Gotterer, Sept. 2, 1956 (div. Apr. 1978); children: Elizabeth Gotterer, Rebecca Gotterer. AB, Bryn Mawr Coll., 1957; MA, U. Md., 1969, JD, 1978. Bar: Md. 1979, N.Mex. 1983. Tchr. English Bryn Mawr Sch., Balt., 1969-75; asst. states atty. Balt. (Md.) City, 1979-83; reporter Santa Fe (N.Mex.) Reporter, 1987-88, Rio Grande Sun, Espanola, N.Mex., 1989; spl. asst. atty. gen. N.Mex. Motor Vehicle Divsn., Santa Fe, 1990—. Office: DWI Legal Sect PO Box 1028 Santa Fe NM 87504-1028

MELNICK, ALICE JEAN (AJ MELNICK), counselor; b. St. Louis, Dec. 25, 1931; d. Nathan and Henrietta (Hausfater) Fisher; BJ, U. Tex., Austin, 1952; MEd, U. North Tex., 1974; m. Harold Melnick, May 24, 1953; children: Susan, Vikki, Patrice. Lic. profl. counselor. Reporter, San Antonio Light, 1952-53; instr. journalism project Upward Bound, So. Meth. U., Dallas, 1967-71; instr. writing El Centro Dallas County Community Coll., Dallas, part time 1972-74; instr. human devel. Richland Community Coll.,

Dallas, part-time 1974-79; tchr. English, journalism and psychology Dallas Ind. Sch. Dist., 1969-81; counselor Ursuline Acad., 1981-94; part-time instr. human devel. Sante Fe C.C. Freelance photographer. Mem. Am. Counseling Assn., Dallas Sports Car Club, N. Mex. Jewish Hist. Soc., Temple Beth Shalom. Jewish. Home: 101 Monte Alto Rd Santa Fe NM 87505-8865

MELOAN, TAYLOR WELLS, marketing educator; b. St. Louis, July 31, 1919; s. Taylor Wells and Edith (Graham) M.; m. Anna Geraldine Leukering, Dec. 17, 1944 (div. 1974); children: Michael David, Steven Lee; m. Jane Innes Bierlich, Jan. 30, 1975. B.S. cum laude, St. Louis U., 1949; M.B.A., Washington U., St. Louis, 1950; D of Bus. Admin., Ind. U., 1953. Advt. mgr. Herz Corp., St. Louis, 1941-42; sales promotion supr. Liggett & Myers Tobacco Co., St. Louis, 1942-43; asst. prof. mktg. U. Okla., Norman, 1953; asst., then assoc. prof. mktg. Ind. U., Bloomington, 1953-59; prof., chmn. dept. mktg. U. So. Calif., Los Angeles, 1959-69, prof. mktg., 1969-92, Robert E. Brooker prof. mktg., 1970-79, Robert E. Brooker disting. prof. mktg. emeritus, 1991—; dean Sch. Bus. Adminstrn. U. So. Calif., L.A., 1969-71, assoc. v.p. acad. adminstrn. and research, 1971-81; prof. bus. adminstrn. U. Karachi, Pakistan, 1962; vis. prof. mktg. Istituto Post U. Per Lo Studio Dell Organizzazione Aziendale, Turin, Italy, 1964, U. Hawaii, 1993, Madrid Bus. Sch., 1993; disting. vis. prof. U. Witwatersrand, Johannesburg, 1978, U. Hawaii, 1993; editl. advisor bus. adminstrn. Houghton Mifflin Co., Boston, 1959-73; cons. to industry and govt., 1953%; bd. dirs Inst. Shipboard Edn. Author: New Career Opportunities, 1978, Innovation Strategy and Management, 1979, Direct Marketing: Vehicle for Department Store Expansion, 1984, Preparing the Exporting Entrepreneur, 1986, The New Competition: Dilemma of Department Stores in the 1980's, 1987, Franchise Marketing: A Retrospective and Prospective View of a Contractual Vertical Marketing System, 1988; co-author: Managerial Marketing, 1970, Internationalizing the Business Curriculum, 1968, Handbook of Modern Marketing, contbg. author, 1986; co-author, co-editor: International and Global Marketing: Concepts and Cases, 1994; bd. editors Jour. Mktg., 1965-72. Trustee World Affairs Coun. Orange County, 1994—. Lt. (j.g.) U.S. Maritime Svc., 1943-46. Mem. Am. Mktg. Assn. (pres. L.A. chpt. 1963-64), Order of Artus, Beta Gamma Sigma, Delta Pi Epsilon, Calif. Yacht Club, Univ. Club, Rotary. Home: 59 Lakefront Irvine CA 92604-4683 Office: U So Calif Dept Mktg Los Angeles CA 90089-1421

MELROSE, ALBERT JOSEPH, investor relations professional; b. Santa Monica, Calif., June 13, 1926; s. Norris Albert and Marguerita Josephine (Menegus) M.; m. Jean Frances Wade, Feb. 14, 1953 (div. Feb. 1987); children: Mark, Dana; m. Marilyn Rausa Jones, May 21, 1987; children: Judith, Malcolm, Barton. AA, Santa Monica City Coll., 1948; AB, U. So. Calif., 1951. From flight test coord. to customer liaison Douglas Aircraft, Santa Monica, 1952-55; from contracts mgr. to mktg. adminstr. Ampex Corp., Santa Monica/Redwood City, Calif., 1955-60; mktg. mgr. Eitel-McCullough Inc., San Carlos, Calif., 1960-62; mktg. rep. Ryan Electronics, San Diego, 1962-63; mktg. analyst Autonetics, Anaheim, Calif., 1963-64; from mktg. mgr. to dir. investor rels. Litton Industries, San Carlos, Beverly Hills, Calif., 1964-79; dir. investor rels. Lockheed Corp., Burbank, Calif., 1979-81; v.p. corp. comms. Kaiser Steel Corp., Fontana, Calif., 1981-83; v.p. internat. mktg. Seidler Amdec Securities, L.A., 1983-88; dir. investor rels. AST Computer, Irvine, Calif., 1988-94; cons. in field, Newport Beach, Calif., 1994—; instr. U. Calif., Irvine, 1978-79; corp. advisor Calif. State U., Fullerton, 1991, U. So. Calif. Grad. Bus. Sch., 1982. Author: Investor Relations Executive Briefings, 1993. Served in U.S. Navy, 1944-46, Pacific/Asia. Mem. IEEE, Assn. Corp. Growth, Nat. Investor Rels. Inst. (pres. L.A. chpt. 1978, officer dir. nat. hdqs. 1979-82, pres. Orange County chpt. 1990). Home and Office: 1048 Irvine Ave Ste 189 Newport Beach CA 92660-4602

MELSHEIMER, HAROLD, obstetrician, gynecologist; b. Legenfeld, Germany, June 11, 1927; came to U.S., 1955; naturalized, 1960; s. Louis and Hella Leonie (Schwehr) Peterman; m. Norma Sykes Sabrina, Nov. 27, 1967; children: Laura, Linda. BS, Marburg U., West Germany, 1951, MD, 1954. Diplomate Am. Bd. Ob-Gyn. Intern Baden County Hosp., West Germany, 1954-55, St. Mary's Hosp. Med. Ctr., Long Beach, Calif., 1955-56; resident Queens Hosp. Med. Ctr., Honolulu, 1956-57, Calif. Hosp. Med. Ctr., L.A., 1957-59; pvt. practice ob-gyn. Encino, Calif., 1959-87; ret.; former dept. chief, now hon. staff mem. Am. Med. Internat. Med. Ctr., Tarzana, Calif., Encino Hosp.; founder Technion Inst. of Tech. Contbr. articles to profl. jours. Operational mem. USCG Aux., 1971. Recipient cert. of honor Wisdom Soc.; named Hon. Citizen, Rep. of Korea, 1966. Fellow ACS (life), Am. Coll. Ob-Gyn., Internat. Coll. Surgeons; mem. AMA, Calif. Med. Assn., L.A. County Med. Assn., Am. Physicians Fellowship for Israel Med. Assn., N.Y. Acad. Scis., Braemar Country Club. Home: 25660 Deertrail Dr Tehachapi CA 93561-9140

MELTEBEKE, RENETTE, career counselor; b. Portland, Oreg., Apr. 20, 1948; d. Rene and Gretchen (Hartwig) M. BS in Sociology, Portland State U., 1970; MA in Counseling Psychology, Lewis and Clark Coll., 1985. Lic. profl. counselor, Oreg.; nat. cert. counselor. Secondary tchr. Portland Pub. Schs., 1970-80; project coord. Multi-Wash CETA, Hillsboro, Oreg., 1980-81; coop. edn. specialist Portland C.C., 1981-91; pvt. practice career counseling, owner Career Guidance Specialists, Lake Oswego, Oreg., 1988—; mem. adj. faculty Marylhurst (Oreg.) Coll., 1989-93, Portland State U., 1994—; assoc. Drake Beam Morin Inc., Portland, 1993-96; career cons. Occupl. Health Svcs. Corp., 1994—, Career Devel. Svcs., 1990—, Life Dimensions, Inc., 1994; presenter Internat. Conf., St. Petersburg, Russia, 1995. Rotating columnist Lake Oswego Rev., 1995—. Pres. Citizens for Quality Living, Sherwood, Oreg., 1989; mem. Leadership Roundtable on Sustainability for Sherwood, 1994-95. Mem. ASTD, Assn. for Psychol. Type, Nat. Career Devel. Assn., Oreg. Career Devel Assn. (pres. 1990), Assn. for Quality Participation, Assn. for Humanistic Psychology, Willamette Writers. Home: 890 SE Merryman St Sherwood OR 97140-9746 Office: Career Guidance Specialists 15800 Boones Ferry Rd # C104 Lake Oswego OR 97035-3456

MELTON, CHERYL ANN, educator, small business owner; b. Bklyn., Jan. 5, 1949; d. Raymond Franklin and Irene Louise (Cotton) Blair; m. Gilbert Edmund Melton, Aug. 26, 1972; children: Byron Adrian, Brandie Alicia. BS in Edn., Ohio State U., 1971; MS in Edn., Nazareth Coll., Rochester, N.Y., 1976. Prof. clear multiple subject teaching credential, Calif. Elem. tchr. N.Y.C. Bd. Edn., Bklyn., 1971-72, Rochester City Sch. Dist., 1973-84; elem. tchr. Long Beach (Calif.) Unified Sch. Dist., 1984-90, lang. arts specialist, 1990—, reading recovery tchr., 1992—, mentor tchr., 1996—; v.p. sales and mktg. Orange County M2 Solutions, 1992—; regional reading specialist Los Angeles County Office of Edn., 1996—; mem. Sch. Program Improvement Leadership Team, Long Beach, 1990—; adv. bd. Scholastic, Inc.-Literacy Place, 1994-95; summer facilitator trainer Early Literacy Inservice Course, 1995; participant Calif. State U.-Long Beach South Basin Writing Project's Think Tank, summer 1996. Chmn. membership devel. Jr. League Long Beach, 1991-92, mem. by-laws task force, 1992-93, adv. future planning, 1989—, selected mentor, 1991—, sustaining advisor placement com., 1994-95, sustainer coun. mem., 1995—; chosen del. Jr. League Dallas. Scholar Calif. literature project Calif. State U., Dominguez Hills, 1992. Mem. Tchrs. Assn. Long Beach, Nat. Coun. Tchrs. English, Nat. Coun. Negro Women, Links (Orange County chpt. Inc., co-chair model initiative youth project 1994, 95, 96, 97, co-chair Journey into Possibilities, Rochester chpt., charter), Jack and Jill of Am. (charter Long Beach chpt.), Internat. Reading Assn., Reading Recovery Coun. N.Am., Beach Cities Reading Assn., Calif. Reading Assn., Nat. Coun. Tchrs. English, English Coun. of Long Beach, Delta Sigma Theta (charter, Long Beach alumnae). Democrat. Baptist. Home: 4508 Hazelnut Ave Seal Beach CA 90740-2918

MELTZOFF, ANDREW N., psychologist, educator; b. N.Y.C., Feb. 9, 1950; s. Julian and Judith (Novikoff) M. BA, Harvard U., 1972; PhD, Oxford U., Eng., 1976. Rsch. instr. U. Wash., Seattle, 1977-80, rsch. asst. prof., 1980-84, assoc. prof., 1984-88, prof., 1988—, adj. prof. psychiatry and behavioral scis., 1988—. Author: Words, Thoughts, and Theories, 1997; contbr. articles to profl. jours.; mem. editorial bd. Infant Behavior and Devel. Grantee NSF, 1983, NIH, 1986; MacArthur Found. grantee, 1984; recipient James McKeen Cattell award, 1990. Fellow AAAS, Am. Psychol. Assn., Am. Psychol. Soc.; mem. Soc. Rsch. and Child Devel., N.Y. Acad. Scis., Western Psychol. Assn., Norwegian Nat. Acad. Sci. and Letters, Phi Beta Kappa. Office: University of Washington Box 357920 Dept of Psychology Seattle WA 98195

MELTZOFF, JULIAN, psychologist; b. N.Y.C., Feb. 16, 1921; s. Nathan G. and Sadie L. (Marcus) M.; m. Judith Novikoff (div. 1975); children: Andrew, Nancy; m. Antonia Ratensky, Oct. 16, 1976. BS, CCNY, 1941; MLitt, U. Pitts., 1946; PhD, U. Pa., 1950. Lic. psychologist, Calif. Clin. psychologist U.S. Army, 1942-46; asst. NYU Testing & Advisement Unit, N.Y.C., 1946; clin. psychology trainee VA Regional Office Mental Hygiene Clinic, Phila., 1946-50, asst. chief psychology, 1950-53; chief psychology sect. VA Hosp., Phila., 1953-54; chief psychology svc. VA Outpatient Clinic, Bklyn., 1954-77; prof., dir. rsch. Calif. Sch. Profl. Psychology, San Diego, 1979-96. Author: Day Treatment Center: Principles, Application & Evaluation, 1966, Research in Psychotherapy, 1970, Critiquing Research: Principles and Practice, 1997; also articles. Staff sgt. U.S. Army, 1942-46, ETO. Fellow APA, Am. Psychol. Soc. Home: 7056 Vista Del Mar Ave La Jolla CA 92037-5339

MELUSO, JOHN, JR., small business owner; b. Watsonville, Calif., June 20, 1949; s. John, Sr. and Diana (Brant) M. BS in Aero. Engring., Calif. Poly. State U., 1971. Cert. in neurolinguistic programming. Salesman George Ball Inc., Chgo., 1972-77; owner Am. Growers Svc., Inc., Sunnyvale, Calif., 1977-82, Corlux Corp., Portland, Oreg., 1982-92; owner, spkr., author Positive Living Inc., Portland, 1992—; coord. Living Enrichment Ctr., Portland, 1992-94. editor Choices, 1982-92; author: The Next Step for Positive Living, 1992, The Next Step, 1993. Mem. Nat. Spkrs. Assn., Oreg. Spkrs. Assn., N.W. Publ. Assn. Home and Office: 5611 SW Corbett Ave Portland OR 97201

MELVIN, JAY WAYNE, computer programmer; b. Oak Park, Ill., Feb. 3, 1946; s. Kendred Wayne and Margarita Alice (Pérez) M.; m. Linda Hansen, Dec. 10, 1980. MA in Urban Studies, Claremont (Calif.) Grad. Sch., 1975, postgrad., 1977. Hot line/prodn. mgr. Forth, Inc., Hermosa Beach, Calif., 1981-85; sr. software engr. Maxtor Corp., San Jose, Calif., 1986-88; computer programmer Tracor-Ultron Labs., San Jose, 1988-90, Comtech Labs., Palo Alto, Calif., 1990-92; programmer, team leader, mgr. software devel. lab. Omnipoint Corp., Colorado Springs, Colo., 1992-96; mgr. applications integration lab. Pacific Bell Mobile Svcs., Pleasanton, Calif., 1996—; cons. phenomenoLOGIC, La Honda, Calif., 1985-92, InfoPath, La Honda, 1990—. Contbr. articles to profl. jours. Peace Corps vol. U.S. State Dept., Begal, India, 1966-68; fire dept. vol. Calif. Dept. Forestry, Kings Mountain, 1986-88; fire dept. lt. Vol. Fire Brigade, La Honda, San Mateo, 1988-94; radio operator Mil. Affiliate Radio Svc., Jackson, Miss., 1962-64. Recipient Beyond War award, 1987; grad. fellowship Law Enforcement Adminstrn. Assn., 1975-77. Mem. IEEE, Amateur Radio Relay League (life), Amateur Satellite Corp. (life), Forth Interest Group, Assn. of Computing Machinery, Pi Sigma Alpha. Home and Office: PO Box 123 La Honda CA 94020-0123

MENDEZ, C. BEATRIZ, obstetrician, gynecologist; b. Guatemala, Apr. 21, 1952; d. Jose and Olga (Sobalvarro) M.; m. Mark Parshall, Dec. 12, 1986. BS in Biology and Psychology, Pa. State U., 1974; MD, Milton Hershey Coll. Medicine, 1979. Diplomate Am. Bd. Ob-gyn.; cert. in advanced operative laparoscopy and hysteroscopy Accreditation Coun. for Gynecologic Endoscopy, Inc. Resident in ob-gyn. George Washington U., Washington, 1979-83; pvt. practice Santa Fe, 1985-95, Locum Tenens, 1996; pvt. practice Lovelace Health Sys., Albuquerque, 1996—; vol. physician Women's Health Svcs., Santa Fe, 1995-96; chair perinatal com. St. Vincent's Hosp., Santa Fe, 1986-89, quality assurance mem., 1986-95, chief ob-gyn., 1992-94; bd. dirs. Milton S. Hershey Coll. Medicine, Hershey, Pa., 1977-82. Vol. Women's Health Svcs., Santa Fe, 1985-95. With USPHS, 1983-85. Mosby scholar Mosby-Hersey Med. Sch., Hershey, 1979. Fellow Am. Coll. Ob-Gyn. (Continuing Med. Edn. award 1986—); mem. AMA (Physician Recognition award 1986—), Am. Assn. Gynecol. Laparascopists, Internat. Soc. Gynecol. Endoscopy, Am. Fertility Soc., Am. Soc. Colposcopy and Cervical Pathology, Residents Assn. George Washington U. (co-founder 1981-83). Democrat. Office: Lovelace-Rio Rancho 3701 Souther Blvd SE Rio Rancho NM 87124

MENDEZ, CELESTINO GALO, mathematics educator; b. Havana, Cuba, Oct. 16, 1944; s. Celestino Andres and Georgina (Fernandez) M.; came to U.S., 1962, naturalized, 1970; BA, Benedictine Coll., 1965; MA, U. Colo., 1968, PhD, 1974, MBA, 1979; m. Mary Ann Koplau, Aug. 21, 1971; children: Mark Michael, Matthew Maximilian. Asst. prof. maths. scis. Met. State Coll., Denver, 1971-77, assoc. prof., 1977-82, prof., 1982—, chmn. dept. math. scis., 1980-82; adminstrv. intern office v.p. for acad. affairs Met. State Coll., 1989-90. Mem. adv. rev. bd. Met. Denver, 1973-79; parish outreach rep. S.E. deanery, Denver Cath. Cmty. Svcs., 1976-78; mem. social ministries com. St. Thomas More Cath. Ch., Denver, 1976-78, vice-chmn., 1977-78, mem. parish council, 1977-78; del. Adams County Rep. Conv., 1972, 74, 1994, Colo. 4th Congl. Dist. Conv., 1974, Colo. Rep. Conv., 1982, 88, 90, 92, 96, Douglas County Rep. Conv., 1980, 82, 84, 88, 90, 92, 94, 96; alt. del. Colo. Rep. Conv., 1974, 76, 84, 5th Congl. dist. conv., 1976, mem. rules com., 1978, 80, precinct committeeman Douglas County Rep. Com., 1976-78, 89-92, mem. cen. com., 1976-78, 89-92; dist. 29 Rep. party candidate Colo. State Senate, 1990; mem. Colo. Rep. Leadership program, 1989-90, bd. dirs., 1990—; Douglas county chmn. Rep. Nat. Hispanic Assembly, 1989—; bd. dirs. Rocky Mountain Better Bus. Bur., 1975-79, Rowley Downs Homeowners Assn., 1976-78; trustee Hispanic U. Am., 1975-78; councilman Town of Parker (Colo.), 1981-84, chmn. budget and fin. com. 1981-84; chmn. joint budget com. Town of Parker-Parker Water and Sanitation Dist. Bds., 1982-84; commr. Douglas County Planning Commn., 1993—; dir. Mile High Young Scholars Program, 1995—. Recipient U. Colo. Grad. Sch. excellence in teaching award, 1965-67; grantee Benedictine Coll., 1964-65, Math. Assn. Am. SUMMA grantee Carnegie Found. N.Y., 1994, NSF, 1995—. Mem. Math. Assn. Am. (referee rsch. notes sect. Am. Math. Monthly 1981-82, gov. Rocky Mountain section 1993—, investment com. 1995—, devel. com. 1995—, task force on reps. 1994—), Am. Math. Soc., Nat. Coun. Tchrs. of Maths., Colo. Coun. Tchrs. of Maths. (bd. dirs. 1994—), Colo. Internat. Edn. Assn., Assoc. Faculties of State Insts. Higher Edn. in Colo. (v.p. 1971-73). Republican. Roman Catholic. Assoc. editor Denver Metro. Jour. Math. and Computer Sci., 1993—; contbr. articles to profl. jours. including Am. Math. Monthly, Procs. Am. Math. Soc., Am. Math. Monthly, Jour. Personalized Instruction, Denver Met. Jour. Math. and Computer Sci., and newspapers. Home: 39 Hummingbird Dr Castle Rock CO 80104 Office: PO Box 173362 Denver CO 80217-3362

MENDIUS, PATRICIA DODD WINTER, editor, educator, writer; b. Davenport, Iowa, July 9, 1924; d. Otho Edward and Helen Rose (Dodd) Winter; m. John Richard Mendius, June 19, 1947; children: Richard, Catherine M. Graber, Louise, Karen M. Chooljian. BA cum laude, UCLA, 1946; MA cum laude, U. N.Mex., 1966. Cert. secondary edn. tchr., Calif., N.Mex. English teaching asst. UCLA, 1946-47; English tchr. Marlborough Sch. for Girls, L.A., 1947-50, Aztec (N.Mex.) High Sch., 1953-55, Farmington (N.Mex.) High Sch., 1955-63; chair English dept. Los Alamos (N.Mex.) High Sch., 1963-86; sr. technical writer, editor Los Alamos Nat. Lab., 1987—; adj. prof. English, U. N.Mex., Los Alamos, 1970-72, Albuquerque, 1982-85; English cons. S.W. Regional Coll. Bd., Austin, Tex., 1975—; writer, editor, cons. advanced placement English test devel. com. Nat. Coll. Bd., 1982-86, reader, 1982-86, project equality cons., 1985-88; book selection cons. Scholastic mag., 1980-82. Author: Preparing for the Advanced Placement English Exams, 1975; editor Los Alamos Arts Coun. bull., 1986-91. Chair Los Alamos Art in Pub. Places Bd., 1987-92; chair adv. bd. trustees U. N.Mex., Los Alamos, 1987-93; pres. Los Alamos Concert Assn., 1972-73, 95—; chair Los Alamos Mesa Pub. Libr. Bd., 1990-94, chair endowment com., 1995—. Mem. Soc. Tech. Communicators, AAUW (pres. 1961-63, state bd. dirs. 1959-63, Los Alamos coordinating coun. 1992-93, pres. 1993-94), DAR, Order Ea. Star, Mortar Bd., Phi Beta Kappa (pres. Los Alamos chpt. 1969-72, v.p. 1996-97), Phi Kappa Phi, Delta Kappa Gamma, Gamma Phi Beta. Home: 124 Rover Blvd Los Alamos NM 87544-3634 Office: Los Alamos Nat Lab Diamond Dr Los Alamos NM 87544

MENDY, SHARON LEE, vocational educator; b. Oakland, Calif., Mar. 17, 1960; d. Jack Ray Mendy and Betty Alma (Goodman) Burke; 1 child, Shane Phillip Young. Student, Sonoma (Calif.) State U., 1984, 85; BA in Psychology, San Jose State U., 1986; postgrad. studies, Sacramento (Calif.) State U., 1994-95. Recreation coord. City of Fremont, Calif., 1987-88; devel. counselor Marin Assn. for Retarded Citizens, San Rafael, Calif., 1981-88; vocat. tng. and edn. coord. Goodwill Industries, Sacramento, 1989-96; vocat. rehab. counselor, site mgr. PRIDE Industries, Roseville and Sacramento, 1996—; active mem. Comty. Resource Coun., 1993—, Hispanic Comty. Coun., Sacramento, 1993—. Active supporter Ctrl. Valley Conditional Release, Sacramento 1992, Spinal Cord Head Injury Prevention, Calif. State U., Sacramento, 1996—. Recipient Cert. of achievement in rehab. adminstrn., U. San Francisco, 1990, Letter of commendation, Sen. Patrick Johnston, Sacramento, 1996. Mem. El Dorado Hills Comty. Svcs. Home: 2582 King Edward Ct El Dorado Hills CA 95762 Office: PRIDE Industries 555 Display Way Sacramento CA 95838

MENEFEE, GERALD ROBERT, writer, management consultant; b. Ft. Dodge, Iowa, June 17, 1936; s. George Victor and Helen Irene Menefee; m. Jilonne Kae Snook, Sept. 3, 1957; children: Jilonne K., Kelly Marie Menefee-Williams. BS in Acctg., Long Beach (Calif.) State Coll, 1964; MBA in Fin., Calif. State U., Long Beach, 1968; EdD, U. So. Calif., 1975. Mgmt. cons. GR Menefee & Assocs., West Covina, Calif., 1972—; writer West Covina, 1981—; pres., CEO Menefee Constrn. Co. Inc., West Covina, 1985-89; assoc. supt. Mpls. Pub. Schs., 1989-93; CFO, sec., fellow Cancer Imaging Targeting & Tech. Consortium, South Pasadena, Calif., 1995—; bd. dirs. CITTCON, Inc.; cons. to bd. Selma (Calif.) Sch. Dist., 1974-76; mem. bd. assocs. Sch. Bus. Assn., N.Y.C., 1989-93; mem. adv. bd. U.S. Colls. & Schs., N.Y.C., 1992. Author: The Gold Run, 1993, Lifeguard On Duty, 1994, Club Cozumel, 1995, Bay of Death, 1996, CITTCON-A Multi Disciplinary Approach to Cancer Research, 1996. Mem., bd. dirs. Queen of Valley Found., West Covina, 1986-89; planning commr. Lakewood (Calif.) Planning Bd., 1965-68. With USN, 1955-59. Named Edn. Adminstr. of Yr., Minn. Sch. Adminstrs., 1990. Mem. Rotary (West Covina chpt. pres., bd. dirs. 1985-89). Home: 1134 S Shasta St West Covina CA 91791-3614

MENGIS, CHRIS LUDWIG, retired internist; b. Monroe, La., July 6, 1924; s. Chris L. and Elizabeth Josephine (Winzerling) M.; children: Robert, Elizabeth, Miranda, Matilda, Sophie (dec.). MD, Tulane U. Rsch. asst. JTF-1, 1946; intern Madigan Army Hosp., Tacoma, Wash., 1951-52; surgeon 370th Amphibious Brigade, Ft. Sherman, Canal Zone, 1952-53; resident in internal medicine Brooke Army Hosp., Fort Sam Houston, Tex., 1953-55; asst. chief medicine Post Hosp., Fort Jay, N.Y., 1955-59; pvt. practice San Juan Clinic, Farmington, N.Mex., 1959-60, St. Vincent Hosp., Santa Fe, N.Mex., 1960-79; asst. chief internal medicine Walla Walla (Wash.) VA Hosp., 1980-93; ret., 1993—. Contbr. articles to profl. jours. Bd. dirs. N.Mex. Tuberculosis Assn., Santa Fe; active Santa Fe Vol. Fire Dept.; pres. Santa Fe Cmty. Coun., 1964. Capt. U.S. Army Med. Corps, 1956-59. Democrat. Home: PO Box 149 Athena OR 97813-0149

MENKIN, CHRISTOPHER (KIT MENKIN), leasing company executive; b. Manhattan, N.Y., Jan. 1, 1942; s. Lawrence and Columbia (Riland) M.; children: Dashiel, Tascha, Ashley. Student, Julliard Sch. of Music, 1960, Santa Monica Coll., 1959-61, UCLA, 1961-64. News editor, dir. Sta. KRFC Radio, San Francisco, 1964-67; adminstrv. asst. to assemblyman Leo J. Ryan South San Francisco, 1967-68; mng. editor Sta. KGO TV News, San Francisco, 1968-69; news producer west coast Sta. ABC TV, Los Angeles, 1969; city mgr. City of San Bruno (Calif.), 1970; owner Menkin & Assocs., Santa Clara, Calif., 1971—; sr. ptnr. Am. Leasing, Santa Clara, 1971—; ptnr. Medallon Leasing, Santa Clara, 1974-80; pres. Monte Sereno Wine Co., Santa Clara, 1978—; dir. Meridian Nat. Bank, 1982-84. Chmn. nominating com. San Jose (Calif.) Symphony, 1988—; sec. Salvation Army, Santa Clara, 1968—, bd. dirs., 1990—, bd. dirs. San Jose chpt., 1990, vice chmn. county adv. bd., 1992; bd. dirs. Cmty. Against Substance Abuse, Los Gatos, Calif., 1988—, Valley Inst. of Theater Arts, Saratoga, Calif., 1987-88, San Jose Trolley, 1988—; vice chmn. Salvation Army Rehab. Bd., 1997. Mem. United Assn. Equipment Leasing (regional chmn. 1992-95, membership chmn. 1994-95, dir. 1996—), Credit Women Internat. (1st male pres.), Santa Clara Valley Wine Soc. (pres. 1988), Credit Profls. Santa Clara Valley (pres. 1990-91), Assn. Credit Grantors (past pres.), Santa Clara C. of C. (pres. 1973-76), Bay Area Exec. Club (sec.), Confrerie de la Chaine de Rotisseurs (charge de presse 1992-95), Royal Rose Soc. Gt. Britain (rep. No. Calif. 1990—). Democrat. Office: Am Leasing 348 Mathew St Santa Clara CA 95050-3114

MENN, LISE, linguistics educator; b. Phila., Dec. 28, 1941; d. David K. and Olga (Cohen) Waldman; m. Michael D. Menn, Dec. 8, 1962 (div. Mar. 1974); children: Stephen Philip, Daniel Joseph; m. William Oliver Bright, Nov. 28, 1986. BA, Swarthmore Coll., 1962; MA, Brandeis U., 1964, U. Ill., 1974; PhD, U. Ill., 1975. Rsch. asst. Boston U. Sch. Medicine, 1977-82, rsch. asst. prof. dept. neurology, 1982-86; assoc. prof. U. Colo., Boulder, 1986-94, prof., 1994—, chair dept. linguistics, 1991-95, 96—; mem. linguistics panel NSF, Wasington, 1983-86; mem. comm. disorders rev. group NIH, Washington, 1992-95. Co-editor: Exceptional Language Linguistics, 1982, Agrammatic Aphasia, 1990, Phonological Development, 1992. Mem. Linguistic Soc. Am. (exec. com. 1994-97), Acad. Aphasia (sec. bd. govs. 1989-92). Office: U Colo Linguistics Dept Box 295 Boulder CO 80309-0295

MENNELLA, VINCENT ALFRED, automotive manufacturing and airplane company executive; b. Teaneck, N.J., Oct. 7, 1922; s. Francis Anthony and Henrietta Vernard (Dickson) M.; B.A. in Acctg., U. Wash., 1948; m. Madeleine Olson, Aug. 18, 1945; children—Bruce, Cynthia, Mark, Scott, Chris. Sales and bus. mgmt. positions Ford div. Ford Motor Co., 1949-55; founder, pres. Southgate Ford, Seattle, 1955-80; pres. Flightcraft, Inc., Seattle, 1973-86; chmn. bd. Stanley Garage Door Co., 1981-86, Zman Magnetics, 1990—. Former chmn. March of Dimes. Served to capt. USNR, 1942-45. Republican. Roman Catholic. Clubs: Rainier Golf, Seattle Tennis, Rotary (past pres.). Home: 1400 SW 171st Pl Seattle WA 98166-3453

MENTZER, RAYMOND A., history educator; b. Pitts., Sept. 20, 1945; s. Raymond A. and Anna M. (Snyder) M.; m. Elizabeth J. Palmer, Sept. 14, 1968; children: Sarah, John. BA, Fordham U., 1967; MA, U. Wis., 1970, PhD, 1973. Prof. history Mont. State U., Bozeman, 1973—. Author: Heresy Proceedings, 1984, Blood and Belief, 1994; editor: Sin and the Calvinists, 1994. Mem. Sixteenth Century Studies (pres. 1996-97), Phi Beta Kappa. Office: Mont State U History Dept Bozeman MT 59717

MERCHANT, ROLAND SAMUEL, SR., hospital administrator, educator; b. N.Y.C., Apr. 18, 1929; s. Samuel and Eleta (McLymont) M.; m. Audrey Bartley, June 6, 1970; children: Orelia Eleta, Roland Samuel, Huey Bartley. BA, NYU, 1957, MA, 1960; MS, Columbia U., 1963, MSHA, 1974. Asst. statistician N.Y.C. Dept. Health, 1957-60, statistician, 1960-63; statistician N.Y. Tb and Health Assn., N.Y.C., 1963-65; biostatistician, adminstrv. coord. Inst. Surg. Studies, Montefiore Hosp., Bronx, N.Y., 1965-72; resident in adminstrn. Roosevelt Hosp., N.Y.C., 1973-74; dir. health and hosp. mgmt. Dept. Health, City of N.Y., 1974-76; from asst. adminstr. to adminstr. West Adams Cmty. Hosp., L.A., 1976; spl. asst. to assoc. v.p. for med. affairs Stanford U. Hosp., Calif., 1977-82, dir. office mgmt. and strategic planning, 1982-85, dir. mgmt. planning, 1986-90; v.p. strategic planning Cedars-Sinai Med. Ctr., L.A., 1990-94; cons. Roland Merchant & Assocs., L.A., 1994—; clin. assoc. prof. dept. family, community and preventive medicine Stanford U., 1986-88, dept. health rsch. and policy Stanford U. Med. Sch., 1988-90. With U.S. Army, 1951-53. USPHS fellow. Fellow Am. Coll. Healthcare Execs., APHA; mem. Am. Hosp. Assn., Nat. Assn. Health Svcs. Execs., N.Y. Acad. Scis. Home: 27335 Park Vista Rd Agoura Hills CA 91301-3639 Office: Roland Merchant & Assocs 27335 Park Vista Rd Agoura Hills CA 91301-3639

MERCKER, MARY ALICE, aviation school administrator; b. Kansas City, Mo., June 29, 1932; d. Kenneth Foster Rhees and Catherine Mary (Tellman) Henel; m. Reid Martin, Nov. 23, 1950 (div. Nov. 1969); children: Reid J., Kenneth C., Mark T., Mary M., Theodore H., Sylvia R., Ben X., Teresa I. Student, Phoenix Coll., 1949-50; AA, Pima Coll., 1990-93; student, U. Ariz., 1994. Fed. aviation adminstr.; comml. pilot; cert. flight instr. Instr. Ariz. Sch. Aviation, Tucson, 1979, Tucson Cmdr., 1980, AVRA Flt. Ctr., Marana, Ariz., 1976-78; pres., founder Alpha Air, Inc., Tucson, 1980—; sec., treas. Manasco Inc., Tucson, 1987—; aviation cons., Tucson, 1987—; adj. profl aviation Pima C.C., Tucson, 1988-94, curriculum cons., 1988-93. Author numerous poems. Recipient 2nd Place Sparrowgrass Poetry Forum, 1996. Mem. Ariz. Pilots Assn., Aircraft Owners and Pilots Assn., 99's (life). Home: 6220 W Belmont Rd Tucson AZ 85743 Office: Alpha Air Inc HC 2 Box 282 Tucson AZ 85735

MERCURIO, EDWARD PETER, natural science educator; b. Orange, Calif., Dec. 28, 1944; s. Peter Amadeo and Jeanne (Monteleone) M.; m. Jeanne Roussel Gable, Oct. 18, 1980 (div. Dec. 1984); 1 child, Katherine Roussel; m. Patricia Ann Kahler, Apr. 12, 1987; children: Peter Edward, Rose Sierra. BA, UCLA, 1967, MA, 1970, CPhil, 1978. Research asst. UCLA, 1971, teaching asst., 1968-71; instructional assoc. Golden West Coll., Huntington Beach, Calif., 1972-73; cons. Monterey County Planning Dept., Salinas, Calif., 1980; prof. Hartnell Coll., Salinas, Calif., 1973—; photographer in field, Calif., 1961—; lectr. in field, Calif., 1970—; cons. in field, 1980—. Fellow Woodrow Wilson Nat. Fellowship Found., 1967. Mem. AAAS, Sierra Club. Democrat. Home: 647 Wilson St Salinas CA 93901-1346 Office: Hartnell Coll 156 Homestead Ave Salinas CA 93901-1628 *Personal philosophy: My personal philosophy can be summarized by five words beginning with the letter H: Hedonism, Holism, Hyperopia, Harmony and Health.*

MEREDITH, RICHARD STEPHEN, psychotherapist, educator; b. Lawrenceburg, Tenn., July 26, 1952; s. Richard and Frances Ellen (Leedy) M.; m. Deborah Ann Powell, Apr. 3, 1982 (div. July 1984). BS, No. Ariz. U., 1974; MA, Adams State Coll., 1990. Lic. profl. counselor, clin. mental health counselor; nat. cert. counselor, cert. criminal justice specialist. Grad. asst. No. Ariz. U., Flagstaff, 1975-76; mental health worker The Guidance Ctr., Flagstaff, 1976-79; case worker Social Svcs., Cortez, Colo., 1979-89; sch. counselor Colo. Timberline, Durango, Colo., 1989-90; psychotherapist S.W. Colo. Mental Health, Cortez, 1990-91; program coord. Sunrise Youth Shelter, Towaoc, Colo., 1991; pvt. practice psychotherapist Cortez, 1991—; mem. grants com. Four Corners Child Advocacy, Cortez, 1993; mem. adv. bd. Ptnrs., Inc., Cortez, 1990, Renew, Cortez, 1980; bd. dirs. Mental Health Assn., Cortez, 1979-80. Bd. dirs. Pinon Project Family Ctrs., 1997—. Mem. ACA, Internat. Assn. Marriage and Family Counselors, Internat. Assn. Addictions and Offender Counselors, Colo. Soc. for Study of Dissociation. Office: Four Corners Counseling Assocs PO Box 1495 Cortez CO 81321

MERENSTEIN, GERALD BURTON, pediatrician, educator; b. Pitts., Feb. 14, 1941; s. Morris and Sarah (Shrinsky) M.; m. Barnetta Maryn, Aug. 21, 1960. BS, U. Pitts., 1962, MD, 1966. Diplomate Am. Bd. Pediatrics; lic. physician, Calif., Colo. Intern then resident Fitzsimons Gen. Hosp., Aurora, Colo., 1966-69; fellow Children's Hosp. San Francisco, 1969-71; program dir. neonatal-perinatal fellowship Fitzsimons Army Med. Ctr., Aurora, Colo., 1975-86, chmn. dept. pediatrics, 1979-86; dir. Lubchenco Perinatal Ctrs. U. Colo./Children's Hosp., Denver, 1986—, acting chmn. dept. pediatrics, 1988-90, dir. child health assoc. program, physician asst., 1994—; prof. of pediatrics, vice chmn. acad. affairs U. Colo./Children's Hosp., 1990—. Co-editor: Handbook of Neonatal Intensive Care, 1985, 2d edit., 1989, 3d edit., 1993, 4th edit. 1997, Handbook of Pediatrics, 16th edit., 1991, 17th edit., 1994, 18th edit. 1997. Bd. dirs. Nat. Cert. Corp., Chgo., 1988-96; mem. steering com., mem. com. on perinatal health March of Dimes, White Plains, N.Y., 1990-93. Col. U.S. Army, 1966-86. Named Outstanding Man of Yr., Denver Jaycees, 1974. Fellow Am. Acad. Pediatrics (chair com. fetus and newborn 1989-93, exec. com. sect. on prenatal pediatrics 1996—); mem. Am. Pediatric Soc., Assn. Pediatric Program Dirs. (exec. com., councilor), Alpha Omega Alpha. Democrat. Jewish. Office: U Colo Health Scis Ctr C219 Denver CO 80262

MERFELD, GERALD LYDON, artist; b. Des Moines, Feb. 19, 1936; m. Carol L. Fiser; 1 child, Elizabeth Ann. Studied with William Mosby, Chgo. Studio asst. Dean Cornwell; combat artist USN. Group exhbns. include Mass. Mus. of Fine Arts, Springfield, Smithsonian Inst., Audubon Artists, N.Y.C., Nat. Acad. of Western Art, others; represented in permanent collections Marietta Coll., USN Archives, John J. McDonough Collection of Am. Art, John Deere & Co. Bd. dirs. Frontier Pathway Scenic Byway, Colo., 1995—. Recipient Gold Medal of Honor, Am. Artist Profl. League, 1989, Am. Artists Mag. award Knickerbocker Artists, 1989, 2 Gold medals Washington Sq. Exhibit, N.Y.S., Painting award Okal. Mus. of Art, 1975, Mainstreams Juror's award of Merit, Marietta Coll., 1976, Mainstreams award of Distinction, 1977, First prize Hope Show, 1980, First prize Butler Inst. of Am. Art. Office: Brookwood Gallery 2302 Muddy Rd Westcliffe CO 81252

MERGL, BETTY MAE, senior center executive director; b. Omaha, Nebr., Aug. 30, 1931; d. Edward Sedlacek and Agnes Marie (Skavril) Swirczek; m. Aldrich Norbert Mergl, Feb. 9, 1951; children: Christine, Kenneth, Gerald, Allan, Brian, Meredith. Grad. h.s., Omaha. Bookkeeping First Nat. Bank, Omaha, 1950-51; claims sec. Lloyd's of London, Tacoma, Wash., 1951-53; payroll supr. Western Paving Co., Denver, 1958-68; exec. dir. Tri Valley Sr. Citizens Assn., Deer Trail, Colo., 1977—; adv. bd. Arapahoe County Transp. Svc., Denver, 1981-84, Arapahoe County C.S.B.G. Funds, Denver, 1983-84. Sch. bd. mem. Deer Trail Sch., Colo., 1979-84; mem. Colo. Congress of Sr. Orgns., Denver, 1982; del. Gov.'s Conf. on Aging, State of Colo., 1980; mem. Sr. Ctrs. of colo., 1982—; adv. bd. mem. Arapahoe Regional Libr., Denver, 1981-84, Gov.'s Vol. Citizen Bd., Denver, 1981-85; mem. Adams County Coun. of Older Ams., Arapahoe County Coun. for Sr. Citizens, Srs. and Lawmen Together-Adams County Sheriff's Dept. and Arapahoe County Sheriff's Dept. Recipient Cert. of Appreciation ARC, 1983, 84, Tri County Health, State of Colo., 1979, award HUD, 1995. Mem. I-70 Corridor C. of C. Home: 8201 S Santa Fe Dr # 197 Littleton CO 80120 Office: Tri Valley Sr Citizens Assn PO Box 776 Littleton CO 80160-0776

MERILAN, JEAN ELIZABETH, statistics educator; b. Columbia, Mo., Sept. 18, 1962; d. Charles Preston and Phyllis Pauline (Laughlin) M. PhD in Statistics, U. Ariz., 1996; AB summa cum laude, U. Mo., 1985, MA in Math., MA in Stats., 1987; PhD in Stats., U. Ariz., 1996. Grad. teaching asst. U. Mo., Columbia, 1985-87; grad. rsch. asst. U. Ariz., Tucson, 1988-89, grad. tchg. asst., 1989-93. Nat. Merit scholar, Univ. Curators scholar U. Mo., 1981-85, Grad. Acad. scholar U. Ariz., 1990-91, Arts and Sci. Grad. scholar U. Mo., 1985-87; Gregory fellow U. Mo., 1985-87, Faculty of Sci. fellow U. Ariz., 1987-88. Mem. Am. Statis. Assn., Inst. Math. Stats., Soc. for Indsl. and Applied Math., Biometric Soc., Am. Math. Soc., Math. Assn. Am., Golden Key Nat. Honor Soc., Sigma Xi, Phi Beta Kappa, Phi Kappa Phi, Phi Eta Sigma, Pi Mu Epsilon.

MERITT, PATRICIA ANNE, early childhood specialist; b. Reno, Jan. 8, 1952; d. William Floyd and Patricia (Goodman) Martinez; m. George Walter Sanders, Feb. 3, 1973 (div. 1977); m. Robert Philo Meritt, Aug. 3, 1979; children: Paul William, Andrew Philo. AA, Sacramento City Coll., 1971; BA in Child Devel., Calif. State U., Chico, 1973; MA in Tchg., U. Alaska, 1984. Exec. dir. Play N Learn Inc., Fairbanks, Alaska; early childhood trainer, cons.; adj. faculty childhood dept. U. Alaska, Fairbanks, asst. prof. early childhood, 1997—; CDA rep. preschool ctrs., Bank St. Coll., N.Y., 1983, infant toddler ctr., 1985, coun. early childhood recognition, Washington, 1996; presenter, cons. in field. Contbr. articles to profl. publ. Commr. Alaska Gov.'s Commn. Children and Youth, chmn.; mem. commn. Alaska's Legis. Children's Commn.; mem. early childhood devel. program rev. com. Tanana Valley C.C.; mem. Mayor's Task Force on Children and Families, Fairbanks; coord. Cmty. Edn. and Training Grants; leader Boy Scouts Am., bd. dirs. Midnight Sun Coun.;sunday sch. tchr. St. Jude's Episcopal Ch., St. Matthew's Episcopal Ch. Recipient Cmty. Svc. award Fairbanks Assn. Edn. Young Children, 1995; named to Panel 100, Beginnings Mag., Panel 200, Child Care Info. Exch. Mag. Mem. Nat. Assn. Edn. Young Children (life), Fairbanks Assn. Edn. Young Children (pres.), KIDPAC (founding, treas.), Rotary. Home: 4581 Drake St Fairbanks AK 99709-3006 Office: U Alaska TVC 8080 Rm 100 510 2nd Ave Fairbanks AK 99701

MERK, ELIZABETH THOLE, sales representative; b. Salt Lake City, July 29, 1950; d. John Bernard and Emily Josephine T.; 1 child, William Lance Ulrich; m. J. Eliot Merk, July 26, 1996. BA, U. Hawaii, Hilo, 1984, paralegal cert. cum laude, 1989; postgrad.in bus. administrn., U. Hawaii, Manoa, 1985-86. Lic. ins. agt. Hawaii. Regional rep. Lightolier, Inc., Salt Lake City, 1978-80; group sales rep. FHP/Utah, Salt Lake City, 1980-81; health net rep. Blue Cross Corp., L.A., 1981-82; v.p. fin. Bus. Support Systems, Hilo, 1983-89; rep. Prudential Ins. and Fin. Svcs., Honolulu, 1989—; registered rep. Pruco Securities Corp. subs. Ins. & Fin. Svcs., 1989—. Docent Lyman House, 1984-85, L.A. County Mus. of Art, 1980-81, S.L.C. Art Mus., 1970-80; bd. dirs. YWCA, Hawaii Island, 1980-91, 1st v.p., 1988. Named YWCA Vol. of Yr., 1991; recipient Nat. Quality award 1991, 92, 93, 94, Nat. Sales Achievement award 1992, 93. Fellow Life Underwriters Tng. Coun.; mem. AAUW (fundraiser chair Kona chpt. 1992, bd. dirs. Hilo chpt. 1987-89, comty. area rep. 1989), Am. Bus. Women's Assn. (past pres. Nani O Hilo chpt. 1995-96, cmty. svc. chair 1993-95, membership chair 1996—, audit com. chair Kanoelani chpt. 1992, program chair Hilo chpt. 1985, expansion com. Hilo Lehua chpt. 1985, Steven Bufton grantee 1985, ways and means com. 1984, memberships chair Lehua chpt. 1983), Nat. Assn. Life Underwriters (legis. rep. West Hawaii 1989—), Million Dollar Round Table (qualifying mem. 1992, 93, 94, 95). Roman Catholic.

MERRELL, ARTHUR NELSON, psychiatrist; b. Tulsa, Jan. 13, 1943; s. Ira Nelson and Rita Noriene (Harris) M.; m. Caro Arlene Doehling, Apr. 22, 1996; children: Kelly, Joshua, Adam, Jacob. BA, Colo. Coll., 1963; MD, U. Colo., 1967. Diplomate Am. Bd. Psychiatry and Neurology. Med. dir. S.E. Wyo. Mental Health Ctr., Cheyenne, 1974—. Col. Wyo. Air Nat. Guard, 1983—. Methodist. Office: 2526 Seymour Ave Cheyenne WY 82001-3159 Home: 6141 Weaves Rd Cheyene WY 82009

MERRIAM, JANET PAMELA, special education educator; b. L.A., Jan. 11, 1958, d. Allen Hugo and Linda (Teagle) Warren; m. Marshal Lockhart Merriam, Aug. 4, 1984 (div. June 1991); 1 child, Jennifer Elizabeth. BA, San Jose State U., 1981. Cert. tchr. learning handicapped, lang. devel. specialist, Calif. Asst. youth edn. dir. Christ Ch. Unity, San Jose, 1988-90; substitute tchr. Santa Clara (Calif.) Unified Sch. Dist., 1990; spl. day class tchr. Oak Grove Sch. Dist., San Jose, 1990—. Sunday sch. tchr. Christ Ch. Unity, San Jose, 1980-92. Mem. Coun. for Exceptional Children, Learning Disabilities Assn. Calif. Republican. Home: 1657 Glenville Dr San Jose CA 95124-3808 Office: 530 Gettysburg Dr San Jose CA 95123

MERRICK, BEVERLY CHILDERS, journalism, communications educator; b. Troy, Kans., Nov. 20, 1944; d. Horace Buchanan Merrick and Vola Yolantha (Clausen) Maul; m. John Douglas Childers, July 10, 1963; children: John Kevin, Pamela Christine, Jessica Faye. BA in Journalism with honors, Marshall U., 1980, BA in English with honors, 1980, M Journalism, 1982; M Creative Writing, Ohio U., 1986, cert. in Women's Studies, 1984, PhD in Comm. with honors, 1989. Reporter, photographer Ashland (Ky.) Daily Ind., 1981; tchr., instr. Albuquerque Pub. Schs., 1986-89; gen. assignment reporter, photographer Rio Rancho (N.Mex.) Observer, 1986; editor, rsch. cons. Ins. Pub. Law, Sch. of Law U. N.Mex., Albuquerque, 1990; asst. prof. Ga. So. U., Statesboro, 1991-94; assoc. prof. dept. mass comm. U. S.D., Vermillion, 1994-95; asst. prof. dept. journalism and mass comm. N. Mex. State U., Las Cruces, 1995—; part-time tchr., tchg. assoc. Ohio U., Athens, 1981-84; part-time copy editor Albuquerque Tribune, 1991; vis. prof. East Carolina U., Greenville, N.C., 1989-90; adj. prof. Embry-Riddle U., Kirtland AFB, N.Mex., 1989, 91; organizer diversity conf., 1st amendment conf. Ga. So. U.; mem. session MIT, 1989; chair campus com. N.Mex. State U. Author: (poetry) Navigating the Platte, 1986, Pearls for the Casting, 1987, Closing the Gate, 1993; contbr. poems to profl. publs., jours. and chpts. to books. Pub. rels. liaison Nat. Convention Bus. and Profl. Women, Albuquerque, 1988; pres. Albuquerque Bus. and Profl. Women, 1986-87, Rio Rancho Civic Assn., 1987-89, So. Ohio Improvement League, 1973-76; pres. bd. dirs. Pine Creek Conservancy Dist., 1976-83. Named Outstanding Citizen, N.Mex. Legislature, Truly Fine Citizen of Ohio, Ohio Gen. Assembly, 1973, Outstanding Homemaker of Ohio, Gov. of Ohio, 1974; grantee Reader's Digest, 1980, 83; John Houk Meml. grantee W.Va. Women's Conf., 1982; fellow Nat. Women's Studies Inst., Lilly Found., 1983, Freedom Forum Ethics, 1995, Am. Newspaper Inst., 1996; E.W. Scripps scholar, 1984; recipient Silver Clover award 4-H, Writing award Aviation/Space Writers Assn., 1981, 1st place open rsch competition Nat. Assn. Women's Dean's, Adminstrs. and Counselors, 1990; rsch. grantee N.Mex. State U., 1996. Mem. Soc. Profl. Journalists, Assn. for Edn. in Journalism and Mass Comm. (mem. nat. conv. com. 1993-94, vice head mag. divsn. 1995-96, head mag. divsn., 1996-97,), N.Mex. State Poetry Soc. (pres. 1987-89), Sigma Tau Delta. Home: 985 Ivydale Las Cruces NM 88005 Office: N Mex State U Dept 3J Box 30001 Las Cruces NM 88003-8001

MERRICK, NICHOLAS GREGORY, photographer; b. Detroit, Apr. 11, 1954; s. Thano and Esther (Lambros) M.; m. Shaun Gilmore, Feb. 27, 1982; children: Athan Gilmore, Benjamin Gilmore, Cole Gilmore. BFA, U. Mich., 1976; MFA, Sch. Art Inst. of Chgo., 1980. Adj. faculty Triton Coll., Riverwoods, Ill., 1977-78; asst. photographer Hedrich-Blessing, Chgo., 1977-79, photographer, 1979-84, ptnr. and prin., 1984—; workshop instr. Santa Fe (N.Mex.) Photo Workshops, 1993, 96; lectr. on photography, 1980—; photograph for archaeol. expdn., Cyrene, Libya, 1973-75, 78-79; photography illustrated various pubs. including Architecture, Archtl. Lighting, Archtl. Record, Chgo. Arch. Ann., Country Home, Designer, Interiors, Interior Design, Iowa Architect, Nikkei Architect, Perspective, Progressive Architecture, Texas Architect, Victoria, Inland Arch., El Croquis, others. One man shows of photographs include: Sill Gallery, Eastern Mich. Univ., 1976, Shade Gallery, Lansing, Mich., 1976, The Studio Gallery, Kirkland, Fine Arts Ctr., Decatur, Ill., 1982, Photographer's Gallery, Tarrant C.C., Dallas, 1984; group shows include: N.A.M.E. Gallery, Chgo., 1976, Art Inst. Chgo., 1977, 83, Ctr. for Creative Studies, Detroit, 1978, Gilbert Gallery, Chgo., 1980, The Studio, San Francisco, 1980, others. Adj. mem. Galisteo (N.Mex.) Vol. Fire and Rescue Dept., 1992—. Home: Hedrich-Blessing HC 75 Box 118 Galisteo NM 87540-9752

MERRILL, COOK, congressman; b. Phila., May 6, 1946; m. Camille Sanders; 5 children. BA in Econs. with high honors, U. Utah, 1969; MBA in Internat. Fin., Harvard U., 1971. Mmgt. cons., profl. budget analyst Arthur D. Little, Inc., Cambridge, Mass., 1971-73; founder, pres. Cook Slurry Co., Utah, 1973-96; mem. 105th Congress from 2nd Utah dist., 1996—; Mem. Transp. and Infrasturcture Com., Banking and Fin. Svcs. Com. mem. transp. and infrastructure com., banking and fin. svcs. com., sci. com. Missionary LDS Ch., Eng., 1965-67; del. Nat. Rep. Conv., 1976-96. Office: 1431 Longworth HOB Washington DC 20515

MERRILL, THOMAS M., produce executive; b. 1929. With Merrill Farms, 1945—, now pres., CEO. Office: Merrill Farms PO Box 659 1067 Merrill St Salinas CA 93901-4420*

MERRILL, THOMAS ST. JOHN, medical photographer; b. Jersey City, N.J., Feb. 21, 1946; s. Willard St. John and Frances Minnie (Havlieck) M.; m. Marie Knoetig, Mar. 19, 1967; children: Monica Marie-Rose, Michelle St. John. Student, Fairleigh Dickenson U., 1963-64, Germain Sch. Photography, 1967-68; AA, Saddleback Coll., 1990; student, Mt. San Antonio Coll., 1990-92; BS in Bus. Adminstrn., U. Phoenix, 1995. Cert. retinal angiographer. Photography asst. VA Hosp., N.Y.C., 1968; dept. head, photography Manhatten Eye, Ear and Throat Hosp., N.Y.C., 1968-69; med. photographer Don Allen Studio, N.Y.C., 1969-71; sr. ophthalmic photographer Mt. Sinai Sch. Medicine, N.Y.C., 1971-76; ophthalmic photographer U. Calif., Irvine, 1976-86; photographer Allergan Inc., Irvine, 1986-89; owner, pres. The Med. Image, Chino, Calif., 1983—; sr. med. photographer Providence St. Joseph Med. Ctr., Burbank, Calif., 1991—. Mem. Luth. Hour Rose Float Com., Pasadena, Calif. With U.S. Army, 1964-67, Vietnam. Mem. Biol. Photographic Assn. (fellow 1991, chmn. so. Calif. chpt. 1990-92), Ophthalmic Photographers' Soc., VFW (life), AMVETS. Home: 4395 Goldenrod Ct Chino CA 91710-1618 Office: Saint Joseph Med Ctr 501 S Buena Vista St Burbank CA 91505-4809

MERRIMAN, EDWARD FRANKLIN, journalist; b. Pendleton, Oreg., May 22, 1952; s. Edward Roy and Virginia Lucille (Livingston) M.; m. Debra Joy Hanna, June 20,1972 (div. Oct. 1978); children: Heath, Raime; m. Sherry Linda Tate, Aug. 25, 1996; stepchildren: Heather, Kristen. AS in Indsl. Tech., Blue Mountain C.C., Pendleton, 1979; BS in Journalism, U. Oreg., 1981. Apprentice in plumbing Merriman Plumbing Co., Pendleton, 1970-75, journeyman plumber, 1975-76, foreman, plumber, 1976-79; freelance writer Eugene, 1979-81; writer ad sales Singles N.W. Magazine, Richland, Washington, 1981-83; reporter Tri-City Herald, Kennewick, Washington, 1983-85; news corr. Statesman Jour., Salem, Oreg., 1985-87; reporter Capital Press, Salem, 1987—. Youth soccer coach Rotary & Stayton (Oreg.) Boys & Girls Club, 1985-90, youth basketball coach, 1986-92; budget com. Stayton Sch. Dist., 1989-95; pres., v.p. Stayton High Booster Club, 1991-95. Mem. Nat. Assn. Agrl. Journalists, Soc. Profl. Journalists. Home: PO Box 131 Stayton OR 97383 Office: Capital Press PO Box 2048 Salem OR 97308

MERRIN, JAMES STEVEN, internist; b. La Crosse, Wis., Mar. 30, 1954; s. Irving and Verna Mae (Borovoy) M.; m. Theresa Suzanne Drapkin, Feb. 23, 1992; 1 child, Abigail Rose. BS, U. Wis., 1976, MS, 1979; MD, La. State U., 1989. Diplomate Am. Bd. Internal Medicine. Resident Cedars Sinai Med. Ctr., L.A., 1989-93; physician Briarwood Ind. Physicians Assn., Thousand Oaks, Calif., 1993—. Eagle Scout, 1969. Named Chancellor's scholar U. Wis., 1972, Mary Shine Peterson scholar in Biochemistry, U. Wis., 1975; recipient Rsch. scholarship Epilepsy Found. of Am., 1987. Mem. AMA, Am. Coll. Physicians, Sierra Club. Office: Briarwood IPA 299 W Hillcrest Dr Thousand Oaks CA 91360-4264

MERRITT, ALAN EDWIN, environmental professional; b. Denison, Tex., Sept. 22, 1952; s. Edwin Herald and Dorothy May (Dooley) M.; m. Cheryl Fields, June 6, 1980. BS, East Tex. State U., 1975, MS, 1980; MBA, Amber U., 1986. Chemist, biologist North Tex. Mcpl. Water Dist., Wylie, 1980-85; field and quality control chemist Laidlaw Environ. Svcs., Clearwater, Fla., 1989-91; environ. scientist State of Idaho Idaho Nat. Engrng. Lab. Oversight Program, Idaho Falls, 1991—. Field support vol. NRA, Idaho Falls, 1992—; pres. libr. bd. Sachse (Tex.) Pub. Libr., 1984-85. Served with U.S. Army, 1975-77. Mem. Sigma Xi (assoc.). Republican. Office: State of Idaho INEL Oversight Program 900 N Skyline Dr Idaho Falls ID 83402-1718

MERROW, WILLIAM WOODROW, management consultant; b. Pitts., Mar. 22, 1956; s. William Hoover and Carol Ann (Defibaugh) M.; m. Susan Lee, July 8, 1974; 1 child, Angela Anne. BA, Ottawa U., 1983; MA, John F. Kennedy U., 1995; cert. project mgmt., Project Mgmt. Inst., Dallas, 1986; cert. applied behavioral sci., National Tng. Lab., Bethel, Maine, 1995. Mktg. mgr. CIGNA Healthplan, Phoenix, 1984-85; fin. dir. CIGNA Healthplan, Hartford, Conn., 1986-87; sys. dir. Am. Express, San Rafael, Calif., 1988-89; sales dir. Am. Express, San Rafael, 1990-93, investment ops. dir., 1994-95; mgmt. cons. Optimizers, Rohnert Park, Calif., 1995—. Fellow Life Mgmt. Inst. Republican.

MERSEREAU, SUSAN S., clinical psychologist; b. Atlanta, Apr. 9, 1947; d. John Andy Jr. and Dorothy Grace (Smith) Smith; m. Peter Roland Mersereau, May 30, 1970; children: Barrett, Travis, Courtney. AB, Vassar Coll., 1969; MSEd, Elmira Coll., 1973; D in Psychology, Pacific U., 1989. Lic. psychologist, Oreg.; diplomate Am. Coll. Forensic Medicine, Nat. Registry of Cert. Group Psychotherapists. Psychology intern Pacific Gateway Hosp., Portland, Oreg., 1987-88, Psychol. Svcs. Ctr., Hillsboro, Oreg., 1988-89; psychology resident Lee Doppelt, Beaverton, Oreg., 1990-91; staff Pac. Gateway Hosp., 1990—; pvt. practice psychologist Beaverton, 1991-93; dir. Pacific Ctr. for Attention and Learning, Beaverton, 1993—; mem. Neuropsychology Delegation to South Africa, 1996. Tchr. Incentive grantee Guam Dept. Edn., 1979. Mem. APA, Oreg. Psychol. Assn., Nat. Register Health Svc. Providers, Am. Coll. Forensic Examiners (diplomate Citizen Amb. program), Nat. Registry Group Psychotherapist (cert. group psychotherapist), Vassar Club Oreg. (admissions com. 1984—, pres. 1984-88). Office: Pacific Ctr Attention & Learning 3800 SW Cedar Hills Blvd Beaverton OR 97005-2027

MERTA, PAUL JAMES, cartoonist, photographer, engineer, restauranteur, real estate developer; b. Bakersfield, Calif., July 16, 1939; s. Stanley Franklin and Mary Ann (Herman) M.; AA, Bakersfield Jr. Coll., 1962; BS in Engring., San Jose State Coll., 1962. Cartoonist nat. mags., 1959—; civilian electronics engr. Air Force/Missiles, San Bernardino, Calif., 1962-65; electronics countermeasures engr., acquisition program mgr. Air Logistics Command, Sacramento, 1965-90; ret.; TV film, video animator, producer, owner Merge Films, 1965—; photographer, owner The Photo Poster Factory, Sacramento, 1971—; owner restaurant La Rosa Blanca, Sacramento, 1979-91; ptnr. Kolinski and Merta Hawaiian Estates, 1981—; polit. cartoonist Calif. Jour., 1958-59, Sacramento Union Newspaper, 1974-94, Sacramento Legal Jour., 1979. Home: 4831 Myrtle Ave Apt 8 Sacramento CA 95841-3621 Office: 1005 12th St Sacramento CA 95814-3920

MESCHKOW, JORDAN MARK, lawyer; b. Bklyn., Mar. 25, 1957; s. Gerald Meschkow and Florence Y. (Katz) Silverman; m. Susan G. Scher, Aug. 10, 1980; children: Sasha Hayley, Alisha Sadie. BS in Biology, SUNY, Stony Brook, 1979; JD, IIT, 1982. Bar: Ariz.z 1982, Fla. 1983; registered U.S. Patent and Trademark Office 1983. Assoc. James F. Duffy, Patent Atty., Phoenix, Ariz., 1982; ptnr. Duffy & Meschkow, Phoenix, 1983-84; sole practice Phoenix, 1984-92; sr. ptnr. Meschkow & Gresham, Plc., Phoenix, 1992—; frequent talk radio guest and spkr. at seminars on patent, trademark and copyright law. Contbr. article series to profl. jours.; patentee in field. Mem. Am. Intellectual Property Law Assn., State Bar Ariz. (intellectual property sect. 1982—), Maricopa County Bar Assn. Office: 5727 N 7th St Ste 409 Phoenix AZ 85014

MESINA, DENNIS G., lawyer; b. Davao City, The Philippines, Nov. 28, 1953; came to U.S., 1984; s. Fermin R. and Gloria (Francisco) M. AB in Philosophy cum laude, U. Philippines, Quezon City, 1976, LLB, 1981; LLM, U. Pa., 1985. Bar: Philippines 1982, Calif. 1988. Lectr. philosophy U. Philippnes, Quezon City, 1980-82; assoc. Siguion Reyna, Montecillo and Ongsiako, Philippines, 1982-84, 86-87, Popella, Allard, McCowan & Jones, San Jose, Calif., 1988-89, Thoits, Hershberger et al, Palo Alto, Calif., 1989-91; pvt. practice San Francisco, 1991—; v.p. Filipino Bar Assn. No. Calif., San Francisco, 1990-91, pres., 1991-92. Founder, steering com. mem. Philippine Environ. & Support Network, Burlingame, Calif., 1990—; v.p. Fil-Am. Coun. of San Francisco, 1992-94. Mem. Fil-Am. C. of C., of San Francisco, Yerba Buena Ctr. for Arts, San Francisco Mus. Modern Art, Sierra Club. Office: Ste 810 433 California St San Francisco CA 94104-1000

MESLOH, WARREN HENRY, civil and environmental engineer; b. Deshler, Nebr., Mar. 17, 1949; s. Herbert Frederick and Elna Florence (Petersen) M.; m. Barbara Jane Anderson, Sept. 7, 1969; children: Christopher Troy, Courtney James. BS, U. Kans., 1975; postgrad., Kans. State U., 1976-77. Registered profl. engr. Colo., Kans., Nebr.; cert. expert witness ACEC. Project mgr. Wilson & Co. Engrs., Salina, Kans., 1975-80, process design dir., 1980-82; engring. dir. Taranto, Stanton & Tagge, Fort Collins, Colo., 1982-85; pres. The Engring. Co., Fort Collins, Colo., 1985—; mem. civil engring. adv. bd. Kans. U., Lawrence, 1982—. Contbg. author (book) Pumping Station Design, 1989, (water pollution control manual) Manual of Practice No. OM-2, 1991, ACEC Certified Exper Witness, 1996; contbr. articles to profl. jours. Cub master Boy Scouts Am., Salina, 1980-81; active Luth. Ch., 1982—; vol. Paralyzed Vets. Orgn., Fort Collins, 1985—; pres. Foothills Green Pool Assn., Fort Collins, 1987-88. Sgt. U.S. Army, 1971-73, Germany. Named Outstanding Engr.-In-Tng. NSPE, 1978. Mem. Am. Pub. Works Assn., Am. Water Works Assn., Water Pollution Control Fedn., Fort Collins Country Club. Republican. Office: The Engring Co 2310 E Prospect Rd Fort Collins CO 80525-9770

MESQUITA, ROSALYN ANAYA, artist, educator; b. Belen, N.Mex., Aug. 21, 1935; d. Trinidad Jose and Margaret Oliva (Aragon) Anaya; m. Theodore Richard Mesquita, Jan. 14, 1956 (div.); children: John, Richard, Larry, Thresa. BA, Calif. State U., Northridge, 1974; MFA, U. Calif., Irvine, 1976. Cert. community coll. credential, Calif. Curator State of N.Mex., Santa Fe, 1968-72; lectr. L.A. Hist. Soc., 1978—; prof. Pasadena (Calif.) City Coll., 1981—; lectr. Non.-Govtl. Orgn. UN PLanning Com., Nairobi, Kenya, and N.Y., 1985—; curator, participant Am. Women in Art, UN World Conf., Nairobi, 1985; curator Mus. Natural History, L.A., 1978; planning com. worldwide women's conf. Global Focus, Beijing, 1995; peer panelist Cultural Affairs Dept. City of L.A., 1995—. Lectr. L.A. BiCentennial and 1985 Olympic Com., 1976-84; mem. Santa Monica Art Commn., 1991—. Recipient Col.-Aide-De Camp award Gov. David F. Cargo, 1972; Ford Found. fellow, 1975. Mem. Coll. Art Assn., Nat. Women's Caucus for Art (affirmative action officer 1980-83, honorarium 1983), Hispanic Faculty Assn. (treas. 1980-90), Assn. Latin Am. Artists (pres. 1982-90), L.A. La Raza Faculty Assn. (sec. 1979-85, v.p. 1988-89). Democrat. Roman Catholic. Home: 1501 Camino Sierra Vista Santa Fe NM 87501 Office: Pasadena City Coll 1370 Colorado Blvd Pasadena CA 90405-1628

MESROBIAN, EDMOND, computer scientist, computer architect; b. Constansa, Romania, May 9, 1960; came to U.S., 1966; s. Ovanes and Aneta (Moshigian) M. BS in Computer Sci., UCLA, 1982, MS in Computer Sci., 1986, PhD in Computer Sci., 1992. Tchg. assoc. in computer sci. UCLA,

1983-87, rsch assoc. in computer sci., 1987-90, prin. devel. engr., 1993-96; sr. scientist Perceptronics, Inc., Woodland Hills, Calif., 1990-92; computer scientist, chief arch. Disney Online, Burbank, Calif., 1996—. Contbr. articles to profl. jours. Mem. IEEE, Assn. Computing Machinery, Optical Soc. Am., Soc. for Computer Simulation. Home: 1014 N Alexandria Ave Los Angeles CA 90029-2518 Office: Disney Online 500 S Buena Visa St Burbank CA 91521-8005

MESSENGER, RON J., health facility administrator; b. 1944. MBA, U. So. Calif., 1968. Engr. CASH, L.A., 1968-73; v.p. Nat. Med. Enterprises, Santa Monica, Calif., 1973-84; pres. L.A. Cmty. Hosp., 1984—, Hollywood (Calif.) Cmty. Hosp., 1984—; pres., sec., CEO Paracelsus Healthcare Corp., Pasadena, Calif., 1984—. Office: Paracelsus Healthcare 155 N Lake Ave Ste 1100 Pasadena CA 91101-1857*

MESSERLI, DOUGLAS, author, publisher; b. Waterloo, Iowa, May 30, 1947; s. John H. and Lorna (Caspers) M.; companion Howard N. Fox. BA in English, U. Md., 1972, MA in English, 1974, PhD in English, 1979. Admissions coord. U. Wis., Madison, 1967-69; asst. head protocol Columbia U., N.Y.C., 1969-70; grad. asst., tchr., coord. interns U. Md., 1973-77; pub. Sun & Moon Press, L.A., 1976—; prof. dept. English Temple U., Phila., 1979-84; dir. The Contemporary Arts Ednl. Project, Inc., 1983—; part-time faculty mem. Calif. Inst. Tech., Pasadena, 1987-89, Otis-Parsons Sch. Arts, L.A., 1989. Author: (poetry) Dinner on the Lawn, 1979, Some Distance, 1982, River to Rivet: A Manifesto, 1985, River to Rivet: A Poetic Trilogy, 1985, Maxims from My Mother's Milk/Hymns to Him: A Dialogue, 1988, An Apple, A Day, 1993, (drama) Silence All Round Marked: An Historical Play in Hysteria Writ, 1992, (as Kier Peters) The Confirmation, 1993, (fiction/film/poetry) Along Without: A Fiction in Film for Poetry, 1993, The Walls Come True: An Opera for Spoken Voices, 1996; editor: From the Other Side of the Century: A New American Poetry 1960-1990, 1994, The Sun & Mood Guide to Eating Through Literature and Art, 1994, 50: A Celebration of Sun & Moon Classics, 1995. Recipient Carey-Thomas award Pubs. Weekly, 1987, Harry Ford Editor's award Nat. Poetry Series, 1994. Mem. MLA, Am. Booksellers Assn. Office: Sun & Moon Press 6026 Wilshire Blvd Los Angeles CA 90036-3607

MESSINGER, J. HENRY, lawyer; b. N.Y.C., Sept. 7, 1944; s. Benjamin and Edna (Balser) M.; m. Karen Gilbert D'Abo, Feb. 5, 1977 (div.); 1 son, Alan Toby. B.A., Union Coll., 1965; J.D., NYU, 1968, M.A. in Polit. Sci., U. N.Mex. 1996. Bar: N.Y. 1968, N.Mex. 1973, U.S. Tax Ct. 1973. Sole practice, Woodstock, N.Y., 1970-72; assoc. Stephen Natelson, Esq., Taos, 1972-73; ptnr. Natelson & Messinger, Taos, 1974-75; sole practice, Taos, 1976-94, Albuquerque, 1994—. Bd. dirs. Taos Sch. Music, 1982—; bd. dirs. R.C. Gorman Found., 1986—, Taos Valley Sch., 1979-82, pres. 1980-81. Mem. ABA, Am. Polit. Sci. Assn., Law and Soc. Assn. Office: 809 Branding Iron St SE Albuquerque NM 87123-4207

MESTAD, ORVILLE LAVERNE, bank executive; b. Decorah, Iowa, Mar. 22, 1923; s. Clarence Benjamen and Edna Belinda (Larson) M.; m. Shirley Gail Matthews, July 20, 1948; children: Cynthia Mestad Johnson, Ronald Matthew. BS, U. So. Calif., 1949, DDS with honors, 1953. Pvt. practice dentistry Arcadia, Calif., 1953-83; instr. clin. dentistry U. So. Calif., Los Angeles, 1953-57; organizer, chmn. Foothill Ind. Bank, Glendora, Calif., 1973—; chmn. Foothill Ind. Bancorp, Glendora, 1986-92. Trustee Foothill Presbyn. Hosp., Glendora, 1972-90, 91—, chmn., 1987-89, 93—; trustee Citrus Valley Health Ptnrs., West Covina, 1995—; mem. exec. com. Citrus Coll. Found., Glendora, 1982-89. Decorated Bronze Star; named Citizen of Yr., City of Glendora, 1990. Mem. ADA, Arcadia Lions Club, Alpha Tau Epsilon. Republican. Presbyterian. Home: 1144 Indian Springs Dr Glendora CA 91741-2334 Office: Foothill Ind Bancorp 510 S Grand Ave Glendora CA 91741-4207

MESTRIL, RUBEN, biochemist, researcher; b. N.Y.C., Jan. 21, 1951; s. Fernando and Renee (Casanova) M.; m. Ilona Erika Brelewski, Dec. 16, 1984; 1 child, Sebastian. BA in Chemistry summa cum laude, St. Thomas U., 1981; PhD in Biochemistry, U. Miami, Coral Gables, Fla., 1986. Postdoctoral fellow German Cancer Rsch. Ctr., Heidelberg, 1986-88; asst. rsch. biochemist U. Calif., San Diego, 1988-92, asst. adj. prof., 1992—. Reviewer Circulation jour., San Diego, 1991—; contbr. revs., articles to profl. jours., chpts. to books. Grantee NSF, 1980, Am. Heart Assn., 1991, NIH, 1994. Mem. AAAS, Am. Inst. Chemists, Am. Soc. Biochemistry and Molecular Biology, Am. Heart Assn. (basic sci. coun. 1991—), Internat. Soc. Heart Rsch. Democrat. Office: U Calif San Diego 9500 Gilman Dr La Jolla CA 92093-5003

METCALF, JACK, congressman, retired state senator; b. Marysville, Wash., Nov. 30, 1927; s. John Read and Eunice (Grannis) M.; m. Norma Jean Grant, Oct. 3, 1948; children: Marta Jean, Gayle Marie, Lea Lynn, Beverlee Ann. Student U. Wash., 1944-45, 47; BA, BEd, Pacific Luth. U., 1951. Tchr., Elma (Wash.) pub. schs., 1951-52, Everett (Wash.) pub schs., 1952-81; mem. Wash. Ho. of Reps., 1960-64; mem. Wash. Senate, 1966-74, 80-92, U.S. congressman, Wash. 2nd Dist., 1995—; chmn. environment and natural resources com., 1988-92; mem. domestic & internat. monetary policy, fin. instns. & consumer credit, aviation, surface transp. coms. Chmn. Honest Money for Am. Mem. Council State Govts., Wash. Edn. Assn. (dir. 1959-61), Wash. Assn. Profl. Educators (state v.p. 1979-81, state pres. 1977-79). Mem. Nat. Conf. State Legislatures, Western States Recycling Coalition, South Whidbey Kiwanis, Deer Lagoon Grange. Republican. Home: 3273 E Saratoga Rd Langley WA 98260-9694 Office: US House Reps House Office Bldg 1510 Longworth Washington DC 20515-4702*

METCALF, VIRGIL ALONZO, economics educator; b. Branch, Ark., Jan. 4, 1936; s. Wallace Lance and Luella J. (Yancey) M.; m. Janice Ann Maples, July 2, 1958; children: Deborah Ann, Robert Alan. BS in Gen. Agr., U. Ark., 1958, MS in Agrl. Econs., 1960; Diploma in Econs., U. Copenhagen, 1960; PhD in Agrl. Econs., U. Mo., 1964. Asst. prof. U. Mo., Columbia, 1964-65, asst. to chancellor, 1964-69, assoc. prof., 1965-69, prof., exec. asst. to the chancellor, 1969-71; prof. econs., v.p. administrn. Ariz. State U., Tempe, 1971-81, prof. Sch. Agribus. and Natural Resources, 1981-88, prof. internat. bus. Coll. of Bus., 1988—; asst. to the chancellor U. Mo., 1964-69, coord. internat. programs and studies, 1965-69, mem. budget com., 1965-71, chmn., co-chmn. several task forces; cons. Ford Found., Bogota, Colombia, 1966-67; mem. negotiating team U.S. Agy. for Internat. Devel., Mauritania, 1982, cons., Cameroon, 1983, agrl. rsch. specialist, India, 1984, agribus. cons., Guatemala, 1987, 88, asst. dir. Reform Coops. Credit Project, El Salvador, 1987-90; co-dir. USIA univ. linkage grant Cath. U., Bolivia, 1984-89; cons. World Vision Internat., Mozambique, 1989. Contbr. numerous articles to profl. jours. Mem. City of Tempe U. Hayden Butte Project Area Com., 1979; bd. commrs. Columbia Redevel. Authority; mem. workable project com. City of Columbia Housing Authority. Econs. officer USAR, 1963, econ. analyst, 1964-66. Fulbright grantee U. Copenhagen, 1959-60, U. Kiril Metodij, Yugoslavia, 1973. Mem. Am. Assn. Agrl. Economists, Soc. for Internat. Devel., Samaritans (chmn. 1976, bd. dirs. 1976, mem. task force of health svc. bd. trustees 1974, health svc. 1974-78, chmn. program subcom. 1975), Kiwanis, Blue Key, Gamma Sigma Delta, Alpha Zeta, Alpha Tau Alpha. Democrat. Home: 1357 W Crystal Spring Dr Gilbert AZ 85233 Office: Ariz State U Coll Bus Tempe AZ 85287

METCALF, WAYNE C., insurance commissioner; m. Shirley Umada Metcalf. BA in Polit. Sci., U. Hawaii, 1975; JD, 1978; student, Tufts U., 1992-93. Atty. pvt. practice, 1979—; spl. cons. UN, 1994; ins. commr. Dept. Commerce and Consumer Affairs State Hawaii, 1994-97; staff Senate Jud. Com., 1973-75; staff dir. Senate Pres.'s Office, 1975-78; vice-chmn. House Com. on Jud., 1984-86; chmn. House Com. on Jud., 1986-92;; mem. house coms. Comsuner Protection and Commerce, 1984-92, Land Use and Hawaiian Affairs Plannong, 1984-86, Labor and Pub. Employment Transp., 1985-88, Housing, Health Humand Svcs, 1988-90, Housing, Health, 1990-92. Recipient Disting. Alumni award U. hawaii, 1988, Disting. Legislator award, Nat. Dem. State LEgis. Leaders Assn., 1988; named one of Hawaii's five best legislators by polit. columnist Dan Boylan, 1990, 92. Office: Insurance Divsn Dept Commerce and Consumer Affairs 250 S King St 5th Fl Honolulu HI 96813

METROS, MARY TERESA, librarian; b. Denver, Nov. 10, 1951; d. James and Wilma Frances (Hanson) M. BA in English, Colo. Women's Coll., 1973; MA in Librarianship, U. Denver, 1974. Adult svcs. libr. Englewood (Colo.) Pub. Libr., 1975-81, adult svcs. mgr., 1983-84; libr. systems cons. Dataphase Systems, Kansas City, Mo., 1981-82; circulation libra. Westminster (Colo.) Pub. Libr. 1983; pub. svcs. supr. Tempe (Ariz.) Pub. Libr., 1984-90, libr. adminstr., 1990—. Mem. ALA, Pub. Libr. Assn., Ariz. Libr. Assn. Democrat. Office: Tempe Pub Libr 3500 S Rural Rd Tempe AZ 85282-5405

METSKER, THOMAS CHARLES, map company executive; b. Tacoma, May 24, 1927; s. Charles Thomas and Emily Rose (Fleming) M.; m. Patricia Jeanne Rossiter; children: Mark F., Thad C., Kimberly J., Ty Thomas. BA in Bus., U. Puget Sound, 1951. Pres. Metsker Map Co., Tacoma, 1942—. Del. Wash. state convs. Rep. Party, 1960-70. With USN, 1945-47. Roman Catholic. Home: 3012 N Narrows Dr Unit 6 Tacoma WA 98407-1556 Office: Metsker Map Co 9616 40th Ave SW Tacoma WA 98499-4302

METTE, JOE, museum director. Dir. California State Capitol Mus., Sacramento, Calif. Office: Calif State Capitol Museum State Capitol Rm B-27 Sacramento CA 95814-4906*

METTEE, STEPHEN BLAKE, publishing executive; b. L.A., Oct. 29, 1947; s. Eugene Blake and Mary Helen (Hustead) M.; m. Suzanne Crawford, Mar. 31, 1969 (div. June 1977); 1 child, Joshua Blake; m. Donna Parker, July 25, 1987. AA, Fresno (Calif.) C.C., 1967; BA, Calif. STate Univ., Fresno, 1984. Pres. Calif. Wholesale Wines, Inc., Fresno, 1970-77; pres., CEO Apple Eddies, Inc., Fresno, 1978-82; owner Calif. Color, The Printing Co., Fresno, 1982-94; pub. Quill Driver Books/Word Dancer Press, Inc., Fresno, 1993—. Editor: The Portable Writers Conference, 1996. Mem. bd. dirs. Fresno Downtown Assn., 1979-82. With U.S. Army, 1969-75. Mem. Writers Internat. Network (bd. dirs.). Republican. Office: Quill Driver Books Word Dancer Press 950 N Van Ness Ave Fresno CA 93728-3428

METTLER, LEEMAN, food executive; b. 1936. Produce insp. USDA, Stockton, Calif., 1958-72; field foreman Demont Packing Co., Victor, Calif., 1973-76; with Delta Packing Co. of Lodi (Calif.), 1976—. Office: Delta Packing Co of Lodi 5950 E Kettleman Ln Lodi CA 95240-6410*

METTY, MICHAEL PIERRE, college dean; b. Pontiac, Mich., Jan. 28, 1942; s. J. Clifford and Rleon (Jacobs) M.; m. Carole Burpee, May 1961 (div. June 1995); children: Kara, Rebecca, Sara; m. Mary R. Currey, Oct. 16, 1995. BA, Antioch Coll., Yellow Springs, Ohio, 1964; MS, Syracuse U., 1969. Prof. Antioch Coll.-Columbia, Columbia, Balt., Md., 1974-78; pres. Northwest C.C., Nome, Alaska, 1979-83, Tanana Valley C.C., Fairbanks, Alaska, 1983-87; dean, cmty. campus U. Alaska, Fairbanks, 1987-88; pres. Logistics, Inc., Fairbanks, 1988-89; dean, continuing edn. C.C. So. Nev., Las Vegas, 1989-96; dean workplace devel. Cerro Coso Coll., Ridgecrest, Calif., 1996—; bd. dirs. Mountain Plains Adult Edn. Assn., 1992-94. Dir. Las Vegas Indian Ctr., 1994-96, Pvt. Industry Coun., Las Vegas, 1994-96. Great Lakes Coll. Assn. traveling fellow, Yugoslavia, 1975; named Adult Educator of Yr., Alaska Vocat. Assn., 1984; recipient Martin Luther King award, Martin Luther King Group of Alaska, Fairbanks, 1985. Unitarian Universalist. Home: 735 N Helena Ridgecrest CA 93555 Office: Cerro Coso Coll 3000 College Heights Blvd Ridgecrest CA 93555

METZ, JAMES ROBERT, secondary education educator; b. Springfield, Ill., June 1, 1949; s. Leonard Thomas and Mary Agnes (Erley) M. BA, St. Louis U., 1971; MA, U. Ill., Springfield, 1977. Cert. tchr. Tchr. math. Griffin H.S., Springfield, 1971-79, Damien H.S., Honolulu, 1979-87; tchr. trainer U.S. Peace Corps, Philippines, 1987-90; tchr. math. Maryknoll H.S., Honolulu, 1990-94, Mid-Pacific Inst., Honolulu, 1994—; editorial cons. U. Hawaii, Honolulu, 1986-87, 90; editorial cons. Instrnl. Materials Corp., Philippines, 1989-90. Contbr. articles to profl. jours.; patentee puzzle. Vol. Results, 1994—. Recipient Excellence in Math. Teaching, Soc. for Indsl. and Applied Math., 1984. Mem. Nat. Coun. Tchr. Math., Ill. Coun. Tchrs. Math., Hawaii Coun. Tchrs. Math. (v.p. 1981-82, pres. 1982-83), Phi Beta Kappa, Pi Mu Epsilon. Democrat. Roman Catholic. Home: 1630 Makiki St C-105 Honolulu HI 96822 Office: Mid-Pacific Inst 2445 Kaala St Honolulu HI 96822-2204

METZ, MARY SEAWELL, university dean, retired college president; b. Rockhill, S.C., May 7, 1937; d. Columbus Jackson and Mary (Dunlap) Seawell; m. F. Eugene Metz, Dec. 21, 1957; 1 dau., Mary Eugena. BA summa cum laude in French and English, Furman U., 1958; postgrad., Institut Phonetique, Paris, 1962-63, Sorbonne, Paris, 1962-63; PhD magna cum laude in French, La. State U., 1966; HHD (hon.), Furman U., 1984; LLD (hon.), Chapman Coll., 1985; DLT (hon.), Converse Coll., 1988. Instr. French La. State U., 1965-66, asst. prof., 1966-67, 1968-72, assoc. prof., 1972-76, dir. elem. and intermediate French programs, 1966-74, spl. asst. to chancellor, 1974-75, asst. to chancellor, 1975-76; prof. French Hood Coll., Frederick, Md., 1976-81, provost, dean acad. affairs, 1976-81; pres. Mills Coll., Oakland, Calif., 1981-90; dean of extension U. Calif., Berkeley, 1991—; vis. asst. prof. U. Calif. Berkeley, 1967-68; mem. commn. on leadership devel. Am. Coun. on Edn., 1981-90, adv. coun. Stanford Rsch. Inst., 1985-90, adv. coun. Grad. Sch. Bus., Stanford U.; assoc. Gannett Ctr. for Media Studies, 1985—; bd. dirs. PG&E, Pacific Telesis, PacTel & PacBell, Union Bank, Longs Drug Stores, S.H. Cowell Found. Author: Reflets du monde francais, 1971, 78, Cahier d'exercices: Reflets du monde francais, 1972, 78, (with Helstrom) Le Francais a decouvrir, 1972, 78, Le Francais a vivre, 1972, 78, Cahier d'exercices: Le Francais a vivre, 1972, 78; standardized tests; mem. editorial bd.: Liberal Edn., 1982—. Trustee Am. Conservatory Theater. NDEA fellow, 1960-62,, 1963-64; Fulbright fellow, 1962-63; Am. Council Edn. fellow, 1974-75. Mem. Western Coll. Assn. (v.p. 1982-84, pres. 1984-86), Assn. Ind. Calif. Colls. and Univs. (exec. com. 1982-90), Nat. Assn. Ind. Colls. and Univs. (govt. rels. adv. coun. 1982-85), So. Conf. Lang. Teaching (chmn. 1976-77), World Affairs Coun. No. Calif. (bd. dirs. 1984-93), Bus.-Higher Edn. Forum, Women's Forum West, Women's Coll. Coalition (exec. com. 1984-88), Phi Kappa Phi, Phi Beta Kappa. Address: PO Box 686 Stinson Beach CA 94970-0686

METZ, STEVEN WILLIAM, small business owner; b. Inglewood, Calif., Nov. 30, 1946; s. Glenn Ludwig and Kathleen Martha (Peterson) M.; m. Michelle Marie McArthur, Aug. 11, 1989; 1 child, Glenn Christian. Student, Fullerton Coll., Calif. Supt. Oahu Interiors, Honolulu, 1969-71, Hackel Bros., Miami, Fla., 1971-73; exec. v.p. Tru-Cut Inc., Brea, Calif., 1974-82; gen. mgr. The Louvre', Grass Valley, Calif., 1983-85; mfg. engring. mgr. Rexnord Aerospace, Torrance, Calif., 1986-87; pres., founder Metz/Calcoa Inc., Torrance, Calif., 1987—; mfg. rep. consul Orange County Spring, Anaheim, 1987—, TALSCO, 1994—, Precision Resources, 1994—, GEMTECH, 1994—; mfg. rep. consul Alard Machine Products, Gardena, Calif., 1988—, v.p. spl. projects, 1997—. Charter mem. Rep. Presdl. Task Force, 1991—; mem. L.A. Coun. on World Affairs, 1991-92. With U.S. Army, 1966-68. Recipient Appreciation awards DAV, 1968, Soc. Mfg. Engrs., 1991. Fellow Soc. Carbide Engrs.; mem. Soc. Carbide and Tool Engrs. (chpt. pres. 1980-82, Appreciation award 1981), Rep. Presdl. Legion of Merit.

METZGER, VERNON ARTHUR, management educator, consultant; b. Baldwin Park, Calif., Aug 13, 1918; s. Vernon and Nellie C. (Ross) M.; BS, U. Calif., Berkeley, 1947, MBA, 1948; m. Beth Arlene Metzger, Feb. 19, 1955; children: Susan, Linda, 1 step-son, David. Estimating engr. C. F. Braun & Co., 1949; prof. mgmt. Calif. State U. at Long Beach, 1949-89, prof. emeritus, 1989—, founder Sch. Bus.; mgmt. cons., 1949-89. Mem. Fire Commn. Fountain Valley, Calif., 1959-60; pres. Orange County Dem. League, 1967-68; mem. State Dept. mgmt. task force to promote modern mgmt. in Yugoslavia, 1977; mem. State of Calif. Fair Polit. Practices Commn., Orange County Transit Com. Served with USNR, 1942-45. Recipient Outstanding Citizens award Orange County (Calif.) Bd. Suprs. Fellow Soc. for Advancement of Mgmt. (life; dir.); mem. Acad. Mgmt., Orange County Indsl. Rels. Rsch. Assn. (v.p.), Beta Gamma Sigma, Alpha Kappa Psi, Tau Kappa Upsilon. Home: 1938 Balearic Dr Costa Mesa CA 92626-3513 Office: 1250 N Bellflower Blvd Long Beach CA 90840-0006

METZNER, JEFFREY LEE, psychiatrist, educator; b. Hagerstown, Md., Mar. 15, 1950; married. BS, U. Md., 1972; MD, U. Md., Balt., 1975. Diplomate Am. Bd. Psychiatry and Neurology, Am. Bd. Forensic Psychiatry; cert. correctional health profl. Intern U. Colo. Health Scis. Ctr., Denver, 1975, resident in psychiatry, 1975-79, chief resident psychiat. liaison div., 1978-79, clin. instr. dept. psychiatry, 1978-81, asst. clin. prof., 1981-89, assoc. clin. prof., 1989-95, clin. prof. psychiatry, 1995—, assoc. dir. forensic psychiatry fellowship program, 1992—; pvt. practice Denver, 1979—; chief psychiatry div. forensic psychiatry Colo. State Hosp., 1978; com. mem. Gov.'s. Criminal Insanity Task Force, 1978-79; lectr.-in-law U. Denver Coll. of Law, 1984-86; co-chmn. Civil Commitment Task Force, 1987-90; examiner Am. Bd. Psychiatry and Neurology, Inc., 1988—; examiner Am. Bd. Forensic Psychiatry, Inc., 1989—, mem. written exam. com., 1989-93, bd. dirs. 1992—, chmn. oral exam. com., 1992-93; chairperson expert panel psychiat. disorders and comml. drivers U.S. Dept. Transp., 1990-91. author: (with others) Psychiatric Decision Making, 1984, Undestanding and Managing Child Sexual Abuse, 1990, Principles in Practice of Forensic Psychitry, 1994; contbr. articles to profl. jours.: reviewer Child Abuse and Neglect: The Internat. Jour., 1986—, Hosp. Community Psychiatry, 1993—. Fellow Am. Psychiat. Assn. (mem. task force on psychiat. svcs. in correctional facilites, 1985-89, mem. coun. on psychiatry and the law 1989-94, vice chmn., 1993-94, mem. task force on sexually dangerous offenders, 1993—); mem. Am. Correctional Health Svcs. Assn. (also Rocky Mountain chpt.), Am. Acad. Psychiatry and the Law (active numerous coms., editor newsletter), Am. Correctional Assn., Am. Coll. Legal Medicine, Am. Acad. Forensic Scis., Colo. Psychiat. Soc.,. Home: 3300 E 1st Ave Ste 590 Denver CO 80206-5808

METZNER, RICHARD JOEL, psychiatrist, psychopharmacologist, educator; b. L.A., Feb. 15, 1942; s. Robert Gerson and Esther Rebecca (Groper) M.; children: Jeffrey Anthony, David Jonathan; m. Leila Kirkley, June 26, 1993. BA, Stanford U., 1963; MD, Johns Hopkins U., 1967. Intern, Roosevelt Hosp., N.Y.C., 1967-68; resident in psychiatry Stanford U. Med. Center, 1968-71; staff psychiatrist div. manpower and tng. NIMH-St. Elizabeths Hosp., Washington, 1971-73; chief audiovisual edn. system VA Med. Center Brentwood, L.A., 1973-79, chmn. VA Dist. 26 Ednl. Task Force, 1976-78; asst. prof. psychiatry UCLA Neuropsychiat. Inst., 1973-80, assoc. clin. prof., 1980-96, clin. prof., 1996—, lectr. Sch. Social Welfare, 1975-84; pvt. practice medicine specializing in psychiatry, Bethesda, Md., 1972-73, L.A., 1973—; dir. Western Inst. Psychiatry, L.A., 1977—; pres. Psychiat. Resource Network, Inc., 1984—; Served with USPHS, 1968-71. Recipient 6 awards for film and videotape prodns., 1976-80; diplomate Am. Bd. Psychiatry and Neurology (cons. 1974-78, producer audiovisual exam. programs 1975-77). Fellow Am. Psychiat. Assn.; mem. So. Calif. Psychiat. Soc., Mental Health Careerists Assn. (chmn. 1972-73), Phi Beta Kappa. Democrat. Jewish. Contbr. numerous articles to profl. publs., 1963—; producer, writer numerous ednl. films and videotapes, 1970—.

MEULI, MINDY DENISE, clinical dietitian; b. Tulsa, June 22, 1963; d. R. Larry and A. Victoria (Parker) M.; m. Bryan F. Clerkin, May 2, 1992. BS in Zoology, U. Wyo., 1985, MS in Food Sci. & Human Nutrition, 1987. Registered dietitian; cert. diabetes educator. Ext. nutrition asst. Expanded Foods and Nutrition Edn. Program, Laramie, Wyo., summer 1986; lab. asst. nutrition lab. U. Wyo., Laramie, 1987; asst. food svc. mgr. U. Wyo. Food Svc., Laramie, 1987-88; clin. dietitian Freeport (Ill.) Meml. Hosp., 1988-89; cons. dietitian Bethesda Care Ctr., Laramie, 1989-93; clin. dietitian Ivinson Meml. Hosp., Laramie, 1989—; mem. Albany County Cmty. Health Awareness Com., Albany County Nutrition Coun., chair comty. benefits coun.; mem. bd. dirs. nom. com. Albany County Heart Assn. Co-author: (video) Centsible Nutrition, 1986. Bd. dirs. Ivinson Meml. Hosp. Found., Laramie, 1994-96. Mem. Am. Dietetic Assn., Am. Assn. Diabetes Educators, Wyo. Dietetic Assn. (legis. network coord. 1990-94, bd. dirs., nominating com. chair 1995-96, Recognized Young Dietitian 1994), Soroptimist Internat. (chair ways and means com.). Republican. Presbyterian. Office: Ivinson Meml Hosp 255 N 30th St Laramie WY 82070-5140

MEYER, C. RICHARD, architect. BArch, U. Calif., Berkeley, 1968. Registered architect, Wash. With The Callison Partnership, Seattle, 1977—, dir. quality assurance; mem. adv. bd. cert. program project mgmt. U. Wash.; contracts rev. panelist Soc. Archtl. Adminstrs.; mem. faculty Pacific real estate symposium N.W. Real Estate Inst.; guest lectr. Archtl. Registration Exam. Seminar; guest lectr. coll. architecture and urban planning U. Wash.; guest panelist Internat. Conf. of Bldg. Ofcls. Nat. Conf., 1991. Mem. AIA (treas. Seattle chpt., mem. steering com. Pacific NW regional conf., vice-chair nat. risk mgmt. com., mem. steering com. nat. practice com., liaison to Am. Arbitration Assn.), Nat. Inst. Bldg. Scis. Office: The Callison Partnership Ltd 1420 5th Ave Ste 2400 Seattle WA 98101-2333*

MEYER, CHARLES G., museum director. Exec. dir. Bakersfield (Calif.) Mus. Art, 1995—. Office: Bakersfield Mus Art 1930 R St Bakersfield CA 93301

MEYER, CHRISTOPHER HAWKINS, lawyer; b. Springfield, Mo., Sept. 29, 1952; s. Richard DeWitt and Nancy (Hawkins) M.; m. Karen Anne Adams, Aug. 8, 1987; 1 child, C. Andrew Meyer. BA in Econs. magna cum laude, U. Mich., 1977, JD cum laude, 1981. Bar: D.C. 1981, U.S. Ct. Appeals (D.C. cir.) 1982, U.S. Ct. Appeals (9th cir.) 1983, Colo. 1985, U.S. Ct. Appeals (10th cir.) 1985, Idaho, U.S. Ct. Appeals (8th cir.). Counsel water resources program Nat. Wildlife Fedn., Washington, 1981-84; assoc. prof. adjoint, counsel Rocky Mountain Natural Resources Clinic Nat. Wildlife Fedn., Boulder, Colo., 1984-91; ptnr. Givens Pursley & Huntley, Boise, 1991—. Contbr. articles to profl. publs. Mem. steering com. Idaho Environ. Profls.; bd. dirs. Idaho Food Bank. Recipient Lawyer of Yr. award Environ. Policy Inst., 1984, Water Conservationist of Yr. Nebr. Wildlife Fedn., 1989. Mem. Phi Beta Kappa. Democrat. Roman Catholic. Home: 2460 E Bergeson St Boise ID 83706-6012 Office: Givens Pursley & Huntley 277 N 6th St Ste 200 Boise ID 83702-7720

MEYER, DANIEL KRAMER, real estate executive; b. Denver, July 15, 1957; s. Milton Edward and Mary (Kramer) M. Student, Met. State Coll., Denver, 1977-78, U. Colo., 1978-80. Ptnr., developer RM & M II (Ltd. Partnership), Englewood, Colo., 1981-87; pres. Centennial Mortgage and Investment, Ltd., Englewood, Colo., 1984-87; prin. Capriole Properties, Greenwood Village, Colo., 1983—. Alumni mem. bd. trustees Kent Denver Country Day Sch., 1981-83; sec. dist. 37 ctrl. and vacancy com. Colo. Ho. of Reps., 1991-92. Recipient Pamela Davis Beardsley devel. award Kent Denver Sch., 1995. Mem. Greenwood Athletic Club. Republican.

MEYER, EDMOND GERALD, energy and natural resources educator, resources scientist, entrepreneur, former chemistry educator, university administrator; b. Albuquerque, Nov. 2, 1919; s. Leopold and Beatrice (Ilfeld) M.; m. Betty F. Knobloch, July 4, 1941; children: Lee Gordon, Terry Gene, David Gary. B.S. in Chemistry, Carnegie Mellon U., 1940, M.S., 1942; Ph.D., U. N.Mex., 1950. Chemist Harbison Walker Refractories Co., 1940-41; instr. Carnegie Mellon U., 1941-42; asst. phys. chemist Bur. Mines, 1942-44; chemist research div. N.Mex. Inst. Mining and Tech., 1946-48; head dept. sci. U. Albuquerque, 1950-52; head dept. chemistry N.Mex. Highlands U., 1952-59; dir. Inst. Sci. Rsch., 1957-63; dean Grad. Sch., 1961-63; dean Coll. Arts and Sci., U. Wyo., 1963-75, v.p., 1974-80, prof. energy and natural resources, 1981-87, prof. and dean emeritus, 1987—; exec. cons. Diamond Shamrock Corp., 1980; bd. dirs. Carbon Fuels Corp., First Nat. Bank, Laramie; sci. adviser Gov. of Wyo., 1964-90; pres. Coal Tech. Corp., 1981—; cons. Los Alamos Nat. Lab., NFS, HHS, GAO, Wyo. Bancorp; contractor investigator Rsch. Corp., Dept. Interior, AEC, NIH, NSF, Dept. Energy, Dept. Edn.; Fulbright exch. prof. U. Concepcion, Chile, 1959. Co-author: Chemistry-Survey of Principles, 1963, Legal Rights of Chemists and Engineers, 1977, Industrial Research & Development Management, 1982; contbr. articles to profl. jours.; patentee in field. Chair, Laramie Regional Airport Bd., 1989-93, treas., 1994-97; mem. Laramie City Coun., 1997—. Lt. comdr. USNR, 1944-46, ret. Recipient Disting. Svc. award Jaycees; rsch. fellow U. N.Mex., 1948-50. Fellow AAAS, Am. Inst. Chemists (pres. 1992-93, chmn. 1994-95); mem. Assoc. Western Univs. (chmn. 1972-74), Am. Chem. Soc. (councilor 1962-90, chmn. Wyo. sect. 1997), Biophys. Soc., Coun. Coll. Arts and Scis. (pres. 1971, sec.-treas. 1972-75), dir. Washington office 1973), Laramie C. of C. (pres. 1984), Sigma Xi. Home: 1058 Colina Dr Laramie WY 82070-5015 Office: U Wyo Coll Arts and Scis Laramie WY 82071-3825

MEYER, FREDERICK G., lawyer; b. Temple, Tex., 1945. BA, Dartmouth Coll., 1967; JD, Columbia U., 1970; LLM, NYU, 1979. Bar: Conn. 1970, N.Y. 1971, Colo. 1979. Mem. Holland & Hart, Denver; vis. lectr. grad. tax program law sch. U. Denver, 1982-83. Co-author: Colorado Probate: Beyond the Basics, 1984, Colorado Probate & Estate Planning, 1986, An Attorney's Look at Tax Planing for the Small Business Owner, Rancher and Farmer: Asset Protection Planning, 1996; co-editor: Colorado Estate Planning Handbook, rev. edit., 1989; editor trust and estate forum Colo. Lawyer, 1981-82; contbr. articles to profl. jours. Fellow Am. Coll. Trust and Estate Counsel, Colo. Bar Found.; mem. ABA (vice chair agrl. tax com. 1996-97), Greater Denver Tax Counsels Assn., Rocky Mountain Estate Planning Counsel (pres. 1987). Office: Holland & Hart PO Box 8749 555 17th St Ste 2900 Denver CO 80201

MEYER, GREG CHARLES, psychiatrist; b. Bismarck, N.D., Aug. 17, 1935; s. Oscar Clarence and Agnes Josephine (Pearson) M. Degree in profl. engring., Colo. Sch. Mines, 1958, Alexander Hamilton Bus. Inst., 1960; MME, U. So. Calif., 1965; MD, Marquette U., 1970. Diplomate Am. Bd. Psychiatry and Neurology. Engr. Minuteman-Thiokol, Brigham City, Utah, 1958-61; sr. engr. Saturn S-II N.Am. Aviation, Downey, Calif., 1962-65; design specialist Titan-Martin, Denver, 1965-66; rotating intern Weld Country Gen. Hosp., Greenly, Colo., 1970-71; psychiatric resident Ariz. State Hosp., Phoenix, 1971-74, psychiatrist, 1974-76; pvt. practice Mesa-Tempe, Ariz., 1975—; psychiatrist Ariz. Ctrl. Med. Ctr., 1994—; psychiatrist Ariz. Ctrl. Med. Ctr.; chmn. psychiatry Desert Samaritan Hosp., Mesa, 1982-86, 90-94, chmn. joint mental health, 1981-83, mem. edn. com., 1979-82, quality assurance com., 1979; mem. exec. com. Desert Vista Hosp., Mesa, 1988-94, chief of staff, 1989; chmn. psychiatry Mesa Luth. Hosp., 1984-85, mem. exec. com., 1984-85; mng. ptnr. Desert Samaritan Med. Bldg. II, Mesa, 1985-86; rsch., edn. com. East Valley Camel Back Hosp., 1989-90, quality assurance com., 1985; psychiatrist Ctrl. Ariz. Med. Ctr., 1995. Co-discoverer Larson-Meyer Transform. Coach Pop Warner Football, 1974. With USMCR, 1953-59. Mem. AMA, Am. Psychiatric Assn., Ariz. Med. Assn., Ariz. Psychiatric Assn., Phoenix Psychiatric Coun., Maricopa Country Med. Assn., Christian Med./Dental Assn., Triple Nine Soc., Sons of Confederate Vets. Republican. Lutheran.

MEYER, HARRY MARTIN, JR., retired health science facility administrator; b. Palestine Tex., Nov. 25, 1928. s. Harry Martin and Marjory Isabel (Griffin) M.; m. Mary Jane Martin, Aug. 19, 1949 (div. 1966); children: Harry, Mary, David; m. Barbara Story Chalfart, Nov. 21, 1966. BS Hendrix Coll., 1949, MD U. Ark., 1953; Diplomate Am. Bd. Pediatrics, 1960. instr. biology Little Rock Coll., 1949, intern. Walter Reed Army Hosp., Washington, 1953-54, med. officer dep. virus and rickettsial diseases, Walter Reed Army Inst. Rsch., 1954-57, asst. resident dep. pediatrics, N.C. Meml. Hosp., Chapel Hill, 1957-59, head virology sect. div. biologics standards, NIH, Bethesda, Md., 1959-64, chief lab. of viral immunol., div. biologics standards, NIH, 1964-72, dir. bur. biologics FDA, Bethesda, 1972-82, dir. Ctr. for Drugs & Biologics FDA, Rockville, Md., 1982-86, pres. med. research div. Am. Cyanamid Co., Pearl River, N.Y., 1986-93; retired 1993. Served to rear admiral USPHS, 1959-86, capt. U.S. Army, 1953-57. Mem. AMA, Am. Epidemiol. Soc., Am. Acad. Pediatrics, Am. Pediatric Soc. Protestant. Avocations: sailing, scuba diving, skiing, back packing. Conbr. articles to profl. jours.; patentee in field.

MEYER, JAROLD ALAN, oil company research executive; b. Phoenix, July 28, 1938; s. Lester M. and Anita (Walker) M.; m. Diane Louise Wheeler; children: Ronald Alan, Sharon Lynne. BSChemE, Calif. Inst. Tech., 1960, MS, 1961. Mgr. process devel. Chevron Rsch., Richmond, Calif., 1978-82; tech. mgr. Chevron U.S.A., El Segundo, Calif., 1982-84; v.p. process rsch. Chevron Rsch., Richmond, 1984-86, pres., 1986—; sr. v.p. Chevron Rsch. and Tech., Richmond, 1990-93; ret., 1993; prin. J.A. Meyer Assocs., Martinez, Calif., 1993—; bd. dirs. Solvent Refined Coal Internat., Inc., San Francisco; mem. adv. bd. Surface Sci. and Catalysis Program Ctr. for Advanced Materials, Lawrence Berkeley Lab., 1988-91; mem. adv. coun. Lawrence Hall Sci., 1989-94; indsl. advisor Accreditation bd. for Engring. and Tech. Inventor petroleum catalysts; contbr. articles to profl. jours. Bd. visitors U. Calif., Davis, 1986-93, trustee found., 1989—. Mem. Nat. Acad. Engring., Am. Chem. Soc., Nat. Petroleum Refining Assn., Indsl. Rsch. Inst., Conf. Bd. Internat. Rsch. Mgmt. Coun., Accreditation Bd. for Engring. and Tech. Indsl. Advisor, Sigma Xi, Tau Beta Pi. Home and Office: 849 Corte Briones Martinez CA 94553-5950

MEYER, JEROME J., diversified technology company executive; b. Caledonia, Minn., Feb. 18, 1938; s. Herbert J. and Edna (Staggemeyer) M.; m. Sandra Ann Beaudoin, June 18, 1960; children—Randall Lee, Lisa Ann, Michelle Lynn. Student, Hamline U., 1956-58; B.A., U. Minn., 1960. Devel. engr. Firestone Tire & Rubber Co., Akron, Ohio, 1960-61; v.p., gen. mgr. Sperry Univac, St. Paul, 1961-79; group v.p. Honeywell, Inc., Mpls., 1979-84; pres., chief operating officer Varian Assocs., Palo Alto, Calif., 1984-86, also bd. dirs.; pres., chief exec. officer Honeywell Inc., 1986-90; from pres. to chmn., CEO Tektronix Inc., Beaverton, Oreg., 1990—; bd. dirs. Portland Gen. Corp., Esterline Tech., Oregon Bus. Coun., AMP. Trustee Oreg. Grad. Inst., Willamette U., Oreg. Children's Found. Mem. Oregon Golf Club. Office: Tektronix Inc PO Box 1000 26600 S W Pky Wilsonville OR 97070*

MEYER, JOHN ANDREW, physicist; b. Waseca, Minn., Aug. 24, 1964; s. Charles Huston and Gladys Marie (Shafer) M.; m. Terrie Ann Wilson, Feb. 17, 1990; children: Lillian Elizabeth, Jacob Andrew. BS, Mankato State U., 1986; MS, U. Iowa, 1989. Design engr. TachTronic Instruments, Inc., New Ulm, Minn., 1985; asst. researcher U. Wis., Madison, 1989-95; assoc. process engr. Tegal Corp., Petaluma, Calif., 1995-96; process. engr. Tegal Corp., Petaluma, —, 1996—. With USAR, 1983—. Mem. IEEE, Am. Phys. Soc., Am. Vacuum Soc., Soc. for Applied Spectroscopy. Office: Tegal Corp PO Box 6020 2201 S McDowell Blvd Petaluma CA 94954

MEYER, JOSEPH B., academic administrator, former state attorney general; b. Casper, Wyo., 1941; m. Mary Orr; children: Vincent, Warren. Student, Colo. Sch. Mines; BA, U. Wyo., 1964, JD, 1967; postgrad., Northwestern U., 1968. Dep. county atty. Fremont County, Wyo., 1967-69; assoc. Smith and Meyer, 1968-71; asst. dir. legis. svc. office State of Wyo., Cheyenne, 1971-87, atty. gen., 1987-95; spl. asst. to pres. Univ. Wyo., Laramie, 1995—; conductor numerous govt. studies on state codes including Wyo. probate, criminal, state adminstrn., banking, domestic rels., game and fish, state instn., employment security, worker's compensation, motor vehicle, others; conductor legis. rev. of adminstrv. rules; negotiator with Office of Surface Mining for Wyo. state preemption; instr. Wyo. Coll. Law, fall 1986; lectr. Rocky Mountain Mineral Law Found., 1977; chmn. Conf. Western Atty. Gen., 1992-93; mem. exec. com. Nat. Assn. Attys. Gen. Bd. dirs. Cheyenne Jr. League, 1982-85, Jessup PTO, 1980-81; instr. Boy Scouts Am. Mem. Rotary. Congregationalist. Office: Univ Wyoming External Rels Box 3315 Laramie WY 82071

MEYER, KEITH JOHN, marketing professional; b. Milw., Sept. 3, 1963; s. John Alan Meyer and Winona Johnston Bell. BS in Bus. Adminstrn., Miami U., Oxford, Ohio, 1985; M of Internat. Mgmt., Thunderbird/Am. Grad. Sch., Glendale, Ariz., 1992. Pub. rels. intern Manning, Selvage, Lee, N.Y.C., 1985; model/actor Tokyo, Milan, Madrid, London,, Paris, Sydney, 1986-90; regional mgr./Asia Sunkist Growers, Inc., Ontario, Calif., 1992-96; product mgr. new markets and new products Calif. State Automobile Assn., San Francisco, 1996—. Home: 1879 Filbert St # 4 San Francisco CA 94123 Office: CSAA/AAA 100 Van Ness Ave 10th Fl San Francisco CA 94102

MEYER, MICHAEL EDWIN, lawyer; b. Chgo., Oct. 23, 1942; s. Leon S. and Janet (Gorden) M.; m. Catherine Dieffenbach, Nov. 21, 1982; children: Linda, Mollie, Patrick, Kellie. BS, U. Wis., 1964; JD, U. Chgo., 1967. Bar: Calif. 1968, U.S. Supreme Ct. 1973. Assoc. Lillick & McHose, L.A., 1967-73, ptnr., 1974-90, mng. ptnr., 1986-87; ptnr. Pillsbury Madison Sutro, 1990—, mem. mgmt. com., 1990-92; judge pro tem Beverly Hills Mcpl. Ct., Calif., 1976-79, Los Angeles Mcpl. Ct., 1980-86; lectr. in field. Bd. dirs. Bldg. Owners and Mgrs. Assn. of Greater L.A., L.A. Coun. Boy Scouts Am.; pub. counsel United Way Greater L.A., Los Angeles County Bar Found. Recipient Good Scout award L.A. coun. Boy Scouts Am., 1992, Man of Yr. award United Way, 1996. Mem. ABA, Am. Arbitration Assn. (arbitrator), Calif. Bar Assn., L.A. Bar Assn., U. Chgo. Alumni Assn. So. Calif. (pres. 1980-82), Calif. Club, U. L.A. Club (dir. 1979-85, pres. 1984-85), L.A. Country Club. Jewish. Home: 4407 Roma Ct Marina Del Rey CA 90292-7702 Office: Pillsbury Madison Sutro 725 S Figueroa St Los Angeles CA 90017-5524

MEYER, PAUL J., food products executive; b. 1947. BA, Stanford U.; MBA, U. Calif., Berkeley, 1969. With Continental Ill. Nat. Bank, Chgo., 1969-71, Bank of Am., San Francisco, 1971-81, Itel Corp., San Francisco, 1981-83, Victoria Sta., Inc., San Francisco, 1983-84; exec. v.p. Maui Land & Pinapple Co., Inc., Kahului, Hawaii, 1984—. Office: Maui Land & Pineapple Co Inc 120 Kane St # 187 Kahului HI 96732*

MEYER, RACHEL ABIJAH, foundation director, artist, theorist, poet; b. Job's Corners, Pa., Aug. 18, 1963; d. Jacob Owen and Velma Ruth (Foreman) M.; children: Andrew Carson, Peter Franklin. Student, Lebanon Valley Coll., 1982-84. Restaurant owner Purcy's Place, Ono, Pa., 1985-87; restaurant mgr. King's Table Buffet, Citrus Heights, Calif., 1987-89; product finalizer TransWorld Enterprises, Blaine, Wash., 1989-91; dir., support svcs. adminstr. Tacticar Found., Sacramento, 1991—; tchr. Tacticar Inst., 1995; chair Conirems, Sacramento, 1996—. Author: Year of the Unicorn, 1994. Studio: 3329 1/2 Douglas St Sacramento CA 95838-4649

MEYER, ROBERT ALLEN, human resource management educator; b. Wisconsin Rapids, Wis., May 31, 1943; s. Charles Harold and Viola Bertha (Stoeckmann) M.; 1 child, Timothy Charles. BA, Valparaiso (Ind.) U., 1966; MA, Mich. State U., 1967, PhD, 1972, postgrad., 1981. Asst. prof. Muskingum Area Tech. Coll., Zanesville, Ohio, 1972-74; adj. prof. U. Fla., Gainesville, 1974-80; dean acad. affairs Santa Fe Community Coll., Gainesville, 1974-80; asst. prof. Purdue U., W. Lafayette, Ind., 1982-84, Ga. State U., Atlanta, 1985-89; assoc. prof., program coord. U. N. Tex., Denton, 1989-91; Fulbright profl. scholar, Bangkok, 1991-92; coord. travel, tourism, hotel, restaurant mgmt. program U. Hawaii Manoa Campus, Honolulu, 1992—; investor, asst. mgr. LaSiene Restaurant, Ann Arbor, Mich., 1970-72; investor, cons. Cafe Brittany St. Thomas, U.S. V.I., 1974-80, owner, operator, Houston, 1980; pres. RTM Cons., Honolulu, Hawaii, 1989—; educator World Tourism Orgn., 1993—; mem. vis. ind. coun. C. of C., 1993—; club mgr. Assn. Am., 1994—. Contbr. articles to profl. jours. Recipient White House Commendation for Partnerships with Industry and Higher Edn.,1984, George Washington Medal of Honor for innovations in higher edn., Freedoms Found., 1985, 86, Achievement award in hospitality edn. Coun. of Hotel, Restaurant & Instl. Edn., 1987. Mem. Tarrant County Hotel and Motel Assn., Dallas Hotel Assn., Am. Soc. Tng. and Devel., Travel Ind. Assn. Tex., Hotel Sales & Mktg. Assn. (bd. dirs. 1985-89), Coun. of Hotel, Restaurant and Instl. Edn. (grad. com. 1989-90). Home: 2611 Ala Wai Blvd Apt 1608 Honolulu HI 96815-3907 Office: U Hawaii Manoa Campus 2560 Campus Rd Honolulu HI 96822-2217

MEYER, ROBERT LEE, secondary education educator; b. St. Joseph, Mo., July 9, 1952; s. Robert James and Jerry Lee (Patterson) M.; m. Barbara Anita Stickles, Aug. 2, 1986. BS in Edn., Mo. Western State Coll., 1974; MA in Edn., U.S. Internat. U., 1988. Cert. tchr., Calif., Mo.; cert. specialist learning handicapped, resource specialist cert., adminstr., Calif. Spl. edn. tchr., learning handicapped Mann Jr. High Sch., San Diego, 1978-80, Serra High Sch., San Diego, 1980-84, Morse High Sch., San Diego, 1984-85; magnet seminar tchr. Bell Jr. High Sch., San Diego, 1985-91; project resource tchr., dir. student activities Serra High Sch., San Diego, 1991-94, resource specialist, 1994-95; magnet coord. Ctr. for Sci., Math. and Computer Tech. Samuel Gompers Secondary Sch., San Diego, 1995—; chmn. resource com. Western Assn. Schs. & Colls. accreditation Serra High Sch., San Diego, 1995, accreditation Gompers Secondary sch., sch. site coun., 1992-95, gov. team mem., 1992-95, chair spl. edn. dept., 1983, mem. sch. leadership team, 1992-95, sr. class advisor, 1994-95; monitor City Schs. Race Human Rels. Monitoring Team, 1991-92, African Am. students program, adminstrv. team mem.; restructuring coord. Senate Bill 1274 Grant, 1993-95, resource specialist, 1994-95; chmn. process com. Western Assn. Schs. and Colls. accreditation Gompers Sec. Sch., adv. com. mem. African Am. students program. Contbr.: (book) History of Andrew Meyer Family, 1989. Alternate del. Dem. Party 6th Dist. and State Conventions, Holt County, Mo., 1976. Mem. Neighborhood House, Delta Chi. Democrat. Roman Catholic.

MEYER, ROBERTA, mediator, communication consultant; b. San Francisco, July 27, 1936; d. Theodore Robert and Virginia (Organ) M.; m. G. William Sheldon; children: Megan McDougall Radeski, Deborah Ann Guerra. Student, U. Utah, 1974. Cert. mediator. Founder, pres., exec. dir. Roberta Meyer Communication Cons., Inc., San Francisco, 1977—; presenter numerous workshops in field of alcoholism and communication; nat. speaker Nat. Found. for Alcohlism Communicaton; keynote speaker Calif. Women's Commn. on Alcoholism, 1981; mem. adv. bd. Soviet Am. Alliance on Alcoholism and Other Addictions. Author: Facts About Booze and Other Drugs, 1980, The Parent Connection: How To Communicate With Your Child About Alcohol and Other Drugs, 1984, Listen to the Heart, 1989, (film) Understanding Addiction, 1988, Better Relationships Through Effective Communication, 1991; numerous radio and TV appearances. Mem. adv. bd. Marin Svcs. for Women, 1980; vol. Pacific Med. Ctr., San Francisco Ballet Aux.; mem. N.Y.C. & San Francisco Ballet Cos., 1950-56; mem. faculty S.G. Ballet Sch., 1956-65; founder, dir. Ballet Arts of San Francisco, 1965-78, San Francisco Ballroom Dance Theatre, 1994—. Recipient award Optimists Club, 1978; named 56th Point of Light, Pres. Bush, 1990. Mem. Nat. Ctr. for Collaborative Planning and Community Svc. (cert.), Nat. Coun. on Alcoholism (co-chmn. pub. info. com. 1985—, v.p. Bay area 1988—, bd. dirs. Teen Kick Off 1987—, Alcoholism and Drug Rsch. Communications Ctr. 1990—; pres. 1988—, creator, cons. youth aware program 1974—), San Francisco Womens Rehab. Assn. (pres. 1975-76), Nat. Coun. on Alcoholism and Drug Dependence Calif. (pres. 1988-91), Childrens Theatre Assn., San Francisco C. of C.

MEYER, ROGER ALLEN, higher education fund raising executive; b. Inglewood, Calif., Oct. 20, 1945; s. Andrew Christian and Margaret Marie (Siemsen) M.; m. Laura Jean Luedders, Apr. 12, 1971; children: Julie Ann, Jared Arnold. BS, Concordia Coll., Seward, Nebr., 1967; MEd, U. Nebr., 1972. Cert. fund raising exec. Tchr. Resurrection Luth. Sch., Chgo., 1967-69; prof. Concordia Coll., Seward, 1969-75, fund raiser, 1975-79; dir. devel. Concordia Sem., St. Louis, 1979-82, UCLA, 1982—. Office: UCLA 10920 Wilshire Blvd Ste 1400 Los Angeles CA 90024-6516

MEYER, ROGER PAUL, physician; b. Atlanta, Mar. 30, 1950; s. Leonard Arthur and Janet Elanor (Miller) M.; children: Seth E., Hilary R. BA in Psychology with honors, U. N.C., 1972; MD, Med. Coll. Ga., 1976; postgrad., U. N.Mex., 1980. Physician in pvt. practice Carson Med. Group, Carson City, Nev., 1980—; chief of staff Carson Tahoe Hosp., 1986-87, chmn. dpt. ob-gyn., 1990-91; v.p. Nev. Physicians Rev. Orgn., 1987; dir. Physicians Managed Care IPA, Nev. Physicians Resources MSO. Fellow Am. Coll. Ob.-Gyn. (Nev. legislature liaison 1991); mem. Am. Acad. Reproductive Medicine, Am. Coll. Physician Execs. Democrat. Jewish. Office: Carson Med Group 1200 N Mountain St Carson City NV 89703-3824

MEYER, RUDOLF X., engineering educator, retired space technology executive; b. Rapperswil, Switzerland, Jan. 13, 1922; came to U.S., 1947; s. Carl and Alice A. (Muller) M.; m. Jeanne A. Meyer, Feb. 8, 1947; children: Jacqueline C. Meyer-Donaher, Dorothy A. Works. Diploma Engr., Swiss Inst. Tech., Zurich, 1945; D of Engring, Johns Hopkins U., 1955. Engr. De Laval Steam Turbine Co., Trenton, N.J., 1947-48; asst. prof. aeronautics U.S. Naval Postgrad. Sch., Annapolis, Md., 1948-52; project mgr. The Hydrofoil Corp., Annapolis, 1952-55; dept. head The Ramo-Wooldridge Corp., L.A., 1955-60; from assoc. dir. phys. rsch. lab. to gen. mgr./chief engr. The Aerospace Corp., L.A., 1960-87; adj. prof. Sch. Engring. UCLA, 1987—; mem. adv. bd. Dept. Def., Washington, 1980-81; invited lectr. MIT, Naval Postgrad. Sch., Naval. Acad., U. So.Calif. Assoc. editor AIAA, 1975-80; contbr. more than 70 articles to profl. jours.; patentee in field. Served with Swiss Army, 1942-45. Recipient Air Force Space div. Excellence awrd USAF, 1985; Regents lectr. U. Calif., 1987. Fellow AIAA. Republican. Roman Catholic. Home: 16966 Livorno Dr Pacific Palisades CA 90272-3229 Office: UCLA MANE Dept M 405 Hilgard Ave Los Angeles CA 90024-1301

MEYEROWITZ, BASIL RALPH, surgeon; b. Johannesburg, South Africa, Sept. 14, 1929; came to U.S., 1960, natuaralized, 1965; m. Miriam Lewinsky, Nov. 1963; children: Robin Marie, Eric Lloyd, Lisa Ann, Jennifer Ray. MB, BCh, Witwatersrand U., 1952. Intern Johannesburg Gen. Hosp., 1953-55; resident Hammersmith Hosp. Postgrad. Sch. of Medicine, 1955-60, Royal Infirmary, Leicester, Eng., 1956-57; spl. fellow, instr. in surgery Albert Einstein Coll. Medicine, 1960-62, asst. prof. surgery, 1962-67; dir. of the Stanford Surg. Svc. San Mateo County Gen. Hosp., 1967-70, chief of surg. svc., 1970-80; clin. assoc. prof. surgery Stanford U. Sch. Medicine, 1967—; assoc. vis. surgeon Bronx Mcpl. Hosp. Ctr., 1967; asst. attending surgeon Mount Sinai Hosp. Divsn. at Elmhurst Hosp., 1967; chief of staff Mills Hosp., 1982-88; chmn. dept. surgery, 1975-77, 90-92, chmn. continuing edn. com., 1974-80, chmn. interdisciplinary com., 1980, chmn. D.R.G. com., 1987-88; chief of staff Chope Community Hosp., San Mateo, 1974-75; hosp. staff Mills Hosp., San Mateo County Gen. Hosp. Contbr. numerous articles to profl. jours. Fellow ACS (No. Calif. chpt.), Royal Coll. Surgeons (Eng.); mem. Calif. Med. Assn., Assn. for Acad. Surgery, Soc. Surgery Alimentary Tract, San Francisco Surg. Soc., Calif. Acad. Medicine, Am. Soc. Bariatric Surgery (founder), San Mateo County Med. Soc. (bd. dirs. 1976-79, 79-82, del. to Calif. Med. Assn. 1979-80, 80-83, many coms.), Calif. Med. Assn. (hosp. surveyor 1980—). Office: 101 S San Mateo Dr Ste 307 San Mateo CA 94401-3844

MEYEROWITZ, ELLIOT MARTIN, biologist, educator; b. Washington, May 22, 1951; s. Irving and Freda (Goldberg) M.; m. Joan Agnes Kobori, June 17, 1984; 2 children. AB, Columbia U., 1973; MPhil, Yale U., 1975, PhD, 1977. Rsch. fellow Stanford U., Calif., 1977-79; asst. prof. biology Calif. Inst. Tech., Pasadena, 1980-85, assoc. prof. 1985-89, prof., 1989—, exec. officer, 1995—. Mem. editl. bd. Trends in Genetics, Current Biology, Cell, Devel.; contbr. articles to profl. jours., 1978—. Recipient LVMH Sci. pour l'Art Sci. prize, 1996; Jane Coffin Childs Meml. Fund fellow, 1977-79, Sloan Found. fellow, 1980-82. Fellow AAAS; mem. NAS, Am. Acad. Arts and Scis., Am. Soc. Plant Physiologists (Gibbs medal 1995), Bot. Soc. Am. (Pelton award 1994), Genetics Soc. Am. (medal 1996), Internat. Soc. Devel. Biology (bd. dirs.), Internat. Soc. for Plant Molecular Biology (pres. 1995-97, bd. dirs.). Office: Calif Inst Tech Divsn Biology Pasadena CA 91125

MEYERS, ANDREW GEORGE, accountant; b. L.A.; s. Andrew George and Aldah Valerie (Willey) M.; m. Holly Noel O'Brien, Mar. 10, 1973; children: Kristin Andrea, Andrew George IV. BS in Fin., Woodbury U., 1968, MS in Fin., 1976; postgrad., Naval War Coll., 1991-93. Tax acct. Security Pacific Bank, L.A., 1968-71; credit analyst United Calif. Bank, L.A., 1971-74, Motorola, L.A., 1975; cons. Stockton, Calif., 1976-83; pub. works fiscal mgr. San Joaquin County, Stockton, 1983—. Dist. com. mem. Boy Scouts Am., Stockton, 1993—, award of merit, 1995. Comdr. USNR. Mem. SAR, U.S. Naval Inst., Navy League U.S., Naval War Coll. Found. Alumni Assn., Stockton Masonic Lodge. Presbyterian. Home: 3868 Fourteen Mile Dr Stockton CA 95219

MEYERS, GENE HOWARD, computer scientist; b. Chgo., Dec. 6, 1942; s. Charles S. and Sara (Miller) M.; m. Carole Esther Terwilliger, May 2, 1971; children: David, Suzanne. BS, U. Ill., 1964; PhD, U. Calif., Berkeley, 1969. Sci. programmer Kaiser Aluminum, Pleasanton, Calif., 1969-77, sr. system analyst, 1977-81, staff system analyst, 1981-88, mgr. computer sci., 1988—. Mem. Assn. Computing Machinery. Democrat. Jewish. Office: Kaiser Aluminum 6177 Sunol Blvd Pleasanton CA 94566-7769

MEYERS, HOWARD CRAIG, lawyer; b. Chgo., Nov. 15, 1951; s. Spencer M. and Joyce L. (Dresdner) M. BA in English, Ariz. State U., 1973, JD, 1977. Bar: Ariz. 1977; cert. bus. bankruptcy specialist Am. Bankruptcy Bd. Cert., cert. bankruptcy specialist State Bar Ariz. Of counsel Burch & Cracchiolo, P.A., Phoenix, Ariz. Mem. ABA, Comml. Law League of Am., Am. Bankruptcy Inst., State Bar Ariz. (debtor-creditor com.), Maricopa County Bar Assn., Internat. Council of Shopping Ctrs., Plaza Club. Republican. Home: 6711 E Camelback Rd Unit 65 Scottsdale AZ 85251-2067 Office: PO Box 16882 702 E Osborn Rd Ste 200 Phoenix AZ 85011

MEYERS, MARLENE O., hospital administrator; m. Eugene Meyers; children: Lori, Lisa, Dean. BSc, U. Sask., 1962; MSc, U. Calgary, Alta., Can., 1976. Instr., chair Mount Royal Coll. Allied Health, Calgary, 1969-82; asst. exec. dir. Rockyview Hosp., Calgary, 1982-85; v.p. patient svcs. Calgary Gen. Hosp., 1985-91, pres., CEO, 1991-95; pres., CEO Meyers and Assocs. Health Care Mgmt. Cons., Calgary, 1995—; surveyor Can. Coun. on Health Facilities Accreditation, 1986—. Rotary Intl. Named Calgary Woman of Yr. in field of Health, 1982; recipient Heritage of Svc. award, 1992. Mem. Alta. Assn. RNs. (hon. mem., 1996), Can. Coll. Health Svcs. Org., Can. Exec. Svcs. Org. Office: Meyers and Assocs, 139 Coleridge Rd NW, Calgary, AB Canada T2K 1X5

MEYERS, RANDAL CURTIS, sculptor; b. Salt Lake City, June 23, 1961; s. C. LaMar and LaRaine (Curtis) M. AAS in Fashion Design, Parsons Sch. Design, 1983; A in Bus. Mgmt. summa cum laude, Salt Lake C.C., 1988; BFA in Sculpture and Painting, U. Utah, 1995; Cert., Skowhegan Sch. Art, 1996; postgrad., Calif. Inst. of the Arts, 1996—. Window designer ZCMI Dept. Store, Salt Lake City, 1978-79, Bergdorf Goodman, N.Y.C., 1979-80; collection designer Geoffrey Beene, N.Y.C., 1983-84; women's collection designer Perry Ellis, N.Y.C., 1984-86; haute couture designer Hanae Mori Paris, 1986-87; women's sportswear designer Hanae Mori, Tokyo, 1987-88; freelance artist, sculptor Salt Lake City, 1988—; instr. drawing Visual Art Inst., Salt Lake City, 1990-91. Author: Fashion Designers Inspired by Painters, 1982; filmmaker (video) ANIMA, 1994; artist/sculptor represented in one-person and group shows at various locations, 1992-94. Recipient Parson Sch. of Design and Fashion Inds. Gold Thimble award, 1983, U. Utah Pres. award, 1991-92, 92-93; Florence Ware scholar Coll. Fine Arts U. Utah, 1992-93, Coll. Fine Arts Adv. Bd. scholar, 1994-95; rsch. grantee U. Utah, 1994. Democrat. Home: 4207 Panorama Dr Salt Lake City UT 84124-2810 Office: R C Meyers Studio PO Box BH-13 24700 McBean Pkwy Valencia CA 91355

MEYERS, THEDA MARIA, textile company executive; b. Bremen, Germany, Feb. 16; came to U.S. 1957; d. Johann-Friedrich and Christophina E.L.J. (Fentrohs) Ficke; m. Laurence Jay Meyers, Oct. 2, 1960 (div. 1970); 1 child, Jayson Bennett. Dipl., U. Bremen, 1956; student, Fashion Inst. Tech., N.Y.C., 1960. Artist-stylist Rosewood Fabrics, N.Y.C., 1960-62; textile stylist Belding Corticelli, N.Y.C., 1962-65; chief designer Jerry Mann of Calif., L.A., 1969-74; fashion designer Sunbow Ltd., Prisma Corp., L.A., 1974-81, Frig & Frag Inc., L.A., 1981-83, Jonathan Martin, L.A., 1983-85; textile stylist, v.p. design E.M.D.A.Y., Inc., L.A., 1985-92; cons. Theda Meyers Consultancy, L.A., 1993—; part-time tchr. Fashion Inst. of Design & Merchandising, L.A., to 1974; part-time judge Trade Tech. Coll., L.A. to 1981; textile designer extensive nat. and internat. experience in womenswear apparel design and textile design. designer Calif. apparel. Mem. NAFE. Office: 600 W 9th St Ste 1003 Los Angeles CA 90015-4328

MEYERSON, BRUCE ELLIOT, lawyer; b. N.Y.C., Apr. 10, 1947. BS, Ariz. State U., 1968; JD, Georgetown U., 1972. Bar: Ariz. 1972. Exec. dir. Ariz. Ctr. for Law in Pub. Interest, 1974-82; judge Ariz. Ct. Appeals, 1982-86; gen. counsel Ariz. State U., 1986-90; atty. Meyer, Hendricks, Victor, Osborn & Maledon, Phoenix; adj. prof. law Ariz. State U., 1985-88. Mem. nat. governing bd. Common Cause, 1978-81; bd. dirs. Community Legal Svcs., 1979-81; chair ad hoc com. on human rels. City of Phoenix, 1984. Office: Meyer Hendricks Victor Osborn & Maledon PO Box 33449 2929 N Central Ave Ste 2100 Phoenix AZ 85012-2765

MEYSENBURG, MARY ANN, principal; b. L.A., Sept. 16, 1939; d. Clarence Henry and Mildred Ethel (McGee) Augustine; m. John Harold Meysenburg, June 17, 1967; children: Peter Augustine, Amy Bernadette. BA magna cum laude, U. So. Calif., 1960; MA Pvt. Sch. Adminstrn. magna cum laude, U. San Francisco, 1995. Cert. elem. tchr., Calif. Auditor, escrow officer Union Bank, L.A., 1962-64; v.p., escro mgr. Bank of Downey, Calif., 1964-66; cons., tchr. Santa Ana (Calif.) Coll. Bus., 1964-66; elem. tchr. St. Bruno's Sch., Whittier, Calif., 1966-70, Pasadena (Calif.) Unified Sch. Dist., 1971-84, Holy Angels Sch., Arcadia, Calif., 1985-89; vice prin., computer coord. Our Mother of Good Counsel, L.A., 1989-93; prin. St. Stephen Martyr, Monterey Park, Calif., 1993—; master catechist religious edn. L.A. Archdiocese, 1988—. Author: History of the Arms Control and Disarmament Organization, 1976; organizer, editor newsletter Cath. Com. for Girl Scouts and Campfire. Eucharistic min. Our Mother of Good Counsel, 1989-95; sec. of senatus Legion of Mary, 1980-85; counselor Boy Scouts Am., 1985—; mem. Cath. com. for Girl Scouts U.S.A. and Campfire, vice chmn. acad. affairs L.A. Archdiocese, 1985-90. Recipient Pius X medal L.A. Archdiocese, 1979, St. Elizabeth Ann Seton award Cath. Com. for Girl Scouts, 1988, St. Anne medal Cath. Com. for Girl Scouts, 1989, Bronze Pelican award Cath. Com. for Boy Scouts, 1989; grantee Milken Family Found., 1989, 92. Mem. Phi Beta Kappa, Phi Delta Kappa (historian 1991-92, founds. rep. 1992-93, treas. 1993-94, 1st v.p. 1994-95, pres. 1995-96), Phi Kappa Phi. Home: 6725 Brentmead Ave Arcadia CA 91007-7708 Office: 119 S Ramona Ave Monterey Park CA 91754-2802

MHAFFEY, MERRILL DEAN, artist; b. Albuquerque, Aug. 12, 1937; s. Dean Elmo and Vera Sarah (McDonald) M.; m. Justine Helm; children: Jerome Dea, Eric Paul; m. Jeanne Michele Shirk, Jan. 1, 1947; 1 child, Spencer Michele. Student, Mesa Coll., Grand Junction, Colo., 1955-57, Calif. Coll. Arts and Crafts, 1983, 89; BA, Sacramento State U., 1959; MFA, Ariz. State U., 1965. Art tchr. pub. schs., Glenwood Springs, Colo., 1959-61; instr. art Western State Coll. Colo., 1965-67; instr. drawing and painting Phoenix Coll., 1967-83; vis. lectr. painting and watercolor Colo. Mountain Coll., Vail, 1983, 89; painting juror Nat. Endowment for Arts, Washington, 1989. Represented in permanent collections at Met. Mus. Art, N.Y.C., Mus. Am. Art, Smithsonian Instns., Washington, Phoenix Art Mus., Denver Art Mus.; pub. art commns. include Colo. State Legislature, 1988, City of Chandler (Ariz.) Art Ctr., 1990, Nat. Ednowment for Arts, Denver, 1993. Home: 4 Puerto Ct Santa Fe NM 87505

MIAN, GUO, electrical engineer; b. Shanghai, Feb. 6, 1957; came to U.S., 1987; s. Wenseng Mian and Guorong Sun; m. Ann Wang, Nov. 1, 1989. BS in Physics, Shanghai U. Sci. & Tech., 1982; MS in Physics, Western Ill. U., 1989; DSc in Elec. Engring., Washington U., 1992. Mgr. Rec. Media Lab. Magnetic Rec. Ctr., Shanghai (China) Ctrl. Chem. Ltd., 1982-85; vis. scientist materials sci. lab. Keio U., Yokohama, Japan, 1985-87; sr. rsch. elec. engring. Quantum Corp., Milpitas, Calif., 1992-93, Conner Peripherals, San Jose, Calif., 1993-95; sr. mgr. HDD R&D Ctr. Samsung Info. Sys. Am., San Jose, Calif., 1995—. Contbr. articles to Jour. Materials Sci., IEEE Trans. Magnetics, Jour. Magnetism & Magnetic Materials, Jour. Applied Physics, Japanese Jour. Applied Physics, Jour. Japanese Magnetic Soc. Recipient C & C Promotion award Found. for C & C Promotion, Tokyo, 1986. Mem. IEEE, IEEE Magnetics Soc., IEEE Computer Soc., Am. Phys. Soc. Home: 105 Serra Way # 362 Milpitas CA 95035-5206

MIAN, LAL SHAH, entomologist; b. Pakistan, Mar. 4, 1945; s. Mohammad Shah M.; m. Judith Anne Conatser, Dec. 26, 1983; children: David Shah and Adam Shah. BSc in Agrl. with honors, U. Peshawar, 1967, MSc in Agrl. with honors, 1972; MS in Agrl., Am. U., Beirut, Lebanon, 1974; PhD in Entomology, U. Calif., Riverside, 1982. Registered Environ. Health Specialist. Tech. asst. forest entomology Forest Rsch. Inst., Peshawar, 1967-68; instr. entomology U. Peshawar, 1969-72, lectr. entomology, 1974-77; vector ecologist San Bernardino (Calif.) County Vector Control Program Pub. Health Dept., 1986—. Author: (with others) Distribution, Transport and Fate of the Insecticides Malathion and Parathion in the Environment, 1981, Interagency Guidelines for the Surveillance and Control of Selected Vector-borne Pathogens in California, 1995; reviewer Environ. Entomology, Jour. of Econ. Entomology, Annals of Entomological Soc.Am., 1980-85; assoc. editor Bull. Soc. Vector Ecology, 1991-92; editl. bd. Wing Beats, 1992-94, Bull. Soc. Vector Ecology, 1992-96. contbr. more than 50 articles to profl. jours.; numerous interviews to newsmedia. Elected mem. U. Senate Lectrs. Constituency, 1976-77, U. Syndicate 23-mem Governing Body, 1976-77; mem. Curriculum Com. Faculty Agrl., 1975-76, Resident Dir. Tchr. Student Ctr., 1975-77, Chancellor's Search Com. for Dean Coll. Natural and Agrl. Scis. U. Calif., 1981, Grad. Student Coun. U. Calif., 1981, Student Mini-Grant Adv. Com. U. Calif. Coop. Ext., 1981-82. Recipient postdoctoral fellow in mosquito rsch. U. Calif., 1982-83, 84-85, 85-86; assistantship in mosquito rsch. U. Calif., 1981-82; Dawood Found. scholar U. Peshawar, 1962-63, Directorate of Edn. scholar, U. Peshawar, 1962-67, Dept. Agrl. scholar U. Peshawar, 1964-67, U.S. Aid scholar Am. U., 1972-74, Ctrl. Overseas scholarship U. Calif., 1977-82. Mem. AAAS, Internat. N.W. Conf. Diseases in Nature Communicable to Man, Am. Registry Profl. Entomologists, Am. Mosquito Control Assn. (recertification and tng. com., 1992-94, recertification com., 1994-95), Entomol. Assn. Am., N.Y. Acad. Scis. (bd. govs. 1997—), Mosquito and Vector Control Assn. Calif. (disease control sub-com. Vector control com., 1990-93, pubs. com., 1990-94, tng. and cert., 1991—, chem. control com., 1993—, Africanized Honey Bee Ad Hoc Com., 1995—), Calif. Environ. Health Assn., Entomological Assn. So. Calif., San Bernardino County Africanized Honey Bee Task Force, State-wide Africanized Honey Bee Stearing Com., Soc. Vector Ecology (pubs. com., 1988, local arrangements com., 1993, program com. ednl. programs in Vector control com., 1993), Big Bear Valley (coordinated resource mgmt. plan group, 1993-94), Sigma Xi. Democrat. Office: San Bernardino County Vector Control Program 2355 E 5th St San Bernardino CA 92410

MICHAEL, ERNEST ARTHUR, mathematics educator; b. Zurich, Switzerland, Aug. 26, 1925; came to U.S., 1939; s. Jakob and Erna (Sondheimer) M.; m. Colette Verger Davis, 1956 (div. 1966); children: Alan, David, Gerard; m. Erika Goodman Joseph, Dec. 4, 1966; children: Hillary, Joshua. B.A., Cornell U., 1947; M.A., Harvard U., 1948; Ph.D., U. Chgo., 1951. Mem. faculty dept. math. U. Wash., Seattle, 1953—; asst. prof. U. Wash., 1953-56, assoc. prof., 1956-60, prof., 1960-93, prof. emeritus, 1993—; mem. Inst. for Advanced Study, Princeton, 1951-52, 56-57, 60-61, 68, Math. Research Inst., E.T.H., Zürich, 1973-74; vis. prof. U. Stuttgart, Ger., 1978-79, U. Munich, Fed. Republic Germany, 1987, 88, 92-93. Editor: Procs. Am. Math. Soc., 1968-71, Topology and Its Applications, 1972-94; contbr. articles to profl. jours. Served with USNR, 1944-46. Grantee AEC; Grantee Office Nav. Research; Grantee NSF; Grantee Guggenheim Found.; Grantee Humboldt Found. Mem. Am. Math. Soc., Math. Assn. Am., ACLU, Amnesty Internat. Jewish. Home: 16751 15th Ave NW Seattle WA 98177-3842 Office: U Washington Dept Math GN 50 Seattle WA 98195

MICHAEL, GARY G., retail supermarket and drug chain executive; b. 1940; married. BS in Bus., U. Idaho, 1962. Staff acct. Ernst & Ernst, CPA's, 1964-66; with Albertson's, Inc., Boise, Idaho, 1966—, acct., 1966-68, asst. controller, 1968-71, controller, 1971-72, v.p., controller, 1972-74, sr. v.p. fin., treas., 1974-76, exec. v.p., 1976-84, vice chmn., CFO, corp. devel. officer, 1984-91, chmn., CEO, 1991—; also dir. Albertson's, Inc. Served to 1st lt. U.S. Army, 1962-64. Office: Albertsons Inc PO Box 20 250 Parkcenter Blvd Boise ID 83726*

MICHAEL, JAMES DANIEL, computer scientist; b. Peoria, Ill., May 27, 1957; s. Thomas Proctor and Mary Lou (Wagner) M.; m. Judith Ann O'Donnell, June 23, 1979. BS in Psychology, U. Calif., Davis, 1978. Teller Bank of Am., Davis, 1978-79, Fresno, Calif., 1979; computer operator Fresno County Computer Svcs., 1979-81; computer programmer Gesco Corp., Fresno, 1981-83, systems programmer, 1983-89; mgr. IBM operating systems Calif. State U., Fresno, 1989—. Co-author: The Porter Tract - An Historical and Architectural Survey, 1990; contbr. articles to profl. publs. Mem. Fresno City and County Hist. Soc., 1989—; founding mem. Landmarks Preservation Coun., Fresno, 1991—, Tree Fresno, 1987—; mem. Fresno Zool. Soc. Mem. Assn. for Computing Machinery, Nat. Systems Programmer Assn. Democrat. Office: Calif State U CCMS 2225 E San Ramon Ave Fresno CA 93740-8029

MICHAELIS, KAREN LAUREE, law educator; b. Milw., Mar. 30, 1950; d. Donald Lee and Ethel Catherine (Stevens) M.; m. Larry Severtson, Aug. 2, 1980 (div. Aug. 1982); 1 child, Quinn Alexandra Michaelis. BA, U. Wis., 1972, BS, 1974; MA, Calif. State U., L.A., 1979; PhD, U. Wis., 1988, MS, 1985, JD, 1989. Bar: Wis., U.S. Dist. Ct. (we. dist.) Wis. Asst. prof. law Hofstra U., Hempstead, N.Y., 1990-93; assoc. prof. law Ill. State U., Normal, 1993-95; asst. prof. law Wash. State U., Pullman, 1995—. Author: Reporting Child Abuse: A Guide to Mandatory Requirements for School Personnel, 1993, Theories of Liability for Teacher Sexual Misconduct, 1996; editor Ill. Sch. Law Quarterly, 1993-95; mem. editl. bd. Nat. Assn. Profs. of Ednl. Adminstrn., 1994-95, Planning and Changing, 1993-95, Jour. Sch. Leadership, 1991—, People & Education: The Human Side of Edn., 1991-96. Mem. ABA, Nat. Coun. Profs. Ednl. Adminstrn. (program com. 1994-95, morphet fund com. 1993—), Nat. Orgn. Legal Problems in Edn. (publs. com. 1993—, program com. 1995). Office: Wash State U Cleveland Hall 351 Pullman WA 99164-2136

MICHAELS, PATRICK FRANCIS, broadcasting company executive; b. Superior, Wis., Nov. 5, 1925; s. Julian and Kathryn Elizabeth (Keating) M.; AA, U. Melbourne, 1943; BA, Golden State U., 1954; PhD, London U., 1964; m. Paula Naomi Bowen, May 1, 1960; children—Stephanie Michelle, Patricia Erin. War corr. CBS; news editor King Broadcasting, 1945-50; war corr. Mid-East Internat. News Service, 1947-49; war corr. MBS, Korea, 1950-53; news dir. Sta. WDSU-AM-FM-TV, 1953-54; fgn. corr. NBC, S. Am., 1954-56; news dir. Sta. KWIZ, 1956-59; commentator ABC, Los Angeles, 1959-62; fgn. corr. Am. News Services, London, 1962-64; news commentator McFadden Bartell Sta. KCBQ, 1964-68; news commentator ABC, San Francisco, 1968-70; news dir. Sta. KWIZ, Santa Ana, Calif., 1970-74, station mgr., 1974-81; pres. Sta. KWRM, Corona, Calif., Sta. KQLH, San Bernardino, Calif., 1981-88; chmn. Michaels Media, Huntington Beach, Calif., 1988—. Bd. dirs. Econ. Devel. Corp. Mem. Nat. Assn. Broadcasters (bd. dirs.), Calif. Broadcasters Assn. (v.p.), Am. Fedn. TV and Radio Artists, Orange County Broadcasters Assn. (pres.), Sigma Delta Chi (ethics com.). Republican. Clubs: Rotary, Balboa Bay (bd. govs.), South Shore Yacht, Internat. Yachting Fellowship of Rotarians (staff commodore). Home: PO Box 832 Corona Del Mar CA 92625-0832

MICHALIK, JOHN JAMES, legal educational association executive; b. Bemidji, Minn., Aug. 1, 1945; s. John and Margaret Helen (Pafko) M.; m. Diane Marie Olson, Dec. 21, 1968; children: Matthew John, Nicole, Shane. BA, U. Minn., 1967, JD, 1970. Legal editor Lawyers Coop. Pub. Co., Rochester, N.Y., 1970-75; dir. continuing legal edn. Wash. State Bar Assn., Seattle, 1975-81, exec. dir., 1981-91; asst. dean devel. & cmty. rels. Sch. of Law U. Wash., 1991-95; exec. dir. Assn. Legal Adminstrs., 1995. Mem. Am. Soc. Assn. Execs., Nat. Assn. Bar Execs., Am. Mgmt. Assn., Nat. Trust Hist. Preservation, Coll. Club Seattle. Lutheran. Office: Assn Legal Adminstrs 175 E Hawthorn Pkwy Vernon Hills IL 60061-1463

MICHALKO, JAMES PAUL, library association administrator; b. Cleve., May 13, 1950; s. Paul James and Lillian (Fanta) M.; 1 child, Alexandra. BA, Georgetown U., 1971; MLS, MBA, U. Chgo., 1974. Asst. to v.p., adminstrn. Technicare Inc. (formerly BCC Industries), Cleve., 1971-72; asst dir., adminstrn. U. Pa. Librs., Phila., 1974-80; dir. bus. and fin. Rsch. Librs. Group, Stanford, Calif., 1980-85, v.p. fin. and adminstrn., 1985-87, acting pres., 1988-89; pres. Rsch. Librs. Group, Mountain View, Calif., 1989—. Contbr. to Libr. Quar., Coll. & Rsch. Librs.; reviewer for Libr. Quar., Coll. & Rsch. Librs., Acad. of Mgmt. Rev., Jour. Acad. Librarianship, Jour. Libr. Adminstrn. Office: Rsch Librs Group Inc 1200 Villa St Mountain View CA 94041-1106*

MICHAUD, DAVID L., protective services official. Student, Met. State Coll., U. Denver, FBI Acad., Quantico, Va., Northwestern U., Denver Police Dept. Tng. Acad. Patrol officer Colo. Police Dept., Ft. Lupton; sgt. Colo. Sheriff's Dept., Weld County; with Denver Police Dept., 1967—, detective, 1970-75, sgt., 1975-83, supr. spl. crime attack team, 1975-80, comdr. spl. crimes bur., 1980-86, lt., 1983-87, capt., 1987-91, comdr. internal investigations and inspection bur., 1987-89, comdr. urban st. crime bur., 1989-91, divsn. chief staff svcs. divsn., 1991-92, divsn. chief traffic divsn., 1991-92, chief of police, 1992—; instr. Denver Police Tng. Acad.; cert. instr. Colo. Law Enforcement Tng. Acad.; speaker in field. Author: (with J.M. MacDonald) The Confession: Interrogation and Criminal Profiles for Police Officers, 1987. Active N.E. Denver Community Youth Forum, City Pk. Pavilion Task Force, N.W. Denver Gang Eradication Task Force, Gov.'s Job Tng. Office Task Force, Denver Pub. Schs. Gang Task Force; bd. dirs. N.E. Denver Coalition Against Drugs. Sgt. USMC. Recipient Cert. of Merit, Manual High Sch., Denver Pub. Schs., 1990, Officer of Yr. award Hispanic Pub. Affairs Com., 1990, Cert. of Appreciation, Pk. Hill Community Safe Neighborhoods, 1991, 58 Letters of Commendation various law enforcement sources. Office: Police Dept 1331 Cherokee St Denver CO 80204-2720

MICHAUDON, ANDRÉ FRANCISQUE, physicist; b. Cavaillon, Vaucluse, France, May 14, 1929; s. Maurice Louis and Jeanne Francoise (Chatal) M.; children: Claire Hello, Helene Caron. Engring. degree, Ecole Supérieure Ingenieurs Arts et Métiers, Paris, 1951, Ecole Supérieure Electricite, Paris, 1953; DSc, U. Paris, 1964. Rsch. engr. Le Materiel Teléphonique, Boulogne, France, 1954-56; group leader Commissariat à Energie Atomique, Cen Saclay, France, 1956-64, 65-72; theorist MIT, Cambridge, 1964-65; div. head Commissariat à Energie Atomique, Bruyeres le Chalel, France, 1972-79; dept. dept. head Commissariat à l'Energie Atomique, Limeil, France, 1979-83; French co-dir. Inst. Laue Langevin, Grenoble, France, 1983-89; prof. Inst. Nat. des Scis. et Techniques Nucléaires, Saclay, Orsay, France, 1969-84; physicist Los Alamos Nat. Lab., 1989—; mem. exec. coun. European Sci. Found., Strasbourg, France, 1987-90; mem. adv. coun. Cen. Bur. for Nuclear Measurements EU, Geel, Belgium, 1990-95; cons. Orgn. for Econ. Cooperation and Devel., Paris, 1989-92. Author, editor: Nuclear Fission, 1981; co-gen. editor: Neutron Sources, 1983, Neutron Radiative Capture, 1984, Probability & Statistics, 1991; contbr. articles to profl. jours. Lt. French Navy, 1953-54. Recipient written congratulations Minister of the Navy, France, 1954, award Acad. des Sciences, Paris, 1980; named knight Order of Merit, Paris, 1984. Fellow Am. Phys. Soc., Am. Nuclear Soc.; mem. Soc. Francaise de Physique, N.Y. Acad. Scis. Home: 211 W Water Sante Fe NM 87501 Office: Los Alamos Nat Lab Lansce 3 MS H 855 Los Alamos NM 87545

MICHEL, MARY ANN KEDZUF, nursing educator; b. Evergreen Park, Ill., June 1, 1939; d. John Roman and Mary (Bassar) Kedzuf; m. Jean Paul Michel, 1974. Diploma in nursing, Little Company of Mary Hosp., Evergreen Park, 1960; BS in Nursing, Loyola U., Chgo., 1964; MS, No. Ill. U., 1968, EdD, 1971. Staff nurse Little Co. of Mary Hosp., 1960-64; instr. Little Co. of Mary Hosp. (Sch. Nursing), 1964-67, No. Ill. U., DeKalb, 1968-69; asst. prof. No. Ill. U., 1969-71; chmn. dept. nursing U. Nev., Las Vegas, 1971-73; prof. nursing U. Nev., 1975—, dean Coll. Health Scis., 1973-90; pres. PERC, Inc.; mgmt. cons., 1993—; mgmt. cons. Nev. Donor Network, 1993; mem. So. Nev. Health Manpower Task Force, 1975; mem. manpower com. Plan Devel. Commn., Clark County Health Sys. Agy., 1977-79, mem. governing body, 1981-86; mem. Nev. Health Coordinating Coun., Western Inst. Nursing, 1971-85; mem. coordinating com. assembly instnl. adminstrs. dept. allied health edn. and accreditation AMA, 1985-88; mem. bd. advisors So. Nev. Vocat. Tech. Ctr., 1976-80; sec.-treas. Nev. Donor Network, 1988-89, bd. dirs., 1986-90, chmn. bd., 1988-90. Contbr. articles to profl. jours. Trustee Desert Spring Hosp., Las Vegas, 1976-85; bd. dirs. Nathan Adelson Hospice, 1982-88, Bridge Counseling Assocs., 1982, Everywoman's Ctr., 1984-86; chmn. Nev. Commn. on Nursing Edn., 1972-73, Nursing Articulation Com., 1972-73, Yr. of Nurse Com., 1978; moderator Invitational Conf. Continuing Edn., Am. Soc. Allied Health Professions, 1978; mgmt. cons. Nev. Donor Network, 1994—, Donor Organ Recovery Svc., Transplant Recipient Internat. Orgn., S.W. Eye Bank, S.W. Tissue Bank. Named Outstanding Alumnus, Loyola U., 1983; NIMH fellow, 1967-68. Fellow Am. Soc. Allied Health Professions, 1991, (chmn. nat. resolutions com. 1981-84, treas. 1988-90, sec's. award com. 1982-83, 92-93, nat. by-laws com. 1985, conv. chmn. 1987); mem. AAUP, Am. Nurses Assn., Nev. Nurses Assn. (dir. 1975-77, treas. 1977-79, conv. chmn. 1978), So. Nev. Area Health Edn. Coun., Western Health Deans (co-organizer 1985, chair, 1988-90), Nat. League Nursing, Nev. Heart Assn., So. Nev. Mem. Hosps. (mem. nursing recruitment com. 1981-83, mem. nursing practice com. 1983-85), Las Vegas C. of C. (named Woman of Yr. Edn.) 1988, Slovak Catholic Sokols, Phi Kappa Phi (chpt. sec. 1981-83, pres.-elect 1983, pres. 1984, v.p. Western region 1989-95, editl. bd. jour. Nat. Forum 1989-93), Alpha Beta Gamma (hon.), Sigma Theta Tau, Zeta Kappa. Office: U Nev Las Vegas 4505 S Maryland Pky Las Vegas NV 89154-9900

MICHEL, VICTOR JAMES, JR., retired librarian; b. St. Louis, Feb. 2, 1927; s. Victor James and Bernadette (Fox) M.; m. Margaret A. Renaud, Feb. 3, 1951; children: Dennis W., Daniel J., Catherine A., Denise M.; student St. Louis U., 1946-48. Asst. librarian McDonnell Aircraft Corp., St. Louis, 1948-55; mgr. Anaheim (Calif.) Information Center, Electronics Ops., Rockwell Internat. Corp., 1955-84; pres. V.J. Michel Inc., Grass Valley, Calif., 1986—; sec. Placentia Devel. Co., 1964-71. Charter mem. Placentia-Tlaquepaque Sister City Orgn., 1964-84; founder, pres. Placentia chpt. St. Louis Browns Fan Club. Planning commr., Placentia, Calif., 1957-60, city councilman, 1960-70, vice-mayor, 1960-64, mayor, 1964-68. Trustee Placentia Library Dist., 1970-79, pres., 1974-79; city historian, Placentia, 1976-84, city treas., 1980-84; chmn. Placentia Fine Arts Commn., 1978-80. Served from pvt. to staff sgt. AUS, 1945-46. Named Placentia Citizen of Yr., 1979. Mem. Placentia C. of C. (v.p. 1960), Placentia Jaycees (hon. life), Calif., Orange County (pres. 1976) library assns. Democrat. Roman Catholic. Club: West Atwood Yacht (hon. yeoman emeritus with citation 1970, ship's librarian). Author: Pictorial History of the West Atwood Yacht Club, 1966; Placentia—Around the World, 1970; also articles in profl. jours. Home: 909 Jack Rabbit Ct Saint Peters MO 63376-5921

MICHELET, JOHN JACOB, JR., advertising agency executive, screenplay writer; b. Madison, Minn., Dec. 23, 1943; s. John Jacob and Vivian Alzeda (Larson) M.; m. Linda Lee Eader, Jan. 28, 1970 (div. June 1994); children: Lindsay Marie, Erik Howard; m. Judith Anne Brymer, Jan. 7, 1995. BA, U. Oreg., 1965; MBA, Stanford U., 1967. Merchandising mgr. Zellerbach Paper Co., San Diego, 1970-72; account exec. Phillips-Ramsey Advt., San Diego, 1972-75, Grey Advt., L.A., 1975; account mgr., v.p. Cole & Weber Advt., Portland, Oreg., 1975-79, 85-87; dir. mktg. Pacific Fireplace Furnishings, Tualatin, Oreg., 1979-82; account mgr. Morton Advt., Portland, 1982-85; pres., creative dir. Genesis, Inc., Portland, 1987—; mem. adv. bd. CODA, Portland, 1995—. Recipient Pica Pole award for best newspaper advt. in Oreg., Oreg. Newspaper Pubs. Assn., 1989, 91, Telly awards for TV commls. and videos, 1989-96, Vision awards, 1990-96, Am. Pub. Transit Assn., Assn. Commuter Transp., Nat. Energy Coun. awards, 1992-96; Silver Microphone award for radio commls., 1992-96. Office: Genesis Inc 14140 SW Chehalem Ct Tigard OR 97223

MICHELI, CHRISTOPHER MICHAEL, lawyer; b. Sacramento, Mar. 14, 1967; s. Paul Lothar and Vima Nina (de Marchi) M.; m. Liza Marie Hernandez, Sept. 4, 1994; 1 stepchild, Morgan. Attended, George Washington U., 1985-86; BA in Polit. Sci. and Pub. Svc., U. Calif., Davis, 1989; JD, McGeorge Sch. Law, 1992. Bar: Calif. 1992, U.S. Dist. Ct. (no. and cen. dists.) 1993, (ea. dist.) 1992, U.S. Ct. Appeals (D.C. and 9th cirs.) 1993. Assoc. Bell & Hiltachk, Sacramento, 1992-93; gen. counsel Calif. Mfrs. Assn., Sacramento, 1993-94; atty., legis. advocate Carpenter, Snodgrass & Assocs., Sacramento, 1994—; mem. editl. adv. bd. State Income Tax Alert, Ga., 1995—, Interstate Tax Report, 1997, The Docket; mem. legis. com. Inst. Govtl. Advocates, Sacramento, 1994-95. Columnist The Daily Recorder, 1994—; contbr. articles to newspapers and profl. jours. Bd. dirs. Jesuit H.S. Alumni Assn., Sacramento, 1992—; soccer referee and coach Del Dayo Sch., Carmichael, Calif., 1994—. Scholar William D. James Found., 1989. Mem. ABA, State Bar Calif., Sacramento County Bar Assn., Phi Delta Phi. Democrat. Roman Catholic. Home: 5511 Ivanhoe Way Carmichael CA 95608-5913 Office: Carpenter Snodgrass Assocs 1121 L St # 210 Sacramento CA 95814

MICHELICH, JOANNA KURDEKA, college dean; b. Twin Falls, Idaho, May 3, 1948; d. John Lawrence and Marjorie (Haight) Kurdeka; m. John Joseph Michelich, July 22, 1972. AA, Cochise Coll., Douglas, Ariz., 1968; BS in English Edn., No. Ariz. U., 1969; MEd in Counseling, U. Ariz., 1970; PhD in Higher Edn., Wash. State U., 1977. Asst. dean of women U. N.D., Grand Forks, 1970-71, dean of women, 1971-72, assoc. dean of students, 1972-73; tchg. and grad. asst. Wash. State U., Pullman, 1973-76; dean of student pers. svcs. West Shore C.C., Scottville, Mich., 1976-78; dean of student affairs Ctrl. Ariz. Coll., Coolidge, 1978-83, v.p. student svcs., 1983-87; dean of instrnl. svcs. Ctrl. Ariz. Coll., Apache Junction, 1992—; co-owner, ptnr. Sun West Ednl. Assocs., Inc., Casa Grande, Ariz., 1987-92. Mem. Casa Grande Elem. Schs. Adv. Task Force, 1985-86, chair sch. facilities and planning com.; del. Casa Grande Town Hall, 1980, 82-87; mem. Citizens' Screening Com. to fill Ariz. legis. vacancy, 1991; del. Apache Junction (Ariz.) Town Hall, 1996; chair Citizens' Screening Com. to fill Apache Junction JP Ct., 1994; active Greater Casa Grande Valley Econ. Devel. Found., 1990-92; co-chair planning com. Pinal County Town Hall, 1988-92, del./facilitator, 1993—; bd. dirs. United Way of Pinal County, 1980-86, v.p., 1981, pres., 1982; bd. dirs. Pinal Gila Behavioral Health Assn., 1997—. Mem. ASTD, Am. Assn. C.C.s, Am. Assn. Higher Edn., Nat. Assn. Student Pers. Adminstrs. (Region IV-West coord. spl. projects 1980-82, editl. bd. jour. 1981-84, Ariz. state dir. 1982-85, nat. task force on C.C.s 1986-87), Nat. Assn. Instrnl. Adminstrs., Nat. Coun. Student Devel. (coord. Region IX 1983-85, vice chair membership 1985-86, sec. 1986-87), Ariz. Acad. Adminstrs. Assn., Ariz. Assn. C.C. Student Pers. Adminstrs. (v.p. 1979-80, pres.-elect 1980-81, chair ann. state conf. 1981, pres. 1981-82), Ariz. C.C. Adminstrs. Assn. (bd. dirs. 1983-87, v.p. 1984-85, chair 1st ann. state conf. 1985), Apache Junction C. of C., Apache Junction Rotary (bd. dirs. 1992-96), Phi Delta Kappa, Phi Kappa Phi. Lutheran. Home: 8389 E Aloe Vera Cir Gold Canyon AZ 85219 Office: Ctrl Ariz Coll 273 Old West Hwy Apache Junction AZ 85219-5231

MICHELSON, SONIA, music educator, author; b. L.A., Feb. 14, 1928; d. Maurice and Elizabeth (Jacobs) Saeta; m. Irving Michelson, Apr. 4, 1954 (div. Aug. 1982); children: Ann Michelson Shoham, Louis F., Hadassah Zelman, Zahava Waldman, Elisheva Levin, Eliyahu Michaeli, Yaacov. BA, U. Calif., Berkeley, 1949. Instr. in guitar Suzuki Music Acad. of Chgo., 1980-81, Music Arts Sch., Highland Park, Ill., 1973-82; dir. in classical guitar Michelson Classic Guitar Studio, Chgo., 1973-88; dir. Michelson Classic Guitar Studio, L.A., 1988—; cons. Music Educators Nat. Conf., Atlantic City, N.J., 1976; columnist Guitar Found. of Am., L.A., 1984—. Author: Easy Classic Guitar Solos, 1977, Classical Guitar Study, 1982, New Dimensions in Classical Guitar for Children, 1984, Young Beginner's First Repertoire for Classical Guitar, 1996; contbr. articles to profl. jours. Mem. Am. String Tchrs. Assn. (spl. cons. 1977-85), Chgo. Classical Guitar Soc. (pres. 1978-88), Guitar Found. of Am. (mem. editorial bd. 1972—), Suzuki Assn. Am., Nat. Music Tchrs. Assn., Music Tchrs. Assn. Calif. Democrat. Jewish. Home: 1465 Reeves St Los Angeles CA 90035-2945

MICK, NEIL MICHAEL, artist, educator; b. N.Y.C., Nov. 22, 1960; s. Michael Fuchs and Corrine Lee (Mick) Tsottles; m. Lori lee Wikkerink, Oct. 31, 1985 (div. Aug. 1991). BFA, Md. Inst., 1983; BA in Human Ecology, Coll. Atlantic, 1985. Counselor Don Webb Nature Camp, Monkton, Md., 1987; art model Md. Inst., Balt., 1988-92; dir., instr. Bay Area Artist's Sch., San Francisco, 1993. Freelance writer Balt. Alternative, 1987, White Wolf Game Studio, Clarkston, Ga., 1996; one-man shows Golden Temple Gallery, Balt., 1990, U. Quincy (Ill.), 1995; group shows La. State U. (Juror's award), Baton Rouge, 1992, Sacramento Fine ARts Ctr. (Best of Show award), 1992, Calif. State Fair (Juror's award), Sacramento, 1993, Slocumb Gallery Ea. Tenn. State U., Johnson City, 1994, Hera Gallery (Best of Show award), 1995. Founding mem. Balt. Greens, 1985-88; vol. intern Am. Friends Svc. Commn., Balt., 1988. Hambidge Art Ctr. fellow, 1991; recipient Juror's award Calif. State Fair, 1993; grantee Ludwig Vogelstein Found., 1994. Mem. Aikido West (Nidan award 1995). Home and Office: 633 York St San Francisco CA 94110

MICKELSON, SIG, broadcasting executive, educator; b. Clinton, Minn., May 24, 1913; s. Olaf and Harriet (Reinholdson) M.; m. Maybelle Brown, June 8, 1940 (dec. Apr., 1985); children: Karen Ann (Mrs. Christiaan De Brauw), Alan; m. Elena Mier y Teran, June 14, 1986. B.A., Augustana Coll., 1934, LLD, 1987; M.A., U. Minn., 1940. With CBS, N.Y.C., 1943-61; pres. CBS News, 1954-61; v.p., dir. Time-Life Broadcast, Inc., N.Y.C., 1961-70, Ency. Brit. Ednl. Corp., Chgo., 1970-72; prof., chmn. editorial dept. Medill Sch. Journalism, Northwestern U., Evanston, Ill., 1972-75; pres. RFE/RL, Inc., Washington, 1975-78; Disting. vis. prof. San Diego State U., 1978-79, exec. dir. Ctr. for Communications, 1979-82, adj. prof, 1984-90, Van Deerlin prof. communications, 1989-90; pres. San Diego Communications Coun., 1989-90; Manship prof. journalism La. State U., 1991-93, disting. prof. comm., 1994—; rsch. fellow Hoover Instn., 1981—; advisor Nat. News Coun., 1973-80; ex-officio Bd. Internat. Broadcasting, 1975-78; dir. Stauffer Comms. Inc., 1979-95. Author: The Electric Mirror, 1972, America's Other Voice, 1983, The First Amendment: The Challenge of New Technology, 1989, From Whistle Stop to Sound Bite, 1989, The Northern Pacific Railroad and the Selling of the West, 1993. Bd. regents Augustana Coll., 1983-95. Mem. Radio TV News Dirs. Assn. (founder, v.p. 1946-48, pres. 1948-49), Internat. Inst. for Comm. (founder, chmn. 1970-71, chmn. exec. com. 1967-70, 71-73), Coun. on Fgn. Rels. Clubs: Century Assn.

(N.Y.C.); Cosmos (Washington). Home: 6443 Pasatiempo Ave San Diego CA 92120-3823

MIDDLETON, ANTHONY WAYNE, JR., urologist, educator; b. Salt Lake City, May 6, 1939; s. Anthony Wayne and Dolores Caravena (Lowry) M.; m. Carol Samuelson, Oct. 23, 1970; children: Anthony Wayne, Suzanne, Kathryn, Jane, Michelle. BS, U. Utah, 1963; MD, Cornell U., 1966. Intern, U. Utah Hosps., Salt Lake City, 1966-67; resident in urology Mass. Gen. Hosp., Boston, 1970-74; practice urology Middleton Urol. Assos., Salt Lake City, 1974—; mem. staff Primary Children's Hosp., staff pres., 1981-82; mem. staff Latter-Day Saints Hosp., chmn. divsn. of Urology, Salt Lake Regional Med. Ctr. 1995—; assoc. clin. prof. surgery U. Utah Med. Coll., 1977—; vice chmn. bd. govs. Utah Med. Self-Ins. Assn., 1980-81, 96—, chmn. 1985-87; med. dir. Uroquest Co., 1996—. Bd. dirs. Utah chpt. Am. Cancer Soc., 1978-86; bishop, later stake presidency Ch. Jesus Christ Latter-day Saints; vice chmn. Utah Med. Polit. Action Com., 1978-81, chmn., 1981-83; chmn. Utah Physicians for Reagan, 1983-84; mem. U. Utah Coll. Medicine Dean's Search Com., 1983-84; bd. dirs. Utah Symphony, 1985—, Primary Children's Found., 1989-96. Capt. USAF, 1968-70. Editor (monthly pub.) AACU-FAX, 1992—; assoc. editor Millenial Star Brit. LDS mag. 1960-61. Mem. ACS, Utah Med. Assn. (pres. 87-88, disting. svc. award 1993), Am. Urologic Assn. (socioecons. com. 1987—, chmn. western sect. socioecons. com. 1989—, western. sect. health policy com. chmn., 1990—), AMA (alt. del. to House of Dels. 1989-92, 94, 96—), Salt Lake County Med. Assn. (sec. 1965-67, pres. liaison com. 1980-81, pres.-elect 1981-83, pres. 1984), Utah Urol. Assn. (pres. 1976-77), Salt Lake Surg. Soc. (treas. 1977-78), Am. Assn. Clin. Urologists (bd. dirs. 1989-90, nat. pres. elect 1990-91, pres. 1991-92, nat. bd. chmn. urologic polit. action com. UROPAC, 1992—), Phi Beta Kappa, Alpha Omega Alpha, Beta Theta Pi (chpt. pres. Gamma Beta 1962). Republican. Contbr. articles to profl. jours. Home: 2798 Chancellor Pl Salt Lake City UT 84108-2835 Office: Hellenic Airforce Com, C-1 Branch, Elefsis Base Greece

MIDDLETON, MICHAEL JOHN, civil engineer; b. N.Y.C., May 14, 1953; s. Vincent Aloysius and Mary Hilda (Lehane) M. BS in Civil Engring., U. Calif., Davis, 1975. Registered profl. engr., Calif., Wash., Hawaii. Project mgr. G.A. Fitch & Assoc., Concord, Calif., 1975-78, v.p., 1978-80; project mgr. Santina & Thompson, Inc., Concord, 1980-83, dir. engring., 1983-88, sr. v.p., 1988—. scholar, Calif. Scholarship Fedn., 1971. Mem. ASCE, Nat. Soc. Profl. Engrs., Soc. Am. Mil. Engrs. Roman Catholic. Home: 1409A Bel Air Dr Concord CA 94521-2802 Office: Santina & Thompson Inc 1355 Willow Way Ste 280 Concord CA 94520-5728

MIDDLETON, RICHARD GEORGE, urologist, educator; b. Salt Lake City, May 7, 1933; s. Richard Palmer and Lucy Jane (Rose) M.; m. Jayne G. Middleton, Sept. 24, 1957; children: Elizabeth, William, Amy. BA, U. Utah, 1955; MD, Cornell U., 1958. Prof. surgery, chmn. divsn. urology U. Utah Sch. Medicine, Salt Lake City, 1968—. Home: 1424 Circle Way Salt Lake City UT 84103-4432 Office: U Utah Sch Medicine 50 N Medical Dr Salt Lake City UT 84132-0001

MIDDLEWOOD, MARTIN EUGENE, technical communications specialist, writer, consultant; b. Galesburg, Ill., Mar. 21, 1947; s. Martin and Bernetta Maxine (Henderson) M.; m. Mona Marie Jarmer, Sept. 10, 1971; children: Erin, Martha, Emily, Margaret. BA, Ea. Wash. U., 1973, MA, 1980. Writer tech. manuals Tektronix, Inc., Beaverton, Oreg., 1976-77, tech. writer, 1977-79, sr. tech. writer, 1979-82, supr. pub. rels., 1982-84, mgr. pub. rels., 1984-85; mgr. mktg. communications Tektronix, Inc., Vancouver, Wash., 1985-87; dir. info. strategy Waggener Edstrom, Portland, Oreg., 1986-96; pub. Cognizer Report, Portland, Oreg., 1990-94; chmn. adv. bd. sci. and tech. writing, Clark Coll., Vancouver, 1984—; owner communications cons. firm, Vancouver, 1978—. Author: (ednl. brochure series) Oscilloscope Measurements, 1979 (award of excellence Willamette Valley chpt. Soc. Tech. Communication, 1980); contbr. articles to profl. jours. Served with USMC, 1967-70. Recipient Cert. Recognition Clark Coll., Vancouver, 1984, 86, 89, 92, 93, 94, 95, award of Excellence Pacific N.W. chpt. Internat. Assn. Bus. Communicators, 1985. Mem. Soc. Tech. Communication (sr., pres. Willamette Valley chpt. 1983-85, award of recognition 1986, chpt. pub. achievement award 1985, 2 awards of distinction 1981). Home: 1107 SE 98th Ave Vancouver WA 98664-4119 Office: Waggener Edstrom 6915 SW Macadam Ave Ste 300 Portland OR 97219-2300

MIDKIFF, DONALD WAYNE, program manager; b. Post, Tex., Sept. 26, 1940; s. Colvert Crockett Midkiff and Judy M. (Poss) Hinckley; m. Olga Maria Androvitch, June 21, 1961 (div. 1968); m. Manbeth Jean Crowell, Apr. 29, 1979. BS in Tech. Mgmt., Denver Tech. Coll., 1988; MS in Mgmt., Colo. Tech. U., 1994. With USAF, 1960, advanced through grades to sgt., 1968; electronics supr. Lockheed Aircraft, Jidda, Saudi Arabia, 1969-71; site mgr. Kentron Hawaii, Ltd., Pleiku, South Vietnam, 1971-73; supr. Kentron, Kwajalein, Marshall Islands, 1973-80, range ops. engr., 1980-84; ops. supr. Kentron PRC, Maui, Hawaii, 1984-87; ops. mgr. Kentron PRC, Colorado Springs, Colo., 1985-87; divsn. security mgr. PRC, Colorado Springs, Colo., 1987-89; program mgr. PRC Inc., Colorado Springs, Colo., 1989—; advisor Denver Tech. Coll., Colorado Springs, 1991—. CPR instr. Am. Red Cross, 1980-86; pres. Kwajalein Dive Club, 1981-83, Kwajalein Tennis Club, 1978-80. Recipient Group Achievement award NASA, 1992. Mem. AFCEA, Mensa, Nat. Contract Mgmt. Assn., Profl. Assn. Diving Instrs. (dive master). Republican. Office: PRC Inc Ste 260 985 Space Center Dr Colorado Springs CO 80915-3638

MIEL, VICKY ANN, municipal government executive; b. South Bend, Ind., June 20, 1951; d. Lawrence Paul Miel and Virginia Ann (Yeagley) Hernandez. BS, Ariz. State U., 1985. Word processing coordinator City of Phoenix, 1977-78, word processing adminstr., 1978-83, chief dep. city clk., 1983-88, city clk. dir., 1988—; assoc. prof. Phoenix Community Coll., 1982-83, Mesa (Ariz.) Community Coll., 1983; speaker in field, Boston, Santa Fe, Los Angeles, N.Y.C. and St. Paul, 1980—. Author: Phoenix Document Request Form, 1985, Developing Successful Systems Users, 1986. Judge Future Bus. Leaders Am. at Ariz. State U., Tempe, 1984; bd. dirs. Fire and Life Safety League, Phoenix, 1984. Recipient Gold Plaque, Word Processing Systems Mag., Mpls., 1980, Green Light Productivity award City of Phoenix, 1981, Honor Soc. Achievement award Internat. Word Processing Assn., 1981, 1st Ann. Grand Prize Records Mgmt. Internat. Inst. Mcpl. Clks., 1990, Olsten Award for Excellence in Records Mgmt., 1991, Tech. Award of Excellence, 1995. Mem. Assn. Info. Systems Profls. (internat. dir. 1982-84), Internat. Inst. Mcpl. Clks. (cert., Tech. award of excellence 1995, 2d v.p. 1996-97, 1st v.p. 1997—), Am. Records Mgrs. Assn., Assn. Image Mgmt., Am. Soc. Pub. Adminstrs., Am. Mgmt. Assn. Office: City of Phoenix 200 W Washington St Ste 1500 Phoenix AZ 85003-1611

MIGDEN, CHESTER L., professional society administrator; b. N.Y.C., May 21, 1921; s. Albert and Louise (Jawer) M.; m. Dina Vohl, July 22, 1944; children: Barbara, Ann, Amy. B.A., CCNY, 1941; LL.B., Columbia U., 1947. Bar: N.Y. State 1947. Atty. NLRB, N.Y.C., 1947-51; various positions Screen Actors Guild Inc., Hollywood, 1952-81; nat. exec. sec. Screen Actors Guild Inc., 1973-81; v.p. Internat. Fedn. Actors, 1973-81, Calif. Labor Fedn., 1974-81, Associated Actors and Artistes Am., 1973-81; exec. dir. Assn. Talent Agts., 1982-94; ret., 1994; officer, trustee Producers-Screen Actors Guild pension, welfare plans, 1960-81; v.p. Motion Picture and TV Fund, 1975—; instr. extension program UCLA. Contbr. articles to profl. jours. Mem. Acad. Motion Picture Arts and Scis., Am. Arbitration Assn. (arbitrator), Labor Rels. Cons. Democrat.

MIKALOW, ALFRED ALEXANDER, II, deep sea diver, marine surveyor, marine diving consultant; b. N.Y.C., Jan. 19, 1921; m. Janice Brenner, Aug. 1, 1960; children: Alfred Alexander, Jon Alfred. Student Rutgers U., 1940; MS, U. Calif., Berkeley, 1948; MA, Rochdale U. (Can.), 1950. Owner Coastal Diving Co., Oakland, Calif., 1950—, Divers Supply, Oakland, 1952—; dir. Coastal Sch. Deep Sea Diving, Oakland, 1950—; capt. and master rsch. vessel Coastal Researcher I; mem. Marine Inspection Bur., Oakland. marine diving contractor, cons. Mem. adv. bd. Medic Alert Found., Turlock, Calif., 1960—. Lt. comdr. USN, 1941-47, 49-50. Decorated Purple Heart, Silver Star. Mem. Divers Assn. Am. (pres. 1970-74), Treasury Recovery, Inc. (pres. 1972-75), Internat. Assn. Profl. Divers, Assn. Diving Contractors, Calif. Assn. Pvt. Edn. (no. v.p. 1971-72), Authors Guild, Internat. Game Fish Assn., U.S. Navy League, U.S. Res. Officers Assn., Tailhook Assn., U.S. Submarine Vets. WWII, Explorer Club (San Francisco), Calif. Assn. Marine Surveyors (pres. 1988—), Soc. Naval Archs. and Marine Engrs. (assoc.), Masons, Lions. Author: Fell's Guide to Sunken Treasure Ships of the World, 1972; (with H. Rieseberg) The Knight from Maine, 1974. Office: 320 29th Ave Oakland CA 94601-2104

MIKEL, THOMAS KELLY, JR., laboratory administrator; b. East Chicago, Ind., Aug. 27, 1946; s. Thomas Kelly and Anne Katherine (Vrazo) M.; BA, San Jose State U., 1973; MA, U. Calif.-Santa Barbara, 1975. Asst. dir. Santa Barbara Underseas Found., 1975-76; marine biologist PJB Labs., Ventura, Calif., 1976-81; lab. dir. CRL Environ., Ventura, 1981-88; lab. dir. ABC Labs, Ventura, 1988—; instr. oceanography Ventura Coll., 1980-81. Chair joint task group, section author 20th edit. Std. Methods Examination Water & Wastewater APHA, 1996. With U.S. Army, 1968-70. Mem. Assn. Environ. Profls., Soc. Population Ecologists, ASTME (rsch. contbr. 10th ann. symposium 1986), Soc. Environ. Toxicology and Chemistry. Biol. coord. Anacapa Underwater Natural trail U.S. Nat. Park Svc., 1976; designer ecol. restoration program of upper Newport Bay, Orange County, Calif., 1978; rsch. contbr. 3d Internat. Artificial Reef Conf., Newport Beach, Calif., 1983, Ann. Conf. Am. Petroleum Inst., Houston. Democrat.

MIKLES, CHRIS, secondary school educator; b. Annapolis, Md., Apr. 23, 1950; d. Robert Edward and Ruth Baier (McBride) Melhorn; m. Scott Allen Mikles, Jan. 5, 1974; children: Andrew Christopher, Allen Scott. AA, Ventura Coll., 1970; BS, Calif. Poly. State Univ., 1972. Cert. tchr., Calif., Idaho, Wash. Tchr. St. Thomas Aquinas Sch., Ojai, Calif., 1972-74, Rio Sch. Dist., El Rio, Calif., 1972-76, Ventura (Calif.) H.S., 1985-95, Univ. Idaho, Coeur d'Alene, 1996-97; co-dir. tchrs. edn. CPM Ednl. Program, Sacramento, 1995—; cons. math. State Calif., Ventura. Bd. dirs. PTA, Am. Youth Soccer Assn., Ventura, 1987-90, soccer coach, 1990-94; chairperson Non-Traditional Career Day, Ventura, 1990-95; coach Ventura Youth Basketball, 1994. Finalist Pres. award NSF, 1994. Mem. AAUW (v.p., Eleanor Roosevelt Tchr. fellow 1994), Nat. Coun. Tchrs. Math., Wash. Math. Coun., Calif. Math. Coun., Idaho Math. Coun., Ventura County Math. Coun. (bd. dirs., Tchr. of Yr. 1993). Republican. Home: 885 Crystal Bay Rd Post Falls ID 83854

MIKO, LESLIE, museum administrator. Mgr., dir. Ctr. for the Arts at Verba Buena Gardens, San Francisco, Calif. Office: Ctr the Arts at Verba Buena Gardens 701 Madison St San Francisco CA 94103*

MIKURIYA, MARY JANE, educational agency administrator; b. Pitts., Oct. 8, 1934; d. Tadafumi and Anna (Schwenk) M.; m. J. Anton Jungherr, June 8, 1977 (div. Dec. 1992); children: Anna Schwenk Mikuriya Jungherr, Anton Jungherr Jr. BA, Brown U., 1956; MA, San Francisco State U., 1970. Cert. tchr. and adminstr., Calif. Tchr. Castilleja Sch. for Girls, Palo Alto, Calif., 1958-60, Mpls. Pub. Schs., 1961-62; tchr. San Francisco Unified Sch. Dist., 1963-68, evaluator, 1968-71, dir. Emergency Sch. Assist. Program, 1971-73; HEW fellow U.S. Dept. of Edn., Washington, 1973-74, edn. program specialist, 1974-76; special asst. to assoc. supt. San Francisco Unified Sch. Dist., 1976-78, grant writer, facilitator, Dept. State & Fed. Projects, 1978—; adv. bd. mem. Far West Lab., San Francisco, 1977-81, Ednl. Testing Svc., Princeton, N.J., 1974-75; cons. U.S. Dept. of Edn., Washington, 1978, 80, 81, 91. Interviewer, bd. dirs. U.S. Servas, 1978—; active Unitarian Ch., 1978—; host Internat. Visitor Ctr., 1985—; mem. coun. Internat. Studies Acad., 1996—. Mem. Japanese-Am. Citizens League. Home: 361 Mississippi St San Francisco CA 94107-2925 Office: San Francisco Unified Sch Dist 20 Cook St San Francisco CA 94118

MILAN, JOHN MAURICE, engineering executive; b. Miami, Ariz.; s. C.M. and Ethel (Jackson) M.; m. Diane Neville, June 28, 1968; children: Andrew, Jeannine. BSEE, U. Ariz., 1967; MSEE, Stanford U., 1968; PhD, UCLA, 1990. Design engr. ITT Gilfillan, Van Nuys, Calif., 1968—, dir. design engr., 1989, v.p. & dir. of engring., 1993. Patentee in field. Mem. IEEE (sr.), Radar Systems Panel. Office: ITT Gilfillan 7821 Orion Ave Van Nuys CA 91406-2027

MILANFAR, PEYMAN, research engineer; b. Tehran, Mar. 1, 1966; came to U.S., 1984; BS, U. Calif., Berkeley, 1988; MS, MIT, 1991, EE, 1992, PhD, 1993. Support engr. Hewlett Packard, Cupertino, Calif., 1988-89; mem. tech. staff Alphatech Inc., Burlington, Mass., 1993-94; rsch. engr. SRI Internat., Menlo Park, Calif., 1994—. Author tech. articles. Pres.'s undergrad fellow U. Calif., Berkeley, 1988; Clement Vaturi fellow MIT, 1992, 93. Mem. IEEE, SIAM, Math. Assn. Am., Sigma Xi. Office: SRI Internat Mailstop 404-69 333 Ravenswood Ave Menlo Park CA 94025-3453

MILANOVICH, NORMA JOANNE, training company executive, occupational educator; b. Littlefork, Minn., June 4, 1945; d. Lyle Albert and Loretta (Leona) Drake; m. Rudolph William Milanovich, Mar. 18, 1943; 1 child, Rudolph William Jr. BS in Home Econs., U. Wis., Stout, 1968; MA in Curriculum and Instrn., U. Houston, 1973, EdD in Curriculum and Program Devel., 1982. Instr. human svcs. dept. U. Houston, 1971-75; dir. videos project U. N.Mex., Albuquerque, 1976-78, dir. vocat. edn. equity ctr., 1978-88, asst. prof. tech. occupational edn., 1982-88, coord. occupational vocat. edn. programs, 1983-88, dir. consortium rsch. and devel. in occupational edn., 1984-88; pres. The Alpha Connecting Tng. Corp., Albuquerque, 1988—; adj. instr. Cen. Tng. Acad., Dept. Energy, Wackenhut; mem. faculty U. Phoenix; mem. adj. faculty So. Ill. U., Lesley Coll., Boston. Author: Model Equitable Behavior in the Classroom, 1983, Handbook for Vocational-Technical Certification in New Mexico, 1985, A Vision for Kansas: Systems of Measures and Standards of Performance, 1992, Workplace Skills: The Employability Factor, 1993; editor: Choosing What's Best for You, 1982, A Handbook for Handling Conflict in the Classroom, 1983, Starting Out. . .A Job Finding Handbook for Teen Parents, Going to Work. . .Job Rights for Teens; author: JTPA Strategic Marketing Plan, 1990, We, The Arcturians, 1990, Sacred Journey to Atlantis, 1991, The Light Shall Set You Free, 1996, JTPA Strategic Mktg. Plan, 1990; editor: Majestic Raise newsletter, 1996, Celestial Voices newsletter, 1991-96. Bd. dirs. Albuquerque Single Parent Occupational Scholarship Program, 1984-86; del. Youth for Understanding Internat. Program, 1985-90; mem. adv. bd. Southwestern Indian Poly. Inst., 1984-88; com. mem. Region VI Consumer Exch. Com., 1982-84; ednl. lectures, tng., tour dir. internat. study tours to Japan, Austria, Korea, India, Nepal, Mex., Eng., Greece, Egypt, Australia, New Zealand, Fed. Republic Germany, Israel, Guatemala, Peru, Bolivia, Chile, Easter Island, Tibet, China, Hong Kong, Turkey, Italy, Russia, Ukraine, Sweden, Norway, Kenya, Tanzania, Zimbabwe, North Pole Arctic Region, Antarctica, Argentina, Ireland, Scotland. Grantee N.Mex. Dept. Edn., 1976-78, 78-86, 83-86, HEW, 1979, 80, 81, 83, 84, 85, 86, 87. Mem. ASTD, Am. Vocat. Assn., Vocat. Edn. Equity Coun., Nat. Coalition for Sex Equity Edn., Am. Home Econs. Assn., Inst. Noetic Scis., N.Mex. Home Econs. Assn., N.Mex. Vocat. Edn. Assn., N.Mex. Adv. Coun. on Vocat. Edn., Greater Albuquerque C. of C., NAFE, Phi Delta Kappa, Phi Upsilon Omicron, Phi Theta Kappa. Democrat. Roman Catholic.

MILANT, JEAN ROBERT, art dealer; b. Milw., Dec. 27, 1943; s. Jacques Jean and Virginia (Zeller) M. BFA, U. Wis., Mils., 1965; cert. master printer, Tamarind Lithography Workshop, L.A., 1969; MA, U. N.Mex., 1970. Tchr. lithograophy U. Calif., Long Beach, 1970; owner, dir. Cirrus Editions Ltd., L.A., 1970—, Cirrus Gallery; lectr., presenter numerous seminars in field, including Art Ctr. Coll. Design, Pasadena, Calif., Otis Art Inst., Alta. Coll. Art, Calgary, Can., San Francisco Mus. Contemporary Art, Santa Barbara (Calif.) Mus. Contemporary Graphics Ctr., others;. Exhibition of Cirrus at L.A. County Mus of Art, 1995-96; author (mus. catalog) Made in L.A.: The Prints of Cirrus Editions. Bd. dirs. Contemporary Art Publs., 1980-83. Mem. Mus. Contemporary Art L.A. (founding), L.A. County Mus. Art, L.A. Inst. Contemporary Art (bd. dirs. 1971-78), New Mus., L.A. Visual Arts (bd. dirs. 1981-85).

MILAVSKY, HAROLD PHILLIP, real estate executive; b. Limerick, Sask., Can., Jan. 25, 1931; s. Jack and Clara M. B in Commerce, U. Sask., Saskatoon, Can., 1953; LLD (hon.), U. Sask., 1995, U. Calgary, 1995. Chief acct., treas., controller Loram Internat. Ltd. div. Mannix Co. Ltd., Calgary, Alta., Can., 1956-65; v.p., chief fin. officer Power Corp. Devels. Ltd., Calgary, Alta., Can., 1965-69; exec. v.p., bd. dirs. Great West Internat. Equities Ltd. (name now Trizec Corp. Ltd.), Calgary, Alta., Can., 1976-94; pres. Trizec Corp. Ltd., Calgary, Alta., Can., 1976-86, bd. dirs., 1976-94, chmn., 1986-93; chmn. Quantico Capital Corp., Calgary, 1994—; bd. dirs. Brascan Ltd., Toronto, Can., Toronto, London Life Ins. Co., London Ins. Group Ltd., London Reins. Group, Wascana Energy Inc., Regina, Nova Corp. Alberta, Calgary, Amoco Can., Calgary, Telus Corp., Edmonton, Encal Energy, Inc., Calgary, Prime West Energy Inc., Calgary. Past dir. Terry Fox Humanitarian Award Program; past dir. Conf. Bd. Can.; past. gov. Acctg. Edn. Found. Alta.; hon. col. 14th Svc. Battalion, Calgary. Recipient Commemorative medal B'nai Brith, 1992. Fellow Inst. Chartered Accts. Alta.; mem. Inst. Chartered Accts. Sask., Can. Inst. Pub. Real Estate Cos. (past pres., bd. dirs.), Can. C. of C. (past chmn.), Internat. Profl. Hockey Alumni (founding dir.), Petroleum Club, Ranchmen's Club. Office: Quantico Capital Corp, 1920-855 Second St SW, Calgary, AB Canada T2P 4J7

MILES, DENNIS GORDON, public affairs executive, consultant; b. Portland, Oreg., Oct. 24, 1944; s. Gordon Dudley and Evelyn Marie (Larkin) M.; m. Hollace Dee Johnson, Sept. 1, 1973 (div. Oct. 1994). BS in Sci. Edn., Oreg. State U., 1967. Educator Oreg. State U., Corvallis, 1971-77; caucus adminstr. Oreg. Legis., Salem, Oreg., 1977; sr. asst., press sec. Gov. Vic Atiyeh, Salem, Oreg., 1979-87; campaign mgr. Atiyeh for Gov., Portland, Oreg., 1982; special asst. Gov. Kay Orr, Lincoln, Nebr., 1987; comm. dir. U.S. Senator David Karnes, Washington, 1987; owner Miles and Assocs., Salem, 1987—. Prodr. (instrnl. film) "Slate it...Slate it Again", 1976; contbr. articles to profl. jours. Mem. state ctrl. com. Oreg. Rep. Party, 1988—; mem. Salem Airport Commn., 1991—, chmn., 1993-96. Recipient Devel. grant Oreg. State U. Found., 1972, Film Prodr. grant Oreg. Edn. Coun., 1975. Mem. Soc. of Profl. Journalists, Acad. of Profl. Cons. and Advisors (cert.), Am. Assn. of Polit. Cons. (election com. 1990-92), Oreg. State U. Alumini Assn. (exec. com., bd. dirs. 1993—). Office: Miles and Assocs 1045 Teviot Pl NW Salem OR 97304-3111

MILES, DON CLIFFORD, architect; b. Ft. Knox, Ky., Sept. 17, 1942; s. Don and Kathrine Eva (Gray) M.; m. Pamela Wait, Aug. 6, 1972; children: Katherine Wait, Lesley Gray, Nicole Conel. BArch with honors, U. Wash., 1966; MArch, M of City Planning in Urban Design, Harvard U., 1971. Registered architect, Wash. Assoc. ptnr. Zimmer, Gunsul, Frasca Partnership, Seattle; cons., lectr. numerous orgns., cities, corps. Prin. projects include Pedestrian Corridor, Major Pub. Open Spaces, CBD Transit Ctr., Bellevue, Wash., Banfield Light Rail Project, Portland, Boise (Idaho) Downtown Major Pub. Open Space, Street Improvements and Transit Malls, Honolulu Rapid Transit Project, Revitalization of State St., Chgo., Midway Corridor Project, Mpls., High Capacity Transit Project, Seattle, Ctrl. Orange County Aerial Fixed Guideway, Mission Valley West Extension Light Rail Project, San Diego, Master Plan for Capitol of State of Wash., Seattle Union Sta. Redevel. Plan, Weyerhauser Corp. Campus, Quadrant Corp. site, Lake Union, Seattle, Whitman Coll. Bd. dirs., founder Project for Pub. Spaces, 1975—; bd. dirs. Seattle Children's Mus., 1978-82; trustee Queen Ann Community Coun., 1978-80. Fellow AIA, Inst. Urban Design. Home: 611 W Comstock St Seattle WA 98119-3422 Office: Zimmer Gunsul Frasca 1191 2nd Ave Ste 800 Seattle WA 98101-2933*

MILES, DONALD F., lawyer; b. Marysville, Calif., Apr. 11, 1949. AB with honors, Stanford U., 1971; JD, U. Calif., San Francisco, 1974. Bar: Calif. 1974, U.S. Dist. Ct. (no. dist.) Calif. 1974, U.S. Dist. Ct. (ea. dist.) Calif. 1977, U.S. Dist. Ct. (so. dist.) Calif. 1986, U.S. Supreme Ct. 1987, U.S. Dist. Ct. (ctrl. dist.) Calif. 1991. Law clk. to Hon. William P. Clark Jr. Supreme Ct. Calif., 1974-75; mem. Howard, Rice, Nemerovski, Canady, Falk & Rabkin, P.C., San Francisco; spl. master U.S. Dist. Ct. (no. dist.) Calif.; instr., adj. faculty mem. Hastings Coll. Law U. Calif.; faculty mem., bd. dirs. Hastings Nat. Coll. Advocacy; mem. adv. com. Calif. Legis. Joint Com. Tort Liability. Author: (with others) Civil Procedure During Trial, vol. II, 1984, 95, California Liability Insurance Practice, 1991, Continuing Education of the Bar Action Guide, 1991; author, narrator: (videotape) Laying a Foundation to Introduce Evidence, 1989; contbr. articles to profl. jours. Mem. ABA (sect. torts and ins. practice), State Bar Calif., Assn. Def. Counsel No. Calif., Bar Assn. of San Francisco, Internat. Assn. Def. Counsel, Def. Rsch. Inst., Thurston Soc., Order of Coif. Office: Howard Rice Nemerovski Canady Falk & Rabkin PC 3 Embarcadero Ctr Ste 7 San Francisco CA 94111-4003

MILES, DONALD GEOFFREY, economist; b. Melbourne, Victoria, Australia, Aug. 26, 1952; s. Harry Raymond and Marian Edith (Lightfoot) M.; m. Judy E. Roberts, Dec. 14, 1991. B. Bus. with distinction, Curtin U. Tech., Muresk, Australia, 1981; MS in Econs., Iowa State U., 1983. Rsch. asst. Iowa State U., Ames, 1980-84; econs. lectr. Curtin U. Tech., Muresk, 1985-87; rsch. economist PRD Consulting Svcs., Pty., Ltd. & Max Christmas Pty. Ltd., Gold Coast, Australia, 1988-89; pres. Miles Internat., Australia and U.S., 1989-96; owner Miles Estate Herb and Berry Farm, Oreg., 1996—; econometric revenue forecaster State of Wash., 1990-96. Inventor environ. wholistic and econ. models, Dept. of Licensing WA/U.S. growth index and transforms, trading day seasonality, copyrights for laws of human ecology, problem shifting analysis, systems econs., wholistic analysis, systems repair, systems improvement, quantifying inefficiency and waste, optimal rates of adjustment, adjustment boxes, events-prices and incomes analysis. Participant World Food Conf., Ames, 1976, Inst. World Affairs, Ames, 1981. Recipient Edwards Prize, Curtin U. Tech., 1987. Mem. World Future Soc. (life). Home and Office: 4308 Marthaler Rd NE Woodburn OR 97071-9543

MILES, RICHARD ROBERT, art historian, writer; b. Tokyo, Apr. 1, 1939; s. Robert Henri and Eleanor Alfrida (Child) Perreau-Saussine. BA, UCLA, 1972. Novelist, screenwriter various, 1965-72; dir. Meilinki Enterprises Ltd., 1980—; pres. Burbank (Calif.) Tchrs. Assn., 1984-85; bd. dirs. Balcom Trading Co., Tokyo, 1979-82. Author: That Cold Day in the Park, 1965 (Dell Book award 1965), Angel Loves Nobody, 1967 (Samuel Goldwyn award UCLA, 1969); (art history) Prints of Paul Jacoulet, 1982, Elizabeth Keith-The Prints, 1989, The Watercolors of Paul Jacoulet, 1992, others. Mem. Internat. Soc. of Fine Art Appraisers, New Eng. Appraisers Assn., Writers Guild of Am. West, Acad. of Am. Poets. Office: Meilinki Enterprises Ltd 214 N Bowling Green Way Los Angeles CA 90049-2816

MILES, SAMUEL ISRAEL, psychiatrist, educator; b. Munich, Mar. 4, 1949; came to U.S., 1949; s. Henry and Renee (Ringel) M.; m. Denise Marie Robey, June 26, 1977; children: Jonathan David, Justin Alexander. BS, CCNY, 1970; MD, N.Y. Med. Coll., 1974; PhD, So. Calif. Psychoanalytic Inst., 1986. Diplomate Am. Bd. Psychiatry and Neurology with added qualifications in forensic psychiatry. Intern D.C. Gen. Hosp., Washington, 1974-75; resident in psychiatry Cedars-Sinai Med. Ctr., Los Angeles, 1975-78; practice medicine specializing in psychiatry Los Angeles, 1978—; ind. med. examiner Calif. Dept. Indsl. Relations, 1984-91, qualified med. examiner, 1991—; asst. clin. prof. psychiatry UCLA Sch. Medicine, 1978—; attending psychiatrist Cedars-Sinai Med. Ctr., 1978—; attending psychiatrist Brotman Med. Ctr., Culver City, Calif., 1978—; mem. faculty So. Calif. Psychoanalytic Inst., 1986—; mem. psychiat. panel Superior Ct. Los Angeles County, 1990—, Fed. Ct., 1990—. Fellow Am. Acad. Psychoanalysis, Am. Orthopsychiat. Assn.; mem. Acad. Psychiatry and the Law, Am. Coll. Legal Medicine, Calif. Psychiat. Assn. (mem. managed care com. 1991-96), So. Calif. Psychiat. Soc. (coun. rep. 1985-88, 92-95, chairperson pvt. practice com. 1988-92, sec. 1991-92, mem. worker's compensation com. 1992—, trea.-elect 1996, treas. 1997), So. Calif. Psychoanalytic Inst. (pres. clin. assocs. orgn. 1981-82, mem. admissions com. 1988-96, mem. ethics stds. com. 1991-92, chairperson ethics stds. com. 1993—, mem. exec. com. 1993—). Jewish. Office: 8631 W 3rd St Ste 425E Los Angeles CA 90048-5908

MILGRIM, DARROW A., insurance broker, recreation consultant; b. Chgo., Apr. 30, 1945; s. David and Miriam (Glickman) M.; m. Laurie Stevens, Apr. 15, 1984; children: Derick, Jared, Kayla. BA, Calif. State U., San Bernardino, 1968; postgrad., U. So. Calif., 1972. Accredited ins. adv.; cert. ins. counselor; cert. sch. adminstr. Tchr. Rialto (Calif.) Unified Sch. Dist., 1969-70, Las Virgenes Unified Sch. Dist., Westlake Village, Calif., 1970-78; instr. Calif. State U., Northridge, Calif., 1980-84; ins. broker, v.p. Speare Ins. Brokers, Blade Ins. Svcs., Brentwood, Calif., 1984—; dir. Calamigos Star C Ranch Summer Camp, Malibu, Calif., Calamigos Environ. Edn. Ctr., Malibu. Editor: Legislation and Regulations for Organized Camps, 1987. Pres. Calif. Camping Adv. Coun., Long Beach, 1985-87; bd. dirs. Calif. Collaboration for Youth, Sacramento, 1985—, Camp Ronald McDonald for Good Times, 1989-95; commr. dept. parks and recreation City of Agoura Hills, Calif., 1987-93; cons. So. Calif. Children's Cancer Svcs.,

L.A., 1986—. Mem. Am. Camping Assn. (bd. dirs. So. Calif. sect., chmn. nat. legis. com. Martinsville, Ind., 1980-97, nat. bd. dirs. 1990-95, legis. liaison, regional honor 1986). Office: Speare and Co Ins Brokers PO Box 250024 Los Angeles CA 90025-9524

MILHEIM, STEPHEN GEORGE, surgeon; b. Phila., Mar. 24, 1961; s. Irvine George and Mary Eleanor (McConnell) M.; m. Sonya Lynn Harder; children: George Harder, Anna Marie. BA, Amherst Coll., 1983; MD, Harvard Med. Sch., 1987. Diplomate Am. Bd. Surgery. Intern, resident U. Colo. Affiliated Hosps., 1987-92; gen. surgeon Kalispell (Mont.) Regional Hosp., 1992—; chmn. Dept. of Surgery Kalispell Regional Hosp., 1996; treas. N.W. Mont. Surg. Assocs. P.C., Kalispell, 1994—. Fellow ACS. Office: NW Mont Surg Assocs PC 1273 Burns Way Kalispell MT 59901

MILHOLLAND, DAVID MARION, writer, editor; b. Greeley, Colo., Oct. 19, 1946; s. Delbert Martin and Alice Olene (Luvaas) M.; m. Theresa Marquez; children: Zachary O., Lola Maria Marquez. BA, Lewis and Clark Coll. With Peace Corps-Guatemala, Aguacatan, 1968-70; rsch. coord. Yaden & Assocs., Portland, Oreg., 1971-75; filmmaker David Milholland & Assocs., Portland, Oreg., 1971-85; mgr., co-owner Clinton St. Theatre, Portland, Oreg., 1979-85; editor, art dir. Clinton St. Quar., Portland, Seattle, 1979-91; prodn. mgr. Nature's Fresh N.W.!, Portland, 1991-93; ptnr. Crackerjack Mktg./Pacific Green, Portland, 1993—. Filmmaker including feature documentaries Blackjack's Family, 1974 (Best of N.W. Film Video festival 1974), The Thorne Family Film, 1977 (N.Y. Film Festival award 1977); editor Clinton St. Quar., 1979-91. Bd. dirs. Media Project, Portland, 1972-77; pres. Local Sch. Adv. Group, Jefferson H.S., Portland, 1988-92, Oreg. Cultural Heritage Commn., 1988-94. Recipient First Pl. in Editorial Writing, Sigma Delta Chi Soc. Profl. Journalists (N.W. chpt.), 1986. Mem. PEN Internat. Office: PO Box 3588 Portland OR 97208-3588

MILLAR, MICHAEL WILLIAM, trombonist; b. N.Y.C., June 22, 1953; s. W. Llewellyn and Janet Josephine (Dean) M.; m. Lisa Rochelle Branch, July 30, 1983 (dec. Aug. 1987); m. Dava Grace Smart, June 25, 1989; children: Emily Ellyn, Matthew Ian. MusB in Performance, U. Colo., Boulder, 1976; MA in Performance Music, Calif. State U., L.A., 1980; studied with, George Roberts, Jeffrey Reynolds, Roy Main, Charlie Shoemake; postgrad., Claremont Grad. U., 1996—. Trombonist Harry James Orch., 1980-85, Les Hooper Grand Band, 1983—; mem. faculty U. Colo., Denver, 1987; has appeared with various brass quintets, brass choirs, trombone choirs, trombone jazz bands, big bands, symphony orchs. and other mus. groups; performed in TV and radio jingles for Sta. KCBS-TV Action News, Budweiser, Toyota, Anheuser Busch, Mountain Dew, IBM, TWA, Gt. Western Bank, Texaco, Am. Express, Home Shopping Network, Honda, Delta Airlines, Qantas, Word Perfect, New Eng. Tel., Sunny Delight, Disney World, AT&T, numerous others. Albums include Blast Off, 1981, Anything Goes, 1989, Singin' With the Big Bands, 1994; appeared in films Hot to Trot, Sing, For the Boys, The Doors, on TV in Hull High, Jerry Lewis MDA Telethon Orch., 1995-96; performed with Steve Allen, Ray Anthony, Tex. Beneke Orch., George Burns, Ray Charles Orch., Warren Covington and Pied Pipers, Rosemary Clooney, Ray Conniff, Colo. Music Festival Orch., Merv Griffin, Jerry Lewis, Shari Lewis, Rich Little, Gordon MacRae, Mills Bros., Liza Minnelli, Helen O'Connell, Patti Page, Debbie Reynolds, Kenny Rogers, The Smothers Brothers, numerous others. Mem. NARAS, Rec. Musicians Assn., Am. Fedn. Musicians. Home: 25430 Via Impreso Valencia CA 91355-2709

MILLAR, ROBERT, artist; b. L.A., Mar. 6, 1958; s. Thomas A. and Josephine E. (Alford) M. BA, Calif. State U., Northridge, 1980. Exhibited work at L.A. Metro Rail Sta., 1990 (progressive Arch. citation 1992), Newport Harbor Art Mus., 1991, Rose Theatre Site, London, 1992, S.D. Alvarado Filtration Plant, 1993. Arts commr. City of Manhattan Beach, Calif., 1985-94, mem. pub. art adv. com. Calif. Arts Coun., 1992. Grantee Pollock-Krasner Found., 1989. Studio: PO Box 515 Manhattan Beach CA 90267-0515

MILLARD, DEREK, industrial organizational development consultant; b. Cortez, Colo., Feb. 6, 1954; s. Arthur Randall and Mildred Mae Millard; m. Janet Marie Klun Lanigan, Feb. 14, 1972 (div. July 1977). Student, U. So. Colo., 1969-70, Lawrence U., Appleton, Wis., 1971-72; degree, U. Wis., Oshkosh, 1976; MS in Human Resource Devel., Am. U., Washington, 1982. Mgr. Culbreath Schs., Colorado Springs, Colo., 1970-71; indsl. engr. Thilmany Pulp and Paper divsn. Hammermill Papers, Kaukauna, Wis., 1971-75; v.p. ops. Rosenow XYZ Corp., Appleton, 1975-76; founder, owner Remarket Industries, Appleton, 1976-79; prin., owner Facilitating Change, Houston, 1979-89, Derek Millard Assocs., San Francisco, 1990—; orgnl. devel. cons. Levi Strauss & Co., San Francisco, 1990-95; cons. Honeywell Corp., Houston, 1988-90, Human Affairs Internat. divsn. Aetna, Houston, 1989-90; cons. and assoc. Designed Learning, Plainfield, N.J., 1993—. Mem. chem. abuse adv. com. Houston-Galveston Area Coun., 1980-84; state co-founder, state chmn. Libertarian Party, Appleton, Wis., 1971-75. Mem. Orgnl. Devel. Network, Am. U./NTL Assn. Libertarian. Home and Office: 308 Shields St San Francisco CA 94132-2734

MILLARD, ESTHER LOUND, foundation administrator, educator; b. Metaline, Wash., June 10, 1909; d. Peter S. and Emily Christine (Dahlgren) Lound; m. Homer Behne Millard, Apr. 25, 1951 (dec. May 1962). BA, U. Wis., 1933, MA, 1935. Cert. tchr., Oreg., Wis. Instr. U. Hawaii, Honolulu, 1938-43; joined USN, 1943, advanced through ranks to lt. commdr., resigned, 1952; dir. Millard Sch., Bandon, Oreg., 1954-81; pres. Millard Found., Bandon, 1984—. Trustee Falcon Found., Colorado Springs, Colo., 1986—; established scholarship fund for med. sch. students, U. Wis. Mem. Bascom Hill Soc. (U. Wis.), Phi Beta Kappa. Republican. Home: 52 Tom Smith Rd Bandon OR 97411-9311

MILLARD, MALCOLM STUART, retired lawyer; b. Highland Park, Ill., Mar. 22, 1914; s. Everett L. and Elizabeth (Boynton) M.; m. Joanne T. Blakeman; 1 child, Anne W. Benjamin. BA, Harvard U., 1936; JD, Northwestern U., 1939. Bar: Ill. 1939, Calif. 1951. Ptnr. Farr & Millard, Carmel, Calif., 1951-55, Millard, Tourangeau, Morris & Staples, P.C., Carmel, 1955-91; ptnr. Millard, Morris & Staples, Carmel, 1991-94, ret., 1994; dir. Leslie Salt Co., 1975-81. Trustee Community Hosp. of Monterey Peninsula, 1982-88, Monterey Inst. Fgn. Studies, 1955-76, Community Found. Monterey County, 1988—; pres. Community Chest of Monterey Peninsula, 1958. Served to lt. USN, 1943-46. Mem. Monterey Inst. Internat. Relations (hon. lifetime trustee 1982—, hon. DHL 1991), Ill. State Bar, Calif. State Bar, Monterey County Bar Assn. (pres.), Old Capital Club, Harvard Club.

MILLARD, NEAL STEVEN, lawyer; b. Dallas, June 6, 1947; s. Bernard and Adele (Marks) M.; m. Janet Keast, Mar. 12, 1994; 1 child, Kendall Layne. BA cum laude, UCLA, 1969; JD, U. Chgo., 1972. Bar: Calif. 1972, U.S. Dist. Ct. (cen. dist.) 1973, U.S. Tax Ct. 1973, U.S. Ct. Appeals (9th cir.) 1987, N.Y. 1990. Assoc. Willis, Butler & Schiefly, Los Angeles, 1972-75; ptnr. Morrison & Foerster, Los Angeles, 1975-84, Jones, Day, Reavis & Pogue, Los Angeles, 1984-93, White & Case, L.A., 1993—; instr. Calif. State Coll., San Bernardino, 1975-76; lectr. Practising Law Inst., N.Y.C., 1983-90, Calif. Edn. of Bar, 1987-90; adj. prof. USC Law Ctr., 1994—. Citizens adv. com. L.A. Olympics, 1982-84; trustee Altadena (Calif.) Libr. Dist., 1985-86; bd. dirs. Woodcraft Rangers, L.A., 1982-90, pres., 1986-88; bd. dirs. L.A. County Bar Found., 1990—; mem. Energy Commn. of County and Cities of L.A., 1995—; bd. dirs. Inner City Law Ctr., 1996—. Mem. ABA, Calif. Bar Assn., N.Y. State Bar Assn., L.A. County Bar Assn. (trustee 1985-87), Pub. Counsel (bd. dirs. 1984-87, 90-93), U. Chgo. Law Alumni Assn. (bd. dirs. So. Calif. chpt. 1981—), Calif. Club, Phi Beta Kappa, Pi Gamma Mu, Phi Delta Phi. Office: White and Case 633 W 5th St Ste 1900 Los Angeles CA 90071-2017

MILLENDER-MCDONALD, JUANITA, congresswoman, former school system administrator; b. Birmingham, Ala., Sept. 7, 1938; d. Shelly and Everlina (Dortch) M.; m. James McDonald III, July 26, 1955; children: Valeria, Angela, Sherryll, Michael, Roderick. BS, U. Redlands, Calif., 1980; MS in Edn., Calif. State U., L.A., 1986; postgrad., U. So. Calif. Manuscript editor Calif. State Dept. Edn., Sacramento; dir. gender equity programs L.A. Unified Sch. Dist.; mem. 104th Congress from 37th Calif. dist. U.S. Ho. of Reps., Washington, 1996—. City councilwoman, Carson; bd. dirs. S.C.L.C. Pvt. Industry Coun. Policy Bd., West Basin Mcpl. Water Dist., Cities Legis. League (vice chmn.; mem. Nat. Women's Polit. Caucus; mem. adv. bd. Comparative Ethnic Tng. U. So. Calif.; founder, exec. dir. Young Advocates So. Calif. Mem. NEA, Nat. Assn. Minority Polit. Women, NAFE, Nat. Fedn. Bus. and Profl. Women, Assn. Calif. Sch. Adminstrs., Am. Mgmt. Assn., Nat. Coun. Jewish Women, Carson C. of C., Phi Delta Kappa. Office: US House of Reps 419 Cannon Washington DC 20515

MILLER, ANNE KATHLEEN, training company executive, technical marketing consultant; b. Denver, Sept. 15, 1942; d. John Henry and Kathryn Elizabeth (Doherty) Meyer; m. Edgar Earle Miller, Aug. 20, 1966 (div. Aug. 1976); children: Sheila Anne, Rebecca Elizabeth; m. Warren Ross Landry, Dec. 11, 1982 (dec. Oct. 1990). BS in Chemistry, St. Mary Coll., Leavenworth, Kans., 1964. Cert. jr. coll., secondary tchr., Calif. Lectr. San Jose (Calif.) State U., 1978-82; product mgr. Jasco Chem., Mountain View, Calif., 1979-82; v.p., gen. mgr. Micropel, Hayward, Calif., 1982-84; product mgr. Cambridge Instruments, Santa Clara, Calif., 1984-86; product mgr. KLA Instruments, Santa Clara, 1986-87; pres., owner Meyland Enterprises, Redwood City, Calif., 1987—, Semiconductor Svc. Tng. Orgn., Redwood City, Calif., 1988—. Inventor formation of optical film. Mem. Soc. Photo Optical Instrumentation Engrs., Am. Chem. Soc., Semiconductor Industry Equipment Materials Internat., Am. Electronics Assn. Office: Meyland/Semiconductor Svcs 735 Hillcrest Way Redwood City CA 94062-3428

MILLER, BARBARA DARLENE, art educator; b. Jarbidge, Nev.; d. Herbert Beard and Gerra Vanetten (Carncross) Beard; 2 children. BA, U. Wash., 1955; MEd, U. Hawaii, 1974. Cert. secondary tchr. Occupational therapist N.D. State Hosp. for Mental Illness, Jamestown, 1954-55; art tchr. Dept. Edn. Hilo (Hawaii) High Sch., 1957-58; art specialist Elem. Intermediate Sch., Kahului, Hawaii, 1964-65; instr. art Maui C.C., Kahului, 1965-96; art dir. Sta. KHVH-TV, Honolulu, 1962-63; ret., 1996. One-woman shows include County Bldg., 1985, 87-90, MCC Libr., 1987, 90; exhibited in group shows at Am. Fac Pla., 1980, 91, Hawaii State Libr., 1980, Honolulu Acad. Arts; commd. numerous portraits. Visual Arts chairperson Maui Community Arts Coun., 1972-80; bd. dirs., past pres. Hui Noeau Art Soc., 1966-90; v.p. Maui Weavers Guild, 1976; planning com., bd. dirs. Art Maui '80-'84, 1979-84; bd. dirs. Maui Symphony Orch., 1984-87; mayor's adv. coun. for culture and the arts Archtl. Art Com., 1986-87; Maui rep. on budget com. Hawaii State Found. on Culture and the Arts, 1991. Recipient Certificate of Appreciation for Beautification of Maui County Council of Maui. Mem. NEA, AAUP, Maui Aikido Ki Soc.

MILLER, BARBARA STALLCUP, development consultant; b. Montague, Calif., Sept. 4, 1919; d. Joseph Nathaniel and Maybelle (Needham) Stallcup; m. Leland F. Miller, May 16, 1946; children: Paula Kay, Susan Lee, Daniel Joseph, Alison Jean. B.A., U. Oreg., 1942. Women's editor Eugene (Oreg.) Daily News, 1941-43; law clk. to J. Everett Barr, Yreka, Calif., 1943-45; mgr. Yreka C. of C., 1945-46; Northwest supr. Louis Harris and Assocs., Portland, Oreg., 1959-62; dir. pub. relations and fund raising Columbia River council Girl Scouts U.S.A., 1962-67; pvt. practice pub. relations cons., Portland, 1967-72; adviser of student publs., asst. prof. communications U. Portland, 1967-72, dir. pub. relations and info., asst. prof. communications, 1972-78, dir. devel., 1978-79, exec. dir. devel., 1979-83; assoc. dir. St. Vincent Med. Found., 1983-88; dir. planned giving Good Samaritan Found., 1988-95; planned giving cons., 1995—. Pres. bd. dirs. Vols. of Am. of Oreg., Inc., 1980-84, pres. regional adv. bd., 1982-84; chmn. bd. dirs. S.E. Mental Health Network, 1984-88; nat. bd. dirs. Vols. of Am., Inc., 1984-96; pres., bd. dirs. Vol. Bur. Greater Portland, 1991-93; mem. U. Oreg. Journalism Advancement Coun., 1991—; named Oasis Sr. Role Model, 1992. Recipient Presdl. Citation, Oreg. Communicators Assn., 1973, Matrix award, 1976, 80, Miltner award U. Portland, 1977, Communicator of Achievement award Oreg. Press Women, 1992, Willamette Valley Devel. Officers award, 1992 (Barbara Stallcup Miller Profl. Achievement award, 1992), Mem. Nat. Soc. Fundraising Execs., Nat. Planned Giving Coun, Women in Comm. (NW regional v.p. 1973-75, Offbeat award 1988), Nat. Fedn. Press Women, Oreg. Press Women (dist. dir.), Pub. Rels. Soc. Am. (dir. local chpt., Marsh award 1989), Oreg. Fedn. Womens Clubs (communications chmn. 1978-80), Alpha Xi Delta (found. trustee, editor 1988-95). Unitarian. Clubs: Portland Zenith (pres. 1975-76, 81-82). Contbr. articles to profl. jours. Home and Office: 1706 Boca Ratan Dr Lake Oswego OR 97034-1624

MILLER, BRIAN ALAN, television production executive; b. Bklyn., Apr. 6, 1961; s. William Jack and Jeanne (Semaria) M.; m. Joanne Marie Lento, June 19, 1982; children: Justin Adam, Brandon Scott, Jeremy Eugene. BA, Calif. State U., Northridge, 1982. Segment prodr. Alan Landsburg Prodns., L.A., 1981-83, Playboy Prodns., L.A., 1984-85; assoc. prodr. DIC Entertainment, Encino, Calif., 1986-89; prodn. supr. DIC Entertainment, Burbank, Calif., 1989-91, v.p. prodn., 1991-95; v.p. Hanna Barbera Prodns., Hollywood, Calif., 1995—. Office: Hanna Barbera Prodns 3400 Cahuenga Blvd Hollywood CA 90068-4301

MILLER, CARL VOSBURGH, artist; b. Waterbury, Conn., Feb. 13, 1932; s. Carl Vosburgh Miller; m. Catherine L. Webb, Aug 22, 1956; children: Craig, Cari. Student, Grand Canyon Coll., Ariz. State Coll. Cert. tchr., Calif. Exhibited watercolor paintings in numerous shows including Adirondacks, N.Y., 1992, West Conn. Watercolor Soc., 1992, Western Colo. Watercolor Soc., 1991, 94, Nat. Watercolor Soc., 1991, Watercolor West, 1986, 87, 88, 90, San Diego Internat., 1988, 90, Rocky Mountain Nat., 1990, many others; contbd. paintings to various books including Painting With the White of Your Paper, 1994, Creative Watercolor, 1995, The Best of Watercolor, 1995. Recipient Pauline Mintz award Audubon Artists, 1989, Gold medal award, 1990, Merit award West Conn. Watercolor Soc., 1992, Mary S. Litt medal Am. Watercolor Soc., 1993, Award of Achievement and Contbns. to Arts Stockton Arts Commn., 1994, award of honor Niagara Frontier Nat. Exhbn., 1996; works included in Creative Watercolor (Mary Ann Beckwith), The Best of Watercolor (Betty Lou Schlemm and Tom Nicholas), Painting with the White of Your Paper (Judi Wagner and Tony Van Hasselt). Mem. Watercolor West, Midwest Watercolor Soc., Am. Watercolor Soc. Home: 334 Paragon Ave Stockton CA 95210-1315

MILLER, CAROLE ANN LYONS, editor, publisher, marketing specialist; b. Newton, Mass., Aug. 1; d. Markham Harold and Ursula Patricia (Foley) Lyons; m. David Thomas Miller, July 4, 1978. BA, Boston U., 1964; bus. cert., Hickox Sch., Boston, 1964; cert. advt. and mktg. profl. UCLA, 1973; cert. retail mgmt. profl. Ind. U., 1976. Editor Triangle Topics, Pacific Telephone, L.A.; programmer L.A. Cen. Area Speakers' Bur., 1964-66; mng. editor/mktg. dir. Teen mag., L.A. and N.Y.C., 1966-76; advt. dir. L.S. Ayres & Co., Indpls., 1976-78; v.p. mktg. The Denver, 1978-79; founder, editor, pub. Clockwise mag., Ventura, Calif., 1979-85; mktg. mgr., mgr. pub. rels. and spl. events Robinson's Dept. Stores, L.A., 1985-87, exec. v.p., dir. mktg. Harrison Svcs., 1987-93; pres. divsn. Miller & Miller Carole Ann Lyons Mktg., Camino, Calif., 1993—; instr. retail advt. Ind. U., 1977-78. Recipient Pres.'s award Advt. Women of N.Y., 1974; Seklemian award 1977; Pub. Svc. Addy award, 1978. Mem. Retail Advt. & Mktg. Assn., Advt. Women N.Y., Calif. Videographers Assn., Retail Advt. & Mktg. Assn., Fashion Group Internat., Bay Area Integrated Mktg., San Francisco Fashion Group, San Francisco Direct Mktg. Assn. UCLA Alumni Assn., Internat. TV Videographer's Assn. (Sacramento chpt.). Editor: Sek Says, 1979. Home: 3709 Carson Rd Camino CA 95709-9593

MILLER, CHARLES DALY, self-adhesive materials company executive; b. Hartford, Conn., 1928; married. Grad., Johns Hopkins U. Sales and mktg. mgr. Yale & Towne Mfg. Co., 1949-59; assoc. Booz, Allen & Hamilton, 1959-64; with Avery Internat. Corp., Pasadena, Calif., 1964—; v.p., mng. dir. Materials Europe, 1965-68; v.p. Fasson Internat. Ops., 1968; group v.p. materials group Avery Internat. Corp., Pasadena, 1969-75, pres., bd. dirs., COO, 1975-77, pres., CEO, 1977-83; chmn., CEO Avery Dennison Corp. (formerly Avery Internat. Corp.), Pasadena, 1983—. Office: Avery Dennison Corp PO Box 7090 Pasadena CA 91109-7090

MILLER, CHARLES MAURICE, lawyer; b. L.A., Sept. 7, 1948; s. Samuel C. and Sylvia Mary Jane (Silver) M.; m. Terri Lee Senesac, Mar. 25, 1979; children: Samuel Mark, Seth Michael. BA cum laude, UCLA, 1970; postgrad., U. So. Calif., L.A., 1970-71; JD, U. Akron, 1975. Bar: Ohio 1975, Calif. 1978, U.S. Dist. Ct. (cen. dist.) Calif. 1978, U.S. Ct. Appeals (9th cir.) 1978, U.S. Supreme Ct. 1981. Gen. atty. U.S. Immigration & Naturalization Svc., U.S. Dept. Justice, L.A., 1976-79; ptnr. Miller Law Offices, L.A., 1979—; adj. prof. law U. West L.A., 1989-90. Co-editor: The Visa Processing Guide: Process and Procedures at U.S. Consulates and Embassies, 4d edit., 1996; articles editor U. Akron Law Rev., 1974-75. Mem. Calif. Bd. Legal Specialization, San Francisco, 1988-89. Mem. Bar of Calif. (chmn. immigration splty. 1988-89, commr. immigration splty. 1987-90), Am. Immigration Law Found. (bd. trustees 1995—), Am. Immigration Lawyers Assn. (chair So. Calif. chpt. 1993-94, co-chair membership 1989-90, co-chair mentor program 1990-91, co-chair visa office liaison 1991-92, vice chair 1994-95, co-chair consular rev. task force 1993-95, Jack Wasserman Meml. award for excellence in immigration litigation 1995). Office: Miller Law Offices 12441 Ventura Blvd Studio City CA 91604-2407

MILLER, CHARLES WALLACE, historian, environmental geologist; b. Phoenix, July 7, 1946; s. Charles W. and Emabel O. Miller; m. Connie Raschke, June 3, 1972; 1 child, Geoffrey Wallace. BA, U. Md., 1969; MA, U. Tex., 1970; BS, SUNY, Albany, 1978; PhD, Union Inst., 1990. Instr. San Antonio Coll., 1972-78, St. Mary's Univ., San Antonio, 1976-78, Cochise Coll., Sierra Vista, Az., 1989-90; environ. geologist U.S. Geol. Survey, Metairie, La., 1978-80; field geologist U.S. Bur. Land Mgmt.; historian U.S. Bur. Reclamation, Salt Lake City, 1990-94; environ. scientist USAF, Tucson, 1994—; mineral cons., Tucson, 1984-89. Author: Stake Your Claim! The Tale of America's Enduring Mining Law, 1991, The Automobile Gold Rushes, 1996. Vol. Christ Comty. Ch., Tucson, 1995, also various youth orgns., 1984-90. Mem. Mining History Assn., Mensa, Phi Alpha Theta, Pi Sigma Alpha. Home: 9501 E Walnut Tree Tucson AZ 85749 Office: USAF 355 CES/CEVA Davis-Monthan AFB AZ 85707

MILLER, CLARA BURR, education educator; b. Higganum, Conn., July 19, 1912; d. Eugene Orlando and Mabel (Clark) Burr; m. James Golden Miller, Sept. 19, 1942; children: Clara Elizabeth, Eugenia Manelle. BA, Mt. Holyoke Coll., 1933; MA, Columbia U., 1942. Cert. tchr., Conn., N.Y., Pa., Ariz. Tchr. Suffield (Conn.) Jr. High Sch., 1934-36, Rockville (Conn.) High Sch., 1936-41, Buckeley High Sch., Hartford, Conn., 1941-42, Pitts. Schs., 1952-55, Winchester-Thurston Sch., Pitts., 1955-58, Vail-Deane Sch., Elizabeth, N.J., 1959-69, Kingman (Ariz.) High Sch., 1971-76; mem. res. faculty Mohave C.C., Kingman, 1978-94; pres. bd. edn., clk. Mohave Union H.S. Dist. 30, 1983-91, bd. dirs., 1983-94; bd. dirs. Mohave Mental Health Clinic, v.p. bd. dirs., 1988, pres. bd. dirs., 1989-90. Author: Trails, Rails and Tales, 1981, (with others) Short Stories, 1984. Bd. dirs. No. Ariz. Comprehensive Guidance Ctr., Flagstaff, 1985-90, Kingman Aid to Abused People; sec. Good Samaritan Assn., Inc., Kingman, 1979-95; pres. Ch. Women United, 1972-74, Presbyn. Women, 1987; elected elder session Kingman Presbyn. Ch., 1983-95; mem. Mojave County Cmty. Action Bd., Western Ariz. Coun. Govts.; coord. League Friendship Indians and Other Americans, 1981-95; co-chmn. Women Making History Com., 1981-95; elected head, Montview Manor social activities, 1996—; elected deacon, Montview Blvd. Presbyn. Ch., 1997—. Recipient Nat. Community Svc. award Mohave County Ret. Tchrs. Assn., 1987, Leta Glancy/Cecil Lockhart-Smith award No. Ariz. Comprehensive Guidance Ctr., 1990; named one of Women Making History Kingman Multi-Club Com., 1985. Mem. NEA, AAUW (pres. 1979-81), Ariz. Edn. Assn., Ariz. Sch. Bds. Assn., Soc. Profl. Journalists, Mohave County Ret. Tchrs. Assn. (v.p. 1991-93, pres. 1993-95), Footprinters. Democrat. Home: Montview Manor Apt 1201 1663 Steele St Denver CO 80206

MILLER, CLIFFORD JOEL, lawyer; b. L.A., Oct. 31, 1947; s. Eugene and Marian (Millman) M.; m. Coco Ando, Apr. 9, 1990. BA, U. Calif., Irvine, 1969; JD, Pepperdine U., 1973. Bar: Calif. 1974, Hawaii 1974, U.S. Dist. Ct. Hawaii 1974. Ptnr. Rice, Lee & Wong, Honolulu, 1974-80, Goodsill Anderson Quinn & Stifel, Honolulu, 1980-89, McCorriston, Miho, Miller & Mukai, Honolulu, 1989—. Mem. ABA, Calif. Bar Assn., Hawaii Bar Assn., Am. Coll. Real Estate Lawyers. Office: McCorriston Miho Miller & Mukai 5 Waterfront Pla 500 Ala Moana Blvd Honolulu HI 96813-4920

MILLER, DANIEL JAMES, systems engineer; b. San Jose, Nov. 6, 1950; s. J.R. and Fay (Boley) M.; m. Laurinda Marie Latino, Dec. 11, 1971; 1 child, Julie Ann. AA, West Valley Coll., Saratoga, Calif., 1971. Frame technician Pacific Bell, San Jose, 1968-72, comm. technician, 1972-95; tech. instr. Pacific Bell, 1995; sys. maintenance engr. Stanford (Calif.) U., 1995—. Author: The Prophet's Candle, 1996. Recipient Positive Place award Internet Positive Living Net, 1996, Path of the Spirit-Award of Excellence, Light of the Spirit WWW, 1997, Webcraft award Collection of Thoughts-WWW, 1997. Office: Stanford University Forsythe Hall Rm 180 Stanford CA 94305-4140

MILLER, DAVID CRAIG, cardiovascular surgeon; b. San Francisco, Dec. 3, 1946; s. Charles Miller; m. Elsann Laws. Student, Dartmouth Coll., 1965-68; BA in Basic Med. Scis., Stanford U., 1969, MD, 1972. Diplomate Am. Bd. Surgery, Am. Bd. Thoracic Surgery, Am. Bd. Gen. Vascular Surgery. Resident in gen. surgery Stanford U. Med. Ctr. and Affiliated Hosps., 1972-75; chief resident in peripheral vascular surgery Stanford U. Med. Ctr., 1975-76, chief resident in cardiovasc. surgery, 1976-77, chief resident in thoracic surgery, 1977, program dir. peripheral vascular surgery residency, 1985-93; chief cardiac surgery section Palo Alto VA Med. Ctr., 1978-86; clin. asst. prof. cardiovasc. surgery sch. medicine Stanford U., 1978, asst. prof., 1978-83, assoc. prof., 1983-89, prof., 1989—; dir. Cardiovasc. Surg. Physiology Rsch. Labs.; staff surgeon cardiac surgery sect. Palo Alto DVA Med. Ctr., 1978-96; mem. various coms. Stanford U.; mem. dean's com. Palo Alto VA Med. Ctr., 1980-88; co-chmn. external rev. com. on cardiac surgery U. Calif. Davis Med. Ctr., 1981-83; mem. strategic planning and mktg. com. and exec. steering subcom. Faculty Practice Plan, 1987-92, bd. dirs., 1989-90, mem. fin. exec. com., 1992-93; mem. VA Rsch. Merit Rev. Bd. Surgery, 1988-91, chmn., 1990-91; mem. surgery, anesthesia and trauma study sect. NIH, 1992-96; presenter in field. Mem. editl. bd. Jour. Cardiac Surgery, 1985—, Jour. Surg. Rsch., 1990-94, Circulation 1991-93, Jour. Heart Valve Disease, 1992—, others; ad hoc referee Circulation, Jour. Clin. Investigation, Jour. Thoracic and Cardiovasc. Surgery, others; contbr. articles to profl. jours. Lt. comdr. M.C., USNR. Grantee Searle Family Found., 1979-82, Upjohn Pharms. Co., 1982-85, NIH, 1983—. Mem. AAAS, ACS (mem. cardiovasc. surgery com. 1986-88, mem. exec. com. 1987-88), AMA, Am. Surg. Assn., Am. Assn. Thoracic Surgery, Am. Coll. Cardiology (mem. sci. abstract rev. com. 1986, 90, mem. peripheral vascular disease com. 1994—), Am. Coll. Chest Physicians, Am. Fedn. Clin. Rsch., Am. Heart Assn. (bd. dirs. Santa Clara County chpt. 1980-82, mem. rsch. com. 1981-83, mem. exec. com. coun. cardiovasc. surgery 1985—, mem. program com. 1988-92, chmn. 1989-92, mem. optimal resources for vascular surgery com. 1985-89, co-chmn. com. sci. sessions program 1992-93, chair coun. cardiovasc. surgery 1995—, grantee Calif. affiliate 1980-82, grantee 1981-83, 91-93), Sociedad Colombiana de Cirugia, Sociedad Chilena de Cardiologia y Cirugia Cardiovasc., Cardiac Soc. Australia and New Zealand (corr.), Calif. Med. Assn., No. Calif. Vascular Soc., San Francisco Surg. Soc., Soc. Clin. Surgery, Santa Clara County Med. Soc. (mem. ethics com. 1980-82), Soc. Univ. Surgeons (mem. publs. com. 1982-85), Soc. Vascular Surgery, Western Thoracic Surg. Assn. (mem. program com. 1983-88, chmn. 1986-88, sec. 1989-93, v.p. 1993-94, pres. 1994-95), Soc. Thoracic Surgeons, Assn. Acad. Surgery, Western Vascular Soc., Internat. Soc. Cardiovasc. Surgery (mem. program com. 1984-87), Soc. Clin. Vascular Surgery, Soc. Thoracic Surg. Edn., Sociedad de Cardiocirujanos (pres. 1987-88), Pan-Pacific Surg. Assn., Stanford U. Med. Sch. Alumni Assn. (bd. govs. 1983-89), Cardiac Surgery Biology Club. Office: Stanford U Sch Medicine Falk Cardiovascular Rsch Ctr Stanford CA 94305-5247

MILLER, DAVID WAYNE, construction inspector, coordinator; b. Yuba City, Calif., June 23, 1949; s. Lloyd Wayne and Beverly Lorene (Ryan) M.; children: Quinlan Kenneth, Erin Patricia, Justin Michael Francis. AA in Constrn. Tech., Delta, 1985; BA in Art, Calif. State U., Hayward, 1989. Cert. tech. transfer and commercialization Internat. Conf. Bldg. Ofcls./Internat. Assn. Plumbing and Mech. Ofcls. Uniform Plumbing Code; cert. mgmt., cert. inspector. Plumber/fitter local 492 United Assn. Pipe Trades, Stockton, Calif., 1972—; plumber/fitter Lawrence Livermore Nat. Lab., Livermore, Calif., 1983-87, estimator, 1987-90; owner Moon Studios, 1976-80, Moonraker, 1991—. Author: (short story) Morgan's Tide, 1982, (Fremont C. of C. lit.) History of Fremont, 1982—; contbr. articles to CitySports, 1982. Sgt. U.S. Army, 1969-71, Vietnam. Mem. Lawrence Livermore Armed Force Vets. Assn., (founder, pres. 1986), Toastmasters.

MILLER, DIANE DORIS, executive search consultant; b. Sacramento, Calif., Jan. 18, 1954; d. George Campbell and Doris Lucille (Benninger) M. BA, U. Pacific, 1976, Golden Gate U., 1985, MBA, 1987. Mgr., A.G. Spanos, Sacramento, 1977-81, Lee Sammis, Sacramento, 1981-83; v.p. Consol. Capital, San Francisco, 1983-86; ptnr. Wilcox, Bertoux and Miller, Sacramento, 1986—. Bd. dirs. Sacramento Symphony En Corps, 1982-84, Sacramento Ballet, 1983-84, 86-92, Sacramento Symphony Assn., 1988-92, Oakland Ballet, Calif., 1984-85, Sacramento Symphony Found., 1994—, Sacramento Reg. Found., 1996—; mem. adv. bd. Golden Gate U., 1995—. Named Vol. of Yr., Junior League, 1983, Bus. Vol. in the Arts, Sacramento C. of C., 1989. Mem. U. Pacific Alumni Assn. (bd. dirs. 1978-85). Republican. Avocations: ballet, water sports.

MILLER, DIANE WILMARTH, human resources director; b. Clarinda, Iowa, Mar. 12, 1940; d. Donald and Floy Pauline (Madden) W.; m. Robert Nolen Miller, Aug. 21, 1965; children: Robert Wilmarth, Anne Elizabeth. AA, Colo. Women's Coll., 1960; BBA, U. Iowa, 1962; MA, U. No. Colo., 1994. Cert. tchr., Colo.; vocat. credential, Colo.; cert. sr. profl. in human resources. Sec.-counselor U. S.C., Myrtle Beach AFB, 1968-69; instr. U. S.C., Conway, 1967-69; tchr. bus. Poudre Sch. Dist. R-1, Ft. Collins, Colo., 1970-71; travel cons. United Bank Travel Svc., Greeley, Colo., 1972-74; dir. human resources Aims Community Coll., Greeley, 1984—; instr. part-time Aims Community Coll., Greeley, 1972—. Active 1st Congl. Ch., Greeley. Mem. Coll. Univ. Pers. Assn., Coll. Univ. Pers. Assn. Colo., No. Colo. Human Resources Assn., Soc. Human Resource Mgmt., Philanthropic Ednl. Orgn. (pres. 1988-89), Women's Panhellenic Assn. (pres. 1983-84), Scroll and Fan Club (pres. 1985-86), WTK Club, Questers. Home: 3530 Wagon Trail Pl Greeley CO 80634-3405 Office: Aims Cmty Coll 5401 W 20th St PO Box 69 Greeley CO 80632-3002

MILLER, DONALD GABRIEL, chemist; b. Oakland, Calif., Oct. 29, 1927; s. Nathan Harry and Edith Eileen (Levy) M.; m. Miriam G. Cohen, Aug. 14, 1949; children: Nancy Gail, Lynne Sandra. BS in Chemistry with honors, U. Calif., Berkeley, 1949; PhD in Phys. Chemistry, U. Ill., 1953. Asst. prof. U. Louisville, Ky., 1952-54; postdoctoral fellow Brookhaven Nat. Lab., Upton, N.Y., 1954-56; chemist Lawrence Livermore (Calif.) Nat. Lab., 1956—; adj. prof. Tex. Christian U., Ft. Worth, 1991—; guest prof. Technische Hochschule, Aachen, Germany, 1985, 88; vis. prof. U. Naples, Italy, 1983, 85, 87, 90, 93. Contbr. articles to profl. jours. and chpts. to books. Planning commr. City of Livermore, 1966-68, councilman, 1968-76, mayor, 1973-74; grand juror County of Alameda, 1992-93. Mem. Am. Chem. Soc., Math. Assn. Am., NRA (life), Nat. Muzzle Loading Rifle Assn. (life), Sigma Xi. Home: 2862 Waverly Way Livermore CA 94550-1740

MILLER, DONNA JEAN, nursing educator; b. L.A., Feb. 9, 1958; d. Lawrence John and Margaret Irene (Mariano) Miller. BA, Creighton U., 1980; diploma, U. So. Calif. Sch. Nursing, 1983; BSN, Calif. State U., 1990, MSN, 1996. RN, Calif.; cert. critical care nurse. Staff nurse ICU/ER Daniel Freeman Meml. Hosp., Inglewood, Calif., 1984-93; edn. specialist Daniel Freeman Meml. Hosp., 1993-97; clin. instr. Mt. St. Mary's Coll., L.A., 1992-93. BLS, ALS instr. Am. Heart Assn. Mem. ACCN, Sigma Theta Tau, Phi Kappa Phi. Office: Daniel Freeman Meml Hosp 333 N Prairie Ave Inglewood CA 90301-4501

MILLER, ELEANOR, English language and literature educator; b. Mill Valley, Calif.. BA, U. Nev., 1966, PhD in English with honors, 1970. Instr. English Valley Coll., San Bernardino, Calif., 1983-84, Crafton Hills Coll., Redlands, Calif., 1984-86, Coll. of the Desert, Palm Springs, Calif., 1986-90; prof. English Composition & Literature So. Nev. C.C., Las Vegas, 1990—; chair teaching-learning excellence com. So. Nev. C.C., Las Vegas, 1991-94, mentor, 1995—. Author: English Placement Grading, 1991, CCSN Writing Across the Curriculum, 1994. Advisor/participant Women's Re-entry Ctr., Palm Springs/Las Vegas, 1989-94; vol. Womyn's Festival Com., U. Nev., Las Vegas, 1994—. Mem. AAUW, Nat. Coun. Tchrs. English, Nev. State Tchrs. English, Nev. Adult Edn. Assn., Nev. Humanities Com., Mountain Plains Adult Edn. Assn., U. Nev. Alumni Assn., Women in Comm., Phi Kappa Phi,. Office: So Nev CC 3200 E Cheyenne Ave North Las Vegas NV 89030

MILLER, ELEANOR LOUISE, lawyer; b. Syracuse, N.Y., Oct. 10, 1947; d. Charles T. and Libby A. (DiNiro) Spuches; m. Roger William Miller, May 1973; children: Cara Christine, Justin Charles. BA in Elem. Edn. cum laude, SUNY, New Paltz, 1969; JD, U. Ariz., 1972. Bar: Ariz. 1972, N.Y. 1973, U.S. Dist. Ct. (no. dist.) N.Y. 1973, U.S. Dist. Ct. Ariz. 1975, U.S. Ct. Appeals (9th cir.) 1978, U.S. Supreme Ct. 1983; cert. criminal law specialist State Bar of Ariz., 1985—. Pvt. practice Syracuse, 1973-74; staff atty. Frank H. Hiscock Legal Aid Soc., Syracuse, 1974-75; pvt. practice Phoenix, 1975-76; law clk. to Hon. Jack D. H. Hays Ariz. Supreme Ct., 1976-77, staff atty., 1977-79; assoc. Goldstein, Flynn & Mason, Phoenix, 1979-80, Thomas A. Thinnes, P.A., Phoenix, 1980-85, 90-91; ptnr. Miller & Miller, P.C., Phoenix, 1985-89, Thinnes & Miller, P.A., Phoenix, 1991-93; pvt. practice Phoenix, 1993—; tchg. participant Nat. Inst. Trial Advocacy, San Diego, 1988; part-time mem. faculty Dept. Justice and Legal Studies, Phoenix Coll., 1994-95. Mem. Ariz. Women Lawyers Assn. (founder and charter mem.), State Bar Ariz. (mem. criminal rules com. 1996—), Ariz. Attys. Criminal Justice (charter mem., mem. bd. govs. 1996—, v.p. north 1997—), N.Y. State Bar Assn., Maricopa County Bar Assn. Democrat. Roman Catholic. Office: 1010 E Jefferson St Phoenix AZ 85034

MILLER, ELIZABETH HEIDBREDER, dean instruction; b. Kansas City, Mo., Dec. 17, 1948; d. Walter Morris and Gunborg Elizabeth (Janson) Heidbreder; m. Thomas Edmund Poley, Jan. 30, 1971 (div. Oct. 1984); children: Brent Matthew Poley, Andrew Morris Poley; m. James Robin Miller, Nov. 24, 1989. BS, Kans. State U., 1970; MS, Emporia State U., 1973; EdD, U. N.Mex., 1996. Tchr. Concordia (Kans.) H.S., 1973-74; coord. and tchr. Kilian C.C., Sioux Falls, S.D., 1980-81; office mgr. Dr. Jess Koons, Liberal, Kans., 1984-86; instr. bus. tech. U. N.Mex., Gallup, 1986-96, dean instrn., 1996—; part-time tchr. Jefferson County Adult Edn., Wheatridge, Colo., 1982-83, Seward County C.C., Liberal, 1984-86; mem. bd. Small Bus. Devel. Ctr., Gallup, 1994—; mem. adv. bd. Sch.-to-Work, Gallup, 1996—. Bd. dirs. Gallup McKinley County C. of C., 1993-96; mem. Leadership McKinley, 1996-97. Mem. Am. Vocat. Assn., Nat. Bus. Edn. Assn., N.Mex. Coun. Chief Instrnl. Officers, Soroptimist Internat. Gallup, Delta Pi Epsilon (bus. hon.). Office: U N Mex 200 College Rd Gallup NM 87301

MILLER, ELIZABETH RODRIGUEZ, city manager; b. Tucson, Feb. 22, 1954; d. Tony S. Martinez and Maria (Corral) Rodriguez; m. Marc Alan Miller, Nov. 5, 1972; children: Andrea Eve, Matthew Luke, Meredith C. BA in Spanish, U. Ariz., 1976, MLS, 1978. Unit mgr. S. Tucson Libr., 1978-80; activities coord. community cable com. City of Tucson, 1980; info./reference mgr. Tucson Pub. Libr., 1981-84, agy. mgr., 1984-85, regional mgr., 1985-87, asst. dir. pub. svcs., 1987-89; dep. exec. dir. divsn. ALA Libr. Adminstrn. & Mgmt. Assn., Chgo., 1990; dep. dir. Tucson Pima Libr., 1990-91, libr. dir., 1991-96; asst. city mgr. City of Tucson, 1996—. Co-editor: Great Library Promotion Ideas V, 1990; contbr. articles to profl. jours. Mem. adv. bd. libr. power grant Tucson Unified Sch. Dist., 1992-95; bd. dirs. Tucson area Literacy Coalition, 1992-95; active Hispanic Profl. Action Com., 1992—. Mem. ALA (mem. pres. program com. 1987, mem. nominating com. 1991-93), REFORMA (chair elections com. 1983-84, 85, chair conf. program 1987, pres. 1987-88), Libr. Adminstrn. and Mgmt. Assn. (mem. cultural diversity com. 1991-92, chair 1992-93, mem. nominating com. 1992-93), Pub. Libr. Assn. (mem. Pub. Libr. Assn.-Libr. Adminstrn. and Mgmt. Assn. cert. com. 1991-92, chair 1992-93, chair Allie Beth Martin Award com. 1987-88, mem. 1989), Ariz. Libr. Assn. (Libr. of Yr. 1995), Ariz. State Libr. Assn. (chair svcs. to Spanish-speaking Roundtable 1980-82, pres. pub. libr. divsn. 1984-85, chair ann. conf. 1986), Internat. City/County Mgmt. Assn. (assoc., participant Comparative Performance Measurement Consortium 1994—), U. Ariz. Hispanic Alumni Assn., Beta Phi Mu. Office: City Mgrs Office City Hall 10th Fl West 255 W Alameda PO Box 27210 Tucson AZ 85726-7210

MILLER, ELLIOT IVAN, editor; b. Inglewood, Calif., July 18, 1951; s. Elliot and Geraldine Miller; m. Corinne Hull, Apr. 25, 1981. BA in Ministry, Anaheim Christian Coll., 1980; MA in Apologetics, Simon Greenleaf U., 1989. Ordained min., Calif. Exec. dir. One Way Help Ctr. and Hotline, Newport Beach, Calif., 1974-76; rschr. Christian Rsch. Inst., Rancho Santa Margarita, Calif., 1976—; bd. dirs. Evang. Ministries to New Religions, St. Louis. Author: A Crash Course on the New Age Movement, 1989; co-author: The Cult of the Virgin, 1992; editor-in-chief Christian Rsch. Jour., 1980—; radio personality The Bible Answer Man, 1994-95. Office: Christian Rsch Inst PO Box 7000 Santa Margarita CA 92688-7000

MILLER, ERIC NATHAN, neuropsychologist; b. Oceanside, Calif., Nov. 21, 1955; s. David Wesley and Nancy Norland (Guinand) M.; 1 child, Bryan Scott. BA in Psychology, U. Va., 1977; MS in Psychology, U. Wis., 1981, PhD in Clin. Psychology, 1986. Lic. clin. psychologist, Calif. Fellow neuropsychology UCLA, 1986-88, asst. rsch. neuropsychologist, 1988-94, assoc. rsch. neuropsychologist, 1994—; owner, proprietor Norland Software, L.A., 1983—; project dir. Divsn. Epidemiology, UCLA, 1987—. Contbr. articles to profl. jours.; consulting editor Psychol. Assessment; reviewer jours. in field. Fellow Wis. Alumni Rsch. Fund. Mem. APA, Internat. Neuropsychol. Soc., Phi Beta Kappa. Office: UCLA Neuropsychiat Inst 760 Westwood Plz Rm C8-747 Los Angeles CA 90024-8300

MILLER, EUGENE H., lawyer; b. Chgo., Dec. 21, 1947; s. Clifford and Birdie (Lubovitz) M.; m. Judith Miriam Bolef, June 15, 1969; children: Adam, Rachel. BS, U. Ill., 1969, JD, 1973. Bar: Ill. 1973, Calif. 1973, U.S. Dist. Ct. (no. dist.) Calif. 1973, U.S. Supreme Ct. 1977, U.S. Tax Ct. 1983. Acct. Lester Witte, Chgo., 1969-70, Price Waterhouse, Oakland, Calif., 1973-74; atty. Heizel, Leighton, Brunn & Deal, Oakland, 1974-79, Miller, Starr & Regalia, Oakland, 1980—; mng. ptnr. Author: (with others) Closely Held Corporations, 1988. Office: Miller Starr & Regalia 5th Fl 1331 N California Blvd Walnut Creek CA 94596

MILLER, FRANCIE LORADITCH, college counselor; b. Avilton, Md., Apr. 18, 1937; d. John William and Agnes Wilda (Broadwater) Loraditch; m. George Aloys Miller, Feb. 27, 1965; children: Peter Raymond, Sandra Patricia. Student, Kent State U., 1955-57; BA in English, Calif. State U., Dominguez Hills, 1978, Ma in English, 1980. Flight attendent Western Airlines, L.A., 1957-65; lectr. English Calif. State U., Carson, 1980-82, asst. coord. learning assistance ctr., 1979-84, asst. dir. univ. outreach svcs., 1984-96; dir. advisement & transfer svcs. Marymount Coll., Palos Verdes, Calif., 1996—; mem. L.A. Regional Intersegmental Adv. Bd., 1996. Editor Campus Staff Newsletter, 1992-96. Mem. edn. com. Palos Verdes (Calif.) C. of C., 1994—; vol. Olympic Games, L.A., 1984; campus rep. Statewide Alumni Coun., Sacramento, 1982-84; participant Civic Chorale, Torrance, Calif., 1993—; apptd. statewide campus adv. com. Project Assist, 1996. Acad. scholar Kent State U., 1955. Mem. Calif. Intersegmental Articulation Coun. (newsletter editor 1993-96, vice chair 1995-96), Nat. Acad. Advising Assn., Western Assn. Coll. Admission Counselors, South Coast Higher Ednl. Coun., Phi Kappa Phi (chpt. pres. 1992—, mem. nat. comm. com. 1996). Republican. Roman Catholic. Office: Marymount Coll 30800 Palos Verdes Dr E Palos Verdes Peninsula CA 90275-6299

MILLER, FRANKLIN EMRICK, software engineer, project engineer; b. Greenville, Ohio, Aug. 12, 1946; s. Rollin Linde and E. Evelyn (Emrick) M.; m. Sandra Lewis, Dec. 20, 1969; children: William Rollin, Rose Mary. BS in Math. and Physics, Otterbein Coll., 1969; MEd in Ednl. Psychology and Counseling, Wayne State U., 1975; PhD in Ednl. Psychology, Computer Stats., U. Denver, 1984. Lic. pvt. pilot FAA. Commd. U.S. Air Force, 1969, advanced through grades to capt.; space surveillance officer SLBM, Maine, 1970-71, BMEWS Thule, Greenland, 1971-72; chief instr./systems analyst, Correlation Ctr. 440L, McGuire AFB, N.J., 1972-73; site space surveillance officer, Aviano, Italy, 1973-75; chief Defense Support Program support programming unit, Colo., 1975-79; chief applications support programming DSP, South Australia, 1979-81, ret., 1988; software engr. Aerojet Electro Systems Corp., Aurora, Colo., 1981-88. Bd. dirs., Aurora Community Mental Health Ctr., 1976-79; vol. counselor Comitis Crisis Ctr., YMCA, Aurora, 1976-78. Mem. Am. Psychol. Assn. (div. Applied Experimental and Engrng. Psychologists), Denver Astron. Soc. (sec.), Soc. Personality Assessment, Phi Delta Kappa. Republican. Author: The Preliminary Online Rorschach Test Manual, 1980; contbr. article to profl. jour. Recipient Corp. award for improving Desert Storm performance, 1991. Office: The Aerospace Corp Buckley Ang Base 18300 E Crested Butte Ave Aurora CO 80011-9518

MILLER, GARY DOUGLAS, aerospace company executive; b. Cleve., Dec. 14, 1942; s. Wells Winton and Ruth Alyce (Noreen) M.; m. Julia Ann Walraven, Aug. 7, 1988; children: Eric, Brooke. AA, Moorpark (Calif.) Coll., 1975; BA in Math. summa cum laude, Calif. State U., Northridge, 1977, MBA in Ops. Rsch. summa cum laude, 1979. Tech. maintenance staff Hughes Aircraft Co., El Segundo, Calif., 1965-72, project dir. tech. pubs., 1972-75, mgr. logistics support, 1975-88, mgr. non-def. initiatives, 1988-94, mgr. internat. studies, 1994—; tech. dir. Sys. Engring. Network, El Segundo, 1993-95; dir. Inst. for Nat. Drug Abuse Rsch., Austin, Tex., 1989-92, Sys. Engring. Adv. Coun., U. So. Calif., L.A., 1993—. Contbr. numerous articles to profl. jours. Sgt. USAF, 1960-64. Mem. AAAS, Am. Def. Preparedness Assn., Nat. Security Indsl. Assn., Internat. Coun. on Sys. Engring., Inst. for Ops. Rsch./Mgmt. Sci., Intertel, Internat. Soc. for Philos. Inquiry, Archaeol. Inst. Am., Mensa, Phi Kappa Phi. Home: 1857 Love Cir Simi Valley CA 93063-4322 Office: Hughes Aircraft Co PO Box 902 2175 Park Pl El Segundo CA 90245

MILLER, GENE FREDERICK, land use planner; b. Seattle, Nov. 29, 1950; s. Robert Gene Miller and Karen Anise (Hansen) Flemmer; m. Deborah June Miller, Dec. 29, 1974 (div. Mar. 1977); 1 child, Jennifer June; m. Pamela Marie Lippold, Aug. 30, 1985; children: Joshua Dart, Amanda Marie, Gene F. Jr. AAS, Everett (Wash.) C.C., 1977. Cert. profl. planner, Wash. Profl. planner Snohomish County, Everett, 1977-95; profl. planner, cons. NORETEP, Arlington, Wash., 1995—. With U.S. Army, 1971-73, Europe. Recipient Nat. Champion Loft award, Thoroughbred Mag., 1990. Mem. Wash. State Racing Pigeon Orgn. (pres. 1984-85), Stilling Racing Club (pres. 1989—), Snohomish County Profl. Consultants. Republican. Presbyterian. Home: 2426 200th St NE Arlington WA 98223-9757

MILLER, GEORGE, mayor; b. Detroit; m. Roslyn Girard; 4 children. BA, U. Ariz., 1947, MEd, 1952. Tchr. high schs., owner, prin. painting contracting co., until 1989; mayor City of Tucson, 1991—. Active mem. Dem. Party So. Ariz., 1960—, treas. Pima County div., state chmn. Presdl. Del. Selection Reform Commn.; bd. dirs. Tucson Jewish Community Ctr., Anti-Defamation League of B'nai B'rith; councilman Tucson City Coun., 1977-91, also vice mayor. With USMC, WWII. Decorated Purple Heart; recipient Recognition award United Way, Cmty. Svcs. Support award Chicano Por La Causa (2), Met. Edn. Commn. Crystal Apple award, cert. appreciation San Ignacio Yaqui Coun., Old Pasqua, Dr. Martin Luther King Jr. Keep the Dream Alive award, 1995; named Father of Yr. 1995, Man of Yr. So. Ariz. Home Builders Assn., Outstanding Pub. Ofcl. Ariz. Parks and Recreation Assn., 1995. Office: Office of Mayor PO Box 27210 Tucson AZ 85726-7210*

MILLER, GEORGE, congressman; b. Richmond, Calif., May 17, 1945; s. George and Dorothy (Rumsey) M.; m. Cynthia Caccavo, 1964; children: George, Stephen. B.A., San Francisco State Coll., 1968; J.D., U. Calif., Davis, 1972. Legis. counsel Calif. senate majority leader, 1969-73; mem. 94th-104th Congresses from 7th Calif. dist., 1975—; chmn. subcom. on oversight and investigations, 1985—, chmn. subcom. on labor stds., 1981-84, chmn. select com. on children, youth and families, 1983-91, chmn. com. on natural resources, 1991-94; mem. com. on edn. and lab., dep. majority whip, 1989-94; vice chair Dem. Policy Com., 1995—. Mem. Calif. Bar Assn. Office: House of Representatives 2205 Rayburn Bldg Washington DC 20515-0005

MILLER, GREGORY KEITH, corporate lawyer; b. Palm Springs, Calif., Mar. 13, 1961; s. Joseph Spear and Mary Ann (McElfresh) M. BA, Colgate U., 1983; JD, U. Va., 1986. Bar: N.Y. 1987, Calif., 1992. Assoc. Brown & Wood, N.Y.C., 1986-90, San Francisco, 1990-95; of counsel Latham & Watkins, San Francisco, 1996—. Notes editor Jour. Law and Politics, Charlottesville, Va., 1985-86. Fellow The Explorers Club; mem. Am. Alpine Club (mem. conservation com.). Office: Latham & Watkins 505 Montgomery St Ste 1900 San Francisco CA 94111-2586

MILLER, HAROLD WILLIAM, nuclear geochemist; b. Walton, N.Y., Apr. 21, 1920; s. Harold Frank and Vera Leona (Simons) M. BS in Chemistry, U. Mich., 1943; MS in Chemistry, U. Colo., 1948, postgrad. Control chemist Linde Air Products Co., Buffalo, 1943-46; analytical research chemist Gen. Electric Co., Richland, Wash., 1948-51; research chemist Phillips Petroleum Co., Idaho Falls, Idaho, 1953-56; with Anaconda (Mont.) Copper Co., 1956; tech. dir., v.p. U.S. Yttrium Co., Laramie, Wyo., 1956-57; tech. dir. Colo. div. The Wah Chang Co., Boulder, Colo., 1957-58; analytical chemist The Climax (Colo.) Molybdenum Co., 1959; with research and devel. The Colo. Sch. of Mines Research Found., Golden, 1960-62; cons. Boulder, 1960—; sr. research physicist Dow Chem. Co., Golden, 1963-73; bd. dirs. Sweeney Mining and Milling Corp., Boulder; cons. Hendricks Mining and Milling Co., Boulder; instr. nuclear physics and nuclear chemistry Rocky Flats Plant, U. Colo. Contbr. numerous articles to profl. jours. Recipient Lifetime Achievement award Boulder County Metal Mining Assn., 1990. Mem. Sigma Xi. Home and Office: PO Box 1092 Boulder CO 80306-1092

MILLER, HARRIET SANDERS, art center director; b. N.Y.C., Apr. 18, 1926; d. Herman and Dorothy (Silbert) S.; m. Milton H. Miller, June 27, 1948; children—Bruce, Jeffrey, Marcie. B.A., Ind. U., 1947; M.A., Columbia U., 1949; M.S., U. Wis., 1962, M.F.A., 1967. Dir. art sch. Madison Art Ctr., Wis., 1963-72; acting dir. Center for Continuing Edn., Vancouver, B.C., 1975-76; mem. fine arts faculty Douglas Coll., Vancouver, 1972-78; exec. dir. Palos Verdes Arts Center, Calif., 1978-84; dir. Junior Arts Center, Los Angeles, 1984—; one woman exhibits at Gallery 7, Vancouver, 1978, Gallery 1, Toronto, Ont., 1977, Linda Farris Gallery, Seattle, 1975, Galerie Allen, Vancouver, 1973. Mem. Calif. Art Edn. Assn., Museum Educators of So. Calif., Arts and Humanities Symposium. Office: Junior Arts Ctr 4814 Hollywood Blvd Los Angeles CA 90027-5302

MILLER, HILLARD CRAIG, physicist; b. Northampton, Pa., Dec. 15, 1932; s. Hillard Alvin and Dorothy Madama (Frantz) M.; m. Ruth Hazel Kingsbury, June 16, 1956; children: Eric, Kent, Curtis, Alice. BA in Physics, Lehigh U., 1954, MS in Physics, 1955; PhD in Physics, Pa. State U., 1960. Physicist GE, Schenectady, 1960-67, Phila., 1967-72; sr. engr. GE, Largo, Fla., 1972-82, prin. physicist, 1982-92; physicist cons., 1993—; adj. instr. St. Petersburg Jr. Coll., Clearwater, Fla., 1974-90. 1st lt. U.S. Army, 1955-57. Mem. AAAS, IEEE, Am. Phys. Soc., Am. Vacuum Soc., European Phys. Soc., Royal Astron. Soc. Can. Home and Office: 16508 NE 27th Pl Bellevue WA 98008-2215

MILLER, JAMES KAY, aerospace engineer; b. Homestead, Pa., Oct. 18, 1939; s. Clarence Russel and Eunice M.; m. Connie J. Weeks, Aug. 19, 1987. BS, Carnegie Mellon Univ., 1961. Engr. Westinghouse Elec., Pitts., 1961-69, Martin Marietta, Balt., 1964-66, Jet Propulsion Lab., Pasadena, Calif., 1966-69, 71—, Logicon, San Pedro, Calif., 1969-71. Contbr. articles to profl. jours. Mem. IEEE, AIAA, Am. Geophys. Union. Home: 19265 Braemore Rd Northridge CA 91326-1206 Office: Jet Propulsion Lab 4800 Oak Grove Dr Pasadena CA 91109-8001

MILLER, JEAN RUTH, librarian; b. St. Helena, Calif., Aug. 4, 1927; d. William Leonard and Jean (Stanton) M. BA, Occidental Coll., 1950; MLS, U. So. Calif., Los Angeles, 1952. Base librarian USAF, Wethersfield, Eng., 1952-55; post librarian USMC Air Sta., El Toro, Calif., 1955-63; data systems librarian Autonetics (Rockwell), Anaheim, Calif., 1963-65; mgr. library services Beckman Instruments, Inc., Fullerton, Calif., 1966-93; mem. adv. com. Library Technician Program, Fullerton Coll., 1969—. Author: (bibliography) Field Air Traffic Control, 1965, Electrical Shock Hazards, 1974. Chair Fullerton Are U. So. Calif. Scholarship Alumni Interview Program, Fullerton, 1974—. Mem. IEEE, So. Calif. Assn. Law Libraries, Med. Library Group of So. Calif., Spl. Libraries Assn. (pres. So. Calif. chpt. 1975-76, chair Sci./Tech. Div. 1985-86). Republican. Home: 3139 E Chapman Ave Apt 4C Orange CA 92869-3742

MILLER, JEREMY MATTHEW, lawyer, legal educator; b. Boston, Apr. 2, 1954; s. Harold Irving and Maida (Rosenberg) M.; children: Rachelle Clara, Peter Jason, Nathaniel Perceval. BA, Yale U., 1976; BS, Meru, Switzerland, 1977; JD cum laude, Tulane U., 1980; LLM, U. Pa., 1981. Bar: Mass. 1980, U.S. Ct. Appeals (1st, 3d and 10th cirs.) 1981, U.S. Supreme Ct. 1985. Law clk. to presiding justice Colo. Supreme Ct., Denver, 1982-83; prof. Western State U. Coll. of Law, Fullerton, Calif., 1983-94; dean, prof. law Chapman U., 1994—; adj. instr. law Calif. State U., 1987—; adj. prof. bar rev. Contbr. to books on criminal law, legal ethics, jurisprudence, articles to profl. jours; editor in chief Orange County Lawyer Mag., 1994—; columnist. Mem. Mass. Bar Assn. Office: Chapman U Sch Law 1240 S State College Blvd Anaheim CA 92806-5150

MILLER, JESSICA LYNN, psychologist, educator, researcher; b. Cleve., Apr. 16, 1966; d. Thomas James and Pauline Joan (Columbo) M. BS, U. Wyo., Laramie, 1989, MS, 1992, PhD in Devel. Psychology, 1994. Asst. prof. psychology Cameron U., Lawton, Okla., 1994-95, Mesa State Coll., Grand Junction, Colo., 1995—; speaker in field. Contbr. articles to profl. jours. Recipient grants in field. Mem. Soc. for Rsch. in Child Devel., Am. Psychology Soc., Rocky Mountain Psychol. Assn., Psi Chi, Phi Kappa Phi. Office: Mesa State Coll PO Box 2464 Grand Junction CO 81502

MILLER, JILL MARIE, psychoanalyst; b. Denver, Mar. 1, 1953; d. Wilbur C. and Viretta Ann (Shaw) M. BA, U. Denver, 1974, MSW, 1979; grad. child and adolescent psychoanalyst, Anna Freud Ctr., London, 1989; PhD, U. London, 1993; grad. adult psychoanalyst, Denver Psychoanalytic Inst., 1996. Bd. cert. diplomate clin. social work. Clin. social worker Cath. Cmty. Svcs., Denver, 1979-83, Mt. Airy Psychiat. Hosp., Denver, 1983-85; pvt. practice clin. social worker Denver, 1982-85, pvt. practice psychoanalyst, 1991—; faculty mem. Denver Psychoanalytic Inst., Colo. Ctr. for Psychoanalytic Studies, 1991—; clin. instr. dept. psychiatry U. Colo. Med. Sch., Denver, 1994—. Contbr. to books. Recipient prize for outstanding clin. paper The Anna Freud Ctr., London, 1987; Dorothy Burlingham scholar The Anna Freud Ctr., London, 1989, 90. Mem. Assn. Child Psychoanalysis (bd. mem., councillor 1996—), Denver Inst. for Psychoanalysis (assoc. dir. child and adolescent tng. 1995—), Colo. Ctr. for Psychoanalytic Studies (bd. mem. 1991-94). Office: 240 Saint Paul St # 315 Denver CO 80206

MILLER, JOANNE LOUISE, middle school educator; b. Milton, Mass., Apr. 4, 1944; d. Joseph Louis and Marion Theresa (Saulnier) Fasci; m. William Frederick Miller, Dec. 4, 1962; 1 child, Robert Joseph. BS, U. Oreg., 1972, MS in Curriculum and Instrn., 1973; EdD, Brigham Young U., 1980; postgrad., Oreg. State U., 1995. Lic. counselor, tchr., adminstr., Oreg. Tchr. South Lane Sch. Dist., Cottage Grove, Oreg., 1973—, lang. arts div. chairperson, 1975-78, 89-90, reading coord., 1978-79, 7th grade block chairperson, 1982-92, mid. sch. talented and gifted coord., 1992-93, counselor, 1991-93; mem. Oreg. State Assessment Content Panel Reading, Salem, 1987-88; mem. Oreg. Lang Arts Curriculum Devel. Com., Salem, 1985-87; del. to Citizen Amb. Program of People to People Internat. 1st U.S.-Russia Joint Conf. on Edn., Moscow, 1994. Vol. Am. Cancer Soc., Am. Diabetes Assn., 1990—; aux.- charter mem. Assistance League of Eugene. Mem. ACA, NEA, Internat. Reading Assn., Am. Sch. Counselor Assn., Oreg. Counseling Assn., Oreg. Edn. Assn., South Lane Edn. Assn., Oreg. Reading Assn., Oreg. Mid. Level Assn., Delta Kappa Gamma, Alpha Rho State (v.p. 1995-97, pres. 1997—). Democrat. Roman Catholic. Home: 85515 Appletree Dr Eugene OR 97405-9738 Office: Lincoln Mid Sch 1565 S 4th St Cottage Grove OR 97424-2955

MILLER, JOHN LAURENCE, professional golfer; b. San Francisco, Apr. 29, 1947; s. Laurence O. and Ida (Meldrum) M.; m. Linda Strouse, Sept. 17, 1969; children: John Strouse, Kelly, Casi, Scott, Brent, Todd. Student, Brigham Young U., 1965-69. Profl. golfer, 1969—; Pres. Johnny Miller Enterprises, Inc.; golf commentator, NBC. Author: Pure Golf, 1976, Johnny Miller's Golf for Juniors, 1987. Named PGA Player of Yr., 1974. Office: PO Box 2260 Napa CA 94558-0060

MILLER, JONATHAN LEWIS, lawyer, computer consultant; b. Boston, Dec. 9, 1947; s. Harold Irving and Maida (Rosenberg) M.; m. Arleen Garfinkle, Nov. 2, 1985; 1 child, Jonah Maxwell. BA in Sociology, Colby

Coll., 1973; BS in Physics, U. Washington, 1980; JD, U. Denver, 1994. Bar: Colo. 1994. Proprietor, cons. J. Miller & Assoc., Colo., 1982-85; pres., atty. J. Miller & Assoc., Inc., Boulder, Colo., 1985-95; assoc. Martin & Mehafty LLC, Boulder, 1995—. Editor: Transp. Law Jour., 1992-94; author: Rocky Mountain Land Use Technical Servia Report, 1994, Orange County Lawyer, 1994. Home: 173 Wild Tiger Rd Boulder CO 80302-9263 Office: Martin & Mehaffy 1655 Walnut St PO Box 1260 Boulder CO 80302

MILLER, JOSEPH ARTHUR, manufacturing engineer, educator, consultant; b. Brattleboro, Vt., Aug. 28, 1933; s. Joseph Maynard and Marjorie Antoinette (Hammerberg) M.; m. Ardene Hedwig Barker, Aug. 19, 1956; children: Stephanie L., Jocelyn A., Shana L., Gregory J. BS in Agrl., Andrews U., Berrien Springs, Mich., 1955; MS in Agrl. Mechs., Mich. State U., 1959; EdD in Vocat. Edn., UCLA, 1973. Constrn. engr. Thornton Bldg. & Supply, Inc., Williamston, Mich., 1959-63, C & B Silo Co., Charlotte, Mich., 1963-64; instr. and dir. retraining Lansing (Mich.) Community Coll., 1964-68; asst. prof./prog. coord./coop coord. San Jose State U., 1968-79; mfg. specialist Lockheed Missiles & Space Co., Sunnyvale, Calif., 1979-81, rsch. specialist, 1981-88, NASA project mgr., 1982-83, staff engr., 1988-96; rsch. staff engr. Lockheed Missiles & Space Co., 1996—; coord. flexible mfg. system simulation project Lockheed Missiles & Space Co., Sunnyvale, Calif., 1994-96, team mem. federally funded AIMS Agile Mfg. project, 1995—; team mem. corp funded machining outsource initative project Lockheed Missles and Space Co., 1995—, coord. productivity improvement program, 1996—; agrl. engring. cons. USDA Poultry Expt. Sta., 1960-62; computer numerical control cons. Dynamechtronics, Inc., Sunnyvale, 1987-90; machining cons. Lockheed, Space Sys. Div., 1986—; instr. computer numerical control DeAnza Coll., Cupertino, Calif., 1985-88, Labor Employment Tng. Corp., San Jose, Calif., 1988-93; instr. computer-aided mfg. and non traditional machining San Jose (Calif.) State U., 1994—. Author: Student Manual for CNC Lathe, 1990; contbr. articles to profl. jours. Career counselor Pacific Union Coll., Angwin, Calif., 1985-92. UCLA fellow, 1969-73. Mem. Soc. Mfg. Engrs. (sr. mem. 1980-92, chmn. edn. com. local chpt. 1984-85, career guidance counselor 1986-88), Nat. Assn. Indsl. Tech. (pres. industry divsn. 1987-88, bd. cert. 1991-92, chmn. accreditation visitation team 1984—), Calif. Assn. Indsl. Tech. (pres. 1974-75, 84-85), Am. Soc. Indsl. Tech. (pres. 1980-81). Seventh-day Adventist. Home: PO Box 190 Berry Creek CA 95916-0190 Office: Lockheed Martin Missiles & Space 1111 Lockheed Way Sunnyvale CA 94089-1212

MILLER, KATHRYN LOUISE, elementary educator; b. Iowa City, Iowa, Oct. 30, 1943; d. Robert Arthur and LaVonne Norma (Lundberg) Haburn; m. Paul Chalmers Miller, Aug. 15, 1964; children: Kelly Sue Miller Mayberry, Matthew Chalmers. BA in Edn., Wayne State Coll., 1965; MA in Edn., U. No. Colo., 1978. Lic. profl. tchr. Tchr. So. Sioux City (Nebr.) Pub. Schs., 1965-68, Jefferson County Pub. Schs., Golden, Colo., 1972-97; insvc. leader Jefferson County Pub. Schs., Golden, 1982-97, staff devel. liaison, 1988-97. Mem. Jefferson County Edn. Assn. Home: 7256 W Clifton Ave Littleton CO 80123

MILLER, KEN C., editor; b. Santa Maria, Calif., Apr. 21, 1965; s. Donald Baird and Sharon Kay (Ackland) M.; m. Annette Marie Albertoni, Aug. 1, 1959; children: Katie Cullum, James Cullum, Shannon Cullum. BS in Journalism, Calif. Poly. Inst., San Luis Obispo, 1988. Editor Santa Maria Times, 1988—. Home: 834 Sierra Madre Ave Santa Maria CA 93454-6747 Office: Santa Maria Times 3200 Skyway Dr Santa Maria CA 93455-1824

MILLER, KEVIN LANE, software engineer/architect, consultant; b. Wichita Falls, Tex., Feb. 2, 1970; s. Dave Lane Miller and Sharon Kay Nixon Silva; m. Victoria J. Weightman, Oct. 4, 1991. BA, Hampden-Sydney Coll., 1991; MBA, U. Phoenix, 1996. Info. systems adminstr. Amity, Inc., Tucson, 1992; software engr. Midak Internat., Tucson, 1992-93; sr. software engr./architect Scottsdale (Ariz.) Ins., 1993—; chief cons. scientist Fionn Enterprises, Scottsdale, 1993—; dir. rsch. Coun. for Energy Rsch., Tucson, 1990-93; mem. bd. publs. Hampden-Sydney, Va., 1990-91. Editor: Wittgenstein's Tractatus Logico-Philosophicus, 1991; author/architect: (software product) Helpdesk, 1993; editor The New Environ. Herald, 1992. Hampden-Sydney Coll. grantee in philosophy, 1990. Mem. IEEE, Phi Beta Kappa, Eta Sigma Phi, Theta Alpha Kappa. Republican. Home: 11772 E Clinton Scottsdale AZ 85259

MILLER, KUBY SUSIE, dance and modeling school owner; b. Romal, Italy, May 14, 1954; d. Stephen and Josette (Jorma) Kuby; m. Lyle G. Miller, Nov. 14, 1988. Grad. high sch., Madison, Wis. Dancer Royal Ballet, London, 1964-70; model Lynette Berit, Paris, 1967-69; dancer Ballet Repertoire, N.Y.C., 1970-75, Southeast Dancing Co., N.Y.C., 1975-76, Bulter Jazz Co., Salt Lake City, 1976-77, Music Ctr., Salt Lake City, 1977-78, Utah Ballet Co., Salt Lake City, 1979-85; model Channel Runway, Paris, 1986-87; dancer Musical Theater Fine Arts, Salt Lake City, 1988-89, TCG Theatre Group, 1993-94, Accop Arts USA, 1994—. Bd. dirs. Mus. Theaters, Salt Lake City, 1988-89, Ballet Dept., Salt Lake City, 1989-90, Susie's Dancing Co., Salt Lake City, 1990—, Susie's Modeling Co., Salt Lake City, 1990-92; mem. Back Stage West, 1994-96, Top Model, 1996, Wake Adoption, North Falmouth, 1991, Nat. Abortion Rights Action League, Salt Lake City, 1990, Nat. Wildlife Fedn., Salt Lake City, 1991. Recipient Susan Kylby-Miller Dance Co. award, 1996-97, Best Acting award Susan Kuby-Miller, 1997, Outstanding Tchg. award, 1996. Mem. Theatre Critics (honor 1991), N.Y. Theatre. Home and Office: 273 East 2100 South Salt Lake City UT 84115

MILLER, LARRY H., professional sports team executive, automobile dealer; b. Salt Lake City; m. Gail Miller; 5 children. Formerly with auto parts bus., Denver and Salt Lake City; now owner auto dealerships, Salt Lake City, Albuquerque, Denver and Phoenix; part-owner Utah Jazz, NBA, Salt Lake City, 1985-86, owner, 1986—. Office: care Utah Jazz 301 W South Temple Salt Lake City UT 84101-1216 Office: Larry H Miller Group 5650 S State St Murray UT 84107-6131*

MILLER, LORRAINE, business owner. BA in History, U. Utah. Lab. technician U. Utah Med. Ctr., 1972-75; pres. Cactus & Tropicals, Inc., Salt Lake City, 1975—; mem. adv. bd. Utah Securities Commn., 1994; panelist Am. Arbitration Assn., 1991; pres., bd. dirs. Phoenix Inst., 1986-87. Vol. VISTA, 1966-69; mem. Gov.'s Task Force Entrepreneurism, 1988, Gov.'s Task Force Work Force Devel., 1994; mentor Women's Network Entrepreneurial Tng., Small Bus. Adminstrn., 1990; mem. adv. bd. Utah Dem. Health Care Task Force, 1991, Women's Bus. Devel. Office State of Utah, 1990-92; employer Supportive Employment for the Handicapped, 1990-92. Recipient Pathfinder award Salt Lake C. of C., 1986, Women of Achievement award YWCA, 1992; named Nat. Small Bus. Person of Yr. by U.S. Small Bus. Adminstrn., 1994. Mem. Nat. Assn. Women's Bus. Owners (pres. Salt Lake chpt. 1992), Utah Assn. Women's Bus. Owners (pres. 1992, 1st v.p. 1991, bd. dirs. 1985, 89-90, named Woman Bus. Owner of Yr. 1987), Wasatch Cactus & Succulent Soc. (co-founder). Office: Cactus & Tropicals of Utah 2735 S 20th St E Salt Lake City UT 84109

MILLER, MARIAN LOFTON, artist, musician; b. Red Willow County, Nebr., Apr. 8, 1922; d. Chester Arthur and Leona Glee (Ellis) Lofton; m. Frank Joseph Haske, Nov. 15, 1949 (dec. Apr. 1968); children: Timothy L. Haske, Gregory F. Haske, Jo Ann Haske, Daniel P. Haske; m. Leopold Sylvan Miller, June 14, 1969. Grad., Nat. Art Sch., Washington, 1946; student, Famous Writers Sch., Westport, Conn., 1970-73; grad., Marion (Nebr.) H.S., 1941. Airbrush artist Reed Rsch., Washington, through 1946; fashion artist Brooks Fine Apparel, Washington, 1947-50, advt. mgr., 1951-53; counselor Leadership Tng. Inst., Halpine Ch., Rockville, Md., 1978-83. Organist, Faith United Ch., Rockville, 1954-72; pianist Halpine Ch., 1977-82; involved in prison ministry New Covenant Ministries, Buena Vista, Colo., 1991—; tchr. Sunday sch. Ch. of God, 1996—, min. of music, 1991—. Republican. Home: 1026 H St Salida CO 81201

MILLER, MAYNARD MALCOLM, geologist, educator, research institute director, explorer, state legislator; b. Seattle, Jan. 23, 1921; s. Joseph Anthony and Juanita Queena (Davison) M.; m. Joan Walsh, Sept. 15, 1951; children: Ross McCord, Lance Davison. BS magna cum laude, Harvard U., 1943; MA, Columbia U., 1948; PhD (Fulbright scholar), St. John's Coll., Cambridge U., Eng., 1957; student, Naval War Coll., Air War Coll., Oak Ridge Inst. Nuclear Sci.; D of Sci. (hon.), U. Alaska, 1990. Registered profl. geologist, Idaho. Asst. prof. naval sci. Princeton (N.J.) U., 1946; geologist Gulf Oil Co., Cuba, 1947; rsch. assoc., coordinator, dir. Office Naval Rsch. project Am. Geog. Soc., N.Y.C., 1948-53; staff scientist Swiss Fed. Inst. for Snow and Avalanche Rsch., Davos, 1952-53; instr. dept. geography Cambridge U., 1953-54, 56; assoc. producer, field unit dir. film Seven Wonders of the World for Cinerama Corp., Europe, Asia, Africa, Middle East, 1954-55; rsch. assoc. Lamont Geol. Obs., N.Y.C., 1955-57; sr. scientist dept. geology Columbia U., N.Y.C., 1957-59; asst. prof. geology Mich. State U., East Lansing, 1959-61, assoc. prof., 1961-63; prof. Mich. State U., 1963-75; dean Coll. Mines and Earth Resources U. Idaho, Moscow, 1975-88, prof. geology, dir. Glaciological and Arctic Scis. Inst., 1975—; dir., state geologist Idaho Geol. Survey, 1975-88; elected rep. Legislature of State of Idaho, Boise, 1992—; prin. investigator, geol. cons. sci. contracts and projects for govt. agys., univs., pvt. corps., geographic socs., 1946—; geophys. cons. Nat. Park Svc., NASA, USAF, Nat. Acad. Sci.; organizer leader USAF-Harvard Mt. St. Elias Expdn., 1946; chief geologist Am. Mt. Everest Expdn., Nepal, 1963; dir. Nat. Geographic Soc. Alaskan Glacier Commemorative Project, 1964—; organizer field leader Nat. Geographic Soc. Joint U.S.-Can. Mt. Kennedy Yukon Meml. Mapping Expdn., 1965, Muséo Argentino de Ciencias Naturales, Patagonian expdn. and glacier study for Inst.. Geologico del Peru & Am. Geog. Soc., 1949-50, participant adv. missions People's Republic of China, 1981, 86, 88, geol. expdns. Himalaya, Nepal, 1963, 84, 87, USAF mission to Ellesmere Land and Polar Sea, 1951; organizer, ops. officer USN-LTA blimp geophysics flight to North Pole area for Office Naval Rsch., 58; prin. investigator U.S. Naval Oceanographic Office Rsch. Ice Island T-3 Polar Sea, 1967-68, 70-73; dir. lunar field sta. simulation program USAF-Boeing Co., 1959-60; co-prin. investigator Nat. Geographic Soc. 30 Yr. Remap of Lemon & Taku Glaciers, Juneau Icefield, 1989-92; exec. dir. Found. for Glacier and Environ. Rsch., Pacific Sci. Ctr., Seattle, 1955-95, chmn., 1992—, pres., 1955-85, trustee, 1960—, organizer, dir. Juneau (Alaska) Icefield Rsch. Program (JIRP), 1946—; cons. Dept. Hwys. State of Alaska, 1965; chmn., exec. dir. World Ctr. for Exploration Found., N.Y.C., 1968-71; dir., mem. adv. bd. Idaho Geol. Survey, 1975-88; chmn. nat. coun. JSHS program U.S. Army Rsch. Office and Acad. Applied Sci., 1982-89; sci. dir. U.S. Army Rsch. Office-Nat. Sci. and Humanities Symposia program, 1991—; disting. guest prof. China U. Geoscis., Wuhan, 1981-88, Changchun U. Earth Scis., People's Republic of China, 1988—; adj. prof. U. Alaska, 1986—. Author: Field Manual of Glaciological and Arctic Sciences; co-author books on Alaskan glaciers and Nepal geology; contbr. over 200 reports, sci. papers to profl. jours., ency. articles, chpts. to books, monographs; prodr., nat. lectr. films and videos. Past mem. nat. exploring com., nat. sea exploring com. Boy Scouts Am.; past mem. nat. adv. bd. Embry Riddle Aero. U.; bd. dirs. Idaho Rsch. Found.; pres. state divsn. Mich. UN Assn., 1970-73; mem. Centennial and Health Environ. Commns., Moscow, Idaho, 1987—. With USN, 1943-46, PTO. Decorated 11 campaign and battle stars; named Leader of Tomorrow Seattle C. of C. and Time mag., 1953, one of Ten Outstanding Young Men U.S. Jaycees, 1954; recipient commendation for lunar environ. study USAF, 1960, Hubbard medal (co-recipient with Mt. Everest expdn. team) Nat. Geog. Soc., 1963, Elisha Kent Kane Gold medal Geog. Soc. Phila., 1964, Karo award Soc. Mil. Engrs., 1966, Franklin L. Burr award Nat. Geog. Soc., 1967, Commendation Boy Scouts Am., 1970, Disting. Svc. commendation plaque UN Assn. U.S., Disting. Svc. commendation State of Mich. Legis., 1975, Outstanding Civilian Svc. medal U.S. Army Rsch. Office, 1977, Outstanding Leadership in Minerals Edn. commendations Idaho Mining Assn., 1985, 87, Nat. Disting. Tchg. award Assn. Am. Geographers, 1996; recipient numerous grants NSF, Nat. Geog. Soc., others, 1948—. Fellow Geol. Soc. Am., Arctic Inst. N.Am., Explorers Club; mem. councilor AAAS (Pacific divsn. 1978-88), AIME, Am. Geophys. Union, Internat. Glaciological Soc. (past councilor), ASME (hon. nat. lectr.), Assn. of Am. State Geologists (hon.), Am. Assn. Amateur Oarsmen (life), Am. Alpine Club (past councilor, life mem.), Alpine Club (London), Appalachian Club (hon. corr.), Brit. Mountaineering Assn. (hon., past v.p.), The Mountaineers (hon.), Cambridge U. Mountaineering Club (hon.), Himalyan Club (Calcutta), English Speaking Union (nat. lectr.), Naval Res. Assn. (life), Dutch Treat Club, Circumnavigators Club (life), Adventurers Club N.Y. (medalist), Am. Legion, Harvard Club (N.Y.C. and Seattle), Sigma Xi, Phi Beta Kappa (pres. Epsilon chpt. Mich. State U. 1969-70), Phi Kappa Phi. Republican. Methodist. Home: 514 E 1st St Moscow ID 83843-2814 Office: U Idaho Coll Mines & Earth Resources Mines Bldg Rm 204 Moscow ID 83843 also: House of Reps Idaho State House Boise ID 83720 also: Found for Glacier & Environ Rsch 4470 N Douglas Hwy Juneau AK 99801

MILLER, MICHAEL, literary arts researcher, writer; b. Colo., May 19, 1949; s. Bryan and Lorraine (Cull) M.; m. Marie Antoinette Montez; 1 child, Estrella Claudine. Student, Inst. Allende, San Miguel, Mex., 1968; BA in History, N.Mex. Highlands U., 1972; MA in Info. Sci., U. Denver, 1974. Mem. faculty N.Mex. Highlands U., Las Vegas, 1974-76; dir. LRC U. N.Mex. No. br., Santa Cruz, 1976-80; archivist N.Mex. State Archives, Santa Fe, 1980-86; dir. N.Mex. State Archives, Santa Cruz, 1986-90; dir., asst. prof. Ctr. S.W. Rsch. U. N.Mex., Albuquerque, 1990-95; dir. rsch. and lit. arts N.Mex. Hispanic Cultural Ctr., Albuquerque, 1995—; mem. editl. adv. bd. S.W. Heritage, Hobbsd, 1980-86, N.Mex. Almanac, Santa Fe, 1990-93; mem. hist. adv. bd. State of N.Mex., 1994—. Author: Monuments of Adobe, 1992 (award of merit), New Mexico Scrapbook, 1991; editor: Hispanic Heroes, 1993. Mem. N.Mex. Cuarto Centennial Com.; vol. Big Bros./Big Sisters, Santa Fe, 1996—; firefighter La Puebla (N.Mex.) Vol. Fire Dept., 1979—; commr. La Puebla Cmty. Ditch, 1995—; mem. La Communidad de la Puebla, 1994—. Grantee Nat. Endowment for Arts, 1990, N.Mex. Arts Coun., 1994; recipient award of excellence Tex. Graphics, 1992, Offcl. Quincentennial Publ. award Archdiocese of Santa Fe, 1992. Mem. N.Mex. Hist. Soc., N.Mex. Libr. Assn., Soc. S.W. Archivists, Chimayo Cultural Preservation Assn., N.Mex. Preservation Alliance (founder). Democrat. Roman Catholic. Home: PO Box 22 Santa Cruz NM 87567 Office: NMex Hispanic Cultural Ctr 1701 4th SW Albuquerque NM 87102

MILLER, MONA JOY DEUTSCH, lawyer; b. Coral Gables, Fla., Feb. 9, 1953; d. Irvin and Freda (Smukler) Deutsch; m. Steven Jeffrey Miller, Aug. 21, 1977; 1 child, Thaïs Helene. AB with distinction, Cornell U., 1973; JD, Stanford U., 1977. Bar: Calif. 1977, U.S. Dist. Ct. (cen. dist.) Calif. 1978, U.S. Dist. Ct. (so. dist.) Calif. 1994, U.S. Supreme Ct. 1994. Assoc. McKenna, Conner & Cuneo, Los Angeles, 1977-83, ptnr., 1983-89; of counsel Blanc, Williams, Johnston & Kronstadt, L.A., 1990-97, Berman, Blanchard, Mausner & Resser, L.A., 1997—. Mem. Univ. Synagogue, Brentwood, Calif., 1980—, sisterhood co-v.p. for programming, 1990-93. Mem. Los Angeles County Bar Assn. (real property and comml. law and bankruptcy sects.), Women Lawyers Assn. L.A. (bd. dirs. 1995-96, chair subcom. status of women in profession 1995—), Calif. Attys. Fed. Credit Union (bd. dirs. 1982), Phi Beta Kappa. Jewish. Office: Berman Blanchard Mausner & Resser 4727 Wilshire Blvd # 500 Los Angeles CA 90010

MILLER, MONICA JEANNE, public relations administrator; b. Laramie, Wyo., Mar. 18, 1948; d. R. Walt and Margaret Louise (Carroll) M.; m. Stephen Lee Spellman, June 3, 1973 (div. Aug. 1980); 1 child, Andrew M. French. BS cum laude in Journalism, U. Wyo., 1971. cert. food safety Nat. Restaurant Assn. Press officer Min. of Agr., Botswana, 1971-73; cmty. rels. officer Colo. Civil Rights Commn., Denver, 1973-80; chief info. officer Colo. Dept. Personnel, Denver, 1980-83, Colo. Divsn. Parks and Recreation, Denver, 1986-88; pub. rels. mgr. Unicover Corp., Cheyenne, Wyo., 1989-91, Taco John's Internat., Inc., Cheyenne, Wyo., 1991—; cons. The Promethean Corp., Denver, 1983-85. Author: (with others) Sexual Harassment in Public Employment, 1983. Dir. Children's Heritage Montessori Sch., Cheyenne, 1993-95, Wyo. Higher Edn. Assistance Authority, 1996—. Mem. ARC (High Plains chpt. dir. 1996—), Soc. Profl. Journalists, Pub. Rels. Soc. Am., Greater Cheyenne C. of C. (vice chair 1995—), Rotary (dir. 1996—). Democrat. Home: 6840 Bomar Dr Cheyenne WY 82009 Office: Taco Johns Internat Inc 808 W 20th St Cheyenne WY 82001-3404

MILLER, NEIL ALLEN, police agent; b. Lincoln, Nebr., Dec. 5, 1952; s. Royce Jordan Miller and Norma Jean (Kahlbau) Poucher; m. C. Susan Wright; children: Sarah Louise, David Allen. AS, Pikes Peak C.C., 1979; BS in Criminology, Met. St. Coll., 1990. Security guard St. Francis Hosp., Colorado Springs, 1977-81; police officer U. Colo. Med. Ctr. Police Dept., Denver, 1981-83, Broomfield (Colo.) Police Dept., 1983-90; police agt. Lakewood (Colo.) Police Dept., 1990—; team watch mem. USN Res., Aurora, 1991—. Coach spl. olympics Fletcher-Miller Sch., Lakewood, 1991—. Sgt. USMC, 1971-78. Recipient Svc. to Handicap award Internat. Toastmasters Club, 1993, World Bench Press Record 198# USPF/World Police-Fire Athletic Assn., 1993, Nat. Bench Press Records 198# NASA Drug Free Assn., 1993, Colo. State Powerlifting Record 198# NASA and Colo. Police and Fire Athletic Assn., 1986-93, Colo. Police/Fire Athletic. Assn. 198#/220# title/record holder powerlifting, 1986-97, NASA Powerlifting Nat. and World Records, Masters, 220 lb., 1996, Colo. Police-Fire Assn. Masters 220 lb. Record Holder Powerlifting, 1996, NASA World Bench Press Record 227#, 1996, Colo. Police-Fire Assn. Record and Title Holder Powerlifting, 1996-97, Colo. ADFPA State Record, BP, Masters 220#, 1995-97. Mem. Vietnam Vets of Am., VFW, Am. Legion, Fraternal Order of Police, Am. Fedn. of Police, Lakewood Police Athletic League. Home: 2958 Will Ave Cir Broomfield CO 80020 Office: Lakewood Police Dept 445 S Allison Pky Lakewood CO 80226-3106

MILLER, NELSON ALVIN, retired army officer, public affairs administrator; b. Bunkie, La., Apr. 26, 1947; s. Nelson Alvin Miller and Barbara Jean (Rarick) Lohman; m. Susan Reed, Jan 13, 1975 (div. Jan. 1976); 1 child, Michael; m. Jeanette A. Christy, Aug 14, 1982; children: Shaine, Jamie. AA, N.Mex. Mil. Inst., 1968; BA in Bus. magna cum laude, U. N.Mex., 1979; MA in Mgmt., Webster U., Kansas City, Mo., 1983. Commd. 2d lt. U.S. Army, 1969, advanced through grades to maj., 1980, ret., 1989; dep. comdt. N.Mex. Mil. Inst., Roswell, 1989-95, pub. affairs officer, 1995—; adj. univ. lectr., 1995—. Author: Leadership Primer, 1995, Co-Author: U.S. Army Nuclear Mission, Area Analysis, 1981. Bd. dirs. Big Brothers-Big Sisters, Gallup, N.Mex., 1985-89, ARC, N.Mex., 1985-93; sec. Rotary, Gallup, 1985-88; basketball coach, Am. Legion, Leavenworth, Kans., 1984; elder Immanuel Luth. Ch., N.Mex., 1985-94. Decorated Legion of Merit, Bronze Star. Republican. Home: 3409 Highland Rd Roswell NM 88201 Office: Pub Affairs Office NMMI 101 W College Blvd Roswell NM 88201-5174

MILLER, O'MALLEY MURRAY, lawyer; b. Sept. 25, 1951; m. Ann W. (Wapple) Miller; children: Brendan, Kevin, Brian, Grady. BA with distinction, Stanford U., 1973; JD, U. So. Calif., 1976. Bar: Calif. 1976. Ptnr. Allen, Matkins, Leck, Gamble & Mallory, 1981-92, Munger, Tolles & Olson, L.A., 1992—; bd. dirs. Skid Row Housing Corp. Contbr. articles to profl. jours. Trustee Good Samaritan Hosp. Mem. ABA, Am. Coll. Real Estate Laywers, Calif. Bar Assn. (exec. com. real property law sect. 1989-90), L.A. County Bar Assn. (exec. com. real property sect. 1980—, chair, 1991-92). Office: Munger Tolles & Olson 355 S Grand Ave Fl 35 Los Angeles CA 90071-1560

MILLER, PAIGE, port executive. Pres. Port of Seattle. Office: Office of the Commn Pier 69 211 Alaskan Way Seattle WA 98121

MILLER, PHILIP GRAY, artist; b. Seattle, Aug. 18, 1947; s. Robert Chester and Angnes Minto (Weston) M. Student, Whitman Coll., Walla Walla, Wash., 1965-69. Artist, musician Gallery Functional Art, Santa Monica, L.A., 1970—; furniture maker Sonrisa Bernice Steinbaum Gallery, N.Y.C.; cons. Inner Cities Murals Project, L.A., 1992—, Met. Transp. Agy., L.A., 1993-94. Author (novella) Death Valley Girls, 1989, (screenplay) Hurt By Love, 1993, (book) Cynic's Guide to Spiritual Awakening, 1993; curator Punch Gallery, L.A., 1993; writer, actor, film maker; works represented in permanent collections Conrado Terasas City Coun., L.A., Laguna Beach (Calif.) Mus., Venice (Calif.) Family Clinic, AIDS Project L.A.; represented in group shows Punch Gallery, 1996, Gallery Function al Art, 1997. Min. Universal Life Ch., Seattle, L.A., 1969—. Recipient Design 100 award Met. Home, 1989.

MILLER, PHOEBE AMELIA, marketing professional; b. Jan. 13, 1948; d. William Prescott and Elizabeth Helen (Lucker) M.. BA in Math., U. Wis., 1970; postgrad., Stanford U., 1973, Golden Gate U., 1975-76. Engr. Bechtel, San Francisco, 1972-77; asst. mgr. Rand Info. Systems, San Francisco, 1977-79; sr. mktg. rep. Computer Sci. Corp., San Francisco, 1979-81; mgr. distbr. sales COGNOS Corp., Walnut Creek, Calif., 1981-86; owner, mgr. P.A. Miller & Assocs., San Francisco, 1986—. Office: PA Miller & Assocs 1750 Montgomery St San Francisco CA 94111-1003

MILLER, RANNE B., lawyer; b. Claremore, Okla., Aug. 22, 1940. BBA, U. Wash., 1963; JD, U. N.Mex., 1967. Bar: N.Mex. 1967. Mem. Miller, Stratvert, Torgerson & Schlenker, Albuquerque. Bd. editors Nat. Resources Jour., 1966-67. Fellow N.Mex. State Bar Found.; mem. Am. Bd. Trial Advocates (pres. N.Mex. chpt. 1976-77), Am. Coll. Trial Lawyers, Fed. Bar Com., State Bar N.Mex., Albuquerque Bar Assn., Phi Kappa Phi. Office: Miller Stratvert Torgerson & Schlenker PO Box 25687 500 Marquette Ave NW Ste 1100 Albuquerque NM 87102

MILLER, RICHARD ALAN, agricultural consultant, hypnotherapist; b. Everett, Wash., Mar. 16, 1944; s. John Harrison and Katheryn Ada (Nelson) M.; m. Patricia Merz, June 30, 1964 (div. 1972); 1 child, Paula Anne. BS in Physics, Washington State U., 1966; Degree in Fluidics (hon.), MIT, 1967; MS in Physics, U. Del., 1968; engr. in tng./profl. engr., U. Wash., 1969. Cert. giophysicist, 1972, hypnotherapist, 1987. Physicist instruments products div. Dupont, Wilmington, Del., 1966-68; physicist The Boeing Co./MASD, Seattle, 1968-71; biophysicist dept. anesthesiology U. Wash., Seattle, 1971-73; owner, mgr. The Beltane Corp., Inc., Seattle, 1973-80; ltd. ptnr. Western Herb Farms/Country Spice, Seattle, 1980-82; owner, mgr., writer Orgn. Advancement of Knowledge, Grants Pass, Oreg., 1983—; owner, mgr., broker Northwest Bots., Inc., Grants Pass, 1987—; ptnr., mgr., telemktg. program Florals, N.W., Grants Pass & Vancouver, B.C., Can., 1994; ptnr., mgr. broker Nat. Collection Co., Grants Pass & Denman, Can., 1992; ptnr., mgr. telemktg. program N.W. Naturals, Inc., Grants Pass, 1991; ptnr., sales mgr. Coltsfoot, Inc., Grants Pass, 1986—; advisor Ariz. Herb Growers Assn., Phoenix, 1988—; mem. New Crops Devel. Oreg. Dept. Agriculture; cons. in field; lectr. in field. Author: The Magical Mushroom Handbook, 1977, The Magical and Ritual Use of Herbs, 1978, The Magical and Ritual Use of Herbs, 1983, German edit., Spanish edit., 1995, The Potential of Herbs as a Cash Crop, 1985, The Magical and Ritual Use of Aphrodisiacs, 1985, German hardback and softback edit., 1992, The Magical and Ritual Use of Perfumes, 1990, German hardback edit., 1991, Spanish softback edit., 1990, Native Plants of Commercial Importance, 1991, The Modern Alchemist, 1991, Pantheon: Archetypal Gods in Daily Living, 1992, The Diamond Body: A Modern Alchemical View of the Philosopher's Stone, 1992, The Modern Alchemist, 1994, spl. hardback edit., 1995; contbr. articles to profl. jours., chpts. to books. Amb. All Am. City, Grants Pass, 1987—. Small Bus. Innovative Rsch. grantee USDA, 1986, Neighborhood Devel. grantee SBA, 1977, USDA grantee, 1985, 95. Mem. Am. Coun. Hypnotist Examiners, Masons. Home and Office: Northwest Botanicals Inc 493 Contant Ln Grants Pass OR 97527

MILLER, RICHARD FRANKLIN, educational consultant, researcher; b. San Francisco, Sept. 9, 1927; s. Henry G. and Hulda M. M. AB, San Francisco State U., 1950; MA, U. Calif.-Berkeley, 1964, EdD, 1970. Cert. secondary tchr., gen. supr. Calif. With San Francisco Unified Sch. Dist., 1956-89, tchr. bus. edn., econs. and social studies Mission H.S., 1967-89, adminstr. career edn. program, 1970-80; ednl. cons., 1989—. Mem. San Francisco Symphony, Fine Arts Mus. Soc. Served to sgt., U.S. Army, 1952-54. Fellow in edn. U. Calif.-Berkeley, 1974-75. Mem. ASCD, United Educators San Francisco, Phi Delta Kappa. Democrat. Unitarian. *Personal philosophy: A quality education must be available to all.*

MILLER, ROBERT CARMI, JR., microbiology educator, university administrator; b. Elgin, Ill., Aug. 10, 1942; s. Robert C. and Melba I. (Steinke) M.; m. Patricia A. Black, Aug. 29, 1964; children: Geoffrey T., Christopher J. BS in Physics, Trinity Coll., Hartford, Conn., 1964; MS in Biophysics, Pa. State U., 1965; PhD in Molecular Biology, U. Pa., 1969. USPHS trainee U. Pa., Phila., 1966-69; postdoctoral fellow U. Wis., Madison, 1969-70; rsch. assoc., Am. Cancer Soc. postdoctoral fellow MIT, Cambridge, 1970-71; asst. assoc. prof. U. B.C., Vancouver, 1971-79, prof. microbiology, 1980—, head dept. microbiology, 1982-85, dean sci., 1985-88, v.p. rsch., 1988-95, univ. senate, 1985-88; assoc. vice provost for rsch., dir. technology transfer U. Wash., Seattle, 1995—; vis. prof. Inst. Molecular Biology, U. Geneva, Switzerland, 1976; mem. grants com. on genetics Med. Rsch. Coun., 1980-82; mem. Grants Panel A Nat. Cancer Inst., 1981-85; biotech. com. B.C. Sci. Coun., 1981-87, univ./industry program grant com., 1987-92; biotech. com. Med. Rsch. Coun., 1983; assoc. com. for biotech. NRC, 1983-86; strategic grant com. biotech. NSERC, 1985-87; bd. dirs. Paprican, Discovery Found.,

Sci. Coun. B.C., TRIUMF. Assoc. editor Virology, 1974-85, Jour. Virology, 1975-84; contbr. 100 articles to profl. jours.; author research papers. Recipient gold medal Nat. Sci. Coun. B.C., 1993; grantee Natural Sci. and Engring. Rsch. Coun., 1971-96, Med. Rsch. Coun., 1981, 86-89, Nat. Cancer Inst., 1982-86. Office: Office Technology Transfer Univ Wash 1107 NE 45th St Seattle WA 98105-4631

MILLER, ROBERT DAVID, forensic psychiatrist; b. Chapel Hill, N.C., Sept. 4, 1941; s. Augustus Taylor and Adeline Helen (Porombovics) M. BS cum laude, Davidson Coll., 1964; PhD in Biochemistry, Duke U., 1972, MD, 1973. Cert. Am. Bd. Psychiatry and Neurology, Am. Bd. Forensic Psychiatry. Resident in psychiatry Duke U., Durham, N.C., 1973-76; with psychiatry dept. Duke U., Durham, 1976-82; staff psychiatrist John Umstead Hosp., Butner, N.C., 1976-78, dir. admissions, 1978-80, resident tng. dir., 1980-82; dir. forensic tng. Mendota Mental Health Inst., Madison, 1982-91; clin. prof. psychiatry, lectr. law U. Wis., 1983-91; prof. psychiatry U. Colo., 1991—; lectr. in law U. Denver Law Sch., 1993—. Contbr. articles to profl. jours. Fellow Am. Acad. Forensic Scis. (program chmn. 1985, sec. psychiat. sect. 1987), Am. Psychiat. Assn.; mem. Am. Acad. Psychiatry and Law (exec. coun., sec. treas., v.p., pres.), Internat. Acad. Law and Mental Health. Democrat. Jewish. Home: 8190 Tempest Ridge Way Parker CO 80134-5866 Office: Colo Health Scis Ctr Box C-249-27 4200 E 9th Ave Denver CO 80220-3706

MILLER, ROBERT G., retail company executive; b. 1944. With Albertson's Inc., 1961-89, exec. v.p. retail ops., 1989-91; chmn. bd., CEO Fred Meyer Inc., Portland, Oreg., 1991—. Office: Fred Meyer Inc 3800 SE 22nd Ave Portland OR 97202-2918*

MILLER, ROBERT JOSEPH, governor, lawyer; b. Evanston, Ill., Mar. 30, 1945; s. Ross Wendell and Coletta Jane (Doyle) M.; m. Sandra Ann Searles, Oct. 17, 1949; children: Ross, Corrine, Megan. BA in Polit. Sci., U. Santa Clara, 1967; JD, Loyola U., Los Angeles, 1971. First legal advisor Las Vegas (Nev.) Met. Police Dept., 1973-75; justice of the peace Las Vegas Twp., 1975-78; dep. dist. atty. Clark County, Las Vegas, 1971-73, dist. atty., 1979-86; lt. gov. State of Nev., 1987-89, acting gov., 1989-90, gov., 1991—. Chmn. Nev. Commn. on Econ. Devel., Carson City, 1987-91, Nev. Commn. on Tourism, Carson City, 1987-91; mem. Pres. Reagan's Task Force on Victims of Crime, 1982; chmn. Nev. divsn. Am. Cancer Soc., 1988-90. Mem. Nat. Dist. Attys. Assn. (pres. 1984-85), Western Govs. Assn. (chmn. 1993-94), Nat. Govs. Assn. (vice chmn. exec. com. 1995-96, chmn. 1996-97, past chmn. com. on justice and pub. safety, chmn. legal affairs com. 1992-94, lead gov. on transp. 1992—), Nev. Dist. Attys. Assn. (pres. 1979, 83). Democrat. Roman Catholic. Home: Gov Mansion 606 N Mountain St Carson City NV 89703-3955 Office: State of Nev Office of Gov Capitol Bldg Carson City NV 89710*

MILLER, ROBERT REUBEN, political science educator; b. Tel Aviv, Sept. 30, 1949; came to U.S., 1977; s. Kalman and Nadia (Davidov) M.; m. Esther F. Farkas, June 22, 1986; children: Nurit S., Adiv K. BA in History and Philosophy, Tel Aviv U., 1976; MA in History, U. Bridgeport, 1979; MA in Internat. Studies, U. Denver, 1982, PhD, 1987. Data analyst Inst. Ct. Mgmt., Denver, 1982; editorial intern U. Denver, 1982-86; asst. prof. U. Colo., Denver, 1990—; rsch. assoc. Abbott Assoc., Inc., Springfield, Va., 1986-87; vis. prof. Old Dominion U., 1988-89, U. No. Colo., 1989-90; instr. Metro. State Coll., Denver, 1981-93, U. Colo., Boulder, 1981-82, St. Francis Coll., Denver, summer, 1982, U. Denver, 1981-86; computer rsch. asst. Grad. Sch. Internat. Studies/U. Denver., 1981-86; cons. Risk Mgmt. Internat., Denver, 1987-88, Moran, Stahl and Boyer, Inc., Boulder, 1985-86; guest lectr. USAF War Coll., Montgomery, Ala., 1994, Air Force Res. Officer Corps., Greeley, 1989, Army-Air Force Ctr. for Low Intensity Conflict, Langley, 1989; presenter in field. Contbr. articles to profl. jours. Sgt. Israel Army, 1967-71. Weinberg fellow Tel Aviv U., 1973, Dr. Irving Vinnick fellow, 1993; Dr. James Halsey internat. scholar U. Bridgeport, 1977; travel grantee Denver U., 1985. Mem. Am. Polit. Sci. Assn. (rsch. travel grantee 1983), Can. Assn. for Security and Intelligence. Home: 520 S Poplar Way Denver CO 80224-1557

MILLER, ROBERT RYAL, history educator; b. Lake Andes, S.D., Oct. 3, 1923; s. John Carroll and Hazel C. (Peck) M.; m. Penelope Handsaker, June 12, 1955. AB, U. Calif., Berkeley, 1948, MA, 1951, PhD, 1960. Asst. prof. history U. Southwestern La., Lafayette, 1959-60; asst. to assoc. prof. N.Mex. State U., Las Cruces, 1960-68; prof. history Ind. U. Southeast, New Albany, Ind., 1970; prof. history Calif. State U., Hayward, 1970-80, prof. emeritus, 1980—; vis. prof. San Marcos U., Lima, Peru, 1966. Author: For Science and National Glory, 1968, Mexico: A History, 1985, Shamrock and Sword, 1989; editor: Mexican War Jour., 1991. Served in U.S. Army Air Corps, 1942-46, Med. Mem. Conf. on Latin Am. History, Calif. Hist. Soc.

MILLER, ROBERT SCOTT, mental health administrator, social worker; b. Seattle, Dec. 12, 1947; s. Bert Lester and Carol Theresa (Gustafson) M.; m. Karen Ann Staake, Nov. 12, 1977; children: Sarah, Megan, Emily. BA in Sociology cum laude, Seattle Pacific U., 1970; AM in Social Work, U. Chgo., 1972; MA in Human Resources Mgmt., Pepperdine U., 1977. Cert. social worker, Wash. Br. supr. Wash. State Dept. Social and Health Svcs., Oak Harbor and Anacortes, 1975-78; supr. casework Wash. State Dept. Social and Health Svcs., Everett, 1973-75; lectr., coord. rural community mental health project U. Wash., Seattle, 1978-83; exec. dir. Armed Svcs. YMCA, Oak Harbor, 1984-86; area dir. United Way of Island County, Oak Harbor, 1986-88, exec. dir., 1988-92; exec. dir. Saratoga Community Mental Health, Coupeville, Wash., 1992-93; outpatient therapist, attention-deficit/hyperactivity disorder mental health specialist Cath. Cmty. Svcs. Northwest, Oak Harbor, Wash., 1993-96; dir. Cath. Cmty. Svcs. Northwest, Oak Harbor and Mount Vernon, Wash., 1996—, Island and Skagit Counties; part-time instr. sociology Chapman U., Orange, Calif., 1988-95; mem. adv. bd. Island Family Health Ctr., Oak Harbor, 1990-91; project mgr. risk mgmt. Com. Associated Provider Network. Contbr. articles to profl. jours. Bd. dirs. Puget Sound chpt. Huntington's Disease Soc. Am., 1989-93, pres., 1991, fundraising chmn., 1989-91, v.p., 1990; mem. adv. bd. United Ways Wash., 1991-92; chmn. Island County bd. emergency food and shelter program Fed. Emergency Mgmt. Agy.; vice chmn. Cmty. Resource Network, Oak Harbor, 1991; mem. steering com. Grater Oak Harbor Econ. Summit, 1991; mem. strategic planning com. Whidbey Gen. Hosp., Coupeville, 1992-93; mem. exec. com. Mt. Baker coun. Boy Scouts Am., 1993; bd. dirs. Opportunity Coun., Bellingham, 1993-94; bd. dirs. Concerts on the Cove, Coupeville, 1993-96, v.p., 1994-95; mem. Oak Harbor Citizen's Comprehensive Plan Task Force, 1994; mem. Readiness to Learn Coupeville Cmty. Team, 1996—; project mgr., risk mgmt. com. Associated Provider Network, 1997—. Recipient outstanding svc. award Armed Svcs. YMCA of U.S., Dallas, 1985, two program merit awards McDonald's Corp., Oak Harbor, 1986; named Alumni of a Growing Vision, Seattle Pacific U., 1991, Diplomat of Yr. Greater Oak Harbor C. of C., 1991. Mem. NASW (bd. dirs. Wash. chpt. 1982-85), Wash. Assn. Social Welfare (pres. 1975-76), Acad. Cert. Social Workers, Rotary. Lutheran. Home: 2450 S Rocky Way Coupeville WA 98239-9610 Office: Cath Community Svcs NW 1121 SE Dock St Oak Harbor WA 98277-4067

MILLER, ROBERT STEVEN, secondary school educator; b. Van Nuys, Calif., Aug. 9, 1963; s. Frederick Earl and Mary (Brash) M. AA, L.A. Valley Coll., 1984; BSBA, Calif. State U., 1987, MA in History, 1990. Cert. substitute tchr., 1993-96. Study group leader, study skills researcher Ednl. Opportunity Program Calif. State U., L.A., 1989-93, faculty mem. History Dept., lectr., 1990-92; sec., treas. Agate/Amethyst World, Inc., Van Nuys, Calif., 1986-91, v.p., 1992—; with Summer Bridge Program Calif. State U., L.A., 1994—; tchr. history Chatsworth (Calif.) H.S., 1996—. Mng. editor (jour.) Perspectives, 1990, editor-in-chief, 1991. Jake Gimbel scholar, 1989. Mem. Am. Historians Assn., The Soc. for Historians of Am. Fgn. Rels., Phi Alpha Theta (v.p. 1990, pres. 1991, Eta Xi chpt., Ledeboer Family scholar 1989), Pi Sigma Epsilon (v.p. 1986-87, pres. 1988 Phi chpt.), Mu Kappa Tau (pres. and founder 1989, Calif State U. LA chpt.). Democrat. Roman Catholic. Home: 13750 Runnymede St Van Nuys CA 91405-1515 Office: Chatsworth HS 10027 Lurline Ave Chatsworth CA 91311

MILLER, ROBERT STEVENS, JR., finance professional; b. Portland, Oreg., Nov. 4, 1941; s. Robert Stevens and Barbara (Weston) M.; m. Margaret Rose Kyger, Nov. 9, 1966; children: Christopher John, Robert Stevens, Alexander Lamont. AB with distinction, Stanford U., 1963; LLB, Harvard U., 1966; MBA, Stanford U., 1968. Bar: Calif. bar 1966. Fin. analyst Ford Motor Co., Dearborn, Mich., 1968-71; spl. studies mgr. Ford Motor Co., Mexico City, 1971-73; dir. fin. Ford Asia-Pacific, Inc., Melbourne, Australia, 1974-77, Ford Motor Co., Caracas, Venezuela, 1977-79; v.p., treas. Chrysler Corp., Detroit, 1980-81, exec. v.p. fin., 1981-90, vice chmn., 1990-92; sr. ptnr. James D. Wolfensohn, Inc., N.Y.C., 1992-93; chmn. bd. dirs. Morrison Knudsen Corp., 1995-96; bd. dirs. Fed.-Mogul, Fluke, Pope & Talbot, Coleman, Symantec, Morrison Knudsen.

MILLER, ROBERT VICTOR, scientific research administrator; b. Batavia, N.Y., Apr. 30, 1936; s. James Joseph and Josephine (Brunovsky) M.; m. Mildred Rose Canne, June 8, 1956; children: Stephen, Cheryl, Eric, Elizabeth. BS, Cornell U., 1958, PhD, 1964; MS, U. Ark., 1961. Rsch. asst. prof. U. Md., Solomons, 1963-65; systematic zoologist U.S. Bureau Comml. Fisheries, Miami, Fla., 1965-71; leader marine mammal rsch. program U.S. Nat. Marine Fisheries Svc., Washington, 1971-80; dep. dir. NOAA/Nat. Marine Fisheries Svc. Nat. Marine Mammal Lab, Seattle, 1980—; mem. affiliate faculty U. Miami, Fla., 1966-71, Fla. Atlantic U., Miami, 1966-71, U. Wash. Sch. Fisheries, Seattle, 1983—; U.S. chair U.S.-Russia Marine Mammal Project, 1973—. Author nat. reports to internat. orgns., papers in field. Coord. blood donor drives NOAA campus Puget Sound Blood Ctr., Seattle, 1990—. Mem. Am. Soc. Ichthyologists and Herpetologists, Am. Soc. Mammalogy, Am. Inst. Fisheries Rsch. Biologists, Soc. Marine Mammalogists, Soc. for Preservation and Encouragement of Barber Shop Quartet Singing in Am. (sec. 1989—). Office: Nat Marine Mammal Lab 7600 Sand Point Way NE Bldg 4 Seattle WA 98115-6349

MILLER, RONALD GRANT, journalist; b. Santa Cruz, Calif., Feb. 28, 1939; s. Fred Robert and Evelyn Lenora (Mosher) M.; m. Darla-Jean Irene Rode, Nov. 2, 1963. AA, Monterey Peninsula Coll., 1958; BA, San Jose State U., 1961. Reporter Santa Cruz (Calif.) Sentinel, 1959-62; reporter, chief news bur. San Jose (Calif.) Mercury News, 1962-77, editor T.V., 1977—; syndicated TV columnist Knight Ridder Syndicate, 1978—; commentator, critic Sta. KLOK, San Jose, 1981-83; panelist, guest speaker various orgns., 1978—; nat. judge Cableace awards, 1987. Author: (foreword) Les Brown's Encyclopedia of Television, 1992; co-author: Masterpiece Theatre, 1995, Author: Mystery! A Celebration, 1996; contbr. articles and short fiction to various mags. Recipient Nat. Spot News Photo award Sigma Delta Chi, 1961, Outstanding Alumnus award San Jose State U. Dept. Journalism and Mass Comm., 1985, Nat. Headline award Press Club Atlantic City, 1994. Mem. TV Critics Assn. (nat. pres. 1981). Democrat. Home and Office: 1554 Arbor Ave Los Altos CA 94024-5913

MILLER, RUTH ELSIE, mathematics educator, industrial designer; b. St. Louis, Mar. 12, 1926; d. Martin Paul Herman and Elizabeth (Houston) Stiller; m. Truman J. Miller, Dec. 28, 1946; children: Stephen J., Gordon T., Marilyn P., Donald T., Ruth A. BS, Utah State U., 1967. Cert. tchr. maths., English, Utah. Indsl. designer Thiokol Chem., Brigham City, Utah, 1958-65; tchr. Ogden (Utah) City Schs., 1967-88. Author: Life & Times of Herman Stiller, 1990, William Houston of Ballygawley, 1992, John Franklin Miller, 1992; contbr. articles to profl. jours. Ch. organist, 1958-88. Mem. 1st Presbyterian Ch., Nat. Republican Senational Comm. Republican. Presbyterian. Home: 1585 Sumac Dr Logan UT 84321

MILLER, SONJA GLAASER, social worker; b. Coos Bay, Oreg., Oct. 16, 1953; d. Edward Glaaser and Gwendolyn (Elrod) Michael; m. David Weston Miller, Oct. 8, 1988; children: Benjamin Frank, Nicolas Johan. BS in Bus. Fin., U. Oreg., 1978; MA in Counseling/Psychology, Lewis & Clark Coll., 1994. cert. nat. counselor. Personal property appraiser Lane County Assessors, Eugene, Oreg., 1979; residential appraiser Jackson County Assessor, Medford, Oreg., 1979-82; camp dir., asst. dir. Silver Sage Girl Scout Coun., Boise, Idaho, summer 1983, 84; young program dir. Ch. of the Good Samaritan, Corvallis, Oreg., 1983-84; youth program cons. Corvallis, Oreg., 1983-86; alcohol and drug abuse counselor DePaul Adolescent Treatment Program, Portland, Oreg., 1987-88; social worker White Shield Ctr., Salvation Army, Portland, Oreg., 1994—. Author: The Director's Handbook for Youth Conferences, 1983. Mem. youth commn. Diocese of Oreg., Portland, 1980-84, chair, 1984-86, program and budget com., 1993-96, Metro-east convocation, pres., 1996—, ministry of all baptise task force, 1995, convocation rep., 1995—; youth dir. vol. St. Mark's Ch., Medford, 1979-83; counselor vol. William Temple House, Portland, 1994; co-pres. MOMS Club Portland, 1993-94; sr. warden St. Michael All Angels Ch., Portland, 1993, mem. vestry, 1990-93, convener women's group, 1994-95. Mem. ACA, Oreg. Counseling Assn. Democrat. Episcopalian. Office: The Salvation Army White Shield Ctr 2640 NW Alexandra Ave Portland OR 97210-1267

MILLER, STANLEY LLOYD, chemistry and biochemistry educator; b. Oakland, Calif., Mar. 7, 1930; s. Nathan Harry and Edith (Levy) M. BS, U. Calif., Berkeley, 1951; PhD, U. Chgo., 1954. F.B. Jewett fellow Cal-Tech., Pasadena, Calif., 1954; asst. prof. Coll. Physicians and Surgeons, N.Y.C., 1955-60; from asst. to full prof. U. Calif., San Diego, 1960—. Mem. Am. Chem. Soc., Am. Soc. Biol. Chemists, Nat. Acad. Scis., Internat. Soc. for the Study of the Origin of Life (pres. 1986-89). Office: Univ Calif San Diego Dept Chemistry 9500 Gilman Dr La Jolla CA 92093-5003

MILLER, STEPHEN HERSCHEL, surgery educator; b. N.Y.C., Jan. 12, 1941; s. Morris Louis and Mildred Lily (Beller) M.; m. Carol Susan Shapiro, Dec. 18, 1965; children: Mark, David. BS, UCLA, 1960, MD, 1964. Diplomate Am. Bd. Surgery, Am. Bd. Plastic Surgery (mem. exec. com. 1985—, chmn. written examination sect. 1985—, bd. dirs. 1984—, chmn. 1989-90). Asst. prof. surgery U. Calif., San Francisco, 1973-74; from asst. prof. to prof. surgery Milton S. Hershey Med. Ctr., Hershey, Pa., 1974-78; chief div. plastic surgery Oreg. Health Scis. U., Portland, 1979-88, Staff Scripps Clinic, La Jolla, Calif., 1988—; clin. prof. surgery U. Calif., San Diego, 1989—. Editor-in-chief Yearbook of Plastic, Reconstructive and Aesthetic Surgery, 1988-95. Physician advisor Boy Scouts Am., dist. chmn. scoutmaster exec. coun., 1983-84; bd. dirs. Temple Beth Israel, Portland, 1984-86. Recipient Physician Recognition award, 1976; grantee Med. Rsch. Found. of Oreg., 1980, Oreg. Health Scis. U., 1980. Mem. ACS (chmn. program com. 1983-87), Am. Soc. Plastic and Reconstructive Surgery (bd. dirs. 1980-89, v.p. 1985-86, pres.-elect 1986-87, pres. 1987-88, grantee 1976), Am. Assn. Plastic Surgeons (chmn. rsch. com. 1983-84, trustee 1988-91, sec. 1990-93, pres. 1994-95), Assn. Acad. Chmn. Plastic Surgery (sec./treas. 1985—). Home: 6555 Caminito Northland La Jolla CA 92037-5823 Office: Scripps Clinic 10666 N Torrey Pines Rd La Jolla CA 92037-1027

MILLER, SUZANNE MARIE, law librarian, educator; b. Sioux Falls, S.D., Feb. 25, 1954; d. John Gordon and Dorothy Margaret (Sabatka) M.; 1 child, Altinay Marie. B.A. in English, U. S.D., 1975; M.A. in Library Sci., U. Denver, 1976; postgrad. in polit. sci. U. LaVerne, 1980, postgrad. in law, 1984. Librarian II, U. S.D. Sch. of Law, Vermillion, 1977-78; law libr. U. LaVerne, Calif., 1978-85, instr. in law, 1980-85; asst. libr. tech. svcs. McGeorge Sch. Law, 1985—, prof. advanced legal rsch., 1994—. Co-author (with Elizabeth J. Pokorny) U.S. Government Documents: A Practical Guide for Library Assistants in Academic and Public Libraries, 1988; contbr. chpt. to book, articles to profl. jours. Recipient Am. Jurisprudence award Bancroft Whitney Pub. Co., 1983. Mem. Am. Assn. Law Librs., So. Calif. Assn. Law Libs. (arrangements com. 1981-82), Innovacq Users Group (chairperson, 1986-88), No. Calif. Assn. Law Librs. (mem. program com., inst. 1988), Western Pacific Assn. Law Librs. (sec. 1990-94, pres. elect 1994-95, pres. 1995-96, local arrangements chair 1997). Roman Catholic. Home: 4030 Jeffrey Ave Sacramento CA 95820-2551 Office: U of the Pacific McGeorge Sch Law Library 3200 5th Ave Sacramento CA 95817

MILLER, THOMAS ALBERT, entomology educator; b. Sharon, Pa., Jan. 5, 1940; s. Stephen Andrew and Amelia (Gorence) Miller (Chmeliar); m. Hollace Lee Gruhn, Dec. 18, 1965 (div. Nov. 1988); children: Remembrance L., Honor C.; m. Soo-ok Johnson, Dec. 13, 1991. BA in Physics, U. Calif., Riverside, 1962, PhD in Entomology, 1967. Rsch. assoc., NIH postdoctoral fellow U. Ill., Urbana, 1967-68; NATO postdoctoral fellow U. Glasgow, Scotland, 1968-69, vis. prof. zoology dept., 1973; NIH fellow U. Calif., 1964-67, asst. prof. entomology, 1969-72, assoc. prof., 1972-76, prof., entomologist, 1976—, acting head div. toxicology and physiology, 1979-80, head div., 1984-86; cons. in residence Wellcome Rsch. Labs., Berkhamsted, Eng., 1973-74, Australian Cotton Growers Rsch. Assn., 1983-84; vis. prof. U. Ariz., 1990; overseas cons. Wellcome Found., London, 1990-93; cons. AID, Ariz. Dept. Agr., Ciba-Geigy, Dow Chem. Co., DuPont Chem. Co., Food Machinery Corp., U. Calif., Berkeley, numerous others; organizer Symposium on Advances in Insect Neurobiology, Entomol. Congress, Hamburg, 1984, organizer, chmn. Symposium on Insect Autonomic Nervous System, Vancouver, 1988. Author: Insect Neurophysiological Techniques, 1979; editor 16 books; founder 2 book series; contbr. over 130 articles and revs. to sci. jours. and proc., including Jour. Analytical Chemistry, Annals Entomol. Soc. Am., Archives Insect Biochem. Physiology, Jour. Econ. Entomology, Jour. Neurochemistry, Pesticide Sci., also chpts. in books. Sgt. Calif. N.G., 1956-62. NAS exch fellow, Hungary, 1978-79, Czechoslovakia, 1986; grantee Nat. Inst. Neurol. Diseases and Stroke, 1969-72, Rockefeller Found., 1970-76, Nat. Inst. Environ. Health Scis., 1972-84; numerous others. Mem. AAAS, Entomol. Soc. Am., Am. Chem. Soc. Office: U Calif Entomology Dept Riverside CA 92521-0134

MILLER, TIMOTHY ALDEN, plastic and reconstructive surgeon; b. Inglewood, Calif., Dec. 11, 1938; s. Henry Bernard and Florence Algena (Maddock) M.; 1 child, Matthew Christopher. Student, U. Calif., Berkeley; MD, UCLA, 1963. Diplomate Am. Bd. Surgery, Am. Bd. Plastic Surgery (bd. dirs. 1991—). Intern Vanderbilt U. Hosp., Nashville, 1963-64; resident in surgery, dept. surg. pathology UCLA, 1966-67, resident, then chief resident gen. and thoracics sugery, 1967-69, acting asst. prof., 1969-70, prof. surgery, 1981—; asst. surg. resident John Hopkins Hosp., 1967; fellow plastic and reconstructive surgery U. Pitts., 1970-72; chief plastic surgery West L.A. VA Med. Ctr., 1973—; dir. Am. Bd. Plastic Surgery, 1991—. Author: (novel) Practice to Deceive, 1991; assoc. editor Jour. Plastic & Reconstructive Surgery, 1987-93, co-editor, 1994—. Trustee Children's Inst. Internat., 1995—. Capt. U.S. Army, 1964-66, Vietnam. Decorated Bronze Star; recipient Thomas Symington award Pitts. Acad. Medicine, 1971. Mem. Am. Soc. for Plastic Surgery (co-editor Jour. Plastic and Reconstructive Surgery), Am. Soc. for Aesthetic Plastic Surgery (bd. dirs. 1990-95), Plastic Surgery Ednl. Found. (bd. dirs. 1991—); trustee Children's Inst. Internat. Office: UCLA Med Ctr 200 Medical Plz Ste 669 Los Angeles CA 90095-6960*

MILLER, VIRGINIA LEE, business owner; b. Columbus, Ohio, Oct. 26, 1941; d. Theodore Irving and Georgiana Mae (Reed) Jones; m. Arthur R. Miller II, Nov. 26, 1960; children: Elizabeth Ann Lilly, William Theodore Miller, Arthur III. Student, Columbus Coll. & Art & Design, 1959-60, Ohio State U., 1960-61. Clerical Sears, Tuscon, Ariz., 1976-84; inventory specialist Sears, Las Vegas, 1984—; sec., owner business Las Vegas, 1989—; inventory specialist, 1996—. Active Weep, Las Vegas, 1992-93; bd. dirs. Luth. Ch., Las Vegas., 1987-94; social events sec. Youth for Internat. Understanding, Las Vegas, 1991-94; active Cheyene H.S. Booster Club, Las Vegas, 1992-96; com. mem. Boy Scouts of Am., advancement chair., 1993-94, sec., 1991-94, com. chair. 1989-90, social chmn., 1991-93 Boys Scout of Am.,(chmn. bd.of review 1995—); com. mem., parent adv., Girl Scouts of Am., 1972-75; com. mem. Cub Scouts, 1984-89; worship com. Holy Spirit Lutheran Ch., 1986-94, youth advisor youth coord., 1993—. Recipient Amb. of Faith award ELCA Luth. Ch., Phoenix, 1993-94. Republican. Office: Sears 4000 Meadows Ln Las Vegas NV 89107-3108

MILLER, WALKER DAVID, judge; m. Susanne Hauk; 3 children. LLB, U. Colo., 1963; LLM, U. Chgo., 1965. Bar: Colo., 1963. Asst. prof. Sch. Law U. Kans., Greeley, Colo., 1966-69; ptnr. Miller & Ruyte, Greeley, Colo., 1969, Miller, Ruyle, Steinmark & Shade, Greeley, 1970-74, Karowsky, Witwer, Miller and Oldenburg, Greeley, 1992-96; pvt. practice U.S. Dist. Ct. Colo., Greeley, 1974-92; judge U.S. Dist. Ct. Colo., Denver, 1996—. Office: US Dist Ct Colo 1929 Stout St Rm C-530 Denver CO 80294

MILLER, WARREN EDWARD, political scientist; b. Hawarden, Iowa, Mar. 26, 1924; s. John Carroll and Mildred Ovedia (Lien) M.; m. Ruth S. Jones, May 1981; children by previous marriage: Jeffrey Ralph, Jennifer Louise. B.S., U. Oreg., 1948, M.S., 1950; Ph.D., Maxwell Sch. Citizenship and Public Affairs, Syracuse U., 1954; Ph.D. (hon.), U. Goteborg, Sweden, 1972. Asst. study dir. Survey Research Ctr., Inst. Social Research, U. Mich., 1951-53, study dir., 1953-56, research assoc., 1956-59, program dir., 1959-68, research coordinator polit. behavior program, 1968-70, prin. investigator nat. election studies, 1977—; dir. Ctr. Polit. Studies, Inst. Social Research, 1970-81; program dir. Ctr. Polit. Studies, 1982-93; asst. prof. polit. sci. Ctr. Polit. Studies, Inst. Social Research, 1956-58, asso. prof., 1958-63, prof., 1963-93, Arthur W. Bromage prof. polit. sci., 1981-82; prof. polit. sci. Ariz. State U., 1981—; fellow Ctr. Advanced Study in Behavioral Scis., 1961-62; exec. dir. Inter-univ. Consortium for Polit. and Social Rsch., 1962-70, assoc. dir., 1978—; vis. prof. U. Tilburg, Netherlands, 1973, U. Geneva, 1973, European U. Inst., Florence, Italy, 1979; vis. Disting. prof. Ariz. State U., 1981; trustee Inst. Am. Univs., 1970—; Regents' prof., Ariz. State U., 1988—. Author: (with others) books including The Voter Decides, 1954, American Voter, 1960, Elections and the Political Order, 1966, (with T.E. Levitin) Leadership and Change: Presidential Elections from 1952-1976, 77, (with M.K. Jennings) Parties in Transition, 1986, Without Consent, 1988, (with others) The American National Election Studies Data Sourcebook, 1952-1978, 80, The American National Election Studies Data Sourcebook, 1952-86, 89; (with J. Merrill Shanks) The New American Voter, 1996; contbr. (with others) articles to profl. pubs.; editl. bd.: (with others) Am. Polit. Sci. Rev, 1966-71, Computers and the Humanities, 1969-71, Social Science History, 1976-91, Social Science Rev., 1973; editorial adv. bd.: (with others) Sage Electoral Studies Yearbook, 1974. Served with USAAF, 1943-46. Recipient Disting. Alumnus award Maxwell Sch. Citizenship and Public Affairs, Syracuse U., 1974, Disting. Faculty Achievement award U. Mich., 1977; honored in the creation of the Warren E. Miller award for Intellectual Accomplishment and Svc. Am. Polit. Sci. Assn. sect. on Elecions, Pub. Opionion and Voting Behavior, 1995, creation of the Warren E. Miller award for Meritorious Svc. to Social Scis. Inter-Univ. Consortium for Polit. and Social Rsch., 1993. Fellow Am. Acad. Arts and Scis.; mem. AAAS, Am. Polit. Sci. Assn. (pres. 1979-80), Internat. Polit. Sci. Assn. (coun. 1969-73), M.W. Polit. Sci. Assn., Internat. Soc. Polit. Psychology, So. Polit. Sci. Assn., Social Sci. History Assn. (pres. 1979-80), Norwegian Acad. Sci. and Letters. Office: Ariz State U Dept Polit Sci Tempe AZ 85287

MILLER, WENDY FRANKLUND, artist; b. Bismarck, N.D., Oct. 11, 1943; d. Clarence David and Gladys Ella (Halseth) Franklund; m. Robert Dewey Miller Jr., July 29, 1977; 1 child, Peter A. Pulliam. AA, Walla Walla (Wash.) C.C., 1974; BS, Ea. Wash. U., 1976. Lic. dental hygienist, Wash. lectr. North Idaho Coll., 1985, 86, 88, Whitworth Coll., Spokane, 1986, 88, Fiber Arts Network, Spokane, 1986, Spokane Art Sch., 1987-88, Spokane Falls C.C., 1987, Seattle Weavers Guild, 1992, Tacoma Weavers Guild, 1994; juror, Western Women's Exhbn., Idaho, 1985, 5th Congl. Dist. Art Competition, 1987, 9th Ann. Edn. Svc. Dist. 101 Regional Art Show, 1988, Spokane Falls C.C., 1989; workshop tchr. Spokane Falls C.C., 1990, Skagit Valley Coll., North Idaho Coll., 1993, Fiber Forum VII, Whidbey Island, Wash., 1993, Bellevue C.C. 1991-94, U. Alaska S.E., 1994-95, Coupeville Arts Ctr., Washington, 1995; art com. Cheney Cowles Mus., 1985-88; panel mem. YWCA, Spokane, 1988; co-curator Buttons, Connections, Bonds, Spokane, 1992, North Idaho Coll., 1993; coord. Wall St. Banner Workshop, C. of C., Spokane, 1995. One-woman shows include: Valley Gallery, North Bend, Wash., 1972, Gallery Dupris, Spokane, 1980, Westside Gallery, Spokane, 1984, Spokane Art Sch., 1985, Wash. State U. Gallery II, 1985, Seattle Pacific U., 1987, Spokane Falls C.C., 1987, U. Montana, Missoula, 1988, North Idaho Coll., 1988, Whitworth Coll., Spokane, 1988, Art Downtown Gallery, 1989, Ea. Wash. U., 1990, Bellevue C.C., 1991, Chase Gallery, Spokane, 1992, Spokane Interplayers Ensemble, 1993, Carriage House Gallery, Cheney Cowles Mus., Hot Flash, Spokane, 1995, Lorinda Knight Gallery, Spokane, 1997; two-person shows include: Miriam Perlman Gallery, Chgo., 1989, Sinclair Coll., Dayton, Ohio, 1994, Allied Arts, Richland, Wash., 1996, Ventura Coll., Calif., 1996; exhibited in group shows at Momentum Gallery, Spokane, 1994, West Coast Paper Co., Seattle, 1995, North Idaho Coll., 1995, Seafirst Gallery, Seattle, 1995, Yakima Valley Coll., 1996, numerous others. Work appears in numerous periodicals, books and catalogs, and pub. and pvt. collections. Recipient Profl. Devel. Program grant Wash. State Arts. Comm., 1996; Women's Studio Workshop fellow, Rosendale, N.Y., 1994. Home and Studio: W 204 Euclid Ave Spokane WA 99205

MILLER, WILLIAM CHARLES, college dean, architect; b. San Francisco, May 11, 1945; s. Francis Leland and Ethel Lorene (Britt) M.; m. Beverly Jean McConnell, Dec. 22, 1968; children: Britt A., David A. BArch, U. Oreg., 1968; MArch, U. Ill., 1970. Registered architect, Ariz., Kans., Utah. Architect various firms, San Francisco, Sacramento, Calif., Tucson and Oak Harbor, Wash.; asst. prof. Coll. Architecture U. Ariz., Tucson, 1970-73, 74-77; assoc. prof. dept. architecture Kans. State U., Manhattan, 1977-86, prof., 1986-92, head dept., 1990-92; dean, prof. Grad. Sch. Architecture U. Utah, Salt Lake City, 1992—; guest lectr. over 36 schs. architecture; presenter to more than a dozen profl. socs. and orgns.; dir. west ctrl. region Assn. Collegiate Schs. Architecture, 1988-91, chair theme paper sessions ann. meeting, San Francisco, 1990, chair regional paper sessions ann. meeting, Washington, 1991, co-chair adminstrv. conf., Milw., 1995; bd. dirs. Nat. Archtl. Accrediting Bd., 1996—. Author: Alvar Aalto: An Annotated Bibliography, 1984; co-editor: The Architecture of the In-Between, 1990, Architecture: Back to Life, 1991; contbr. articles to profl. jours., chpts. to books. Bd. dirs. Assist, Inc., Artspace, Inc., Contemporary Arts Group. Recipient Svc. awards Assn. Collegiate Schs. Architecture, Nat. Coun. Archtl. Registration Bds. Fellow AIA (architects in edn. com., com. on design, Kans. profl. edn. com., pres-elect Flint Hills, treas. Utah, exec. com., treas., exec. com. Western Mountain region); mem. Am.-Scandinavian Found., Soc. for Advancement Scandinavian Studies, Tau Sigma Delta. Office: U Utah Grad Sch Architecture Salt Lake City UT 84112

MILLER, WILLIAM ELWOOD, mining company executive; b. Bend, Oreg., May 9, 1919; s. Harry Adelbert and Sarah (Heyburn) M.; B.A., Stanford, 1941, M.B.A., 1947; m. Constance Alban Crosby, July 2, 1955; children: William, Constance, Harold, Mary, Sarah Crosby, Charles Crosby, Helen, Harry. Owner and operator Central Oregon Pumice Co., Bend, 1948—; pres. The Miller Lumber Co., Bend, The Miller Ranch Co., Bend, Miller Tree Farm. Commr., City of Bend, 1959-62, mayor, 1960. Bd. dirs. Central Oreg. Coll.; pres. Central Oreg. Coll. Found., 1956-57; dir. Central Oregon Coll. Area Ednl. Dist., 1961-65, chmn., 1964-65; bd. govs. Ore. Dept. Geology and Mineral Industries, 1971-75. Served with A.C., USNR, 1942-45. Decorated D.F.C., Air medal. Mem. Central Oreg. (v.p. 1954), Bend (pres. 1954) C. of C., Bend Golf Club, Rotary (dir. Bend 1955-56), Kappa Sigma. Republican. Episcopalian. Home: 527 NW Congress St Bend OR 97701-2509 Office: 110 NE Greenwood Ave Bend OR 97701-4602

MILLER, WILLIAM FREDERICK, research company executive, educator, business consultant; b. Vincennes, Ind., Nov. 19, 1925; s. William and Elsie M. (Everts) M.; m. Patty J. Smith, June 19, 1949; 1 son, Rodney Wayne. Student, Vincennes U., 1946-47; BS, Purdue U., 1949, MS, 1951, PhD, 1956; D.Sc., 1972. Mem. staff Argonne Nat. Lab., 1955-64, assoc. physicist, 1956-59, dir. applied math. div., 1959-64; prof. computer sci. Stanford U., Palo Alto, Calif., 1965—; Herbert Hoover prof. pub. and pvt. mgmt. Stanford U., 1979—, assoc. provost for computing, 1968-70, v.p. for research, 1970-71, v.p., provost, 1971-78; mem. Stanford Assocs., 1972—; pres., chief exec. officer SRI Internat., Menlo Park, Calif., 1979-90; chmn. bd., chief exec. officer SRI Devel. Co., Menlo Park, David Sarnoff Research Ctr., Inc., Princeton, N.J.; bd. dirs. Borland Internat., Inc., 1996—; chmn. bd. dirs. Whowhere, Inc., 1997; professorial lectr. applied math. U. Chgo., 1962-64; vis. prof. math. Purdue U., 1962-63; vis. scholar Ctr. for Advanced Study in Behavioral Scis., 1976; bd. dirs. Wells Fargo and Co., McKenna Group; mem. adv. coun. BHP Internat.; mem. computer sci. and engring bd. NAS, 1968-71; mem. Nat. Sci. Bd., 1982-88; mem. corp. com. computers in edn. Brown UU., 1971-79; mem. policy bd. EDUCOM Planning Coun. on Computing in Edn., 1974-79, chmn., 1974-76; mem. ednl. adv. bd. Guggenheim Meml. Found., 1976-80; mem. com. postdoctoral and doctoral rsch. staff NRC, 1977-80, mem. computer sci. and telecom. Assoc. editor: Pattern Recognition Jour, 1968-72, Jour. Computational Physics, 1970-74. Served to 2d lt. F.A. AUS, 1943-46. Recipient Frederic B. Whitman award United Way Bay Area, 1982, Sarnoff Founders medal, 1997. Fellow IEEE, Am. Acad. Arts and Scis., AAAS; mem. Am. Math. Soc., Am. Phys. Soc., Soc. Indsl. and Applied Math., Assn. Computing Machinery, Nat. Acad. Engring., Sigma Xi, Tau Beta Pi. Office: Stanford U Grad Sch Bus Stanford CA 94305

MILLER, ZOYA DICKINS (MRS. HILLIARD EVE MILLER, JR.), civic worker; b. Washington, July 15, 1923; d. Randolph and Zoya Pavlovna (Klementinovska) Dickins; m. Hilliard Eve Miller, Jr., Dec. 6, 1943; children: Jeffrey Arnot, Hilliard Eve III. Grad. Stuart Sch. Costume Design, Washington, 1942; student Sophie Newcomb Coll., 1944, New Eng. Conservatory Music, 1946, Colo. Coll., 1965; grad. Internat. Sch. Reading, 1969. Instr. Stuart Summer Sch. Costume Design, Washington, 1942; fashion coord. Julius Garfinckel, Washington, 1942-43; fashion coord., cons. Mademoiselle mag., 1942-44; star TV show Cowbelle Kitchen, 1957-58, Flair for Living, 1958-59; model mags. and comml. films, also nat. comml. recs., 1956—; dir. devel. Webb-Waring Inst. for Biomedical Rsch., Denver, 1973—. Contbr. articles, lectures on health care systems and fund raising. Mem. exec. com., bd. dirs. El Paso County chpt. Am. Lung Assn., Colo., 1954-63; mem. exec. com. Am. Lung Assn. Colo., 1965-84, bd. dirs. 1965-87, chmn. radio and TV coun., 1963-70, mem. med. affairs com., 1965-70, pres., 1965-66, procurer found. funds, 1965-70; developer nat. radio ednl. prodns. for internat. use Am. Lung Assn., 1963-70, coord. statewide pulmonary screening programs Colo., other states, 1965-72; chmn. benefit fund raising El Paso County Cancer Soc., 1963; co-founder, coord. Colorado Springs Debutante Ball, 1967—; coord. Nat. Gov.'s Conf. Ball, 1969; mem. exec. com. Colo. Gov.'s Comprehensive Health Planning Coun., 1967-74, chmn., 1971-72; chmn. Colo. Chronic Care Com., 1969-73, chmn. fund raising, 1970-72, chmn. spl. com. congl. studies on nat. health bills, 1971-73; mem. Colo.-Wyo. Regional Med. Program Adv. Coun., 1969-73; mem. Colo. Med. Found. Consumers Adv. Coun., 1972-78; mem. decorative arts com. Colorado Springs Fine Arts Ctr., 1972-75; founder, state coord. Nov. Noel Pediatrics Benefit Am. Lung Assn., 1973-87; founder, corp. pres. Newborn Hope, Inc., 1987—; mem. adv. bd. Wagon Wheel Girl Scouts, 1991—, Cmty. in Schs., 1995—. Zoya Dickins Miller Vol. of Yr. award established Am. Lung Assn. of Colo., 1979; recipient James J. Waring award Colo. Conf. on Respiratory Disease Workers, 1963, Nat. Pub. Rels. award Am. Lung Assn., 1979, Gold Double Bar Cross award, 1980, 83, Jefferson award Am. Inst. Pub. Svc., 1991, Thousand Points of Light award The White House, 1992, Recognition award So. Colo. Women's C. of C., 1994, Silver Spur Community award Pikes Peak Range Riders, 1994, Silver Bell award Assistance League Colorado Springs, 1996, Svc. to Mankind award Centennial Sertoma Club, 1997, Help Can't Wait award Pikes Peak chpt. ARC, 1997; named Humanitarian of Yr., Am. Lung Assn. of Colo., 1987, One of 50 Most Influential Women in Colorado Springs by Gazette Telegraph Newspaper, 1990, One of 6 Leading Ladies Colo. Homes & Lifestyles Mag., 1991. Lic. pvt. pilot. Mem. Colo. Assn. Fund Raisers, Denver Round Table for Planned Giving, Nat. Soc. Fund Raising Execs., Nat. Cowbell Assn. (El Paso county pres. 1954, TV chmn., chmn. nat. Father of Yr. contest Colo. 1956-57), Broadmoor Garden Club. Home: 74 W Cheyenne Mountain Blvd Colorado Springs CO 80906-4336

MILLET, BLAINE WILLIAM, sales and marketing executive; b. Salt Lake City, Sept. 9, 1954; s. C. Wayne and Iona Gayle (Jensen) M.; m. Lorrie Adele Slaughter, July 28, 1984; children: Krystal Ashley, Jason Blaine, Katrina Ann. BS in Biology cum laude, U. Utah, 1976, MBA in Fin. Mktg., 1979. Ski instr. U. Utah, Salt Lake City, 1973-78; asst. mgr. Millet's Inc., Salt Lake City, 1975-79; bus. mgr. U. Utah Chronicle, Salt Lake City, 1978-79; mktg. rep. IBM Corp., Seattle, 1979-83; mng. dir. Source EDP, Bellevue, Wash., 1983-92; dir. enterprise consulting Arthur Andersen & Co., Seattle, 1992—; pres. Fin. and Personal Cons., Salt Lake City, 1978-79; cons. Millets Inc., 1979-86. Supr. Big Bros. of Am., Salt Lake City, 1978; leader Boys Ranch, Salt Lake City, 1979. Named to Peformers Bd., Source Svcs., 1983-91, Hundred Percent Club, IBM, 1980-82. Mem. Data Processing Mgmt. Assn., The Million Dollar Forum, Soc. for Info. Mgmt. Home: 12826 197th Pl NE Woodinville WA 98072-5666 Office: 801 2nd Ave Ste 800 Seattle WA 98104-1509

MILLEY, JOHN ROSS, neonatologist, educator; b. Hartford, Conn., Oct. 10, 1946; s. Chesley Ross and Muriel Frances (Potter) M.; m. Donna Beatrice Scholts, June 11, 1968; 1 child, Jeffrey Ross. BA in Chemistry, Ill. Wesleyan U., 1967; PhD in Chemistry, U. Chgo., 1974, MD, 1975. Diplomate Am. Bd. Pediats., Neonatal Perinatal Medicine, Nat. Bd. Med. Examiners; lic. physician, Md., Pa., Utah. Intern in pediats. Johns Hopkins U., Balt., 1975-76, resident in pediats., 1976-78, fellow in perinatal medicine, 1978-80, asst. in pediats., 1979-80; from asst. prof. to assoc. prof. ob-gyn. U. Pitts. Sch. Medicine, 1980-88; mem. med. staff Primary Children's Med. Ctr., Salt Lake City, 1988—, U. Utah Med. Ctr., Salt Lake City, 1988—; assoc. prof. pediats. U. Utah Sch. Medicine, Salt Lake City, 1988—; dir. neonatal fellowship program U. Pitts., 1987-88; dir. neonatal fellowship program U. Utah, Salt Lake City, 1988—, assoc. dir. div. neonatology; mem. med. staff Johns Hopkins Hosp., Balt., 1979-80, Children's Hosp. Pitts., 1980-88, Children's Home of Pitts., 1985-88, LDS Hosp., Salt Lake City, 1988—, Magee-Womens Hosp., Pitts., 1980-88, mem. quality assurance com., 1985-88, perinatal morbidity and mortality com., 1984-88; vis. prof. dept. pediatrics U. Cin. Sch. Medicine, 1987; mem. instnl. rev. bd. Primary Children's Med. Ctr., Salt Lake City, 1989—, chmn. instnl. rev. bd., 1991—; mem. ad hoc subcom. for decentralized lab. testing U. Utah Sch. Medicine, Salt Lake City, 1990—; prin. investigator numerous grants, programs Nat. Inst. Child Health and Human Devel. Ad hoc reviewer: Pediats. Rsch., Diabetes, Am. Jour. Physiology; contbr. articles to profl. publs. Mem. med. adv. com. Pitts. Planned Parenthood, 1982-86. Rsch. grantee Children's Hosp. Pitts., 1980-85, Magee-Womens Hosp. Rsch. Fund, 1980-81, 81-84, 82-85, 84-85, 86-87, Ann Ricketson Loftberg Fund, 1981-85, Western Pa. Heart Assn., Inc., 1981-82, Ross Labs., 1984-86, 84-88, U. Utah Sch. Medicine, 1988-89. Fellow Am. Acad. Pediats. (dist. VIII perinatal sect. 1988—), Am. Physiol. Soc., Intermountain Pediat. Soc., Soc. for Pediat. Rsch., Perinatal Rsch. Soc., Utah Perinatal Assn., Study Group for Complications of Perinatal Care. Office: Univ Utah Sch Medicine 50 N Medical Dr Salt Lake City UT 84132-0001

MILLIGAN, RONALD EDGAR, journalist; b. Oakland, Calif.; s. Edgar Dewitt and Arline Claudia (Mahar) M.; m. Damita Esperanza Prado, July 12, 1952 (dec. Dec. 1983); children: Marina, Erin. BS, U. Calif., Berkeley, 1951; cert. internat. reporting, Columbia U., 1970. Fgn. corr. Reuters News Agy., Madrid, Spain, 1963-66, Group W News, Saigon, Vietnam, 1966-69; radio TV news corr. ABC, N.Y.C., 1970-71; prof. journalism Calif. State U., Long Beach, 1986-89, Dominguez Hills, 1989-90; copy editor Wave Publs., L.A., 1991—. Mem. Radio TV News Assn., Soc. Profl. Journalists. Home: 8401 23rd St Westminster CA 92683-3352

MILLIKEN, JOHN GORDON, research economist; b. Denver, May 12, 1927; s. William Boyd and Margaret Irene (Marsh) M.; m. Marie Violet Machell, June 13, 1953; children: Karen Marie, Douglas Gordon, David Tait, Anne Alain. BS, Yale U., 1949, BEng, 1950; MS, U. Colo., 1966, PhD, 1969. Registered profl. engr., Colo. Engr. U.S. Bur. Reclamation, Denver, 1950-55; asst. to plant mgr. Stanley Aviation Corp., Denver, 1955-56; prin. mgmt. engr., dept. mgr. Martin-Marietta Aerospace Divsn., Denver, 1956-64; mgmt. engr. Safeway Stores, Inc., Denver, 1964-66; sr. rsch. economist, prof., assoc. div. head U. Denver Rsch. Inst., 1966-86; pres. Univ. Senate, 1980-81; prin. Milliken Chapman Rsch. Group, Inc., Littleton, Colo., 1986-88, Milliken Rsch. Group, Inc., Littleton, 1988—; vis. fellow sci. policy rsch. unit U. Sussex, Eng., 1975-76; bd. dirs. Sci. Mgmt. Corp.; cons. mgmt. engr. Author: Aerospace Management Techniques, 1971, Federal Incentives for Innovation, 1974, Recycling Municipal Wastewater, 1977, Water and Energy in Colorado's Future, 1981, Metropolitan Water Management, 1981, Technological Innovation and Economic Vitality, 1983, Water Management in the Denver, Colorado Urban Area, 1988, Benefits and Costs of Oxygenated Fuels in Colorado, 1990, Water Transfer Alternatives Study, 1994, Colorado Springs Water Resources Plan Alternative Assessment Study, 1995; contbr. articles to profl. jours. Bd. dirs. S.E. Englewood Water Dist., 1963—, South Englewood San. Dist., 1965—; bd. dirs. South Suburban Pk. and Recreation Dist., 1971-96, chmn., 1990-92; chmn. Dem. Com. of Arapahoe County, 1969-71, 5th Congl. Dist. Colo., 1972-73, 74-75; mem. exec. com. Colo. Faculty Adv. Coun., 1981-85; mem. Garrison Diversion Unit Commn., 1984; trustee Colo. Local Govt. Liquid Asset Trust, 1986—, chmn., 1991-93; bd. dirs. Colo. Spl. Dist. Assn. Property and Liability Pool, 1989—, pres. 1997—. With M.C., U.S. Army, 1945-46. Recipient Adlai E. Stevenson Meml. award, 1981, hon. title "Amicus Universitatis," U. Denver, 1994, Disting. Svc. award Spl. Dist. Assn. Colo., 1995; Milliken Park named in his honor for svcs. to Littleton cmty., 1996. Mem. Acad. Mgmt., Nat. Assn. Bus. Economists, Yale Sci. and Engring. Assn., Am. Water Works Assn., Sigma Xi, Tau Beta Pi, Beta Gamma Sigma, Sigma Iota Epsilon. Congregationalist. Home and Office: 6502 S Ogden St Littleton CO 80121-2561

MILLIN, LAURA JEANNE, museum director; b. Elgin, Ill., June 11, 1954; d. Douglas Joseph and PAtricia Ruth (Feragen) M. BA in Interdisciplinary Studies, The Evergreen State Coll., 1978. Dir. On The Boards, Seattle, 1979; art dir. City Fair Merocenter YMCA, Seattle, 1980; dir. Ctr. on Contemporary Art, Seattle, 1981; co-owner Art in Form Bookstore, Seattle, 1981-89; co-dir. 3d internat festical of films by women dirs. Seattle Art Mus.. & 911 Contemporary Arts, 1988; auction coord. Allied Arts of Seattle, 1989; dir. Missoula (Mont.) Mus. of the Arts, 1990—; dir. Visual AIDS Missoula Missoula Mus. of the Arts, 1989; curator Radio COCA, Ctr. on Contemproary Art, Seattle, 1986, co-curator, 1981, 83; lectr. in field. Co-editor: AnOther (ind. feminist newspaper), Seattle, 1989, editor: (exhibition catalog) James Turrell: Four Light Installations, 1981. Bd. dirs. Internat. Festival of Films by Women Dirs., Seattle, 1987, 89, Nine One One Comtemporary Arts Ctr., Seattle, 1981-87, bd. chmn. 1981-85; bd. advisors REFLEX (art mag.), Seattle, 1988-89, Ctr. on Contemporary Art, Seattle, 1983-86; state vis. Mont. Arts. Coun., Missoula, 1991, NEA, Mpls., 1988, Chgo., 1987; ; panelist Mont. Arts Coun., Helena, 1990; cons. Seattle Arts Commn., 1989, juror, 1985. Home: 1721 S 9th St W Missoula MT 59801-3432 Office: Missoula Mus of the Arts 335 N Pattee St Missoula MT 59802-4520*

MILLMAN, PAUL RICHARD, fundraiser; b. Hartford, Conn., Nov. 5, 1959; s. Richard B. and Marion (Kopcych) M. BA, U. Hartford, 1981. Cert. fund raising exec. Nat. Soc. Fund Raising Profls. Projects coord. Orlando Regional Med. Ctr., Orlando, Fla., 1981-83; assoc. dir. ann. giving Rollins Coll., Winter Park, Fla., 1983-86; dir. ann. giving Art Ctr. Coll. of Design, Pasadena, Calif., 1986-89; dir. ann. fund U. Ctrl. Fla., Orlando, 1989-91; dir. adminstrn. PUENTE Learning Ctr., L.A., 1991—. Recipient Fund Raising Improvement award CASE, 1988. Mem. Nat. Soc. Fund Raising Execs. (chair fund raising com. 1994, bd. dirs. Greater L.A. chpt. 1994, 96-98, vice-chair Fund Raising Day in L.A. 1996, profl. fund raiser of the yr. award com. 1997, Mem. of Month award 1994). Democrat. Office: PUENTE Learning Ctr 501 S Boyle Ave Los Angeles CA 90033-3816

MILLS, BASIL E., food products executive. Attended, U. Colo., 1948-50. Broker Walter S. Markham Co., Salinas, Calif., 1953-55; with Royal Packing Co., Salinas, 1955-58; pres. Mills Distributing Co., Salinas, 1958—; ptnr. MIVCO Packing Co., Salinas, 1973—. With U.S. Army, 1951-53. Office: Mills Distributing Co 375 W Market St Salinas CA 93901-1423*

MILLS, BECKY, park administrator. BA, Swarthmore Coll.; MSW, U. Calif., Berkeley. Cmty. and individual social work, 1963-69; adminstrv. analyst Statewide Pres.'s Office U. Calif., 1969-72; exec. dir. Advocates for Women Econ. Devel. Ctr., 1972-76; cons. in fundraising and tng. Stanford U., Girl Scouts USA, others, 1976-78; equal opportunity mgr., chief youth programs Western Regional Nat. Park Svc., 1978-95; supr. Gt. Basin Nat. Park, 1995—. Office: Great Basin Nat Pk Hwy 488 Baker NV 89311

MILLS, CAROL MARGARET, business consultant, public relations consultant; b. Salt Lake City, Aug. 31, 1943; d. Samuel Lawrence and Beth (Neilson) M.; BS magna cum laude, U. Utah, 1965. With W.S. Hatch Co., Woods Cross, Utah, 1965-87, corp. sec., 1970-87, traffic mgr., 1969-87, dir. publicity, 1974-87; cons. various orgns., 1988—; dir. Hatch Service Corp., 1972-87, Nat. Tank Truck Carriers, Inc., Washington, 1977-88; bd. dirs. Intermountain Tariff Bur. Inc., 1978-88, chmn., 1981-82, 1986-87; bd. dirs. Mountainwest Venture Group. Fund raiser March of Dimes, Am. Cancer Soc., Am. Heart Assn.; active senatorial campaign, 1976, gubernatorial campaign, 1984, 88, congl. campaign, 1990, 92, 94, vice chair voting dist., 1988-90, congressional campaign, 1994; chmn. 1990-92, chmn. party caucus legis. dist.; witness transp. com. Utah State Legislature, 1984, 85; apptd. by gov. to bd. trustees Utah Tech. Fin. Corp., 1986—, corp. sec., mem. exec. com., 1988—; mem. expdn. to Antarctica, 1996, Titanic '96 expdn. Recipient svc. awards W. S. Hatch Co., 1971, 80; mem. Pioneer Theatre Guild, 1985—; V.I.P. capt. Easter Seal Telethon, 1989, 90, recipient Outstanding Vol. Svc. award Easter Seal Soc. Utah, 1989, 90. Mem. Nat. Tank Truck Carriers Transp. Club Salt Lake City, Am. Trucking Assn. (pub. rels. coun.), Utah Motor Transport Assn. (dir. 1982-88), Internat. Platform Assn., Traveler's Century Club, Titanic Internat., Beta Gamma Sigma, Phi Kappa Phi, Phi Chi Theta. Home and Office: 77 Edgecombe Dr Salt Lake City UT 84103-2219

MILLS, DON HARPER, pathology and psychiatry educator, lawyer; b. Peking, China, July 29, 1927; came to U.S., 1928; s. Clarence Alonzo and Edith Clarissa (Parrett) M.; m. Lillian Frances Snyder, June 11, 1949; children: Frances Jo, Jon Snyder. BS, U. Cin., 1950, MD, 1953; JD, U. So. Calif., 1958. Diplomate Am. Bd. Law in Medicine. Intern L.A. County Gen. Hosp., 1953-54, admitting physician, 1954-57, attending staff pathologist, 1959—; pathology fellow U. So. Calif., L.A., 1954-55, instr. pathology, 1958-62, asst. clin. prof., 1962-65, assoc. clin. prof., 1965-69, clin. prof., 1969—, clin. prof. psychiatry and behavioral sci., 1986—; asst. in pathology Hosp. Good Samaratian, L.A., 1956-65, cons. staff, 1962-72, affiliating staff, 1972-91; dep. med. examiner Office of L.A. County Med. Examiner, 1957-61; instr. legal medicine Loma Linda (Calif.) U. Sch. Medicine, 1960-66, assoc. clin. prof. humanities, 1966-95; cons. HEW, 1972-73, 75-76, Dept. of Def., 1975-80; bd. dirs. Am. Bd. Law in Medicine, Inc., Chgo., 1980-86; med. dir. Profl. Risk Mgmt. Group, 1989—. Column editor Newsletter of the Long Beach Med. Assn., 1960-75, Jour. Am. Osteopathic Assn., 1965-77, Ortho Panel, 1970-78; exec. editor Trauma, 1964-88, mem. editl. bd., 1988—; mem. editl. bd. Legal Aspects of Med. Practice, 1972-90, Med. Alert Comms., 1973-75, Am. Jour. Forensic Medicine and Pathology, 1979-87, Hosp. Risk Control, 1981-96; contbr. numerous articles to profl. jours. Bd. dirs. Inst. for Med. Risk Studies, 1988—. Recipient Ritz Heerman award Calif. Hosp. Assn., 1986, Disting. fellow Am. Acad. Forensic Scis., 1993, Genesis award Pacific Ctr. for Health Policy and Ethics, 1993, Founder's award Am. Coll. Med. Quality, 1994. Fellow Am. Coll. Legal Medicine (pres. 1974-76, bd. govs. 1970-78, v.p. 1972-74, chmn. malpractice com. 1973-74, jour. editl. bd. 1984—), Am. Acad. Forensic Sci. (gen. program chmn. 1966-67, chmn. jurisprudence sect. 1966-67, 73-74, exec. com. 1971-74, 84-88, v.p. 1984-85, pres. 1986-87, ethics com. 1976-86, 91—, chmn. ethics com. 1994—, strategic planning com. 1990—, jour. editl. bd. 1965-79); mem. AMA (jour. editl. bd. 1973-77), AAAS, ABA, Calif. Med. Assn., L.A. County Med. Assn., L.A. County Bar Assn., Am. Soc. Hosp. Attys., Calif. Soc. Hosp. Attys. Home: 700 E Ocean Blvd Unit 2606 Long Beach CA 90802-5039 Office: 911 Studebaker Rd Ste 250 Long Beach CA 90815-4900

MILLS, LAWRENCE, lawyer, business and transportation consultant; b. Salt Lake City, Aug. 15, 1932; s. Samuel L. and Beth (Neilson) M. BS, U. Utah, 1955, JD, 1956. Bar: Utah 1956, ICC 1961, U.S. Supreme Ct. 1963. With W.S. Hatch Co. Inc., Woods Cross, Utah, 1947-89, gen. mgr., 1963-89, v.p., 1970-89, also dir.; bd. dirs. Nat. Tank Truck Carriers, Inc., Washington, 1963—, pres., 1974-75, chmn. bd., 1975-76; mem. motor carrier adv. com. Utah State Dept. Transp., 1979—; keynote speaker Rocky Mountain Safety Suprs. Conf., 1976; mem. expedition to Antartica, 1996, Titanic Expedition, 1996. Contbr. articles to legal publs. Del. to County and State Convs., Utah, 1970-72; v.p. Utah Safety Coun., 1979-82, bd. dirs., 1979—, pres., 1983-84; mem. Utah Gov's Adv. Com. on Small Bus.; capt. Easter Seal Telethon, 1989, 90; state vice chmn. High Frontier, 1987—; mem. adv. com. Utah State Indsl. Commn., 1988—, chmn. com. studying health care cost containment and reporting requirements 1990—; mem. expdn. to Antarctica, 1996, Titanic '96 expedition. Recipient Safety Dir. award Nat. Tank Carriers Co., 1967, Outstanding Svc. and Contbn. award, 1995, Trophy award W.S. Hatch Co., 1975, Disting. Svc. award Utah State Indsl. Commn., 1992, Outstanding Svc. award Utah Safety Coun., 1994. Mem. Salt Lake County Bar Assn., Utah Motor Transport Assn. (dir. 1967—, pres. 1974-76, Outstanding Achievement Award 1989), Utah Hwy. Users Assn. (dir. 1981—), Indsl. Rels. Coun. (dir. 1974—), Salt Lake City C. of C., U.S. Jaycees (life Senator 1969—, ambassador 1977—, pres. Utah Senate 1979-80, Henry Giessenbier fellow 1989), Nat. Petroleum Coun., Utah Associated Gen. Contractors (assoc. 1975-77, 88—), Silver Tank Club, Hillsdale Coll. President's Club, Traveler's Century Club. Home and Office: 77 Edgecombe Dr Salt Lake City UT 84103-2219 *Personal philosophy: Excessive government regulation stifles individual initiative. We should learn from the downfall of communism.*

MILLS, RICHARD PENCE, ophthalmologist; b. Evanston, Ill., Sept. 13, 1943; s. Glen Earl and Ruth Arlene (Pence) M.; m. Catherine Louise Baily, June 1, 1966 (div. Sept. 1975); 1 child, Lianne Louise; m. Karen Elisabeth, Aug. 1, 1976; children: Elisabeth Ruth, Emily Carole. BA magna cum laude, Yale U., 1964, MD cum laude, 1968. Clin. instr. dept. ophthalmology U. Wash., Seattle, 1972-75, clin. asst. prof., 1975-80, clin. assoc. prof. depts. ophthalmology, medicine, 1980-84, assoc. prof. dept. ophthalmology, 1984-87, prof., vice-chmn. dept. ophthalmology, 1987—; adj. prof. depts. medicine and neurol. surgery, U. Wash., 1987—; pres. St. Peter Hosp. Med. Staff, Olympia, Wash., 1982; trustee Bishop Found., Seattle, 1996. Author: (books) Glaucoma Surgical Techniques, 1991, Perimetry Update: 1990-91, 1991, Perimetry Update: 1992-93, 1993, 94-95, 95. Surgeon USPHS, 1969-73. Recipient Optic Neuritis Treatment Trial award Nat. Eye Inst., Washington, 1988-91, Collaborative Initial Glaucoma Treatment Study, 1993-96, Collaborative Normal Tension Glaucoma Study award Glaucoma Rsch. Found., San Francisco, 1988-96. Fellow Am. Acad. Ophthalmology (pres. 1995, Honor award 1989, Sr. Honor award 1996), Wash. Acad. Eye Physicians and Surgeons (pres. 1983, Spl. Honor 1993), Wash. State Med. Assn. (trustee 1996), Am. Glaucoma Soc. (dir. 1993-94), No. Am. Neuro-Ophth. Soc., Internat. Perimetric Soc. (sec. 1988-94). Office: Univ Wash Dept Ophthalmology Box 356485 1959 NE Pacific Seattle WA 98195

MILLS, ROBERT CHARTERS, retired oil company executive; b. Park River, N.D., Jan. 18, 1928; s. David and Myrtle (Finneseth) M.; m. Josephine Shaw, Sept. 25, 1954 (dec. Oct. 1995); children: Laura Akhavan, Juliana Oswald, Anne Gaultier. BE in Petroleum Engring., U. So. Calif., 1952. Gen. mgr. Mobil Producing Nigeria, Lagos, 1972-75, chmn., mng. dir., 1975-77; gen. mgr. Mobil Denver Exploration and Prodn. Divsn., Denver, 1977-81; pres., gen. mgr. Mobil Oil Indonesia, Inc., Jakarta, 1981-85, Mobil Oil Exploration and Prodn. S.E., Inc., New Orleans, 1985-87, Mobil Exploration and Prodn. Svc., Inc., Dallas, 1987-89; bd. dirs. Identi-Graphics, Portland, Oreg.; chmn. bd. dirs. Heaven, Inc., POrtland, 1996. Bd. dirs., chmn. oil sector United Way, New Orleans, 1985-86, bd. dirs., Dallas, 1987-88; bd. dirs. Found. Advanced Christian Tng., Menlo Park, Calif., 1995-96; vol. Cmty. Hosp., Monterey, Calif., 1991-96. 1st lt. USAF, 1950-53. Republican. Presbyterian. Home: 2996 Franciscan Way Carmel CA 93923-9216

MILLS, ROGER E., food products executive; b. 1935. Exec. v.p. Mills Distbg. Co., Inc., Salinas, Calif., 1958—; ptnr. Mivco Packing Co., Salinas, Calif., 1973—. Office: Mills Distributing Co Inc 375 W Market St Salinas CA 93901-1423*

MILLS, SHERRY RAE, training and conference planning; b. Colorado Springs, Colo., Apr. 3, 1940; d. Ray Edwin and Lorena Marguerite (Ferguson) Gregory; m. Ronald Keith Mills, July 22, 1962; children: Tracy Rae, Darren Keith. B in Music Edn., U. Colo., 1962; MA, U. Colo., Colorado Springs, 1979. Tchr. Harrison Dist. 2, Colorado Springs, 1962-66; music tchr. Rocky Mountain Rehab. Ctr., Colorado Springs, 1969-72; music specialist Colorado Springs Dist. 11, Colorado Springs, 1972-75; pres., exec. dir. Colo. Arts for the Handicapped, Colorado Springs, 1975-85; owner, gen. ptnr. Creative Tng. Assocs., Colorado Springs, 1985—; presented papers Colo. State Conf. of the Coun. for Exceptional Children, 1976, 77, 78, 79, 80, Chgo., 1976; conducted numerous workshops for Mile High Consortium, Denver, 1976, Head Start, Colorado Springs, 1977, Nat. Assn. of Music Therapy, Anaheim, Calif., 1977, Butte (Mont.) Silverbow Anti-Poverty Coun.-Head Start, 1978, Nat. Conf. for Citizens with Down Syndrome, Boston, 1976, St. Louis, 1978, Washington, 1987, Fla. Learning Resource Sys., Pensacola, 1980, Pueblo Sch. Dist. 60 Music Tchrs., 1979, Internat. Conf. Coun. Exceptional Children, Dallas, 1979, Phila., 1980, Houston, 1982; instr. U. Colo., Colorado Springs, Chapman Coll., Pikes Peak C.C., Adams State Coll., Ft. Lewis Coll., Morgan C.C., Trinidad State Jr. Coll., Mesa State Coll., Aurora U., New Berlin, Wis.; leader workshops nat. leadership conf. Am. Soc. Tng. and Devel., 1991, 92, 95, 96; presenter in field. Author: Fun with Instruments: An Instrumental Method for the Special Child, 1976-78, A Source Guide for the Special Child: Learning Activities and Music, 1978; contbr. articles to profl. jours. Vol. grant writer Colo. Springs Police Dept. Grantee Colo. Coun. for Exceptional Children Dept. Edn., 1980-81, 81-82, Found. for Exceptional Children, 1981, Arts for the Handicapped program. Mem. ASCD, ASTD (treas. Pike's Peak chpt. 1988, v.p. 1989, pres. 1990, 91, chair region VI conf. 1991, rep. region VI coun. 1991, 92, region VI rep. nat. chpt. award com. 1993, nat. awards com. 1994, asst. regional dir. Train Am.'s Workforce program 1992, v.p. membership 1994, 95), Nat. Staff Devel. Coun., Meeting Planners and Conf. Suppliers of So. Colo. (pres. 1991, 92, 96, other bd. positions 1985—), Meeting Planners Assn. Colorado Springs (treas. 1989, pres. 1990, immediate past pres. 1991, conf. chair 1990-91, 1st v.p. 1992, pres. 1993, 2d v.p. 1994, co-pres. 1995, membership chair 1996, Meeting Planner of Yr. award 1990), Coun. for Exceptional Children (sec. chpt. 403 1976-77, pres. elect 1977-78, pres. 1978-79, membership chair 1984-88; state chmn. com. for direct svc. to children 1977-79, v.p. Colo. fedn., 1979-80, pres. elect 1980-81, pres. 1981-82, immediate past pres. 1982-83, chmn. grants com. 1983-86), Down Syndrome Congress, Am. Assn. Mental Deficiency, Found. for Exceptional Children, Internat. Platform Assn., Music Edn. for Handicapped. Baptist. Home: 2220 Glenwood Cir Colorado Springs CO 80909-1555 Office: Creative Tng Assocs PO Box 25806 Colorado Springs CO 80936-5806

MILLS, TIMOTHY IGNATIUS, logistics officer, East-Asian culture consultant; b. Boston, May 7, 1960; s. Thomas Francis and Daphene Mary (McLaughin) M.; m. Denise Joan Pelletier, Oct. 5, 1985; children: Katherine, Ian, Emily. BS in Psychology, U. Mass., 1983; MS in Logistics Mgmt., Air Force Inst. of Tech., 1988; BA in East Asian Studies, U. Md., Tokyo, 1994; MBA in Internat. Mgmt., Golden Gate U., 1996. Commd. 2d. lt. USAF, 1985, advanced through grades to maj.; program mgr. Electronic Sys. Divsn., Hanscom AFB, Mass., 1988-91; chief def. coop. divsn. USAF Head Quarters, Tokyo, Japan; dep. F-111 program mgr. Sacramento, Air Logistics Ctr., Sacramento, 1994—; East Asian bus. cons., Sacramento, 1994—; Total Quality Mgmt. facilitator USAF, Tokyo, 1991-94. Mem. Soc. of Logistics Engrs. (cert. profl. logistician), Air Force Assoc., Logistics Assoc. (pres., 1992-93), KC (3rd degree Knight). Republic. Catholic. Home: 7848 Teton Way Sacramento CA 95843 Office: Sacramento Air Logistics Ctr Sacramento CA 95843

MILLSTEAD, SUSAN, mortgage loan officer; b. Tokyo, Dec. 3, 1949; parents Am. citizens; d. Ira Franklin Crigger and Sumiko Watanabe Teramoto; m. Larry Millstead, Dec. 30, 1990. Student, U. Utah. Credit mgr. Savage Bros. Transport, American Fork, Utah, 1982-84; loan officer Western Savs. & Loan, Yuma, Ariz., 1984-88, Zions Mortgage Co., Orem, Utah, 1990-94; br. mgr. Norwest Mortgage, Orem, 1994—. Mem. Mortgage Bankers of Utah County (v.p. 1992-94), Women's Coun. Realtors (Affiliate of Month 1996), Utah Valley Home Builders Assn. (program com. 1994-96), Mortgage Bankers of Ariz. (v.p. 1985-86). Office: Norwest Mortgage Inc 313 East 1300 South Orem UT 84058

MILNE, JAMES DAVID, educator; b. Duluth, July 28, 1926; s. John Fitzpatrick and Margaret (Sullivan) M. BA, U. Minn., 1957; MA, Long Beach State U., 1953; PhD, Mich. State U., 1963. Asst. prof. edn. U. Detroit; assoc. prof. edn. Marquette U., Milw.; assoc.prof., asst. dir. U. Wis., Wausau; dir. summer sessions & continuing edn. Humboldt State U., Arcata, Calif.; dir. projects for advancement of creativity in edn. Humboldt, Del Monte and Mendicino Counties, Eureka, Calif.; assoc. prof. edn., dir. continuing edn. U. Portland; dir. adult edn. State Operated Schs., Anchorage; pres. Inupiat U. Arctic, Barrow, Alaska; dir. funding & fisheriesfunding & devel. Aleutian Probiloff Islands Assn. Awareness House Internat., Berkeley, Calif.; dir. Cmty. Problems Ctr. Anchorage & Mats Valley; dir. Funding & Devel. for Heartbeat Alaska and One Sky Internat. Prodns. With USN, 1943-48. Fellow U. Minn., Mich. State U. Mem. Nat. Assn. Adult Edn., Nat. Assn. Elem. Prins., Nat. Sci. Tchrs. Assn., British Interplanetary Soc. Democrat. Roman Catholic. Home: PO Box 3821 Palmer AK 99645-3821 Office: Cmty Problems Ctr 6701 Homebuilt Cir Wasilla AK 99654

MILNER, JOE W., journalism educator; b. Winnsboro, Tex., Jan. 2, 1929; s. O.K. and Annie (Boyd) M.; children: Derek Jeffrey, Brent Martin. BS, East Tex. State U., 1954; MA, U. Okla., 1955; EdD, U. Wyo., 1963. Reporter Commerce (Tex.) Daily Jour., 1947-49; reporter Dallas Times Herald, 1949-51, Greenville (Tex.) Herald, 1953-54; journalism instr. Eastern N.Mex. U., Portales, 1955-57; head journalism dept. Miss. State Coll. for Women, Columbus, 1957-58; prof. U. Wyo., Laramie, 1960-67; dir. Journalism Sch. Ariz. State U., Tempe, 1970-79, prof., 1967—; vis. prof. Angelo State U., San Angelo, Tex., 1992-93; sec. Walter Cronkite Journalism Endowment, 1992—. Editor Wyo. Press, Laramie, 1960-67, Journalism Roundtable, 1965-76, 80-81. Recipient Disting. Newspaper Advisor award, Nat. Coun. Coll. Advisors, 1965; Fulbright scholar, East Pakistan, 1963-64. Mem. Soc. Profl. Journalists, Nat. Conf. Editl. Writers, Am. Soc. Journalism Adminstrs. (nat. pres. 1978). Home: 2095 E Manhatton Dr Tempe AZ 85282-5967 Office: Sch of Journalism Ariz State U Tempe AZ 85287

MILONE, ANTHONY M., bishop; b. Omaha, Sept. 24, 1932. Grad., North American Coll. (Rome). Ordained priest Roman Catholic Ch., 1957. Ordained titular bishop of Plestia and aux. bishop Diocese of Omaha, 1982; apptd. bishop Mont. Diocese, Great Falls-Billings, 1987—. Office: PO Box 1399 121 23rd St S Great Falls MT 59403-1399*

MILONE, EUGENE FRANK, astronomer, educator; b. N.Y.C., June 26, 1939; arrived in Can., 1971; s. Frank Louis and Vera Christine (Joeckle) M.; m. Helen Catherine Louise (Ligor), Mar. 1, 1959; children: Bartholomew Vincenzo Llambro, Marie Christina Milone Jack. AB, Columbia U., 1961; MSc, Yale U., 1963, PhD, 1967. Astronomer space sci. div. rocket spectroscopy br. Naval Rsch. Lab., Washington, 1967-84; asst. prof. Gettysburg (Pa.) Coll., 1968-71; asst. prof. dept. physics and astronomy U. Calgary, Alta., Can., 1971-75, assoc. prof., 1976-81, prof., 1981—; co-dir. Rothney Astrophys. Obs., 1975—; Organizer Internat. Symposium on the Origins, Evolution and Destinies of Binary Stars in Clusters, U. Calgary, June 1995; chair rsch. grants com. U. Calgary, 1995-96. Editor: Infrared Extinction and Standardization, 1989; co-author: Challenges of Astronomy, 1991, Exploring Ancient Skies, 1997; editor: Light Curve Modeling of Eclipsing Binary Stars, 1993, The Origins, Evolution, and Destinies of Binary Stars in Clusters, 1996; contbr. more than 150 articles to profl. jours. Elected mem. com. for coll. and univ. svcs. Evang. Luth. Ch. in Can., Synod of Alberta and the Territories, Edmonton, Alta., 1989-93. Operating and Equipment grantee Natural Scis. and Engring. Rsch. Coun. Can., 1972—; Killam Resident fellow Killam Found. U. Calgary, 1982, 88. Mem. Internat. Astron. Union (mem. organizing com., commn. 25 1985-91, 94—), Am. Astron. Soc. (chmn. local organizing com. Calgary meeting 1981), Can. Astron. Soc., Sigma Xi (pres. U. Calgary chpt. 1979-80). Democrat. Lutheran. Home: 1031 Edgemont Rd NW, Calgary, AB Canada Office: U Calgary Dept Physics and Astronomy, 2500 University Dr NW, Calgary, AB Canada T2N 1N4

MILOSZ, CZESLAW, poet, author, educator; b. Lithuania, June 30, 1911; came to U.S., 1960, naturalized, 1970; s. Aleksander and Weronika (Kunat) M. M Juris, U. Wilno, Lithuania, 1934; LittD (hon.), U. Mich., 1977; honoris causa, Brandeis U., 1985, Harvard U., 1989, Jaqellonian U., Poland, 1989, U. Rome, Italy, 1992. Programmer Polish Nat. Radio, 1935-39; diplomatic service Polish Fgn. Affairs Ministry, Warsaw, 1945-50; vis. lectr. U. Calif., Berkeley, 1960-61; prof. Slavic langs. and lits. U. Calif., 1961-78, prof. emeritus, 1978—. Author: The Captive Mind, 1953, Native Realm, 1968, Post-War Polish Poetry, 1965, The History of Polish Literature, 1969, Selected Poems, 1972, Bells in Winter, 1978, The Issa Valley, 1981, Separate Notebooks, 1984, The Land of Ulro, 1984, The Unattainable Earth, 1985, Collected Poems, 1988, Provinces, 1991, Beginning With My Streets, 1992, A Year of the Hunter, 1994, Facing the River, 1995, A Book of Luminous Things, 1996, Striving Towards Being, 1996. Recipient Prix Littéraire Européen Les Guildes du Livre, Geneva, 1953, Neustadt Internat. prize for lit. U. Okla., 1978, citation U. Calif., Berkeley, 1978, Nobel prize for lit., 1980, Nat. Medal of Arts, 1990; Nat. Culture Fund fellow, 1934-35; Guggenheim fellow, 1976. Mem. AAAS, Am. Acad. Arts and Scis., Am. Acad and Inst. Arts and Letters, Polish Inst. Letters and Scis. in Am., PEN Club in Exile. Office: U Calif Dept Slavic Langs Lits Berkeley CA 94720

MILTON, JOHN P., ecologist, educator, author, photographer; b. Jersey City, N.J., Nov. 30, 1938; s. John Jr. and Barbara (Potter) M. BS, U. Mich., 1962, MS, 1963. Dir. internat. programs divsn. Conservation Found., Washington, 1963-72; pres., chmn. Threshold Found., Washington, 1973—; vis. scholar Woodrow Wilson Internat. Sch. for Scholars, Washington, 1972-73; vis. prof. U. Ill., Springfield, 1978-80; pres. Sacred Passage and the Way of Nature, Bisbee, Ariz., 1985—. Author: Future Environments of North America, 1966, Nameless Valleys, Shining Mountains, 1970, The Careless Technology: Ecology and International Development, 1972, Ecological Principles for Economic Development, 1973, Alaska, The Last Great Wilderness, 1973, The Future of America, 1977, The Galapagos, 1980, Ecological Planning in the Nepalese Terai, 1981. Mem. NAS (com. mem.), Am. Assn. Scis. (com. mem.), Ecol. Soc. Am. Office: Sacred Passage The Way of Nature PO Box CZ Main St Bisbee AZ 85603

MINAMI, ROBERT YOSHIO, artist, graphic designer; b. Seattle, May 1, 1919; s. Kichitaro and Suma (Fujita) M.; m. Shizu Tashiro, May 30, 1953; 1 child, Ken. Artist; student, Art Inst., Chgo., 1957, Am. Acad. Art, Chgo., 1980-81. Graphic artist Filmack Studios, Chgo., 1945-48, S. Taylor & Leavitt Assocs., Chgo., 1949-50; head graphic designer NBC-TV, Chgo., 1950-82; fine artist Robert Minami's Studio, Oceanside, Calif., 1983—; artist Goodman Theatre Design, Chgo., 1955-56; mem. Oceanside Mus. Art Exhbn. Com.; art instr. Mus. Sch. Art, Oceanside, 1997-98. Exhibits include Oceanside Mus. Art, 1996. Active Supporters for City Couns., Oceanside, 1984—. Recipient Merit award Artist Guild Chgo., 1956, People's Choice award Carlsbad Oceanside Art League, 1986, Dick Blick award, 1992, 1st place award Mixed Media Collage, 1993, Nat. Watercolor award Watercolor West, 1994. Mem. San Diego Watercolor Soc., United Scenic Artists (life), Am. Fine Art Connection, San Diego Art Inst., Nat. Watercolor Soc. (assoc.), Watercolor West Juried Assn.

MINAR, PAUL G., design consultant; b. Phoenix, July 12, 1932; s. Aaron Crowther and Ione Anna (Schmid) Mortensen. Student, Ariz. State U., 1950-54, John F. Kennedy U., 1978-80, Antioch West U., 1980. Sound effects technician, TV stage mgr. Sta. KHJ-AM-TV, L.A., 1955-63; displayer W.&J. Sloane Furniture Co., Beverly Hills, Calif., 1963-66, Bullock's Dept. Store, L.A., 1966-68, Macy's Dept. Store, San Francisco, 1968-70; interior designer Lloyd's Furniture Co., San Diego, 1970-7l, Bonynge's Furniture Co., Oakland, Calif., 1971-72, Breuner's Furniture Co., Oakland, 1972-74; design cons. The Other Artist, San Francisco, 1974—; archival rschr. and conservation Petaluma Hist. Mus., 1994—; profl. numerologist; lectr. in onomatology. Author: Numerology For People Who Dont Understand It, 1997. Writer, producer (documentary) The Modern Nursing Home, 1959. Vol. talent agt. San Francisco Symphony Black and White Ball, 1983. Mem. Inst. Noetic Scis., Petaluma Mus. Assn. Democrat. Roman Catholic. Office: The Other Artist 3200 Buchanan St San Francisco CA 94123-3517

MINARD, EUGENE WATKINS, consulting forensic psychiatrist; b. Villisca, Iowa, Mar. 28, 1924; s. Jess Ernest and Iva Eda (Watkins) M.; m. Joyce Almira Smith, Dec. 13, 1947 (div. May 1966); children: Diane, Scott, Kurt, Mark, Elizabeth; m. Doris Marie Cameron-Minard, July 6, 1982. BA, Stanford (Calif.) U., 1946, MD, 1949; MPH, U. Calif., Berkeley, 1956. Diplomate Am. Bds. Preventive Medicine, Psychiatry and Neurology; lic. Calif., Oreg. Rotating intern San Francisco City and County Hosp., 1948-49; psychiatric resident VA Hosp., Palo Alto, Calif., 1949-50; public health resident San Joaquin Local Health Dist., Stockton, Calif., 1953-55; asst. dir. pub. health County San Bernardino, 1956-59; pvt. practice San Bernardino, 1959-60, 63-70; staff psychiatrist, psychiatric resident Patton State Hosp., San Bernardino, Calif., 1960-63; pvt. practice San Diego, 1970-80; staff psychiatrist Northwest Permanente, Portland, Oreg., 1980-82; psychiatrist II Western State Hosp., Ft. Steilacoom, Wash., 1982; staff psychiatrist Dammasch State Hosp., Wilsonville, Oreg., 1982-84; pvt. practice Portland, 1983-86, Salem, Oreg., 1985-89; supervising and staff psychiatrist Dammasch State Hosp., 1989-94, Oreg. State Hosp. Forensic, 1994-95; cons. State Vocat. Rehab. Dept., Family Svcs. Agy., Calif. Medi-Cal Program, Mental Health Assn., San Bernardino, 1963-70; part-time San Diego County Mental Health Svcs., Douglas Young Clinic, State of Calif. Medi-Cal, 1970-80; mem. mental health adv. bd. Oreg. Advocacy Ctr., Portland, 1986-89; mem. provider panel Capitol health Care, Salem. Disability Determinations, Oreg. and Wash. Presenter and author in field. With U.S. Army, 1943-46; capt. USAF, 1951-53. Mem. Am. Psychiat. Assn., Am. Neuropsychiat. Assn., Am. Acad. Psychiatry and the Law, World Psychiat. Assn., World Fedn. for Mental Health, Oreg. Psychiat. Assn., North Pacific Soc. for Neurology and Psychiatry, Oreg. Med. Assn., Clackamas County Med. Assn., Amnesty Internat., Internat. Physicians for Prevention of Nuclear War.

MINCIN, KARL JOHN, nutritionist, educator; b. Pitts., Jan. 3, 1960; s. John Alfred and Connie (Ricci) M.; m. Dianna Kay Lindberg; children: Brook, Hannah. AA, Bellevue (Wash.) C.C., 1983; BS, Evergreen State Coll., Olympia, Wash., 1984; BS in Nutrition, Bastyr U., Seattle, 1986. Chief nutritionist Health Resource Inst., Bellevue, 1985-86; clin. nutritionist Tahoma Clinic, Kent, Wash., 1985-89; nutrition cons. Nutrition Resource Ctr., Concrete, Wash., 1981—; clin. nutritionist Osteo. Med. Svcs., Inc., Bellevue, 1997—; instr. Bastyr U., 1991-95, Puget Consumers Coop., Seattle, 1982—, Brian Utting Sch. of Massage, Seattle, 1989—; lectr. in field. Contbr./cons.: (books) Optimal Wellness, 1996, Stevia: Nature's Sweet Secret, 1996; contbr. articles to profl. jours. Mem. Ctr. for Sci. in the Pub. Interest, Wash. Food and Nutrition Coun., Internat. Assn. of Cancer Victors and Friends (Seattle chpt.). Jehovah's Witness. Office: Nutrition Resource Ctr PO Box 126 419A Leonard Pl Concrete WA 98237

MINDELL, EARL LAWRENCE, nutritionist, author; b. St. Boniface, Man., Can., Jan. 20, 1940; s. William and Minerva Sybil (Galsky) M.; came to U.S., 1965, naturalized, 1972; BS in Pharmacy, N.D. State U., 1963; PhD in Nutrition, Pacific We. U., 1985; masner herbalist Dominion Herbal Coll., 1995; m. Gail Andrea Jaffe, May 16, 1971; children: Evan Louis-Ashley, Alanna Dayan. Pres. Adanac Mgmt. Inc., 1979—; instr. Dale Carnegie course; lectr. on nutrition, radio and TV. Mem. Beverly Hills, Rancho Park, Western Los Angeles (dir.) regional chambers commerce, Calif., Am. pharm. assns., Am. Acad. Gen. Pharm. Practice, Am. Inst. for History of Pharmacy, Am. Nutrition Soc., Internat. Coll. Applied Nutrition, Nutrition Found., Nat. Health Fedn., Orthomolecular Med. Assn., Internat. Acad. Preventive Medicine. Clubs: City of Hope, Beverly Hills Rotary, Masons, Shriners. Author: Earl Mindell's Vitamin Bible, Parents Nutrition Bible, Earl Mindell's Quick and Easy Guide to Better Health, Earl Mindell's Pill Bible, Earl Mindell's Shaping Up with Vitamins, Earl Mindell's Safe Eating, Earl Mindell's Herb Bible, Mindell's Food as Medicine, Earl Mindell's Soy Miracle, 1995, Anti-Aging Bible, 1996, Secret Remedies, 1997; columnist Let's Live mag., The Vitamin Supplement (Can.), The Vitamin Connection (U.K.), Healthy N' Fit; contbr. articles on nutrition to profl. jours. Fellow Brit. Homeopathic Inst., Scottish Inst. Homeopathy. Home: 244 S El Camino Dr Beverly Hills CA 90212-3809 Office: 107 S Beverly Dr Beverly Hills CA 90212-3020

MINER, JOHN BURNHAM, industrial relations educator, writer; b. N.Y.C., July 20, 1926; s. John Lynn and Bess (Burnham) M.; children by previous marriage: Barbara, John, Cynthia, Frances; m. Barbara Allen Williams, June 1, 1979; children: Jennifer, Heather. AB, Princeton U., 1950, PhD, 1955; MA, Clark U., 1952. Lic. psychologist, N.Y. Rsch. assoc. Columbia U., 1956-57; mgr. psychol. svcs. Atlantic Refining Co., Phila., 1957-60; faculty mem. U. Oreg., Eugene, 1960-68; prof., chmn. dept. orgnl. sci. U. Md., College Park, 1968-73; rsch. prof. Ga. State U., Atlanta, 1973-87; pres. Orgnl. Measurement Systems Press, Eugene, Oreg., 1976—; prof. Human Resources SUNY, Buffalo, 1987-94, chmn. dept. orgn. and human resources, 1989-92; profl. practice Eugene, Oreg., 1995—; cons. McKinsey & Co., N.Y.C., 1966-69; vis. lectr. U. Pa., Phila., 1959-60; vis. prof. U. Calif., Berkeley, 1966-67, U. South Fla., Tampa, 1972; researcher on orgnl. motivation, theories of orgn., human resource utilization, bus. policy and strategy, entrepreneurship. Author many books and monographs including Personnel Psychology, 1969, Personnel and Industrial Relations, 1969, 73, 77, 85, The Challenge of Managing, 1975, (with Mary Green Miner) Policy Issues Personnel and Industrial Relations, 1977, (with George A. Steiner) Management Policy and Strategy, 1977, James A. Hamilton-Hosp. Adminstrs. Book award 1982, 86), (with M.G. Miner) Employee Selection Within the Law, 1978, Theories of Organizational Behavior, 1980, Theories of Organizational Structure and Process, 1982, People Problems: The Executive Answer Book, 1985, The Practice of Management, 1985, Organizational Behavior: Performance and Productivity, 1988, Industrial-Organizational Psychology, 1992, Role Motivation Theories, 1993, (with Donald P. Crane) Human Resource Management: The Strategic Perspective, 1995, The 4 Routes to Entrepreneurial Success, 1996, (with Michael H. Capps) How Honesty Testing Works, 1996; contbr. numerous articles, papers to profl. jours. Served with AUS, 1944-46, ETO. Decorated Bronze Star, Combat Infantryman's Badge; named Disting. Prof. Ga. State U., 1974. Fellow APA, Acad. of Mgmt. (editor Jour. 1973-75, pres. 1977-78), Soc. for Personality Assessment, Am. Psychol. Soc.; mem. Soc. for Human Resource Mgmt., Indsl. Rels. Rsch. Assn., Internat. Coun. for Small Bus., Strategic Mgmt. Soc., Internat. Pers. Mgmt. Assn., Human Resource Planning Soc. Republican. Home and Office: 34199 Country View Dr Eugene OR 97408

MINER, JOHN EDWARD, city manager; b. Wabash, Ind., Feb. 6, 1937; s. Carlos Monroe and Mary Rebecca (Hoover) M.; m. Sharon Rose Craft, Mar. 24, 1961; children: Carla Marie Crowfoot, Heather Lynet. BS, Manchester Coll., North Manchester, Ind., 1962, Ind. U., 1972; MPA, Ind. U., 1978. Reg. adminstr. Ind. Criminal Justice, Lafayette, Ind., 1970-73; chief rsch. Allen County Sheriff's Dept., Ft. Wayne, Ind., 1973-75; city adminstr. City of Wabash, Ind., 1976-79; exec. budget analyst State of Ariz., Phoenix, 1980; prof. pub. adminstrn. Western Internat. U., Phoenix, 1981-83; city mgr. City of Benson, Ariz., 1981-84; pres., chief exec. officer Municipal MegeTrends, 1984—; govt./environ. affairs specialist Laurent Bouillet-Howard, Phoenix and Paris, 1985-90; city mgr. City of Quartzsite, Ariz., 1990-93; cmty. devel. dir. Town of Camp Verde, Ariz., 1994-95. With USMC, 1957-59. Gov.'s fellow in pub. adminstrn., State of Ind., 1976-78; recipient Award of Excellence in Energy Conservation, Govt., State of Ariz., 1983. Mem. Masons, Elks, Am. Criminal Justice Assn. Home: 2311 W Tuckey Ln Phoenix AZ 85015-1041

MINER, ROBERT FREDERICK, consulting engineer; b. Seattle, Feb. 27, 1957; s. Jack Manning and Wilhelmina Long (Taylor) M.; m. Karen Joy Thiessen, Aug. 22, 1980; children: Jonathan, Rebekah, Javan, Joel. BS in Engring., Case Western Res. U., 1983; MS in Engring., U. Tex., 1989. Registered profl. engr., Wash. Fishing guide Big Bay (B.C., Can.) Marina, 1973-79; engr. GRL & Assocs., Inc., Cleve., 1982-86; sr. engr. GRL & Assocs., Inc., Seattle, 1989—. Contbr. articles to profl. jours. Mem. ASCE, Am. Geophys. Union, Can. Geotech. Soc. Office: GRL & Assocs Inc PO Box 340 Manchester WA 98353

MINES, MICHAEL, lawyer; b. Seattle, May 4, 1929; s. Henry Walker and Dorothy Elizabeth (Bressler) M.; m. Phyllis Eastham, Aug. 24, 1957; children: Linda Mines Elliott, Sandra, Diane Paull, Michael Lister. Student Whitman Coll., 1947-49; BA, U. Wash., 1951, JD, 1954. Bar: Wash. 1954, U.S. Dist. Ct. (we. dist.) Wash. 1957, U.S. Dist. Ct. Mont. 1970, U.S. Ct. Appeals (9th cir.) 1961, U.S. Supreme Ct. Assoc. Skeel, McKelvy, Henke, Evenson & Uhlman, Seattle, 1956-66, ptnr., 1966-68, Hullin, Roberts, Mines, Fite & Riveland, Seattle, 1968-75, Skeel, McKelvy, Henke, Evenson & Betts, Seattle, 1975-79, Betts, Patterson & Mines, Seattle, 1978—. Moderator Wash.-No. Idaho conf. United Ch. of Christ, 1975-76; bd. trustees Plymouth Housing Group, 1991-97. With U.S. Army, 1954-56. Mem. ABA, Wash. State Bar Assn., Seattle-King Bar Assn., Am. Coll. Trial Lawyers (state chair 1982-83, Internat. Assn. Def. Counsel, Wash. Assn. Def. Counsel (pres. 1971-72), Internat. Acad. Trial Lawyers (bd. dirs. 1991-96), U. Wash. Law Sch. Alumni Assn. (trustee, pres. bd. dirs. 1995—). Home: 2474 Crestmont Pl W Seattle WA 98199-3714 Office: Betts Patterson Mines PS 800 Financial Ctr 1215 4th Ave Seattle WA 98161-1090

MINETA, NORMAN YOSHIO, aerospace transportation exescutive, former congressman; b. San Jose, Calif., Nov. 12, 1931; s. Kay Kunisaku and Kane (Watanabe) M.; m. Danealia; children: David, K., Stuart S. B.S., U. Calif.-Berkeley, 1953; D of Pub. Svc., Santa Clara U., 1989; HHD (hon.), Rust Coll., 1993. Agt./broker Mineta Ins. Agy., San Jose, 1956-89; mem. adv. bd. Bank of Tokyo in Calif., 1961-75; mem. San Jose City Council, 1967-71; vice mayor City of San Jose, 1969-71, mayor, 1971-75; mem. 94th-104th Congresses from 13th (now 15th) Calif. dist., 1975-95; subcom. surface transp., 1989-92, former dep. Dem. whip, ranking minority mem. transp. and infrastructure com.; sr. v.p., mng. dir. transp. sys. & srvs. Lockheed Martin, Washington, 1995—; chmn. fin. com. Santa Clara County (Calif.) Council Chs., 1960-62; commr. San Jose Human Relations Commn., 1962-64, San Jose Housing Authority, 1966—. Precinct chmn. Community Theater Bond Issue, 1964; mem. spl. gifts com. Santa Clara County council Boy Scouts Am., 1967; sec. Santa Clara County Grand Jury, 1964; bd. dirs. Wesley Found., San Jose State Coll., 1956-58, Pacific Neighbors, Community Council Cen. Santa Clara County, Japan Soc., San Francisco, Santa Clara County chpt. NCCJ, Mexican-Am. Community Services Agy.; mem. exec. bd. No. Calif.-Western Nev. dist. council Japanese Am. Citizens League, 1960-62, pres. San Jose chpt., 1957-59; bd. regents Smithsonian Instn., 1979-95 ; chmn. Smithsonian vis. com. for Freer Gallery, 1981-95; mem. bd. regents Santa Clara U. Served to lt. AUS, 1954-56. Mem. Greater San Jose C. of C., Nat. Assn. Indsl. Ins. Agts., Calif. Assn. Indsl. Ins. Agts., San Jose Assn. Ind. Ins. Agts. (dir. 1960-62), North San Jose Optimists Club (pres. 1956-58), Jackson-Taylor Bus. and Profl. Assn. (dir. 1963). Methodist. Office: Lockheed Martin 1200 K St NW Fl 12 Washington DC 20005
Personal philosophy: My two greatest responsibilities are accountability and accessibility to everyone I represent, and to anyone who comes to me for help.

MINGER, TERRELL JOHN, public administration institute executive; b. Canton, Ohio, Oct. 7, 1942; s. John Wilson and Margaret Rose M.; m. Judith R. Arnold, Aug. 7, 1965; 1 child, Gabriella Sophia. BA, Baker U., 1966; MPA, Kans. U., 1969; Urban Exec. Program, MIT, 1975; Loeb fellow Harvard U., 1976-77; Exec. Devel. Program, Stanford U., 1979; MBA, U. Colo., 1983. Asst. dir. admissions Baker U., 1966-67; asst. city mgr. City of Boulder, Colo., 1968-69; city mgr. City of Vail, Colo., 1969-79; pres., chief exec. officer Whistler Village Land Co., Vancouver, B.C., Can., 1979-81; v.p., gen. mgr. Cumberland S.W. Inc., Denver, 1981-83; exec. asst., dep. chief of staff to Gov. Colo., 1983-87; pres., chief exec. officer Sundance (Utah) Inst. for Resource Mgmt., 1986—; pres., chief exec. officer Sundance Enterprises Ltd., 1988-91; adj. prof. grad. sch. pub. affairs U. Colo., 1983—, Sch. Bus. U. Denver, 1992—; bd. dirs. Colo. Open Lands, Inc., 1986—; participant UN Conf. on Environment and Devel., Rio de Janeiro, 1992; chmn. environ. adv. bd. Wal-Mart, Inc., 1990—; bd. dirs. Piton Found., 1996. Editor: Greenhouse/Glasnost—The Global Warming Crisis, 1990. Spl. del. UN Habitat Conf. Human Settlements, spl. rep. to UN Environment Program, 1992, coord. UN Global Youth Forum, 1993, 94, co-chmn. conf. on environment and marketing, N.Y.C., 1993; founder Vail Symposium; co-founder, bd. dirs. Colo. Park Found., 1985—; founding mem. Greenhouse/Glasnost U.S./USSR Teleconf. with Soviet Acad. Scis., 1989—; mem. pres. task force Commn. on Sustainable Devel., 1994—; co-chmn. Golf and Environ. Conf., Pebble Beach, Calif., 1995; founder, pres. Western Rendezvous, 1995—. Nat. finalist White House Fellowship, 1978; named one of B.C.'s Top Bus. Leaders for the '80's, 1980. Mem. Urban Land Inst., Colo. Acad. Pub. Adminstrn. (charter, founding mem. 1988), Colo. City Mgmt. Assn., Internat. City Mgrs. Assn. (Mgmt. Innovation award 1974-76), Western Gov.'s Assn. (staff coun., chmn. adv. com. 1985-86), Flatirons Athletic Club. Editor: Vail Symposium Papers, 1970-79; author, editor: Growth Alternatives for Rocky Mountain West, 1976; Future of Human Settlements in the West, 1977. Home: 785 6th St Boulder CO 80302-7416 Office: Ctr for Resource Mgmt 1410 Grant St Ste 307C Denver CO 80203-1846

MINK, PATSY TAKEMOTO, congresswoman; b. Paia, Maui, Hawaii, Dec. 6, 1927; d. Suematsu and Mitama (Tateyama) Takemoto; m. John Francis Mink, Jan. 27, 1951; 1 child, Gwendolyn. Student, Wilson Coll., 1946, U. Nebr., 1947; BA, U. Hawaii, 1948; LLD, U. Chgo., 1951; DHL (hon.), Chaminade Coll., 1975, Syracuse U., 1976, Whitman Coll., 1981. Bar: Hawaii. Pvt. practice Honolulu, 1953-65; lectr. U. Hawaii, 1952-56, 59-62, 79-80; atty. territorial Ho. of Reps., 1955; mem. Hawaii Ho. of Reps., 1956-58, Ter. Hawaii Senate, 1958-59, Hawaii State Senate, 1962-64, 89th-94th Congresses from 2nd Hawaii dist., 101st-105th Congresses from 2d dist. Hawaii, 1990—; mem. econ. and ednl. opportunity com., mem. budget com.; mem. U.S. del. to UN Law of Sea, 1975-76, Internat. Woman's Yr., 1975, UN Environ. Program, 1977, Internat. Whaling Commn., 1977; asst. sec. of state U.S. Dept. State, 1977-78. Charter pres. Young Dem. Club Oahu, 1954-56, Ter. Hawaii Young Dems., 1956-58; del. Dem. Nat. Conv., 1960, 72, 80; nat. v.p. Young Dem. Clubs Am., 1957-59; v.p. Ams. for Dem. Action, 1974-76, nat. pres., 1978-81; mem. nat. adv. com. White House Conf. on Families, 1979-80; mem. nat. adv. coun. Federally Employed Women. Recipient Leadership for Freedom award Roosevelt Coll., Chgo., 1968, Alii award 4-H Clubs Hawaii, 1969, Nisei of Biennium award, Freedom award Honolulu chpt. NAACP, 1971, Disting. Humanitarian award YWCA, St.

Louis, 1972, Creative Leadership in Women's Rights award NEA, 1977, Human Rights award Am. Fedn. Tchrs., 1975, Feminist of Yr. award Feminist Majority Found., 1991, Margaret Brent award ABA, 1992, Outstanding Woman of Yr. award Nat. Assn. Profl. Am. Women, 1992, Environ. Leadership award Nat. League Conservation Voters, 1993, Jessie Bernard Wise Women award Ctr. for Women Policy Studies, 1993, Hawaii's Health Mother award, 1994, Hispanic Health Leadership award, 1995, Women Work! Nat. Network for Women's Employment, 1995, Women at Work Pub. Policy award, 1995, Justice in Action award Asian Am. Legal Def. and Edn. Fund, 1996, Daniel K. Inouye award Hawaii Psychol. Assn., 1996, Indsl. Union Dept. Lewis-Murray-Reuther Social Justice award AFL-CIO, 1996, Top Rating for Global Internat. Trade Watch, Pub. Citizens/Nat. Farmers Union/Friends of the Earth, 1996, award Inferfaith IMPACE for Justice and Peace, 1996, Hawaii Coun. on Lang. Planning and Policy cert. for opposition to English-only legislation, 1996. Office: US Ho of Reps 2135 Rayburn HOB Washington DC 20515

MINNERLY, ROBERT WARD, retired headmaster; b. Yonkers, N.Y., Mar. 21, 1935; s. Richard Warren and Margaret Marion (DeBrocky) M.; m. Sandra Overmire, June 12, 1957; children: Scott Ward, John Robert, Sydney Sue. AB, Brown U., 1957; MAT, U. Tex., Arlington, 1980. Tchr., coach Rumsey Hall Sch., Washington Conn., 1962-64; tchr., coach Berkshire Sch., Sheffield, Mass., 1964-70, asst. head, 1969-70, headmaster, 1970-76; dir. Salisbury (Conn.) Summer Sch. Reading and English, 1970; prin. upper sch. Ft. Worth Country Day Sch., 1976-86; headmaster Charles Wright Acad., Tacoma, Wash., 1986-96; ednl. cons. The Educators' Group, 1996—; cons. Tarrant County Coalition on Substance Abuse, 1982-84; mem. mayor's task force Tacoma Edn. Summit, 1991-92. Contbr. articles to profl. jours. Bd. dirs. Tacoma/Pierce County Good Will Games Art Coun., 1989; mem. exec. com. Am. Leadership Forum, 1991-95; bd. dirs. Broadway Ctr. for Performing Arts, Tacoma, 1988-94, 96-97, mem. exec. com., 1990-93; elected Wash. State Bd. Edn., 1996—. Named Adminstr. of Yr. Wash. Journalism Edn. Assn., 1991. Mem. Pacific N.W. Assn. Ind. Schs. (chmn. long-range planning com. 1989-92, exec. com. 1990-92, 91, v.p. 1994). Republican. Presbyterian. Home and Office: 4214 39th Avenue Ct NW Gig Harbor WA 98335-8029

MINNICH, DIANE KAY, state bar executive; b. Iowa City, Feb. 17, 1956; d. Ralph Maynard Minnich and Kathryn Jane (Obye) Tompkins. BA in Behavioral Sci., San Jose State U., 1978. Tutorial program coord./instr. Operation SHARE/La Valley Coll., Van Nuys, Calif., 1979-81; field exec. Silver Sage Girl Scout Coun., Boise, Idaho, 1981-85; continuing legal edn. dir. Idaho State Bar/Idaho Law Found. Inc., Boise, 1985-88, dep. dir., 1988-90, exec. dir., 1990—. Mem. Assn. CLE Adminstrs., Chgo., 1985-90; bd. dirs. Silver Sage coun. Girl Scouts, Boise, 1990-93, nominating com. mem., 1990-94, chair nominating com., 1991-92. Named one of Outstanding Young Women in Am., 1991. Mem. Nat. Orgn. Bar Execs. (membership com. 1992), Zonta Club Boise (prs. 1991-92, bd. dirs. 1989-93, chair long range planning com.), Rotary Club Boise (chair mem. com. 1994-96, bd. dirs. 1996—). Office: Idaho State Bar/Idaho Law Found PO Box 895 525 W Jefferson St Boise ID 83702-5931

MINNICH, JOSEPH EDWARD, tourist railway consultant; b. Swanton, Ohio, Sept. 13, 1932; s. Charles and Leila (Gaiman) M.; m. Frances Katherine Searcy, Feb. 6, 1977; children: Christopher, Susan, Teresa. Student, U. Toledo, 1956-58, Am. U., 1969. Ins. broker Wright Russell & Bay Co., Toledo, 1961-67; ch. adminstr. St. Paul's Luth. Ch., Toledo, 1968-80; pres. Toledo Lake Erie & Western R.R., 1978-81, Heritage R.R. Co., 1981-83; exec. v.p. Centennial Rail, Ltd., Denver, 1981-94, chmn. bd. dirs., 1994—; v.p. Airpower West Ltd., 1992-95. Author: Steam Locomotives in the United States, 1985, Historic Diesels in the United States, 1988; editor Trainline mag., 1979-95. V.p. Airpower West, Ltd., 1992-95. Sgt. USAF, 1951-55. Nat. Assn. Ch. Bus. Adminstrs. fellow, 1971. Mem. Tourist Ry. Assn. (bd. dirs. 1984-95, Disting. Svc. award 1991), Colo. Ry. Mus. Republican. Lutheran. Home: 3641 S Yampa St Aurora CO 80013-3527 Office: Centennial Rail Ltd PO Box 460393 Aurora CO 80046-0393

MINNIE, MARY VIRGINIA, social worker, educator; b. Eau Claire, Wis., Feb. 16, 1922; d. Herman Joseph and Virginia Martha (Strong) M. BA, U. Wis., 1944; MA, U. Chgo., 1949, Case Western Reserve U., 1956. Lic. clin. social worker, Calif. Supr. day care Wis. Children Youth, Madison, 1949-57; coordinator child study project Child Guidance Clinic, Grand Rapids, Mich., 1957-60; faculty, community services Pacific Oaks Coll., Pasadena, Calif., 1960-70; pvt. practice specializing in social work various cities, Calif., 1970-78; ednl. cons. So. Calif. Health Care, North Hollywood, Calif., 1978—; med. social worker Kaiser Permanente Home Health, Downey, Calif., 1985-87; assoc. Baby Sitters Guild, Inc., 1987-94; cons. Home Health, 1987-90; pres. Midwest Assn. Nursery Edn., Grand Rapids, 1958-60; bd. dirs., sec. So. Calif. Health Care, North Hollywood; bd. dirs., v.p. Baby Sitters Guild Inc., South Pasadena, 1986-94; cons. project Head Start Office Econ. Opportunity, Washington, 1965-70. Mem. Soc. Clin. Social Workers, Nat. Assn. Social Workers, Nat. Assn. Edn. Young Children (1960-62). Democrat. Club: Altrusa (Laguna Beach, Calif.) (pres. 1984-87). Home and Office: 2225 Silver Oak Way Hemet CA 92545-8126

MINOR, LARRY J., food products executive; b. 1945. With Agri-Empire, pres. Office: Agri-Empire 630 W 7th St San Jacinto CA 92583-4015*

MINOR, TOM, mayor. Mayor City of San Bernardino, Calif. Office: City of San Bernardino 300 N D St San Bernardino CA 92418

MINOR, WILLIE, college dean; b. Navasota, Tex., Jan. 31, 1951; s. Carl Jr. and Marjorie (Williams) M. BS, Prairie View A&M U., 1973, MS, 1974; MA, U. Phoenix, 1980; EdD, Ariz. State U., 1976. Assoc. prof. bus. Pairie View (Tex.) A&M U., 1976-77; coord., prof. bus. Phoenix Coll., Phoenix, 1977-87, prof. bus., dept. chair, 1987-89, assoc. dean of instrn., 1989—. Bd. dirs. Jr. Achievement, Phoenix, 1995-96, Future Devel. Edn. & Performing Arts Acad., Phoenix, 1995-96. Mem. Ariz. Occupational Adminstrn. Coun. (pres. 1989—), Maricopa Coun. on Black Am. Affairs, Phi Delta Kappa, Delta Mu Delta, Pi Omega Pi, Phi Beta Lambda. Democrat. Home: 6442 W Fremont Rd Laveen AZ 85339 Office: Phoenix Coll 1202 W Thomas Rd Phoenix AZ 85013-4208

MINOT, MARK MORTON, engineering executive; b. L.A., Dec. 26, 1958; s. Robert M. and Marcia Minot; m. Katharine Minot, 1982; children. BSEE, U. Calif., 1981, MSEE, 1982, PhD, 1990, MBA, 1996. Con. engr. Sputered Films Inc., Santa Barbara, Calif., 1979-82; cons. engr. ECS, Santa Barbara, 1979-82; sr. design engr. Avantek Microwave Inc., Santa Clara, Calif., 1982-85; cons. engr. ECS, Irvine, Calif., 1985-91; engring. mgr. R&D Baxter Healthcare, Irvine, 1991—. Contbr. articles to profl. jours. Mem. IEEE, Am. Vacuum Soc., Optical Soc. Am., Assn. Advancement Med. Instrumentation, Soc. Photometric Instrumentation Engrs. Office: Baxter Healthcare 17221 Red Hill Ave Irvine CA 92614-5627

MINTS, GRIGORI EFROIM, specialist in mathematical logic; b. Leningrad, USSR, June 7, 1939; s. Efroim B. and Lea M. (Novick) M.; m. Maryanna Rozenfeld, July 21, 1987; 1 child, Anna. Diploma, Leningrad U., 1961, PhD, 1965, ScD, 1989. Rsch. assoc. Steklov Inst. Math., Leningrad, 1961-79; with Nauka Pubs., Leningrad, 1979-85; sr. rsch. assoc. Inst. Cybernetics, Tallinn, Estonia, 1985-91; prof. dept. philosophy Stanford (Calif.) U., 1991—; mem. adv. bd. Jour. Symbolic Logic, 1987-90; mem. editorial bd. Jour. Symbolic Computation, 1983-96, Jour. of Functional Programming, 1990-95; mem. program orgn. com. Logic in Computer Sci., 1991-94, ASL mtg. March 1997, Conf. on Automated Deduction, Logic Programming and Automated Reasoning. Editor: Mathematical Investigation of Logical Deduction, 1967, COLOG-88, 1989, Logic Colloquium, 1996; Jour. Logic and Computation, 1991—; contbr. articles to profl. jours. Mem. Assn. Symbolic Logic (mem. coun. 1990-93), Internat. Union History and Philosophy and Sci. (assessor 1991-95), Annals of Pure and Applied Logic (mem. editorial bd. 1980-89).

MINTZ, DENA MARLENE, optometrist; b. Aug. 29, 1957. Student, Calif. State U., Fullerton, 1980-83; BS in Visual Sci. cum laude, So. Calif. Coll. Optometry, 1985, OD, 1987. Ind. contractor Sun City (Calif.) Vision Clinic, 1987-89; sole propr. optometric practice Corona, Calif., 1988—; asst. prof. Optometric Ctr. So. Calif. Coll. Optometry, Fullerton, 1987—, lab. instr., 1989; supr. optometric interns Baldwin Park Optometric Ctr., 1987; instr. Calif. State U., Fullerton, 1991; rschr. in field. Vol. career conf. YWCA, 1991, 92, Women's Wellness Cay, Circle City Hosp./Charter Hosp. of Corona, 1991, Kids' Care Fair, 1994. Fellow Am. Acad. Optometry (diplomate candidate cornea and contact lens sect., trustee Calif. chpt. 1993, sec. 1994, pres.-elect 1996); mem. Calif. Optometric Assn. (ocular disease symposium com. 1995, edn. com. 1996), Am. Optometric Assn. (contact lens sect.), Assn. Optometric Educators, Corona C. of C., Am. Bus. Women's Assn. (v.p. 1991-92, chmn. scholarship com. 1991-92, chmn. membership com. 1992-93, Woman of Yr. 1993), Rotary. Office: 800 Magnolia Ave Ste 113 Corona CA 91719-3123

MINTZ, MARSHALL GARY, lawyer; b. Detroit, May 28, 1947. BA, UCLA, 1968, JD, 1971. Bar: Calif. 1972. Law clk. appellate dept L.A. County Superior Ct., 1971-72; ptnr. Kelly & Lytton, L.A., Calif., 1995—; moderator, panelist Calif. Continuing Edn. of Bar, 1980—; mem. arbitration adminstrv. com. L.A. County Superior Ct., 1979, mem. 1984 Olympics spl. settlement panel. Mem. ABA, State Bar Calif., L.A. County Bar Assn. (arbitrator arbitration and client rels. com. 1978-90), Assn. Bus. Trial Lawyers (bd. govs. 1976-77, program chmn. 1976). Office: Kelly & Lytton Ste 1450 1900 Avenue Of The Stars Los Angeles CA 90067-4405

MINUDRI, REGINA URSULA, librarian, consultant; b. San Francisco, May 9, 1937; d. John C. and Molly (Halter) M. BA, San Francisco Coll. for Women, 1958; MLS, U. Calif.-Berkeley, 1959. Reference libr. Menlo Park (Calif.) Pub. Libr., 1959-62; regional libr. Santa Clara County (Calif.) Libr., 1962-68; project coord. Fed. Young Adult Libr. Svcs. Project, Mountain View, Calif., 1968-71; dir. profl. services Alameda County (Calif.) Libr., 1971, asst. county libr., 1972-77; libr. dir. Berkeley Pub. Libr., 1977-94; lectr. U. San Francisco, 1970-72, U. Calif., Berkeley, 1977-81, 91-93; lectr. San Jose State U., 1994—; cons., 1975—; adv. bd. Miles Cutter Ednl., 1992—. Bd. dirs. No. Calif. ACLU, 1994-96, Cmty. Memory, 1989-91, Berkeley Cmty. Fund, 1994—, chair youth com., 1994—, Berkeley Pub. Libr. Found. Bd., 1996—; mem. bd. mgrs. cen. br. Berkeley YMCA, 1988-93. Recipient proclamation Mayor of Berkeley, 1985, 86, 94, Citation of Merit Calif. State Assembly, 1994; named Woman of Yr. Alameda County North chpt. Nat. Women's Polit. Caucus, 1986, Outstanding Alumna U. Calif. Sch. Libr. and Info. Scis., Berkeley, 1987. Mem. ALA (pres. 1986-87, exec. bd. 1980-89, coun. 1979-88, 90-94, Grolier award 1974), Calif. Libr. Assn. (pres. 1981, coun. 1965-69, 79-82), LWV (dir. Berkeley chpt. 1980-81, v.p. comm. svcs. 1995—). Author: Getting It Together, A Young Adult Bibliography, 1970; contbr. articles to publs. including School Libr. Jour., Wilson Libr. Bull. Office: Reality Mgmt 836 The Alameda Berkeley CA 94707-1916*

MINZNER, DEAN FREDERICK, aviation company executive; b. Winchester, Mass., July 20, 1945; s. Frederick Louis and Winifred (Hughes) M.; B.A., Franklin and Marshall Coll., 1967; M.B.A., Columbia U., 1972. Dist. exec. Greater N.Y. councils Boy Scouts Am., N.Y.C., 1972-76; sales exec. Coast Avia, Long Beach, Calif., 1976-78, Performance Aircraft, Inc., Hayward, Calif., 1978; owner, pres. Western Aviation Consultants, Inc., Hayward, 1978-82, Cal-Pacific Assocs., Inc., Hayward, 1979—, Cal-Pacific Enterprises, Hayward, 1982—. Mem. Assn. M.B.A. Execs., Columbia U. Grad. Sch. Bus. Alumni Assn., Aircraft Owners and Pilots Assn. Office: PO Box 6206 Hayward CA 94540-6206

MINZNER, PAMELA B., judge; b. Meridian, Miss., Nov. 19, 1943. BA cum laude, Miami U., 1965; LLB, Harvard U., 1968. Bar: Mass. 1968, N.Mex. 1972. Pvt. practice Mass., 1968-71, Albuquerque, 1971-73; adj. prof. law U. N.Mex., Albuquerque, 1972-73, asst. prof., 1973-77, assoc. prof., 1977-80, prof. law, 1980-84; judge N.Mex. Ct. Appeals, Albuquerque, 1984; now justice N.Mex. Supreme Ct., Sante Fe; mem. faculty Inst. Preparativo Legal U., N.Mex. Sch. Law, 1975, 79; participant NEH Summer Seminar for Law Tchrs. Stanford Law Sch., 1982, U. Chgo. Law Sch., 1978. Co-author (Robert T. Lawrence) A Student's Guide to Estates in Land and Future Interests: Text, Examples, Problems & Answers, 1981, 2d edit. 1993. Mem. ABA, State Bar N.Mex. (co-editor newsletter 1979-83, bd. dirs. 1978-79, 83-84, sect. on women's legal rights and obligations), Gamma Phi Beta. Democrat. Office: PO Box 848 Santa Fe NM 87504-0848

MION, PIERRE RICCARDO, artist, illustrator; b. Bryn Mawr, Pa., Dec. 10, 1931; s. Bernardo and Katherine (Newbaker) M.; m. Dorothy Marie Smith, Dec. 29, 1961 (div. June 1980); children: Keith, Tina Affeldt, Nicole McCorgary; m. Sandra Lee Brenton, Apr. 1, 1995. Student, George Washington U., 1950-52, 56, Corcoran Sch. Art, Washington, 1950-52, Montgomery Coll., Rockville, Md., 1980-83. Art dir. Creative Arts Studio, Washington, 1956-60; v.p. No. Sci. Industries, Washington, 1964-66; artist-illustrator Chevy Chase, Md., Arlington, Va., Lovettsville, Va., 1960—. Author, photographer, illustrator: Smithsonian Fire of Life, 1981; illustrator Nat. Geographic mag., 1961-97 (numerous awards), others; executed murals for Smithsonian Inst., 1970, Mus. Natural History, 1979, Air and Space Mus., 1981; designed 12 postage stamps/postcards U.S. Postal Svc., 1987-93; represented in permanent collections for Smithsonian Air & Space mus., NASA Fine Arts Collection, USMC Combat Art Collection, others; work commd. for Newmont Gold Co., Denver. 1007. Stone Mountain Park, Atlanta, 1996. With USMC, 1952-54, temporary lt. col. (combat artist), 1968, Vietnam. Recipient merit awards Soc. Illustrators, Art Dirs. Club, N.Y.C.; named Outstanding Citizen, Town of Lovettsville, Va., 1990; nat. champion race car driver, 1959, 61, regional champion 1962, 63, 64. Home and Office: 59 Cascade Pagosa Springs CO 81147

MIRANTE, KATHLEEN MARIE, cardiologist; b. Seattle, Apr. 8, 1940; d. Dominic and Frances (Drew) M. BS, Coll. Notre Dame, 1967; MD, Med. Coll. Pa., 1971. Diplomate Am. Bd. Internal Medicine, Am. Bd. Cardiovascular Disease. Resident Montefiore Hosp. & Med. Ctr., Bronx, N.Y., 1971-73, Mercy Hosp. & Med. Ctr., San Diego, 1973-74; fellow in cardiology Pacific Med. Ctr., San Francisco, 1974-76; attending physician Kaiser Found. Hosp., Fontana, Calif., 1976—; dir. cardiac rehabilitiation Kaiser Found. Hosp., Fontana, 1978—, dir. CCU, 1994. Named Physician of Yr., So. Calif. Permanente Med. Group, Fontana, 1987. Fellow Am. Coll. Cardiology, Am. Coll. Chest Physicians. Office: Kaiser Hosp Dept Cardiology 9981 Sierra Ave Fontana CA 92335-6720

MIRIKITANI, JOHN MASA, foundation administrator; b. Honolulu, Nov. 24, 1962; s. Clifford Kunio and Helene M. AB, U. Calif., Berkeley, 1985; JD, U. Mich., 1990; postgrad., U. Hawaii. Policy analyst intern Sloan Found. for Pub. Policy and Mgmt./U. Calif., Berkeley, 1984; policy analyst legis. bus. devel. com. State of Hawaii, Honolulu, 1988-89; founder, pres. John and Clifford Mirikitani Found., Honolulu, 1988—; sponsor Mirikitani Lectrs. in law and econs. edn., U. Hawaii, Manoa, Honolulu, 1989—. Candidate for State Bd. Edn., State Hawaii, 1992, 94. Recipient fellowship Harvard Kennedy Sch. of Govt., 1985. Mem. Am. Law and Econs. Assn., Phi Beta Kappa. Home: 2336 Oahu Ave Honolulu HI 96822-1965

MIRK, JUDY ANN, elementary educator; b. Victorville, Calif., June 10, 1944; d. Richard Nesbit and Corrine (Berghoefer) M. BA in Social Sci., San Jose (Calif.) State U., 1966, cert. in teaching, 1967; MA in Edn., Calif. State U., Chico, 1980. Cert. elem. edn. tchr., Calif. Tchr. Cupertino (Calif.) Union Sch. Dist., 1967-95; lead tchr. lang. arts Dilworth Sch., San Jose, 1988-90, mem. supt.'s adv. team, 1986-90, mem. student study team, 1987-95; mem. student study team, 1987-95; mem. Dilworth Sch. Site Coun., 1981-95. Mem. The Camp Fellowship. Mem. Daytime Drama Guild (charter), Phi Mu. Republican. Home: 4132 Valerie Dr Campbell CA 95008-3728

MIRRASOUL, ROBIN STUART, first aid safety products executive; b. Portland, Oreg., May 11, 1959; d. George Stuart and June Valentine (Park) Hutchison; m. Gerald James Craig, Aug. 27, 1977 (div. Apr. 1980); m. Marc Girard Mirrasoul, July 2, 1988. Cert. EMT, Oreg. Clerical sales rep. PC Dayton Tire, Portland, Oreg., 1977-80; territory rep. Schmunks Tire Ctr., Springfield, Oreg., 1980-84; sales rep. Evergreen Distbg., Bend, Oreg., 1984-86; truck driver Intermountain Bldg. Supply, Bend, 1986-87; sales rep. Zee Med., Portland, 1987-90; owner Cascade First Aid and Safety, LaPine, Oreg., 1990—. Mem. Am. Legion Aux. Office: Cascade First Aid & Safety PO Box 1470 La Pine OR 97739

MIRSKY, PHYLLIS SIMON, librarian; b. Petach Tikva, Israel, Dec. 18, 1940; d. Allan and Lea (Prizant) Simon; m. Edward Mirsky, Oct. 21, 1967; 1 child, Seth. BS in Social Welfare, Ohio State U., 1962; postgrad., Columbia U., 1962-63; AMLS, U. Mich., 1965. Caseworker field placement Children's Aid Soc., N.Y.C., 1962-63; hosp. libr. hosp. and instns. divsn. Cleve. Pub. Libr., 1963-64; reference libr. UCLA Biomed. Libr., 1965-68, reference/acquisitions libr., 1968-69, head cons./continuing edn. Pacific S.W. Regl. Med. Libr. Sv., 1969-71, asst. dir. Pacific S.W. Regl. Med. Libr. Sv., 1971-73, faculty coord. Biomed. Libr. program Cen. San Joaquin Valley Area Health Edn. Ctr., 1973-77, assoc. dir. Pacific S.W. Regl. Med. Libr. Sv., 1973-79; head reference sect., coord. libr. assoc. program Nat. Libr. of Medicine, Bethesda, Md., 1979-81; asst. univ. libr., scis. U. Calif.-San Diego, La Jolla, 1981-86, acting univ. libr., 1985, 92-93, asst. univ. libr. adminstrv. and pub. svcs., 1986-87, assoc. univ. libr. adminstrv. and pub. svcs., 1987-92, assoc. univ. libr., 1993-95; dep. univ. libr., 1995—; guest lectr. Libr. Schs. UCLA and U. So. Calif., 1967-78, Grad. Sch. Libr. Sci. Cath. U., Washington, 1980, Grad. Sch. Libr. and Info. Sci. UCLA, 1984; mem. task force on role of spl. libr. nationwide network and coop. programs Nat. Commn. on Libr. and Info. Svcs./Spl. Libr. Assn., 1981-83; facilitator AASLD/MLA Guidelines Scenario Writing Session, L.A., 1984; mem. users coun. OCLC Online Computer Libr. Ctr., Inc., 1991-94; U. Calif.-San Diego rep. Coalition for Networked Info., 1992—; instr. Assn. Rsch. Librs., Office Mgmt. Studies, Mgmt. Inst., 1987; peer reviewer Coll. Libr. Tech. and Cooperation Grant Program U.S. Dept. Edn., 1988-94; cons. Nat. Libr. Medicine, Bethesda, Md., 1988, San Diego Mus. Contemporary Art Libr., La Jolla, Calif., 1993, Salk Inst., 1995; mem. Libr. of Congress Network Adv. Com., 1994—, chair steering com., 1995—. Contbr. articles to profl. jours. and bulls. NIH fellow Columbia U., 1962-63; sr. fellow UCLA/Coun. on Libr. Resources, 1987. Mem. ALA (site visitors panel com. on accreditation 1990-92, libr. adminstrn. and mgmt. assn. 1990-92), Med. Libr. Assn. (bd. dirs. 1977-80), Med. Libr. Group Soc. Calif. and Ariz. (sec. 1970-71, v.p. 1971-72, pres. 1972-73), Documentation Abstracts, Inc. (bd. dirs. 1985-90, vice chair bd. dirs. 1988-90), Med. Libr. Assn. (pres. 1984-85), U. Mich. Sch. Libr. Sci. Alumni Assn. Office: U Calif-San Diego Univ Libr 0175G 9500 Gilman Dr La Jolla CA 92093-0175

MISA, KENNETH FRANKLIN, management consultant; b. Jamaica, N.Y., Sept. 24, 1939; s. Frank J. and Mary M. (Soszka) M.; BS cum laude in Psychology, Fairfield U., 1961; MS in Psychology, Purdue U., 1963; PhD in Psychology (Fellow 1963-66), St. John's U., 1966. Staff psychologist Rohrer, Hibler & Replogle, Los Angeles, 1966-67; assoc. A.T. Kearney, Inc., Los Angeles, 1968-71, sr. assoc., 1972-74, prin., 1975-78, v.p., partner, 1979-86; pres. HR Cons. Group, 1987—. Cert. mgmt. cons.; lic. psychologist, Calif. Mem. Am. Psychol. Assn., Am. Psychol. Soc., Calif. State Psychol. Assn., Soc. for Human Resources Mgmt., Human Resources Planning Soc., Indsl. Rels. Rsch. Assn., Soc. for Indsl. and Organizational Psychology, World Affairs Coun. of L.A., Town Hall of So. Calif., Glendale C. of C., Jonathan Club. Republican. Roman Catholic. Home: 924C S Orange Grove Blvd Pasadena CA 91105-1741 Office: HR Cons Group 100 N Brand Blvd Ste 200 Glendale CA 91203-2614

MISCHER, DONALD LEO, television director and producer; b. San Antonio, Mar. 5, 1940; s. Elmer Frederick and Lillian Alma. B.A., U. Tex., 1961, M.A., 1963. Mem. faculty U. Tex., 1962-63; producer/dir. USIA, Washington, 1965-68; with Charles Guggenheim Prodns., 1969-71; pres. Don Mischer Prodns., pres. Mischer Enterprises, Inc., Beverly Hills, Calif., prodr., dir., and program packager for network television programs, 1971—. Television programs include: The Opening and Closing Ceremonies of the 1996 Centennial Olympic Games, Atlanta, The Kennedy Center Honors: A Celebration of the Performing Arts (Emmy Awards 1981, 87); The Tony Awards (Emmy Awards 1987-88); Michael Jackson's Super Bowl XXVII Halftime Show; Baryshnikov by Tharp (Emmy Award 1985); Gregory Hines, Tap Dance America; Carnegie Hall: Live at 100; It's Garry Shandling's Show; Mowtown 25: Yesterday, Today, Tomorrow (Emmy Award 1983); The Muppets Celebrate Jim Henson; Motown Returns to the Apollo (Emmy Award 1985); Baryshnikov in Hollywood, Goldie and Liza Together, Shirley MacLaine—Illusions, Making Television Dance with Twyla Tharp, An Evening with Robin Williams, Am. Film Inst. Salute to Gene Kelly; producer additional programs with Bob Hope (Bob Hope: The First 90 Years - Emmy award Outstanding Variety, Music or Comedy Special, 1993), Barbara Walters, Goldie Hawn, others. Recipient: Primetime Emmy awards (10), Director's Guild awards for Outstanding Directorial Achiement (8), NAACP Image awards (3), Peabody award, Golden Rose of Montreux award, Gabriel award, Ohio State award. Mem. Dirs. Guild Am., Nat. Acad. TV Arts and Scis. Gov., Am. Film Inst. Office: Brillstein-Grey Entertainment 9150 Wilshire Blvd Ste 350 Beverly Hills CA 90212-3430

MISHKIN, MARJORIE WONG, aviation and marketing consultant; b. Los Angeles, Oct. 28, 1940; d. Thomas A. and Mayme M. (Moe) Wong; children: Barbara Joanne, Cynthia Anne; m. David Gordon Mishkin, Jan. 6, 1991. BA, Goucher Coll., 1962; MA, U. Calif. at Berkeley, 1965. Research economist Fed. Reserve Bank San Francisco, 1964-65; bus. cons., travel industry, 1968-74; marketing analyst The Flying Tiger Line Inc., Los Angeles, 1974-76, systems analyst, 1976-77, mgr. mgmt. reporting and performance analysis, 1977-78; dir. passenger pricing and fare devel. Continental Airlines, 1978-80, dir. internat. pricing, 1980-83; aviation and mktg. cons. Chen & Assocs., 1983—, dir. practice devel. Greenberg, Glusker, Fields, Claman & Machtinger, 1989-90; fin. cons. Shearson Lehman Hutton; bd. dirs. Continental Fed. Credit Union. Trustee, chmn. devel. Marlborough Sch.; trustee, deacon 1st Congl. Ch. of Los Angeles; mem. evaluation com. Am. Heart Assn. Danforth Found. assoc., 1968-79. Mem. Nat. Mgmt. Assn. (membership chmn.), World Affairs Council L.A., L.A. Libr. Assn. (v.p., treas.), Town Hall Calif., U. Calif. Alumni Assn., Marlborough Alumni Assn. Republican. Home: Ste 406 10430 Wilshire Blvd Los Angeles CA 90024

MISIASZEK, JOHN J., psychiatrist; b. London, Dec. 10, 1948; came to U.S., 1951; s. Walter Peter and Maria Elizabeth Misiaszek; m. Jenifer Davis George; children: Julie, Michael. BS with distinction, U. Ariz., 1971, MD, 1975. Diplomate Nat. Bd. Med. Examiners; bd. cert. psychiatry; lic. psychiatrist, Ariz.; cert. controlled substances registration. Intern in medicine Santa Barbara (Calif.) Gen. Hosp., 1975-76; resident in psychiatry Ariz. Health Scis. Ctr., Tucson, 1976-79; coord. consultation-liaison svc. dept. psychiatry U. Ariz., Tucson, 1978; asst. prof. psychiatry dept. psychiatry Ariz. Health Scis. Ctr.-U. Ariz., Tucson, 1979-85, dir. consultation-liaison svc., 1979-90, clin. asst. prof. psychiatry, 1985, assoc. prof. clin. psychiatry, 1985—; dir. med. psychiatry Outpatient Clinic, Tucson, 1993—; cons. psychiatrist VA Hosp., Tucson, So. Ariz. Mental Health Ctr., Tucson. Contbr. articles to med. and sci. jours. Fellow Am. Psychiat. Assn.; mem. Assn. for Academic Psychiatry, Acad. Psychosomatic Medicine. Office: Ariz Health Scis Ctr 1501 N Campbell Ave Tucson AZ 85724-0001

MISNER, CHARLOTTE BLANCHE RUCKMAN, community organization administrator; b. Gifford, Idaho, Aug. 30, 1937; d. Richard Steele and Arizona (Hill) Ruckman; m. G. Arthur Misner, Jr., Aug. 29, 1959; children: Michelle, Mary, Jennifer. BS in Psychology, U. Idaho, 1959. Vol. numerous orgns. India, Mexico, The Philippines, 1962-70; sec., v.p., pres., trustee St. Luke's Hosp., Manila, 1970-84; founding mem., 3d v.p., pres. Am. Women's Club of Philippines, 1980-84; exec. adminstr. Friends of Oakland (Calif.) Parks and Recreation, 1986-92, exec. dir., 1992—. Active Lincoln Child Ctr., Oakland, 1984—. Recipient Vol. Svc. award Women's Bd. St. Luke's Hosp., 1977, Mid. Sch. Vol. award Internat. Sch.-Manila, 1980. Me. Alpha Gamma Delta (alumnae treas., pres. East Bay 1985-89, province dir. alumnae 1989—), Cum Laude Soc. (hon.). Home: 481 Ellita Ave Oakland CA 94610-4808 Office: Friends of Oakland Parks & Recreation 1520 Lakeside Dr Oakland CA 94612-4521

MISNER, GERVASE ARTHUR, personnel analyst; b. Lewiston, Idaho, Nov. 21, 1935; s. Gervase A. and Blenda (Westerlund) M.; m. Charlotte B. Ruckman, Aug. 29, 1959; children: Michelle, Mary, Jennifer. BS in Agr. with high honors, U. Idaho, 1958; B Fgn. Trade, Am. Inst. for Fgn. Trade, 1960; MBA cum laude, U. Ams., Mexico City, 1970; postgrad., Laney Coll., 1990. Pres. Philippines Rohm and Haas Co., Phila., 1971-78, area dir. East Asia, 1976-80, area dir. South Asia, 1981-83; v.p. Corp. Fin. Assocs., Atlanta, 1984-86; co-founder UCAM Corp., San Jose, Calif., 1987-89; pers. adminstr. City of Oakland, Calif., 1990—; bd. dirs. Envirozone Techs., Inc.,

Tracy, Calif. Mem. Ateneo de Manila (prof., chmn. exec. com. 1976-77), Rotary Club (pres. 1975-76), Lake Merritt Breakfast Club. Home: 481 Ellita Ave Oakland CA 94610-4808 Office: City of Oakland 505 14th St Oakland CA 94612-1406

MISSETT, KATHRYN MCANDREW, public relations expert; b. Suffolk, Va., Mar. 9, 1949; d. William Joseph and Kathryn Rose (McAndrew) M.; m. Randall T. Cox, July 16, 1983; 1 child, Matthew. BA, U. Wyo., 1973. Editor Wyo. Issues mag. U. of Wyo., Laramie, 1979-82; asst. editor Wyo. Game & Fish, Cheyenne, 1983-85; pub. rels. coord. Campbell County Pub. Libr., Gillette, 1993-96; gen. ptnr. Mountain States Mediation, Gillette, 1996—; v.p. editl. affairs High Country News, Paonia, Colo., 1985-87, bd. dirs. Mem. Wyo. C.C. Commn., Cheyenne, 1986-92, Wyo. Commn. on Women, Cheyenne, 1984-86; bd. dirs. Johnson County Children's Ctr., Buffalo, Wyo., 1987-88, Johnson County Pub. Libr., Buffalo, 1989-92; mem. Wyo. State Bd. Edn., 1997—. Mem. Nat. Fedn. Press Women.

MITCHELL, CARL JACK, medical entomologist, research scientist; b. Sallisaw, Okla., Dec. 3, 1936; s. George and Vera (Walters) M.; m. Barbara M. Williams, Dec. 14, 1961; children: Katherine Ann, Samuel Joseph, Thomas Owen. BS, Northeastern State U., Tahlequah, Okla., 1959; MS, U. Hawaii, 1963; ScD, Johns Hopkins U., 1966. Postdoctoral fellow NIH, Hamilton, Mont., 1966-67; chief Tex. activities U.S. CDC, Plainview, 1967-70; project leader WHO, Taipei, Taiwan, 1970-72; scientist, biologist WHO, Geneva, Switzerland, 1972-73; extension entomologist U. Calif., Davis, 1973-75; rsch. entomologist U.S. CDC, Ft. Collins, Colo., 1974-85, chief Vector Virology Lab., 1984-89, chief med. entomology-ecology br., 1989-95; supervisory rsch. entomologist Arbovirus Diseases Br. U.S. CDC, 1995—; entomologist U.S. Antarctic Rsch. Project, McMurdo Sound, 1961-62; cons. Pan Am. Health Orgn., Dominican Republic and Argentina, 1977, 84, WHO, Geneva, 1986, U.S. AID, Kathmandu, Nepal, 1989; mem. joint Soviet/U.S.A. expdns. to western Siberia, 1990, 91. Author or co-author book chpts. and numerous sci. articles. Recipient Antarctic Svc. medal Dept. Def., 1962, Meritorious Citation, Republic of China, 1972. Mem. Am. Mosquito Control Assn. (chair editl. bd.), Am. Soc. Tropical Medicine and Hygiene, Soc. for Vector Ecology, Entomol. Soc. Am. Office: US CDC PO Box 2087 Fort Collins CO 80522

MITCHELL, DAVID CAMPBELL, inventor, corporate executive; b. Sacramento, Dec. 11, 1957; s. Alan Campbell and Lorraine May (Grant) M.; m. Lanette Pearson; children: David Kirk, Travis, Holly Ann. Student, U. Utah, 1973-74, Brigham Young U. Rsch. dir. Flex Inc., Williston, N.D., 1976-78; with Deseret Industries, Salt Lake City, 1978-81; head R&D Pro Biotiks Labs., Ogden, Utah, 1981—, Melaleuca, Idaho Falls, Idaho, 1987-89; pres., chmn. David C. Mitchell Med. Rsch. Inst., Salt Lake City, 1980—; rsch. cons. U. Utah Rsch. Park, Salt Lake City, 1981—; environ. cons. Hi-Valley Chem., Salt Lake City, 1988—; v.p. Mitchell Products, Orem, Utah, 1989—. Inventor, 125 patents in vitamins, cosmetics, pharmaceuticals, arthritis, cancer, psoriasis, scars and wounds, artificial sweeteners, pain killers, anti-depressants and related biochemistries. Vol. Freeman Inst., Salt Lake City, 1980-87; vol. supr. Granite Bakery (Feed the Poor), Salt Lake City, 1982-87; active rehab. handicapped Deseret Industries, Salt Lake City, 1978-81; pres., young adults rep. Latter-day Saints Ch., Salt Lake City, 1977-78. Scholar NSF, 1973; named one of Outstanding Young Men of Am., 1989. Fellow AAAS, ACS, N.Y. Acad. Scis. Home and Office: 3594 Little Cottonwood Ln Sandy UT 84092

MITCHELL, DAVID VOKES, editor, publisher; b. San Francisco, Nov. 23, 1943; s. Herbert Houston and Edith (Vokes) M. B in English, Stanford U., 1965, M in Comm., 1967. Instr. Upper Iowa Coll., Fayette, 1968-70; reporter Council Bluffs (Iowa) Nonpareil, 1970, Union Dem., Sonora, Calif., 1971-73; editor Sebastopol (Calif.) Times, 1973-75; editor, pub. Point Reyes Light, Point Reyes Station, Calif., 1975-81, 84—; reporter San Francisco Examiner, 1981-83. Author: The Light on Synanon, 1980 (made into a CBS tv movie Attack on Fear). Adv. bd. mem. Calif. Marine Mammal Ctr., 1984-85. Recipient Pulitzer prize for pub. svc. Columbia U., N.Y., 1979, numerous regional, state and nat. journalism awards, 1973—. Mem. Calif. Newspaper Pubs. Assn. (dir. 1985-86), Point Reyes Bus. Assn., Environ. Action Com. of West Marin, West Marin C. of C. Democrat. Home: PO Box 786 Point Reyes Station CA 94956-0786 Office: Point Reyes Light Box 210 Point Reyes Station CA 94956

MITCHELL, GENEVA BROOKE, hypnotherapist; b. Ringgold, Tex., Feb. 15, 1929; d. Roy Banks and Willie Jewel (Lemons) Shaw; m. Roy David Mitchell, Nov. 30, 1947; children: Ronald, Donald, Joel, Pamela, Annette. Cert. master hypnotist Hypnosis Tng. Inst., L.A., 1980, cert. hypnotherapist, 1983; cert. in advanced investigative and forensic hypnosis Tex. A&M U., 1982; D. Clin. Hypnosis, Am. Inst. Hypnotherapy, Calif., 1989. Chiropractic asst. Alamogordo, N.Mex., 1962-79; hypnotherapist Alamogordo Hypnosis and Counseling Ctr., 1980-92; mgr. Shaw Mobile Home Park, 1986—; mng. ptnr. Shaw, Mitchell & Mallory, Albuquerque, 1986, mgr., 1987-88; hypnotherapist M&M Horses Corp., Tularosa, N.Mex., 1985-92; owner A New Image Hypnosis Ctr., Albuquerque, retired, 1992; pres. N.Mex. Chiropractic Aux., 1984-85; mem. Am. Council Hypnotist Examiners, 1980-85; hypnotist for tape series; instr. New Forever Trim Life Loss Program. Author: Take The Power, 1991. Charter pres. La Sertoma, Alamogordo, 1957; pres. Oregon sch. PTA, Alamogordo, 1958, La Luz Sch. Parents Club, N.Mex., 1962; sec. N.Mex. Jr. Rodeo Assn., 1964; co-founder Pre-Sch. La Luz, 1969; mem. N.Mex. Gov.'s Council on Youth, 1969; bd. dirs. Otero County Jr. Rodeo Assn., N.Mex., 1968; dir. self-hypnosis sch.; speaker Am. Bd. Hypnotherapy Conv., 1991. Recipient Speakers award Life Found., 1984. Mem. Am Assn. Profl. Hypnotherapists, Ladies for Life (Appreciation award 1984, 90), N.Mex. Ladies Life Fellowship (pres. 1983, bd. dirs. 1985), S.W. Hypnotherapy Examining Bd., Internat. Chiropractic Assn. Aux. (pres. 1994—, conv. chmn. 1993), Ladies for Life Chiropractic Orgn. (pres. elect 1993). Avocations: golf, painting, swimming, martial arts, writing.

MITCHELL, GUY, singer, entertainer, actor; b. Detroit, Feb. 22, 1927; m. Betty J. Mitchell. Recorded 16 songs, each selling over 1,000,000 copies each, including Singing the Blues (Columbia Hall of Fame), Heartaches by the Number, My Heart Cries for You, My Truly, Truly, Fair, The Roving Kind, Pittsburgh Pennsylvania, Belle, Belle, My Liberty Belle, Sparrow in the Tree Top, She Wears Red Feathers, Feet Up, Pat Him on the Po Po, A Beggar in Love, Unless, Christopher Columbus, Rock-a-Billy, Knee Deep in the Blues, Pretty Little Black Eyed Susie, Cloud Lucky Seven, Chicka-Boom; starred in movies Red Garters, Those Red Heads from Seattle; co-star TV series Whispering Smith; star The Guy Mitchell Show, 1957-58; host, also numerous guest appearances on Arthur Godfrey Show, The Milton Berle Show, Ed Sullivan Show; guest star Dinah Shore Show, Bob Hope Show, Perry Mason Show, also others; command performance before Queen Elizabeth II, London Paladium, 1953. With USN, 1945-46. Mem. AFTRA, SAG, Soc. Singers. Office: GMI care John Elizondo PO Box 42536 Las Vegas NV 89116

MITCHELL, HERBERT EUGENE, management consultant, marketing specialist; b. Elkhart, Ind., July 25, 1929; s. Charles Nathaniel and Beulah Mae (McDonald) M.; m. Roberta Marie Blesie, Oct. 22, 1949; children: Robert, Debra, Kimbra, Candi, Melissa. BS, Iowa State U., 1949. Cert. mgmt. cons. Retail bus. owner J.W. Rodgers Florist, Dayton, Ohio, 1949-65; dir. product devel. The John Henry Co., Lansing, Mich., 1965-67; dir. wholesale mktg. Harry & David/Jackson & Perkins, Newport Beach, Calif., 1967-69; v.p. mktg. Teleflora div. D&B, Redondo Beach, Calif., 1969-75; pvt. practice cons. Creative Mktg., Newport Beach, 1975—. Author: The Fundamentals of Visual Presentation, 1987, Design With Flowers Premier Edition, 1991; editor-in-chief Teleflora Spirit, 1965-67, Design for Profit, 1981-84, The Profl. Floral Designer, 1984-91, Design With Flowers, 1991-92; sr. editor Floriculture Directions, 1975-91. Recipient Floriculture Hall of Fame award Soc. Am. Florists, 1984. Fellow Am. Inst. Floral Designers (bd. dirs. 1976-78, pres. 1978-80, award of disting. svc. 1983); mem. Inst. Mgmt. Cons. Republican. Office: Creative Mktg Specialists 28 Auvergne Newport Coast CA 92657-1026

MITCHELL, JERRY MICHAEL, biologist; b. Borger, Tex., Nov. 24, 1955; s. James C. and JoAnn (Huffine) M.; m. Cassy Ann Mulford, Apr. 2, 1949; 1 child, Hanna Carry. BS in Wildlife Biology, West Tex. A&M U., 1977, MS in Biology, 1979. Resource mgmt. technician Nat. Park Svc., Zion Nat. Park, Utah, 1979, resource mgmt. specialist, to 1988; chief planning and backcountry programs Nat. Park Svc., Grand Canyon Nat. Park, Ariz., 1988-93, acting chief resources mgmt. divsn., 1990-91; chief cultural resource mgmt. Nat. Park Svc., Yosemite Nat. Park, Calif., 1993-96, chief gen. mgmt. plan implementation office of supt., 1997—; Nat. Park Svc. coord. Interagy. Glen Canyon Environ. Studies, 1989-93; park coord. Yosemite Valley Implementation Plan, 1995—; tech. writer Colo. River Mgmt. Plan, 1989, Grand Canyon R.R. Els, 1989-93, Glen Canyon Dam Els, 1989-93. Contbr. articles to profl. jours. Mem. George Wright Soc., Park Steward Assn. Office: National Park Service Yosemite National Park CA 95389

MITCHELL, JOHN HENDERSON, retired army officer, management consultant; b. Atlanta, Sept. 9, 1933; s. William Lloyd and Jessie (Henderson) M.; m. Joan Ann Cameron, Apr. 8, 1961; children: John Cameron, Christopher Lloyd, Colin MacKenzie. BABA, St. Bonaventure U., 1956, PhD in Sci., 1991; MA in Pub. Adminstrn., Shippensburg State U., 1973. Commd. 2nd lt. U.S. Army, 1956, advanced through grades to maj. gen., 1982; comdr. 8th Bn., 6th Arty., 1st Inf. divsn. U.S. Army, Vietnam, 1968; chief officer assignments Field Arty. br. Officer Pers. Directorate, U.S. Army, Washington; chief of staff 8th divsn. U.S. Army, 1973-75; asst. dept. chief of staff for personnel, Hdqrs. U.S. Army Europe and 7th Army U.S. Army, Heidelberg, Germany, 1975-77; comdr. Arty. divsn., chief of staff 1st Inf. divsn. U.S. Army, Ft. Riley, Kans., 1977-79; comdr., Field Command, Def. Nuclear Agy. U.S. Army, Kirtland AFB, N.Mex., 1979-81; dir. Human Resources Devel. Office, dept. chief staff for pers. U.S. Army, Washington; U.S. comdr. Berlin, 1984-88; ret., 1989; pres. Intersys., Inc., Englewood, Colo., 1989-94, Pease, Orr, Mitchell Enterprises, Colorado Springs, Colo., 1994—. Bd. dirs. Nat. Safety Coun., 1982-84. Decorated D.S.M. with oak leaf cluster, Legion of Merit with oak leaf cluster, D.F.C. with oak leaf cluster, Bronze Star with oak leaf cluster and V., Air medals. Mem. Assn. U.S. Army, VFW, Army Navy Club, Army War Coll. Alumni, Soc. of First Inf. Div. Republican. Roman Catholic. Home: 375 Hidden Creek Dr Colorado Springs CO 80906-4386

MITCHELL, JOHN NOYES, JR., electrical engineer; b. Pownal, Maine, Dec. 16, 1930; s. John Noyes and Frances (Small) M.; m. Marilyn Jean Michaelis, Sept. 1, 1956; children: Brian John, Cynthia Lynn Mitchell Tumbleson, Stephanie Lee Mitchell Judson. BSEE, Milw. Sch. Engring., 1957. Registered profl. engr., Ohio. Elec. rsch. engr. Nat. Cash Register Co., Dayton, Ohio, 1957-65; sr. engr. Xerox Corp., Rochester, N.Y., 1965-70, area mgr., 1970-73; area mgr. Xerox Corp., Dallas, 1973-76; area mgr. Xerox Corp., El Segundo, Calif., 1976-79, tech. program mgr., 1979-85, competitive benchmarking mgr., 1985-92, quality mgr., 1992—. With USN, 1949-53. Mem. IEEE, Mason. Republican. Episcopalian. Home: 11300 Providencia St Cypress CA 90630-5351 Office: Xerox Corp ESC1-16W Xerox Centre Dr El Segundo CA 90245-4806

MITCHELL, JOHN WILLIAM, economist; b. New Haven, Conn., July 13, 1944; s. Frank Sprague and Martha Louise (Bridge) M.; m. Susan Catherine Lewis, Aug. 27, 1966 (div. 1983); children: Heather, Kiandra; m. Carol Diane Overlund, Sept. 11, 1988. BA in Econs., Williams Coll., Williamstown, Mass., 1966; MA in Econs., U. Oreg., 1968, PhD in Econs., 1970. Prof. econs. Boise (Idaho) State U., 1970-83; chief econ. U.S. Bancorp, Portland, Oreg., 1983—; prin. M&H Econ. Cons., Boise, 1973-83. Chmn. leadership coun. N.W. Policy Ctr., Seattle, 1990-95; active Emanuel Found. Bd., Portland, 1989-95. Fellow U. Oreg. Coll. Arts and Scis., 1995. Mem. Nat. Assn. Bus. Econs. (chmn.), Oreg. Coun. Econs. Advisors, Phi Beta Kappa. Office: US Bancorp 111 SW 5th Ave Portland OR 97204-3604

MITCHELL, JOSEPH PATRICK, architect; b. Bellingham, Wash., Sept. 29, 1939; s. Joseph Henry and Jessie Delila (Smith) M.; student Western Wash. State Coll., 1957-59; BA, U. Wash., 1963, BArch, 1965; m. Marilyn Ruth Jorgenson, June 23, 1962; children: Amy Evangeline, Kirk Patrick, Scott Henry. Assoc. designer, draftsman, project architect Beckwith Spangler Davis, Bellevue, Wash., 1965-70; prin. J. Patrick Mitchell, AIA & Assoc./Architects/Planners/Cons., Kirkland, Wash., 1970—. Chmn. long range planning com. Lake Retreat Camp, 1965-93; bldg. chmn. Northshore Baptist Ch., 1980-96, elder, 1984-90; mem. bd. extension and central com. Columbia Baptist Conf., 1977-83; Northshore Bapt. Ch. del. Bapt. World Alliance 16th Congress, Seoul, Korea, 1990, 17th Cong., Buenos Aires, Argentina, 1995; trustee Bakke Libr./Cultural Ctr., 1994-96; vice moderator Columbia Baptist Conf., 1995-96, moderator, 1996-97, ch. ministries overseer bd., 1997—; chartered mem., Cascade Cmty. Ch., 1997—. Recipient Internat. Architectural Design award St. John Vianney Parish, 1989. Cert. Nat. Council Archtl. Registration Bds. Mem. AIA, Constrn. Specification Inst., Interfaith Forum Religion, Art, and Architecture, Nat. Fedn. Ind. Bus., Christian Camping Internat., Wash. Farm Forestry Assn., Rep. Senatorial Inner Circle, Woodinville C. of C., Kirkland C. of C. Republican. Office: 12620 120th Ave NE Ste 208 Kirkland WA 98034-7511 *Personal philosophy: Look to God for inspiration and direction; pursue higher education; be a strong family person; plan wisely for today and the future; work hard yet take time to smell the roses; be firm yet kind; do it right the first time; take care of the details, and the big things will take care of themselves.*

MITCHELL, KATHLEEN ANN, illustrator, graphic designer; b. Cin., July 27, 1948; d. Gerald Paige and Velma Alice (Bleier) Clary; m. Terence Nigel Mitchell, Feb. 2, 1977; children: Jessica Rose, Alexander Christien. BSc in Design, U. Cin., 1971. Graphic designer Lippincott & Margulies, N.Y.C., 1971, Allied Internat., London, 1972, Moura-George Briggs, London, 1973-75; art dir., photographer Phonograph Record Mag., L.A., 1976-77; ptnr. Walter Morgan Assocs., Santa Monica, Calif., 1977-80; illustrator Artists Internat., L.A. and N.Y.C., 1983—. Illustrator: (books) Once Upon a Cat, 1983, Jane Eyre, 1983, Alice in Wonderland, 1986, The Wizard of Oz, 1987, The Secret Garden, 1987, Kittens, Kittens, Kittens, 1987, My Bible Alphabet, 1987, The Christmas Story, 1989, Silent Night, 1989, The First Christmas, 1992, Aladdin and the Magic Lamp, 1993, Cinderella, 1993, Cats, 1994, Friendships, 1994, Thoughts, 1994, Beauty and the Beast, 1995, Joseph and the Dream Coat, 1995, Dogs, 1995, My Little Flower, 1995, The Joy of Christmas, 1995, There's a Ghost in the House, 1996, Puss in Boots, 1997, My Secret Valentine, 1997, Valentine Thoughts, 1997, Sleeping Beauty, 1997. Democrat. Home: 1040 22nd St Santa Monica CA 90403-4518

MITCHELL, LAURA REMSON, public policy analyst, writer; b. Mpls., May 12, 1945; d. Sidney and Dora (Blustein) Remson; m. Neil Jay Mitchell, June 25, 1967; 1 child, Brian Jason. BA in Journalism magna cum laude, San Fernando Valley State Coll., 1967. Reporter, copy editor Valley News, Van Nuys, Calif., 1967-71; freelance writer, 1971—; instr. journalism Calif. State Univ., Northridge, 1970-71;. Columnist San Fernando Valley Mag., Calif., 1980. Legis. cons. gov. fin. LWV Calif., 1976-84, cons. emeritus, 1984; adv. econ. Joy Picus for City Coun. campaign, L.A., 1977; mem. Assessment Practices Adv. Coun., L.A. County, 1978-85; govt. issues coord. So. Calif. chpt. Nat. Multiple Sclerosis Soc., Glendale, 1988-89, Multiple Sclerosis Calif. Action Network, 1990—; co-chmn. health and welfare com. Californians for Disability Rights, 1991-95; chair health com., legis. com. Calif. Disability Leadership Forum, 1991-95; mem. steering com. Health Access, Calif., 1991—, Calif. Citizens for Right to Know, 1994—; coord. So. Calif. Disability Campaign for Health-Care Reform, 1994; bd. dirs. Western Law Ctr. for Disability Rights, L.A., 1995—. Recipient Shevy Healey Outstanding Achievement award So. Calif. chpt. Nat. Multiple Sclerosis Soc., 1990, MS Pub. Edn. award Nat. Multiple Sclerosis Soc., 1990, Access award Los Angeles County Commn. on Disabilities, 1996. Mem. Soc. Profl. Journalists (bd. dirs. L.A. chpt. 1970-71).

MITCHELL, LINDELL MARVIN, financial planner; b. Hagerman, N.Mex., July 11, 1937; s. Marvin P. and Lillie (Collom) M.; children: Lisa A. Purdy, Leah J. Student, N.Mex. State U., 1954-61. CFP; CLU; ChFC; registered rep., investment advisor. Owner, ins. broker, fin. planner, investment advisor Lindell M. Mitchell & Assocs., Albuquerque, 1971—; broker dealer Brokers Transaction Svcs., Inc., Dallas, Tex. Mem. N.Mex. Life Underwriters Assn. (pres. 1977-90), N.Mex. Soc. of Inst. Cert. Fin. Planners (founding pres.), Nat. Assn. Life Underwriters, Million Dollar Round Table. Republican. Home: 8800 Osuna Rd NE Albuquerque NM 87111-2142 Office: 5907 Alice Ave NE Ste F Albuquerque NM 87110-6560

MITCHELL, MARTHA L., library director; b. Oregon City, Oreg., Nov. 4, 1958; d. James M. and Betty L. (Sampsel) Manning; m. Byron D. Mitchell, Sept. 26, 1981; children: Aaron Lee Mitchell, Ashley Marie Mitchell. Student, Portland State U., 1976-78, Columbia Christian Coll., Portland, 1978-79. Security K-Mart, Tualatin, Oreg., 1976-77; ins. coder Farmers Ins., Tigard, 1977-79; nanny Rafter Q Cattle Co., Paulina, Oreg., 1979-81; mainstream facilatator Umatilla E.S.D., Pendleton, Oreg., 1989-92; libr. dir. Helix (Oreg.) Pub. Libr., 1992—; substitute Pendleton Sch. Dist., 1996—. Vol. aide in schs., Helix, 1990-94; coach Little League Baseball, Helix, 1991-94; mem. Helix Park and Recreation Bd., 1991-93. Republican. Mem. Christian Ch. Office: Helix Pub Libr PO Box 324 Helix OR 97835-0324

MITCHELL, MARY MCELWAIN, art therapist art educator; b. Chgo., Apr. 12, 1933; d. Walter and Eloise Stevens. m. John McElwain IV, 1958 (div. 1982); m. Harold Mitchell, June 30, 1984; children: Brian T. McElwain, Robert S. McElwain, John F. McElwain, Allison M. Schallert. BS in Applied Arts, U. Wis., 1955; BS in Art Edn., N. Ctrl. Coll., 1958; grad. cert. Art Therapy, Art Inst. Chgo., 1983. Cert. tchr. art, Ill., art therapist, 1986. Window display designer Marshall Fields & Co., Chgo., 1955-58; tchr. elem. art Hinsdale, Ill., 1969-70; interior display designer Homemakers Divsn. John M. Smyth, Downers Grove, Ill., 1978-79; draftsperson N.Am. Graphics, Chgo., 1981-82; art therapist Wyler Children's Hosp. U. Chgo., 1983; art therapist Riveredge Hosp., 1984-87; art tchr., art therapist DuPage Cmty. Sch., Downers Grove, 1985-86; art therapist for elderly King Bruwaert House, Hinsdale, 1986-90; art therapist Bartlett (Ill.) Learning Ctr., 1990-93, Carino Art Therapy Found., 1993-95; art therapist for elderly St. Vincent's Hosp., Santa Fe, 1995-96; lectr. in field. Exhibited at Door County, Wis., 1990, 94, Neuville Mus., Green Bay, Wis., 1990, DuPage Art League, Wheaton, Ill., 1987-93, Founders Square Gallery, Fish Creek, Wis., 1991-93, Hardy Gallery, Ephraim, Wis., 1993, 94, 96, Downers Grove Heritage Fest, Downers Grove Pub. Libr., Unitarian Ch., Hinsdale, Std. Fed. Bank, Downers Grove, Riveredge Hosp., Forest Park, Ill. Mem. Am. Art Theraphy Assn., Networking Therapists of Santa Fe, Nat. Garden Club, Kappa Kappa Gamma, N.Mex. Watercolor Soc., Door County Art League, Self Help for the Hard of Hearing. Home: 1 via Magdalene Santa Fe NM 87501-9670

MITCHELL, MICHAEL ERNST, pediatric urologist, educator; b. Montclair, N.J., Apr. 11, 1943; s. William Alexander and Ruth (Cobbey) M.; m. Constance Wormser, June 25, 1967; children: Michael, Emily, Nicole, Hallie. BS, Princeton U., 1965; MD, Harvard U., 1969. Diplomate Am. Bd. Urology. Intern PBBH, Boston, 1989-74, resident; urologist Mass. Gen. Hosp., Boston, 1974-78, pediatric urologist; chief pediatric urology Ind. U., Indpls., 1984-89, prof. urology, 1985-89; chief pediatric urology, prof. urology U. Wash., Seattle, 1989—; sec. faculty Ind. Med. Sch., Indpls., 1988. Contbr. articles to profl. jours. Fellow Am. Acad. Pediatrics, Am. Coll. Surgeons; mem. Am. Urol. Soc., Genito Urinary Surgeons, Soc. Pediatric Urology (sec./treas. 1993—), Soc. Pediatric Urologis Surgeons. Office: Childrens Hosp and Med Ctr Box C5371 Seattle WA 98105

MITCHELL, ROBERT CAMPBELL, nuclear consultant; b. West Point, N.Y., Mar. 28, 1940; s. Herbert V. and Beatrice Cheeseman (Campbell) M.; m. Mardeene Burr, Aug. 19, 1963 (div. Dec. 1983); children: Wendolyn, Dawnelle; m. Patricia Johnson, Aug. 17, 1987. B of Engring., Stevens Inst. Tech., 1962; MEE, Rensselaer Poly. Inst., 1965. Registered profl. engr., Calif. Design/ops. engr. Knolls Atomic Power Lab., Schenectady, N.Y., 1962-67; prin. tng. engr. Nuclear Energy Div. Gen. Electric Co., San Jose, Calif., 1967-72, project engr., 1972-75, mgr. advanced projects, 1975-77, project mgr., 1977-87, licensing mgr., 1987-95; pvt. cons. San Jose, 1995—. Contbr. articles to profl. jours. Nominee White House fellow Gen. Electric Co., San Jose, 1973. Mem. Elfun Soc. Republican. Home and Office: 2140 E Bighorn Mt Dr Tucson AZ 85737

MITCHELL, ROBIN, artist, educator; b. L.A., Sept. 29, 1951; d. Lee and Libby (Besser) M. Student, Calif. State U., Northridge, 1968-70, UCLA, 1970-71; BFA, Calif. Inst. of Arts, 1972, MFA, 1974. Lectr. Calif. State U., Northridge, 1977-80; lectr. Sch. Fine Arts U. So. Calif., L.A., 1981—; lectr. Claremont (Calif.) Grad. Sch., 1979-80, U. So. Calif., 1981—, U. Calif., Irvine, 1987-92, Santa Barbara, 1991, 93-94, 94—. One-woman shows include Jan Baum Gallery, L.A., 1984, 83, 93, Baum-Silverman Gallery, L.A., 1981, Comsky Gallery, L.A., 1994; exhibited in group shows at Selby Gallery of Ringling Sch. of Art and Design, 1994, U. Calif. Santa Barbara, 1993, Otis Sch. Art and Design Gallery, L.A., 1992, Dorothy Goldeen Gallery, Santa Monica, Calif., Jan Turner Gallery, L.A., 1991, Sant Barbara Contemporary Arts Forum, 1995, Sweeny Art Gallery, U. Calif., Riverside, 1996, Skirball Cultural Ctr., L.A., 1996, Lace-L.A. Cont. Exhbns., L.A., 1996, Shoshana Wayne Gallery, Santa Monica, 1997. Grantee Nat. Endowment for Arts, 1987, Anonymous Was A Woman Award, 1996; Cultural grantee for artists City of L.A., 1997-98. Home: 2614 Euclid St Apt E Santa Monica CA 90405-4735

MITCHELL, SERETTE ELIZABETH, law enforcement official; b. Chgo., July 24, 1953; d. Otis Joseph and Luna Mae (Lucas) M. AA, Compton Community Coll., 1976; BA in Sociology, Calif. State U., L.A., 1980. Cert. motorcycle mechanic. Profl. roller skater Nat. Skating Derby, Hollywood, Calif., 1970-77; mail carrier, clk. U.S. Postal Service, L.A., 1977-78; tutor Compton (Calif.) Community Coll., 1979-80; recreation leader Lynwood (Calif.) Parks & Recreation, 1980-81; sub. tchr. Compton (Calif.) Sch. Dist., 1981-82; police officer Compton Police Dept., 1982—; poet. Boxing coach Sheriff's Amateur Athletic League, Lynwood, 1988—; rape/crisis intervention counselor YWCA, Compton, 1989—; guest speaker annual career awareness day, Lynwood Unified Sch. Dist., 1982; speaker career day, L.A. Unified Sch. Dis.t, 1983, Compton Unified Sch. Dist., 1979; social change accessor, Calif. State Coll. Dominguez Hills., City of Lynwood, 1977; Christian Sunday Sch. Tchr. Mem. Compton Police Officers Assn., Peace Officers Rsch. Assn. Calif., Internat. Union Police Assn., Alpha Gamma Sigma Tau (membership chmn. 1975-76), Calif. State U. Giving Club. Democrat. Office: PO Box 180 West Covina CA 91793-0180

MITCHELL, SUSAN E., editor, desktop publisher; b. Fairbanks, Alaska, Aug. 14, 1960; d. Leslie Gerard and Mary Margaret Swartz; m. Russell C. Mitchell, Sept. 19, 1987; 1 child, Ellen Elizabeth. BA in English, U. Hawaii-Manoa, Honolulu, 1982; MA in Profl. Writing, U. Alaska, Fairbanks, 1991. Writer/editor Bur. Land Mgmt., Fairbanks, 1985-91; editor U. Alaska, Fairbanks, 1991—; owner Inkworks, Fairbanks, 1985—. Chmn., mem. Goldstream Alaska Rd. Commn., Fairbanks, 1991-95. Recipient Natural Resource Response award U.S. Dept. Interior, 1990, Commendation, Regional Dir. of Nat. Park Svc., 1990. Mem. Vanessa Press (editl. com. 1996—). Home and Office: 2324 Waterford Rd Fairbanks AK 99709

MITCHELL, THOMAS, journal editor; m. Janice Mitchell; children: Jeffery, Jay. Grad., Colo. State U. City editor Mid-Cities Daily News, Hurst, Tex.; editor Lewisville (Tex.) Daily Leader; city editor Shreveport (La.) Jour.; night city editor The Miami News; mng. editor Las Vegas Rev.-Jour., 1989-92, editor, 1992—. Recipient First place prize for editl. writing Best of the West journalism competition, 1990, First place prize Nev. Press Assn., 1995. Mem. Am. Soc. Newspaper Editors, Investigative Reporters and Editors. Office: 111 W Bonanza Las Vegas NV 89125-0070

MITCHELL, THOMAS EDWARD, JR., communications cabling executive; b. Sacramento, Apr. 12, 1946; s. Thomas Edward and Violet Mae (Southall) M.; m. Terri Kathleen Vance, Apr. 20, 1969; children: Anthony E., Brian C. BA, Nat. U., 1987, MBA, 1988. Enlisted USMC, 1966, advanced through grades to maj., 1980, retired, 1989; sr. exec. Nat. Decision Sys., Encinitas, Calif., 1989-90, Equifax Mktg. Decision Sys., San Dieto, 1990-93; pres., COO Holocomm Sys. Inc., San Diego, 1993—; bd. dirs. Cal-Pacific Steel Structure Inc., Hawaii, Calif. Contbr. articles to profl. jours.; patentee in field. Dir. Toys for Tots, L.A./ORange Counties, Calif., 1974-77. Recipient Silver Star medal U.S. Pres., 1968, Meritorious Svc. medal, Joint Chiefs of Staff Commendation medal, others. Mem. World Trade Assn. (assoc. 1989—), Am. Legion, Internat. Platform Assn. Home: 3264 Chase Ct Oceanside CA 92056-3809 Office: Holcomm Sys Inc 6540 Lusk Blvd Ste C252 San Diego CA 92121-2771

MITCHELL, THOMAS GEORGE, real estate company executive; b. July 2, 1944; s. Charles Henry and Loraine (Hauber) M.; divorced, 1 child, Erik. BBA, U. Cin., 1967; postgrad., U. Cin., Santa Clara U. Corp. acct., computer systems mktg. exec. Litton Industries, Cin., 1970-73, Burroughs Corp., Cin., 1973-75; founder, mng. gen. pgnr. Mitchell & Co. Real Estate, Inc., 1979-89; pres. Elite Properties Inc., 1989—; pres. PRD Realty Group, Inc. Author: The Commercial Lease Guidebook; Learn how to win the leasing game!, 1992, (software) Real Estate Devel. System, 1984. Home: 3870 Mahinahina St Lahaina HI 96761-9346 Office: PO Box 5273 Lahaina HI 96761-5273

MITCHELL, THOMAS SOREN, urologist; b. Santa Monica, Calif., Feb. 15, 1941; s. Cyril Louis and Florence Jeanette (Mortensen) M.; m. Michal Jane Lawrence, June 19, 1963; children: Thomas Soren Jr., Lee Delphine. BA, Loma Linda U., 1962, MD, 1966. Diplomate Am. Bd. Urology. Resident U. Wash. Hosp., Seattle, 1966-67, Loma Linda (Calif.) Univ. Hosp., 1967-68; resident in urology U. Calif. Hosp., San Diego, 1970-74; pvt. practice urology Santa Monica, Calif., 1974-96; chief urology St. John's Hosp., Santa Monica, 1990-94; asst. clin. prof. urology UCLA Med. Sch., 1976—. Capt. USAF, 1968-70, Vietnam. Mem. Pacific Oncology Soc. (exec. bd. dirs., sec. 1994—), Am. Urol. Assn., Bay Surg. Soc. Office: 2021 Santa Monica Blvd Ste 510E Santa Monica CA 90404-2206

MITCHELL, WAYNE LEE, health care administrator; b. Rapid City, S.D., Mar. 25, 1937; s. Albert C. and Elizabeth Isabelle (Nagel) M.; m. Marie Galletti; BA, U. Redlands (Calif.), 1959; MSW, Ariz. State U., 1970, EdD, 1979. Profl. social worker various county, state, and fed. agys., 1962-70, Bur. Indian Affairs, Phoenix, 1970-77, USPHS, 1977-79; asst. prof. Ariz. State U., 1979-84; with USPHS, Phoenix, 1984—. Bd. dirs. Phoenix Indian Cmty. Sch., 1973-75, ATLATL, 1995; bd. dirs. Phoenix Indian Ctr., 1974-79, Cmty. Svc. award, 1977; mem. Phoenix Area Health Adv. Bd., 1975; mem. Community Behavioral Mental Health Bd., 1976-80; mem. bd. trustees Heard Mus. of Anthropology, Phoenix, Ariz., 1996; mem. bd. dirs. Partnership for Cmty. Devel. Ariz. State U.-West, 1996—; lectr. in field. Bd. dirs. Ctrl. Ariz. Health Sys. Agy., 1982-85; mem. Fgn. Rels. Com. Phoenix. With USCG, 1960-62. Recipient Cmty. Svc. award Ariz. Temple of Islam, 1980, Ariz. State U., 1996, Dir. Excellence award Phoenix Area IHS Dir., 1992, 93. Mem. NASW, NAACP, Fgn. Rels. Coun., Am. Hosp. Assn., Asia Soc., U.S.-China Assn., Kappa Delta Pi, Phi Delta Kappa, Chi Sigma Chi, Nucleus Club. Congregationalist. Democrat. Contbr. articles to publs. Home: PO Box 9592 Phoenix AZ 85068-9592 Office: 3738 N 16th St Phoenix AZ 85016-5947

MITIO, JOHN, III, state agency administrator; b. Michigan City, Ind., Jan. 15, 1950; s. John Mitio Jr. and Bonnie Gloria (Pearce) Morse; stepson of Eugene A. Morse; m. Judy Sena, Nov. 25, 1971 (div. 1985); m. Gail Stefl, Sept. 5, 1987 (div. 1995); 1 child, Kevin Michael. AA in Liberal Arts, N.Mex. State U., Alamogordo, 1976; BA in Anthropology, N.Mex. State U., Las Cruces, 1979. Engr. aide U.S. Civil Service, Alamogordo, 1974-75, Dynalectron Corp., Alamogordo, 1976; law enforcement campus police N.Mex. State U., Las Cruces, 1977-79; eligibility worker human svcs. dept. State of N. Mex., Albuquerque, 1984-86; medicaid planner human svcs. dept. State of N. Mex., Santa Fe, 1986—. Sgt. USAF, 1969-73, 1st lt., 79-83. Decorated Nat. Def. Svc. medal, Armed Forces Expeditionary medal, Air Force Overseas Svc. medal, Air Force Good Conduct medal. Mem. Planetary Soc., World Future Soc., Nat. Space Soc. Republican. Roman Catholic. Home: PO Box 16094 Santa Fe NM 87506 Office: Human Svcs Dept PO Box 2348 2500 Cerrillos Rd Santa Fe NM 87504-2348

MITLIN, VLADIMIR SOLOMON, chemical engineer, researcher; b. Moscow, Feb. 24, 1959; came to U.S., 1990; s. Solomon and Mina (Yermakov) M.; 1 child, Victoria. MS in Applied Math., Gubkin Oil and Gas Inst., Moscow, 1981; PhD in Petroleum Engring., Nat. Rsch. Inst. Gas Industry, Moscow, 1987. Project engr. Computation Ctr. of Ministry Pub. Health of Russia, Moscow, 1977-79; rsch. assoc., group supr. Nat. Rsch. Inst. for Gas Industry, Moscow, 1981-87; rsch. assoc. Inst. of Earth Physics Russian Acad. Sci., Moscow, 1987-90; rsch. assoc. U. Tex., Austin, 1990-94; cons. Nielsen Mktg. Rsch., Schaumburg, Ill., 1994-95; mgr. fluid mechs. rsch. TerraTek Rsch., Salt Lake City, 1995—; cons. Inst. Chem. Physics, Russian Acad. Sci., Moscow, 1981-90. Author: Nonlinear Dynamics of Reservoir Mixtures, 1993; contbr. chpt. to Encyclopedia of Fluid Mechanics, 1993; contbr. numerous articles to profl. jours. Recipient 1st Prize award Nat. Conf. Young Petroleum Engrs., Uchkeken, USSR, 1984, Best Young Investigator award Nat. Rsch. Inst. for Gas Industry, Moscow, 1987, 2d Prize award Nat. Conf. Young Geophysicists, Pereslavl', Russia, 1990. Mem. AIChE. Jewish. Home: 470 S 1300 E # 911 Salt Lake City UT 84102 Office: TerraTek Inc University Research Park 400 Wakara Way Salt Lake City UT 84108-1211

MITMAN, GRANT GREGORY, biology educator; b. Easton, Pa., July 9, 1958; s. Robert Clay and Marilyn Louise Mitman; m. Kimberley Anne MacHardy, Jan. 5, 1964. BS in Marine Biology, U. Mass., Dartmouth, 1980; MS in Phycology, Oreg. State U., 1983; PhD in Algal Genetics, Dalhousie U., Halifax, N.S., 1992. Lectr. St. Mary's U., Halifax, N.S., 1988-90; asst. prof. biology St. Francis Xavier U., Antigonish, N.S., 1990-93, Am. Internat. Coll., Springfield, Mass., 1993-94; assoc. prof. biology Mont. Tech. of U. Mont., Butte, 1994—. Editor-in-chief genetics sect. Am. Jour. Botany, 1991—; editor Am. Jour. Phycology Newsletter, 1996—. Mem. Little Basin Creek Vol. Fire Co., Butte, 1994—. Mem. Sigma Xi. Home: 614 Little Basin Creek Rd Butte MT 59701 Office: Mont Tech of U Mont Dept Biol Scis 1300 W Park St Butte MT 59701

MITNICK, SCOTT W., municipal administrator; b. Inglewood, Calif., Nov. 20, 1964; s. Michael E. Mitnick and Donna E. (Rappaport) Lundquist; m. Miriam E. Crane, Aug. 22, 1988. Student, Bristol (Eng.) U., 1985-86; BA in Polit. Sci. with honors, Calif. State U., Fullerton, 1987; MPA, Syracuse U., 1989. Budget officer/adminstrv. asst. City of Brea, Calif., 1987-88; teaching asst. Syracuse (N.Y.) U., 1988-89; adminstrv. analyst City of Burbank, Calif., 1989-91, project mgr., 1991-92, asst. to city mgr., 1992-94, budget adminstr., 1994-96; adminstrv. svcs. dir. Yuba City, Calif., 1996—. Mem. ASPA (v.p. fin. L.A. chpt. 1993—), Internat. City Mgmt. Assn., Govt. Fin. Officers Am. (nat. budget reviewer 1994—), Calif. Soc. Mcpl. Fin. Officers (state budget reviewer 1994—), Mcpl. Mgmt. Assts. So. Calif. (bd. dirs., pres. regional chpt. 1987-94). Office: 1201 Civic Ctr Blvd Yuba City CA 95993

MITRA, SANJIT KUMAR, electrical and computer engineering educator; b. Calcutta, West Bengal, India, Nov. 26, 1935; came to U.S., 1958; MS in Tech., U. Calcutta, 1956; MS, U. Calif., Berkeley, 1960, PhD, 1962; D of Tech. (hon.), Tampere (Finland) U., 1987. Asst. engr. Indian Statis. Inst., Calcutta, 1956-58; from teaching asst. to assoc. Univ. Calif., Berkeley, 1958-62; asst. prof. Cornell U., Ithaca, N.Y., 1962-65; mem. tech. staff Bell Telephone Labs., Holmdel, N.J., 1965-67; prof. U. Calif., Davis, 1967-77; prof. elec. and computer engring. U. Calif., Santa Barbara, 1977—, chmn. dept. elec. and computer engring., 1979-82; dir. Ctr. for Info. Processing Rsch., 1993-96; cons. Lawrence Livermore (Calif.) Nat. Lab., 1974-95; cons. editor Van Nostrand Reinhold Co., N.Y.C., 1977-88; mem. adv. bd. Coll. Engring. Rice U., Houston, 1986-89; mem. adv. coun. Rsch. Inst. for Math. and Computing Sci., U. Groningen, The Netherlands, 1995—. Author: Analysis and Synthesis of Linear Active Networks, 1969, Digital and Analog Integrated Circuits, 1980; co-editor: Modern Filter Theory and Design, 1973, Two-Dimensional Digital Signal Processing, 1978, Miniaturized and Integrated Filters, 1989, Multidimensional Processing of Video Signals, 1992, Handbook for Digital Signal Processing, 1993, Digital Signal Processing: A Computer-Based Approach, 1997. Named Disting. Fulbright Prof., Coun. for Internat. Exch. of Scholars, 1984, 86, 88, Disting. Sr. Scientist, Humboldt Found., 1989. Fellow AAAS, IEEE (Edn. award Crcts. and Systems Soc. 1988, disting. lectr. Crcts. and Systems Soc. 1991—, Tech. achievement award Signal Processing Soc. 1996), Internat. Soc. Optical Engring.; mem. Am. Soc. for Engring. Edn. (F.E. Terman award 1973, AT&T Found. award 1985), European Assn. for Signal Processing. Office: Univ Calif Dept Elec Computer Eng Santa Barbara CA 93106

MITRY, DARRYL JOSEPH, educator, writer, strategic advisor; b. Pitts., Feb. 25, 1943; s. Joseph David and Lorraine Marion (Viale) de Mitry; m. Sue Ellen McMaster (div.); 1 child, Eden Michelle de Mitry. BA, Calif. State U., L.A., 1967; MA, U. So. Calif., 1968, DPhil, 1971. Pres. S.M.I. Corp., L.A., 1968-70; prof. Calif. State U., San Francisco, 1970-71, U. Redlands, Calif., 1971-73, West Coast U., San Deigo, 1996-97; rsch. dir. U. Ky. Med. Ctr., Lexington, 1973-76; lectr. med. econs., dir. bur. bus., econs. San Diego State U., 1976-78, 88-90; pres. Crossover Corp., L.A., 1979-85; consulting dir. Mirchandani Assocs., Beverly Hills, Calif., 1986-94; pres. Writers Web Global Internet, 1997—; prof. Nat. U., LaJolla, Calif., 1997—; exec. cons. StereoMedia Inc., Burbank, Calif., 1992-94. Author: Profiles in Price Theory, 1972, Synoptic Guide in Political Economics, 1985, Strategic Initiatives, 1996; editor Bus. Inquiry jour., 1976-78. Exec. dir. Nat. Living History Inst., San Diego, 1996; co-chair soc. club Am. Cancer Soc., San Diego, 1996; bd. dirs. Animal Rights Legal Fund, Mission Viejo, Calif., 1996. Recipient Golden Baton award San Diego Orch. Assn., 1985, Gallery Honor award Art Assn., San Diego, 1984. Mem. Omicron Delta Epsilon (Disting. Merit award 1971). Home: 10840 Queen Ave La Mesa CA 91941-7124 Office: Nat U 11255 North Torrey Pines Rd La Jolla CA 92037-1011

MITTERER, BRUCE ALAN, government agency administrator; b. Aurora, Colo., Dec. 14, 1966; s. John J. and Sharon K. (Moyle) M. BS, Colo. State U., 1989. Contract specialist USN, Washington, 1989-94; contract adminstr. Dept. Def. Office Civilian Health and Med. Program of Uniformed Svcs., Aurora, 1995; contracting officer Dept. Def. OCHAMPUS, Aurora, 1996—. Mem. Nat. Contract Mgmt. Assn. Home: 14024 E Radcliff Cir Aurora CO 80015

MIYAMOTO, CRAIG TOYOKI, public relations executive; b. Joliet, Ill., Oct. 14, 1944; s. Robert Mitsuo and Dorothy Toyoko (Okumura) M.; BBA, Woodbury Coll., 1967; MA, U. So. Calif., 1972; m. Diana Chie Ueda, Mar. 24, 1966; children: James Anthony Kazuyuki, Carleton Alan Yasuo. Reporter, Alhambra (Calif.) Post-Advocate, 1968-70; editor Monterey Park Californian, 1970-71; mng. editor So. Calif. Pub. Co., 1971-72; dep. pub. rels. dir. Honolulu Bd. Water Supply, 1972-76, pub. rels. dir., 1976-77; pres. Miyamoto Advt./Pub. Relations, Honolulu, 1977-87; v.p. Profl. Communications, Inc., 1987-92; exec. v.p., 1995—; asst. prof. U. Hawaii, 1992-95; Pineapple Post, Honolulu, 1977—, Aura Publs., Honolulu, 1980-83, instr. pub. rels. U. Hawaii, 1978-80, 95—. Pres., Honolulu Jaycees, 1975-76; mem. exec. com. 50th State Fair, 1974-76; dir. pub. rels. Hawaii Jaycees, 1974-75, Monterey Park C. of C., 1970-71; bd. dirs. San Gabriel Valley YMCA, 1971-72, Garfield Community Sch. Bd., 1971-72; mem. Jaycees Internat. Senate, 1976—; treas. Alzheimer's Assn. of Hawaii, 1991-92; bd. dirs. Am. Heart Assn. Hawaii affiliate. Named Man of Yr., Honolulu, 1974; recipient John Armbruster award, 1974, State Svc. award Hawaii Jaycees, 1974, Gregg Perry Pub. Rels. Profl. of the Year, Hawaii, 1992. Fellow Pub. Rels. Soc. Am. (accredited, bd. dirs. Hawaii chpt., pres., v.p., sec. Hawaii chpt., chmn. South Pacific dist., sec. environ. sect., nat. bd. dirs. 1997—); mem. Am. Advt. Fedn., Am. Mktg. Assn. (v.p. comm. group Honolulu chpt. 1996-97), Internat. Acad. Bus. Disciplines, Hawaii Advt. Fedn. (bd. dirs.), Mensa, Am. Philatelic Soc., Am. Topical Assn., Internat. Soc. for Japanese Philately, Bur. Issues Assn., Hawaiian Philatelic Soc., Hawaii Stamp and Coin Dealers Assn. (pres., v.p.). Democrat. Author: How to Earn $2,000 or More Without Hardly Working At All, 1979, The Pineapple Post Catalogue, 1984, Environmental Public Relations: A Primer on the Hottest Growth Area of the 90's, 1991, U.S. Corporate Environmental Policy: Philosophy vs. Practice at the Dawnof a New Millenium, 1995, Environmental Public Relations and the PRSA Code of Ethics, 1995, Public Relations Ethics 201: Challenges We Just Can't Ignore, 1996. Office: Pacific Tower 19th Fl 1001 Bishop St Honolulu HI 96813-3429

MIYAMOTO, OWEN, transportation consultant. Airport adminstr. Hawaii State Dept. of Transp., Honolulu, until 1996; cons. Hawaii State Dept. of Transp., 1996—. Office: Honolulu Internat Airport 400 Rodgers Blvd Ste 700 Honolulu HI 96819-1880*

MIYAMOTO, WAYNE AKIRA, painter, printmaker, educator; b. Honolulu, Sept. 6, 1947; s. James Masato and Thelma Kimiko (Ito) M.; children: Tyler Iolani, Akira Oakaokalani, Yasuo Iomaka. Studied Rensselaer Poly. Inst., Troy, N.Y., 1965-68; BA, BFA, U. Hawaii, 1970, MFA, 1974. Asst. prof. dept. art Fla. Tech. U. (U. Central Fla.), Orlando, 1976-78; asst. prof. art Calif. State U., Sacramento, 1980-81; prof. art dept. U. Hawaii, Hilo, 1981—, chair, 1983-85, 86-92, 94—, dir. printmaking seminar, 1982, 84; mem. nat. painting jury Scholastic Mag., Inc., N.Y.C., 1977; guest artist Art Inst. Chgo., 1978; mem. selection com. State Found. for Culture and Arts, Hilo, 1981—; mem. adv. panel, Honolulu; cons. East Hawaii Cultural Ctr., Hilo, 1981-82; dir. Pacific States Exhbn. Series, 1982—, Pacific Rim Internat. Series, 1993—; artist-in-residence Fellowship 11th Asilah Internat. Festival, Morocco, 1988. Group shows include Pacific State Regional, 1984 (purchase award), 30th Ann. Ball State Small Sculpture and Drawing Exhibit, Muncie, Ind., 1984, 9th Kans. Nat., 1984 (purchase award), 7th Hawaii Nat., 1984, Boston Printmakers 34th Nat., 1985, 17th Dulin Nat., Knoxville, Tenn., 1985, 19th Dixie Ann., Montgomery, Ala., 1985, Pacific States Regional Juror's award 1985, Art-USA, Grand Junction, Colo., 1986, 1st Internat Bienniel, Somers, N.Y., 1986, Pacific Coastline Drawing Competition, Salem, Oreg., 1986, 58th Ann. Honolulu Printmakers Exhibit, 1986, 14th Boston Printmakers Members Show, 1986., 37th Artists fo Hawaii, 1987, 19th Dulin Nat., Knoxville, 1987, 15th Boston Printmakers, 1987, 13th Kans. Nat., Hays, 1988, 21st Bradley Nat., Peoria, Ill., 1988, 17th Boston Printermakers, Duxbury, Mass., 1989, N.W. Print Coun. Print Biennial, Portland, Oreg., 1989, Art Inst. of the Permian Basin, Odessa, Tex, 1989, Pa. Sch. of Art and Design, Lancaster, 1989, 22nd Bradley Nat., 1989, Print Club of Phila., Princeton, N.J., 1989, 64th Internat. Competition, Phila., 1989, 2nd Internat. Biennial, Somers, N.Y., 1989, 16th Boston Printmakers, 1989, Baylor U., Tex., 1990, Hui No'eau Visual Arts Ctr. Maui, Hawaii, 1990, 3rd Internat., Somer, 1990, 18th Ann. Boston Printmakers, 1990, Wash. State U., Spokane, 1990, Morehead State U., Ky., 1990, N.D. Ann., Grand Forks, 1990, Thirty-Fourth Hunterdon Nat., Clinton, N.J., 1990, 62nd Ann. Honolulu Printmakers, Hawaii, 1990, Silvermine Internat., New Canaan, Conn., 1990, Nat. Mus. of Fine Arts, Veitnam, 1991, 2nd Bharat Bhavan Internat. Biennial of Prints, Bhopal, India, 1991, 23rd Bradley Nat., 1991, U. of Cen. Arks., 1991, Nat. Mus., Hanoi, 1991, 34th N.D. Ann., Grand Forks, 1992, Silvermine Internat. Exhibit, New Canaan, Conn., 1992, N.Am. Print Exhibit, Boston, 1993, 7th Parkside Nat., Kenosha, Wis., 1993, 65th Soc. Am. Graphic Artists Nat., N.Y.C., 1993, Silvermine Art Guild, New Canaan, Conn., 1994, Internat. Print Triennial, Kracow, Poland, 1994, Dakotas Internat., Vermillion, S.D., 1994, Hui No'eau Visual Arts Ctr., Makawao, Hawaii, 1994, Gallery 206, St. Joseph, Mo., 1994, Univ. Art Galleries, U. S.D., Vermillion, 1994, Consumenta '95, Internat. Triennial Krakow-Nuremburg (Germany) '95, 45th No. Am. Print Exhbn., Boston Printmakers, Duxbury, Mass., 1995, Inter-Kontakt-Grafik '95, Prague (Czech Republic)-Cracow, Internat. Triennial Graphic Art, 1995, 39th Nat. Juried Print Exhbn., Hunterdon Art Ctr., Clinton, N.J., 1995, Contemporary Prints '95, Beasley Art Mus., No. Ariz. U., Flagstaff, 3rd Bharat Bhavan Internat. Biennial of Prints, Roopankar, Mus. Fine Arts, Bhopal, India, 1995. Recipient Regional award Nat. Soc. Arts and Letters, Purchase award State Found. for Culture and the Arts, 1971, 74, 75, 87, 91, 92, Ft. Hays State U., 1984, Knoxville Mus. of Art, 1987, Juror's award Eugene Feldman Meml., 1988, award Hawaiian Graphics Corp., 1990; travel grantee U. Hawaii, 1988, 90, 92, Univ. Rsch. Coun. Travel grantee, 1992; guest artist fellow The Printmaking Workshop, 1990. Mem. N.W. Print Coun., Coll. Art Assn. Am., Soc. Am. Graphic Artists, Boston Printmakers, Print Club Phila., So. Graphics Coun. Office: U Hawaii At Hilo Art Dept 200 W Kawili St Hilo HI 96720-4075

MIYATA, KEIJIRO, culinary arts educator; b. Tokyo, Mar. 8, 1951; came to U.S., 1967; s. Yataro Miyata and Hekkiken (Liu) Choy; m. Connie Joyce Nelson, Mar. 8, 1976; children: Michelle, Kelly, Adam. Assoc. in Occupational Study, Culinary Inst. Am., Hyde Park, N.Y., 1972, cert. of nutrition, 1991; cert., Seattle Wine Sch., 1991. Cert. exec. chef; cert. culinary educator. Garde mgr. Mid-Pacific Country Club, Kailua, Hawaii, 1972; working chef Waikiki Yacht Club, Honolulu, 1972-74, Sagano Japanese Restaurant, New Rochelle, N.Y., 1974-76; asst. pastry chef Rye Town (N.Y.) Hilton Hotel, 1976-77; working chef The Explorer, Everett, Wash., 1977-79; exec. chef Holiday Inn, Everett, 1979-81, Mill Creek (Wash.) Country Club, 1981; culinary art instr. Everett Community Coll., 1981-85, North Seattle (Wash.) Community Coll., 1985-90, Seattle Cen. Community Coll., 1990—; cons. Chalon Corp., Redmond, Wash., Chiang-Mai Restaurant, Mukilteo, Wash., 1988, Holiday Inn Crown Plaza, Seattle, Satsuma Japanese Restaurant, 1996. Recipient Gold awards Am. Culinary Fedn., Oreg. State Chef's Assn., Portland, 1983, Gold and Bronze medals World Culinary Olympic, Frankfurt, Germany, 1984, 88, Grand Champion award U.S. Nat. Ice Carving Contest, N.Y.C., 1986, 2d place award All Japan Ice Carving Assn., Asahikawa, 1988, Ednl. Excellence award Oreg. and Wash. Community Coll. Couns. Wash. Fedn. of Tchrs. & Am. Fedn. of Tchrs., AFL-CIO, 1988, 89; ACF Seafood Challenge State finalist, Charlotte, N.C., 1989, New Orleans, 1990; 1st place Pacific Rim Invitational World Ice Sculpting Classic, 1989; 1st place Seymour Ice Sculpting Competition, 1991; 1st place 3d Ann. Internat. Ice Sculpting Competition, Lake Louise, Alta., Can., 1993, Award of Excellence Wash. Fedn. Tchrs./Am. Fedn. Tchrs./AFL-CIO, 1993, 1st place Wash. State Seafood Festival Recipe Contest, Shelton, Wash., 1993, Grand Cahmpion, 1994, 1st place ICE ART'94 Ice Sculpting Competition, Fairbanks, Alaska, 1994, Most Artistic award AsahiKawa Internat. Ice Sculpting Competition, 1996, 1st place IceCarver's Choice, People's Choice Awards--8th Internat. Ice Carving Championship, Anchorage, Alask, 1997; selected as Snow Sculpting Team Mem. of Sister City of Portland, Internat. Snow Sculpting Competition, Sapporo, Japan, 1997. Mem. Wash. State Chefs Assn. (bd. dirs. 1982, 83, 86, 87, 88, cert. chmn. 1986-92, Chef of Yr. 1986), Am. Acad. Chefs, Nat. Ice Carving Assn. Office: Seattle Cen Community Coll 1701 Broadway Seattle WA 98122-2413

MIYOSHI, DAVID MASAO, lawyer, international investment consultant; b. Overton, Nev., Jan. 2, 1944; s. Joseph Masaru and Jean Michiye (Horikiri) M.; m. Teruko Ochiai, July 16, 1977; children: Mark Masahiro, Brandon Kohei. BS, U. So. Calif., 1966; JD, U. Calif., San Francisco, 1973; cert. completion, Waseda U., Tokyo, 1976; MBA, Harvard U., 1978. Bar: Calif. 1973, U.S. Dist. Ct. (cen. dist.) Calif. 1973. Fgr. assoc. atty. Matsuo and Kosugi Law Offices, Tokyo, 1974-76; assoc. atty. Matsuo Law Office, Tokyo, 1976-78; assoc. Mori & Ota, L.A., 1978-80, Morgan, Lewis & Bockius, L.A., 1980-82; pres., chief exec. officer Trans-Continental Investment, L.A., 1982-84; sr. atty. Miyoshi Law Office, L.A., 1983—; pres. Dai-Ichi Mortgage Co., L.A., 1984-86; sr. atty. Law Offices of David Miyoshi, L.A., 1986-93; pres. Global Fin. Corp., L.A., 1988-93, Miyoshi & Kitamura, Inc., 1995—; legal, investment cons. Itoman (U.S.A.) Inc., L.A., 1979-83; bd. dirs. Yozya Devel. Co., Garden Grove, Calif., MOS Foods West, SantaMonica, Calif.; chmn. Sports Connection U.S.A., 1993—. Author: U.S. Condominium Regulations, 1976, U.S. Real Property Investment, 1986, Gingrich, America's De Gaulle; editor: U.S. trade Laws newsletter, 1978, U.S. Real Estate Report, 1987-93; contbr. articles to profl. jours. Bd. dirs. Am. Bapt. Soc., Los Angeles, 1986, Palos Verdes (Calif.) Bapt. Ch., 1986. Served to capt. USMC, 1966-69, Vietnam. Mem. ABA, Calif. Bar Assn., L.A. County Bar Assn. Republican. Office: 3250 Wilshire Blvd Ste 1610 Los Angeles CA 90010-1606

MIYOSHI, MASAO, English literature educator, writer; b. Tokyo, May 14, 1928; came to U.S., 1952; s. Katsunai Miyoshi and Hisae Takahama; m. Elizabeth Ann Lester, July 27, 1953 (div. 1977); m. Martha L. Archibald, Apr. 8, 1977; children: Kathy Michel, Owen Malcolm, Melina Cybele. BA, U. Tokyo, 1951; MA, NYU, 1955, PhD, 1963. Instr., lectr. Gakushin U., Tokyo, 1951-52, 54-55; from asst. prof. to assoc. prof. to prof. English U. Calif., Berkeley, 1963-87; Edwin O. Reischauer prof. Japanese studies Harvard U., Cambridge, Mass., 1984-85; Hajime Mori prof. lit. U. Calif., San Diego, 1986—; vis. prof. U. Chgo., 1978-81; ; dir. regional seminar and Japanese studies U. Calif., Berkeley, 1980-86; dir. program and Japanese studies U. Calif., San Diego, 1989-95. Author: The Divided Self, 1969, Accomplices of Silence, 1975, As We Saw Them, 1979, Off Center, 1991; editor: Postmodernism and Japan, 1989, Japan in the World, 1993, (book series) Asia-Pacific: Culture, Politics, and Society. Guggenheim fellow, 1971-72, 75-76. Mem. MLA, Assn. for Asian Studies, Internat. Comparative Lit. Assn. Office: U Calif 9500 Gilman Dr La Jolla CA 92093-5003

MIZER, RICHARD ANTHONY, technology company executive; b. San Francisco, Jan. 7, 1952; s. Conrad Xavier and Sally Jo (Hagan) M. BA in Bioengring. and Econs., U. Calif., San Diego, 1977. Founding ptnr. Microdoctors, Palo Alto, Calif., 1974-94; mgr., ptnr. K-Family Corp. dba Harlow's Night Club, Fremont, Calif., 1977-79, Restaurants Unique Inc. dba Bourbon St., Mountain View, Calif., 1980-83; engring. mgr. Pacific Bell, San Ramon, Calif., 1983-89; tech. staff advanced tech. Pacific Bell, 1989-92, developer advanced video svcs., 1992-96; asst. v.p. Nuko Info. Sys., Inc., San Jose, Calif., 1996—. Exec. prodr.: Cinema of the Future sm, 1992; assoc. prodr. Soccer Fest: World Cup Soccer Final in HDTV to Europe and U.S. theaters from Pasadena Rose Bowl, 1994; exec. in chg. prodn. 50th Anniversary of Signing of UN Charter, 1995. Mem. security staff Republican Task Force, San Francisco, 1984, tech. staff U.S. Olympic Com., Los Angeles, 1984. Mem. IEEE, Nat. Assn. Broadcasters, Soc. Motion Picture and TV Engrs. Roman Catholic. Office: Nuko Info Sys Inc 2391 Qume Dr San Jose CA 95131

MIZOKAMI, IRIS CHIEKO, mechanical engineer; b. Honolulu, Oct. 19, 1953; d. Takeo and Muriel Yae (Maeda) M.; m. Joseph John Nainiger, Nov. 27, 1976 (div. June 1987). BSME, Case Inst. Tech., 1975. Project engr. Aluminum Co. of Am., Cleve., 1975-77; engr. machine, tool and die dept. Chevrolet-Parma, Ohio, 1977-81; engr. facilities Pearl Harbor (Hawaii) Naval Shipyard, 1988-90, acting drydock engr., 1990-91, design engr. facilites, 1991—. Vol. Manor Care Nursing Home, North Olmsted, Ohio, 1986-87; mem. Honolulu Community Band, 1987-90. Mem. ASME, ASHRAE, Nat. Fire Protection Assn., Shetland Sheepdog Club Hawaii (bd. dirs.), Chopin Club, Eta Kappa Nu. Mem. LDS Ch. Home: 94-523 Ahaula St Mililani HI 96789-2544 Office: Pearl Harbor Naval Shipyard PO Box 400 Honolulu HI 96809-0400

MIZRAHI, YVES, retail executive; b. Paris, France, Nov. 22, 1954; came to U.S., 1959; s. Maurice and Fanny (De Leon) M.; m. Deborah Anne Mizrahi, May 20, 1978; children: Lauren, Amanda. BA in Biology, U. Wash., 1977; MBA in Fin., U. Puget Sound, 1980. Registered real estate broker, Wash. Pers. officer U. Wash., Seattle, 1977-80; sr. treasury analyst ENI Exploration Co., Seattle, 1980-81; sr. fin. analyst Seafirst Bank, Seattle, 1981-83; sr. econ. cons. The NBBJ Group, Seattle, 1983-85; sr. investment analyst Composite Rsch., Seattle, 1985-86; v.p. Wahl & Assocs., Seattle, 1986-90; v.p. real estate and store development Starbucks Coffee, Seattle, 1990—. Mem. com. Downtown Seattle Assn., 1983-85; mem. fin. com. Villa Acad., Seattle, 1992-93. Mem. Internat. Conf. Shopping Ctrs., NACORE. Office: 2401 Utah Ave S Seattle WA 19134

MO, ROGER SHIH-YAH, electronics engineering manager; b. Shanghai, Rep. of China, Mar. 10, 1939; s. Maurice Chun-Dat and Mary (Shen) M.; m. Amy Chun-Muh Chang, June 21, 1964; 1 child, Karen Voong-Tsun. BSEE, MIT, 1962; MSEE, Northeastern U., Boston, 1964, PhD, 1967; MBA, Pepperdine U., 1980. Engr. Raytheon Corp., Sudbury, Mass., 1967-69; on tech. staff Xerox, El Segundo, Calif., 1969-74, mgr. memory, 1974-77, mgr. cirs. and subsystems, 1977-81, area mgr., 1981-87, program mgr., 1987-89, imaging systems mgr., 1989-92, systems design mgr., 1992—; sr. lectr. West Coast U., L.A., 1978-87, chmn. acad. standards com., 1981-82. Contbr. articles to profl. jours. Bd. dirs. The Wellness Community So. Bay Cities, 1989-96. Mem. IEEE, Chinese Am. Assn. of So. Calif. (bd. dirs. 1983-87). Democrat. Roman Catholic. Lodge: Flip Flap (local chmn. 1974, nat. chmn. 1976). Home: 6852 Verde Ridge Rd Palos Verdes Penin CA 90275-4638 Office: Xerox Corp 701 S Aviation Blvd El Segundo CA 90245-4806

MOBERLY, LINDEN EMERY, educational administrator; b. Laramie, Wyo., Jan. 4, 1923; s. Linden E. and Ruth (Gathercole) M. BS, Coll. Emporia, 1952; MS, Kans. State Tchrs. Coll., 1954; m. Viola F. Mosher, Apr. 29, 1949. Tchr. sci., Florence, Kans., 1952-54, Concordia, Kans., 1954-56, Grand Junction, Colo., 1957-60; asst. prin. Orchard Mesa Jr. High Sch., Grand Junction, 1960-66, prin., 1967-84; field cons. Nat. Assn. Secondary Sch. Prins., 1985—. Sgt. USMC, 1941-46. Recipient Outstanding Secondary Prin. award Colo. Assn. Sch. Execs., 1978. Mem. NEA, VFW, Nat. Assn. Secondary Prins. (bd. dir. 1979-83), Colo. Edn. Assn. (bd.dir. 1968-71), Colo. North Central Assn. Colls. and Secondary Schs., Colo. Assn. Secondary Sch. Prins. (bd. dir. 1974-77), Lions, Sons of the Revolution, Marine Corps League (life), VFW (life), Masons (award of Excellence 1990). Home: 2256 Kingston Rd Grand Junction CO 81503-1221

MOBLEY, CHARLES MURRAY, archaeologist; b. Paulding, Ohio, Feb. 18, 1954; s. Charles Richard and Theresa (Bradley) M.; divorced; 1 child, Charles Ottar Carlson Mobley. BA in Anthropology, Case Western Res. U., 1974; MA in Conservation Archaeology, So. Meth. U., 1978, PhD in Anthropology, 1981. Cert. Soc. Profl. Archeologists. Prof. anthropology Sheldon Jackson Coll., Sitka, Alaska, 1986-88; dir. Exxon Cultural Resource Program, Anchorage, 1989-90; pres. Charles M. Mobley & Assocs., Anchorage, 1982—; adj. prof. U. Alaska, Anchorage, 1982, 83, 85, 91. Author: The Campus Site: A Prehistoric Camp, 1991; contbr. articles to profl. jours. Grantee Inst. for Study of Earth and Man, 1978, Alaska Hist. Commn., 1983, 84, Sheldon Jackson Coll., 1986, 87; Geist Fund grantee U. Alaska Mus., 1982. Mem. Soc. for Am. Archaeology, Alaska Anthrop. Assn., Soc. Profl. Archaeologists. Office: Charles M Mobley & Assocs 200 W 34th Ave # 534 Anchorage AK 99503-3969

MOBLEY, KAREN RUTH, art gallery director; b. Cheyenne, Wyo., Aug. 26, 1961; d. David G. and Marlene G. (Franz) M. BFA, U. Wyo., 1983; MFA, U. Oka., 1987. Sales assoc. Morgan Gallery, Kansas City, Mo., 1984-85; grad. asst. U. Okla. Mus. Art, Norman, 1985-87; dir. Univ. Art Gallery N.Mex. State U., Las Cruces, 1988-93; exec. dir. Nicolaysen Art Mus., Casper, Wyo., 1993—; guest artist Okla. City Community Coll., 1986. Paintings exhibited in numerous exhbns. including Phoenix Triennial, 1990, New Am. Talent, Laguna Gloria Art Mus., Austin, Tex., 1992, Adair Margo Gallery, El Paso, 1992, 93, 94, Wyo. Arts Coun. Gallery and Casper Coll., 1995, Mont. State U., 1996. Wyo. Arts Coun. Individual Artist grantee 1994, Lit. fellow, 1995, 96; named Outstanding Young Women Am. Mem. Am. Assn. Mus., Mountain Plains Mus. Assn., N.Mex. Mus Assn., Coll. Art Assn., Phi Beta Kappa, Phi Kappa Phi. Home: PO Box 1574 Casper WY 82602-1574 Office: Nicolaysen Art Mus 400 E Collins Dr Casper WY 82601-2815

MOCCIA, MARY KATHRYN, social worker; b. Harrisburg, Pa.; d. John Joseph and Winifred Louise Trephan. BEd, U. Hawaii, 1978, MSW with distinction, 1980; postgrad., Fuller Theol. Sem., 1987. Diplomate clin. social work. Intern Koko Head Mental Health Clinic, Honolulu, 1978-79, Dept. Social Services and Housing, Honolulu, 1979-80; vol. worker, group co-leader Waikiki Mental Health Ctr., Honolulu, 1979, social worker, 1980; workshop facilitator St. Louis-Chaminade Edn. Ctr. Dept. Insts. and Workshops, Honolulu, 1980-83; founding mem. Anorexia and Bulimia Ctr. Hawaii, Honolulu, 1983, pvt. practice psychotherapy and cons., 1983—; personal counselor Chaminade U. Honolulu, 1980-88; clin. social worker Queen's Med. Ctr., 1988—; practicum instr. U. Hawaii, 1992—; guest lectr. U. Hawaii Sch. Social Work, Honolulu, 1980-81; vol. telephone specialist Suicide and Crisis Ctr. and Info. and Referral Service, Honolulu, 1981-83; group leader obesity program Honolulu Med. Group, 1988-96; mem. Hawaii Coun. Self Esteem, 1993; condr. various workshops on anorexia and bulimia. Guest appearances on local tv and radio programs. Mem. Manoa Valley Ch. Mem. NASW, Nat. Assn. Christians in Social Work, Acad. Cert. Social Workers, Registry Clin. Social Workers, Mortar Bd. (pres., nat. del. 1978), Phi Kappa Phi, Pi Lambda Theta, Alpha Tau Delta (pres. 1970). Office: Queens Med Ctr Dept Social Work 1301 Punchbowl St Honolulu HI 96813-2413

MOCK, STANLEY CLYDE, financial planner, investment advisor; b. Seattle, Nov. 7, 1946; s. Darrell O. and Elsie (Broeckel) M.; m. Deloris J. Weis, June 4, 1967; children: Shannon Mock Frohardt, Kristin Ann Hagen. Student, Columbia Basin U., 1965-67; CFP, Coll. Fin. Planning, 1987. CFP; registered fin. advisor, registered investment advisor. Agt. Met. Life Ins. Co., Eugene, Oreg., 1969-73; sales mgr. Met. Life Ins. Co., Spokane, 1973-76; advanced underwriting advisor Met. Life Ins. Co., Bellevue, Wash., 1976; dist. sales mgr. Met. Life Ins. Co., Boise, Idaho, 1976-78; gen. agt. Ohio Nat. Cos., Boise, 1978—; fin. planner Fin. Planning Svcs., Boise, 1978—. Author: Life Insurance Selling, 1992; contbr. articles to mags. With USNR, 1967-69. Named One of Best Fin. Planners in Am., Money Mag., 1987. Mem. Internat. Assn. Fin. Planning (pres. 1988-89), Distributive Edn. Club Am. (pres. 1965), Rotary. Republican. Home: 10246 W Cranberry Ct Boise ID 83704-1999 Office: Fin Planning Svcs 3050 N Lakeharbor Ln Ste 200 Boise ID 83703-6243

MOCKARY, PETER ERNEST, clinical laboratory scientist, researcher; b. Zghorta, Lebanon, Jan. 6, 1931; came to U.S., 1953; s. Ernest Peter and Evelyn (Kaddo) M.; m. Yvette Fadlallah, Aug. 27, 1955; children: Ernest, Evelyn, Paula, Vincent, Marguerite. BA in Philosophy, Coll. des Freres, Tripoli, Lebanon, 1948; BA in Medicine, Am. U. Beirut, 1950, postgrad., 1950-52. Cert. clin. lab. technologist, Calif.; cert. clin. lab. scientist Nat. Certification Agy. Chief hematology unit VA Wadsworth Med. Ctr., West Los Angeles, Calif., 1956-81; CEO Phoenicia Trading Co., 1981-88; dir. Coagulation Lab., Orthopaedic Hosp., L.A., 1988—; lab. supr. Westside Hosp., L.A., 1964-79; lectr. hematology UCLA, West Los Angeles, 1970-78. Pres. World Lebanese Cultural Union, L.A., 1978-79. With U.S. Army, 1954-56. Recipient outstanding performance award lab. svc. VA Wadsworth Med. Ctr., 1972-76. Republican. Roman Catholic. Home: 3103 Gilmerton Ave Los Angeles CA 90064-4319 Office: Orthopaedic Hosp 2400 S Flower St Los Angeles CA 90007-2629

MOE, ANDREW IRVING, veterinarian; b. Tacoma, Jan. 2, 1927; s. Ole Andrew and Ingeborg (Gordham) M.; BS in Biology, U. Puget Sound, 1949; BA, Wash. State U., 1953, DVM 1954; m. Dorothy Clara Becker, June 25, 1950; children: Sylvia Moe McGowan, Pamela Moe Barker, Joyce. Meat cutter Art Hansen, Tacoma, 1943-48; gen. practice as veterinarian Baronti Vet. Hosp., Eugene, Oreg., 1956-57; veterinarian, regulatory Calif. Animal Health br. Calif. Dept. Food and Agr. Resident veterinarian II, Modesto, Calif., 1957-64, acting veterinarian-in-charge Modesto Dist. Office (veterinarian III), 1976-77, ret., 1990—. Watersafety instr. ARC, 1958-61. Capt., Vet. Corps., 1954-56, 62; comdr. 417th Med. Svc. Flight Res. (AFRES), 1965-66, 71-73; lt. col. Biomed. Scis. Corps USAF, ret., 1982. Recipient Chief Veterinarian badge, 1975. Mem. VFW (life), AVMA, Calif. Vet. Med. Assn., No. San Joaquin Vet. Med. Assn. (pres. 1979), Calif. Acad. Vet. Medicine (charter), Res. Officers Assn. (life), Ret. Officers Assn. (life), Assn. Mil. Surgeons U.S. (life), U.S. Animal Health Assn., Sons of Norway, Shriners (bd. dirs., dir. Modesto Shrine 1995), Masons (Illustrious Master Modesto chpt. 1983, Allied Masonic degrees, pres. Modesto Masonic Luncheon Club 1991, Meritorious Svc. medal 1992), Scottish Rite, Internat. Order of the Rainbow for Girls, Theta Chi, Alpha Psi. Lutheran (del. 102d Synod 1961). Home: 161 Norwegian Ave Modesto CA 95350-3542 *Personal philosophy: Try to be comparatively good.*

MOE, ORVILLE LEROY, racetrack executive; b. Spokane, Wash., Nov. 26, 1936; s. Clarence Orville and Georgia Maria (Lombard) M.; m. Deonne Wesley Schultz, Jan. 11, 1953; children: Kathleen June, Susan Marie, Terry Ann. Co-owner Moe's Sudden Svc. Fuel Co., Spokane, Wash., 1956-74; sec. Gold Res. Mining Corp., Spokane, 1973-89, Bonanza Gold Corp., Spokane, 1973-85; pres., founder Spokane Raceway Park, Inc., 1971—; regional v.p. Am. Hot Rod Assn., Kansas, Mo., 1968-84, mktg. dir., 1978-84; co-producer Internat. Car Show Assn., Spokane, 1969-90. Co-producer Spokane Auto Boat Speed Show, 1964—. Mem. Nat. Rep. Senatorial Com., 1984—; mem., trustee Rep. Presdl. Task Force, mem. 1992 Presdl. Trust Rep. Nat. Com. Mem. ISCA, Eagles, Am. Hot Rod Assn. (exec. v.p. Spokane, Wash. 1986—), Internat. Footprint Assn., Am. Auto Racing Assn. (regional v.p.). Republican. Office: Spokane Raceway Park Inc 101 N Hayford Rd Spokane WA 99224-9510

MOE, STANLEY ALLEN, architect, consultant; b. Fargo, N.D., May 28, 1914; s. Ole Arnold and Freda Emily (Pape) M.; m. Doris Lucille Anderson, May 25, 1937; children: Willa Moe Crouse, Myra Moe Galther. BArch, U. Minn., 1936; D of Engring. (hon.), U. N.D., 1993. lic. architect several states; cert. Nat. Coun. Archl. Registration Bds. Project architect several firms in Midwest, 1936-42; project architect U.S. Army Corps Engrs., Africa, 1942-43; ptnr. H.S. Starin, Architects & Engrs., Duluth, Minn., 1943-47; sr. ptnr. Moe & Larsen, Architects & Engrs., L.A., 1947-54; ptnr., gen. mgr., exec. v.p. Daniel, Mann, Johnson & Mendenall, L.A., 1954-71, corp. v.p., 1972-79; prin. Stanley A. Moe, AIA, L.A., 1979—; dir. design of major mil. projects in Eritrea, Sudan, Egypt, Yemen for Allied Forces, 1942-43; chmn. control com. DMJM & Assocs., 1958-63; project dir. Space Shuttle facilities Kennedy Space Ctr., 1973; project dir. for design of aircraft maintenance complex Iranian Aircraft Industries, 1978; project mgr. for design of major med. facility program Min. of Def. and Aviation, Saudi Arabia, 1975-76; project mgr. design of Boufarik Internat. Airport, Algeria, 1983. Pres. San. Fernando Valley Young Reps., 1952, Van Nuys (Calif.) Jaycees, 1950. Recipient Dsiting. Svc. award for cmty. svc. Van Nuys Jaycees, 1949, Sioux award U. N.D. Alumni Assn., 1985, Trustees Soc. award U. Minn., 1992. Mem. AIA (Calif. coun.), Delta Tau Delta. Republican. Presbyterian. Home and Office: 447 S Plymouth Blvd Los Angeles CA 90020-4706

MOELLER, BONNIE JEAN, elementary school educator; b. New Prague, Minn., May 31, 1969; d. William Fredrick and Donna Mae (Segler) Busacker; m. Louis Daniel Moeller, Aug. 20, 1994. BS in Elem. Edn., Concordia Tchr.'s Coll., 1991. Cert. elem. tchr. Music tchr. 5th and 6th grades Amazing Grace Luth. Sch., Seattle, 1991-92; music tchr. 6th and 7th grades Pilgrim Luth. Sch., Beaverton, Oreg., 1992-94; music tchr. 3d and 4th grades Forest Hills Luth. Sch., Cornelius, Oreg., 1994—. Mem. Luth. Edn. Assn. Home: 4018 19th Ave Forest Grove OR 97116-2204

MOELLER, D(OUGLAS) JOE, development professional; b. Ft. Madison, Iowa, Aug. 12, 1969; s. Clarence and Helen (Merschman) M. BA, U. S.D., 1991. Coord. ann. fund U. S.D. Found., Vermillion, 1991-92; assoc. dir. devel. U. S.D. Found., 1992-94; dir. alumni and devel. N.E. Mo. State U., Kirksville, 1994-95; dir. devel. Ariz. State U. Coll. Edn., Tempe, 1995—; fund-raising cons. Com. to Protect Mo.'s Future, Kirksville, 1995, United Way of Adair County, Kirksville, 1995, Kirksville Kiwanis, 1995, Com. to Elect Jim Seward, Vermillion, 1993. Bd. dirs. Vermilion 2000, 1992, Kirksville Ambs., 1994-95, Scottsdale (Ariz.) Prevention Inst., 1995—; mem. exec. bd. Farber Fund, Vermilion, 1994—. Mem. Nat. Soc. Fund Raising Execs., Coun. for Advancement and Support of Edn., Pi Omega Pi. Office: Ariz State U Coll Edn PO Box 870211 Tempe AZ 85287

MOELLER, JAMES, state supreme court justice; b. Valley, Nebr., Nov. 14, 1933; s. Hans and Marie Grace (Shumaker) M.; m. Nancy Lee Kiely, Dec. 16, 1961; children: Amy Jo, Linda Anne. BA, Nebr. Wesleyan U., 1954; JD with high distinction, George Washington U., 1959. Bar: Ariz. 1959, U.S. Dist. Ct. Ariz. 1959, U.S. Ct. Appeals (9th cir.) 1961. Assoc. Lewis and Roca, Phoenix, 1959-64, ptnr., 1964-70; ptnr. Moeller Hover Jensen & Henry, Phoenix, 1970-77; judge Maricopa County Superior Ct., Phoenix, 1977-87; assoc. justice Ariz. Supreme Ct., Phoenix, 1987-92, vice chief justice, 1992-96, assoc. justice, 1996—. Editor-in-chief George Washington U. Law Rev., 1958-59. Bd. dirs. Found. for Blind Children, Scottsdale, Ariz., 1964-70, Ariz. Found. Prevention of Blindness, Phoenix, 1966-70; Rep. committeeman, Phoenix and Scottsdale, 1965-69. Served with U.S. Army, 1954-56. Mem. ABA, Am. Judicature Soc., Ariz. Bar Assn., Maricopa County Bar Assn. Methodist. Office: Ariz Supreme Ct 432 Ariz Courts Bldg 1501 W Washington St Phoenix AZ 85007-3231

MOELLER, SCOTT RUSSELL, psychologist; b. Milw., Sept. 14, 1968; s. Roy Paul and Barbara Scott Moeller. BA in Sociology and Psychology, UCLA, 1992; postgrad., Victoria U., Wellington, N.Z., 1993, Cambridge (Eng.) U., 1989. Pub. policy staff Nat. Mental Health Assn., Alexandria, Va., 1994; exec. dir. Helpline of Am., San Diego, 1994—; counselor San Diego Crisis Team; exec. dir., trainer UCLA Counseling Helpline. Bd. dirs. United Way of San Diego Info Line, 1996—. Rotary Found. scholar. Office: Helpline of America 2640 Del Mar Heights Rd Ste 195 Del Mar CA 92014-3110

MOELLER, WALTER EUGENE, management consultant; b. Spokane, Wash., Mar. 4, 1944; s. William Fredrick and Chlorene (Myers) M.; children: Jeffrey William, Jonathan Edward, Jennifer Marie. AA, Maple Woods Cmty. Coll., Kansas City, Mo., 1973; BBA, U Mo., 1975, MBA, 1978. Sr. mgr. Arthur Young, 1985-89; regional mgr. Axiom Info. Cons., Inc., 1990-91; pres., sr. cons. Walter E. Moeller Consulting, Inc., Concord, Calif., 1992-96; regional dir. Data Warehouse Practice; dir. KPMG Cons., Palo Alto, Calif., 1996—; dir. Marcus Software Designs, Davis, Calif., 1991—; founder, pres. San Francisco Case Users Group, 1987-88; founding bd. mem. Internat. Case User's Group; co-founder San Francisco Entity Relationship Diagrammers Group. Contbr. articles to profl. jours. Mem. San Francisco Data Adminstr. Mgmt. Assn. (past pres. 1986-88). Office: KPMG Peat Marwick 3460 Bayshore Rd Palo Alto CA 94303-4227

MOENS, DAVID BRIAN, manufacturing company executive; b. Burlington, Vt., Jan. 23, 1958; s. Albert John Moens and Helen Lillian (Parsons) Wildman; m. Rebecca Marie Reilly, Oct. 1, 1983 (div. Jan. 1996); children: Kaitlyn Elizabeth, Colleen Patricia. Student, U. Pa., 1975-76. Programmer Germantown Savs. Bank, Bala Cynwyd, Pa., 1977-79; sr. programmer Minicom Corp., Cherry Hill, N.J., 1979-80; ptnr. Bus. Sys. Software, Haddonfield, N.J., 1980-86; software engr. Commodore Semiconductor Sys., Norristown, Pa., 1986-87; sr. programmer, analyst Franklin Mint, Franklin Center, Pa., 1988-89; cons. Integral Systems, Inc., Albuquerque, 1989-91; sr. cons. Computer Methods Corp., Marlton, N.J., 1991-95; decision support mgr. Intel Corp., Chandler, Ariz., 1995—.

MOERBEEK, STANLEY LEONARD, lawyer; b. Toronto, Ont., Can., Nov. 12, 1951; came to U.S., 1953; s. John Jacob and Mary Emily (Giroux) M.; m. Carol Annette Mordaunt, Apr. 17, 1982; children: Sarah, Noah. BA magna cum laude, Calif. State U., Fullerton, 1974; student, U. San Diego-Sorbonne, Paris, 1977; JD, Loyola U., 1979. Bar: Calif. 1980; cert. in internat. bus. transactions, bankruptcy and bus. rehab., and civil trial practice. From law clk. to assoc. McAlpin Doonan & Seese, Covina, Calif., 1977-81; assoc. Robert L. Baker, Pasadena, Calif., 1981-82, Miller Bush & Minnott, Fullerton, 1982-83; prin. Law Office of Stanley L. Moerbeek, Fullerton, 1984—; judge pro tem Orange County Superior Ct., Calif., 1984—; notary pub., lt. gov. 9th cir. law student divsn. ABA, 1979. Mem. Heritage Found., Washington, 1989—. Calif. Gov.'s Office scholar, 1970; recipient Plaque of Appreciation, Fullerton Kiwanis, 1983. Mem. Calif. Assn. Realtors (referral panel atty. 1985—), Orange County Bar Assn. (Coll. of Trial Advocacy 1985), Orange L.A. County Bar Assns., Calif. C. of C., Phi Kappa Phi. Roman Catholic. Office: 1370 N Brea Blvd Ste 210 Fullerton CA 92835-4128

MOERNER, WILLIAM ESCO, physicist; b. Pleasanton, Calif., June 24, 1953; s. William Alfred and Bertha Frances M.; m. Sharon Judith Stein, June 19, 1983; 1 child, Daniel Everett. BS in Physics and Elec. Engring., Washington U., St. Louis, 1975, AB in Math., 1975; MS in Physics, Cornell U., 1978, PhD in Physics, 1982. Langsdorf engring. fellow Washington U., St. Louis, 1971-75; NSF grad. fellow Cornell U., Ithaca, N.Y., 1975-78; rsch. asst. Cornell U., 1978-81; mem. rsch. staff IBM Rsch. Div., Almaden, San Jose, Calif., 1981-88; mgr. IBM Rsch. Div., Almaden, San Jose, 1988-89; project leader IBM Rsch. Div. Almaden, San Jose, 1989-95; disting. prof. phys. chemistry and biochemistry U. Calif., San Diego, 1995—; gen. chair Topical Meeting on Persistent Spectral Hole-Burning, 1991; vis. guest prof. Swiss Inst. Tech., 1993-94. Patentee, strain-sensitive spectral features detection method, device, photorefractive polymers; author, editor: Persistent Spectral Hole-Burning: Science and Applications, 1988, Single Molecule Optical Detection, Imaging, and Spectroscopy, 1997; contbr. articles to tech. publs. Tenor San Jose Symphonic Choir, 1983-91; ofcl. observer Am. Radio Relay League, Santa Clara Valley, Calif., 1987-88, asst. tech. coord., 1990-95. Named Outstanding Young Elec. Engr., Eta Kappa Nu, 1984. Fellow Am. Phys. Soc., Optical Soc. Am.; mem. IEEE (sr., treas. Lasers and Electro-Optics Soc. ann. meeting 1989), Am. Chem. Soc., IBM Amateur Radio Club (pres. 1987-88). Office: UCSD Dept Chem and Biochem Mail Code 0340 9500 Gilman Dr La Jolla CA 92093-0340

MOFFATT, HUGH MCCULLOCH, JR., hospital administrator, physical therapist; b. Steubenville, Ohio, Oct. 11, 1933; s. Hugh McCulloch and Agnes Elizabeth (Bickerstaff) M.; m. Ruth Anne Colvin, Aug. 16, 1958; children: David, Susan. AB, Asbury Coll., 1958; cert. in phys. therapy, Duke U., 1963. Lic. in phys. therapy and health care adminstrn. Commd. officer USPHS, 1964, advanced through grades to capt.; therapist USPHS, N.Y.C., 1964-66, Sitka, Alaska, 1970-72; therapist cons. USPHS, Atlanta, 1968-70; clinic adminstr. USPHS, Kayenta, Ariz., 1972-73; hosp. dir. USPHS, Sitka, 1973-78; therapist cons. Idaho Dept. Health, Boise, 1966-68; contract health officer USPHS, Anchorage, 1978-89, ret., 1989; phys. therapy cons. Ocean Beach Hosp., Ilwaco, Wash., 1989—, Harbors Home Health Svcs., Aberdeen, Wash., 1990—; therapist cons. Our Lady of Compassion Care Ctr., Anchorage, 1979—, Alaska Native Med. Ctr., Anchorage, 1988—. With U.S. Army, 1955-57. Mem. Am. Phys. Therapy Assn., Commd. Officers Assn. USPHS, Res. Officers Assn., Ret. Officers Assn., Am. Assn. Individual Investors, Am. Assn. Ret. Persons, Eagles.

MOFFATT, ROBERT HENRY, accountant, publisher, writer, consultant; b. Montreal, Que., Can., June 30, 1930; came to U.S., 1968, naturalized, 1973; s. James Bigelow and Edwige Edith M.; m. Hannelore Mann, Jan. 7, 1989. Student Loyola Coll., Montreal, Que., 1948-52, Acadia U., 1962, UCLA, 1970, 72. Lic. in air navigation, Can.; enrolled agt., Dept. Treasury. Mng. editor, pub. Kings-Annapolis Wings, 1961-66; pres., Valley Pubs. Ltd., Kingston, N.S., Can., 1961-67 exec. dir. Maritime Motor Transport Assn. and editor Maritime Truck Transport Rev., Moncton, N.B., Can., 1967-68; dir. spl. products div. Wolf-Brown Inc., Los Angeles, 1968-77; newsletter pub, writer, 1980—; pvt. practice tax acctg., Los Angeles, 1970—; noetic ethicist. Columnist, author editorials in mags. Clk., author constn. Village of Greenwood, N.S., 1961-63; chmn. bd. commrs., 1963-66; publicity chmn. Voluntary Econ. Planning Program, province N.S., 1965-66. Served to lt. Can. Air Force, 1954-60. Mem. Nat. Assn. Enrolled Agts. (newsletter editor, bd. dirs.), Nat. Soc. Pub. Accts (accredited in taxation), Calif. Soc. Enrolled Agts. Home and Office: 7509 W 88th St Los Angeles CA 90045-3408

MOFFETT, FRANK CARDWELL, architect, civil engineer, real estate developer; b. Houston, Dec. 9, 1931; s. Ferrell Orlando and Jewell Bernice (Williams) M.; BArch, U. Tex., 1958; m. Annie Doris Thorn, Aug. 1, 1952 (div.); children: David Cardwell (dec.), Douglas Howard; m. Darlene Adele Alm Sayan, June 7, 1985 (div.); m. Jennie Bob Hays Bergstrom, July 4, 1995 (div.). Architect with archtl. firms, Seattle, Harmon, Pray & Detrich, Arnold G. Gangnes, Ralf E. Decker, Roland Terry & Assocs., 1958-64; ptnr. Heideman & Moffett, AIA, Seattle, 1964-71; chief architect Wash. State Dept. Hwys., Olympia, 1971-77, Wash. State Dept. Transp., 1977-87; owner The Moffett Co., Olympia, 1974—; founder, treas. TAA, Inc., Olympia, 1987-90, pres., 1991—; advisor Wash. State Bldg. Code Council, 1975-95; instr. civil engring. tech. Olympia Tech. Community Coll., 1975-77; adv. mem. archtl. barriers subcom. Internat. Conf. Building Ofcls.; presenter in field; archtl. works include hdqrs. Gen. Telephone Directory Co., Everett, Wash., 1964; Edmonds Unitarian Ch., 1966; tenant devel. Seattle Hdqrs. Office, Seattle-First Nat. Bank, 1968-70; Wash. State Dept. Transp. Area Hdqrs. Offices, Mt. Vernon, Selah, Raymond, Colfax and Port Orchard 1973-87; Materials Lab., Spokane, Wash., 1974; Olympic Meml. Gardens, Tumwater, Wash., 1988, City Anacortes emergency power stas., 1989, L. Albert Residence, 1990, F. Gasperetti Residence, 1991; archtl. barriers cons. State of Alaska, 1978, State of Wash., 1972-94. Chmn. Planning Commn. of Mountlake Terr., Wash., 1963, 64, mem., 1961-67; mem. State of Wash. Gov.'s Task Force on Wilderness, 1972-75, Heritage Park Task Force, Olympia, Wash., 1986—; trustee Cascade Symphony Orch., 1971; incorporating pres. United Singles, Olympia, 1978-79; capt. CAP, pub. affairs officer Olympia Squadron; mem. nat. panel profl. advisors to Nat. Multiple Sclerosis Soc., 1993—; bd. dirs. Wash. Coalition Citizens with Disabilities, 1997—. With USN, 1951-54. Registered architect, Alaska, Calif., Wash., profl. engr., Wash.; cert. Nat. Council Archtl. Registration Bds., U.S. Dept. Def., Fallout Shelter Analysis, environ. engring. Mem. AIA (dir. S.W. Wash. chpt. 1980-82, pres.-elect 1985, pres. 1986, dir. Wash. council 1986, architects in govt. nat. com. 1978-87, chmn. N.W. and Pacific region conf. 1991), Am. Public Works Assn., Inst. Bldgs. and Grounds, ASCE, Constrn. Specifications Inst., Am. Arbitration Assn. (invited panelist), Gen. Soc. Mayflower Descs. (gov. Wash. Soc. 1982-83), Nat. Huguenot Soc. (pres. Wash. Soc. 1981-83, 85-87, 95—), Olympia Geneal. Soc. (pres. 1978-80), SAR (state treas. 1984-85), SCV, Sons and Daus. of Pilgrims, (gov. Wash. Soc. 1984), Order of Magna Charta, Aircraft Owners' and Pilots' Assn., Rotary (pres. Edmonds, 1969-70), Olympia, Coll. Club of Seattle. Co-author: An Illustrated Handbook for Barrier-Free Design, 4th Edit., 1989, Accessibility Design for All, 1992, 2nd edit., 1995, Housing and Building Accessibility: The Law in Washington, 1992. Republican. Baptist. Home and Office: PO Box 2422 Olympia WA 98507-2422

MOFFITT, DONALD EUGENE, transportation company executive; b. Terre Haute, Ind., May 22, 1932; s. James Robert and Margaret Mary (Long) M.; m. Billie Duffy, Feb. 21, 1989; 1 child, Jaime. BA, Ind. State U., 1954; postgrad., Ind. U., 1956; grad., Advanced Mgmt. Program, Harvard U., 1972. Acct. Foster Freight Lines, Indpls., 1955-56; with Consol. Freightways Inc., San Francisco, 1956-88, v.p. planning, 1961-69; v.p. fin., motor carrier subs. Consol. Freightways Corp. Del., 1969-75; v.p. fin., treas. parent co. Consol. Freightways Inc., San Francisco, 1975-81; exec. v.p. Consol. Freightways Inc., Palo Alto, Calif., 1981-86; vice chmn. parent co. bd. Consol. Freightways, Inc., Palo Alto, Calif., 1986-88; chmn., CEO Circle Express, Indpls., 1988-90; pres., CEO Consol. Freightways, Inc., Palo Alto, Calif., 1990-96, chmn., CEO, 1995-96, also bd. dirs.; chmn. bd. dirs. all subsidiaries CNF Transport, 1990—; chmn., pres., CEO CNF Transp. Inc., 1996—. Bd. dirs. Bay Area Coun., Calif. Bus. Roundtable, Conf. Bd., Boy Scouts Am., ARC; bd. dirs., exec. com. Hwy. Users Fedn.; bd. trustees Automotive Safety Found.; bus. adv. coun. Northwestern U. Transp. Ctr. Mem. Nat. C. of C. (Washington) (bd. dirs.). Office: Consol Freightways Inc 3240 Hillview Ave Palo Alto CA 94304-1201

MOFFITT, KEVIN DAVID, food products executive; b. Portland, Oreg., Apr. 23, 1957. BSBA, U. Oreg., 1980. Mgr. new product Dole Food Co., San Francisco, 1981-86; sales mgr. Agrl. Mktg. and Devel., Florence, N.J., 1986-88; internat. mktg. svcs. mgr. Sun Diamond Growers of Calif., Pleasant, Calif., 1988-89; v.p. internat. mktg. Oreg.-Wash.-Calif. Pear Bur., Portland, 1989—. Contbr. articles to profl. jours. Mem. Produce Mktg. Assn. (chmn. internat. trade conf. com. 1996-98), Moffat Clan Soc. N.Am., Chi Psi. Office: Oreg-Wash-Calif Pear Bur 4382 SE International Way Milwaukie OR 97222

MOGENSEN, ERIC, lawyer; b. San Jose, Calif., Apr. 4, 1961; s. Kaj and Margareth June Mogensen; m. Terri Lynn Curtis. B of Sci. and Commerce, Santa Clara U., 1983, JD, 1987; LLM in Tax, Golden Gate U., 1991. Bar: Calif. 1988; cert. tax specialist Calif. Bar. Acct., computer programmer FMC, San Jose, 1980-87; ptnr. Miller, Morton, Caillat & Nevis, San Jose, 1988—. Mem. Santa Clara County Bar Assn. Office: Miller Morton et al Ste 1300 50 W San Fernando San Jose CA 95113

MOGER, COLETTE ANN, planning engineer; b. Mott, N.D., Dec. 19, 1950; d. Val L. and Dorotheia I. (Hardmeyer) Hoerner; m. Michael Norman Moger, July 15, 1972. BS, N.D. State U., 1972; MS in Mgmt., U. of Mary, Bismarck, N.D., 1988. Credit analyst Beneficial Loan, St. Cloud, Minn., 1972-74; svc. rep. U.S. West, St. Cloud, Minn., 1974-81; sr. clk. U.S. West, Bismarck, 1981-85, facility specialist, 1985-87, credit cons., 1987-90, planning engr., 1990-94; infrastructure planner, 1994—; instr. U. of Mary, Bismarck, 1989-94; project assoc. U. Denver, 1996. Mem. Refuge Settlement Program, Bismarck; Eucharistic minister Pax Christi Ch., Highlands Ranch, Colo. Mem. Bus. and Profl. Women's Club, N.D. State U. Alumni Assn., U. of Mary Alumni Assn., Phi Upsilon Omicron. Roman Catholic. Home: 9955 Bronti Circle Littleton CO 80124 Office: US West 700 W Mineral Littleton CO 80120

MOGG, DONALD WHITEHEAD, chemist; b. La Grange, Ill., Feb. 11, 1924; s. Harold William and Margaret (Whitehead) M.; B.S., Allegheny Coll., 1944; postgrad. Harvard U., 1946-47. Asst. chemist Gt. Lakes Carbon Corp., Morton Grove, Ill., 1947-48, chemist, 1948-53, research chemist, 1953-56, project supr., 1956-59, sect. head, 1959-63; sect. head Gt. Lakes Research Corp., Elizabethton, Tenn., 1963-66; research and devel. mgr. bldg. products div. Grefco, Inc., Torrance, Calif., 1966-68, corp. research and devel. mgr., 1968-72, group mgr., 1972-81, sr. research assoc., 1981-82. Served with U.S. Army, 1944-46. Mem. Am. Chem. Soc., AAAS, Phi Beta Kappa, Phi Kappa Phi. Presbyterian. U.S. and fgn. patentee in field of bldg. products. Home: 3823 Ingraham St Apt B202 San Diego CA 92109-6436

MOGHADAM, AMIR, consultant, educational administrator. BSME, U. London, 1983; PhD in Aeronautical Engring., U. Cambridge, 1987. Rsch. assoc. U. Calif., Santa Barbara, 1987-88; asst. prof. Northrop U., L.A., 1988-92, v.p. faculty senate, 1990-91; assoc. prof. Northrop-Rice Aviation Inst. of Tech., Inglewood, Calif., 1992-94, dir. engring. tech., 1994-95, dean of academics, prof. engring. tech., 1995-96, dean/campus dir., 1996—; pres., CEO Aeronautics Innovation Inc., Marina del Rey, Calif., 1993—; ind. cons., Woodland Hills, Calif., 1988-93. Contbr. articles to profl. jours. Mem. AIAA, ASME, Soc. Automotive Engrs., Am. Soc. Engring. Edn., Sigma Xi, Tau Alpha Pi, Tau Beta Pi, Sigma Gamma Tau. Office: Northrop-Rice Aviation Inst Tech 8911 Aviation Blvd Inglewood CA 90301-2904

MOGREN, PAUL ANDREW, librarian; b. Fort Collins, Colo., Aug. 31, 1950; s. Edwin W. and Arle Mae (Arnason) M.; m. Ann Marie Breznay, Aug. 16, 1980; 1 child, Christian Andrew. BA, Colo. State U., 1972; MA, U. Denver, 1973; PhD, U. Utah, 1980. Reference libr. Marriott Libr., U. Utah, Salt Lake City, 1973-82, head of reference, 1982-96, collection specialist, 1996—; cons. Gov.'s Mansion Libr., Salt Lake City, 1995—, Dixie Coll. Libr., St. George, Utah, 1990; adj. prof. Emporia (Kans.) State U., 1996—. Mem. AAUP (pres. U. Utah chpt. 1986-89), ALA (coun. 1992-96), Utah Libr. Assn. (pres. 1988-89). Office: U Utah Marriott Libr Salt Lake City UT 84112

MOHAI, PETER, internist, educator; b. Linz, Austria, June 20, 1949; came to U.S., 1950; s. Karl and Hermine (Kronixfeld) M.; m. Lynda Glynne, Feb. 18, 1978. BA, Northwestern U., 1971; MD, Emory U., 1975. Diplomate Am. Bd. Internal Medicine. Intern in medicine U. Wash., Seattle, 1975-76, resident in medicine, 1976-78, fellow in rheumatology, 1978-80; pvt. practice, Seattle, 1980—; pres. Minor & James Med. Group, 1995—; clin. assoc. in medicine U. Wash., Seattle, 1980—; cons. region X, HHS, Seattle, 1983—, Seattle VA Hosp., 1984—. Bd. dirs. Wash. chpt. Arthritis Found., Seattle, 1994—. Mem. N.W. Rheumatism Soc., Wash. State Med. Soc., King County Med. Soc. (trustee 1995-96), Seattle Acad. Medicine. Office: Minor & James Med PLLC 515 Minor Seattle WA 98104

MOHANTY, BINAYAK PRASAD, hydrologist, environmental engineer; b. Bhubaneswar, Orissa, India, June 23, 1964; came to U.S., 1989; s. Harish Chandra and Indulata Mohanty; m. Deepanwita Mohanty, July 14, 1991. B in Engring., Orissa U. Agr. and Tech., 1985; M in Engring., Asian Inst. Tech., 1987; PhD, Iowa State U., 1992. Instr. Orissa U. Agr. and Tech., Bhubaneswar, India, 1985; rsch. assoc. Asian Inst. Tech., Bangkok, Thailand, 1987-88; rsch. asst., postdoctoral rschr. Iowa State U., Ames, 1989-93; rsch. scientist U.S. Salinity Lab. USDA-ARS, Riverside, Calif., 1993—. Assoc. editor: Paddy Field Engineering, 1988, 92; contbr. articles to profl. jours. Mem. Am. Geophys. Union, Am. Soc. Agrl. Engrs., Soil Sci. Soc. Am., Agronomy Soc. Am., Nat. Ground Water Assn., Soil and Water Conservation Soc., Alpha Epsilon, Gamma Sigma Delta. Office: US Salinity Lab 450 W Big Springs Rd Riverside CA 92507-4617

MOHLER, GEORGIA ANN, geriatrics nurse practitioner; b. Iowa Falls, Iowa, Mar. 11, 1941; d. George Edward and Norma Dorothy (Wolf) M. Diploma, Meth.-Kahler, Rochester, Minn., 1962; BSN, U. Wash., 1971. RN, Wash.; cert. geriatric nurse practitioner. Relief charge nurse, team leader Swedish Hosp., Seattle, 1963-72; pub. health nurse Vis. Nurse Svc., Seattle, 1971-72; relief charge nurse and medicare coord. Restorative Care Ctr., Seattle, 1972-81; unit coord. Tacoma Luth. Home and Retirement Ctr., Tacoma, 1981-82; nurse practitioner Tacoma Luth. Home, 1983—, dir. home health agy. and nurse practitioner, 1993—. Contbr. to profl. jours. Mem. Pierce County Nurse Practitioner Group, Nat. Conf. Gerontol. Nurse Practitioners. Lutheran. Home: 909 N I St Apt 401 Tacoma WA 98403-2136

MOHR, JOHN LUTHER, biologist, environmental consultant; b. Reading, Pa., Dec. 1, 1911; s. Luther Seth and Anna Elizabeth (Davis) M.; m. Frances Edith Christensen, Nov. 23, 1939; children: Jeremy John, Christopher Charles. AB in Biology, Bucknell U., 1933; student, Oberlin Coll., 1933-34; PhD in Zoology, U. Calif., Berkeley, 1939. Research asso. Pacific Islands Research, Stanford, 1942-44; rsch. assoc. Allan Hancock Found., U. So. Calif., 1944-46, asst. prof., 1946-47, asst. prof. dept. biology, 1947-54, asso. prof., 1954-57, prof., 1957-77; chmn. dept., 1960-62, prof. emeritus, 1977—; vis. prof. summers U. Wash. Friday Harbor Labs., 1956, '57; rsch. assoc. vertebrate zoology Natural History Mus., Los Angeles County, 1996—; marine borer and pollution surveys harbors So. Calif., 1948-51, arctic marine biol. research, 1952-71; chief marine zool. group U.S. Antarctic research ship Eltanin in Drake Passage, 1962, in South Pacific sector, 1965; research deontology in sci. and academia; researcher on parasitic protozoans of anurans, crustaceans, elephants; analysis of agy. and industry documents, ethics and derelictions of steward agy., sci. and tech. orgns. as they relate to offshore and coastal onshore oil activities, environ. effects of oil spill dispersants and offshore oil industry discharges and naturally occurring radioactive material NORMs. Active People for the Am. Way; mem. Biol. Stain Commn., 1948-80, trustee, 1971-80, emeritus trustee, 1981—, v.p., 1976-80. Recipient Guggenheim fellowship, 1957-58. Fellow AAAS (coun. 1964-73), So. Calif. Acad. Scis., Sigma Xi (exec. com. 1964-67, 68, 69, chpt.-at-large bd. 1968-69); mem. Am. Micros. Soc., Marine Biol. Assn. U.K. (life), Am. Soc. Parasitologists, Western Soc. Naturalists (pres. 1960-61), Soc. Protozoologists, Soc. Integrative and Comparative Biology, Ecol. Soc. Am., Calif. Native Plant Soc., Assn. Forest Svc. Employees Environ. Ethics, Common Cause, Huxleyan, Sierra Club, Phi Sigma, Theta Upsilon Omega. Home: 3819 Chanson Dr Los Angeles CA 90043-1601

MOHR, SIEGFRIED HEINRICH, mechanical and optical engineer; b. Vöhrenbach, Baden, Fed. Republic Germany, Sept. 20, 1930; came to U.S., 1958.; s. Adolf and Luise (Faller) M.; m. Gloria P. Vauges, Apr. 25, 1959 (div. 1972); children: Michael S., Brigitte M.; m. Jeani Edith Hancock, Mar. 24, 1973; 1 child, Suzanne A. Diplom-Ingenieur, Universität Stuttgart, Fed. Republic Germany, 1957; MS in Optical Engring., SUNY, 1971. Thesis researcher Daimler Benz AG, Stuttgart, 1957; design engr. Russell, Birdsall & Ward B & Nut Co., Port Chester, N.Y., 1958-59; devel. engr. IBM Advanced Systems Devel. divsn., San Jose, Calif., 1960-64; rsch. engr., inventor Precision Instrument Co., Palo Alto, Calif., 1964-67; prin. engr. RCA Instructional Systems, Palo Alto, 1967-70; rsch. engr., scientist Singer Simulation Products, Sunnyvale, Calif., 1971-73; project leader Dymo Industries Tech. Ctr., Berkeley, Calif., 1973-77; leader, adv. rsch. & devel. NCR Corp. Micrographic Systems Div., Mountain View, Calif., 1977-89; advanced project mgr. electro-optics dept. (U.S.A.) Angénieux, Santa Clara, Calif., 1989—; translator for books in English, French and German; corr., writer for European jazz publs. Patentee, author in field. Bicycle activist League of Am. Wheelmen, Balt., 1975—; del. mem. U.S. Del. ISO Conf., Paris, 1988. Mem. Soc. Photo-Optical Instrumentation Engrs., Assn. Info. and Image Mgmt., Internat. Soc. Optical Engring. Home: 3311 Benton St Santa Clara CA 95051-4420

MOHRDICK, EUNICE MARIE, nurse, consultant, health educator; b. Alameda, Calif.; d. Walter William and Eunice Marie (Connors) M. BS in Nursing Edn., U. San Francisco, 1955; MA in Edn. spl interest, San Francisco State Coll., 1967; Pub. Health Cert., U. Calif., San Francisco, 1968; EdD, Western Colo. U., 1977. RN, Calif. Supr. oper. rm. St. John's Hosp., Oxnard, Calif., 1947-50, supr. maternity, delivery and nursery rms., 1950-53; nurse, supr. St. Mary's Hosp., San Francisco, 1943-45, supr., instr., 1955-60, 62-65; asst. dir. nursing, tchr. nursing history St Mary's Coll. of Nursing, San Francisco, 1953-55; tchr. home nursing Mercy High Sch., San Francisco, 1960-61; tchr. Health, Family Life San Francisco Unified Schs., 1968-83; tchr. holistic health Contra Costa Coll., 1981-86; cons. pvt. practice Albany, Calif., 1986—; tchr. El Cerrito (Calif.) Senior Ctr., 1986-88. Author: Elementary Teacher Handbook, How to Teach Sex Education, Grades, 4,5,6, 1977. Mem. Madonna Guild, San Francisco, 1986—, v.p., 1989—; mem. Half Notes' Singing Club to Sick and Spl. Needy, 1970—. Recipient Title I Grant U. Calif. San Francisco, 1968, Workshop Grant for Culture Inter-relationship Study, Singapore, UNESCO, Washington U., St. Louis, 1973. Mem. AAUW, San Francisco State U. Alumna, U. San Francisco Nursing Alumni (charter mem., bd. dirs. 1974-88), Mensa. Republican. Roman Catholic. Home & Office: 555 Pierce St Apt 129 Albany CA 94706-1011

MOIR, ALFRED KUMMER, art history educator; b. Mpls., Apr. 14, 1924; s. William Wilmerding and Blanche (Kummer) M. A.B. cum laude, Harvard U., 1948, A.M., 1949, Ph.D., 1953. From instr. to assoc. prof. Newcomb Coll., Tulane U., 1952-62; mem. faculty U. Calif., Santa Barbara, 1962-91, prof. art history, 1964-91, prof. emeritus, 1991—, chmn. dept., 1963-69; dir. Edn. Abroad Program U. Calif., Italy, 1978-80; cons. for acquisitions Isaac Delgado Mus. Art, 1953-57; v.p. Friends La. State Mus., 1959-62, Friends New Orleans Pub. Libr., 1959-62; pres. So. Calif. Art Historians, 1964-66, 67-69; chmn. Tri-Counties Com. to Rescue Italian Art, 1967-68; art historian in residence Am. Acad. Rome, 1969-70, 80; cons. NEH, 1971-78; vis. prof. U. Minn., 1973; hon. curator of drawings U. Calif.-Santa Barbara Art Mus., 1985-94, cons. curator of drawings, 1997—. Author: (with others) Art in Italy, 1600-1700, 1965, The Italian Followers of Caravaggio, 2 vols, 1967, Caravaggio's Copyists, 1976, Caravaggio, 1982, Van Dyck, 1994; editor: (with others) Seventeenth Century Italian Drawings in the Collection of Janos Scholz, 1974, European Drawings in the Santa Barbara Museum of Art, 1976, Regional Styles of Drawing in Italy 1600-1700, 1977, Old Master Drawings from the Feitelson Collection, 1983, Old Master Drawings from the Collection of John and Alice Steiner, 1985, (with others) Van Dyck's Antwerp, 1991. Trustee Santa Barbara Free Sch., 1968-71; gov. Brooks Inst. Art Gallery, 1968-69. Served with AUS, 1943-46. Named hon. alumnus Tulane U., 1963, Outstanding Alumnus of 1993, The Blake Sch., Mpls., 1993. Mem. Coll. Art Assn., Medieval Acad. Am., Soc. Archtl. Historians, Renaissance Acad. Am., Soc. Fellows of Am. Acad. in Rome, Ateneo Veneto (fgn. mem.). Clubs: Harvard (La. pres. 1959-62, Boston), University Calif. at Santa Barbara Faculty (pres. 1968). Office: U Calif Dept Art History Santa Barbara CA 93106

MOJAS, KATHLEEN MARIE, psychologist; b. Santa Monica, Calif., July 1, 1961; d. Peter William and Mary Elizabeth Mojas. BA in Comms., UCLA, 1987; PhD in Clin. Psychology, Calif. Grad. Inst., 1992. Lic. psychologist, Calif., 1994. Intern, tutor, counselor Dr. Gardner Child Psychologist, Brentwood, Calif., 1988-90; psychol. asst. Calif. Grad. Inst. Counseling Ctr., L.A., 1988-89; psychol. asst. Options Counseling Ctr., Beverly Hills, Calif., 1989-94, seminar leader, spkr., writer, 1989—; rsch. asst. UCLA, 1987, Artists and Educators for Self-Esteem, L.A., 1987-89, Dick Clark Prodns., L.A., 1987; behavior edn. counselor Nutrisys., Northridge, Calif., 1986-87; media psychologist nat. talk, news shows. Contrb. articles to profl. jours., mags. Assoc. mem. APA, Golden Key. Democrat. Office: 449 S Beverly Dr Ste 212 Beverly Hills CA 90212-4428

MOLANDER, GLENN M., human resources executive; b. L.A., Feb. 26, 1940; s. Glenn M. and Ethel Louise (Reicherter) M.; m. Barbara H. Fanderlik, June 21, 1960 (div. Aug. 1964); 1 child, Lloyd Bryan Molander-Adams; m. Sara Rahauser, Apr. 18, 1974; 1 child, Leif Douglas. BA in Bus. Adminstrn., U. Hawaii, 1984; Cert. in Mgmt., Kauai C.C., 1978. Mgr. data processing Dyn Corp., Barking Sands, Hawaii, 1971-86, mgr. range ops., 1986-87; mgr. human resources Dyn Corp., Holloman AFB, N.Mex., 1987-92, mgr. adminstrv. svcs., 1992-94, mgr. human resources, 1994—. Mem. vocat. adv. bd. Kauai c.C., Lihue, 1984; mem. Hawaii Libr. Commn., 1985-87; mem. budget and allocations com. United Way of Otero County, N.Mex., 1990-91; pres. West Kauai Rotary, 1981-82. Recipient Bronze award United Way of Otero County, 1991. Mem. Nat. Contract Mgmt. Assn. (pres. 1995-96), So. N.Mex. Soc. Human Resources Mgmt. (Pinicle award 1995-96), Assn. of U.S. Army. Home: PO Box 1831 Alamogordo NM 88311 Office: Dyn Corp PO Drawer R Holloman AFB NM 88330

MOLASKY, ALICE, state insurance commissioner. Commr. ins. State of Nev. Office: Divsn Ins 1665 Hot Springs Rd Ste 152 Carson City NV 89710

MOLINA, RAFAEL ANTONIO, investment company executive; b. Sept. 5, 1963; s. Rafael Antonio and Rosa Isabel (Villacorta) M.; m. Maria Asuncion Cornejo, Sept. 28, 1985; children: Elisa Maria, Rafael Augusto, Cristia Adolfo, Leonardo Paolo. AA, Sacramento City Coll., 1983; BS, Golden Gate U., 1994. Cert. adminstr. Calif. State Auto Assn. CFO MVM Investments, Sacramento, 1983-85; adminstr. State of Calif., Sacramento, 1985-93; CEO, mng. dir. C & T Investments, Dixon, Calif., 1988—; dir. MAM Co., Sacramento, 1985—; CEO, dir. Del Sol Investments, Dixon, 1989—. Mem. Calif. State Employees Assn., Sacramento, 1985, Am. Mgmt. Assn., Sacramento, 1991; pres. St. Peter's Ch., Dixon, 1992. Recipient Outstanding Achievement award Calif. Dept. Health Svcs., 1988, Primary Clinics, 1990. Mem. Am. Mgmt. Assn., Network Profl. Assn., Tele-Comms. Assn., Calif. Microcomputers Users. Roman Catholic. Office: C & T Investments Co 358 East A St Dixon CA 95620

MOLINARI, CAROL V., writer, investment company executive, educator; b. Bklyn., Oct. 14, 1931; d. Sabino and Anna (Mancusi) M. BS, Douglass Coll., 1953; MEd, Rutgers U., 1962; postgrad., U. Alaska, Anchorage, 1963—. Tchr. Bridgewater Twp. Schs., Bridgewater, N.J., 1953-56, Somerville (N.J.) H.S., 1956-59; tchr. phys. edn., guidance counselor Bridgewater H.S., Raritan, N.J., 1959-62; guidance counselor Anchorage Borough Sch. Dist., 1962-63, Air Force Dependent Sch., Tokyo, 1963-64, Arcturus Jr. H.S., Ft. Richardson, Alaska., 1965-67; asst. dir. student coll. ctr. Douglass Coll., Rutgers U., New Brunswick, N.J., 1967-69; cons., counselor Native Head Start program Alaska Meth. U., Anchorage, 1967-69; adminstr. asst., counselor U. Alaska, Anchorage, 1969-70; office sales mgr. Alcan Realty, Anchorage, 1971-74; dir. Ctr. for Alcohol and Addiction Studies U. Alaska, Anchorage, 1975-79; sales assoc. Century 21 Royal Realty, Anchorage, 1970-83; cons. in the devel. of Now Dimensions Holistic Health Ctr.; pres., dir. Molinari Investments Inc., Anchorage, 1982—. Author: The Magic of Financing and Investing, 1987, America's Wakeup, 1996, (cookbook) Mom's Italian Recipes; co-author: Out of Nowhere; contbr. articles to Alaska Tchr., This Alaska, Alcohol Health and Research World, others. Bd. dirs. Alaska region Nat. Coun. on Alcohol, Morning Song; mem. adv. bd. Salvation Army; mem. ch. coun. Holy Family Cathedral. Rutgers U. schoalr, 1975. Mem. NAFE, NEA, Alaska Edn. Assn., Bd. Realtors, Women of Vision and Action, Soroptimist. Home: PO Box 101696 Anchorage AK 99510 Office: Molinari Investment Inc 520 W 19th St Anchorage AK 99503

MOLINSKY, BERT, tax consultant; b. Bronx, N.Y., Feb. 25, 1938; s. Joseph and Ida G. (Rosenberg) M.; m. Donna L. Thurman, June 26, 1964; children: Avery, Lucy, Lois, Sarah. Student, U. Ariz., 1956-61, Diablo Valley Coll., 1986-88, Calif. State U., Hayward, 1988-92. CFP; CLU; ChFC; Enrolled Agt. Field supt. INA Life, Phoenix, 1968-72; regional life mgr. Sentry Life Ins. Co., Oklahoma City, 1972-73, Mpls., 1973-75, San Francisco, 1975-78; mgr. Acacia Mutual Life, Oakland, Calif., 1978-80; gen. agt. Am. United Life, Concord, Calif., 1980-82; owner East Bay Triple Check Tax Svcs., Walnut Creek, Calif., 1982—, Triple Check Tax and Fin. Svc., Peoria, Ariz., 1993—; instr. Golden Gate U. CPD, San Francisco, 1983-93, Mt. Diablo Sch. Dist., Concord, 1986-93; faculty Coll. for Fin. Planning, Denver, 1983—; bd. dirs. Triple Check Licensee Coun. Contbr. articles to profl. jours. Nat. dir. U.S. Jaycees, Phoenix, 1967; pres. Bnai Brith Coun. of Lodges, San Francisco, 1986. With USNR, 1955-72. Named Jaycee of Yr. Ariz. Jaycees, 1967. Fellow Nat. Tax Practice Inst.; mem. Enrolled Agts., East Bay Assn Life Underwriters (pres. 1985-86), Nat. Assn. Enrolled Agts., Peoria Sunset Lions (pres. 1996—), Ariz. State Enrolled Agts. Assn. (v.p. 1996—). Office: Plaza Del Rio Ctr 9401 W Thunderbird Rd Ste 140 Peoria AZ 85381-4817 also: PO Box 100 Peoria AZ 85380-0100

MOLL, DEBORAH ADELAIDE, lawyer; b. Wilmington, Del., Jan. 19, 1946. BA, St. John's Coll., Annapolis, Md., 1969; MA, U. Tex., 1972, JD, 1975. Bar: N.Mex. 1977. Law clk. Tex. Ct. Criminal Appeals, Austin, 1975-76, U.S. Ct. Appeals (10th cir.), Santa Fe, N.Mex., 1977-78; asst. atty. gen. N.Mex. Atty. Gen., Santa Fe, 1978-84; asst. appellate defender N.Mex. Pub. Defender Dept., Santa Fe, 1984-87; staff atty. N.Mex. Taxation and Revenue Dept., Santa Fe, 1987-92; shareholder Kemrer-Hayes & Moll, P.A., Albuquerque, 1992; gen. counsel N.Mex. Gen. Svcs. Dept., Santa Fe, 1993—. Mem. N.Mex. State Bar (bd. dirs. pub. law sect. 1996—, bd. dirs. bankruptcy sect. 1992, mem. adv. opinoin com. 1993-96). Office: NMex Gen Svcs Dept 715 Alta Vista Santa Fe NM 87503

MOLLETT, DAVID L., artist; b. Portland, Oreg., Mar. 5, 1950; s. Donald Lee and Shirley (Gordon) M.; m. Nina Dee Schectman, Nov. 3, 1976 (div.); 1 child, Tobin Lee. Student, N.Y. Studio Sch., N.Y.C., 1970-71; BA, Reed Coll., Portland, Oreg., 1975. Instr. studio art courses U. Alaska, Fairbanks, 1985—; curator paintings from the Arctic Refuge Civic Ctr. Gallery, Fairbanks, 1991. Exhibited in one-man shows at Anchorage Hist. and Fine Arts Mus., 1981, 89, Alaska State Mus., Juneau, 1991, Civic Ctr. Gallery, Fairbanks, 1980, 85, 94, Alaska Pacific U., Anchorage, 1994, Espace Reduit Gallerie, Cassis, France, 1992, Stonington Gallery, Anchorage, 1987, 92; exhibited in group shows at Chaffey Coll., Rancho Cucamonga, Calif., 1994, Norway-L.A. Print Exch. Exhbn., Oslo, 1993. Panelist for grants and budgets Alaska State Coun. on the Arts, 1990, 94. Resident fellow Camargo Found., Cassis, 1992; Alaska State Coun. on Arts fellow, 1982, 88. Mem. N.W. Print Coun., L.A. Printmaking Soc. Democrat. Office: Site 250 Fine Art 250 Cushman St Ste 2A Fairbanks AK 99701-4665

MOLLMAN, JOHN PETER, book publisher, consultant electronic publishing; b. Belleville, Ill., Feb. 8, 1931; s. Kenneth John and Maurine (Farrow) M.; children—Sarah Chase, Eric Cleburne. B.Arts, Washington U., St. Louis, 1952. Advt. specialist Gen. Electric Co., Schenectady and Boston, 1952-54; mgr. Enterprise Printing Co., Millstadt, Ill., 1956-66; gen. mgr. Monarch Pub. Co., N.Y.C., 1966-67; dir. prodn. Harper & Row Pubs., N.Y.C., 1967-74; pub. Harper's Mag. Press, N.Y.C., 1971-74; v.p. prodn. Random House Inc., N.Y.C., 1974-81; sr. v.p. World Book-Childcraft Inc., Chgo., 1981-88; pres. World Book Pub., 1988-91; pub. cons., 1991-92; dir. intellectual property devel. Multimedia Publishing Microsoft, 1992-96; cons. in electronic pub. Carmel, Calif., 1996—. Chmn. graphics standards rsch. com. NEH; mem. vis. com. Washington U., pub. com. Art Inst. of Chgo. With U.S. Army, 1954-56. Mem. Assn. Am. Pubs., Siwanoy Club (Bronxville, N.Y.), Sigma Delta Chi, Omicron Delta Kappa. Unitarian. Home: 25340 Vista Del Pinos Carmel CA 93923

MOLLNER, FREDERICK RICHARD, director publications, graphic designer; b. L.A., Aug. 21, 1946; m. Virginia Donahoo, Jan. 6, 1973. BA, Calif. State U., L.A., 1971, MA, 1972; postgrad., Art Ctr. Coll. Design, L.A. Graphic designer Calif. State U., L.A., 1972-77; art dir. Amb. Coll., Pasadena, Calif., 1977-78; art dir. Pepperdine U., Malibu, Calif., 1978-80, creative dir., 1980-84, dir. pubs., 1984—; tchr. Calif. State U., 1983-84, Pepperdine U., 1988; freelance graphic designer. Mem. Coun. for Advancement and Support of Edn., Univ. and Coll. Designers Assn. (sec. 1980), Advt. Club Ventura County, Art Dir. Club L.A., Am. Inst. Graphic Artists. Office: Pepperdine U 24255 Pacific Coast Hwy Malibu CA 90263-4181

MOLNAR, JOSEPH, retired clinical social worker; b. Detroit, Jan. 5, 1928; s. Joseph Jr. and Julia (Tomasi) M.; m. Claire Miriam Fitzgerald, Jan. 23, 1960 (div. Dec. 1988); children: Cecilia Anne, Elizabeth J. Baker, Patricia, Joseph J.; m. Elvira Arzaga, May 1, 1993. PhB, U. Detroit, 1951; MSW, U. So. Calif., 1955. Lic. clin. social worker. Chief social worker Juniper Serra Boys Club, L.A., 1957-68, Tri-City Mental Health, Pomona, Calif., 1968-79; mental health clinician IV San Bernardino (Calif.) County Mental Health, 1979-94; v.p. U. So. Calif. Alumni Assn., L.A., 1959; 2d/3d v.p. NAACP, Pomona, 1959-63. Contbr. papers to profl. jours. Bd. dirs. Calif. Assn. Children of Alcoholics, 1982-89. With U.S. Army, 1946-47. Named Social Worker of Yr., NASW, 1989. Democrat. Roman Catholic. Home: 31182 Nice Ave Mentone CA 92359-1381 *Died March 20, 1997.*

MOLONEY, STEPHEN MICHAEL, lawyer; b. L.A., July 1, 1949; s. Donald Joseph and Madeline Marie (Sartoris) M.; m. Nancy Paula Barile, Jan. 15, 1972; children: Michael, John, Kathleen. Student, St. John's Sem., Camarillo, Calif., 1967-69; BS, U. Santa Clara, 1971, JD, 1975. Bar: Calif. 1975, U.S. Dist. Ct. (cen. dist.) Calif. 1976, U.S. Supreme Ct. 1990. Assoc. Gilbert, Kelly, Crowley & Jennett, L.A., 1975-80, from ptnr. to sr. ptnr., 1980—; arbitrator, settlement officer Los Angeles Superior Ct., 1985—. Contbr. articles to profl. jours. Dir. Calif. Def. Polit. Action Com., Sacramento, 1991—. With USAR. Recipient Svc. award to Pres. of So. Calif. Def. Counsel, Def. Rsch. Inst., Chgo., 1992. Mem. Assn. So. Calif. Def. Counsel (pres. 1992-93), Calif. Def. Counsel (dir. 1991—), L.A. County Bar Assn. (vols. in parole, 1976-77, exec. com. alternative dispute resolution com. 1992—), Jonathan Club, Oakmont Country Club, La Quinta Hotel Golf Club. Democrat. Roman Catholic. Office: Gilbert Kelly Crowley & Jennett 1200 Wilshire Blvd Ste 6 Los Angeles CA 90017-1908

MOMENT, JOAN, artist, educator; b. Sellersville, Pa., Aug. 22, 1938; d. Robert Joseph and Margaret Velma (Adams) Ingham; m. Roger Lloyd Moment, May 27, 1962 (div. 1970); 1 child, Benjamin Robert. BS and RN, U. Conn., 1960; MFA, U. Colo., 1970. Psychiat. nurse Yale Med. Ctr., New Haven, 1960-61; pub. health nurse Vis. Nurse Assn., New Haven, 1961-62; grad. assistantship U. Colo., Boulder, 1968-69; lectr. U. Colo., Denver, 1970; from asst. prof. to full prof. Calif. State U., Sacramento, 1970—; vis. assoc. prof. East Carolina U., Greenville, N.C., 1984; vis. artist, lectr. Syracuse (N.Y.) U., 1985, U. N.C., Chapel Hill, 1986, Princeton U., 1987; guest lectr. Crocker Art Mus., 1994. One woman shows include Candy Store Gallery, Folsom, Calif., 1973, Wenger Gallery, San Francisco, 1974, La Jolla, 1975, 82, Whitney Mus. Am. Art, N.Y.C., 1974, La Jolla, 1975, 82, Galerie Simonne Stern, New Orleans, 1979, Crocker Art Mus, Sacramento, 1981, Quay Gallery, San Francisco, 1982, Southeastern Ctr. for Contemporary Art, Winston Salem, N.C., 1984, Gray Art Gallery, E. Carolina U., Greenville, N.C., 1984, Rena Bransten Gallery, San Francisco, 1985, Calif. State U., Sacramento, 1985, Galerie Hirondelle, N.Y.C., 1987, Jennifer Pauls, 1978, 89, Solomon Dubnick Gallery, Sacramento, 1992; group exhbns. include Calif. State U., Sacramento, 1971, 76, 88, 94, San Francisco Art Inst., 1972, Oakland Mus., 1972, 83, 92, 94, Crocker Mus., 1972, 85, 88, 91, 94, 95, Whitney Mus. of Am. Art, N.Y.C., 1973, Walnut Creek Civic Arts Gallery, Calif., 1977, Portland Ctr. Visual Arts, Oreg., 1977, L.A.C.E., L.A., 1979, Palo Alto Cultural Ctr., Calif., 1979, San Jose Mus. Art, 1981, Quay Gallery, San Francisco, 1981-84, Long Beach Mus. Art, Long Beach, Ca., 1982, Chan Elliot Gallery, 1983, San Francisco Arts Commn. Gallery, 1983, Auckland Mus., Chapel Hill, N.C., 1987, Fresno Art Mus., Calif., 1987, Jennifer Pauls Gallery, 1988, CSU, Long Beach, Calif., 1989, Richard Nelson Gallery, U. Calif. Davis, 1990, 94, 95, 96, San Francisco Mus. Modern Art Rental Gallery, 1990, U. Colo. Art Mus., 1991, Pence Gallery, 1991, 94, Ctr. for Contemporary Art, Sacramento, Calif., 1991, William Sawyer Gallery, 1993, Bergen Mus. Art, Paramus, N.J., 1993, Alza Corp., Vacaville, Calif., 1991, Oakland Mus., 1992, 94, Somona State U., Rohnert Park, Calif., 1995, Temporary/Contemporary, Las Vegas, 1995, others; collections include Crocker Art Mus., U. Colo., Boulder, Oakland Mus., N.Y. State Devel. Corp., Allen Meml. Art Mus., Oberlin, Ohio, others. Juror selection panelist Art in Pub. Places Meml. Auditorium, Sacramento, 1991; juror Calif. Exposition and State Fair, Sacramento, 1991. Recipient Meritorious Performance award Calif. State U., 1986; Rockefeller artist-in-residency fellow, 1984. Mem. Coll. Artists Assn. Home: 1424 35th St Sacramento CA 95825-6811 Office: Calif State Univ Dept Art 6000 J St Sacramento CA 95819-2605

MONACO, DANIEL JOSEPH, lawyer; b. Easton, Pa., May 12, 1922; s. Federico and Maria (Romano) M.; m. Marian P. Monaco, June 25, 1953 (div.); children: Denise E., Mimi D. AB, Lafayette Coll., 1943; MA, U. Chgo., 1946; JD, Stanford U., 1950; postgrad., U. Mich., 1944-45. Bar: Calif. 1951, U.S. Dist. Ct. (no. dist.) Calif. 1951, U.S. Sup. Ct. 1961. Faculty U. Miami, Fla., 1946-47; founder, sr. ptnr. Monaco, Anderlini & Finkelstein, San Mateo, 1953—; probate judge State of Calif., 1963-67; real estate broker, 1960-67; judge pro-tem Calif. Mcpl. and Superior Cts. Chmn. San Mateo County Dem. Cen. Com., 1960-61, mem. Calif. State Exec. Bd.; founder, pres. Circlon Internat., 1980-81; chmn. World Peace Through Law Conf. com. to establish a Citizens World Ct.; mem. No. Calif. Coun. Fgn. Affairs. With U.S. Army, 1943-46; lt. USAR, 1946-50. Mem. ABA, Calif. State Bar Assn., Assn. Trial Lawyers Am., Calif. Trial Lawyers Assn. (bd. govs.), San Mateo County Trial Lawyers Assn. (pres.), San Mateo County Hosp. Found. Bd., World Jurist Assn. (pres. of Ams. 1991-93, 2d v.p. 1995—, fin. chmn. 1995—), Am. Bd. Trial Advocates, Am. Soc. Internat. Law, Assn. World Citizens, Gorbachev Found., The Commonwealth Club, Peninsula Golf and Country Club. Democrat. Avocations: travel, internat. law, peace endeavors. Home: 295 Darrell Rd Hillsborough CA 94010-7109 Office: 400 S El Camino Real Ste 700 San Mateo CA 94402-1708

MONACO, DICK STEVEN, mail order vendor; b. San Diego, Oct. 12, 1956; s. Louis Antonio and Judith Ann (Frank) M.; m. Anne Raylene Hoover, Sept. 26, 1989; children: Teresa Anne, Michele Dawn. BA in Journalism, Nat. U., 1990. Copywriter, artist Interstate Mktg., San Diego, 1979-93; owner Dicks of Am., San Diego, 1986—; cons. computer graphics, San Diego, 1990-94. Author: I Love Peanut Butter Cookbook, 1985 (Best Self Pub. award Am. Bookdealer's Exch. 1987), Dick Liquers, 1994. Office: Sunsponges Pub PO Box 600782 San Diego CA 92160-0782

MONACO, PAUL, academic administrator, educator, artist, writer; b. Niskayuna, N.Y., Sept. 11, 1942; s. Angelo M. and Birdena (O'Melia) M.; m. Victoria O'Donnell, 1993. BS, Columbia U., 1965; MA, U. N.C., 1966; PhD, Brandeis U., 1974. Asst. prof. hist. Brandeis U., Waltham, Mass., 1973-75; prof. arts and humanities U. Tex., Dallas, 1975-85, dir. grad. studies arts and humanities, 1976-80; dept. head, prof. media and theatre arts Mont. State U., Bozeman, 1985—; bd. dirs. U. Film and Video Assn., 1988-91, 95-96, Bozeman Film Festival, 1985— (pres. 1987-90); mem. Hist. Preservation Com., Bozeman, 1988-90, Mont. Com. for Humanities, Missoula, 1989-93; regional coord. Nicholls Screenwriting Awards, 1989-91.

Author: Cinema and Soc., Modern Europe Culture..., 1993, Ribbons in Time, 1988 (ALC Outstanding Acad. Book award 1988); prodr., dir.: Montana: 2d Century, 1990-96 (Mont. broadcasters award 1991), Bison in the Killing Fields, 1996; prodr., dir., co-writer: Home to Montana, 1988; dir. I Often Thought of Berlin, 1989, Women, War and Work, 1994, Way of the Trout, 1994, Gary Strobel: A Portrait, 1996. Bd. dirs. Mont. Ballet Co., Bozeman, 1986-90; mem. selection com. Fulbright Found., Germany, 1996, 97. Recipient Fulbright Prof. award U.S., Germany, 1982-83, 92. Home: 290 Low Bench Rd Gallatin Gateway MT 59730-9741 Office: Mt State Univ Visual Communications Bldg Bozeman MT 59717

MONACOS, STEVE PERRY, electrical engineer; b. Arcadia, Calif., July 23, 1959; s. Perry and Helen Monacos. AA, Pasadena (Calif.) City Coll., 1979; BS, UCLA, 1981, MS, 1984; diploma in elec. engring., U. So. Calif., L.A., 1990, PhD in Elec. Engring., 1996. Tech. staff Jet Propulsion Lab., Pasadena, 1982-96, tech. group leader, 1996—. Contbr. articles to profl. jours.; patentee in field. Treas. St. Nectarios Ch., Covina, Calif., 1993-95. Mem. Optical Soc. Am. Greek Orthodox. Office: Jet Propulsion Lab 4800 Oak Grove Dr Pasadena CA 91109

MONAHAN, RITA SHORT, nursing educator; b. Waterloo, Iowa, Sept. 16, 1954; d. Andrew T. and Lillian R. (Weber) Short; m. W. Gregory Monahan, Jr., June 2, 1976; children: Andrew G., Catherine R. BSN, U. Iowa, 1976; MS in Nursing, Duke U., 1980; EdD, W.Va. U., 1986. Cert. gerontology clin. nurse specialist. From instr. to asst. prof. sch. nursing W.Va. U., Morgantown, 1981-86; assoc. prof. sch. nursing Oreg. Health Scis. U., LaGrande, 1986—. Contbr. articles to profl. jours. Mem. ANA, AAUW, Am. Diabetes Assn., Oreg. Nurses Assn., Sigma Theta Tau. Office: Oreg Health Scis U Sch Nursing 1410 L Ave La Grande OR 97850-2899

MONARCHI, DAVID EDWARD, management scientist, information scientist, educator; b. Miami Beach, Fla., July 31, 1944; s. Joseph Louis and Elizabeth Rose (Muller) M.; BS in Engring. Physics, Colo. Sch. of Mines, 1966; PhD (NDEA fellow), U. Ariz., 1972; 1 child by previous marriage, David Edward. Asst. dir. of Bus. Rsch. Divsn., U. Colo., Boulder, 1972-75, asst. prof. mgmt. sci./info. systems, 1972-75, assoc. prof. mgmt. sci. and info. systems, 1975—; assoc. dir. Bus. Rsch. Divsn., 1975-80, dir. Divsn. Info. Sci. Rsch., 1982-84; prin. investigator of socio-econ. environ. systems for govtl. agys., and local govt. orgns., State of Colo., also info. systems for pvt. firms, 1972-77. Mem. Gov.'s Energy Task Force Com., 1974. Mem. IEEE, Inst. for Mgmt. Sci., Assn. Computing Machinery, Am. Assn. Artificial Intelligence. Contbr. numerous articles on socio-econ. modeling, object-oriented systems and artificial intelligence to profl. jours. Home: 32 Benthaven Pl Boulder CO 80303-6210 Office: U Colo Grad Sch Bus Boulder CO 80309-0419

MONDA, MARILYN, quality improvement consultant; b. Paterson, N.J., Aug. 11, 1956; d. Thomas John and Lydia Mary (Dal Santo) M.; m. Lawrence G. Gifford, Jr., Aug. 25, 1984. BA, San Diego State U., 1980; MA, Baylor U., 1984. Math. statistician Navy Personnel Rsch. and Devel. Ctr., San Diego, 1984-86; quality engr. Info. Magnetics, Inc., San Diego, 1986-87; mgmt. cons. Process Mgmt. Inst., Inc., Mpls., 1987-89; staff assoc. Luftig & Assocs., Inc., Detroit, 1989-92; founder Quality Disciplines, San Diego, 1992—; bd. dirs. Deming Users Group, San Diego, 1985-87; lecturer in the field. Contbr. articles to profl. jours. Mem. San Diego Deming Users Group, Am. Soc. Quality Consultants, Am. Statistical Assn., Phi Beta Kappa.

MONDAVI, ROBERT MICHAEL, vintner; b. 1943. Grad., Santa Clara U. Prin. Robert Mondavi Winery; pres., CEO Robert Mondavi Corp., Oakville, Calif. Office: Robert Mondavi Corp 841 Latour Ct Napa CA 94558*

MONDAY, JON ELLIS, music publishing company executive; b. San Jose, Calif., Oct. 6, 1947; s. John Lang Monday and Marjorie (Meinecke) Licht; m. Anna Genia Hochman, Nov. 6, 1968; 1 child, Rachel. V.p., gen. mgr. Takoma Records, L.A., 1970-79; dir. mktg. Chrysalis Records, Inc., L.A., 1979-82; v.p. product devel. Romox, Inc., Campbell, Calif., 1982-85; v.p. mgmt. info. systems Epyx, Inc., Redwood City, Calif., 1985-89; pres., co-founder MusicWriter, Inc., Los Gatos, Calif., 1989—. Producer various records including Gospel Nights, 1979, Last Chance..., 1978, A Christmas Yet to Come, 1975; co-inventor NoteStation music distribution system. Mem. Vedanta Soc. (bd. dirs.). Office: MusicWriter Inc 170 Knowles Dr Ste 203 Los Gatos CA 95030-1833

MONDAY, MARK JAMES ALBERT, author; b. Phoenix, Sept. 4, 1946; s. Albert James and Shirley Ann (Schmidt) M.; m. Anne Callahan. BA in Edn., Ariz. State U., 1968. Reporter Am. Newspaper Group/KALF Radio, Phoenix, 1961-66; proofreader Republic & Gazette, Phoenix, 1966; reporter Ariz. Republic, Phoenix, 1968-71; reporter/columnist San Diego Tribune, 1971-92; pub./editor Terrorism, Violence & Insurgency Jour., San Diego, 1979-81, Briefing: Terrorism and Law Intensity Conflict, San Diego, 1989-92; dir. info. svcs. Vantage Systems, Inc., San Diego, Phoenix, 1992—. Author: A Summer of Sunshine, 1976, Killing Zone, 1994. Mem. info. com. San Diego Crime Commn., 1991—. Co-recipient Pulitzer Prize in Journalism for best local reporting, 1979; recipient Resolution of Commendation, Rules Com., Calif. State Legis., 1972, Info. award Civil Air Patrol, Ariz. Wing, 1971. Mem. Soc. Profl. Journalists, San Diego Newspaper Guild (sec. 1986-89). Democrat. Home: PO Box 14685 Scottsdale AZ 85267 Office: 1027 Cherry Orchard Loop Hamilton MT 59840

MONE, LOUIS CARMEN, clinical social worker; b. Bklyn., July 10, 1936; s. Louis Anthony and Carmella (Guidone) M.; BA, U. Ariz., 1962; MSW, Rutgers U., 1965; PhD in Clin. Social Work, 1985. Diplomate Am. Bd. Clin. Social Workers. m. Elinor Sypniewski, Sept. 28, 1958; children: Marc, Lisa. Detention supr. Pima County Detention Home, Tucson, 1959-60; social worker N.J. Neuro-Psychiat. Inst., Princeton, 1961-63; psychiat. social worker Alcoholism Treatment Ctr., Roosevelt Hosp. Metuchen, N.J., 1963-66; caseworker Family Counseling Svc. of Somerset County, Bound Brook, N.J., 1965-67, group cons., 1965-69; prin. psychiat. social worker Raritan Bay Mental Health Ctr., Middlesex County Mental Health Clinic, Perth Amboy, N.J., 1966-69; social work cons. Borough of Spotswood, Spotswood (N.J.) Pub. Schs., 1967-69; pilot project dir., group therapist Heart Assn. Middlesex County, Edison, N.J., 1968-69; chief psychiat. social worker Insts. Religion and Health, N.Y.C., 1969-71; pvt. practice adolescent and adult psychotherapy, marriage and family counseling, East Brunswick, N.J., 1965-71, Del Mar, Calif., 1972-78, individual, marriage, family and child therapy, San Diego, 1973-78, La Jolla, Calif., 1978-86, San Diego, Del Mar, Calif., 1986—; instr. nursing programs Rutgers U., New Brunswick, N.J., 1970; dir. profl. svcs. Family Svcs. Assn. San Diego, 1971-75; instr. Calif. Sch. Profl. Psychology, 1974, 76-80; lectr. San Diego State U., 1989—. Dem. candidate Calif. 78th Assembly Dist., 1995-96; site coord. dept. psychaitry Children's Hosp. and Health Ctr., San Diego, 1997. With AUS, 1955-57. Mem. Am. Group Psychotherapy Assn., Nat. Fedn. Cin. Social Workers (com. psychoanalysis), San Diego Group Psychotherapy Soc. (past pres.), Calif. Soc. for Clin. Soc. Work (past pres., Clin. Social Worker of Yr. San Diego dist. 1995), Delta Chi. Author: Private Practice: A Professional Business. Home: 40 Kingston Ct S Coronado CA 92118-3343 Office: 3130 5th Ave San Diego CA 92103-6624

MONEY, RUTH ROWNTREE, child development specialist, consultant; b. Brownwood, Tex.; m. Lloyd Jean Money; children: Jeffrey, Meredith, Jeannette. BA in Biology, Rice U., 1944; MA in Devel. Psychology, Calif. State U., Long Beach, 1971; BA in Early Childhood Edn., U. D.C., 1979. Rsch. psychologist Early Edn. Project, Capitol Heights, Md., 1971-73; lectr. No. Va. C.C., Anandale, 1973-74; tchr. preschs. Calif. and Va., 1979-81; dir. various preschs., Washington and Va., 1981-85; instr. guided studies Pacific Oaks Coll., Pasadena, Calif., 1986-88; cons. parent/infant programs Resources for Infant Educarers, L.A., 1986—; founder, dir. South Bay Infant Ctr., Redondo Beach, Calif., 1988-92; instr. child devel. Harbor Coll., L.A., 1992-93; bd. dirs. Resources for Infant Educarers, 1986—; pres. bd. dirs. South Bay Infant Ctr., Redondo Beach, 1988-94, treas., 1994—. Producer (ednl. videos) Caring for Infants, 1988—. Mem. League of Women Voters, 1956—, v.p., 1972-76. Mem. Nat. Assn. for Edn. of Young Children, Assn. for Childhood Edn. Internat. Home: 904 21st St Hermosa Beach CA 90254-3105 Office: Resources for Infant Educarers 1550 Murray Cir Los Angeles CA 90026-1644

MONFERRATO, ANGELA MARIA, entrepreneur, investor, writer, designer; b. Wissembourg, Alsace-Loraine, France, July 19, 1948; came to U.S., 1950; d. Albert Carmen and Anna Maria (Vieri) M. Diplomate, Pensionnat Florissant, Lausanne, Switzerland, 1966-67; BS in Consumer Related Studies, Mktg., Pa. State U., 1971, postgrad. in speech and comms., 1971-72. Simultaneous translator fgn. langs. Inst. for Achievement of Human Potential, Phila., 1976-78; art dir. The Artworks, Sumneytown, Pa., 1975-76; asst. productionist Film Space, State College, Pa., 1976; real property mgr. Pla. 15 Condominium, Ft. Lauderdale, Fla., 1979-80; legal asst. Ft. Lauderdale, Fla., 1981-85; owner Rising Sun the Real Estate Corp. South Fla., Ft. Lauderdale, 1986—; pres. Kideos Video Prodns., 1985—; designer Colo. Remodel & Design, 1988-92; owner, designer Monferrato Designs, 1993-97; designer homes, interiors, furniture and landscapes. Office: Monferrato Designs Telluride 200 Front St Placerville CO 81430

MONFILS-CLARK, MAUD ELLEN, analyst; b. Amstelveen, The Netherlands, June 7, 1955; d. Wouter William Frederic and Jeane Albertina (Verbauwen) Monfils; m. Harry Carl Clark, Nov. 26, 1983 (div. 1993). BSBA, Calif. State U., L.A., 1990. Physicians assocs. mgr. L.A. County Health Dept., L.A., 1990-92, fin. mgr., 1992-93, health planning analyst, 1993-95; contract officer Gen. Relief Health Care Program, 1995—; active Comm. Strategy Group, L.A., 1994—, Workforce Devel., L.A., 1994—; mem. staff Strategic Planning Leadership Team, L.A., 1994—, High Desert Hosp. Strategic Planning Com., L.A., 1994—. Co-recipient Nat. Assn. Counties award, 1994, Pub. Svc. Excellence award, 1994.

MONGOLD, MICHAEL RAY, psychologist; b. Fresno, Calif., Aug. 18, 1951; s. Elton Conway and Carol (McKinsey) M.; m. Kathleen Washburn, July 17, 1987; children: Michael David, Sarah Michelle, Allison Carol. BA in Recreation Therapy, Calif. State U., Fresno, 1973; MA in Counseling, Pepperdine U., 1976; MA in Clin. Psychology, Calif. Sch. Profl. Psychology, 1981, PhD in Clin. Psychology, 1983. Lic. psychologist, Calif. Dir./therapist 8th Jud. Ct. of Conciliation, Great Falls, Mont., 1977-79; psychology intern Youth City Am., Mariposa, Calif., 1979-80, U. Calif. Davis Med. Ctr., Sacramento, 1980-81; crisis worker Valley Med. Ctr., Fresno, Calif., 1981-82; predoctoral intern in clin. and cmty. psychology Shasta County Mental Health Svcs., Redding, 1982-83, crisis intervention coord., 1985-86, program mgr., 1986-87; exec. dir., staff psychologist Mat-Su Cmty. Counseling Ctr., Wasilla, Alaska, 1983-85; pvt. practice clin. psychology Redding, 1985, 87—; dir. psychiat. programs Redding (Calif.) Specialty Hosp., 1990-92, dir. psychol. svcs., 1992—; mem. staff Valley Hosp., Palmer, Alaska, 1985, Shasta Psychiat. Hosp., Redding, 1986—, Mercy Med. Ctr., Redding, 1990—, Redding Med. Ctr., 1990—, Redding Specialty Hosp., 1991—; tchr. U. San Francisco, 1986-88, Mat-Su C.C., 1984-85; chief acad. officer U. for Humanistic Studies, Redding, Calif. campusclin. supr. social work, counseling psychology and psychiat. nurse students U. Alaska, Anchorage, 1983-85; clin. supr. Mat-Su Cmty. Counseling Ctr., Wasilla, 1984-85, Shasta County Mental Health Svcs., 1986-88, Redding Specialty Hosp., 1991—. Mem. adv. bd. No. Valley Cath. Social Svcs.; active Shasta Symphony Orch., Redding Symphony Orch., Shasta County Performing Arts Soc. Capt. USAF, 1973-77. Mem. APA, Calif. State Psychol. Assn., Shasta County Psychol. Assn. (chair hosp. practice com., Outstanding Psychologist of Yr. 1992). Office: Redding Specialty Hosp 2801 Eureka Way Redding CA 96001-0222

MONK, DIANA CHARLA, artist, stable owner; b. Visalia, Calif., Feb. 25, 1927; d. Charles Edward and Viola Genevieve (Shea) Williams; m. James Alfred Monk, Aug. 11, 1951; children: Kiloran, Sydney, Geoffrey, Anne, Eric. Student, U. Pacific, 1946-47, Sacramento Coll., 1947-48, Calif. Coll. Fine Arts, San Francisco, 1948-51, Calif. Coll. Arts & Crafts, Oakland, 1972. Art tchr. Mt. Diablo Sch. Dist., Concord, Calif., 1958-63; pvt. art tchr. Lafayette, Calif., 1963-70; gallery dir. Jason Aver Gallery, San Francisco, 1970-72; owner, mgr. Monk & Lee Assocs., Lafayette, 1973-80; stable owner, mgr. Longacre Tng. Stables, Santa Rosa, Calif., 1989—. One-person shows include John F. Kennedy U., Orinda, Calif., Civic Arts Gallery, Walnut Creek, Calif., Vallery Art Gallery, Walnut Creek, Sea Ranch Gallery, Gualala, Calif., Jason Aver Gallery, San Francisco; exhibited in group shows at Oakland (Calif.) Art Mus., Crocker Nat. Art Gallery, Sacramento, Le Salon des Nations, Paris. Chair bd. dirs. Walnut Creek (Calif.) Civic Arts, 1972-74, advisor to dir., 1968-72; exhibit chmn. Valley Art Gallery, Walnut Creek, 1977-78; juror Women's Art Show, Walnut Creek, 1970, Oakland Calif. Art. Home and Office: Longacre Tng Stables 1702 Willowside Rd Santa Rosa CA 95401-3922

MONK, GORDON RAY, recreation therapist; b. Jacksonville, N.C., Feb. 15, 1955; s. George Delma Monk and Annie Mae (Hucks) Dixon; m. Gwendolyn Deloris Barkley, Dec. 26, 1978 (div. June 1990); children: Earnest, Natasha; m. Ahmia Unique Boyd, Oct. 16, 1994; children: Adrienne, Lovie, Johnny. AA and AS, Ft. Steilacoom C.C., Tacoma, 1983; BA in Liberal Arts, Evergreen State Coll., 1985; M in Guidance Counseling, City U., 1996. Recreation therapist Western State Hosp., Lakewood, Wash., 1987—; vol. supr. Western State Hosp., Lakewood, 1987-90, 96; counselor intern Steilacoom (Wash.) H.S., 1995-96. Alumni Evergreen State Coll., Tacoma, 1990, Al Davies Boys and Girls Club, Tacoma, 1990; mem. com. Tacoma Ministerial Alliance Scholarship, 1991. Sgt. U.S. Army, 1973-81. Mem. Toastmasters (edn. planner and sgt. at arms 1986-87, pub. rels. com. 1987-88, v.p. 1988-89, pres. 1989-90, Competent Toastmaster 1987, Advanced Toastmaster 1988, Advanced Toastmaster Bronze 1989). Home: 7227 S Wapato St #D-9 Tacoma WA 98409 Office: Western State Hosp 9601 Steilacoom Blvd SW Lakewood WA 98498-7213

MONK, JANICE JONES, women's studies researcher, university program administrator; b. Sydney, Australia, Mar. 13, 1937; came to U.S., 1961; d. Harold Frederick and Edith Emily (Collins) J.; m. David Monk, July 31, 1964. BA with honors, U. Sydney, 1958; MA, U. Ill., 1963, PhD, 1972. Instr. geography U. Ill., Urbana, 1967-72, asst. prof., 1972-80; assoc. dir. S.W. Inst. for Rsch. on Women U. Ariz., Tucson, 1980-83, exec. dir., 1983—; cons. Nat. Geog. Soc., 1979-81, 86, 87; mem. U.S. Nat. Com. Internat. Geog. Union, Washington, 1980-88, vice chairperson gender study group, 1988-92, Commn. on Gender, 1992-96; bd. dirs. Ctr. for Geography in Higher Edn., Oxford, Eng. Co-editor: Women and the Arizona Economy, 1987, The Desert is No Lady, 1987, Western Women: Their Land, Their Lives, 1988, Full Circles: Geographies of Women over the Life Course, 1993, Women of the European Union: The Politics of Work and Daily Life, 1996; exec. producer The Desert is No Lady, 1995; contbr. articles to various publs. Bd. dirs. Prescott Coll., 1990-96. Mem. Assn. Am. Geographers (councilor 1978-81, meritorious svc. award perspectives on women group 1988, honors award 1992, award named in her honor 1997), Nat. Coun. Geog. Edn. (sec. 1984-86, bd. dirs. 1980-83), Soc. Woman Geographers (Washington, nat. councilor 1987-90), Nat. Coun. Rsch. on Women (bd. dirs. 1995—). Office: U Ariz SW Inst Rsch Women 102 Douglas Bldg Tucson AZ 85711

MONKE, J. VICTOR, psychiatrist, health services administrator; b. Litchfield, Ill., Mar. 24, 1914; s. William Henry and Amanda (Niemann) M.; m. Beulah Elizabeth Wilson, Nov. 4, 1944; children: Carlisle, Kevin. MA, U. Tenn., 1937; PhD, U. Md., 1941; MD, U. Minn., 1949; PhD, So. Calif. Psychiat. Inst., Beverly Hills, 1959. Diplomate Am. Bd. Psychiatry and Neurology. Chief human svcs. VA, L.A., 1992-95; chief svcs. Mt. Sinai Hosp., L.A., 1995—; pvt. practice. Maj. USAF, 1992-95. Mem. Am. Psychoanalytic Assn. (dir. 1990-96). Democrat. Home: 1331 Linda Flora Dr Los Angeles CA 91049-1733 Office: 6500 Wilshire Blvd Los Angeles CA 90048-4939

MONROE, CECIL R., securities trader. Adminstr. Divsn. Fin. and Corp. Securities, Salem, Oreg. Office: Divsn Fin and Corp Securities Rm 110 21 Labor & Industries Bldg Salem OR 97310

MONROE, MARY-LYNNE, computer consultant, special education educator; b. Chgo., Sept. 30, 1954; d. Clarence Anthony and Edna Ruth (Waleski) M.; m. Richard Neilan McPartland, Nov. 19, 1994; 1 child, Alyssa Joy McPartland. BS in Edn., Ill. State U., Normal, 1977; MS in Edn., Portland (Oreg.) State U., 1991. Cert. tchr., Oreg., Ill. Spl. educator Higbee Jr. H.S., Pittsfield, Ill., 1977-78, Bloomington (Ill.) Alternative Sch., 1978-83, Woodstock Sch., Portland, Oreg., 1983-84; from spl. educator to English educator Franklin H.S., Portland, 1984-93; computer coord. Am. Internat. Sch., Cairo, Egypt, 1991-92; computer cons. Matrix Cons., Wilsonville, Oreg., 1994—; computer instr. Whitaker Mid. Sch., Portland, 1995—. Mem. Fellowship of Reconciliation, Portland, 1990—; PAL, speaker Cascade AIDS Project, Portland, 1989—; local rep. UN NGO Forum on Women, Beijing, 1995. Mem. Internat. Soc. for Tech. Edn., NEA, Internat. Soc. Tech. Edn., Women's Internat. League for Peace and Freedom, Nat. Journalism Edn. Assn., Nat. Coun. Tchrs. English, Journalism Educators Assn., Oreg. Edn. Assn., Portland Assn. Tchrs., Oreg. Journalism Edn. Assn.

MONROE, SIDNI MCCLUER, special education educator; b. Alexandria, Minn., Mar. 11, 1949; d. Frank and Catharine (Peterson) Shapiro; m. Larry K. Monroe, July 21, 1973; 1 child, Colin Yung Hwan. BA in Math., SUNY, Buffalo, 1971; postgrad., Pitts. State U., 1976-78; MA in Spl. Edn., Marshall U., 1984; postgrad., Columbia U., 1984-85. Cert. secondary math., learning and severely handicapped, gifted tchr., Calif. Insvc. tchr. trainer math. U.S. Peace Corps, 1971-75; tchr. spl. edn. Unified Sch. Dist. # 250, 1976-78, Joplin (Mo.) Regional Ctr., 1978-80; grad. teaching asst., cons. asst. Marshall U., Huntington, W.Va., 1982; program dir. Ohio Ctr. for Youth and Family Devel., Ironton, Ohio, 1982-84; office mgr. Ctr. for Study and Edn. of Gifted Columbia U., N.Y., 1984-85; dir. residential assessment, diagnostic edn. specialist State. Dept. Edn. Diagnostic Ctr., L.A., 1986-92; del. Citizen Amb. Program Early Childhood Spl. Edn. to Russia and Ea. Europe, 1992. Mem. Coun. Exceptional Children.

MONSMA, STEPHEN VOS, political scientist, educator; b. Pella, Iowa, Sept. 22, 1936; s. Martin and Marie (Vos) M.; m. Mary Carlisle, Dec. 19, 1964; children: Martin S., Kristin J. AB, Calvin Coll., Grand Rapids, Mich., 1958; MA, Georgetown U., 1961; PhD, Mich. State U., 1965. Asst. prof. SUNY, Plattsburgh, 1964-67; prof. Calvin Coll., Grand Rapids, 1967-74; rep. State Legis., Lansing, Mich., 1974-78; senator State of Mich., Lansing, 1978-82; dir. office quality rev. Dept. Social Svcs., Lansing, 1985-87; prof. Pepperdine U., Malibu, Calif., 1987—, prof. and chair social sci. divsn., 1996—. Author: Pursuing Justice in a Sinful World, 1984, Positive Neutrality, 1993, When Sacred and Secular Mix, 1996; corr. editor Christianity Today, 1993—. Mem. Natural Resources Commn., Lansing, 1983-85; bd. dirs. Ctr. for Pub. Justice, Annapolis, Md., 1996—, Bread for the World, Washington, 1991-93. Am. Polit. Sci. Assn. grantee, 1995, Earhart Found., 1985; Calvin Ctr. for Christian Scholarship vis. scholar, 1993-94. Mem. Am. Polit. Sci. Assn., Christians in Polit. Sci. (pres. 1994-96). Presbyterian. Office: Pepperdine University Social Science Divsn Malibu CA 90263

MONSON, ARVID, food products executive; b. 1941. With Munson & Son Cattle Co., Sunnyside, Wash., 1959-84; pres. Munson Ranches, Inc., Outlook, Wash., 1984—. Office: 2330 Outlook Rd Outlook WA 98938-9200*

MONSON, JANET MARLENE, biochemist; b. Mondovi, Wis., July 31, 1944; d. Sigvald and Velma Lillian (Nyre) M. BS in Chemistry, Gonzaga U., 1969; PhD in Biochemistry, U. Wash., 1974. Postdoctoral fellow U. Wash., Seattle, 1974; Eidgenössische Techische Hochschule U. Zurich, ETH Molecular Biology Inst., Hönggerberg, Switzerland, 1975; postdoctoral fellow U. Calif., San Francisco, 1975-78; postgrad. rsch. scholar, 1978; asst. rsch. biochemist U. Calif., 1979-82; sr. rsch. scientist, project leader Zymos Corp., Seattle, 1982; vis. scientist U. Wash. and Fred Hutchinson Cancer Rsch. Inst., Seattle, 1982-83; asst. prof. dept. surgery McGill U., Montreal, 1983-89; freelance writer Hayward, Calif. Contbr. articles to profl. jours. Cmty. chair biohazard com. U. Calif., San Francisco, 1975-78; sr. biohazard safety officer USPHS, San Francisco, 1975-78. Recipient Individual Postdoctoral fellowship Am. Cancer Soc., 1975, Nat. Rsch. Svc. award, Individual Postdoctoral fellowship USPHS, 1975-78, Chercher-bousier sr. Fonds de la recherche en sante du Quebec, 1984-87, Sr. Scientist award Med. Rsch. Coun. Can., 1984-89; USPHS co-grantee, 1979-82, Med. Rsch. Coun. Can., grantee, 1984-89. Mem. AAAS.

MONSON, THOMAS SPENCER, church official, publishing company executive; b. Salt Lake City, Aug. 21, 1927; s. George Spencer and Gladys (Condie) M.; m. Frances Beverly Johnson, Oct. 7, 1948; children—Thomas L., Ann Frances, Clark Spencer. BS with honors in mktg, U. Utah, 1948; MBA, Brigham Young U., 1974, LLD (hon.), 1981. With Deseret News Press, Salt Lake City, 1948-64; mgr. Deseret News Press, 1962-64; mem. Council Twelve Apostles, Ch. of Jesus Christ of Latter Day Saints, 1963-85, mem. first presidency, 1985—, bishop, 1950-55; pres. Canadian Mission, 1959-62; chmn. bd. Deseret News Pub. Co., 1977-96; vice chmn. Deseret Mgmt. Corp.; pres. Printing Industry Utah, 1958; bd. dirs. Printing Industry Am., 1958-64; mem. Utah exec. bd. U.S. West Communications. Mem. Utah Bd. Regents; mem. nat. exec. bd. Boy Scouts Am.; trustee Brigham Young U.. With USNR, 1945-46. Recipient Recognition award, 1964, Disting. Alumnus award U. Utah, 1966; Silver Beaver award Boy Scouts Am., 1971; Silver Buffalo award, 1978; Bronze Wolf award World Orgn. of the Scout Movement, 1993. Mem. Utah Assn. Sales Execs., U. Utah Alumni Assn. (dir.), Salt Lake Advt. Club, Alpha Kappa Psi. Club: Exchange (Salt Lake City). Office: LDS Ch 47 E South Temple Salt Lake City UT 84150-1005

MONTAG, DAVID MOSES, telecommunications company executive; b. Los Angeles, Apr. 30, 1939; s. Gustave and Esther (Kessler) M.; children: Daniel Gershon, Esther Yael, Michael Menachem. student UCLA, 1957-61. Tech. writer L.H. Butcher Co., Los Angeles, 1961; phys. sci. lab. technician East Los Angeles Coll., Monterey Park, 1961—, planetarium lectr., 1963-78; pres., dir. Or Chadash, Inc., Monterey Park, 1968—; owner EDUCOMP, Monterey Park, Calif., 1980—; cons. David M. Montag & Assocs., Monterey Park, 1993—; pres. Aquinas Computer Corp.; chief scientist FCC Co., Monterey Park, 1996—; CEO Infrared Telecomms., Monterey Park, 1996—. ednl. cons. for computer-assisted instrn.; v.p., bd. dirs. Coll. Religious Conf., 1968-92. Mem. AIAA, Assn. of Orthodox Jewish Scientists, Laser Inst. Am., Internat. Soc. Tech. in Edn., Physics Instructional Resource Assn. Home and Office: PO Box 384 Monterey Park CA 91754-0384

MONTAGNE, JOHN, geology educator, consulting geologist; b. White Plains, N.Y., Apr. 17, 1920; s. Henry and Ella Tappey (Spurgeon) de la Montagne; m. Phoebe Morris Corthell, Dec. 23, 1942; children: Clifford, Mathew Hagen. BA, Dartmouth Coll., 1942; MA, U. Wyo., 1951, PhD, 1955. Cert. profl. geologist. Instr., Colo. Sch. Mines, Golden, 1953-55, asst. prof., 1955-57; asst. prof. Mont. State U., Bozeman, 1957-60, assoc. prof., 1960-63, prof. dept. earth scis., 1963-83, prof. emeritus, 1983—; chmn. Internat. Snow Sci. Workshop, Bozeman, 1981-82. Pres. Mont. Wilderness Assn., 1965; pres. bd. Bridger Bowl Ski Area, Inc., Bozeman, 1973. Served to capt. U.S. Army, 1942-46, MTO. Named Rotarian of Yr., 1989; recipient Gold and Blue award Mont. State U., 1987. Fellow Geol. Soc. Am. (sr., chmn. Rocky Mountain sect. 1982); mem. Am. Assn. Petroleum Geologists, Internat. Glaciol. Soc., Am. Inst. Profl. Geologists, Am. Assn. Avalanche Profls. (pres. 1991-94). Lodge: Rotary (pres. Bozeman 1967-68, dist. gov. 1979). Home: 1201 Highland Blvd Apt 120 Bozeman MT 59715-5983 Office: Mont State U Dept Earth Scis Bozeman MT 59717

MONTAGUE, GARY LESLIE, newspaper advertising executive; b. Mullan, Idaho, Apr. 4, 1939; s. William Bryan and Gladys Viola (Finkbeiner) M.; m. Dorothy Barclay, Feb. 14, 1959 (div. 1973); children: Teresa Montague Scofield, Douglas; m. Mikael Jones, Mar. 13, 1982. Grad., Am. Press Inst. Columbia U., 1973; postgrad., Cen. Wash. U., 1977. Classified advt. rep. The Wenatchee World, 1957-71, classified advt. mgr., 1971—; sr. ptnr. Leslie/Bryan/Jones, Wenatchee, 1992—; cons., lectr. arts adminstrn. Chmn. Wash. State Arts Commn., Olympia, 1985-88, commr., 1974-78, 82-88; trustee Wash. State Arts Alliance Found., 1981-88, Western States Arts Found., Santa Fe, N.M., 1982-88; pres. Cen. Wash. Hosp. Found., Wenatchee, 1987-88, Wenatchee Area Visitor and Conv. Bur., 1980-81, Allied Arts Coun. of North Cen. Wash., 1973-74, Music Theater of Wenatchee, 1970-71, Wenatchee Valley Dance Found., Gallery '76 art gallery Wenatchee Valley Coll.; commr. City of Wenatchee Arts Commn., 1975-78; exec. com. Wash. State Rep. Cen. Com., 1975-77; dir. Better Bus. Bur., 1993—; bd. dirs. Am. Lung Assn. Wash., 1997—. Mem. Assn. Newspaper Classified Advt. Mgrs., Western Classified Advt. Assn. (pres. 1990-91), Pacific N.W. Assn. of Newspaper Classified Advt. Mgrs. (pres. 1981-82), Wenatchee Area C. of C. (pres. 1978-79). Mem. Unity Ch. Lodge: Rotary. Home: 2142 Sunrise Cir Wenatchee WA 98801-1047 Office: World Pub Co 14 N Mission St Wenatchee WA 98801-2250 also: Leslie Bryan Jones PO Box 4644 Wenatchee WA 98807-4644

MONTAGUE, SIDNEY JAMES, real estate developer; b. Denver, Oct. 3, 1950; s. Jerome Edward and Donna Sherrill (Nixon) M.; m. Mary Francis Terry, Dec. 26,1987; stepchildren: Jonathan Ramsey Shockley, Britt Elizabeth Shockley; children: Noah Reimer. BA in Econs., Midland Luth. Coll., Fremont, Nebr., 1972. Loan counselor Am. Nat. Bank, Denver, 1972-74; loan officer First Nat. Bank Denver, 1974-79; exec. v.p. Buell Devel. Corp., Denver, 1979-84; v.p. The Writer Corp., Denver, 1985-86; pres. Mondevco Inc., Littleton, Colo., 1986-87; devel. mgr. Perini Land & Devel. Co., Phoenix, 1987-91; v.p. Perini Land & Devel. Co., San Francisco, 1991-94; prin. Farrmont Realty Group, Inc., 1994-96; v.p. Orsett Properties Ariz., 1996—. Republican.

MONTALI, LAWRENCE RICHARD, JR., religious newspaper editor; b. Somerset, Bermuda, Nov. 30, 1962; s. Lawrence Richard and Sammie Louise (Brocato) M.; m. Veronica Bavestrello, Aug. 10, 1991; children: Lorenzo Antonio and Stefano Samuel (twins). Student, U. Exeter, Eng., 1983-84; BA in Psychology, U. Calif., San Diego, 1985; MS in Mag. Journalism, Syracuse U., 1989. Founder, dir. Project Rainbow-Newton Coll., Lima, Peru, 1989-91; editor The Southern Cross, San Diego, 1991—; freelance writer, photographer Nat. Cath. Register, Encino, Calif., 1993—, Our Sunday Visitor, Huntington, Ind., 1994—. Exhbn. photographs Grove Gallery, San Diego. Recipient Best Story award NCCJ, 1993. Mem. San Diego Press Club (Best Story award 1994, Best Feature Story award 1994), Cath. Press. Assn. Roman Catholic. Office: The So Cross PO Box 81869 San Diego CA 92138-1869

MONTANDON, ARTHER RONALD, municipal lawyer; b. San Diego, Oct. 11, 1952; s. Francis Hammond and Sayoko (Kutazume) M.; m. Cathleen Elizabeth Conway, Nov. 24, 1986 (div. July 1981); m. Carol Lynn McCraw, Dec. 25, 1950; 1 child, Matthew Arther; stepchildren: Michael Balais, Debra Michelle Hawley, Amber Balais-Montandon, Amy Montandon. BS in Bus. Mgmt. with honors, San Diego State U., 1975; JD, U. Pacific, Sacramento, 1979. Bar: Calif. 1979. Assoc. McLean & McLean, San Diego, 1980-82; asst. city atty. City of Gardena, Calif., 1982-84; dep. city atty. City of Santa Maria, Calif., 1984-85, city atty., 1985—; city atty. City of Atascadero, Calif., 1989—. Editor: California Municipal Law Handbook, 1993. Mem. Ethnic Minority Rels. Com. of State Bar, San Francisco, 1991-94, Santa Barbara County Pvt. Industry Coun., 1991-93. Recipient Excellence in Practice of Pub. Law award Santa Barbara County Judges, 1992. Mem. U.S. Jr. C. of C. (amb.). Office: City Hall 204 E Cook St Santa Maria CA 93454-5136

MONTANEZ, MARY ANN CHAVEZ, vocational rehabilitation counselor, writer, producer; b. Pasadena, Calif., July 16, 1936; d. Vincent Chavez-Trujillo-Mendibles and Trinidad (Huerta-Molina) Chavez; m. R.E. Montanez, Nov. 17, 1956 (div. June 1976); children: Robert, Eric, (twins) Michael and Manuel. AA in Human Devel.; BA, Pacific Oaks Coll., 1988; cert. counseling, Calif. State U., L.A., 1994. Life cert. C.C. counseling and instrn. Placement officer Pasadena (Calif.) C.C. Dist., 1981-90, coll. instr., 1986-90; vocat. rehab. counselor Calif. Dept. Rehab., L.A., 1990—; mem. outreach bd. Pasadena Mental Health Assn., 1976-79; field rep. El Centro De Accion Social, Inc., 1976-77; dir. program Pasadena Unified Sch. Dist., 1977-78; coord. outreach, crisis counselor Pasadena Mental Health, 1978-81; cons., field reader Women's Ednl. Equity Act, Washington, 1981; outplacement coord. PCC, 1984; staff recruitment program Pasadena C.C., 1987-88; acad. counselor Multi Cultural Ctr.-Cerritos Coll. Dist., 1990-91. Mem. ACT, Pasadena, 1980-95; commr. Commn. on Disabilities, 1990—; adv. bd. mem. Fiesta Educativa, 1991—; bd. mem. West Side Ctr. on Ind. Living, L.A., 1993—; mem. credit com. Pasadena Employees Credit Union, 1996; active Huntington Libr. Democrat. Roman Catholic. Home: 2533 Glenrose Ave Altadena CA 91001-5049

MONTERO, DARREL MARTIN, sociologist, social worker, educator; b. Sacramento, Mar. 4, 1946; s. Frank and Ann Naake; m. Tara Kathleen McLaughlin, July 6, 1975; children: David Paul, Lynn Elizabeth, Laura Ann, Emily Kathryn. AB, Calif. State U., 1970; MA, UCLA, 1972, PhD, 1974. Postgrad. researcher Japanese-Am. Research Project UCLA, 1971-73, dir. research, 1973-75; assoc. head Program on Comparative Ethnic Studies, Survey Research Ctr. UCLA, 1973-75; asst. prof. sociology Case Western Res. U., Cleve., 1975-76; asst. prof. urban studies, research sociologist Pub. Opinion Survey, dir. urban ethnic research program U. Md., College Park, 1976-79; assoc. prof. Ariz. State U., Tempe, 1979—; cons. rsch. sect. Viewer Sponsored TV Found., Los Angeles, Berrien E. Moore Law Office, Inc., Gardena, Calif., 1973, Bur. for Social Sci. Research, Inc., Washington, Friends of the Family, Ltd., Nat. Sci. Found. Author: Japanese Americans: Changing Patterns of Ethnic Affiliation Over Three Generations, 1980, Urban Studies, 1978, Vietnamese Americans: Patterns of Resettlement and Socioeconomic Adaptation in the United States, 1979, Social Problems, 1988; mem. editorial bd. Humanity and Society, 1978-80; contbr. articles to profl. jours. Served with U.S. Army, 1966-72. Mem. Am. Sociol. Assn., Am. Assn. Pub. Opinion Research (exec. council, standards com.), Am. Ednl. Research Assn., Council on Social Work Edn., Soc. Study of Social Problems, D.C. Sociol. Soc., Am. Soc. Pub. Adminstrn., Nat. Assn. Social Workers, Pacific Sociol. Assn. Office: Ariz State Univ Sch Social Work Tempe AZ 85281

MONTGOMERY, JAMES FISCHER, savings and loan association executive; b. Topeka, Nov. 30, 1934; s. James Maurice and Frieda Ellen (Fischer) M.; m. Diane Dealey; children: Michael James, Jeffrey Allen, Andrew Steven, John Gregory. BA in Acctg., UCLA, 1957. With Price, Waterhouse & Co., C.P.A.'s, Los Angeles, 1957-60; controller Conejo Valley Devel. Co., Thousand Oaks, Calif., 1960; asst. to pres. Gt. Western Fin. Corp., Beverly Hills, Calif., 1960-64; pres. United Financial Corp of Calif., Los Angeles, 1964-75; chmn., CEO Great Western Financial Corp., Chatsworth, Calif., 1975—, now chmn. bd. dirs.; fin. v.p., treas. United Fin. Corp., Los Angeles, 1964-69, exec. v.p., 1969-74, pres., 1975; pres. Citizens Savs. & Loan Assn., Los Angeles, 1970-75. Served with AUS, 1958-60. Office: Great Western Fin Corp 9200 Oakdale Ave Chatsworth CA 91311-6519*

MONTGOMERY, ROBERT LEMUEL, county official; b. Flat Rock, Ill., July 25, 1936; s. Lemuel Merton and Virginia Louise (Miles) M.; m. Deanna Jean Tenerelli, July 11, 1959; children—Deborah, David, DeAnn Kay. Student Portland State Coll., 1958, Clark Coll., 1959. Lic. real estate salesperson, Oreg. Asst. sales mgr. Nicolai Door Mfg. Co., Portland, Oreg., 1959-65; sales mgr. Wood Mosaic Corp., Louisville, 1965-68; v.p. Treeco Veneers Co., Lake Oswego, Oreg., 1968-69; owner Montgomery Supply Co., Bend, Oreg., 1969-75; county commr. Deschutes County, Bend, 1975-79; adminstr. State of Oreg., Salem, 1979-87, county adminstr. Hood River, Oreg., 1987-88, gen. mgr., Port of Cascade Locks, 1989-94, Legislature, Oreg. State, 1995—; mem. adv. com. Oreg. State U. Sea Grant; bd. dirs. Hood River Meml. Hosp., Discovery Ctr., The Dalles, Oreg., Mt. Hood C.C. Found. Bd.; active Republican Party. Served with USCG, 1954-58. Mem. Am. Legion, VFW, Lodges: Masons, Shriners, KT, Elks. Home: PO Box 65 Cascade Locks OR 97014-0065 Office: Port Office Cascade Locks OR 97010

MONTGOMERY, ROBERT LOUIS, chemical engineer; b. San Francisco, Nov. 20, 1935; s. Louis Clyde and Fay Elythe (Myers) M.; m. Patricia Helen Cook, Mar. 17, 1962; children: Cynthia Elaine, Jeanette Louise, Cecelia Irene, Howard Edwin. BS in Chemistry, U. Calif., Berkeley, 1956; PhD in Phys. Chemistry, Okla. State U., 1975. Registered profl. engr., Kans., Tex., Colo. Phys. chemist U.S. Bur. Mines, Reno, 1956-62; NSF predoctoral fellow Okla. State U., Stillwater, 1963-66; sr. engr. Boeing Co., Wichita, Kans., 1966-75; postdoctoral fellow Rice U., Houston, 1975-77, sr. research assoc., 1982-84; tech. data engr. M.W. Kellogg Co., Houston, 1977-82; staff engr. Martin Marietta, Denver, 1984-94. Contbr. articles to profl. jours. Mem. Am. Chem. Soc., Am. Soc. for Metals, Profl. Engrs. Colo., Sigma Xi. Home: 9933 Fairwood St Littleton CO 80125-8811

MONTGOMERY, SETH DAVID, retired state supreme court chief justice; b. Santa Fe, Feb. 16, 1937; s. Andrew Kaye and Ruth (Champion) M.; m. Margaret Cook, Oct. 29, 1960; children: Andrew Seth, Charles Hope, David Lewis. AB, Princeton U., 1959; LLB, Stanford U., 1965. Bar: N.M. 1965. Ptnr. Montgomery & Andrews, P.A., Santa Fe, 1965-89, of counsel, 1994—; justice N.Mex. Supreme Ct., 1989-94, chief justice, 1994; adj. prof. law U. N.Mex. Sch. Law, Albuquerque, 1970-71; chmn. N.Mex. adv. coun. Legal Svcs. Corp., Santa Fe, 1976-89. Bd. visitors Stanford U. Sch. Law, 1967-70, 82-85, U. N.Mex. Sch. Law, 1982-89; pres., chmn. Santa Fe Opera, 1981-86; pres. Santa Fe Opera Found., 1986-89; chmn., vice chmn. Sch. Am. Rsch., Santa Fe, 1985-89; bd. dirs. New Vistas, Santa Fe, 1986-89, First Interstate Bank of Santa Fe, 1977-89, Old Cienega Village Mus., 1980-89. Lt. (j.g.) USN, 1959-62. Named Citizen of Yr., Santa Fe C. of C., 1986, Sunwest Bank of Santa Fe, 1994; recipient Disting. Cmty. Svc. award Anti-Defamation League, 1991, Western Area Outstanding Achievement award Nat. Multiple Sclerosis Soc., 1992, award for advancement of law N.Mex. Trial Lawyers, 1994, Award for Outstanding Judge Albuquerque Bar Assn., 1994. Fellow Am. Coll. Trial Lawyers, Am. Coll. Trust and Estate Counsel, Am. Bar Endowment, N.Mex. Bar Assn. (bd. bar commrs. 1986-89, sec., treas. 1988-89, Professionalism award 1993); mem. ABA, Am. Judicature Soc. Democrat.

MONTNEY, MARVIN RICHARD, writer, poet, playwright; b. Leavenworth, Wash., July 20, 1937; s. Iness Marshal Montney and Marian Woodruff Gonser Montney Johnson; m. Eugenia Magdalene Méndez, Dec. 6, 1966 (div. Nov. 1972). BA in Philosophy, Reed Coll., Portland, Oreg., 1961; MA, U. Chgo., 1970; postgrad., U. Hawaii, 1975-78, 80-85. Instr. philosophy William Rainey Harper Coll., Palatine, Ill., 1970-71; grad tchg. asst. Asian and western philosophy U. Hawaii, Honolulu, 1982-84. Author: (novel) The Countersexual, 1997, (book of poetry) diving into flesh, 1994, (play) Sophronicsus' Son, 1991; co-author: (memoir) Card Times, 1992. Recipient John Billings Fiske prize in poetry U. Chgo. English Dept. Chmn., 1970. Mem. Nat. Writers Assn. Democrat. Home: 1462 44th Ave San Francisco CA 94122-2929

MONTONE, KENNETH ALAN, art director, creative director, consultant; b. Chgo., Aug. 30, 1938; s. George Joseph and Beatrice Mabel (Calcott) M.; m. Patricia Joan Klapperich, Feb. 1, 1964; children: James Paul, Ian Andrew, Paul Matthew, Anne Elizabeth. BFA with honors, U. Ill., 1963. Graphic designer U. Ill. Press, Champaign, 1962-63; staff graphic designer ABC-TV, Chgo., 1963-65; art dir. McCann-Erickson, Inc., Sydney, Australia, 1965-67; staff graphic designer CBS-TV, Chgo., 1967-69; syndicated cartoonist, "Kiwi" Chgo. Tribune-N.Y. News Syndicate; art dir. McCann-Erickson, Inc., Portland, Oreg., 1969-80; creative dir. Morton Advt., Portland, 1980-84, Ken Montone & Assocs., Portland, 1984—. Art dir.: "Celebrate" series, 1980. With USN, 1956-59. Recipient Reata Howard Trombley award Portland Ad Fedn., 1983, Art Dirs. Club award N.Y. Ad, 1983, Best in West award Am. Advt. Fedn., 1983. Mem. Advt. Industry Emergency Fund (bd. dirs.), Portland Ad Fedn., Advt. Museum. Home and Office: Ken Montone & Assocs 165 NW 95th Ave Portland OR 97229-6303

MONTOYA, MICHAEL A., state treasurer, accountant; b. Albuquerque, May 4, 1952; s. Orlando (Reno) and Nancy (Maestas) M. BS, U. Colo., 1982. CPA, N.Mex. Tax mgr. Ernst and Young, Albuquerque, 1985-90; dep. state auditor State of N.Mex., Santa Fe, 1993-94, treas., 1995—. V.p., bd. dirs. Albuquerque Hispano C. of C., 1986-90; bd. dirs. Belen (N.Mex.) C. of C., 1986-90; bd. dirs. Healthnet of N.Mex., Albuquerque, 1987-90, Recreational Health Occupl. Ctr., Inc., Albuquerque, 1986-90. Mem. AICPAs, Assn. Hispanic CPAs. Democrat. Home: PO Box 414 Los Lunas NM 87031 Office: NMex State Treasurer PO Box 608 Santa Fe NM 87504-0608

MONTOYA, PAUL ANTHONY, accountant; b. Santa Fe, Dec. 20, 1962; s. Joe G. and Rebecca (Romero) M.; m. Myrna M. Peña, July 2, 1994; children: Estevan, Desiree, Adrianna. B in Accountancy, Coll. of Santa Fe, 1989. CPA, N.Mex. Chief fin. bur. Office Atty. Gen. N.Mex., Santa Fe, 1989-90; adminstr. N.Mex. Forestry Dept., Santa Fe, 1990; staff acct. Los Alamos County, Los Alamos, N.Mex., 1990-91; staff auditor, acct. Daymon & Assocs., CPA's, Santa Fe, 1991-92; fin. specialist 3 N.Mex. Corrections Dept., Santa Fe, 1992-93; fin. mgmt. cons. adminstrv. svcs. div. N.Mex. Human Svcs. Dept., Santa Fe, 1993-94, audit mgr. Office Ins. Gen., 1994—. Home: 5972 Sierra Nevada Santa Fe NM 87505 Office: NMex Human Svcs Dept Office Insp Gen PO Box 2348 Santa Fe NM 87504-2348

MONTROSE, DONALD W., bishop; b. Denver, May 13, 1923. Grad., L.A. Coll., 1943; student, St. John's Sem., Camarillo. Ordained priest Roman Cath. Ch., 1949. Tchr. Mater Dei H.S., Santa Ana, Calif., 1960-64, prin., 1960-64; supt. Cath. H.S. Archdiocese of L.A., 1964-77; adminstr. Resurrection Parish, 1970-73, pastor, 1973—; Aux. bishop Roman Cath. Ch., Los Angeles, 1983; bishop Diocese of Stockton, Calif., 1985—. Office: Diocese of Stockton PO Box 4237 1105 N Lincoln St Stockton CA 95203-2410

MOODY, BRENT, protective services official. Dir. law enforcement City of Fairbanks (Alaska). Office: 656 7th Ave Fairbanks AK 99701

MOODY, HELEN F., training and consulting company executive, writer; b. Palo Alto, Calif., Feb. 6, 1949; d. Dwight L. and Bobbie J. (Naugher) M.; m. Richard A. Borthwick, Oct. 1, 1988; 1 child from a previous marriage: Amy Stroud Jackson. BA with honors, San Jose State U., 1971; PhD, U. Calif., Berkeley, 1981. Dir. ops. Comm. Strategies, Inc., Albuquerque, 1980-84; pres. Comm. Strategies, Inc., Corrales, N.Mex., 1984—; cons. Albuquerque C. of C., 1986, U. N.Mex., Albuquerque, 1987. Author: The Debate of the Rose, 1981, Good Grammar, Good Style, 1994, Writing by Design, 1995, Communication Strategies for the Internet, 1996. Mem. Village Planning Task Force, Corrales, 1988. Grantee Ford Found., 1974. Mem. Internat. Soc. for Performance Improvement (pres. N.Mex. chpt. 1995), Medieval Acad. Am., Soc. Tech. Comm. (sr.). Office: Comm Strategies Inc PO Box 2578 Corrales NM 87048

MOODY, KATE LADD, composer, music educator; b. Washington, Aug. 17, 1955; d. Graham Blair Moody and Dorothy Mills Field. BA, Sonoma State U., 1987. Pvt. instr. piano Poulsbo, Wash. Composer symphony, 1996, (music book) Playing and Composing/Circle of Fifths, 1992; composer, prodr. CDs Grateful Heart, 1993, Incurable Romantic, 1995. Office: Frog Rock Prodns 14410 Sandy Hook Rd Poulsbo WA 98370

MOODY, PATRICIA ANN, psychiatric nurse, artist; b. Oceana County, Mich., Dec. 16, 1939; d. Herbert Ernest and Dorothy Marie (Allen) Baesch; m. Robert Edward Murray, Sept. 3, 1960 (div. Jan. 1992); children: Deanna Lee Cañas, Adam James Murray, Tara Michelle Murray, Danielle Marie Murray; m. Frank Alan Moody, Sept. 26, 1992. BSN, U. Mich., 1961; MSN, Washington U., St. Louis, 1966; student, Acad. of Art, San Francisco, 1975-78. RN; lic. coast guard, ocean operator. Psychiat. staff nurse U. Mich., Ann Arbor, 1961-62, Langley-Porter Neuro-Psychiat. Inst., San Francisco, 1962-63; instr. nursing Barnes Hosp. Sch. Nursing, St. Louis, 1963; psychiat. nursing instr. Washington U., St. Louis, 1966-68; psychiat. nurse instr. St. Francis Sch. Nursing, San Francisco, 1970-71; psychiat. staff nurse Calif. Pacific Med. Ctr., San Francisco, 1991—; psychiat. staff nurse Charter Heights Behavioral Health Sys., Albuquerque, 1996-97; owner, cruise cons. Cruise Holidays Albuquerque, 1995—. Oil and watercolors included in various group exhbns., 1982-93. V.p. Belles-Fundraising Orgn., St. Mary's Hosp., San Francisco, 1974; pres. PTO, Commodore Sloat Sch., 1982. Recipient Honor award Danforth Found., 1954, Freshman award Oreon Scott Found., 1958; merit scholar U. Mich., 1957. Mem. San Francisco Women Artists (Merit award for oil painting 1989), Artist's Equity (bd. dirs. No. Calif. chpt. 1987-89, pres. No. Calif. chpt. 1990), Met. Club. Republican. Lutheran. Home: 219 Spring Creek Ln NE Albuquerque NM 87122 Office: Cruise Holidays Albuquerque 11032 Montgomery Blvd NE Albuquerque NM 87111-3962

MOODY, RAYMOND ALBERT, foreign language educator; b. San Diego, Oct. 28, 1936; s. Glen and Florence (Skiles) M.; divorced; children: Donna, Kevin. AA, Bakersfield Coll., 1956; BA, Stanford U., 1958; PhD, UCLA, 1967. Tchg. asst. UCLA, 1959-61; asst. prof. Ind. U., Bloomington, 1964-71; assoc. prof. European langs. U. Hawaii, Honolulu, 1971—; vis. lectr. U. Wis., Madison, 1968, vis. prof., 1970; vis. prof. U. Iberoamericana, Mex., 1969; organizer Symposium on Psychol. Type and Culture-East and West, Honolulu, 1993, 96. Author: (procs.) Personality and Ethnic Differences, 1995; contbr. articles to profl. jours. Coord. Radio Amateur Civil Emergency Svc., Honolulu, 1996—. Recipient award for best pedagogical article MLA, 1970-75; rsch. grantee U. Hawaii, 1979, 82, 87, 89, Ctr. for Applications Psychol. Type, Gainesville, Fla., 1991-92, 96-97. Home: PO Box 11099 Honolulu HI 96828 Office: U Hawaii European Langs Dept Honolulu HI 96822

MOON, RONALD T. Y., state supreme court chief justice; b. Sept. 4, 1940; m. Stella H. Moon. B in Psychology and Sociology, Coe Coll., 1962; JD, U. Iowa, 1965. Bailiff, law clk. to Chief Judge Martin Pence U.S. Dist. Ct., 1965-66; dep. prosecutor City and County of Honolulu, 1966-68; assoc. Libkuman, Ventura, Ayabe, Chong & Nishimoto (predecessor firm Libkuman, Ventura, Moon & Ayabe), Honolulu, 1968-72, ptnr., 1972-82; judge 9th div. 1st cir., Cir. Ct., State of Hawaii, Honolulu, 1982-90; assoc. justice Supreme Ct., State of Hawaii, Honolulu, 1990-93; chief justice Supreme Ct., State of Hawaii, 1993—; apptd. arbitration judge 1st cir. cir. ct.; adj. prof. law U. Hawaii, 1986, 87, 88; lectr., guest spkr. numerous events. Mem. ABA, Hawaii Bar Assn., Assn. Trial Lawyers Am., Am. Bd. Trial Advocates (pres. 1986-93, nat. sec. 1989-91), Am. Inns of Cts. IV (bencher 1983-90), Am. Judicature Soc., Hawaii State Trial Judges' Assn. (seminar orgn. com. 1987, exec. com. 1985-90, liaison supreme ct. 1990). Office: Supreme Ct Hawaii 417 S King St Honolulu HI 96813-2912

MOON, WILLIAM LAWRENCE, sales representative; b. Kenniwick, Wash., May 8, 1958; s. William R. and Barbara A. (Hills) M. BSEE magna cum laude, U. Lowell, 1981; MSEE, U. So. Calif., 1983, MBA, 1989. Project engr. Hughes Aircraft Co., L.A., 1981-91; field sales rep. Zeus Electronics, Irvine, Calif., 1995-97; regional sales mgr. Lambda Physik, Irvine, Calif., 1997—; owner, mgr. Dive Trip & Instrn. Co., L.A., 1983—; prin. sys. engr. Litton Laser Sys., Orlando, Fla., 1991-95. Contbr. numerous articles to scuba diving publs. Mem. dean's adv. bd U. So. Calif., L.A., 1987. Hughes Aircraft Co. fellow, 1981. Mem. Nat. Assn. Underwater Instrs., Hughes Aircraft Scuba Club (v.p. 1982-85, pres. 1986-88), Eta Kappa Nu, Beta Gamma Sigma. Office: Zeus Electronics 6 Cromwell Ste 100 Irvine CA 92618-1816

MOONEY, JEROME HENRI, lawyer; b. Salt Lake City, Aug. 7, 1944; s. Jerome Henri and Bonnie (Shepherd) M.; m. Carolyn Lasrich, Aug. 10, 1965 (div. Dec. 1978); 1 child, Dierdre Nicole; m. Kaitlyn Cardon, Sept. 23, 1995. BS, U. Utah, 1966, JD, 1972. Bar: Utah 1972, U.S. Ct. Appeals (10th cir.) 1974, U.S. Supreme 1984. Sole practice Salt Lake City, 1972-75, 79-83; sr. ptnr. Mooney, Jorgenson & Nakamura, Salt Lake City, 1975-78, Mooney & Smith, Salt Lake City, 1983-87, Mooney & Assoc., Salt Lake City, 1987-94, Mooney Law Firm, Salt Lake City, 1995—; bd. dirs. Mooney Real Estate, Salt Lake City. Mem. Gov.'s Coun. on Vet. Affiars, Salt Lake City, 1982-89; trustee Project Realty, Salt Lake City, 1976—, P.E.A.C.E.; FDA sponsor Project Reality, 1994—; vice chair State Mil. Acad. Assoc., 1992-93. Mem. ABA (criminal justice sect. U.S. Sentencing Commn. com.), Utah Bar Assn. (chmn. criminal bar sect. 1987-88), Utah NG Assn. (trustee 1976), 1st Amendment Lawyers Assn. (v.p. 1986-88, pres. 1988-89), Nat. Assn. Criminal Def. Lawyers (adv. com. Familys Against Mandatory Minimums), VFW. Democrat. Jewish. Home: 128 I St Salt Lake City UT 84103-3418 Office: Mooney Law Firm 4th Floor 50 W Broadway Fl 4 Salt Lake City UT 84101-2006

MOONEY, STEVE, food products executive; b. 1957. With Mooney Constrn. and Farms, Chico, Calif., 1978-88; ptnr. Mooney Farms, Chico, Calif., 1988—. Office: Mooney Farms 1220 Fortress St Chico CA 95973-9029*

MOONEY, WILLIAM OLIVER, retired military officer, corporation executive; b. Pulaski, Tenn., Apr. 21, 1948; s. Oliver D. and Auleen (Simpson) M.; m. Paula Gilliam, Sept. 5, 1969; children: Ashley Brooke, Wesley Brent. AA, Martin Coll., 1968; BS, Mid. Tenn. State U., 1970; MS, La. Tech. U., 1974. Commd. 2d lt. USAF, 1970, advanced through grades to col.; comdr. cadet squadron USAF, Colorado Springs, Colo., 1980-83; F-4 pilot USAF, 1983-92; vice comdr. Cheyenne Mt. Ops. USAF, Colorado Springs, 1992-94; dir. ops. Cheyenne Mt. Ops. USAF, 1994-96, ret., 1996; program mgr. Betac Corp., Colorado Springs, 1996—; ptnr. Locktight Storage, Pulaski, 1995—, Southpointe Manor, Pulaski, 1996—; cons. Gen. Mills, Inc., Mpls., 1995. Coach youth football and basketball, Colorado Springs, 1987-92; bd. dirs. Liquor Licensing Bd., Colorado Springs, 1996—. Recpient Cert. of Merit, Def. Intelligence Agy., 1992. Fellow Ret. Officer Assn., Air Force Assn., Colorado Springs C. of C. Republican. Home: 1235 Allegheny Dr Colorado Springs CO 80919 Office: Betac Corp 985 Space Center Dr Colorado Springs CO 80915

MOOR, ANTHONY JAMES, reporter; b. Evanston, Ill., Apr. 13, 1960; s. Donell Deloss and Lynne (Holliday) M. BA, Williams Coll., 1982. Desk asst. ABC, Tokyo, 1982-84; morning anchor JCTV, Tokyo, 1982-84; freelance reporter CNN, Tokyo, 1983-84; reporter KOB-TV, Santa Fe, 1985-87, WKBW-TV, Buffalo, 1987-89, KRON-TV, San Francisco, 1989—. Office: KRON-TV 1001 Van Ness Ave San Francisco CA 94109-6913

MOOR, WILLIAM CHATTLE, industrial engineering educator; b. St. Louis, Jan. 17, 1941; s. William A. and M. Carmen (Cross) M.; m. Marilyn E. Nichols, Sept. 19, 1964; children: Kathryn E., William E. BS in Indsl. Engring., Washington U., St. Louis, 1963, MS, 1965; PhD, Northwestern U., 1969. Indsl. engr. GSA, St. Louis, 1963-64; assoc. prof. Ariz. State U., Tempe, 1968—. Contbr. articles to profl. jours. Bd. dirs. Mesa (Ariz.) Bowling Assn., 1977-80, 89—. Mem. Inst. Indsl. Engrs. (sr.), Am. Soc. for Engring. Mgmt. (charter), Am. Soc. for Engring. Edn., Internat. Assn. for Mgmt. Tech. Methodist. Office: Ariz State U Dept Indsl Engring Tempe AZ 85287-5906

MOORE, ALISON LYNN, English educator, author; b. Pittsfield, Mass., Nov. 6, 1951; d. Herbert Samuel and Audley Elaine (Thomas) Moore; m. Robert Bruce von Liski, July 28, 1973 (div. Feb. 1982) Student, Marlboro (Vt.) Coll., 1970-72; MFA in Creative Writing, Warren Wilson Coll., 1990. Adj. lectr. Pima C.C., Tucson, 1990-94; asst. prof. English U. Ariz., Tucson, 1994—; dir. Writers at Work reading series, Tucson, 1995—. Author: Synonym for Love (novel), 1995, Small Spaces Between Emergencies (short stories), 1992 (Notable Book ALA 1993). Bd. dirs. Arts Reach, Tucson, 1991—. Nat. Endowment for the Arts fellow, 1993. Office: University of Arizona Dept English Modern Lang 445 Tucson AZ 85721

MOORE, ARLENE JOY, elementary school educator; b. San Diego, Aug. 28, 1951; married, two children. BA, San Diego State U., 1975, MA, 1986. Cert. elem., secondary sch. tchr., choral music, adminstrv. svcs., Calif. Tchr., music coord. La Mesa (Calif.) Schs., 1975-82; visual, performing arts specialist grades 1-6 Santa Rosa (Calif.) City Schs., 1986, summer sch. prin., 1988-91, tchr. grade 5, 1987—, visual, performing arts mentor, 1993—; ednl. cons. Sonoma County Office of Edn., Santa Rosa, Calif., 1988—; mem. educators' adv. bd. Sonoma County Cultural Arts Coun., Santa Rosa, 1994—; visual and performing arts profl. devel. series coord. The Calif. Arts Project, 1995-96; co-dir. Tng. Inst. The Calif. Arts Project, San Rafael and Arcadia, Calif., 1995-96; visual and performing arts trainer Sch. Leadership Acad., Santa Rosa, 1996. Author: Summer School Adminstrators Handbook, 1991, Integrating Arts Across the Curriculum, 1994. Mem. Youth Adv. Bd. Beth Ami Synagogue, Santa Rosa, 1993-94; sec. PTA Montgomery H.S., Santa Rose, 1995-96, co-chairperson Project grad.-security Montgomery H.S. Santa Rosa, 1995-96. Mem. Assn. Calif. Sch. Adminstrs., Calif. Tchrs. Assn., Calif. Alliance for Arts Edn., Calif. Arts Project (coord., trainer 1995—), Sonoma County Folk Song Soc. Office: Santa Rosa City Schs 211 Ridgeway Ave Santa Rosa CA 95402

MOORE, BOBBIE FAY, geriatrics nurse practitioner, nurse administrator; b. Woodward, Okla., Jan. 21, 1943; d. Marion Byron and Lelah Catherine (Anderson) Carey; m. Donald Kent Strickland, Apr. 2, 1959 (div. June 1968); children: Donald, Michael; m. Myrl Lynn Moore, Apr. 15, 1988. ADN, N.Mex. State U., Carlsbad, 1983; geriatric nurse practitioner, U. Colo., Denver, 1985. Cert. geriatric nurse practitioner, Am. Nurses Credentialing Ctr., N.Mex. Charge nurse Landsun Homes, Carlsbad, 1971-76; office nurse Dr. C. Munkers, Marquette, Mich., 1976-78; staff and treatment rm. nurse Guadalupe Med. Ctr., Carlsbad, 1978-83; nursing supr., nurse practitioner Landsun Homes, Carlsbad, 1985—, lic. nursing home adminstr., 1990—; mem. nursing adv. bd. N.Mex. State U., 1985—. Tchr. Sunday sch. Meth. Ch., Carlsbad; treas. Continuing Edn. Commn., Carlsbad, 1988—; counselor Boy Scouts Am., Carlsbad, 1989—; youth spnosor 1st

United Meth. Ch., Carlsbad, 1990—. Mem. N.Mex. Nurse Practitioner Coun. Home: 1401 Chico Dr Carlsbad NM 88220-5231

MOORE, CARLETON BRYANT, geochemistry educator; b. N.Y.C., Sept. 1, 1932; s. Eldridge Carleton and Mabel Florence (Drake) M.; m. Jane Elizabeth Strouse, July 25, 1959; children—Barbara Jeanne, Robert Carleton. BS, Alfred U., 1954, DSc (hon.), 1977; PhD, Cal. Inst. Tech., 1960. Asst. prof. geology Wesleyan U., Middletown, Conn., 1959-61; mem. faculty Ariz. State U., Tempe, 1961—; nat. rsch. coun. rsch. assoc. NASA Ames Rsch. Ctr., 1974; prof., dir. Ctr. for Meteorite Studies Ariz. State U., Regents' prof., 1988—; vis. prof. Stanford U., 1974; Prin. investigator Apollo 11-17; preliminary exam. team Lunar Receiving Lab., Apollo, 12-17. Author: Cosmic Debris, 1969, Meteorites, 1971, Principles of Geochemistry, 1982, Grundzügeder Geochemie, 1985; editor: Researches on Meteorites, 1961, Jour. Meteoritical Soc.; contbr. articles to profl. jours. Fellow Ariz.-Nev. Acad. Sci. (pres. 1979-80), Meteoritical Soc. (life hon., pres. 1966-68), Geol. Soc. Am., Mineral. Soc. Am., AAAS (council 1967-70); mem. Geochem. Soc., Am. Chem. Soc., Am. Ceramic Soc., Sigma Xi. Home: 507 E Del Rio Dr Tempe AZ 85282-3764 Office: Ariz State U Ctr for Meteorite Studies Tempe AZ 85287

MOORE, CHARLES AUGUST, JR., psychologist; b. Medford, Oreg., Feb. 22, 1944; s. Charles August and Bernadine (Newlun) M. BS, Lewis and Clark Coll., 1965; MA, U. Colo., 1967, PhD, 1972. Lic. psychologist, Calif., Oreg. Teaching asst. U. Colo., Boulder, 1965-66, 70-71, rsch. asst., counselor, practicum supr., 1966-67, 71-72; asst. psychologist State Home and Tng. Sch., Grand Junction, Colo., 1967; intern in psychology Camarillo (Calif.) State Hosp., 1968-69; psychology assoc., program psychologist Camarillo Drug Abuse Program (The Family), 1969-70; intern in psychology Oxnard (Calif.) Mental Health Ctr., 1969; clin. psychologist, dir. intern tng. Rural Clinics, Reno, 1972; clin. psychologist Kern County Mental Health Svcs., Bakersfield, Calif., 1972-74; clin., cons. psychologist San Diego County Mental Health Svcs., 1974-88; pvt. practice La Jolla (Calif.) Clinic, 1976-78; August Ctr., Chula Vista, Calif., 1978-85; staff psychologist Dept. Vet.'s Affairs Domiciliary, White City, Oreg., 1988—; guest lectr. Calif. State Coll., Bakersfield, 1973-74; mem. Health Systems Agy. Mental Health Task Force, 1979; mem. doctoral dissertation com. U.S. Internat. U., 1975-76; mem. mental health task force San Diego County Bd. Suprs., 1979. Contbr. articles to profl. jours. Mem. Univ. City Community Coun., San Diego, 1976-78; bd. dirs. Pub. Employees Assn., 1976-77. Recipient Experiment in Internat. Living European Study award Lewis and Clark Coll., 1962; USPHS fellow, 1967-68; U. Colo. Grad. Sch. Rsch. grantee, 1971; recipient Hands and Heart award Dept. Vets. Affairs, 1989-90, Domiciliary Spl. Contbn. and Outstanding Performance awards, 1990, 91. Mem. APA, Am. Psychology and Law Soc., Calif. Psychol. Assn., Western Psychol. Assn., San Diego County Psychol. Assn., Assn. County Clin. Psychologists San Diego, San Diego Psychology and Law Soc., San Diego Soc. Clin. Psychologists. Office: Dept VA Domiciliary Psychology Svc 8495 Crater Lake Hwy White City OR 97503-3011

MOORE, DAN STERLING, insurance executive, sales trainer; b. Lincoln, Nebr., June 27, 1956; s. Jack Leroy and Carolyn Marie (Bachman) M.; m. Marla Janine Collister, June 2, 1979; children: Tyler David, Anna Rose. Student, Red Rocks Coll., 1977. Lic. ins. exec. Asst. mgr. European Health Spa, Englewood, Colo., 1975-78; sales mgr. Colo. Nat. Homes, Westminster, 1979-80; sales assoc. Dale Carnegie, Denver, 1981; sales mgr. Paramount Fabrics, Denver, 1981-84; sales assoc. Mighty Distbg., Arvada, Colo., 1984-87; dist. mgr. Nat. Assn. for Self Employed/United Group Assn., Englewood, Colo., 1987—; dist. mgr. Communicating for Agr. Assn., 1993—, Am. Soc. Women Entrepreneurs, 1997—. Leader, trainer Alpine Rescue Team, Evergreen, Colo., 1971-74; minister Jehovah's Witnesses, 1972—. Mem. Am. Soc. Women Entrepreneurs (dist. mgr. 1997—). Home: 892 Nob Hill Trl Franktown CO 80116-8716 Office: Nat Assn Self Employed/United Group 10579 Bradford Pl Suite 100 Littleton CO 80127

MOORE, DANIEL ALTON, JR., retired state supreme court justice; b. 1933. BBA, U. Notre Dame, 1955; JD, U. Denver, 1961. Dist. ct. magistrate judge Alaska, 1961-62; pvt. practice law, 1962-80; judge 3d Jud. Dist. Superior Ct., 1980-83; justice Alaska Supreme Ct., Anchorage, 1983-92, chief justice, 1992-95; ret., 1995.

MOORE, DEBORAH, environmental scientist and advocate; b. Charlottesville, Va., June 27, 1963; d. Oliver Semon Moore and Dina Downing DuBois; m. Adam Cheney Dawson, Aug. 13, 1988. BA in Physics, Reed Coll., 1985; MS in Energy and Resources, U. Calif., Berkeley, 1989. Rsch. asst. dept. epidemiology Sloan-Kettering Meml. Hosp., N.Y.C., 1982; asst. mgr. Metaresearch Inc., Portland, Oreg., 1983; instr. dept. physics Reed Coll., Portland, 1983-85; rsch. assoc. dept. biology Brookhaven Nat. Labs., Upton, N.Y., 1985-86; staff scientist Environ. Def. Fund, Oakland, Calif., 1986—. Editor The Water Calendar, 1988-89; contbr. articles to newspapers and jours. Vol. Exploratorium Sci. Mus., San Francisco, 1987—. Mem. Am. Water Resources Assn., Internat. Secretariat for Water (bd. mem.). Office: Environ Def Fund 5655 College Ave Ste 304 Oakland CA 94618-1583

MOORE, DERRITH RACHELLE, environmental engineer; b. Flagstaff, Ariz., Feb. 5, 1964; d. Leo Chester Sr. and Pauline Mae (Yellowhair) Watchman; m. Henry Kee Moore, June 12, 1987; children: Chantal, Callan, Cheyenne, Cierra. BS in Animal Sci., Colo. State U., 1986. Extension agt. The Navajo Nation Dept. Agrl., Window Rock, Ariz., 1988; environ. specialist The Navajo Nation, EPA, Window Rock, 1988-92; asst. dir., site assessment mgr. all Indian Pueblo coun. Pueblo Office Environ. Protection, Albuquerque, 1992-95; environ./safety engr. Packard-Hughes Interconnect, Ft. Defiance, Ariz., 1995—. Recipient scholarship Am. Indian Sci. and Engring. Soc., Boulder, Colo., 1984; named Outstanding Young Women of Am., 1988. Democrat. Roman Catholic. Home: PO Box 207 Navajo NM 87328-0207 Office: Packard-Hughes Interconnect PO Box 679 Fort Defiance AZ 86504

MOORE, DONALD WALTER, academic administrator, school librarian; b. Culver City, Calif., June 9, 1942; s. Raymond Owen and Jewel Elizabeth (Young) M.; m. Dagmar Ulbrich, Mar. 28, 1968; 1 child, Michael. AA, L.A. Valley Coll., 1967; BA in History, Calif. State U., Northridge, 1970; MA in Learning Disability, Calif. State U., 1973; MLS, U. So. Calif., 1974. Part time librarian L.A. Pierce Coll., Woodland Hills, Calif., 1974—; instr. vocat. edn. act program L.A. Trade Tech. Coll., 1978-80, pres.'s staff asst., 1983-87; instr. learning skills L.A. City Coll., 1987-88, dir. amnesty edn., 1988-92, dir. Citizenship Ctr., 1992—; adj. instr. computer sci. L.A. Trade-Tech. Coll., 1983—, Coll. of the Canyons, Valencia, Calif., 1996—. Author: Cavalrymen, 1983; contbr. fiction, articles, revs. to various publs. Mem. Ednl. Writers Am., Co. Mil. Historians, Edpress, Little Big Horn Assn. Republican. Roman Catholic. Office: LA City Coll Citizenship Program 855 N Vermont Ave Los Angeles CA 90029-3500 *Personal philosophy: To survive in this world you must believe in yourself and know what's worth fighting for and what's not. But never despair, despair is the greatest sin.*

MOORE, ELAINE ANN, medical technologist; b. Toledo, July 19, 1948; d. Chester Anthony and Mary Felicia (Matuszek) Pacer; m. Richard M. Moore Jr., Nov. 13, 1971; children: Brett Lee, Lisa Marie. BS in Med. Tech., Toledo State U., 1970; MA in Sociology, U. Colo., 1993. Med. technologist Mercy Hosp., Toledo, 1970-72; toxicologist St. Francis-Penrose Hosp., Colorado Springs, 1972-94; med. technologist Bannock Regional Med. Ctr., Pocatello, Idaho, 1994—. Vol. Namaste Alzheimer Ctr., Colorado Springs, 1990-92. Mem. Am. Soc. Clin. Pathologists (cert. med. technician), Soc. Children's Book Writers, Columbia U. Parents Club. Democrat. Roman Catholic. Home: 88 N 3167 East Idaho Falls ID 83402

MOORE, ELIZABETH JANE, banker; b. Long Branch, N.J., Dec. 14, 1940; d. Robert William and Ruth Elizabeth (Dunphy) Marton; m. Gerard George Moore, Mar. 3, 1962; children: Christine Marie, Stephanie Ann, Gerard Marton, Paul Henry George, Barbara Jean. BBA, U. Phoenix, 1987. Charge card specialist Valley Nat. Bank, Phoenix, 1971-74, corp. trust specialist, 1974-80; trust specialist Valley Nat. Bank, Prescott, Ariz., 1980-84, 84-86, trust adminstr., sr. client svcs. officer, 1986-89, asst. v.p., 1989-93; v.p. Bank One Ariz., Phoenix, 1993-96; sr. trust officer Bank One Ariz. Advantage Trust, Phoenix, 1994-96. Bd. dirs. Cen. Yavapai County (Ariz.) Fire Dist., 1988-89, clk., 1989—, chmn. bd., 1990-91; bd. dirs. Yavapai Humane Soc., 1989-91, 97, 1st v.p., treas., 1990-91; bd. dirs. Vol. Firefighters Relief and Pension Fund, 1989-91, Prescott Fine Arts Assn., 1997; chmn. bd. dirs. Cen. Yavapai Pub. Safety Pers., 1991. Recipient 1st Place Photo Contest award Parade mag., 1992. Mem. Yavapai County Legal Secs. Assn. (treas. 1983-85, gov. 1985-86, Legal Sec. of Yr. 1984), U. Phoenix Network for Profl. Devel. (chartered), Friday Club, Phoenix Pub. Libr. Home: 3002 Pleasant Valley Ct Prescott AZ 86301-4150 *Personal philosophy: Always be willing to learn something new. Accept growth and changes as a normal part of life.*

MOORE, EVERETT LEROY, library administrator; b. Eugene, Oreg., May 24, 1918; s. Clinton L. Moore and Elsie LaVerne (Crowder) Morgan; m. Fern Irene Owen, July 13, 1942; children: David LeRoy, Richard Eugene, Patricia Elaine. BA, Wheaton Coll., 1949; MA, Pasadena Coll., 1954; MA in Libr. Sci., Vanderbilt U., 1960; PhD, U. So. Calif., 1973. Cert. C.C. chief adminstrv. officer, Calif. Libr. Evangel Coll., Springfield, Mo., 1955-57; head tech. svcs. North Coastal Regional Libr., Tillamook, Oreg., 1957-60; head social sci. and bus. libr. Calif. State U., Chico, 1960-62; dir. libr. svcs. Coll. of the Desert, Palm Desert, Calif., 1962-75; dir. univ. libr. Am. U. Cairo, 1970-72; dir. libr. svcs. Woodbury U., L.A., 1976-87, dir. libr. svcs., prof. emeritus, 1987—; pres. so. region Jr. Coll. Round Table, Calif. Libr. Assn., Sacramento, 1965-66; chair tech. svcs. com. Calif. C.C. Libr. Coop., 1968-70, chmn. Desert area, 1974-75. Contbr. to profl. jours. Home: 1322 E Ave Q12 Palmdale CA 93550

MOORE, FRANK JAMES, artist, educator; b. Columbus, Ohio, June 25, 1946; s. James F. and Constance (Chidester) M.; 1 child, Koala Bear. BA, Univ. N.M., 1972; MA in Psychology, Univ. Without Walls, Berkeley, Calif., 1976; MFA in Performanc, Video, San Francisco Art Inst., 1983. Tchr. univ. possibilities Inter-Rels., Inc., Berkeley, 1988—; dir. Theater Human Melting, Berkeley, 1975-82; mgr. Blind Lemon Theatre, Berkeley, 1977-81. Author: Cherotic Magic, 1990, Art of a Shaman, 1991; co-author: Vision Theater, 1994; editor (mags.) The Cherotic Revolutionary, 1991—; pub., editor Inter-Rels., Inc., Berkeley, 1993—; contbr. (anthologies) Range of Motion, 1993, Consider the Alternatives, 1996; contbr. articles to jours., periodicals, mags., newspapers. Performance Art fellow NEA, 1985; recipient Showcase award Cleve. Pub. Theatre Performance Art Festival, 1990, Honorable Mention, East Bay Video Festival, 1991, Second place, 1992, Best of Bay Performance Artist, Bay Guardian, San Francisco, 1992. Office: Inter Rels Inc PO Box 11445 Berkeley CA 94712

MOORE, GEORGE BARNARD, poet, educator; b. Pasadena, Calif., July 12, 1950; s. George Crosby and Jessica Francis (Barnard) M. BS, Lewis and Clark Coll., 1975; MA, U. Colo., 1981, PhD, 1990. Instr. dept. English U. Colo., Boulder, 1980-90, instr. dept. continuing edn., 1983—, instr. Sewall acad. program, 1987, 88, 91—; judge, panelist Arts and Humanities Assembly of Boulder, 1995-96; judge Colo. Coun. on Arts, Boulder, 1994. Author: (books) Long Way Around, 1992, Petroglyphs at Wedding Rocks, 1998, Gertrude Stein's The Making of Americans, 1997, A Thousand Frontiers, 1997. Recipient Creative Work award Arts and Scis. U. Colo., 1986, Covisions Recognition award Colo. Coun. on Arts, 1996. Mem. MLA, Am. Culture Assn. (area chair politics and lit. 1996), Am. Soc. for Aesthetics (v.p. Rocky Mountain divsn. 1996), Western Lit. Assn., Rocky Mountain Modern Lang. Assn. Office: U Colo Sewall Acad Program Boulder CO 80309

MOORE, GEORGE W(ILLIAM), geologist; b. Palo Alto, Calif., June 7, 1928; s. George Raymond and Grace Amy (Hauch) M.; m. Ellen Louise James, Nov. 27, 1960; children: Leslie Ann, Geoffrey. BS, Stanford U., 1950, MS, 1951; PhD, Yale U., 1960. Geologist U.S. Geol. Survey, Menlo Park, Calif., 1951-94; courtesy prof. geology, Oreg. State U., Corvallis, 1987—; geologist in charge La Jolla (Calif.) Marine Geology Lab., 1966-75; rsch. assoc. Scripps Instn. Oceanography, La Jolla, 1972-75; participant Deep Sea Drilling Project, Japan, 1977; chmn. arctic panel Circum-Pacific Map Project, 1979—; invited lectr. USSR Acad. Sci., 1980, Indonesian Marine Geol. Inst. and Nat. Petroleum Co., 1986, City of Corvallis Da Vinci Days, 1989-96; rapporteur UN com. for coordination of offshore prospecting, Peoples Republic of China, 1985; advisor Calif. Coastal Commn., 1970-75; chmn. Earth and Space Scis. Awards, Internat. Sci. Fair, 1978. Author: Speleology—Caves and the Cave Environment, 1997 (Sci. Book Club award 1997); editor Geodynamic Map of the Circum-Pacific Region, 1990, Plate-Tectonic Map of the Circum-Pacific Region, 1992. Exhibit com. mem. San Diego Natural History Mus., 1968-75. Fellow AAAS, Geol. Soc. Am.; mem. Nat. Speleol. Soc. (hon., pres. 1963), Am. Assn. Petroleum Geologists (com. chmn. 1977), Am. Geophys. Union, Palo Alto Hist. Assn., Peninsula Geol. Soc. (pres. 1986). Democrat. Home: 3324 SW Chintimini Ave Corvallis OR 97333-1529 Office: Dept Geosciences Oreg State U Corvallis OR 97331-5506

MOORE, GORDON E., electronics company executive; b. San Francisco, Jan. 3, 1929; s. Walter Harold and Florence Almira (Williamson) M.; m. Betty I. Whittaker, Sept. 9, 1950; children: Kenneth, Steven. BS in Chemistry, U. Calif., 1950; PhD in Chemistry and Physics, Calif. Inst. Tech., 1954. Mem. tech. staff Shockley Semicondr. Lab., 1956-57; mgr. engring. Fairchild Camera & Instrument Corp., 1957-59, dir. research and devel., 1959-68; exec. v.p. Intel Corp., Santa Clara, Calif., 1968-75; pres., chief exec. officer Intel Corp., 1975-79, chmn., chief exec. officer, 1979-87, chmn., 1987—; bd. dirs. Varian Assocs. Inc., Transamerica Corp. Fellow IEEE; mem. Nat. Acad. Engring., Am. Phys. Soc. Office: Intel Corp 2200 Mission College Blvd Santa Clara CA 95054-1537*

MOORE, JAMES C., museum director. Dir. Albuquerque Mus. Office: Albuquerque Mus 2000 Mountain Rd Albuquerque NM 87104

MOORE, JAMES R., lawyer; b. Longview, Wash., Sept. 14, 1944; s. James Carlton and Virginia (Rice) M.; m. Patricia Riley, Aug. 25, 1967 (div. 1978); 1 child, Katherine M.; m. Christine M. Monkman, July 14, 1979 (div. 1996); stepchildren: Amy McKenna, John McKenna; 1 foster child, Zia Sunseri; m. Kathryn Lindquist, Aug. 26, 1996; stepchildren: Matthew Elggren, Adam Elggren, Erin Elggren, David Heilner. BA, Whitman Coll., 1966; JD, Duke U., 1969. Bar: Wash. 1970, U.S. Ct. Appeals (4th cir.) 1972, U.S. Supreme Ct. 1973, U.S. Ct. Appeals (9th cir.) 1974, D.C., 1995. Law clk. to Hon. J. Barnes U.S. Ct. Appeals (9th cir.), L.A., 1969-70; trial atty. pollution control, land/natural resources div. U.S. Dept. Justice, Washington, 1970-74; asst. U.S. atty. U.S. Atty.'s Office, Seattle, 1974-82; regional counsel U.S. EPA Region 10, Seattle, 1982-87; counsel Perkins Coie, Seattle, 1987-88, ptnr., 1989—; trainer, speaker on environ. litigation, negotiation and law. Contbr. articles to profl. jours. Bd. dirs. Environ. Law Inst., 1995—; chair audit com. Whitman Coll., 1994—. Mem. ABA (sect. natural resources 1987—), Wash. State Bar Assn. (environ. and land use sect. 1974—, spl. dist. coun. 1988-95). Democrat. Office: Perkins Coie 1201 3rd Ave Ste 4100 Seattle WA 98101-3000 also: 607 14th St NW Washington DC 20005-2007

MOORE, JOHN D., management consultant; b. Mt. Pleasant, Iowa, Apr. 7, 1937; s. Burris P. and Esther I. (Copenhaver) M.; m. Karen K. Kriegel, June 19, 1957; children: Charles A., Michael J., Susan K., David J. AB, Muscatine Community Coll., 1961; BBA, Augustana Coll., 1966; postgrad. U. Iowa, 1966-68. Office mgr. Stanley Engring., Muscatine, Iowa, 1956-64; pers. mgr. Oscar Mayer & Co., Davenport and Perry, Iowa, 1964-68; Midwest regional mgr. A. S. Hansen, Lake Bluff, Ill., 1968-73; legal adminstr. Gardner, Carton & Douglas, Chgo., 1973-78, Heller Ehrman White & McAuliffe, San Francisco, 1978-84; v.p. and dir. Hildebrandt, Inc., Walnut Creek, Calif., 1984-90; pres. Moore Cons. Inc., 1990—. Pres., Libertyville (Ill.) High Sch. Bd., 1974, Libertyville Ecumenical Council, 1975; bd. dirs. Libertyville YMCA, 1969-71. Recipient Muscatine Disting. Service award, 1963; named Outstanding State V.P., Iowa Jaycees, 1964; Outstanding Nat. Dir., U.S. Jaycees, 1965. Mem. Assn. of Legal Adminstrs. (regional v.p. 1977-78, nat. v.p. 1979-81, nat. pres. 1982-83), Found. Assn. of Legal Adminstrs. (pres. 1986-88), Golden Gate Assn. Legal Adminstrs. Republican. Methodist. Home and Office: 2632 Quiet Place Dr Walnut Creek CA 94598-4440

MOORE, JUDITH LYNN, animal scientist; b. Pitts., May 3, 1946; d. Carl Emil Joseph and Edris Christine (Ott) Hoffmann; m. James Lynn Moore, Dec. 28, 1968; children: Aaron, Jeremy. BS in Zoology, Colo. State U., 1968; MS in Environ. Comm., U. Wis., 1969. Editor U. Wis., Madison, 1969-70; pvt. practice horse and dog trainer Oregon, Wis., 1970-76, Buena Vista, Colo., 1976—; co-owner Insolar Homes, Inc., 1979—; animal control officer Chaffee County Govt., Colo., 1977-78. Editor: Wisconsin's Recreation-Tourism Industry: An Annotated Bibliography, 1970; author Chaffee County animal control ordinances. Founder, dir. Pet Assistance League, Chaffee County, 1978. Home and Office: 17900 Vista Dr Buena Vista CO 81211-9618

MOORE, JUSTIN EDWARD, data processing executive; b. West Hartford, Conn., June 17, 1952; s. Walter Joseph and Victoria Mary (Calcagni) M. BS in Mgmt. Sci., Fla. Inst. Tech., 1974. Systems assoc. Travelers Ins., Hartford, Conn., 1974-77; data processing programmer R.J. Reynolds Inc., Winston-Salem, N.C., 1977-78; programmer/analyst Sea-Land Svc., Elizabeth, N.J., 1978-79; mgr. market analysis Sea-Land Svc., Oakland, Calif., 1979-82; asst. v.p., dir. application systems Fox Capital Mgmt. Corp., Foster City, Calif., 1982-86; mgr. bus. svcs. dept mktg. and pricing Am. Pres. Cos., Ltd., Oakland, 1987-88, dir. mktg. and pricing systems, 1988-89; dir. systems devel. The Office Club, Concord, Calif., 1989-91; dir. MIS Revo, Inc., Mountain View, Calif., 1992-93; account mgr. Imrex Computer Systems, Inc., South San Francisco, 1993-94; project mgr. Exigent Computer Group, Inc., San Ramon, Calif., 1994—. Democrat. Roman Catholic. Home: 5214 Jomar Dr Concord CA 94521-2343 Office: Exigent Computer Group Inc 4000 Executive Pky San Ramon CA 94583-4257 *Personal philosophy: Strive always to do the right things, at the right time, the right way for the right reasons.*

MOORE, MARIANNA GAY, law librarian, consultant; b. La Grange, Ga., Sept. 12, 1939; d. James Henry and Avanelle (Gay) M. AB in French, English, U. Ga., 1961; MLS, Emory U., 1964; postgrad., U. Ga., 1965-66, U. Ill., 1967-68. Asst. law libr. U. Ga., Athens, 1964-66; asst. libr. Yavapai Coll. Libr., Prescott, Ariz., 1969-72; libr. U. Ill. Law Libr., Urbana, 1966-68; law libr. Leva, Hawes, Symington, Washington, 1972-75; libr. project coord. Wash. Occupational Info. Svc., Olympia, 1976-80, Wash. State Health Facilities Assn., Olympia, 1981-82; mgr. Wash. State Ret. Tchrs. Assn., Olympia, 1982-83, exec. dir., 1984-89; exec. dir. Wash. State Retired Tchrs. Found., Olympia, 1986-89; law libr. Solano County Law Libr., Fairfield, Calif., 1989—; libr. LIBRARY/USA N.Y. World's Fair, N.Y.C., 1965; consulting law libr. Dobbins, Weir, Thompson & Stephenson, Vacaville, Calif., 1989—; law libr. cons. Coconino County Law Libr., Flagstaff, Ariz., 1968-70. Author: Guide to Fin. Aid for Wash. State Students, 1979; tng. package to introduce librs. to Wash. State Info. Svc., 1980. Bd. dirs. Thurston County Sr. Ctr., Olympia, 1976-84, Thurston-Mason Nutrition Program, Olympia, 1977-79, Wash. Soc. Assn. Execs., Edmonds, 1987-89. Mem. Am. Assn. Law Librs., No. Calif. Assn. Law Librs., Calif. Coun. of County Law Librs. Office: Solano County Law Libr Hall of Justice 600 Union Ave Fairfield CA 94533-6324

MOORE, MARY FRENCH (MUFFY MOORE), potter, community activist; b. N.Y.C., Feb. 25, 1938; d. John and Rhoda (Teagle) Walker French; m. Alan Baird Minier, Oct. 9, 1982; children: Jonathan Corbet, Jennifer Corbet, Michael Corbet. BA cum laude, Colo. U., 1964. Ceramics mfr., Wilson, Wyo., 1969-82, Cheyenne, Wyo., 1982—; commr. County of Teton (Wyo.), 1976-83, chmn. bd. commrs., 1981, 83, mem. dept. pub. assistance and social svc., 1976-82, mem. recreation bd., 1978-81, water quality adv. bd., 1976-82. Bd. dirs. Teton Sci. Sch., 1968-83, vice chmn., 1979-81, chmn., 1982; bd. dirs. Grand Teton Music Festival, 1963-68, Teton Energy Coun., 1978-83, Whitney Gallery of Western Art, Cody, Wyo., 1995—; mem. water quality adv. bd. Wyo. Dept. Environ. Quality, 1979-83; Dem. precinct committeewoman, 1978-81; mem. Wyo. Dem. Cen. Com., 1981-83; vice chmn. Laramie County Dem. Cen. Com., 1983-84, Wyo. Dem. nat. committewoman, 1984-87; chmn. Wyo. Dem. Party, 1987-89; del. Dem. Nat. Conv., 1984, 88, mem. fairness commn. Dem. Nat. Com., 1985, vice-chairwoman western caucus, 1986-89; chmn. platform com. Wyo. Dem. Conv., 1982; mem. Wyo. Dept. Environ. Quality Land Quality Adv. Bd., 1983-86; mem. Gov.'s Steering Com. on Troubled Youth, 1982, dem. nat. com. Compliance Assistance Commn., 1986-87; exec. com. Assn. of State Dem. Chairs, 1989; mem. Wyo. Coun. on the Arts, 1989-95, chmn., 1994-95, Dem. Nat. Com. Jud. Coun., 1989—; legis. aide for Gov. Wyo., 1985, 86; project coord. Gov.'s Com. on Childrens' Svcs., 1985-86; bd. dirs. Wyo. Outdoor Coun., 1984-85; polit. dir., dep. mgr. Schuster for Congress, 1994-95. Recipient Woman of Yr. award Jackson Hole Bus. and Profl. Women, 1981, Dem. of Yr. Nellie Tayloe Ross award, Wyo. Dems., 1990. Mem. Alden Kindred of Am., Jackson Hole Art Assn. (bd. dirs., vice chmn. 1981, chmn. 1982), Assn. State Dem. Chairs, Soc. Mayflower Descendents, Pi Sigma Alpha. Home: 8907 Cowpoke Rd Cheyenne WY 82009-1234

MOORE, MATTHEW EMERSON, environmental program planning management specialist; b. Tuscaloosa, Ala., Aug. 5, 1964; s. Charles Thomas Moore Sr. and Annabel (Owens) Moore Allen; m. Anne Goldthwaite Dorr, March 20, 1993. BS, No. Ariz. U., 1987; MA, Claremont Grad. Sch., 1989. Mem. policy clinic team Ctr. for Politics and Policy, Claremont (Calif.) Grad. Sch., 1987-89; rsch. asst. Rose Inst. State and Local Govt., Claremont, 1989; analyst, asst. planner LSA Assocs., Inc., Irvine, Calif., 1989-90; project mgr. Urban Vision, Irvine, 1991-93; regional water quality mgmt. planning coord. Ariz. Dept. Environ. Quality, Phoenix, 1994; sr. air quality analyst Idaho Divsn. Environ. Quality, Boise, 1994—; mem. Sch. Renewable Natural Resources master's thesis com. U. Ariz., Tucson, 1994. Author: Lead Agency CEQA Procedures Survey Results, 1991; co-author: Taxes, Trees and Transit; California's Response to CO2-Induced Climate Change, 1990, Curbing Air Pollution in the South Coast Air Basin, 1989; editor-at-large: Multiple Resource Mgmt. Plan for El Cipres, Ensenada, Mex., 1994. Founding pres. Explorer Post 477, Boy Scouts Am., Tempe, Ariz., 1980-82; interpretive specialist Walnut Canyon Nat. Monument, Flagstaff, Ariz., 1987; mem. drought planning adv. bd. City of Claremont, 1988-89; mem. leadership coun. First United Meth. Ch., Boise. Mem. Am. Planning Assn., Am. Polit. Sci. Assn., Nat. Assn. Environ. Profls., Internat. Assn. Impact Assessment. Methodist.

MOORE, OMAR KHAYYAM, experimental sociologist; b. Helper, Utah, Feb. 11, 1920; s. John Gustav and Mary Jo (Crowley) M.; m. Ruth Garnand, Nov. 19, 1942; 1 child, Venn. BA, Doane Coll., 1942; MA, Washington U., St. Louis, 1946, PhD, 1949. Instr. Washington U., St. Louis, 1949-52; teaching assoc. Northwestern U., Evanston, Ill., 1950-51; rsch. asst., prof. sociology Tufts Coll., Medford, Mass., 1952-53; researcher Naval Rsch. Lab., Washington, 1953-54; asst. prof. sociology Yale U., New Haven, 1954-57, assoc. prof. sociology, 1957-63; prof. psychology Rutgers U., New Brunswick, N.J., 1963-65; prof. social psychology, sociology U. Pitts., 1965-71, prof. sociology, 1971-89, prof. emeritus, 1989—; scholar-in-residence Nat. Learning Ctr.'s Capital Children's Mus., Washington, 1989-90; pres. Responsive Environ. Found., Inc., Estes Park, Colo., 1962—; assessor of rsch. projects The Social Scis. and Humanities Rsch. Coun. Can., 1982—; adj. prof. U. Colo., Boulder, 1992—. Contbg. editor Educational Technology; contbr. numerous articles to profl. jours.; patentee in field; motion picture producer and director. Recipient Award The Nat. Soc. for Programmed Instruction, 1965, Award Doane Coll Builder Award, 1967, Ednl. Award Urban Youth Action, Inc., 1969, Award House of Culture, 1975, Cert. of Appreciation, 1986, Cert. of Appreciation D.C. Pub. Schs., 1987, da Vinci Award Inst. for the Achievement of Human Potential, 1988, Cert. of Appreciation Capital Children's Museum, 1988, award Jack & Jill of America Found., 1988, Cert. of Appreciation U.S. Dept. of Edn., 1988, Cert. of Appreciation D.C. Pub. Schs., 1990, Person of Yr. in Ednl. Tech. award Ednl. Tech. mag., 1990. Mem. AAAS, Am. Math. Soc., Am. Psychol. Assn., Internat. Sociol. Assn., Am. Sociol. Assn., Assn. for Symbolic Logic, Assn. for Anthrop. Study of Play, Philosophy Sci. Assn., Psychonomics Soc., Soc. for Applied Sociology, Soc. for Exact Philosophy, Math. Assn. Am. Republican. Home and Office: 2341 Upper High Dr PO Box 1673 Estes Park CO 80517

MOORE, RICHARD, academic administrator; m. Susan Moore; children: Betsy, Parker. BS in Econs., Claremont Men's Coll., 1955, PhD, 1965; MBA, U. Calif., 1956. Asst. prof. mktg. San Jose (Calif.) State U., 1959-61; instr., divsn. dir. San Bernardino Valley (Calif.) Coll., 1961-66; dean instrn. Moorpark Coll., Calif., 1966-74; pres., supt. Santa Monica (Calif.) Coll., 1974-94; pres. C.C. So. Nev., Las Vegas, 1994—. Active C.C. H.S. program Clark County Sch. Dist., Boys & Girls Clubs, Learning and Earning Program, Weekend Coll., Silver Sage Coll., Peace Officers Acad., Video

Distance Edn., other acad. programs. Lt. U.S. Army, 1957-59. Office: C C So Nev 820 Shadow Ln Ste 307 Las Vegas NV 89106*

MOORE, ROBERT HORTON, physician; b. Jonesboro, Ark., Dec. 29, 1924; s. Robert Horton and Macie Terra (Galloway) M.; m. Joan Brown, Mar. 27, 1954; children: Robert Harold, Pamela Ann. BA, Vanderbilt U., 1947, MD, 1951. Diplomate Am. Bd. Preventive Medicine, Occupational Medicine. Resident in internal medicine Northwestern U., 1956; chief, admitting svc. VA Rsch. Hosp., Chgo., 1956-60; pvt. practice Decatur, Ill., 1960-65; asst. med. dir. Pacific Mut. Life Ins. Co., L.A., 1965-68; v.p. Hanford Environ. Health Found., Richland, Wash., 1968-78; dir. U.S. Uranium Registry, Richland, 1978-88; v.p. Northwest Health Svc., Richland, 1988-89; occupational physician USN, San Diego, Calif., 1989—. Editor: (proceedings) Biokinetics and Analysis of Uranium in Man, 1984; contbr. articles to Health Physics jour., 1978-88. d. dirs. Am. Coll. Occupation and Envrion. Med., Chgo., 1989-92, del. 1972-89. With U.S. Army inf., 1943-45, ETO. Fellow Am. Coll. Occupl. and Environ. Medicine, Am. Acad. Occupl. Medicine, Am. Occupl. Med. Assn.; mem. AMA. Presbyterian. Home: 1258 Santa Barbara St San Diego CA 92107-3960

MOORE, ROGER ALBERT, JR., archaeologist; b. Tampa, Fla., Dec. 18, 1946; s. Roger Albert Moore and Frieda E. (Heil) Hutchison; m. Susan Kay Waters, Sept. 8, 1978; children: Tabitha Rose, Roxie Ann. BA in Anthropology, Ohio State U., 1972; student, U. Tenn., 1974-75; MA in Anthropology, Ea. N.Mex. U., 1981. Lic. archael. surveyor, N.Mex., Colo., Utah, Wyo., Ariz. Crew chief, field foreman U. Tenn., Knoxville, 1973-74, excavator, lab. asst., 1974-75; excavator, lab. asst. Cahokia Mounds State Park, Collinsville, Ill., 1974; lithic analyst Ea. N.Mex. U., Portales, 1975-78; lab. dir. U. Colo., Cortez, 1978-79; field dir. ESCA-Tech, Inc., Ridgeway, Colo., 1980; lab. dir. Navajo Nat. Archaeology Dept., Farmington, N.Mex., 1980-82; supervisory archaeologist San Juan County Mus. Assn., Bloomfield, N.Mex., 1982-88; owner, prin. investigator Moore Anthropol. Rsch., Aztec, N.Mex., 1988—; owner Southwest Archaeol. Svcs., Aztec, N.Mex., 1996—; instr. San Juan Coll., Farmington, 1983; mem. strategic action team Aztec Mcpl. Sch. Dist., 1995. Co-author: Old Dallas Historical Archaeology Project, 1987; contbr. articles to profl. jours. Vol. Portales (N.Mex.) Food Coopr., 1976-78, Salmon Ruin Mus., Bloomfield, 1982-88, Bonds for Books Plus Com., Aztec, 1994; mem. lithic dictionary com. N.Mex. Archaeol. Coun., 1989—; chmn. com. B.L.M. Cultural Adv. Group, Farmington, 1991—; mem. Aztec H.S. parent adv. com., 1996-97. Mem. Soc. Am. Archaeology (life), N.Mex. Archaeol. Coun., Archaeol. Soc. N.Mex. (cert., Archaeol. Achievement award 1994), Ariz. Archaeol. and Hist. Soc., Tenn. Anthropol. Assn. (life), San Juan County Mus. Assn. (bd. dirs. 1993-95), Nat.Trust for Hist. Preservation, Aztec C. of C. (bd. dirs. 1995—), San Juan Archaeol. Soc., Phi Kappa Phi. Republican. Presbyterian. Office: Moore Anthropol Rsch 102 N Main Aztec NM 87410-1156

MOORE, RONALD MELVILLE, Philosophy educator; b. Framingham, Mass., May 4, 1943; s. Albert Melville and Edith (Snyder) M.; m. Nancy Anne; 1 child, Alice. AB, Stanford U., 1964; PhD, Columbia U., 1971. Preceptor Columbia Coll., N.Y.C., 1966-68; asst. prof. U. Hawaii, 1971-74, assoc. prof., 1974-79; assoc. prof. U. Wash., 1979—; dir. U. Wash. Ctr. for Humanitites, 1987-94. Author: Legal Norms and Legal Science, 1978; co-author: Puzzles About Art, 1989; editor: Aesthetics for Young People, 1995; book rev. editor: Jour. Aesthetics and Art Criticism, 1994—. Recipient Liberal Arts fellowship in law and philosophy Harvard Law Sch., 1976. Mem. Internat. Soc. Philosophy of Law Am. Soc. Polit. and Legal Philosophy, Am. Soc. Aesthetics (trustee 1993-96), U. Wash. Med. Ctr. (trustee 1988—). Democrat. Unitarian. Office: U Wash Dept Philosophy PO Box 353350 Seattle WA 98195-3350

MOORE, TERRY WAYNE, high technology venture management consultant; b. North Kingston, R.I., Feb. 26, 1957; s. Robert Wendell and Marilyn (Rose) M. BS in Engring., U. Fla., 1981; MBA, U. San Diego, 1993; postgrad., U. Calif., San Diego, 1994. Sr. materials engr. U.S. Dept. Def., Alameda, Calif., 1981-85, program mgr., 1985-87; staff engr., scientist Gen. Atomics, La Jolla, Calif., 1987-89, project mgr., 1989-92, mktg. program mgr., 1992-93; owner Moore Consulting Co., San Diego, 1994—; entrepreneur Venture Mgmt., Moore Cons. Co., San Diego, 1990—; new high tech. ventures cons. for emerging growth and start up cos., 1991—; mem. dirs. database com. Internat. Forum Corp. Dirs., 1995—, program com., 1995—, membership com., 196—, improving dir. effectiveness cert.; mem. San Diego Regional Tech. Alliance, Calif. State Office Strategic Tech. Devel. Trade and Commerce; mem. Team Dennis Conner's Am.'s Cup Syndicate, 1995, crew mem. Stars and Stripes, winner Pacific Class Nat. Championships, 1995. Judge San Diego Sci. Fair, 1989—; rep. Neighborhood Watch, La Costa, Calif., 1989—; vol. fund raiser Am. Cancer Soc., Epilepsy Soc., United Way, U. Calif. San Diego Cancer Ctr. Found. Mem. Am. Soc. for Materials Internat. (sec.-treas. 1990-92, vice chmn. 1993-94, chmn. 1994-95, past chmn. 1995-96, bd. dirs. 1989—, mem. chpt ops. com., chmn. computer subcom. 1991—, chmn. 1994-95), Project Mgmt. Inst. (sec. 1993-94, treas. 1994-95, bd. dirs. 1993—), Nat. Bd. Cert. Project Mgmt. Profl. (cert.), San Diego Engring. Soc. (program chmn. bd. dirs. 1995-96), Soc. Advancement of Material and Process Engring., San Diego Venture Mgmt. Group, MIT Enterprise Forum (mem. panel selection com.), Found. for Enterprise Devel., San Diego Yacht Club. Republican. Presbyterian. Home and Office: 905 Orchid Way Carlsbad CA 92009-4830

MOORE, THOMAS SCOTT, lawyer; b. Portland, Oreg., Nov. 17, 1937; s. Harry Alburn and Geraldine Elizabeth (Scott) M.; m. Saundra L. Wagner, Sept. 7, 1957 (div. 1974); children: Cindy, Kristin, Thomas, Victoria, Wendy; m. Alice H. Zeisz, Nov. 5, 1976; 1 child, Alice G. BA, Willamette U., 1959, JD cum laude, 1962. Bar: Oregon 1962. Pvt. practice Portland, 1962—. Contbr. articles to law jours. Republican. Office: 4512 SW Kelly Ave Portland OR 97201-4257

MOORE, TODD ALLEN, poet; b. Freeport, Ill., Nov. 14, 1937; s. John Earl and Helen Marie (Babcock) M.; m. Barbara Diane Mayfield, Dec. 21, 1963. BS in Edn., No. Ill. U., 1962, MA in L.S., 1968. Cert. tchr. English secondary level, Ill. English tchr. Forreston (Ill.) Schs., 1962-63, Freeport (Ill.) Schs., 1963-68; Libr. No. Ill. U., DeKalb, 1968-70; English tchr. Belvidere (Ill.) Schs., 1970-93. Contbr. poetry to numerous publs. and anthologies, including Poets on Photography, 1981, Prairie Smoke, 1990, Gildzen at 50: A Celebration, 1990, A New Geography of Poets, 1992, A Gathering of Poets, 1992; also critical studies. Mem. Great Plains Writers Assn. Home: 3216 San Pedro NE Albuquerque NM 87110

MOORE, TONI F., elementary education educator; b. West Berlin, Jan. 22, 1948; (parents Am. citizens); d. Harry Donald and Theresa Elizabeth (Picollo) M.; m. Donald F. Teeguarden, Apr. 1, 1968 (div. Nov. 1984); children: Kurt Patrick Teeguarden, Deanna Kathleen Teeguarden. BA in Elem. Edn., Western State Coll., 1970. Tchr. Ordot (Guam)-Chalen Pago Elem., 1970-72, Harmon Loop Elem., Dededo, Guam, 1972-73; tchr. physical edn. George Washington H.S., Mangilao, Guam, 1973-74; tchr. Finegayan Elem., Agana, Guam, 1974-75; tchr. physical edn. Iditarod Elem., Wasilla, Alaska, 1975-84, tchr., 1984—. Mem. Gold Dust Dancers ($1000 Am.'s Funniest Home Videos 1995). Vol. EMT, Wasilla Ambulance, 1979-93, Talkeetna (Alaska) Ambulance, 1993—; instr. and presenter Nat. Sci. Tchrs. Conv., Houston, 1991, Boston, 1992. Democrat. Lutheran. Home: FIC 89 Box 8550 Talkeetna AK 99676 Office: Mat Su Borough Sch Dist Iditarod Elem 801 N Wasilla Fishhook Rd Wasilla AK 99654

MOORE, WALTER DENGEL, rapid transit system professional; b. Chgo., Sept. 16, 1936; s. Walter D. and Velma Louise (Rhode) M.; m. Sandra M. Stetzel, Jan. 23, 1965 (div. 1980); children: Thomas, Timothy. BA in Liberal Arts and Scis., U. Ill., 1958; BSEE, Ill. Inst. Tech., 1972. Supt. maintenance of way Chgo. Transit Authority, 1963-89; supr. of rail activation and rail tech. support Met. Transp. Assn. Los Angeles County, L.A., 1989—. With U.S. Army, 1958-60. Mem. Am. Pub. Transp. Assn. (vice chmn. power com. 1974-75), Am. Ry. Engring. Assn. (vice chmn. subcom. on power signals and comm. 1990—), Underwater Soc. Am. (N.Am. record in spear-fishing 1988), Calif. Pub. Utilities Commn. (gen. order 1995), Nat. Rsch. Coun., NAS (transp. rsch. bd.), Nat. Acad. Engrs. (project C3 and D6 light rail track manual). Home: 12741 Andy St Cerritos CA 90703-6044 Office: Met Transp Assn L A County 320 S Santa Fe Ave Los Angeles CA 90013-1812

MOORE, WILLIAM CULLEN, retired electronics company executive; b. Portland, Oreg., Nov. 17, 1912; s. William Cullen and Lillian (Rodé) M.; m. Helen Hays Edgar, Aug. 8, 1936; children: Shirley Carol, Ronald Cullen, Paul Alan, Katherine Leone. BA in Physics, Reed Coll., Portland, 1936; MA in Physics, Boston U., 1949. Electronics engr. United Airlines, Chgo., 1937-38; project leader Motorola, Inc., Chgo., 1938-47; sect. head govt. electronics group Motorola, Inc., Scottsdale, Ariz., 1958-78; ret.; project supr./instr. Upper Air Lab., Boston U., 1947-51; chief engr. Tracerlab, Inc., Boston, 1951-53; engring. mgr. Boonton (N.J.) Radio Corp., 1953-58; cons./facilitator (space) Motorola Mus. of Electronics, Schaumburg, Ill., 1987-90; investigator Apollo comms. NASA, Madrid, Spain, 1971. Contbr. articles to profl. jours. Mem. sch. bd. Lombard (Ill.) Sch. Dist., 1946-47, Mountain Lakes (N.J.) Sch. Dist., 1956-58; mem. allocations panels United Way, 1977-94. Fellow AIAA (assoc.; sect. chair 1963-64); mem. IEEE (sr.; sect. chair 1940—). Home: Apt 346 10015 W Royal Oak Rd Sun City AZ 85351-3186

MOORE, WILLIAM HOWARD, history educator, writer; b. Harriman, Tenn., June 26, 1942; s. Lonnie Henry and Goldie Myrtle (Williams) M.; m. Mary Elizabeth Galvan, Sept. 27, 1969 (div. 1980); 1 child, Adam William; m. June Uvalda Vialpando, Mar. 8, 1986. BS, U. Tenn., 1964, MA, 1965; PhD, U. Tex., 1971. Instr. Southwest Tex. State U., San Marcos, 1971-72; asst. prof. Ohio U., Athens, 1972-73; from asst. prof. to prof. U. Wyo., Laramie, 1973—, chair dept. history, 1992—; cons. Harper Collins Pubs., N.Y.C., 1991-92, McGraw Hill Pubs., N.Y.C., 1992. Author: Kefauver Committee, 1974, Company Town, 1989; article referee Jour. American History, Bloomington, Ind., 1989; mem. editorial adv. bd. Annals of Wyoming, Cheyenne, 1990—; contbr. articles to profl. jours. Cons. Albany County Sch. Bd., Laramie, 1989, 91. Grantee Nat. Endowment Humanities, 1977, 90, Eisenhower World Affairs Inst., 1990, Hoover Pres. Libr. Assn., 1992. Mem. Orgn. Am. Historians, Ctr. Study Presidency. Home: 802 University Ave Laramie WY 82070 Office: U Wyo Dept History PO Box 3198 Laramie WY 82071-3198

MOORE, WILLIAM JAMES, newspaper editor; b. Corpus Christi, Tex., Oct. 7, 1943; s. Edwin R. and Mary Wilson (Clokey) Ross M.; m. Ann Sarae Bancroft, May 2, 1976 (div. Dec. 1990); 1 child, Matthew. BA in Comm. and Polit. Sci., Stanford U., 1965, MA in Comm., 1966. Reporter Ariz. Daily Star, Tucson, Ariz., 1962; editor Stanford (Calif.) Daily, 1964; reporter San Francisco Chronicle, 1967-79; news editor Oakland (Calif.) Tribune-Eastbay Today, 1979-81; met. editor Sacramento Bee McClatchy Newspapers, 1982, editor Forum, 1982—. Press asst., vol. Robert F. Kennedy Presdl. campaign, San Francisco, 1968; vol. VISTA, San Juan, P.R., 1966-67. Served with USCGR, 1967-73. Recipient Silver award Assn. of Opinion Page Editors, 1993. Democrat. Office: Sacramento Bee PO Box 15779 Sacramento CA 95852-0779

MOORE, WILLIAM JOSEPH, retired educator; b. Siloam Springs, Ark., Feb. 19, 1932; s. Robert Alexander and Nelle Elizabeth (Donly) M.; m. Peggy Jo Perkins, Aug. 24, 1952; children: Christopher D., Kevin W., Lisa M. BA, U. Redlands, 1954, MA, 1955; postgrad., Hong Kong U., 1955-56; PhD, Claremont Grad. Sch., 1963. Prof. San Bernardino (Calif.) Valley Coll., 1956-69, dean instrn., 1969-74; v.p., provost U. of Redlands, Calif., 1974-76; pres. Crafton Hills Coll., Yucaipa, Calif., 1976-81; pres., supt. Chabot Coll./South County C.C. Dist., Hawyard, Calif., 1981-85; pres. Assn. Ind. Calif. Colls. and Univs., Sacramento, 1985-91; ret., 1991; vice chmn. bd. dirs. Calif. Casualty Indemnity Exch., San Mateo, 1995; cons. TRW Sys., El Segundo and San Bernardino, 1964-71; labor mgmt. mediator, arbitrator Bd. Supervisors and Employees San Bernardino County, 1972-92. Trustee U. of Redlands, 1976-95; pres. bd. dirs. World Affairs Coun. of Inland So. Calif., Riverside, 1980-81; bd. dirs. Nat. Assn. Ind. Colls. and Univs., Washington, 1990-91; chmn. bd. dirs. Calif. Higher Edn. Policy Inst., San Jose, 1992—. Fellow Ford Found., 1954-55, Rotary Found., 1955-56. Democrat. Home: 5160 Wild Horse Valley Rd Napa CA 94558 also: PO Box 414 West Yellowstone MT 59758

MOORE, WILLIS HENRY ALLPHIN, history and geography educator; b. N.Y.C., Dec. 14, 1940; s. Carl Allphin and Mary Catherine (Moody) M.; children: Patrick Kakela, Michael Kirby, Catherine Malia. BA Letters, U. Okla., 1962; MEd in Adminstrn., U. Hawaii, 1971. Teaching asst. dept. history U. Hawaii, 1962-64; dir. edn. Bernice P. Bishop Mus., Honolulu, 1967-76; pres. Hawaii Geog. Soc., Honolulu, 1976-78, exec. sec., editor, 1978—; mem. Hawaii Com. for Humanities, 1976-78; producer, narrator film-lecture programs Nat. Aududon Soc. and travelogue forums; instr. in history, geography and polit. sci. Chaminade U. of Honolulu, 1986—; lectr. elderhostel U. Hawaii, Hawaii Pacific U., Lewis and Clark State Coll., Idaho. Co-author/co-editor: Hawaii Parklands, Sociological History of Honolulu, Total Solar Eclipse over Hawaii, 1991; contbr. articles to Honolulu Advertiser, Pacific Daily News, Guam, Pacific Mag., Honolulu Star-Bull. Lay reader St. Andrew's Cathedral; active Nat. Mus. Am. Indian. Mem. Internat. Map Trade Assn., Am. Assn. State & Local History, Am. Mus. Assn., Pacific Sci. Assn., Hawaii Mus. Assn. (pres. 1972-74), Hawaii Pub. Radio, Am. Guild Organists, Soc. Prfs. Dispute Resolution, Sierra Club (chmn. Hawaii chpt. 1973-75), Hawaiian Hist. Soc., Nat. Soc. of Arts and Letters. Office: PO Box 1698 Honolulu HI 96806-1698

MOORHEAD, CARLOS J., former congressman; b. Long Beach, Calif., May 6, 1922; s. Carlos Arthur and Florence (Gravers) M.; m. Valery Joan Tyler, July 19, 1969; children: Theresa, Catharine, Steven, Teri, Paul. BA, UCLA, 1943; JD, U. So. Calif., 1949. Bar: Calif. 1949, U.S. Supreme Ct. 1973. Pvt. practice law Glendale, Calif., 1949-72; dir. Lawyers Reference Service, Glendale, 1950-66; mem. 93d-104th Congresses from 22d (now 27th) Dist. Calif., 1973-96; mem. judiciary com., chmn. subcom. on cts. and intellectual property, vice chmn. commerce com., mem. subcom. on energy & power, subcom. on telecomm. & fin.; dean Calif. Congl. Rep. Delegation; apptd. to Fed. Cts. Study Com. Pres. Glendale Hi-Twelve Club; mem. Verdugo Hills council Boy Scouts Am.; mem. Calif. Assembly, 1967-72; mem. Calif. Law Revision Commn., 1971-72; pres. 43d Dist. Republican Assembly, Glendale Young Republicans; mem. Los Angeles County Rep. Central Com., Calif. Rep. Central Com.; pres. Glendale La Crescenta Camp Fire Girls, Inc. Served to lt. col. AUS, 1942-46. Recipient Man of Yr. award USO, 1979. Mem. Calif. Bar Assn. L.A. County Bar Assn., Glendale Bar Assn. (past pres.), Glendale C. of C., Masons, Shriners, Lions, Moose, VFW. Presbyterian. Office: 420 N Brand Blvd # 304 Glendale CA 91203*

MOORHOUSE, MARY FRANCES, rehabilitation nurse; b. Seattle, Sept. 13, 1947; d. Francis E. and Frances L. (Ranus) McGlothlin; m. Jan G. Moorhouse, Feb. 3, 1968; children: Paul, Jason. Diploma, Beth El Sch. Nursing, Colorado Springs, Colo., 1968. CRRN; cert. legal nurse cons. Patient care coord. critical care Penrose Community Hosp., Colorado Springs, 1974-79; dir. nursing Nurses PRN of Denver, Inc., Colorado Springs, 1985; owner, cons. TNT-RN Enterprises, Colorado Springs, 1985—; nurse cons. Fortis Corp., Colorado Springs, 1989-92. Author: Nursing Care Plans: Nursing Diagnosis in Planning Patient Care, 4th edit., 1997, The Nurses' Pocket Guide: Nursing Diagnosis with Interventions, 5th edit., 1996, Care Plans for Critical Care, 1987. Recipient Outstanding Book of Yr. award Nursing, 1984, AJN Book of Yr. award, 1989; named Nurse of Yr., Colo. Nurses Assn., 1987, So. Colo. Woman of Yr. in Health Field So. Colo. Womens Life Festival and Sta. KOAA-TV, 1988. Mem. AACN, Colo. Nurses Assn. (Sustained Contbn. to Nursing Profession honor 1992, Improvement of Health Status and Well-being of Citizens of Colo. honor 1994), Nat. League for Nursing, N.Am. Nursing Diagnosis Assn., Nursing Found. Colo. Assn. Rehab. Nurses, Internat. Assn. Forensic Nurses. Home and Office: 1219 E Bijou St Colorado Springs CO 80909-5515

MOORMAN, LAWRENCE ALAN, humanities educator; b. San Francisco, Feb. 28, 1940; s. Charles Carroll and Margaret (Gormlu) M.; m. Marilyn Petanatti Jones, Apr. 3, 1969 (div. June 1976). AA in English, St. Josephs Coll., Menlo Park, Calif., 1961; BA, St. Patricks Coll., Menlo Park, Calif., 1963; MA in Humanities, San Francisco State U., 1966. Instr. humanities Yuba C.C., Marysville, Calif., 1966—; instr. Core Coll., 1971-73. Author: Value Sources, 1974, Synthesis, 1985; one-man shows include San Francisco State U., 1983, 92, Sacramento State U., 1984, Consumes River Coll., 1989, Sonoma State U., 1988. Singer with Sacramento Symphony all Beethoven concert, 1991, Christmas concert, 1990, 92. Mem. Pioneer Art Gallery. Roman Catholic. Home: 862 Clark Ave Yuba City CA 95991-3815 Office: Yuba C C 2088 N Beale Rd Marysville CA 95901-7605

MOOSE, CHARLES A., state official; b. Aug. 11, 1953. BA in U.S. History, U. N.C., 1975; MA in Pub. Adminstrn., Portland State U., 1984, PhD in Urban Studies and Criminology, 1993; grad., FBI Nat. Acad. Patrol officer Portland Police Dept., 1975-81, sergeant, 1981-84, lieutenant, 1984-91, capt. of No. Precinct, 1991-92, dep. chief of Ops. Branch, 1992-93, chief of police, 1993—. Bd. dirs. Boys and Girls Club of Portland, Comprehensive Options for Drug Abusers; mem. funding allocation com. Black United Fund Oreg.; mem. Multnomah County Cmty. Action Commn., Police Exec. Rsch. Forum, Bd. Pub. Safety Standards and Tng., Gov.'s Drug and Violent Crime Policy Bd., Gov.'s Juvenile Justice Task Force; bd. dirs. Portland State U. Mem. Am. Soc. Criminology, Nat. Orgn. of Black Law Enforcement Execs., Soc. of Police Futurists Internat., Internat. Assn. Chiefs of Police. Address: Police Bureau 1111 SW 2nd Ave Portland OR 97204-3232*

MOOSER, STEPHEN, author; b. Fresno, Calif., July 4, 1941; s. Joseph Nathan and Lillian Ruth (Davidson) M.; m. Etta Karlovec, Dec. 29, 1972 (div. Dec. 1994); children: Chelsea, Bryn. BA, UCLA, 1963, MA in Journalism, 1968. Reporter Dodge Svcs., L.A., 1964-66; freelance film maker Utah, 1966-68; author children's books SWRL, L.A., 1969-75; freelance author children's books L.A. and N.Y.C., 1975—. Author: New York Kids Book, 1979, 101 Black Cats, 1979, Elvis Is Back and He's in the Sixth Grade, 1994, many others. With U.S. Army, 1963-68. Mem. Soc. Childrens Book Writers and Illustrators (co-founder, pres. 1971—). Home and Office: 1342 Wellesley # 102 Los Angeles CA 90025

MOOSSA, A. R., surgery educator; b. Port Louis, Mauritius, Oct. 10, 1939; s. Yacoob and Maude (Rochecoute) M.; m. Denise Willoughby, Dec. 28, 1973; children: Pierre, Noel, Claude, Valentine. BS, U. Liverpool, Eng., 1962, MD (hon.), 1965; postgrad., Johns Hopkins U., 1972-73, U. Chgo., 1973-74. Intern Liverpool Royal Infirmary, 1965-66; resident United Liverpool Hosps. and Alder Hey Children's Hosp., 1966-72; from asst. prof. surgery to assoc. prof. U. Chgo., 1975-77, prof., dir. surg. rsch., chief gen. surgery svc., vice chmn. dept., 1977-83; chmn. dept. surgery U. Calif.-San Diego Med. Ctr., 1983—; Litchfield lectr. U., Oxford, Eng., 1978; praelector in surgery U. Dundee, Scotland, 1979; Hampson Trust vis. prof. U. Liverpool, Eng., 1992, G.B. Ong. vis. prof. U. Hong Kong, 1993, Philip Sandblon vis. prof. U. Lund, Sweden. Editor: Tumors of the Pancreas, 1982, Essential Surgical Practice, 1983, 3d edit., 1995, Comprehensive Textbook of Oncology, 1985, 2d edit., 1991, Gastrointestinal Emergencies, 1985, Problems in General Surgery, 1989, Operative Colorectal Surgery, 1993. Fellow Royal Coll. Surgeons (Hunterian prof. 1977); mem. ACS, Am. Surg. Assn., Soc. Univ. Surgeons, Am. Soc. Clin. Oncology. Office: U Calif San Diego Med Ctr 200 W Arbor Dr San Diego CA 92103-1911

MORA, DAVID RICHARD, city manager; b. L.A., Feb. 18, 1945; s. David Mora and Bessie Saavedra; m. Judith Anne Crawford, June 10, 1972; children: Teresa, Gabriela. BA, Calif. State U., L.A., 1967; MPIA, U. Pitts., 1971. Vol. U.S. Peace Corps, Philippines, 1967-70; planning chief Jobs for Progress, Inc., L.A., 1972-73; community rels. dir. City of Santa Barbara, Calif., 1973-77, dep. city adminstr., 1977-80; town mgr. Town of Los Gatos, Calif., 1981-85; city mgr. City of Oxnard, Calif., 1985-90, City of Salinas, Calif., 1990—. Contbg. author (book) Reflections of Local Government Professionals, 1987. Chair govt. campaign United Way, Salinas, 1993. Fellow Nat. Acad. Pub. Adminstrn.; mem. Itnerant. City Mgmt. Assn. (pres. ICMA Hispanic Network 1990-92, chair ICMA Coun.-Mgr. Task Force 1992-94, mem. ICMA-Cmty. Oriented Police Svcs. Adv. 1994—, mem. Model City charter com. 1986-88, West Coast regional v.p.), Calif. City Mgrs. Dept. (pres. 1991-92). Office: City of Salinas 200 Lincoln Ave Salinas CA 93901-2639

MORALES, CYNTHIA TORRES, clinical psychologist, consultant; b. L.A., Aug. 13, 1952; d. Victor Jose and Lupe (Pacheco) Torres; m. Armando Torres Morales, June 30, 1989. BA, UCLA, 1975, M in Social Welfare, 1978, D in Counseling Psychology, 1986. Lic. psychologist, Calif. Clin. social worker VA, Brentwood, Calif., 1977-78; med. social worker Harbor-UCLA Med. Ctr., Carson, Calif., 1978-79; psychotherapist San Fernando Valley Child Guidance Clinic, Northridge, Calif., 1979-80; psychiat. social worker L.A. County Dept. Mental Health, 1980-81; child welfare worker L.A. County Dept. Children's Svcs., 1981-86; cons. psychologist, organizational devel. mgr. UCLA, 1986—; pvt. practice and consultation, 1992—; cons. Dept. Children Svcs., Health Svcs. Divsn., 1994—; cons. Hispanic Family Inst., L.A., 1989—, U. Calif., Calif. Youth Authority, Project Info.; mem. diversity com. UCLA, 1988—, mem. mental health emergency task force, 1986-89. Mem. Centro de Ninos Bd. Dirs., L.A., 1984-88; lobbyist self devel. people United Presbyn. Ch. Synod, L.A., 1982-88; chair Inner City Games Acad. Contest Hollenbeck Police Bus. Coun., L.A., 1992; co-chair Inner City Games Acad. Essay Contest, 1993; commr. L.A. County Commn. Children and Family Svcs., 2nd Supervisorial Dist. Recipient Cert. of Appreciation, Children's Bapt. Home, 1984, Cert. of Appreciation, Hollenbeck Police Bus. Coun. 1992, Spl. Recognition award Fed. Judge Takasugi, Pro Bono Bar Rev. and L.A. City Atty. 1993, Cert. of Appreciation, Hollenbeck Youth Ctr., 1992, commendation L.A. County Commn. for Children and Families, 1996. Mem. APA, L.A. County Psychol. Assn. Office: 1100 Glendon Ave Ste 1701 Los Angeles CA 90024-3521

MORAN, RITA JANE, music, drama, restaurant critic, travel writer; b. St. Louis, Aug. 23, 1934; d. Victor Robert Sr. and Margaret Lillian (Oliver) Witte; m. P. Joseph Moran, July 9, 1960; 1 child, Patrick J. BA in English, Writing, Webster U., 1956; MA in English, St. Louis U., 1958. Tchr. English Webster U., Webster Groves, Mo., 1956-58; feature writer St. Louis U. Alumni Mag., 1958-60; feature writer Ventura (Calif.) Star-Free Press, 1961, 65-78, feature editor, 1978-92; music, drama and restaurant critic, feature/travel writer Ventura County Star, 1992—. Selected for Arts critics seminar NEH, 1977. Mem. Kappa Gamma Pi, Alpha Sigma Mu. Roman Catholic. Office: Ventura County Star 5250 Ralston St Ventura CA 93003

MORAN, THOMAS HARRY, university administrator; b. Milw., Oct. 21, 1937; s. Harry Edward and Edna Agnes Moran; BS, U. Wis., 1964, MA, 1972, PhD, 1974; m. Barbara Ellen Saklad, June 10, 1969; children: David Thomas, Karen Ellen. Dir. capital budgeting Wis. Dept. Adminstrn., 1962-64; exec. dir. Wis. Higher Edn. Aids Bd., 1964-69; spl. cons. tax policy Wis. Dept. Revenue, 1973-74; dep. dir. Wis. Manpower Coun., Office of Gov., 1974-76; v.p. bus. and fin., treas. U. Detroit, 1976-78; exec. assoc. v.p. health affairs U. So. Calif., L.A., 1979-87; v.p. bus. affairs, 1988—. USN fellow, 1957-59; U.S. Office Edn. rsch. fellow, 1973. Mem. Am. Assn. Higher Edn., Phi Kappa Phi. Office: U So Calif 200 Town & Gown University Park Los Angeles CA 90007

MORAND, BLAISE E., bishop; b. Tecumseh, Ont., Can., Sept. 12, 1932. Ordained priest Roman Cath. Ch., 1958. Ordained coadjutor bishop Diocese of Prince Albert, Sask., Can., 1981, bishop, 1983—. Office: Diocese of Prince Albert, 1415 4th Ave W, Prince Albert, SK Canada S6V 5H1*

MORANG, DIANE JUDY, writer, television producer, business entrepreneur; b. Chgo., Apr. 28, 1942; d. Anthony Thomas Morang and Laura Ann Andrzejczak. Student, Stevens Finishing Sch., Chgo., 1956, Fox Bus. Coll., 1959-60, UCLA, 1967-69. Mem. staff Chgo. Sun Times, Daily News, 1957, Drury Ln. Theatre, Chgo., 1961-62, AM Show ABC-TV, Hollywood, Calif., 1970-71; chair, mem. judging panel Regional Emmy awards, 1989, judge 2 categories, 1985. Author: How to Get into the Movies, 1978; author, creator: The Rainbow Keyboard, 1991; creator: The Best Kids' Show in the World; contbr. numerous articles to newspapers, mags. Bd. dirs., mem. scholarship com. Ariz. Bruins UCLA Alumni Assn. Mem. NATAS (mem. Hollywood Emmy-award winning team Hollywood, Calif. 1971), Ariz. Authors Assn. (bd. dirs.). Roman Catholic.

MORE, BLAKE, writer, poet; b. West Covina, Calif., Sept. 16, 1965; d. Robert Lawrence and Shirley Ann Blakemore. BA, UCLA, 1987. Cert. yoga tchr. writer/cons./designer, San Francisco, 1996. Author: Definitive Guide to Headaches, 1996; contbg. poet: Hard Love, 1996; editor Insights mag., 1993-94; contbr. articles to Yoga Jour., Tokyo Time Out. Recipient Source Ctr. for Spiritual Devel. Poetry award, 1995. Mem. Marin Dance Collective, Marin Poetry Ctr., Burning Man Collective, Phi Beta Kappa. Home and Office: 218 N Glendora Ave Covina CA 91724

MOREIRA, ALLAN, urologist; b. Managua, Nicaragua, Sept. 30, 1937; came to U.S., 1955; s. Gilberto and Esther (Conrado) M.; m. Laila I.B. Olsson, Oct. 15, 1960; children: Ingrid, Linda, Kerstin, Alan. AA, U. Calif., Berkeley, 1957; MD, Creighton U., 1962. Intern Mercy Hosp., Des Moines, 1962-63; gen. practice Cogley Clinic, Council Bluffs, Iowa, 1963-64; resident Mt. Zion Hosp., San Francisco, 1966-67, U. Calif., San Francisco, 1967-70; urologist pvt. practice, Fremont & San Francisco, Calif., 1970-76; urologist Kaiser Permanente, Honolulu, 1984-94, chief dept. urology, 1994—. Col. U.S. Army, 1964-84. Mem. AMA, Calif. Med. Assn., Hawaii Urological Soc., Assn. Mil. Surgeons U.S., Soc. Govt. Svc. Urologists. Republican. Roman Catholic. Office: Kaiser Permanente 3288 Moanalua Rd Honolulu HI 96819-1469

MOREL-SEYTOUX, HUBERT JEAN, civil engineer, educator; b. Calais, Artois, France, Oct. 6, 1932; came to U.S., 1956; s. Aimé and Suzanne Claire (Rousseau) M.-S.; m. Margery K. Keyes, Apr. 16, 1960; children: Aimée, Claire, Sylvie, Marie-Jeanne. BS, Ecole St. Genevieve, Versailles, France, 1953; MS, Ecole Nationale des Ponts et Chaussées, Paris, 1956; PhD, Stanford U., 1962. Research engr. Chevron Oil Field Research Co., La Habra, Calif., 1962-66; prof. Colo. State U., Ft. Collins, 1966-91, prof. emeritus, 1991—; chargé de recherches U. Grenoble, France, 1972-73; maitre de recherches Ecole des Mines de Paris, Fontainebleau, France, 1982; directeur de recherches ORSTOM, Montpellier, France, 1991—; cons. hydrology Atherton, Calif., 1992—; cons. AID, Dakar, Senegal, 1985-86, 88, Ministry of Agriculture and Water, Riyadh, Saudi Arabia, 1978-83, City of Thornton, Colo., 1986-88, King Abdulaziz U., Jeddah, Saudi Arabia, 1987, 89—, Ford Found., India, 1976, 79, South Fla. Water Mgmt. Dist., West Palm Beach, 1991—, Battelle Pacific Northwest Labs., Richland, Wash., 1991—, City of Paris, France, 1992—, Agence de l'Eau Seine-Normandie, 1992—, Utah State U., Logan, 1994-95, Reservoir Engrng. Rsch. Inst., Palo Alto, 1994-95; vis. prof. Ecole Polytechnique Federale de Lausanne, 1987; vis. scholar Stanford U., 1992—; adj. prof. U. Colo., Boulder, 1992—; lectr. U. Calif., Berkley, 1993. Editor: Hydrology Days, 1981—, 3d Internat. Hydrology Symposium, 1977, Unsaturated Flow in Hydrologic Modeling, 1989. Pres. Internat. Ctr., Ft. Collins, 1984-86. Served to lt. French Army Marine Corps Engrs., 1959-62. Sr. Fulbright scholar, France, 1972-73; recipient Abell Faculty Rsch. award Colo. State U. Coll. Engring., 1985. Mem. Am. Geophys. Union, ASCE, Soc. Petroleum Engrs., Am. Meteorol. Soc., Am. Soc. Agrl. Engrs. Home: 57 Selby Ln Atherton CA 94027-3926 Office: Hydrology Days Publs 57 Selby Ln Atherton CA 94027-3926

MORENO, MANUEL D., bishop; Educator U. of Calif., L.A., St. John's Sem., Camarillo, Calif. Ordained priest Roman Cath. church, 1961. Ordained aux. bishop of Los Angeles, titular bishop of Tanagra, 1977; installed as bishop of Tucson, 1982—. Office: PO Box 31 192 S Stone Ave Tucson AZ 85702*

MORENO-CABRAL, CARLOS EDUARDO, cardiac surgeon; b. Zacatecas, Mex., Nov. 4, 1951; s. Manuel Julio Moreno and Dominga Cabral; children: Rodrigo, Iza, Daniel. MD, Nat. U. Mex., 1976. Diplomate Am. Bd. Surgery, Am. Bd. Thoracic Surgery. Resident in gen. surgery U. Hawaii, 1977-80, Mich. State U., 1980-82; fellow in cardiac surgery Stanford (Calif.) U., 1982-84, 86-88; tng. in thoracic surgery SUNY, Bklyn., 1984-86; dir. cardiac transplant program St. Francis Hosp., Honolulu, 1989—. Author: Postoperative Management in Adult Cardiac Surgery, 1988. Fellow ACS; mem. Soc. Thoracic Surgeons. Office: 1380 Lusitana St Ste 912 Honolulu HI 96813-2448

MOREY, ROBERT HARDY, communications executive; b. Milw., Sept. 5, 1956; s. Lloyd W. and Ruby C. (McElhaney) M. AA, Ricks Coll., 1978; BA, Brigham Young U., 1983. Program dir. Sta. KABE-FM, Orem, Utah, 1982-83, sales mgr., 1983; nat. mgr. ops. Tiffany Prodns. Internat., Salt Lake City, 1983-84; account exec. Osmond Media Corp., Orem, 1984; corp. sec., bd. dirs. Positive Communications, Inc., Orem, 1984—, chief exec. officer, 1987—; gen. mgr. Sta. KSRR, Orem, 1985—; pres. K-Star Satellite Network, Orem, 1986—, Broadcast Media Svcs., Orem, 1989-93; gen. mgr. Sta. KMGR, Salt Lake City, 1993; ops. mgr. KQMB-FM, Salt Lake City, 1994-95, gen. mgr., 1995—; guest lectr. various colls. and univs., 1981—. Chmn. Rep. voting dist., Orem, 1984. Recipient Community Service award Utah Valley Community Coll., 1983; named one of Outstanding Young Men in Am. U.S. Jaycees, 1983. Home: PO Box 828 Orem UT 84059-0828 Office: Sta KSRR Ventura Media Ctr 1240 E 800 N Orem UT 84097-4318

MORGAN, AUDREY, architect; b. Neenah, Wis., Oct. 19, 1931; d. Andrew John Charles Hopfensperger and Melda Lily (Radtke) Anderson; m. Earl Adrian Morgan (div); children: Michael A. Morgan, Nancy Lee Morgan, Diana Lou Hansen, Susan Lynn Heiner. BA, U. Wash., 1955. Registered architect, Wash., Oreg.; cert. NCARB. Project mgr. The Austin Co., Renton, Wash., 1972-75; med. facilities architect The NBBJ Group, Seattle, 1975-79; architect constrn. rev. unit Wash. State Divsn. Health, Olympia, 1979-81; project dir., med. planner John Graham & Co., Seattle, 1981-83; pvt. practice architecture, Ocean Shores, Wash., 1983—, also health care facility cons., code analyst. Contbg. author: Guidelines for Construction and Equipment of Hospitals and Medical Facilities; Co-editor: Design Consideration for Mental Health Facilities; contbr. articles to profl. jours. and govt. papers; prin. works include quality assurance coord. for design phase Madigan Army Med. Ctr., Ft. Lewis, Wash.; med. planner and code analyst Rockwood Clinic, Spokane, Wash., Comprehensive Health Care Clinic for Yakima Indian Nation, Toppenish, Wash.; code analyst S.W. Wash. Hosps., Vancouver; med. planner Pacific Cataract & Lazer Inst. Chehalis & Kennewick, Wash; med. planner facilities for child, adult, juvenile and forensic psychiatric patients., States of Wash. and Oreg. expert witness litigation cases involving mental health facilities. Cons. on property mgmt. Totem council Girl Scouts U.S.A., Seattle, 1969-84, troop leader, cons., trainer, 1961-74; mem. Wash. State Bldg. Code Coun., tech. adv. group for non-residential bldgs., Barier Free Com. Tech. adv. group for Ams. with Disabilties Act; assoc. mem. Wash State Fire Marshals Tech. Adv. Group. Mem. AIA (nat. acad. architecture for health 1980—, subcoms. codes and standards, chair mental health com., 1989-92, and numerous other coms., founding mem. Wash. council AIA architecture for health panel 1981—, recorder 1981-84, vice chmn., 1987, chmn. 1988, bd. dirs. S.W. Wash. chpt. 1983-84), Nat. Fire Protection Assn., Soc. Am. Value Engrs., Am. Hosp. Assn., Assn. Western Hosps., Wash. State Hosp. Assn., Wash. State Soc. Hosp. Engrs. (hon.), Seattle Womens Sailing Assn., Audubon Soc., Alpha Omicron Pi. Lutheran. Clubs: Coronado 25 Fleet 13 (Seattle) (past sec., bull. editor); GSA 25 Plus. Home and Office: PO Box 1990 Ocean Shores WA 98569-1990 also: 904 Falls Of Clyde Loop SE Ocean Shores WA 98569-9542

MORGAN, CHARLES EDWARD PHILLIP, bank executive; b. Wichita, Kans., Nov. 3, 1916; s. Wells C. Morgan and Mary E. (Brown) Allredge; m. Elizabeth Ann Brown, Oct. 14, 1943 (div. Dec. 1972); children—Valerie Donahue, Renee Tompkins. Student U. Wichita, 1935; student bus. adminstrn., U. Calif.-Berkeley, 1963. Teller First Nat. Bank, Santa Fe, 1938-42; safety officer Libby-McNeil-Libby, Sacramento, 1946-48; from teller to v.p./br. mgr. Wells Fargo Bank, Sacramento, 1948-76; sr. v.p. Capitol Bank of Commerce, Sacramento, 1976-86. Served to 1st lt. USAF, 1942-45. Mem. Masons, Shriners. Democrat. Mem. Christian Ch. Home: 1111 Alvarado Ave Apt F362 Davis CA 95616-5918

MORGAN, DAN L., manufacturing company executive; b. Hutchinson, Kans., Feb. 1, 1957; s. Lester Herbert and Marjorie Maxine (Allen) M. Student, Hutchinson C.C., 1977; BBA, Bartlesville Wesleyan U., 1980. Head clk. Safeway Stores, Hutchinson, 1973-76; supr. Chevron Affiliates, Dallas, 1982-90; asst. dist. mgr. Chevron Corp. USA, Pleasanton, Calif., 1990-92; CEO, pres. Creative Designs Internat., Riverside, Calif., 1992—. Office: 17450 Blue Water Ct Riverside CA 92503

MORGAN, DAVID FORBES, minister; b. Toronto, Ont., Can., Aug. 3, 1930; came to U.S., 1954; s. Forbes Alexander and Ruth (Bamford) M.; m. Delores Mae Storhaug, Sept. 7, 1956; children—Roxanne Ruth, David Forbes II. BA, Rocky Mt. Coll.; ThB, Coll. of the Rockies, MDiv; postgrad. Bishop's Sch. Theology; LittD (hon.), Temple Coll., 1956, D.C. Nat. Coll. Ordained priest. Pres., Coll. of the Rockies, Denver, 1960-73; founder and rector Prior Order of Christ Centered Ministries, Denver, 1973—; canon pastor St. John's Cathedral, Denver, 1982-96, canon at large, 1996— ; bd. dir. Alpha Inc., Denver, 1981—. Author: Christ Centered Ministries, A Response to God's Call, 1973; Songs with A Message, 1956. Clubs: Oxford, Denver Botanic Garden. Home: 740 Clarkson St Denver CO 80218-3204 Office: St Johns Cathedral 1313 Clarkson St Denver CO 80218-1806

MORGAN, DIRCK, broadcast journalist; b. L.A., Feb. 3, 1954; s. Phillip Barton and Katherine (Ramirez) Segall; m. Ellen Tomoye Matsumoto, Dec. 1, 1993; 1 child, Makena Sunao. AA, Pierce Coll., 1973. Assignment editor KFWB/Group W. Westinghouse, L.A., 1972-74; corp. comm. specialist Northrop Corp., L.A., 1975-78; news dir. KARM, KFIG, Fresno, Calif., 1978-84; editor, anchor KGIL, L.A., 1984-85; fin. anchor KWHY-TV, L.A., 1985-87; cmty. resources specialist Optimist Boys Home, L.A., 1985-87; reporter KFWB/CBS, L.A., 1988—; media crisis mgmt. specialist L.A. County Fire Dept., 1990—, L.A. Police Dept., 1991—, LAUSD, 1996, Calif. State Mil. Res., L.A., 1990-95. Helicopter Airborne reporter broadcast series on L.A. riots, 1992 (L.A. Press Club award), L.A. Police Dept. Ballistics, 1994 (L.A. Press Club award), Radio TV News Assn: 14 golden mikes. Instr., announcer Kenkojuku Junko World Karate, L.A., 1984-92; host Nissei Week, L.A., 1990-95. Mem. L.A. Police Protective League (hon. life). Office: KFWB/CBS 6230 Yucca St Los Angeles CA 90028

MORGAN, GARY B., journalism educator; b. San Diego, Nov. 5, 1943; s. Howard Wilson and Loyola Elizabeth (Heiberger) M.; m. Sharon Kay Traylor, June 16, 1965 (div. 1974); children: Stephen William Laurence, David Nathan Robert. BA, N.Mex. Highlands U., Las Vegas, 1966; MA, Colo. State U., 1968; DA, U. No. Colo., 1990. So. Calif. prep sports editor L.A. Examiner, 1959-61; sports editor Star-News, National City, Calif., 1960-61; announcer KFUN Radio, Las Vegas, N.Mex., 1963-66; sports info. dir. New Mex. Highlands U., 1964-66; grad. teaching asst. dept. English Colo. State U., 1966-68; info. dir. Mt. Plains Intercollegiate Athletic Assn., 1968-71, 74-76; asst. dir. info. svc. U. No. Colo., 1968-77; asst. prof. journalism Met. State Coll., Denver, 1977-84; prof. journalism Oxnard Coll., Calif., 1984—, pres. acad. senate, 1993-96. Author: Yes You Can, 1990, The Georgetown Loop, 1976, Sugar Tramp, 1975, Three Foot Rails, 1970, There Was So Much Laughter, 1984; contbr. articles to profl. jours. Pres. Oxnard Coll. Acad. Senate, 1993-96. Recipient Mark Dever award for excellence in teaching, Oxnard Coll., 1985-86. Mem. Nat. Collegiate Baseball Writers Assn. (pres. 1976), Coll. Sports Info. Dirs. Am. (bd. dirs.), Journalism Assn. C.C. (state pres. 1989-90, So. Calif. pres. 1988-89), C.C. Journalism Assn. (nat. pres. 1992), Assn. for Edn. in Journalism and Mass Comm., Calif. Newspaper Pubs. Assn. Office: Oxnard College 4000 S Rose Ave Oxnard CA 93033-6699

MORGAN, GLEN, college official; b. Marquette, Mich., Oct. 28, 1946; s. Glen and Margaret Morgan; m. Connie Jean Engman, Sept. 23, 1967; children: Michelle, Kristin. BA in Speech and English, No. Mich. U., 1970; MA in Teaching, U. Wis., 1973, MEd in Curriculum and Instrn., 1979. Instr. comm. dept. Lakeshore Tech. Coll., Cleveland, Wis., 1970-78, assoc. dean, 1978-83; mgr. staff devel. and tng. dept. human resources Mt. Sinai Med. Ctr., Milw., 1983-84; cons., mgr. mgmt. and human resources The Mgmt. Bd. div. Modern Mgmt., Inc., Lake Bluff, Ill., 1984-86; procurement assistance, tng. and devel. cons. Coll. Lake County Ctr. for Econ. Devel., Grayslake, Ill., 1986-87, assoc. dean Ctr. for Econ. Devel., 1987-89; dir. Bus.-Industry Support Ctr. and Small Bus. Devel. Ctr. Seminole C.C., Sanford, Fla., 1989-95; deam cmty. & econ. devel., exec. dir. Colo. Ctr. Profl. Devel. Arapahoe C.C., Englewood, Colo., 1995—; edit. reviewer Pers. Adminstr.; text reveiwer William C. Brown and Co. Author: Passport to Successful Exporting, 1989, The Nursing Professional, Support Staff Development/Training Program Handbook, 1982; guest editor Herald Times Reporter; also articles. Loaned profl. United Way Lake County, 1987, account exec., Seminole County, Fla. chpt., 1993; mem. Fla. Econ. Devel. Coun., Econ. Devel. Commn. Mid-Fla.; bd. dirs. Manitowoc Expo/County Fair; mem. bd. appeal Nat. League Nursing; pres., v.p. St. Andrew Athletic Assn.; pres., v.p., sec.-treas. St. Andrew Home and Sch. Assn.; co-exec. Lakeshore Marriage Encounter. Roepke-Cassel scholar, 1995. Recipient Challenge award Community Field Svcs., 1982. Mem. ASTD, NEA, Am. Assn. Cmty. Colls., Assn. Govt. Mktg. Assistance Specialists, Am. Soc. for Healthcare Edn. and Tng., Coun. Vocat. Educators, Am. Vocat. Assn., Internat. Listening Assn. (charter, founding), Fla. Assn. C.C.'s, Speech Comm. Assn., Kappa Delta Pi. Office: Arapahoe Cmty Coll Ste 105 9201 E Mississippi Ave Englewood CO 80111

MORGAN, GWENDOLYN JEAN, minister, writer; b. Portland, Oct. 28, 1963; d. Robley King and Mary Jean (McCallum) M.; m. Matthew Jon Morgan-Jones, Aug. 15, 1987; children: Carmen Elizabeth Quishpe, Christian Andrés Quishpe. AA, Sheldon Jackson Coll., 1984; BA, Whitworth Coll., 1986; MDiv, San Francisco Theol. Sem., 1992; MFA, Goddard Coll. Ordained to ministry Presbyn. Ch., 1993. Vol. Internat. Youth Exch., Monrovia, Liberia, 1984-85; staff mem., vol. Providence Hospitality House, Seattle, 1986-87; tentmaker First Presbyn. Ch., Moorcroft, Wyo., 1993-96. Author: poems. Bd. dirs. N.W. Coalition Against Malicious Harrassment, Seattle, 1994-96. Mem. Bear Lodge Writers, Wyoming Writers, Women Writing the West. Home: 5745 NW Sewell Rd Hillsboro OR 97124

MORGAN, JACK M., lawyer; b. Portales, N.Mex., Jan. 15, 1924; s. George Albert and Mary Rosana (Baker) M.; BBA, U. Tex., 1948; LLB, 1950; m. Peggy Flynn Cummings, 1947; children: Marilyn, Rebecca, Claudia, Jack. Admitted to N.Mex. bar, 1950; sole practice law, Farmington, N.Mex., 1956—; mem. N.Mex. State Senate, 1973-88 . Served with USN, 1942-46. Mem. Am. Bar Assn., N.Mex. Bar Assn., S.W. Regional Energy Council (past chmn.), Kiwanis, Elks. Republican. Office: PO Box 2151 Farmington NM 87499-2151

MORGAN, JACOB RICHARD, cardiologist; b. East St. Louis, Ill., Oct. 10, 1925; s. Clyde Adolphus and Jennie Ella Henrietta (Van Ramshorst) M.; m. Alta Eloise Ruthruff, Aug. 1, 1953; children: Elaine, Stephen Richard. BA in Physics, BBA, U. Tex., 1953; MD, U. Tex., Galveston, 1957. Diplomate Am. Bd. Internal Medicine, Am. Bd. Cardiology. Ensign USN, 1944, advanced through grades to capt., 1969; intern U.S. Naval Hosp., Oakland, Calif., 1957-58; chief medicine U.S. Naval Hosp., Taipei, Republic of China, 1962-64; internal medicine staff San Diego, 1964-67, chief cardiology, 1969-73; ret., 1973; dir. medicine R.E. Thomas Gen. Hosp., El Paso, Tex., 1973-75; asst. clin. prof. medicine U. Calif., San Diego, 1970-73; prof. medicine, assoc. chmn. dep. Tex. Tech U. Sch. Medicine, Lubbock and El Paso, 1973-75; pvt. practice National City, Calif., 1976—; dir. cardiology Paradise Valley Hosp., National City, 1976-88; presenter in field. Contbr. articles on cardiology to sci. jours. Recipient Casmir Funk award, 1972. Fellow ACP, Am. Coll. Cardiology, Am. Coll. Chest Physicians, Am. Heart Assn. (coun. on clin. cardiology). Home: 9881 Edgar Pl La Mesa CA 91941-6833 Office: 2409 E Plaza Blvd National City CA 91950-5101

MORGAN, JAMES FREDERICK, lawyer, educator; b. Chico, Calif., Sept. 26, 1954; s. Jack Francis and Joan Claudia (Nedry) M.; m. Sheryl Diane Lewis, June 6, 1987. BS, Calif. State U., Chico, 1976; JD, U. Calif., Davis, 1980. Bar: Calif. 1980, U.S. Dist. Ct. (ea. dist.) Calif. 1980, U.S. Ct. Appeals (9th cir.) 1983, U.S Supreme Ct. 1989. Lectr. Calif. State U., Chico, 1981-83, asst. prof., 1983-86, assoc. prof., 1986-92, prof., 1992—, chair dept. mgmt., 1992-97; assoc. Peters, Fuller, Rush & Carter, 1988-90, Carter & Hendrin, Chico, 1991-92; adj. prof. law Calif. No. U., 1986; course designer Real Estate Depository, Modesto, Calif., 1986-92, cons. Tri-Counties Bank, Chico, 1987; state-wide seminar dir. Calif. State U. Inst. for Teaching and Learning, 1988-90. Co-editor: Legislation and Recent Development for California Business Lawyers, 1986; contbr. articles to profl. jours. Pres. Butte County Dep. Sheriff's Assn., 1983-84; chmn. Pacific Gas & Electric Consumer Adv. Commn., N. Cen. Calif., 1984-85; 1st vice chair Butte County Rep. Cen. Com., 1987-90. Mem. ABA (com. on the scope uniform comml. code 1985—), Am. Bus. Law Assn., Western Bus. Law Assn., Chico Area C. of C. (bd. dirs. 1992—), Butte County Family Svc. Assn. (bd. dirs. 1990-93), SAR (pres. Butte County chpt. 1988-90, 1st v.p. Calif. State Soc., pres. 1990-91), Greater Chico C. of C. (pres. 1997). Republican. Office: Calif State U Dept Mgmt & Bus Chico CA 95929

MORGAN, JOE LEONARD, investment company executive, former professional baseball player; b. Bonham, Tex., Sept. 19, 1943. Student, Oakland City (Ind.) Coll.; BA in Phys. Edn., Calif. State U.-Hayward, 1990. Infielder Houston Astros, 1962-71, 2nd baseman, 1980; 2nd baseman Cin. Reds, 1972-79, San Francisco Giants, 1981-82, Phila. Phillies, 1983, Oakland A's, 1984; pres. Joe Morgan Investments Inc., Oakland, 1984—; baseball analyst Sta. WLWT-TV, Cin., 1985; college baseball analyst ESPN, 1985-88, analyst ESPN Sunday Night Baseball, 1990—; analyst GiantsVision, 1986-90, ABC-TV, 1988, NBC-TV, 1994—; analyst Oakland Athletics Baseball Sports Channel, 1995—; owner, pres. Joe Morgan Beverage Co., 1988—. Named Most Valuable Player Tex. League, 1964; Rookie of Yr. in Nat. League Sporting News, 1965; Most Valuable Player Nat. League, 1975, 76; Maj. League Player of Year. Sporting News, 1975, 76; named to Nat. League All-Star Team, 1970, 72-79, Nat. League Comeback Player of the Year Sporting News, 1982, Nat. League Player of the Year Sporting News, 1975, Nat. League All Star Team Sporting News, 1972, 73-77; recipient Silver Slugger award Sporting News, 1982; elected to Baseball Hall of Fame, 1990; recipient CableACE award, 1990. also: ESPN ESPN Plz Bristol CT 06010 Address: 3239 Danville Blvd #A Alamo CA 94507-1913*

MORGAN, KAT C., political activist; b. Bklyn., Aug. 4, 1963; d. David Morgan and Cordelia Katherine (Wagner) Reimers. BA in Women's Studies, U. Colo., 1988; MSW, U. Denver, 1992. Resource specialist Prevention Ctr., Boulder, Colo., 1988-91; cmty. support program coord. SafeHouse for Battered Women, Denver, 1992; exec. dir. Gay, Lesbian & Bisexual Cmty. Svcs. Ctr. of Colo., Denver, 1993-94; program dir. Shelter Against Violent Environments, Fremont, Calif., 1995—; trainer Valuing Diversity Project, Boulder, 1992-94. Bd. editors Empathy jour., Columbia, S.C., 1990—. Bd. dirs. Chinook Fund, Denver, 1992-94, Cmty. Shares of Colo., Denver, 1993-94; founder, pres. Equal Protection Coalition, Boulder, 1985-87. Recipient Making a Difference award Colo. Gay and Lesbian Task Force, 1990. Dean Emil Sunley award U. Denver Grad. Sch. Social Work, 1992, Susan B. Anthony award Boulder NOW, 1993, cert. of appreciaiton for victim svcs. Dept. of Justice, 1996; day named in her honor, Boulder, 1995. Mem. NASW, NCADV, Emergency Svcs. Network of Alameda County.

MORGAN, LANNY, musician; b. Des Moines, Mar. 30, 1934; s. Harold Ira and Ruth (Maddick) M.; m. Marty Shelton Morgan; children: Breck, Wynter. Student, L.A. (Calif.) City Coll., 1952. instr. Stanford U. Summer Jazz Workshops, L.A. Jazz Workshop, Grove Sch. Music, Many others; guest artist, instr. at coll., high schs. throughout U.S.; played on recordings, films, TV; guest solo U.K. clubs, festivals. Played lead alto saxophone with Maynard Ferguson, Rey De Michele Orch., Oliver Nelson, Bill Holman Band, Bob Florence Band, Supersax; appeared, recorded Steely Dan, Natalie Cole, Diane Schurr, Shirley Horn, Andy Williams, Mel Torme, Frank Sinatra, Julie Andrews, and many others; lead quartet/quintet in L.A.; recordings include Lanny Morgan Quartet, 1993, Pacific Standard, 1997. With U.S. Army, 1957-59. Home: 6470 Gaviota Ave Van Nuys CA 91406-6401

MORGAN, MARK QUENTEN, astronomer, astrophysics educator; b. Topeka, Dec. 27, 1950; s. Walter Quenten and Barbara Gene (Haynes) M. BA in Astronomy, San Diego State U., 1972; PhD in Astronomy, U. Addison, Ont., Can., 1976. Jet engine and power plant engr. N.Am. Aviation, Palmdale, Calif., 1966-68; astron. observer San Diego State U., 1970-74; engr., solar observer U. Md.-Clark Lake Radio Obs., Borrego Springs, Calif., 1978-82; engr., lectr. Sci. Atlanta, San Diego, 1979—. Inventor continuous wave laser, 1965, high intensity sound acoustic screening system, 1979. Mem. Inst. Environ. Scis., Acoustic Soc. Am., Astrophys. Soc. Am., Union Concerned Scientists, Planetary Soc. Office: Sci Atlanta PO Box 4254 San Diego CA 92164-4254

MORGAN, MEREDITH WALTER, optometrist, retired educator; b. Kingman, Ariz., Mar. 22, 1912; s. Meredith Walter and Florence (Forsyth) M.; m. Ida Marcia Engelking, Mar., 7, 1937 (dec. Nov. 1990); 1 child, Linda Morgan-Outhisack. AB, U. Calif., Berkeley, 1934, MA, 1939, PhD, 1942; DOS (hon.), Ill. Coll. Optometry, 1968; DSc, So. Calif. Coll. Optometry, 1974, Pa. Coll. Optometry, 1976, SUNY, 1989. Pvt. practice optometry Richmond, Calif., 1934-60; from instr. to prof. U. Calif., 1942-75, dean Sch. Optometry, 1960-73, prof. and dean emeritus, 1975—; vis. prof. U. Waterloo, Ont., 1974, U. Ala., Birmingham, 1977; mem. const. rev. com. USPHS, Washington, 1964-65, Nat. Adv. Coun. on Med., Dental, Optometric and Podiatric Edn., 1966-67; mem. adv. coun. Nat. Eye Inst., NIH, Washington, 1969-71; adminstrv. cons. SUNY, 1976; hon. chmn. Diamond Jubilee Com. Sch. Optometry, U. Calif., 1996—. Author: Optics of Ophthalmic Lenses, 1978; co-editor: Vistion and Aging, 1986, rev. edit., 1993, Pediatric Optometry, 1990; contbr. articles to sci. jours. Pres., mem. West Contra Costa County YMCA, Richmond, Calif., 1940-70, Meml. Youth Ctr. Bd., Richmond, 1950-68, Union High Sch. Bd., Richmond, 1950-55, Bd. Edn., Richmond, 1954-61. Recipient Berkeley citation U. Calif., 1968. Fellow Am. Acad. Optometry (life, awards com., pres. 1953-54, Prentice medal 1967); mem. Am. Optometric Assn. (Apollo medal 1975), Sons in Retirement, Rotary. Democrat. Presbyterian. Home: 1217 Skycrest Dr # 4 Walnut Creek CA 94595-1811 Office: U Calif Sch Optometry Berkeley CA 94720

MORGAN, MICHAEL BREWSTER, publishing company executive; b. L.A., Dec. 30, 1953; s. Brewster Bowen and Eleanor (Boysen) M.; m. Debra Hunter, July 20, 1986. BA, Conn. Coll., 1975. Coll. sales rep. Addison Wesley Pub. Co., Chapel Hill, N.C., 1977-81; sponsoring editor Addison Wesley Pub. Co., Reading, Mass., 1981-84; chief exec. officer Morgan Kaufmann Pubs., San Francisco, Calif., 1984—. Mem. Am. Assn. for Artificial Intelligence, Assn. for Computing Machinery. Office: Morgan Kaufmann Pubs 340 Pine St San Francisco CA 94104-3205

MORGAN, NEIL, author, newspaper editor, lecturer, columnist; b. Smithfield, N.C., Feb. 27, 1924; s. Samuel Lewis and Isabelle (Robeson) M.; m. Caryl Lawrence, 1945 (div. 1954); m. Katharine Starkey, 1955 (div. 1962); m. Judith Blakely, 1964; 1 child, Jill. AB, Wake Forest Coll., 1943. Columnist San Diego Daily Jour., 1946-50; columnist San Diego Evening Tribune, 1950-92, assoc. editor, 1977-81, editor, 1981-92; assoc. editor, sr. columnist San Diego Union-Tribune, 1992—; syndicated columnist Morgan Jour., Copley News Service, 1958—; lectr.; cons. on Calif. affairs Bank of Am., Sunset mag. Author: My San Diego, 1951, It Began With a Roar, 1953, Know Your Doctor, 1954, Crosstown, 1955, My San Diego 1960, 1959, Westward Tilt, 1963, Neil Morgan's San Diego, 1964, The Pacific States, 1967, The California Syndrome, 1969, (with Robert Witty) Marines of Margarita, 1970, The Unconventional City, 1972, (with Tom Blair) Yesterday's San Diego, 1976, This Great Land, 1983, Above San Diego, 1990, (with Judith Morgan) Dr. Seuss & Mr. Geisel, 1995; conbr. non-fiction articles to Nat. Geog., Esquire, Redbook, Reader's Digest, Holiday, Harper's, Travel and Leisure, Ency. Brit. Lt. USNR, 1943-46. Recipient Ernie Pyle Meml. award, 1957, Bill Corum Meml. award, 1961, Disting. Svc. citation Wake Forest U., 1966, grand award for travel writing Pacific Area Travel Assn., 1972, 78, Fourth Estate award San Diego State U., 1988, The Morgan award Leadership Edn. Awareness Devel. San Diego, 1993; co-recipient Ellen and Roger Revelle award, 1986; named Outstanding Young Man of Yr. San Diego, 1959. Mem. Authors Guild, Am. Soc. Newspaper Editors, Soc. Profl. Journalists, Explorers Club, Soc. of Am. Travel Writers, Bohemian Club, Phi Beta Kappa, Omicron Delta Kappa. Home: 7930 Prospect Pl La Jolla CA 92037-3721 Office: PO Box 191 San Diego CA 92112-4106

MORGAN, PATRICK MICHAEL, political science educator; b. Syracuse, N.Y., Dec. 6, 1940; s. George Amos and Mary Kathleen (Cartin) M.; m. Marilyn Adele Kelly, Aug. 24, 1963; children: Kelly Sue, Christopher, Kimberly. BA, Harpur Coll., 1962; MA, Yale U., 1964, PhD, 1967. Asst. prof. Wash. State U., Pullman, 1967-72, assoc. prof., 1972-76, prof., 1976-91; vis. prof. U. Wash., 1980-82, Coll. of Europe, Bruges, Belgium, 1985, 87-88, 1989—; vis. prof. Katholieke Universiteit, Leuven, Belgium, 1992—; Tierney prof., chair Peace Rsch. U. Calif., Irvine, 1991—; cons. Sloan Found., 1977, Am. Coun. on Edn., Washington, 1979. Author: Deterrence: A Conceptual Analysis, 2d edit., 1983, Theories and Approaches to International Politics, 4th edit., 1987; co-author: Strategic Military Surprise, 1983; co-editor: Security and Arms Control, 2 vols., 1989, Regional Orders, 1997. Fulbright fellowship U.S. Govt., 1985; fellowship Am. Coun. on Edn., U. Calif., 1976-77, Woodrow Wilson Ctr., 1973-74. Mem. Internat. Studies Assn. (v.p. 1988-89), Am. Polit. Sci. Assn., Coun. on U.S.-Korean Security Studies (co-coord. 1984—). Democrat. Home: 5 Whitman Ct Irvine CA 92612-4056 Office: U Calif Dept Politics & Soc Irvine CA 92717

MORGAN, RICHARD THOMAS, accountant, county official; b. Pocatello, Idaho, Apr. 17, 1968; s. Sylvan Lowell and Carma Jean (Povey) M.; m. Sandra Sudbury, Aug. 7, 1992; 1 child, Madison. BBA, Idaho State U., 1994. CPA, Idaho. Tax acct. Morgan & Morgan LLP, Pocatello, 1994—; dep. auditor Bannock County, Pocatello, 1996—; cons. 1st Security State Games, Pocatello, 1995—; bookseller Deseret Book, Pocatello, 1996—. Editor newsletter Morgan's Moments, 1995-96. Counselor, fin. clk. LDS Ch., Pocatello, 1996—. Recipient Hope of Am. award Kiwanis, Pocatello. Democrat. Home: 646 Boyd Chubbuck ID 83202 Office: Bannock County 624 E Center Rm 104 Pocatello ID 83201

MORGAN, RONALD WILLIAM, sales executive; b. Redlands, Calif., May 9, 1951; s. Liberty W. and Eleanor L. (Creech) M.; m. Debra Ann Lein, Nov. 30, 1991. AA in Machine Shop, Valley Coll., 1973; BA in Bus., Calif. State U., San Bernardino, 1977. Sales mgr. Combined Ins., Redlands, 1976-77; ter. sales mgr. Bullard Safety, L.A., 1977-79; sales engr. H.E.S. Machine Tool, Whittier, Calif., 1979-81, Machinery Sales, L.A., 1981-89; regional mgr. Ingersoll Rand Water Jet, Yorba Linda, Calif., 1989-91; ter. sales mgr. Machinery Sales, L.A., 1991-93; dist. mgr. Ellison Machinery, L.A., 1993-94; regional mgr. Daewoo Machinery, L.A., 1995—. With USCGR. Mem. Soc. Mfg. Engrs., Sons Am. Revolution.

MORGAN, STANLEY CHARLES, plastic and reconstructive surgeon; b. Phoenix, July 23, 1935; s. Fred Charles and Hazel (King) M.; m. Doris Anne Duke, Sept. 8, 1956; children: Pamela Anne, Cheryl Lynn, Mark Thomas. BS, U. Ariz.; MD, St. Louis Sch. Medicine. Diplomate Am. Bd. Plastic Surgery. Intern UCLA Ctr. Health Svcs., 1961-62, resident plastic surgery, 1966-68; resident gen. surgery Wadsworth Vets. Hosp., L.A., 1962-66; practice medicine specializing in plastic surgery Pasadena, Calif., 1970—; asst. clin. prof. U. So. Calif. Sch. Medicine, Los Angeles, 1981—, UCLA Ctr. Health Scis., 1970-81. Lt. col. U.S. Army, 1968-70. Fellow ACS, Am. Soc. Plastic and Reconstructive Surgeons, Am. Soc. Aesthetic Plastic Surgery, Calif. Soc. Plastic Surgeons. Office: 10 Congress St Ste 407 Pasadena CA 91105-3023

MORGAN-FADNESS, CORRINA MAY, staff charge nurse; b. Longview, Wash., Jan. 12, 1963; d. Arthur Dallas and Dorothy Irene (Ellis) Miller; 1 child, Michael Patrick. AA, Lower Columbia Coll., 1982; BSN, U. Portland, 1987. RN, Wash.; cert. gerontol. nurse, cert. dir. nursing. Staff nurse Centralia (Wash.) Gen. Hosp., 1987; charge nurse Walker Care Ctr., Centralia, 1987-89, Park Royal Med. Ctr., Longview, Wash., 1987, 89; house supr. WHCC Riverside, Centralia, 1989-92; staff nurse Auburn (Wash.) Gen. Hosp., 1992—, WHCC Riverside, Centralia, 1996—; IV cons. on-call Evergreen Pharms., Inc., 1990—; unit mgr. Oakhurst Convalescent Ctr., Elma, Wash., 1992-93; patient care coord. Rehab. Sharon Care Ctr., Centralia, Wash., 1993—; staff nurse Morton (Wash.) Long Term Care, 1994-96; staff/charge nurse WHCC Riverside, Centralia, 1996—. Home: 403 2nd Ave NE Napavine WA 98565

MORGENROTH, EARL EUGENE, entrepreneur; b. Sidney, Mont., May 7, 1936; s. Frank and Leona (Ellison) M.; m. Noella Nichols, Aug. 2, 1958; children: Dolores Roxanna, David Jonathan, Denise Christine. BS, U. Mont., 1961. From salesman to gen. mgr. Sta. KGVO-AM Radio, Missoula, Mont., 1958-65; sales mgr. Stas. KGVO-TV, KTVM-TV and KCFW-TV, Missoula, Butte, Kalispell, Mont., 1965-66, gen. mgr., 1966-68; gen. mgr. Sta. KCOY-TV, Santa Maria, Calif., 1968-69; v.p., gen. mgr. Western Broadcasting Co., Missoula, 1966-69, gen. mgr., pres., 1969-81; gen. mgr., pres. numerous cos., Mont., Calif. Idaho, P.R., Ga., 1966-84; pres., chmn. Western Broadcasting Co., Missoula, 1981-84, Western Communications, Inc., Reno, 1984-90; prin. Western Investments, Reno, 1984—; chmn. Western Fin., Inc., Morgenroth Music Ctrs., Inc., Mont., Mont. Band Instruments, Inc.; chmn. E & B Music Inc., Times Square, Inc. Mem. Mont. Bank Bd., Helena; commencement spkr. U. Mont., 1988; bd. dirs. U. Mont. Found., 1985-95. With U.S. Army, 1954-57. Named Boss of Yr. Santa Maria Valley J.C.s, 1968. Mem. U. Mont. Century Club (pres.), Missoula C. of C. (pres.), Rocky Mountain Broadcasters Assn. (pres.), Craighead Wildlife-Wildlands Inst. (bd. dirs.), Boone and Crockett Club (bd. dirs., v.p. comm.), Grizzly Riders Internat. (bd. dirs., v.p.), Bldg. A Scholastic Heritage (bd. dirs.). Republican. Methodist.

MORGENSEN, JERRY LYNN, construction company executive; b. Lubbock, Tex., July 9, 1942; s. J.J. and Zelline (Butler) M.; m. Linda Dee Austin, Apr. 17, 1965; children: Angela, Nicole. BCE, Tex. Tech U., 1965. Area engr. E.I. Dupont Co., Orange, Tex., 1965-67; div. engr. E.I. Dupont Co., La Place, La., 1967-73; project mgr. Hensel Phelps Constrn. Co., Greeley, Colo., 1973-78, area mgr., 1978-80, v.p., 1980-85, pres., 1985—. Office: Hensel Phelps Constrn Co 420 Sixth Ave PO Box O Greeley CO 80632*

MORGENSTERN, LEON, surgeon; b. Pitts., July 14, 1919; s. Max Samuel and Sarah (Master) M.; m. Laurie Mattlin, Nov. 27, 1967; 1 son, David Ethan. Student, CCNY, 1936-37; B.A. magna cum laude, Bklyn. Coll., 1940; M.D., N.Y. U., 1943. Diplomate: Am. Bd. Surgery. Intern Queens Gen. Hosp., Jamaica, N.Y., 1943-44; fellow, asst. resident in pathology Queens Gen. Hosp., 1947-48, resident in surgery, 1948-52; practice medicine, specializing in surgery Los Angeles, 1953-59, 60—, Bronx, N.Y., 1959-60; dir. surgery Cedars of Lebanon Hosp., Los Angeles, 1960-73; dir. surgery Cedars-Sinai Med. Center, Los Angeles, 1973-88, emeritus dir. surgery, 1989—; dir. Bioethics Program Cedars-Sinai Med. Ctr., L.A., 1995—; emeritus prof. surgery UCLA Sch. Medicine, 1973-85, prof. in residence, 1985—; dir. bioethics program Cedars-Sinai Med. Ctr., 1995—; asst. prof. surgery Albert Einstein Coll. Medicine, N.Y.C., 1959-60; adj. prof. bioethics U. Judaism, L.A., 1996—. Assoc. editor Mount Sinai Jour. Medicine, 1984-88; contbr. articles to profl. publs. Served to capt. M.C. U.S. Army, 1944-46. Mem. Soc. for Surgery Alimentary Tract, Soc. Am. Gastrointestinal Endoscopic Surgeons (hon.), Am. Gastroent. Assn., L.A. Surg. Soc. (pres. 1977), ACS (sec.-treas. 1976-77, pres. 1978, bd. dirs. So. Calif. chpt. 1976-78, gov.-at-large), Internat. Soc. Surgery, Western Surg. Assn., Pacific Coast Surg. Assn., AMA, Calif. Med. Assn., Los Angeles County Med. Assn., Am. Surg. Assn., others. Home: 5694 Calpine Dr Malibu CA 90265-3812

MORGENSTERN, NORBERT RUBIN, civil engineering educator; b. Toronto, Ont., Can., May 25, 1935; s. Joel and Bella (Skornik) M.; m. Patricia Elizabeth Gooderham, Dec. 28, 1960; children: Sarah Alexandra, Katherine Victoria, David Michael Gooderham. BASc, U. Toronto, 1956, DEng h.c., 1983; DIC, Imperial Coll. Sci., 1964; PhD, U. London, 1964; DSc h.c., Queen's U., 1989. Research asst., lectr. civil engring. Imperial Coll. Sci. and Tech., London, 1958-68; prof. civil engring. U. Alta., Edmonton, Can., 1968-83, Univ. prof., 1983—, chair dept. civil engring., 1994—; cons. engr., 1961—. Contbr. articles to profl. jours. Bd. dirs. Young Naturalists Found., 1977-82, Edmonton Symphony Soc., 1978-85. Athlone fellow, 1956; recipient prize Brit. Geotech. Soc., 1961, 66, Huber prize ASCE, 1971, Legget award Can. Geotech. Soc., 1979, Alta. order of Excellence, 1991. Fellow Royal Soc. Can., Can. Acad. Engring.; mem. U.S. Nat. Acad. Engring. (fgn. assoc.), Royal Acad. Engring. (fgn. mem.), Canadian Geosci. Coun. (pres. 1983), Can. Geotechnical Soc. (pres. 1989-91), Internat. Soc. for Soil Mechanics and Found. Engring. (pres. 1989-94), Royal Glenora Club, Athenaeum (London), various other profl. assns. Home: 106 Laurier Dr, Edmonton, AB Canada T5R 5P6 Office: U Alta, Dept Civil Engring, Edmonton, AB Canada T6G 2G7

MORGENTHALER, ALISA MARIE, lawyer; b. St. Louis, June 3, 1960; d. Gerald Thomas and Mary Louise (Neece) M. BA, S.W. Mo. State U., 1982; JD, Cornell U., 1985. Bar: N.Y. 1986, D.C. 1988, Calif. 1990. Law clk. City of Springfield, Mo., 1981; bd. govs. FRS, Washington, 1984; staff atty. Fed. Res. System, Washington, 1985-86; assoc. Kirkpatrick & Lockhart, Washington, 1986-88, Stroock & Stroock & Lavan, Washington, 1988-89, Christensen, Miller, Fink, Jacobs, Glaser, Weil & Shapiro, L.A., 1989—. Mem. ABA, Calif. Bar Assn., D.C. Bar Assn., N.Y. Bar Assn., L.A. County Bar Assn., Beverly Hills Bar Assn., Century City Bar Assn., Women Lawyers Assn. of L.A. (bd. dirs.), 3019 Third St. Owners Assn. (bd. dirs.), Alpha Iota House Corp. (bd. dirs.), Order of Omega, Phi Alpha Delta, Rho Lambda, Phi Kappa Phi, Pi Sigma Alpha, Gamma Phi Beta. Office: Christensen Miller Et Al 2121 Ave of Stars 18th Fl Los Angeles CA 90067-5010

MORI, MARYELLEN TOMAN, language educator, translator, literature educator; b. Chgo., July 10, 1950; d. John Charles and Helen Veronica (Kelley) Toman; m. Shozo Mori, Feb. 18, 1978; 1 child, Jonathan Masami. BA in English, Yale U., 1972; student, Tokyo Sch. Japanese Lang., 1973-76; MA, Harvard U., 1978, PhD, 1988. Instr. English Kansai Lang. Group, Itō and Tokyo, Japan, 1972-76; instr. Japanese studies, modern Japanese lit. in translation Harvard U., Cambridge, Mass., 1982-83; assoc. prof. Japanese, head Japanese sect. Santa Clara (Calif.) U., 1988—. Contbr. chpt. to book The Woman's Hand: Gender and Theory in Japanese Women's Writing, 1996; contbr. articles to profl. jours.; translator (book) Kangaroo Notebook, 1996 (PEN US West Translation award, 1997), numerous short stories. Fellow Harvard U., 1976-77, Stanford U., 1978; scholar Nat. Def. Fgn. Lang., 1977-78; recipient NEH summer stipend, 1997. Mem. AAUW (Dissertation fellow 1987-88), Am. Literary Translators Assn., Assn. Asian Studies, Assn. Tchrs. Japanese, Midwest Assn. Japanese Literary Studies, The Japan Soc., MLA, So. Comparative Lit. Assn., PEN Am. Soc., Phi Sigma Iota. Democrat. Office: Santa Clara U Dept Modern Langs and Lit 500 the Alameda Santa Clara CA 95053

MORIE, G. GLEN, manufacturing company executive, corporate lawyer. BA, Bowdoin Coll., 1964; LLB, U. Pa., 1967. Bar: Wash. 1968. Pvt. practice law Wash., 1970-73; asst. counsel PACCAR, Inc., Bellevue, Wash., 1973-79, asst. gen. counsel, 1979-82, gen. counsel, 1983-85, v.p., gen. counsel, corp. sec., 1985—. Office: PACCAR Inc PO Box 1518 Bellevue WA 98009-1518*

MORIMOTO, CARL NOBORU, computer system engineer, crystallographer; b. Hiroshima, Japan, Mar. 31, 1942; came to U.S., 1957, naturalized, 1965; s. Toshiyuki and Teruko (Hirano) M.; m. Helen Kiyomi Yoshizaki, June 28, 1969; children: Matthew Ken, Justin Ray. BA, U. Hawaii, 1965; PhD, U. Wash., 1970. Research assoc. dept. chemistry Mich. State U., East Lansing, 1970-72; postdoctoral fellow dept. biochemistry and biophysics Tex. A&M U., College Station, 1972-75; sr. sci. programmer Syntex Analytical Instruments Inc., Cupertino, Calif., 1975-78; prin. programmer analyst, software engring. mgr. Control Data Corp., Sunnyvale, Calif., 1978-83; mem. profl. staff GE Aerospace, San Jose, Calif., 1983-93; prin. engr. GE Nuclear Energy, San Jose, 1993—. Mem. Am. Crystallographic Assn., Assn. Computing Machinery, Am. Chem. Soc., Sigma Xi. Am. Baptist. Home: 4003 Hamilton Park Dr San Jose CA 95130-1223

MORIN, PAULA MARIE YVETTE (MARYAN MORIN), photographer, artist, photo researcher; b. Hollywood, Calif., Feb. 4, 1945; d. Charles Eugene Robert Anthony Joseph and Mary Elsa (Hoffmann) M.; m. Robert C. McCamey, 1970 (div. 1974); children: Marc Richard McCamey, Ian Eugene McCamey. BA in Fine Art magna cum laude, So. Oreg. State Coll., Ashland, 1978; cert. secondary tchr., So. Oreg. State Coll./U. Wash., Ashland and Seattle, 1990. Photographer, oral historian Circle Sky Prodns., Talent, Oreg., 1979-81; photographer U. Mont., Missoula, 1981-82; owner, photographer Heritage Photo Works LLC, Prescott, Ariz., 1991-96, Hamilton, Mont., 1991-96; artist, photographer Paula Morin Photo Art LLC, Missoula, 1997—; field rschr. Oreg. Folk Arts, Oreg. Art Commn., Salem, 1979; mem. adj. faculty Prescott (Ariz.) Coll., 1993; founding dir. N.W. Exposure Photography Inc., Ashland, Oreg., 1979. Represented in permanent collections of Casa Grande (Ariz.) Mus., 1993 and Mt. Angel Abbey (Oreg.). Profl. devel. grantee Ariz. Commn. on Arts, Phoenix, 1993. Mem. Profl. Photographers Am., Mont. Hist. Soc. Roman Catholic. Office: Paula Morin Photo Art LLC PO Box 8222 Missoula MT 59802

MORITA, JOHN TAKAMI, artist; b. Honolulu, Apr. 10, 1943; s. Takaichi and Miyako (Shiraishi) M. BA in History, Chaminade Coll., Honolulu, 1965; BFA in Photography, San Francisco Art Inst., 1974; MA in Printmaking, San Francisco State U., 1976. Lectr. in art U. Hawaii-Manoa, Honolulu, 1982-83, Windward C.C., Kaneohe, Hawaii, 1991-92. Exhibited in one-man shows at Galerie Marina Dinkler, Berlin, 1978, San Francisco Mus. Modern Art, 1979, Contemporary Art Ctr., Honolulu, 1982, Soker/Kaseman Gallery, San Francisco, 1983, Alternative Mus., N.Y.C., 1987, Intergrafic 90, Berlin, 1990, Print Club, Phila., 1990, Honolulu Acad. Arts, 1977; group exhbns. include Intergrakif, Berlin, 1984, 87, 90, Alternative Mus., N.Y.C., 1988, 90, 91, Wakayama Internat. Print Biennial, Japan, 1989, 93, Varna (Bulgaria) Internat. Print Biennale, 1991-93; represented in collections. Bd. dirs., mem. program adv. bd. Kapiolani C.C., Honolulu, 1992-94. Served with U.S. Army, 1966-69, West Germany. Recipient 1st prize Internat. Print Triennial, Berlin, 1987, Print Club Selection award Print Club, Phila., 1988, Fellowship Merit award Hawaii State Found. Culture and Arts, 1995; NEA fellow in printmaking, 1986, other awards. Mem. Honolulu Printmaking Workshop (bd. dirs. 1992-94, v.p. 1994-95), N.W. Print Coun., Am. Print Alliance. Democrat. Home: 1640 Ahihi St Honolulu HI 96819-3773

MORITA, TOSHIYASU, technical manager; b. Tokyo, Feb. 8, 1967; s. Hiroshi and Fusako (Ishikawa) M. Grad. high sch., 1985. Programmer Origin Systems, Inc., Austin, Tex., 1987; engr. Cyclops Electronics, Boerne, 1988-90; programmer Taito R&D, Bothell, Wash., 1990; mgr. new tech. Lucas Arts Entertainment, San Rafael, Calif., 1990-93; tech. dir. Sega Tech. Inst., Redwood City, Calif., 1993-94, Sega of Am., Redwood City, 1994-96, SegaSoft, Redwood City, 1996—. Mem. IEEE Computer Soc. (affiliate), Mensa.

MORITZ, TIMOTHY BOVIE, psychiatrist; b. Portsmouth, Ohio, July 26, 1936; s. Charles Raymond and Elisabeth Bovie (Morgan) M.; m. Joyce Elizabeth Rasmussen, Oct. 13, 1962 (div. Sept. 1969); children: Elizabeth Wynne, Laura Morgan; m. Antoinette Tanasichuk, Oct. 31, 1981; children: David Michael, Stephanie Lysbeth. BA, Ohio State U., 1959; MD, Cornell U., 1963. Diplomate Am. Bd. Psychiatry and Neurology. Intern in medicine N.Y. Hosp., N.Y.C., 1963-64, resident in psychiatry, 1964-67; spl. asst. to dir. NIMH, Bethesda, Md., 1967-69; dir. Community Mental Health Ctr., Rockland County, N.Y., 1970-74, Ohio Dept. Mental Health, Columbus, Ohio, 1975-81; med. dir. psychiatry Miami Valley Hosp., Dayton, Ohio, 1981-82; med. dir. N.E. Ga. Community Mental Health Ctr., Athens, Ga., 1982-83, Charter Vista Hosp., Fayetteville, Ark., 1983-87; clin. dir. adult psychiatry Charter Hosp., Las Vegas, Nev., 1987-94; pvt. practice psychiatry Las Vegas, Nev., 1987—; prof. Wright State U., Dayton, Ohio, 1981-82; asst. prof. Cornell U., N.Y.C., 1970-73; cons. NIMH, Rockville, Md., 1973-83. Author: (chpt.) Rehabilitation Medicine and Psychiatry, 1976; mem. editorial bd. Directions in Psychiatry, 1981—. Dir. dept. mental health and mental retardation Gov.'s Cabinet, State of Ohio, Columbus, 1975-81. Recipient Svc. award Ohio Senate, 1981, Svc. Achievement award Ohio Gov., 1981. Fellow Am. Psychiat. Assn. (Disting. Svc. award 1981); mem. AMA, Nev. Assn. Psychiat. Physicians, Nev. State Med. Assn., Clark County Med. Soc., Cornell U. Med. Coll. Alumni Assn. Office: Timothy B Moritz MD 3815 S Jones Blvd # 7 Las Vegas NV 89103-2289

MORLOCK, WALTER O'MALLEY, marketing professional; b. Aurora, Ill., Mar. 22, 1965; s. David and Katherine (O'Malley) M.; m. Kirsten K. Stone, Sept. 1, 1990. Grad., N. Ctrl. Coll., 1987. Mktg. dir. Paramount Arts Ctr., Cerritos, Calif., 1989-92; mktg. dir. Cerritos (Calif.) Ctr. for Performing Arts, 1992-96, asst. dir., 1996—. Mem. Internat. Soc. Performing Arts Adminstrs., Am. Mktg. Assn., Assn. Performing Arts Presenters, Western Assn. Arts Adminstrs. Office: Cerritos Ctr Performing Art 12700 Center Court Dr S Cerritos CA 90701-4552

MORNES, AMBER J. BISHOP, consultant, computer software trainer, analyst; b. Ft. Rucker, Ala., Oct. 20, 1970; d. David Floyd and Holly Brooke (Decker) Bishop; m. David Michael Mornes, May 22, 1993. BA in Psychology, U. Colo., Boulder, 1992. Asst. dir. admissions Rocky Mountain Coll. Art and Design, Denver, 1992-94, placement and alumni svcs. coord., 1995-96; computer software instr. Knowledge Alliance, Aurora, Colo., 1996—; analyst, cons. Andersen Cons., Denver, 1997—. Vol. Colo. Art Educator Assn., 1993—. Mem. APA (student affiliate), Nat. Art Edn. Assn., Colo. Art Edn. Assn. Home: 8288 S Emerson Way Littleton CO 80122 Office: Andersen Cons 1225 17th St Ste 3200 Denver CO 80202

MOROZ, ANDREW, chemical engineer; b. Warsaw, Poland, Sept. 13, 1949; came to U.S., 1988; s. Wlodzimierz and Nina (Karmelit) M.; m. Eva Anna Paczesna, Feb. 15, 1975 (div. June 20, 1987); children: Sylvia, Anna; m. Bozena Krystyna Bekasiewicz, Nov. 21, 1987. BSChemE, Poly. Warsaw, 1973; MSChemE, Tech. U., Lodz, Poland, 1977. Prof. asst. Poly. Warsaw, 1971-73; rsch. engr., lab supr. Polski Fiat/Fiat Corp., Warsaw, 1973-83; prodn. mgr. Poltrade Fgn. Trade Co., Warsaw, 1983-87; pilot plant supr. Borzynski Rsch. Inst., Houston, 1987-90; chief chemist Appropriate Technologies II, Chula Vista, Calif., 1990-92; lab dir. Southland Labs, Inc., National City, Calif., 1992-94; prin. Andrew Moroz Consulting, San Diego, 1992-94; ABM Environ. Labs. Inc., San Diego, 1994—; cons. Polcargo, Warsaw, 1977-81; gen. dir. advisor Polski Fiat, Warsaw, 1981; vis. scientist Bayer Rsch. Ctr., Leverkusen, Germany, 1979, Fiat Rsch. Ctr., Torino, Italy, 1980. Contbr. articles to profl. jours. Pres. Solidarnośc, Warsaw, 1980-81; v.p. Auto Club SKM, Warsaw, 1976-80. Mem. Am. Chem. Soc. Democrat. Roman Catholic. Office: 1123 W Morena Blvd Ste B San Diego CA 92110

MORRELL, JUNE ELIZABETH, elementary educator; b. Yakima, Wash., June 20, 1925; d. Robert Enoch Faw and Birdie Ethel Nead; m. Lawrence Reed Morrell, June 22, 1947; 1 child, Janice Ellen. BA in Edn., Ea. Wash. U., 1969. Tchr. Twisp (Wash.) Pub. Sch., 1969-70; substitute tchr. Springdale and Loon Lake (Wash.) pub. schs., 1971-73; tchr. presch. June's Pre-sch., Springdale, Wash., 1979-81; prin., tchr. Camas Valley Christian Sch., Springdale, 1981—. Home: 4972 Bowler Rd Springdale WA 99173

MORRIN, THOMAS HARVEY, engineering research company executive; b. Woodland, Calif., Nov. 24, 1914; s. Thomas E. and Florence J. (Hill) M.; m. Frances M. Von Ahn, Feb. 1, 1941; children: Thomas H., Diane, Linda, Denise. *My wife, Frances, and I recently moved to the Gold Country Retirement Community, out of Placervill, California. We are gradually getting adjusted to the pleasant environment and prepared meals. We will look forward to visits by our four children and ten grandchildren .* BS, U. Calif., 1937; grad., U.S. Navy Grad. Sch., Annapolis, Md., 1941. Student engr. Westinghouse Electric Mfg. Co., Emeryville, Calif., 1937; elec. engr. Pacific Gas & Electric Co., 1938-41; head microwave engring. div. Raytheon Mfg. Co., Waltham, Mass., 1947-48; chmn. elec. engring. dept. Stanford Research Inst., 1948-52, dir. engring., research, 1952-60, gen. mgr. engring., 1960-64, vice pres. engring., sci., 1964-68; pres. University City Sci. Inst., Phila., 1968-69; pres., chmn. bd. Morrin Assos., Inc., Wenatchee, Wash., 1968-72. Trustee Am. Acad. Transp. Served as officer USNR, 1938-58, comdr. USN, 1945-48. Decorated Bronze Star; recipient Bank Am. award for automation of banking during 1950's, 1992. Fellow IEEE, AAAS; mem. Sci. Research Soc. Am., U.S. Naval Inst., Navy League, Marine Meml. Club (San Francisco). Home: Gold Country Retirement Cty 6081 Golden Center Ct # 115 Placerville CA 95667 *In my 82nd year I look back at the many accomplishments made in science and engineering and their contributions to business and industry as well as to many lives. However, when I look forward to the many things yet to come, I wish I were fifty years younger. In my 82nd year I feel privileged in having lived through the greatest advances made in the world: from the horse and buggy to people traveling 17,000 miles per hour in an earth orbit and sending probes throughout the solar system; from the pony express to world-wide instantaneous communications; from the one-room school to world-wide web. Although it has been a wonderful ride, as I expressed to my wife many years ago, our advances in technology have exceeded society's ability to match it with moral and cultural values. There is always such a time lag but in due time it always adjusts.*

MORRIS, BONNIE S., education director; b. Providence, Aug. 6, 1957; d. Earl and Barbara (Parness) Sharfman; m. Roger N. Morris; children: Stephanie, Erica, Rebecca. BA in History, Hebrew U., Jerusalem, 1979, BA in Edn., 1979, MEd, 1980. Dir. edn. The Solel Sch., Paradise Valley, Ariz., 1990—; conf. chair Pardes, Scottsdale, Ariz., 1995, v.p., 1996—; apptd. commn. Jewish Ed., 1997. Contbr. articles to profl. jours. Recipient Reform Jewish Educator Title award Union Am. Hebrew Congregations, 1993. Mem. Nat. Assn. Temple Educators (conf. co-chair kallah San Diego 1996, family edn. chair 1996-97, accreditation sch. chair 1997). Office: Temple Solel 6805 E McDonald Dr Paradise Valley AZ 85253

MORRIS, BRIAN, advertising executive. Pres. Dailey & Assoc., L.A., Calif. Office: 3055 Wilshire Blvd Los Angeles CA 90010*

MORRIS, BRUCE DORIAN, technical writer, literary historian, educator; b. San Francisco, July 10, 1947; s. William and Helen S. (Jorgensen) M. AA, Coll. San Mateo, Calif., 1968; BA in English and Linguistics, San Francisco State Coll., 1969; MA in English Lit., San Francisco State U., 1972; PhD, U. Denver, 1977. Grad. teaching fellow dept. English U. Denver, 1973-77; asst. instr. Pacific Crest Outward Bound Sch., Portland, Oreg., 1978; jr. tech. writer Harris-Farinon, San Carlos, Calif., 1979-82; sr. tech. writer Verilink Corp., San Jose, Calif., 1985-88, Tektronix Corp., Mountain View, Calif., 1988-90, MorComm Tech. Writing Svcs., Palo Alto, Calif., 1991—, MorComm Press, Palo Alto, Calif., 1992—; sr. tech writer Alpha Lab Telco Syss., Fremont, Calif., 1994-96. Author: Sport Climber's Guide to Skyline Boulevard, 1995; editor: Arthur Symons: Letters to Yeats, 1989. Calif. State grad. fellow. Mem. MLA, Internat. Platform Soc., Soc. for Tech. Comm., Irish-Am. Cultural Inst., Am. Alpine Club, Access Fun, Alpha Gamma Sigma. Home and Office: MorComm Press and Tech Writing Svcs 2221 Thurm Ave Belmont CA 94002-1547

MORRIS, DAVID BROWN, writer; b. N.Y.C., Aug. 11, 1942; s. Allston J. and Emily (Brown) M.; m. Ruth Cohen, May 25, 1979; 1 child, Ellen Greene. BA, Hamilton Coll., Clinton, N.Y., 1964; PhD, U. Minn., 1968. Asst. prof. U. Va., Charlottesville, 1968-72; assoc. prof. Am. U., Washington, 1972-74; prof. U. Iowa, Iowa City, 1974-82. Author: Religious Sublime, 1972 (Samla award 1973), Alexander Pope, 1984 (Gottschalk award 1984), Culture of Pain, 1991 (PEN award 1992), Earth Warrior, 1995; assoc. editor Literature and Medicine, 1992—. Home and Office: 4908 Northern Trail NW Albuquerque NM 87120-2027

MORRIS, DAVID JOHN, mining engineer, consultant, mining executive; b. Seattle, May 6, 1945; s. Jack Abraham and Alice Jean (Hanson) M.; m. Melania F. Kearney, July 28, 1978; children: Whitney Elizabeth, Benton James, Sienna Elise. BA in Math. and Physics, Whitman Coll., 1968; BS in Mining Engring., Columbia U., 1968. Registered profl. engr., Colo., Utah, Wash. Mining engr. Union Oil of Calif., Los Angeles, 1968-69; mining engr. John T. Boyd Co., Denver, 1974-76, sr. mining engr., 1976-78, v.p., mgr., 1978-87; mng. ptnr. Palmer Coaking Coal Co., Black Diamond, Wash., 1976-82, 90—; pres. Pacific Coast Coal Co., Black Diamond, Wash., 1982—, Pacific Hydropower Devel., Inc., Seattle, Wash., 1995—. Mem. Bd. Overseers Whitman Coll., Walla Walla, Wash., 1986—, vice chair, 1993-95, chmn. Rep. campaign for Whitman, Denver, 1985; coach youth athletics. Served as lt. USN, 1969-74, Vietnam. Henry Krumb scholar Columbia U., N.Y.C., 1967-68. Mem. NSPE, Soc. Mining Engrs. (admissions com. 1985-88, Howard Eavenson award com. 1984-87, Woomer award com. 1990-93, chair 1993—, Ramsay award com. 1992-95, chair 1995—), Nat. Coal Assn. (bd. dirs. 1990—, exec. com. 1993-94, 96—), Nat. Coal Coun. (appointed by Sec. of Energy 1992, 94), Nat. Mining Assn. (bd. dirs. 1995—), Seattle C. of C. (chmn. energy com. 1991-94), Western Rugby Football Union (sec. 1980), Broadmoor Golf Club, Rotary. Republican. Home: 3711 E Madison St Seattle WA 98112-3838 Office: Pacific Coast Coal Co Inc 900 4th Ave Ste 3625 Seattle WA 98164-1001

MORRIS, DEANNA RUTH, mathematics tutor; b. Shelbyville, Tenn., Nov. 21, 1943; d. Henry Franklin and Dorothy Ann (Evans) Shriver; m. Dwight Eduard Morris, June 18, 1967; children: Gregory Dwight, Melody Deanna, Holly Michelle, Gerald R. S. BA, Adams State Coll., 1964, MA in Sec. Edn., History & Math, 1965. Math. tchr. Fairbanks (Alaska) NOrth Star/Borough Schs., 1965-68, homebound tutor, 1987-93, substitute tchr., 1989-94, spl. edn. tutor for expelled students, 1993—; census worker U.S. Census Bur., Fairbanks, 1990. Election worker State of Alaska, Fairbanks, 1992—; precinct chmn. North Star Borough/City of Fairbanks. Named Homemaker of Yr., Tanana Valley Homemakers, Fairbanks, 1974, State Homemaker of Yr., Alaska Homemakers Assn., 1974; recipient Blue Ribbon Svc. award Tanana Valley State Fair Assn., Fairbanks, 1986. Mem. Order Ea. Star (sec. 1989—), Order of Amaranth (treas. 1984—), Grand Ct. Order of Amaranth (treas. 1992—), Grand Assembly Alaska (grand mother 1989-90, 93-94, Grand Cross Color 1990), Internat. Order Rainbow for Girls (adult mem., advisor). Presbyterian. Home: 206 Slater Dr Fairbanks AK 99701-3430

MORRIS, DONALD ARTHUR ADAMS, college president; b. Detroit, Aug. 31, 1934; s. Robert Park and Margaret Lymburn (Adams) M.; m. Zella

Mae Stormer, June 21, 1958; children: Dwight Joseph, Julie Adams. B.A., Wayne State U., 1961; M.P.A., U. Mich., 1966, Ph.D., 1970; LLD (hon.), Olivet Coll., 1987. Copy boy Detroit Times, 1952-55, reporter, 1955-57, edn. writer, 1957-60; adminstrv. asst. Wayne State U., Detroit, 1960-62; mng. editor news service U. Mich., 1962-64, mgr. spl. programs, 1964-68; mgr. Met. Detroit Devel. Program, 1968-71; v.p. for devel. Hobart and William Smith Colls., Geneva, N.Y., 1971-76; exec. v.p. Hobart and William Smith Colls., 1976-77; pres., prof. polit. sci. Olivet (Mich.) Coll., 1977-92; pres. emeritus Olivet Coll., Mich., 1992—, cons., 1992-93; trustee Mich. Intercollegiate Athletic Assn., 1977-92, Assn. Ind. Colls. and Univs. Mich., 1977-92, chair, 1984-85; cons. evaluator North Ctrl. Assn. Colls. and Schs., 1986-92; mem. Mich. Jud. Tenure Commn., 1991-94; mem. Newspaper Guild of Detroit, 1952-60, exec. bd., 1958-60. Contbr. articles to profl. jours. Trustee Olivet Coll., 1977-92, Mich. Coll. Found., 1977-92, exec. com., 1989-92; mem. Mich. Higher Edn. Assistance and Student Loan Authorities, 1986—, chair, 1989-94; bd. dirs. Planned Parenthood of Finger Lakes, N.Y., 1973-77, pres., 1975-77; bd. dirs., treas. Genesee Regional Family Planning Program N.Y., 1975-77; trustee Coun. Higher Edn., United Ch. of Christ, 1977-92, mem. exec. com., 1982-92, chair, 1986-88; trustee Glen Lake Cmty. Libr. Bd., 1993—, pres., 1994—; mem. Sleeping Bear Noontiders, 1993—, sec., 1995, v.p. 1996-97, pres., 1997-98, South Manitou Meml. Soc., 1980—, chair nominating com., 1997. Mem. Am. Assn. for Higher Edn., Sigma Delta Chi, Omicron Delta Kappa, Alpha Lambda Epsilon, Kappa Sigma Alpha, Gamma Iota Sigma, Alpha Mu Gamma, Phi Mu Alpha Sinfonia, Rotary (local pres. 1987-88, Paul Harris fellow). Congregationalist. Home: 8330 S Dunns Farm Rd Maple City MI 49664-8721 also: 6551 E Dorado Blvd Tucson AZ 85715-4705

MORRIS, DONALD CHARLES, real estate developer; b. Iowa City, Nov. 15, 1951; s. Lucien Ellis and Jean (Pinder) M.; m. Barbara Louise Small, Apr. 28, 1973 (div. Apr. 1980); m. Jana Susan Moyer, Aug. 28, 1982; children: Alexander Charles, Elisa Jean. Student, Cantab Coll., Toronto, Can., 1970-71; BSC, U. Guelph, Can., 1974; MSC, U. Guelph, 1975; PhD, U. B.C., Vancouver, 1978. Instr. U. B.C., Vancouver, 1975-77; pres. Morley Internat., Inc., Seattle, 1976-81; self-employed Comml. Investment Real Estate, Seattle, 1981-83; v.p., regional mgr. DKB Corp., Seattle, 1983-86; pres. Morris Devel. Svcs., Inc., Seattle, 1986—, Washington Group, Inc., Seattle, 1986—. Bd. dirs. Perservation Action, Washington, 1985-90; mem. Nat. Trust for Historic Preservation. Mem. Nat. Assn. Realtors, Wash. Assn. Realtors, Pioneer Square Assn. Seattle, Pioneer Square Property Owners Assn. Seatte, Meydenbauer Yacht Club. Office: Wash Group Morris Devel PO Box 4584 Rollingbay WA 98061-0584

MORRIS, EDWARD J(AMES), JR., insurance agent, small business owner; b. Jersey City, Jan. 9, 1936; s. Edward James Sr. and Mary Alice (Carr) M.; m. Joan M. O'Keefe, Sept. 17, 1955; children: Edward James III, Glenn D., Gary J. Student, Drakes Bus. Coll., 1953; cert. ins. broker, Vale Tech. Inst., 1962. CLU, Chartered Fin. Cons. Part-time salesperson Stanley Home Products, Jersey City, 1958-60; selector Am. Stores, South Kearny, N.J., 1957-62; owner Ed Morris State Farm Agy., Jersey City, 1962-72; owner, mgr., restauranteur E&J Morris Enterprises, Inc., New Bern, N.C., 1972-79; owner, mgr. Morris Ins. Agy., Jackson, N.J., 1979-82; spl. agt., reg. rep. Morris Fin. and Ins. Agy., Matawan, N.J., 1982-92; owner, mgr. Sunset Selections, Scottsdale, Ariz., 1992—; agt. emeritus Prudential Ins. Cos., Scottsdale, 1992—. Contbr. articles to profl. jours. Mem. com. Boy Scouts Am., Jersey City, 1966-72; basketball coach Our Lady of Mercy Ch., Jersey City, 1967-69; treas., basketball coach Coll. Little League, Jersey City, 1966-71; mcpl. chmn. Citzens for Goldwater, Jersey City, 1963-64. Sgt. USMC, 1954-57.

MORRIS, ELIZABETH TREAT, physical therapist; b. Hartford, Conn., Feb. 20, 1936; d. Charles Wells and Marion Louise (Case) Treat; BS in Phys. Therapy, U. Conn., 1960; m. David Breck Morris, July 10, 1961; children: Russell Charles, Jeffrey David. Phys. therapist Crippled Children's Clinic No. Va., Arlington, 1960-62, Shriners Hosp. Crippled Children, Salt Lake City, 1967-69, Holy Cross Hosp., Salt Lake City, 1970-74; pvt. practice phys. therapy, Salt Lake City, 1975—. Mem. nominating com. YWCA, Salt Lake City. Mem. Am. Phys. Therapy Assn., Am. Congress Rehab. Medicine, Am. Alliance for Health Phys. Edn. Recreation & Dance, Nat. Speakers Assn., Utah Speakers Assn., Salt Lake Area C. of C., Friendship Force Utah, U.S. Figure Skating Assn., Toastmasters Internat., Internat. Assn. for the Study Pain, Internat. Platform Assn., World Confederation Phys. Therapy, Medart Internat. Home: 4177 Mathews Way Salt Lake City UT 84124-4021 Office: PO Box 526186 Salt Lake City UT 84152-6186

MORRIS, HENRY MADISON, III, software manufacturing executive, minister; b. El Paso, Tex., May 15, 1942; s. Henry Madison and Mary Louise (Beach) M.; m. Janet Deckman, July 25, 1964; children: Henry M., Scotta Marie. BA summa cum laude, Christian Heritage Coll., 1976; MDiv, Luther Rice Sem., 1977, DMin, 1978; MBA Pepperdine U., 1989. Ordained to ministry Bapt. Ch., 1968. Regional mgr. Integon Ins. Co., Greenville, S.C., 1969-75; pastor Hallmark Bapt. Ch., Greenville, 1969-75; assoc. prof. Bible, Christian Heritage Coll., El Cajon, Calif., 1977-78, adminstrv. v.p., 1978-80; pastor First Bapt. Ch., Canoga Park, Calif., 1980-86; chief adminstrv. officer, CFO SunGard Fin. Systems Inc., Canoga Park, 1986-94, v.p. sales and mktg., 1994-96; adminstrv. pastor Ch. at Rocky Peak, Chatsworth, Calif., 1996—; lectr. in field; cons. World Pubs., 1995. Republican. Author: Baptism: What is It?, 1977; Explore the Word, 1978, Churches: History and Doctrine, 1980; co-author: Many Infallible Proofs, 1996; contbg. editor: The Defenders Bible, 1995. Served with U.S. Army, 1959-66. Office: The Church at Rocky Peak 22601 Santa Susana Pass Rd Chatsworth CA 91311

MORRIS, JANET ELOISE, controller, poet; b. Lincoln, Nebr., May 10, 1952; d. Robert D. and Jessie E. (Hillhouse) M.; m. John W. Tucker, Aug. 1, 1973 (div. Mar. 1, 1979); 1 child, Jon W. Tucker. Grad., So. H.S., Wymore, Nebr., 1970. Contr. Ideus Constrn. Co., Lincoln, 1976-82; acct. Coopers & Lybrand, Lincoln, 1984-94; CFO Innovative Design Techs., Burbank, Calif., 1995—. Author: (poetry poster) A New Epitaph for Pere Lachaise, 1993 (33d best seller in world 1995); contbg. author The Doors Collectors Mag., 1993-96. Office: Innovative Design Techs 3099 N Lima St Burbank CA 91504-2013

MORRIS, JOHN THEODORE, planning official; b. Denver, Jan. 18, 1929; s. Theodore Ora and Daisy Allison (McDonald) M.; BFA, Denver U., 1955; m. Dolores Irene Seaman, June 21, 1951; children: Holly Lee, Heather Ann, Heidi Jo, Douglas Fraser. Apprentice landscape architect S.R. DeBoer & Co., Denver, summer 1949, planning technician (part-time), 1954-55; sr. planner and assoc. Trafton Bean & Assocs., Boulder, Colo., 1955-62; prin. Land Planning Assocs., planning cons., Boulder, 1962-65; planning dir. and park coord. Boulder County, 1965-67; sch. planner Boulder Valley Sch. Dist., 1967-84, also dir. planning and engrng., 1967-84, supr. facility improvement program, 1969-84; pvt. sch. planning cons., 1984—; cons. U. Colo. Bur. Ednl. Field Svcs., 1974. Bd. dirs. Historic Boulder, 1974-76; mem. parks and recreation adv. com. Denver Regional Coun. Govts., 1975-84. Served with USCG, 1950-53. Mem. Am. Inst. Cert. Planners, Am. Planning Assn., Longmont Artist Guild. Home and Office: 7647 32nd St Boulder CO 80302-9327

MORRIS, RICHARD WARD, author; b. Milw., June 16, 1939; s. Alvin Harry and Dorothy Lydia (Wissmueller) M. BS, U. Nev., 1962, PhD, 1968; MS, U. N.Mex., 1964. Exec. dir. COSMEP, Inc., San Francisco, 1968-95. Author: Poetry Is a Kind of Writing, 1975, Light, 1979, The End of the World, 1980, The Fate of the Universe, 1982, Evolution and Human Nature, 1983, Dismantling the Universe, 1983, Time's Arrows, 1985, The Nature of Reality, 1987, The Edges of Science, 1990, Assyrians, 1991, (with others) The Word and Beyond, 1982, Cosmic Questions, 1993, Achilles in the Quantum Universe, 1997.

MORRIS, RUSTY LEE, architectural consulting firm executive; b. Glenwood Springs, Colo., Nov. 28, 1940; d. Raymond M. and Raylene Pearl Marie (Hendrick) Morris; m. Robert W. Sosa, Nov. 20, 1995; children: Thomas John, Michael Joseph (dec.), Michelle Renee Bentley. Student, York Christian Coll., 1974-75, U. Nebr., 1975-76, Mesa State Coll., 1992-95; BS in Orgnl. Mgmt. summa cum laude, Colo. Christian U., 1996; postgrad., Union Inst., 1996—; MS in Mgmt., Colo. Christian U., Cin., 1997. Specialist comm. security Martin-Marietta Corp., Larson AFB, 1962-63; communications security specialist classified def. project Boeing Aerospace Div., Larson AFB, Wash., 1963-64; with F.W. Sickles div. Gen. Instrument Corp., Chicopee, Mass., 1965-68; adminstr. judicial affairs J. Arthur Hickerson, Judge, Springfield, Mass., 1969-71; researcher Mont. United Indian Assn., Helena, 1970-72; adminstrv. asst. Vanderbilt U. Hosp., Nashville, 1980-82; paid bus. supr. Sears Svc. Ctr., Grand Junction, Colo., 1987-89; founder, chief exec. officer Vast Spl. Svcs., Grand Junction, 1988—; courier U.S. Census Bur., Grand Junction, 1990; spl. program coord. Colo. Dept. Parks and Recreation, Ridgway, 1990-91; acad. athletic program founder, coord. Mesa State Coll., 1992-93, math. and sci. rep., student govt., 1992—, athletic coun., 1993—, student health ctr. com., 1993—, faculty search com., 1993; founder, CEO Rolling Spokes Assn.; world cons. on archtl. contracts for structural and/or outdoor recreational facilities. Author: Abuse of Women with Disabilities, 1996. Vol. Easter Seals Soc., 1964-67, vol. instr. Adult Literacy Program, 1984-87; vol. T.V. host Muscular Dystrophy Assn. Am., 1975-94; bd. dirs. Independent Living Ctr., 1985-87, Handicap Awareness Week, 1989; trails com. Colo. State Parks and Outdoor Recreation, 1988—; condr. seminars Ams. With Disabilites Act, 1989—; cons. Bur. Reclamation, 1988—, Bur. Land Mgmt., 1989—; staff trainer Breckenridge Outdoor Recreation Ctr., 1989-90; emergency svcs. officer Colo. Civil Air Patrol, Thunder Mountain Squadron, 1989—; bd. dirs. Handicap Awareness, 1989; dir. com. Colo. State Trails Commn., 1989-90; mem. Dem. Nat. Com., 1991—; dist. com. Grand Junction Sch. Dist., 1992—; mem. Restore the Com., Avalon, 1993—; bd. dirs., presenter No. Colo. chpt. Colo. Orgn. of Victim Assistance; with victim assistance Mesa County Sheriff's Dept., 1993—. Recipient Hometown Hero award, 1993. Mem. AAUW, Internat. Platform Assn., Handicap Scholarship Assn. (bd. dirs. 1994, award 1993), Nat. Orgn. Victim Assistance (presenter 1988—), Nat. Coun. Alcoholism and Drug Abuse (vol. 1987—), Mother's Against Drunk Driver's (bd. dirs. Mesa County chpt., v.p. 1985—), Concerns of Policy Survivors, Club 20 of Western Colo. (mem. com. status), Great Outdoor Colo., Grand Junction C. of C., Grand Junction Symphony, Mus. Western Colo., Mesa State Coll. Geology Club, Toastmasters (Able Toastmaster, winner speech contests 1985-87). Home and Office: Vast Spl Svcs 612 N 15th St Grand Junction CO 81501-4422

MORRIS, STEPHEN EUGENE, surgery educator; b. Murray, Utah, May 18, 1955; s. Douglas and Marilyn Morris; m. Marie Kuhni. BA in Chemistry magna cum laude, U. Utah, 1978, MD, 1982. Diplomate Am. Bd. Surgery, Am. Bd. Surg. Critical Care. Burn fellow Shriner's Burns Inst., Galveston, Tex., 1987-89; resident in surgery U. Utah, Salt Lake City, 1982-87, asst. prof. surgery, 1989-96, assoc. prof. surggery, 1996—; assoc. dir. Intermountain Burn Ctr., Salt Lake City, 1989—; co-dir. Intermountain Tissue Ctr., Salt Lake City, 1994—. Recipient Meritorious Rsch. award AMA, 1980; Winthrop rsch. fellow Am. Assn. Surgery for Trauma, 1988. Fellow ACS; mem. Am. Burn Assn. (rehab. com. 1993-95), Assn. Acad. Surgeons, Surg. Infection Soc., Am. Assn. Tissue Banks, Southwestern Surg. Congress, Alpha Omega Alpha. Office: Univ Hosp Dept Surgery 50 N Medical Dr Rm 3b-316 Salt Lake City UT 84132-0001

MORRIS, SYLVIA MARIE, university official; b. Laurel, Miss., May 6, 1952; d. Earlene Virginia (Cameron) Hopkins Stewart; m. James D. Morris, Jan. 29, 1972; children: Cedric James, Taedra Janae. Student, U. Utah, 1970-71. From adminstrv. sec. to adminstrv. mgr. mech. engrng. U. Utah, Salt Lake City, 1972—. Mem. Community Devel. Adv. Bd., Salt Lake City, Utah, 1984—; nom. chmn. and del. to Dem. Mass Meeting, 1988. Recipient Presdl. Staff award, 1994. Mem. NAACP, NAFE, Consortium Utah Women in Higher Edn. Baptist. Home: 9696 Pinebrook Dr South Jordan UT 84095 Office: U Utah 2202 MEB Mech Engr Dept Salt Lake City UT 84112

MORRISON, CRAIG SOMERVILLE, physical education educator; b. Montreal, Que., Can., Sept. 14, 1946; came to U.S., 1982; s. Samuel and Olive Somerville (Cameron) M. BPE, U. N.B., 1970; MS, Springfield Coll., 1976; EdD, Brigham Young U., 1982. Tchr., high sch. Dept. Edn. Geelong, Victoria, Australia, 1971-72, Ea. Twps. Regional Sch. Bd., Que., Can., 1972-73, Gladstone, Queensland Dept. Edn., 1974; lectr. Charles Stuart U., 1974-79; grad. teaching asst. Brigham Young U., Provo, Utah, 1980-82; temporary asst. prof. U. Louisville, 1982-84; tchr., physical edn. Laurel Sch., Cleve., 1985-86; asst. prof. U. Tex., Div. Edn., San Antonio, 1987-89, Okla. State U., Stillwater, So. Utah U.; acting coord. phys. edn. U. Tex., 1988-89; lectr. Ballarat Coll. Advanced Edn., Ballant Victoria, Australia, 1986-87, U. Wyo., Laramie, 1984-85, vis. lectr. U. Victoria, B.C., 1979-80; coord. sports medicine symposium Utah Summer Games, 1991-93. Mem. edit. rev. bd. The Physical Educator, 1992-95; (textbook) Qualities Analysis of Human Movement; contbr. articles to profl. jours. Mem. AAHPERD, Utah AHPERD, Nat. Assn. Phys. Edn. in Higher Edn., Triathlon Fedn. USA, Can. AHPERD, Tex. AHPERD, Phi Kappa Phi. Office: So Utah U Dept Phys Edn Cedar City UT 84720

MORRISON, GUS (ANGUS HUGH MORRISON), mayor, engineer; b. Buffalo, Sept. 13, 1935; s. John Weir and Mary (Norton) M.; m. Joy Rita Hallenbarter, Feb. 7, 1959; children: Frank, Gloria, Heather. Technician Bell Aircraft Corp., Niagara Falls, N.Y., 1956-58; technician Lockheed Missiles and Space Corp., Sunnyvale, Calif., 1958-63, test. engr., 1963-78, group engr., 1978-86, dept. mgr., 1986—. Mayor Fremont, Calif., 1985—, council mem., 1978-85, planning commr., 1977-78; bd. dirs. Tri City Ecology Ctr., 1976—. Served with USN, 1953-56. Democrat. Roman Catholic. Office: Office of Mayor PO Box 5006 Fremont CA 94537*

MORRISON, JAMES IAN, research institute executive; b. Irvine, Scotland, Dec. 22, 1952; came to U.S., 1985; s. James Morrison and Janet Miller (McCondach) Munro; m. Nora Cadham, Dec. 6, 1980; children: David, Caitlin. BPhil, U. Newcastle-upon-Tyne, Eng., 1976; MA, U. Edinburgh, Scotland, 1974; PhD, U. B.C., Can., 1985. Isntr. B.C. Inst. Tech., Vancouver, 1980-85; rsch. assoc. U. B.C., Vancouver, 1980-85; rsch. fellow Inst. for the Future, Menlo Park, Calif., 1985-86, dir. health care rsch. program, 1986-91, pres., 1990-96, sr. fellow, 1996—; chmn. Health Futures Forum Andersen Consulting; bd. dirs. Interim Svcs., Ft. Lauderdale, Fla.; mem. corp. adv. bd. Bristol-Myers Squibb, Princeton, N.J., 1992—; mem. UNIS Press Adv. Bd., 1990—. Co-author: Looking Ahead at American Health Care, 1988, Directing the Clinical Laboratory, 1990, System in Crisis: The Case for Health Care Reform, 1991, Reforming the System: Containing Health Care Costs in an Era of Universal Coverage, 1992, Future Tense: The Business Realities of the Next Ten Years, 1994, The Second Curve: Managing the Velocity of Change, 1996; contbr. articles to profl. jours. Mem. environ. scanning com. United Way of Am., 1990-92. Social Sci. Rsch. Coun. scholar U. Newcastle-upon-Tyne, 1974-76. Address: 1635 Bay Laurel Dr Menlo Park CA 94025

MORRISON, JOHN CARL, ophthalmologist, educator; b. Portland, Oreg., July 13, 1951; s. Carl Vincent and Dorothy Grace (Nafus) M.; m. Lynne Lorraine Hubbell, Aug. 24, 1974; children: Steven, Elizabeth. BA, U. Oreg., 1973; MD, U. Oreg., Portland, 1977. Diplomate Am. Bd. Ophthalmology, Nat. Bd. Med. Examiners. Intern U. Calif. Davis Med. Ctr., Sacramento, 1977-78; emergency rm. physician St. Vincent Hosp., Portland, Oreg., 1978-80; resident in ophthalmology Oreg. Health Scis. U., Portland, 1982-85, preresidency fellow, 1980-82, fellow in glaucoma, 1985-86; fellow in glaucoma Johns Hopkins Med. Ctr., Balt., 1986-88; asst. prof. ophthalmology Oreg. Health Scis. U., 1988-93, assoc. prof., 1993—. Contbr. chpts. to books, articles to Am. Jour. Ophthalmology, Ophthal. Surgery, Current Opinion in Ophthalmology, others; patentee microneedle for injecting ocular vessels. Recipient Miriam and Benedict Wolfe award Rsch. to Prevent Blindness, 1991; NIH grantee, 1991, 93. Mem. Am. Acad. Ophthalmology (honor award 1994), Assn. for Rsch. in Vision and Ophthalmology, Oreg. Acad. Ophthalmology, Am. Glaucoma Soc., West Coast Glaucoma Soc., Friedenwald Glaucoma Soc. (charter mem.), Phi Beta Kappa, Alpha Omega Alpha. Office: Casey Eye Int 3375 SW Terwilliger Blvd Portland OR 97201-4146

MORRISON, JOY SOUTH, journalist; b. Montpelier, Idaho, June 3; d. Edward Marshall and Ruth Eldora (Heath) South; m. Thomas Lamar Morrison, Mar. 25, 1950; 1 child, Michele Ann Morrison Heuser. BA in Journalism, U. Wis., 1946; postgrad., U. Utah, 1951, U. Mo., 1983. Office mgr. Uncle Ray's Mag., Cleve., 1947; journalism tchr. East High Sch., Salt Lake City, 1952--53; copywriter KWIK Radio, Pocatello, 1952-55; Life and Times editor Idaho State Jour., Pocatello, feature, food and religion editor, 1955—. Chmn. publicity com. Am. Heart Assn., Bannock, Idaho, Pocatello High Sch. Found.; bd. dirs. March of Dimes; mem. Smile Fest Com. Recipient numerous state and nat. awards including Penney-Mo. award, 1987, 88, 1st place family living pages award AP, 1983-90, Athena award, Cmty. Svc. award Gate City Rotary, Paul Harris award Pocatello Rotary, Disting. Svc. award Soroptimist, Svc. award Alpha Omicron Pi Alumnae. Mem. Idaho Press Women, Idaho State U. Alumni Assn. (Friend of Idaho State U. award, Bartz Svc. award), Phi Kappa Phi. Home: 1015 E Elm St Pocatello ID 83201-3953 Office: Idaho State Jour 305 S Arthur Ave Pocatello ID 83204-3306

MORRISON, MARCY, state legislator; b. Watertown, N.Y., Aug. 9, 1935; m. Howard Morrison; children: Liane, Brenda. BA, Queens Coll., 1957; student, Colo. Coll., U. Colo. Mem. Colo. Ho. of Reps., 1992—, mem. judiciary, health, environ., welfare and instns. coms. Mem. Manitou Springs (Colo.) Sch. Bd., 1973-83, pres., 1980-82, County Park Bd., 1976-83, State Bd. Health, 1985-93, pres., 1988-90, Mountain Scar Commn., 1989, Future Pub. Health, 1989-90, Health Policy Commn., 1990-92; commr. El Paso County, 1985-92, chmn., 1987-89; active Citizens Goals, United Way. Named Outstanding Sch. Bd. Mem., Pikes Peak Tchrs. Assn., 1978, Woman of Spirit, Penrose-St. Francis Hosp. Sys., 1991. Mem. LWV, Health Assn. Pikes Peake Area, Women's Edn. Assn., El Paso Mental Health Assn. Republican. Jewish. Home: 302 Sutherland Pl Manitou Springs CO 80829-2722 Office: Colo Ho of Reps State Capitol Denver CO 80203*

MORRISON, MICHELLE WILLIAMS, nursing educator, administrator, author; b. Reno, Feb. 12, 1947; d. Robert James and Dolores Jane (Barnard) Williams; m. Harrison Russell Morrison, Dec. 29, 1974. BSN, U. Nev., Reno, 1973; M Health Svc., U. Calif., Davis, 1977. RN, Oreg. Staff nurse VA Hosp., Reno, 1973-77; family nurse practitioner Tri-County Indian Health Svc., Bishop, Calif., 1977-78; instr. nursing Roque C.C., Grants Pass, Oreg., 1978-82; psychiat. nurse VA Hosp., Roseburg, Oreg., 1982; dir. edn. Josephine Meml. Hosp., Grants Pass, 1983-84; geriat. nurse practitioner Hearthstone Manor, Medford, Oreg., 1984-86; chmn. nursing dept. Roque C.C., Grants Pass, Oreg., 1986-89, instr. social scis., 1997—; prin. Health and Ednl. Cons. Inc., Grants Pass, 1989—; DON Highland House Nursing Ctr., Grants Pass, 1990; bd. dirs. Tri-County Indian Health Svc.; cons. for nursing svcs. in long-term care facilities. Author: Professional Skills for Leadership, Foundations of Mental Health Nursing, 1997; contbr.; Fundamental Nursing: Concepts and Skills. Mem. Josephine County Coalition for AIDS, Grants Pass, 1990. With USN, 1965-69. Mem. NAFE, Nat. League Nursing, Oreg. Ednl. Assn., Oreg. State Bd. Nursing (mem. re-entry nursing com. 1992-93). Office: PO Box 89 Williams OR 97544-0089

MORRISON, MURDO DONALD, architect; b. Detroit, Feb. 21, 1919; s. Alexander and Johanna (Macaulay) M.; BArch, Lawrence Inst. Tech., 1943; m. Judy D. Morrison; children from previous marriage—Paula L., Reed A., Anne H. Individual practice architecture, Detroit, 1949, Klamath Falls, Oreg., 1949-65, Oakland, Calif., 1965-78; ptnr. Morrison Assocs., San Francisco, 1978-85, Burlingame, Calif., 1985-89, Redwood City, Calif., 1989—; v.p. Lakeridge Corp., 1968—; chmn. Oreg. Bd. Archtl. Examiners, 1961-65, chmn., 1964. Mem. Town Council Klamath Falls, 1955-57; co-chmn. Oakland Pride Com., 1968-77; mem. Redwood City Gen. Plan Com., 1986, Redwood City Design REv. Com., 1991—, Emerald Hills Design Rev. Bd., 1990—. Served with USN, 1943-46. Recipient Progressive Architecture award, 1955, Alumni of Yr. award Lawrence Inst., 1965. Mem. AIA (treas. East Bay, chmn. Oakland chpt.). Presbyterian. Architect: Gilliam County Courthouse (Progressive Architecture design award), 1955, Chiloquin (Oreg.) Elem. Sch., 1963, Lakeridge Office Bldg., Reno, 1984, Provident Cen. Credit Union Bldg., Monterey, Calif., 1986, Embarcadero Fed. Credit Union, San Francisco, 1991, Warrick Residence, The Sea Ranch, Calif., 1996, Spectre Industries Office Bldg., Milpitas, Calif., 1997, others. Home and Office: 3645 Jefferson Ave Redwood City CA 94062-3137 *Personal philosophy: Life presents many challenges--and I enjoy them all!.*

MORRISON, ROBERT LEE, physical scientist; b. Omaha, Nov. 22, 1932; s. Robert Alton and Lulu Irene (Ross) M.; m. Sharon Faith Galliher, Feb. 19, 1966; children: Dennis, Karyn, Cheryl, Tamara, Traci. BA, U. Pacific, Stockton, Calif., 1957, MS, 1960. Chief chemist Gallo Winery, Modesto, Calif., 1957-66; rsch. scientist Lawrence Livermore Nat. Lab., Livermore, Calif., 1966-69, sr. rsch. scientist, 1973-93; pres. Poolinator, Inc., Gardena, Calif., 1970-72; owner R.L. Morrison Techs., Modesto, 1993—; cons., speaker, presenter in field. Contbr. numerous articles to profl. jours.; patentee in field. Recipinet Excellence in Nuclear Weapons award U.S. Dept. Energy, 1990, others. Mem. Am. Chem. Soc. Home: 1117 Springcreek Dr Modesto CA 95355-4820

MORRISON, ROGER BARRON, geologist; b. Madison, Wis., Mar. 26, 1914; s. Frank Barron and Elsie Rhea (Bullard) M.; BA, Cornell U., 1933, MS, 1934; postgrad. U. Calif., Berkeley, 1934-35, Stanford U., 1935-38; PhD, U. Nev., 1964; m. Harriet Louise Williams, Apr. 7, 1941 (deceased Feb. 1991); children: John Christopher, Peter Hallock and Craig Brewster (twins). Registered profl. geologist, Wyo. Geologist U.S. Geol. Survey, 1939-76; vis. adj. prof. dept. geoscis. U. Ariz., 1976-81, Mackay Sch. Mines, U. Nev., Reno, 1984-86; cons. geologist; pres. Morrison and Assocs., Ltd., 1978—; prin. investigator 2 Landsat-1 and 2 Skylab earth resources investigation projects NASA, 1972-75. Fellow Geol. Soc. Am.; mem. AAAS, Internat. Union Quaternary Rsch. (mem. Holocene and paleopedology commns., chmn. work group on pedostratigraphy), Am. Soc. Photogrammetry, Am. Soc. Agronomy, Soil Sci. Soc. Am., Internat. Soil Sci. Soc., Am. Quaternary Assn., Am. Water Resources Assn., Colo. Sci. Soc., Sigma Xi. Author 3 books, co-author one book, co-editor 2 books; editor: Quaternary Nonglacial Geology, Conterminous U.S., Geol. Soc. Am. Centennial Series, vol. K-2, 1991; mem. editorial bd. Catena, 1973-88; contbr. over 150 articles to profl. jours. Research includes Quaternary geology and geomorphology, hydrogeology, environ. geology, neotectonics, remote sensing of Earth resources, paleoclimatology, pedostratigraphy. Office: 13150 W 9th Ave Golden CO 80401-4201

MORRISON, SAMUEL FERRIS, secondary school educator; b. Glasgow, Scotland, Oct. 7, 1941; came to U.S., 1949; s. Thomas Green and Susan (McCaskill) M.; m. Kathryn Emily Schnaible, Aug. 14, 1971; 1 child, Ian James. BA, U. Wyo., 1968, MEd, 1985. Tchr. social studies Platte County Sch. Dist. 1, Wheatland, Wyo., 1968—, athletic dir., 1987—. With U.S. Army, 1963-65. Mem. NEA, Wyo. Edn. Assn., Platte County Edn. Assn. (pres. 1972-73). Democrat. Presbyterian. Home: 200 Front Rd Wheatland WY 82201-9158 Office: Wheatland Jr High Sch 13 And S Oak St Wheatland WY 82201

MORRISON, WILLIAM FOSDICK, business educator, retired electrical company executive; b. Bridgeport, Conn., Mar. 14, 1935; s. Robert Louis and Helen Fosdick (Mulroney) M.; m. E. Drake Miller, Dec. 14, 1957 (div. Sept. 1972); children: Donna Drake, Deanne Fosdick, William Fosdick; m. Carol Ann Stover, Nov. 20, 1972. BA in Econs., Trinity Coll., 1957. Mgr. purchasing dept. Westinghouse Electric Co., Lima, Ohio, 1960-68; mgr. mfg. Westinghouse Electric Co., Upper Sandusky, Ohio, 1969; gen. mgr. Westinghouse Electric Co., Gurabo, P.R., 1970-71; mgr. tng. Westinghouse Electric Co., Pitts., 1972-84; program mgr. Westinghouse Electric Co., Sunnyvale, Calif., 1984-89, procurement project dir., 1990-94; prof. San Jose State U., Calif., 1993—, Golden Gate U., San Francisco, 1995—; procurement cons., lead negotiator Advanced Micro Devices, Santa Clara, Calif., 1995—; prof. U. Calif., Berkeley, 1996—; negotiation cons. and trainer, 1969—. Author: The Pre-Negotiation Planning Book, 1985, The Human Side of Negotiations, 1994; contbr. articles to profl. jours. Bd. dirs. Valley Inst. of the Theatre Arts, Saratoga, Calif., 1986-90, Manhattan Playhouse, 1989-94; chmn. Sensory Access Found. Golf Tournament, 1995-96. Served to capt. USAFR, 1958-64. Named Man of the Yr. Midwest Lacrosse Coaches Assn., 1983, recipient Service award U.S. Lacrosse Assn., 1982. Mem. Nat. Assn. Purchasing Mgmt. (pres. Lima chpt. 1966-67, dir. nat. affairs 1967-68, dist. treas. 1968-70). Club: Sunnyvale Golf Assn. (vice-chmn. 1985, chmn. 1986, 93, handicap scorer 1992-93). Lodge: Elks. Home: 3902 Duncan Pl Palo Alto CA 94306-4550 Office: San Jose State U Coll of Bus 1 Washington Sq San Jose CA 95112-3613

MORRISSEY, JOHN CARROLL, lawyer; b. N.Y.C., Sept. 2, 1914; s. Edward Joseph and Estelle (Caine) M.; m. Eileen Colligan, Oct. 14, 1950; children: Jonathan Edward, Ellen (Mrs. James A. Jenkins), Katherine, John, Patricia, Richard, Brian, Peter. BA magna cum laude, Yale U., 1937, LLB, 1940; JSD, N.Y. U., 1951; grad., Command and Gen. Staff Sch., 1944. Bar: N.Y. State 1940, D.C. 1953, Calif. 1954, U.S. Supreme Ct. 1944. Asso. firm Dorsey and Adams, 1940-41, Dorsey, Adams and Walker, 1946-50; counsel Office of Sec. of Def., Dept. Def., Washington, 1950-52; acting gen. counsel def. Electric Power Adminstrn., 1952-53; atty. Pacific Gas and Electric Co., San Francisco, 1953-70; assoc. gen. counsel Pacific Gas and Electric Co., 1970-74, v.p., gen. counsel, 1975-80; individual practice law San Francisco, 1980—; dir. Gas Lines, Inc. Bd. dirs. Legal Aid Soc., San Francisco; chmn. Golden Gate dist. Boy Scouts Am., 1973-75; commr. Human Rights Commn. of San Francisco, 1976-89, chmn., 1980-82; chmn. Cath. Social Svc. of San Francisco, 1966-68; adv. com. Archdiocesean Legal Affairs, 1981—; regent Archdiocesan Sch. of Theology, St. Patrick's Sem., 1994; dir. Presidio Preservation Assn., 1995—. Served to col. F.A. U.S. Army, 1941-46. Decorated Bronze star, Army Commendation medal. Mem. NAS, AAAS, ABA, Calif. State Bar Assn., Fed. Power Bar Assn., N.Y. Acad. Scis., Calif. Conf. Pub. Utility Counsel, Pacific Coast Electric Assn., Pacific Coast Gas Assn., Econ. Round Table of San Francisco, World Affairs Council, San Francisco C. of C., Calif. State C. of C., Harold Brunn Soc. Med. Rsch., Electric Club, Serra Club, Commonwealth Club, Yale Club of San Francisco (pres. 1989-90), Pacific-Union Club, Sometimes Tuesday Club, Sovereign Mil. Order Malta, Phi Beta Kappa. Roman Catholic. Home: 2030 Jackson St San Francisco CA 94109-2840 Office: PO Box 77000 123 Mission St Rm 1709 San Francisco CA 94177

MORROW, BRUCE WILLIAM, educational administrator, business executive, consultant; b. Rochester, Minn., May 20, 1946; s. J. Robert and Frances P. Morrow; m. Jenny Lea Morrow. BA, U. Notre Dame, 1968, MBA with honors in Mgmt., 1974, MA in Comparative Lit., 1975; grad. U.S. Army Command and Gen. Staff Coll., 1979. Co-mg. Wendy's Old Fashioned Hamburgers, South Bend Ind., 1976-77; adminstrn. mgr. Eastern States Devel. Corp., Richmond, Va., 1977; v.p. JDB Assos., Inc., Alexandria, Va., 1976-78; owner Aardvark Prodns., Alexandria, Va., 1980-82; sr. cons. Data Base Mgmt., Inc., Springfield, Va., 1979-80; sys. analyst/staff officer Hdqrs., Dept. Army, Washington, 1980-84; chmn. bd. Commonwealth Dominion Corp., Sierra Vista, Ariz., 1982—; co-founder Southwest Bus. Group, Tucson, 1995—; pres. Sierra Vista Golf, Inc., Ariz., 1994-95; dir. continuing edn. Southside Va. C.C., Alberta, Va., 1989-91; Cochise County team leader Ariz. Coun. Econ. Conversion, 1994-95; mem. com. Ariz. Small Bus. Initiative, 1994—. Author: (radio series) Survival in the Computer Jungle, 1986; (classroom text) Introduction to Computers, 1988, Defense Conversion Handbook, 1995, Business Assessment Manual, 1996, Employee Manual Guide, 1996, Business Plan Guide, 1996, Marketing Plan Guide, 1996; contbg. columnist Notre Dame mag., 1974-86; composer songs. Active Boy Scouts Am., 1960-69; chmn. elem. German, U. Notre Dame, 1973-75; mem. Roanoke Wildwood Vol. Fire Dept., 1991-93. Lt. col. USAR, ret. Decorated Bronze Star, Army Commendation medals, Army Achievement medal, Meritorious Svc. medals, Parachutist's badge. Mem. VFW (life), Nat. Eagle Scout Assn., Lake Gaston C. of C. (bd. dirs.), Am. Legion, Sierra Vista Area C. of C., Lions (v.p. local club), Beta Gamma Sigma, Delta Phi Alpha. Clubs: Friends Internat. (Am. v.p. 1969-71, Boeblingen, Germany), Order of DeMolay. Office: Commonwealth Dominion Corp 2160 E Fry Blvd Ste 400 Sierra Vista AZ 85635-2736

MORROW, MARK JAY, neurologist, educator; b. Methuen, Mass., May 13, 1959; s. Hugh III and Marlen Patricia (McAuliffe), M ; m. Valerie Minna Dessau, Apr. 19, 1986; children: Keith Michael, Kendra Margaret. BA, Boston U., 1982, MD, 1982. Intern internal medicine U. So. Calif. L.A. (Calif.) County Med. Ctr., 1982-83; resident neurology UCLA Med. Ctr., L.A., 1983-85, chief resident neurology, 1985-86; clin. and rsch. fellow neuro-ophthalmology The Toronto (Ont.) Hosp., 1986-89; acting chief dept. neurology Olive View/UCLA Med. Ctr., Sylmar, 1989-90, chief dept. neurology, 1990—; asst. prof. UCLA Sch. Medicine, 1989-96, assoc. prof., 1996—; cons. physician UCLA Med. Ctr., L.A., 1989—, Sepulveda (Calif.) VA Med. Ctr., 1989—. Contbr. to various med. texts and articles to profl. jours. Recipient Nat. Rsch. Svc. award NIH/Nat. Eye Inst., Bethesda, 1987-89, F.I.R.S.T. award NIH/Nat. Eye Inst., 1994—. Fellow Am. Acad. Neurology (chair sect. neuro-ophthalmology and neuro-oncology 1995—); mem. Soc. for Neurosci., Assn. for Rsch. in Vision and Ophthalmology, N.Am. Neuro-Ophthalmology Soc., Olive View Profl. Staff Assn. (pres. 1994-96), Frank B. Walsh Soc., Olive View UCLA Edn. and Rsch. Inst. (pres.-elect 1996—). Office: Olive View/UCLA Med Ctr Dept Neurology 14445 Olive View Dr Sylmar CA 91342-1438

MORROW, SHARON R., financial advisor; b. Mechanicsburg, Pa., Oct. 2, 1963; d. Samuel David Morrow and Jeanette Elizabeth (Sgrignoli) Boisvert; m. Christopher Oscar Pumarejo, Sept. 7, 1985 (div. feb. 1988); m. Kevin David Guertin, Aug. 25, 1990. AA, Harrisburg Area (Pa.) C.C., 1983; BBA, Pa. State U., Middletown, 1985. Pers. fin. advisor Am. Express Fin. Advisors, Walnut Creek, Calif., 1991—. Mentor, Fulfillment Fund, L.A., 1989-94; counselor vol. Navy and Marine Corps Relief Soc., Concord, Calif., 1996—. Lt. USN, 1985-91, USRN, 1991—. Mem. NAFE (bd. dirs. 1996—), NOW, Women's Referral Svc. (bd. dirs., treas.), Bus. and Profl. Women. Democrat. Roman Catholic. Office: American Express Financial Advisors Ste 200 1333 N California Blvd Walnut Creek CA 94596

MORROW, WINSTON VAUGHAN, financial executive; b. Grand Rapids, Mich., Mar. 22, 1924; s. Winston V. and Selma (von Egloffstein) M.; m. Margaret Ellen Staples, June 25, 1948 (div.); children: Thomas Christopher, Mark Staples; m. Edith Burrows Ulrich, Mar. 2, 1990. AB cum laude, Williams Coll., 1947; JD, Harvard U., 1950. Bar: R.I. 1950. Assoc. atty. Edwards & Angell, Providence, 1950-57; exec. v.p., asst. treas., gen. counsel, bd. dirs. Avis, Inc. and subs., 1957-61; v.p., gen. mgr. Rent A Car div. Avis, Inc., 1962-64, pres., bd. dirs., 1964-75; chmn., chief exec. officer, bd. dirs. Avis, Inc. and Avis Rent A Car System, Inc., 1965-77; chmn., pres., bd. dirs. Teleflorists Inc. and subs., 1978-80; pres. Westwood Equities Corp., L.A., 1981-95, CEO, 1984-95, also bd. dirs.; chmn., pres., chief exec. officer Ticor Title Ins. Co., 1982-91, also bd. dirs.; chmn. TRTS Data Svcs. Inc., 1985-91; bd. dirs. AECOM Tech. Corp., L.A., 1990—; dir. William & Scott, Inc., 1994-96; mem. Pres.'s Industry and Govt. Spl. Travel Task Force, 1968, travel adv. bd. U.S. Travel Svcs., 1966-76, L.A. City-wide Airport Adv. Com., 1983-85; co-chmn. L.A. Transp. Coalition, 1985-91. Mem. juvenile delinquency task force Nat. Coun. Crime and Delinquency, 1985-86, L.A. Mayor's Bus. Coun., 1983-86, Housing Roundtable, Washington, 1983-85; chmn., pres. Spring St. Found., 1991—; bd. dirs. Police Found., Washington, 1983-91; trustee Com. for Econ. Devel., Washington, 1987-91. Decorated Stella Della Solidarieta Italy, Gold Tourism medal Austria). Mem. Fed. Bar Assn., R.I. Bar Assn., Car and Truck Rental Leasing Assn. (nat. pres. 1961-63), Am. Land Title Assn. (bd. govs. 1989-90), L.A. Area C. of C. (bd. dirs. 1983-90), Williams Club, L.A. Tennis Club, Phi Beta Kappa, Kappa Alpha. Home: 4056 Farmouth Dr Los Angeles CA 90027-1314 also: Meadowview Farm Cushing Corners Rd Freedom NH 03836-0221

MORRY, G. RICHARD, lawyer; b. Seattle, Mar. 2, 1943. BA cum laude, U. Wash., 1965, JD with honors, 1970. Bar: Wash. 1971, Hawaii 1973, U.S. Ct. Appeals (9th cir.) 1973, U.S. Supreme Ct. 1974. Ptnr. Rush Moore Craven Sutton Morry & Beh, Honolulu; pres. Hawaii Inst. for CLE, 1996. Exec. editor Wash. Law Rev., 1969-70; bd. editors Hawaii Bar Jour., 1975-97. Mem. ABA, Wash. State Bar Assn., Hawaii State Bar Assn., Am. Judicature Soc., Maritime Law Assn. of U.S. Address: Rush Moore Craven Sutton Morry & Beh 20th Fl Hawaii Tower Amfac Ctr 745 Fort Street Mall Honolulu HI 96813-3823

MORSBERGER, ROBERT EUSTIS, English language educator; b. Balt., Sept. 10, 1929; s. Eustis Espey and Mary Virginia (Burgess) M.; m. Katharine Miller, June 17, 1955; 1 child, Grace Anne. BA, Johns Hopkins U., 1950; MA, U. Iowa, 1954, PhD, 1956. Instr., asst. prof. Miami U., Oxford, Ohio, 1956-59; asst. prof. English Utah State U., Logan, 1959-61; asst. prof., assoc. prof. Mich. State U., East Lansing, 1961-68; assoc. prof., dept. head U. Nigeria, Nsukka, 1964-66; prof. English Eastern Ky. U., Richmond, 1968-69; assoc. prof., prof. English, dept. head Calif. State Polytech U., Pomona, 1969—. Author: James Thurber, 1964, (with wife) Lew Wallace: Militant Romantic, 1980; editor: Steinbeck, ZAPATA, 1993; co-editor: American Screenwriters, 1984, vol. 2, 1986; contbr. articles, books and short stories. Chmn. bd. dirs. Claremont (Calif.) Playhouse, 1978-81; bd. dirs. CAMASU, Claremont, 1992—. Mem. Modern Lang. Assn., Internat. John Steinbeck Soc. (edit. bd. 1970—, Burkhardt award Outstanding Contbn. 1991), Am. Assn. 18th Century Studies. Democrat. Home: 1530 Berea Ct Claremont CA 91711-3505 Office: Calif State Polytech U 3801 W Temple Ave Pomona CA 91768-2557

MORSE, CHRISTIENNE, counselor; b. South Bend, Ind., Dec. 27, 1959; d. John Philip and Cheryl Margaret (Cone) Morse. BA in Linguistics & French, U. Calif., Irvine, 1981; MA, John F. Kennedy U., 1991. Office mgr. Rotech, Berkeley, Calif., 1986-88; adminstr., property mgr. Loc-n-Stor Svcs., Berkeley, Calif., 1988-92; counselor San Leandro (Calif.) Cmty. Ctr., 1991-92, Mercy Adolscent Care Unit, Nampa, Idaho, 1992-93, Starting Point Svcs., Nampa, 1992-94, Boise (Idaho) State U., 1993—; instr. Knowledge Alliance, San Francisco, 1996; high sch. counselor Meridian Acad., 1996—. Mem. Am. Counseling Assn., Am. Mental Health Counselors Assn., Idaho Counseling Assn. (membership chair 1996—), Idaho Mental Health Counselors Assn. (pres. 1995-96), Calif. Assn. Marriage & Family Therapists. Office: Boise State U Counseling Ctr 1910 University Dr Boise ID 83725-0001

MORSE, FLO, writer; b. June 21, 1921; m. Joseph Morse, Oct. 1, 1943; children: Joel N., Jonathan. BA, Barnard Coll., 1943. Author: Yankee Communes: Another American Way, 1971, How Does It Feel to Be a Tree?, 1976, The Shakers and the World's People, 1980, rev. edit., 1987, The Story of the Shakers, 1986; contbr. poetry to various books, jours, mags., articles to newspapers. Trustee Friends of the Shakers, New Gloucester, Maine, 1976—; corporator United Soc. of Shakers, New Gloucester.

MORSE, HELVISE GLESSNER, physical and life sciences educator; b. Frederick, Md., Sept. 17, 1925; d. George Edward and Rosa May (Durphy) Glessner; m. Melvin Laurance Morse, Jan. 25, 1949; children: Margaret Louise, Laurance Clinton. BA, Hood Coll., 1946; MS, U. Ky., 1949, U. Colo., Denver, 1963; PhD, U. Colo., Denver, 1966. Supr. cytogenetics lab. Children's Hosp., Denver, 1978-79; postdoctoral fellow U. Colo. Med. Ctr., Denver, 1966-67, rsch. assoc., 1968-73, rsch. cytogeneticist, 1974-78, asst. prof. biochemistry, biophysics and genetics, 1979-88, assoc. prof., 1988—; dir. Core cytogenetics lab. U. Colo. Cancer Ctr., Denver, 1988—; Eleanor Roosevelt Inst. Cancer Rsch. fellow U. Colo., Denver, 1979—; mem. cytogenetics subcom. Nat. Children's Cancer Study Group, U.S.A. and Can., 1980-87. Contbr. articles on gene mapping, cytogenetics and Leukemia research to profl. publs., 1970—. Active So. Poverty Law Ctr. Mem. NAACP, Mortar Bd., Sigma Xi. Democrat. Home: 254 S Jasmine St Denver CO 80224-1033 Office: Univ Colo Health Scis Ctr Dept Biochem/Biophys/Genet 4200 E 9th Ave Denver CO 80220-3706

MORSE, JACK CRAIG, lawyer; b. Evanston, Ill., Aug. 11, 1936; s. Leland Robert and Pauline (Pettibone) M.; children by past marriage: David Leland, Katherine Malia. BA, Beloit Coll., 1958; JD, Northwestern U., 1965. Bar: Hawaii 1967, U.S. Dist. Ct. Hawaii 1969, U.S. Ct. Appeals (9th cir.) 1977. Legal staff Bishop Estate, Honolulu, 1966-68; dep. atty. gen. State of Hawaii, Honolulu, 1968-71; ptnr. Saunders & Morse, Honolulu, 1971-73; assoc. Chuck & Wong, Honolulu, 1974-75; officer, dir. Morse, Nelson & Ross, Honolulu, 1976-85; mem. Hawaii Med. Claim Conciliation Panel, Honolulu, 1977—, chmn., 1980—; mem. panel of arbitrators First Judicial Cir., Hawaii, 1986—. Lt. USN, 1959-62. Hardy scholar Northwestern U., 1962. Mem. Am. Judicature Soc., Assn. Trial Lawyers Am., Omicron Delta Kappa. Office: 700 Richards St Apt 1706 Honolulu HI 96813-4619

MORSE, JOHN MOORE, architect, planner; b. Brookline, Mass., Aug. 23, 1911; s. Arthur Moore and Helen (Stearns) M.; m. Emily Hall (dec. 1988); children: David Hall, Catherine Morse Wikkerink; m. Helen Taverniti, Aug. 5, 1989. AB, Harvard U., 1934, MArch, 1940. Registered architect, Wash. Tchr. Loomis Sch., Windsor, Conn., 1934-36; ptnr. Bassetti & Morse, Seattle, 1947-62; prin. John Morse & Assocs., Seattle, 1962-78; ptnr. Morse Stafford Ptnrship., Seattle, 1978-85; prin. John Morse Architect & Planner, Seattle, 1985—. Mem. King County (Wash.) Planning Commn., 1965-70, Design Rev. Bd., Mill Creek, Wash., 1987-89; chmn. Seattle Urban Design Bd., 1966; bd. dirs. Cornish Coll. Arts, Seattle, 1974-80. Fellow AIA (pres. Seattle chpt. 1969, Seattle chpt. medal, various local and nat. awards). Democrat. Office: 7027 32nd Ave NE Seattle WA 98115-5906

MORSE, JUDY, science foundation administrator. Ceo Arboretum Foundation, Los Angeles County Arboreta and Botanic Gardens, Arcadia, Calif. Office: Los Angeles County Arboretum Found 301 N Baldwin Ave Arcadia CA 91007-2628

MORSE, KAREN WILLIAMS, academic administrator; b. Monroe, Mich., May 8, 1940; m. Joseph G. Morse; children: Robert G., Geoffrey E. BS, Denison U., 1962; MS, U. Mich., 1964, PhD, 1967; DSc (hon.), Denison U., 1990. Rsch. chemist Ballistic Rsch. Lab., Aberdeen Proving Ground, Md., 1966-68; lectr. chemistry dept. Utah State U., Logan, 1968-69, from asst. to assoc. prof. chemistry, 1969-83, prof. chemistry dept., 1983-93, dept. head Coll. Sci., 1981-88, dean Coll. Sci., 1988-89, univ. provost, 1989-93; pres. Western Wash. U., Bellingham, 1993—; mem., chair Grad. Record Exam in chemistry com., Princeton, N.J., 1980-89, Gov.'s Sci. Coun., Salt Lake City, 1986-93, Gov.'s Coun. on Fusion, 1989-91, ACS Com. on Profl. Tng., 1984-92; cons. 1993; nat. ChemLinks adv. com. NSF, 1995; bd. advisor's orgn. com. 2008 summer Olympic Games, Seattle, 1995; faculty Am. Assn. State Colls. and Univs. Pres.'s Acad., 1995, 96; chair Wash. Coun. of Pres., 1995-96; bd. dirs. Whatcom State Bank. Contbr. articles to profl. jours. Mem. Cache County Sch. Dist. Found., Cache Valley, Logan, 1988-93; swim coach, soccer coach; trustee First United Presbyn. Ch., Logan, 1979-81, 82-85; adv. bd. Sci. Discovery Ctr., Logan, 1993, KCTS-TV, Bellingham, 1996—; mem. bd. dirs. United Way, Whatcom County, 1993—; exec. com. Bellingham-Whatcom Econ. Devel. Com., 1993—. Recipient Disting. Alumni in Residence award U. Mich., 1989. Fellow AAAS; mem. Am. Chem. Soc. (Utah award Salt Lake City and Cen. dists. 1988, Garvan-Olin medal 1997), Am. Assn. State Colls. and Univs. (mem. policy and purposes com. 1995, chair 1996), Bus. and Profl. Women Club (pres. 1984-85), Philanthropic Edn. Orgn., Phi Beta Kappa, Sigma Xi, Phi Beta Kappa Assocs., Phi Kappa Phi, Beta Gamma Sigma. Office: Western Washington Univ Office of Pres Bellingham WA 98225-5996

MORSE, LOWELL WESLEY, banking and real estate executive; b. West Palm Beach, Fla., May 1, 1937; s. Alton and Blanche (Yelverton) M.; B.S., U. Santa Clara, 1968; grad. Def. Lang. Inst., Monterey, Calif., 1959; m. Vera Giacalone, June 22, 1958; children: Lowell Wesley, Stephen D., Michael S. Russian linguist U.S. Army Security Agy., 1957-60; asst. city mgr. City of Pacific Grove (Calif.), 1961-66; city mgr. Town of Los Altos Hills (Calif.), 1967-69; chmn. Morse & Assos., Inc., Portland, Oreg., 1972—; founder, dir. Comerica Bank Calif., San Jose, 1979—; dir. Internat. Family Entertainment; chmn. Cypress Ventures Inc., Portland, The Bagel Basket, Inc.; chmn. bd. trustees Regent U. Served with U.S. Army, 1957-60. Home: 21042 SW Wyndham Hill Ct Tualatin OR 97062-7711 Office: 5335 Meadows Rd Ste 365 Lake Oswego OR 97035-3114

MORSE, MICHAEL DAVID, chemistry educator, researcher; b. New Martinsville, W.Va., Oct. 6, 1952; s. Harold Lane and Opal Geneva (Nichols) M.; m. Cynthia Jo Brandt, Nov. 26, 1983; children: Lauren E., Samuel E., Matthew B. BS, Haverford Coll., 1974; MS, U. Chgo., 1977, PhD, 1980. Vis. asst. prof. Rice U., Houston, 1981-83, rsch. assoc., 1983-84; asst. prof. U. Utah, Salt Lake City, 1985-90, assoc. prof., 1990-93; prof., 1993—. Contbr. articles to profl. jours. Fellow AAAS; mem. Am. Phys. Soc., Am. Chem. Soc. Office: Univ Utah Dept Chemistry Salt Lake City UT 84112

MORSE, RICHARD, social scientist; b. Boston, Oct. 12, 1922; s. Stearns and Helen Ward (Field) M.; m. Romola Thomas Chowdhry, June 23, 1949; children: Ashok Daniel, Martha Sunita Kelly. A.B., Dartmouth Coll., 1946; postgrad., Banaras Hindu U., Aligarh Muslim U., Gokhale Inst. Politics and Econs., India, 1947, Columbia, 1950; A.M., ABD, Harvard, 1958. Edn. officer ECA, Burma, 1950-53; asst. rep. Ford Found., Burma, 1954-56; sr. internat. economist Stanford Research Inst., Menlo Park, Calif., 1958-64, 66-69; cons. Ford Found., India, 1964-66; indsl. devel. cons. Andover, Mass., 1969-74; rsch. assoc., sr. fellow, co-coord. Participatory Devel. Group East West Ctr., Honolulu, 1974-94; sr. fellow emeritus East West Ctr., Honolulu, 1994—; study dir. NAS and Nat. Acad. Engring. Internat. Panel on Internat. Industrialization Inst., 1972-73; chmn. bd. govs. Inst. Current World Affairs, 1972-74, trustee, 1988-91; bd. dirs. Inst. World Affairs, 1988-91, mem. adv. coun., 1992—; co-founder, dir. Hawaii Entrepreneurship Tng. and Devel. Inst., 1977—; mem. adv. com. Immigrant Ctr. Enterprise Project, Honolulu, 1992—; ptnr.-founder Kalimat Moosilauke Pubs., 1996—. Co-author (with Eugene Staley): Modern Small Industry for Developing Countries, 1965, Village Voices in Rural Development and Energy Planning, 1987; co-editor: Grassroot Horizons: Connecting Participatory Development Initiatives East and West, 1995. Served with AUS, 1942-45. Fellow Inst. Current World Affairs, 1946-49; recipient certificate of honor Hawaii Ho. of Reps., 1994. Mem. Am. Econ. Assn., Am. Agrl. Econs. Assn., Am. Assn. Asian Studies, Economists Allied for Arms Reduction, Nitrogen Fixing Tree Assn., UN Assn. (exec. bd. Hawaii divsn.). Home: 1621 Halekoa Dr Honolulu HI 96821-1126 Office: 1777 E West Rd Honolulu HI 96822-2323

MORSE, RICHARD JAY, human resources and organizational development consultant, manufacturers' representative company executive; b. Detroit, Aug. 2, 1933; s. Maurice and Belle Rosalyn (Jacobson) M. BA, U. Va., 1955; MA in Clin. Psychology, Calif. State U., L.A., 1967. Area pers. adminstr. Gen. Tel. Co. of Calif., Santa Monica, 1957-67; sr. v.p. human resources The Bekins Co., Glendale, Calif., 1967-83; pvt. cons. human resources and orgn. devel. Cambria, 1983—. Contbr. articles to profl. jours. Fund raiser various orgns., So. Calif., 1970—. Mem. Internat. Soc. Performance Improvement (founding mem. 1958—). Republican. Jewish. Home and Office: 6410 Cambria Pines Rd Cambria CA 93428-2009

MORT, GARY STEVEN, physical education educator; b. San Francisco, Jan. 2, 1959; s. Robert Joseph and Antoinette Patricia (Dominguez) M.; m. Rochelle Ann Dias, Aug. 02, 1980; children: Aaron Nicholas, Courtney Faith. BS Phys. Edn., San Jose State, 1983; MS Ednl. Adminstrn., Nat. Univ., Fresno, Calif., 1989. Cert. tchr. phys. edn., Calif. Tchr. phys. edn. Alum Rock Unified, San Jose, Calif., 1984-85, Clovis (Calif.) Unified Schs., 1985—, 1993—. Found. grantee Clovis Found., 1993-94; named Coach of the Yr., North Yosemite League, Fresno area, 1990. Mem. AAHPERD (presenter nat. conv. 1992, 93, 95), Calif. Assn. Health, Phys. Edn., Recreation and Dance), U.S. Water Polo (dist. sec. 1974—), Calif. Consortium of Ind. Study. Home: 8564 Chickadee Ln Clovis CA 93611-9461 Office: Gateway High Sch Enterprise High Sch 1550 Herndon Ave Clovis CA 93611-0569

MORTEN, RALPH EDWARD, police officer, bomb technician; b. Yankton, S.D., Aug. 23, 1950; s. Claude Leslie and Evelyn Madeline (Steele) M.; m. Alison Joan Squire, Apr. 3, 1982; children: Joshua, Lauren, Sarah, Erin. BS in Criminal Justice Adminstrn., Calif. State U., 1983. Cert. tchr. C.C. level, Calif. Police officer Phoenix Police Dept., 1974-79, L.A. Police, 1979—; pres. The Morten Group, Upland, Calif., 1995—; firearms cons. Nat. Tactical Officers Assn., LaMirada, Calif., 1986-90, Internat. Assn. Chiefs Police, Washington, 1986-91; firearms, security cons. R.M. Consulting, Upland, Calif., 1989—; del., union rep., LA Police Protective League, 1994—. Inventor: Robotic Forklift (remote control), 1995. Baseball coach Little League, Upland, Calif., 1994—. With USMC, 1971-73. Recipient medal of valor L.A. Police Dept., 1990; named Officer of Yr. Internat. Footprint Assn., L.A., 1990. Mem. Internat. Assn. Bomb Technicians and Investigations, Peace Officers Assn. L.A. County. Republican. Methodist. Office: LA Police Dept 150 N Los Angeles St Los Angeles CA 90012-3309

MORTENSEN, ARVID LEGRANDE, lawyer; b. Bremerton, Wash., July 11, 1941; s. George Andrew and Mary Louise (Myers) M.; m. Elaine Marie Mains, Aug. 2, 1968; children: Marie Louise, Anne Catherine, Joseph Duncan. BS in English and Psychology, Brigham Young U., 1965, MBA in Mktg. and Fin., 1967; JD cum laude, Ind. U., 1980. Bar: Ind. 1980, U.S. Supreme Ct. 1983, Mo. 1985, D.C. 1985; CLU, 1971; Accredited Estate Planner, 1995. Agt. Conn. Mut. Life Ins. Co., Salt Lake City, 1967-68, agt. and br. mgr., Idaho Falls, Idaho, 1968-74; with Rsch. and Rev. Svc. Am., Inc./Newkirk Assocs., Inc., Indpls., 1974-83, sr. editor, 1975-79, mgr. advanced products and seminars, 1979-80, sr. mktg. exec., 1980-83; tax and fin. planner, Indpls., 1980-85, St. Louis and Chesterfield, Mo., 1985-90, Tampa Bay, Fla., 1990-91, Orange County, Calif., 1991—. mem. sr. mgmt. com., v.p. Allied Fidelity Corp., 1983-85, Allied Fidelity Ins. Co., 1983-85, Tex. Fire and Casualty Ins. Co., 1983-85; v.p., bd. dirs. Gen. Am. Ins. Co., St. Louis, 1985-86; v.p. Gen. Am. Life Ins. Co., St. Louis, 1985-90; pvt. practice law, Indpls., 1980-85, St. Louis, Chesterfield and Bridgeton, Mo., 1985-90, Tampa Bay, 1990-91, Orange County, 1991—; active with Ch. Jesus Christ of Latter-day Saints, Denver, Idaho Falls, Idaho, Indpls., St. Louis, Chesterfield, Tampa Bay Area and Orange County, Calif., Profl. Assn. Diving Instrs. cert. Divemaster, 1989—; lic. amateur radio operator FCC, 1994—, amateur extra class, 1996. Mem. Assn. Advanced Life Underwriting, Mo. Bar Assn., Bar Assn. Met. St. Louis, D.C. Bar Assn., Ind. Bar Assn., Am. Soc. CLU's, Nat. Assn. Life Underwriters, Orange County. Author: Employee Stock Ownership Plans, 1975, Fundamentals of Corporate Qualified Retirement Plans, 1975, 78, 80, Buy-Sell Agreements, 1988, The Key Executive Sale, 1989, (with Norman H. Tarver) The IRA Manual, 1975-87 edits., (with Norman H. Tarver) The Keogh Manual, 1975, 77, 78, 80 edits., (with Norman H. Tarver) The Section 403 (b) Manual, 1975, 77, 78, 80, 84, 85, 87 edits., sole author 1991,93 , 94, edit., (with Leo C. Hodges) The Life Insurance Trust Handbook, 1980; contbr. articles to profl. jours.; editor-in-chief various tax and fin. planning courses; bd. editors Ind. Law Rev., 1977-78. Office: 620 Newport Center Dr Ste 1100 Newport Beach CA 92660-8011 also: PO Box 6362 Laguna Niguel CA 92607-6362

MORTENSEN, GLEN ALBERT, chemical engineer; b. Moscow, Idaho; s. William A. and Frances (Nicholson) M; m. Patricia L. Harkness; children: Keith, Wayne, Hans, Mark. BSChemE, U. Idaho, 1955; PhD, U. Calif., Berkeley, 1963. Diploma Oak Ridge Sch. Reactor Tech., 1956; engr. Atomic Energy Commn., 1956-58, Nat. Reactor Test Sta., 1963-75, Intermountain Techs. Inc., 1975-86; consulting engr. Idaho Nat. Engring. Lab., Idaho Falls, 1986—. Mem. Am. Nuclear Soc., Assn. Computer Machinery. Home: 2975 Balboa Dr Idaho Falls ID 83404-7499 Office: INEL PO Box 1625 Idaho Falls ID 83415-3808

MORTENSEN, RICHARD HAROLD, data processing executive; b. St. Anthony, Idaho, Oct. 23, 1953; s. Richard and Wanda Rae (Green) M.; m. Marva Dawn Storer; children: Kimberli, Dane, Erik. BS in Math./Computer Sci., U. Idaho, 1977. Programmer Billing Computer Corp., Provo, Utah, 1977-79; programmer/sr. analyst HEW, Boise, Idaho, 1979-82; data processing mgr. Boise Cascade Corp., 1982—; computer cons. Computer Ptnrs. Inc., Boise, 1982. Author software GS-STAT, Master, 1989. Coach Little League Baseball, Boise, 1989-93, umpire, 1994. Mem. Data Processing Mgmt. Assn. Home: 11807 W Dason Ct Boise ID 83713-1755 Office: Boise Cascade Corp 1 Jefferson Sq Boise ID 83728-0001

MORTENSEN, WILLIAM S., banking executive; b. 1932. Chmn. bd., pres., CEO 1st Fed. Bank Calif., Santa Monica, 1955—, CEO, until 1997. Office: 1st Fed Bank Calif 401 Wilshire Blvd Santa Monica CA 90401-1416*

MORTIMER, KENNETH P., academic administrator. Pres. Western Wash. U., Bellingham, 1988—. Office: Western Wash U Office of President 516 High St Bellingham WA 98225-5946

MORTIMER, WENDELL REED, JR., superior court judge; b. Alhambra, Calif., Apr. 7, 1937; s. Wendell Reed and Blanche (Wilson) M.; m. Cecilia Vick, Aug. 11, 1962; children: Michelle Dawn, Kimberly Grace. AB, Occidental Coll., 1958; JD, U. So. Calif., L.A., 1965. Bar: Calif. 1966. Trial atty. legal divsn. Legal div. State of Calif., L.A., 1965-73; assoc. Thelen, Marrin, Johnson & Bridges, L.A., 1973-76, ptnr., 1976-93; pvt. practice San Marino, Calif., 1994-95; judge L.A. Superior Ct., 1995—. With U.S. Army, 1960-62. Mem. ABA, Los Angeles County Bar Assn., Pasadena Bar Assn., Calif. Judges Assn., Am. Judicature Soc., Am. Judges Assn., Legion Lex. Home: 1420 San Marino Ave San Marino CA 91108-2042

MORTIMER, WILLIAM JAMES, newspaper publisher; b. Provo, Utah, June 26, 1932; s. William Earl and Margaret (Johnson) M.; m. Paula Ann Deline, Sept. 17, 1956; children: Jeffrey, David, Gregory, Bradley, Judy, William James II, Jennifer. BS, Utah State U, 1954; MS, Columbia U., 1957. Reporter Deseret News, Salt Lake City, 1957-59, pres., pub., 1985—; sales mgr. Deseret News Press, Salt Lake City, 1959-63; gen. mgr. Deseret News Press, 1979-80, Deseret Book Co., Salt Lake City, 1966-79; sr. account exec. Wheelwright Lithographing, Salt Lake City, 1963-66; dir. LDS Ch. Printing Svcs., Salt Lake City, 1980-85; v.p., dir. Newspaper Agy. Corp., Salt Lake City, 1985—; pres. Printing Industries of Utah, 1964-65, Utah Retail Mchts. Assn., Salt Lake City, 1977-79. Author: How Beautiful Upon the Mountains, 1963. Campaign chmn. Salt Lake Area United Way, 1987; hon. col. Utah N.G.; chmn. Utah Partnership Ednl. and Econ. Devel., 1995-97; mem. exec. com. Salt Lake Conv. and Visitors Bur.; chmn. bd. Pioneer State Theatre, 1990-93; bd. dirs. Utah Symphony; chmn. bd. dirs. Prevent Blindness, Utah. 1st lt. U.S. Army, 1954-56, Korea. Named Disting. Citizen of Yr., Salt Lake City, 1995. Mem. Utah-Idaho-Spokane AP Assn. (pres. 1993-94), Utah Press Assn. (pres. 1994-95), Salt Lake Area C. of C. (chmn. bd. 1988-89), Alta Club. Mem. LDS Ch. Home: 8763 Kings Hill Dr Salt Lake City UT 84121-6135 Office: Deseret News Pub Co PO Box 1257 Salt Lake City UT 84110-1257

MORTON, GEORGE THOMAS, reporter; b. Cin., Jan. 25, 1954; s. George Thomas and Marian Elizabeth (Wilt) M. BA in English, Miami U., Oxford, Ohio, 1976; MDiv, Gordon-Conwell Theol. Sem., South Hamilton, Mass., 1983. Reporter Beaumont (Tex.) Enterprise, 1983-88, Colorado Springs (Colo.) Gazette Telegraph, 1988-90; freelance writer Colorado Springs, 1991-92; reporter Casper (Wyo.) Star-Tribune, 1992—; instr. sociology of religion U. Colo., Colorado Springs, 1989, 90; fgn. corr. Hearst News Svc., N.Y.C., 1986. Author: The Survivor's Guide to Unemployment, 1992; ghostwriter: Parenting Teens with Love and Logic, 1992; freelance reporter Religion News Svc., 1989-93, Christianity Today, 1991-93; actor Casper Coll. Theatre, 1996, Stage III Theatre, Casper, 1996. Recipient Comm. award Bapt. Gen. Conv. of Tex., El Paso, 1986, Thomas Stokes award Washington Journalism Ctr., Beaumont, Tex., 1988, Media award Am. Acad. Nursing, Phoenix, 1994, Pacemaker award Wyo. Press Assn., 1993, 96. Mem. Religion Newswriters Assn., Soc. Profl. Journalists, Soc. Am. Bus. Editors and Writers, Soc. Environ. Journalists, Investigative Reporters and Editors. Av.

MORTON, LAUREL ANNE, elementary education educator; b. Cin., July 27, 1954; d. James William and Rosemary (Danner) M. BA in Social Sci., Calif. State U.-Stanislaus, Turlock, 1978; teaching credential, Calif. State Polytech U., Pomona, 1986; MA in Edn., Calif. State Poly. U., Pomona, 1992. Cert. tchr., Calif., Colo. Sr. loan clk. Shearson Am. Express Mortgage Corp., Newport Beach, Calif., 1978-82; adminstrv. asst. Investco Corp., Santa Barbara, Calif., 1982-83; supr. loan servicing dept. County Savs. Bank, Santa Barbara, 1983-84; comm. asst. Fuller Theol. Sem., Pasadena, Calif., 1984-85; elem. tchr. Howard Sch., Ontario, Calif., 1986-91; tchr. Bon View Elem. Sch., Ontario, 1992—, 4th grade team leader, 1993-94, track leader, 1995-96. Tchr. sponsor Performing Arts Club, Bon View Elem. Sch., 1996-97. Mem. Nat. Honor Soc., Phi Kappa Phi, Zeta Tau Alpha. Home: 1919 Stonehouse Rd Sierra Madre CA 91024-1409 Office: Bon View Elem Sch 2121 S Bon View Ave Ontario CA 91761-5530

MORTON, LINDA, mayor; b. Dec. 7, 1944; married; 2 children. BA with honors, U. Nebr., 1966. Lic. real estate broker. Tchr. Sunnyvale (Calif.) Elem. Sch., 1967-69, Jefferson County (Colo.) Sch. Dist., 1966-67, 69-70; real estate agt. Crown Realty, Lakewood, Colo., 1979-82, Van Schaack & Co., Lakewood, 1982-83, Re-Max Profls., Lakewood, 1983-91. Mem. city coun. City of Lakewood, 1981-91, mayor, 1991—; chair Denver Metro Mayors Caucus; appts. by Gov. to Blue Ribbon Panel on State Transp. Needs, 1995; represented Lakewood on Bd. Denver Regional Coun. of Govts., from 1981, chair, 1986-87; chair Jefferson City C. of C., 1989-90; apptd. by Gov. Colo. to Met. Air Quality Coun., 1985; bd. dirs. Nat. Assn. Regional Coun. Govts., 1986-90, CML, 1993—. Office: City of Lakewood 445 S Allison Pky Lakewood CO 80226-3106*

MORTVEDT, JOHN JACOB, soil scientist; b. Dell Rapids, S.D., Jan. 25, 1932; s. Ernest R. and Clara (Halvorson) M.; m. Marlene L. Fodness, Jan. 23, 1955; children: Sheryl Mortvedt Jarratt, Lori Mortvedt Klopf, Julie Mortvedt Stride. BS, S.D. State U., 1953, MS, 1959; PhD, U. Wis., 1962. Soil chemist TVA, Muscle Shoals, Ala., 1962-87, sr. scientist, 1987-92, regional mgr. field programs dept., 1992-93; ext. soils specialist Colo. State U., Ft. Collins, 1994-95, ext. environ. and pesticide edn. specialist, 1996. Editor: Micronutrients in Agriculture, 1972, 2d edit., 1991; contbr. articles to profl. jours. 1st lt. U.S. Army, 1953-57. Fellow AAAS, Soil Sci. Soc. Am. (pres. 1988-89, editor-in-chief 1982-87, Profl. Svc. award 1991), Am. Soc. Agronomy (exec. com. 1987-90); mem. Internat. Soil Sci. Soc., Colombian Soil Sci. Soc. (hon.), Exch. Club (pres. Florence, Ala. chpt. 1987-88), Toastmasters (pres. Florence chpt. 1964-65), Phi Kappa Phi. Office: Colo State U Dept Soil and Crop Scis Fort Collins CO 80523

MOSBY, DOROTHEA SUSAN, municipal official; b. Sacramento, Calif., May 13, 1948; d. William Laurence and Esther Ida (Lux) M. AA in Sociology, Bakersfield (Calif.) Coll., 1966-69; BS in Recreation, San Jose State U., 1969-72; MPA, Calif. State U. Dominguez Hills, Carson, 1980-82. Asst. dept. pers. officer San Jose Pks. and Recreation Dept., 1972-73, neighborhood ctr. dir., 1973-74; sr. recreation leader Santa Monica Recreation and Pks. Dept., 1974-76, recreation supr., 1976-83; head bus. divsn. Santa Monica Recreation and Parks Dept., 1983-88; bus. adminstr. Santa Monica Cultural & Recreation Svcs., 1988-91; dir. pks. and recreation City of South Gate, Calif., 1991—; bd. dirs., officer Santa Monica City Employees Fed. Credit Union, 1980-89, pres. 1986-87; mem. citizens adv. com. L.A. Olympic Organizing Com., 1982-84. Mem. choir, flute soloist Pilgrim Luth. Ch., Santa Monica, 1974—, treas. Luth. ch. coun., 1984-86; vol. driver XXIII Olympiad, Los Angeles, 1984; contbr. local housing assistance U.S. Olympic Com., Los Angeles, 1984; mem. adv. com. Windsor Sq. Hancock Park Hist. Soc., Los Angeles, 1983, dir. Christmas carolling, 1980—, chmn. Olympic com., 1984, bd. trustees, 1984-90, chmn. pub. programs, 1985, co-chmn. pub. programs, 1986, co-vice chair, 1987, chmn., 1988, 89—; L.A. Philharm. Bus. & Profl. Com.; mem. Samuel C. May Grad. Student Rsch. Paper Judging Com., Western Govt. Rsch. Assn., 1994. Recipient Outstanding Profl. of Yr. award Los Angeles Basin Pk. and Recreation Commrs. and Bd. Mems., 1993. Mem. Calif. Pk. and Recreation Soc. (bd. dirs. 1979-82, 86, mem. Calif bd. pk. and recreation pers. 1990-92, Scholarship Found. Bd. 1992—, chair 1996, dist. 10 v.p. 1994, 95, 96), Nat. Recreation and Pk. Assn., Mgmt. Team Assocs. (sec., treas. 1979-83), L.A. World Affairs Coun., Western Govtl. Rsch. Assn., Nat. Assn. Univ. Women, South Gate C. of C., Kiwanis Club (pres. elect), Chi Kappa Rho (pres. 1986), Pi Alpha Alpha. Home: 9329 Elm Vista Dr Apt 103 Downey CA 90242-2992 Office: City of South Gate Dept Pks and Recreation 4900 Southern Ave South Gate CA 90280-3462

MOSER, C. THOMAS, lawyer; b. Seattle, Aug. 10, 1947; s. Carl Thomas and Helen Louise (Felton) M.; m. Deborah J. St. Clair, Sept. 25, 1976; children: Nicole, Lauren. BA, Cen. Wash. U., 1972; M in Pub. Adminstrn., George Washington U., 1974; JD, Gonzaga U., 1976. Bar: Wash. 1977; U.S. Dist. Ct. (we. dist.) Wash. 1977, U.S. Dist. Ct. (ea. dist.) Wash. 1980, U.S. Ct. Appeals (9th cir.) 1980, U. S. Supreme Ct. 1981. Dep. pros. atty. Skagit County Pros. Atty., Mount Vernon, Wash., 1976-77, chief civil dep., 1979-80, pros. atty., 1980-86; pros. atty. San Juan County Pros. Atty., Friday Harbor, Wash., 1977-79; pvt. practice Mount Vernon, 1987—; hearing examiner pro tem Skagit County, 1992—. Author: Gonzaga Law Review, 1975. Bd. dirs. Wash. Environ. Coun., Seattle, 1971-72, Padilla Bay Found., Skagit County, Wash., 1988; bd. trustees Wash. Assn. County Officials, Olympia, 1983; exec. bd. North Pacific Conf. Evang. Covenant Ch., vice sec. 1991-96. Sgt. U.S. Army, 1967-69, Korea. Recipient Silver Key award ABA Student Law Div., 1976, Legion of Honor award Internat. Order DeMolay, Kansas City, Mo., 1982, Chevalier award 1982. Mem. ATLA, Nat. Coll. Advocacy (advocate), Wash. State Trial Lawyers Assn. (bd. govs. 1990-92, 96—), Wash. Assn. Pros. Attys. (bd. dirs. 1983-85), Skagit County Bar Assn. (pres. 1995-96), Kiwanis Club Mt. Vernon, Affiliated Health Svc. (ethics com.), Christian Legal Soc. Democrat. Evangelical. Office: 411 Main St Mount Vernon WA 98273

MOSES, ELBERT RAYMOND, JR., speech and dramatic arts educator; b. New Concord, Ohio, Mar. 31, 1908; s. Elbert Raymond Sr. and Helen Martha (Miller) M.; m. Mary Miller Sterrett, Sept. 21, 1933 (dec. Sept. 1984); 1 child, James Elbert (dec.); m. Caroline Mae Entenman, June 19, 1985. AB, U. Pitts., 1932; MS, U. Mich., 1934, PhD, 1936. Instr. U. N.C., Greensboro, 1936-38; asst. prof. Ohio State U., Columbus, 1938-46; assoc. prof. Ea. Ill. State U., Charleston, 1946-56; asst. prof. Mich. State U., E. Lansing, Mich., 1956-59; prof. Clarion (Pa.) State Coll., 1959-71, chmn. dept. speech and dramatic arts, 1959—, emeritus prof., 1971—; Fulbright lectr. State Dept. U.S. Cebu Normal Sch., Cebu City, Philippine Islands, 1955-56; vis. prof. phonetics U. Mo., summer 1968; hon. sec.'s advocate dept. of aging State of Pa., Harrisburg, 1980-81. Author: Guide to Effective Speaking, 1957, Phonetics: A History and Interpretation, 1964, Three Attributes of God, 1983, Adventure in Reasoning, 1988, Beating the Odds, 1992, In Pursuit of Life, 1996; poems included in Best Poems of the 90s, 1992, in two web pages; contbr. articles to profl. jours.. Del. 3d World Congress Phoneticians, Tokyo, 1976; mem. nat. adv. com. fng. students and tchrs. HEW; del. to Internat. Congress Soc. Logopedics and Phoniatre, Vienna, 1965; liaison rep. to Peace Corps; pres. County Libr. Bd.; past exec. dir. Clarion County United Way; commr. Boy Scouts Am., 1976-77; pres. Venango County Adv. Coun. for Aging, 1978-79. Maj. AUS, 1942-46, lt. col. AUS, ret. Recipient Ret. Sr. Vol. Program Vol. of Yr. award No. Ariz. Coun. Govts., 1989, Spl. award Speech Comm. Assn., 1989, Endowment Benefactor award, 1991; 6 Diamong Pin of Melvin Jones Found., Internat. Lions, Best Male Songwriter, Poet of Yr. awards Entertainer Network Nashville, 1994, Listing Achievement in Entertainer-Indi-Assn. as Most Consistent Golden Poet of Nashville, 1995, EIA Platinum Poet, 1995, 96, Best Legendary Poet, 1996; named to Internat. Poetry Hall of Fame. Fellow United Writers Assn.; mem. Ariz. Comm. Support System, Quarter Century Wireless Assn., Soc. Wireless Pioneers, Mil. Affiliate Radio System, Hospitalier Order of St. John of Jerusalem, Knights Hospitalier, Knightly and Mil. Order of St. Eugene of Trebizond (chevalier), Soverign and Mil. Order of St. Stephen the Matyr (comdr.), Knightly Assn. of St. George the Matyr, Ordre Chevaliers du Sinai, Hist. File, VFW (comdr.), Am. Legion (comdr.), Rotary (pres. 1966-67, dist. gov. 1973-74), Order of White Shrine of Jerusalem, Niadh Nask (Marshall of Kilbonane), Internat. Chivalric Inst., Confedn. of Chivalry (life, mem. grand coun.), Ordre Souverain et Militaire de la Milice du Saint Sepulcre (chevalier grand cross), Sovereign World Order of White Cross (lord of knights, dist. commdr. Ariz.), Prescott High Twelve Club (pres. 1990), Morse Telegraph Club, Inc., 21st Century Club (charter), The Old Old Timers Club, Phi Delta Kappa (Svc. Key 1978). Republican. Methodist. Home: 2001 Rocky Dells Dr Prescott AZ 86303-5685

MOSES-FOLEY, JUDITH ANN, special education educator; b. Steubenville, Ohio, Sept. 1, 1936; d. Joseph and Katherine Ann (Pavich) Moses; m. John P. Foley, 1958 (div. 1986); children: Katherine Ann Foley, John Joseph Foley, Sean Michael Foley, Judith Kristina Foley; m. John H. Murphy, 1986 (dec. 1992). BS in Edn., Ohio U., 1958; MA in Ednl. Adminstrn., Fresno Pacific U., 1981; postgrad., Brigham Young U., 1982-84, U. San Francisco, 1985-86; student, U. N.Mex., 1993-94. Cert. in ednl. adminstrn., Calif.; lang. arts, phys. edn., history, govt., health, social studies K-12, Ohio; spl. edn., bilingual/TESOL, and as transition resource specialist, N.Mex. Adminstr., tchr. health and social sci., coach Madera (Calif.) Unified Schs., 1958-81; chair dept. phys. edn. Dos Palos (Calif.) H.S., 1963-64; prin. Chowchilla (Calif.) Elem. Schs., 1981-85; instr. phys. edn. Merced (Calif.) C.C., 1981-85; supt./prin. St. Luke's Sch., Merced, 1985-86; instr. polit. sci. and bus. adminstrn. West Hills C.C., Lemore, Calif., 1985-86; instr. phys. edn. Mohave C.C., Kingman, Ariz., 1989-90; transition resource specialist Silver Consol. Sch., Silver City, N.Mex., 1993—; adj. prof. early childhood edn. Western N.Mex. U., Silver City; spl. edn. resource specialist Silver H.S., Silver City, 1990—, coach U.S. acad. decathlon, 1991—; grant writer Circle of Life, 1994—; coord., grant writer R.E.: Learning; mem. North Ctrl. Accreditation Steering Com., 1992-95; v.p. Divsn. of Transition and Curriculum Devel., State of N.Mex.; mem. N.Mex. State Bd. com. U.S. Acad. Decathlon, 1993—; developer lang. arts, social studies transition curriculum 9-12 Silver Consolidated Schs., N.Mex. Pres. Bobby Sox Softball League, Madera, 1975-78; head coach track and field Jr. Olympics, Madera County, 1970-81; coord. Gathering of War Birds Airshow, Madera, 1976-79. Recipient Master Tchr. award Calif. State U., Fresno, 1978-79; recipient scholarships and grants. Mem. AAHPER, AAUW, Am. Assn. Ret. Persons, Coun. for Exceptional Children. Mem. ASCD. Home: PO Box 2 Buckhorn NM 88025-0002 Office: Silver Consol Schs 3200 N Silver St Silver City NM 88061-7283

MOSHER, SALLY EKENBERG, lawyer; b. N.Y.C., July 26, 1934; d. Leslie Joseph and Frances Josephine (McArdle) Ekenberg; m. James Kimberly Mosher, Aug. 13, 1960 (dec. Aug. 1982). MusB, Manhattanville Coll., 1956; postgrad., Hofstra U., 1958-60, U. So. Calif., 1971-73; JD, U. So. Calif., 1981. Bar: Calif., 1982. Musician, pianist, tchr., 1957-74; music critic Pasadena Star-News, 1967-72; mgr. Contrasts Concerts, Pasadena Art Mus., 1971-72; rep. Occidental Life Ins Co., Pasadena, 1975-78; v.p. James K. Mosher Co., Pasadena, 1961-82, pres., 1982—; pres. Oakhill Enterprises, Pasadena, 1984—; assoc. White-Howell, Inc., Pasadena, 1984—; real estate broker, 1984—; harpsichordist, lectr., composer, 1994—. Contbr. articles to various publs. Bd. dirs. Jr. League Pasadena, 1966-67, Encounters Concerts, Pasadena, 1966-72, U. So. Calif. Friends of Music, L.A., 1973-76, Calif. Music Theatre, 1988-90, Pasadena Hist. Soc., 1989-91, I Cantori, 1989-91; bd. dirs. Pasadena Arts Coun., 1986-92, pres., 1989-92, chair adv. bd., 1992-93; v.p., bd. dirs. Pasadena Chamber Orch., 1986-88, pres., 1987-88; mem. Calif. 200 Coun. for Bicentennial of U.S. Constn., 1987-90; mem. Endowment Adv. Commn., Pasadena, 1988-90; bd. dirs. Foothill Area Cmty. Svcs., 1990-95, treas., 1991, vice chair, 1992-94, chair, 1994-95. Manhattanville Coll. hon. scholar, 1952-56. Mem. ABA, Calif. Bar Assn., Assocs. of Calif. Inst. Tech., Athenaeum, Kappa Gamma Pi, Mu Phi Epsilon, Phi Alpha Delta. Home: 1260 Rancheros Rd Pasadena CA 91103-2759 Office: 711 E Walnut St Ste 407 Pasadena CA 91101-4403

MOSHIER, MARY BALUK, patent lawyer; b. Pitts., Aug. 20, 1905; d. Andrew and Johanna (Hlebasko) Baluk; m. Ross Warren Moshier; children: Thomas, Stephen. BA, U. Ark., 1929; postgrad., U. Chgo., 1945-46; JD, No. Ky. U., 1962. Bar: U.S. Patent Office 1944, Ohio 1962. Tchr. Gary (Ind.) Pub. Schs., 1930-35; tech. libr. Monsanto Co., Dayton, Ohio, 1936-41, patent chemist, 1942-45, agt., atty., 1949-66; patent adviser U.S. Office of Naval Rsch., San Francisco, 1948-49; patents cons., pvt. practice, 1969—. Co-author: Anydrous Aluminum Chloride in Organic Chemistry, 1941. Mem. AAAS, AAUW, NOW, Lawyers Club of Sun City, Nat. Assn. Ret. Fed. Employees, U.S. Chess Fedn., Phi Alpha Delta Legal Frat. Internat. Democrat. Episcopalian. Home and Office: 17300 N 88th Ave Apt 238 Peoria AZ 85382-3505

MOSK, STANLEY, state supreme court justice; b. San Antonio, Sept. 4, 1912; s. Paul and Minna (Perl) M.; m. Edna Mitchell, Sept. 27, 1937 (dec.); 1 child, Richard Mitchell; m. Susan Hines, Aug. 27, 1982 (div.); m. Kaygey Kash, Jan. 15, 1995. Student, U. Tex., 1931; PhB, U. Chgo., 1933; postgrad., U. Chgo. Law Sch., 1934; JD, Southwestern U., 1935; postgrad., The Hague Acad. Internat. Law, 1970, U. Pacific, 1970; LLD, U. San Diego, 1971, U. Santa Clara, 1976, Calif. Western U., 1984, Whittier Coll. Law, 1993, Pepperdine U., 1995, Western State U., San Diego, 1995. Bar: Calif. 1935, U.S. Supreme Ct. 1956. Practiced in Los Angeles, until 1939; exec. sec. to gov. Calif., 1939-42; judge Superior Ct. Los Angeles County, 1943-58; pro tem justice Dist. Ct. Appeal, Calif., 1954; atty. gen. Calif., also head state dept., justice, 1959-64; justice Supreme Ct. Calif., 1964—; mem. Jud. Coun. Calif., 1973-75, Internat. Commn. Jurists. Chmn. San Francisco Internat. Film Festival, 1967; mem. Dem. Nat. Com, Calif., 1960-64; mem. bd. regents U. Calif., 1940; pres. Vista Del Mar Child Care Svc., 1954-58; bd. dirs. San Francisco Law Sch., 1971-73, San Francisco Regional Cancer Found., 1980-83. With AUS, WWII. Recipient Disting. Alumnus award U. Chgo., 1958, 93. Mem. ABA, Nat. Assn. Attys. Gen. (exec. bd. 1964), Western Assn. Attys. Gen. (pres. 1963), L.A. Bar Assn., San Francisco Bar Assn., Am. Legion, Manuscript Soc., Calif. Hist. Soc., Am. Judicature Soc., Inst. Jud. Adminstrn., U. Chgo. Alumni Assn. No. Calif. (pres. 1957-58, 67), Order of Coif, B'nai B'rith, Hillcrest Country Club (L.A.), Commonwealth Club, Beverly Hills Tennis Club. Office: Supreme Ct Calif 303 2nd St San Francisco CA 94107-1366

MOSK, SUSAN HINES, lawyer; b. Pitts., Dec. 14, 1946; d. William James and Catherine Elizabeth (Cook) Hines; m. Stanley Mosk, Aug. 27, 1982 (div. Jan. 1995). B in Music Edn., Fla. State U., 1968, M in Music Edn., 1970; JD, U. Calif., San Francisco, 1990. Bar: Calif. 1990, U.S. Dist. Ct. (no. dist.) Calif. 1990, U.S. Ct. Appeals (9th cir.) 1990. Assoc. Payne, Thompson & Walker, San Francisco, 1990-94; of counsel Knecht, Haley, Lawrence & Smith, San Francisco, 1994-95; prin. Law Offices of Susan H. Mosk, San Francisco, 1995—; commr. Jud. Nominees Evaluation Commn., 1992-96. Author/editor: Rainmaking Guide to Corporate Counsel, 1993. Mem. steering com. Women's Leadership Coun. for U.S. Senator Diane Feinstein, 1992—; chair No. Calif. Women's Cabinet for Kathleen Brown Gubernatorial Campaign, San Francisco, 1994; co-chair fin. Willie L. Brown Mayoral Campaign, 1995. Mem. State Bar of Calif., Calif. Women Lawyers (bd. govs. 1992-94, 1st v.p. 1993-94), Queen's Bench. Democrat. Office: Law Offices of Susan H Mosk 57 Post St Ste 604 San Francisco CA 94104

MOSKOWITZ, ROBERT ARTHUR, publishing executive; b. Newark, Oct. 27, 1946; m. Francine Reese Levy, June 30, 1968; children: Jake, Alex. B of Am. Civilization, U. Pa., 1968; postgrad., New Sch. Social Rsch., 1969-71. Editorial dir.exec. reports divsn. Prentice Hall Pub., Englewood Cliffs, N.J., 1968-70; freelance writer, 1970-75; pres. Personal Productivity Ctr., Phila., 1975-83; sr. cons. Hill and Knowlton, L.A., 1983-84; sr. acct. supr. Madison Fielding Pub. Rels., L.A., 1984-87; pres. Crown Communications Group, Woodland Hills, Calif., 1981—, Key Publs., Woodland Hills, Calif., 1991—. Author: How to Organize Your Work and Yout Life, 1981, Parenting Your Aging Parents, 1991, The Small Business Computer Book-A Guide to Plain English, 1993, Out On Yout Own-Everything You Need to Know Before, During and After Leaving the Nest, 1994. Mem. Am. Telecommuting Assn., Authors Guild, Ind. Writers So. Calif., PEN.

MOSLEY, CYNTHIA LISA, marketing professional; b. Culver City, Calif.; d. Robert Eugene and Elizabeth Jane (Jeffers) Haynie; m. James David Mosley. BA cum laude, U. Portland, 1987; MBA, Calif. State U., Fullerton, 1992; advanced mgmt. cert., U. Calif., Riverside, 1995, exec. mgmt. cert., 1996. Intern YWCA, Portland, Oreg., 1986-87; cons. Comprehensive Care Corp., Orange, Calif., 1987-89; referral coord. Corona (Calif.) Cmty. Hosp., 1989-92; dir. cmty. programs Valley Health Sys., Hemet, Calif., 1992—; bd. dirs. Valley Youth Found., Hemet; mem. Valley Health Mag., Hemet, 1995—. Mem. ways and means com. First Congl. Ch., Corona, 1996—. Mem. Corvettes of So. Calif. (hospitality com. 1989-90). Office: Valley Health Sys 1117 E Devonshire Ave Hemet CA 92543-3083

MOSQUEIRA, CHARLOTTE MARIANNE, dietitian; b. L.A., July 26, 1937; d. Leo and Magdalene Tollefson; children: Mark, Michael. BS, St. Olaf Coll., 1959; postgrad. U. Oreg. Med. Sch., 1959-60; MA, Central Mich. U., 1980. Registered dietitian. Dir. food svc. Holy Cross Hosp., Salt Lake City, 1973-77; dir. dietetics Riverside Meth. Hosp., Columbus, Ohio, 1977-79; dir. nutrition and food svc. Fresno (Calif.) Community Hosp. and Med. Ctr., 1980-91; mem. faculty Dept. Enology and Food Sci., Calif. State U., Fresno, 1984-93; dir. nutritional svc. Emanuel Med. Ctr., Turlock, Calif., 1991—. Mem. Am. Dietetic Assn., Calif. Dietetic Assn. Lutheran.

MOSS, DEBRA LEE, special education educator; b. L.A., June 15, 1952; d. Boris and Mildred Rose (Volk) Elkin; divorced; children: Ryan Adam, Lauren Nicole, Rebecca Anne. BA in Psychology, UCLA, 1973; MA in Spl. Edn., Calif. State U., L.A., 1977. Cert. elem. tchr. severely handicapped, learning handicapped and jr. coll. tchr., Calif. Tchr. spl. edn. UCLA Neuropsychiat. Inst., 1972-75, demonstration tchr., curriculum coord., 1975-78; edn. specialist Harbor Regional Ctr. for Developmentally Disabled, Torrance, Calif., 1978-82; ednl. cons. North L.A. Regional Ctr. for Developmentally Disabled, Panorama City, Calif., 1982-87; behavior specialist L.A. Unified Sch. Dist., 1987-91, program specialist, 1991-92, support staff spl. edn. mid. schs., 1992-93; inclusion facilitator, 1993—; hon. lectr. West Valley Occupational Ctr., 1986—; tutor spl. edn., L.A., 1973—; behavior specialist to families, 1985—. Contbr. articles to profl. jours. Mem. Am. Assn. on Retardation, Nat. Assn. for Autistic Children and Adults, Coun. for Exceptional Children. Democrat. Office: LA USD West Valley Spl Edn Svc Unit 6505 Zelzah Ave Reseda CA 91335-6221

MOSS, ELIZABETH LUCILLE (BETTY MOSS), transportation company executive; b. Ironton, Mo., Feb. 13, 1939; d. James Leon and Dorothy Lucille (Russell) Rollen; m. Elliott Theodore Moss, Nov. 10, 1963 (div. Jan. 1984); children: Robert Belmont, Wendy Rollen. BA in Econs. and Bus. Adminstrn., Drury Coll., 1960. Registrar, transp. mgr. Cheley Colo. Camps, Inc., Denver and Estes Park, 1960-61; office mgr. Washington Nat. Ins. Co., Denver, 1960-61; sec. White House Decorating, Denver, 1961-62; with Ringsby Truck Lines, Denver, Oakland, Calif., and L.A., 1962-67, System 99 Freight Lines, L.A., 1967-69; terminal mgr. System 99 Freight Lines, Stockton, Calif., 1981-84; with Yellow Freight System, L.A., 1969-74, Hayward, Calif., 1974-77; ops. mgr. Yellow Freight System, Urbana, Ill., 1977-80; sales rep. Calif. Motor Express, San Jose, 1981; regional sales mgr. Schneider Nat. Carriers, Inc., No. Calif., 1984-86; account exec. TNT-Can., Nev. and Cen. Calif., 1986-88; mgr. Interstate-Intermodal Divs. HVH Transp., Denver, 1988-89; regional sales mgr. MNX, Inc., Northern Calif., 1989-91; dir. sales Mountain Valley Express, Manteca, Calif., 1992—; chmn. op. coun. for San Joaquin and Stanislaus Counties Calif. Trucking Assn., 1983-84; planning adv. com. Truck Accident Reduction Projects, San Joaquin County, 1987-88. Mem. Econ. Devel. Coun. Stockton C. of C., 1985-86; active Edison High Sch. Boosters, 1982-88. Mem. Nat. Def. Transp. Assn. (bd. dirs. 1986-87), Stockton Traffic Club (bd. dirs. 1982-84, Trucker of Yr.), Ctrl. Valley Traffic Club, Oakland Traffic Club, Delta Nu Alpha (bd. dirs. Region 1 1982-84, v.p. chpt. 103 1984-85, pres. 1985-86, chmn. bd. 1985-87, regional sec. 1987-88, Outstanding Achievement award 1986, 88), Coun. Logistics Mgmt. Methodist. Home: 455 E Ocean Blvd Apt 602 Long Beach CA 90802-4940

MOSS, ERIC OWEN, architect; b. L.A., July 25, 1943. BA, UCLA, 1965; MArch with honors, U. Calif., Berkeley, 1968, Harvard U., 1972. Prof. design So. Calif. Inst. Architecture, 1974—; prin. Eric Owen Moss Archs., Culver City, Calif., 1975—; Eliot Noyes chair Harvard U., Cambridge, Mass., 1990; Eero Saarinen chair Yale U., New Haven, 1991; lectr. Hirshhorn Mus. Symposium, Washington, 1990, Nat. AIA Conv., 1990, Mus. Contemporary Art, L.A., 1991, N.Y. Archtl. League, 1991, Archtl. Assn. Ireland, Dublin, Archtl. Assn., London, 1991, Royal Coll. Art, London, 1991, Smithsonian Inst., Washington, 1992, U. Calif., Berkeley, 1992, Osterreichisches Mus. fur Angewandte Kunst, Vienna, Austria, 1992, UCLA, 1992, Royal Danish Acad. Fine Arts, Copenhagen, 1993, U. Lund, Sweden, 1993, Mus. Finnish Architecture, Helsinki, 1993, Royal Acad. Arts, London, 1993, U. Pa., Phila., 1994, others; tchr. U. Tex., Austin, 1983, Wash. U., St. Louis, 1984, U. Ill., Chgo., 1985, Tulane U., New Orleans, 1985, U. Minn., Mpls., 1985, Columbia U., N.Y.C., 1986, Rice U., Houston, 1988; participant various confs. Exhbns. of work include World Biennial of Architecture, Sofia, Bulgaria, 1989, Salle des Tirages du Credit Foncier de France, Paris, 1990, Bartlett Sch. Architecture and Urban Design, London, 1991, Gallery of Functional Art, Santa Monica, Calif., 1992, GA Gallery, Tokyo, 1992, Mus. fur Gestaltung Zurich, Switzerland, 1993, Santa Monica (Calif.) Mus. Art, 1993, Fonds Regional D'Art Contemporain du Centre, 1993, Aspen (Colo.) Art Mus., 1993, Centro de Arte y Comunicacion, Buenos Aires, 1993, Contemporary Arts Ctr., Cin., 1993, Philippe Uzzan Galerie, Paris, 1993, Contemporary Arts Ctr., Tours, France, 1993, Internat. Exhbn. Contemporary Architecture, Havana, Cuba, 1994, others. Recipient Progressive Architecture Design award, 1978, 92, Winning Interior Archtl. Record award, 1984, Interiors Design award, 1991. Fellow AIA (L.A. awards 1977, 79, 83, 88, 90, Calif. Coun. awards 1981, 86, 88, L.A. Honor awards 1991, Nat. Honor awards 88, 89, Calif. Coun. Urban Design/Adaptive Re-Use awards 1991, Nat. Interior Design awards 1992, 94, L.A. Design awards 1992, 93). Office: 8557 Higuera St Culver City CA 90232-2535*

MOSS, JACK, print shop executive, textile chemist, consultant; b. Bklyn., Aug. 29, 1928; s. Sol and Rose (Cohen) M.; m. Phyllis Y. Resnick, June 29, 1952; children: William, Michael A. BS in Chemistry, U. Mass., 1951. Plant supt. Vitromar Piece Dye, Paterson, N.J., 1951-58; supt. Sudamtex de Uruguay, Colonia, Uruguay, 1958-61; rsch. chemist GAF Corp., Easton, Pa., 1961-66; tech. rep. Sandoz, Inc., East Hanover, N.J., 1966-70, Ventron Corp., Beverly, Mass., 1970-77; cons. Whittaker Textiles, Marysville, N.B., Can., 1977-78; sales mgr., asst. to pres. Apex Chem Corp., Elizabeth, N.J.,

1975-77; pres. Jack-B-Quick, Inc., Millburn, N.J., 1978-92; ret., 1992; chmn. bd. JBQ Printing Svcs., Inc., Livingston, N.J., Mikie's Inc., Redmond, Wash.; cons. in field; perfectum mondonaire, Mexico City, 1965. Contbr. material on disperse dyes, fiber blends to Chem. Encyc., 1965. Mem. Nat. Assn. Quick Printers, N.J. Assn. Quick Printers (sec., advt. mgr.), C. of C., Masons (master of lodge 1992, 97).

MOSS, LYNDA BOURQUE, museum director. Dir. Western Heritage Ctr., Billings, Mont. Office: Western Heritage Ctr 2822 Montana Ave Billings MT 59101

MOSS, MELODY ANN, history educator, researcher; b. Traverse City, Mich., Sept. 3, 1963; d. Arlo Frederick and Dolores Mary Ann (Rhoades) M. AA in Liberal Arts, Northwestern Mich. Coll., 1985; BA in History, U. Calif., Santa Cruz, 1990, MA in History, 1992, postgrad., 1993. Tchg. asst. in history and women's studies U. Calif., 1989-92, tchg. fellow in history and writing, 1993; lectr. medieval and early modern European history Seattle U., 1994—. Rsch. on witch hunts in early modern England. Mem. Am. Hist. Assn. Office: Seattle U Broadway and Madison Seattle WA 98122

MOSS, MYRA E. See ROLLE, MYRA MOSS

MOSS, RICHARD B., pediatrician; b. N.Y.C., Oct. 30, 1949. MD, SUNY, Downstate, 1975. Intern Children's Meml. Hosp., Chgo., 1975-76, resident, 1976-77; fellow Stanford (Calif.) U. Med. Sch., 1977-79, 80-81; now pediatrician Lucile Salter Packard Children's Hosp., Palo Alto, Calif.; prof. pediats. Stanford U. Med. Sch. Office: Stanford U Sch Med Ctr Dept Pediats Stanford CA 94305-5119

MOSS, STANLEY W., orthopedic surgeon; b. Salt Lake City, Apr. 20, 1949; s. Lee W. and Loraine (Law) M.; m. Diane Gillespie, May 30, 1973; children: Brian, Eric, Mark, Lisa, Craig. BS in Med. Biology, U. Utah, 1971, MD, 1973. Diplomate Am. Bd. Orthopedic Surgery. Straight surg. intern U. Calif., San Diego, 1973-74; resident in orthopaedic surgery U. Utah Med. Ctr., Salt Lake City, 1977-81; pvt. practice, Boise, Idaho, 1981—. Capt. M.C., U.S. Army, 1974-77. Fellow Am. Acad. Orthopedic Surgery, Western Orthopedic Assn. Office: 333 N 1st St Ste 240 Boise ID 83702-6132

MOSTELLER, JAMES WILBUR, III, data processing executive; b. Ft. Riley, Kans., June 21, 1940; s. James Wilbur, Jr., and Ruth Renfro (Thompson) M.; B.S. in Econs., Rensselaer Poly. Inst., 1962; M.B.A., Temple U., 1971; m. Sandra Josephine Stevenson, Oct. 13, 1962; children—Margaret, Steven, Michael. Data processing systems analyst, Philco-Ford, Ft. Washington, Pa., 1966-69; data processing analyst and supr., Merck Sharp & Dohme, West Point, Pa., 1969-75, dir. mgmt. info. systems KELCO div. Merck and Co., San Diego, 1975-87; dir. info. mgmt. Advanced Systems div. United Technologies, San Diego, 1987-88; computer scientist Navy Personnel Research and Devel. Ctr., San Diego, 1988—. Bd. dirs. New Horizons Montessori Sch., Ft. Washington, Pa., 1974-75; leader youth programs North County YMCA, 1977-81; mem. San Diego Research Park Com., 1978-86; 1st. v.p., mem. exec. com. San Diego Space and Sci. Found., 1985-92. With USN, 1962-66, capt. Res., 1966-93. Cert. in data processing. Mem. Data Processing Mgmt. Assn., Assn. Systems Mgmt., Naval Res. Assn. (life), U.S. Naval Inst. (life), Beta Gamma Sigma, Sigma Alpha Epsilon (chpt. pres. 1961-62). Office: Navy Pers R & D Ctr San Diego CA 92152-6800

MOTE, CLAYTON DANIEL, JR., mechanical engineer, educator, administrator; b. San Francisco, Feb. 5, 1937; s. Clayton Daniel and Eugenia (Isnardi) M.; m. Patricia Jane Lewis, Aug. 18, 1962; children: Melissa Michelle, Adam Jonathan. BSc, U. Calif., Berkeley, 1959, MS, 1960, PhD, 1963. Registered profl. engr., Calif. Asst. specialist U. Calif. Forest Products Labs., 1961-62; asst. mech. engr., 1962-63; lectr. mech. engring. U. Calif., Berkeley, 1962-63, asst. prof., 1967-69, asst. research engr., 1968-69, assoc. prof., assoc. research engr., 1969-73, prof., 1973—, vice chmn. mech. engring. dept., 1976-80, 83-86, chmn. mech. engring. dept., 1987-91, vice chancellor univ. rels., FANUC chair mech. systems, 1991—; research fellow U. Birmingham, Eng., 1963-64; asst. prof. Carnegie Inst. Tech., 1964-67; vis. prof. Norwegian Inst. Wood Tech., 1972-73, vis. sr. scientist, 1976, 78, 80, 84, 85; cons. in engring. design and analysis; sr. scientist Alexander Von Humboldt Found., Fed. Republic Germany, 1988, Japan Soc. for Promotion of Sci., 1991; mem. adv. bd. for mech. engring. Ga. Inst. Tech., Carnegie Mellon U.; pres. U. Calif. Berkeley Found.; trustee Behring-Hofmann Ednl. Inst. Mem. editl. bd. Soma Jour. Sound and Vibration, Machine Vibration; contbr. articles to profl. jours.; patentee in field. NSF fellow, 1963-64; recipient Disting. Teaching award, U. Calif., 1971, Pi Tau Sigma Excellence in Teaching award, U. Calif., 1975, Humboldt Prize, Fed. Republic Germany, 1988, Frederick W. Taylor Rsch. medal. Soc. Mfg. Engrs., 1991, Hetenyi award Soc. Exptl. Mechanics, 1992. Fellow NAE, AAAS, ASME (Blackall award 1975, v.p. environ. and transp. 1986-90, nat. chmn. noise control and acoustics 1980-84, chmn. San Francisco sect. 1978-79, Disting. Svc. award 1991, Charles Russ Richards award 1994, Rayleigh lectr. 1994), Internat. Acad. Wood Sci., Acoustical Soc. Am.; mem. ASTM (com. on snow skiing F-27 1984-87), Am. Acad. Mechanics, Am. Soc. Biomechanics, Orthopaedic Rsch. Soc., Internat. Soc. Skiing Safety (v.p., sec. 1977-85, bd. dirs. 1977—, chmn. sci. com. 1985—), Sigma Xi, Pi Tau Sigma, Tau Beta Pi. Office: U Calif 2440 Bancroft Way Berkeley CA 94704-1603

MOTLEY, MICHAEL TILDEN, communication educator; b. Salt Lake City, Jan. 4, 1945; s. Henry Lee and Lyda Edyth (Simpson) M.; m. Deirdre Mary Sullivan, Dec. 15, 1973; children: Shannon, Shane. BA, U. Tex., 1965, MA, 1967; PhD, Pa. State U., 1970. Asst. prof. Calif. State U., Fresno, 1970-71; asst. prof., assoc. prof. Calif. State U., L.A., 1971-77; assoc. prof. Ohio State U., Columbus, Ohio, 1977-82; prof. U. Calif., Davis, 1982—. Author: Orientations to Language and Communication, 1978, Overcoming Your Fear of Public Speaking: A Proven Method, 1995; contbr. articles to profl. jours. Mem. Western Speech Communication Assn. (chair lang. behavior divsn. 1974-76), Speech Communication Assn. (chairlang. sci. divsn. 1976-77). Office: U Calif Dept Communication Davis CA 95616

MOTOYAMA, CATHERINE TOMOKO, communications educator; b. Honolulu, Apr. 7, 1955; d. Iwao and Sumie (Kubota) M. BA, U. Hawaii, 1977; MA, U. Wash., 1982, PhD, 1987. Lectr. U. Wash., Seattle, 1987-88; vis. asst. prof. Ariz. State U., Tempe, 1988-90; assoc. prof. Coll. San Mateo, Calif., 1990—; founder, dir. Student Tchr.Excellence Through Mentoring, San Mateo, 1992—; v.p. governing coun. acad. senate Coll. San Mateo, 1996—. Scriptwriter, dir.: Overblown with Hope, 1996; contbr. articles to jours. Bd. dirs. Japanese Am. Citizens League, San Mateo, 1992—; pres., bd. dirs. Talespinners Theatre, San Francisco, 1994—. Recipient Exemplary Program award Bd. Govs. Calif. C.C.s, Ventura, 1995. Mem. Speech Comm. Assn. (rep. legis. coun. 1996—), Pacific Asian Comm. Assn. (editl. bd. 1996—), Asian Pacific Am. Caucus (chair exec. bd. 1995-96), Western States Comm. Assn. (del.-at-large legis. assembly, Master Tchr. award 1997). Office: Coll San Mateo 1700 W Hillsdale Blvd San Mateo CA 94402

MOTT, JUNE MARJORIE, school system administrator; b. Faribault, Minn., Mar. 8, 1920; d. David C. and Tillie W. (Nelson) Shifflett; m. Elwood Knight Mott, Oct. 18, 1958. BS, U. Minn., 1943, MA, 1948. Tchr. high schs. in Minn., 1943-46, 48-53, 54-57; script writer, Hollywood, Calif., 1953-54; tchr. English, creative writing and journalism Mt. Miguel High Sch., Spring Valley, Calif., 1957-86, chmn. English dept., 1964-71, chmn. Dist. English council, 1967-68; mem. Press Bur., Grossmont (Calif.) High Sch. Dist., 1958-86; elected to Grossmont Union High Sch. Governing Bd., 1986—, clk. sch. bd., 1989, v.p. governing bd., 1989-90, 93, pres. sch. bd., 1991-92, v.p., 1992-93, pres. governing bd., 1993-94, v.p., 1996—; script-writer TV prodn. Lamp Unto My Feet, Jam Dandy Corp.; free-lance writer, cons. travel writer, photographer; editor, publ Listening Heart, 1989. Author, editor in field. Vice chmn. polit. action San Diego County Regional Resource Ctr., 1980-81; mem. S.D. Bd. of Alcohol and Drug Abuse Prevention, 1990—, Curriculum Com. Grossmont Dist., 1990—, Site Facilities Com., Master Planning Com., 1992—, East County Issues and Mgmt. Com., 1990—, East County Women in Edn.; apptd. del. Calif. Sch. Bds. Assn., 1992—, del. assembly, 1992—, elected to region 17 del. assembly, 1993—; v.p., pub. rels. chmn. Lemon Grove Luth. Ch., 1962-78, 89—, v.p., 1993, pres. 1994. Writing project fellow U. Calif., San Diego, 1978; named Outstanding Journalism Tchr., State of Calif., Outstanding Humanities Tchr., San Diego County, Tchr. of Yr. for San Diego County, 1978; U. Cambridge scholar, 1982; Woman of Yr. Lemon Grove Soroptimists, 1990. Mem. ASCD, NEA, AAUW, Nat. Council Tchrs. English, Nat. Journalism Assn., Calif. Assn. Tchrs. English, Calif. Tchrs. Assn., So. Calif. Journalism Assn., Calif. Sch. Bds. Assn. (elected del. region 17, del. assembly 1993—), Calif. Elected Women's Assn. for Edn. Rsch. (ednl. cons. 1990), San Diego County Journalism Educators Assn. (pres. 1975-76), Grossmont Edn. Assn. (pres. 1978-80), Greater San Diego Council Tchrs. English, Nat. Writers Club, Am. Guild Theatre Organists, Am. Guild Organists, Calif. Retired Tchrs. Assn. (membership chairwoman 1986-89, pres. chpt. # 69 1989-94, parlimentarian 1992-93), Lemon Grove C. of C. (mem. econ. devel. com. 1994—), Nat. Sch. Bds. Assn., Order Ea. Star, Kiwanis (pres. elect Lemon grove chpt. 1992, program chmn., pres. 1993-94), Sigma Delta Chi, Delta Kappa Gamma (pres. Theta Gamma chpt. 1993—). Democrat. Home and Office: 2885 New Jersey Ave Lemon Grove CA 91945-2826 *Personal philosophy: Christian principles have sustained me all my life; my topmost priority is to love others and promote peace.*

MOTTRAM, ROBERT HUGH, journalist; b. Yonkers, N.Y., June 12, 1940; s. John Wilbur and Fay (Burak) M.; m. Karen Ann Melick, Aug. 7, 1962; children: Cheryl Ann, Dianna Marie, John Forrest. BS, S.D. State U., 1962. State editor Rapid City (S.D.) Daily Jour., 1963-66; reporter, corres. Associated Press, 1966-73; reporter, chief editorial writer, outdoor writer, columnist The News Tribune, Tacoma, Wash., 1973—. Author: Saltwater Salmon Angling, 1989 (Excellence in Craft award 1990). Recipient Inspirational award Wash. State Sportsmen's Coun., 1990, Spl. award Trout Unltd., 1993. Mem. N.W. Outdoor Writers Assn. pres. 1993-94, chmn. bd. 1994-95, Best of the Best award in newspaper category 1995-96), Outdoor Writers Assn. of Am. Office: News Tribune PO Box 11000 Tacoma WA 98411-0008

MOTULSKY, ARNO GUNTHER, geneticist, physician, educator; b. Fischhausen, Germany, July 5, 1923; came to U.S., 1941; s. Herman and Rena (Sass) Molton; m. Gretel C. Stern, Mar. 22, 1945; children: Judy, Harvey, Arlene. Student, Cen. YMCA Coll., Chgo., 1941-43, Yale U., 1943-44; BS, U. Ill., 1945, MD, 1947, DSc (hon.), 1982, MD (hon.), 1991. Diplomate Am. Bd. Internal Medicine, Am. Bd. Med. Genetics. Intern, fellow, resident Michael Reese Hosp., Chgo., 1947-51; staff mem. charge clin. investigation dept. hematology Army Med. Service Grad. Sch., Walter Reed Army Med. Ctr., Washington, 1952-53; research assoc. internal medicine George Washington U. Sch. Medicine, 1952-53; from instr. to assoc. prof. dept. medicine U. Wash. Sch. Medicine, Seattle, 1953-61, prof. medicine, prof. genetics, 1961—; head div. med. genetics, dir. genetics clinic Univ. Hosp., Seattle, 1959-89; dir. Ctr. for Inherited Diseases, Seattle, 1972-90; attending physician Univ. Hosp., Seattle; cons. Pres.'s Commn. for Study of Ethical Problems in Medicine and Biomed. and Behavioral Research, 1979-83; cons. various coms. NRC, NIH, WHO, others. Editor Am. Jour. Human Genetics, 1969-75, Human Genetics, 1969—. Commonwealth Fund fellow in human genetics Univ. Coll., London, 1957-58; John and Mary Markle scholar in med. sci., 1957-62; fellow Ctr. Advanced Study in Behavioral Scis., Stanford U., 1976-77, Inst. Advanced Study, Berlin, 1984. Fellow ACP, AAAS; mem. NAS, Internat. Soc. Hematology, Am. Fedn. Clin. Research, Genetics Soc. Am., Western Soc. Clin. Research, Am. Soc. Human Genetics, Am. Soc. Clin. Investigation, Am. Assn. Physicians, Inst. of Medicine, Am. Acad. Arts and Scis. Home: 4347 53rd Ave NE Seattle WA 98105-4938 Office: U Wash Divsn Med Genetics Box 356423 Seattle WA 98195-6423

MOU, THOMAS WILLIAM, physician, medical educator and consultant; b. Phila., May 17, 1920; s. Thomas Simonsen and Ellen Marie (Mathiesen) M.; m. Marie Elizabeth Hartmann, Dec. 29, 1945 (div. Oct., 1976); children: Susan, Roberta; m. M. Delma Jane Schreiber, Nov. 11, 1976. BSc in Bacteriology, Phila. Coll. Pharm & Sci., 1941; MD, U. Rochester, 1950. Diplomate Nat. Bd. Med. Examiners. Instr. medicine and bacteriology U. Rochester (N.Y.) Sch. of Medicine, 1954-56; asst. prof. preventive medicine to prof. cmty. medicine SUNY at Syracuse, 1956-70; exec. dean to assoc chancellor health sci. SUNY Ctrl. Adminstrn., Albany, 1970-77; dean clin. campus W. Va. U., Charleston, 1977-85; pres. Ednl. Commn. for Fgn. Med. Grads., Phila., 1986-88; dean emeritus W. Va. U. Med. Ctr., Morgantown, 1986—; geriatric practice Adult Medicine Specialists, Pueblo, Colo., 1990—; cons. Carnegie Commn. for Advancement of Tchg., Princeton, N.J., 1987-88, Charles A. Dana Found., N.Y.C., 1988, Geriatric Pharmacy Inst. of Phila. Coll. of Pharmacy and Sci., 1988. Contbr. 36 article or presentations to profl. jours or sci. confs. Capt. Sanitary Corps, 1941-45. Recipient Disting. Alumnus award Phila. Coll. Pharmacy and Sci., 1975, award of distinction and honor Ben Franklin Soc. SUNY, N.Y.C., 1975, Koch medal Am. Optometric Soc., N.Y.C., 1976; T.W. Mou Endowed Lectureship W. Va. U., Charleston, 1985. Fellow Am. Coll. Physicians, Am. Coll. Preventive Medicine, Phila. Coll. Physicians. Home: 3050 Valleybrook Ln Colorado Springs CO 80904 Office: Adult Medicine Specialists 314 W 16th St Pueblo CO 81003

MOUCHIZADEH, JOSEPH, urologist; b. London, Dec. 19, 1955; s. David and Bertha (Horesh) M. MB BS, U. London, 1979. Diplomate Am. Bd. Urology. Resident in urology U. N.Mex. Albuquerque, 1987-91; urologist Cigna Health Plans (now Friendly Hills Healthcare Network), L.A., 1991-95; clin. attending urologist L.A. County Hosp./U. So. Calif., 1992-95; urologist Friendly Hills Hosp., L.A., 1996—. Office: Friendly Hills Clinic 450 E Huntington Dr Arcadia CA 91006-3748

MOUFFE, DAVID H., woodworker, sculptor; b. Boulder, Colo., May 11, 1955; s. Frank E. and Barbara S. (Swann) M.; m. Erika M. Mattekowitsch, May 30, 1993. Head chef Old West Steak House, Steamboat Springs, Colo., 1983-87; owner Maui Motion Photography, Kihei, Maui, Hawaii, 1988-92, Tropical Woodworks, Kihei, Maui, Hawaii, 1992—; woodwork studios cons. Lahaina Arts Soc., 1995-96. Artist: Wave Cave wood sculpture, 1996. Democrat.

MOULAKIS, ATHANASIOS, philosopher, educator; b. Athens, Greece, July 11, 1945; came to U.S., 1986; s. Michael and Frosso (Nassiakou) M.; m. Eleanor Gail Durham, July 9, 1969; 1 child, Anne. PhD, Ruhr U., Bochum, Germany, 1969, habilitation, 1979. Instr. U. Cologne, Germany, 1969; asst. prof. Ruhr U., Bochum, 1970-78; lectr. London Sch. Econs., 1978-79; prof. European Univ. Inst., Florence, Italy, 1979-86; guest prof. U. Calif., San Diego, 1986-87; rsch. assoc. Harvard U., Cambridge, Mass., 1988; tutor St. John's Coll., Annapolis, Md., 1988-89; Herbst prof. of Humanities, dir. Herbst program U. Colo., Boulder, 1989—; hon. rsch. fellow Univ. Coll. London. Author: Homonoia, 1972, Simone Weil, Die Politik der Askese, 1981, Beyond Utility, 1993 (Choice Outstanding Book of Yr., Ness Book prize Am. Assn. Colls. and Univs.); editor: The Promise of History, 1986. Vice chmn. bd. advisers Am. Sch., Florence, Italy, 1981-83. Named Olin Disting. Lectr. in Philosophy of Free Instns., Harvard U., 1981. Mem. Inst. Internat. de Philosophie Polit. (bd. dirs.), Hellenic Philosophic Soc. (corr.), Circolo dell' Unione, Florence. Mem. Greek Orthodox Ch. Home: 600 Cascade Ave Boulder CO 80302-7428 Office: Univ Colo Campus Box 422 Boulder CO 80309

MOULE, WILLIAM NELSON, electrical engineer; b. Highland Park, Mich., Sept. 13, 1924; s. Hollis Creager and Kate DeEtte (Hill) M.; m. Barbara Ann Bagley, June 27, 1953; children: Janice Louise, Robert Hollis (dec.), Linda Anne, Nancy Lynn Moule Moles. BSEE, Mich. State U., 1949; MSEE, U. Pa., 1957. Reg. profl. engr., N.J. Design engr. Radio Corp. of Am., Camden, N.J., 1949-59; sr. design engr. Radio Corp. of Am., Moorestown, N.J., 1959-67; sr. engr. Emerson Elec. Co., St. Louis, 1967-70, Emerson Elec. Rantec Divsn., Calabasas, Calif., 1970; sr. staff engr. Raytheon Co., Santa Barbara, Calif., 1970-73, ITT Gilfillan, Van Nuys, Calif., 1973, Jet Propulsion Lab., Pasadena, Calif., 1973-79; sr. rsch devel. engr. Lockheed Advanced Devel. Co., Burbank, Calif., 1979—. Patentee numerous inventions, 1956—. Dir. nat. alumni bd. Mich. State U., East Lansing, 1984-87; pres. Big Ten Club of So. Calif., L.A., 1992. Staff sgt. USAAF, 1943-46. Mem. IEEE (sr., L.A. chpt. sec., treas. Antennas and Propagation soc. 1987-89, vice chmn. 1989-90, chmn. 1990-91), 305th Bombardment Group Meml. Assn. (life). Democrat. Presbyn. Home: 5831 Fitzpatrick Rd Calabasas CA 91302-1104 Office: Lockheed Martin Skunk Works 1011 Lockheed Wy Palmdale CA 93599

MOULTON-GERTIG, SUZANNE CAREY LEROY, musician, educator; b. Exeter, N.H., Feb. 26, 1950; d. Gerald Baker and Leah Margaret (Colby) LeRoy; m. John King Gertig, Oct. 13, 1990; 1 child, Christina Ann. B in Music Edn., James Madison U., 1974; MLS, Kent State U., 1979, M in Musicology, 1982. Music libr. Wallace Libr., Fitchburg Mass., 1982-83; assoc. prof. Univ. Denver, 1985—; assoc. dir. Reznicek Soc., Indian, Alaska, 1993—. Editor Ars Musica Denver, 1990-91. mem. Am. Musicol. Soc. (chpt. pres. 1987-88), Music Libr. Assn., Am. Harp Soc. (editor jour. 1994-96), Beta Phi Mu, Pi Kappa Lamda. Office: U Denver Lamont Sch Music 7111 Montview Blvd Denver CO 80220

MOUSEL, CRAIG LAWRENCE, lawyer; b. St. Louis, July 22, 1947; s. George William and Charlotte (Howard) M.; m. Polly Deane Burkett, Dec. 21, 1974; children: Donna, Dennis, D'Arcy. AB, U. So. Calif., 1969; JD, Ariz. State U., 1972. Bar: Ariz. 1973, U.S. Dist. Ct. Ariz. 1973, U.S. Ct. Appeals (9th cir.) 1973, Colo. 1993. Adminstrv. asst. to Hon. Sandra O'Connor Ariz. State Senate, Phoenix, 1971-72; asst. atty. gen. Ariz. Atty. Gen.'s Office, Phoenix, 1973-75; ptnr. Sundberg & Mousel, Phoenix, 1975—; spl. counsel City of Chandler, 1991; varsity baseball coach Valley Luth. H.S.; lectr. Ariz. State U. Coll. Bus., 1993—. Hearing officer Ariz. State Personnel Bd., 1976-80, spl. appeals counsel, 1978—; hearing officer Ariz. Outdoor Recreation Coordinating Commn., 1975; dep. state land commr. Ariz. State Land Dept., 1978; precinct capt. Rep. Com. Fellow Ariz. Bar Found.; mem. ABA, ATLA, Ariz. Bar Assn., Sports Lawyer's Assn., Internat. Platform Assn., Ariz. Club, Am. Baseball Coaches Assn., USC Ptnrs. Alumni Group. Office: Sundberg & Mousel 934 W Mcdowell Rd Phoenix AZ 85007-1730

MOUSKOS, ANDREAS ALEXANDER, psychotherapist; b. London, Jan. 28, 1953; came to U.S., 1976; s. Alexandros and Augusta (Elia) M.; m. Christy Ioannou, Oct.9, 1992 (div. Apr. 1993); children: Socrates, Mirabelle; m. Rhodora Vidal, May 31, 1994. MA, Boulder (Colo.) Grad. Sch., 1989. Carrier U.S. Postal Svc., Niles, Mich., 1977-81; mktg. dir. Golden Lotus Inc., Englewood, Colo., 1981-84; owner Spiritual Integration Ctr., Denver, 1985-94; co-owner Infinite Human Potential, Lakewood, Colo., 1994—; meditation tchr. Aurora (Colo.) Presbyn. Hosp., 1987-91. Author: (audio tapes) Minding Your Sound Health, 1990. Ridhwan. Office: Infinite Human Potential 3005 Xenon St Lakewood CO 80215-6560

MOUSSEUX, RENATE, language educator; b. Stuttgart, Germany, Oct. 27, 1942; came to U.S., 1964; d. Emile and Gertrud Muller; m. Patrick Mousseux, Dec. 12, 1963; 1 child, Marc. BA, Padagogische Hochschule, Germany; MA, Grand Canyon U.; BL French, German, ESL, Phoenix U. Cert. French, German, psychology, bilingual French, ESL, secondary grades 7-12, Ariz., Calif. Prof. German Berlitz Sch. Lang., Sherman Oaks, Calif., 1966-67, Thunderbird Grad. Sch. Internat. Mgmt., Glendale, Ariz., 1968-72; prof. German and French Scottsdale Dist. H.S., 1980—; prof. French and German Rio Salado C.C., 1976-86; prof. French Scottsdale C.C., 1990-96, U. Phoenix, 1991—, 1991—; lit. and talent agt., co-producer for film, 1991—; distbr. Native Am. Music; bus. lang. trainer , course developer various corps.; trainer student tchrs. Ariz. State U., Ottawa U. Author: Accellerated French (Vive le Francais), 1989, Accellerated German (Wilikommen Deutsch), 1990, Accellerated Spanish (Viva el Espanol), 1991, Accellerated Japanese (Moshi Moshi), 1991, Accellerated English (Hello English), 1992. With Essential Skills Com. Ariz. State Bd. Edn. Recipient Ariz. Fgn. Lang. Tchr. of Yr. award Ariz. Assn. Fgn. Lang. Tchrs., 1986, Exceptional Mentorship Skills award Ariz. State U., 1994, Excellence in Mentorship cert. Ariz. State Coll., 1995; named Tchr. of Yr. U.S. West Outstanding Tchr. Program, 1989. Mem. NEA, Nat. Geographic Soc., Am. Assn. Tchrs. German, Alliance Francaise, French Tchrs. Assn., Cultural Heritage Alliance, Ariz. Fgn. Lang. Assn., Scottsdale Edn. Assn. Home: 15611 N Boulder Dr Fountain Hill AZ 85268 Office: Chaparral High School 6935 E Gold Dust Ave Scottsdale AZ 85253-1447

MOWAT, GREG THOMAS, state official; b. Bellingham, Wash., Dec. 11, 1948; s. Jack Thomas and Marjorie June (Vandemark) M.; m. Meiman Liu, Apr. 12, 1971; 1 child, Lisa Meiling. BA, Western Wash. U., 1976. Labor rep. Retail Clks. Union, Bellingham, 1976-78; labor rep. Svc. Employees Union, Bellingham, 1978-83, Tacoma, 1983-88; dir. Svc. Employees Internat. Union, Tacoma, 1988-91; program mgr. employment stds. Wash. Dept. Labor and Industries, Tumwater, 1991—. Bd. dirs. Wash. Citizen Action, Seattle, 1982—, United Way Pierce County, Tacoma, 1988—; mem. Am. Leadership Forum, Tacoma, 1991—; chmn. Pierce County Dems., 1992—. Recipient G. Ginnis Cmty. Svc. award Pierce County Labor Coun., 1992. Mem. Elks. Home: 4108 N 28th St Tacoma WA 98407 Office: Dept Labor and Industries 7273 Linderson Way Olympia WA 98505

MOWER, MELISSA BEE, magazine editor, writer; b. South Weymouth, Mass., July 16, 1959; d. Robert Ellis and Virginia Keith. BA, Calif. State U., Chico, 1982. Reporter Lassen Advocate, Susanville, Calif., 1983-84; reporter Oakdale (Calif.) Leader, 1984; reporter/editor MPG Newspapers, Plymouth, Mass., 1986-89; mng. editor Massage Mag., Davis, Calif., 1990-93; sr. editor Massage Mag., Davis, 1993-94; southwestern editor Massage Mag., Tucson, 1994-96; sr. editor Massage Mag., Santa Rosa, Calif., 1996—, media rels. coord. Sohnen-Moe Assocs., Tucson, 1994—. Democrat. Office: 1223 College Ave Ste 2 Santa Rosa CA 95404

MOWER, WILLIAM REX, medical educator, researcher; b. Ogden, Utah, Jan. 16, 1956; s. William R. Jr. and Paula (Blanch) M. BS in Math. and Physics, U. Utah, 1977, M in Engring., 1979, MD, 1985; MS, UCLA, 1994. Diplomate Am. Bd. Med. Examiners, Am. Bd. Emergency Medicine. Sci. analyst, programmer Hercules, Inc., Salt Lake City, 1979-81; tech. analyst, programmer BSL Techs., Salt Lake City, 1981-83; resident in surgery U Utah, Salt Lake City, 1985-87; resident in emergency medicine UCLA Emergency Medicine Ctr., 1987-90; cons. specialist Olive View Med. Ctr., L.A., 1990-92; rsch. fellow in emergency medicine UCLA Sch. Medicine, 1990-92, asst. prof. medicine and emergency medicine, 1992—. Contbr. articles to med. jours. Recipient various awards. Mem. Soc. Acad. Emergency Medicine, Alpha Omega Alpha. Christian. Office: UCLA Emergency Medicine Ctr 10833 Le Conte Ave Los Angeles CA 90024-1602

MOYEMONT, TERRY WALTER, video producer, videographer; b. Joplin, Mo., Aug. 28, 1943; s. Taylor Eugene and Geraldine Irene (Frederisy) M.; m. Mary Carol Van Houtte, May 22, 1987. BA in Philosophy, U. Chgo., 1966; postgrad., U. Ill., 1974-76, U. Ill., Chgo., 1978. Rsch. asst. U. Ill. Edn., Urbana, 1973-77; prodr., videographer Afterimage Video, Chgo., 1979-81; prodr., mktg. profl. Automotion Opticals, San Francisco, 1981-85; mktg. dir. Optimotion Co., San Francisco, 1986-88; prodr., videographer Head of Steam Video, Bainbridge Island, Wash., 1988-92; edn. dir. Mont. Pub. TV Assn., Helena, 1992-95; tech. adv. bd. Seattle Ctrl. C.C., 1990-91; cons. prodr. Cultural Affairs Dept., City of Chgo., 1990-91; ednl. cons. Young Audiences Film Festival, Helena, 1993, 95; dir. prodn. Bainbridge Island Broadcasting, 1996. Prodr. (feature film) Stereopticon, 1969, (videos) Running a Steam Locomotive, 1979, The Glass Dimension, 1994. Home and Office: 7873 Fletcher Bay Rd NE Bainbridge Island WA 98110

MOYER, CRAIG ALAN, lawyer; b. Bethlehem, Pa., Oct. 17, 1955; s. Charles Alvin and Doris Mae (Schantz) M.; m. Candace Darrow Brigham, May 3, 1986; 1 stepchild, Jason; 1 child, Chelsea A. BA, U. So. Calif., 1977; JD, U. Calif., L.A., 1980. Bar: Calif. 1980, U.S. Dist. Ct. (cen. dist.) Calif. 1980. Assoc. Nossaman, Krueger et al, L.A., 1980-83, Finley, Kumble et al, Beverly Hills, Calif., 1983-85; ptnr. Demetriou, Del Guercio, Springer & Moyer, L.A., 1985—; instr. Air Resources Bd. Symposium, Sacramento, 1985—, U. Calif., Santa Barbara, 1989—; lectr. Hazmat Conf., Long Beach, Calif., 1986—, Pacific Automotive Show, Reno, Nev., 1989—; lectr. hazardous materials, environ. law UCLA; lectr. environ. law U. Calif., Santa Barbara; lectr. hazardous materials regulatory framework U. Calif., Santa Barbara. Co-author: Hazard Communication Handbook: A Right to Know Compliance Guide, 1990, Clean Air Act Handbook, 1991; contbr. articles to profl. jours. Pres. Calif. Pub. Interest Rsch. Group, L.A., 1978-80. Mem. ABA (natural resources sect.), Calif. Bar Assn., L.A. County Bar Assn. (environ. law sect., chmn. legis. rev. com., mem. exec. com.), Tau Kappa Epsilon (pres. L.A. chpt. 1975-76, Outstanding Alumnus 1983). Republican. Office: Demetriou Del Guercio et al Chase Plz 801 S Grand Ave Fl 10 Los Angeles CA 90017-4613

MOYER, J. KEITH, newspaper editor. Exec. editor The Fresno (Calif.) Bee. Office: The Fresno Bee 1626 E St Fresno CA 93786

MOYER, LINDA LEE, artist, educator; b. Niles, Mich., Feb. 11, 1942; d. Roy Delbert and Estelle Leona (Beaty) Moyer; m. Brock David Williams Dec. 3, 1994; 1 child from previous marriage, Metin Ata Gunsay. Student, Occidental Coll., 1959-61; BA, UCLA, 1964; MA, Calif. State U., Long Beach, 1977, MFA, 1980. Cert. tchr. secondary edn., cert. instr. C.C., Calif. Instr. art. Huntington Beach (Calif.) Union High Sch., 1967-81, Calif. State U., Long Beach, 1981-85, Saddleback Coll., Mission Viejo, Calif., 1986-88, Fullerton (Calif.) Coll., 1990, 94, Goldenwest Coll., Huntington Beach, 1990; artist in residence St. Margaret's Episcopal Sch., San Juan Capistrano, 1993; lectr., workshop presenter Santa Barbara (Calif.) C.C., 1992; series lectr. Rancho Santiago Coll., 1985, 90; lectr. Cypress Coll., 1986, Watercolor West, 1987, 94, others. One-woman shows include Laguna Beach (Calif.) Mus. Art, 1982, Orlando Gallery, Sherman Oaks, Calif., 1983, Long Beach City Coll., 1983, Orange County Ctr. Contemporary Art, 1982, 85, Cerritos Coll., Norwalk, Calif., 1986, Louis Newman Galleries, Beverly Hills, 1986, 88, 90, Westmont Coll., Santa Barbara, Calif., 1992, Maturango Mus., Ridgecrest, Calif., 1996; exhibited in group shows at Owensboro (Ky.) Mus. Fine Arts, 1979, Burpee Art Mus., Rockford, Ill., 1981, Newport Harbor Art Mus., Newport Beach, Calif., 1981, Nat. Acad. Galleries, N.Y.C., 1982, Leslie Levy Gallery, Scottsdale, Ariz., 1983, Art Inst. So. Calif., 1984, Saddleback Coll., Mission Viejo, Calif., 1988, Riverside (Calif.) Art Mus., 1989, Ch. of Jesus Christ of LDS Mus. Art and History, Salt Lake City, 1988, 91, Mt. San Antonio Coll., Calif., 1996, others; represented in permanent collections Home Savings Bank of Am., Nat. Bank of La Jolla, Greenburg Deposit Bank, Ashland, Ky., INMA Gallery, Saudi Arabia, pvt. collectors. Recipient Gold Medal of Honor, Am. Watercolor Soc., 1982, Walser S. Greathouse medal, 1988, Gold Medal of Honor for watercolor Allied Artists Am., 1982, cash merit award Ch. of Jesus Christ Latter Day Saints Mus. Art and History, 1991. Signature mem. Nat. Watercolor Soc., Watercolor West (1st award 1984), West Coast Watercolor Soc.; mem. Women Painters West. Mormon. Home and Office: 9622 Zetland Dr Huntington Beach CA 92646-6026

MOYES, TERENCE E., publishing executive; b. London, Apr. 22, 1942; came to U.S., 1963; s. Ronald A. and Eileen E.R. (Knight) M.; m. Irene Spencer, Sept. 25, 1942; children: Douglas, Stuart. Classified advt. mgr. George Newnes Ltd., London, 1960-63; advt. dir. Camping Jour., N.Y.C., 1965-70; advt. dir. World Tennis mag. CBS Mags., N.Y.C., 1978-79; advt. dir. Ski Mag. Times Mirror Mags., N.Y.C., 1970-77, 79-81, pub. Popular Sci. Mag., 1981-86; v.p. advt. Ski Bus. Mag., Darien, Conn., 1986-89; v.p., gen. mgr. Ski Racing Internat., Waitsfield, Vt., 1989-91; gen. mgr. Bicycle Retailer Mag. divsn. Miller Freeman Inc., Santa Fe, N.Mex., 1992-96; publisher Bicycle Retailer Mag. & Wintersport Bus. divsn., Santa Fe, 1997—; pub. cons. N.Y.C., 1986-89. Office: Miller Freeman Inc 502 W Cordova Santa Fe NM 87501

MOYS, JACK J., sales and advertising executive; b. Idaho Falls, Idaho, Sept. 19, 1918; s. John E. and Zouva Zelma (Benham) M.; m. Marian I. Frauen, June 18, 1949 (div. Apr. 1980); children: Michele, Milo. Grad., h.s., Seattle, 1936. Local freelance radio drama KOL Radio, Seattle, 1933-36; network freelance radio drama CBS, L.A., 1937-41; v.p., gen. sales mgr. KPOJ Radio, Portland, Oreg., 1961-66; pres., gen. mgr. KXA Radio, Seattle, 1967-70; v.p., gen. sales mgr. KPOJ and KPOK Radio, Portland, 1970-73; exec. v.p., mgr. Evans Pacific Advt., Portland, 1973-82; mktg. dir. KXL Radio, Portland, 1983-90; owner Jack Moys Enterprises, Milwaukie, Oreg., 1991—; chmn. Oreg. bd. Am. Assn. Advt. Agys., 1977. Chmn. programs United Fund, Portland, 1964. Sgt. U.S. Army, 1945-46, Okinawa. Mem. Advt. Golf Assn. Oreg. (pres. bd., nat. exec. bd. 1988-92, Outstanding Svc. award 1987), Inspirators of Oreg. (pres., bd. dirs., First Ann. Inspirator of Yr. award 1981), Elks. Home: 2710 SE Courtney # 27 Milwaukee OR 97222

MOZENA, JOHN DANIEL, podiatrist; b. Salem, Oreg., June 9, 1956; s. Joseph Iner and Mary Teresa (Delaney) M.; m. Elizabeth Ann Hintz, June 2, 1979; children: Christine Hintz, Michelle Delaney. Student, U. Oreg., 1974-79; B in Basic Med. Scis., Calif. Coll. Podiatric Medicine, D in Podiatric Medicine, 1983. Diplomate Am. Bd. Podiatric Surgery. Resident in surg. podiatry Hillside Hosp., San Diego, 1983-84; pvt. practice podiatry Portland, Oreg., 1984—; dir. residency Med. Ctr. Hosp., Portland, 1985-91; lectr. Nat. Podiatric Assn. Seminar, 1990, Am. Coll. Gen. Practitioners, 1991, Am. Coll. Family Physician, 1995. Cons. editor Podiatry Mgmt. mag., 1994—; contbr. articles to profl. jours.; patentee sports shoe cleat design, 1985. Podiatric adv. coun. Oreg. Bd. Med. Examiners. Fellow Am Coll. Ambulatory Foot Surgeons, Am. Coll. Foot Surgeons. Republican. Roman Catholic. Office: Town Ctr Foot Clinic 8305 SE Monterey Ave Ste 101 Portland OR 97266-7728

MRACKY, RONALD SYDNEY, marketing and promotion executive, travel consultant; b. Sydney, Australia, Oct. 22, 1932; came to U.S., 1947, naturalized, 1957; s. Joseph and Anna (Janousek) M.; m. Sylvia Frommer, Jan. 1, 1960; children: Enid Hillevi, Jason Adam. Student, English Inst., Prague, Czechoslovakia, 1943-47; grad., Parsons Sch. Design, N.Y.C., 1950-53; postgrad., NYU, 1952-53. Designer D. Deskey Assocs., N.Y.C., 1953-54; art dir., designer ABC-TV, Hollywood, Calif., 1956-57; creative dir. Neal Advt. Assocs., L.A., 1957-59; pres. Richter & Mracky Design Assocs., L.A., 1959-68; pres., CEO Richter & Mracky-Bates div. Ted Bates & Co., L.A., 1968-73, pres., CEO Regency Fin., Internat. Fin. Svcs., Beverly Hills, Calif., 1974-76; sr. ptnr. Sylron Internat., L.A., 1973—; mgmt. dir. for N.Am. Standard Advt.-Tokyo, L.A., 1978-91; CEO Standard/Worldwide Cons. Group, Los Angeles and Tokyo, 1981-87; officer, bd. dirs. Theme Resorts, Inc., Denver, 1979—; prin., officer Prodn. Travel & Tours, Universal City, 1981—, Eques Ltd., L.A., 1988—; mng. ptnr. GO! Pubs., 1993—; cons. in field; exec. dir. Inst. for Internat. Studies and Devel., L.A., 1976-77;. Contbr. articles to profl. jours.; mem. editl. bd., mktg. dir. The African Times and Africa Quar., 1990—. With U.S. Army, 1954-56. Recipient nat. and internat. awards design and mktg. Mem. Am. Mktg. Assn., African Travel Assn. (amb.-at-large, pres. So. Calif. chpt.), L.A. Publicity Club, Pacific Asia Travel Assn., S.Am. Travel Assn., Am. Soc. Travel Agents. Office: 10554 Riverside Dr Toluca Lake CA 91602-2441

MUCH, KATHLEEN, editor; b. Houston, Apr. 30, 1942; d. C. Frederick and Ortrud V. (Lefevre) M.; m. W. Robert Murfin, Aug. 17, 1963 (div. 1981); children: Brian C., Glen M.; m. Paul Stanley Peters Jr., Jan. 1, 1988. BA, Rice U., 1963, MA, 1971, postgrad., 1978. Tchr. Kinkaid H.S., Houston, 1964-66; editor Rice U., 1969-81; freelance writer, Calif., 1971—; dir. info. Meth. Hosp., Houston, 1981-84; sr. editor Addison-Wesley Pub. Co., Menlo Park, Calif., 1984-86; editor Ctr. for Advanced Study in Behavioral Scis., Stanford, Calif., 1986—; dir. Tex. Wordworks, Inc., Assn. Rice Alumni. Mem. Houston Ballet Guild, Rice U. Fund Coun., Friends of Stanford String Quartet. Mem. Internat. Assn. Bus. Communicators, Soc. Tech. Comm., Phi Beta Kappa. Editor, contbr. profl. jours. Office: Ctr for Advanced Study 202 Junipero Serra Blvd Stanford CA 94305-8006

MUDD, MICHAEL EDWARD, communications educator; b. Orange, N.J., Nov. 23, 1954; s. Oscar and Ola (Toomer) M.; m. Milly McBride, June 27, 1980 (div. 1990); children: Kevon, John; m. Joy Johnson, June 13, 1991; 1 child, Angie. BE, U. Hawaii, 1975, MS in Comm., 1990. Journalist The Daily Journal, Hilo, Hawaii, 1980-88; tchr. comm. Dane Barse Sch., Honolulu, 1988-92, Durand Werik C.C., Kailua, Hawaii, 1992—. Author: The Easy Way to Becoming a Good Writer, 1995, How to Make Writing Fun, 1996; contbr. articles to various newspapers and mags.; cons., lectr. in field. Pres. Kailua Little League, 1994—; troop leader Kailua coun. Boy Scouts Am., 1995—. With USAFR, 1975-90. Recipient Maurice Johnson award Hawaii Tchrs. Assn., 1993. Mem. ARC, NAE, NEA, Nat. Assn. Black Journalists, Soc. Profl. Journalists. Baptist. Office: Durand Werik CC 1384 Kahili St Kailua HI 96734-4062

MUDGE, JEAN MCCLURE, writer, filmmaker; b. Fort Benning, Ga., Dec. 4, 1933; d. Robert Battey and Eva Eugenia (Colby) McClure; m. Lewis Seymour Mudge, June 15, 1957; children—Robert Seymour, William McClure, Anne Evelyn. B.A., Stanford U., 1955; M.A., U. Del., 1957; Ph.D., Yale U., 1973. Reader, Smith Coll., Northampton, Mass., 1963-65, lectr., 1972-73; curator Amherst (Mass.) Coll., 1965-76; filmmaker, Amherst, 1971—; vis. scholar China Trade Mus., Milton, Mass., 1977—; cons. Peabody Mus., Salem, Mass., 1980—, Essex Inst., Salem, 1980—; lectr. Field Mus., Chgo., 1982—. Author: Chinese Export Porcelain for the American Trade, 1785-1835, 1962, rev. edit., 1987; Emily Dickinson and the Image of Home, 1975; Chinese Export Porcelain in North America, 1986; author films: Emily Dickinson, 1978; Herman Melville, 1982; Sanctuary in Chicago, 1985, Seminary: The Word at Work, 1989, Mary Lyon: Precious Time, 1987, Edgar Allan Poe: Architect of Dreams, 1991, Edgar Allan Poe: Architect of Dreams, 1991. Winterthur fellow H. F. duPont Mus., Wilmington, Del., 1955-57; Danforth Found. fellow, 1969-71; recipient Red Ribbon, N.Y. Film Festival, 1978, finalist, 1982; Chris Plaque, Columbus Film Festival, 1978, 82. Mem. NOW, MLA, Oriental Ceramic Soc., Winterthur Grads. Assn., Soc. Values in Higher Edn. Democrat. Home: 2444 Hillside Ave Berkeley CA 94704

MUEGGE, LYN, advertising executive. CFO, exec. v.p. Hal Riney & Ptnrs. Inc., San Francisco. Office: 735 Battery St San Francisco CA 94111*

MUELLER, GERHARD G(OTTLOB), financial accounting standard setter; b. Eineborn, Germany, Dec. 4, 1930; came to U.S., 1952, naturalized, 1957; s. Gottlob Karl and Elisabeth Charlotte (Hossack) M.; m. Coralie George, June 7, 1958; children: Kent, Elisabeth, Jeffrey. AA, Coll. of Sequoias, 1954; BS with honors, U. Calif.-Berkeley, 1956, MBA, 1957, PhD, 1962; D Econs. (hon.), Swedish Sch. Econs. and Bus. Adminstrn., 1994. CPA, Wash. Staff accountant FMC Corp., San Jose, Calif., 1957-58; faculty dept. accounting U. Wash., Seattle, 1960-96, assoc. prof., 1963-67, prof., 1967-96, chmn. dept., 1969-78, dir. grad. profl. acctg. program, 1979-90, sr. assoc. dean, 1990-95, acting dean, 1994, Hughes M. Blake prof. internat. bus. mgmt., 1992-95, Julius A. Roller prof. acctg., 1995-96; dir. U. Wash. Acctg. Devel. Fund, Overlake Hosp. Med. Ctr., Bellevue, 1984-96, chmn. bd. trustees, 1991-93; cons. internat. tax matters U.S. Treasury Dept., 1963-68; cons. Internat. Acctg. Rsch., 1964-96; vis. prof. Cranfield Sch. Mgmt., Eng., 1973-74, U. Zurich, Switzerland, 1973-74; lectr. in field. Author: International Accounting, 1967; co-author: Introductory Financial Accounting, 3d edit., 1991, A Brief Introduction to Managerial and Social Uses of Accounting, 1975, International Accounting, 1978, 2nd edit., 1992, Accounting: An International Perspective, 1987, 3rd edit., 1994, 4th edit., 1997; editor: Readings in International Accounting, 1969, Accounting-A Book of Readings, 2d edit., 1976, A New Introduction to Accounting, 1971, A Bibliography of Internat. Accounting, 3d edit., 1973, Essentials of Multinational Accounting—An Anthology, 1979, Frontiers of International Accounting, 1986, AACSB Curriculum Internationalization Resource Guide, 1988; contbr. numerous articles to profl. jours. Expert legal witness, IRS, 1991-93. Recipient U. Wash. Disting. Teaching award, 1983, Disting. Service award, 1984; Price Waterhouse internat. accounting research fellow, 1962-64; Ford Found. fellow, 1958-59. Fellow Acad. Internat. Bus.; mem. AICPAs (internat. practice exec. com. 1972-75, exec. coun. 1987-89), Am. Acctg. Assn. (pres. 1988-89, acad. v.p. 1970-71, chmn. adv. bd. internat. acctg. sect. 1977-79, Wildman medal 1986, Nat. Outstanding Educator 1981, Disting. Internat. Lectr. in Black Africa 1987, Outstanding Internat. Acctg. Educator 1991), Fin. Execs. Inst., Wash. Soc. CPAs (pres. 1988-89, Outstanding Educator award 1985, Pub. Svc. award 1995), Acctg. Edn. Change Commn. (chmn. 1994-96), Beta Alpha Psi (Acad. Acct. of Yr. 1987), Beta Gamma Sigma (Disting. scholar 1978-79), Alpha Gamma Sigma. Home: 40 Breed's Hill Pl Wilton CT 06897-1538 Office: Fin Acctg Standards Bd 401 Merritt 7 PO Box 5116 Norwalk CT 06856-5116 *It has always been important to me to associate with people and tangible and intangible things of the highest quality. I make it a practice to set clear goals and then pursue them actively. A broad world view on all aspects of life engenders more success and happiness than special interest perspectives. I welcome change in professional matters, but seek constancy in personal and family affairs. Fate has played a role in my successes. I believe in God, Protestant ethics, and the merits of classical academic scholarship.*

MUFTIC, FELICIA ANNE BOILLOT, consumer relations professional; b. Muskogee, Okla., Feb. 27, 1938; d. Lowell Francois and Geneva Margaret (Halstead) Boillot; m. Michael Muftic, Sept. 6, 1961; children: Tanya Muftic-Streicher, Theodore B., Mariana C. BA, Northwestern U., 1960. Exec. dir. Metro Dist. Atty.'s Consumer Office, Denver, 1973-79; talk show host KNUS, Denver, 1981-83; clk., recorder City and County of Denver, Colo., 1984-91; spl. projects dir. Consumer Credit Counseling, Denver, 1991-95; cons. consumer affairs pvt. practice, Denver, 1995—; pres. Muftic and Assocs., Denver, 1980-83; commr. Uniform Consumer Credit Code, Colo., 1991—. Author: Colorado Consumer Handbook, 1982. Candidate for mayor, Denver, 1979. Named Media person of Yr., NASW, Colo., 1982; recipient Outstanding Contbrn. in Consumer Affairs award Denver (Colo.) Fed. Exec. Bd., 1982. Mem. Am. Arbitration Assn. (chmn. regional dispute settlement bd. 1993-96), Inst. Internat. Edn. (bd. mem. 1980—), Rotary Internat. Democrat. Home and Office: 3671 S Pontiac Way Denver CO 80237-1326

MUGLER, LARRY GEORGE, regional planner; b. Chgo., June 22, 1946; s. Warren Franklin and Elaine Mae (Mittag) M.; m. Judy Ann Allison, Aug. 3, 1968; children: Jonathan, Allison. BSCE, Northwestern U., 1968; postgrad., Evang. Theol. Sem., 1968-70; MS in Urban and Regional Planning, U. Wis., 1972. Planning analyst State of Wis., Madison, 1970-72; dir. community devel. Cen. Okla. Econ. Devel. Dist., Shawnee, 1972-74; planner Denver Regional Council of Govts., 1974-80, dir. environ. services, 1980-83, dir. devel. services, 1983—. Contbr. chpt. on pub. works mgmt. to book. Pres. bd. dirs. Leawood Met. Recreation and Park Dist., Littleton, Colo., 1978—; chair planning and rsch. com., bd. stewards Rocky Mountain Conf. The United Meth. Ch. Named one of Outstanding Young Men in Am., Jaycees, 1974; Lasker Found. fellow, 1971; recipient Disting. Svc. award Spl. Dist. Assn. of Colo., 1989. Mem. Am. Planning Assn. (sec. Colo. chpt. 1970-96), ASCE (subcom. chmn. 1985-86, 88-91, div. exec. com. 1991—, vice chair 1994-96, chair 1996), Urban Land Inst. Republican. Methodist. Office: Denver Regional Coun Govts 2480 W 26th Ave Ste 200B Denver CO 80211-5304

MUGRIDGE, DAVID RAYMOND, lawyer; b. Detroit, Aug. 6, 1949; s. Harry Raymond and Elizabeth Lou (Aldrich) M.; m. Sandra Lee Jackson, June 25, 1988; children: James Raymond, Sarah Lorraine. BA, U. of Ams., Puebla, Mex., 1970; MA, Santa Clara U., 1973; JD, San Joaquin Coll. of Law, 1985. Bar: Calif. 1986, U.S. Dist. Ct. (ea. dist.) Calif. 1986, U.S. Ct. Appeals (9th cir.) 1987, U.S. Supreme Ct. 1996. Staff atty. to presiding justice 5th Dist. Ct. Appeals, Fresno, Calif., 1985-87; assoc. Law Office of Nuttall, Berman, Magill, Fresno, 1987-88; pvt. practice Fresno, 1988—; tchr. civil litigation Fresno City Coll., 1988—; tchr. Spanish for legal profession, Fresno, 1994; arbitrator Fresno County Bar Assn., 1988-96; judge pro-tem Fresno County Juvenile Ct., 1992-96, Fresno Mcpl. Ct., 1994-96. Contbg. author: Practical Real Estate Law, 1995. Mem. ABA, Calif. Attys. for Criminal Justice, Nat. Assn. Criminal Def. Lawyers, Calif. Trial Lawyers Assn. Republican. Roman Catholic.

MUHAMMAD, KHALEEDAH, entrepreneur, sales and marketing consultant, community activist; b. Berkeley, Calif., Nov. 2, 1943; d. Samuel Taylor Odom and Robbie Lee (Taylor) Gordon; children: Raymie, Jamal; m. Ansar El Muhammad, June 12, 1974; children: Tamishi, Ansar El II. BA, Los Angeles State Coll., 1965; postgrad., Calif. State, Hayward, 1971-72. Caseworker Pacoima (Calif.) Child Guidance Clinic, 1965-68; probation officer Los Angeles Probation Dept., 1968-72; ednl. opportunity program counselor U. Calif., Berkeley, 1974-79; community cons. YWCA, Richmond, Calif., 1979-81; owner, sales mgr. Touch of Class Boutique, Richmond, 1981-84; owner, mktg. cons. Nature's Co., Richmond, 1982-84; owner Unique Home Services, Richmond, 1984—; part-owner, mktg. cons. Cora's Kitchen, Oakland, Calif., 1987—, Halal Mktg. Services, Oakland, 1987—; sales, mktg. cons. The Fox Factory, Richmond, 1985-87. Author: (pamphlet) It's Not Easy Being a Parent, 1979. Vice chairperson Unity Orgn., Richmond, 1979-83; founder People United For Coops., Richmond, 1983; bd. dirs. Richmond chpt. Reading Is Fundamental, 1979-83, Minority Arts Network, Contra Costa, Calif., 1987; ct. apptd. spl. rep. Adv. for Wards of the Ct., 1990-91; co-founder Loving Care Inc.; exec. dir. Ansari House Residential Treatment Facility for Teenage Girls. Mem. Nat. Assn. Female Execs. Democrat. Islam. Home: 147 Downie Dr Vallejo CA 94589 Office: 123 12th St Richmond CA 94801

MUHLBACH, ROBERT ARTHUR, lawyer; b. Los Angeles, Apr. 13, 1946; s. Richard and Jeanette (Marcus) M.; m. Kerry Eldene Mahoney, July 26, 1986. BSME, U. Calif., Berkeley, 1967; JD, U. Calif., San Francisco, 1976; MME, Calif. State U., 1969; M in Pub. Adminstrn., U. So. Calif., 1976. Bar: Calif. 1976. Pub. defender County of Los Angeles, 1977-79; assoc. Kirtland & Packard, Los Angeles, 1979-85, ptnr., 1986—. Chmn. Santa Monica Airport Commn., Calif., 1984-87. Served to capt. USAF, 1969-73. Mem. ABA, AIAA, Internat. Assn. Def. Counsel, Am. Bd. Trial Advs. Office: Kirtland & Packard Ste 2600 1900 Avenue Of The Stars Los Angeles CA 90067-4507

MUICO-MERCURIO, LUISA, critical care nurse; b. Caloocan, Manila, Philippines, Nov. 17, 1955; d. Amado B. and Eustaquia (Buenavista) Muico; m. Wilfred Tongson Mercurio, Dec. 28, 1974; children: Elyjah Matthew, Kristoffer Ross, Mercurio. ADN, Harbor City Coll., 1978; BSN, Calif. State U., 1990, postgrad., 1992—. Cert. ACLS instr., BLS instr; CCRN; cert. pub. health nurse. Staff nurse ICU Long Beach (Calif.) Meml. Med. Ctr., 1978-80; staff nurse CVT/ICU Cedar Sinai Med. Ctr., L.A., 1980-84; staff nurse ICU, critical care unit, emergency rm., cath. lab. Long Beach Community Hosp., 1982-86; ICU, CCU coord. Pioneer Hosp., Artesia, Calif., 1986-87; staff nurse CSU Kaiser-Permanente, L.A., 1988-90, pub. health nurse, 1990, asst. dept. adminstr., 1990-92; asst. dept. adminstr. Kaiser-Permanente, Sunset and Bellflower, Calif.; cardiovascular/thoracic surgery nurse coord. Kay Med. Group/Hosp. Good Samaritan, L.A., 1992—; adminstrv. supr. Barlow Respiratory Hosp., L.A., 1993; staff nurse critical care unit UCLA, 1994—; nursing faculty Pacific Coast Coll., 1994—, ICU-Kaweah Delta Dist. Hosp., Visalia, Calif., 1996—; adminstr., cons. Welco Guest Homes, Porterville, Calif., 1996—. Named to Dean's list Harbor City Coll., 1976-78, Dean's list Calif. State U., 1988-90. Mem. AACN (cert.), Nat. Golden Key Honor Soc., Nursing Honor Soc., Sigma Theta Tau (Nu Mu chpt.). Republican.

MULASE, MOTOHICO, mathematics educator; b. Kanazawa, Japan, Oct. 11, 1954; came to U.S., 1982; s. Ken-Ichi and Mieko (Yamamoto) M.; m. Sayuri Kamiya, Sept. 10, 1982; children: Kimihico Chris, Paul Norihico, Yurika. BS, U. Tokyo, 1978; MS, Kyoto U., 1980, DSc, 1985. Rsch. assoc. Nagoya (Japan) U., 1980-85; JMS fellow Harvard U., Cambridge, Mass., 1982-83; vis. asst. prof. SUNY, Stony Brook, 1984-85; Hedrick asst. prof. UCLA, 1985-88; asst. prof. Temple U., Phila., 1988-89; assoc. prof. U. Calif., Davis, 1989-91, prof., 1991—, vice chair dept. math., 1995—; mem. Math. Scis. Rsch. Inst., Berkeley, Calif., 1982-84, Inst. for Advanced Study, Princeton, N.J., 1988-89; vis. prof. Max-Planck Inst. for Math., Bonn, Germany, 1991-92, Kyoto U., 1993, 94, Humboldt U., Berlin, Germany, 1995, 96. Contbr. articles to profl. jours. Treas. Port of Sacramento Japanese Sch., 1990-91. Mem. Math. Soc. Japan, Am. Math. Soc. (com. on internat. affairs 1993-96). Office: U Calif Dept Math Davis CA 95616

MULL, JOCELYN BETHE, school administrator; b. Nassau, N.Y., Oct. 21, 1968; divorced; 1 child, Eron Michael. BA, SUNY, Buffalo, 1981, MA, 1989. Dir. edn. Ctr. for Positive Thought, Mus. African Am. Arts and Antiquities, Buffalo, 1978-83; tchr. English, Buffalo Bd. Edn., 1980—, cons. tchr. inclusion project, 1991-93, fed. magnet curriculum specialist Futures Acad., 1993—; case mgr. spl. edn., gifted and comprehensive programs Crenshaw H.S., L.A., 1995, case mgr., coord. spl. edn., GATE coord., peer tutoring coord., 1996—; case mgr. spl. edn. and GATE coord. Crenshaw H.S. Author: (poetry) Goti, Paja, Mguu-The Knee, A Thigh and The Leg, 1980, Strength in the Water, 1995. Rec. coord., publicist Lighthouse Interdenominational Choir, 1988-94; project coord. Performing Artists Collective, Western N.Y. United Against Drugs, Buffalo, 1993—; mem. Mayor's Arts and Adv. Coun. Against Drugs and Violence, 1995. Recipient Educator of Excellence award PUSH Excel, Operation PUSH, 1981, N.Y. State English Coun., 1994, Creative Arts award, 1980, citation Martin Luther King Jr. Arts and Scis. award, 1986—, Outstanding Commemorative Youth award for performing arts and cmty. svc., 1980. Mem. ASCD, NEA (spl. edn. com.), Buffalo Tchrs. Fedn. (multicultural com.), AAUW, Phi Delta Kappa. Office: Crenshaw High School 5010 11th Ave Los Angeles CA 90043-4816

MULLARKEY, MARY J., state supreme court justice; b. New London, Wis., Sept. 28, 1943; d. John Clifford and Isabelle A. (Steffes) M.; m. Thomas E. Korson, July 24, 1971; 1 child, Andrew Steffes Korson. BA, St. Norbert Coll., 1965; LLB, Harvard U., 1968; LLD (hon.), St. Norbert Coll., 1989. Bar: Wis. 1968, Colo. 1974. Atty.-advisor U.S. Dept. Interior, Washington, 1968-73; asst. regional atty. EEOC, Denver, 1973-75; 1st atty. gen. Colo. Dept. Law, Denver, 1975-79, solicitor gen., 1979-82; legal advisor to Gov. Lamm State of Colo., Denver, 1982-85; ptnr. Mullarkey & Seymour, Denver, 1985-87; justice Colo. Supreme Ct., Denver, 1987—. Recipient Alumni award St. Norbert Coll., De Pere, Wis., 1980, Alma Mater award, 1993. Fellow ABA Found., Colo. Bar Found.; mem. ABA, Colo. Bar Assn., Colo. Women's Bar Assn. (recognition award 1986), Denver Bar Assn., Thompson G. Marsh Inn of Ct. (pres. 1993-94). Office: Supreme Ct Colo 2 E 14th Ave Denver CO 80203-2115

MULLEN, ROBERT CHARLES, school system administrator; b. Muskogee, Okla., Nov. 13, 1944; s. Charles W. and Kathryn B. (Hunt) M.; m. Celesta Rose Schmidt, June 25, 1966; children: Charles, Robert, Michael, Kevin. BS, Minot (N.D.) State U., 1966, MS, 1967; EdD, U. No. Colo., Greeley, 1981. Speech pathologist Benton-Tama-Iowa-Poweshiek Dept. Spl. Edn., Toledo, Iowa, 1967-68, hearing clinician, 1968-69, coord. speech and hearing, 1969-73; dir. ACCA Speech and Hearing Ctr., Fairbanks, Alaska, 1973-75; asst. dir. Alaska Treatment Ctr., Anchorage, 1975-76, exec. dir., 1976-79; dir. Reno County Edn. Coop. USD #610, Hutchinson, Kans., 1981-85, Rio Blanco Bd. Endl. Svcs., Rangely, Colo., 1985-89; supt. Rangely Pub. Schs. RE-4, 1989—; v.p. bd. dirs. Horizon Inc., Steamboat, Colo.; pres. Vocat. Edn. Adv. Bd., Colo. No. Community Coll., Rangely, 1988. Co-author: Exceptional Individuals: An Introduction, 1993. Commr. Mayor's Health Commn., Anchorage, 1976-79; Alaska rep. Nat. Conf. on Aging, Washington; bd. mem. Spl. Edn. Adv. Bd., U. No. Colo., 1988; state com. mem. Colo. Parent/Profl. Partnership, Denver, 1988-90; mem. planning com. White house Conf. on Handicapped; mem. bd. govs. Colo. Alliance for Sci., 1996. U.S. Office Edn. grantee, Greeley, Colo., 1980, 81. Mem. Am. Assn. Sch. Adminstrs., Coun. Exceptional Children, Colo. Assn. Sch. Execs. Roman Catholic. Office: Rangely Pub Schs 402 W Main St Rangely CO 81648-2408

MULLEN, ROD GORDEN, nonprofit organization executive; b. Puyallup, Wash., Aug. 2, 1943; s. Charles Rodney and Grace Violet (Fritsch) M.; m. Lois Fern Tobiska, May 3, 1963 (div. Jan. 1977); children: Cristina, Charles, Moneka; m. Naya Arbiter, Oct. 17, 1977. Student, U. Idaho, 1961-63; AB in Polit. Sci., U. Calif., Berkeley, 1966; postgrad., San Francisco Art Inst., 1968. Dir. Oakland (Calif.) facility Synanon Found., Inc., Badger, 1971-73; dir. San Francisco facility Synanon Found., Inc., 1972-73, dir. Tomales Bay (Calif.) facility, 1976-78, dir. Synanon edn. programs, 1973-76; treatment dir. nat. programs Vision Quest, Inc., Tucson, 1981-82; dir. resources and devel. Amity, Inc., Tucson, 1982-84, exec. dir., 1984-95; pres., CEO Amity Found. of Calif., Miramonte, Calif., 1995—; mem. Nat. Adv. Com. on Substance Abuse Prevention, 1990-92, 93-96; mem. sci. adv. bd. Ctr. for Therapeutic Cmty. Rsch., Narcotic and Drug Rsch., Inc., N.Y.C., 1991-96; program mgr. Drug Abuse Treatment Waiting Period Reduction Program, 1990-91; dir. Coop. Program between Amity, Inc. and Pima County Probation Dept., 1990-92; cons. Calif. Office Criminal Justice Planning, Sacramento, 1993; prin. investigator program Nat. Inst. on Drug Abuse, 1990-93. Contbr. numerous articles to profl. publs., chpts. to books. Mem. Internat. Coun. on Alcoholism and Addictions, Am. Jail Assn., Am. Psychol. Soc., Nat. Assn. Perinatal Addiction Rsch. and Edn., Nat. Assn. State Alcohol and Drug Abuse Dirs., World Fedn. Therapeutic Comtys., U.S.-Mex. Border Health Assn., Nat. Coun. La Raza, Therapeutic Comtys. of Am. (exec. coun. 1988-94). Office: Amity Found of Calif PO Box 44319 Lemon Cove CA 93244-0449

MULLEN, WILLIAM KEMP, JR., contract management executive; b. San Bernardino, Calif., Feb. 11, 1958; s. William Kemp and Doris Martha (Gray) M. Student, U. Calif., Santa Barbara, 1976-78; BS in Mgmt., Calif. State U., Long Beach, 1980; Cert. in Contract Mgmt., U. Calif., Irvine, 1988. Account exec. Automatic Data Processing, La Palma, Calif., 1981-83; sr. acct. Northrop Corp., Anaheim, Calif., 1985-89; sr. contract analyst Northrop

Corp., El Segundo, Calif., 1989-91; contract adminstr. Teledyne Electronic Tech., Marina del Rey, Calif., 1991-95; mgr. contracts Tech. Svc. Corp., Santa Monica, Calif., 1995—. Mem. Nat. Contract Mgmt. Assn. Office: Technology Service Corp 2950 31st St # 200 Santa Monica CA 90405

MULLER, DAVID WEBSTER, architectural designer; b. Norwich, Conn., Aug. 25, 1956; s. Richard Johnson and Barbara Alice (Reading) M.; m. Susan Akers, Dec. 31, 1989; 1 stepchild, Shannon. BA in Polit. Sci., George Washington U., 1978. Rsch. assoc. Rep. Nat. Com., Washington, 1978-80, dep. dir. spl. projects, 1981-83; western field dir. Nat. Rep. Congl. Com., Washington, 1983-85; v.p. Russo Watts & Rollins, Sacramento, Calif., 1985-86; campaign mgr. Chavez for U.S. Senate, Silver Spring, Md., 1986; v.p. Russo Watts & Rollins, Sacramento, 1987-89; cons. Sacramento, 1989, pvt. investor, 1990—; archtl. design and restoration Muller/West, 1990—. Mem. Nat. Coun. for Arts and Scis. Home and Office: Muller/West 380 Wyndgate Rd Sacramento CA 95864-5945

MULLER, JEROME KENNETH, photographer, art director, editor; b. Amityville, N.Y., July 18, 1934; s. Alphons and Helen (Haberl) M.; m. Nora Marie Nestor, Dec. 21, 1974. BS, Marquette U., 1961; postgrad., Calif. State U., Fullerton, 1985-86; MA, Nat. U., San Diego, 1988; postgrad., Newport Psychoanalytic Inst., 1988-90. Comml. and editorial photographer N.Y.C., 1952-55; mng. editor Country Beautiful mag., Milw., 1961-62, Reprodns. Rev. mag., N.Y.C., 1967-68; editor, art dir. Orange County (Calif.) Illustrated, Newport Beach, 1962-67, art editor, 1970-79, exec. editor, art dir., 1968-69; owner, CEO Creative Svcs. Advt. Agy., Newport Beach, 1969-79; founder, CEO Mus. Graphics, Costa Mesa, Calif., 1978—; tchr. photography Lindenhurst (N.Y.) High Sch., 1952-54; tchr. comic art U. Calif., Irvine, 1979; guest curator 50th Anniversary Exhbn. Mickey Mouse, 1928-78, The Bowers Mus., Santa Ana, Calif., 1978; organized Moving Image Exhbn. Mus. Sci. and Industry, Chgo., Cooper-Hewitt Mus., N.Y.C., William Rockhill Nelson Gallery, Kansas City, 1981; collector original works outstanding Am. cartoonists at major mus. One-man shows include Souk Gallery, Newport Beach, 1970, Gallery 2, Santa Ana, Calif., 1972, Cannery Gallery, Newport Beach, 1974, Mus. Graphics Gallery, 1993, White Gallery Portland State U., 1996, U. Calif., Irvine, 1997; author: Rex Brandt, 1972; contbr. photographs and articles to mags. Served with USAF, 1956-57. Recipient two silver medals 20th Ann. Exhbn. Advt. and Editorial Art in West, 1965. Mem. APA, Mus. Modern Art (N.Y.C.), Met. Mus. Art, Art Mus. Assn. Am., L.A. Press Club, Newport Beach Tennis Club, Orange County Mus. Art, Alpha Sigma Nu. Home: 2438 Bowdoin Pl Costa Mesa CA 92626-6304 Office: PO Box 10743 Costa Mesa CA 92627-0234

MULLIN, CHRIS(TOPHER) PAUL, professional basketball player; b. N.Y.C., July 30, 1963. Student, St. John's U., 1981-85. Basketball player Golden State Warriors, 1985—; mem. U.S. Olympic Team (received Gold medal), 1984, 92. Recipient Wooden award, 1985; named to Sporting News All-Am. First Team, 1985, NBA All-Star team, 1989-93, NBA First Team, 1992.. Office: Golden State Warriors 1221 Broadway 20th Flr Oakland CA 94612-1918*

MULLINS, RUTH GLADYS, nurse; b. Westville, N.S., Can., Aug. 25, 1943; d. William G. and Gladys H.; came to U.S., 1949, naturalized, 1955; student Tex. Womans U., 1961-64; BS in Nursing, Calif. State U.-Long Beach, 1966; MNursing, UCLA, 1973; m. Leonard E. Mullins, Aug. 27, 1963; children: Deborah R., Catherine M., Leonard III. Pub. health nurse, L.A. County Health Dept., 1967-68; nurse Meml. Hosp. Med. Center, Long Beach, 1968-72; dir. pediatric nurse practitioner program Calif. State U., Long Beach, 1973—, asst. prof., 1975-80, assoc. prof., 1980-85, prof., 1985—; health svc. credential coord. Sch. Nursing Calif. State U., Long Beach, Calif., chmn., 1979-81, coord. grad. programs, 1985-92; mem. Calif. Maternal, Child and Adolescent Health Bd., 1977-84; vice chair Long Beach/Orange County Health Consortium, 1984-85, chair 1985-86. Tng. grantee HHS, Divsn. Nursing Calif. Dept. Health; cert. pediatric nurse practitioner. Fellow Nat. Assn. Pediatric Nurse Assocs. and Practitioners (exec. bd., pres. 1990-91), Nat. Fedn. Nursing Specialty Orgns. (sec. 1991-93); mem. Am. Pub. Health Assn., Nat. Alliance Nurse Practitioners (governing body 1990-92), Assn. Faculties Pediatric Nurse Practitioner Programs, L.A. and Orange County Assn. Pediatric Nurse Practitioners and Assocs., Am. Assn. U. Faculty, Ambulatory Pediatric Assn. Democrat. Methodist. Author: (with B. Nelms) Growth and Development: A Primary Health Care Approach; contbg. author: Quick Reference to Pediatric Nursing, 1984; asst. editor Jour. Pediatric Health Care. Home: 6382 Heil Ave Huntington Beach CA 92647-4232 Office: Calif State U Dept Nursing 1250 N Bellflower Blvd Long Beach CA 90840-0006

MULLIS, KARY BANKS, biochemist; b. Lenoir, N.C., Dec. 28, 1944; s. Cecil Banks Mullis and Bernice Alberta (Barker) Fredericks; children: Christopher, Jeremy, Louise. BS in Chemistry, Ga. Inst. Tech, 1966; PhD in Biochemistry, U. Calif., Berkeley, 1973; DSc (hon.), U. S.C., 1994. Lectr. biochemistry U. Calif., Berkeley, 1972; postdoctoral fellow U. Calif., San Francisco, 1977-79, U. Kans. Med. Sch., Kansas City, 1973-76; scientist Cetus Corp., Emeryville, Calif., 1979-86; dir. molecular biology Xytronyx, Inc., San Diego, 1986-88; cons. Specialty Labs, Inc., Amersham, Inc., Chiron Inc. and various others, Calif., 1988—; chmn. StarGene, Inc., San Rafael, Calif.; v.p. Histotec, Inc., Cedar Rapids, Iowa; Disting. vis. prof. U. S.C. Coll. of Sci. and Math. Contbr. articles to profl. jours.; patentee in field. Recipient Preis Biochemische Analytik award German Soc. Clin. Chem., 1990, Allan award Am. Soc. of Human Genetics, 1990, award Gairdner Found. Internat., 1991, Nat. Biotech. award, 1991, Robert Koch award, 1992, Chiron Corp. Biotechnology Rsch. award Am. Soc. Microbiology, 1992, Japan prize Sci. and Tech. Found. Japan, 1993, Nobel Prize in Chemistry, Nobel Foundation, 1993; named Calif. Scientist of Yr., 1992, Scientist of Yr., R&D Mag., 1991. Mem. Am. Chem. Soc., Am. Acad. Achievement, Inst. Further Study (dir. 1983—). Office: 6767 Neptune Pl Apt 5 La Jolla CA 92037-5924*

MULTHAUP, MERREL KEYES, artist; b. Cedar Rapids, Iowa, Sept. 27, 1922; d. Stephen Dows and Edna Gertrude (Gard) Keyes; m. Robert Hansen Multhaup, Apr. 7, 1944; children: Eric Stephen, Robert Bruce. Student fine art, State U. of Iowa, 1942-43; student color theory, Rice U., 1971. Mem. teaching faculty Summit (N.J.) Art Assn., 1956-60; art instr. studio classes Springfield, N.J., 1954-55, Bloomfield (N.J.) Art Group, 1955-56, Westport, Conn., 1962-63; mem. teaching faculty Hunterdon Art Ctr., Clinton, N.J., 1985-92. One woman exhbns. include Coriell Gallery, 1995; exhibited in group shows at Nat. Assn. Women Artists, N.Y.C., 1957-93 (awards in figure painting), Hartford (Conn.) Athanaeum Mus., 1961 (1st prize), Highgate Gallery, N.Y.C., Waverly Gallery, N.Y.C., Leicester Gallery, London, Silvermine Gallery, Conn., Pendut Gallery, Tex., Benedict Gallery, Sidney Rothman Gallery, N.J., Stamford (Conn.) Mus., Bridgeport (Conn.) Mus., Montclair (N.J.) Mus., Newark Mus., Coriell Gallery, Albuquerque; included in traveling exhibit Nat. Assn. Women Artists, 1996—, Gallery Art 54, N.Y.C., 1997. Bd. dirs., exhbn. chmn. Summit Art Assn., 1950-60, Silvermine Guild of Art, New Canaan, Conn., 1960-64; bd. dirs. Artist's Equity of N.J., 1977-84, chmn. state-wide event, 1983, 86; artist's adv. coun. Hunterdon Art Ctr., Clinton, 1988-92. Recipient awards in juried exhbns. in Iowa, Pa., N.J., Conn., N.Y.C. Mem. Nat. Mus. for Women in Arts (charter mem.), Nat. Assn. Women Artists Inc. (awards for figure painting 1957, 80, 89), Albuquerque United Artists. Home and Studio: 1321 Stagecoach Rd SE Albuquerque NM 87123-4320

MULTZ, CARTER VICTOR, rheumatologist; b. Billings, Mont., June 4, 1934; s. Victor William and Charlotte Deneice (Waddeu) M. BS, Gonzaga U., 1955; MD, Loyola U., Chgo., 1959. Diplomate Am. Bd. Internal Medicine. Intern St. Mary's Hosp., San Francisco, 1959-60, resident, 1960-61; fellow, clin. asst. medicine Robert Breck Brigham Hosp., Boston, 1961-62; fellow Lanhey Clinic, Boston, 1962-63; pvt. practice San Jose, 1963-66, 68—; asst. chief rheumatology Walter Reed Gen. Hosp., Washington, 1966-68; clin. assoc. medicine dir. Syntex Rsch., Palo Alto, Calif., 1968-85; med. dir. DDI Pharm., Inc., Mountain View, Calif., 1985-88; pres., med. dir. Personal Choice Med. Group, Inc., San Jose, 1987—; mem. active staff O'Connor Hosp., San Jose; mem. courtesy staff Santa Clara Valley Med. Ctr., San Jose, Good Samaritan Hosp., San Jose, San Jose Hosp.; chmn. utilization rev. com. O'Connor Hosp., 1974, chmn. profl. activities com., 1975, mem. staff exec. com., 1975, 77, chmn. arthritis com., 1985-87; dir. Santa Clara Valley Profl. Standards Rev. Com., 1975-78, chmn., 1977; dir. O'Connor Physician's Assn., 1986-88; dir., chmn. quality assurance com. Silicon Valley Med. Group, 1986-88, v.p., 1988-89; dir. San Jose Med. Group, 1994—; presenter in field. Contbr. numerous articles to profl. jours. Mem. med. and sci. com. No. Calif. chpt. Arthritis Found., 1965-85, chmn. med. adv. com. Santa Clara County br., 1985-87, chmn. adv. bd. 1988—, dir. San Jose br., 1976-84; dir. Calif. Arthritis Inst., 1981-83. Fellow Am. Coll. Physicians, Am. Coll. Rheumatology; mem. Am. Coll. Physician Execs., Calif. Soc. Internal Medicine (membership com. 1986-88, trustee 1990—), Santa Clara County Soc. Internal Medicine (sec., treas. 1985-87, pres. 1987-90). Office: Arthritis Care Ctr Inc 1835 Park Ave San Jose CA 95126-1650

MULVANEY, JANELLE WILLIAMS, development professional; b. Billings, Mont., July 20, 1959; d. John F. Williams and N. Karen (Young) Musgrave; 1 child, Jason; m. Doug Mulvaney, July 24, 1993. BSBA with honors in Bus. Adminstrn., Ea. Mont. Coll., 1993. Asst. mgr. Size 5.7.9 Shop, Billings, 1977-78; retail mgr. Satin Garter, Billings, 1978-79; night mgr. lounge Dos Machos, Billings, 1979-81; sales rep. US West Communications, Billings, 1981-90; program devel. coord. Ea. Mont. Coll., Billings, 1990-92; stockbroker Dean Witter Reynolds, Billings, 1992-95; dir. devel. Mont. Spl. Olympics, Inc., 1995—; team leader fund drive Ea. Mont. Coll. Found. Achievement, 1992, 93. Mem. telethon com. Arthritis Found., Billings, 1986-87; sec. bd. dirs. Billings Citizens advocacy, 1987-91; dir. spl. events summer games Mont. Spl. Olympics, Billings, 1987-88; mem. Spl. Olympics outreach program, 1988-90; mem. 1977 reunion com. Billings West High Sch., 1986-90; mem. Ea. Mont. Coll. Ivy Honor Guard, 1991—; mem. Leadership Great Falls, 1996—. Named 1991 CASE Dist. VIII Student del. Mem. NAFE, U.S. West Women, Mont. Devel. Officers Assn., Am. Bus. Womens Assn. (charter Billings chpt., treas., chmn. ednl. scholarship com., mktg. com., program com.), Ea. Mont. Coll. Alumni Assn. (amb. edn. 1994, chair alumni awards program 1994-95). Republican. Methodist. Home: 329 28th Ave NW Great Falls MT 59404

MULVIHILL, PETER JAMES, fire protection engineer; b. Honolulu, Jan. 24, 1956; s. James H. and Jane A. (Norton) M. BSCE, Worcester (Mass.) Poly. Inst., 1978. Registered profl. engr. Fire Protection, Nev. Sr. engr. Indsl. Risk Insurers, San Francisco, 1978-84; fire protection engr. Aerojet Gen. Corp., Sacramento, 1984-87, Reno Fire Dept., 1987-93; bn. chief Boise (Idaho) Fire Dept., 1993-95; cons. Rolf Jensen & Assocs., Inc., Lehi, Utah, 1995-96; fire protection engr. Rolf Jensen & Assocs., Inc., Las Vegas, Nev., 1996—; part-time instr. univ. extension U. Calif., Davis, 1993-95, Truckee Meadows Community Coll., Reno, 1988-93. Commr. Gov.'s Blue Ribbon Commn. to Study Adequacy of State Regulations Concerning Highly Combustible Materials, Carson City, Nev., 1988. Mem. Soc. Fire Protection Engrs., No. Nev. Fire Marshal's Assn. (pres. 1992-93), Nat. Fire Protection Assn., Internat. Assn. Fire Chiefs, Calif. Fire Chiefs' Assn. (fire prevention officers sect. No. divsn.), Fire M arshals' Assn. N. Am.

MUMFORD, CHRISTOPHER GREENE, corporate financial executive; b. Washington, Oct. 21, 1945; s. Milton C. and Dorothea L. (Greene) M.; B.A., Stanford U., 1968, M.B.A., 1975. Cons., Internat. Tech. Resources Inc., 1974; asst. v.p. Wells Fargo Bank, San Francisco, 1975-78; v.p., treas. Arcata Corp., San Francisco, 1978-82, v.p. fin., 1982-87, exec. v.p. fin., 1987-94. gen. ptnr. Scarff, Sears & Assocs., San Francisco, 1986-95, mng. dir. Questor Ptnrs. Fund, L.P., San Francisco, 1995—; v.p. bd. dirs. Triangle Pacific Corp., Dallas, 1986-88, Norton Enterprises Inc., Salt Lake City, 1988-90; bd. dirs. Community Home Med. Enterprises, Inc., Grass Valley, Calif., Crown Pacific Ltd., Portland, Oreg., Ryder TRS, Inc., Miami, Fla., Ockham Personal Ins. Agy., PLC, London, Union Security Mortgage, Inc., Santa Ana, Calif., 1993-94. Office: 601 California St Ste 1800 San Francisco CA 94108-2823

MUNCH, WILLIAM DAVID, information systems consultant; b. Jamaica, N.Y., Mar. 21, 1938; s. William F. and Madeline (Eisenbarth) M.; m. Sigrid M. Loffler, Oct. 9, 1960; children: Lilo, William K., Kurt E. BBA in Indsl. Mgmt., Adelphi U., 1960. Mem. internat. banking group Bankers Trust, N.Y.C., 1974-79; v.p., mgr. br. on-line banking Wells Fargo, San Francisco, 1979-82; info. systems cons. in pvt. practice, Pleasant Hill, Calif., 1982—. Mem. Assn. for Systems Mgmt. (bd. dirs. 1985-88, exec. com. 1989-94, internat. pres. 1993-94, Meritorious Svc. award 1994, Systems Profl. of Yr. award 1984, 86). Home and Office: 178 Devon Ave Pleasant Hill CA 94523-2529

MUND, GERALDINE, bankruptcy judge; b. L.A., July 7, 1943; d. Charles J. and Pearl (London) M. BA, Brandeis U., 1965; MS, Smith Coll., 1967; JD, Loyola U., 1977. Bar: Calif. 1977. Bankruptcy judge U.S. Ctrl. Dist. Calif., 1984—, bankruptcy chief judge, 1997—. Past pres. Temple Israel, Hollywood, Calif.; mem. bd. Jewish Fedn. Coun. of Greater L.A. Mem. ABA, L.A. County Bar Assn. Office: 21041 Burbank Blvd Woodland Hills CA 91367

MUNERA, GERARD EMMANUEL, manufacturing company executive; b. Algiers, Algeria, Dec. 2, 1935; s. Gabriel and Laure (Labrousse) M.; m. Paule A. Ramos, July 28, 1959; children: Catherine, Philippe, Emmanuelle, Jean-Marie. M in Math., M in Physics, M in Chemistry, Ecole Polytechnique, Paris, 1956; CE, Ecole des Ponts et Chaussees, Paris, 1959. Chief county engr. Dept. Rds. and Bridges, South Algiers, 1959-62; cons. French Ministry Fgn. Affairs, Argentina, 1962-66; sr. v.p. fin. Camea Group Pechiney Ugine Kuhlmann, Buenos Aires, 1966-70, chmn. bd., chief exec. officer, 1976-77; exec. v.p. Howmet Aluminum Corp., Greenwich, Conn., 1976-77, pres., chief operating officer, 1977-79, pres., chief exec. officer, 1980-83; corporate v.p. nuclear fuels Pechiney, Brussels, 1983-85; vice chmn., chief exec. officer Union Minière, Brussels, 1985-89; head corp. planning and devel. RTZ, London, 1989-90; pres., CEO Minorco USA, Englewood, Colo., 1990-94, also bd. dirs.; chmn. and CEO Latin Am. Gold, Inc., N.Y.C., 1994-96, Synergex Inc., 1996—; bd. dirs. Arcadia Inc., Scaltech, Inc., Latin Am. Gold, Inc., Nevsun Resources, Inc.; chmn., CEO Synergex, Inc. Patentee low-income housing system. Served with French Air Force, 1956-57. Decorated Legion of Honor. Roman Catholic.

MUNIAIN, JAVIER P., computer company executive, physicist, researcher; b. Madrid, Apr. 4, 1966; came to U.S., 1989.; s. Luis Perez De Muniain y Leal and Crescencia Mohedano Hernandez. BSc, U. Complutense of Madrid, 1990; M. in Physics, U. Calif., Riverside, 1992, PhD in Theoretical Physics, 1996. Rsch., teaching asst. U. Calif., Riverside, 1992-96; pres., CEO Surfernet, San Diego, 1996—. Author: Gauge Fields, Knots and Gravity, 1994; contbr. articles to profl. jours. Mem. Am. Phys. Soc., Riverside Wine Tasing Soc. (co-founder 1994). Home: C/Alcala 236, Madrid Spain 28027 Office: Surfernet 3239 Caminito Ameca La Jolla CA 92037

MUNITZ, BARRY, university administrator, English literature educator, business consultant; b. Bklyn., July 26, 1941; s. Raymond J. and Vivian L. (LeVoff) M.; m. Anne Tomfohrde, Dec. 15, 1987. BA, Bklyn. Coll., 1963; MA, Princeton U., 1965, PhD, 1968; cert., U. Leiden, Netherlands, 1962. Asst. prof. lit. and drama U. Calif., Berkeley, 1966-68; staff assoc. Carnegie Commn. Higher Edn., 1968-70; mem. presdl. staff, then assoc. provost U. Ill. System, 1970-72, acad. v.p., 1972-76; v.p., dean faculties Central campus U. Houston, 1976-77, chancellor, 1977-82, chmn. coordinating bd. faculty workload, 1976-80; chmn. Tex. Long Range Planning, 1980-82; pres., COO Federated Devel. Co., 1982-91; vice chmn. Maxxam Inc., L.A., 1982-91; chancellor Calif. State U. System, Long Beach, Calif., 1991—; prof. English lit. Calif. State U., L.A., 1991—; bd. dirs. Sta. KCET-TV, Am. Coun. on Edn., Nat. Bus. Higher Edn. Forum, SunAmerica Inc.; cons. in presdl. evaluation and univ. goverance. Author: The Assessment of Institutional Leadership, 1977, also articles, monographs. Mem. task force NSF. Recipient Disting. Alumnus award Bklyn. Coll., 1979, U. Houston Alumni Pres.'s medal, 1981; Woodrow Wilson fellow, 1963. Mem. Young Pres. Orgn., Heritage Club, Phi Beta Kappa. Office: Calif State U System Office of Chancellor 400 Golden Shore St Long Beach CA 90802-4209

MUNN, WILLIAM CHARLES, II, psychiatrist; b. Flint, Mich., Aug. 9, 1938; s. Elton Albert and Rita May (Coykendall) M.; student Flint Jr. Coll., 1958-59, U. Detroit, 1959-61; M.D., Wayne State U., 1965; children by previous marriage—Jude Michael, Rachel Marie, Alexander Winston. Intern David Grant USAF Med. Center, Travis AFB, Calif., 1965-66; resident in psychiatry Letterman Army Hosp., San Francisco, 1967-70; practice medicine, specializing in psychiatry, Fairfield, Calif., 1972—; chief in-patient psychiatry David Grant Med. Center, 1970-71, chmn. dept. mental health, 1971-72; psychiat. cons. Fairfield-Suisun Unified Sch. Dist., 1971—, Fairfield Hosp. and Clinic, 1971, N. Bay Med. Ctr.(formerly Intercommunity Hosp.), Fairfield, 1971—, Casey Family Program, 1980—, Solano County Coroner's Office, 1981; asst. clin. prof. psychiatry U. Calif., San Francisco, 1976—; cons. Vaca Valley Hosp., Vacaville, Calif., 1988—, VA Hosp., San Francisco, 1976, David Grant USAF Hosp., 1976. Served to maj., M.C., USAF, 1964-72, flight surgeon, chief public health, chief phys. exam. center McGuire AFB, N.J., 1966-67. Diplomate Am. Bd. Psychiatry and Neurology (examiner). Mem. Am. Psychiat. Assn., No. Calif. Psychiat. Soc., E. Bay Psychiat. Assn. Office: 1245 Travis Blvd Ste E Fairfield CA 94533-4842

MUNOZ, JOHN JOSEPH, retired transportation company executive; b. Salinas, Calif., Jan. 18, 1932; s. John Fernando and Naomal (Smith) M.; m. Phyllis Taylor, Feb. 6, 1961 (div. 1978); children: Sam, Kathy, Toni; m. Rachel Canales, Nov. 24, 1979; children: Michelle, Monique. AA, Allan Hancock Coll., 1956; student, San Jose State U., 1981, Western Sierra Law Sch. Ops. mgr. So. Pacific Milling Co., Santa Maria, Calif., 1971-77; cons. Govt., Venezuela, 1977-78; fleet supt. Granite Rock Co., San Jose, Calif., 1978-80; plant mgr. Granite Constrn. Co., Greenfield, Calif., 1980-85; mgr. transpn. Ball, Ball & Brosmer Inc., Danville, Calif., 1985-86; ops. mgr., bd. dirs. Sorrento Ready Mix Co., Del Mar, Calif., 1986-89; trans. cons. Greenfield, Calif., 1991-96; ret., 1996; cons. Dept. Agrl. Devel., Maricaibo, Venezuela, 1976—. Commr. Planning Commn., Greenfield, Calif., 1982-85; mem. fund raising com. Broccoli Festival, Greenfield, 1983-85; dir. Soledad Prison Vocat. Tng., 1982-85. Lt. 11th Ranger Airborne, U.S. Army, 1950-52, Korea. Mem. Am. Concrete Inst., Calif. Trucking Assn., Los Californianos, Rotary, Lions, Elks. Republican. Home and Office: PO Box 3654 Greenfield CA 93927-3654

MUÑOZ-SANDOVAL, ANA F., Language educator; b. Chillan, Chile, Jan. 31, 1947; came to U.S., 1970; d. Washington del Carmen Muñoz Canales and Alicia del Carmen Sandoval de Muñoz; m. Frederick Mitronovas, Feb. 24, 1971 (div. Feb. 1988); m. Richard W. Woodcock, June 14, 1991. Student, Tribhuvan U., Katmandu, Nepal, 1979-80, Goethe-Inst., Poona, India; BA in Anthropology, SUNY, Buffalo, 1982, MS in Student Pers. Adminstrn., 1984; EdD in Intercultural/Internat. Edn., U. So. Calif., 1992. Developer, implementer Spanish lang. manual and tapes Buffalo Student Health Clinic, 1982-84; bilingual social svcs. worker Puerto Rican/Chicano Cmty. Svcs. Ctr., Buffalo; tchr. Spanish U. Ariz., 1986-88, U. So. Calif., 1989-91; with Measurement/Learning/Conss., Tolovana Park, Oreg., 1987—. Home: PO Box 22786 Nashville TN 37202 Office: Measurement/Learning/Conss PO Box 161 Tolovana Park OR 97145-0161

MUNRO, MALCOLM GORDON, obstetrician, gynecologist, educator; b. Woodstock, Ont., Can., Mar. 22, 1952; came to U.S., 1991; s. Charles Gordon and Maribelle (Logie) M.; m. Sandra June Brander-Smith, Nov. 17, 1990; children: Tyler Gordon, Megan Danielle. MD, U. Western Ont., London, 1975. Diplomate Am. Bd. Ob-Gyn. Intern Royal Columbian Hosp., New Westminster, B.C., 1975-76; resident ob.-gyn, U. Western Ont., London, 1976-77; resident U. B.C., Vancouver, 1978-80, clin. fellow gyneolgic. oncology, 1980-81, clin. instr. ob-gyn., 1981-83; asst. clin. prof. UCLA, Vancouver, 1983-89; assoc. clin. prof. U. B.C., 1988-92; assoc. prof. UCLA, 1991-95, prof., 1995—, assoc. chmn. dept. ob/gyn., 1994-95; chmn. ob/gyn sect. B.C. Med. Assn., Vancouver, 1984-88, Rsch. Coordinating Com. Grace Hosp., Vancouver; founding co-chair Gynecologic Studies Group, Washington, 1993—; cons. Cancer Control Agy., B.C., 1981-91, Ethicon Endosuture Core Cons. Group, 1992—; chair STOP-DUB Clin. Trial, 1996-2001. Author: (book) Gynecology, A Practical Approach, 1990; contbr. articles to profl. jours., chpts. to books; inventor, patentee laparoscopic loop electrodes, 1993; mem. editl. bd. Treating the Female Patient, 1988-94, Jour. of Gynecologic Technique, 1993—; reviewer Obstetrics and Gynecology, 1990—, Fertil Steril, 1993—, Am. Jour. Managed Care, 1996—; mem. ad hoc rev. com. Jour. Am. Assn. Gynecologic Laparoscopists, 1994—. Med. dir. Planned Parenthood, Vancouver, 1980-85; founding dir. U. B.C. Coop. Osteoporosis Program, 1987-91, Multidisciplinary Osteoporosis Clinic, U. Hosp., Vancouver, 1987-91. Recipient Appreciation cert. Planned Parenthood of B.C., 1991; grantee Vancouver Found., 1988, P.W. Woodward Found., 1988, Ethicon Endosurgery, 1992, NIH/NIAID AIDS and Cervical Neoplasia co-investigator, 1992-94, 96, study chair AHCPR/GSG. Fellow Royal Coll. Surgeons Can., Soc. Obstetricians and Gynecologists Can.; mem. Can. Fertility and Andrology Soc., Am. Fertility Soc., Am. Assn. Gynecologic Laparoscopists, Am. Coll. Obstetricians and Gynecologists (vice-chair B.C. section VIII 1987-90). Office: UCLA Med Ctr 14445 Olive View Dr Sylmar CA 91324-1495

MUNRO, RALPH DAVIES, state government official; b. Bainbridge Island, Wash., June 25, 1943; s. George Alexander and Elizabeth (Troll) M.; m. Karen Hansen, Feb. 17, 1973; 1 son, George Alexander. BA in History and Edn. (scholar), Western Wash. U. Successively indsl. engr. Boeing Co.; sales mgr. Continental Host, Inc.; asst. dep. dir. ACTION Agy.; spl. asst. to gov. of Wash.; gen. mgr. Tillicum Enterprises & Food Services Co.; dir. Found. for Handicapped; pres. Northwest Highlands Tree Farm; now sec. of state State of Wash. Chmn. community service com. Seattle Rotary Club 4; founder 1st pres. Rotary Youth Job Employment Center, Seattle. Named Man of Yr. Assn. Retarded Citizens, Seattle, 1970. Mem. Nat. Assn. Secs. State (pres.), Nat. Assn. Retarded Children, Wash. Historic Mus. (dir.), Wash. Trust Historic Preservation (founder), Nature Conservancy. Republican. Lutheran. Office: Sec of State Legislative Bldg PO Box 40220 Olympia WA 98504-0220

MUNROE, MARY HILLS, preschool and daycare operator; b. Nantucket Island, Mass., Dec. 11, 1931; d. Isaac III and Hilda Susan Hills; m. Willard Noble Munroe, June 28, 1952 (div. 1975); children: Susan Willard, David, Bruce, Elizabeth. AA, Pima C.C., Tucson, Ariz., 1976. Real estate broker. Co-owner, operator Green Harbor Village, West Yarmouth, Mass., 1955-69; real estate assoc./broker Richard H. Huff, Tucson, 1971-76; founder, dir. Mis Hijitos Presch., Tucson, 1976-94; founder, owner La Palomita de Patagonia, Patagonia, Ariz., 1993—; adv. bd. Ariz. Dept. Health, Phoenix, 1984, Ariz. Dept. Edn. Security, Phoenix, 1980—. Editor: (monthly newspaper) Patagonia Press. Bd. dirs. Community Action Com., Tucson, 1983; mem. panel/polit. interviews C. of C., Tucson, 1992-94. Mem. Ariz. Child Care Assn. (pres. 1978-83, bd. dirs. 1983-93), Patagonia Community Assn.

MUNSELL, JONI ANNE, middle school educator; b. San Diego, Sept. 14, 1954; d. George Clifton and Mary Jo (Hisaw) Nuttall; m. Donald Eugene Munsell, Jan. 15, 1977; children: Jeffrey Ryan, Steven Donald. BA, Calif. State U., Long Beach, 1977; MS in Ednl. Adminstrn., Calif. State U., Fullerton, 1993. Educator Wintersburg High Sch., Huntington Beach, Calif., 1985-86, Newhart Jr. High, Mission Viejo, Calif., 1986-94; Colinas Mid. Sch., Laguna Niguel, Calif., 1994-95; educator Niguel Hills Mid. Sch., 1995—. Office: Niguel Hills Mid Sch 29070 Paseo Escuela Laguna Niguel CA 92677

MUNSON, LUCILLE MARGUERITE (MRS. ARTHUR E. MUNSON), real estate broker; b. Norwood, Ohio, Mar. 26, 1914; d. Frank and Fairy (Wicks) Wirick; R.N., Lafayette (Ind.) Home Hosp., 1937; A.B., San Diego State U., 1963, student Purdue U., Kans. Wesleyan U.; m. Arthur E. Munson, Dec. 24, 1937; children—Barbara Munson Papke, Judith Munson Andrews, Edmund Arthur. Staff and pvt. nurse Lafayette Home Hosp., 1937-41; indsl. nurse Lakey Foundry & Machine Co., Muskegon, Mich., 1950-51, Continental Motors Corp., Muskegon, 1951-52; nurse Girl Scout Camp, Grand Haven, Mich., 1948-49; owner Munson Realty, San Diego, 1964—. Mem. San Diego County Grand Jury, 1975-76, 80-81, Calif. Grand Jurors Assn. (charter). Office: 2999 Mission Blvd Ste 102 San Diego CA 92109-8070

MUNSTERTEIGER, KAY DIANE, speech and language pathologist; b. Newcastle, Wyo., June 2, 1956; d. Donald Francis and Janice Mathilda (Emerson) M. BS, U. Wyo., 1978; MS, U. Nev., Reno, 1980. Speech lang. pathologist No. Nev. Speech lang. Clinic, Reno, 1980-82, Washakie County Sch. Dist. 1, Worland, Wyo., 1982—; pvt. practice speech pathologist Worland, 1982—; speech lang. pathologist, cons. Washakie County Sch. Dist. 2, Tensleep, Wyo., 1984-85; speech lang. pathologist Spl. Touch Presch., Worland, 1985-86, 89-93, Rehab Visions, 1995—; pres. bd. examiners Speech Pathology and Audiology, 1988-93. Mem. Pub. Sch. Caucus. Mem. NEA,

State Edn. Assn., Am. Speech Lang. Hearing Assn., Wyo. Speech Lang. Hearing Assn., Nat. Stuttering Project, Pub. Sch. Caucus, Assn. Childhood Edn. Internat., Phi Kappa Phi. Democrat. Roman Catholic. Office: Washakie County Sch Dist # 1 1200 Culbertson Ave Worland WY 82401-3520

MUNTZ, J(OHN) RICHARD, clergyman; b. Buffalo, Dec. 14, 1927; s. J. Palmer and Laura Estelle (Wedekindt) M.; m. Marietta Hayden, June 22, 1951; children: Palmer Hayden, Laura Marie St. Clair. BS, Wheaton (Ill.) Coll., 1949; BDiv, We. Conservative Bapt. Sem., Portland, Oreg., 1953; MA, Wayne State U., Detroit, 1964; ThM, No. Bapt. Sem., Chgo., 1964; MA in Libr., San Jose State U., 1976. Ordained to ministry Bapt. Ch. Pastor Grace Bapt. Ch., Rochelle, Ill., 1954-56, West Bloomfield Bapt Ch., Orchard Lake, Mich., 1957-62; prof., libr. San Francisco Bapt. Theol. Sem., 1964-72, Denver Bible Bapt. Sem., 1972-75; libr., prof. We. Bapt. Coll., Salem, Oreg., 1975—; accreditation team mem. Am. Assn. Bible Colls., Fayetteville, Ark., 1977-94. Author: A Suggested Theological Bibliography for AABC Colleges, Supplement I, 1994. Deacon, tchr. Bethany Bapt. Ch., Salem, Oreg. Mem. Assn. Christian Librs., So. Bapt. Hist. Soc., Beta Phi Mu. Republican. Baptist. Home: 1095 Cayuse Cir SE Salem OR 97306-1396 Office: Western Bapt Coll 5000 Deer Park Dr SE Salem OR 97301-9330

MURANE, WILLIAM EDWARD, lawyer; b. Denver, Mar. 4, 1933; s. Edward E. and Theodora (Wilson) M.; m. Rosemarie Palmerone, Mar. 26, 1960; children: Edward Wheelock, Peter Davenport, Alexander Phelps. AB, Dartmouth Coll., 1954; LLB, Stanford U., 1957. Bar: Wyo. 1957, Colo. 1958, Calif. 1958, D.C. 1978, U.S. Supreme Ct. 1977. Assoc. then ptnr. Holland & Hart, Denver, 1961-69; dep. gen. counsel U.S. Dept. Commerce, Washington, 1969-71; gen. counsel FDIC, Washington, 1971-72; ptnr. Holland & Hart, Denver, 1972—, chmn. litigation dept., 1986-90; pub. mem. Adminstrv. Conf. of the U.S., Washington, 1978-81. Bd. dirs. Ctr. for Law and Rsch., Denver, 1973-76, Acad. in the Wilderness, Denver, 1986—; trustee Colo. Symphony Orch., 1994—; mem. bd. visitors Stanford U. Law Sch. Capt. USAF, 1958-61. Fellow Am. Coll. Trial Lawyers; mem. ABA (ho of dels. 1991-96), U. Club, Cactus Club. Republican. Office: Holland & Hart 555 17th St Ste 3200 Denver CO 80202-5555

MURATA, MARGARET KIMIKO, music educator; b. Chgo., July 29, 1946; d. Yoshinori and Mikiko Murata. AB, U. Chgo., 1967, AM, 1971, PhD, 1975. From asst. to assoc. prof. U. Calif., Irvine, 1973-84, prof. music, 1984—, chair dept. music, 1995-96; music subject test com. Grad. Record Examination, Princeton, 1995—. Author: Operas for the Papal Court, 1981, revised edit., 1997; contbr. articles to profl. jours. Recipient Disting. Tchg. award U. Calif. Irvine Alumni Assn., 1984, Sch. Arts, 1996; hon. fellow Woodrow Wilson Found., 1967, Dissertation fellow AAUW, 1972-73. Mem. Internat. Musicol. Soc., Am. Musicol. Soc. (bd. dirs., v.p. 1994-96), Coll. Music Soc., Società Italiana di Musicologia, Japanese-Am. Citizens League. Office: U Calif Irvine 292 Music Bldg 714 Irvine CA 92697-2775

MURATORE, MARILYN ANN, contractor; b. San Francisco, June 26, 1941; d. Thomas James and Camille Catherine (Bacigalupi) Dennison; m. Richard Peter Muratore, Oct. 25, 1959; 1 child, Tamara Ann. Treas. Peter D. Scatena, Inc., San Francisco, 1974-84; v.p., sec. Muratore Corp., San Francisco, 1985-91, chmn. bd., sec., 1991—. Active Com. to Reelect Dick Claire for Mayor, Redwood City, Calif., 1991. Mem. Am. Bldg. Contractors Assn. (bd. dirs. 1992—), San Francisco C. of C. Office: Muratore Corp 250 Alameda de las Pulgas Redwood City CA 94062

MURDOCH, PAUL ALLAN, architect; b. Phila., Nov. 6, 1956; s. Roderick Graeme and Mae Ellen (Helfrich) M.; m. Milena Iancovici, Sept. 2, 1985; children: Tess, Graham. BS in Architecture, U. Va., 1978; MArch, UCLA, 1984. Registered architect, Calif., Ariz. Designer Geddes Brecher Qualls & Cunningham, Phila., 1981-82, Urban Innovations Group, 1983; designer, project mgr., architect Arthur Erickson Architects, L.A., 1984-91; founder, pres. Paul Murdoch Architects, L.A., 1991—; Mem. L.A. Eco-Cities Coun., Design Profls. Coalition Steering Com., Rebuild L.A. Urban Planning Task Force, Environ. Design Group City L.A.; guest critic Undergrad. Design Studio, Sch. Architecture and Urban Planning, Ahmedabad, India, 1979, Design Studio, UCLA, 1990, 91, 92; teaching asst., initiator grad. seminar UCLA, 1983; teaching asst. grad. design studio UCLA, 1984; UCLA rep. Internat. Lab. Architecture and Urban Design, Siena, Italy, 1983; lectr. U. So. Calif. Sch. Architecture, 1993-97. Contbg. author: Man and His House in the Himalaya, 1981; contbg. architect: Growth and Integration, 1984, Architecture California, 1982, LA Architect, 1981, GA Houses 33, Tokyo, 1992, House & Garden, N.Y.C., 1992, GA Houses 35, Tokyo, 1992; prin. projects include Donald Bruce Kaufman Brentwood Br. Libr., L.A., Wilson Student Ctr., UCLA Sch. Medicine, Biol. Scis. Bldg. U. Calif., Irvine, Civic Ctr. Metrorail Sta., L.A., Pershing Square Metrorail Sta., L.A., others. Recipient Best Pub. Use of Architecture award L.A. Bus. Coun., 1995, AIA Rsch.-Nat. Renewable Energy Lab. merit award, 1996; UCLA Found. fellow, 1982, 83, 84, UCLA traveling fellow, 1983, McGuire fellow UCLA, 1983, AIA Found. fellow UCLA, 1983; UCLA grad. rsch. grantee, 1982. Mem. AIA. Office: Paul Murdoch Architects 1250 S Lucerne Blvd Los Angeles CA 90019-6805

MURDOCK, DAVID H., diversified company executive; b. Kansas City, Apr. 10, 1923; m. Maria Ferrer, Apr., 1992. LLD (hon.), Pepperdine U., 1978; LHD (hon.), U. Nebr., 1984, Hawaii Loa Coll., 1989. Sole proprietor, chmn., chief exec. officer Pacific Holding Co., L.A.; chmn., chief exec. officer Dole Food Co. (formerly Castle & Cooke, Inc.), L.A., 1985—, also bd. dirs. Trustee Asia Soc., N.Y.C., L.A.; founder, bd. dirs. Found. for Advanced Brain Studies, L.A.; bd. visitors UCLA Grad. Sch. Mgmt.;bd. govs. Performing Arts Coun. of Music Ctr., L.A.; bd. govs. East-West Ctr., L.A.; patron Met. Opera, N.Y.C. With USAAC, 1943-45. Mem. Regency Club (founder, pres.) Bel-Air Bay Country Club, Sherwood Country Club (founder, pres.), Met. Club (N.Y.C.). Office: Dole Food Co Inc 31355 Oak Crest Dr Westlake Village CA 91361-4633 also: Pacific Holding Co 10900 Wilshire Blvd Ste 1600 Los Angeles CA 90024-6535*

MURDOCK, PAMELA ERVILLA, travel and advertising company executive; b. Los Angeles, Dec. 3, 1940; d. John James and Chloe Conger (Keefe) M.; children: Cheryl, Kim. BA, U. Colo., 1962. Pres., Dolphin Travel, Denver, 1972-87; owner, pres. Mile Hi Tours, Denver, 1973—, MH Internat., 1987—, Mile-Hi Advt. Agy., 1986—. Bd. dirs. Rocky Mountain chpt. Juvenile Diabetes Found. Internat. Named Wholesaler of Yr., Las Vegas Conv. and Visitors Authority, 1984. Recipient Leadership award Nat. Multiple Sclerosis Soc., 1996. Mem. NAFE, Am. Soc. Travel Agts., Nat. Fedn. Independent Businessmen. Republican. Home: 5565 E Vassar Ave Denver CO 80222-6239 Office: Mile Hi Tours Inc 2160 S Clermont St Denver CO 80222-5007

MURI, JOHN IMRE, mechanical engineer; b. Szerencs, Hungary, Aug. 20, 1964; came to U.S., 1987; s. Istvan and Julia (Toth) M. MSME, Budapest Tech. U., 1987. Chief design engr. Accudyne Engring., Bell Gardens, Calif., 1988-90; devel. engr. Alcon Surgical, Irvine, Calif., 1990-92; sr. engr. Birtcher Medical Systems, Irvine, Calif., 1992-95; cons. R&D Med. Devices Orgn., Irvine, 1993—, Internat. Bus., Budapest, 1992—. Inventor in field. Pres. Youth Dance Club, Budapest, 1987. Mem. Soc. Plastic Engrs. Roman Catholic.

MURIAN, RICHARD MILLER, book company executive; b. East St. Louis, Ill., Sept. 17, 1937; s. Richard Miller Jr. and Margaret Keyes (Gregory) M.; m. Judith Lee, Aug. 11, 1961 (dec. apr. 1992); 1 child, Jennifer Ann. BA, U. Calif., Davis, 1969; MLS, U. Calif., Berkeley, 1972; MA, Calif. State U., Sacramento, 1975; MDiv, Trinity Evang., 1977. Cert. history instr., libr. sci. instr., Calif. History reader Calif. State U., Sacramento, 1965-66; history reader U. Calif., Davis, 1966-68, philosophy researcher, 1968-69; bibliographer Argus Books, Sacramento, 1970-71; rsch. dir. Nat. Judical Coll., Reno, 1971-72; libr. Calif. State U., Sacramento, 1972-76; tv talk show host Richard Murian Show, L.A., 1979-80; pres. Alcuin Books, Ltd., Phoenix, 1981—; bd. mem. Guild of Ariz. Antiquarian Books; pres. East Valley Assn. Evangs., Mesa, Ariz., 1984-86; cons. Ariz. Hist. Soc., 1993—; cons. Ariz. Hist. Soc. Contbr. articles to profl. jours. Active U. Calif. Riverside Libr., 1981-83, KAET (PBS), 1988—, Ariz. State U., 1989—. Recipient Sidney B. Mitchell fellowship U. Calif., Berkeley, 1971. Mem. Am. Assn. Mus., Ariz. Preservation Found., Grand Canyon Nature Assn., Internat. Platform Assn., Phi Kappa Phi. Democrat. Presbyterian. Office: Alcuin Books Ltd 115 W Camelback Rd Phoenix AZ 85013-2519

MURILLO, VELDA JEAN, social worker, counselor; b. Miller, S.D., Dec. 8, 1943; d. Royal Gerald and Marion Elizabeth (Porter) Matson; m. Daniel John Murillo, June 25, 1967 (div. Dec. 1987); 1 child, Damon Michael. BS, S.D. State U., 1965; MA, Calif. State U., Bakersfield, 1980. Cert. marriage, family and child counselor. Social worker adult svcs. Kern County Dept. Welfare, Bakersfield, 1965-78, social worker child protective svcs., 1978-84; asst. coord. sexual abuse program Kern County Dist. Atty., Bakersfield, 1985-91, coord. sexual abuse program, 1991—; Mem. Calif. Sexual Assault Investigators, 1982-84, Kern Child Abuse Prevention Coun., Bakersfield, 1982-84; co-developer, presenter Children's Self Help Project, Bakersfield, 1982-87; cons. mem. Sexual Assault Adv. Com., Bakersfield, 1991-96. Democrat. Office: Kern County Dist Atty 1215 Truxtun Ave Bakersfield CA 93301

MURKOWSKI, FRANK HUGHES, senator; b. Seattle, Mar. 28, 1933; s. Frank Michael and Helen (Hughes) M.; m. Nancy R. Gore, Aug. 28, 1954; children: Carol Victoria Murkowski Sturgulewski, Lisa Ann Murkowski Martell, Frank Michael, Eileen Marie Murkowski Van Wyhe, Mary Catherine Murkowski Judson, Brian Patrick. Student, Santa Clara U., 1952-53; BA in Econs, Seattle U., 1955. With Pacific Nat. Bank of Seattle, 1957-58, Nat. Bank of Alaska, Anchorage, 1959-67; asst. v.p., mgr. Nat. Bank of Alaska (Wrangell br.), 1963-66; v.p. charge bus. devel. Nat. Bank of Alaska, Anchorage, 1966-67; commr. dept. econ. devel. State of Alaska, Juneau, 1967-70; pres. Alaska Nat. Bank, Fairbanks, 1971-80; mem. U.S. Senate from Alaska, Washington, D.C., 1981—; chmn. Com. on Energy and Natural Resources; mem. Com. on Fin., Vets Affairs Com., Indian Affairs Com., Japan-US Friendship Com.; Rep. nominee for U.S. Congress from Alaska, 1970. Former v.p. B.C. and Alaska Bd. Trade; mem. U.S. Holocaust Mus. Coun. Served with U.S. Coast Guard, 1955-57. Mem. AAA, AMVETS, NRA, Am. Legion, Polish Legion Am. Vets., Ducks Unltd., Res. Officer's Assn., Alaska Geog. Soc., Alaska World Affairs Coun., Fairbanks Hist. Preservation Found., Coalition Am. Vets., Alaska Native Brotherhood, Naval Athletic Assn., Am. Bankers Assn., Alaska Bankers Assn. (pres. 1973), Young Pres.'s Orgn., Alaska C. of C. (pres. 1977), Anchorage C. of C. (bd. dirs. 1966), B.C. C. of C., Fairbanks C. of C. (bd. dirs. 1973-78), Pioneers of Alaska, Internat. Alaska Nippon Kai, Capital Hill Club, Shilla Club, Army Athletic Club, Congl. Staff Club, Diamond Athletic Club, Washington Athletic Club, Elks, Lions. Office: US Senate 322 Hart Senate Bldg Washington DC 20510

MURPHEY, MARGARET JANICE, marriage and family therapist; b. Taft, Calif., July 24, 1939; d. Glen Roosevelt Wurster and Lucile Mildred (Holt) Lopez; m. Russell Warren Murphey, June 20, 1959; children: Lucinda Kalbfleisch, Rochelle Murphey, Janice Sorenson. BA in Social Sci., Calif. State U., Chico, 1986, MA in Psychology, 1989; postgrad., La Salle U. Sec. Folson State Prison, Calif., 1963-66; tchr. Desert Sands Unified Schs., Indio, Calif., 1969-72; claims determiner Employment Development Dept., Redding, Calif., 1976-78; sec. Shasta County Pers., Redding, 1978-79; welfare worker Shasta County Welfare Office, Redding, 1979-85; therapy intern Counseling Ctr. Calif. State U., Chico, 1989-90; therapist Family Svc. Assn., Chico, 1987-90, Butte County Drug and Alcohol Abuse Ctr., Chico, 1989-90; mental halth counselor Cibecue (Ariz.) Indian Health Clinic, 1990—; mem. Kinisba Child Abuse Com., 1994—. Vol. Pacheco Sch., Redding, 1972-76; Sunday sch. tchr., dir. vacation Bible sch. Nazarene Ch., Sacramento, Indio and Redding, 1958-85. Recipient Sch. Bell award Pacheco Sch. Mem. APA, ACA, Am. Assn. Christian Counselors, Am. Assn. Multi-Cultural Counselors, Internat. Assn. Trauma Counselors. Home: PO Box 1114 Show Low AZ 85901-1114 Office: Cibecue Health Ctr Apache Behavioral Health PO Box 1089 Whiteriver AZ 85941-1089

MURPHY, CATHERINE MARIA, public affairs consultant; b. Columbus, Ga., May 11, 1967; d. John Edward Murphy Jr. and Lynette (Albertazzie) Crosby. BA in Comms., Ohio State U., 1989. Constituent liaison Ohio rep. Mike Stinziano, Columbus, 1989; account assoc. Solem & Assocs., San Francisco, 1990-91; polit. cons. San Francisco, 1991-93; pub. rels. assoc. Working Assets, San Francisco, 1993-94; sr. mgmt. assoc. Pacific/West Comms., San Francisco, 1994-95; sr. account exec. Kearns & West Pub. Rels., San Francisco, 1996—; mem. adv. bd. Airport Noise Abatement Com., San Francisco, 1996—. Bd. dirs. San Francisco chpt. Nat. Women's Polit. Caucus, 1994—. Mem. Pub. Rels. Soc. Am. Roman Catholic. Office: Kearns & West 235 Pine St # 1675 San Francisco CA 94104-2701

MURPHY, DAVID HAZLETT, geologist; b. Ann Arbor, Mich., Sept. 11, 1954; s. Richard J. and Janice (Kerlin) M. B.A., Albion Coll.; M.S., U. Mich. Lic. profl. geologist, Wyo. Geologist, Amoco Prodn. Co., Houston, 1978-81, Mobil Oil Corp., Denver, 1981-86; consulting geologist, Denver, 1986-89; geologist The Mark Group, Pleasant Hill, Calif., 1989; cartographer Def. Mapping Agy., 1989-91; geologist U.S. Bur. Land Mgmt., 1991—. Asst. scoutmaster, Boy Scouts Am., Aurora, Colo., 1981-84, scoutmaster, 1984-87, unit commr., Winnemucca, Nev., 1992, dist. commr., 1993-94, coun. commr., Reno, 1995—. Recipient Dist. Award of Merit, Boy Scouts Am., 1993, Silver Beaver award, 1997. Mem. Am. Assn. Petroleum Geologists, Nev. Petroleum Soc., Geothermal Resources Coun., Sigma Gamma Epsilon.

MURPHY, FRANCIS SEWARD, journalist; b. Portland, Oreg., Sept. 9, 1914; s. Francis H. and Blanche (Livesay) M.; BA, Reed Coll., 1936; m. Clare Eastham Cooke, Sept. 20, 1974. With The Oregonian, Portland, 1936-79, TV editor, Behind the Mike columnist, 1952-79. Archeol. explorer Mayan ruins, Yucatan, Mex., 1950—, mem. Am. Quintana Roo Expdn., 1965, 66, 68. With U.S. Army, 1942-46. Author: Dragon Mask Temples in Central Yucatan, 1988. Mem. Am. Philatelic Soc. (life), Royal Asiatic Soc., City Club (bd. govs. 1950, 64-66), Explorers Club, Am. Club of Hong Kong, Oreg. Hist. Soc., Soc. Am. Archeaology, Am. Philatelic Soc., Hong Kong Philatelic Soc., World Wide Fund Nature, Royal Hong Kong Jockey Club. Democrat. Congregationalist. Home: 4213 NE 32nd Ave Portland OR 97211-7149

MURPHY, LINDA S., city official; b. Lynchburg, Va., June 7, 1948; d. Carter P. and Dorothy L. (Clark) Tucker; m. Daniel K. Murphy, Mar. 25, 1972; 1 child, Krystal. Student, Longwood Coll., 1966-68. Exec. sec. First Nat. Bank of Anchorage, Seward, Alaska, 1976-80; clk. of ct., asst. magistrate Alaska Ct. System, Seward, 1980-81; city clk. City of Seward, 1981—. Sec., Seward Concert Assn., 1982; chmn. Seward Sch. Adv. Bd., 1983; v.p. bd. dirs. Seward Life Action Coun., 1983-84, pres. bd. dirs., 1984-86; chmn. Seward-Obihiro Sister City Com., 1984; lt. gov. Transition Team, 1995; chmn. local United Way, 1995. Named Alaska Mcpl. Official of Yr., 1992. Mem. Internat. Inst. Mcpl. Clks. (bd. dirs. 1992-95, 2d v.p. 1995-96, 1st v.p. 1996-97, pres. 1997—), Alaska Assn. Mcpl. Clerks (sec. 1984-85, v.p. 1985-86, pres. 1986-87), Alaska Women in Govt. (v.p. 1985-87), Bus. and Profl. Women's Club (v.p. 1988-89, pres. 1989-90), Rotary (bd. dirs. 1989-96, treas. 1991-93, v.p. 1993-94, pres. 1994-95). Democrat. Home: Salmon Rd Seward AK 99664 Office: Seward City Hall PO Box 167 Seward AK 99664-0167

MURPHY, MARY ANN, human services administrator; b. Salt Lake City, Feb. 13, 1943; d. Wallace L. and Irene (Hummer) Matlock; m. Robert A. Glatzer, Dec. 31, 1977; children: Gabriela, Jessica, Nicholas. BA, U. Wash., 1964; MS, Ea. Wash. U., 1975. House counselor Ryther Child Ctr., Seattle, 1966-67; tchr. presch. Head Start, L.A. and Seattle, 1967-70, Children's Orthopedic Hosp., Seattle, 1970-72; faculty Ea. Wash. U., Cheney, 1973-82; exec. dir. Youth Help Assn., Spokane, Wash., 1983-88; mgr. regional ctr. for child abuse and neglect Deaconess Med. Ctr., Spokane, 1988—; pres. Wash. State Alliance for Children, Youth and Families, Seattle, 1985-87; chairperson Gov.'s Juvenile Justice Adv. Commn., Olympia, Wash., 1987—. Mem. Nat. Coun. on Juvenile Justice, 1994. Recipient Alumni Achievement award Ea. Wash. U., 1994; named Outstanding Women Leader in Health Care YWCA, 1992, Outstanding Children's Advocate, Wash. State Children's Alliance, 1996. Home: 1950 W Clarke Ave Spokane WA 99201-1306 Office: Deaconess Med Ctr 604 W 6th Ave Spokane WA 99204-2708 *Personal philosophy: "Take the first step in faith. You don't have to see the whole staircase, just take the first step." Dr. Martin Luther King, Jr.*

MURPHY, MICHAEL JOSEPH, county official; b. Seattle, May 24, 1947; s. John Anthony and Helen Elizabeth (Domick) M.; m. Theresa Ann Smith. BA in History, Seattle U., 1969; MBA, Pacific Luth. U., 1978. Chief adjudicator vet.'s program Office of the State Treas., Olympia, Wash., 1972-75, adminstr. pub. deposit protection commn., 1975-81, internal auditor to state treas., 1981-87; treas. Thurston County, Olympia, 1987—; mem. adv. bd. asset/liability com. Twin County Credit Union, Olympia, 1987—; instr. profl. orgns., govt. Treas. Thurston County Dems., 1973-77. Mem. Wash. Assn. County Treasurers (bd. dirs., officer 1987—, legis. coord. 1989—, Pres. award 1994), Wash. Assn. County Officials (bd. dirs. 1989-90), Wash. Mcpl. Treasurers Assn. (bd. dirs. 1990—, Cert. Excellence for investment policy 1992), Wash. Fin. Officers Assn. (profl. fin. officer 1988-94), Olympia Yacht Club, Olympia Country and Golf Club, Valley Athletic Club. Roman Catholic. Home: PO Box 1342 Olympia WA 98507-1342 Office: Thurston County Treas 2000 Lakeridge Dr SW Olympia WA 98502-6045*

MURPHY, MICHAEL R., federal judge; b. Denver, Aug. 6, 1947; s. Roland and Mary Cecilia (Maloney) M.; m. Maureen Elizabeth Donnelly, Aug. 22, 1970; children: Amy Christina, Michael Donnelly. BA in History, Creighton U., 1969; JD, U. Wyo., 1972. Bar: Wyo. 1972, U.S. Ct. Appeals (10th cir.) 1972, Utah 1973, U.S. Dist. Ct. Utah 1974, U.S. Dist. Ct. Wyo. 1976, U.S. Ct. Appeals (5th cir.) 1976, U.S. Tax Ct. 1980, U.S. Ct. Appeals (9th cir.) 1981, U.S. Ct. Appeals (fed. cir.) 1984. Law clk. to chief judge U.S. Ct. Appeals (10th cir.), Salt Lake City, 1972-73; with Jones, Waldo, Holbrook & McDonough, Salt Lake City, 1973-86; judge 3d Dist. Ct., Salt Lake City, 1986-95, pres. judge, 1990-95; judge U.S. Ct. Appeals (10th cir.), Salt Lake City, 1995—; mem. adv. com. on rules of civil procedure Utah Supreme Ct., Salt Lake City, 1985-95, mem. bd. dist. ct. judges, 1989-90; mem. Utah State Sentencing Commn., 1993-95, Utah Adv. Com. on Child Support Guidelines, 1989-95, chair 1993-95; mem. Utah Child Sexual Abuse Task Force, 1989-93. Recipient Freedom of Info. award Soc. Profl. Journalists, 1995, Utah Minority Bar Assn. award, 1995; named Judge of Yr., Utah State Bar, 1992. Fellow Am. Bar Found.; mem. ABA, Utah Bar Assn. (chmn. alternative dispute resolution com. 1985-88), Salt Lake County Bar Assn., Sutherland Inn of Ct. II (past pres.). Roman Catholic. Office: 6012 Federal Bldg 125 S State St Salt Lake City UT 84138

MURPHY, MIRIAM BRINTON, editor, writer; b. Salt Lake City, Nov. 10, 1933; d. Edward Augustus and Julia Irene (Maxfield) Brinton; m. William Hunt Murphy, Dec. 31, 1964 (div. 1970); 1 child, William Augustus. BA in English, U. Utah, 1956. Pub. rels. asst. Blue Cross/Blue Shield, Salt Lake City, 1956-58; copywriter trainee J. Walter Thompson, N.Y.C., 1958-59; adv. copywriter ZCMI, Salt Lake City, 1960-62, Smith's & Emporium, Oakland and San Francisco, 1962-69; assoc. editor Utah Hist. Quar., editor Beehive History Utah State Hist. Soc., Salt Lake City, 1970—; mem. lit. adv. panel Utah Arts Coun., Salt Lake City, 1977-79, 85-89; mem. spkrs. bur. Utah Humanities Coun., Salt Lake City, 1988-89; pres. Wasatch Westerners, Salt Lake City, 1994-95. Contbr. poetry to anthologies, articles to encys. and hist. pubs. Office: Utah State Hist Soc 300 Rio Grande St Salt Lake City UT 84101-1106

MURPHY, PHILIP EDWARD, broadcast executive; b. Chgo., May 11, 1945; s. Edward Curtis and Mary Francis (D'Incecco) M.; m. Carol Jean Sefton, Mar. 11, 1967 (div. 1985); children: Mandy Jean, Patrick Jeffrey. BS, Ind. U., 1967. Prodn. mgr. Sta. WFIU-FM, Bloomington, Ind., 1968; news reporter, photographer, editor Sta. WTHR-TV, Indpls., 1969, sr. account exec., 1970-80; acct. exec. Blair TV, L.A., 1980-81; pres. Am. Spot Cable Corp., Hollywood, Calif., 1981-82; sr. v.p. TV group ops. Paramount Pictures, Hollywood, 1982—; head ops. United Paramount Network; responsible United Paramount Network Ops.; spkr. film preservation, in field; advisor Libr. of Congress, Washington, Nat. Archives, Washington. Lighting designer Civic Theatre, Indpls., 1979; tech. dir. Footlite Mus., Indpls., 1970-78; bd. dirs. Cathedral Arts, Indpls., 1978-80. Mem. Assn. Moving Image Archivists, Human Rights Campaign (Washington), Gay and Lesbian Alliance Against Defamation L.A., Hollywood Supports Assn., Soc. Motion Picture and TV Engrs. Office: Paramount Pictures TV Stage 3/212 5555 Melrose Ave Hollywood CA 90038-3197

MURPHY, ROBIN ROBERSON, computer science educator; b. Mobile, Ala., Aug. 25, 1957; d. Fred Blakely and Ada Lee (Wills) Roberson; m. Kevin Eddy Murphy, Aug., 27, 1982; children: Kathleen Freebern, Allan Roberson. B in Mech. Engring., Ga. Inst. Tech., 1980, MS in Computer Sci., 1989, PhD in Computer Sci., 1992. Project engr. Dow Chem. USA, Plaquemine, La., 1980-84; software project engr. Turbitrol Co., Atlanta, 1984-86; asst. prof. dept. math. and comp. sci. Colo. Sch. Mines, Golden, 1992—, assoc. dir. Ctr. Robotics and Intelligent Systems, 1994-95; mem. NSF vis. com. on computer sci. curriculum U. Va., Charlottesville, 1992-95. Author: (with others) The Handbook of Brain Theory and Neural Networks, 1995; contbr. articles to profl. jours. Rsch. grantee NSF, 1994—, Advanced Rsch. Projects Agy., 1994—, NASA, 1994—. Mem. AAAI, IEEE, AIAA, Assn. Computing Machinery. Office: Colo Sch Mines Dept Math and Computer Sci Golden CO 80401-1887

MURPHY, SARA JO, library director; b. St. Louis, Nov. 20, 1942; d. Richard O. and Helen F. (Cross) Colvin; m. Dennis R. Murphy, Sept. 5, 1964; children: Thomas R., JoEllen, Andrew R. BA, Emporia State U., 1964. Self-employed ins. agt. Webster Ins., La Veta, Colo., 1978-88; real estate agt. Spoon River Real Estate, La Veta, 1979-88; columnist Huerfano World, Walsenburg, Colo., 1987-90; dir. Carnegie Pub. Libr., Trinidad, Colo., 1990—. County chmn. Rep. Party, Huerfano, Colo., 1988-90. Mem. ALA, AAUW, Colo. Libr. Assn., Santa Fe Trail Assocs., Trinidad Hist. Soc. (bd. dirs.). Office: Carnegie Public Library 202 N Animas St Trinidad CO 81082-2643

MURPHY, THOMAS JOSEPH, archbishop; b. Chgo., Oct. 3, 1932; s. Barthomew Thomas and Nellie M. AB, St. Mary of the Lake Sem., 1954, STB, 1956, MA, 1957, STL, 1958, STD, 1960. Ordained priest Roman Cath. Ch., 1958. Various positions with Archdiocese of Chgo.; bishop of Great Falls-Billings Mont., 1978-87; coadjutor archbishop of Seattle, 1987-91, archbishop of Seattle, 1991—. Office: Archdiocese of Seattle 910 Marion St Seattle WA 98104-1274*

MURPHY, TIM, food products executive; b. 1954. With USDA Farmers Adminstrn, 1975-79; now pres., treas. APIO Inc., Guadalupe, Calif. Office: APIO Inc PO Box 627 Guadalupe CA 93434*

MURRAY, COLETTE MORGAN, healthcare executive, fundraising consultant; b. San Francisco, July 28, 1935; d. Thomas Ralph and Althea L. (Bail) Morgan; m. J. Roger Samuelsen, Sept. 14, 1959 (div. 1969); 1 child, Thea S. Kano; m. Richard Arlan Murray, Nov. 4, 1983. AB, U. Calif., Berkeley, 1959; JD, U. San Francisco, 1964; cert. in mgmt., U. Calif., Davis, 1975, U. Tex., 1989. Cert. fund raising exec. Pvt. practice law Walnut Creek, Calif., 1965-73; exec. dir. Calif. Alumni Assn., Berkeley, 1973-78; asst. chancellor univ. rels. U. Calif., Santa Cruz, 1978-85; v.p. for devel. and alumni U. Louisville, Ky., 1985-88; v.p. for devel. and univ. rels. Tex. Tech. U., Lubboch, 1988-90; corp. v.p. for philanthropy and community devel. Henry Ford Health System, Detroit, 1990-95; CEO Sharp Healthcare Found., San Diego, 1995—; cons. Coun. for the Advancement and Support of Edn., Washington, 1980—, bd. dirs. NSFRE, Wash., Leadership Detroit, Leadership Calif., LEAD San Diego; pres. Leadership Am. Assn., Washington, 1993-94. Bd. dirs. CATCH, Detroit, 1990-95, bd. dirs., Ladership, Calif., 1996—. Mem. LEAD San Diego, Class of 1996-97. Recipient Dorothy Shaw award Alpha Delta Pi, 1958; named Citizen of Yr., Santa Cruz C. of C., 1981. Mem. NSFRE (chpt. pres. 1994, sec. nat. bd. 1997), Coun. for Advancement and Support of Edn. (chair bd. 1981-82, Hesburgh award 1984), Univ. Club, San Diego Country Club. Office: Sharp Healthcare Found Ste 302 8525 Gibbs Dr San Diego CA 92123

MURRAY, DONALD EUGENE, plasic surgeon; b. Dillon, Mont., May 30, 1937; s. Ned Charles and Ruth Adelaide (McFarland) M.; m. Charla Leavens Murray, June 18, 1961; children: Thomas Allan, Carol Ann. BS in Quantitative Biology, MIT, 1959; MD, Stanford Sch. of Medicine, 1964. Diplomate Am. Bd. Plastic Surgery, Nat. Bd. Med. Examiners; lic. Mont. Straight surgery internship Palo Alto-Stanford Med. Ctr., Calif., 1964-65; asst. resident gen. surgery Stanford U. Sch. of Medicine, Palo Alto, Calif., 1965-66, fellow in rehabilitaion surgery, 1966-67, resident gen. surgery, 1967-

68, chief resident plastic and reconstructive surgery, 1969-70; chief resident gen. surgery San Mateo Gen. Hosp./Stanford U. Sch. of Medicine, Calif., 1968; chief resident head and neck surgery Roswell Park Meml. Inst., Buffalo, N.Y., 1969; fellow plastic and reconstructive surgery Royal Melbourne Hosp., Australia, 1970-71; honorary plastic and reconstructive surgeon Middlemore Hosp., Auckland, New Zealand, 1971; pvt. practice Missoula, Mont., 1971—; chief of surgery Missoula Cmty. Hosp., 1974, St. Patrick's Hosp., 1977; trainee in VRA summer Clin. Tng. Program Rehab. Medicine Stanford Med. Ctr., 1962; clin. clk. St. Thomas' Hosp. Cardiovasc. Surgery, London, England, 1963; mem. Mont. State Comprehensive Health Planning Coun., Mont. Fedn. for Med. Care (instl. rev. steering com. 1976-86, bd. dirs. 1982-88), Mont. Physicians' Svc. Adjudication Com., 1979, Mont. Medicare Adv. Com., 1992-95; surgery com. Missoula Cmty. Hosp., 1973, 86, surgery com. St. Patrick's Hosp., 1975-78, 88-89, pres. elect med. staff, 1981, pres. med. staff, 1982, quality assurance com., 1981 (chmn. 1983), by-laws revision com., 1985; chmn. Health Facilities Com. State of Mont. Dept. of Health & Environ. Scis., 1973-75, credentials com. St. Patrick's Hosp., 1986-88; faculty affiliate Dept. Comm. Sci. & Disorders U. Mont., 1975-90; adv. com. Missoula Tech. Ctr., 1977; orgnl. com. Mont. Health Sys. Agy., 1977; burn chmn. Western Mont. Emergency Med. Svcs. Coun., 1978; assoc. mem. Am. Soc. of Clin. Hypnosis, 1982. Mem. Missoula Symphony Assn. (bd. dirs. 1980-87, pres. 1986). Fellow ACS (com. on applicants 1980—); mem. AMA, Am. Soc. of Plastic and Reconstructive Surgeons (annotated bibliography com. 1979-82), Am. Cleft Palate Assn., Northwest Soc. of Plastic Surgeons, Rocky Mountain Assn. of Plastic and Reconstructive Surgeons (nominating com. 1979, pres. elect 1989, pres. 1990), Mont. Cleft Palate Assn. (pres. 1974), Mont. Med. Assn. (joint med. legal panel 1976-78, malpractice panel 1978, profl. liability com. 1980-86), Western Mont. Med. Soc. (v.p. 1974, pres. elect 1975, pres. 1976). Office: 614 W Spruce St Missoula MT 59802-4002

MURRAY, JAMES ALAN, urban and environmental consultant, investor; b. Evansville, Ind., Oct. 2, 1942; s. William Dewey and Dorothy Marie (Gleason) M.; BS, U. N.Mex., 1964; MBA, Harvard U., 1969; MA (NDEA fellow), U. Oreg., 1971, PhD, 1972; children: Heidi Lynn, Paul Alan, Kendra Leigh. Dir. fin. City of Boulder (Colo.), 1972-73, dir. adminstrv. svcs., 1973-74; v.p. Briscoe, Maphis, Murray & Lamont, Inc., Boulder, 1974-78, pres., 1978-84, also dir.; dir. fin. City and County of Denver, 1984-86, chief exec. officer, 1986-87, asst. to mayor, 1987-89; pres., dir. Murray Lamont & Assocs., Inc., 1990—; pres., dir. Colo. Scientific Investments, Inc., 1993—; chmn. Lanhou Murray Eletronics Co., Ltd., China, 1994-95, chmn. Lanzhou Murray Clothing Co., China, 1995—; adj. assoc. prof. Grad. Sch. Public Affairs, U. Colo., Boulder, 1972-80, Denver, 1985-91. Mem. open space adv. com. City of Boulder, 1972-74; bd. dirs. Met. Denver Sewage Authority, 1984-85; Colo. Baseball Commn., 1989-93. Mem. ASPA, Am. Econ. Assn., Western Econ. Assn., Water Pollution Control Fedn., Denver Athletic Club, Kappa Mu Epsilon, Pi Alpha Alpha. Home: 99 S Downing St Apt 602 Denver CO 80209-2407 Office: 1660 Wynkoop St Ste 1060 Denver CO 80202-1146

MURRAY, JAMES PATRICK, newspaper columnist; b. Hartford, Conn., Dec. 29, 1919; s. James and Molly (O'Connell) M.; m. Geraldine Norma Brown, Oct. 20, 1945 (dec. Apr. 1984); children: Theodore, Anthony, Pamela, Eric (dec.). AB, Trinity Coll., Hartford, 1943, LittD honoris causa, 1981; LLD honoris causa, Pepperdine U., 1987. Mem. staff New Haven Register, 1943, Los Angeles Examiner, 1944-48, Time, Inc., 1948-61; sports columnist Los Angeles Times, 1961—. Author: The Best of Jim Murray, 1965, The Sporting World of Jim Murray, 1968, The Jim Murray Collection, 1988, Jim Murray: An Autobiography, 1993. Recipient Sportswriter of Yr. award Nat. Assn. Sportscasters and Sportswriters, 1964, 66-77, 79, Headliners Club award, 1965, 76, Alumni medal Trinity Coll., 1972, J.G. Taylor Spink award Baseball Hall of Fame, Cooperstown, N.Y., 1988, Pulitzer prize for disting. commentary, 1990. Mem. Time-Life Alumni Assn., L.A. Press Club (v.p. 1953), PGA West Club, Riviera Country Club, Bel Air Country Club. Office: Los Angeles Times Times Mirror Sq Los Angeles CA 90053

MURRAY, JOHN FREDERIC, physician, educator; b. Mineola, N.Y., June 8, 1927; s. Frederic S. and Dorothy Murray; m. Diane Lain, Nov. 30, 1968; children—James R., Douglas S., Elizabeth. A.B., Stanford, 1949, M.D., 1953; D.Sc. (hon.), U. Paris, 1983. From instr. to asso. prof. medicine U. Calif. at Los Angeles, 1957-66; mem. sr. staff Cardiovascular Research Inst., U. Calif., San Francisco, 1966-94; asso. prof. medicine Cardiovascular Research Inst., U. Calif. (Sch. Medicine), 1966-69, prof., 1969-94; chief chest service San Francisco Gen. Hosp., 1966-89; Vis. prof. Brompton Inst. for Diseases of the Chest, London, 1972-73; Macy faculty scholar Inst. Nat. de la Santé et de la Recherche Medicale, Paris, 1979-80; mem. adv. council and pulmonary disease adv. com. Nat. Heart, Lung and Blood Inst.; mem. clin. studies panel NRC; bd. govs. Am. Bd. Internal Medicine, Am. Bd. Emergency Medicine. Author: The Normal Lung, 1976, 2d edit., 1986; co-author: Diseases of the Chest, 5th edit., 1980; co-editor: Textbook of Respiratory Medicine, 1988, 2d edit., 1994; editor: Am. Rev. Respiratory Disease, 1973-79; contbr. articles to profl. jours. Chmn. Internat. Union Against Tb and Lung Disease. Served with USNR, 1945-46. Sr. Internat. fellow Fogarty Inst.; recipient Pres.'s award European Respiratory Soc., 1996. Fellow Royal Coll. Physicians; mem. Assn. Am. Physicians, Am. Soc. Clin. Investigation, Am. Physiol. Soc., Western Soc. Clin. Research, Western Assn. Physicians, Am. Thoracic Soc. (pres. 1981-82, Trudeau medal 1994), Académie Nationale de Médecine Francaise. Home: 24 Edith St San Francisco CA 94133-2913 Office: U Calif PO Box 0841 San Francisco CA 94143

MURRAY, LYNNETTE R., elementary education educator; b. Spokane, Oct. 23, 1966; d. Robert J. and G. Marian (Benson) M. BA in Edn., Ea. Wash. U., 1989; MA in Edn., U. Wash., 1995. Pre-sch. tchr. Small World Learning Ctr., Spokane, 1983-87; reconciliation clk., trainer Toys R Us, Spokane, 1987-89; tchr., grades 6 and 7 Wilsona Sch. Dist., Challenger Middle Sch., Lancaster, Calif., 1989-92, coord. Open House, 1990; advisor Challenger Middle Sch. Cheerleaders, Lancaster, 1990-91; tchr. grade 7 Franklin Pierce Sch. Dist., Ford Mid. Sch.; mem. PTSA, coord. cultural fairs 1993, 94, 95; mentor tchr., 1993-94; coord. earthquake preparedness plan; mem. sch. and cmty. involvement group, 1994—; spkr. St. Martin's Coll., 1993—. Mem. Calif. Tchrs. Assn., Calif. Coun. for the Social Studies, U. Wash. Tacoma Alumni Assn., Phi Kappa Phi, Delta Kappa Phi. Methodist. Office: Ford Middle School 1602 104th St E Tacoma WA 98445-3812

MURRAY, PATTY, senator; b. Seattle, Wash., Oct. 11, 1950; d. David L. and Beverly A. (McLaughlin) Johns; m. Robert R. Murray, June 2, 1972; children: Randy P., Sara A. BA, Wash. State U., 1972. Sec. various cos., Seattle, 1972-76; citizen lobbyist various ednl. groups, Seattle, 1983-88; legis. lobbyist Orgn. for Parent Edn., Seattle, 1977-84; instr. Shoreline Community Coll., Seattle, 1984—; mem. Wash. State Senate, Seattle, 1989-92, U.S. Senate, Washington, 1993—; ranking minority mem. Appropriations Legis Br.; vice chmn. Senate Dem. Policy Com.; mem. Com. on Banking, Housing and Urban Affairs, Budget Com., Senate Dem. Tech. and Comms. Com., Com. on Vets. Affairs, Select Com. on Ethics. Mem. bd. Shoreline Sch., Seattle, 1985-89; mem. steering com. Demonstration for Edn., Seattle, 1987; founder, chmn. Orgn. for Parent Edn., Wash., 1981-85; lst Congl. rep. Wash. Women United, 1983-85. Recipient Recognition of Svc. to Children award Shoreline PTA Coun., 1986, Golden Acorn Svc. award, 1989; Outstanding Svc. award Wash. Women United, 1986, Outstanding Svc. to Pub. Edn. award Citizens Ednl. Ctr. NW, Seattle, 1987. Democrat. Office: US Senate 111 Russell Senate Office Bldg Washington DC 20510-4704*

MURRAY, ROBERT HENRY, technical manager; b. San Antonio, Aug. 15, 1955; s. Robert H. and Fay C. (Temple) M.; m. Marion McGarrity, Aug. 24, 1990; children: Nicola J., Craig T. BSc in Math., U. Houston, 1982. With CSX (formerly Tex. Gas Exploration Corp.), Houston, 1982-86; pvt. cons. PT Badak NGL Co., Bontang, Indonesia, 1986-89, PT Cal Tex, Jakarta, Indonesia, 1989-90, Eczacibi Bilgi Illetim, Istanbul, Turkey, 1990, Brit. Steel, plc, Glasgow, Scotland, 1990, Panhandle Ea. Corp., Houston, 1990-91, Cell-Tech, Houston, 1991, ARCO Alaska, Inc., Anchorage, 1991-93, LGL Alaska Rsch. Assocs., Anchorage, 1993-94; sr. software engr. Computer Task Group, Inc., Anchorage, 1994-95, Alyeska Pipeline Svc. Co., BP Exploration (Alaska) Inc., Anchorage, 1995, Alyeska Pipeline Svc. Co., Anchorage, 1996—; ptnr. Wilkinson Murray & Assocs., Anchorage, 1993—; bd. dirs. CRX Internat. Ltd., Edinburgh, Scotland. Author computer program Inventory Simulation for Maintenance and Repair Operations and Disposal Economics, 1993, 94. Mem. Inst. Data Processing Mgmt. Republican. Episcopalian. Home: 19120 Sarichef Loop Eagle River AK 99577 Office: RH Murray & Assocs PO Box 242145 Anchorage AK 99524-2145

MURRAY, ROBERT MICHAEL, telecommunications executive; b. N.Y.C., Jan. 5, 1961; s. Thomas Patrick and Ida Michelle (Di Persia) M.; m. Heidi Kristine Kingston, June 25, 1988; 1 child, Erin Taylor. BS, U. So. Calif., 1983. CPA, Calif. Acct. Ernst & Young, L.A. and San Diego, 1983-87; account rep. Digital Equipment Corp., San Diego, 1987-90; regional mktg. officer Bank of Am., San Diego, 1990-92; v.p., gen. mgr. PageNet Inc., San Diego, 1992—. Office: PageNet Inc 11455 El Camino Real San Diego CA 92130

MURRAY, STEPHEN O., sociologist consultant; b. St. Paul, Minn., May 4, 1950; s. Omer K. M. and Una C. Peterson; m. Keelung Hong, July 15, 1981. BA, Michigan State U., 1972; MA, U. Ariz., 1975; PhD, U. Toronto, Ont., Can., 1979. Cons. Social Network Conss., San Francisco, 1978-80; postdoctoral fellow U. Calif., Berkeley, 1980-82; rsch. dir. El Instituto Obregón, San Francisco, 1982—. Author: Theory Groups and the Study of Language, 1994, Latin American Male Homosexualities, 1995, American Gay, 1996, Angkor Life, 1996; co-author: Taiwanese Culture, Taiwanese Society, 1994, Islamic Homosexualities, 1996; editl. bd. Journal of Homosexuality, 1987—, History of Sociology, 1985—, Encyclopedia of Homosexuality, 1986-89, Sexualities, 1996—. Bd. dirs. Life Ctr., San Francisco, 1992. Recipient theory devel. award Internat. Gay Acad. Union, 1982, Iong Otik awrd Taiwan Found., 1995. Mem. Acad. for Rsch. on Male Sexualities, Am. Sociol. Assn., Am. Anthropol. Assn., Am. Ethnol. Soc., Sociologists' Lesbian and Gay Caucus (editor 1977-79), Soc. Lesbian and Gay Anthropologists (editor 1989-92). Office: El Instituto Obregón 1360 De Haro San Francisco CA 94107-3239

MUSCIO, RICHARD J., accountant; b. Berkeley, Calif., June 3, 1958; s. Robert D. and Dolores Jean (Kowalchick) M.; m. Mari C. O'Donnell, Oct. 18, 1987; children: Evan Dante, Mia Catherine, Demi Michelle. BA, U. San Diego, 1980. CPA, Calif. Staff acct. Krauss & Co., San Diego, 1979-82; acct. Richard Muscio CPA, San Diego, 1983-88, Carter, Polito & Muscio, Inc., Vista, Calif., 1989—. Contbr. articles to profl. jours. Bd. dirs. Susan Scott Found., San Diego, 1994—, CPA/Law Forum, San Diego, 1992—; mem. planned giving bd. Salk Inst., La Jolla, Calif., 1993—. Mem. Salk Inst. Pres.' Club, Lomsa Santa Fe Country Club. Home: PO Box 8090 Rancho Santa Fe CA 92067 Office: Carter Polito & Muscio Inc 1800 Thibodo Rd Ste 200 Vista CA 92083

MUSGRAVE, LEE, artist, museum administrator; b. Perth, Australia, June 13, 1944; came to U.S., 1946; s. Cecil Beryl and Dulse Joan (Aldersea) M.; m. Heidi Orbitz, Dec. 19, 1964; children: Timothy Devon, Christopher Kim. AA, L.A. Valley Coll., 1965; BA, Calif. State U., Northridge, 1967; MA, Calif. State U., L.A., 1970. Cert. secondary art tchr., Calif. Prof. art. L.A. Mission Coll., Sylmar, Calif., 1974-95; dir. L.A. Mission Coll. Campus Gallery, San Fernando, Calif., 1974-82, Mcpl. Gallery, Agoura Hills, Calif., 1983-86, Merging One Gallery, Santa Monica, Calif., 1986-88; curator County of Los Angeles Century Gallery, Sylmar, 1983-86, dir., 1991-95; curator of contemporary art Maryhill Mus. Art, Goldendale, Wash., 1996—. One man shows include Heritage Gallery, L.A., 1985, Orlando Gallery, L.A., 1986, Chemetka Gallery, Salem, Oreg., 1986, Ersgard Gallery, Santa Monica, Calif., 1992. Founding pres. Santa Monica/Venice Art Dealers Assn., 1987-88, Cultural Affairs Commn., Agoura Hills, 1983-86; dir. N.E. Valley Arts Coun., Sylmar, 1991-95. Fellow Wash. Arts Commn., 1996; recipient cert. of appreciation Calif. Art Edn. Assn., 1992, Calif. Legis. Assembly, 1987, cert. of recognition Calif. State Senate, 1987. Mem. Nat. Art Educators Assn., Wash. Art Educators Assn., Columbia Gorge Regional Arts Assn. Home: PO Box 256 Lyle WA 98635 Office: Maryhill Mus Art 35 Maryhill Mus Dr Goldendale WA 98620

MUSICH, ROBERT LORIN, motivational speaker; b. Glendale, Calif., Feb. 15, 1969; s. Richard and Zola (Nickel) M. Student, Mt. San Antonio Coll., Walnut, Calif., 1987-88, Rio Hondo Coll., Whittier, Calif., 1989-91. Sr. asst. mgr. Am. Gen. Fin., Upland, Calif., 1988-89; mgmt./corp. trainer Mortgage Link, Pasadena, 1989-94; mgr. AT&T, L.A., 1994-96; owner Musich & Assocs., West Covina, Calif., 1989—. Singer (tenor) So. Calif. Mormon Choir, 1994—; cand. Calif. State Assembly, 59th Dist., 1995; vol. Am. Cancer Soc., 1994-96; coach Youth League Football, 1987-92; elder's quorum pres. LDS Ch., sec., 1992-93, 2d and 1st counselor, 1995-96, mem. stake single adult com., 1993-95, mem. regional single adult com. bi-regional chmn., 1993-95. Republican. Home: 3447 E Hillhaven Dr West Covina CA 91791-1718 Office: Musich and Associates 3447 E Hillhaven Dr West Covina CA 91791-1718

MUSIHIN, KONSTANTIN K., electrical engineer; b. Harbin, China, June 17, 1927; s. Konstantin N. and Alexandra A. (Lapitsky) M.; m. Natalia Krilova, Oct. 18, 1964; 1 child, Nicholas; came to U.S., 1967, naturalized, 1973; student YMCA Inst., 1942, North Manchurian U., 1945, Harbin Poly. Inst., 1948. Registered profl. engr., Calif., N.Y., Pa., Ill., Wash. Asst. prof. Harbin Poly. Inst., 1950-53; elec. engr. Moinho Santista, Sao Paulo, Brazil, 1955-60; constrn. project mgr. Caterpillar-Brazil, Santo Amaro, 1960-61; mech. engr. Matarazzo Industries, Sao Paulo, 1961-62; chief of works Vidrobras, St. Gobain, Brazil, 1962-64; project engr. Brown Boveri, Sao Paulo, 1965-67; sr. engr. Kaiser Engrs., Oakland, Calif., 1967-73; sr. engr. Bechtel Power Corp., San Francisco, 1973-75; supr. power and control San Francisco Bay Area Rapid Transit, Oakland, 1976-78; chief elec. engr. L.K. Comstock Engrng. Co., San Francisco, 1978-79; prin. engr. Morrison Knudsen Co., San Francisco, 1979-84; prin. engr. Brown and Caldwell, Cons. Engrs., Pleasant Hill, Calif., 1984-85; cons. engr. Pacific Gas and Electric Co., San Francisco, 1986-89; sr. engr. Bechtel Corp., San Francisco, 1989—. Mem. IEEE (sr.), Nat., Calif. socs. profl. engrs., Instituto de Engenharia de Sao Paulo. Mem. Christian Orthodox Ch. Clubs: Am.-Brazilian. Home: 320 Park View Ter Apt 207 Oakland CA 94610-4653

MUSMANN, KLAUS, librarian; b. Magdeburg, Germany, June 27, 1935; came to U.S., 1957; s. Ernst Hans and Eva (Grunow) M.; m. Gladys H. Arakawa, June 15, 1963 (div. 1973); children: Carlton, Michelle; m. Lois Geneva Steele, Dec. 27, 1986. BA, Wayne State U., 1962; MALS, U. Mich., 1963; MA, Mich. State U., 1967; PhD, U. So. Calif., 1981. Libr. Detroit Pub. Libr., 1962-65; asst. serials libr. Mich. State U., East Lansing, 1965-67; head of acquisitions Los Angeles County Law Libr., L.A., 1968-84; coll. devel. libr. U. Redlands, Calif., 1984—, acting dir., 1994-96, dir., 1996—. Author: Helen and Vernon Farquhar Collection: A Bibliography, 1987, Diffusion of Innovations, 1989, Technological Innovations in Libraries, 1850-1950, 1993; contbr. articles to profl. jours. Grantee Coun. on Libr. Resources, 1990. Mem.ALA, Assn. Coll. and Rsch. Librs., Soc. for History of Tech. Home: 220 W Highland Ave Redlands CA 92373-6768 Office: Univ of Redlands Redlands CA 92374

MUSOLF, LLOYD DARYL, political science educator, institute administrator; b. Yale, S.D., Oct. 14, 1919; s. William Ferdinand and Emma Marie (Pautz) M.; m. Berdyne Peet, June 30, 1944; children—Stephanie, Michael, Laura. B.A., Huron Coll., 1941; M.A., U. S.D., 1946; Ph.D., Johns Hopkins U., 1950. Mem. faculty Vassar Coll., Poughkeepsie, N.Y., 1949-59, assoc. prof. polit. sci., 1955-59; chief of party adv. group Mich. State U., Republic South Vietnam, 1959-61; prof. polit. sci. Mich. State U., East Lansing, 1961-63; prof. polit. sci. U. Calif.-Davis, 1963-87, dir. Inst. Govtl. Affairs, 1963-84, prof. emeritus, 1988—; vis. prof. Johns Hopkins U., Balt., 1953, U. Del., 1954, U. Mich., 1955-56; U.S. Nat. rapporteur for Internat. Congress Adminstrv. Scis., Berlin, 1983; cons. and lectr. in field. Author: Federal Examiners and the Conflict of Law and Administration, 1953, Public Ownership and Accountability: The Canadian Experience, 1959, Promoting the General Welfare, Government and the Economy, 1965, (with others) American National Government-Policies and Politics, 1971, Mixed Enterprise-A Developmental Perspective, 1972, (with Springer) Malaysia's Parliamentary System-Representative Politics and Policymaking in a Divided Society, 1979, Uncle Sam's Private Profitseeking Corporations-Comsat, Fannie Mae, Amtrak and Conrail, 1983; editor: (with Krislov) The Politics of Regulation, 1964, Communications Satellites in Political Orbit, 1968, (with Kornberg) Legislatures in Developmental Perspective, 1970, (with Joel Smith) Legislatures in Development-Dynamics of Change in New and Old States, 1979; contbr. monographs, chpts. to books, articles to profl. jours. Served to lt. USNR, 1942-45. Johnston scholar Johns Hopkins U., 1946-48; Faculty fellow Vassar Coll., 1954-55; sr. assoc. East-West Ctr., Honolulu, 1968-69; vis. scholar Brookings Instn., Washington, 1980. Mem. Am. Soc. Pub. Adminstrn. (exec. council 1967-70), Nat. Assn. Schs. Pub. Affairs and Adminstrn. (exec. council 1972-75), Western Govtl. Research Assn. (exec. bd. 1966-68), Am. Polit. Sci. Assn., Nat. Assn. State Univs. and Land Grant Colls. (rsch. com. fdiv. urban affairs 1980-81). Home: 844 Lake Blvd Davis CA 95616-2611 Office: U Calif Dept Polit Sci Davis CA 95616

MUSSEHL, ROBERT CLARENCE, lawyer; b. Washington, May 1, 1936; s. Chester Carl and Clara Cecelia (Greenwalt) Mussehl; children: Debra Lee, David Lee, Omar Chung; spouse: Misook Chung, Mar. 22, 1987. BA, Am. U., 1964, JD, 1966. Bar: Wash. 1967, U.S. Dist. Ct. (we. dist.) Wash. 1967, U.S. Ct. Appeals (9th cir.) 1968, U.S Supreme Ct. 1971. Sr. ptnr. Thom, Mussehl, Navoni, Hoff, Pierson & Ryder, Seattle, 1967-78, Neubauer & Mussehl, Seattle, 1978-80, Mussehl & Rosenberg, Seattle, 1980—; speaker law convs. and other profl. orgns.; moot ct. judge Nat. Appelate Advocacy Competition, San Francisco, 1987; panel mem. ABA Symposium on Compulsory Jurisdiction of World Ct., San Francisco, 1987; chmn. bd., chief exec. officer The Seattle Smashers profl. volleyball club, 1976-80. Contbr. numerous articles to legal publs. Mem. Wash. Vol. Lawyers for Arts, 1976-80; statewide chair Lawyers for Durning for Gov., 1976; mem. task force on the single adult and ch. Ch. Coun. Greater Seattle, 1976-78; bd. dirs. Wash. State Pub. Interest Law Ctr., 1976-81; founder, chair Wash. State Lawyers Campaign for Hunger Relief, 1991—. Fellow Am. Bar Found., Am. Acad. Matrimonial Lawyers; mem. ABA (ho. of dels. 1979-91, spl. adv. com. on internat. activities 1989-91, chair marriage and family counseling and conciliation com. family law sect. 1981-83, mem. world order under law standing com. 1983-89, chair, 1986-89, chair ad hoc com. on the assembly 1986-89, mem. assembly resolutions com. 1979-91, mem. blue ribbon com. for world ct. 1987-88, mem. standing com. on dispute resolution, 1992-93; exec. coun. sect. dispute resolution 1993-95, asst. budget officer, 1995—, others, Achievement award), Wash. State Bar Assn. (exec. com. family law sect. 1973-75, chmn. internat. law com. 1974-76, sec.-treas., exec. com. world peace through law sect. 1980—, chair 1981-82, mem. edit. bd. Family Law Deskbook 1987-89), Wash. State Trial Lawyers Assn., Seattle-King County Bar Assn. (family law sect. 1971-90, other coms. 1970—, chmn. young lawyers sect. 1971-72, sec. 1972-73, trustee), Am. Arbitration Assn. (panel arbitrators), World Assn. Lawyers of World Peace Through Law Ctr. (founding mem.), Heritage Club YMCA Greater Seattle (charter 1977—), UN Assn. U.S.A. (bd. dirs. Seattle chpt. 1989-91). Home: One Pacific Tower 2000 1st Ave Apt 902 Seattle WA 98121-2167 Office: 1111 3rd Ave Ste 2626 Seattle WA 98101-3207

MUSSER, GEORGE S., editor, astronomer. ScB, Brown U., 1988; MS, Cornell U., 1994. Editor: (mag.) Mercury, 1994—. Mem. Nat. Assn. Sci. Writers, Sigma Xi. Office: Astron Soc of Pacific 390 Ashton Ave San Francisco CA 94112

MUSTACCHI, PIERO, physician, educator; b. Cairo, May 29, 1920; came to U.S., 1947; naturalized, 1962; s. Gino and Gilda (Rieti) M.; m. Dora Lisa Ancona, Sept. 26, 1948; children: Roberto, Michael. BS in Humanities, U. Florence, Italy, 1938; postgrad. in anatomy, Eleve Interne, U. Lausanne, Switzerland, 1938-39; MB, ChB, Fouad I U., Cairo, Egypt, 1944, grad. in Arabic lang. and lit., 1946; D Medicine and Surgery, U. Pisa, 1986; D Honoris Causa, U. Aix-Marseilles, France, 1988; hon. degree, U. Alexandria, Egypt, 1985. Qualified med. examiner, Calif. Indsl. Accident Commn., 1994. House officer English Hosp., Ch. Missionary Soc., Cairo, Egypt, 1945-47; clin. affiliate U. Calif., San Francisco, 1947-48; intern Franklin Hosp., San Francisco, 1948-49; resident in pathology U. Calif., San Francisco, 1949-51; resident in medicine Meml. Ctr. Cancer and Allied Diseases, N.Y.C., 1951-53; rsch. epidemiologist Dept. HEW, Nat. Cancer Inst., Bethesda, Md., 1955-57; cons. allergy clinic U. Calif., San Francisco, 1957-70, clin. prof. medicine and preventive medicine, 1970-90, clin. prof. medicine and epidemiology, 1990-96, head occupl. epidemiology, 1975-90, head divsn. internat. health edn. dept. epidemiology and internat. health, 1985-90; médecin agréé, official physician Consulate Gen. of France, San Fransisco, 1995—; med. cons., vis. prof. numerous edn. and profl. instns., including U. Marseilles, 1981, 82, U. Pisa, Italy, 1983, U. Gabon, 1984, U. Siena, Italy, 1985, work clinic U. Calif., 1975-84, Ctr for Rehab. and Occupl. Health U. Calif., San Francisco, 1984-93; cons. numerous worldwide govtl. agys.; ofcl. physician French Consulate Gen., San Francisco, 1995. Contbr. chpts. to books, articles to profl. jours. Editorial bd. Medecine d'Afrique Noire, Ospedali d'Italia. Served with USN, USPHS, 1953-55. Decorated Order of Merit (Commander) (Italy), Ordre de la Legion d'Honneur (France), Medal of St. John of Jerusalem, Sovereign Order of Malta, Order of the Republic (Egypt); Scroll, Leonardo da Vinci Soc., San Francisco, 1965; award Internat. Inst. Oakland, 1964; Hon. Vice Consul. Italy, 1971-90. Fellow ACP, Am. Soc. Environ. and Occupational Health; mem. AAAS, Am. Assn. Cancer Rsch., Calif. Soc. Allergy and Immunology, Calif. Med. Assn., San Francisco Med. Soc., West Coast Allergy Soc. (founding), Mex. Congress on Hypertension (corr.), Internat. Assn. Med. Rsch. and Continuing Edn. (U.S. rep.), Acad. Italiana della Cucina. Democrat. Home: 3344 Laguna St San Francisco CA 94123-2208 Office: U Calif Parnassus Ave San Francisco CA 94143

MUTAFOVA-YAMBOLIEVA, VIOLETA NIKOLOVA, pharmacologist; b. Svishtov, Bulgaria, Apr. 18, 1954; d. Nikola Anastassov Mutafov and Bogdanka Ivanova (Boteva) Mutafova; m. Ilia Angelov Yamboliev, Mar. 24, 1984; children: Irena, Kalina. MD, Med. Acad., Sofia, Bulgaria, 1978, splty. Pharmacology, 1985, PhD, 1987. Physician Dept. Internal Medicine Dist. Hosp., Svishtov, Bulgaria, 1979-82; rsch. asst. prof. pharmacology Med. Acad., Sofia, 1982-87, Bulgarian Acad. Scis., Sofia, 1987-93; Fogarty Internat. fellow Sch. Medicine Univ. Nev. Reno, 1993-95. Co-author: Trends in Pharmacology and Pharmacotherapy; contbr. articles to profl. jours. Mem. AAAS, Bulgarian Pharmacol. Soc. (exec. com., Best Young Pharmacologist award 1988), Soc. Bulgarian Physicians, N.Y. Acad. Scis.

MUTCH, JAMES DONALD, pharmaceutical executive; b. Portland, Oreg., Mar. 6, 1943; s. Keith William and Dorothy (Wones) M.; m. Judith Ann Thompson, June 12, 1965; children: William James, Alicia Kathleen. BS in Pharmacy, Oreg. State U., 1966. Registered pharmacist, Calif., Oreg.; cert. regulatory affairs profl. Mgr. regulatory affairs Syntex Labs., Palo Alto, Calif., 1970-72, assoc. dir. regulatory affairs, 1972-76, dir. regulatory affairs, 1976-80; dir. regulatory affairs and clin. devel. Cooper Vision, Inc., Mt. View, Calif., 1980-86; dir. regulatory affairs and pre-clin. devel. Salutar, Inc., Sunnyvale, Calif., 1987-89, v.p. product devel., 1990-91; pres. Altos Biopharm. Inc., Los Altos, 1991-92; v.p. regulatory affairs and product devel. Pharmacyclics, Inc., Mountain View, Calif., 1992-96; Reiki master, tchr., cons., herbal pharmacist Palo Alto, Calif., 1996—. Contbr. articles to profl. jour. Pres. bd. Woodland Vista Swim & Racquet Club, Los Altos, Calif., 1982-83. With USPHS, 1966-68. Mem. AAAS, Am. Pharm. Assn., Regulatory Affairs Profl. Soc. Democrat.

MUTH, JOHN WILLIAM, economics educator; b. Atlanta, Dec. 20, 1948; s. William Franklin and Edith Maxine (Powell) M. BA summa cum laude, Colo. Coll., Colorado Springs, 1970; MA in Econs., U. Colo., 1974, PhD in Econs., 1978. Staff assoc. Acad. Ind. Scholars, Boulder, Colo., 1980; field coord. Instnl. Devel. and Econ. Affairs Svc., Boulder, 1979; asst. prof. U. Colo., Denver, 1982-83; dir. divsn. bus. Regis U., Denver, 1989-92, 97—, assoc. prof., 1983—; vis. lectr. Richmond Coll., London, 1985; cons. Colo. Office Regulatory Reform, Denver, 1985, U.S. Dept. Edn., Washington, 1988—; field evaluator Assn. Collegiate Bus. Schs. and Programs, 1992—; asst. dir. Regis U. Forensics Program, Denver, 1991—. Editor, co-author: (curriculum guides) Community Social Profiles, 1976-78; author curriculum module econs., internat. trade, 1984-86; co-author, editor profl. exam rev. Micromash CMA Rev., 1992-93; author computer interactive tutorial Friendly Finance, 1996. Pres. bd. dirs. Parkway Towers Condo Assn., Denver, 1991—. Mem. Phi Beta Kappa. Office: Regis U Divsn Bus 3333 Regis Blvd Denver CO 80221-1154

MUTO, SHEILA NOBUKO, journalist; b. San Jose, Calif., Nov. 4, 1967; d. Reginald Takayoshi and Celia Danielle (Izu) M. BA in Sociology and Mass Comm., U. Calif., Berkeley, 1990, MS in Journalism, 1995. Libr. asst. Edn.-Psychology Libr., U. Calif., Berkeley, 1987-90; staff writer, assoc. editor

Asian Week, San Francisco, 1990-91; head technical svcs. Edn.-Psychology Libr., U. Calif., Berkeley, 1991-95; editl. asst. Wired Mag., San Francisco, 1994; staff writer The Oakland (Calif.) Tribune, 1994-95, The Wall Street Journal, L.A., 1995; stringer The New York Times, L.A., 1995-96; reporter The Wall St Journal, San Francisco, 1996—; bd. mem. Nat. Japanese Am. Hist. Soc., San Francisco, 1992-94, Japanese Cultural & Cmty. Ctr., San Francisco, 1992-93; editl. bd. mem. Nikkei Heritage, San Francisco, 1993-94. Rschr. (TV documentaries) Loyalty and Betrayal, Fox Network, 1994, The Way It Was, PBS, 1994-95. Mem. Nat. Coalition for Redress/Reparations, San Francisco, 1990-94. Recipient Eugene Block journalism award, Human Rights Commn., San Francisco, 1992, McClatchy prize for in-depth reporting, McClatchy Newspapers, 1995. mem. Asian Am. Journalists Assn. (Scholarship of Achievement 1994-95), Soc. Profl. Journalists (treas. Berkeley chpt. 1993—, Mark of Excellence, TV Feature 1994), mem. Nat. Coalition for Redress Reparations, 1990-94. Office: The Wall St Journal 100 California St Ste 725 San Francisco CA 94111

MUTSCHLER, HERBERT FREDERICK, retired librarian; b. Eureka, S.D., Nov. 28, 1919; s. Frederick and Helena (Oster) M.; m. Lucille I. Gross, Aug. 18, 1945; 1 dau., Linda M. B.A., Jamestown Coll., 1947; M.A., Western Res. U., 1949, M.S., 1952. Tchr. history high sch. Lemmon, S.D., 1947-48; asst. librarian Royal Oak (Mich.) Libr., 1952-55; head librarian Hamtramck (Mich.) Libr., 1955-56; head public svcs. Wayne County Libr. System, Wayne, Mich., 1956-59; asst. county librarian Wayne County Libr. System, 1960-62; dir. King County Libr. System, Seattle, 1963-89; library bldg. cons. Wayne County Libr., 1956-62, Wash. State Libr., 1966—; cons. Salt Lake County Libr., Pierce County Libr., North Olympic Libr.; lectr. U. Wash. Sch. Librarianship, 1970-71; bldg. cons. Hoquiam (Wash.) Libr., Olympic (Wash.) Regional Libr., Camas (Wash.) Pub. Libr., N. Cen. (Wash.) Regional Libr., Spokane (Wash.) County Libr., Enumclaw (Wash.) Libr., Puyallup (Wash.) Pub. Libr., Kennewick (Wash.) Pub. Libr., Lopez Island (Wash.) Libr. Contbr. articles profl. jours. Mem. Foss Home and Village Bd. Trustees, 1989—; bd. dirs. King County Libr. Sys. Found. With AUS, 1941-45; to capt. 1950-52. Decorated Silver Star, Bronze Star with cluster, Purple Heart, Presdl. Unit Citation. Mem. ALA (councilor at large 1965-69, chpt. councilor 1971-75, pres. library adminstrv. div. 1974-75), Pacific N.W. Library Assn., Wash. Library Assn. (exec. bd. 1964-65, 69-71, pres. 1967-69). Republican. Lutheran. Club: City, Municipal League. Lodge: Kiwanis. Home: 5300 128th Ave SE Bellevue WA 98006-2952

MUTTART, SUSAN CHAMBLESS, corporate communications manager; b. Tallahassee, Aug. 3, 1957; d. Henry I. and Carrie L. (Anderson) Chambless; m. Daniel H. Muttart, Oct. 9, 1982. BS in Journalism, Fla. A&M U., 1979. Account exec. Manning, Selvage & Lee, Inc., N.Y.C., 1980-81, Lobsenz-Stevens, Inc., N.Y.C., 1982-83; dir. mktg. The Achieve Group divsn. Zenger-Miller, Inc., Mississauga, Ont., Can., 1985-86; mgr. pub. rels. Zenger-Miller, Inc., San Jose, Calif., 1986-90, mgr. publ. rels. & client comms., 1990-93, mgr. corp. comms., 1993-95; public rels. cons. Dallas, Tex., 1995—; dir. mktg. Universal Tng., Chgo., 1997—. Vol. mktg. cons. Bay Area Homeless Vets. Rehab. Program, Menlo Park, Calif., 1988-89. Mem. Pub. Rels. Soc. Am., No. Calif. Songwriters Assn., Gospel Music Assn. (assoc.), Dallas Songwriters Assn. (v.p. spl. events 1995-96), San Francisco Jr. C. of C. (v.p. adminstrn. 1987-88), N.Y. Jr. C. of C. (dir. publicity and spl. events 1981-82, Outstanding Publicity Support award 1981).Dallas Songwriters Assn.(v.p. spl. event, 1996). Presbyterian.

MUZYKA-MCGUIRE, AMY, marketing professional, nutrition consultant; b. Chgo., Sept. 24, 1953; d. Basil Bohdan and Amelia (Rand) Muzyka; m. Patrick J. McGuire, June 3, 1977; children: Jonathan, Elizabeth. BS, Iowa State U., 1975, postgrad., 1978—; registered dietitian, St. Louis U., 1980. Cert. dietitian. Home economist Nat. Livestock and Meat Bd., Chgo., 1975-77; dietary cons. various hosps. and nursing homes, Iowa, 1978-79; supr. foodsvc. Am. Egg Bd., Park Ridge, Ill., 1980-83; assoc. dir., mgr. foodsvc. Cole & Weber Advt., Seattle, 1984-85; prin., owner Food and Nutrition Comms., Federal Way, Wash., 1986—. Co-author: Turkey Foodservice Manual, 1987; editor: (newsletter) Home Economists in Business, 1975-77, Dietitians in Business and Industry, 1982-85; Food Net on Internet, 1995—; contbr. articles to profl. jours. Active Federal Way Women's Network, 1986-87. Named Outstanding Dietitian of Yr. North Suburban Dietetic Assn., 1983. Mem. Am. Dietetic Assn., Internat. Foodsvc. Editorial Coun., Consulting Nutritionists, Vegetarian Nutrition, Home Economists in Bus. Home: 5340 SW 315th St Federal Way WA 98023-2034

MYBECK, RICHARD RAYMOND, lawyer; b. Chgo., Dec. 5, 1928; s. Walter Raymond and Genevieve Lucille (Carlsten) M.; m. Betty Jane Engle, Aug. 23, 1952; children: Walter R. II, Wendy Sue, Lucinda Jeanne, Amanda Jane (dec.), Candace Christine, Sara Melinda. BChE, Purdue U., 1950, BS in Engring. Law, 1953; JD, Ind. U., 1953. Bar: Ind. 1953, Wis. 1954, Ill. 1962, Ariz. 1973; registered U.S. patent atty., patent agt., Can. Patent trainee, atty. Allis Chalmers Mfg. Co., West Allis, Wis., 1953-57, patent atty., 1957-62; atty. Koehring Corp., Milw., 1957; patent atty. Armour and Co., Chgo., 1962-71; sr. patent atty. Greyhound Corp., Chgo., Phoenix, 1971-77; sr. counsel Armour Pharmaceutical Co., Phoenix, Scottsdale, Ariz., 1977-81; pvt. practice Scottsdale, 1981—; pres., bd. dirs. Farmakeia, Inc., Scottsdale, Hoosier Investment Co., Scottsdale; dir. Ariz. State Rsch. Inst., 1988-97. Councilman Town of Paradise Valley, Ariz., 1988-92, commr., chmn. planning and zoning commn., 1981-88, mem. chmn. bd. adjustment, 1974-81; lay speaker United Meth. Ch., 1954—. Named to Hall of Fame Oak Park (Ill.) Youth Baseball, 1987; recipient Degentesh award Forest Park (Ill.) VFW, 1969. Mem. ABA, Ariz. Bar Assn. (chmn. various sects.), Ill. Bar Assn., Wis. Bar Assn., Intellectual Property Assn. Chgo., Ariz. Patent Law Assn., Purdue Alumni Assn. (dir. region 15 1993-95), Culver Legion, Ind. U. Alumni Assn., Elks, Masons, Tau Kappa Epsilon, Sigma Delta Kappa. Methodist. Home: 4901 E Tomahawk Trl Paradise Valley AZ 85253-2030 Office: Mybeck Law Office 8010 E Morgan Trl Ste 10 Scottsdale AZ 85258-1234 *Personal philosophy: If it ain't broke, don't fix it. It's amazing what you can accomplish when you don't worry about who gets credit for it.*

MYER, WARREN HITESH, mortgage broker, internet advertising executive; b. New Delhi, India, Sept. 8, 1961; s. Hana N.S. and Veena Myer; m. Suki Myer, Aug. 15, 1991. MS, U. Del., 1986; MBA, U. Chgo., 1990. Instr. U. Del., Newark, 1984-86; mem. tech. staff Lachman Assoc., Naperville, Ill., 1986-88; sys. mgr. Pyramid Tech., San Jose, Calif., 1988-91; pres. Myers Equity Express, San Jose, Calif., 1991—, Myers Fin. Group, Inc., Colorado Springs, 1994—, Myers Internet Svcs., San Jose, Calif., 1995—. Inventor in field. Home: 1421 Old Piedmont Rd San Jose CA 95132-2417 Office: Myers Equity Express 1590 Oakland Rd Ste B-207 San Jose CA 95131-2443

MYERS, CAROL MCCLARY, retired sales administrator, editor; b. Dawson, N.Mex.; d. Joseph Franklin and Alberta Lenore (McGarvey) McClary; m. Dwight Andrew Myers, Sept. 16, 1950 (dec. Sept. 1995); children: Robert Andrew, Debra Ann, James Allen. MusB, U. Redlands, 1950. Cert. tchr., Calif. Tchr. music Barstow (Calif.) Pub. Schs., 1950-52; sec./acct. U.S. Army, Columbus, Ga., 1952-54; part-time sec. Robert Lafollette, Atty., Albuquerque, 1954-57; sec./acct. Midland Specialty Co., Albuquerque, 1957-60; pvt. tchr. piano Oakland, N.J., 1960-70; organist, choir dir., ch. sec. Ramapo Valley Bapt., Oakland, N.J., 1965-70; order fulfillment/invoicing U. N.Mex. Press, Albuquerque, 1974-76, sales mgr., 1976-88; ret., 1988. Editor (mag.) Book Talk, 1971-96, (7 books) In Celebration of the Book: Literary New Mexico, 1982. Recipient Edgar Lee Hewett award Hist. Soc. N.Mex., 1985, Paso Por Aqui award Rio Grande Hist. Collections, 1990. Mem. N.Mex. Libr. Assn. (hon. life, treas. 1989-91, bd. dirs. 1992-94), Rocky Mountain Book Pubs. Assn. (Jack D. Rittenhouse award 1994), Mountains and Plains Booksellers Assn. Republican. Home: 8632 Horacio Pl NE Albuquerque NM 87111

MYERS, CINDY L., museum director. Exec. dir. Phoenix Mus. History, 1996—. Office: Phoenix Mus History 105 N 5th St PO Box 926 Phoenix AZ 85001

MYERS, DOUGLAS GEORGE, zoological society administrator; b. L.A., Aug. 30, 1949; s. George Walter and Daydeen (Schroeder) M.; m. Barbara Firestone Myers, Nov. 30, 1980; children: Amy, Andrew. BA, Christopher Newport Coll., 1981. Tour and show supr. Annheuser-Busch (Bird Sanctuary), Van Nuys, Calif., 1970-74, mgr. zool. ops., 1974-75, asst. mgr. ops., 1975-77, mgr. ops., 1977-78; gen. services mgr. Annheuser-Busch (Old Country), Williamsburg, Va., 1978-80, park ops. dir., 1980-81; gen. mgr. wild animal park Zool. Soc. San Diego, 1981-83, dep. dir. ops., 1983-85, exec. dir., 1985—; cons. in field. Bd. dirs. San Diego Conv. and Visitors Bur.; mem. adv. com. of pres.' assn. Am. Mgmt. Assn. Fellow Am. Assn. Zool. Parks and Aquariums (profl.), Internat. Union Dirs. Zool. Gardens; mem. Internat. Assn. Amusement Parks and Attractions, Calif. Assn. Zoos and Aquariums, Mus. Trustee Assn. Lodge: Rotary. Office: San Diego Zoo PO Box 551 San Diego CA 92112-0551

MYERS, ELIZABETH ROUSE, management consultant; b. Grand Island, Nebr., July 14, 1923; d. William Wayne Rouse and Lulu Zella Trout; m. Richard Roland Myers, June 25, 1943; children: Diane Marie Berndt, Richard Wayne. Student, Kearny State Tchrs. Coll., Nebr., 1942-43. Draftsman Borg-Warner Corp., Kalamazooo, 1944; acct. CFI Steel Corp., Pueblo, Colo., 1950-52; sec., treas. Standard Paint, Yakima, Wash., 1954-86; pres. Pied Piper Childrens Books, Yakima, Wash., 1985-96; federal oil leases, 1980—; docent Yakima Valley Mus. & Gilbert House, Wash. 1984—. Editor: H.S. Paper. Tchr., supt. First Presbyn. Ch., Yakima, Wash., 1958-70; mem. bd. Parent Tchrs.; bd. dirs., teen chmn. YWCA; pres. Gilbert House. Mem. Yakima Valley Mus. (awarded Doll 1985, Show 1986, vol. of yr. 1994). Republican. Presbyterian. Home: 106 N 25th Ave Yakima WA 98902-2807

MYERS, ELMER, psychiatric social worker; b. Blackwell, Ark., Nov. 12, 1926; s. Chester Elmer Myers and Irene (Davenport) Lewis; widowed; children: Elmer Jr., Keith, Kevin. BA, U. Kans., 1951, MA, 1962; student, U. Calif., Santa Barbara, 1977-78. Psychiat. social worker Hastings (Nebr.) State Hosp., 1960-62; psychiat. social worker State of Calif., Sacramento, 1962-75, supr. psychiat. social worker, 1975-80; supr. psychiat. social worker Alta Calif. Regional Ctr., Sacramento, 1980-85; exec. dir. Tri-County Family Services, Yuba City, Calif., 1966-69; cons. to 3 convalescent Hosps., Marysville, Calif., 1969-71; lectr. Yuba Coll., Marysville, 1971-76; assoc. prof. Calif. State U., Chico, 1972-73; cons. in field, Marysville, 1985—; group therapist Depot Homeless Shelter, 1996—. Juror Yuba County Grand Jury, Marysville, 1965, 87-88; sec. Y's Men's Club, Yuba City, 1964-65; chmn. Tri-County Home Health Agy., Yuba City, 1974-76; vice-chmn. Gateway Projects, Inc., Yuba City, 1974-75; bd. dirs. Christian Assistance Network, 1993, Habitat for Humanity, 1993, Yuba County Truancy Bd., Marysville, 1964-67, Golden Empire Health Sys. Agy., Sacramento, 1972-76, Youth Svcs. Bur., Yuba City, 1967, Bi-County Mental Retardation Planning Bd., Yuba City, 1972, Yuba County Juvenile Justice Commn., Marysville, 1982-90, Am. Cancer Soc., Marysville, 1985-92, Yuba County Rep. Ctrl. Com., 1983-90, Salvation Army, 1990, facilitator care project, 1992; asst. dir. Marysville Adult Activity Ctr., 1990; active Yuba-Sutter United Way, 1971-73, 91—, Tri-County Ethnic Forum, sec., 1991—; sec. steering com. Yuba County Sr. Ctr. Assn., 1992, 95—; chmn. Yuba County Cmty. Svcs. Commn., 1997; v.p. Yuba-Sutter Gleaners, 1995—, Yuba-Sutter Commn. on Aging, 1996. Recipient Cert. Spl. Recognition Calif. Rehab. Planning Project, 1969, Cert. Spl. Recognition State of Calif., 1967; Cert. Spl. Recognition Alta Calif. Regional Ctrs., 1985. Mem. Nat. Assn. Social Workers (cert.), Kern County Mental Health Assn. (chmn. 1978-79). Lodge: Rotary (bd. dirs. Marysville club 1975-76). Home and Office: 3920 State Highway 20 Marysville CA 95901-9003

MYERS, GREGORY EDWIN, aerospace engineer; b. Harrisburg, Pa., Jan. 1, 1960; s. Bernard Eugene and Joyce (Calhoun) M.; m. Susan Ann Hayslett, Dec. 30, 1983; children: Kimberly, Benjamin. BS in Aerospace Engring., U. Mich., 1981; MS in Aerospace Engring., Air Force Inst. Tech., 1982. Aerospace engr. Sperry Comml. Flight Systems group Honeywell, Inc., Phoenix, 1987-90; sr. project engr. satellite systems ops. Honeywell, Inc., Glendale, Ariz., 1990-92; sr. project engr. air transport systems Honeywell, Inc., Phoenix, 1992-93, prin. engr., 1993-97; prin. software engr. Orbital Scis. Corp., Chandler, Ariz., 1997—; presenter in field. Contbr. articles to profl. jours. Mem. Aviation Week Rsch. Adv. Panel, 1990-91. Recipient Certs. of Recognition and Appreciation Lompoc Valley Festival Assn., Inc., 1983, Arnold Air Soc. (comdr. 1979), Cert. of Appreciation Instrument Soc. Am., 1991. Mem. AIAA (sr.). Lutheran. Office: Orbital Scis Corp 3380 S Price Rd Chandler AZ 85027-2708 *Personal philosophy: My 3 principles to live by: ask questions, be honest and try.*

MYERS, MARK D., petroleum geologist, researcher; b. Monroe, Wis., Apr. 24, 1955; s. Rhea Bowman and Ardelle Ione (Van Matre) M.; m. Alice Reding Myers, April 30, 1983; children: Justine Alice, Nathan Mark. BS in Geology and Geophysics with honors, U. Wis., 1977, MS in Geology, 1981; PhD in Geology, U. Alaska, 1994. Petroleum geologist ARCO Oil & Gas, Lafayette, La., 1981-83, ARCO Alaska, Inc., Anchorage, 1983-87, divsn. of oil & gas, State of Alaska, Anchorage, 1988—. Contbr. articles to scientific jours. lt. USAF, 1979-80. Mem. Am. Assn. Petroleum Geologists (del. 1992—), Alaska Geological Soc. (v.p. 1993, mem. bd. dirs. 1993-95), Soc. Sedimentary Geology, Eagle River Presbyn. Ch. (pres. bd. trustees 1993—). Office: State of Alaska Divsn Oil & Gas 3601 C St Ste 1380 Anchorage AK 99503-5948

MYERS, RHONDA JAN, allergist; b. North Hollywood, Calif., Feb. 15, 1954; d. Seymour Leslie and Charlotte Sara (Fradin) M.; m. Klaus Peter Rosebrock, May 14, 1986; children: Laina Emily Myers, Daniel Thomas Myers. BSc, UCLA, 1975; PhD, U. Edinburgh, Scotland, 1980; MD, Albany Med. Coll., 1984. Postdoctoral fellow U. Conn., Farmington, 1979-80, U. Calif., Irvine, 1989-91; pvt. practice Irvine, 1991—. Fellow ACP, Am. Coll. Allergy, Asthma and Immunology; mem. Am. Acad. Allergy and Immunology, Sigma Xi. Office: 4902 Irvine Center Dr Ste 108 Irvine CA 92604-3334*

MYERS, SHARON DIANE, auditor; b. Lawrence, Kans., Sept. 18, 1955; d. Richard Paul and Helen Carol (Overbey) M. AA, Mt. San Antonio Coll., Walnut, Calif., 1981; BSBA, Calif. State U., Pomona, 1983, MBA, 1986. Cert. fraud examiner; cert. govt. fin. mgr. Revenue agt. IRS, Glendale, Calif., 1984-85; auditor Def. Contract Audit Agy., L.A., 1985-92; auditor Office Inspector Gen. FDIC, Newport Beach, Calif., 1992—; instr. Azusa (Calif.) Pacific U., 1987, 88, West Coast U., San Diego, 1992. Musician, Sunday sch. supt. Covina (Calif.) Bapt. Temple, 1975-95, Liberty Bapt. Ch., Irvine, Calif., 1995—. Mem. Assn. Govt. Accts. Republican. Home: 2702 44th Ave NW Olympia WA 98502

MYERS, WALTER E., protective services official. Chief of police Salem, Oreg. Office: 555 Liberty St SE Rm 130 Salem OR 97301

MYERS, WILLIAM ELLIOTT, investment company executive; b. Balt., Jan. 4, 1935; s. Jacob Ross Myers Jr. and Roberta Cockrill (Laudeman) M.; m. Caren Kay Westphal, Nov. 5, 1977; children: William E. Jr., John G. AB in Econs., Dartmouth Coll., 1957, MBA in Fin., 1959. Founder, pres. Myers Rsch. Corp., L.A., 1961-67, Air Calif., Newport Beach, 1966-69; founder, CEO, chmn. Cable Commuter Airlines, Upland, Calif., 1966-69; founder, pres. Myers Bldg. Industries, Ltd., Claremont, Calif., 1973-93; owner Myers Investment Co., Bermuda Dunes, Calif., 1995—; chmn. Braswell Engerprises, Pomona, Calif., 1975-88. Author: Real Estate Central, 1966. With U.S. Army, 1958-66. Mem. Jonathan Club, 20th Century Econ. Roundtable (chmn. 1963), Bermuda Dunes Country Club. Republican. Presbyterian. Home and Office: 79-154 Buff Bay Court Bermuda Dunes CA 92201

MYERS, WILLIAM HARDY, attorney general; b. Electric Mills, Miss., Oct. 25, 1939; m. Mary Ann Thalhofer, 1962; children: Hardy III, Christopher, Jonathan. AB with distinction, U. Miss., 1961; LLB, U. Oreg., 1964. Bar: U. S. Dist. Ct. Oreg., U.S. Ct. Appeals (9th cir.). Law clk to Hon. William G. East U.S. Dist. Ct., 1964-65; pvt. practice, 1965-96; atty. gen. State of Oreg., Salem, 1997—. Mem. editl. bd. Oreg. Law Rev. Pres. Portland City Planning Comm., 1973-74; com. mem. Commn. on the Judicial Br., 1983-85; chmn. Citizens Task Force on Mass Transit Policy, 1985-86, Oreg. Jail Project, 1984-86, Oreg. Criminal Justice Coun., 1987-91, Portland Future Focus, 1990-91, Metro Charter Com., 1991-92, Govs. Task Force on State Employee Benefits, 1994; co-chmn. Govs. Task Force on State Employee Compensation, 1995. Mem. Oreg. State Bar Assn., Multnomah County Bar Assn., Phi Eta Sigma, Phi Kappi Phi, Omicron Delta Kappa. Office: 1162 Court St NE Salem OR 97310

MYERSON, ALAN, director, film and television writer; b. Cleve., Aug. 8, 1936; s. Seymour A. and Vivien I. (Caplin) M.; m. Irene Ryan, June 2, 1962; 1 son, Lincoln; m. Leigh French, Apr. 15, 1977; children: Sierra Jasmine French-Myerson, Darcy Anna French-Myerson. Student, Pepperdine Coll., 1956-57, UCLA, 1957. mem. drama faculty U. Calif., Berkeley, 1966, San Francisco State U., 1967. Dir. Broadway and Off Broadway Prodns., 1958-64, including This Music Crept By Me Upon the Waters, The Committee; dir.: Second City, N.Y.C. and Chgo., 1961, 62; founder, producer, dir. The Committee, San Francisco, L.A. and N.Y., 1963-74; dir.: (films) Steelyard Blues, 1972, Private Lessons, 1981, Police Academy 5, 1988, It's Showtime, 1976; numerous TV shows, 1975—, including Laverne and Shirley, Rhoda, Bob Newhart Show, Welcome Back, Kotter, Fame, Crime Story, Dynasty, Miami Vice, Hunter, Sisters, Picket Fences, The Larry Sanders Show, Frazier, Friends; TV films The Love Boat, 1976, Hi, Honey, I'm Dead, 1991, Bad Attitudes, 1991, Holiday Affair, 1996. Active in civil rights, anti-war, anti-nuclear power movements, 1957—. Mem. Acad. Motion Picture Arts and Scis., Acad. TV Arts and Scis., Dirs. Guild Am., Writers Guild Am. West.

MYERSON, RAYMOND KING, investment counseling company executive; b. Chgo., Oct. 21, 1917; s. Harry J. and Minnie (King) M.; m. Natalie Salter, Feb. 20, 1943; children: Bette Kay, Toby Salter. BA, U. Chgo., 1940. Gen. sales mgr. Helene Curtis Industries Inc., Chgo., 1946-60; v.p., dir. mktg. Solo Cup Co., Chgo., 1961-62; v.p. internat. div. Max Factor & Co., Hollywood, Calif., 1963-69; pres., chief exec. officer Myerson Van Den Berg & Co., Santa Barbara, Calif., 1969—. Trustee, treas. Santa Barbara Mus. Natural History, 1975—; bd. dirs., treas. Rec. for Blind, Santa Barbara, 1975-90, U. Calif.-Santa Barbara affiliates, 1990—. treas., active various local polit. campaigns. Lt. USNR, 1942-45. Republican. Office: 3336 Campanil Dr Santa Barbara CA 93109-1017

MYHRE, KATHLEEN RANDI, nurse; b. Everett, Wash., Apr. 18, 1952; d. Richard Alvin and Beverley Jeanette (Nesbit) M. LPN, Bellingham (Wash.) Tech. Sch., 1970; ADN, Lane C.C., Eugene, Oreg., 1988. RN, Oreg. LPN night charge nurse Island's Convalescent Ctr., Friday Harbor, Wash., 1970-75; LPN float Sacred Heart Gen. Hosp., Eugene, Oreg., 1975-87; charge nurse urgent care unit Eugene Clinic, 1987—. Democrat. Home: 80687 Lost Creek Rd Dexter OR 97431-9742

MYHREN, TRYGVE EDWARD, communications company executive; b. Palmerton, Pa., Jan. 3, 1937; s. Arne Johannes and Anita (Blatz) M.; m. Carol Jane Enman, Aug. 8, 1964; children: Erik, Kirsten, Tor; m. 2d Victoria Hamilton, Nov. 14, 1981; 1 stepchild, Paige. BA in Philosophy and Polit. Sci., Dartmouth Coll., 1958, MBA, 1959. Sales mgr., unit mgr. Procter and Gamble, Cin., 1963-65; sr. cons. Glendinning Cos., Westport, Conn., 1965-69; pres. Auberge Vintners, 1970-73; exec. v.p. Mktg. Continental, Westport, 1969-73; v.p., gen. mgr. CRM, Inc., Del Mar, Calif., 1973-75; v.p. mktg. Am. TV and Communications Corp., Englewood, Colo., 1975-78, sr. v.p. mktg. and programming, 1978-79, exec. v.p., 1980, pres., 1980, chmn. bd., chief exec. officer, 1981-88; v.p., then exec. v.p. Time Inc., N.Y.C., 1981-88; mem. exec. com., treas., vice chmn., then chmn. bd. dirs. Nat. Cable TV Assn., Washington, 1982-91; mem. adv. com. on HDTV, FCC, 1987-89; bd. dirs. Advanced Mktg. Sys., Inc., La Jolla, Calif., Providence (R.I.) Jour. Co., pres., 1990-96; bd. dirs. Founders Funds, Inc., J. D. Edwards, Inc., Verio, Inc., Denver; pres. Myhren Media, 1989—, Greenwood Cable Mgmt., 1989-91; pres., CEO King Broadcast Co., 1991-96. Vice chmn. Pub. Edn. Coalition; mem. Colo. Forum, 1984-91, chmn. higher edn. com., 1986; bd. dirs., co-founder Colo. Bus. Com. for the Arts, 1985-91; mem. exec. coun. Found. for Commemoration U.S. Constn., 1987-90; mem. Nat. GED Task Force, 1987-90, Colo. Baseball Commn., 1989-91, Colo. Film Commn., 1989-91; trustee Nat. Jewish Hosp., 1989— (Humanitarian award 1996), R.I. Hosp., 1991-95, Lifespan Health Sys., 1994-97, U. Denver, 1996—; chmn. Local Organizing Commn. 1995 NCAA Hockey Championship. Lt. (j.g.) USNR, 1959-63. Recipient Disting. Leader award Nat. Cable TV Assn., 1988, ann. humanitarian award Nat. Jewish Hosp., 1996. Mem. Cable TV Adminstrn. and Mktg. Soc. (pres. 1978-79, Grand Tam award 1985, One of A Kind award 1994), Cable Adv. Bur. (co-founder 1978), Cable TV Pioneers, Crohns and Colitis Found. Am. (trustee Rocky Mountain chpt.). Episcopalian.

MYLNECHUK, LARRY HERBERT, financial executive; b. Littlefork, Minn., Mar. 9, 1948; s. William and Marjorie (Raco) M.; m. Sandy L. Henderson, Mar. 14, 1970; children: Kendra Elizabeth, Scott William. BA, Lewis & Clark Coll., Portland, 1970; JD, Lewis & Clark Coll., 1974. Legal specialist Oreg. Dept. Edn., Salem, 1976-82; sr. v.p., dir. Morley Capital Mgmt. Inc., Portland, 1982-89; founder, pres. Integra Assocs., Inc., Lake Oswego, Oreg., 1989—; exec. dir. The Stable Value Assn., Inc., Lake Oswego, 1990-96; cons. Hueler Analytics, Inc., Mpls., 1989—; conf. chmn. GIC Nat. Forum Conf., Washington, 1993-95; guest lectr. Portland State U., 1978. Contbr. articles to profl. jours. Founder Woodstock Neighborhood Assn., 1975; mem. Multnomah County (Oreg.) Charter Rev. Commn., 1978, Tualatin (Oreg.) City Coun., 1980-84, Portland Com. on Fgn. Rels., 1976—, bd. dirs., 1993—; mem. Gov.'s Commn. on Adminstrv. Hearings, State of Oreg., 1988-89; trustee St. Francis of Assisi Endowment Fund, 1993; vestry mem., lay eucharistic min., del. State Episcopal Conv., 1996; mem. Diocesan Coun., 1996—; chmn. corp. fundraising Lake Oswego Children's Choir. Fellow NEH, 1979, ednl. policy fellow George Washington U., 1980. Mem. SAR (pres. Lewis and Clark chpt.), Western Pension Conf., Assn. Soc. Execs., World Affairs Coun. Oreg., Citizen Amb. Program to Western Europe, Gen. Soc. The War of 1812, Soc. Colonial Wars, Sons and Daus. of Pilgrims, Oreg. Soc. Sons of the Revolution (co-founder, treas. 1996), Internat. Bus. Forum (mem. adv. bd. 1996), Sons of the Bench and Bar (charter), SAR (pres. Oreg. State Soc. 1997). Democrat. Episcopalian. Office: Integra Assocs Inc PO Box 1594 Lake Oswego OR 97035-0013

NACARIO, ROBERT JOHN, educational administrator; b. Hayward, Calif., Mar. 27, 1955; s. Jules and Madge (Asuncion) N.; m. Vickie Lynn Nacario, June 27, 1981; 1 child, Adam Robert. AA, Chabot Jr. Coll., Hayward, Calif., 1976; BA in Liberal Studies, Calif. State U., Hayward, 1979, MS in Edn., 1994. Cert. in adminstrv. svcs., Calif. Tchr. New Haven Unified Sch. Dist., Union City, Calif., 1979-90, adminstr., 1991—; analyst World Airways Inc., Oakland, Calif., 1981-88; adv. K-12 linkage com. Calif. State U., Hayward, 1996—. Exec. bd. Asian Am. Fedn. of Calif., Union City, 1996; bd. dirs. Friends of the Filipiniana Collection, Union City, 1995-96. Mem. ASCD, Assn. Filipino Am. Educators (Achievement in Edn. award 1996), Assn. of Calif. Sch. Adminstrs., Calif. League of Mid. Schs., Nat. Assn. Secondary Sch. Prins., Alumni Assn. of Calif. State U. Hayward, Golden Key. Christian Evang. Ch. Home: 1810 Egret Ln Hayward CA 94545-4910 Office: New Haven Unified School Dist 34200 Alvarado Niles Rd Union City CA 94587-4402

NACHMAN, RICHARD JOSEPH, management training executive; b. Washington, Sept. 18, 1944; s. Joseph Frank and Rosemary (Anderson) N.; m. Nancy Ruth Hodgson, Feb. 4, 1966 (div. Oct. 1975); children: Russell J., Kirk L.; m. Christina Maria Schulz, Jan. 2, 1979; 1 child, William C. Hoff. BA, U. Colo., 1968. Program dir. mgmt. edn. Grad. Sch. Bus. U. Mich., Ann Arbor, 1968-70; dir. Ctr. Mgmt. and Tech. Programs Sch. Bus. U. Colo., Boulder, 1970-74; pres. Mgmt. Rsch. Corp., Loveland, 1974—, RJN and Assocs., Loveland, 1977—. Contbr. articles to profl. pubs.; prodr. seminars, video tng. materials The One Minute Manager, The Art of Negotiating, Japanese Manufacturing Techniques, World Class Manufacturing. Advisor bd. dirs. World Missionary Press; bd. dirs. Hand of Help, Inc. Republican.

NACHMANOVITCH, STEPHEN, violinist, composer, author and educator. BA, Harvard U., 1971; PhD in History of Consciousness, U. Calif., Santa Cruz, 1975. violinist performing internationally, numerous appearances on radio, TV and at music and theater festivals. Author: Free Play: Improvisation in Life and Art, 1990; author compositions: The Four Zoas, 1978, Doors of Perception, 1979, Music From Before the Beginning, 1980, Minding the Earth, 1981, Blake's Vision, 1982, Earth's Answer, 1982, Training the Mind Ox, 1984, Path of Light, 1986, First Life, 1986, Music for Rachel's Brain, 1987, Music for Death Valley Jour., 1988, Mesopotamiah Spring, 1990, Providence, 1990, Ishartûin, 1990, Ain Soph, 1991, Wheel of Time, 1991, Merging at Merging One, 1992, The Magic Number 7, 1992, also recordings; composer computer music software: The World Music Menu,

Visual Music. Office: Free Play Prodns PO Box 265 Pacific Palisades CA 90272-0265

NACHT, SERGIO, biochemist; b. Buenos Aires, Apr. 13, 1934; came to U.S., 1965; s. Oscar and Carmen (Scheiner) N.; m. Beatriz Kahan, Dec. 21, 1958; children: Marcelo H., Gabriel A., Mariana S., Sandra M. BA in Chemistry, U. Buenos Aires, 1958, MS in Biochemistry, 1960, PhD in Biochemistry, 1964. Asst. prof. biochemistry U. Buenos Aires, 1960-64; asst. prof. medicine U. Utah, Salt Lake City, 1965-70; rsch. scientist Alza Corp., Palo Alto, Calif., 1970-73; sr. investigator Richardson-Vicks Inc., Mt. Vernon, N.Y., 1973-76; asst. dir., dir. rsch. Richardson-Vicks Inc., Mt. Vernon, 1976-83; dir. biomed. rsch. Richardson-Vicks Inc., Shelton, Conn., 1983-87; sr. v.p. rsch. and devel. Advanced Polymer Systems, Redwood City, Calif., 1987-93, sr. v.p. sci. and tech., 1993—; lectr. dermatology dept. SUNY Downstate Med. Ctr., Blkyn., 1977-87. Contbr. articles to profl. jours.; patentee in field. Mem. Soc. Investigative Dermatology, Soc. Cosmetic Chemists (award 1981), Dermatology Found., Am. Physiological Soc., Am. Acad. Dermatology. Democrat. Jewish. Home: 409 Wembley Ct Redwood City CA 94061-4308

NACHT, STEVE JERRY, geologist; b. Cleve., July 8, 1948; s. Max and Elfrida (Kamm) N.; m. Patricia Katherine Osicka, Aug. 3, 1976; 1 child, David Martin. BS in Geology, Kent State U., 1971, MS in Geology, 1973; MS in Urban Studies, Cleve. State U., 1979. Registered geologist, S.C., Va., Wyo.; environ. assessor, Calif.; cert. geologist, Ind.; lic. drinking water treatment class III, Ohio; cert. environ. mgr., Nev. Geologist Cleve. Utilities Dept., 1974-78; geologist, hydrologist Dalton, Dalton & Newport, Cleve., 1979-82; prin. scientist Lockheed-Emsco, Las Vegas, Nev., 1983-86; sr. geologist, project mgr. Earth Tech. Inc., Long Beach, Calif., 1986-87, The MARK Group, Las Vegas, 1987-90; dir. waste tech., sr. geologist Reynolds Elec. & Engring. Co., Las Vegas, 1990-92, chief environ. remediation sect., 1992-95; asst. project mgr. Bechtel Nev. Corp., Las Vegas, 1996—. Contbr. articles to profl. jours. Mem. AAAS, ASTM (groundwater com., past chmn. sect., well maintenance, rehab. and decommissioning sect.), Am. Inst. Profl. Geologists (cert.), Assn. Ground Water Scientists and Engrs., Assn. Engring. Geologists, Project Mgmt. Profl. (cert.), Project Mgmt. Inst. Home: 4184 Del Rosa Ct Las Vegas NV 89121-5011 Office: Bechtel Nev PO Box 98521 Las Vegas NV 89193-8521

NADEL, ANN HONIG, sculptor, educator; b. San Francisco, May 9, 1940; d. Louis and Miriam (Anixter) Honig; m. Joseph Nadel, June 10, 1962; children: Marcia, David. BA in Humanities, San Francisco State U., 1962, M in Edn., 1970; studied with Peter Voulkos, 1976. One woman shows include Judy Kay, Burlingame, 1978, Irene Drori Gallery, L.A., 1979, Bluxome Gallery, San Francisco, 1983, 85, Temple Emanu-El, San Francisco, 1988, Grad. Theol. Union, Berkeley, Calif., 1988, Earl McGrath Gallery, L.A., 1988, 90, 92, Jewish Mus., San Francisco, 1994; exhibited in group shows at Am. Crafts Coun., Kitchen Show, San Francisco, 1976, Gump's Gallery, San Francisco, 1981, No. Calif. Craft Exhbn., Mendocino (Calif.) Art Ctr., 1982, The San Francisco Arts Festival, 1983, San Francisco Internat. Airport Commn. Exhbn., 1985, Frederick Weisman Found. of Art, 1986, Cedars-Sinai Med. Ctr., L.A., 1986, Judah L. Magnes Mus., Berkeley, 1987, Jewish Cmty. Mus., San Francisco, 1987, Bluxome Gallery, San Francisco, 1995, Earl McGrath Gallery, N.Y.C., 1992, Grad. Theol. Union, Berkeley, 1995, Bolinas (Calif.) Art Mus., 1995, Jewish Mus., San Francisco, 1995; represented in permanent collections at Residence of U.S. Vice Pres., Washington, Frederick Weisman Found. of Art, Advanced Micro Devices Corp., Hewlett-Packard Co., Fireman's Fund Ins., Koll Co., Steefel, Levitt & Weiss, Grad. Theol. Union, Berkeley, Cedars-Sinai Med. Ctr., L.A., Deloitte and Touche, San Francisco, Coudert Bros., Grad. Theol. Sem., Dr. Carl Djerassi, Palo Alto, Calif.; contbr. to various catalogs, revs., online, including Ceramic Monthly, Am. Craft, Libr. of Congress Catalog, Jewish Bull. of San Francisco.

NADER, KATHLEEN OLYMPIA, psychotherapist, consultant in childhood trauma; d. S. and E. Nader. BA, Duke U., 1970; MSW, Tulane U., 1974, DSW, 1989. Lic. clin. social worker; bd. cert. clin. social worker. Psychotherapist Youth Svcs. Program, Fountain Valley, Calif., 1976-82; pvt. practice psychotherapy Two Suns, Laguna Hills, Calif., 1978—; program dir., cons. UCLA, 1985-94. Appeared in films and videotapes; contbr. numerous articles to profl. jours. Mem. bd. advisors Gift from Within. Mem. Nat. Registry of Social Workers, Internat. Soc. for Traumatic Stress Studies, Trauma Grief and Mourning Interest Group, Consortium for Children in War and Cmty. Violence, Intergenerational Effects of Trauma Interest Group. Office: Two Suns PO Box 2251 Laguna Hills CA 92654

NADLER, JUDY, mayor. Mayor City of Santa Clara, Calif. Office: City of Santa Clara 1500 Warburton Ave Santa Clara CA 95050

NADY, JOHN, electronics company executive; b. Agfalva, Hungary, Feb. 13, 1945; came to U.S., 1951; s. John and Hermine Nady. BSEE, Calif. Inst. Tech., 1965; MSEE, U. Calif., Berkeley, 1968. Elec. engr. Lawrence Radiation Lab., Livermore, 1966-71, Westinghouse Corp., Oakland, Calif., 1971-72; owner, chief exec. officer Nady Systems, Inc., Oakland, Calif., 1976—, Calif. Concerts, Inc., Oakland, Calif., 1985-93. Patentee in field. Recipient Emmy award Pioneering Devel. Wireless Microphones, 1996. Mem. Nat. Assn. Broadcasters, Audio Engring. Soc., Nat. Assn. Music Merchants. Office: Nady Systems Inc 6701 Bay St Emeryville CA 94608-1023

NAEF, WESTON JOHN, museum curator; b. Gallup, N.Mex., Jan. 8, 1942; s. Weston John and Kathleen Winifred (Skerry) N.; m. Mary Dawes Meghan, Apr. 4, 1964; children: Edward Weston, Ella Dawes. B.A., Claremont Men's Coll., 1964; M.A., Ohio State U., 1966; postgrad., Brown U., 1966-69. Vis. scholar Boston Pub. Library, 1968; dir. art gallery Wheaton Coll., Mass., 1969; staff dept. prints and photographs Met. Mus. Art, N.Y.C., 1970-84; asst. curator Met. Mus. Art, 1971-81, curator, 1981-84; curator photographs J. Paul Getty Mus., Malibu, Calif., 1984—; cons. in field. Author, exhbn. dir. Behind the Great Wall of China, 1971, The Painterly Photograph, 1973, The Truthful Lens: A Survey of Victorian Books Illustrated with Photographs, 1974, Era of Exploration, The Rise of Landscape Photography in the American West 1860-1885, 1975, Pioneer Photographers of Brazil 1939-1914, 1976, The Collection of Alfred Stieglitz, 1978, Georgia O'Keeffe by Alfred Stieglitz, 1978, Eliot Porter, The Intimate Landscapes, 1979, After Daguerre: Masterworks of 19th Century French Photography from the Bibliotheque Nationale, Paris, 1980, Counterparts: Form and Emotion in Photographs, 1982, Whisper of the Muse: Photographs by Julia Margaret Cameron, 1986, Edward Weston in Los Angeles: The Home Spirit and Beyond, 1986, Rare States and Unusual Subjects: Photographs by Paul Strand, Andre Kertesz and Man Ray, 1987, Capturing Shadows: Notable Acquisitions, 1985-1990, 1990; August Sander: Faces of the German People, 1991; Atget's Magical Analysis; Photographs, 1915-27, 91, Two Lives: O'Keeffe by Stieglitz, 1917-23, 1992, Being and Becoming: Photographs by Edmund Teske, 1993, André Kentesz: A Centennial Tribute, 1994, Palette of Light: Handcrafted Photographs, 1898-1914, 1994, Frederick Sommer: Poetry and Logic, 1994, Hidden Witness: African Americans in Early Photography, 1995, Carrie Mae Weems Reacts to Hidden Witness, 1995, Alfred Stieglitz: Seen and Unseen, 1995, The J. Paul Getty Museum Handbook of the Photographs Collection, 1995, In Focus: Andre Kertesz, 1994, In Focus: Alfred Stieglitz, 1995, The Eye of Sam Wagstaff, 1997, Time Not in Motion, 1997. Kress fellow, 1968. Club: Grolier (N.Y.C.). Office: J Paul Getty Mus Dept Photographs 1000 Getty Ctr Dr Los Angeles CA 90049

NAEGLE, SHIRL R., museum director. Dir. Nev. State Mus. and Hist. Soc., Las Vegas, 1991—. Office: Nev State Mus & Hist Soc State Mail Complex Las Vegas NV 89158

NAFPLIOTIS, CINDY HERMAN, editor, publisher; b. Olean, N.Y., Nov. 27, 1955; d. James Lloyd and Natalie Elaine (Tucker) Herman; m. Michael C. Nafpliotis, Apr. 31, 1979 (div.); children: Natalie, Constantinos, Peter, Stephanie, Cara. Student, U. Alaska. Libr. mgr., publ. asst. Publ. Ctr., Fairbanks, Alaska, 1993-94; mng. editor Sun Star, Fairbanks, 1994; pub. rels. intern Alaska Space Grant Program, Fairbanks, 1994-95; freelance desktop pub., editor, writer Fairbanks, 1995—; cons. Alaska Family Health and Birth Ctr., Fairbanks, 1989-95, Lighthouse Ministries Internat., Fairbanks, 1988-95. Editor (mag.) Alaska Space Ventures, 1994, (newsletter) The Pioneer, 1994; co-creator, author (travel newspaper) Chena Trailmarker, 1993. Cmty. resource specialist Alaska Family Health & Birth Ctr., Fairbanks, 1990-92; mental health lands trust specialist Advocacy of Alaska, Fairbanks, 1992. Mem. Soc. Profl. Journalists, Phi Alpha Theta. Pentecostal. Home and Office: PO Box 71715 Fairbanks AK 99707

NAFZIGER, JAMES ALBERT RICHMOND, lawyer, educator; b. Mpls., Sept. 24, 1940; s. Ralph Otto and Charlotte Monona (Hamilton) N.; BA, U. Wis., 1962, MA, 1969; JD, Harvard U., 1967. Bar: Wis. 1967. Law clk. to chief judge U.S. Dist. Ct. (ea. dist.) Wis., 1967-69; fellow Am. Soc. Internat. Law, Washington, 1969-70, adminstrv. dir., 1970-74; exec. sec. Assn. Student Internat. Law Socs., 1969-70; lectr. Sch. Law, Cath. U. Am., Washington, 1970-74; vis. assoc. prof. Sch. Law, U. Oreg., 1974-77; vis. prof. Nat. Autonomous U. Mex., 1978; assoc. prof. law Coll. Law, Willamette U., Salem, Oreg., 1977-80, prof., 1980-95, Thomas B. Stoel prof., 1995—, assoc. dean, 1985-86, dir. China program, 1984—; scholar-in-residence Rockefeller Found. Ctr., Bellagio, Italy, 1985; lectr., tutor Inst. Pub. Internat. Law and Internat. Relations, Thessaloniki, Greece, 1982; cons. Adminstrv. Conf. U.S., 1988-90; mem. bd. advisors Denver Jour. Internat. Law and Policy, Am. Jour. Comparative Law (bd. dirs. 1985—); bd. dirs. N.W. Regional China Coun., 1987-89. Served to 1st lt. U.S. Army, 1962-64. Recipient Burlington No. Faculty Achievement award, 1988. Mem. ABA (legal specialist ctrl. and east European law initiative 1992—), Am. Soc. Internat. Law (exec. coun. 1983-86, 92—, exec. com. 1994—, chmn. ann. meeting 1988, chmn. nominating com. 1989), Am. Soc. Comparative Law (bd. dirs. 1985—), Internat. Law Assn. (rapporteur cultural heritage law com. 1990—, Am. br. exec. com. 1986—, v.p. 1994—, co-dir. studies 1991-95, chmn. human rights com. 1983-88), UNA-USA (pres. Oreg. divsn. 1987-90, bd. govs., nat. coun. 1990—, exec. com. coun. chpt. and divsn. pres., v.p. 1990-94), Washington Fgn. Law Soc. (v.p. 1973-74), Internat. Studies Assn. (exec. bd. 1974-77, internat. law sect.), ACLU (pres. chpt. 1980-81, mem. state bd. 1982-88, sec. 1983-87), Assn. Am. Law Schs. (chmn. law and arts sect. 1981-83, 89-91, chmn. immigration law sect. 1990-91, chmn. internat. law sect. 1984-85, com. on sects. and ann. meeting 1995—, chmn. internat. law workshop, 1995), Am. Law Inst., Oreg. Internat. Coun. (pres. 1990-92), Internat. Sports Law Assn. (v.p. 1992—), Phi Beta Kappa, Phi Kappa Phi. Editor Procs. of Am. Soc. Internat. Law, 1977; Am. author: Conflict of Laws: A Northwest Perspective, 1985, International Sports Law, 1988; contbr. articles to profl. jours. Home: 3775 Saxon Dr S Salem OR 97302-6041 Office: Willamette U Coll Law Salem OR 97301

NAGANO, KENT GEORGE, conductor; b. Morro Bay, Calif.. B.A. Sociology & Music (high honors), U of Calif., Santa Cruz; MA in Composition, San Francisco State U.; studied with, Laszlo Varga. Former asst. Opera Co. Boston; former prin. guest condr. Ensemble InterContemporain & the Dutch Radio Orch.; mus. dir. & condr. Berkeley Symphony, 1978—; mus. dir. Opéra de Lyon, 1989—; assoc. prin. & guest condr. LSO, London, England, 1990; mus. dir., prin. condr. designate Hallé Orch., England, 1991-94; mus. dir., prin. condr. Hallé Orch., 1994—. has performed with numerous orchestras around the world; recordings include: Songs of the Auvergne, Peter and the Wolf, Turandot and Arlecchino (Grammy nom.), La Boheme, Dialogues of the Carelites, The Death of Klinghoffer (Grammy nom.), Love for Three Oranges (Grammy nom.), Susannah (Grammy award), La damnation de Faust, The Rite of Spring, Rodrgue et chimene. Recipient Seaver/NEA Conducting award, 1985; Record of Yr. award Gramophone; named "officer" of France's Order of Arts and Letters, 1993. Office: care Vincent & Farrell Asso 157 W 57th St Ste 502 New York NY 10019*

NAGASAMY, VIJAY, mechanical and aerospace engineer; b. Thane, Maharashtra, India, Apr. 3, 1961; s. S. and Parvathi (Swamy) N.; m. Kamala Tyagarajan, Mar. 31, 1993; 1 child, Priya. B.Tech. in Mech. Engring., Indian Inst. Tech., Bombay, 1982; MS in Mech. and Aerospace Engring., Rutgers U., 1985, PhD in Mech. and Aerospace Engring., 1988. Rsch. and teaching asst. in mech. and aerospace engring. Rutgers U., 1982-88; sr. engr., project leader LSI Logic Corp., Milpitas, Calif., 1988-91, staff engr. in software R&D divsn., 1991-96; sr. mgr. VSIS Inc., Sunnyvale, Calif., 1996—. Contbr. articles to profl. jours.; patentee methodology for deriving executable low-level structural descriptions and valid physical implementations of circuit and systems from semantic specifications and descriptions thereof; holder 4 patents. Merit scholar Bd. of Edn., Govt. of India, 1971. Mem. IEEE, Am. Soc. Mech. Engrs., Tau Beta Pi. Home: 34361 Zircon Ter Fremont CA 94555-3817 Office: VSIS Inc 1060 E Arques Ave Sunnyvale CA 94086

NAGEL, JEROME KAUB, architect; b. Denver, Dec. 26, 1923; s. Fritz Andrew and Josephine (Gaylord) N.; m. Cynthia Fels, Sept. 1, 1951; children—Peter Barry, James Gaylord. B.Arch., Yale U., 1949. Registered architect, Colo. Prin. J.K. Nagel Architect, Denver, 1953-61, Rogers & Nagel, Denver, 1961-66, Rogers, Nagel, Langhart, Architects, 1966-77, Interplan Inc., 1969-77; pres. Nagel Investment Co.; dir. Bank Western, Denver, Field Devel. Corp., Denver. Mem. Colo. Hwy. Commn., chmn., 1982-83; bd. dirs. Planned Parenthood Fed. Am. Inc., N.Y.C., 1974-78, Rocky Mountain Planned Parenthood, Denver, 1972-76, Colo. chpt. ARC, 1957-60, 80-81, Denver Santa Claus Shop, 1987-91; mem. panel arbitrators Am. Arbitration Assn., 1962—; chmn. Colo. Bicycling Adv., Denver Bicycling Adv. Bd. Bd. Served to 1st lt. AC U.S. Army, 1943-45. Decorated D.F.C., Air medal with 11 oak leaf clusters. Mem. AIA (nat. life; sec. chpt. 1960-61, pres. 1962-63), Denver Country Club (bd. dirs. 1983-86), Univ. Club (bd. dirs. 1962-66) Mile High Club, Denver Rotary Club Found. (pres. 1992-93), Denver Athletic Club. Episcopalian. Home: 67 Eudora St Denver CO 80220-6311

NAGEL, STANLEY BLAIR, retired construction and investment executive; b. Bklyn., Mar. 19, 1928; s. Robert Arthur and Renee Ann Nagel; children: Scott Alan, Robert Arthur. BBA, U. Oreg., 1950. With constrn. dept. Nagel Investment, Portland, Oreg., 1955-58, pres., 1956—; pres. R.A. Constrn., Portland, 1956—; buyer May Co., Portland, 1958-72; gen. mgr. Portland Outdoor Store, 1972-75; owner Nagels Nursery & Greenhouses, Portland, 1975—; pres. E & S Distbrs., Portland, 1982—; ret., 1996. Coinventor pizza machine (patent pending). 2d lt. U.S. Army, 1952-55. Republican. Jewish. Home and Office: 5353 SW Martha St Portland OR 97221-1840

NAGHI, LADISLAU-GEORGE, priest; b. Timisoara, Romania, June 16, 1950; came to U.S., 1992; children: Christian, Diana. Diploma in theology, U. Theol. Inst., Sibiu, Romania, 1973. Ordained priest Romanian Orthodox Ch., 1975. Parish priest Holy Resurrection Romanian Orthodox Parish, Hayward, Calif., 1996—; sec. Casa Romana & Capela, Hayward, 1992—. Asst. editor Romanian Home Bull, 1992—; contbr. articles to profl. publs.

NAGLE, ROBERT DAVID, therapist, educator, author; b. Gowanda, N.Y., Sept. 13, 1935; s. Carl and Sarah (Zabatinsky) N.; m. Eugenia S. Karabacz, Nov. 20, 1956; children: Carl, Sonya, Paula. BA, N.Mex. Highlands U., 1960, MA, 1961; PhD, Union U., 1977. Cert. addictions specialist Am. Acad. Health Scis. Providers Addictive Disorders; cert. clin. hypnotherapist. Psyciat. therapist N.Mex. State Hosp., Las Vegas, 1961-63; grad. fellow U. Nebr., Lincoln, 1963-64, U. Miami, Fla., 1964-65; prof. Inst. of Discourse, Kansas City, Mo., 1967—, pres., 1968—; prof. emeritus Northwest Mo. State U., Maryville, 1965-85; dir. ednl. programming Acad. for Counseling and Change, Kansas City, 1981—, dir. profl. hypnotherapy-psychotherapy svcs., 1992—; prof., therapist Ottowa U., Overland Park, Kans., 1987—; adj. prof. psychology, clin. hypnotherapy Union Inst., Cin., 1990-94; bd. dirs. Rsch. Data Analysis. Author: When Moses Last in the Dooryard Laughed, 1978, Men Freeing Men, 1985; contbr. poetry to revs., collections and mags. Bd. dirs. Ariz. Addiction Treatment Program, 1993. Mem. AACD, ACLU, Soc. Philosophy and Psychology, Am. Philos. Assn., Henry Miller Lit. Soc., Mo. Assn. Counseling and Devel., Am. Assn. Profl. Hypnotherapists, Soc. Advanced Philos. Rsch., Inst. Advanced Philos. Rsch. (coun. advisors), The Cousteau Soc., Ariz. State Poetry Soc. (pres. 1995-97). Home: 2327 E Geneva Dr Tempe AZ 85282 Office: 525 W Southern Ave Ste 11 Mesa AZ 85210-5009 also: Ste 1 McCormick Ranch 8075 E Morgan Trail Scottsdale AZ 85258

NAGLER, MICHAEL NICHOLAS, classics and comparative literature educator; b. N.Y.C., Jan. 20, 1937; s. Harold and Dorothy Judith (Nocks) N.; m. Roberta Ann Robbins (div. May 1983); children: Jessica, Joshua. BA, NYU, 1960; MA, U. Calif., Berkeley, 1962, PhD, 1966. Instr. San Francisco State U., 1963-65; prof. classics, peace studies and comparative lit. U. Calif., Berkeley, 1966-91, prof. emeritus, 1991—. Author: Spontaneity and Tradition, 1974, America Without Violence, 1982; co-author: The Upanishads, 1987; contbr. articles to profl. publs. Pres. bd. dirs. METTA Ctrs. for Nonviolence Edn. Fellow Am. Coun. Learned Socs., NIH; MacArthur Found. grantee, 1988. Mem. Am. Philolog. Soc. (editor Oral Tradition). Office: U Calif Classics Dept Berkeley CA 94720

NAGLESTAD, FREDERIC ALLEN, legislative advocate; b. Sioux City, Iowa, Jan. 13, 1929; s. Ole T. and Evelyn Elizabeth (Erschen) N.; student (scholar) U. Chgo., 1947-49; m. Beverly Minnette Shellberg, Feb. 14, 1958; children—Patricia Minnette, Catherine Janette. Pub. affairs, pub. relations, newscaster, announcer KSCJ-radio, Sioux City, Iowa, 1949-51; producer, dir., newscaster, announcer WOW-TV, Omaha, 1953-57; program mgr. WCPO-TV, Cin., 1957-58; mgr. KNTV-TV, San Jose, Calif., 1958-61; owner Results Employment Agy., San Jose, 1961-75; legis. advocate Naglestad Assocs., Calif Assn. Employers, Calif. Automotive Wholesalers Assn., Air Quality Products, Calif. Assn. Wholesalers-Distbrs., State Alliance Bd. Equalization Reform, Quakemaster, many others, 1969—. Pres. Calif. Employment Assn., 1970-72. Asst. concertmaster Sioux City Symphony Orch., 1945-47. Sgt. AUS, 1951-53. Recognized for outstanding contbn. to better employment law, Resolution State Calif. Legislature, 1971. Office: 3991 Fair Oaks Blvd Sacramento CA 95864-7254 *Personal philosophy: Tell the truth, persevere and follow through.*

NAGTALON-MILLER, HELEN ROSETE, humanities educator; b. Honolulu, June 27, 1928; d. Dionicio Reyes and Fausta Dumbrigue (Rosete) N.; m. Robert Lee Ruley Miller, June 15, 1952. BEd, U. Hawaii, 1951; Diplôme, The Sorbonne, Paris, 1962; MA, U. Hawaii, 1967; PhD, Ohio State U., 1972. Cert. secondary education educator. Tchr. humanities Hawaii State Dept. Edn., Honolulu, 1951-63; supr. student tchrs. French lab. sch. Coll. of Edn. U. Hawaii, Honolulu, 1963-66, instr. French, coord. French courses Coll. Arts and Scis., 1966-69; teaching asst. Coll. Edn. Ohio State U., Columbus, 1970-72; instr. French lab. sch. Coll. Edn. U. Hawaii, Honolulu, 1974-76; adminstr. bilingual-bicultural edn. project Hawaii State Dept. Edn., Honolulu, 1976-77; coord. disadvantaged minority recruitment program Sch. Social Work, U. Hawaii, Honolulu, 1977-84; coord. tutor tng. program U. Hawaii, Honolulu, 1984-86; program dir. Multicultural Multifunctional Resource Ctr., Honolulu, 1986-87; vis. prof. Sch. Pub. Health, ret. U. Hawaii, Honolulu, 1987-92; bd. dirs. Hawaii Assn. Lang. Tchrs., Honolulu, 1963-66, Hawaii Com. for the Humanities, 1977-83; mem. statewide adv. coun. State Mental Health Adv. Com., Honolulu, 1977-82; task force mem. Underrepresentation of Filipinos in Higher Edn., Honolulu, 1984-86. Author: (with others) Notable Women in Hawaii, 1984; contbr. articles to profl. jours. Chairperson edn. and counseling subcom. First Gov.'s Commn. on Status of Women, Honolulu, 1964; vice chairperson Honolulu County Com. on the Status of Women, 1975-76, Hawaii State Dr. Martin Luther King Jr. Commn., Honolulu, 1982-85; pres. Filipino Hist. Soc. of Hawaii, 1980—; mem. Hawaii State Adv. Com. to U.S. Commn. on Civil Rights, 1981—, chairperson, 1982-85; bd. dirs. Japanese Am. Citizens League Honolulu chpt., 1990—, mem. Hawaiian Sovereignty com., 1994—. Women of Distinction, Honolulu County Com. on Status of Women, 1982; recipient Nat. Edn. Assn. award for Leadership in Asian and Pacific Island Affairs, NEA, 1985, Alan F. Saunders award ACLU in Hawaii, 1986, Disting. Alumni award U. Hawaii Alumni Affairs Office, 1994. Mem. Filipino Am. Nat. Hist. Soc., Filipino Coalition for Solidarity, Gabriela Network (Hawaii chpt.), Filipino Cmty. Ctr., NOW, Alliance Française of Hawaii. Democrat. Home and Office: 3201 Beaumont Woods Pl Honolulu HI 96822-1423

NAGY, STEPHEN MEARS, JR., physician, allergist; b. Yonkers, N.Y., Apr. 1, 1939; s. Stephen Mears and Olga (Zahoruiko) N.; m. Branda Yu Nagy, 1966; children: Catherine, Stephen III. BA, Princeton U., 1960; MD, Tufts U., 1964. Diplomate Am. Bd. Internal Medicine, Am. Bd. Allergy and Immunology. Pvt. practice Sacramento, Calif., 1971-95; prof. Sch. Medicine U. Calif., Davis, 1974—. Author, editor Evaluation & Management of Allergic and Asthmatic Diseases, 1981; mem. editl. bd. Clinical Reviews in Allergy; creator Famous Teachings in Modern Medicine-Allergy Series slide collection. Capt. U.S. Army, 1966-68, Vietnam. Fellow Am. Acad. Allergy, Am. Coll. Allergy; mem. AMA, Sacramento-El Dorado Med. Soc. (bd. dirs. 1971-95). Office: 4801 J St Ste A Sacramento CA 95819-3746

NAHMIAS, VICTOR JAY, architect; b. Woodside, N.Y., May 2, 1951; s. Leon and Judith (Haupt) N.; m. Michal Caspi, June 24, 1975; children: Ariel, Tamar. BA, U. Pa., 1973; BArch, U. B.C., Vancouver, 1977. Registered profl. architect. Carpenter's asst. Weir Constrn., Vancouver, 1973; designer, draftsman Kenn Butts, Northridge, Calif., 1977-78; project mgr. B. Robert Axton, Sherman Oaks, Calif., 1978-79, Howard R. Lane, Woodland Hills, Calif., 1979-81; project architect Rochlin & Baran Assocs., Los Angeles, 1981-84; area architect Kaiser Permanente, Pasadena, 1984-90; ptnr. Wendland-Nahmias AIA & Assocs., Westlake Village, Calif., 1990-96; prin. Envision Architecture, L.A., 1996—; bd. dirs. Kosmic Kids. Bd. dirs., pres. Cameo Woods Home Owners Assn.; co-convener L.A. City Coun. 8th Dist. West Area Assembly; past chmn. Purim Carnival, libr. com. Temple Israel; mem. Nature Conservancy, World Wildlife Fund, Statue of Liberty/Ellis Island Found., L.A. County Mus. Art, Natural History Mus. of L.A., Mus. Contemporary Art, Skirball Cultural Ctr., Mus. of Tolerance. Mem. AIA (past co-chmn. L.A. com. on govt. rels., mem. com. on health), AIA/L.A. Calif. Coun. (past mem. bd. dirs., steering com., past legis. rev. com.), Cmty. Assns. Inst., Am. Planning Assn., Assn. Facility Engrs., Am. Soc. Hosp. Engrs., World Future Soc., Congress for New Urbanism, Am. Philatelic Soc., Nat. Trust for Hist. Preservation, Nat. Audubon Soc., Sierra Club, Beverly Hills C. of C., Culver City C. of C., Century City C. of C., L.A. C. of C., World Affairs Coun. Democrat. Jewish. Home: 3647 Kalsman Dr Apt L Los Angeles CA 90016-4447 Office: Ste 260 3000 S Robertson Blvd Los Angeles CA 90034

NAIDORF, LOUIS MURRAY, architect; b. Los Angeles, Aug. 15, 1928; s. Jack and Meriam (Abbott) N.; m. Dorise D. Roberts, June 1948 (div.); children: Victoria Beth Naidorf-Slifer; m. Patricia Ann Shea, June 1, 1968 (div.); m. Patricia Ruth Allen, Dec. 6, 1992. BA, U. Calif., Berkeley, 1949, MA, 1950. Registered architect, Calif. Designer Welton Becket Assocs., L.A., 1950-51, Pereira and Luckman, L.A., 1951-52; project designer Welton Becket Assocs., L.A., 1952-55, sr. project designer, 1955-59, v.p. asst., dir. design, 1959-70, sr. v.p., dir. rsch., 1970-73; sr. v.p., design prin. Ellerbe Becket Assocs., L.A., 1973-95; dean Sch. Architecture and Design Woodbury U., L.A., 1990—; mem. peer rev. panel Nat. Endowment Arts, 1995—; vis. lectr. Calif. Poly. Sch. Architecture, San Luis Obispo, 1975-82; instr. UCLA Sch. Architecture, 1985, UCLA Landscape Archtl. Program, 1980-85, Otis-Parsons, L.A., 1986-92. Prin. works include Capitol Records Bldg., Century City, Los Angeles, Hyatt Regency, Dallas, Restoration Calif. State Capitol Bldg. Bd. dirs. Inst. for Garden Studies, L.A., 1986—. Recipient Honor award Nat. Trust for Hist. Preservation, 1985. Fellow AIA (bd. dirs. Los Angeles chpt. 1977-79, Silver Medal 1950, Nat. Honor award 1985). Office: Woodbury Univ 7500 N Glenoaks Blvd Burbank CA 91504-1052 *Leadership often requires decisions based on limited information. Course corrections can be made but only after action is taken because you can't steer a car that isn't moving.*

NAJJAR, TAMARA LITCHFIELD, mail order business owner; b. Elgin, Ill., June 2, 1958; d. Kelmar Thomas and Betty Joan (Light) Litchfield; m. Idris M. Najjar, Jan. 5, 1986; children: Zakariya, Suraya, Ali. AS in Fire Protection, AS in Safety, We. Ky. U., Bowling Green, 1983. Lic. cosmetologist. Asst. supr. Opryland USA Inc., Nashville, 1983-86; asst. mgr. Hitachi Am., Nashville, 1986-91; owner, mgr. TJ Designs, Riverside, Calif., 1993—. Author, pub.: Beauty Shop in A Book, 1993. Fundraising chair Islamic Acad., Riverside, 1993-94, yearbook organizer, 1993. Mem. Mosque of Riverside. Democrat. Muslim. Home and Office: 273 Newell Dr Riverside CA 92507-3106

NAKABAYASHI, NICHOLAS TAKATERU, retired retail executive; b. Honolulu, Feb. 25, 1920; s. Denji and Ume (Teraoka) N. BS, Utah State U., 1949; MS, U. Ill., 1953, PhD, 1959. Rsch. asst. U. Ill., Urbana, 1953-59; jr. rsch. physiologist UCLA, 1959-61, asst. rsch. physiologist, 1961-64; rsch. fellow Calif. Inst. Tech., Pasadena, 1961-64; sec.-treas. Underwater Rsch.

Corp., L.A., 1962-64; rsch. asst. dept. ob/gyn U. Mich. Med. Ctr., Ann Arbor, 1964-70; biologist VA Hosp., Wadsworth, 1971-72; instr. San Gabriel Adult Sch., Calif., 1971-78; supr. serology VA Hosp., Long Beach, Calif., 1972-74; owner Regent Liquor Store, L.A., 1974-79; pres., treas. Regent Liquor, Inc., L.A., 1979-85; ret. NIH grantee, 1967, 69. Mem. N.Y. Acad. Sci., 100th Inf. Battalion Vets. Club. Home: 516 Kamoku St Apt 302 Honolulu HI 96826-5102

NAKAGAWA, ALLEN DONALD, radiologic technologist; b. N.Y.C., Mar. 14, 1955; s. Walter Tsunehiko and Alyce Tsuneko (Kinoshita) N. BS in Environ. Studies, St. John's U., Jamaica, N.Y., 1977; MS in Marine Biology, C.W. Post Coll., 1980. Cert. radiologic technologist, in fluoroscopy, Calif.; cert. Am. Registry Radiol. Technologists. Research asst. environ. studies St. John's U., 1976-78; lab. asst. Bur. Water Surveillance, Nassau Co. of Health Dept., Wantaugh, N.Y., 1978; clin. endocrinology asst. U. Calif. VA Hosp., San Francisco, 1981-83; student technologist St. Mary's Hosp., San Francisco, 1985-86; radiologic technologist Mt. Zion Hosp., San Francisco, 1986-88; sr. radiologic technologist U. Calif., San Francisco, 1989—, urosurg. radiologic technologists, 1988-89; attendee U. Calif. San Francisco Trauma and Emergency Radiology Conf., 1995, U. Calif. San Francisco Musculoskeletal MRI Conf., 1996. Mem. AAAS, ACLU, Calif. Soc. Radiologic Technologists, Marine Mammal Ctr., Calif. Acad. Scis., Japanese-Am. Nat. Mus., World Affairs Coun., San Francisco, Sigma Xi. Democrat. Methodist. *If you know, believe and have faith in yourself first, only then can you endeavor to assist someone else. Otherwise, you have wasted your efforts and may have even caused a loss of life.*

NAKAHATA, TADAKA, retired consulting engineer, land surveyor; b. Kauai, Hawaii, Nov. 24, 1924; s. Tadao and Yae (Ohta) N.; BS in Civil Engring., U. Hawaii, 1951; m. Clara S. Sakanashi, June 23, 1956; children—Leanne A. Nikaido, Holly E. Chung, Merry Y. Ifuku. Engr./surveyor B.H. McKeague & Assos., Honolulu, 1951-55, Harland Bartholomew & Assos., Honolulu, 1955-56, Paul Low Engring. Co., Honolulu, 1956-59, Nakahata, Kaneshige, Imata & Assos., 1959-63; owner T. Nakahata, Honolulu, 1964-83, ret., 1983; mem. Hawaii Bd. Registration of Architects, Engrs. and Land Surveyors, 1980-83. With AUS, 1946-47. Mem. ASCE, Am. Congress Surveying and Mapping, Nat. Soc. Profl. Engrs. Mem. Makiki Christian Ch.

NAKAMOTO, CAROLYN MATSUE, principal; b. Hilo, Hawaii, Jan. 28, 1947; d. Matsuichi and Kiyoko Sugimoto; m. Glenn Sunao Nakamoto, June 15, 1985. BEd in Secondary Edn., U. Hawaii, 1969, MEd in Ednl. Adminstrn., 1994. Cert. prof. sch. adminstr., Hawaii; cert. profl. tchr. secondary tchr. phys. sci. and gen. sci., Hawaii. Tchr. sci. Kalani H.S., Honolulu, 1971-77, Kaiser H.S., Honolulu, 1977-87; vice-prin. McKinley H.S., Honolulu, 1987-90; acting prin. Royal Elem., Honolulu, 1989; prin. Hahaione Elem., Honolulu, 1990—. Mem. ASCD, Nat. Assn. Secondary Sch. Prins., Phi Delta Kappa, Delta Kappa Gamma.

NAKASHIMA, MITSUGI, state agency administrator. Chmn. Edn. divsn., Honolulu. Office: Education Dvsn PO Box 2360 Honolulu HI 96804-2360*

NAKAYAMA, PAULA AIKO, justice; b. Honolulu, Oct. 19, 1953; m. Charles W. Totto; children: Elizabeth Murakami, Alexander Totto. BS, U. Calif., Davis, 1975; JD, U. Calif., 1979. Bar: Hawaii 1979. Dep. pros. atty. City and County of Honolulu, 1979-82; ptnr. Shim, Tam & Kirimitsu, Honolulu, 1982-92; judge 1st Cir. Ct. State of Hawaii, Oahu, 1992-93; justice State of Hawaii Supreme Ct., Honolulu, 1993—. Mem. Am. Judicature Soc., Hawaii Bar Assn., Sons and Daughters of 442. Office: Ali'iolani Hale 417 S King St Honolulu HI 96813-2902 Address: PO Box 2560 Honolulu HI 96804-2560*

NAKAYAMA, RANDALL SHIGE, English language educator; b. Oakland, Calif., Aug. 20, 1957; s. Shigenobu and Helen (Wada) N. AB in English, U. Calif., Berkeley, 1979, MA in English, 1982, PhD in English, 1986. Vis. asst. prof. San Jose (Calif.) State U., 1988-90; asst. prof. English San Francisco State U., 1991—. Author introduction, editor: The Life and Death of Mrs. Mary Frith, 1993. Mem. Phi Beta Kappa. Home: 314 Garces Dr San Francisco CA 94132-2137 Office: San Francisco State U Dept English San Francisco CA 94132

NAKRA, NARESH KUMAR, food products executive; b. New Delhi, India, Jan. 8, 1946; came to U.S. in 1967; s. Tilak Raj and Eimla K. (Kalra) N.; m. Kavita Nakra, Aug. 16, 1971; children: Neal, Navin. BSME, U. Delhi, India, 1967; MSME, U. Iowa, 1970, PhD, 1975. Sr. process engr. Quaker Oats, Chgo., 1973-78, mgr. env. and energy, 1978-80, mgr. ops. pkg., 1980-84, mgr. engring., 1984-86; v.p. engring. Sunshine Biscuits, Inc., Woodbridge, N.J., 1986-88, v.p. plant ops., 1988-89, sr. v.p. ops., 1989-91; COO Gruma Corp., L.A., 1991-93, pres., CEO, 1993—, sr. v.p. ops., 1994. Cmty. Leadership, L.A., 1995. Mem. ASME, Packaging Inst. Office: Gruma Corp 5750 Grace Pl Ste A Los Angeles CA 90022-4121*

NALDER, ERIC CHRISTOPHER, investigative reporter; b. Coulee Dam, Wash., Mar. 2, 1946; s. Philip Richard and Mibs Dorothy (Aurdal) N.; m. Jan Christiansen, Dec. 20, 1968; 1 child, Britt Hillary. BA in Communications, U. Wash., 1968. News editor Whidbey News-Times, Oak Harbor, Wash., 1971; reporter Lynnwood (Wash.) Enterprise, 1972, Everett Herald, Lynnwood, 1972-75; gen. assignment reporter Seattle Post-Intelligencer, 1975-78, edn. writer, 1977-78, investigative reporter, 1978-83; chief investigative reporter Seattle Times, 1983—. Author: Tankers Full of Trouble, 1994. Recipient Edn. Writers Assn. award Charles Stewart Mott Found., 1978, Hearst Cmty. Svc. award, 1978, C.B. Blethen awards (13), Outstanding Govt. Reporting award Seattle Mcpl. League, Pub. Svc. in Journalism award Sigma Delta Chi, 1987, Edward J. Meeman award Scripps Howard Found., 1987, Thomas Stokes award, Washington Journalism Ctr., 1990, Pulitzer prize for nat. reporting, 1990, Nat. Headline award, 1991, AP Sports Editors' Investigative Reporting award, 1992, Pub. Svc. award AP Mags. Editors Assn., 1992, Goldsmith prize for investigative reporting, 1992, Worth Bingham prize for investigative reporting, 1992, Headliner award, 1992, Investigative Reporters and Editors award, 1992, 95, Silver Gavel award ABA, 1995, Pulitzer prize for investigative reporting, 1997. Mem. Investigative Reporters and Editors, Pacific N.W. Newspaper Guild. Office: Seattle Times Fairview Avenue St N Seattle WA 98109

NAMBA, KATHRYN ELIZABETH, elementary educator; b. San Francisco, Mar. 23, 1958; d. Richard Anthony and Kathryn Elizabeth (Mares) Torres; children: Tetsuro, Kan, Yohta. BA magna cum laude, San Francisco State U., 1980; postgrad., U. N.Mex., 1992-94, Coll. Santa Fe, 1995—. Cert. elem. tchr., N.Mex. Owner, mgr., instr. Pvt. Jyuku for ESL, Kanzaki-cho, Japan, 1980-89; pers. mgmt. specialist EPA, San Francisco, 1990-91; Spanish tchr. grades 1-8 Taos (N.Mex.) Valley Sch., 1991-92, elem. tchr., 1995-96; elem. tchr. Questa (N.Mex.) Ind. Sch. Dist., 1992-95; founder, dir., instr. Listos Cmty. Edn. Ctr. for Children, San Cristóbal, N.Mex., 1996—; organizer, instr. Wild About Reading, Costilla, N.Mex., summer, 1994; presenter in field. Mem. ASCD. Home: PO Box 188 San Cristobal NM 87564

NAMEN, ANTHONY EUGENE, biochemist, immunologist; b. Helena, Mont., Aug. 3, 1943; s. Anthony James and Kathryn Marie (Morris) N. BS, Mont. State U., 1977, MS, 1979; PhD, Wash. State U., 1984. Sr. staff scientist Immunex Corp., Seattle, 1984—. Contbr. articles to profl. jours. Served with U.S. Navy, 1965-70, Egypt. Mem. N.Y. Acad. Sci. Democrat. Roman Catholic. Home: 1135 4th Ave E Kalispell MT 59901-5818

NANCE, ROBERT LEWIS, oil company executive; b. Dallas, July 10, 1936; s. Melvin Renfro Nance and Ruth Natlie (Seibert) Nowlin; m. Penni Jane Warfel; children: Robert Scott, Amy Louise, Catherine Leslie. BS, So. Meth. U., 1959; LLD (hon.), Rocky Mountain Coll., 1989. V.p. geology Oliver & West Cons., Dallas, 1960-66; ptnr. Nance & Larue Cons., Dallas, 1966-69; pres., CEO Nance Petroleum Corp., Billings, Mont., 1969—; bd. dirs. First Interstate Bank Commerce, MDU Resources, Rocky Mountain Coll., Billings, chmn., 1986-91; mem. Nat. Petroleum Coun., 1992-94; chmn. Petroleum Technology Transfer Coun. Coun. pres. Am. Luth. Ch., Billings, 1980; trustee, chmn. Deaconess Med. Ctr., Billings; chmn. Deaconess Billings Clinic Healty Sys. Recipient Hall of Fame award Rocky Mountain Coll. Alumni, 1987, Disting. Svc. Trusteeship, Assn. Governing Bds. Univs. Colls., 1988. Mem. Am. Assn. Petroleum Geologists, Ind. Petroleum Assn. Am. (exec. com., nat. bd. govs.), Ind. Petroleum Assn. Mountain States (v.p. Mont. 1977-79), Mont. Petroleum Assn., Hilands Golf Club, Billings Petroleum Club. Office: Nance Petroleum Corp PO Box 7168 550 N 31st St Billings MT 59103

NANDAGOPAL, MALLUR R., engineer; b. Kolar, Karnataka, India, May 14, 1938; came to U.S., 1976; s. M. Ramanuja Iyengar and Garudammal; m. Sreedharani K. Ramamurthy; children: Radha, Meena, Sudha. BS, Cen. Coll., Bangalore, India, 1958; B of Tech., Indian Inst. Tech., Bombay, 1962; ME, Indian Inst. Sci., Bangalore, 1963, PhD, 1974. Registered profl. engr., Wash. Mem. faculty Indian Inst. Sci., 1963-77; engr. City of Spokane, Wash., 1977—; coord. summer sch. Indian Inst. Sci., 1974-75. Contbr. articles to profl. jours. Mem. restoration adv. bd. Fairchild AFB. Mem. IEEE (sr., Engr. of Yr. award 1995), Inst. Sci. (sec. Staff Club 1972-74), Fed. Emergency Mgmt. Agy. (mitigation com.). Hindu. Home: 410 E Shiloh Hills Dr Spokane WA 99208-5819 *Motto: "It is better that managers lose face than the public lose money."*

NANTO, ROXANNA LYNN, marketing professional, management consusltant; b. Hanford, Calif., Dec. 17, 1952; d. Lawson Gene Brooks and Bernice (Page) Jackson; m. Harvey Ken Nanto, Mar. 23, 1970; 1 child, Shea Kiyoshi. AA, Chemeketa Community Coll., 1976; BSBA, Idaho State U., 1978. PBX operator Telephone Answer Bus. Svc., Moses Lake, Wash., 1965-75; edn. coord. MimiCassia Community Edn., Rupert, Idaho, 1976-77; office mgr. Lockwood Corp., Rupert, Idaho, 1977-78; cost acct. Keyes Fibre Co., Wenatchee, Wash., 1978-80; acctg. office mgr. Armstrong & Armstrong, Wenatchee, Wash., 1980-81; office mgr. Cascade Cable Constrn. Inc., East Wenatchee, Wash., 1981-83; interviewer, counselor Wash. Employment Security, Wenatchee, 1983-84; pres. chief exec. officer Regional Health Care Plus, East Wenatchee, 1986-88; dist. career coord. Eastmont Sch. Dist., East Wenatchee, 1984-90; prin. Career Cons., 1988-90; exec. dir. Wenatchee Valley Coll. Found., 1990-91; ednl. cons. Sunbelt Consortium, East Wenatchee, 1991-93; cons. CC Cons. Assocs., 1993—; ptnr. Cmty. Devel. Mktg. and Mgmt. Resource Group, Wenatchee, Wash., 1994—; also bd. dirs. Cmty. Devel. Mktg. and Mgmt. Resource Group, Wenatchee; speaker North Cen. Washington Profl. Women, Wenatche, 1987, Wen Career Women's Network, Wenatchee, 1990, Wenatchee Valley Rotary, 1990, Meeting the Challenge of Workforce 2000, Seattle, 1993; cons., speaker Wash. State Sch. Dirs., Seattle, 1987; speaker Wenatchee C. of C., 1989; sec. Constrn. Coun. of North Cen. Washington, Wenatchee, 1981-83; bd. dirs. Gen. Vocat. Adv. Bd., Wenatchee, 1986-88, Washington Family Ind. Program, Olympia, 1989—; mem. econ. devel. coun. Grant County, 1992—; ptnr. low income housing devel. Bus. Cons. & Rsch., Wenatchee, 1996—. Mem. at large career Women's Network, 1984—, mem. Econ. Devel. Coun. of No. Cen. Washington; mem. Steering Com. to Retain Judge Small. Recipient Nat. Paragon award, 1991; grantee Nat. Career Devel. Guidelines Wash. State, 1989; named Wenatchee Valley Coll. Vocat. Contbr. of Yr., 1991. Fellow Bem. Women's Club; mem. Nat. Assn. Career Counselors, Nat. Assn. Pvt. Career Counselors, Nat. Coun. Resource Devel., NCW Estate Planning Coun. Home and Office: 2961 Riviera Blvd Malaga WA 98828-9733

NAPLES, CAESAR JOSEPH, public policy educator, lawyer, consultant; b. Buffalo, Sept. 4, 1938; s. Caesar M. and Fannie A. (Occhipinti) N.; children: Jennifer, Caesar; m. Sandra L. Harrison, July 16, 1983. AB, Yale U., 1960; JD, SUNY, 1963. Bar: N.Y. 1963, Fla. 1977, Calif. 1988, U.S. Supreme Ct. 1965. Assoc. Moot & Sprague, Buffalo, 1965-69; asst. dir., employee rels. N.Y. Gov. Office, Albany, 1969-71; asst. v. chancellor SUNY, Albany, 1971-75; vice chancellor and gen. counsel Fla. State U. System, 1975-82; v. chancellor Calif. State U. System, 1983-92; vice chancellor emeritus Calif. State U., 1992—; prof. law and fin. Calif. State U. System, Long Beach, 1983—; gen. counsel Walden U., Mpls. and Naples, Fla., 1993—; cons. Govt. of Australia, U. Nev. Sys., Assn. Can. Colls. and Univs., Que., also other univs. and colls. Contbr. articles to profl. jours.; co-author: Romanov Succession, 1989 with J.Victor Baldridge. Mem. Metlife Resources Adv. Bd., 1986—, chmn., 1992—; mem. heart bd. Long Beach Meml. Hosp., 1993—; bd. dirs. Calif. Acad. Math. and Scis., 1995—. Capt. U.S. Army, 1963-65. Mem. Acad Pers. Adminstrn. (founder), Nat. Ctr. for Study Collective Bargaining Higher Edn. (bd. dirs.). Office: 816 N Juanita Ave Ste B Redondo Beach CA 90277-2200

NAPOLITANO, GRACE F., state legislator; b. Brownsville, Tex., Dec. 4, 1936; d. Miguel and Maria Alicia Ledezma Flores; m. Frank Napolitano, 1982; 1 child, Yolando M., Fred Musquiz Jr., Edward M., Michael M., Cynthia M. Student, Cerritos Coll., L.A. Trade Tech, Tec Southwest Coll. Mem. Calif. Assembly, 1993—. Councilwoman City of Norwalk, Calif., 1986-92, mayor, 1989-90; active Cmty. Family Guidance. Mem. Cerritos Coll. Found., Lions Club. Democrat. Roman Catholic. Home: 12946 Belcher St Norwalk CA 90650-3328 Office: Calif Assembly State Capitol Rm 4005 Sacramento CA 95814-4906 also: PO Box 942849 Sacramento CA 94249-0001*

NAPOLITANO, JANET ANN, prosecutor; b. N.Y.C., Nov. 29, 1957; d. Leonard Michael and Jane Marie (Winer) N. BS, U. Santa Clara, Calif., 1979; JD, U. Va., 1983. Bar: Ariz. 1984, U.S. Dist. Ct. Ariz. 1984, Ct. Appeals (9th cir.) 1984, U.S. Ct. Appeals (10th cir.) 1988. Law clk. to hon. Mary Schroeder U.S Ct. Appeals (9th Cir.), 1983-84; ptnr. Lewis & Roca, Phoenix, 1984-93; U.S. atty. Dist. Ariz., Phoenix, 1993—; mem. Atty. Gen.'s Adv. Com., 1993—, chair, 1995-96. Vice-chair Ariz. Dem. Party, 1991-92; mem. Dem. Nat. Com., 1991-92; State Bd. Tech. Registration, 1989-92; Phoenix Design Standards Rev. Com., 1989-91; bd. dirs. Ariz. Cmty. Legal Svcs. Corp., 1987-92; bd. regents Santa Clara U., 1992—. Truman Scholarship Found. scholar, 1977. Mem. ABA, Am. Law Inst., Ariz. Bar Assn., Maricopa County Bar Assn., Am. Judicature Soc., Ariz. State Bar (chmn. civil practice and procedure com. 1991-92), Phi Beta Kappa, Alpha Sigma Nu. Office: US Attys Office 4000 US Courthouse 230 N 1st Ave Phoenix AZ 85025-0230

NARAMORE, JAMES JOSEPH, family practice physician, educator; b. Gillette, Wyo., Nov. 29, 1949; s. Kenneth Chester and Joan (Biggerstaff) N.; m. Karen Rae Buttermore, July 9, 1972; children: Lindsay, Marissa, Jessica, Marcus. BA with highest achievement in Biology, John Brown U., Siloam Springs, Ark., 1972; MD with family practice honors, U. Utah, 1977. Diplomate Am. Bd. Family Practice. Resident in family practice U. Nebr., Omaha, 1977-80, chief resident; pvt. practice, Gillette, 1981—; mem. staff Campbell County Meml. Hosp., Gillette, 1980—, chief staff, 1986, chief dept. family practice, 1990-91; instr. dept. human medicine U. Wyo., 1983-86, clin. assoc. prof. family practice, 1986—; ptnr., co-founder Med. Arts Lab., Gillette, 1981—; med. dir. Campbell County Detention Ctr., 1988—; med. dir. Pioneer Manor Nursing Home, Gillette, 1989—; aviation med. examiner FAA, Oklahoma City, 1986—; cons. on occupational medicine to numerous industries, Campbell County, 1986—. Charter mem. Gillette Area Leadership Inst., 1986-87; chmn. missions com. Grace Bible Ch., Gillette, 1983—, chmn. bd. elders, 1989—. Mem. Am. Acad. Family Physicians, Wyo. Med. Soc., Campbell County Med. Soc. (pres. 1983-84), Gillette C. of C. (bd. dirs. 1987-90), Toastmasters (pres. Gillette 1992, Competent Toastmaster award 1986—). Republican. Home: 1214 Hilltop Ct Gillette WY 82718-5625 Office: Family Health 407 S Medical Arts Ct Ste D Gillette WY 82716-3372

NARAYAN, BEVERLY ELAINE, lawyer; b. Berkeley, Calif., June 19, 1961; d. Jagjiwan and Alexandra (Mataras) N.; m. James Dean Schmidt, Jan. 7, 1989; children: Sasha Karan, Kaiya Maria. Student, San Francisco State U., 1979-80; BA, U. Calif., Berkeley, 1983; JD, U. Calif., San Francisco, 1987. Bar: Calif. 1987, U.S. Dist. Ct. (no. dist.) Calif. 1987, U.S. Dist. Ct. (ctrl. dist.) 1988. Atty. Daniels Barratta & Fine, L.A., 1988-89, Kornblum Ferry & Frye, L.A., 1990-91, Clapp Moroney Bellagamba Davis & Vucinich, Menlo Park, Calif., 1991-93, pvt. practice, Burlingame, Calif., 1993—; arbitrator Nat. Assn. Securities Dealers, San Francisco, 1987—, Pacific Stock Exch., San Francisco, 1994—; mediator Peninsula Conflict Resolution Ctr., San Mateo, Calif., 1995—; judge pro tem San Mateo Superior Ct., Redwood City, Calif., 1994—. Candidate Sch. Bd. San Mateo (Calif.) Unified Sch. Dist., 1993. Recipient U. Calif. Hastings Coll. Law Achievement award, 1986; named Barrister of Yr., San Mateo County, 1996. Mem. ABA, San Mateo County Bar Assn. (co-chair women lawyers 1995, bd. dirs. 1994-96), Nat. Women's Polit. Caucus (bd. dirs., diversity chair 1993—), San Mateo County Barristers Club (bd. dirs. 1993—, child watch chair 1995—). Office: 1508 Howard Ave Burlingame CA 94010-5216

NARAYANAMURTI, VENKATESH, research administrator; b. Bangalore, Karnataka, India, Sept. 9, 1939; came to U.S., 1961; s. Duraiswami and Janaki (Subramaniam) N.; m. Jayalakshmi Krishnayya, Aug. 23, 1961; children: Arjun, Ranjini, Krishna. BSc, MSc, St. Stephen's Coll., Delhi, India, 1958; PhD, Cornell U., 1965. Instr., rsch. assoc. Cornell U., Ithaca, N.Y., 1965-68; mem. tech. staff AT&T Bell Labs., Murray Hill, N.J., 1968-76, dept.head, 1976-81, dir., 1981-87; v.p. rsch. Sandia Nat. Labs., Albuquerque, 1987-92; dean engring. U. Calif., Santa Barbara, 1992—; chmn. microelectric bd. Jet Propulsion Lab., Pasadena, Calif., 1988—; chmn. condensed matter and materials phys. panel NRC, 1996; mem. U. Calif. Pres.' Coun. for Nat. Labs., 1995—; bd. dirs. Serpal Interface, Inc., Santa Clara, Calif., 1997—; mem. NAE Pub. Info. Adv. Bd., 1993—, NSF Dir.'s Strategic Planning Bd., 1994—, Los Alamos Nat. Lab. Adv. Bd. for Materials and Indsl. Partnerships, 1994—. Author more than 130 publs.; patentee in field. Fellow IEEE, AAAS, Am. Phys. Soc., Indian Acad. Scis.; mem. NAE, Royal Swedish Acad. Engring. Scis. (fgn.). Office: U Calif Dept Engring Santa Barbara CA 93106

NARDI, WILLIAM ANTHONY, aerospace executive, consultant; b. Cleve., Apr. 16, 1942; s. William Anthony and Ann (Peritore) N.; m. Judy Arlene Hampsten, Apr. 20, 1974; children: Lisa, Dario, Chris. BA, U. So. Calif., 1964, MBA, 1968. Cert. in contract mgmt.; cert. tchr., Calif. Underwriter Allstate Ins. Cos., Pasadena, Calif., 1966-68; in contracts Hughes Aircraft, Culver City, Calif., 1968-70; cons. EMSCO, Woodland Hills, Calif., 1970-72, Northrop Grumman, Hawthorne, Calif., 1972—; tchr. various colls., L.A. and Bishop, Calif., 1965—; cons. Gates Mfg., Hawthorne, 1977-86; cons., bd. dirs. Bailly Mfg., Hawthorne, 1979—, Micron Mfg., Missions Hills, Calif., 1995—. Author: Work Breakdown Structure, 1985, (manual) Intracompnay Procurement, 1992. Scoutmaster, Boy Scouts Am., Encino, Calif., 1968—. Mem. Nat. Contract Mgmt. Assn., Mgmt. Club. Office: Bus Mgmt 3520 E Ave M Palmdale CA 93550

NARELL, IRENA, freelance writer, history educator; b. Sanok, Poland, Sept. 17, 1923; came to U.S., 1939; d. Abraham and Antonina Penzik; m. Murray Narell, June 29, 1945 (dec. Jan. 1991); children: Jeff, Andrew. BS, Columbia U., 1969. Asst. to Polish UN Delegation, N.Y.C., 1945-51; owner Art Originals Gallery, N.Y.C., 1961-63, 1964-69; co-mgr. The Steel Bandits—a mus. group; project dir. San Francisco Jews-Old Traditions on a New Frontier, bicentennial exhibit Judah L. Magnes Mus., Cmty. and Diversity, Bay Area Jewish Families, 1989. Mem. editl. bd.: Western States Jewish History; author: Ashes to the Taste, 1961, The Invisible Passage, 1969, Joshua Fighter for Bar Kochba, 1978 (Nat. Jewish Book award 1979), Our City: The Jews of San Francisco, 1981, History's Choice, 1996; contbr. numerous short stories, revs. and articles to profl. jours. and mags.; translator: Holy Week (Jerzy Andrzejewski) Samson (Kazimierz Brandys), Summer in Nohant (Jaroslaw Iwaszkiewicz), Poetry by Julian Tuwim. Mem. Jewish Arts Cmty. of the Bay, San Francisco, 1975-96. Mem. Inst. Hist. Study. Jewish. Home: 5949 Estates Dr Oakland CA 94611-3113

NARULA, MOHAN LAL, realtor; b. Ferozepur, India, Feb. 2, 1939; came to U.S., 1962; s. Ram Dyal and Pemeshwari Narula; m. Sylvia Conway, Aug. 31, 1968; children: Rabinder, Rajinder. BS, Panjab U., India, 1960; BSME, Calif. Poly. State U., San Luis Obispo, 1965; MS in Engring., Calif. State U., Northridge, 1970. Engr. Abex Corp., Oxnard, Calif., 1965-69; salesman, realtor Walker & Lee, Oxnard, Calif., 1970-73; owner, realtor Narula Co. Realtors, Oxnard, Calif., 1973—. Mem. Cert. Comml. Investment Mem. (designate 1979), Oxnard Harbor Bd. Realtors (mem. profl. standard com. 1980-89), Los Angeles Cert. Comml. Investment Mem. (bd. dirs., treas. 1985). Home: 2830 W Hill St Oxnard CA 93035-2522 Office: Narula Co Realtor 3201 Samuel Ave Ste 7 Oxnard CA 93033-5334

NASH, CLARICE ALDINE HAYES, family nurse practitioner, critical care nurse; b. Chgo., May 12, 1952; d. Clarence Jesse and Beatrice Ann (Bevers) Hayes; m. Robert James Nash, Aug. 8, 1981; children: Christopher Robert, Jesse Daniel, Sara April. BSN, U. Tex., El Paso, 1974; MSN, U. South Ala., 1991; FNP, Miss. U. for Women, 1991. RN, Tex., Calif., Miss., Wash.; cert. FNP, ANCC. Staff nurse Sun Towers Hosp., El Paso, Tex., 1974-76; head nurse CCU, St. Joseph Hosp., El Paso, 1976-77; staff nurse MICU/SICU Grossmont Dist. Hosp., La Mesa, Calif., 1984-86; staff nurse CCU, Sharp Meml. Hosp., San Diego, 1984-86, Gulf Coast Community Hosp., Biloxi, Miss., 1987-89; staff nurse critical care Analytical Med. Enterprises, Gulfport, Miss., 1991; nurse practitioner Kitsap County Health Dist., Bremerton, Wash., 1991-93; family nurse practitioner Peninsula Family Med. Ctr., Gig Harbor, Wash., 1994—; adj. faculty ADN program Olympic Coll., Bremerton, 1991-94; clin. faculty grad. nursing programs U. Wash., Pacific Luth. U. With Nurse Corps USN, 1977-83, comdr. USNR. Mem. ANA, AACN, Wash. Nurse's Assn., Nat. League for Nursing, Am. Acad. Nurse Practitioners, Assn. Mil. Surgeons of U.S. Lutheran. Office: Peninsula Family Med Ctr 4700 Point Fosdick Dr NW Gig Harbor WA 98335-1706

NASH, K(IM) ALAN, public information executive; b. Midland, Mich., Nov. 15, 1956; s. Oliver F. and Betty June (Case) N.; m. Mary Sue Gangel, Sept. 4, 1982 (div. June 1991); m. Sharon Waddell Bentley, May 15, 1993 (div. Feb. 1996). AS, Ferris State Coll., 1977, BS in TV, 1980; MS in Journalism, Iowa State U., 1985. Announcer WFRS/WRKX campus radio, Big Rapids, Mich., 1976-79, WMPX radio, Midland, Mich., 1978; news and farm dir. KSCB/KEZS radio, Liberal, Kans., 1980; reporter/anchor WOI-TV, Des Moines, 1980-82; prodr. KSNW/Kans. State Network, Wichita, Kans., 1982-83; asst. news dir. KTIV-TV, Sioux City, Iowa, 1983-86; adj. prof. Morningside Coll., Sioux City, Iowa, 1986; news dir. KTVQ-TV/Mont. TV Network, Billings, Mont., 1986-93; dir. news and ops. Sta. KMID-TV, Midland, Tex., 1993-94; dir. devel. Billings (Mont.) Symphony, 1995-96; pk. ranger Yellowstone Nat. Pk., Wyo., 1995-96; pub. info. officer Yosemite (Calif.) Nat. Pk., 1996—; vis. asst. prof. U. Mont., 1994. Address: PO Box 778 Yosemite National Park CA 95389

NASH, REFORD BROOKS, minister; b. Chickasha, Okla., June 17, 1944; s. Cheston Alfred and Gladys Marion (Brooks) N.; m. Rosemarie Benziger, Mar. 20, 1971 (div. Sept. 1983); 1 child, Aaron Alfred; m. Marilyn Carol Konkol, Aug. 31, 1984; children: Trevor James McLellan, Shelley Elizabeth. BA, Okla. Bapt. U., 1966; MDiv, San Francisco Theol. Sem., 1969; ThM, Princeton Theol. Sem., 1978; D of Ministry, McCormick Theol. Sem., 1985. Ordained, 1969. Assoc. pastor Pasadena (Calif.) Presbyn. Ch., 1969-71, First Presbyn. Ch., Oceanside, Calif., 1971-74; chaplain, chair religion dept. The Hun Sch., Princeton, N.J., 1975-78; pastor First Presbyn. Ch., Grapevine, Tex., 1978-80, West Side Presbyn. Ch., Wichita, Kans., 1980-88; sr. pastor Federated Cmty. Ch., Flagstaff, Ariz., 1988-96, Presbyn. Ch. of the Roses, Santa Rosa, Calif., 1996—; mediator Superior Ct., Flagstaff, Ariz., 1994—, Ariz. Atty. Gen., Flagstaff, 1989-96; com. on ministry mem. Grand Canyon Presbytery, Ariz., 1993-96; commr. Presbyn. Synod of Southwest, Phoenix, 1994. Bd. dirs. Cath. Social Svc., Flagstaff; mem. adv. bd. Grand Canyon Coun. Boy Scouts Am., Phoenix, 1992-96. Mem. N.Am. Acad. Liturgy (assoc.), Acad. Family Mediators (cert. mediator), Santa Rosa Rotary Club. Home: 5780 Corbett Circle Santa Rosa CA 95403 Office: Presbyn Ch of the Roses 2500 Patio Ct Santa Rosa CA 95405

NASH, RICHARD EUGENE, aerospace engineer; b. San Diego, Feb. 18, 1954; s. Clifford Arthur Jr. and Dorothy Fay (Johnson) N.; m. Lynn Elora Martin, Aug. 5, 1978. BSCE, U. Ky., 1981; MSCE, U. So. Calif., 1988; MSEM, West Coast U., 1995. Registered profl. civil engr., Calif.; cert. profl. mgr. Mem. tech. staff Rockwell Internat., Downey, Calif., 1982—, lead engr. space shuttle propulsion systems, 1986-88; engr. Nat. Aero-Space Plane, Long Beach, Calif., 1988-89, space shuttle orbiter project engr., 1989-95; project mgr. problem action ctr., orbiter shuttle program Rockwell Internat., Downey, Calif., 1995—; pvt. practice civil engring., Calif., 1985—. Scoutmaster Boy Scouts Am., Covington, Ky., 1972-74, Williamstown, Ky., 1976-82, asst. scoutmaster, Ft. Hood, Tex., 1975-76. Sgt. U.S. Army, 1976. Recipient Eagle Scout award Boy Scouts Am., 1972, Space Flight Awareness award, 1995, Manned Space Flight Awareness award 1996; named to Hon. Order of Ky. Cols., 1985. Mem. Nat. Mgmt. Assn., Nat. Eagle Scout Assn. (advisor 1983), Masons (32 degree, sr. warden), Chi Epsilon. Republican. Office: Rockwell Internat Space Transp and Systems Div 12214 Lakewood

Blvd Downey CA 90242-2655 *Personal philosophy: If you want to be a doctor; talk to a doctor, she has already done it. If you want to be an engineer; talk to an engineer, he has already done it. If you want to be a success; talk to yourself, for only you know how to define it.*

NASH, STEVEN ALAN, museum curator, art historian; b. Wadsworth, Ohio, Apr. 8, 1944; s. Frank W. N. and LaDema (Siffert) N.; m. Carol Ostrowski, June 14, 1969; children: Colin H., Jessica K. BA, Dartmouth Coll., 1966; PhD, Stanford U., 1973. Curator Albright-Knox Art Gallery, Buffalo, 1973-80; dep. dir., chief curator Dallas Mus. Art, 1980-88; assoc. dir., chief curator, European Arts Fine Arts Mus. of San Francisco, 1988—; panelist Nat. Endowment for the Arts, Washington, 1986—, Inst. Mus. Svcs., Washington, 1979—; bd. dirs. Oberlin (Ohio) Intermus. Conservation Labs., 1976-80. Author: Catalogue: Albright-Knox Art Gallery, 1976, Ben Nicholson, 1977, Naum Gabo: Constructivism, 1986, Century of Modern Sculpture, 1987. Bd. dirs. Lakehill Prep. Sch., Dallas, 1987-88, Buffalo Archtl. Guidebook, 1979-80. Mus. Profl. fellow Nat. Endowment for Arts, 1980; fellow Mabelle McLeod Lewis Found., 1970-71. Mem. Coll. Art Assn., Am. Assn. Mus., Dartmouth Alumni Club. Office: Fine Arts Mus San Francisco Lincoln Pk San Francisco CA 94121*

NASH, WILLIAM KELLY, lawyer; b. Preston, Idaho, Mar. 10, 1959; s. William Isaac and Lois Jean (Meyers) N.; m. Karen Lynn Fox, June 24, 1984; children: Amanda Lynn, Lindsay Katherine, Erika Jean, William Brady, Amy Katherine. BS, Brigham Young U., 1983, JD, 1986. Bar: Utah 1986, U.S. Dist. Ct. Utah 1986. Summer assoc. Jones, Waldo, Holbrook & McDonough, Salt Lake City, 1985, assoc., 1987-90; ptnr. Holme Roberts & Owen, 1990-96; jud. clk. U.S. Dist. Ct., Salt Lake City, 1986-87; v.p. and counsel First Health/First Data Corp., 1996—; judge pro tem small claims div. 5th Cir. Ct., Murray, Utah, 1988—. Mormon missionary Kobe/Osaka, Japan, 1978-80. Brigham Young U. scholar, 1977-78, J. Reuben Clark Law Sch. scholar, 1984-86. Mem. Utah Bar Assn. (young lawyers and litigation sect., chmn. membership support com.), Profl. Ski Instrs. Assn. (cert. instr.). Republican. Home: 1709 Haven Chase Ln Salt Lake City UT 84121-6517 Office: First Health 6975 Union Park Center # 600 Midvale UT 84047

NASON, DOLORES IRENE, computer company executive, counselor, eucharistic minister; b. Seattle, Jan. 24, 1934; d. William Joseph Lockinger and Ruby Irene (Church) Gilstrap; m. George Malcolm Nason Jr., Oct. 7, 1951; children: George Malcolm III, Scott James, Lance William, Natalie Joan. Student, Long Beach (Calif.) City Coll., 1956-59; cert. in Religious Edn. for elem tchrs., Immaculate Heart Coll., 1961, cert. teaching, 1962, cert. secondary teaching, 1967; attended, Salesian Sem., 1983-85. Buyer J. C. Penney Co., Barstow, Calif., 1957; prin. St. Cyprian Confraternity of Christian Doctrine Elem. Sch., Long Beach, 1964-67; prin. summer sch. St. Cyprian Confraternity of Christian Doctrine Elem. Sch., Long Beach, 1965-67; pres. St. Cyprian Confraternity Orgn., Long Beach, 1967-69; dist. co-chmn. L.A. Diocese, 1968-70; v.p. Nason & Assocs., Inc., Long Beach, 1978—; pres. L.A. County Commn. on Obscenity & Pornography, 1984—; eucharistic minister St. Cyprian Ch., Long Beach, 1985—; bd. dirs. L.A. County Children's Svcs., 1988—; part-time social svcs. counselor Disabled Resources Ctr., Inc., Long Beach, 1992—; vol. Meml. Children's Hosp., Long Beach, 1977—; mem. scholarship com. Long Beach City Coll., 1984-90, Calif. State U., Long Beach, 1984-90. Mem. devel. bd. St. Joseph High Sch., 1987—; pres. St. Cyprian's Parish Coun., 1962—; mem. Long Beach Civic Light Opera, 1973—, Assistance League of Long Beach, 1976—. Mem. L.A. Fitness Club, U. of the Pacific Club, K.C. (Family of the Month 1988). Republican. Roman Catholic.

NASVIK-DENNISON, ANNA, artist; b. St. Paul; d. Peter Olson and Hattie Mathilda (Swenson) Nasvik; m. Roger Bennett, Nov. 7, 1936 (dec. 1996); children: Lynne, Kristin. Student, Coll. of St. Catherine, St. Paul, 1925, St. Paul Sch. of Art, 1927, Art Student's League, 1932. Tchr. art St. Joseph's Acad., St. Paul, 1926-30; freelance fashion illustrator N.Y.C., 1930-64; artist syndicated page The Fashion Syndicate, N.Y.C., 1934-38; mem. nat. art bd. Nat. League Am. Pen Women, 1990-92. One woman shows include Colbert Galleries, Sherbrooke St., Mont., Can., 1979, Gallery Milhalis, Sherbrooke St., Mont., 1984, T. Eaton Foyer des Arts, Mont., 1982-87, Venable-Neslage Gallerie, Washington, 1979-84, Lido Galleries, Scottsdale, Ariz., 1988, Hilltop Galleries, Nogales, Ariz., 1991 (top painting award, People's Choice award), 1995, Maiden Ln. Gallery, San Francisco, 1991, Hilltop Gallery, Nogales, 1995 (hon. mention Tubac Ctr. of Arts 1995), 96. Named Woman of Art, Foyer des Arts, 1982; winner 3 top awards Ariz. juried show, Nat. League Am. Pen Women, 1989; recipient 3 People's Choice award Hilltop Galleries, 1991. Mem. Nat. Mus. Women in Arts, Santa Cruz Valley Art Assn., Lakeshore Assn. of Art, Nat. League of Pen Women (3 Top awards 1989, nat. bd. dirs. 1990—), Pen Women Sonora Desert. Home and Office: 231 W Paseo Adobe Green Valley AZ 85614-3462

NATARAJAN, RAMA, research scientist; b. Bangalore, India, June 30, 1952; came to U.S., 1980; d. Jayaraman Narayaswamy and Kameswari (Natesan) Jayaraman; m. Rajan Natarajan, June 27, 1979; 1 child, Pradeep. BS, Bangalore U., 1971, MS, 1973; PhD, Indian Inst. Sci., 1977. Sci. Rsch. Coun. rsch. assoc. Salford (Eng.) U., 1979-80; rsch. assoc. U. So. Calif. Med. Sch., L.A., 1980-87, asst. prof. rsch. medicine, 1987-90; asst. rsch. scientist City of Hope Med. Ctr., Duarte, Calif., 1990-96, assoc. rsch. scientist, 1996—. Contbr. rev. articles to profl. jours. Mem. grant rev. study sect. Am. Heart Assn., L.A., 1994, 95, Am. Cancer Soc., 1996. Recipient R29 1st award NIH, 1993—, Losartan award in rsch. DuPont Merck, 1992, Young Investigator award Am. Heart Assn., 1992. Fellow Am. Heart Assn. (high blood pressure coun. 1995—); mem. Endocrine Soc., Am. Diabetes Assn., Am. Fedn. Clin. Rsch. (Henry Christian award for excellence rsch. 1991). Office: City of Hope Med Ctr 1500 Duarte Rd Duarte CA 91010-3012

NATHAN, LAWRENCE CHARLES, chemistry educator; b. Corning, Calif., Nov. 26, 1944; s. Jules Morris and Mildred (Wood) N.; m. Frieda Ruth Bjornson, Aug. 29, 1966 (div. Dec. 1987); children: Kristine M., Cheryl L.; m. Linda Lou Hartman Crabb, June 17, 1988; stepchildren: Anthony W. Crabb, Tammy J. Crabb. BA, Linfield Coll., 1966; PhD, U. Utah, 1971. From asst. prof. to assoc. prof. Santa Clara (Calif.) U., 1970-88, prof., 1988—, chmn. chemistry dept., 1992—; vis. assoc. prof. U. Utah, Salt Lake City, 1976, 77. Contbr. articles to profl. jours. Recipient Disting. Faculty awd. Santa Clara U., 1979. Mem. Am. Chem. Soc., Sigma Xi. Office: Santa Clara U Chemistry Dept Santa Clara CA 95053

NATHAN, LEONARD EDWARD, writer, educator; b. Los Angeles, Nov. 8, 1924; s. Israel and Florence (Rosenberg) N.; m. Carol Gretchen Nash, June 27, 1949; children: Andrew Peter, Julia Irene, Miriam Abigail. Student, Ga. Tech., 1943-44, UCLA, 1946-47; BA summa cum laude, U. Calif.-Berkeley, 1950, MA, 1952, PhD, 1961. Instr. Modesto (Calif.) Jr. Coll., 1954-60; prof. dept. rhetoric U. Calif., Berkeley, 1960-91, ret., 1991, chmn. dept., 1968-72. Author: Western Reaches, 1958, The Glad and Sorry Seasons, 1963, The Matchmaker's Lament, 1967, The Day The Perfect Speakers Left, 1969, The Tragic Drama of William Butler Yeats, 1963, Flight Plan, 1971, Without Wishing, 1973, The Likeness, 1975, Coup, 1975, Returning Your Call, 1975, The Transport of Love: The Meghaduta by Kalidasa, 1976, Teachings of Grandfather Fox, 1977, Lost Distance, 1978, Dear Blood, 1980, Holding Patterns, 1982, Carrying On: New and Selected Poems, 1985, Diary of a Left-Handed Bird Watcher, 1996; also record: Confessions of a Matchmaker, 1973, De Meester van Het WinterLandschap, Selected Poems in Dutch transl. by Cees Nooteboom, Uitgeverij de Arbiedspers, Amsterdam, 1990; translator: Songs of Something Else, 1982, Grace and Mercy in Her Wild Hair, 1982, (with Czeslaw Milosz) Happy As a Dog's Tail: Poems by Anna Swir, 1985, (with Czeslaw Milosz) With the Skin: Poems of Aleksander Wat, 1989, (with Czeslaw Milosz) Talking to My Body, poems of Anna Swir, 1996, (with Arthur Quinn) The Poet's Work: Study of Czeslaw Milosz, 1991; (with Czeslaw Milosz) Talking To My Body: Poems by Anna Swir, 1996. With U.S. Army, 1943-45, ETO. Recipient Phelan award, 1955; Longview prize, 1961; award in lit. Nat. Inst. Arts and Letters, 1971; Poetry medal Commonwealth Club, 1976, 81; U. Calif. Creative Arts fellow, 1961-62, 73-74; U. Calif. Humanities research fellow, 1983-84; Am. Inst. Indian Studies fellow, 1966-67; Guggenheim fellow, 1976-77. Mem. Assn. of Lit. Scholars and Critics. Home: 40 Beverly Rd Kensington CA 94707-1304

NATHAN, ROBERT A., allergist, educator; b. Miami, Fla., Aug. 11, 1948; m. Leslie Lewis, July 2, 1970; children: Brett Andrew, Douglas Adam. BA cum laude, Tulane U., 1970; MD, U. Miami, 1974. Diplomate Nat. Bd. Med. Examiners, Am. Bd. Internal Medicine, Am. Bd. Allergy and Immunology. Intern dept. medicine Jackson Meml. Hosp. and U. Miami Affiliated Hosps., 1974-75, asst. resident, 1975-76, sr. resident, 1976-77; fellow in allergy and clin. immunology Nat. Jewish Hosp. and Rsch. Ctr., Denver, 1977-79; pvt. practice Asthma & Allergy Assocs., P.C., and Rsch. Ctr., Colorado Springs, Colo., 1979—; mem. courtesy staff Penrose/St. Francis Healthcare Sys., 1979-82, mem. active staff, 1982—; mem. courtesy staff Meml. Hosp., 1979-86, mem. active staff, 1986; clin. instr. divsn. allergy and immunology, dept. internal medicine U. Colo. Health Scis. Ctr., Denver, 1981-83, asst. clin. prof., 1983-90, assoc. clin. prof., 1990—; dir. W.C. Service Allergy and Asthma Rsch. Found., Inc., 1981—; chmn. pharmacy com. Penrose Hosp., 1984-86; pres. So. Colo. Med. Practice Assoc., 1985-89; mem. interspecialty adv. panel Physicians Payment Rev. Commn., 1991; mem. reimbursement com. and non-govt. programs subcom. Joint Coun. Allergy and Immunology, 1991-93; mem. Wellpoint Nat. Pharmacy and Therapeutics Com., 1994—; presenter in field. Author: (with others) Understanding Asthma, A Blueprint for Breathing, 1989; mem. editl. bd. The New Eng. and Regional Allergy Procs., 1982-86, Jour. Asthma, 1991—, Allergy Procs., 1994—; contbr. articles to profl. jours. Vol. physician Champ Camp Colo., 1985—; trustee Temple Shalom, 1987-94, pres., 1990-92; bd. dirs. Colo. Found. Med. Care, 1990-94, El Paso County Med. Soc. Found., 1991—, pres., 1991—. Fellow ACP, Am. Coll. Chest Physicians, Am. Coll. Allergy, Asthma, and Immunology (chmn. local, state and regional allergy socs. 1984-86, vice-spkr. ho. of dels. 1988-91, spkr. 1991-94, mem. bd. regents 1991-94), Am. Acad. Allergy and Immunology (bd. govs. Fedn. SLR Socs. 1992—, chmn. physicians pub. svc. coun. 1994—), Am. Assn. Clin. Immunology and Allergy, Am. Assn. Cert. Allergists; mem. AMA, Am. Lung Assn. of Colo. (chmn. com. profl. edn. Pikes Peak regional coun. 1984-87, v.p. 1985-87, pres. 1987-89, bd. dirs. nat. assn. 1987-93, mem. exec. coun. 1990-92, treas. 1991-92, Pres. award 1990, Asthma Rsch. and Vol. Svcs. award Pikes Peak chpt. 1993), Colo. Med. Soc. (mem. jud. coun. 1987-89, bd. dirs. 1989—), Colo. Allergy Soc. (mem. exec. coun. 1981-85, sec./treas. 1981-82, pres. 1982-84), Western Soc. Allergy and Immunology (mem. exec. coun. 1987-95, sec./treas. 1989-90, 94-95, pres.-elect 1990-92, pres. 1992-93), El Paso County Med. Soc. (alt. del. to Colo. Med. Soc., 1981-83, del. 1984-87, mem. exec. coun. 1989—, chmn. med./legal com. 1989-90, chmn. credentials com. 1990-91, v.p. 1990-91, pres.-elect 1991-92, chmn. physicians/nurse collaborative com. 1992-93, pres. 1992-93), Medallion Soc., Phi Delta Epsilon, Phi Beta Kappa. Home: 312 Lake Ave Colorado Springs CO 80906 Office: 2709 N Tejon St Colorado Springs CO 80907-6231

NATHANSON, JOSEPH S., media relations company executive; b. N.Y.C., June 23, 1930; s. Abraham I and Rachel (Holtzberg) N.; divorced; 1 child, Julie. BA, Hobart Coll., Geneva, N.Y., 1952; postgrad., Oxford U., 1953, UCLA, 1970-93. Reporter, editor Reuters Ltd., N.Y.C., UN and London, 1952-57; pub. info. and pub. rels. profl. N.Y. Stock Exch., N.Y.C., 1957-59; account exec., v.p., dir. West Coast ops. Ruder & Finn, N.Y.C. and L.A., 1959-75; chmn. Working Press, Inc., Santa Monica, Calif., 1975—. Mem. Pub. Rels. Soc. Am., L.A. Press Club, Los Angeles County Mus. Art, B'nai B'rith, French Am. C. of C. Office: Working Press Inc 2525 Main St Santa Monica CA 90405-3517

NATHANSON, THEODORE HERZL, aeronautical engineer, architect; b. Montreal, Que., Can., Apr. 20, 1923; came to U.S., 1949; naturalized, 1983; s. Henry and Minnie (Goldberg) N.; student McGill U., 1940-42; SB in Aero. Engring., MIT, 1944; MArch, Harvard U., 1955. Research engr. Noorduyn Aviation Ltd., Montreal, 1944-45; stress engr. Canadair Ltd., Montreal, 1945-46; structural engr. A.V. Roe (Can.) Ltd., Malton, Ont., 1946-47; with Mies van der Rohe, Chgo., summer 1949, R. Buckminster Fuller, Forest Hills, N.Y., summer 1951; cons. engr. and architect, Montreal, Boston, Los Angeles, 1955—; mem. tech. staff Rockwell Internat., 1979-92, structural analysis and advanced design Space Transp. Systems div., Downey, Calif., 1979-86, mission ops. and advanced concepts Space Sta. Systems div., 1986-87, space sta. elec. power system Rocketdyne div., Canoga Park, Calif., 1987-92; cons. Aerospace Engr., L.A., 1992—; lectr. architecture, McGill U., 1967-68. Fellow Brit. Interplanetary Soc.; mem. Order Engrs. Que., Order Architects Que., Soc. Am. Registered Architects, Nat. Soc. Profl. Engrs., AIAA, AIA (assoc.), Royal Archtl. Inst. Can., Nat. Mgmt. Assn., Copley Soc. of Boston, MIT Club of So. Calif. (bd. govs.), Can. Soc. (Los Angeles). Projects and models included in group shows: Mus. Fine Arts, Springfield, Mass., 1961, N.Y. World's Fair, 1965, Winterfest, Boston, 1966, Boston Artists' Project '70. Jewish. Home: 330 Cliff Dr # 208 Laguna Beach CA 92651

NATHWANI, BHARAT NAROTTAM, pathologist, consultant; b. Bombay, Jan. 20, 1945; came to U.S., 1972; s. Narottam Pragji and Bharati N. (Lakhani) N. MBBS, Grant Med. Coll., Bombay, 1969, MD in Pathology, 1972. Intern Grant Med. Coll., Bombay U., 1968-69; asst. prof. pathology Grant Med. Coll., 1972; fellow in hematology Cook County Hosp., Chgo., 1972-73; resident in pathology Rush U., Chgo., 1973-74; fellow in hematopathology City of Hope Med. Ctr., Duarte, Calif., 1975-76, pathologist, 1977-84; prof. pathology, chief hematopathology U. So. Calif., L.A., 1984—. Contbr. numerous articles to profl. jours. Recipient Grant awards Nat. Libr. Medicine, Bethesda, Md., Nat. Cancer Inst., 1991. Mem. AAAS, Internat. Acad. Pathology, Am. Soc. Clin. Pathology, Am. Soc. Hematology, Am. Soc. Oncology. Office: U So Calif Sch Medicine HMR 209 2011 Zonal Ave Los Angeles CA 90033-1034

NAUGHTEN, ROBERT NORMAN, pediatrician; b. Stockton, Calif., Oct. 13, 1928; s. Norman Stafford and Junetta (Doherty) N.; m. Ann Louise Charkins, June 26, 1954; children: Robert James, Annette Marie Naughten-Dessel, Patricia Louise Schoof. AA, San Jose City Coll., San Jose, Calif., 1948; BA, U. Calif., Berkeley, 1950; MA, Stanford U., 1955; MD, Hahnemann U., 1959. Lic. physician and surgeon, Calif. Intern Highland-Alameda County Hosp., Oakland, Calif., 1959-60; rsch. fellow Nat. Cancer Inst., Stanford, Calif., 1960-61; resident pediat. Stanford Med. Ctr., 1961-63; pvt. practice specializing in pediat. Los Gatos, Calif., 1963—; instr. Santa Clara Valley Med. Ctr., San Jose, 1963—, Dept. of Pediat., Stanford, 1963-73; cons. drug abuse San Jose Police Dept., 1963-68; cons. child abuse Dist. Atty., San Jose, 1984—; cons. dept. social svcs. State of Calif., 1989—. Contbr. articles to profl. jours. Bd. dirs., v.p. Outreach and Escort, Inc., San Jose, 1985-88. Named Alumnus of Yr. San Jose City Coll., 1967, Chef of the West Sunset Mag., 1989; fellow Coll. of Physicians, Phila., 1986. Mem. AMA, Calif. Assn., Santa Clara Med. Assn. (v.p. 1986-88), Am. Acad. Pediatrics, Am. Acad. Allergy and Clin. Immunology, Calif. Alumni Assn. (Berkeley), Stanford Alumni Assn., Commonwealth Club (San Francisco), Soc. of the Sigma Xi. Democrat. Roman Catholic. Home: 13601 Riverdale Dr Saratoga CA 95070-5229 Office: 777 Knowles Dr Ste 14 Los Gatos CA 95030-1417

NAUGLE, CHARLOTTE JUNE, principal, educator; b. Long Beach, Calif., June 1, 1938; d. Robert F. and Florence A. (Smith) Ballenger; A.A., San Bernardino Valley Coll., 1959; BA, Calif. State U., 1966, MA, 1978; children: Roberta Lynn, Marina Rae. Tchr., Barstow (Calif.) Sch. Dist., 1966, U.S. Dependent Sch., Kenitra, Morocco, 1967-69; tchr., bilingual coordinator, state demonstration tchr. Colton (Calif.) Sch. Dist., 1970-81, state compensation project dir., 1981-83; prin. Smith Demonstration Sch., Bloomington, Calif., 1984-87, Walter Zimmerman Sch., Bloomington, 1987-94, Wilson Elem. Sch., Colton, Calif., 1994—; ednl. cons.; extension instr. U. Calif., Riverside, 1975-77. Pub. edn. chmn. San Bernardino-Riverside Counties, Am. Cancer Soc., 1979-81; bd. dir. Cedar House Rehab. Ctr.; steering com. Island Empire Quality Improvement Network. Recipient, Able Toastmasters award, 1982; Outstanding Tchr. of Writing award Inland Area Writing Project, U. Calif., Riverside, 1980. Mem. Nat. Assn. Exec. Women, Assn. Supervision and Curriculum Devel., Mgmt. Assn. Colton Educators (pres. 1990), Assn. Calif. Sch. Adminstrs. (sec. region 12 1992-93), Phi Delta Kappa. Republican. Club: Toastmasters (internat. pres. 1980, div. ednl. v.p. 1981). Home: 25590 Prospect Ave Apt 41E Loma Linda CA 92354-3154 Office: 750 S 8th St Colton CA 92324-3573

NAULIN, JOHN ARTHUR, entertainment company executive; b. Euclid, Ohio, Mar. 21, 1956; s. Arthur Arnold and Verne Lou Naulin; m. Shayna Lin Klickstein, Jan. 3, 1976; children: Daniel Patrick, Juliet Christine. AA in Theatre arts, Phoenix (Ariz.) Coll., 1976; student, Sherwood Oaks Coll., Hollywood, Calif., 1978. Mgr. Shop of 1000 Faces Universal Studios, Inc., University City, Calif., 1976-78; supr. R&D Don Post Studios, Inc., North Hollywood, Calif., 1978-83; owner M.T.S.D. Design, Granada Hills, Calif., 1983—; supr. 3-D design Landmark Entertainment, North Hollywood, 1989-92; co-owner M.B.C. Entertainment, Oxnard, Calif., 1993-95; supr. practical design and devel. Santa Monica (Calif.) Pictures, 1996—; design cons. Walt disney Imagineering, Burbank, Calif., 1990, Sci-Fi Cafe, Inc., Thousand Oaks, Calif., 1995-96; design submissions to NASA Mars Program, Washington, 1990. West Coast editor: Questar, 1983-85; scriptwriter Ghosts, 1986, Magic and Mischief, 1987, The Wolf Pack, 1987, Soapbox, 1989, Scared Witless, 1995; co-scriptwriter Corporate States, 1990, The Oath, 1994. Float design and coun. mem. YMCA, Thousand Oaks, 1996. Recipient Tech. Achievement award for film spl. effects Canne Film Festival, 1985; named Hon. Congl. Mem. U.S. Congress, 1972. Republican. Home: 133 Hope Rd Newbury Park CA 91320 Office: Santa Monica Pictures 3025 Olympic Blvd Santa Monica CA 90404

NAVA, CYNTHIA D., state legislator. BS, Western Ill. U.; MA, Ea. Ill. U. Dep. supt. Gadsden Schools; mem. N.Mex. Senate; mem. rules com., fin. com. Home: 3002 Broadmoor Dr Las Cruces NM 88001-7501 Office: N Mex Senate State Capitol Santa Fe NM 87503*

NAVA, YOLANDA MARGOT, public relations and communications consultant; b. L.A., Nov. 23, 1944; d. Roberto Nava and Consuelo (Chavira) Stepsis; m. Art Torres, May, 1975 (div. July 1993); children: Joaquin Nava Torres, Danielle Nava Torres. BA, UCLA, 1967, postgrad., 1968-70. Credentialed C.C. educator. Tchr. h.s. L.A. Unified Sch. Dist., 1968-70; instr. sociology Santa Monica (Calif.) Coll., 1970-71; project dir. Neighborhood Youth Corps United Way, L.A., 1971-73; career opportunity devel. specialist Calif. State Univs.-Colls., L.A., 1973-74; host "Impacto" KNBC-TV, Burbank, Calif., 1973-74; prodr., host "Saturday" KNBC-TV, Burbank, 1974-75, co-host "Sunday", 1983-85; news anchor, reporter KTXL-TV, Sacramento, Calif., 1977-79, KXTV-TV, Sacramento, 1979-81; west coast reporter, nat. host "Latin Tempo" La Raza Prodn. Ctr., Washington, 1983-86; news reporter, host "2-the-Point" KCBS-TV, L.A., 1987-89; v.p., owner Ponce Nicasio Broadcasting, Inc./KCMY Channel 29, Sacramento, 1990-95; cons. pub. info. L.A. Unified Sch. Dist., 1990—. Author: Chicanas in the Media, 1981, Hispanics in the Media, 1986; weekly columnist Eastern Group Publs., L.A., 1995—; columnist Eastern Group Publs. Bd. dirs. YWCA Greater L.A., 1993—, L.A. Area Boy Scout Coun., 1992—, Bella Lewitsky Dance Co., L.A., 1991—; mem. adv. com. L.A. Chamber Orch., 1992—. Recipient Emmy award Acad. TV Arts & Scis., 1988; named one of 5 Women of Achievement, L.A. Times, 1986, one of 25 Top Hispanic Leaders, L.A. Herald Examiner, 1983, one of 100 Top Women in Calif., 1983. Mem. Trusteeship for Women, Women in Film, Nat. Assn. Hispanic Journalists, Calif. Coun. Adult Educators, Comision Femenil Mexicana Nacional (founder, pres. 1973-75). Democrat. Mem. Ch. Religious Sci. Office: Eastern Group Publs 2500 S Atlantic Blvd Bldg B Los Angeles CA 90040-2004

NAVARRO, EDWARD, historic site administrator. Dist. supt. Old Town San Diego State Park. Office: c/o San Diego Coast Dist 9609 Naples Ste 2000 San Diego CA 92121

NAVARRO, MANUEL, protective services official; b. Oakland, Calif.. AA in Fire Sci., BA in Pub. Adminstrn. Cert. master fire instr., Colo. Fire fighter, 1966-67, Lawrence Radiation Lab. Fire Dept., 1967-72; various positions to asst. chief Oakland (Calif.) Fire Dept., 1972-93; fire chief Colorado Springs (Colo.) Fire Dept., 1993—; mem. FEMA Urban Search and Rescue Mgmt. and Control Com. Mem. Mex.-Am. Polit. Assn. (chairperson). Office: Colorado Springs Fire Dept 31 S Weber St Colorado Springs CO 80903-1913*

NAVRATIL, GREG ALLAN, artist; b. Denver, Oct. 14, 1946; s. Hans and Mollie (Schell) N.; m. Judith Winifred Leonard, Jan. 2, 1986. BFA, Met. State Coll., Denver, 1974. Former signpainter, screenprinter, book illustrator, art dir.; artist-in-residence Rocky Mountain Nat. Park, 1995. One-man shows Nat. Ctr. for Atmospheric Rsch., Boulder, Colo., 1993, U. Mont., 1996, Courthouse Gallery, 1997, Koelbel Libr., 1997; 2-person show The Lincoln Ctr., Ft. Collins, Colo., 1993; exhibited in over 40 group shows, including Nat. Arts Festival, Louisville, Colo., 1991, Arts for Parks, Jackson Hole, Wyo., 1991, 93, Colo. State Fair, Pueblo, 1992, 93, Fremont Ctr. for Arts, Canon City, Colo., Contemporary Realism V, Scottsdale, Ariz., Confluence, Ingram, Tex., 1994, Salon Internat., Jackson, Miss., 1994, The New West Sangri de Cristo Arts Ctr., Pueblo, Colo., 1996; represented in numerous corp. and pvt. collections, including Texaco, Adams Mark Hotels; represented by Saxon Mountain Gallery, 1/1 Gallery, Max'ims Galleries. With U.S. Army, 1963-66. Recipient hon. mention 7-State Regional, Cheyenne, 1990, best of show and hon. mention, 1991, 2d place and hon. mention, 1992, merit award Nat. Arts Festival, 1991, purchase award Am. Realism 91, 1992, jurors award 45th Ann., Central City, Colo., 1992, jurors choice award 46th Ann., 1993, hon. mention Santa Fe Trail Art Show, Trinidad, Colo., 1991, meritorious award Colo. State Fair, 1991, 3d place and People's Choice awards Fremont Ctr. for Arts, 1993, purchase award 33d Ann., 1993, Top award Artist's Mag., 1993, Top 100, Arts for the Parks, 1995. Home and Studio: 6801 W Eldorado Pl Lakewood CO 80227-5206

NAYLOR, BRUCE GORDON, museum director; b. Midale, Sask., Can., Aug. 19, 1950; s. John Raymond Naylor and Mary Lynn (Frisby) Redeberg; m. Marlene Johnstone, Dec. 19, 1981 (dec. July 1992); m. Judith Jeune, June 11, 1994; 1 child: John Raymond. BS with high honors, U. Sask., 1972; PhD, U. Alta., 1978. Postdoctoral fellow U. Toronto, Ont., 1978-80; lectr. U. Calif., Berkeley, 1979; asst. prof. U. Alta., Edmonton, 1980-82; curator Tyrrell Mus., Drumheller, Alta., 1982-86; asst. dir. Royal Tyrrell Mus., Drumheller, 1986-92, dir., 1992—; adj. prof. U. Alta., 1983—; sen. U. Calgary, Alta., 1989-90; bd. dirs. Yoho-Burgess Shale Rsch. Found. Contbr. articles to sci. publs. Operating grantee Nat. Sci. & Engring. Rsch. Coun., Ottawa, 1981-82. Fellow Geol. Assn. Can.; mem. Soc. Vertebrate Paleontology, Rotary Club Drumheller. Office: Royal Tyrrell Mus, Box 7500, Drumheller, AB Canada T0J 0Y0

NAYLOR-JACKSON, JERRY, public relations consultant, retired, entertainer; b. Chalk Mountain, Tex., Mar. 6, 1939; s. William Guy and Mary Bernice (Lummus) Jackson; m. Pamela Ann Robinson, Jan. 30, 1966; children: Geoffrey K. Naylor, Kelli A. Naylor-Dobazinski, Gregory K. Naylor. Grad., Elkins Electronics Inst., Dallas, 1957; student, U. Md., Fed. Republic of Germany, 1957-58. Life first class radio/TV engring. lic. FCC. Broadcaster various local TV and AM radio stas., San Angelo, Texas, 1955-57; mem. Buddy Holly and the Crickets, 1960-65, lead singer, 1960-65; solo entertainer, performer, recording artist and producer, 1965-87; sr. v.p. corp. devel. Newslink Internat. Satellite Broadcast Comms. Co., Inc., Washington, 1986-88; pres. Internat. Syndications, Inc. subs. Newslink, Inc., Washington, 1986-88; pres., CEO, owner The Jerry Naylor Co., McMinnville, Oreg., 1984—; v.p. capital programs, sr. cons. Calif. Luth. Univ., Thousand Oaks, 1990-92; sr. cons., dir. ann. fund Calif. Luth. U., 1989-90; polit./media cons. various Rep. candidates and orgns., 1968-93; spl. cons. to Violeta Barrios de Chamarro, Pres. of Republic of Nicaragua, 1990-92; disc jockey Sta. KHEY-AM, Sta. KINT-AM, El Paso, Tex., 1959; on-air personality Sta. KRLA-AM, Sta. KDAY-AM, L.A., 1960; on-air disc jockey, air personality, celebrity host KLAC-AM, L.A., 1974-83; on-camera and voice-over spokesman for Safeway Stores, Inc., Avis Rent-a-Car, Mut. of Omaha, Wrigley Co., 1968-83; U.S. presdl. appointee, chmn. Job Tng. Partnership Act work group/youth at risk subcom. Nat. Commn. for Employment Policy, 1985-91; nat. dir. spl. events Reagan for Pres., 1979-81; apptd. mem. commn. for employment policy Pres. Ronald Reagan, 1985-91. Recording artist maj. labels including CBS Records, Motown Records, Warner Bros. Records, EMI Records, 1965-84; host weekly nat. and internat. radio program Continental Country (Number 1 syndicated country music radio show in Am., Billboard Mag., Country Music Assn., 1974), (weekly variety show) Music City, USA, 1966-67. Nat. dir. spl. events Reagan for Pres., 1975-76, 79-80; sr. cons. to White House, 1981-88, 89-92. With U.S. Army, 1957-58. Named to Top 40 Male Vocalists of Yr., Billboard Mag., 1970, named #1 Rock Group (Crickets), Billboard Mag./New Musical Express Mag., 1958, 62. Mem. NARAS, Country Music Assn., Acad. Country Music (Telly award for TV documentary 1991, 92), Phi Kappa Phi (alumni). Home and Office: Jerry Naylor Co 1279 SW Russ Ln Mcminnville OR 97128 *Know no boundaries. Experience the world and become enriched from its varied inhabitants.*

NAZAIRE, MICHEL HARRY, physician; b. Jérémie, Haiti, Sept. 29, 1939; s. Joseph and Hermance N.; m. Nicole N., Dec. 28, 1968 (div.); children: Hanick and Carline (twins). *Daughters Carline and Hanick, born in 1970, are living in New York: Carline is currently employed as administrative assistant by Rheinbraun Thyssen Inc.; Hanick is a student at City College, studying education-early childhood.* Grad., Coll. St. Louis de Gonzague, 1959; MD Faculty of Medicine and Pharmacology, State U. Haiti, 1966. Intern, State U. Hosp., Port-Au-Prince, Haiti, 1965-66; resident physician Sanitarium, Port-Au-Prince, Haiti, 1966-68; practice medicine specializing in pneumology, 1966-68; practice medicine specializing in pneumo-physiology, Port-Au-Prince, 1966—; physician fellow Klinik Havelhohe, West Berlin, 1969-70, 89-91; attending physician Sanitarium, Port-Au-Prince, 1976-91. Dep. mem. Internat. Parliament for Safety and Peace; envoy-at-large Internat. State Parliament; mem. global environ. technol. network Who. Contbr. articles to Jour. Indsl. Hygiene, Pneumology and Respiratory Protection. Fellow Internat. Soc. for Respiratory Protection, Am. Coll. Chest Physicians (assoc.); mem. Am. Pub. Health Assn., Am. Conf. Govtl. Indsl. Hygienists, Internat. Union Against Tuberculosis, Internat. Platform Assn. Address: 6407 S 12th St Apt 1711 Tacoma WA 98465 also: 1115-25 Dorchester Rd #3C Brooklyn NY 11218

NAZZARO, DAVID ALFRED, sales executive; b. Malden, Mass., Sept. 15, 1940; s. Alfred Anthony and Louise (Cunningham) N.; m. Jane Valentine, June 26, 1971; one child, David Thomas. BME, U.S. Mcht. Marine Acad., 1962; MS, Columbia U., 1965; MBA, Pepperdine U., 1975. Regional mgr. Turbo Power and Marine Systems divsn. United Techs., Hardford, Conn., 1965-74; mgr. bus. devel S & Q Corp., San Francisco, 1974-78; v.p. and gen. mgr. Con-Val, Oakland, Calif., 1978-85; pres. and chief exec. officer Dasa Controls, Belmont, Calif., 1985-87; mgr. bus. devel Johnson Yokogawa Corp., San Francisco, 1987-94; ptnr. Alexander Mortgage, Mortgage Banker, San Carlos, Calif., 1994—; bd. dirs. Peninsula Exch. Contbr. papers to profl. publs. Bd. dirs. Clearview Homeowners Assn., San Mateo, 1976; pres. St. Bartholomew's Parish Council, San Mateo, 1986. Lt. USNR, 1963-69. Sr. Mem. Instrument Soc. Am. (pres. No. Calif. Sec. 1987-88); mem. ASME, Am. Water Works Assn., Elks, Jaycees, St. Bartholomew's Mens Club (pres. 1977). Home: 30 Tollridge Ct San Mateo CA 94402-3730

NEACSU, MARIA, artist; b. Manoleasa, Romania, Aug. 15, 1948; d. Ioan and Valeria (Busuioc) Grosu; m. Marius C. Neacsu, Aug. 15, 1970; 1 child, George Mircea. BSBA, Acad. Econ. Study, Bucharest, 1973; BS in Art, U. Calif., Berkeley, 1993; MFA, U. Calif., 1995. Econ. Iprochim, Bucharest, 1973-81; sr. acct. Bechtel, Inc., San Francisco, 1981-83; acctg. mgr. West Mgmt. Co., Oakland, Calif., 1983-86; sr. acct. Kaiser Engring. Inc., Oakland, 1986-89; artist Walnut Creek, Calif., 1989—. Jack K. and Gertrude Murphy fine arts fellow San Francisco Found., 1994. Republican. Home: 505 Pimlico Ct Walnut Creek CA 94596-3677

NEAL, JAMES MADISON, JR., retired editor and educator; b. Oklahoma City, Aug. 6, 1925; s. James Madison and Tillie Belle (Milliken) N.; m. Caroline Dorothy Becker (dec. Dec. 1974); children: Charles, James W., Jody, Carolyn. BA, U. Colo., 1949; MA, S.D. State U., 1970. Editor various newspapers, Colo., Nebr. and Okla., 1949-59; wire editor Rapid City Journal, Rapid City, S.D., 1959-67; instr. S.D. State U., Brookings, S.D., 1967-71; asst. prof. U. Nebr., Lincoln, 1971-73, assoc. prof., 1973-90; S.D. chmn. AP Mng. Editors Assn., 1962-64. Mem. ACLU (bd. dirs. Nebr. affiliate 1979-82, Ariz. affiliate 1994), VFW, Soc. Profl. Journalists, Investigative Reporters and Editors. Unitarian. Home: Apt 7207 4700 N Kolb Rd Tucson AZ 85750-6187

NEAL, MICHAEL RENN, software engineer; b. Augusta, Ga., June 15, 1960; s. James Allen and Grace (Runyan) N.; m. Teresa Jean Schreibeis, Apr. 7, 1990; 1 child, Rianna Michele. BS in Computer Sci., U. S.C., 1983. Sr. software engr. Lockheed Corp., Burbank, Calif., 1983-90, Auto-trol Tech., Thornton, Colo., 1992-93; sr. applications engr. Template Graphics Software, San Diego, 1990-92; project dir. software devel. CogniSeis Devel., Boulder, Colo., 1993-95; sr. mem. tech. staff CADIS, Inc., Boulder, 1995—; instr. Xhibition Conf., San Jose, Calif., 1993-94. Contbr. articles to profl. jours. State treas. S.C. Young Reps., 1980; chmn. Lexington County (S.C.) Young Reps., 1980. Mem. Assn. for Computing Machinery (spl. interest group on graphics 1987-95, spl. interest group on human computer interface 1993—, course organizer and instr. SIGGRAPH Conf. 1994). Office: CADIS Inc 1909 26th St Boulder CO 80302

NEAL, PHILIP MARK, diversified manufacturing executive; b. San Diego, Aug. 28, 1940; s. Philip Mark and Florence Elizabeth (Anderson) N.; children: Brian, Kevin. B.A., Pomona Coll., 1962; M.B.A., Stanford U., 1964. Mgr. financial planning and analysis CBS, Hollywood, 1964-66; cons. McKinsey & Co., Los Angeles, 1966-73; v.p., controller Avery Internat. Corp., Los Angeles, 1974-78; sr. v.p. fin. Avery Internat. Corp., Pasadena, 1979-88, group v.p. materials group, 1988-90; exec. pres. Avery Internat. Corp., 1990, pres., chief operating officer, 1990—; bd. dirs. Ind. Colls. of So. Calif. Trustee Pomona Coll; gov. Town Hall of Calif. Bd. Govs. Mem. Fin. Execs. Inst. Republican. Episcopalian. Office: Avery Dennison Corp PO Box 7090 150 N Orange Grove Blvd Pasadena CA 91103*

NEARY, PATRICIA ELINOR, ballet director; b. Miami, Fla.; d. James Elliott and Elinor (Mitsitz) N. Corps de ballet Nat. Ballet of Can., Toronto, Ont., 1957-60; prin. dancer N.Y.C. Ballet, 1960-68; ballerina Geneva Ballet (Switzerland), 1968-70, ballet dir., 1973-78; guest artist Stuttgart Ballet, Germany, 1968-70; asst. ballet dir., ballerina West Berlin Ballet, 1970-73; ballet dir. Zurich Ballet (Switzerland), 1978-86, La Scala di Milano ballet co., Italy, 1986-88; tchr., Balanchine ballets, Balanchine Trust, 1987—.

NEBELKOPF, ETHAN, psychologist; b. N.Y.C., June 13, 1946; s. Jacob and Fannie (Carver) N.; m. Karen Horrocks, July 27, 1976; children: Demian David, Sarah Dawn. BA, CCNY, 1966; MA, U. Mich., 1969; PhD, Summit U., 1989. Social worker Project Headstart, N.Y.C., 1965; coord. Project Outreach, Ann Arbor, 1968-69; program dir. White Bird Clinic, Eugene, Oreg., 1971-75; counseling supr. Teledyne Econ. Devel. Corp., San Diego, 1976-79; dir. planning and edn. Walden House, San Francisco, 1979-89, dir. tng., 1990-93; program evaluator United Indian Nations, Oakland, Calif., 1994-96; clin. dir. Indian Health Ctr. Santa Clara Valley, San Jose, Calif., 1997—; adj. prof. dept. social work San Francisco State U., 1982-87; cons. Berkeley (Calif.) Holistic Health Ctr., 1979-84, Medicine Wheel Healing Co-op, San Diego, 1976-79; alternate del. Nat. Free Clinic Coun., Eugene, 1972-74. Author: White Bird Flies to Phoenix, 1973, The New Herbalism, 1980, The Herbal Connection, 1981, Hope Not Dope, 1990. Mem. Mayor's Task Force on Drugs, San Francisco, 1988; mem. treatment com. Gov.'s Policy Coun. on Drugs, Sacramento, 1989; task force Human Svcs. Tng., Salem, Oreg., 1972; organizer West Eugene Bozo Assn., 1973; founder Green Psychology, 1993. Named Outstanding Young Man of Am., U.S. Jaycees, 1980; recipient Silver Key, House Plan Assn., 1966. Fellow Am. Orthopsychiat. Assn.; mem. Calif. Assn. Family Therapists, World Fedn. of Therapeutic Communities, Nat. Writer's Club, N.Y. Acad. Scis., Internat. Assn. for Human Rels. Lab. Tng., Calif. Assn. of Drug Programs and Profls. (pres. 1988-90), Phi Beta Kappa. Office: 6641 Simson St Oakland CA 94605-2220

NECHIS, BARBARA, artist; b. Mt. Vernon, N.Y., Sept. 25, 1937; d. Rudolph and Anna (Sincoff) Friedman; m. Malvin Nechis, June 22, 1958 (div. 1982); children—Barry, Steven, Sharon; m. Andrew D'Anneo, Oct. 22, 1988. B.A., U. Rochester, 1959; M.S., Alfred U. Mem. faculty Parsons Sch. Design, N.Y.C., 1980-92; condr. watercolor workshops for museums, arts groups and colls including Pratt Inst., N.Y., U. Alaska, Am. Acad. Art, Chgo.; juror Watercolor West, Mid-West Watercolor, Nat. Arts Club, Am. Watercolor Soc. Exhibited one-woman shows including: New Sch.-Parsons Sch. Design, 1984; group shows include: Am. Watercolor Soc., Canton Mus., Ohio, 1985; represented in permanent collecion Butler Inst. Am. Art. Author: Watercolor, The Creative Experience, 1979, Watercolor From the Heart, 1993. Mem. Am. Watercolor Soc. (bd. dirs. 1983-86) Lena Newcastle award 1985. Home and Studio: 1085 Dunaweal Ln Calistoga CA 94515-9799

NEE, CHRISTOPHER CHI-HUANG, computer software engineer; b. Taipei, Taiwan, Apr. 4, 1951; came to U.S., 1994; s. Yen-Yuan and Shu-Yuan (Cheng) N.; m. Pauline B. Jaw, June 6, 1991; 1 child, Jasmine. BS in Chemistry, Nat. Chung-Hsing U., 1974; MS in Organic Chemistry, Wash. State U., 1979; postgrad., Ohio State U., 1983; MS in Computer Sci., Tex. A&M U., 1985. Patent exam. officer Organic Synthesis divsn. Nat. Bur. Patents, Taipei, 1974-77; software sys. engr. Columbia Presbyn. Med. Ctr., N.Y.C., 1985-87, Commodore Electronics Ltd., Taipei, 1987-89; sr. software engr. Chroma Ate Inc., Taipei, 1989-91, Leegood Automatic Sys. Inc., Taipei, 1991-94; founder, ind. cons. SESC, Santa Clara, 1004—. Author: Introductin to DCS, 1987. Chinese cultural and natural sci. scholar Republic of China Govt., 1975. Office: 2537 Rose Way Santa Clara CA 95051-5331

NEEDHAM, CAROL ANN, lawyer, educator; b. Chgo., Nov. 1, 1957; d. Robert Michael and Loretta Ann (Grabowy) Needham; m. Thomas Joseph Timmermann, July 23, 1994. BA in English, Northwestern U., 1979, JD, 1985; MA in English, U. Va., 1982. Bar: Calif. 1987, D.C. 1990, Ill. 1985. Jud. law clk. U.S. Dist. Ct., Honolulu, 1985-86; atty. Gibson, Dunn & Crutcher, L.A., 1986-90, Chadbourne & Parke, L.A., 1990-91; prof. law St. Louis U. Sch. Law, 1992—. Contbr. articles to profl. jours. Chair scholarship com. Verbum Dei H.S., L.A., 1987-95. Mem. ABA, Ctrl. States Law Assn. (treas. 1995-96, v.p. 1996-97), Mo. Bar (vice chair com. on lawyers' advt. 1995—), Am. Assn. Law Schs. (profl. responsibility exec. com. 1995—). Office: St Louis U Sch Law 3700 Lindell Blvd Saint Louis MO 63108

NEEDLEMAN, JACOB, philosophy educator, writer; b. Phila., Oct. 6, 1934; s. Benjamin and Ida (Seltzer) N.; m. Carla Satzman, Aug. 30, 1959 (div. 1989); children: Raphael, Eve; m. Gail Anderson, Dec. 1990. BA, Harvard U., 1956; grad., U. Freiburg, 1957-58; PhD, Yale U., 1961. Clin. psychology trainee West Haven (Conn.) Veterans Hosp. Adminstrn., 1960-61; rsch. assoc. Rockefeller Inst., N.Y., 1961-62; from asst. prof. to assoc. prof. philosophy San Francisco State U., 1962-66, prof philosophy, 1967—, chair dept. philosophy, 1968-69; vis. scholar Union Theol. Seminary, 1967-68; dir. Ctr. Study New Religions, 1977-83; lectr. psychiatry, cons. med. ethics U. Calif., 1981-84. Author: Being-in-the-World, 1963, The New Religions, 1970, Religion for a New Generation, 1973, A Sense of the Cosmos, 1975, On the Way to Self-Knowledge: Sacred Tradition and Psychotherapy, 1976, Lost Christianity, 1980, Consciousness and Tradition, 1982, The Heart of Philosophy, 1982, Sorcerers, 1986, Sin and Scientism, 1986, Lost Christianity: A Journey of Rediscovery to the Centre of Christian Experience, 1990, Money and the Meaning of Life, 1991, Modern Esoteric Spirituality, 1992, The Way of the Physician, 1993, The Indestructible Question, 1994, A Little Book on Love, 1996; (trans.) The Primary World of Senses, 1963, Essays on Ego Psychology, 1964; editor Care of Patients with Fatal Illness, 1969, The Sword of Gnosis, 1973, Sacred Tradition and Present Need, 1974, Understanding the New Religions, 1978, Speaking of My Life: The Art of Living in the Cultural Revolution, 1979, Real Philosophy: An Anthology of the Universal Search for Meaning, 1991; contbr. Death and Bereavement, 1969, To Live Within, 1971, My Life with a Brahmin Family, 1972, The New Man, 1972, The Universal Meaning of the Kabbalah, 1973, The Phenomenon of Death. Grantee Religion in Higher Edn., 1967-68, Marsden Found., Ella Lyman Cabot Trust, 1969, Marsda Found, Far West Inst., 1975; Fulbright scholar Germany, 1957-58; Fels Found. fellow Munich, 1959; fellow Rockefeller Found. Humanities, 1977-78. Office: San Francisco State U Dept Philosophy 1600 Holloway Ave San Francisco CA 94132-1722

NEELD, MICHAEL EARL, legislative staff administrator; b. Portland, Oreg., May 13, 1955; s. Carl Eugene and Frances Karlene (Riggers) N. BA in Journalism and Polit. Scis., U. Oreg., 1977. Advt. rep. Post Publs., Camas, Wash., 1977; chpt. cons. Kappa Sigma Internat. Fraternity, Charlottesville, Va., 1977-79; fundraising dir. Am. Cancer Soc., Richmond, Va., 1979-80; news editor, polit. rep. Sta. KYXI, Portland, 1980-84; comms. dir. Moshofsky for Congress, Portland, 1984; pub. info. officer Wash. State Ho. of Reps., Olympia, 1984-85; comms. dir. Paulus for Gov., Portland, 1985-86; sr. info. officer Wash. State Ho. of Reps., Olympia, 1986-91, rep. staff coord., 1991-96, pub. rels. coord., 1996—; founder, ptnr. Pacific N.W. Advocates Pub. Affairs Cons., Olympia, 1989—; instr. polit. strategy, tactics, fundraising and media Wash. State Rep. Party, Tukwila, 1991-92; campaign dir. House Rep. Orgnl. Com., Olympia, 1991-92. Recipient Best Coverage of Breaking News award Oreg. AP/Broadcast, 1982. Mem. U. Oreg. Alumni Assn., Trumpeters, City Club of Portland, Fremont Grove Soc. (founder), Indian Summer Golf and Country Club, Kappa Sigma (alumni, housing corp. bd. dirs. 1980-84). Presbyterian. Home: 7224 Deerfield Park Dr NE Olympia WA 98516 Office: Wash Ho of Reps 410 John L O'Brien Bldg PO Box 40600 Olympia WA 98504-0600

NEELEY, JAMES K., credit agency executive; b. Visalia, Calif., Dec. 4, 1955; s. James M. and Dorothy Neeley; m. Lynn Travioli, Aug. 13, 1977; children: Janessa, Jimmy. BS in Bus. Adminstrn., Calif. State U., Fresno, 1978. Lic. personal property appraiser. Loan officer Visalia Prodn. Credit Assn., Tipton, Calif., 1978-82; asst. br. mgr. Visalia (Calif.) Prodn. Credit Assn., 1982-83; v.p., br. mgr. Valley Prodn. Credit Assn., Visalia, 1983-91, Valley Farm Credit, Visalia, 1991—; advisor Redwood Future Farmers of Am., Visalia, 1988-90; advisor computer software devel. Western Farm Credit Bank, Sacramento, 1990-91; mem., advisor Kit Fox Adv. Com., Visalia, 1995-96. Mem. Ctrl. Dem. Com., Visalia, 1975-77; soccer coach Am. Youth Soccer Orgn., Tulare, Calif., 1990-96; coach Tulare Little League, 1996; parent vol. St. Alyosios Sch., Tulare, 1993-96; mem. coun. on fin., head audit com. Calif./Nev. United Meth., 1990-96; layleader Tulare United Meth. Ch., 1994-96, mem. adminstrv. bd., 1996—. Scholar So. Calif. Edn., 1974. Fellow Calif. Agrl. Leadership Program; mem. Tulare Host Lions Club (pres. 1982-83), Phi Kappa Phi. Office: Valley Farm Credit Svcs PO Box 4379 Visalia CA 93278

NEFF, FRANCINE IRVING (MRS. EDWARD JOHN NEFF), former federal government official; b. Albuquerque, Dec. 6, 1925; d. Edward Hackett and Georga (Henderson) Irving; m. Edward John Neff, June 7, 1948; children: Sindle, Edward Vann. AA, Cottey Coll., 1946; BA, U. N.Mex., 1948. Divsn. and precinct chmn. Republican Party, Albuquerque, 1966-71; mem. ctrl. com. Bernalillo County (N.Mex.) Republican Party, 1967-74, mem. exec. bd., 1968-70; mem. N.Mex. State ctrl. com. Republican Party, 1968-74, 77-82, mem. exec. bd., 1970-74, 81-83; Rep. nat. committeewoman State of N.Mex., 1970-74; also mem. exec. com.; Treas. of U.S. U.S. Dept. Treasury, Washington, 1974-77; nat. dir. U.S. Savs. Bonds, 1974-77; mktg. v.p. Rio Grande Valley Bank, Albuquerque, 1977-81; bd. dirs. La.-Pacific Corp., Portland, Oreg., D.R. Horton, Inc., Arlington, Tex. N.Mex. state adviser Teenage Reps., 1967-68; del. Rep. Nat. Conv., Miami, 1968, 72; campaign coord. Congressman Lujan of N.Mex., 1970; pres. Albuquerque Federated Rep. Women's Club, 1977; Leader Camp Fire Girls, Albuquerque, 1957-64; pres. Inez (N.Mex.) PTA, 1961; den mother Cub Scouts Am., Albuquerque, 1964-65; former mem. exec. bd. United Way of Albuquerque; former mem. adv. coun. Mgmt. Devel. Ctr., Robert O. Anderson Grad. Sch. Bus. and Adminstrv. Scis., U. N.Mex.; former mem. Def. Adv. Com. on Women in the Svcs., 1980-83; trustee Cottey Coll., Nevada, Mo., 1982-89. Recipient Exceptional Svc. award U.S. Dept. Treasury, 1976, Horatio Alger award Horatio Alger Assn. Disting. Americans, Inc., 1976. Mem. P.E.O. (pres. Albuquerque chpt. 1958-59, 63-64), Albuquerque City Panhellenic Assn. (pres. 1959-60), Greater Albuquerque C. of C. (bd. dirs. 1978-81), Alpha Delta Pi, Sigma Alpha Iota, Phi Kappa Phi, Pi Lambda Theta, Phi Theta Kappa. Episcopalian.

NEFF, JOHN, recording engineer, producer; b. Birmingham, Mich., Mar. 13, 1951; s. Robert Leslie Joseph and Mary Therese (McElvarr) N.; m. Nancy Louise Boocks, Aug. 29, 1987; children: Jennifer Lyn Neff, Bryan C. Groves, Kenneth John Neff. Student, Oakland Community Coll., Auburn Hills, Mich., 1970-72. Freelance recording artist, session musician Detroit, 1965-73; freelance record producer Toronto, Phoenix, L.A., 1974-79; radio announcer, engr. Stas. KVIB, KHEI, KMVI, KLHI, KAOI, 1981-88; record producer Maui Recorders, Kula, Hawaii, 1986-92; cons. studio design Roadrunner Audio Svcs., Glendale, Ariz., 1993—; rec. engr. for Walter Becker, Donald Fagen (Steely Dan), Buffy Ste Marie, Willie Nelson, Sagan Lewis; touring musician Detroit, Toronto, Phoenix, L.A., 1969-79; engring. cons. TEC & Ton, L.A.; studio monitor design for Kenny "Baby Face" Edmonds, Brian Austin Green; tech. cons. to David Lynch, Fox Scoring Stage. Recipient Grammy award nomination for Kamakiriad, 1994. Mem. ASCAP, Audio Engring Soc. (cert.), Am. Fedn. Musicians. Home and Office: Roadrunner Audio Svcs 23846 N 38th Dr Glendale AZ 85310-4113

NEGLEY, FLOYD ROLLIN, genealogist, retired army officer and civilian military employee; b. Ashland, Nebr., Apr. 26, 1924; s. Floyd Carroll and Margaret (Miners) N.; m. Teresa Mitsuko Ohashi, Mar. 12, 1954; children: Teresa Kei, Caroline Yumi. Japanese lang. student, U.S. Army Lang. Sch., Monterey, Calif., 1956-57; student in computer scis., U. Ariz., 1959-61; BS in Econs., Sophia U., Tokyo, 1965. Intelligence analyst U.S. Army, Tokyo, Okinawa, Japan, 1949-59; automated comm. maintenance officer U.S. Army, various cities, 1960-69; automated comm. analyst U.S. Army, Ft. Huachua, Ariz., 1970-92; genealogist Tucson, 1970—; advisor Armed Forces Comm.-Electronics Assn., Tokyo/Ft. Huachuca, 1961-92; computer advisor Japanese Army/Air Force, Tokyo, 1963-67; owner Japan Food Mart, Tucson, 1971-80; owner, property mgr. Negley Svcs., Tucson, 1970—. Author 5 books on Negley U.S. history and genealogy, 1986-88; author, indexer 2 books, 1994-96; translator (Japanese fiction) A Bamboo Doll, 1967. Pres. Pima-Cochise Commuters, Inc., Tucson, 1988, advisor, 1971-91; various offices Aztec Toastmasters, Tucson, 1992—, Thunder Mountain Toastmasters, Ft. Huachuca, 1982-91. Named Disting. Toastmaster, Toastmasters Internat., 1995, state 4-H champion, Nebr. 4-H Clubs, Lincoln, 1943. Mem. SAR, Ariz. Geneal. Soc. (pres. 1985-87, editor Copper State Bull. 1987—). Office: Negley Svcs PO Box 41984 Tucson AZ 85717

NEIL, J. MEREDITH, museum director; b. Boise, Ida., June 2, 1937; s. Carl Hurst and Ellen Addie (Hurt) N.; m. Virginia Mary Bivens, Aug. 16, 1958 (div. July 1992); children: John-Marcus Moore. AB, Yale U., 1959; MS, U. Wis., 1963; PhD, Wash. State U., 1966. Asst. prof. history Sam Houston State Coll., Huntsville, Tex., 1966-67; assoc. prof. Am. studies U. Hawaii, Honolulu, 1967-72; exec. dir. Idaho Bicentennial Commn., Boise, 1972-76; guest lectr. art history U. Victoria, B.C., 1976-77; city conservator Seattle, 1978-81; dir. Nicolaysen Art Mus., Casper, Wyo., 1983-89; realtor White-Riedel & Co., Boise, Idaho, 1992—. Author: Paradise Improved, 1972; Toward a National Taste, 1975; Saints and Odd Fellows, 1976; editor (with M. Fishwick): Popular Architecture, 1974; editor: Will James: THe Spirit of the Cowboy, 1985. Bd. dirs. KTWO Community Adv. Bd., Casper, 1984-85, Boise Allied Arts Council, 1975-76, Idaho Historic Sites Rev. Bd., 1974-79; mem. Wyo. Coun. Arts, 1985-89. Mem. Soc. Archtl. Historians, Popular Culture Assn., Democrat. Methodist Club: Morey's (New Haven). Home: 300 S Straughan Ave Apt 402 Boise ID 83701 Office: White-Riedel & Co 1500 W Bannock Boise ID 83702

NEILL, MARY GARDNER, museum administrator. Dir. Seattle Art Mus., Wash. Office: Seattle Art Museum PO Box 22000 Seattle WA 98122*

NEIMAN, TANYA MARIE, legal association administrator; b. Pitts., June 28, 1949; d. Max and Helen (Lamaga) N. AB, Mills Coll., 1970; JD, U. Calif. Hastings Coll. of Law, San Francisco, 1974. Bar: Calif. 1975. Law assoc. Boalt Hall U. Calif., Berkeley, 1974-76; pub. defender State of Calif., San Francisco, 1976-81; assoc. gen. counsel, dir. vol. legal services Bar Assn. San Francisco, 1982—; bd. dirs. Jack Berman Advocacy Ctr. Tanya Neiman Day proclaimed in her honor by Mayor of San Francisco, 1991; recipient Disting. Citizen award Harvard Club San Francisco, 1995, Kutka-Dodds prize Nat. Legal Aid and Defender Assn., 1996. Mem. ABA (mem. ABA Commn. on Homelessness 1993-96, speaker 1985—, Harrison Tweed award 1985), Calif. Bar Assn. (exec. com. 1984—, legal svcs. sect., chair steering com. State Bar Legal Corps), Golden Gate Bus. Assn. Found. (v.p. grant making 1985—), Nat. Conf. Women and Law (speaker 1975—), Nat. Lawyers Guild. Office: Bar Assn San Francisco 685 Market St San Francisco CA 94105-4200

NEIMANN, ALBERT ALEXANDER, mathematician, business owner; b. Torrington, Wyo., Nov. 29, 1939; s. Alexander and Lydia (Temple) N.; m. Barbara Jean Maw, May 6, 1962; children: Debbie, Todd, Amy, Kelly.. BA, Willamette U., 1967. Mathematician Keyport (Wash.) Naval Torpedo Sta., 1968-70; math. statistician Concord (Calif.) Naval Weapons Sta., 1970-85, engring. statistician, 1985-94; bus. owner Antioch Sports Cards and Collectibles, A&T Sports Cards, Calif., 1994—. Mgr. Little League Baseball, Antioch, Calif., 1977-84, Little League Softball, Antioch, 1984-87; Sunday sch. tchr. Grace Bapt. Ch., 1979-90; statistician Antioch H.S., 1985-89. Recipient Performance award Concord Naval Weapons Sta., 1978, 88-94. Mem. Am. Statis. Assn., Math. Assn. Am., Am. Soc. for Quality Control, Nat. Coun. Tchrs. Math. Office: Antioch Sports Cards & Collectibles 2550 Somersville Rd Ste 51 Antioch CA 94509-8704

NEINAS, CHARLES MERRILL, athletic association executive; b. Marshfield, Wis., Jan. 18, 1932; s. Arthur Oscar and Blanche Amelia (Reeder) N.; children: Andrew, Toby. B.S., U. Wis., 1957. Asst. exec. dir. Nat. Collegiate Athletic Assn., Kansas City, Mo., 1961-71; commr. Big Eight Conf., Kansas City, 1971-81; exec. dir. Coll. Football Assn., 1981—; Dr. Patricia L. Pacey prof. econs. U. Colo., Boulder, 1981—, econ. cons., 1981—; adviser Am. Football Coaches Assn., 1997—. Served with USNR, 1952-54. Home: 4977 Idylwild Trl Boulder CO 80301-3651 Office: College Football Assoc 6688 Gunpark Dr Boulder CO 80301-3372

NEINSTEIN, LAWRENCE STEVEN, physician, educator; b. L.A., Dec. 26, 1949; m. Debra Barak, Dec. 17, 1972; children: Yael, Aaron, David. BS, UCLA, L.A., 1971, MD, 1974. Diplomate Am. Bd. Internal Medicine, Am. Bd. Adolscent Medicine. Resident Cedars Sinai Med. Ctr., L.A., 1974-78; asst. prof. clin. pediatrics and medicine U. So. Calif., L.A., 1979-84, assoc. prof. clin. pediatrics and medicine, 1984-89, tenure assoc. prof. pediatrics and medicine, 1989—; assoc. dir. dovsn. adolscent medicine Children Hosp. L.A., 1988-95, mem. med. exec. com., 1994—; exec. dir. U. So. Calif. Univ. Park Health and Counseling Ctr., 1995—. Author: Adolescent Health Care Practical Guide, 3rd edit., 1996, Issues in Reproductive Health, 1994. Bd. dirs. L.A. Hebrew H.S., 1994—, Temple Ari El, North Hollywood, Calif., 1994—. Adolscent Med fellow Childrens Hosp. L.A., 1978-79; Regents scholar, 1972. Fellow ACP; mem. AMA, Soc. Adolescent Medicine (exec. bd. 1990-93, Jefferson abstract selection com. 1994—), Phi Beta Kappa. Office: Children Hosp LA 4650 W Sunset Blvd Los Angeles CA 90027-6062

NEKIMKEN, JUDY MARIE, secondary school educator; b. Janesville, Wis., May 9, 1960; d. Robert Leroy and Wanda Maureen (Reeder) Lilburn; m. Howard Lewis, July 30, 1983; children: Kyle James, Adam Lee. BA in Humanistic Studies, U. Wis., Green Bay, 1992. Cert. tchr. secondary math., N.Mex. Tchr. Rankin (Ill.) H.S., 1984-85; tchr. math. Los Alamos H.S., 1985—, curriculum writer, 1988, 94; faculty U. N.Mex., Los Alamos, 1988-90. Mem. Nat. Coun. Tchrs. Math., Beta Sigma Phi (pres., corr. sec. 1992—). Office: Los Alamos High School 1300 Diamond Dr Los Alamos NM 87544-2209

NELIPOVICH, SANDRA GRASSI, artist; b. Oak Park, Ill., Nov. 22, 1939; d. Alessandro and Lena Mary (Ascareggi) Grassi; m. John Nelipovich Jr., Aug. 19, 1973. BFA in Art Edn., U. Ill., 1961; postgrad., Northwestern U., 1963, Gonzaga U., Florence, Italy, 1966, Art Inst. Chgo., 1968; diploma, Accademia Universale Alessandro Magno, Prato, Italy, 1983. Tchr. art Edgewood Jr. High Sch., Highland Park, Ill., 1961-62, Emerson Sch. Jr. High Sch., Oak Park, 1962-77; batik artist Calif., 1977—; illustrator Jolly Robin Publ. Co., Anaheim, Calif., 1988—; supr. student tchrs., Oak Park, 1970-75; adult edn. tchr. ESL, ceramics, Medinah, Ill., 1974; mem. curriculum action group on human dignity, EEO workshop demonstration, Oak Park, 1975-76; guest lectr. Muckenthaler Ctr., Fullerton, Calif., 1980, 92, Niguel Art Group, Dana Point, Calif., 1989, Carlsbad A.A., 1990, ARt League, Oceanside Art Group, 1992; 2d v.p. Anaheim Hills Women's Club, 1990-91, rec. sec. 1991-92; fabric designer for fashion designer Barbara Jax, 1987. One-Woman shows include Lawry's Calif. Ctr., L.A., 1981-83, Whittier (Calif.) Mus., 1985-86, Anaheim Cultural Ctr., 1986-88, Ill. Inst. Tech., Chgo., 1989, Muckenthaler Cultural Ctr., Fullerton, 1990; also gallery exhibits in Oak Brook, 1982, La Habra, Calif., 1983, Millard Sheets Gallery, Pomona, Calif., 1996; represented in permanent collections McDonald's Corp., Oak Brook, Glenkirk Sch., Deerfield, Ill., Emerson Sch., Oak Park, galleries in Laguna Beach, Calif., Maui, Hawaii, Mich., N.J.; poster designer Saratoga Fine Arts. Active Assistance League, Anaheim, Calif., 1992—, 2d v.p. ways and means com., 1995-96, 97—. Recipient numerous awards, purchase prizes, 1979—; featured in Calif. Art Rev., Artists of So. Calif.,

Vol. II, Nat. Artists' Network, 1992. Mem. AAUW (hospitality chmn. 1984-85), Soc. Children's Book Writers and Illustrators, Assistance League Anaheim, Oak Park Art League, Orange Art Assn. (jury chairperson 1980), Anaheim Art Assn., Muckenthaler Ctr. Circle, Anaheim Hills Women's Club. Roman Catholic. Home and Office: 5922 E Calle Cedro Anaheim CA 92807-3207

NELL, JANINE MARIE, metallurgical and materials engineer; b. Milw., Jan. 15, 1959; d. Joseph Frank (Gabrhel) and Joyce Cecelia (Jans) Clendening; m. Michael Paul Nell, Aug. 19, 1978. SB in Materials Sci. and Engring., MIT, 1981, PhD in Metallurgy, 1989. Rsch. asst. MIT, Cambridge, 1981-89; sr. engr., asst. to pres. Failure Analysis Assocs., Inc., Menlo Park, Calif., 1989-91, sr. engr. exec. office, 1991-92, mgr. corp. lab. and testing svcs., 1992-94, sr. engr. materials and mechanics group, 1994—; mem. vis. com. for undergrad. edn. and student affairs MIT, 1992—. Author: Progress in Powder Metallurgy, 1986, Superalloys 92, 1992; contbr. articles to profl. jours. Recipient Karl Taylor Compton award MIT, 1986; Cabot Corp. fellow, 1981-85. Mem. ASME, ASM Internat., The Metall. Soc., Am. Inst. Mining, Metall. and Petroleum Engrs., Soc. Plastics Engrs., Am. Welding Soc., The Human Factors and Ergonomics Soc., Sigma Xi, Tau Beta Pi. Office: Failure Analysis Assocs Inc 149 Commonwealth Dr Menlo Park CA 94025-1133

NELLERMOE, LESLIE CAROL, lawyer; b. Oakland, Calif., Jan. 26, 1954; d. Carrol Wandell and Nora Ann (Conway) N.; m. Darrell Ray McKissic, Aug. 9, 1986; 1 child, Devin Anne. BS cum laude, Wash. State U., 1975; JD cum laude, Willamette U., 1978. Bar: Wash. 1978, U.S. Dist. Ct. (ea. dist.) Wash. 1979, U.S. Dist. Ct. (we. dist.) Wash. 1983. Staff atty. Wash. Ct. Appeals, Spokane, 1978-79; asst. atty. gen. Wash. Atty. Gen. Office, Spokane, 1979-83, Olympia, 1983-85; assoc. Syrdal, Danelo, Klein, Myre & Woods, Seattle, 1985-88; ptnr. Heller Ehrman White & McAuliffe, Seattle, 1989—. Bd. dirs. N.W. Environ. Bus. Coun., 1996—, Campfire Boys & Girls, Seattle, 1991—. Mem. ABA, Wash. State Bar Assn., King County Bar Assn., Wash. Environ. Industry Assn. (bd. dirs.). Office: Heller Ehrman White & McAuliffe 701 5th Ave 6100 Columbia Ctr Seattle WA 98104

NELSEN, KEVIN KIRK, contracts and proposals executive; b. Brigham City, Utah, June 16, 1963; s. Kirk Richard and Joan (Smoot) N.; m. Karen John, Nov. 2, 1972; children: Jason, Marcie Nelsen Alcorn, Russell, Phillip. BS in Bus. Mgmt., Weber State U., 1978; MBA, U. Phoenix, 1988. Internat. contracts specialist Sperry Corp., Salt Lake City, 1976-78; contacts mgr. E-Sys., Salt Lake City, 1978-87; program mgr. Thiokol Corp., Brigham City, 1987-90; dir. contracts and proposals Barnes Group Inc., Ogden, Utah, 1990—; pres. The Transnat. Group, Ogden, 1995—; mem. faculty U. Phoenix, Salt Lake City, 1991-95; lectr. on internat. bus., 1996—. Author: Risks of Contracting with the Federal Government, 1989. Mem. Am. Def. Preparedness Assn. (v.p. 1991—), Nat. Contracts Mgrs. Assn. (mem. adv. bd. 1990-94), Internat. Bus. Assn. (pres. 1996—), No. Utah Touring Assn. (pres. 1986—), Weber Wildlife Fedn. Republican. Mem. LDS Ch. Office: Transnat Group LLC 4126 N 950 W Pleasant View UT 84414

NELSON, ALAN CURTIS, government official, lawyer; b. Oakland, Calif., Oct. 18, 1933; s. Albert C. and Martha (Peters) N.; m. JoAnn Wallen, Jan. 31, 1960; children: Kristine Ann, Kathryn Donna, Karin Martha. BS, U. Calif., Berkeley, 1955, JD, 1958. Bar: Calif. 1959, U.S. Dist. Cts. Calif. 1959, U.S. Supreme Ct. 1984. Atty. Rogers, Clark & Jordan, San Francisco, 1959-64; dep. dist. atty. Alameda County (Calif.), 1964-69; asst. dir. State of Calif. Human Resource Dept., Sacramento, 1969-72; dir. State of Calif. Dept. Rehab., Sacramento, 1972-75; gen. atty. Pacific Telephone & Telegraph, San Francisco, 1975-81; dep. commr. Immigration and Naturalization Service, Washington, 1981-82, commr., 1982-89; cons. fed. Am. immigration reform U.S. Dept. Justice, Washington, 1989-90; gen. counsel Employment Devel. Dept. State of Calif., 1990-91; atty. and cons. on immigration Sacramento, 1994—; adj. prof. McGeorge Sch. Law, U. Pacific. Chmn. Calif. Gov. Com. for Employment of Handicapped, 1981-82. Recipient Alumnus of Yr. award Tau Kappa Epsilon, 1987; Border Patrol Sta., Imperial Beach, Calif. dedicated to Commr. Nelson, 1988. Mem. State Bar Calif., Assn. Calif. Tort Reform (dir.), Bar Assn. San Francisco, Legal Aid Soc. San Francisco (dir.), Assn. Fed. Investigators (pres. 1987). Republican. Club: Commonwealth. Office: Law Offices of Alan Nelson 835 Shoreside Dr Sacramento CA 95831-1422 *Four Key Personal and Management Concepts: Pride, Integrity, Innovation and Persistence. Pride: pride in ones country, family and traditions are a foundation for all meaningful personal actions. Integrity: most individuals have an innate sense of integrity; this plus integrity which is learned in one's life experience must also form the foundation for all actions. Innovation: constantly pursue new challenges and approaches; innovation, which makes our system so effective, is essential in all business and government. Persistence: in any bureacratic setting a lack of persistence can often equate to failure because most obstacles must be overcome with some difficulty.*

NELSON, ALBERT LOUIS, III, finance executive; b. St. Louis, Apr. 29, 1938; s. Albert Louis and Mildred Mary (Bischoff) N.; m. Pamela Eakins, Mar. 14, 1970; children: Holly Reid, Amy Bischoff. BSME, Washington U., St. Louis, 1960, MBA, 1962; LLB, George Washington U., 1964. Exec. v.p. Equity Research Assocs., Inc., N.Y.C., 1967-69; pres. The Westwood Group, Inc., Los Angeles, 1969-73; dir. chem. plastics Gen. Tire & Rubber Co., Akron, Ohio, 1973-75; sr. v.p., dir. corp. service dept. Prescott, Ball & Turben, Cleve., 1975-86; pres. Albert Nelson Investment Co., Inc., Tucson, 1986—. With U.S. Army, 1964-66. Mem. N.Y. Stock Exch. Lunch Club, Portage Country Club.

NELSON, ALLEN F., investor relations and proxy solicitation company executive; b. Portland, Oreg., Oct. 17, 1943; s. Roy August and Mildred Mary (Jensen) N.; BS, U. Iowa, 1965, MA, 1968; m. Johanna Molenaar, Dec. 8, 1973. V.p. Shareholder Communications Corp., N.Y.C., 1970-72, Trafalgar Capital Corp., N.Y.C., 1973; pres. Nelson, Lasky & Co., Inc., N.Y.C., 1974-76; account exec. Corp. Communications Inc., Seattle, 1976-77; pres. Allen Nelson & Co., Inc., Seattle, 1977—. Mem. Fin. Analysts Fedn., Nat. Investor Relations Inst., Nat. Security Traders Assn., Practising Law Inst., Pub. Relations Soc. Am., Am. Soc. Corporate Secs., Can. Corp. Shareholder Svcs. Assn. (pres.), Can. Soc. Corp. Secs., Rainier Club, Montana Club. Home: 4400 Beach Dr SW Seattle WA 98116-3937 Office: Allen Nelson & Co Inc PO Box 16157 Seattle WA 98116-0157

NELSON, BARBARA LOUISE, secondary education educator; b. Indpls., Apr. 18, 1935; d. Dennis Arthur Chandler and Bertha Louise (Drane) Hill; children: Edwin Robert Swanson, III, Patricia Marie Swanson, Barbara Michelle Swanson Clure. BA, Ind. U., 1956; tchrs. cert., Millikin U., 1964; MA, U. Denver, 1969. Cert. English tchr. Tchr. AL Jr. High Sch., Jefferson Co.; tchr., dept. chair O'Connell Jr. High, Jefferson Co.; tchr. Alameda High Sch., Jefferson County R-1, Lakewood, Colo.; exch. tchr. ITF, Melbourne, Australia, 1976, Lakewood-Sutherlandshire Sister City Tchr. Visitation Exch., 1989; mem. writing com. Jefferson County;. Stephen min., mem. stewardship commn., mem. evangelism commn., Christ Episcopal Ch. Mem. NEA, Nat. Coun. Tchrs. English, Colo. Internat. Tchr. Exch. League, Colo. Edn. Assn., Colo. Lang. Arts Soc., Jefferson County Edn. Assn., Delta Kappa Gamma (past pres., v.p., rec. sec. and treas., corr. sec. Pi chpt.), Phi Delta Kappa (scholarship chmn.), Delta Delta Delta. Home: 3100 S Race St Englewood CO 80110-3032

NELSON, BARBARA SECREST, educational developer; b. Reidsville, N.C., Jan. 7, 1949; d. Edgar B. and Mary Elizabeth (Slate) Trent; m. Michael William Nelson, Dec. 31, 1985. BA in Edn., U. N.C., 1971, MA in Curriculum and Instrn., 1975. Cert. K-3 tchr., N.C. Kindergarten and primary tchr. Wake County Schs., Raleigh, N.C., 1971-74; rsch. and evaluation cons. N.C. Dept. Pub. Instrn., Raleigh, 1974-84; mktg. and sales mgr. edn. div. Computer South, Charlotte, N.C., 1984-85; mktg. support rep. Apple Computer, Inc., Charlotte, 1985-87; K-8 solutions mgr. Apple Computer, Inc., Cupertino, Calif., 1987-89; account exec. Apple Computer, Inc., Culver City, Calif., 1989-92, ednl. devel., 1990—; S.E. mktg./solutions mgr. Apple Computer, Inc., Charlotte, N.C., 1994—; com. mem. N.C. Effective Teaching Com., Raleigh, 1984; program chmn. N.C. Instrnl. Microcomputing Conf., Greensboro, 1985. Co-author Apple Learning Series for K-2, 1986. Mem. ASCD. Home and Office: 4908 Carmel Club Dr Charlotte NC 28226-8020

NELSON, BRYAN H(ERBERT), non-profit agency administrator; b. Yakima, Wash., July 3, 1956; s. Herbert B. and Marilyn A. (Cupper) N.; m. Sandra Exley, June 11, 1993; children from previous marriage: Christofer A., Bryanne E. BEd, Ea. Wash. U., 1977, MS in Speech Pathology, 1978. Speech pathologist Ednl. Svc. Dist. 101, Spokane, Wash., 1978-83, coord. speech pathology, 1983-84, coord. inservice tng., 1985; processor fruit broker Herb Nelson Inc., Yakima, 1985-88; coord. early childhood and spl. edn. programs Selah (Wash.) Sch. Dist., 1989-92, coord. spl. edn., 1989-92; dir. New Directions, EPIC, 1992—; gen. ptnr. Nelson Perkins Assocs., Yakima, 1990-93; dir. New Directions-Epic, Yakima, Wash., 1992—; guest lectr. Ea. Wash. U., Cheney, 1984-85; chmn. very spl. arts festival Ednl. Svc. Dist 101, 1985, on-site coord. IDEAS conv., 1983. Bd. dirs., chmn. citizens adv. bd. Yakima Vocat. Skill Ctr., 1988-89; mem. gen. adv. com. Yakima Vocat. Coop.; mem. allocation panel United Way, Yakima, 1974, loaned exec., 1990; mem. exec. com. Yakima County Birth to Six, 1989-90. Home: 7303 Perry St Yakima WA 98908-2013 Office: New Directions-Epic 14S S 6th Ave Yakima WA 98901

NELSON, DARRYL ALLAN, television cameraman; b. Corning, Calif., Oct. 15, 1959; s. Jack Donald and Patricia Ann (Siemens) N. Student, Butte Coll., Oroville, Calif., 1979; BA, Calif. State U., Chico, 1986. Chief photographer Sta. KHSL-TV, Chico, 1986-87; news photographer Sta. KOLO-TV, Reno, Nev., 1987, Sta. KLAS-TV, Las Vegas, Nev., 1987-96; chief photographer Sta. KLAS-TV, Las Vegas, 1993-96; profl. camera operator, Las Vegas, 1990—. Recipient Spot/Feature News award UPI, 1987, 88, 89. Mem. NATAS, Nat. Press Photographers Assn., Soc. Profl. Journalists, Am. Legion (medal of honor 1973, 77), Rotary (Citizen of Yr. 1977). Home: 1806 Navarre Ln Henderson NV 89014

NELSON, DAVID SAMUEL, public relations executive; b. LaGrande, Oreg., Dec. 20, 1941; s. Roy K. and Anne Cecila (Barkman) N.; m. Leah Marie Thom, Nov. 7, 1969; children: Barry, Molly, Amy. BA in Agrl., Oreg. State U., 1964, BSBA, 1967. Field rep. Oreg. Farm Bur. Fedn., Salem, 1967-69, exec. v.p., 1969-75; v.p. Agrl. Commodity Promotions, Salem, 1975-77; pres. Dave Nelson & Assocs., Inc., Salem, 1977—; co-founder, v.p. Agri-Comp, Inc., Salem, 1979-82; mem. adv. com. Workmans Compensation Bd., Salem, 1973-83. Mem. Turner (Oreg.) Elem. Sch. Bd., 1974-82, chmn., 1978. Named Seedsmen of Yr. Oreg. Seed Coun., Salem, 1991. Mem. Am. Quarter Horse Assn., Oreg. Quarter Horst Racing Assn. (chmn. 1974-97), Capitol Club. Republican Methodist. Home: 7479 Nelson Ln SE Turner OR 97392-9768 Office: Dave Nelson & Assocs 1193 Royvonne Ave SE Ste 11 Salem OR 97302-6501

NELSON, DOROTHY WRIGHT (MRS. JAMES F. NELSON), federal judge; b. San Pedro, Calif., Sept. 30, 1928; d. Harry Earl and Lorna Amy Wright; m. James Frank Nelson, Dec. 27, 1950; children: Franklin Wright, Lorna Jean. B.A., UCLA, 1950, J.D., 1953; LL.M., U. So. Calif., 1956; LLD honoris causa, Western State U., 1980, U. So. Calif., 1983, Georgetown U., 1988, Whittier U., 1989, U. Santa Clara, 1990; LLD (honoris causa), Whittier U., 1989. Bar: Calif. 1954. Research assoc. fellow U. So. Calif., 1953-56; instr., 1957, asst. prof., 1958-61, assoc. prof., 1961-67, prof., 1967, assoc. dean., 1965-67, dean., 1967-80; judge U.S. Ct. Appeals (9th cir.), 1979—; cons. Project STAR, Law Enforcement Assistance Adminstrn.; mem. select com. on internal procedures of Calif. Supreme Ct., 1987—; co-chair Sino-Am. Seminar on Mediation and Arbitration, Beijing, 1992; dir. Dialogue on Transition to a Global Soc., Weinacht, Switzerland, 1992. Author: Judicial Adminstration and The Administration of Justice, 1973, (with Christopher Goelz and Meredith Watts) Federal Ninth Circuit Civil Appellate Practice, 1995; Contbr. articles to profl. jours. Co-chmn. Confronting Myths in Edn. for Pres. Nixon's White House Conf. on Children, Pres. Carter's Commn. for Pension Policy, 1974-80, Pres. Reagon's Madison Trust; bd. visitors U.S. Air Force Acad., 1978; bd. dirs. Council on Legal Edn. for Profl. Responsibility, 1971-80, Constnl. Right Found., Am. Nat. Inst. for Social Advancement; adv. bd. Nat. Center for State Cts., 1971-73; chmn. bd. Western Justice Ctr., 1986—; mem. adv. com. Nat. Jud. Edn. Program to promote equality for woman and men in cts. Named Law Alumnus of Yr. UCLA, 1967; recipient Profl. Achievement award, 1969; named Times Woman of Yr., 1968; recipient U. Judaism Humanitarian award, 1973; AWARE Internat. award, 1970; Ernestine Stalhut Outstanding Woman Lawyer award, 1972; Pub. Svc. award Coro Found., 1978, Pax Orbis ex Jure medallion World Peace thru Law Ctr., 1975, Hollzer Human Rights award Jewish Fedn. Coun., L.A., 1988, Medal of Honor UCLA, 1993; Lustman fellow Yale U. 1977. Fellow Am. Bar Found., Davenport Coll., Yale U.; mem. Bar Calif. (bd. dirs. continuing edn. bar commn. 1967-74), Am. Judicature Soc. (dir., Justice award 1985), Assn. Am. Law Schs. (chmn. com. edn. in jud. adminstrn.), Am. Bar Assn. (sect. on jud. adminstrn., chmn. com. on edn. in jud. adminstrn. 1973-89), Phi Beta Kappa, Order of Coif (nat. v.p. 1974-76), Jud. Conf. U.S. (com. to consider standards for admission to practice in fed. cts. 1976-79). Office: US Ct Appeals Cir 125 S Grand Ave Ste 303 Pasadena CA 91105-1621

NELSON, DOUGLAS MICHAEL, school system administrator, educator; b. Seattle, Wash., Feb. 20, 1948, s. Donald Edgar and Helen Thomasina (Manarino) N.; m. Virginia Jude Smith, Aug. 4, 1973; children: Kourtney, Karly, Jenna. BA, Whitman Coll., 1970; MEd, U. Puget Sound, 1974; EdD, Seattle U., 1986. Tchr. history Auburn (Wash.) Sr. H.S., 1970-75; asst. prin. Pioneer Jr. H.S., Walla Walla, Wash., 1975-78; prin. Highland Middle Sch., Kennewick, Wash., 1978-80, Meridian Jr. H.S., Kent, Wash., 1980-85; asst. supt. Franklin Pierce Sch. Dist., Tacoma, Wash., 1985-89; supt. Pullman (Wash.) Sch. Dist., 1989—; adj. prof. Wash. State U., Pullman, 1990—. pres. Wash. Sch. Admin. Polit. Action Com., State of Wash., 1996. Recipient Excellence in Edn. award, State of Wash., 1994, Outstanding Adminstr. award Wash. State PTA Region 9, Kent, Wash., 1985. Mem. Pullman (Wash.) C. of C. (pres. 1994), Parkland-Spanaway (Wash.) C. of C. (exec. bd., pres. elect 1986-89, community growth award 1988), Wash. Assn. Sch. Adminstrs. (regional officer 1988-89), Future of Wash. Schs. (exec. comm. 1995—), Wash. ASCD (outstanding educator award 1984), Rotary Club, Phi Delta Kappa (scholarship award 1985). Roman Catholic. Home: 555 SE Water St Pullman WA 99163 Office: Pullman Sch Dist PO Box 429 Pullman WA 99163

NELSON, DREW VERNON, mechanical engineering educator; b. Elizabeth, N.J., Oct. 11, 1947; s. Andrew K. and Myra G. (Kempson) N. BSME, Stanford U., 1968, MSME, 1970, PhDME, 1978. Research asst. Stanford U., Calif., 1971-74, asst. prof., 1978-83, assoc. prof., 1983-96; prof. Stanford U., 1996—; engr. Gen. Electric Co., Sunnyvale, Calif., 1975-76, sr. engr., 1977-78; cons. in field. Co-editor: Fatigue Design Handbook, 1989; contbr. articles to profl. jours. Recipient Spergel Meml. award for Most Outstanding Paper, 32d Internat. Wire and Cable Symposium, 1984, Hetenyi award for Best Rsch. Paper Pub in 1994 in the jour. Exptl. Mechanics. Mem. ASTM, Soc. Automotive Engrs., Soc. for Exptl. Mechanics, Sigma Xi, Tau Beta Pi. Home: 840 Cabot Ct San Carlos CA 94070-3464 Office: Stanford U Dept Mech Engring Stanford CA 94305-4021

NELSON, FRANCES PATRICIA, food service executive; b. Denver, Jan. 15, 1948; d. Wilbur Jordan and Margaret Emma Anna (Kruger) Cannon; m. Kenneth Roy Nelson, Sept. 2, 1972; children: Krista, Erin, Michael. BS, Colo. State U., 1970; MA, U. No. Colo., 1981. Asst. dir. child nutrition Colo. Dept. Edn., Denver, 1971-77; dir. nutrition svc. Denver Head Start, 1981-83; dir. food svc. Englewood (Colo.) Pub. Schs., 1988-91, Jefferson County Schs., Golden, Colo., 1991—; cons. Wildwood Child Care, Englewood, 1984-88, Mile High Child Care Assn., Denver, 1981-83, Colo. Dept. Edn., Denver, 1976, Denver Pub. Schs., 1979. Contbr. articles to profl. jours. Leader Girl Scouts Am., Denver, 1982-88, Boy Scouts Am., 1991; team adminstr. Aurora (Colo.) Soccer Club, 1981-88. Mem. Am. Dietetic Assn., Am. Sch. Food Svc. Assn., Colo. Sch. Food Svc. Assn. (pres.-elect 1991-92, pres. 1992-93). Home: 6227 S Netherland Cir Aurora CO 80016-1323 Office: Jefferson County Pub Schs 1829 Denver West Dr # 27 Golden CO 80401-3120

NELSON, HAROLD BERNHARD, museum director; b. Providence, R.I., May 14, 1947; s. Harold B. and Eleanor (Lavina) N. BA, Bowdoin Coll., 1969; MA, U. Del., 1972. Rsch. fellow NMAA Smithsonian Inst., Washington, 1976-77; curator Am. art Mus. Art & Archeol., U. Mo., Columbia, 1977-79; registrar Solomon R. Guggenheim Mus., N.Y.C., 1979-83; exhibition program dir. Am. Fedn. Arts, N.Y.C., 1983-89; dir. Long Beach (Calif.) Mus. of Art, 1989—; juror Annual Art Exhibition Mus. Art, Sci. & Industry, Bridgeport, Conn., 1988, Annual Art Exhibition, Clark County Dist. Libr., Las Vegas, Nev., 1984; speaker Am. Assn. Mus. Annual Conf., Detroit, 1985, annual meeting Western Mus. Conf., Portland, Oreg., 1987, Grantmakers in Art Symposium, N.Y.C., 1986, annual meeting Western Mus. Conf., Salt Lake City, 1985; mem. adv. com. APA, Assn. Sci. and Tech. Ctrs.; panelist Aid to Spl. Exhibitions, NEA, Washington, 1986; participant Am. Legal Assn., ABA Conf., San Francisco, 1986; observer, respondent Mus. Symposium, NEA, Dallas, 1985. Author: Sounding the Depths: 150 Years of American Seascape, 1989, New Visions: Selina Trieff, 1997. Office: Long Beach Mus Art 2300 E Ocean Blvd Long Beach CA 90803-2442

NELSON, HARRY, journalist, medical writer; b. Interlachen, Fla., Apr. 18, 1923; s. Knut Alfred and Edith Farr (Wilkes) N.; m. Diane Gabriella Meerschaert, Aug. 29, 1948 (div. 1977); children—Tanya Ann, Lawrence Stephen, Ronald Gerard, James Anthony, John Christopher; m. Gita Doris Wheelis, Jan. 29, 1984. B.A., U. So. Calif., 1949. Reporter, photographer Bakersfield Press, Calif., 1949; reporter, photographer Bakersfield Community Chest, Calif., 1949; promotion writer Los Angeles Times, 1949-57, reporter, 1957-58, med. writer, 1958-88, sr. writer, 1977-80; freelance med. writer, 1988—; staff writer Milbank Meml. Fund, 1993—. Charter mem. bd. dirs. Los Angeles County Comprehensive Health Planning Assn., Los Angeles, 1968-69. Served with USAAF, 1941-45. Recipient spl. commendation AMA, 1974, John Hancock award John Hancock Ins. Co., 1978, Journalism award Am. Acad. Pediatrics, 1979, Disting. Svc. by non-physician award Calif. Med. Assn., 1988, Lifetime Achievement in med. writing award AMA, 1988, Peter Lisagor award for exemplary journalism Chgo. Headliners Club, 1988. Mem. Nat. Assn. Sci. Writers (pres. 1966). Address: Med Writers Internat PO Box N 14016 Yellowstone Dr Frazier Park CA 93222

NELSON, HELEN MARTHA, retired library director; b. Anaconda, Mont., Dec. 20, 1929; d. Ole Bertin and Caroline Helen (Massey) N. BA with honors, U. Mont., 1951; MLS, U. Wash., 1960. Asst. documents and serials libr. U. Mont., Missoula, 1951-52; tchr. English and history, libr. Laurel H.S., 1952-54; tchr. English, libr. Beaverhead County H.S., 1954-56; tchr. English, journalism Anaconda Sr. H.S., 1956-59; libr., adminstr. U.S. Army, 1960-68; libr. dir. Oceanside (Calif.) Libr., 1968-94; chmn. Serra Coop. Libr., 1973-74, 84-85, 90-91; mem. coun. Serra Coop. Sys., 1969-94. Chmn. Christian Sponsors, Oceanside, 1975; congl. pres. King of Kings Luth. Ch., Oceanside, 1974, 77, 84, mem. coun. 1971-77, 82-84, 92-94; bd. dirs. Oceanside/Carlsbad ARC, 1970-71; del. Calif. Gov.'s Conf. Librs. and Info. Sci. Mem. ALA, AAUW, LWV, Mont. Libr. Assn., Calif. Libr. Assn. (coun. 1978-80, v.p. Palomar chpt. 1978), Pub. Libr. Execs. of So. Calif., Oceanside C. of C., Calif. Inst. Libr. (bd. dirs. 1978-80).

NELSON, IVORY VANCE, academic administrator; b. Curtis, La., June 11, 1934; s. Elijah H. and Mattie (White) N.; m. Patricia Robbins, Dec. 27, 1985; children: Cherlyn, Karyn, Eric Beatty, Kim Beatty. BS, Grambling (La.) State U., 1959; PhD, U. Kans., 1963. Assoc. prof. chemistry So. U., Baton Rouge, 1963-67, head div. sci., 1966-68; prof. chemistry Prairie View (Tex.) A&M U., 1968-83, asst. acad. dean, 1968-72, v.p. rsch., 1972-82, acting pres., 1982-83; exec. asst. Tex. A&M U. System, College Station, 1983-86; chancellor Alamo C.C. Dist., San Antonio, 1986-92; pres. Cen. Wash. U., Ellensburg, 1992—; DuPont teaching fellow U. Kans., 1959; rsch. chemist Am. Oil Co., 1962; sr. rsch. chemist Union Carbide Co., 1969; vis. prof. U. Autonomous Guadalajara, Mex., 1966, Loyola U., 1967; Fulbright lectr., 1966; cons. evaluation coms. Oak Ridge (Tenn.) Assoc. Univs., NSF, Nat. Coun. for Accreditation Tchr. Edn., So. Assn. Colls. and Schs.; mem. regional policy coms. on minorities Western Interstate Com. on Higher Edn., 1986-88; mem. exec. com. Nat. Assn. State Univs. and Land Grant Colls., 1980-82. Contbr. articles to profl. jours. Bd. dirs. Target 90, Goals San Antonio, 1987-89, coun. of pres.NAIDA,(1993-96) Commn. on Student Learning, Wash., 1992—, United Way San Antonio, 1987-89, Alamo Area coun. Boy Scouts Am., 1987-89, San Antonio Symphony Soc., 1987-91, Key Bank of Wash.; mem. bd. dirs. assn. Western U., (1995—) mem. com. fir jud. reform State of Tex., 1991; mem. edn. adv. bd. Tex. Rsch. Park, 1987-89; bd. givs. Am. Inst. for character Edn., Inc., 1988-91; mem. adv. com. Tex. Ho. of Reps., 1978; chmn. United Way Campaign Tex. A&M U. System, 1984, others. Staff sgt. USAF, 1951-55, Korea. T.H. Harris scholar Grambling State U., 1959; fellow Nat. Urban League, 1969. Mem. AAAS, Am. Chem. Soc., Tex. Acad. Sci., NAACP, Phi Beta Kappa, Sigma Xi, Phi Lambda Upsilon, Beta Kappa Chi, Alpha Mu Gamma, Kappa Delta Pi, Sigma Pi Sigma, Omega Psi Phi, Sigma Pi Phi, Phi Kappa Phi. Home: 211 E 10th Ave Ellensburg WA 98926-2911 Office: Office of Pres Cen Wash U Ellensburg WA 98926

NELSON, JAMES ALONZO, radiologist, educator; b. Cherokee, Iowa, Oct. 20, 1938; s. Joe George and Ruth Geraldine (Jones) N.; m. Katherine Metcalf, July 16, 1966; children: John Metcalf, Julie Heaps. AB, Harvard U., 1961, MD, 1965. Asst. prof. radiology U. Calif., San Francisco, 1972-74; assoc. prof. U. Utah, Salt Lake City, 1974-79, prof., 1979-86; prof. U. Wash., Seattle, 1986—; dir. radiol. rsch. U. Calif./Ft. Miley VA Hosp., 1973-74, U. Utah, 1974-85, U. Wash., 1986—; mem. bd. sci. advisors NeoVision, 1995—, Oreg. Life Scis.; co-founder Circulation, Inc., 1996; mem. adv. panel on non-radioactive diagnostic agts. USP, 1984-96. Contbr. chpts. to books, articles to Am. Jour. Roentgenology, Radiology, Investigative Radiology, others. Capt. USAF, 1967-69. John Harvard scholar, 1957-61, James Picker Found. scholar, 1973-77; recipient Mallinkrodt prize Soc. Body Computerized Tomagraphy, 1990, Roscoe Miller award Soc. Gastrointestinal Radiology, 1991. Fellow Am. Coll. Radiology (diplomate); mem. Radiol. Soc. N.Am., Assn. Univ. Radiology. Office: U Wash Dept Radiology Diagnostic Imaging Sci Ctr Box 357115 Seattle WA 98195

NELSON, JAMES C, justice; m. Chari Werner; 2 children. BBA, U. Idaho, 1966; JD cum laude, George Washington U., 1974. Fin. analyst SEC, Washington; pvt. practice Cut Bank; county atty. Glacier County; justice Mont. Supreme Ct., 1993—; former mem. State Bd. Oil and Gas Conservation, also chmn.; former mem. State Gaming Adv. Counsel, Gov. Adv. Coun. on Corrections and Criminal Justice Policy; liaison to Commn. of Cts. of Ltd. Jurisdiction, mem. adv. com. Ct. Assessment Program. Served U.S. Army. Office: Justice Bldg 215 N Sanders St Rm 323 Helena MT 59620-3003*

NELSON, JIM, chemicals executive; b. 1942. Degree, U. Utah. Prof. U. Utah, Salt Lake City; pres. Datacem Labs., Salt Lake City, 1972—. Office: Datacem Labs 960 W Levoy Dr Salt Lake City UT 84123-2547*

NELSON, JOHN GUSTAF, lawyer; b. Denver, Jan. 29, 1965; s. Carl R. and Dorothy M. (Harris) N. BA, U. Colo., 1987, JD, 1990. Bar: Colo. 1990, U.S. Dist. Ct. Colo. 1991, U.S. Ct. Appeals (10th cir.) 1992, U.S. Fed. Claims Ct. 1993, Tribal Ct. Omaha Tribe Nebr. 1996. Staff atty. Mountain States Legal Found., Denver, 1990-94; atty. Law Offices of John D. Musick Jr. and Assocs., Denver, 1994—. Contbr. articles to profl. jours. Mem. The Centennial Soc., 1994—; vice-chair Colo. Com. for Equal Opportunity, Denver, 1995—; bd. dirs. Freedom Republican, Denver, 1995—. Mem. Colo. Bar Assn., Denver Bar Assn., The Federalist Soc., Rocky Moutain Mineral Law Found., Highlands Lodge No. 86. Lutheran. Home: 10574 Pierson Circle Denver CO 80021 Office: Law Offices John D Musick Jr and Assocs 1775 Sherman St Ste 2500 Denver CO 80203-4322

NELSON, KENNETH ARTHUR, electrical engineer; b. Coeur d'Alene, Idaho, Apr. 18, 1942; s. Elton Arthur and Maxine Edna (Barnes) N.; m. Sharon Fay Paynter, Sept. 2, 1962; children: Neva Kenine, Krena Krista, Kelina Kara, Kimberly Kay. BSEE, U. Idaho, 1965; cert., Alaxander Hamilton Inst., 1970. Registered profl. engr., Calif., Idaho. With GE, various locations, 1965-75; sr. mfg. engr. Jenn-Air Corp., Indpls., 1975-79; plant engr. A.O. Smith Corp., Newark, Calif., 1979-82; dir. facilities Memorex Corp., Santa Clara, Calif., 1982-88; with Scenic Mgmt. Corp., Tracy, Calif., 1988—; instr. Profl. Engring. Inst., San Carlos, Calif., 1985-88, ITT Ednl. Svcs., Inc., Hayward, Calif.; founder Scenic Mgmt., Livermore, Calif., 1985—. Inventor in field. Mem. IEEE, Am. Soc. Metals Internat. Republican. Lutheran. Home: 1585 Hoot Owl Ct Tracy CA 95376-4396

NELSON, LAVERN C., mayor. Mayor City of Greeley, Colo. Office: City of Greeley 1000 10th St Greeley CO 80631

NELSON, MARGARET ROSE, tourism executive; b. Juneau, Alaska, Apr. 18, 1958; d. James M. and Ruth I. (Gray) N. Student, U. Santa Clara, 1976-77, U. Bridgeport, 1977-78; BA, U. Alaska, 1980. Reporter Fairbanks (Alaska) Daily News Miner, 1980-86; communications cons. Fairbanks, 1985-86; pub. information officer Alaska Fedn. of Natives, Anchorage, 1986; spl. asst. to exec. dir., corp. communications officer Alaska Housing Fin. Corp., Anchorage, 1986-94; pres. Nelson Communications, 1994-96; v.p. tourism Goldbelt, Inc., Juneau, Alaska, 1996—; bd. dir Goldbelt, Inc. 1991-94. Mem. Alaska Visitors Assn., Am. Indian Bus. Assn., S.E. Alaska Tourism Assn.

NELSON, MARY CARROLL, artist, author; b. Bryan, Tex., Apr. 24, 1929; d. James Vincent and Mary Elizabeth (Langton) Carroll; m. Edwin Blakely Nelson, June 27, 1950; children: Patricia Ann, Edwin Blakely. BA in Fine Arts, Barnard Coll., 1950; MA, U. N.Mex., 1963. Juror Am. Artist Golden Anniversary Nat. Art Competition, 1987, Don Ruffin Meml. Art Exhbn., Ariz., 1989, N.Mex. Arts and Crafts Fair, 1989, 96; guest instr. continuing edn. U. N.Mex., 1991; conf., organizer Affirming Wholeness, The Art and Healing Experience, San Antonio, 1992, Artists of the Spirit Symposium, 1994. Group shows include N.Mex. Mus. Fine Arts Biennial, 1987, N.Mex. Lightworks, 1990, Level to Level, Layering, Ohio, 1987, Artist as Shaman, Ohio, 1990, The Healing Experience, Mass., 1991, A Gathering of Voices, Calif., 1991, Art is for Healing, The Universal Link, San Antonio, Tex., 1992, Biennial, Fuller Lodge Art Ctr. Los Alamos, N.Mex., 1993, Layering, Albuquerque, 1993, Crossings, Bradford, Mass., 1994, The Layered Perspective, Fayetteville, Ark., 1994, Tree of Life, San Miguel de Allende, Mex., 1996, Honoree, Magnifico, Albuquerque, 1997; represented in pvt. collections in: U.S., Fed. Republic of Germany, Eng. and Australia; author: American Indian Biography Series, 1971-76, (with Robert E. Wood) Watercolor Workshop, 1974, (with Ramon Kelley) Ramon Kelley Paints Portraits and Figures, 1977, The Legendary Artists of Taos, 1980, (catalog) American Art in Peking, 1981, Masters of Western Art, 1982, Connecting, The Art of Beth Ames Swartz, 1984, Artists of the Spirit, 1994, Doris Steider, A Vision of Silence, 1996, (catalog) Layering, An Art of Time and Space, 1985, (catalog) Layering/Connecting, 1987; contbg. editor Am. Artist, 1976-91, Southwest Art, 1987-91; editor (video) Layering, 1990; arts correspondent Albuquerque Jour., 1991-93. Mem. Albuquerque Arts Bd., 1984-88. Mem. Soc. Layerists in Multi-Media (founder 1982). Home: 1408 Georgia St NE Albuquerque NM 87110-6861

NELSON, NANCY ELEANOR, pediatrician, educator; b. El Paso, Apr. 4, 1933; d. Harry Hamilton and Helen Maude (Murphy) N. BA magna cum laude, U. Colo., 1955, MD, 1959. Intern, Case Western Res. U. Hosp., 1959-60, resident, 1960-63; pvt. practice medicine specializing in pediats., Denver, 1963-70; clin. prof. U. Colo. Sch. Medicine, Denver, 1988—, assoc. dean, 1988—. Mem. Am. Acad. Pediats., AMA (sect. med. schs. governing coun. 1994-96), Denver Med. Soc. (pres. 1983-84), Colo. Med. Soc. (bd. dirs. 1985-88, mem. jud. coun. 1992—, mem. liason com. med. edn. 1995—). Home: 1140 Columbine St # 406 Denver CO 80206 Office: 4200 E 9th Ave Denver CO 80262

NELSON, NEVIN MARY, interior designer; b. Cleve., Nov. 5, 1941; d. Arthur George Reinker and Barbara Phyllis (Gunn) Parks; m. Wayne Nelson (div. 1969); children: Doug, Brian. BA in Interior Design, U. Colo., 1964. Prin. Nevin Nelson Design, Boulder, Colo., 1966-70, Vail, Colo., 1970—; program chmn. Questers Antique Study Group, Boulder, 1969. Coord. Bob Kirscht for Gov. campaign, Eagle County, Colo., 1986; state del. Rep. Nat. Conv., 1986-88; county coord. George Bush for U.S. Pres. campaign, 1988, 92; chmn. Eagle County Reps., 1989-93; v.p. bd. dirs. Park Lane Condo Assn., Denver, 1995-96. Mem. Am. Soc. Interior Designers. Episcopalian. Home: PO Box 1212 Vail CO 81658-1212 Office: 2498 Arosa Dr Vail CO 81657-4276

NELSON, PAULA MORRISON BRONSON, educator; b. Memphis, Mar. 26, 1944; d. Fred Ford and Julia (Morrison) Bronson: m. Jack Marvin Nelson, July 13, 1968; children: Eric Allen, Kelly Susan. BS, U. N.Mex., 1967; MA, U. Colo., Denver, 1985. Physical edn. tchr. Grant Union Sch. Dist., Sacramento, 1967-68; physical edn. tchr. Denver Pub. Schs., 1968-74, with program for pupil assistance, 1974-80, chpt. 1 reading specialist, 1983-96; computer/reading specialist Denver Pub. Schs., Parker, Colo., 1996—; tchr. ESL Douglas County Pub. Schs., Parker, Colo., 1982-83; demonstration tchr. Colo. Edn. Assn., 1970-72; mem. curriculum com. Denver Pub. Schs., 1970-72; mem. Douglas County Accountability Com., Castle Rock, Colo., 1986-92; mem. educators rev. panel Edn. for Freedom; computer trainer Denver Pub. Schs. Tech. Team, 1992—. Co-author: Gymnastics Teacher's Guide Elementary Physical Education, 1973, Applauding Our Constitution, 1989; editorial reviewer G is for Geography, Children's Literature and the Five Themes. 1993; producer slide shows Brotherhood, 1986, We the People...Our Dream Lives On, 1987, Celebration of Cultures, 1988. Named Pub. Edn. Coalition grantee, Denver, 1987, 88, 89, 90, grantee Rocky Mountain Global Edn. Project, 1987, Wake Forest Law Sch., Winston-Salem, N.C., 1988, 89, 90, 92; recipient chpt. II grant, 1991, Tech. grant, 1993, Three R's of Freedom award State Dept. Edn., 1987, Nat. Recognition award Commn. on Bicentennial of Constitution., 1987, Distinguished Tchr. award City of Denver, 1994. Mem. Windstar Found., Colo. Coun. Internat. Reading, Internat. Reading Assn., Nat. Soc. for Study of Edn., Colo. Coun. for the Social Studies, Tech. in Edn., Am. Fedn. Tchrs., Denver Fedn. Tchrs. Republican. Methodist. Home: 10488 E Meadow Run Parker CO 80134-6220

NELSON, RANDALL ERLAND, surgeon; b. Hastings, Nebr., Dec. 28, 1948; s. Marvin Erland and Faith Constance (Morrison) N.; m. Carolyn Joy Kaufman, Feb. 28, 1976. BS in Chemistry cum laude, So. Nazarene U., 1971; MD, U. Nebr., 1975; MS in Surgery, U. Ill., Chgo., 1979. Diplomate Nat. Bd. Med. Examiners, Am. Bd. Surgery. Intern in gen. surgery Strong Meml. Hosp., Rochester, N.Y., 1975-76; resident in gen. surgery U. Rochester Affiliated Hosps., 1976-78, Rush-Presbyn.-St. Luke's Med. Ctr., Chgo., 1978-81; gen. surgeon Surg. Group San Jose, Calif., 1981—; instr. gen. surgery U. Rochester Sch. Medicine and Dentistry, 1975-78, Rush Med. Coll., Chgo., 1978-80; adj. attending surgeon Rush-Presbyn.-St. Luke's Med. Ctr., 1980-81. Mem. Rep. Nat. Com., Washington, 1984—. Fellow ACS, Southwestern Surg. Congress; mem. Calif. Med. Assn., Santa Clara County Med. Soc., San Jose Surg. Soc., U.S. C. of C., Circle-K Club, Phi Delta Lambda. Republican. Office: Surg Group of San Jose 2101 Forest Ave Ste 124 San Jose CA 95128-1424

NELSON, ROBERT EARL, mental health counselor; b. Hardtnar, Kans., Sept. 13, 1952; s. Robert and Elsie (Brennon) N.; m. Mary K. Burton, Apr. 24, 1976; children: Nathan, Heber, Rebekah, David. BS, Brigham Young U., 1976, MEd, 1985; PhD, Calif. Coast U., 1994. Cert. mental health counselor, Wash. Fin. mgr. Southwestern Investment Co., Amarillo, Tex., 1978-80; officer USMC, 1980-84; sch. counselor Elk Grove (Calif.) H.S., 1985; crisis counselor Sacramento (Calif.) Cmty. Mental Health, 1985-87; chaplain U.S. Army, 1987-92; mental health profl. Columbia River Mental Health, Vancouver, Wash., 1993—; pvt. practice counseling, Vancouver, 1992—; adv. bd. Parents Anonymous, Vancouver, 1993. Author: W.I.N.N. Against Suicide, 1993; contbr. articles to profl. jours. Vol. The Share House, Vancouver, 1993—; mentor The Homeless Coun., Vancouver, 1994; chmn. precinct com. Dem. Party, Vancouver, 1993—; participant Leadership Clark County C. of C. Program, Vancouver, 1994; bd. trustees Cascade Disability Resources, Inc. Mem. ACA, Internat. Brotherhood of Magicians, Am. Mental Health Counselors Assn., Nat. Eagle Scout Assn., The Augustine Soc., Toastmasters Internat. (club pres., area gov. 1992—). Mormon. Home and Office: Nelson Counseling & Cons 1211 Manzanita Way Vancouver WA 98661-6356

NELSON, RONALD JOHN, cardiothoracic surgeon, educator; b. St. Paul, Nov. 20, 1934; s. Clarence Oscar and Magnhild Marie (Anderson) N.; m. L. Ruth Needels, June 10, 1961; children: Daniel G., Peter J., Kristen A. B.A. magna cum laude, U. Minn., 1956, B.S., 1957, M.D., 1959. Diplomate Am. Bd. Surgery, Am. Bd. Thoracic Surgery. Intern King County Hosp., Seattle, 1959-60; resident in surgery U. Wash., Seattle, 1961-68, instr. dept. surgery, 1967-68; asst. chief cardiovascular surgery Harbor/UCLA Med. Ctr., Torrance, 1968-73, chief cardiovascular surgery, 1973-76, chief div. thoracic and cardiovascular surgery, 1976-89; chief cardiac surgery St. John's Heart Inst., 1989-93, cardiac surgeon, 1989—; dir. Research and Edn. Inst., 1981-82; asst. prof., assoc. prof. surgery UCLA Sch. Medicine, 1970-80, prof. surgery, 1981-89, clin. prof. surgery, 1989—; mem. staff UCLA Med. Ctr., Santa Monica. Contbr. chpts. to books, articles to sci. jours. Chmn., Rolling Hills Covenant Ch., Rolling Hills Estates, Calif., 1975-77; mem. bd. reference Fuller Theol. Sem. Extension, Pasadena, Calif., 1978-83. Postdoctoral fellow NIH, 1964-65, research grantee, 1978—. Fellow ACS, Council of Cardiovascular Surgery of Am. Heart Assn.; mem. Pacific Coast Surg. Assn., Am. Assn. Thoracic Surgery, Soc. Thoracic Surgeons, other profl. orgns., Phi Beta Kappa, Alpha Omega Alpha. Home: 603 Ocean Ave 2N Santa Monica CA 90402 Office: St Johns Place 1301-20th St Ste # 590 Santa Monica CA 90404

NELSON, SCOTT HAVILAND, psychiatrist, administrator; b. Cleve., July 31, 1940; s. Albert S. and Jane (Sutton) N.; children; Todd, Riley, Chad. BA, Yale U., 1962; MD, Harvard U., 1966, MPH, 1970. Diplomae Am. Bd. Psychiatry and Neurology (examiner 1981—). Mental health dir. Job Corps. Dept. Labor, Washington, 1970-72, med. dir., 1972-73; dir. planning and evaluation Alcohol, Drug Abuse and Mental Health Adminstrn., Rockville, Md., 1973-76; dir. mental health divsn. Dept Hosps. and Isntns. State of New Mex., Santa Fe, 1976-78; dir. behavioral health divsn. Dept. Health and Environment State of New Mex., Santa Fe, 1978-80; dept. sec. and commr. of mental health Dept. Pub. Welfare, State of Pa., Harrisburg, 1980-87; chief mental health, social svcs. Indian Health Svc., Albuquerque, New Mex., 1987—; clin. prof. psychiatry U. N. Mex., dept. psychiatry, Albuquerque, 1990—; reviewer Hosp. and Cmty. Psychiatry, 1982—, Am. Jour. Psychiatry, 1978—; mem. editorial bd. Cmty. Mental Health Jour., 1984-88, invited reviewr, 1988—; cons. NIMH for Medicare Survey, 1978-84; psychiat. cons. Santa Fe Indian Hosp., Taos, Santa Clara and Dulce Health Clinics. Author: A Collector's Guide to Van Briggle Pottery, 1986; contbr. chpts. to books, monographs for sci. meetings and articles to profl. jours. Past pres. Los Arroyos Home Owners Assn., Santa Fe, 1992-95. Capt. USPHS, 1970—. Recipient Pres.' award Pa. Assn. of Mental Health/Mental Retardation Providers, Harrisburg, 1986, commendation Pa. Alliance for the Mentally Ill, Harrisburg, 1986. Fellow Am. Psychiat. Assn. (mem. many coms. including chmn. task force on involuntary commitment 1979-81, Gold award 1991); mem. Nat. Assn. State Mental Health Dirs. (many coms. and offices including pres. 1981-83), Psychiat. Med. Assn. N.Mex. (pres. 1993-94).

NELSON, SONJA BEA, paralegal; b. Calif., Jan. 20, 1961; d. John Bruce and Anita Pauline (Dean) Nelson. BA in Spanish with honors, U. Calif., Santa Barbara, 1983. Cert. paralegal, corp. specialist, 1984, litigation specialist, 1988. Paralegal Lawler, Felix & Hall, L.A., 1985-88, Adams, Duque & Hazeltine, L.A., 1988-89, Schramm & Raddue, Santa Barbara, 1989-92, Seed, Mackall & Cole LLP, Santa Barbara, 1992—; mem. adv. bd. and instr. Paralegal program U. Calif., Santa Barbara, 1993—. Com. mem. Semana Nautica Masters Volleyball, Santa Barbara, 1995—. Recipient Affiliates award Nat. Assn. Legal Assts., 1997. Mem. Legal Assts. Assn. Santa Barbara (pres. 1993-95, 1st v.p. 1992-93, treas., seminar chair, membership sec. 1989-92). Democrat. Office: Seed Mackall & Cole LLP 1332 Anacapa St Ste 200 Santa Barbara CA 93101-2090

NELSON, THOMAS G., federal judge; b. 1936. Student, Univ. Idaho, 1955-59, LLB, 1962. Ptnr. Parry, Robertson, and Daly, Twin Falls, Idaho, 1965-79, Nelson, Rosholt, Robertson, Tolman and Tucker, Twin Falls, from 1979; judge U.S. Cir. Ct. (9th cir.), Boise, Idaho, 1990—. With Idaho Air N.G., 1962-65, USAR, 1965-68. Mem. ABA (ho. of dels. 1974, 87-89), Am. Bar Found., Am. Coll. Trial Lawyers, Idaho State Bar (pres., bd. commrs.), Idaho Assn. Def. Counsel, Am. Bd. Trial Advocates (pres. Idaho chpt.), Phi Alpha Delta, Idaho Law Found. Office: US Ct Appeals 9th Circuit 304 N Eighth St PO Box 1339 Boise ID 83701-1339*

NELSON, THOMAS WILFRED, computer network company executive; b. Milw., Sept. 13, 1954; s. Marvin W. and Margaret (Tobin) N.; m. Carla I. Halverson, Aug. 7, 1981; children: Catherine I., Tobin J., Tyler T. BSBA in Mgmt., Acctg., U. Denver, 1976, MBA, 1977. Cons. U. Denver, 1976-77; mgr. acctg., systems and planning Infolink, Northbrook, Ill., 1977-78; cash adminstr. Congoleum Corp., Milw., 1979; fin. analyst corp. planning JI Case, Racine, Wis., 1979-83; sr. fin. analyst No. Telecom, Nashville, 1983-85, mgr. ops. support, 1985-86; controller New Eng. area No. Telecom, Waltham, Mass., 1986-89; dir. fin. and adminstrn. No. Telecom, West Palm Beach, Fla., 1989-91; group mgr. fin. planning analysis and reporting Johnson Controls, Inc., Milw., 1991-94; contr. JC Network Integration Svcs. Inc., Pitts., 1994-96; sr. v.p. fin. Fiber Optic Techs., Inc., Englewood, Colo., 1996—. Mem. Nat. Assn. Accts. (local dir. 1981-82), Jefferson Sq. Assn. (dir. 1984-86), Racine Zool. Soc. (dir. com. 1992—). Home: 5662 S Hannibal Way Aurora CO 80015 Office: ICG Fiber Optic Techs Inc Ste 308 6555 S Kenton St Englewood CO 80111

NELSON, WALTER WILLIAM, computer programmer, consultant; b. Seattle, May 7, 1954; s. Arne A. and Helen R. (Truitt) N.; m. Paula E. Truax, Dec. 21, 1985. BA in Zoology, U. Wash., 1976, BS in Psychology, 1977; PhC in Psychology, U. Minn., 1982. Systems analyst Dept. of Social and Health Svcs., State of Wash., Seattle, 1986-89; computer info. cons. Dept. of Health, State of Wash., Seattle, 1989-90; pres. Data Dimensions, Inc. (name now Nelson Consulting, Inc.), Seattle, 1990—; pres. Tech. Alliance, Renton, Wash., 1990-91, Nelson Family Homes, Inc., 1996—. Contbr. articles to profl. jours. Mem. Tech Alliance, Berkeley Macintosh Users Group, Seattle Downtown Macintosh Bus. Users Group, 4th Dimension Spl. Interest Group (founder, pres. 1990—). Office: Nelson Consulting Inc 6729 20th Ave NW Seattle WA 98117-5707

NELSON, WARREN JAMES, III, oil company executive, accountant; b. L.A., Sept. 16, 1950; s. Warren James Jr. and Mary Louise (Simmons) N.; m. Maria Louise Stuebinger, Jan. 5, 1980; 1 child, Trevor Carl. BS in Acctg. with honors, Calif. Poly., San Luis Obispo, 1972; MBA, U. Calif., Berkeley, 1974. CPA, Calif., Tex. Audit mgr. Price Waterhouse, Newport Beach, Calif., 1974-82; acting CFO, chief acctg. officer, contr. Smith Internat., Inc., Houston, 1982-90; exec. v.p., CFO, Everest & Jennings Internat., Ltd., Camarillo, Calif., 1990-92, Huntway Ptnrs., L.P., Newhall, Calif., 1993—. Treas. Salem Luth. Ch., Orange, Calif., 1985-88; treas. troop 0775 Boy Scouts Am., Thousand Oaks, Calif., 1993—. Mem. AICPA, Calif. Soc. CPA's. Republican. Presbyterian. Office: Huntway Ptnrs LP 25129 The Old Rd Ste 322 Newhall CA 91381-2249

NELSON, WILLIAM RANKIN, surgeon, educator; b. Charlottesville, Va., Dec. 12, 1921; s. Hugh Thomas and Edith (Rankin) N.; m. Nancy Laidley, Mar. 17, 1956 (div. 1979); children: Robin Page Nelson Russel, Susan Kimberly Nelson Wright, Anne Rankin Nelson Cron; m. Pamela Morgan Phelps, July 5, 1984. BA, U. Va., 1943, MD, 1945. Diplomate Am. Bd. Surgery. Intern Vanderbilt U. Hosp., Nashile, 1945-46; resident in surgery U. Va. Hosp., Charlottesville, 1949-51; fellow surg. oncology Meml. Sloan Kettering Cancer Ctr., N.Y.C., 1951-55; instr. U. Colo. Sch. Medicine, Denver, 1955-57; asst. clin. prof. U. Colo. Sch. Medicine, 1962-87, clin. prof. surgery, 1987—; asst. prof. Med. Coll. Va., Richmond, 1957-62; mem. exec. com. U. Colo. Cancer Ctr.; mem. nat. bd., nat. exec. com. Am. Cancer Soc. Contbr. articles to profl. jours. and chpts. to textbooks. Capt. USAAF, 1946-48. Recipient Nat. Div. award Am. Cancer Soc., 1979. Fellow Am. Coll. Surgeons (bd. govs. 1984-89); mem. AMA, Internat. Soc. Surgery, Brit. Assn. Surg. Oncology, Royal Soc. Medicine (U.K.), Soc. Surg. Oncology (pres. 1975-76), Soc. Head and Neck Surgeons (pres. 1986-87), Am. Cancer Soc. (pres. Colo. div. 1975-77, exec. com., nat. bd. dirs., del. dir. from Colo. div. 1975—), Am. Soc. Clin. Oncology, Western Surg. Assn. Colo. Med. Soc., Denver Med. Soc., Denver Acad. Surgery, Rocky Mt. Oncology Soc., Univ. Club, Rotary. Republican. Episcopalian.

NELSON-RODRIGUEZ, CATHERINE LYNN, artist, writer, American Indian basket weaver; b. Oceanside, Calif., Oct. 2, 1953; d. Theodore and Dorothy Nelson; m. Gary A. Rodriguez Sr., Aug. 4, 1978 (dec. Apr. 1983); children: David J. Nelson, Gary A. Rodriguez II; m. John A. Rodriguez, June 1, 1993. Student, Palomar Coll., San Marcos, Calif., 1984-86. Grant writer La Jolla Band of Indians, Valley Center, Calif., 1984-93, water park mgr., 1985-90; tchr. basket weaving La Jolla Indian Reservation, 1996; guest speaker on art. Exhibited in one woman shows at Calif. Sch. Profl. Psychology, San Diego, 1996, Santa Ysabel (Calif.) Art Gallery, 1996; group shows include Centro Cultural de la Raza, Balboa Park, Calif., 1987, Am. Indian Contemporary Arts, San Francisco, 1995, Robert Freeman Art Gallery, Rincon Indian Reservation, 1995, 95. Mem. Tribal Coun., La Jolla Band of Indians, 1989-91, housing chair, 1984-90. Lassen County Arts Coun. fellow, 1994. Christian. Office: PO Box 894 Valley Center CA 92082

NEMAN, EDWARD LOUIS, III, hospital administrator; b. Land O'Lakes, Wis., Mar. 16, 1951; s. Edward Louis Jr. and Helen Eusibia (Lawler) N.; m. Nancy Mitchell Fleming, Sept. 27, 1980. BA in Journalism, Marquette U., 1973, BA in Polit. Sci., 1973, MA in Journalism, 1975; MA in Habitational Resources, U. Wis., Menomonie, 1979. Cert. alcoholism and substance abuse counselor, Ariz. News anchor/prodr. WITI TV-6, Milw., 1972-74; news dir. WRIT Newsradio, Milw., 1974-76; counselor Pasar, Inc., Tucson, 1979-81; mgr. Thanet Hotel, London, 1981-82; anchor/talk show host KNST Newstalk Radio, Tucson, 1982-84; dir. pub. rels. Owens Advt., Tucson, 1984; pub. rels. dir. Miles Advt. & Pub. Rels., Tucson, 1985; owner, exec. v.p. Lauer-Neman Advt., Tucson, 1986-88; owner, pres. Media Plus Advt. and Pub. Rels., Tucson, 1986-88; psychiat. program dir. Kino Hosp., Tucson, 1988-91; pres. Quality Enhancement Assocs., Inc., Scottsdale, Ariz., 1992—; program cons. Chrysalis Shelters Victims of Domestic Violence, Phoenix, 1993-94; crisis counselor Terros, Inc., Phoenix, 1994—; supervisory mem. Kino Improvement Coun., Kino Hosp., 1990-91, chmn. commn. coun., 1991; cert. instr. W. Edwards Deming-Theories of Mgmt. Tng., Tucson, 1989-91. Editor, writer, producer documentary film for AMA, 1974; food editor Tucson Mag., 1984-86; food/restaurant critic Am. Restaurant Rev., 1978. Vice chmn. Democrats of Greater Tucson, 1983; dep. voter registrar Pima County, Ariz., Tucson; fundraising chair United Way Pima County, Tucson, 1989, 90; mem. Sunsounds of Ariz.; dep. voter registrar Maricopa County, Ariz.; precinct committeeman, Scottsdale; candidate Ariz. State Ho. of Reps., 1992. Recipient Gov.'s Cup Best Newscast Ariz. Press Club, 1984; named Outstanding Citizen of the Yr. Goodwill Industries, Milw., 1974. Mem. Tucson Press Club, London Press Club, Milw. Press Club (gov. 1976-78), Sigma Delta Chi (pres. 1972-73). Democrat. Home: 4354 N 82nd St Apt 109 Scottsdale AZ 85251 Office: Terros Inc 320 E Virginia Phoenix AZ 85004

NEMETZ, PETER NEWMAN, policy analysis educator, economics researcher; b. Vancouver, B.C., Can., Feb. 19, 1944; s. Nathan Theodore and Bel Nemetz; m. Roma E.S. Kellock, July 16, 1994; 1 stepchild, Fiona Susan. BA in Econs. and Polit. Sci., U. B.C., 1966; AM in Econs., Harvard U., 1969, PhD in Econs., 1973. Teaching fellow, tutor Harvard U., Cambridge, Mass., 1971-73; lectr. Sch. Planning, U. B.C., Vancouver, 1973-75, asst. prof. to assoc. prof. policy analysis, 1975-96, prof., 1996—, chmn., 1984-90; non-resident faculty Green Coll., 1993-94, 95-97; postdoctoral fellow Westwater Rsch. Centre, Vancouver, 1973-75; vis. scientist, dept. med. stats. and epidemiol. Mayo Clinic, 1986-88, sr. visiting scientist Dept. of Health Scis. Rsch. Mayo Clinic, 1988—; cons. consumer and corp. affairs, Can., 1977-80; program chmn. The Vancouver Inst., 1990—; mem. rsch. mgmt. com. Ctr. Health Svcs and Policy Rsch., U. B.C., 1990—, mgmt. com. Ctr. Southeast Asia Rsch., 1992—; bd. dirs. U. B.C. Press, 1993—; faculty assoc. U. B.C. dept. resource mgmt. and envirin. studies, 1979—, Ctr. Japanese Studies, 1992—, dept. healthcare and epidemiology; selection com. U. B.C. Rhodes Scholarship, 1991-97; assoc. Ctr. Pacific Basin Monetary and Econ. Studies, Econ. Rsch. Dept., Fed. Reserve Bank of San Francisco, 1991—. Mem. bd. mgmt. BC-Yukon divsn. Can. Nat. Inst. for Blind., 1992-94; mem. Earthquake Engring. Rsch. Inst. Editor Jour. Bus. Adminstrn., 1978—. Contbr. articles to sci. jours. Grantee Natural Scis. and Engring. Rsch. Coun. of Can., 1976-92, Consumer and Corp. Affairs Can., 1978-80, Econ. Coun. of Can., 1979-80, Max Bell Found., 1982-84. Mem. Am. Econ. Assn., AAAS. Jewish. Clubs: Harvard of B.C. (pres. 1986-94), Vancouver Club. Avocations: swimming; photography. Office: Univ British Columbia, Faculty of Commerce, Vancouver, BC Canada V6T 1Z2

NEMIR, DONALD PHILIP, lawyer, commodities trader; b. Oakland, Calif., Oct. 31, 1931; s. Philip F. and Mary (Shavor) N. AB, U. Calif., Berkeley, 1957, JD, 1960. Bar: Calif. 1961, U.S. Dist. Ct. (no. dist.) Calif. 1961, U.S. Ct. Appeals (9th cir.) 1961, U.S. Dist. Ct. (ctrl. dist.) Calif. 1975, U.S. Supreme Ct. 1980. Pvt. practice, San Francisco, 1961—; pres. Law Offices Donald Nemir. Mem. Calif. State Bar Assn. Home: PO Box 1089 Mill Valley CA 94942-1089

NEMIROFF, MAXINE CELIA, art educator, gallery owner, consultant; b. Chgo., Feb. 11, 1935; d. Oscar Bernard and Martha (Mann) Kessler; m. Paul Rubenstein, June 26, 1955 (div. 1974); children: Daniel, Peter, Anthony; m. Allan Nemiroff, Dec. 24, 1979. BA, U. So. Calif., 1955; MA, UCLA, 1974. Sr. instr. UCLA, 1974-92; dir., curator art gallery Doolittle Theater, Los Angeles, 1985-86; owner Nemiroff Deutsch Fine Art, Santa Monica, Calif.; leader of worldwide art tours; cons. L'Ermitage Hotel Group, Beverly Hills, Calif., 1982—, Broadway Dept. Stores, So. Calif., 1979—, Security Pacific Bank, Calif., 1978—, Am. Airlines, Calif. Pizza Kitchen Restaurants; art chmn. UCLA Thieves Market, Century City, 1960—, L.A. Music Ctr. Mercado, 1982—; lectr. in field. Apptd. bd. dirs. Dublin (Calif.) Fine Arts Found., 1989; mem. Calif. Govs. Adv. Coun. for Women, 1992. Named Woman of Yr. UCLA Panhellenic Council, 1982, Instr. of Yr. UCLA Dept. Arts, 1984. Mem. L.A. County Mus. Art Coun., UCLA Art Coun., UCLA Art Coun. Docents, Alpha Epsilon Phi (alumnus of yr. 1983). Democrat. Jewish.

NEMO, GINA, actress, producer, photographer, recording executive; b. N.Y.C., Mar. 22, 1965; d. Henry and Carol (Holt) N.; m. Peter DeLuise, 1988 (div. 1992); m. Justin Page, 1995. AA, Santa Monica (Calif.) Coll., 1985. Pub. Indano Music Co., Pacific Palisades, Calif., 1991—; owner Gina Nemo Photography, Santa Monica, 1992—; ptnr. Omen Fiction, Santa Monica, 1995—; owner Omen Fiction Pub., Santa Monica, 1995—; freelance cons. for various record labels, L.A., 1994—. photographs published in People Mag. Named Best Actress in a Fgn. TV Series, 1989. Mem. SAG, AFTRA, ASCAP. Office: Omen Fiction 1223 Wilshire Blvd # 411 Santa Monica CA 90403

NEPPE, VERNON MICHAEL, neuropsychiatrist, author, educator; b. Johannesburg, Transvaal, Rep. South Africa, Apr. 16, 1951; came to U.S., 1986; s. Solly Louis and Molly (Hesselsohn) N.; m. Elisabeth Selima Schachter, May 29, 1977; children: Jonathan, Shari. BA, U. South Africa, 1976; MB, BCh, U. Witwatersrand, Johannesburg, 1973, diploma in psychol. medicine, 1976, M in Medicine, 1979, PhD in Medicine, 1981; MD, U.S., 1982. Diplomate Am. Bd. Psychiatry and Neurology, Am. Bd. Geriatric Psychiatry, Am. Bd. Forensic Psychiatry, Am. Bd. Forensic Examiners, Am. Bd. Forensic Medicine; registered psychiatry specialist U.S., Republic of South Africa, Can. Specialist in tng. dept. psychiatry U. Witwatersrand, Johannesburg, 1974-80; sr. cons. U. Witwatersrand Med. Sch., Johannesburg, 1980-82, 83-85; neuropsychiatry fellow Cornell U., N.Y.C., 1982-83; div. dir. U. Wash. Med. Sch., Seattle, 1986-92; dir. Pacific Neuropsychiat. Inst., Seattle, 1992—; mem. clin. faculty dept. psychiatry and behavioral scis. U. Wash. Med. Sch., 1992—; adj. prof. psychiatry St. Louis U. Sch. of Medicine, dept. psychiatry and human behavior, 1994—; attending physician N.W. Hosp., 1992—; neuropsychiatry cons. South African Brain Rsch. Inst., Johannesburg, 1985—; chief rsch. cons. Epilepsy Inst., N.Y.C., 1989; mem. faculty lectr. Epilepsy: Refining Med. treatment, 1993-94. Author: The Psychology of Déjà Vu, 1983, Innovative Psychopharmacotherapy, 1990, (text) BROCAS SCAN, 1992; (with others) 31 book chpts.; editor 14 jours. issues; contbr. articles to profl. jours. Recipient Rupert Sheldrake prize for rsch. design (2d prize) award New Scientist, 1983, Marius Valkhoff medal South African Soc. for Psychical Rsch., 1982, George Elkin Bequest for Med. Rsch., U. Witwatersrand, 1980; named Overseas Travelling fellow, 1982-83. Fellow Psychiatry Coll. South Africa (faculty), Royal Coll. Physicians of Can., North Pacific Soc. for Neurology, Neurosurgery and Psychiatry, Coll. Internat. Neuropharmacologicum, Am. Coll. Forensic Examiners; mem. AMA, Parapsychologic Assn., Am. Psychiat. Assn. (U.S. transcultural collaborator diagnostic and statis. manual 1985-86, cons. organic brain disorders 1988—), Am. Epilepsy Soc., Soc. Biol. Psychiatry, Can. Psychiat. Assn., Soc. Sci. Exploration, Am. soc. Clin. Psychopharmacology, Am. Neuropsychiat. Assn. Jewish. Office: Pacific Neuropsychiat Inst 10330 Meridian Ave N Ste 380 Seattle WA 98133-9463

NESBITT, PAUL EDWARD, historian, author, educator; b. Balt., Dec. 25, 1943; s. William Ervin and Margaret Caroline (Shaw) N.; m. Donna Jean Coppock, Aug. 15, 1966 (dec. 1972); children: Erik-Paul A., Janelle M., m.

Pamela Jean Lichty, May 25, 1974 (div. 1983); m. Anita Louise Wood, Dec. 8, 1984 (div. 1989); m. Paula Jane Sawyer, May 7, 1994. AB, U. Wash., 1965; MA, Wash. State U., 1968, PhD (hon.), 1970; PhD, U. Calgary, 1972. Reader in Anthropology, U. Wash., 1965, grad. research-tchr. Wash. State U., 1966-68, instr., Tacoma Community Coll., Wash., 1968-69; grad. research-tchr. U. Calgary, Alta., Can., 1969-71; exec. Hudson's Bay Co., Calgary, 1971; prof. Western Oreg. U., Monmouth, 1971-74; state historian State of Calif., Sacramento, 1974—; dir. Am. Sch. of Interior Design, San Francisco, 1974, HBC Bow Fort Rsch., Morley, Atla., 1970-71; instr. Am. River Coll., Sacramento, 1980-86; exec. mgr. Calif. State Govt. United Way Campaign, 1986, 87, also bd. dirs., mem. fiscal and communication coms., El Dorado County and Sacramento chpts., 1988—; designer, cultural rsch. cons. pvt. contracts western states, 1960—; exec. dir. Heritage Areas Assn., 1993—, pres. bd. dir., 1994—. Contbr. articles to prof. jours. Fellow Am. Anthropl. Assn.; mem. Calif. Hist. Soc., Am. Inst. of Interior Designers (profl. 1974-77, bd. dirs. energy planning and devel. cos. 1986-88), AIA (Cen. Valley chpt. 1975-77), Rotary. Home: 3177 Clark St Placerville CA 95667-6405 Office: PO Box 942896 Sacramento CA 94296-0001

NESHEIM, DENNIS WARREN, art educator, artist, writer, instructional materials producer; b. Decorah, Iowa, Nov. 24, 1948; s. Kenneth H. and Adelle T. (Amundson) N.; m. Lavonne Selene Jones, Mar. 29, 1968. AA, Rochester State Jr. Coll., Minn., 1970; BS in Art/Art Edn., Winona (Minn.) State U., 1972. cert. art tchr. K-12, Minn., Wis., Dept. Def. Dependent Schs. Tchr. art Cassville (Wis.) Pub. Schs., 1972-74, Franklin Mid. Sch., Shawano, Wis., 1974-76; substitute tchr., tchr. 4th grade Dept. Def. Dependent Schs., Neu Ulm, Germany, 1977-78; tchr. art Ulm. Am. Sch. Dept. Def. Dependent Schs., Neu Ulm, 1978-80, tchr. art and video arts, 1980-87; tchr., artist art ctrs., Fla., 1987-89; owner, producer Nesheim Arts & Video, Lakeland Fla., Lakewood, Colo., 1989—; tchr. art, tchr. aide Synergy Sch., Denver, Colo.; presenter workshops and seminars, 1980-86; video tng., cons., Lakeland, 1988-93. Author, illustrator: (workbook) Making Waves, An Imagination Starter, 1994; creator, producer: (instrnl. video/handbook kits) Look and Draw series, 1990—; editor lit. quar. Onionhead, 1989-93, others; cons. writer, editor Frugal Times, 1992; part-time writer, editor Free Shopping News, 1985-87, S&N Advertising, 1985-87; prodr. (videos) Fantastic Realism, The Video, 1989, Epic Silence, 1989, Verbal Science, 1989, October 26, 1970, 1990, See in the Dark, 1990, Look and Draw, 1990, Head in the Clouds, 1990, Look and Draw Faces and Figures, 1991, Look and Draw Space In Perspective, 1992; prodr. (with David Lee Jr.) Produce Better Video, 1989; one-man shows include Donau Casino, Neu Ulm, Germany, 1977, Maas Brothers Gallery, Lakeland, 1990; exhibited in group shows Wurzburg (Germany) Milcom, 1979, Oberstube Gallery, Ulm, Germany, 1985, 86, Ridge Art, Winter Haven, Fla. (Merit award), 1988, Arts on the Park, Lakeland, (Honorable Mention award) 1988, 89, 90, 91, Arts Ctr., St. Petersburg, Fla. 1989, Art League Manatee, Bradenton, Fla., 1989, Ridge Art Assn., Winter Haven, Fla., 1990, Mt. Dora (Fla.) Ctr. for the Arts, 1990, Imperial Artists Gallery, Lakeland, 1990, 1991; contbr. articles to profl. jours. Mem. Arts on Park, Lakeland Ctr. for Creative Arts, 1987-95, bd. dirs., 1991-93; mem. Green Mountain Park Vols. Recipient various commendations and appreciation awards from schs. and cmty. orgns. Mem. Nat. Art Edn. Assn., Fine Art Forum, Compuserve. Office: Synergy Sch 4123 S Julian Way Denver CO 80236-3101

NESS, BRYAN DOUGLAS, biologist, educator; b. Seattle, June 6, 1961; s. Iver L. and Nancy J. (Anderson) N.; m. Judy Lynn Egnew, June 7, 1981; children: Tara Lynn, Reuben David. BS in Biology, Walla Walla Coll., 1983, MS in Biology, 1985; PhD in Botany, Wash. State U., 1992. Assoc. prof. biology Pacific Union Coll., Angwin, Calif., 1989—. Editl. cons. Calochortus Soc., Berkeley, Calif., 1992—; contbr. articles to profl. jours.; contbg. author: The Jepson Manual, 1993. Recipient N.W. Sci. Assn. award, 1986; Sigma Xi grantee, 1986, NSF grantee, 1987-89; Hannah Aase fellow, 1986-88. Mem. Am. Soc. Plant Taxonomists, Bot. Soc. Am., audubon Soc., Adventist Sci. Educators Soc., Nature Conservancy, Am. Philatelic Soc. Home: 46 Mobile Manor Angwin CA 94508 Office: Pacific Union College 1 Angwin Ave Angwin CA 94508

NESS, JAMES JOSEPH, law enforcement educator; b. Stevens Point, Wis., July 6, 1941; s. Lawrence Joseph and Eleanor Thresa (Hojnacki) Niespodziani; m. Sandra Jean Peters Feverston, Apr. 11, 1964 (div. Sept. 1985); 1 child, Peter James; m. Ellyn Katherine Buikema, Nov. 29, 1986; 1 child, Jamie (dec.). BA in Liberal Arts, Northeastern Ill. U., 1975; MS in Law Enforcement, So. Ill. U., 1979, PhD in Ednl. Admin., 1989. Patrol officer Wis. Dells Police, 1964-66, Drake U. Police, Des Moines, 1966-69; police lt. Triton Police Dept., River Grove, Ill., 1969-77; rschr. So. Ill. U., Carbondale, 1977-79, dir. police mgmt. study, 1979-81, prof. law enforcement, 1983-89; chief of police Villa Grove (Ill.) Police, 1981-83; dir. AJ programs Barton County C.C., Great Bend, Kans., 1989-95; dean of academics Haitian Nat. Police Tng. Ctr., Port-au-Prince, Haiti, 1995; internat. police task force UN, Bosnia, Yugoslavia, 1996—. Author: Introduction to Law Enforcement, 1994; contr. articles to profl. jours. Staff sgt., USAF, 1959-64. Mem. Internat. Assn. Chiefs of Police, Central Kans. CASA (pres. 1990-94), Ctrl. Kans. Cmty. Corrections (pres. 1993-95). Home: 1111 N 64th # 9 Mesa AZ 85205 Office: Ness Ness & Assoc Ltd PO Box 20562 Mesa AZ 85272-0562

NESTER, ROBBI LYNNE KELLMAN, writing and literature educator; b. Phila., Oct. 26, 1953; d. Morris David and Lydia Gertrude (Horvitch) Kellman; m. Richard Harrison Nester, May 30, 1976; 1 child, Jeremy Leigh. BA in English, Hollins Coll., 1975, MA in English, 1976; MFA in Creative Writing, U. Calif., Irvine, 1982, PhD in Comparative Lit., 1993. Career libr. U. Mass., Amherst, 1978-80; instr. composition Calif. State U., Long Beach, 1982-83; tchg. asst., assoc., instr. U. Calif., Irvine, 1980-89, 95; tutor Hyperlearning, Irvine, 1993—; tutor, freelance editing, 1976—; co-editor: GradTimes, U. Calif., Irvine, 1986; speaker in field. Publs. include book revs., L.A./The Agitator, 1987, Prodigal Sun, Irvine, 1984, The Greenfield Review, Greenfield, N.Y., others. Sec. Cousin's Club, Irvine, 1988-89; mem. New Jewish Agenda, Irvine, 1986-88. Travel grantee U. Calif., Irvine, 1988. Mem. MLA, Am. Comparative Lit. Assn., Vladimir Nabakov Soc. Democrat. Jewish. Home: 196 Streamwood Irvine CA 92620

NESTOR, JOHN JOSEPH, JR., pharmaceutical executive; b. Miami, Fla., Jan. 21, 1945; s. John J. and Marion (Sexton) N.; m. Janet Francis, Aug. 14, 1976; 1 child, James. BS in Chemistry, Poly. Inst. Bklyn., 1966; PhD in Organic Chemistry, U. Ariz., 1971; postgrad. in peptide chemistry, Cornell U., Ithaca, N.Y., 1972-74. Staff rschr. I/II/sr. Syntex Rsch., Palo Alto, Calif., 1974-83, dept. head, 1983-85, asst. dir. Inst. Bioorganic Chemistry, 1985-87, v.p., inst. dir., 1987-95, Roche Biosci. disting. scientist, v.p., 1995-96; exec. v.p., chief sci. officer Helios Pharms., Inc., Louisville, 1996—. Editor: LHRH and Its Analogs, part I, 1984, part II, 1987. Mem. indsl. adv. bd. U. Calif.-San Diego, 1990-96. Mem. AAAS, Internat. Soc. Quantum Biology, Am. Peptide Soc., Am. Chem. Soc.

NESWITZ, MARGYE FULGHAM, newspaper columnist; b. Brownsboro, Tex., Oct. 15, 1920; d. Ivy Thomas and Nannie Savannah (Brewer) Fulgham; m. David Ross Thompson, Sept. 11, 1942 (dec.); children: Ivy Victor, (twins) Rhonda Ruth and Dennis Manning (dec.); m. Philip Neswitz, Apr. 9, 1955. AA, Lon Morris Coll., 1939; BA, Baylor U., 1942. Clk. Lockheed, San Diego, 1942-44; prof. drama Lon Morris Coll., Jacksonville, Tex., 1947; tchr. Oxnard (Calif.) H.S., 1949-52; theater critic Chgo. newspapers, 1963-69; freelance travel writer Chgo., 1959—; society columnist Monterey (Calif.) County Herald; society editor KSBW-TV, Monterey; past adv. bd. Ctr. for Performing Arts, Monterey Bay. Chair Art al Fresco of Monterey Peninsula, Pebble Beach, Calif., East Meets West, Pebble Beach. Recipient Monterey County benefactor award Cultural Coun. Monterey County, 1993, disting. alumni award Lon Morris Coll., 1994, spl. commendations: March of Dimes, ARC, Am. Diabetes Assn., Am. Heart Assn., Quota Club Monterey/Pacific Grove, Monterey County United Vol. Svc. Mem. Soroptimists, Monterey County Symphony Guild. Home and Office: PO Box 1131 Pebble Beach CA 93953-1131

NETHERCUTT, GEORGE RECTOR, JR., congressman, lawyer; b. Spokane, Wash., Oct. 4, 1944; s. George Rector and Nancy N.; m. Mary Beth Socha Nethercutt, Apr. 2, 1977; children: Meredith, Elliott. BA in English, Wash. State U., 1967; JD, Gonzaga U., 1971. Bar: D.C. 1972. Law clk. to Hon. Raymond Plummer U.S. Dist. Ct. Alaska, Anchorage, 1971; staff counsel to U.S. Senator Ted Stevens Washington, 1972, chief of staff to U.S. Senator Ted Stevens, 1972-76; pvt. practice Spokane, Wash., 1977-94; mem. 104th Congress from 5th Wash. dist., Washington, 1994—; mem. agriculture, interior, nat. security coms. Chmn. Spokane County Rep. Party, 1990-94, co-founder Vanessa Behan Crisis Nursery, pres. Spokane Juvenile Diabetes Found., 1993-94. Mem. Masons (lodge #34), Lions Club (Spokane Ctrl.), Sigma Nu. Republican. Presbyterian. Office: US House Reps 1527 Longworth House Office Bldg Washington DC 20515-4705*

NETTLESHIP, LOIS ELLEN, history educator; b. Bklyn., June 14, 1942; d. Charles and Ethel (Bernstein) Shankman; m. William. A. Nettleship, Aug. 14, 1966; children: Elizabeth, Anna. BA, Sarah Lawrence Coll., 1964; MA, Columbia U., 1966; DPhil., U. Sussex, Eng., 1976. Mem. faculty Johnson County Community Coll., Overland Park, Kans., 1975-91, Fullerton (Calif.) Coll., 1991—; dir. Johnson County Ctr. for Local History, Overland Park, Kans., 1983-91; tchr. Great Plains and Western U.S. history Columbia U., summer 1990. Author numerous books on local Kans. history, 1986-91; contbr. articles to profl. jours. Mem. Johnson County Bicentennial Commn., 1987-88. Woodrow Wilson Found. fellow 1964, NEH fellow 1980, 82; named Innovator of Yr. League for Innovation, 1984. Mem. Kans. Com. for the Humanities (bd. dirs. 1987-90), Kans. Hist. Tchrs. Assn. (pres. 1987-88), Kans. State Hist. Soc. (editorial com. 1988-90). Home: 526 Pinehurst Ave Placentia CA 92870-4450

NETTLESHIP, WILLIAM ALLAN, sculptor; b. Indpls., Dec. 2, 1944; s. Anderson Nettleship and Mollie (Markley) O'Kane; m. Lois Ellen Shankman, Aug. 14, 1966; children: Elizabeth, Anna. BA, Columbia U., 1967; MFA, U. Ark., 1972. Instr. art Avila Coll., Kansas City, Mo., 1974-76; mem. collaborative design teams mcpl. agencies of Kansas City, Mo., 1988, Phoenix, 1991-95; lectr. various mus., arts coun. and univ./colls. Exhbns. include 17 solo and two person shows, 27 group shows including Kyoto Gallery, Japan, 1993; pub. commns. include Hyde Park Neighborhood Markers, Kansas City, 1978, 49/63 Neighborhood Markers, Kansas City, 1982, Alden Weber Meml. Plaza, John Brown Park, Osawatomie, Kans., 1982, Lake Overlook, William Woods Coll., Fulton, Mo., 1983, Playground, The New Sch., Fayetteville, Ark., 1984, Poletno Veselje (The Summer Pleasure), Maribor, Slovenia, 1986, Ursa Major, William Christman H.S., Independence, Mo., 1987, A Meditation Place, Whitebook Garden, U. Judaism, L.A., 1988, Incomplete/A Stage, McCune Sch., Independence, 1988, Progression, Kansas City Mid. Sch. for the Arts, 1988, As Smart As I Am., Kan. Sch. for Visually Handicapped, 1989, Entrace walk, Audubon Art Ctr., New Haven, 1990, Amy Frets Meml., Rosedale Sharing Cmty., Mennontie, Kansas City, Kans., 1991, The Queen of the Prairie, Liberty Ctr. Theater, Sedalia, Mo., 1991, Seven Tactile Navigation Sculptures, The Exploratorium, San Francisco, 1992, Sophron, Alameda County Pub. Works Dept. Bldg., Hayward, Calif., 1993, Alluvium, Concession facility, Folsom Lake State Recreation Area, Granite Bay, Calif., 1994, Shell and Beach, Toll Plaza, Zuma Beach County Park, Malibu, Calif., 1995, Siauruju Juru Centre (At the Center of the Narrow Seas), Vilnius, Lithuania, 1995, The Black Swamp, Bowling Green State U., 1996. Commn. grantee Nat. Endowment for the Arts, 1992, Kans. Arts Commn., 1989, 91, Mo. Arts Coun., 1987, 88, 91. Home and Office: 526 Pinehurst Ave Placentia CA 92870

NETZEL, PAUL ARTHUR, fund raising management executive, consultant; b. Tacoma, Sept. 11, 1941; s. Marden Arthur and Audrey Rose (Jones) N.; BS in Group Work Edn., George Williams Coll., 1963; m. Diane Viscount, Mar. 21, 1963; children: Paul M., Shari Ann. Program dir. S. Pasadena-San Marino (Calif.) YMCA, 1963-66; exec. dir. camp and youth programs Wenatchee (Wash.) YMCA, 1966-67; exec. dir. Culver-Palms Family YMCA, Culver City, Calif., 1967-73; v.p. met. fin. devel. YMCA Met. Los Angeles, 1973-78, exec. v.p. devel., 1979-85; pres. bd. dirs. YMCA Employees Credit Union, 1977-80; chmn. N.Am. Fellowship of YMCA Devel. Officers, 1980-83; adj. faculty U. So. Calif. Coll. Continuing Edn., 1983-86, Loyola Marymount U., L.A., 1986-90, Calif. State U., L.A., 1991-92, UCLA Extension, 1991—; chmn., CEO Netzel Assocs., Inc., 1985—; pvt. practice cons., fund raiser. Chmn. Culver-Palms YMCA, Culver City, 1991-93, chmn. 1989-91, bd. mgrs. 1985—; pres. bd. Culver City Guidance Clinic, 1971-74; mem. Culver City Bd. Edn., 1975-79, pres., 1977-78; mem. Culver City Edn. Found., 1982-91; bd. dirs. Los Angeles Psychiat. Svc., 1971-74, Goodwill Industries of So. Calif., 1993—; mem. Culver City Council, 1980-88, vice-mayor, 1980-82, 84-85, mayor, 1982-83, 86-87; mem. Culver City Redevel. Agy., 1980-88, chmn., 1983-84, 87-88, vice chmn, 1985-86; bd. dirs. Los Angeles County Sanitation Dists., 1982-83, 85-87, Western Region United Way, 1986-93, vice chmn, 1991-92; chmn. bd. dirs. Calif. Youth Model Legislature, 1987-92; mem. World Affairs Coun., 1989—; mem. adv. bd. Automobile Club of So. Calif., 1996—. Recipient Man of Yr. award Culver City C. of C., 1972. Mem. Nat. Soc. Fund Raising Execs. (nat. bd. dirs. 1989-91, vice chmn. 1994, v.p. bd. dirs. Greater L.A. chpt. 1986-88, pres. bd. dirs. 1989-90, Profl. of Yr. 1983), Calif. Club, Rotary (L.A. # 5, pres. 1992-93, treas. L.A. found. 1995-96), Rotary Internat. (gov. dist. 5280 1997—), Mountain Gate Country. Address: Netzel Assocs Inc 9696 Culver Blvd Ste 204 Culver City CA 90232-2753

NEU, CARL HERBERT, JR., management consultant; b. Miami Beach, Fla., Sept. 4, 1937; s. Carl Herbert and Catherine Mary (Miller) N.; BS, MIT, 1959; MBA, Harvard U., 1961; m. Carmen Mercedes Smith, Feb. 8, 1964; children—Carl Bartley, David Conrad. Cert. profl. mgmt. cons. Indsl. liaison officer MIT, Cambridge, 1967-69; coord. forward planning Gates Rubber Co., Denver, 1969-71; pres., co-founder Dyna-Com Resources, Lakewood, Colo., 1971-77; pres., founder Neu & Co., Lakewood, 1977—; mng. dir. Pro-Med Mgmt. Systems, Lakewood, 1981—; lectr. Grad. Sch. Pub. Affairs, U. Colo. Denver, 1982-84. Mem. exec. coun. Episcopal Diocese Colo., 1974; mem. Lakewood City Coun., 1975-80, pres., 1976; chmn. Lakewood City Charter Commn., 1982, Lakewood Civic Found., Inc., 1986—; pres. Lakewood on Parade, 1978, bd. dirs., 1978-80; pres. Classic Chorale, Denver, 1979, bd. dirs., 1978-83; pres. Lakewood Pub. Bldg. Authority, 1983—; bd. dirs. Metro State Coll. of Denver Found., 1990—, treas., 1994—; bd. dirs. Kaiser Permanente Health Adv. Com., 1990—, chair, 1997. With U.S. Army, 1961-67. Decorated Bronze Star medal, Army Commendation medal; recipient Arthur Page award AT&T, 1979; Kettering Found. grantee, 1979-80. Mem. World Future Soc., Internat. City Mgrs. Assn., Lakewood-So. Jefferson County C. of C. (bd. dirs. 1983-89, chmn. 1988, chmn. 1987-88), Jefferson County C. of C. (chmn. 1988). Republican. Episcopalian. Contbr. articles to profl. jours. Home: 8169 W Baker Ave Denver CO 80227-3129

NEUDECKER, STEPHEN K., marine ecologist, museum professional. BS in Zoology, U. Ky., 1974; MS in Biology, U. Guam, 1978; PhD in Marine Ecology, U. Calif., Davis, 1982; grad. Mus. Mgmt. Inst., U. Calif., Berkeley, 1993. Project scientist U. Guam Marine Lab., Mangilao, 1975-77; marine environ. cons. Santa Fe Engrs. and Yamada Engrs., Guam and Tokyo, 1977-78, Dames and Moore, Inc., San Francisco, 1983; cons., sr. scientist Ecol. Analysts, Inc., Concord and Lafayette, Calif., 1979-80, 82-84; sr. scientist, lab. coord. Lockheed Engring. and Mgmt. Svcs. Co., Las Vegas, 1984; cons., sr. project mgr. Henwood Energy Svcs., Sacramento, 1985-86; prin. Environ. Cons. Svcs., Davis and Bonita, Calif., 1984—; exec. dir. Bayfront Conservancy Trust, Chula Vista, Calif., 1984—. Contbr. numerous articles to profl. jours. Mem. AAAS, Am. Assn. Mus., Am. Zoo and Aquarium Assn., Ecol. Soc. Am. (cert. sr. ecologist), Am. Soc. Icthyologists and Herpetologists, Bonita Sunrise Rotary (past pres.), Internat. Wine and Food Soc. (past pres. Chula Vista chpt.), Sigma Xi. Office: Chula Vista Nature Ctr 1000 Gunpowder Point Dr Chula Vista CA 91910-1201

NEUDORF, HOWARD FRED, family physician; b. Milw., Nov. 26, 1954; s. Herman David and Bella (Silberman) N.; m. Rebecca Neudorf; 1 child, Samantha Lea. BA with honors, U. Ill., 1976; MD, U. Autonoma de C. Juarez, Mex., 1983. Diplomate Am. Bd. Family Practice. Resident Ravenswood Hosp., Chgo., 1983-84, 86, Edgewater Hosp., Chgo., 1984-85, Bronx (N.Y.) - Lebanon Med. Ctr., 1987-89; fellow St. Luke's Med. Ctr., Chgo., 1989-90; fellow U. Hawaii, Honolulu, 1990-91, resident, 1991-92; clinician Hawaii Med. Clinic, Honolulu, 1992; staff physician Pace of Hawaii, Honolulu, 1992-94; house physician St. Francis Med. Ctr. West, Ewa Beach, Hawaii, 1992—; staff physician Waianae (Hawaii) Coast Comp. Health Ctr., 1994-96; pvt. practice Ewa Beach, 1996—; utilization rev. com. St. Francis Med. Ctr. West, Ewa Beach, 1994—. Mem. AMA, Am. Geriat. Soc., Am. Acad. Family Physicians, Hawaii Med. Assn. (ethics com. 1992-94, long term care com. 1994-96). Democrat. Jewish. Home: 94-83OA Lelepua St Waipahu HI 96797 Office: 91-2139 Fort Weaver Rd Ste 307 Ewa Beach HI 96706-3610

NEUHARTH, DANIEL J., II, psychotherapist; b. Sioux Falls, S.D., Nov. 10, 1953; s. Allen Harold and Loretta Faye (Helgeland) N. BA, Duke U., 1975; MS in Journalism, Northwestern U., 1978; MA, John F. Kennedy U., 1988; PhD in Clin. Psychology, Calif. Sch. Profl. Psychology, 1992. Lic. marriage, family and child counselor. Reporter USA Today, Washington, 1982-83; lectr. San Diego State U., 1983-84; talk show host KSDO-AM, San Diego, 1983-84; pres. Dialogues, San Francisco, 1987—; psychotherapist pvt. practice, San Francisco, 1992—; vis. prof. U. Fla., Gainesville, 1980-81, U. Hawaii, Honolulu, 1981-82; adj. faculty U. San Francisco, 1989—. Host, producer radio talk show Saturday Night People, 1984; contbg. author: Confessions of an S.O.B., 1989. Office: Dialogues PO Box 1022 Fairfax CA 94978-1022

NEUHOFF, PHILIP STEPHEN, geochemist, researcher; b. Dubuque, Iowa, Nov. 26, 1970; s. Alfred Louis and Marion Loretta (Underwood) N.; m. Christine Louise Shero, June 18, 1994. BS, U. Iowa, 1993; postgrad., Stanford U., 1993—. Rsch. asst. Oak Ridge (Tenn.) Nat. Lab., 1991-93, Iowa Geol. Survey, Iowa City, 1992, Stanford (Calif.) U., 1993—; cons. Danish Lithosphere Ctr., Copenhagen, 1995—, Geol. Survey Denmark and Greenland, Copenhagen, 1997. Grad. fellow NSF, 1993. Mem. Geol. Soc. Am. (Rsch. award 1995), Am. Assn. Petroleum Geologists, Am. Geophysical Union, Mineral. Soc. Am., Sigma Xi (assoc.). Roman Catholic. Office: Stanford U Dept Geol & Environ Sci Stanford CA 94305-2115

NEUMAN, JAMES BURTON, land company executive; b. Concord, Calif., Dec. 11, 1943; s. Charles and Virginia Lee (Jones) N. BS, U. Calif., Berkeley, 1966, MBA, 1968. Pres. Mobil Oil Redwood, Redwood City, Calif., 1969-78, Western Internat. Properties, Portland, Oreg., 1979-88, Stanly Land Co., Napa, Calif., 1989-96, Corp. Realty Resources, Napa, 1996—. Bd. dirs. Napa Valley Coll. Found., Napa, Calif., Napa Valley Econ. Devel. Corp., Napa, Napa Valley Opera House, Napa. Mem. Univ. Club, Napa Valley C. of C. Office: 1142 1st St Napa CA 94558

NEUMANN, HARRY, philosophy educator; b. Dormoschel, Germany, Oct. 10, 1930; came to U.S., 1937, naturalized, 1948; s. Siegfried and Frieda (Lion) N.; m. Christina Sopher, Sept. 25, 1959. B.A., St. John's Coll., 1952; M.A., U. Chgo., 1954; Ph.D., Johns Hopkins U., 1962; postgrad., U. Heidelberg, Germany, 1956-58. Mem. faculty Mich. State U., 1962-63, Lake Forest Coll., 1963-65; prof. philosophy, and govt. Claremont Grad. Sch. Scripps Coll., Claremont (Calif.) Grad. Sch., 1966—; research assoc. Rockefeller Inst., N.Y.C., 1963. Author: Liberalism, 1991; contbr. articles profl. jours. With AUS, 1954-56. Classical Philosophy fellow Ctr. Hellenic Studies, Dumbarton Oaks, Washington, 1965-66, rsch. fellow Salvatori Ctr. for Study of Individual Freedom in the Modern World, 1970; rsch. fellow Earhart Found., 1973-74, 78, 82, 86, 90, 94. Mem. AAUP, Univ. Ctrs. Rational Alternatives, Univ. Profs. for Acad. Order, John Brown Cook Assn. for Freedom (advisor). Office: Scripps Coll Claremont CA 91711

NEUMANN, HERMAN ERNEST, elementary and special education educator; b. Winona, Minn., Nov. 11, 1931; s. Herman Ferdinand and Dena Matilda (Peterson) N.; m. Juanita Evelyn, Sept. 11, 1954; children: Mary Evelyn, Herman Ernest Jr., Martin Andrew, Amy Louise. BS, Winona State U., 1961; MA, Calif. State U., Bakersfield, 1976; postgrad., San Jose U., 1977, Calif. State U., San Barbara, 1978. Cert. early childhood, spl. edn., elem. edn., ESL instr. Classroom tchr. grades K-6, resource specialist Bakersfield (Calif.) City Schs., 1980-82; classroom tchr. Kern County, Bakersfield, 1982-84; resource specialist Bakersfield (Calif.) City Schs., 1984-92; lectr. in edn. Calif. State U., Bakersfield, 1995—. Contbr. articles to profl. jours. 1st class airman USAF, 1952-56. NSF fellow, 1966, Internat. Biog. Assn. fellow, Cambridge, Eng., 1993; named to Hall of Fame Teaching Excellence Kern County, 1990, Tchr. of Yr., 1990. Mem. NEA (grantee 1969), Bakersfield Elem. Tchrs. Assn., ASCD, Calif. Tchrs. Assn. Home: 5219 Cedarbrook Ln Bakersfield CA 93313-2719 Office: Bakersfield City Schs 1300 Baker St Bakersfield CA 93305-4326

NEUMANN, NORBERT PAUL, immunochemist; b. Chgo.. BS in Chemistry cum laude, St. Peter's Coll., Jersey City, 1953; MS in Biochemistry, Okla. State U., 1955; PhD in Biochemistry, U. Wis., 1958. Teaching asst., rsch. asst. Okla. State U., 1953-55; rsch. asst. U. Wisc., 1955-58; rsch. assoc. The Rockefeller Inst. for Med. Rsch., N.Y.C., 1958-61; from rsch. assoc. to asst. prof. Inst. Microbiology, Rutgers, The State U. N.J., 1961-64, 64-67; asst. prof. exptl. medicine, assoc. dir. tchg. labs. U. Medicine and Dentistry of N.J., Rutgers Med. Sch., 1967-69; sr. scientist immunol. devel. Ortho Diagnostic Sys., Inc., Raritan, N.J., 1969-70; dir. biochemistry Ortho Diagnostic Sys., Inc., Raritan, 1970-74, asst. dir. rsch., 1974-80, prin. scientist clin. immunology, 1980-81, dir. immunol. rsch., 1981-82; dir. biology The Purdue Frederick Co., Norwalk, Conn., 1982-85; dir. product devel. Allergy and Immunotechnology, Inc., Newport Beach, Calif., 1987-88; rsch. assoc. Reagent Applications, Inc., San Diego, 1988-90; sr. immunochemist Internat. Enzymes, Inc., Fallbrook, Calif., 1990—. Contbr. articles to profl. jours. Mem. AAAS, Am. Chem. Soc., Am. Men Sci., N.Y. Acad. Scis., Soc. for Complex Carbohydrates, Soc. Human Genetics, Parenteral Drug Assn., Phi Lambda Upsilon, Sigma Xi. Office: Internat Enzymes 772 F N Twin Oaks Valley Rd N San Marcos CA 92069

NEUMANN, PETER GABRIEL, computer scientist; b. N.Y.C., Sept. 21, 1932; s. J.B. and Elsa (Schmid) N.; 1 child, Helen K. AB, Harvard U., 1954, SM, 1955; Dr rerum naturarum, Technische Hochschule, Darmstadt, Fed. Republic Germany, 1960; PhD, Harvard U., 1961. Mem. tech. staff Bell Labs, Murray Hill, N.J., 1960-70; Mackay lectr. Stanford U., 1964, U. Calif., Berkeley, 1970-71; computer scientist SRI Internat., Menlo Park, Calif., 1971—. Author: Computer-Related Risks, 1995. Fulbright fellow, 1958-60. Fellow AAAS, IEEE, Assn. for Computing Machinery (editor jour. 1976-93, chmn. com. on computers and pub. policy 1985—). Office: SRI Internat EL-243 333 Ravenswood Ave Menlo Park CA 94025-3493

NEUTRA, DION, architect; b. Los Angeles, Oct. 8, 1926; s. Richard Joseph and Dione (Niedermann) N.; children: Gregory, Wendy, Haig, Nicholas. Student, Swiss Inst. Tech., 1947-48; B.Arch. cum laude, U. So. Calif., 1950. With Richard J. Neutra (architect), Los Angeles, 1942-55; assoc. Neutra & Alexander, Los Angeles, 1955-60; asso. Robert E. Alexander, Los Angeles, 1960-62; prin. Richard & Dion Neutra, Architects and Assos., Los Angeles, 1962—; pres. Richard J. Neutra, Inc., 1970—; exec. con. Inst. for Survival Through Design, L.A.; lectr. Calif. State U., L.A., Sacramento City Coll., Mira Costa State U., Cabrillo State U., Soka U., Tokyo, San Diego City Coll., Germany, Switzerland, Eng., Austria; vis. prof. Calif. State U.-Pomona, 1970, 85-86; vis. lectr. U. So. Calif. Prin. works include various residential, ednl., religious and instnl. facilities including Am. Embassy Karachi, Pakistan, Gettysburg Meml., Simpson Coll. Libr., Adelphi Coll. Libr., Libr. and Resource Ctr. for City of Huntington Beach, Calif., Treetops Townhouses, 1980; exhbns. "View from Inside", 1984, 86, 92, "Visions & Exiles", Vienna, 1995. Mem. Silver Lake-Echo Park Dist. Plan Adv. Com., Master Plan City of Los Angeles, 1970-71; mem. Citizens to Save Silver Lake, 1973-76; dir. Child Care and Devel. Services, 1970-71, Preservation and Maintenance of Existing Neutra Projects. Served with USNR, 1944-46. Street named Neutra Pl. in firm's honor, Silverlake, 1992; Neutra Centennial, 1992. Mem. AIA, Nat. Council Archtl. Registration Bds., Alpha Rho Chi. Studio: Richard & Dion Neutra 2440 Neutra Pl Los Angeles CA 90039-3141

NEVILLE-HARRIS, ALICE ALMEDA (ALICE ALMEDA AHNA), retired critical care nurse; b. N.Y.C., Nov. 19, 1933; d. Anthony and Bessie Beatrice (Brown) Harris; m. James Edward Neville, May 21, 1951 (dec. June 30, 1963); children: Mary Ann, Wallace Lee, Denise Leona, James Edward, Clyde Leo. AA, West L.A. C.C., 1981; BA, John Jay Coll., N.Y.C., 1983. CCCN. Psychiat. nurse Bronx Mcpl. Hosp., N.Y.C., 1956-67; thoracic surgery nurse Sloane Kettering, N.Y.C., 1968-69; prison health nurse N.Y.C., 1968-77; home care nurse Norrell Registry, Van Nuys, Calif., 1979-78; CCRN Crenshaw Hosp., L.A., 1982-93. Author-dir.: (play) God's Watchin' You, 1995; contbr. poetry to anthologies. with NAACP, SCLC, Vols. Am., Mayor Lindsey Prison Health Task Force, 1969. Inducted World of Poets Hall of Fame World of Poetry Press, 1986. Mem. Internat. Poet

Soc. (life), Internat. Black Writers and Artists (bd. dirs. 1995—). Democrat. Home: 1124 W 82d St Los Angeles CA 90044

NEVIN, DAVID WRIGHT, real estate broker, mortgage broker; b. Culver City, Calif., July 27, 1947; s. Wilbur D. and Anita J. (Hulderman) N.; m. Shirley Grimes, Nov. 12, 1977; children: Jenny, David Wright Jr. BA, Calif. State Poly. U., 1974. Rural manpower asst. employment devel. State Calif., Riverside, 1970-74; pers. mgr. Lindsay Olive Growers, Calif., 1974-79; employee rels. mgr. Morton Salt Co., Newark, Calif., 1979-80; real estate salesman Valley Realty, Fremont, Calif., 1980, The Property Profls., Fremont, Calif., 1980-85; owner Nevin & Nevin, Inc., 1984-88, CitiDesign, 1989—; co-owner Brokers Exch., Inc., 1985-86; dir., officer CitiBrokers Real Estate, Inc., 1986-94; owner Nevin Fin/Mortgage Exchange 1992—; br. mgr. Brandt Property Mgmt. Group, 1994-95; mgr. Internat. Trade Corp., Saigon, Vietnam, 1997—. Sustaining mem. Rep. Nat. Com., Washington, 1984; mem. Presdl. Task Force, Washington, 1984, Fremont Cmty. Ch. Served with U.S. Army, 1967-69. Mem. Realtors Nat. Mktg. Inst. (real estate brokerage coun.), Internat. Real Estate Fedn., So. Alameda County Bd. Realtors (local govt. rels. com. 1983-86). Address: PO Box 3191 Fremont CA 94539-0319

NEVINS, KEITH PATRICK, municipal consultant; b. Leavenworth, Kans., Aug. 11, 1936; s. Lloyd William and Dorothy Helen (Weatherford) N.; m. Marilyn Ann Gottschalk, Jan. 29, 1941; children: David Scott, Kristine Koy, Jill Colleen. BA in Math., St. Benedict's Coll., Atchison, Kans., 1957; BS in Civil Engring., Kans. State U., 1960. Registered profl. engr., Wash. Assoc. John W. Smith, cons. engrs., Hays, Kans., 1960-63; asst. city engr. City of Walla Walla, Wash., 1963-65; city engr., dir. pub. works City of Moses Lake, Wash., 1965-69; dir. pub. works City of Auburn, Wash., 1969-85; city engr., city supr. City of Oak Harbor, Wash., 1985-96; cons. to municipalities Oak Harbor, 1996—; past pres. Auburn Credit Union; legis. rep. City Engrs. Assn. and Assn. Washington Cities. Contbr. articles to profl. jours. mem. Oak Harbor Sch. Dist. Cmty. Budget Adv. Com.; bd. dirs. Island County Econ. Devel. Coun. Named Pub. Employee of Yr. Island County Econ. Devel. Coun., 1993. Mem. NSPE, Internat. City Mgmt. Assn., Wash. City Mgmt. Assn., Wash. Soc. Profl. Engrs., Navy League, Greater Oak Harbor C. of C., Am. Pub. Works Assn. (pres., v.p., sec.-treas., bd. dirs. 1961—, James Robertson award Wash. state chpt. 1981, one of top 10 pub. works leader in U.S. and Can. 1982), Inst. Adminstrv. Mgmt. (past pres.). Roman Catholic. Home and Office: 847 SW Echo Loop Oak Harbor WA 98277-2434

NEVLING, HARRY REED, health care human resources executive; b. Rochester, Minn., Sept. 15, 1946; s. Edwin Reid and Ruth Margaret (Mulvihill) N.; m. Joanne Carol Meyer, Nov. 26, 1976; 1 son, Terry John. AA, Rochester Community Coll., 1973; BA cum laude, U. Winona, 1974; MBA, U. Colo., 1990. Pers. rep. Rochester Meth. Hosp., 1974-75; dist. mgr. Internat. Dairy Queen Corp., 1975-76; with David Realty Corp., Littleton, Colo., 1976-83, v.p., 1979-83, gen. mgr., 1981-83, Longmont (Colo.), United Hosp., 1977—; pers. dir., 1977-87, dir. human resources, 1988-95, v.p. human resources, 1995—; cons. Front Range Community Coll. of Denver, 1983-85; prin. Harry R. Nevling-Broker, 1983-85, 95—; v.p. Realty Mart Internat., Inc., 1985-93, Dist. chmn. Am. Party, 1973-74, St. Vrain Valley Sch. Dist., Health Occupations Adv. Com. 1977—, chmn. 1979-85, Vocat. Edn. Adv. Coun. 1986-91, pres. 1986-91; citizen amb. People to People program, Hungary, Czech Republic, Germany, 1991; mem. exec. com. Nat. Health Care Skills Stds. Project, 1993-95; spkr. in field. Co-author: Healthcare Reform: The Human Resources Cornerstone to Successful Reform, 1992. Served to capt. U.S. Army, 1965-72; Vietnam. Decorated D.F.C., Bronze Star with oakleaf cluster, Air medal (22, valor device); recipient Rescue citation for lifesaving Boeing Co., 1969, Helping Hand award United Way, 1974, Outstanding Service award, 1979, cert. of appreciation, 1982, Disting. Young Alumni award Winona State U., 1989. Mem. VFW (past post comdr.), Longmont Area Human Resources Assn., 1980-89, Boulder Area Human Resource Assn., 1978—, Mountain States VHA (pers. com. 1989—, chmn. 1989-93), Colo. Healthcare Assn. for Human Resource Mgmt. (sec. 1980, pres. elect 1981, pres. 1981-82, exec. com. 1986—), Am. Soc. for Healthcare Human Resources Adminstrn. (ann. meeting chmn. 1985-86, regional dir. 1986-90, legis. and labor liaison 1988-90, chpt. rels. com. 1990-91, pres. elect 1991-92, pres. 92-93, immediate past pres. 1993-95, exec. com. 1991-95, chmn. nominating com. 1994-95, chmn. conflict of interest com., 1994-95, orgnl. transition task force 1994-95, nat. nominating com. 1996, Bylaws com. 1992-93, 96-97, Disting. Svc. award 1996), Soc. Human Resource Mgmt., Human Resource Cert. Inst. (sr. profl.); bd. mem. Boulder Bus. Dependent Care assn., 1995—, pres. 1996. Home: 2346 Eagleview Cir Longmont CO 80501-7797 Office: Longmont United Hosp 1950 Mountain View Ave Longmont CO 80501-3129

NEWACHECK, DAVID JOHN, lawyer; b. San Francisco, Dec. 8, 1953; s. John Elmer and Estere Ruth Sybil (Nelson) N.; m. Dorothea Quandt, June 2, 1990. AB in English, U. Calif., Berkeley, 1976; JD, Pepperdine U., 1979; MBA, Calif. State U., Hayward, 1982; LLM in Tax, Golden Gate U., 1987. Bar: Calif. 1979, U.S. Dist. Ct. (no. dist.) Calif. 1979, U.S. Ct. Appeals (9th cir.) 1979, U.S. Supreme Ct. 1984, Washington D.C. 1985. Tax cons. Pannell, Kerr and Forster, San Francisco, 1982-83; lawyer, writer, editor Matthew Bender and Co., San Francisco, 1983—; instr. taxation Oakland (Calif.) Coll. of Law, 1993—; lawyer, tax cons., fin. planner San Leandro, Calif., 1983—; bd. dirs. Aztec Custom Co., Orinda, Calif., 1983—; cons. software Collier Bankruptcy Filing Sys., 1984. Author/editor: (treatises) Ill. Tax Service, 1985, Ohio State Taxation, 1985, N.J. Tax Service, 1986, Pa. Tax Service, 1986, Calif. Closely Held Corps., 1987, Texas Tax Service, 1988; author: (software) Tax Source 1040 Tax Preparation, 1987, Texas Tax Service 1988, California Taxation, 1989, 2d edit., 1990, Bender's Federal Tax Service, 1989, Texas Litigation Guide, 1993, Family Law: Texas Practice & Procedure, 1993, Texas Transaction Guide, 1994, Ohio Corporation Law, 1994, Michigan Corporation Law, 1994, Massachusetts Corporation Law, 1994. Mem. youth com. Shepherd of the Valley Luth. Ch., Orinda, 1980-85, ch. coun., 1980-82. Mem. ABA, Internat. Platform Assn., State Bar Assn. Calif., Alameda County Bar Assn., U. Calif. Alumni Assn., U. Calif. Band Alumni Assn., Mensa. Republican. Club: Commonwealth (San Francisco). Home: 5141 Vannoy Ave Castro Valley CA 94546-2558 Office: 438 Estudillo Ave San Leandro CA 94577

NEWBERG, DOROTHY BECK (MRS. WILLIAM C. NEWBERG), portrait artist; b. Detroit, May 30, 1919; d. Charles William and Mary (Labedz) Beck; student Detroit Conservatory Music, 1938; m. William C. Newberg, Nov. 3, 1939; children: Judith Bookwalter Bracken, Robert Charles, James William, William Charles. Trustee Detroit Adventure, 1967-71, originator A Drop in Bucket Program for artistically talented inner-city children. Cmty. outreach coord. Reno Police Dept.; bd. dirs. Bloomfield Art Assn., 1960-62, trustee 1965-67; bd. dirs. Your Heritage House, 1972-75, Franklin Wright Settlement, 1972-75, Meadowbrook Art Gallery, Oakland U., 1973-75, Sierra Nevada Mus. Art, 1978-80, NCCJ; mem. adv. bd. Gang Alternatives Partnership Adv. Bd. Recipient Heart of Gold award, 1969; Mich. vol. leadership award, 1969, Outstanding Vol. award City of Reno, 1989-90. Mem. Nevada Mus. Art, No. Nev. Black Cultural Awareness Soc. (bd. dirs.), Hispanic 500 C. of C. No. Nev. Roman Catholic. Home: 2000 Dant Blvd Reno NV 89509-5193

NEWBERG, WILLIAM CHARLES, stock broker, real estate broker, automotive engineer; b. Seattle, Dec. 17, 1910; s. Charles John and Anna Elizabeth (Anderson) N.; BSME, U. Wash., 1933; MME, Chrysler Inst. Engring., 1935; LLB (hon.), Parsons Coll., 1958; m. Dorothy Beck, Nov. 3, 1939; children: Judith N. Newberg Bookwalter, Robert Charles, James William, William Charles. Salesman, Am. Auto Co., Seattle, 1932-33; student engr. Chrysler Corp., Detroit, 1933-35, exptl. engr., 1935-42, chief engr. Chgo. plant, 1942-45, mem. subs. ops. staff, Detroit, 1945-47, pres. airtemp. divsn., Dayton, Ohio, 1947-50, v.p., dir. Dodge divsn., Detroit, 1950-51, pres. Dodge divsn., 1951-56, group v.p., Detroit, 1956-58, exec. v.p., 1958-60, pres., 1960; corp. dir. Detroit Bank & Trust, Detroit, 1955-60; corp. cons., Detroit, 1960-76; realtor Myers Realty, Inc., Reno, 1976-79; owner Bill Newberg Realty, 1979—; account exec. Allied Capital Corp., Reno, 1980—; chmn. Newberg Corp., 1982; treas. Perfect "10" Industries. Elder, St. John's Presbyn. Ch., Reno, 1976—; mem. exec. bd. Detroit Area coun. Boy Scouts Am., 1955-74, Nev. Area coun. Boy Scouts Am., 1976—; Mich. state chmn. March of Dimes, 1967-68. Mem. Soc. Automotive Engrs., Am. Def. Preparedness Assn. (life), Automotive Orgn. Team (life), U. Wash. Alumni Assn. (life), Newcomen Soc., Franklin Inst., Alpha Tau Omega. Clubs: Prospectors, Harley Owners Group. Home: 2000 Dant Blvd Reno NV 89509-5193

NEWBERRY, CONRAD FLOYDE, aerospace engineering educator; b. Neodesha, Kans., Nov. 10, 1931; s. Ragan McGregor and Audra Anitia (Newmaster) N.; m. Sarah Louise Thonn, Jan. 26, 1958; children: Conrad Floyde Jr., Thomas Edwin, Susan Louise. AA, Independence Jr. Coll., 1951; BEME in Aero. Sequence, U. So. Calif., 1957; MSME, Calif. State U., Los Angeles, 1971, MA in Edn., 1974; D.Environ. Sci. and Engring., UCLA, 1985. Registered profl. engr., Calif., Kans., N.C., Tex. Mathematician L.A. divsn. N.Am. Aviation Inc., 1951-53, jr. engr., 1953-54, engr., 1954-57, sr. engr., 1957-64; asst. prof. aerospace engring. Calif. State Poly. U., Pomona, 1964-70, assoc. prof. aerospace engring., 1970-75, prof. aerospace engring., 1975-90, prof. emeritus, 1990—; staff engr. EPA, 1980-82; engring. specialist space transp. systems div. Rockwell Internat. Corp., 1984-90; prof. aeronautics and astronautics Naval Postgrad. Sch., Monterey, Calif., 1990—, acad. assoc. space systems engring., 1992-94. Recipient John Leland Atwood award as outstanding aerospace engring. educator AIAA/Am. Soc. Engring. Edn., 1986. Fellow AIAA (dep. dir. edn. region VI 1976-79, dep. dir. career enhancement 1982-91, chmn. L.A. sect. 1989-90, chmn. Point Lobos sect. 1990-91, chmn. acad. affairs com. 1990-93, dir. tech.-aircraft sys. 1990-93), Inst. Advancement Engring., Brit. Interplanetary Soc.; mem. IEEE, AAAS, ASME, NSPE, Royal Aero. Soc., Calif. Soc. Profl. Engrs., Am. Acad. Environ. Engrs. (cert. air pollution control engr.), Am. Soc. Engring. Edn. (chmn. aerospace divsn. 1979-80, divsn. exec. com. 1976-80, 89-94, exec. com. ocean and marine engring. divsn. 1982-85, 90-97, program chmn. 1991-93, chmn. 1993-95, chmn. PIC II 1995-97), Am. Soc. Pub. Adminstrn., Am. Meteorol. Soc., U.S. Naval Inst., Am. Helicopter Soc., Soc. Naval Architects and Marine Engrs., Air and Waste Mgmt. Assn., Inst. Environ. Scis., Exptl. Aircraft Assn., Water Environ. Fedn., Soc. Automotive Engr., Soc. Allied Weight Engrs., Assn. Unmanned Vehicle Sys., Calif. Water Pollution Control Assn., Nat. Assn. Environ. Profls., Am. Soc. Naval Engrs., SAFE, SID, Planetary Soc., Tau Beta Pi, Sigma Gamma Tau, Kappa Delta Pi. Democrat. Mem. Christian Ch. (Disciples of Christ). Home: 9463 Willow Oak Rd Salinas CA 93907-1037 Office: Naval Postgrad Sch Dept Aeronautics and Astronautics AA/Ne 699 Dyer Rd Monterey CA 93943-5106

NEWBERRY, ELIZABETH CARTER, greenhouse and floral company owner; b. Blackwell, Tex., Nov. 25, 1921; m. Weldon Omar Newberry, Sept. 24, 1950 (dec. Nov. 1984); 1 child. Student Hardin Simmons U., 1938-39. Office mgr. F. W. Woolworth, Abilene, Tex., 1939-50; acct. Western Devel. & Investment Corp., Englewood, Colo., 1968-72; owner, operator Newberry Bros. Greenhouse and Florist, Denver, 1972—; bd. dirs. Western Devel. and Investment Corp. Englewood, Colo., 1979-87. Pres. Ellsworth Elem. Sch. PTA, Denver, 1961-62; v.p. Hill Jr. High Sch. PTA, Denver. Home: 201 Monroe St Denver CO 80206-5505 Office: Newberry Bros Greenhouse 201 Garfield St Denver CO 80206-5518

NEWBILL, KAREN MARGARET, elementary school educator, education educator; b. East Orange, N.J., Oct. 6, 1945; d. Richard Oliver and Edna Mae (Crook) Jacobson; m. Gary C. Newbill, Aug. 18, 1965; children: Kari L., Erick D. BA, Seattle Pacific U., 1968; MEd, City U., Bellevue, Wash., 1993. Cert. tchr., Wash. Tchr. Shoreline Pub. Schs., Seattle, 1969-71, Northshore Sch. Dist., Bothell, Wash., 1971-74; tutor, substitute tchr. Issaquah (Wash.) Sch. Dist., 1980-89, tchr., 1989—, tech. and curriculum integration cons., 1991—; adj. prof. N.W. Coll., Kirkland, Wash., 1994—, mem. profl. edn. adv. bd., 1994—; adj. prof. Seattle Pacific U., 1994—; student tchr. supr. U. Wash., Seattle, 1991—. Children's choir dir. Westminster Chapel, Bellevue, Wash., 1980-88; children's worship leader Evergreen Christian Fellowship, Issaquah, 1993-94. Mem. ASCD, NEA, Wash. Edn. Assn., Nat. Coun. Tchrs. Math., Internat. Reading Assn. Home: 420 Kalmia Pl NW Issaquah WA 98027-2619 Office: Issaquah Sch Dist. 565 NW Holly St Issaquah WA 98027-2834

NEWBY, IDUS ATWELL, historian, educator; b. Hawkinsville, Ga., Oct. 3, 1931; s. Idus A. and Nomie Bell (Floyd) N. BS, Ga. So. U., 1951; MA, U. S.C., 1957; PhD, UCLA, 1962. Asst. prof. history Western Wash. U., Bellingham, 1962-63, Calif. State U., Fullerton, 1963-66; asst. prof. U. Hawaii, Honolulu, 1966-68, assoc. prof., 1968-70, prof., 1970—, grad. chmn. dept. history, 1993-94, dept. chmn., 1994—. Author: Jim Crow's Defense, 1965, Challenge to the Court, 1968, Black Carolinians, 1971, The South: A History, 1978, Plain Folk in the New South, 1989. Sgt. USAF, 1951-55. Mem. Am. Hist. Assn., Orgn. Am. Historians, So. Hist. Assn., Am. Studies Assn. Home: 2533 Ala Wai Blvd Honolulu HI 96815 Office: U Hawaii Dept History 2530 Dole St Honolulu HI 96822-2303

NEWELL, CLAYTON, media professional, writer; b. Denver, May 16, 1958; s. John William and Suzann Allison (Boardman) N.; m. Cindy Jo Gehrig, Aug. 18, 1981; 7 children. BA in Journalism, Colo. State U., 1990. Media rels. officer Ch. of Jesus Christ of Latter-Day Saints, Salt Lake City, 1993—; staff writer, cons. Right at Home mag., Salt Lake City, 1995—; dir., spokesman Utah Home Edn. Assn., Salt Lake City, 1995—. Author: Dying Words—Colombian Journalists and the Cocaine Warlords, 1990, Cowchips Aren't for Dippin'—A Guide to Life in the New Wild West, 1996; contbr.: The Mission: Inside the Church of Jesus Christ of Latter-day Saint, 1996; editor: (book) A House of Learning, A House of God: Latter-day Saint Perspectives on Home-based Education, 1997; contbr. articles to profl. publs. Dir. Utah Home Edn. Assn., 1995-99. Scripps Howard scholar, 1988, 89, 90; Reader's Digest rsch. grantee Reader's Digest Edn. Found., 1989-90. Mem. Soc. Profl. Journalists (profl. mem.), Phi Beta Kappa, Phi Kappa Phi. Office: Ch of Jesus Christ of Latter-day Saints 15 E S Temple Salt Lake City UT 84150

NEWELL, DONI LEONARD, elementary school principal; b. Lexington, N.C., Nov. 1, 1946; d. Roland Webster and Nellie Frances (Thomason) Leonard; m. Eugene Bruce Newell, July 8, 1967; 1 child, Joseph Brett. BA in Elem. Edn., Catawba Coll., Salisbury, N.C., 1970; MEd, U. Mont., 1991, postgrad., 1993—. Cert. and classified pers. supervision and evaluation. Tchr. Pickett Elem. Sch., Lexington, 1969-70, Sch. Dist. #6, Missoula, Mont., 1970-71, Franklin Elem. Sch., Missoula, 1971-74, Sch. Dist. #1, Missoula, 1974-76, Hegen-Nelson Kindergarten, Columbia Falls, Mont., 1976-77, Columbia Falls Elem. Sch., 1977-79; tchr.'s aide Trout Creek Elem. Sch., 1979-80, tchr., 1980-92, prin., curriculum dir., Title IX coord., 1992-96; asst. prin. Unalaska (Alaska) City Sch., 1996—. Bd. dirs. Sanders County Fair Bd.; rep. Mont. 4-H Found.; orgnl. and project leader 4-H Club. Recipient Gold Star Tchr. award Sta. KECI-TV, 1996; named Educator of the Yr., Mont. Tree Farmers Assn., 1996; Wash. Water Power grantee, 1993, 95; NASA scholar, 1989. Mem. ASCD, Nat. Assn. Elem. Sch. Prins., Sch. Adminstrs. Mont., N.W. Prins. Assn., Nat. Sci. Tchrs. Assn., Young Astronauts of Am., Mont. Puppet Guild, Five Valleys Reading Coun., Phi Delta Kappa, Delta Kappa Gamma. Office: Unalaska City Sch PO Box 570 Unalaska AK 99685

NEWELL, GREGORY JOHN, international business advisor; b. Geneseo, Ill., Aug. 30, 1949; s. Eugene Earl Sr. and Ima Delores (Stamper) Newell; m. Candilyn Jones, Oct. 2, 1978; children: David, Kendall, Catherine, Michael, Mattson, Thomas. BA in Internat. Rels. Polit. Sci., Brigham Young U., 1988. Staff asst. to the Pres. White House, Washington, 1974-77; adminstrv. staff Lang. Tng. Mission, Provo, Utah, 1977-78; polit. aide U.S. Senator Dole, Washington, 1978-79; dep. adminstr. Gov. of Pa., Harrisburg, 1979-81; spl. asst. to the Pres. White House, Washington, 1981-82; U.S. asst. sec. of state U.S. Dept. State, Washington, 1982-85; U.S. amb. U.S. Dept. State, Stockholm, 1985-89; pres. Dow, Lohnes & Albertson, Washington, 1989-91, Internat. Commerce Devel. Corp., Provo, 1993—; bd. dirs. Landmark Legal Found., Kansas City, Mo.; adj. fellow Ctr. for Strategic and Internat. Studies, Washington, 1989-90. Voluntary missionary LDS Ch., France, Belgium, Luxembourg, 1968-71; bd. mem. Bachauer-Internat. Piano Competition, Salt Lake City, 1991—. Named Hon. Consul Gen., Govt. Sweden, Hon. Chmn. Am. Scandinavian Assn., Washington, Swedish Am. Cultural Union, Washington. Mem. Coun. Am. Ambs., Internat. Soc. Mormon. Office: Internat Commerce Devel 2696 N University Ave Ste 130 Provo UT 84604-3863

NEWELL, L. JACKSON, education educator; b. Dayton, Ohio, Oct. 11, 1938; s. Leonard J. and Henrietta (Wahlenmaier) N.; m. Linda King, June 15, 1963; children: Christine, Jennifer, Eric, Heather. Student Deep Springs Coll., Calif., 1956-59; B.A. in History, Ohio State U., 1961, Ph.D. in Higher Edn., 1972; M.A. in History, Duke U., 1964. Instr. history Deep Springs Coll., Calif., 1965-67, bd. trustees, 1987-95, chair, 1994-95; asst. dean Coll. Liberal Arts, U. N.H., 1967-70; assoc. dir. Univ. Council for Ednl. Adminstrn., Columbus, Ohio, 1970-74; successively asst. prof., assoc. prof., prof. higher edn., then univ. prof. U. Utah, Salt Lake City, 1974—, Case prof., 1991-92, dean liberal edn., 1974-90; pres. Deep Springs Coll., Calif., 1995—. vis. prof. Anglican Mgmt. Ctr., Danbury, Essex, Eng., 1978, U. Victoria, B.C., Can., 1989-91, U. Auckland, New Zealand, 1993; World Bank cons. to Govt. Bahamas, 1990-91; cons. Budapest, Hungary, 1993; prin. investigator curricular devel. fund for improvement of post-secondary Nat. Inst. Edn., 1981-83; Co-author: A History of Thought and Practice in Educational Administration, 1987, Under Scrutiny, 1988, Creating Distinctiveness: Lessons From Uncommon Colleges, 1992, (with Sterling M. McMurrin) Matters of Conscience, 1996; editor Rev. of Higher Edn., 1986-91; co-editor: Dialogue: A Journal of Mormon Thought, 1982-87. Bd. dirs. Bennion Ctr. Community Svc., 1988—. Thomas Holy fellow Ohio State U., 1971, Hatch prize U. Utah, 1993, Joseph Katz award Nat. Assn. for Gen. and Liberal Studies, 1994, Presdl. Teaching scholar U. Utah, 1994—. Mem. Assn. Gen. and Liberal Studies (pres. 1988-89), Am. Ednl. Rsch. Assn. (assoc. program chmn. 1986—), Assn. Study of Higher Edn. (program chair 1994, bd. dirs.), Assn. Am. Colls. (instl. rep. 1983—), Phi Beta Kappa, Phi Kappa Phi (chpt. pres. 1985), Phi Alpha Theta, Phi Delta Kappa. Home and Office: 1218 Harvard Ave Salt Lake City UT 84105-1906

NEWELL, MICHAEL STEPHEN, finance company executive, international finance, security-protection consultant; b. Denver, Dec. 22, 1949; s. Henry Michael and Marlene (McRae) N.; m. Linda Margaret Wolfe, Sept. 19, 1987; children: Katherine Margaret, Brittany Nicole; children from previous marriage: Troy, Angela, Michael, Jennifer. Grad., Denver Police Acad., 1972; CO Real Estate Lic., Real Estate Prep., 1977. Cert. peace officer, Colo. Police officer Denver Police Dept., 1972-79; prin. Michael Newell & Assocs., Denver, 1979-82; sr. account exec. Am. Protection Industries, Los Angeles, 1982-84; chief exec. officer Newco Fin., Huntington Beach, Calif., 1984—; chmn. The Newco Internat. Group/Newco Fin., Huntington Beach; founder, bd. dirs. EDEN Philanthropic Found., Fountain Valley, Calif., VALUES Self Improvement Program, Fountain Valley; cofounder, bd. dirs. Self-Love, Sexuality & Spirituality seminars, Fountain Valley; bd. dirs. Lifesong Self-Esteem workshops, Huntington Beach.; chmn. bd., bd. dirs. Steel Head Investment Group; proprietor Steel Head Inn, Michael's Supper Club; expert witness stalking crimes and preadtor control techniques; condr. seminars on stalker suppression, stalking survival, threat mgmt. in the workplace. Author: The Security Manual, 1995, Stalker Suppression, 1996, (video prodns.) The Personal Protection Technique, 1995, Stalking Survival, 1995, The Sting, 1995, Legal Fencing for the Insurance Industry, 1995. Founder, bd. dirs. Law Enforcement Support Assn., Denver, 1981; bd. dirs. Crisis Action Network/Stalking Rescue. Served with U.S. Army, 1968-71, Viet Nam. Decorated Bronze Star, Viet Svc. medal with clusters; recipient Pres.'s Nat. Patriotism medal Am. Police Hall of Fame, Nat. Assn. Chiefs Police, 1996, others. Republican. Mem. Religious Sci. Ch. Office: Internat Risk Cons PO Box 558 Littleton CO 80160

NEWHOUSE, ERIC, newspaper editor; b. Madison, Wis., Mar. 4, 1945; s. John Newhouse and Frances (Herrick) Myers; m. Susie Newhouse; children: Erica, Sarah. BS, U. Wis., 1967; MA, U. Md., 1970; MS, Columbia U., 1972. Corr. AP, Chattanooga, 1976-78, Pierre, S.D., 1976-80, St. Louis, 1978-80; chief bur. AP, Charleston, W.Va., 1984-88; news editor Great Falls (Mont.) Tribune, 1988-91, editl. editor, 1991—. Internat. fellow Columbia U., N.Y.C., 1972. Office: Great Falls Tribune 205 River Dr S Great Falls MT 59405-1854

NEWKIRK, RAYMOND LESLIE, management consultant; b. Shreveport, La., July 13, 1944; s. Raymond Clay and Dorothy Emily (Parker) N.; m. Felicisima Guese Calma, Jan. 19, 1985. AA, Dayton Community Coll., 1973; BS in Behavioral Sci., N.Y. Inst. Tech., 1976; MS in Philosophy, Columbia Pacific U., 1980, PhD in Behavioral Sci., 1982; PhD in Human Sci., Saybrook Inst., 1992. Clin. intern Fielding Inst., 1995; chief exec. officer, cons. Newkirk & Assocs., Ft. Lauderdale, Fla., 1980-84; head dept. ADP Royal Saudi Naval Forces, Jeddah, 1984-86; pres., cons. Internat. Assn. Info. Mgmt., Santa Clara, Calif., 1984; cert. quality analyst Quality Assurance Inst., Orlando, Fla., 1986—; prin. cons. Info. Impact Internat., Nashville, 1988—; pres., CEO Sys. Mgmt. Inst., Pleasant Hill, Calif., 1987; pres., COO P.Q. Info. Group, Egmont ann Hoeff, The Netherlands, 1992-94; pres., CEO Systems Mgmt. Inst., 1994—; prin. Forum 2000, 1996—; dep. gov. Am. Biog. Inst., 1995. Author: Chronicles of the Making of A Philosopher, 1983; contbr. articles to profl. jours. Speaker, mem. Union for Concerned Scientists, San Francisco, 1988. Fellow Brit. Inst. Mgmt., Internat. Biog. Assn.; mem. Assn. Systems Mgmt., Assn. Profl. Cons., Planetary Soc., Columbia Pacific Alumni Assn. (pres. Mid-east chpt. 1985), Assn. Computing Machinery, IEEE Computer Soc., Am. Biograph. Inst. (dep. gov. 1995), Phi Theta Kappa (outstanding scholar award 1973), Confedn. of Chivalry (knight). Roman Catholic. Home: 95 Greenock Ln Pleasant Hill CA 94523-2083

NEWLAND, RUTH LAURA, small business owner; b. Ellensburg, Wash., June 4, 1949; d. George J. and Ruth Marjorie (Porter) N. BA, Cen. Wash. State Coll., 1970, MEd, 1972; EdS, Vanderbilt U., 1973; PhD, Columbia Pacific U., 1981. Tchr. Union Gap (Wash.) Sch., 1970-71; ptnr. Newland Ranch Gravel Co., Yakima, Wash., 1970—, Arnold Artificial Limb, Yakima, 1981-86; owner, pres. Arnold Artificial Limb, Yakima and Richland, Wash., 1986—; ptnr. Newland Ranch, Yakima, 1969—. Contbg. mem. Nat. Dem. Com., Irish Nat. Caucus Found.; mem. Pub. Citizen, We The People, Nat. Humane Edn. Soc.; charter mem. Nat. Mus. Am. Indian. George Washington scholar Masons, Yakima, 1967. Mem. NAFE, NOW, Am. Orthotic and Prosthetic Assn., Internat. Platform Assn., Nat. Antivisection Soc. (life), Vanderbilt U. Alumni Assn., Peabody Coll. Alumni Assn., Columbia Pacific U. Alumni Assn., World Wildlife Fund, Nat. Audubon Soc., Greenpeace, Mus. Fine Arts, Humane Soc. U.S., Wilderness Soc., Nature Conservancy, People for Ethical Treatment of Animals, Amnesty Internat., The Windstar Found., Rodale Inst., Sierra Club (life), Emily's List. Democrat. Home: 2004 Riverside Rd Yakima WA 98901-9526 Office: Arnold Artificial Limb 9 S 12th Ave Yakima WA 98902-3106 *Personal philosophy: God first. Then be politically and socially conservative but liberal in your concern for others.*

NEWLIN, DOUGLAS RANDAL, learning products engineer; b. Denver, Mar. 26, 1940; s. Loren Randall and Nola Berniece (Paris) N.; m. Sandra Temple, June 22, 1968; children: Jason Britt, Jeremy Owen. BS in Journalism, U. Colo., 1968. Advt. prodn. mgr. Am. Sheep Producers Council, Denver, 1968-70; promotion dir. Sta. KLZ-AM-FM, Denver, 1970-71; account mgr. Curran-Morton Advt., Denver, 1971-72; advt. and sales promotion specialist Gates Rubber Co., Denver, 1972-78; mktg. communications mgr. Hewlett Packard Co., Ft. Collins, Colo., 1978-90; learning products engr., 1990—; vis. lectr. U. Colo., Boulder, 1972-73, statis. quality control course George Washington U., Washington, 1984. Author hardware and software catalogs, 1984-90, UNIX Tech. Documentation, 1990—; contbr. articles to profl. jours. Pres. Lake Sherwood Homeowners Assn., Ft. Collins, 1982; treas. Lake Sherwood Lake Com., Ft. Collins, 1983-85. Served with U.S. Army, 1959-61. Recipient Gold Key award Bus. and Profl. Advt. Assn., 1976. Republican. Home: 4112 Mt Vernon Ct Fort Collins CO 80525-3335 Office: Hewlett Packard Co 3404 E Harmony Rd Fort Collins CO 80525-9544

NEWLIN, L. MAX, parks and recreation director; b. June 4, 1942. BS, Wilmington Coll., 1968. Mgr. Massacre Rocks State Pk., American Falls, Idaho, 1996—. Exec. dir. Friends Massacre Rocks Inc.; v.p. S.E. Idaho Travel Coun. Idaho Parks and Recreation Assn. fellow, 1990. Mem. Power County/Am. Falls Hist. Soc. (chmn.). Office: Massacre Rocks State Pk 3592 Park Ln American Falls ID 83211-5555

NEWMAN, ANITA NADINE, surgeon; b. Honolulu, June 13, 1949; d. William Reece Elton and Margie Ruth (Pollard) Newman; m. Frank E.X. Ward, Sept. 9, 1995; children: Justin Ellis, Chelsea Newman, Andrew Frank, Tyler William. AB, Stanford U., 1971; MD, Dartmouth Coll., 1975.

Diplomate Am. Bd. Otolaryngology. Intern, then resident in gen. surgery Northwestern Meml. Hosp., Chgo., 1975-77, resident in otolaryngology, 1977-78; resident UCLA Hosp. and Clinics, 1979-82, assoc. prof., 1982-96; staff surgeon Wadsworth VA Hosp., L.A., 1982-84; rsch. fellow in neurotology UCLA, 1984-88. Contbr. articles to med. jours. Mem. alumni admissions support com. Darmouth Med. Sch. Alumni Coun., 1983-87. Fellow ACS; mem. Am. Acad. Otolaryngology, Am. Med. Women's Assn., Los Angeles County Med. Women's Assn., Assn. Rsch. in Otolaryngology, Stanford Women's Honor Soc. Democrat. Office: UCLA Hosp and Clinics Div Head And Neck Surg Ucla CA 90095

NEWMAN, CAROL L., lawyer; b. Yonkers, N.Y., Aug. 7, 1949; d. Richard J. and Pauline Frances (Stoll) N. AB/MA summa cum laude, Brown U., 1971; postgrad. Harvard U. Law Sch., 1972-73; JD cum laude, George Washington U., 1977. Bar: D.C., 1977, Calif., 1979. With antitrust div. U.S. Dept. Justice, Washington and L.A., 1977-80; assoc. Alschuler, Grossman & Pines, L.A., 1980-82, Costello & Walcher, L.A., 1982-85, Rosen, Wachtell & Gilbert, 1985-88, ptnr., 1988-90; ptnr. Keck, Mahin & Cate, 1990-94; pvt. practice, L.A., 1994—; adj. prof. Sch. Bus., Golden Gate U., spring 1982. Candidate for State Atty. Gen., 1986; L.A. city commr. L.A. Bd. Transp. Commrs., 1993—, v.p., 1995-96; bd. dirs. Women's Progress Alliance, 1996—. Mem. ABA, State Bar Calif., L.A. County Bar Assn., L.A. Lawyers for Human Rights (co. pres. 1991-92), Log Cabin (bd. dirs. 1992—, pres. 1996—), Calif. Women Lawyers (bd. dirs., bd. govs. 1991-94), Order of Coif, Phi Beta Kappa.

NEWMAN, DEAN GORDON, business consultant; b. North Branch, Iowa, Mar. 17, 1929; s. Floyd William and Hazel Jane (Covault) N.; m. Maggie; B.A., Simpson Coll., 1950; M.B.A. (Hicks fellow), Stanford U., 1952; children—Gary Dean, Craig William. Trainee, Gen. Electric, Schenectady, 1952, Syracuse, N.Y., 1955-56, Chgo., 1956-58; mem. employee and community relations staff, Chgo., 1958-62, mgr. employee and community relations, Milw., 1962-67, DeKalb, Ill., 1967-69; v.p. employee and pub. relations United Nuclear Corp., Elmsford, N.Y., 1969-71; v.p. employee and indsl. relations Apache Corp., Mpls., 1971-83, v.p. human resources and communications, 1983-87 . Pres. Apache Found., 1973-87 ; v.p., bd. dirs. Boys Clubs of Mpls., 1978-85; chmn. Boys and Girls Club of Mpls., 1985-88, exec. com., 1988-89; v.p. fin., bd. dirs. Boys and Girls Club Larimer County, 1993-96; vice chmn. Bus. Econs. Edn. Found., 1986-88, chmn. fin. com., 1988-89; Served with USNR, 1952-55; Korea. Mem. Nat. Assn. Mfrs. (dir. 1981-87), Alpha Tau Omega, Epsilon Sigma, Sigma Tau Delta, Pi Gamma Mu. Republican. Methodist. Home and Office: 125 County Rd 84W Allenspark CO 80510

NEWMAN, EDGAR LEON, historian, educator; b. New Orleans, Jan. 21, 1939; s. Isidore and Anna (Pfeifer) N.; children: Jonathan, Suzanne; m. Linda Loeb Clark, Apr. 21, 1989. BA, Yale U., 1962; PhD, U. Chgo., 1969. Asst. prof. N.Mex. State U., Las Cruces, 1969-75, assoc. prof. history, 1975—; lectr. U. Peking, 1985. Fulbright fellow, 1965-66; Am. Philos. Soc. fellow, 1971; Nat. Endowment for Humanities fellow, 1975-76. Mem. Western Soc. for French History (pres. 1977-78, governing coun. 1990-92, 96—), Societe d'histoire de la Revolution de 1848 (comite directeur), Soc. Scis. History Assn., French Hist. Studies Assn., Am. Hist. Assn. (annotator for France bibliographical survey 1815-52). Editor: Historical Dictionary of France from the 1815 Restoration to the Second Empire; contbr. Dictionnaire de Biographie Française, Dictionnaire du Movement Ouvrier Français, Jour. of History of Ideas, Dictionary of Am. Biography. Office: NMex State U PO Box 3H Las Cruces NM 88003-0001

NEWMAN, FRANK NEIL, bank executive; b. Quincy, Mass., Apr. 20, 1942; m. Lizabeth Newman. B.A. in Econs. magna cum laude, Harvard U., 1963. Exec. v.p., CFO Wells Fargo & Co. and Wells Fargo Bank, San Francisco, 1980-86; CFO, vice-chmn. bd. dirs. Bank Am. Corp, Bank of Am., San Francisco, 1986-93; under sec. domestic fin. Dept. Treasury, Washington, 1993-94, dep. sec., 1994-95; sr. vice chmn. Bankers Trust, 1995—, pres., 1996—, CEO, chmn., 1996—. Office: Bankers Trust 130 Liberty St New York NY 10006

NEWMAN, KATHARINE DEALY, author, consultant; b. Phila., Aug. 17, 1911; d. Creswell Victor and Harriet Elizabeth (Hetherington) Dealy; m. Morton Newman, May 11, 1946 (div. 1968); children: Deborah Silverstein, Blaze. BS in Edn. summa cum laude, Temple U., 1933; MA in English, U. Pa., 1937, PhD in English, 1961. Cert. secondary and coll. English educator, Commonwealth of Pa. Tchr. Phila. High Schs., 1933-46, 49-50; asst. prof. U. Minn., Mpls., 1946-47, Temple U. C.C., Phila., 1959; assoc. prof. Moore Coll. Art, Phila., 1961-63; tchr. Abington (Pa.) High Sch., 1963-67; prof. West Chester (Pa.) State U., 1967-77; cons. Inst. for Ethnic Studies, West Chester U., 1975-77; exch. prof. Cheyney State (Pa.) U., 1971, San Dieguito Adult Sch., 1993-94; cons. in field. Author: The Gentleman's Novelist: Robert Plumer Ward, 1765-1846, 1961, The American Equation: Literature in a Multi-Ethnic Culture, 1971, Ethnic American Short Stories, 1975, The Girl of the Golden West, 1978, Never Without a Song, 1995; contbr. articles to profl. jours. Named Outstanding Bd. Mem. Jr. League, 1987; Coordinating Coun. Literary Mags. Editor fellow, 1980. Mem. MLA (emeritus), Soc. for Study of Multi-Ethnic Lit. of U.S. (founder, officer 1973, editor newsletter 1973-77, editor MELUS jour. 1977-81, editor emeritus 1983—, Contbn. award 1982), Inst. for Ethnic Studies (founder, chmn. 1975-77), Episc. Svc. Alliance (co-founder 1978, bd. dirs. 1978-87, v.p. 1982, 86, pres. 1983-84, cert. appreciation 1987). Democrat. Episcopalian. Home: 910 Bonita Dr Encinitas CA 92024-3805

NEWMAN, MARC ALAN, electrical engineer; b. Jasper, Ind., Nov. 21, 1955; s. Leonard Jay and P. Louise (Shainberg) N.; m. Shelley Jane Martin, Aug. 13, 1977; 1 child, Kelsey Renée. BSEE, Purdue U., 1977, MSEE, 1979. Sr. elec. engr. Sperry Corp. Flight Systems, Phoenix, 1979-85; staff engr. Motorola Inc., Tempe, Ariz., 1985-88, Quincy St. Corp., Phoenix, 1988-89; prin. staff scientist Motorola Inc., Chandler, Ariz., 1989-91, Scottsdale, Ariz., 1991—; Prolog and artificial intelligence expert Motorola Inc., Tempe, Chandler and Scottsdale, 1985—. Patentee in field. Mem. IEEE, The Assn. for Logic Programming (London), Am. Assn. Artificial Intelligence, Ariz. Artificial Intelligence Assn. (founder), Internat. Platform Assn., Phi Sigma Kappa, Eta Kappa Nu. Home: Estate 110 7411 S Rita Ln Tempe AZ 85283 Office: Motorola Inc 8201 E Mcdowell Rd Scottsdale AZ 85257-3812

NEWMAN, MICHAEL RODNEY, lawyer; b. N.Y.C., Oct. 2, 1945; s. Morris and Helen Gloria (Hendler) N.; m. Cheryl Jeanne Anker, June 11, 1967; children: Hillary Abra, Nicole Brooke. Student NASA Inst. Space Physics, Columbia U., 1964; BA, U. Denver, 1967; JD, U. Chgo., 1970. Bar: Calif. 1971, U.S. Dist. Ct. (cen. dist.) Calif. 1972, U.S. Ct. Appeals (9th cir.) 1974, U.S. Dist. Ct. (no. dist.) Calif. 1975, U.S. Supreme Ct. 1978, U.S. Dist. Ct. (so. dist.) Calif. 1979, U.S. Tax Ct. 1979, U.S. Dist. Ct. (ea. dist.) Calif. 1983. Assoc. David Daar, 1971-76; ptnr. Daar & Newman, 1976-78, Miller & Daar, 1978-88, Miller, Daar & Newman, 1988-89, Daar & Newman, 1989—; judge pro tem L.A. Mcpl. Ct., 1982—, L.A. Superior Ct., 1988—. Lectr. Ea. Claims Conf., Ea. Life Claims Conf., Nat. Health Care Anti-Fraud Assn., AIA Conf. on Ins. Fraud; mem. L.A. Citizens Organizing Com. for Olympic Summer Games, 1984, mem. govtl. liaison adv. commn. 1984; mem. So. Calif. Com. for Olympic Summer Games, 1984; cert. ofcl. Athletics Congress of U.S., co-chmn. legal com. S.P.A-T.A.C, chief finish judge; trustee Massada lodge B'nai Brith. Recipient NYU Bronze medal in Physics, 1962, Maths. award USN Sci., 1963. Mem. ABA (multi-dist. litigation subcom., com. on class actions), Los Angeles County Bar Assn. (chmn. attys. errors and omissions prevention com., mem. cts. com. litigation sect.), Conf. Ins. Counsel, So. Pacific Assn., TAC (bd. dirs., Disting. Svc. award 1988), Porter Valley Country Club. Office: 865 S Figueroa St Ste 2500 Los Angeles CA 90017-2567

NEWMAN, MURRAY ARTHUR, aquarium administrator; b. Chgo., Mar. 6, 1924; emigrated to Can., 1953, naturalized, 1970; s. Paul Jones and Virginia (Murray) N.; m. Katherine Greene Rose, Aug. 8, 1952; 1 child, Susan. B.Sc., U. Chgo., 1949; postgrad., U. Hawaii, 1950; M.A., U. Calif., Berkeley, 1951; Ph.D., U. B.C. (Can.), Vancouver, 1960. Curator fisheries UCLA, 1951-53, Ichthyology Museum, U. B.C., 1953-56; curator Vancouver Public Aquarium, 1956-66, dir., 1966-93; pres. Mana Aquarium Cons.; fgn. adv. Nat. Mus./Aquarium Project, Taiwan; past chmn. adv. com. Western Can. Univs. Marine Biol. Soc.; co-chmn. Enoshima (Japan) Internat. Aquarium Symposium, 1997. Author: Life in a Fishbowl: Confessions of an Aquarium Director, 1994. Served with USN, 1943-46. Decorated Order of Can.; recipient Man of Yr. award City of Vancouver, 1964; Centennial award Govt. Can., 1967, cert. of merit, 1988; Harold J. Merilees award Vancouver Visitors Bur., 1976, 75 Achievers award, 1987, Silver Bravery medal Royal Soc. Canada, 1992, Canada 125 medal, 1992. Mem. Am. Assn. Zool. Parks and Aquariums, Internat. Union Dirs. Zool. Gardens, Can. Assn. Zool. Parks and Aquariums (pres. 1978-79), Vancouver Club, Round Table Club. Office: Vancouver Pub Aquarium, PO Box 3232, Vancouver, BC Canada V6B 3X8

NEWMAN, RICHARD, engineering executive. With Cahn Gengr Inc., L.A., 1960-77; pres. of subsidiary Daniel Mann Johnnson & Mendenhall, L.A., 1977-88; pres. Aecom Tech Corp., L.A., 1989—, now chmn. bd. dirs., pres., CEO. Office: Aecom Tech Corp 3250 Wilshire Blvd # 5 Los Angeles CA 90010-1502*

NEWMAN, RICHARD D., computer resources professional, software developer; b. Puyallup, Wash., Nov. 20, 1964; s. Rovaughn Drone and Beverly Joan (Vehrs) N.; m. Manuela Erickson, June 24, 1984 (div. 1986); m. Jodi Irene Kortman, July 27, 1991; 1 child, Alexander Rovaughn. Grad. high sch., Spanaway, Wash. cert. computer profl. Computer output control specialist Weyerhaeuser Co., Tacoma, Wash., 1983, records specialist, 1983-84, sr. records specialist, 1984-85; programmer/analyst IPC Pension Svcs. Co., Seattle, 1986-88, sr. programmer/analyst, 1988-89, adminstr., 1989-90, sr. adminstr., 1990-91, sr. adminstrv. programmer, 1991-93; programmer/analyst Idaho Lottery, 1994-95; cons. Meridian, Idaho, 1994-96; software engr. lead Spur Products Corp., 1996. Advocate, counselor Seattle Rape Relief, 1987; campaign worker Dem. Ctrl. Com., Seattle, 1988; computer cons. ACLU of Idaho, 1995-96.

NEWMAN, RICHARD STEPHEN, pathology educator; b. L.A., Oct. 13, 1951; s. Emanuel and Pauline Newman. BS with honors, Calif. Inst. Tech., 1973; MD, U. Calif., Irvine, 1980. Resident Coll. Medicine U. Calif., Irvine, 1980-81, fellow in bloodbanking Coll. Medicine, 1981-83, resident Coll. Medicine, 1983-84; asst. clin. prof. pathology U. Calif. Irvine, 1984-90, assoc. clin. prof. pathology, 1990—; assoc. dir. blood bank U. Calif. Irvine Med. Ctr., Orange, Calif., 1984—, dir. coagulation lab., 1984—, dir. Histocompatibility Lab., 1984-96; cons. ARC Blood Svcs., L.A., Orange County, 1991-92. Contbr. chpts. to books and articles to profl. jours. Mem. Am. Assn. Blood Banks, Am. Soc. Histocompatibility and Immunogenetics, Am. Soc. Hematology, Calif. Blood Bank Sys. Office: U Calif Irvine Med Ctr 101 The City Dr S Orange CA 92868

NEWMAN, SHARON ANN, principal; b. Denver, Sept. 25, 1946; d. Paul G. and Agnes J. (Hillesheim) Schneible; m. John G. Newman, June 30, 1973; children: Michael, Lisa. BA in Speech, Coll. Mt. St. Joseph, Cin., 1969; MAT in Liberal Studies, Lewis and Clark Coll., Portland, Oreg., 1992. Textbook editor Nat. Textbook Co., Chgo., 1972; tchr. speech and drama Seton High Sch., Cin., 1968-69; tchr. 6th grade St. Therese Sch., Aurora, Colo., 1979-70; tchr. speech and English Seton High Sch., Pueblo, Colo., 1970-71; tchr., head speech dept. Jefferson County Pub. High Schs., Denver, 1971-74; tchr. grades 7 and 8 Shakopee (Minn.) Cath. Middle Sch., 1983-84; tchr., team leader Regis High Sch., Denver, 1985-87; dir. admissions Jesuit High Sch., Portland, 1988-90; prin. St. Thomas More Sch., Portland, 1992—; speaker, cons. in field. Author newspaper columns, booklets, books for local use. Mem. Cin. Human Rels. Commn., 1967. Recipient Oreg. Disting. Pvt. Sch. Prin. award Oreg. Elem. & Secondary Prins. Assn., 1995. Mem. ASCD, AAUW, Nat. Assn. Elem. and Secondary Prins., Nat. Cath. Edn. Assn., Nat. Middle Level Assn., N.W. Women in Ednl. Adminstrn., Confedn. Oreg. Sch. Adminstrs., Oreg. Middle Level Assn. Office: St Thomas More Sch 3521 SW Patton Rd Portland OR 97221-4124

NEWMAN, STANLEY RAY, oil refining company executive; b. Milo, Idaho, Mar. 5, 1923; s. Franklin Hughes and Ethel Amelda (Crowley) N.; student Tex. A&M U, 1944-45; B.S., U. Utah, 1947, Ph.D., 1952. m. Rosa Klein, May 27, 1961 (div. Mar. 1980); children: Trudy Lynn, Susan Louise, Karen Elizabeth, Paul Daniel, Phillip John; m. Madelyn Wycherly, Jan. 10, 1991; children: Heidi, Heather, Amy. With Texaco Res. Ctr., Beacon, N.Y., 1951-82, technologist, 1973-77, sr. technologist research mfg.-fuels, 1977-82, profl. cons. on fuels and chems., 1983-91. Chmn., Planning Bd., Village of Fishkill, N.Y., 1973- 77; village trustee, 1990-92; mem. Dutchess County Solid Waste Mgmt. Bd., 1974-76. With inf. Signal Corps U.S. Army, 1944-46. Mem. AAAS, N.Y. Acad. Sci., Dutchess County Geneal. Soc. (pres. 1981-87, exec. v.p. 1987-88), N.Y. Fruit Testing Assn., Sigma Xi (pres. Texaco Res. Ctr. br. 1980-81). Republican. Mormon. Patentee in field. Home: 285 Plantation Cir Idaho Falls ID 83404-7990 *I was born of humble parents in Idaho. Life was hard and difficult so early in my life at considerable sacrifice I went the extra distance to go to a good high school to prepare for college. By working at night and weekends, I was able to complete college with a Ph.D. Blessed with an inquiring mind, a strong will to work, and a desire to learn, I moved to the east coast, worked hard both at my job and in the community, always retaining the honesty, integrity and strong religious values taught by my humble parents. At retirement, I had numerous patents, publications, and had world wide responsibility for fuels for Texaco.*

NEWMARK, MILTON MAXWELL, lawyer; b. Oakland, Calif., Feb. 24, 1916; s. Milton and Mary (Maxwell) N.; m. Marion Irene Johnson, July 31, 1941 (dec.), children—Mari Newmark Anderson, Lucy Newmark Sammons, Grace Newmark Lucini; m. Aylene Pruett Rosselli, June 21, 1991. A.B., U. Calif.-Berkeley, 1936, J.D., 1947. Bar: Calif. 1940, U.S. Supreme Ct. 1944. Ptnr. Milton Newmark, San Francisco, 1941-56; sole practice, 1956-62; sole practice, Lafayette, Calif., 1962-80, Walnut Creek, Calif., 1980-94; lectr. bankruptcy State Bar of Calif. Continuing Edn. Program. Served with U.S. Army, 1942-46; to lt. col. USAR. Mem. Alameda County Rep. Cen. Com., 1940-41; pres. Alameda County Rep. Assembly, 1950. Mem. Am. Legion, ABA, San Francisco Bar Assn., Contra Costa Bar Assn., Alameda County Bar Assn., Scabbard and Blade. Lodges: Masons, Shriners, Rotary. Home: 609 Terra California Dr Apt 6 Walnut Creek CA 94595-3344

NEWMILLER, WILLIAM ERNEST, English educator; b. Chgo., Dec. 6, 1947; s. Walter George and Gladys Marie (Anderson) N.; m. Gloria Louise Freehling, June 24, 1967; children: Tracy Lippard, Todd Newmiller, Joel Newmiller. BA, Mich. State U., 1969; MA, U. Mich., 1977; BS, Chapman U., 1993. Tchr. Reeths-Puffer H.S., Muskegon, Mich., 1969-70; commd. 2d lt. USAF, 1970, advanced through grades to lt. col., 1987; ret., 1993; unit chief FBI, Washington, 1993-94; prof. English, USAF Acad., Colorado Springs, 1994—. Mem. bd. edn. St. Paul Sch., Wichita Falls, Tex., 1975-76, Redeemer Luth. Sch., Colorado Springs, 1988-92, Amazing Grace Luth. Sch., Seattle, 1982-84. Mem. Alliance for Computers and Writing. Home: 7645 Hickorywood Dr Colorado Springs CO 80920 Office: USAF Acad Dept English 2354 Fairchild Dr Ste 6D35 Colorado Springs CO 80840

NEWQUIST, DONALD STEWART, designer, technical director, consultant; b. Frankfort, Ky., May 25, 1953; s. Edward Wallace N. and Jeanne Gayle (Utterback) Caddy; m. Linda Susan Carter, Oct. 10, 1987. BA, Centre Coll. of Ky., Danville, 1975; MA, U. Nev., Las Vegas, 1979; postgrad., U. Nev., 1987—. Grad. fellow Ctr. Coll. of Ky., 1975-76; grad. teaching asst. U. Nev., Las Vegas, 1976-78; instr. tech. theater Clark County Community Coll., N. Las Vegas, Nev., 1978-80; tech. supr. City of Las Vegas, 1979-91; adminstr. Las Vegas Civic Ballet, 1988-90; engring. analyst City of Las Vegas Project Unit, 1991; lighting designer T.J. Krob Cons. Engrs., Las Vegas, 1991—; tech. dir. USAF Base Talent Show, Davis-Monthan AFB, Ariz., 1986, 87; tech. cons. USAF Recreation Ctr., Nellis AFB, Nev., 1982-85; resident designer Ecdysis Dance Theater, Las Vegas, 1980-84; mem. Lorenzi Park Amphitheater Task Force, Las Vegas, 1988. Designer: stage renovation, Reed Whipple Cultural Ctr., 1981; stage addition, Charleston Heights Arts Ctr., 1980. Lic. lay reader, Christ Episcopal Ch., Las Vegas, 1981—. Mem. Illuminating Engring. Soc. N.Am. (sect. treas. 1989-90, sect. pres. 1990-92, bi-regional conf. chmn., regional v.p. 1994-96, dir. 1995-96). Republican. Office: TJ Krob Cons Engrs 1919 S Jones Blvd Ste B Las Vegas NV 89102-1299

NEWSHAM, DAVID P., protective services official; b. Long Beach, Calif., Oct. 11, 1942. BA in Mgmt., U. Redlands. From police res. officer to capt. Burbank (Calif.) Police Dept., 1970-90, chief of police, 1990—; chmn. dept. master plan task force Burbank Police Dept., 1990-95. Bd. dirs. YMCA, Burbank, ARC, Boy Scouts Am., Am. Heart Assn. With USAF, 1960-64. Mem. Internat. Assn. Chiefs Police, Calif. Peace Officers Assn., L.A. County Police Chiefs Assn., San Gabriel Valley Police Chiefs Assn., Burbank Police Officers Assn., Profl. Helicopter Pilots Assn. Office: Office Chief of Police 272 E Olive Ave Burbank CA 91510

NEWSTEAD, ROBERT RICHARD, urologist; b. Detroit, Sept. 16, 1935; s. Oran Henry and Agnes Audery (Lewandowski) N.; m. Marie Carmela LiPuma, Aug. 5, 1961; children: Elizabeth Marie, Peter Joseph, Angela Agnes, Paul Michael. Student, Coll. Idaho, 1955-57, Quincy Coll., 1957-58; MD, Loyola U., Chgo., 1963. Intern Walter Reed Gen. Hosp., Washington, 1963-64; resident U. Iowa, Iowa City, 1967-71; urologist Urology Clinic Yakima, Wash., 1971-84, pres., 1984—; chief of staff Yakima Valley Meml. Hosp., 1995—; chief of surgery St. Elizabeth Med. Ctr., Yakima, 1980-81, Yakima Valley Hosp., 1978-79. Bd. dirs. St. Elizabeth Found., Yakima, 1983-93, The Capital Theater, 1987-93, Boy Scouts Am., Yakima, 1982-86. Capt. U.S. Army, 1962-67. Fellow Am. Cancer Soc., Iowa City, 1969-70, Am. Cancer Soc., 1961; named one of Outstanding Young Men Am., 1968. Fellow Am. Bd. Urology, ACS, Am. Urol. Assn., Wash. State Urol. Bd. (mem. at large exec. com.); mem. AMA, Rubin Flocks Soc. (pres. 1985-86), Yakima Surgical Soc. (pres. 1982-83), Yakima County Med. Soc. (pres. 1989-90), Rotary. Roman Catholic. Home: 814 Conestoga Blvd Yakima WA 98908-2419 Office: Urology Clinic Yakima 206 S 11th Ave Yakima WA 98902-3205

NEWTON, BARBARA BESS, artist, educator; b. Puyallup, Wash., Oct. 25, 1943; d. Andrew Joseph and Ethel Vivian (Heimsoth) Benedetti; m. Charles William Iles, Jr., June 26, 1965 (div. 1983); children: Tobin William, Andrea Elisabeth-Rose; m. Jay Newton, Apr. 25, 1987. Grad., Burnley Art sch., Seattle, 1966. Owner Bina Designs, Renton, Wash., 1988—; instr./owner Colored Pencil Workshops, Renton, Wash., 1993—. Editor Colored Pencil Soc. DC207 Am. newsletter, 1991—; artwork pub. in all edits. of: Best of Colored Pencil series (4 books), Creative Colored Pencil, 1996, The Best of Flower Painting, 1997; solo exhibits include Renton (Wash.) Arts Commn. Closing Artist, 1995, Kent Arts Commn. Opening Artist, 1995, PACCAR Inc., Bellevue, Wash., 1994, Auburn Arts Commn. Visual Arts Exhbn., Wash., 1993; group shows include Catharine Lorillard Wolfe Art Club 100th Ann. Juried Exhibit, N.Y.C., 1996, Bellevue Art Mus., 1996, Realism, 1996, 97, Parkersburg (W.Va.) Art Ctr., 1996, Oreg. State U., 1996, Internat. Colored Pencil Exhbn., Oreg., 1994, Ohio, 1995, Calif., 1996, Gango Gallery, Portland, 1994, 95, 96, Sidney Gallery, Port Orchard, Wash., 1996, Sitka Art Invitational, Portland, 1996, Sidney Gallery, Port Orchard, 1995, Artsplash, Redmond, Wash., 1995—, Pacific Gallery, Wash., 1994, Eastside Assn. Fine Arts, 1994, 95, 97, Seahurst Gallery, Burien, Wash., 1993, Western Wash. State Fair art Show, 1992, others. Recipient Ridgewood Art Inst. award, 1996, Best of Show award Eastside Assn. Fine arts, 1994, 95. Colored Pencil Soc. Am. (charter mem. 1990, signature mem., 1996, nat. membership dir. 1993-94, pres. 1994-95, advisor to bd. 1995-96), Knickerbocker Artists of N.Y. (assoc.), Allied Artists of Am. (assoc.), Eastside Assn. Fine Arts.

NG, ASSUNTA, newspaper publisher; b. Canton, China, Oct. 5, 1951; came to U.S., 1970; d. Eric and Hoi Sai (Wong) Woo; m. George Liu, July 6, 1974; children: Ho-Yin, Ho-Ghan. BA, U. Wash., 1974, MA, 1979. Tchr. Seattle Pub. Sch., 1974-79; pub. Seattle Chinese Post, 1982—, Northwest Asian Weekly, Seattle, 1983—; judging panelist Leadership Tomorrow, 1992; founding mem. Seattle Chinese Voice, KRAB Radio program; bd. dir. Stellar Connection; founding mem. Chinese Info. and Svc. Ctr. Newspaper columnist. Adv. bd. First Lady of Seattle; com. mem. Gov.-elect Mike Lowry's Transition Team; bd. dirs. YWCA Nominating Com., awards judge; organize, chair numerous fundraising campaigns for civic orgns. Recipient Small Bus. award Mayor Charles Royer, 1984, The Best of Men and Women Under 40 award Esquire mag., 1984, The Brightest Under 40 award Pacific Northwest mag., 1986, Mentor award Network Managerial and Profl. Women, 1989, Influential People Under 40 award Seattle Weekly, 1989, Matrix Table Women of Achievement award Women in Comm., 1990, Cmty. Svc. award Japanese Am. Citizens League, 1991, Cultural Diversity award Nordstrom's, 1991, Women of Enterprise awards Avon and Small Bus. Adminstrs., 1991, Influential People Under 40 award Eastside Week, 1991; named Western Wash. Woman Bus. Advocate of Yr., Small Bus. Adminstrs., 1992, Minority Bus. Advocate of Yr., 1992, Region X's Bus. Advocate of Yr., 1993; featured in Remarkable People of the Northwest, Sta. KCTS, Wash. Mem. Rotary Internat., Minority Pub. Assn. (pres. 1988—), Greater Seattle C. of C. (bd. trustees 1992-95), Chinatown C. of C., Taiwan C. of C., Internat. Women's Forum (Women Making a Difference in Corp. World award 1992). Buddhist. Office: Seattle Chinese Post Inc 414 8th Ave S Seattle WA 98104-3002

NG, CHOON MENG, design engineer, consultant; b. Kuala Lumpur, Malaysia, Nov. 27, 1961; came to U.S., 1975; s. Kok Toong and Choong Kam (Lau) N. BS, Poly. Inst. N.Y., 1985; MS, U. Cin., 1989. Registered profl. engr., Calif. Coop. engr. Johnson Space Ctr. NASA, Houston, 1982-84; nozzle engr., combustor design engr., aerospace propulsion controls engr. GE, Cin., 1985-89; design engr. space propulsion and space power systems Rocketdyne Rockwell Internat., Canoga Park, Calif., 1989—; computer cons. CMN Microsystems, Simi Valley, Calif., 1993—. Inventor, patentee convergent nozzle, coal combustor. Mem. AIAA (sr.), Sigma Gamma Tau, Tau Beta Pi. Home: 1733 Empty Saddle Ave Simi Valley CA 93063-6431 Office: Rocketdyne PO Box 7922 MS 902/LB03 Canoga Park CA 91309

NG, LAWRENCE MING-LOY, pediatric cardiologist; b. Hong Kong, Mar. 21, 1940; came to U.S., 1967, naturalized, 1977; s. John Iu-cheung and Mary Wing (Wong) N.; m. Bella May Ha Kan, June 25, 1971; children: Jennifer Wing-mui, Jessica Wing-yee. B in Medicine, U. Hong Kong, 1965, B in Surgery, 1965. House physician Queen Elizabeth Hosp., Hong Kong, 1965-66, med. officer, 1966-67; resident physician Children's Hosp. of Los Angeles, 1967-68; resident physician Children's Hosp. Med. Center, Oakland, Calif., 1968-70, fellow in pediatric cardiology, 1970-72, now mem. teaching staff; practice medicine, specializing in pediatrics and pediatric cardiology, San Leandro, Calif., 1972—, Oakland, Calif., 1982—; mng. ptnr. Pediatric Med. Assocs. of East Bay, 1990—; chief of pediatrics Oakland Hosp., 1974-77; chief of pediatrics Vesper Meml. Hosp., 1977-79, sec. staff, 1984, v.p. staff, 1985; chief pediatrics Meml. Hosp., San Leandro, 1986-88; founder Pediatric Assocs. of East Bay, 1990. Active Republican Party. Diplomate Am. Bd. Pediatrics. Fellow Am. Acad. Pediatrics; mem. AMA, Calif. Med. Assn., Am. Heart Assn., Alameda County Assn. Primary Care Practitioners (membership chmn. 1993—, sec. treas 1994—), Los Angeles Pediatric Soc., East Bay Pediatric Soc., Smithsonian Assocs., Nat. Geog. Soc., Orgn. Chinese Ams. (chpt. pres. 1984), Chinese-Am. Physicians Soc. (co-founder, sec. 1980, pres. 1983), Chinese-Am. Polit. Assn. (life), Oakland Mus. Assns., Oakland Chinatown C. of C. (bd. dirs. 1986-91); Oakland Asian Cultural Ctr. (dir. 1996—, treas. 1996—), Hong Kong U. Alumni Assn. (sec. No. Calif. chpt. 1992-96, pres. 1997—), Stanford U. Alumni Assn. (life), Chancellor's Assocs. U. Calif. at Berkeley, Commonwealth Club, Consumers' Union (life); Chinese Am. Golf Club. Buddhist. Office: 345 9th St Ste 204 Oakland CA 94607-4206 also: 101 Callan Ave Ste 401 San Leandro CA 94577-4519

NG, WING CHIU, accountant, computer software consultant, educator, activist; b. Hong Kong, Hong Kong, Oct. 14, 1947; came to U.S., 1966; s. Bing Nuen and Oi Ying (Lee) Ng. BS, Yale U., 1969, MS, 1969; PhD, NYU, 1972. CPA, Hawaii. Rsch. assoc. SUNY, Stony Brook, 1972-74; asst. prof. U. Md., College Park, 1974-76; rsch. physicist U. Bonn, Fed. Republic of Germany, 1976-78; chartered acct. Richter, Usher & Vineberg, Montreal, Can., 1978-80; pvt. practice Honolulu, Hawaii, 1980—; pres. Bowen, Ng & Co., Honolulu, 1983-84, Asia-Am. Investment, Inc., Honolulu, 1983—, Mathematica Pacific, Inc., Honolulu, 1984—; part-time prof. U. Hawaii, Honolulu, 1982—; ptnr. Advance Realty Investment, Honolulu, 1980—; dir. S & L Internat., Inc., Honolulu, 1987—. Creator: (computer software) Time Billing, 1994, Dbase General Ledger, 1987, Dbase Payroll, 1987, Dbase Accounts Receivable, 1989; co-author: Draft Constitution of the Federal Republic of China, 1994. Dir. Orgn. of Chinese Ams., Honolulu, 1984-86, Fedn. for a Dem. China, Honolulu, 1990—, Hong Kong, 1991—.

Included in Prominent People of Hawaii, Delta Pub. Co., 1988. Mem. AICPA, Hong Kong Soc. Accts., Hawaiian Trail & Mountain Club (auditor 1987—). Democrat. Buddhist. Office: 1149 Bethel St Ste 306 Honolulu HI 96813-2210

NGUYEN, ANN CAC KHUE, pharmaceutical and medicinal chemist; b. Sontay, Vietnam; came to U.S., 1975; naturalized citizen; d. Nguyen Van Soan and Luu Thi Hieu. BS, U. Saigon, 1973; MS, San Francisco State U., 1978; PhD, U. Calif., San Francisco, 1983. Teaching and research asst. U. Calif., San Francisco, 1978-83, postdoctoral fellow, 1983-86; research scientist U. Calif., 1987—. Contbr. articles to profl. jours. Recipient Nat. Research Service award, NIH, 1981-83; Regents fellow U. Calif., San Francisco, 1978-81. Mem. AAAS, Am. Chem. Soc., N.Y. Acad. Scis., Bay Area Enzyme Mechanism Group, Am. Assn. Pharm. Scientists. Roman Catholic. Home: 1488 Portola Dr San Francisco CA 94127-1409 Office: U Calif Box 0446 San Francisco CA 94143

NGUYEN, EDWARD DUY, real estate financier; b. Saigon, Vietnam, May 26, 1963; came to U.S., 1975; BSEE summa cum laude, Calif. State U., L.A., 1982; MSEE, Calif. Inst. Tech., 1983; postgrad. in Elec. Engring., U. So. Calif., 1983-87; postgrad in Law, U. West L.A., 1990-91. Lic. real estate broker, Calif. Comm. systems engr. Hughes Aircraft Co., El Segundo, Calif., 1983-88; pres. Far East Devel. Co., Beverly Hills, Calif., 1988-91; mng. dir. Global Devel. Group, L.A., 1991-95, Windsor Capital, Beverly Hills, 1995—. Recipient Howard Hughes Doctoral fellowship, 1983-87, Am. Jurisprudence awards on Tort and Contracts, 1990-91; named to Dean's Honor list, 1990-91. Home: 1440 Veteran Ave Apt 607 Los Angeles CA 90024-4877 Office: Windsor Capital Ste 211 499 N Canon Dr Beverly Hills CA 90210

NGUYEN, HAN VAN, mechanical engineer; b. Danang, Vietnam, June 10, 1956; came to U.S., 1974; s. Tien Van and Dieu Anh Khoa Nguyen; m. Thien-Tam Trang, Jan. 7, 1995; 1 child, Huy. BSME with distinction, Iowa State U., 1979; MSME, Purdue U., 1981, PhD, 1986. Registered profl. engr., Calif. Grad. rsch. asst. Purdue U., West Lafayette, 1979-83; sr. engr. Westinghouse Electric Corp., Sunnyvale, Calif., 1983-87; sr. engring. specialist Boeing North American, Inc., Downey, Calif., 1987—; mem. adj. faculty Calif. State Poly. U., Pomona, 1995—. Contbr. articles to profl. jours. Recipient NASA award, Rockwell Internat. awards 1992, 94; Iowa State U. scholar; Purdue U. fellow;. Mem. AIAA (sr.), Am. Soc. Engring. Edn., Golden Key, Sigma Xi, Phi Kappa Phi, Tau Beta Pi, Pi Tau Sigma, Eta Kappa Nu, Pi Mu Epsilon, Phi Eta Sigma. Office: Boeing North Am Inc MS AE70 12214 Lakewood Blvd Downey CA 90241-7009

NGUYEN, JOSEPH KIM QUY, foreign language educator; b. Nhatrang, Vietnam, Sept. 10, 1939; came to the U.S., 1985; m. Marie-Therese Tran Thanh Loan, 1996. BA in French Lit., U. Saigon, 1963; MA in Tchg., Portland State U., 1986; PhD in Romance Langs., U. Oreg., 1990. Tchr. Nhatrang (Vietnam) H.S., 1963-68; asst. prof. French U. Dalat, Vietnam, 1973-75; grad. tchg. fellow U. Oreg., Eugene, 1986-90; asst. prof. French Ea. Wash. U., Cheney, 1990-92; health info. specialist Multnomah County Health Dept., Portland, 1993—; vis. prof. French Portland (Oreg.) State U., summer 1988; participant MLA Convs., Washington and San Francisco, 1989, 91; spkr. in field. Recipient recognition award Portland (Oreg.) State U., 1986, recognition award Refugee Forum of Oreg. & Southwest Wash., 1994; Gilbert Chinard scholar Inst. Francais de WA, Chapel Hill, N.C., 1989; recipient grad. student award U. Oreg., 1989. Mem. Confedn. Oreg. Fgn. Lang. Tchrs., Soc. des Professeurs Francais et Francophones en Amerique, Phi Kappa Phi. Home: 7006 SE 76th Ave Portland OR 97206-7211

NGUYEN, KING XUAN, language educator; b. Hue, Vietnam, Dec. 20, 1930; came to U.S., 1975; s. Duong Xuan Nguyen and Thi Thi Ton-Nu. BA, U. Saigon, 1960, LLB, 1963; MEd, Boise State U., 1980. Tchr. Boise Sch. Dist., 1975-95; lectr. S.E. Asian Studies Summer Inst./U. Wash., 1992, 93, U. Wis., 1994, Ariz. State U., 1996, 97; spl. lectr. Boise State U., 1975-77. Col. Vietnamese Air Force to 1975. Recipient Red Apple Award for Outstanding Svc. to Edn., Boise, 1990. Mem. NEA, Idaho Edn. Assn., Boise Edn. Assn., Consortium Tchrs. Southeast Asian Langs., Assn. of TESOL. Home: 9674 W Pattie Ct Boise ID 83704-2824

NGUYEN, LAM DUC, business executive, consultant; b. Ninh Binh, Vietnam, July 20, 1945; came to the U.S., 1975; s. Phuong-Duc and Thien-Thi Nguyen; m. Trang Thu Nghiem, June 17, 1978; children: Katherine, Andrew, Alexander. BA, U. Saigon, 1968; diploma in TEFL, U. Sydney, Australia, 1973; postgrad., Furman U., 1977, San Jose State U., 1980; AS in Computer Sci., Condie Coll., 1981; MS in Telecomm. Sys. Mgmt., Nat. U., Calif., 1996, postgrad., 1997—. Cert. Emergency Specialist Tchg. credential ESL grades K-12; Calif. C.C. tchg. credential for ltd. svcs. in basic edn.; Calif. C.C. instr. credential in computer scis. Materials/mfg. sys. analyst, project leader Shugart Corp., Sunnyvale, Calif., 1979-84; mgr. programming and sys. devel. Televideo Sys., Inc., San Jose, Calif., 1984-86; sales and mktg. sys. analyst, project leader Spectra-Physics, San Jose, 1986; project mgr. U.S. Wind Power, Livermore, Calif., 1986-87; asst. mgr. ops. Burger King Corp., San Jose, 1987-88; dir. programs, dep. exec. dir. IRCC Inc., San Jose, 1988-93; pres., founder WIN-Visions, San Jose, 1993—; asst. chief tng. team Combined Document Exploitation Ctr., 1965-68; lang. instr. Military Asst. Command Civil Ops. for Rural Devel. Strategies/USAID, Bien Hoa, Vietnam, 1968-69; tchr. ESL/EFL Vietnamese-Am. Assn., Saigon, 1970-75; lectr. med. English U. Saigon-Med. Coll., 1974-75; spl. asst. to dir. refugee liaison officer, chief interpreter staff Refugee Camp, Eglin AFB, Fla., 1975; refugee camp mgmt. counselor Indochinese Inter-Agy. Task Force, U.S. State Dept., Indiantown Gap Refugee Camp, Pa., 1975; statis. quality control Michelin Tire Corp., S.C., 1976-78, others; part-time ESL instr. Foothill-De Anza Coll., San Jose, Calif., 1979-80; bilingual elem. and ESL tchr. San Jose Unified Sch. Dist., 1979-80; spkr., panelist in field. Editor VIET mag., Thi Truong Tu Do mag.; co-editor, reporter Tin Bien News; contbr. articles to profl. jours. Active Nat. Asian Pacific Islanders Am. Adv. Coun., Democratic Nat. Com., 1991—, San Jose City Mayor's Gang Prevention Policy Team, 1992—, Coalition of Asian Pacific-Ams., No. Calif., 1992—, Nat. Immigration Forum, 1994; nat. co-chair Nat. Vietnamese-Am. Voter's League, 1992—, Nat. League Indochinese Am. Voters, 1992—; pres. Vietnamese-Ams. Civic Action Com., 1992—; mem., contbr. World Affairs Coun., 1993—; mem. adv. com. on voter registration and Get Out To Vote, Santa Clara County, co-chair, 1993, 94; mem. Dem. Congl. Campaign Com., 1992—; charter mem. Senate Task Force, 1992—; mem. Dem. Nat. Com.; mem. nat. steering com. Clinton/Gore, 1996; mem. Calif. State Adv. Coun. Refugee Assistance, 1992—, mem. various coms.; chair Vietnamese-Ams. Com. for Clinton/Gore, No. Calif., 1992; chair Tet Festival, 1988-91; leader Vietnamese Ams. Dukakis' Presdl. Campaign, 1988. Recipient Appreciation cert. Nat. ARC, 1975, Appreciation cert. and letter of commendation Refugee Liaison Office, USAF, 1975, Achievement cert. Dept. Army, 1975, Outstand Svc. to Refugee citation World YMCA, 1975, Peter Casey Asian Am. Leadership award, 1987, Letter of Commendation, Senator Art Torres, 1989, Letter Commendation, Santa Clara County Greater Ave. for Independence/Refugee Employment and Social Svcs. Adminstrn., 1990, Appreciation cert. State Calif. Dept. Social Svcs., 1990, Appreciation Cert. Calif. Dept. Health Svcs., Tobacco Control, 1991, Appreciation cert. U. Berkeley, Extended Foods and Nutrition Edn. Program, 1991, Merit award Coalition of Nationalist Vietnamese Orgns. of No. Calif., 1991, Leadership award No. Calif. Asian Pacific Americans, 1992, Cmty. Svc. award City of San Jose, 1993, Spirit of Democracy award State of Calif., 1994. Democrat. Buddhist. Home and Office: WIN-Visions 4864 Miramar Ave San Jose CA 95129-1004

NGUYEN, TAI ANH, minister. Supt. Vietnamese Ministry Dist. of the Christian and Missionary Alliance. Office: 2275 W Lincoln Ave Anaheim CA 92801-6551*

NGUYEN, THINH VAN, physician; b. Vietnam, Apr. 16, 1948; came to U.S., 1971; s. Thao Van and Phuong Thi (Tran) N.; m. Phi Thi Ho, Jan. 2, 1973; children: Anh-Quan, Andrew. BS, U. Saigon, 1970; MS, U. Mo., 1973; MD, U. Tex., 1982. Diplomate Am. Bd. Internal Medicine, Am. Acad. Pain Mgmt., Fed. Lic. Examination. Rsch. asst. U. Tex. Med. Sch., Dallas, 1974-78; intern U. Tex. Med. Br., Galveston, 1982-83, resident, 1983-85; internist Family Health Plan, Inc., Long Beach, Calif., 1985-88, internist, area chief, 1988-89; pvt. practice San Jose, Calif., 1990—; chmn. quality assurance/UM com. Premier Care of No. Calif. Med. Group, Inc., 1996—; chmn. interdisciplinary com. Charter Cmty. Hosp., Hawaiian Gardens, Calif., 1988-89, San Jose Med. Ctr., 1993—. Fellow Am. Acad. Otolaryngic Allergy (affiliate); mem. ACP, AMA, Am. Acad. Pain Mgmt., Calif. Assn. Med. Dirs. (bd. dirs. 1988-92), Calif. Med. Assn., Santa Clara County Med. Assn. Office: 2470 Alvin Ave Ste 5 San Jose CA 95121-1664

NGUYEN, THOMAS, computer executive; b. 1958; came to U.S., 1983; Grad., U. Calif., Berkeley, 1987. With electronics and mech. field Vietnam, 1975-83; with IBM, San Jose, Calif., 1983-87, U. Calif., 1983-87, Olivetti, Cupertino, Calif., 1988; pres. Advanced Integrated Rsch., 1989—. Office: Advanced Integrated Research 2188 Del Franco St San Jose CA 95131-1575*

NGUYEN, TIEN MANH, communications systems engineer; b. Saigon, Vietnam, Apr. 5, 1957; came to the U.S., 1975; s. Hung The and Bi Thi (Luu) N.; m. Thu Hang Thi, Dec. 28 1986. BS in Engring., Calif. State U., Fullerton, 1979, MS in Engring., 1980; MSEE, U. Calif., San Diego, 1982; PhD in Elec. Engring., Columbia Pacific U., 1986; MA in Math., Claremont Grad. Sch., 1993, PhD in Engring. Math., 1995. Cert. electro magnetic compatibility engr., mfg. technologist. Tchg. asst. U. Calif., San Diego, 1982-83; chief automated mfg. dept. ITT Ednl. Svcs., West Covina, Calif., 1983-85; tech. staff Jet Propulsion Lab., Pasadena, Calif., 1985-96; engring. specialist The Aerospace Corp., El Segundo, Calif., 1996—; prin. tech. advisor Internat. Consultative Com. for Space Data Systems (CCSDS), Pasadena, 1985-90, 93-96. Editor: Proceedings of CCSDS RF & Modulation, 1989, 94, VACET Tech. Jour., 1996—; contbr. over 60 articles to profl. jours. Grad. rep. EECS dept. U. Calif., San Diego, 1982-83; NASA del. to internat. CCSDS, 1986—. San Diego fellow, 1980-82, Long Beach Found. scholar Calif. State U.; recipient Bendix Mgmt. Club award, 1987, NASA Hon. award, 1988, over 23 NASA monetary awards, 1989-96, 2 NASA Hon. awards, 1993, Vest Bond prize award for best PhD dissertation, 1995. Mem. IEEE (sr., vice chmn. 1987-94, session chmn. internat. symposium on electro magnetic compatibility 1986, internat. conf. on telecomm. 1995, session organizer, award 1986, 95, student activities chair Orange County Sect., 1997—), AIAA (sr.), AAAS, Soc. Mfg. Engrs., Am. Math. Soc., Armed Forces Commn. and Electronics Assn., Vietnamese-Am. Sci. and Profl. Engring. Soc. (chmn. bd. dirs. 1995-96, planning chair and tech. program chair conf. 1996, presenter in field, editor VASPES '96 Conf. Proc.), Vietnamese Assn. for Computing, Engring., Tech., and Sci. (gen. co-chmn. Viet-Tech. Internat. Conf. 1996 (editor-in-chief VACETS Tech. Jour. 1996-97), N.Y. Acad. Scis., U.S. Naval Inst., Phi Kappa Phi, Sigma Xi. Republican. Buddhist. Home: 1501 Maxzim Ave Fullerton CA 92833-4511 Office: Jet Propulsion Lab 4800 Oak Grove Dr Pasadena CA 91109-8001

NGUYEN-ELY, DARLENE, sculptor; b. Saigon, Vietnam, May 27, 1958; came to U.S., 1975; d. Hue Thie Tran; m. Paul Ely, May 22, 1992. BFA, Calif. State U., Long Beach, 1992. One-woman shows include Long Beach Pub. Main Libr., Calif., 1992, 93, Acme Art Co., Columbus, Ohio, 1984, Creative Arts Ctr. Mcpl. Gallery, Burbank, Calif., 1994, FireHouse Gallery Rogue C.C., Grants Pass, Oreg., 1995, Sinclair C.C., Dayton, Ohio, 1995, U. Pacific, Stockton, Calif., 1995, Chico Art Ctr., Calif., 1995, Bachman Gallery, Munster, Ind., 1995, U. Ala., Huntsville, 1996, Sun Cities Mus.of Art, Phoenix, 1997; exhibited in group shows at Spring Street Gallery, L.A., 1995, Hunsaker Schlesinger Gallery, Santa Monica, Calif., 1996, Ariana Gallery, Royal Oak, Mich., 1996, Orlando Gallery, Sherman Oaks, Calif., 1996, Sonia Zaks Gallery, Chgo., 1996, Site Gallery, L.A., 1997, numerous others; contbr. articles to profl. mags. Recipient award The Drawing Room Studios and Gallery, 1993, Assn. Viet Arts, 1993, Creative Arts Ctr. 1993, 94, 95, Calif. Discovery Gold award, 1993, Gallery 57, 1994, Calif. Works, 1994, Thousand Oaks Art Assn., 1994, Riviera Fine Arts Ctr., 1994, Baystreet Galleria, 1995, Michael Levy Gallery, 1996; (honorarium paid) Sinclair C.C., 1995, Rogue C.C., 1995, Royals Gallery, 1995, Assn. for Viet Arts, 1995, Chico Art Ctr., 1995, U. Ala., 1996, Palos Verdes Art Ctr., Mcpl. Art Ctr., 1996; Individual Artist fellow, 1996-97; Elizabeth Greenshield Found. grantee, 1996-97, Ruth Chenven Found. grantee, 1995-96, Pollock-Krasner Found. grantee, 1994-95.

NGUYEN TRUNG, B., plastic surgeon; b. Saigon, Vietnam, June 19, 1937; s. Buu and Thinh (Ngo) Nguyen; m. Hang B. Nguyen, June, 1966; children: Alison, Amy, Johnny, Andy. MD, Saigon Med. Sch., 1966. Bd. cert. plastic rehab. surgery. Chief resident plastic surgery N.Y. Cornell Hosp., N.Y.C., 1982-83; attending plastic surgeon Kaiser Bellflower (Calif.) Med. Ctr., 1983-85, chief plastic surgery dept., 1985-95. Capt. South Vietnamese Army, 1966-75. Decorated Valiant medal Vietnamese Army, 1968; recipient N.Y. Hosp. Corp. award, 1980. Mem. Am. Soc. Plastic and Reconstructive Surgery, L.A. Calif. Med. Assn. Office: Bellflower Kaiser Med Ctr 9600 Rosecran Bellflower CA 90706

NIBLEY, ROBERT RICKS, retired lawyer; b. Salt Lake City, Sept. 24, 1913; s. Joel and Teresa (Taylor) N.; m. Lee Allen, Jan. 31, 1945 (dec.); children—Jane, Annette. A.B., U. Utah, 1934; J.D., Loyola U., Los Angeles, 1942. Bar: Calif. bar 1943. Accountant Nat. Parks Airways, Salt Lake City, 1934-37, Western Air Lines, Los Angeles, 1937-40; asst. mgr. market research dept. Lockheed Aircraft Corp., Burbank, Calif., 1940-43; asso. firm Hill, Farrer and Burrill, Los Angeles, 1946-53; partner Hill, Farrer and Burrill, 1953-70, of counsel, 1971-78. Served from ensign to lt. comdr. USNR, 1943-46. Mem. ABA, L.A. Bar Assn., Calif. Club, Phi Delta Phi, Phi Kappa Phi, Phi Delta Theta. Home: 4860 Ambrose Ave Los Angeles CA 90027-1866

NICHOLAS, FREDERICK M., lawyer; b. N.Y.C., May 30, 1920; s. Benjamin L. and Rose F. (Nechols) N.; m. Eleanore Berman, Sept. 2, 1951 (div. 1963); children: Deborah, Jan, Tony; m. Joan Fields, Jan. 2, 1983. AB, U. So. Calif., 1947; postgrad., U. Chgo., 1949-50; JD, U. So. Calif., 1952. Bar: Calif. 1952, U.S. Dist. Ct. Calif. 1952, U.S. Ct. Appeals (9th cir.) 1952. Assoc. Loeb & Loeb, L.A., 1952-56; ptnr. Swerdlow, Glikbarg & Nicholas, Beverly Hills, Calif., 1956-62; pvt. practice Beverly Hills, 1962-80; pres., atty. Hapsmith Co., Beverly Hills, 1980—; bd. dirs. Malibu Grand Prix, L.A., 1982-90; gen. counsel Beverly Hills Realty Bd., 1971-79; founder, pres. Pub. Counsel, L.A., 1970-73. Author: Commercial Real Property Lease Practice, 1976. Chmn. Mus. Contemporary Art, L.A., 1987-93, chmn. com. Walt Disney Concert Hall, L.A., 1987-95; trustee Music Ctr. L.A. County, 1987-95, L.A. Philharm. Assn., 1987-95; chmn. Calif. Pub. Broadcasting Commn., Sacramento, 1972-78; pres. Maple Ctr., 1977-79. Recipient Citizen of Yr. award Beverly Hills Bd. Realtors, 1978, Man of Yr. award Maple Ctr., 1980, Pub. Svc. award Coro Found., 1988, The Medici award L.A. C. of C., 1990, Founders award Pub. Counsel, 1990, Trustees award Calif. Inst. Arts, 1993, City of Angels award L.A. Ctrl. Bus. Assn.; named Outstanding Founder in Philanthropy, Nat. Philanthropy Day Com., 1990. Mem. Beverly Hills Bar Assn. (bd. govs. 1970-76, Disting. Svc. award 1974, 81, Exceptional Svc. award 1986), Beverly Hills C. of C. (Man of Yr. 1983). Home: 1011 Cove Way Beverly Hills CA 90210-2818 Office: Hapsmith Co 9300 Wilshire Blvd Beverly Hills CA 90212

NICHOLS, CARL MICHAEL, interactive media executive; b. Springfield, Mass., Sept. 19, 1961. BS, Brown U., 1983; MBA, Harvard U., 1987. Mgr. Aarhus Olrefabrik, Aarhus, Denmark, 1983; project mgr. Booz Allen & Hamilton, San Francisco, 1983-85, 87-91; mgr. AT&T Internat., Morristown, N.J., 1986; v.p. strategic bus. mgmt. Scrivner Inc., Oklahoma City, 1991-94; asst. v.p. Pacific Telesis, San Francisco, 1994-96; v.p., CFO Interactive Minds, San Francisco, 1996—; COO Internat Fin. Network Corp., 1996—; v.p. bus. devel. Net Channel, Inc., 1996—. Editor: Technology in Business, 1983 (award 1984). Cons. Jr. Achievement, Edmond, Okla., 1991-93; vol. Okla. Sch. Sci. and Math., Oklahoma City, 1992-94; bd. dirs. San Francisco Edn. Fund, 1996—. Mem. Sigma Xi.

NICHOLS, JAMES RAYMOND, JR., civil engineer; b. Holyoke, Mass., Mar. 14, 1966; s. James Raymond and Donna Jean (Riley) N. BSCE, Northeastern U., 1989; MS in Environ. Engring., U. Conn., 1994. Registered profl. engr., Wash. Staff engr. N.L. Jacobson & Assocs., Chester, Conn., 1989-95; project engr. II City of Olympia (Wash.) Pub. Works Dept., 1995—; instr. South Puget Sound C.C., Olympia, 1997—; speaker Am. Filtration & Separations Soc. conf., Nashville, 1995, Impervious Surface Reduction Rsch. Symposium, Olympia, Wash., 1996, Western Regional Urban Streams Conf., Arcata, Calif., 1996. Contbr. articles to profl. jours. Mem. Chester Inland Wetlands Commn., 1993-95. Mem. ASCE. Home: 5500 Park Place Loop SE Lacey WA 98503-4339 Office: City Olympia Pub Works Dept 520 Pear St P O 1967 Olympia WA 98507

NICHOLS, JOHN ROGER, county official; b. Des Moines, Dec. 11, 1949; s. John Woodrow and Mary Ann (West) N.; m. Terry Lynn Huffman (div. June 1985); children: Lauren Ashley, John Clarke; m. Terrie Lynne Jacobson, Apr. 17, 1989 (div. Nov. 1994); 1 child, Anthony. BS in Bus. Adminstrn., Drake U., 1974. Project supt. Weitz Corp., Des Moines, 1979-84; project mgr. maj. projects E.G. Bowen Co. Inc., L.A., 1987-92, Hussmann Corp., Sacramento, 1992-93; bldg. insp. comml. constrn. County of Sacramento, Calif., 1994—; bd. dirs. J-T Publs., Sacramento; trustee T's Calif. Trust, Sacramento, 1993—. Author: How to Inspect Homes, 1992; editor: Do it yourself inspections, 1992. Tchr. Cath. Sch., St. John the Evangelist Ch., Carmichael, Calif. Mem. Internat. Coun. Bldg. Ofcls. (profl. mem.), Carpenters Union 1147 (master carpenter), Masons. Republican. Home: 8048 Hidden View Cir Fair Oaks CA 95628

NICHOLS, LEE ANN, library media specialist; b. Denver, Apr. 27, 1946; d. Bernard Anthony and Margaret Mary (Pughes) Wilhelm; m. Robert Joseph Nichols, July 12, 1975; children: Rachel, Steven, Sarah. BS in Edn., St. Mary of the Plains, Dodge City, Kans., 1968; MA in Edn., Colo. U., 1978. Cert. type B profl. tchr., Colo. Tchr. So. Tama Sch. Dist. Montour, Iowa, 1968-70, Strasburg (Colo.) Sch. Dist., 1970-73; svc. rep. Montain Bell, Denver, 1973-75; libr., tchr. Simla (Colo). Sch. Dist., 1976-78; dir. Simla Br. Libr., 1978-81; dir. Christian edn. St. Anthony's Ch/, Sterling, Colo., 1983-84; libr. cons. Rel Valley Sch., Iliff, Colo., 1984—, Plateau Sch. Dist., Peetz, Colo., 1986—; mem. Colo. Coun. for Libr. Devel., Denver, 1986-92, chmn. 1991; instr. Northeastern Jr. Coll., Sterling; del. Gov.'s Conf. on Libr. and Info. Scis., 1990. Contbr. articles to profl. jours. Active Sterling Arts Coun., sec., 1982-85, v.p., 1985, pres., 1986-87; chair Northeastern Jr. Coll. Found., Sterling, 1983-87, mem. 1981-91; mem. community adv. coun. Northeastern Jr. Coll., 1991-93, chair, 1993; bd. dirs. Wagon Wheel chpt. Girl Scouts Am., 1975-78. Mem. ALA, Am. Assn. Sch. Librs., Assn. Libr. Svcs. to Children, Colo. Ednl. Media Assn., Colo. Libr. Coun., Internat. Reading Assn. (Colo. Coun.). Home: 12288 County Road 370 Sterling CO 80751-8421 Office: Caliche Jr High Sch RR 1 Iliff CO 80736-9801

NICHOLS, MARK EDWARD, engineer; b. Schenectady, N.Y., Sept. 3, 1950; s. John Burton and Betty Jane (Paulsen) N.; m. Cornelia Rocas. BS in Engring. Physics, U. Calif., Berkeley, 1972; MS in Sci. and Engring. Mgmt., West Coast U., 1984; postgrad., Ind. Coll. Armed Forces, 1977. Cert. in Nat. Security Mgmt. Inst. and mech. technician Wetzel-Moreau Engring. Co., Inglewood, Calif., 1970-71; sales engr., supr. United Tech. Industries/Turbocooler Divsn., Manhattan Beach, Calif., 1972-73; wind tunnel test engr. Space Divsn. Rockwell Internat., Downey, Calif., 1973-76; flight and sys. engr. Space Sys. Divsn. Rockwell Internat., Palmdale, Calif., 1976-78; aero. test engr. Space Sys. Divsn. Rockwell Internat., Downey, 1980-85, project engr. payloads-cargo integration Aerospace Divsn., 1985-96; flight test integration engr. Gen. Dynamics/Convair, San Diego, 1978-80; project engr. mission/manifest integration requirements Boeing N.Am., 1996—; instr. Aerodynamics and Aeronautics, Adv. Career Tng., Downey, 1986—; instrnl. aide, lectr. Discover-E, Downey, 1992—. Columnist, Long Beach Press-Telegram, 1987-90. With USN, 1968-69. Judge L.A. County and Calif. State Sci. and Engring. Fairs, 1987—. Recipient Achievement award Bank of Am., 1968, Silver Snoopy Achievement award NASA, 1978; Gov.'s scholar, 1968. Mem. ASME, AIAA, Nat. Mgmt. Assn., Am. Legion #270, Planetary Soc., Moose #1739, Los Amigos Men's Club. Republican. Home: 11682 Lakewood Blvd Downey CA 90241-5272 Office: Boeing NAm 12214 Lakewood Blvd Downey CA 90242-2693

NICHOLS, MIKE, stage and film director; b. Berlin, Nov. 6, 1931; s. Nicholaievitch and Brigitte (Landauer) Peschowsky; m. Patricia Scott, 1957 (div.); m. Margot Callas, 1974 (div.); m. Annabel Davis-Goff (div.); m. Diane Sawyer, Apr. 29, 1988. Student, U. Chgo., 1950-53; student acting, Lee Strasberg. Ptnr. with Elaine May in comedy act; first appeared at Playwrights Theatre Club, Compass Theatre, Chgo.; N.Y. debut An Evening with Mike Nichols and Elaine May, 1960; acted in A Matter of Position, Phila., 1962; dir.: (plays) Barefoot in the Park, 1963 (Tony award best dir.), The Knack, 1964, Luv, 1964 (Tony award best dir.), The Odd Couple, 1965 (Tony award best dir.), The Apple Tree, 1966, The Little Foxes, 1967, Plaza Suite, 1968 (Tony award best dir.), The Prisoner of 2d Avenue, 1971 (Tony award best dir.), Uncle Vanya (co-adapted), 1973, Streamers, 1976, Comedians, 1976, The Gin Game, 1977, (L.A. Drama Critics award), Drink Before Dinner, 1978, Lunch Hour, 1980, Fools, 1981, The Real Thing, 1984 (Tony award 1984,), Hurlyburly, 1984, Social Security, 1984, Elliot Loves, 1990, Death and the Maiden, 1992; (films) Who's Afraid of Virginia Woolf?, 1966, (Academy award nomination best director 1966), The Graduate, 1967 (Academy award best director 1967), Catch-22, 1970, Carnal Knowledge, 1971, The Day of the Dolphin, 1973, The Fortune, 1975, Silkwood, 1983 (Academy award nomination best director 1983), Heartburn, 1986, Biloxi Blues, 1987, Working Girl, 1988 (Academy award nomination best director 1988), Postcards From the Edge, 1990, Regarding Henry, 1991, Wolf, 1994, The Bird Cage, 1995; producer: (musical) Annie, 1977; performed at N.Y. musical Pres. Johnson's Inaugural Gala, 1965; TV appearances include Today Show. Office: care Bryan Lourd CAA 9830 Wilshire Blvd Beverly Hills CA 90212-1804

NICHOLS, ROBIN ANN, accountant; b. Tacoma, Wash., Nov. 27, 1959; d. Shirley Ann (Heggen) LaVelle; m. Gordon L. Nichols, Aug. 20, 1983; children: Melinda Ann, Angela Elizabeth, Lindsey Katherine. BBA cum laude, Pacific Luth. U., 1985. CPA, Wash. V.p. acctg. and fin. Sorrento Enterprises, Inc., Spanaway, Wash., 1980-85; accountant, audit mgr. Ernst & Young, Seattle, 1985-90; audit. mgr. Dwyer, Pemberton & Coulson, Tacoma, Wash., 1990-92; pvt. practice Tacoma, 1992—; v.p. fin. and support Steel Systems Tech., Inc., Tacoma, 1996—. Treas., bd. dirs. Clover Creek Riders 4-H Club, 1996—. Mem. AICPA, Wash. Soc. CPAs, Inst. Mgmt. Accts. (dir. acquisition 1985-87, dir. tech. programs 1989-90, v.p. profl. devel. 1990-91, Outstanding Achievement Mem. Acquisition award 1985-86, v.p. membership and mktg. 1991-92, v.p. fin. and adminstrn., 1993-94, chair corp. and acad. devel., chair audit com. 1996—), Pacific Luth. U. Bus. Alumni Assn. (founding bd. dirs.), Wash. State Horseman Assn., Beta Alpha Psi (pres. Delta Rho chpt.). Home and Office: 4104 145th St E Tacoma WA 98446-1674

NICHOLSON, MARILYN LEE, arts administrator; b. San Jose, Calif., Feb. 7, 1949; d. John Hart Nicholson and Betty Ann (Price) Shepardson; m. Neal Luit Evenhuis. BA in English and History, U. Ariz., 1972; BFA in Studio, U. Hawaii-Manoa, Honolulu, 1977, MA in English, 1977, AS, 1984. Edn. coord., dir. Bishop Mus. Arts and Crafts Sch., Honolulu, 1977-79; owner Fiber Arts Store, Kailua, Hawaii, 1978-82; field coord. Hawaii State Found. on Culture and Arts, Honolulu, 1981-85; exec. dir. Sedona (Ariz.) Arts Ctr., 1986-92, Volcano (Hawaii) Art Ctr., 1992—; mem. bd. artist selection com. Ariz. Indian Living Treasures, 1988-92; bd. dirs., treas. Sedona Cultural Arts Ctr., 1987-92; conf. speaker Nat. Assembly Arts Agys., 1988. Founding Chmn. Sedona Gallery Assn., 1990-92; mem. com. Sedona Acad., 1986-92; mem. steering com. community plan City of Sedona, 1989-91; commr. Arts & Cultural Ctr., Sedona, 1989-91; mem. exec. com. planning Volcano Community Assn., 1993—. Recipient Mayor's award for Disting. Svc., Sedona City Coun., 1992. Mem. Hawaii Mus. Assn. (bd. dirs. 1995—), Cooper Ctr. Coun. (bd. dirs. 1992—), Aloha Festivals-Hawaii Island (bd. dirs. 1992—). Office: Volcano Art Ctr PO Box 104 Hawaii National Park HI 96718-0104

NICHOLSON, WILLIAM JOSEPH, forest products company executive; b. Tacoma, Aug. 24, 1938; s. Ferris Frank and Athyleen Myrtle (Fesenmaier) N.; m. Carland Elaine Crook, Oct. 10, 1964; children: Courtney, Brian, Kay, Benjamin. SB in ChemE, MIT, 1960, SM in ChemE Practice, 1961; PhD in ChemE, Cornell U., 1965; MBA, Pacific Luth. U., 1969. Registered profl. chem. engr., Wash. Sr. devel. engr. Hooker Chem. Co., Tacoma, 1964-69, Battelle N.W., Richland, Wash., 1969-70; planning assoc. Potlatch Corp., San Francisco, 1970-75, mgr. corp. energy service, 1976-94, dir. corp. energy and environ. svcs., 1994—; chmn. electricity com. Am. Forest and Paper Assn., 1977—, mem. solid waste task force, 1988-91, air quality com., 1989—, mem. environ. policy and oversight com., 1994—, vice-chmn. life cycle analysis work group, 1994—, chmn. wood products environ. task force, 1994—; U.S. expert on environ. labelling to Internat. Stds. Orgn., 1994—; chmn., mem. adv. bd. Forest Products Lab., U. Calif., Richmond, 1992-95; mem. adv. bd. Coll. of Natural Resources, U. Calif., Berkeley, 1993-95; mem. U.S. tech. adv. group. environ. stds. Mem. AAAS, AIChE (assoc.), Am. Chem. Soc., Tech. Assn. Pulp and Paper Industry, Sigma Xi, Commonwealth Club (San Francisco), Cornell Club (N.Y.). Republican. Home: PO Box 1114 Ross CA 94957-1114 Office: Potlatch Corp 244 California St Ste 610 San Francisco CA 94111-4351

NICKEL, ROSALIE JEAN, reading specialist; b. Hooker, Okla., Oct. 10, 1939; d. Edwin Charles and Esther Elizabeth (Wiens) Ollenburger; m. Ted W. Nickel, June 3, 1960; 1 child, Sandra Jean. BA, Tabor Coll., 1961; MA, Calif. State U., Fresno, 1970. Cert. tchr., Calif. Elem. tchr. Visalia (Calif.) Pub. Schs., 1961-62; overseas tchr. Kodaikanal Internat. Sch., Madras State, India, 1963-65; tchr. Mendota (Calif.) Jr. High Sch., 1966; elem. tchr. Fresno Pub. Schs., 1966-68, Inglewood (Calif.) Pub. Schs., 1968-73; spl. reading tchr. Tulsa Pub. Schs., 1974-81; salesperson, mgr. Compaq, Marion, Kans., 1981-85; gifted student tchr. Wichita (Kans.) Pub. Schs., 1986; reading specialist and resource tchr., 1987—, sch. technology coord., 1989—, dist. K-3 literacy task force, 1995—, dist. lang. arts adoption com. 1995——; evaluator State Textbook Com., Tulsa, 1976, 78; mem. quality rev. team Birney Elem. Sch., Fresno. Newsletter editor Marion County Arts Council, 1981-82. Co-dir. Am. Field Svc., Tulsa, 1980-81; v.p. Women's Federated Clubs Am., Marion, 1985-86; pres. Butler Mennonite Brethern Women's Fellowship, 1989-91. Mem. Internat. Reading Assn., Fresno Area Reading Council. Home: 2821 W Compton Ct Fresno CA 93711-1181 Office: Fresno Unified Schs Tulare And M St Fresno CA 93701

NICOL, NOREEN HEER, nursing administrator, dermatology nurse practitioner, educator; b. Jamestown, N.D., July 16, 1955; d. Clifford Howard and Lois Ann (Smith) Heer; m. Robert Bruce Nicol, June 18, 1983; children: Brent Jeffrey, Erica Marie. BSN, U. No. Colo., 1977; MS in Nursing, U. Utah, 1981. RN, Colo., N.D., Utah; lic. nurse practitioner, Utah; cert. tchr., Colo. Sch. nurse, tchr. health Weld County Sch. Dist. 6, Greeley, Colo., 1977-78; nurse coord. emotionally disturbed summer camp program, charge nurse chem. dependency unit N.D. State Hosp., Jamestown, 1978-79; pediatric clin. specialist, charge nurse U. Utah Med. Ctr., Salt Lake City, 1979-81, dir. pediatric dialysis dept., nurse practitioner, adminstr., intermountain pediatric and adolescent renal disease program, 1981-84; instr. clin. nursing, DON Loretto Heights Coll., Denver, 1984-86; dermatology clin. specialist, nurse practitioner Nat. Jewish Med. and Rsch. Ctr., Denver, 1986—, DON, 1995—; clin. instr. Coll. Nursing, U. Utah, 1982-85, assoc. instr. dept. pediatrics Coll. Medicine, 1983-85; mem. adj. faculty Loretto Heights Coll., Denver, 1987-88; clin. sr. instr. U. Colo. Health Sci. Ctr. Sch. Nursing, Denver, 1989—; nurse clinician home intravenous therapy and nutrition Travenol Labs., Inc., Denver, 1984-86; speaker, presenter in field. Contbr. articles to profl. jours., chpts. to books. Mem. Weld County Drug and Alcohol Coun., 1977-78, health adv. com. Douglas County (Colo.) Schs., 1993—. Nursing scholar U. No. Colo., 1975-77. Mem. Nat. Fedn. for Splty. Nursing Orgns. (edn. com. 1991, health policy com. 1991-92, treas. 1992-93, pres. 1993-94), Colo. Nurses Assn. (Garnet Milhone scholar 1976-77), Dermatology Nurses Assn. (edn. com. 1987, liaison for Colo. 1987-88, nat. edn. vice chmn. 1988, chmn. nat. conv. 1988, nat. bd. dirs. western region dir. 1989-90, nat. bd. dirs. 1991—, nat. pres. elect, 1991, nat. pres. 1992—, edn. com. core curriculum chmn., 1993—), Am. Acad. Allergy and Immunology, Skin Photorauma Found., Sigma Theta Tau (hosp. liason 1991—). Office: Nat Jewish Med and Rsch Ctr 1400 Jackson St Denver CO 80206-2761

NICOL, ROBERT DUNCAN, architect; b. La Jolla, Calif., Sept. 16, 1936; s. Duncan and Catherine (Muffly) N.; m. Susann Kay Larson; 1 child, Jennifer E. AA, Principia Coll., 1956; BArch, U. Calif., Berkeley, 1961. Registered arch., Ariz., Calif., Mont., Wash. Designer Kawneer Mfg. Co., Richmond, Calif., 1961-62, Claude Oakland, San Francisco, 1962-64; project arch. David T. Johnson, Oakland, Calif., 1964-68; pvt. practice Oakland, Calif., 1968—. Mem. bd. appeals City of Alameda, 1971-73, vice chair planning commn., 1973-77, founder, chair, vice chair design rev. bd., 1974-80, founder, chair, vice chair hist. adv. bd., 1976—, co-founder, chair, vice chair mayor's com. for handicapped, 1980-86; mem. Calif. State Access Bd., 1995—. Recipient Design award Am. Registered Archs., 1969, Harper Plz. Design award Calif. Bldg. Ofcls. Assn., 1985. Fellow AIA; mem. Soc. Am. Registered Archs., Nat. Coun. Archtl. Registration Bds. (sr.), Alexander Graham Bell Assn. for Deaf (lectr.), Oral Hearing Impaired Sec., San Leandro Hist. Railway Soc. (founder, charter mem., chair, vice-chair), Alameda Jr. C. of C. (project dir. 1969), Alameda Victorian Preservation Soc. Republican. Office: 455 17th St Oakland CA 94612-2101

NICOLAI, EUGENE RALPH, public relations consultant, editor, writer; b. Renton, Wash., June 26, 1911; s. Eugene George and Josephine (Heidinger) N.; student U. Wash., 1929, Whitman Coll., 1929-30; B.A., U. Wash., 1934; postgrad. Am. U., 1942; M.A., George Washington U., 1965; m. Helen Margaret Manogue, June 5, 1935; 1 son, Paul Eugene. Editor, U. Wash. Daily, Seattle, 1934; asst. city editor, writer, nat. def. editor Seattle Times, 1934-41; writer Sta. KJR, Seattle, 1937-39; writer, editor, safety edn. officer Bur. Mines, Washington, 1941-45; news dir. Grand Coulee Dam and Columbia Basin Project, Washington, 1945-50; regional info. dir. Bur. Mines, Denver and Pitts., 1950-55, asst. chief mineral reports, Washington, 1955-61, news dir. office of oil and gas, 1956-57; sr. info. officer, later sr. public info. officer Office Sec. Interior, Washington, 1961-71, staff White House Nat. Conf. on Natural Beauty, spl. detail to White House, 1971, ret.; now public relations cons., tech. editor, writer. Formerly safety policy adviser Interior Dept.; com. mem. Internat. Cooperation Year, State Dept., 1971. With George Washington U. Alumni Found.; founder, mng. dir. Josephine Nature Preserve; pres. Media Assocs. Bd. dirs. Wash. State Council on Alcoholism; adviser Pierce Transit Authority, Pierce County Growth Mgmt., Pierce County Ethics Commn. Named Disting. Alumnus, recipient Penrose award, both Whitman Coll., 1979. Mem. Nature Conservancy, Wash. Environ. Council, Nat. Audubon Soc. (Am. Belgian Tervuren dist. rep.), Crook County (Oreg.) Hist. Soc., Washington State Hist. Soc., Emerald Shores Assn, Sigma Delta Chi, Pi Kappa Alpha. Presbyn. Clubs: George Washington U., Purdy (pres.). Lodge: Masons. Author: The Middle East Emergency Committee; editor: Fed. Conservation Yearbooks. Home: 9809 N Seminole Dr Spokane WA 99208-8608

NICOLAI, THOMAS R., lawyer; b. Frazer, Mich., Dec. 1, 1943. BA cum laude, Kalamazoo Coll., 1965; JD, U. Mich., 1970. Bar: Ill. 1972, Oreg. 1973. Fellow in Econs. U. Bonn., Germany, 1965-67; fellow Alexander von Humbolt Found. at Max Planck Inst. for Fgn. and Internat. Patent, Copyright and Unfair Competition Law, Munich, West Germany, 1970-72; mem. Stoel Rives LLP, Portland, Oreg. Mem. ABA (mem. real property, probate and trust law, bus. law and internat. law and practice sects.), Phi Beta Kappa, Phi Alpha Delta. Office: Stoel Rives LLP 900 SW 5th Ave Ste 2300 Portland OR 97204-1232

NICOLAS, KENNETH LEE, international financial business executive; b. San Francisco, Feb. 7, 1944; s. Norman L. and Bernice L. (Hameister) N.; m. Anne Vanderwielen, July 5, 1992; children: Juliana M., Camille G. BA in Polit. Sci., Calif. State U., Fullerton, 1968; MA in Legis. Affairs/Econs., George Washington U., 1975. Exec. asst. Congressman Richard T. Hanna, Washington, 1970-72; sr. staff assoc. Nat. Assn. Ednl. Broadcasters, Washington, 1972-74; founder, pres. Nicolas Assocs. Internat., Inc., 1972; exec. dir. Am. Coll. Nuclear Physicians, Washington, 1974-77; aide to the Pres. White House, Washington, 1977-80; v.p. McSweeney & Co. Consulting, Newport Beach, Calif., 1980-83, L.E. Peterson & Co. Investment Banking, Costa Mesa, Calif., 1983-85; pres. Fin. Strategies Group, Inc., Newport Beach, 1985—; CEO Tradex Internat., Inc., Newport Beach, 1988-94; founder, CEO Trade Access Group, Inc., 1994—; bd. dirs. Amtrex Corp., Irvine, Calif.; adj. prof. Orange Coast Coll., Costa Mesa, 1983—, internat. MBA program U. So. Calif., 1989-90, Thunderbird Sch. Internat. Bus., Orange County, 1990-92, U. Calif., Riverside and Irvine, 1996—, internat. bus. edn. U. Calif.-Riverside, 1996—; adj. prof. U. Calif., Riverside and Irvine, 1996—. Author: (article series) Business to Business Mag., 1984-87 (Excellence award 1984-87). 10K race dir. Leukemia Soc. Am., Orange County, Calif., 1982-86, bd. dirs., v.p., 1982-88; chmn. Holiday Project, 1992-94. With U.S. Army, 1968-70, Vietnam. Recipient Outstanding Svc. award Nat. Holiday Project, 1993, Nat. Svc. Appreciation award Pres. Jimmy Carter, 1980, Excellence award Leukemia Soc. Am., 1988. Mem. Internat. Mktg. Assn. (corp. mem., Outstanding Export award 1993), Export Mgrs. Assn. Calif. (bd. dirs. 1990—, Excellence award 1992), World Trade Ctr. Assn. of Orange County (corp. mem., com. chmn. 1983-85, Outstanding Achievement award 1983, 84), Japan Am. Soc. (Orange County chpt. exec. bd. dirs. 1995—), Japan Am. Soc. So. Calif. (exec. bd. 1996—).

NICOLETTI, WILLIAM WALTER, pharmaceutical company executive; b. Phila., Dec. 30, 1952; s. Louis Joseph and Jessie B. (Geddes) N.; m. Patricia Ellen Berry; 1 child, Jessica. BA in Sci., Temple U., 1974, BS in Pharmacy, 1977, MBA in Mktg., 1984. Registered pharmacist Pa., Nev. Dir. pharmacy St. Joseph's Villa, Flourtown, Pa., 1980-83, Booth Maternity Ctr., Salvation Army, Phila., 1980-83; nat sales mgr. Boiron Labs., Norwood, Pa., 1983-87; pres. DoLisos Homeopathy, Las Vegas, 1987—. Mem. Am. Assn. Homeopathic Pharmacists (treas. 1993, pres. 1995), Am. Pharm. Assn., Nev. Pharm. Assn., Homeopathic Pharmacopeia U.S., Internat. des Pharmaciens Homeopathes Com. Office: DoLisos America 3014 Rigel Ave Las Vegas NV 89102-0709

NICOSIA, GERALD MARTIN, author, freelance writer; b. Berwyn, Ill., Nov. 18, 1949; s. Peter and Sylvia Anna (Fremer) N.; m. Marcia Selene Vincent, Oct. 16, 1989 (div. Jan. 15, 1992; m. Ellen Louise Wilson, July 5, 1992. BA, U. Ill., Chgo., 1971, MA, 1973. Cert. H.S. tchr., Ill. Tchr. Cook County high schs., Chgo., Ill., 1971-77; freelance writer, 1978—; prof. nonfiction writing U. Ill., Chgo., 1986-87; guest lectr. Naropa Inst., U. Wis., New Coll. Calif., U. Wash., Columbia Coll., others, 1983—; extension lectr. UCLA, 1991-92; advisor (movie) Kerouac, San Francisco, 1983-84; playwright in residence, advisor Am. Blues Theatre, Chgo., 1986-87; creator Vietnam Vet. Peace Archive, Santa Cruz, Caif., 1993; advisor, organizer Cafe Arts Week, San Francisco; organizer Jan Kerouac Benefits, San Francisco, 1995. Author: Memory Babe: A Critical Biography of Jack Kerouac (disting. young writer award Nat. Soc. Arts and Letters 1978), 1983, Bughouse Blues, 1977, Lunatics, Lovers, Poets, Vets and Bargirls, 1990; playwright: Jack in Ghost-town, 1986. Mem. PEN (bd. dirs. midwest 1986-88, west 1991—), Authors Guild. Office: care Gelfman/Schneider Agy 250 W 57th St New York NY 10107

NIDEFFER, ROBERT FOSTER, artist, educator; b. Ventura, Calif., Feb. 3, 1964; s. Robert Morse Nideffer and Elvira (Daunhauer) Barthelemy. BA in Cultural Anthropology, U. Calif., Santa Barbara, 1988, MA in Sociology, 1990, PhD in Sociology, 1994, postgrad. Rsch. asst., tchg. asst. U. Calif., Santa Barbara, 1988-94, tchg. assoc., instr. sociology, 1991-95; cons. Social Sci. Computing Facility, U. Calif., Santa Barbara, 1992-95. Contbr. articles to profl. jours. Organizer, presider Siggraph 93, L.A., 1993, Virtual Incs., Villanova, Pa., 1995, Social Theory, Politics and the Arts, U. Calif., Santa Barbara, 1995. Grantee Regents of U. Calif., 1992—, 94, U. Calif., Santa Barbara, 1993, 94; Calif. State U. grad. fellow, 1993—, 94. Mem. Am. Sociol. Assn., Assn. for Computing Machinery, Pacific Sociol. Assn. Office: U Calif Art Studio Santa Barbara CA 93106-9430

NIEDERAUER, GEORGE H., bishop; b. Los Angeles, CA, June 14, 1936; s. George and Elaine N. B.A. Philosophy, St. John's Seminary, Camarillo, CA, 1959; B.A. Sacred Theology, Catholic U., Washington, DC, 1962; M.A. English Lit., Loyola U., Los Angeles, CA, 1962; Ph.D. English Lit., USC, 1966. ordained priest April 30, 1962; named prelate of honor (monsignor) 1984; named bishop of Diocese of Salt Lake City, Nov. 3, 1994. Asst. pastor Our Lady of the Assumption Parish, Claremont, CA, 1962-63; priest in residence Holy Name of Jesus Parish, Los Angeles, CA, 1963-65; instr. English Lit. St. John's Seminary Coll., Camarillo, CA, 1965-79; instr. of English Lit. Mt. St. Mary's Coll., Los Angeles, CA, 1967-74; English Dept. chmn. St. John's Seminary Coll., Camarillo, CA, 1968-77; spiritual dir. St. John's Seminary Coll., 1972-79; part-time instr. of Spiritual Theology St. John's Seminary Theologate, 1976-79, full-time instr. of Spiritual Theology, 1979-87; part-time instr. of English Lit. St. John's Seminary Coll., 1979-92; rector St. John's Seminary, 1987-92, spiritual dir., 1979—; co-dir. Cardinal Manning House of Prayer for Priests, Los Angeles, CA, 1992—; mem. Nat. Fedn. of Spiritual Dirs. (pres. 1975-77); mem. Alpha Sigma Nu (Jesuit Honor Soc. - LMU Chapter); pres. Western Assn. of Spiritual Dirs., 1973-75; mem. bd. of the Comm. of Priests' Retreat, Archdiocese of Los Angeles; mem. select comm. for the revision of the U.S. Catholic Conf. "Program for Priestly Formation" 3rd edition; mem. Vatican Visitation Team for Theologates; speaker World Vision Internat, Fuller Theological Seminary, Calif. Lutheran Coll.; mem. Camarillo Ministerial Assn. Office: Chancery Office 27 C St Salt Lake City UT 84103-2302*

NIEDZIELSKI, HENRI ZYGMUNT, French and English language educator; b. Troyes, France, Mar. 30, 1931; came to U.S., 1956, naturalized, 1963; s. Zygmunt and Anna (Pelik) N.; children: Henri Zygmunt, Daniel Domenic, Robert Nicholas, Anna-Pia Irene. B.A., U. Conn., 1959, M.A., 1963, Ph.D., 1964. Instr. U. Mass., 1962-64, asst. prof., 1965-66; free-lance interpreter, 1960—; asst. prof. U. Laval, Quebec, Can., 1964-65; assoc. prof. U. Hawaii, 1966-72, prof., 1972-90, chmn. div. French, 1968-70, prof. emeritus; linguistic specialist NDEA, Edn. Profl. Devel. Act, 1963-69; Fulbright lectr. linguistics and TESL Krakow, Poland, 1972-74, Bujumbura, Burundi, 1980-81, Poznan, Poland, 1990-92; guest prof. Avignon, France, 1983-84, Bonn, Fed. Republic Germany, 1986-87; Disting. fellow Auckland U., New Zealand, 1989. Author: Le Roman de Helcanus, 1966, Basic French: A Programmed Course, 1968, Handbook of French Structure; A Systematic Review, 1968, Intermediate French: An Individualized Course, 1972, The Silent Language of France, 1975, French Sound Visuals, 1976; Films on Polish Body Language, 1989; editor: Language and Literature in Hawaii, 1968-72, Jean Misrahi Memorial Volume: Studies in Medieval Languages and Literature, 1977, Studies on the Seven Sages of Rome, 1978; assoc. editor: The Phonetician, 1994—. Pres. Family Counseling Center Hawaii, 1968-70; chmn. bd. Family Edn. Centers Hawaii, 1969-72. Served with French Armored Cav., 1951-53. Mem. MLA, Am. Translators Assn., Am. Assn. Tchrs. French (pres. Hawaii chpt. 1981-83), Am. Coun. Tchg. Fgn. Langs. (dir. 1970-72), Internat. Sociol. Assn., Hawaii Assn. Lang. Tchrs. (pres. 1968-69), Chopin Soc. Hawaii (dir. 1990—), Alliance Française Hawaii (pres. 1978-80), Hawaii Assn. Translators (founding pres.s 1982—), Hawaii Second Lang. Articulation Com. (chmn. 1986-89), Rotary, Elks, Phi Beta Kappa, Pi Delta Phi, Phi Kappa Phi, Sigma Delta Pi. *There is more than one way to help people but there is only one way to live: Help people.*

NIELSEN, DAVID EDWARD, history and physical education educator; b. Pasadena, Calif., Apr. 22, 1946; s. David Stjerne and Ruth (Norvell) N.; m. Faye Ann Brough, June 4, 1970; children: David, Kirsten, Kelli, Chris. BA, Brigham Young U., 1971; MA, Calif. State U., L.A., 1975. Cert. secondary, elem. edn., adminstrn. Tchr. secondary edn. Brigham Young U., Provo, Utah, 1970-72; tchr. history San Gabriel H.S., Alhambra, Calif., 1973; tchr. history and phys. edn. Repetto Sch., Monterey Park, Calif., 1973-84, Mark Keppel H.S., Alhambra, 1984—; athletic dir. LDS Ch., Arcadia, Calif., 1982-84; teen club. advisor Repetto Sch., Monterey Park, 1972-84, student govt. advisor, 1983-84; coach football, softball, basketball, cross country, track Mark Keppel H.S., Alhambra, 1984-96. Sports editor Banyan, 1969-71; author: (syllabus) I Step - BYU, 1971. 2nd v.p. PTA, Monterey Park, 1983-84; pres. Duarte Parks & Recreation Commn., 1989-96. Recipient Hon. Svc. award PTA, Monterey Park, 1976, 80, 82, Cmty. Svc. award Duarte Parks & Recreation Commn., 1993. Mem. NEA, Nat. Coaches Assn., Calif. Tchrs. Assn., Alhambra Tchrs. Assn., Calif. Commrs. Assn., Calif. Hist. Soc., Duarte Hist. Soc., U.S. Olympic Soc. Democrat. Mem. LDS Ch. Home: 87 Cedarwood Ave Duarte CA 91010-3604 Office: Mark Keppel HS 501 E Hellman Ave Alhambra CA 91801-5716

NIELSEN, DONALD RODNEY, soil and water science educator; b. Phoenix, Oct. 10, 1931; s. Irven Roy and Irma Evelyn (Chase) N.; m. Joanne Joyce Locke, Sept. 26, 1953; children: Cynthia, Pamela, Barbara, Wayne, David. BS, U. Ariz., 1953, MS, 1954; PhD, Iowa State U., 1958; DSc (hon.), Ghent (Belgium) State U., 1986. Asst. prof. soil and water sci. U. Calif., Davis, 1958-63, assoc. prof., 1963-68, prof., 1968-94, dir. Kearney Found. of Soil Sci., 1970-75, assoc. dean, 1970-80, dir. Food Protection and Toxicology Ctr., 1974-75, chmn. dept. land, air and water resources, 1975-77, exec. assoc. dean Coll. Agrl. Environ. Scis., 1986-89, chmn. dept. agronomy and range sci., 1989-91; cons. Davis, 1994—; cons. corps. and govtl. agys. Editor Nitrogen in the Environment; co-editor Water Resources Research, 1985-88; mem. editorial bd. Jour. Soil Sci., Soil Sci., Soil Technology; contbr. articles to profl. jours. NSF fellow, 1965-66. Fellow Am. Geophys. Union (pres. hydrology sect. 1990-92), Soil Sci. Soc. Am. (pres. 1983-84), Am. Soc. Agronomy (pres. 1990-91); mem. Sigma Xi, Phi Kappa Phi, Gamma Sigma Delta, Phi Lambda Upsilon, Alpha Zeta. Democrat. Home and Office: 1004 Pine Ln Davis CA 95616-1728

NIELSEN, PAMELA JEANNE, artist, writer; b. Austin, Tex., Mar. 15, 1953; d. Robert Allen and Marjorie Lenore (Peterson) Newstrom; m. Scott Robert Nielsen, July 9, 1970 (div. Jan. 1980). Student, U. Md., Heidelberg, Germany, 1976-77, U. Tex., El Paso, 1979-80, Otis Parsons Sch. Design, L.A., 1985-86. Pvt. tchr. art, Long Beach, Calif., 1988—. One-woman show Long Beach Cmty. Players Gallery, 1991, Gaga's, Long Beach, 1991; exhibited in group shows Long Beach Arts, 1992, Long Beach City Coll., 1993; rec. artist Disclosure-Voices of Women, New Alliance Records, 1992; writer, performer Royal Theater, Queen Mary, Long Beach, 1993; contbr. poetry to various publs. Juvenile counselor Los Padrinos Prison, Downey, Calif., 1989; spkr. high schs., Long Beach, 1993—; mem. arts and cultural edn. subcom. City of Long Beach, 1994. Scholar and grantee Otis Parsons Sch. Design, 1985-86. Mem. Long Beach Arts, Sierra Club. Home and Studio: 205 Pomona Ave Long Beach CA 90803

NIELSEN, WILLIAM FREMMING, federal judge; b. 1934. BA, U. Wash., 1956, LLB, 1963. Law clk. to Hon. Charles L. Powell U.S. Dist. Ct. (ea. dist.) Wash., 1963-64; mem. firm Paine, Hamblen, Coffin, Brooke & Miller, 1964-91; judge to chief of judge U.S. Dist. Ct. (ea. dist.) Wash., Spokane, 1991—. Lt. col. USAFR. Fellow Am. Coll. Trial Lawyers; mem. ABA, Wash. State Bar Assn., Spokane County Bar Assn. (pres. 1981-82), Fed. Bar Assn. (pres. 1988), Spokane County Legal Svcs. Corp. (past pres.), Lawyer Pilot Bar Assn., Assn. Trial Lawyers Am., Wash. State Trial Lawyers Assn., Assn. Def. Trial Attys., Am. Inns of Ct., Charles L. Powell Inn (pres. 1987), The Spokane Club, Rotary, Alpha Delta Phi, Phi Delta Phi. Office: US Dist Ct PO Box 2208 920 W Riverside Ave 9th Fl Spokane WA 99210-2208*

NIELSON, THEO GILBERT, law enforcement official, university official; b. Roosevelt, Utah, June 29, 1938; s. John Gilbert and Mazie (Alexander) N.; m. Martha Perez, May 22, 1961; children: Lucille Marie, Sherry Lou, Mark Andrew, Rex Alexander, Theo Gilbert Jr., Cristal Ina, Gregory Angus, Mazie Leah, Rosanna Alma. Grad., FBI Nat. Acad., 1970; BA, Ariz. State U., 1975, MS, 1977. Officer Univ. Police, Ariz. State U., Tempe, 1963-67, sgt., 1967-70, lt., 1970-79; chief police Douglas (Ariz.) Police Dept., 1979-82; div. adminstr. Ariz. Criminal Intelligence Systems Agy., Tucson, 1982-84; dir. campus safety and security No. Ariz. U., Flagstaff, 1984-92; chief police Ariz. Dept. Adminstrn., 1992—. Mem. Am. Soc. for Indsl. Security (chmn. No. Ariz. chpt. 1987), Internat. Assn. Chiefs Police, Internat. Assn. Campus Law Enforcement Adminstrs., Ariz. Assn. Campus Law Enforcement (pres. 1989-90). Republican. Mormon. Home: 3335 E Hampton Ave Mesa AZ 85204-6410 Office: Ariz State Capitol Police 1700 W Washington St Ste B15 Phoenix AZ 85007-2812

NIELSON, THOMAS ALLEN, mental health company executive; b. Twin Falls, Idaho, May 27, 1962; s. Blaine James and Karen Roberta (Arment) N.; m. Annette Elizabeth Rowe, Sept. 6, 1986; children: Katie Rosemarie, Conner Thomas. BS, Boise State U., 1989; MA, Coll. of Idaho, 1992. Children's mental health designated examiner; qualified mental retardation profl.; lic. profl. counselor. Mgr. night and weekend ops. student union bldg. Boise State U., 1985-86; asst. facility dir. Idaho Youth Rance, Boise, 1986-89; tchr. Idaho Youth Rance, Rupert, 1989-90; facility dir. Nampa Boys home Idaho Youth Ranch, 1990-92; facility dir. family preservation svcs. Idaho Youth Ranch, Nampa, 1992-93; regional juvenile justice supr. Idaho Dept. Health and Welfare, Twin Falls, 1993-95; clin. dir., owner McNiel & Assocs., Twin Falls, 1995—; Twin Falls, 1996; clin. cons. W.D.B., Inc., Twin Falls, 1995—, Adult and Child Devel. Ctr., Twin Falls, 1995—, Dept. Juvenile Corrections, Boise, 1995—. Mem. parish coun. St. Edward Cath. Ch., Twin Falls, 1995—; treas. Twin Falls Child Protection Team, 1995—. Roman Catholic. Office: McNiel & Associates 1426 Addison Ave E Ste A Twin Falls ID 83301-5229

NIEMI, JANICE, lawyer, former state legislator; b. Flint, Mich., Sept. 18, 1928; d. Richard Jesse and Norma (Bell) Bailey; m. Preston Niemi, Feb. 4, 1953 (divorced 1987); children—Ries, Patricia. BA, U. Wash., 1950, LL.B., 1967; postgrad. U. Mich., 1950-52; cert. Hague Acad. Internat. Law, Netherlands, 1954. Bar: Wash. 1968. Assoc. firm Powell, Livengood, Dunlap & Silverdale, Kirkland, Wash., 1968; staff atty. Legal Service Ctr., Seattle, 1968-70; judge Seattle Dist. Ct., 1971-72, King County Superior Ct., Seattle, 1973-78; acting gen. counsel, dep. gen. counsel SBA, Washington, 1979-81; mem. Wash. State Ho. of Reps., Olympia, 1983-87, chmn. com. on state govt., 1984; mem. Wash. State Senate, 1987-95; sole practice, Seattle, 1981-94; superior ct. judge King County, 1995—, chief criminal judge, 1997; mem. White House Fellows Regional Selection Panel, Seattle, 1974-77, chmn., 1976, 77; incorporator Sound Savs. & Loan, Seattle, 1975. Bd. dirs. Allied Arts, Seattle, 1971 , Ctr. Contemporary Art, Seattle, 1981-83, Women's Network, Seattle, 1981-84, Pub. Defender Assn., Seattle, 1982-84; bd. visitors dept. psychology U. Wash., Seattle, 1983-87, bd. visitors dept sociology, 1988— . Named Woman of Yr. in Law, Past Pres.'s Assn., Seattle, 1971; Woman of Yr., Matrix Table, Seattle, 1973, Capitol Hill Bus. and Profl. Women, 1975. Mem. Wash. State Bar Assn., Wash. Women Lawyers, Allied Arts of Seattle Bd. Democrat. Home: PO Box 20516 Seattle WA 98102-1516

NIERENBERG, NORMAN, urban land economist, retired state official; b. Chgo., May 8, 1919; s. Isadore Isaac and Sadie Sarah (Dorfman) N.; m. Nanette Joyce Fortgang, Feb. 9, 1950; children: Andrew Paul, Claudia Robin. AA, U. Chgo., 1939; AB, Calif. State Coll., L.A., 1952; MA, U. So. Calif., 1956. Lic. real estate broker, Calif.; cert. supr. and coll. instr., Calif. Right-of-way agt. Calif. Dept. Transp., L.A., 1951-61, 85-88; sr. agt. Calif. Dept. Transp., San Francisco, 1988-89; instr. UCLA, 1960-61, 67-75, 81-85; coord. continuing edn. in real estate U. Calif., Berkeley, 1961-64; coord. econ. benefits study Salton Sea, Calif. Dept. Water Resources, L.A., 1968-69; regional economist L.A. dist. CE, 1970-75, chief economist, 1981-85; regional economist Bd. Engrs. for Rivers and Harbors, Ft. Belvoir, Va., 1975-81; faculty resource person Oakland Project, Ford Found., U. Calif., Berkeley, 1962-64; project reviewer EPA, Washington, 1972-73. Editor: History of 82d Fighter Control Squadron, 1945; assoc. editor Right of Way Nat. Mag., 1952-55. Capt. USAAF, 1942-46, ETO, Lt. Col. USAFR ret. Mem. NEA, Am. Econ. Assn., Calif. Tchrs. Assn., Calif. Assn. Real Estate Tchrs. (bd. dirs. 1962), L.A. Coll. Tchrs. Assn., Res. Officers Assn., Ret. Officers Assn., Omicron Delta Epsilon. Democrat. Jewish. Home: Unit 4 21931 Burbank Blvd Woodland Hills CA 91367-6464 *Personal philosophy: Strive for excellence. Honorable in all endeavors.*

NIERENBERG, WILLIAM AARON, oceanography educator; b. N.Y.C., Feb. 13, 1919; s. Joseph and Minnie (Drucker) N.; m. Edith Meyerson, Nov. 21, 1941; children—Victoria Jean (Mrs. Tschinkel), Nicolas Clarke Eugene. Aaron Naumberg scholar, U. Paris, 1937-38; B.S., CCNY, 1939; M.A., Columbia U., 1942, Ph.D. (NRC predoctoral fellow), 1947. Tutor CCNY, 1939-42; sect. leader Manhattan Project, 1942-45; instr. physics Columbia U., 1946-48; asst. prof. physics U. Mich., 1948-50; assoc. prof. physics U. Calif. at Berkeley, 1950-53, prof., 1954-65; dir. Scripps Instn. Oceanography, 1965-86, dir. emeritus, 1986—; vice chancellor for marine scis. U. Calif. at San Diego, 1969-86; dir. Hudson Labs., Columbia, 1953-54; assoc. prof. U. Paris, 1960-62; asst. sec. gen. NATO for sci. affairs, 1960-62; spl. cons. Exec. Office Pres., 1958-60; sr. cons. White House Office Sci. and Tech. Policy, 1976-78. Contbr. papers to profl. jours. E.O. Lawrence lectr. Nat. Acad. Sci., 1958, Miller Found. fellow, 1957-59, Sloan Found. fellow, 1958, Fulbright fellow, 1960-61; mem. U.S. Nat. Commn. UNESCO, 1964-68, Calif. Adv. Com. on Marine and Coastal Resources, 1967-71; adviser-at-large U.S. Dept. State, 1968—; mem. Nat. Sci. Bd., 1972-78, 82-88, cons., 1988-89; chmn. USNC/PSA, NRC, 1988—; mem. Nat. Adv. Com. on Oceans and Atmosphere, 1971-77, chmn., 1971-75; mem. sci. and tech. adv. Council Calif. Assembly; mem. adv. council NASA, 1978-83, chmn. adv. council, 1978-82. NATO Sr. Sci. fellow, 1969; Decorated officer Nat. Order of Merit France; recipient Golden Dolphin award Assn. Artistico Letteraria Internazionale, Disting. Pub. Service medal NASA, 1982, Delmer S. Fahrney medal The Franklin Inst., 1987, Compass award Marine Tech. Soc., 1975. Fellow Am. Phys. Soc. (coun., sec. Pacific Coast sect. 1955-64); mem. Am.

Acad. Arts and Scis., NAE, NAS (coun. 1973—), Am. Philos. Soc., Sigma Xi (pres. 1981-82, Procter prize 1977). Home: PO Box 927269 San Diego CA 92192-7269 Office: U Calif Scripps Instn Oceanography 0221 La Jolla CA 92093

NIERMEYER, SUSAN, medical educator; b. Indpls., July 24, 1953; d. John H. and Elnora Lorraine (Eissler) N.; m. John Allen Brett, Apr. 25, 1987. BA in Zoology/Chemistry, Butler U., 1975; MD, Vanderbilt U., 1979. Diplomate Am. Bd. Pediatrics. Cert. sub-bd. Nat. Bd. Med. Examiners, Colo. State Bd. Med. Examiners. Neonatologist The Children's Hosp. Neonatal Group, Denver, 1984-85; neonatologist Neonatal Consultants, P.C., Denver, 1985-90; assoc. prof. pediat., neonatology U. Colo. Sch. Medicine, Denver, 1990—; doctoral program grad. faculty, health and behavioral scis. U. Colo. Denver, 1994—; med. dir. Perinatal Outreach Edn. program, Denver, 1986-94, dir. Neonatal Edn., 1994—; steering com. Nat. Neonatal Resuscitation Program, editor NRP Instr. Update, 1995—. Contbr. book chpt., articles to profl. jours. Com. mem. Colo. Dept. Health Am. Stop Smoking Intervention Study, Denver, 1992—. Grantee WHO, Chiapas, Mexico, 1991-92, Am. Heart Assn., 1994-95, Kempe Rsch. Ctr., Denver, 1989-90, Global Change and Environ. Quality Program, 1996. Fellow Am. Acad. Pediatrics (chair Colo. chpt. 1992—, internal. pediatrics com.); mem. Western Soc. for Pediatric Rsch., Am. Anthropol. Assn., Denver Med. Soc. Office: The Childrens Hosp 1056 E 19th Ave Denver CO 80218-1007

NIESLUCHOWSKI, WITOLD S., cardiovascular and thoracic surgeon; b. Warsaw, Poland, Mar. 2, 1944; came to U.S., 1975; s. Stanislaw Leon and Izabela Anna (Swierczynska) N.; m. Bonnie Jean Thomas, Apr. 15, 1978; children: Jason Brian, Christopher Thomas, Megan Jean, Jennifer Anne. MD, Warsaw Med. Sch., 1967. With Akademicki Zwiazek Sportowy, Warsaw, 1961-75; cardiovascular surgeon Oxnard (Calif.) Hosp., 1975—. Mem. Oxnard Humanitarians, 1987—; bd. dirs. Am. Heart Assn., Camarillo, Calif., 1988—. Fellow ACS, Am. Coll. Cardiologists; mem. Soc. for Thoracic Surgeons. Club: Cabrillo Tennis (Camarillo). Office: 1700 N Rose Ave Ste 420 Oxnard CA 93030-3793

NIJENHUIS, ALBERT, mathematician, educator; b. Eindhoven, Netherlands, Nov. 21, 1926; came to U.S., 1952, naturalized, 1959; s. Hendrik and Lijdia (Koornneef) N.; m. Marianne Dannhauser, Aug. 14, 1955; children: Erika, Karin, Sabien, Alaine. Candidaat, U. Amsterdam, Netherlands, 1947, Doctorandus, 1950, Doctor cum laude, 1952. Assoc. Math. Ctr., Amsterdam, Netherlands, 1951-52; asst. Inst. Advanced Study, Princeton, N.J., 1955; mem. Inst. Advanced Study, 1953-55, 61-62; instr., rsch. assoc. U. Chgo., 1955-56; faculty U. Wash., Seattle, 1956-63, prof., 1961-63, affiliate prof., 1988—; prof. math. U. Pa., Phila., 1963-87, prof. emeritus, 1987—; Fulbright lectr. U. Amsterdam, 1963-64; vis. prof. U. Geneva, Switzerland, 1967-68, Dartmouth Coll., 1977-78; researcher and author publs. on subjects including differential geometry, deformation theory in algebra, combinatorics, especially tensors, holonomy groups, graded lie algebras, algorithms. Co-author: Combinatorial Algorithms, 1975, 78; editor: Jour. Algorithms. Postdoctoral fellow Princeton, 1952-53; Fulbright grantee, 1952-53, 63-64; Guggenheim fellow, 1961-62. Mem. Am. Math. Soc., Math. Assn. Am., Netherlands Math. Soc., Assn. for Computing Machinery, AAUP, Royal Netherlands Acad. Scis. (corr.). Office: U Wash Dept Math Box 354350 Seattle WA 98195-4350

NIJINSKY, TAMARA, actress, puppeteer, author, librarian, educator; b. Vienna; came to U.S., 1961; d. Waslaw and Romola (de Pulszky) N.; widowed; 1 child, Kinga Maria Szakats-Gaspers. Ed. in Europe, postgrad. studies in U.S. Mem., actress Nat. Theater of Budapest; owner, tchr. Tamara Nijinsky Performing Art Studio, Montreal; tchr. speech/drama, French and German, libr. Cath. H.S., Phoenix; established non-profit internat. orgn. The Waslaw and Romola Nijinsky Found., Inc., 1991, exec. dir., 1991—; lectr. on Nijinsky, U.S., Can. and Europe. Author: Nijinsky and Romola, 1991. Decorated Chevalier Order Arts and Letters (France); recipient Nijinsky medal, Pagart, Poland. Roman Catholic. Office: Nijinsky Foundation Inc 4925 N 43d St Phoenix AZ 85018

NIKIDES, BILL, military officer; b. N.Y.C., Dec. 16, 1954; s. Diomides and Martha N.; m. Cheryl Ocilla Meredith, May 21, 1977; children: Meredith Irene, Mary Elizabeth, Martha Leigh. BA in History, The Citadel, 1977; MA in European History, Webster U., 1986; postgrad., Fla. State U., 1990—, Samford U., 1994—. Ordained to ministry So. Baptist Ch., 1994. Commd. 2nd lt. USAF, 1977, advanced through grades to maj., 1988; chief target intelligence br. 23 Tactical Fighter Wing/HQ Rapid Deployment Air Force, Alexandria, La., Sumter, S.C., 1978-80, 80-83; intelligence instr. The NATO Sch., Oberammergau, Germany, 1983-85; master instr./supr. Air Intelligence Sch., Denver, 1985-87; chief spl. program/covert targeting HQ Tactical Air Command, Hampton, Va., 1987-90; chief of intelligence 325 Fighter Wing, Panama City, Fla., 1990-93, 4440 Composite Wing, Dhahran, Saudi Arabia, 1992; chief electronic combat targeting HQ Cen. Air Forces, Riyadh, Saudi Arabia, 1991; target intelligence flight comdr. 12th Air Force, Tucson, Ariz., 1993-94. Contbr. articles to jours. Counselor Spl. Olympics, Panama City, 1990-93; guest tchr. Panama City Pub. Schs., 1992. Decorated various mil. medals including Liberation of Kuwait medal, Humanitarian Svc. medal, others. Mem. Am. Hist. Assn., Am. Soc. Church Historians, Air Force Assn., Phi Alpha Theta. Republican. Baptist. Home: 148 E Glenwood Dr Birmingham AL 35209-3950 Office: 12th Air Force/AIF Tucson AZ 85707

NIKULA, KRISTEN JAN, veterinary and experimental pathologist; b. Fitchburg, Mass., May 15, 1954; d. Peter Eugene and Phyllis Beverly (Burger) N.; m. Tony Lynn Lantzer, Aug. 7, 1982. BS, U. Calif., Davis, 1977, DVM, 1979, PhD, 1986. Diplomate Am. Coll. of Vet. Pathologists; lic. vet. Calif., N.Mex. Vet. Jamul, Calif., 1979-82; postdoctoral fellow Nat. Cancer Inst./Univ. Calif., Davis, 1982-84; environmental pathology trainee Nat. Inst. Environ. Health Scis./U. Calif., Davis, 1984-85; postdoctoral fellow Am. Lung Assn./U. Calif., Davis, 1985-86; asst. prof. Coll. of Vet. Med. and Biomed. Scis./Colo. State U., Fort Collins, 1986-88; clin. assoc. prof. Coll. of Pharmacy/U. N.Mex., Albuquerque, 1992—; exptl. pathologist Inhalation Toxicology Rsch. Inst., Albuquerque, 1988—; presenter sci. meetings; cons., participant in pathology peer-rev. panels. Contbr. articles to profl. jours.; contbr. book chpts. to Biological Reactive Intermediate IV, 1990, Handbook of Toxicologic Pathology, 1991, Proceedings of 8th International Radiation Protection Association, 1992, Toxic and Carcinogenic Effects of Solid Particles in Respiratory Tract, 1994, Concepts in Inhalation Toxicology, 1995. Recipient Sch. Vet. Medicine medal, 1979; Regents scholar U. Calif., 1972. Mem. AAAS, Am. Coll. Vet. Pathologists, Am. Vet. Med. Assn., Soc. Toxicol. Pathologists, Phi Zeta, Phi Kappa Phi, Alpha Zeta. Office: Inhalation Toxicology Rsch Inst PO Box 5890 Albuquerque NM 87185

NILLES, DARRELL LERAD, artist, inventor, architect, b. Madison, Wis., Nov. 30, 1957; s. Fred and Agnes Nilles. BArch., U. Minn., 1981. Architect LKA Ptnrs., Colorado Springs, Colo., 1983-86; architect, designer Wolff Lang Christopher, Rancho Cucamonga, Calif., 1986-89, Hill Pinkert, Irvine, Calif., 1989, Wimberly Allison Tony Goo, Newport Beach, Calif., 1989-91; owner, artist, inventor Nilles Studios, Orange, Calif., 1991-95; architect, curator art exhibits RTKL Internat., L.A., 1994—; owner, artist LeRad Studios, L.A., 1995—; student project juror U. Calif., Fullerton, 1993-94. Exhibited in shows at L.A. Art Assn., 1991, Fine Arts Inst., San Bernardino County Mus., Redlands, Calif., 1993, Irvine (Calif.) Fine Art Ctr., 1994, numerous others. Mem. Internat. Sculpture Ctr., L.A. Contemporary Exhbns.

NILLES, JOHN MATHIAS (JACK NILLES), futurist; b. Evanston, Ill., Aug. 25, 1932; s. Elmer Edward and Hazel Evelyn (Wickum) N.; m. Laila Padorr, July 8, 1957. BA magna cum laude, Lawrence Coll., 1954; MS in Engring., UCLA, Los Angeles, 1964. Sr. engr. Raytheon Mfg. Co., Santa Barbara, Calif., 1956-58; section head. Ramo-Woodridge Corp., L.A., 1958-59; project engr. Space Technology Lab., L.A., 1960; dir. The Aerospace Corp., L.A., 1961-67; sr. systems engr. TRW Systems, L.A., 1967-69; assoc. group dir. The Aerospace Corp., L.A., 1969-72; dir. interdisciplinary programs U. So. Calif., L.A., 1972-81, dir. info. technology program, 1981-89; pres. JALA Internat. Inc., L.A., 1980—; coord. EC Telework Forum, Madrid, 1992—; dir. Telecommuting Adv. Coun., L.A., 1991—, pres., 1993-94; chmn. Telecommuting Rsch. Inst., Inc., L.A., 1990—. Author: The Telecommunications Transportation Tradeoff, 1976, Japanese edit., 1977, Exploring the World of the Personal Computer, 1982, French edit., 1985, Micros and Modems, 1983, French edit., 1986, Making Telecommuting Happen, 1994, Portuguese edit., 1997. Capt. USAF, 1954-56. Recipient Rod Rose award Soc. Rsch. Adminstrs., 1976, Environ. Pride award L.A. Mag., 1993, Environ. Achievement award Renew Am., 1994-96. Mem. IEEE, IEEE Computer Soc., AAAS, Assn. Computing Machinery, Inst. Ops. Rsch. and Mgmt. Scis., World Future Soc., Calif. Yacht Club. Office: JALA Internat Inc 971 Stonehill Ln Los Angeles CA 90049-1412

NIMMAGADDA, RAO RAJAGOPALA, materials scientist, researcher; b. Donepudi, Andhra Pradesh, India, July 1, 1944; came to U.S., 1967; s. Suryaprakasa Rao and Bullemma (Venigalla) N.; m. Usha Rani Chava, Nov. 7, 1965 (div. Nov. 1980); children: Sandhya Rani, Pramada Shree; m. Jhansi Rani Talluri, Dec. 18, 1980; children: Sai Chandra and Sri Spandana. B Tech. with honors, Indian Inst. Tech., Bombay, 1965; MS, Mich. Tech. U., 1970; PhD, UCLA, 1975. Jr. sci. officer Def. Metall. Rsch. Labs., Hyderabad, India, 1965-67; postdoctoral scholar UCLA, 1975-78, rsch. engr., 1978-81; rsch. scientist Smith Tool, Irvine, Calif., 1981-83, Burroughs, Westlake Village, Calif., 1983-84; rsch. engr. Memorex Corp., Santa Clara, Calif., 1984-86; staff scientist Lockheed Missiles & Space Co., Palo Alto, Calif., 1986-93; sect. head Akashic Memories Corp., San Jose, Calif., 1993—. Contbr. articles to profl. jours. Pres. Telugu Assn. So. Calif., 1977, dir. Hindu Temple Soc. So. Calif., 1977-80, pres., 1980. Recipient of Outstanding Tech. Achievement award Strategic Def. Initiative Orgn., Washington, 1989. Mem Am. Vacuum Soc., Materials Rsch. Soc. Republican. Hindu. Home: 120 Gilbert Ave Santa Clara CA 95051-6705 Office: Akashic Memories Corp 305 W Tasman Dr San Jose CA 95134-1704

NING, XUE-HAN (HSUEH-HAN NING), physiologist, researcher; b. Peng-Lai, Shandong, People's Republic of China, Apr. 15, 1936; came to U.S., 1984; s. Yi-Xing and Liu Ning; m. Jian-Xin Fan, May 28, 1967; 1 child, Di Fan. MD, Shanghai 1st Med. Coll., People's Republic of China, 1960. Rsch. fellow Shanghai Inst. Physiology, 1960-72, leader cardiovasc. rsch. group, 1973-83, head, assoc. prof. cardiovasc. rsch. unit, 1984-87, prof. and chair hypoxia dept., 1988-90, vice chairperson academic com., 1988-90; NIH internat. rsch. fellow U. Mich., Ann Arbor, 1984-87, vis. prof., hon. prof., rsch. investigator, 1990-95; prof. and dir. Hypoxia Physiology Lab. Academia Sinica, Shanghai, 1989—; acting leader, High Altitude Physiology Group, Chinese mountaineering and sci. expdn. team to Mt. Everest, 1975; leader High Altitude Physiology Group, Dept. Metall. Industry of China and Ry. Engring. Corps, 1979; vis. prof. dept. physiology Mich. State U., East Lansing, 1989-90; vis. prof. dept. pediat. U. Wash., Seattle, 1994—. Author: High Altitude Physiology and Medicine, 1981, Reports on Scientific Expedition to Mt. Qomolungma, High Altitude Physiology, 1980, Environment and Ecology of Qinghai-Xizang (Tibet) Plateau, 1982; mem. editl. bd. Chinese Jour. Applied Physiology, 1984—, Acta Physiologica, 1988—; contbr. articles to profl. jours. Recipient Merit award Shanghai Sci. Congress, 1977, All-China Sci. Congress, Beijing, 1978, Super Class award Academia Sinica, Beijing, 1986, 1st Class award Nat. Natural Scis., Beijing, 1987, # 1 Best Article award Tzu-Chi Med. Jour., Taiwan, 1995. Mem. Am. Physiol. Soc., Internat. Soc. Heart Rsch., Royal Soc. Medicine, Shanghai Assn. Physiol. (bd. dirs. 1988—), Chinese Assn. Physiol. (com. applied physiology 1984—, com. blood, cardiovascular, respiratory and renal physiology 1988—), Chinese Soc. Medicine, Chinese Soc. Biomed. Engring. Home: 7033 43rd Ave NE Seattle WA 98115-6015 Office: U Wash Dept Pediatrics Box 356320 1959 NE Pacific St Seattle WA 98195

NINKOVICH, THOMAS, owner research firm, consultant; b. Fresno, Calif., Dec. 26, 1943; s. Howard Sydney Davis and Louise Metkovich Ninkovich; stepfather: Dan Ninkovich. Student, U. Calif., Berkeley, 1961-65. Owner Reunion Rsch., Auberry, Calif., 1982—. Author: Reunion Handbook, 1988, Military Reunion Handbook, 1991, Family Reunion Handbook, 1992; editor: Fun and Games for Family Gatherings, 1996; rschr. demograhics as well as sociol. and psychol. aspects of group reunions. With USN, 1965-67. Office: Reunion Rsch 40609 Auberry Rd Auberry CA 93602

NINNEMAN, THOMAS GEORGE, broadcast educator; b. Chgo., Apr. 13, 1950; s. Milton Charles and Bernice Helen (Sharp) N.; m. Nancy Gail Rogers, Aug. 12, 1972; children: Stephanie Christine, Peter Christopher. BA, U. No. Colo., 1972. Dir. news. Sta. KGLN, Glenwood Springs, Colo., 1972-73; program mgr. Sta. KKEP, Estes Park, Colo., 1973-74; ops. mgr. Sta. WMST-AM-FM, Mt. Sterling, Ky., 1974-75; dir. news Sta. KPIK-AM-FM, Colorado Springs, Colo., 1975-77; news stringer AP, UPI, various stas., Colorado Springs, Colo., 1977-78; mgr. driver edn., safety dept. Am. Automobile Assn., Denver, 1978-81; pres. mkt. rschr. Rampart Range Broadcasting Inc., Castle Rock, Colo., 1981-83; news editor Sta. KDEN, Denver, 1983-84; dir. news Stas. KSGT and KMTN-FM, Jackson, Wyo., 1984-94; instr. TV/prodr. dist. TV programming Teton County Sch. Dist., Jackson, 1989—; panelist Yellowstone Fire Rev., Yellowstone Nat. Pk., 1989; contract spokesperson on fire safety Bridger-Teton Nat. Forest, Jackson, 1990—; seasonal pub. affairs specialist Grand Teton Nat. Park, summers 1995, 96—. Asst. scoutmaster, then scoutmaster Boy Scouts Am., Castle Rock, Colo., 1979-84, mem. dist. com., 1984-93; vice chair Teton County Centennial Com., Jackson, 1989; co-founder, mgr. Jackson Hole Cmty. Band, 1989—; charter mem., mem. coun. Shepherd of the Mountains Luth. Ch.; active Jackson Hole Brass Quintet, 1985—; mem. local com. Christian Ministry in Nat. Parks, 1988-96; mem. pub. adv. com. Wyo. Pub. Radio, 1990—; com. mem. Jackson divsn. Am. Heart Assn., 1994-95. Recipient Tony Bevinette Friend of Wyo. Tourism award Wyo. Travel Commn., 1993; co-recipient Wyo. News Station of Yr. award AP, 1990; named Broadcast Newsman of Yr. AP, 1976. Home: PO Box 105 Jackson WY 83001-0105 Office: Jackson Hole HS PO Box 568 Jackson WY 83001-0100

NINOS, NICHOLAS PETER, retired miliatry officer, physician; b. Chgo., May 11, 1936; s. Peter Spiros and Ann (Lesczynsky) N. BA in Art, Bradley U., 1958, BS in Chemistry, 1959; MD, U. Ill., Chgo., 1963. Diplomate Am. Bd. Internal Med., Am. Bd. Cardiology, Am. Bd. Critical Care Medicine. Intern Cook County Hosp., Chgo., 1963-64, resident in internal medicine, 1964-67, fellow in cardiology, 1967-68; commd. capt. U.S. Army, 1968, advanced through grades to col., 1979; chief dept. medicine U.S. Army Community Hosp. U.S. Army, Bremerhaven, Fed. Republic Germany, 1968-69, Wurzberg, Fed. Republic Germany, 1969-72; chief critical care Letterman Army Med. Ctr., San Francisco, 1976-91; dep. comdr. San Francisco med. command Letterman Army Med. Ctr./Naval Hosp. of Oakland, San Francisco and Oakland, Calif., 1988-90; ret., 1991; assoc. prof. medicine and surgery Uniformed Svcs. U. Health Scis., Bethesda, Md., 1981-91; critical care medicine cons. to U.S. Army Surgeon Gen., 1981-91; lectr. in field. Author: (jour.) Ethics, 1988; co-editor: Nutrition, 1988, Problems in Critical Care, Nutrition Support; mem. editl. bd. Jour. Critical Care Medicine, 1988-91; illustrator: Medical Decision Making, 1988. 2d v.p. Twin Springs Condominium Homeowners Assn., Palm Springs, Calif., 1993-94, sec., 1994-96; ch. bd. councilman St. George Orthodox Ch. of the Desert, Palm Desert, Calif., 1993-95; active Palm Springs Comm., 1993—; bd. dirs. Mizell Sr. Ctr., Palm Springs, 1996—. Decorated Legion of Merit, Meritorious Svc. medal with oak leaf cluster. Fellow Am. Coll. Critical Care Medicine (mem. bd. regents 1989-94, chmn. 1989-91); mem. AMA, Soc. Critical Care Medicine (pres. uniformed svcs. sect. 1987-90, Shubin/Weil award 1988), Soc. Med. Cons. to Armed Forces (assoc.), Inst. Critical Care Medicine (exec. v.p. 1991-92), Toastmasters Internat. (sec.-treas. Palm Springs chpt. 1993-94, pres. 1994, gov. area D-3 1994-95, divsn. gov. 1995-96).

NISH, ALBERT RAYMOND, JR., retired newspaper editor; b. San Bernardino, Calif., Mar. 16, 1922; s. Albert Raymond and Mabel Claire (Shay) N.; m. Lois Maxine Ringgenberg, June 21, 1942; children: Steven Raymond, Richard Henry, Kathleen Lorie Jenner. Student San Bernardino Valley Jr. Coll., 1939-41, U. Calif., Berkeley, 1941-42, Wash. State Coll., 1943; Am. Press Inst., 1977. Pony wire editor AP, San Francisco, 1941-42; reporter Chico Record, Calif., 1945-46, Berkeley Daily Gazette, Calif., 1946-48; valley editor Modesto Bee, Calif., 1948-60, asst. mng. editor, 1960-62, mng. editor, 1962-85. Served as fighter pilot USAAC, 1942-45, PTO. Decorated DFC.

NISHIMURA, ROBERT NEAL, physician, medical educator, researcher; b. Spokane, Wash., Feb. 12, 1947; s. Roy Y. and Masako Nishimura. BS, Wash. State U., 1968; MD, Johns Hopkins U., 1972. Diplomate Am. Bd. Neurology and Psychiatry. Intern in medicine U. Calif., San Diego, 1972-73; resident in neurology U. Calif., San Francisco, 1973-76; rsch. fellow NIH, Bethesda, Md., 1976-79; asst. prof. U. Oreg., Portland, 1979-81; asst. prof. UCLA, 1981-87, assoc. prof. neurology, 1987—; com. for protection of human subjects State of Calif., Sacramento, 1994—. Contbr. articles to profl. jours. Rsch. fellow United Cerebral Palsy Fedn., 1971, postdoctoral fellow Nat. Multiple Sclerosis Soc., 1976-78. Mem. Am. Acad. Neurology, Soc. for Neurosci., Am. Soc. for Neurochemistry, Royal Soc. Medicine. Office: VA Med Ctr 16111 Plummer St Sepulveda CA 91343-2036

NISHIOKA, TERUO (TED NISHIOKA), electrical engineer; b. Crystal City, Tex., Sept. 6, 1945; s. Kazuto Benjamin and Kofumi (Shinkawa) N.; m. Suzanne Nayeko Hayashi, June 24, 1978; 1 child, Stephanie. BSEE, Calif. State Poly. U., 1970. Engr. Salt River Project, Phoenix, 1970-72, Pacific Gas and Electric, San Francisco, 1972-74; power plant engr. Wismer and Becker, Sacramento, 1975-78; sr. elec. engr. Ariz. Pub. Svc., Phoenix, 1978—. Author: Underground Cable Thermal Backfill, 1981. Active Japanese-Am. Citizens League, Phoenix, 1978—, bd. dirs. 1991—; v.p. Ariz. Buddhist Ch., Phoenix, 1987-88, pres., 1989-91; mem. Matsuri steering com., 1992—. With U.S. Army, 1966-68. Mem. IEEE, Power Engring. Soc., Elec. Insulation Soc. Office: Ariz Pub Svc PO Box 53999 Phoenix AZ 85072-3999

NISHITANI, MARTHA, dancer; b. Seattle, Feb. 27, 1920; d. Denjiro and Jin (Aoto) N. B.A. in Comparative Arts, U. Wash., 1958; studied with, Eleanor King, Mary Ann Wells, Perry Mansfield, Cornish Sch., Conn. Coll. Sch. Dance, Long Beach State U. Founder, dir. Martha Nishitani Modern Dance Sch. and Co., Seattle, 1950—; dance dir. Helen Bush Sch. and Central YWCA, 1951-54; choreographer U. Wash. Opera Theater, 1955-65, Intiman Theater, 1972—; dance instr. Elementary and Secondary Edn. Act Program, 1966; dance specialist spl. edn. program Shoreline Pub. Schs., 1970-72; condr. workshops and concerts King County Youth Correctional Instns., 1972-73; Dance adv. counsel Wash. Cultural Enrichment Program; dance adv. bd. Seattle Parks and Recreation. Dancer Eleanor King Co., Seattle, 1946-50, dance films, 1946-51, Channel 9, Ednl. TV, 1967-68; lectr. demonstrator numerous colls., festivals, convs., childrens theater.; author articles on dance; one of the subjects: A Celebration of 100 Years of Dance in Washington, 1989. Trustee Allied Arts Seattle, 1967. Recipient Theta Sigma Phi Matrix Table award, 1968, Asian Am. Living Treasure award Northwest Asian Am. Theater, 1984; listed Dance Archives, N.Y.C. Libr., 1991, N.Y.C. Lincoln Ctr. Dance Archives, 1991, U. Wash. Libr. Archives, 1993, exhibit of Japanese Am. Women of Achievement, Burke Mus., 1994, 43d Anniversary of Martha Nishitani Modern Dance Sch. Mem. Am. Dance Guild (exec. com. 1961-63), Com. Research in Dance, Seattle Art Mus., Internat. Dance Alliance (adv. council 1984), Smithsonian Assos., Progressive Animal Welfare Soc. Address: 4205 University Way NE PO Box 45264 Seattle WA 98145-0264 *Until a few years ago a compelling force within me would let nothing interfere with performing, teaching, and directing dance. My belief: "I must be selfish about that which means most to me." This dedication was in constant battle with loneliness, frugality and neglect of loved ones. My first solo dance was Credo in Conflict. I have earned a degree of success, satisfaction, joy and recognition. My thoughts are now that I have learned to pursue a balance in life as I battle. The scars of selfishness persist but the broader view brings validity to my beliefs.*

NISKANEN, PAUL MCCORD, travel company executive; b. Bend, Oreg., July 6, 1943; s. William Arthur and Nina Elizabeth (McCord) N.; m. Christine Campbell; 1 son, Tapio. Student U. Freiburg, Germany, 1963-64; BA, Stanford U., 1965; MBA, U. Chgo., 1966. Fin. analyst Kimberly-Clark Corp., Neenah, Wis., 1966-68; bus. mgr. Avent Inc. subs. Kimberley-Clark Corp., Tucson, 1968-70; v.p., gen. mgr. Pacific Trailways Bus. Line, Portland, Oreg., 1970-81; chmn. bd., owner Niskanen & Jones, Inc., Moab, Utah, 1982—, Perspectives, Inc., Portland; co-owner Cruise Masters, Beaverton, Oreg., 1989—. Apptd. consul for Finland, 1980—; active Gov.'s Travel Adv. Com., Salem, Oreg., 1976-81; 1st pres. Oreg. Hospitality and Visitors Assn., Portland, 1977-78; bd. dirs. Suomi Coll., Hancock, Mich., 1981—; nat. co-chmn. Dole for Pres. Com., 1987; co-chmn. Vistory 88. Decorated knight 1st Class Order White Rose Republic of Finland. Mem. Travel Industry Assn. Am., Am. Assn. Travel Agts., Pacific Northwest Travel Assn. (chmn. 1978-79), Scandinavian Heritage Found. (bd. dirs. 1984). Republican. Home: 4366 SW Hewett Blvd Portland OR 97221-3107 Office: Cruise Masters 2730 SW Cedar Hills Blvd Beaverton OR 97005-1356

NISSEL, MARTIN, radiologist, consultant; b. N.Y.C., July 29, 1921; s. Samuel David and Etta Rebecca (Ostrie) N.; m. Beatrice Goldberg, Dec. 26, 1943; children: Philippa Lyn, Jeremy Michael. BA, NYU, 1941; MD, N.Y. Med. Coll., 1944. Diplomate Am. Bd. Radiology. Intern Met. Hosp., N.Y.C., 1944-45, Lincoln Hosp., N.Y.C., 1947-48; resident in radiology Bronx Hosp., 1948-50, attending radiologist, 1952-54; resident in radiotherapy Montefiore Hosp., Bronx, 1950-51, attending radiotherapist, 1954-65; attending radiologist Buffalo (N.Y.) VA Hosp., 1951-52; attending radiotherapist Univ. Hosp. Boston City Hosp., 1965-69; asst. prof. radiology Boston U. Sch. of Medicine, 1965-69; chief radiotherapist,dir. radiation ctr. Brookside Hosp., San Pablo, Calif., 1969-77; group leader, radiopharm. drugs FDA, Rockville, Md., 1977-86; pvt. cons. radiopharm. drug devel., 1986—. Contbr. articles to profl. jours. Lectr. Am. Cancer Soc., Contra Costa County, Calif., 1973-76. Capt. MC AUS, 1945-47, Korea. Recipient Contra Costa County Speakers Bur. award Am. Cancer Soc., 1973, 76, Responsible Person for Radiol. Health Program for Radiopharm. Drugs award FDA, 1980-86. Mem. Am. Coll. Radiology, Radiol. Soc. N.Am. Office: PO Box 5537 Eugene OR 97405-0537

NISULA, LARRY WILLIAM, artist; b. Phoenix, Oct. 10, 1960; s. William Elmer and Mavis Marie (Ball) N. Student, Glendale C.C., 1979-81. Artist, 1985—; lectr. in field. One-man shows include Phoenix Coll. Art Gallery, 1985, Fagen-Peterson Fine Art, 1987-96, Glendale C.C., 1992, 95; exhibited in group shows Mars Gallery, 1986, Hospice of Valley, 1986, Galleria Mesa, 1988; works represented in collections throughout U.S. and Europe. Mem. Phoenix Blues Soc., Mus. Modern Art N.Y. Home and Studio: 1506 W Fillmore St Phoenix AZ 85007-2213

NITZ, FREDERIC WILLIAM, electronics company executive; b. St. Louis, June 22, 1943; s. Arthur Carl Paul and Dorothy Louise (Kahm) N.; m. Kathleen Sue Rapp, June 8, 1968; children: Frederic Theodore, Anna Louise. AS, Coll. Marin, 1970; BS in Electronics, Calif. Poly. State U., San Luis Obispo, 1972. Electronic engr. Sierra Electronics, Menlo Park, Calif., 1973-77, RCA, Somerville, N.J., 1977-79; engring. mgr. EGG-Geometrics, Sunnyvale, Calif., 1979-83; v.p. engring. Basic Measuring Insts., Foster City, Calif., 1983-91; exec. v.p. Reliable Power Meters, Los Gatos, Calif., 1991—; cons. in field, Boulder Creek, Calif., 1978—. Patentee in field. Bd. dirs. San Lorenzo Valley Water Dist., Boulder Creek, 1983—, Water Policy Task Force, Santa Cruz County, Calif., 1983-84. With U.S. Army, 1965-67. Democrat. Lutheran. Home: 24 Taryn Ct Scotts Valley CA 95066-3837 Office: Reliable Power Meters 400 Blossom Hill Rd Los Gatos CA 95032-4511

NITZ, GARY LEE, psychiatrist; b. Goodland, Kans., Mar. 3, 1936; s. Gilbert Benjamin and Marjorie (Wilcox) N.; m. Judith Hood, June 3, 1958; children: Brenda Nitz Vanderberry, Daren Hood. BA, U. Kans., 1958, MD, 1962. Postgrad. Strong Meml. Hosp./U. Rochester, 1962-65, Johns Hopkins Hosp., 1965-67; clin. psychiatrist U.S. Army, Tex. and Colo., 1967-69; pvt. practice psychiatrist Colorado Springs, Colo., 1969-81, Scottsdale, Ariz., 1981—, Litchfield Pk., Ariz., 1996—. Fellow Am. Psychiat. Assn. Office: 501 E Plaza Cir Ste 15 Litchfield Park AZ 85340

NIVEN, WILLIAM JOHN, historian, educator; b. Bklyn., Oct. 26, 1921; s. William John and Marion (Fredricks) N.; m. Elizabeth Thomson, Sept. 11, 1948; children: John Drake, Katherine Pope. BA, U. Conn., 1943; MA, Columbia U., 1947, PhD, 1954. Instr. Mitchell Coll., New London, Conn., 1949-51; supr. employee rels. Electric Boat divsn. Gen. Dynamics Corp., Groton, Conn., 1951-54; asst. to v.p. comm. Gen. Dynamics Corp., N.Y.C., 1954-55, asst. to CEO and pres., 1955-57, dir. pubs., 1955-60; assoc. prof., prof. Claremont (Calif.) Grad. Sch., 1965-90; prof. emeritus, 1990—; cons. in field. Co-author: Dynamic America, 1960; author: Connecticut for the

Union, 1965, Years of Turmoil: The Civil War and Reconstruction, 1969, Gideon Welles, Lincoln's Secretary of the Navy, 1973, Connecticut Hero: Israel Putnam, 1977, Martin Van Buren and the Romantic Era of American Politics, 1983, The American President Lines and Its Forebears, 1848-1984: From Paddle Wheelers to Container Ships, 1986, The Coming of the Civil War, 1989, John C. Calhoun and the Price of Union, 1987, Salmon P. Chase, A Study in Paradox, 1995; editor: The Salmon P. Chase Papers,. Lt. USNR, 1942-46, WWII. Grantee Am. Philos. Soc., 1962, Am. Coun. Learned Socs., 1962; recipient Award of Merit, Nat. Assn. State and Local History, 1966, Jules and Frances Landry award, 1987; Commonwealth Club Calif. Silver medal, 1974. Fellow Smithsonian Inst. (sr. 1965-66), Soc. Am. Historians; mem. Am. Hist. Assn. (chmn. Avery Craven award com. 1985, Beveridge-Dunning award com. 1974, 75, chmn. 1976, Pacific Coast Br. award 1966), Orgn. Am. Historians, So. Hist. Assn. (chmn. Charles Sydnor prize com. 1983, 84), Zamorano Club, Coffee House. Home: 2275 Forbes Ave Claremont CA 91711-1749 Office: Claremont Grad Sch 170 E 10th St Claremont CA 91711-5909

NIX, NANCY JEAN, librarian, designer; b. Denver; d. James Frederik and Josephine (Britt) N. AB in History, U. So. Calif., L.A., 1959, MLS, 1960. Exhibited in group shows including Iemoto Historical Flower Arrangement Exhibit, 1992. Mem. guiding com. Art Assn. Egg and the Eye Gallery and Restaurant, 1973—; participant Arts & Humanities Symposium, Palm Desert, Calif., 1974; patron cultural symposium L.A. Garden Club, 1975. Recipient Kakan Monpyo award Ikenobo Ikebana Soc. Floral Art, 1988; named Woman of Yr. L.A. Nikkei Cmty. So. Calif. Japanese-Am. Soc., L.A. Japanese-Am. Cultural League, 1997. Mem. Ikebana Internat. (bd. dirs. L.A. chpt. 1978-82, mem. chmn. 1980-82), Japanese Am. Citizens League (historian, exec. bd. L.A. Downtown chpt. 1990—, chpt. historian), Japanese Am. Nat. Mus., Japanese Am. Cultural and Cmty. Ctr., Libr. Assocs./Libr. Found. L.A., L.A. Jazz Soc. Republican. Jewish.

NIXON, JOHN HARMON, economist; b. Mpls., Apr. 7, 1915; s. Justin Wroe and Ida Elisabeth (Wickenden) N. AB, Swarthmore Coll., 1935; AM, Harvard U., 1949, PhD, 1953. Analyst U.S. R.R. Retirement Bd., Washington, 1938-41; economist U.S. Office of Price Adminstrn., Washington, 1941-46; teaching fellow, sr. tutor Harvard Coll., Cambridge, Mass., 1947-50; asst. prof. econs. CCNY, 1953-56; dir. econ. devel. N.Y. State Dept. Commerce, Albany, 1956-59; dir. area devel. Com. for Econ. Devel., N.Y.C., 1959-65; dir. tech. assistance U.S. Econ. Devel. Adminstrn., Washington, 1966-67; urban economist U.S. AID, Saigon, Vietnam, 1967; economist Ralph M. Parsons Co., Washington, 1968-70; chief economist/systems Ralph M. Parsons Co., Pasadena, Calif., 1971-82; mem. adv. bd. U.S. Area Devel. Adminstrn., Washington, 1963-65. Co-author, editor: Community Economic Development Efforts, 1964, Living Without Water (Cairo), 1980. Vice chmn. Mayor's Com. on Econ. Devel., L.A., 1974-75; pres. Pasadena Devel. Corp., 1982-84. Mem. Nat. Economists Club, Nat. Assn. Bus. Economists, Harvard Club N.Y.C., Phi Beta Kappa. Democrat. Presbyterian. Office: PO Box 76267 Los Angeles CA 90076-0267

NIXON, NORA, educational director; b. Alexandria, Va., Sept. 19, 1956; d. Robert Tharp and Alice Mary Nixon; m. Alexander Paul Vertikoff, Dec. 24, 1984; children: Cole Robert, Carmen Kira. BA in Spanish/Portuguese, U. N.Mex., 1981; MA in TESL/Applied Linguistics, UCLA, 1986. Lang. lab. asst. dept. modern and classical langs. U. N.Mex., 1981-82, English instr., 1981-82; ednl. aide II Venice High Sch., L.A. Unified Sch. Dist., 1981-82; teaching asst. intermediate ESL UCLA, 1984, teaching assoc. advanced composition ESL, 1985-86; fgn. expert/researcher Zhongshan U., People's Republic China, 1984-85; ESL instr. West L.A. C.C., 1986-87, UCLA Extension, 1983-87; asst. dir. English, asst. prof. English, EAP, ESP West Coast U., L.A., 1987-91; assoc. dir. acad. yr. programs Ednl. Resource Devel. Trust, Marina Del Rey, Calif., 1991-94. Author: Advanced Writing in EST: A Coursebook for Graduate Students of Science and Technology, 1985; contbr. articles to profl. publs. Grantee Fulbright Found., 1988, USIA, 1991. Mem. TESOL, CATESOL.

NIXON, ROBERT OBEY, SR., business educator; b. Pitts., Feb. 14, 1922; s. Frank Obey and Margurite (Van Buren) N.; m. Marilyn Cavanagh, Oct. 25, 1944 (dec. 1990); children: Nan Nixon Friend, Robert Obey, Jr., Dwight Cavanagh. BS in bus. adminstrn., U. Pitts., 1948; MS, Ohio State U., 1964; MBA, U. Phoenix, 1984. Commd. 2d lt. USAF, 1943, advanced through grades to col., 1970, master navigator WWII, Korea, Vietnam; sales, adminstrn. U.S. Rubber Corp., Pitts., 1940-41; asst. engr. Am. Bridge Corp., Pitts., 1941-42; underwriter, sales Penn Mutual Life Ins. Corp., Pitts., 1945-50; capt., nav. instr. USAF Reserves, 1945-50; ret. USAF Col., divsn. chief Joint Chiefs of Staff, 1973; educator, cons. U. Ariz., 1973-79; bus. dept. chmn., coord., founder weekend coll. Pima Community Coll., Tucson, 1979-90, prof. mgmt., coord. Weekend Coll. program, 1991—; founder, pres. Multiple Adv. Group ednl. cons., Tucson, 1978—. Author: Source Document: On Accelerated Courses and Programs at Accredited Two- and Four-Year Colleges and Universities, 1996; contbr. articles to profl. jours. Mem. Soc. Logistics Engrs. (sr., charter mem.), Phi Delta Theta. Presbyterian. Home: 1824 S Regina Cleri Dr Tucson AZ 85710-8664

NIXON, SCOTT SHERMAN, lawyer; b. Grosse Pointe, Mich., Feb. 7, 1959; s. Floyd Sherman and Marjorie Jane (Quermann) N.; m. Cathryn Lynn Starnes, Aug. 27, 1983; children: Jeffry Sherman, Kelsy Jane, James Robert. BABA, Mich. State U., 1981; JD, U. Denver, 1984. Bar: Colo. 1984, U.S. Dist. Ct. Colo. 1984, U.S. Ct. Appeals (10th cir.) 1984. Assoc. Pryor, Carney & Johnson, P.C., Englewood, Colo., 1984-89, shareholder, 1990-95; shareholder Pryor, Johnson, Montoya, Carney & Karr, P.C., Englewood, 1995—. Officer, bd. dirs. Luth. Brotherhood Br. 8856, Denver, 1993—, Mark K. Ulmer Meml. Native Am. Scholarship Found., Denver, 1994—; officer, mem. coun. Bethan Luth Ch., Englewood, 1993-95. Mem. ABA, Colo. Bar Assn., Denver Bar Assn., Colo. Def. Lawyers Assn. Home: 6984 S Pontiac Ct Englewood CO 80112 Office: Pryor Johnson Montoya et al Ste 1313 6400 S Fiddler's Green Cir Englewood CO 80111

NIZZE, JUDITH ANNE, physician assistant; b. L.A., Nov. 1, 1942; d. Robert George and Charlotte Ann (Wise) Swan; m. Norbert Adolph Otto Paul Nizze, Dec. 31, 1966. BA, UCLA, 1966, postgrad., 1966-76; grad. physician asst. tng. program, Charles R. Drew Sch. Postgrad., L.A., 1979; BS, Calif. State U., Dominguez, 1980. Cert. physician asst., Calif. Staff rsch. assoc. I-II Wadsworth Vet. Hosp., L.A., 1965-71; staff rsch. assoc. III-IV John Wayne Clinic Jonsson Comprehensive Cancer Ctr., UCLA, 1971-78; clin. asst. Robert S. Ozeran, Gardena, Calif., 1978; physician asst. family practice Fred Chasan, Torrance, Calif., 1980-82; sr. physician asst. Donald L. Morton prof., chief surg. oncology Jonsson Comprehensive Cancer Ctr., UCLA, 1983-91; adminstrv. dir. immunotherapy John Wayne Cancer Inst., Santa Monica, Calif., 1991—. Contbr. articles to profl. jours. Fellow Am. Acad. Physician Assts., Am. Assn. Surgeons Assts., Calif. Acad. Physician Assts.; mem. AAUW, Assn. Physician Assts. in Oncology. Republican. Presbyterian. Home: Ste J 13243 Fiji Way Marina Dl Rey CA 90292-7079 Office: John Wayne Cancer Inst St John's Hosp & Health Ctr 1328 22d St 2 West Santa Monica CA 90404-2032

NOBLE, DONALD CHARLES, geologist, educator; b. N.Y.C., Mar. 2, 1937; s. Oliver Donald and Ella DeCoursey (Kratz) N.; m. Bettie Eleanor Hardy, 1955 (div. 1971); children: Jean Elizabeth, William Hardy, Thomas Charles; m. Carol Jane Rasmussen, 1973. BS, Cornell U., 1958; MS, Stanford U., 1961, PhD, 1962. Geologist U.S. Geol. Survey, Denver, 1962-66; asst. prof. Harvard U., Cambridge, Mass., 1966-71; vis. prof., rsch. prof. U. Nev., Reno, 1972-75; geol. cons. Reno, also Peru, 1971-75; from assoc. prof. to prof. geology Mich. Technol. U., Houghton, 1975-80; prof. geology and econ. geology Mackay Sch. Mines, U. Nev., Reno, 1980—; cons. econ. geologist we. N.Am. and S.Am., 1980—. Contbr. more than 100 articles to Econ. Geology, Geology, Bull. of Geol. Soc. Am., Earth and Planetary Sci. Letters, Jour. Geophys. Rsch., Lithos, Am. Jour. Sci., others. 1st lt. USAR, 1958-59. Recipient numerous NSF grants, 1960s-1980s; Nev. Nuclear Waste Project Office grantee, numerous others. Fellow Soc. Econ. Geologists, Mineral. Soc. Am.; mem. Sociedad Geologica del Peru, Soc. Mining, Metallurgy and Exploration, Geol. Soc. Am., Geol. Soc. Nev. Home: 3450 Rolling Ridge Rd Reno NV 89506-9776 Office: Mackay Sch Mines MS 172 U Nev Reno Reno NV 89557

NOBLE, HELEN BONNER, artist; b. Northville, Mich., Mar. 27, 1922; d. George Coburn and Helen Josephine (McCambridge) Harper; m. Morton Noble, Jr., June 27, 1943; children: Martha, Kathryn, Elizabeth, John. Student, Wayne State U., We. Res. U., 1939-43, Santa Barbar Art Inst. One-woman shows include Gallery 932, Ventura, Calif., 1983, The Oaks Gallery, Ojai, Calif., 1988; group shows include Bradley Galleries, Santa Barbara, Calif., 1978, 79, Meredith Niles Gallery, Santa Barbara, 1980-83, Merida-Rapp Graphics, Louisville, 1986; other exhibits include 3rd Women in Art Exhbn., Springfield, Ill., 1983, 2nd Ann. Nat. Print Exhbn. of Springfield Art Assn., 1982, 24th Ann. Nat. Exhbn. of Prints & Drawings, Oklahoma City, 1982, 40th Ann Nat. Juried Print Exhbn., Clinton, N.J., 1996, others; represented in collections.

NOBLE, PHILLIP D., lawyer; b. Oakland, Calif., Aug. 1, 1946. BA, AD in Bus., U. Wash., 1968, JD, 1971. Bar: Wash. 1971. Law clk. to Hon. Morell Sharp Wash. State Supreme Ct., 1971, U.S. Dist. Ct. (we. dist.) Wash., 1972; with Helsell, Fetterman LLP, Seattle. Editor: Justice on Trial, 1971. Mem. ABA, Wash. State Bar Assn., Seattle-King County Bar Assn. Office: Helsell Fetterman LLP 1500 Puget Sound Plz 1325 4th Ave Seattle WA 98101-2509

NOBLE, RICHARD LLOYD, lawyer; b. Oklahoma City, Oct. 11, 1939; s. Samuel Lloyd and Eloise Joyce (Millard) N. AB with distinction, Stanford, 1961, LLB, 1964. Bar: Calif. 1964. Assoc. firm Cooper, White & Cooper, San Francisco, 1965-67; assoc., ptnr. firm Voegelin, Barton, Harris & Callister, Los Angeles, 1967-70; ptnr. Noble & Campbell, Los Angeles, San Francisco, 1970—; dir. Langdale Corp., L.A., Gt. Pacific Fin. Co., Sacramento; lectr. Tax Inst. U. So. Calif., 1970; mem. bd. law and bus. program Stanford Law Sch. Contbr. articles to legal jours. Bd. govs. St. Thomas Aquinas Coll. Recipient Hilmer Dehlman Jr. award Stanford Law Sch., 1962; Benjamin Harrison fellow Stanford U., 1967. Mem. ABA, State Bar Calif., L.A. Bar Assn., San Francisco Bar Assn., Commercial Club (San Francisco), Petroleum Club (L.A.), Capitol Hill Club (Washington), Pi Sigma Alpha. Republican. Home: 2222 Ave Of Stars Los Angeles CA 90067-5655 Office: Noble & Campbell 333 N Grand Ave Los Angeles CA 90012-2622

NOBLIT, BETTY JEAN, publishing technician; b. St. Elmo, Ill., June 12, 1948; d. Clyde W. and Lucille M. (Haggard) N. Grad. in restaurant and club food mgmt., LaSalle U., 1973; grad., Am. Sch. Travel, 1975. Teletype puncher Sarasota (Fla.) Herald-Tribune, 1968-70, Pueblo Chieftain, 1970—; unified composer; pagination operator Star Jour. Pub. Co., Pueblo, Colo.; personal corr. Prime Min. Indira Gandhi. Sec. Pueblo Chieftain and Star-Journal Credit Union. Mem. Nat. Geog. Soc., Colo. Hist. Soc., Pueblo Hist. Soc. Home: 1 Cambridge Ave Apt 4B Pueblo CO 81005-2024

NOETH, LOUISE ANN, journalist; b. Evergreen Park, Ill., Nov. 17, 1954; d. Cy John and Alice Rose (Bobrovich) N.; m. Michael T. Lanigan, Aug. 29, 1992. Editor Petersen Pub. Co., Inc., Calif., 1980; assoc. pub., editor Autoscene Mag., Westlake Village, Calif., 1981; investigative editor Four Wheeler Mag., Canoga Park, Calif., 1982—; owner, founder Landspeed Productions, 1985—; automotive writer, columnist Press-Courier Newspaper, Oxnard, Calif., 1992-94, Ventura County Newspapers, 1994-95, L.A. Times, 1995; Car Craft Mag., 1994—; with EG&G, Inc., 1992; auto writer, columnist Ventura County Newspapers, 1994-95; adminstr. Spirit of Am. World Land Speed Record Team, 1996—; cons. Spirit Am. World Speed Record Team, Pontiac Motor divsn. Land Rover N.Am., others; mem. Green Mamba Racing Team, Reseda, Calif., 1978—; graphic art commns. for Wallenius Lines, Harbortown Resort, GTE, Ferro Corp., Nikon Profl. Svcs., Kodak Profl. Network, Forbes mag., SEA, Sailing. Author: Ventura County Destination Guide: Channel Islands Harbor Retrospect; editor: Hot Rod Performance and Custom, 1979; prodr.: Renewing Pride, Schoolroom in Paradise, Heritage Square; contbr. articles to numerous automotive mags.; photography exhibited at Ventura Village Art Gallery, 1994, Ventura County Mus. History and Art, 1991, Ventura County Nat. Bank, 1990, 92, Ventura County Fair, 1990 (spl. non-competition award profl. category), The New-West, 1996; represented in permanent collection Harbor Town Marina Resort Gallery. Mem. project R.A.F.T. Russians and Ams. for Teamwork, Buffalo Bill's West Show; mem. bd. dirs., pub. chair Carnegie Art Mus., 1995—. Recipient Moto award in investigative news category, Automotive Journalism Conference, 1983-84, 86. Mem. Tallship Californian Quarter deck Comm., Oxnard C. of C., Edn. Comm. Youth Edn. Motivation Program, Internat. Motor Press Assn. (sec. 1986—), Specialty Equipment Market Assn. (pub. relations com. 1983, suspension and tire com. 1984-85), Am. Auto Racing Writers and Broadcasters Assn.

NOHRDEN, PATRICK THOMAS, lawyer; b. Santa Cruz, Calif., Mar. 7, 1956; s. Thomas Allen and Roberta Eugenia (Brydon) N.; m. Debora Ann Heintz, Sept. 19, 1981; children: Steven, Laura, Maranda, Patricia. AS, SUNY, Albany, 1980; BA in English, San Jose State U., 1984; JD, U. Akron, 1992. Bar: Nev. 1993, U.S. Dist. Ct. Nev. 1993. Regional dir. CareerPro, Inc., Roseville, Calif., 1984-91; cons. Patrick T. Nohrden & Assocs., Youngstown, Ohio, 1991-93; pvt. practice, Las Vegas, Nev., 1993 ; bd. dirs. Profl. Resume Svc., Inc., Las Vegas, Las Vegas Diamondbacks, Inc., Old Nev. Fin., Inc., Las Vegas. Sgt. U.S. Army, 1975-81. Recipient Spirit of Pro Bono award. Mem. ATLA, ABA (family law sect.), Fed. Bar Assn., Nev. Trial Lawyers Assn., State Bar Nev. (family law and bankruptcy sects.), Clark County Bar Assn., Phi Kappa Phi. Republican. Roman Catholic. Office: 608 S 8th St Las Vegas NV 89101

NOKES, JOHN RICHARD, retired newspaper editor, author; b. Portland, Oreg., Feb. 23, 1915; s. James Abraham and Bernice Alfaretta (Bailey) N.; m. Evelyn Junkin, Sept. 13, 1936; children: Richard Gregory, William G., Gail (Mrs. William M. Hulden), Douglas J., Kathy E. B.S., Linfield Coll., 1936, LHD (hon.), 1988. With The Oregonian, Portland, 1936-82, city editor, 1950-65, asst. mng. editor, 1965-71, mng. editor, 1971-75, editor, 1975-82; disting. vis. prof. journalism Linfield Coll., 1982-85; cons. editor The Hong Kong Standard, 1994. Author: American Form of Government, 1939, Columbia's River: The Voyages of Robert Gray 1787-1793, 1991; editor Oreg. Edn. Jour., 1944. Bd. dirs. Portland U.S.O., 1968-72, U.S. Coast Guard Acad. Found., 1972-74, Portland Opera Assn., 1976-78; trustee Linfield Coll., 1977-93; v.p. Oreg. UN Assn., 1983-85, chmn. Oreg. UN Day, 1983. Lt. (j.g.) USNR, 1944-46; comdr. Res. (ret.). Mem. Navy League U.S. (pres. Portland coun. 1969-71), Linfield Coll. Alumni Assn. (pres. 1940), World Affairs Coun. Oreg. (pres. 1973-74), AP Mng. Editors Assn. (dir. 1973-80), Am. Soc. Newspaper Editors, N.W. China Coun., Sigma Delta Chi (pres. Willamette Valley chpt. 1975-76). Republican. Methodist. Club: Multnomah Athletic (Portland). Home: 14650 SW 103rd Ave Tigard OR 97224-4740

NOLAN, JAMES MICHAEL, fire chief; b. Orlando, Fla., Sept. 30, 1943; s. James Douglas and Marjorie Kathleen (Rouse) N.; m. Patricia Ann Fenwick Nolan, Jan. 31, 1969; children: Michael Douglas, Teresa Kathleen. AA in Fire Sci., U. Alaska, 1977; exec. fire officer, Nat. Fire Acad., 1993. Hazardous Materials Incident Mgr. Fed. Emergency Mgmt. Agency. Computer technician KLM Office Machines, Anchorage, Alaska, 1969-73; firefighter Anchorage Fire Dept., 1973-76, fire apparatus engr., 1976-80, fire capt., 1980-84, sr. fire capt., 1984-86, battalion chief, tng., 1986-88, battalion chief, 1988, deputy chief, chief of ops., 1988-94, fire chief, 1994—; chmn. Anchorage Police & Fire Ret. Bd., 1982; mem. Anchorage Regional Fire Tng. Ctr. Bd., 1984-89; mem. State of Alaska Fire Svc. Tng. award Com., 1986-90; adj. instr. in Fire Sci. U. Alaska, Anchorage, 1982-85. Contbr. articles and photographs to book. Chmn. 457 Deferred Compensation Bd., Anchorage, 1995—; mem . Local Chpt. Am. Red Cross, 1995—; mem. Emergency Planning Commn., 1995, Environ. Quality Control Com., 1994—. Mem. Nat. Fire Protection Assn., Alaska State Fire Chiefs Assn., Internat. Assn. of Fire Chiefs, Anchorage Area Interagnecy Emergency Mgmt. Assn. (pres. 1994—). Office: Anchorage Fire Dept 1301 E 80th Ave Anchorage AK 99518-3308*

NOLAN, MARK GREGORY, advertising executive; b. San Francisco, July 3, 1958; m. Robyn Lynn Nolan, June 7, 1980. Founder, chief exec. officer Mark Nolan & Assocs., Inc., Citrus Heights, Calif., 1981-87; v.p., ptnr. Nolan Mktg. Group Inc., Citrus Heights, 1987—; mktg. dir., ptnr. Fin. Mktg. Corp., Citrus Heights, 1989—; keynote speaker Marin Self-Pubs. Assn., Ross, Calif., 1986; featured speaker Community Entrepreneurs Assn., Sacramento, 1986, home-based bus. conf., 1991; treas. COSMEP, San Francisco, 1986-88; lectr. UCLA, 1987. Author: The Instant Marketing Plan, 1995; editor: Info. Mktg., 1985-87. Mem. Better Bus. Bur., Eagle Scouts. Mem. S.C. Publicists Assn., Community Entrepreneurs Assn., Internat. Assn. Self-Pubs. (treas. 1986-88), Com. of Small Mag. Editors and Pubs., C. of C., Turtles, Oregon Advt. Club, Entrepreneurs Am., Active 20-30 Club. Office: Nolan Mktg Group Inc PO Box 2570 Fair Oaks CA 95628-9570

NOLAN, ROBERT R., mayor. Mayor City of Upland, Calif. Office: City of Upland 460 N Euclid Ave Upland CA 91786

NOLAN, RUTH MARIE, writer; b. San Bernardino, Calif., Nov. 13, 1962; d. Joseph Michael and Beverly Sue (Pinkerton) N.; 1 child, Tarah Jo. AA in Liberal Arts, Victor Valley Coll., 1985; BA in English, Calif. State U., San Bernardino, 1988; MA in English, No. Ariz. U., 1995. Cert. cmty. and secondary tchr., Calif., Ariz. Wildland firefighter U.S. Forest Svc., Big Bear Road, Calif., 1982-85; with Bur. Land Mgmt., Apple Valley, Calif., 1986-87; tchr. English Victor Valley HSD, Victorville, Calif., 1989-91, South Mountain H.S., Phoenix, 1991-93; instr. English No. Ariz. U., Flagstaff, 1993-95; writer Victorville, 1995—. Author numerous poems. Mem.. Calif. State U. Alumni Assn., No. Ariz. U. Alumni Assn., Phi Kappa Phi. Home: 19455 Corwin Road Apple Valley CA 92307

NOLLE, RICHARD, writer, astrological consultant; b. Orlando, Fla., Mar. 13, 1950; s. Frank Richard and Jeannie (Gilham) N.; m. Maria Barbara Standish, Sept. 29, 1974; children: Dylan R., Jonah B. BA, U. Fla., 1971. Cert. profl. astrologer Am. Fedn. Astrologers. Urban planner Planning Office of Orange County, Orlando, 1971-73; free-lance astrolog. cons. Orlando, 1973-84; free-lance writer, columnist Dell Pub. Co. Horoscope Mag., N.Y.C., 1975-92; editor Am. Fedn. Astrol. Rsch. Jour., Tempe, Ariz., 1984-86, Star*Tech Mag., Tempe, 1987-89; feature writer, cons. numerous nat. periodicals, Tempe, 1984—. Author: Critical Astrology, 1981, Chiron, 1983, Interpreting Astrology, 1986; co-author: Astrology of the Macrocosm, 1990; webmaster astropro World Wide Website, 1996—. Mem. Assn. for Astrol. Networking (chmn. legal com. 1989-90). Office: PO Box 26599 Tempe AZ 85285-6599

NOLTE, JOHN MICHAEL, lawyer, consultant; b. England, Mar. 20, 1941; s. Ernest H. Nolte and Katheryn A. (Reinhart) Robertson; m. S.K. Marren (div. 1979); children: Stephanie Ann, Jennifer Lee, Sarah Sookwang; m. Diane L. Staufenbeil, Apr. 1982. BS, Ariz. State U., Tempe, 1963; MBA in Fin., U. Calif., Berkeley, JD, 1966. Bar: Oreg. 1966, Calif. 1973. Assoc. Keane, Haessler, Bauman & Harper, Portland, Oreg., 1966-71; assoc. gen. counsel Boise Cascade Corp., Palo Alto, Calif., 1972-73, Larwin Group, L.A., 1973-74; mng. ptnr. Leahy, O'Dea & Givens, San Francisco, 1974-81; pvt. practice law and cons. Canterbury and Tunbridge Wells, Eng., 1981-88, Montecito, Calif., 1988—; assoc. mng. dir. Staufenbeil Co., A.G., Boppard, Germany; officer Larwin Co., Encino, Calif.; mem. adv. bd. dirs. ID, Inc., Savo Electronics Divsn., Corvallis, Oreg. Hon. mem. East Sussex Conservative Party, Buxted, Eng., 1986—; pres. Glen Oaks Comty. Assn., Montecito, 1990-92; bd. trustees Castaic Union Edn. Found. With USMC, 1960-66; lt. comdr. USNR, 1966-70. Mem. ABA, Calif. Bar Assn., Oreg. Bar Assn., L.A. Bar Assn., Am. Judicature Soc., Order of Coif, Phi Kappa Phi. Republican. Home: 167 Pomar Ln Montecito CA 93108-2631 Office: PO Box 5493 Santa Barbara CA 93150-5493

NOLTE, SCOTT LLOYD, artistic director, actor; b. Aberdeen, Wash., Oct. 13, 1954; s. Lloyd Lester and Jaquelyn Fern (Edwards) N.; m. Pamela Baldwin Bailey, Aug. 17, 1974; children: Peter, Lisa. BA in Dramatic Arts, Seattle Pacific U., 1976. Artistic dir. Taproot Theatre Co., Seattle, 1976—; adj. faculty Seattle Pacific U., 1980-82, comml. actor. Pres. Greenwood C. of C., Seattle, 1992. Recipient Alumni Medallion award Seattle Pacific U., 1979, Howard E. Cummings Meml. award Greenwood C. of C. Presbyterian. Office: Taproot Theatre Co 204 N 85th St Seattle WA 98103-3604

NOONAN, DANIEL CHRISTOPHER, consultant; b. Conn., Dec. 17, 1950; s. Daniel Alexander and Eleanor Noonan; children: Erin, Teresa, Sean, Beth. Student, Loyola U., L.A., 1971. Project mgr. Loyola U., L.A., 1968-71; prin. CBIS, L.A., 1969-71; dir. Continental Airlines, L.A., 1971-82; sr. mgr. Coopers & Lybrand, L.A., 1982-84; sr. v.p. Security Pacific Corp., Denver and San Diego, 1984-90; chief info. officer Com Systems, L.A., 1991; exec. cons. The Genessee Group, Thousand Oaks, Calif., 1991—. Address: 1144 El Monte Ave Thousand Oaks CA 91362

NOONAN, EDWARD JAMES, student activity director; b. Butte, Mont., Mar. 11, 1949; s. Edward J. and Sara L. (McCartan) N. BA in Speech, Lewis U., 1971; MA in Speech (Theatre), Ball State U., 1983. Tchr. Cantwell High Sch., Montebello, Calif., 1971-75, Brother Rice High Sch., Chgo., 1975-79; dir., performer After Church Players, Helena, Mont., 1979—, Last Chance Storytellers, Helena, Mont., 1979—; resident dir. Carroll Coll., Helena, Mont., 1986-90, student activity dir., 1990—, adj. theatre prof., 1986—; bd. dirs. Grandstreet Theatre, Helena. Author: (play) War of the Copper Kings, 1989, Warren Street House, 1992, Frontier Justice, 1994, Taking History, 1995, Quartet, Edinburg Theatre Festival, 1997. Chmn. Spring Meadow Resources, Helena, 1994—. Recipient award to publish (book of poetry) Fresh Recognition, 1994, (novel) Missing Pieces, 1994; playwrighting fellow Mont. Arts Coun., 1995. Democrat. Roman Catholic. Home: 409 Dearborn Ave Helena MT 59601-6146 Office: Carroll Coll Box 102 Carroll Coll Helena MT 59625

NOONAN, JOHN T., JR., federal judge, legal educator; b. Boston, Oct. 24, 1926; s. John T. and Marie (Shea) N., m. Mary Lee Bennett, Dec. 27, 1967; children: John Kenneth, Rebecca Lee, Susanna Bain. B.A., Harvard U., 1946, LL.B., 1954; student, Cambridge U., 1946-47; M.A., Cath. U. Am., 1949, Ph.D., 1951, LHD, 1980; LL.D., U. Santa Clara, 1974, U. Notre Dame, 1976, Loyola U. South, 1978; LHD, Holy Cross Coll., 1980; LL.D., St. Louis U., 1981, U. San Francisco, 1985; student, Holy Cross Coll., 1980, Cath. U. Am., 1980, Gonzaga U., 1986, U. San Francisco, 1986. Bar: Mass. 1954, U.S. Supreme Ct. 1971. Mem. spl. staff Nat. Security Council, 1954-55; pvt. practice Herrick & Smith, Boston, 1955-60; prof. law U. Notre Dame, 1961-66; prof. law U. Calif., Berkeley, 1967-86, chmn. religious studies, 1970-73, chmn. medieval studies, 1978-79; judge U.S. Ct. Appeals (9th cir.), San Francisco, 1985—; Oliver Wendell Holmes, Jr. lectr. Harvard U. Law Sch., 1972, Pope John XXIII lectr. Cath. U. Law Sch., 1973, Cardinal Bellarmine lectr. St. Louis U. Div. Sch., 1973, Baum lectr. U. Ill., 1988, Strassberger lectr. U. Tex., 1989; chmn. bd. Games Rsch., Inc., 1961-76; overseer Harvard U., 1991—. Author: The Scholastic Analyst of Usury, 1957; Contraception: A History of Its Treatment by the Catholic Theologians and Canonists, 1965; Power to Dissolve, 1972; Persons and Masks of the Law, 1976; The Antelope, 1977; A Private Choice, 1979; Bribes, 1984; editor: Natural Law Forum, 1961-70, Am. Jour. Jurisprudence, 1970, The Morality of Abortion, 1970. Chmn. Brookline Redevel. Authority, Mass., 1958-62; cons. Papal Commn. on Family, 1965-66, Ford Found., Indonesian Legal Program, 1968; NIH, 1973, NIH, 1974; expert Presdl. Commn. on Population and Am. Future, 1971; cons. U.S. Cath. Conf., 1979-86; sec., treas. Inst. for Research in Medieval Canon Law, 1970-88; pres. Thomas More-Jacques Maritain Inst., 1977—; trustee Population Council, 1969-76, Phi Kappa Found., 1970-76, Grad. Theol. Union, 1970-73, U. San Francisco, 1971-75; mem. com. theol. edn. Yale U., 1972-77; exec. com. Cath. Commn. Intellectual and Cultural Affairs, 1972-75; bd. dirs. Ctr. for Human Values in the Health Scis., 1969-71, S.W. Intergroup Relations Council, 1970-72, Inst. for Study Ethical Issues, 1971-73. Recipient St. Thomas More award U. San Francisco, 1974, Christian Culture medal, 1975, Laetare medal U. Notre Dame, 1984, Campion medal Cath. Book Club, 1987; Guggenheim fellow, 1965-66, 79-80, Laetare medal U. Notre Dame, 1984, Campion medal, 1987, Alemany medal Western Dominican Province, 1988; Ctr. for advanced Studies in Behavioral Scis. fellow, 1973-74; Wilson Ctr. fellow, 1979-80. Fellow Am. Acad. Arts and Scis., Am. Soc. Legal Historians (hon.); mem. Am. Soc. Polit. and Legal Philosophy (v.p. 1964), Canon Law Soc. Am. (gov. 1970-72), Am. Law Inst., Phi Beta Kappa (senator United chpts. 1970-72, pres. Alpha of Calif. chpt. 1972-73). Office: US Ct Appeals 9th Cir 121 Spear St San Francisco CA 94103*

NOORDA, RAYMOND J., computer software company executive; b. Ogden, Utah.. BSEE, Utah, 1949. CEO Novell Inc., 1982—; chmn. MTI

Inc, Anaheim, Calif. Office: MTI Technology Corp 4905 E La Palma Ave Anaheim CA 92807-1915*

NOORZOY, MOHAMMAD SIDDIEQ, economist, educator; b. Kabul, Afghanistan, July 5, 1934; came to the U.S., 1954; s. Noor Ul and Bibi Aisha Haq; m. V. Elizabeth Haviside, Aug. 30, 1957 (div. 1984); children: Shah Hamid, Aisha Aryana, Zia Jamal; m. Farkhunda Fakhri, Mar. 30, 1990; 1 child, Zala Farkhunda. BA, U. Calif., Berkeley, 1957, MA, 1960; PhD, U. Wash., 1965. Instr. U. Calif., U. Wash., Berkeley, 1959-63; mem. rsch. dept. Fed. Res. Bank San Francisco, 1963; asst. prof. Calif. State U., San Luis Obispo, 1963-64; asst. prof. U. Alberta, 1965-69, assoc. prof., 1971-80, prof., 1981-87, emeritus prof. econs., 1988—; rsch. assoc. inst. internat. studies U. Calif., Berkeley, 1986-90; vis. scholar Hoover Instn. Stanford U., 1984, 91; adj. prof. Naval Postgrad. Sch., Monterey, Calif., 1989-90; fellow Ctr. for Middle Eastern Studies U. Calif., Berkeley, 1992—. Contbr. articles to profl. jours. Pres. Afghanistan Assistance Coun. Grantee Earhart Found., 1986-87; recipient rsch. award in humanities and social scis. Can. Coun., 1969-70; scholar U. Wash., 1961-62. Mem. Am. Econ. Assn., Middle East Studies Assn., Western Econ. Assn. Home: 3070 Lopez Rd Pebble Beach CA 93953-2930

NOPAR, ALAN SCOTT, lawyer; b. Chgo., Nov. 14, 1951; s. Myron E. and Evelyn R. (Millman) N. BS, U. Ill., 1976; JD, Stanford U., 1979. Bar: Ariz. 1979, U.S. Dist. Ct. Ariz. 1980, U.S. Ct. Appeals (9th cir.) 1980, U.S. Supreme Ct. 1982, Calif. 1989; CPA, Ill. Assoc. O'Connor, Cavanagh, Anderson, Westover, Killingsworth & Beshears P.A., Phoenix, 1979-85, ptnr., 1985-87; of counsel Tower, Byrne & Beaugureau, Phoenix, 1987-88; ptnr. Minutillo & Gorman, San Jose, Calif., 1989-91, Bosco, Blau, Ward & Nopar, San Jose, 1991-96; exec. v.p., gen. counsel, dir. AmeriNet Fin. Systems, Inc., Ontario, Calif., 1996—. Mem. Ariz. Rep. Caucus, Phoenix, 1984-88. Mem. AICPA, ABA (bus. law and law practice mgmt. sects., mem. forum com. on franchising), Ariz. Bar Assn. (bus. law sect.), Calif. State Bar Assn. (bus. law sect.). Office: AmeriNet Fin Systems Inc 2166 The Alameda San Jose CA 95126-1144

NORA, JAMES JACKSON, physician, author, educator; b. Chgo., June 26, 1928; s. Joseph James and May Henrietta (Jackson) N.; m. Barbara June Fluhrer, Sept. 7, 1949 (div. 1963); children: Wendy Alison, Penelope Welbon, Marianne Leslie; m. Audrey Faye Hart, Apr. 9, 1966; children: James Jackson Jr., Elizabeth Hart Nora. AB, Harvard U., 1950; MD, Yale U., 1954; MPH, U. Calif., Berkeley, 1978. Intern Detroit Receiving Hosp., 1954-55; resident in pediatrics U. Wis. Hosps., Madison, 1959-61, fellow in cardiology, 1962-64; fellow in genetics McGill U. Children's Hosp., Montreal, Can., 1964-65; assoc. prof. pediatrics Baylor Coll. Medicine, Houston, 1965-71; prof. genetics, preventive medicine and pediatrics U. Colo. Med. Sch., Denver, 1971—; dir. genetics Rose Med. Ctr., Denver, 1980—; dir. pediatric cardiology and cardiovascular tng. U. Colo. Sch. Medicine, 1971-78; mem. task force Nat. Heart and Lung Program, Bethesda, Md., 1973; cons. WHO, Geneva, 1983—; mem. U.S.-U.S.S.R. Exchange Program on Heart Disease, Moscow and Leningrad, 1975. Author: The Whole Heart Book, 1980, 2d rev. edit., 1989; (with F.C. Fraser) Medical Genetics, 4th rev. edit., 1994, Genetics of Man, 2d rev. edit., 1986, Cardiovascular Diseases: Genetics, Epidemiology and Prevention, 1991; (novels) The Upstart Spring, 1989, The Psi Delegation, 1989, The Hemingway Sabbatical, 1996. Com. mem. March of Dimes, Am. Heart Assn., Boy Scouts Am. Served to lt. USAAC, 1945-47. Grantee Nat. Heart, Lung and Blood Inst., Nat. Inst. Child Health and Human Devel., Am. Heart Assn., NIH; recipient Virginia Apgar Meml. award. Fellow Am. Coll. Cardiology, Am. Acad. Pediatrics, Am. Coll. Med. Genetics; mem. Am. Pediatric Soc., Soc. Pediatric Rsch., Am. Heart Assn., Teratology Soc., Transplantation Soc., Am. Soc. Human Genetics, Authors Guild, Authors League, Acad. Am. Poets, Mystery Writers Am., Rocky Mountain Harvard Club. Democrat. Presbyterian.

NORBECK, JANE S., nursing educator; b. Redfield, S.D., Feb. 20, 1942; d. Sterling M. and Helen L. (Williamson) N.; m. Paul J. Gorman, June 28, 1970; 1 child Sara J. Gorman. BA in Psychology, U. Minn., 1965, BSN, 1965; MS, U. Calif., San Francisco, 1971, DNSc, 1975. Psychiat. nurse Colo. Psychiat. Hosp., Denver, 1965-66, Langley Porter Hosp., San Francisco, 1966-67; pub. health nurse San Francisco Health Dept., 1968-69; prof. U. Calif. (San Francisco) Sch. of Nursing, 1975—, dept. chair, 1984-89, dean, 1989—; chair study sect. Nat. Inst. of Nursing Rsch., 1990-93, mem. editl. bd. Archives of Psychiat. Nursing, 1985-95, Rsch. in Nursing and Health, 1987—. Co-editor: Annual Review of Nursing Research, 1996-97; contbr. articles to profl. jours. Mem. ANA, Am. Acad. Nursing, Am. Orgn. Nursing Exec., Am. Assn. Coll. Nursing, Inst. of Medicine, Sigma Theta Tau. Office: U Calif Sch Nursing 501 Parnassus Ave San Francisco CA 94122-2722

NORBY, CHRISTOPHER, mayor; b. Fullerton, Calif., Dec. 3, 1949; m. Charlotte Norby; 1 child. BA in Religious Studies, Occidental Coll., 1972; MA in History, Calif. State U., Fullerton, 1989. With Fullerton Transp. Commn., Fullerton Bicentennial Commn.; jr. high sch. tchr. Brea-Olinda Unified Sch. Dist.; mem. City Coun. of Fullerton, since 1984; mayor City of Fullerton, 1990—; bd. govs. Occidental Coll. Active Titan Athletic Found., Amnesty Internat., Fullerton First Presbyn Ch. Mem. Pres.'s Circle Calif. State U. Fullerton, Fullerton C. of C. Office: Office of Mayor 303 W Commonwealth Ave Fullerton CA 92632-1710*

NORBY-LOUD, MARIE BARBARA, secondary education educator; b. Chgo., Sept. 14, 1947; d. Walter Carl and Emma Dell (Fowler) Norby; m. Robert Thiel, Mar. 17, 1967 (div. Dec. 1988); children: William, Steven, Christopher; m. Bennie Lee Loud, Mar. 20, 1992. BS, U. Minn., 1985; MA, U. No. Colo., 1991, EdD, 1996. Cert. English and lang. arts, Minn.; cert. fgn. lang., Colo. English instr. Ea. Wyo. Coll., Douglas, 1986-89; tchg. asst. U. No. Colo., Greeley, 1989-91; exec. dir. Right to Read, Greeley, 1991-92; adj. faculty Aims C.C., Greeley, 1992-93; Spanish tchr. R.E. 5J Sch. Dist., Johnstown, Colo., 1993-96; prin. Idalia (Colo.) Schs., 1996—; mem. student fees allocation com. U. No. Colo., Greeley, 1991-93. Mem., v.p. Wyo. Child Care Cert. Adv. Commn., Cheyenne, 1979-82; mem. Planning Commn., Douglas, 1980-82; unit commr. Boy Scouts Ctrl. Wyo. Coun., Casper, 1984-85. Colo. Grad. fellow U. No. Colo., Greeley, 1990. Mem. Phi Delta Kappa, Sigma Tau Delta. Home: PO Box 67 Idalia CO 80735 Office: PO Box 40 Idalia CO 80735

NORCROSS, CATHERINE BELLE, elementary education educator; b. Worcester, Mass., Jan. 20, 1964; d. George Linwood and Edith Marilyn (Tourtellotte) N. BS, Westfield (Mass.) State Coll., 1986; MA, U. Conn., 1990. Tchr. grade 3 Oxford, Mass., 1986-91; tchr. grade 6 Tonopah, Nev., 1991—; chairperson Computers for Kids, Oxford, 1990-91; head girls' varsity softball coach, 1993; mid. sch. volleyball coach, 1992, 94, 95, student coun. advisor, 1993, 94. Mem. NEA, Assn. Supervision and Curriculum Devel., Internat. Reading Assn., Nev. State Ednl. Assn., Nev. Reading Assn., Mass. Tchrs. Assn., Oxford Edn. Assn., Kappa Delta Pi. Home: PO Box 3467 1310 Globemallow # 6A Tonopah NV 89049 Office: Tonopah Mid Sch Utah St Tonopah NV 89049

NORD, HAROLD EMIL, JR., small business owner, consultant; b. Manistee, Mich., Dec. 28, 1928; s. Harold Emil Nord and Anna Margaret (Simmons) Chase; m. Dolores Lillian Matistic, Apr. 26, 1952; children: Harold Emil III, Karen. BS in Hotel Adminstrn., Mich. State U., 1950; M Aero. Sci. Mgmt., Embry-Riddle Aero. U., 1993. Cert. air transport pilot. Capt. Eastern Airlines, Miami, Fla., 1957-88; owner, operator Golden Gate Cottages, Laconia, N.H., 1969-73, Seaplane Svcs., Inc., Laconia, 1969-73; pres. Aviation Mgmt. Advisors, Inc., West Palm Beach, Fla., 1978—; gen. ptnr. Airports Mgmt. Group, Tucson, 1993; bd. dirs. Tucson U.; nat. chmn. Aviators Legal Fund, Inc.; v.p. pub. rels. and govt. affairs Air Boston Airlines; sales and mktg. Alpine Air of Am., Blaine, Minn.; ptnr., dir. Jeriko Corp., Tucson; bd. dirs., founding mem. So. Skies Airgroup, Inc., Tucson, Starship Airlines, Atlanta. Mem. U.S. Rep. Senatorial Club, Washington, 1977—, Futures Group of Palm Beach, 1984, Pundits of Palm Beach, 1983, Safety, Health and Environ. Resource Ctr. Internat., Vets. of Safety, 1993; nat. chmn. com. Postal Commemorative Stamp for Capt. Edward V. Rickenbacker; sr. advisor CAP; v.p. N.E. region Violence Rsch. Found., Tustin, Calif. Named Master Bush Pilot, Ladd Air Force Base, Fairbanks, Alaska, 1955; Paul Harris fellow Palm Beach Rotary Club, 1987—. Mem. Airline Pilots Assn., Internat. Fellowship Flying Rotarians, Mich. State U. Alumni Assn. (pres. Atlanta chpt. 1959-61, pres. N.H. chpt.), Ret. Ea. Pilots Assn., Ea. Airlines Retirees Assn., Early Birds Aviation, Nat. Eagle Scout Assn., Nat. Seaplane Pilots Assn., Nat. Aero. Assn., Exptl. Aircraft Assn., Dadaelians Assn., N.J. Rotary Club, Quiet Birdmen, Toastmasters, Silver Wings Club, Delta Upsilon. Home and Office: Aviation Mgmt Advisors Inc PO Box 425 Rye Beach NH 03871-0425 also: Apt 2502 5200 Poinsettia Ave West Palm Beach FL 33407 also: 5128 E 2nd St Tucson AZ 85711-1309 also: 44 Cocoanut Row A-310 Palm Beach FL 33480

NORD, RICHARD, film editor; b. Bronx, May 3, 1952; s. Jack William N. and Michelline (Couche) Menetrey; m. Lisa Robin Feldman, Aug. 25, 1978 (div. Sept. 1980); m. Sharon Anne Wong, June 3, 1984; children: Sean Alexander, Jason Eric, Lauren Marie. BA, CUNY, 1974; MA, NYU, 1976. Asst. editor Orion Pictures, N.Y.C., 1981-86; assoc. editor Paramount Pictures, N.Y.C., 1986-88; film editor Universal Pictures, N.Y.C., 1988, Warner Bros., L.A., 1993, Metro Golden Mayer, L.A., 1995-96; chmn.health & welfar com. Local 771 IATSE, N.Y.C., 1990-92. Editor: (films) Biloxi Blues, 1988, Working Girl, 1989, A Fine Romance, 1990, Strictly Business, 1991, Veronica & Me, 1992, Passenger 57, 1992, Fugitive, 1993, Renaissance Man, 1993, Getting Away With Murder, 1994-95, Fled, 1995-96. Nominated Eddie award, 1994, British Acad. award, 1994, Acad. award, 1994. Home: 4008 Knobhill Dr Sherman Oaks CA 91403-4617 Office: Metro Golden Mayer 1450 Broadway Santa Monica CA 90404-2712

NORDEL, PATRICIA A. OLMSTEAD, medical/surgical, critical care, and obstetrical nurse; b. New Britain, Conn., Jan. 19, 1965; d. Lester B. and Patricia (Tufts) Olmstead; m. David R. Nordel; children: David M., Dominic X. BSN, U. Conn., 1987. Cert. med.-surg. nurse. Commd. 2d lt. USAF, 1987, advanced through grades to capt., 1991; staff nurse med.-surg. USAF, Scott AFB, Ill., Travis AFB, Calif.; charge nurse outpatient USAF, RAF Greenham Common, Eng.; staff nurse obstetrics USAF, RAF Upper Heyford, Eng., 1987-94; staff nurse Travel Nurse Broker Svc., Napa, Calif., 1994-95; RN Profl. Nursing Svcs., Suisun City, Calif., 1995-96; staff nurse Lake Meade Med. Ctr., Las Vegas, 1996—.

NORDGREN, WILLIAM BENNETT, engineering executive; b. Salt Lake City, Mar. 5, 1960; s. Kent Widstoe and Eliza (Schmuhl) N.; m. Carolyn B. Erickson, June 26, 1981; children: William Tyson, Cameron Lynn. BS, Brigham Young U., 1986, MS, 1989. Engr. Boeing Airplanes Co., Seattle, 1986-88; pres. CIM Engring. Assocs., Orem, Utah, 1988-89; v.p. engring. Prodn. Modeling Corp., Orem, 1989-93; pres. F & H Simulations, Inc., Orem, 1993—. Developer, polar coordinant mill. Mem. Soc. Mfg. Engrs., Inst. Indsl. Engrs. Republican. Mormon. Office: PO Box 658 Orem UT 84059-0658

NORDMEYER, MARY BETSY, vocational educator; b. New Haven, May 19, 1939; d. George and Barbara Stedman (Thompson) N. ABPhil, Wheaton Coll., Norton, Mass., 1960; MA, San Jose State U., 1968; AS in Computer Sci., West Valley Coll., 1985. Cert. tchr. spl. edn., Calif.; cert. secondary tchr., Calif. Instr. English Santa Clara (Calif.) Unified Sch. Dist., 1965-77, vocat. specialist, 1977—, dir. project work ability, 1984—, also mem. community adv. com.; facilitator Project Work-Ability, Region 5, 1985-86, sec., 1988-90. Author poetry, 1960, Career and Vocat. Edn. for Students With Spl. Needs, 1986; author/designer Career English, 1974, Career Information, 1975. Recipient Outstanding Secondary Educator award, 1975, Award of Excellence, Nat. Assn. Vocat. Edn., 1984; named Tchr. of Yr. in Spl. Edn., Santa Clara Unified Sch. Dist., 1984-85. Mem. Calif. Assn. Work Experience Educators, Sierra Club, Epsilon Eta Sigma. Democrat. Home: 14920 Sobey Rd Saratoga CA 95070-6236 Office: Santa Clara Unified Sch Dist 1889 Lawrence Rd Santa Clara CA 95051-2162

NORDSTROM, BRUCE A., department store executive; b. 1933; married. BA, U. Wash., 1956. With Nordstrom, Inc., Seattle, 1956—, v.p., 1964-70, pres., 1970-75, chmn., 1975-77, co-chmn., 1977—, dir. Office: Nordstrom Inc 1501 5th Ave Seattle WA 98101-1603*

NORDSTROM, JOHN N., department store executive; b. 1937; married. BA, U. Wash., 1958. With Nordstrom, Inc., Seattle, 1958—, v.p., 1965-70, exec. v.p., 1970-75, pres., 1975-77, co-chmn., 1977—, dir.; bd. dirs. Fed. Res. Bank San Francisco. Office: Nordstrom Inc 1501 5th Ave Seattle WA 98101-1603*

NOREM, MARGARET ALICE, agronomist, editor; b. Butte, Mont., May 12, 1953; d. William C. and Alice J. (Ellsworth) N.; m. Rick Allen Unklesbay, May 5, 1984; children: Nancy Beth, Laura Meghan. BS in Biology, Ariz. State U., 1975; MS in Agronomy, U. Ariz., 1980, PhD in Agronomy, 1982. Rsch. assoc. dept. plant scis. U. Ariz., Tucson, 1984-85, rsch. assoc. Office Arid Land Studies, 1985-88, rsch. assoc. Biosphere II project Environ. Rsch. Lab., 1986-89, program specialist gen. project Office Internat. Agr. Progs., 1989, rsch. specialist Arboretum Affairs, 1990—, editor Desert Plants-Boyce Thompson Arboretum, 1993—; rsch. assoc. Gambian Mixed Farming project Colo. State U.-The Gambia, Banjul, 1985. Editor jour. Desert Plants, 1993—; contbr. articles to profl. publs. Bd. mem., v.p. fin. Tucson Comty. Sch., 1995-97; bd. mem. Desert Survivors, 1996—. Fellow Office of Surface Mining, Washington and Tucson, 1979-80, 80-81, Rsch. fellow Women in Devel., The Gambia, 1985. Mem. Ariz. Native Plant Soc., Boyce Thompson Southwestern Arboretum. Democrat. Episcopalian. Office: Desert Plants 2120 E Allen Rd Tucson AZ 85719

NORGAARD, RICHARD BRUCE, economist, educator, consultant; b. Washington, Aug. 18, 1943; s. John Trout and Marva Dawn (Andersen) N.; m. Marida Jane Fowle, June 19, 1965 (div.); children—Kari Marie, Marc Anders; m. Nancy A. Rader, June, 5, 1993. B.A. in Econs., U. Calif.-Berkeley, 1965; M.S. in Agrl. Econs. Oreg. State U., 1967; Ph.D. in Econs., U. Chgo., 1971. Instr. Oreg. Coll. Edn., 1967-68; asst. prof. agrl. and resource econs. U. Calif.-Berkeley, 1970-76, assoc. prof., 1976-77, 80-87, assoc. prof. energy and resources, 1987-92, prof. energy and resources, 1992—; project specialist Ford Found., Brazil, 1978-79; cons. Ford Found., Calif. Dept. Water Resources, Pub. Interest Econs., Ind. Petroleum Producers of Calif., Plan Sierra Dominican Republic, UN Food & Agrl. Orgn., UN Environment Program, USAID-Thailand, The World Bank; mem. sci. com. on problems of the environment U.S. Nat. Rsch. Coun. Author: Development Betrayed: The End of Progress and a Coevolutionary Revisioning of the Future, 1994; contbr. numerous articles to acad. jours. Active civil rights, environ, and peace orgns. Mem. AAAS, Assn. Pub. Policy and Mgmt., Latin Am. Studies Assn., Am. Econs. Assn., Internat. Soc. Ecol. Econs. (pres.-elect, chmn. bd. redefining progress), Fedn. Am. Scientists, Assn. Environ. and Resource Econs. Home: 1198 Keith Ave Berkeley CA 94708-1607 Office: U Calif Energy & Resources Program 310 Barrows Berkeley CA 94720-3050

NORIEGA, DOROTHY LORRAINE, nursing educator; b. San Bernardino, Calif., Jan. 9, 1927; d. Emmett C. and Dagmar D. (Nelson) Hert; m. William E. Noriega; children: Robert, Lynda, Merridee. AA, San Bernardino Valley Coll., 1961; BS, Loma Linda U., 1968; MS, Calif. State U., L.A., 1972. Staff nurse psychiatry Patton (Calif.) State Hosp., 1961-62, unit supr., 1962-64, supr. nurse psychiatry, 1964-66, dir. psychiatric edn., 1966-68; cons. mental health State of Calif., Sacramento, 1968-76; coord. nursing Patton State Hosp., 1976-79, dir. nursing, 1979-81; dir. nursing Lanternon Behavioral Ctr., Pomona, Calif., 1981-87; instr. psychiatric nursing San Bernardino (Calif.) Valley Coll., 1987—; v.p. adv. bd. Mental Health Soc., San Bernardino, 1980-92; mem. adv. bd. U.A.W., San Bernardino, 1989-90; vol. RSVP, Ojai, Calif., 1990—. Col. ARC, 1993; bd. dirs. Vis. Nurses Assn., Riverside, Calif., 1979; vol. tchr. Am. Cancer Soc., 1980. Democrat. Mem. LDS Ch. Home: 304 Topa Topa Dr Ojai CA 93023-3232

NORKIN, MARK MITCHELL, sales executive; b. Whittier, Calif., Nov. 19, 1955; s. Cleo Donald and Carol Ann (Stewart) Mathis. Grad., Gemmological Inst. Am., 1976. Gemmologist Slavicks Jewelers, Newport Beach, Calif., 1976-77; apprentice Troy Sheet Metal Works, Montebello, Calif., 1977-79, journeyman, 1979-80, foreman, 1980-82, project engr., 1982-85, v.p. sales and engring., 1985—; bd. dirs. Troy Sheet Metal. Republican. Office: 1026 S Vail Ave Montebello CA 90640-6020

NORLING, LLOYD IVER, insurance agency owner; b. Mpls., July 3, 1934; s. Albert Arvid and Lillian Frances (Pehrson) N.; m. Janice Ilene Sandberg, Feb. 11, 1962; 1 child, Deidre Kae. MBA, U. Beverly Hills, 1982. Installer Western Electric, Mpls., 1953-64; cons. Proudfoot, Chgo., 1964-66; staff engr. Wofac, Palo Alto, Calif., 1966-69; dir. mdsg. Mode O'Day, Burbank, Calif., 1969-80; owner Lloyd's Fin. Svcs., Vacaville, Calif., 1982—. With U.S. Army, 1956-58. Fellow IOOF (sec. 1996-97); mem. C. of C. (treas. 1993-94, dir. 1994-97, pres. 1995-96), Rotary (charter pres. 1991-93, Paul Harris fellow 1994). Republican. Lutheran. Home: 4100 Orchard Canyon Ln Vacaville CA 95688

NORMAN, ARNOLD MCCALLUM, JR., engineer; b. Little Rock, May 1, 1940; s. Arnold McCallum and Ann Carolyn (Gibson) N.; m. Sylvia Burton, July 1, 1962 (div. 1967); m. Marisha Irene Malin, June 7, 1969; children: Frank Lee, Paul James. BS in Physics, Ga. Inst. Tech., 1962. Test engr. Rocketdyne div. Rockwell Internat., Canoga Park, Calif., 1962-64, engr. in charge of various programs, 1964-75, engr. in charge, project engr. large chem. lasers, 1975-85, project engr. space sta. propulsion system, 1985-87, project engr. nat. launch system health mgmt. systems, 1987-92, project engr. kinetic energy weapons, 1993-94; project engr. advanced propulsion systems Rockwell Internat., Canoga Park, Calif., 1994-95, sr. engring. specialist, 1995-96; health mgmt. sys. team head, x-33 Aerospike rocket engine Boeing-N.Am. Rocketdyne Divsn., Canoga Park, Calif., 1996-97; cons. rocket propulsion sys., ops. and health mgmt., 1997—; mem. ops. com. health mgmt. ctr. U. Cin., 1988-94; mem. program com. Ann. Internat. Conf. on Engring. Applications of Artificial Intelligence, 1988-90; presenter in field. Mem. editorial bd. Jour. Applied Intelligence, 1990-94; author numerous papers in field. Fellow AIAA (assoc., sect. chair sr. adv. com. 1991-93, San Fernando Valley sect., chmn. 1989-90, sys. effectiveness & safety com. 1995—), Inst. Advancement Engring; mem. Tau Beta Pi. Home: 4053 Bones Rd Sebastopol CA 95472

NORMAN, DANIEL WILEY, computer technician, programmer; b. High Point, N.C., June 20, 1961; s. Jerry William and Christine Eugenia (Steed) N.; m. Debra Kloss, June 23, 1984; children: Thomas William, Kathryn Elizabeth. BS in Math., Mars Hill Coll., 1986. Data control lead Tymshare, Garden Grove, Calif., 1982-84; sys. technician GI Trucking Co., La Mirada, Calif., 1986-95; LAN adminstr. Union Pacific R.R., 1995—; scorekeeper/programmer NRA/Charlton Heston Celebrity Shoot, Irvine, Calif., 1993, 94; owner A.H.C. Computer Solutions, La Mirada, 1993—. Ind. instr. gun safety, Whittier, Calif., 1993—. Mem. IEEE, NRA (instr.), Gun Owner's Action Com. Republican. Baptist. Office: PO Box 10 La Mirada CA 90637-0010

NORMAN, E. GLADYS, business computer educator, consultant; b. Oklahoma City, June 13, 1933; d. Joseph Eldon and Mildred Lou (Truitt) Biggs; m. Joseph R.R. Radeck, Mar. 1, 1953 (div. Aug. 1962); children: Jody Matti, Ray Norman, Warren Norman (dec. May 1993), Dana Norman; m. Leslie P. Norman, Aug. 26, 1963 (dec. Feb. 1994); 1 child, Elayne Pearce. Student, Fresno (Calif.) State Coll., 1951-52, UCLA, 1956-59, Linfield Coll., 1986-95. Math. aid U.S. Naval Weapons Ctr., China Lake, Calif., 1952-56, computing systems specialist, 1957-68; systems programmer Oreg. Motor Vehicles Dept., Salem, 1968-69; instr. in data processing, dir. Computer Programming Ctr., Salem, 1969-72; instr. in data processing Merritt-Davis Bus. Coll., Salem, 1972-73; sr. programmer, analyst Teledyne Wah Chang, Albany, Oreg., 1973-79; sr. systems analyst Oreg. Dept. Vets. Affairs, Albany, 1979-80; instr. in bus. computers Linn-Benton Community Coll., Albany, 1980-95; ret., 1995; computer cons. for LBCC Ret. Sr. Vol. Program, 1995—; presenter computer software seminars State of Oreg., 1991-93, Oreg. Credit Assoc. Conf., 1991, Oreg. Regional Users Group Conf., 1992; computer tchr. Linn-Benton C.C., 1996-97; computer cons. Oremet Titanium, 1996-97; computer cons. in field. Mem. Data Processing Mgmt. Assn. (bd. dirs. 1977-84, 89-95, region sect. 1995-96, assoc. v.p. 1988, Diamond Individual Performance award 1985). Democrat.

NORMAN, JOHN BARSTOW, JR., designer, educator; b. Paloa, Kans., Feb. 5, 1940; s. John B. and Ruby Maxine (Johnson) N.; m. Roberta Jeanne Martin, June 6, 1967; children: John Barstow III, Elizabeth Jeanne. BFA, U. Kans., 1962, MFA, 1966. Designer and illustrator Advt. Design, Kansas City, Mo., 1962-64; asst. instr. U. Kans., Lawrence, 1964-66; art dir. Hallmark Cards, Inc., Kansas City, Mo., 1966-69; instr. dept. art U. Denver, 1969-73, asst. prof., 1973-78, assoc. prof., 1978-93, Disting. prof., 1980 , prof. emeritus, 1993—; sr. designer Mo. Coun. Arts and Humanities, 1966-67; cons. designer Rocky Mountain Bank Note Corp., Denver, 1971—, Signage Identity System, U. Denver; bd. dirs. communications U. Denver; tech. cons. Denver Art Mus., 1974—, designed exhbns., 1974-75; adv., cons. Jefferson County (Colo.) Sch., System, 1976—; chmn. Design and Sculpture Exhbn., Colo. Celebration of the Arts, 1975-76. One man shows include: Gallery Cortina, Aspen, Colo., 1983; commd. works include: Jedda, Saudi Arabia, Synegistics Corp., Denver; represented in permanent collections Pasadena Ctr. for the Arts, N.Y. Art Dirs. Club, Calif. State U./Fiber Collection, Pasadena (Calif.) Ctr. for the Arts, 1984, N.Y. Art Dirs. Club, 1985 Midland Art Coun./Fiber Collection, 1985, Geologic Soc. Am.; represented in traveling exhbns. L.A. Art Dirs. Show and N.Y. Art Dirs. Show, U.S., Europe, Japan, 1985; featured in Denver Post, 1984, Post Electric City Mag., 1984, Rocky Mt. News, 1984, Douglas County Press, 1984, Mile High Cable Vision, 1985, Sta. KWGN-TV, 1985, Les Krantz's Am. Artists, 1988, Illustrated Survey of Leading Contemporaries, 1988, U.S. Surface Design Jour., 1988; co-work represented in film collection Mus. Modern Art, N.Y.C.; selected fashion show designs displayed to Sister City dels., Denver, 1987. Co-recipient Silver Medal award N.Y. Internat. Film and Video Competition, 1976, Design awards Coun. Advancement and Support of Edn., 1969, 71, 73, 76, Honor Mention award L.A. Art Dirs. Club, 1984, Honor Mention award N.Y. Art Dirs. Club, 1984, Native Am. Wearable Art Competition, 1985, 5th pl. Nat. Wind Sail Am. Banners Competition, Midland, Mich., 1985, also awards for surface designs in Colo. Ctr. for the Arts Wearable Art Competition, 1984-85, Foothills Art Gallery Nat. Wearable Art Competition, 1984-85, Fashion Group of Denver Competition, 1984-85. Mem. Art Dirs. Club Denver (Gold medals 1974-82, Best of Show Gold medal 1983, Honor Mention award, 1984, 3 Gold medals 1989), Univ. Art Dirs. Assn. Home: PO Box 302 751 Willow Lake Dr Franktown CO 80116 Office: U Denver Sch Art 2121 E Asbury Ave Denver CO 80210-4303

NORMAN, JOHN EDWARD, petroleum landman; b. Denver, May 22, 1922; s. John Edward and Ella (Warren) N.; m. Hope Sabin, Sept. 5, 1946; children—J. Thomas, Gerould W., Nancy E., Susan G., Douglas E. BSBA, U. Denver, 1949, MBA, 1972. Clk., bookkeeper Capitol Life Ins. Co., Denver, 1940-42, 45-46; salesman Security Life and Accident Co., Denver, 1947; bookkeeper Central Bank and Trust Co., Denver, 1947-50; automobile salesman H.A. Hennies, Denver, 1950; petroleum landman Continental Oil Co. (name changed to Conoco Inc. 1979), Denver, 1950-85; ind. petroleum landman, 1985; ind. investor 1985—. Lectr. pub. lands Colo. Sch. Mines, 1968-85; lectr. mineral titles and landmen's role in oil industry Casper Coll., 1969-71. Mem. Casper Mcpl. Band Commn., 1965-71, mem. band, 1961-71, mgr., 1968-71; former musician, bd. dirs. Casper Civic Symphony; former bd. dirs. Jefferson Symphony, performing mem., 1972-75. Served with AUS, World War II. Mem. Am. Assn. Petroleum Landmen (dir. at large, chmn. publs. for regional dir.), Wyo. Assn. Petroleum Landmen (pres.), Denver Assn. Petroleum Landmen, Rocky Mountain Oil and Gas Assn. (pub. lands com. 1981-85), Rocky Mountain Petroleum Pioneers. Episcopalian (mem. choir, vestryman, past dir. acolytes). Club: Elks. Home and Office: 2710 S Jay St Denver CO 80227-3856

NORMAN, NITA VEGAMORA, librarian, educator, storyteller; b. Sariaya, Philippines, Aug. 29; came to U.S., 1968; d. Romualdo and Leoncia (Cereza) Vegamora; m. Michael B. Norman, June 15, 1972. BS in Edn., U. Santo Tomas, 1965; Rosary Coll.MLS, 1975, 1975; M in Edn., Storytelling, Reading, Eastern Tenn. State U., 1995. Sch. tchr. Quiapo Parochial Sch., Manila, 1965-68; asst. libr. Cen. States Inst. of Addiction, Chgo., 1970-75; out-reach libr. Chgo. Pub. Libr., 1975-77, branch head, 1977-83; branch mgr. Phoenix Pub. Libr., 1983—. Speaker in field. Named Libr. of the Year., Friende of the Chgo. Pub. Libr., 1980; recipient Outstnading Pub. Svc. award City of Phoenix , 1985, Disting. Svc. award Murphy Elem. Sch., Phoenix, 1990; Contbn. to Literacy award Hamilton Sch., Phoenix, 1993-94. Mem. ALA (local program com. Chgo. 1978), Pub. Libr. Assn. (alternative edn. program com. 1985—, multilingual libr. svcs. com. 1985—), Reforma (libr. svcs. to Spanish speaking), Ariz. State Libr. Assn. (libr. svcs. to Spanish speaking round table 1983—), Asian Pacific Am. Library Assn. Democrat. Home: 1513 W Culver St Phoenix AZ 85007-1823 Office: Mesquite Br Libr 4525 Paradise Valley Pkwy N Phoenix AZ 85000 *Nita Norman is a storyteller, teacher, and librarian, with more than 15 years of experience sharing stories with children and adults of all ages. Last year, she became a professional storyteller after receiving a Masters degree in Storytelling from East Tennessee State University, Johnson City, Tennessee. Nita has been active in promoting the art of storytelling with her involvement in the National Association of Storytelling. She is listed in the Artist Roster 1996-97, of the Arizona Commission of the Arts, and in Who's Who in the West, 1996-97. Nita's repertoire includes folktales, fairytales, participatory stories and songs, and personal experiences.*

NORRIS, JAMES LEO "JIM", historian, editor, publisher; b. Salt Lake City, July 7, 1930; s. Leo H. and Erma B. (Davis) N.; m. Lynne Oldmen, Apr., 1951; children: Michael, John, Jean, Jane Suzanne. BS, U. So. Calif., L.A., 1952; MA, Calif. State U., L.A., 1960. Cert. Marriage Family Child Counselor. Tchr., counselor, coach El Segundo H.S., L.A., 1957-61, Palos Verdes H.S., L.A., 1961-64; prof. El Camino Coll., L.A., 1964-81; pub. Olive Press Publs., L.A. and Santa Barbara, Calif., 1981—; historian L.A. and Santa Barbara, 1981—; pres. El Comino Coll. Faculty Assn., L.A., 1975, Calif. C.C. Counseling Assn., 1972. Editor, pub.: Can a Woman Over Forty?, 1980, Be Careful What You Dream (It Might Come True), 1985, Women of My Other Worlds, 1985, Mattei's Tavern, 1986, Urho Saari: Olympian, 1986, San Ramon Chapel Pioneers & Their California Heritage, 1990, Smut, 1992, It Don't Hurt To Laugh: Cowboy Poetry, 1993, Around the World in Sixty Years, 1993, Let Me Tell You, 1993, History of Zaca Lake, 1994, Don't Get Me Started, 1995, Ho! For The Foxen Canyon Wine Trail, 1996, Tour Of Los Alamos Historic District, 1996, Knights Of The Oblong Table, 1996, Santa Maria Style Barbeque, 1997; reader Huntington and Bancroft Librs.; contbr. numerous articles to hist. publs. Editor Santa Ynez (Calif.) Valley Hist. Soc., 1984-94; pres. Los Olivos Imporovement Assn., Los Olivos, 1981-83; chmn. Santa Barbara County Landmark Com., Santa Barbara, 1990-92. Lt. (j.g.) USN, 1952-55, PTO. Mem. Santa Barbara Corral Westeners (keeper of the chips 1983—), Los Californianos, Wet Noodle (pres. 1980). Home: Box 99 Los Olivos CA 93441 Office: Olive Press Publs PO Box 99 Los Olivos CA 93441-0099

NORRIS, JOHN STEVEN, healthcare company executive; b. Chgo., Apr. 25, 1943; s. Norris Dale and Olive (Grissinger) N. BA, U. Ariz., 1967; B in Fgn. Trade, Am. Grad. Sch. Internat. Mgmt., 1968; MPH, U. Ariz., 1995; diplomate Am. Coll. Healthcare Execs.; lic. nursing home adminstr., gen. contractor, real estate broker; m. Susan Jean Armstrong, May 3, 1975; children: Lindsey Jean, Whitney Ann, John Scott. Inspection officer Citicorp, Brazil, Colombia, Mex., 1968-72, asst. cashier, N.Y.C., 1972-74; pres., gen. mgr. Phoenix Athletic Club, 1974-76; bus. mgr. Phoenix Pub. Inc., 1976-77; project mgr. Environ. Constrn. Co., Phoenix, 1977-79; pres. AGN Devel. Corp., Phoenix, 1979—, Valley View Realty, Inc., 1981-87; exec. v.p., sec., pres. RGW Constrn. Co., Inc.; pres. Norris/Roberts Group, Inc., Phoenix, 1987-90; CEO Christian Care Cos., Inc., Phoenix, 1990—. Bd. dirs. Christian Care Inc.; deacon christian ch.; adv. bd. dirs. Area Agy. Aging; pres. elect Phoenix Rotary (Paul Harris fellow). Fellow Am. Assn. Home Svcs. Aging; mem. Am. Coll. Healthcare Adminstrs, Phi Delta Theta. Republican. Avocations: golf, skiing, racquetball. Home: 111 W Tam O'Shanter Dr Phoenix AZ 85023-6241 Office: Christian Care Cos 2002 W Sunnyside Dr Phoenix AZ 85029-3534

NORRIS, LOIS ANN, elementary school educator; b. Detroit, May 13, 1937; d. Joseph Peter and Marguerite Iola (Gourley) Giroux; m. Max Norris, Feb. 9, 1962 (div. 1981); children: John Henry, Jeanne Marie, Joseph Peter. BS in Social Sci., Ea. Mich. U., 1960, MA, 1960; cert. adminstr., Calif. State U., Bakersfield, 1983. Kindergarten tchr. Norwalk-LaMirada Unified Sch. Dist., 1960-62; tchr. various grades Rialto Unified Sch. Dist., 1962-66; kindergarten tchr. Inyokern (Calif.) Sch., 1969-82; 1st grade tchr. Vieweg Basic Sch, 1982-92, kindergarten tchr., 1992-96; retired, 1996; head tchr. Sierra Sands Elem. Summer Sch.; adminstrv. intern Sierra Sands Adult Sch., master tchr., head tchr., counselor. Ofcl. scorekeeper, team mother, snack bar coord. China Lake Little League; team mother, statistician Indian Wells Valley Youth Football; bd. mem. PTA; pres. Sch. Site Coun.; treas. Inyokern Parents Club; run coord. City of Hope; timekeeper, coord. Jr. Olympics; mem. planning com. Sunshine Festival; active Burros Booster Club. Recipient Hon. Svc. award PTA, 1994. Mem. Calif. Tchrs. Assn., NEA, Desert Area Tchrs. Assn., Assn. Calif. Sch. Adminstrs., Inyokern C. of C. (sec.), Am. Motorcycle Assn., NRA, Bakersfield Calif. Diamond Club. Republican. LDS Ch. Home: PO Box 163 201 N Brown Rd Inyokern CA 93527

NORRIS, MARGOT CHRISTA, English language educator; b. Baden, Austria, Dec. 23, 1944; came to the U.S., 1954; d. Josef Hofstaetter and Helga (Hochberger) Barisits; m. m. Thomas Elfred Norris, Aug. 22, 1964 (div. Sept. 1967); 1 child, A. Josef; m. Rowland Hallowell Davis, June 5, 1994. BA, U. Fla., 1967; PhD, SUNY, Buffalo, 1972. Asst. prof. English U. Tulsa, Okla., 1972-76; asst. to full prof. English U. Mich., Ann Arbor, 1976-87; prof. English and comparative lit. U. Calif., Irvine, 1987—; vis. prof. English U. Basel, Switzerland, 1982-83; mem. adv. com. Publ. of the MLA, N.Y.C., 1990-94. Author: The Decentered Universe of Finnegans Wake, 1976, Beasts of the Modern Imagination, 1985, Joyce's Web, 1992. Fellow Am. Coun. Learned Socs., Heidelberg, Germany, 1977-78, Guggenheim Meml. fellow, 1988-89. Mem. MLA (chair divsn. for 20th century British lit. 1990-94). Democrat. Office: Dept English & Comparative Lit Univ Calif Irvine Irvine CA 92697

NORRIS, WILLIAM ALBERT, federal judge; b. Turtle Creek, Pa., Aug. 30, 1927; s. George and Florence (Clive) N.; m. Merry Wright, Nov. 23, 1974; children: Barbara, Donald, Kim, Alison; m. Jane Jelenko. Student, U. Wis., 1945; B.A., Princeton U., 1951; J.D., Stanford U., 1954. Bar: Calif. and D.C. 1955. Assoc. firm Northcutt Ely, Washington, 1954-55; law clk. to Justice William O. Douglas U.S. Supreme Ct., Washington, 1955-56; sr. mem. firm Tuttle & Taylor, Inc., L.A., 1956-80; judge U.S. Ct. Appeals (9th cir.), L.A., 1980-94, sr. judge, 1994—; spl. counsel Pres.' Kennedy's Com. on Airlines Controversy, 1961; mem., v.p. Calif. State Bd. Edn., 1961-67. Trustee Calif. State Colls., 1967-72; pres. L.A. Bd. Police Commrs., 1973-74; Democratic nominee for atty. gen. State of Calif., 1974; founding pres. bd. trustees Mus. Contemporary Art, L.A., 1979—; trustee Craft and Folk Art Mus., 1979—. With USN, 1945-47. Home: 1473 Oriole Dr West Hollywood CA 90069-1155 Office: US Ct Appeals 9th Cir 312 N Spring St Los Angeles CA 90012-4701*

NORRIS, WILLIAM SCOTT, retired career officer, automotive educator; b. Bainbridge, Md., May 8, 1957; s. William Arthur and Florinda May (Hartley) n.; m. Cathy Lynn Norris, Mar. 17, 1979; children: Shasta, Lauren, Skyler. BS in Aero., Embrey Riddle U., 1981; BS in Workforce Edn., So. Ill. U., 1994. Cert. automotive master. Enlisted U.S. Army, 1975, advanced to chief warrant officer 2; technician 1st cav. divsn. U.S. Army, Ft. Hood, Tex., 1975-78; cobra pilot AH-1 101 ABN divsn. U.S. Army, Ft. Campbell, Ky., 1979-82; commd. 2nd lt. USAF, 1981, advanced through grades to capt., 1985; forward air contr. 21st Tactical Air Support Squadron USAF, Shaw AFB, S.C., 1982-85; F-16 pilot 80th TAC FTR WG USAF, Kunsan A.B., Korea, 1986-87; F-16 pilot 401st TAC FTR WG USAF, Torrejon ABS, Spain, 1988-90; unit comdr. OLE 501 TACW USAF, Ansbach, Germany, 1990-92; A-10 pilot 354 FTR SQ USAF, McChord AFB, Wash., 1991-95; instr. Renton (Wash.) Tech. Coll., 1995—. Contbr. articles to profl. jours. Bd. dirs. J.A. Scholarship Fund, Puyallup, Wash. Decorated Bronze Star. Mem. Am. Vocat. Edn. Assn., Masons. Republican. Home: 6220 81st St E Puyallup WA 98371-5520 Office: Renton Coll Ford Asset Program 3000 NE 4th St Renton WA 98056-4123

NORSBY, KIMBERLY LYN, tax specialist, consultant; b. Tacoma, Wash., Aug. 3, 1962; d. Donald F. and Nancy L. (Getty) Westcott; m. Jeffrey David Norsby, Nov. 29, 1980; 1 child, Kenneth Donald. Student, Tacoma C.C., 1986, Rancho Santiago Coll., Santa Ana, Calif., 1987-89, Calif. State U., Fullerton, 1989. Property mgr. Am. Republic Realty Corp., Dallas and Milw., 1981-84, Victor L. Lyon Realtors, Tacoma, 1985-86; acctg. mgr. Robotronics, Stanton, Calif., 1986-88; staff acct. Harold Dilbeck Accts., Inc., Tustin, Calif., 1988-93; co-owner Coast Mobile Wash, Garden Grove, Calif., 1987—; agt., owner Tax Tyme, Garden Grove, Calif., 1992—; co-owner Dirt Blaster Equipment Co., Garden Grove, Calif., 1995—. del. White House Conf. Small Bus., 1995. Mem. Nat. Assn. Enrolled Agts., Orange County Soc. Enrolled Agts., Garden Grove C. of C. (pres. 1996-97, CFO 1994-96). Republican. Home and Office: 11381 Jerry Ln Garden Grove CA 92840-3447

NORTON, DUNBAR SUTTON, economic developer; b. Hoquiam, Wash., Jan. 30, 1926; s. Percy Dunbar and Anna Fedelia (Sutton) N.; m. Kathleen Margaret Mullarky, Dec. 21, 1948 (dec. Apr. 1994); children: Priscilla K., Rebecca C., Jennifer A., Douglas S.; m. Mary Ethel Wolff, May 25, 1996. Student, U. Oreg., 1946-48; diploma, U.S. Army Command & Gen. Staff, 1964. Enlisted U.S. Army, 1944, commd. 2d lt., 1948, advanced through grades to lt. col., ret., 1974; dir. econ. devel. dept. Yuma (Ariz.) County C. of C., 1974-83; exec. v.p. Lakin Enterprises, Yuma, 1983-87; owner Norton Cons., Yuma, 1987—; corp. mem. Greater Yuma Econ. Devel. Corp., 1984-96, vice chmn., 1993-95. Mem. Yuma County Indsl. Devel. Authority, 1984-90, 92—, pres. 1992—; chmn. fundraising com. Yuma Cross Park Coun., 1984-88, sec. 1988-90, v.p. 1990-92, bd. dirs. 1982-96; bd. dirs. Yuma Leadership, Inc., 1978-88, Yuma Youth Leadership, , 1990-93; chmn. devel. com. Yuma County Airport Authority, 1985-92, v.p. 1992—; vice chmn. Yuma Main St. Bd., 1988-90, Yuma County Geog. Info. Sys. Task Force, 1991-95, Yuma Kids Voting, 1990-91, bd. dirs. Ariz. Partnership Air Transp., 1990-96, v.p. 1993-95; bd. dirs. Yuma County Civic Trusteeship, 1993-95; chmn. The Southwest Inst., 1995-96, What's Best for Our Kids, 1995-96, Yuma Sch. Dist. No. 1 New Elem. Sch. Planning Com., 1996-97; mem. bd. trustees Yuma County Libr., 1996—. Decorated Legion of merit with oak leaf cluster, Bronze Star. Mem. Ariz. Assn. for Econ. Devel. (bd. dirs. 1975-82, pres. 1982-83, legis. affairs com. 1987—, Developer of Yr. 1977), Yuma Execs. Assn. (sec.-treas., exec. dir. 1987—). Republican. Episcopalian. Home: 12267 E Del Norte Yuma AZ 85367-7356 Office: 11411 S Fortuna Rd Ste 205 Yuma AZ 85367-7827

NORTON, GALE A., state attorney general; b. Wichita, Mar. 11, 1954; d. Dale Bentsen and Anna Jacqueline (Lansdowne) N.; m. John Goethe Hughes, Mar. 26, 1990. BA, U. Denver, 1975, JD, 1978. Bar: Colo. 1978, U.S. Supreme Ct. 1981. Jud. clk. Colo. Ct. of Appeals, Denver, 1978-79; sr. atty. Mountain States Legal Found., Denver, 1979-83; nat. fellow Hoover Instn. Stanford (Calif.) U., 1983-84; asst. to dep. sec. U.S. Dept. of Agr., Washington, 1984-85; assoc. solicitor U.S. Dept. of Interior, Washington, 1985-87; pvt. practice law Denver, 1987-90; atty. gen. State of Colo., Denver, 1991—; Murdock fellow Polit. Economy Rsch. Ctr., Bozeman, Mont., 1984; sr. fellow Ind. Inst., Golden, Colo., 1988-90; policy analyst Pres. Coun. on Environ. Quality, Washington, 1985-88; lectr. U. Denver Law Sch., 1989; transp. law program dir. U. Denver, 1978-79. Contbr. chpts. to books, articles to profl. jours. Participant Rep. Leadership Program, Colo., 1988, Colo. Leadership Forum, 1989; past chair Nat. Assn. Attys. Gen. Environ. Com.; co-chair Nat. Policy Forum Environ. Coun.; candidate for 1996 election to U.S. Senate, 1995—. Named Young Career Woman Bus. and Profl. Wome, 1981, Young Lawyer of Yr., 1991. Mem. Federalist Soc., Colo. Women's Forum, Order of St. Ives. Republican. Methodist. Office: Colo Dept of Law 1525 Sherman St Fl 5 Denver CO 80203-1760

NORTON, GOLDY See GOLDSTEIN, NORTON MAURICE

NORTON, KAREN ANN, accountant; b. Paynesville, Minn., Nov. 1, 1950; d. Dale Francis and Ruby Grace (Gehlhar) N. BA, U. Minn., 1972; postgrad. U. Md., 1978; cert. acctg. U.S. Dept. Agr. Grad. Sch., 1978; MBA, Calif. State Poly. U.-Pomona, 1989. CPA, Md. Securities transactions analyst Bur. of Pub. Debt., Washington, 1972-79, internal auditor, 1979-81; internal auditor IRS, Washington, 1981; sr. acct. World Vision Internat., Monrovia, Calif., 1981-83, acctg. supr., 1983-87; sr. systems liaison coord., Home Savs. Am., 1987-97, sys. auditor, 1997—; cons. (vol.) info. systems John M. Perkins Found., Pasadena, Calif., 1985-86. Author (poetry): Ode to Joyce, 1985 (Golden Poet award 1985). Second v.p. chpt. Nat. Treasury Employees Union, Washington, 1978, editor chpt. newsletter; mem. M-2 Prisoners Sponsorship Program, Chino, Calif., 1984-86. Recipient Spl. Achievement award Dept. Treasury, 1976, Superior Performance award, 1977-78; Charles and Ellora Alliss scholar, 1968. Mem. Angel Flight, Flying Samaritans. Avocations: flying, chess, racquetball, whitewater rafting.

NORTON, STEVEN DAVID, immunologist, researcher; b. Endicott, N.Y., Aug. 14, 1965; s. David Gibbons and Ro Jean (Reeves) N.; m. Lynette Dayton, Sept. 30, 1987; children: Jonathan Steven, Gregory Dayton, James David. BS, Brigham Young U., 1988; PhD, U. Minn., 1992. Predoctoral fellow U. Minn., Mpls., 1988-92; postdoctoral fellow U. Chgo., 1992-93; sr. staff scientist Paradigm Biosciences, Inc., Salt Lake City, 1993—; adj. faculty dept. pathology U. Utah, Salt Lake City, 1993—, dept. biology Salt Lake C.C., 1996—. Contbr. articles to sci. jours.; contbr. chpt. to Encyclopedia of Immunology. Recipient Rsch. award 20th Midwest Immunology Conf., 1991. Mem. Am. Assn. Immunologists, Fedn. Am. Socs. Exptl. Biology, Phi Kappa Phi.

NORVELLE, JOAN WILSON, forensic accountant, educator, consultant; b. Shreveport, La., May 14, 1939; d. Alexander Culberson and Ruby (Crouch) Wilson; m. Larry Cole Thompson (div.); 1 child, Cole; m. Michael E. Norvelle (div.). BS in Bus. Adminstrn., Centenary Coll. of La., 1966; MS in Bus. Adminstrn., Acctg., Va. Commonwealth U., 1968; PhD of Higher Edn. Adminstrn., U. Ariz., 1978. Instr. Smithdeal-Massey Bus. Coll., Richmond, Va., 1965-67; divsn. chmn. bus. scis. John Tyler C.C., Richmond, Va., 1967-70; asst. prof. dept. acctg. Va. State Coll., Petersburg, 1970-71; grad. teaching assoc. in acctg. U. Ariz., Tucson, 1971-73; rsch. assoc. dean's office, Coll. Bus. and Pub. Adminstrn. instr. acctg. U. Ariz., Tucson, 1973-75; lectr. dept. acctg. U. Ariz., Tucson, 1975-77; rsch. assoc., acctg. cons. Bur. Indian Affairs Contract, Office Lands and Studies, U. Ariz., Tucson, 1977-78; instr. dept. acctg. U. Ariz., Tucson, 1978-79, assoc. dept. head and lectr., 1979-96; mem. adj. faculty Va. Commonwealth U., Richmond, 1967-70, So. Ariz. Law Enforcement Inst., Tucson, 1973-77, Pima Coll., Tucson, 1975-77; presenter on Fund Acctg. U. Ariz., CPA Rev. Course, 1981, 87, 89; fiscal officer Divsn. Indsl. Coop., U. Ariz. Found., 1981-87; mgmt. cons. several agrl. projects in Ariz., 1979-82; presenter workshops 1978—; tng. various tribes for Bur. Indian affairs, 1977-78; acad. decathelon judge State Ariz., 1984, 86; cons. to many law enforcement agys. nationwide; conducted numerous seminars fin. and fraud exposure. Author: Introduction to Fund Accounting, fifth edit., 1994; co-author: (with Richard A. Nossen) The Detection, Investigation and Prosecution of Financial Crimes, 2d edit., 1993, (with Larry C. Thompson) Writer's Guide to Educational Periodicals, 1973; contbr. articles to profl. jours. in legal prosecution and acctg. Mem. Assn. Cert. Fraud Examiners (cert. fraud examiner, rsch. com. 1992, bd. regents 1993). Office: PO Box 85151 Tucson AZ 85754-5151

NOSLER, ROBERT AMOS, sports company executive; b. Ashland, Oreg., Apr. 21, 1946; s. John Amos and Louise (Booz) N.; m. Joan Kathleen Hilliard, July 15, 1967; children: Christie Lynn, Jill Ann, John Robert. Student, U. Oreg., 1965. V.p., gen. mgr. Nosler Bullets, Inc., Bend, Oreg., 1974-88; pres., chief exec. officer Nosler Bullets, Inc., 1988-90; pres., CEO Nosler, Inc., Bend, 1990—. Editor: Nosler Reloading Manual #1, 1976. Bd. dirs. Bend C. of C., 1984-88, treas., 1988; chmn. Central Oreg. Welcome Ctr. Steering Com., 1988. With USN, 1966-70; trustee Ctrl. Oreg. Community Coll. Found., 1992—; trustee Nat. Rifle Assn. Found., 1997—. Recipient Pres.' award Bend C. of C., 1984, 87, 88. Mem. Nat. Reloading Mfrs. Assn. (bd. dirs. 1982-86, 90-93, pres. 1984-86), Oreg. Grad. Inst. Sci. & Tech. Chief Exec. Roundtable, Greater Bend Rotary (dir. 1989-91). Republican. Lutheran. Office: Nosler Inc 107 SW Columbia St Bend OR 97702-1014

NOTHERN, MARJORIE CAROL, nursing administrator; b. Bonners Ferry, Idaho, June 23, 1936; d. Carl John and Ione Faye (Hobson) Frank; m. Abbott Burton Squire, Dec. 15, 1956 (div. Aug. 5, 1972); m. William Thomas Nothern, Aug. 5, 1972. Diploma, Deaconess Hosp. Sch. Nursing, Spokane, Wash., 1956; BA, Stephens Coll., Columbia, Mo., 1981; MBA, Golden Gate U., San Francisco, 1987. Cert. nursing adminstrn. advanced ANCC. Relief head nurse Deaconess Hosp., Spokane, Wash., 1956-57; staff nurse Kadlec Meth. Hosp., Richland, Wash., 1957-58, Southern Pacific Hosp., San Francisco, 1958-59; relief evening supr. The Gen. Hosp., Eureka, Calif., 1959-60; med. office nurse Eley & Davis, Eureka, Calif., 1960-66; head nurse Redbud Cmty. Hosp., Clear Lake, Calif., 1968-72, dir. nurses, 1972-77; supr. Hosp. Nursing Kaiser Found. Hosp., Martinez, Calif., 1977-78; dir. med. ctr. nursing Kaiser Permanente Med. Ctr., Richmond, Calif., 1978-80; asst. hosp. administr. Kaiser Found. Hosp., Hayward, Calif., 1980-94; assoc. M2, Inc., San Francisco, 1996—; nurse evaluator II Calif. Dept. Health Svcs., San Francisco, 1996—. Mem. health sci. adv. commn. Ohlone Coll., Fremont, Calif., 1980-94; mem. med. aux. and nursing adv. com. Chabot Coll., Hayward, Calif., 1980-94; mem. Grad. Coll. Nursing adv. bd. San Francisco State U., 1986—; mem. Stephens Coll. Alumnae Coun., 1996-98. Recipient Leadership award Sigma Theta Tau, Alpha Gamma, San Jose State U., 1990. Mem. ANA-Calif., Orgn. Nurse Execs.-Calif., East Bay Orgn. Nurse Execs., Assistance League Diablo Valley, Blackhawk Country Club, Blackhawk Bus. Women, Sigma Theta Tau., Alpha Gamma, Nu Xi. Republican. Home: 363 Jacaranda Dr Danville CA 94506-2124

NOTHMANN, RUDOLF S., legal researcher; b. Hamburg, Fed. Republic of Germany, Feb. 4, 1907; came to U.S., 1941, naturalized, 1943; s. Nathan and Henrietta G. (Heymann) N. Referendar, U. Hamburg, 1929, PhD in Law, 1932; postgrad. U. Liverpool Law Sch. (Eng.), 1931-32. Law clk. Hamburg Cts., 1929-31, 32-33; export, legal adviser, adviser ocean marine ins. various firms, Ger., Eng., Sweden, Calif., 1933-43, 46-47; instr. fgn. exchange, fgn. trade Extension div. UCLA, 1947-48, vis. assoc. prof. UCLA, 1951; asst. prof. econs. Whittier Coll., 1948-50, assoc. prof., 1950-51; contract work U.S. Air Force, U.S. Navy, 1953-59; contract negotiator space projects, space and missile systems orgn. USAF, L.A., 1959-77; pvt. researcher in internat. comml. law, Pacific Palisades, Calif., 1977—. With U.S. Army, 1943-45; ETO. Recipient Gold Tape award Air Force Systems Command, 1970. Mem. Internat. Bar Assn. (vice chmn. internat. sales and related comml. trans. com. 1977-82), Am. Econ. Assn., Calif. Bar Assn. (internat. law sect.), Am. Soc. Internat. Law, Uebersee Club (Hamburg, Germany). Author: The Insurance Certificate in International Ocean Marine Insurance Law and Foreign Trade, 1932; The Oldest Corporation in the World: Six Hundred Years of Economic Evolution, 1949. Home: PO Box 32 Pacific Palisades CA 90272-0032

NOTTAGE, JAMES H., museum administrator, curator, historian; b. Laramie, Wyo., 1950; s. Harold J. and Frieda (Oliver) N.; m. Mary Ellen Hennessey, 1976. BA in History, U. Wyo., 1972; MA in Mus. Studies, SUNY, Oneonta, 1976; MA in Am. Studies, U. Wyo., 1978. Curator exhibits Kans. State Hist. Soc., Topeka, 1977-79, asst. mus. dir., 1979-81, supervisory historian, 1981-85; chief curator Autry Mus. Western Heritage, L.A., 1985-95, v.p. and chief curator, 1995—. Author: (monograph) Stagecoach!, 1990; (book) Saddlemaker to the Stars, 1996. Certification insp. U.S. Army Mus. Sys., 1983-84. Smithsonian Inst. fellow, 1973; Team Planning fellow Kellogg Seminars, 1982. Mem. Am. Assn. Mus. (mus. assesment cons. 1980-85), Western History Assn. Office: Autry Mus Western Heritage 4700 Western Heritage Way Los Angeles CA 90027

NOTTINGHAM, EDWARD WILLIS, JR., federal judge; b. Denver, Jan. 9, 1948; s. Edward Willis and Willie Newton (Gullett) N.; m. Cheryl Ann Card, June 6, 1970 (div. Feb. 1981); children: Amelia Charlene, Edward Willis III; m. Janis Ellen Chapman, Aug. 18, 1984; 1 child, Spencer Chapman. AB, Cornell U., 1969; JD, U. Colo., 1972. Bar: Colo. 1972, U.S. Dist. Ct. Colo. 1972, U.S. Ct. Appeals (10th cir.) 1973. Law clk. to presiding judge U.S. Dist. Ct. Colo., Denver, 1972-73; assoc. Sherman & Howard, Denver, 1973-76, 78-80, ptnr., 1980-87; ptnr. Beckner & Nottingham, Grand Junction, Colo., 1987-89; asst. U.S. atty. U.S. Dept. Justice, Denver, 1976-78; U.S. dist. judge Dist. of Colo., Denver, 1989—. Bd. dirs. Beaver Creek Met. Dist., Avon, Colo., 1980-88, Justice Info. Ctr., Denver, 1985-87, 21st Jud. Dist. Victim Compensation Fund, Grand Junction, Colo., 1987-89. Mem. ABA, Colo. Bar Assn. (chmn. criminal law sect. 1983-85, chmn. ethics com. 1988-89), Order of Coif, Denver Athletic Club, Delta Sigma Rho, Tau Kappa Alpha. Episcopalian. Office: US Dist Ct 1929 Stout St Denver CO 80294-0001

NOURSE, THOMAS MILLER, consulting company executive; b. Greenville, Ohio, Aug. 24, 1922; s. John Darlington and Louise Anderson (Miller) N.; m. Dorothy Ann Beale, Apr. 3, 1945; children: James Gregory, Daniel Miller, William Beale. BSChemE, Purdue U., 1943. Registered profl. engr., N.Y. Sales mgr. Hagan Chems. & Controls, Pitts., 1947-62; mktg. mgr. Daystrom Control Systems Div., La Jolla, Calif., 1962-63, Foxboro-Digital Systems Div., Foxboro, Mass., 1963-65; strategic planning Gen. Electric, Charlottesville, Va., 1965-68; v.p., gen. mgr. Interactive Scis. Corp., Braintree, Mass., 1968-70; pres. Nourse Assocs., Inc., San Diego, Calif., 1970—; task force mem. Fin. Acctg. Standards Bd.-Cash Flow Reporting, Stamford, Conn., 1985-87. Pres. San Diego Hall of Sci., 1975-78. Lt. USNR, 1943-46. Mem. Instrument Soc. Am., Assn. Iron and Steel Engrs. Republican. Episcopalian. Home and Office: 17632 Fonticello Way San Diego CA 92128-1816

NOVAK, JOE, artist; b. Springfield, Mass., Oct. 15, 1930; s. Benjamin D. and Mae (Lavitt) N. BA, Dartmouth Coll., 1952; JD, Harvard U., 1955. Solo exhbns. include Vered Gallery, East Hampton, N.Y., 1985, 87, 88, Milari Ltd., N.Y.C., 1989, Light Emanations, Tesuque, N.Mex., 1992, The Bank of Santa Fe, 1996, Davidson & Daughters, Portland, Maine, 1997; exhibited in group shows at Parrish Art Mus., Southampton, N.Y., Guild Hall Mus., East Hampton, Vered Gallery, Milari, Ltd., Olaf Clasen Gallery, Cologne, Germany, numerous others; works included in collections including Guild Hall Mus., U. Tex.-Pan Am., Mus. Fine Arts, Santa Fe, Mus. Art, Ft. Lauderdale, Fla., Hood Mus., Dartmouth Coll.; subject of articles. Lt. USN, 1955-58. Recipient awards for art. Home: PO Box 393 Tesuque NM 87574

NOVICK, STUART ALLAN, publishing executive; b. Savannah, Ga., Aug. 21, 1944; s. Jehiel and Dorothy Ruth (Selicovitz) N.; m. Francesca Julita Lim, June 22, 1986 (div. Mar. 1993); 1 child, Casey Adam. Grad., Stanford U., 1967. Mgr. Chico-San, Inc., Seattle, 1969-72; bus. mgr. Seventh Inn, Boston, 1972-74; owner, mgr. Simulsense, Seattle, 1974-77, More Time! Good Time!, Honolulu, 1977-80; pres. Foodpower, Honolulu, 1980-83, Profitability Cons., Honolulu, 1983-88, Novick and Einstein Advt., Honolulu, 1988—; owner Environ. Mktg. Sys., Honolulu, 1994—; cons. WorkHawaii, Honolulu, 1990, Am. Lung Assn., Honolulu, 1991. Pub. Hawaii Environ. Gazette, 1994-95. Coord. Gov.'s Energy Awards Program, 1991; chmn. Hunger Project Found., Honolulu, 1977-80; coord. Pau Hunger Found., Honolulu, 1980-81; co-founder, coord. Partnership for the Environment, 1992-95. Mem. Exch. Club (coord. Hilo 1990-91). Office: 1487 Hiikala Pl Apt 8 Honolulu HI 96816-5633

NOWOSATKO, JEROME RAYMOND, software engineer; b. Detroit, Apr. 30, 1965; s. Raymond Peter and Sophie Helen (Pendzik) N. AA in Computer Sci., U. Md., Naples, Italy, 1989, BS in Info. Systems, 1989; MS in Software Engring., Colo. Tech., 1996. Cert. data processor, sys. profl., computing profl. Commd. E-4 U.S. Army, 1984; software engr. Compuware Corp., Detroit, 1990-91, Columbus, Ohio, 1991-92, Colorado Springs, 1992—. Mem. Data Processing Mgmt. Assn., Inst. for Certification of Computing Profls., Project Mgmt. Inst., Buckley Sch. Forensic Soc., Project Mgmt. Inst. Republican. Roman Catholic. Home: 7215 Big Valley Ct Colorado Springs CO 80919-1035 Office: Compuware Corp 5575 Tech Center Dr Ste 212 Colorado Springs CO 80919-2349

NUCE, MADONNA MARIE, military officer; b. Denver, Jan. 15, 1952; d. Donald William and Marie Dorothy (Ruscio) N.; m. Edward Ray Geron, Oct. 9, 1982; 1 child, Maria Louise. BA, U. No. Colo., 1974; grad., Command and Gen. Staff Coll., Ft. Leavenworth, 1993. Enlisted U.S. ANG, 1973; commd. 2d lt. U.S. Army, 1981, advanced through grades to lt. col., 1993; adminstrv. supply tech. Colo. Army Nat. Guard, Denver, 1974-79; supply technician Colo. Army Nat. Guard, Golden, Colo., 1979-81; tng. officer Colo. Army Nat. Guard, Aurora, Colo., 1981-84, adminstrv. officer, 1984-85; maintenance officer Colo. Army Nat. Guard, Golden, Colo., 1985-86, asst. supply officer, 1986-91, data processing chief, 1991-92, supply mgmt. officer, 1992-93, comptr., 1993-94, dir. maintenance, 1994-96; logistics officer Colo. Army Nat. Guard, Golden, 1996—; Mem. Colo. Nat. Guard Assn. (sec. 1981-83, bd. dirs. 1983-85), Assn. of the U.S. Army (treas. 1986-88), Colo. Artists Assn. Group leader 5th grade Archdiocese of Denver Jr. Great Books Program, St. Anne Sch., 1987-89, group leader 7th grade Holy

Family, 1991-92; bd. dirs. 9 Health Fair, Denver, 1985-90. Decorated Meritorious Svc. medal, Army Commendation medal, Army Achievement medal, Air Force Achievement medal. Mem. Colo. Nat. Guard Assn. (sec. 1981-83, bd. dirs. 1983-85), Assn. of U.S. Army (treas. 1986-88). Roman Catholic. Office: Colo Army Nat Guard 6848 S Revere Pky Englewood CO 80112-3904

NUGENT, CONSTANCE MARIE JULIE, health facility administrator; b. Lewiston, Maine, July 3, 1933; d. Joseph E.W. Sr. and Beatrice M.J. (Levasseur) Lessard; m. John Thomas Nugent Sr., Jan. 2, 1954 (dec. Feb. 27, 1982); children: John Thomas Jr., Michael Joseph. Diploma in nursing, Maine Gen. Hosp., 1953; BA, St. Joseph's Coll., Windham, Maine, 1974; family nurse practitioner cert., U. Maine Sch. of Nursing, 1976; M in Health Svc. Adminstrn., St. Joseph's Coll., Windham, Maine, 1995. RNNP, Maine, Calif., Ariz. Staff nurse med. surg., peds., gyn. Maine Med. Ctr., Portland, 1953-57; staff nurse ob-gyn. Mercy Hosp., Portland, Maine, 1957-59; emergency rm. nurse Huntington Meml. Hosp., Pasadena, Calif., 1959-63; supr. critical care unit Osteopathic Hosp. of Maine, Portland, 1963-69; clin. instr. sch. nursing Mercy Hosp., Portland, 1969; supr. ICU Dallas (Tex.) Osteopathic Hosp., 1970; adminstr. Nat. Med. Care of Portland, 1970-80; dir. nursing svcs. Lassen Cmty. Hosp., Susanville, Calif., 1980-87, Hospice of Monterey Peninsula, Carmel Valley, Calif., 1987; adminstr. Ukiah (Calif.) Convalescent Hosp., 1988—; cons. Office of Alcohol Drug Abuse Prevention, Augusta, Maine, 1975-77; mem. adv. com. Home Health Care, Portland, 1974-76, adv. coun. Bur. of Elderly, Portland, 1975-80, Provider Health Forum, Susanville, 1983-87. Sec. Lassen County Mental Health Bd., Susanville, 1980-81; co-facilitator Diabetic Clinic, Susanville, 1983-87; vice-chair Lassen County Health Human Svcs. Bd., Susanville, 1985-87. Mem. Bus. and Profl. Women (treas., v.p. 1990-94), Calif. Assn. Health Facilities, Coun. of Long Term Care Nurses of Calif. (pres. Redwood Empire chpt. 1989-92). Republican. Roman Catholic. Office: Ukiah Convalescent Hosp 1349 S Dora St Ukiah CA 95482-6512

NUGENT, DANIEL FREDERICK, social anthropologist, educator; b. Salt Lake City, May 29, 1954; s. Charles Arter and Margaret (Flint) N.; m. Ana Maria Alonso Zaldivar, Mar. 20, 1983 (div. Jan. 1995); 1 child, Carlos Alonso; m. Eva Concepcion Zorrilla Tessler, Jan. 23, 1995; 1 child, Gabriella Zorrilla. BA, U. Chgo., 1976, MA, 1980, PhD, 1988. Maitenance of way laborer Union Pacific R.R., Wyo., Utah and Idaho, 1976-78; lectr. U. Chgo., 1986; vis. rschr. fellow Ctr. U.S.-Mex. Studies U. Calif.-San Diego, La Jolla, 1986-87; faculty assoc. Brown U., Providence, 1988; lectr., rsch. assoc. Inst. Latin Am. Studies U. Tex., Austin, 1988-90; asst. prof. U. Ariz., Tucson, 1990—; cons. Borderlands Theater, Tucson, 1994—. Author: Spent Cartridges of Revolution, 1993; editor: Rural Revolt in Mexico and U.S. Intervention, 1988; co-author: (play) 13 Dias/13 Days: How the New Zapatistas Shook the World, 1996; responsible editor: Jour. Hist. Sociology, 1994-95. Grad. fellow NSF, 1979-82; writing grantee Am. Coun. Learned Socs., 1989. Communist. Office: U Ariz Dept Anthropology Tucson AZ 85721-0030

NUGENT, DENISE SMITH, holistic nurse; b. Winston Salem, N.C., July 27, 1959; d. Richard Delane and Betty Jean (Williams) Smith; m. Francis William Nugent Jr., Sept. 19, 1980. RN, Cabarrus Hosp. Sch. Nursing, Concord, N.C., 1980; cert., Internat. Inst. Reflexology, St. Petersburg, Fla., 1990, cert. in reflexology, 1996. RN, N.C., Va., Pa., Mass., Ariz., Calif. Staff nurse oncology dept. Bapt. Hosp., Winston Salem, 1980-82; staff nurse diabetes dept. Lehigh Valley Hosp., Allentown, Pa., 1982-83; staff nurse home health Berks Vis. Nurse Assn., Reading, Pa., 1983-85; staff nurse diabetic educator Moses Taylor Hosp., Scranton, Pa., 1990-93; staff nurse, supr. In Home Health, San Mateo, Calif., 1993-94; holistic nurse, cons. in pvt. practice Foster City, Calif., 1995—; dir. profl. svcs. Olsten Health Care, Scranton, 1992-93; cons., 1995—; tchg. Reiki, 1995—. Mem. Am. Holistic Nurses Assn. (cert. program holistic nursing, bd. cert. holistic nurse), Inst. Noetic Sci., Calif. Connection-Holistic Nurses, Foster City C. of C. Home: 44 Rock Harbor Ln Foster City CA 94404-3565 Office: 969G Edgewater Blvd # 764 Foster City CA 94404-3760

NUGENT, FRANK ANTHONY, psychology educator; b. Lyndhurst, N.J., Jan. 5, 1921; s. Anthony Joseph and Edith Ida (Volpe) N.; m. Ann Van Arsdel, Dec. 20, 1955; children: Ellen, Laura, Michael, David. BS, William Paterson Coll., Wayne, N.J., 1942; MA, Columbia U., 1947; PhD in Counseling Psychology, U. Calif., Berkeley, 1959. Lic. psychologist. Supervising counselor Counseling Ctr., U. Calif., Berkeley, 1947-50, Stanford U., Palo Alto, Calif., 1950-53; counselor Pleasant Hill (Calif.) Sch., 1956-58; asst. prof. edn. L.A. State Coll., 1959-61; dir. counseling Western Wash. U., Bellingham, 1962-73, prof. psychology, 1961-86, prof. emeritus psychology, 1986—. Author: Professional Counseling, 1981, Introduction to Counseling, 1990, 2nd edit., 1994. Bd. dirs. Cmty. Mental Health, Bellingham, Residential Treatment, Bellingham. Fulbright sr. rsch. scholar, Cologne, Germany, 1982-83. Mem. APA, ACA, Am. Soc. Aging, Wash. Psychol. Assn. (pres. 1968-69), Wash. Counseling Assn. (pres. 1980-82, Hank Bertness award 1994). Home: 4146 Ridgewood Ave Bellingham WA 98226-2560 Office: Western Wash U Dept Psychology Bellingham WA 98225

NUGENT, ROBERT J., JR., fast food company executive; b. 1942. BBA, U. Cin., 1964. loan officer Citizens Savs., 1964-67; asst. v.p. Gem City Savs., 1967-69; v.p. Ponderosa System Inc., 1969-78, Ky. Fried Chicken, 1978-79; v.p. Foodmaker Inc., San Diego, from 1979, exec. v.p. ops., mktg., 1985-95; CEO, pres. Foodmaker Inc., 1995—. Office: Foodmaker Inc 9330 Balboa Ave San Diego CA 92123-1516*

NUMANO, ALLEN STANISLAUS MOTOYUKI, musician, writer; came to U.S., 1974; Grad., St. Joseph's Coll., Colombo, Ceylon, 1929; postgrad., Worcester Coll., Oxford, Eng., 1940, Royal Coll. Music, London, 1940. Sr. examiner, translator Gen. Hdqs. Supreme Comdr. for Allied Powers, Tokyo, 1945-47; cons., chief tech. translator U.S.-Japanese joint venture Pfizer Taito Co. Ltd., Tokyo, 1954-68; lectr. English composition Sophia U., Tokyo, 1967-68; founder Safilta Tech. Translation Svc., 1969—. Author: (as A.L.A. Corenanda) Music and Reminiscences, 1982-83; translator: All About Christmas (Maymie R. Krythe), 1962; pioneering originator in new field of study Mentalogy; contbr. concert revs., recital critiques and mus. news briefs Nippon Times (now Japan Times), also articles to Times of Ceylon, Organic Forum, Indian Labour Rev.; pencil sketches exhibited at 55th Ann. Exhbn. of Ceylon Soc. of Arts, Colombo, 1952; performed as violinist at Royal Coll. Hall, Colombo, 1940; inventor tech. innovations. Del. Sr. Citizens of Honolulu to Gov.'s State Conf. on Aging. Recipient Gov.'s Cert. of Appreciation, 1980, certs. of appreciation Pres. Ronald Reagan and Pres. George Bush; named Citizen of Yr. 1994 Principality of Hutt River Province Australia. Fellow Inst. Linguists; mem. Soc. Authors, London (assoc.), Translator's Assn., London, Smithsonian Instn. (nat. mem.).

NUNES, FRANK R., JR., food products executive; b. 1952. BA in English, Sacramento State U., 1975. Carpenter various gen. contractors, Lake Tahoe, Calif., 1975-79; pvt. practice as carpenter Lake Tahoe, Calif., 1979-82; with The Nunes Co., Inc., Salinas, Calif., 1982—; v.p. Nunes Vegetables, Inc., 1992—. Office: Nunes Vegetables Inc 929 Johnson Ave Salinas CA 93901*

NUNES, THOMAS P., food products executive; b. 1951. BA, Calif. Polytech. Inst., 1973. With Nunes Farms, Salinas, Calif., 1973-74; owner Nunes Ranches, Salinas, Calif., 1975-78; pres. Nunes Vegetables Inc., Salinas, Calif., 1978—. Office: Nunes Vegetables Inc 929 Johnson Ave Salinas CA 93901*

NUSE, DELAND LYNN, film director, writer, producer; b. Las Vegas, N.Mex., June 20, 1946; s. Herbert C. and Magdalena L. (Landrum) N.; m. Angela June Allaire, Jan. 22, 1994. BA in Psychology, Calif. State U., Stanislaw, 1969; postgrad., U. N.Mex., 1970-72; MA in Film, San Francisco State U., 1983. Lectr. in film San Francisco State U., 1980-82; cinematographer Hausberg Prodns., L.A., 1987-89; dir. Transbay Prodns., L.A., 1989-90; writer, dir. Screenplayers Co., L.A., 1991-93; prodr., dir. Matador Prodns., Palmdale, Calif., 1994—. Dir. photography (documentary) The Other Bridge, 1982 (Sci. Film award 1983); dir. photography (feature) War Birds, 1988; dir. films (short) City of Death, 1983, (feature) The Chilling, 1990; writer film (feature) M.M., 1992; dir. photography (feature) Millennium Day, 1996. Democrat. Home: 37211 Oak Hill St Palmdale CA 93552-4407

NUSSINOW, JILL ANNE, nutritionist; b. Bklyn., Apr. 13, 1955; d. Bernard L. and Mary Lou (Siegel) N.; m. Timothy J. Marchel, June 1, 1985 (div. Aug. 1991); m. Richard B. Cratty Jr., Oct. 1, 1992; 1 child, Shane Scott. BBA in Mktg., U. Miami, 1976; MS in Dietetics and Nutrition, Fla. Internat. U., 1981. Registered dietitian. Bd. dirs., purchasing coord. South Dade Food Coop, South Miami, Fla., 1978-80; dietitian Mercy Hosp., Miami, 1980-81; nutritionist trainee dept. pediatrics The Mailman Ctr. for Child Devel., U. Miami (Fla.) Med. Sch., 1981-82; dietitian in pvt. practice Calif., 1982—; nutrition cons. Control Data Corp., Westchester, Calif., Montecito Heights Health and Racquet Club, Santa Rosa, Calif., The Airport Club, Santa Rosa, Amy's Kitchen, Natural Frozen Food Mfr., Petaluma, Calif., others; instr. Calif. State U. Northridge, 1987-88, West L.A. Coll. Cmty. Svcs., Bay Cities Jewish Cmty. Ctr., Mont. Mercantile Cooking Sch.; nutritionist Maxicare, Inc., L.A., 1985-88, others; adj. faculty Santa Rosa Jr. Coll., 1989—; presenter in field. Author, editor: Vegetarian Cooking For Everyone, Vol. 1, 1993; pub.: Vegetarian Times, The Vegetarian Jour., Delicious Mag. Past. pres. Westside Consumers Edn. Found. Mem. Am. Dietetic Assn. (registered mem., vegetarian practice group), Soc. for Nutrition Edn., Dietitians in Bus. and Industry Practice Group, Sports and Cardiovascular Nutritionists Practice Group, Internat. Food, Wine and Travel Writers Assn., Internat. Assn. Culinary Profls., Sonoma County Culinary Guild (founder, past pres., pub. rels. chairperson). Home: 1988 Respite Pl Santa Rosa CA 95403-7947 Office: The Vegetarian Connection PO Box 218 Petaluma CA 94953-0218

NUSZ, PHYLLIS JANE, fundraising consultant, meeting planner; b. Lodi, Calif., Dec. 16, 1941; d. Fred Henry and Esther Emma (Enzminger) N. BA, U. Pacific, 1963, MA, 1965; EdD, Nova Southeastern U., 1987. Cert. fund raising exec. Prof. speech comm. Bakersfield (Calif.) Coll., 1965-86; from asst. dir. student activites to found. exec. dir. Bakersfield (Calif) Coll., 1965-86; mgmt. seminar dir. Delta Kappa Gamma Soc. Internat., Austin, Tex., 1983-86; loaned exec. United Way San Joaquin County, Stockton, Calif., 1990; fund raising cons. PJ Enterprises, Lodi, Calif., 1987—. Bd. dirs. U. Calif. Sch. Medicine Surg. Found., San Francisco, 1989—; mem. Heritage Circle and Chancellor's Assn., U. Calif. San Francisco, 1987—. Recipient archives award of merit Evang. Luth. Ch. in Am., 1988; fellow Calif. Luth. U., 1985—; Packer Internat. scholar, 1986-87. Mem. NEA, Nat. Soc. Fund Raising Execs. (chmn. mentor program Calif. Capital chpt. 1991, bd. dirs. 1988-91, chmn. acad. fund raising 1991, chmn. mentor program Golden Gate chpt. 1991, founding, pres. San Joaquin chpt. 1992-93, Pres.'s award for Meritorious Svc., Golden Gate chpt. 1991), U. Pacific Alumni Assn. (bd. dirs. 1974-82), Nat. Assn. Parliamentarians, Rotary (North Stockton bd. dirs. 1993—, treas. 1994-96, found. treas. 1994-96, pres.-elect 1996-97, pres. 1997—), Delta Kappa Gamma (internat. scholar 1986, chpt. pres. 1976-78). Republican. Lutheran. Office: PJ Enterprises 1300 W Lodi Ave Ste A11 Lodi CA 95242-3000

NUTTALL, MICHAEL LEE, engineer, educator; b. Salem, Mass.; s. Leonard John IV and Ethel (Pecukonis) N.; m. Susan Patricia Wade, July 12, 1988; children: Leonard John VI, Andrew Norman, Michelle Leigh, Patricia Katherine. BSChemE, Brigham Young U., 1987; MEE, U. Utah, 1994. Japanese linguist Utah Army N.G., Provo, 1984-87; math tutor Utah Valley C.C., Provo, 1987; engr. Micron Tech., Boise, Idaho, 1988-89, lead engr., 1989-91, process devel. engr., 1994—; instr. Salt Lake C.C., Salt Lake City, 1991-92. Patentee in field. Home: 1469 N Deep Creek Way Meridian ID 83642-4215 Office: Micro Tech 8000 Federal Way Boise ID 83716-9632

NUTZLE, FUTZIE (BRUCE JOHN KLEINSMITH), artist, author, cartoonist; b. Lakewood, Ohio, Feb. 21, 1942; s. Adrian Ralph and Naomi Irene (Rupert) Kleinsmith; children: Adrian David, Arielle Justine and Tess Alexandra (twins). Represented by The Pope Gallery, Santa Cruz, Calif. Author: Modern Loafer, Thames and Hudson, 1981, (autobiography) Futzie Nutzle, 1983, Earthquake, 1989, Run the World: 50 Cents Chronicle Books, 1991; illustrator: The Armies Encamped Beyond Unfinished Avenues (Morton Marcus), 1977, Box of Nothing, 1982, The Duke of Chemical Birds (Howard McCord), 1989, Book of Solutions, 1990, Fact and Friction, 1990, Managing for the 90s, 1992, Soundbites for Success, 1994; feature cartoonist Rolling Stone, N.Y.C., 1975-80, The Japan Times, Tokyo and L.A., 1986—, The Prague Post, Czechoslovakia, 1991—; contbr. exhbns. include Inaugural, 1966, Cupola, 1967, Rolling Renaissance, San Francisco, 1968, 100 Acres, O.K. Harris 1971, N.Y.C., San Francisco Mus. Art, 1972, Indpls. and Cin. Mus. Art, 1975, Leica, L.A., 1978, Santa Barbara Mus. Annex, Calif., 1978, Swope, Santa Monica, West Beach Cafe, Venice, Calif., 1985, Les Oranges, Santa Monica, Correspondence Sch., 1970-78, 1st Ann. Art-A-Thon, N.Y.C., 1985, Am. Epiphany with Phillip Hefferton, 1986, Polit. Cartoon Show, Braunstein, San Francisco, Komsomolskaya Pravda, 1988, retrospective Eloise Packard Smith, 1990, exemplary contemporary, Cowell, U. Calif. Santa Cruz, 1991, Silicon Graphics Inc., Computer Graphics for NAB, Las Vegas, 1993, Prague Eco-Fair, 1991; represented in pvt. and pub. collections (complete archives) Spl. Collections, McHenry Libr., U. Calif., Santa Cruz, Mus. Modern Art, N.Y.C., San Francisco Mus. Modern Art, Oakland Mus., San Francisco Mus. Cartoon Art, Whitney Mus. Am. Art, N.Y.C. regular contbr. The Japan Times. Ltd., Tokyo. Address: PO Box 325 Aromas CA 95004-0325

NUWER, MARC ROMAN, neuroscientist, physician; b. Buffalo, July 8, 1948; s. Donald Charles and Arlene Ruth (Ebert) N.; m. Beverly Ann Jones, Oct. 12, 1978; children: Jamie Marie, Charles Marc, Stephen John, Catherine Ann. BA, Stanford U., 1970, MSEE, 1972, PhD, 1975, MD, 1975. Diplomate Am. Bd. Psychiatry and Neurology. Asst. prof. neurology UCLA, 1979-87, assoc. prof. neurology, 1987-93, prof. neurology, 1993—, chief evoked potential lab., 1979—, chief EEG lab., 1986—; dept. head for clin. neurophysiology UCLA Med Ctr.; chmn. UCLA Neurology Profl. Group, 1985-90. Author: Evoked Potential Monitoring in the Operating Room, 1986; mem. editorial bd. Electroencephalography and Clin. Neurophysiology, Brain Topography. Med. research grantee NIH, 1980—, FDA Adv. Panel, 1994—. Fellow Am. Acad. Neurology (mem. practice com. 1991—), Am. EEG Soc. (pres. 1993-94), Am. Epilepsy Soc., Am. Soc. Neurol. Investigation (pres. 1984-85), Am. Neurol. Assn., Internat. Fedn. Clin Neurophysiology (exec. bd. 1993—, pres. 1997—), Western EEG Soc. (pres. 1990-91). Office: UCLA Dept Neurology 710 Westwood Plz Los Angeles CA 90024-8300

NWASIKE, CHIKE OKECHUKWU, computer industry executive, engineering and computer consultant; b. Envou, Nigeria, Nov. 29, 1955; came to U.S., 1974; s. Edmund Philip and Maud Odinchezo (Mbanuoo) N.; m. Noni Adadbi Nwabueze, Aug. 9, 1986; children: Chinedu, Kaylee, Ugo. BA in Engring., UCLA, 1978. Cert. Microsoft systems engr. Engr. Mobil Oil Corp., Lagos, Nigeria; CEO, pres. Optimized Tech., Inc., Chatsworth, Calif., 1985—. Mem. IEEE (computer soc.). Office: Optimized Tech Inc 9566 Topanga Canyon Blvd Chatsworth CA 91311

NYARADY, STEFAN ALAN, analytical chemist; b. Ft. Ord, Calif., May 11, 1950; s. Stefan Albert and Wanda Helen (Heltman) N.; m. Barbara Jean Millage, June 2, 1973; 1 child, Claire Kathryn. BS in Chemistry, Stanford U., 1972; MS in Chemistry, Naval Postgrad. Sch., 1973; PhD in Chemistry, U. Colo., 1985. Analytical chemist Tenn. Eastman Co., Kingsport, 1978-81; grad. rsch. asst. U. Colo., Boulder, 1982-85; devel. scientist Pfizer Pharm. Co., Groton, Conn., 1985-88; sr. devel. chemist Coors Brewing Co., Golden, Colo., 1988—. Inventor in field; contbr. articles to profl. jours. Lt. USN, 1972-78. Mem. AAAS, Am. Chem. Soc. (analytical divsn.), Am. Soc. Brewing Chemists (tech. subcom. chair 1988-94), Sigma Xi. Office: Coors Brewing Co M/S BC 600 Golden CO 80401

NYCUM, SUSAN HUBBELL, lawyer. B.A., Ohio Wesleyan U., 1956; J.D., Duquesne U., 1960; postgrad., Stanford U. Bar: Pa. 1962, U.S. Supreme Ct. 1967, Calif. 1974. Sole practice law Pitts., 1962-65; designer, adminstr. legal research system U. Pitts., Aspen Systems Corp., Pitts., 1965-68; mgr. ops. Computer Ctr., Carnegie Mellon U., Pitts., 1968-69; dir. computer facility Computer Ctr., Stanford U., Calif., 1969-72, Stanford Law and Computer fellow, 1972-73; cons. in computers and law, 1973-74; sr. assoc. MacLeod, Fuller, Muir & Godwin, Los Altos, Los Angeles and London, 1974-75; ptnr. Chickering & Gregory, San Francisco, 1975-80; ptnr.-in-charge high tech. group Gaston Snow & Ely Bartlett, Boston, NYC, Phoenix, San Francisco, Calif., 1980-86; mng. ptnr. Palo Alto office Kadison, Pfaelzer, Woodard, Quinn & Rossi, Los Angeles, Washington, Newport Beach, Palo Alto, Calif., 1986-87; sr. ptnr., chmn. U.S. IP/IT practice group Baker & McKenzie, Palo Alto, 1987—, mem. U.S. leadership team, 1987-96, mem. Asia Pacific regional coun., 1995—; trustee EDUCOM, 1978-81; mem. adv. com. for high tech. Ariz. State U. Law Sch., Santa Clara U. Law Sch., Stanford Law Sch., U. So. Calif. Law Ctr., law sch. Harvard U., U. Calif.; U.S. State Dept. del. OECD Conf. on Nat. Vulnerabilities, Spain, 1981; invited speaker Telecom, Geneva, 1983; lectr. N.Y. Law Jour., 1975—, Law & Bus., 1975—, Practicing Law Inst., 1975—; chmn. Office of Tech. Assessment Task Force on Nat. Info. Systems, 1979-80. Author:(with Bigelow) Your Computer and the Law, 1975, (with Bosworth) Legal Protection for Software, 1985, (with Collins and Gilbert) Women Leading, 1987; contbr. monographs, articles to profl. pubs. Mem. Town of Portola Valley Open Space Acquisition Com., Calif., 1977; mem. Jr. League of Palo Alto, chmn. evening div., 1975-76. NSF and Dept. Justice grantee for studies on computer abuse, 1972—. Mem. ABA (sect. on sci. and tech. chmn. 1979-80, chmn. elect 1978-79), Internat. Bar Assn. (U.S. mem. computer com. of corps. sect.), Assn. Computing Machinery (mem. at large of council 1976-80, nat. lectr. 1977—, chmn. standing com. on legal issues 1975—, blue ribbon com. on rationalization of internat. proprietary rights protection on info. processing devel. in the '90s, 1990—), Computer Law Assn. (v.p. 1983-85, pres. 1986—, bd. dirs. 1975—), Calif. State Bar Assn. (founder first chmn. econs. of law sect., vice chmn. law and computers com.), Nat. Conf. Lawyers and Scientists (rep. ABA), Strategic Forum on Intellectual Property Issues in Software of NAS. Home: 35 Granada Ct Portola Valley CA 94028-7736 Office: Baker & McKenzie PO Box 60309 Palo Alto CA 94306

NYDAM, RONALD DANIEL, manufacturing executive; b. Grand Junction, Colo., Feb. 5, 1969; s. Russel John and Vandetta Joy (Miller) N. BS in Telecom Mgmt., DeVry Coll., L.A., 1990. Chief technician Centel Comm., Anaheim, Calif., 1988-90; account exec. MCI Telecomm., L.A., 1990-92; cons. video sys. Studio Spectrum, Burbank, Calif., 1992-93; mgr. bus. tng. Omni Internat., Seattle, 1993-95; nat. sales mgr. Pinnacle Sys., Mountain View, Calif., 1995—. Mem. Internat. TV Assn. Republican. Home: 415 S Bernard Ave # 311 Sunnyvale CA 94086 Office: Pinnacle Sys Inc 280 N Bernardo Ave Mountain View CA 94043

NYE, ERIC WILLIAM, English language and literature educator; b. Omaha, July 31, 1952; s. William Frank and Mary Roberta (Lueder) N.; m. Carol Denison Frost, Dec. 21, 1980; children: Charles William, Ellen Mary. BA, St. Olaf Coll., 1974; MA, U. Chgo., 1976, PhD, 1983; postgrad., Queens' Coll., Cambridge, England, 1979-82. Tutor in coll. writing com. U. Chgo., 1976-79, tchg. intern, 1978; tutor Am. lit. Cambridge (Eng.) U., 1979-82; asst. prof. English U. Wyo., Laramie, 1983-89, assoc. prof., 1989—; v.p., bd. dirs. Plainview Tel. Co., Nebr.; hon. vis. fellow U. Edinburgh (Scotland) Inst. for Advanced Studies in the Humanities, 1987; guest lectr. NEH summer Inst., Laramie, Wyo., 1985, Carlyle Soc. of Edinburgh, 1987, Wordsworth summer Conf., Grasmere, Eng., 1988, cons. NEH. Contbr. articles and reviews to profl. jours. Mem. Am. Friends of Cambridge U., Gen. Soc. Mayflower Descendants; elected mem. Wyo. Coun. for Humanities, 1992-96, mem. exec. com., 1993-94; mem. adv. bd. Wyo. Ctr. for the Book, 1995—. Named Nat. Merit Scholar St. Olaf Coll., 1970-74; recipient Grad. Fellowship, Rotary Found., 1979-80, grant Am. Coun. of Learned Socs., 1988, Disting. Alumnus award, Lincoln (Neb.) E. High Sch., 1986. Mem. MLA (del. assembly 1991-93), Assn. for Documentary Editing, Bibliog. Soc. London, Assn. for Computers and the Humanities, Assn. for Lit. and Linguistic Computing, Coleridge Soc. (life), Friends of Dove Cottage (life), Charles Lamb Soc., Carlyle Soc., Rsch. Soc. for Victorian Periodicals, Soc. for History of Authorship, Reading and Pub., The Victorians Inst., Gen. Soc. Mayflower Descs., The Tennyson Soc., Penn Club (London), Queens Coll. Club (Cambridge) Phi Beta Kappa (pres., v.p., sec. Wyo. chpt. 1988—). Home: 1495 Apache Dr Laramie WY 82070-6966 Office: U Wyo Dept English PO Box 3353 Laramie WY 82071-3353

NYE, GENE WARREN, art educator; b. Sacramento, July 3, 1939; s. Charles Frederick and Dorthy Dell Nye; m. Alena Mae Nye, Sept. 20, 1974; children: Dirk, Ronni, Anthony, Timothy. AA, American River Coll., Sacramento, 1962; AB, Sacramento State U., 1964; cert. Secondary Art Tchr., U. Calif., Berkeley, 1966. Printer Roseville (Calif.) Press Tribune, 1957-60; typographer Oakland (Calif.) Tribune, 1960-65; tchr. art Long Beach (Calif.) Unified Sch. Dist., 1965-67; tchr., chair art dept. Woodland (Calif.) Unified Sch. Dist., 1967—; freelance artist Wildcat Art, Sacramento, 1985—; cons. N.Mex. Ctrl. Coun. Student Activities, 1991; workshop presenter. Author: (workbook set and video) Posters Made EZ, 1990. Mem. task force Constn. Revision of CADA, L.A., 1988-89. Named to Calif. Assn. Dirs. of Activities Hall of Fame, 1992. Mem. NEA (life), Calif. Tchrs. Assn., Woodland Edn. Assn. (v.p. 1971-72), Calif. Art Edn. Assn., Nat. Art Edn. Assn., Calif. League Mid. Schs., U. Calif.-Berkeley Alumni Assn. (life). Home: 2200 Eastern Ave Sacramento CA 95864-0805 Office: Lee Jr HS 520 West St Woodland CA 95695-3705

NYE, MARY JO, historian, humanities educator; b. Nashville, Dec. 5, 1944; d. Joe Allen and Mildred (Heath) Mann; m. Robert Allen Nye, Feb. 17, 1968; 1 child, Lesley Noel. Student, Vanderbilt U., 1962-64; BA, U. Wis., 1964-65, PhD, 1965-70. From asst. prof. to assoc. prof. then prof. U. Okla., 1970-94; prof. humanities and history Oreg. State U., Corvallis, 1994—; assoc. fellow ctr. for Hist. Study Rutgers U., New Brunswick, N.J., 1989-90; mem. sch. hist. studies Inst. Advanced Study, Princeton, N.J., 1981-82; vis. prof. Harvard U., Cambridge, Mass., 1988. Author: Molecular Reality, 1972, Science in the Provinces, 1986, From Chemical Philosophy to Theoretical Chemistry, 1993, Before Big Science, 1996; editor: The Question of the Atom, 1984, The Invention of Physical Science, 1992. Fellow AAAS; mem. Hist. Sci. Soc. (pres. 1988-89), Am. Hist. Assn., Internat. Union of History and Philosphy of Sci. (U.S. nat. com. 1986-89), Internat. Union of History and Philosophy of Sci. (2d v.p. divsn. history and sci. 1993—), Phi Beta Kappa.

NYE, W. MARCUS W., lawyer; b. N.Y.C., Aug. 3, 1945; s. Walter R. and Nora (McLaren) N.; m. Eva Johnson; children: Robbie, Stephanie, Philip, Jennifer. BA, Harvard U., 1967; JD, U. Idaho, 1974. Bar: Idaho 1974, U.S. Dist. Ct. Idaho 1974, U.S. Ct. Appeals (9th cir.) 1980; lic. pilot. Ptnr. Racine, Olson, Nye, Cooper & Budge, Pocatello, Idaho, 1974—; vis. prof. law U. Idaho, Moscow, 1984; adj. prof. Coll. Engring. Idaho State U., 1993—; bd. dirs. Idaho State U. Found. Recipient Alumni Svc. award U. Idaho, 1988. Fellow ABA (mem. ho. dels. 1988—, state chmn. ho. of dels. 1991—, bd. of govs. 1997—), Am. Bar Found. (stat. chmn. 1992-95); mem. Am. Bd. Trial Advs., Am. Coll. Trial Lawyers, Idaho Bar Assn. (commr. 1985—, pres. bd. commrs. 1987-88), Idaho Def. Counsel Assn. (pres. 1982), Idaho State Centennial Found. (commr. 1985-90), 6th Dist. Bar Assn. (pres. 1982). Home: 173 S 15th Ave Pocatello ID 83201-4056 Office: Racine Olson Nye Cooper & Budge PO Box 1391 Pocatello ID 83204-1391

NYGAARD, MARY PAYNE, primary school education; b. Rome, Ga., Dec. 27, 1948; d. Julian Wesley and Mary Kate Payne; m. Steven Jay Nygaard, Apr. 5, 1975; children: Mandy Lee Nygaard Herreid, Carrie Ann. BA, Berry Coll., 1969; M in Ednl. Leadership, U. Portland, 1994. Lifetime tchg. cert. Wash. First grade tchr. Goldendale (Wash.) Primary Sch., 1969-73, kindergarten tchr., 1973-76; sch. bd. mem. Goldendale (Wash.) Christian Sch., 1981-82, kindergarten tchr., 1982-86, tchr. grades 1-3, 1986-87; home sch. tchr. grades 4 and 6 Goldendale, 1987-88; substitute tchr. grades K-8 Centerville Sch. Goldendale (Wash.) Primary Sch., 1988-90, tchr. grade 1, 1990-94, title I coord., 1994—. Mem. Delta Kappa Gamma (pres. 1992-94). Baptist. Office: Goldendale Primary Sch 820 S Schuster Ave Goldendale WA 98620-9038

NYIRI, JOSEPH ANTON, sculptor, art educator; b. Racine, Wis., May 24, 1937; s. Joseph Anton Nyiri and Dorothy Marion (Larson) Zink; m. Laura Lee Primeau, Aug. 29, 1959 (dec. Mar. 1982); children: Krista, Nicole, Page; m. Melissa Trent, July 28, 1985. BA, U. Wis., 1959, MS, 1961. Tchr. art Madison (Wis.) Sch. Dist., 1959-62; art cons. San Diego Unified Schs., 1962-65, dist. resource tchr., 1965-73, regional tchr. occupational art, 1973-76, mentor tchr., 1985-95; sculptor San Diego, 1962—, fine arts cons., 1966—; head dept. art edn. Serra H.S., San Diego, 1976-95; tchr. art Zool. Soc. San Diego, 1991-95; ret., 1995; cons. gifted and talented edn. program San Diego City Schs., 1995—, gifted programs Escondido, Calif. and Poway, Calif. Schs., 1995—, Boston Schs., 1996, Romana, Calif. Pub. Schs., 1997—; instr. art U. Calif. at San Diego, La Jolla, 1967-80, San Diego State U. Extension,

1969—; fine art restorer, 1963—, lectr. art and art edn., 1963—; pvt. art tchr. San Diego City Zoo. Exhibited sculpture in numerous one-man, two-person, juried and invitational shows, 1960—, U. Mex.-Baja Calif., 1983; rev. Calif. Art Rev., 1989. Active Art Guild San Diego Mus. Art; bd. dirs. San Diego Art Inst. Sgt. Wis. N.G., 1955-61. Named One of 3 Tchrs. of Yr., San Diego County, 1983, One of Outstanding Art Tchrs. in U.S., RISD, 1984, Secondary Tchr. of Yr., San Diego City Schs., 1982; recipient creativity award Pacific Inst., 1969. Mem. Arts/Worth: Nat. Coun. Art (charter), Allied Craftsmen San Diego, Internat. Platform Assn., San Diego Art Inst. (bd. dirs.), San Diego Mus. Art (mem. Art Guild). Democrat. Mem. Christian Ch. Office: 3525 Albatross St San Diego CA 92103-4807 Also: Zool Soc San Diego Edn Dept PO Box 551 San Diego CA 92112 *Personal philosophy: Love others, exercise everyday, be creative, live life and enjoy, be able to receive pleasure and give pleasure and live life as if you are going to die tomorrow.*

NYMAN, DAVID HAROLD, retired nuclear engineer; b. Aberdeen, Wash., May 21, 1938; s. Carl Victor and Elsie Ingagord (Laaksonen) N. Assoc., Grays Harbor Coll., 1958; BSMetE, U. Wash., 1961, MSMetE, 1963. Engr. Gen. Electric Co., Richland, Wash., 1963-68; engrng. specialist United Nuclear Corp., New Haven, 1968-73; mgr. Westinghouse Hanford subs. Westinghouse Corp., Richland, 1973-96; ret., 1996. Contbr. articles to profl jours. Mem. Robotics Internat. of Soc. Mfg. Engrs. (div. chmn. 1985-86, tech. v.p. 1986-88), Robots West Conf. (adv. com. 1984, vice-chmn. 1986, Pres.'s award 1989), Am. Nuclear Soc. (chmn. meetings, proceedings, and transactions com. 1992—), Am. Soc. Metals., Inst. Nuclear Materials Mgmt., Columbia Basin Dog Tng. Club (pres. 1982-84), Richland Kennel Club, West Highland White Terrier Club of Puget Sound, West Highland White Terrier Club Am. (obedience com. 1982-88), Am. Kennel Club (judge tracking dog excellent tests). Republican. Lutheran.

NYQUIST, MAURICE OTTO, government agency administrator and scientist; b. Fairmont, Minn., May 30, 1944; s. Carl Arther and Wilda Yvette (Freitag) N.; m. Mary Maud Magee, Aug. 8, 1977; children: Gretchen, Beth. BS in Biology, Hamline U., 1966; MA in Biology, Mankato State U., 1968; PhD in Zoology, Wash. State U., 1973. Asst. prof. zoology Wash. State U., Pullman, 1973-74; scientist Nat. Park Svc., Lakewood, Colo., 1974-76, mgr., 1979-93; mgr., scientist Nat. Biol. Svc., Denver, 1993-96, USGS, Denver, 1996—; mem. peer rev. coms. for academia, govt. and pvt. industry; agy. rep. Fed. Geographic Data Com. Dir. prodn. interactive computer exhibit on remote sensing for Denver Mus. Nat. History; contbr. sci. articles to profl. jours. Bd. dirs. Nat. Park Service Equal Employment Opportunity Com., Denver, 1981, chmn., 1982. Recipient Mgrs. award Nat. Park Service, Lakewood, 1981, Performance Commendation award, 1988; research grantee Nat. Rifle Assn., 1972. Fellow Am. Soc. Potogrammetry and Remote Sensing (exec. com., bd. dirs. 1988-90, v.p. 1992, pres.-elect 1993, pres. 1994, asst. dir. remote sensing applications divsn. 1985-87); mem. Am. Congress on Surveying and Mapping (joint satellite mapping and remote sensing com.), The Wildlife Soc., GRASS Users Group (steering com. 1986—, treas. 1987—), ELAS Users Group (co-chmn. 1985-86, chmn. 1986-87), Sigma Xi. *Personal philosophy: We need to view the land as a community to which we all belong, instead of a commodity for individual gain. (adopted from Aldo Leopold's A Sand County Almanac, 1949).*

NYQUIST, MICHAEL S., civil engineer; b. Marquette, Mich., Oct. 22, 1949; s. George R. and Hazel (Moyle) N.; m. Valda M. Marais, July 31, 1982. BME, GM Inst., 1972; MPA, No. Ariz. U., 1983. With engrng. staff Gen. Motors, 1967-73; with Frederic R. Harris, Inc., Ft. Lauderdale, Fla., and Haiti, Trinidad, Lesotho, 1976-82; constrn. engr. Bur. of Indian Affairs, Phoenix and Keams Canyon, 1983-85, highway design sect. leader, 1985-87; highway design engr. Evans, Kuhn and Assocs., Phoenix, 1987-88; roads advisor, head of roads sect. Chemonics Internat., Cairo, Egypt, 1988-90; road/traffic engr. Burrow Binnie Ltd. (formerly John Burrow and Ptnrs.), Mbabane, Swaziland, 1990-92; civil engr. Louis Berger Internat., General Santos City, Philippines, 1990, 92-93; chief of party Mozambique, 1993-95; hwy. design engr. Post Buckley, Swaziland, 1996—; mem. U.S. Peace Corps, Lesotho, Swaziland, 1973-76.

OAK, CLAIRE MORISSET, artist, educator; b. St. Georges, Quebec, Can., May 31, 1921; came to U.S., 1945; d. Louis and Bernadette (Coulombe) Morisset; m. Alan Ben Oak, July 2, 1947. Student, Ecole des Beaux Arts, 1938-42, Parsons Sch. Design, N.Y.C., 1945, Art Students League, N.Y.C., 1945-46. Staff artist Henry Morgan & R. Simpson, Montreal, 1942-45; artist illustrator W.B. Golovin Advt. Agy., N.Y.C., 1947-49; freelance illustrator Arnold Constable & Advt. Agy., N.Y.C., 1948-50, Le Jardin des Modes, Paris, 1950-51, May & Co., L.A., 1956, Katten & Marengo Advt., Stockton, Calif., 1962-84; pvt. practice illustrator, designer San Joaquin Valley, Calif., 1984-92; art instr. San Joaquin Delta Coll., Stockton, 1973—; owner Fashion Illustrator's Workshop, N.Y.C., 1953-54; instr. Bauder Coll., Sacramento, 1975-76; painting workshop leader Lodi Art Ctr., 1991—; watercolor workshop leader D'Pharr Painting Adventures, Virginia City, Nev., 1992; ongoing watercolor workshop Galerie Iona, Stockton, Calif., 1993—. Named S.B. Anthony Woman of Achievement in the Arts, U. Pacific, 1982. Mem. Stockton Art League, Lodi Art Ctr., Ctrl. Calif. Art League, The League of Carmichael Artists, Delta Watercolor Soc. (bd. mem. 1988—). Home: 2140 Waudman Ave Stockton CA 95209-1755 *You are a success in the visual arts if you teach others how to see.*

OAKES, DUWAYNE EARL, retired principal; b. Fillmore, N.D., May 28, 1926; s. Ralph William Oakes and Ella Catherine (Anderson) Baril; m. Elva Jean Jacobsen, Nov. 6, 1948; children: Jon, Robert, Kathleen, Mary. BA in Edn., Pacific Luth. U., 1952, MA, 1972. Tchr. DuPont Ft. Lewis Sch. Dist., Wash., 1952-59; prin. DuPont Ft. Lewis Sch. Dist., 1959, Clover Park Sch. Dist., Lakewood, Wash., 1959-71. Author: God's Call to Communion, 1982; contbr.: National Poetry Library Anthology, 1995-96; inventor fishing rod socket. Vol. Red Cross Mealsite. Inductee Internat. Poetry Hall of Fame, 1996. Mem. Norwegian Lodge, Eagles Club. Christian Socialist. Lutheran. Home: 8515 94th St SW Lakewood WA 98498

OAKES, ROBERT GIBSON, retired electronics company executive, management consultant; b. Oyster Bay, N.Y., Mar. 20, 1918; s. George Nettleton and Sarah (Thornton) O.; m. Delores Marie Cook, June 12, 1954 (div. Oct. 1962); 1 child, Robert Jr. BBA, Manhattan Coll., 1941; postgrad., Harvard U., 1942-43; MBA, NYU, 1954; cert. in profl. contracts mgmt., UCLA, 1969. Cert. profl. contracts mgr. Enlisted USN, 1943, advanced through grades to comdr.; asst. naval attache USN, Rome, 1949-50; retired USN, 1965; adminstrv. buyer N. Am. Aviation Co., Downey, Calif., 1966-68; subcontract mgr. Rockwell Internat. Corp., Downey, 1968-72; head cost analysis group Hughes Aircraft Co., El Segundo, Calif., 1973-80, mgr. cost analysis, 1980-85, procurement mgr., spl. projects (Hughes-Gen. Motors), 1986-88; mgmt. cons., 1988—. Pres. Sunset Rep. Club, Sherman Oaks, Calif., 1988-89, 96, 97. Fellow Nat. Contract Mgmt. Assn.; mem. Res. Officers Assn. (bd. dirs. chpt. 14, treas. 1996, sec., treas.), Ret. Officers Assn. (2nd v.p. San Fernando Valley chpt. 1994), Hughes Mgmt. Club, Mil. Order World Wars, Navy League U.S. Republican. Roman Catholic. Home and Office: 15153 Otsego St Sherman Oaks CA 91403-1204

OAKES, TERRY LOUIS, retail clothing store executive; b. Denver, June 12, 1953; s. Robert Walter and Stella Marie (Ray) O.; m. Cynthia Alison Bailey, Jan. 10, 1981; children: Madeleine Bailey, Robert Alan. BBA, So. Meth. U., 1975. Dept. mgr. Wolff Bros., Dallas, 1975-76; buyer I.K.O. Dry Goods, Denver, 1976-79, gen. sales mgr., 1979-81, exec. v.p., mdse. mgr., 1981-86; nat. sales mgr. Fresh Squeeze div. Bayly Corp., Denver, 1986-88; owner, pres. Bolderdash, Denver, 1988—; tchr., mem. adv. bd. fashion mdse. divsn. Colo. Inst. Art., Denver, 1991—. Bd. dirs. Vail Racquet Club, Vail, Colo. Mem. Vail Racquet Club (bd. dirs.). Democrat. Presbyterian. Home: 5390 S Geneva St Englewood CO 80111-6219 Office: Bolderdash 2817 E 3rd Ave Denver CO 80206-4905

OAKES, THOMAS CHAPAS, financal analyst; b. Elizabeth, N.J., Dec. 7, 1960; s. John H. and Effie C. O.; Claudia B. Barros, Sept. 17, 1985. BA in Econ., Rutgers U., 1983, BS in Engring., 1983; MBA in Fin. cum laude, U. Chgo., 1992; postgrad., Ariz. State U., 1993—. Regional sales mgr. Vibra Screw, Inc., Totowa, N.J., 1984-86; investment specialist NML/Baird Securities, Princeton, N.J., 1986; fin. cons. Merrill Lynch & Co., Princeton, N.J., 1987-88; nat. sales mgr. Roscom, Inc., Trenton, N.J., 1988-90; pres. OMOT, Inc., Chgo., 1991-92; pres., dir., chmn. OMOT Cons., Inc., Mesa, Ariz., 1994—; lectr. fin. Ariz. State U., Tempe, 1995—. Author: Understanding Financial Institutions, Markets and Instruments, 1996; editor: (newsletter) General Investment, 1995. Sr. examiner Ariz. Govs. Quality award, Phoenix, 1992. Am. Collegiate Schs. Bus. fellow, 1993. Mem. Omicron Delta Epsilon. Republican. Home: 7420 E Knowles Ave Mesa AZ 85208 Office: Ariz State Univ Dept Fin Tempe AZ 85287

OAKLEY, CAROLYN LE, state legislator, small business owner; b. Portland, Oreg., June 28, 1942; d. George Thomas and Ruth Alveta Victoria (Engberg) Penketh; children: Christine, Michelle. BS in Edn., Oreg. State U., 1965. Educator Linn County (Oreg.) Schs., 1965-76; owner Linn County Tractor, 1965-90; mem. Oreg. Legis. Assembly, Salem, 1989—, asst. majority leader, 1993—, majority whip, 1994; mem. exec. bd. Oreg. Retail Coun., 1987-90. Chmn. Linn County Rep. Ctrl. Com., 1982-84; chmn. bd. dirs. North Albany Svc. Dist., 1988-90; chair Salvation Army, Linn and Benton Counties, 1987—; vice chmn. bd. trustees Linn-Benton C.C. Found., 1987—; pres. Women for Agr., Linn and Benton Counties, 1984-86; mem. STRIDE Leadership Round Table, 1991—; state chair Am. Legis. Exch. Coun., 1991-96; nat. bd. dirs., 1993, exec. com., 1995, nat. 2d vice chair, 1996; mem. Edn. Commn. of the States, 1991—, com. policies and priorities, 1993—; mem. Leadership Coun. on Higher Edn., 1995—; mem. nat. policy bd. Danforth Found., 1995—; state dir., Women in Govt., 1996; state dir., Nat. Order Women Legislators, 1993—; hon. mem. Linn-Benton Compact Bd., 1993—; active Linn County Criminal Justice Coun., 1994—. Named Woman of Yr. Albany chpt. Beta Sigma Phi, 1970. Mem. Nat Conf. State Legislators (chmn. edn. com. 1992—), Albany C. of C. (bd. dirs. 1986-93, 96—), Linn County Rep. women (legis. chmn. 1982-91). Republican. Methodist. Home: 3197 NW Crest Loop Albany OR 97321-9627 Office: Oreg Legis Assembly State Capital Salem OR 97310

OAKLEY, JOHN BILYEU, law educator, lawyer, judicial consultant; b. San Francisco, June 18, 1947; s. Samuel Heywood and Elsie-Maye (Bilyeu) O.; m. Fredericka Barvitz, May 25, 1969; children: Adélie, Antonia. BA, U. Calif., Berkeley, 1969; JD, Yale U., 1972. Bar: Calif. 1972, U.S. Dist. Ct. (no. dist.) Calif. 1974, U.S. Dist. Ct. (ctrl. and ea. dists.) Calif. 1975, U.S. Supreme Ct. 1977, U.S. Ct. Appeals (5th cir.) 1979, U.S. Ct. Appeals (9th cir.) 1992. Rsch. atty. chief justice Donald R. Wright Supreme Ct. of Calif., 1972-73, sr. rsch. atty. chief justice Donald R. Wright, 1974-75; sr. law clk. chief judge M. Joseph Blumenfeld U.S. Dist. Ct. Conn., Hartford, 1973-74; acting prof. law U. Calif., Davis, 1975-79, prof. law, 1979—; reporter Speedy Trial Planning Group, U.S. Dist. Ct., Sacramento, 1977-82, Civil Justice Reform Act Adv. Group, 1991-94, U.S. Jud. Conf. Com. on Fed.-State Jurisdiction, 1991-96, Western Regional Conf. on State-Fed. Jud. Relationships, 1992-93; scholar-in-residence, sr. trial atty. Civil Rights Divsn., U.S. Dept. Justice, Washington, 1979-80; vis. scholar U. Coll., Oxford (Eng.) U., 1982-83; apptd. counsel death penalty appeal Supreme Ct. Calif., 1984-96; cons. Calif. Jud. Coun. Commn. on the Future of the Cts., 1992-93. Co-author: Law Clerks and the Judicial Process, 1980, An Introduction to the Anglo-American Legal System, 1980, 2d edit., 1988, Civil Procedure, 1991, 2d edit., 1996; contbr.: Restructuring Justice, 1990. Pub. mem. New Motor Vehicle Bd. Calif., Sacramento, 1976-82; bd. dirs. Fallen Leaf Lake (Calif.) Mutual Water Co., 1980-82, 94—; western regional assoc., field assoc. Duke U. Primate Ctr., 1986-91. With U.S. Merchant Marine, 1969, Vietnam. Nat. Merit scholar, 1964. Mem. Am. Law Inst. (reporter project on revision of fed. jud. code 1995—), Assn. Am. Law Schs. (chair sect. on civil procedure 1979-80, 96-97), Phi Beta Kappa. Office: Univ Calif Sch Law Davis CA 95616

OAKS, M(ARGARET) MARLENE, minister; b. Grove City, Pa., Mar. 30, 1940; d. Allen Roy and Alberta Bell (Pinner) Eakin; m. Lowell B. Chaney, July 30, 1963 (dec. Jan. 1977); children: Christopher Allen, Linda Michelle; m. Harold G. Younger, Aug. 1978 (div. 1986); m. Gilbert E. Oaks, Aug. 3, 1987. BA, Calif. State U., L.A., 1972; religious sci. studies with several instrs. Ordained to ministry Cmty. Ch., 1978. Tchr. Whittier (Calif.) Sch. Dists., 1972-74, Garden Grove (Calif.) Sch. Dist., 1974-78; instr. Fullerton Coll., 1974-75; founding min. Community Ch. of the Islands (now Ch. of Religious Sci.), Honolulu, 1978-80; min. Ch. of Divine Sci., Pueblo, Colo., 1980-83; founding min. Ch. Religious Sci., Palo Alto, Calif., 1983-86; min. First ch. Religious Sci., Fullerton, Calif., 1986-94, min. emeritus, 1994—; 2d v.p., chmn., corp. sec. VCC Internat., Anaheim, Calif., 1994—; founder, pres. LaVida Inst., Inc., 1994—; pres. Lavida Inst.; sr. pastor Lavida A Ch. for Today's World; 2nd v.p., vorp. sec. VCC Internat.; workshop leader Religious Sci. Dist. Conv., San Jose, Calif., 1985, Internat. New Thought Alliance Conf., Las Vegas, 1984, 92, Calgary, Alta., Can., 1985, Washington, 1988, Denver, 1989, Anaheim, Calif., 1990, Golden Valley Unity Women's Advance, Mpls., 1986, 87, Qume Corp., San Jose, 1985; presenter SANTI Conf., 1992-94; guest workshop leader Ctr. for Life Enrichment, 1990-92; speaker to cmty. of Tartarstan, 1993. Author: The Christmas in You, 1983, rev. edit., 1994, Ki Aikido the Inner Martial Art, 1984, Old Time Religion Is a Cult, 1985, 2d rev. edit., 1992, Service the Sure Path to Enlightenment, 1985, Stretch Marks on My Aura, 1987, rev. edit., 1995, Beyond Addiction, 1990, 10 Core Concepts of Science of Mind, 1991, Forgiveness and Beyond, 1992, rev. edit. Christmas for All Seasons, 1994, 21 Seeds, Miracle Grow For the Soul, 1995, Values Remembered, 1995, 21 Seeds-Miracle Grow for Your Soul, Values Remembered, Forgiveness and Beyond, The Alsone in English and in Russian. Del. Soviet and Am. Citizens Summit Conf., 1988, 89; pres. Soviet-Am. New Thought Initiatives, 1991, chmn. conf. St. Petersburg, 1992, Moscow, 1992, weekly radio program Radio Moscow, The Philippines, 1992—; founder Operation K.I.D.S., La Vida Inst., 1994; founder, bd. dirs. Awakening Oaks Found., 1990; pres. SANTI, 1991-94, founder and pres. La Vida Inst., 1994. Named Outstanding Businesswoman, Am. Business-women's Assn., 1989. Mem. Fullerton Interfaith Ministerial Assn. (sec.-treas. 1987-89, pres. 1991-92), United Clergy of Religious Sci. (treas. 1991-92, sec. 1992-93, treas. So. Calif. chpt. 1991-92, v.p. 1993-94, pres. 1994-95), Internat. New Thought Alliance (O.C. chpt. pres. 1990), Soroptomists (chair com. internat. coop. and goodwill 1987-88), Kappa Delta Pi. Republican. Office: LaVida Inst Awakening Oaks Press 1775 E Lincoln Ave Ste 101 Anaheim CA 92805-4300

OARD, MICHAEL JOHN, meteorologist; b. Seattle, Sept. 23, 1945; s. John Lionel and Frances (Vawter) O.; m. Beverly Maureen Muoth, June 18, 1969; children: David, Tara, Amy, Nathan. BS, U Wash., 1969; MS, U. Wash., 1973. Researcher U. Wash., Seattle, 1969-70; agrl. meteorologist Nat. Weather Svc., Bakersfield, Calif., 1975-77; aviation forecaster Nat. Weather Svc., Great Falls, Mont., 1977-80, lead forecaster, 1980—. Author: An Ice Age Caused by the Genesis Flood, 1990, Ancient Ice Ages or Gigantic Submarine Landslides?, 1996, The Weather Book, 1997; co-author: Life in the Great Ice Age, 1993; contbr. articles to profl. jours. With USN, 1964-66. Mem. Am. Meteorol. Soc., Creation Rsch. Soc., Bible-Sci. Assn. Republican. Home: 3600 7th Ave S Great Falls MT 59405-3409

OATES, CATHERINE ANNE, writer, editor; b. Inglewood, Calif., Feb. 21, 1962; d. William Frederick and Vicki Susan (Mott) Oates; m. Thomas Allen Knotts, Sept. 10, 1990; 1 child, Stephen William Jesse Knotts. BA, Calif. State U., Hayward, 1987; MA, Stanford U., 1989. Assoc. editor Sequoia Jour., Stanford, Calif., 1988-89; tchg. asst. dept. English Stanford U., 1988-89; writer, 1989—. Contbr. poetry to Ceilidh, Painted Bride, So. Humanities Rev., Art Times, Anthology of Mag. Verse. Democrat.

OATES, JOYCE MARIE, psychiatrist; b. Salt Lake City, Mar. 31, 1948; d. Douglas Francis and Lois Joy (Allgaier) O. BS magna cum laude, U. Utah, 1970, MD, 1974. Diplomate Am. Bd. Psychiatry and Neurology. Intern Pa. Hosp., Phila., 1974-75; resident in psychiatry Inst. of Pa. Hosp., Phila., 1975-78; physician Intensive Treatment unit Copper Mountain Community Mental Health Ctr., Salt Lake City, 1978-79; pvt. practice psychiatry Salt Lake City, 1980-88; med. dir. psychiatry Yuma (Ariz.) Reg. Med. Ctr., 1988-90; psychiatrist locum tenens CompHealth, Salt Lake City, 1990; pvt. practice psychiatrist Las Vegas, 1990—; med. dir. Cinnamon Hills residential treatment, 1993—; med. dir., part owner Vista Treatment Ctr., St. George, Utah, 1995-96. Mem. Latter Day Saints.

O'BANION, TERRY UNDERWOOD, academic administrator, consultant; b. La Belle, Fla., Aug. 19, 1936; s. Terry Hugh and Olney Cuthbert (Blount) O'Banion; m. Yolande Ringoot, June 27, 1980; children: Kerry, Erin. BA, U. Fla., 1958, MEd, 1961; PhD, Fla. State U., 1966. Dean of students Ctrl. Fla. Jr. Coll., Ocala, 1960-64; dean of students Santa Fe C.C., Gainesville, Fla., 1964-67; prof. higher edn. U. Ill., Urbana, 1967-75; exec. dir. League for Innovation in the C.C., L.A., 1975-80, League for Innovation, Mission Viejo, Calif., 1982—; vice chancellor Dallas C.C.s, 1980-82; cons. 500 c.c. and univs, 46 states, 1985—; vis. prof. U. Calif., Berkeley, Fla. State U., U. Hawaii; disting. vis. prof. U. Tex. Author: (11 books) including Teaching and Learning in the Community College, 1994, Innovation in the Community College, 1991; contbr. articles, book chpts. to profl. publs. Recipient Nat. Leadership award Am. Assn. C.C.s, 1994. Home: 26 Vienna Newport Beach CA 92660-6832 Office: League for Innovation 26522 La Alameda Ste 370 Mission Viejo CA 92691-6330

O'BERG, ROBERT MYRON, minister; b. Long Beach, Calif., Apr. 21, 1961; s. Robert Ronald and Carolyn Ruth (Smith) O'B.; m. Kristen Johnson, Mar. 22, 1986; children: Erin Kristine, Robert William. BA, U. Calif., Riverside, 1983; MA, Claremont Grad. Sch., 1990; MDiv, Pacific Luth. Theol. Sem., 1991. Ordained to ministry Luth. Ch., 1991. Assoc. pastor Our Saviour Luth. Ch., Evang. Luth. Ch. in Am., Simi Valley, Calif., 1991—; book reviewer Augsburg Fortress Pub. House; initial interviewer multi-synodical candidacy com. Evang. Luth. Ch. in Am.; relief chaplain Simi Valley Hosp. and Health Care Svcs.; convener Simi Valley Ecumenical Coun. (Luth., Episcopal and Roman Cath.), 1993-95. Mem. steering com. Luth. Social Svcs. Ctrl. Coast, 1993. Recipient Disting. Svc. award Luth. Social Svcs., 1993; named Pastor of Day, Sta. KKLA-FM, 1995. Mem. Aid Assn. for Lutherans, Luth. Brotherhood, U. Calif.-Riverside Alumni Assn., Claremont Grad. Sch. Alumni Assn., Pacific Luth. Theol. Sem. Alumni Assn. Democrat. Home: 6439 Sibley St Simi Valley CA 93063-3857 Office: Our Savior Luth Ch 4191 Cochran St Simi Valley CA 93063-2347

OBERLANDER, CORNELIA HAHN, landscape architect; b. Muelheim-Ruhr, Germany, June 20, 1924; arrived in U.S., 1939; d. Franz and Lotte Beate (Jastrow) H.; m. H. Peter Oberlander, Jan. 2, 1953; children: Judith A., Timothy A., Wendy E. BA, Smith Coll., 1944; B of Landscape Architecture, Harvard U., 1947; LLD (hon.), U. British Columbia, 1991. guest prof. U. B.C. Dept. Landscape Architecture, 1992; lectr. for guided tour Renaissance Gardens of No. Italy, Smith Coll. Alumni Assn., 1988; mem. adv. com. on design Nat. Capital Commn., 1975-82; mem. adv. panel, co-founder Children's Play Resource Centre, Vancouver, 1978—; lectr. in field. Prin. works include C.K. Choi Bldg., U. B.C., 1992-96, New Pub. Library, 1992—, Asian Inst., U. B.C., 1993—, Thunderbird Housing, U. B.C., 1992—, Kwantlen Coll., 1991—, Cariboo Coll., 1991—, N.W. Territories Legis. Bldg., 1991—, UN Peacekeeping Meml., 1990—, Ritsumeikan U. B.C. Ho., 1990—, Ottawa City Hall, 1989—, Environ. Sci. Bd., Ward Environ. Garden, Trent U., 1989—, Nat. Gallery Can., 1983-88, Canadian Chancery, Washington D.C., 1983-89. Recipient medal Smith Coll., 1982, Regional Honor award and Nat. Merit award Christopher Phillips Landcape Architects, Inc., 1992, Allied Arts medal Royal Archtl. Inst. Can., 1995, Cathedral Place, 1983-88, Nat. Gallery of Can., Ottawa, Ontario, Can. Chancery Am. Assn. of Nurseymen, 1990, Grand award for L'Ambassade du Can., Landscape Contractors Assn., 1989, Can. Architect award of Excellence, Matsuzaki Wright Architects, Inc., 1989, Amenity award City of Vancouver for Robson Square, 1986, Citation award Can. Soc. of Architects for Chancery & Nat. Gallery, 1990. Fellow Am. Soc. Landscape Architects, Can. Soc. Landscape Architects; mem. Order of Can., Royal Can. Acad. Arts, Archtl. Inst. B.C. (hon.). Home: 1372 Acadia Rd, Vancouver, BC Canada V6T 1P6

OBERLINK, JAMES RICHARD, environmental association executive, lawyer; b. Vandalia, Ill., Feb. 20, 1953; s. James Wendell and Gladys Mae (Stine) O. AB, U. Ill., 1976; JD, U. Calif., Berkeley, 1980. Bar: Calif. 1981. Law clk. Sierra Club Legal Def. Fund, San Francisco, 1979; atty. Law Office of Robert Lane, Oakland, Calif., 1982-83, Law Office of Garrett Riegg, Oakland, 1989-92; exec. dir. Californians for Population Stabilization, Sacramento, 1992—; mem. Chancellor's Com. on Conservation and Environ. Quality, Berkeley, 1978-79; spkr., writer in field. Served with U.S. Army, 1971-73, Germany. Mem. Sierra Club, East Bay Bicycle Coalition. Office: Californians for Population Stabilization 926 J St Ste 915 Sacramento CA 95814-2707

OBERSTEIN, MARYDALE, geriatric specialist; b. Red Wing, Minn., Dec. 30; d. Dale Robert and Jean Ebba-Marie (Holmquist) Johnson; children: Kirk Robert, Mark Paul, MaryJean. Student, U. Oreg., 1961-62, Portland State U., 1962-64, Long Beach State U., 1974-76. Cert. geriatric specialist, Calif. Florist, owner Sunshine Flowers, Santa Ana, Calif., 1982—; pvt. duty nurse Aides in Action, Costa Mesa, Calif., 1985-87; owner, activity dir., adminstr. Lovelight Christian Home for the Elderly, Santa Ana, 1987—; activity dir. Bristol Care Nursing Home, Santa Ana, 1985-88; evangelist, speaker radio show Sta. KPRZ-FM, Anaheim, Calif., 1985-88; adminstr. Leisure Lodge Resort Care for Elderly in Lake Forest, Lake Forest, Calif., 1996—; nursing home activist in reforming laws to eliminate bad homes, 1984-90; founder, tchr. hugging classes/laughter therapy terminally ill patients, 1987—; founder healing and touch therapy laughter Therapy, 1991-93; bd. dirs. Performing Arts Ctr.; speaker for enlightenment and healing. Author (rewrite) Title 22 Nursing Home Reform Law, Little Hoover Commn.; model, actress and voiceovers. Bd. dirs. Orange County Coun. on Aging, 1984—; chairperson Helping Hands, 1985—, Pat Robertson Com., 1988, George Bush Presdl. Campaign, Orange County, 1988; bd. dirs., v.p. Women Aglow Orange County, 1985—; evanglist, pub. spkr., v.p. Women Aglow Huntington Beach; active with laughter therapy and hugging classes for terminally ill. Recipient Carnation Silver Bowl, Carnation Svc. Co., 1984-85, Gold medal Pres. Clinton, 1994; named Woman of Yr., Kiwanis, 1985, ABI, 1990, Woman of Decade, Am. Biog. Soc., 1995, Little Hoover Commn., 1995; honored AM L.A. TV Show, Lt. Gov. McCarthy, 1984. Mem. Calif. Assn. Residential Care Homes, Orange County Epilepsy Soc. (bd. dirs. 1986—), Calif. Assn. Long Term Facilities. Home: 2722 S Diamond St Santa Ana CA 92704-6013

OBERTI, SYLVIA MARÎE ANTOINETTE, rehabilitation counselor and administrator, career advisor, textile consultant; b. Fresno, Calif., Dec. 29, 1952. BA in Communicative Disorders, Calif. State U.-Fresno, 1976, MA in Rehab. Counseling, 1977. Cert. rehab. counselor Commn. Rehab. Counselors; cert. life tchr. community coll., nat. cert. counselor; Diplomate Am. Bd. Disability Analysts. Sr. rehab. cons. Crawford Rehab. Services, Inc., Emeryville, Calif., 1978-80; vocat. rehab. counselor Rehab. Assocs., Inc., San Leandro, Calif., 1980-81; owner, textile cons. Rugs and Carpets of the Orient, Oakland, Calif., 1979—; exec. dir. TheOberti Co., Oakland and San Jose, Calif., 1981—; cons. to industry, ins. cos., disabled, ADA; tchr. job seeking skills to the disabled; expert witness in the field. Bd. dirs., treas. Pacific Basin Sch. Textile Arts, 1982-86; active Calif. Assn. Physically Handicapped, Inc., 1976—; fundraising chairperson CARP, 1990; fund raiser Special Olympics, 1992-95; fund raiser Nat. Breast Cancer Coalition, 1996. HEW grantee, 1976-77; first woman to solo and finish Mille Miglia, 1992; recipient Pacific Region Community Svc. Trophy Ferrari Club Am., 1992, Silver award Musical Watch Veteran Car Club Mille Miglia Organizers, 1992, 93, 3d of U.S.A., 1993; named to Women's Hall of Fame-Outstanding Woman of Yr. in Sports and Athletics, Alameda County, 1996. Mem. Am. Counseling Assn., Am. Rehab. Counseling Assn. , Internat. Round Table Advancement of Counseling, Nat. Rehab. Counseling Assn., LWV. Office: 3629 Grand Ave Ste 101 Oakland CA 94610-2009

OBNINSKY, VICTOR PETER, lawyer; b. San Rafael, Calif., Oct. 12, 1944; s. Peter Victor and Anne Bartholdi (Donston) O.; m. Clara Alice Bechtel, June 8, 1969; children: Mari, Warren. BA, Columbia U., 1966; JD, U. Calif., Hastings, 1969. Bar: Calif. 1970. Sole practice, Novato, Calif., 1970—; arbitrator Marin County Superior Ct., San Rafael, 1979—; superior ct. judge pro tem, 1979—; lectr. real estate and partnership law. Author: The Russians in Early California, 1966. Bd. dirs. Calif. Young Reps., 1968-69, Richardson Bay San. Dist., 1974-75, Marin County Legal Aid Soc., 1976-78; baseball coach Little League, Babe Ruth League, 1970-84; mem. nat. panel consumer arbitrators Better Bus. Bur., 1974-88; leader Boy Scouts Am., 1970-84; permanent sec. Phillips Acad. Class of 1962, 1987—; mem. Phillips Acad. Alumni Council, 1991-95; bd. community advisors Buck Ctr. for Rsch. on Aging. Mem. ABA, State Bar Calif., Marin County Bar Assn. (bd. dirs. 1985-91, treas. 1987-88, pres.-elect 1989, pres. 1990), Phi Delta Phi, Phi Gamma Delta. Republican. Russian Orthodox. Office: 2 Commercial Blvd Apt 103 Novato CA 94949-6121 *An all-out intellectual attempt to* *understand baseball thoroughly may give sufficient insight to understand oneself; the so-called "designated hitter" rule shoold be abolished immediately.*

O'BRIAN, BONNIE JEAN, library services supervisor; b. Great Bend, Kans., Oct. 19, 1940; d. Claude Marion and Mildred Geraldine (Schmaider) Baker; m. Patrick Gilbert Gibson (div.); 1 child, Debra Kathleen; m. John Robinson O'Brian, Nov. 2, 1968. BS, UCLA, 1961; MS, Calif. State U., Northridge, 1977; Credential in Libr. Media Svcs., Calif. State U., Long Beach, 1978. Libr. L.A. Unified Sch. Dist., Northridge, 1978-84; supr. chpt. 2 L.A. Unified Sch. Dist., L.A., 1984, coord. field libr., 1984-87, supr. libr. svcs., 1987—; asst. prof. libr. sci. Calif. State U., L.A.; condr. workshops in field. Recipient N.W. Valley Parent Tchr. Student award 1978, San Fernando Valley Reading Assn. Myrtle Shirley Reading Motivation award 1986. Mem. ALA, Am. Assn. Sch. Librs., Calif. Sch. Libr. Assn. (pres.), So. Calif. Coun. on Lit. for Children and Young People, White House Conf. on Libr. and Info. Svcs. Republican. Office: Los Angeles Unifed Sch Dist 1320 W 3rd St Los Angeles CA 90017-1410

O'BRIEN, ANNMARIE, education educator; b. N.Y.C., Nov. 10, 1949; d. Hugh and Margaret (Doherty) O'B.; m. William James McGinty, Dec. 30, 1976; children: Michael Hugh, Liam Patrick. BS in Elem. Edn., Boston U., 1971; MS in Early Childhood Edn., Queens Coll., 1976; EdD in Ednl. Leadership, Portland State U., 1994. Tchr. St. Gerard Majella Elem. Sch., Hollis, N.Y., 1972-76, Lower Kuskokwim Sch. Dist., Bethel, Alaska, 1977-85; child sexual abuse prevention coord. Resource Ctr. for Parents and Children, Fairbanks, Alaska, 1986; grad. asst., project evaluator Portland (Oreg.) State U., 1989-92, student tchr. supr., 1992; prof. edn., rsch. assoc. Inst. Social and Econ. Rsch. U. Alaska, Anchorage, 1993-96; prin. Old Harbor Sch., Kodiak Island Borough Sch. Dist., Kodiak, Alaska, 1996—. Author: A Child Abuse Prevention Training Manual for Educators, 1976; co-author: The Academy for Future Educators Guidebook, 1992. Recipient scholarship Portland State U., 1991. Mem. AAUW, Kappa Delta Pi. Office: Old Harbor Sch PO Box 49 Old Harbor AK 99643

O'BRIEN, DAVID KERAN, marine geologist, environmental scientist; b. Queens, N.Y., Oct. 2, 1962; s. Keran and Barbara Hope (Zwickel) O'B.; m. Irene Marie Russell, May 18, 1988; children: Thomas Matthew, Daniel Kenneth. BS Earth and Space Sci. magna cum laude, SUNY, Stony Brook, 1983; MS in Geology, U. Calif., Berkeley, 1985; PhD in Geology and Geophysics, U. Hawaii, Manoa, 1990. Teaching asst. U. Calif., Berkeley, 1983-84, rsch. asst., 1984-85; rsch. asst. U. Hawaii, Manoa, Honolulu, 1985-90; phys. properties specialist Ocean Drilling Program, College Station, Tex., 1988; marine geologist, environ. scientist EMCON Alaska, Inc., Anchorage, 1990—; adj. instr. U. Alaska, Anchorage, 1991, 95, Alaska Pacific U., Anchorage, 1990, 92. Contbr. chpts. to books, articles to profl. jours. Mem. Alaska Geol. Soc., Am. Geophys. Union, Geol. Soc. Am., Am. Assn. Environ. Profls., Sigma Xi, Sigma Gamma Epsilon (chpt. pres. 1983). Home: 8651 Swiss Pl Anchorage AK 99507-3646 Office: EMCON Alaska Inc Ste 36 4701 Business Park Blvd Anchorage AK 99503-7166

O'BRIEN, HAROLD ALOYSIUS, JR., nuclear chemist, physics researcher, consultant; b. Dallas, May 17, 1936; s. Harold Aloysius and Adelaide (Esser) O'B.; m. Ann Akard, Aug. 22, 1958; children: Walter, Sheri, Matthew. BA, U. Tex., 1959; MS, N.Mex. State U., 1961; PhD, U. Tenn., 1968. Hon. diplomate Am. Bd. Sci. in Nuclear Medicine. Rsch. scientist Oak Ridge (Tenn.) Nat. Lab., 1962-68; mem. rsch. staff Los Alamos Nat. Lab., 1968-74, 86-93, asssoc. group leader, 1974-80, group leader, 1980-85; sr. tech. mgr. Sci. Applications Internat. Corp., Los Alamos, 1994—; pres. O'Brien & Assocs., Los Alamos, 1994—; vis. scientist Lawrence Berkeley (Calif.) Lab., 1985-86, Lawrence Livermore (Calif.) Lab., 1985-86, U. Calif., Davis, 1985-86; bd. dirs. Am. Bd. Sci. in Nuclear Medicine, 1976-85, pres., 1983-85; bd. dirs. Rho Med, Inc., Albuquerque, 1987-95; mem. subcom. on nuclear and radio chemistry NAS-NRC, 1974-78; mem. spl. study sect. NIH, 1976. Contbr. numerous articles to profl. jours., chpts. to books; patentee in field. Chmn. N.Mex. Radiation Tech. Adv. Coun., Santa Fe, 1974-85, 90—. Mem. Am. Chem. Soc. (exec. com. 1981-84), AAAS, Soc. Nuclear Medicine (trustee 1975-76, bd. dirs. Edn. and Rsch. Found. 1985—). Home: 107 La Senda Rd Los Alamos NM 87544-3819 Office: O'Brien & Assocs 107 La Senda Rd Los Alamos NM 87544-3819

O'BRIEN, JACK GEORGE, artistic director; b. Saginaw, Mich., June 18, 1939; s. J. George and Evelyn (MacArthur Martens) O'B. A.B., U. Mich., 1961, M.A., 1962. Asst. dir. APA Repertory Theatre, N.Y.C., 1963-67; asso. dir. APA Repertory Theatre, 1967-69; worked with San Diego Nat. Shakespeare Festival, 1969-82, A.C.T., 1970-80, Loretto Hilton, 1975, Ahmanson, Los Angeles, 1978-80, San Francisco Opera, Houston Grand Opera, Washington Opera Soc., N.Y.C. Opera. Lyricist: Broadway prodn. The Selling of the President, 1972; dir.: on Broadway Porgy and Bess (Tony award nominee 1977), Most Happy Fella, Street Scene, Two Shakespearean Actors, 1993, Damn Yankees, 1994, Hapgood, 1994, others; artistic dir.: Old Globe Theatre, San Diego, 1981. Mem. Actors' Equity, Am. Soc. Composers and Performers, Soc. Stage Dirs. and Choreographers, Dirs. Guild Am. *

O'BRIEN, KEVIN E., lawyer; b. Teaneck, N.J., Nov. 22, 1952. BA, U. Notre Dame, 1975; JD, U. Denver, 1977. Bar: Colo. 1980. Atty. Hall & Evans, L.L.C., Denver; instr. Nat. Inst. Trial Advocacy, 1987. With USAR, 1972-78. Office: Hall & Evans LLC 1200 17th St Ste 1700 Denver CO 80202-5835

O'BRIEN, MARGE ETT, museum administrator; b. Hazleton, Pa., July 14, 1938; d. Gideon E. and Margurite (Pryor) Davis; m. Robert W. O'Brien, June 6, 1958; children: Robert D., Kevin J., William G. Student, Pa. State U., 1956-57; AA, Calif. State U., Dominquez Hills, 1978, BA, 1981, MA, 1983. Tchr. Pre-Sch. Co-op., San Pedro, Calif., 1977-79; dir. Drum Barracks Civil War Mus., Wilmington, Calif., 1986—; cons. Wilmington (Calif.) Hist. Soc., 1989—. Editor Highlands Homeowners newspaper, 1973. Mem. Am. Mus. Assn., Southwestern Mus. Assn., USAF Space Div. Wife's Club (pres. 1976-77). Republican. Lutheran. Office: Drum Barracks Civil War Mus 1052 N Banning Blvd Wilmington CA 90744-4604

O'BRIEN, MARK DAVID, poet, journalist; b. Boston, July 31, 1949; s. Walter Francis and Helen Agnes (Kelly) O'B. BA in English, U. Calif., Berkeley, 1982. Author: Breathing, 1990; author poems; contbr. articles to popular mags. Ingram-Merril Found. grantee, N.Y.C., 1987. Democrat. Roman Catholic. Home: 1849 Shattuck Ave Apt 306 Berkeley CA 94709

O'BRIEN, PATRICIA ANN, history educator; b. Cambridge, Mass., Dec. 29, 1945; d. Maurice Joseph and Elizabeth Mary (Sullivan) O'B. BA, Regis Coll., 1967; MA, Columbia U., 1968, PhD, 1973. Instr. Yale U., New Haven, 1971-73; asst. prof. Yale U., 1973-74, U. Calif., Irvine, 1974-80; assoc. prof. U. Calif., 1980-93, prof., 1993—; acting assoc. dean undergrad. studies U. Calif., Irvine, 1981, acting chair history dept., 1983-84, chair history dept., 1985-88, assoc. vice chancellor for rsch., 1990-94, acting vice chancellor for rsch., dean grad. studies, 1993; NSF, NEH referee. Author: The Promise of Punishment: Prisons in Nineteenth-Century France, 1982 (French translation, 1988); co-author: Civilization in the West, 1991, Unfinished Legacies, 1992, Societies and Cultures in World History, 1995; contbr. articles to profl. jours. Woodrow Wilson fellow, 1968, NEH fellow, 1973, Nat. Humanities Ctr. Rsch. fellow, 1988. Office: U Calif Humanities Rsch Inst Irvine CA 92697

O'BRIEN, RAYMOND FRANCIS, transportation executive; b. Atchison, Kans., May 31, 1922; s. James C. and Anna M. (Wagner) O'B.; m. Mary Ann Baugher, Sept. 3, 1947; children: James B., William T., Kathleen A., Christopher R. B.S. in Bus. Adminstrn., U. Mo., 1948; grad., Advanced Mgmt. Program, Harvard, 1966. Accountant-auditor Peat, Marwick, Mitchell & Co., Kansas City, Mo., 1948-52; contr., treas. Riss & Co., Kansas City, Mo., 1952-58; regional contr. Consol. Freightways Corp. of Del., Indpls., also, Akron, Ohio, 1958-61; contr. Consol. Freightways, Inc., San Francisco, 1961—; v.p., treas. Consol. Freightways, Inc., 1962-63, bd. dirs., 1966, v.p. fin., 1967-69, exec. v.p., 1969-75, pres., 1975—, chief exec. officer, 1977-88, 90-91, chmn., 1988—, now chmn. emeritus; pres. CF Motor Freight subs. Consol. Freightways, Inc., 1973; dir. Transam. Corp., Watkins-Johnson, Inc.; past chmn. WesternHwy. Inst., Champion Road Machinery, Ltd. Former mem. bus. adv. bd. Northwestern U., U. Calif., Berkeley; bd. dirs., regent, former chmn. bd. trustees St. Mary's Coll.; bd. dirs., regent Charles Armstrong Sch., 1991—; mem. Pres.'s Adv. Herbert Hoover Boys and Girls Club; dir. Boy Scouts Am. Bay Area Coun.; adv. coun. Nat. Commn. Agaisnt Drunk Driving. Served to 1st lt. USAAF, 1942-45. Recipient Disting. Svc. Citation Automotive Hall Fame, 1991; named Outstanding Chief Exec. five times Financial World Mag. Mem. Am. Trucking Assn. (bd. dirs. Found., exec. com.), Pacific Union Club, World Trade Club, Commonwealth Club (San Francisco), Burning Tree Country Club, Menlo Country Club. Home: 26347 Esperanza Dr Los Altos CA 94022-2601 Office: Consol Freightways Inc 3000 Sand Hill Rd Ste 130 Menlo Park CA 94025-7116

O'BRIEN, THOMAS JOSEPH, bishop; b. Indpls., Nov. 29, 1935. Grad., St. Meinrad Coll. Sem. Ordained priest Roman Catholic Ch., 1961. Bishop of Phoenix, 1982—. Office: Catholic Diocese 400 E Monroe St Phoenix AZ 85004-2336*

OBSTFELD, MAURICE, economics educator and consultant; b. N.Y.C., Mar. 19, 1952; s. George Eliakim and Selma Giselle O. BA, U. Pa., 1973; MA, Cambridge U. (Eng.), 1975; PhD, MIT, 1979. Asst. prof. Columbia U., N.Y.C., 1979-81, assoc. prof. dept. econs., 1981-85, prof., 1985-86; prof. U. Pa., Phila., 1986—; prof. U. Calif., Berkeley, 1989—; Class of 1958 prof. U. Calif., Berkeley, 1995—. vis. scholar Fed. Res., Washington, 1981, 94, MIT, Cambridge, 1982, Stockholm U., 1988, 93, IMF, 1989; vis. prof. Tel-Aviv U., Israel, 1984, Harvard U., 1989-90; mem. econs. adv. panel NSF, 1983-84. Author: (with others) International Economics: Theory and Policy, 1987, 4th edit., 1997, Foundations of International Macroeconomics, 1996; co-editor: Financial Policies and the World Capital Market, 1983; editl. bd. Jour. Monetary Econs., 1983—, Jour. Internat. Econs., 1985—, Internat. Econ. Rev., 1986—, Rev. Internat. Econs., 1992—; rsch. assoc. Nat. Bur. Econ. Rsch., Cambridge, Mass.; rsch. fellow Ctr. Econ. Policy Rsch., London; author articles. Danforth Found. grad. fellow, 1973; NSF research grantee, 1981, 84, 86, 88, 91, 94; Alfred P. Sloan Found. rsch. fellow, 1984. Fellow Econometric Soc.; mem. Am. Econ. Assn. (editorial bd. jour. 1987—). Office: Univ Calif Dept Econs Berkeley CA 94720

O'BYRNE, MICHAEL, management consultant; b. Butte, Mont., Dec. 26, 1938; s. Michael E. and Margaret F. (Turner) O'B.; m. Penny L. Graham, Nov. 14, 1964; children: Jennifer L. McLellan, Gregory M. O'Byrne, Andrew G. O'Byrne. BSME, U. Wash., 1961. Cert. engr., Wash. V.p. PACCAR, Inc., Bellevue, Wash., 1969-84; pres. Mobi-Dock, Inc., Mercer Island, Wash., 1985-86; ptnr. The Catalyst Group, Mercer Island, 1986-89; pres. Raima Corp., Bellevue, 1988-89, Pacific North Equiptment Co., Kent, Wash., 1990-95; cons. Master Performance, Inc., Bellevue, 1995—. Council mem. Hunts Point, Wash., 1980-97; mem. bd. dirs. Mcpl. League of King County, Seattle, 1994-95; dist. chmn. Boy Scouts Am., Seattle, 1994—. Lt. comdr. USN, 1961-69. Mem. Soc. Automotive Engrs., Assoc. Equipment Distributors (chpt. pres. 1994-95), Rotary Internat., Seattle Yacht Club. Republican. Home and Office: 4224 Hunts Point Rd Bellevue WA 98004-1106

O'BYRNE, PAUL J., bishop; b. Calgary, Alta., Can., Dec. 21, 1922. Ordained priest Roman Catholic Ch., 1948; bishop of Calgary, 1968—. Office: Cath Pastoral Care Ctr, 120 17th Ave SW, Calgary, AB Canada T2S 2T2*

OCCHIATO, MICHAEL ANTHONY, city official; b. Pueblo, Colo.; s. Joseph Michael and Joan Occhiato; m. Peggy Ann Stefonowicz, June 27, 1964 (div. Sept. 1983); children: Michael, James, Jennifer; m. Patsy Gay Payne, June 2, 1984; children: Kim Carr, Jerry Don Webb. BBA, U. Denver, 1961; MBA, U. Colo., 1984; postgrad., U. So. Colo. Sales mgr. Tivoli Brewing co., Denver, 1965-67, acting brewmaster, prodn. control mgr., 1967-68, plant mgr., 1968-69; adminstrv. mgr. King Resources Co., Denver, 1969-70; ops. mgr. Canners Inc., Pepsi-Cola Bottling Co., Pueblo, 1970-76; pres. Pepsi-Cola Bottling Co., Pueblo, 1978-82; gen. mgr. Pepsi-Cola Bottling Group div. PepsiCo., Pueblo, 1982, area v.p., 1982-83; ind. cons. Pueblo, 1983—; broker assoc. Sound Venture Realty, Pueblo, 1996—; v.p. Colo. Soft Drink Assn., 1978, pres., 1979; regional dir. Pepsi Cola Mgmt. Inst. divsn. Pepsi Co., 1979-82; pres. Ethnic Foods Internat. dba Taco Rancho, Pueblo; chmn. Weifang (China) Sister City Del., 1991—; bd. dirs. HMO So. Colo. Health Plan, 1988-93; rancher, 1976—; land devel. real estate broker assoc., 1996—. V.p. Colo. Soft Drink Assn., 1979-80, pres., 1980-81; mem. coun. City of Pueblo, 1978-93, pres., 1986, 87, 90, 91; mem. bd. health, 1978-80, regional planning commn., 1980-81, Pueblo Action Inc., 1978-80, Pueblo Planning and Zoning Commn., 1985; chmn. Pueblo Area Coun. Govts., 1980-82; mem. Pueblo Econ. Devel. Corp., 1983-91; chmn. fundraising Pueblo chpt. Am. Heart Assn., 1983—; bd. dirs. El Pueblo Boys Ranch, 1971-73; del. 1st World Conf. Local Elected Orcls. to 1st UN Internat. Coun. for Local Environ. Initiative; active Earth Wise Pueblo, 1991. Lt. USN, 1961-65. Mem. So. Colo. Emergency Med. Technicians Assn. (pres. 1975), Am. Saler Assn., Am. Quarter Horse Assn., Colo. Cattle Assn., Pueblo C. of C., Rotary, Pi Kappa Alpha (v.p. 1960). Home and Office: 11 Harrogate Ter Pueblo CO 81001-1723

OCCHIPINTI, CARL JOSEPH, broadcasting executive; b. New Orleans, Feb. 11, 1931; s. Victor and Anne (Maenza) O.; m. Ila M. Fanning, Nov. 22, 1939; children—Vickie, Michael, Diane. B.S., U. Wyo., 1956. Bus. and advt. mgr. Laramie (Wyo.) Newspapers, Inc., 1957-63; gen. mgr. Sta. KTVS-TV, Sterling, Colo., 1963-75; gen. mgr., v.p. Wyneco Communications, Inc., including Stas. KYCU-TV, Cheyenne, Wyo., KSTF-TV, Scottsbluff, Nebr., KTVS-TV, Sterling, Colo., 1975-86; gen. mgr. Sta. KGWN TV Cheyenne, 1986-96, Sta. KSTF TV, Scottsbluff, Nebr., 1986-96, Sta. KTVS TV, Sterling, Colo., Sta. KGWC TV, Casper Wyo., 1986-96, Sta. KGWL TV., Lander-Riverton, Wyo., Sta. KGWR TV, Rock Springs, Wyo., 1986-96; cons. in field, 1997—. With USAF, 1950-53. Mem. Advt. Assn. Denver, Colo. Broadcasters Assn. (past v.p.), Am. Legion, Cheyenne C. of C. (past 1st v.p.). Roman Catholic. Clubs: Cheyenne Country, Sterling Country, Elks. Office: Sta KGWN-TV 2923 E Lincolnway Cheyenne WY 82001-6149

OCHITILL, HERBERT NOLAN, psychiatrist, educator; b. Phila., May 27, 1946; s. Samuel Joseph and Gertrude Ochitill; m. Sally Thresher, Apr. 20, 1974; children: Emily, Sarah. BS in Natural Sci., Muhlenberg Coll., 1968; MD, Jefferson Med. Coll., 1972. Diplomate Am. Bd. Neurology and Psychiatry (bd. examiner 1983—). Intern Med. Coll. Pa., Phila., 1972-73; resident in psychiatry Johns Hopkins Hosp., Balt., 1973-76; fellow in psychosocial medicine med. ctr. U. Rochester, N.Y., 1976-77; staff cons. San Francisco Gen. Hosp., 1977-81, chief consultation svc., 1981—, asst. med. chief med. staff devel. and quality assurance program of psychiatry svc., 1989—; assoc. clin. prof. dept. psychiatry sch. medicine U. Calif., San Francisco, 1992—; lectr. San Francisco chpt. Am. Heart Assn., 1980—; mem. com. physician hiring and compensation Dept. Pub. Health, 1990—; cons. Laguna Honda Hosp., 1990-92; mem. various univ. and hosp. coms.; presenter in field. Author: (with others) Treatment of Mental Disorders, 1982, Assaults within Psychiatric Facilities, 1983, Review of General Psychiatry, 1984, AIDS Knowledge Base, 1986, AIDS and the Nervous System, 1988, San Francisco AIDS Knowledgebase, 1988; ad hoc referee Psychosomatics, 1983—, Psychiatry in Medicine, 1985—, N.Y. State Jour. Medicine, 1989—. Reviewer behavioral sci. topics Burke Sch., 1985—. Mem. AAAS, Am. Psychosomatic Soc. (exec. coun. 1997—), Acad. Psychosomatic Medicine (edn. com.). Office: San Francisco Gen Hosp 1001 Potrero Ave San Francisco CA 94110-3518

OCHOA, ARMANDO, bishop; b. Oxnard, Calif., Apr. 3, 1943. Grad., Ventura (Calif.) Coll., St. John's Coll., Camarillo, Calif. Ordained priest Roman Cath. Ch., 1970. Titular bishop of Sitifi Calif.; aux. bishop, vicar gen. L.A., 1987-96; bishop Diocese of Tex., El Paso, 1996—. Office: 3424 Wilshire Blvd Los Angeles CA 90010-2241*

OCHS, HANS DIETER, pediatrics educator; b. Spaichingen, Germany, Sept. 29, 1936; came to U.S., 1968; s. Anton and Anna (Braun) O.; m. Ute Hanna Brintzinger, June 20, 1963; children: Oliver D., Ulrike I. BS, Gymnasium, 1956; MD, U. Freiburg, 1961, U. Wash., 1969. Intern Flower Hosp., Toledo, Ohio, 1963-64; resident Children's Hosp., Honolulu, 1964-65, Children's Hosp., U. Tuebingen, Germany, 1967-68, Children's Hosp., U. Wash., Seattle, 1968-69; asst. prof. pediatrics U. Wash., Seattle, 1972-75, assoc. prof., 1975-80, prof., 1980—, fellow immunology dept. pediatrics, 1969-72. Contbr. over 200 scientific articles to profl. jours. Howard Hughes Med. Inst. grantee, 1972-80. Mem. Am. Assn. Immunologists, Soc. Pediatric Rsch., Clin. Immunology Soc. Office: U Wash Sch Medicine Dept Pediatrics Box 356320 Seattle WA 98195-6320

OCKER, CHRISTOPHER MICHAEL, historian, educator; b. Queens, N.Y., Nov. 23, 1958; s. Ralph Franz and Christa Gertrud (Holder) O.; m. Varda Koch, Aug. 29, 1987; children: Gabriel, Tanya, Stella. MDiv, Fuller Theol. Sem., 1983; ThM, Princeton Theol. Sem., 1985, PhD, 1991. Rsch. fellow Institut für Europäische Geschichte, Mainz, Germany, 1988-91; asst. prof. history San Francisco Theol. Sem., San Anselmo, 1991-95; assoc. prof. history San Francisco Theol. Sem., San Anselmo, Calif., 1995—; mem. core doctoral faculty Grad. Theol. Union, Berkeley, Calif., 1991—; assoc. dir. Ctr. for Hermeneutical Studies, Berkeley, 1991-94; vis. fellow Max-Planck-Inst. Geschichte, Göttingen, Germany, 1995. Author: Johannes Klenkok: A Friar's Life, 1993; editor: Protocol of the Colloguy of the Center for Hermeneutical Studies, 1992-94. Bd. dirs. San Anselmo Organ Festival, 1994. Recipient Theol. Scholarship and Rsch. award Assn. Theol. Schs., 1995, Rsch. award Deutscher Akademischer Austauschdienst, 1987; Alexander von Humboldt-Stiftung fellow, 1995. Mem. Am. Hist. Assn., Am. Soc. Ch. History, Medieval Acad. Am., Am. Acad. Religion. Presbyterian. Office: San Francisco Theol Sem 2 Kensington Rd San Anselmo CA 94960-2905

OCKEY, RONALD J., lawyer; b. Green River, Wyo., June 12, 1934; s. Theron G. and Ruby O. (Sackett) O.; m. Arline M. Hawkins, Nov. 27, 1957; children: Carolyn S. Ockey Baggett, Deborah K. Ockey Christiansen, David, Kathleen M. Ockey Hellewell, Valerie Ockey Sachs, Robert. B.A., U. Utah, 1959, postgrad. 1959-60; J.D. with honors, George Washington U., 1966. Bar: Colo. 1967, Utah 1968, U.S. Dist. Ct. Colo. 1967, U.S. Dist. Ct. Utah 1968, U.S. Ct. Appeals (10th cir.) 1969, U.S. Ct. Claims 1987. Missionary to France for Mormon Ch., 1954-57; law clk. to judge U.S. Dist. Ct. Colo., 1966-67; assoc. ptnr., shareholder, v.p., treas., dir. Jones, Waldo, Holbrook & McDonough, Salt Lake City, 1967-91, pres., IntelliTrans Internat. Corp., 1992-94; mem. Utah Ho. Reps., 1988-90, Utah State Senate, 1991-94; of counsel Mackey Price & Williams, Salt Lake City, 1995—; trustee SmartUTAH, Inc., 1995—, Utah Tech. Fin. Corp., 1966—; lectr. in securities, pub. fin. and bankruptcy law. State govtl. affairs chmn. Utah Jaycees, 1969; del. state Rep. Convs., 1972-74, 1976-78, 1980-82, 84-86, del. Salt Lake County Rep. Conv., 1978-80, 88; sec. Wright for Gov. campaign, 1980; legis. dist. chmn. Utah Rep. Party, 1983-87; trustee Food for Poland, 1981—, pres., trustee, Unity to Assist Humanity Alliance, 1992—; bd. dirs. Utah Opera Co., 1991-94; trustee Utah Info. Tech. Assn., 1991—; bd. dir., mem. exec. com. Smart Utah, Inc., 1995—. Lt. U.S. Army, 1960-66; to capt. Judge Adv. Gen. USAR, 1966-81. Mem. Utah State Bar Assn. (various coms.), , Nat. Assn. Bond Lawyers (chmn. com. on state legislation 1982-85), George Washington U. Law Alumni Assn. (bd. dirs. 1981-85), Order of Coif, Salt Lake Rotary, Phi Delta Phi. Contbr. articles on law to profl. jours.; mem. editorial bd. Utah Bar Jour., 1973-75; mem. staff and bd. editors George Washington Law Rev., 1964-66. Home: 4502 Crest Oak Cir Salt Lake City UT 84124-3825

O'CONNELL, HUGH MELLEN, JR., retired architect; b. Oak Park, Ill., Nov. 29, 1929; s. Hugh M. and Helen Mae (Evans) O'C.; m. Frances Ann Small, Apr. 13, 1957; children—Patricia Lynn, Susan Marie, Jeanette Maureen. Designer, John Mackel. Student mech. engring., Purdue U., 1948-50; B.S. in Archtl. Engring, U. Ill., 1953. Registered architect, Ariz., Calif., La., Nev., Nat. Council Archtl. Registration Bds. Structural engr. Los Angeles, 1955-57; architect Harnish & Morgan & Causey, Ontario, Calif., 1957-63; self-employed architect Ventura, Calif., 1963-69; architect Andrews/O'Connell, Ventura, 1970-78; dir. engring. div. Naval Constrn. Bn. Center, Port Hueneme, Calif., 1978-91; supervisory architect Naval Constrn. Bn. Center, Port Hueneme, 1991-93; ret., 1993; mem. tech. adv. com. Ventura Coll., 1965-78; sec. Oxnard Citizens' Adv. Com., 1969-79, v.p., 1970-72, pres., 1972—; chmn. Oxnard Beautification Com., 1969, 74, Oxnard Cmty. Block Grant adv. com., 1975-76; mem. Oxnard Planning Commn., 1976-86, vice chmn., 1978-79, chmn., 1980-81. Mem. Oxnard Art-in-Pub. Places Commn., 1988—. Served with AUS, 1953-55. Mem. AIA (emeritus, pres. Ventura chpt. 1973), Am. Concrete Inst., Soc. Am. Registered Architects (Design award 1968, dir. 1970), Am. Legion, Soc. for Preservation and Encouragement of Barbershop Quartet Singing in Am. (chpt. pres. 1979, chpt. sec. 1980-83), Acad. Model Aeros. (#9190 1948—), Channel Islands Condors Club (treas. 1986—), Sports Flyers Assn., Alpha Rho Chi. Presbyterian (elder 1963, deacon 1967). Lodges: Kiwanis (pres. 1969, div. sec. 1974-75), Elks. Home and Office: 520 Ivywood Dr Oxnard CA 93030-3527

O'CONNELL, KENNETH ROBERT, artist, animator, educator; b. Ogden, Utah, Jan. 22, 1945; s. Daniel D. and Virginia N. (Kyle) O'C.; m. Gwyneth P. Jones, June 21, 1969; children: Anneka, Marlika, Sean. BS in Art Edn., U. Oreg., 1966, MFA in Graphic Design with honors, 1972. Mem. faculty Treasure Valley C.C., Ontario, Oreg., 1973-78, chair dept. art, 1975-78; adj. faculty (multi-image) Goddard Coll., Plainfield, Vt., 1980-81; asst. prof. fine and applied arts U. Oreg., Eugene, 1978-82, assoc. prof., head fine and applied arts, 1983-91, prof., head fine and applied arts, 1991-96; prof., dir. fine arts dept New Media Design Lab., 1996—; vis. faculty in film, animation, photography Evergreen State Coll., Olympia, Wash., 1976; art gallery chair SIGGRAPH 95 Conf., 1994-95; cons., workshop facilitator, lectr., presenter in field. Exhibited works at Ann Arbor (Mich.) Film Festival, 1974, Coos Art Mus., Coos Bay, Oreg., 1977, 78, USA Film Festival, Dallas, 1980, Hong Kong Film Festival, 1981, Athens (Ohio) Internat. Film Festival, 1981, Internat. Animation Festival of Japan, Hiroshima, 1985, Zagreb (Yugoslavia) World Animation Festival, 1986, Portland Art Mus., 1987, Sapporo (Japan) Art Park, 1989, Chgo. Internat. Festival of Children's Films, 1991, Toyoma (Japan) Mus. Art, 1992, others; featured in mag. articles. Recipient award First N.W. Film and Video Festival, 1973, 3d prize USA Film FEstival, Dallas, 1980, Dirs. Choice award Sinking Creek Film Celebration, Nashville, 1986, others; Horseshoe grantee Grad. Sch. U. Oreg., 1982, 84,86, 89; Getty grantee, 1988, others; named to Outstanding Young Men of Am., 1977. Mem. Found. Art, Theory and Edn., Assn. for Computer Machinery/SIGGRAPH, Coll. ARt Assn., Nat. Coun. Art Adminstrs., Soc. for Animation Studies. Office: U Oreg Dept Fine and Applied Arts Eugene OR 97403

O'CONNELL, MARY ANN, state senator, business owner; b. Albuquerque, Aug. 3, 1934; d. James Aubrey and Dorothy Nell (Batsel) Gray; m. Robert Emmett O'Connell, Feb. 21, 1977; children: Jeffery Crampton, Gray Crampton. Student, U. N.Mex., Internat. Coun. Shopping Ctrs. Exec. dir. Blvd. Shopping Ctr., Las Vegas, Nev., 1968-76, Citizen Pvt. Enterprise, Las Vegas, 1976; media supr. Southwest Advt., Las Vegas, 1977—; owner, operator Meadows Inn, Las Vegas, 1985—, 3 Christian bookstores, Las Vegas, 1985—; state senator Nev. Senate, 1985—; chmn. govtl. affairs; vice chmn. commerce and labor; mem. taxation com.; vice chmn. Legis. Commn., 1985-86, 95-96; mem., 1987-88, 91-93; commr. Edn. Commn. States; rep. Nat. Conf. State Legislators; past vice chair State Mental Hygiene & Mental Retardation Adv. Bd. Pres. explorer div. Boulder Dam Area coun. Boy Scouts Am., Las Vegas, 1979-80, former mem. exec. bd.; mem. adv. bd. Boy Scouts Am.; pres., bd. dirs. Citizens Pvt. Enterprise, Las Vegas, 1982-84, Secret Witness, Las Vegas, 1081-82; vice chmn. Gov.'s Mental Health-Mental Retardation, Nev., 1983—; past mem. community adv. bd. Care Unit Hosp., Las Vegas; past mem. adv. bd. Kidney Found., Milligan Coll., Charter Hosp.; tchr. Young Adult Sunday Sch. Recipient Commendation award Mayor O. Grayson, Las Vegas, 1975, Outstanding Citizenship award Bd. Realtors, 1975, Silver Beaver award Boy Scouts Am., 1980, Free Enterprise award Greater Las Vegas C. of C., Federated Employers Assn., Downtown Breakfast Exch., 1988, Award of Excellence for Women in Politics, 1989, Legislator of Yr. award Bldg. and Trades, 1991, Legislator of Yr. award Nat. ASA Trade Assn., 1991, 94, Guardian of Liberty award Nev. Coalition of Conservative Citizens, 1991, Internat. Maxi Awards Promotional Excellence, Guardian of Small Bus. award Nat. Fedn. Ind. Bus., 1995-96; named Legislator of Yr., Nev. Retail Assn., 1992. Mem. Retail Mchts. Assn. (former pres., bd. dirs.), Taxpayers Assn. (bd. dirs.), Greater Las Vegas C. of C. (past pres., bd. dirs., Woman of Achievement Politics women's coun. 1988). Republican. Mem. Christian Ch. Home: 7225 Montecito Cir Las Vegas NV 89120-3118 Office: Nev Legislature Senate 401 S Carson St Carson City NV 89701-4747

O'CONNELL, MICHAEL ALEXANDER, social worker; b. Dayton, Ohio, May 28, 1948; s. William J. and Aida May (Duncan) O'Co. BS in econ., U. Pa., 1970; MSW, U. Wash., 1977. Cert. social worker, Wash. Dir. Second Chance Youth Alcoholism Program, Seattle, 1977-78; social worker Riverton Hosp., Burien, Wash., 1979-80; therapist Robinson William & Assocs., Seattle, 1981-82; therapist & cons. Althean Assocs., Seattle, 1982-83, Everett, 1983—. Author: Working With Sex Offenders, 1990. Pres. Wash. State Chpt., Assn. for the Treatment of Sexual Abusers, 1997—. Mem. Acad. Cert. Social Workers, Assn. Treatment of Sexual Abusers, Am. Profl. Soc. on the Abuse of Children. Office: Michael A O'Connell & Assocs 8625 Evergreen Way Ste 203 Everett WA 98208-2620

O'CONNELL, ROBERT HOUSTON, religious educator, writer, editor; b. Kitchener, Ont., Can., Dec. 4, 1955; s. Ronald J. O'Connell and Joan H. (Roberts) Molloy; m. Mina M. Fain, Aug. 14, 1982; children: Nathan H., Sean M. BA in music, U. Western Ont., 1978; ThM in Old Testament, Dallas Theological Sem., 1982, ThD in Old Testament, 1989; PhD in Divinity, U. Cambridge, Cambridge, Eng., 1993. Assoc. prof. Old Testament Colo. Christian U., Lakewood, Colo., 1991-96; freelance writer, editor, 1996—. Author: Concentricity and Continuity: The Literary Structure of Isaiah, 1994, The Rhetoric of the Book of Judges, 1996. Shipley scholarship Fitzwilliam Coll., 1988-89, Crosse scholarship U. Cambridge, 1989-91, Overseas Rsch. Student award, London, Eng., 1988-91. Mem. Soc. Bibl. Lit., Nat. Assn. Profs. of Hebrew, Soc. for Old Testament Studies (U.K.), Am. Acad. Religion. Home and Office: 3250 S Lafayette St Englewood CO 80110-2924

O'CONNER, LORETTA RAE, lawyer; b. Denver, Dec. 23, 1958; d. Ronald Lee and Norma Jareene (Warner) Barkdoll; m. George Ellis Bentley, Dec. 31, 1976 (div. 1979); m. Donald Hugh O'Conner, Feb. 3, 1987; children: Justin Lee, Brandon Craig. AS, Denver Acad. Ct. Reporting, 1983; BA summa cum laude, Regis U., 1992; JD, U. Colo., 1996. Bar: Colo., 1996. Ct. reporter Denver, 1983-87; dist. ct. reporter Judicial Dept., State of Colo., Pueblo, 1987-91; ct. reporter Pueblo, 1991-93; student atty. Pueblo County Legal Svcs.; pvt. practice Pueblo, 1996—. Chief justice Student Govt. Ct., U. So. Colo., Pueblo, 1992; trained facilitator Kettering Found., Pub. Policy Inst., Dayton, Ohio, 1992; sec. So. Colo. Registered Interpretors for Deaf, Pueblo, 1991. President's scholar U. So. Colo., 1991-92, Alumni Assn. scholar, 1991-92; grantee Kettering Found., 1992; Colo. Legislature grantee and scholar Regis U., 1992; Colo. Legislature grantee U. Colo. Sch. Law, 1993-95, Dean's scholar, Dazzo Scholar, King scholar U. Colo. Sch. Law, 1993-96. Mem. ATLA, ABA, Nat. Ct. Reporters Assn., Colo. Trial Lawyers Assn., Colo. Bar Assn., Colo. Womens Bar Assn., Colo. Ct. Reporters Assn., Boulder Bar Assn., Golden Key Soc., Phi Delta Phi (clk. 1994-95). Home and Office: 1911 N Santa Fe Ave Pueblo CO 81003

O'CONNOR, JOHN EDWARD, physician; b. Sidney, Nebr., Dec. 28, 1928; s. Daniel Edward and Lenore (Gilbert) O'C.; m. Beverly L. O'Connor, Jan. 31, 1956; children: Daniel L. John D., William E. BS, U. Nebr., 1951, DDS, 1954; MD, U. Nebr., Omaha, 1961. Diplomate Am. Bd. Plastic Surgery, Am. Bd. Otolaryngology. Pvt. practice. Lt. Commdr. USNR, 1951-63. Fellow ACS; mem. Am. Cleft Palate Assn., Am. Soc. Maxillofacial Surgeons. Office: 2519 13th Ave S Great Falls MT 59405-5155

O'CONNOR, KEVIN THOMAS, archdiocese development official; b. Dubuque, Iowa, Oct. 9, 1950; s. Francis John and Marion Helen (Rhomberg) O'C.; m. Abbie J. O'Connor, July 17, 1993; 1 child, Sean Francis. BS, Regis Coll., Denver, 1973. Spl. agt. Northwestern Mut. Life, Denver, 1973-78; account exec. Blue Cross/Blue Shield of Colo., Denver, 1978-82; pres., owner O'Connor Ins. Cons., Denver, 1982-92; dir. devel. Archdiocese of Denver, 1992-95, mgr. Cath. appeal, 1995-96; dir. devel. Archdiocese L.A., 1996—. Chmn. Regis Coll. Telefund, Denver, 1987-88, 90-91; treas., 1st vice chmn. Serra Trust Fund for Vocations, 1988-93, chmn., 1993-96; mem. fin. coun. St. James Parish, 1988-95, chmn. autumn bazaar, 1985, 87, mem. choir, 1993-95; sec. Mother Teresa Com., 1989. Recipient Share Serra Comm. award Serra Internat., 1989, Spl. Project award Dist. 6, 1986, 88, Spl. Recognition award, 1989, Outstanding Serran award, 1995, Jan Berbers award, 1996, Alumni Svc. award Regis Coll., 1990, Disting. Alumnus award Wahlert H.S., 1994. Mem. Serra Club of Denver (sec. 1986-89, v.p. membership 1989-90, pres. 1991-92, trustee 1992-95, chmn. founders com. Colorado Springs chpt. 1994-95, dist. 6 gov. 1995-96, U.S. and Can. Coun. for membership 1990—), Serra Club Greeley (chmn. founders com. 1996), Serra Club Pueblo (co-chmn. founders com. 1992), Serra Internat. (bd. trustees 1997—), Serra Club L.A. Roman Catholic. Home: 3510 Fallenleaf Pl Glendale CA 91206 Office: Archdiocese LA 3424 Wilshire Blvd Los Angeles CA 90010

O'CONNOR, PAM, mayor. Mayor City of Santa Monica, Calif. Office: City of Santa Monica 1685 Main St Santa Monica CA 90401

O'CONNOR, SHEILA ANNE, freelance writer; b. Paisley, Scotland, Jan. 20, 1960; came to the U.S., 1988; d. Brian Aubrey Witham and Margaret Kirk (Reid) Davies; m. Frank Donal O'Connor, Aug. 9, 1986; children: David Michael, Andrew James, Christine Charlotte. BA in French and German, Strathclyde U., 1980, postgrad. diploma in office studies, 1981, MBA, 1992. Office asst. BBC, London, 1982-83; asst. to mng. dir. Unimatic Engrs. Ltd., London, 1983-84; freelance word processing operator London, 1984-88; staff asst. Internat. Monetary Fund, Washington, 1988-94; prin. Internat. Media Assn., Washington, 1988—. Contbr. numerous articles to various publs. Mem. Am. Mktg. Assn., Bay Area Travel Writers Assn., Calif. Writers Club. Home and Office: 2531 39th Ave San Francisco CA 94116-2752

ODA, YOSHIO, physician, internist; b. Papaaloa, Hawaii, Jan. 14, 1933; s. Hakuai and Usako (Yamamoto) O.; AB, Cornell U., 1955; MD, U. Chgo., 1959. Diplomate Am. Bd. Internal Medicine. Intern U. Chgo. Clinics, 1959-60; resident in pathology U. Chgo., 1960-62, Queen's Hosp., Hawaii, 1962-63, Long Beach (Calif.) VA Hosp., 1963-65; resident in allergy, immunology U. Colo. Med. Center, 1966-67; pvt. practice, L.A., 1965-66; pvt. practice internal medicine, allergy and immunology, Honolulu, 1970—; asst. clin. prof. medicine U. Hawaii, Honolulu, 1970—. Maj., AUS, 1968-70. Mem. ACP, Am. Acad. Allergy. Office: Piikoi Med Bldg 1024 Piikoi St Honolulu HI 96814-1925

ODAHL, CHARLES M., history and languages educator; b. Fresno, Calif., July 1, 1944; s. Albert Charles and Audrey Ruth (Weinberg).; m. Linda Kay, Dec. 20, 1968 (div. June 1979); 1 child, Charlynn Anne. BA, Fresno State U., 1966; MA, Calif. State U., Fresno, 1968; PhD, U. Calif., San Diego, 1976. Instr. Palm Springs (Calif.) H.S., 1968-71; grad. tchg. asst. U. Calif.-San Diego, La Jolla, 1971-75; prof. history and Latin Boise (Idaho) State U., 1975—; vis. prof. U. Avignon, France, 1981, Bath (Eng.) Coll. Higher Edn., 1988; dir., guide Classical and Christian study tours, Rome and Istanbul, 1995. Author: Early Christian Latin Literature, 1993; contbr. articles to profl. jours. Mem. Am. Hist. Assn., Assn. Ancient Historians, Classical Assn. of Pacific N.W., Soc. for Ancient Numismatics, Am. Cath. Hist. Assn., Am. Soc. Ch. History, U.S. Nat. Com. for Byzantine Studies, Medieval Acad. of Am., Medieval Soc. Idaho, Medieval Assn. of Pacific, Rocky Mountain Medieval and Renaissance Assn. (pres. 1986-87), Phi Kappa Phi (pres. Boise State U. chpt. 1992-95), Pi Gamma Mu. Roman Catholic/Lutheran. Home: Laurel Park 455 Ave H Boise ID 83712 Office: Boise State U History and Classics Boise ID 83725

O'DANIEL, DAMON MARK, government relations administrator; b. San Antonio, Nov. 2, 1970; s. Don Mark and Elaine (Brinkley) O'D. BS in Pub. Adminstrn., U. So. Calif., 1993. Commerce and trade asst. Calif. Gov.'s Office, Washington, 1992; govt. rels. program dir. Los Angeles Area C. of C., 1994—; mem. adv. bd. First Break, L.A., 1994—; mem. ednl. and telecomms. network Los Angeles County, L.A., 1994—. Mem. Kappa Sigma. Republican. Home: 4444 Via Marina Apt 801 Marina Del Rey CA 90292-6875 Office: LA Area C of C 350 S Bixel St Los Angeles CA 90017-1418

ODEL, FRANKLIN DAVID, photography educator, publisher; b. L.A., June 12, 1945; s. Murray and Jenny (Berman) O. BA, Calif. Inst. of the Arts, MFA, 1990. Pub. Oversight Mag., L.A., 1988—; tchr. photography and digital arts Otis Coll. of Art, L.A., 1990—, UCLA, 1993—. Bd. mem. Found. for Art Resources, L.A., 1992-95. Office: Oversight Mag Box 29292 Los Angeles CA 90029

ODELL, JOHN H., construction company executive; b. Toledo, Oct. 31, 1955; s. John H. and Doris Irene (Haskell) O.; m. Kathryn Lau, Oct. 1, 1988; children: Ceara, Heather, Victoria. B of Environ. Design, U. Miami, Oxford, Ohio, 1977. Staff architect Richard Halford and Assocs., Santa Fe, 1978-79; ptnr. B.O.A. Constrn., Santa Fe, 1980-84; assoc. Stanley Design Works, Santa Fe, 1984-85; owner John H. Odell Constrn., Santa Fe, 1985—; v.p. Los Pintores Inc., Santa Fe, 1990-92; pres. Uncle Joey's Food Svcs. Inc., 1991—, John H. Odell Assocs. Inc., Santa Fe, 1995—. Musician Santa Fe Community Orch., 1982, Huntington Community Orch., Huntington, W.Va., 1972-73. Mem. AIA (assoc. mem., treas., bd. dirs. Santa Fe chpt. yearly 1988-95, mem. liaison com. on design 1987—, Cmty. Svc. award 1993), Vine and Wine Soc. (N.Mex. No. Rio Grande chpt. pres., bd. dirs., v.p.). Home: PO Box 2967 Santa Fe NM 87504-2967 Office: John H Odell Assn 729 Dunlap St Santa Fe NM 87501-2541

ODEN, ROBERT RUDOLPH, surgeon; b. Chgo., Dec. 2, 1922; s. Rudolph J.E. and Olga H. (Wahlquist) O.; m. Nancy Clow; children: Louise, Boyd, Beach, Lisbeth. BS, U. Ill., 1943; MD, Northwestern U., 1947, MS in Anatomy, 1947. Intern Augustana Hosp., Chgo., 1947-48, resident in surgery, 1948-49; resident in orthopaedics Hines Vets. Hosp., Chgo., 1949-51; resident in children's orthopaedics Shriner's Hosp., 1953-54; pvt. practice Chgo., 1954-57, Aspen, Colo., 1957—; clin. assoc. prof. in orthopaedics U. Colo.; orthopaedic surgeon U.S. Olympic Com., 1960, 72, 76, 80. Assoc. editor: Clin. Orthopaedics and Related Rsch. Trustee U.S. Ski Ednl. Found., 1967-82, Aspen Valley Hosp., 1978-86; founder Aspen Orthopaedic and Sports Medicine Pub. Found., 1985, Aspen Inst. for Theol. Futures, 1978, Great Tchrs. and Preachers Series Christ Episc. Ch., 1989; mem. organizing com. Aspen World Cup, 1976-92; founder, trustee Pitkin County Bank, 1983—; founder Aspen Pitkin Employee Housing, 1975. Recipient Blegan award for most outstanding svc. to U.S. skiing, 1985, Halsted award U.S. Ski Assn., 1987, inducted into Aspen Hall of Fame, 1996. Mem. Am. Acad. Orthopaedic Surgeons, ACS, Internat. Coll. Surgeons, Western Orthopaedic Assn., SICOT, Am. Assn. Bone & Joint Surgeons, Rocky Mountain Traumatologic Soc., Canadian Orthopaedic Assn., Am. Orthopaedic Soc. for Sports Medicine, Internat. Ski Safety Soc., ACL Study Group, Internat. Soc. Knee, Internat. Knee Inst., Phi Beta Kappa. Home: PO Box 660 Aspen CO 81612-0660 Office: 100 E Main St Aspen CO 81611-1778

ODER, BROECK NEWTON, school emergency management consultant; b. Highland Park, Ill., Apr. 20, 1953; s. Bruce Newton and Mary Louise (Roe) O.; m. Jolene Marie Peragine, June 28, 1975 (dec. June 1979). BA in History, U. San Diego, 1974, MA in History, 1975; postgrad., U. N.Mex., 1976-79. Life C.C. teaching credential, Calif. Rsch. asst. to pres. U. San Diego, 1975; grad. asst. U. N.Mex., Albuquerque, 1976-79; tchr. history, chmn. dept. Santa Catalina Sch., Monterey, Calif., 1979—, asst. dean students, 1981-83, dir. ind. study, 1981-95, dean students, 1983-91, dir. emergency planning, 1986—, dean campus affairs, 1991-94, dir. security, 1994—; mem. disaster preparedness coun. Monterey County Office Edn., 1988—; chair Diocesan Sch. Emergency Preparedness Coun., 1991—. Mem. bd. of tchrs. The Concord Rev.; contbr. articles to profl. publs. Participant Jail and Bail, Am. Cancer Soc., Monterey, 1988, 89; reviewer sch. emergency plans, Monterey, 1989—. Recipient award of merit San Diego Hist. Soc., 1975, Outstanding Tchr. award U. Chgo., 1985, Outstanding Young Educator award Monterey Peninsula Jaycees, 1988, resolution of commendation Calif. Senate Rules Com., 1988, cert. of commendation Calif. Gov.'s Office Emergency Svcs., 1991, nat. cert. of achievement Fed. Emergency Mgmt. Agy., 1991. Mem. ACLU, NRA (life), Congress Racial Equality, Am. Hist. Assn., Orgn. Am. Historians, Nat. Coun. on History Edn., Soc. for History Edn., Second Amendment Found., Individual Rights Found., Phi Alpha Theta. Office: Santa Catalina Sch 1500 Mark Thomas Dr Monterey CA 93940-5238

ODERKIRK, WENDELL W., nursing educator; b. Glendale, Calif., Mar. 17, 1944; s. Dorn S. and Edith Eileen O.; m. Diana Oderkirk; children: Shimane, Shonda. BSN, Mt. Mercy Coll., Cedar Rapids, Iowa, 1976; MS, U. Nebr., Omaha, 1982; PhD, U. Nebr., Lincoln, 1987; MSN, Clarkson Coll., 1994. Assoc. prof. N.Mex. State U., Las Cruces. Contbr. articles to profl. jours. Mem. ANA, Sigma Theta Tau. Office: NMex State U Dept Nursing Box 3185 Las Cruces NM 88001

ODERMAN, JEFFREY M., lawyer; b. Orange, N.J., Oct. 30, 1949. BA summa cum laude, UCLA, 1971; JD, Stanford U., 1974. Bar: Calif. 1975, U.S. Supreme Ct., U.S. Ct. Appeals (9th cir.), U.S. Dist. Ct. (ctrl. and no. dists.) Calif. Mem. Rutan & Tucker, Costa Mesa, Calif. Mem. State Bar Calif., Phi Beta Kappa, Order of Coif. Office: Rutan & Tucker PO Box 1950 611 Anton Blvd Ste 1400 Costa Mesa CA 92626-1904

ODLAND, ROBERT OLIVER, land use consultant; b. Yankton, S.D., Aug. 27, 1939; s. Orlando Marion and Dorothy (Oliver) O.; m. Charlotte Kelly. BS in Engring., U.S. Mil. Acad., West Point, N.Y., 1963; JD, U. Calif., Berkeley, 1972, M in City Planning, 1973. Bar: Calif. 1974; cert. land use planner. Regional planner Assn. Bay Area Govts., Berkeley, 1973-74; legis. staff Calif. Legislature, Sacramento, Calif., 1974-75; assoc. planner Sedway/Cooke, Planning Cons., San francisco, 1975-78; br. chief Nat. Renewable Energy Lab., Golden, Colo., 1978-81; cons. Odland Assocs., Livermore, Calif., 1981-85; sr. assoc. Sedway Cooke Assocs. Planning Cons., San Francisco, 1985-94; cons. Russian Federation, Eastern European Countries, 1994—; lectr. in field. Contbr. numerous articles to profl. jours. Mem. state task force to draft changes Calif. Environ. Quality Act. Capt. U.S. Army, 1963-69. Mem. ABA, AAAS, AICP, Am. Planning Assn. (former chair environ. natural resources and energy divsn.), Am. Solar Energy Soc., State Bar Calif., Assn. Environ. Profls., World Future Soc., Urban Ecology (bd. dirs.). Unitarian. Home: 7530 Terrace Dr El Cerrito CA 94530-3017

O'DONNELL, LESLIE ANN, newspaper editor; b. Worcester, Mass., July 19, 1947; d. Jack and Beverly (Silverman) Kadis; m. L. Michael O'Donnell, Feb. 14, 1988; children: Christopher J. Glode, Jeremy G. Glode. AB, Barnard Coll., 1969; MSW, W.Va. U., 1975. News corr. Statesman Jour., Salem, Oreg., 1981-83; reporter Polk County Itemizer-Observer, Dallas, Oreg., 1984-85; trend editor News-Times, Newport, Oreg., 1985-89; freelance writer Oreg. Coast Mag., Florence, Oreg., 1987-90; entertainment editor News-Times, Newport, 1989-90, assoc. editor, 1990, mng. editor, 1990—. Sch. bd. mem. Falls City (Oreg.) Sch. Dist., 1981-85. Recipient Best Editl. First Pl. award Nat. Fedn. Press Women, 1993, 95, 1st Pl. Best Editl. award Oreg. Newspaper Pubs. Assn., 1993, 95, 1st Pl. Best News Coverage, 1993, seven 1st pl. awards Oreg. Press Women, 1987, 89, 90, 91, 92, 94, 95, Hazel Brannon Smith award for editl. excellence Nat. Fedn. Press Women, 1995. Mem. Oreg. Press Women, Oreg. Coast Coun. for the Arts, U. OReg. Seminar for Profl. Journalists (Wendell Webb fellow, 1987, 90). Office: News-Times PO Box 965 Newport OR 97365-0075

O'DONNELL, VICTORIA J., communications educator; b. Greensburg, Pa., Feb. 12, 1938; d. Victor C. and Helen A. (Detar) O'D.; children from previous marriage: Christopher O'Donnell Stupp, Browning William Stupp; m. Paul M. Monaco, Apr. 9, 1993. BA, Pa. State U., 1959, MA, 1961, PhD, 1968. Asst. prof. comm. Midwestern State U., Wichita Falls, Tex., 1965-67; prof. dept. chair comm. U. No. Tex., Denton, 1967-89; prof., dept. chair comms. Ore. State U., Corvallis, 1989-91; prof. comm., basic course dir. Mont. State U., Bozeman, 1991-93, prof. comm., dir. honors program, 1993—; prof. Am. Inst. Fgn. Studies, London, 1988; cons. Arco Oil & Gas, Dallas, 1983-86, Federal Emergency Mgrs. Agy., Salt Lake City, 1986; speechwriter Sen. Mae Yih, Salem, Ore., 1989-91; steering com. Ore. Alliance Film & TV Educators, 1990-91. Author: Introduction to Public Communication, 1992, 2d edit., 1993; co-author: Persuasion, 1982, Propaganda and Persuasion, 1986, 2d edit., 1992; producer: (video) Women, War and Work, 1994; mem. editl. bd. Am. Comm. Jour. Bd. dirs. Friends of the Family, Denton, 1987-89, Bozeman Film Festival, 1991—; del. Tex. Dem. Convention, Denton, 1976. Grantee Mont. Com. for the Humanities, 1993, Oreg. Coun. for the Humanities, 1991, NEH, 1977. Mem. Nat. Collegiate Honors Coun., Speech Comm. Assn., Internat. Comm. Assn., Western States Comm. Assn. Home: 290 Low Bench Rd Gallatin Gateway MT 59730-9741 Office: Univ Honors Program Mont State U Bozeman MT 59717

O'DONNELL, WILLIAM THOMAS, management consultant; b. Latrobe, Pa., Feb. 22, 1939; s. William Regis and Kathryn Ann (Coneff) O'D.; m. Judith Koetke, Oct. 1, 1965; children: William Thomas, William Patrick, Allison Rose, Kevin Raymond. Student Ea. N.Mex. U., 1958-61; student in mktg. John Carroll U., 1961-65, Ill. Inst. Tech., 1965-66; BSBA, U. Phoenix, 1982, MBA with distinction, 1984; postgrad. Union Inst., 1996. Various sales positions Hickok Elec. Instrument Co., Cleve., 1961-65, Fairchild Semicondr., Mpls., 1965-67; Transitron Semicondr., Mpls., 1967-69; regional sales mgr. Burroughs Corp., Plainfield, N.J., 1967-71; mktg. mgr. Owens-Ill. Co., 1972-73, v.p. mktg. Pantek Co., subs. Owens-Ill. Co., Lewistown, Pa., 1973-75, v.p. mktg., nat. sales mgr., Toledo, 1975-76; mktg. mgr. Govt. Electronics div. group Motorola Co., Scottsdale, Ariz., 1976-80, U.S. mktg. mgr. radar positioning systems Motorola Govt. Electronics Group, 1981—; gen. mgr. J.K. Internat., Scottsdale, 1980-81; mgmt. cons. Pres. Cambridge Group, 1987—; v.p. mktg. Pinnacle Surg. Products, 1989; v.p. mktg., Kroy, Inc., 1992-94; mgmt. cons., 1994—; v.p. mktg. and bus. devel. Kroy Inc., 1992, v.p. mktg. Process Control Tech., Inc., 1996—; adj. prof. Union Grad. Sch.; guest lectr. U. Mich. Grad. Sch. Bus. Adminstrn.; instr., chair strategic mgmt. U. Phoenix, 1988, pres. faculty, 1989—, area chair mktg., 1995—; Scottsdale Community Coll., Paradise Valley Community Coll.; talk show host Sta. KFNN, 1992-95. Area chair-gen. mgmt. Union Grad. Sch. Maricopa Community Coll., U. Phoenix. Chmn., Rep. Precinct, Burnsville, Minn., 1968-70; city fin. chmn., Burnsville; dir. community devel. U.S. Jaycees, Mpls., 1968-69; mem. Scottsdale 2000 Com. With USAF, 1957-61. Recipient Outstanding Performance award Maricopa Community Coll. System, 1987, Faciliation award, Maricopa Community Coll., Citation for Faciliation Ability U. Phoenix, 1986, 90, 93; named Hon. Citizen, Donaldsville, La., 1978; others. Mem. Am. Mktg. Assn., Afro-Am. Small Bus. Assn. (bd. dirs.), Phoenix Indian Ctr., Inc. (bd. dirs. 1994), Amateur Athletic Union (swimming ofcl. 1980-82), Phoenix Execs. Club, U. Phoenix Faculty Club (bd. dirs., pres. 1988-91, recipient Presdl. Designation award, officer), North Cape Yacht Club, Scottsdale Racquet Club, Toftnees Country Club. Roman Catholic. Home: 8650 E Via Del Arbor Scottsdale AZ 85258-3526

O'DOWD, DONALD DAVY, retired university president; b. Manchester, N.H., Jan. 23, 1927; s. Hugh Davy and Laura (Morin) O'D.; m. Janet Louise Fithian, Aug. 23, 1953; children: Daniel D., Diane K., James E., John M. BA summa cum laude, Dartmouth Coll., 1951; postgrad. (Fulbright fellow), U. Edinburgh, Scotland, 1951-52; MA, Harvard U., 1955, PhD, 1957. Instr., asst. prof. psychology, dean freshmen Wesleyan U., Middletown, Conn., 1955-60; assoc. prof., prof. of psychology, dean Univ. Oakland Univ., Rochester, Mich., 1960-65, provost, 1965-70; pres. Oakland U., Rochester, Mich., 1970-80; exec. vice chancellor SUNY, Albany, 1980-84; pres. U. of Alaska Statewide System, 1984-90. Sr. cons. Assn. Governing Bds. Univs. and Colls. Carnegie Corp. fellow, 1965-66. Mem. APA, AAAS, Phi Beta Kappa, Sigma Xi. Home and Office: 1550 La Vista Del Oceano Santa Barbara CA 93109-1739

OEDEKOVEN, BYRON FRANK, protective services official; b. Gillette, Wyo., Feb. 15, 1955; s. Charles Robert and Rhyllis Rae (Richmond) O.; m. Marjorie Grace Orvalla, Feb. 1, 1985. Student, Black Hills State Coll., 1974; AS in Criminal Justice, Sheridan C.C., 1980. Animal control officer Gillette Police Dept., 1974-75, police officer I, 1975-77, police officer II, 1977-78, police sgt., 1978-83, police lt., 1983-86; sheriff Campbell County Sheriff's Dept., Gillette, 1987—. Mem. Wyo. Com. Employer Support of the Guard and Res. Named Outstanding Young Law Enforcement Officer, Gillette Jaycees, 1977, 80, Outstanding Young Men in Am., Nat. Jaycees, 1977; recipient Dale Carnegie Impromptu Speaking award, 1983, Dale Carnegie Human Rels. Achievement award, 1983, Svc. to the City award Mayor of Gillette, 1986, Friend of Edn. award Campbell County Sch. Dist., 1989. Mem. NRA (life), SAR, Wyo. Assn. Sheriffs and Chiefs (2d v.p.), Internat. Assn. Chiefs of Police, Nat. Sheriffs' Assn., FBI Nat. Acad. Assocs., Wyo. Peace Officers' Assn., Wyo. Sheriffs' Assn., Mont. Snowmobile Assn., S.D. Snowmobile Assn., Wyo. Snowmobile Assn., Am. Quarter Horse Assn., Mayflower Soc., Thomas Rogers Soc., Gillette Jaycees, Masons, Shriners, Order Ea. Star, Valley of Orient of Sheridan, Kalif Temple Sheridan. Republican. Office: Campbell County Sheriff 600 W Boxelder Rd Gillette WY 82718-5219

OELCK, MICHAEL M., plant geneticist, researcher; b. Münster, Fed. Republic of Germany, July 26, 1954; s. Max and Ursula (Swiderski) O.; m. Elke Steinmann, Oct. 15, 1983; children: Fabian, Alexandra, Florian, Victoria. Diploma in Plant Genetics and Agronomy, U. Agr., Bonn., Fed. Republic of Germany, 1981; PhD in Molecular Genetics, U. Cologne, Fed. Republic of Germany, 1984. Leader rsch. lab. Hoechst AG, Frankfurt, Fed. Republic of Germany, 1984-88; vis. scientist Agriculture Can., Ottawa, Ont., 1988-90; group leader biotech. Hoechst Can., Saskatoon, Sask., Can., 1990-93; leader biotech AgrEvo Can., Saskatoon, 1994—. Contbr. articles to Jour. Plant Breeding, Jour. Plant Physiology, Biotech., Internat. Rapeseed Congress. Emergency ambulance officer Malteser Hilfsdienst, Kelkheim, Germany, 1987-88. Grad. grantee Max Planck Inst., Cologne, 1980-83. Mem. Deutsche Landwirtschaftsgesellschaft, Verein für Angestellte Akademiker, Deutsche Gesellschaft für Angewandte Botanik, Internat. Assn. Plant Cell Tissue Culture, Canadian Seed Trade Assn. Office: AgrEvo Can Inc, 106 Research Dr, Saskatoon, SK Canada S7N 3R3

OESTING, DAVID W., lawyer; b. Chgo., Aug. 6, 1944. AB, Earlham Coll., 1967; JD, Wash. U., 1970. Bar: Wash. 1970, Alaska 1981. Mem. Davis Wright Tremaine, Anchorage. Editor-in-chief Wash. U. Law Quarterly, 1969-70. Mem. ABA, Wash. State Bar Assn., Alaska Bar Assn., Anchorage Bar Assn., Order of Coif. Office: Davis Wright Tremaine 550 W 7th Ave Ste 1450 Anchorage AK 99501-3566

OESTING, SUSAN CAROLYN, education counselor; b. Washington, Jan. 31, 1945; d. Lawrence Alan and Virginia Carolyn (Harper) Seymour; m. David Winslow Oesting, Sept. 10, 1965; children: Aaron David, Sarah Kimberly, Erica Susan. BA, Earlham Coll., 1967; M in Counseling in Edn., U. Alaska, Anchorage, 1991. Cert. counseling in edn., Alaska. Sci. tchr. Whitfield Sch., Ladue, Mo., 1967-70; career resource technician Anchorage Sch. Dist., 1988-91, H.S. counselor, 1991—; mem., sec. Parent Adv. Com., Dimond H.S., Anchorage, 1986-88; mem. curriculum adv. com. Anchorage Sch. Dist., 1987. Bd. mem. Chugach Coun. Campfire, Anchorage, 1982-84; amb. coord. Anchorage Olympic Organizing Com., 1985-88. Mem. Alaska Sch. Counselors Assn., Anchorage Edn. Assn. Office: Dimond HS 2909 W 88th Ave Anchorage AK 99502-5363

OESTMANN, IRMA EMMA, minister; b. Auburn, Nebr., May 6, 1930; d. Martin Edward and Magdalene Augusta (Volkman) O.; m. Allister Roland Behrends, July 29, 1948 (div. 1968); children: John, Allan, Patricia, William, Michael, Russell, Kurt. BS in Edn., U. Nebr., 1972. Ordained min. Unity Ch., Unity Village, Mo., 1982. Dairy farm pvt. farmer Johnson, Nebr., 1948-68; art tchr. Burke High Sch., Omaha, 1972-73, L.A. (Calif.) Pub. Schs., 1974-77; mgr. U-Rent Furniture, Canoga Park, Calif., 1978-80; min. There Is A Way TV Ministry, Palm Springs, Calif., 1982-83, Unity Ch. of Truth, Pomona, Calif., 1983-85, Unity of Del Ray Beach, Fla., 1986-87, Unity of Jupiter, Fla., 1988-90, Unity Ch. of San Gabriel, Calif., 1991-94, United Fellowship of Grants Pass, Oreg., 1994-95; asst. min. Unity Ch., Ventura, Calif., 1995-96; cert. hypnotist, self-instr., therapist Encino, Calif., 1978-80; pvt. children's art tchr., Upland, Calif., 1986-87; seminar/workshop presenter, 1980. Artist oil and watercolor paintings, 1968—; author, artist: (audio tapes) Methods of Relaxation, 1980, Inner-Space Meditations, 1994; producer, host: (tv panel series) The Truth Is, 1989; contbr. poems and articles to mags. Mem. San Gabriel (Calif.) Cmty. Coun., 1991-93. Home: 300 Rossmore Dr Oxnard CA 93035

OFFEN, KAREN MARIE, historian, educator; b. Pocatello, Idaho, Oct. 10, 1939; d. Norman V. and Ella Mae (McAlister) Stedtfeld; m. George R. Offen, Dec. 30, 1965; children: Catherine, Stephanie. BA, U. Idaho, 1961; AM, Stanford U., 1963, PhD, 1971. Lectr. History U. Santa Clara, Calif., 1973, U. San Francisco, 1975-76, Stanford (Calif.) U., 1978, 82, 84, 86, 89, 92; ind. scholar affiliated with Inst. Rsch. Women & Gender, Stanford U., 1978—; dir. summer seminar NEH, 1984, 86, 89, 92; founding mem., sec.-treas. Internat. Fedn. Rsch. Women's History, 1987-95; pres. Western Assn.

Women Historians, 1991-93. Mem. editl. adv. bd. French Hist. Studies, Arenal, L'Homme, Jour. Women's History, History European Ideas, Hist. Reflections; contbr. articles to profl. jours. Recipient Disting. Alumni Achievement award U. Idaho, 1994, Sr. Scholar award, 1995; NEH Ind. Study & Rsch. fellow, 1980-81, Rockefeller Found. Humanities fellow, 1985-86, J.S. Guggenheim fellow, 1995-96. Mem. Am. Hist. Assn. (com. women historians 1983-86, chair com. internat. hist. activities 1986-90), Soc. French Hist. Studies (exec. com. 1983-86), P.E.O., Kappa Kappa Gamma. Democrat. Office: Stanford U Inst Rsch Women & Gender Stanford CA 94305-8640

OFFEN, RONALD CHARLES, school librarian; b. Chgo., Oct. 2, 1930; s. Charles Henry and Ellen (Shirreffs) O.; m. Sharon Rae Nealy, Mar. 17, 1951 (div.); children: Deirdre, Eric; m. Rosine J. Franke, Aug. 20, 1966; children: Michele, Darren P. AA, Wright Jr. Coll., Chgo., 1950; MA, U. Chgo., 1967. Ins. investigator various ins. cos., Chgo., 1952-68; mng. editor Chicagoland Mag., Chgo., 1968-70; editor Automotive Fleet, Glenview, Ill., 1970-71; freelance editor, writer, author Chgo., 1971-78; sch. libr. Capistrano Unified Sch. Dist., Laguna Niguel, Calif., 1983—; adminstr. theater co. The Peripatetic Task Force, Chgo., 1975-78. Co-editor Odyssey: Explorations in Poetry, 1956-58; exec. editor Lit. Times, 1975-78; co-author: (non-fiction) Dillinger: Dead or Alive?, 1970; author: (biographies) Cagney, 1973, Brando, 1974; (poetry) Poet as Bad Guy, 1963, Instead of Gifts, 1995, Questions, Answers, 1996; editor: The Starving Poet's Cookbook, 1994; editor Free Lunch, 1996—. Mem. Acad. Am. Poets (1st prize 1958), Authors Guild. Office: Free Lunch PO Box 7647 Laguna Niguel CA 92607-7647

OFFENKRANTZ, WILLIAM CHARLES, psychiatrist; b. Sept. 2, 1924. BS in Biol. Sci., Rutgers U., 1945; MD, Columbia U., 1947; cert. in psychoanalysis, William Alanson White Inst., N.Y.C., 1957, Chgo. Inst. Psychoanalysis, 1966. Diplomate Am. Bd. Psychiatry and Neurology, Nat. Bd. Med. Examiners. Intern Jersey City Med. Ctr., 1947-48; resident in neuropsychiatry VA Hosp., Lyon, N.J., 1948-50; resident in psychiatry N.Y. State Psychiat. Inst.-Columbia-Presbyn. Med. Ctr., N.Y.C., 1950-51; pvt. practice N.Y.C., 1951-53; assoc. rsch. scientist in psychiatry Creedmoor Inst. for Psychobiologic Studies, Queens Village, N.Y., 1955-56; pvt. practice San Diego, 1956-57; chief cons. and liaison svc. psychiatry U. Chgo. Hosps. and Clinics, 1957-58; from asst. to assoc. prof. dept. psychiatry sch. medicine U. Chgo., 1957-71, prof., 1971-79, dir. residency tng. in psychiatry Sch. Medicine, 1958-69; prof. psychoanalysis and psychiatry dept. psychiatry and mental health scis., dir. divsn. psychoanalysis Med. Coll. Wis., Milw., 1979-87; pvt. practice Milw., 1979-87; dir. consultation and liaison svc. Milwaukee County Gen. Hosp., Milw., 1979-80; dir. out-patient svcs. Milwaukee County Mental Health Complex, Milw., 1980-81; dir. psychotherapy ctr. Columbia Hosp., Milw., 1981-87; pvt. practice Scottsdale, Ariz., 1987—; chief psychotherapy tng. Maricopa Med. Ctr., Phoenix, 1987—; asst. psychiatrist Vanderbilt Clinic Columbia-Presbyn. Med. Ctr., N.Y.C., 1950-51; cons. Family Svc. Assn., San Diego, 1956-57, TV series Sleep and Dreaming ABC-TV, Chgo., 1960, Peace Corps, Malaya Project, 1960, Youth Guidance Agy., Chgo., 1959-66, U. Chgo. Svc. at Ill. State Psychiat. Inst., 1959-70; mem. attending staff dept. psychiatry Maricopa Med. Ctr., 1988—. Mem. editl. bd. Jour. Nervous and Mental Disease, 1965-71; reviewer Am. Jour. Psychiatry, 1965—, Archives of Gen. Psychiatry Vol. 30, 1974, Am. Handbook of Psychiatry, Vol. 5, 1975, Psychoanalytic Psychotherapy, Manual of Psychiatric Peer Rev., 1976, 3d edit., 1980; (with John Crayton) The Psychiatric Formulation: A Handbook for Board Candidates, 1992. Capt. U.S. Army Med. Corps, 1953-55. Fellow Am. Psychiat. Assn. (life, therapy com. 1968-69, nat. adv. com. for CHAMPUS-APA peer rev. contract 1977-83, peer rev. com. 1980-86, com. on practice of psychotherapy 1986-90), Am. Psychoanalytic Assn. (life, co-chmn., peer rev. com. 1974-82, chmn. joint DSM-III com. 1978-81, dir. Wis. psychoanalytic new tng. facility 1985-87), So. Calif. Psychoanalytic Inst. (geog. rule tng. analyst Ariz. 1989—); mem. Internat. Psychoanalytic Assn., Group Advancement Psychiatry (therapy com. 1962—, bd. dirs. 1981-83), Chgo. Inst. Psychoanalysis (faculty 1966-87, progression com. 1974-75, chmn. dream rsch. workshop 1964-79, tng. and supervising analyst 1978-87, geog. rule tng. analyst Wis. psychoanalytic new tng. facility 1979-87). Home: PO Box 6002 Carefree AZ 85377-6002 Office: 6619 N Scottsdale Rd Scottsdale AZ 85250-4421

OFNER, WILLIAM BERNARD, lawyer; b. L.A., Aug. 24, 1929; s. Harry D. and Gertrude (Skoss) Offner; m. Florence Ila Maxwell, Apr. 13, 1953 (div. 1956). AA, L.A. City Coll., 1949; BA, Calif. State U., L.A., 1953; LLB, Loyola U., L.A., 1965; postgrad. Sorbonne, 1951, cert. de Langue Francaise, 1987; postgrad. U. So. Calif., 1966, Glendale Community Coll., 1986-92. Bar: Calif. 1966, U.S. Dist. Ct. Calif. 1966, U.S. Supreme Ct. 1972. Assoc. Thomas Moore and Assocs., L.A., 1967-69; pvt. practice, L.A., 1969-70, 74—; assoc. Peter Lam, L.A., 1981-94, mgn. atty. 1993—; assoc. C.M. Coronel, 1986-87, Jack D. Janofsky, 1987-89, Mario P. Gonzalez, 1990-92; lectr. Van Norman U., 1975. With USNR, 1947-54. Mem. Inst. Gen. Semantics, Inst. for Antiquity and Christianity, Soc. des Amis De l'Universite de Paris, Safari Athletic Club, Toastmasters. Democrat. Avocations: painting, photography, linguistics, French tutoring, travel. Office: 23441 Golden Springs Dr # 357 Diamond Bar CA 91765-2030

OFTE, DONALD, retired environmental executive, consultant; b. N.Y.C., Aug. 23, 1929; s. Sverre and Ingeborg Ofte; m. Margaret Mae McHenney, July 23, 1955; children: Marc Christian, Nancy Carolyn Ofte Appleby, Kirk Donald Jr. BA in Chemistry, Dana Coll., 1952; postgrad. study metall. engring., Ohio State U., 1958-60. Jr. chemist Inst. Atomic Research, Ames, Iowa, 1952-53; sr. research chemist Monsanto Research Corp., Miamisburg, Ohio, 1958-66; ops. engr. AEC, Miamisburg, 1966-69; br. chief, div. dir. ops. office AEC, Albuquerque, 1969-73; mgr. Pinellas area office AEC, Largo, Fla., 1973-79; mgr. Rocky Flats area office Dept. Energy, Golden, Colo., 1979-82; asst. mgr. devel. and prodn. Dept. Energy, Albuquerque, 1982-83, dep. mgr. ops. office, 1983-84; prin. dep. asst. sec. Dept. Energy Defense Programs, Washington, 1984-87; mgr. ops. office Dept. Energy, Idaho Falls, Idaho, 1987-89; mgmt. cons. Idaho Falls, 1989-92; v.p. govt. ops. United Engrs. and Constructors, Denver, 1992-93; v.p. Adv. Scis., Inc., Albuquerque, 1993-94; pres. FERMCO, Cin., 1994-96; ret., 1996; v.p. Fluor-Daniel, Inc., 1994-96; affiliate prof. Idaho State U., 1990-92; bd. dirs. Denver Fed. Exec. Bd., 1979-82. Author: (with others) Plutonium 1960, 1965, Physicochemical Methods in Metallurgical Research; contbr. articles to profl. jours. on metallurgy and ceramics. Campaign chmn. United Way Pinellas, St. Petersburg, Fla., 1978; bd. dirs. Bonneville County United Way, Idaho Rsch. Found.; mem. adv. bd. Teton Peaks Council Boy Scouts of Am., 1987-92, Eastern Idaho Tech. Coll.; chmn. Excellence in Edn. Fund Com., 1990-92; vice chmn., bd. dirs. Rio Grande Ch. ARC, Albuquerque, 1982-84. Served to lt. (j.g.) USN, 1953-57. Recipient citation AEC for Apollo 12 SNAP 27 Radioisotope Generator, 1969, High Quality Performance award AEC, 1968, Group Achievement award NASA, 1972; Meritorious Svc. award Dept. Energy, 1985, Disting. Career Svc. award, 1989. Mem. Am. Chem. Soc., Am. Nuclear Soc., Am. Soc. Metals, Nat. Contract Mgmt. Assn., Am. Soc. Pub. Adminstrs., Suncoast Archeol. Soc., Idaho Falls C. of C. (bd. dirs., cmty. svc. award 1990), Rotary Internat. (Paul Harris fellow). Home: 1129 Salamanca NW Albuquerque NM 87107

OGAN, CHESTER VANCE, wildlife biologist; b. Needles, Calif., Mar. 22, 1947; s. Reginald Treloar and Donna May (Buker) O.; m. Mary Ellen Sullivan, Sept. 1970 (div. 1973); m. Barbara Buckman, Aug. 9, 1980; children: Jonathan Allan, Katherine Louise. A.Biol.Sci., Santa Barbara City Coll., 1967; B.Biology, Humboldt State U., 1970. Forestry technician fire control U.S. Forest Svc., San Fernando, Calif., 1970-74; forestry technician hydrology, fire sci. Pacific S.W. Exptl. Sta., San Dimas, Calif., 1974-77; forestry technician silviculture Pacific S.W. Exptl. Sta., Arcata, Calif., 1981-82, wildlife technician rsch., 1982-86, wildlife technician endangered species rsch., 1986—; biol. sci. asst. electron microscopy, parasitology Walter Reed Army Inst. Rsch., Washington, 1977-81; adv. com. Arcata Marsh & Wildlife Sanctuary, 1984-92. Contbr. articles to profl. jours. Mem. sch. site coun. com. Washington Elem. Sch./Eureka City Schs., 1994-96; mem. com. troop 27 Boy Scouts Am., 1994—. Sgt. U.S. Army, 1977-81; Calif. Army N.G., 1981—. Decorated Army Commendation medal. Fellow The Wildlife Soc. (bd. dirs. 1996—, sec. 1996—), Am. Birding Assn., Redwood Region Audubon Soc. (program chmn. 1988-90, publicity chmn. 1984-88, bd. dirs. 1984-93, conservation com. 1986—). Republican. Methodist. Home: 811 O St Eureka CA 95501 Office: Redwood Sciences Lab 1700 Bayview Dr Arcata CA 95521

O'GARA, BARBARA ANN, soap company executive; b. Newark, Aug. 8, 1953; d. Frank Percy and Rose Stevens. AA, Keystone Jr. Coll., 1973; BS, U. Ariz., 1976. Media buyer Wells, Rich, Green/Townsend, Irvine, Calif., 1977-80; dist. sales mgr. Dial Corp., Phoenix, 1980-82; regional sales mgr. Guest Supply, Inc., North Brunswick, N.J., 1982-85; dir. hotel mktg. and sales Neutrogena Corp., L.A., 1985-92, v.p. hotel mktg. and sales, 1992-96; cons. Bath and Body Works, 1996—. Keystone Jr. Coll. scholar, 1972, Morris County scholar, 1971; recipient Outstanding Sales Accomplishment award Armour-Dial, 1981. Mem. Am. Mktg. Assn., Am. Mgmt. Assn., Am. Hotel and Motel Assn., Network Exec. Women in Hospitality. Republican. Roman Catholic. Avocations: tennis, aerobics, running, skiing, photography. Home and Office: Penthouse A 2218 Main St Santa Monica CA 90405-2273

OGBURN, GREGORY ALLEN, accountant; b. Detroit, Nov. 21, 1961; s. Donald Allen and Ruby Juanita (Robbins) O.; m. Jobie Jaelyn Cabbell, Aug. 22, 1987; children: Haley Jaelyn, Preston Allen, Parker Allen. BBA in Acctg., Harding U., Searcy, Ark., 1983. CPA, Tex., N.Mex. Audit staff Arthur Young & Co., Dallas, 1983-86; sr. acct. Martin Trachta Hunter & Co., Dallas, 1987-88; supr. Hallquist Thurman & Assocs., Santa Fe, 1989-91; pres. Gregory A. Ogburn, P.C., Los Alamos, N.Mex., 1991—; mem. adv. bd. U. N.Mex.-Los Altos Small Bus. Devel. Ctr., 1994—. Pres. Los Alamos Econ. Devel. Corp., 1996-97; chmn. Econ. Devel. Orgn. Team, Los alamos, 1996-97; bd. dirs. Ponderosa Christian Camp, Albuquerque, 1991—. Mem. N.Mex. Soc. CPAs (bd. dirs. 1994—, pres. Los Alamos chpt. 1994—), Tex. Soc. CPAs, Los Alamos C. of C. (bd. dirs. 1996—), Kiwanis. Republican. Mem. Ch. of Christ. Office: 1460 Trinity Ste 1 Los Alamos NM 87544

OGDEN, JEAN LUCILLE, sales executive; b. Chgo., Jan. 20, 1950; d. George William and Mary Elizabeth (MacKenzie) Anderson; m. Michael Jude Ogden, Aug. 27, 1977 (div. Dec. 1983). BA with honors, U. Calif., Santa Barbara, 1971. Sales rep. Am. Hosp. Supply Co., Irvine, Calif., 1975-77, Abbott Labs., HPD, L.A., 1977-78, Gillette Co., Albququerque, 1978-79, Unitek Corp., Monrovia, Calif., 1979-86, Nat. Patent Dental Products, San Diego, 1986-87; area mgr. Branson Ultrasonics Corp., L.A., 1987—. Mem., co-chair Nat. Multiple Sclerosis Soc., San Diego, 1983—; mem. Am. Cancer Soc., San Diego, 1985—, Zool. Soc., San Diego, 1984-85. Named one of Outstanding Young Women in Am., 1984. Mem. AAUW, NAFE, Med. Mktg. Assn., Salesmasters Albuquerque, Soroptimist Internat. (officer Carlsbad and Oceanside, Calif. chpt. 1983-85), Alpha Phi (house corp. bd. Long Beach chpt. 1974-75, chpt. advisor 1975-76). Republican. Office: Branson Ultrasonics Corp 12955 E Perez Pl La Puente CA 91746-1414

OGDEN, STEVEN KEVIN, recording industry executive, producer; b. San Diego, Aug. 27, 1960; s. Jack Lindley and Roseann (Rhapps) O. Student, Art Ctr. Coll. Design, Pasadena, Calif., 1980-82. Owner Third St. Sound, Hollywood, Calif., 1986-96. Mem. Inter Documentary Assn. (bd. dirs. 1993-96). Address: 7095 Hollywood Blvd #650 Hollywood CA 90028-8903

OGDEN, VALERIA JUAN, management consultant, state representative; b. Okanogan, Wash., Feb. 11, 1924; d. Ivan Bodwell and Pearle (Wilson) Munson; m. Daniel Miller Ogden Jr., Dec. 28, 1946; children: Janeth Lee Ogden Martin, Patricia Jo Ogden Hunter, Daniel Munson Ogden. BA magna cum laude, Wash. State U., 1946. Exec. dir. Potomac Coun. Camp Fire, Washington, 1964-68, Ft. Collins (Colo.) United Way, 1969-73, Designing Tomorrow Today, Ft. Collins, 1973-74, Poudre Valley Community Edn. Assn., Ft. Collins, 1977-78; pres. Valeria M. Ogden, Inc., Kensington, Md., 1978-81; nat. field cons. Camp Fire, Inc., Kansas City, Mo., 1980-81; exec. dir. Nat. Capital Area YWCA, Washington, 1981-84, Clark County YWCA, Vancouver, Wash., 1985-89; pvt. practice mgmt. cons. Vancouver, 1989—; mem. Wash. Ho. of Reps., 1991—; mem. adj. faculty pub. adminstrn. program Lewis and Clark Coll., Portland (Oreg.) State U., 1979-94; mem. Pvt. Industry Coun., Vancouver, 1986-95; mem. regional Svcs. Network Bd. Mental Health, 1993—. Author: Camp Fire Membership, 1980. County vice chmn. Larimer County Dems., Ft. Collins, 1974-75; mem. precinct com. Clark County Dems., Vancouver, 1986-88; mem. Wash. State Coun. Vol. Action, Olympia, 1986-90; treas. Mortar Bd. Nat. Found., Vancouver, 1987-96; bd. dirs. Clark County Coun. for Homeless, Vancouver, 1989—, chmn., 1994; bd. dirs. Wash. Wil life and Recreation Coalition, 1995—, Human Svcs. Coun., 1996—; chair arts and tourism com. Nat. Coun. State Legis., 1996-97; bd. Wash. State Hist. Soc., 1996—. Named Citizen of Yr. Ft. Collins Bd. of Realtors, 1975; recipient Gulick award Camp Fire Inc., 1956, Alumna Achievement award Wash. State U. Alumni Assn., 1988. Mem. Internat. Assn. Vol. Adminstrs. (pres. Boulder 1989-90), Nat. Assn. YWCA Exec. Dirs. (nat. bd. nominating com. 1988-90), Sci. and Society Assn. (bd. dirs. 1993—), Women in Action, Philanthropic and Ednl. Orgn., Phi Beta Kappa. Democrat. Home: 3118 NE Royal Oak Dr Vancouver WA 98662-7435 Office: John L O'Brien Bldg Rm 342 State Ave NE Olympia WA 98504-1134

OGG, WILSON REID, lawyer, poet, retired judge, lyricist, curator, publisher, educator, philosopher, social scientist, parapsychologist; b. Alhambra, Calif., Feb. 26, 1928; s. James Brooks and Mary (Wilson) O. Student Pasadena Jr. Coll., 1946; A.B., U. Calif. at Berkeley, 1949, J.D., 1952; Cultural D in Philosophy of Law, World Univ. Roundtable, 1983. Bar: Calif. Assoc. trust Dept. Wells Fargo Bank, San Francisco, 1954-55; pvt. practice law, Berkeley, 1955—; adminstrv. law judge, 1974-93; real estate broker, cons., 1974—; curator-in-residence Pinebrook, 1964—; owner Pinebrook Press, Berkeley, Calif., 1988—; rsch. atty., legal editor dept. of continuing edn. of bar U. Calif. Extension, 1958-63; psychology instr. 25th Sta. Hosp., Taegu, Korea, 1954; English instr. Taegu English Lang. Inst., Taegu, 1954. Trustee World U., 1976-80; dir. admissions Internat. Soc. for Phil. Enquiry, 1981-84; dep. dir. gen. Internat. Biographical Centre, Eng., 1986—; dep. gov. Am. Biographical Inst. Research Assn., 1986—; ind. rep. Excel Comm., Inc. Served with AUS, 1952-54. Cert. community coll. instr. Mem. VFW, AAAS, ABA, ASCAP, State Bar Calif., San Francisco Bar Assn., Am. Soc. Composers, Am. Arbitration Assn. (nat. panel arbitrators), World Future Soc. (profl. mem.), Calif. Soc. Psychical Study (pres., chmn. bd. 1963-65), Internat. Soc. Unified Sci., Internat. Soc. Poets, (life), Internat. Platform Assn., Amnesty Internat., Am. Civil Liberties Union, Intertel, Internat. Soc. Individual Liberty, Triple Nine Soc., Wisdom Soc., Inst. Noetic Scis., Men's Inner Circle of Achievement, Truman Libr. Inst. (hon.), Am. Legion, Faculty Club (U. Calif.), City Commons Club (Berkeley), Commonwealth Club of Calif., Town Hall Club of Calif., Marines Meml. Club, Masons, Shriners, Elks. Unitarian. Contbr. numerous articles profl. jours; contbr. poetry to various mags. including American Poetry Anthology Vol. VI Number 5, Hearts on Fire: A Treasury of Poems on Love, Vol. IV, 1987, New Voices in American Poetry, 1987, The Best Poems of the 90's, Distinguished Poets of America, The Poetry of Life A Treasury of Moments Am. Poetry Anthology, Vol. VII, 1988, Nat. Libr. Poets, 1992, Disting. Poets Of Am., 1993, The Best Modern Writer of 1994, Parnassus of World Poets, 1994, 95, 96, Best Poems of 1995, 96. Home: Pinebrook 8 Bret Harte Way Berkeley CA 94708-1609 Office: 1104 Keith Ave Berkeley CA 94708-1607 also: 39193 Liberty St Fremont CA 94538-1501 *Judge Ogg's career combines outstanding achievement in the legal profession with a major analysis of the problems of distinguishing co-existence from causality in medicine and science. He has also formulated the two-way flow theory of matter and consciousness under which principles of quantum mechanics, black notes, light, suppression and contraction of manifestation, and physical and biological evolutions are derivative from the basic postulates of the theory.*

OGLE, EDWARD PROCTOR, JR., investment counseling executive; b. Inglewood, Calif., Dec. 20, 1935; s. Edward Proctor and Allene Emma (Blumenthal) O.; m. Elizabeth Lovejoy Myers, Mar. 28, 1958; children: Kathryn Ogle Nava, Terry Ogle Nelson, Wendy Ogle Reeves. BA, U. So. Calif., 1964; MA, Claremont Grad. Sch., 1980. Cert. fin. planning practitioner. Zone mgr. Investors Diversified Svcs., Pasadena, Calif., 1964-66; asst. mgr. Merrill Lynch Pierce Fenner Smith, Pasadena, 1966-72; mgr. Clark Dodge & Co-Capital Place Dept., L.A., 1972-74; sr. v.p. Security Pacific Bank - Pacific Century Group, L.A., 1974-86; mgr., registered prin. Brown Bros. Harriman & Co., L.A., 1986—. Author: (booklet) Role of Bank Trust Department, 1981; editor (booklet) Parade Operations Manual, 1992, 93. Com. sec. Tournament of Roses Assn., Pasadena, 1976—; mem. Town Hall of Calif., L.A., 1977—; mem. Rep. Presdl. Task Force, Orange County, Calif., 1984—; mem. L.A. World Affairs Coun., 1985—; elder Presbyn. Ch. Recipient Corp. Fund Raising Cert. United Way, L.A., 1978-80, Exec. Mgmt. Cert. Claremont Grad. Sch., 1979, Mgmt. and Exec. Cert. Security Pacific Bank, L.A., 1981. Mem. Internat. Assn. Fin. Planners, Drucker Ctr. Mgmt. Assn., Claremont Grad. Sch. Alumni Assn. (pres. 1984-86), Pasadena Bond Club, Bond Club L.A., Jonathan Club. Republican. Office: Brown Bros Harriman & Co 355 S Grand Ave Ste 3250 Los Angeles CA 90071-1592

OGLE, JAMES, performing company executive; m. Mary Davis; children: Matthew, Ryan. Student, Nat. ConservatoryMusic; studied with Seiji Ozawa, Leonard Bernstein, Andre Previn, Sir Collin Davis, Boston. Music dir. Boise Philharmonic Assn., Idaho; assoc. condr. N.C. Symphony; condr.-in-residence Appalachian State U. Cannon Music Camp; guest condr. Music from Bear Valley, Winston-Salem Symphony, South Bend Symphony, Nebr. Chamber Orchestra; guest clinician and condr. La. State U. Symphony Orchestra and Wind Ensemble; guest artist-in-residence U. N.C.; founder, condr., artistic dir. summer residence N.C. Symphony, 1982-94,. Recipient James Bland Meml. Scholarship, Malko Internat. Condr. award, 1974. Mem. Downtown Rotary Club. Office: Boise Philharmonic Assn 516 S 9th St Ste C Boise ID 83702*

OH, SEHO, research engineer; b. Daejeon, Korea, Sept. 12, 1957; s. In-Sung and Un-Ok Oh; m. Suk-Yeon Chung, Apr. 21, 1985; children: Daniel Chun-Suk, David Hyung-Suk. BS, Seoul Nat. U., 1979; MS, KAIST, Seoul, 1981; PhD, U. Wash., 1989. Rsch. engr. Goldstar Co., Seoul, 1981-86; rsch. assoc. U. Wash., Seattle, 1990-93, affiliate asst. prof., 1993—; sr. rsch. engr. NeoPath Inc., Redmond, Wash., 1993—. Assoc. editor IEEE Trans. on Neural Networks, 1992-93. Christian. Office: NeoPath Inc 8271 154th Ave NE Redmond WA 98052-3878

O'HAGAN, WILLIAM GORDON, state agency administrator; b. Allentown, N.J., Oct. 12, 1943; s. Forrest Allen and Voncile Arline (Linton) O'H.; m. Marcia Helen Beck, Aug. 12, 1947 (div. Oct. 1985). Grad. high sch., Azusa, Calif., 1962. Owner Richfield Oil Co., Baldwin Park, Calif., 1970-72; mgr. Am. Teaching Aids, Covina, Calif., 1972-88; owner Bill's Auto Repair Co., Covina, 1988-93; mechanic, 1993-95; supr./foreman Public Auction Agy. of Calif., 1996—. Block commander Neighborhood Watch, Covina. Republican. Baptist. Home: 163 N Marcile Ave Glendora CA 91741-2453 *Personal philosophy: The clock of life is wound but once - don't wait until tommorrow for the hands may be still.*

O'HALLORAN, THOMAS ALPHONSUS, JR., physicist, educator; b. Bklyn., Apr. 13, 1931; s. Thomas Alphonsus Sr. and Nora (Sheehan) O'H.; m. Barbara Joyce Hug, June 4, 1954; children: Theresa Joyce, Maureen Ann, Kevin Thomas, Patrick Joseph. Student, San Jose State U., 1948-50; BS in Physics & Math., Oreg. State U., 1953, MS in Physics, 1954; PhD, U. Calif., Berkeley, 1963. Rsch. asst. Lawrence Berkeley Lab., U. Calif., 1963-64; rsch. fellow Harvard U., Cambridge, Mass., 1964-66; asst. prof. physics U. Ill., Urbana, 1966-68, assoc. prof., 1968-70, prof., 1970-93, prof. emeritus, 1993—; vis. scholar U. Utah, Salt Lake City, 1990-93, rsch. prof. physics, 1993—; mem. program adv. com. Argonne Nat. Lab., Lemont, Ill., Fermi Lab., Batavia, Ill., Brookhaven Nat. Lab., Upton, L.I.; vis. scientist Lawrence Berkeley Lab., U. Calif., 1979-80. Contbr. numerous articles on elem. particle physics to profl. jours. Lt. USN, 1954-58. Guggenheim fellow, 1979-80. Fellow Am. Phys. Soc.; mem. Molly Green Club. Home: 4614 Ledgemont Dr Salt Lake City UT 84124-4735 Office: U Utah Physics Dept 201 Jfb Salt Lake City UT 84112

OHANIAN, EDWARD, psychologist; b. Selma, Calif., Nov. 14, 1922; s. Benjamin and Mary (Gorouzian) O.; m. Martha Loraine Taylor, Aug. 17, 1950; chidlren: Valerie Gay, Lee Edward. BA, U. So. Calif., 1947, MA, 1950, PhD, 1952. Lic. psychologist, Calif. Instr. U. Mont., Missoula, 1953-54; asst. prof. Pepperdine U., L.A., 1954-57, assoc. prof., co-dir. psychology-speech clinic, 1958-61; pvt. practice L.A., 1961-67, Carmel, Calif., 1967—; cons. Freeman Clinic, L.A., 1952-53; vis. prof. U. Calif., L.A., Santa Barbara, Santa Cruz, Riverside, 1956-82; dir. Parent Tng. Ctr., L.A., 1957-59; lectr. Loyola U., L.A., 1961-67. With USNR, 1942-45, PTO. Mem. APA, Wine and Food Soc. Monterey Peninsula (pres. 1973-74), Brotherhood Knights of the Vine (master knight). Home and Office: PO Box 1392 Pebble Beach CA 93953

O'HARA, MICHAEL J(AMES), physicist; b. Winthrop, Mass., Aug. 7, 1956; s. George J. and Gilda A. (Capone) O. BS in Physics, U. Lowell (Mass.), 1978; MS in Physics, U. Ill., 1980, MS in Computer Sci., 1984. Mem. tech. staff I Hughes Aircraft Co., El Segundo, Calif., 1984-86, mem. tech. staff II, 1986-87; tech. supr. Hughes Aircraft Co., 1987-89, sect. head, 1989-91, asst. dept. mgr., 1991-94, project mgr., 1994—; software cons. Duosoft Corp., Urbana, 1982-83; bd. dirs. Ednl. Scis. Corp. Am., L.A., 1986—; CEO Ednl. Scis. Corp. Am., L.A., 1996—. Mem. N.Y. Acad. Sci., Planetary Soc., Soc. Photo-Optical Instrumentation Engrs., U. Ill. Alumni Club, Soc. Physics Students, Sigma Pi Sigma. Republican. Roman Catholic. Office: Hughes Aircraft Co Space and Comms 909 N Sepulveda Blvd El Segundo CA 90245

O'HEARN, MICHAEL JOHN, lawyer; b. Akron, Ohio, Jan. 29, 1952; s. Leo Ambrose and Margaret Elizabeth (Clark) O'H. BA in Econs., UCLA, 1975; postgrad., U. San Diego, 1977; JD, San Fernando Valley Coll. Law, 1979. Bar: Calif. 1979, U.S. Dist. Ct. (cen. dist.) Calif. 1979. Document analyst Mellonics Info. Ctr., Litton Industries, Canoga Park, Calif., 1977-79; pvt. practice Encino, Calif., 1979-80; atty. VISTA/Grey Law Inc., L.A., 1980-81; assoc. Donald E. Chadwick & Assocs., Woodland Hills, Calif., 1981-84, Law Offices of Laurence Ring, Beverly Hills, Calif., 1984-85; atty., in-house counsel Coastal Ins. Co., Van Nuys, Calif., 1985-89; atty. Citrus Glen Apts., Ventura, Calif., 1989-92; pvt. practice Ventura County, Calif., 1992—. Recipient Cert. of Appreciation, Agy. for Vol. Svc., 1981, San Fernando Valley Walk for Life, 1988, Cert. of Appreciation, Arbitrator for the Superior and Mcpl. Cts., Ventura County Jud. Dist., 1996. Mem. KC, Ventura County Bar Assn., Ventura County Trial Lawyers Assn., Secular Franciscan Order. Republican. Roman Catholic. Home: 1741 Fisher Dr Apt 201 Oxnard CA 93035 Office: 3650 Ketch Ave Oxnard CA 93035-3029

OHLSEN, GERALD G., real estate developer, lawyer, physicist; b. Eugene, Oreg., May 1, 1933; s. Glenn Randolph and Doris Louise (Perry) O.; m. Sally Slaughter, Sept. 1958 (div.); m. Linnea Delores Carlson McGehee, Mar. 1974. BA, U. Oreg., 1955; MS, Stanford U., 1957, PhD, 1960; JD, U. N.Mex., 1992. Bar: N.Mex. 1992; lic. real estate broker, N.Mex. Asst. prof. U. Tex., Austin, 1960-61; fellow Australian Nat. U., Canberra, 1961-65; mem. staff Los Alamos (N.Mex.) Nat. Lab., 1965-80; real estate developer Santa Fe, N.Mex., 1980—. Contbr. articles to profl. publs. Home and Office: 1169 E Alameda St Santa Fe NM 87501-2286

OHMAN, DIANA J., state official, former school system administrator; b. Sheridan, Wyo., Oct. 3, 1950; d. Arden and Doris Marie (Carstens) Mahin. AA, Casper Coll., 1970; BA, U. Wyo., 1972, MEd, 1977, postgrad., 1979—. Tchr. kindergarten Natrona County Sch. Dist., Casper, Wyo., 1971-72; tchr. rural sch. K-8 Campbell County Sch. Dist., Gillette, Wyo., 1972-80, rural prin. K-8, 1980-82, prin. K-6, 1982-84, assoc. dir. instrn., 1984-87; dir. K-12 Goshen County Migrant Program, Torrington, Wyo., 1988-89; prin. K-2 Goshen County Sch. Dist., Torrington, Wyo., 1987-90; state supt. pub. instrn. State of Wyo., Cheyenne, 1991-94, secretary of state, 1995—; chmn. Campbell County Mental Health Task Force, 1986-87; mem. Legis. Task Force on Edn. of Handicapped 3-5 Yr. Olds, 1988-89. State Committeewoman Wyo. Rep. Party, 1985-88. Recipient Wyo. Elem. Prin. of Yr. award, 1990; named Campbell County Tchr. of Yr. 1980, Campbell County Profl. Bus. Woman of Yr. 1984, Outstanding Young Woman in Am., 1983. Mem. Coun. of Chief of State Sch. Officers (Washington chpt.), Internat. Reading Assn., Wyo. Assn. of Sch. Adminstrs., Kappa Delta Pi, Phi Kappa Phi, Phi Delta Kappa. Republican. Lutheran. Office: Sec State Office State Capitol Cheyenne WY 82002-0020

OISHI, CALVIN SHIZUO, orthopedic surgeon; b. Honolulu, Mar. 2, 1961; s. Masaichi and Kazumae (Ichiuji) O.; m. Selma Hiroko Yonamine, Feb. 1, 1992; 1 child, Sarah. BA in Biology, Pomona Coll., 1983; MD, U. Calif., San Diego, 1987. Diplomate Am. Bd. Orthopedic Surgery. Intern in surgery U. Calif., San Francisco, resident in orthop.; fellow in total joint replacement Scripps Clinic and Rsch. Found.; orthop. surgeon Orthop. Assocs. of Hawaii Inc., Honolulu, 1993—; asst. clin. prof. orthop. surgery, U. Hawaii, Manoa,

1993—; mem. knee design team Exactech, Gainesville, Fla., 1994—. Contbr. articles to profl. jours. NCAA scholar Pomona Coll., 1983; U. Calif. med. sch. grantee, 1984. Fellow Am. Acad. Orthop. Surgeons; mem. Hawaii Orthop. Assn., Hawaii Med. Assn., Leroy C. Abbott Orthop. Soc. Methodist. Office: Orthop Assocs of Hawaii Inc Ste 604 1380 Lusitana St Honolulu HI 96813-2492

OIZUMI, JUN, pediatrician, geneticist; b. Tokyo, 1948; m. Ann Reid Cronin, May 28, 1994. MD, Tokyo-Jikei Med. Sch., 1973, PhD, 1982. Diplomate Am. Bd. Pediats., Am. Bd. Med. Genetics. Pediat. intern Children's Hosp., L.A., 1978, pediat. resident, 1979-80, fellow in genetics, 1980-81, asst. prof. med. staff, 1981-84; dir. Nat. Children's Med. Rsch. Ctr., Tokyo, 1985-93; dir. pediats. Orthop. Hosp., L.A., 1993—. Contbr. articles to profl. jours. Fellow Am. Coll. Med. Genetics (founding fellow), Am. Acad. Pediats.; mem. AMA, Calif. Med. Assn., L.A. County Med. Assn. Office: Orthop Hosp 2400 S Flower St Los Angeles CA 90007-2629

O'JACK, HELEN MARGARET, clinical social worker; b. Denver, Jan. 31, 1951; d. Herbert Henry and Lillian Anna (Meyer) Thimm; m. William Allan Schmeling, Jr., July 24, 1982 (div. Dec. 1992); children: Dustin William Schmeling, Alexander Thimm Schmeling; m. Stanislav G. O'Jack, June 16, 1995. BA in Psychology, U. Colo., 1973; MSW, U. Denver, 1982. Lic. profl. social worker, Wyo. Peer counselor Met. Community Coll., Omaha, 1975-76; outreach worker South Omaha Crisis Ctr., 1976-77; child care worker Mt. St. Vincent's Youth Home, Denver, 1978-81; social work intern health scis. ctr. U. Colo., Denver, 1981-82; coord. crisis line Vol. Info. Referral Service, Rock Springs, Wyo., 1983-85; clin. social worker, coord. elderly svcs. S.W. Counseling Svc., Rock Springs, 1985-92; med. social worker Wyo. Home Health Care, Rock Springs, 1986-95; pvt. practice, 1992—; facilitator Alzheimer's Family Support Group, Rock Springs, 1983-92; social work cons. Castle Rock Convalescent Ctr., Green River, Wyo., 1990, Sage View Care Ctr., 1992-95; sch. counselor Desert View Sch., 1992—. Mem. NEA, NASW (regional rep. on bd. dirs. Wyo. chpt. 1991-92). Democrat. Office: Desert View Elem Sweetwater Sch Dist # 1 PO Box 1089 Rock Springs WY 82902-1089

OKADA, RONALD MASAKI, insurance agent; b. Tokyo, Oct. 23, 1941; s. Robert M. Okada and Betty (Nakai) Chung; m. Barbara Moo Ching Lau, May 1, 1971; 1 child, Evie Michi. BBA, U. Hawaii, 1964. CLU; ChFC; CFP, Coll. for Fin. Planning. Ops. supr. Cen. Pacific Bank, Honolulu, 1964-66; mgmt. trainee Bank of Hawaii, Honolulu, 1968-70; life ins. agt. Conn. Mut. Life, Honolulu, 1970-96, Mass. Mutual, Honolulu, 1996—. Chmn. bd. dirs. Hawaii Bapt. Found., Honolulu, 1993—; exec. bd. dirs. Hawaii Bapt. Conv., Honolulu, 1977-80; deacon, tchrs., various coms., Sunday Sch. dir. Mililani Bapt. Ch., Mililani Town, Hawaii, 1975—. Mem. Hawaii State Assn. Life Underwriters (pres. 1994-95, Life Ins. Profl. of Yr. runner-up 1984), Nat. Assn. Life Underwriters (nat. sales achievement award, nat. quality award, Million Dollar Round Table), Am. Soc. CLU's and ChFC's (com. chmn. 1984-87, 91-92), West Honolulu Assn. Life Underwriters (bd. dirs. 1982-87), Hawaii Estate Planning Coun., Assn. Health Ins. Agts. Office: MassMutual City Financial Tower 201 Merchant St Ste 2200 Honolulu HI 96813

OKAWA, ANTONIA CAMACHO, primary school educator; b. Saipan, Mar. 13, 1949; d. Rafael and Thomasa (Aguon) Camacho; m. Ryo Okawa, June 25, 1973; children: Chamie, Lanelle, Ray. AA in Elem. Edn., No. Marianas Coll., Saipan, 1986; BA in Elem. Edn., U. Guam, 1991. Tchr. 4th grade Chalan Kanoa Elem. Sch., Saipan, 1968-69; tchr. of deaf Chalan Kanoa Spl. Edn., Saipan, 1969-75; substitute tchr. Saipan Cmty. Sch., 1977-79; tchr. 1st grade William S. Reyes Sch., Saipan, 1985-90; tchr. kindergarten Pub. Sch. Sys., Saipan, 1990—; chairwoman task force math. William S. Reyes Sch., Saipan, 1992-93; owner Okawa's Elec. Svcs., 1973—. Author: (project proposals) Enriched Integrated Curriculum with Thematic Units, Effective School Practices Kindergarten Integrated Thematic Experience, 1993-95. Leader Girl Scouts, Daisy Scouts, William S. Reyes Sch., Saipan, 1988—; chairwoman Chamoro/Carolinian lang. policy commn. Saipan Mcpl., 1991-92; tchr. catechetical Christian discipline Chalan Kanoa Parish Coun., 1992-95. Mem. ASCD, Nat. Coun. Tchrs. Math. Home: Chalan Kanoa PO Box 141 Saipan MP 96950 Office: Pub Sch Sys PO Box 1370 Saipan MP 96950

O'KEEFE, MARK DAVID, state official; b. Pittston, Pa., July 10, 1952; s. Gervase Frances and Anne Regina (Faltyn) O'K.; m. Lucy Bliss Dayton, Sept. 24, 1983; children: Margaret, Angus, Greer. BA in Environ. Studies, Calif. State U., Sacramento, 1977; MS in Environ. Studies, U. Mont., 1984. Mgr. adjudication program Mont. Dept. Nat. Resources, Helena, 1979-81, dir. water devel., 1981-83; owner, operator Glacier Wilderness Guides, West Glacier, Mont., 1983-89; mem. Mont. Ho. Reps., Helena, 1989-92; state auditor State of Mont., Helena, 1993—. Bd. dirs. Boyd Andrew Chem. Dependency Treatment Ctr., Helena, 1991—. With U.S. Army, 1971-73. Democrat. Home: 531 Power St Helena MT 59601-6115 Office: State Auditors Office PO Box 4009 Helena MT 59604-4009*

OKEN, RICHARD LESLIE, pediatrician; b. Balt., May 24, 1945; s. Louis E. and Rosa E. (Hudson) O.; m. Judith Carolyn Faulkner, July 15, 1967; children: Erik Richard, April Kelly. BS cum laude in Biology, Boston Coll., 1963-67; MD, U. Calif., San Francisco, 1967-71. Diplomate Am. Bd. Pediatrics. Pediatrician, mng. ptnr. East Bay Pediatric Med. Group, Berkeley, Calif., 1975—; clin. prof. Pediatrics U. Calif., San Francisco, 1991—; bd. dirs. Alta Bates Health Sys., Emeryville, Calif. Trustee The Coll. Prep. Sch., Oakland, Calif., 1991—; trustee, bd. dirs. Alta Bates Med. Ctr., Berkeley, 1987-90; mem. med. adv. bd. Found. for Osteoporosis Rsch. and Edn., Oakland, 1993—. Fellow Am. Acad. Pediatrics; mem. Calif. Med. Assn., Alameda Contra Costa Med. Assn. Home: 224 Pala Ave Piedmont CA 94611-3741 Office: East Bay Pediatric Med Group 2999 Regent St Ste 325 Berkeley CA 94705-2118

OKI, BRIAN MASAO, software engineer; b. Inglewood, Calif., Oct. 17, 1958; s. Masao and Chiyoe (Yata) O. BS summa cum laude, U. Calif., Irvine, 1980; MS, MIT, 1983, PhD, 1988. Mem. rsch. staff Xerox Palo Alto (Calif.) Rsch. Ctr., 1988-92; sr. mem. tech. staff Teknekron Software Systems, Inc., Palo Alto, 1992-94; sr. tech. staff Oracle Corp., Redwood Shores, Calif., 1994-96; staff engineer, software Sun Microsystems, Inc., Menlo Park, Calif., 1996—. Mem. IEEE, Assn. Computing Machinery, Phi Beta Kappa, Sigma Xi. Home: 493 Mill River Ln San Jose CA 95134-2420 Office: Sun Soft Inc 2550 Garcia Ave Mountain View CA 94043-1109

O'KIERSEY, PATRICK M., artist, company executive; b. Chgo., Mar. 27, 1944; s. Michael M. and Cora Louise (Erp) O'K. BA, Roosevelt U., Chgo., 1969; MFA, Mills Coll., Oakland, Calif., 1985. Paper handler Chgo. Sun Times, 1968-70; tchr. Search Sch., Chgo., 1970-72; paper handler San Francisco Newspaper Agy., 1973-93; corp. pres. Weststar Inc., Oakland, Calif., 1994—; exhibiting artist Triangle Gallery, San Francisco, 1990—; advt., distbn. coord. for open studios project Pro-Arts, Oakland, 1993-94. Artist expressionist landscape. Clinic intake vol. Fritzie Englestein Free Clinic, Chgo., 1970-72. Mills Coll. Alumni scholar, 1984-85, Trefethen award, 1984-85. Mem. San Francisco Paper Handlers Union (exec. bd. 1992).

OKRASINSKI, RICHARD JOSEPH, meteorologist; b. Kingston, Pa., Dec. 24, 1951; s. Joseph and Catherine (Conway) O. BS in Meteorology, U. Utah, 1974, MS in Meteorology, 1977. Phys. scientist Phys. Sci. Lab., Las Cruces, N.Mex., 1977—. Mem. Am. Meteorol. Soc. Office: Phys Sci Lab PO Box 30002 Las Cruces NM 88003-8002

OKUMA, ALBERT AKIRA, JR., architect; b. Cleve., Feb. 10, 1946; s. Albert Akira Sr. and Reiko (Suwa) O.; m. Janice Shirley Bono, July 17, 1971; children: Reiko Dawn, Benjamin Scott. BS in Archtl. Engring, Calif. Poly. State U., San Luis Obispo, 1970, BArch, 1975; edn. facility planning cert., U. Calif., Riverside, 1990. Lic. architect, Calif., Mont., Ariz., Ill., Nev., N.Mex., Oreg., Maine; cert. Nat. Coun. Archtl. Bds. Architect USN, Point Mugu, Calif., 1975-76; designer Wilson Stroh Wilson Architects, Santa Paula, Calif., 1976-79; architect, project mgr. W.J. Kulwiec AIA & Assocs., Camarillo, Calif., 1979-83, Wilson & Conrad Architects, Ojai, Calif., 1983-84, Dziak, Immel & Lauterbach Services Inc., Oxnard, Calif., 1984-85; ptnr. Conrad & Okuma Architects, Oxnard, 1985-96; architect So. Calif. Edison/Edison Internat., Ventura, 1996—; commr. Calif. Bd. Archtl. Examiners, 1985—, City of San Buenaventura Hist. Preservation Commn., 1990-94, chmn., 1991-93, City of San Buenaventura Planning Commn., 1994—, City of San Buenaventura Design Rev. Com., 1994—, vice chair 1994—; peer reviewer Am. Cons. Engrs. Coun., 1987—; lectr. U. Calif. Ext., Riverside, 1991—. Prin. works include Hobson Bros. Bldg. (reconstrn. and preservation), Ventura, Calif., (Design for Excellence award 1991, Historic Bldg. of Yr. award 1992, Archtl. Rev. Design award 1993), Oxnard (Calif.) Main Post Office Renovation (Design for Excellence award 1994). Mem. Spiritual Assembly Baha'is of Ventura, Calif., 1978—, treas., 1978-79, 84, 86-88, chmn., 1992-93; treas.'s rep. Nat. Spiritual Assembly Baha'is U.S., Wilmette, Ill., 1981-91, dist. tchg. com., 1992-93; treas. Parents and Advs. for Gifted Edn., 1988-89; chmn. Ventura Unified Sch. Dist. Citizens Budget Adv. Com., 1990-92, adult edn. adv. com., 1992; mem. City of San Buenaventura specific plan citizens com., 1990-93, multicultural/cmty. heritage task force of the cultural arts plan com., 1991-92, strategic planning citizens adv. com., 1992-93; emergency svcs. vol. State of Calif., 1994—. 1st lt. U.S. Army, 1971-73. Mem. AIA (chpt. bd. dirs. 1976-79, 81—, chpt. sec. 1981, v.p. 1982, pres. 1983, Intern Devel. Program Outstanding Firm award 1993), Am. Planning Assn., Internat. Conf. Bldg. Ofcls., Nat. Trust for Hist. Preservation, Calif. Preservation Found., Constrn. Specifications Inst., Design Methods Group, Coalition for Adequate Sch. Housing, Coun. Ednl. Facility Planners Internat., Structural Engrs. Assn. So. Calif. (affiliate), Ventura County Econ. Devel. Assn. (impact II adv. com. 1993-94, edn. com. 1992-94), Calif. Polytech. State U. Alumni Assn. (life), Toastmasters Internat. Office: So Calif Edison/Edison Internat New Constrn Svcs/EE 10180 Telegraph Rd Ventura CA 93004 *Personal philosophy: Live a life of service to others while keeping a global perspective on life and maintaining a clear vision of one's future goals. This service must be balanced among our own faith, family, and career.*

OKUMURA, MITCHIO, chemical physics educator; b. Columbia, Mo., Sept. 1, 1957; s. Koji and Akiko O. BS, MS, Yale U., 1979; cert. postgrad. study, Cambridge (Eng.) U., 1980; PhD, U. Calif., Berkeley, 1986. Postdoctoral rsch. assoc. U. Chgo., 1987-88; asst. prof. chem. physics Calif. Inst. Tech., Pasadena, Calif., 1988-94, assoc. prof. chem. physics, 1994—. Recipient Churchill scholarship U.S. Winston Churchill Found., 1979-80, Newly Apptd. Faculty award Camille & Henry Dreyfus Found., 1981; named Presdl. Young investigator NSF, 1989-95. Mem. AAAS, Am. Phys. Soc., Am. Chem. Soc., Am. Geophys. Union. Office: Calif Inst Tech Chemistry Dept MC 127-72 Pasadena CA 91125

OLAH, GEORGE ANDREW, chemist, educator; b. Budapest, Hungary, May 22, 1927; came to U.S., 1964, naturalized, 1970; s. Julius and Magda (Krasznai) O.; m. Judith Agnes Lengyel, July 9, 1949; children: George John, Ronald Peter. PhD, Tech. U. Budapest, 1949, D (hon.), 1989; DSc (hon.), U. Durham, 1988, U. Munich, 1990, U. Crete, Greece, 1994, U. Szeged, Hungary, 1995, U. Veszprem, Hungary, 1995, Case Western Res. U., 1995, U. So. Calif., 1995, U. Montpellier, 1996. Mem. faculty Tech. U. Budapest, 1949-54; assoc. dir. Ctrl. Chem. Rsch. Inst., Hungarian Acad. Scis., 1954-56; rsch. scientist Dow Chem. Can. Ltd., 1957-64, Dow Chem. Co., Framingham, Mass., 1964-65; prof. chemistry Case Western Res. U., Cleve., 1965-69, C.F. Mabery prof. rsch., 1969-77; Donald P. and Katherine B. Loker disting. prof. chemistry, dir. Hydrocarbon Rsch. Inst., U. So. Calif., L.A., 1977—; vis. prof. chemistry Ohio State U., 1963, U. Heidelberg, Germany, 1965, U. Colo., 1969, Swiss Fed. Inst. Tech., 1972, U. Munich, 1973, U. London, 1973-79, L. Pasteur U., Strasbourg, 1974, U. Paris, 1981; hon. vis. lectr. U. London, 1981; cons. to industry. Author: Friedel-Crafts Reactions, Vols. I-IV, 1963-64; (with P. Schleyer) Carbonium Ions, Vols. I-V, 1969-76, Friedel-Crafts Chemistry, 1973, Carbocations and Electrophilic Reactions, 1973, Halonium Ions, 1975; (with G.K.S. Prakash and J. Somer) Superacids, 1984; (with Prakash, R.E. Williams, L.D. Field and K. Wade) Hypercarbon Chemistry, 1987; (with R. Malthotra and S.C. Narang) Nitration, 1989, Cage Hydrocarbons, 1990; (with Wade and Williams) Electron Deficient Boron and Carbon Clusters, 1991; (with Chambers and Prakash) Synthetic Fluorine Chemistry, 1992; (with Molnar) Hydrocarbon Chemistry, 1995; also chpts. in books, numerous papers in field; patentee in field. Recipient Alexander von Humboldt Sr. U.S. Scientist award, 1979, Calif. Scientist of Yr. award, 1989, Pioneer of Chemistry award Am. Inst. Chemists, 1993; Mendeleev medal Russian Acad. Scis., 1992, Kapitsa medal Russian Acad. Natural Scis., 1995; Nobel prize in Chemistry, 1994; Guggenheim fellow 1972, 88. Fellow AAAS, Chem. Inst. Can.; mem. NAS, Italian NAS, European Acad. Arts, Scis. and Humanities, Italy Chem. Soc. (hon.), Hungarian Acad. Sci. (hon.), Am. Chem. Soc. (award petroleum chemistry 1964, Leo Hendrik Baekeland award N.J. sect. 1966, Morley medal Cleve. sect. 1970, award synthetic organic chemistry 1979, Roger Adams award in organic chemistry 1989), German Chem. Soc., Brit. Chem. Soc. (Centenary lectr. 1978). Home: 2252 Gloaming Way Beverly Hills CA 90210-1717 Office: U So Calif Labor Hydrocarbon Rsch Inst Los Angeles CA 90007 *America still is offering a new home and nearly unlimited possibilities to the newcomer who is willing to work hard for it. It is also where the "main action" in science and technology remains.*

OLDERMAN, MURRAY, columnist, cartoonist; b. N.Y.C., Mar. 27, 1922; s. Max and Jennie (Steinberg) O.; m. Nancy J. Calhoun, Feb. 28, 1945; children: Lorraine Imlay, Marcia Lynn, Mark. BJ, U. Mo., 1943; BS in Humanities, Stanford U., 1944; MJ, Northwestern U., Evanston, Ill., 1947. Sports editor Rockland Leader, Spring Valley, N.Y., 1938-40; cartoonist, writer McClatchy Newspapers, Sacramento, 1947-51, Mpls. Star-Tribune, 1951-52; cartoonist, writer, exec. editor Newspaper Enterprise Assn., N.Y.C., 1952-87; asst. prof. San Francisco State U., 1974-80, U. Redlands, Calif., 1987, U. Oreg., Eugene, 1991-97; sr. editor Palm Springs (Calif.) Life, 1995-97; project dir. Hall of Fame, Oakland (Calif.) Raiders, 1995-97. Author: (books) The Pro Quarterback, 1966, The Running Back, 1969, The Defenders, 1972, Tennis Clinic, 1979, Super: "Just Win, Baby", 1984, Starr, 1987; (book series) My Best Year, 1969-71. Pres. Calif. Alliance for Mentally Ill, Sacramento, 1994-95. Lt. M.I., U.S. Army, 1944-45, ETO. Recipient Bert McGrane award Football Writers Assn. Am., 1991; named to Nat. Sportswriters and Sportscasters Hall of Fame, Salisbury, N.C., 1993, Internat. Jewish Sports Hall of Fame, Netanya, Israel, 1997. Mem. Nat. Cartoonists Soc. (Best Sports Cartoonist 1973, 78), Golf Writers Assn. Am. (Best Feature 1982), Pro Football Writers Assn. (Dick McCann award 1979, Best Feature 1983), Baseball Writers of Am., Basketball Writers of Am. (Best Feature 1959), Football Writers Assn. Am. (pres. 1960-61), Phi Beta Kappa. Democrat. Home: 832 Inverness Dr Rancho Mirage CA 92270

OLDHAM, ELAINE DOROTHEA, retired elementary and middle school educator; b. Coalinga, Calif., June 29, 1931; d. Claude Smith Oldham and Dorothy Elaine (Hill) Wilkins. AB in History, U. Calif., Berkeley, 1953; MS in Sch. Adminstrn., Calif. State U., Hayward, 1976; postgrad. U. Calif., Berkeley, Harvard U., Mills Coll. Tchr. Piedmont Unified Sch. Dist., Calif., 1956-94, ret., 1994. Pres., bd. dirs. Camron-Stanford House Preservation Assn., 1979-86, adminstrv. v.p., bd. dirs., 1976-79, 86—; mem. various civic and community support groups; bd. dirs. Anne Martin Children's Ctr., Lincoln Child Ctr., Acacia br. Children's Hosp. Med. Ctr., No. Light Sch. Aux., East Bay League II of San Francisco Symphony, Piedmont Hist. Soc., pres. Children's Hosp. Med. Ctr. Mem. Am. Assn. Museums, Am. Assn. Mus. Trustees, Internat. Council Museums, Inst. Internat. Edn., Am. Assn. State and Local History, Am. Decorative Arts Forum, Oakland Mus. Assn. (women's bd.), DAR (regent, Outstanding Tchr. Am. History award), Colonial Dames Am., Magna Charta Dames, Daus. of Confederacy (bd. dirs.), Hugeunot Soc. (bd. dirs.), Plantagenent Soc., Order of Washington, Colonial Order of Crown, Americans of Royal Descent, Order St. George and Descs. of Knights of Garter, San Francisco Antiques Show (com. mem.), U. Calif. Alumni Assn. (co-chmn. and chmn. of 10th and 25th yr. class reunion coms.), Internat. Diplomacy Coun. (San Francisco chpt.), Internat. Churchill Soc., English Speaking Union, Pacific Mus. Soc., Prytanean Alumnae Assn. (bd. dirs.), Phi Delta Kappa, Delta Kappa Gamma. Republican. Episcopalian. Clubs: Harvard (San Francisco), Bellevue.

OLDHAM, MAXINE JERNIGAN, real estate broker; b. Whittier, Calif., Oct. 13, 1923; d. John K. and Lela Hessie (Mears) Jernigan; m. Laurance Montgomery Oldham, Oct. 28, 1941; 1 child, John Laurence. AA, San Diego City Coll., 1973; student Western State U. Law, San Diego, 1976-77, LaSalle U., 1977-78; grad. Realtors Inst., Sacramento, 1978. Mgr. Edin Harig Realty, LaMesa, Calif., 1966-70; tchr. Bd. Edn., San Diego, 1959-66; mgr. Julia Cave Real Estate, San Diego, 1970-73; salesman Computer Realty, San Diego, 1973-74; owner Shelter Island Realty, San Diego, 1974—. Author: Jernigan History, 1982, Mears Geneology, 1985, Fustons of Colonial America, 1988, Sissoms. Mem. Civil Svc. Commn., San Diego, 1957-58. Recipient Outstanding Speaker award Dale Carnegie. Mem. Nat. Assn. Realtors, Calif. Assn. Realtors, San Diego Bd. Realtors, San Diego Apt. Assn., Internationale des Professions Immobilieres (internat. platform speaker), DAR (vice regent Linares chpt.), Colonial Dames 17th Century, Internat. Fedn. Univ. Women. Republican. Roman Catholic. Avocations: music, theater, painting, geneology, continuing edn. Home: 3348 Lowell St San Diego CA 92106-1713 Office: Shelter Island Realty 2810 Lytton St San Diego CA 92110-4810

OLDKNOW, ANTONY, English educator, writer, publisher; b. Peterborough, Eng., Aug. 15, 1939; came to U.S., 1966, naturalized, 1995; s. William Fleming and Gertrude Ada (Webster) G.; m. Meriel Dorothy Batchelor Steines, Aug. 18, 1962 (div. Apr. 1969). BA in English with honors, U. Leeds, Eng., 1961; MEd, U. Leeds, 1963; MS in Phonetics, U. Edinburgh, Scotland, 1964; PhD in English, U. N.D., 1983. Cert. tchr. English and history K-12, U.K. Ministry of Edn. Lectr. English Cowdenbeath (Scotland) Tech. Coll., 1962-64; asst. prof. linguistics Université Laval, Que., Can., 1964-66; asst. prof. English N.D. State U., Fargo, 1966-72; grad. tchg. asst. dept. English U. N.D., Grand Forks, 1972-76; instr. English U. N.D., 1976; instr. English U. Wis., Stevens Point, 1976-79, acad. coord., 1980-84; instr. English U. Kans., Lawrence, 1984-87; asst. prof. Eastern N.M. U., Portales, 1987-90; assoc. prof. English Eastern N.M. U., 1990-94, prof. English, 1994—; gen. editor, pub. The Scopcraeft Press, Portales, 1966—; traveling writer Great Plains Book Bus, Fargo, 1980-81; vis. asst. prof. English Mankato (Minn.) State U., 1982-83; poetry reader Cottonwood Mag., Lawrence, Kans., 1985-87; chair dept. lang. and lit. Eastern N.M. State U., 1991—. Author: (short story collection) The Rod of the Lord, 1971, (poems) Anthem for Rusty Saw and Blue Sky, 1975, Consolation for Beggars, 1978, Miniature Clouds, 1981, Wanderers, 1995, (with Cynthia Hendershoe, Jesse Swan) A Short Book of Literary Terms, 1995; translator Clara d'Ellebeuse, 1992 (Jammes); editor Scopcraeft Mag., 1966-72, The Fifth Horseman Mag., 1967-68, The Mainstreeter Mag., 1971-79, Blackwater Mag., 1995—. Office: Eastern NMex Univ Dept Langs & Lit Portales NM 88130

OLDKNOW, CONSTANTINA W., art historian; b. L.A., June 10, 1955; d. William Henry and Constantina (Skouras) O.; m. Peter Jansen Herzberg, June 9, 1984. BA in Art History, UCLA, 1978; MA in Art History, U. Pa., 1982. Photo archivist J. Paul Getty Mus., Malibu, Calif., 1978-79; curatorial asst. Southwest Mus., L.A., 1981-82; assoc. curator ancient and Islamic art L.A. County Mus. Art, 1982-89; devel. assoc. Henry Art Gallery, U. Wash., Seattle, 1990-91; dir. Donald Young Gallery, Seattle, 1991-96; writer/ind. curator Seattle, 1996—; curatorial cons. Seattle Art Mus., 1990—, Tacoma (Wash.) Art Mus., 1996—. Author: Pilchuck: A Glass School, 1996, Chihuly: Persians, 1997; editor Glass Art Soc. Jour.; author: (catalogue) Josh Simpson: New Work, New Worlds, 1994. Mem. gifts and deaccession panel Seattle Arts Commn., 1994—. Mem. Glass Art Soc., Internat. Assn. for History of Glass, Archaeol. Inst. Am. Home and Office: 5240 18th Ave NE Seattle WA 98105

OLDSHUE, PAUL FREDERICK, financial executive; b. Chgo., Nov. 4, 1949; s. James Young and Betty Ann (Wiersema) O.; m. Mary Elizabeth Holl, July 12, 1975; children: Emily Jane, Andrew Armstrong, Abigail Anne. BA, Williams Coll., Williamstown, Mass., 1971; MBA, NYU, 1978. With Chem. Bank, N.Y.C., 1973-78, asst. sec., 1976-78; with Orbanco Fin. Svc. Corp., 1978-83, v.p., treas., 1980-83; exec. v.p. Oreg. Bank, Portland, 1984-88; v.p. syndications PacifiCorp Fin. Svcs., Inc., 1988-90; exec. v.p. U.S. Bancorp, Portland, 1991—. Mem. Fin. Execs. Inst., Multnomah Athletic Club (Portland). Republican.

O'LEARY, DENNIS, museum director. Exec. dir. Boise (Idaho) Art Mus., 1980—. Office: Boise Art Mus 670 Julia Davis Dr Boise ID 83702

O'LEARY, JOHN JOSEPH, security firm executive; b. St. Paul, Mar. 31, 1934; s. Edward Michael and Gertrude Cecilia (Connell) O'L.; m. Sheila Maria Dudley, May 15, 1957 (div. Aug. 1984); children: Michael Patrick, Mareen Shannon, Kevin Timothy, Patrick John; m. Maria Lourdes Lavalle, Apr. 29, 1990. AA, U. Minn., St. Paul, 1960. Factory rep. U.S. The Lindsay Co., St. Paul, 1955-61; owner Motorette Corp., Reseda, Calif., 1961-68; mgr. nat. accounts The Anderson Co., Gary, Ind., 1968-78; v.p. and ops. mgr. Ameripak, San Dimas, Calif., 1978-80; regional sales mgr. Carter Carburator, L.A., 1980-83; regional sales rep. cons. J.S. Paluch Co., Santa Fe Springs, Calif., 1983-93; owner O'Leary Enterprises, San Diego, 1993-97. Inventor: Electric Wheel Chair (sold), Aloud Alarm System, Tops for Turbines. Mayorial bid City of San Diego, 1990; County Sch. Dist. bid City of San Diego, 1992. Sgt. USMC, 1952-55, Korea. Mem. Marine Corp. League (treas.), Ancient Order Hibernians in Am., KC. Republican. Roman Catholic. Office: O Leary Enterprises PO Box 7353 San Diego CA 92167

O'LEARY, MICHAEL JOSEPH, surgeon, neurotologist; b. Denver, May 17, 1954; s. Denis J. O'Leary and Audrey M. Ryan; m. Leslie S. West, Jan. 5, 1985; children: Claire Michael, Dorian Marie, Graden Joseph. BA cum laude, U. Rochester, 1976; MD magna cum laude, Georgetown U., 1980. Diplomate Nat. Bd. Med. Examiners, Am. Bd. Otolaryngology. Commd. ensign USN, 1976, advanced through grades to capt., 1995; intern specialized medicine Balboa Naval Hosp., San Diego, 1980-81; med. officer USS Bainbridge, 1981-82; resident otolaryngology, head and neck surgery Balboa Naval Hosp., San Diego, 1982-86; chief otolaryngology, head and neck surgery Navy Hosp., Newport, R.I., 1986-89; neurotology clin. fellow skull base surgery House Ear Clinic, L.A., 1989-90; microvascular surgery fellow Washington U., St. Louis, 1990-91; asst. clin. prof. surgery Uniformed Svcs. U. Health Scis., Bethesda, Md., 1992—; chief neurotology and skull base surgery divsn. otolaryngology, head and neck surgery dept. Navy Hosp. Balboa, San Diego; chmn. med. records and utilization rev. com. Naval Hosp., Newport, 1987-88, ACLS affiliate faculty mem. mil. tng. network, 1988-89; ATLS instr. Naval Hosp. San Diego, 1992—; med. news reporter Archives of Otolaryngology, 1991—; book reviewer Mil. Medicine, Bethesda, 1989—; mem. computers com. Am. Acad. Otolaryngology, 1992—, mem. skull base surgery com., 1992; invited guest instr. St. Louis U. Med. Ctr., 1991, 92, 93; guest instr. House Ear Inst., L.A., 1991, 93; tchr. various courses Naval Hosp., Newport, 1987, So. Calif. Health Coalition, San Diego, 1992, NHSD, 1992, NAB Coronado, Calif., 1993, AAOA, San Francisco, Boston, 1988, AFIP, Washington, 1985, Johns Hopkins, Balt., 1987, NNMC, Bethesda, 1987, Washington U., St. Louis, 1991, Ear Inst., Nashville, 1988, Naval Hosp. Oak Knoll, Oakland, Calif., 1983, 88, Navy Hosp., San Diego, 1991—, Mt. Sinai Sch. Medicine, N.Y.C., 1991; presenter in field. Author: (with others) Insights in Otolaryngology, 1991, Facial Plastic and Reconstructive Surgery, 1992, Otolaryngology - Head and Neck Surgery, 1992, Proceedings of the 4th International Tinnitus Seminar, 1992; contbr. articles to med. jours. Decorated Navy Commendation medal, Navy Achievement medal; recipient 1st prize San Diego Assn. Otolaryngology/Head & Neck Surgery, 1984, 86, 1st prize Mil. Assn. Otolaryngology/Head & Neck Surgery, 1984, 86. Fellow Am. Acad. Otolaryngology/Head and Neck Surgery (chmn. teleconsultation sub-group Navy Hosp.); mem. AMA, Am. Soc. Mil. Surgeons, Soc. Mil. Otolaryngologists (treas./sec. 1991-92, 92-93, pres. 1993-94), San Diego Acad. Otolaryngology/Head and Neck Surgery (treas./sec. 1995-96, v.p. 1996-97), Alpha Omega Alpha. Home: 14030 Crest Way Del Mar CA 92014-3010 Office: Navy Hosp Balboa Otolaryngology/Head & Neck Surgery Dept San Diego CA 92134

O'LEARY, PRENTICE L., lawyer; b. L.A., May 6, 1942. BA, UCLA, 1965, JD, 1968. Bar: Calif. 1969. With Sheppard, Mullin, Richter & Hampton, L.A. Bd. dirs. Legal Aid Found. L.A., 1987-93. Mem. ABA (bus. bankruptcy com.), State Bar Calif., Los Angeles County Bar Assn. (chmn. bankruptcy com., chmn. comml. law and bankrupt sect. 1985-86), Am. Coll. Bankruptcy Profls., Order of Coif. Office: Sheppard Mullin Richter & Hampton 333 S Hope St Fl 48 Los Angeles CA 90071-1406

O'LEARY, STEPHANIE SMITH, occupational therapist, educational therapist; b. San Francisco, Jan. 5, 1949; d. Edmund Thomas and Wilda Ann (Siebenthal) Smith; m. Kevin Donald O'Leary, July 4, 1970 (div. May

1977). BA, U. Ariz., 1972; MS in Occupl. Therapy, San Jose State U., 1986. Cert. occupl. therapist. Staff occupl. therapist Santa Clara Valley Med. Ctr., San Jose, Calif., 1985-88; program mgr. spinal cord injury computer program VA Palo Alto (Calif.) Health Care Sys., 1988—. Author: Computer Access for Persons with SCI, 1996; author monthly column Computer Bits in Paraplegia News, 1991—; designer hand typing aid; contbr. articles to profl. jours. Mem. Am. Occupl. Therapy Assn. Calif. 1982—, (com. 1994—, Santa Clara chpt. bd. dirs. 1986-88, Pres.'s award 1990). Home: 9 E Middlefield Rd # 25 Mountain View CA 94043-3858 Office: VA Palo Alto Health Care Sys 3801 Miranda Ave Palo Alto CA 94304-1207

O'LEARY, THOMAS HOWARD, resources executive; b. N.Y.C., Mar. 19, 1934; s. Arthur J. and Eleanor (Howard) O'L.; m. Cheryl L. Westrum; children: Mark, Timothy, Thomas, Denis, Daniel, Mary Frances. A.B., Holy Cross Coll., 1954; postgrad., U. Pa., 1959-61. Asst. cashier First Nat. City Bank, N.Y.C., 1961-65; asst. to chmn. finance com. Mo. Pacific R.R. Co., 1966-70, v.p. finance, 1971-76, dir., 1972-82, chmn. finance com., 1976-82; treas. Mo. Pacific Corp., St. Louis, 1968-71; v.p. finance Mo. Pacific Corp., 1971-72, exec. v.p., 1972-74, dir., 1972-82, pres., 1974-82; chmn. bd., CEO Mississippi River Transmission Corp., 1974-82; vice chmn. Burlington No., Inc., Seattle, 1982-89; chmn., CEO Burlington Resources, 1989—; bd. dirs. BF Goodrich, Kroger Co. Served to capt. USMC, 1954-58. Mem. Blind Brook Club (N.Y.C.), Chgo. Club. Office: Burlington Resources Inc 999 3rd Ave Ste 2810 Seattle WA 98104-4001

OLES, STUART GREGORY, lawyer; b. Seattle, Dec. 15, 1924; s. Floyd and Helen Louise (La Violette) O.; B.S. magna cum laude, U. Wash., 1947, J.D., 1948; m. Ilse Hanewald, Feb. 12, 1954; children: Douglas, Karl, Stephen. Admitted to Wash. bar, 1949, U.S. Supreme Ct. bar, 1960; dep. pros. atty. King County (Wash.), 1949, chief civil dept., 1949-50; gen. practice law, Seattle, 1950-95; sr. partner firm Oles, Morrison & Rinker and predecessor, 1955-90, of counsel, 1991-95. Author: A View From the Rock, 1994. Chmn. Seattle Community Concert Assn., 1955; pres. Friends Seattle Pub. Library, 1956; mem. Wash. Pub. Disclosure Commn., 1973-75; trustee Ch. Div. Sch. of Pacific, Berkeley, Calif., 1974-75; mem. bd. curators Wash. State Hist. Soc., 1983; former mem. Seattle Symphony Bd.; pres. King County Ct. House Rep. Club, 1950, U. Wash. Young Rep. Club, 1947; Wash. conv. floor leader Taft, 1952, Goldwater, 1964; Wash. chmn. Citizens for Goldwater, 1964; chmn. King County Rep. convs., 1966, 68, 76, 84, 86, 88, 90, 92, 96, Wash. State Rep. Conv., 1980. Served with USMCR, 1943-45. Mem. ABA (past regional vice chmn. pub. contract law sect.), Wash. Bar Assn., Order of Coif, Scabbard and Blade, Am. Legion, Kapoho Beach Club (pres.), Am. Highland Cattle Assn. (v.p. and dir.), Phi Beta Kappa, Phi Alpha Delta. Episcopalian (vestryman, lay-reader), Home: 22715 SE 43rd Ct Issaquah WA 98029-5200 Office: Oles Morrison & Rinker 701 5th Ave Ste 3300 Seattle WA 98104-7016

OLIPHANT, CHARLES ROMIG, physician; b. Waukegan, Ill., Sept. 10, 1917; s. Charles L. and Mary (Goss) R.; student St. Louis U., 1936-40; m. Claire E. Canavan, Nov. 7, 1942; children: James R., Cathy Rose, Mary G., William D. Student, St. Louis U., 1936-40, MD, 1943; postgrad. Naval Med. Sch., 1946. Intern, Nat. Naval Med. Ctr., Bethesda, Md., 1943; pvt. practice medicine and surgery, San Diego, 1947—; pres., CEO Midway Med. Enterprises; former chief staff Balboa Hosp., Doctors Hosp., Cabrillo Med. Ctr.; chief staff emeritus Sharp Cabrillo Hosp.; mem. staff Mercy Hosp., Children's Hosp., Paradise Valley Hosp., Sharp Meml. Hosp.; sec. Sharp Sr. Health Care, S.D.; mem. exec. bd., program chmn. San Diego Power Squadron, 1985-93, 95. Charter mem. Am. Bd. Family Practice. Served with M.C., USN, 1943-47. Recipient Golden Staff award Sharp Cabrillo Hosp. Med. Staff, 1990. Fellow Am. Geriatrics Soc. (emeritus), Am. Acad. Family Practice, Am. Assn. Abdominal Surgeons; mem. AMA, Calif. Med. Assn., Am. Acad. Family Physicians (past pres. San Diego chpt., del. Calif. chpt.), San Diego Med. Soc., Public Health League, Navy League, San Diego Power Squadron (past comdr.), SAR. Clubs: San Diego Yacht, Cameron Highlanders. Home: 4310 Trias St San Diego CA 92103-1127

OLIVA, STEPHEN EDWARD, resource conservationist, lawyer; b. San Rafael, Calif., Jan. 31, 1946; s. George Verdelli Jr. and Dorothy Margaret (Austin) O.; m. Susan Rebecca Ellis, May 5, 1984; children: Stephanie, Mary. BA, U. Calif., Santa Barbara, 1972; JD, U. of the Pacific, 1992. Bar: Calif. 1993, U.S. Dist. Ct. (ea. dist.) Calif. 1993, U.S. Dist. Ct. (fed. dist.) Calif. Naturalist Calif. Dept. Transp., San Francisco, 1973-76; planner Calif. Energy Commn., Sacramento, 1976, Calif. Air Resources Bd., Sacramento, 1976-79; spl. asst. to sec. The Resources Agy., Sacramento, 1979-80; spl. asst. Calif. Dept. Conservation, Sacramento, 1980, mgr. land conservation unit, 1981-87; spl. asst. Calif. Dept. Forestry, Sacramento, 1980-81; chief Office Land Conservation Calif. Dept. Conservation, Sacramento, 1987-89, dep. chief Calif. div. of recycling, 1989-91, environ. coord., 1991-92, staff counsel, legal office, 1992—; mem. governing bd. Calif. Tahoe Regional Planning Agy., South Lake Tahoe, 1979-81; mem. policy adv. com. Sacramento County Local Agy. Formation Commn., 1988-89. Served with U.S. Army, 1966-68, Vietnam. Mem. ABA, Calif. State Bar, Sacramento County Bar Assn. Democrat. Office: Calif Dept Conservation 801 K St # 03 Sacramento CA 95814-3500

OLIVEIRA, MARY JOYCE, middle school education educator; b. Oakland, Calif., Feb. 16, 1954; d. Joseph and Vivian (Perry) O. BA, U. Calif., Berkeley, 1978; student, Holy Names Coll., Oakland, 1992; grad. in math., Calif. State U., Hayward, 1994. Cert. tchr., Calif.; cert. single subject math. credential, Hawaii. Recreation specialist Oakland Parks and Recreation, 1977-89; substitute tchr. Diocese of Oakland, 1989-90; tutor Oakland Pub. Schs., 1991; substitute tchr. Alameda (Calif.) Unified Sch. Dist., 1991—, Piedmont (Calif.) Unified Sch. Dist., 1993-96; tchr. summer program Wood Mid. Sch., Alameda, 1993, 96, Chipman Mid. Sch., Alameda, 1994, Encinal H.S., Alameda, 1995; math. tutor Calif. State U., Hayward, 1996, Intersession, Bay Farm Sch., Alameda, 1996; math tutor, 1996-97. Creator children's sock toys Oliveira Originals, 1985. Vol. in art therapy oncology ward Children's Hosp., Oakland, 1985; vol. Berkeley Unified Sch. Dist., 1990-91. Mem. Nat. Coun. Tchrs. Math., Calif. Math. Coun., Math. Assn. Am., Alameda Swimming Pool Assn.

OLIVER, DAN DAVID, banker; b. Walla Walla, Wash., Mar. 11, 1952; s. Harold Allen and Nydia Jane (Munns) O.; children: Ana Mary, Whitney Leigh. Univ. Coll., Cardiff, Wales, 1972-73; BA in Pre-Law, Wash. State U., 1974; MBA in Taxation, Golden Gate U., 1979; JD, Western State U., 1978; grad. with trust specialization, Pacific Coast Banking Sch., U. Wash., Seattle, 1987; grad. Banking Law Sch., George Mason U., Washington, 1993; grad. Nat. Compliance Sch., U. Okla., 1994. Tax acct. John F. Forbes & Co., San Francisco, 1979-81; cat skinner James Francis Munns Farms, Inc., Prescott, Wash., 1981-82; law clk. Sherwood, Tugman, Gose & Reser, Walla Walla, 1975-79; trust adminstrv. asst. Baker-Boyer Nat. Bank, Walla Walla, 1982-83, asst. trust officer, 1984, trust officer, 1985, asst. v.p., legal counsel, 1986, asst. v.p., legal/complaince officer, 1987, v.p. and legal/compliance officer, 1988—, v.p., legal counsel, compliance mgr., 1996; vice chmn. bd. dirs. Elite Turf Farm, Inc., West Richland, Wash., sr. v.p., sec., legal counsel, 1988-92. Commr. Walla Walla City Housing Authority, 1992—; mem. Homeless Coalition, 1994—; bd. dirs. Prescott Sch. Dist., 1983-87, vice chmn., 1985, chmn., 1986; vol. spirits religious program St. Patrick's Cath. Ch., 1990-94; mem. Walla Walla Park and Recreation Adv. Bd., 1991-92, vice chmn., 1992; chmn. Park Improvement Com. for Irrigation, 1992; chmn. Walla Walla Area Com. for Housing, 1991-94; linesman Youth Soccer League; sch. vol. Prospect Point Elem. Sch.; mem. panel govt. and politics seminar Leadership Walla Walla, 1994; vice-chmn. Walla Walla City-County Regional Housing Com., 1997—. Mem. Am. Bankers Assn., Nat. Assn. Housing and Redevel. Ofcls., Wash. Bankers Assn. (symposium panelist 1996, compliance com. 1990—, vice chmn. 1994-95, cmty. reinvestment act panel 1994, compliance symposium panelist of local experts), Walla Walla Valley Estate Planning Coun. (bd. dirs. 1986-87, treas. 1987-88, sec. 1988-89, v.p. 1989-90, pres. 1990-91), Nat. Arbor Day Found., Columbia Rural Elec. Assn., Nat. Assn. Underwater Instrs. (open water I and II, advanced certs., cert. CPR, first aid, and oxygen provider, advanced cert. 1993—, ref. environ. edn. found. 1994—), Bergevin Family Reunion and Edn. Assn. (treas. 1993-96), Frenchtown Found. (charter), Walla Walla Men's Group (treas.), Walla Walla Exch. Club, Beta Sigma Phi. Office: Baker-Boyer Nat Bank Main and 2d Sts Walla Walla WA 99362 *Personal philosophy: I believe we need to try to be all that we can be, with compassion for those who can not.*

OLIVER, JOHN EDWARD, bank training consultant; b. Bedford, Eng., Apr. 14, 1951; came to U.S., 1978; s. Fred K. and Marjorie F. (Brown) O.; m. Jacqueline L. Alcock, Oct. 7, 1972; 1 child, Sophie Rose. Student, Mander Coll., Bedford, 1968-71. Mgr.'s asst. Nat. Westminster Bank, Bedford, 1971-73; credit analyst Kleinwort Benson Ltd., London, 1973-76; mktg. coord. Amex Bank Ltd., London, 1976-78; v.p. Continental Ill. Energy Devel. Corp., Houston, 1978-85; pres. Laurel Mgmt. Systems Inc., San Francisco, 1986—; cons. various U.S. and internat. banks including Merita Bank, London, 1985—; bank edn. cons. Bank Am., San Francisco, 1986—; advisor Am. Inst. Banking, San Francisco, 1994—. Author: What Really is Expected of Me?-The Role of the Community Bank Director, 1995. Mem. ASTD, Assn. Bank Trainers and Cons. Office: Laurel Mgmt Systems Inc 3933 20th St San Francisco CA 94114-2906

OLIVER, JOYCE ANNE, journalist, editorial consultant, columnist; b. Coral Gables, Fla., Sept. 19, 1958; d. John Joseph and Rosalie Cecile (Mack) O. BA in Communications, Calif. State U., Fullerton, 1980, MBA, 1990. Corp. editor Norris Industries Inc., Huntington Beach, Calif., 1979-82; pres. J.A. Oliver Assocs., La Habra Heights, Calif., 1982—; corp. editorial cons. Norris Industries, 1982, Better Methods Cons., Huntington Harbour, Calif., 1982-83, Summit Group, Orange, Calif., 1982-83, UDS, Encinitas, Calif., 1983-84, MacroMarketing, Costa Mesa, Calif., 1985-86, PM Software, Huntington Beach, Calif., 1985-86, CompuQuote, Canoga Park, Calif., 1985-86, Nat. Semicondr. Can. Ltd., Mississauga, Ont., Can., 1986, Maclean Hunter Ltd., Toronto, Ont., 1986-90; Frame Inc., Fullerton, Calif., 1987-88, The Johnson-Layton Co., L.A., 1988-89, Corp. Rsch. Inc., Chgo., 1988, Axon Group, Horsham, Pa., 1990-91, Am. Mktg. Assn., Chgo., 1990-92, Kenzaikai Co., Ltd., Tokyo, 1991, Penton Pub., Cleve., 1991, Bus. Computer Pub., Inc., Peterborough, N.H., 1991-92, Helmers Pub., Inc., Peterborough, 1992, Schnell Pub., Co., Inc., N.Y.C., 1992-93, Diversified Pub. Group, Carol Stream, Ill., 1993; mem. Rsch. Coun. of Scripps Clinic and Rsch. Found., 1987-92. Contbg. editor Computer Merchandising/ Resell, 1982-85, Computer Reselling, 1985, Reseller Mgmt., 1987-89; contbg. editor Can. Electronics Engring., 1986-90, west coast editor, 1990, Chem. Bus. mag., 1992-93; spl. feature editor Cleve. Inst. Electronics publ. The Electron, 1986-89; bus. columnist Mktg. News, 1990-92; contbr. articles to profl. jours. and mags. Bd. dirs. Action Comms., 1993—. Mem. IEEE, Internat. Platform Assn., Soc. Photo-optical Instrumentation Engrs., Inst. Mgmt. Scis., Nat. Writers Club (profl.), Internat. Mktg. Assn., Soc. Profl. Journalists, L.A. World Affairs Coun. Republican. Roman Catholic. Office: 2045 Fullerton Rd La Habra CA 90631-8213

OLIVER, LEON EUGENE, building and development designer, consultant; b. Seattle, Jan. 28, 1949; s. James Norman and Bertha Marie (Gaston) O.; m. Christine Margaret Douglas, Dec. 13, 1970 (div. July 1988); 1 child, Travis; m. Diana Louise Eliot, Sept. 15, 1989. Grad. high sch., Redlands, Calif. Gen. contractor, Portland, 1976-85; realtor various brokers, Portland and Lincoln City, Oreg., 1978-82; constrn. mgr. Hoover Constrn., Beaverton, Oreg., 1985-86; bldg. designer, Portland, 1986-88, Grants Pass, Oreg., 1988—; land use cons., Grants Pass. Contbr. bldg. plans Riverside West Park, Grants Pass, 1991, Habitat for Humanity, Grants Pass, 1994; mem. steering com. Housing Needs Assessment, Grants Pass, 1996; mem. Grants Pass City Coun., 1996—. Recipient awards for bldg. design City of gRants Pass, 1993, for project design, 1995. Mem. Am. Inst. Bldg. Design (cert. profl. bldg. designer, past pres. So. Oreg. chpt. 1995-96, bldg. design awards 1988, 91), Internat. Conf. Bldg. Ofcls., Oreg. Bldg. Industry Assn. (chmn. codes and tech. 1996-97), Oreg. Homebuilders Assn. (com. chmn. 1988-96, bd. dirs. 1989-96), Homebuilders Assn. Josephine County (v.p., pres.-elect 1996-97, bd. dirs. 1989-96). Republican. Home and Office: 1183 Ironwood Dr Grants Pass OR 97526

OLIVER, MARY ANNE MCPHERSON, religion educator; b. Montgomery, Ala., Nov. 21, 1935; d. James Curtis and Margaret Sinclair (Miller) McPherson; m. Raymond Davies Oliver, Aug. 28, 1959; children: Kathryn Sinclair, Nathan McPherson. BA, U. Ala., Tuscaloosa, 1956; cert., Sorbonne, Paris, 1958; MA, U. Wis., 1959; PhD, Grad. Theol. Union, Berkeley, Calif., 1972. Vol. tchr., preacher, counselor, 1972—; instr. U. Calif., Berkeley, St. Mary's Coll., Moraga, Calif., 1973; adj. faculty San Francisco Theol. Sem., San Anselmo, 1977-81; prof. Ctr. Anglican Learning & Life Grad. Theol. Union, Berkeley, Calif., 1995—; lectr. San Jose (Calif.) State U., 1980-81, San Francisco State U., 1985-86; adj. prof. dept. liberal arts John F. Kennedy U., Orinda, Calif., 1987-95; vis. prof. Gen. Theol. Sem., N.Y.C., 1995. Author: History of Good Shepherd Episcopal Mission, 1978, Conjugal Spirituality: The Primacy of Mutual Love in Christian Tradition, 1994; contbr. articles to profl. jours. Rep. Ala. Coun. on Human Rels., Mobile, 1958; active deanery, conv. Good Shepherd Episc. Ch., Berkeley, Calif., 1970-75; rep. U. Calif. Fgn. Student Hospitality, Berkeley, 1965-70; vol. tchr. Berkeley pub. schs., 1965-73; bd. dirs. Canterbury Found., Berkeley, 1972-75; chmn. bd. dirs. West Berkeley Parish, Berkeley, 1976-78, adult edn. program St. Mark's Episc. Ch., 1992-93; mentor Edn. for Ministry, Univ. of the South, 1993—. Recipient award French Consulate, New Orleans, 1956; Fulbright grantee, 1956, grantee Mabelle McLeod Lewis Found., 1969. Mem. Am. Acad. Religion, Conf. on Christianity and Lit. Democrat. Home: 1632 Grant St Berkeley CA 94703-1356 *Wherever two are gathered, there is the Holy One.*

OLIVER, ROBERT WARNER, economics educator; b. L.A., Oct. 26, 1922; s. Ernest Warner and Elnore May (McConnell) O.; m. Darlene Hubbard, July 1, 1946 (dec. Mar. 1987); children: Lesley Joanne Oliver McClelland, Stewart Warner; m. Jean Tupman Smock, July 15, 1989. AB, U. So. Calif., 1943, AM, 1948; AM, Princeton U., 1950, PhD, 1958. Tchg. asst. U. So. Calif., 1946-47; instr. Princeton U., 1947-50, Pomona Coll., L.A., Calif., 1950-52; asst. prof. U. So. Calif., L.A., 1952-56; economist Stanford Rsch. Inst., South Pasadena, Calif., 1956-59; mem. faculty dept. econs. Calif. Inst. Tech., 1959-88, prof. econs., 1973-88, prof. emeritus, 1988—; urban economist World Bank, Washington, 1970-71; cons. Brookings Instn., 1961, OECD, Paris, 1979; vis. prof. U. So. Calif., 1985; vis. scholar Pembrook Coll., Cambridge (Eng.) U., 1989-90. Author: An Economic Survey of Pasadena, 1959, International Economic Cooperation and the World Bank, 1975, reissued with new intro., 1996, Bretton Woods: A Retrospective Essay, 1985, Oral History Project: The World Bank, 1986; contbg. author: Ency. of Econs., 1981, 93, George Woods and the World Bank, 1995. Mem. Human Rels. Com. City of Pasadena, 1964-65, Planning Commn., 1972-75, 91-95; bd. dirs. Pasadena City Coun., 1965-69; mem. Utilities Adv. Commn., 1984-88, 96—, Strategic Planning Com., 1985; pres. Pasadena Beautiful Found., 1972-74; bd. dirs. Pasadena Minority History Found., 1984—, Jackie Robinson Meml. Found., 1994—, UN Assn., Pasadena chpt., 1996—; trustee Pasadena Hist. Soc., 1992-94. Lt. (j.g.) USN, 1942-46. Social Sci. rsch. fellow London Sch. Econs., 1954-55; Rockefeller Found. fellow, 1974, 91; Danforth assoc., 1981; recipient Outstanding Tchg. award, 1982, Master of the Student Houses, 1987; Hon. Alumnus, 1987—. Mem. Am. Econs. Assn., Royal Econs. Assn., Athenaeum Club, Phi Beta Kappa, Phi Kappa Phi, Delta Tau Delta. Democrat. Methodist. Home: 3197 San Pasqual St Pasadena CA 91107-5330 Office: 1201 E California Blvd Pasadena CA 91125-0001 *The world is so full of beauty, natural and man-made, that human intelligence should seek to comprehend and enjoy it. Observation and reflection which lead to understanding are more important than performance, and the most important performance is service to others. The greatest human virtue is love, which is why family is important. If there be a God, I believe He works His will amongst civilized men through love, and He manifests His works through beauty.*

OLLANDER-KRANE, JASON ERIC, management consultant; b. New Haven, Apr. 14, 1955; s. Sherman Morton and June Carol (Pickus) Krane; life ptnr. Robert Ollander, May 7, 1980; 1 child, Craig Scott Ollander-Krane. BA, Rutgers Coll., 1978. Tng. exec. Macy's, N.Y.C., 1979-82; asst. to pres. Bus. Careers, N.Y.C., 1982-83; mgr. tng. devel. Young & Rubicam, N.Y.C., 1983-88; dir. human resources Wells Fargo Bank, San Francisco, 1988-89; v.p. tng. and staff devel. Adia Svcs. Inc., Menlo Park, Calif., 1989-90; owner, chief exec. Ollander-Krane/Johnson, San Francisco, 1990—; owner, pres., CEO Ceres, The Ctr. for Relationship and Cmty. Bldg., 1997—. Author (book) Goodbye Willy Loman: Selling in the 90's, 1990. Mem. adv. com. Pres.'s Nat. Svc. Program, San Francisco, 1993; commr. Blue Ribbon Commn. for Nat. Svc., San Francisco, 1993—; chmn. Neil Johnson Meml. Fund, San Francisco, 1993—; cons. The Names Project/AIDS Meml. Quilt, San Francisco, 1993—, Glide Meml. Ch., 1994—. Eder Bros. Inc. scholar, 1973-78.

OLLMAN, ARTHUR LEE, museum director, photographer; b. Milw., Mar. 6, 1947; s. Benn and Shirley O. B.A., U. Wis., 1969; student, San Francisco Art Inst., 1974; M.F.A., Lone Mountain Coll., 1977. Instr. San Francisco Mus. Modern Art, 1976-78, Chabot Coll., 1977-83; mus. dir. Mus. Photog. Arts, San Diego. Founder, dir., producer Photo History Video Project; author: Samuel Bourne, Images of India, 1983, Arnold Newman, Five Decades, 1986, William Klein: An American in Paris, 1987, Revelaciones, The Art of Manuel Alvarez Bravo, 1990, Fata Morgana: The American Way of Life, 1992, Seduced by Life: The Art of Lou Stoumen, 1992, Points of Entry: A Nation of Strangers, 1995; exhibited in one-man shows including Grapestake Gallery, San Francisco, 1979, Centre Georges Pompidou, Musee Nat. D'Art et De Culture, Paris, 1979, Inst. Contemporary Art, Boston, 1985, Night: Photograph Gallery, N.Y.C., 1981, Kodak Gallery, Tokyo, 1988; exhibited in group shows at Milw. Art Ctr., 1979, U. Hawaii, 1979-81, San Francisco Mus. Modern Art, 1980, Monas Heiroglyphicas, Milan, Italy, 1978, Mus. Modern Art, N.Y.C., 1978, Whitney Mus. Am. Art, N.Y.C., 1981, Detroit Inst. Arts, 1994, Mus. Contemporary Art, L.A., 1994, Tower of David Museum, Jerusalem, 1996; represented in permanent collections, including, Mus. Modern Art, N.Y.C, Centre Georges Pompidou, Bibliotheque Nationale, Paris, Tokyo Inst. Polytechnics, Met. Mus. Art, N.Y.C., Nat. Mus. Am. Art, Washington, Chase-Manhattan collection, N.Y.C., J. Paul Getty Mus., L.A. NEA fellow, 1979; Calif. Arts Council grantee, 1977-78, NEA grantee, 1978, exhbn. aid grantee, 1979-80. Mem. San Francisco CAMERAWORK (pres. bd. dirs. 1978-83), Am. Assn. Mus. Jewish. Address: 4310 Goldfinch St San Diego CA 92103-1315 also: Mus Photographic Arts Balboa Park San Diego CA 92101

OLLSON, MICKEY LOUIS, zoo owner; b. Phoenix, May 12, 1941; s. William Archie and Edith Iris (Curnow) O.; m. Donna Marie Ollson, Dec. 5, 1965 (div. Feb. 1975); children: Micalin, Louis Michael. AA, Phoenix Coll., 1961; BS, Ariz. State U., 1963. Owner, dir. Ollson's Exotic Animal Farm, Glendale, Ariz., 1965-83, Wildlife World Zoo, Glendale, 1983—. Contbr. articles to profl. publs. Mem. Am. Assn. Zool. Parks and Aquariums (profl.), Am. Fedn. Aviculture (v.p. 1976-77), Am. Game Bird Fedn. (bd. dirs. 1988--, pres. 1984-89, Outstanding Mem. of Yr. award 1968), Internat. Soc. Zooculturists (charter; treas. 1987-88), Am. Pheasant and Waterfowl Soc. (bd. dirs. 1972-78), Avondale-Goodyear-Litchfield Park C. of C. (bd. dirs. 1985-88), Kappa Sigma (pres. Rho chpt. 1964). Republican. Office: Wildlife World Zoo 16501 W Northern Ave Litchfield Park AZ 85340-9466*

OLMSTEAD, RICHARD GALE, JR., engineering manager; b. Cheyenne, Wyo., Sept. 13, 1950; s. Richard Gale and Dorothy Fern (Willis) O.; m. Patricia Ann Smith Olmstead Boultinghouse, July 21, 1974 (div. Sept. 1986); children: Melissa Michelle, Richard Gale III; m. Cheryl Anne Reichel Sherman, June 25, 1993. BS in Gen. Bus., U. Wyo., 1973; MA in Human Resource Mgmr., Pepperdine U., 1978; postgrad., Woodbury U. Cert. profl. mgr. Engring. asst. Wyo. Hwy. Dept., Cheyenne, 1969-72; asst. mgr. Gen. Fin. Corp. of Wyo., 1980-81; office mgr. Cheyenne Country Club, 1981; owner, operator Sweet Tymes Ice Cream Parlour, Cheyenne, 1980-82; electronic systems engr. Lockheed Aeronautical Systems Co., Burbank, Calif., 1981-86; group engr. Lockheed Advanced Devel. Co., Palmdale, Calif., 1986-94; chief engr. Lockheed Martin Skunk Works, Palmdale, Calif., 1994—; supr. and mgmt. skills facilitator, Lockheed Mgmt. Assn., Palmdale, 1989—;. Lt. USN, 1967-80; cmdr. USNR, 1980-95. Mem. Nat. Mgmt. Assn., Lockheed Mgmt. Assn. (dir. SMS tng. 1991-92, v.p. profl. devel. 1994-96), Inst. Cert. Profl. Mgrs., Naval Res. Assn., Kiwanis (club pres, div. sec.-treas., bd. dirs., leadership devel. trainer Burbank 1990—, Kiwanian of Yr. award 1982, 89, 91). Republican. Home: 3850 Paula Ln Lancaster CA 93535-5866 Office: Lockheed Martin Skunk Works 1011 Lockheed Way Palmdale CA 93599-0001

OLMSTEAD-ROSE, LESTER MORTON, social welfare administrator; b. Grass Valley, Calif., Dec. 13, 1960; s. David Morton Rose and Patricia Jean (Olmstead Rose) Baker. BA, Stanford U., 1983. Cmty. organizer Cmty. United Against Violence, San Francisco, 1988-90; exec. dir. Cmty. United Against Violence, 1993—; legis. asst. Supr. Angela Alioto, San Francisco, 1990-93. Mem. Lesbian/Gay Adv. Panel to Human Rights Commn., San Francisco, 1984-88; bd. dirs., co-chair Intergroup Clearinghouse, San Francisco, 1989—; mem. exec. com. Alice B. Toklas Lesbian/Gay Dem. Club, San Francisco, 1986-90. Office: Cmty United Against Violence 973 Market St Ste 500 San Francisco CA 94103-1717

OLMSTED, RONALD DAVID, foundation executive, consultant; b. Portland, Oreg., June 27, 1937; s. Clifford Wolford and Ruth Emily (Driesner) O.; m. Susan Mary Spare, Dec. 27, 1961 (div. June 1972); 1 child, Craig William. Student, Lewis and Clark Coll., 1955-57, U. So. Calif., L.A., 1959-62. V.p., exec. dir. L.A. Ctr. for Internat. Visitors, 1961-67; assoc. dir. devel. U. Chgo., 1967-71; v.p. devel. and pub. affairs Northwestern Meml. Hosp., Chgo., 1971-79; dir. devel. Marimed Found., Honolulu, 1989-93; exec. dir. Alzheimer's Assn., Honolulu, 1995-96; cons. on health, edn. and human svc. orgns., Ill., Mich., Oreg., Hawaii, 1979—; mem. Honolulu Mayor's Com. on People with Disabilities, 1995-96. Contbr. articles on African travels and African affair to profl. publs. Co-founder, treas. Civil Found. of Chelsea, Mich., 1982-83; treas. Chelsea Area C. of C., 1981-83; trustee Harris Sch., Chgo., 1972-73, Ogden Dunes (Ind.) Town Bd.; bd. dirs. United Way Porter County, Ind., 1969-71; mem. L.A. Com. on Fgn. Rels., 1965-69; bd. dirs. Am. Friends of Africa, 1965-68, Nat. Coun. for Cmty. Svcs. to Internat. Visitors, 1965-67; mem. exec. com. L.A. Mayor's Coun. for Internat. Visitors and Sister Cities, 1964-68; vice chmn. Greater L.A. Com. Internat. Student Svcs., 1966; mem. Honolulu Mayor's Com. on People with Disablities, 1995. Recipient Koa Anvil award Pub. Rels. Soc. Am.-Honolulu, 1992, multiple awards Assn. Am. Colls., 1975-79, multiple MacEachern awards Am. Acad. Hosp. Pub. Rels., 1974-79, multiple awards Nat. Assn. for Hosp. Devel., 1975-79. Mem. Nat. Soc. Fund Raising Execs. Presbyterian. Home and Office: 469 Ena Rd Apt 1506 Honolulu HI 96815-1710

OLMSTED, SUZANNE M., photographer; b. Palo Alto, Calif., Apr. 15, 1956; d. Gerald W. and Frances M. (Barnett) O.; m. Edward A. Gillum, July 6, 1982; children: Gerald, James. BA, U. Calif., Santa Cruz, 1979; MFA, So. Ill. U., 1982. Lectr. in photography Ea. Mont. Coll., Billings, 1983-87; exec. dir. Artlink, Phoenix, 1991; artist-in-residence The City of Tempe, Ariz., 1990-92; photo editor The Current, Phoenix, 1993-94; gallery mgr., asst. prof. art U. Nev., Reno, 1994-95; lectr. in photography U. Calif., Santa Cruz, 1996—; vis. artist San Francisco Art Inst., 1997. One-woman exhibition at Northcutt Steele Gallery, Mont. State U., Billings; group exhibitions include Ea. N.Mex. U., Portales, 1993, Szabo Fine Arts Gallery, Phoenix, 1992, Tempe Art Ctr., 1992, So. Ill. U., Carbondale, 1991, Photo Art Gallery, Burbank, Calif., 1991, Gallery of Art, Rockford (Ill.) Coll., 1991, Red River Exhbn./Silver Anniversary, Plains Art Mus., Moorhead, Minn., 1990, John Michael Kohler Art Ctr., Sheboygan, Wis., 1990, UN Women's Conf., Beijing, numerous others; contbr. photographs to numerous publs. including Northern Lights, New Times, Quantum Metaphysics and more. Recipient Eben Demarest award Eben Demarest Trust, Pitts., 1987, Outstanding Young Women of Am. award, 1984. Home: 9 Plaza Dr Berkeley CA 94705-2413

OLPIN, ROBERT SPENCER, art history educator; b. Palo Alto, Calif., Aug. 30, 1940; s. Ralph Smith and Ethel Lucille (Harman) O.; m. Mary Florence Catharine Reynolds, Aug. 24, 1963; children: Mary Courtney, Cristin Lee, Catharine Elizabeth, Carrie Jean. BS, U. Utah, 1963; AM, Boston U., 1965, PhD, 1971. Lectr. art history Boston U., 1965-67; asst. prof. U. Utah, Salt Lake City, 1967-72, assoc. prof., 1972-76, prof., 1976—, chmn. dept., 1975-82, dir. art history program, 1968-76, 83-84, dean Coll. Fine Arts, 1987—; cons. curator Am. and English art Utah Mus. Fine Arts, 1973—. Grantee U. Utah, 1972, 85, Utah Mus. Fine Arts, 1975, Utah Bicentennial Commn., 1975, Ford Found., 1975, Utah Endowment for Humanities, 1984, 85, Quinney Found., 1986, U. Utah, 1987, State Utah, 1989, Christensen Found., 1993, Eccles Found, 1994, 95; trustee Pioneer State Theatre Found., 1988—; vice chair Utah Arts Coun., 1993-95, chair, 1995—, Utah Sci. Ctr. Authority, 1995-97; vice chair adv. bd. U. Utah Fine Arts, 1996-97, chair, 1997—. Mem. NASULGC (commn. on the arts, 1989-93), Utah Arts Coun., Utah Sci. Authority, Archives Am. Art Smithsonian Instn., Coll. Art Assn. Am., Utah Acad. Scis. Arts Letters, Assn. Historians Am. Art, Internat. Coun. Fine Arts Deans, Phi Kappa Phi, Sigma Nu. Republican. Mormon. Author: Alexander Helwig Wyant, 1836-92, 1968, Mainstreams/Reflections-American/Utah Architecture, 1973, American

Painting Around 1850, 1976, Art-Life of Utah, 1977, Dictionary of Utah Art, 1980, A Retrospective of Utah Art, 1981, Waldo Midgley: Birds, Animals, People, Things, 1984, A Basket of Chips, 1985, The Works of Alexander Helwig Wyant, 1986, Salt Lake County Fine Arts Collection, 1987, Signs and Symbols...Utah Art, 1988, J.A.F. Everett, 1989, George Dibble, 1989, Utah Art, 1991; contbd. articles to profl. jours. including Utah, State of the Arts, 1993, Utah History Ency., 1994, Garland's Dutch Art Ency., 1997, Macmillan's Dictionary of Art, 1996. Home: 887 Woodshire Ave Salt Lake City UT 84107-7639 Office: U Utah Coll Fine Arts 250 Art & Architecture Ctr Salt Lake City UT 84112 *Personal philosophy: Not to reduce what I think about life to a motto.*

OLSCHWANG, ALAN PAUL, lawyer; b. Chgo., Jan. 30, 1942; s. Morton James and Ida (Ginsberg) O.; m. Barbara Claire Miller, Aug. 22, 1965; children: Elliot, Deborah, Jeffrey. B.S., U. Ill., 1963, J.D., 1966. Bar: Ill. 1966, N.Y. 1984, Calif. 1992. Law clk. Ill. Supreme Ct., Bloomington, 1966-67; assoc. Sidley & Austin, and predecessor, Chgo., 1967-73; with Montgomery Ward & Co., Inc., Chgo., 1973-81, assoc. gen. counsel, asst. sec., 1979-81; ptnr. Seki, Jarvis & Lynch, Chgo., 1981-84, dir., mem. exec. com.; exec. v.p., gen. counsel, sec. Mitsubishi Electric Am., Inc., N.Y.C., 1983-91, Cypress, Calif., 1991—. Mem. ABA, Am. Corp. Counsel Assn., Calif. Bar Assn., Ill. Bar Assn., Chgo. Bar Assn., N.Y. State Bar Assn., Bar Assn. of City of N.Y., Am. Arbitration Assn. (panel arbitrators). Office: Mitsubishi Electric Am 5665 Plaza Dr Cypress CA 90630-5023

OLSEN, CLIFFORD WAYNE, consultant, retired physical chemist; b. Placerville, Calif., Jan. 15, 1936; s. Christian William and Elsie May (Bishop) O.; m. Margaret Clara Gobel, June 16, 1962 (div. 1986); children: Anne Katherine Olsen Cordes, Charlotte Marie; m. Nancy Mayhew Kruger, July 21, 1990 (div. 1994). AA, Grant Tech. Coll., Sacramento, 1955; BA, U. Calif.-Davis, 1957, PhD, 1962. Physicist, project leader, program leader, task leader Lawrence Livermore Nat. Lab., Calif., 1962-93; ret., 1993, lab. assoc., 1993-95, 96—; cons. Keystone Internat., 1996-97, Am. Techs. Inc., 1997—; mem. Containment Evaluation Panel, U.S. Dept. Energy, 1984—, mem. Cadre for Joint Nuclear Verification Tests, 1988; organizer, editor procs. for 2nd through 7th Symposiums on Containment of Underground Nuclear Detonations, 1983-93. Contbr. articles to profl. jours. Mem. bd. convocators Calif. Luth. U., 1976-78. Recipient Chevalier Degree, Order of DeMolay, 1953, Eagle Scout, 1952. Mem. AAAS, Am. Radio Relay League, Seismol. Soc. Am., Livermore Amateur Radio Klub (pres. 1994-96), Sigma Xi, Alpha Gamma Sigma (life), Gamma Alpha (U. Calif.-Davis chpt. pres. 1960-61). Democrat. Lutheran.

OLSEN, DAVID MAGNOR, chemistry and astronomy educator; b. Deadwood, S.D., July 23, 1941; s. Russell Alvin and Dorothy M. Olson; m. Muriel Jean Bigler, Aug. 24, 1963; children: Merritt, Chad. BS, Luther Coll., 1963; MS in Nat. Sci., U. S.D., 1967. Instr. sci., math. Augustana Acad., Canton, S.D., 1963-66; instr. chemistry Iowa Lakes Community Coll., Estherville, Iowa, 1967-69; instr. chemistry Merced (Calif.) Coll., 1969—, instr. astronomy, 1975—, div. chmn., 1978-88, coord. environ. hazardous materials tech., 1989—. Trustee Merced Union High Sch. Dist., 1983—, pres., 1986-87, 97. Mem. NEA, Am. Chem. Soc., Astron. Soc. of the Pacific, Calif. Tchrs. Assn., Planetary Soc., Calif. State Mining and Mineral Mus. Assn. (bd. dirs., sec. 1990-93), Nat. Space Soc., Merced Coll. Faculty Assn. (pres. 1975, 93, 94, treas. 1980-90, 96—, bd. dirs., sec. 1990-91), Castle Challenger Learning Ctr. Found. (bd. dirs.), Merced Track Club (exec. bd. 1981), M Star Lodge, Sons of Norway (v.p. 1983), Rotary Internat. Democrat. Lutheran. Home: 973 Idaho Dr Merced CA 95340-2513 Office: Merced Coll 3600 M St Merced CA 95348-2806

OLSEN, GREG SCOTT, chiropractor; b. Anaheim, Calif., June 28, 1968; s. John Carlos and Gloria (Brownmiller) Frazier. D Chiropractic, L.A. Coll. Chiropractic, Whittier, Calif., 1994. Pvt. practice, Huntington Beach, Calif., 1994; postgrad. tchg. asst. Internat. Coll. Applied Kinesiology, L.A., 1995—. Mem. Am. Chiropractic Assn., Internat. Chiropractic Assn., Internat. Coll. Applied Kinesiology, Calif. Chiropractic Assn. Office: GO Chiropractic 16168 Beach Blvd Ste 135 Huntington Beach CA 92647-3814

OLSEN, HARRIS LELAND, real estate and international business executive, educator, diplomat; b. Rochester, N.H., Dec. 8, 1947; s. Harries Edwin and Eva Alma (Turmelle) O.; m. Mimi Kwi Sun Yi, Mar. 15, 1953; children: Garin Lee, Gavin Yi, Sook Ja. AS, SUNY, Albany, 1983, BS, 1988; MA in Polit. Sci., U. Hawaii, 1990; PhD in Internat. Bus. Adminstrn., Kennedy Western U., Idaho, 1993. Enlisted USN, 1967, advanced through grades to; served in various nuclear power capacities USN, Conn., 1971-76, Hawaii, 1976-87; ret. USN, 1987; v.p. Waiono Land Corp., Honolulu, 1981-92, dir., 1993-95; v.p. Asian Pacific Electricity, Honolulu, 1988-89, Kapano Land Assocs., Honolulu, 1988-92, 94-95, MLY Networks, Inc., Honolulu, 1989—, THO Consultants Cor., 1991—, Clarix Internat. Corp., 1994; staff cons. Mariner-Icemakers, Honolulu, 1982-84, Transpacific Energy Corp., Honolulu, 1982-84; dir. Asian Pacific Devel. Bank, 1983; sr. cons. Western Rsch. Assocs., Honolulu, 1984-87, 94-95; quality assurance cons. Asian Pacific, Inc., Hoholulu, 1987-88; instr., lectr. Asian history and culture U. Chaminade in Honolulu, 1991; nuclear reactor plant specialist Pearl Harbor Emergency Recall Team, 1991-95; instr. nuclear reactor theory Pearl Harbor, Hawaii, 1992-95; v.p. Schwartz, inc., 1992—, dir. Schwartz Jewelry Sch., 1996—; cons. Waiono/Kapano Devel. Co., 1993; bd. dirs., sec. Pacific Internat. Engring. Corp., 1994-95; Keiretsu sec. Global Ocean Cons., Inc. and Assocs., 1994-95; joint venture Premier Fisheries Pty. Ltd., Papua New Guinea, 1995—; cons. BFD Devel. Group, 1995-96; co-drafter Nat. Tuna Industry Devel. Plan for Papua New Guinea, 1995; quality analyst, Pearl Harbor, 1995; rep. for Min. for Fisheries, Papua New Guinea, Bi-lateral Fisheries Access Rights Japan and Papua New Guinea, 1996—, drafter Bi-Lateral Fishing Treaty Japan and Papua New Guinea, 1996; U.S. del. to 4th World Tuna Conf., Manila, 1995, U.S. del. to 5th Aquatic Continent Conf., Maui, Hawaii, 1995, 6th, 1996; apptd. rep. Abau Electorate, Papua New Guinea Timber Sales, 1995—; apptd. hon. counsel gen. and trade rep. for Govt. of Papua New Guinea in Honolulu, 1996—. Inventor, alternate power supply system; contbr. articles to profl. publs. Head coach USN Men's Softball, Honolulu, 1978-79; pres. Pearl Harbor (Hawaii) Welfare and Recreation Com., 1983-84; mem. Bishop Mus, Rep. Senatorial Inner Cir.; commd. hon. consul gen. Ind. State Papua, New Guinea, 1996. Named Alumnus of Yr., Kennedy Western U., 1993; recipient Citation of Leadership, Rep. Nat. Com., 1996. Mem. ASCD, AAAS, Internat. Fedn. Profl. and Tech. Engrs., Am. Polit. Sci. Assn., Semiotic Soc. Am., N.Y. Acad. Scis., Toronto Semiotics Cir., USCG Aux., Am. Legion, Fleet Res. Assn., Internat. Platform Assn., Navy League, U.S. Naval Inst., UN Assn., U.S. Submarine Vets., Honolulu Acad. Arts, U. Hawaii Founders Assn., U. Hawaii Coll. Arts and Sci. Found., Delta Epsilon Sigma. Republican. Buddhist. Home: 94-1025 Anania Cir Apt 56 Mililani HI 96789-2045 Office: Ban of Am Bldg 1357 Kapiolani Blvd # 1440 Honolulu HI 96814

OLSEN, HELEN MAY, author; b. Parma, Idaho, Apr. 12, 1914; d. Frank Curlette and Pearl Frances (Mussell) Lynch; m. Cloyd Henry Olsen, Nov. 8, 1935; children: Evelyn, Jay. With J.R. Simplot Co., Caldwell, Idaho, 1956-79, field dept. mgr., 1959-61, sec. to pres., 1961-71, sec. to pres., office mgr., 1971-75, divsn. pers. mgr., 1975-79. Author poetry, short fiction nat. newspapers and mags.; contbr. articles to profl. jours. Asst. sec. Gov.'s Campaign, Wilder, Idaho, 1982; tutor Laubach Literacy Program, Homedale, Idaho, 1991-92; transcriber oral histories Caldwell Libr., 1975-78; judge poetry contest Idaho Writers League, 1993. Named Sec. of the Yr., Nat. Secs. Assn. (Can/Ida chpt.), 1970, Profl. Secs. Internat., 1981. Mem. Family Scanners Soc. (v.p. 1989), Native Daus. of Idaho, Idaho Hist. Soc., Owyhee County Hist. Soc. Republican. Methodist. Home: 23289 Homedale Rd Wilder ID 83676

OLSEN, MARK NORMAN, small business owner; b. Seattle, Mar. 3, 1947; s. Norman Henry and Agnes Carolyn (Hansen) O.; m. Antoinette Marie Korman, June 20, 1991. Student, U. Wash., Western Wash. U., 1965-67, BHM Tech. Coll., 1968. Cert. autobody journeyman, estimator, inter-industry conf. auto collision repair. Mgr. body shop Fraser Chevrolet, Bellingham, Wash., 1967-83; owner Olsen Auto Body, Bellingham, 1983—. Bd. dirs. Bellingham Tech. Coll. Mem. Auto Body Craftsman (treas.). Home: 1117 N Shore Dr Bellingham WA 98226-9420 Office: Olsen Auto Body 1919 Humboldt St Bellingham WA 98225-4204

OLSEN, NAYANTARA MARIETTA, human resources executive, marketing consultant; b. Colombo, Sri Lanka, May 30, 1969; came to U.S., 1989; d. Alexander Bastian and Nirmali Moreen (Corea) Jayasekera; m. Rudy Earl Olsen, Aug. 10, 1990; children: Alexander Earl, Joseph Bastian. BS in Bus. Mktg. and Human Resources, U. Idaho, 1994. Dir. human resources Latah Health Svcs., Moscow, Idaho. Democrat. Lutheran. Home: 633 East F Moscow ID 83843 Office: Latah Health Svcs 510 W Palouse River Dr Moscow ID 83843

OLSEN, PHILLIP BUCK, corporate pilot, retired educator; b. Duluth, Minn., Feb. 28, 1931; s. Henry Jomar Olsen and Hjordis (Buck) Henley; m. Frances Ann MacKay, May 22, 1961 (div. Dec. 1984); m. Minnie Eiko Komagome, Aug. 19, 1988 (div. Oct. 1994). AB, Wesleyan U., Middletown, Conn., 1953; MS in Journalism, UCLA, 1959. Cert. flight instr. FAA. Commd. 2d lt. USAF, 1953, advanced through grades to capt., 1961; pilot various locations, U.S. and Europe, 1953-63; vol. U.S. Peace Corps, Philippines, 1962-64; regional dir. Mindanao/Sulu, Philippines, 1964-66; desk officer Washington, 1966-67; dir., assoc. dean Coll. Arts and Scis. U. Hawaii/Manoa, Honolulu, 1967-86; capt., asst. chief pilot Alexander & Baldwin, Inc., Honolulu, 1986-94; pres., ptnr. Aviation Holding, Ltd., Honolulu, 1983—; capt. Avant Aire, Honolulu, 1995—; v.p., bd. dirs. Honolulu Marathon Assn., 1976-80. adj. instr. Embry Riddle Aeronautical U., Hickam AFB, Hawaii, 1992. Editor jour. Western Airlines, 1959-60. Comdr. Aloha State Search and Rescue Squadron, Honolulu, 1972-79; active Honolulu Symphony Guild. Recipient Estella della Solidarieta, Republic of Italy, 1956. Mem. Asian Studies Assn., Aircraft Owners and Pilots Assn., Elks. Home: 2080 Mauna Pl Honolulu HI 96822-2502

OLSEN, RODNEY WAYNE, business development manager, technical consultant; b. Provo, Utah, July 24, 1951; s. Wayne B. and Charleen (Chase) O.; m. Esther Lee Holmstead, Mar. 30, 1981 (div. Sept. 1993); children: Tiffanie Ann, Mathew Wayne; m. Anna Przybylska, Oct., 1995. BSEE, U. Utah, 1981. Electronic technician Sperry Univac, Salt Lake City, 1978-79; electronic technician Evans & Sutherland, Salt Lake City, 1979-82, design engr., 1982-85, project engr., 1985-92, computer graphics bus. devel. mgr., 1992—. Home: 2977 S Alamo St West Valley City UT 84120 Office: Evans & Sutherland 600 Komas Dr Salt Lake City UT 84108-1229

OLSHEN, ABRAHAM CHARLES, actuarial consultant; b. Portland, Oreg., Apr. 20, 1913; m. Dorothy Olds, June 21, 1934; children: Richard Allen, Beverly Ann Jacobs. AB, Reed Coll., 1933; MS, U. Iowa, 1935, PhD, 1937. Chief statistician City Planning Commn., Portland, Oreg., 1933-34; rsch. asst. math. dept. U. Iowa, 1934-37; biometrics asst. Med. Ctr., 1936-37; actuary, chief examiner Oreg. Ins. Dept., 1937-42, 45-46; actuary West Coast Life Ins. Co., San Francisco, 1946—, chief actuary, 1953-63, v.p., 1947—, 1st v.p., 1963-67, senior v.p., 1967-68, bd. dirs., 1955-68; cons. actuarial and ins. mgmt., pres. Olshen & Assocs., San Francisco, 1979—; bd. dirs. Home Federal Savs. & Loan Assn., San Francisco, 1972-85, vice-chmn. bd. 1979-85, bd. chmn. 1985-86; guest lectr. various univs. Contbg. writer Ency. Britannica, Underwriters' Report, The Nat. Underwriter, Life Underwriters Mag., Annals of Math. Stats., other publs. Mem. Calif. com. Health Ins. Coun., U. Calif. Med. Care Adminstrn. com., San Mateo County Retirement Bd. (1975-77). Rsch. assoc. Div. of War Rsch., 1942-44, Ops. Rsch. Gp., H/Q Comdr.-in-Chief, U.S. Fleet, 1944-45. Recipient U.S. Navy Ordnance Devel. award, 1945, Disting. Service award U.S. Office of Sci. Rsch. & Devel., 1945, Presdl. Cert. Merit, 1947. Fellow AAAS, Sigma Xi; mem. Health Ins. Assn. Am. (mem., past chmn. Blanks Com., actuarial & stat. com.), Actuarial Club of Pacific States (past pres.), Actuarial Club of San Francisco (past pres.), Am. Acad. of Actuaries (charter), Am. Math. Soc., Am. Risk and Ins. Assn., Calif. Math. Coun., Commonwealth Club (life), Fellow Conf. of Actuaries in Public Practice, Inst. Mgmt. Scis., Inst. Math. Stats., Internat. Actuarial Assn., Internat. Assn. Consulting Actuaries, Internat. Cong. Actuaries, Ops. Rsch. Soc. (charter), San Francisco Press Club (life). Office: Olshen & Assocs 760 Market St Ste 739 San Francisco CA 94102-2302

OLSON, EARLE OLIVER, marketing and sales executie, consultant; b. Fargo, N.D., Feb. 12, 1959; s. Daniel Elias and Ellen Marie (Endersbee) O.; m. Patricia Ann McManus, Mar. 14, 1987; children: Melissa Anne, Danielle Marie. BS, St. Cloud (Minn.) State U., 1982; MBA, U. Redlands, 1996. Product mgr. divsn. electronic components Deutsch, Banning, Calif., 1981-83; product mgr. Sourrau Inc., Paris and Valencia, Calif., 1987-89; sales exec. Electronic Supply, Riverside, Calif.; corp. market mgr. Cypress Electronics, Buena Park, Calif., 1983-87; v.p. N.Am. market AB Electronics Ltd., South Wales, 1989-92; sales exec. AMP Inc., Diamond Bar, Calif., 1992-95; regional product mgr. AMP Inc., Cupertino, Calif., 1995—; cons. on mil. and aerospace electronics and optics. Named Supplier of Yr., Delco-Hughes Electronics, 1994. Mem. Optical Soc. Am., World Airline Entertainment Assn., Airlines Electronic Engring. Com., Aero. Radio. Home: 37333 Morning Cir Palmdale CA 93550 Office: AMP Inc 3333 Corporate Ter Diamond Bar CA 91765

OLSON, KENNETH HARVEY, computer company executive; b. Souris, N.D., May 7, 1927; s. Oscar L. and Clara (Haugen) O.; m. Darlene R. Gronseth, Aug. 19, 1950 (div. 1987); children: Kenneth David, Martha C., Marie K. BA, Concordia Coll., Moorhead, Minn., 1950; MS, U. N.D., 1953; postgrad., U. Minn., 1955. Instr. math. U. N.D., Grand Forks, 1952-54; programming supr. Convair, San Diego, 1955-59; mgr. software Control Data Corp., Mpls., 1959-61, product mgr., 1961-62; sales mgr. Control Data Corp., San Diego, 1962-70; v.p. Automated Med. Analysts, San Diego, 1970-90; pres., dir. Focus 010 Group, San Diego, 1975—; pres., dir. Health Care Svcs. Corp., San Diego, 1971-74, H.C.S. Corp., San Diego, 1972-75; v.p., trustee Calif. Prepaid Health Plan Coun., 1971-74; trustee HMO Assn. Am., 1974-75; bd. dirs. Touch Techs., Inc., San Diego. Editor: Approximations for the 1604 Computer, 1960; contbr. papers to Computer Applications, 1957-61. Pres. Lemon Grove (Calif.) Luth. Ch., 1957-59; treas. St. Luke's Luth. Ch., La Mesa, Calif., 1992-93; founder San Diego Nat. Bank, 1980, mem. bus. adv. com., 1981-85. Named Subcontractor of Yr., Small Bus. Assn. and SAI Corp., 1985; day proclaimed in his honor Mayor of San Diego, 1986; recipient Pres.'s award for disting. svc. Concordia Coll., 1991. Mem. Assn. for Computing Machinery, Sons of Norway. Republican.

OLSON, KENNETH PAUL, rehabilitation counselor; b. Providence, June 26, 1935; s. Gustave Frederick and Beatrice Evelyn (Backstrom) O.; m. Judith Luellan Hazard, Nov. 12, 1965; children: Glenn Edward Johnson. BA in Sociology, U. Denver, 1960; MA in Sociology, U. Colo., 1973. Cert. rehab. counselor, vocat. specialist; lic. profl. counselor, Colo. Exec. dir. Goodwill Industries, Colorado Springs, Co., 1960-65, San Francisco, 1965, Ft. Worth, 1966-70; counselor II Colo. Div. Rehab., Colorado Springs, 1972-83; pres. Olson Vocat. Svcs., Colorado Springs, 1983—; vocational expert Social Security Adminstn., Denver, 1984—; rehab counselor U.S. Dept. Labor, Denver, 1984-89. V.p. Bus. Arts Ctr., Manitou Springs, 1988-89; councilman Manitou Springs, 1975-78; mem. Econ. Devel. Com., Manitou Springs, 1984-86; chmn. Health Adv. Coun., Pikes Peak Region, 1979-80; mem. Commn. for Rehab. Counselor Cert., 1979-85, Bd. for Rehab. Cert., 1984-86; pres. Manitou Art Project, 1994-95; mem. acountability com. Cmty. Prep. Sch. Fellow Nat. Rehab. Counseling Assn.; mem. Colo. Rehab. Counseling Assn. (pres. 1979, named Counselor of Yr. 1976), Great Plains Rehab. Assn. (pres. 1982-83), Colo. Rehab. Assn., Colo. Vocat. Evaluation Work Adjustment Assn., El Paso County Assn. Lic. Profl. Counselors (treas. 1994-96), Colorado Springs C. of C. (Small Bus. Person of Yr. award 1991), Manitou Springs C. of C. (pres. 1986). Home: PO Box 226 Manitou Springs CO 80829-0226 Office: Olson Vocat Svcs 701 S Cascade Ave Colorado Springs CO 80903-4003

OLSON, LENORA MARY, health facility administrator, epidemiologist; b. Hutchinson, Kans., Mar. 17, 1959; d. Harry Harper and Mary Agnes (Little) O.; m. James Michael Brandi, Oct. 21, 1989. BA in Anthropology, U. N.Mex., 1981, MA in Anthropology, 1988. Infection control practitioner Univ. Hosp., Albuquerque, 1989-90; program mgr. Emergency Dept. U. N.Mex., Albuquerque, 1990-94, dir. injury prevention, 1994—; mem. grant rev. panel Maternal Child Health, Rockville, Md., 1991—; mem. disability prevention adv coun. N.Mex. Dept. Health, Santa Fe, 1992—; mem. child abuse prevention com. N.Mex. Dept. Health, Santa Fe, 1991-93. Contbr. articles to profl. jours. Mem. APHA (com. chair injury control sect. 1991-93, challenge fund program grantee 1994, chair injury control sec. 1996-97), N.Mex. Health Assn. Office: U NMex-Sch Medicine Dept Emergency Medicine ACC 4 West Albuquerque NM 87131

OLSON, LUTE, university athletic coach; b. Mayville, N.D., Sept. 22, 1934; s. Albert E. and Alinda E. (Halvorson) O.; m. Roberta R. Russell, Nov. 27, 1953; children: Vicki, Jodi, Gregory, Christi, Steven. B.A., Augsburg Coll., Mpls., 1956; M.A., Chapman Coll., Orange, Calif., 1964. Cert. counselor. Head basketball coach Mahonomen High Sch., Minn., 1956-57, Two Harbors High Sch., Minn., 1957-61; dean of boys Baseline Jr. High Sch., Boulder, Colo., 1961-62; head basketball coach Loara High Sch., Anaheim, Calif., 1962-64, Marine High Sch., Huntington Beach, Calif., 1964-69, Long Beach City Coll., Calif., 1969-73, Long Beach State U., 1973-74, U. Iowa, Iowa City, 1974-83; head basketball coach U. Ariz. Wildcats, 1983—, head coach NCAA Divsn. 1A basketball, ranked #10, 1992, head coach NCAA Tournament winner West Region, semifinalist (overall), 1994. Author: Passing Game Offense, 1980, Multiple Zone Attack, 1981, Pressure Defense, 1981, Match-up Zone, 1983. Crusade chmn. Am. Cancer Soc., Iowa, 1982. Named Coach of Yr. Orange League, 1964; named Coach of Yr. Sunset League, 1968, Coach of Yr. Met. Conf. Calif., 1970-71, Coach of Yr. PCAA, 1974, Coach of Yr. Big Ten Conf., 1979, 80. Mem. Nat. Assn. Basketball Coaches (Coach of Yr. 1980). Lutheran. Office: U Ariz Mckale Ctr Tucson AZ 85721*

OLSON, MARIAN KATHERINE, emergency management executive, consultant, publisher, information broker; b. Tulsa, Oct. 15, 1933; d. Sherwood Joseph and Katherine M. (Miller) Lahman; m. Ronald Keith Olson, Oct 27, 1956, (dec. May 1991). BA in Polit. Sci., U. Colo., 1954, MA in Elem. Edn., 1962; EdD in Ednl. Adminstrn., U. Tulsa, 1969. Tchr. public schs., Wyo., Colo., Mont., 1958-67; teaching fellow, adj. instr. edn. U. Tulsa, 1968-69; asst. prof. edn. Eastern Mont. State Coll., 1970; program assoc. research adminstrn. Mont. State U., 1970-75; on leave with Energy Policy Office of White House, then with Fed. Energy Adminstrn., 1973-74; with Dept. Energy, and predecessor, 1975—, program analyst, 1975-79, chief planning and environ. compliance br., 1979-83; regional dir. Region VIII Fed. Emergency Mgmt. Agy., 1987-93; exec. dir., Search and Rescue Dogs of the U.S., 1993—; pres. Western Healthclaims, Inc., Golden, Co.; pres. Marian Olson Assocs., Bannack Pub. Co.; mem. Colo. Nat. Hazards Mitigation Coun., Colo. Urban Search and Rescue Task Force. Contbr. articles in field. Grantee Okla. Consortium Higher Edn., 1969, NIMH, 1974. Mem. Am. Soc. for Info. Sci., Am. Assn. Budget and Program Analysis, Assn. of Contingency Planners, Internat. Assn. Ind. Pubs., Assn. of Contingency Planners, Nat. Inst. Urban Search and Rescue (bd. dirs.), Nat. Assn. for Search and Rescue, Colo. Search and Rescue, Search and Rescue Dogs of U.S., Colo. Emergency Mgmt. Assn., Front Range Rescue Dogs, Colo. State Fire Chiefs Assn., Kappa Delta Pi, Phi Alpha Theta, Kappa Alpha Theta. Republican. Home: 203 Iowa Dr Golden CO 80403-1337 Office: Western Healthclaims Inc 203 Iowa Dr Ste B Golden CO 80403-1337

OLSON, PAUL S., nuclear engineer; b. Cambridge, Mass., May 2, 1933; s. Charles Louis and Mary Agnis (Navin) O.; m. Elaine Marylyn Selvitella, Nov. 25, 1956; children: Cheryl McCarthy, Christine Baginski, Karen Barbarick. BSChemE, Northeastern U., 1957; MS Nuclear Engring., U. Cin., 1962. Registered prof. engr. Calif. Commd. 2d lt. Rockwell, 1952; advanced through ranks to col. U.S. Army, 1978, retired, 1985; engr. GE, Cin., 1958-62, Rockwell, Canoga Park, Calif., 1962—. Bd. dirs. Univ. Mo. NE, Rolla, 1994-97, St. Anthony Home for Troubled Youngsters, Canoga Park, 1983-89. Fellow ASTM (chmn. 1958—, Merit award 1983); mem. K.C. (Grand Knight 1980—, Merit award 1985), Tau Beta Pi, Sigma Xi. Democrat. Roman Catholic. Home: 1365 Van Antwerp Rd # M-128 Niskayuna NY 12309-4441 Office: Rockwell 6633 Canoga Ave Canoga Park CA 91303-2703

OLSON, PHILLIP DAVID LEROY, agriculturist, chemist; b. Anchorage, Feb. 3, 1940; s. Marvin Willard and Bernadette (McName) O.; m. Deborah Andreé Butler, Apr. 10, 1982; children from a previous marriage: Jamie Kay, Samuel Phillip, Jill Andre. BS, U. Idaho, 1963; MS, Oreg. State U., 1972. Technician U. Calif., Riverside, 1963-65; rsch. staff Oreg. State U., Corvallis, 1965-75; mgr. R & D, Hoechst-Roussel Agri-Vet Co., Somerville, N.J., 1975-91; owner, pres. Profl. Agrl. Cons., Indio, Calif., 1991—; R & D cons. and quality assurance rsch. contractor Elf Atochem N.A., Bryan, Tex., 1991—, Dupont, Wilmington, Del., 1991—, Ciba-Geigy, Greensboro, N.C., 1991—, BASF, Research Triangle Park, N.C., 1991, ISK-Bioscis., Fresno, Calif., 1992—, Rhone-Plulenc, Durham, N.C., 1992—, Sandoz Agro, Inc., Des Plaines, Ill., 1992—, Zeneca, Inc., Richmond, Calif., 1992—, Stewart AG, Macon, Mo., 1995—; cons. in field. Mem. Soc. Quality Assurance, Pacific Regional Quality Assurance Soc., Oreg. State U. Found. (hon.), Smithsonian Instn., Archaeol. Soc. Am., Acad. Model Aeronautics, Elks.

OLSON, ROBERT HOWARD, lawyer; b. Indpls., July 6, 1944; s. Robert Howard and Jacquline (Wells) O.; m. Diane Carol Thorsen, Aug. 13, 1966; children: Jeffrey, Christopher. BA in Govt. summa cum laude, Ind. U., 1966; JD cum laude, Harvard U., 1969. Bar: U.S. Dist. Ct. (no. dist.) Ohio 1970, U.S. Dist. Ct. (no. Dist.) Ind. 1970, U.S. Dist. Ct. (so. Dist.) Ohio 1971, U.S. Supreme Ct. 1973, Ariz. 1985. Assoc. Squire, Sanders & Dempsey, Cleve., 1969, 70-71, 76-81, ptnr., 1981—, ptnr., Phoenix, 1985—; sr. law clk. U.S. Dist. Ct., No. Dist. Ind. 1969-70; chief civil rights div. Ohio Atty. Gen.'s Office, Columbus, 1971-73, chief consumer protection, 1973-75, chief counsel, 1975, 1st asst. (chief of staff), 1975-76; instr. Law Sch., Ohio State U., Columbus, 1974; mem. Cen. Phoenix com. to advise city council and mayor, 1987-89; bd. dirs. Orpheum Theater Found., 1989—, sec., 1989-90, pres., 1990-97; bd. dirs. The Ariz. Ctr. for Law in the Pub. Interest, 1988—, mem. exec. com., 1990-94, treas. 1992-93, v.p., 1993-94; mem. Ariz. Ctr. for Disability Law, 1994-96, treas. 1994-95; mem. Valley Leadership Class XIV, Ariz. Town Hall, 1977. Author monograph on financing infrastructure, 1983; also law rev. articles on civil rights, consumer protection. Bd. dirs. 1st Unitarian Ch. Phoenix, v.p., 1987-89; bd. dirs. 1st Unitarian Ch. Found., 1987-93, pres., 1990-93. Mem. Ariz. State Bar Assn., Phi Beta Kappa. Democrat. Home: 5201 E Paradise Dr Scottsdale AZ 85254-4746 Office: Squire Sanders & Dempsey 40 N Central Ave Ste 2700 Phoenix AZ 85004-4424

OLSON, RONALD CHARLES, aerospace executive; b. Sioux Falls, S.D., Jan. 23, 1937; s. Arthur Helmer and Myrtle Esther (Gustafson) O.; m. Barbara Jean Newcomb, Apr. 7, 1957; children: Bradley Charles, Jodi Lynn. AA, North Idaho Coll., 1956; BS in EE, U. Idaho, 1958; grad. sr. exec. mgmt. program, MIT, 1988. Design engr. Boeing Aerospace, Seattle, 1958-72, engring. mgr., 1973-83; postgrad. in mgmt. MIT, Seattle, 1988; program mgr. Boeing Defense and Space Group, Seattle, 1985-95; pres., gen. mgr. Sea Launch Co., LDC, Seattle, Cayman Islands, 1995-97; v.p. Boeing Comml. Space Co., Seattle, Cayman Islands, 1995-97; exec. v.p. Boeing Comml. Space Co., Seattle, 1997—; mem. engring. adv. bd. U. Idaho Coll. Engring., Moscow, 1988-95, chmn. bd., 1991-95. Recipient Gen. Ira C. Eaker, Air Force Assn., Vandenburg AFB, 1985. Mem. Boeing Mgmt. Assn. (sec. 1981-85), Big Band Dance Club (instr. 1980-85), Twin Lakes Golf & Country Club. Republican. Lutheran. Home: 1206 184th Avenue Ct E Sumner WA 98390-9419 Office: Boeing Defense Space Group PO Box 3999 Seattle WA 98124-2499

OLSON, STEVEN STANLEY, social service executive; b. Longview, Wash., Aug. 5, 1950; s. Robert Martin and Martha Virginia (Duffin) O.; 1 child, Derek Thomas Dailey. BA, Wash. State U., 1972; MEd, Auburn U., 1977; postgrad., Seattle U., 1981-83. Cert. rehabilitation mgmt. Agrl. extensionist Action/Peace Corps, Popayan, Colombia, 1972-73; supr. Stonebelt Ctr. for the Mentally Retarded, Bloomington, Ind., 1974; adjustment counselor Exceptional Industries, Bowling Green, Ky., 1974-75; vocat. evaluator Exceptional Industries, 1975-76; alcohol counselor E. Ala. Mental Health, Opelika, 1976; intern Auburn Univ./Ptnrs. of the Americas, Guatemala City, Guatemala, 1976; planner, researcher Marion County Mental Health, Salem, Oreg., 1977-78; assoc. dir. Reliable Enterprises, Centralia, Wash., 1979-80; exec. dir. Reliable Enterprises, 1980—; v.p. govt. affairs Rehab. Enterprises Wash., Olympia, 1984-86, chmn. regional rep., 1986-89, pres., 1990-91; treas. Arc of Wash., Olympia, 1983-85, govt. affairs chmn., 1983-89, v.p., 1989-90, sec., 1996-97; adv. coun. Lewis/Mason/Thurston Area Agy. on Aging, 1993—. Contbr. articles to Vocat. Evaluation and Work Adjustment Bull., 1976, Rehab. World, 1977. Treas. Communities United for Reponsible Energy, Lewis County, Wash., 1979—; vice chairperson Wash. Solar Coun., Olympia, Wash., 1980-83; co-chair Early Childhood Help Orgn., Olympia, 1988. Home: 4333 Maytown Rd SW Olympia WA 98512-9239 Office: Reliable Enterprises 203 W Reynolds Ave Centralia WA 98531-3313

OLSON, WILLIAM THOMAS, business executive, educator, consultant; b. Coeur d'Alene, Idaho, May 1, 1940; s. William Anthony and Julia Glenn (Hunter) O.; BA, U. N.Mex., 1968; postgrad. U. Va., 1968-72; m. Diana Jean Dodds, Aug. 22, 1962; children: Kristin Ann (dec.), Kira Lynn. Cert. mgmt. cons. Intelligence agt. U.S. Army, 1962-65; asso. editor Newspaper Printing Corp., Albuquerque, 1965-66; news and pub. affairs dir. Sta. KUNM-FM, U. N.M., 1966-68; news person KOAT-TV, Albuquerque, 1968; news dir. WCHV Radio, Charlottesville, Va., 1968-69; moderator, producer Radio-TV Center, U. Va., 1969-73; columnist The Jefferson Jour., Charlottesville, Va., 1972; instr. history U. Va., 1971-73; information specialist Wash. State U. Cooperative Ext. Service, Pullman, 1973-77, instr. Sch. Communications, 1976-77, asst. dir., Wash. Energy Ext. Service, 1977-79; founder, pres. Inland N.W. Soc. Consulting Profls., 1995-96; dir. Spokane County Head Start, 1979-84; adminstr. Community Colls. of Spokane, 1984-89, dir. critical Thinking Project, 1988-89; pres. Effective Mgmt. Systems Corp., 1987-92, CEO, chmn., bd. dirs., 1992—. Dir. Connoisseur Concerts Assn., 1983-86, pres. 1985-86; dir. West Cen. Community Devel. Assn., pres., 1985-86; dir. Spokane Community Ctrs. Found., 1986—; mem. Mayor's budget com. City of Spokane, 1988-89. Served with AUS, 1962-65. Mem. Am. Soc. Quality Ctrl., advisory bd. Goal/QPC, Wash. Family Independence Program 1990-92, Inst. Mgmt. Conss. (mem. 1995—); founding pres., mem. Inland Northwest Soc. of Consulting Profls., 1995—; Author TV documentary (with Ken Fielding): The Golden Years?, 1973; film (with B. Dale Harrison and Lorraine Kingdon) New Directions Out of the Culture of Poverty, 1974. Home: 2018 E 14th Ave Spokane WA 99202-3562 Office: Stewart Bldg W-427 First Ave Spokane WA 99204

OLSSON, RONALD ARTHUR, computer science educator; b. Huntington, N.Y., Nov. 16, 1955; s. Ronald Alfred and Dorothy Gertrude (Hofmann) O. BA and MA, SUNY, 1977; MS, Cornell U., 1979; PhD, U. Ariz., 1986. Teaching asst. Cornell U., Ithaca, N.Y., 1977-79, rsch. asst., 1979; lectr. SUNY, Brockport, 1979-81; rsch. assoc. U. Ariz., Tucson, 1981-86; prof., vice chair Computer Sci. Dept. U. Calif., Davis, 1986—. Author (book) The SR Programming Language: Concurrency in Practice, 1993; contbr. articles to profl. jours. Grantee MICRO U. Calif., 1987, 92, NSF, 1988, 96, Dept. Energy, 1988-92, Advanced Rsch. Projects Agy., 1993—. Mem. Assn. for Computing Machinery. Home: 2741 Brandywine Pl Davis CA 95616-2904 Office: U Calif Dept Computer Sci Davis CA 95616-8562

OLVER, MICHAEL LYNN, lawyer; b. Seattle, June 22, 1950; s. Manley Deforest and Geraldine (Robinson) O.; m. Wendy Kay, July 6, 1974; children: Erin, Christina. BA, U. Wash., 1972; JD, Calif. Western Sch. of Law, 1976. Assoc. Robbins, Merrick & Kraft, Seattle, 1976-77; lawyer, sole practitioner Michael L. Olver, Seattle, 1977-80; ptnr., pres. Merrick & Olver, P.S., Seattle, 1980—; bd. dirs. Found. for Handicapped, Seattle, 1988-93; commr. pro tem Ex part Dept. King County Superior Ct., Seattle, 1992—. Author: Wills and Trusts for the Disabled, 1989, Living Trusts--Pros and Cons, 1992, Special Needs Trusts After OBRA '93, 1994, Bascomb's Rogue, 1994, others; editor Calif. Western Internat. Law Jour., 1975-76. Chmn. Ann. Cath. Appeal, Assumption Parish, Seattle, 1989-90. Mem. Nat. Acad. Elder Law Attys. (dir. Wash. chpt. 1994—), Wash. State Trial Lawyers Assn. Office: Merrick & Olver PS 9222 Lake City Way NE Seattle WA 98115-3268

O'MAHONY, TIMOTHY KIERAN, writer; b. Cork City, Cork, Ireland, Feb. 16, 1953; came to U.S., 1982; s. Michael John and Bridget (Horan) O'M.; m. Mary Bernadette O'Leary, June 11, 1975; children: Darragh Shane, Roman Daniel, Madelein Caoimhe Anne. BA, Nat. U. Ireland, 1973, HDE, 1974, MEd, 1981. Tchr. H.S., Cork, Ireland, 1973-82; writer, pub. Educare Press, Seattle, 1983—; pub. Glen Abbey Books, Seattle, 1990-93. Author: (short stories) To the Woods and Waters Wild, 1992, (trilogy) Geography, Education, 1988-94; editor: Valiant Captains, 1992. Fellow Royal Geog. Soc.; mem. PMA., (Pub. Weekly Assn. Office: Educare Press PO Box 4802 Seattle WA 98104

O'MALLEY, PETER, professional baseball club executive; b. N.Y.C., Dec. 12, 1937; s. Walter F. and Kay (Hanson) O'M.; m. Annette Zacho, July 10, 1971; children: Katherine, Kevin, Brian. B.S. in Econs, U. Pa., 1960. Dir. Dodgertown, Vero Beach, Fla., 1962-64; pres., gen. mgr. Spokane Baseball Club, 1965-66; v.p. Los Angeles Dodgers Baseball Club, 1967-68, exec. v.p., from 1968; pres. Los Angeles Dodgers, Inc., 1970—, also bd. dirs.; bd. dirs. Tidings newspaper. Bd. dirs. L.A. Police Meml. Found., L.A. World Affairs Coun., Jackie Robinson Found., L.A.-Gungzhou (Republic of China) Sister City Assn., Amateur Athletic Found.; pres. Little League Found.; active L.A. County Bd. Govs., Music Ctr., So. Calif. Com. for the Olympic Games. Mem. Korean-Am. C. of C. of L.A. Office: LA Dodgers 1000 Elysian Park Ave Los Angeles CA 90012-1112*

O'MALLEY, THOMAS PATRICK, academic administrator; b. Milton, Mass., Mar. 1, 1930; s. Austin and Ann Marie (Feeney) O'M. BA, Boston Coll., 1951; MA, Fordham U., 1953; STL, Coll. St.-Albert de Louvain, 1962; LittD, U. Nijmegen, 1967; LLD (hon.), John Carroll U., 1988. Entered Soc. of Jesus, 1952. Instr. classics Coll. of Holy Cross, Worcester, Mass., 1956-58; asst. prof., chmn. dept. classics Boston Coll., 1967-69, assoc. prof., chmn. dept. theology, 1969-73; dean Boston Coll. (Coll. Arts and Scis.), 1973-80; pres. John Carroll U., Cleve., 1980-88; vis. prof. Cath. Inst. W. Africa, 1988-89; assoc. editor AMERICA, N.Y.C., 1989-90; rector Jesuit Com. Fairfield U., 1990-91; pres. Loyola Marymount U., L.A., 1991—. Author: Tertullian and the Bible, 1967. Trustee Boston Theol. Inst., 1969-73, Fairfield U., 1971-82, 89-91, John Carroll U., 1976-88, Xavier U., 1980-86, U. Detroit, 1982-88, Boston Coll. H.S., 1986-88, Boys Hope, 1986-88, Loyola Marymount U., 1991—, St. Joseph's U., 1996—. Mem. AAUP, Soc. Bibl. Lit., N.Am. Patristic Soc.

OMAN, HENRY, retired electrical engineer, engineering executive; b. Portland, Oreg., Aug. 29, 1918; s. Paul L. and Mary (Levonen) O.; m. Winifred Eleanor Potter, June 17, 1944 (dec. Nov. 1950); m. Earlene Mary Boot, Sept. 11, 1954; children: Mary Janet, Eleanor Eva, Eric Paul. BSEE, Oreg. State U., 1940, MSEE, 1951. Registered profl. engr., Wash. Application engr. Allis Chalmers Mfg. Co., Milw., 1940-48; rsch. engr. Boeing Co., Seattle, 1948-63, engrng. mgr., 1963-91. Author: Energy Systems Engineering Handbook, 1986; contbr. numerous articles to profl. jours. Mem. team that restarted amateur radio communication to the outside world from the People's Republic of China, 1981. Recipient prize paper award Am. Inst. Elec. Engrs., 1964. Fellow IEEE (founder power electronics systems confs., 1970—, v.p. Aerospace and Electronics Systems Soc. 1984-88, Harry Mimno award 1989, editor-in-chief IEEE Aerospace and Electronic Sys. mag. 1995—/rated in top two by Inst. for Scientific Info.), AIAA (assoc.); mem. AAAS (bd. dir. Pacific divsn. 1992—). Republican. Methodist. Home: 19221 Normandy Park Dr SW Seattle WA 98166-4129

OMANG, BONITA ELLA, artist; b. Balt., Mar. 12, 1950; d. William Frederick and gwendolyn Olive (Dean) Baumann; m. William Harold Mooney, Nov. 4, 1967 (div. Aug. 1974); children: Scott everette, Shelly gwendolyn Mooney Diaz; m. Keith Allen Omang, July 24, 1982. Student, Black Hills State U., 1995. Heavy equip. operator Bear creek Uranium, Douglas, Wyo., 1979-87, Golden reward Mining, Lead, S.D., 1988-91. Artist leather sculpture: Wyoming Woman, 1995, stone sculpture: Fantisy Flower, 1993; represented in galleries in Wyoming and South Dakota. With USAF, 1974-75. Mem. Dakota artists Guild, Northeastern Wyo. Artists Guild. Home: 22 Nathan Hale Rd Gillette WY 82718-9431

O'MEARA, SARA, nonprofit organization executive; b. Knoxville, Tenn., Sept. 9; m. Robert O'Meara (dec.); children: John Hopkins, Charles Hopkins (dec.); m. Robert Sigholtz, Nov. 1986; stepchildren: Taryn, Whitney. Attended, Briarcliff Jr. Coll.; BA, The Sorbonne, Paris; D (hon.), Endicott Coll. Co-founder, chmn. bd., CEO CHILDHELP USA/Internat. (formerly Children's Village USA), Scottsdale, Ariz., 1960—. Bd. dirs. Internat. Soc. Prevention Child Abuse and Neglect, Children to Children, Inc.; hon. com. mem. Learning Disabilities Found., Inc.; mem. Mayor's adv. bd., Defense for Children Internat., Nat. Soc. Prevention Cruelty to Children, World Affairs Coun.; adv. bd. mem. Ednl. Film Co.; bd. dirs. Internat. Alliance on Child Abuse and Neglect; sustaining mem. Spastic Children's League, past pres.; mem., past recording sec. Assistance League So. Calif. Recipient Cross of Merit, Knightly Order of St. Brigitte, 1967, Victor M. Carter Diamond award Japan-Am. Soc., 1970, Dame Cross of Merit of Order of St. John of Denmark, 1980, Official Seal of 34th Gov. Calif., 1981, Woman of Achievement award Career Guild, 1982, Women Making History award Nat. Fedn. Bus. Profl. Women's Clubs, 1983, Disting. Am. award for svc., 1984, Humanitarian award Nat. Frat. Eagles, 1984, Nat. Recognition award outstanding leadership Am. Heritage Found., 1986, Notable Am. award svc. to Calif., 1986, Dove of Peace award Pacific Southwest and Ctrl. Pacific Regions B'nai B'rith, 1987, Paul Harris fellow award Rotary Found., 1989, Internat. Collaboration to Prevention Child Abuse award HRH Queen of Eng., 1989, Living Legacy award Women's Internat. Ctr., 1989, Love and Help the Children award, 1990, Presdl. award, 1990, Kiwanis World Svc. medal, 1991, Family Circle award Family Circle Mag., 1992, Outstanding Woman for Tenn. award Nat. Mus. Women in Arts, 1993, Nat. Caring award Nat. Caring Inst., 1993, Hubert Humphrey award Touchdown Club Washington, 1994, numerous others. Mem. SAG, AFTRA, Victory Awards (exec. com.), Am. Biographical Inst. (nat. bd. advisors), Alpha Delta Kappa (hon.). Office: Childhelp USA 15757 N 78th St Scottsdale AZ 85260-1737

OMEL, HAROLD, protective services official; m. Patti, 1962; 2 children. A in Fire Sci., Long Beach City Coll. Joined Long Beach (Calif.) Fire Dept., 1964—, from firefighter to bn. chief, 1964-94, fire chief, 1994—; apptd. State Bd. Fire Svcs., 1986—, chmn. freeway sigh com. 1988, mem. hose thread com. 1988—; former chmn. joint apprenticeship com. Calif. State Marshal's Office Calif. Profl. Firefighters. Trustee Long Beach Police & Fire Meml. Trust Fund, 1979—. Recipient L.A. Cmty. Protectors award, 1985. Mem. Internat. Assn. Firefighters (chmn. grievance com. 1978-94, So. Calif. state rep. 1980-86), Long Beach Firefighter Union (pres. 1972-94, former bd. dirs., former treas.), Calif. State Firemen's Assn., Calif. State Fedn. Labor, L.A. County Fedn. Labor, Calif. Profl. Firefighters (1st dist. v.p. 1982-89, mem. legis. com. 1982-94, sec.-treas. 1989-94). Office: Long Beach Fire Dept 925 Harbor Plz Ste 100 Long Beach CA 90802-6411*

OMENN, GILBERT STANLEY, university dean, physician; b. Chester, Pa., Aug. 30, 1941; s. Leonard and Leah (Miller) O.; m. Martha Darling; children: Rachel Andrea, Jason Montgomery, David Matthew. AB, Princeton U., 1961; MD, Harvard U., 1965; PhD in Genetics, U. Wash., 1972. Intern Mass. Gen. Hosp., Boston, 1965-66; asst. resident in medicine Mass. Gen. Hosp., 1966-67; research assoc. NIH, Bethesda, Md., 1967-69; fellow U. Wash., 1969-71, asst. prof. medicine, 1971-74, assoc. prof., 1974-79, investigator Howard Hughes Med. Inst., 1976-77, prof., 1979—, prof. environ. health, 1981—, chmn. dept., 1981-83, dean Sch. Pub. Health and Community Medicine, 1982—; bd. dirs. Rohm & Haas Co., Amgen, BioTechniques Labs. Inc., Immune Response Corp., Clean Sites, Inc., Population Svcs. Internat., Pacific N.W. Pollution Prevention Rsch. Ctr.; White House fellow/spl. asst. to chmn. AEC, 1973-74; assoc. dir. Office Sci. and Tech. Policy, The White House, 1977-80; assoc. dir. human resources Office Mgmt. and Budget, 1980-81; vis. sr. fellow Wilson Sch. Pub. and Internat. Affairs, Princeton U., 1981; sci. and pub. policy fellow Brookings Instn., Washington, 1981-82; cons. govt. agys., Lifetime Cable Network; mem. Nat. Com. on the Environment, environ. adv. com. Rohm & Haas, Rene Dubos Ctr. for Human Environments, AFL-CIO Workplace Health Fund., Electric Power Rsch. Inst., Carnegie Commn. Task Force on Sci. and Tech. in Jud. and Regulatory Decision Making, adv. com. to dir., Ctrs. Disease Control, 1992—, adv. com. Critical Technologies Inst., RAND; mem. Pres.'s Coun., U. Calif., 1992—. Co-author: Clearing the Air, Reforming the Clean Air Act, 1981. Editor: (with others) Genetics, Environment and Behavior: Implications for Educational Policy, 1972; Genetic Control of Environmental Pollutants, 1984; Genetic Variability in Responses to Chemical Exposure, 1984, Environmental Biotechnology: Reducing Risks from Environmental Chemicals through Biotechnology, 1988, Biotechnology in Biodegradation, 1990, Biotechnology and Human Genetic Predisposition to Disease, 1990, Annual Review of Public Health, 1991, 92, 93, 94, Clinics in Geriatric Medicine, 1992; assoc. editor Cancer Rsch., Cancer Epidemiology, Biomarkers and Prevention, Environ. Rsch., Am. Jour. Med. Genetics, Am. Jour. Preventive Medicine; contbr. articles on cancer prevention, human biochem. genetics, prenatal diagnosis of inherited disorders, susceptibility to environ. agts., clin. medicine and health policy to profl. publs. Mem. President's Council on Spinal Cord Injury; mem. Nat. Cancer Adv. Bd., Nat. Heart, Lung and Blood Adv. Council, Wash. State Gov.'s Commn. on Social and Health Services, Ctr. for Excellence in Govt.; chmn. awards panel Gen. Motors Cancer Research Found., 1985-86; chmn. bd. Environ. Studies and Toxicology, Nat. Rsch. Coun., 1988-91; mem. Bd. Health Promotion and Disease Prevention, Inst. Medicine; mem. adv. com. Woodrow Wilson Sch., Princeton U., 1978-84; bd. dirs. Inst. for Sci. in Society; trustee Pacific Sci. Ctr., Fred Hutchinson Cancer Research Ctr., Seattle Symphony Orch., Seattle Youth Symphony Orch., Seattle Chamber Music Festival, Santa Fe Chamber Music Festival; mem. Citizens for a Hunger-Free Washington; chmn. rules com. Democratic Conv., King County, Wash., 1972. Served with USPHS, 1967-69. Recipient Research Career Devel. award USPHS, 1972; White House fellow, 1973-74. Fellow ACP, AAAS, Nat. Acad. Social Ins., Western Assn. Physicians, Hastings Ctr., Collegium Ramazzini; mem. Inst. Medicine of NAS, White House Fellows Assn., Am. Soc. Human Genetics, Western Soc. Clin. Rsch. Jewish. Home: 5100 NE 55th St Seattle WA 98105-2821 Office: U Wash Dean Sch Pub Health Box 357230 Seattle WA 98195-7230

ONAK, THOMAS PHILIP, chemistry educator; b. Omaha, July 30, 1932; s. Louis Albert and Louise Marie (Penner) O.; m. Sharon Colleen Neal, June 18, 1954. BA, Calif. State U., San Diego, 1954; PhD, U. Calif., Berkeley, 1957. Research chemist Olin Mathieson Chem. Corp., Pasadena, Calif., 1957-59; asst. prof. Calif. State U., Los Angeles, 1959-63, assoc. prof., 1963-66, prof. chemistry, 1966—. Author: Organoborane Chemistry, 1975; Contbr. articles to profl. jours., chpts. to books. Recipient Rsch. Career award NIH, 1973-78, Nat. award Am. Chem. Soc., 1990, Outstanding Prof. award Calif. State U., System, 1993-94; named Calif. Prof. of Yr. Carnegie Found. and Coun. for the Advancement and Support of Edn., 1995; Fulbright Rsch. fellow U. Cambridge, Eng., 1965-66. Home: PO Box 1477 South Pasadena CA 91031-1477 Office: Calif State U Dept Chemistry 5151 State U Dr Los Angeles CA 90032

ONCKEN, ELLEN LORRAINE, minister, speaker; b. Dallas, Dec. 28, 1957; d. Keith Loren and Mary Helen (Games) Riffe; m. Bradley Paul Oncken, Dec. 15, 1983; children: Michael, Tiffany, Stephen. BA in Psychology, Socialogy, English, Calif. Bapt. Coll., Riverside, 1980; MDiv, Midwestern Bapt. Theology Sem., Kansas City, Mo., M in Religious Edn. Min. Glen Avon Cmty. Ch., Riverside, Calif., 1980-81; min. spl. mission ministry Northgate Bapt. Ch., Kansas City, 1982-83; missionary Ch. of the Redeemer, Birmingham, Eng., 1985, 87; min., counselor Yucuipa Coll. Redlands (Calif.) U., 1988-90; tchr. John Jenkins Christian Acad., Santa Paula, Calif., 1990-91; min. Pleasant Valley Bapt. Ch., Camarillo, Calif., 1991-93; min., owner Value Power Sems. and Publs., Camarillo, 1993—; associational min. Blue River Bapt. Assn., Kansas City, 1981-84; staff mem. Midwestern Bapt. Sem., 1993—. Author: Arcade Ministry Manual, 1982, Value Power Study Bible, 1997. Mem. Am. Entrepreneurs Assn. (pres. 1994—), Phi Beta Kappa. Home and Office: 770 Marigras Ct Camarillo CA 93010

O'NEAL, SHAQUILLE RASHAUN, professional basketball player; b. Newark, Mar. 6, 1972; s. Philip A. Harrison and Lucille O'Neal. Student, La. State U. Center Orlando Magic, 1992-96, L.A. Lakers, 1996—. Appeared in movie Blue Chips, 1994, Kazaam, 1996. Named to Sporting News All-American first team, 1990-91; recipient Rookie of the Yr. award NBA, 1993; mem. NBA All-Star team, 1993, 94, Dream Team II, 1994; first pick overall, 1992 draft. Office: LA Lakers PO Box 10 Inglewood CA 90306

O'NEIL, W. SCOTT, publishing executive. Publ. Investor's Bus. Daily, L.A., 1992—. Office: Investor's Bus Daily 12655 Beatrice St Los Angeles CA 90066

O'NEILL, BRIAN, landmark administrator. Dir. Golden Gate Nat. Recreation Area, San Francisco. Office: Golden Gate Nat Rec Area Bldg 201 Fort Mason San Francisco CA 94117

O'NEILL, MAUREEN ANNE, city administrator, arts administrator; b. Seattle, Nov. 11, 1948; d. Robert P. and Barbara F. (Pettinger) O. BA in Sociology cum laude, Wash. State U., 1971; MA, Bowling Green State U., 1972. Grad. asst. dept. coll. student personnel Bowling Green (Ohio) State U., 1971-72; asst. coordinator coll. activities SUNY-Geneseo, 1972-75, acting coordinator coll. activities, 1975-76; regional mgr. northeast Kazuko Hillyer Internat. Agy., N.Y.C., 1976-77; mgr. lectures and concerts Meany Theater U. Wash., Seattle, 1977-81; mgr. performing and visual arts Parks and Recreation, City of Seattle, 1981-83, recreation dist. mgr., 1983-92, recreation mgr. north divsn., 1992—; cons. Nat. Endowment for Arts: Site Evaluator, 1980; interarts panel 1981; multi-music panel 1988, 89, 90; workshop presenter Washington Parks and Recreation, 1989, Washington Recreation and Parks to Washington State Arts Commn., 1988, 89, 90, bd. dirs. liaison; mem. program and edn. com. Seattle Art Mus., 1981—; workshop presenter Nat. Recreation and Parks Assn. Regional Confs., 1985-86; mem. conf. com. Internat. NW Parks and Recreation Assn. Conf., 1986. Bd. dirs. Bumbershoot-Seattle Arts Festival, 1979, 80; bd. dirs. Northwest Folklife Inc., 1982—, treas., 1985, 86, pres. 1986-89, chmn. edn. com., 1991-94, chair ad hoc com. NEA Advancement Grant, 1994-96; cantor Sacred Heart Ch., Seattle, 1982—; mem. Seattle Art Mus. Mem. Phi Beta Kappa, Mu Phi Epsilon, Alpha Delta Pi. Roman Catholic. Home: PO Box 19278 Seattle WA 98109-1278 Office: 100 Dexter Ave N Seattle WA 98109-5102

O'NEILL, MICHAEL, academic administrator; b. Washington, Sept. 2, 1938; s. John Patrick and Mary Lou (Maginnis) O'N.; m. Elfrieda Langemann, Apr. 10, 1993; 1 child, Susan Ewens. BA, St. Thomas Coll., 1960; MA, Cath. U., 1964; EdD, Harvard U., 1967. Supt. Cath. Diocese of Spokane (Wash.), 1967-76; assoc. prof., dir. pvt. sch. adminstrn. U. San Francisco, Sch. Edn., 1976-78, dean, prof., 1978-81, prof., 1981-82; dir. fundraising No. Calif. Nuclear Weapons Freeze, 1982; prof., dir. inst. non-profit orgn. mgmt. U. San Francisco, Coll. Profl. Studies, 1983—; tchr. Boston Coll., 1984, Ft. Wright Coll., 1970, 75, U. Notre Dame, 1968, 69. Author: How Good are Catholic Schools?, 1967, New Schools in a New Church, 1971, The Third America: Emergence of the Nonprofit Sector in the United States, 1989, Ethics in Nonprofit Management: A Collection of Cases, 1990; co-author: (with Dennis R. Young) Educating Managers of Nonprofit Organizations, 1988, (with Herman Gallegos) Hispanics and the Nonprofit Sector, 1991, (with Teresa Odendahl) Women and Power in the Nonprofit Sector, 1994; assoc. editor Nonprofit Mgmt. and Leadership, 1989—; mem. editl. bd. Harvard Ednl. Review, 1965-67; contbr. articles to profl. jours. Mem. membership com. Ind. Sector, 1993—, rsch.com., 1989-92; bd. dirs. Nat. Acad. Ctrs. Coun., 1991—, Support Ctr./Cmty. Tng. and Devel., 1984-88. Teaching fellow Harvard U., 1965-67. Mem. Assn. for Rsch. Non-profit Orgns. and Vol. Action (bd. dirs. 1993—, pres. 1996—). Roman Catholic. Office: U San Francisco Coll Profl Studies 2130 Fulton St San Francisco CA 94117-1080

O'NEILL, MICHAEL FOY, business educator; b. Milw., Apr. 16, 1943; s. Edward James and Marcellian (Wesley) O'N.; m. Karen Lynn Shoots, June 13, 1968; children: Kristine, Brenna. BBA, Ohio State U., 1966; PhD in Bus. Adminstrn., U. Oreg., 1978. Cons. Robert E. Miller and Assocs., San Francisco, 1969-73; mem. faculty Calif. State U., Chico, 1971-73, 1980—, U. Oreg., Eugene, 1974-77, U. Ariz., Tucson, 1977-79; pres. Decision Sci. Inst., Atlanta, 1986-87, v.p., 1985-86. Contbr. articles to profl. jours. Served with U.S. Army, 1962-68. Recipient Dean's Research award Calif. State U., Chico, 1981. Home: 2819 North Ave Chico CA 95973-0916 Office: Calif State U Dept Fin and Mktg Chico CA 95926

O'NEILL, SALLIE BOYD, education educator, business owner, sculptor; b. Ft. Lauderdale, Fla., Feb. 17, 1926; d. Howard Prindle and Sarah Frances (Clark) Boyd; AA, Stephens Coll., 1945; m. Roger H. Noden, July 8, 1945; children: Stephanie Ann Ballard, Ross Hopkins Noden; m. Russell R. O'Neill, June 30, 1967. Course coord. UCLA Extension, 1960-72, specialist continuing edn. dept. human devel., acad. appointment, 1972-83; pres. Learning Adventures, Inc., 1985-86; v.p., CFO The Learning Network, Inc., 1985-86; ednl. cons., 1986—; sculptor, 1987—. Bd. dirs. Everywoman's Village, Sherman Oaks, Calif., 1988—, v.p. 1993-95. Mem. Women in Bus. (v.p., bd. dirs. 1976-77, 86-87), Golden State Sculpture Assn., UCLA Assn. Acad. Women. Democrat. Home and Studio: 15430 Longbow Dr Sherman Oaks CA 91403-4910

ONG, ERNEST GRANT, auditor, researcher, accountant; b. Phoenix, Ariz., Sept. 12, 1951; s. Samuel and Chack (Yee) O. AA, Solano C.C., 1977; BS, Ariz. State U., 1976; MPA, U. Ariz., 1981. Cert. C.C. instr. Math. aide Ames Rsch. Ctr., Moffett Field, Calif., 1979; program analyst EPA, San Francisco, 1982; auditor State of Calif.-Contr., Sacramento, 1983-92. Treas. Davis (Calif.) Chinese Christian Ch., 1988-92, Grad. Pub. Adminstrn. Community, L.A., 1993-96; mem. Asian Pacific Policy and Planning Coun., L.A., 1993—; Asian Pacific Am. Cmty. Rsch. Roundtable, 1995—. Staff sgt. USAF, 1974-77.

ONISHI, YASUO, environmental researcher; b. Osaka, Japan, Jan. 25, 1943; came to U.S., 1969; s. Osamu and Tokiko (Domukai) O.; m. Esther Anna Stronczek, Jan 22, 1972; children: Anna Tokiko and Lisa Michiyo. BS, U. Osaka Prefecture, 1967, MS, 1969; PhD, U. Iowa, 1972. Rsch. engr. U. Iowa, Iowa City, 1972-74; sr. rsch. engr. Battelle Meml. Inst., Richland, Wash., 1974-77, staff engr., 1977—, mgr. rsch. program office, 1984-92; adj. grad. faculty Wash. State U., Tri-Cities, 1993—. Co-author: Principles of Health Risk Assessment, 1985, several other environ. books; contbr. articles to profl. jours.; featured in TV program NOVA. Recipient Best Platform Presentation award ASTM, 1979. Mem. ASCE (chmn. task com. 1986—), IAEA (advisor on environ. issues, U.S. coord. water and soil assessment bilateral joint work on Chernobyl nuclear accident), Nat. Coun. Radiation Protection and Measurements (adj., mem. task com. 1983-96), Sigma Xi. Lutheran. Home: 144 Spengler Rd Richland WA 99352-1971 Office: Battelle Pacific NW Labs Batelle Blvd Richland WA 99352

ONOFRIO, JOE FREDERICK, III, piano company executive; b. Denver, Nov. 26, 1955; s. Joe Frederick Jr. and Vivien C. (Piogossi) O.; m. Paula Marie Vann, Dec. 23, 1963; children: Stephania, Olivia, Angelica, Sylvana Rosa. BS in Acctg., Bus. Adminstrn., Regis U., 1981. Outfitter, horse wrangler Colo., Ariz., Colo., Mont., Ariz., 1969-77; piano tech. Onofrio Piano Co., Denver, 1977-81; mfrs. rep. J&B Importers, Denver, 1981-91; pres. Onofrio Piano Co., Denver, 1991—. Sponsor Opera Colo., Denver, Colo. Ballet, Denver, 1993—, Ctrl. City (Colo.) Opera, 1993—. Recipient Joseph A. Ryan Excellence in Bus. Adminstrn. award Regis U., 1981. Mem. Alpha Sigma Nu. Republican. Roman Catholic. Office: Joe Onofrio Piano Co 1332 S Broadway Denver CO 80210-2205

ONOPA, ROBERT LAWRENCE, English language educator; b. Chgo., Jan. 5, 1943; s. Alexander and Anna (Gacioch) O.; m. Janet Kemble, Mar. 15, 1980; children: Ryder Kalani, Alexi Kaikaina. BA, U. Ill., 1964; MA, U. Conn., 1966; PhD, Northwestern U., 1974. Asst. prof. English U. Hawaii, Honolulu, 1974-80, assoc. prof., 1980—; Fulbright lectr. West Africa, 1970. Author: Pleasure Tube, 1979; co-editor: Triquar. Mag., 1979-80. Creative fellowship Nat. Endowment for the Arts, 1987. Home: 1040 Maunawili Loop Kailua HI 96734-4621 Office: U Hawaii at Manoa Dept English Honolulu HI 96822

ONYEADOR, EMMANUEL OSITA, mathematics and computer educator; b. Okigwe, Imo, Nigeria, Mar. 4, 1957; came to U.S., 1985; s. Felix Anitche and Justina Mbokwo (Ezumah) O. BS in Physics with honors, U. Ife, Ile-Ife, Nigeria, 1982; BS in Computer Sci., San Francisco State U., 1991, MA in Edn., Computer Applications, 1993. Cert. tchr., Calif. Math. educator Oakland (Calif.) Unified Sch. Dist., 1987—, technology curriculum specialist, 1993—; exec. com. mem. Oakland Unified Sch. Dist./U. Calif. Partnership for Math., 1992-94; chmn. acad. achievement com. Comer process King Estates, Oakland, 1992—; rsch. assoc. Stanford Linear Accelerator Ctr., Palo Alto, Calif., 1992; advisor Leadership Inst. Chabot Observatory & Sci. Ctr., Oakland, 1994; physics/calculus educator Mills Coll., Oakland, 1991; curr. developer Oakland Unified Sch. Dist., 1991—; dir. Computer Comm. and Repair Acad., 1996—; ednl. software developer King Estates, Oakland, 1991-94; curr. adviser KDOL-TV, Oakland, 1994—; instr. computer techs. in edn. U. Calif. Extension, Berkeley, 1995—; chmn. telecom. com. SMARTNET project Chabot Obs. and Sci. Ctr., 1994—. Editor/developer: (curriculum) Math A, 1991, Math B, 1991; developer: (interactive software)

Algebra Project Software, 1992, (activity software) Fractals Activity for Math., 1994. Bd.dirs. East Bay Computer Using Edn., 1996—; cons. on various projects. Mem. NEA, Am. Phys. Soc., Assn. Computing Machinery, Physic and Engring. Physic Assn., Calif. Tchrs. Assn. (Educators award 1991), Oakland Edn. Assn. (Super Tchr. 1992). Roman Catholic. Home: 1083 45th St Emeryville CA 94608-3329 Office: Oakland Unified Sch Dist 8251 Fontaine St Oakland CA 94605-4109

OOLIE, DARLENE, advertising executive; b. Rochester, N.Y., Nov. 14, 1961. BBA in Mktg. cum laude, Pace U., 1983. Coder, norms mgr., project dir. ASI Market Rsch., L.A., 1983-86; sr. rsch. project dir. Phillips-Ramsey Advt., San Diego, 1986—. Mem. Am. Mktg. Assn. Office: Phillips-Ramsey Advt 6863 Friars Rd San Diego CA 92108-1121

OPFELL, JOHN BURTON, chemical engineer, educator; b. Cushing, Okla., July 24, 1924; s. Edward Uriah and Carrie Evelyn (Walker) O.; m. Olga Anna Strandvold, Sept. 10, 1954; children: Christopher Kaj, Thane Fredrick, Jon Guido. BS, U. Wis., 1945; MS, Calif. Inst. Tech., 1947, PhD, 1954; MBA, Stanford U., 1951. Registered profl. engr., Calif. Engr. Stanolind Oil and Gas Co., Tulsa, 1947-49, Cutter Labs., Berkeley, Calif., 1955-61, Dynamic Sci. Corp., South Pasadena, Calif., 1961-64, Philco-Ford Corp., Newport Beach, Calif., 1964-69; asst. mgr. corp. planning Sunkist Growers, Sherman Oaks, Calif., 1970-73; asst. to exec. v.p. Henningson, Durham and Richardson, Santa Barbara, Calif., 1980-83; engr. AiResearch Mfg. Co., Torrance, Calif., 1973-80, AlliedSignal Aerospace Co., Torrance, Calif., 1983-93; v.p. Ideation Internat., Santa Monica, Calif., 1993-95; lectr. Calif. Inst. Tech., Pasadena, 1954, U. Calif., Santa Barbara, 1973, 82, Calif. State U., Northridge, 1986. Author: (with others) Momentum Transfer in Fluids, 1956, Equations of State for Hydrocarbons, 1959; contbr. articles to profl. jours. Lt. (j.g.) USNR, 1944-54. Fellow AAAS, Royal Soc. Health (London); mem. AIChE, Ops. Rsch. Soc. Am., Masons, Sigma Xi. Democrat. Home: 1007 Park Circle Dr Torrance CA 90502-2817

OPFER, NEIL DAVID, construction educator, consultant; b. Spokane, Wash., June 3, 1954; s. Gus Chris and Alice Ann (Blom) O. BS in Bldg. Theory cum laude, Wash. State U., 1976, BA in Econs. cum laude, 1977, BA in Bus. cum laude, 1977; MS in Mgmt., Purdue U., 1982. Cert. cost engr., cert. project mgr. Estimator Standard Oil (Chevron), Richmond, Calif., 1975; gen. carpenter forman Opfer Constrn. Corp., Spokane, 1976; assoc. engr. Inland Steel Corp., East Chgo., Ind., 1977-78; millwright supr. Inland Steel Corp., 1978-79, field engr., 1979-82, project engr., 1982-84, sr. engr., 1984-87; asst. prof. construction and construction mgmt. Western Mich. U., Kalamazoo, 1987-89; asst. prof. construction and construction mgmt. U. Nev., Las Vegas, 1989-95, assoc. prof. construction and construction mgmt., 1995—. Contbr. articles to publs. Bd. dirs. Christmas in April, 1993—, Habitat for Humanity, 1991—. Mem. Am. Welding Soc. (bd. dirs. 1982-87), Am. Inst. Constructors, Am. Assn. Cost Engrs. (nat. bd. dirs. 1995-97, Order of Engr. award 1989), Project Mgmt. Inst., Constrn. Mgmt. Assn., Tau Beta Pi (life), Phi Kappa Phi (life). Methodist. Home: 1920 Placid Ravine Las Vegas NV 89117 Office: Univ Nev 4505 S Maryland Pkwy Las Vegas NV 89154-4015

OPITZ, BERNARD FRANCIS, JR., postal service administrator; b. Springfield, Mass., Dec. 9, 1947; s. Bernard Francis and Bertha Margaret (Diamond) O.; m. Elena Louise Cotti, Oct. 10, 1970 (div. 1979); children: Bernard Francis III, Douglas Richard; m. Patricia Ann Menzer, Feb. 29, 1980 (div. May 1994); 1 stepchild, Karyn Renee Beaty. AAS, Springfield Tech. Inst., 1968. Sr. detail draftsman Combustion Engring., Windsor, Conn., 1968-71; distbn. clk. U.S. Post Office, 1966-68; with U.S. Postal Svc., Springfield, 1971-89, supr. prodn. planning, 1978-80, customer requirements specialist, 1980-89; dir. city ops. U.S. Postal Svc., Stamford, Conn., 1989-92; sr. ops. performance analyst U.S. Postal Svc. Hdqrs., Washington, 1992-94; ops. support specialist U.S. Postal Svc. Pacific Area Office, San Bruno, Calif., 1994—. Mem. Am. Mgmt. Assn., Am. Softball Assn. (umpire 1993—), Sacred Heart Alumni Assn., Springfield Tech. Alumni Assn. Roman Catholic. Office: US Postal Svc In-Plant Support 400 Oyster Point Blvd South San Francisco CA 94099-1100

OPITZ, JOHN MARIUS, clinical geneticist, pediatrician; b. Hamburg, Germany, Aug. 15, 1935; came to U.S., 1950, naturalized, 1957; s. Friedrich and Erica Maria (Quadt) O.; m. Susan O. Lewin; children: Leigh, Teresa, John, Chrisanthi, Emma. BA, State U. Iowa, 1956, MD, 1959; DSc (hon.), Mont. State U., 1983; MD (hon.), U. Kiel, Germany, 1986. Diplomate Am. Bd. Pediatrics, Am. Bd. Med. Genetics. Intern, State U. Iowa Hosp., 1959-60, resident in pediatrics, 1960-61; resident and chief resident in pediatrics U. Wis. Hosp., Madison, 1961-62; fellow in pediatrics and med. genetics U. Wis., 1962-64, asst. prof. med. genetics and pediatrics, 1964-69, assoc. prof., 1969-72, prof., 1972-79; dir. Wis. Clin. Genetics Ctr., 1974-79; clin. prof. med. genetics and pediatrics U. Wash., Seattle, 1979—; adj. prof. medicine, biology, history and philosophy, vet. rsch. and vet. sci. Mont. State U., Bozeman, 1979-94, McKay lectr., 1992, Univ. prof. med. humanities MSU. Bozeman, 1994—; adj. prof. pediatrics, med. genetics U. Wis., Madison, 1979—, Class of 1947 Disting. prof., U. of Wis., 1992; coordinator Shodair Mont. Regional Genetic Svcs. Program, Helena, 1979-82; chmn. dept. med. genetics Shodair Children's Hosp., Helena, 1983-94; dir. Found. Devel. and Med. Genetics, Helena, Mont.; pres. Heritage Genetics P.C., Helena, 1996; Farber lectr. Soc. Pediatric Pathology, 1987; Joseph Garfunkel lectr. So. Ill. U., Springfield, 1987, McKay lectr. Mont. State U., 1992; Warren Wheeler vis. prof. Columbus (Ohio) Children's Hospital, 1987; Bea Fowlow lectr. in med. genet. U. Calgary, 1996; 1st vis. prof. Hanseatic U. Found. of Lübeck, 1996. Editor, author 14 books; founder, editor in chief Am. Jour. Med. Genetics, 1977—; mng. editor European Jour. Pediatrics, 1977-85; contbr. numerous articles on clin. genetics. Chair Mont. Com. for Humanities, 1991. Recipient Pool of Bethesda award for excellence in mental retardation rsch. Bethesda Luth. Home, 1988, Med. Alumni Citation U. Wis., 1989, Col. Harlan Sanders Lifetime Achievement award for work in the field of genetic scis. March of Dimes, Purkinje medal Czech Soc. Medicine, Mendel medal Czech Soc. Med. Genetics, 1996, Internat. prize Phoenix-Anni Verdi for Genetic Rsch., 1996. Fellow AAAS, Am. Coll. Med. Genetics (founder); mem. German Acad. Scientists Leopoldina, Am. Soc. Human Genetics, Am. Pediatric Soc., Soc. Pediatric Rsch., Am. Bd. Med. Genetics, Birth Defects Clin. Genetic Soc., Am. Inst. Biol. Scis., Am. Soc. Zoologists, Teratology Soc., Genetic Soc. Am., European Soc. Human Genetics, Soc. Study Social Biology, Am. Acad. Pediatrics, German Soc. Pediatrics (hon.), Western Soc. Pediatrics Rsch. (emeritus), Italian Soc. Med. Genetics (hon.), Israel Soc. Med. Genetics (hon.), Russian Soc. Med. Genetics (hon.), So. Africa Soc. Med. Genetics (hon.), Japanese Soc. Human Genetics (hon.), Sigma Xi. Democrat. Roman Catholic. Home: 2930 E Craig Dr Salt Lake City UT 84109 Office: U Utah Sch Medicine Primary Childrens Med Ctr 100 N Medical Dr Salt Lake City UT 84113

OPOTOWSKY, MAURICE LEON, newspaper editor; b. New Orleans, Dec. 13, 1931; s. Sol and Fannie (Latter) O.; m. Madeleine Duhamel, Feb. 28, 1959 (dec.); children: Didier Sol Duhamel, Joelle Duhamel, Arielle Duhamel (dec.); m. Bonnie Feibleman, May 4, 1991. Student, Tulane U., 1949-51; B.A. cum laude, Williams Coll., 1953. Reporter Berkshire Eagle, Pittsfield, Mass., 1951-53; pub. Sea Coast Echo, Bay St. Louis, Miss., 1953-54; reporter U.P.I., 1956-62; feature editor Newsday, Ronkonkoma, N.Y., 1962-64; Suffolk day editor Newsday, 1964-65, Nassau night editor, 1965-67, nat. editor, 1967-70, Suffolk editor, 1970-72; dir. L.I. Mag., 1972; day editor Press-Enterprise, Riverside, Calif., 1973-84, mng. editor features/adminstrn., 1984-87, sr. mng. editor, 1987-92, mng. editor, 1992—; chief N.Y. State Syndicate Service, 1961-74; mem. Calif. Freedom of Info. Exec. Com., sec., 1979-80, treas., 1980-81, v.p., 1981-82, pres., 1982-83. Trustee Harbor Country Day Sch., 1970-72; bd. dirs. Calif. Newspaper Editor Conf. Bd., 1978-83; mem. Smithtown (N.Y.) Hunt, 1970-73, West Hills Hunt, 1976-80, Santa Fe Hunt, Whip, 1985—; co-chmn. Calif. Bench-Bar Media Com.; mem. adv. coun. dept. comm. Calif. State U., Fullerton, 1995—. Served with AUS, 1954-56. Recipient Lifetime Achievement award Calif. 1st Amendment Assembly, 1997. Mem. AP News Execs. Calif. (chmn. 1986-87), Calif. 1st Amendment Coalition (pres., treas.), Calif. Soc. Newspaper Editors (bd. dirs., vice chmn. steering com. 1983), AP Mng. Editors Assn., Am. Soc. Newspaper Editors. Office: Press Enterprise Co 3512 14th St Riverside CA 92501-3814

OPPEDAHL, PHILLIP EDWARD, computer company executive; b. Renwick, Iowa, Sept. 17, 1935; s. Edward and Isadore Hannah (Gangstead) O.; B.S. in Naval Sci., Navy Postgrad. Sch., 1963, M.S. in Nuclear Physics, 1971; M.S. in Systems Mgmt., U. S.C., 1978; m. Sharon Elaine Ree, Aug. 3, 1957 (dec. Aug. 1989); children: Gary Lynn, Tamra Sue, Sue Ann, Lisa Kay. Commd. ensign U.S. Navy, 1956, advanced through grades to capt., 1977; with Airborne Early Warning Squadron, 1957-59, Anti-Submarine Squadron, 1959-65; asst. navigator USS Coral Sea, 1965-67; basic jet flight instr., 1967-69; student Armed Forces Staff Coll., 1971; test group dir. Def. Nuclear Agy., 1972-74; weapons officer USS Oriskany, 1974-76; program mgr. for armament Naval Air Systems Command, Washington, 1977-79; test dir. Def. Nuclear Agy., Kirtland AFB, N.Mex., 1979-82, dep. comdr. Def. Nuclear Agy., 1982-83; pres., chief exec. officer Am. Systems, Albuquerque, 1983—; dir., bd. dirs. BASIS Internat., 1991—. Pres., bd. dirs. Casa Esperanza, 1990-92. Decorated Disting. Service medal. Mem. Naval Inst., Am. Nuclear Soc., Aircraft Owners and Pilots Assn., Assn. Naval Aviation Navy League. Lutheran. Author: Energy Loss of High Energy Electrons in Beryllium, 1971; Understanding Contractor Motivation and Incentive Contracts, 1977. Home and Office: 5850 Eubank Blvd NE # B 49 Albuquerque NM 87111 *Personal philosophy: The remainder of my life is dedicated to giving back to the universe the life, love and energy that the universe has given me.*

OPPEL, ANDREW JOHN, computer systems consultant; b. Kerrville, Tex., Dec. 22, 1952; s. Wallace Churchill and Anne Kathryn (Smith) O.; m. Laura Lee Partridge, Aug. 26, 1972; children: Keith Andrew, Luke Andrew. BA in Computer Sci., Transylvania U., 1974. Computer programmer Johns Hopkins U., Balt., 1974-77; data base programmer Equitable Trust Co., Balt., 1977-78; sr. programmer, analyst Md. Casualty Co., Balt., 1978-79; sr. programmer, analyst Levi Strauss & Co., San Francisco, 1979-82, sr. requirements mgr., 1982-84, tech. cons., 1984-91, tech. advisor, 1991-93, mgr. database mgmt. sys., 1994-96, sr. sys. architect, 1996-97; sr. cons. Triadigm Internat., San Francisco, 1997—; instr. U. Calif. Extension, Berkeley, 1983—. Ops. officer Alameda County Radio Amateur Civil Emergency Svc., San Leandro, Calif., 1980-92; cub master Boy Scouts Am., Alameda, Calif., 1991-92; referee U.S. Soccer Fedn., Alameda, 1988—, referee instr., 1996—. Democrat. Episcopalian. Home: 1308 Burbank St Alameda CA 94501-3946 Office: Triadigm Internat Ste 1220 345 California St San Francisco CA 94104-2621

OPPELT, NORMAN THEODORE, park researcher, retired psychology educator; b. Chgo., Feb. 1, 1930; s. Norman Theodore Sr. and Jeannette (Willey) O.; m. Patricia Louise Bast, June 6, 1954; children: Eric Theodore, Karen Elizabeth. BS in Zoology, Colo. State U., 1954; MA in Psychology, U. No. Colo., 1955; PhD in Counseling Psychology, Mich. State U., 1962. Lic. psychologist, Colo. Dean of men U. No. Colo., Greeley, 1960-64, v.p. student affairs, 1964-70, prof. psychology, 1967-87, asst. to pres., 1970-72, chair dept. coll. student pers. adminstrn., 1972-83, prof. emeritus, 1987—; park ranger, rschr. Mesa Verde Nat. Park, Colo., 1987—. Author: Guide to Prehistoric Ruins, 1981, Southwestern Pottery, 1988, Tribal Indian Colleges, 1990, Earth, Water and Fire, 1991. Advisor Blue Key, 1960; v.p. Nat. Assn. Student Pers. Adminstrs., 1970-72; candidate City Coun., Greeley, 1973. Sgt. USMC, 1950-52, Korea. Mem. High Plains Archaeol. Soc. (pres. 1975-76), Colo. Psychol. Assn., Colo. Archaeol. Soc. (adv. com. 1964—), Phi Delta Kappa, Sigma Alpha Epsilon (regional v.p. 1964-68). Home: 2218 25th St Greeley CO 80631

OPPERMAN, HAL N., art historian; b. Kansas City, Mo., Oct. 18, 1938; s. Halbert Hoover and Anna Clara (Niedermeyer) O.; m. Isabelle Catherine Noiret, July 4, 1966 (div. Jan. 1985); children: Anne Elisabeth Opperman Reese, F. Lucien; m. JoLynn Edwards, Sept. 5, 1989. BA, Knox Coll., 1960; AM, U. Chgo., 1963, PhD, 1972. Asst. prof. art history U. Wash., Seattle, 1967-74, assoc. prof. art history, 1974-83, prof. art history, 1983-94, prof. emeritus, 1994—, chair comparative history of ideas, 1979-82; gen. editor fine arts Corbis Corp., Bellevue, Wash., 1991-96; mem. Art Bull. Adv. Bd., 1990-94; mem. Gottschalk Prize Com., 1985, chair, 1986; mem. nat. screening com. Fulbright Grant Program, 1992-94; mem. editorial adv. bd. Eighteenth-Century Studies, 1993-96. author: Jean-Baptiste Oudry, 1977 (Prix Cailleux), (exhbn. catalogue) Jean-Baptiste Oudry, 1982-83; contbr. numerous articles to profl. publs. Fulbright scholar, 1965-67, Nat. Merit scholar, 1956. Mem. Wash. Ornithol. Soc. (editor jour., bd. dirs. 1989—), Am. Soc. Eighteenth-Century Studies, Coll. Art Assn., Société de l'Histoire de l'Art Français. Home: PO Box 286 Medina WA 98039-0286

ORBACH, RAYMOND LEE, physicist, educator; b. Los Angeles, July 12, 1934; s. Morris Albert and Mary Ruth (Miller) O.; m. Eva Hannah Spiegler, Aug. 26, 1956; children: David Miller, Deborah Hedwig, Thomas Randolph. BS, Calif. Inst. Tech., 1956; PhD, U. Calif., Berkeley, 1960. NSF postdoctoral fellow Oxford U., 1960-61; asst. prof. applied physics Harvard U., 1961-63; prof. physics UCLA, 1963-92, asst. vice chancellor acad. change and curriculum devel., 1970-72, chmn. acad. senate L.A. divsn., 1976-77, provost Coll. Letters and Sci., 1982-92; chancellor U. Calif., Riverside, 1992—; mem. physics adv. panel NSF, 1970-73; mem. vis. com. Brookhaven Nat. Lab., 1970-74; mem. materials rsch. lab. adv. panel NSF, 1974-77; mem. Nat. Commn. on Rsch., 1978-80; chmn. 16th Internat. Conf. on Low Temperature Physics, 1981; Joliot Curie prof. Ecole Superieure de la Physique et Chimie Industrielle de la Ville de Paris, 1982, chmn. Gordon Rsch. Conf. on Fractals, 1986; Lorentz prof. U. Leiden, Netherlands, 1987; Raymond and Beverly Sackler lectr. Tel Aviv U., 1989; faculty rsch. lectr. UCLA, 1990; Andrew Lawson lectr. U. Calif., Riverside, 1992; mem. external rev. com. Nat. High Magnetic Fields Lab., 1994—. Author: (with A.A. Manenkov) SpinLattice Relaxation in Ionic Solids, 1966; Div. assoc. editor Phys. Rev. Letters, 1980-83, Jour. Low Temperature Physics, 1980-90, Phys. Rev., 1983—; contbr. articles to profl. jours. Alfred P. Sloan Found. fellow, 1963-67; NSF sr. postdoctoral fellow Imperial Coll., 1967-68; Guggenheim fellow Tel Aviv U., 1973-74. Fellow Am. Phys. Soc. (chmn. nominations com. 1981-82, counselor-at-large 1987-91, chmn. divsn. condensed matter 1990-91); mem. AAAS (chairperson steering group physics sect.), NSF (mem. rsch. adv. com. divsn. materials 1992-93), Phys. Soc. (London), Univ. Rsch. Assn. (chair coun. pres. 1993), Sigma Xi, Phi Beta Kappa, Tau Beta Pi. Home: 4171 Watkins Dr Riverside CA 92507-4738 Office: U Calif Riverside Chancellor's Office Riverside CA 92521-0101

ORCUTT, JAMES CRAIG, ophthalmologist; b. Holyoke, Colo., July 22, 1946; s. John Potter and Irene M. (Falk) O.; m. Barbara McCallum, Feb. 9, 1974; children: John, Gale. BPh in Pharmacy, U. Colo., Boulder, 1969; PhD in Pharmacology, U. Colo., Denver, 1976, MD, 1977. Diplomate Am. Bd. Ophthalmology. Intern U. Wash., Seattle, 1977-78, resident, 1978-81; fellow in orbital disease Moorfields Eye Hosp., London, 1981-82; fellow in neuro-ophthalmology Hosp. for Nervous Diseases and Great Ormond St. Hosp., London, 1982; asst. prof. ophthalmology U. Wash., Seattle, 1983-88, adj. prof. otolaryngology, 1987-88, assoc. prof. ophthalmology/adj. assoc. prof. otolargyngology, 1988-95, prof. ophthalmology, 1995—; chief ophthalmology Seattle Vets. Affairs Ctr., 1983—; ophthalmology cons. Vets. Affairs Ctrl. Office, Washington, 1993—. Pres. bd. trustees Northwest Sch., Seattle, 1996—. Office: U Wash Dept Ophthalmology Box 356485 Seattle WA 98195

ORD, LINDA BANKS, artist; b. Provo, Utah, May 24, 1947; d. Willis Merrill and Phyllis (Clark) Banks; m. Kenneth Stephen Ord, Sept. 3, 1971; children: Jason, Justin, Kristin. BS, Brigham Young U., 1970; BFA, U. Mich., 1987; MA, Wayne State U., 1990. Asst. prof. Sch. Art U. Mich., Ann Arbor, 1994—; juror Southeastern Mich. Scholastic Art Award Competition, Pontiac, 1992, Scarab Club Watercolor Exhbn., Detroit, 1991, Women in Art Nat. Exhbn., Farmington Hills, Mich., 1991, U. Mich. Alumni Exhbn., 1989-90. One-woman shows Atrium Gallery, Mich., 1990, 91; group shows include Am. Coll., Bryn Mawr, Pa., Riverside (Calif.) Art Mus., Kirkpatrick Mus., Oklahoma City, Montgomery (Ala.) Mus. Fine Arts, Columbus (Ga.) Mus., Brigham Young U., Provo, Utah, Kresge Art Mus., Lansing, Mich., U. Mich., Ann Arbor, Detroit Inst. Arts, Kirkpatrick Ctr. Mus. Complex, Oklahoma City, 1994, Riverside (Calif.) Art Mus., 1995, San Bernadino County Mus., Redlands, Calif., 1996, Neville Mus., Green Bya, Wis., 1996, Downey Mus. Art, Calif., 1996, Detroit Inst. Arts, 1996, Gallery Contemporary Art, U. Colo., Colorado Springs, 1996; works in many pvt. and pub. collections including Kelly Svcs., Troy, Mich., FHP Internat., Fountain Valley, Calif., Swords Into Plowshares Gallery, Detroit; work included in: (books) The Artistic Touch, 1995, Artistic Touch 2, 1996; (mag.) Watercolor, An Am. Artist, 1996. Chairperson nat. giving fund Sch. Art, U. Mich., 1993; Sch. Art rep. Coun. Alumni Socs., U. Mich., 1992—. Recipient 1st Pl. award Swords Into Plowshares Internat. Exhbn., Detroit, 1989, Silver award Ga. Watercolor Soc. Internat. Exhbn., 1991, Pres.'s award Watercolor Okla. Nat. Exhbn., Oklahoma City, 1992, Flint Jour. award Buckham Gallery Nat. Exhbn., 1993, Ochs Meml. award N.E. Watercolor Soc. Nat. Exhbn., Goshen, N.Y., 1993, Color Q award Ga. Watercolor Soc., 1994, St. Cuthberts award Tex. Watercolor Soc., 1996, many state and nat. painting awards. Mem. U. Mich. Alumni Assn. (bd. dirs. 1992—, Sch. Art rep.), U. Mich. Sch. Art Alumni Soc. (bd. dirs. 1989-91, pres.), Mich. Watercolor Soc. (chairperson 1992-93, bd. dirs. adv. 1993-94).

ORDUNO, ROBERT DANIEL, artist, painter, sculptor; b. Ventura, Calif., Sept. 5, 1933; s. Octavio and Mary G.; children: Patrice Schulman, Nicole Franco. Pvt. and group tchr., Santa Fe, 1990—, Australia, 1993; guest lectr. Australian Coun. on Adult Edn., 1993; interviewed on local radio stas., 1996. Exhibited in Great Falls Tribune, J.M. Swanson, 1985, Gazette, Cody Bur, Wyo., Tom Howard, 1987, Aurora, Great Falls, Mont., Shirley Edam Diaz, 1988, S.W. Art Mag., J.M. Swanson, 1990; featured artist Shaman's Drum, 1992, The Advocate, Tasmania, Australia, 1993, The New Mexican, Santa Fe, 1994, Wheelright Mus. Am. Indian, Santa Fe, 1995, The World Times, 1995, Seasons Quarterly, 1996; featured artist and cover image Internat. Fine Art Collector, 1992, cover and featured artist Informart Mag., 1994. Recipient Best Oil, Denver Indian Mkt., Pine Ridge S.D., 1985, 86, 87, 1st and 2d graphics Red Cloud Indian Sch., Best Painting artists choice Great Falls Native Am. Exhibit, James Bama award Best of Show, Best Contemporary Painting Buffalo Bill Hist. Ctr., Cody, Wyo., 1987, Best Painting Artists Choice award Great Falls Native Am. Exhibit, 1989, Best Show award, 1993. Home: 153 Calle Don Jose Santa Fe NM 87501-2391

O'REGAN, DEBORAH, association executive, lawyer; b. New Prague, Minn., Aug. 30, 1953; d. Timothy A. and Ermalinda (Brinkman) O'R.; m. Ron Kahlenbeck, Sept. 29, 1984; 1 child, Katherine. BA, Coll. of St. Catherine, 1975; JD, William Mitchell Coll. of Law, 1980. Bar: Ala. 1982, Minn. 1980. Asst. city atty. City of Bloomington, Minn., 1978-81, asst. city mgr., 1981-82; CLE dir. Alaska Bar Assn., Anchorage, 1982-84, exec. dir., 1985—; mem. task force on gender equality State Fed. Joint Commn., Anchorage, 1991—; mem. selection com. U.S. Magistrate Judge, U.S. Dist of Ala., 1992; mem. adv. bd. Anchorage Daily News, 1991-93. Mem. Nat. Assn. Bar Execs. (mem. exec. com.). Office: Alaska Bar Assn 510 L St Ste 602 Anchorage AK 99501-1964

O'REILLY, SEAN JOSEPH, editor; b. Bradford, Eng., Feb. 22, 1952; s. Sean and Anne (Hillam) O'R.; m. Brenda Sue Davis, Dec. 8, 1990; children: Clement Matthew, Seumas Xavier, Liam David, Tobias Joseph. BA in Psychology and Philosophy, U. Dallas. Author: Politics and the Soul, 1993; editor: Travelers' Tales: France, 1995, Travelers' Tales: Hong Kong, 1996, Travelers' Tales: San Francisco, 1996, Travelers' Tales: Paris, 1997; publisher The National Organ, 1995. With USN, 1987-95. Republican. Roman Catholic. Home: 19616 N 51st Dr Glendale AZ 85308 Office: Travelers' Tales 10 Napier Ln San Francisco CA 94133

O'REILLY, T. MARK, real estate executive; b. Cleve., Apr. 10, 1944; s. Wilfred Philip and Mary Alice (Conger) O'R. BA, Middlebury Coll., 1966; JD, U. Denver, 1974; MS, U. Vt., 1982. Lic. real estate broker, Colo.; bar: Colo., 1973. Assoc. atty. Office of Charles D. Burg, Denver, 1973-76; staff atty. Forest Oil Corp., Denver, 1976-77; dir. pub. affairs U.S. Ski Assn., Denver, 1977-79; asst. v.p. Sherburne Corp., Killington, Vt., 1979-81; v.p. Talley Corp., Denver, 1982-85; sr. v.p. Mission Viejo Co., Denver, 1986-95; v.p. Highlands Mgmt. Group, Breckenridge, Colo., 1996—. Vice pres. Colo. Ski Mus., Vail, 1995. Capt. USAF, 1967-71. Mem. Nat. Assn. Indsl. and Office Parks (v.p. 1996), S.E. Denver and Douglas County E.D.C. (chmn. 1993-94). Office: Highlands Mgmt Group PO Box 8029 Breckenridge CO 80424

ORENSTEIN, (IAN) MICHAEL, philatelic dealer, columnist; b. Bklyn., Jan. 6, 1939; s. Harry and Myra (Klein) O.; m. Linda Turer, June 28, 1964; 1 child, Paul David. BS, Clemson U., 1960; postgrad., U. Calif., Berkeley, 1960-61. Career regional mgr. Minkus Stamp & Pub. Co., Calif., 1964-70; mgr. stamp div. Superior Stamp & Coin Co., Inc., Beverly Hills, Calif., 1970-90; dir. stamp divsn. Superior Galleries, Beverly Hills, Calif., 1991-94; dir. space memorabelia Superior Stamp and Coin. Co., Inc., Beverly Hills, Calif., 1992-94; dir. stamp and space divsn. Superior Stamp & Coin an A-Mark Co., Beverly Hills, 1994—; stamp columnist L.A. Times, 1965-93, Brookman Times, 1997—, Scott Stamp Monthly, 1997—; bd. Adelphi U. N.Y. Inst. Philatelic and Numismatic Studies, 1978-81. Author: Stamp Collecting Is Fun, 1990; philatelic advisor/creator The Video Guide To Stamp Collecting, 1988; writer The Brookman Times, Scott Stamp Mo. With AUS, 1962-64. Mem. Am. Stamp Dealers Assn., C.Z. Study Group, German Philatelic Soc., Confederate Stamp Alliance, Am. Philatelic Soc. (writers unit 1975-80, 89-93), Internat. Fedn. Stamp Dealers, Internat. Soc. Appraisers: Stamps, Space Memorabilia. Republican. Office: Superior Stamp & Coin An A-Mark Co 9478 W Olympic Blvd Beverly Hills CA 90212-4246

ORENSTEIN, PEGGY JO, writer, editor; b. Mpls., Nov. 22, 1961; d. Melvin Israyl and Beatrice (Dolf) O.; m. Steven Okazaki, June 4, 1992. BA, Oberlin Coll., 1983. Asst. editor Esquire mag., N.Y.C., 1983-86; assoc. editor, then sr. editor Manhattan, Inc. mag., N.Y.C., 1986-87; sr. editor 7 Days mag., N.Y.C., 1987-88; mng. editor Mother Jones mag., San Francisco, 1988-91. Author: Schoolgirls: Young Women, Self Esteem and the Confidence Gap, 1994; contbr. numerous articles to popular jours.

ORFIELD, ADRIENNE ADAMS, judge; b. Memphis, June 14, 1953. BA, Cal. State Coll., San Bernardino, 1975; JD, U. San Diego, 1979. Bar: Calif. 1979, U.S. Dist. Ct. 1979. Assoc. Shifflet & Sharp, San Diego, 1980-82, Ault, Deuprey, Jones, and Gorman, San Diego, 1982-87; ptnr. Ault, Deuprey, Jones & Gorman, San Diego, 1987-95; appointed to San Diego Mcpl. Ct., San Diego, 1995. Republican. Office: San Diego Mcpl Ct 220 W Broadway San Diego CA 92101

ORLEBEKE, WILLIAM RONALD, lawyer; b. El Paso, Tex., Jan. 5, 1934; s. William Ronald and Frances Claire (Cook) O.; m. Barbara Raye Pike, Aug. 29, 1954 (div. 1988); children: Michelle, Julene, David; m. Kathie Waterson, 1989; 1 stepson, Jack D. Waterson. BA, Willamette U., 1956; MA, Kans. U., 1957; JD, Willamette U., 1966. Bar: Calif. 1966, U.S. Dist. Ct. (no. dist.) Calif. 1967, U.S. Ct. Appeals (9th cir.) 1967, U.S. Ct. Appeals (7th cir.) 1989, U.S. Dist. Ct. (no. dist.) Ill. 1989, U.S. Dist. Ct. (cen. dist.) Calif. 1989. Assoc. Eliassen & Postel, San Francisco, 1966-69; ptnr. Coll, Levy & Orlebeke, Concord, Calif., 1969-77, Orlebeke & Hutchings, Concord, 1977-86, Orlebeke, Hutchings & Pinkerton, 1986-88, Orlebeke & Hutchings, 1988-89; prin. Law Offices W. Ronald Orlebeke, 1989—; hearing officer Contra Costa County, Calif., 1981—; arbitrator Contra Costa County Superior Ct., 1977—, U.S. Dist. Ct. No. Calif., 1978—, Mt. Diablo Mcpl. Ct., 1987—; judge pro tem Mt. Diablo Mcpl. Ct., 1973-77. Alumni bd. dirs. Willamette U., 1978-81, trustee, 1980-81; scholarship chmn. Concord Elks, 1977-79; del. Joint U.S/China Internat. Trade Law Conf., Beijing, Peoples Republic of China, 1987. Served with USMCR, 1952-59. Sr. scholar, Willamette U., 1955-56; Woodrow Wilson fellow, Kans. U., 1956-57; U.S. Bur. Nat. Affairs fellow, 1966, others. Mem. SAR, Sons of Confederate Vets. (Award of Merit 1989), Sons of Union Veterans Civil War, U.S. Navy League, First Marine Divsn. Assn. Republican. Lodges: Order Ea. Star (worthy patron 1980), Masons, Shriners, Elks, Rotary (charter pres. Clayton Valley/Concord Sunrise club 1987-88, chmn. dist. 5160 Calif. membership devel. 1989-90, dist. govs. liaison dist. 5160 1990-92, dist. 5160 Rotarian of Yr. 1989-90, Paul Harris fellow 1988, 1992 dist. conf. chmn. benefactor 1990, award of merit 1990). Office: 3330 Clayton Rd Ste B Concord CA 94519-2894

ORLOFF, CHET, cultural organization administrator; b. Bellingham, Wash., Feb. 22, 1949; s. Monford A. and Janice (Diamond) O.; m. Wendy Lynn Lee, Sept. 20, 1970; children: Callman Labe, Hannah Katya, Michele Alison. BA, Boston U., 1971; MA, U. Oreg., 1978; postgrad., Portland State U. Tchr. Peace Corps, Afghanistan, 1972-75; asst. dir. Oreg. Hist. Soc., Portland, 1975-86, dir., 1991—; dir. Ninth Cir. Hist. Soc., Pasadena, Calif., 1987-91. Editor: Western Legal History, 1987-91, Law for the Elephant, 1992; sr. editor: Oreg. Hist. Quar.; contbr. articles to profl. jours. Commr. Met. Arts Commn., Portland, 1981-84, Portland Planning Commn., 1989-92; pres. Nat. Lewis and Clark Bicentennial Coun., 1996—. Mem. Phi Alpha Theta. Office: Oregon Historical Society 1200 SW Park Ave Portland OR 97205-2441

ORLOFF, NEIL, lawyer; b. Chgo., May 9, 1943; s. Benjamin R. and Annette (Grabow) O.; m. Jan Krigbaum, Oct. 9, 1971 (div. 1979); m. Gudrun Mirin, Oct. 2, 1992. BS, MIT, 1964; MBA, Harvard U., 1966; JD, Columbia U., 1969. Bar: D.C. 1969, N.Y. 1975, Calif. 1989, Utah 1993. Ops. officer World Bank, Washington, 1969-71; dir. regional liaison staff EPA, Washington, 1971-73; legal counsel Pres.'s Council on Environ. Quality, Washington, 1973-75; prof. dept. environ. engring. Cornell U., Ithaca, N.Y., 1975-88, sch. law UCLA, 1992; dir. Ctr. for Environ. Research, 1984-87, Am. Ecology Corp., 1986-88; of counsel Morgan, Lewis & Bockius, N.Y.C., 1986-87; ptnr. Irell & Manella, Los Angeles, 1986-92, Parsons, Behle & Latimer, Salt Lake City, 1992—; vice chmn. bd. dirs. S.W. Research and Info. Ctr., Albuquerque, 1975-84; vice chmn. air quality commn. ABA, Chgo., 1983-92, co-chmn. intensive course in environ. law ABA, 1994—, co-chmn. roundtable sr. environ. lawyers ABA, 1996—. Author: The Environmental Impact Statement Process, 1978, The National Environmental Policy Act, 1980, Air Pollution-Cases and Materials, 1980, Community Right-to-Know Handbook, 1988; mem. editorial bd. Natural Resources and Environment, 1984-87. Adviser Internat. Joint Com. Can., 1979-81; governing bd. N.Y. Sea Grant Inst., 1984-87; vice chmn. City of Ithaca Environ. Commn., 1976-77; adviser N.Y. Dept. Environ. Conservation, 1984-87.

ORMAN, JOHN LEO, software engineer, writer; b. San Antonio, Mar. 19, 1949; s. Alton Woodlee and Isabel Joan (Paproski) O. BS in Physics, N.Mex. Inst. Mining & Tech., 1971, BS Math., MS Physics, 1974. Rsch. asst. N.Mex. Inst. Mining & Tech., Socorro, 1967-74; computer programmer State of N.Mex., Santa Fe, 1974-76; computer analyst Dikewood Corp., Albuquerque, 1976-83; nuclear engr. Sandia Nat. Labs., Albuquerque, 1983-88, software engr., 1988—. Author numerous poems. NSF fellow, 1971-74; recipient 2d place award N.Mex. State Postry Soc., 1987. Mem. IEEE Computer Soc., Am. Assn. Physics Tchrs., Assn. for Computing Machinery, Nat. Writer's Club (poetry award 1987), Southwest Writers Workshop (3d place award non-fiction 1987), N.Mex. Mountain Club. Home: 900 Solar Rd NW Albuquerque NM 87107-5750 Office: Sandia Nat Labs MS 0974 PO Box 5800 Albuquerque NM 87185

ORMASA, JOHN, retired utility executive, lawyer; b. Richmond, Calif., May 30, 1925; s. Juan Hormaza and Maria Inocencia Olondo; m. Dorothy Helen Trumble, Feb. 17, 1952; children: Newton Lee, John Trumble, Nancy Jean Davies. BA, U. Calif.-Berkeley, 1948; JD, Harvard U., 1951. Bar: Calif. 1952, U.S. Supreme Ct. 1959. Assoc. Clifford C. Anglim, 1951-52; assoc. Richmond, Carlson, Collins, Gordon & Bold, 1952-56, ptnr., 1956-59; with So. Calif. Gas Co., L.A., 1959-66, gen. atty., 1963-65, v.p., gen. counsel, 1965-66; v.p., sys. gen. counsel Pacific Lighting Service Co., Los Angeles, 1966-72; v.p., gen. counsel Pacific Lighting Corp., Los Angeles, 1973-75, v.p., sec., gen. counsel, 1975. Acting city atty., El Cerrito, Calif., 1952. Served with U.S. Navy, 1943-46. Mem. ABA, Calif. State Bar Assn., Richmond (Calif.) Bar Assn. (pres. 1959), Kiwanis (v.p. 1959). Republican. Roman Catholic.

ORME, MELISSA EMILY, mechanical engineering educator; b. Glendale, Calif., Mar. 12, 1961; d. Myrl Eugene and Geraldine Irene (Schmuck) O.; m. Vasilis Zissis Marmarelis, Mar. 12, 1989; children: Zissis Eugene and Myrl Galinos (twins). BS, U. So. Calif., L.A., 1984, MS, 1985, PhD, 1989. Rsch. asst. prof. U. So. Calif., 1990-93; asst. prof. U. Calif., Irvine, 1993-96, assoc. prof., 1996—; panel reviewer NSF, Arlington, Va., 1993—; cons. MPM Corp., Boston, 1993—. Contbr. articles to profl. jours. Recipient Young Investigator award NSF, 1994, Arch T. Colwell Merit award SAE, 1994. Mem. AAUW, AIAA, ASME, Am. Phys. Soc., Minerals, Metals and Materials Soc. Office: U Calif Dept Mech Engring Irvine CA 92697-3975

OROPALLO, DEBORAH, artist, educator; b. Hackensack, N.J., Nov. 29, 1954. BFA, Alfred (N.Y.) U., 1979; MA, U. Calif., Berkeley, 1982, MFA, 1983. Teaching asst. Alfred (N.Y.) U., 1979, U. Calif., Berkeley, 1982-83; instr. San Francisco Art Inst., 1984-85, San Francisco Art Acad. Coll., 1986, 87-92; vis. prof. San Francisco Art Inst., 1993; artist C. O. Stephen Wirtz Gallery, San Francisco, 1994—. One-woman shows include Media Gallery, N.Y., 1979, Stephen Wirtz Gallery, San Francisco, 1986, 88, 90, 93, Meml. Union Art Gallery, Davis, Calif., 1987, Raab Gallerie, Berlin, 1987, Inst. Contemporary Art, Boston, 1990, Artspace, San Francisco, 1990, Greenville County Mus. Art, Greenville, S.C., 1991, Germans van Eck Gallery, N.Y.C., 1991, Weatherspoon Gallery, Greensboro, N.C., 1992, Ann Jaffee Gallery, Bay Harbor Island, Fla., 1992, Kate Block Fine Arts, Boston, 1993, Stephen Wirtz Gallery, San Francisco, 1993, 95, 97, San Jose Mus. Art, 1994, Zolla Lieberman Gallery, Chgo., 1996; exhibited in group shows at Fosdick Nelson Gallery, Alfred, N.Y., 1979, Albright Knox Mus., Buffalo, 1980, Richmond (Calif.) Art Ctr., 1980, Civic Ctr., San Francisco, 1981, Calif. State Fair Art Exhbn., Sacramento, 1981, San Jose Inst. Contemporary Art, 1981, Worth Ryder Gallery, Berkeley, Calif., 1981, 1982, Annual Conf. of Mus. Assn. Am., 1983, Berkeley Art Mus., 1983, San Francisco Art Inst., 1984, San Francisco Arts Commn. Gallery, 1985, Acad. Art Gallery, San Francisco, 1986, Freson (Calif.) Art Ctr., 1987, Allport Gallery, San Francisco, 1988, Whitney Mus. Am. Art, N.Y.C., 1989, Stephen Wirtz Gallery, San Franscisco, 1989, 91, 95, Am. Acad. and Inst. Arts and Letters, N.Y.C., 1989, Cleve. Ctr. Contemporary Art, 1990, Milw. Art Mus., 1990, Okla. Mus. Art, Oklahoma City, 1990, Contemporary Art Mus., Houston, 1990, Oakland Mus., 1991, Molica Guidarte Gallery, N.Y.C., 1991, Susan Cummins Gallery, Mill Valley, Calif., 1992, Calif. Coll. Arts and Crafts, Oakland, 1992, Krakow Gallery, Boston, 1992, Kate Block Fine Art, Boston, 1992, Corcoran Gallery of Art, Washington, 1992, San Jose Mus., 1993, Galleria de Arte, Sao Paulo, Brazil, 1994, Palo Alto (Calif.), Cultural Ctr., 1994, Michael Kohler Arts Ctr., Sheboygan, Wis., 1994, Okeanos Press, Berkeley, Calif., 1994, CAPP Street Project, San Francisco, 1994, The Artists Contemporary Gallery, Hyatt Regency Plz., Sacramento, 1995, Gallery Concord, Concord, Calif., 1995, Natural Mus. Am. Art, Washington D.C., 1996, others. Recipient F.C.-J.C. Fine Art award Alfred U., 1977, Michael Cory Levins Sculpture award Alfred U., 1978, N.Y. Coll. Register Cert. of Recognition, 1977, Hon. mention Calif. State Fair Art Exhbn., 1981, Second Pl. award, 1981, Richmond (Calif.) Art Ctr. award, 1982, Ann Bremer award U. Calif., 1982, 22nd Ann. Art Exhibit Second Pl. award, 1983, Engelhard award Inst. Contemporary Art, Boston, 1987, Art Space Support grant, 1988, 90, NEA award, 1991, Fleishhacker award, 1993. Office: 49 Geary St Fl 3 San Francisco CA 94108-5705

O'ROURKE, DENNIS, advertising executive. CFO, sr. v.p. Goldberg, Moser & O'Neill, San Francisco, Calif. Office: 77 Maiden Ln San Francisco CA 94108*

O'ROURKE, J. TRACY, manufacturing company executive; b. Columbia, S.C., Mar. 14, 1935; s. James Tracy and Georgia Adella (Bridges) O'R.; m. Lou Ann Turner, Mar. 19. 1954; 1 son, James Tracy. BSME, Auburn U., 1956. Teflon specialist duPont Co., Wilmington, Del., 1957-62; pres., chief exec. officer LNP Corp., Malvern, Pa., 1962-72; v.p. Carborundum, Niagara Falls, N.Y., 1972-76; exec. v.p. Chemetron, Chgo., 1976-78; sr. v.p. Allen Bradley Co. subs. Rockwell Internat. Corp., Milw., 1978-81, pres., chief oper. officer, 1981-86, also chief exec. officer, dir., 1986-90; chmn., chief exec. officer Varian Assocs., Palo Alto, Calif., 1990—. Served as 1st lt. USAF, 1957-59. Office: Varian Assocs PO Box 10800 3050 Hansen Way Palo Alto CA 94304-1000*

O'ROURKE, JOAN B. DOTY WERTHMAN, educational administrator; b. N.Y.C., June 7, 1933; d. George E. Doty and Lillian G. Bergen; 10 children, 8 stepchildren. BA summa cum laude, Marymount Coll., Manhattan, N.Y., 1953; MA, Columbia U., 1958; PhD, St. John's U., 1971. Tchr. History Marymount High Sch., N.Y.C., 1953-55; hist. instr. Marymount Manhattan Coll., 1957-59; acting chmn. hist. dept. Nassau Community Coll., Mineola, N.Y., 1959-60; prof. history Westchester Community Coll., Valhalla, N.Y., 1963-74; prin. Pius X Sch., Scarsdale, N.Y., 1974-77; assoc. dir. alumni relations Fordham U., N.Y.C., 1980-84; co-founder, dir. Assn. for Profl. Psychol. and Ednl. Counseling, Wilmette, Ill., 1987—; ptnr. O'Rourke and Assocs., 1993—; pres. O'Rourke and Assocs., mgmt. cons., 1993—; dir., writer Sta. WFAS Radio, White Plains, 1963-64; adj. prof. social sci. Fordham U., 1974-76. Teaching fellow St. John's U., Jamaica, N.Y., 1968; recipient Alumni award Marymount Coll., 1987-88. Mem. Soc. Mayflowers Descs. Ill., Michigan Shores Club. Democrat. Roman Catholic. Office: 78614 Blooming Ct Palm Desert CA 92211-1401

O'ROURKE, MICHAEL, artistic director; b. Denver, July 31, 1949; s. Lee and Patricia (O'Rourke) Leberer; children: Toby Jarius, Morgan, Tansi Grant. AA, Casper (Wyo.) Coll., 1969; BA, U. Wyo., 1971, MA, 1973. Founder, artistic dir. Casper Coll. Amateur Dramatic Soc., 1967-69, Poor Yorick Players, Laramie, Wyo., 1970-73; dir., actor Oreg. Shakespeare Festival, Ashland, 1973-77; co-founder, artistic dir. Actors' Theatre, Talent, Oreg., 1982-95; artistic dir. emeritus Actors' Theatre, Talent, 1995—; co-founder Theatre IK'CE'CA'SA, 1996; actor Colo. Shakespeare Festival, Boulder, 1971; dir., producer Prodn. Co., Portland, Oreg., 1979; dir. Skid Road Theatre, Seattle, 1980; editor: In Passing, 1968-69; playwright: Pinocchio, Tom Sawyer, Fellowship of the Ring, Count of Monte Cristo, The Seven Dreams of Icarus; co-author: Walking on Turtle Island; producer, dir. more than 100 prodns., 1982-94. Named Best Dir. Sneak Preview News, 1990; recipient Outstanding Achievement award Arts Coun. So. Oreg., 1993, 2d prize Nat. Libr. Poetry, 1996. Office: Actors Theatre PO Box 780 Talent OR 97540

ORR, GREGORY THOMAS, restaurant manager, business studies educator; b. Richmond, Calif., May 23, 1952; s. William Thomas and Bernadine (Smith) O.; m. Patricia Doncan, Aug. 14, 1972 (div. Apr. 15, 1992); children: Jason Thomas, Kelly Rose, Tim P.; m. Kristin Eileen Snyder, Nov. 19, 1992. BA, U. of the Pacific, 1974; MBA, Sul Ross U., 1989. Cert. post-secondary tchr., Nev. Commd. 2d lt. USAF, 1979, advanced through grades to capt., 1992; bus. prof. Truckee Meadows Coll., Reno, 1992-94; gen. mgr. Washoe Zephyr Coop., Reno, 1993-94, Home Town Buffet, San Jose, Calif., 1995—. Active Jaycees, Walnut Creek, 1975-80. Recipient Air Force Commendation medal. Mem. Culinary Inst. Am., Air Force Assn. Democrat. Presbyterian. Home: PO Box 67181 Scotts Valley CA 95067-7181 Office: Home Town Buffet 3085 Meridian Ave San Jose CA 95124

ORR, JOHN CHRISTOPHER, English language educator; b. Fruita, Colo., Dec. 4, 1949; s. E. Robert and Florence Marion (Ree) O.; m. Lynne Norma Jenkins, Oct. 6, 1979; children: Caitlin, Theresa, Lauren. BA magna cum laude, Amherst Coll., 1972; MA in English and Am. Lit., Claremont Grad. Sch., 1976; postgrad., U. Calif., Irvine, 1981, U. Rochester, 1983, Calif. Polytechnic U., 1984, 87, 92,, U. Edinburgh, Scotland, 1993. Instr. in English Walnut (Calif.) H.S., 1973-85; instr. in English Fullerton (Calif.) Coll., 1985, coord. proficiency exam. program, 1988-95, coord. engring. dept., 1997—; lectr., presenter in field; reader Coll. Bd./Edn. Testing Svc., Princeton, N.J., 1986—; chief writer Cleve. Project, Hoffman Custom Products, Duarte, Calif., 1989. NEH grantee, 1983; U. Calif.-Irvine fellow, 1981. Mem. NEA, Calif. Tchrs. Assn., Am. Studies Assn., Calif. Assn. Tchrs. English, English Coun. Calif. Two Yr. Colls., Faculty Assn. Calif. C.C. Democrat. Office: Fullerton Coll 321 E Chapman Ave Fullerton CA 92632-2011

ORR, ROBERT DAVID, clinical ethicist, educator, physician; b. Mooers, N.Y., Mar. 16, 1941; s. Willard Joseph and Nina Elizabeth (Bell) O.; m. Joyce Lorraine Wirick, June 9, 1962; children: Shirley Ann, Ronald Lee, Robin Lisabeth. BS cum laude, Houghton Coll., 1962; MD, Chirurgee Magistrum, McGill U., Montreal, Que., Can., 1966. Diplomate Am. Bd. Family Practice. Intern U.S. Naval Hosp., Bethesda, Md., 1966-67; resident U.S. Naval Hosp., Jacksonville, Fla., 1967-69; med. officer U.S. Naval Hosp., Roosevelt Roads, P.R., 1969-71; pvt. practice Brattleboro, Vt., 1971-89; fellow clin. ethics U. Chgo., 1989-90; assoc. prof. Loma Linda (Calif.) U., 1990-95, prof., 1995—; clin. co-dir. Ctr. for Christian Bioethics, Loma Linda, 1991—; mem. adv. bd. Ctr. for Bioethics and Human Dignity, Bannockburn, Ill., 1994—. Co-author: Life and Death Decisions, 1990; author 8 book chpts.; contbr. numerous articles to profl. jours. Elder Bethany Reformed Ch., Redlands, Calif., 1995-97; pres. Brattleboro Area Hospice, 1981-84. Lt. comdr. USN, 1966-71. Named Vt. Family Dr. of Yr., Vt. State Med. Soc., 1989. Mem. AMA, Christian Med. and Dental Soc. (mem. ethics commn., chmn. ethics commn. 1991-94), Calif. Med. Assn. (mem. com. on bioethics), Soc. for Bioethics Cons. (bd. dirs. 1996—). Mem. Reformed Ch. Am. Office: Loma Linda U Ste C 11340 Mountain View Ave Loma Linda CA 92354

ORR, STANLEY CHI-HUNG, financial executive; b. Shanghai, China, May 19, 1946; s. Chiu-Lai and Chiu-Chun (Ma) O.; children: Simon K., Edmund K., Norman K. Grad., Hong Kong Bapt. U., 1966; M in Econs., Chu Hoi Coll., Hong Kong, 1973; post grad., East Anglia U., Eng., 1975; MBA, Bradford U., Eng., 1977, West Coast U., L.A., 1980. CPA, Calif.; CMA, Eng.; notary pub. Chief acct. Cordial Knitting Factory Ltd., Hong Kong, 1966-69, mgr., 1969-71; chief acct. for Asia Mark Holding Co. Ltd., Hong Kong, 1971-74; chief fin. officer Knits-Cord Ltd., Montebello, Calif., 1977—; broker Dept. of Real Estate, 1992—. Treas., sec. World Univs. Svc., Hong Kong, 1965-66. Mem. AICPA, Chinese-Am. CPA Soc. (chmn., pres. 1991), Calif. Soc. CPAs. Republican. Office: Knits-Cord Ltd 1600 Date St Montebello CA 90640-6371

ORTEGA, CYNTHIA, financial analyst; b. L.A., Mar. 31, 1971; d. Javier Francisco and Andrea Maria (Esparza) O. BA, UCLA, 1993; postgrad., Calif. State U., L.A., 1994—. Fin. analyst, divsn. chief Compton Mcpl. Ct., Lynwood, Calif., 1991—. Campaign vol. Lambros for Assembly, Bellflower, Calif., 1996. Mem. Female Mgrs. Network of L.A. County. Republican.

ORTIZ, ANTONIO IGNACIO, public relations executive; b. Mexico City, Feb. 22, 1961; came to U.S., 1988; s. Antonio and Sylvia (Vega) O.; m. Socorro Chinolla, June 12, 1982. B in Bus., Universidad Autonoma de Baja Calif., Tijuana, 1984. With acctg. dept. Bank of the Atlantic, Tijuana, 1979-83; mgr. Aldaco, Tijuana, 1983-84; dir. pub. rels. Oh! Laser Club, Tijuana, 1984-88, Iguanas, Tijuana, 1988-90, Euebe, S.A., Tijuana, 1990—; cons. DDBSA Corp., Chula Vista, Calif., Calif. Alson Ltd., San Diego, Exim Trading Co., San Diego, R.P. Noble Enterprises, La Jolla, Ca.; dir. pub. rels. R. Noble Enterprises. Home: PO Box 431859 San Diego CA 92143-1859 Office: Exim Trading Corp PO Box 435108 San Diego CA 92143-5108

ORTIZ, BEVERLY RUTH, ethnographic consultant; b. L.A., Feb. 5, 1956; d. Joseph Antonio and Beverly Rae (Miller) O. BS, U. Calif., Davis, 1974; postgrad, U. Calif., Berkeley, 1993—. Dist. historian Plumas Nat. Forest, Greenville, Calif., 1976; park technician Yosemite Nat. Park, Wawona, Calif., summers 1978-81; naturalist Bay Regional Park Dist., Oakland, Calif., 1980—; ethnographic cons. Walnut Creek, Calif., 1986—; cons. Mount Diablo State Park, Walnut Creek, 1990-93, Healdsburg (Calif.) Mus., 1989, Sonoma State U. Acad. Found., Inc., Calif., 1993-95. Author: It Will Live Forever, 1991; writer: (video documentary) Pomo Basketweavers: A Tribute to Three Elders, 1996 (Best Feature Length Videotape Am. Indian Film Festival 1996); contbr. articles to profl. jours. Pres., bd. mem. Miwok Archeol. Preserve of Marin, 1985-89; chair, commr. Walnut Creek Park and Recreation Commn., 1988-92; founder, bd. dirs., pres. Friends of Creeks in Urban Settings, Walnut Creek, 1984—; mem. adv. com. Oyate, Berkeley, 1990—; mem. Citizens Task Force on Creeks Restoration and Trails Master Plan, 1992-93, Contra Costa County Urban Creeks Task Force, 1986-88, Drainage Area 46 Task Force, 1986-87, Walnut Creek in the Yr. 2000 Subcom. on Open Space and Recreation, 1986. Recipient Cert. of Achievement and Profl. Merit East Bay Regional Pks., 1988, 95; named Outstanding Grad. Student Instr., U. Calif., Berkeley, 1995-96. Mem. Phi Kappa Phi. Office: Coyote Hills Regional Park 8000 Patterson Ranch Rd Fremont CA 94555-3502

ORTIZ, DIANA M., curriculum coordinator. BA in Polit. Sci./History, The Colo. Coll., 1976; M. Cmty./Regional Planning/Pub. Adminstn, U. N.Mex., 1995. Co-dir. Tonantzin Land Inst., Albuquerque, 1984-88; field dir. women's vote N.Mex. Conf. of Chs., Albuquerque, 1988; coord. recreation dept. Pueblo of Acoma, N.Mex., 1989-90; cons. Rural Econ. Assistance Link U.S. West Found., Albuquerque, 1991; grad. asst. cmty. and regional planning U. N.Mex., Albuquerque, 1991; intern Ctr. for the New West, Albuquerque, 1993; learning ctr. coord. Futures for Children, Albuquerque, 1994-95; curriculum and tng. coord. Nat. Indian Youth Leadership Devel. Project, Inc., Gallup, N.Mex., 1995—; cons. levi Strauss Found. Sec., bd. mem. Bd. of Edn., Pueblo of Laguna. Recipient Spl. Acad. award Am. Indian Grad. Ctr., 1991, Parent Involvement award Laguna Elem. Sch., 1991, 92, U. N.Mex. Alumni Assn. Recognition award, 1993-94. Mem. Am. Planning Assn., Am. Soc. Pub. Adminstrs., Internat. Assn. Facilitators, Pi Alpha Alpha. Home: PO Box 443 Casa Blanca NM 87007-0443

ORTIZ, DIANE THORMAN, librarian, management analyst; b. Mpls., July 22, 1945; d. Edward Francis and Florence Eleanor (Thorman) O. BA in Polit. Sci., U. Nev., 1967; MA in Librarianship, San Jose (Calif.) State U., 1970; student, Am. U., 1973; MPA, U. Nev., 1977. Cert. secondary tcrh. and specialized libr., Caif., NCIC instr., Nev. Sub. tchr. Clark County (Nev.) Sch. Dist., Las Vegas, 1967; asst. law libr. Georgetown U. Law Ctr. Libr., Washington, 1970-71; head cataloger, cataloging supr. Xerox BiblioGraphics, Cheverly, Md., 1971-74; audiovidsual cataloger Xerox BiblioGraphics, Cheverly, 1974; project mgr. Automated Typographics, Inc., Arlington, Va., 1974; from mgmt. analyst trainee to mgmt. analyst I and II City of Las Vegas, 1978-88; bus. office mgr. Alt. Sentencing and Edn. divsn. Las Vegas Mcpl. Ct., 1988—. Mem. Clark County Dem. Cen. Com., Las Vegas. Mem. ALA, Am. Soc. Pub. Adminstrn., Am. Assn. Law Librs., Spl. Librs. Assn., Nev. Libr. Assn., Western Govtl. Rsch. Assn., Assn. of Records Mgrs. and Adminstrs., Alumni Assn. U. Nev. Las Vegas, Alumni Assn. San Jose State U., Beta Phi Mu, Pi Sigma Alpha. Democrat. Jewish/Unitarian. Office: Las Vegas Mcpl Ct Alt Sentencing & Edn Divsn Las Vegas NV 89101

ORTIZ, GEOFFREY, stock broker, retirement planning specialist; b. L.A., Nov. 19, 1958; s. Ben B. and Cecelia (Baca) O. AA in Liberal Arts, Santa Monica Coll., 1980; BA in Econs., UCLA, 1981. Registered commodities agt., registered investment advisor, registered rep.; lic. in life, disability and annuities, Calif. Sales mgr. Friden/Alcatel Corp., Union City, Calif., 1979-82; maj. accounts exec. Olympia U.S.A., Somerville, N.J., 1982-83; nat. sales trainer Panasonic Indsl. Co., Secaucus, N.J., 1983-85; regional dealer mgr. Velobind Inc., Sunnyvale, Calif., 1985-88; investment cons. Municicorp, Woodland Hills, Calif., 1988-90; assoc. v.p. investments Dean Witter Reynolds, Malibu, Calif., 1990—. Dir. Malibu Cmty. Aid Golf Tournament, 1994—; Gold sponsor Dolphin Run, Malibu, 1996. Recipient various awards; Dick Gustave Meml. scholar, 1976. Mem. Rotary Club of Malibu (investment adv. bd. 1995—, bd. dirs. 1994—, pres.-elect 1997—, Dist. Gov. award 1995), Surfrider Found., Heal the Bay, Pacific Sailing Club, Pt. Dume Club Park (pres. acquisition com. 1994—). Home: 29500 Heathercliff Rd Spc 169 Malibu CA 90265-4185 Office: Dean Witter Reynolds 22917 Pacific Coast Hwy Malibu CA 90265-4934

ORTIZ, JAMES GEORGE, data information services company executive; b. Boston, June 6, 1961. BA suma cum laude, Monterey Inst. Internat. Studies, 1989, MA, 1990. Instr. lang. Blue Mountain C.C., Pendleton, Oreg., 1990—; pres., CEO, Data Info. Svc., Inc., Toppenish, Wash., 1991-93; safety dir. Marlette Homes, Inc., Hermiston, Oreg., 1993—. Regional dir. CASA of Oreg., Hermiston, 1990. Scholar Chevron Co., 1988-89. Mem. Am. Soc. Safety Engrs. Republican. Adventist.

ORTIZ, KATHLEEN LUCILLE, travel consultant; b. Las Vegas, N.Mex., Feb. 8, 1942; d. Arthur L. and Anna (Lopez) O. BA, Loretto Hghts. Coll., 1963; MA, Georgetown U., 1966; cert. tchg., Highlands U., 1980; cert. travel, ABQ Travel Sch., 1984. Mgr. Montezuma Sq., Las Vegas, 1966-70; office mgr. Arts Food Market, Las Vegas, 1971-75; tchr. Robertson H.S., Las Vegas, 1976-80; registered rep. IDS Fin. Svcs., N.Mex., 1980-84; travel cons. VIP Travel & Tours, Albuquerque, 1985-86, New Horizons Travel, Albuquerque, 1986-87, All World Travel, Albuquerque, 1987-90, Premium Travel Svcs., Albuquerque, 1990-91; travel cons., group tours Going Places Travel, Albuquerque, 1991—. Contbr. 100 articles to newspapers. Founding mem. Citizens Com. for Hist. Preservation, Las Vegas, 1977-79; fund raiser St. Anthony's Hosp., Las Vegas, 1969-75; mem. Hispanic Geneol. Rsch. Ctr., 1996—. Mem. LWV (numerous positions), Internat. Airlines Travel Agent Network, Airlines Reporting Corp. Agent, Georgetown Club of N.Mex. (bd. dirs. at large 1991-94). Home: 7600 Adele Pl NE Albuquerque NM 87109-5362 Office: Going Places Travel 6400 Uptown Blvd NE Ste 429E Albuquerque NM 87110-4203

ORTMEYER, CARL EDWARD, retired demographer; b. Charles City, Iowa, Mar. 12, 1915; s. Arthur Herman and Sarah Emilie (Stoeber) O.; 1 child, Kerry Michael; m. Ruth Sandlin, Oct. 5, 1996. BA, U. Iowa, 1939; MS, Iowa State U., 1948, PhD in Rural Sociology, Demography, 1954. Rsch. assoc. bur. pub. health Sch. Pub. Health U. Mich., Ann Arbor, 1954-56; demographer social security adminstrn. Libr. Congress, Washington, 1956-57; rsch. assoc. Sch. Medicine Howard U., 1958-59; demographer Nat. Ctr. Health Statistics Pub. Health Svc. U.S. Dept. H.E.W., 1959-68; demographer Nat. Inst. Occpl. Safety and Health CDC U.S. Dept. H.E.U., 1968-80, ret., 1980. Vol. caregiver Benedictine Nursing Ctr., Mt. Angel, Oreg., 1990-96, Wesley Hanes Health Ctr., Des Moines, Wash., 1996—; mem. Wesley Found., Ams. for Democratic Action. Sgt. U.S. Army, 1941-45. Travel grantee London Sch. Econs. Rockefeller Found., 1969. Fellow Am. Pub. Health Assn., AAAS. Democrat. Mem. United Meth. Ch. Home: Apt 203 815 S 216th St Des Moines WA 98198-6396

ORTON, EVA DOROTHY, volunteer; b. San Jose, Calif., Aug. 21, 1921; d. George Alfred and Marguerite Carolyn (Del Ponte) Prudhomme. AB in Dietitics, San Jose State Coll., 1943. Intern Highland-Alameda Hosp., Oakland, Calif., 1944; dietitian Providence Hosp., Oakland, 1944-46; relief dietitian Santa Clara Valley Med. Ctr., San Jose, 1949-51, 52-53, sr. dietitian, 1953-63; food adminstr., dir. nutrition and food svc. Santa Clara Valley Ctr., San Jose, 1963-86; ret., 1986—. Bd. dirs., vol. YWCA, San Jose, 1984-93; adv. legis. com. chair Adv. Coun. to Coun. on Agy., San Jose, 1987-95; fin. com. Cmty. Kids to Camp, San Jose, 1987-93, adv. bd., current; active Hunger Coalition, 1992—. Named Disting. Alumni, San Jose State U., 1982, Vol. of Yr. Silicon Valley Charity Ball Found., 1991-92; recipient disting. citizen award Exch. Club and City Coun. San José, Cert. of Appreciation Calif. Sr. Legislature, 1996. Mem. LWV (exec. com., v.p., pres. 1993-95), Am. Dietitic Assn. (registered dietitian), State and Local Dietitic Assn. (chmn. various coms.), Interagency Nutrition Coun. (various coms.). Roman Catholic. Home: 4925 Bel Escou Dr San Jose CA 95124-5441

ORTON, MARY C., nonprofit administrator; b. Prince George's County, Md., Oct. 28, 1954; d. Richard Earl and Shirley Mae (Johnson) O.; m. Michael David Paulson, Jan. 16, 1988. BA in Polit. Sci., Ariz. State U., 1993. Office mgr. Tex. Women's Polit. Caucus, Austin, 1976-77; coord. Austin (Tex.) Women's Ctr., 1977-78; organizer Assn. of Community Orgns. for Reform Now, Austin, Tex., Colorado Springs and Reno, Nev., 1979-81; voter registration coord. Maricopa County Dem. Party, 1982; asst. to congressman U.S. Rep. Morris K. Udall, Phoenix, 1982-84; field dir. Bill Schulz Gubernatorial Campaign, Phoenix, 1984-85; exec. dir. Cen. Ariz. Shelter Svcs., Inc., Phoenix, 1985—. Bd. dirs. Cen. Ariz. Shelter Svcs., Inc., 1984-85, Interfaith Coop. Ministries, 1987-88, Labor's Community Svc. Agy., 1987-93, Ariz. Coalition for Tomorrow, 1992-96, pres.-elect 1993-94, pres. 1994-95; bd. dirs. Ariz. Town Hall, 1993—, Nucleus Club, 1992—, Mercy Housing, 1993-96; mem. joint legis. com. to study the homeless, apptd. by Gov. Bruce Babbitt, 1986; mem. police protection subcom. City of Phoenix Citizens Bond Com., 1988, numerous others. Recipient Social Svcs. Citizen of Yr. award NASW Ariz. chpt. dist. 1, 1987. Mem. Am. Soc. Pub. Adminstrn. (Superior Svc. award 1990). Democrat. Home: 101 N 7th St Unit 259 Phoenix AZ 85034-1040 Office: Cen Ariz Shelter Svcs 1209 W Madison St Phoenix AZ 85007-3123

ORTON, WILLIAM H. (BILL ORTON), former congressman, lawyer; b. North Ogden, Utah, Sept. 22, 1948. BS, Brigham Young U., 1973, JD, 1979. Adj. prof. Portland (Oreg.) State U./Portland C.C., 1974-76, Brigham Young U., Provo, Utah, 1984-85; tax auditor IRS, 1976-77; corp. counsel WI Forest Products, Inc., Portland, Oreg., 1980-81; of counsel Merritt & Tenney, Atlanta, 1986-90; tax atty. pvt. practice, Utah, 1986-90, Washington, 1986-90; atty., 1980-90; mem. 102d-104th Congresses from 3f Utah dist., 1990-97; mem. budget com., mem. banking and fin. svcs. com. Democrat. Mormon. address: 411 Constitution Ave NE Washington DC 20002*

OSADA, STAN, construction executive; b. 1936. With Dillingham Constrn. Pacific Ltd., 1966—, now sr. v.p. Office: Dillingham Cnstr Pcf Ltd 614 Kapahulu Ave Honolulu HI 96815-3846

OSBORN, LUCIE P., library director; b. Cheshire, Conn., June 20, 1949; m. Harry L. Osborn II, Aug. 28, 1971. BA in Sociology, Wittenberg U., 1971; MA in Secondary Edn., Wright State U., 1978; MLS, Kent State U., 1979. Asst. county libr. Laramie County Libr. Sys., Cheyenne, Wyo., 1979-87, county libr., 1990—; libr. dir. Frederick C. Adams Pub. Libr., Kingston, Mass., 1988-90. Office: Laramie County Libr Sys 2800 Central Ave Cheyenne WY 82001-2799

OSBORN, MARIJANE, English language professional/educator; b. Cornwall-on-the-Hudson, N.Y., Nov. 18, 1934; d. D. Remington and Idella (Purnell) Stone; children: David, Desiree. BA, U. Calif., Berkeley, 1962; MA, Stanford U., 1965; postgrad., Oxford U., 1965-66; PhD, Stanford U., 1969. Vis. lectr., asst. prof., fellow various univs., 1968-81; asst. prof. U. Calif., Davis, 1981-83, assoc. prof., 1983-94, prof., 1994—; Fulbright scholar U. Iceland, Reykjavik, 1987; dir. medieval studies program U. Calif., Davis, 1991-92, 93-94. Translator: (book) Beowulf: A Verse Translation, 1983; co-author: (book) Landscape of Desire, 1994. Named Fulbright prof. Fulbright Assn., Iceland, 1978, 79, 87. Mem. Phi Beta Kappa (pres. PBK-UC Davis 1993-94). Office: U Calif at Davis Dept of English Davis CA 95616

OSBORNE, LEO EWELL, artist; b. Marshfield, Mass., Nov. 26, 1947; s. Walter Thomas and Judith May (Ewell) O.; m. Lee Madsen, Aug. 16, 1970 (div. 1989); m. Terri Malec, Dec. 29, 1990; 1 child, Rachel E. Grad., New Eng. Sch. of Art & Design, Boston. instr. Ward Mus., Salisbury, Md., Ultima Workshops. Exhibns. include Soc. Animal Artists, 1986, 87, 88, 89, 91, 92, 93, 94, 95, 96, Shore Village Mus., Rockland Maine, Phila. Mus. Natural Scis., 1984, Frye Mus. Art, Seattle, 1986, Cape Cod (Mass.) mus. Natural History, 1982, 84, 87, Sculpture in the Park, Loveland, Colo., 1991, 92, 93, 94, 95, 96, Rocky Mountain Art Assn., Park City, Utah, 1993, nat. Acad. We. Artists, Oklahoma City, 1993, Tacoma (Wash.) Mus. Art, 1995, numerous others; represented in permanent collections Leigh Yawkey Woodson Art Mus., Genesee Country Mus., So. Alleghenies Mus. Art., Maine Audubon Soc., Worcester Poly. Inst., Loveland (Colo.) High Plains Art Coun., Nature Ctr. Snake Lake, Ward Mus. Wildfowl Art; work featured in Southwest Art Mag., Internat. Wildlife Fedn. Mag., Wildfowl Carving and Collecting Mag., Wildlife Art Mag., Equine Images Mag., Internat. Fine Art Collecting Mag., Taos Mag. Revue Art Mag. Recipient Best of Show awards Ward Mus. Wildfowl Carving Internat. Bird Carving Annual, awards Northwest Wildlife Ea. Oreg. State Coll., Pacific Rim Wildlife Art Exposition, Dremel/DU Masters Carving Competition, Mpls. We. and Wildlife Art Show, Southeastern Wildlife Art Exposition, 1st, 2nd, 3rd Place awards Ward Found. World Bird Carving Competition. Mem. Nat. Sculpture Soc., Soc. Animal Artists (6 Awards of Excellence, 3 Don Miller Sculpture awards, Margaret Hexter prize). Home: 656 West Shore Dr Anacortes WA 98221

OSBORNE, REBECCA J., state agency administrator; b. Oregon City, Oreg., Aug. 16, 1956; d. John Walter and Betty Ruth (Merz) Cox; m. Allen Lee Osborne. BS, City U., 1983; JD, Northwestern Sch. Law, 1987. Bar: Oreg. 1989. Hearing officer Ins. Divsn. State of Oreg., Salem, 1988-89, supr. hearings Ins. Divsn., 1989-94, supr. hearings Employment Dept., 1994-95, mgr. hearings Employment Dept., 1995—. Democrat. Lutheran. Office: State of Oreg Employment Divsn 875 Union St NE Room 208 Salem OR 97311

OSBORNE, THOMAS JEFFERSON, chiropractor; b. Palo Alto, Calif., June 4, 1970; s. George Baynard Osborne and Linda Jane (Mariani) Du Hamel; m. Melanie Therese Botsch, June 25, 1996. Student, Saddleback Coll., Mission Viejo, Calif., 1990-91; D Chiropractic, Palmer Coll Chiropractic, San Jose, Calif., 1995. Occupational and rehab. supr. Palmer U., San Jose, 1995; team physician Griffen Sports, San Jose, 1995—; med. dir. Laidlaw Transport, San Jose, 1995—; resident Palmer Chiropractic Coll. Clinics, San Jose, 1994-95; staff doctor Sport Centre Chiropractic Group, San Jose, 1995-96; clinic dir. COR Chiropractic, San Jose, 1996—; sr. cons. Calif. Health Cons., Menlo Park, 1991-96; corp. coord. Peak Performance Internat., Orange, Calif., 1990-92; corp. trainer Bus. Safety Solution, San Luis Obispo, Calif., 1988-90. Author: Ergo Office, 1994; (tng. program) Save-A-Back, 1995. Fellow Palmer Chiropractic Coll. West, 1995. Mem. Am. Chiropractic Sports Coun., Am. Coll. Sports Medicine, World Chiropractic Assn., Am. Chiropractic Assn., Calif. Chiropractic Assn. (New Doctor of Yr. award 1995), Santa Clara Chiropractic Assn. (v.p. 1995—). Republican. Roman Catholic. Office: COR Chiropractic 1305 N Bascom Ave San Jose CA 95128-1206

OSBURN, MELVIN L., psychotherapist, realtor; b. Slaton, Tex., Nov. 6, 1938; s. James Leroy and Donnie Ovetra (Sanders) O.; m. Joyce Elaine Osburn, June 23, 1963; children: Julie Ann (dec.), Blaine Alan, Brenda Joyce. AA with honors, San Bernardino Valley Coll., 1975; BA with honors, Calif. State Coll., San Bernardino, 1977; MA, Chapman Coll., 1981. Lic. marriage, family and child counselor, Calif.; cert. hypnotherapist, Calif.; lic. marriage and family therapist, Nev. Therapist Knollwood Psychiatric Hosp., Riverside, Calif.; dir., therapist Merrill Community Svc., Fontana, Calif.; vol. therapist Parents United, San Bernardino; pvt. practice Colton, Calif., 1983—. With U.S. Army, 1956-59. Mem. AACD, Psi Chi. Home: PO Box 621 Highland CA 92346-0621 Office: 1420 E Cooley Dr Ste 200B Colton CA 92324

O'SCANNLAIN, DIARMUID FIONNTAIN, judge; b. N.Y.C., Mar. 28, 1937; s. Sean Leo and Moira (Hegarty) O'S.; m. Maura Nolan, Sept. 7, 1963; children: Sean, Jane, Brendan, Kevin, Megan, Christopher, Anne, Kathleen. BA, St. John's U., 1957; JD, Harvard U., 1963; LLM, U. Va., 1992. Bar: Oreg. 1965, N.Y. 1964. Tax atty. Standard Oil Co. (N.J.), N.Y.C., 1963-65; assoc. Davies, Biggs, Strayer, Stoel & Boley, Portland, Oreg., 1965-69; dep. atty. gen. Oreg., 1969-71; public utility commr. of Oreg., 1971-73; dir. Oreg. Dept. Environ. Quality, 1973-74; sr. ptnr. Ragen, Roberts, O'Scannlain, Robertson & Neill, Portland, 1978-86; judge, U.S. Ct. Appeals (9th cir.), San Francisco, 1986—, mem. exec. com., 1988-89, 1993-94, mem. Jud. Coun. 9th Cir., 1991-93; mem. U.S. Judicial Conf. Com. on Automation and Tech., 1990—; cons. Office of Pres.-Elect and mem. Dept. Energy Transition Team (Reagan transition), Washington, 1980-81; chmn. com. adminstrv. law Oreg. State Bar, 1980-81. Mem. council of legal advisers Rep. Nat. Com., 1981-83; mem. Rep. Nat. Com., 1983-86, chmn. Oreg. Rep. Party, 1983-86; del. Rep. Nat. Convs., 1976, 80, chmn. Oreg. del., 1984; Rep. nominee U.S. Ho. of Reps., First Congl. Dist., 1974; team leader Energy Task Force, Pres.'s Pvt. Sector Survey on Cost Control, 1982-83, trustee Jesuit High Sch.; mem. bd. visitors U. Oreg. Law Sch., 1988—; mem. citizens adv. bd. Providence Hosp., 1986-92. Maj. USAR, 1955-78. Mem. Fed. Bar Assn., ABA (sec. Apellate Judges Conf. 1989-90, exec. com. 1990—, chmn.-elect 1994—), Arlington Club, Multnomah Club. Roman Catholic. Office: US Ct Appeals 313 Pioneer Courthouse 555 SW Yamhill St Portland OR 97204-1336*

OSCARSON, KATHLEEN DALE, writing assessment coordinator, educator; b. Hollywood, Calif., Sept. 16, 1928; d. Chauncey Dale and Hermine Marie Rulison; m. David Knowles Leslie, June 16, 1957 (div. Aug. 1970); m. William Randolph Oscarson, Apr. 27, 1974. AB, UCLA, 1950, MA, 1952; Cert. Advanced Study, Harvard U., 1965; Diplomé Elementaire, Le Cordon Bleu U. Paris, 1972. Gen. secondary life credential, Calif. Cons. Advanced Placement English Calif. Dept. Edn., Sacramento, 1968-70; reader Calif. Assessment Program, Sacramento, 1989—; instr. individual study U. Calif. Extension, Berkeley, 1979-92; reader, reader Ednl. Testing Svc., Princeton, N.J. and Emeryville, Calif., 1967—; reader San Jose (Calif.) State U., 1991—; tchr. English, counselor Palo Alto (Calif.) Unified Sch. Dist., 1954-90, H.S. writing assessment coord., 1987—; adj. lectr. English Santa Clara (Calif.) U., 1990-91; commr. Curriculum Study Commn., San Francisco Bay Area, 1978—; chair tchrs. English Spring Asilomar Conf., Pacific Grove, Calif., 1992, Asilomar 44, Pacific Grove, 1994; presenter Conf. on English Leadership, Chgo., 1996. Mem. lang. arts assessment adv. com. Calif. State Dept. Edn., Sacramento, 1975-90; mem.-at-large exec. bd. Ctrl. Calif. Coun. Tchrs. English, Bay Area, 1969-71; mem. Medallion Soc. San Francisco Opera, 1984—; mem. ann. summer event com., membership com. Internat. Diplomacy Coun. Mem. MLA, Nat. Coun. Tchrs. English (group leader conf. San Francisco), Calif. Assn. Tchrs. English, Internat. Diplomacy Coun. San Francisco (membership and events coms. 1996), Harvard Club San Francisco, Christopher Marlowe Soc. Home: 230 Durazno Way Portola Valley CA 94028-7411

OSEGUEDA, LAURA MARGARET, librarian; b. Oakland, Calif., Mar. 25, 1955; d. Eugene Walter and Elizabeth Victory (Mahan) O. BS in Biol. Scis., Calif. State U., 1979; MLS, U. Calif., Berkeley, 1980. Sci. libr. San Jose (Calif.) State U., 1981-84; agrl. and life scis. libr. N.C. State U., Raleigh, 1984-88; head Chemistry Libr. U. Calif., Berkeley, 1988-95; head Vet. Med. Libr. N.C. State U., Raleigh, 1995—. Author: (with others) End Users in Libraries, 1988; contbr. articles to profl. jours. Pres. Friends of Melrose Libr., Oakland, 1994—. Mem. ALA (chmn. Assn. Rsch. Librs. sci. and tech. section 1989-90), Am. Chem. Soc., Nat. Audubon Soc., SLA, Med. Libr. Assn. Office: NC State U 4700 Hillsborough St Raleigh NC 27606

OSEGUERA, PALMA MARIE, marine corps officer, reservist; b. Kansas City, Mo., Dec. 29, 1946; d. Joseph Edmund and Palma Louise (Utke) O'Donnell; m. Alfonso Oseguera, Jan. 1, 1977; stepchildren: Kristie M. Daniels, Michelle L. Nielson, Lori A. Kelley. BA in Phys. Edn., Marycrest Coll., 1969. Commd. 2d lt. USMC, 1969, advanced through grades to col., 1991; asst. marine corps exch. officer Hdqs. and Hdqs. Squadron, Marine Corps Air Sta., Beaufort, S.C., 1969-71; classified material control officer Hdqs. and Svcs. Battalion, Camp S.D. Butler, Okinawa, 1971-73; adminstrv. officer, asst. Marine Corps exch. officer Marine Corps Air Sta., El Toro, Santa Ana, Calif., 1973-76; Marine Corps exch. officer Marine Corps Air Sta., Yuma, Ariz., 1976-77; asst. marine corps exch. officer Hdqrs. and Support Bat., Marine Corps Devel. & Edn. Command, Quantico, Va., 1977-79; marine corps exch. officer Hqrs. Marine Corps, Washington, 1979-80; adminstrv. officer Marine Air Base Squadon 46, Marine Air Group 46, Marine Corps Air Sta., El Toro, Santa Ana, 1981-83, Hdqs. and Maintanence Squadron 46, Marine Air Group 46, Marine Corps Air Sta., El Toro, Santa Ana, 1983-85, Mobilization Tng. Unit Calif. 53, Landing Force Tng. Command, Pacific, San Diego, 1985-89, 3d Civil Affairs Group, L.A., 1989; dep. asst. chief of staff G-1 I Marine Expeditionary Force, Individual Mobilization Augumentaee Detachment, Camp Pendleton, Calif., 1990-91; assoc. mem. Mobilization Tng. Unit Del. 01, Del., 1992-94; adminstrn. officer Mobilization Tng. Unit, CA-53, EWTG Pac, NAB, Coronado, San Diego, 1994-96; exch. officer MWRSPT ACT IMA Det MCB, Camp Pendleton, Calif., 1996—. Mem. choir St. Elizabeth Seaton, Woodbridge, Va., 1978-80, St. Patricks, Arroyo Grande, Calif., 1990-94; vol. Hospice, San Luis Obispo, 1995—; mem. Los Osos (Calif.) veteran's events com. Mem. AAUW (past libr.), Marine Corps Assn., Marine Corps Res. Officer Assn., Marine Corps Aviation Assn. (12 dist. dir. 1987), Women in Mil. Svc. for Am. Republican. Roman Catholic. Home: 728 Scenic Cir Arroyo Grande CA 93420-1617

OSGOOD, FRANK WILLIAM, urban and economic planner, writer; b. Williamston, Mich., Sept. 3, 1931; s. Earle Victor and Blanche Mae (Eberley) O.; children: Ann Marie, Frank William Jr. BS, Mich. State U., 1953; M in City Planning, Ga. Inst. Tech., 1960. Prin. planner Tulsa Met. Area Plnning Commn., 1958-60; sr. assoc. Hammer & Co. Assocs., Washington, 1960-64; econ. cons. Marvin Springer & Assocs., Dallas, 1964-65; sr. assoc. Gladstone Assocs., Washington, 1965-67; prof. urban planning Iowa State U., Ames, 1967-73; pres. Frank Osgood Assoc./Osgood Urban Rsch., Dallas, 1973-84; dir. mktg. studies MPSI Americas Inc., Tulsa, 1984-85, Comarc Systems/Roulac & Co., San Francisco, 1985-86; pres. Osgood Urban Rsch., Millbrae, Calif., 1986-95; freelance writer Millbrae, Calif., 1994-95; VISTA vol. coord. Chrysalis, Santa Monica, Calif., 1995-96; pres. Osgood Urban Rsch., L.A., 1996—; adj. prof. U. Tulsa, 1974-76; lectr. U. Tex., Dallas, 1979, U. Tex., Arlington, 1983. Author: Control Land Uses Near Airports, 1960, Planning Small Business, 1967, Continuous Renewal Cities, 1970; contbr. articles to profl. jours. Chmn. awards Cub Scouts Am., Ames, 1971-73; deacon Calvary Presbyn. Ch., San Francisco, 1987-90. 1st lt. USAF, 1954-56. Recipient Community Leaders and Noteworthy Americans award 1976. Mem. Am. Planning Assn. (peninsula liaison 1987-89, dir. pro-tem 1990 No. Calif. sect., edn. coord. 1991-92, Calif., dir. N. Cen. Tex. sect., Tex. chpt. 1983), Am. Inst. Planners (v.p. Okla. chpt. 1975-77), Okla. Soc. Planning Cons. (sec., treas. 1976-79), Urban Land Inst., Le Club. Republican. Presbyterian. Home: Ter Trousdale 11400 National Blvd Los Angeles CA 90064-3729

O'SHAUGHNESSY, ELLEN CASSELS, writer; b. Columbia, S.C., Oct. 1, 1937; d. Melvin O. and Grace Ellen (Cassels) Hemphill; m. John H. Sloan (dec.); children: John H., Anne H.; m. John F. O'Shaughnessy, Dec. 8, 1979 (div. Mar. 1990). BA, Internat. Coll., L.A., 1977; MA in Counseling Psychology, Fielding Inst., Santa Barbara, Calif., 1980. Tchr.'s aide, art instr. Monterey Peninsula (Calif.) Unified Sch. Dist., 1968-74; tchr. adult sch. Pacific Grove (Calif.) Unified Sch. Dist., 1974-82, spl. edn. cons., 1984-85; sustitute tchr. Monterey County Office Edn., Salinas, Calif., 1983-84; owner, writer, pub. Synthesis, Pacific Grove, Calif., 1984—. Author: Teaching Art to Children, 1974, Synthesis, 1981, You Love to Cook Book, 1983, I Could Ride on the Carousel Longer, 1989, Somebody Called Me A Retard Today...And My Heart Felt Sad, 1992, Walker & Co., N.Y.C. Episcopalian. Home: PO Box 51063 Pacific Grove CA 93950-6063

OSHEROFF, DOUGLAS DEAN, physicist, researcher; b. Aberdeen, Wash., Aug. 1, 1945; s. William and Bessie Anne (Ondov) O.; m. Phyllis S.K. Liu, Aug. 14, 1970. B.S. in Physics, Calif. Inst. Tech., 1967; M.S., Cornell U., 1969, Ph.D. in Physics, 1973. Mem. tech. staff Bell Labs., Murray Hill, N.Y., 1972-82, head solid state and low temperature physics research dept., 1982-87; prof. Stanford (Calif.) U., 1987—, J.G. Jackson and C.J. Wood prof. physics, 1992—; chair physics, 1993-96. Researcher on properties of matter near absolute zero of temperature; co-discoverer of superfluidity in liquid 3He, 1971, nuclear antiferromagnetic resonance in solid 3He, 1980. Co-recipient Simon Meml. prize Brit. Inst. Physics, 1976, Oliver E. Buckley Solid State Physics prize, 1981, Nobel prize in physics, 1996; John D. and Catherine T. MacArthur prize fellow, 1981. Fellow Am. Phys. Soc., Am. Acad. Arts and Scis., Nat. Acad. Scis. Office: Stanford U Dept Physics Stanford CA 94305-4060

OSMAN, MARVIN PHILLIP, psychiatrist and psychoanalyst; b. Mpls., Apr. 15, 1924; s. Samuel S. and Rose Marie (Bouis) O.; m. Patricia Diener, June 4, 1967; children: Suzanne G., Daniel S. BS, U. Minn., 1946, BA, 1947, MB, 1949, MD, 1950. Diplomate Am. Bd. Psychiatry and Neurology. Intern Los Angeles County Gen. Hosp., 1949-50; resident in psychiatry VA Hosp., Brentwood, Calif., 1950-51, 53-54; tng. in psychoanalysis So. Calif. Psychoanalytic Inst., 1951, 54-63; from instr. to assoc. clin. prof. psychiatry U. So. Calif. Med. Sch., L.A., 1957-84, clin. prof. psychiatry, 1984—; mem. faculty So. Calif. Psychoanalytic Inst., L.A., 1967—, tng. and supervising analyst, 1981—, pres., 1986-87, 92-94, dir advanced tng. program in psychodynamic psychotherapy, 1990—; pvt. practice psychiatry and psychoanalysis Beverly Hills, 1955—. Contbr. articles to profl. jours. Trustee L.A. Mental Health Assn., 1962-65, Resthaven Psychiat. Hosp., 1964-70. 1st lt. M.C., U.S. Army, 1951-53. Recipient Outstanding Tchr. award Clin. Assocs. of So. Calif. Psychoanalytic Inst., 1980. Fellow Am. Psychiat. Assn.; mem. Calif. Med. Assn., Los Angeles County Med. Assn., Am. Psychoanalytic Assn., Internat. Psychoanalytic Assn., So. Calif. Psychoanalytic Soc. and Inst. Office: 9735 Wilshire Blvd Beverly Hills CA 90212

OSMAR, NILS ARNOLD, visual artist; b. Seward, Alaska, Dec. 28, 1952; s. Per Eric and Frances (Liverance) O. AA, Seattle Ctrl. C.C., 1976. Art instr. ASUW Exptl. Coll., Seattle, 1979—; freelance visual artist Seattle, 1986—; dir. Wonder Sch. of the Arts, Seattle, 1992—. Author: (fiction) The Hungry Time, 1996; (play) Demea, 1992. Bd. trustees ASUW Exptl. Coll., Seattle, 1990-92. Mem. Graphic Artists Guild, Nat. Cartoonists Soc.

OSSANA, DIANA LYNN, screenwriter, author; b. St. Louis, Aug. 24, 1949; d. Livio Aldo and Marian Yvonne O.; 1 child, Sara Maria. Pres. Saria Co., Inc., Tucson, 1993—. Co-author: (novel) Pretty Boy Floyd, 1994, Zeke and Ned, 1996, (teleplay miniseries) Streets of Laredo, 1995, Deadman's Walk, 1995. Recipient Teleplay of Yr. award Cowboy Hall of Fame, 1996, Teleplay of Yr. award Dallas Film Critics Assn., 1996. Mem. Pen Am. West (Tex. affiliation), Am. Acad. Poets, Internat. Crime Writers Assn., Women in Film.

OSTER, CYNTHIA ANN, critical care nurse; b. Monmouth, Ill., Oct. 11, 1958; d. Paul Eugene and Carol Marlene (Isaacson) Hennenfent; m. Lewis Henry Oster, Jr., Mar. 14, 1981; children: Kristen, Jonathan. BSN, U. Iowa, 1980; MS in Nursing, U. Nebr., Omaha, 1985; postgrad. in nursing, U. Colo., 1995—. RN, Colo.; cert. CCRN. Rsch. nurse U. Nebr. Med. Ctr. Coll. Nursing, 1985; clin. nurse specialist I, case mgr. U. Iowa Hosps. and Clinics, Iowa City, 1987-88; critical care clin. specialist Columbia Aurora Med. Ctr., 1988—. Mem. ANA, AACN, Sigma Theta Tau. Office: Columbia Aurora Presbyn Hosp 700 Potomac St Aurora CO 80011-6701

OSTERHOFF, JAMES MARVIN, retired telecommunications company executive; b. Lafayette, Ind., May 18, 1936; s. Abel Lyman and Mildred Paulene (Post) O.; m. Marilyn Ann Morrison, Aug. 24, 1958; children—Anne Michelle Bitsie, Amy Louise Olmsted, Susan Marie. B.S.M.E., Purdue U., 1958; M.B.A., Stanford U., 1963. Staff asst. FMC Corp., San Jose, Calif., 1963-64; with Ford Motor Co., Dearborn, Mich., 1964-84; v.p. fin. Ford Motor Credit Co., Dearborn, 1973-75; controller car ops. N. Am. Automotive Ops., Ford Motor Co., Dearborn, 1975-76; asst. controller N. Am. Automotive Ops., Ford Motor Co., 1976-79; controller tractor ops. Ford Motor Co., Troy, Mich., 1979-84; v.p. fin., CFO Digital Equipment Corp., Maynard, Mass., 1985-91; exec. v.p., CFO U.S.West Inc., Englewood, Colo., 1991-95; bd. dirs. GenCorp, Inc., FSA Holdings, Ltd., Pvt. Sector Coun., Colo. Neurol. Inst., Goodwill Industries of Denver. Bd. dirs. Colo. Neurol. Inst., Goodwill Industries of Denver. Served to lt. (j.g.) USN, 1958-61. Recipient Disting. Engring. Alumnus award Purdue U.; named Outstanding Mech. Engring. Alumnus, Purdue U. Mem. Fin. Execs. Inst.

OSTLER, DAVID VAL, engineering executive; b. Cambridge, Mass., Jan. 22, 1957; s. David Sorenson and Sharon (Scott) O.; m. Cynthia Hale, Dec. 17, 1982; children: Andrew Hale, Sarah, Carly. BS in Computer Sci. cum laude, U. Utah, 1981, BS in Elec. Engring. cum laude, 1981, MS in Med. Biophysics and Computing, 1984. Summer intern R & D Hewlett Packard Corp., Corvallis, Oreg., 1981; applications programmer med. biophysics and computing U. Utah, Salt Lake City, 1978-81, rsch. asst. med. biophysics and computing, 1981-84; programmer, analyst Computer Sci. Rsch., Regenstrief Inst., Indpls., 1984-85; computer sys. engr. NASA/Johnson Space Ctr. Med. Ops. Br. Krug Internat., Houston, 1985-88; interface software engr. Motorola/EMTEK Health Care Sys., Phoenix, 1988, tech. mgr. interface devel., 1988-90, tech. mgr. product configuration, 1989-90, engring. mgr. integration and support, 1990, product mgr. integration products and platform, 1990-92, program mgr., engring. mgr., 1992-95, dir. computer tech., 1995—; presenter in field. Contbr. articles to profl. jours. Mem. IEEE, IEEE Computer Soc., IEEE Engring. in Medicine and Biology Soc. (stds. com. chmn. 1989-93), Am. Nat. Stds. Inst., Eta Kappa Nu. Home: 3627 E Summerhaven Dr Phoenix AZ 85044-4523 Office: EMTEK Health Care Systems #190 1501 W Fountainhead Pkwy Tempe AZ 85282-1846

OSTROM, PHILIP GARDNER, computer company executive; b. New Haven, Aug. 8, 1942; s. David McKellar and Barbara (Kingsbury) O.; m. Toni Hammons, Dec. 21, 1965; m. Nancy Jean Kahl, Apr. 2, 1983; children: Eric Craig, Paige Lynne. BS, U. Ariz., 1965; postgrad., U. Calif., 1992-94. Cert. sr. examiner quality control, Calif. Sales mgr. Procter & Gamble Co., Louisville, 1968-70, Dun & Bradstreet, L.A., 1970-71; internat. sales mgr. Memorex Corp., Santa Clara, Calif., 1971-82; dir. ops. Memtek Products, Campbell, Calif., 1982-86, Victor Techs., Scotts Valley, Calif., 1986-88; ops. mgr. Apple Computer, Cupertino, Calif., 1988-93; pres./CEO Ostrom & Assocs., San Jose, Calif., 1993—; ISO9000 lead assessor, 1992—. Spl. examiner CCQS, State of Calif., 1994—, presiding judge; examiner Malcolm Baldridge award, 1993—. Home: 1099 Maraschino Dr San Jose CA 95129-3317 Office: Ostrom & Assocs 1099 Maraschino Dr M/S07PG0 San Jose CA 95129-3317

OSWALD, DELMONT RICHARD, humanities organization executive, writer; b. Idaho Falls, Idaho, Oct. 7, 1940; s. Philip Fredrick and Lucille (Andrus) O.; m. Jean Stringam, June 17, 1967 (div. Jan. 1979); children: Sarah Mary, Benjamin Philip. BA, Idaho State U., 1962; MA, Brigham Young U., 1967. Instr. history Brigham Young U., Provo, Utah, 1967-71, asst. to dean social sci., 1971-74; exec. dir. Utah Humanities Coun., Salt Lake City, 1974—; pres. elect Utah Acad. Sci., Arts, Letters, Salt Lake City, 1989-90, pres. 1991-93; nat. bd. dirs. Nat. Fedn. State Humanities Couns., Washington 1988-93, chmn. Nat. meeting, Portland, Oreg., 1990. Author: Autobiography of James Beckwourth, 1972 (U.S. Amb. Book 1972); mem. editorial bd. Dialogue Mag., 1992—. U.S. Senate Reauthorization N.E.H. testifier Fedn. State Humanities Coun., Washington, 1990, mem. gov.'s Martin Luther King Jr./Human Rights Commn.; mem. edn. com. Project 2000, 1989-90; bd. dirs. Utah Alliance for Arts and Humanities. Recipient N.E.H. Merit awards 1984, 86, 88, Exemplary award, 1990, 91, Gov.'s award in the arts Utah Arts Coun., 1994, award for arts and humanities Cathedral of the Madeline, 1995, Excellence in Ethics award Utah Valley State Coll., 1996; Dedicatory Address Jewitt Ctr. Humanities, Salt Lake City, 1989. Mem. Nat. Fedn. State Humanities Coun. (bd. dirs.), Utah Hist. Assn., Mormon Hist. Assn., Salt Lake City C. of C. (Honors in Arts 1990). Home: 209 4th Ave Salt Lake City UT 84103-2484 Office: Utah Humanities Coun 350 S 400 E Ste 110 Salt Lake City UT 84111-2946

OSWALD, DONALD JAMES, economics educator; b. Tacoma, Oct. 15, 1946; s. George Oswald and Arlene Patricia (Cowling) Wills; m. Christine Anna Lien, Sept. 9, 1967; children: Michael G., Brent A. BA in Econs., Wash. State U., 1968, MA in Econs., 1969, PhD in Econs., 1974; postgrad., Lincoln (Ill.) Christian Sem., 1979-81. Grad. rsch. asst. Wash. State U., Pullman, 1968-71; sr. cons. transp. program Ernst & Ernst, Washington, 1976-79; vis. lectr. econs. Lincoln Christian Coll. and Sem., 1979-81; asst. prof. econs. Calif. State U., Bakersfield, 1981-87, assoc. prof., 1987-96, prof., 1996—, gen. studies fellow, 1981—, assoc. dir. Ctr. for Study Classical Econs., 1986-88; professorial lectr. Am. U., Washington, 1975; lectr. George Mason U., Fairfax, Va., 1976. Contbr. articles to profl. jours. Capt. USAF, 1971-76. Mem. Am. Econs. Assn., Western Econ. Assn. (conf. presenter, 1983, 92), Assn. Social Econs., Am. Sci. Affiliation. Home: 3800 Club Run Bakersfield CA 93309-7746

O'TOOLE, JAMES JOSEPH, business educator; b. San Francisco, Apr. 15, 1945; s. James Joseph and Irene (Nagy) O'T.; m. Marilyn Louise Burrill, June 17, 1967; children: Erin Kathleen, Kerry Louise. BA, U. So. Calif., L.A., 1966; DPhil, Oxford (Eng.) U., (Eng.), 1970. Corr. Time-Life News Service, L.A., 1967-68, Nairobi, Kenya, 1967-68; mgmt. cons. McKinsey & Co., San Francisco, 1969-70; coordinator field investigations Pres.'s Comm. on Campus Unrest, Washington, 1970; spl. asst. to sec. HEW, Washington, 1970-73; prof. mgmt. U. So. Calif.-Los Angeles, 1973-93, Univ. Assocs. Chair of Bus., 1982-93; v.p. Aspen Inst., 1994-97; mng. dir. Booz-Allen & Hamilton Leadership Ctr., San Francisco, 1997—; chmn. sec.'s com. work in Am. HEW, Washington, 1971-72; exec. dir. The Leadership Inst., 1990-93; bd. dirs. Radica Games. Prin. author: Work in America, 1973, Energy and Social Change, 1976; author: Work, Learning and the American Future, 1977, Making America Work, 1982 (Phi Kappa Phi prize 1982), Vanguard Management, 1985, The Executive's Compass, 1993, Leading Change, 1995; bd. editors: Ency. Britannica, Chgo., 1981-87; editor: New Management, Los Angeles, 1983-89, The American Oxonian, 1996—. Mem. Project Paideia, Chgo., 1981-83. Rhodes scholar, 1966; recipient Mitchell prize Woodlands Conf., 1979. Mem. Phi Beta Kappa. Home: 23715 Malibu Rd # 552 Malibu CA 90265-4628 Office: Booz Allen Hamilton 101 California St San Francisco CA 94111-5855

O'TOOLE, ROBERT JOHN, II, telemarketing consultant; b. Binghamton, N.Y., Mar. 24, 1951; s. Robert John and Joan Ceclia (Martin) O'T.; m. Donna Sue Stevenson, Jan. 28, 1978 (div. 1984); 1 child, Irene Grace; m. Karen Irene Cady, Dec. 21, 1994. Student, Corning (N.Y.) C.C., 1969-71, SUNY, Brockport, 1970-71; BA, Wake Forest U., 1973; MBA, Southwestern Coll., 1986. Asst. dir. devel. Duvall Home for Children, DeLand, Fla., 1978-81; gen. mgr. Royale Art Advt., Odessa, Tex., 1981-82; v.p. Barnes Assocs. Advt., Odessa, 1982-84, Tex. Assn. for Blind Athletes, Austin, 1985-86; sales mgr. Los Amables Pub., Albuquerque, 1987-88; dir. devel. Albuquerque (N.Mex.) Help for the Homeless, 1988-91; chmn., CEO Advantage Ventures, Inc. (formerly Advantage Mktg., Inc.), Albuquerque, 1991—; CEO LaCourt, Medina & Sterling, Albuquerque, 1993—; cons. Nat. Child Safety Coun., Austin, 1985, Assn. Profl. Fire Fighters, Austin, 1985, Reynolds Aluminum, Austin, 1986, N.Mex. State Legis., 1990, Children's Charity Fund, 1996,

N.Am. Found. for AIDS Rsch., 1992-93, N.Am. Pediatric AIDS Found., 1995. Author: Telemarketing Tickets, 1988; founder, editor: (newspaper) Albuquerque Street News, 1990; publisher: (newspaper) The New Mexican, 1991; contbr. articles to jours. Founder Permian Basin Rehab. Ctr., Odessa, 1983, Albuquerque (N.Mex.) Help for the Homeless, Inc., 1988. Recipient Cert. of Merit, Small Bus. Adminstrn., Odessa, 1984. Mem. Direct Mktg. Assn., Amnesty Internat. Home: Historic Coke House 1023 2nd St SW Albuquerque NM 87102-4124 Office: Advantage Ventures Inc 201 Pacific Ave SW Albuquerque NM 87102-4176

OTOROWSKI, CHRISTOPHER LEE, lawyer; b. Teaneck, N.J., Nov. 20, 1953; s. Wladyslaw Jerzy and Betty Lee (Robbins) O.; m. Shawn Elizabeth McGovern, Aug. 4, 1978; children: Kirsten, Hilary. BSBA cum laude, U. Denver, 1974, MBA, 1977, JD, 1977. Bar: Wash. 1977, Colo. 1977, U.S. Dist Ct. (we. dist.) D.C. 1977, U.S. Dist. Ct. (we. dist.) Wash. 1978. Asst. atty. gen. Wash. State Atty. Gen., Spokane, 1978-79; atty. Bassett, Gemson & Morrison, Seattle, 1979-81; pvt. practice Seattle, 1981-88; atty. Sullivan, Golden & Otorowski, Seattle, 1988-91, Morrow & Otorowski, Bainbridge Island, 1996—; pvt. practice Morrow and Otorowski, Bainbridge Island, Wash., 1991-96. Contbr. articles to profl. jours. Bd. dirs. Bainbridge Edn. Support Team, Bainbridge Island, 1991—. Mem. Fed. Bar Assn. We. Dist. Wash. (sec. 1979-82, trustee 1990-93), Wash. State Trial Lawyers Assn. (bd. govs. 1991-93), Assn. Trial Lawyers Am., Seattle Tennis Club, Seattle Yacht Club. Office: 298 Winslow Way W Bainbridge Island WA 98110

OTOSHI, TOM YASUO, electrical engineer, consultant; b. Seattle, Sept. 4, 1931; s. Jitsuo and Shina Otoshi; m. Haruko Shirley Yumiba, Oct. 13, 1963; children: John, Kathryn. BSEE, U. Wash., 1954, MSEE, 1957. With Hughes Aircraft Co., Culver City, Calif., 1956-61; sr. mem. tech. staff Jet Propulsion Lab., Calif. Inst. Tech., Pasadena, 1961—; cons. in field. Recipient NASA New Tech. awards, Exceptional Svc. medal NASA, 1994. Mem. Wagner Ensemble of Roger Wagner Choral Inst., L.A. Bach Festival Chorale. Fellow IEEE (life); mem. Sigma Xi, Tau Beta Pi. Contbr. articles to profl. jours; patentee in field. Home: 3551 Henrietta Ave La Crescenta CA 91214-1136 Office: Jet Propulsion Lab 4800 Oak Grove Dr Pasadena CA 91109-8001

OTT, ROBERT WILLIAM, publishing executive, corporate trainer, author; b. Cleve., Feb. 13, 1945; s. R.W. Ott and Mary Jane (Evar) Sahle; 1 child, Noelle. Grad. high sch., Cleve., 1964; BA, U. Calif., 1969, U. Calif., 1969; ind. studies Ea. and We. traditions, 1971-95. Mem. core staff Krishnamurti Found. Am., Ojai, Calif., 1975-79; v.p. Ojai Found., 1980-81; co-founder Sacred Arts, San Francisco, 1986; pres. The Terma Co., Santa Fe, Calif., 1990-96; founding ptnr. Living Systems, 1992—; bd. dirs. Ojai Found., 1993-95. Author: The Box: Remember the Gift, 1993. Bd. dirs. Concerned Citizens for Nuclear Safety, Santa Fe, 1991. Buddhist. Office: Living Systems, LTD CO PO Box 5495 Santa Fe NM 87502

OTT, WAYNE ROBERT, environmental engineer; b. San Mateo, Calif., Feb. 2, 1940; s. Florian Funstan and Evelyn Virginia (Smith) O.; m. Patricia Faustina Bertuzzi, June 28, 1967 (div. 1983). BA in Econs., Claremont McKenna Coll., 1962; BSEE, Stanford U., 1963, MS in Engring, 1965, MA in Comm., 1966, PhD in Environ. Engring., 1971. Commd. lt. USPHS, 1966, advanced to capt., 1986; chief lab. ops. br. U.S. EPA, Washington, 1971-73, sr. systems analyst, 1973-79, sr. rsch. engr., 1981-84, chief air toxics and radiation monitoring rsch. staff, 1984-90; vis. scientist dept. stats. Stanford (Calif.) U., 1979-81, 90—; vis. scholar Ctr. for Risk Analysis and dept. stats., civil engring., 1990-93; sr. environ. engr., EPA Atmospheric Rsch. and Exposure Assessment Lab, 1993-95; consulting prof. of civil engring. Stanford (Calif.) U., 1995—; dir. field studies Calif. Environ. Tobacco Smoke Study, 1993-95. Author: Environmental Indices: Theory and Practice, 1976, Environmental Statistics and Data Analysis, 1995; contbr. articles on indoor air pollution, total human exposure to chems., stochastic models of indoor exposure, motor vehicle exposures, personal monitoring instruments, and environ. tobacco smoke to profl. jours. Decorated Commendation medal USPHS, 1977; recipient Nat. Statistician award for outstanding contribution to environ. statistics EPA, 1995, Commendable Svc. Bronze medal for assessing human exposure from motor vehicle pollution, 1996. Mem. Internat. Soc. Exposure Analysis (v.p. 1989-90, Jerome J. Weselowski Internat. award for career achievement in exposure assessmemt 1995), Am. Statis. Assn., Am. Soc. for Quality Control, Air and Waste Mgmt. Assn., Internat. Soc. Indoor Air Quality and Climate, Phi Beta Kappa, Sigma Xi, Tau Beta Pi, Kappa Mu Epsilon. Democrat. Clubs: Theater, Jazz, Sierra. Avocations: hiking, photography, model trains, jazz recording. Developer nationally uniform air pollution index, first total human exposure activity pattern models. Home: 1008 Cardiff Ln Redwood City CA 94061-3678 Office: Stanford U Dept Stats Sequoia Hall Stanford CA 94305

OTTEN, ARTHUR EDWARD, JR., lawyer, corporate executive; b. Buffalo, Oct. 11, 1930; s. Arthur Edward Sr. and Margaret (Ambrusko) O.; m. Mary Therese Torri, Oct. 1, 1960; children: Margaret, Michael, Maureen Staley, Suzanne Hoodecheck, Jennifer. BA, Hamilton Coll., 1952; JD, Yale U., 1955. Bar: N.Y. 1955, Colo. 1959. Assoc. Hodges, Silverstein, Hodges & Harrington, Denver, 1959-64; ptnr. Hodges, Kerwin, Otten & Weeks (predecessor firms), Denver, 1964-73, Davis, Graham & Stubbs, Denver, 1973-86; gen. counsel Colo. Nat. Bankshares, Inc., 1973-93; pres., mem. Otten, Johnson, Robinson, Neff & Ragonetti, P.C., Denver, 1986—; rec. sec. Colo. Nat. Bankshares, Inc., Denver, 1983-93; gen. counsel Regis U., Denver, 1994—; com. bd. Centura Health, Denver, St. Anthony Hosps., Denver. Lt. USN, 1955-59. Mem. ABA, Colo. Bar Assn., Denver Bar Assn., Am. Arbitration Assn. (panel arbitrators, large complex case panel, mediator panel), Nat. Assn. Securities Dealers (bd. arbitrators), Law club, Univ. Club, Denver Mile High Rotary (pres. 1992-93), Phi Delta Phi. Republican. Roman Catholic. Home: 3774 S Niagara Way Denver CO 80237-1248 Office: Otten Johnson Robinson Neff & Ragonetti PC 1600 Colorado National Bldg 950 17th St Denver CO 80202-1056

OTTEN, THOMAS, zoological park director. Student, El Camino Coll., 1965-68, Brigham Young U., 1969. Animal keeper, aquarist Marineland, Rancho Palos Verde, Calif., 1969-70, lead dolphin trainer, 1970-73, curator of mammals, 1973; gen. curator, dep. dir. Point Defiance Zoo & Aquarium, Tacoma, Wash., 1981, zoo dir., 1985—; mem. adj. faculty U. Puget Sound, Tacoma, 1985-90. Contbr. articles to profl. jours. Mem. Am. Assn. Zool. Parks and Aquariums, Internat. Assn. Aquatic Animal Medicine, Internat. Soc. Zooculturalists, Marine Mammal Interest Group (chmn. 1990). Office: Point Defiance Zoo & Aquarium 5400 N Pearl St Tacoma WA 98407-3218

OTTENSMEYER, DAVID JOSEPH, healthcare consultant, retired neurosurgeon; b. Nashville, Tenn., Jan. 29, 1930; s. Raymond Stanley and Glenda Jessie (Helpingstein) O.; m. Mary Jean Langley, June 30, 1954; children: Kathryn Joan, Martha Langley. BA, Wis State U., Superior, 1951; MD, U. Wis., Madison, 1959; MS in Health Svcs. Adminstrn., Coll. St. Francis, 1985. Diplomate Am. Bd. Neurological Surgery. Intern then resident in gen. surgery Univ. Hosps., Madison, Wis., 1959-61; resident in neurol. surgery Univ. Hosps., 1962-65; staff neurosurgeon Marshfield Clinic, Wis., 1965-76; from instr. of neurol. surgery to clin. asst. prof. U. Wis. Med. Sch., Madison, 1964-77; CEO Lovelace Med. Ctr., Albuquerque, 1976-86, chmn., 1986-91; clin. prof. community medicine U. N.Mex., Albuquerque, 1977-79, clin. prof. neurol. surgery, 1979-92; exec. v.p., chief med. officer Equicor, 1986-90; part-time cons. pvt. practice, 1996; bd. dirs. Exogen Inc., Ultrasite Inc., United Clin. Rsch.; v.p. Marshfield Clinic, 1970-71, pres., CEO, 1972-75; pres., CEO The Lovelace Insts., 1991-96; sr. v.p., chief med. officer Travelers Ins. Co., 1990-91; served on numerous adv. and com. posts. Contbr. articles to profl. jours. Col. USAR, 1960-90. Fellow ACS, Am. Coll. Physician Execs. (pres. 1985-86); mem. Am. Group Practice Assn. (pres. 1983-84), Am. Bd. Med. Mgmt. (bd. dirs. 1989-95, chmn. 1995). Republican. Episcopalian. Home: 2815 Ridgecrest Dr SE Albuquerque NM 87108-5132

OTTER, CLEMENT LEROY, lieutenant governor; b. Caldwell, Idaho, May 3, 1942; s. Joseph Bernard and Regina Mary (Buser) O.; m. Gay Corinne Simplot, Dec. 28, 1964; children: John Simplot, Carolyn Lee, Kimberly Dawn, Corinne Marie. BA in Polit. Sci., Coll. Idaho, 1967; PhD, Mindanao State U., 1980. Mgr. J.R. Simplot Co., Caldwell, Idaho, 1971-76, asst. to v.p. adminstrn., 1976-78, v.p. adminstrn., 1978-82, internat. pres., from 1982, now v.p.; lt. gov. State of Idaho, Boise, 1987—. Mem. Presdl. Task Force-AID, Washington, 1982-84; com. mem. invest tech. devel. State Adv. Council, Washington, 1983-84; mem. exec. council Bretton Woods Com., 1984—; mem. U.S. C. of C., Washington, 1983-84. Mem. Young Pres.' Orgn., Sales and Mktg. Execs., Idaho Assn. Commerce and Industry, Idaho Agrl. Leadership Council, Idaho Ctr. for Arts, Idaho Internat. Trade Council, Pacific N.W. Waterways Assn., N.W. Food Producers, Ducks Unltd. Republican. Roman Catholic. Clubs: Arid, Hillcrest Country. Lodge: Moose, Elks. Office: Office of the Lt Gov PO Box 83720 Boise ID 83720-0057*

OTTO, CHARLES WILSON, anesthesiologist, educator; b. Omaha, Dec. 3, 1941; s. Claude W. and Mary A. (Adams) O.; m. Carol Elaine Todd, May 24, 1969; children: Christopher Wade, Deborah Anne. BA, Swarthmore Coll., 1963; MD, U. Mo., Columbia, 1968. Diplomate Am. Bd. Anesthesiology, Am. Bd. Internal Medicine. Intern, resident internal medicine U. Ky., Lexington, 1968-70; resident in anesthesiology and critical care Harvard U./ Mass. Gen. Hosp., Boston, 1972-75; asst. prof. anesthesia and medicine U. Ariz. Coll. Medicine, Tucson, 1975-82, assoc. prof. anesthesia and medicine, 1982-88, prof. anesthesia, assoc. prof. medicine, 1988—; assoc. examiner Am. Bd. Anesthesiology, Hartford, Conn., 1986—; cons. FDA, Washington, 1986-88, NIH, Washington, 1991—. Assoc. editor Survey of Anesthesiology, Balt., 1984—; contbr. articles to profl. publs., chpts., to textbooks. Fellow Am. Coll. Critical Care Medicine; mem. AMA, Ariz. Med. Assn., Am. Soc. Anesthesiologists (alt. dir. 1989—), Ariz. Soc. Anesthesiologists (pres. 1984-85), Soc. Critical Care Medicine (dir. anesthesiology sect. 1991—), Assn. Univ. Anesthesiologists, Am. Soc. Critical Care Anesthesiologists. Office: U Ariz Dept Anesthesiology 1501 N Campbell Ave Tucson AZ 85724-0001

OTTO, JOSEPH CLAIR, information systems educator; b. Carroll, Iowa, Nov. 4, 1955; s. Clair Joseph and Lou Ann (Wolterman) O.; children: Tyler, Abigail, Hayley, Taylor. BS, Iowa State U., 1978; MS, Ea. Ill. U., 1982; EdD, Memphis State U., 1987. Rsch. asst. Ea. Ill. U., Charleston, Ill., 1979-80; instr. Sparks Coll., Shelbyville, Ill., 1980-84, Memphis State U., 1984-86; prof. Calif. State U., L.A., 1986—; cons. Riverside C.C., Norco, Calif., 1992—. Author: (textbooks) A Mastery Approach to Lotus 1-2-3, 2.3, 2.4, 1993, Spreadsheet Applications Job-Based Tasks, 1992, A Mastery Approach to Lotus 1-2-3, 2.2, 1991, Power Up With Lotus 5 for Windows, 1996. Mem. Nat. Bus. Edn. Assn., Calif. Bus. Edn. Assn. (cert. of recognition 1994, Profl. Svc. award 1991; conf. com. 1986—, state legis. com., strategic planning com., past pres.), Delta Pi Epsilon (cert. of merit Nat. Coun. 1992). Home: 12916 Saratoga Pl Chino Hills CA 91709-1103 Office: Calif State U 5151 State University Dr Los Angeles CA 90032-4221

OTTO, KLAUS, physicist, physical chemist; b. Friedrichroda, Germany, Sept. 18, 1929; came to U.S., 1960, naturalized, 1967; s. Theodor M.W.A. and Gertrud (Gohla) O.; m. Christa Thomsen, Nov. 16, 1962; children: Ina N., Peter N. Vordiplom, U. Hamburg, Fed. Republic of Germany, 1954, Diplom, 1957, D of Natural Scis., 1960. Rsch. asst. U. Hamburg, 1959-60; postdoctoral fellow Argonne (Ill.) Nat. Lab., 1960-62; sr. rsch. scientist Ford Motor Co., Dearborn, Mich., 1962-73, prin. rsch. scientist assoc., 1973-81, staff scientist, 1981-95; ret., 1995; adj. prof. Mich. State U., 1986-95. Contbr. articles to profl. jours. Recipient Parravano award for excellence in catalysis rsch. and devel., 1986. Mem. AAAS, Am. Chem. Soc., German Bunsen Soc. of Electrochemistry, Mich. Catalysis Soc. (pres. 1980-81), N.Y. Acad. Scis., Sigma Xi (pres. Ford chpt. 1985-86). Home: 201 E Tonto Dr Sedona AZ 86351-7323

OUELLETTE, DEBRA LEE, administrative assistant, policy and procedure consultant; b. Butte, Mont., Aug. 1, 1962; d. Eugene George and Avonne Gail (Smeltzer) O.; m. Anthony Lee Jaeger, Aug. 27, 1994. BA in Soc. and Tech., Mont. Tech. Inst., 1985. Photographer, trainer Mountain States Energy, Butte, 1984-85; lab. asst. Western Energy, Butte, 1985-86, receptionist, 1986; acctg. data entry clk. N.Am. Resources, Butte, 1986, lease and oil data entry clk., 1986-87; data entry clk. Spl. Resource Mgmt., Butte, 1987-89; adminstrv. asst. N.Am. Indian Alliance, Butte, 1989—. Designer chem. dependency forms. Mem.-at-large Vol. Ctr., Butte, 1995-96. Outstanding Pub. Svc. award Soc. Security Adminstrn., Proctective Payee Program.Personnal Invitation to Pres. Inauguration. Mem. VFW Ladies Aux. (sr. v.p. 1994-96). Office: NAm Indian Alliance 100 E Galena Butte MT 59701

OUSLEY, PAMELA DARLENE, legal assistant; b. Norman, Okla., June 26, 1956; d. Gary Lee and Edna Elmira (Horn) O. BA in Psychology, Phillips U., 1978; cert. paralegal, Denver Paralegal Inst., 1989. Office clk., sec. Marley Cooling Tower Co., Overland Park, Kans., 1980-81; acctg. clk. Colorado Springs (Colo.) Cablevision, 1981-84; check proofer-acctg. Current, Inc., Colorado Springs, 1985-86; accounts receivable clk. Garden of the Gods Club, Colorado Springs, 1986-89; paralegal intern Dist. Atty. 4th Jud. Dist., Colorado Springs, 1989; office clk. Western Temp. Svcs., Colorado Springs, 1989-90; legal researcher, writer Prestige Paralegal Svcs., Colorado Springs, 1990-91; office mgr. Queen & Co., Colorado Springs, 1990-91; legal asst. Wiley Hurst & Assocs., Yakima, Wash., 1991-95, Law Offices Robert W. Warren, Seattle, 1996—. Author: Legal Dentistry = Toxic Free Dentistry, 1994, The Law and Mercury-Free Dentistry, 1994. Parliamentarian, v.p. Comet Club, Enid, Okla., 1975-78; v.p., pres. Circle K, Enid, 1976-78. Democrat.

OUTTERBRIDGE, JOHN WILFRED, artist, art administrator; b. Greenville, N.C., Mar. 12, 1933; s. John Ivery and Olivia (Northern) O.; m. Beverly Marie Outterbridge, Jan. 23, 1960 (div. Sept. 1991); 1 child, Tami Lynn. Student, Agrl. & Tech. U., Greensboro, 1952-53, Am. Acad. Art, Chgo., 1956-59; DFA (hon.), Otis Coll. Art and Design, L.A., 1994. Cert. tchr., Calif., 1970. Artist/designer Aircraft, a divsn. Traid Corp., L.A., 1964-68; art instr., fine art installer Pasadena Mus. Art, 1967-72; co-founder, artistic dir. Communicative Arts Acad., Compton, Calif., 1969-75; lectr. arts and humanities dept. Calif. State U., Carson, 1970-73; artist/dir. Watts Towers Art Ctr., Cultural Affairs Dept., City of L.A., 1975-92. Exhbns. include Long Beach (Calif.) Mus. Art, 1968, 71, 90, LaJolla (Calif.) Mus. Art, 1970, L.A. County Mus. Art, 1972, Brockman Gallery, L.A., 1972, Renshaw Gallery, McMinnville, Oreg., 1973, Mcpl. Arts Gallery, 1976, E.B. Crocker Art Gallery, Sacramento, 1974, N.C. Mus. Art, 1980, Calif. Afro-Am. Mus., 1984, 89, 93, Everson Mus. Art, 1986, Armory Ctr. for the Arts, Pasadena, 1989, Wight Art Gallery, UCLA, 1989, The Patrick and Beatrice Haggerty Mus. Art, Milw., 1993, Haggerty Mus. Art/Marquette U., 1993, Calif. Afro-Am. Mus. Art, L.A., 1993, L.A. Mcpl. Arts Gallery, 1994, Transitional Met. Coun., South Africa, 1994, Studio Mus. of Harlem, 1995; solo shows include Rancho Santiago Coll. Art Gallery, 1992; contbr. articles to profl. jours. Mem. Gov.'s selection com. for directorship Calif. State Arts Coun., 1978; adv. com. getty Inst. for Arts Edn., 1978-80; visual arts panelist Nat. Endowment of the Arts, 1978-80, others in past. Fulbright fellow to Nat. Conf. of Maori Artists N.Z., 1988, J.R. Hyde Vis. Artist fellow Memphis Inst. of the Arts, 1994, J. Paul Getty fellow for visual arts, 1994, Nat. Ednowment for the Arts fellow, 1994. Home: 5838 Woodlawn Ave Los Angeles CA 90003-1226

OUZTS, EUGENE THOMAS, minister, secondary education educator; b. Thomasville, Ga., June 7, 1930; s. John Travis and Livie Mae (Strickland) O.; m. Mary Olive Vineyard, May 31, 1956. BA, Harding U., 1956, MA, 1957; postgrad., Murray State U., U. Ark., U. Ariz., Ariz. State U., No. Ariz. U. Cert. secondary tchr., Ark., Mo., Ariz.; cert. c.c. tchr., Ariz.; ordained minister Church of Christ, 1956. Min. various chs., Ark., Mo., 1957-65; tchr. various pub. schs., Ark., Mo., 1959—; min. Ch. of Christ, Clifton and Morenci, Ariz., 1965—; 1st lt. CAP/USAF, 1980, advanced through grades to lt. col., 1989; chaplain CAP/USAF, Ariz., 1982—; asst. wing chaplain CAP/USAF, 1985—; adviser student activities Clifton (Ariz.) Pub. Schs., 1965-92; bd. dirs. Ariz. Ch. of Christ Bible Camp, Tucson, 1966—. Mem. airport adv. bd. Greenlee County, Clifton, Ariz., 1992—. Mem. Mil. Chaplains Assn., Disabled Am. Vets., Am. Legion, Elks. Democrat. Home and Office: HC 1 Box 557 Duncan AZ 85534-9720

OVENS, MARI CAMILLE, school system administrator, dietitian; b. Spokane, Wash., June 18, 1954; d. Harold Chester and May Eloise (Gundry) Chapman; m. Dana Preston Ovens, Dec. 18, 1985; children: Dylan Preston, Delaney Camille. BS in Dietetics, Ea. Wash. U., 1976; MS in Home Econs., Wash. State U., 1979. Registered dietitian, Wash. Dietary coord. City of Vancouver, Wash., 1978-83; clin. dietitian Eastmoreland Gen. Hosp., Portland, Oreg., 1983; supr. child nutrition Vancouver Sch. Dist. 37, 1983—; mem. culinary arts adv. bd. Clark Coll., Vancouver, 1983—; mem. task force Am. Heart Assns., Seattle, 1988—. Mem. Am. Sch. Food Svc. Assn., (registered dir., adminstr. III), Am. Dietetic Assn. (Recognized Young Dietitian of Yr. Wash. State 1983), Wash. Sch. Food Svc. Assn. (treas. 1989-91, trainer 1993—), Wash. State Dietetic Assn., Soroptimists (pres. Vancouver 1990-92). Office: Vancouver Sch Dist 37 PO Box 8937 Vancouver WA 98668-8937

OVERBY, MONESSA MARY, clinical supervisor, counselor; b. Staples, Minn., Sept. 7, 1932; d. Joseph Melvin Overby and Marie Frances (Fellman) Vollstedt. BS, Coll. of St. Teresa, 1964; MS, Winona State U., 1978. Entered Franciscan Sisters, Roman Cath. Ch., 1953; nat. cert. counselor, Gestalt therapist, trainer. Elem. and jr. high tchr. Cath. Sch. System, Austin, Tracy, Lake City, Minn., 1955-67; sch. adminstr. McCahill Inst., Lake City, 1964-70; pastoral counselor and adult educator St. Edward's, Austin, Minn., 1970-76; adj. faculty and campus minister Winona (Minn.) State U., 1976-84; psychotherapist Family & Children's Ctr. and Human Devel. Assocs., La Crosse, Wis., 1978-84; family counselor Betty Ford Ctr., Rancho Mirage, Calif., 1987-89, dir. family and outpatient svcs., 1990—; workshop presenter in field. Mem. Am. Counseling Assn., Assn. for Specialists in Group Work, Minn. Assn. Specialists in Group Work (founding pres.). Democrat. Roman Catholic. Office: Betty Ford Ctr 39000 Bob Hope Dr Rancho Mirage CA 92270-3221

OVERBY, PAUL, writer, political analyst; b. Hazelcrest, Ill., Nov. 27, 1942; m. Jane Leung Larson, June 21, 1980. BA, Reed Coll., Portland, Oreg., 1966. Founder Pub. Power Action Group, Portland, 1978-85. Author: Holy Blood: An Inside View of the Afghan War, 1993; contbr. articles to profl. jours.

OVERELL, WILLIAM LAWRENCE, finance executive; b. Bismarck, N.D., Dec. 30, 1947; s. Lawrence V. and M. Helen (Hynes) O.; m. Patricia Miskimen, June 7, 1969; children: Edward, Michael, Mary. BS, Purdue U., 1969; MBA, Stanford U., 1971. CPA, Calif. Cons. Arthur Andersen & Co., San Francisco, 1971-74; v.p., contr. Spectra Physics, San Jose, Calif., 1974-89; v.p. fin. and adminstrn., CFO Gamma Microwave, Santa Clara, Calif., 1989-90; cons. Los Altos, Calif., 1990-92; sr. v.p. fin., CFO Ins. Auto Auctions, North Hollywood, Calif., 1992-96; v.p. fin., CFO Software Techs. Corp., Arcadia, Calif., 1996—. Mem. Fin. Execs. Inst., AICPA, Assn. Computing Machinery. Roman Catholic. Home: 2120 Monterey Rd South Pasadena CA 91030-3939 Office: Software Techs Corp PO Box 661090 Arcadia CA 91066

OVERGAARD, WILLARD MICHELE, retired political scientist, jurisprudent; b. Montpelier, Idaho, Oct. 16, 1925; s. Elias Nielsen and Myrtle LaVerne (Humphrey) O.; m. Lucia Clare Cochrane, June 14, 1946; children: Eric Willard, Mark Fredrik, Alisa Claire. B.A., U. Oreg., 1949; Fulbright scholar, U. Oslo, 1949-50; M.A. (non-resident scholar 1954-55), U. Wis., Madison, 1955; Ph.D. in Polit. Sci. (adminstrv. fellow 1955-56, research fellow 1962-64), U. Minn., 1969. Instr., Soviet and internat. affairs Intelligence Sch., U.S. Army, Europe, 1956-62; dir. intelligence rsch. tng. program Intelligence Sch., U.S. Army, 1958-61; asst. prof. internat. affairs George Washington U., 1964-67; sr. staff polit. scientist Ops. Research Inst., U.S. Army Inst. Advanced Studies, Carlisle, Pa., 1967-70; assoc. prof. polit. sci., chmn. dept., dir. Internat. Studies Inst., Westminster Coll., New Wilmington, Pa., 1970-72; prof. polit. sci. and pub. law Boise (Idaho) State U., 1972-94, chmn. dept., 1972-87, acad. dir. M.P.A. degree program, personnel adminstr., mem. humanities council interdisciplinary studies in humanities, 1976-87, prof. of pub. law emeritus, 1994—, dir. Taft Inst. Seminars for Pub. Sch. Tchrs., 1985-87, coord. Legal Asst. Program, 1990-95; mem. comml. panel Am. Arbitration Assn., 1974—; mem. Consortium for Idaho's Future, 1974-75; adv. com. Idaho Statewide Tng. Program Local Govt. Ofcls., 1974-78; adv. group Gov. Idaho Task Force Local Govt., 1977; co-dir. Idaho State Exec. Inst., Office of Gov., 1979-83; grievance hearing officer City of Boise, 1981-85; arbitrator U.S. Postal Svc., 1988-90; cons. in field. Author: The Schematic System of Soviet Totalitarianism, 3 vols, 1961, Legal Norms and Normative Bases for the Progressive Development of International Law as Defined in Soviet Treaty Relations, 1945-64, 1969; co-author: The Communist Bloc in Europe, 1959; editor: Continuity and Change in International Politics, 1972; chief editor: Idaho Jour. Politics, 1974-76. Served with USAAF, 1943-45; with AUS, 1951-54; ret. maj. USAR. Named Disting. Citizen of Idaho Idaho Statesman, 1979; named Outstanding Prof. of Sch. Social Scis. and Pub. Affairs, Boise State U., 1988. Mem. ABA (assoc.), Res. Officers Assn. (life). Home: 2023 S Five Mile Rd Boise ID 83709-2316

OVERHOLT, MILES HARVARD, cable television consultant; b. Glendale, Calif., Sept. 30, 1921; s. Miles Harvard and Alma Overholt; A.B., Harvard Coll., 1943; m. Jessie Foster, Sept. 18, 1947; children: Miles Harvard, Keith Foster. Mktg. analyst Dun & Bradstreet, Phila., 1947-48; collection mgr. Standard Oil of Calif., L.A., 1948-53; br. mgr. RCA Svc. Co., Phila., 1953-63, ops. mgr. Classified Aerospace project RCA, Riverton, N.J., 1963; pres. CPS, Inc., Paoli, Pa., 1964-67; v.p. Gen. Time Corp.; mem. pres.'s exec. com. Gen. Time Corp., Mesa, Ariz., 1970-78; gen. mgr., dir. svc. Talley Industries, Mesa, 1967-78; v.p., gen. mgr. Northwest Entertainment Network, Inc., Seattle, 1979-81; v.p., dir. Cable Communication Cons., 1982—; mcpl. cable cons., 1981—; pub. The Mcpl. Cable Regulator. Served with USMCR, 1943-46. Decorated Bronze Star, Purple Heart (two). Mem. Nat. Assn. TV Officers and Advisors. Home: 8320 Frederick Pl Edmonds WA 98026-5033 Office: Cable Communication Cons 502 E Main St Auburn WA 98002-5502

OVERLY, FREDERICK DEAN, civilian military employee, entrepreneur; b. Miami, Fla., Jan. 2, 1953; s. Harry Robert and Beverly Beryl (Dengler) O.; m. Cheryl Diane Battle, June 23, 1975 (div. Aug. 1976); Joanne Elizabeth Smart, Dec. 28, 1979; children: Heidi Johanna, Melissa Elizabeth Emma. AA in Forestry, Fla. Jr. Coll., Jacksonville, 1975; BS in Ethology, So. Ill. U., 1980. Pers. officer First Interstate Bank, Anchorage, Alaska, 1985; pers. mgmt. Alaska NG, Anchorage, 1986-89, mgmt. analyst, 1989—; cons. Kaladi Bros. Coffee Co., Inc., Anchorage, 1989—. Participant Alaska Pacific rim issue, Commonwealth North, Anchorage, 1993. Maj. USAF, 1980-84; maj. Alaska Air N.G., 1984—. Mem. Res. Officers Assn., Air Force Assn. (past pres. chpt. 103), Found. N.Am. Wild Sheep, Alaska NG Officer Assn., Safari Club Internat., Roll-Royce Owners Club, Rotary Internat. Lutheran. Office: Alaskan NG 176 Wing 5005 Raspberry Rd Anchorage AK 99502-1982

OVERMAN, LARRY EUGENE, chemistry educator; b. Chgo., Mar. 9, 1943; s. Lemoine Emerson and Dorothy Jane Overman; m. Joanne Louise Dewey, June 5, 1966; children: Michael, Jackie. BA in Chemistry, Earlham Coll., 1965; PhD in Organic Chemistry, U. Wis., 1969. Asst. prof. chemistry U. Calif., Irvine, 1971-76, assoc. prof. chemistry, 1976-79, prof. chemistry, 1979—, chair dept. chemistry, 1990-93, disting. prof. chemistry, 1994—; mem. sci. adv. bd. Pharmacopeia, Inc., 1993—. Bd. editors Organic Reactions, 1984—, Organic Syntheses, 1986-94; mem. editl. adv. bd. Ann. Reports in Hetero Chem., 1989—, Synlett, 1989—, Jour. Am. Chem. Soc., 1996—, Chem. Revs., 1996—, Accounts Chem. Rsch., 1996—; mem. cons. editors Tetrahedron Publs., 1995—. NIH fellow, 1969-71, A.P. Sloan Found. fellow, 1975-77; Arthur C. Cope scholar, 1989; Guggenheim fellow, 1993-94; recipient Sr. Scientist award Alexander von Humboldt Found., 1985-87, Jacob Javits award Nat. Inst. Neurol. Sci., 1985-91, 92—. Fellow NAS, Am. Acad. Arts and Scis.; mem. Am. Chem. Soc. (exec. com. organic divsn., Cope Scholar award 1989, Creative Work in Synthetic Organic Chemistry award 1995), Royal Soc. Chemistry. Office: U Calif Irvine Dept Chemistry 516 Physical Scis 1 Irvine CA 92697-2025

OVERSON, BRENT C., municipal official, former state senator; b. Nephi, Utah, Apr. 18, 1950; s. Fay Dean and Elda Rae (Huntsman) O.; m. Joanne Robison, Nov. 18, 1971; 3 children. A.A., U. Md., 1978; B.S. in Fin., U. Utah, 1982. Lic. real estate broker. Sales agt., office mgr. Envirowest Realty, Inc., Salt Lake City, 1978-82, 85-87; v.p. real estate and devel. Trailside Gen. Stores, Bountiful, Utah, 1982-85; chmn. County Salt Lake City office of Bd. County Commrs., 1995—; mem. Utah Senate, 1983-86; chief dep. assessor, Salt Lake County, 1987—. Served with USN, 1972-78. Mem. Nat. Assn. Realtors, Internat. Assn. Assessing Officers (bd. dirs. Utah chpt.) Republican. Mormon. Office: Office Bd County Commrs 2001 S State St Ste N 2100 Salt Lake City UT 84910-1000*

OVERSTREET, HON. KAREN A., federal bankruptcy judge. BA cum laude, Univ. of Wash., 1977; JD, Univ. of Oregon, 1982. Assoc. Duane, Morris & Heckscher, Phila., 1983-86; ptnr. Davis Wright Tremaine, Seattle, 1986-93; bankruptcy judge U.S. Bankruptcy Ct. (we. dist.) Wash., Seattle, 1994—; assoc. editor Oregon Law Review; dir. People's Law Sch.; mem. advisory com. U.S. Bankruptcy Ct. (we. dist.) Wash. Mem. Nat. Conf. of Bankruptcy Judges, Wash. State Bar Assn. (creditor-debtor sec.), Seattle-King County Bar Assn. (bankruptcy sec.), Am. Bar Assn., Wash. Women Lawyers Assn. Office: US Bankruptcy Ct Park Place Bldg 1200 6th Ave Ste 424 Seattle WA 98101-1128*

OVERTON, EDWIN DEAN, campus minister, educator; b. Beaver, Okla., Dec. 2, 1939; s. William Edward and Georgia Beryl (Fronk) O. BTh, Midwest Christian Coll., 1963; MA in Religion, Eastern N.Mex. U., 1969, EdS, 1978; postgrad. Fuller Theol. Sem., 1980. Ordained to ministry Christian Ch., 1978. Minister, Christian Ch., Englewood, Kans., 1962-63; youth minister First Christian Ch., Beaver, Okla., 1963-67; campus minister Central Christian Ch., Portales, N.Mex., 1967-68, Christian Campus House, Portales, N.Mex., 1968-70; tchr. religion, philosophy, counseling Eastern N.Mex. Univ., Portales, 1970—, campus minister, Christian Campus House, 1968—, dir., 1980—; farm and ranch partner, Beaver, Okla., 1963—. State dir. Beaver Jr. C. of C., 1964-65; pres. Beaver High Sch. Alumni Assn., 1964-65; elder Cen. Christian Ch., Portales, 1985-88, 1990-93; chmn. Beaver County March of Dimes, 1966; pres. Portales Tennis Assn., 1977-78. Mem. U.S. Tennis Assn., Am. Assn. Christian Counselors, Ea. N.Mex. U. Faith in Life Com. Republican. Club: Lions. Home: 1129 Libra Dr Portales NM 88130-6123 Office: 223 S Avenue K Portales NM 88130-6643

OVIATT, LARRY ANDREW, retired secondary school educator; b. Boone, Iowa, Mar. 13, 1939; s. Eli Charles and T. Mae (Lathrop) O.; children: Julia, Vanessa, Dana. BA, Drake U., Des Moines, 1962; MS, San Diego State U., 1975. Tchr. art San Diego City Schs., 1969-96, mentor tchr., 1992-96; owner Perfect Travel of La Jolla, 1989—. San Diego dir. Anderson for Pres., 1976; dist. coord. Hedgecock for Mayor, San Diego, 1984; dir. elder Help Corp., San Diego, 1988; v.p. Afrian Am. Mus., 1989-92; pres. Sushi Gallery, 1980-82; bd. dirs. Mingei Internat. Mus., 1983-87; pres. Cmty. Svc. Assn., 1984-88; past pres. Diversionary Theatre, African Am. Mus.; dir. AIDS Walk for Life, 1988, 89; bd. dirs. AIDS Art Alive. Named 1986 Tchr. of Yr. Urban League, 1986, Sec. Art Tchr. of Yr. Calif. Art Tchrs. Assn., 1988, Art Tchr. of Yr. Calif. Art Tchrs. Assn., 1992, Vol. of Yr. San Diego City Schs., 1993. Mem. So. Calif. Art Tchrs. Assn. (pres. 1984-89), Calif. Art Edn. Assn. (dir. 1984-89, conf. adminstr., Art Edn. Tchr. of Yr. award 1992), Nat. Art Edn. Assn. (dir. 1987-93). Home: 1571 E Orange Grove Pasadena CA 91104-4727 Office: San Diego City Schs 4100 Normal St San Diego CA 92103-2653

OVITZ, MICHAEL S., communications executive; b. 1946; m. Judy Reich, 1969; 3 children. Grad., UCLA, 1968. With William Morris Agy., 1968-75; co-founder, chmn. Creative Artists Agy., L.A., 1975-95; pres. Walt Disney Co., Burbank, Calif., 1995-97; mem. bd. advisors Med. Sch. UCLA, bd. dirs. Sch. Theatre, Film and TV. Trustee St. John's Hosp. and Health Ctr., Santa Monica, Calif., Mus. Modern Art, N.Y.C.; bd. govs. Cedars-Sinai Hosp., L.A.; mem. exec. adv. bd. Pediatric AIDS Found.; bd. dirs. Calif. Inst. Arts, Sundance Inst. Mem. Zeta Beta Tau. Office: Dreyer Edmonds & Assocs 355 S Grand Ave Ste 4150 Los Angeles CA 90071*

OWEN, BRADLEY SCOTT, lieutenant governor; b. Tacoma, May 23, 1950; s. Laural Willis; m. Linda Owen; children: Shanie, Dana, Mark, Sherrie, Adam, Royce. Student pub. sch., Germany. State rep. Wash. Ho. Rep., Olympia, 1976-82; state senator Wash. State Senate, Olympia, 1983-96; lt. gov. State Wash., Olympia, 1997—. Mem. Wash. State substance abuse coun., 1997—. Mem. Elks, Kiwanis. Democrat. Office: Wash State Lt Gov PO Box 40400 Olympia WA 98504-0400

OWEN, CAROL THOMPSON, artist, educator; b. Pasadena, Calif., May 10, 1944; d. Sumner Comer and Cordelia (Whittemore) Thompson; m. James Eugene Owen, July 19, 1975; children: Kevin Christopher, Christine Celese. Student, Pasadena City Coll., 1963; BA with distinction, U. Redlands, 1966; MA, Calif. State U., L.A., 1967; MFA, Claremont Grad. Sch., 1969. Cert. community coll. instr., Calif. Head resident Pitzer Coll., Claremont, Calif., 1967-70; instr. art Mt. San Antonio Coll., Walnut, Calif., 1968-96, prof. art, 1996—, dir. coll. art gallery, 1972-73. Group shows include Covina Pub. Libr., 1971, U. Redlands, 1964, 65, 66, 70, 78, 88, 92, Am. Ceramic Soc., 1969, Mt. San Antonio Coll., 1991, The Aesthetic Process, 1993, Separate Realities, 1995, San Bernardino County Mus., 1996, 97, others; ceramic mural commd. and installed U. Redlands, 1991. Recipient award San Bernardino County Mus., 1996, Past Pres.'s Monetary award, 1997. Mem. Am. Ceramic Soc. (design divsn.), Calif. Scholarship Fedn., Faculty Assn. Mt. San Antonio Coll., Coll. Art Assn. Am., Calif. Tchrs. Assn., Friends of Huntington Library, L.A. County Mus. Art, Redlands Art Assn., Heard Mus. Assn., Sigma Tau Delta. Republican. Presbyterian. Home: 534 S Hepner Ave Covina CA 91723-2921 Office: Mt San Antonio Coll Grand Ave Walnut CA 91789

OWEN, JOHN, retired newspaper editor; b. Helena, Mont., June 10, 1929; s. John Earl and Ella Jean (McMillian) O.; m. Alice Winnifred Kesler, June 9, 1951; children—David Scott, Kathy Lynn. B.A. in Journalism, U. Mont., 1951. Sports editor Bismarck (N.D.) Tribune, 1953-55; wire editor Yakima (Wash.) Herald, 1956; with Seattle Post-Intelligencer, 1956-94, sports editor, 1968-80, assoc. editor, 1980-94, columnist, 1968-94. Author: Intermediate Eater Cookbook, 1974, Gourmand Gutbusters Cookbook, 1980, Seattle Cookbook, 1983, Great Grub Hunt Cookbook, 1989, Press Pass, 1994; also short stories. Served with AUS, 1951-52. Named Top Sports Writer in Wash. Nat. Sportswriters Orgn., 1966, 68, 69, 71, 74, 85, 88. Home: 611 Bell St Apt 4 Edmonds WA 98020-3065

OWEN, WILLIAM FREDERICK, engineering and management consultant; b. Pontiac, Mich., July 27, 1947; s. Webster Jennings and Elizabeth (Hayes) W.; m. Delores T. Owen, Mar. 30, 1974 (div. Dec. 1978); m. Janice L. Pierce, July 29, 1983. BS, Mich. Tech. U., 1972; MS, U. Mich., 1973; PhD, Stanford U., 1978. Research engr. Neptune Microfloc, Corvallis, Oreg., 1973-75, process applications engr., 1975-76; process applications engr. Dr. Perry McCarty, Stanford, Calif., 1976-78; sr. engr. Culp/Wesner/Culp, Cameron Park, Calif., 1978-82; pres. Owen Engring. and Mgmt. Cos., Denver, 1982—. Author: Energy in Wastewater Treatment, 1982, Turbo Mainenance Manager. Del. People-to-People, People's Republic China, 1986. Served with USN, 1965-68. Recipient Local Govt. Innovations award Denver Regional Council Govt., 1983, Boettcher Innovations award Denver Regional Council Govt., 1984, Energy Innovations award Colo. Council Energy Ofcls., 1983. Club: Pinehurst Country (Denver). Home: 3829 S Chase St Denver CO 80235-2953 Office: Owen Engring and Mgmt Cons Inc 5353 W Dartmouth Ave Denver CO 80227-5515

OWENS, B. RAYDEAN, retired oil company field service executive; b. Brownfield, Tex., Aug. 26, 1934; s. Burnis Franklin and Nellie Florence (Van Noy) O.; m. Verna Joyce Pounds, Jan. 2, 1956; children: Lonnie Bruce, Brooke Alan. Student, U. N.Mex., 1953-54. Assoc. sponsor Dale Carnegie Courses, various locations, N.Mex., 1962-72; v.p. sales and gen. mgr. Permian Basin, Peabody Vann, Inc., Houston, 1972-78; gen. sales mgr. Bearing Svc. and Supply, Artesia, N.Mex., 1978-92; ret. With U.S. Army, 1956-58. Republican. Baptist. Home: 1305 E Castleberry Rd Artesia NM 88210-9725

OWENS, BILL, state treasurer; m. Frances Owens; children: Monica, Mark, Brett. With Touche Ross & Co., Gates Corp.; legis. State of Colo., state treas., 1994—; guest host Mike Rosen, Ken Hamblin and Chuck Baker talk shows; lectr. Russia. Contbr. more than 50 articles to profl. jours. Named One of Country's Ten Up-and-Coming leaders Robert Novak. Office: 140 State Capitol Bldg Denver CO 80203

OWENS, BILLY DON, martial arts educator; b. San Francisco, Feb. 9, 1961. Student, Laney Coll., Oakland, Calif., Alameda (Calif.) Coll. Founder, pres. Art of Mind and Body, Berkeley, Calif. Author: Getting to Know Yourself, 1992; lyricist Negative Frame of Mind, 1995; photographer. Mem. Internat. Glamour Photographers Assn., Internat. Assn. Fitness Profls., Seven Shadows Assn. Home and Office: Art of Mind and Body 1442A Walnut St Ste 79 Berkeley CA 94709-1405

OWENS, ROBERT PATRICK, lawyer; b. Spokane, Wash., Feb. 17, 1954; s. Walter Patrick and Cecile (Phillippay) O.; m. Robin Miller, Aug. 12, 1978; children: Ryan Barry, Meghan Jane. BA, Wash. State U., 1976; JD, Gonzaga U., 1981; LLM in Admiralty Law, Tulane U., 1983. Bar: Wash. 1982, Alaska 1984, U.S. Dist. Ct. (ea. dist.) Wash. 1982, U.S. Dist. Ct. Alaska 1984, U.S. Ct. Appeals (5th cir.) 1983. Assoc. Groh, Eggers & Price, Anchorage, 1983-88; mng. atty. Taylor & Hintze, Anchorage, 1988-90; Anchorage office mgr. Copeland, Landye, Bennett and Wolf, Anchorage, 1990—; bd. dirs. Hope Cottages, Inc. Coord. supplies Insight Seminars, Anchorage, 1985-86. Mem. ABA (dist. 27 rep. young lawyers div. 1988-90), Alaska Bar Assn., Wash. State Bar Assn., Anchorage Bar Assn. (pres. 1991-92, v.p. 1990-91, pres. young lawyers sect. 1986-88), Alaska Fly Fishers, Phi Alpha Delta. Roman Catholic. Office: Copeland Landye Bennett & Wolf 550 W 7th Ave Ste 1350 Anchorage AK 99501-3565

OWINGS, DONALD HENRY, psychology educator; b. Atlanta, Dec. 7, 1943; s. Markley James and Loyce Erin (White) O.; m. Sharon Elizabeth Calhoun, Jan. 29, 1966; children: Ragon Matthew, Anna Rebekah. BA in Psychology, U. Tex., 1965; PhD, U. Wash., 1972. Asst. prof. psychology U. Calif., Davis, 1971-78, assoc. prof., 1978-83, prof., 1983—, chair dept., 1989-93. Contbr. articles to profl. jours., book chpts. NSF rsch. grantee, 1978-80, 82-84. Fellow Animal Behavior Soc.; mem. Internat. Soc. for Ecol. Psychology, Internat. Soc. for Behavioral Ecology, Internat. Soc. for Comparative Psychology, Am. Psychol. Soc. Democrat. Home: 815 Oeste Dr Davis CA 95616-1856 Office: U Calif Dept Psychology Davis CA 95616-8686

OWINGS, MARGARET WENTWORTH, conservationist, artist; b. Berkeley, Calif., Apr. 29, 1913; d. Frank W. and Jean (Pond) Wentworth; m. Malcolm Millard, 1937; 1 child, Wendy Millard Benjamin; m. Nathaniel Alexander Owings, Dec. 30, 1953. A.B., Mills Coll., 1934; postgrad., Radcliffe Coll., 1935; LHD (hon.), Mills Coll., 1993. One-woman shows include Santa Barbara (Calif.) Mus. Art, 1940, Stanford Art Gallery, 1951, stitchery exhbns. at M.H. De Young Mus., San Francisco, 1963, Internat. Folk Art Mus., Santa Fe, 1965. Commr. Calif. Parks, 1963-69, mem., Nat. Parks Found. Bd, 1968-69; bd. dirs. African Wildlife Leadership Found., 1968-80, Defenders of Wildlife, 1969-74; founder, pres. Friends of the Sea Otter, 1969-90; chair Calif. Mountain Lion Preservation Found., 1987; trustee Environmental Def. Fund, 1972-83; Regional trustee Mills Coll., 1962-68. Recipient Gold medal, Conservation Svc. award U.S. Dept. Interior, 1975, Converation award Calif. Acad. Scis., 1979, Am. Motors Conservation award, 1980, Joseph Wood Krutch medal Humane Soc. U.S., Nat. Audubon Soc. medal, 1983, A. Starker Leopole award Calif. Nature Conservancy, 1986, Gold medal UN Environment Program, 1988, Conservation award DAR, 1990, Disting. Svc. award Sierra Club, 1991. Home: Grimes Point Big Sur CA 93920

OWINGS, THALIA KELLEY, elementary school educator; b. Franklin, N.H., Apr. 11, 1948; d. James Warren and Elizabeth Louise (Chadwick) Kelley; m. Alan Morritt, June 25, 1966 (div. June 25, 1990); children: Manderlee, Tiffany, Brooke; m. Frederick Richard Owings, Dec. 31, 1994; children: Jennifer, Lisa. AA, Harvard U. Ext., 1982, BA, 1989; postgrad., Calif. State U., San Bernardino. Cert. tchr., Calif. Instr. CEA Internat., Providence, 1971-77; adminstrv. asst. Gulf Oil/Cumbeland Farms, Norwood, Mass., 1989-91, So. Calif. Edison Co., Rosemead, Calif., 1991-96; substitute tchr. Palm Springs (Calif.) Unified Sch. Dist., 1996—; tchr. credentialling program Calif. State U., San Bernardino. Tutor Calif. for Literacy!, Pasadena, Chino, and Palm Springs, Calif., 1991—. Mem. So. Calif. Harvard/Radcliff Club, Toastmasters Internat. (v.p. pub. rels. 1995-96), Edison's Roundtable (comm. chair 1994-96). Home: 407 E Laurel Cir Palm Springs CA 92262-2236

OWNBEY, LENORE F. DALY, real estate investment specialist; b. Fremont, Nebr., Feb. 24; d. Joseph E. and Anna R. (Godel) Daly; m. Amos B. Ownbey, June 18, 1948; children: Kenton, Stephen. BBA, U. Nebr. Cert. comml. investment mem. Real estate and comml. investment specialist, 1976—; lectr. in field. Writer, speaker Investment, Business and Personal Skills, Motivational and Inspirational. Recipient Ptnrs. in Excellence Achievement award Colo. Chpt. Nat. Speakers Assn., 1988, Cert. of Proclamation Internat. Women of Yr., 1992-93, 96. Mem. Nat. Assn. Realtors, Colo. Assn. Realtors, Denver Bd. Realtors (life mem.), Comml. Investment Real Estate Inst. (life mem., cert. comml. investment mem.).

OYER, SARAH ELIZABETH, lawyer; b. Elkhart, Ind., July 2, 1957; d. John Stanley and Carol Joyce (Schertz) O. Student, U. Vienna, Acad. of Music, 1978-79; BA in German and Music, Goshen Coll., 1980; MusM in Violin, Hartt Sch. Music, 1983; JD, Yale U., 1993. Bar: Wash. 1993. Libr. asst. Robinson & Cole, Hartford, Conn., 1983-85; instr. violin and viola Hartford Camerata Conservatory, 1985-90; assoc. Ctr. for Internat. Environ. Law, Washington, summer 1991, Preston, Thorgrimson, Shidler, Gates & Ellis, Seattle, summer 1992, Preston, Gates & Ellis, Seattle, 1993-95, Bennett & Bigelow, Seattle, 1995—. Sr. editor Yale Jour. Internat. Law. Violinist Hartford Symphony Orch., 1983-90, com. mem., 1985-89, musician's rep. to bd. of dirs., 1987-89, vice-chair negotiating com., 1988, chair orch. com., 1988-89. Conn. Bar Found. Pub. Interest fellow, 1991-93. Mem. Wash. Women Lawyers Assn., Sierra Club. Office: Bennett & Bigelow Ste 2150 999 3d Ave Seattle WA 98104

OZANICH, CHARLES GEORGE, real estate broker; b. Fayette County, Pa. Aug. 11, 1933; s. Paul Anthony and Alma Bertha (Sablotne) O.; student Am. River Coll., Sierra Coll.; m. Betty Sue Carman, Feb. 20, 1955; children: Viki Lynn, Terri Sue, Charles Anthony, Nicole Lee. Owner, broker Terrace Realty, Basic Realty, Grass Valley, Calif., 1971—; compliance inspector Dept. Vets. Affairs. Mem. Grass Valley Vol. Fire Dept., 1965-93. Served with USAF, 1951-55; Korea. Decorated Bronze Star with three oak leaf clusters, Korean Presdl. citation, UN citation. Mem. Neveda County Bd. Realtors (dir. 1973-74). Lodges: Am. Legion, Masons, Shriners, Moose (charter mem.). Nat. Champion award Truck Drivers Roadeo class 5 semi-trailer 18 wheeler div., 1954. Home and Office: 15053 Chinook Ln Grass Valley CA 95945-8846

OZI, ELIZABETH, private school administrator; b. Sáo Paulo, Brazil, Aug. 5, 1959; d. Heni and Firmina O. BA in Psychology, U. Las Vegas, 1987; postgrad., NOVA U., Fla., 1989—; cert. of continuing profl. edn., U. Nev., 1988. Cert. tchr. Tchr. Clark County Sch. Dist., Las Vegas, Nev., 1990-94; owner, sch. dir. Parent's Choice, Las Vegas, Nev., 1993—; dir. Home Base Bus., Las Vegas, Nev., 1993—. Interviewer (Radio Show Series) Recognizing Signs to Prevent Suicide, 1990. Counselor Suicide Prevention, Nev., 1988-90. Recipient Cert. of Leadership award Nat. U., Las Vegas, 1990. Mem. Psi Chi. Home: 4646 Grasshopper Dr Las Vegas NV 89122

ÖZKARAGÖZ, INCI ZÜHRA, linguist; b. Ankara, Turkey, Aug. 29, 1954; came to U.S., 1959; d. Ethem and Nihal (Aksoy) Ö. BA, U. Bosphorus, Istanbul, Turkey, 1976; MA, U. Calif., La Jolla, 1979, PhD, 1986. Tech. writer SoftCraft, Inc., San Diego, 1987-88; linguist Systran, La Jolla, 1988-89, Emerson & Stern Assocs., San Diego, 1989-90; tech. writer Sci. Applications Internat. Corp., San Diego, 1990-92; lectr. English, U Calif. San Diego Ext., La Jolla, 1992; asst. v.p. Chicks Franchising Ltd., San Diego, 1992-93; linguist Davidson, Torrance, Calif., 1994—. Contbr. articles to profl. jours. Mem. Linguistics Soc. Am., Assn. Computational Linguists.

OZMINKOWSKI, MARIUSZ, journalist, educator; b. Kowal, Poland, Mar. 26, 1956; came to the U.S., 1981; s. Jan and Jolanta Ozminkowski. BA in Philosophy, Warsaw U., 1981; MA in Pub. Policy, Calif. State U., L.A., 1995; postgrad., Claremont Grad. Sch., 1993—. Journalist various papers and radios, Poland, 1980-90; prof. Calif. State U., L.A., 1990-94; corr. in L.A. Gazeta Wyborcza, Warsaw, 1991—. Editor (underground jour. in Poland) Yes, But..., 1976-81. Activist in anti-communist student movement, 1976-81. Named Best of Show in the annual Art Competition, Oceanside/Carlsbad Art League, 1987. Office: 293 Ohio St Apt 11 Pasadena CA 91106-4269

PAAUW, DOUGLAS STEPHEN, medical educator, primary care physician; b. Lake Forest, Ill., Nov. 16, 1958; s. Douglas Seymour and Helen Kaye (Horan) P.; m. Kathryn Ann Wells, Aug. 15, 1981; 1 child, Carly. BA, Macalaster Coll., St. Paul, 1980; MD, U. Mich., 1985. Diplomate Am. Bd. Internal Medicine. Assoc. prof. dept. medicine U. Wash. Sch. Medicine, Seattle, 1989—. Fellow ACP, Clerkship Dirs. in Internal Medicine (mem. coun. 1996—); mem. Soc. Gen. Internal Medicine (regional coun. 1993-94). Home: 2617 185th Ave NE Redmond WA 98052-5922 Office: U Wash Med Ctr Box 356420 Seattle WA 98195

PACE, R(ALPH) WAYNE, organizational leadership educator; b. Wanship, Utah, May 15, 1931; s. Ralph W. and Elda (Fernelius) P.; m. Gae Tueller, Mar. 19, 1953; children: Michael, Rebecca, Lucinda, Gregory, Angela, Lavinia. BS, U. Utah, 1953; MS, Brigham Young U., 1957; PhD, Purdue U., 1960. Assoc. prof. Parsons Coll., Fairfield, Ia., 1960-62; vis. prof. Bowdoin Coll., Brunswick, Maine, 1961; asst. prof. Calif. State U., Fresno, 1962-66; prof., chmn. dept. speech communication U. Mont., 1966-72; lectr. Sch. Adminstrv. Leadership, 1968-72; prof., chmn. dept. speech communication U. N.Mex., 1972-78; prof. dept. communication, dir. Communication Research Ctr., coordinator human resource devel. program Brigham Young U., 1978-85, prof. orgnl. behavior Sch. Mgmt., 1986-96, prof. emeritus, 1996—; prof. human resource devel. Brigham Young U., Laie, Hawaii, 1987-88; sr. ptnr. Organizational Assocs., 1970—; cons. editor HRD series Prentice Hall Pub. Co., 1989—; disting. vis. prof. Boise State U., 1992; faculty rsch. fellow So. Cross U., Lismore, N.S.W., Australia, 1995, adj. prof. soc. and workplace devel. rsch. fellow, workplace rsch., learning, and devel. World Inst., 1996—. Author: (with R.R. Boren) The Human Transaction: Facets, Functions and Forms of Interpersonal Communication, 1973, (with Boren and B.D. Peterson) Communication Behavior: A Scientific Approach, 1975, Communication Experiments: A Manual for Conducting Experiments, 1975; co-editor: (with B.D. Peterson and T.R. Radcliffe) Communicating Interpersonally: A Reader, 1973, (with B.D. Peterson and G.M. Goldhaber) Communication Probes, 3d edit, 1982, (with B.D. Peterson and M.D. Burnett) Techniques for Effective Communication, 1979, Organizational Communication, 1983, (with G.E. Mills) Bibliography of Management Development Literature, 1987, Supplement, 1990, (with G.E. Mills and B.D. Peterson) Analysis in Human Resource Training and Organizaton Development, 1989, (with D.F. Faules) Organizational Communication, 1989, 2d edit., 1994, (with E. Stephan) The Perfect Leader, 1990, (with P.C. Smith and G.E. Mills) Human Resource Development, 1991, (with D. F. Faules) Organizational Communication, 3d edit., 1994, (with E. Stephan) Me Mum Sez, 1994. Served with AUS, 1953-55. Fellow AAAS, Acad. Human Resource Devel. (pres. 1993); mem. ASTD (Mgmt. Devel. award of Excellence 1987, Profs. Human Resource Devel. Disting. Scholar award 1992), Internat. Com. Assn. (pres. 1970-71, Divsn. IV Outstanding Mem. award 1986), Western States Comm. Assn. (pres. 1978), Internat. Soc. Gen. Semantics, Am. Bus. Comm. Assn., Speech Comm. Assn., Acad. Mgmt., Sons Utah Pioneers (nat. v.p. 1986-87, pres. Brigham Young chpt. 1986, Disting. Svc. award 1987). Republican. Mem. LDS Ch.

PACHECO, MANUEL TRINIDAD, academic administrator; b. Rocky Ford, Colo., May 30, 1941; s. Manuel J. and Elizabeth (Lopez) P.; m. Karen M. King, Aug. 27, 1966; children: Daniel Mark, Andrew Charles, Sylvia Lois Elizabeth. BA, N.Mex. Highlands U., 1962; MA, Ohio State U., 1966, PhD, 1969. Prof. edn., univ. dean Tex. A&I U., Laredo, 1972-77, exec. dir. Bilingual Edn. Ctr., Kingsville, 1980-82; prof. multicultural edn., chmn. dept. San Diego State U., 1977-78; prof. Spanish and edn. Laredo State U., 1978-80, pres., 1984-88; assoc. dean Coll. Edn. U. Tex., El Paso, 1982-84, exec. dir. for planning, 1984; chief policy aide for edn. to gov. N.Mex., 1984; pres. U. Houston-Downtown, 1988-91, U. Ariz., Tucson, 1991—; cons. lang. div. Ency. Britannica, 1965-72; bd. dirs. Valley Nat. Bank Corp., Nat. Security Edn. Program.; mem. exec. com. Bus.-Higher Edn. Forum. Co-editor: Handbook for Planning and Managing Instruction in Basic Skills for Limited English Proficient Students, 1983; producer: (videotapes) Teacher Training, 1976. Treas. adv. com. U.S. Commn. on Civil Rights, L.A., 1987-91; trustee United Way of Houston, 1988-91; chmn. pub. rels. Buffalo Bayou Partnership, Houston, 1988-91; bd. dirs. Ctr. for Addiction and Substance Abuse, Greater Tucson Econ. Coun., Ariz. Econ. Coun., Ariz. Town Hall. Recipient Disting. Alumnus award Ohio State U., Columbus, 1984; named Most Prominent Am.-Hispancis Spanish Today mag., 1984, one of 100 Outstanding Hispanics Hispanic bus., 1988, Man of Yr. Hispanic Profl. Action Com., 1991; Fulbright fellow U. de Montepellier, France, 1962. Mem. Am. Assn. State Colls. and Univs., Nat. Acad. of Pub. Adminstrn., Hispanic Assn. Colls. and Univs., Tex. Assn. of Chicanos in Higher Edn., Rotary, Phi Delta Kappa. Office: U Ariz Office of Pres Tucson AZ 85721*

PACIFIC, JOSEPH NICHOLAS, JR., educator; b. Honolulu, Oct. 27, 1950; s. Joseph Nicholas Sr. and Christine Mary (Mondelli) P.; m. Paulette Kay Miller, July 7, 1975. BA in Math., BS in Biology, BSEE, Gonzaga U., 1974; MMSc in Clin. Microbiology, Emory U., 1978. Cert. tchr., Hawaii, Wash. Rsch. specialist Ctr. Disease Control, Atlanta, 1978-82; supr. Joe Pacific Shoe Repair, Honolulu, 1983; lab. technician Mont. State U., Bozeman, 1984; sci. tchr. Hawaii Preparatory Acad., Kamuela, 1985-87; unit mgr. Hawaii Med. Service Assn., Honolulu, 1987-88; tchr. biology St. Andrew's Priory Sch., Honolulu, 1988—. Mem. Nat. Registry Microbiologists, Sigma Xi, Pi Mu Epsilon, Phi Sigma, Kappa Delta Pi, Alpha sigma Nu. Office: St Andrew's Priory Sch 224 Queen Emma Sq Honolulu HI 96813-2304

PACK, PHOEBE KATHERINE FINLEY, civic worker; b. Portland, Oreg., Feb. 2, 1907; d. William Lovell and Irene (Barnhart) Finley; student U. Calif., Berkeley, 1926-27; B.A., U. Oreg., 1930; m. Arthur Newton Pack, June 11, 1936; children: Charles Lathrop, Phoebe Irene. Layman referee Pima County Juvenile Ct., Tucson, 1958-71; mem. pres.'s council Menninger Found., Topeka; mem. Alcoholism Council So. Ariz., 1960—; bd. dirs. Kress Nursing Sch., Tucson, 1957-67, Pima County Assn. for Mental Health, 1958—, Ariz. Assn. for Mental Health, Phoenix, 1963—, U. Ariz. Found., Casa de los Niños Crisis Nursery; co-founder Ariz.-Sonora Desert Mus., Tucson, 1975—, Ghost Ranch Found., N.Mex.; bd. dirs. Tucson Urban League, Tucson YMCA Youth Found. Mem. Mt. Vernon Ladies Assn. Union (state vice regent, 1962-84),Mt. Vernon One Hundred (founder), Nature Conservancy (life), Alpha Phi. Home: Villa Compana 6653 E Carondelet Dr Apt 415 Tucson AZ 85710-2153

PACK, RUSSELL T., theoretical chemist; b. Grace, Idaho, Nov. 20, 1937; s. John Terrell and Mardean (Izatt) P.; m. Marion Myrth Hassell, Aug. 21, 1962; children: John R., Nathan H., Allen H., Miriam, Elizabeth, Quinn R., Howard H. BS, Brigham Young U., 1962; PhD, U. Wis., 1967. Postdoctoral fellow U. Minn., Mpls., 1966-67; asst. prof. Brigham Young U., Provo, 1967-71; assoc. prof. Brigham Young U., 1971-75, adj. prof., 1975-88; staff scientist Los Alamos (N.Mex.) Nat. Lab., 1975-83, fellow, 1983—, assoc. grp. leader, 1979-81; vis. prof. Max Planck Institut, Gottingen, 1981; chmn. Gordon Rsch. Conf., 1982; lectr. in field. Contbr. articles to profl. jours. Named Sr. U.S. Scientist, Alexander Vol Humboldt Found., 1981. Fellow Am. Phys. Soc. (sec.-treas. div. Chem. Physics 1990-93); mem. Am. Chem. Soc., Sigma Xi. Mem. Ch. of Jesus Christ of Latter Day Saints. Home: 240 Kimberly Ln Los Alamos NM 87544-3526 Office: Los Alamos National Lab T-12 Ms # B268 Los Alamos NM 87545

PACKARD, ROBERT GOODALE, III, planner; b. Denver, Apr. 12, 1951; s. Robert and Mary Ann (Woodward) P.; m. Jane Ann Collins, Aug. 25, 1973; children: Jessica Nelson, Robert Gregg. BA, Willamette U., 1973; M in Urban and Regional Planning/Community Devel., U. Colo., 1976. Project mgr. Environ. Disiciplines, Inc., Portland, Oreg., 1973-75; asst. dir. planning Portland Pub. Schs., 1976-78; dir. planning Bur. of Parks, Portland, 1978-79; dir. planning and urban design Zimmer Gunsul Frasca, Portland, 1979-81, dir. project devel., 1981-84, mng. ptnr., 1984—. Co-author: The Baker Neighborhood/Denver, 1976. Contbr. articles to profl. jours. Trustee Willamette U., 1994; mem. City of Portland Waterfront Commn., 1982-83; mem. Mayor's Task Force for Joint Use of Schs., Portland, 1979-80; mem. Washington Park Master Plan Steering com., Portland, 1980-81; bd. dirs. Washington Park Zoo, 1983-86, pres. Arts Celebration Inc./Artquake, 1986—, New Rose Theatre, 1981-83; dir., pres. Grant Park Neighborhood Assn., Portland, 1981-83; mem. Pioneer Sq. Bd., 1992, Archtl. Found. Oreg., 1992; mem. crafts bd. Oreg. Sch. Arts. Recipient Spl. Citation, Nat. Sch. Bds. Assn., 1978; Meritorious Planning Project award Am. Planning Assn., 1980,

Nat. Am. Planning Assn., 1981; Meritorious Design award Am. Soc. Landscape Architects, 1981; Honor award Progressive Arch., 1983. Mem. AIA (Architecture Firm award 1991, assoc.), Am. Planning Assn., Young Pres. Assn., Racquet Club, Arlington Club, City Club, Racquet Club. Home: 3313 SW Fairmount Blvd Portland OR 97201-1478 Office: Zimmer Gunsul Frasca Ptnrship 320 SW Oak St Ste 500 Portland OR 97204-2735

PACKARD, RONALD, congressman; b. Meridian, Idaho, Jan. 19, 1931; m. Jean Sorenson, 1952; children: Chris, Debbie, Jeff, Vicki, Scott, Lisa, Theresa. Student, Brigham Young U., 1948-50, Portland State U., 1952-53; D.M.D., U. Oreg., Portland, 1953-57. Gen. practice dentistry Carlsbad, Calif., 1959-82; mem. 98th-105th Congresses from 43rd (now 48th) Dist. Calif., 1983—; chmn. appropriations legis. subcom., former mem. pub. works and transp. com., sci., space, tech., also mem. appropriations fgn. ops. and transp. subcoms. Mem. Carlsbad Sch. Dist. Bd., 1962-74; bd. dirs. Carlsbad C. of C., 1972-76; mem. Carlsbad Planning Commn., 1974-76, Carlsbad City Coun., 1976-78; Carlsbad chmn. Boy Scouts Am., 1977-79; mayor City of Carlsbad, 1978-82; mem. North County Armed Svcs. YMCA, North County Transit Dist., San Diego Assn. Govts., Coastal Policy Com., Transp. Policy Com.; pres. San Diego div. Calif. League of Cities. Served with Dental Corps USN, 1957-59. Republican. Mem. Ch. LDS. Office: US Ho of Reps 2372 Rayburn HOB Washington DC 20515

PACKER, MARK BARRY, lawyer, financial consultant, foundation official; b. Phila., Sept. 18, 1944; s. Samuel and Eve (Devine) P.; m. Donna Elizabeth Ferguson (div. 1994); children: Daniel Joshua, Benjamin Dov, David Johannes; m. Helen Margaret (Jones) Klinedinst, July, 1995. AB magna cum laude, Harvard U., 1965, LLB, 1968. Bar: Wash. 1969, Mass. 1971. Assoc. Ziontz, Pirtle & Fulle, Seattle, 1968-70; pvt. practice, Bellingham, Wash., 1972—; bd. dirs., corp. sec. BMJ Holdings (formerly No. Sales Co., Inc.), 1977—; trustee No. Sales Profit Sharing Plan, 1977—; bd. dirs. Whatcom State Bank, 1995—. Mem. Bellingham Planning and Devel. Commn., 1975-84, chmn., 1977-81, mem. shoreline subcom., 1976-82; mem. Bellingham Mcpl. Arts Commn., 1986-91, landmark rev. bd., 1987-91; chmn. Bellingham campaign United Jewish Appeal, 1979-90; bd. dirs. Whatcom Community Coll. Found., 1989-92; trustee, chmn. program com. Bellingham Pub. Sch. Found., 1991—; Heavy Culture classic lit. group, 1991—, Jewish studies group, 1993—; trustee Kenneth L. Kellar Found., 1995—; mng. trustee Bernard M. & Audrey Jaffe Found; trustee, treas. Congregation Eytz Chaim, Bellingham, 1995—. Recipient Blood Donor award ARC, 1979, 8-Gallon Pin, 1988, Mayor's Arts award City of Bellingham, 1993. Mem. Wash. State Bar Assn. (sec. environ. and land use law, sec. bus. law, sec. real property, probate and trust, com. law examiners 1992-94). Office: PO Box 1151 Bellingham WA 98227-1151

PACKMAN, VICKI SUE, human services assessment analyst; b. Piqua, Ohio, Dec. 8, 1948; d. Charles Richard Packman and Norma Gene (Zimpher) Westerveld. BA in Psychology, Calif. State U., Long Beach, 1977, MS in Indsl. Psychology, 1983. Ind. contractor, cons. L.A., Lafayette and Rosemead, Calif., 1981-83; sr. assessment analyst Salt River Project, Phoenix, 1983—. Pres. Tempe (Ariz.) Soroptimists, 1986. Mem. ACA, APA, Nat. Career Devel. Assn., Pers. Testing Coun. Ariz. (co-founder, past pres., bd. dirs. 1984—), Ariz. Career Devel. Assn. (sec. 1993-94, v.p. edn. 1995, pres.-elect 1996, pres. 1997), Soc. Indsl. and Orgnl. Psychology, Phi Kappa Phi. Home: 6333 E Carolina Dr Scottsdale AZ 85254-1933 Office: Salt River Project CRF 205 PO Box 52025 Phoenix AZ 85072-2025

PACKWOOD, BOB, retired senator; b. Portland, Oreg., Sept. 11, 1932; s. Frederick William and Gladys (Taft) P.; children: William Henderson, Shyla. BA, Willamette U., 1954; LLB, NYU, 1957; LLB (hon.), Yeshiva U., 1982, Gallaudet Coll., 1983. Bar: Oreg. Law clerk to Justice Harold J. Warner Oreg. Supreme Ct., 1957-58; pvt. atty., 1958-68; chmn. Multnomah County Rep. Cen. Com., 1960-62; mem. Oreg. Legislature, 1963-69; U.S. senator from Oreg., 1969-95, chmn. small bus. com., 1981-84, chmn. commerce com., 1981-85, chmn. fin. com., 1985-86, ranking min. mem. fin. com., 1987-94, chmn. fin. com., 1995, resigned, 1995. Mem. Internat. Working Group of Parliamentarians on Population and Devel., 1977; mem. Pres.'s Commn. on Population Growth and the Am. Future, 1972; chmn. Nat. Rep. Senatorial Com., 1977-78, 81-82; bd. dirs. NYU, 1970; bd. overseers Lewis and Clark Coll., Portland, 1966. Named One of Three Outstanding Young Men of Oreg., 1967; Portland's Jr. 1st Citizen, 1966; Oreg. Speaker of Yr., 1968; recipient Arthur T. Vanderbilt award NYU Sch. Law, 1970; Anti-Defamation League Brotherhood award, 1971; Torch of Liberty award B'nai B'rith, 1971; Richard L. Neuberger award Oreg. Environ. Coun., 1972; Conservation award Omaha Woodmen Life Ins. Soc., 1974; Monongahela Forestry Leadership award, 1976; Solar Man of Yr., Solar Energy Industries Assn., 1980; Guardian of Small Bus. award Nat. Fedn. Ind. Bus., 1980; Forester of Yr., Western Forest Industries Assn., 1980; Am. Israel Friendship award B'nai Zion, 1982; Grover C. Cobb award Nat. Assn. Broadcasters, 1982; Religious Freedom award, Religious Coalition for Abortion Rights, 1983; 22d Ann. Conv. award, Oreg. State Bldg. and Constrn. Trade Council, 1983; United Cerebral Palsy Humanitarian award, 1984; Am. Heart Assn. Pub. Affairs award, 1985; Margaret Sanger award Planned Parenthood Assn., 1985; Worth his Wheat in Gold award for leadership on tax reform Gen. Mills., 1986; Am. Assn. Homes for the Aging for Outstanding Svc. in cause of elderly, 1987; NARAL award for congrl. leadership, 1987; James Madison award Nat. Broadcast Editorial Assn., 1987; Pub. Excellence award First Ann. Jacob K. Javits, 1987; Golden Bulldog award Watchdogs of Treasury, Inc., 1988, 90; Sound Dollar award, 1989; Golden Eagle award Nurse Anesthetists, 1990; John F. Hogan Disting. Svc. award Radio-TV News Dirs. for def. of First Amendment, 1991; Nat. Conf. Soviet Jewry recognition, 1992, Space Shuttle Endeavor recognition, 1993, Spirit of Enterprise award U.S. C. of C., 1994, numerous others. Mem. Oreg. Bar Assn., D.C. Bar Assn., Beta Theta Pi. Office: 2201 Wisconsin Ave NW Ste 120 Washington DC 20007

PADEREWSKI, CLARENCE JOSEPH, architect; b. Cleve., July 23, 1908. BArch, U. Calif., 1932. Chief draftsman Sam W. Hamill, 1939-44; with Heitschmidt-Matcham-Blanchard-Gill & Hamill (architects), 1943; then practiced as C.J. Paderewski, 1944-48; pres. Paderewski, Dean & Asso., Inc. (and predecessor), San Diego, 1948-78; instr. adult edn. San Diego city schs., 1939-44, U. Calif. extension div., 1945, 56; Lectr. in field. Prin. works include Charactron Labs, Gen. Dynamics Corp., Convair, S.D., 1954, South Bay Elem. Schs., S.D., 1948-74; additions to El Cortez Hotel; including first passenger glass elevator in the world and New Travolator Motor Hotel, S.D., 1959, Palomar Coll., San Marcos, 1951-80, San Diego County U. Gen. Hosp., San Diego Internat. Airport Terminal Bldgs., Fallbrook Elem. Schs., 1948-74, Silver Strand Elem. Sch., Coronado, Tourmaline Terrace Apt. Bldg., San Diego Salvation Army Office Bldg. Mem. adv. bd. Bayside Social Service Center, 1953-75, San Diego Polonia Newspaper, 1994—; mem. San Diego Urban Design Com.; mem. adv. bd. Camp Oliver, 1963—, pres., 1975-76; bd. dirs. San Diego Symphony Orch. Assn., 1954-62, San Diego chpt. ARC, 1971-74; bd. dirs., chmn. coms., pres. San Diego Downtown Assn., 1963—; bd. dirs. Nat. Council Archtl. Registration Bds., 1958-66, bd. dirs. other offices, 1961-64, pres., 1965-66, chmn. internat. relations com., 1967-68, Salvation Army, vice chmn., 1989, life mem. adv. bd., 1993—, Copernicus Found., 1994—; mem. Calif. Bd. Archtl. Examiners, 1949-61, past pres., commr., 1961—; mem. Nat. Panel Arbitrators, 1953—, Nat. Council on Schoolhouse Constrn.; bd. dirs. Salvation Army, vice chmn., 1989, mem. coms., life mem. adv. bd., 1993—; hon. chmn. Ignacy Jan Paderewski Meml. Com., 1991; adv. bd. S.D. Balboa Park Cmty. Endowment Fund, 1995—. Decorated Knight Order Polonia Restituta, Polish govt. in exile, 1982; recipient Award of Merit for San Diego County Gen. Hosp., San Diego chpt., AIA, 1961, Honor award for San Diego Internat. Airport Terminal, Honor award Portland Cement Co., Golden Trowel award Plastering Inst., 1958-60, 4 awards Masonry Inst., 1961, award Prestressed Concrete Inst., 1976, Outstanding Community Leadership award San Diego Downtown Assn., 1963, 64, 65, 80. Fellow AIA (pres. San Diego chpt. 1948, 49, bd. dirs. 1947-53, chmn. several coms., spl. award 1977, Calif. Coun. Spl. award 1979, Calif. Coun. Disting. Svc. award 1982); mem. San Diego C. of C. (bd. dirs. 1959-62, 64-67), Am. Arbitration Assn. (San Diego adv. coun. 1969—), Sister City Soc. (bd. dirs.), Lions (past pres. Hillcrest Club, Lion of Yr. 1990, fellow internat. found. 1991), Father Serra Club (charter, past pres.), Outboard Boating Club San Diego, Chi Alpha Kappa, Delta Sigma Chi.*. Home: 2837 Kalmia Pl San Diego CA 92104-5418

PADGET, JOHN E., management consultant; b. L.A., Aug. 26, 1948; s. LeRoy and Gladys (Black) P. BA, U. Kans., 1969, postgrad., 1970. Instr. bridge Am. Contract Bridge League, 1971-77; owner Hectors, Kirkland, Wash., 1978-84; producer TV show Sta. 2, Oakland, 1985-88; regional mgr. Keithwood Agy.-Am. Health Care Adv., Pleasanton, Calif., 1991—; exec. v.p. J. & J. Warren Co., Walnut Creek, Calif., 1991—. Author: Winning Style, 1977. Mem. AAAS, Mensa, Internat. Platfrom Soc. Jewish. Office: PO Box 271403 Concord CA 94527-1403

PADILLA, DONALD LORENZO, state records manager, consultant; b. Lemitar, N.Mex., May 27, 1951; s. Perfecto Padilla de la Serna and Maria Ascension (Lopez) Padilla. BGS, N.Mex. Inst. Mining and Tech., Socorro, 1973; MA, U. Wyo., 1976. Archivist N.Mex. Commn. Pub. Records, Santa Fe, 1983-86, mgmt. analyst, 1986-94, dir. records mgmt. divsn., 1994—. Republican. Roman Catholic. Office: State Records Ctr/Archives Records Mgmt Divsn 404 Montezuma Santa Fe NM 87501-2502

PADILLA, ELSA NORMA, school system administrator; b. Guines, Havana, Cuba, Feb. 25, 1947; came to U.S., 1962; d. Regulo and Esther (Beato) Cuesta; m. Pedro Manuel Padilla, June 10, 1967; children: Jorge Alberto, Alejandro Manuel. BA, U. Ariz., 1970, MEd, 1972, cert. administration, 1982. Cert. elem. tchr. bilingual endorsement, spl. edn., adminstrn., Ariz. Spl. edn. tchr. Tucson Unified Sch. Dist., 1970, 1972-76, spl. edn. program specialist, 1976-78, spl. edn. tchr., 1978-81, bilingual diagnostician, 1981-84, asst dir spl. edn., 1984-89; principal Ochoa Elem. Sch. Tucson Unified Sch. Dist., 1989-96, compliance coord., 1996—; part time instr. Ariz. Dept. Edn., 1980-87, No. Ariz. U., 1983-89, U. Ariz., Tucson, 1983-88; mem. Bilingual Diagnostic Team, Tucson Sch. Dist., 1978, author Bilingual Spl. Edn. Program, 1980; prin. in restructuring of sch. project funded by Charles Stewart Mott Found.; cons. in field. Co-author: Courage to Change. Bd. dirs. TETRA Corp., Tucson, 1988-94, Vista Adv. Coun., Tucson, 1990-93; mem. City of South Tucson Econ. Devel. Adv. Bd. Grantee: U.S. Dept. Edn., Tucson, 1984; recipient NEA Excellence award, 1994. Mem. ASCD, Tucson Assn. for Bilingual Edn., Tucson Adminstrs. Inc., Nat. Assn. for Bilingual Edn., Assn. Cubana de Tucson. Democrat. Office: Morrow Edn Ctr 1010 E 10th St Tucson AZ 85719-5813

PADILLA, MARIO RENÉ, literature educator, writer, actor; b. Detroit, Oct. 4, 1949; s. Marcelino Ramos and Nina Consolata (Macioce) P.; m. Maureen Leigh Gates, Dec. 16, 1978 (div. Feb. 1996); children: Francesca, Miguel, Marcello. BS, Ohio State U., 1971; MA, Loyola Marymount U., 1987; PhD, U. So. Calif., 1993. Prodn. supr. CBS TV, L.A., 1972-78; actor L.A., 1980—; prof. Latin Am. lit. Antioch U., Marina Del Rey, Calif., 1994—; prof. English lit. Santa Monica (Calif.) Coll., 1994—; writer U. So. Calif., L.A., 1995-96. Author: Reaching Back for the Neverendings, 1993, Borges, Faulkner, Hemingway: Young Poets of Prose, 1993 (Fulbright award 1993); composer (ballet) The Harbinger of Evolution, 1980 (ASCAP award 1981), (song) I Found Love, and numerous other songs and ballets. Capt. U.S. Army, 1971-72. Mem. ASCAP, MLA, Screen Actors Guild, Am. Fedn. TV Radio Artists, Actor's Equity. Home: 1211 Vienna Way Venice CA 90291-4026

PADRICK, KEVIN D., lawyer; b. Seattle, Aug. 25, 1955. BS with honors, USAF Acad., U. Santa Clara, 1976, MBA with honors, 1979, JD magna cum laude, 1979. Bar: Oreg. 1979, Wash. 1988, Alaska 1990, Colo. 1993. Formerly ptnr. Miller, Nash, Wiener, Hager & Carlsen, Portland, Oreg.; now sole practitioner Silverton, Colo. Mem. Oreg. State Bar (contbg. editor newsletter 1982-84, chair debtor-creditor sect. 1987-88), Wash. State Bar Assn., Alaska Bar Assn., Colo. Bar Assn. Office: Miller Nash Wiener Hager Carlsen PO Box 116 Silverton CO 81433

PADRÓ, FERNANDO FRANCISCO, history and education educator, administrator; b. San Juan, P.R., Mar. 9, 1957; s. Fernando Agustin and Helen Marie (Krabbe) P. BA, U. Ariz., 1977, MEd, 1981, PhD in Secondary and Higher Edn., 1988. Cert. Comty Coll. tchr. in History, Ariz., K-12 substitute tchr., Ariz. Instr. Resource Effectiveness Tng., Nogales, Ariz., 1991-9; adj. faculty Prescott Coll., Tucson and Nogales, 1992, 96—; staff coord., mem. Crismon & Assocs., Houston, 1992—; dir. edn. programs Esmor Houston STISF, Houston, 1993-94; edn. mgr. NACE Internat., Houston, 1994-95; adj. faculty Houston C.C., 1994-95; adjunct faculty N.E. Ariz. U., Flagstaff and Tucson, 1996—; adj. faculty Vt. Coll. of Norwich U., Burlington, Vtr., Tucson, 1996—; dean of students Ariz. State Schs. for the Deaf and the Blind, Tucson, 1995—; chief adminstrv. officer, bd. dirs. USCI Adv. Group, Tucson, 1987-93; 1st vice chair, bd. dirs. Tucson Residence Found., 1996—; asst. to dir. Estudios Hispanicos, Tucson and Segovia, Spain, 1979-81; adj. acad. advisor Coll. Arts and Scis., U. Ariz., 1987-88; adj. faculty Downtown campus Pima C.C., 1988-89. Author: (in-svc. manuals) Esmore STISF Notes, 1993-94, ASDB Residence Notes, 1995-96; also articles. Co-chair candidate info. network, Pima County Rep. Party, Tucson, 1989-91, County chair cand. com. Tucson, 1991; interim chmn. Ariz. Hispanic Republican Assn., Pima County, Tucson, 1991-92; cons. Internat. Christian Inst., Houston, 1993-95. Office: Ariz State Schs for the Deaf & Blind PO Box 85000 Tucson AZ 85754

PADVE, MARTHA BERTONNEAU, urban planning and arts consultant, fundraiser; b. Scobey, Mont., Feb. 22; d. Henry Francis and Marie (Vaccaro) Bertonneau; m. Jacob Padve, May 9, 1954 (div. 1980). Student, Pasadena Jr. Coll., 1938-40; cert., S.W. U. Bus. Coll., L.A., 1940-41, Pasadena Inst. for Radio, 1946-47; student, Claremont Colls., 1972-74, U. So. Calif., 1983-84, Community Coll., Pasadena, 1987-88. Juvenile roles Pasadena (Calif.) Community Playhouse, 1935-37; ptnr., bus. mgr. restaurant devel. ventures, Pasadena, 1940-50; club dir. Red Cross, Nfld., Can., 1944-45; leading roles Penthouse Theatre, Altadena, Calif., 1946-48; club dir. armed forces spl. svcs. Red Cross, Austria, 1949-52; head dept. publs. Henry E. Huntington Libr., San Marino, Calif., 1953-57; cons. art planning Model Cities program, Omaha, 1975; founding instr. contemporary art collecting class, 1979-80; dir. devel. Bella Lewitzky Dance Found., L.A., 1980-81; instr. Art. Ctr. Coll. Design, Pasadena, 1981-82, assoc. dir. devel., 1981-83; instr. Coll. Continuing Edn. U. So. Calif., L.A., 1983-84; urban planning and arts cons. The Arroyo Group, Pasadena, 1979-94; freelance writer, journalist, playwright, 1994—; developer edn. program Mus. Contemporary Art, L.A., 1984-86; freelance writer, 1990—; author arts segment Pasadena Gen. Plan, 1980-83. Columnist Pasadena Star, 1996—; contbr. articles to newspapers. Trustee, v.p. Pasadena Art Mus., 1967-74; co-chmn. bldg. fund Norton Simon Mus. Art, Pasadena 1968-70; chmn. Pasadena Planning Commn., 1973-81, Pasadena Street Tree Plan, 1975-76, Pasadena High Rise Task Force, 1979, San Gabriel Valley Planning Coun., 1977-78; mem. Pasadena Downtown Urban Design Plan, 1980-83; founding mem. Arts, Pks. & Recreation Task Force, 1978-80; vice-chmn. Pasadena Design Review Commn., 1974-78; founding chmn. So. Calif. Fellows of Contemporary Art, 1976-78; mem. adv. com. U. So. Calif. Art Galleries, 1976-82, UCLA oral history program contemporary art, 1983-94; chmn. audit com. L.A. County Grand Jury, 1986-87; founder Pasadena Robinson Meml., Inc., 1990-92, bd. dirs. 1992-93; curator Vroman's Art on the Stairwell, 1992—; mem. exec. com. St. Andrew's Sch. Bd., 1993-94; co-chmn. restoration adv. com. St. Andrew's Ch., 1994; judge Pasadena Tournament of Roses, 1994. Named Woman of the Yr., Pasadena Women's Civic League, 1980; recipient Gold Crown award Tenth Muse, Pasadena Arts Coun., 1983, Commendation awards Pasadena City Dirs., 1975, 80, 82, 83, Commendation award L.A. County Bd. Suprs., 1987, Graphic Arts award Southern Calif. Fellows Contemporary Art, 1978. Republican. Roman Catholic. Home and Office: 350 Olympic View Ln Friday Harbor WA 98250-9662 *Personal philosophy: I have come to believe that nothing is a coincidence; that our lives are a series of interconnections with people and events; that our destiny is controlled by exterior forces. A lesson to remember is that we never know where or when a chance acquaintance (or subordinate) may become a major player in our lives.*

PAGE, CATHERINE JO, chemistry educator; b. Portland, Oreg., Aug. 21, 1958; d. Urlin Scott and Barbara Ann (Williams) P.; m. David Charles Johnson, Aug. 22, 1981; children: Daniel Robert, Emily Page. BA in Chemisty cum laude, Oberlin Coll., 1980; PhD in Inorganic Chemistry, Cornell U., 1984. Researcher Rockwell Internat., Thousand Oaks, Calif., 1979; rsch. asst. Oberlin (Ohio) Coll., 1979-80, Cornell U., Ithaca, N.Y., 1981-84; rsch. chemist E.I. DuPont de Nemours & Co., Inc., Wilmington, Del., 1984-86; rsch. asst. prof. U. Oreg., Eugene, 1986-89, asst. prof., 1989-96, assoc. prof., 1996—; mem. small bus. innovative rsch. rev. panel NSF, 1989, mem. materials synthesis and processing rev. panel, 1992; presenter papers Reed Coll., 1991, Portland State U., 1991, Lewis and Clark Coll., 1992, Fla. Advanced Materials Conf., 1992, Solid State Gordon Conf., 1992, Oreg. State U., 1992, Am. Crystallographic Assn., Albuquerque, 1993. Author: (with others) Better Ceramics Through Chemistry, 1992; contbr. articles to profl. jours.; patentee in field. Fellow NATO, 1982, 83, Oberlin Coll., 1979, 80. Mem. Am. Chem. Soc. (paper presenter), Materials Rsch. Soc. (paper presenter), Sigma Xi, Iota Sigma Pi. Office: U Oreg Dept Chemistry Eugene OR 97403

PAGE, CURTIS MATTHEWSON, minister; b. Columbus, Ohio, Oct. 24, 1946; s. Charles N. and Alice Matthewson P.; m. Martha Poitevin, Feb. 12, 1977; children: Allison, Charles, Abigail. BS, Ariz. State U., 1968; MDiv, San Francisco Theol. Sem., 1971, D Ministry, 1985. Ordained to ministry Presbyn. Ch., 1971. Pastor Ketchum (Idaho) Presbyn. Ch., 1972-80, Kirk O'The Valley Presbyn. Ch., Reseda, Calif., 1980-90; campaign dir. Kids 1st Edn. Reform Partnership, L.A., 1990-91; sr. pastor Orangewood Presbyn. Ch., Phoenix, 1991-93, First Meridian Heights Presbyn. Ch., Indpls., 1993—; mem. com. Ch. Devel., Ind., 1995—; bd. dirs. Express Pub., Ketchum. Bd. dirs. Mary Magdalene Home, Reseda; chmn. com. on preparation for the ministry, San Fernando, Calif., 1988-90; chmn. Ketchum City Zoning Commn., 1979-80; mem. Ketchum Master Planning Commn., 1974, L.A. Mayor's Citizen's Adv. Task Force on Ethics, 1990; co-chmn. Voice Cmty. Orgn. in San Fernando Valley, 1988-90; chair Family Cares, Indpls., 1995—. Office: First Meridian Heights Pres 4701 Central Ave Indianapolis IN 46205-1828

PAGE, DON NELSON, theoretical gravitational physics educator; b. Bethel, Alaska, Dec. 31, 1948; s. Nelson Monroe and Zena Elizabeth (Payne) P.; m. Catherine Anne Hotke, June 28, 1986; children: Andrew Luke Nelson, John Paul Weslie, Anna Joy Claire. AB in Physics and Math., William Jewell Coll., 1971; MS in Physics, Calif. Inst. Tech., 1972, PhD in Physics and Astronomy, 1976; MA, U. Cambridge, Eng., 1978. Rsch. asst., assoc. Calif. Inst. Tech., Pasadena, 1972-76, 87; rsch. asst., NATO fellow U. Cambridge, 1976-79; rsch. fellow Darwin Coll., Cambridge, 1977-79; asst. prof. physics Pa. State U., University Park, 1979-83, assoc. prof., 1983-86, prof., 1986-90; prof. U. Alta., Edmonton, Can., 1990—; vis. rsch. faculty, assoc. U. Tex., Austin, 1982, 83, 86; vis. rsch. assoc. Inst. Theoretical Physics, U. Calif., Santa Barbara, 1988; vis. prof. U. Alta, Edmonton, Can., 1989-90; mem. Inst. Advanced Study, Princeton, N.J., 1985; assoc. Can. Inst. Advanced Rsch., Toronto, 1987-91, fellow, 1991—; cons. Time-Life, Alexandria, Va., 1990—. Editorial bd. jour. Classical and Quantum Gravity, 1988-91; assoc. editor Can. Jour Physics, 1992—; contbr. articles to The Phys. Rev., Physics Letters, Phys. Rev. Letters, Nuclear Physics. U.S. Presdl. scholar, 1967; Danforth Found. grad. fellow, 1971-76; Alfred P. Sloan Found. rsch. fellow, 1982-86; John Simon Guggenheim Found. fellow, 1986-87. Fellow Am. Sci. Affiliation, Can. Inst. Advanced Rsch.; mem. Am. Phys. Soc. Baptist. Home: 5103-126 St, Edmonton, AB Canada T6H 3W1 Office: U Alta, 412 Physics Lab, Edmonton, AB Canada T6G 2J1

PAGE, JAKE (JAMES K. PAGE, JR.), writer, editor; b. Boston, Jan. 24, 1936; s. James Keena Page and Ellen Van Dyke (Gibson) Kunath; m. Aida de Alva Bound, Nov. 28, 1959 (div. 1974); children: Dana de Alva Page, Lea Gibson Page Kuntz, Brooke Bound Page; m. Susanne Calista Stone, Mar. 10, 1974; stepchildren: Lindsey Truitt, Sally Truitt, Kendall Barrett. BA, Princeton U., 1958; MA, NYU, 1959. Asst. sales promotion mgr. Doubleday & Co., 1959-60; editor Doubleday Anchor Books, 1960-62, Natural History Press, Doubleday, N.Y.C., 1962-69; editorial dir. Natural History Mag., N.Y.C., 1966-69; editor-in-chief Walker & Co., N.Y.C., 1969-70; sci. editor Smithsonian Mag., Washington, 1970-76; founder, dir. Smithsonian Books, Washington, 1976-80; start-up editor Smithsonian Air & Space Mag., Washington, 1985; pvt. practice as writer Waterford, Va., Corrales, N.Mex., 1980—; mag. cons. Denver Mus. Nat. History, 1989-90; contract text editor Doubleday, 1992. Author: (with Richard Saltonstall Jr.) Brown Out & Slow Down, 1972, (with Larry R. Collins) Ling-Ling & Hsing Hsing: Year of the Panda, 1973, Shoot the Moon, 1979, (with Wilson Clark) Energy, Vulnerability and War: Alternatives for America, 1981, Blood: River of Life, 1981, (with Susanne Page) Hopi, 1982, Forest, 1983, Arid Lands, 1984, Pastorale: A Natural History of Sorts, 1985, Demon State, 1985, (with Eugene S. Morton) Lords of the Air: The Smithsonian Book of Birds, 1989, Smithsonian's New Zoo, 1990, Zoo: The Modern Ark, 1990, Animal Talk: Science and the Voice of Nature, 1992, The Stolen Gods, 1993, Songs to Birds, 1993 (with Chalres B. Officer) Tales of the Earth, 1993, The Deadly Canyon, 1994 (with David Leeming) Goddess: Mythology of the Female Divine, 1994, The Knotted Strings, 1995, Smithsonian Guides to Natural America: Arizona and New Mexico, 1995, (with Susanne Page) Navajo, 1995, (with David Leeming) God: Mythology of the Male Divine, 1996, The Lethal Partner, 1996, (with Charles Officer) The Great Dinosaur Extinction Controversy, 1996, Operation Shatterhand, 1996; editor: (with Malcolm Baldwin) Law and the Environment, 1970; contbg. editorships Science Mag., 1980-86, Oceans Mag., 1987, Mother Earth News, 1990, National Geographic Traveler, 1990-93, TDC (Destination Discovery), 1991-95; contbg. author to numerous books and mags. Mem. nat. bd. advisors Futures for Children, Albuquerque, 1980—. Democrat. Home and Office: PO Box 78 644 Dixon Rd Corrales NM 87048

PAGE, LESLIE ANDREW, disinfectant manufacturing company executive; b. Mpls., June 5, 1924; s. Henry R. and Amelia Kathryn (Steinmetz) P.; m. DeEtte Abernethy Griswold, July 6, 1952 (div. Sept. 1975); children: Randolph, Michael, Kathryn, Caroline; m. Mary Ellen Decker, Nov. 26, 1976. BA, U. Minn., 1949; MA, U. Calif., Berkeley, 1953; PhD, U. Calif., 1956. Asst. microbiologist, lectr. U. Calif., Davis, 1956-61; cons. San Diego Zoological Soc. Zoo Hosp., 1957-60; microbiologist, research leader Nat. Animal Disease Ctr., USDA, Ames, Iowa, 1961-79; ret., 1979, specialist in Chlamydial nomenclature and disease; med. text cons. Bay St. Louis, Miss., 1979-85; founder, pres., chmn. bd. Steri-Derm Corp., San Marcos, Calif., 1987—; cons. McCormick Distilling Co., Weston, Mo., 1994-95. Editor: Jour. Wildlife Diseases, 1965-68, Wildlife Diseases, 1976; contbr. chpts. to med. texts, over 70 articles to profl. jours.; patentee Liquid Antiseptic Composition, 1989. Pres. Garden Island Cmty. Assn., Bay St. Louis, Miss., 1980-81; chief commr. East Hancock Fire Protection Dist., Bay St. Louis, 1982-83; treas. Woodridge Escondido Property Owners Assn., 1986-88. Fellow Am. Acad. Microbiology (emeritus); mem. Wildlife Disease Assn. (pres. 1972-73, Disting. Svc. award 1980, Emeritus award 1984), Am. Soc. for Microbiology, Zool. Soc. San Diego, Sigma Xi, Phi Zeta (hon.). Home and Office: 1784 Deavers Dr San Marcos CA 92069-3359

PAGE, RICHARD EDWARD, entertainment company executive, business owner; b. Providence, R.I., May 11, 1947; s. Clayton E. and Cherry C. (Ballard) P.; m. Joan L. Summers, Jan. 13, 1973. Student, Westmont Coll., 1967-69. Dir. Areopagus, Inc., Santa Barbara, Calif., 1970-74; founder, pres. R. Page Enterprises, Santa Barbara, Calif., 1974-81; dir. mktg. CBS Inc., Priority Records, Nashville, 1981; dir. artist devel. RCA Records, Nashville, 1981-85; founder, pres. Page Mgmt. Group, Malibu, Calif., 1985—; co-owner Casa Malibu Inn on the Beach, Malibu, 1992—. Bd. dirs. Malibu C. of C., 1992—. Presbyterian. Office: Page Management Group 22752 Pacific Coast Hwy Malibu CA 90265-5039

PAGET, JOHN ARTHUR, mechanical engineer; b. Ft. Frances, Ont., Can., Sept. 15, 1922; s. John and Ethel (Bishop) P.; B. in Applied Sci., Toronto, 1946; m. Vicenta Herrera Nunez, Dec. 16, 1963; children: Cynthia Ellen, Kevin Arthur, Keith William. Chief draftsman Gutta Percha & Rubber, Ltd., Toronto, Ont., 1946-49; chief draftsman Viceroy Mfg. Co., Toronto, 1949-52; supr., design engr. C.D. Howe Co. Ltd., Montreal, Que., Can., 1952-58, sr. design engr. Combustion Engring., Montreal, 1958-59; sr. staff engr. Gen. Atomic, Inc., La Jolla, 1959-81. Mem. ASME, Soc. for History Tech., Inst. Mech. Engrs., Brit. Nuclear Energy Soc. Patentee in field. Home: 3183 Magellan St San Diego CA 92154-1515

PAGON, ROBERTA ANDERSON, pediatrics educator; b. Boston, Oct. 4, 1945; d. Donald Grigg and Erna Louise (Goettsch) Anderson; m. Garrett Dunn Pagon Jr., July 1, 1967; children: Katharine Blye, Garrett Dunn III, Alyssa Grigg, Alexander Goettsch. BA, Stanford U., 1967; MD, Harvard U., 1972. Diplomate Am. Bd. Pediatrics, Am. Bd. Med. Genetics. Pediatric intern U. Wash. Affiliated Hosp., Seattle, 1972-73, resident in pediatrics, 1973-75; fellow in med. genetics U. Wash. Sch. Medicine, Seattle, 1976-79, asst. prof. pediatrics, 1979-84, assoc. prof., 1984-92, prof., 1992—; supr. Helix: A Directory of Medical Genetics Labs., Seattle, 1992—. Sponsor N.W. region U.S. Pony Club, 1985-94. Mem. Am. Soc. Human Genetics, Phi Beta Kappa. Office: Children's Hosp Med Ctr Divsn Med Genetics CH 25 4800 Sand Point Way NE Seattle WA 98105-0371

PAGOTTO, LOUISE, English language educator; b. Montreal, June 22, 1950; came to U.S., 1980; d. Albert and Elena (Tibi) P. BA, Marianopolis Coll., Montreal, 1971; TESL Diploma, U. Papua New Guinea, 1975; MA, McGill U., 1980; PhD, U. Hawaii at Manoa, Honolulu, 1987. Tchr. Yarapos High Sch., Wewak, Papua New Guinea, 1971-73, Electricity Commn. Tng. Coll., Port Moresby, Papua New Guinea, 1975-76, Coll. of the Marshall Islands, Majuro, summers 1983-91, Leeward C.C., Pearl City, Hawaii, 1988-89, Kapiolani C.C., Honolulu, 1989—; presenter at confs. Contbr. articles to profl. jours. McConnell fellow McGill U., 1979, Can. Coun. fellow, 1980-83; recipient Excellence in Teaching award Bd. of Regents, 1993. Mem. AAUW, Linguistic Soc. Am., Nat. Coun. Tchrs. English, Hawaii Coun. Tchrs. English. Office: Kapiolani CC 4303 Diamond Head Rd Honolulu HI 96816-4421

PAI, GREGORY GI YONG, public utilities official; b. Washington, Mar. 4, 1945; s. Edward Ei Whan and Inez (Kong) P. BA, U. Hawaii, 1967; MArch, Harvard U., 1974; PhD, MIT, 1979. Economist Dept. Commerce, Washington, 1979-82; v.p., chief economist First Hawaiian Bank, Honolulu, 1983-89; spl. asst. to gov. for econ. affairs State of Hawaii, Honolulu, 1989-94, dir. office of state planning, 1994-96; commr. Pub. Utilities Commn., Honolulu, 1996—. Author: Rural to Urban Migration Squatter Settlements and Low-Income Housing: The Case of Seoul, Korea, 1973. Pres. First Night of Honolulu, 1993-96; chmn. rsch. com. Hawaii Visitors' Bur., Honolulu, 1985, social action com. econ. justice task force Cath. Diocese of Honolulu, 1985, human resources task force Dept. Labor and Indsl. Rels., 1987; mem. gov.'s blue ribbon panel on healthcare in Hawaii, 1993; bd. dirs. Honolulu Symphony Orch., 1988, Hawaii Pub. Radio, v.p., 1994-96. Catherine Bauer Wurster fellow Harvard/MIT Joint Ctr. for Urban Studies, 1978, Bemis Fund fellow MIT, 1978, NSF fellow, 1979. Mem. Am. Statistical Assn. (pres. Hawaii chpt. 1988), Hawaii-Korean C. of C. (pres. 1986). Office: Pub Utilities Commn 465 S King St #103 Honolulu HI 96813

PAIEMENT, GUY DARIUS, orthopedic surgeon, educator; b. St. Benoit, Que., Can., Sept. 1, 1953. BSc, U. Ottawa, Ont., Can., 1975; MD, U. Montreal (Que.), 1979. Diplomate Am. Bd. Orthopedic Surgeons. Intern, resident U. Montreal (Can.) Affiliated Hosp., 1979-84; asst. clin. prof. orthopedic surgery U. Montreal, 1987-92; assoc. prof. Orthopedic Surgery U. Calif., San Francisco, 1993—; chief Orthopedic Surgery San Francisco Gen. Hosp., San Francisco, 1993—. Rsch. fellow Harvard Med. Sch., 1984-87. Office: San Francisco Gen Hosp 1001 Potrero Ave # 3a36 San Francisco CA 94110-3518

PAINE, HERBERT, ballet administrator. Exec. dir. Oakland (Calif.) Ballet. Office: Oakland Ballet Alice Arts Ctr 1428 Alice St Oakland CA 94612

PAINTER, JOEL H., psychologist; b. Ashland, Ohio, July 3, 1936; s. Harold D. and Margaret R. (Stone) P.; m. Saundra Sue Brunn, Nov. 28, 1958 (div.); children: Daniel Joel, Jeremy Jon; m. Saundra Belle Gray, July 6, 1996; step-children: Douglass Gray, Julia Gray Hines. Student, Westmont Coll., Santa Barbara, Calif., 1954-57; BS, Old Dominion U., 1967; PhD, Ariz. State U., 1972. Lic. psychologist, Calif. Tchg. asst. Ariz. State U., Tempe, 1966-69; intern VA Hosp., Phoenix, 1969-71; staff psychologist VA Hosp., Atlanta, 1971-74; program coord. VA Med. Ctr., Long Beach, Calif., 1974-80; chief psychologist VA Outpatient clinic, Santa Barbara, 1980-95; psychologist in pvt. practice Santa Barbara, 1982-96; clin. dir. Minirth Meier New Life Clinic, Santa Barbara, 1996—. Sgt. U.S. Army, 1961-64. Republican. Methodist. Home: 958 Cocopah Dr Santa Barbara CA 93110 Office: Minirth Meier New Life Clinic 5290 Overpass Rd #231 Santa Barbara CA 93111

PAL, PRATAPADITYA, museum curator; b. Bangladesh, Sept. 1, 1935; came to U.S., 1967; s. Gopesh Chandra and Bidyut Kana (Dam) P.; m. Chitralekha Bose, Apr. 20, 1968; children—Shalmali, Lopamudra. M.A., U. Calcutta, 1958, D.Phil., 1962; Ph.D. (U. K. Commonwealth Scholar), U. Cambridge, Eng., 1965. Research assoc. Am. Acad. of Benares, India, 1966-67; keeper Indian collections Mus. Fine Arts, Boston, 1967-69; sr. curator Indian and Southeast Asian art Los Angeles County Mus. Art, L.A., 1970-95, acting dir., 1979; vis. curator Indian and S.E. Asian art Art Inst. Chgo., 1995—; cons. curator Norton Simon Mus., Pasadena, Calif., 1995—; adj. prof. fine arts U. So. Calif., 1971-89; vis. prof. U. Calif., Santa Barbara, 1980, Irvine, 1994-95; William Cohn lectr. Oxford U., 1983; Catherine Mead meml. lectr. Pierpont Morgan Libr., N.Y.C., 1986; Ananda K. Coomaraswamy meml. lectr. Prince of Wales Mus., Bombay, 1987; D.J. Sibley prehistoric art lectr. U. Tex., Austin, 1989; Anthony Gardner meml. lectr. Victoria and Albert Mus., London, 1993, keynote spkr. 1st Internat. Conf. on Tibetan Art, 1994; mem. commr.'s art adv. panel IRS, Washington. Author: The Arts of Nepal, vol. 1, 1974, vol. 2, 1979, The Sensuous Immortals, 1977, The Ideal Image: Gupta Sculptures and its Influence, 1978, The Classical Tradition in Rajput Painting, 1978, Elephants and Ivories, 1981, A Buddhist Paradise: Murals of Alchi, 1982, Art of Tibet, 1983, Tibetan Painting, 1984, Art of Nepal, 1985, From Merchants to Emperors, 1986, Indian Sculpture, vol. 1, 1986, Icons of Piety, Images of Whimsey, 1987, Indian Sculpture, vol. 2, 1988, Buddhist Book Illuminations, 1988, Romance of the Taj Mahal, 1989, Art of the Himalayas, 1991, Pleasure Gardens of the Mind, 1993; Indian Painting, vol. 1, 1993, The Peaceful Liberators: Jain Art from India, 1994; gen. editor: Marg mag., 1993—. Bd. dirs. Music Circle, Pasadena, Calif. John D. Rockefeller III Fund fellow, 1964, 69, fellow NEA, 1974; Getty scholar, 1995-96. Fellow Asia Soc. (Bombay, hon.); mem. Asiatic Soc. (Calcutta, B.C. Law gold medal 1993). *The guiding principles of my life have been hard work, total commitment to everything I do, whether work or play, fairness in all my dealings and treat everybody equally, whether a prince or a pauper.*

PALACIOS, PEDRO PABLO, lawyer; b. Santo Tomas, N.Mex., June 29, 1953; s. Luis Flores and Refugio (Hernandez) P.; m. Kelle Haston, July 2, 1983; children: Pedro Pablo II, Charles Rey, Jose Luis. BA, Yale U., 1975; JD, U. N.Mex., 1979. Bar: N.Mex. 1979. Pvt. practice Las Cruces, N.Mex., 1983—. Mem. N.Mex. State Bar Assn. Democrat. Roman Catholic. Home: PO Box 16335 Las Cruces NM 88004-6335 Office: 1980 E Lohman Ave Ste D-3 Las Cruces NM 88001-3194

PALADE, GEORGE EMIL, biologist, educator; b. Jassy, Romania, Nov. 19, 1912; came to U.S., 1946, naturalized, 1952; s. Emil and Constanta (Cantemir) P.; m. Irina Malaxa, June 12, 1941 (dec. 1969); children—Georgia Teodora, Philip Theodore; m. Marilyn G. Farquhar, 1970. Bachelor, Hasdeu Lyceum, Buzau, Romania; M.D., U. Bucharest, Romania. Instr., asst. prof., then assoc. prof. anatomy Sch. Medicine, U. Bucharest, 1935-45; vis. investigator, asst. assoc., prof. cell biology Rockefeller U., 1946-73; prof. cell biology Yale U., New Haven, 1973-83; sr. research scientist Yale U., 1983-89; prof.-in-residence, dean sci. affairs Med. Sch., U. Calif., San Diego, 1990—. Author sci. papers. Recipient Albert Lasker Basic Research award, 1966, Gairdner Spl. award, 1967, Horwitz prize, 1970, Nobel prize in Physiology or Medicine, 1974, Nat. Medal Sci., 1986. Fellow Am. Acad. Arts and Scis.; mem. Nat. Acad. Sci., Pontifical Acad. Sci., Royal Soc. (London), Leopoldina Acad. (Halle), Romanian Acad., Royal Belgian Acad. Medicine. *

PALAFOX, MARI LEE, private school educator; b. Des Moines, Sept. 22, 1952; d. Ronald Lester and Maxine Lucille (Miller) Watts; m. René Jose Palafox, July 13, 1974; 1 child, Rebecca Leigh. BA, U. Calif.-San Diego, La Jolla, 1975. Multiple subjects credential, Calif., Assn. Christian Schs. Internat. Teaching credential, 1990. Mid. sch. tchr. Santee (Calif.) Sch. Dist., 1975-80; tchr. math., softball coach Christian Jr. High Sch., El Cajon, Calif., 1980-89, Christian High Sch., El Cajon, 1989-95; math. specialist Christian Unified Schs. San Diego. Recipient cert. of recognition Ednl. Testing Svc., 1991; named Disting. Tchr., U. Calif., San Diego, 1996. Mem. Calif. Tchrs. Math., Greater San Diego Math. Coun. (pvt. sch. rep. 1982-83), Nat. Coun. Tchrs. Math. Home: PO Box 2067 El Cajon CA 92021-0067 Office: Christian High Sch 2100 Greenfield Dr El Cajon CA 92019-1161

PALEY, ALFRED IRVING, value engineering and consulting company executive, lecturer; b. Monticello, N.Y., Apr. 12, 1927; s. Max and Dora (Gutkin) P.; m. Sylvia Tiffel, June 26, 1949; children: Maureen, Howard, Doreen. BEE, Poly. Inst. Bklyn., 1949. Sr. engr. W.L. Maxson Corp., N.Y.C., 1950-58; chief engr. Acoustica Assocs., Mineola, N.Y., 1958-60; staff scientist in acoustics Am. Bosch Arma Corp., Garden City, N.Y., 1960-62; chief engr. in elec. acoustics Janus Products, Syosset, N.Y., 1962-63; mgr. Anti-Submarine Warfare systems Gyrodyne Co. of Am., St. James, N.Y., 1963-67; mgr. cost and value control Loral Electronic Systems, Yonkers, N.Y., 1967-80; v.p. program mgmt. FEL Corp., Farmingdale, N.J., 1980-84; pres. NRI Assocs., Ltd., 1984—; value engrng. program mgr. CECOM, U.S. Army, Ft. Monmouth, N.J., 1985-95, ret. 1995; assoc. prof. Poly. Inst. Bklyn., 1955-65, Hofstra U., Hempstead, N.Y., 1974-79; lectr. Am. Mgmt. Assn., N.Y.C., 1973-80. Contbr. articles to profl. jours. Patentee in field. Bd. dirs. Suburban Temple, Wantagh, N.Y., 1964-80, Monmouth Reform Temple, Tinton Falls, N.J., 1983-91; bd. dirs. Miles Value Found., sec., 1996—. Served with USN, 1945-46. Recipient Outstanding Achivement Through Value Engring. award Dept. Def., 1995. Mem. Project Mgmt. Inst., Soc. Info. Display, (sec. 1978), Nat. Mgmt. Assn. (pres. chpt. 1975-76), SAVE Internat. (Value Engr. of Yr. 1985-86, 88-89, Disting. Svc. award 1991). Democrat. Jewish. Home and Office: 5442 N Whitethorn Pl Tucson AZ 85704-2634

PALIA, ASPY PHIROZE, marketing educator, researcher, consultant; b. Bombay, Nov. 27, 1944; came to U.S., 1973; s. Phiroze E. and Homai P. (Irani) P. BE in Mech. Engring., U. Bangalore, 1966; MBA, U. Hawaii at Manoa, 1976; DBA, Kent State U., 1985. Sales engr. Larsen & Toubro Ltd., 1966-72, export sales engr., 1972-73; teaching fellow Coll. Bus. Adminstrn. Kent State U., 1977-80, instr. Coll. Bus. Adminstrn., 1982-84; asst. prof. Coll. Bus. Adminstrn. U. Hawaii, Manoa, 1984-89, assoc. prof., 1990-95, prof., 1996—, pres. faculty coun., 1995-96; senator U. Hawaii Manoa Faculty Congress, 1996—; vis. prof. Coll. Mgmt. Nat. Sun Yat-sen U., Kaohsiung, Taiwan, 1992, Chulalongkorn U., Bangkok, Thailand, 1992, 93, U. Otago, New Zealand, 1995, Adminstrv. Staff Coll. India, Hyderabad, 1992; mem. U. Hawaii Manoa Ctr. for Teaching Excellence Faculty Adv. Group, 1991; mem. mktg. plan adv. com. U. Hawaii, Manoa, 1994, mem. honors and awards com., 1990-91, pres. faculty coun. 1995-96; vis. scholar faculty bus. adminstrn. Nat. U. Singapore, 1991, Mktg. Inst. Singapore Exec. Devel. Seminars, 1991, 94-95, Hong Kong Inst. Mktg. Exec. Devel. Seminar, 1996, others; affiliate faculty Japan Am. Inst. Mgmt. Sci., Honolulu, 1989—; vis. prof. Grad. Sch. Internat. Mgmt., Internat. U. Japan, Uhrasa, Yamatomachi, 1991, U. Internat. Bus. and Econs., Beijing, 1991, U. Kebangsaan Malaysia, Bangi-Selangor, Kuala Lumpur, Malaysia, 1991, 92; lectr., cons., presenter in field. Editor: (with Dennis A. Rondinelli) Project Planning and Implementation in Developing Countries, 1976; contbr. conf. procs. and articles to profl. jours. and books, including Indsl. Mktg. Mgmt., Internat. Bus. Jour., Asia-Pacific Jour. Mgmt., Internat. Mktg. Rev., Fgn. Trade Rev., Internat. Rev. Econs. & Bus., others; contbr. to numerous confs. and symposia in field; developer various mktg. decision support systems and decision-making tools for use in strategic market planning and in marketing simulations. Mem. various program rev. coms. Pacific and Asian Mgmt. Inst., Acad. Internat. Bus., Assn. Bus. Simulation and Exptl. Learning, others; bd. examiners Nat. U. Singapore Sch. Postgrad. Mgmt. Studies, 1991; mem. adv. bd. Soc. Coll. of Bus. Adminstrn. Alumni and Friends Exec. Com., 1991-93; adv. bd. Salvation Army Resdl. Treatment Facilities for Children and Youth Adv. Coun., 1989-96, vice chair, 1987-89; chair Salvation Army Family Treatment Svcs. Adv. Coun., 1997—; mem. Salvation Army Honolulu Adv. Bd., 1997—; treas., bd. dirs. Kings Gate Homeowners Assn., 1994-96. Univ. fellow Kent State U., 1983; East-West Ctr. scholar East-West Ctr., 1973-75; Ednl. Improvement Fund grantee, 1989, Instrl. Travel and Devel. Fund grantee Office Faculty Devel. and Acad. Support, 1991, 95, joint rsch. grants U. Kebangsaan Malaysia, Nat. U. Singapore, U. So. Queensland, Australia, U. Otago, New Zealand; recipient Internat. Agreements Fund award Office Internat. Programs and Svcs., 1990-91, 91-92, ORA travel award U. Rsch. Coun., 1986, 88, 89, 91, 92, 94, 95, 96, 97. Mem. Am. Mktg. Assn. (academia editor Honolulu chpt. 1986-87), Acad. Internat. Bus. (chair Pacific Basin Region 1995, chair Pacific Basin chpt. 1996—, co-chair Asia Pacific Conf. 1997), Pacific Asian Consortium for Internat. Bus. Edn. and Rsch., Assn. for Bus. Simulation and Exptl. Learning, Pan-Pacific Bus. Assn. (charter), Mortar Bd. (Outstanding Educator award 1993, Mentor award 1995), East-West Ctr. Alumni Assn. U.S. (v.p. Hawaii chpt. 1987-89, ad campaign com. 1987-88), Beta Gamma Sigma (faculty advisor, sec.-treas. Alpha of Hawaii chpt. 1990—, Outstanding Svc. award 1992-93, Bd. Gov. Commitment to Excellence award 1997), Mu Kappa Tau, Pi Sigma Epsilon. Home: 2724 Kahoaloha Ln Apt 1605 Honolulu HI 96826-3337 Office: U Hawaii Manoa Dept Mktg 2404 Maile Way Honolulu HI 96822-2223

PALINKAS, LAWRENCE ALBERT, anthropologist, educator; b. Hamilton, Ont., Can., Jan. 10, 1953; came to U.S., 1964; s. Alexander Joseph and Elizabeth Margaret (Toth) P.; m. Terri Lee Stayner McLees, Oct. 26, 1984; children: Ashleigh, Jonathan. BA, U. Chgo., 1974, postgrad., 1975-76; MA, U. Calif., San Diego, 1975, PhD, 1981. Instr. U. Calif., San Diego, 1981-82; NRC postdoctoral rsch. assoc. U.S. Naval Health Rsch. Ctr., San Diego, 1982-84, dep. head environ. medicine, 1984-89; assoc. prof. U. Calif., San Diego, 1989—; U.S. rep. Human Biology and Medicine Working Group, Sci. Com. Antarctic Rsch., 1996—; mem. NRC Com. Space Biology and Medicine, Space Studies Bd., 1997—; grant proposal reviewer NSF, Naval Med. Rsch. and Devel. Command, Natural Scis. and Engring. Rsch. Coun. Can., Natural Environment Rsch. Coun. of Gt. Britain, Am. Acad. Family Physicians Found., Am. Acad. Family Physicians, Am. Inst. Biol. Scis.; editl. cons. Westview Press, Soc. Sci. and Medicine, Med. Anthropology Quar., Internat. Jour. Obesity, Human Orgn., Annals of Behavioral Medicine, Brit. Med. Jour., Life Support and Biosphere Sci.; book reviewer Am. Anthropologist, Social Sci. and Medicine; cons. U.S. Dept. Interior. 1985-87, 87-89, 88-89, San Diego Coun. Community Clinics, 1986, Wash. State Dept. Ecology, 1987-88, Calif. Dept. Health Svcs., 1988, NASA, 1994—; presenter papers in field. Author: A Systems Approach to Social Impact Assessment, 1985, Rhetoric and Religious Experience, 1989; author: (with others) Women and the World of Work, 1982, The Many Faces of Psychohistory, 1984, Measurement Strategies in Health Psychology, 1985, Transformations of Christianity: An Anthropological Approach, 1988, Engineering, Construction, and Operations in Space, 1988, From Antarctica to Outer Space: Life in Isolation and Confinement, 1990; contbr. articles to profl. jours. Regents fellow U. Calif., 1974-75, dissertation rsch. fellow, 1980-81, NRC fellow, 1982-84; named Swift scholar U. Chgo., 1971-74; recipient AFL-CIO scholarship, 1970-71, Philips scholarship, U. Calif., 1976-77; dissertation rsch. grantee U. Calif., 1979-80; grantee Naval Med. Rsch. and Devel. Command, 1980-82, Dept. Interior, 1981, 82, 83-84, NRC/Naval Med. Rsch. and Devel. Command, 1982-84, 84-85, 84-86, 84-87, NSF, 1988—, Navy Sci. Adv. program, 1987-88, NIH, 1993-95, NASA, 1997—. Fellow Am. Anthropol. Assn., Soc. for Applied Anthropology; mem. APHA, AAAS, N.Am. Primary Care Rsch. Group (bd. dirs. 1990—, Master's Presentation award 1991), Soc. for Med. Anthropology, Soc. for Psychol. Anthropology, Coastal Rsch. Group, Soc. for Behavioral Medicine. Democrat. Office: U Calif-San Diego 9500 Gilman Dr La Jolla CA 92093-5003

PALLOTTI, MARIANNE MARGUERITE, foundation administrator; b. Hartford, Conn., Apr. 23, 1937; d. Rocco D. and Marguerite (Long) P. BA, NYU, 1968, MA, 1972. Asst. to pres. Wilson, Haight & Welch, Hartford, 1964-65; exec. asst. Ford Found., N.Y.C., 1965-77; corp. sec. Hewlett Found., Menlo Park, Calif., 1977-84, v.p., 1985—; bd. dirs. Overseas Devel. Network. Bd. dirs. N.Y. Theatre Ballet, N.Y.C., 1986—, Consortium for Global Devel., 1992, Miramonte Mental Health Svcs., Palo Alto, Calif., 1989, Austin Montessori Sch., 1993. Mem. Women in Founds., No. Calif. Grantmakers, Peninsula Grantmakers. Home: 532 Marine World Pky # 6203 Redwood Shores CA 94065 Office: William & Flora Hewlett Found 525 Middlefield Rd Ste 200 Menlo Park CA 94025-3448

PALL-PALLANT, TERI, paleontologist, inventor, behavioral scientist, design engineer, advertising agency executive; b. Somerville, N.J., Jan. 6, 1931; d. Stanley and Milicent P.-P.; BA, Imperial Coll., London, 1948, MS, 1949; PhD, London U., 1954; postgrad. Warren Sch. Aeros., Los Angeles, 1950, Calif. Inst. Tech., 1951; PhD Columbia U., 1963, London U., 1966, ScD, London Inst. Applied Rsch., 1973; cert. rehab. counselor U. So. Calif., 1975; student UCLA, 1955. Design engr. Simmonds Aerocessories Ltd., London, 1949, dir. vocat. rehab., 1950; founder, owner Teri Pall Advt. Agy., Los Angeles, 1951—, Pall Indsl. Surveys, Pasadena, Calif., 1952—, Pall Tech. Industries, Tarzana, Calif., 1979—; chmn. bd. Pall Industries, Ltd., Taipei, Taiwan and Tarzana, Calif., 1980—; vertebrate paleontologist Am. Mus. Natural History, N.Y.C., 1965-69; leader Teri Pall Trio, L.A., 1951-69; exec. dir. Hoffman House, Long Beach, Calif., 1970-72; sr. adminstrv. analyst Econ. and Youth Opportunities, Los Angeles County, 1973-74; dep. dir. Head Start Program L.A. County, 1974-75; assoc. dir. Casa de las Amigas, Pasadena, dir. rsch. and evaluation projects Nat. Inst. Alcohol Abuse and Alcoholism, Washington, 1977; pvt. practice vocat. rehab. counseling, Beverly Hills, Calif., 1977; exec. dir. Little House L.A. County, 1978; robotics cons. JPL, Pasadena, 1974-95. Fossil exhibit contbr. Los Angeles County Mus., 1968-77; chmn. Mayor's Commn. on Barrier-Free Architecture, 1978—; vice chmn. research and coordinating com. Gov.'s Commn. on Safe Energy Alternatives, 1979—; mem. Cancer Research Coordinating Com., 1979—; lectr. Long Beach Hosp., 1978; office bd. Inventor's Workshop Internat. Edn. Found., 1980—, Am. Guild of Inventors, 1990—; bd. dirs. Commn. Conserve Chinese Culture. Recipient Spl. Contbns. award Engrng. and Grading Constructors Assn., 1968, Interkamera Gold award Cannes Art Festival, 1969, Speaker of Year award Toastmasters Calif., 1971, Woman of Year for Civic Leadership award Long Beach, 1971, Outstanding Achievement award Am. Cancer Soc., 1979, others. Mem. Statis. Quality Control Engrs. (sec. 1951—), Assoc. Bus. Publs., AAUW, Nat. Rehab. Counseling Assn., Architects and Engrs. Inst., Nat. Soc. Vertebrate Paleontologists, MENSA, Phi Beta Kappa. Republican. Episcopalian. Author: (play) El Rancho Verde, 1951; (novel) With Banners Flying, 1953; Chinese and Western Worlds from 1800 B.C. to Modern Times, 1950; 4000 Years of Egyptian History, 1950; The Integrating Power Meter, 1956; About the Mammoth, 1962; Look, a Travelogue in Time, 1967; The History of Our Calendar, 1977; designer robotics exhibit Calif. Mus. of Sci. and Industry, L.A., 1990. Developer 2-mile cordless telephone, 1978, wrist chronograph calculator, 1979, Etch-A-Sketch, 1962, AC-DC multimeters, 1954, Miniaturized transcutaneous nerve stimulator, 1969, Electronic remote control system, 1972.

PALMA, JACK D., lawyer; b. N.Y.C., Sept. 15, 1946. BA, Allegheny Coll., 1968; JD with honors, U. Denver, 1974. Bar: Colo. 1975, Wyo. 1976. Mem. Holland & Hart, Cheyenne, Wyo. Mem. ABA, Colo. Bar Assn., Wyo. State Bar, Order St. Ives. Office: Holland & Hart PO Box 1347 2020 Carey Ave Ste 500 Cheyenne WY 82003-1347

PALMATIER, MALCOLM ARTHUR, editor, consultant; b. Kalamazoo, Nov. 11, 1922; s. Karl Ernest and Cecile Caroline (Chase) P.; m. Mary Elizabeth Summerfield, June 16, 1948 (dec. Oct. 1982); children: Barnabus, Timothy K., Duncan M.; m. Marie-Anne Suzanne van Werveke, Jan. 12, 1985. BS in Math., Western Mich. U., 1945; MA in English, UCLA, 1947; MA in Econs., U. So. Calif., 1971. Instr. English Pomona Coll., Claremont, Calif., 1949-51; editor Naval Ordnance Test Sta., Pasadena, Calif., 1951-54; head editorial unit Rocketdyne, L.A., 1954-55; editor The RAND Corp., Santa Monica, Calif., 1955-87; cons. editor The RAND Corp., Santa Monica, 1987—; instr. English UCLA, L.A., summer 1950. Mng. editor, cons. editor Jour.: Studies in Comparative Communism, L.A., 1968-80; co-editor Perspectives in Economics, 1971; contbr. chpts. to book, book revs. and articles to profl. jours. Chmn. bd. New Start, West L.A., 1982-84. With USNR, 1943-45. Mem. Jonathan Club. Home: 516 Avondale Ave Los Angeles CA 90049-4804 Office: The RAND Corp 1700 Main St Santa Monica CA 90407-2138

PALMER, BEVERLY BLAZEY, psychologist, educator; b. Cleve., Nov. 22, 1945; d. Lawrence E. and Mildred M. Blazey; m. Richard C. Palmer, June 24, 1967; 1 child, Ryan Richard. PhD in Counseling Psychology, Ohio State U., 1972. Lic. clinical psychologist, Calif. Adminstrv. assoc. Ohio State U., Columbus, 1969-70; rsch. psychologist Health Svcs. Rsch. Ctr. UCLA, 1971-77; commr. pub. health L.A. County, 1978-81; pvt. practice clin. psychology Torrance, Calif., 1985—; prof. psychology Calif. State U., Dominguez Hills, 1973—. Reviewer manuscripts for numerous textbook pubs; contbr. numerous articles to profl. jours. Recipient Proclamation County of L.A., 1972, Proclamation County of L.A., 1981. Mem. Am. Psychol. Assn. Office: Calif State U Dominguez Hills Dept Psychology Carson CA 90747

PALMER, CHARLES RAY, retired graphics specialist, investor; b. New Orleans, Oct. 17, 1940; s. Zack and Amy Cecilia Palmer; m. Jeanette Francis Smith, Oct. 24, 1964; 1 child, Bridgette Latrice. AA in Art, Southwest City Coll., 1975; BA in Art with honors, Calif. State U., Dominguez Hills, 1979. Binderyman System Devel. Corp., Santa Monica, Calif., 1964-66; duplicator operator System Devel. Corp., Santa Monica, 1966-73, Northrop Corp., Hawthorne, Calif., 1973-75; printing press operator Northrop Corp., Hawthorne, 1975-79, visual aid artist, 1979-83, graphics prodn. control specialist, 1983-87, graphic art service mgr., 1987-93; graphics specialist, 1994-95, ret., 1994; ltd. partnership, Crenshaw Graphics, L.A., 1979-82; pres. Palmer's Profiters Investment Club, 1996—. With USAF, 1960-64. Mem. Palmer's Profiteers Investment Club (founder, pres.), Am. Legion. Democrat. Roman Catholic. Home: 7630 Cimarron St Los Angeles CA 90047-2319 Office: Northrop Corp One Northorne Ave Orgn Zone 1553 # 87 Hawthorne CA 90250

PALMER, CRAIG M., anesthesiologist, educator; b. Wilmington, Del., Feb. 17, 1956; s. Cutter D. Palmer; m. Cassa Coulter, Oct. 22, 1983; children: Aileen Coulter, Ian Prosper. BA in Econs. with honors, U. Del., 1979; MD, Thomas Jefferson U., 1983. Diplomate Am. Bd. Med. Examiners, Am. Bd. Anesthesiology. Intern and resident in gen. surgery The Grad. Hosp., Phila., 1983-85; resident dept. anesthesiology Thomas Jefferson U. Hosp., Phila., 1987-88, fellow dept. anesthesiology, obstet. and cardiac anesthesia, 1987-88; asst. prof. clin. anesthesiology U. Ariz., Tucson, 1988-95, assoc. prof. clin. anesthesiology, 1995—, dir. obstet. anesthesia, 1990—. Contbr. to profl. jours. Mem. Am. Soc. Anesthesiologists (com. on obstet. anesthesia 1993-95, 96-97), Internat. Anesthesia Rsch. Soc., Ariz. Soc. Anesthesiologists (bd. dirs. 1995—), Soc. Obstetric Anesthesia and Perinatology (bd. dirs. 1993-97), Childbirth Edn. Assn. of Tucson (cons.). Office: U Ariz Health Sci Ctr 1501 N Campbell Ave # 5319 PO Box 245114 Tucson AZ 85724-5114

PALMER, DOUGLAS S., JR., lawyer; b. Peoria, Ill., Mar. 15, 1945. AB cum laude, Yale U., 1966; JD cum laude, Harvard U., 1969. Bar: Wash. 1969. Mem. Foster Pepper & Shefelman, Seattle. Office: Foster Pepper & Shefelman 1111 3rd Ave Fl 34 Seattle WA 98101-3207

PALMER, EARL A., ophthalmologist, educator; b. Winchester, Ohio, July 2, 1940; m. Carolyn Mary Clark, June 13, 1963; children: Andrea, Aaron, Genevieve. BA, Ohio State U., 1962; MD, Duke U., 1966. Diplomate Am. Bd. Pediatrics, Am. Bd. Ophthalmology. Resident in pediatrics U. Colo. Med. Ctr., Denver, 1966-68; resident in ophthalmology Oreg. Health Scis. U., Portland, 1971-74; fellow Baylor Coll. Medicine, Houston, 1974-75; asst. prof. Pa. State U., Hershey, 1975-79; prof. Oreg. Health Scis. U., 1979—; chmn. Multicenter Outcome Study of Retinopathy of Prematurity. Contbr. articles to profl. jours. Fellow Am. Acad. Pediatrics, Am. Acad. Ophthalmology (Honor award); mem. Am. Assn. Pediatric Ophthalmology and Strabismus (pres. 1996-97). Office: Casey Eye Inst 3375 SW Terwilliger Blvd Portland OR 97201-4146

PALMER, GILBERT CHARLES, insurance company executive; b. Milw., Feb. 4, 1944; s. Lawrence Edward and Helen Katarine (Szemerelo) P.; m. Susan Marie Kloehn, Aug. 26, 1966; children: Lawrence Edward, Jennifer Ann. Grad., Messmer H.S., Milw., 1963. Cert. assoc. in claims, fraud claims law specialist, fraud claims law assoc. Claim mgr. Allstate Ins., Milw., 1967-73; svc. dir. Hall Chevrolet, Milw., 1973-75; spl. projects dir. Allstate Ins., Northbrook, Ill., 1975-94; divsn. mgr. Auto Club of So. Calif., Costa Mesa, 1995—; bd. dirs. Collision Industry Electronic Comms. Assn., Detroit, 1992-93; cons. Nat. Ins. Crime Bur., Chgo., 1991-94, Am. Ins. Group, N.Y.C., 1994-95. Recipient Cert. of Achievement, Inter Industry Coun. on Auto Collision Repair, 1987. Republican. Roman Catholic. Home: 20 Alcott Pl Laguna Niguel CA 92677-4700 Office: Automobile Club So Calif 3333 Fairview Rd # P307 Costa Mesa CA 92626-1610

PALMER, HANS CHRISTIAN, economics educator; b. N.Y.C., Sept. 21, 1933; s. Hans P. and Dagny E. (Stockel) P.; m. Beverly Wilson, June 28, 1963; children: Margaret D., David E. B.A., U. Calif.-Berkeley, 1954, M.A.,

1955, Ph.D., 1965. Instr. econs. Pomona Coll., Claremont, Calif., 1962-65, asst. prof., 1965-70, assoc. prof., 1970-77, prof. econs., 1977—. Co-author: Financial Barrier to Higher Education in California, 1965; co-author, co-editor: Long-Term Care: Perspectives from Research and Demonstrations, 1983. Served to 1st lt. U.S. Army, 1955-57. Grantee NSF, 1975-76. Mem. Am. Econs. Assn., Assn. Health Services Research, Econ. History Assn., Econ. History Soc. (U.K.), History of Econs. Soc., Assn. Comparative Econ. Studies. Office: Pomona Coll Dept Econs Dept Econs 425 N College Dr Claremont CA 91711

PALMER, HOLLIS MARIE, public relations executive; b. Seattle, Aug. 13, 1952; d. Marshall Truman and Artis Loretta (Brown) P.; m. Robert Leslie Perlman, Dec. 20, 1985; 1 child, Hannah Palmer Perlman. BA in Art History, Yale U., 1976; MA in English, San Francisco State U., 1979. Cert. tchr. C.C., Calif. Prof. English Internat. Christian U., Tokyo, 1980-81; comm. specialist Saitama Bank, Tokyo, 1981-82; comm. mgr. Boeing Comml. Airplane Co., Seattle, 1982-86; account exec. Davis Group, Seattle, 1986-87, Cole & Weber, Seattle, 1987; comm. cons. Seattle, 1987-94; dir. mktg. and pub. rels. Mus. of Flight, Seattle, 1994—. Dir. Yale Alumni Schs. Com., Western Wash., 1994—. Mem. Pub. Rels. Soc. Am. Office: Mus of Flight 9404 E Marginal Way S Seattle WA 98108-4046

PALMER, JAMES DANIEL, inspector; b. Oklahoma City, Okla., Aug. 11, 1936; s. Athol Ford and Marjorie Lorraine (Ward) P.; m. Gail Dorothy Myers, June 1954 (div. Sept. 1956); 1 child, James Douglas; m. Gloria Jean West, Dec. 14, 1963; children: Diana Lorraine, Elana Louise, Sheri Francis. AB in Police Sci. with honors, San Jose (Calif.) State U., 1963, AB in Psychology, 1964; MPA, Golden Gate U., 1972. Cert. Calif. police officers standards and tng. Asst. foreman Hunts Foods, Inc., Hayward, Calif., 1959-64; spl. investigator Dept. A.B.C. State of Calif., Oakland, 1964-67; criminal inspector Contra Costa County Dist. Atty., Martinez, Calif., 1967-72, lt. of inspectors, 1972-92; ret., 1992; pres. Contra Costa County Peace Officers, Richmond, 1974-75; past v.p. Contra Costa County Dist. Atty's Inv. Assn., Martinez, 1971, tng. officer, 1990-92. Contbr. articles to profl. jours. Past pres. South Hayward (Calif.) Dem. Club, 1976, 77, San Leandro (Calif.) Dems., 1975; mem. Gov's Law Enforcement Adv. Commn., Sacramento, Calif., 1972-76, Calif. Dem. Coun., 1972-73; rev. Am. Fellowship Protestant Ch., 1990—, min., 1990—. With USAF, 1955-58. Home: 2788 Sydney Way Castro Valley CA 94546-2738

PALMER, KIM MICHAELE, mental health counselor, consultant; b. Dayton, Ohio, Sept. 5, 1957; m. John Richard Palmer, Oct. 28, 1989; children: Scott Richard, Alexis. BA, Wright State U., 1987, MS, 1989; postgrad., Saybrook Inst., 1996—. Cert. nat. Interpreter for the Deaf. Counselor Layh & Assocs., Dayton, 1985-89; pvt. practice counselor Ogden, Utah, 1990—; cons. Rocky Mountain Cons., Ogden, 1995-96; bd. mem. Utah Alcohol Found., Ogden, 1992-94; v.p. Trauma Found., Salt Lake City, 1994-96. Mem. ACA, PEO, Registry of Interpreters for the Deaf. Office: PO Box 9301 Ogden UT 84409-0301

PALMER, LYNNE, writer, astrologer; b. El Centro, Calif., Dec. 14, 1932; d. Clarence Lee and Paquita Mae (Hartley) Hafer; m. Bruno Cazzaniga, Mar. 13, 1964 (div. 1965). Student, Ch. of Light, 1957-62, Calif. Sch. Escrows, L.A., 1960; theatre mgmt. degree, Mus. Arenas Theatres Assn., N.Y.C., 1963. Asst. teller Western Mortgage, L.A., 1957-58; head teller Sutro Mortgage Svc., L.A., 1958-61; freelance astrologer N.Y.C., 1961-92, Las Vegas, Nev., 1962—; owner, operator, tchr. astrology sch. N.Y.C., 1970-72; owner Star Bright Pubs., Las Vegas, 1996—; spkr. women's clubs, indsl. shows, astrol. orgns. Author: Signs for Success, Prosperity Signs, Nixon's Horoscope, Astrological Almanac, Astrological Compatibility (Profl. Astrologers ann. award for outstanding contbn. to art and sci. of astrology 1976), Horoscope of Billy Rose, ABC Basic Chart Reading, ABC Major Projgressions, ABC Chart Erection, Pluto Ephemeris (1900-2000), Daily Positions, Use Astrology and Change Your Name, Do-It-Yourself Publicity Directory, Your Lucky Days and Numbers, Money Magic, Astro-Guide to Nutrition and Vitamins, Gambling to Win, The Astrological Treasure Map, Dear Sun Signs; columnist mags. and newsletters including Self, House Beautiful, Gold; record album: Cast and Read Your Horoscope; TV appearances include The Johnny Carson Tonight Show, What's My Line, 60 Minutes, CBS News Night Watch; contbr. articles to mags. and newspapers. Mem. AFTRA, Am. Fedn. Astrologers (cert. astrologer). Home: # 912 850 E Desert Inn Rd Las Vegas NV 89109 Office: Star Bright Pubs 2235 E Flamingo Rd Las Vegas NV 89119

PALMER, MADELYN STEWART SILVER, family practice physician; b. Denver, July 18, 1964; d. Barnard Stewart and Cherry (Bushman) Silver; m. James Michael Palmer, Sept. 26, 1992; children: Adoniram Jacob, Benjamin Kern. BA cum laude, Wellesley (Mass.) Coll., 1986; MD, U. Utah, 1990. Family practice resident Mercy Med. Ctr., Denver, 1990-93; physician South Fed. Family Practice, Denver, 1993-95, South West Family Pracice, Littleton, Colo., 1995, Family Medicine Clinic, P.C., 1996—; staff St. Anthony Ctrl. Hosp., Denver, Porter Hosp., Denver, Swedish Hosp., Littleton Hosp. Ward Young Women's pres. LDS Ch., Littleton, ward primary sec., choir dir., Englewood. Mem. Am. Acad. Family Practice, Colo. Acad. Family Practice, Colo. Med. Soc. Home: 543 E Maplewood Dr Littleton CO 80121 Office: 6169 S Balsam Way Ste 220 Littleton CO 80123-3062

PALMER, MARSHA KAY, special services administrator; b. Centerville, Iowa, Sept. 28, 1944; d. James Dale and Velma (Liggett) Gibbs; m. Larry Reed Palmer, Jan. 10, 1969; children: Shawn Dale, Mary Latisha. Student, Centerville Community Coll., 1962-63; BS in Edn., N.E. Mo. State U., 1968; MS in Spl. Edn., Drake U., 1976; cert., No. Ariz. U. Cert. elem. edn., spl. edn., learning disabilties and emotional disabilities tchr., Mo., Iowa, Ariz. Tchr. 3d grade Cambria (Iowa) Corydon Community Schs., 1965-67; tchr. 2d and 3d grades Des Moines Pub. Schs., 1968-71; tchr. learning disabilities Clarke Community Schs., Osceola, Iowa, 1976-78, Colfax (Iowa) Community Schs., 1978-81; skills tchr. Washington Elem. Dist. Sch., Phoenix, 1981-82, tchr. learning disabilities, 1982-86, program specialist, 1986-91; adminstr. Washington Elem. Dist. Sch., 1991-95; dir. spl. svcs. Buckeye (Ariz.) Union High Sch. Dist., 1995—; instr. Chapman Univ., Phoenix Ctr. Vol. Kids Voting, Glendale, Ariz., 1990. Grantee Drake U. Mem. Coun. for Exceptional Children, Spl. Edn. of Ariz. Adminstrs. Republican. Methodist. Office: Buckeye Union High Sch Dist 902 E Eason Ave Buckeye AZ 85326

PALMER, PATRICIA ANN TEXTER, English language educator; b. Detroit, June 10, 1932; d. Elmer Clinton and Helen (Rotchford) Texter; m. David Jean Palmer, June 4, 1955. BA, U. Mich., 1953; MEd, Nat.-Louis U., 1958; MA, Calif. State U.-San Francisco, 1966; postgrad. Stanford U., 1968, Calif. State U.-Hayward, 1968-69. Chmn. speech dept. Grosse Pointe (Mich.) Univ. Sch., 1953-55; tchr. South Margarita Sch., Panama, 1955-56, Kipling Sch., Deerfield, Ill., 1955-56; grade level chmn. Rio San Gabriel Sch., Downey, Calif., 1957-59; tchr. newswriting and devel. reading Roosevelt High Sch., Honolulu, 1959-62; tchr. English, speech and newswriting El Camino High Sch., South San Francisco, 1962-68; chmn. ESL dept. South San Francisco Unified Sch. Dist., 1968-81; dir. ESL Inst., Millbrae, Calif., 1978—; adj. faculty New Coll. Calif., 1981—, Skyline Coll., 1990—; Calif. master tchr. ESL Calif. Coun. Adult Edn., 1979-82; cons. in field. Past chair Sister City Com. Millbrae. Recipient Concours de Francais Prix, 1947; Jeanette M. Liggett Meml. award for excellence in history, 1949. Mem. AAUW, NAFE, TESOL, ASCD, Am. Assn. of Intensive English Programs, Internat. Platform Assn., Calif. Assn. TESOL, Nat. Assn. for Fgn. Student Affairs, Computer Using Educators, Speech Commn. Assn., Faculty Assn. of Calif. C.C., U. Mich. Alumnae Assn., Nat.-Louis U. Alumnae Assn., Ninety Nines (chmn. Golden West chpt.), Cum Laude Soc., Soroptimist Internat. (Millbrae-San Bruno Women Helping Women award 1993), Peninsula Lioness Club (pres.), Rotary Club (sec. Millbrae, pres.-elect), Chi Omega, Zeta Phi Eta. Home: 2917 Franciscan Ct San Carlos CA 94070-4304 Office: 450 Chadbourne Ave Millbrae CA 94030-2401

PALMER, RAYETTA J., technology coordinator, educator; b. Tribune, Kans., Dec. 9, 1949; d. Raymond H. and Helen Jean (Whittle) Helm; children: Carol Lynn, Eric Lee. BA in Bus. Edn., U. No. Colo., 1970; MA in Computer Edn., Lesley Coll., 1990. Bus./computer tchr. Dept. Def. Schs., Mannheim, Germany, 1983-87; computer tchr./coord. Cheyenne County Sch. Dist., Cheyenne Wells, Colo., 1987—; part-time instr. Lamar Community Coll., 1987—. Treas. Cheyenne County Rep. Cen. Com., Colo., 1989—. Mem. Internat. Soc. for Tech. in Edn., Pi Omega Pi. Republican. Home: PO Box 771 Cheyenne Wells CO 80810-0771 Office: Cheyenne County Sch Dist PO Box 577 Cheyenne Wells CO 80810-0577

PALMER, ROBERT ARTHUR, private investigator; b. St. Augustine, Fla., May 20, 1948; m. Christine Lynn Creger, May 14, 1974. AA, Glendale C.C., 1975; BS, U. Phoenix, 1981; MA, Prescott Coll., 1993. Lic. pvt. investigator, Ariz.; bd. cert. forensic examiner. Dep. sheriff Maricopa County Sheriff's Office, Phoenix, 1971-79; owner Palmer Investigative Svcs., Prescott, Ariz., 1980-90; pres. The Magnum Corp., Prescott, 1990—. V.p. Mountain Club Homeowners, Prescott, 1986—. Mem. Internat. Assn. Chem. Testing, World Assn. Detectives, Nat. Assn. Legal Investigators, Nat. Assn. Profl. Process Servers, Am. Coll. Forensic Examiners, Ariz. Assn. Lic. Pvt. Investigators (pres. 1984), Ariz. Process Servers Assn. (pres. 1985-86), Prescott C. of C. (v.p. 1987-90). Office: Palmer Investigative Svcs PO Box 10760 Prescott AZ 86304-0760

PALMER, ROBERT FIELDS, neurosurgeon, educator; b. Portland, Oreg., Mar. 5, 1922; cons. Bur. of Hearings and Appeals, Social Security Adminstrn., Disability Evaluation, Oakland, Calif., 1967—; mem. neurosurgery adv. bd. Kentfield (Calif.) Rehab. Hosp., 1990—; s. Arvis Richard and Capitola Georgia (Fields) P.; m. Mary Bernice Johnson, Oct. 5, 1944 (div. 1971); children: Elizabeth Ann, Ellen, Scott, Eileen, Eric, Edward; m. Melanie Marie Soares, Aug. 11, 1971; children: Anne Marie, Robert F. III, Georgia L., Margaret B., James W. BA in Med. Scis., U. Calif., Berkeley, 1943; MD, U. Calif., San Francisco, 1946. Diplomate Am. Bd. Neurol. Surgery. Intern U. Calif. Hosp., San Francisco, 1946; post-doctoral rsch. fellow Atomic Energy Commn., NRC, The Rice Inst., Houston, 1949; asst. resident in gen. surgery U. Calif. Hosp., San Francsico, 1949-52, asst. resident in neurol. surgery, 1953-56, sr. resident in neurol. surgery, 1955-56; pvt. practice neurol. surgeon San Francisco, 1956—; clin. instr. dept. neurosurgery U. Calif., San Francisco, 1956-64, asst. clin. prof. dept. neurosurgery, 1964—; chief neurol. surgery Childrens Hosp., San Francisco, 1969-92. Contbr. articles to profl. jours. Physician San Francisco Giants, 1960-70; candidate for city coun., Mill Valley, 1963; participating subject Buck Ctr. for Rsch. on Aging, Mill Valley, 1991; vol. St. Anthony's Kitchen, San Francisco, 1991. Col. U.S. Army, 1938—. Recipient Presdl. Meritorious Svc. medal, 1972, 82, Commendation medal, cert. of appreciation U.S. Army, Operation Desert Storm, 1991; named one of Best Doctors, San Francisco Focus Mag., 1992. Office: 3600 California St San Francisco CA 94118-1702

PALMER, ROBERT L., lawyer; b. Bryn Mawr, Pa., Aug. 15, 1946. BA, Georgetown U., 1968; JD, Columbia U., 1971. Bar: D.C. 1972, Ariz. 1976. Law clerk to Hon. Harold Leventhal U.S. Ct. Appeals (D.C. cir.), 1971-72; with Covington & Burling, Washington, 1972-73, 75; asst. spec. prosecuter Watergate spec. prosecution force U.S. Dept. Justice, 1973-74; mem. Meyer, Hendricks, Victor, Osborn & Maledon, Phoenix, Ariz., 1976-95, Hennigan, Mercer & Bennett, L.A., 1995—; adj. prof. law U. Ariz., 1983.; bd. dirs. Ariz. Ctr. for Law in Pub. Interest, 1990-96, pres., 1990-92. Notes and comments editor Columbia Law Rev., 1970-71. Mem. ABA (assoc. editor litigation jour. sect. litigation 1979-82). Office: Hennigan Mercer & Bennett 601 S Figueroa St Ste 3300 Los Angeles CA 90017-5704

PALMER, ROGER CAIN, information scientist; b. Corning, N.Y., Oct. 14, 1943; s. Wilbur Clarence and Eleanor Louise (Cain) P. AA, Corning (N.Y.) C.C., 1964; BA, Hartwick Coll., 1966; MLS, SUNY, Albany, 1972; PhD, U. Mich., 1978. Tchr. Penn Yan (N.Y.) Acad., 1966-68, 70-71; dep. head, grad. libr. SUNY, Buffalo, 1972-75; asst. prof. UCLA, 1978-83; sr. tech. writer Quotron Sys., Culver City, 1984; sr. sys. analyst Getty Art History Info., Santa Monica, Calif., 1984-90, mgr. tech. devel., 1990-93; mgr. internal cons. group The J. Paul Getty Trust, Santa Monica, 1993-96; mgr. ITS Infrastructure Ops. The J. Paul Getty Trust, L.A., 1996—; gen. ptnr. Liu-Palmer, L.A., 1989—. Author: Online Reference and Information Retrieval, 1987, dBase II and dBase III: An Introduction, 1984, Introduction to Computer Programming, 1983. With U.S. Army, 1968-70. Mem. IEEE Computer Soc., ALA, Am. Soc. for Info. Scis., Spl. Librs. Assn., Art Librs. Soc. of N.Am., Assn. for Computing Machinery, Pi Delta Epsilon, Beta Phi Mu. Home: 1045 N Kings Rd Apt 310 West Hollywood CA 90069-6027 Office: The J Paul Getty Trust 1200 Getty Ctr Dr Ste 200 Los Angeles CA 90049-1679

PALMER, THOMAS PHILIP, lawyer; b. Wilmington, Del., Jan. 24, 1951; s. Albert Montgomery and Betty (Arbuckle) P.; m. Ann C. Carter, Sept. 18, 1982; children: Allegra Foster, Charles Carter Montgomery. AB in Govt., Hamilton Coll., Clinton, N.Y., 1973; JD, Cornell U., 1976. Assoc. Kaye, Scholer, Fierman, Hayes & Handler, N.Y.C., 1976-79, Shearman & Sterling, N.Y.C., 1979-87; ptnr. Tonkon, Torp, Galen, Marmaduke & Booth, Portland, Oreg., 1988—. Chmn. Portland Com. on Fgn. Rels., 1995-96. Office: Tonkon Torp Galen Marmaduke & Booth 888 SW Fifth St #1600 Portland OR 97204

PALMER, VINCENT ALLAN, construction consultant; b. Wausa, Nebr., Feb. 18, 1913; s. Victor E. and Amy (Lindquist) P.; AA, Modesto Jr. Coll., 1933; BSCE, U. Calif., Berkeley, 1936; m. Louise V. Cramer, Mar. 12, 1938 (dec. June 1979); children: Margaret, Georgia, Vincent Allan; m. 2d, Hope Parker, Jan. 23, 1982. Constrn. engr. Kaiser Engrs., 1938-63, constrn. mgr., 1963-69, mgr. constrn., 1970-75, project mgr., 1975-76; project mgr. reef runway Universal Dredging Corp., Honolulu, 1975-76; pvt. practice constrn. cons., Walnut Creek, Calif., 1976—. Mem. ASCE (life), Project Mgmt. Inst. Home and Office: 1356 Corte Loma Walnut Creek CA 94598-2904

PALMER, WILLIAM EARL, private school educator; b. Oak Park, Ill., Oct. 11, 1961; s. Warren Everett and Leone Anne (Homan) P.; m. Jody Lynette Story, June 6, 1987; children: William Elijah, Jessy Katherine. BS in History, Coll. Great Falls, 1987. Dir. student life Mont. Wilderness Bible Coll., Augusta, Mont., 1983-84; social studies tchr., dept. head Tri-City Christian Sch., Vista, Calif., 1987—; art tchr., dept. head Tri-City Christian Sch., Vista, 1989—; guitar tchr., 1994—; art, music and drama ministry Ramona (Calif.) First Bapt. Ch., 1991-94; art tchr. Wasatch Acad., Mt. Pleasant, Utah, 1993; seminar leader on memory/study skills Tri-City Christian Sch. Home Sch., Vista, 1994. Econs. for Leaders scholar Found. for Tchg. Econs., Davis, Calif., 1994. Mem. Chess Club Suprs. Republican. Baptist. Office: Tri City Christian Sch 302 N Emerald Dr Vista CA 92083-6112

PALMER, WILLIAM JOSEPH, accountant; b. Lansing, Mich., Sept. 3, 1934; s. Joseph Flammin Lacchia and Henrietta (Yagerman) P.; m. Judith Pollock, Aug. 20, 1960 (div. Nov. 1980); children: William W., Kathryn E., Leslie A., Emily J.; m. Kathleen Francis Booth, June 30, 1990. BS, U. Calif., Berkeley, 1963; stepchildren: Blair T. Manwell, Lindsay A. Manwell. CPA. With Coopers and Lybrand, 1963-80, mng. ptnr., Sacramento, 1976-80; ptnr. Arthur Young & Co., San Francisco, 1980-89; ptnr. Ernst & Young, San Francisco, 1989-94; guest lectr. Stanford U. Engring. Sch., 1976; lectr. Golden Gate Coll., 1975; prof. U. Calif., Berkeley, 1994—. Author: (books) Businessman's Guide to Construction, 1981, Construction Management Book, 1984, Construction Accounting & Financial Management 5th Edition, 1994, Construction Litigation-Representing The Contractor, 1992, Construction Insurance, Bonding and Risk Management, 1996. Bd. dirs. Sacramento Met. YMCA, 1976-82, v.p., 1979-82; bd. dirs. Sacramento Symphony Found., 1977-80; asst. state fin. chmn. Calif. Reagan for Pres., 1980. Served to Lt. USN, 1953-59. Mem. AICPA (vice chmn. com. constrn. industry, 1975-81), Nat. Assn. Accts. (pres. Oakland/East Bay chpt. 1972, Man of Yr. 1968), Calif. Soc. CPAs., Assn. Gen. Contractors Calif. (bd. dirs. 1971-74), World Trade Club, Commonwealth Club (San Francisco), Del Paso Country Club, Sutter Club, Lambda Chi Alpha. Presbyterian. Avocations: antique boats, sailing, tennis, book collecting, pipe collecting. Home: 6 Heather Ln Orinda CA 94563-3508 Office: Ernst & Young 555 California St San Francisco CA 94104-1502

PALMIERI, RODNEY AUGUST, state agency administrator, pharmacist; b. Santa Rosa, Calif., July 12, 1944; s. August John and Olga P.; m. Phyllis Scott, Aug. 14, 1965; children: Christopher August, Joshua Scott. AA, Santa Rosa Jr. Coll., 1964; B of Pharmacy, U. Colo., 1968. Pvt. practice pharmacy, Santa Rosa, 1968-71; pharm. cons. State of Calif., San Jose, 1971-75; chief pharm. cons. State of Calif., Sacramento, 1975-80, sr. mgr., 1991-95; project dir. Vital Record Improvement Project, 1991—; gen. ptnr. Cold Springs Office Devel., Placerville, Calif., 1984—; chief Office Vital Records, 1995—; dep. state registrar State of Calif., 1995—. Mem. El Dorado County Grand Jury, 1990; Webelos leader Boy Scouts Am., 1976-77, scoutmaster, 1977-82; referee, coach El Dorado (Calif.) Youth Soccer League, 1977-83; dir. El Dorado County Fair; chmn. City of Placerville Pers. Bd., 1995—; cert. profl. guide and instr. for whitewater rafting. Mem. Rho Chi (pres. 1967-68), Phi Delta Chi. Office: Cold Springs Cons 2900 Cold Springs Rd Placerville CA 95667-4220

PALOIAN, RENATA DIANA, elementary art educator, writer; b. Chgo., June 2, 1959; d. Lucio Fedele and Barbara Jean (Heath) Savoia; m. David Wayne Paloian, June 5, 1982; children: Cassandra Anne, Malia Lynn. BFA in Visual Comm., Northern Ill. U., 1982. Sr. graphic designer Baxter-Travenol, Deerfield, Ill., 1982-85; freelance designer Chandler, Ariz., 1988-93; chair, Masterpiece Art Program St. Mary-Basha Elem. Sch., Chandler, Ariz., 1993—; co-writer arts curriculum stds. com., Diocese of Phoenix, Ariz., 1993-95; tchr. Summer Art for Kids, Chandler, 1995—. Author (books) K-8 Masterpiece Studies with Projects, 1994. Home: 1154 E Dublin St Chandler AZ 85225

PALUMBO, DENNIS JAMES, political scientist, educator; b. Chgo., Nov. 18, 1929; s. Richard Anthony and Nora (Griffin) P.; m. Sachiko Onishi, Apr. 15, 1954; children: Jean, Dennis, Linda. MA in Social Sci., U. Chgo., 1957, MA in Polit. Sci., 1958, PhD of Polit. Sci., 1960. Asst. prof. Mich. State U., East Lansing, 1960-62; asst. prof. dept. polit. sci., asst. rschr. U. Hawaii, Honolulu, 1962-63; asst. prof. polit. sci. U. Pa., Phila., 1963-66; assoc. prof., prof. polit. sci. CUNY, Bklyn. Coll., 1966-76; prof. Pub. and Environ. Affairs Ind. U., Bloomington, 1976-77; prof. polit. sci., exec. dir. Ctr. for Pub. Affairs U. Kans., Lawrence, 1977-83; prof. pub. affairs, dir. Morrison Inst. for Pub. Policy Ariz. State U., Tempe, 1983-86, prof. justice studies, 1986-88, Regents' prof. justice studies, 1988—; guest lectr. U. Ga., 1975, SUNY Stony Brook, 1975, U. Ala., 1976; cons. Ford Found. Evaluation of Minority Support Program, 1974, N.Y.C. Police Dept., 1975, Ctr. for Law and Poverty, Indpls., Hamilton-Pabinowitz, Inc., Pub. Mgmt. Svcs., Okla. Crime Commn., Shawnee County Kans. Comprehensive Plan for Cmty. Corrections, 1978-79; cons. Home Arrest in Ariz. Project Intervention, Gang Resistance Edn. and Tng., Project Care, Shock Incarceration, Cmty. Partnership of Phoenix, EMPOWER Welfare Reform in Ariz., cmty. punishment program in Ariz., injury prevention team Ariz. Dept. Health Svcs.; expert witness various law firms in discrimination cases.; presenter papers in field; panelist profl. meetings; participant workshops. Author: Workbook to Accompany Statistics in Political and Behavioral Science, 1969, Statistics in Political and Behavior Science, 1969, 2d edit., 1977, American Politics, 1973, American Politics Instructor's Manual, 1973, Public Policy In America: Government in Action, 1989, 2d edit., 1994, Workbook to Accompany Statistics in Political and Behavioral Science, 1969, (with J. Levine and M. Musheno) Criminal Justice A Public Policy Approach, 1980, Criminal Justice in America: Law in Action, 1986 (with Steven Maynard-Moody) Contemporary Public Administration, 1991; editor: The Politics of Program Evaluation, 1987, Optimizing, Implementing and Evaluating Public Policy, 1980, (with Mike Harder) Implementing Public Policy, 1981, (with Steve Fawcett and Paula Wright) Optimizing and Evaluating Public Policy, 1981, Implementation: What Have We Learned and Still Need to Know, 1987, (with Donald Calista) Implementation and the Policy Process: Opening up the Black Box, 1990; co-editor: Introduction to Social Sciences, 11 vols., 1962, (with George Taylor) Urban Policy, 1979; contbr. chpts. to books, numerous articles to profl. jours.; author monographs; founding editor, editor-in-chief Policy Studies Review, 1981-87, editor with Michael Musheno, 1987-90. Grantee Pub. Health Svs. Rsch. Project, 1965-67, Kans. Dept. Revenue, 1979-81, Nat. Inst. Justice, 1981-83, Nat. Highway Traffic and Safety Adminstrn., 1982-84, Ariz. Dept. Corrections, 1989-90. Mem. APHA (health programs evaluation com. 1971-73), Am. Polit. Sci. Assn., Am. Soc. Criminology, Am. Evaluation Assn., Assn. of Mgmt. in Pub. Health, Evaluation Rsch. Soc. (chair awards com. 1981), N.Y. State Polit. Sci. Assn. Office: Sch Justice Studies Ariz State Univ Tempe AZ 85287

PAMPLIN, ROBERT BOISSEAU, JR., agricultural company executive, minister, writer; b. Augusta, Ga., Sept. 3, 1941; s. Robert Boisseau and Mary Katherine (Reese) P.; m. Marilyn Joan Hooper; children: Amy Louise, Anne Boisseau. Student Va. Poly. Inst., 1960-62; BSBA Lewis and Clark Coll., 1964, BS in Acctg., 1965, BS in Econs., 1966, LHD (hon.), 1995, DHL (hon.), 1995; MBA U. Portland, 1968, MEd, 1975, LLD (hon.), 1972, Western Bapt. Coll., 1989; MCL Western Conservative Bapt. Sem., 1978, DMin, 1982, PhD Calif. Coast U., DHL (hon.) Warner Pacific Coll., 1988, LLD (hon.) Western Bapt. Coll., 1989; cert. in wholesale mgmt. Ohio State U., 1970; cert. in labor mgmt. U. Portland, 1972; cert. in advanced mgmt. U. Hawaii, 1975; DD (hon.) Judson Bapt. Coll., 1984; DBA (hon.) Marquis Giuseppe Scicluna Internat. U. Found., 1986; LittD (hon.) Va. Tech. Inst. and State U., 1987, LHD (hon.); D of Sacred Letter (hon.) Western Conservation Bapt. Sem., 1991; DD Western Evang. Sem., 1994; DBA (hon.) U. S.C., 1996. Pres., COO R.B. Pamplin Corp., Portland, Oreg., 1964—; chmn., CEO Columbia Empire Farms, Inc., Lake Oswego, Oreg., 1976—, United Tile Co., Pamplin Comms., Oreg. Wilbert Vault; chmn., CEO Mt. Vernon Mills Inc.; lectr. bus. adminstrn. Lewis and Clark Coll., 1968-69, trustee, 1989—; adj. asst. prof. bus. adminstrn., U. Portland, 1973-76; pastor Christ Cmty. Ch., Lake Oswego; lectr. in bus. adminstrn. and econs. U. Costa Rica, 1968, Va. Tech. Found., 1986; chmn. bd. dirs. United Tile Co., Christian Supply Ctrs., Inc. Author: Everything is Just Great, 1985, The Gift, 1986, Another Virginian: A Study of the Life and Beliefs of Robert Boisseau Pamplin, 1986, (with others): A Portrait of Colorado, 1976, Three in One, 1974, The Storybook Primer on Managing, 1974, One Who Believed, Vol. I, 1988, Vol. II, 1991, Climbing the Centuries, 1993, Heritage The Making of an American Family, 1994, American Heroes, 1995, Prelude to Surrender, 1995; editor Oreg. Mus. Sci. and Industry Press, 1973, trustee, 1971, 74—; editor Portrait of Oregon, 1973, (with others) Oregon Underfoot, 1975; hon. life pres. Western Conservative Bapt. Seminary; chmn. regents Western Sem., 1994. Mem. Nat. Adv. Coun. Vocat. Edn., 1975—; mem. Western Interstate Com. Higher Edn., 1981-84; co-chmn. Va. Tech. $50 million Campaign for Excellence, 1984-87, Va. Tech. Found., 1986—, Va.-Oreg. State Scholarship Commn., 1974—, chmn., 1976-78; mem. Portland dist. adv. coun. SBA, 1973-77; mem. rewards rev. com., City of Portland, 1973-78, chmn., 1973-78; bd. regents U. Portland, 1971-79, chmn. bd., 1975-79, regent emeritus, 1979—; trustee Oreg. Episc. Schs., 1979, Linfield Coll., U. Puget Sound, 1989—; chmn. bd. trustees Lewis and Clark Coll., 1991. Recipient Disting. Alumnus award Lewis and Clark Coll., 1974, ROTC Disting. Svc. award USAF, 1974, Albert Einstein Acad. Bronze medal, 1986, Disting. Leadership medal Freedoms Found., Disting. Bus. Alumnus award U. Portland, 1990, Nat. Caring award Caring Inst., 1991, Pride of Portland award Portland Lions Club, Hero Athlete award, 1994, Herman Lay Entrepreneurship award 1995; Va. Tech Coll. Bus. Adminstrn. renamed R.B. Pamplin Coll. Bus. Adminstrn. in his honor; Western Conservative Bapt. Sem. Lay Inst. for Leadership, Edn., Devel. and Rsch. named for R.B. Pamplin, Jr., 1988. Mem. Acad. Mgmt., Delta Epsilon Sigma, Beta Gamma Sigma, Sigma Phi Epsilon, Waverley Country Club, Arlington, Multnomah Athletic Club, Capitol Hill Club, Greenville Country Club, Poinsett Club, Eldorado Country Club, Thunderbird Country Club, Rotary. Republican. Episcopalian. Office: R B Pamplin Corp Inc 900 SW 5th Ave Portland OR 97204-1235

PAN, WILLIAM JIAWEI, import and export company executive, consultant; b. Shanghai, People's Republic of China, July 24, 1935; came to U.S., 1985; s. You-Yuan Pan and Ruth Li Tien; m. Lena Fengqiu Liu, Dec. 26, 1965; 1 child, Song. BS, Peking U., People's Republic of China, 1958. Cert. sr. engr., People's Republic of China. Engr. Beijing Radio Factory, 1958-78, Dong Feng TV Factory, Beijing, 1978-80; asst. gen. mgr. Beijing br. China Nat. Electronics Import/Export Corp., 1980-91; mgr. electronics dept. China Resource Products, N.Y.C., 1985-91; pres., chief exec. officer King Trading, Inc., San Francisco, 1987-91; pres., CEO Kings Internat., Inc., San Jose, Calif., 1991—. Office: Kings Internat Inc 467 Saratoga Ave Ste 150 San Jose CA 95129-1326

PANDER, HENDRIK PIETER (HENK PANDER), artist; b. Haarlem, Netherlands, Nov. 21, 1937; came to the U.S., 1965; s. Jacob and Henderica (Smedes) P.; m. Marcia Lynch, 1964 (div.); children: Jacob, Arnold. Cert. completion, Rijksacademie van Beeldende, Amsterdam, 1961. co-founder, bd. mem. Storefront Theatre, Portland, 1970-87; founder, mem. selection com. Visual Chronicle Portland, 1985-91; commr. Met. Arts Commn., Portland, 1992-93, mem. pub. art adv. com., 1993-96; presenter in field. One-person shows include Elizabeth Leach Gallery, Portland, 1993, 94, 95, 96, Davidson Galleries, Seattle, 1994, 97, Index Gallery, Clark Coll., Vancouver, Wash., 1994; group shows include Seattle Art Mus., 1992-93, Seattle (Wash.) Art Fair, 1992, 93, 94, 95, U. Oreg. Mus. Art, Eugene, 1993, Tacoma (Wash.) Art Mus., 1993, Nordic Heritage Mus., Seattle, 1994, Artquake, Portland, 1994, Chgo. Art Fair, 1995, Art Initiatives, N.Y.C., 1996, Av Holdings, Leeuwarden, The Netherlands, 1997, Mus. Flight, Seattle; represented in permanent collections including City of Amsterdam, Netherlands, City of Portland, Oreg., NASA, others. Recipient Prix de Rome, Dutch Govt., 1961, Talens prize Talens Art Supply Factory, 1961, Therese van Duyl Schwarze award, Amsterdam, 1964, Drammy award for best set Willamette Week Newspaper, Portland, 1992; Master fellow Oreg. Arts Commn., Salem, 1991. Mem. ARTNET, N.W. Figurative Art Alliance, Netherlands Bus. and Cultural Assn. Studio: 1801 NW Upshur St Portland OR 97209-1700

PANDO, LEO, mayor; b. June 10, 1945; m. Sharon Pando, Jan. 27, 1979; children: Jeff, Todd. Police officer Cheyenne, Wyo.; mem. Cheyenne City Coun., 1989-92; mayor City of Cheyenne, 1993—; mem. steering com. Nat. League of Cities Cmty. and Econ. Devel. With Wyo. Army Nat. Guard, 6 yrs. Mem. Wyo. Assn. Municipalities, Greater Cheyenne C. of C. Democrat. Roman Catholic. Home: 6510 Armant Ct Cheyenne WY 82009 Office: 2101 O'Neil Ave Ste 310 Cheyenne WY 82001

PANDOL, JACK J., food products executive; b. 1952. With Pandol & Sons Inc., 1973—. Office: Pandol & Sons 192 County Line Rd Delano CA 93215-9560*

PANDOL, MATT, food products executive; b. 1927. With Pandol & Sons, 1948—. Office: Pandol & Sons 192 County Line Rd & 401 Rd Delano CA 93215-9560*

PANEC, DONALD JOHN, marketing executive; b. Oak Park, Ill., Mar. 24, 1955; s. Donald Otto and Sherry (Heflin) P. BA, U. Calif., L.A., 1981; MBA, Harvard U., 1984. Profl. actor various children's theater and tv commls., 1975-78; adminstrv. dir. TNRC Prodns., Studio City, Calif., 1978-79; tv prodr. ednl. children's programming TNRC Prodns., Studio City, 1980-82; asst. mktg. mgr. He-Man (Masters of the Universe) Mattel Toys, Hawthorne, Calif., 1984-85; assoc. mktg. mgr. He-Man, BraveStarr Mattel Toys, Hawthorne, 1985-86, product mktg. mgr. Mad Scientist, BraveStarr, 1986-87; mgr. toy devel. and mktg. DIC, Burbank, 1987-88; mktg. mgr. video game hardware and software Epyx, Inc., Redwood City, 1988-89, Broderbund Software, San Rafael, 1989-90; from mktg. dir. to v.p. mktg. OddzOn Products, Campbell, 1990-92, 92—. Office: OddzOn Products 1696 Dell Ave Campbell CA 95008-6901

PANETTA, JOSEPH DANIEL, biotechnology executive; b. Syracuse, N.Y., Mar. 1, 1954; s. Salvatore and Josephine Mary (Sbardella) P.; m. Karin Ann Hoffman, Oct. 21, 1978; children: Lauren Marie, Christopher Daniel. BS, LeMoyne Coll., 1976; MPH, U. Pitts., 1979. Environ. protection specialist U.S. EPA, Washington, 1979-82, sr. policy analyst, 1982-84; project leader Schering Corp./NorAm Chem Co., Wilmington, Del., 1984-85; mgr. regulatory affairs agrchems. divsn. Pennwalt Corp., Phila., 1985-88; mgr. corp. regulatory affairs Mycogen Corp., San Diego, 1988-90; dir. corp. regulatory affairs and quality assurance Mycogen Corp., 1990-92; dir. corp. regulatory, environ. affairs Mycogen Corp., San Diego, 1992—; chmn. agr. and environment subcom. Internat. Bioindustry Forum; chmn. maneb data task force Inter-industry, Washington, 1985-88; guest lectr. biotech. U. Calif., San Diego, and Calif. Western Law Sch.; advisor bd. on agr. NAS. Contbr. articles to profl. jours. Mem. Rep. State Com. Del., 1987. Mem. Nat. Agrl. Chems. Assn. (mem. registrations com. 1986-89), Biotech. Industy Orgn. (mem. food and agr. steering com., chmn. bipesticides com., internat. affairs com.), Calif. Indsl. Biotech. Assn. (mem. agrl. affairs com.), Am. Chem. Soc. (mem. agrl. div.). Roman Catholic. Home: 4324 Corte Al Fresco San Diego CA 92130-2160 Office: Mycogen Corp 5501 Oberlin Dr San Diego CA 92121-1736

PANG, HERBERT GEORGE, ophthalmologist; b. Honolulu, Dec. 23, 1922; s. See Hung and Hong Jim (Chuu) P.; student St. Louis Coll., 1941; BS, Northwestern U., 1944, MD, 1947; m. Dorothea Lopez, Dec. 27, 1953. Intern Queen's Hosp., Honolulu, 1947-48; postgraduate course ophthalmology N.Y.U., Med. Sch., 1948-49; resident ophthalmology Jersey City Med. Ctr., 1949-50, Manhattan Eye, Ear, & Throat Hosp., N.Y.C., 1950-52; practice medicine specializing in ophthalmology, Honolulu, 1952-54, 56—; mem. staffs Kuakini Hosp., Children's Hosp., Castle Meml. Hosp., Queen's Hosp., St. Francis Hosp.; asst. clin. prof. ophthalmology U. Hawaii Sch. Medicine, 1966-73, now asso. clin. prof. Cons. Bur. Crippled Children, 1952-73, Kapiolani Maternity Hosp., 1952-73, Leahi Tb. Hosp., 1952-62. Capt. M.C., AUS, 1954-56, Diplomate Am. Bd. Ophthalmology. Mem. AMA, Am. Acad. Ophthalmology and Otolaryngology, Assn. for Rsch. Ophthalmology, ACS, Hawaii Med. Soc. (gov. med. practice com. 1958-62, chmn. med. speakers com. 1957-58), Hawaii Eye, Ear, Nose and Throat Soc. (pres. 1960), Pacific Coast Oto-Ophthalmological Soc., Pan Am. Assn. Ophthalmology, Mason, Shriner, Eye Study Club (pres. 1972—). Home: 346 Lewers St Honolulu HI 96815-2345

PANICCIA, PATRICIA LYNN, television news reporter, lawyer; b. Glendale, Calif., Sept. 19, 1952; d. Valentino and Mary (Napoleon) P.; m. Jeffrey McDowell Mailes, Oct. 5, 1985; children: Alana Christine, Malia Noel. BA in Communication, U. Hawaii, Honolulu, 1977; JD, Pepperdine U., Malibu, Calif., 1981. Bar: Hawaii 1981, Calif. 1982, U.S. Dist. Ct. Hawaii 1981. Extern law clk. Hon. Samuel P. King U.S. Dist. Ct., Honolulu, 1980; reporter, anchor woman Sta. KEYT-TV, Santa Barbara, Calif., 1983-84; reporter Sta. KCOP-TV, Los Angeles, 1984-88; reporter CNN L.A., 1989-93; instr. communications law Pepperdine Sch. Law, 1987, 94—, adj. prof.; profl. surfer, 1977-81. Recipient Clarion award Women In Communication, Inc., 1988. Mem. ABA (chair of law and media com. young lawyers div., 1987-88, nat. conf. com. lawyers and reps. of media, 1987-91), Calif. State Bar (mem. com. on fair trial and free press 1983-84, pub. affairs com. 1985-87), Hawaii Bar Assn., Phi Delta Phi (historian 1980-81). Avocations: surfing, skiing, piano, guitar. Office: 1313 Foothill Blvd Ste 11 La Canada CA 91011-2146

PANKRATZ, ROBERT LEE, psychologist; b. Hemet, Calif., Nov. 11, 1946; s. Otto J. and Emily (Frantz) P.; m. Karen Pankratz, July, 1971 (div. 1982); children: Aaron T., Loren D.; m. Saundra D. Morgan, Aug. 3, 1985; children: Brian P. Fleming, Jana N. Fleming. BA, Occidental Coll., 1968; MDiv, Am. Bapt. Seminary West, 1971; M in Counseling, Calif. State U., Fresno, 1982, postgrad., 1982-83. Lic. ednl. psychologist, Calif.; credentialed sch. psychologist, Calif. Youth and music pastor 1st Bapt. Ch., Bellflower, Calif., 1969-71, Stockton, Calif., 1971-74; sr. pastor East Princeton Bapt. Ch., Fresno, 1975-80; high sch. vocat. counselor Madera (Calif.) Unified Sch. Dist., 1981-83; sch. psychologist Los Banos (Calif.) Unified Sch. Dist., 1983-84, Fresno Unified Sch. Dist., 1984—. Min. of music Ch. of Brethren, Fresno, 1981-85. Mem. Calif. Assn. Sch. Psychologists, Nat. Assn. Sch. Psychologists, Am. Bapt. Mins. Assn. (pres. Ctrl. Valley chpt. 1978). Home: 1284 E Cromwell Ave Fresno CA 93720-2681

PANNER, OWEN M., federal judge; b. 1924. Student, U. Okla., 1941-43, LL.B., 1949. Atty. Panner, Johnson, Marceau, Karnopp, Kennedy & Nash, 1950-80; judge, now sr. judge U.S. Dist. Ct. Oreg., Portland, 1980—. Office: US Dist Ct 335 US Courthouse 620 SW Main St Portland OR 97205-3037

PANSKY, EMIL JOHN, entrepreneur; b. Manhattan, N.Y., June 1, 1921; s. Stanislaus and Anna (Jankovic) P.; m. Billie B. Byrne, May 27, 1955; 1 adopted child, Jimmy. BME, Cooper Union Coll., 1941; MBA, Harvard U., 1949; MADE, NYU, 1950. Registered profl. engr., Mich. Chief insp. flight line Republic Aviation, Farmingdale, L.I., 1941-45, salvage engr., 1946-47; product control supr. to product control mgr. Ford Motor, Detroit, 1949-51; asst. plant mgr. Anderson Brass, Birmingham, Ala., 1951-53; asst. v.p. to v.p. mfg. Cummins Engine, Columbus, Ind., 1953-54; pvt. practice Emil J. Pansky Assoc., San Leandro, Calif., 1954—; pres. Calif. Mfrs. Tech. Assn., San Francisco, 1978-80; ind. tech. cons. to small bus., 1994—. Patentee die cast auto wheels, 1965. Pres. Menlo Circus Club, Menlo Park, Calif., 1974-81, Home Owners Assn., Kanuela, Hawaii, 1989-95; bd. dirs. No. Calif. Tennis Assn., San Francisco, 1984-87. Mem. ASME (life), Harvard Club San Francisco (bd. dirs. 1986-92), Harvard Bus. Sch. Club San Francisco (bd. dirs. 1970-73, cons. 1994-95). Democrat. Home: 901 Jackling Dr Hillsborough CA 94010-6127 Office: Emil J Pansky Assoc 1666 Timothy Dr San Leandro CA 94577-2312

PANTALEO, JACK, playwright, composer, social worker; b. Melrose Park, Ill., Nov. 30, 1954; s. Jack Sam Pantaleo and Sophia Carmelita Mannozzi Cicero. Psychiat. Tech., C.C., San Francisco, 1981; BA in Humanities, New Coll. Calif., San Francisco, 1986; MA in Writing, U. San Francisco, 1988. Lic. psychiat. technician. Asst. to dean U. San Francisco Sch. Nursing, 1984-88; grammar sch. tchr. St. Michael's Cath. Sch., San Francisco, 1989-91; instr. English Vista C.C., Berkeley, Calif., 1990-93; social worker City and County of San Francisco, 1991—; founder, dir. Evangelicals Concerned, San Francisco, 1978-85; co-founder, co-dir. AIDS InterFaith Network, San Francisco, 1983-88. Playwright/composer musical The Gospel According to the Angel Julius; contbg. author: (collection of meditations) The Road to Emmaus, 1990; author booklet and articles. Caregiver for babies with AIDS, The Bridge, San Francisco, 1989-93. Work included in Silver Quill, The David Ross Meml. Competition, Wichita, 1996. Mem. Social Workers Union, Nat. Writers Union. Democrat. Episcopalian. Office: Child Protection Ctr San Francisco Gen Hosp 995 Potrero St San Francisco CA 94110

PANTOS, WILLIAM PANTAZES, mechanical engineer, consultant; b. Ann Arbor, Mich., May 15, 1957; s. William Van and Lillian William (Skinner) P. BS in Mech. Engring., Northwestern U., Evanston, Ill., 1979; MS in Mech. Engring., San Diego State U., 1991. Registered profl. engr., Calif. Owner Signs & Symbols, Niles, Ill., 1975-80; engr. Hughes Aircraft, El Segundo, Calif., 1980-83, Gen. Dynamics, San Diego, 1983-85; staff engr. TRW, San Diego, 1985-90; pres. Tekton Industries, Carlsbad, Calif., 1990—. NROTC scholar USN, 1975. Mem. Am. Soc. Mech. Engrs., Nat. Soc. Profl. Engrs., Alpha Delta Phi. (pres. 1978). Greek Orthodox. Home: 6857 Seaspray Ln Carlsbad CA 92009-3738

PAPAMARCOS, MARK STANLEY, electronic design automation consultant; b. Elgin, Ill., Sept. 24, 1962; s. John and Barbara Ann (Johnson) P.; m. Barbara Joan Bauer. BS in Computer Engring., U. Ill., 1982, MS in Elec. Engring., 1984; MBA, U. Calif., Berkeley, 1993. Sr. engr. Valid Logic Systems, Inc., San Jose, Calif., 1985-87; dir. hardware devel. Modeling Systems, Inc., Milpitas, Calif., 1987-90; mgr. process integration Valid Logic Systems, Inc., San Jose, 1991; mgr. design methodology Cadence Design Systems, San Jose, 1991-93; owner, prin. EDA Assocs., San Jose, 1990-91, 93-95; mgr. emulation hardware Synopsys, Mountain View, Calif., 1995—. Patentee in field. Mem. IEEE (P896.2 standards com. 1984-87). Office: Synopsys 700 AE Middlefield Rd Mountain View CA 94043

PAPARIAN, WILLIAM M., mayor. Mayor dist. 4 City of Pasadena, Calif. Office: City of Pasadena 100 N Garfield Ave Rm 237 Pasadena CA 91109-7215

PAPATHAKIS, PEGGY CALLAGHAN, registered dietitian; b. L.A., Sept. 29, 1955; d. Joseph Molnar and Jacqueline Ann Callaghan; m. John Anthony Papathakis, Apr. 12, 1980; children: Sean, Eric, Caitlin. BS in Dietetics, Calif. Poly. State U., 1977. Registered dietitian; cert. specialist in pediatric nutrition. Dietetic intern Alton Ochsner Med. Found., New Orleans, 1978-79; clin. nutritionist U. Calif. Davis Med. Ctr., Sacramento, 1979-81, pediatric nutritionist, 1981—; area dir. and instr. Shapers Nutrition Class, Kaiser, Sacramento and Roseville, Calif., 1985-88, 95-96; mem. med. adv. bd. Hinckley and Schmitt Bottled Water Group, 1995—. Author articles; interviewed on TV, radio and in newspapers. Bd. dirs., fundraising chair, pub. rels. chair Cedar Springs Waldorf Sch., Placerville, Calif., 1992-96. Mem. NOW, Am. Dietetic Assn. (Young Dietitian of Yr. 1984), Calif. Dietitian Assn. (media spokesperson 1989—, legis. steering com. 1990—, dist. pres., sec. nominating com. 1983-90, Excellence in Clin. Practice award 1992, Jane Pirkey award 1992), Am. Soc. Parenteral and Enteral Nutrition. Office: U Calif Davis Med Ctr 2516 Stockton Blvd Sacramento CA 95817-2208

PAPE, ARNIS WESTON, minister; b. Portales, N.Mex., Dec. 24, 1950; s. Arnis Wilson and Lella Mae (Berry) P.; m. Lucena Ann Molzen, May 31, 1975; children: John Dayton, Jennifer Marie. BA in Psychology, U.N.Mex., 1974; MS in Biblical and Related Studies, Abilene Christian U., 1995. Ordained to ministry Church of Christ, 1972. Assoc. minister Ch. of Christ, Plainview, Tex., 1974-76; pulpit minister Ch. of Christ, Artesia, N.Mex., 1976-85, Ft. Collins, Colo., 1985—; tchr. Pepperdine U., Malibu, 1991, 93. Editor bull. Meadowlark Messenger, 1985—; contbr. articles to profl. jours.; author booklet: Happy Though Married, 1988, rev. edit., 1992. Co-founder Am. Children's Transplant Fund, Ft. Collins, 1987; mem. Parent Adv. Bd., Artesia, 1983-84; mem. pres.'s coun. Lubbock Christian U., 1985—. Recipient award for outstanding svc. Ch. of Christ, 1985. Home: 2212 Shawnee Ct Fort Collins CO 80525-1849 Office: Church of Christ 2810 Meadowlark Ave Fort Collins CO 80526-2838 *A principle I have tried to hold to in my adult life is found in the old axiom, "Attitude is Everything". A positive mind brings a brighter idea, a more noble solution, and a happier day.*

PAPE, BARBARA KAREN, administrative assistant; b. Compton, Calif., Jan. 31, 1950; d. Louis and Theresa Carolyn (Gallup) Aprea; m. Jack William Pape, Dec. 31, 1969; children: Jack Lewis, Chad William. Diploma in med. assisting, Blair Coll. Med. and Dental; student, Orange Coast Coll., Saddleback Coll., U. Calif., Irvine. Lic. x-ray technician, Calif. Instrnl. aide remedial reading grades 7 and 8 Placentia (Calif.) Unified Sch. Dist., 1974-79; proficiency test coord. grades 9 to 12 Irvine (Calif.) Unified Sch. Dist., 1979-85; part time adminstrv. asst. Cirello Magnetos and Racing, Costa Mesa, Calif., 1972—; part time clerical specialist Fluor Daniel, Irvine, 1993—. Co-author, publisher: How to Begin a Successful Acting Career, 1993. Active Irvine (Calif.) Unified Sch. Dist. Adv. Com., 1983-84, 85; mem. citizens adv. com. Orange County Transit Dist., 1984-91; bd. mem., vol. Sutton Found., 1993—. Republican. Roman Catholic. Home: 11 Longstreet Irvine CA 92620-3368

PAPERNY, DAVID MARK N., pediatrician; b. L.A.; 1 child, Jerald. BS magna cum laude in Biochemistry, UCLA, 1973, MD, 1977. Diplomate Am. Bd. Pediatrics, Nat. Bd. Med. Examiners. Resident in pediat. Kapiolani-Children's Med. Ctr., Honolulu, 1977-80; fellow in adolescent medicine U. Wash., Seattle, 1980-81; from assoc. to asst. prof. pediat. and adolescent medicine U. Hawaii Sch. Medicine, Honolulu, 1981—; dir. Kaiser-Permanente Adolescent Svcs., 1981—, health promotion and preventive svcs. com., 1984—, project dir. pediat. patient edn. video, 1989, audio-visual task force/ednl. media task force, 1990, founder newborn drug abuse task force and drug intervention subcom. health promotion and preventive svcs. com., 1990, staff well-being com., 1989, ad hoc teen intervention adv. com., 1989; attending physician Hawaii Sex Abuse Treatment Ctr., 1979—; mem. adv. com. Hawaii State Dept. Commerce and Consumer Affairs, Regulated Industries Complaint Office, 1988—; mem. adv. coun. Cmty.-Based Teenage Health Clinic for Waikiki Health Ctr., Hawaii, 1990—. Dir. March of Dimes Teen Health Computer Project, 1984; med. affairs com. Hawaii Planned Parenthood, 1988—; mem. Hawaii Teen Parenting and Pregnancy Coun., 1980, Nat. Com. for Prevention Child Abuse, 1988. Recipient L.A. C. of C. Cmty. Svc. award, 1973. Fellow Am. Acad. Pediat. (chmn. com. on adolescence Hawaii chpt. 1986, Hawaii chpt. liaison to task force and provisional com. on substance abuse 1988, chpt. rep. to Hawaii family health svcs. divsn. task force drug edn. and prevention adv. com. 1987, exec. com. Sect. on Computer Tech. 1995); mem. Am. Soc. Clin. Hypnosis (cert. cons.), Soc. for Adolescent Medicine, Hawaii Acad. Hypnosis (founder), Phi Beta Kappa, Sigma Xi, Phi Eta Sigma. Office: Kaiser Permanente 1010 Pensacola St Honolulu HI 96814-2118

PAPILE, LUCILLE ANN, pediatrician, educator; b. Quincy, Mass., June 10, 1943; d. John Peter and Madeline Catherine (Jancaterino) P.; m. Stephen Francis Lawless, May 16, 1969 (div. Dec. 1987). BA in Chemistry, Albertus Magnus Coll., 1965; MD, Med. Coll. Pa., 1969. Diplomate Am. Bd. Neonatal/Perinatal Medicine. From instr. to assoc. prof. dept. pediatrics U. N.Mex., Albuquerque, 1972-89, from asst. prof. to assoc. prof. ob-gyn., 1974-89, prof. pediatrics and ob-gyn., 1989—; vis. scientist U. Calif., San Francisco, 1980-81; Congl. fellow U.S. Ho. of Reps., Washington, 1992; mem. sub-bd. com. Am. Bd. Pediatrics, 1988-94. Contbr. numerous articles to profl. jours. Grantee Thrasher Rsch. Found., 1980-83, U.S. Dept. Edn., 1988-91, 91-94, NIH, 1991-96, 96—. Mem. Am. Acad. Pediatrics (tech. com. bd. 1993—), Am. Pediatric Soc., Soc. for Pediatric Rsch. Office: U NMex ACC 3 West 8131 UNMH/BCMC Dept Pediatrics Albuquerque NM 87131

PAPP, HENRY, science association administrator. Pres. Ariz. Zool. Soc., The Phoenix Zoo, 1995—. Office: Phoenix Zoo 455 N Galvin Pkwy Phoenix AZ 85008

PAPPAS, JIM D., judge. Chief judge U.S. Bankruptcy Ct., Boise. Office: US Bankruptcy Ct Fed Bldg and US Courthouse 550 W Fort St Box 039 Boise ID 83724

PAPPAS, LEAH AGLAIA, civic worker, political consultant, educator; b. Ogden, Utah, Mar. 23, 1936; d. George Thomas and Maria (Harames) P. BA, Coll. St. Mary of the Wasatch, 1959. Tchr. Bishop Gorman High Sch., Las Vegas, Nev., 1959-64; with Dist. Atty.'s staff, Las Vegas, 1972-75; tchr. Weber State Coll., Las Vegas, 1985. Civic worker various orgns., including Opera Guild, Heart Fund, City of Hope, March of Dimes, also groups for prevention of blindness, sr. citizens' groups, others, Ogden and Las Vegas, 1955—; cons. numerous polit. campaigns, Ogden, Las Vegas and Boston, L.A., John F. Kennedy campaign, 1959; alt. del. Chgo. Nat. Conv.; vol. Senator Robert Kennedy Campaign, 1968; supr. Senator Edward M. Kennedy Campaign, Boston, 1970, 76, Presdl. Campaign, 1980; campaign worker Gov. Jerry Brown, L.A., 1978, Pres. Bill Clinton, 1996. Greek Orthodox. Home: 1323 Marilyn Dr Ogden UT 84403-0424

PAPPAS, MARIA ELENI, nurse; b. Encino, Calif., Oct. 1, 1960; d. Nicholas Constantine and Helen Cleo (Tannors) P. BSN, U. San Francisco, 1985; M in Nursing, UCLA, 1991. Cert. critical care nurse, pub. health nurse. Staff med./surg. nurse VA Med. Ctr., West L.A., 1985-87; staff nurse ICU VA Med. Ctr., San Francisco, 1987-88; staff nurse SICU St. Mary's Hosp., San Francisco, 1988-89; staff nurse ICU St. Joseph's Hosp., Burbank, Calif., 1989-91; clin. nurse specialist Northridge (Calif.) Hosp. Med. Ctr., 1991-95; asst. clin. prof. Sch. Nursing, UCLA, 1993—. Co-author: (manual) Brain Death Policy Manual, 1993. VA scholar U. San Francisco, 1984, Reynolds Estate scholar UCLA, 1991. Mem. Sigma Theta Tau (Outstanding Contbn. award 1989). Greek Orthodox. Home: 8012 Comanche Ave Winnetka CA 91306-1832 Office: Raytel Heart Ctr 10445 Balboa Blvd Granada Hills CA 91394-9400

PAQUETTE, RICHARD, airport executive. V.p. airport devel. Calgary Airport, AB, Can. Mem. Calgary Conv. and Visitors Bureau, Alta. Aviation Coun. Mem. Am. Assn. Airport Execs., Calgary C. of C., Calgary Rotary Club. Office: Calgary International Airport, 2000 Airport Rd NE, Calgary, AB Canada T2E 6W5*

PARCEL, RANDY LYNN, lawyer; b. Chgo., July 2, 1945; s. Roland E. and LaVera M. (Ervin) P.; m. Judith C. Carroll, Jan. 30, 1971 (div. Jan. 1991); 1 child, Andrew. BS in Mining Engring., S.D. Sch. Mines & Tech., Rapid City, 1967; JD, Northwestern U., 1970. Assoc., ptnr. Holland & Hart, Denver, 1970-78; ptnr., shareholder Parcel, Mauro, Hultin & Spaanstra, P.C., Denver, 1978—; pres. Rocky Mountain Mineral Law Fedn., Denver, 1993-94; chmn. mineral law sect. Colo. Bar Assn., Denver, 1982-83. Trustee Colo. Sch. Mines, Golden, 1995-96, S.D. Sch. Mines & Tech. Found., Rapid City, 1993-96. Named Disting. Practitioner in Residence, U. Denver Coll. Law, 1992. Mem. Soc. Mining Engrs. Office: Parcel Mauro Hultin & Spaanstra PC # 3600 1801 California Denver CO 80202

PARDUE, A. MICHAEL, plastic and reconstructive surgeon; b. Nashville, June 23, 1931; s. Andrew Peyton and Ruby (Fly) P.; m. Lilavati Sharma, Dec. 1996. BS, U. of the South, 1953; MD, U. Tenn., 1957. Resident in gen. surgery Pittsfield (Mass.) Affiliated Hosps., 1966; resident in plastic surgery N.Y. Hosp./Cornell Med. Ctr., 1968; plastic surgeon A. Michael Pardue, M.D., Thousand Oaks, Calif., 1968—. Lt. comdr. USN, 1956-62. Fellow ACS; mem. Am. Soc. Plastic and Reconstructive Surgeons, Am. Soc. Aesthetic Plastic Surgery, Calif. Soc. Plastic Surgeons. Episcopalian.

PARDUE, KAREN REIKO, elementary education educator; b. Honolulu, June 13, 1947; d. Rex Shinzen and Ruth Fujiko (Arakawa) Ishiara; m. Jerry Thomas Pardue, Oct. 21, 1978 (dec. Sept. 1994); 1 child, Holly. BS, Western Ill. U., 1969; MA, U. No. Colo., 1971, 72. Tchr. home econs. Galesburg (Ill.) High Sch., 1969-70; tchr. spl. edn. Jefferson County Pub. Schs., Golden, Colo., 1973-85, 87-94; tchr. 3d & 3d grades Englewood (Colo.) Christian Sch., 1985-86; tchr. 2d grade Jefferson County Pub. Schs., 1994—; adj. instr. Colo. Christian U., Lakewood, 1989—; mem. recommended basic list com. Jefferson County Pub. Schs., 1993-95. Colo. Dept. Edn. Mini grantee, 1976, Jefferson Found. Venture grantee, 1988. Mem. ASCD, Colo. Coun. LEarning Disabilities, Jefferson County Ednl. Assn., Jefferson County Internat. Reading Assn., Delta Kappa Gamma (rec. sec. 1988-89, pres. 1990-92, treas. 1994—).

PAREDES, BERT (NORBERT PAREDES), computer systems engineer; b. Frankfurt, Germany, Dec. 27, 1947; s. George and Elfriede (Kleebach) P.; m. Linda L. Stubblefield, July 5, 1968 (div. 1986); m. Katherine Blacklock, Feb. 4, 1989. BS in Computer Sci., SUNY, Albany, 1970; postgrad., U. Colo., 1977-78. Enlisted U.S. Army, 1970, programmer/analyst, 1970-79, resigned, 1979; staff engr. Martin Marietta, Denver, 1979-81, sr. staff engr., 1984-92; regional analyst, mgr. Gould Computer Systems, Denver, 1981-84; mgr. tech. analysis and support Denelcor, Inc., Aurora, Colo., 1984; v.p. C-Quad Systems, Inc., Littleton, Colo., 1992-94, pres., 1994—; Pres., chief exec. officer A.C.T., Inc., Denver, 1982-84. Contbr. articles to profl. jours. Nat. Merit scholar, 1966. Mem. Assn. Computing Machinery, Armed Forces Communications and Electronics Assn., Am. Rose Soc., Mensa, Denver Bot. Gardens. Lutheran. Home: 6859 N Beaver Run Littleton CO 80125-9202 Office: C-Quad Systems Inc 26 W Dry Creek Cir Ste 600 Littleton CO 80120-4475

PARENT, EDWARD ALPHONSE, psychologist, consultant, publishing company executive; b. Vernal, Utah, Nov. 8, 1940; s. Joseph A. and Dorthea R. (Frost) P.; m. Sydney Minnette Brown, June 14, 1967; children: A. Roger, Sydney M., Ephraim E., Alexander A., Bethany A. BS in Physics, Math. and French, Brigham Young U., 1967, MBA in Bus., 1969, PhD in Counseling and Personnel Svcs., 1982. Lic. psychologist. Instr. in orgnl. behavior Brigham Young U., Provo, Utah, 1969-70; mktg. analyst Exxon Internat., Inc., N.Y.C., 1970-72; adminstr. Bonneville Med. Group, Salt Lake City, 1972-84; adminstr., counselor Dennis W. Remington, MD, Provo, 1984-88; pres. Vitality House Internat., Provo, 1982—; resident in psychology Utah Valley Regional Med. Ctr., Provo, 1988-90, staff psychologist, 1990—; cons. Green Valley Health Resort, St. George, Utah, 1987-90, Nat. Inst. of Consulting Svcs., Salt Lake City, 1992-94; mem. adv. bd. doctoral program com. ednl. psychology dept. Brigham Young U., Provo, 1993-94; chmn. staff psychologists Utah Valley Reg. Med. Ctr., Provo, Utah, 1995—. Co-author: How to Lower Your Fat Thermostat, 1982, Recipes for Kids to Lower their Fat Thermostat, 1994, (audio tape) The Neuropsychology of Weight Control, 1985, 12 Steps to Lower Your Fat Thermostat, 1993. Cub master pack 738 Boy Scouts Am., Provo, 1986-90, chmn. scout com., 1994. Mem. Utah Psychol. Assn. (membership com. 1990). Office: Vitality House Internat Inc 1675 N Freedom Blvd Ste 11C Provo UT 84604-2570

PARENTI, KATHY ANN, sales professional; b. Gary, Ind., Sept. 24, 1957; d. Lee Everett Huddleston and Barbara Elizabeth (Daves) Tilley; m. Michael A. Parenti, Mar. 31, 1979 (div. Sept. 1990); m. S. Curtis McCoy, Sept. 6, 1996. Student, Ind. U., Gary, 1977; cert., U. Nev., Las Vegas, 1978; diploma, Interior Design Inst., Las Vegas, 1984. Supr. Circus Circus Hotel, Las Vegas, 1980-87; owner Interior Views, Las Vegas, 1984-87; sales rep. Win-Glo Window Coverings, 1987-88; owner Dimension Design, 1988-90; sales rep. Sidney Goldberg & Assoc., Las Vegas, 1990—; sales rep., Parenti & Assocs., 1990—. Mem. NAFE, Am. Soc. Interior Designers, Internat. Interior Design Assn., Network of Exec. Women in Hospitality, Design Inst. Soc., Rep Network.

PARER, JULIAN THOMAS, obstetrics and gynecology educator; b. Melbourne, Australia, Sept. 2, 1934; m. Robin M.W. Fletcher, Apr. 23, 1962; 1 child, William John. B Agr. Sci., U. Melbourne, 1959; M Rural Sci. in Bioclimatology, U. New Eng., Australia, 1962; PhD, Oreg. State U., 1965; MD, U. Wash., 1971. Diplomate Am. Bd. Ob-Gyn, Am. Bd. Maternal and Fetal Medicine. Grad. fellow and asst., summer and rsch. fellow U. Oreg. Med. Sch., Portland, 1961-63; vis. scientist Oreg. Regional Primate Rsch. Ctr., Portland, 1964-66; instr. dept. ob-gyn U. Wash., Seattle, 1966-68, sr. fellow, mem. med. rsch. unit, mem. Anesthesia Rsch. Ctr., 1969-71; resident Los Angeles County-U. So. Calif. Sch. Medicine, L.A., 1971-74; asst. prof., assoc. prof. U. Calif., San Francisco, 1974-82, prof., 1982—, dir. obstetrics, 1980-87, dir. maternal-fetal medicine fellowship tng. program, 1983—; rsch. affiliate Regional Primate Ctr., Seattle, 1969-71; assoc. staff Cardiovascular Rsch. Inst., U. Calif., 1976—; vis. scientist Nuffield Inst. for Med. Rsch., Oxford (Eng.) U., 1981-82; vis. scientist U. Chile, Santiago, 1985-96, Devel. Physiology Lab., U. Auckland, New Zealand, 1988-90, Perinatal Rsch. Group, U. Plymouth, Eng., 1995-96. Author: Handbook of Fetal Heart Rate Monitoring, 1983, 2d edit., 1997; editor: (with P.W. Nathanielsz) Research in Perinatal Medicine, 1984; Antepartum and Intrapartum Management, 1989; contbr. numerous articles and abstracts to med. jours. Fellow Am. Coll. Obstetricians and Gynecologists; mem. Am. Physiol. Soc., Australian Perinatal Soc., Soc. for Gynecol. Investigation, Soc. Perinatal Obstetricians (bd. dirs. 1988-91), Soc. for Study Fetal Physiology, Chilean Soc. Ob-Gyn (fgn. corr.), Phi Kappa Phi, Phi Sigma. Office: U Calif 505 Parnassus Ave San Francisco CA 94143-0550

PAREZO, NANCY JEAN, anthropologist, curator; b. Buffalo, Jan. 8, 1951; d. Charles William and Georgia Leon (Pierce) P.; m. Richard V.N. Ahlstrom, Oct. 23, 1983. BA in Anthropology, Sociology cum laude, Miami U., 1973; MA, U. Ariz., 1976, PhD in Cultural Anthropology, 1981. Student registrar Elma Pratt Folk Art Collection Miami U., 1970-71, lab technician, teaching asst. dept anthropology, 1972-73; ceramic restorer Musee de l'Etat, Luxembourg, 1971-72; grad. rsch. asst. Bur. Ethnic Rsch. U. Ariz., 1974-75, grad. rsch. asst. dept. anthropology, v.p. rsch., 1975-78, from grad. teaching asst. to instr. dept. anthropology, 1979-81, instr. Elderhostel program divsn. continuing edn., 1982-83, rsch. prof. Am. Indian studies, anthropology, 1992—; instr. internship tng. program Nat. Mus. Natural History/Smithsonian Instn., 1981-82; ethnologist Ariz. State Mus., 1983-85, assoc. curator ethnology, 1985-90, curator ethnology, 1990—; instr. dept. landscape architecture U. Ariz., 1976, instr. divsn. continuing edn., 1979-81, dir. mus. studies program dept. anthropology, 1985-90, cons. agrl. ext., 1989, rsch. prof. Am. Indian Studies and Anthropology, 1992—, D'Arcy McNickle Indian fellow Newberry Libr., 1994-95; rschr. collections divsn. Ariz. State Mus., 1977; instr. Pima C.C., 1979-81; regents loaned exec. Ariz. Bd. Regents, 1990-91; assoc. program dir. anthropology NSF, 1987-88; field reviewer Inst. for Mus. Svcs., 1988-89; panel mem. NEH, 1986, 90; cons. and lectr. in field. Editor: Hidden Scholars. Women Anthropologists and the Native American Southwest, 1993; co-editor: Preserving the Anthropological Record, 1992; curator numerous exhibits in Anthropology and Native Am. studies; contbr. articles to profl. jours. Grantee Wenner-Gren Found., 1985-86, 89-91, 92-95, U. Ariz., 1977-80, 86-87, 92, NEH, 1985-86, 89, 92, Ednl. Commn. of States, 1990, Smithsonian Instn., 1986-90, Mus. No. Ariz., 1978, Ariz. Humanities Coun., Ind. Prodrs. Svcs., Haffenreffer Mus.; Undergrad. Rsch. fellow Miami U., 1971-72, Postdoctoral fellow Smithsonian Instn., 1981-82; Weatherhead Resident scholar Sch. Am. Rsch., 1978-79, Sigma Xi scholar, 1979, Grad. scholar U. Ariz., 1973-75, Alumni scholar Miami U., 1971-72, Nat. Purchasing Agts. scholar, 1971-72, N.Y. State regents scholar, 1969. Fellow AAAS, Am. Antrhop. Assn.; mem. AAUW, Am. Ethnological Assn., Soc. for Am. Archaeology, Soc. for Applied Anthropology, Soc. for Feminist Anthropology, Am. Assn. Mus. (accreditation com. 1989-90, MAP advisor and reviewer 1989-93), Coun. for Mus. Anthropology (bd. dirs. 1988-92, program chair 1992, treas. 1985-88), History Anthropology Network, Assn. for Women Faculty (sec. 1990-91, com. acad. profl. 1985-87), Southwestern Anthrop. Assn., Coun. for Preservation of Anthrop. Records (pres. 1994—), Phi Beta Kappa (bd. dirs. 1990-91), Alpha Kappa Delta. Democrat. Office: Univ Ariz Ariz State Mus Tucson AZ 85721

PARHAM, LINDA DIANE, occupational therapist, researcher, educator; b. Guantanamo, Cuba, Aug. 28, 1952; d. Gerald Dathel and Shirley (Melzer) P.; m. Harry Edward Trigg III, June 1, 1985; 1 child, Dorothy Helen Trigg, Oct. 28, 1993. BS, U. Fla., 1974; MA, U. So. Calif., L.A., 1980; PhD, UCLA, L.A., 1989. Asst. dir. occupational therapy Bayberry Psychiat. Hosp., Hampton, Va., 1974-75; sr. occupational therapist Maryview Community Mental Health Ctr., Portsmouth, Va., 1975-78; pvt. practice L.A., 1980-84; asst. prof. U. So. Calif., L.A., 1986-92, assoc. prof., 1992—; adj. instr. U. So. Calif., 1979-80, 85-86; dir. edn. Ayres Clinic, Torrance, Calif, 1985-96. Author: (chpt.) Sensory Integration and Children with Learning Disabilities; editor: Play in Occupational Therapy for Children; mem. editorial rev. bd. Occupational Therapy Jour. of Rsch., 1988-90; contbr. numerous articles to profl. jours. Ctr. for Study of Sensory Integrative Dysfunction scholar, 1980; Am. Occupational Therapy Found. fellow, 1988. Fellow Am. Occupational Therapy Assn.; mem. Occupational Therapy Assn. Calif., World Fedn. Occupational Therapists, Sensory Integration Internat. (faculty emeritus, sec. 1986-87), Soc. for Rsch. in Child Devel., The Assn. for the Study of Play. Office: U So Calif 1540 Alcazar St # 133 Los Angeles CA 90033-4500

PARHAM, ROBERT BRUCE, archivist; b. Denver, June 4, 1948; s. James Monroe and Doris Demetral (Lands) P.; m. Meredith Howard, May 20, 1989; 1 stepchild, Gwendolyn. BA cum laude, Western State Coll., Gunnison, Colo., 1970; MA, U. Wis., 1974, U.Colo., 1981. Cert. archivist. Rsch. analyst Pub. Records Bd. Wis., Madison, 1974; manuscripts curator U. Ark., Fayetteville, 1974-77; film archivist Denver Mus. Natural History, 1979-80; archivist Boulder (Colo.) Hist. Soc., 1979-82; instr. history dept. Calif. State U.-Dominguez Hills, Carson, 1983-84, archivist, asst. prof. libr. sci., 1982-85; asst. prof. libr. sci., ast. archivist U. Alaska, Fairbanks, 1985-89; archivist Nat. Pers. Records Ctr., St. Louis, 1989-90; asst. dir. Nat. Archives-Alaska region, Anchorage, 1990-97; archivist Nat. Archives-Pacific Alaska Region, Anchorage, 1997—; sec.-treas. Alaska at War, Anchorage, 1992-96. Author: (book rev.) Alaska History, 1994; contbr. articles to profl. jours. Mem. Soc. Am. Archivists, Nat. Assn. Govt. Archives and Records Adminstrs., N.W. Archivists (Alaska rep. 1992—), Alaska Hist. Soc. (bd. dirs. 1995—), Cook Inlet Hist. Soc. Democrat. Home: 4310 Seeley Ct Anchorage AK 99502-1957 Office: US Nat Archives & Records Adminstrn Pacific Alaska Region 654 West 3d Ave Anchorage AK 99501-2145

PARICH, BEATRICE ANN, secondary school educator; b. Dickinson, N.D., Mar. 15, 1954; children: Michael, Steven. BS, Univ. Oreg., 1978; MA in Tchg., Lewis and Clark Coll., 1984; student, Oreg. State Univ. Cert. health educator, sch. counselor. Health educator Evergreen Jr. H.S., Hillsboro, Oreg., 1979—; tchr. health edn. Hillsboro H.S., 1979-90; coach volleyball, track, girl's basketball, girl's softball Hillsboro Jr. H.S. Good will ambassador Sister City Del. Students, Japan, 1990; group facilitator Dougy Ctr. Grieving Children, 1991-93; fundraiser Greater Portland Tennis Coun., 1996; vol. coach Hillsboro Soccer Club, 1996. Mem. NEA, Oreg. Edn. Assn., Hillsboro Edn. Assn., Oreg. Assn. Advancement Health Edn., Univ. Oreg. Alumni Assn., Lewis and Clark Coll. Alumni Assn., Multnomah Athletic Club (chairperson soccer 1993-95, adv. jr. events 1994-95, budget sub-com. 1995, chmn. mem. athlete sub-com. 1996), Kappa Kappa Gamma Alumni Assn. Democrat. Roman Catholic. Home: 1241 NE Oleander Ln Hillsboro OR 97124-2653 Office: Hillsboro Sch Dist 759 SE Washington St Hillsboro OR 97123-4229

PARIGIAN, MICHAEL JOHN, forensic scientist; b. Culver City, Calif., July 22, 1960; s. Abraham and Ann Louis Parigian; m. Trelene Tracey Fitzgerald, May 4, 1989; 1 child, Nichelle Ann. BS, U. Calif., Irvine, 1982; MS, Calif. State U., L.A., 1989. Chemist trainee Met. Water Dist., La Verne, Calif., 1980; chemist Day-Glo Color Corp./Pacific Dispersions, Cudahy, Calif., 1983-87; criminalist Ventura County (Calif.) Sheriff's Crime Lab, 1987—. Contbr. articles to profl. jours. Mem. Am. Acad. Forensic Scis., Calif. Assn. Criminalists (treas., sec. com. endowment com.), Calif. Homicide Investigators Assn., L.A. Soc. Coating Tech. Republican. LDS Ch. Office: Ventura County Sheriffs Lab 800 S Victoria Ave Ventura CA 93009-0001

PARIKH, ANJAN, electronics company executive; b. Devgadhbaria, Gujrat, India, Feb. 19, 1957; came to U.S., 1983; s. Rajnikant and Surbala (Modi) P.; m. Rita Mehta, Dec. 6, 1982; children: Pranay, Raxit. BSEE, S.P. Univ., India., 1979; MSEE, Santa Clara (Calif.) U., 1988. Sr. test engr. Hindustan Brown Boveri, Bombay, India, 1980-83, Signetics (Philips), Sunnyvale, Calif., 1983-88; mgr. test engr. Harris Semiconductor, Santa Clara, 1988-92, Siliconix, Santa Clara, 1992—. Home: 3809 Ashridge Ln San Jose CA 95121-1402 Office: Siliconix 2201 Laurelwood Rd Santa Clara CA 95054-1516

PARIS, EDWARD MARVIN, education administrator; b. Denver, Oct. 7, 1951; s. Marvin E. and Winifred A. (West) P.; m. Carol L. Powell, Aug. 2, 1975; 1 child, Julia. BA, U. Colo., Boulder, 1973, MPA, 1979; postgrad., U. Colo., Denver. Adminstrv. officer Colo. Dept. Revenue, Denver, 1979-80, Colo. Dept. Social Svc., Denver, 1980; budget analyst U. Colo., Boulder, 1980-84; instl. analyst U. Colo., Colorado Springs, 1984-89, dir. instl. rsch., 1989-94, interim dir. fin. svcs., 1991-94, assoc. vice chancellor adminstrn. and fin., 1994—; cons. in info. systems, Colorado Springs; instl. rep. Am. Coll. Testing prog. Mem. Assn. Instnl. Rsch. (mem. workshop selection com. for nat. conv. 1989), Pi Alpha Alpha. Home: 2614 Farragut Cir Colorado Springs CO 80907-6406 Office: U Colo PO Box 7150 Colorado Springs CO 80933-7150

PARIS, RICHARD WAYNE, forester; b. Corning, N.Y., July 22, 1956; s. Robert Lee and Ann (Seeley) P.; m. Alberta E. Blanchard, Mar. 21, 1992. BS in Forest Resource, Iowa State U., 1978; postgrad., Everett C.C., 1984. Forester Colville Tribal Forestry, Nespelem, Wash., 1979-81, U.S. Bur. Indian Affairs, Nespelem, 1986—; fire warden, forester State of Utah, Kamas, 1982; law enforcement park technician U.S. Nat. Park Svc., Coulee Dam N.R.A., Wash., 1983-85; park technician U.S. Corps Engrs., Somerset, Ky., 1985-86; instr. Inland Empire EMS Tng. Coun. EMT, ambulance dir., fire chief Grand Coulee (Wash.) Vol. Fire Dept., 1981—; first aid instr. ARC, Ephrata, Wash., 1980-94; instr.-trainer CPR, Am. Heart Assn., Grant Countym Wash., 1980—; mem. Wash. State EMS, Edn. Com.; vol. Boy Scouts Am., 1983-96. Recipient Outstanding Svc. award ARC, 1982. Mem. Soc. Am. Foresters, Am. Forestry Assn., Coulee Med. Found. (sec. 1987-88), Grant County EMS Coun. (pres. 1984-86, sec. 1987-94), North Ctrl. Wash. Regional EMS Coun. (pres. 1990—, EMS Adminstr. of Yr. 1989, 91). Baptist. Office: US Bur Indian Affairs Colville Indian Agy Nespelem WA 99155

PARIS, VREDA, artist, educator; b. Manhattan, N.Y., Mar. 20, 1928; d. Jacob and Sarah (Meltzer) Alpert; m. Harold Persico Paris, Mar. 20, 1953 (div. May 1969); m. Vernon Clarence Zimmerman, Aug. 26, 1972. BA, Pratt Inst., 1949; MFA in Painting, Lone Mountain Coll., 1976. Assoc. prof. Calif. Coll. Arts and Crafts, Oakland, 1964-78; pvt. art tchr. Orange Cove, Calif., 1978-90; asst. prof. U. Calif., Santa Barbara, 1969; creative dir. Ad Fried Assocs., Oakland, 1965-69; art dir. Vernon Cash Assocs., Oakland, 1969-72; lectr. U. Sonora, Hermacillo, Mexico, 1970, U. Calif., Berkeley, 1971; artist-in-residence U. Nev., Las Vegas, 1972-73, Santa Rosa (Calif.) Jr. Coll., 1974-75; mktg. cons. Zico Mktg., San Francisco, 1973-75; pvt. practice art cons., 1977-79; presenter in field. One-person shows include Gumps Art Gallery, San Francisco, 1987, Merced (Calif.) Coll., 1988, Banco de Patricios, Buenos Aires, 1988, Fresno (Calif.) State U., 1996, numerous others; group exhbns. include Am. Embassy, Buenos Aires, 1989, Am. Embassy, Santiago, Chile, 1989, Hilton Hotel Art Gallery, Buenos Aires, 1989, Ankrum Gallery, L.A., 1989, numerous others; represented in permanent collections including U. Tex., Austin, Phoenix Art Mus., La Jolla (Calif.) Mus., Ft. Worth Mus. Modern Art, numerous others. Adminstr. for handicapped Moss Wood Park Sch., Oakland, 1967; creator graphic studio Walnut Creek (Calif.) Art Ctr., 1968. Mem. Coll. Art Assn. Am. Jewish. Home: 12293 Avenue 460 Orange Cove CA 93646-9502

PARK, DALE LEE, stand-up comedian, author; b. Pueblo, Colo., July 30, 1956; s. Robert Griffith and Eva Jean (Shackelford) P.; m. Katherine Le-Anne Waller, May 29, 1992; children: Joshua Scott Waller, Robyn Griffith. Acctg. diploma, Electronic Tech. Inst., 1986. Delivery and warehouse man Sturgeon Electric, Pueblo, 1973-76; chmn., rodman Hanten Surveying, Pueblo, 1977-78; salesman Am. Electric, Pueblo, 1979-81, C.E.D., Pueblo, 1981-82; outside salesman Nelectric Supply, Pueblo, 1981-82; clk., cashier Loaf N Jug, Pueblo, 1982-83, 7-11 Stores, Pueblo, 1983-84; with lighting, sound and videotaping dept. Comedy Corner, Colorado Springs, Colo., 1987-89; standup comedian, Pueblo, 1987—. Author: Humor on the Halfshell, 1992, Adlibs, Abstract Absurdities, 1993, The Celestial Brain Warp, 1994, Operation Funny Bone, 1994; contbr. poetry to various publs.; country music singer, songwriter, TV and radio comml. writer. Speaker Keating Alternative Sch., Pueblo, 1993. Home and Office: 1825 Iroquois Rd Pueblo CO 81001-1640

PARK, EDWARD CAHILL, JR., retired physicist; b. Wollaston, Mass., Nov. 26, 1923; s. Edward Cahill and Fentress (Kerlin) P.; m. Helen Therese O'Boyle, July 28, 1951. AB, Harvard U., 1947; postgrad., Amherst Coll., 1947-49; PhD, U. Birmingham, Eng., 1956. Instr. Amherst (Mass.) Coll., 1954-55; mem. staff Lincoln Lab., Lexington, Mass., 1955-57, Arthur D. Little, Inc., Cambridge, Mass., 1957-60; group leader electronic systems Arthur D. Little, Inc., Santa Monica, Calif., 1960-64; sr. staff engr., head laser system sect. Hughes Aircraft Co., Culver City, Calif., 1964-68; sr. scientist Hughes Aircraft Co., El Segundo, Calif., 1986-88; mgr. electro optical systems sect. Litton Guidance and Control Systems, Woodland Hills, Calif., 1968-70; sr. phys. scientist The Rand Corp., Santa Monica, 1970-72; sr. scientist R&D Assocs., Marina Del Rey, Calif., 1972-1986, cons., 1986-89; sr. tech. specialist Rockwell Internat., N.Am. Aircraft, Seal Beach, Calif., 1988-94. Contbr. articles to profl. jours.; patentee in field. Served to 1st lt. USAAF, 1943-46. Grantee Dept. Indsl. and Sci. Research, 1953. Fellow Explorers Club (sec. So. Calif. chpt. 1978-79); mem. IEEE, Optical Soc. Am., N.Y. Acad. Scis., Armed Forces Communications and Electronics Assn., Assn. Old Crows, Sigma Xi. Democrat. Clubs: 20-Ghost (Eng.), Harvard (So. Calif.). Home: 932 Ocean Front Santa Monica CA 90403-2410

PARK, JAMES EDWARD, SR., former city administrator, materials management consultant; b. Cheyenne, Wyo., Sept. 6, 1939; s. John William Dewey and Dorothea Mabel (Werblow) P.; m. Ruta Akmentins, Oct. 25, 1958 (div. Apr. 21, 1996); children: Lynn Ann, James Edward, Andrea Lee. BA in Polit. Sci., U. Nev., Las Vegas, 1979. Cert. profl. contracts mgr.; cert. pub. purchasing ofcl. Buyer Catalytic Constrn., Phila., 1960-65; buyer City of Las Vegas, 1965-68, sr. contract adminstr., 1968-76, chief purchasing/contracts, 1976-85, dep. dir. gen. svcs., 1985-86, dir. gen. svcs., 1986-92; instr. Nat. Inst. Govtl. Purchasing, Reston, Va., also auditor. Author: (poetry) Of Sunshine and Dreams, 1996. Sgt. U.S. N.G., 1957-63. Democrat. Lutheran. Home: 1275 Westwind Rd Las Vegas NV 89102

PARK, JONG HWAN, educational company executive; b. Seoul, Korea; s. Soon-Chul and Young Sook (Kim) P.; m. Shannon Cho, Mar. 29, 1987; children: Rina, Alexander. BS, U. Calif., Irvine, 1988; postgrad., Pacific State U., 1996—. CEO, pres. Elite Ednl., Inc., Rowland Heights, Calif., 1987—; founder, owner Elite Ednl. Inst., Redland Heights, L.A., Cerritos, Arcadia, Anaheim Hills, Calif.; mem. adv. bd. bus. sch. Pacific State U., L.A., 1996—. Columnist The Korean Times, 1995—. mem. Rhema Evang. Mission, 1992—. Mem. Am. Cons. Assn., Astra. Office: Elite Edn Inst 19280 ColimaRd #100 Rowland Heights CA 91748

PARK, JOSEPH CHUL HUI, computer scientist; b. Seoul, Korea, Aug. 6, 1937; s. Don Gil and Eui Kyung (Shin) P.; m. Young Ja Yoon, Aug. 17, 1968; children: Esther Y.J., Maria Y.S., David Y.W., Jonathan Y.S. BA, Coll of Wooster, Ohio, 1959; BS, MIT, 1959; MS, U. Ill., 1961, PhD, 1967. Mem. rsch. staff Stanford Linear Accelerator Ctr Stanford U., 1969-72, 73-75; assoc. prof., then prof. computer sci. Korea Advanced Inst. of Sci., Seoul, 1975-82; head Computer Sci. Rsch. Ctr. Korea Advanced Inst. Sci., Seoul, Korea, 1980-82; mem. tech. staff Braegen Corp., Milpitas, Calif., 1982-86, Hewlett-Packard Labs., Palo Alto, Calif., 1986-92; tech mgr. compiler Advanced Processor div. Intergraph Corp., Palo Alto, 1992-93; sr. staff engr. Sun Microelectronics, Sun Microsystems Compter Corp., Mountain View, Calif., 1993—; lectr. in computer engring. Santa Clara (Calif.) U., 1987-94. Mem. IEEE, Assn. Computing Machinery. Baptist. Home: 14800 Masson Ct Saratoga CA 95070-9715

PARK, RODERIC BRUCE, academic administrator; b. Cannes, France, Jan. 7, 1932; came to U.S., 1932; s. Malcolm Sewell and Dorothea (Turner) P.; m. Marijke DeJong, Aug. 29, 1953; children: Barbara, Marina, Malcolm. AB, Harvard U., 1953; PhD, Calif. Inst. Tech., 1958. Postdoctoral fellow Calif. Inst. Tech., 1958, Lawrence Radiation Lab., Berkeley, Calif., 1958-60; prof. botany U. Calif., Berkeley, 1960-89, prof. plant biology, 1989-93, prof. emeritus, 1993—; chmn. dept. instrn. in biology U. Calif., 1965-68; provost, dean U. Calif. (Coll. Letters and Sci.), 1972-80, vice chancellor, 1980-90; chancellor U. Colo., Boulder, 1994-97; pres. Brickyard Cove Harbors, Inc., 1975-77; dir. William Kaufmann, Inc., 1976-86; mem. corp. Woods Hole Oceanographic Instn., 1974-80; mem. Harvard Vis. Com. on Biochemistry and Molecular Biology, 1990-93. Co-author: Cell Ultrastructure, 51967, Papers on Biological Membrane Structure, 1968; Biology editor, W.H. Freeman & Co., 1966-74; Contbr. articles to profl. jours. Trustee Athenian Sch., 1980—, U. Calif.-Berkeley Found., 1986-90; pres. Jepson Endowment, 1992—, pres., 1994—; bd. dirs. Assoc. Harvard Alumni, 1976-79; bd. overseers Harvard U., 1981-87; mem. exec. com. Coun. Acad. Affairs, 1986-90, chmn., 1988-89; mem. exec. com. Nat. Assn. State Univs. and Land Grant Colls., 1988-90; mem. vis. com. Arnold Arboretum, 1981-88, chmn., 1986-88; acting dir. Univ. and Jepson Herbaria, 1991-93; co-chair Colo. Combined Campain, 1996-97. Recipient New York Bot. Gardens award, 1962. Fellow AAAS; mem. Am. Soc. Plant Physiologists, Am. Bot. Soc., Am. Soc. Photobiology, Danforth Assn. (pres. San Francisco chpt. 1972), Richmond Yacht Club (commodore 1972, dir. found. 1992—), Transpacific Yacht Club, Pacific Cup Yacht Club, Explorers Club. Home: 531 Cliffside Ct Port Richmond CA 94801 Office: U Colo Office of the Chancellor Boulder CO 80309-0017

PARK, U. YOUNG, nuclear engineer; b. Seoul, Republic of Korea, Oct. 12, 1940; came to U.S., 1968; s. Myung W. and Duk-Jo (Chang) P.; children: Tara Lynne, Thomas Robert, Kyung Gi. BS, Seoul Nat. U., 1963; MS, U. Cin., 1970. Registered profl. engr., Ohio, Calif. Nuclear engr. State of Ohio, Columbus, 1975-78, Batelle Columbus (Ohio) Labs., 1978-81, Bechtel, San Francisco, 1981-88; program mgr. Savannah River Site U.S. Dept. Energy, Aiken, S.C., 1988-95; Bechtel nuclear project advisor Korea Electric Power Corp, Seoul, 1993—. Mem. Am. Nuclear Soc. Office: c/o Bechtel Korea 50 Beale St San Francisco CA 94105-1813

PARKER, ALAN DALE, financial development executive; b. Yonkers, N.Y., Mar. 2, 1935; s. Edward Frederick Charles and Olga Frieda (Turrian) P.; m. Hjördis Birgitta Maria Anderson, Sept. 14, 1963; children: Joakim Erik, Douglas Byron, Jenny Maria. BA, Stanford U., 1957; 2MA, UCLA, 1960; cert., U. Paris, 1962. V.p. devel. Sta. KCPB, pub. radio, Santa Barbara, Calif., 1978-82, Santa Barbara YMCA, 1982-85; dir. devel. Inst. of Ams., La Jolla, Calif., 1985-86, Army and Navy Acad., Carlsbad, Calif., 1986-90; cons. A.D. Parker Assocs., Carlsbad, 1990—; dir. devel. Santa Barbara Mus. Art, 1975-78; cons. Boojum Inst., Carlsbad, 1991—, 1991—, San Luis Rey Mission, Oceanside, Calif., 1992—. Contbr. numerous articles on European affairs to profl. publs. Pres. R.S.V.P., Santa Barbara, 1980-83, Santa Barbara chpt. UN Assn., 1982-84; dir. San Diego Internat. Children's Festival, 1987-89. Mem. San Diego Planned Giving Roundtable. Home and Office: 3111 La Costa Ave Carlsbad CA 92009-7523

PARKER, BARRY RICHARD, physics educator; b. Penticton, B.C., Can., Apr. 13, 1935; came to U.S., 1960; s. Gladstone and Olive (Young) P.; m. Gloria Parker, 1960; 1 child, David. BA in Physics with honors, U. B.C., Vancouver, 1959, MSc, 1961; PhD, Utah State U., 1967. Asst. prof. physics Weber State Coll., Ogden, Utah, 1963-66, Idaho State U., Pocatello, Idaho, 1967—. Author: Einstein's Dream, 1986, Search for a Supertheory, 1987, Creation, 1988, Invisible Matter, 1989, Colliding Galaxies, 1990, Cosmic Time Travel, 1991, Vindication fo the Big Bang, 1993, Stairway to the Stars, 1994, Chaos in the Cosmos, 1996. Recipient Writing award U. Tex.-McDonald Obs. Home: 750 Fairway Dr Pocatello ID 83201-2014 Office: Idaho State Univ Dept Physics Pocatello ID 83209

PARKER, BRIAN PRESCOTT, forensic scientist; b. Norfolk, Va., Aug. 31, 1929; s. Milton Ellsworth and Louise Randall (Smith) P.; BS in Quantitative Biology, M.I.T., 1953; JD, Northwestern U., 1957; M.Criminology, U. Calif., Berkeley, 1961, D.Criminology, 1967; m. Sonia Garcia Rosario, Dec. 23, 1960; children: Robin Marie, Augustin Keith. Research asst. U. P.R. Med. Sch., 1961; cons. P.R. Justice Dept., 1961-63; spl. asst. FDA, Washington, 1964; lectr., then asst. prof. criminology U. Calif., Berkeley, 1964-70; sr. criminalist, then sr. forensic scientist Stanford Research Inst., Menlo Park, Calif., 1971-73; prof. forensic sci. and criminal justice Calif. State U., Sacramento, 1973-92; prof. emeritus, 1988—; project dir. phys. evidence Dept. Justice, 1969-70; vis. fellow Nat. Police Research Unit, Australia, 1985; vis. prof. Elton Mayo Sch. Mgmt., South Australia Inst. Tech., 1985. Mem. Am. Chem. Soc. Co-author: Physical Evidence in the Administration of Criminal Justice, 1970, The Role of Criminalistics in the World of the Future, 1972; asso. editor Law, Medicine, Science—and Justice, 1964; contbr. to Ency. Crime and Justice, 1983. Home: 5117 Ridgegate Way Fair Oaks CA 95628-3603

PARKER, CATHERINE SUSANNE, psychotherapist; b. Norwood, Mass., Nov. 4, 1934; d. George Leonard and Hazel Olga (Remmer) P. BA, Bates Coll., 1956; MSW, U. Denver, 1961. Diplomate Acad. Cert. Social Workers; cert. social worker, Colo. Social worker Taunton (Mass.) State Hosp., 1956-59; social worker Ft. Logan Mental Health Ctr., Denver, 1961-66, clin. team leader, 1966-72; dir. adult services Western Inst. Human Resources, Denver, 1973-74; pvt. practice psychotherapy Denver, 1974—; workshop facilitator Arapahoe C.C., 1986-90. Mem. NASW. Home: 6453 S Downing St Littleton CO 80121-2517 Office: Denver Mental Health 165 Cook St Ste 100 Denver CO 80206-5308

PARKER, CHARLES EDWARD, lawyer; b. Santa Ana, Calif., Sept. 9, 1927; s. George Ainsworth and Dorothy P.; m. Marilyn Esther Perrin, June 23, 1956; children—Mary, Catherine, Helen, George. Student, Santa Ana Coll., U. So. Calif.; J.D., S.W. U.-La. Bar: Calif. 1958, U.S. Dist. Ct. (cen. dist.) Calif. 1958, U.S. Supreme Ct. 1969, D.C. 1971, U.S. Dist. Ct. (no. and so. dists.) Calif. 1981. Prof. law Western State U., Fullerton, Calif., 1973-83; spl. counsel Tidelands, First Am. Title Co., 1980-82; dir. First Am. Fin. Corp., 1981-82. Served to sgt. U.S. Army, 1951-53. Author: (book) Tidelands and The Public Trust, 1991. Mem. ABA (com. improvement land records, sect. real property, mem. com. on title ins. sect. real property), Orange County Bar Assn., Calif. Bar Assn., D.C. Bar Assn. Club: Santa Ana Kiwanis, Lodge: Elks (Santa Ana). Contbr. articles in field to profl. jours. Office: 18101 Charter Rd Orange CA 92861-2638

PARKER, EDWIN BURKE, communications executive; b. Berwyn, Alta., Can., Jan. 19, 1932; m. Frances G. Spigai, 1976; children—David Kendall, Karen Liane. B.A., U. B.C., Can., 1954; M.A., Stanford U., 1958, Ph.D. in Mass Communications, 1960. Staff reporter Vancouver Sun, B.C., Can., 1954-55; info. officer U. B.C., Vancouver, 1955-57; research asst. Inst. Communications Research, Stanford U., 1957-60, asst. prof., 1962-63, assoc. prof., 1963-71, prof., 1971-79; v.p. Equatorial Communications Co., 1979-85, chmn. bd. dirs., 1986-87; pres. data networks divsn. CONTEL, 1987-88; pres. Parker Telecomm., Gleneden Beach, Oreg., 1989—; asst. prof. Communications U. Ill., Urbana, 1960-62. Ctr. for Advanced Studies in Behavioral Sci. fellow, 1969-70. Office: Parker Telecommunications PO Box 402 Gleneden Beach OR 97388

PARKER, HAROLD ALLEN, lawyer, real estate executive; b. Denver, Sept. 14, 1924; s. Hyman and Sophia P.; m. Gertrud Parker; children: David, Rodney, Diana, Jesse, Jonathan. JD, Golden Gate U., 1971. Bar: Calif. 1972. Pvt. practice San Francisco; gen. ptnr. Harold Parker Properties, San Francisco; legal cons. San Francisco Craft and Folk Art Mus.; past mem. Bay Area Lawyers for the Arts; spkr. in field; prime developer Union St. Comml. Corridor, San Francisco, 1963—. Author: Wolfgang Paalen, His Art and His Writings, 1980, Richard Bowman, Forty Years of Abstract Painting, 1986. Chmn. Fine Arts Commn., Tiburon, Calif., 1976-78. Mem. Family Club (San Francisco). Office: 1844 Union St San Francisco CA 94123

PARKER, HARRY S., III, art museum administrator; b. St. Petersburg, Fla., Dec. 23, 1939; s. Harry S. Parker and Catherine (Baillie) Knapp; m. Ellen McCance, May 23, 1964; children: Elizabeth Day, Thomas Baillie,

Samuel Ferguson, Catherine Allan. A.B. magna cum laude, Harvard U., 1961; M.A., NYU, 1966. Exec. asst., adminstrv. asst. to dir. Met. Mus. Art, N.Y.C., 1963-66, exec. asst. to pres., 1966-67, exec. asst. to dir., 1967, chmn. dept. edn., 1967-71, vice dir. edn., 1971-73; dir. Dallas Mus. Art, 1974-87, Fine Arts Mus. San Francisco, 1987—. Mem. Am. Assn. Mus. (v.p.) Assn. Art Mus. Dirs., Century Assn., Bohemian Club. Home: 171 San Marcos Ave San Francisco CA 94116-1462 Office: Fine Arts Mus of San Francisco Golden Gate Pk San Francisco CA 94118*

PARKER, JAMES AUBREY, federal judge; b. Houston, Jan. 8, 1937; s. Lewis Almeron and Emily Helen (Stuessy) P.; m. Florence Fisher, Aug. 26, 1960; children: Roger Alan, Pamela Elizabeth. BA, Rice U., 1959; LLB, U. Tex., 1962. Bar: Tex. 1962, N.Mex. 1963. With Modrall, Sperling, Roehl, Harris & Sisk, Albuquerque, 1962-87; judge U.S. Dist. Ct. N.Mex., Albuquerque, 1987—; mem. Standing Commn. on Rules of Practice and Procedures of U.S. Cts., N.Mex. Commn. on Professionalism, 1986—. Articles editor Tex. Law Rev., 1961-62. Mem. ABA, Fed. Judges Assn., Am. Judicature Soc., Am. Bd. Trial Advocates, Tex. Bar Assn., N.Mex. Bar Assn., Albuquerque Bar Assn., Order of Coif, Chancellors, Phi Delta Phi. Office: US Dist Ct PO Box 566 Albuquerque NM 87103-0566

PARKER, JOHN CARLYLE, retired librarian and archivist, editor; b. Ogden, Utah, Oct. 14, 1931; s. Levi and Marietta (Parkinson) P.; m. Janet C. Greene, May 31, 1956; children: Denise, Nathan, Bret. BA, Brigham Young U., 1957; MLS, U. Calif., Berkeley, 1958. Cert. jr. coll. life credential, Calif. Spl. svcs. libr. Humboldt State U., 1958-60; cataloger, reference libr. Ch. Coll. Hawaii, 1960-62, acting libr., 1962-63; head Pub. svcs. Calif. State U. Libr., Stanislaus, 1963-68, head pub. svcs., asst. libr. dir., 1968-83, 84-90, acting libr. dir., 1983-84, univ. archivist, 1990-94, libr. and univ. archivist emeritus, 1994—; s ctr. reference svc. for genealogists and geneal. rsch. for genealogists, 1966—; cons. Bailey's Moving and Storage Co., Allied Van Lines, Bountiful, Utah, 1983-85, Gale Rsch. Co., Detroit, 1986, 92, E & J Gallo Winery, Modesto, Calif., 1990; editor Marietta Pub. Co., 1985—. Author: Library Service for Genealogists, 1981, Going to Salt Lake City to Do Family History Research, 3d rev. and expanded edit., 1996; compiler numerous books, including Directory of Archivist and Librarian Genealogical Instructors, 2d edit., 1990, Rhode Island Biographical and Genealogical Sketch Index, 1991; contbr. articles and book revs. to profl. jours. Founder, vol. libr. Modesto Family History Ctr., 1968-90, Turlock (Calif.) Family History Ctr., 1990—; chmn. Stanislaus County United Way campaign Calif. State U., Stanislaus Campus, 1980-81; sec. bd. dirs. Turlock Centennial Found., 1971-75; pres. Turlock Cmty. Concert Bd., 1973-75; trustee Turlock Libr., 1969-70; merit badge counselor Yosemite coun. Boy Scouts Am., 1973—. With U.S. Army, 1953-55. Fellow Utah Geneal. Assn., 1984. Mem. ALA (chmn. genealogy com. 1989-92, award reference and adult svcs. divsn., history sect.-geneal. pub. co. award 1994, fellow 1965), AAUP, Nat. Geneal. Soc. (award of merit 1984), Calif. Libr. Assn. (pres. Redwood dist. 1959-60, state coll. librs. divsn. 1969, chmn. geneal. librs. round table 1994,, 96-97), Calif. Geneal. Alliance (historian 1991—), Stanislaus County Hist. Soc. (v.p., program chmn. 1972-73), Geneal. Soc. Stanislaus County (hon.), Turlock Hist. Soc. Democrat. Me. LDS Ch. Home: 2115 N Denair Ave Turlock CA 95382-1821

PARKER, JOHN MARCHBANK, consulting geologist; b. Manhattan, Kans., Sept. 13, 1920; s. John Huntington and Marjorie Elizabeth (Marchbank) P.; m. Agnes Elizabeth Potts, Mar. 17, 1978; m. Jan Goble, July 18, 1941 (div. 1968); children—Susan Kelly, Elizabeth Douglass, Deirdre Parker, John Eric; m. Nancy Booth, Jan. 24, 1970 (div. 1974). Student U. Minn., 1937, U. Wyo., 1938; B.S., Kans. State U., 1941. Cert. petroleum geologist Am. Inst. Profl. Geologists. Geologist, U.S. Pub. Roads Adminstrn., Alaska Hwy., Can., 1942-43; Field geologist Imperial Oil Ltd., Northwest Ter., Can., 1943-44; dist. geologist Stanolind Oil & Gas Co., Casper, Wyo., 1944-52; v.p. exploration Kirby Petroleum Co., Houston, 1952-74; v.p. exploration Northwest Exploration Co., Denver, 1974-75; cons. geologist Denver, 1975—. Contbr. articles to profl. jours. Recipient Disting. Service in Geology award Kans. State U., 1983. Fellow AAAS, Geol. Soc. Am.; mem. Am. Assn. Petroleum Geologists (pres. 1982-83, adv. council Tulsa 1983-84, Hon. Mem. award), Rocky Mountain Assn. Geologists (explorer of yr. 1979; pres. 1980-81). Home: 2615 Oak Dr No 32 Lakewood CO 80215

PARKER, JOHN WILLIAM, pathology educator, investigator; b. Clifton, Ariz., Jan. 5, 1931; s. Vilas William and Helen E. Parker; m. Barbara A. Atkinson, June 8, 1957; children: Ann Elizabeth, Joy Noelle, John David, Heidi Susan. BS, U. Ariz., 1953; MD, Harvard U., 1957. Diplomate Am. Bd. Pathology. Clin. instr. pathology U. Calif. Sch. Medicine, San Francisco, 1962-64; asst. prof. U. So. Calif. Sch. Medicine, L.A., 1964-68, assoc. prof., 1968-75, prof., 1975—, dir. clin. labs., 1974-94, vice chmn. dept. pathology, 1985—, dir. pathology reference labs., 1991-94; assoc. dean sci. affairs U. So. Calif., 1987-89; co-chmn. 15th Internat. Leucocyte Culture Conf., Asilomar, Calif., 1982; chmn. 2d Internat. Lymphoma Conf., Athens, Greece, 1981; v.p. faculty senate U. So. Calif., 1991-92; bd. dirs. ann. meeting Clin. Applications of Cytometry, Charleston, S.C., 1988—. Founding editor (jour.) Hematological Oncology, 1982-93; assoc. editor Jour. Clin. Lab. Analysis, 1985—; co-editor: Intercellular Communication in Leucocyte Function, 1983; founding co-editor (jour.) Communications in Clin. Cytometry, 1993—; contbr. over 150 articles to profl. jours., chpts. to books. Named sr. oncology fellow Am. Cancer Soc., U. So. Calif. Sch. Medicine, 1964-69, Nat. Cancer Inst. vis. fellow Walter and Eliza Hall Inst. for Med. Research, Melbourne, Australia, 1972-73. Fellow Coll. Am. Pathologists, Am. Soc. Clin. Pathologists; mem. Am. Assn. Pathologists, Am. Soc. Hematology, Internat. Acad. Pathology, Clin. Cytometry Soc. (v.p. 1994-95, pres. 1995-97), Phi Beta Kappa, Phi Kappa Phi. Office: U So Calif Sch Medicine CSC 108 2250 Alcazar St Los Angeles CA 90033-4523

PARKER, JOYCE STEINFELD, social worker; b. Neptune, N.J., Dec. 11, 1946; d. Milton Donald and Lillian (Sonia) Steinfeld; m. Lawrence Neil Parker, Sept. 18, 1970 (div. Sept. 1990); children: Jill Monica, Gregory Robert. MEd, Boston U., 1969; MSW, UCLA, 1976; PhD, U.S.C., 1992. Lic. social worker. Tchr. spl. edn. Dearborn Sch., Boston, 1969-70, Christ Ch. Child Ctr., Bethesda, Md., 1970-71; tchr. 1st grade Hiroshima (Japan) Internat. Sch., 1971-72; clin. social worker Orange County Mental Health, Westminster, Calif., 1976-80; employee asst. affiliate Human Affairs Internat., L.A., 1987—; instr. U. So. Calif. Sch. Social Work, L.A., 1988-90; pvt. practice clin. social work Torrance, Calif., 1981—; community speaker parenting, marriage, psychol. topics, So. Bay of La., 1983—. Fellow NASW, Soc. Clin. Social Work (cert. employee assistance profl.).

PARKER, LARRY BENSON, judge; b. Harmony, N.C., July 29, 1947; s. Benson Thedford and Grace Agnes (Johnson) P.; m. Jayne Marie Miller, July 16, 1977; 2 children. AB in Econs., Pfeiffer Coll., Misenheimer, N.C., 1969; JD, U. N.C., 1973; LLM, U. Va., 1986. Bar: N.C. 1974, Calif. 1991, Wash. 1992. Law clk. N.C. Ct. Appeals, Raleigh, N.C., 1973-74; commd. 1st lt. USMC, 1974, advanced through grades to maj., jduge adv., 1979-92; litigation assoc. Copy Hatch & Blanchard, Inc., Lynnwood, Wash., 1992-93; dep. atty. gen. Atty. Gen. Calif., San Diego, 1993-95; U.S. adminstrv. law judge Office of Hearings and Appeals, San Diego, 1995-96, 1996—. Author: Handbook for Summary Courts, 1979, Victim Witness Assistance Guide, 1992. Mem. ABA, San Diego County Bar Assn., Ret. Officers Assn., Am. Legion, Disabled Am. Vets. Democrat. Presbyterian. Home: 5219 Silver Bluff Dr Oceanside CA 92057-6334 Office: US Adminstrv Law Judge Office of Hearings/Appeals 750 B St Ste 1100 San Diego CA 92101-5266

PARKER, LARRY LEE, electronics company executive, consultant; b. St. Paul, Oct. 21, 1938; s. Clifford Leroy and Evelyn Elaine (McArtor) P.; m. Esperanza Victoria Delgado, Aug. 7, 1965; children: Sean Lawrance, Nicole Kathleen. AA in Engring., Antelope Valley Coll., Lancaster, Calif., 1964; BS in Indsl. Engring., U. Calif., Berkeley, 1966, MS in Ops. Rsch., 1968. Prin., cons. Ted Barry & Assocs., L.A., 1968-73; v.p. mfg. Pacific divsn. Mark Controls, Long Beach, Calif., 1973-79; v.p. world ops. ARL divsn. Bausch & Lombe, Sunland, Calif., 1979-84; pres. control products divsn. Leach Corp., Buena Park, Calif., 1984-88, exec. v.p., chief operating officer parent co., 1988-90, pres., COO, 1990-96; pres.bd. dirs. Leach Internat., Asia-Pacific, 1996—; advisor engring. coun. U. Calif., Long Beach, 1990—; bd. dirs. So. Calif. Tech. Exec. Network. With USN, 1956-59. Recipient Outstanding Achievement award Los Angeles County Bd. Suprs., 1964. Mem. Am. Prodn. Inventory Control Soc. (mem. exec. com. mfg.), Am. Electronics Assn. (pres.'s roundtable), Calif. Coalition U.S.-China Rels. Home: 2711 Canary Dr Costa Mesa CA 92626-4747 Office: Leach Corp PO Box 5032 Buena Park CA 90622-5032

PARKER, LAWRENCE NEIL, medical educator; b. N.Y.C., Nov. 8, 1943; s. Norman Samuel and Lee (Shapiro) P.; m. Joyce Parker, July 18, 1970 (div. 1988); children: Jill, Gregory. BA, Columbia Coll., 1964; MD, Stanford (Calif.) U., 1969. Diplomate Am. Bd. Internal Medicine: Internal Medicine, Endocrinology and Metabolism. Intern Boston City Hosp., 1969-70; resident in internal medicine U. Calif., San Diego, 1972-74; fellowship in endocrinology UCLA-Harbor Gen. Hosp., 1974-77; internist and endocrinologist Ross Loos Cigna Med. Group, Torrance, 1977; asst. chief of endocrinology VA Med. Ctr., Long Beach, Calif., 1977—; asst. prof. medicine Coll. of Medicine, U. Calif., Irvine, 1978-82, assoc. prof. medicine, 1982-88, prof. medicine, 1988—; edn. evaluation com. VA Med. Ctr., 1978-80, residency selection com., 1978, nutrition com., 1980—, med. libr. com., 1981-85, human studies com., 1981-84, med. svc. morbidity rev. com., 1983-89, clin. activity quality of care subcom., 1989—, quality assurance bd. of investigation, 1990, quality mgmt. team, 1992, chmn. drug usage evaluation subcom., 1991—; rsch. grant reviewer Dept. Vet. Affairs Merit Rev. Bd., Med. Rsch. Coun., Vancouver, Can.; lectr. in field; physician Marshall Islands Med. Program, 1994. Author: Adrenal Androgens in Clinical Medicine, 1989; jour. reviewer Jour. Clin. Endocrinology and Metabolism, Metabolism: Clin. and Exptl., Ob-Gyn., Acta Endocrinologica, Jour. Nat. Cancer Inst., Jour. Endocrinol. Investigation, Western Jour. Medicine, N.Y. State Jour. Medicine; guest editor Radioimmunoassay for Physicians; contbr. articles to profl. jours., chpts. to books. Mem. Atomic Bomb Casualty Commn. Hiroshima, Japan, 1971-72. Surgeon (lt. comdr.) USPHS, 1970-72. Grantee VA Rsch. Adv. Group, 1978-80, VA Merit Rev., 1980-82, 82-86, 86-88, 90-93. Fellow ACP; mem. Endocrine Soc., Am. Fedn. Clin. Rsch., Amnesty Internat., Union of Concerned Scientists. Office: VA Med Ctr 5901 E 7th St Long Beach CA 90822-5201

PARKER, LEANNE, nursing educator, nurse practitioner; b. Ogden, Utah, Jan. 6, 1961; d. Samuel LeGrande and Edith JoAnne (Dewey) P.; 1 child, Clinton D. Willard. AS, Weber State U., 1985; BS, U. Utah, 1987, MSc, 1994. Cert. women's health care nurse practitioner, ob-gyn. nurse practitioner, Nat. Certification Corp. for Obstetric and Neonatal Nursing. RN St. Benedict's Hosp., Ogden, 1986-87; nurse practitioner Planned Parenthood of Utah, Salt Lake City, 1989-96; asst. prof. Weber State U., Ogden, 1993—; pvt. practice Layton, Utah, 1997—. Author (videotape) Clinical Teaching of Nurse-Midwifery and Nurse Practitioner Students: Teaching Strategies for Preceptors, 1993. Chair breast/cervical cancer task force Am. Cancer Soc., Ogden, 1994-96, mem. breast/cervical cancer task force, 1996—. Recipient Faculty Vitality award Hemingway Found., 1995, Internat. Activities grant Weber State U., 1996. Mem. ANA, Utah Nurses Assn., , Nat. Assn. Nurse Practitioners Reproductive Health, Sigma Theta Tau. Office: Weber State Univ 3903 University Cir Ogden UT 84408-3903

PARKER, MARILYN ADELE, paralegal; b. San Diego, May 5, 1945; d. James Ralph and Hazel Adele (Scofield) Walton; div.; children: Adrianna Maria, Charles Edward, HEather Anne, Nicole Marie. AA, San Diego City Coll., 1968; JD, Nat. U., 1980; cert. real estate, Cuyamaca Coll., 1986. Tchr. Century Coll., San Diego, 1983-88; paralegal Defenders Inc., San Diego, 1980-84; rsch. libr. San Diego County Law Libr., San Diego, 1984-87; exec. dir. Pub. Paralegal Svs., El Cajon, Calif., 1987—. Mem. Better Bus. Bureau. Mem. Alliance of Paralegals. Office: Pub Paralegal Svcs 8685 N Magnolia Ave Ste C Santee CA 92071

PARKER, MARSHA L., nutrition services director; b. Mpls., Sept. 2, 1954; d. Gordon George and Sylvia Helene (Miller) Gartland; m. Anthony James Parker, Mar. 15, 1980; children: Elizabeth, Susan, Nancy. BS, U. Wis., Menomonie, 1976. Asst. dir. food svc. Walker Meth. Residence & Health Ctr., Mpls., 1979-80; pers. mgmt. dietitian St. Paul Ramsey Med. Ctr., 1980-84, food prodn. and svc. dietitian, 1984-85; clin. dietitian St. Mary-Corwin Regional Med. Ctr., Pueblo, Colo., 1985-89, chief clin. dietitian, 1990-91, dir. nutrition svcs., 1991—; cons. dietitian Villa Pueblo Towers, Pueblo, 1988-90, So. Colo. Clinic, Pueblo, 1989-90, So. Colo. Nephrology Assn., Pueblo, 1990. Sec. Belmont Elem. PTO, Pueblo, 1992; coach Odessey Mind, Pueblo, 1993-94, site coord. and coach, 1994—; co-facilitator site based decision team Belmont Elem., 1994—. Mem. Am. Dietetic Assn. (registered dietitian), Am. Soc. Hosp. Food Svc. Assn., Colo. Dietetic Assn. (mem. nominating com. 1992), Pueblo Dietetic Assn. (treas. 1991-93, pres. 1993-94). Home: 7 Briargate Ter Pueblo CO 81001-1707 Office: St Mary Corwin Regional Med Ctr 1008 Minnequa Ave Pueblo CO 81004-3733

PARKER, ROBERT GEORGE, radiation oncology educator, academic administrator; b. Detroit, Mich., Jan. 29, 1925; s. Clifford Robert and Velma (Ashman) P.; m. Diana Davis, June 30, 1977; children by previous marriage: Thomas Clifford, James Richardson. BS, U. Wis., 1946, MD., 1948. Diplomate Am. Bd. Radiology (trustee 1978-90, pres. 1988-90). Intern U. Nebr. Hosp., Omaha, 1948-49; resident in pathology Western Res. U., Cleve., 1949-50; resident in radiology U. Mich., Ann Arbor, 1950, 52-54, instr. in radiology, 1954-55; staff radiotherapist Swedish Hosp. Tumor Inst., Seattle, 1955-58; prof. radiology U. Wash., Seattle, 1958-77; prof. radiation oncology UCLA, 1977—. Lt. USNR, 1950-52. Fellow Am. Coll. Radiology; mem. AMA (radiology residence rev. com.), Am. Soc. Therapeutic Radiologists (pres. 1975-76), Radiol. Soc. N.Am. (bd. dirs. 1984-90, pres. 1991-92), Am. Radium Soc. (bd. dirs. 1988-92, pres. 1992). Office: UCLA Ste B265 200 UCLA Medicine Plz Los Angeles CA 90095-6951

PARKER, ROBIN, mayor. Mayor Sunnyvale, Calif. Address: PO Box 3707 Sunnyvale CA 94088-3707

PARKER, ROY ALFRED, transportation engineer, planner; b. Conway, Ark., Apr. 6, 1930; s. Walter Lane and Harriett Mae (Diffee) P.; m. Dixie Anna Dean, June 9, 1953; children: Walter Lane II, David Dean, Shauna Amyr. BS, U. Idaho, 1953; cert. in hwy. traffic, Yale U., 1958. Registered profl. traffic engr., Calif. Asst. planning programming engr. Bur. Pub. Roads (now Fed. Hwy. Adminstrn.), Sacramento, 1958-59; asst. city traffic engr. City of Phoenix, 1959-62; city traffic engr. Palo Alto, Calif., 1962-66; sr. transp. engr. Wilbur Smith & Assocs., London, 1966-68; project mgr. Wilbur Smith & Assocs., Sacramento, 1980; sr. transp. engr. F.R. Harris Engring. Corp., São Paulo, Brazil, 1968-69; prin. assoc. R.W. Crommelin & Assocs., Los Angeles, 1969-70; dep. transp. dir. City and County of Honolulu, 1970-75, dir. dept. transp. services, 1981-83; exec. dir. Oahu Met. Planning Orgn., Honolulu, 1975-79; sr. traffic engr. Lyon Assocs., Inc., Damascus, Syrian Arab Republic, 1979; pres. Roy A. Parker and Assocs., La Jolla, Calif., 1980; transp. engr. City of Concord, Calif., 1983-84, dep. pub. works dir., 1984-88; transp. adminstr. City San Leandro (Calif.), Calif., 1988-90, 91-93; acting dir. dept. engring. and transp. City San Leandro (Calif.), 1990-91; pres. Roy A. Parker and Assocs., Pismo Beach, Calif., 1994—; lectr. dept. civil engring. Coll. Engring., U. Hawaii, 1971-75; lectr. Inst. Transp. Studies, U. Calif., Berkeley, 1983-91. Served with USAF, 1953-57. Fellow Inst. Transp. Engrs. (pres. western dist. 1975-76, pres. San Francisco Bay Area sect. 1991-92); mem. Phi Eta Sigma, Sigma Tau. Democrat. Home and Office: 64 La Garza Pismo Beach CA 93449-2838

PARKER, SUE TAYLOR, anthropologist, educator; b. Seattle, Jan. 1, 1938; d. Sidney Beverly Taylor and Kathryn Jane (Ivey) Plumb; m. Andrew Wilson, Sept. 7, 1995 ; 1 child, Aron. AB, U. Calif., Berkeley, 1966, MA, 1969, PhD, 1973. Asst. prof. Sonoma State U., Rohnert Park, Calif., 1971-78, assoc. prof., 1978-82, prof., 1982—, chair, 1992—. Reviewer numerous jours. including Current Anthropology, Internat. Jour. Primatology, Am. Jour. Primatology; author, co-editor: Language and Intelligence in Monkeys and Apes, 1990, Self-Awareness in Animals and Humans, 1994; co-editor: Naming Our Ancestors, 1994, Reaching Into Thought, 1996; contbr. articles to profl. jours. Commr. transp. City of Berkeley, Calif., 1993—. Fulbright rsch. scholar, 1986; grantee Sch. for Am. Rsch., 1995. Mem. Am. Primatological Soc., Internat. Soc. Primatologists, Calif. Acad. Scis., Jean Piaget Soc. (plenary speaker 1995). Office: Sonoma State U 1801 E Cotati Ave Rohnert Park CA 94928-3613

PARKER, THEODORE CLIFFORD, electronics engineer; b. Dallas, Oreg., Sept. 25, 1929; s. Theodore Clifford and Virginia Bernice (Rumsey) P.; BSEE magna cum laude, U. So. Calif., 1960; m. Jannet Ruby Barnes, Nov. 28, 1970; children: Sally Odette, Peggy Claudette. V.p. engring. Telemetrics, Inc., Gardena, Calif., 1963-65; chief info. systems Northrop-Nortronics, Anaheim, Calif., 1966-70; pres. AVTEL Corp., Covina, Calif., 1970-74, Aragon, Inc., Sunnyvale, Calif., 1975-78; v.p. Teledyne McCormick Selph, Hollister, Calif., 1978-82; sr. staff engr. FMC Corp., San Jose, Calif., 1982-85; pres. Power One Switching Products, Camarillo, Calif., 1985-86; pres. Condor D.C. Power Supplies, Inc., 1987-88, pres. Intelligence Power Tech. Inc., Camarillo, 1988—. Mem. IEEE (chmn. autotestcon '87), NRA (life), Am. Prodn. and Inventory Control Soc., Am. Def. Preparedness Assn., Armed Forces Communications and Electronics Assn., Tau Beta Pi, Eta Kappa Nu. Home: 250 E Telegraph Rd Spc 47 Fillmore CA 93015-2145 Office: Intelligence Power Tech Inc PO Box 3158 Camarillo CA 93011-3158

PARKER, WAYNE CHARLES, municipal finance official; b. Sacramento, Nov. 14, 1956; s. Allen B. and Marilyn Kay (Alt) P.; m. Julie Ann Fife, June 29, 1979; children: Spencer, Alycia, Kara, Taylor, Grant. BA, Brigham Young U., 1979, MPA, 1981. Adminstrv. intern City of Santa Ana, Calif., 1981; pub. mgmt. intern City of Kansas City, Mo., 1981-82; city adminstr. City of Smithville, Mo., 1982-85, City of Merriam, Kans., 1985-88; city mgr. City of Roy, Utah, 1988-93; dir. state and local planning Utah Gov.'s Office, 1993-95; dir. mgmt. svcs. City of Ogden, Utah, 1995—; adj. prof. Mo. Internat. U., Kansas City, 1987-88. Bd. dirs. Merrian C. of C., 1987-88; chmn. Fire Dept. Consolidation Task Force, Ogden, Utah, 1989-93; exec. com. Weber Econ. Devel. Corp., Ogden, 1990; LDS Bishop 1992-97; exec. adv. coun. U. Phoenix, 1995—; pres. Roy Utah West Stake, LDS Ch. David M. Kennedy scholar, 1980. Mem. Internat. City Mgmt. Assn., Utah City Mgmt. Assn. (sec. 1990-93), Govt. Fin. Officer's Assn., Kiwanis, Beta Gamma Sigma (life). Office: City of Ogden 2484 Washington Blvd Ste 500 Ogden UT 84401-2319

PARKER, WILLIAM ELBRIDGE, consulting civil engineer; b. Seattle, Mar. 18, 1913; s. Charles Elbridge and Florence E. (Plumb) P.; m. Dorris Laurie Freeman, June 15, 1935; children—Dorris Laurie, Jane Elizabeth. B.S., U.S. Naval Acad., 1935. Party chief King County Engrs., 1935-39; exec. sec., cons. engr. State Wash., 1946-49; city engr., chmn. Bd. Pub. Works, City of Seattle, 1953-57; cons. City of San Diego, 1957; ptnr. Parker-Fisher & Assocs., 1958-66; cons. engr. Minish & Webb Engrs., Seattle, 1966-70; city engr. City of Bremerton (Wash.), 1970-76; owner Parker & Assocs., Seattle, 1976—. Served to capt. C.E.C., USNR, 1939-45, 51-53. Named to Broadway Hall of Fame. Registered profl. engr., Wash. Mem. Am. Pub. Works Assn., U.S. Naval Inst., Pioneers of State Wash. (pres.), U.S. Naval Acad. Alumni Assn. (chpt. pres.), College Club (Seattle). Lodges: Masons, Shriners.

PARKER, WILMA JOAN, artist; b. Springfield, Mass., May 15, 1941. BFA, R.I. Sch. Design, 1963; MFA, Sch. of the Art Inst., 1966. Solo exhibits include NAS Alameda Hist. Mus., 1996, Officer's Club, 1996, San Diego Maritime Mus., 1996, Maritime and Yachting Mus., Jensen Beach, Fla., 1996, Salmagundi Club, 1996, Frye Art Mus., Seattle, 1997, Commonwealth Club, San Francisco, 1994, 95, Nautilus Meml., Groton, Conn., 1993, Mus. of Fine Art, Springfield, Mass., 1992, Lyman Allyn Art Mus., New London, 1992, Mus. of the Hudson Highlands, 1989, others; group shows includ U.S. Coast Guard, Governor's Island, N.Y.C. (COGAP prize '94), Mus. Naval Aviation, Pensacola, Fla., 1994, Columbia River Maritime Mus., Astoria, Oreg., 1994, others; works collected in various museums/corps. Mem. Salmagundi Club, Am. Soc. Marine Artists, Internat. Soc. of Marine Painters, Internat. Diplomacy Council, Tailhook Assn., Alliance Francaise.

PARKER-FAIRBANKS, DIXIE, artist; b. Cedar Rapids, Iowa, Aug. 1, 1936; d. James N. and Mary Louise (Mussell) Parker; m. Richard Fairbanks, Aug. 26, 1966 (dec. Mar. 1989). *Husband Richard Fairbanks, born in Yakima, Washington, 1929, received a BA from the University of Washington in 1953 and an MA from Mills College in 1955. Fulbright 1959-60 study Taideteollinen Oppilaitos, guest artist OY Wärtsilä-Arabia, Helsinki, Finland. Professor Drake University, Des Moines, Iowa, 1956-63, Central Washington University, Ellensburg, Washington 1963-89. Ceramics in Renwick Gallery, American Craft Museum, Everson Museum, Alfred University, Museum of Applied Arts, Helsinki. Private collections in United States, Japan, Finland. Permanent exhibit at Arabia Museum. Eleven national, international posthumous exhibits.* BFA, Drake U., 1958, MFA, 1959. Craft instr. State of Wis., Waukesha, 1960-61; asst. dir. dept. edn. Des Moines Art Ctr., 1961-66; art lectr. Ctrl. Wash. U., Ellensburg, 1967-69; coord./dir. Richard Fairbanks Project, Ellensburg, 1991-95. Prodr./editor: (biography) Richard Fairbanks, American Potter, 1993; exhibited in one-person shows, 1962-96, two-person shows, 1970-95; gallery affiliations include Galerie Pelin, Helsinki, Finland, City of Sanda, Japan, Galerie Prisma, Vienna, C.G. Rein, Scottsdale, Ariz., Maxwell Galleries, Inc., San Francisco, Des Moines Art Ctr., Percival Galleries, Inc., Des Moines, Greenwood Galleries, Seattle, PANACA, Bellevue, Wash., Louise Matzke Gallery, Seattle, N.W. Craft Ctr., Bellevue, Lynn McAllister Gallery, Seattle, Seattle Art Mus., Richard White Gallery, Seattle, Gallery One, Ellensburg, Allied Arts, Yakima, Wash., Oak Hollow Gallery, Yakima, Larson Gallery, Yakima. Home and Office: 1011 E First Ave Ellensburg WA 98926

PARKINSON, THOMAS BRIAN, marketing executive; b. Lytham-St. Annes, Lancashire, Eng., Oct. 14, 1935; came to U.S., 1966; s. Alfred and Marjorie (Wright) P.; m. Margaret Moore, Oct. 12, 1957; children: Karen, Lynn, Stephen David. Cert. Mech. Engring., Harris Coll. Further Edn., Preston, Lancashire, Eng., 1962. Apprentice tool maker English Electric Co. Ltd., Preston, Lancashire, Eng., 1951-57; designer aircraft structure British Aircraft Corp., Warton, Lancashire, Eng., 1957-63, stress engr. aircraft, 1963-66; stress engr. aircraft Douglas Aircraft Co., Long Beach, Calif., 1966-76, sales engr. commercial mktg., 1976-78, project mgr. commercial mktg., 1978-85, sales mgr. comml. mktg. Pacific and Asia, 1985-89, exec. asst. comml. mktg. Pacific and Asia, 1989-91, sr. prin. specialist analyst mkt. devel., 1991-94; ret., 1994; cons. aircraft mktg. and performance field. Commr. Planning Commn., City of Huntington Beach (Calif.), 1975-77, Underground Utilities Commn., Huntington Beach, 1975-77; chmn. City Charter Revision Com., Huntington Beach, 1977; campaign mgr. Com. to Re-Elect Jerry Matney, Huntington Beach, 1973; fire chief Kellogg Vol. Fire Dept., 1996—; bd. dirs. Kellogg Vol. Fire Dist., 1997—. With Royal Navy, 1953-55. Mem. Instn. Engring. Designers (assoc.), Pacific Area Travel Assn. (chmn. rsch. authority, bd. dirs. 1983-85, award of merit 1985). Episcopalian. Home: 944 Cattle Dr Roseburg OR 97470-9309

PARKS, DEBORA ANN, principal; b. Homestead, Fla., July 23, 1954; d. Jack Wesley and Blanche Margaret (Shawver) Hardin; m. Lewis O'Dell Parks, Apr. 12, 1970 (div. May 1980); 1 child, Kerri Shane. BS in Early Childhood Edn., U. Ala., Tuscaloosa, 1983, MA in Spl. Edn., 1984, MA in Early Childhood Edn., 1987, PhD in Elem. Edn., 1991. Kindergarten tchr. Martin Luther King Jr. Elem. Sch., Tuscaloosa, 1983-85; tchr. gifted grades 2-5 Martin Luther King Jr. Elem. Sch. and Univ. Place Elem. Sch., Tuscaloosa, 1985-86; early childhood edn. instr. Shelton State C.C., Tuscaloosa, 1985-88; instr. U. Ala., Tuscaloosa, 1987; elem. tchr. 1st grade Martin Luther King Jr. Elem. Sch., Tuscaloosa, 1988-89; tchr. gifted grades 3-6 Carthay Elem. Sch., L.A. Unified Sch. Dist., 1991; faculty-in-residence Sunset Village Residence Halls and Hitch Stes. UCLA, 1991-95; tchr. gifted grades K-8 Maimonides Acad., L.A., 1992-94; asst. rschr. So. Calif. Injury Prevention Rsch. Ctr. Sch. Pub. Health, UCLA, 1993-95; facuty liaison on campus housing com.'s darkroom UCLA, 1993-95, instr. dept. edn., 1994, 95, instr., rschr., 1989-95; tchr. gifted grades 2-8 Maimonides Acad., L.A., 1995—, gen. studies prin., 1995—; grad. tchg. asst. elem. edn. U. Ala., Tuscaloosa, 1986-87; field coord., instr. Tchr. Edn. Lab., Grad. Sch. Edn., UCLA, 1989-93; enrichment tchr. grades 3-5 The Buckley Sch., Sherman Oaks, Calif., summer, 1991, 92, 93; evaluation coach/cons. Stanford Rsch. Inst., SB 620 Statewide Healthy Start Initiative Program, L.A., 1993-95; spl. faculty advisor UCLA Photographic Soc., 1993-95; evaluator lang. arts program, curriculum and tchrs. Maimonides Acad., L.A., 1994; enrichment tchr. grades 4-5 Buckley Sch., Sherman Oaks, Calif., summer 1994, enrichment tchr., summer 1995; evaluation coach, cons. Stanford Rsch. Inst., L.A., 1993-95; mem. governing bd. Nat. Assn. Creative Children and Adults, Ohio, 1992-94; rsch. adviser Phi Delta Kappa, UCLA chpt., 1992-94; mem. Adopt-A-Sch. Coun., L.A. Unified Sch. Dist., 1990-95; chairperson Tuscaloosa City Sch.'s Kindergarten Math. Com., 1984; presenter confs. and workshops. Author: The Newspaper Workbook, 1983, Pedestrian and Bicyclist Safety Curriculum for Grades K-5, 1994, Adopt-A-School Programs: A Guide for Pre-Service Teachers, 1995; manuscript asst. editor Am. Mid. Sch. Edn., 1986-87; asst. editor Adopt-A-School Newsletter, 1993; contbr. articles to profl. jours. Vol. Rebuild L.A., 1992-93. Recipient award NEA and Kodak, N.Y. and Ala., 1985, scholarships Am. Bus. Women's Assn., Ala., 1988, Beta Chi of Delta Kappa Gamma, 1983, Epsilon chpt. Alpha Delta Kappa, 1984, Yewell R. Thompson Endowed scholarship, 1988; designee Ala. Tchr. of Yr. Program, 1984-85, 85-86. Mem. Phi Delta Kappa. Democrat. Home: 4308 Via Marina Apt C Marina del Rey CA 90292-6228 Office: Maimonides Acad 310 N Huntley Dr Los Angeles CA 90048-1919

PARKS, DONALD LEE, mechanical engineer, human factors engineer; b. Delphos, Kans., Feb. 23, 1931; s. George Delbert and Erma Josephine (Boucek) P.; student Kans. Wesleyan U., 1948-50; BSME, Kans. State U., 1957, BS in Bus. Adminstrn., 1957, MS in Psychology, 1959; cert. profl. Ergonomist; m. Bessie Lou Schur, Dec. 24, 1952; children: Elizabeth Parks Anderson, Patricia Parks-Holbrook, Donna, Charles, Sandra. Elem. tchr., 1950-51; with Kans. State U. Placement Svc., 1957-59; human factors engr., systems engr. Boeing Co., Seattle, 1959-90, sr. specialist engr., 1972-74, sr. engring. supr., 1974-90; pres. D-Square Assocs. Engring. Cons., 1990-95; pres. Venture Worlds, 1995—; adj. lectr. UCLA Engring. Extension, 1989—; cons., lectr. in field; participant workshops on guidelines in profl. areas, NATO, NSF, Nat. Acad. Sci., NRC. Mem. Derby (Kans.) Planning Commn., 1961-62, chmn., 1962; del. King County (Wash.) Republican Conv., 1972. With AUS, 1952-54. Mem. Human Factors Soc. (Puget Sound Pres.'s award 1969), ASME, Am. Psychol. Assn., Elks. Presbyterian. Contbr. over 80 articles to publs., chpts. to 8 books. Home: 6232 127th Ave SE Bellevue WA 98006-3943

PARKS, FREDRICK SCOTT, systems engineer; b. Phoenix, Ariz., Jan. 7, 1961; s. David Walker and Carrie Ellen (Abbott) P.; m. Kimberly Louise Kubeja, May 8, 1993. BS, Rensselaer Poly. Inst., 1982, MS, 1984. Rsch. material physicist DSM, Geleen, The Netherlands, 1982; sr. engr. analyst Anser Inc., Arlington, Va., 1983-93; sr. systems engr. Lockheed Missiles and Space Co., Inc., Sunnyvale, Calif., 1993-96; assoc. systems engr. Steven Myers & Assocs, Newport Beach, Calif., 1996—. Contbr. articles to profl. jours. Emergency Planning Coun. ARC, Arlington, 1985-92; EMT, 1990-91. Mem. AIAA, Internat. Coun. Systems Engring., Am. Def. Preparedness Assn. Home: 663 S Bernardo Ave Ste M Sunnyvale CA 94087-1020 Office: 1301 Dove St Fl 7 Newport Beach CA 92660-2412

PARKS, HAROLD RAYMOND, mathematician, educator; b. Wilmington, Del., May 22, 1949; s. Lytle Raymond Jr. and Marjorie Ruth (Chambers) P.; m. Paula Sue Beaulieu, Aug. 21, 1971 (div. 1984); children: Paul Raymond, David Austin; m. Susan Irene Taylor, June 6, 1985; 1 stepchild, Kathryn McLaughlin. AB, Dartmouth Coll., 1971; PhD, Princeton U., 1974. Tamarkin instr. Brown U., Providence, 1974-77; asst. prof. Oreg. State U., Corvallis, 1977-82, assoc. prof., 1982-89, prof. math., 1989—; vis. assoc. prof. Ind. U., Bloomington, 1982-83. Author: Explicit Determination of Area Minimizing Hypersurfaces, vol. II, 1986, (with Steven G. Krantz) A Primer of Real Analytic Functions, 1992, (with G. Musser, R. Burton, W. Siebler) Mathematics in Life, Society and the World, 1997; contbr. articles to profl. publs. Cubmaster Oregon Trail Coun. Boy Scouts Am., 1990-92. NSF fellow, 1971-74. Mem. Am. Math. Soc., Math. Assn. Am., Soc. Indsl. and Applied Math., Phi Beta Kappa. Republican. Mem. Soc. of Friends. Home: 33194 Dorset Ln Philomath OR 97370-9555 Office: Oreg State U Dept Math Corvallis OR 97331-4605

PARKS, MICHAEL CHRISTOPHER, journalist; b. Detroit, Nov. 17, 1943; s. Robert James and Rosalind (Smith) P.; m. Linda Katherine Durocher, Dec. 26, 1964; children: Danielle Anne, Christopher, Matthew. AB, U. Windsor, Ont., Can., 1965. Reporter Detroit News, 1962-65; corr. Time-Life News Service, N.Y.C., 1965-66; asst. city editor Suffolk Sun, Long Island, N.Y., 1966-68; polit. reporter, foreign corr. The Balt. Sun, Saigon, Singapore, Moscow, Cairo, Hong Kong, Peking, 1968-80; fgn. corr. L.A. Times, L.A., Peking, Johannesburg, Moscow, Jerusalem, 1980-95, dpty. fgn. editor, 1995-96; mng. editor, 1996—; v.p. L.A. Times, 1996-97, sr. v.p., 1997—. Recipient Pulitzer Prize, 1987. Mem. Royal Commonwealth Soc. London, Soc. Profl. Journalists, Fgn. Corr. Club (Hong Kong). Office: L A Times Times Mirror Sq Los Angeles CA 90012

PARKS, MICHAEL JAMES, publisher, editor; b. Spokane, Wash., June 3, 1944; s. Floyd Lewis and C. Marie (McHugh) P.; m. Janet K. Holter, Aug. 12, 1967; children: Michael J., Gregory F., Sarah M. BA, Seattle U., 1966. Reporter The Seattle Times, 1966-74, fin. editor, 1974-77; pub., editor Marple's Bus. Newsletter, Seattle, 1977—. Bd. govs. Seattle U. Alumni Assn.; trustee Seattle Rotary Service Found. Fellow Am. Press Inst., N.Y.C., 1973. Roman Catholic. Lodge: Rotary. Office: Marples Bus Newsletter 117 W Mercer St Ste 200 Seattle WA 98119-3953

PARKS, RICHARD CAMERON, outdoor sports professional, small business owner; b. Cloquet, Minn., June 20, 1943; s. Merton James and Ellen Laura (Nightingale) P. BS, Mont. State U., 1966. Owner Parks Fly Shop, Gardiner, Mont., 1970—. Co-author: Tying and Fishing the West's Best Day Flies, 1978. Sec. No. Plains Resource Coun., Billings, 1988-90, vice chmn., 1990-91, chmn., 1991-93; chmn. Western Orgn. Resource Coun., 1994. Mem. Fishing Outfitters Assn. of Mont. (pres. 1986-90). Democrat. Unitarian.

PARKS, RICHARD KEITH, clinical social worker; b. Rock Springs, Wyo., Oct. 13, 1947; s. Keith Andrew and Mildred Ann (Matkovich) P.; m. Debra D. Thomas, Sept. 21, 1968 (div. Nov. 1971); m. Alberta Dea Henderson, Feb. 26, 1974; children: Heather, Richell. AA, Western Wyo. Coll., 1969; BSW, U. Wyo., 1985; MSW, Denver U., 1988. Lic. social worker. Owner, mgr. Rich's Britches, Rock Springs, 1974-77; asst. mgr. Wyo. Bearing, Rock Springs, 1976-82; residential counselor Southwest Wyo. Rehab. Ctr., Rock Springs, 1983-85; community care worker, therapist Southwest Counseling Svc., Rock Springs, 1985-89; sch. social worker Sch. Dist. #1, Rock Springs, 1989-90; mental health counselor State of Nev. Rural Clinics, Fernley, 1990-92; inpatient clin. social worker Nev. Mental Health Inst., Reno, 1992-93; social work cons. Pershing Gen. Hosp., Lovelock, Nev., 1991-93; clin. social worker Human Affaire Internat.-Aetna, Salt Lake City, 1993—; program mgr. Transitional Living Ctr., 1985-87; workshop presenter in field, 1986. Vol. counselor Sweetwater Crisis Intervention Ctr., Rock Springs, 1973-83, bd. dirs., 1979-83; v.p. Downtown Mchts. Assn., 1975. Mem. NASW, Alumni Assn. U. Wyo. Congregationalist.

PARKS, THOMAS NORVILLE, neurobiologist; b. Berkeley, Calif., May 27, 1950; s. Herbert Otho and Wilma Jean (Strong) P.; m. Patricia Legant, July 6, 1980; 1 child, Anna Legant. B.S., U. Calif., Irvine, 1972; Ph.D., Yale U., 1978. Lectr. psychology Yale U., New Haven, 1977; postdoctoral fellow U. Va., Charlottesville, 1977-78; asst. prof. anatomy U. Utah, Salt Lake City, 1978-83, assoc. prof., 1983-87, prof., 1987—, George and Lorna Winder prof. Neuroscience and chair, dept. Neurobiology and Anatomy, 1992—; bd. dirs. NPS Pharmaceuticals Inc., v.p., 1987-88. Sci. rev. com. Nat. Orgn. Hearing Rsch., 1996—. Mem. NIH (hearing rsch. study sect. 1986-90, Claude pepper award 1993—). Office: U Utah Sch Medicine Dept Neurobiology Anatomy Salt Lake City UT 84132

PARLANTE, DIANE GOULLARD, interpreter, translator; b. Verdun, Que., Can.; came to U.S., 1979; BA in Music, U. Montreal, Que., 1979; paralegal cert., St. Mary's Coll., Moraga, Calif., 1984. Registered interpreter of non-designated langs. Calif. Jud. Coun., 1996. Legal sec., logistics coord. Honeywell, Inc., San Francisco, Brisbane, Calif., 1984-96; interpretor, translator Calif. and Ariz., 1984—; paralegal Levine Newton & Irvine, L.A., Law Offices James Thierney, Santa Monica, Calif., Pillsbury Madison & Sutro, San Francisco, Aguiree & Eckmann, San Diego, 1984-91; real estate saleswoman Century 21, Fallbrook, 1991. Mem. Ariz. Prodns. Assn., etc.

PARMA, FLORENCE VIRGINIA, magazine editor; b. Kenilworth, N.J., Aug. 30, 1940; d. Howard Frank and Mildred Faye (Lister) von Finkel; m. Wilson Henry Parma, June 15, 1973 (div. Aug. 1986). Studies with pvt. tutor, Chaumont, France, 1961-62; student, NYU, 1962-63. Copywriter Schless & Co., N.Y.C., 1963-65; editor, researcher Barchas Lab., Stanford, Calif., 1969-73; adminstrv. exec. Crater Inc., Honolulu, 1974-79; mgr., editor Off Duty mag., Honolulu, 1979—; v.p. Mapasa, Inc. (dba The Prides of New Zealand), 1992—. Editor: Welcome to Hawaii Guide, 1985—; co-editor: Serotonin and Behavior, 1972; freelance columnist. Republican. Episcopalian. Home and Office: Off Duty Hawaii 3771 Anuhea St Honolulu HI 96816-3849

PARMAN, MICHAEL J., publishing executive. Pub. Press Democrat, Santa Rosa, Calif. Office: Press Democrat 427 Mendocino Ave Santa Rosa CA 95402

PARMAN, SUSAN MORRISSETT, anthropologist, writer; b. Middletown, Conn., Aug. 17, 1945; d. Lee Ferguson and Edith Rosalie (Morrissett) Parman; m. Jacob Pandian, May 11, 1972; 1 child, Georgina Morrissett Pandian. BA, Antioch Coll., 1967; PhD, Rice U., 1972. Asst. prof. anthropology Calif. State U., Hayward, 1972-76; lectr. anthropology various colls. and univs., Calif., 1976-88; prof. anthropology Calif. State U., Fullerton, 1988—, chair dept. anthropology, 1996—; cons. Holt, Rinehart & Winston, 1985—, Harcourt, Brace Jovanovich Pubs., 1985—. Author: Scottish Crofters, 1990, Dream and Culture, 1991, Europe in the Anthropological Imagination, 1997; contbr. articles to Am. Anthropologist, Folklore, Ethnos. Founding mem., v.p. Placentia (Calif.) Pride Coun., 1992—. NEH rsch. fellow, Scotland, 1983, 92; Calif. State U. Found. grantee, 1991, 92, 93, 94, 95, NSF grantee, 1995. Fellow Soc. Antiquarians of Scotland; mem. Am. Anthrop. Assn., Soc. for the Anthropology of Europe (publs. chair 1992-96), Pacific Coast Conf. on Brit. Studies. Democrat. Home: 4931 Hamer Dr Placentia CA 92870-3021 Office: Calif State U Fullerton Dept Anthropology Fullerton CA 92634

PARONI, GENEVIEVE MARIE SWICK, retired secondary education educator; b. Eureka, Nev., July 27, 1926; d. William Jackson and Myrtle Rose (Smith) S.; m. Walter Andrew Paroni, Dec. 26, 1954; 1 child, Andrea Marie. BA, U. Nev., Reno, 1948; MEd, U. Idaho, 1978; postgrad., MIT, Oreg. State U., U. Oreg., U. Wash., Ft. Wright Coll., U. Portland. Cert. elem. and secondary sect., Nev. Tchr., vice prin. Eureka County H.S., 1948-66; coast geodetic U.S. Govt., Eureka, 1950's; tchr. biol. and phys. scis., facilitator Pub. Schs. Dist. # 393, Wallace, Idaho, 1968-91; ret., 1991; regional dir. NSTA, Idaho, Panhandle, 1982-90; chmn. in svc. adv. State Dept. Edn., Boise, Idaho, 1980-83, mem. state sci. commn., 1981-82; mem. Idaho Sci. Curriculum Guide Com., 1987, Univ. Idaho Commn. on Math/Sci. Edn., 1988-89, Inland Empire Physics Alliance, 1989-90, Idaho Sci. Alliance Com., 1990. Contbr. history articles to profl. jours. Active Wallace City Coun., 1970-80; bd. dirs. Wallace Pub. Libr., 1983—, chmn., 1995—; bd. dirs. Silver Valley Arts and Crafts Assn., 1991, Greater Wallace, 1980-93, Wallace Dist. Arts Coun., 1993—; mem. citizen's adv. bd. Idaho Nat. Engring. Lab., 1994-96; facilitator Panhandle Area Ecolab., 1995; Rep. precinct chairperson, Wallace, 1970-80; bishop's warden area Episc. Ch., 1990-94; mem. coun. Episc. Diocese Spokane, 1992-96. Grantee Idaho Power, 1985; named Outstanding Tchr., Dist. #393. 1975; finalist Presdl. awards in High Sch. Sci. Teaching. Mem. NEA, AAUW (pres. 1970s), Wallace Edn. Assn. (sec. 1970s), Bus. and Profl. Women Assn. (v.p. Nev. chpt. 1953-55), Pythian Sisters (Grand Guard 1950), Order Ea. Star (matron Nev. chpt.), Delta Kappa Gamma (pres. 1980-82), Phi Delta Kappa. Home: PO Box 229 Wallace ID 83873-0229

PARRIS, ANNE WITMER, secondary education educator, writer; b. East Orange, N.J., Oct. 24, 1960; d. Paul Sutherland and Hannah Steele (Calkin) Parris; m. Andrew Patrick Murray, Aug. 14, 1982; m. Douglas K. Rogers, July 19, 1991. BA in English, U. Calif., Davis, 1983; postgrad., Mills Coll., 1990—. Cert. tchr., Calif. Tchr. English Castro Valley (Calif.) H.S., 1984—; mentor tchr. Castro Valley Unified Sch. Dist., 1989-91. Mem., faculty advisor Amnesty Internat., 1990—. NEH summer seminar study grantee, 1990, 93, 96. Mem. Nat. Coun. Tchrs. English, Calif. Tchrs. Assn. (state coun. rep. 1990-96), Delta Kappa Gamma. Office: Castro Valley HS 19400 Santa Maria Ave Castro Valley CA 94546-3400

PARRISH, JEANNE ELAINE, former mayor, city councilwoman, former health services administrator, nurse; b. Great Falls, Mont., Sept. 7, 1921; d. Robert Edwin and Golda Mae (Jones) Cunningham; m. Charles Edward Parrish, Nov. 9, 1940; children: Charles Edwin, Carol Jean Parrish Wixted. BA, Calif. State Coll., San Diego, 1957, MA, 1959; MPH, U. Calif., Berkeley, 1962. RN, Calif. Staff nurse Rsch. Hosp., Kansas City, Mo., 1945, VNA, 1946; office nurse Rsch. Hosp., San Diego, 1947-50, pub. health nurse, 1950-52; supr. pediatrics San Diego County Hosp., 1952-54, clin. instr. pediatrics, 1955-58; dir. vocat. nurse program Grossmont, Calif., 1958-59; adminstrv. resident Cedars Sinai Hosp., L.A., 1962; exec. asst. nursing L.A. County Hosp., 1962-65; sr. asst. adminstr. Hollywood Presbyn. Hosp., L.A., 1965-75; med./legal analyst Farmers Ins., L.A., 1975-77; mental health cons. Calif. State Dept. of Mental Health, L.A., 1977-78, pub. health cons., 1978-84, med. area mgr., 1984-87; ret., 1987; elected city councilwoman City of Rancho Mirage, Calif., 1992-93; mayor City of Rancho Mirage, Calif., 1993-96; dir. pub. affairs Inst. Critical Care Medicine, Palm Springs, Calif., 1996—. Mem. Womens Club of Rancho Mirage, 1992; mem. Rep. Womens Fedn., Rancho Mirage, 1991; bd. dirs., past pres. Desert Coun. for Aging, Riverside, 1990; bd. dirs., sec. Retired Sr. Vol. Program, Palm Desert, 1992; bd. dirs. Coachella Valley ARC, 1990. Republican. Home: 65 Colgate Dr Rancho Mirage CA 92270-3703 Office: Inst Critical Care Medicine 1695 N Sunrise Way Palm Springs CA 92262

PARRISH, STANLEY GLENISTER, real estate broker; b. L.A., Oct. 5, 1913; s. Marion Fay and Helen (Stonaker) P.; children: Judith E., Stephen S., Nathan A., Julia E., Janine E., Jeri E., Jill E., Jon S. Ordained to ministry Bapt. Ch., 1940; lic. real estate broker, Oreg. Min. Federated Chs., Central Point, Oreg., 1937-39, Am. Bapt. Ch., Burns & Carlton, Oreg., 1939-42; field svc. rep. N.Am. Aviation, L.A., 1943-45; owner constrn. co. Medford, 1945-67; owner real estate co. Portland, 1973—; owner, pres. Converta Hoist Corp., 1960-64. Author: Inventions, Etc., 1994, Stuff & Nonsense, 1994; patentee child safety buckle. Part-time vol. EMT. Home & Office: 3737 SW 117th Ave Unit 40 Beaverton OR 97005-2290

PARROTT, DENNIS BEECHER, sales executive; b. St. Louis, June 13, 1929; s. Maurice Ray and Mai Ledgerwood (Beecher) P.; m. Vivian Cleveland Miller, Mar. 24, 1952; children: Constance Beecher, Dennis Beecher, Anne Cleveland. BS in Econs., Fla. State U., Tallahassee, 1954; postgrad. Princeton U., 1964; MBA, Pepperdine U., 1982. With Prudential Ins. Co. Am., 1954-74, v.p. group mktg., L.A., 1971-74; sr. v.p. Frank B. Hall Cons. Co., L.A., 1974-83; v.p. Johnson & Higgins, L. A., 1983-95; exec. v.p. Arthur J. Gallagher & Co., L.A., 1995—; speaker in field. Chmn. Weekend with the Stars Telethon, 1976-80; chmn. bd. dirs. United Cerebral Palsy/Spastic Children's Found. Los Angeles County, 1979-82, chmn. bd. govs., 1982-83; bd. dirs. Nat. United Cerebral Palsy Assn., 1977-82, pres., 1977-79; bd. dirs. L.A. Emergency Task Force, 1992; mem. community adv. council Birmingham High Sch., Van Nuys, Calif., 1982-85 ; sect. chmn. United Way, Los Angeles, 1983-84; bd. dirs. The Betty Clooney Found. for Brain Injured, 1986-88; mem. com. to fund an endowed chair in cardiology at Cedars-Sinai Med. Ctr., 1986-88; adv. council Family Health Program Inc., 1986-88; bd. Deacons Bel Air Presbyn. Ch., 1990-92, chmn. 1991-92; elder Bel Air Presbyn. Ch. 1993-96; mem. adv. coun. Blue Cross Calif., 1996—. Served to 1st lt. AUS, 1951-53. C.L.U. Mem. Am. Soc. C.L.U.s, Internat. Found. Employee Benefits, Merchants and Mfrs. Assns. 44th Annual Mgmt. Conf. (chmn. 1986), Employee Benefits Planning Assn. So. Calif. Republican. Presbyterian. Clubs: Los Angeles, Woodland Hills Country, Jonathan (Los Angeles). Office: Warner Ctr Plaza Ste 400 21650 Oxnard St Woodland Hills CA 91367-4945

PARROTT, JOEL, zoo director; b. Lake George, N.Y., Aug. 21, 1952; married; 2 children. BS in Biology, Colo. State U., 1975, DVM, 1980. Intern Denver Zoo, 1979; veterinarian in pvt. practice Castro Valley, Calif., 1980-84; asst. dir. Oakland (Calif.) Zoo, 1984, exec. dir., 1985—. Office: The Oakland Zoo PO Box 5238 9777 Golf Links Rd Oakland CA 94605

PARRUCK, BIDYUT, electrical engineer; b. Calcutta, W. Bengal, India, Oct. 31, 1958; came to U.S., 1981; s. Birendra Singh and Jyotsna (Kothari) P. B in Tech., Indian Inst. Tech., Kharagpur, 1981; MS in Elec. Engring., Va. Poly. Inst., 1983. Mem. tech. staff ITT Advanced Tech. Ctr., Shelton, Conn., 1983-86; R & D engr. Contel Fin. Systems, Stamford, Conn., 1987-89; sr. design engr. TranSwitch Corp., Shelton, 1989-93; sect. head II Farinon divsn. Harris Corp., San carlos, Calif., 1993; prin. engr. Network Equipment Techs., Redwood City, Calif., 1993-94; v.p. asynchronous transfer mode sonet CorEl MicroSystems, Fremont, Calif., 1994—, also bd. dirs.; founder, advisor Next Generation Systems, Matawan, N.J., 1986—; advisor, cons. OSS Corp., Shelton, Conn., 1988—. Contbr. articles to profl. jours.; patentee in field. Vol. Ourhouse-North, Daly City, Calif., 1993-94, Holiday Project, San Francisco, 1995-96. Mem. IEEE. Home: 1325 Buckthorne Way San Jose CA 95129

PARRY, ELLWOOD COMLY, III, art history educator; b. Abington, Pa., Aug. 9, 1941; s. Ellwood Comly Jr. and Elizabeth (Graham) P.; m. Carol Jaqueline Newman, Feb. 1, 1964 (div. Nov. 1971); m. Pamela Gay Jeffcott, Nov. 20, 1971; children: Janna Jeffcott, Evan Graham, Taylor Jeffcott. BA cum laude, Harvard U., 1964; MA in Art History, UCLA, 1966; PhD in Art History, Yale U., 1970. Asst. prof. art history Columbia U., N.Y.C., 1969-75; fellow for ind. study and rsch. NEH, 1975-76; assoc. prof. U. Iowa, Iowa City, 1976-81; prof. U. Ariz., Tucson, 1981—. Author: Image of the Indian and the Black Man, 1974, (monograph) The Art of Thomas Cole, 1988. Home: 3775 N Bear Creek Cir Tucson AZ 85749-9454 Office: U Ariz Dept Art Tucson AZ 85721

PARRY, RICHARD GITTINGS, plastic and reconstructive surgeon, writer; b. Chgo., July 6, 1942; s. Norman Gittings and Lillian (Koudelka) P.; m. Katherine Sue Peck, June 12, 1965; children: David, Matthew. MD, U. Ill., Chgo., 1966. Intern in surgery, jr. resident Johns Hopkins U., Balt., 1966-68; surg. resident Boston City Hosp., 1968-72; plastic and reconstructive resident Harvard Med. Sch., Cambridge, Mass., 1974-76; plastic and reconstructive surgeon Lahey Clinic, Boston, 1976-78; pvt. practice Fairbanks, Alaska, 1978—. Author: (novels) Ice Warrior, 1991, Venom Victim, 1992; contbr. articles to profl. jours. Lt. comdr., surgeon USN, 1972-74. Mem. Alaska State Med. Assn. (pres. 1983-84), Fairbanks Med. Assn. (pres. 1982-83), Am. Cancer Soc. (pres. Alaska divsn. 1987-88), Phi Beta Pi, Alpha Omega Alpha. Home: 2111 Cowles St # 3 Fairbanks AK 99701-5918 Office: 2111 Cowles St Ste 3 Fairbanks AK 99701-5962*

PARSA, FEREYDOUN DON, plastic surgeon; b. Tehran, Iran, May 20, 1942; came to U.S., 1970; s. Issa and Zahra (Bismark) P.; m. Touri Akhlaghi, June 17, 1972; children: Natalie, Alan, Sean. MD, Lausanne U., Switzerland, 1969. Diplomate Am. Soc. Plastic Surgery. Chif of plastic surgery, prof. surgery U. Hawaii, Honolulu, 1981—. Contbr. articles to profl. jours. Mem. Am. Cancer Soc. (chmn., early detection and treatment com. 1993—). Office: U Hawaii Sch Med Surg 1356 Lusitana St Honolulu HI 96813-2421 Office: U Hawaii 1329 Lusitana St Honolulu HI 96813-2429

PARSELL, ROGER EDMUND, retired educator, civic worker; b. Elkhart, Ind., Feb. 8, 1929; s. Abijah Dunnell and Eula Maud (Golden) P.; m. Hazel Mae Stratton, June 11, 1955; children: Reed Dunnel, Portia Ellen Parsell Hainzelin. BA, Wabash Coll., 1951; MA, Butler U., Indpls., 1956; PhD, U. Denver, 1972. Tchr. The Leelenau Schs., Glen Arbor, Mich., 1954-56; instr. Northwestern Mich. Coll., Traverse City, Mich., 1956-57; Fulbright asst. Tulle Schule, Mannheim, Germany, 1957-58; asst. prof. Ill. State U., Normal, 1958-68, Western State Coll., Gunnison, Colo., 1968-69; grad. asst. U. Denver, 1969-73; sr. lectr. James Cook U., Townsville, Australia, 1974-82; adv. bd. Samuel Butler Soc. newsletter, 1985-92. Co-editor: Samuel Butler: An Annotated Bibliography, 1990; author: (monograph) In the Wild with Samuel Butler, 1981, (study guide) Butler's The Way of All Flesh, 1974. Mem. Common Cause, Denver, 1983—, Handgun Control, Washington, 1985—. Fulbright Found. assistantship, 1957-58. Mem. MLA. Home: 4176 S Reading Way Denver CO 80237

PARSLEY, STEVEN DWAYNE, title company executive; b. Monrovia, Calif., Dec. 31, 1959. BBA magna cum laude, U. Albuquerque, 1985. Lic. agt. to issue title ins., N.Mex. Data processing asst. The Orion Corp., Albuquerque, 1978-79; title searcher N.Mex. Title, Albuquerque, 1979; various positions Rio Grande Title Co., Albuquerque, 1979-84, v.p., mgr. title ops., 1984-91, sr. v.p., escrow officer, 1992-94, exec. v.p., 1994—. Recipient Presdl. scholarship U. N.Mex., Albuquerque, 1978. Mem. N.Mex. Land Title Assn. (past v.p., pres.-elect), Albuquerque Bd. of Realtors (mem. affiliate rels. com.). Home: 5417 Rayito Del Luna Ln NE Albuquerque NM 87111-1647 Office: Rio Grande Title Co 6400 Indian School Rd NE Albuquerque NM 87110-5305

PARSON, SCOTT W., construction company executive; b. Ogden, Utah, Feb. 3, 1968; s. Jack B. Jr. and DeAnne (Wilson) P.; m. Allison Steed, Dec. 17, 1992. BA, Brigham Young U., 1991; MBA, U. Chgo., 1993. Missionary Ch. of Jesus Christ of Latter-Day Sts., Tokyo, 1987-89; intern Mitsui Fire and Marine Ins. Co., Tokyo, 1992; v.p. human resources, planning and devel. Jack B. Parson Cos., Ogden, Utah, 1992—. Mem. cabinet Hill/DOO '95, Ogden, 1994; asst. scoutmaster Boy Scouts Am., Layton, Utah, 1993-94. Mem. Assoc. Gen. Contractors Am. (closely held bus. com., open shop com.). Republican. Mem. LDS Ch. Office: Jack B Parson Cos PO Box 3429 2350 South 1900 West Ogden UT 84040

PARSONS, ADRIENNE MARY, principal; b. Worcester, Mass., Oct. 18, 1956; d. James F. and Adrienne M. (Morris) P.; m. John Scheinfeld, Feb. 11, 1979 (div. June 1993). BS in Edn., Northwestern U., 1978; MEd, UCLA, 1988. Elem. tchg. cert. Tchr. grade 2 The Buckley Sch., Sherman Oaks, Calif., 1988-93; asst. prin. The Buckley Sch., Sherman Oaks, 1993—. Editor Lower Sch. Friday newsletter, 1993—. Vol. Make-A-Wish, L.A., 1995, 96. Fellow UCLA Writing Project; mem. Nat. Coun. Tchrs. English, Calif. Reading Assn. Home: 1103 Raintree Cir Culver City CA 90230

PARSONS, C. LOWELL, surgery educator; b. Troy, N.Y., Sept. 21, 1944; s. H. Kenwood and Elsie (Herrick) P.; m. JoEllen Noonan, Mar. 28, 1967; 1 child, J. Kellogg Parsons. BS, Manhattan Coll., 1966; MD, Yale U., 1970. Intern Yale-New Haven Hosp., 1970-71; Resident in urology U. Pa., Phila., 1973-77; asst. prof. surgery U. Calif., San Diego, 1977-81, assoc. prof., 1981-88, prof., 1988—. Contbr. articles to profl. jours. Grantee USPHS-NIH, 1984-89, 89-94, 90-95, VA, 1979-84, 84-89, 89-92, 92-94, 95—. Fellow ACS, Am. Urol. Assn. Home: 6699 Avenida Andorra La Jolla CA 92037-6403 Office: UCSD Hosp 200 W Arbor Dr San Diego CA 92103-1911

PARSONS, CHRISTINA MARIE, science writer, education consultant; b. San Diego, Oct. 16, 1953; d. Virgil and Margaret (Binau) P. BA in Biology, U. San Diego, 1975; MA in Edn., San Diego State U., 1983; MBA, U. San Francisco, 1996. Field biologist, scuba diver Dept. Fish and Game State of Calif., San Diego, 1975-77; asst. edn. researcher Sea World, San Diego, 1978-80; educator Zool. Soc. San Diego Wild Animal Pk., 1982-84; edn. specialist Monterey (Calif.) Bay Aquarium, 1984-87; assoc. dir. CHPP Stanford U., Salinas, Calif., 1986-88; faculty Dept. of Mus. Studies J.F.K. U., Orinda, Calif., 1991-93; owner/mgr. Word Craft, Monterey, 1987—; bd. dirs., publs. chair Visitor Studies Assn., Jacksonville, Ala., 1993-95; bd. dirs. Western Mus. Assn., L.A. Author: Dangerous Marine Animals of Pacific, 1985, Monterey Bay Aquarium Coloring Book, 1988; contbr. articles to Ranger Rick mag., 1986, 90. Vol., 1988 grad. Leadership Monterey Peninsula. Mem. Am. Assn. Museums, Assn. Sci-Tech. Ctrs. Office: Word Craft 480 Calle Principal #2 PO Box 1271 Monterey CA 93942

PARSONS, DONALD D., bishop. Bishop of Alaska Evang. Luth. Ch. in Am., Anchorage. Office: Synod of Alaska 1847 W Northern Lights Blvd # 2 Anchorage AK 99517-3343

PARSONS, ELMER EARL, retired clergyman; b. Cloverland, Wash., Oct. 4, 1919; s. Claud Solomon and Bessie Lillian (Campbell) P.; m. Marjorie Emma Carlson, Aug. 29, 1942; children—Karl Elmer, James Myron, Helen Joy, Ann Elizabeth, Lois Marie, Louise Melba. B.A., Seattle Pacific U., 1942; S.T.B., N.Y. Theol. Sem., 1945; S.T.M., Asbury Theol. Sem., Wilmore, Ky., 1955; D.D. (hon.), Greenville (Ill.) Coll., 1958. Ordained to ministry Free Methodist Ch., 1944; acad. dean Wessington Springs (S.D.) Coll., 1945-47; missionary to China, 1947-49, missionary to Japan, 1949-54; supt. Japan Free Meth. Mission, 1950-54; pres. Central Coll., McPherson, Kans., 1955-64, Osaka (Japan) Christian Coll., 1964-74; Asia area sec., Free Meth. Ch., 1964-74; bishop Free Meth. Ch. N.Am., 1974-85. Author: Witness to the Resurrection, 1967. Chmn. Free Meth. Study Commn. on Doctrine, 1990-

95. Named Alumnus of Year Seattle Pacific U., 1976. Mem. Wesleyan Theol. Soc.

PARSONS, J. A., paper and wood products company executive; b. 1935. BS, Portland State U., 1961. With Peat Marwick Mitchell & Co., 1961-66, sr. acct.; with Willamette Industries Inc., 1966—, contr., 1969-83, v.p., contr., from 1983, now exec. v.p., CFO. Office: Willamette Industries Inc 1300 SW 5th Ave Ste 3800 Portland OR 97201-5644*

PARSONS, POLLY ELSBETH, internist; b. Bennington, Vt., Jan. 30, 1954; married; 2 children. AB in Biology magna cum laude, Harvard U., 1975; MD, U. Ariz., 1978. Diplomate Nat. Bd. Med. Examiners, Am. Bd. Internat. Medicine, Am. Bd. Pulmonary Medicine, Am. Bd. Critical Care Medicine. Intern, then resident in internal medicine U. Colo. Med. Ctr., 1978-81; rsch. fellow Nat. Jewish Hosp. and Rsch. Ctr., 1981-82; fellow in pulmonary medicine U. Colo. Health Scis. Ctr., 1982-85, instr. pulmonary medicine, 1985-86, asst. prof., 1986-92; staff physician Denver Gen. Hosp., 1985—, co-dir. med. ICU, 1991-93, dir. med. ICU, 1993—; assoc. prof. Sch. Medicine U. Colo., 1992—; mem. rsch. grant rev. com. Am. Lung Assn., 1991-95; mem. critical care medicine test and policy com. Am. Bd. Internal Medicine, 1995—; presenter nat. meetings NIH, 1987, 91, 92, 93, 95, mem. task force on rsch. in cardiopulmonary dysfunction, critical care medicine Nat. Heart, Blood and Lung Inst., 1993-94; presenter various profl. confs., 1989-96. Co-editor: Critical Care Secrets, 1992, Pulmonary and Respiratory Therapy Secrets, 1996; contbr. chpts. to several books, most recently: Seminars in Respiratory Medicine, Endotoxin and the Lung, The Adult Respiratory Distress Syndrome, Emergency Medicine Secrets; contbr. articles to profl. publs.; contbr. revs. to Critical Care Medicine, Chest, Alcoholism: Clin. and Exptl. Rsch., Jour. Lab. and Clin. Investigation, Jour. Clin. Investigation, Am. Rev. of Respiratory Disease. Bd. dirs. Biomed. Rsch. Found., 1995—; sec.-treas. Colo. Trudeau Soc., 1996. Mem. Am. Thoracic Soc. (mem. long-range planning com. 1993-97), Western Soc. Clin. Medicine. Office: Denver Gen Hosp 777 Bannock St Denver CO 80204-4507

PARSONS-PETERSEN, PAMELA ANNE, publishing executive. BA in Econs., UCLA, 1983. Sr. clk. L.A. Times, 1983-85; bus. mgr. The Chronicle, St. Helens, Oreg., 1985-91, pub., 1991—. Mem. St. Helens C. of C. (bd. dirs. 1994—), Jaycees (pres. 1987). Office: The Chronicle PO Box 1153 Saint Helens OR 97051-8153

PARTHEMORE, JACQUELINE G., physician, educator; b. Harrisburg, Pa., Dec. 21, 1940; d. Philip Mark and Emily (Buvit) Parthemore; m. Alan Morton Blank, Jan. 8, 1967; children: Stephen Eliot, Laura Elise. BA, Wellesley Coll., 1962; MD, Cornell U., 1966. Rsch. edn. assoc. VA Hosp., San Diego, 1974-78; staff physician VA Med. Ctr., San Diego, 1978-79, asst. chief, med. svc., 1979-80, acting chief, med. svc., 1980-81, chief of staff, 1984—; asst. prof. medicine U. Calif. Sch. Medicine, San Diego, 1974-80, assoc. prof. medicine, 1980-85, prof. medicine, assoc. dean, 1985—; mem. nat. rsch. resources coun. NIH, Bethesda, Md., 1990-94. Contbr. articles to profl. jours., chpts. to books. Bd. dirs. San Diego Vets. Med. Rsch. Found.; mem. adv. bd. San Diego Opera. Recipient Bullock's 1st Annual Portfolio award, 1985, San Diego Pres.'s Coun. Woman of Yr. award, 1985, YWCA Tribute to Women in Industry award, 1987. Fellow ACP; mem. Endocrine Soc., Am. Fedn. Clin. Rsch., Am. Bone and Mineral Soc., Nat. Assn. VA Chiefs Staff (pres. 1989-91), Am. Assn. Clin. Endocrinologists, Wellesley Coll. Alumnae Assn. (1st v.p. 1992-95). Office: VA Med Ctr 3350 La Jolla Village Dr San Diego CA 92161-0002

PARTLOW, MARIANNE FAIRBANK, artist, consultant, curator; b. Cleve., May 19, 1947; d. Robert Louis and Dorothy (Tomkinson) Fairbank; m. Kenneth Lawrence Partlow III, Apr. 7, 1973; children: Liza Katherine, Joshua Fairbank. BA in Art History, Cornell U., 1969; MA in Art History, U. Va., 1971. Prodn. asst. Hill Holliday Connors Cosmopulos, Boston, 1966-70; rsch. assoc. Adams Davison Gallery, Washington, 1971-73; instr. art history U. R.I., Kingston, 1973-74; advt. mgr. Foster Parents Plan, Warwick, R.I., 1973-74; dir. Galerie Royale, Vancouver, B.C., Can., 1974-79; cons. Olympia, Wash., 1978-84; owner, dir. Marianne Partlow Gallery, Olympia, 1984-92; adj. curator N.W. collection Tacoma Art Mus., 1995; painter Olympia. Bd. dirs. Wash. State Capital Mus., Olympia, 1980, Patrons of South Sound Cultural Activities, Olympia, 1980-95; art commr. City of Olympia Art Commn., 1986-95; drafter preservation ordinance City of Olympia, 1982.

PARTON, BRAD, mayor. Mayor Redondo Beach, Calif. Office: 415 Diamond St Redondo Beach CA 90277-0270

PARTRIDGE, CATHLEEN FLANAGAN, library director; b. St. Paul, Apr. 21, 1945; d. John Theodore and Virginia Helen (McGuigan) Flanagan; m. Lyman Clark Partridge, Oct. 8, 1983; stepchildren: Elizabeth Partridge Mills, Erica Maren, Robert Edward. BA, U. Ill., 1967, MLS, 1969, PhD in Libr. Sci., 1976. Audio-visual libr. Marriott Libr. U. Utah, Salt Lake City, 1969-71, asst. prof. edn., 1976-82; supr. info. svcs. Hercules Aerospace, Magna, Utah, 1982-92; dir. learning resources Salt Lake C.C., 1992—. Author: Books and Other Printed Materials, 1980; editor: Utah Governors Conference on Libraries and Information Services, 1979; co-editor: American Folklore: A Bibliography, 1950-74. Mem. ALA, Utah Libr. Assn. (chair legis. com. 1994-95, pres. 1986-87, Disting. Svc. award 1994), Wasatch Mountain Club, Sierra Club, Phi Beta Kappa, Beta Phi Mu, Phi Kappa Phi, Pi Delta Phi, Phi Delta Kappa. Office: Salt Lake C C Markosian Lib PO Box 30808 4600 S Redwood Rd Salt Lake City UT 84130-0808

PARTRIDGE, L(LOYD) DONALD, science educator; b. Phila., May 10, 1945; s. Lloyd D. and Jean Marie (Rutledge) P.; m. Susan Patrick, May 25, 1984; children: Erika Morgan, Daniella Partridge, Rachel Conover. BS, MIT, 1967; PhD, U. Wash., 1973. Asst. prof. U. N.M., Albuquerque, 1976-84, assoc. prof., 1984-92, prof., 1992—; researcher Max-Planck Inst., Göttingen, Germany, 1991. Author: The Nervous System: Its Function and Its Interaction with the World, 1992; editor: Calcium Channels: Their Properties, Functions, Regulation and Clinical Relevance, 1991. Pres. Friends of Music, Albuquerque, 1988-92. 1st lt. U.S. Army Med. Svc. Corps, 1967-69. Welcome Rsch. fellow U. Bristol, Eng., 1973-74; NIH postdoctoral fellow U. Wash., 1974-76; Fulbright scholar Max-Planck Inst., Munich, Germany, 1985-86. Mem. Soc. for Neuroscience. Home: 3405 Mackland Ave NE Albuquerque NM 87106-1216 Office: U NMex Dept Neurosci Albuquerque NM 87131

PARTRIDGE, LOREN WAYNE, art historian, educator; b. Raton, N.Mex., Apr. 11, 1936; s. Don F. and Ruth (Isaacson) P.; widowed; children: Wendy, Amy. BA in English Lit., Yale U., 1958; cert. in L.Am. lit., U. Buenos Aires, 1959; diploma in Russian, U.S. Army Lang. Sch., Monterey, Calif., 1961; MA in Fine Arts, Harvard U., 1965, PhD in Fine Arts, 1969. Tchg. fellow Harvard U., Cambridge, Mass., 1964-66; lectr. U. Calif., Berkeley, 1968, acting asst. prof., 1969-70, asst. prof., 1970-76, assoc. prof., 1976-80, prof., 1980—, chmn. dept. history of art, 1978-87, 90-93; resident in art history Am. Acad. in Rome, 1985; reviewer Art Bull, 1972, 78, 80, 83, Renaissance Quar., 1984, 87, 90, Design Book Rev., 1987, Master Drawings, 1987, Am. Hist. Rev., 1993, Apollo, 1996. Author: John Galen Howard and the Berkeley Campus: Beaux-Arts Architecture in the Athens of the West, 1978, Caprarola, Palazzo Farnese, 1988, (with Randolph Starn) A Renaissance Likeness: Art and Culture in Raphael's Julius II, 1980, Arts of Power: Three Halls of State in Italy 1300-1600, 1992, The Art of Renaissance Rome, 1400-1600, 1996, Michelangelo: The Sistine Chapel Ceiling, Rome, 1996; contbr. author: Ency. of Italian Renaissance, 1981, Internat. Dictionary Art and Artists, 1990, Dictionary of Art, 1994; contbr. articles to profl. jours. With U.S. Army, 1960-63. Scholar Yale U., 1955-58, Harvard U., 1964-66; Fulbright fellow, 1958-59, 75, Am. Acad. in Rome fellow, 1966-68, Kress fellow Inst. for Advanced Studies, 1974-75, U. Calif., 1971-71, 88-89, Guggenheim fellow, 1981-92; grantee Kress Found., 1968-69, 71-72, Getty. sr. rsch. grantee, 1988-89. Office: U Calif Dept History of Art 6020 405 Doe Libr Berkeley CA 94720-6020

PASCALE, ANTONINA SUSANNA, marketing professional, writer; b. Hoboken, N.J., Jan. 19, 1968; d. Mario Anthony and Catherine Antonina (Rogowski) P.; m. Steven Benjamin Lalim Falcone, Nov. 16, 1996. BA in English, U. Calif., Berkeley, 1990; MFA in Creative Writing, Mills Coll., 1993. Account exec. Blattel Assocs., San Francisco, 1990-92; mktg. coord. Ratcliff Archs., Emeryville, Calif., 1992-94; mktg. mgr. William Turnbull Assoc., San Francisco, 1994-95; mktg. dir. Archtl. Resources Group, San Francisco, 1995—. Mem. Berkeley Archtl. Heritage Assn., 1995—. Mem. Soc. Mktg. Profl. Svcs. (mem. pub. rels. com. 1995—, editor newsletter 1995—), Calif. Alumni Assn. (mem. scholarship selection 1993-94). Democrat. Office: Acrhtl Resources Group The Embarcadero Pier 9 San Francisco CA 94111

PASCOE, PATRICIA HILL, state senator, writer; b. Sparta, Wis., June 1, 1935; d. Fred Kirk and Edith (Kilpatrick) Hill; m. D. Monte Pascoe, Aug. 3, 1957; children: Sarah, Ted, Will. BA, U. Colo., 1957; MA, U. Denver, 1968, PhD, 1982. Tchr. Sequoia Union High Sch. Dist., Redwood City, Calif. and Hayward (Calif.) Union High Sch. Dist., 1957-60; instr. Met. State Coll., Denver, 1969-75; instr. Denver U., 1975-77, 81, research asst. bur. ednl. research, 1981-82; tchr. Kent Denver Country Day, Englewood, Colo., 1982-84; freelance writer Denver, 1985—; mem. Colo. Senate, Denver, 1989-93, 95—; commr. Edn. Commn. of the States, Denver, 1975-82. Contbr. articles to numerous publs. and jours. Bd. dirs. Samaritan House, 1990-94, Cystic Fibrosis Found., 1989-93; pres. East H.S. Parent Tchr. and Student Assn., Denver, 1984-85; mem. Moore Budget Adv. Com., Denver, 1966-72; legis. chmn. alumni bd. U. Colo., Boulder, 1987-89; del. Dem. Nat. Conv., San Francisco, 1984, N.Y.C., 1992; mem. Denver Woman's Press Club, 1986—; bd. dirs. Opera Colo., 1996—. Mem. Soc. Profl. Journalists, Common Cause (bd. dirs. Denver chpt. 1986-88), Colo. Endowment for Humanities, Phi Beta Kappa. Presbyterian.

PASCOTTO, ALVARO, lawyer; b. Rome, Mar. 8, 1949; came to U.S., 1984; s. Antonio and Anna Ludovica (Habig) P.; m. Linda Haldan, July 20, 1985. JD, U. Rome, 1973. Bar: Italy 1976, Calif. 1987, U.S. Dist. Ct. (cen. dist.) Calif. 1987, U.S. Ct. Appeals (9th cir.) 1987. Ptnr. Studio Legale Pascotto, Rome, 1976-86, Pascotto, Gallavotti & Gardner, L.A. and Rome, 1986-90, Pascotto & Gallavotti, L.A., 1990—; of counsel Irell & Manella, L.A.; counsel, cons. Quantum Inc., Reno, Nev., 1980-87, Execucorp Mgmt. Cons., Miami, Fla., 1980-85; official counsel Consulate Gen. Italy, L.A., 1987—. Mem. ABA, Calif. Bar Assn., Italian-Am. Bar Assn., Am. Mgmt. Assn., Consiglio dell'Ordine Degli Avvocati e Procuratori di Roma. Clubs: Circolo del Golf (Rome); Malibu (Calif.) Racquet Club, Regency Club (L.A.). Home: 6116 Merritt Dr Malibu CA 90265-3847 Office: Pascotto & Gallavotti 1800 Avenue Of The Stars Los Angeles CA 90067-4212*

PASHGIAN, MARGARET HELEN, artist; b. Pasadena, Calif., Nov. 7, 1934; d. Aram John and Margaret (Howell) P. BA, Pomona Coll., 1956; MA in Fine Arts, Boston Univ., 1958; student, Columbia U., 1957. Art instr. Harvard-Newton Program Occidental Coll., Newton, Mass., 1959-62, instr. art, 1977-78; artist in residence Calif. Inst. Tech., 1970-71; grants panelist Calif. Arts Coun., Sacramento, 1993. Artist: solo shows include Rex Evans Gallery, L.A., 1965, 67, Occidental Coll., 1967, Kornblee Gallery, N.Y.C., 1969-72, U. Calif., Irvine, 1975, U. Calif. Santa Barbara, 1976, Stella Polaries Gallery, L.A., 1981, 82, Kaufman Galleries, Houston, 1982, Modernism Gallery, San Francisco, 1983, Works Gallery, Long Beach, Costa Mesa, Calif., 1986, 87, 88, 89, 90, 91, 92, Malka Gallery, L.A., 1997; group exhibitions include Pasadena Art Mus., 1965, Carson Pirie Scott, Chgo., 1965, Calif. Palace of Legion of Honor, San Francisco, 1967, Esther Bear Gallery, Santa Barbara, 1967, 69, Lytton Ctr. of the Visual Arts, L.A., 1968, Salt Lake Art Inst., Salt Lake City, 1968, Mus. Contemporary Crafts, Internat. Plastics Exhibition, 1969, Second Flint (Mich.) Invitational, 1969, Milw. Art Ctr., 1969, U.S.I.S. Mus., N.Y.C., Mus. Contemporary Art, Chgo., 1970, Studio Merconi, Milan, 1970, Calif. Inst. Tech., Baxter Art Galley, 1971, 1980, Calif. Innovations, Palm Springs Dessert Mus., 1981, Calif. Internat. Arts Found. Mus. of Modern Art, Paris, 1982, L.A. Artists in Seoul, Donsangbang Gallery, 1982, An Artistic Conversation, 1931-82, Poland, USA, Ulster Mus., Belfast, Ireland, 1983, Madison (Wis.) Art Ctr., 1994, Calif. State U., Fullerton, 1995, Oakland (Calif.) Mus., 1995; represented in pub. collections at River Forest (Ill.) State Bank, Atlantic Richfield Co., Dallas, Frederic Weisman Collection, L.A., Security Pacific Bank, L.A., Singapore, Andrew Dickson White Mus. of Art, Cornell U., Ithaca, N.Y., L.A. County Mus. of Art, Santa Barbara Art Mus., Laguna Beach Mus. of Art. Trustee, Pomona Coll, Claremont, Calif., 1987—; parade judge Tournament of RosesCentennial Parade, Pasadena, 1987; bd. dirs. L.A. Master Chorale, 1992—. NEA grantee, 1986. Home and Studio: 731 S Grand Ave Pasadena CA 91105-2424

PASICH, KIRK ALAN, lawyer; b. La Jolla, Calif., May 26, 1955; s. Chris Nick and Iva Mae (Tormey) P.; m. Pamela Mary Woods, July 30, 1983; children: Christopher Thomas, Kelly Elizabeth, Connor Woods. BA in Polit. Sci., UCLA, 1977; JD, Loyola Law Sch., L.A., 1980. Bar: Calif. 1980, U.S. Dist. Ct. (no., so., ea. and cen. dists.) Calif. 1981, U.S. Ct. Appeals (9th cir.) 1982, U.S. Ct. Appeals (1st cir.) 1992. Assoc. Paul, Hastings, Janofsky & Walker, L.A., 1980-88, ptnr., 1988-89; ptnr. Troop Meisinger Steuber & Pasich (formerly Hill Wynne Troop & Meisinger), L.A., 1989—. Author: Casualty and Liability Insurance, 1990, 96; entertainment law columnist, ins. law columnist L.A. and San Francisco Daily Jour., 1989—; contbr. articles to profl. jours. Active bd. dirs. Nat. Acad. Jazz, L.A., 1988-89, chmn. bd. dirs. Woody Herman Found., L.A., 1989-92, active L.A. City Atty's. Task Force for Econ. Recovery, 1992-93. Named to Calif's. Legal Dream Team as 1 of state's top 25 litigators, Calif. Law Bus., 1992, as one of the nation's top 45 lawyers under age 45, The Am. Lawyer, 1995. Mem. ABA (mem. Task Force on Complex Insurance Coverage Litigation). Office: Troop Meisinger Steuber & Pasich 10940 Wilshire Blvd Los Angeles CA 90024-3902

PASQUA, THOMAS MARIO, JR., journalism educator; b. L.A., Aug. 13, 1938; s. Thomas Mario and Ann Ione (Anderson) P.; m. Sandra Mae Liddell; children: Bruce Burks, Julie Burks, Geoffrey, Alexis. BA, Whittier (Calif.) Coll., 1960; MA, UCLA, 1961; PhD, U. Tex., 1973. Cert. secondary tchr. Reporter, photographer Whittier Daily News, 1954-65; tchr. LaSerna High Sch., Whittier, 1961-63, 64-65; lectr. Calif. State U., Fullerton, 1973-75, Mesa Coll., San Diego, 1978-83, U. San Diego, 1979-80, San Diego State U., 1985; prof. Southwestern Coll., Chula Vista, Calif., 1965—; staff writer San Diego Mag., 1997. Co-author: Excellence in College Journalism, 1983, Mass Media in the Information Age, 1990, Historical Perspectives in Popular Music, 1993; editor C.C. Journalist, 1983—; bibliographer Journalism Quar., 1974-92; contbr. articles to profl. jours. Mem. ch. coun. St. Andrew Luth. Ch., Whittier, 1965; mem. Chula Vista Bd. of Ethics, 1978-86; mem. Chula Vista Charter Rev. Com., 1969; mem. adv. bd. Bay Gen. Hosp., Chula Vista, 1985-87; mem. ch. coun. Victory Luth. Ch., Chula Vista, 1989-90; adv. com. Otay Valley Regional Park, 1990—. Wall St. Jour. Newspaper Fund fellow U. Wash., 1962; recipient Nat. Teaching award Poynter Inst. Media Studies, 1987. Mem. C.C. Journalism Assn. (archivist 1989—, charter inductee Hall of Fame, 1994), Journalism Assn. C.C.'s (exec. sec. 1975-81), Assn. for Edn. in Journalism and Mass Comm. (Markham prize 1974), Internat. Comm. Assn., Coll. Media Advisers, Am. Fedn. Tchrs. (pres. Southwestern Coll. 1977-78, 81-87), Phi Kappa Phi, Kappa Tau Alpha, Pi Sigma Alpha. Democrat. Home: 760 Monterey Ave Chula Vista CA 91910-6318 Office: Southwestern Coll 900 Otay Lakes Rd Chula Vista CA 91910-7223

PASQUALE, JOSEPH, computer scientist, educator; b. Weehawken, N.J., Feb. 12, 1958; s. Carlo and Maria Pasquale; m. Barbara Katherine Bittel. BSEE, MSEE, MIT, 1982; PhD in Computer Sci., U. Calif., Berkeley, 1988. Computer systems cons. La Jolla, Calif., 1980—; asst. prof. U. Calif., San Diego, 1987-93, assoc. prof., 1993-96, prof., 1996—, J. Robert Beyster Endowed Chair in Engring., 1996—; dir. Sequoia 2000 Project, 1994—; chmn. NASA Sci. User Network Working Group, 1993—; sr. fellow San Diego Supercomputer Ctr., La Jolla, 1990—. Contbr. articles to profl. jours. Recipient Presdl. Young Investigator award NSF, 1989, IBM Faculty Devel. award, 1991; named Outstanding Teaching Asst. of Yr. Eta Kappa Nu, 1983. Mem. Assn. Computing Machinery, IEEE. Office: U Calif San Diego Dept Computer Sci Engring La Jolla CA 92093-0114

PASSANTINO, HEATHER ANN, special education educator; b. San Jose, Nov. 27, 1962; d. Ronald Walter and Joan DeBruler (Norton) Riffe; m. David Thomas Passantino, Aug. 11, 1984; children: Robert, Julie, Anthony, Anna. BA in Liberal Studies, U. of the Pacific, 1983; MA in Edn., U.S. Internat. U., 1990. Cet. learning handicapped tchr., Calif. Educator Sunnyvale (Calif.) Sch. Dist., 1984—; v.p. Sunnyvale Edn. Assn., chmn. diversity com., rep. curriculum coun. Mem. NEA, Nat. Coun. on Self Esteem, Coun. for Exceptional Children, Calif. Tchr.'s Assn., Order of Eastern Star (Ruth 1981, Adah 1986, conductress 1986, assoc. matron 1987, worthy matron 1988, Esther 1989, dep. grand matron 1991. Republican. Office: Columbia Middle Sch 739 Morse Ave Sunnyvale CA 94086-3010

PASSMAN, STEPHEN LEE, theoretical mechanics scientist; b. Suffolk, Va., Sept. 3, 1942; s. Milton Lawrence and Jean (Lehrman) P.; children: Michael, Rebecca, Sara, Rachel. BSEM, Ga. Inst. Tech., 1964, MSEM, 1966, PhD, 1968. Instr. U.S Naval Acad., Annapolis, Md., 1968-70; postdoctoral fellow Johns Hopkins U., Balt., 1970-71; from asst. to assoc. prof. Ga. Inst. Tech., Atlanta, 1971-78; sr. mem. tech. staff Sandia Nat. Labs., Albuquerque, 1978—; lectr. George Washington U., Washington, 1969-70; vis. mem. Math. Rsch. Ctr., U. Wis., Madison, 1972, Inst. Math. and Its Applications, U. Minn., Mpls., 1984, 89, Math. Sci. Inst., Cornell U., 1987-90; cons. Bell Labs., Norcross, Ga., 1975-78; vis. scientist Pitts. Energy Tech. Ctr., 1988-90, cons., 1990-96; vis. scientist U.S. Dept. Energy, Washington, 1995—; vis. scholar Carnegie Mellon U., 1988-90; adj. prof. engring. U. Pitts., 1990-96; U.S. rep. multiphase flow com., Internat. Energy Agy., 1992-96; U.S. rep. G-7 Nuclear Experts Meeting, Paris, 1996; mem. steering com. U.S.-Russian Plutonium Disposition Program, 1995—. Contbr. articles to profl. jours. Served to capt. U.S. Army, 1968-70. Recipient Monie A. Ferst Rsch. award, 1968; scholar Johns Hopkins U., 1990. Mem. ASME (elasticity com. 1987—, multiphase flow com. 1990-96), Soc. Natural Philosophy (treas. 1977-78, dir. 1978-96, chmn. bd. dirs. 1985-86), Soc. Engring. Sci. (bd. dirs. 1986-96, treas. 1987-96), Am. Acad. Mechanics, Am. Phys. Soc., Soc. Rheology, Sigma Xi. Office: Sandia Nat Labs MS 1393 Box 5800 Albuquerque NM 87185

PASTEGA, RICHARD LOUIS, retail specialist; b. Klamath Falls, Oreg., Mar. 25, 1936; s. Louie and Jennie (Borgialli) P. BS, So. Oreg. State Coll., 1960; MS, Mont. State U., Bozeman, 1961. Tchr. social studies Henley High Sch., Klamath Falls, Oreg., 1962-63, Juneau (Alaska) Douglas High Sch., 1964-67, Thessaloniki (Greece) Internat. High Sch., 1967-69; editor, pub. Breakdown Newspaper, Klamath Falls, Oreg., 1971-73; mgr. Pastega's Market, Klamath Falls, 1975—. Del. dem. Nat. Conv., N.Y.C., 1976, Oreg. Dem. Platform conv., Eugene, Beaverton and Ashland, 1978-80, 82; councilor City of Klamath Falls, 1986-88; bd. dirs. Basin Transit Svc., Klamath Falls, 1981-87; chair Klamath County Dem. Ctrl. Com., 1983-86, sec. 1992-94. Mem. Sons of Italy. Democrat. Home: 428 S 9th St Klamath Falls OR 97601-6126

PASTERNACK, ROBERT HARRY, school psychologist; b. Bklyn., Nov. 30, 1949; s. William and Lillian Ruth (Levine) P.; m. Jeanelle Livingston, Apr. 10, 1980; children: Shayla, Rachel. BA, U. South Fla., 1970; MA, N.Mex. Highlands U., 1972; PhD, U. N.Mex., 1980. Dir. Eddy County Drug Abuse Program, Carlsbad, N.Mex., 1972-73; adminstrv. intern U.S. Office Edn., Washington, 1975-76; exec. dir. Villa Santa maria, Cedar Crest, N.Mex., 1976-78; clin. dir. Ranchos Treatment Ctr., Taos, N.Mex., 1978-79; sch. psychologist N.Mex. Boys Sch., Springer, 1980—, supt., 1991; pres. Ensenar Health svcs., Inc., Taos, 1980—; exec. dir. Casa de Corazon, Taos, N.Mex., 1994—; instr. N.Mex. Highlands U., Las Vegas, 1980—, U. N.Mex., Albuquerque, 1980—; cons. N.Mex. Youth Authority, Santa Fe, 1988—, N.Mex. Devel. Disabilities Bur., Santa Fe, 1986—, various sch. dists. Author: Growing Up: The First Five Years, 1986; contbr. articles to profl. publs. Pres., bd. dirs. Children's Lobby, N.Mex., 1978, N.Mex. Spl. Olympics, 1986-88, Child-Rite, Inc., Taos, 1990; mem. Gov.'s Mental Health Task Force, Albuquerque, 1988—. Mem. Nat. Assn. Sch. Psychologists, Correctional Edn. Assn., Nat. Alliance Mentally Ill, N.Mex. Coun. on Crime and Delinquency. Home and Office: Enseñar Inc PO Box 3126 Taos NM 87571-3126 Office: Casa de Corazon PO Box 73 Taos NM 87571-0073

PASTERNAK, BILL, amateur radio newswriter; b. Feb. 7, 1942; m. Sharon (Wagner) Pasternak. Student, NYCC; grad., RCA Inst., N.Y.C. Maintenance technician Rupat Electronic Svc. Ctr., Bklyn., 1960-62; consumer electronics mgmt. field svc. rep. GE Corp., N.Y.C., 1962-68; co-owner, v.p. Mind Garden Electronics, Inc., Bklyn., 1968-71; VCR maintenance specialist Sears Consumer Svc., Chattsworth, Calif., 1971-79; tech. dir. "Alive 'n Well" DBA Entertainment Corp., Hollywood, Calif., 1979-80; broadcast engr. KTTV-Fox Television, L.A., 1980—; co-founder, prodr., writer Amateur Radio Newsline, Saugus, Calif., 1976—; broadcast cons., 1979—; ednl. TV film writer, prodr., dir., 1974—; cons. in 2-way radio sys. installation and svc., 1962—. Author: The Practical Handbook of Amateur Radio FM and Repeaters, 1980, VCRs - Buying, Using and Maintaining, 1983; vol. editor The Westlink Report, 1981-87; columnist 73 Mag., 1972-92; contbr. numerous articles to spl. interest publs. Recipient DARA Spl. Achievement award, 1981, DARA Radio Amateur of Yr. award, 1989, AMSAT Outstanding Contributions award, 1990. Mem. Radio Club Am., Quarter Century Wireless Assn., Am. Radio Relay League (Southwestern Divsn. Meritorious Svc. award 1988, Nat. Cert. Merit, 1995). Office: Amateur Radio Newsline 28197 Robin Ave Saugus CA 91350-2066

PASTIN, MARK JOSEPH, executive consultant, association executive; b. Ellwood City, Pa., July 6, 1949; s. Joseph and Patricia Jean (Camenite) P.; m. Joanne Marie Reagle, May 30, 1970 (div. Mar. 1982); m. Carrie Patricia Class, Dec. 22, 1984 (div. June 1990); m. Christina M. Brecto, June 15, 1991. BA summa cum laude, U. Pitts., 1970; MA, Harvard U., 1972, PhD, 1973. Asst. prof. Ind. U., Bloomington, 1973-78, assoc. prof., 1978-80; founder, bd. Compliance Resource Group, Inc., 1983—; chmn., CEO, pres. Coun. Ethical Orgns., Alexandria, Va., 1986—; prof. mgmt., dir. Ariz. State U., Tempe, 1988-92, prof. emeritus, 1996—; prof. emeritus, 1996—; chair Health Ethics Trust, 1995—; adv. bd. Aberdeen Holdings, San Diego, 1988-90; dir. Sandpiper Group, Inc., N.Y.C., 1987—, S.W. Projects, Inc., San Diego, 1988-90, Learned Nicholson, Ltd., 1990-91; bd. Japan Am. Soc. Phoenix, Found. for Ethical Orgns.; cons. GTE, Southwestern Bell, 1987-89, Tex. Instruments, MicroAge Computers, Med-Tronic, Blood Sys., Inc., Opus Corp., GTE, NyNex, Am. Express Bank, Kaiko Bussan Co., Japan, Arex Co., Japan, Century Audit Co., Japan, Scottsdale Meml. Hosp., Consanti Found., Lincoln Electric Co., Tenet Healthcare Corp., The Williams Co.; vis. faculty Harvard U., 1980; invited presenter Australian Inst. Mgmt., Nippon Tel. & Tel., Hong Kong Commn. Against Corruption, 1984, Young Pres.'s Orgn. Internat. U., 1990, Nat. Assn. Indsl. & Office Parks, 1990, ABA, 1991, Govt. of Brazil, 1991, Tzuzuki Edn. Sys., 1995. Author: Hard Problems of Management, 1986 (Book of Yr. award Armed Forces Mil. Comtrs. 1986, Japanese edit. 1994), Power by Association, 1991, The Hotline Handbook, 1996, The State of Ethics in Arizona, 1991, Planning Forum, 1992; editor: Public-Private Sector Ethics, 1979; columnist Bus. Jour. Founding bd. mem. Tempe Leadership, 1985-89; bd. mem. Ctr. for Behavioral Health, Phoenix, 1986-89, Tempe YMCA, 1986—, Valley Leadership Alumni Assn., 1989—; mem. Clean Air Com., Phoenix, 1987-90. Nat. Sci. Found. fellow, Cambridge, Mass., 1971-73; Nat. Endowment for the Humanities fellow, 1975; Exxon Edn. Found. grant, 1982-83. Mem. Strategic Mgmt. Soc. (invited presenter 1985), Am. Soc. Assn. Execs. (invited presenter 1987-95), Bus. Ethics Soc. (founding bd. dirs. 1983), Found. Ethical Orgns. (chmn. 1988, pres.), Pres.'s Assn., Am. Mgmt. Assn., Golden Key, Harvard Club D.C., Phi Beta Kappa. Home: 7206 Park Terrace Dr Alexandria VA 22307-2035 Office: 1216 King St Ste 300 Alexandria VA 22314-2825

PASTOR, ED, congressman; b. June 28, 1943. Mem. Maricopa County Bd. Suprs., Phoenix, Ariz., 1976-91; mem. 102nd-105th Congresses from Ariz. 2nd dist., 1991—; mem. appropriations com. Office: House of Reps 2465 Rayburn Washington DC 20515*

PASTORE, THOMAS MICHAEL, telecommunications sales executive; b. Bronx, N.Y., Jan. 25, 1959; s. Philip J. and Olga E. (DeGenito) P.; m. Kimberly A. Coppersmith, Dec. 13, 1986; children: Gabriela Maria, Thomas John. BA in Bus., Western State Coll., 1981. Sales rep. Victor Technologies Inc., Denver, 1981-84; account mgr. No. Telecom Inc., Denver, 1984-87, v.p. sales coun., 1985—, sales engr., 1987-92, dist. sales mgr., 1992—. Mem. Better Air Campaign, 1990—; sec. Warren Sq. Homeowners Assn., Denver, 1987-92; player, contbr. Dale Tooley Tennis Tournament, 1991-92; fundraiser Am. Cancer Soc., Denver, 1991—; mem. Denver Art Mus., 1991-92. Republican. Roman Catholic. Home and Office: No Telecom Inc 16095 Quarry Hill Dr Parker CO 80134-9553

PASTREICH, PETER, orchestra executive director; b. Bklyn., Sept. 13, 1938; s. Ben and Hortense (Davis) P.; m. Jamie Garrard Whittington; children by previous marriages: Anna, Milena, Emanuel, Michael. A.B. magna cum laude, Yale Coll., 1959; postgrad., N.Y. U. Sch. Medicine, 1959-60; studied trumpet, with Robert Nagle at Yale U., with Raymond Sabarich, Paris. Asst. mgr. Denver Symphony, Balt. Symphony; mgr. Greenwich Village Symphony, N.Y.C., 1960-63; gen. mgr. Nashville Symphony, 1963-65, Kansas City Philharmonic, 1965-66; asst. mgr., mgr. St. Louis Symphony, 1966-78, exec. dir., 1966-78; exec. dir. San Francisco Symphony, 1978—; instr. orch. mgmt. Am. Symphony Orch. League; bd. dirs. Nat. Com. for Symphony Orch. Support; founder San Francisco Youth Orch.; rep. planning and constrn. Davies Symphony Hall, San Francisco Symphony, 1980. Author: TV comml., 1969 (CLIO award); contbr. articles to various newspapers. Mem. recommendation bd. of the Avery Fisher Artist Program, Yale U. Council com. on music; past mem. adv. panel Nat. Endowment for the Arts, co-chmn. music panel, 1985; founding mem. bd. dirs. St. Louis Conservatory, mem. policy com. Maj. Orch. Mgrs. Conf., chmn., 1980; bd. dirs. Laumeier Sculpture Park, St. Louis, Stern Grove Festival, San Francisco Conv. and Visitors Bur.; chmn. fund campaign French-Am. Internat. Sch., San Francisco. Served with U.S. Army, 1960. Recipient First Disting. Alumnus award Yale U. Band, 1977, cert. Merit Yale Sch. Music, 1984. Mem. Am. Symphony Orch. League (dir., chmn., former chmn. task force on mgmt. tng.; mem. exec. and long-range planning com., chmn. standing com. on adminstrv. policy), Assn. Calif. Symphony Orchs. (dir.), Bankers Club of San Francisco. Club: Yale (N.Y.C.). Office: San Francisco Symphony Davies Symphony Hall San Francisco CA 94102

PATANO, PATRICIA ANN, health and fitness professional, marketing and public relations specialist; b. Chgo., June 14, 1950; d. Thomas Vincent and Gladys Estelle (Olejniczak) P. Student, Los Angeles Pierce Coll., 1968-70, UCLA, 1974-84; BS in Bus. and Mgmt. summa cum laude, U. Redlands, 1995. Pub. relations mgr. Motel 6, Inc., Century City, Calif., 1974-77; mgr. corp. communications 1st Travel Corp., Van Nuys, Calif., 1977-79; mktg. pub. relations mgr. Unitours, Inc., Los Angeles, 1979-81; asst. v.p. pub. relations Los Angeles Olympic Com., 1981-84; pres., co-owner PaVage Fitness Innovations, Playa del Rey, Calif., 1984-88; dir. spl. projects J.D. Power and Assocs., Agoura Hills, Calif., 1988—; trustee Nat. Injury Prevention Found., San Diego, 1983—; cons. Dick Clark Productions, Burbank, Calif., 1985, Reebok USA Ltd., Boston, 1983—. Co-author: MuscleAerobics, 1985; contbr. articles to profl. jours. Vol. Motion Picture Hosp., Woodland Hills, Calif., 1968-70; bd. dirs. Los Angeles Boys and Girls Club, 1984—; mem. council San Fernando Natural History Mus., 1987-89; big sister Pride House, Van Nuys, 1987-89; active juvenile delinquent program Pride House. Recipient Corp. award Pres.'s Council Phys. Fitness, 1983; fellow Alfred North Whitehead Leaderships Soc.-U. Redlands, 1995. Mem. L.A. Advt. Club, Nat. Injury Prevention Found. (trustee 1984-87), Child Shelter Homes: A Rescue Effort (bd. dirs.), Mid Valley Athletic Club (Reseda, Calif.), Marina City (Marina del Rey, Calif.). Republican. Presbyterian. Clubs: Mid Valley Athletic (Reseda, Calif.); Marina City (Marina del Rey, Calif.). Office: JD Power & Assocs 30401 Agoura Rd Agoura Hills CA 91301-2084

PATE, SUSAN LEE HARGRAVE, theater arts educator, choreographer; b. Ithaca, N.Y., Mar. 5, 1950; d. Haas M. and Margaret Jean (Gladstone) Hargrave; m. Ronald D. Pate, Aug. 24, 1985; 1 child, Cameron D. BA in Theatre Arts, Cornell U., 1972; MA in Theatre, SUNY, Binghamton, 1974; PhD in Dance/Theatre History, Cornell U., 1980. Grad. teaching asst. SUNY, Binghamton, 1972-74; fine arts coord., theatre instr. SUNY, Brockport, 1974-76; grad. teaching asst. theatre arts Cornell U., Ithaca, N.Y., 1976-79; assoc. prof. theatre arts San Jose (Calif.) State U., 1979-84; prof. performance in theatre arts Calif. State U., Chico, 1986—; guest artist, tchr. of mime Fairbanks (Alaska) Summer Arts Festival, 1987-90, Pribilof Sch. Dist., Alaska, 1994; guest artist, choreographer, tchr. Fairbanks Summer Arts Camp, 1988, 89; instr. dance gymnastics camp Houston Bapt. U., 1980; artistic dir. Chico Dance Theatre, 1996—; adjudicator Region VIII, Am. Coll. Theatre Festival, 1995—. Co-author: The Beginning Actor's Companion, 1989; dir. 41 plays and musicals, 1969—; choreographer more than 50 dances and musicals, 1979—, Miriam Liturgical Dance Co., 1996—; mime choreographer, 1979—. Home missionary So. Bapt. Conv., Chico, 1991-94; music team singer, soloist New Life Christian Fellowship and Esplanade Baptist, Chico, 1986-96; group leader eating disorder recovery groups, Chico, 1992-93. Affirmative Action grantee Calif. State U., Chico, 1989; Cornell U. Grad. Sch. summer fellow, 1977, 78. Mem. Calif. Edn. Theatre Assn. Republican. Christian. Office: Calif State U Chico Theatre Arts Dept PAC 217 Chico CA 95929-8100

PATEL, CHANDRA KUMAR NARANBHAI, communications company executive, educator, researcher; b. Baramati, India, July 2, 1938; came to U.S., 1958, naturalized, 1970; s. Naranbhai Chaturbhai and Maniben P.; m. Shela Dixit, Aug. 20, 1961; children: Neela, Meena. B.Engring., Poona U., 1958; M.S., Stanford U., 1959, Ph.D., 1961. Mem. tech. staff Bell Telephone Labs., Murray Hill, N.J., 1961-93, head infrared physics and electronics rsch. dept., 1967-70, dir. electronics rsch. dept., 1970-76, dir. phys. rsch. lab., 1976-81, exec. dir. rsch. physics and acad. affairs div., 1981-87, exec. dir. rsch., materials sci., engring. and acad. affairs div., 1987-93; trustee Aerospace Corp., L.A., 1979-88; vice chancellor rsch. UCLA, 1993—; mem. governing bd. NRC, 1990-91; bd. dirs. Accuware Corp., Santa Monica, Calif., chmn. bd. Contbr. articles to tech. jours. Chmn. Calif. Biomed. Found., 1994—; mem. exec. bd. Calif. Healthcare Inst., 1995—. Recipient Ballantine medal Franklin Inst., 1968, Coblentz award Am. Chem. Soc., 1974, Honor award Assn. Indians in Am., 1975, Founders prize Tex. Instruments Found., 1978, award N.Y. sect. Soc. Applied Spectroscopy, 1982, Schawlow medal Laser Inst. Am., 1984, Thomas Alva Edison Sci. award N.J. Gov., 1987, William T. Ennor Manufacturing Technology award ASME, 1995, Nat. Medal of Sci., 1996. Fellow AAAS, IEEE (Lamme medal 1976, medal of honor 1989), Am. Acad. Arts and Scis., Am. Phys. Soc. (coun. 1987-91, exec. com. 1987-90, George E. Pake prize 1988, pres. 1995), Optical Soc. Am. (Adolph Lomb medal 1966, Townes medal 1982, Ives medal 1989), Indian Nat. Sci. Acad. (fng.); mem. NAS (coun. 1988-91, exec. com. 1989-91), NAE (Zworykin award 1976), Gynecol. Laser Surgery Soc. (hon.), Am. Soc. for Laser Medicine and Surgery (hon.), Third World Acad. Scis. (assoc.), Calif. Biomed. Found. (pres. 1994—), Calif. Healthcare Inst. (exec. com. 1995—), Sigma Xi (pres. 1994-96). Home: 1171 Roberto Ln Los Angeles CA 90077-2302 Office: UCLA Vice Chancellor Rsch PO Box 951405 Los Angeles CA 90095-1415

PATEL, DINESH C., business executive; b. Kabwe, Zambia, Sept. 6, 1950; came to U.S., 1973; naturalized, 1981; s. Chhotubhai A. and Savitaben C. P.; B.S., Gujarat U., India, 1973; M.S., Phila. Coll. Pharmacy, 1975; Ph.D., U. Mich., 1978; m. Kalpana Patel, June 28, 1973; children: Ashish, Avni. Research asst. U. Mich., 1976-78; research scientist Lederle Labs., Am. Cyanamid Co., Pearl River, N.J., 1978-81; head dermatology product devel. Alcon Labs., Ft. Worth 1981-83, head drug delivery group, 1983-85; founder, pres. and CEO TheraTech Inc., Salt Lake City, 1985—. Mem. Am. Pharm. Assn., AAUP, Sigma Xi, Rho Chi, Phi Lambda Upsilon. Home: 5839 Meadowcrest Dr Murray UT 84107-6512 Office: Research Park 417 Wakara Way Ste 100 Salt Lake City UT 84108-1255

PATEL, MARILYN HALL, federal judge; b. Amsterdam, N.Y., Sept. 2, 1938; d. Lloyd Manning and Nina J. (Thorpe) Hall; m. Magan C. Patel, Sept. 2, 1966; children: Brian, Gian. B.A., Wheaton Coll., 1959; J.D., Fordham U., 1963. Bar: N.Y. 1963, Calif. 1970. Mng. atty. Benson & Morris, Esq., N.Y.C., 1962-64; sole practice N.Y.C., 1964-67; atty. U.S. Immigration and Naturalization Svc., San Francisco, 1967-71; sole practice San Francisco, 1971-76; judge Alameda County Mcpl. Ct., Oakland, Calif., 1976-80, U.S. Dist. Ct. (no. dist.) Calif., San Francisco, 1980—; adj. prof. law Hastings Coll. of Law, San Francisco, 1974-76. Author: Immigration and Nationality Law, 1974; also numerous articles. Mem. bd. visitors Fordham U. Sch. Law. Mem. ABA (litigation sect., jud. adminstrn. sect.), ACLU (former bd. dirs.), NOW (former bd. dirs.), Am. law Inst., Am. Judicature Soc. (bd. dirs.), Calif Conf. Judges, Nat. Assn. Women Judges (founding mem.), Internat. Inst. (bd. dirs.), Advs. for Women (co-founder), Assn. Bus. Trial Lawyers (bd. dirs.). Democrat. Office: US Dist Ct PO Box 36060 450 Golden Gate Ave Rm 19-5356 San Francisco CA 94102

PATINO, HUGO, food science research engineer; b. Monterey, Nuevo Leon, Mex., Oct. 1, 1952; came to U.S., 1982; s. Francisco De Paula and Aurora (Leal) P.; m. Leslie Ellen Nickels, May. 20, 1978; children: Erica, Laura Elizabeth. B of Engring., Monterrey Inst. Tech., 1974; PhD, U. Waterloo, 1979. Asst. prof. Monterrey (Mex.) Inst. Tech., 1975-76; mgr. brewing product engring. Cuauhtemoc Breweries, Monterey, 1979-82; asst. prof. U. Calif., Davis, 1982-84; dept. head rsch. Coors Brewing Co., Golden, Colo., 1984-91, dir. rsch. & devel., 1991-93, v.p., R & D, 1993—; bd. govs. Colo. Alliance for Sci., Boulder. Co-author: Quality Control in Commercial Vegetable Processing, 1989; contbr. articles to profl. jours. Recipient Nat. Hispanic Employers Assn. Profl. Achievement award, 1997. Mem. Am. Soc. Brewing Chemists (edit. bd. mem. 1991—), Master Brewers Assn. Am. (tech. com. mem. 1991—, Presdl. award Best Paper 1990), Am. Inst. Chem. Engring., Inst. Food Technologists. Roman Catholic. Office: Coors Brewing Co BC600 Golden CO 80401

PATINO, ISIDRO FRANK, law enforcement educator; b. San Antonio, Mar. 10, 1943; s. Isidro F. and Maria (Narro) P.; children: Michael, Rebecca, Karleen. BS, Calif. State U., L.A., 1973; MBA, U. Redlands, 1995. Records comdr. Placentia (Calif.) Police Dept., 1980-85; asst. dean Criminal Justice Tng. Ctr. Golden West Coll., Huntington Beach, Calif., 1986-89, assoc. dean instrn., 1989-92; divsn. dean dept. pub. svc. Rio Hondo Coll., Whittier, Calif., 1992—; pres., mem. State Chancellors Adv. Com. Pub. Safety Edn., 1991—; chmn. So. Calif. Pub. Safety Tng. Consortium, 1994—, active, 1993—; bd. suprs. L.A. County Spl. Task Force on Pub. Safety Tng., 1995—; mem. Hispanic male adv. com. Dept. Edn. Connections Project. Kellogg C.C. Diversity Leadership fellow, 1996-97. Mem. Calif. Law Enforcement Assn. Records Suprs. (pres. so. chpt. 1985-87, state pres. 1986-87), Calif. Acad. Dirs. Assn. (chmn. 1988-89), Am. Soc. Criminologists, Acad. Criminal Justice Scis., Western and Pacific Assn. Criminal Justice Educators, Calif. Assn. Adminstrn. of Justice Educators (v.p. 1996-97, state pres. 1997—), Calif. Peace Officers Stds. and Tng. Basic Course Consortium (chmn. instrn. com. 1987-88),World Future Soc. (pres. Orange County-Long Beach chpt. 1988- 92), Nat. Assn. Field Tng. Officers (nat. pres. 1992-93), Nat. Assn. Chiefs of Police, Internat. Assn. Chiefs of Police, Soc. Law Enforcement Trainers. Roman Catholic.

PATKAU, JOHN, architect; b. Winnipeg, Man., Can., Aug. 18, 1947; s. Abe John and Bertha (Klassen) P.; m. Patricia Frances Gargett, Aug. 10, 1974. BA, U. Manitoba, 1969, BA in Environ. Studies, 1969, MArch, 1972. Registered architect, B.C., Ont. Prin. John Patkau Architect Ltd., Edmonton, Can., 1977-83; ptnr. Patkau Archs. Inc., Vancouver, B.C., Can., 1984—; chmn. edn. com. Alta. Assn. Architects, 1981; vis. critic U. Calgary, 1981, 92, U. Waterloo, 1987, 89, U. Pa., 1987, Tech. U. N.S., 1987, U. B.C., 1988, 89, UCLA, 1989; design critic U. B.C., 1985-86; urban design panel Vancouver, 1990-92; vis. prof. William Lyon Somerville Lectureship U. Calgary, 1994; Eliot Noyes vis. design critic Harvard U., 1995. Recipient Progressive Architecture citation, 1981, Progressive Architecture award, 1993, 95, Can. Architects award, 1983, 86, 87, 89, 90, 92, 94, Wood Coun. First award, 1984, Gov. Gen. medal, 1986, 90, 92, 94, Gov. Gen. award, 1990, Lt. Gov. Archtl. medal, 1992, Honor award, 1992. Fellow Royal Archtl. Inst. Can. (chmn. design com. 1987); mem. Archtl. Inst. B.C., Royal Can. Coll. Art, Ont. Assn. Architects. Office: Patkau Archs, 560 Beatty St Ste L110, Vancouver, BC Canada V6B 2L3

PATKAU, PATRICIA, architect, architecture educator; b. Winnipeg, Manitoba, Can., Feb. 25, 1950; d. John Frederick and Aileen Constance (Emmett) Gargett; m. John Robert Patkau, Aug. 10, 1974. BA in Interior Design, U. Manitoba, 1973; MA in Architecture, Yale, New Haven, Conn., 1978. Ptnr. Patkau Archs., Vancouver, B.C., Can., 1983—; asst. prof. Sch. Architecture UCLA, U.S.A., 1988-90; assoc. prof. Sch. Architecture U. B.C., Can., 1992—; vis. critic U. Calgary, 1981, 87, U. Waterloo, 1987, U. Pa., U.S.A., 1987, U. Toronto, 1988, Southern Calif. Inst. Architecture, U.S.A., 1990, UCLA, 1991, U. Oreg., U.S.A., 1992, MIT, U.S.A., 1993, Yale U., 1993; design critic U. B.C., 1984-87; vis. prof. Harvard U., U.S.A., 1993, U. Calgary, 1994. Ctrl. Mortgage and Housing fellow, 1977, 78; recipient Manitoba Gold medal, 1973, Progressive Architecture citation, 1981, 93, Can. Architect Excellence award, 1983, 86, 87, 89, 90, 92, 94, Can. Wood Coun. First award, 1984, Honor award, 1992, Gov. Gen. Architecture medal, 1986, 90, 92, 94, Gov. Gen. Architecture award, 1990, Lt. Gov. Architecture medal, 1992, Can. Wood Coun. award, 1991. Fellow Royal Archtl. Inst. Can.; mem. Archtl. Inst. B.C. (Honor award 1988). Office: Patkau Archs, 560 Beatty St Ste L110, Vancouver, BC Canada V6B 2L3

PATNODE, DARWIN NICHOLAS, academic administrator, professional parliamentarian; b. Mpls., June 20, 1948; s. Arthur T. and Agnes M. (Oeffling) P. BA, St. Mary's U., Winona, Minn., 1968; MA, U. Minn., 1970, PhD, 1974. Cert. profl. parliamentarian. Corp. rels. coord. Stanford (Calif.) U., 1983-87; dir. of devel. Foothill Coll., Los Altos Hills, Calif., 1987-94; assoc. dean West Valley-Mission C.C. Dist., Saratoga, Calif., 1994-96; exec. dir. The Found. for San Mateo (Calif.) County C.C. Dist., 1996—; vis. lectr. in English, Santa Clara (Calif.) U., 1982-83. Author: History of Parliamentary Procedure, 1982; co-author: Robert's Rules of Order, Modern Edition, 1989. Bd. dirs. Nonprofit Devel. Ctr., San Jose, Calif., 1993-96. Mem. Parliamentarians Internat. (pres. 1982—), Am. Inst. of Parliamentarians (pres. 1994-95), Nat. Assn. of Parliamentarians. Home: 3353 Brittan Ave Apt 13 San Carlos CA 94070-3431 Office: Foundation for San Mateo County CC Dist 3401 CSM Dr San Mateo CA 94402

PATNOE, SHELLEY ELIZABETH, psychologist, writer; b. Cardston, Alta., Can., Aug. 25, 1945; d. Carl William and Helen Rae (Nelson) Poll; m. Herbert Darrell Patnoe, Feb. 29, 1968 (dec. Mar. 1981); children: Christoper David, Geoffrey Brian. BA, San Jose State U., 1979, MA, 1981; PhD, U. Calif., Santa Cruz, 1986. Lectr. dept. psychology San Jose State U., 1987-96; sch. psychologist Fairfield (Calif.) Unified Sch. Dist., 1993—; lectr. dept. edn. Calif. State U., Sacramento, 1996—. Author: A Narrative History of Experimental Social Psychology, 1988, The Jigsaw/Classroom, 1997. Recipient grant Sigma Xi, 1985. Mem. APA, Am. Psychol. Soc., Calif. Assn. Sch. Psychologists. Home: 1105 Marina Circle Davis CA 95616 Office: CSU Sacramento Dept Edn 6000 J St Sacramento CA 95819-6079

PATON, SCOTT MADISON, publisher; b. Miami, Fla., Aug. 18, 1963; s. Robert Wishart and Mary Ann (Hinson) P.; m. Heidi Mae Kellar, June 8, 1996. BS in Bus. Adminstrn., Calif. State U., Chico, 1986. Asst. editor Quality Digest, Red Bluff, Calif., 1984-86; editor in chief Quality Digest, Red Bluff, 1986-95; publisher Quality Digest, Chico, Calif., 1996—, Paton Press, Red Bluff, 1995—. Publisher, editor: (book) The QS-9000 Answer Book, 1996; also contbr. articles to mags. Republican. Episcopalian. Home: 153 Beverly Ave Red Bluff CA 96080 Office: Quality Digest 40 Declaration Dr Ste 100-C Chico CA 95973

PATRICK, LESLIE DAYLE, hydrologist; b. Grand Island, Nebr., Nov. 20, 1951; d. Robert Norman and Charlotte Ruth (Thomas) Mayfield; m. Jeffrey Rogan Patrick, July 1, 1972 (div. Feb. 1995). BA in Geology, U. Alaska, Anchorage, 1975, MS in Mgmt., 1991. Data base mgr. U.S. Geol. Survey, Anchorage, 1975-78, with digital modeling, 1980-85, with water use studies, 1978-91, chief computer sect., systems analyst, 1985-91, asst. dist. chief mgmt. ops., 1991—. Mem. NAFE, Am. Mgmt. Assn., Am. Soc. Quality Control, Alaska Groundwater Assn. (sec., treas. 1980). Office: US Geol Survey Water Resources Div 4230 University Dr Ste 201 Anchorage AK 99508-4664 *Personal philosophy: Greet each day with a stretch and a smile.*

PATRICK, LUCILLE NICHOLS, artist, rancher; b. Oak Park, Ill., Apr. 23, 1924; d. James Calvin and Mary Lucille (Sullivan) Nichols; children: Patricia Lucille Patrick Williams Harter, James Nichols, John Michael, Barbara Jo Patrick Knight. U. Minn., U. Ariz., U. Wyo. Author: Best Little Town By a Dam Site, 1968, The Candy Kid J.C. Nichols, 1969, Carolina Lockhart, 1984. Pres., sec. Park County Hist. Soc., Cody, Wyo, 1950-70, Cody (Wyo.) Country Art League, 1960-80. Republican. Episcopalian. Home: 2117 Southfork Rd Cody WY 82414-8006

PATRICK, WENDY LYNN, lawyer; b. Orange, Calif., Oct. 19, 1968. BA, UCLA, 1990; JD, Calif. Western Sch. of Law, 1994. Bar: Calif. 1994, U.S. Dist. Ct. (so. dist.) Calif. 1994, U.S. Ct. Appeals (9th cir.) 1995. Lawyer San Diego Pub. Defender's Office, 1994-97, San Diego Dist. Atty.'s Office, 1997—. Mem. Law Review Calif. Western Law Sch. Mem. San Diego County Bar Assn. Roman Catholic. Office: San Diego Dist Atty 410 S Melrose Dr Ste 200 Vista CA 92083

PATTEN, BEBE HARRISON, minister, chancellor; b. Waverly, Tenn., Sept. 3, 1913; d. Newton Felix and Mattie Priscilla (Whitson) Harrison; m. Carl Thomas Patten, Oct. 23, 1935; children: Priscilla Carla and Bebe Rebecca (twins), Carl Thomas. D.D., McKinley-Roosevelt Coll., 1941; D.Litt., Temple Hall Coll. and Sem., 1943. Ordained to ministry Ministerial Assn. of Evangelism, 1935; evangelist in various cities of U.S., 1933-50; founder, pres. Christian Evang. Chs. Am., Inc., Oakland, Calif., 1944—, Patten Acad. Christian Edn., Oakland, 1944—, Patten Bible Coll., Oakland, 1944-83; chancellor Patten Coll., Oakland, 1983—; founder, pastor Christian Cathedral of Oakland, 1950—; held pvt. interviews with David Ben-Gurion, 1972, Menachim Begin, 1977, Yitzhak Shamir, 1991; condr. Sta. KUSW world-wide radio ministry, 70 countries around the world, 1989-90, Stas. WHRI and WWCR world coverage short wave, 1990—. Founder, condr.: radio program The Shepherd Hour, 1934—; daily TV, 1976—, nationwide telecast, 1979—; Author: Give Me Back My Soul, 1973; Editor: Trumpet Call, 1953—; composer 20 gospel and religious songs, 1945—. Mem. exec. bd. Bar-Ilan U. Assn., Israel, 1983; mem. global bd. trustees Bar-Ilan U., 1991. Recipient numerous awards including medallion Ministry of Religious Affairs, Israel, 1969; medal Govt. Press Office, Jerusalem, 1971; Christian honoree of yr. Jewish Nat. Fund of No. Calif., 1975; Hidden Heroine award San Francisco Bay coun. Girl Scouts U.S.A., 1976, Golden State award Who's Who Hist. Soc., 1988; Ben-Gurion medallion Ben-Gurion Rsch. Inst., 1977; Resolutions of Commendation, Calif. Senate Rules Com., 1978, 94, Disting. Leadership award Ch. of God Sch. of Theology, 1996; hon. fellow Bar-Ilan U., Israel, 1981; Dr. Bebe Patten Social Action chair established Bar-Ilan U., 1982. Mem. Am. Assn. for Higher Edn., Religious Edn. Assn., Am. Acad. Religion and Soc. Bibl. Lit., Zionist Orgn. Am., Am. Assn. Pres. of Ind. Colls. and Univs., Am. Jewish Hist. Soc., Am.-Isreal Pub. Affairs Com. Address: 2433 Coolidge Ave Oakland CA 94601-2630 *He that labors in any great or laudable undertaking has his fatigues first supported by hope, and afterwards rewarded by joy. To strive with difficulties, and to conquer them, is the highest human felicity. I am not afraid of tomorrow for I have seen yesterday and I love today.*

PATTEN, RICHARD E., personnel company owner; b. Seattle, May 17, 1953; s. Donald Wesley and Lorraine Louise (Kienholz) P.; m. Monica Rose Bourg, Mar. 20, 1976; children: Richard Douglas, Wesley Bourg, Melinda Rose. BA, U. Wash., 1976. Exec. v.p. Microfilm Svc. Co., Seattle, 1976-84, gen. mgr., 1985-87, chmn. bd., 1988-90; pres. Express Svcs. Temporary and Permanent Pers., Seattle, 1990—. Candidate for U.S. Ho. of Reps., 1982; deacon Bethany Bapt. Ch., Seattle, 1983-86; co-chmn. fin. com. Wash. State Billy Graham Crusade, 1990-91. Mem. Nat. Micrographics Assn. (pres. N.W. chpt. 1979-80, bd. dirs. 1978-79), Assn. Image and Info. Mgmt. (chmn. svc. co. 1987), Assn. Records Mgrs. and Adminstrs., Wash. Athletic Club, Rotary (bd. dirs. 1996—). Republican. Baptist. Home: 7012 NE 161st St Bothell WA 98011-4265 Office: Express Pers Svcs Ste 101 1201 4th Ave Seattle WA 98134-1531

PATTERSON, AGNES STARK, author; b. L.A., Mar. 27, 1930; d. Rudolph and Yolan (Fischer) Stark; m. Richard J. Patterson, Oct. 20, 1950 (dec. Jan. 1976); 1 child, Michael Patrick. Student, L.A. City Coll., 1948, Glendale (Calif.) Coll., 1985. Ins. underwriter Atlas Assurance cos., L.A., 1952-57, Cravens, Dargan Co., L.A., 1958-60, John topham & Sons, L.A., 1961-62, Planned Ins. Assocs., L.A., 1962-73; legal transcriber L.A., 1973-81; legal sec. Pacific Bell, L.A., 1981-94. Editor, biographer: Pacific Bell Dept. Newsletter, 1993-94; author: Romanian Rhapsody, 1984, 2d edit. 1994; contbr. short stories, poetry to profl. jours. Den mother Boy Scouts Am., L.A., 1957-60, den mother trainer, 1960-64; fundraiser United Way, Pacific telesis, L.A., 1986-89. Named Den Mother of the Yr., Boy Scouts Am., L.A., 1963, Award of Appreciation, United way, 1986. Mem. Am. Mensa. Democrat. Home and Office: 916 Dexter St Los Angeles CA 90042

PATTERSON, DANIEL WILLIAM, dentist; b. Minot, N.D., Aug. 12, 1948; s. Girdell William and Fern Lemay (Sullivan) P. DDS, Northwestern U., 1972; Alumnus degree (hon.), U. Colo., 1977; BS in Biology, U.N.Y., 1993; M in Healthcare, U. Denver, 1994. Cert. health industry orgn., ops. U.Denver, 1993, cert. gerontology, 1996. Dentist Dan L. Hansen, DDS, P.C., Lakewood, Colo., 1974-75; pvt. practice dentistry Littleton, Colo., 1975-88; clin. instr. dept. applied dentistry U. Colo., Denver, 1981-83, lectr., 1983, clin. asst. prof. depts. restorative and applied dentistry, 1989-91, dir. advanced dentistry program, 1989-90, asst. prof. clin. track dept. restorative dentistry, 1991—. Mem. editorial adv. panel Dental Econs. Jour., 1981; also articles. Active Chatfield Jaycees, Littleton, 1976-81; vocal soloist, mem. Denver Concert Chorale, 1978-82. Lt. USN, 1968-74. Fellow Acad. Gen. Dentistry (bd. eligible certifying bd. gen. dentistry 1991); mem. ADA, Met. Denver Dental Soc., Colo. Dental Assn. (Pres.'s Honor Roll 1982-84), Mensa, Sedalia Wild Game Club. Lutheran. Home: 6984 N Fargo Trl Littleton CO 80125-9270 Office: U Colo Health Scis Ctr Sch Dentistry Box C-284 4200 E 9th Ave Denver CO 80262-0284

PATTERSON, DONALD SCOTT, psychiatrist; b. Detroit, Jan. 4, 1916; s. Glenn Scott and Leola Catherine (Atkinson) P.; m. Jane Carrard Rodman Ketron, July 23, 1950. AB, U. Mich. Lit. Sci. & Arts Coll, 1937; MD, U. Mich., 1940. Diplomate Am. Bd. Psychiatry, Am. Bd. Forensic Psychiatry; qualified med. evaluator for State of Calif. Intern Kings County Hosp., Bklyn., 1940-41; resident Neuropsychiatric Inst., Ann Arbor, Mich., 1945-46, VA, Palo Alto, Calif., 1946-48; psychiatrist pvt. practice, Santa Barbara, Calif., 1948—; hon. staff mem. St. Francis Hosp., Santa Barbara, Santa Barbara Cottage Hosp., dept. chair, 1948-88; attending psychiatrist VA Regional Office, Santa Barbara, 1948-49; cons. Calif. Youth Authority Ventura Sch. for Girls, 1948-50, cons. adminstrv. law judge Office of Hearings and Appleas, Santa Barabra, 1984—; mem. med. panel-ct. psychiatrists Cos. of Santa Barbara Venture, 1949—; clin. dir. Santa Barbara Gen. Hosp., 1949-78. Lt. col. U.S. Army Med. Corps, 1941-46. Mem. Am. Psychiat. Assn. (life), So. Calif. Psychiatris Assn. (life), Am. Acad. Psychiatry & Law, Alpha Omega Alpha, Phi Kappa Phi. Home and office: 835 San Ysidro Ln Santa Barbara CA 93108-1324

PATTERSON, FRANCINE G. P., foundation administrator; b. Chgo., Feb. 13, 1947; d. Cecil H. and Frances L. (Spano) P. AB in Psychology, U. Ill., 1970; PhD in Devel. Psychology, Stanford U., 1979. Rsch. asst. U. Ill. Children's Rsch. Ctr., Urbana, 1969-70; pres., rsch. dir. The Gorilla Found., Woodside, Calif., 1976—; adj. rsch. assoc. dept. anthropology and ctr. anthrop. rsch. San Jose (Calif.) State U., 1982—; adj. assoc. prof. dept. psychology U. Santa Clara (Calif.), 1984—; bd. consultants Ctr. for Cross-Cultural Communications, Washington. Author: Koko's Kitten, 1985 (Tex. Bluebonnet award 1987), Koko's Story, 1987 (N.J. Libr. Assn. award 1990); co-author: The Education of Koko, 1981. Grantee for gorilla lang. rsch. Nat. Geog. Soc., 1976-83, 85; recipient Rolex award for enterprise Rolex, Geneva, 1978, Award for Outstanding Profl. Svc., Preservation of the Animal World Soc., 1986. Mem. Am. Soc. Primatologists, Am. Ednl. Rsch. Assn. Am. Assn. Zool. Parks and Aquariums, Am. Assn. Zookeepers, Animal Behavior Soc., Phi Beta Kappa. Office: The Gorilla Found PO Box 620530 Woodside CA 94062-0530

PATTERSON, JAMES, mayor; b. San Mateo, Calif., Feb. 18, 1948; m. Sharon LeTourneau, 1968; children: B.J., Jason, Lindsay. BA in Polit. Sci. summa cum laude, Calif. State U., Fresno, 1992. Radio broadcasting exec. Sta. KIRV-AM, Fresno, Calif., 1968—; mayor City of Fresno, 1993—. Chair San Joaquin River Conservancy; vice chair Fresno County Transp. Authority; bd. mem. Fresno City-County Consortium Agy.; chmn. NO on Measure H Com., 1989, Criminal Justice and Law Enforcement Commn., 1990-91; vice chmn. YES on Measure E Com., 1988; mem. Human Rels. Commn., City of Fresno, 1987-91; bd. dirs. Leadership Fresno Alumni Assn., 1989-91, Fresno County YFC/Campus Life, 1984-88. Mem. Fresno City and County C. of C. (chmn. local govt. affairs com. 1990-91, bd. dirs. FRESPAC 1990-91, city budget rev. com. 1989-91, privatization task force 1988-89, charter sect. 809 rev. task force 1987-88). Office: Office of the Mayor City Coun City Hall 2600 Fresno St Fresno CA 93721-3620*

PATTERSON, JAMES FRANKLYN, physics educator; b. Mountain View, Calif., May 28, 1970; s. Robert James and Carole Gertrude (Hudson) P. BS, Harvey Mudd Coll., 1992; MEd, U. LaVerne, 1996. Tchr. Harvard Westlake Sch., Studio City, Calif., 1994—. Home: 17933 Santa Rita St Encino CA 91316-3602 Office: Harvard Westlake Sch 3600 Coldwater Canyon Ave North Hollywood CA 91604-4043

PATTERSON, LLOYD CLIFFORD, psychiatrist; b. Toronto, Ont., Can., Jan. 16, 1917; came to U.S., 1942; s. William Henry and Florence May (Sonley) P.; m. Gloria May Patterson, Nov. 12, 1943; children: Diane Meisenheimer, Pamela DeBarr. MD, U. Western Ont., London, 1942. Diplomate Am. Bd. Psychiatry; cert. Am. Psychoanalytic Assn. Intern Hollywood Presybn. Hosp., L.A., 1942-43; fellow in intern medicine U. Calif. Hosp., San Francisco, 1943-44; resident in psychiatry Langley Porter Neuropsychiat. Inst., San Francisco, 1944-48; cons. psychiatrist student health U. Calif., Berkeley, 1960-70; assoc. clin. prof. U. Calif. Med. Sch., San Francisco, 1972—; dir. med. edn. Alta Bates Med. Ctr., Berkeley, 1988—; program chair Western Divisional Psychoanalytic meetings, San Francisco, 1966. Mem. East Bay Psychiat. Assn. (pres. 1962), No. Calif. Psychiat. Assn. (pres. 1968-69), San Francisco Psychoanalytic Soc. (pres. 1972-73), Am. Psychiat. Soc., Am. Psychoanalytic Soc., Calif. Med. Assn. (hosp. surveyor, mem. continuing med. edn. com. 1985-91, cons. CME com. 1992), Alameda Contra Costa Med. Assn. Home: 409 Cola Ballena Alameda CA 94501-3608 Office: 3021 Telegraph Ave Berkeley CA 94705-2013

PATTERSON, MARION LOUISE, photographer, educator; b. San Francisco, Apr. 24, 1933; d. Morrie Leslie and Esther Elizabeth (Parker) P. BA, Stanford U., 1955; MA, Calif. State U., San Francisco, 1970. Clk. Best's Studio (Ansel Adams Gallery), Yosemite, Calif., 1958-61; asst. to photography editor Sunset mag., Menlo Park, Calif., 1961-64; freelance photographer, Oaxaca, Mex., 1964-66; comm. cons. Projects to Advance Creative in Edn., San Mateo, Calif., 1966-68; instr. photography, chmn. dept. Foothill Coll., Los Altos Hills, Calif., 1968—; instr. U. Calif., Santa Cruz, 1984—. One woman shows include West German Embassy in the Hague, Bayreuth, Republic of Germany, Kasteel Hoensbroeck, Netherlands, Daxaca, Mex., San Francisco Mus. of Modern Art, Focus Gallery, San Francisco, Oakland Mus., Monterey County Mus., Stanford U., Ansel Adams Gallery, Yosemite, and others; exhibited in group shows MIT, George Eastman House, Polaroid Corp., Art in the Embassies, Ind. U., U. of Ala., Critics Choice Traveling Exhibit, New Light, New Directions, Reclaiming Paradise, and others; contbr. photographs and articles in books and magazines. Mem. Soc. for Photographic Edn.

PATTERSON, MARK JEROME, computer software designer; b. Inglewood, Calif., July 23, 1960; s. Jerry Lee Patterson and Robin Helen McCracken Steely; m. Jenny Anne Lynn, Dec. 31, 1995. Programmer Green & Assocs., L.A., 1985-87; systems analyst The Software Works, Glendale, Calif., 1987-90; programmer Snow Software, Clearwater, Fla., 1990; pres. Atomic Software, Altadena, Calif., 1990-94; mgr. KPMG Peat Marwick, Palo Alto, Calif., 1994—; design cons. Prestige Station, Inc., 1990-93, Petro-Can., Inc., Calgary, Alta., 1988-90. Author computer programs: Set of Dataflex Macros, 1990, Ultimate File Viewer, 1992, Data Communications and Client/Server Systems, 1993-97. Libertarian. Scientologist. Home: 814 N Mentor Ave Pasadena CA 91104

PATTERSON, PAUL EDWARD, minister; b. Columbus, Ohio, Sept. 10, 1946; s. George William and Janice Rae (Mueller) P. AA, Miami U., Oxford, Ohio, 1981; BS, SUNY, Albany, 1996. Ordained to ministry Unity Ch., 1991; cert. vocat. and elem. tchr., authority in delinquent youth and dysfunctional family. Victim's advocate, victim's awareness tchr. State of Calif., Calif. Youth Authority, 1985—; min. Unity Ch., Sonora, Calif., 1992; founder, min. Motherlode Cmty. Ch., Sonora, 1996, group leader inner child workshops Survivors of Sexual Abuse. Past bd. dirs. Parents United of Stanislaus County. Sgt. U.S. Army, 1966-69. Office: Motherlode Cmty Ch PO Box 4074 Sonora CA 95370

PATTERSON, RUSSELL ALFRED, business valuation consultant; b. Roslyn, N.Y., June 27, 1947; s. Thomas Russell and Sarah Marion (Roberts) P.; m. Joan Ellen McGlynn, Dec. 20, 1975; children: Thomas Russell, Edward Joseph. BS, The Citadel, 1969; MBA, NYU, 1975. Cert. bus. appraiser. Mgr. Arthur Young, N.Y.C., 1985; sr. cons. A.D. Little Valuation, Inc., Edison, N.J., 1984-85; prin. R.A. Patterson & Assocs., N.Y.C., 1983-84; mgr. W.R. Grace & Co., N.Y.C., 1970-82; dir. Deloitte & Touche (formerly Deloitte Haskins & Sells), N.Y.C., 1985-88; sr. mgr. in charge Deloitte & Touche (formerly Deloitte Haskins & Sells), L.A., 1988-91; prin. Fin. Valuation and Consulting, L.A., 1991—; exec. fellow Civil Aeronautics Bd., Washington, 1978-79. Author: Handbook of Strategic Planning, 1986, Know How to Sell Your Business, 1990. Chmn. Citizenship Budget Adv. Com. to Sch. Bd., West Islip, N.Y., 1980-83; committeeman Dem. Party Election Dist. #1, Islip, 1980-86; pres., v.p. N.Y. Citadel Club, Inc., 1982-84. 1st lt. USAR, 1970. Mem. Assn. of Citadel Men (life), The Bridgadier Club (bd. dirs. 1983-86), Am. Soc. Appraisers (sr.), Inst. of Bus. Appraisers (cert.). Episcopalian. Home: 2050 Sunnybank Dr La Canada Flintridge CA 91011-1355 Office: Fin Valuation and Consulting 333 S Grand Ave Los Angeles CA 90071-1504

PATTERSON, TOM C., state legislator. Senator Ariz. State, 1989—. Office: 4811 E Camelhead Dr Phoenix AZ 85018

PATTIE, STEVEN NORRIS, advertising executive, artist, author; b. Alexandria, Va., Aug. 26, 1952; s. Frank Norris and Mary Jane (Shunk) P.; m. Sage Lenhart, Jan. 13, 1980; children: Nathan Norris, Lucas Ohio. Student, Stanford U.; BA, Westmont Coll., 1974; MDiv, Fuller Theol. Sem., 1978. Adminstr., tchg. fellow Carmen Deo Ctr. Christian Study, Santa Barbara, Calif., 1978-80; area dir. Fuller Extended Edn., Santa Barbara, 1978-83; author, visual artist Poppyfields Studio, Pleasanton, Calif., 1980—; supr. cultural arts divsn. City of San Buenaventura Pks. and Recreation, Ventura, Calif., 1982-83; asst. to pres. Fuller Theol. Sem., Pasadena, Calif., 1983-87; sr. acct. exec. Russ Reid Co., Pasadena, 1987-93, 94—; pres. New Coll. Berkeley, Calif., 1993-94. Author: For Fathers of Sons, 1995; mem. editl. bd. La Paz Mag., 1990—; contbg. articles, essays, poems and mags.; exhbns. include Arlington Gallery, Santa Barbara, Nanny Goat Hill Gallery, San Francisco, Faulkner Gallery, Santa Barbara, Springville (Utah) Mus. Art, Canton (China) Inst. Art, Santa Barbara Arts Festival, Good Earth Restaurants, Santa Barbara, Santa Cruz Art League, Arroyo Arts Collective, L.A., Gallery 52, Pasadena, Casillas, Compean and Williams, Inc., L.A., Bade Mus., Berkeley, Kerrwood Gallery, Santa Barbara, Melrose Village Gallery, West Hollywood, Peconic Gallery, N.Y.C., Weingart Galleries, L.A., Boise (Idaho) State Univ. Galleries, City of L.A. Cultural Affairs Dept., Santa Barbara Mus. Nat. History, Dirs. Guild Am., L.A., Hole in the Wall Gallery, West Hollywood, San Diego Art Inst., First St. Gallery, Danville, Calif. Recipient Fine Arts award Bank Am., 1970, Program of Yr. award Calif. Dept. Parks & Recreation, 1983, Gold Medal Echo award Direct Mktg. Assn., 1992, 1st Place award Santa Barbara Art Assn., 1983, 1st Place award Pleasanton Art Assn., 1994. Mem. L.A. Art Assn., Christians in the Visual Arts, Arroyo Arts Collective, Nat. Soc. Fund Raising Execs., Omicron Delta Kappa. Democrat. Office: Russ Reid Co 2 N Lake Ave Ste 600 Pasadena CA 91101-1868

PATTON, ANNE JEWELL, elementary school counselor; b. New Haven, Nov. 22, 1941; d. Dominic A. and Immaculata M. (Lucarelli) Messina; m. John Beacham Patton, Aug. 24, 1966; children: John Alan, Michele Anne, Elisabeth Ellen. BS in Edn., So. Conn. State U., 1964; MA in Edn., No. Ariz. U., 1967; M. Counseling Edn., Idaho State U., 1994; postgrad., U. Ariz., 1966-69. Lic. profl. counselor, Idaho; nat. cert. counselor. Tchr. grade 3 Branford (Conn.) Sch. Dist., 1964-65; tchr. grades 3-6 Amphitheater Pub. Schs., Tucson, 1966-69; tchr. grade 6 Sierra Sands Sch. Dist., Ridgecrest, Calif., 1979-80; tchr. grade 1 Holy Rosary Sch., Idaho Falls, Idaho, 1982-94; counselor Blackfoot (Idaho) Sch. Dist., 1994—; asst. prin. Holy Rosary Sch., Idaho Falls, 1988-89, dept. chair, 1989-94. Vol. Girl Scouts Am., Idaho Falls, 1980—, Boy Scouts Am., Idaho Falls, 1980—, Civil Air Patrol, Idaho Falls, 1988—. Mem. Assn. for Play Therapy, Am. Counseling Assn., Am. Sch. Counselor Assn., Idaho Sch. Counselor Assn., Idaho Counseling Assn., Idaho Soc. Individual Psychology. Office: Blackfoot Sch Dist 55 270 Bridge St Blackfoot ID 83221

PATTON, MARILYN JANICE, state agency administrator. BS, Skidmore Coll., 1977; MSW, SUNY, Albany, 1982. Cert. social worker, Wyo. Patient support svcs. coord. Warren Washington Cmty. Mental Health Ctr., 1977-79; adminstrv. asst. Glens Falls Hosp. Human Resource Ctr., 1979-80; edn!. cons., staff trainer Bur. Tng. and Resource Devel., N.Y.C., 1979-83; pvt. practice Albany, N.Y., 1982-89; outpatient psychotherapist S.W. Counseling, Rock Springs, Wyo., 1989-91; mental health program cons. divsn. behavioral health State of Wyo., Cheyenne, Wyo., 1991-95; adminstr. divsn. behavioral health cmty. programs State of Wyo., Cheyenne, 1995—; exec. dir. Oasis, Inc., Saratoga Springs, N.Y., 1983-86; cons., facilitator displaced homemaker program N.Y.S. Dept. Labor, 1986-87; ptnr. A League Enterprises, Albany, 1985-87; program mgr. S.W. Counseling, Rock Springs, 1990-91; Wyo. mental health negotiating team State of Wyo., 1994; adj. faculty Hudson Valley C.C., 1987-89, Adirondack C.C., 1979-89, Skidmore Coll., 1982-89; field instr. SUNY, Albany, 1985-88, Skidmore Coll., 1985-86. Cmty. funding bd. Honding Our Own, Inc., 1987. Ford Found. scholar Skidmore Coll., 1974-77. Mem. NASW (S.E. rep. Wyo. bd. dirs. 1994-95). Office: Divsn Behavioral Health Hathaway Bldg 4th Fl Cheyenne WY 82002

PATTON, STUART, biochemist, educator; b. Ebenezer, N.Y., Nov. 2, 1920; s. George and Ina (Neher) P.; m. Colleen Cecelia Lavelle, May 17, 1945; children—John, Richard, Gail, Thomas, Mary Catherine, Patricia, Joseph. B.S., Pa. State U., 1943; M.S., Ohio State U., 1947, Ph.D., 1948. Chemist Borden Co., 1943-44; research fellow Ohio State U., Columbus, 1946-48; mem. faculty Pa. State U., University Park, 1949-80, prof., 1959-80; Evan Pugh rsch. prof. agr. Pa. State U., 1966-80; adj. prof. neurosci. Sch. Medicine U. Calif., San Diego, 1981—; vis. scientist Scripps Instn. Oceanography; cons. in field, 1950—. Author: (with Robert Jenness) Principles of Dairy Chemistry, 1959, (with Robert G. Jensen) Biomedical Aspects of Lactation, 1975. Served to lt. (j.g.) USNR, 1944-46. Recipient Borden award chemistry milk Am. Chem. Soc., 1957, Agrl. and Food Chemistry award, 1975; Alexander von Humboldt sr. scientist award, 1981, Macy-Gyorgy award Internat. Soc. for Rsch. on Human Milk and Lactation, 1997. Mem. Am. Chem. Soc., Am. Dairy Assn., Am. Soc. Biochemistry and Molecular Biology, Am. Soc. Cell Biology. Home: 6208 Avenida Cresta La Jolla CA 92037-6510 Office: U Calif San Diego Ctr Molecular Genetics 0634-J La Jolla CA 92093

PAUL, BENJAMIN DAVID, anthropologist, educator; b. N.Y.C., Jan. 25, 1911; s. Phillip and Esther (Kranz) P.; m. Lois Fleischman, Jan. 4, 1936; children: Robert Allen, Janice Carol. Student, U. Wis., 1928-29; AB, U. Chgo., 1938, PhD in Anthropology, 1942. Lectr., rsch. dir. Yale U., 1942-44; community orgn. expert Inter-Am. Ednl. Found., 1946; from lectr. to assoc. prof. anthropology Harvard U., 1946-62, dir. social sci. program Sch. Pub. Health, 1951-62; prof. anthropology Stanford (Calif.) U., 1963—, chmn. dept., 1967-71, dir. program in medicine and behavioral sci., 1963-70; cons. NIH, 1957—. Editor: Health, Culture and Community: Case Studies of Public Reactions to Health Programs, 1955, Changing Marriage Patterns in a Highland Guatemalan Community, 1963, The Maya Midwife as Sacred Professional, 1975, Mayan Migrants in Guatemala City, 1981, The Operation of a Death Squad in San Pedro la Laguna, 1988. 2d lt. AUS, 1944-46. Travelling fellow Social Sci. Rsch. Coun., 1940-41, Ctr. Advanced Study Behavioral Scis. fellow, 1962-63. Mem. Am. Anthropol. Assn. (Disting. Svc. award 1994), Phi Beta Kappa, Sigma Xi. Home: 622 Salvatierra St Palo Alto CA 94305-8538 Office: Stanford U Dept Anthropology Stanford CA 94305

PAUL, DON, writer, musician; b. Amherst, N.S., Can., July 14, 1950; s. Paul Murphy and Elizabeth Ford (Cannon) Hulme. Student, Stanford U., 1971-72. Author: (poems) AmeriModern, 1982, (novel) Good Intentions, 1984; songwriter, prodr.: We Could Use the Rain, 1991; prodr.: America Fears the Drum, 1992. Stegner Creative Writing fellow, 1971-72; World's Best 50-Kilometer run, U.S. Road Running Info. Ctr., Santa Barbara, Calif., 1982-94. Mem. Track and Field Writers Assn. Office: PO Box 33-0178 San Francisco CA 94133

PAUL, FLORENCE JOSEPH, writer; b. N.Y.C.; d. Solomon and Stella (Kass) Joseph; m. Les Baer Paul, Nov. 4, 1939; children: Glenn Scott Paul, Kenneth Dean Paul. Student, Rancho Santiago Coll., Santa Ana, Calif. Clk. N.Y. State Unemployment Svc., N.Y.C., 1962—; writer, 1976—. Author: A Dream Betrayed, 1995, He Never Pulled the Trigger, 1996; contbr. over 50 mag. articles. Vol. Children's Hosp., 1967—; active one mile pk. constrn. Bd. Supt. Recipient 4 certs. Calif. Press Women, 1990, 95, 96, 97, bronze plaque for constrn. one mile pk. Mem. New Horizons, Hadassah (v.p. edn.). Home: 13222 Eton Pl Santa Ana CA 92705-2148

PAUL, PAULA GRIFFITH, writer; b. Lubbock County, Tex., July 31, 1938; d. George Franklin and Sarah Julia (Bailey) Griffith; m. W. Kenneth Paul, May 31, 1959; children: Timothy Shain, Kristen Sarah. BA in Journalism, Ea. N.Mex. U., 1960. Reporter Morton (Tex.) Tribune, 1957-58, Portales (N.Mex.) News Tribune, 1960-61, Albuquerque Tribune, 1961-63, 80-87; substitute tchr. Albuquerque pub. schs. Author: Inn of the Clowns, 1976, The Wail of La Llorona, 1977, Geronimo Chino, 1980, You Can Hear A Magpie Smile, 1980, Dance With Me, Gods, 1982, Sarah, Sissy Weed, And The Ships of the Desert, 1985, Silent Partner, 1986, Last Summer I Got In Trouble, 1987, Night Of The Jaguar, 1987, Lady Of the Shadows, 1992, The Mistress At Blackwater, 1993, Sweet Ivy's Gold, 1993, A Bad Girl's Money, 1993; numerous free-lance mag. articles on bus., health, family interest, environment, religion and people. Recipient Most Outstanding Alumni award Ea. N.Mex. U., 1988, N.Mex. Zia award for fiction, 1984, 87, Tex. Inst. of Letters award for children's lit., 1987, Nat. Edn. Writers First Place award, 1985, N.Mex. Med. Soc. award for excellence in med. journalism, 1984, AP/Mng. Editors' award for feature writing, 1984, N.Mex. Press Assn. Cmty. Svc. award for investigative reporting, 1981, others. Mem. Nat. Authors Guild, S.W. Writers Workshop, N.Mex. Assn. Press Women (awards for feature writing and news writing 1981-87), Na.t Assn. Press Women (Award for Book-length fiction 1982). Democrat. Presbyterian.

PAUL, VIRGINIA O., writer, administrator; b. Easton, Wash., Mar. 18, 1917; d. Clarence and Anne Marie (Streigel) Otto; m. Philip Henry Paul, May 19, 1940 (dec. Oct. 1992); children: Philip O., J. Stephen, Joseph H., Jeananne. Diploma in efficiency, Peterson's Tech. Sch., 1938. State office sec. Wash. Farm Bur. Fed., Ellensburg, 1957-62, Wash. Cattlemen's Assn., Ellensburg, 1962-65; state sec.-treas., dir. comm. Wash. State Beef Coun., Ellensburg, 1962-69; exec. sec. Wash. State Beef Commn., Ellensburg, 1969-80; spkr. various cities in the West, 1950-85; state dir. edn., promotion and mktg. Wash. Beef Coun. and Commn., Ellensburg, 1962-80; radio program Wash. radio stas., 1963-80; exec. dir. and news photo features United Way Kittitas County, Ellensburg, 1968-69. Author: This was Cattle Ranching, 1973, This was Sheep Ranching, 1976, The Homestead Cookbook, 1976, The History of Ferrers and their Connections in England and Colonial America, Vol. 1, 1991, Vol. 2, 1996, Standing by the Side of Your Arm: An Illustrated History of the City of Kittitas, Washington, A Western Railroad Cow Town, 1996. Mem. Wash. State Farm Bur. Fedn., Ellensburg, 1950-75, Kittitas County Farm Bur., Ellensburg, 1950-75. Recipient 1st Pl. non-fiction Nat. Fedn. Press Women, 1974, Women of Achievement award Wash. State Press Assn., 1979, honorarium Wash. State U., 1976, Outstanding Svc. award Home and Family Life Tchrs., 1980, Cmty. Svc. award Kittitas County Centennial Com., 1983. Mem. Nat. Cattlewomen, Wash. State Cattlewomen (Cattlewoman of the Yr. 1990), Kittitas County Cattlewomen, Kittitas County Genealogical Soc. (v.p. 1982, publicity chmn. 1984-95, editor Kittitas Kinfolk 1988-95). Home: 109 N Anderson St Ellensburg WA 98926

PAULES, PAUL MICHAEL, city manager; b. Oakland, Calif., June 22, 1956; m. Elena Angela De Jesus, Oct., 1980; children: Gregory David, Kathleen Diane. BA in Polit. Sci., Calif. State U., Fullerton, 1978; MPA, U. So. Calif., 1980. Adminstrv. intern City of Anaheim, Calif., 1977; adminstrv. aide City of La Mirada, Calif., 1978; asst. to city mgr. City of Stanton, Calif., 1978-81; asst. city mgr. Alhambra, Calif., 1991—; city mgr. City of San Gabriel, Calif., 1992—. Bd. dirs. Wysong Pla. Sr. Citizen Housing Complex; regional campaign coord. United Way; active in Am. Youth Soccer, Immaculate Conception Ch. and Sch. Mem. Internat. City/County Mgmt. Assn. (internat. affairs com. 1990-93, U.S. rep. to 1990 mgmt. exchange with Australia; scholarship Pacific Rim Symposium, Fletcher Bowron award), San Gabriel Valley City Mgrs. Assn., Assn. Cities Transp. Com., Mcpl. Mgmt. Assts. of So. Calif. (past chmn.) West Snn Gabriel Valley Planning Coun. Office: City of San Gabriel 532 W Mission Dr San Gabriel CA 91776-1202

PAULEY, RICHARD HEIM, real estate counselor; b. Cleve., Dec. 14, 1932; s. Kenneth H. and Romaine (Heim) P.; m. Jan E. Minnick, Oct. 26, 1957; children: Tyler Kent, Elysa Pauley Del Guercio. BA in Polit. Sci., Stanford U., 1954; postgrad. U. So. Calif., 1956-57. Sr. cons. Coldwell Banker & Co., Newport Beach, Calif., 1963-77; owner Richard H. Pauley Co., Investment Realtors, Newport Beach, and Tustin, Calif., 1977—; sr. mktg. exec. The Seeley Co., Irvine, Calif., 1986-89. Bd. dirs. Orange Coast YMCA, 1973-78. Capt. USAFR, 1965. Recipient Cert. of Appreciation City of Newport Beach, 1975-76; Disting. Svc. award Rehab. Inst. Orange County, 1973. Mem. Am. Soc. Real Estate Counselors (chmn. internat. activities com.), Internat. Real Estate Fedn., Calif. Assn. Realtors, Nat. Assn. Realtors, SAR, The Ctr. Club (bd. govs., Costa Mesa, Calif.), Stanford Club Orange County (past pres.), Lambda Alpha Internat. Hon. Real Estate Soc. (bd. dirs. Orange County chpt.), Beta Theta Pi, Phi Delta Phi. Republican. Home: 22 Morning Sun Irvine CA 92612-3715 Office: 100 Pauley Bldg 17371 Irvine Blvd Tustin CA 92780-3045

PAULSEN, RICHARD WALLACE, counselor; b. Blue Island, Ill., Aug. 9, 1945; s. Richard W. and Betty L. (Frobish) P.; m. Mildred Baker Ewoldt, July 16, 1964 (dec. Jan. 1977); children: Kristen Irene, David, John, Clair O'Neil. BS, U. Nev., 1972, MBA, 1980; postgrad., Whitworth Coll., Spokane, Wash., 1995—. Cert. data processor; registered counselor, Wash. Programmer, engr. State of Nev., Carson City, 1964-74; 2nd v.p. Continental Bank, Chgo., 1974-81; sr. v.p. Wells Fargo Bank, San Francisco, 1981-84; dir., COO, exec. v.p. First Interstate Svcs., Torrance, Calif., 1985-90; founder, owner Whimsy Wear, Carson City, 1989-95; dir., CEO, pres. Recovery Technologies, Spokane, Wash., 1994; dir. Praxis Internat., Framingham, Mass., 1988-94; co-founder, counselor Survivor Support Svcs., Spokane, 1995—; vice chmn. City Gate Inner City Ministry, Spokane, 1995-96; mem. steering com. Workplace Connection, Spokane, 1995-96; mem. adv. bd. Inner City Juvenile Ministries, Spokane, 1995-96; mem. governing bd. Garland Ave. Alliance Ch., Spokane, 1996; guest spkr. Calif. Psychol. Assn., San Diego, 1995. Bd. trustees Athenian Sch., Danville, Calif., 1982-83, Avery Coonley Sch., Downers Grove, Ill., 1980-81. Recipient Outstanding Grad. award State of Nev., Carson City, 1969. Mem. ACA, Internat. Soc. for Study of Dissociation, Am. Assn. Christian Counselors, Christian Soc. for Healing Dissociative Disorders, Assn. for Spiritual, Ethical and Religious Values in Counseling, Spokane County Domestic Violence Consortium. Office: Survivor Support Svcs PO Box 10657 Spokane WA 99209

PAULSEN, SUSAN STEENBAKKERS, counselor; b. Stanford, Calif., Sept. 17, 1952; m. Wim Steenbakkers, Apr. 29, 1972 (div. July 1986); children: Trevor, Jon-Paul, Anneke; m. Richard W. Paulsen, Aug. 15, 1992. Student, Foothill Jr. Coll., Los Altos Hills, Calif., 1970-72, Meadows Inst., Wickenburg, Ariz., 1996. Registered counselor, Wash. Camp hostess Stanford Sierra Camp, Fallen Leaf Lake, Calif., 1982-85; real estate agt. Coldwell Banker, Minden, Nev., 1987-90; nat. mktg. dir. Whimsy Wear, Carson City, Nev., 1990-95; co-founder, counselor Survivor Support Svcs., Spokane, Wash., 1995—; mem. cmty. mission outreach Missions Com. Garland Ave Alliance Ch., Spokane, 1995; mem. svc. com. Spokane County Domestic Violence Consortium, 1995. Athlete's rep. U.S. Olympic Com., Lake Placid, N.Y., 1971. Jr. nat. champion U.S. Synchronized Assn., 1968-69, sr. nat. champion, 1970, 71, champion synchronized swimming World Invitational, Osaka, Japan, 1970, Pan Am. Games, Cali, Columbia, 1971. Mem. ACA, Internat. Soc. for Study of Dissociation, Am. Assn. Christian Counselors, Christian Soc. for Healing of Dissociative Disorders, Assn. for Specialists in Group Work, Spokane County Domestic Violence Consortium. Office: Survivor Support Svcs PO Box 10657 Spokane WA 99209

PAULSEN, VIVIAN, magazine editor; b. Salt Lake City, May 10, 1942; d. Paul Herman and Martha Oline (Blattman) P. B.A., Brigham Young U., 1964, postgrad., 1965; postgrad., U. Grenoble, France, 1966. Cert. tchr., Utah. Tchr. French Granite Sch. Dist., Salt Lake City, 1966-67; assoc. editor New Era mag., Salt Lake City, 1970-82; mng. editor Friend mag., Salt Lake City, 1982—. Am. Field Service scholar, 1959; grad. fellow Brigham Young U., 1964-66. Mem. Soc. Children's Book Writers. Republican. Mem. Ch. of Jesus Christ of Latter-day Saints. Office: The Friend 50 E North Temple Salt Lake City UT 84150-0002*

PAULSON, DENNIS ROY, museum director, biology educator, curator; b. Chgo., 1937. BS in Zoology, U. Miami, 1958, PhD in Zoology, 1966. Asst. curator vertebrate rsch. collection U. Miami, Fla., 1954-64; instr. zoology U. N.C., Chapel Hill, 1964-65, USPHS fellow, 1966; rsch. assoc. dept. zoology U. Wash., Seattle, 1966-69, 74-76, asst. prof., 1969-74, affiliate curator vertebrates Burke Mus., 1976-82, acting curator zoology, 1982-83, affiliate curator birds, 1983—; dir. Slater Mus. Natural History, instr. biology dept. U. Puget Sound, Tacoma, 1990—; instr. Orgn. for Tropical Studies, U. Costa Rica, 1967, 69, 70, 75; vis. instr. Evergreen State Coll., 1976-77; resource assoc. Jones & Jones, archs., landscape archs., planners, Seattle, 1976-89, Inst. for Field Ornithology, U. Maine, Machias, 1988, Resource Inst., Seattle, 1984-90, Seattle Audubon Soc., 1991—, Nat. Audubon Soc. Camp, Maine, 1993, also others; field experience on all continents. Author: Exotic Birds, 1989, Shorebirds of the Pacific Northwest, 1993, (with others) A Guide to Bird Finding in Washington, 1991; editor Wash. Birds, 1988-92; mem. editl. bd. Western Birds and Odonatologica; contbr. articles to sci. jours., also popular pubs. Rsch. grantee NSF, 1970, 72-74, Burke Mus. Modern Vertebrates Fund, 1989. Mem. Am. Ornithologists Union, Cooper Ornithol. Soc., Wilson Ornithol. Soc., Assn. Field Ornithologists, Western Field Ornithologists, Wash. Ornithol. Soc., Am. Birding Assn., Soc. Internat. Odonatologica, Dragonfly Soc. Ams. Home: 1724 NE 98th St Seattle WA 98115-2327 Office: U Puget Sound Slater Mus Natural His Tacoma WA 98416

PAULSON, LARRY A., protective services official. Chief of police Boise. Office: 7200 Barrister Dr Boise ID 83704

PAULSON, RICHARD JOHN, obstetrician, gynecologist, educator; b. Prague, Czech Republic, Feb. 2, 1955; came to U.S., 1966, naturalized citizen, 1972.; m. Lorraine M. Cummings, Oct. 11, 1987; children: Jessica, Jennifer, Philip, Erika, Josef. BS in Physics magna cum laude, UCLA, 1976, MD, 1980; postdoctoral study Sch. Medicine, U. So. Calif., 1992—. Diplomate Am. Bd. Ob-Gyn. Rotating intern Harbor-UCLA Med. Ctr., Torrance, 1980-81, resident in ob-gyn., 1981-84; clin. rsch. fellow dept. ob-gyn. Los Angeles County/U. So. Calif. Med. Ctr., L.A., 1984-86, mem. staff, 1984—; clin. instr. ob-gyn. Sch. Medicine U. So. Calif., L.A., 1984-86, asst. prof., 1986-91, assoc. prof., 1991-96, prof., 1996—; affiliate staff mem. Calif. Med. Ctr., L.A., 1986—; staff mem. L.A. Clin. & U. So. Calif. Med. Ctr., 1986—, dir. clin. infertility program, 1986—; chief divsn. reproductive endocrinology and infertility Sch. Medicine U. So. Calif., L.A., 1995—; vis. prof. in vitro fertilization lecture series Clinica Kennedy, Guayaquil, Ecuador, 1980; presenter at numerous profl. confs., symposia and grand rounds. Co-editor Infertility, Contraception and Reproductive Endocrinology, 4th edit., 1996; contbr. chpt. to Management of Common Problems in Obstetrics and Gynecology, 2nd. edit., 1988, 3rd edit., 1994, Infertility, Contraception and Reproductive Endocrinology, 1991; co-author 10 book chpts.; contbr. or co-contbr. over 100 articles to sci. jours.; mem. editl. bd. Jour. of Assisted Reprodn. and Genetics, Jour. Soc. for Gynecologic Investigation; mem. ad hoc editl. bd. Fertility and Sterility, Am. Jour. Ob-Gyn., Jour. of AMA, Contraception, Am. Jour Reproductive Immunology, others. Co-recipient Wyeth award 1985, recipient, 1989; co-recipient Serono award, 1991, 92, 93, Poster award 1994; rsch. grantee Ortho Pharm. Corp., 1986-87, Tap Pharmas., 1989-91, Irvine Sci., 1990-91, Syntex, 1990-92, Serono, 1992-93. Fellow ACOG (mem. PROLOG task force for reproductive endocrinology 1993), L.A. Obsetrical and Gynecologic Soc.; mem. Pacific Coast Fertility Soc. (bd. dirs. 1992—), Am. Fertility Soc., Soc. Reproductive Surgeons, Soc. for Assisted Reproductive Tech., Soc. Reproductive Endocrinologists, Endocrine Soc. Office: Womens Hosp 1240 N Mission Rd Rm 1M2 Los Angeles CA 90033-1078

PAULSON-EHRHARDT, PATRICIA HELEN, laboratory administrator; b. Moses Lake, Wash., June 10, 1956; d. Luther Roanoke and Helen Jane (Baird) Paulson; m. Terry Lee Ehrhardt, Mar. 12, 1983. Student, Pacific Luth. U., 1974-76; BS in Med. Tech., U. Wash., 1976; BS in Biology, MS in Biology, Eastern Wash. U., 1982. Med. technologist Samaritan Hosp., Moses Lake, 1979-81; lab. supr. Moses Lake Clinic, Kalispell (Mont.) Regional Hosp., 1982-88; med. technologist Kalispell Regional Hosp., 1987; account exec. Pathology Assocs. Med. Lab., Spokane, Wash., 1988—; mem. med. lab. tech. adv. com. Wenatchee (Wash.) Valley Coll., 1984-85, chmn., 1985-86; spkr. in field. Mem. Flathead Valley Community Band, 1987-90. Mem. Am. Soc. Clin. Lab. Scientists, Clin. Lab. Mgmt. Assn. (pres. Inland

N.W. chpt. 1993-94, bd. dirs. 1994-95), Am. Soc. Clin. Pathologists (cert.), Pan Players Flute Soc., Flathead Tennis Assn., Sigma Xi, Kappa Delta (pledge class pres. 1976). Republican. Lutheran. Home: 26 Cub Dr Great Falls MT 59404-6425

PAULUS, NORMA JEAN PETERSEN, lawyer, state school system administrator; b. Belgrade, Nebr., Mar. 13, 1933; d. Paul Emil and Ella Marie (Hellbusch) Petersen; LL.B., Willamette Law Sch., 1962; LL.D., Linfield Coll., 1985; LittD (hon.), Whitman Coll., 1990; LHD (hon.), Lewis & Clark Coll., 1996; m. William G. Paulus, Aug. 16, 1958; children: Elizabeth, William Frederick. Sec. to Harney County Dist. Atty., 1950-53; legal sec., Salem, Oreg., 1953-55; sec. to chief justice Oreg. Supreme Ct., 1955-61; admitted to Oreg. bar, 1962; of counsel Paulus and Callaghan, Salem, mem. Oreg. Ho. of Reps., 1971-77; sec. state State of Oreg., Salem, 1977-85; of counsel firm Paulus, Rhoten & Lien, 1985-86; supt. pub. instrn. State of Oreg., 1990—; Oreg. exec. bd. US West, 1985—; adj. prof. Willamette U. Grad. Sch, 1985; mem. N.W. Power Planning Com., 1986-89. Fellow Eagleton Inst. Politics, 1971; mem. Pacific NW Power Planning Council, 1987-89; adv. com. Defense Adv. Com. for Women in the Service, 1986, Nat. Trust for Hist. Preservation, 1988—; trustee Willamette U., 1978—; bd. dirs. Benedictine Found. of Oreg., 1980—, Oreg. Grade. Instn. Sci. and Tech., 1985—, Mid Willamette Valley coun. Camp Fire Girls, 1985-87, Edn. Commn. States, 1991—, Coun. Chief State Sch. Officers, 1995—, Nat. Assessment Governing Bd., 1996—; overseer Whitman Coll., 1985—; bd. cons. Goodwill Industries of Oreg.; mem. Salem Human Relations Commn., 1967-70, Marion-Polk Boundary Commn., 1970-71; mem. Presdl. Commn. to Monitor Philippines Election, 1986, Nat. Assessment Governing Bd. .Recipient Distinguished Service award City of Salem, 1971, LWV, 1995; Path Breaker award Oreg. Women's Polit. Caucus, 1976; named One of 10 Women of Future, Ladies Home Jour., 1979. Woman of Yr., Oreg. Inst Managerial and Profl. Women, 1982, Oreg. Women Lawyers, 1982, Woman Who Made a Difference award Nat. Women's Forum, 1985. Mem. Oreg. State Bar, Nat. Order Women Legislators, Women Execs. in State Govt., Women's Polit. Caucus Bus. and Profl. Women's Club (Golden Torch award 1971), Zonta Internat., Delta Kappa Gamma.

PAUP, MARTIN ARNOLD, real estate and securities investor; b. Seattle, Aug. 30, 1930; s. Clarence Jacob and Emaline Ethel (Lodestein) P.; m. Mary Jean Iske, Apr. 4, 1959; children: Barbara Ann Paup Soriano, Jennifer Marie, Elizabeth Paup Gail. BS, U. Wash., 1952. Indsl. engr. Boeing Airplane Co., Seattle, 1954-60; owner Coopers Unfinished Furniture, Seattle, 1960-63; claims rep. Unigard Ins., Seattle, 1963-66; asst. benefits mgr. Equitable Life Assurance, Seattle, 1966-85; owner Paup Ventures, Seattle, 1974--, Paup Investment Co., Seattle, 1963--, Ella Paup Properties, Seattle, 1963--. Bd. dirs. Denny Regrade Property Owners' Assn., Seattle, Denny Regrade Bus. Assn., Seattle, First Ave. Assn., Seattle. Seattle Dept. Community Devel. grantee, 1980. Mem. Greenwood C. of C., Seattle Opera Guild. Democrat. Roman Catholic. Home: 2021 1st Ave Ste 4G Seattle WA 98121-2135 Office: Paup Co 2021 1st Ave # 4G Seattle WA 98121-2135

PAUPP, TERRENCE EDWARD, legal research associate, educator; b. Joliet, Ill., Aug. 10, 1952; s. Edward Theodore and Mary Alice (Combs) P. BA in Social Scis., San Diego State U., 1974; ThM, Luth. Sch. Theology, 1978; JD, U. San Diego, 1990. Instr. philosophy San Diego City Coll., 1983-86, Southwestern Coll., Chula Vista, Calif., 1980-83; law clerk Sch. Law U. San Diego, 1987-88; law clerk Office of Atty. Gen., San Diego, 1988-89; rsch. assoc. Frank & Milchen, San Diego, 1989, Dougherty & Hildre, San Diego, 1990-95; sr. rsch.-assoc. Inst. for Ctrl. and Ea. European Studies, San Diego State U., 1996—; cons. Cmty. Reinvestment Act, San Diego, 1993-95; sr. rsch. assoc. Inst. Ctrl. and Ea. European Studies San Diego State U., 1994-95. Contbr. articles to law jours. Cons. Neighborhood House 5th Ave., 1994-95, Bethel Baptist Ch., 1994-95, PBS Frontline documentary The Nicotine Wars, 1994. Mem. ATLA, N.Y. Acad. Scis. Democrat. Lutheran. Office: San Diego State University Inst Ctrl and Ea Europ Stud 4430 North Ave Apt 9 San Diego CA 92116-3941

PAURA, CATHERINE, marketing professional. With Louis Harris Orgn., N.Y.C., 1973-77; with Nat. Rsch. Group Inc., 1977—, now pres. Office: Nat Research Group Inc 5900 Wilshire Blvd Los Angeles CA 90036-5013*

PAVA, ESTHER SHUB, artist, educator; b. Hartford, Conn., June 29, 1921; d. Jacob H. and Rose (Rietkop) Shub; m. Jacob Pava, June 16, 1946; children: David Lauren, Jonathan Michael, Daniel Seth, Nathaniel Alexander. BFA, R.I. Sch. of Design, 1944; MA, San Francisco State U., 1971. Artist New Eng. Roto Engraving Co., Holyoke, Mass., 1944-46, Wyckoff Advt. Agy., San Francisco, 1947-48; tchr. San Francisco Unified Sch. Dist., 1963-66, Laguna Salada Sch. Dist., Pacifica, Calif., 1966-83; artist, educator Belmont, Calif., 1983—; tchr. pvt. students Manor House, Belmont, Caif. Recipient numerous awards for artwork. Mem. Nat. League Am. Pen Women, Burlingame Art Soc. (pres. 1983-84), Thirty and One Artists (pres. 1992-93), Soc. Western Artists (signature mem. and juror), Calif. Watercolor Assn., others. Home: 2318 Hastings Dr Belmont CA 94002-3318 Studio: Manor House 1219 Ralston Ave Belmont CA 94002-1902

PAVLIK, MICHAEL, management consultant; b. Louisville, Dec. 1, 1940; s. George Michael and Isabelle (Travis) P.; m. Mary Ann Albenze, Dec. 16, 1964 (div. Dec. 1975); 1 child, Dominick; m. Julie Faye Smith, June 25, 1977; children: Marisa, Tiffany, Travis. BA, U. Pitts., 1973; MBA, City U., Seattle, 1985; cert. quality sys. auditor, U. Phoenix, 1994. Mgmt. cons. Sci. Mgmt. Corp., Basking Ridge, N.J., 1973-77; indsl. engr. and mgr. The Boeing Co., Seattle, 1977-91; dir. mgmt. consulting Ariz. Dept. Transp., Phoenix, 1991-93; mgmt. cons. Interstate Assessment Techs., Tempe, Ariz., 1993-95; account cons. Transworld Sys. Inc., Phoenix, 1996—. Rep. precinct committeeman, Seattle, Phila., Phoenix, 1980—; tchr. Jr. Achievement, Phoenix, 1995; vol. Bus. Vols. Arts, Phoenix, 1995—; bd. dirs. Winterwood Home Owners Assn., Kent, Wash., 1986-87. Recipient Morgan Doughton award Pa. Jaycees, 1974. Mem. Internat. Assn. Hospitality Accts., Am. Soc. Quality Control, Assn. Quality and Participation (bd. dirs. 1992-93), Inst. Mgmt. Cons., Inst. Indsl. Engrs. (pres. 1979-80, v.p. 1994-95, Indsl. Engr. Yr. 1983). Lutheran. Home: 4968 E Paradise Ln Scottsdale AZ 85254 Office: Transworld Sys Inc 5090 N 40th St Ste 170 Phoenix AZ 85018

PAVLIK, NANCY, convention services executive; b. Hamtramck, Mich., July 18, 1935; d. Frank and Helen (Vorobojoff) Phillips; m. G. Edward Pavlik, June 30, 1956; children: Kathleen, Christine, Laureen, Michael, Bonnie Jean. Student, U. Ariz., 1956-80. Exec. sec. Mich. Bell, Detroit, 1951-56, RCA, Camden, N.J., 1956-58; owner, pres. S.W. Events Etc., Scottsdale, Ariz., 1969—. Chmn. hospitality industry com. Scottsdale City Coun., 1989—; bd. dirs. Scottsdale Curatorial Bd., 1987-89. Mem. Soc. Incentive Travel Execs., Meeting Planners Internat., Am. Soc. Assn. Execs., Indian Arts and Crafts Assn., Scottsdale C. of C. (bd. dirs., tourism steering com. 1984-88), Contemporary Watercolorists Club. Democrat. Roman Catholic. Home: 15417 Richwood Fountain Hills AZ 85268 Office: SW Events Etc 3200 N Hayden Ste 100 Scottsdale AZ 85251

PAVLOVICH, ROBERT J., small business owner, state legislator; b. Butte, Mont., June 6, 1929; s. John and Stella (Knego) P.; m. Joyce Driscoll, June 1953 (div. 1960); m. Kathleen M. Murphy; children: Kathy, Dennis, Robert, Marcy, Julie, John, Maureen. Grad., Butte H.S., 1947. Owner tavern Met Tavern, Butte, 1951—; mem. Mont. Ho. of Reps., Helena, 1979—. Mem. Elks. Democrat. Roman Catholic. Home: 2751 Yale Ave Butte MT 59701 Office: Met Tavern 1375 Harrison Ave Butte MT 59701

PAWULA, KENNETH JOHN, artist, educator; b. Chgo., Feb. 4, 1935; s. John and Clara (Brzezinski) P.; student Northwestern U., 1956, Art Inst. Chgo., 1956; B.F.A., U. Ill., 1959; M.A. in Painting, U. Calif., Berkeley, 1962. Graphic designer Motorola, Inc., Chgo., 1959-60; grad. asst. printmaking U. Calif., Berkeley, 1961-62, asso. in art, 1962-63; archaeol. delineator for Islamic excavation Am. Research Center, Egypt, 1964-65; instr. Sch. of Art, U. Wash., Seattle, 1965-67, asst. prof., 1967-73, asso. prof., 1974—; participant artist-in-residence program of Ecole Superieure Des Beaux-Arts D'Athenes at Rhodos Art Center, Greece, 1978; cons. to Wydawnictwo Interpress, Warsaw, Poland, 1978; mem. art jury ann. painting, drawing and sculpture show Art Mus. of Greater Victoria, Can., 1971, Unitarian Art Gallery, Seattle, 1968, Cellar Gallery, Kirkland, Wash., 1968, Lakewood Artist's Outdoor Exhibit, Tacoma, Wash., 1968; participant Painting Symposium, Janow Podlaski, Poland, 1977. One-man shows of paintings include: Univ. Unitarian Fine Arts Gallery, Seattle, 1970, Polly Friedlander Gallery, Seattle, 1970, Lynn Kottler Galleries, N.Y.C., 1971, U. Minn. Art Gallery, Mpls., 1971, Art Mus. of Greater Victoria, Can., 1972, Second Story Gallery, Seattle, 1972, Yuuhigaoka Gallery Osaka, Japan, Universidade Federal Fluminense Niteroi, Rio de Janiero, Brazil, 1990, Pyramid Gallery, N.Y.C., 1991; group shows include: Worth Ryder Gallery, U. Calif., Berkeley, 1962, Seattle Art Mus., 1964, 70, 65, 66, Frye Art Mus., Seattle, 1966, San Francisco Art Ins., 1966, Henry Gallery, U. Wash., Seattle, 1966, 67, 70, State Capitol Mus., Olympia, Wash., 1967, Attica Gallery, Seattle, 1967, 69, Sec. of State's Office, Olympia, 1968, Eastern Mich. U., Ypsilanti, 1968, Rogue Gallery, Medford, Oreg., 1968, Marylhurst Coll., Oreg., 1968, Spokane Art Mus., 1968, Cheney Cowles Mus., Spokane, 1969, Jade Gallery, Richland, Wash., 1969, Alaska U., 1970, Polly Friedlander Gallery, Mpls., 1971, Anchorage Art Mus., 1972, U. Nev. Art Gallery, 1972, Juneau (Alaska) Art Mus., 1972, Springfield (Mo.) Art Mus., 1973, U. N.D., Grand Forks, 1974, Washington and Jefferson Coll., Washington, Pa., 1975, MacMurray Coll., Jacksonville, Ill., 1976, Gallery of Fine Arts, Eastern Mont. Coll., 1976, Inst. of Culture, Janow Podlaski, Poland, 1977, Seattle Arts Commn., 1978, Polish Cultural Center, Buffalo, 1979, Cabo Frio Internat. Print Biennial, Brazil, 1983, Sunderland (Eng.) Poly. U. Faculty Exchange Exhbn., 1984, Internat Art Biennial Mus. Hosio Capranica-Viterbo, Italy, 1985; represented in permanent collections: San Francisco Art Mus., Seattle Art Mus., Henry Gallery, U. Wash., Seattle, Highline Coll., Midway, Wash., Marylhurst Coll., Art Mus., Janow Podlaski, Poland, Tacoma Nat. Bank, Fine Arts Gallery of San Diego. Mem. Coll. Art Assn., AAUP. Home: 2242 NE 177th St Seattle WA 98155-5241 Office: U Wash Coll Arts & Scis Sch Art Dm # 10 Seattle WA 98195

PAXMAN, DAVID BROCKBANK, English literature educator; b. Salt Lake City, Dec. 31, 1946; s. Monroe Junior and Shirley (Brockbank) P.; m. Susan Wear, Apr. 1, 1970 (div. Dec. 1989); children: Isaac, Jonathan, Jane, Judith; m. Kathryn Hoopes, Aug. 9, 1996. BA, Brigham Young U., 1971; MA, U. Chgo., 1972, PhD, 1982. Asst. prof. Brigham Young U.-Hawaii campus, Laie, 1976-82, assoc. prof., 1982-88; assoc. prof. Brigham Young U., Provo, Utah, 1988—. Author: A Newcomer's Guide to Hawaii, 1993; contbr. articles to profl. jours. Mem. Am. Soc. for Eighteenth-Century Studies. Mem. LDS Ch. Office: Brigham Young Univ English Dept Provo UT 84602

PAYEA, NORMAN PHILIP, II, plastic surgeon, lawyer; b. Detroit, May 11, 1949; s. Norman Philip and Helen (Kucera) P.; 1 child, Heather Marie. BS in Biology, Mich. State U., 1970, MD, 1974; JD, U. Denver, 1991, MBA, 1992. Diplomate Am. Bd. Plastic Surgery; cert. hand surgeon. Intern, gen. surgery Loyola U. Med. Ctr., Chgo., 1974-75, resident, gen. surgery, 1975-77; resident, plastic/reconstructive and hand surgery McGill U. Teaching Hosps., Montreal, Que., Can., 1977-79; plastic surgeon East Tawas, Mich., 1979-81, Wheat Ridge, Colo., 1981-82, Lakewood, Colo., 1983—; aviation med. examiner Fed. Aviation Agy.; lectr. in field. Contbr. articles to profl. jours. Active numerous civic orgns. and founds. including Denver Art Mus., Denver Botanical Gardens, Denver Art Mus., Denver Mus. of Natural History, Denver Zool. Found., Internat. Soc. for Athletic Plastic Surgery, others. Fellow Royal Coll. Physicians and Surgeons of Can., Am. Coll. of Surgeons, Internat. Coll. of Surgeons, Coll. of Legal Medicine; mem. ABA, AMA, ATLA, Can. Med. Assn., Can. Soc. Surgery of the Hand, Can. Soc. Aesthetic Cosmetic Plastic Surgery, Flying Physicians Assn., Am. Coll. Physician Execs., Am. Acad. Healthcare Attys., Am. Burn Assn., Am. Assn. Hand Surgery, Am. Soc. Plastic and Reconstructive Surgeons, Am. Coll. Legal Medicine, Nat. Health Lawyers Assn., Wilderness Med. Soc., Rocky Mountain Hand Surgery, Colo. Med. Soc., Colo. Bar Assn., Colo. Trial Lawyers Assn., Colo. State Soc. Plastic and Reconstructive Surgeons (various offices), Clear Creek Valley Med. Soc. (various offices). Home: 3470 Ward Rd Wheat Ridge CO 80033-5225 Office: Lakewood Med Ctr 8805 W 14th Ave Denver CO 80215-4848

PAYNE, ANCIL HORACE, retired broadcasting executive; b. Mitchell, Oreg., Sept. 5, 1921; s. Leslie L. and Pearl A. (Brown) P.; m. Valerie Dorrance Davies, Apr. 6, 1959; children: Anne Sparrow, Alison Louise, Lucinda Catherine. Student, Willamette U., 1939-41, U. Oreg., 1941, U. Notre Dame, Ohio State U., 1943; B.A., U. Wash., 1947; postgrad., Am. U., 1950-51; hon. PhD, Willamette Univ., 1991. Adminstrv. asst. to congressman, Washington, 1949-52; gen. mgr. Martin Van Lines, Anchorage, 1952-56; mgr. Frontiers-Oreg. Ltd., Portland, Oreg., 1956-59; asst. v.p. bus. div. King Broadcasting Co., Seattle, 1959-63, v.p., 1963-70, exec. v.p., 1970-71, pres., 1971-87; chmn. bd. affiliates NBC, 1975-80. Mem. Oreg. Bd. Higher Edn., 1966-70; bd. trustees Whitman Coll., 1985-90; bd. dirs. Centrum Found., Cobalt Inc., Film Com, Inc. Lt. (j.g.) USNR, 1942-45, PTO. Mem. Monday Club, Rainier Club, Columbia Tower Club, Phi Beta Kappa Assocs., Alpha Delta Sigma. Episcopalian. Home: 1107 1st Ave Apt 2001 Seattle WA 98101-2948 Office: Ancil H Payne & Assocs 1107 1st Ave Apt 606 Seattle WA 98101-2944

PAYNE, JAMES RICHARD, environmental chemist; b. Anaheim, Calif., Sept. 3, 1947; s. Theodore L. and Laura P. (Schutz) P.; m. Marinee J. Pavlovich, June 29, 1968; children: Clayton Bennett, Taylor Sierra. BA with honors, Calif. State U., Fullerton, 1969; PhD, U. Wis., 1974. Chemist in engrng. coll. unit N.Am. Rockwell Corp., Downey, Calif., 1968-69; tchg. asst., rsch. asst., and NIH predoctoral fellow U. Wis., Madison, 1969-74; postdoctoral scholar Woods Hole (Mass.) Oceanographic Inst., 1974-75; asst. rsch. chemist U. Calif. Bodega Marine Lab., Bodega Bay, 1975-78; sr. chemist, asst. v.p. Sci. Applications Internat. Corp., La Jolla, Calif., 1978-91; sr. v.p., dir. rsch. SOUND Environ. Svcs., Inc., Carlsbad, Calif., 1991-96; mgr. chem. tech. br. Ogden Environ. & Energy Svcs. Co., Inc., San Diego, 1996—; also bd. dirs. SOUND Environ. Svcs., Inc., Carlsbad; mem. exec. sci. and tech. coun. Sci. Applications Internat. Corp., La Jolla, 1985-91; mem. NAS/NRC Marine Bd.: Com. on Effectiveness of Oil Spill Dispersants, Washington, 1985-88; ind. oil spill cons., Encinitas, Calif., 1991—. Co-author: Fate and Weathering of Petroleum Spills in the Marine Environment: A Literature Review and Synopsis, 1980, Petroleum Spills in the Marine Environment: The Chemistry and Formation of Water-in-Oil Emulsions and Tar Balls, 1985, Oil Spill Dispersants: Mechanisms of Action and Laboratory Tests, 1993. Home: 1651 Linda Sue Ln Encinitas CA 92024-2427 Office: Ogden Environ & Energy Svcs Co Inc 5510 Morehouse Dr San Diego CA 92121

PAYNTER, HOWARD LAGER, mechanical engineer, educator, consultant; b. West Allis, Wis., Jan. 3, 1931; s. Raymond Grey and Helen Emilie (Lager) P.; m. Janet Alice Trushinski, Apr. 9, 1949; children: Pamela Dawn Wright, Howard Jon, David Ray. BS in Mech. Engring., U. Wis., 1955; postgrad., UCLA, San Diego, 1956-60; MS in Mech. Engring., U. Denver, 1965. Reg. profl. engr., Colo. Jr. engr. York (Pa.) Corp., 1954; sr. thermodynamics engr. Convair Divsn. Gen. Dynamics, San Diego, 1955-60; rsch. chief thermodynamics and fluid mechanics sect. Martin Marietta Corp., Denver, 1960-74; assoc. prof. mech. engr. tech. Met. State Coll. Denver, 1974-82, prof., 1982—, dept. chair, 1977-80, prog. coord., 1990-93, prog. dir., 1994-96, chair, 1996—, interim dir. engring. tech. divsn., 1996—; pres. H. Lager Engring., Littleton, Colo., 1975—; invited lectr. U. Stuttgart, Germany, 1973, Sperry Rand, Ltd., Bracknell, Eng.; advisor engring. and engring. tech. bd. No. Ariz. U., Flagstaff, 1991-93; mem. invited faculty Chinese Assn. Sci. and Tech., Beijing., May 1989. Co-author: Rocket Propellant and Pressurization Systems, 1964; patentee in field. Precinct leader Republican party, Littleton, Colo., 1975-86. NASA/Am. Soc. Engring. Edn. Summer Faculty fellow, 1977, 79, 84. Mem. Am. Soc. Mech. Engrs. (v.p. Rocky Mountain region), Nat. Soc. Profl. Engrs., Am. Soc. Engring. Edn., Colo. Symphony Assn., Planetary Soc. Home: 3 Meadowbrook Rd Littleton CO 80120

PAYTON, DANIEL NELSON, III, physicist; b. Lamar, Mo., July 2, 1940; s. Daniel Nelson Jr. and L. Gay (Evilsizer) P.; m. H. Jane Whitting, July 30, 1960; 1 child, Janna Nicole Morter. PhD, U. Mo., Rolla, 1966. Staff mem. Los Alamos (N.Mex.) Nat. Lab., 1963-67; tech. dir. Air Force Weapons Lab., Albuquerque, N.Mex., 1967-84; v.p., systems engr. Eos Techs., Inc., Albuquerque, 1984-92; v.p., N.Mex. ops. Sci. Applications Internat., Albuquerque, 1992—; mem. adv. bd. AAMPEC Industry, Albuquerque, 1992—. Contbr. articles to profl. jours. Active Econ. Forum, Albuquerque, 1993—; pres. N.Mex. Zool. Soc., Albuquerque, 1980-88. Recipient Civilian Disting. Svc. award USAF, 1982. Mem. Am. Phys. Soc., AIAA, Greater Albuquerque C. of C., Hispano C. of C. Office: Sci Applications Internat 2109 Airpark Rd SE Albuquerque NM 87106-3258

PAYTON, GARY DWAYNE, professional basketball player; b. Oakland, Calif., July 23, 1968; m. Monique Payton; children: Raquel, Gary Dwayne. Grad., Oreg. State U., 1990. Drafted NBA, 1990; guard Seattle Supersonics, 1990—. Named mem. All-Am. First Team, The Sporting News, 1990, Pacific-10 Conf. Player of Yr., 1990, NBA All-Star, 1994, 95, NBA Player of the Week; named to NBA All-Def. 1st Team, 1994, 95. Office: Seattle Supersonics 190 Queen Anne Ave N Ste 200 Seattle WA 98109-4926*

PEACOCK, HARRY RICHARD, city manager; b. Portsmouth, Va., July 16, 1941; s. Harry Peacock and Hazel Ward (Hunning) Hansen; m. Barbara Elias, June 13, 1964; 1 child, Rebecca Jean. AB, UCLA, 1964; MPA, U. So. Calif., 1969, DPA, 1993. Adminstrv. asst. City of West Covina, Calif., 1966-69; asst. adminstrv. officer, adminstrv. officer City of Gardena, Calif., 1969-72; city mgr. City of Rolling Hills Estates, Calif., 1973-85, City of Saratoga, Calif., 1985-95. Contbr. articles to profl. jours. Lt. USN, 1964-66. Named City Mgr. of Yr. Mcpl. Mgmt. Assts., 1985. Mem. Internat. City Mgmt. Assn. (mem. internat. exchange program 1993-94), Am. Soc. Pub. Adminstrn. (Outstanding Govt. Program award 1986), Rotary Internat., UCLA Alumni Assn., Alpha Phi Alpha. Republican. Presbyterian. Office: City of Saratoga 13777 Fruitvale Ave Saratoga CA 95070-5151

PEARCE, HUGH MORRIS, engineering executive; b. Tillsonburg, Ont., Can., Jan. 12, 1943; came to U.S., 1965; s. Harold Wilfred and Catherine Ada (Broad) P.; m. Julie Ann Jackson, Aug. 26, 1967; children: David Andrew, Brian Scott. BSc in Engring. Physics, Queen's U., Kingston, Ont., 1965; MS in Elec. Engring., MIT, 1966, EE in Elec. Engring., 1967; PhD in Elec. Engring., U. Mich., 1970. Rsch. engr. Calspan Corp., Buffalo, N.Y., 1971-73; v.p. Sys. Control Inc., Palo Alto, Calif., 1973-81; exec. v.p. Sys. Control Tech., Palo Alto, 1981-84; divsn. mgr. Tech. Svc. Corp., Los Gatos, Calif., 1984-88; pres. Advanced Def. Techs., Mountain View, Calif., 1988-90; v.p., gen. mgr. Radar/Digital Sys., Auburn, Calif., 1990; cons. Los Altos Hills, Calif., 1991-93; pres., CEO Wireless Transactions Corp., Sunnyvale, Calif., 1993—. Pres. Los Altos Edn. Found., 1984-85. Mem. IEEE, AIAA. Office: Wireless Transactions Corp 1183 Bordeaux Dr Ste 22 Sunnyvale CA 94089-1201

PEARL, JUDEA, computer scientist, educator; b. Tel-Aviv, Sept. 4, 1936; U.S. citizen; married; 3 children. BSc, Israel Inst. Tech., 1960; MSc, Newark Coll. Engring., 1961; PhD in Elec. Engring., Poly. Inst. Bklyn., 1965. Rsch. engr. Dental Sch., NYU, 1960-61; mem. tech. staff RCA Rsch. Labs., 1961-65; dir. advanced memory devices Electronic Memories, Inc., Calif., 1966-69; prof. engring. sys. and computer scis. UCLA, 1969—; instr. Newark Coll. Engring., 1961; cons. Rand Corp., 1972, Integrated Sci. Corp., 1975, Hughes Aircraft, 1989. Recipient Outstanding Achievement award RCA Labs., 1965. Fellow IEEE, Am. Assn. Artificial Intelligence; mem. Nat. Acad. Engring. Office: UCLA Dept Computer Sci 4731 Boelter Hall Los Angeles CA 90024

PEARLMAN, NANCY SUE, environmental broadcaster; b. Huntington, W.Va., Apr. 17, 1948. BA in Anthropology cum laude, UCLA, 1971; MA in Urban Studies and Planning, Antioch U., 1979; postgrad., U. So. Calif., 1979. Cert. secondary, C.C. and adult edn. tchr. Former secondary social studies tchr. pub. and pvt. schs.; pres. Multi-City Svcs.; exec. prodr., host Ednl. Comm., 1972—; host, exec. prodr., dir. radio series Environ. Directions, 1977—; exec. prodr., host, TV series ECONEWS, 1984—; co-host Femininist Mag. radio series Sta. KPFK; lectr., spkr., talk show guest; instr. San Diego State U., 1989, Calif. State U., Fullerton, 1990, L.A. C.C., 1977—; adminstr., cons. Calif. League Conservation Voters, 1973-75, Zero Population Growth, L.A., 1973-75, others; mem. adv. coun. Californians for Population Stabilization. Dir., prodr., writer, host for numerous video and TV prodns. including Using the Apple IIe, Santa Susana: Where the Past is Present, The Great East Mojave, Gem in the Heart of the City, Wind: Energy for the 90's and Beyond, Population Crisis, USA; narrator, host, prodr. radio prodns. including Environ. Directions, Sta. KPWR, 1977-93; editor The Compendium Newsletter, 1972—; co-editor: Directory of Environmental Organizations, 1972—; contbr. articles to newspapers and mags. Founder Ecology Ctr. of So. Calif., Project Eco-Tourism; mem. career network program UCLA; citizen diplomat Internat. Visitors Coun. L.A.; founding co-coord. Earth Day 1970; mem. adv. bd. Carry Capacity Network, 1990—, Ballona Lagoon Marine Preserve, 1992-93, Let's Live, 1990—, L.A. Earth Day, 1990, Earth Summit Fast, 1992; past bd. dirs. Calif. State U. Network for Environ. Sci. Tng., Task Force on Calif. Recycling, Calif. Wilderness Coalition, Calif. Desert Alliance, Citizens for Mojave Nat. Park, numerous other civic and environ. orgns.; judge Chevron Conservation Awards, 1989—, Acad. TV Arts and Scis. EMMY awards, 1986-95, Nat. Acad. Cable Programming Nat. ACE Awards, 1986-93. Recipient numerous awards, including Commendation Resolutions, City of West Hollywood, 1986, County of L.A., 1986, City of L.A., 1986, State of Calif., 1986, Best of the West Spl. Merit award Western Ednl. Soc. for Telecomms., 1987, ACE nomination Nat. Acad. Cable Programming, 1987, Diamond award So. Calif. Cable Assn., 1989, Emmy award nomination, 1987, 88, 93, Buccaneer award for Excellence in Pub. Svc., Pub. Interest Radio and TV Ednl. Soc., 1988, 89, 91, Earth Harmony Achievement award 1st Ann. Earth Harmony Expo, 1991, others; laureate Global 500 Roll of Honour, UN Environ. Programme, 1989; honoree Chevron Conservation awards. Mem. Calif. Wilderness Coalition (adv. coun.), Universal Pantheist Soc. (bd. dirs.). Office: Ednl Comms PO Box 351419 Los Angeles CA 90035-9119

PEARSALL, THOMAS PERINE, physics and electronics educator; b. Richmond, Va., Nov. 2, 1945. BEng, Dartmouth Coll., 1968; MSc in Solid-State Physics, U. London, 1970; PhD in Applied Physics, Cornell U., 1973. With Bell Labs., Holmdel, N.J., 1973-76, Laboratoire Central de Recherches, Thomson/CSF, Orsay, France, 1976-80; program mgr. optical electronics systems Bell Labs., Murray Hill, N.J., 1980—, mgr. European mktg. for optical communications, 1986-88, mgr. internat. bus. devel. Far East, 1988-89; Boeing chair semiconductor electronics U. Wash., Seattle, 1989—; dir. Ctr. for Compound Semicondr. Tech. Wash. Tech. Ctr., Seattle; sr. rsch. fellow CNRS, Grenoble, France, 1996—. Patentee GaInAsP long wave LED, 1976; long-wavelength GaInAs photodiode, 1978; noise-free, high temperature photodetector, 1980; developer long distance optical fiber telecommunications. Recipient Design News award; NSF Fellow to India, 1983-87; James B. Reynolds fellow; Fulbright scholar, 1996-97; fellow IEEE, Am. Phys. Soc. Office: U Wash Dept Elec Engring Seattle WA 98195

PEARSON, APRIL VIRGINIA, lawyer; b. Martinsville, Ind., Aug. 11, 1960; d. Clare Grill and Sheila Rosemary (Finch) Rayner; m. Randall Keith Pearson, Dec. 10, 1988; children: Randall Kyle, Austin Finch, Autumn Virginia. BA, Calif. State U., Long Beach, 1982; JD, Pepperdine U., 1987. Bar: Calif. 1987, Idaho 1993, D.C. 1989. Assoc. counsel Union Oil of Calif., L.A., 1988—; v.p. Pa's Bier, Long Beach, Calif., 1988—; bd. dirs. Unocal Chems. Internat., The Hague, The Netherlands, 1993-95, Ammonia Safety Tng. Inst., 1995—, sec., 1997—. Mem. Women Lawyers of Long Beach (v.p. 1990-93), Orange County Bar Assn., Chem. Industry Coun. Calif. (chair regulatory affairs com. 1995, cert. indsl. fire brigade and HAZWOPER team mem.). Office: Union Oil Co care Unocal 376 S Valencia Brea CA 92823

PEARSON, BELINDA KEMP, economist, consultant; b. Kansas City, Mo., Apr. 14, 1931; d. William Ewing and Margaret Norton (Johnson) Kemp; m. Carl Erik Pearson, Sept. 15, 1953; children: Erik, Frederick, Margaret. BA, Wellesley Coll., 1952; MA, Tufts U., 1954, PhD, 1958. Rsch. asst. Harvard U., Cambridge, Mass., 1954-55; instr. econs. Suffolk U., Boston, 1956-59; lectr. econs., Wellesley Coll., Mass., 1964-65; econ. analyst, asst. econs. Seafirst Bank, Seattle, 1966-79, v.p., 1974-85; chief economist, 1979-85; dir. Lektor, Inc., Issaquah, Wash., 1984—, pres., 1987—; mem. Wash. Gov's. Coun. Econ. Advisors, Olympia, 1979—; dir. Pacific N.W. Regional Econ. Conf., 1979—, chair, Seattle Conf., 1987; mem. Western Blue Chip Econ. Forecast Panel, 1988—; mem. King County, Wash., Land Capacity Task Force, 1995-96; mem. bd. regents Wash. State U., Pullman, 1985-90, v.p., 1988-90, Regents Found. Investment Com. of Wash. State U., 1987-91; mem. Wash. State Libr. Commn., Olympia, 1976-84. Fulbright scholar London Sch. Econs., 1952-53. Mem. Am. Econ. Assn., Nat. Assn. Bus. Economists (chmn. arrangements 1982 ann. meeting), Seattle

Economists Club (pres. 1973-74), Mcpl. League, City Club (Seattle) (chmn. reports com. 1986-88), pres. LWV, Lake Wash. East, 1993-95. Office: Lektor Inc 4227 Providence Point Dr SE Issaquah WA 98029-7217

PEARSON, CLAUDE MEREDITH, legal consultant; b. Hudson, Wyo., Dec. 20, 1921; s. Claude Meredith and Golda May (King) P.; m. Helen Lucille Adams, Feb. 1, 1947; children: Susan Mae Pearson-Davis, Marcia Kay Pearson Vaughan. BA, Jamestown Coll., 1943; JD, U. Mich., 1948. Bar: Wash. 1949, U.S. Dist. Ct. (we. dist.) Wash., 1950. Ptnr. Pearson & Anderson, Tacoma, 1946-52, Pearson Anderson & Pearson, Tacoma, 1953-60, Davies Pearson & Anderson, Tacoma, 1960-72; shareholder Davies Pearson P.C., Tacoma, 1972-91, legal cons., 1991—; chair bus. sect. Wash. State Bar, Seattle, 1972, chair specialization bd., 1985-87, chair alt. dispute resolution sect., 1990; bd. dirs. Law Fund, 1993-94, 96-97; adj. instr. McChord campus Chapman U., 1992-93; bd. dirs., v.p. N.W. Justice Project, 1995, pres., 1997. Pres. United Good Neighbor Fund, Tacoma, 1964. With USNR, 1942-73, capt. 1966. Mem. Mich. Alumni Assn. (past dir.-at-large, 1st v.p., citation 1984). Home: 3419 N 24th St Tacoma WA 98406-5805 Office: Davies Pearson PC 920 S Fawcett Ave Tacoma WA 98402-5606

PEARSON, DENNIS LEE, optometrist; b. Portland, Oreg., June 21, 1951; s. Alvin Wesley and Pharaby Iva (Barnett) P.; m. Corinne Elaine Boggs, Aug. 27, 1972; children: Kathleen Erin, Erik Edward. BS in Chemistry, Portland State U., 1974; OD, Pacific U., Forest Grove, Oreg., 1978. Optometrist Drs. Diederich & Pearson, St. Helens, Oreg., 1979-83; pvt. practice Lebanon, Oreg., 1983—; adv. panel mem. managed care Vision Svc. Plan, Rancho Cucamunga, Calif., 1995—; adv. panel mem. laser refraction Laser Vision Ctr. at Pacific U., Portland, 1995—. Sch. bd. mem. Sodaville Sch. Dist., Oreg., 1989-93; bd. dirs. Lebanon Boys & Girls Club, 1989-91, 93-94; elder Lebanon Presbyn. Ch., 1992—. Mem. Am. Optometric Assn., Oreg. Optometric Assn. (bd. dirs. 1988—, past pres.), Kiwanis Club of Lebanon, Lebanon C. of C. Office: 90 Market St Ste 20 Lebanon OR 97355-2328

PEARSON, JOHN, mechanical engineer; b. Leyburn, Yorkshire, U.K., Apr. 24, 1923; came to U.S., 1930, naturalized, 1944; s. William and Nellie Pearson; m. Ruth Ann Billhardt, July 10, 1944 (wid. Nov. 1984); children: John, Armin, Roger; m. Sharoll L. Chisolm, Sept. 8, 1993. B.S.M.E., Northwestern U., 1949, M.S., 1951. Registered profl. engr., Calif. Rsch. engr. Naval Ordnance Test Sta., China Lake, Calif., 1951-55, head warhead rsch. br., 1955-58, head solid dynamics br., 1958-59, head detonation physics group, 1959-67; head detonation physics div. Naval Weapons Ctr., China Lake, Calif., 1967-83, sr. rsch. scientist, 1983—; cons., lectr. in field; founding mem. adv. bd. Ctr. for High Energy Forming, U. Denver; mem. bd. examiners Sambalpur U., India, 1982-83. Author: Explosive Working of Metals, 1963; Behavior of Metals Under Impulsive Loads, 1954; contbr. articles to profl. publs; patentee impulsive loading, explosives applications. Charter mem. Sr. Exec. Svc. U.S., 1979. With C.E., U.S. Army, 1943-46, ETO. Recipient L.T.E. Thompson medal, 1965, William B. McLean medal, 1979, Superior Civilian Svc. medal USN, 1984, Haskell G. Wilson award, 1985, cert. of recognition Sec. Navy, 1975, merit award Dept. Navy, 1979, cert. of commendation Sec. Navy, 1981, Career Svcs. award Sec. Navy, 1988, John A. Ulrich award Am. Def. Preparedness Assn., 1991; 1st disting. fellow award Naval Weapons Ctr., 1989. Fellow ASME; mem. Am. Soc. Metals, Am. Phys. Soc., AIME, Fed. Exec. League, Sigma Xi, Tau Beta Pi, Pi Tau Sigma, Triangle. Home and Office: PO Box 1390 858 N Primavera St Ridgecrest CA 93555-7907

PEARSON, KEITH LAURENCE, retired environmental scientist; b. Chgo., Apr. 1, 1929; s. Victor R. and Ingeborg E. (Olson) P.; m. Ellen M. O'Dell, May 28, 1955; 1 child, Brian V. BA, Augustana Coll., 1951; MA, U. Ariz., 1965, PhD, 1969. Asst. prof. U. Wis., Superior, 1967-68; assoc. prof. No. Ariz. U., Flagstaff, 1968-76; environ. analyst Bur. Land Mgmt., Washington, 1976-78; environ. planner Bur. Land Mgmt., Phoenix, 1979-95, ret., 1995. Author: The Indian in American History, 1973; contbg. author: A Slice of Life, 1975; contbr. articles to profl. jours. Fellow Am. Anthropol. Assn.; mem. Soc. for Applied Anthropology. Democrat. Episcopalian. Home: 6370 W Donald Dr Glendale AZ 85310

PEARSON, RICHARD JOSEPH, archaeologist, educator; b. Kitchener, Ont., Can., May 2, 1938; s. John Cecil and Henrietta Anne (Wallwin) P.; m. Kazue Miyazaki, Dec. 12, 1964; 1 child, Sarina Riye. B.A. in Anthropology with honours, U. Toronto, 1960; Ph.D., Yale U., 1966. Asst. prof., then assoc. prof. archaeology U. Hawaii, 1966-71; mem. faculty U. B.C., Vancouver, 1971—; now prof. archaeology U. B.C. Author: The Archaeology of the Ryukyu Islands, 1969, Higashi Ajia no Kodai Shakai to Kokogaku, 1984, Windows on the Japanese Past, Studies in Archaeology and Prehistory, 1986, Ancient Japan, 1992; contbr. articles to profl. jours. Guggenheim fellow. Mem. Am. Anthrop. Assn., Soc. Am. Archaeology, Indo-Pacific Prehistory Assn., Assn. Asian Studies. Office: U BC, Dept Anthropology-Sociology, Vancouver, BC Canada V6T 1Z1

PEARSON, ROBERT ALLEN, optometrist; b. Scottsbluff, Nebr., Dec. 8, 1946; s. William Franklin and Hope Jacqueline (Williams) P.; m. Sue Ione Parmelee, Sept. 6, 1969. BS, BA, U. Wyo., 1970; OD, So. Calif. Coll. Optometry, 1986. Microbiologist State of Nev., Las Vegas, 1970-82; optometrist S.W. Vision, Las Vegas, 1986—. Mem. LIGA Internat., Inc., Santa Ana, Calif., Vision U.S.A., St. Louis, VOSH-Calif. Mem. APHA, Nev. Pub. Health Assn., Am. Optometric Assn., Nev. Optometric Assn. (Optometrist of Yr. 1988), Nev. State Bd. Optometry. Home: 3404 El Cortez Ave Las Vegas NV 89102-3925 Office: SW Vision PO Box 15645 Las Vegas NV 89114-5645

PEARSON, THOMAS CARLETON, management executive; b. Somerville, Mass., Sept. 11, 1941; s. Thomas and Dorothy Gertrude (White) P.; m. Carol Louise Baird, June 15, 1962; children: Thomas David, Deborah Anne, Sheri Lynn. BSBA, Calif. State Poly. U., Pomona, 1964; MBA, Calif. State U., Long Beach, 1971; MA in Mgmt., Claremont (Calif.) Grad. Sch., 1983, PhD in Exec. Mgmt., 1986. Ops. analyst Douglas Oil Divsn. Conoco, L.A., 1968-72; mgr. spl. projects Douglas Oil Divsn. Conoco, Costa Mesa, Calif., 1979-84; dist. mgr. bus. devel. Am. Appraisal Co., L.A., 1972-76; mgr. ops. analysis Amtrak, Washington, 1976-79; dir. supplies bus. CalComp, Inc., Anaheim, 1984-89, dir. team 90 product devel., 1989-90; dir. product devel. Harman/JBL, Northridge, Calif., 1991-93; pres. Competitive Improvement Cons., Laguna Hills, Calif., 1993-96; sr. v.p. Littoral Co., L.A., 1996—. Lt. USN, 1964-68. Mem. Train Collector's Assn., Assn. Naval Aviation. Home: 10 Autumn Hill Ln Laguna Hills CA 92653-6016

PEARSON, VELVET D., English and composition educator; b. Bakersfield, Calif., Mar. 13, 1964; d. Timothy Tilden and Nelda S. (Collins) P.; m. Hiroshi Sasaki, May 26, 1995. BA in English, U. Calif., Santa Barbara, 1987; MA in English, San Diego State U., 1989; postgrad., U. So. Calif., L.A. Grad. tchg. asst. San Diego State U., 1987-89; vis. lectr. Universite de Provence, Aix-En-Provence, France, 1989-90; adj. lectr. Bakersfield C.C., 1991; asst. lectr. U. So. Calif., L.A., 1991—; instrnl. coord. U. So. Calif., L.A., 1993-95. Mem. editl. bd. The Writing Instructor, 1991-95, asst. mng. editor, 1995-96, mng. editor, 1996—, editor (issue), 1992, 93, 94; contbr. articles to popular mags. and newspapers. Active NOW, L.A., 1992—, Greenpeace, L.A., 1992—, Amnesty Internat., L.A., 1989—. Mem. MLA, AAUW, 16th Century Conf., Nat. Coun. Tchrs. English, Assn. English Grad. Students. Democrat.

PEARSON, WARREN THOMAS, surgeon; b. Burlington, Iowa, Dec. 8, 1929; s. George John and Elma Ann (Pollock) P.; m. Margaret Louise Kofoed, Sept. 5, 1965; children: George Maxwell, Ralph Warren. MD, U. Iowa, 1955. Diplomate Am. Bd. Surgery, Am. Bd. Thoracic Surgery. Intern Grasslands Hosp., Valhalla, N.Y., 1955-56; resident in gen. surgery Bronx (N.Y.) VA Hosp., 1956-60; resident in thoracic and cardiovascular surgery Walter Reed Army Hosp., Washington, 1963-65; fellow dept. cardiovascular surgery Upstate Med. Ctr., Syracuse, N.Y., 1960-61; instr. surgery NYU, N.Y.C., 1968-79; pvt. practice N.Y.C., 1968-79; asst. clin. prof. Mt. Sinai Coll. Medicine, CUNY, 1974-79; pvt. practice Encino, Calif., 1979-86; pvt. practice, Santa Monica, Calif., 1986—; clin. instr. cardiothoracic surgery UCLA, 1989—. Contbr. articles to med. jours. Maj. M.C., U.S. Army, 1961-67. Fellow ACS, Am. Coll. Chest Physicians, Am. Coll. Cardiology; mem. AAAS, AMA, Soc. Thoracic Surgeons, N.Am. Soc. for Pacing and Electrophysiology, Internat. Soc. for Study Lung Cancer, Am. Thoracic Soc., Am. Heart Assn. (coun. on cardiovascular surgery), Pan-Am. Med. Assn., Calif. Med. Assn., N.Y. Acad. Medicine, N.Y. Acad. Scis., Los Angeles County Med. Assn., L.A. Trudeau Soc., Internat. Soc. for Heart and Lung Transplantation, Am. Coll. Angiology, Longmire Surg. Soc. Republican. Episcopalian. Home: 1701 Midvale Ave Los Angeles CA 90024-5512 Office: 2021 Santa Monica Blvd Santa Monica CA 90404-2208

PEASE, ROBERT ALLEN, electrical engineer; b. Rockville, Conn., Aug. 22, 1940; s. Mahlon Harold and Beulah May (Kammer) P.; m. Nancy Jean Baker, Aug. 12, 1961; children: Benjamin, Jonathan. BSEE, MIT, 1961. Chief engr. Teledyne PhilBrick, Dedham, Mass., 1961-75; staff scientist Nat. Semiconductor Corp., Santa Clara, Calif., 1976—; cons. editor EDN CAHNERS, Newton, Mass., 1978—. Contbr. numerous articles to profl. jours.; monthly colunist "Pease Porridge" Electronic Design, 1990—; holder 15 U.S. patents. Mem. IEEE. Episcopalian. Home: 682 Miramar Ave San Francisco CA 94112-1232 Office: Nat Semiconductor MS-D 2597A 2900 Semiconductor Dr Santa Clara CA 95051-0606

PEASLAND, BRUCE RANDALL, financial executive; b. Buffalo, N.Y., Mar. 24, 1945; s. Kenneth Arthur and Edith Grace (Bristow) P.; m. Debra Myers Peasland, June 13, 1981; children: Michael John, Timothy Scott, Amanda Jean. BS, U. So. Calif., 1971, MBA in Fin., 1978; JD, Western St. U., 1983. Price and cost analyst McDonnell Douglas Corp., Long Beach, Calif., 1966-70; cost mgr. The Gillette Co., Santa Monica, Calif., 1971-78; controller Lear Siegler Inc., Santa Ana, Calif., 1978-85, British Petroleum, Hitco, Newport Beach, Calif., 1986-87; v.p. fin., dir. Control Components Inc., Rancho Santa Margarita, Calif., 1987-90; chief fin. officer MacGillivray Freeman Films, Laguna Beach, Calif., 1990-91; exec. v.p., chief fin. officer Intervest Industries Inc, Carlsbad, Calif., 1992—. Youth advisor YMCA, Dana Point, Calif., 1985—. With USMC, 1963-69. Recipient of Mgr. of Yr. award Nat. Mgmt. Assn., 1984. Fellow U. So. Calif. MBA Assn.; mem. Nat. Assn. of Accts., Nat. Mgmt. Assn. (dir. 1978-85), U. So. Calif. Trojan Club, U. So. Calif. Alumni Club. Republican. Episcopalian. Home: 25211 Yacht Dr Dana Point CA 92629-1439 Office: Intervest Industries Inc 7720B El Camino Real Ste 201 Carlsbad CA 92009-8506

PEAVEY, CHARLES CARMAN, engineering executive; b. Westfield, Mass., Apr. 10, 1955; s. John Forrest and Ann Gordon (Carman) P.; m. Pockhui Kara Kim, Nov. 16, 1979; children: Russell Kim, Sarah Kim. BSE, Princeton U., 1977; MS, Stanford U., 1978. Sr. engr./scientist aerodynamics Douglas Aircraft Co., Long Beach, Calif., 1978-85; engr. specialist aerodynamics Northrop Advanced Sys. Divsn., Pico Rivera, Calif., 1985-88; mgr. CFD devel. B-2 divsn. Northrop Grumman Corp., Pico Rivera, 1988—. Stanford Engring. Grad. fellow, 1977. Mem. AIAA (sr. mem., fluid dynamics tech. com. 1988-91). Republican. Home: 4795 Via Corona Yorba Linda CA 92887-1823 Office: Northrop Grumman Corp 8900 Washington Blvd Pico Rivera CA 90660-3765

PEAVY, FRANK, management consultant; b. Columbus, Ga., Oct. 16, 1957. BA, U. Wash., 1979; MBA, U. So. Calif., L.A., 1984. Sr. cons. Deloitte Haskins & Sells, San Francisco; mgr. GE Cons. Svcs., San Francisco; dir. corp. info. svcs. Visa Internat., San Mateo, Calif.; prin. I.T.M. Group, Foster City, Calif. Author: Client Server Technology: Management Essentials, 1994. Mem. Japan Soc. No. Calif., Commonwealth Club.

PECK, CHRISTOPHER, editor; b. Wyo., Aug. 2, 1950; m. Kate Duignan Peck; children: Sarah, Cody. Degree in Comms., Standord U., 1972. Editor The Wood River Jour., Sun Valley, Idaho; city editor, edtl. oage editor, mng. editor Times-News, Twin Falls, Idaho, 1975-79; columnist, 1979, editor, 1982—; dir. Nat. Assn. Press Mng. Editors Assn.; mem. Soc. Am. Soc. Newspaper Editors; Pulitzer prize nominating judge. Office: The Spokane Review/Cowles Pub Co Western Farmer Stockman PO Box 2160 Spokane WA 99210-1615

PECK, DONALD HARVEY, chiropractor; b. Oak Park, Ill., July 18, 1945; s. Donald Ray and Dorothy Sylvia (LaFlamme) P.; m. Mary Evelyn Lamb, June 15, 1964 (div. 1971); children: Donald Lee, Nancy Ellen; m. Cheryl Jean Cox, July 7, 1973; children: Richard Krom Watkins Jr., Bradley Alan, Steven Edward. AA, Mt. San Antonio Coll., 1966; DC, Palmer Coll. of Chiropractic, 1970. Diplomate Nat. Bd. Chiropractic Examiners. Engring. technician Besteel Corp., Industry, Calif., 1965-66, City of Ontario, Calif., 1966-67; supr. Mercy Hosp., Davenport, Iowa, 1967-70; pvt. practice chiropractor San Bernardino and Redlands, Calif., 1971-81; pvt. practice Cottonwood, Ariz., 1981—; instr. Yavapai Coll. Clarkdale, Ariz., 1982-88. Scoutmaster Calif. Inland Empire coun. Boy Scouts Am., 1974-81, Grand Canyon coun. Boy Scouts Am., 1981—; active Am. Youth Soccer Orgn., Cottonwood, 1977-92, regional commr., 1984-88; asst. varsity soccer coach Mingus Union High Sch., 1989-93; instr. trainer, chief instr. Ariz. Game and Fish Dept., Cottonwood, 1983—. Recipient Award of Merit Boy Scouts Am., 1980, Silver Beaver award, 1988; named Vol. of Yr. Verde Valley C. of C., 1987. Mem. Kiwanis (bd. dirs. 1985-87), Order of Arrow (vigil honor mem., Cert. Merit Boy Scout Am. Nat. Ct. of Honor 1990). Republican. Office: 703 S Main St Cottonwood AZ 86326-4615

PECK, ELLIE ENRIQUEZ, retired state administrator; b. Sacramento, Oct. 21, 1934; d. Rafael Enriquez and Eloisa Garcia Rivera; m. Raymond Charles Peck, Sept. 5, 1957; children: Reginaldo, Enrico, Francisca Guerrero, Teresa, Linda, Margaret, Raymond Charles, Christina. Student polit. sci. Sacramento State U., 1974. Tng. services coord. Calif. Div. Hwys., Sacramento, 1963-67; tech. and mgmt. cons., Sacramento, 1968-78; expert examiner Calif. Pers. Bd., 1976-78; tng. cons. Calif. Pers. Devel. Ctr., Sacramento, 1978; spl. cons. Calif. Commn. on Fair Employment and Housing, 1978; cmty. svcs. rep. U.S. Bur. of Census, No. Calif. counties, 1978-80; spl. cons. Calif. Dept. Consumer Affairs, Sacramento, 1980-83, project dir. Golden State Sr. Discount Program, 1980-83; dir. spl. programs for Calif. Lt. Gov., 1983-90, ret., 1990; pvt. cons., 1990—; cons., project dir. nat. sr. health issues summit Congress Calif. Srs. Edn. and Rsch. Fund, 1995; project dir. various post-White House Conf. on Aging seminars and roundtables, 1995—; coord. Calif. Sr. LEgis., 1995—; project dir. SSI/QMB Outreach Project, 1993-94. Author Calif. Dept. Consumer Affairs publ., 1981, U.S. Office Consumer Edn. publ., 1982. Bd. dirs Sacramento/Sierra Am. Diabetes Assn., 1989-90. Author: Diabetes and Ethnic Minorities: A Community at Risk. Trustee, Stanford Settlement, Inc., Sacramento, 1975-79; bd. dirs. Sacramento Emergency Housing Ctr., 1974-77, Sacramento Cmty. Svcs. Planning Coun., 1987-90, Calif. Advs. for Nursing Home Reform, 1990—, Calif. Human Devel. Corp., 1995—; campaign workshop dir. Chicano/Latino Youth Leadership Conf., 1982-95; v.p. Comision Femenil Nacional, Inc., 1987-90; del. Dem. Nat. Conv., 1976; mem. exec. bd. Calif. Dem. Cen. Com., 1977-89; chairperson ethnic minority task force Am. Diabetes Assn., 1988-90; steering com. Calif. Self-Esteem Minority Task Force, 1990-93; del. White House Conf. Aging, 1995. Recipient numerous awards including Outstanding Cmty. Svc. award Comuicaciones Unidos de Norte Atzlan, 1975, 77, Outstanding Svc. award, Chicano/Hispanic Dem. Caucus, 1979, Vol. Svc. award Calif. Human Devel. Corp., 1981, Dem. of Yr. award Sacramento County Dem. Com., 1987, Outstanding Advocate award Calif. Sr. Legis., 1988, 89, Calif. Assn. of Homes for Aging, Advocacy award, 1989, Resolution of Advocacy award, League Latin-Ams. Citizens, 1989, Meritorious Svc. to Hispanic Cmty. award Comite Patriotico, 1989, Meritorious Svc. Resolution award Lt. Gov. of Calif., 1989, Cert. Recognition award Sacramento County Human Rights Commn., 1991, Tish Sommers award Older Women's League/Joint Resolution Calif. Legislature, 1993, Latino Eagle award in govt. Tomas Lopez Meml. Found., 1994. Mem. Hispanic C. of C., Older Women's League, CongressCalif. Srs., Sacramento Gray Panthers, Latino Dem. Club Sacramento County (v.p. 1982-83). Home and Office: 2667 Coleman Way Sacramento CA 95818-4459

PECK, GAILLARD RAY, JR., aerospace and business consultant, business owner; b. San Antonio, Oct. 31, 1940; s. Gaillard Ray and Lois (Manning) P.; m. Jean Adair Hilger, Dec. 23, 19662 (div. Oct. 1969); children: Scott, Gaillard III, Katherine Adair; m. Peggy Ann Lundt, July 3, 1975; children: Jennifer Caroline, Elizabeth Ann. BS, Air Force Acad., 1962; MA, Cen. Mich. U., 1976; MBA, U. Nev. Las Vegas, 1990. Lic. comml. pilot, flight instr. Commd. 2d lt. USAF, 1962, advanced through grades to col., 1983, ret., 1988, air force instr. pilot, fighter pilot, 1963-72; instr. Fighter Weapons Sch. USAF, Nellis AFB, 1972-75; fighter tactics officer Pentagon, Washington, 1975-78; aggressor pilot, comdr. 4477th Test & Evaluation Squadron, Nellis AFB, Nev., 1978-80; mil. advisor Royal Saudi Air Force, Saudi Arabia, 1980-82; student Nat. War Coll., Washington, 1982-83; dir. ops., vice comdr. Kadena Air Base, Japan, 1983-85; wing comdr. Zweibrucken Air Base, Germany, 1985-87; dep. dir. Aerospace Safety directorate USAF, Norton AFB, Calif., 1987-88; rsch. asst. U. Nev., Las Vegas, 1988-90; mktg. cons. Ctr. for Bus. & Econ. Rsch. U. Nev., Las Vegas, 1990; adminstr. Lung Ctr. of Nev., Las Vegas, 1991-93; bus. owner, cons. Las Vegas, 1993—; owner Great Western Aircraft Parts, LLC. Author: The Enemy, 1973, As Best I Recall, 1994. Recipient Silver Star, Legion of Merit (2), DFC (3), Air Medal (11). Mem. Phi Kappa Phi Nat. Honor Soc., Order of Daedalians, Red River Fighter Pilots Assn., Air Force Assn., Ky. Col., U. Nev. Las Vegas and Air Force Acad. Alumni Assn., The Ret. Officers Assn. Home: 1775 Sheree Cir Las Vegas NV 89119-2716

PECK, GEORGE HOLMES, public relations executive; b. Altoona, Pa., May 11, 1946; s. George Heckler and Regina (Jackson) P.; m. Barbara Ann Izydorczak, Feb. 21, 1970; children: Mark David, Heather Anne. BA, U. Montana, 1968; MA, Ball State U., 1978. Staff announcer KDRG Radio, Deer Lodge, Mont., 1963-66; staff announcer, producer KUFM Radio-TV, Missoula, Mont., 1965-68; commd. 2d lt. USAF, 1968; info. officer 4621st Air Base Group, Niagara Falls, N.Y., 1968-70; film writer, editor Aerospace Def. Command, Colorado Springs, 1970-72; chief info. Incirlik Common Def. Inst., Adana, Turkey, 1973-75; sr. pub. affairs rep. Camp New Amsterdam, Soesterberg, The Netherlands, 1975-78; dir. pub. affairs Wurtsmith AFB, Oscoda, Mich., 1978-80; spl. asst. pub. affairs Strategic Sys./B-1B Sys. Program, Dayton, Ohio, 1980-84; asst. to vice cmdr. HQ Air Force Sys. Command, Washington, 1984-86; dir. pub. affairs Aeronautical Sys. Divsn., Dayton, Ohio, 1986-88; chief media and civil affairs Hqrs. Strategic Air Command, Omaha, 1988-91; dep. pub. affairs officer UN Command, Seoul, South Korea, 1991-92; dir. pub. affairs Lowry Tng. Ctr., Denver, 1992-94; dir. pub. rels. Lowry Redevel. Authority, Denver, 1994-96; dir. cmty. rels. Columbia Presbyn./St. Luke's Med. Ctr., Denver, 1996—. Author: Understanding the Media, 1991. Bd. dirs. Aurora (Colo.) Edn. Found., 1991—, Leadership Aurora, 1991—; bd. mgrs. Aurora YMCA, 1992-96. Mem. Pub. Rels. Soc. Am. (accredited), Air Force Assn., Soc. Strategic Air Command, Colo. Healthcare Communicators, Aurora Rotary, Aurora C. of C. Roman Catholic. Home: 13250 E Center Ave Aurora CO 80012-3514 Office: Columbia Presbyn/St Lukes Med Ctr 1719 E 19th Ave Denver CO 80218

PECK, PAUL LACHLAN, minister; b. Glens Falls, N.Y., Sept. 11, 1928; s. Paul Lee and Caroline Jeannette (Stanton) P.; children: Paul Barrett, Kathryn Elizabeth Peck Kadick. BS, U. Conn., 1952; ThD, Bernadean U., 1976; MEd, Westfield State Coll., 1983. Ordained to ministry Truth Ctr., 1972. With Proctor and Gamble Co., Watertown, N.Y., 1956-60; dir. deferred giving programs Syracuse (N.Y.) U., 1960-68, v.p., 1968-70; v.p. Fairleigh-Dickinson U., N.J., 1970-71, Manhattan Coll., Bronx, N.Y., 1971-75; founder, pastor Arete' Truth Ctr., San Diego, 1975—. Author: Footsteps Along the Path, 1978, Inherit the Kingdom, 1978, Milestones of the Way, 1978, Freeway to Health, 1980, Freeway to Work and Wealth, 1981, Freeway to Human Love, 1982, Freeway to Personal Growth, 1982, Your Dreams Count, 1990, Heroic Love Poems, 1990. Bd. dirs. Girl Scouts U.S.A., Syracuse, 1967-70; trustee, bd. dirs. Erickson Ednl. Found., 1970-75; vol. chaplain Auburn (N.Y.) State Prison, 1967-68; mem. chaplains' coun. Syracuse U., 1960-70; co-founder suicide and drug abuse prevention program Syracuse U., 1968-71, Fairleigh-Dickinson U., 1970-71, Manhattan Coll., 1971-75. Staff sgt. USNG, 1947-50. Mem. Internat. New Thought Alliance, SAR, Rotary, Knights of Malta (svc. award 1973), Masons, Shriners, Spiritual Frontiers Fellowship. Home and Office: 6996 Camino Revueltos San Diego CA 92111-7642

PECK, RAYMOND CHARLES, SR., driver and traffic safety research specialist; b. Sacramento, Nov. 18, 1937; s. Emory Earl and Margaret Helen (Fiebiger) P.; m. Ellie Ruth Enriquez, Sept. 5, 1957; children: Teresa M. Peck Montijo, Linda M. Peck Heisler, Margaret H. Peck Henley, Raymond C., Christina M. Peck Reich. BA in Exptl. Psychology, Calif. State U., Sacramento, 1961, MA in Exptl. Psychology, 1968. Rsch. analyst Calif. Dept. Motor Vehicles, Sacramento, 1962-71, sr. rsch. analyst, program mgr., 1971-80, rsch. program specialist II, 1980, acting, chief rsch., 1980-81, rsch. program specialist II, 1981-84, chief of rsch., 1984—; statis. cons. to pvt. and pub. orgns., 1970—. Chmn. com. on operator regulation Transp. Rsch. Bd., Nat. Acad. Scis., 1976-82; past mem. editl. adv. bd. Traffic Safety Evaluation Rsch. Review; mem. editl. bd. Jour. Safety Rsch., Accident Analysis and Prevention; contbr. articles to profl. jours. Recipient Met. Life award of Hon., Nat. Safety Council, 1970, Met. Life Cert. of Commendation, 1972, A.R. Lauer award Human Factor Soc., 1981, award of Hon., award of Merit Traffic Safety Evaluation Rsch. Rev., 1983. Mem. APHA, AAAS, Am. Statis. Assn., Am. Assn. Automotive Medicine, Internat. Coun. Alcohol, Drugs and Traffic Safety, Human Factors Soc.. Democrat. Home: 2667 Coleman Way Sacramento CA 95818-4459 Office: Calif Dept Motor Vehicles 2415 1st Ave Sacramento CA 95818-2606

PECK, RICHARD EARL, academic administrator, playwright, novelist; b. Milw., Aug. 3, 1936; s. Earl Mason and Mary Amanda (Fry) P.; m. Donna Joy Krippner, Aug. 13, 1960; children: Mason, Laura. AB magna cum laude, Carroll Coll., Waukesha, Wis., 1961; MS, U. Wis., 1962, PhD, 1964. Asst. prof. U. Va., Charlottesville, 1964-67; assoc. dean, prof. Temple U., Phila., 1967-84; dean arts and scis. U. Ala., 1984-88; provost, v.p. academic affairs Ariz. State U., Tempe, 1988-89, interim pres., 1989-90; pres. U. N.Mex., Albuquerque, 1990—. Editor: Poems/Nathaniel Hawthorne, 1967, Poems/Floyd Stovall, 1967; author: (books) Final Solution, 1973 (nominated for John W. Campbell award as Best Sci. Fiction Novel of 1973 by Sci. Fiction Rsch. Assn.), Something for Joey, 1978, Passing Through, 1982, (plays) Sarah Bernhardt and the Bank, 1972, Don't Trip over the Money Pail, 1976, The Cubs Are in fourth Place and Fading, 1977, Phonecall, 1978, Bathnight, 1978, Prodigal Father, 1978, Lovers, Wives and Tennis Players, 1979, Curtains, 1980, A Party for Wally Pruett, 1982, Allergy Tests, 1982, Your Place or Mine, 1987, (films) Starting over Again, 1982, What Tangled Webs, 1974, Tutte le Strade Portanno a Roma, 1974, Il Diritto, 1974; contr. numerous scholarly articles to lit. jours., book revs., travel articles and humor columns to newspapers and mags., papers to univ. orgns. and witers' confs. Bd. dirs. East Valley Partnership (Econ. Devel. Orgn.), Sci. and Tech., Samaritan Health Svcs.; gubernatorial appointee, bd. dirs. Ala. Humanities Found.; mem. Nat. Found. for Post-Secondary Edn.; bd. dirs. Phila. Alliance for Teaching Humanities in the Schs., Dela. Valley Faculty Exch.; adv. bd. Ea. Pa. Theater Coun.; chmn. Temple U. Bicentennial Festival of Am. Arts, 1976; mem. Univ. Negotiating Team in re: Temple-AAUP faculty contract. Capt. USMC, 1954-59. Recipient Whitman Pub. scholarship, 1959-63, Woodrow Wilson fellowship, 1961-62, Knapp Found. fellowship, 1962-63, C. Brooks Fry award Theater Americana, Altadena, Calif., 1979. Mem. MLA, Northeast MLA. Conf. Univs. and Colls. Arts, Letters and Scis., Coun. Colls. Arts and Scis., Nat. Assn. State Univs. and Land-Grant Colls. Home: 1901 Roma Ave NE Albuquerque NM 87106-3824 Office: U NMex Office of Pres Scholes Hall Rm 160 Albuquerque NM 87131*

PECK, ROBERT DAVID, educational foundation administrator; b. Devil's Lake, N.D., June 1, 1929; s. Lester David and Bernice Marie (Peterson) P.; m. Lylia June Smith, Sept. 6, 1953; children: David Allan, Kathleen Marie. BA, Whitworth Coll., 1951; MDiv, Berkeley (Calif.) Bapt. Div. Sch., 1958; ThD, Pacific Sch. Religion, 1964; postgrad., U. Calif., Berkeley, 1959-60, 62-63, Wadham Coll., Oxford U., Eng., 1963. Music tchr. pub. schs. Bridgeport, Wash., 1954-55; prof., registrar Linfield Coll., McMinnville, Oreg., 1963-69; asst. dir. Ednl. Coordinating Coun., Salem, Oreg., 1969-75; assoc. prof. Pacific Luth. U., Tacoma, 1976-79, U. Puget Sound, Tacoma, 1977; v.p. John Minter Assocs., Boulder, Colo., 1979-81, Coun. Ind. Colls., Washington, 1981-84; adminstrv. v.p. Alaska Pacific U., Anchorage, 1984-88; pres. Phillips U., Enid, Okla., 1988-94, chancellor, 1994-95; chmn. The Pres. Found. for Support of Higher Edn., Washington, 1995—; pres. Phillips U. Ednl. Enterprises Inc., 1994-95; cons. Higher Edn. Exec. Assocs., Denver, 1984—; owner Tyee Marina, Tacoma, 1975-77; yacht broker Seattle, 1977-79. Author: Future Focusing: An Alternative to Strategic Planning, 1983, also articles. Dem. county chmn., McMinnville, 1968, Dem. candidate for state Ho. of Reps., McMinnville, 1969; pres. McMinnville Kiwanis, 1965-69. Cpl. Signal Corps, U.S. Army, 1952-54. Carnegie Corp. grantee, 1982, 84. Mem. Okla. Ind. Coll. Assn. (sec. 1989—). Mem. Christian Ch.

PECKOL, JAMES KENNETH, consulting engineer; b. Cleve., Oct. 24, 1944; s. William John and Elinor Elizabeth (Bustard) P.; children: Erin, Robyn. BS Engring., Case Inst. Tech., 1966; MSEE, U. Wash., 1975, PhDEE, 1985. Cons. GE, Raytheon, Ling Temco Vought, RCA, Boeing Co., 1966-72; sr. staff engr. indsl. products bus. unit John Fluke Mfg. Co., Seattle, 1972-83, sr. staff engr. automated systems bus. unit, 1983-86, sr. staff engr. MR&D Bus. unit, 1986-93; founder Oxford Cons., Edmonds, Wash., 1987—; affiliate asst. prof. dept. elec. engring., affiliate asst. prof. dept. computers and software sys. U. Wash., Seattle, 1984-87, 95—; sr. lectr., assoc. prof. dept. elec. engring. U. Aberdeen, Scotland, 1987; lectr. dept. math. and sci. Shoreline C.C., Seattle, 1989—; lectr. dept. computer sci. Edmonds (Wash.) C.C., 1992—; assoc. prof. dept. engring./computer sci. U. Nantes, Frances, 1993, 96; mem. computer sci. and elec. engring. curriculum adv. bd. Wash. State U., 1990—; lectr. various confs. and univs. Contbr. articles to profl. jours.; patentee in field. Mem. IEEE, Am. Assn. Artificial Intelligence, Assn. Computing Machinery, Tau Beta Pi. Home and Office: Oxford Cons Ltd 859 14th St SW Edmonds WA 98020-6611

PECSOK, ROBERT LOUIS, chemist, educator; b. Cleve., Dec. 18, 1918; s. Michael C. and Katherine (Richter) P.; m. Mary Bodell, Oct. 12, 1940 (dec. Apr. 1996); children: Helen Pecsok Wong, Katherine, Jean Pecsok Nagle, Michael, Ruth Pecsok Hughes, Alice Pecsok Tominaga, Sara Pecsok Lima; m. Marcella Beeman, Apr. 23, 1997. S.B. summa cum laude, Harvard, 1940, Ph.D., 1948. Prodn. foreman Procter & Gamble Co., Balt., 1940-43; instr. chemistry Harvard, 1948; asst. prof. chemistry U. Calif. at Los Angeles, 1948-55, asso. prof., 1955-61, prof., 1961-71, vice chmn. dept., 1965-70; prof., chmn. dept. U. Hawaii, Honolulu, 1971-80; dean natural scis. U. Hawaii, 1981-89; sci. adviser FDA, 1966-69. Author: Principles and Practice of Gas Chromatography, 1959, Analytical Methods of Organic and Biochemistry, 1966, Modern Methods of Chemical Analysis, 1968, 2d edit., 1976, Modern Chemical Technology, 1970, rev. edit. 1989, Physicochemical Applications of Gas Chromatography, 1978. Served as lt. USNR, 1943-46. Recipient Tolman medal, 1971; Guggenheim fellow, 1956-57; Petroleum Research Fund Internat. fellow, 1963-64. Mem. Am. Chem. Soc., Am. Inst. Chemists, Phi Beta Kappa, Alpha Chi Sigma, Phi Lambda Upsilon. Home: 13855 Riverhead Ct San Diego CA 92129-3222

PEDDY, JULIE ANN, federal agent; b. Chicago Heights, Ill., Apr. 2, 1959; d. Ronald Ryno and Myra Jean (Clark) P. MPA, Ind. U., Gary, 1984. Benefit authorizer trainee U.S. HHS, Chgo., 1979-80; investigator U.S. Office of Personnel Mgmt., Chgo., 1980-81, Def. Investigative Svc., Chgo., 1981-83; investigator, sr. resident agt. Def. Investigative Svc., Hammond, Ind., 1983-84; supervisory investigator, team chief Def. Investigative Svc., Chgo., 1984-89; spl. agt. in charge Def. Investigative Svc., Seattle, 1989—; mem. Seattle Fed. Exec. Bd., 1990—, chairwoman, 1995-96. Bd. dirs. Civic Light Opera, Seattle, 1996—, Lynwood (Ill.) Terr. Condominium Assn., 1989. Mem. ASPA, Ind. U. Alumni Assn. (life), Pi Alpha Alpha. Methodist. Office: Def Investigative Svc PO Box 33520 Seattle WA 98133-0520

PEDEN, LYNN ELLEN, marketing executive; b. L.A., Mar. 1, 1946; d. Orlan Sidney and Erna Lou (Harris) Friedman; m. Ernest Peden, Aug. 1994. Student UCLA, 1963-65, 71-72, Willis Bus. Coll., 1965-66, Fin. Schs. Am., 1982, Viewpoints Inst., 1970-71. Office mgr. Harleigh Sandler Co., L.A., 1965-67; customer svc. Investors Diversified Svcs., West L.A., Calif., 1968-76; exec. sec. McCulloch Oil Corp., West L.A., 1976; mgr. publs. Security 1st Group, Century City, Calif., 1976-80; office mgr. Morehead & Co., Century City, 1980-81; dir. mktg., mgr. customer svc. Ins. Mktg. Services, Santa Monica, Calif., 1981-82; v.p. Decatur Petroleum Corp., Santa Monica, 1982-83; asst. v.p., broker svcs., dir. Angeles Corp., L.A., 1984-87; asst. to pres. Pacific Ventures, Santa Monica, 1988-90; asst. to pres. La Grange Group, West L.A., 1990-95. Mem. Migi Car Am. Club (sec., newsletter editor). Fin. and ins. writer; contbr. poetry to UCLA Literary Mag., 1964. Home: 4365 Mclaughlin Ave Apt 12 Los Angeles CA 90066-5957

PEDERSEN, GAYLEN, genealogy organization administrator; b. Salt Lake City, Mar. 4, 1934; s. Oliver Cowdery and Phoebe Gold (Gedge) P.; m. Mary Ann Hunter, Sept. 13, 1957; children: Mark Alan, Gordon Hunter, Gay Lynn, Eric David, Scott Douglas, Julie Ann, Dale Ryan. BS in Physics, Brigham Young U., 1959. Missionary Ch. of Jesus Christ of Latter-day Saints, New England states, 1954-56; instr. math. Cen. Utah Vocat. Sch., Provo, Utah, 1958-59; assoc., design engr. Boeing Co., Seattle, Washington, 1959-62; gen. mgr. Ogden Air Logistics Ctr., Hill Air Force Base (Utah), 1962-87; sr. instr. Shipley Assocs., Bountiful, Utah, 1987-89; pres., CEO Pedersen Pub., Bountiful, 1987-89; pres., chmn. bd. Gaylen Pedersen Family Orgn., Bountiful, 1976—; dir. mktg. Redcon-Resource Data Consultants, Bountiful, 1989-90; USAF sr. mgmt. staff Ogden Air Logistics Ctr., Hill Air Force Base, 1983-87, USAF mid. mgr., 1976-83; pvt. cons., 1990—. Author: System Level, Post Production Support: Tendencies, Conditions and Principles, 1988; editor: Nutritional Herbology, Vol. I, 1987, Vol. II, 1988. Instl. rep. Boy Scouts Am., Bountiful, 1965-67, basketball coach Explorer Scouts, 1980-87; bishop Ch. Jesus Christ Latter-day Saints, 1969-73. With U.S. Army, 1956-58. Republican. Office: Gaylen Pedersen Family Orgn 1311 Indian Trail Cir Bountiful UT 84010-1461

PEDERSEN, JEAN JORGENSON, mathematician, educator; m. Kent A. Pedersen. B.S., Brigham Young U., 1955. M.S. in Math., U. Utah, 1958. Cert. secondary tchr., Utah. Tchr. math., public jr. and sr. high schs., Utah, 1958-59; instr. math. U. Utah, 1959-65; asst. prof. U. Santa Clara, 1965-72, lectr., 1972-85; sr. lectr. 1985-89, asst. prof., 1989-90, assoc. prof., 1990—; lectr. NSF Vis. Scientist Program, 1963-65, and active various other NSF programs, 1959-79; dir. Bay Area Women and Math. Lectureship Program, 1975-80. Mem. Am. Math. Soc., Math. Assn. Am. (lectr. women and math. lectureship program mem. panel vis. lectrs., gov. No. Calif. sect. 1981-84), Calif. Math. Council, Nat. Council Tchrs. Math, Santa Clara Valley Math. Assn. (pres. 1976-77). Author: (with E. Allan Davis) Essentials of Trigonometry, 1969, 2d edit., 1973, 74; (with Kent A. Pedersen) Geometric Playthings, 1973, 3rd edit., 1986; (with Allan Davis) Essentials of Trigonometry, 1975; (with Franz O. Armbruster) A New Twist (To Arithmetic Drill Through Problem Solving), 1979; (with Peter J. Hilton) Fear No More, An Adult Approach to Mathematics, 1983, (with Peter Hilton) Build Your Own Polyhedra, 1988, 94, (with Peter Hilton) College Preparatory Mathematics, 1994 (with Peter Hilton and Derek Holton) Mathematical Reflections: In a Room with Many Mirrors, 1997; contbr. numerous articles to profl. publs.; assoc. editor Math. Mag., 1981-84. Home: PO Box 26 New Almaden CA 95042-0026

PEDERSEN, KIM AASBERG, newsletter publisher, video producer; b. Bakersfield, Calif., Feb. 11, 1952; s. Gill Aasberg Pedersen and Gerda Lykke (Petersen) Bishop; m. Carol Ellen Stephens, May 31, 1981; children: Kory Carl, Skyler Drew. AA, Cañada Coll., Redwood City, Calif., 1972. Cook Spaghettory, Redwood City, 1972; car washer Genie Car Wash, San Diego, 1973-75; aerospace artist Foster City, Calif., 1976-78; accounts receivable clk. Beechcraft West, Hayward, Calif., 1978-85; fin. asst. II City of Fremont, Calif., 1985—; pres., editor, owner The Monorail Soc., Calif., 1989—. Editor Monorail Newsletter, 1989—; prodr. (video) Roller Coaster Films of Kim Pedersen, 1989, Monorails of Japan, 1992.

PEDERSEN, MARTIN ALBERT, consulting land surveyor; b. Rawlins, Wyo., Dec. 2, 1946; s. Rasmus and Ella (Rasmussen) P.; m. Karen Louise Bond, Aug. 26, 1967 (div. 1978); children: David Frank, Jennifer Louise; m. Patricia Ann Smith, Mar. 1, 1980; 1 child, Hans Rasmus. Student, U. Wyo., 1965. Registered land surveyor, Wyo., Mont., Idaho, Nev., Ariz., N.Mex., N.D., S.D., Colo., Calif., U.S. mineral surveyor. Surveyor Robert Jack Smith & Assocs., Rawlins, 1966-75, prin., 1975—. Scoutmaster Boy Scouts Am., Rawlins, 1969-75, dist. chmn., 1975-81; active Rawlins Search and Rescue Dive Team; mem. Christ Luth. Ch., Rotary. Mem. Wyo. Assn. Cons. Engrs. and Surveyors (pres. 1978), Wyo. State Bd. for Registration for Profl. Engrs. & Profl. Land Surveyors, Profl. Land Surveyors Wyo. (pres. 1980-81), Am. Congress Surveying and Mapping, Wyo. Engring. Soc. (sec.-treas. 1988-96), Ducks Unltd., Elks. Home: 207 E Heath St Rawlins WY 82301-4307 Office: Robert Jack Smith Assocs Inc PO Box 1104 1015 Harshman St Rawlins WY 82301-1104

PEDERSEN, MOGENS HINGEBERG, software engineer; b. Skive, Denmark, Jan. 18, 1947; came to U.S., 1979; s. Bjarne H. and Signe R. (Christensen) P.; children: Glenn, Ian, Brian. Student pub. schs., Denmark. Systems programmer Data Centralen, Copenhagen, 1967-68, Eaton's, Toronto, Ont., Can., 1969-71; cons. Can. Systems Group, Mississauga, Can., 1971-79; engr. Storage Tech. Corp., Louisville, Colo., 1979-84; sr. adv. engr. Storage Tech. Corp., Louisville, 1987—; software engr. Intelli Store, Longmont, Colo., 1984-87. Co-author: (inventions) DDSR, 1993, Snapshot Application Group, 1995. Home: 1233 Brookfield Dr Longmont CO 80501 Office: Storage Tech Corp 2270 S 88th St Louisville CO 80028-0001

PEDESKY, GERALDINE GOLICK, design project professional; b. Hayward, Calif., Oct. 27, 1935; d. Charles Anthony and Dolores Irene (Lemon) Golick; m. Charles Francis Pedesky, Nov. 10, 1960. BA, San Jose State Coll., 1957. Flight attendant Trans Continental Airlines, Burbank, Calif., 1958-62; office mgr. The Hertz Corp., L.A., 1964-77; v.p. adminstr. Vitousek Real Estate Sch., Honolulu, 1977-94; project mgr. Philpotts & Assoc., Honolulu, 1994—; mem. sec. Hawaii Assn. Real Estate Schs., Honolulu, 1977-93. Trustee Bernice Pauahi Bishop Mus., Honolulu, 1988-94, mem. exec. com., 1994; mem. Bishop Mus. Assn., Honolulu, 1983-87 (past pres.), Bishop Mus. Svc. League, Honolulu, 1977-83 (pres. 1982); bd. dirs. Outrigger Duke Kahanamoku Found., Honollulu, 1986-94 (pres.1989). Mem. Outrigger Canoe Club (bd. dirs., sec.-treas., v.p. ops.), Honolulu Acad. Arts, Contemporary Mus. Art, Nature Conservancy, Bishop Mus. Assn. Office: Philpotts & Assocs 925 Bethel St Ste 200 Honolulu HI 96813-4307

PEDITTO, CHRISTOPHER NATALE, humanities, English and communications educator; b. Riverside, N.J., Dec. 3, 1943; s. Christopher Natale and Constance (LaFreda) P.; m. Cathleen Hughes, May 1978 (div. 1982); m. Barbara Levin Romain, Aug. 1995. BA, Rutgers U., 1966; MA, Calif. State U., Northridge, 1990. Instr., coord. Graterford prison writing program Montgomery County C.C., Norristown, Pa., 1984-85; instr. cmty. outreach writing program La Salle U., Phila., 1985; instr. Bus. Comm. Adelphi Bus. Coll., Van Nuys, Calif., 1985-87; instr. Bus. English and Comm., Proofreading Barclay Coll., L.A., 1987-90; adj. instr. civic outreach program L.A. Trade-Tech Coll., L.A., 1990—; instr. Columbia Coll., Hollywood, Calif., 1990-91; asst. prof. Charles R. Drew U. of Medicine & Sci., L.A., 1990—; lectr. pub. speaking/interpersonal comm. Loyola Marymont U., L.A., 1990-91. Contbg. editor: Home Planet News, 1985—; publ., gen. editor: Heat Press, 1993—; artistic dir.: (theatrical) Gray Pony Prodns., 1990—; dir. (poetry series) Open Mouth Poetry, 1982-85. NEH fellow, 1993, 94. Mem. Speech Comm. Assn., Nat. Coun. Tchrs. English, Conf. Coll. Composition and Comm., Am.-Italian Hist. Assn., Arba Sicula. Home: 1521 Sargent Pl Los Angeles CA 90026-2539

PEEBLES, CAROL LYNN, immunology researcher; b. Wellington, Kans., Jan. 20, 1941; d. Harry Alexander and Phyllis Dorothy (Pyle) P. BA, Kans. State Coll. of Pittsburg, 1962, MS, 1964; cert. med. technology, St. Francis Hosp., Wichita, Kans., 1965. Med. technologist St. Francis Hosp., Wichita, 1965-74; lab. supr. allergy and immunology Scripps Clinic and Rsch. Found., La Jolla, Calif., 1974-77; sr. rsch. asst. Autoimmune Disease Ctr. Scripps Clinic and Rsch. Found., La Jolla, 1982—; lab. supr. rheumatology lab. U. Colo. Health Scis. Ctr., Denver, 1977-82. Author workshop manual; contbr. articles to sci. publs. Mem. Am. Coll. Rheumatology, AAAS, Am. Soc. Microbiology, Am. Soc. Med. Tech., Am. Soc. Clin. Pathology. Office: Scripps Rsch Inst Rm SBR6 10550 N Torrey Pines Rd La Jolla CA 92037-1027

PEEL, FRED WELCH, JR., law educator, writer; b. Junction City, Ky., Aug. 5, 1918; s. Fred Welch and Bessie Prudence (Rogers) P.; m. Evelyn Osovitz, Dec. 21, 1948; 1 child, Ellen Susan. BS, Harvard U., 1939, LLB, 1942. Bar: D.C. Cons. War Dept., Washington, 1946; bus. specialist U.S. Housing Agy., Washington, 1946-47; economist U.S. Treasury, Washington, 1947; rsch. clk. Senate Fin. Com., Washington, 1947-48; atty. Joint Taxation Com., Washington, 1948-52; atty., ptnr. Alvord & Alvord, Washington, 1952-65, Miller & Chevalier, Washington, 1965-76; prof. law U. Ark. Little Rock Sch. Law, 1976-87, Altheimer Disting. prof., 1986-87; vis. prof. Gonzaga Law Sch., Spokane, summer 1979, So. Meth. Law Sch., Dallas, 1980, William and Mary Law Sch., Williamsburg, Va., 1982-83; adj. prof. Santa Clara (Calif.) Law Sch., 1997; mem. adv. coun. Ark. Tax Reform Commn., Little Rock, 1987-88. Author: Consolidated Tax Returns, 1959, 3d edit., 1984, Understanding the Federal Income Tax, 1988; co-author: Readings and Materials on Tax Policy, 1996. Capt. U.S. Army, 1945-46, ETO. Mem. ABA, D.C. Bar, Nat. Tax Assn., Nat. Press Club, Harvard Club of San Francisco, Phi Beta Kappa. Democrat. Home: 4 Mariposa Ct Burlingame CA 94010-5731

PEELER, STUART THORNE, petroleum industry executive and independent oil operator; b. Los Angeles, Oct. 28, 1929; s. Joseph David and Elizabeth Fiske (Boggess) P.; m. Sylvia Frances Townley, Nov. 5, 1985. B.A., Stanford U., 1950, J.D., 1953. Bar: Calif. 1953. Ptnr. Musick, Peeler & Garrett, Los Angeles, 1958-73; with Santa Fe Internat. Corp., Orange, Calif., 1973-81; v.p., sec., assoc. gen. counsel Santa Fe Internat. Corp., 1973-74, sr. v.p., gen. counsel, dir., 1975-81; vice-chmn. bd., chmn. exec. com. Supron Energy Corp., 1978-82; chmn. bd., chief exec. officer Statex Petroleum, Inc., 1982-89; chmn., pres. and chief exec. officer Putumayo Prodn. Co., 1989—; bd. dirs. Cal Mat Co., Homestake Mining Co., Chieftain Internat. Inc. Trustee J. Paul Getty Trust; mem. U.S. Tuna Team, 1957-67, capt., 1966. Served with U.S. Army, 1953-55. Decorated Army Commendation medal. Mem. AIME, State Bar Calif., Am. Judicature Soc., Theta Chi, Phi Delta Phi, Tucson Country Club, Skyline Country Club. Republican. Congregationalist. Office: PO Box 35852 Tucson AZ 85740-5852

PEERSEN, OLVE BREIEN, biochemist; b. Bergen, Norway, Nov. 20, 1965; came to U.S., 1978; s. Svend Eilif Peersen and Lajla Auguste (Breien) Ryen; m. Rebecca Lynn Finkel. BS, Carnegie Mellon U., 1988; MPhil, Yale U., 1991, PhD, 1994. Rsch. assoc. U. Colo., Boulder, 1994—. NSF grantee, 1987; NIH tng. grantee, 1988, NIH postdoctoral fellow, 1994.

PEFLEY, NORMAN GORDON, financial analyst; b. Eugene, Oreg., Dec. 15, 1955; s. Gordon Vergne Pefley and Jean Pefley (Lee) Hawley; m. Emma Ginete Lacuesta, July 5, 1986. BA, U. Calif., Davis, 1977; MA, Johns Hopkins U., 1979; MBA, U. Chgo., 1981. CFA. Rsch. analyst Chgo. Bd. Options Exch., 1981-83; sr. fin. analyst Bank of Am., San Francisco, 1983-89, v.p., 1989—; referee Jour. Futures Market, N.Y.C., 1984-87. Mem. Am. Fin. Assn., Am. Econ. Assn., Assn. for Investment Mgmt. and Rsch., The Security Analysts of San Francisco, Commonwealth Club of Calif., Toastmasters Internat., Phi Beta Kappa, Delta Phi Alpha, Omicron Delta Epsilon.

PEI, YAZHONG, chemist; b. Yushu, Jilin, China, July 26, 1962; came to the U.S., 1985; s. Guanghui and Runxian (Fu) P.; m. Min Teng, July 7, 1988; 1 child, Bradley Minxing. BS in Chemistry, Jilin U., ChangChun, China, 1984; PhD in Chemistry, SUNY, Stony Brook, 1990. Post-doctoral fellow Parke-Davis/Warner-Lambert Co., Ann Arbor, Mich., 1990-92; scientist Chiron Corp., Emeryville, Calif., 1992-94; sr. scientist Cortex Pharmaceuticals, Inc., Irvine, Calif., 1994-95; sr. rsch. scientist Houghten Pharms., Inc., San Diego, 1995—. Patentee in field. Chemistry Grad. Program fellow Ministry of Edn., China, 1985. Mem. Am. Chem. Soc. Office: Houghten Pharms Inc 3550 Gen Atomics Ct San Diego CA 92121

PEIRANO, LAWRENCE EDWARD, civil engineer; b. Stockton, Calif., May 13, 1929; s. Frank Lloyd and Esther Marie (Carigiet) P.; m. Mary Ellen Alabaster, July 26, 1952; children: Thomas Lawrence, Ellen Marie. BSCE, U. Calif., Berkeley, 1951, MSCE, 1952. Registered profl. engr., Calif., Nev.; diplomate Am. Acad. Environ. Engrs. Assoc. civil engr. Calif. Div. Water Resources, 1952-53; with Kennedy Engrs., Inc., San Francisco, 1955-94, project mgr., 1960-79, v.p., chief environ. engr., 1974-79; dir. ops. Kennedy/Jenks Engrs., Inc., San Francisco, 1979-86; sr. v.p., regional mgr. Kennedy/Jenks/Chilton, Inc., San Francisco, 1986-90; exec. v.p., chief tech. officer Kennedy/Jenks Cons., Inc. (formerly Kennedy Engrs., Inc.), San Francisco, 1990-94, also bd. dirs., chmn. bd., 1972-94; ret., 1994; spl. lectr. san. engring. U. Calif., Berkeley, 1976. Served in U.S. Army, 1953-55, Korea, Okinawa. James Monroe McDonald scholar, 1950-51. Fellow ASCE (life); mem. Water Environ. Fedn., U. Calif. Alumni Assn., Sierra Club, Tau Beta Pi, Chi Epsilon. Republican. Roman Catholic. Home: 3435 Black Hawk Rd Lafayette CA 94549-2326 *Focus on serving clients and rewards will follow.*

PEIRSON, GEORGE EWELL, film producer, art director, educator; b. L.A., May 16, 1957; s. Malcolm Alan and Beth (Wanlass) P. BFA, Art Ctr. Coll. of Design, Pasadena, Calif., 1986. Photographer Griffith Park Observatory, L.A., 1981-84; owner, art dir. Peirson to Peirson Studio, West Hills, Calif., 1983—; instr. Art Workshops, L.A., 1988-89, Learning Tree U., Chatsworth, Calif., 1990-93. Art dir., films include Valentine's Day, 1986, Private Demons, 1986, The Courtyard, 1987, Hope of the Future, Escape from Lethargia, 1988, Time Scrambler, 1988, Star Quest, 1988, Star Runner, 1989, The World of Early Bird, 1989, Dominic's Castle, 1991, The Deadly Avenger, 1991, Hell Comes to Frogtown II, 1991, The Minister's Wife, 1991, Eye of the Stranger, 1992, Showtime, 1992, Star Runners, 1992, Monty, 1992, Guyver, Dark Hero, 1993, Tiger Mask, The Star, 1994, Dragon Fury, 1994, Arizona Werewolf, 1994, Drifting School, 1994; prodr., films include Jurassic Women, 1994, Wolves Carnival, 1995, King of Hearts, 1995, Rollergator, 1995, Lord Protector, 1996, Lancelot: Guardian of Time, 1997. Mem. Assn. for Astron. Arts (bd. mem., v.p. 1987-89), Costumers Guild West, Assn. of Sci. Fiction and Fantasy Artists. Republican. Office: Peirson to Peirson Studio 23409 Gilmore St West Hills CA 91307-3314

PEKAR, PETER, JR., business professional; b. Chgo., June 15, 1942; s. Peter Paul and Mildred (Samec) P.; m. Michele McFaull; children: Michele, Erik, William, Patrick. MA in Math., U. Ill., 1969; PhD in Bus. and Econs., Ill. Inst. Tech., 1974. V.p. Michael Allen Co., Conn., 1980-83; head bus. devel. Dun & Bradstreet, N.Y.C., 1983-87; pres. U.S.A. Bührmann-Tetterode N.V., Greenwich, Conn., 1987-91; sr. advisor Booz Allen & Hamilton, L.A., 1992—; pres., mng. dir. Claremont (Calif.) Alliance Group, 1991; vis. assoc. prof. London Bus. Sch., 1996. Author: Planning for Non-Planners, 1980 (Top 5 Book award Am. Mgmt. Assn. 1980); contbg. editor Planning Rev., 1983-86; contbr. articles to profl. jours. Active Chgo. United Way, Am. Cancer Soc., Chgo. Mem. Am. Mgmt. Assn., The Planning Forum, Univ. Club, N.Y.C. and Chgo., Nat. Assn. Corp. Dirs. Home: 2272 N Indian Hill Blvd Claremont CA 91711-1726 Office: Booz Allen & Hamilton 5220 Pacific Con Dr 390 Los Angeles CA 90045

PELKING, MARIAN VIRGINIA, early childhood educator; b. Fort Thomas, Ky., Aug. 19, 1929; d. William Fred and Marian Mattie (Ward) Wahlert; m. Douglas C.R. Pelking, Aug. 25, 1950; children: Scott Irwin, Holly Lynne. BS in Edn., Ind. U., South Bend, 1972; MEd, Ind. State U., 1976. Cert. tchr., N.Mex. 3d grade tchr. Mishawaka (Ind.) Schs., 1973-74, 81-82; 2d grade tchr. Las Cruces (N.Mex.) Pub. Schs., 1984-85, 88-89, 1st grade tchr., 1989-95, ret., 1995; co-dir. Exxon Math Grant, Las Cruces, 1989—; cooperating tchr. Las Cruces Pub. Schs., N.Mex. State U., 1984—; edn. cons., 1995—. Named Outstanding Math. Tchr. N.Mex. Acad. Sci., 1992; recipient Nat. Educator award Milkew Family Found., 1994. Mem. Nat. Coun. Tchrs. Math. (Presdl. citation NSF/Nat. Coun. Tchrs. Math. 1991, 93, Las Curces Tchr. Yr. 1994), Nat. Assn. Edn. Young Children, Phi Delta Kappa. Democrat. Presbyterian. Home: 1967 Cummings Ct Las Cruces NM 88001-2502

PELLEGRINI, CARLOS ALBERTO, surgeon, educator; b. Freye, Argentina, June 23, 1946. MD, U. Rosario Med. Sch., 1971. Intern in surgery Rosario U. Hosp., Argentina, 1970-71; resident in gen. surgery Rosario U. Hosp., 1971-75; fellow in surgery U. Chgo., 1975-76, resident in surgery, 1976-79; asst. prof. U. Calif., San Francisco, 1979-84; assoc. prof. U. Calif., 1984-89, prof., 1989-92; prof., chmn. dept. surgery U. Wash., Seattle, 1993-96, Henry N. Harkins prof., chmn. dept. surgery, 1996—; staff physician VA Med. Ctr., San Francisco, 1979-92, chief surgical outpatient clinics, 1979-89, chief exptl. surgery, 1980-89; attending physician U. Calif., San Francisco, 1979-92, chief blue surgery svc., 1987-92, asst. chief surgery faculty practice, 1988-92, dir. ctr. for study of gastrointestinal motility and secretions, 1989-92; attending surgeon, U. Wash., 1993—; surgery physician VA Med. Ctr., Seattle, 1993—; attending surgeon Harborview Med. Ctr., Seattle, 1993—. Fellow ACS (internat. rels. com. 1983—, subcom. on guest scholars 1985-88, chmn. 1988-89, liaison and rep. to Latin Am. Congress of Fellows 1989-92, com. on motion pictures 1988—, exec. com. mem. 1991, chmn. 1993-95, chmn. gen. surgery program com. No. Calif. chpt. 1980-83, councilor San Francisco 1984-86, sec.-treas. 1986-89, pres.-elect 1989-90, pres. 1990, chmn. No. Calif. dist. #1 com. on applicants 1987-92); mem. AAAS, AMA (cons. diagnostic & therapeutic tech. assessment 1992), Am. Assn. Study of Liver Disease, Am. Motility Soc., Am. Gastroenterological Assn., Am. Surg. Assn., Am. Bd. Surgery (guest examiner 1985, 88), ACGME (residency review com., rep.), Soc. Surgery of Alimentary Tract (mem. membership com. 1985-89, trustee 1994—), Collegium Internationale Chirurgiae Digestivae (U.S.A. sect., pres. 1992-94, chmn. edn. com., 1995—), Pan Pacific Surg. Assn. (v.p. 1993), Assn. Acad. Surgery, H.C. Naffziger Surg. Soc., San Francisco Med. Soc., Assn. Argentina de Cirugia, hon. mem. Soc. Univ. Surgeons, Western Surg. Assn., Pacific Coast Surg. Assn., Soc. Am. Gastrointestinal Endoscopy Surgeons, Soc. Argentina de Cirugia Digestiva (hon.), Internat. Hepato-Biliary-Pancreatic Assn., Soc. Internat. de Chirugie, Soc. Clin. Surgery, Southwestern Clin. Congress, Soc. Colombiana de Cirugia, Calif. Acad. Medicine, North Pacific Surg. Assn., Soc. Surg. Chmn., James IV Assn. Surgeons, Surg. Biology Club, Esophageal Surg. Club, The Pancreas Club (chmn. local arrangements com. 1986, 92). Home: 11755 NE 36th Pl Bellevue WA 98005-1234 Office: U Wash Dept Surgery PO Box 356410 1959 NE Pacific St Seattle WA 98195-0004

PELLETIER, KENNETH R., behavioral physician, educator, author; b. Nashua, N.H., Apr. 27, 1946; s. Roger Norman and Lucy Barbara (Leonetti) P.; m. Elizabeth Anne Berryhill, Oct. 28, 1980. BA in Psychology, U. Calif., Berkeley, 1969, PhD in Clin. Psychology, 1974; MD, Ministry of Health, 1985. Lic. clin. psychologist, Calif. Assoc. clin. prof., dept. medicine and dept. psychiatry Univ. Calif., Sch. of Medicine, San Francisco, 1974-90; clin. assoc. prof. Stanford Ctr. for Disease Prevention Stanford U. Sch. Medicine, Calif., 1990—, dir. Stanford Corp. health program, 1990—; dir. complementary and alternative medicine program Stanford U., 1995—; v.p. Healthtrac, Inc., Menlo Park, Calif., 1995—; sr. clin. assoc. Johnson & Johnson Health Mgmt. Inc., New Brunswick, N.J., Santa Monica, Calif., 1985-95; advisor U.S. Dept. Health and Human Svcs.; bd. Nat. Resource Ctr. on Worksite Health Promotion, Blue Shield, The Can. Ministry of Health, World Health Orgn.; bd. dirs. Health Sys. Internat., Health Net, Am. Inst. of Stress, Conservation Internat., Calif. Wellness Found., Nat. Health Mgmt. Found., Am. Holistic Med. Assn. Co-author: Consciousness: East and West, 1976; author: Mind as Healer, Mind as Slayer, 1977, rev. edit., 1992, Toward a Science of Consciousness, 1978, Holistic Medicine: From Stress to Optimum Health, 1979, Longevity: Fulfilling our Biological Potential, 1981, rev. edit., 1991, Health People in Unhealthy Places: Stress and Fitness at Work, 1984, Sound Mind, Sound Body, 1994, A New Model for Lifelong Health; mem. editl. bd. Medical Self-Care Mag., Am. Jour. Health Promotion, Longevity, Am. Health; contbr. over 250 articles to jours. Named Woodrow Wilson fellow Woodrow Wilson Found., 1970, USPHS Svc. fellow, 1973-74. Mem. AAAS, Am. Psychol. Assn., Washington Bus. Group on Health, Soc. Behavioral Medicine, Am. Heart Assoc. Office: Stanford Univ Sch Medicine 1000 Welch Rd Stanford CA 94304-1825

PELLONE, DAVID THOMAS, financial executive; b. Ashtabula, Ohio, Mar. 15, 1944; s. Frank Joseph and Shirley Edna (Foster) P.; m. Sunny Jewel Unfug, May 28, 1977; children: Todd Gary, Michelle Christine. BBA in Indsl. Mgmt., Kent State U., 1967; MBA in Acctg. and Fin., U. Santa Clara, 1973. Product supr., indsl. engr. Owens Corning Fiberglass, Santa Clara, Calif., 1970-72; line contr. Fairchild Semiconductor, Mountain View, Calif., 1973-74; corp. contr. Cermetek, Inc., Mountain View, 1974-76; various mgmt. positions 3M Co., Ventura, Calif., 1976-83; cons. J&P Assocs., Menlo Park, Calif., 1983-84; area fin. mgr. GenRad, Inc., Milpitas, Calif., 1984-86; v.p., contr. Genus, Inc., Mountain View, 1986-90; v.p. fin. and adminstrn. AG Assocs. Inc., Sunnyvale, Calif., 1990-93; prin. Auburn Cons. Group, Menlo Park, Calif., 1993-95; contr. Duel Systems Inc., San Jose, Calif., 1995—; instr. U. San Francisco, 1990-91, DeAnza Coll., 1991, Golden Gate U., 1994—, Menlo Coll., Calif., 1997—. With U.S. Army, 1967-69. Mem. Am. Mgmt. Assn., Am. Acctg. Assn., Inst. Internal Auditors, Inst. Indsl. Engrs. (sr.), U. Santa Clara MBA Alumni (bd. dirs.), Churchill Club, Commonwealth Club (Calif.), World Forum of Silicon Valley. Republican. Episcopalian.

PELOQUIN, LOUIS OMER, lawyer; b. Tracy, Quebec, Can., June 15, 1957; came to U.S., 1986; s. Gilles and Andree (Gelinas) P.; m. Carole Plante, Aug. 21, 1987; children: Louis-Alexandre, Valerie. BBA, Laval U.,

Quebec City, Can., 1980; LLB, U. Montreal, Can., 1984; LLM, NYU, 1987. Bar: Que. 1985, N.Y. 1988. Assoc. Martineau Walker, Montreal, Que., Can., 1985-86, Paul, Weiss, Rifkind, Wharton & Garrison, N.Y.C., 1987-89, Shearman & Sterling, N.Y.C., 1989-91, McCarthy Tetrault, Montreal, 1991-93; v.p., gen. counsel, sec. Golden Star Resources Ltd., Denver, 1993—. Contbr. articles to profl. jours. Recipient Richard de Boo prize in Taxation, 1984. Mem. ABA, N.Y. Bar Assn., Quebec Bar Assn., Assn. Am. Corp. Counsel, Rocky Mountain Mineral Law Found. Home: 5300 E Nichols Dr Littleton CO 80122-3892 Office: Golden Star Resources Ltd 1700 Lincoln St # 1950 Denver CO 80203-4501

PELOSI, NANCY, congresswoman; b. Balt., Mar. 26, 1941; d. Thomas J. D'Alesandro Jr.; m. Paul Pelosi; children: Nancy Corinne, Christine, Jacqueline, Paul, Alexandra. Grad., Trinity Coll. Former chmn. Calif. State Dem. Com., 1981; committeewoman Dem. Nat. Com., 1976, 80, 84; fin. chmn. Dem. Senatorial Campaign Com., 1987; mem. 99th-102d Congresses from 5th Calif. dist., 1987-1992, 103rd Congress from 8th Calif. dist., 1993—; mem. appropriations com., subcoms. on labor, HHS and edn., fgn. ops., mem. intelligence select com. Office: US House of Rep 2457 Rayburn Washington DC 20515-0508

PELOTTE, DONALD EDMOND, bishop; b. Waterville, Maine, Apr. 13, 1945; s. Norris Albert and Margaret Yvonne (LaBrie) P. AA, Eymard Sem. and Jr. Coll., Hyde Park, N.Y., 1965; BA, John Carroll U., 1969; MA, Fordham U., 1971, PhD, 1975. Ordained priest Roman Cath. Ch., 1972. Provincial superior Blessed Sacrament, Cleve., from 1978; ordained coadjutor bishop Diocese of Gallup, N.Mex., 1986-90, bishop, 1990—; nat. bd. dirs. Maj. Superiors of Men, Silver Spring, Md., 1981-86, Tekakwitha Conf., Great Falls, Mont., 1981—. Author: John Courtney Murray: Theologian in Conflict, 1976. 1st native Am. bishop. Mem. Cath. Theol. Soc. Am., Am. Cath. Hist. Soc. *

PELTASON, JACK WALTER, former university president, educator; b. St. Louis, Aug. 29, 1923; s. Walter B. and Emma (Hartman) P.; m. Suzanne Toll, Dec. 21,1946; children: Nancy Hartman, Timothy Walter H., Jill K. BA, U. Mo., 1943, MA, 1944, LLD (hon.), 1978; AM, Princeton U., 1946, PhD, 1947; LLD (hon.), U. Md., 1979, Ill. Coll., 1979, Gannon U., 1980, U. Maine, 1980, Union Coll., 1981, Moorehead (N.D.) State U., 1980; LHD (hon.), 1980, Ohio State U., 1980, Mont. Coll. Mineral Scis. and Tech., 1982, Buena Vista Coll., 1982, Assumption Coll., 1983, Chapman Coll., 1986, U. Ill., 1989. Asst. prof. Smith Coll., Mass., 1947-51; asst. prof. polit. sci. U. Ill., Urbana, 1951-52, assoc. prof., 1953-59, dean Coll. Liberal Arts and Scis., 1960-64, chancellor, 1967-77; vice chancellor acad. affairs U. Calif., Irvine, 1964-67, chancellor, 1984-92; pres. U. Calif. System, Oakland, 1992-95, Am. Coun. Edn., Washington, 1977-84; prof. emeritus dept. politics and soc. U. Calif., Irvine, 1995—; Cons. Mass. Little Hoover Commn., 1950. Author: The Missouri Plan for the Selection of Judges, 1947, Federal Courts and the Political Process, 1957, Fifty-eight Lonely Men, 1961, Understanding the Constitution, 14th edit., 1997, orig. edition, 1949, (with James M. Burns) Government By the People, 16th edit., 1995, orig. edit., 1952; contbr. articles and revs. to profl. jours. Recipient James Madison medal Princeton U., 1982. Fellow Am. Acad. Arts and Scis.; mem. Am. Polit. Sci. Assn. (council 1952-54), Phi Beta Kappa, Phi Kappa Phi, Omicron Delta Kappa, Alpha Phi Omega, Beta Gamma Sigma. Home: 18 Whistler Ct Irvine CA 92612-4069 Office: U Calif Dept Politics and Society 18 Whistler Ct Irvine CA 92612-4069

PELTON, HAROLD MARCEL, mortgage broker; b. Montreal, Que., Can., Jan. 24, 1922; s. Grover Cleveland and Denise (Pigeon) P.; m. Frances Farley, June 1947 (div. 1968); children: Mary Virginia Joyner, Diane Jean Slagowski; m. Virginia L. King, July 11, 1970. Student, L.A. City Coll., 1948-49, Anthony Schs., Van Nuys, Calif., 1966. Lic. real estate real broker, Calif. Stockbroker, agt. Mitchum, Jones, Templeton Assurance Co., L.A., 1957-60; owner Assurance Investment Co., Van Nuys, Calif., 1960-65; sales syndicator TSI Investment Co., L.A., 1965-69; pres., owner Univest Co., Beverly Hills, Calif., 1970-72, Am. Oil Recovery, L.A., 1973-79; v.p. Newport Pacific Funding Co., Newport Beach, Calif., 1979-81; chmn. bd. dirs. TD Publs., El Toro, Calif., 1981-83; pres., broker HP Fin., Inc., Laguna Hills, Calif., 1983--. Contbg. editor Am. Oil Recovery newspaper, 1973-79; editor Trust Deed Jour., 1981-83. Served with U.S. Army, 1942-46, PTO. Mem. L. A. Mus. Art, Laguna Hills C. of C., Kiwanis, Toastmasters. Republican. Office: HP Fin Inc 24942 Georgia Sue Laguna Hills CA 92653-4323

PELTZER, DOUGLAS LEA, semiconductor device manufacturing company executive; b. Clinton, Ia., July 2, 1938; s. Albert and Mary Ardelle (Messer) P.; m. Nancy Jane Strickler, Dec. 22, 1959; children: Katharine, Eric, Kimberly. BA, Knox Coll., 1960; MS, N.Mex. State U., 1964; MBA, U. Phoenix, 1990. Rsch. engr. Gen. Electric Co., Advanced Computer Lab., Sunnyvale, Calif., 1964-67; large scale integrated circuit engr. Fairchild Camera & Instrument, Rsch. & Devel. Lab., Palo Alto, Calif., 1967-70, bipolar memory divsn., Mountain View, Calif., 1970-83, tech. dir., 1977-83; v.p. tech. ops. Trilogy Systems Corp., Cupertino, Calif., 1983-85; pres. Tactical Fabs, Inc., 1985-89; v.p. process devel. Chips and Techs. Inc., 1989-92; pres, CEO Camlan, Inc., San Jose, Calif., 1992-94; staff Chip Express, Santa Clara, Calif., 1994—; prin. Corp. Tech. Devel., 1994—. NSF fellow, 1962-63; recipient Sherman Fairchild award for tech. excellence, 1980, Semiconductor Equipment and Materials Inst. award, 1988; Inventor of Yr. award Peninsula Patent Law Assn., 1982. Mem. AAAS, IEEE, Sigma Pi Sigma. Inventor in field; patentee in field. Home: 10358 Bonny Dr Cupertino CA 95014-2908

PEMBERTON, BOBETTE MARIE (HARMAN), nursing administrator; b. San Mateo, Calif., Oct. 20, 1952; d. William Adolph and Agnes Marie (Costa) Harman; m. William Charles Pemberton (div. Sept. 1993). BSN, U. San Francisco, 1975, PHN. RN, Calif., Hawaii, Fla., Ind.; cert. pub. health nurse, flight nurse, oper. rm. nurse. Recreation supr. Burlingame (Calif.) Recreation Ctr., 1968-74; nursing asst. III Stanford U. Med. Ctr., Palo Alto, Calif., 1974-75, staff nurse, 1976-78; clin. edn. supr., mobile ops. supr. Irwin Meml. Blood Bank, San Francisco Med Soc., 1978-87; OR staff nurse U. Calif., Davis, 1987-88; asst. dir. blood svcs. ARC, Farmington, Conn., 1988-89; coord. blood bank St. Anthony's Med. Ctr., St. Petersburg, Fla., 1989-90; dir. donor svcs. Hunter Blood Ctr., Clearwater, Fla., 1990-93; dir. nursing svcs. Blood Bank of Hawaii, Honolulu, 1993-95; dir. nursing Peninsula Blood Bank, 1995—; chairperson nursing edn. com. Calif. Blood Bank System, No. Calif. region seminar Irwin Meml. Blood Bank; mem. sci. com. Blood Bank Nurses Calif., Calif. Blood Bank System; nursing rep. Local 535; lectr. in field. With USAFR, 1983—. Mem. NAFE, Am. Bus. Women's Assn. (rec. sec., chairperson spring conf. Burlingame charter chpt., del. Kansas City conv.), Am. Assn. Blood Banks, Calif. Blood Bank Soc. (nursing and donor svcs. com., continuing edn. com.), Air Force Assn., Air Force Res. Officers Assn. Republican. Roman Catholic. Home: 512 Marin Dr Burlingame CA 94010-2727

PEMBERTON, CINDY LEE A., physical education educator; b. Portland, Oreg., Oct. 2, 1958; d. Ronald E. and Patricia E. (Schars) Pemberton. BS in Biology and Psychology, Willamette U., 1980; MS in Interdisciplinary Studies, So. Oreg. State U., 1983; EdD, Portland State U., 1996. Instr. Trucker Meadows Community Coll., Nev., 1985-87; instr., swimming coach U. Nev., Reno, 1984-89; asst. athletic dir. women's sports Linfield Coll., McMinnville, Oreg., 1989-95, assoc. prof., aquatics dir., 1989—. Hannah Kennan scholar, Peck scholar. Mem. AAUW, NOW, Am. Swim Coaches Assn., Coll. Swim Coaches Assn., U.S. Swimming Assn., Alpha Chi Omega, Omicron Delta Kappa, Psi Chi, Kappa Delta Pi, Pi Kappa Phi. Office: Linfield Coll 900 South Baker Mcminnville OR 97128

PEMBERTON, RANDALL GRANT, industrial engineer; b. Sacramento, Jan. 29, 1953; s. Rodney Olson and Diana Joyce (Button) Kohrs; m. Vivian Lee Koirtyohann, May 29, 1976; children: Grant Austin, Travis Andrew, Carly Anne. Student, Purdue U., 1971-73; BS in Indsl. Engring., U. Mo., 1976; MSE in Indsl. Engring., Ariz. State U., 1992. Indsl. engr. B F Goodrich, Akron, Ohio, 1976-78; aero systems engr. Gen. Dynamics, Ft. Worth, 1978-79; sr. indsl. engr. Am. Airlines, Ft. Worth, 1979-83, mgr. fleet planning, 1983-87; sr. rsch. analyst United Airlines, Chgo., 1987-89; cons. Integrated Systems Solutions, Phoenix, 1989-92; cons. supr. Univ. Tech. Assistance Program, Bozeman, Mont., 1993-95; sr. process engr. Motorola, Scottsdale, Ariz., 1995—. Coach Gilbert (Ariz.) Youth Soccer Assn., 1993-94; vol. musician Morning Sounds, Bozeman, 1994; musician Psalm 100, Gilbert, 1995—. U. Mo. Honors scholar, 1975. Mem. Inst. Indsl. Engrs. (chpt. pres. 1973—, award of Excellence 1983), Soc. Mfg. Engrs., Tau Beta Pi, Alpha Pi Mu. Democrat. Home: 1640 E Heather Ave Gilbert AZ 85234-8233 Office: Motorola Space and Sys Technology Group 8220 E Roosevelt Rd MDR2215 Scottsdale AZ 85257

PEÑA, FEDERICO FABIAN, federal official; b. Laredo, Tex., Mar. 15, 1947; s. Gustavo J. and Lucille P.; m. Ellen Hart, May 1988. BA, U. Tex., Austin, 1969, JD, 1972. Bar: Colo. 1973. Ptnr. Pena & Pena, Denver, 1973-83; mayor City and County of Denver, 1983-91; pres. Peña Investment Advisors, Inc., Denver, 1991-93; sec. U.S. Dept. of Energy, Washington, 1993—; assoc. Harvard U. Ctr. for Law and Edn., Cambridge, Mass.; mem. Colo. Bd. Law Examiners. Mem. Colo. Ho. of Reps., 1979-83, Dem. leader, 1981. Named Outstanding House Dem. Legislator, Colo. Gen. Assembly, 1981. Roman Catholic. Home: 3517 Sterling Ave Alexandria VA 22304-1834 Office: Dept of Energy Office Sec 1000 Ind Ave SW Washington DC 20585-0001*

PEÑA, JUAN JOSÉ, interpreter; b. Hagerman, N.Mex., Dec. 13, 1945; s. Rosa Peña; m. Petra Cervantes, Dec. 22, 1974 (div. 1982); children: Federico Ezequiel, Margarita María Blea. BA, N.Mex. Highlands U., 1968, MA, 1972, postgrad. With Albert Garcia Gen. Contr., Las Vegas, N.Mex., 1955-67; teaching asst. N.Mex. Highlands U., Las Vegas, 1971-72, prof. Spanish, Chicano studies, 1972--78; teaching asst. U. N.Mex., Albuquerque, 1978-79; attendant N.Mex. State Mental Hosp., Las Vegas, 1982-83; staff and supervisory interpreter U.S. Dist. Ct. N.Mex., Albquerque, 1983—; head Raza Unida del to PLO in Lebanon, 1981, head negotiator with Iranians for release of 2 Chicanos and 1 Indian; supr ct. interpreters and reporters sect. U.S. Dist. Ct. N.Mex.; co-chmn. Cuatro-Centennial Com., Inc.; mem. exec. com. N.Mex. Human Rights Coalition. Author collection of poetry: Angustias y Remembranzas; contbr. articles to profl. jours.; author play: Canto a La Raza, 1978. Pres. Dads Against Discrimination, Albuquerque, 1993—; chmn. bd. trustees No. N.Mex. Legal Svcs., Las Vegas, 1972-81; mem. exec. com. Ind. Socialist Parties of Latin Am.; exec. commn. N.Mex. Human Rights Coalition. Decorated Bronze Star medal. Mem. N.Mex. Translator and Interpreters Assn. (pres. 1984-86), Nat. Assn. Judiciary Interpreters (sec. 1986-88), Nat. Partido Raza Unida (pres. 1976-81), N.Mex. Partido Raza Unida (pres. 1972-75, 77-78), Vietnam Vets. Am. (vice chmn. chpt. 1993—), Vietnam Vets. N.Mex., Am. GI Forum (Albuquerque Chpt. 1 comdr. 1993—), N.Mex. GI Forum (comdr. 1996), Nat. Assn. Chicano Studies (founding mem.), N.Mex. Chicano Studies Assn. (pres. 1972-78), Hispanic Round Table of N.Mex. (chmn. 1995), Barelas Neighborhood Assn. (pres.), Phi Sigma Iota. Democrat. Roman Catholic. Home: 1115 9th St SW Albuquerque NM 87102-4027 Office: US Dist Ct Dist of NM 421 Gold Ave SW Rm 108 Albuquerque NM 87102-3254

PENCE, MARTIN, federal judge; b. Sterling, Kans., Nov. 18, 1904; m. Eleanor Fisher, Apr. 12, 1975. Bar: Calif. 1928, Hawaii 1933. Practice law Hilo, Hawaii, 1936-45, 50-61; judge 3d Circuit Ct., Hawaii, 1945-50; chief judge U.S. Dist. Ct., Hawaii, 1961-74; sr. judge U.S. Dist. Ct., 1974—. Office: US Dist Ct Rm C-426 PO Box 50128 Honolulu HI 96850

PENDERGHAST, THOMAS FREDERICK, business educator; b. Cin., Apr. 23, 1936; s. Elmer T. and Dolores C. (Huber) P.; BS, Marquette U., 1958; MBA, Calif. State U., Long Beach, 1967; D in Bus. Adminstrn. Nova U., 1987; m. Marjorie Craig, Aug. 12, 1983; children: Brian, Shawna, Steven, Dean, Maria. Sci. programmer Autonetics, Inc., Anaheim, Calif., 1960-64; bus. programmer Douglas Missile & Space Ctr., Huntington Beach, Calif., 1964-66; computer specialist N.Am. Rockwell Co., 1966-69; asst. prof. Calif. State U., Long Beach, 1969-72; prof. Sch. Bus. and Mgmt., Pepperdine U., Los Angeles, 1972—; spl. adviser Commn. on Engring. Edn., 1968; v.p. Visual Computing Co., 1969-71; founder, pres. Scoreboard Animation Systems, 1971-77; exec. v.p. Microfilm Identification Systems, 1977-79; pres. Data Processing Auditors, Inc., 1981—; data processing cons. designing computer system for fin. health and mfg. orgns., 1972—. Mem. Orange County Blue Ribbon Com. on Data Processing, 1973; mem. Orange County TEC Policy Bd., 1982-87; mgmt. and organization devel. cons. Assn. Psychological Type, 1993—. Served to lt. USNR, 1958-60. Cert. in data processing. Mem. Users of Automatic Info. Display Equipment (pres. 1966). Author: Entrepreneurial Simulation Program, 1988. Home: 17867 Bay St Fountain Valley CA 92708-4443

PENDLETON, JOAN MARIE, microprocessor designer; b. Cleve., July 7, 1954; d. Alvin Dial and Alta Beatrice (Brown) P. BS in Physics, Elec. Engring., MIT, 1976; MSEE, Stanford U., 1978; PhDEE, U. Calif., Berkeley, 1985. Sr. design engr. Fairchild Semiconductor, Palo Alto, Calif., 1978-82; staff engr. Sun Microsystems, Mountain View, Calif., 1986-87; dir. engring. Silicon Engring. Inc., Scotts Valley, Calif., 1994-95; cons., designer computer sci. dept. U. Calif., Berkeley, 1988-90. Contbr. articles to profl. jours.; inventor, patentee serpentine charge transfer device. Recipient several 1st, 2d and 3d place awards U.S. Rowing Assn., Fairchild Tech. Achievement award, 1982, 1st place A award Fed. Internat. Soc Aviron, 1991. Mem. IEEE, Assn. for Computing Machinery, Lake Merritt Rowing Club, Stanford Rowing Club, U.S. Rowing Assn.

PENDLETON, OTHNIEL ALSOP, fundraiser, clergyman; b. Washington, Aug. 22, 1911; s. Othniel Alsop and Ingeborg (Berg) P.; m. Flordora Mellquist, May 15, 1935; children: John, James (dec.), Thomas, Ann, Susan. AB, Union Coll., Schenectady, N.Y., 1933; BD, Eastern Bapt. Theol. Sem., 1936; MA, U. Pa., 1936, PhD, 1945; postgrad., Columbia U., 1937-38. Ordained to ministry Bapt. Ch., 1936. Pastor chs. Jersey City, 1935-39, Phila., 1939-43; dean Sioux Falls Coll., S.D., 1943-45; fund raiser Am. Bapt. Ch., N.Y.C., 1945-47; fund-raiser Mass. Bapt. Ch., Boston, 1947-54; fund-raiser Seattle, Chgo., Boston, Washington, N.Y.C. and Paris, France, 1955-64, Westwood, Mass., 1971-84; staff mem. Marts & Lundy, Inc., N.Y.C., 1964-71; lectr. Andover-Newton (Mass.) Sem., 1958, Boston U. Sch. Theology, 1958, Harvard U., Cambridge, Mass., 1977-84; cons. Grant MacEwan Coll., Edmonton, Alta., Can. Author: New Techniques for Church Fund Raising, 1955, Fund Raising: A Guide to Non-Profit Organizations, 1981; contbr. articles in field to profl. jours. Address: 529 Berkeley Ave Claremont CA 91711-4539

PENG, ZHONG, electrical engineer; b. Tianjin, China, May 20, 1946; came to U.S. 1981; s. Shichang and Rungeng (Bu) P. BSEE, Tianjin U., 1968; MSEE, Purdue U., 1982; MS in Computer Engring., U. So. Calif., 1984. Registered profl. engr., Calif. Elec. engr. Henan Power Adminstrn., Anyang, China, 1968-78; rsch. assoc. Electric Power Rsch. Inst., Beijing, 1980-81; lectr. Calif. State U., L.A., 1985; power system analyst CAE Electronics, Montreal, Que., Can., 1987-89; power system engr. Pacific Gas & Electric, San Francisco, 1985-87, elec. engr., 1989-94; utility engr. Nev. Pub. Svc. Commn., Las Vegas, 1994—. Contbr. articles to profl. jours. Coord. alumni svcs. Grad. Sch. Chinese Acad. Scis., 1991—. Mem. IEEE (sr., prize paper award 1987, 88). Office: State Nev Pub Svc Commn 555 E Washington Ave Ste 4600 Las Vegas NV 89101-1049

PENISTON, LORRAINE CAROL, special education educator, therapeutic recreation specialist; b. East Orange, N.J., July 12, 1959; d. Leonard and Carol Elaine (Harris) P. BA, Kean Coll. N.J., 1981, MA, 1983; PhD, U. N.Mex., 1990. Activity therapist Newark Extended Care, 1981-82; activity therapy program asst. Green Brook (N.J.) Regional Ctr., 1982-83; vocat. counselor Occupational Ctr. Essex County, Orange, N.J., 1983-84; latch key coord. YMCA Mountainside, Albuquerque, 1984-85; asst. supr. therapeutic site City of Albuquerque, 1985; dir. recreation therapy Manor Care Heights, Albuquerque, 1985-88; coord. therapeutic recreation svcs. Care Unit Hosp., Albuquerque, 1988-89; therapeutic recreation specialist Lovelace Hosp., Albuquerque, 1988-94, 96—; learning disabilities specialist U. N.Mex. Ctr. for Acad. Program Support, Albuquerque, 1989—. Author: Developing Recreation Skills in Persons with Learning Disabilities, 1997; editor Learning Disability Newsbriefs, 1991-94; reviewer Therapeutic Recreation Jour., 1990-94; assoc. editor Therapeutic Recreation Jour., 1996—. Mem. Nat. Parks and Recreation Assn., Nat. Therapeutic Recreation Assn., N.Mex. Parks and Recreation Assn. (br. pres. 1988), Coll. Reading and Learning Assn. (chair learning disabilities Spl. Interest Group 1991-94), Orton Dyslexia Soc. (bd. dirs. S.W. br. 1995—), Phi Epsilon. Office: Univ NMex CAPS 3d Fl Zimmerman Library Albuquerque NM 87131

PENLEY, LARRY EDWARD, management educator; b. Bristol, Va., Feb. 9, 1949; s. William Edward and June (Caudill) P.; m. Yolanda Elva Sanchez, Nov. 25, 1977; children: Jonathan Andrew, Josephine Anna. BA, Wake Forest U., 1971, MA, 1972; PhD, U. Ga., 1976. Assoc. dean U. Tex., San Antonio, 1980-85; vis. prof. ITESM, Monterey, Mex., 1977, Universidad de Carobobo, Valencia, Venezuela, 1978; prof., chmn. dept. Ariz. State U., Tempe, 1985—; chair dept of mgmt. Ariz. State U., 1985-90; dean Coll of Bus., Ariz. State U., 1985-90. Contbr. articles to profl. jours.; mem. editorial rev. bd. Borderlands Jour., 1985—. Mem. Acad. Mgmt. (chmn. div. program 1986), Southwestern Council Latin Am. Studies, Internat. Communication Assn., Am. Soc. Personnel Adminstrn., Acad. Internat. Bus. mem. bd. dirs., Greater Phoenix Coun., Well Fargo Bank, Ariz., mem. bd. Adv.Inroads Ariz.,First Interstate Svs. Marketing., mem. Fin. Co. Coun. Diocese of Phoenix. Democrat. Roman Catholic. Home: 14052 S 24th Way Phoenix AZ 85048-9002 Office: Ariz State U Office of The Dean Coll Business Tempe AZ 85287

PENN, ARTHUR HILLER, film and theatre producer; b. Phila., Sept. 27, 1922; s. Harvy and Sonia (Greenberg) P.; m. Peggy Maurer, Jan. 27, 1955; children: Matthew, Molly. Student, Joshua Logan's Stage Co., Black Mountain Coll., Asheville, N.C., U. Perugia, Florence, Italy, Actors Studio, Los Angeles; studied with Michael Chekhov. Joined Army Theatre Co. during World War II; worked in TV, 1951-53; producer plays for Broadway theatre including The Miracle Worker (Tony award 1960), All The Way Home, Toys in the Attic, Two for the Seesaw, In the Council House, Wait Until Dark, Sly Fox, Monday After the Miracle; films include The Left-Handed Gun, 1957, The Miracle Worker, 1962, Mickey One, 1964, The Chase, 1965, Bonnie and Clyde, 1967, Alice's Restaurant, 1969, Little Big Man, 1971, Night Moves, 1975, The Missouri Breaks, 1976, Four Friends, 1981, Target, 1985, Dead of Winter, 1987; co-dir. film Visions of Eight, 1973; dir. theatre: Golden Boy, Hunting Cockroaches. Office: care Sam Cohn Internat Creative Mgmt 40 W 57th St New York NY 10019-4001 Address: Bell and Co Pc 535 Fifth Ave 21st Fl New York NY 10017*

PENN, BARBARA A(NNE), artist, educator; b. Pitts., Jan. 10, 1952; d. John Newton III and Jean (Schlafer) P. BS in Art Edn., SUNY, New Paltz, 1973; BFA in Painting, San Francisco Art Inst., 1983; postgrad., Showhegan Sch. Painting, Maine, 1985; MFA in Painting, U. Calif., Berkeley, 1986. K-12 tchr. art Delaware Acad. and Ctrl. Sch., N.Y., 1974-77; mem. installation crew San Francisco Mus. Modern Art, 1987-89; instr. extended univ. studio program U. Calif., Berkeley, 1988; instr. San Francisco Art Inst., 1989; vis. resident artist, lectr. Middlebury (Vt.) Coll., 1990-91; asst. prof. painting and drawing U. Ariz., Tucson, 1991—, coord. 2D Founds., 1991-95; dean students Showkegan Sch. Painting and Sculpture, summers 1987, 89; juror Ctrl. Arts Collective, Tucson, 1995, Dinnerware Artists' Coop. Gallery, 1995; lectr. Tucson Mus. Art, 1994; conf. planner, panelist, lectr. Women and Creative Process, Tucson, 1994; panel lectr. Women's Caucus for The Arts, 1997; artist resident Millay Colony for Arts, Inc., Austerlitz, N.Y., 1990, Yaddo, Saratoga Springs, N.Y., 1990. One-woman shows include Gallery Paule Anglim, San Francisco, 1990-91, Galerie Nalepa, Berlin, 1991, Univ. Art Mus., Tucson, 1995, Artemisia Gallery, Chgo., 1996, Gallery A., Chgo., 1997; exhibited in group shows at Galerie im Haus am Lutzowplatz, Berlin, 1992, Mead Art Mus., Amherst, Mass., 1997, Ariz. State Mus., Tempe, Ariz., 1997; represented in permanent collections Art Source, San Francisco, Merrill Lynch, San Francisco, Mary Zlot and Assocs., San Francisco, numerous pvt. collections. Recipient juror's award Galeria Mesa, Mesa Ctr. for Arts, 1995; Seymour H. Knox scholar Showhegan Sch. Painting and Sculpture, 1985; Regent's fellow U. Calif., 1985-86; rsch. grantee U. Ariz., 1995, 96. Mem. Coll. Art Assn., Emily Dickinson Internat. Soc.

PENN, MEADE LOVE THOMAS, social sciences researcher, library assistant; b. New Roads, La., Nov. 18, 1967; d. Windsor Pipes Jr. and Alice (Brasfield) Thomas; m. Douglas Robert Penn, Apr. 22, 1995. BS in Psychology and Polit. Sci., U. of the South, 1989; MA in Internat. Studies, U. Denver, 1992, postgrad., 1992—. Intern Brit. Consulate, Boston, 1988; asst. mgr. Japanese macaque rsch. facility U. Colo. Health Sci. Ctr., Denver, 1989-92; rsch. asst. Sierra Club Legal Def. Fund, Denver, 1990; mgr. rsch. fellowship program Wildlife Conservation Internat., Bronx, N.Y., 1992; rsch. asst. policy agendas project U. Denver, 1993, asst. pub. svc. desk Penrose Libr., 1989—, asst. to reference dept. Penrose Libr., 1993—; facilitator Environ. Policy Clinics, Grad. Sch. Internat. Studies, U. Denver, 1991—. Editor: (conf. procs.) Conservation and Environment in Papua New Guinea, 1991. Student rep. Sewanee (Tenn.) Women's Coun., 1988-89; spkr. internat. environ. issues UN Modelling Group, Cherry Creek H.S., Denver, 1993. Mem. AAAS, Soc. Conservation Biology. Office: Penrose Libr Reference Dept 2150 E Evans Ave Denver CO 80210-4704

PENNAK, ROBERT WILLIAM, biologist, educator; b. Milw., June 13, 1912; s. William Henry and Ella Sophia (Clemeson) P.; m. Alberta Vivian Pope, Sept. 7, 1935; children: Richard Dean, Cathy Ann. BS, U. Wis., 1934, MS, 1935, PhD, 1938. Instr. biology U. Colo., Boulder, 1938-40, prof. biology, 1941-74, prof. emeritus, 1974—; cons. numerous nat. and internat. corps. Author: Fresh-water Invertebrates of the U.S., 1953, Collegiate Dictionary of Zoology, 1964; contbr. over 120 articles to profl. jours. Rsch. grantee various orgns. Mem. Am. Microscopical Soc., Am. Benthological Soc. (Excellence in Benthic Sci. award 1991), Am. Soc. Limnology and Oceanography, Am. Soc. Zoologists, Internat. Assn. Meiobenthologists. Home: 14215 E Marina Dr Aurora CO 80014-3761 Home: 2501 E 104th Ave Apt 3 1201 Thornton CO 80233

PENNER-SEKERA, CYNTHIA DAWN, secondary education educator; b. Stockton, Calif., Mar. 23, 1959; d. Donald Dean and Frances Lee (Cox) Penner; m. Carl Joseph Sekera, June 21, 1981; children: Matthew Carl, Samantha Dawn. BA, Calif. State U., 1981, postgrad., 1983, MA in Edn., 1984, postgrad., 1991. Cert. tchr., Calif. Tchr. KinderCare Schs., Santa Ana, Calif., 1981-84, Long Beach (Calif.) Sch. Dist., 1984-87, Tracy (Calif.) Adult/Elem. Dist., 1987-95; tech. tchr. Tracy High Sch. Dist., 1995-96; math. tchr. San Ramon Valley Sch. Dist., 1996—; mem. Tracy Dist. Tech. Steering Com., 1991-96; tech. mentor tchr. Tracy Elem. Dist., 1992-95; pub. C.U.E. (Computer Using Educators) Newsletter, 1994-95. Contbr. articles to profl. jours. Tchr. McHenry House for the Homeless, Tracy, 1990-93. Mem. AAUW (vol. coord. 1988-90, v.p. 1990-91). Office: Charlotte Wood Mid Sch 600 El Capitan Dr Danville CA 94526

PENNEY, ROGER LEE, artist; b. Boston, Nov. 19, 1939; s. Frank E. and Ann (Lee) P.; m. Gale Ensie, May 19, 1968 (div. May 1974); m. Elizabeth Swegle, June 12, 1978; 1 child, Spencer Swegle Penney. Artist murals Circle's Cup Coffee House, San Diego, 1961-62; artist painting and talk Madmen & Fools, San Francisco, L.A.,, 1963-66; artist portraits Madmen & Fools, L.A., San Diego, 1966-75; artist shipyard signs Madmen & Fools, San Diego, 1975-86, artist painting and books, 1975—; artist Unindurable Pleasure Infinitly Prolonged, San Diego, 1966—. Prin. works include Homotopic Soviet Surrealism, 1963-68, An Unknown Magic, 1968-69, Human Dominiums, 1970—. Pvt. 1st class U.S. Army, 1958-60. Home: 8089 Hillandale Dr San Diego CA 92120-1512 Office: Unindurable Pleasure Infinitly Prolonged 8089 Hillandale Dr San Diego CA 92120-1512

PENNINGTON, ARTHUR STEWART, systems consultant; b. Jersey City, Apr. 25, 1959; s. Douglas Alfred and Ellen Lilies (Stewart) P.; m. Karen Louise McCormack, Nov. 21, 1981; children: David, Daniel, Amy. BS in Mgmt. Sci., U. Lowell, 1981. CPA, Tex. Acct. Mown & Mown PC, Woburn, Mass., 1981-82, Oppenheim Appel Dixon, Dallas, 1982-88; sys. and revenue analyst ANCO, Dallas and Midland, Tex., 1988-94; sys. cons. Paradigm Techs., Denver, 1994—. Mem. Toastmasters (divsn. gov. 1996—). Home: 7950 W 72d Pl Arvada CO 80005

PENNINO, PHIL, mayor; b. Mpls., Apr. 2, 1955; m. Melanie Pennino; children: Bryan Phillip, Summer Nichol. AA in Bus., San Joaquin Delta Coll., 1982; BS in Orgnl. Behavior, U. San Francisco, 1989; cert. econ. devel., U. Okla., 1991. Harbormaster Tower Park Marina, 1971-77; from helper gas transmission & distbn. to econ. devel. coord Pacific Gas & Electric Co., 1977-93, clean air transp. coord., 1993—; mayor City of Lodi, Calif., 1993—. Vice-mayor City of Lodi, 1992, coun. mem., 1990-91; chmn. San Joaquin Coun. Govts., 1992-93; pres. Lodi Lions Club, 1988-89; com. mem. San Joaquin County Retention Task Force, Tracy Econ. Devel. Corp., San

Joaquin Partnership-Mktg. Mem. Am. Econ. Devel. Coun., Calif. Assn. Local-Econ. Devel., Lodi C. of C. (com. mem.). Office: PO Box 3006 Lodi CA 95241

PENNY, AUBREY JOHN, painter, sculptor; b. London, July 30, 1917; came to U.S., 1939, naturalized; s. Samuel Arthur Duncan and Edith May (Payne) P. A.B. in Art History and Application, UCLA, 1953, M.A. in Art, 1955. Ptnr. Penny Bros., London and Los Angeles, 1934—; owner, operator Penny Studio, Los Angeles, 1955—, Penny Fine Art, Los Angeles, 1979—, Geneva, 1973—. One-man shows UCLA, 1955, Mt. San Jacinto Coll., Calif., 1972, 82; group shows include Los Angeles County Mus., 1955, 56, 57, Corcoran Gallery, Washington, 1957, Pa. Acad., 1959, Madison Gallery, N.Y.C., 1962, Internat. Art Festival Los Angeles, 1965, Palmer Gallery Los Angeles, 1967, Palais des Beaux-Arts, Rome, 1972, Chautauqua, N.Y., 1978, Los Angeles Inst. Contemporary Art, 1981; represented in permanent collections Edward Dean Mus., Cherry Valley, Calif., Mt. San Jacinto Coll. Mem. UCLA Art Council, 1956—. Recipient awards, including Selectionne, Internat. de Deauville, France, 1972. Mem. Am. Soc. Aesthetics, Los Angeles Inst. Contemporary Art (Gold Seal award 1981), Contemporary Art Soc. of Tate Gallery. Republican. Home: 17400 Haynes St Van Nuys CA 91406-5353 Office: Penny Fine Art PO Box 7796 Van Nuys CA 91409 also: Montserrat Gallery 584 Broadway New York NY 10012 also: Penny Fine Art 17400 Haynes St Van Nuys CA 91406-5353

PENNY, ROBERT, pediatrician, educator, researcher; b. Cin., June 6, 1935; s. Ralph and Marie (Cottrell) P.; m. Joselyn Baily, May 21, 1971; 1 child, Angline. BS, U. Cin., 1959; MD, Ohio State U., 1963. Diplomate Am. Bd. Pediatrics, Am. Bd. Pediatric Subspecialty in Pediatric Endocrinology. Intern Children's Hosp., Columbus, Ohio, 1963-64; resident in pediatrics Children's Hosp., Cin., 1964-66; instr. pediatrics Loma Linda (Calif.) U., 1967-68; fellow pediatric endocrinology John Hopkins Hosp., Balt., 1968-71; asst. prof. pediatrics U. So. Calif., L.A., 1971-75, assoc. prof. pediatrics, 1975-81, prof. pediatrics, 1981—, prof. rsch. medicine, 1991—; sabbatical molecular biology U. Calif., Riverside, 1990-91. Mem. editorial bd. Am. Jour. Disease of Childhood, 1988-93, Archives of Pediatrics and Adolescent Medicine, 1993—; contbr. over 103 articles to profl. jours. V.p. Rancho Palos Verdes (Calif.) Coun. Homeowners Assn., 1994—; oral examiner Am. Bd. Pediatrics, 1987, mem. com. programs for renewal of certification in pediatrics, 1989-91. Capt. USAF, 1966-68. Fellow Am. Acad. Pediatrics; mem. Am. Fedn. Clin. Rsch., Am. Pediatric Soc., Endocrine Soc., Soc. Pediatric Rsch., Lawson Wilkins Pediatric Endocrine Soc. Home: PO Box 427 904 Silver Spur Rd Rolling Hills CA 90274 Office: U Soc Calif Med Ctr 2025 Zonal Ave Unit I Los Angeles CA 90033-4526

PENNY, STEVE, media producer, speaker; b. L.A., Sept. 12, 1951. BA in Comm. Studies, U. Calif., Santa Barbara, 1974. Ind. media producer, 1974—; condr. selection programs U.S. State Dept., Santa Barbara, 1974; frequent speaker Soc. for Human Resource Mgmt. Author: How to Get Grants to Make Films and Videos, 1978, Seven Ways to Motivate People That Don't Cost Money, 1997; producer audio cassette and book Hiring the Best People, 1993, The Information Revolution: How to Make It Work, 1984; prodr. (video) The Island in the Sky, The Magic of Bali, Dreamtime, The Cave Paintings of the Chumash Indians. Film prodn. grantee James Irvine Found., 1976; Project Pakistan grantee, 1973. Office: Hiring the Best People 7960 Soquel Dr # 377 Aptos CA 95003-3945

PENSO, PIERPAOLO, ship repair company executive; b. Venice, Italy, Aug. 3, 1942; came to U.S., 1968; s. Silvano and Margherita (Maestri) P. BS in Marine Engring., Nautical U., Camogli, Italy, 1961. Cadet engr. F.LLI Cosulich, Genoa, Italy, 1961-62; 3d engr. Filli Cosulich, Genoa, Italy, 1962-63, 2d engr., 1963-64, 1st engr., 1964-67, chief engr., 1967-78; tech. dir. Panteknik SRL, Milan, 1978-80; pres. Internat. Wine Imports, Jacksonville, Fla., 1980-88; gen. mgr. Marine and Indsl. Repairs, Long Beach, Calif., 1980—; cons. various fleet operators, 1988—. Mem. L.A./Long Beach Port Engrs. Roman Catholic. Home: 200 McNeil Ln Apt 217 Newport Beach CA 92663-2650

PENWELL, DONNA CAROL, museum director; b. Waltham, Mass., Oct. 22, 1954. BA in Am. History and Art History, U. N.C., 1976; MA in Mus. Adminstrn., SUNY, 1977. Curator art Mus. Collection Mgmt. Unit Calif. Dept. Parks and Recreation, Sacramento, 1977-78, chief curator, 1978-79; historic cons. Pine Lodge, Ehrman Manson, Lake Tahoe, Tahoma, Calif., 1979-80; exhibit designer State Capitol Restoration Project, Sacramento, 1980-82; exhibit designer mus. devel. unit Calif. Dept. Parks and Recreation, Sacramento, 1982-84; mus. dir., cultural arts mgr. Colton Hall Mus. of City of Monterey, Calif., 1984-90; mus. dir. Maritime Mus. Monterey, 1990—. Bd. mem. Monterey County Hospitality Assn., 1993—, Monterey County Cultural History Assn., 1994—. Nat. Mus. Art scholar, 1977. Mem. Am. Assn. Museums, Calif. Assn. Museums, Coun. Maritime Museums. Office: Maritime Mus Monterey 5 Custom House Plz Monterey CA 93940-2430*

PENWELL, JONES CLARK, real estate appraiser, consultant; b. Crisp, Tex., Dec. 19, 1921; s. Clark Moses and Sarah Lucille (Jones) P.; BS, Colo. State U., 1949; m. A. Jerry Jones, July 1, 1967; children: Dale Maria, Alan Lee, John Steven, Laurel Anne, Tracy Lynn. Farm mgmt. supr. Farmers Home Adminstrn., Dept. Agr., 1949-58; rancher 1958-61; real estate appraiser/realty officer Dept. Interior, Tex., Calif., Ariz., Colo., Washington, 1961-78, chief appraiser Bur. Reclamation, Lakewood, Colo., 1978-80; ind. fee appraiser, cons., 1980-94; ret., 1995. Served with USN, 1940-46. Accredited rural appraiser; cert. review appraiser, gen. appraiser; recipient Outstanding Performance awards U.S. Bur. Reclamation, 1964, 75, 80. Mem. Am. Soc. Farm Mgns. and Rural Appraisers, Internat. Right-of-Way Assn., Nat. Assn. Rev. Appraisers (regional v.p. 1978-79), Jefferson County Bd. Realtors. Democrat. Presbyterian. Clubs: Elks, Rotary, Mt. Vernon Country. Author: Reviewing Condemnation Appraisal Reports, 1980; The Valuation of Easements, 1980. Home and office: 10100 W 21st Pl Lakewood CO 80215-1406 *Personal philosophy: Great personal satisfaction and benefit to society follows a person's development, constant improvement and marketing of talents in a line of work which is enjoyable and most comfortable for him to deliver.*

PEOPLES, DONALD R., research scientist; b. 1939. Athletic dir. Butte (Mont.) Ctrl. High Sch., 1967-69; dir. info. and evaluation Butte Model Cities Program, 1969-70; dir. pub. works, model cities and cmty. devel. Butte, 1970-77; dir. pub. works dept. Butte-Silver Bow City-County Govt., 1977-79, CEO, 1979-89; with Mont. Tech. Cos., Butte, 1989—, now pres., CEO. Office: Montana Tech Companies 220 N Alaska St Butte MT 59701-9212*

PEOPLES, ESTHER LORRAINE, elementary education educator; b. Ames, Iowa, Sept. 18, 1933; d. Henry Francis and Hildred Cecile (Jacques) Gulliver; m. Graydon Peoples, Dec. 11, 1970; children: Cathryn Louise Hill, Charles Henry Hill, Stephen Edward Hill; 6 stepchildren. BS in Elem. Edn., Drake U., 1962, MS in Edn., Curriculum and Instruction, 1967, postgrad., 1978. Cert. elem. tchr., Iowa; cert. elem. tchr., elem. prin., Ariz. Primary tchr. Fisher Elem. Sch., 1962-78, student tchr., coop. tchr., 1966-77, 90; intern prin. Fisher Elem. Sch., Marshalltown, Iowa, 1978; elem. program dir. Tesseract, Paradise Valley, Ariz., 1988-91; elem. tchr. Phoenix Country Day Sch., 1978-88; acting head lower sch. K-5 Phoenix Country Day, Paradise Valley, Ariz., 1985; tchr. grade 2 Tesseract, Paradise Valley, Ariz., 1988-96; ret., 1996. Contbr. articles to profl. jours. Mem. NEA, Iowa State Edn. Assn., Moble In Svc. Tng. Lab., Mortar Bd. Home: 7760 E Hywy 69 C-5 #333 Prescott Valley AZ 86314

PEPLINSKI, DANIEL RAYMOND, project engineer; b. Chgo., Sept. 23, 1951; s. Alex J. and Florence (Turkowski) P. BS in Chemistry, Loyola U., Chgo., 1973; MS in Chemistry, Ill. Inst. Tech., 1977. Rsch. asst. Rsch. Inst., ADA, Chgo., 1978; rsch. assoc. The Aerospace Corp., El Segundo, Calif., 1978-80, mem. tech. staff, 1980-90, project engr., 1990—. Contbr. articles to profl. jours. Mem. Am. Phys. Soc., Soc. Info. Display. Republican. Roman Catholic. Office: The Aerospace Corp Mail Sta M6/722 PO Box 92957 Los Angeles CA 90009-2957

PEPPER, DAVID M., physicist, educator, author, inventor; b. L.A., Mar. 9, 1949; s. Harold and Edith (Kleinplatz) P.; m. Denise Danyelle Koster, Mar. 19, 1992. BS in Physics summa cum laude, UCLA, 1971; MS in Applied Physics, Calif. Inst. Tech., 1974, PhD in Applied Physics, 1980. Mem. tech. staff Hughes Rsch. Labs., Malibu, Calif., 1973-87, sr. staff physicist, 1987-91, head nonlinear and electro-optic devices sect., 1989-91, sr. scientist, 1991-94; sr. rsch. scientist Hughes Rsch. Labs., Malibu, 1994—; adj. prof. math. and physics Pepperdine U., Malibu, 1981—; mem. adv. panel NSF, Washington, 1997. co-author: Optical Phase Conjugation, 1983, Laser Handbook, Vol. 4, 1985, Optical Phase Conjugation, 1995, Spatial Light Modulator Technology, 1995, CRC Handbook of Laser Science and Technology, 1995; tech. referee profl. jours.; contbr. articles to tech. jours. including Sci. Am.; holder 18 patents. Mem. Sons and Daughters of 1939 Club, 2d Generation of Martyrs Meml., Mus. Holocaust. Recipient Rudolf Kingslake award Soc. Photo-Optical Instrumentation Engrs., 1982, Publ. of Yr. award Hughes Rsch. Lab., 1986; NSF trainee Calif. Inst. Tech., 1971; Howard Hughes fellow Hughes Aircraft Co., 1973-80. Fellow Optical Soc. Am. (conf. adv. com. 1996; mem. adv. bd. topical conf. on nonlinear optics, Hawaii 1996); mem. AAAS, IEEE (guest editor, assoc. editor; mem. program com. lasers and electro-optics, Balt. 1997), SPIE (guest editor), N.Y. Acad. Scis., Am. Phys. Soc., Laser Inst. Am., Internat. Coun. Sci. Unions (com. on sci. and tech. in developing countries), Sigma Xi (v.p. 1986-87, chpt. pres. 1987-88, 90-91, 91-92), Sigma Pi Sigma. Jewish. Office: Hughes Rsch Labs 3011 Malibu Canyon Rd Malibu CA 90265-4737 *Personal philosophy: We all have a profound, meaningful purpose and mission in life—the challenge is to identify, appreciate, realize and embrace our dreams and goals.*

PEPPER, JOHN ROY, oil and gas executive; b. Denver, Feb. 24, 1937; s. Wesley Wayne and Lucille (Stith) P.; m. Sallie K. Force, Dec. 13, 1958 (div. July 1970); m. Judithea Lawrence Douglas, Sept. 24, 1977; stepchildren: Sarah Douglas-Broten, Kenneth R. Douglas. BBA, U. Denver, 1961; postgrad., UCLA, 1962, U. Denver, 1965. Analyst Texaco, Inc., L.A., 1962-63; landman Texaco, Inc., Bakersfield, Calif., 1963-65; prin. John Pepper, Landman, Denver, 1965-75; owner, operator John R. Pepper Oil & Gas Co., Denver, 1975—; bd. dirs. Trans-Telecom, Miami, Fla.; cons. Organizer Friends of Bob Crider campaign, Denver, 1985. Mem. Ind. Petroleum Assn. Mountain States, Ind. Petroleum Assn. of Ams. (pub. lands com. 1968-74). Republican. Lutheran. Home: 2499 S Colorado Blvd Apt 608 Denver CO 80222-5926 Office: John R Pepper Oil & Gas Co 1800 Glenarm Pl Ste 200 Denver CO 80202-3829

PERALTA, RICHARD CARL, groundwater engineer; b. Enid, Okla., Nov. 8, 1949; s. John Francis and Christina Margareta (Reinl) P.; m. Ann Wilson Blanchard, Mar. 27, 1972; children: Dia, Samantha, Nancy, Hugh. BS, U. S.C., 1971; MS, Utah State U., 1977; PhD, Okla. State U., 1979. Registered profl. engr., Ark. Grad. rsch. assoc. Oklahoma State U., Stillwater, 1977-79; from asst. prof. to assoc. prof. agrl. engring. U. Ark., Fayetteville, 1980-88; assoc. prof. dept. biol. and irrigation engring. Utah State U., Logan, 1988-91, prof., 1991—; cons. hydrologist U.S. Geol. Survey, Fayetteville, 1985-87; cons. engr. Mid-Am. Internat. Agrl. Consortium, Lima, Peru, 1986-87; cons. engr. ARD, FAO, 1989-94. Contbr. articles to sci. jours. Co-dir. Citizens for Responsible Legis., Stillwater, 1979; elders quorum, pres., exec. sec., fin. asst. clk., activities com. chmn. LDS Ch., 1979—, elders quorum, counsellor, 1992-94; scoutmaster Boy Scouts Am., 1988-89, cubmaster, 1989-91, 94-95. 1st lt. USAF, 1971-75; col. Res. Mem. ASCE, Am. Soc. of Agrl. Engrs., Am. Water Resources Assn., Gamma Sigma Delta, Sigma Xi. Home: 522 N 350 E Hyde Park UT 84318 Office: Utah State U Dept Biol & Irrigation Engring Logan UT 84322

PERCY, ROBERT WAYNE, dentist; b. San Bernardino, CA, Aug. 31, 1933; s. Charles Roland and Alma Irene (Garrett) P.; m. Janet Ann Hawley, Mar. 14, 1953; children: Gerald Keith, Kenneth Wayne, Charles Robert, Cathie Dee. Student, Kans. State U., 1954; AA, San Bernardino C.C., 1956; student, UCLA, 1956-57; DDS, U. So. Calif., 1961. Dentist pvt. practice, San Bernardino, Calif., 1961-66; ptnr. Wildwood Dental Group, San Bernardino, 1966-79, sole owner, 1979-93; cons. Highland, Calif., 1993—; cons. various ins. cos. and dental group practices; adj. instr. UCLA, So. Calif. U., Canadian Dental Group Assn., Am. Acad. Dental Group Practice, Numerous Dental Soc. Orgns. Mem. Human Rels. Commn., 1965-68, San Bernardino Sch. Bd., 1968-71, U. So. Calif. Scholarship Com., 1961-73, Calif. State Bd. Pub. Health, 1972-74 (Reagan appointee), Calif. State Health Adv. Coun. (Gov. Reagan appointee), 1974-76, Calif. State U. San Bernardino Pres. adv. bd., 1992—, chmn., 1995-97; mem. San Bernardino C.C. Found., 1996—; co-chmn. Citizens for Better Edn.; bd. dirs. Jr. C. of C., San Bernardino; bd. dirs. VNA, Goodwill Industries, YMCA, United Fund; county chmn. Salk Inst.; campaign co-chmn. Senator George Murphy, Calif., 1964; campaign chmn. assemblyman Jerry Lewis, 1968, 70, 72, 74, 76, polit. cons. and fin. chmn. Congressman Jerry Lewis, 1978—. With U.S. Army Med. Corps, 1953-55. Recipient Hon. Citation U.S. Congress, Nov. 15, 1993. Mem. Am. Dental Assn., Calif. Dental Assn., Tri-County Dental Assn., Western Acad. Dental Group Practice (bd. dirs.), Am. Acad. Group Practice (bd. dirs.), Am. Acad. Gen. Dentistry, Am. Soc. for Preventive Dentistry, U. So. Calif. Trojan Alumni Club (pres. 1965-72), U. So. Calif. Skull and Dagger Men's Honor Soc., Alpha Tau Epsilon. Home: 26248 Glenmare St Highland CA 92346-1632

PEREGRINE, DAVID SEYMOUR, astronomer, consultant; b. Telluride, Colo., June 9, 1921; s. William David and Ella Bethea (Hanson) P. AB, UCLA, 1950; postgrad., U. Calif., Berkeley, 1956-59. Leadman N.Am. Aviation, Inglewood, Calif., 1940-44; sr. physicist N.Am. Aviation, Downey, Calif., 1960-66; photogrammetric cartographer U.S. Geol. Survey, Denver, 1950-56; exec. and sci. specialist space div., Chrysler Corp., New Orleans, 1966-68; cons. Denver, 1970—. Co-author: (environ. manuals) Moon, 1963, Mars, 1965, Venus, 1965. Served with U.S. Army, 1944-46, PTO. Mem. Am. Astron. Soc., Am. Soc. Photogrammetry, Sigma Xi. Home: 190 S Marion Pky Denver CO 80209

PEREL, MICHAEL JOSEPH, dermatologist, inventor; b. Memphis, Oct. 29, 1947; s. Philip Alexander and Dorothy Louise (Dansby) P.; m. Georgia Chris Roberts, Nov. 20, 1973; 1 child, Eric. BS, Tulane U., 1969; MD, U. Tenn., Memphis, 1972. Diplomate Am. Bd. Dermatology. Pvt. practice dermatology Oxnard, Calif., 1977-89; dermatologist Riverside (Calif.) Med. Clinic, 1989—; owner Dreamscape Masonry & Landscaping Co., 1995—. Songwriter for rock group Killing Culture; inventor electronic med. record, 1993, Dr. Perel's hair regrowth formula, 1995. Mem. Inland Counties Dermatologic Soc., Calif. Med. Soc. Libertarian. Home: 2328 Caserta Ct Henderson NV 89014-5316

PERENCHIO, ANDREW JERROLD, film and television executive; b. Fresno, Calif., Dec. 20, 1930; s. Andrew Joseph and Dorothea (Harvey) P.; m. Robin Green, July 16, 1954 (div.); children: Candace L., Catherine M., John Gardner; m. Jacquelyn Claire, Nov. 14, 1969. BS, UCLA, 1954. V.p. Music Corp. Am., 1958-62, Gen. Artists Corp., 1962-64; pres., owner theatrical agy. Chartwell Artists, Ltd., L.A., from 1964; chmn. bd. Tandem Prodns., Inc. and TAT Communications Co., L.A., 1973-83; pres., CEO Embassy Pictures, L.A., from 1983; now pres. Chartwell Partnerships Group, L.A. Promoter Muhammad Ali-Joe Frazier heavyweight fight, 1971, Bobby Riggs-Billie Jean King tennis match, 1973. Served to 1st lt. USAF, 1954-57. Clubs: Bel-Air Country (Los Angeles); Westchester (N.Y.) Country; Friars (N.Y.C.). Office: Chartwell Partnerships Group 1999 Ave Of The Stars Ste 3050 Los Angeles CA 90067-6001*

PERER, MARVIN A., gastroenterologist; b. Pitts., Dec. 18, 1939; s. William A. and Ethel R. (Green) P.; m. Irene S. Waldman; Sept. 13, 1972; children: Elise, Michael. BA, Washington & Jefferson Coll., 1961; MD, Northwestern U., 1965. Intern U. Mich., Ann Arbor, 1965-66, resident in internal medicine, 1966-69; gastroenterology fellow U. Wis., Madison, 1971-73; gastroenterologist Fallon Clinic, Inc., Worcester, Mass., 1973-82; pvt. practice Las Vegas, Nev., 1982—. Pres. Jewish Fedn. Las Vegas, 1990-92. Maj. M.C., U.S. Army, 1969-71, Vietnam. Mem. ACP, Am. Coll. Gastroenterology, Am. Gastroent. Assn., Am. Soc. for Gastrointestinal Endoscopy. Office: PO Box 81560 Las Vegas NV 89180-1560

PERERA, VICTOR HAIM, journalism educator, writer; b. Guatemala City, Guatemala, Apr. 12, 1934; came to U.S., 1946; s. Salomon and Tamar (Nisim) P.; m. Padma Hejmadi, Aug. 8, 1960 (div. 1974). BA, Bklyn. Coll., 1956; MA, U. Mich., 1958. Fact editor, reporter The New Yorker, N.Y.C., 1963-66; lectr. English dept. Vassar Coll., Poughkeepsie, N.Y., 1968-70; freelance reporter The N.Y. Times Mag., N.Y.C., 1971-75; program specialist, lit. Nat. Endowment for the Arts, Washington, 1983-84; lectr. lit. & creative writing U. Calif., Santa Cruz, 1972-88; lectr. grad. sch. journalism U. Calif., Berkeley, 1992—; peer panelist NEA, Washington, 1983-96; sr. editor IVRI Mag., 1997—. Author: Rites: A Guatemalan Boyhood, 1986, Unfinished Conquest: The Guatemalan Tragedy, 1993, The Cross and the Pear Tree: A Sephardic Journey, 1995; co-author: Last Lords of Palenque: The Lacandon Mayas of the Mexican Rain Forest, 1982; contbr. articles to L.A. Times, Sunday Opinion, and Washington Post Book World. Recipient Lila Wallace Readers Digest Fund Writing award, 1992-94, Creative Writing award NEA, 1980, Major Essay award Avery Hopwood U. Mich., 1961. Mem. PEN Am. Ctr. Jewish. Office: 1534 Campus Dr Berkeley CA 94708-2060

PERETZ, PAUL, political economist, educator; b. London, Oct. 13, 1942; came to U.S., 1969; s. Edward and Lillian (Aaronson) P.; m. Jean Reith Schroedel; 1 child, John Alexander. BA with 1st class honours, Victoria U., 1969; MA, U. Chgo., 1972, PhD, 1978. Lectr. U. Chgo., 1974-75, U. Tex., Dallas, 1975-78; asst. prof. SUNY, Fredonia, 1978-79, Columbia U., N.Y.C., 1979-80, U. Wash., Seattle, 1980-88, Cornell U., Ithaca, 1988-89; prof. polit. econs. Calif. State U., Fullerton, 1989—. Author: The Political Economy of Inflation in the U.S., 1983, The Politics of American Economic Policy Making, 1987, 2d edit., 1996; contbr. articles to profl. jours. Recipient Orange County Acad. Excellence award ASPA, 1991; Culpepper fellow Brown U., 1984-85. Home: 725 Santa Barbara Dr Claremont CA 91711-3444 Office: Calif State Univ Dept Political Econs Fullerton CA 92634

PEREY, RON, lawyer; b. Cleve., Feb. 2, 1943; s. John Perecinsky and Anne (Nagy) Disman; 1 child, Page Suzanne; m. Janice Ash, Aug. 19, 1995. BA in Polit. Sci., Miami U., Oxford, Ohio, 1965; JD cum laude, Ohio State U., 1968. Bar: Wash. 1968, U.S. Dist. Ct. (we. dist.) Wash. 1968, U.S. Ct. Appeals (9th cir.) 1973, U.S. Supreme Ct. 1985. Assoc. Reed McClure, Seattle, 1968-71, ptnr., 1971-82; ptnr. Perey & Smith, Seattle, 1982-86, Perey Langley, Seattle, 1986-92; owner Law Offices of Ron Perey, Seattle, 1992—; lectr. in field of personal injury and trial practice. Contbr. articles to profl jours. Roscoe Pound Found. fellow. Fellow Roscoe Pound Found.; mem. ATLA (state del. 1989-90), ABA (litigation sect.), King County Bar Assn. (chmn. med.-legal com. 1989-90), Wash. State Trial Lawyers Assn. (bd. govs. 1983-85, 89-91), Am. Bd. Trial Advs. (diplomate; nat. bd. rep. 1996—), Wash. State Bar Assn. (bd. govs. 1994—), Damage Attys. Round Table. Democrat. Office: Market Place Tower 2025 1st Ave Ste 350 Seattle WA 98121-2100

PEREYRA-SUAREZ, CHARLES ALBERT, lawyer; b. Paysandu, Uruguay, Sept. 7, 1947; came to U.S., 1954, naturalized, 1962; s. Hector and Esther (Enriquez-Sarano) P.-S.; m. Susan H. Cross, Dec. 30, 1983. BA in History magna cum laude, Pacific Union Coll., 1970; postgrad., UCLA, 1970-71; JD, U. Calif., Berkeley, 1975. Bar: Calif. 1975, D.C. 1980. Staff atty. Western Ctr. Law and Poverty, Inc., Los Angeles, L.A., 1976; trial atty. civil rights div. U.S. Dept. Justice, Washington, 1976-79; asst. U.S. atty., criminal div. U.S. Dept. Justice, Los Angeles, L.A., 1979-82; sr. litigation assoc. Gibson, Dunn & Crutcher, Los Angeles, L.A., 1982-84; sole practice Los Angeles, L.A., 1984-86; ptnr. McKenna & Cuneo, Los Angeles, L.A., 1986-95, Davis Wright Tremaine, L.A., 1995—. Democrat.

PEREZ, MARK, food products executive; b. 1953. With Perez Packing Inc., Firebaugh, Calif., 1974—. Office: Perez Packing Inc 5879 N Washoe Ave Firebaugh CA 93622-9509*

PEREZ, REINALDO JOSEPH, electrical engineer; b. Palm River, Cuba, July 25, 1957; came to U.S., 1975; s. Reinaldo I. and Palminia Ulloa (Rodriguez) P.; m. Madeline Kelly Reilly, Mar. 11, 1989; children: Alexander, Laura-Marie, Richard Kelly. BSc in Physics, U. Fla., 1979, MSc in Physics, 1981; MScEE, Fla. Atlantic U., 1983, PhD, 1989. Comms. engr. Kennedy Space Ctr., NASA, Cape Canaveral, Fla., 1983-84; chief reliability engr. jet propulsion lab. JPL Calif. Inst. Tech., Pasadena, 1988—, chief engr. Mars surveyor program, 1988—; instr. engring. UCLA, 1990-94. Author, editor: Handbook of Electromagnetic Compatibility; contbr. articles to profl. publs. Mem. AAAS, IEEE (sr. mem., book rev. editor 1990—), NSPE, Electromagnetic Compatibility Soc. (assoc. editor jour.), Am. Soc. Physics Tchrs., N.Y. Acad. Scis., Applied Computational Electromagnetic Soc. (assoc. editor jour., chief editor newsletter, bd. dirs.), Phi Kappa Phi. Republican. Baptist. Office: JPL Calif Inst Tech 4800 Oak Grove Dr # 301 460 Pasadena CA 91109-8001

PEREZ, RICHARD LEE, lawyer; b. L.A., Nov. 17, 1946; s. Salvador Navarro and Shirley Mae (Selbrede) P.; m. Yvonne Perez; children: Kristina, Kevin, Ryan. BA, UCLA, 1968; JD, U. Calif., Berkeley, 1971. Bar: U.S. Dist. Ct. (no. dist.) Calif. 1974, U.S. Ct. Appeals (9th cir.) 1974, U.S. Dist. Ct. (ea. dist.) Calif. 1982, U.S. Dist. Ct. (no. dist.) Tex. 1984, U.S. Dist. Ct. (so. dist.) Calif. 1991. Assoc. McCutchen, Doyle, Brown & Enersen, San Francisco, 1972-74, John R. Hetland, Orinda, Calif., 1974-75; ptnr. Lempres & Wulsfberg, Oakland, Calif., 1975-82, Perez & McNabb, Orinda, 1982—; speaker real estate brokerage and computer groups and seminars; mem. adv. bd. Computer Litigation Reporter, Washington, 1982-85, Boalt Hall High Tech. Law Jour., 1984-90. Assoc. editor U. Calif. Law Rev., 1970-71. Served to capt. U.S. Army, 1968-79. Mem. ABA, Alameda County Bar Assn., Contra Costa County Bar Assn. Office: Perez & McNabb 140 Brookwood Rd Orinda CA 94563

PEREZ, THOMAS, food products executive; b. 1925. Officer Perez Ranches, Inc., Crows Landing, Calif., 1946—; with Perez Packing, Inc., 1972—. With U.S. Army, 1945-46. Office: Perez Packing Inc 6879 N Washoe Ave Firebaugh CA 93622-9502*

PEREZ-CASTRO, ANA VERONICA, developmental biology researcher; b. Lima, Peru, Jan. 27, 1962; came to U.S., 1986; d. Cesar Antonio and Ines Gladys (Marquina) P.; m. Alonso Castro, June 11, 1988. BS, Cayetano Heredia U., Lima, 1984, licentiate in chemistry and biology, 1985; MA, Columbia U., 1988, MPhil, 1990, PhD in Microbiology, 1992. Jr. prof. dept. chemistry Cayetano Heredia U., 1985-86; teaching asst. dept. microbiology U. Ga., Athens, 1987, Columbia U., N.Y.C., 1989; postdoctoral fellow life scis. div. Los Alamos (N.Mex.) Nat. Lab., 1992-95; rsch. assoc. dept. biology U. N.Mex., Albuquerque, 1996—; speaker Fedn. Am. Socs. for Exptl. Biology, 1992, Baylor Coll. Medicine, Houston, 1992, Mexican Soc. Genetics, Guanajuato, 1993, Mexico City 1994. Contbr. articles to sci. jours. Recipient young scientist award Fedn. Am Socs. for Exptl. Biology, 1992; Nat. Coun. Sci. and Tech. grad. fellow Cayetano Heredia U., 1985-86; Fieger predoctoral scholar Norris Comprehensive Cancer Ctr., U. So. Calif., 1991-92. Mem. AAAS, Am. Soc. Microbiology, Am. Soc. Human Genetics. Home: 2546 Camino San Patricio Santa Fe NM 87505 Office: Univ NMex Dept Biology Castetter Hall Albuquerque NM 87131

PERILLOUX, BRUCE EDGAR, optical engineer; b. New Orleans, Mar. 24, 1961; s. Louis Francis and Edna Eloise P.; m. Anne Mary Jeansonne, Jan. 29, 1985; 1 child, Katherine. BSEE, U. New Orleans, 1983, MS in Engring., 1984. Grad. teaching asst. U. New Orleans, 1983-84, grad. rsch. asst., 1984-85; thin film engr. I Coherent, Inc., Auburn, Calif., 1985-86, thin film engr. II, 1986-87, sr. thin film engr., 1988, product line mgr., 1989-93, staff thin film engr., 1994—. Holder 5 optical engring. patents; author 12 tech. publs. Mem. Optical Soc. Am. (editing referee 1984—), Sigma Xi, Phi Kappa Phi. Office: Coherent Inc 2301 Lindberg St Auburn CA 95602-9562

PERINE, ROBERT HEATH, artist, writer; b. L.A., Nov. 30, 1922; s. Theo Wesley and Irma Barnes (Heath) P.; m. La Dorna Larson, Mar. 12, 1947 (div. Sept. 1970); children: Jorli, Lisa, Terri; m. Blaze Newman, Dec. 31, 1979. Student, U. So. Calif., 1945, 56; cert., Chouinard Art Inst., L.A., 1947-50. Pres. Artra Pub., Inc., Encinitas, Calif., 1985—. Author: Chouinard: An Art Vision Betrayed, 1986, The California Romantics, 1987, San Diego Artists, 1988; contbr. articles to Arts Mag., The Publ. Mag., Vintage Guitar Mag., San Diego Mag. With USN, 1942-46. Mem. Nat. Watercolor Soc. (bd. dirs. 1949-51, 71-88, purchase award 1972), Butler Inst. Am. Art (purchase award 1972), Nat. Watercolor Soc. (hon. mention 1973), San Diego Art Inst. (1st pl. award 1974). Home and Office: Artra Pub 910 Bonita Dr Encinitas CA 92024-3805

PERITO, JOSEPH GERALD, JR., educator, musician, counselor, consultant; b. Denver, Feb. 9, 1927; s. Joseph and Rose (Comnillo) P.; B.A. in Music Edn., Denver U., 1950, M.A., 1955; Ed.D., U. No. Colo., 1967. Tchr. music, instrumental, vocal, theory Jefferson County (Colo.) Pub. Schs. Dist. R-1, Lakewood, 1950-57, supr. music, 1957-64, rsch. specialist, 1964-65; prin. Carmody Jr. High Sch., Lakewood, 1965-78; adminstr., counselor Fundamental Mid. Alternative Sch., Lakewood, 1976-78, adminstrv. asst. in ctrl. adminstrn., 1978-81; adminstr., cons., counselor 1983—. Mem. NEA, Am. Ednl. Rsch. Assn., Am. Acad. Polit. and Social Scis., Nat., Colo. Assns. Secondary Sch. Prins., Music Edn. Nat. Conf., Am. Choral Dirs. Assn., Am. String Tchrs. Assn., Colo. Edn. Assn., Kappa Delta Pi, Phi Delta Kappa. Home: 430 N Garrison St Lakewood CO 80226-1125 Office: 430 N Garrison St Lakewood CO 80226

PERITORE, LAURA, law librarian; b. San Francisco, Nov. 28, 1945; d. Attilio and Anita (Firenzi) Marcenaro; children: Victor Anthony, Phillip Michael. BA, U. Calif., Santa Barbara, 1967, MA, 1970; MLS, U. Mo., 1974. Asst. libr. Mo. Hist. Soc., Columbia, 1971-74, 77-79; asst. libr. Hastings Law Libr., San Francisco, 1980-86, assoc. libr., 1986—; part-time tchr. legal rsch. City Coll., San Francisco, 1990-91. Author: Guide to California County Probate and Vital Records, 1994; contbr. articles and monographs to profl. jours. Mem. Am. Assn. Law Librs., No. Calif. Assn. Law Librs. (asst. editor newsletter 1984-86, workshop com. 1988, advt. editor 1990-91, sec. 1993-94, grantee 1984). Office: Hastings Law Libr 200 Mcallister St San Francisco CA 94102-4707

PERKES, KIM SUE LIA, journalist; b. Breese, Ill., Jan. 19, 1957; d. Jupe and Betty Jane (Schwarz) P. BS in Mass Comm., Ill. State U., Normal, 1979. Lifestyle editor Daily News-Sun, Sun City, Ariz., 1979-81; news editor Glendale (Ariz.) Star/Peoria Times, 1981-82; lifestyle editor The Scottsdale (Ariz.) Progress, 1983-87; religion editor The Ariz. Republic, Phoenix, news reporter, 1987—. Recipient Spl. Recognition award Scottsdale Women in Partnership, 1986, Outstanding Journalism award Nat. Order Women Legislators, 1993, over 70 writing awards AP, Religion Newswriters Assn., Ariz. Newspaper Assn., Ariz. Press Club, Nat. Fedn. Press Women, Ariz. Press Women; named Woman of Achievement IMPACT for Enterprising Women, 1988; named to Outstanding Young Women of Am., 1986. Mem. Nat. Fedn. Press Women, Religion Newswriters Assn., Soc. Profl. Journalists, Ariz. Press Women (polit. liaison 1992-93), Ariz. Press Club (pres., v.p., contest chairwoman 1992-96). Office: The Ariz Republic Phoenix Gazette 200 E Van Buren St Phoenix AZ 85004-2238

PERKINS, FLOYD JERRY, theology educator; b. Bertha, Minn., May 9, 1924; s. Ray Lester and Nancy Emily (Kelley) P.; m. Mary Elizabeth Owen, Sept. 21, 1947 (dec. June 1982); children: Douglas Jerry, David Floyd, Sheryl Pauline; m. Phyllis Genevra Hartley, July 14, 1984. AB, BTh, N.W. Nazarene Coll., 1949; MA, U. Mo., 1952; MDiv, Nazarene Theol. Sem., 1952; ThM, Burton Sem., 1964; PhD, U. Witwatersrand, Johannesburg, South Africa, 1974; ThD, Internat. Sem., 1994. Ordained to Christian ministry, 1951. Pres. South African Nazarene Theol. Sem., Florida Transvaal, Africa, 1955-67; pres. Nazarene Bible Sem., Lourenzo Marques, Mozambique, 1967-73, Campinas, Brazil, 1974-76; prof. missions N.W. Nazarene Coll., Nampa, Idaho, 1976; prof. theology Nazarene Bible Coll., Colorado Springs, Colo., 1976—; chmn., founder com. higher theol. edn. Ch. of Nazarene in Africa, 1967-74; sec. All African Nazarene Mission Exec., 1967-74; ofcl. Christian Council Mozambique, 1952-74. Author: A History of the Christian Church in Swaziland, 1974. Served with USN, 1944-46. Mem. Soc. Christian Philosophers, Evang. Theol. Soc., Am. Schs. Orientan Rsch., Am. Soc. Missiology, Assn. Evang. Missions Profs. Republican. Home: 1529 Lyle Dr Colorado Springs CO 80915-2009 Office: Nazarene Bible Coll 1111 Chapman Dr Colorado Springs CO 80916-1901 *Personal philosophy: Be cheerful, hopeful, courageous, honest, candid, faithful, committed, loyal, and the whole world will be yours!.*

PERKINS, LINDA GILLESPIE, real estate executive; b. Albany, Calif., Sept. 17, 1944; d. Leonard Leroy and Cloie Vivian (Howard) Gillespie; m. Harold Michael Morgan, Sept. 18, 1965 (div. Oct. 1978); 1 child, Trisha Leigh Morgan Franz; m. Donald Anthony Perkins, June 1, 1996. BA with honors, N.Mex. State U., 1967, MA in English Lit. with honors, 1972. Social worker N.Mex. Human Svcs., Santa Fe, 1967-78, adoption dir., 1978-81, adolscent crisis counselor, 1978-81; exec. Yablon Real Estate, Santa Fe, 1981—; aerobics instr. Tom Young's Spa, Sante Fe, 1980-85; cons. in field. Author of poems. Foster parent judicial rev. panel Dist. Ct. N.Mex., Sante Fe, 1992-95, permanancy planning project, 1992-95; mem. YMCA. Mem. Planned Parenthood, Mensa, Alpha Chi Omega. Democrat. Methodist. Home: 808 Vassar NE Albuquerque NM 87106 Office: Yablon Real Estate PO Box 1794 Santa Fe NM 87504

PERKINS, NANCY ANN, nurse; b. American Fork, Utah, Jan. 31, 1961; d. George Thorvald and Ann Elizabeth (Williamson) Gardner; m. Layne Todd Perkins, Sept. 6, 1986; children: Christian H., Nathaniel B. BSN, Westminster Coll., 1982. RN, BLS, AHA, Utah. LPN med./surg. unit staff nurse Holy Cross Hosp., Salt Lake City, 1980-81; RN staff nurse renal St. Marks Hosp., Salt Lake City, 1982-86, RN charge nurse diabetic unit, 1986-87, RN diabetic educator, 1986-87, RN, charge nurse med. psych. unit, 1987-93, RN, community educator, 1991-94; RN resource nurse IHC, Salt Lake City, 1992—. Author/educator: (class design syllabus) Adoptive Parenting, 1991. Active Prenatal Boarding Home, Children's Aid Soc., Ogden, Utah, 1992-94; jr. leader Girl Scouts U.S., Salt Lake City, 1984-86; charge first aid clinic Presbyn. USA Gen. Assembly, Salt Lake City, 1990. Mem. Utah Nurses Assn. (Clin. Nurse Practice award 1988). Democrat. Presbyterian. Home: 3682 S 2110 E Salt Lake City UT 84109-4320 Office: IHC Telehealthcare Svc. PO Box 25547 Salt Lake City UT 84125-0547

PERKINS, RICHARD DALE, police official, state legislator; b. Boulder City, Nev., Nov. 15, 1961; s. Daniel Kenneth and Shirley Joan (Williams) P.; m. Terri Jo Campbell, Feb. 24, 1989; children: Nicole, Stephanie, Brian, Ashley,, Rikki. Student, U. Nev., Las Vegas, 1979—. Police officer Henderson (Nev.) Police Dept., 1984-91, sgt., 1991-95, capt., 1995—; state assemblyman Nev. Legis., Carson City, 1993—, majority floor leader, 1996—. Mem. adv. bd. McCaw Sch., Henderson, 1996—; mem. Nev. Sentencing Adv. Commn., 1995—, Indsl. Adv. Panel, Henderson, 1996; v.p. Henderson Dem. Club, 1992—. Recipient Meritorious award Clark County Dist. Atty., 1991, Silver State Citizen award Nev. Atty. Gen., 1991, Freshman Legislator of Yr. award Nev. Conf. Police/Sheriffs, 1993, Excellence award Nev. Trial Lawyers, 1995. Home: 408 Glasgow St Henderson NV 89015 Office: Henderson Police Dept 223 Lead St Henderson NV 89015

PERKINS, THOMAS JAMES, venture capital company executive; b. Oak Park, Ill., Jan. 7, 1932; s. Harry H. and Elizabeth P.; m. Gerd Thune-Ellefsen, Dec. 9, 1961; children: Tor Kristian, Elizabeth Siri. B.S.E.E., M.I.T., 1953; M.B.A., Harvard U., 1957. Gen. mgr. computer div. Hewlett Packard Co., Cupertino, Calif., 1965-70, dir. corp. devel., 1970-72; gen. partner Kleiner & Perkins, San Francisco, 1972-80; sr. ptnr. Kleiner Perkins Caufield & Byers, San Francisco, from 1980; chmn. bd. Tandem Computers, Inc., Cupertino, Calif.; chmn. bd. Tandem Computers, Genentech; dir. Spectra Physics., Corning Glass Works, Collagen Corp., LSI Logic Corp., Hybritech Inc., Econics Corp., Vitalink Communications Corp. Author: Classic Supercharged Sports Cars, 1984. Trustee San Francisco Ballet, 1980—. Mem. Nat. Venture Capital Assn. (chmn. 1981-82, pres. 1980-81). Clubs: N.Y. Yacht, Links, Am. Bugatti (pres. 1983—). Office: Tandem Computers Inc 10435 Tantau Ave Cupertino CA 95014-3548 also: Genentech Inc 460 Point San Bruno Blvd South San Francisco CA 94080-4918*

PERKINS, WENDY FRANCES, author, speaker; b. Chgo., May 9, 1953; d. Francis Joseph and Elaine (Birmingham) P. BA, Bradley u., 1975; M in Internat. Mgmt., Am. Grad. Sch., 1978. Cert. stockbroker. Temporary worker different agys., L.A., 1987-90; lectr., speaker Permanently Collectible, L.A. and Phoneix, 1990—; stockbroker and bond trader, Beverly Hills, Calif., 1983-86. Author, pub.: Temporarily Yours, 1989; contbr. articles to profl. jours. Temporary worker adv. OWN, 1990-94; testified to U.S. Senate Labor Com., Washington, 1993. Democrat. Office: PR Prose 7121 N 45th Ave Glendale AZ 85301

PERKINS, WILLIAM CLINTON, company executive; b. Decatur, Ill., Mar. 7, 1920; s. Glen Rupert and Frances Lola (Clinton) P.; m. Eunice Cagle, Sept. 7, 1939 (div. 1954); stepchildren: William Rea Cagle, Howard Christy Cagle; 1 child, Clinton Colcord; m. Lillian Wuollet, Sept. 7, 1955 (div. 1965); m. Shirley Thomas, Oct. 24, 1969. BS Mil. Sci. and Meteorology, U. Md., 1954; MS in Bus. and Pub. Adminstrn., Sussex Coll., Eng., 1975. Commd. USAF, 1943-73, advanced through grades to col.; with Ship Systems div. Litton Ind., Culver City, Calif., 1973-75; dir. material Hughes Aircraft Co., Tehran, Iran, 1974-78; mgr. internat. s/c Northrop Corp., Dahran, Saudi Arabia, 1978-81; dir. materiel CRS, Riyadh, Saudi Arabia, 1981-83; head major subcontracts Lear Ziegler Corp., Santa Monica, Calif., 1984-88; pres., chmn. bd., CEO Snowtech, Inc., L.A., 1984—; bd. dirs. Ice Village Ctrs., Inc., L.A., Forefront Industries, Maywood, Calif. Bd. dirs. World Children's Transplant Fund, L.A., 1987-95; mem. Mayor's Space Adv. Com., L.A., 1970-74; mem. aerospace hist. com. Mus. Sci. and Industry, L.A., 1988—. Mem. AIAA (sec. chmn. 1970), Ret. Officers Assn. (pres. 1992-95), Soc. for Non-destructive Testing (program chmn. 1973), Am. Soc. Quality Control, Am. Meterol. Soc., Sigma Alpha Epsilon (alumni chpt. pres. 1974-76). Home: 8027 Hollywood Blvd Los Angeles CA 90046-2510

PERKOWSKI, MAREK ANDRZEJ, electrical engineering educator; b. Warsaw, Poland, Oct. 6, 1946; came to U.S., 1981; s. Adam Perkowski and Hanna (Zielinska) Mystkowska; m. Ewa Kaja Wilkowska, Oct. 26, 1974; 1 child, Mateusz Jan. MS in Electronics with distinction, Tech. U. Warsaw, 1970, PhD in Automatics with distinction, 1980. Sr. asst. Inst. Automatics, Tech. U. Warsaw, 1973-80, asst. prof., 1980-81; vis. asst. prof. dept. elec. engring. U. Minn., Mpls., 1981-83; assoc. prof. elec. engring. Portland (Oreg.) State U., 1983-94, prof., 1994—. Co-author: Theory of Automata, 3d edit., 1976, Problems in Theory of Logic Circuits, 4th edit., 1986, Theory of Logic Circuits-Selected Problems, 3d edit., 1984; contbr. 134 articles to profl. jours., 11 chpts. to books. Mem. Solidarity, Warsaw, 1980-81. Recipient Design Automation award SIGDA/ACM/DATC IEEE, 1986-91; Rsch. grantee NSF, 1991, 94, Commn. for Familites Roman Cath. Ch., Vatican, 1981, Air Force Office Sci. Rsch., 1995. Mem. IEEE (Computer Soc.), Polish Nat. Alliance, Assn. for Computing Machinery, Am. Soc. for Engring. Edn. Roman Catholic. Home: 15720 NW Perimeter Dr Beaverton OR 97006-5391 Office: Portland State U Dept Elec Engring PO Box 751 Portland OR 97207-0751

PERLMAN, JANET, indexer; b. Bklyn.; m. Gerald M. Perlman, Jan. 21, 1962; children: Eric S., Joshua N. BS in Chemistry, CUNY, 1961; MA in Mgmt., U. Phoenix, 1990. Editorial asst. Crowell Collier Pub., N.Y.C., 1961-62; editorial supr. John Wiley & Sons, N.Y.C., 1962-65; indexer, pvt. practice N.Y.C., 1965-77; adminstrv. asst. Jewish Community Ctr., Phoenix, 1978-80, Jewish Fedn. Greater Phoenix, 1980-83, City of Phoenix Parks Dept., 1983-94; free-lance indexer, owner Southwest Indexing, Phoenix, 1991—. Mem. AAUW, Am. Soc. Indexers (nat. bd. dirs.), Am. Med. Writers Assn., Ariz. Book Pubs. Assn., Women's Am. ORT (pres. Phoenix region 1992-94). Home: 2114 E Escuda Rd Phoenix AZ 85024-1250

PERLMUTTER, MILTON MANUEL, chemist, paralegal, private investigator, accountant, financial consultant, property manager, real estate appraiser; b. Montreal, Que., Can., July 21, 1956; s. Max and Edith (Liszauer) P. Student, Dawson Coll., Montreal, 1975; BSC, McGill U., Montreal, 1978; PhD, Queen's U., Kingston, Ont., 1984. Cert. profl. chemist. Lectr./tutor Queen's U., Kingston, 1984-85; postdoctoral scholar UCLA Sch. Medicine, 1986-89; sr. chemist P.G. & E. Co., L.A., 1989-92; pres., chief exec. officer MMP Chem. and Environ. Cons. Svcs. Co., L.A., 1992—; sr. rsch. scientist U. So. Calif. Sch. Dentistry, L.A., 1993—; cons. in field. Contbr. articles to profl. jours. Vol. UCLA Sch. Medicine, 1989—, Chabad House, L.A., 1986—. R. Samuel McLaughlin scholar, 1978-79, Natural Scis. and Engring. Rsch. Coun. scholar, 1979-82, 92—. Fellow Am. Inst. Chemists, Am. Biog. Inst., Internat. Biog. Inst.; mem. AAAS, Am. Chem. Soc., Internat. Union Pure and Applied Chemists, N.Y. Acad. Sci., Soc. Nuclear Medicine. Jewish. Office: MMP Chem Environ Cons Svcs Co 1015 Gayley Ave Ste 1260 Los Angeles CA 90024-3424

PERLOFF, JEAN MARCOSSON, lawyer; b. Lakewood, Ohio, June 25, 1942; d. John Solomon and Marcella Catherine (Borngen) Marcosson; m. Lawrence Storch, Sept. 8, 1991. BA magna cum laude, Lake Erie Coll., 1965; MA in Italian, UCLA, 1967; JD magna cum laude, Ventura Coll. Law, 1976. Bar: Calif. 1976, U.S. Dist. Ct. (cen. dist.) Calif. 1978. Assoc. in Italian U. Calif.-Santa Barbara, 1967-70; law clk., paralegal Ventura County Pub. Defender's Office, Ventura, Calif., 1975; sole practice, Ventura, 1976-79; co-prin. Clabaugh & Perloff, A Profl. Corp., Ventura, 1979-82; sr. jud. atty. to presiding justice 6th div. 2d Dist. Ct. Appeals, L.A., 1982-97; instr. Ventura Coll. Law, 1976-79. Pres., bd. dirs. Santa Barbara Zool. Gardens, 1987-88; bd. trustees Lake Erie Coll., 1993—. Named Woman of Yr., 18th Senatorial dist. and 35th Assembly dist. Calif. Legislature, 1992; recipient Disting. Alumnae award Lake Erie Coll., 1996. Mem. ABA, Calif. Bar Assn. (mem. appellate ct. com. 1993-95), Kappa Alpha Sigma. Democrat. Club: Fiesta City. Avocations: tennis, jogging, biking, reading, music. Home: 1384 Plaza Pacifica Santa Barbara CA 93108-2877

PERNELL, ROBERT, municipal official. Pres. bd. dirs. Sacramento (Calif.) Mcpl. Utility Dist. Office: Sacramento Utility Dist MS B407 6201 S St PO Box 15830 Sacramento CA 95852

PERRAULT, CHARLES RAYMOND, computer scientist; b. Arvida, Que., Can., Mar. 7, 1949; came to U.S., 1983; s. Charles H. and Lucette (Benington) P.; m. Elizabeth J. Trueman, Mar. 12, 1983; 1 child, Andrew. BSc, McGill U., Montreal, Can., 1969; MA, U. Mich., 1971, PhD, 1975. Asst. to assoc. to full prof. U. Toronto, Ont., Can., 1974-83; sr. computer scientist SRI Internat., Menlo Park, Calif., 1983-85, dir. natural lang. program, 1985-88, dir. artificial intelligence ctr., 1988—; cons. prof. Stanford U., 1983—. Fellow Am. Assn. for Artificial Intelligence; mem. AAAS, Assn. Computing Machinery, Internat. Joint Confs. on Artificial Intelligence (chair of trustees), Assn. for Computational Linguistics, Sigma Xi. Office: SRI Internat 333 Ravenswood Ave Menlo Park CA 94025-3453

PERRIN, CHARLES LEE, chemist; b. Pitts., July 22, 1938; s. Samuel Robert and Ethel (Katz) P.; m. Marilyn B. Heller, June 14, 1964; children: David M., Edward J. AB summa cum laude, Harvard U., 1959, PhD, 1963. NSF postdoctoral fellow U. Calif., Berkeley, 1963; asst. prof. chemistry U. Calif. San Diego, La Jolla, 1964-71, assoc. prof., 1971-80, prof., 1980—; cons. in field; NIH spl. research prof. Gothenburg U., Sweden, 1972-73; NATO prof. U. Padua, Italy, 1986. Author: Mathematics for Chemistry, 1969, Organic Polarography, 1970; contbr. articles to profl. jours.; patentee in field. NSF grantee. Fellow AAAS; mem. Am. Chem. Soc. (grantee), Phi Beta Kappa, Sigma Xi. Home: 8844 Robinhood Ln La Jolla CA 92037-2137 Office: U Calif San Diego Dept Chemistry 0358 La Jolla CA 92093-0358

PERRIN, CYNTHIA SUZANNE, secondary education educator; b. Colorado Springs, Colo., Oct. 9, 1958; d. Oliver William and Jean Louise (MacDonald) P. BS in English, U. No. Colo., 1981; MEd, Lesley Coll., 1996. Cert. secondary tchr., Colo. Tchr., coach Unified Sch. Dist. 242, Weskan, Kans., 1981-86, Fremont Sch. Dist, Canon City, Colo., 1986—. Home: 314 W Circle Canon City CO 81212 Office: Fremont Sch Dist RE-1 101 North St Canon City CO 81212

PERRIN, HAL See **HALPERN, LEON**

PERRIN, KENNETH LYNN, university chancellor; b. L.A., July 29, 1937; s. Freeman Whitaker and Lois Eileen (Bowen) P.; m. Shirley Anne Cupp, Apr. 2, 1960; children: Steven, Lynne. BA, Occidental Coll., 1959; MA, Calif. State U., Long Beach, 1964; PhD, Stanford U., 1969. Lic. in speech pathology, Calif. Chmn. dept. communicative disorders U. Pacific, Stockton, Calif., 1969-77; dir. edn. and sci. programs Am. Speech-Lang.-Hearing Assn., Rockville, Md., 1977-80; dean Faculty Profl. Studies West Chester U., Pa., 1980-82; acting acad. v.p. West Chester U., 1982, pres., 1983-91; pres. Coun. on Postsecondary Edn., Washington, 1991-93; chancellor, system sr. v.p. U. Hawaii, Hilo and West Oahu, 1993-97; chancellor Ind. U. South Bend, 1997—; cons. in field, 1969-76; pres. north region Calif. Speech Hearing Assn., 1975-76. Co-author: monograph Prevalence of Communicative Disorders, 1981; contbr. articles to profl. jours.; editor: Guide to Graduate Education Speech Pathology and Audiology, 1980. Chmn. Southeastern chpt. Greater Brandywine Br. ARC; trainee Vocat. Rehab. Adminstrn., 1965-69. Named Disting. Alumnus Sch. Humanities Calif. State U., Long Beach, 1988. Fellow Am. Speech-Lang.-Hearing Assn. (vice chmn. edn. tng. bd. 1975-77 cert. clin. competence in speech pathology); mem. West Chester C. of C. (pres. 1988). Home: 543 Kaanini St Hilo HI 96720 Office: Indiana U South Bend 1700 Wishawaka Ave PO Box 7111 South Bend IN 46634*

PERROT, PAUL NORMAN, museum director; b. Paris, France, July 28, 1926; came to U.S., 1946, naturalized, 1954; s. Paul and K. Norman (Derr) P.; m. Joanne Stovall, Oct. 23, 1954; children—Paul Latham, Chantal Marie Claire, Jeannine, Robert. Student, Ecole du Louvre, 1945-46, N.Y. U. Inst. Fine Arts, 1946-52. Asst. The Cloisters, Met. Mus. Art, 1948-52; asst. to dir. Corning (N.Y.) Mus. Glass, 1952-54, asst. dir. mus., 1954-60, dir., 1960-72; editor Jour. Glass Studies, 1959-72; asst. sec. for mus. programs Smithsonian Instn., Washington, 1972-84; dir. Va. Mus. Fine Arts, 1984-91; dir. Santa Barbara Mus. Art, 1991-94, mus. cons., 1995—; lectr. glass history, aesthetics, museology; past v.p. Internat. Coun. Mus. Found.; past pres. N.E. Conf. Mus.; past pres. Internat. Centre for Study of Preservation and Restoration of Cultural Property, Rome, mem. coun., 1974-88. Author: Three Great Centuries of Venetian Glass, 1958, also numerous articles on various hist. and archael. subjects. Former trustee Winterthur Mus.; former trustee, treas. Mus. Computer NEtwork; mem. Internat. Cons. Com. for the Preservation of Moenjodaro; chmn. adv. com. World Monuments Fund; chmn. vis. com. Getty Conservation Inst. Mem. Am. Assn. Mus. (past v.p., coun. 1967-78), N.Y. State Assn. Mus. (past pres.), Internat. Assn. History Glass (past v.p.) Corning Friends of Library (past pres.), So. Tier Library System (past pres.).

PERROTTO, GLEN ROGERS, artist, teacher; b. Forest, Miss., Jan. 15, 1953; d. Carl Henry and Mary Alice (McCrory) Rogers; m. Nicholas Joseph Perrotto Jr., Dec. 16, 1977. BA, U. Fla., 1977; MA, San Francisco State U., 1982; MFA, San Jose (Calif.) State U., 1992. Instr. San Francisco State U., 1988, 90, 92, 94; project mgr., art dir. Marketshare, Inc., Milpitas, Calif., 1988-93; dir. Citadel Print Ctr., San Jose, Calif., 1991-93; instr. Calif. State Summer Sch. for Arts, L.A., 1995, 96; artist cons. Campbell (Calif.) Union Sch. Dist., 1995—; artist Citadel, San Jose, 1997—. One woman shows include Pacific Internat. Art Gallery, Palo Alto, Calif., 1992, dp Fong Galleries, San Jose, 1996; exhibited in group shows at Singapore Mus. Art, 1990, de Saisset Mus., Santa Clara, Calif., 1993; prin. works include (collaborative pub. art) Lyrical Animation, 1996. Bd. dirs. Inst. Contemporary Art, San Jose, 1995—, San Jose Art League, 1985. New Works grantee Arts Coun. Santa Clara County, 1996, Artist-in-Residence grantee Calif. Arts Coun., 1985-88; Printmaking fellow Kala Inst., Berkeley, Calif., 1992; Named Disting. Artist of Yr., Cupertino (Calif.) Arts Commn., 1990. Mem. Calif. Soc. Printmakers, L.A. Soc. Printmakers, Women's Caucus for Art. Home: 18595 Ralya Ct Cupertino CA 95014 Office: Citadel 199 Martha St San Jose CA 95112

PERRY, DALE LYNN, chemist; b. Greenville, Tex., May 12, 1947; s. Francis Leon and Violet (Inabinette) P. BS, Midwestern U., 1969; MS, Lamar U., 1972; PhD, U. Houston, 1974. NSF fellow dept. chemistry Rice U., Houston, 1976-77; Miller Research fellow dept. chemistry U. Calif.-Berkeley, 1977-79; prin. investigator solid state chemistry and spectroscopy Lawrence Berkeley Lab. U. Calif., 1979—, sr. scientist, 1987—; lectr. Ana G. Mendez Ednl. Found., 1988; rsch. mem. G.T. Seaborg Inst. for Transactinium Sci. Author, editor: Instrumental Surface Analysis of Geologic Materials, 1990, Applications of Analytical Techniques to the Characterization of Materials, 1992, Applications of Synchrotron Radiation Techniques to Materials Science, 1993, II, 1995, III, 1996; contbr. articles to profl. jours. Fellow Royal Soc. Chemistry (London); mem. Am. Chem. Soc. (chmn. materials chemistry and engring. subdivsn., indsl. and engring. chemistry divsn., 1992-96), Soc. Applied Spectroscopy, Coblentz Soc., Materials Rsch. Soc. (corp. participation com. 1991—), Sigma Xi (nat. rsch. award 1994). Office: U Calif Lawrence Berkeley Lab Mail Stop 70A-1150 Berkeley CA 94720

PERRY, DAVID NILES, public relations executive; b. Utica, N.Y., Mar. 7, 1940; s. Francis N. and Marion H. P.; B.S., Utica Coll. Syracuse U., 1962; m. Jacqueline J. Adams, Dec. 21, 1962. Pub. affairs rep. Allstate Ins. Co., Pasadena, Calif., 1966-67; dir. press rrels. L.A. C. of C., 1968; rep. pub. rels. Lockheed Propulsion Co., Redlands, Calif., 1968-70; mgr. pub. rels. Bozell & Jacobs Inc., L.A., 1970-73, Phoenix, 1974; pres. David Perry Pub. Rels. Inc., Scottsdale, Ariz.; exec. dir. Ariz. Water Quality Assn. Served with USNR, 1962-65. Office: 6819 E Diamond St Scottsdale AZ 85257-3233

PERRY, DONALD LESTER, II, venture capitalist; b. Culver City, Calif., Jan. 21, 1958; s. Donald Lester Sr. and Joyce Estella (Kirklin) P.; m. Michael Albert Behn, July 24, 1982. BA in Econs. and Polit. Sci., Williams Coll., 1979; MBA in Strategic Mgmt., Claremont (Calif.) Grad. Sch., 1990. Fgn. exch. trader Morgan Guaranty Trust Co., N.Y.C., 1979-80; exec. recruiter Benson-McBride & Assoc., Beverly Hills, Calif., 1980-82; asst. v.p. money markets divsn. Nat. Australia Bank, L.A., 1982-86; v.p. eurodollar trader Sanwa Bank of Calif., L.A., 1986-88; v.p. comml. loans Union Bank, L.A., 1989-90; mng. ptnr. Pine Cobble Ptnrs., L.A., 1990—; speaker Pacific Coast Regional SBDC, L.A., 1989—, Nat. Assn. Black MBAs, L.A., 1990—, So. Calif. Edison/Joint Coun., L.A., 1990—. Contbr. articles to mags. Mem. Town Hall of Calif., L.A., 1990. Recipient Outstanding Entrepreneur of Yr., Peter F. Drucker Ctr. at Claremont Grad. Sch., 1995; named Positive Black Role Model, Assn. Black Women Entrepreneurs, 1993. Mem. L.A. Venture Assn., L.A. Urban Bankers, Pacific Coast Regional Small Bus. Devel. Corp. (mem. loan com. 1990-94), L.A. World Affairs Coun. Republican. Office: 811 W 7th St Ste 1000 Los Angeles CA 90017-3421

PERRY, ELISABETH SCHERF, psychologist; b. Kasel-Trier, Germany, Aug. 24, 1952; came to U.S., 1976; d. Willibald and Brigitta (Jakobs) Scherf; m. R. T. Perry. AA in Maths., Columbia Basin Coll., Pasco, Wash., 1978; BS in Psychology with honors, U. Wis., 1982; MA in Psychology, Calif. Sch. Prof. Psychology, L.A., 1985, PhD in Clin. Psychology, 1988. Lic. psychologist, N.Mex.; cert. Am. Bd. Forensic Examiners. Psychologist Psychol. Health Inc., Albuquerque, 1988-91, Los Lunas (N.Mex.) Sch. Dist., 1990-91; psychologist, dir. S.W. Psychol. Svcs., Santa Fe, 1991—; police psychologist Gallup (N.Mex.) Police Dept., 1992—, McKinley County Sheriff's Dept., Gallup, 1992—; psychologist, supr. Mesilla Valley, Gallup, 1995; sch. psychologist Los Alamos Schs., 1995. V.p. Santa Fe Child abuse Coun., 1991. Mem. APA, N.Mex. Psychol. Assn., Phi Kappa Phi. Office: SW Psychol Svcs 125 E Palace Ave Ste 62 Santa Fe NM 87501-2042 also: 800 Trinity Dr Ste I Los Alamos NM 87544

PERRY, JAMES GREGORY, sales and marketing executive; b. Missoula, Mont., Oct. 4, 1952; s. Joseph Tarsisus and Mary Cathrine (Schneider) P.; m. Diana Sue Coen, May 24, 1974; 1 child, Natalie Shureé. Student, Yuba Coll., Marysville, Calif., 1970-72. Credit supr. CBS Mus. Instruments, Fullerton, Calif., 1975-76, mktg. rep., 1976-80, sales rep., 1980-82; mktg. rep. Paiste Am., Inc., Brea, Calif., 1982-85, nat. sales mgr., 1985-91; field sales mgr. Am. Med. Sales, 1991-93; dir. sales and mktg., 1993—; caption chief percussion So. Calif. Judges Assn., 1983—; percussion judge So. Calif. Sch. Band Orch. Assn., 1985-93. With USN, 1972-75. Mem. Mu Sigma Kappa (pres. 1972), Jaycees (pres. Castleton, Ind. chpt. 1981), Am. Drum Line Assn. (v.p. 1994—). Office: Am Med Sales Inc 4928 W Rosecrans Ave Hawthorne CA 90250-6616

PERRY, JOHN RICHARD, philosophy educator; b. Lincoln, Nebr., Jan. 16, 1943; s. Ralph Robert and Ann (Roscow) P.; m. Louise Elizabeth French, Mar. 31, 1962; children: James Merton, Sarah Louise, Joseph Glenn. BA, Doane Coll., Crete, Nebr., 1964; PhD, Cornell U., Ithaca, N.Y., 1968; DLitt (hon.), Doane Coll., 1982. Asst. prof. philosophy UCLA, 1968-72; vis. asst. prof. U. Mich., Ann Arbor, 1971-72; assoc. prof. UCLA, 1972-74, Stanford (Calif.) U., 1974-77; prof. Stanford U., 1977-85, Henry Waldgrave Stuart prof., 1985—, chmn. dept. philosophy, 1976-82, 90-91, dir. ctr. study lang. and info., 1985-86, 93—, resident fellow Soto House, 1985-91. Author: Dialogue on Identity and Immortality, 1978, (with Jon Barwise) Situations and Attitudes, 1983, The Problem of the Essential Indexical, 1993. Pres. Santa Monica Dem. Club, Calif., 1972-74. Woodrow Wilson fellow, 1964-65, Danforth fellow, 1964-68, Guggenheim fellow, 1975-76, NEH fellow, 1980-81. Mem. Am. Philos. Assn. (v.p. Pacific divsn. 1992-93, pres.

1993-94). Office: Stanford U Ctr Study Language & Information Stanford CA 94305

PERRY, JOSEPHINE, secondary education educator, writer; b. Weymouth, Mass., Aug. 20, 1950; d. John Frederick and Maria Rose (Folino) P. BA, U. Mass., 1981; MFA, Ohio U., 1983; MA, Calif. State U., Long Beach, 1988. Cert. C.C. instr., Calif. Tchr. Long Beach (Calif.) Unified Sch. Dist., 1983-87, Sedona (Ariz.) Unified Sch. Dist., 1989-91; instr. English, mythology and lit. Cerritos C.C., Norwalk, Calif., 1987-89; instr. English, Lit. Los Medanos Coll., Pittsburg, Calif., 1991—; reader, script cons. L.A. Theatre Ctr., 1983-85; asst. lit. mgr. Pa. State Co., Allentown, 1982-83. Prodr. film God Talk, 1996; author: (screenplays) Blueberry Hill, 1995, Presumed Dead, 1996, Amazing Grace, 1997 (play) My Movie Star, 1995.

PERRY, JOYCE FITZWILLIAM, secondary school educator; b. San Francisco, Aug. 12, 1946; d. Leo Matthew and Mildred E. (McBain) Fitzwilliam; m. Robert James Perry, June 21, 1969 (div. Apr. 1980); children: Dominic Matthew, Alex Michael. BA, Gonzaga U., 1968; M in Counseling, U. Phoenix, 1995. Cert. tchr., nat. cert. counselor, Ariz. Middle sch. lang. arts and social studies tchr. Frank Odle Jr. High, Bellevue, Wash., 1969-72, Greenway Middle Sch., Phoenix, 1979-82, Sunrise Middle Sch., Scottsdale, Ariz., 1982—; mem. evaluation team North Ctrl. Schs. Accreditation, Ariz., 1988-90. Author: Seasons of the Heart, 1982. Named Middle Level Educator of Yr., Ctrl. Ariz. Middle Level Assn., 1994. Mem. ACA, Phi Delta Kappa.

PERRY, LORI, preschool educator; b. Alameda, Calif., Apr. 10, 1962; d. Arnold Charles and Virginia Minnie (Pimintel) P. AA, Chabot Coll., Hayward, Calif., 1984, postgrad., 1993—; BS in Human Devel., Calif. State U., Hayward. Receptionist Animal Hosp., Hayward, 1986-87, 91-93; Hollywood artist Lyric Composer, L.A., 1991—; pre-sch. tchr. Christian Ministry, Castro Valley, Calif., 1995—. Author poetry: Hearts on Fire, 1991 (Silver Poet award 1991), Fair, 1996 (Silver medallion 1996), Internat. Poet, 1995 (merit award 1995). Mem. Internat. Poets Assn. Republican. Roman Catholic. Home: 18667 Times Ave San Lorenzo CA 94580

PERRY, MICHAEL DEAN, professional football player; b. Aiken, S.C., Aug. 27, 1965. Student, Clemson. Defensive tackle Cleveland Browns, 1988-94, Denver Broncos, 1994—. Voted to Pro Bowl, 1989-91, 93, 94-96; named defensive tackle The Sporting News All-Pro team, 1989-93. Office: Denver Broncos 13655 Broncos Pkwy Englewood CO 80112-4150

PERRY, PHILLIP EDMUND, middle school educator; b. Kalispell, Mont., Oct. 4, 1951; s. Joseph T. and Mary C. (Schneider) P.; m. Janette Adele Miller, June 18, 1977; children: Jennifer, Joseph. AA in Liberal Arts, Yuba C.C., 1971; BA in Drama, Calif. State U., Chico, 1974; MA in Ednl. Adminstrs., Calif. State U., Sacramento, 1990. Store owner Perry's Music, Marysville, Calif., 1979-83; tchr. 8th grade Notre Dame Sch., Marysville, 1980-84; tchr. Woodlake Elem. Sch., Sacramento, 1985-97, Gray Ave Middle Sch., Yuba City, 1997—. Coach Yuba Sutter Youth Soccer League, 1990—; instr. Am. Red Cross; actor, dir., technician, bd. dirs. The Acting Co., Yuba City, 1995—. Mem. ASCD, PTA, KC, Calif. Tchr.'s Assn., Assn. of Calif. Sch. Adminstrs., North Sacramento Ednl. Assn. Home: 1192 Hobart Dr Marysville CA 95901-3537 Office: Gray Ave Middle Sch 808 Gray Ave Yuba City CA 95991

PERRY, RAYMOND CARVER, education educator; b. Anaheim, Calif., July 6, 1906; s. Arthur Raymond and Helen (Carver) P.; m. Evelyn Lucile Wright, July 7, 1940; children: Douglas Wright, David Wright. AB, Stanford U., 1926; MA, U. So. Calif., L.A., 1928, EdD, 1933. Cert. psychologist, Calif. Secondary tchr. Mexia (Tex.) Sch. Dist., 1926-27; elem. tchr. Artesia (Calif.) Sch. Dist., 1927-28; tchr. jr. high L.A. Sch. Dist., 1928-30, tchr. jr. coll., 1930-35; prof. and dean San Diego State Coll., 1935-40; divsn. chief Calif. Dept. Edn., Sacramento, 1940-45; prof. edn. U. So. Calif., L.A., 1945-72, prof. edn. emeritus, 1972—; curriculum cons., psychologist Fontana (Calif.) Sch. Dist., 1947-51; curriculum survey staff Melbo Assocs., L.A., 1948-71; curriculum cons. Sulphur Springs Sch. Dist., L.A. County, 1965-69. Author: Basic Mathematics for College Students, 1957, Group Factor Analysis of Adjustment Questionnaire, 1934, Cross My Heart, 1990; co-author: Review of Educational Research, 1965. Svc. group rep. City Coordination Coun., Long Beach, Calif., 1933-35. Lt. comdr. USNR, 1942-45. Mem. Nat. Coun. Tchrs. Math., Andrus Ctr. Assocs., U. So. Calif. Ret. Faculty, Phi Delta Kappa (San Diego chpt. pres. 1935-40). Republican. Presbyterian.

PERRY, TEKLA SHELESTAK, editor, writer; b. San Francisco, Feb. 17, 1958; d. James W. and Helen (Barna) P.; m. Eric C. Nee, Nov. 11, 1989; children: Alexander B., Nadya K. BA, Mich. State U., 1979. Assoc. editor IEEE Spectrum, N.Y.C., 1979-85, mng. editor, 1985-87, sr. editor, 1987—. Contbr. articles to mags. Pres. parent bd. Downtown Children's Ctr., Palo Alto, Calif., 1995-96.

PERRY-CRUMRINE, LORI FRANCES, special education educator, administrator; b. Denver; d. Lawrence John and Bernice Marie (DiLorenzo) Perry; m. Christopher David Crumrine, Aug. 19, 1995; children: Nathan Dennis Crumrine, Frannie Marion Crumrine. BA in Spl. Edn., U. No. Colo., 1981; MA in Curriculum, U. Denver, 1992. Cert. Type A tchr.-spl. edn., type D adminstr.-prin. K-12, Colo. Tchr. spl. edn. Sabin Sch., Denver, 1981-85, Barnum Sch., Denver, 1985-90, Lincoln H.S., Denver, 1990-94, Skinner Mid. Sch., Denver, 1994-96; asst. prin. D'Evelyn Jr.-Sr. H.S., Jefferson County Pub. Schs., Golden, Colo., 1996—. Mem. NEA, ASCD, Nat. Assn. Secondary Sch. Prins. Office: D'Evelyn Jr-Sr HS 13200 W 32d Ave Golden CO 80401

PERSCHBACHER, DEBRA BASSETT, lawyer; b. Pleasanton, Calif., Oct. 28, 1956; d. James Arthur and Shirley Ann (Russell) Bassett; m. Rex Robert Perschbacher, June 4, 1989. BA, U. Vt., 1977; MS, San Diego State U., 1982; JD, U. Calif., Davis, 1987. Bar: Calif. 1987, D.C. 1990, U.S. Dist Ct. (no. and ea. dists.) Calif. 1988, U.S. Ct. Appeals (9th cir.), 1988, U.S. Supreme Ct., 1991. Guidance counselor Addison Cen. Supr. Union, Middlebury, Vt., 1982-83, Milton (Vt.) Elem. Sch., 1983-84; assoc. Morrison & Foerster, San Francisco, 1986; jud. clk. U.S. Ct. Appeals (9th cir.), Phoenix, 1987-88; assoc. Morrison & Foerster, San Francisco and Walnut Creek, Calif., 1988-92; sr. atty. Calif. Ct. Appeal (3d appellate dist.), Sacramento, 1992—; tutor civil procedure, rsch. asst. U. Calif., Davis, 1985-87; instr. U. Calif. at Davis Ext., 1995—; vis. prof. law U. Calif., Davis, 1996—. Sr. articles editor U. Calif. Law Rev., Davis, 1986-87; editor, 1985-86. Bd. dirs. Samaritan Counseling Ctr., 1994—. Mem. AAUW, ABA (vice chmn. ethics com. young lawyers divsn. 1989-91, exec. com. labor and employment law com. 1989-90), Sacramento County Bar Assn., Women Lawyers of Sacramento. Democrat. Home: 1541 39th St Sacramento CA 95816 Office: Ct Appeal 914 Capitol Mall Sacramento CA 95814-4802

PERSE, ARIA LEON, international business advanced technologies executive; b. L.A., Dec. 30, 1962; s. Constante A. and Marianne (Cobetti) P. PhD, UCLA, 1989. Chmn., CEO Advanced Tech. USA, Inc., Wilmington, Del., 1991—. Mem. exec. campaign bd. Republican Party, L.A., 1992. Mem. AAAS, Nat. Aero. Assn., Pacific Wings (Van Nuys, Calif.), Planetary Soc. (Pasadena, Calif.), L.A. World Affairs Coun. Home: 17311 Castellammare Dr Pacific Palisades CA 90272-4139

PESIC, PETER DRAGAN, liberal arts educator; b. San Francisco, May 11, 1948; s. Paul Sviatoslavovic and Milena Ljubomirovna (BoyoviĆ) Pesic; m. Ssu Isabel Weng, June 2, 1984; children: Andrei Petrovic, Alexei Petrovic. AB, Harvard U., 1969; MS, Stanford U., 1970, PhD, 1975. Lectr. Stanford (Calif.) U., 1976-80; tutor St. John's Coll., Santa Fe, 1980—, musician-in-residence, 1984—. Contbr. articles to profl. jours. Danforth fellow Danforth Found., 1969-75. Democrat. Orthodox. Office: Saint John's Coll 1160 Camino de la Cruz Blanca Santa Fe NM 87501

PETER, ARNOLD PHILIMON, lawyer; b. Karachi, Pakistan, Apr. 3, 1957; came to U.S., 1968; s. Kundan Lal and Irene Primrose (Mall) P. BS, Calif. State U., Long Beach, 1981; JD, Loyola U., L.A., 1984; MS, Calif. State U., Fresno, 1991. Bar: Calif. 1985, U.S. Dist. Ct. (ea., so., no. and cen. dists.) Calif. 1986, U.S. Ct. Appeals (9th cir.) 1989, U.S. Ct. Appeals (11th cir.) 1990. Law clk. appellate dept. Superior Ct., L.A., 1984-85, U.S. Dist. Ct. (ea. dist.) Calif., Fresno, 1986-88; assoc. Pepper, Hamilton & Scheetz, L.A., 1988-89, McDermott, Will & Emery, P.A., L.A., 1989-90, Cadwalader, Wickersham & Taft, L.A., 1990-91; labor and employment counsel City of Fresno, Calif., 1991-94; v.p. labor rels. and litigation Universal Studios, Hollywood, Calif.; adj. prof. law San Joaquin (Calif.) Sch. Law, 1993—, Calif. State U., Fresno, 1993—, acad. inquiry officer, 1993—, Calif. State U., Fresno. Contbr. articles to profl. jours. Mem. ABA, L.A. County Bar Assn. (mem. conf. of dels., com. on fed. cts.), Calif. State Bar Assn. (chmn. com. on fed. cts., chmn. exec. com. labor and employment law sect.), L.A. Athletic Club. Office: Universal Studios 100 Universal City Plz Universal City CA 91608

PETERS, BARBARA HUMBIRD, writer, editor; b. Santa Monica, Calif., Sept. 26, 1948; d. Philip Rising and Caroline Jean (Dickason) P. AA, Santa Monica Coll., 1971; BS, San Diego State U., 1976; postgrad. UCLA, 1981-82, 84. Ptnr. Signet Properties, L.A., 1971-85; tech. editor C. Brewer & Co., Hilo, Hawaii, 1975; editor The Aztec Engineer mag., San Diego, 1976-77; regional publicist YWCA, San Diego, 1977-78; campaign cons. Rep. Congl. and Assembly Candidates San Diego; pollster L.A. Times, 1983; pres., dir. Humbird Hopkins Inc., San Clemente, Calif., 1978-91; pub. rels. cons. ASCE, San Diego, 1975-76, Am. Soc. Mag. Photographers, San Diego, 1980. Author: The Layman's Guide to Raising Cane: A Guide to the Hawaiian Sugar Industry, 1975, The Students' Survival Guide, 1976, 2d edit. 1977. Mem. Mayor's Coun. on Librs., L.A., 1969; mem. Wilshire Blvd. Property Owners Assn., Santa Monica, 1972-78; docent Mus. Sci. and Industry, L.A., 1970; founding mem. Comml. and Indsl. Properties Assn., Santa Monica, 1982-89. Recipient Acting award Santa Monica Coll., 1970. Mem. NAFE, Internat. Assn. Bus. Communicators, Sales and Mktg. Execs. Assn. Avocations: travel, opera, puns.

PETERS, CAL ANTHONY, engineer; b. Lebannon, Oreg., Oct. 28, 1957; s. Cecil Laverne and Shirley Ann (Swem) P.; m. Laurel Ann Hubert, Aug. 11, 1988. Cert. mechanic, small engine repair. Gen. machine operator South Bay Cable, Idyllwild, Calif., 1974-77, asst. engr., 1977-84, chief engr., 1984—. Mem. Marine Tech. Soc. Office: South Bay Cable PO Box 67 54125 Maranatha Dr Idyllwild CA 92549

PETERS, CLAIRE LEILA, public relations, advertising executive; b. Tulsa, Okla., July 12, 1948; d. Elmer Ernest and Eleanor Claire (Wyvell) Hogg.; m. Glen Allen Bluemel, July 26, 1969 (div. Apr. 1977); m. William Robert Peters, Dec. 2, 1977. BA in Journalism, Advt. Sequence, Tex. Tech. U., 1970. Account exec. Wm. Golden Avt., Stockton, Calif., 1973-77; asst. dir. mktg. Stockton (Calif.) Savings & Loan Assn., 1977-78; account exec. Press Courier Newspaper, Oxnard, Calif., 1979-81; asst. v.p. mktg., pub. and mem. rels. Farm Credit Banks of Sacramento (Calif.) and Tex,, 1981-86; mgr. pub. rels. Sunkist Growers, Inc., Sherman Oaks, Calif., 1986—. mem. Internat. Assn. Bus. Comms. (v.p. membership 1991—), Pub. Rels. Soc. Am., Nat. Coun. Farmer Coops. (pub. rels. com.), Agrl. Coun. Am. (pub. rels. com.), Nat. Agri-mktg. Assn. (pres. So. Calif. chpt.). Office: Sunkist Growers 14130 Riverside Dr Sherman Oaks CA 91423-2313

PETERS, DOUGLAS CAMERON, mining engineer, geologist; b. Pitts., June 19, 1955; s. Donald Cameron and Twila (Bingel) P. BS in Earth and Planetary Sci., U. Pitts., 1977; MS in Geology, Colo. Sch. Mines, 1981, MS in Mining Engring., 1983. Technician, inspector Engring. Mechanics Inc., Pitts., 1973-77. Rsch. asst. Potential Gas Agy., Golden, Colo., 1977-78; geologist U.S. Geol. Survey, Denver, 1978-80; cons. Climax Molybdenum Co., Golden, 1981-82; cons., Golden, 1982-84; mining engr., prin. investigator U.S. Bur. Mines, Denver, 1984-96; owner Peters Geoscis., 1996—; bur. rep. to Geosat Com., 1984-95; program chmn. GeoTech Conf., Denver, 1984-88, mem. long. range planning subcom., 1989-92, gen. chmn., 1991; engr. in tng. #11800, Colo., profl. geologist, Wyo., #367, Pa., 2365. Author: Physical Modeling of Draw of Broken Rock in Caving, 1984, Bur. Mines Articles and Reports; editor COGS Computer Contbns., 1986—, Geology in Coal Resource Utilization, 1988-91; assoc. editor Computers & Geosciences, 1989—; contbr. articles to profl. jours.; guest editor various jours. Am. Inst. Profl. Geologists, 1984, 85, 86, Appreciation award, 87, Spl. award Denver Geotech Com., 1988, Appreciation award, 1989. Mem. Computer Oriented Geol. Soc. (charter, com. chmn. 1983-95, pres. 1985, dir. 1986, contbg. editor newsletter 1985-96), Geol. Soc. Am., Rocky Mountain Assn. Geologists, Am. Inst. Profl. Geologists (cert. profl. geologist #8274), Soc. Mining Metallurgy and Exploration, Am. Assn. Petroleum Geologists (astrogeology com., 1984—, pubs. com. 1995—, remote sensing com. 1990—, Energy Mineral div. v.p. 1990-91, pres. 1991-92, Cert. of Merit award 1992, 93, Pres.'s award 1993, Disting. Svc. award 1995), Am. Soc. Photogrammetry and Remote Sensing, Nat. Space Soc., Colo. Mining Assn., Pitts. Geol. Soc., Planetary Soc., Space Studies Inst., Soc. Exploration Geochemists. Republican.

PETERS, JOHN U., English language educator; b. Snohomish, Wash., June 20, 1945; s. John and Virginia Jean (Eagle) Ursulescu. BA, UCLA, 1967; MA, Johns Hopkins U., 1970; PhD, U. Wis., 1973. Lectr. in English L.A. C.C. Dist., 1972—, Calif. State U., Northridge, 1977—; textbook cons., 1984—. Author: The Elements of Critical Reading, 1991; contbr. articles, revs. to profl. jours. Mem. MLA. Home: PO Box 416 Sunland CA 91041-0416 Office: Calif State U Dept English Northridge CA 91330

PETERS, JOSEPH DONALD, filmmaker; b. Montebello, Calif., Mar. 7, 1958; s. Donald Harry and Anna Lucia (Suarez) P.; m. Anna Marie Cervantes-Peters, Oct. 3, 1992. BA in Comm., U. So. Calif., L.A., 1982. Tech. support staff Xerox Corp., La Palma, Calif., 1985—; filmmaker Renaissance Prodns., Ltd., Glendora, Calif., 1986—. Writer, prodr., dir. films: Seniors and Alcohol Abuse, 1986, Eskimo Ice Cream Shoes, 1990 (Gold award 1991), Rachel, 1994 (Silver and Bronze award 1995), Emotions, 1996; writer A Breath of Life, 1997. Mem. Am. Film Inst., Assn. Ind. Video and Filmmakers, Ind. Feature Project, Cinewomen. Office: Renaissance Productions Ltd 1050 E Ivy St Glendora CA 91740

PETERS, KEVIN CASEY, interactive multimedia producer; b. L.A., Nov. 14, 1952; s. Edwin Dale Peters and Marylee (Loftus) Green. AA in Speech, L.A. City Coll., 1975; BA in Govt. and Social Rels., Immaculate Heart Coll., 1980; MA in Film and TV, UCLA, 1992. cer. multimedia prodn., Pratt Coll., 1996. Nat. sec. People's Party, Washington, 1976-79; office mgr., statewide campaign hdqrs. Californians for a Bilateral Nuclear Weapons Freeze, 1982; studio transp. driver Teamsters # 399, L.A., 1979-89; libr. gifts coord. UCLA Univ. Rsch. Libr., 1989-95; interactive multimedia prodr. Pixel Prose, 1996—. Author: C-SPAN: Congress on Television, 1992, (poems) Atoms for Peace, 1984. Mem. state exec. com. Peace and Freedom Party, Calif., 1980— South State Chairperson Peace and Freedom Party, 1996, mem. exec. com. AFSCME local 3235, UCLA, 1990—; campaign treas. Gerald Horne for U.S. Senate, Calif., 1992; candidate for trustee L.A. C.C., 1993; apptd. Libr. Com. for Diversity, UCLA, 1990-93, pres. Peoples Campaign, 1996. Mem. ACLU, Union for Dem. Comms., Ctr. for Voting and Democracy. Home: 446 S Van Ness Ave Los Angeles CA 90020-4615

PETERS, RAY JOHN, surveyor; b. St. Louis, Feb. 10, 1931; s. John Henry and Pearl Minnie Peters; m. Barbara Mary Linacre, June 18, 1955; children: Alison Elizabeth, Andrew James, Gwendoline Joy. Student, Mo. Sch. Mines, 1952-53. Cert. land surveyor, Calif., Nev., N.D. Surveyor State of Calif., San Francisco, 1955-60; pres. Peters, Verdugo & Hull, Lafayette, Calif., 1960-88; ptnr. Peters & Hull, Lafayette, 1988—. Author: Real Estate Handbook, 1993, The Lafitte Case, 1997. With U.S. Army, 1948-52. Recipient Disting. Cmty. Svc. award Lafayette Sun., 1978; named Citizen of Yr. Lions Club, 1983. Mem. ASCE (Calif. coun.), Calif. Land Surveyors Assn., Calif. Writers club. Republican. Congregational. Home: 1324 Martino Rd Lafayette CA 94549

PETERS, RAYMOND EUGENE, computer systems company executive; b. New Haven, Aug. 24, 1933; s. Raymond and Doris Winthrop (Smith) P.; m. Millie Mather, July 14, 1978 (div. Nov. 1983). Student, San Diego City Coll., 1956-61; cert., Lumbleau Real Estate Sch., 1973, Southwestern Coll., Chula Vista, Calif., 1980. Cert. quality assurance engr. Founder, pub. Silhouette Pub. Co., San Diego, 1960-75; co-founder, news dir. Sta. XEGM, San Diego, 1964-68; news dir. Sta. XERB, Tijuana, Mex., 1973-74; founder, chief exec. officer New World Airways, Inc., San Diego, 1968-77; co-founder, exec. vice chmn. bd. San Cal Rail, Inc.-San Diego Trolley, San Diego, 1974-77; founder, pres. Ansonia Sta., micro systems, San Diego, 1986—; cons. on multimedia and electronic commerce sys., 1995—; co-founder, dir. S.E. Cmty. Theatre, San Diego, 1960-68; commr. New World Aviation Acad., Otay Mesa, Calif., 1971-77; co-founder New World Internat. Trade and Commerce Commn., Inc., 1991-94. Author: Black Americans in Aviation, 1971, Profiles in Black American History, 1974, Eagles Don't Cry, 1988; founder, pub., editor Oceanside Lighthouse, 1958-60, San Diego Herald Dispatch, 1959-60. Co-founder, bd. dirs. San Diego County Econ. Opportunity Commn., 1964-67; co-founder Edn. Cultural Complex, San Diego, 1966-75; co-founder, exec. dir. S.E. Anti-Poverty Planning Coun., Inc., 1964-67; mem. U.S. Rep. Senatorial Inner Circle Com., Washington, 1990—; mem. bus. adv. bd. Value Add Reseller, 1995. With U.S. Army, 1950-53, Korea. Decorated (2) Bronze stars, UN medal. Mem. Am. Soc. Quality Control, Nat. City C. of C., Afro-Am. Micro Sys. Soc. (exec. dir. 1987—), Negro Airmen Internat. (Calif. pres. 1970-75, nat. v.p. 1975-77), Tuskegee Airmen (charter, bd. dirs. Benjamin O. Davis San Diego chpt. 1995—), Internat. Platform Assn., U.S. C. of C., Greater San Diego Minority C. of C. (bd. dirs. 1974—, past chmn. bd.), Masons (most worshipful grand master, supreme coun.), Shriners (Al Kadosh Disting. Cmty. Svc. award 1975). Republican. Home: Meadowbrook Estates # 245 8301 Mission Gorge Rd Santee CA 92071-3500

PETERS, RICHARD, lawyer; b. Bklyn., June 6, 1945; s. Edmund Richard and Louise (Parks) P. BA, Tulane U., 1967; MA, Fla. State U., 1968, PhD, 1985; JD, Calif. Western, 1988. Bar: Calif. 1989. Instr. English U. San Diego, 1991, San Diego City Coll., 1989—, San Diego Mesa Coll., 1989—; panel atty. Appellate Defenders, Inc., San Diego, 1989—. Author: (poetry) On Aging, 1991. Mem. ABA, San Diego County Bar Assn. Office: Richard Peters Atty 5690 Greenshade Rd San Diego CA 92121

PETERS, RITA, university administrator; b. Riverhead, N.Y., Sept. 1, 1953; d. Herbert E. and Loni S. Peters. BA, Lycoming Coll., Williamsport, Pa., 1974; MS, U. Calif., Davis, 1990. Cert. fund raising exec. Cons. Winning Edge, Stockton, Calif., 1984-92; dir. grants and founds. U. of the Pacific, Stockton, 1992—. Lilly Endowment Rsch. awardee, 1991. Mem. Nat. Soc. Fund Raising Execs., Rotary. Home: PO Box 9020 Stockton CA 95208-1020 Office: Univ of Pacific 2d Floor Burns Tower 3601 Pacific Ave Stockton CA 95211-0110

PETERS, ROBERT WAYNE, direct mail and catalog sales specialist; b. LaPorte, Ind., Jan. 2, 1950; s. Harry Carl and Dorothy May (Fischer) P.; m. Frances Kay Cooley, Aug. 21, 1971; children: Carolyn Marie, Angela Lynn. BA, Purdue U., 1972. CLU. Mgr. pension adminstrn. Gen. Life Ins. Corp., Milw., 1973-75; dir. qualified plan devel. Cen. Life Assurance Co., Des Moines, 1976-84; v.p. individual ops. First Farwest Ins. Co., Portland, Oreg., 1984-90; pres. CAF Enterprises, Inc., Portland, 1990—; lectr. various govt. agys. Contbr. articles to profl. jours. Mem. N.W. Vintage Thunderbird (v.p. 1988, pres. 1989-90, exec. bd. 1991, sec. 1992-93, treas. 1995-96), Optimists (treas. West Des Moines chpt. Iowa Club 1983-84). Office: CAF Enterprises Inc 9997 SW Avery St Tualatin OR 97062-9517

PETERS, ROBERT WOOLSEY, architect; b. Mpls., Mar. 24, 1935; s. John Eugene and Adelaide Elizabeth (Woolsey) P. BArch., U. Minn., 1958; MArch., Yale U., 1961. Registered architect, N.Mex., Ariz. Dir. design Schaefer & Assocs., Wichita, Kans., 1975-76; participating assoc. Skidmore Owings & Merrill, Chgo., 1961-74; ptnr. Addy & Peters, Albuquerque, 1979-82; owner Robert W. Peters AIA Architect, Albuquerque, 1982—. Exhibited work Centre Georges Pompidou, Paris, 1980; Univ. Art Mus., Albuquerque, 1982, 92, Albuquerque Mus., 1988. Bd. dirs. Contemporary Art Soc. N.Mex. Contbr. articles to Century Mag., Progressive Architecture, House & Garden, House Beautiful, also others. Recipient honor awards N.Mex. Soc. Architects, 1980-83, 86, 87, 92; honor award HUD, 1980, 5th Nat. Passive Solar Conf., Amherst, Mass., 1981. Fellow AIA. Democrat. Roman Catholic. Club: Yale of N.Mex.

PETERS, SHIRLEY ANN, pediatrics nurse; b. Burbank, Calif., July 25, 1948; d. Frank F. and Marion Belle (Thorn) P. Diploma, Kaiser Found. Sch. Nursing, 1970; BS in Health Sci., Chapman Coll., 1978, MS in Health Sci., 1981. RN, Calif.; cert. pediatric nurse practitioner. Pediatric nurse practitioner Kaiser-Permanente Med. Ctr., Panorama City, Calif., 1974-87; rsch. nurse practitioner Pharmacology Rsch. Inst., Van Nuys, Calif., 1987-88; pediatric nurse practitioner, infection control practitioner Granada Hills (Calif.) Community Hosp., 1988-89; pediatric nurse practitioner Med. Ctr. of North Hollywood, Calif., 1989-90, CIGNA Health Plans of Calif., North Hollywood, 1990-92; patient care coord., quality improvement/utilization rev. Alternative Health Care, Chatsworth, Calif., 1992-94; pediatric nruse practitioner Childrens Hosp. of L.A., L.A., 1994-95; maternal child health supr. home health Queen of Angels-Hollywood-Presbyn. Hosp., L.A., 1995—. Mem. United Nurse's Assn. Calif. (clinic co-chair, parliamentarian, negotiator, NAPNAP, Assn. Infection Control Practitioners.

PETERS, WILLIAM FRANK, art educator; b. Oakland, Calif., Nov. 8, 1934; s. Clifford Leslie and Gladys Fay (Parrish) P.; m. Patricia Ann Redgwick, June 3, 1956 (div. 1973); 1 child, David William. B. Art Edn. with honors, Calif. Coll. Arts & Crafts, 1961; postgrad., various schools, various locations. Cert. spl. secondary art edn. life, gen. jr. high life. Summer campus art dir., instr. Richmond (Calif.) Unified Sch. Dist., 1961-66, Sch. of Fine Arts, Mt. Diablo Unified Sch. Dist., Concord, Calif., 1967-74; instr. Liberty Union H.S. Dist., Brentwood, Calif., 1961—, chmn. arts & crafts dept., 1976-91; dist. rep. Pacific Art Assn., East Contra Costa County, Calif., 1967-70, Calif. Art Assn., East Contra Costa County, 1970-74; accreditation team mem. Western Assn. Schs. and Colls., Albany, Calif., 1981; film evaluator Contra Costa County Schs., 1965-84. Exhibited in group shows at Contra Costa County Fair (oil painting Best of Show 1968, watercolor Best of Show 1990, 1st pl. photography 1987-95), Delta Art Show, Antioch, Calif. (1st pl. jewelry 1979), Festival of Color, Concord, Calif. (1st pl. ceramic 1963);. Fundraiser United Crusade, Brentwood, Calif., 1980-83; publicity vol. East Contra Costa County Soroptimist Club, East County Rape/Crisis Ctr., Kappa Beta, John Marsh Meml. Assn., Knightsen 4-H, Delta Rotary Club, Delta Recreation Dept., Oakley Women's Club, Town of Byron, others. Named Contra Costa County Tchr. of Yr. AAUW, 1981; postgrad scholar Calif. Coll. of Arts and Crafts, 1962-63. Mem. NEA, Calif. Tchrs. Assn., Liberty Edn. Assn. (chmn. salary com., past v.p., chmn. evaluation com., chmn. pers. policies com., chmn. scholarship com.), Delta Art Assn. (past bd. dirs.), Brentwood C. of C. (dir. Brentwood Christmas decorations 1968-94). Democrat. Office: Liberty Union HS Dist 104 Oak St Brentwood CA 94513-1335

PETERSEN, AIMEE BERNICE, interior designer, artist, landscape designer; b. North Vancouver, B.C., Can., Apr. 13, 1939; d. Samuel Nathaniel and Aimee Selena (Topping) Hadley; m. Gary Andrew Petersen, May 1, 1959; children: Todd William, Troy Andrew. Student, U. Wash., 1957-59, Edmonds (Wash.) C.C., 1967-74. Owner, designer The Designing Woman, Edmonds, 1979 . Pres. Ballinger Elem. PTA, 1969-71, Madrona Jr. H.S., 1973, 74; deaconess United Presbyn. Ch., Edmonds, 1967-75. Recipient Golden Acorn award Ballinger Sch. PTA, 1972; named Woman of Yr., Jr. Women Federated Women's, 1967. Mem. Nat. Fedn. Ind. Bus. People, Better Bus. Bur., Bus. and Profl. Women, Women Investing Now (founder 1991), Edmonds C. of C., Sons of Norway (Lodge 130 social chmn. 1987—). Presbyterian. Home: 5528 173rd Pl SW Lynnwood WA 98037-3034 Office: The Designing Woman 9691 Firdale Ave Edmonds WA 98020-6519

PETERSEN, ANN NEVIN, computer systems administrator, consultant; b. Mexico City, Aug. 7, 1937; parents Am. citizens; d. Thomas Marshall and Gerry (Cox) Nevin; m. Norman William Petersen, Aug. 24, 1956; children: Richard, Robert, Thomas, Anita, David. AS in Electronics, Monterey Peninsula Coll., Monterey, Calif., 1962; student, U. N.Mex., 1956, Las Positas Coll., Livermore, Calif., 1992. Cert. computer profl. CAD mgr. Naval Air Rework Facility, Alameda, Calif., 1979-80; computer systems analyst Space and Naval Warfare System Command, Washington, 1980-84, Facilities Computer Systems Office, Port Hueneme, Calif., 1984-86; systems mgr. Lawrence Livermore Nat. Lab., Livermore, 1986-89; data base mgr. Clayton Environ. Cons., Pleasanton, Calif., 1989-90; computer systems mgr. Waltrip & Assocs., Sacramento, 1990-94; dir. computer systems, CFO Innovative Techs. Inc., Pleasanton, 1992—. Author databases. Bd. dirs. Am. Field Svc., Port Hueneme, 1976-78; mem. various adv. bds. U.S. Navy, 1957-86; mem. adv. bd. Calif. Deaf/Blind Regional Ctr., Sacramento, 1976-80; bd. dirs. ARC Alameda County, Hayward, Calif., 1992—. Recipient Superior Performance award U.S. Navy, 1980, Speaker of Month award Toastmasters, 1985. Mem. Data Processing Mgmt. Assn., bd. dirs., sec.), Assn. for Computing Machinery, Tri Valley MacIntosh Users Group, Inst. for Cert. of Computer Profls. Office: Innovative Techs Inc 5238 Riverdale Ct Pleasanton CA 94588-3759

PETERSEN, ARNE JOAQUIN, chemist; b. L.A., Jan. 27, 1932; s. Hans Marie Theodore and Astrid Maria (Pedersen) P.; m. Sandra Joyce Sharp, Aug. 12, 1961; children: Christina Lynn, Kurt Arne. AA, Compton Coll., 1957; BS, Calif. State U., Long Beach, 1959; BA, U. Calif., Irvine, 1975. Comml. pilots lic. Chemist/scientist Beckman Instruments, Inc., Fullerton, Calif., 1959-62, engr., scientist, 1962-65, project, sr. project engr., 1965-74; project/program mgr. Beckman Clin. Ops., Fullerton/Brea, Calif., 1974-80; ops. mgr. Graphic Controls Corp., Irvine, 1980-82; engr./rsch. and devel. mgr. Carle Instruments Chromatography, Anaheim, Calif., 1982-84; ops. mgr. Magnaflux/X-Ray Devel., L.A., 1984-85; rsch. and devel. dir., new products Am. Chem. Systems, Irvine, Calif., 1985-86; rsch. assoc. U. Calif., Irvine, 1987-88; ind. cons., contractor, sales real estate investment, 1989—; career guidance counselor U. Calif., Irvine, 1976; bus. cons. electronics co. Internat. Exec. Svc. Corps, Egypt, 1993-94. Author scientific papers in field; patentee in field. Vol. F.I.S.H., Costa Mesa and Newport Beach, Calif.; basketball coach Boys-Girls Club, Newport Beach, 1975-78, baseball coach Newport Beach Parks, 1975-78; adv. com. Newport/Costa Mesa Sch. Bd., 1974-75. Sgt. USAF, 1951-55. Mem. Biomed. Engring. Soc., Am. Mgmt. Assn., Internat. Exec. Svc. Corps (exec. svc. with Agy Internat. Devel., 1993, 94), U. Calif. Irvine Univ. Club (bd. dirs.), Kappa Sigma (founder Calif. State. U., Long Beach).

PETERSEN, BENTON LAURITZ, paralegal; b. Salt Lake City, Jan. 1, 1942; s. Lauritz George and Arleane (Curtis) P.; m. Sharon Donnette Higgins, Sept. 20, 1974 (div. Aug. 9, 1989); children: Grant Lauritz, Tashya Eileen, Nicholas Robert, Katrina Arleane. AA, Weber State Coll., 1966, BA, 1968; BA, Weber State Coll., 1968; M of Liberal Studies, U. Okla., 1980; diploma, Nat. Radio Inst. Paralegal Sch., 1991. Registered paralegal. Announcer/news dir. KWHO Radio, Salt Lake City, 1968-70, KDXU Radio, St. George, Utah, 1970-73, KSOP Radio, Salt Lake City, 1973-76; case worker/counselor Salvation Army, Midland, Tex., 1976-84; announcer/news dir. KBRS Radio, Springdale, Ark., 1984-86; case worker/counselor Office of Human Concern, Rogers, Ark., 1986-88; announcer KAZM Radio, Sedona, Ariz., 1988-91; paralegal Benton L. Petersen, Manti, Utah, 1991—; cons. Sanpete County Srs., Manti, 1992—. Award judge Manti City Beautification, 1992-96; treas. Manti Destiny Com., 1993—; tourism com. Sanpete County Econ. Devel., Ephraim, Utah, 1993-96. Served with U.S. Army N.G., 1959-66. Mem. Am. Soc. Notaries, Nat. Assn. Federated Tax Preparers, Nat. Paralegal Assn., Am. Legion. Mem. LDS Ch. Home: 470 E 120 N Manti UT 84642-0011 Office: Benton L Petersen ND Paralegal Svcs 470 E 120 N Manti UT 84642-0011

PETERSEN, DONALD FELIX, consultant; b. Centralia, Wash., Nov. 16, 1928; s. Otto Anders and Martha Hilda (Peck) P.; m. Norma Ingeborg Wise, Jan. 17, 1954; children: Marilyn, Ronald, Kenneth. BBA, U. Wash., 1950. Transp. rate analyst Pub. Utility Commr., Salem, Oreg., 1953-57; mgmt. effectiveness analyst Dept. of Fin. and Adminstrn., Salem, 1958, mgmt. analyst, 1958-61, supr., fiscal analyst, 1962-67; prin. fiscal analyst Legis. Budget Com., Olympia, Wash., 1967-79, legis. auditor, 1980-85; program analysis mgr. Dept. Social and Health Svcs., Olympia, 1986-91; cons. on state, fed. and local govt. Olympia, 1991—; mem. state career exec. program dept. pers. State of Wash., Olympia, 1986-89; team mem. Price-Waterhouse, Olympia, 1987. Freeholder Thurston County Bd. Freeholders, 1978-79; chmn. Tanglewilde Park and Recreation Dist., Lacey, 1987, 89-90, vice-chmn., 1988; active Dem. Party, Thurston County, 1987-94; vol. RSVP, 1988-92. Cert. of Appreciation, North Thurston Kiwanis, 1988, State of Wash., 1988, Dept. Social and Health Svcs., 1989, ACTION, 1990. Mem. AARP (3d congl. dist. coord. Vote Program 1990-94, mem. state legis. com. Wash. 1994—, Capital City task force coord. 1995-96, vice-chair 1996—), Nature Conservancy, Masons, Kiwanis (pres. 1973-74, sec. 1970-71). Democrat. Home and Office: 423 Ranger Dr SE Olympia WA 98503-6728

PETERSEN, FINN BO, oncologist, educator; b. Copenhagen, Mar. 26, 1951; came to U.S., 1983; s. Jorgen and Ebba Gjeding (Jorgensen) P.; m. Merete Secher Lund, Mar. 7, 1979; children: Lars Secher, Thomas Secher, Andreas Secher. BA, Niels Steensen, Copenhagen, 1971; MD, U. Copenhagen, 1978. Intern in internal medicine Copenhagen, 1978-79, resident in hematology, 1980-83; fellow oncology Fred Hutchinson Cancer Rsch. Ctr. U. Wash., Seattle, 1983-85, assoc. researcher oncology, 1985-87, asst. mem. in clin. rsch., 1987-91, asst. prof., 1988-91, prof. medicine, 1992—; clin. dir. bone marrow transplant program U. Utah Sch. Medicine, 1992—. Author: Hematology, 1977; contbr. articles to profl. jours. Mem. AMA, AAAS, Internat. Soc. Exptl. Hematology, Am. Soc. Clin. Oncology, Am. Soc. Hematology, Assn. Gnotobiology. Office: U Utah Bone Marrow Transplant Program Div of Hematology and Oncology Salt Lake City UT 84132

PETERSEN, GERALD MICHAEL, city official; b. Cheltenham, Eng., Sept. 25, 1953; (parents Am. citizens); s. Iner Leroy and Ann Estelle Peterson; m. Valerie Jacobson, July 22, 1978; children: Julia Rose, Andrea, Estelle. Student, Mont. State U., 1975-78, Missoula Vocat.-Tech. Sch., 1979-81. Desk clk. Palace Hotel, Missoula, Mont., 1979-81; bench technician Dana Corp., Bozeman, Mont., 1981-82; wastewater treatment operator City of Bozeman, 1982-91, operator water plant, 1991—. 3d class petty officer USN, 1971-75. Mem. Beall Park Art Ctr., Folklore Soc. Bozeman, Big Sky Wind Drinkers. Home: 201 N Western Dr Bozeman MT 59718-2667 Office: City of Bozeman Water Treatment Plant 7022 Sourdough Canyon Rd Bozeman MT 59715-8020

PETERSEN, JAMES NIELS, chemical engineering educator; b. Great Falls, Mont., July 26, 1954; s. Theodore Peter and Mary Elenor (Murphy) P.; m. Renee Karla Barnes, June 9, 1975; children: Matthew, Jonathan, Johanna, Michaela. BSChemE, Mont. State U., 1976; PhD in Chem. Engring., Iowa State U., 1979. Vis. prof. Weyerhaeuser Co., Tacoma, 1980, Chevron Rsch. Co., Richmond, Calif., 1981; asst. prof. Wash. State U., Pullman, 1979-85; vis. rsch. assoc. Oak Ridge (Tenn.) Nat. Lab., 1989-90; faculty rsch. assoc. Battelle Pacific Northwest Labs., Richland, Wash., 1992—, affiliate staff scientist, 1994—; assoc. prof. Wash. State U., Pullman, 1985-94, prof., 1994—; cons. Chevron, U.S.A., San Francisco, 1982, Martin Marietta Energy System, Oak Ridge, 1993; mem. INEEL Univ. rsch. consortium, 1995—. Patentee continuous fluidited bed contactor; author: (book chpt.) Immobilized Biosorbents for Dissolved Metals, 1991. Grantee Battelle PNL, 1990-97, Martin Marietta Energy Systems, 1990-95, NSF, 1993-96, Nat. Supercomputer Ctr. for Energy and the Environment, 1993, Inel Univ. Rsch. Consortium, 1996—. Mem. AIChE, Am. Soc. Engring. Edn. (Outstanding Young Faculty mem. 1985), Am. Chem. Soc., Sigma Xi. Office: Wash State U Chem Engring Dept Pullman WA 99164-2710

PETERSEN, MARGARET SARA, civil engineering consultant, retired civil engineering educator; b. Moline, Ill., Apr. 28, 1920; d. Charles and Alvena Catherine (Fischer) P. BS in Civil Engring., U. Iowa, 1947, MS in Mechanics and Hydraulics, 1953. Registered civil engr., Iowa. Hydraulic engr. Waterways Experiment Sta. C.E., U.S. Army, Jackson, Miss., 1947-52; hydraulic engr. Mo. River Divsn. C.E., U.S. Army, Omaha, 1953-55; hydraulic engr. Little Rock Dist. C.E., U.S. Army, 1955-64; hydraulic engr. Waterways Experiment Sta. C.E., U.S. Army, Vicksburg, Miss., 1964; hydraulic engr. Sacramento Dist. C.E., U.S. Army, 1964-77; assoc. prof. dept. civil engring. U. Ariz., Tucson, 1981-91, assoc. prof. emerita, 1991—; mem. adjudication commn. Ariz. Navigable Streams, Phoenix, 1992-94; cons. Vicksburg Dist. Corps of Engrs., 1985-89; lectr. U. Witwatersrand, Johannesburg, South Africa, 1988, 93, Morocco, China. Author: Water Resources Planning and Development, 1984, River Engineering, 1986, Monograph on Island Navigation and Canalization, 1996; co-author: Water Resources Development in Developing Countries, 1991; contbr. chpts. to books, articles to profl. jours. Recipient Disting. Alumni award U. Iowa, 1987. Mem U. Iowa Disting Engrings Alumni Acad; mem. Adv. bd. of Huntington Libr. fund for the Heritage of Civil Engring. Mem. (hon.) ASCE (sec. com. on metrication 1978-94, mem. water resources engring. rsch. and edn. com. 1993—, mgmt. group D 1978-80, hydraulics divsn. exec. com. 1972-76), U.S. com. Internat. Commn. Large Dams, Permanent Internat. Assn. of Navigation Congresses, Internat. Assn. for Hydraulic Rsch., Internat. Water Resources Assn., Assn. Arid Lands, Sigma Xi, Chi Epsilon. Office: U Ariz Dept Civil Engring Tucson AZ 85721

PETERSEN, MARK L., public relations executive; b. Ogden, Utah, Jan. 3, 1959; s. Ronald L. and Charlene Mary (Moore) P.; m. Becky Lyn Stott, Mar. 12, 1981; children: Melissa, Julie, Derek, Adam, Kalynn, Nathan. BS in Theatre Arts/Comm., Weber State U., 1985. Asst. bus./pub. rels. mgr. Weber State Theatre, Odgen, 1980-82, bus./pub. rels. mgr., 1982-84; dir. mktg., pub. rels. Coll. of Arts and Human, Weber State U., Odgen, 1984-86; mktg. coord. Area Tech. Ctr., Odgen, 1986-87; dir. pub. rels. Dixie Coll., St. George, Utah, 1987-95; cons. KIWI Pub., St. George, 1993—; biographer, family histories, St. George, 1989—. Contbr. articles to profl. jours. Bd. dirs. Utah's Dixie Internat. Folkfest, St. George, 1991-95, Washington County Children's Safety Coun., St. George, 1993-95; pres-elect Chamber Pub. Rels. Group, St. George, 1995-96, pres., 1996—; mem. Spirit of Dixie Com., St. George, 1987-90. Recipient Community Svc. award City of St. George, 1990, 4 First Pl. Publ. award, 1995-96, 1st Pl. Nat. Paragon award, 1996. Mem. Nat. Coun. for Mktg. and Pub. Rels., Nat. Sch. Pub. Rels. Assn. (Merit award 1991), Nat. Assn. of Vocat. Tech. Edn. Communicators (3rd Pl. 1987), Dixie Coll. Staff Assn. (pres. 1995), St. George C. of C. Home: 1761 N Centennial Dr Saint George UT 84770-5616 Office: Dixie Coll 225 S 700 East Saint George UT 84770

PETERSEN, MARTA JEAN, dermatologist, educator; b. Spokane, Wash., Feb. 13, 1953; d. William Harry and Patricia Ann (Gramling) P.; m. Harold Hume Sears, Oct. 9, 1982; 1 child, Madeleine Rose Helen. BA, U. Minn., 1975; MD, U. Utah, 1979. Diplomate Am. Bd. Dermatology, Am. Bd. Internal Medicine. Intern in internal medicine Strong Meml. Hosp., U. Rochester, N.Y., 1979-80; resident U. Utah Hosps., Salt Lake City, 1980-82; rsch. fellow in dermatology U. Utah, Salt Lake City, 1982-84; resident in dermatology Sch. Medicine U. N.C., Chapel Hill, 1984-87, asst. prof., 1987-89; asst. prof. U. Utah, Salt Lake City, 1989-95, assoc. prof., 1995—; sec.-treas. Sulzberger Inst. for Dermatologic Edn., Schaumburg, Ill., 1994—. Contbr. articles to profl. jours. Fellow Am. Acad. Dermatology; mem. Soc. Investigative Dermatology, Dermatology Found., Am. Soc. Cell Biology, Alpha Omega Alpha. Office: U Utah Sch Medicine 50 N Medical Dr Salt Lake City UT 84132-0001

PETERSEN, MARTIN EUGENE, museum curator; b. Grafton, Iowa, Apr. 21, 1931; s. Martin S. and Martha Dorothea (Paulsen) P. B.A., State U. Iowa, 1951, M.A., 1957; postgrad., The Hague (Netherlands), 1964. Curator San Diego Mus. Art, 1957-96; advisor Olaf Wieghorst Mus., El Cajon, Calif., 1996—; extension instr. U. Calif., 1958, lectr., 1960. Author art catalogues, books, articles in field. Served with AUS, 1952-54. Mem. So. Calif. Art Historians. Home: 4571 Narragansett Ave San Diego CA 92107-2915

PETERSEN, NORMAN WILLIAM, naval officer, engineering facility administrator; b. Highland Park, Ill., Aug. 26, 1933; s. Jens Edlef and Marie (Wenderling) P.; m. Ann Nevin, Aug. 24, 1956; children: Richard Nevin, Robert William, Thomas Marshall, Anita, David Arthur. BEE, U. N.Mex., 1956; MEE with distinction, Naval Postgrad. Sch., Monterey, Calif., 1962; postgrad., Harvard Bus. Sch., 1982. Registered profl. engr., Mass., Calif. Shops engr. Naval Station, Key West, Fla., 1956-59; personnel dir. Bur. Yards and Docks, Washington, 1959-60; pub. works officer Fleet Anti-Air Warfare Ctr., Dam Neck, Va., 1962-64; engring. coord. Southwest div. Naval Facilities Engring. Command, San Diego, 1964-66; exec. officer Amphibious Constrn. Battalion 1, San Diego, 1966-67; force civil engr. Comdr. Naval Air Force Pacific, San Diego, 1967-70; pub. works officer Naval Air Sta. Miramar, San Diego, 1970-73; exec. officer Pub. Works Ctr., Great Lakes, Ill., 1973-75; comdg. officer Navy Civil Engring. Rsch. Lab., Port Hueneme, Calif., 1975-78, Pub. Works Ctr. San Francisco Bay Area, Oakland, Calif., 1978-80; comptroller, programs dir. Naval Facilities Engring. Command, Washington, 1980-84; pub. works officer Pacific Missile Test Ctr., Point Mugu, Calif., 1984-86; deputy assoc. dir. for plant engring. Lawrence Livermore (Calif.) Nat. Lab., 1986-91, sr. facilities advisor, 1991-94; v.p. Innovative Techs. Inc, Pleasanton, Calif., 1994—. Contbr. articles to profl. jours. Bd. dirs. CBC Fed. Credit Union, Port Hueneme, 1984-86, Ventura County United Way, Oxnard, Calif., 1976-78, strategic planning com., Camarillo, Calif., 1984-86; guest mem. Ventura County Assn. Govts., 1984-86; pres. Garnet Austin chpt. ARC, 1992-94, v.p. Alameda County chpt. Decorated (twice) Legion of Merit; Gallantry Cross (Republic Vietnam); recipient 2 Meritorious Svc. medals, Navy Commendation medal, Navy Unit citation, 2 Meritorious Unit commendations. Mem. Am. Soc. Mil. Comptrollers, Soc. Am. Mil. Engrs., Assn. Phys. Plant Adminstrs. (affiliate), Navy League, Oxnard Gem and Mineral Soc. (2d v.p.), Sigma Xi, Lambda Chi Alpha. Office: Innovative Techs Inc 5238 Riverdale Ct Pleasanton CA 94588-3759

PETERSEN, PHIL BRENT, psychiatrist, educator; b. Tempe, Ariz., Oct. 13, 1945; mm. Carol Jean Gold, June 2, 1972; children: Ryan C., Amy, Barr J., Camie. AB in Zoology, San Diego State U., 1968; MD, U. Utah, 1972. Diplomate Am. Bd. Psychiatry and Neurology. Resident in gen. psychiatry U. Utah, Salt Lake City, 1972-74; fellow in child psychiatry U. Utah Coll. Medicine-Primary Children's Med. Ctr., Salt Lake City, 1974-76; clin. instr. in med. hypnosis U. Utah, Salt Lake City, 1972-73, instr. psychiatry, 1976-80, clin. instr., 1981-90, clin. assoc. prof., 1990—; child psychiatrist Salt Lake Cmty. Mental Health Ctr., 1976—; child psychiatrist Primary Children's Mental Ctr., 1976-80, acting. clin. dir. outpatient Children's Psychiat. Ctr., 1977-78, clin. dir. outpatient dept. child psychiatry, 1978-80; pvt. practice Salt Lake City, 1981—; assoc. dir. children's specialty svcs. Salt Lake Valley Mental Health Ctr., 1982-93; psychiat. cons. Odyssey House, 1973-75; med. cons. Salt Lake Drug/Alchol Detoxification Ctr., 1975-82; dir. children's svcs. Salt Lake Cmty. Mental Helath Ctr., 1976-81, clin. dir. children's behavior therapy unit, 1976—, chmn. children's com., 1976-81; asst. clin. dir. inpatient unit Children's Psychiat. Ctr. of Primary Children's Med. Ctr., 1976-78; mem. ad hoc com. State Divsn. to Mental Health, 1976-78; mem. Utah State Mental Adv. Coun., 1977-79; assoc. clin. prof. psychiatry U. Utah, 1990; presenter in field. Contbr. articles to profl. jours. Fellow Am. Psychiat. Assn.; mem. Utah State Med. Assn. (com. on psychiat. emergencies 1976-78), Utah Soc. for Autistic Children (mem. adv. bd. 1979—), Salt Lake County Med. Soc. (del. ho. dels.), Utah Psychiatry Assn., Am. Acad. of Child Psychiatry (alt. del.), Intermountain Acad. Child Psychiatry (sec. 1976-78, pres. 1978-80). Office: 1414 E 4500 S Salt Lake City UT 84117-4208

PETERSEN, ROBERT E., publisher; b. Los Angeles, Sept. 10, 1926; s. Einar and Bertha (Putera) P.; m. Margie McNally, Jan. 26, 1963. Founder, chmn. bd. emeritus Petersen Pub. Co. (pubs. Hot Rod, Motor Trend, Car Craft, Motorcyclist, Photog., Skin Diver, Teen, Hunting, Guns & Ammo, Circle Track, Dirt Rider, Los Angeles, 1948—; owner, chmn. bd. Petersen Properties, L.A., 1996—; owner Petersen Aviation, Van Nuys, Calif., 1996—. Mem. Los Angeles Library Commn., 1963-64; Bd. dirs. Boys Club Am., past pres. Hollywood br.; bd. dirs. Thalians; founder Petersen Automotive Mus., L.A. Served with USAF. Clubs: So. Calif Safari, Balboa Bay, Catalina Island Yacht, Confrerie de la Chaine des Rotisseurs, Chevaliers du Tastevin. Office: Petersen Publishing Co 6420 Wilshire Blvd Los Angeles CA 90048-5502

PETERSEN, THOMAS SE TIENNE, orthopedic surgeon; b. Seattle, May 22, 1938; s. Ralph Clarence and Harriet May (De Tienne) P.; m. Mary Gail Beerman, June 23, 1962; children: Donald Williams, Michael Charles, Laura Christine, Theresa Michelle. BS, Stanford U., 1960; MD, Washington U., St. Louis, 1964. Diplomate Am. Bd. Orthop. Surgery. Intern U. Calif., San Diego, 1964-65, orthop. resident, 1965-69; pvt. practice orthop. surgeon Alvarado Orthop. Med. Group, San Diego, 1969—; mem. adv. implant panel Zimmer Corp., Warsaw, Ind., 1980-90; chief or orthop. Alvarado Hosp., 1972-74, 78-80. Contbr. articles to profl. jours.; patentee in field (20). Maj. U.S. Army, 1965-73. Fellow Am. acad. Orthopedics; mem. Knee Soc. Office: Alvarado Orthopedic Medical Group 5555 Reservoir Dr San Diego CA 92120

PETERSEN, VERNON LEROY, communications and engineering corporation executive; b. Mason, Nev., Nov. 3, 1926; s. Vernon and Lenora Eloise (Dickson) P.; children: Anne C., Ruth F. Cert. naval architecture, U. Calif., 1944, cert. in plant engring., adminstrn. and supervision UCLA, 1977; cert. in real estate exchanging Orange Coast Coll., 1978. Philippines Real Estate Office, U.S. C.E., 1950-55; pres., gen. mgr. Mason Merc. Co., 1956-62; pres., gen. mgr. Mason Water Co., 1956-62; pres. Petersen Enterprises, Cons. Engrs., Nev. and Calif., Downey, 1962-79, Vernon L. Peterson, Inc., 1980—; pres., chief exec. officer Castle Communications Co. Inc., 1985—; Sta. KCCD-TV, 1985-89; installation mgr. Pacific Architects & Engrs., L.A. and South Vietnam, 1969-72, facilities engr., ops. supr., acting contract mgr. L.A. and Saudi Arabia, 1979-82; bldg. engr. Purex Co., Inc., Lakewood, Calif., 1975-79; lectr. plant engring., various colls. in Calif., 1975—. Candidate for U.S. Congress, 1956, del. Rep. State Conv., 1960-64; candidate for U.S. Presidency, 1980. With AUS, 1944-47. Inducted into the Order of the Engrs. Fellow Soc. Am. Mil. Engrs. (life mem., named Orange County Post's Engr. of Year 1977, founder Da Nang Post 1969, Orange County Post 1977, pres. 1978-79, Red Sea Post, Jeddah, Saudi Arabia 1980), Internat. Platform Assn., Orange County Engr. Coun. (pres. 1978-79), Am. Inst. Plant Engrs. (chpt. 38 Engring. Merit award 1977-78), Soc. Women Engrs. (assoc.), AIAA. Mormon. Office: Castle Communications PO Box 787 Temecula CA 92593-0787

PETERSON, ANDREA LENORE, law educator; b. L.A., July 21, 1952; d. Vincent Zetterberg and Elisabeth (Karlsson) P.; m. Michael Rubin, May 29, 1983; children: Peter Rubin, Eric Rubin, Emily Rubin. AB, Stanford U., 1974; JD, U. Calif., Berkeley, 1978. Bar: Calif., 1979, U.S. Dist. Ct. (no. dist.) Calif., 1979. Law clk. to Judge Charles B. Renfrew U.S. Dist. Ct. (no. dist.) Calif., San Francisco, 1978-79; lawyer Cooley, Godward, Castro, Huddleson & Tatum, San Francisco, 1979-80; law clk. to Justice Byron R. White U.S. Supreme Ct., Washington, 1980-81; lawyer Heller, Ehrman, White & McAuliffe, San Francisco, 1981-83; prof. law Boalt Hall U. Calif., Berkeley, 1983—. Contbr. articles to profl. jours. Office: U Calif Sch Law Boalt Hall Berkeley CA 94720

PETERSON, BARBARA ANN BENNETT, history educator, television personality; b. Portland, Oreg., Sept. 6, 1942; d. George Wright and Hope (Chatfield) Bennett; m. Frank Lynn Peterson, July 1, 1967. BA, BS, Oreg. State U., 1964; MA, Stanford U., 1965; PhD, U. Hawaii, 1978; PhD (hon.), London Inst. Applied Rsch., 1991, Australian Inst. Coordinated R, 1995. Prof. history U. Hawaii, Honolulu, 1967-96; prof. emeritus history, 1996—; chmn. social scis. dept. U. Hawaii, Honolulu, 1971-73, 75-76, asst. dean, 1973-74; prof. Asian history and European colonial history and world problems Chapman Coll. World Campus Afloat, 1974, European overseas exploration, expansion and colonialism U. Colo., Boulder, 1978; assoc. prof. U. Hawaii-Manoa Coll. Continuing Edn., 1981; Fulbright prof. history Wuhan (China) U., 1988-89; Fulbright rsch. prof. Sophia U., Japan, 1978; rsch. assoc. Bishop Mus., 1995—; lectr. Capital Spkrs., Washington, 1987—; tchr. Hawaii State Ednl. Channel, 1993—. Co-author: Women's Place is in the History Books, Her Story, 1962-1980: A Curriculum Guide for American History Teachers, 1980; author: America in British Eyes, 1988; editor: Notable Women of Hawaii, 1984, (with W. Solheim) The Pacific Region, 1990, 91, American History: 17th, 18th and 19th Centuries, 1993, America: 19th and 20th Centuries, 1993, John Bull's Eye on America, 1995; assoc. editor Am. Nat. Biography; contbr. articles to profl. publs. Participant People-to-People Program, Eng., 1964, Expt. in Internat. Living Program, Nigeria, 1966; chmn. 1st Nat. Women's History Week, Hawaii, 1982; pres. Bishop Mus. Coun., 1993-94; active Hawaii Commn. on Status of Women. Fulbright scholar, Japan, 1967, China, 1988-89; NEH-Woodrow Wilson fellow Princeton U., 1980; recipient state proclamations Gov. of Hawaii, 1982, City of Honolulu, 1982, Outstanding Tchr. of Yr. award Wuhan (China), U., 1988, Medallion of Excellence award Am. Biog. Assn., 1989, Woman of Yr. award, 1991; inducted into the Women's Hall of Fame, Seneca Falls, N.Y., 1991; named Hawaii State Mixed Doubles Tennis Champion, 1985. Fellow World Literacy Acad. (Eng.), Internat. Biog. Assn. (Cambridge, Eng. chpt.); mem. AAUW, Am. Hist. Assn. (mem. numerous coms.), Am. Studies Assn. (pres. 1984-85), Fulbright Alumni Assn. (founding pres. Hawaii chpt. 1984-88, mem. nat. steering com. chairwomen Fulbright Assn. ann. conf. 1990), Am. Coun. on Edn., Maison Internat. des Intellectuals, France, Hawaii Found. History and Humanities (mem. editl. bd. 1972-73), Hawaii Found. Women's History, Hawaii Hist. Assn., Nat. League Am. Pen Women (contest chairperson 1986), Women in Acad. Adminstrn., Phi Beta Phi, Phi Kappa Phi.

PETERSON, CHASE N., university president; b. Logan, Utah, Dec. 27, 1929; s. E.G. and Phebe (Nebeker) P.; m. Grethe Ballif, 1956; children: Erika Elizabeth, Stuart Ballif, Edward Chase. A.B., Harvard U., 1952, M.D., 1956. Diplomate: Am. Bd. Internal Medicine. Asst. prof. medicine U. Utah Med. Sch., 1965-67; assoc. Salt Lake Clinic; dean admissions and fin. aids to students Harvard U., 1967-72, v.p. univ., 1972-78; v.p. health scis. U. Utah, Salt Lake City, 1978-83, prof. medicine, 1983—, pres., 1983-91, clin. prof. medicine, 1991—; pres. emeritus U. Utah, Salt Lake City, 1992—; bd. dirs. First Security Corp., Utah Power & Light Co., D.C. Tanner Co., OEC Med. Systems. Mem. Nat. Assn. State Univs. and Land-Grant Colls. (chmn. 1988-89, chair U.S. Ofc. Tech. Assessment adv. bd. 1990-92). Home: 66 Thaynes Canyon Dr Park City UT 84060-6711 Office: U Utah 1C26 Sch Medicine Salt Lake City UT 84112

PETERSON, CRAIG A., state senator; b. Salt Lake City, May 23, 1947; m. Annette Peterson; 5 children. BS Mfg. Engring. Tech., Weber State Coll.; postgrad., Tex. State U. V.p. cons. engring. firm; mem. Utah Ho. of Reps., 1986-88; mem. Utah State Senate, 1988—, majority whip, 1993-94, majority leader, 1995-96; mem. various coms. including mgmt., retirement, and human svcs. Republican. Office: 1687 North 200 Orem UT 84057

PETERSON, EDWIN CUTHBERT, counselor, educational administrator, adult educator; b. Sault Ste. Marie, Mich., Feb. 11, 1936; s. Edwin B. and Gladys M. (Cuthbert) P. B.S., No. Mich. U., 1958, M.A. in Sch. Adminstrn., 1965; M.S. in Guidance, U. Wis., 1962; cert. in guidance, U. Mass., 1967; cert. in urban affairs, U. So. Calif., 1972, Ed.D. in Supervision Adminstrn., 1977; cert. in resource mgmt., Indsl. Coll. Armed Forces, 1979; cert. edn. Harvard U., 1985; nat. cert. counselor, 1983. Edn. adviser 507th Fighter Wing, Aerospace Def. Command, Kincheloe AFB, Mich., 1958-60, 327th Fighter Wing, Truax Field, Wis., 1961-62; edn. services officer, 410th Bombardment Wing, SAC, K. I. Sawyer AFB, Mich., 1963-65; chief edn. br. 8th AF Hdqrs, Westover AFB, Mass., 1965-67; chief of edn. and tng. div. Aerospace Def. Command Hdqrs., Colorado Springs, Colo., 1967-72; chief edn. and tng. br., Hdqrs., Pacific Air Forces, Hickam AFB, Hawaii, 1972—; participant Hawaii Edn. Summit, 1990; co-chmn. 1st Community Coll. of the Air Force Adv. Panel, 1977-78, 83-84, chmn. 1984-85; mem. Veteran's Edn. Adv. Council, Chaminade U., Hawaii, 1972-74. Recipient Disting. Alumni award, No. Mich. U., 1981; Outstanding Service award, Community Coll. of the Air Force, 1979, 85; Career Edn. award U.S. Civil Service Commn., 1971; Outstanding Achievement in Aerospace Edn. award, SAC, 1967, Disting Edn. Achievement award, 1966, Ednl. Achievement award, 1965; award for Meritorious Civilian Service Dept. of Air Force, 1983, Outstanding Individual award Nat. Continuing Edn. Assn. 1986; Outstanding Alumni award Lake Superior State U., 1992; named to Internat. Adult and Continuing Edn. Hall of Fame, 1996. Mem. Am. Assn. for Adult and Continuing Edn. (v.p. for programs, 1978-79, Hawaii del. 1975-77, Meritorious Service award 1979, Tilton Davis Jr. Mil. Educator of Yr. 1986), Am. Counseling Assn., Nat. Univ. Continuing Edn. Assn., Hawaii Counseling Assn., Phi Delta Kappa. Home: PO Box 592 Honolulu HI 96809-0592 Office: HQ Pacific Air Forces/Edn & Tng Br 25 E St Ste D208 Hickam AFB HI 96853-5400

PETERSON, EDWIN J., retired supreme court justice, law educator; b. Gilmanton, Wis., Mar. 30, 1930; s. Edwin A. and Leora Grace (Kitelinger) P.; m. Anna Chadwick, Feb. 7, 1971; children: Patricia, Andrew, Sherry. B.S., U. Oreg., 1951, LL.B., 1957. Bar: Oreg. 1957. Assoc. firm Tooze, Kerr, Peterson, Marshall & Shenker, Portland, 1957-61; mem. firm Tooze, Kerr, Peterson, Marshall & Shenker, 1961-79; assoc. justice Supreme Ct. Oreg., Salem, 1979-83, 91-93, chief justice, 1983-91; ret., 1993; disting. jurist-in-residence, adj. instr. Willamette Coll. of Law, Salem, Oreg., 1994—; chmn. Supreme Ct. Task Force on Racial Issues, 1992-94; mem. standing com. on fed. rules of practice and procedure, 1987-93; bd. dirs. Conf. Chief Justices,

1985-87, 88-91. Chmn. Portland Citizens Sch. Com., 1968-70; vice chmn. Young Republican Fedn. Orgn., 1951; bd. visitors U. Oreg. Law Sch., 1978-83, 87-93, chmn. bd. visitors, 1981-83. Served to 1st lt. USAF, 1952-54. Mem. ABA, Am. Judicature Soc., Oreg. State Bar (bd. examiners 1963-66, gov. 1973-76, vice chmn. profl. liability fund 1977-78), Multnomah County Bar Assn. (pres. 1972-73), Phi Alpha Delta, Lambda Chi Alpha. Episcopalian. Home: 3365 Sunridge Dr S Salem OR 97302-5950 Office: Willamette Univ Coll Law 245 Winter St SE Salem OR 97301-3900

PETERSON, EILEEN M., state agency administrator; b. Trenton, N.J., Sept. 22, 1942; d. Leonard James and Mary (Soganic) Olschewski; m. Lars N. Peterson, Jr., 1970 (div. 1983); children: Leslie, Valerie, Erica. Student, Boise State U. Adminstrv. sec. State Ins. Fund, Boise, 1983-85; legal asst. Bd. Tax Appeals, Boise, 1985-87, exec. asst., 1987-92, dir., 1992—; ind. distbr. for USANA nutritional products; outside referring travel agt. Travelmax Intenrat. Vol. Boise Art Mus., Idaho Refugee Svc. Recipient Gov's. Cert. of Recognition for Outstanding Achievement, 1995. Mem. Mensa, Investment Club (pres.), Mountains West Outdoor Club, Idaho Rivers United. Democrat. Home: 3317 Mountain View Dr Boise ID 83704-4638 Office: Idaho State Bd Tax Appeals 1109 Main St Boise ID 83702-5640

PETERSON, ERLE VIDAILLET, retired metallurgical engineer; b. Idaho Falls, Idaho, Apr. 29, 1915; s. Vier P. and Marie (Vidaillet) P.; m. Rosemary Sherwood, June 3, 1955; children: Kent Sherwood, Pamela Jo. BS in Mining Engring., U. Idaho, 1940; MS in Mining Engring., U. Utah, 1941. Tech. advisor Remington Arms Co., Salt Lake City, 1941-43; constrn. engr. plutonium plant duPont, Hanford, Wash., 1943-44; R & D engr. exptl. sta. duPont, Wilmington, Del., 1944-51; plant metallurgist heavy water plant duPont, Newport, Ind., 1951-57; rsch. metallurgist metals program duPont, Balt., 1957-62, prin. project engr. USAF contracts, 1962-68; devel. engr. duPont, Wilmington, 1969-80; ret., 1980. Patentee in field; contbr. articles to profl. jours. Candidate for State Senate-Am. Party, Wilmington, 1974; com. chmn. Boy Scouts Am., Wilmington, 1975-78; treas. Local Civic Assn., Wilmington, 1977-79. Rsch. fellow U. Utah, 1940. Mem. Am. Soc. Metallurgists Internat., Del. Assn. Profl. Engrs. Republican. Home: PO Box 74 Rigby ID 83442-0074 *It matters not that you grow up on homestead and graduate from a country high school in a class of five during a great depression. With persistence and dedication toward your objectives, you can achieve goals that appear impossible.*

PETERSON, GARY TAYLOR, English educator; b. Hayward, Calif., Dec. 18, 1939; s. Ernst Wilhelm and Joyce Dean (Taylor) P.; m. Patricia Cottam, Feb. 9, 1963; children: Eric Gregory, Christopher Scott, Kurt Sven. BA, San Jose State U., 1962, MA, 1965; EdD, Ind. U., 1971. Dir. media Canal Zone Coll., La Boca, Canal Zone, Panama, 1966-68; assoc. dean instrn. De Anza Coll., Cupertino, Calif., 1971-77; dean instrn. West Valley Coll., Saratoga, Calif., 1977-79; v.p., dean instrn. Coll. of Siskiyous, Weed, Calif., 1979-84; exec. v.p. Coll. of Redwoods, Eureka, Calif., 1984-90; acting pres. Coll. of Redwoods, Eureka, 1987-88, chmn. dept. English, 1990—. Author: The Learning Center, 1975; contbr. chpt. to book and articles to profl. jours. Mem., pres. Lions, Weed and Eureka, 1979-87; bd. mem. Hospice of Humboldt, Eureka, 1987-90. Writing grantee various orgns. Home: 201 Stafford Rd Scotia CA 95565-9702 Office: College of Redwoods Eureka CA 95501

PETERSON, GERALD JOSEPH, aerospace executive, consultant; b. Decatur, Ill., Oct. 27, 1947; s. Raymond Gerald and Mary Louise (Johnson) P. AA, Lincolnland Community Coll., Springfield, Ill., 1969; student, Schiller Coll., Heidelberg, Germany, 1971, Sangamon State U., Springfield, 1972, U. Minn., 1976. Cert. aircraft pilot, engring. tech. Author LOGIC IV commodities futures trading program, 1996; patentee in field. Served with USAF, 1965, French Foreign Legion, 1979. Mem. U.S. Naval Inst. (life). Home and Office: 2117 Kinoole St Hilo HI 96720-5327

PETERSON, HOWARD COOPER, lawyer, accountant; b. Decatur, Ill., Oct. 12, 1939; s. Howard and Lorraine (Cooper) P.; BEE, U. Ill., 1963; MEE, San Diego State Coll., 1967; MBA, Columbia U., 1969; JD, Calif. Western Sch. Law, 1983; LLM in Taxation NYU, 1985. Bar: Calif., cert. fin. planner.; CPA, Tex.; registered profl. Engr., Calif.; cert. neuro-linguistic profl. Elec. engr. Convair divsn. Gen. Dynamics Corp., San Diego, 1963-67, sr. electronics engr., 1967-68; gen. ptnr. Costumes Characters & Classics Co., San Diego, 1979-86; v.p., dir. Equity Programs Corp., San Diego, 1973-83; pres., dir. Coastal Properties Trust, San Diego, 1979-89, Juno Securities, Inc., 1983-96, Juno Real Estate Inc., 1974—, Scripps Mortgage Corp., 1987-90, Juno Transport Inc., 1988—; CFO, dir. Imperial Screens of San Diego, 1977-96, Heritage Transp. Mgmt. Inc., 1989-91, A.S.A.P. Ins. Svcs. Inc., 1983-85. Mem. ABA, Interam. Bar Assn., Nat. Soc. Public Accts., Internat. Assn. Fin. Planning, Assn. Enrolled Agts.

PETERSON, KEVIN BRUCE, newspaper editor, publishing executive; b. Kitchener, Ont., Can., Feb. 11, 1948; s. Bruce Russell and Marguerite Elizabeth (Hammond) P.; m. Constance Maureen Bailey, Feb. 11, 1975 (dec. May 1975); m. Sheila Helen O'Brien, Jan. 9, 1981. B.A., U. Calgary, Alta., Can., 1968. Chief bur. Calgary Herald, 1972-75, city editor, 1976-77, news editor, 1977-78, bus. editor, 1978, mng. editor, 1978-86, editor, asst. pub., 1986-87, gen. mgr., 1987-88, pub., 1989-96; pres. Canadian Univ. Press, Ottawa, Ont., Can., 1968-69; dir. New Directions for News. Harry Brittain Meml. fellow Commonwealth Press Union, London, 1979. Mem. Can. Mng. Editors (bd. dirs. 1983-87), Am. Soc. Newspaper Editors, Horsemen's Benevolent and Protective Assn., Alta. Legis. Press Gallery Assn. (v.p. 1971-76), Can. Daily Newspaper Assn. (bd. dirs. 1990-96, vice chmn. , treas 1992, chmn. 1993-96), Calgary Petroleum Club, Ranchmen's Club, 100-t-1 Club, (Arcadia, Calif.).

PETERSON, LAURENCE ROBERT, pathologist; b. Mpls., July 30, 1947; s. Robert E. and Beverly J. (Robinson) P.; m. Carol Ann Seeburger, June 20, 1970; children: Nathaniel Dow, Alexander Jorgan. BA, Carleton Coll., 1969; MD, U. Chgo., 1973. Diplomate Am. Bd. Pathology. Residency pathology U. Wash., Seattle, 1973-77; pathologist, owner Skagit Pathology Inc., P.S., Mount Vernon, Wash., 1977—. Fellow Coll. of Am. Pathologists, Am. Soc. Clin. Pathologists; mem. AMA, Pacifi N.W. Soc. Pathologists. Office: Skagit Valley Labs Inc 1310 E Division St Mount Vernon WA 98273-4133

PETERSON, LEROY, retired secondary education educator; b. Fairfield, Ala., Feb. 15, 1930; s. Leroy and Ludie Pearl (Henderson) P.; m. Theresa Petite, Apr. 6, 1968 (div. Oct. 1984); children: Leroy III, Monica Teresa; m. Ruby Willodine Hopkins, July 21, 1985 (div. Apr. 1995). Cert. in piano, Bavarian State Acad., Wuerzburg, Fed. Republic Germany, 1954; BS in Music Edn., Miami U., Oxford, Ohio, 1957. Life credential music tchr., Calif. Tchr. music Cleve. Pub. Schs., 1957-62, L.A. Unified Schs., 1963-94; retired, 1994. Song composer. With U.S. Army, 1952-54. Mem. Alpha Phi Alpha, Phi Mu Alpha Sinfonia. Republican. Home: 2646 Lime St Riverside CA 92501-2215

PETERSON, LOWELL, cinematographer; b. L.A., Feb. 1, 1950; s. Lowell Stanley and Catherine Linda (Hess) P.; m. Deanna Rae Terry, Aug. 2, 1981. Student, Yale U., 1968; BA in Theater Arts, UCLA, 1973. Asst. cinematographer, Hollywood, Calif., 1973-83; camera operator Hollywood, 1983-92, dir. photography, 1992—. Asst. cinematographer various prodns. including Blind Ambition, 1979, Hawaii Five-O, 1979-80, White Shadow, 1980-81, Lou Grant, 1981-82, Two of a King, 1982, Remington Steele, 1982-83, Something About Amelia, 1983; camera operator various prodns. including Tourist Trap, 1979, Newhart, 1983, Scarecrow and Mrs. King, 1983-85, Children in the Crossfire, 1984, Stranded, 1986, Knots Landing, 1986-87, 89-92, Like Father Like Son, 1987, Star Trek: The Next Generation, 1987-89, Coupe de Ville, 1990, Show of Force, 1990, Postcards from the Edge, 1990, Guilty by Suspicion, 1991, The Mambo Kings, 1992, Dracula, 1992; dir. photography Knots Landing, 1992-93, Second Chances, 1993-94 (Am. Soc. Cinematographers award nomination), Galaxy Beat, 1994, Hotel Malibu, 1994, Lois and Clark, 1995, The Client, 1995-96, Moloney, 1996—; contbr. articles to Film Comment, 1974, Internat. Photographer, 1984—. Mem. Soc. Motion Picture and TV Engrs., Internat. Photographers Guild, L.A. Music Ctr. Opera League, Friends of UCLA Film Archive, Am. Cinematheque, U.S. Chess Fedn., Acad. TV Arts & Scis. Home and Office: 3815 Ventura Canyon Ave Sherman Oaks CA 91423-4710

PETERSON, MARTIN LYNN, public administrator; b. Lewiston, Idaho, Apr. 22, 1943; s. Conrad E. and Charlotte K. (Hoffman) P.; m. Barbara Ann Dodson, May 31, 1975; children: Julia Beata, Emily Ann. AAS, Columbia Basin Coll., 1964; BA, U. Idaho, 1968. Asst. to Senator Frank Church U.S. Senate, Washington, 1968-71; dir. manpower planning State of Idaho, Boise, 1971-74; dir. govt. rels. Assn. Idaho Cities, Boise, 1975-78, exec. dir., 1978-83; budget dir. State of Idaho, Boise, 1983-88; pres. Idaho Centennial Found., Boise, 1988-91; cons. Boise, 1991-92; asst. to pres. U. Idaho, Boise, 1992—. Author: Celebrating Idaho, 1991. Founding incorporator Idaho Heritage Trust, Boise, 1989-92; trustee Idaho Bicentennial Trust Fund; mem. Boise Art Mus.; mem. Hemingway Soc.; pres. Silver City Homeowners Assn.; dir. Idaho Epilepsy League; co-dir. 1996 Internat. Hemingway Conf. Recipient Cert. of Appreciation Gov. of Idaho, 1979, 82, Boyd A. Martin award Assn. Idaho Cities, 1989. Mem. North Idaho C. of C., Boise C. of C. Home: 743 Hearthstone Dr Boise ID 83702-1823 Office: U Idaho/Boise Ctr 800 Park Blvd Boise ID 83712-7742

PETERSON, PAMELA CARMELLE, principal, educator; b. Bakersfield, Calif., Sept. 24, 1954; d. Bob Eugene and Carmelita Denyse (Coodey) York; m. Robert Leroy Peterson, Feb. 9, 1979; children: Aimee, Sara, Matthew, Hannah. Assoc., Bakersfield Coll., 1992; BA in History, Calif. State U., Bakersfield, 1994. Exec. adminstr. Kern Bldg. Materials, Bakersfield, 1973-95; prin. Rosewall Christian Acad., Bakersfield, 1994—; prin., tchr. Dynasty Christian Schs., Bakersfield, 1995—; pres. bd. Dynasty Christian Schs., 1995; exec. sec. bd. dirs. Kern Bldg. Materials, 1983-95. Mem. Assn. Christian Schs., Inc., Assn. Christian Sch. Adminstrs., Phi Alpha Theta (sec. 1994-95, v.p. 1995-96). Home: 4213 Rosewall St Bakersfield CA 93313-2529 Office: Dynasty Christian Schs Inc 18210 Rosedale Hwy Bakersfield CA 93312-9488

PETERSON, RALPH R., engineering executive; b. 1944. BS in Civil Engring., Oreg. State U., 1969; MS in Environ. Engring., Stanford U., 1970; AMP, Harvard Bus. Sch., 1991. Engring. aide Johnson, Underkofler & Briggs, Boise, 1962-63; surveyor Smith, Keyes & Blakely, Caldwell, Idaho, 1963-64; with Chronic & Assocs., Boise, 1964-65; with CH2M Hill Cos., Ltd., 1965—, sr. v.p., dir. tech., 1988, pres., CEO, 1990. Office: CH2M Hill Cos Ltd 6060 S Willow Dr Greenwood Village CO 80111

PETERSON, RICHARD ALLAN, pediatrician; b. Oak Park, Ill., Aug. 10, 1934; s. Otto Stewart and Catherine Helen (Esin) P.; m. Sue Anne Schaefer, Sept. 15, 1956 (div. Sept. 1972); children: Ben, Andrew, Jennifer, Dan. AB, Grinnell Coll., 1956; BS, MD, U. Ill., 1960. Diplomate Am. Bd. Pediatrics. Intern Ind. U. Med. Ctr., Indpls., 1960-61; resident in pediatrics Mayo Clinic, Rochester, Minn., 1961-64; pediatrician Anchorage Pediatric Group, 1967-71, The Children's Clinic, Anchorage, 1971-76; pediatric neurology fellow UCLA, 1976-77; pvt. practice Templeton, Calif., 1977—; bd. dirs. Affiliated Health Providers North County, Templeton. Chmn. health educator curriculum com. Anchorage Borough Sch. Dist., 1968-70; bd. dirs. Mozart Festival, San Luis Obispo, Calif., 1988-91. Capt. USAF, 1964-67. Fellow Am. Acad. Pediatrics (Alaska state chmn. 1972-73); mem. AMA, North Pacific Pediatric Soc., Calif. Med. Assn., San Luis Obispo County Med. Soc., L.A. Pediatric Soc. Home: 294 Via San Blai San Luis Obispo CA 93401 Office: 1050 Las Tablas Rd Templeton CA 93465-9729

PETERSON, RICHARD HERMANN, history educator, retired; b. Berkeley, Calif., Jan. 16, 1942; s. William Martin and Dorothy Jean (Heyne) P.; m. Nora Ann Lorenzo, June 21, 1970; 1 child, Nina Elizabeth. AB, U. Calif., Berkeley, 1963; MA, San Francisco State U., 1966; PhD, U. Calif., Davis, 1971. Calif. community coll. teaching credential. Asst. prof. history Ind. U., Kokomo, 1971-76; instr. social studies Coll. of Redwoods, Ft. Bragg, Calif., 1976-78; assoc. prof. history San Diego State U., 1978-82, prof. history, 1982-96, prof. emeritus, 1996—; freelance writer, 1996—. Author: Manifest Destiny in the Mines, 1975, The Bonanza Kings, 1977, 91, Bonanza Rich, 1991; book rev. editor Jour. of San Diego History, 1978-82, editorial cons., 1980-82; contbr. articles to profl. jours. Judge for papers Internat. History Fair, San Diego, Tijuana, Mex., 1983-88. Faculty Summer fellow Ind. U., 1975, 76, San Diego State U., 1980; rsch. grantee Sourisseau Acad., 1977, Am. Assn. State/Local History, 1988; named Golden Poet of Yr., World of Poetry, 1987-89. Mem. Am. Hist. Assn., Calif. Hist. Soc., Western History Assn., Calif. Studies Assn. Home: 7956 Lake Adlon Dr San Diego CA 92119-3117

PETERSON, RONALD ARTHUR, business law educator; b. Valley, Nebr., June 21, 1920; s. Arthur Lawrence and Hazel McClellan (Foster) P.; m. Patricia Marguerite North, Aug. 29, 1942; children: Ronald, Kathleen, Patrick, James, John, Thomas, Mary, Joseph. B.A. in Poly. Sci., U. Omaha, 1943; J.D. in Law, Creighton U., 1948; postgrad. U. Wash., 1963-64. Bar: Nebr. 1948, Wash. 1949. Asst. prof. Seattle U., 1963-76, dir. legal studies, 1973-83, assoc. prof., 1976-84, prof. emeritus dept. bus. law, 1984—. Author: The Old English Year Books. Dir. high sch.-coll. and alumni rels. Seattle U., 1950-58, dir. admissions, 1958-73; founding mem. Wash. State Coun. on High Sch.-Coll. Rels., 1953-73, chmn., 1962-63; founding mem. Seattle Archdiocese Sch. Bd., Western Wash., 1969; mem. Spl. Task Force on Legis. for Wash. System of Pub. Librs., 1971-73; assoc. dir. Wash. Criminal Justice Edn. and Tng. Ctr., 1973; mem. editorial bd. Introduction to Law and the Legal Process, 1980, mem. Oreg.-Wash. Commn. on the Pub. of Mapping Your Education; vol. chaplain juvenile ct. King County Dept. Youth Svcs., 1991; bd. dirs. Cath. Community Svcs. Legal Action Ctr., 1994—. Lt. USNR, 1943-46. Recipient Exemplary Tchr. award Alpha Kappa Psi, 1964. Mem. Am. Bus. Law Assn. (del. 1980), Pacific Northwest Bus. Law Assn. (pres. 1984-85), Seattle U. Alumni Assn. (Campus Svc. award 1989), Beta Gamma Sigma. Roman Catholic. Home: 1625 Mcgilvra Blvd E Seattle WA 98112-3119 *Personal philosophy: We should strive for faith in God, ourselves and others, for hope in God's providence and for love of God, ourselves, our families, and all other persons as expressed in the giving of one's self.*

PETERSON, STANLEY LEE, artist; b. Viborg, S.D., Mar. 26, 1949; s. Norman and Neva Jean (Harns) P.; m. Katherine Anne Burnett. BFA, U. S.D., 1971. Artist W.H. Over Museum, Vermillion, S.D., 1971-72; graphic artist S.D. Pub. TV, Brookings, 1972-76; free lance artist San Francisco, 1976-77; engring. technician City of Tracy, Calif., 1977-85; artist Stanley Peterson Graphics, Los Banos, Calif., 1985—; contract engring. technician, system mgr. City of Tracy, 1985-89, system mgr., 1989-90; engring. technician IV County of Sacramento, 1991, prin. engring. technician, 1991—; cons. in field. Artist/designer Nat. History Diorama, W.H. Over Museum, 1972. Democrat. Home: 427 N Santa Monica St Los Banos CA 93635-3223

PETERSON, SUSAN HARNLY, artist, writer; b. McPherson, Kans., July 21, 1925; d. Paul Witmore and Iva Wilda (Curtis) Harnly; m. Jack L. Peterson, Oct. 8, 1949 (div. 1972); children: Jill Kristin, Jan Sigrid, Taäg Paul; life ptnr. Robert Schwarz Jr. AA, Monticello Coll., Alton, Ill., 1944; AB, Mills Coll., 1946; MFA, Alfred U., 1950. Cert. tchr. sec. schs. Head of ceramics Wichita Art Assn. Sch., 1947-49, Chouinard Art Inst., L.A., 1951-55; prof. of ceramics U. So. Calif., L.A., 1955-72; head of ceramics Idyllwild (Calif.) Sch. of Music and Art, 1957-1987; prof. of ceramics Hunter Coll. CUNY, 1972-1994. Author: Shoji Hamada, A Potter's Way and Work, 1974, (re-issued) 1996, The Living Tradition of Maria Martinez, 1978, Lucy M. Lewis, American Indian Potter, 1984, The Craft and Art of Clay, 1992, 2d edit., 1995, Pottery by American Indian Women, Legacy of Generations; exhibited in nat. and internat. group shows, 1950—; 54 half-hour CBS TV shows, Wheels, Kilns and Clay, 1969-70. Recipient Critics award Nat. Endowment for the Arts, Washington, 1985, Wrangler ward, Nat. Cowboy Hall of Fame, 1978. Fellow Am. Craft Coun.; mem. World Craft Coun., Nat. Ceramic Educators Coun. Am., Am. Ceramic Soc., PEO, Phi Beta Kappa. Home and Studio: 38800 Spanish Boot Rd Carefree AZ 85377

PETERSON, VANCE TULLIN, academic administrator, educator; b. Santa Monica, Calif., Nov. 4, 1944; s. William Tullin and Chanuth Joy (Griggs) P.; m. Anne Rose Breck, Apr. 7, 1968; children: Sara Rose, Theresa Pauline. BA, Occidental Coll., 1966; MS, George Washington U., 1971; PhD, Stanford (Calif.) U., 1976. Instr. Stanford U., 1972-73; researcher Carnegie Commn. on Higher Edn., Berkeley, Calif., 1973-74; asst. prof. U. Toledo, 1974-77; exec. dir. univ. rels. U. So. Calif., L.A., 1977-83; assoc. provost UCLA, 1983-89; v.p. Occidental Coll., L.A., 1989-96; pres. Sierra Nevada Coll., Incline Village, Nev., 1996—. Editor: The Law & Higher Education, 1976; contbr. articles to profl. jours. Trustee CASE, 1996—; trustee Arcadia Ednl. Found., 1989-93; mem. Pasadena (Calif.) 2000 Commn., 1988. Capt. USNR (ret.). World ranked track 400m IH, 1965-66. Mem. Nat. Soc. Fundraising Execs., Coun. for Advancement and Support of Edn., Jonathan Club, Rotary, Alpha Tau Omega. Republican. Episcopalian. Office: Sierra Nevada Coll PO Box 4269 Incline Village NV 89450

PETERSON, WAYNE TURNER, composer, pianist; b. Albert Sea, Minn., Sept. 3, 1927; s. Leslie Jules and Irma Thelma (Turner) P.; m. Harriet Christiansen, 1948 (div. 1978); children: Alan, Craig, Drew, Grant. BA, U. Minn., 1951, MA, 1953; postgrad., Royal Acad. Music, London, 1953-54; PhD, U. Minn. Instr. music U. Minn., 1955-59; asst. prof. music Chico (Calif.) State U., 1959-60; prof. music San Francisco State U., 1960—; vis. prof. composition U. Ind., Bloomington, 1992, Stanford U., 1992-94; artist in residence Briarcombe Found., Bolinas, Calif., 1983; vis. artist Am. Acad. in Rome, 1990. Composer: Allegro for String Quartet, 1952, Introduction and Allegro, 1953, Free Variations for Orch., 1954-58, Can Death Be Sleep, 1955, Earth, Sweet Earth, 1956, (cappella chorus) Cape Ann, 1957, Three Songs for Soprano and Piano, 1957, (cappella chorus) Psalm 56, 1959, Exaltation, Dithyramb and Caprice, full orchestra, 1959-60, (cappella chorus) An e e Cummings Triptych, 1962, Tangents for flute, clarinet, horn and violin, 1963, An e e Cummings Cantata, 1964, Fantasy Concertante for violin and piano, 1965, Reflections, ballet, full orchestra, 1965, Metamorphosis for Wind Quintet, 1967, Phantasmagoria for flute, clarinet, double bass, 1968, Cataclysms, full orchestra, 1968, Clusters and Fragments for string orch., 1969, Ceremony After a Fire Raid, Soprano and piano, 1969, Sinfonia and Canticle for baritone voice and organ, 1969, Capriccio for Flute and Piano, 1973, Transformations for String Quartet, 1974, Trialogue for violin, cello and piano, 1975, Diatribe for violin and piano, 1975, Encounters mixed ensemble of mini instrument, 1976, Rhapsody for Cello and Piano, 1976, An Interrupted Serenade for flute, harp and cello, 1978, Dark Reflections (cycle of four songs for high voice, violin and piano), 1980, Mallets Aforethought (symphony for percussion ensemble), 1981, Sextet for flute, clarinet, percussion, harp, violin and cello, 1982, Doubles for 2 flutes and 2 clarinets, 1982, Debussy Song Cycle transcribe for voice and small orchestra, 1983, String Quartet, 1983-84, Ariadne's Thread for harp, flute, clarinet, horn, percussion and violin, 1985, Transformations for chamber orch., 1986, Duo for viola and cello, 1986-87, Trilogy for Orch., 1987, Labyrinth for flute, clarinet, violin and piano, 1987, The Widening Gyre for full orch., 1991, The Face of the Night, the Heart of the Dark for full orch., 1991 (Pulitzer prize for music 1992), Mallets Aforthought percussion symphony revision, 1991, String Quartet # 2, 1992, Diptych, fl, cl, pec., po, rn,vc, 1992, Janus, mixed ensemble of ten instrument, 1993, Duo for Violin and Piano, 1993, And the Winds Shall Blow, a fantasy for saxophone quartet, symphony winds, brass and percussion, 1994; Theseus for smaller orchestra, Vicissiyude (fl, cl, perc, po, vn, vc, 1995, A Robert Herrick Motley (five a capella Choruses) Windup Saxaphone Quartet, Peregrinations (solo clarinet) 1996; recs. with Mercury Records, Desto Records, Arch Records, Grenadilla Records, Koch Internat. CRI, Innova, Foghorn, Centur, San Francisco Chamber Singers; Recordings commd. Am. Music Ctr., 1959, Virtuosi of San Francisco, 1968, Unitarian Ch., 1969, Paul Mason, Inc., 1974, 87, NEA Consortium Commn., 1982, Charles Wuorinen and San Francisco Symphony, 1985, Am. Composers Symphony, Inc., 1987, San Francisco Symphony, 1991, Gerbode Found., 1990, Koussevitzky Found., 1990, Fromm Music Found., 1992, Philharmonic Orch. of Freiburg in Breisgau, Germany, 1993, U. Minn., 1995, Neel the Composer (Consortium, Comm.) 1996, Allen Blustine, 1996. Recipient 11th Ann. Norman Fromm Composer's award, 1982, Meritorious Svc. award Calif. State U. System, 1984, Top award Am. Harp Soc., 1985, Composer's award Am. Acad. and Inst. Arts and Letters, 1986, Pulitzer Prize for music, 1992; Fulbright scholar, Royal Acad. Music, 1953-54; NEA grantee, 1976; Guggenheim fellow, 1989-90, Djerassi Found. fellow, 1989-91. Home: 140 S Lake Merced Hill San Francisco CA 94132-2935

PETICOLAS, WARNER LELAND, physical chemistry educator; b. Lubbock, Tex., July 29, 1929; s. Warner Marion and Beulah Francis (Lowe) P.; m. Virginia Marie Wolf, June 30, 1969; children—Laura M., Alicia B.; children by previous marriage—Cynthia M., Nina P., Phillip W. B.S., Tex. Technol. Coll., 1950; Ph.D., Northwestern U., 1954. Research asso. DuPont Co., Wilmington, Del., 1954-60; research div. IBM, San Jose, Calif., 1960-67; cons. IBM, 1967-69, mgr. chem. physics group, 1965-67; prof. phys. chemistry U. Oreg., 1967—; vis. prof. U. Paris-Pierre and Marie Curie, 1980-81; vis. prof. Weizmann Inst. Sci., Rahovat, Israel, 1991, vis. prof. U. Reims, 1996. Committeeman Democratic party, Eugene, Oreg., 1967-70. Served with USPHS, 1955-57. Recipient Alexander von Humboldt award, W. Ger., 1984-85. Guggenheim fellow Max von Laue-Paul Langevin Inst., Grenoble, France, 1973-74. Fellow Am. Phys. Soc.; mem. Am. Chem. Soc., Am. Phys. Soc., Sigma Xi, Alpha Chi Sigma, Tau Beta Pi. Episcopalian. Home: 2829 Arline Way Eugene OR 97403-2527 Office: U Oregon Dept Of Chemistry Eugene OR 97403

PETILLON, LEE RITCHEY, lawyer; b. Gary, Ind., May 6, 1929; s. Charles Ernest and Blanche Lurene (Mackay) P.; m. Mary Anne Keeton, Feb. 20, 1960; children: Andrew G., Joseph R. BBA, U. Minn., 1952; LLB, U. Calif., Berkeley, 1959. Bar: Calif. 1960, U.S. Dist. Ct. (so. dist.) Calif. 1960. V.p. Creative Investment Capital, Inc., L.A., 1969-70; corp. counsel Harvest Industries, L.A., 1970-71; v.p., gen. counsel, dir. Tech. Svcs. Corp., Santa Monica, Calif., 1971-78; ptnr. Petillon & Davidoff, L.A., 1978-92, Gipson Hoffman & Pancione, 1992-93; pvt. practice Torrance, Calif., 1993-94; ptnr. Petillon & Hansen, Torrance, Calif., 1994—. Co-author: R&D Partnerships, 2d edit., 1985, Representing Start-Up Companies, 1992, 3d edit., 1996, California Transaction Forms, 1996. Chmn. Neighborhood Justice Ctr. Com., 1983-85, Middle Income Co., 1983085; active Calif. Senate Commn. on Corp. Governance, State Bar Calif. Task Force on Alternative Dispute Resolution, 1984-85; chmn. South Bay Sci. Found., Inc.; vice-chmn. Calif. Capital Access Forum, Inc. Recipient Cert. of Appreciation L.A. City Demonstration Agy., 1975, United Indian Devel. Assn., 1981, City of L.A. for Outstanding Vol. Svcs., 1984. Mem. ABA, Calif. State Bar Assn. (pres., Pro Bono Svcs. award 1983), L.A. County Bar Found. (bd. dirs. 1986-89), L.A. County Bar Assn. (chmn. law tech. sect., alt. dispute resolution sect. 1992-94, trustee 1984-85, Griffin Bell Vol. Svc. award 1993). Home: 1636 Via Machado Palos Verdes Estates CA 90274-1930 Office: Petillon & Hansen 21515 Hawthorne Blvd # 1260 Torrance CA 90503

PETIT, SUSAN YOUNT, French educator; b. Fairfield, Ohio, Aug. 25, 1945; d. Howard Wesley and Elizabeth Rosina (Rummel) Yount; m. John M. Gill, June 22, 1984. BA in English, Knox Coll., 1966; MA in English, Purdue U., 1968; MA in French, Coll. of Notre Dame, Belmont, Calif., 1983. Prof. French and English Coll. of San Mateo, Calif., 1968—; mem. exec. com. Calif. C.C. Acad. Senate, Sacramento, 1984-86; pres. acad. senate San Mateo County C.C. Dist., 1981-82, Coll. of San Mateo, 1978-79. Author: Michel Tournier's Metaphysical Fictions, 1991; contbr. articles to profl. publs., chpts. to books. Mem. MLA, Am. Assn. Tchrs. French, Simone de Beauvoir Soc., Women in French, Calif. Fgn. Lang. Tchrs. Assn., Phi Beta Kappa. Home: 777-64 San Antonio Rd Palo Alto CA 94303 Office: Coll of San Mateo 1700 W Hillsdale Blvd San Mateo CA 94402

PETOW, JOAN CLAUDIA, orthopedic nurse; b. Spokane, Wash., Mar. 5, 1946; d. August and Ella (McHargue) P. Diploma summa cum laude, Deaconess Hosp. Sch. Nursing, Spokane, 1967; BSN cum laude, Pacific Luth. U., 1969. RN, Wash.; cert. orthopedic nurse. Staff nurse orthopedic unit Deaconess Med. Ctr., Spokane, 1969-70, nurse ICU, 1970-72, asst. head nurse adult surg. unit, 1972-73, head nurse orthopedics unit, 1973-83; orthopedic staff nurse Valley Hosp. and Med. Ctr., Spokane, 1984-96; nurse N.W. Orthopedic and Fracture Clinic, Spokane, 1995—; orthopedic quality assurance rep. Valley Hosp. and Med. Ctr., Spokane, 1988-90. Chmn. Spokane Coun. Christian Bus. and Profl. Women, 1976-77. Mem. Nat. Assn. Orthopedic Nurses (cert.), Sigma Theta Tau.

PETRILLO, LISA MARIE, newspaper reporter; b. Wilmington, Del., June 27, 1958; m. Robert Scally, Sept. 12, 1987; 1 child, Clark. Student, U. Del., 1980. Part-time reporter News-Jour., Wilmington, Del., 1979; reporter, photographer Oakdale (Calif.) Reader, 1980; reporter Turlock (Calif.) Jour., 1980-81, Visalia (Calif.) Times-Delta, 1981-84, Stockton (Calif.) Record, 1984-85, San Diego Union, 1985-92, San Diego Union -Tribune, 1992—; stringer N.Y. Times, 1991. Author: Badge of Betrayal, 1992; contbr. articles to popular mags. Recipient Deadline Writing award Calif. Newspaper Pub. Assn., 1989, Maggie award Planned Parenthood, 1994, 1st Pl. award for short story writing Am. Assn. Festures and Sunday Editors, 1996. Mem. Soc. Profl. Journalists (officer, bd. dirs. 1995-96, numerous writing awards 1985—), San Diego Newspaper Guild (pres. 1996-97). Office: San Diego Union-Tribune 350 Camino de la Reina San Diego CA 92112

PETRINOVICH, LEWIS F., psychology educator; b. Wallace, Idaho, June 12, 1930; s. John F. and Ollie (Steward) P. BS, U. Idaho, 1952; PhD, U. Calif., Berkeley, 1962. Asst. prof. San Francisco State Coll., 1957-63; from assoc. to prof. SUNY, Stony Brook, 1963-68; prof. U. Calif., Riverside, 1968-91, chmn. psychology, 1968-71, 86-89, prof. emeritus, 1991—. Author: Understanding Research in Social Sciences, 1975, Introduction to Statistics, 1976, Human Evolution, Reproduction and Mortality, 1995, Living and Dying Well, 1996; editor: Behavioral Development, 1981, Habituation, Sensitization and Behavior, 1984; cons. editor Behavioral and Neural Biology, 1972-90, Jour. Physiol. and Comparative Psychology, 1980-82, Jour. Comparative Psychology, 1983-90. Fellow Am. Psychol. Assn., Am. Psychol. Soc., Calif. Acad. Scis., Human Behavior and Evolution Soc., Western Psychol. Assn.; mem. Am. Ornithological Union (elected), Animal Behavior Soc., Sigma Xi. Home: 415 Boynton Ave Berkeley CA 94707-1701 Office: U Calif Riverside Dept of Psychology Riverside CA 92521

PETROCHILOS, ELIZABETH A., writer, publisher; b. Blytheville, Ark., Aug. 11, 1943; d. James Alfred Clark and Macie Lee Burris; m. Cleomenis Matheos Petrochilos, Oct. 26, 1961 (div. Mar. 1966); children: Matthew C., Raquel D. Grad., Fresno H.S. Cashier Family Owned Markets, Fresno, 1961-64; med. receptionist Dr. Floyd E. Lee, Lemoore, Calif., 1964-65; pub., author E.A. Prodns., Fresno, 1965—; Author: (poetry) Stone the Poet, 1964. Home: 1155 E Bullard # 206 Fresno CA 93710

PETRONE, JOSEPH ANTHONY, business consultant, writer; b. N.Y.C., July 6, 1956; s. Louis Richard and Catherine Amelia (DeVito) P.; m. Deborah Bernice Steele, Sept. 24, 1983. BS in Chemistry, Muhlenberg Coll., 1978. Sales rep. Calgon Corp., San Francisco, 1978-82; mktg. mgr. Calgon Corp., Pitts., 1982-85; sales engr. Nicolet Corp., Pitts., 1985-88; regional sales mgr. Nicolet Corp., San Francisco, 1988-91, gen. mgr., 1992-95; bus. author, cons. Joe Petrone & Assocs., Pleasanton, Calif., 1995—. Author: Building the High Performance Sales Force, 1994 (Top Book ranking Soundview Exec. Book Summaries, Fortune & Newgridge Bus. Book Club selection); contbr. articles to profl. publs. Vol. Big Bros./Big Sisters, Oakland, Calif.; hospice vol., Sewickley, Pa., 1985. Mem. Inst. Mgmt. Cons. Home: 3649 Dunsmuir Cir Pleasanton CA 94588

PETROVICH, PETER YUROSH, English and foreign language educator, writer; b. Tuzla, Bosnia-Herzegovina, Feb. 20, 1960; came to the U.S., 1985; s. Drago and Yovanka Petrovich. M in English and Spanish, U. Bosnia, Sarajevo, 1983. English/Spanish tchr. Rudarski Školski Ctr. Titovo Velenje, Slovenia, 1983-85; English tchr., translator Inst. Argentino de Edn. Am. Schs., L.A., 1988-95; English/Spanish tchr. Lexicon, L.A., 1992—. Author: Step by Step 1, 1994, Step by Step 2, 1995, Step by Step 3, 1995, Advanced Conversational English, 1995, Modern English Grammar, 1996. Mem. YMCA, Downey, Calif. Home and Office: 13032 Blodgett Ave Downey CA 90242

PETRUZZI, CHRISTOPHER ROBERT, business educator, consultant; b. Peoria, Ill., July 28, 1951; s. Benjamin Robert and Mary Katherine (Urban) P.; m. Therese Michele Vaughan, Aug. 21, 1982 (div.1987); m. Georgina Sailer, June 20, 1992; 1 child, Lillian Caroline. BA, Wabash Coll., 1972; MBA, U. Chgo., 1974; PhD, U. Southern Calif., 1983. Lectr. bus. U. Wis., Milw., 1975-77; cons. H.C. Wainwright, Boston, 1978-79; lectr. U. So. Calif., 1978-81; prof. bus. U. Pa., Phila., 1981-84; prof. acctg. NYU, 1984-89, Calif. State U., Fullerton, 1989—; pres. ECON, N.Y.C., L.A., 1987—. Earhart fellow, 1972-73; U. Chgo. fellow, 1974-76. Libertarian. Christian. Home: 1527 Via Tulipan San Clemente CA 92673-3717

PETTERSEN, THOMAS MORGAN, accountant, computer company executive; b. Poughkeepsie, N.Y., Nov. 9, 1950; s. Olsen Thomas and Reva Frances (Palmer) P. BS, U. Albany, 1973. CPA, N.Y. Sr. acct. Arthur Andersen and Co., N.Y.C., 1973-76; sr. ops. auditor Gulf and Western Inc., N.Y.C., 1977, fin. analyst, 1978; adminstr. auditing NBC, N.Y.C., 1979; mgr. auditing NBC, Burbank, Calif., 1980, dir. auditing, 1981-88, dir. acctg. systems and ops. analysis, 1988-90; v.p. fin. and adminstrn. Data Dimensions, Inc., Culver City, Calif., 1991-92; cons. Westwood One, Inc., Culver City, 1992-93; CFO Computer Image Sys., Inc., Torrance, Calif., 1993—. Mem. AICPA, Fin. Execs. Inst. Republican. Roman Catholic. Home: 217 1st Pl Manhattan Beach CA 90266-6503 Office: Computer Image Sys Inc 20030 Normandie Ave Torrance CA 90502-1210

PETTEY, JANICE GOW, fund raising executive non profit organization; b. San Francisco, Dec. 16, 1944; d. Edward William and Mildred (Hee) Gow; m. Marvin Allen Pettey, Mar. 28, 1968; children: Jonathan, Matthew, Marvin Aaron. BA, Park Coll., 1966; postgrad. studies in Arts, Colo. State U., 1966-67, postgrad studies in Pub. Adminstrn., Calif. State U., Hayward, 1975-77. Area exec. Girl Scouts of U.S., San Francisco, 1970-79; campign dir. United Way, San Francisco, 1979-88; v.p. fin. devel. YMCA of San Francisco, 1988-93; dir. devel. San Francisco Ballet, 1993; v.p. membership San Francisco C. of C., 1994; chief advancement officer Am. Red Cross, San Francisco, 1995—; cons. Cameron House, San Francisco, 1993—, Strybing Arboretum, San Francisco, 1993—, Ingleside Ch., San Francisco, 1993—, Ctr. for Improvement Integration of Journalism, San Francisco, 1993—. Bd. mgrs. YMCA, San Francisco, 1995—. Mem. LWV (bd. dirs. San Francisco), Nat. Soc. Fund Raising Execs. (cert. fund raising exec., bd. dirs. 1994-96, found. bd., 1995—), City Club San Francisco, Commonwealth Club. Office: Am Red Cross 85 Second St 8th Flr San Francisco CA 94105

PETTIGREW, EDWARD W., lawyer; b. Aurora, Ill., July 16, 1943. AB, Kenyon Coll., 1965; JD, U. Mich., 1968. Bar: Wash. 1970, Mich. 1971, U.S. Ct. Appeals (9th cir.) 1971, U.S. Dist. Ct. (we. and ea. dists.) Wash. 1971. Mem. Graham & Dunn, Seattle. Mem. Fed. Bar Assn. (pres. western dist. Wash. 1987-88). Office: Graham & Dunn 1420 5th Ave Fl 33 Seattle WA 98101-2333

PETTIGREW, STEVEN LEE, healthcare management consultant; b. Colorado Springs, May 8, 1949; s. Wesley N. and Mary Ellen (Howard) P.; m. Elise Woodcock, Dec. 12, 1987. BS in Mech. Engring., Colo. State U., 1972. Regional dir. Mgmt. Engring. Svcs. Assn. Program, Inc., Phoenix, 1972-76; v.p. Ariz. Hosp. Assn., Phoenix, 1976-79; corp. exec. dir. Samaritan Health Svc., Phoenix, 1979-96; prin. Ragan Pettigrew LLC, 1996—; lectr. Ariz. State U., Tempe, 1976-78, 93-94. Contbr. articles to tech. publs. Bd. dirs. Hospice of Valley, Phoenix, 1981-88, pres., 1986-88, trustee endowment fund, 1983—; Valley Leadership Class XII, 1990-91; mem. adv. bd. Chandler Hist. Mus., 1994—, vice-chair, 1995-96, chair, 1996-97. NSF rsch. grantee, 1971-72. Fellow Healthcare Info. and Mgmt. Sys. Soc. (bd. dirs. 1980-81); mem. Instn. Indsl. Engrs. (sr.), Sigma Tau, Kiwanis (bd. dirs. Phoenix chpt. 1985-86, 94-95, treas. 1994-95, Spl. Svc. award 1986, 92, 93, 94, 96). Methodist.

PETTIS-ROBERSON, SHIRLEY MCCUMBER, former congresswoman; b. Mountain View, Calif.; d. Harold Oliver and Dorothy Susan (O'Neil) McCumber; m. John J. McNulty (dec.); m. Jerry L. Pettis (dec. Feb. 1975); m. Ben Roberson, Feb. 6, 1988; children: Peter Dwight Pettis, Deborah Neil Pettis Moyer. Student, Andrews U., U. Calif., Berkeley. Mgr. Audio-Digest Found., L.A., Glendale; sec.-treas. Pettis, Inc., Hollywood, 1958-68; mem. 94th-95th Congresses from 37th Calif. Dist., mem. coms. on interior, internat. rels., edn. and labor; pres. Women's Rsch. and Edn. Inst., 1979-80; bd. dirs. Kemper Nat. Ins. Cos., 1979—, Lumbermines Mut. Ins. Co. Mem. Pres.'s Commn. on Arms Control and Disarmament, 1980-83, Commn. on Presdl. Scholars, 1990-93; trustee U. Redlands, Calif., 1980-83, Loma Linda (Calif.) U. and Med. Ctr., 1990-95; chair Loma Linda U. Children's Hosp. Found.; mem. Former Mems. Congress, 1988-94. Mem. Morningside Country Club (Rancho Mirage, Calif.), Capitol Hill Club (Washington).

PETTIT, GEORGE ROBERT, chemistry educator, cancer researcher; b. Long Branch, N.J., June 8, 1929; s. George Robert and Florence Elizabeth (Seymour) P.; m. Margaret Jean Benger, June 20, 1953; children: William Edward, Margaret Sharon, Robin Kathleen, Lynn Benger, George Robert III. B.S., Wash. State U., 1952; M.S. Wayne State U., 1954, Ph.D., 1956. Teaching asst. Wash. State U., 1950-52, lecture demonstrator, 1952; rsch. chemist E.I. duPont de Nemours and Co., 1953; grad. teaching asst. Wayne State U., 1952-53, rsch. fellow, 1954-56; sr. rsch. chemist Norwich Eaton Pharms., Inc., 1956-57; asst. prof. chemistry U. Maine, 1957-61, assoc. prof. chemistry, 1961-65, prof. chemistry, 1965; vis. prof. chemistry Stanford U., 1965; chmn. organic div. Ariz. State U., 1966-68, prof. chemistry, 1965—; vis. prof. So. African, Univs., 1978; dir. Cancer Rsch. Lab., 1974-75, Cancer Rsch. Inst., 1975—; lectr. various colls. and univs.; cons. in field. Contbr. articles to profl. jours. Mem. adv. bd. Wash. State U. Found., 1981-85. Served with USAFR, 1951-54. Recipient Disting. Rsch. Professorship award Ariz. State U., 1978-79, Alumni Achievement award Wash. State U., 1984; recipient Rsch. Achievement award Am. Soc. Pharmacolgnosy, 1995; named Dalton Prof. Medicinal Chemistry and Cancer Rsch., 1986—, Regents Prof. Chemistry, 1990—. Fellow Am. Inst. Chemists (Pioneer award 1989, Ariz. Gov.'s Excellence award 1993); mem. Am. Chem. Soc. (awards com. 1968-71, 78-81), Chem. Soc. (London), Pharmacognosy Soc., Am. Assn. Cancer Rsch., Sigma Xi, Phi Lambda Upsilon. Office: Ariz State U Cancer Rsch Inst Tempe AZ 85287

PETTIT, GHERY DEWITT, retired veterinary medicine educator; b. Oakland, Calif., Sept. 6, 1926; s. Hermon DeWitt Pettit and Marion Esther (St. John) Menzies; m. Frances Marie Seitz, July 5, 1948; children: Ghery St. John, Paul Michael. BS in Animal Sci., U. Calif., Davis, 1948, BS in Vet. Sci., 1951, DVM, 1953. Diplomate Am. Coll. Vet. Surgeons (recorder 1970-77, pres., chmn. bd. dirs. 1978-80). Asst. prof. vet. surgery U. Calif., Davis, 1953-61; prof. vet. surgery Wash. State U., Pullman, 1961-91, prof. emeritus, 1991—; mem. Wash. State Vet. Bd. Govs., 1981-88, chmn., 1987; vis. fellow Sydney (Australia) U., 1977. Author/editor: Intervertebral Disc Protrusion in the Dog, 1966; cons. editoral bd. Jour. Small Animal Practice, Eng., 1970-88; mem. editoral bd. Compendium on C.E., Lawrenceville, N.J., 1983-86, editoral rev. bd. Jour. Vet. Surgery, Phila., 1984-86, editor 1987-92; contbr. articles to profl. jours., chpts. to books. Elder Presbyn. Ch., Pullman, 1967—. Served with USN, 1944-46. Recipient Norden Disting. Tchr. award Wash. State U. Class 1971, Faculty of Yr. award Wash. State U. Student Com., 1985. Mem. AVMA, Am. Legion, Kiwanis Internat., Sigma Xi, Phi Zeta, Phi Kappa Sigma (chpt. advisor 1981-93, 2d v.p. 1993-98). Republican.

PETTITE, WILLIAM CLINTON, public affairs consultant; b. Reno, Nev.; s. Sidney Clinton and Wilma (Stibal) P.; m. Charlotte Denise Fryer; children: Patrick Keane, William Ellis, Joseph Clinton. Owner, Market Lake Citizen & Clark County Enterprise Newspapers, Roberts, Idaho, 1959-70, pub., 1959-61; publicity dir. Golden Days World Boxing Champs, Reno, 1970; pub. Virginia City (Nev.) Legend newspaper, 1970; public affairs cons., Fair Oaks, Calif., 1966—, owner PT Cattle Co., Firth, Idaho; cons. in Ireland, Wales, Korea, Japan, France, Czech Republic, Scotland, Alberta, British Columbia, New Brunswick, Prince Edward Island, Nova Scotia, Can., Channel Islands, Costa Rica, Macau, Hong Kong, 1984—. County probate judge, Idaho, 1959-61; acting County coroner, 1960-61; sec., trustee Fair Oaks Cemetery Dist., 1963-72; bd. dir. Fair Oaks Water Dist., 1964-72, v.p., 1967-68, pres., 1968-70; dir., v.p. San Juan Cmty. Svcs. Dist., 1962-66, 68-72; exec. sec. Calif. Bd. Landscape Archs., 1976-78, Calif. Assn. Collectors, 1966-68. Cons. Senate-Assembly Joint Audit Com. Calif. Legislature, 1971-73; exec. officer Occupational Safety and Health Appeals Bd., 1981-83; mem. regulatory rev. commn. Calif. FabricCare Bd., 1981-82; mem. Sacramento County Grand Jury, 1973-74, 1981-82, cons. bd. supvs. Sacramento County, 1985-87; chmn. bus. adv. bd. East Lawn Corp, 1991—; devel. coord. Sacramento Diocese Cath. Cemeteries, 1996—. Election campaign coord. for E.S. Wright, majority leader Idaho Senate, 1968, Henry Dworshak, U.S. Senator, 1960, Hamer Budge, U.S. Rep., 1960, Charles C. Gossett, former Gov. Idaho, 1959-74; asst. sgt. at arms Rep. Nat. Conv., 1956; chmn. Rep. County Cen. Com., 1959-61; del. Rep. State Conv., 1960. Chmn. Idaho County Centennial Commn., 1959-61. Recipient Idaho Centennial award, 1968, 69. Mem. Assn. Sacramento County Water Dists. (bd. dir. 1967-72, pres. 1970-72), No. Calif. Peace Officers Assn., Nat. Coun. Juvenile Ct. Judges (com. 1959-61). Club. Author: Memories of Market Lake, Vol. I, 1965; A History of Southeastern Idaho, Vol. II, 1977, Vol. III, 1983, Vol. IV, 1990; contbr. articles to newspapers, profl. jours. Home: PO Box 2127 Fair Oaks CA 95628-2127 Office: 2631 K St Sacramento CA 95816-5103 *Personal philosophy: Proverbs 3:3 "Never forget to be truthful and kind. Hold these virtues tightly. Write them deep within your heart."*

PETTY, LEONORA KATHLEEN, psychiatrist. BA, Mt. Holyoke Coll., 1970; MD, U. Pa., 1973. Diplomate Am. Bd. Psychiatry and Neurology, Am. Bd. Quality Assurance and Utilization Review Physicians. Psychiatry residency U. Pa. Hosp., 1973-75; assoc. medical dir. intramural program Phila. Child Guidance Clinic, 1977, acting medical dir. intramural program, 1977-78; child psychiatrist, unit dir. neuropsychiatric inst. U. Calif., L.A., 1978-91; asst. prof. in resident in psychiatry & bio-behavioral scis. Neuropsychiatric Inst. U. Calif., L.A., 1978-82, adj. asst. prof., 1982-87; clinical asst. prof. psychiatry U. Calif., L.A., 1987-91; medical dir. Preferred Health Care, LTD, Irvine, Calif., 1987-88, Life Link Inc, Pasadena, Calif., 1988-91; medical dir. adolescent unit Spartanburg (S.C.) Regional Medical Ctr., 1991; clin. dir. children's unit Montevista Hosp., Las Vegas, 1992; pvt. practice Las Vegas, 1992—; consulting psychiatrist Behavioral Health Care Options, Las Vegas, 1992—; physician adv. Southern Calif. Edison, 1988-91, Boys Republic, Chino, Calif., 1987-91, Southern Nev. Child and Adolescent Mental Health Svcs., 1987-91; cons. to adolescent program Montevista Hosp., Las Vegas, 1987, Charter Hosp., Las Vegas, 1986-87. Contbr. articles to profl. jours. Appointed to chair APA com. in psychiatric svcs. in military, 1986, 87-88, com. psychiatric svcs. in the military, 1984-90. Recipient Nat. Sci. Found. fellowship, 1970, CIBA-Geigy, 1970, Falk fellowship Am. Psychiatry Assn., 1975-77. Mem. Am. Psychiatric Assn. (task force Changing Family Patterns, 1980), Southern Calif. Psychiatric Soc., Sigma Xi. Office: 4045 Spencer St Ste 109 Las Vegas NV 89119-5246

PEZESHKI, KAMBIZ A., metallurgical engineer; b. Tabriz, Iran, Sept. 30, 1949; came to U.S., 1970, naturalized; s. Amir Aziz and Azam (Mazi) P.; m. Shiron Cashmir Wisenbaker, Apr. 7, 1976; children: Shahene A., Shahla J. BS in Metall. Engring., U. Utah, 1977; MBA in Mktg. and Human Rels., U. Phoenix, 1983. Cert. tchr., Ariz. Process metallurgist Amax, Inc., Golden, Colo., 1977-79; process, rsch. engr. Cities Svcs. Co./Oxidental, Miami, Ariz., 1979-84; tech. svcs. engr. Am. Cyanamid, Wayne, N.J., 1984-87; mgr. western mining Rhone-Poulenc, Inc., Salt Lake City, 1987-93; nat. sales engr. Hychem, Inc., Salt Lake City, 1993—; polymerization cons. RTZ/Kennecott Copper, Salt Lake City, 1989—. Fund raiser Jake Garn for Senate, Salt Lake City, 1976; fund raiser, motivator Barry Goldwater for Senate re-election, 1980-81; vol. Ted Wilson for Gov., Salt Lake City, 1988. Mem. Am. Mining Engrs. Soc. Republican. Presbyterian.

PFAELZER, MARIANA R., federal judge; b. L.A., Feb. 4, 1926. AB, U. Calif., 1947; LLB, UCLA, 1957. Bar: Calif. 1958. Assoc. Wyman, Bautzer, Rothman & Kuchel, 1957-69, ptnr., 1969-78; judge U.S. Dist. Ct. (ctrl. dist.) Calif., 1978—; mem. Jud. Conf. Adv. Com. on Fed. Rules of Civil Procedure. pres., v.p., dir. Bd. Police Commrs. City of L.A., 1974-78; bd. vis. Loyola Law Sch. UCLA Alumnus award for Profl. Achievement, 1979, named Alumna of Yr., UCLA Law Sch., 1980, U. Calif. Santa Barbara Disting. Alumnus award, 1983. Mem. ABA, Calif. Bar Assn. (local adminstrv. com., spl. com. study rules procedure 1972, joint subcom. profl. ethics and computers and the law coms. 1972, profl. ethics com. 1972-74, spl. com. juvenile justice, women's rights subcom. human rights sect.), L.A. County Bar Assn. (spl. com. study rules procedure state bar 1974), mem. Judicial Conf. Advisory Comm. on Federal Rules of Civil Procedure. Office: US Dist Ct 312 N Spring St Rm 152 Los Angeles CA 90012-4701

PFAFF-HARRIS, KRISTINA LEE, management and computer consultant; b. Reno, Nev., Oct. 30, 1966; d. Donald Chesley and Nancy (Watson) Pfaff; m. Charles Macloren Harris, Nov. 14, 1989. BS, Thomas Edison State Coll., 1993; MA in Linguistics, U. Nev., 1996. Lic. air traffic contr. Ops. officer, cons. Mylan's Enterprises Mgmt., Inc., 1993-94; pres. Apogee Self-Mktg. Cons., Reno, Nev., 1993-94; computer systems adminstr., webmaster U. Nev. Math. Ctr., 1993-96; systems adminstr. Gt. Basin Internet Svcs., 1996—. Contbg. author, editor The Eclectic Collection, 1993-94; contbg. writer home computiing, Reno Gazette-Jour., 1993-95. With U.S. Army, 1986-90.

PFALMER, CHARLES ELDEN, secondary school educator; b. Trinidad, Colo., Aug. 9, 1937; s. Arthur Joseph and Nettie Mildred (Powell) P.; m. Margaret Christine La Duke, June 25, 1964; children: Betholyn Ann, Garret. AA, Trinidad State Jr. Coll., 1957; BA, Adams State Coll., 1959, MA, 1962. Cert. tchr., Colo. Tchr. Olathe (Colo.) H.S., 1959-60, Yuma (Colo.) H.S., 1960—; instr. Northeastern Jr. Coll., Sterling, Colo., 1990-97. Precinct chmn. Dem. Orgn., Yuma, 1992-96, del. to state conv., 1984-86, 88-90, 92-94, 96; ch. treas. Yuma Episcopal Ch., 1985—; v.p. Citizens Action Com., Yuma, 1994. Recipient Outstanding Educator award West Yuma Sch. Dist., 1987, Colo. State Ho. of Reps., 1987, Local Disting. Svc. award Colo. H.S. Activities Assn., 1991, Outstanding Cmty. Svc. award Colo. Athletic Dirs. Assn., 1990. Mem. NEA, Am. Polit. Collectors, Nat. Coun. for the Social Studies, Colo. Edn. Assn., Phi Delta Kappa. Home: 321 E 10th Ave Yuma CO 80759-3001 Office: Yuma HS 1000 S Albany St Yuma CO 80759-3008

PFEIFFER, GEOFFREY E., financial company executive; b. Cin., Nov. 21, 1949; s. Elmer and Alice Ruth (Stout) P.; m. Lea Marie Pfeiffer, June 4, 1976; children: Erin Marie, Victoria Lynn, Alicia Anne. BBA, U. Cin., 1972, JD, 1975. Bar: Ohio, 1975. Pvt. practice law Cin., 1975-78; advanced mktg. cons. Hartford (Conn.) Life, 1978-83; dir. advanced mktg. Nat. Life of vt., Montpelier, 1983-90; brokerage mgr. Mass. Mut. Life, Phoenix, 1991-93; devel. specialist Prudential Ins., Phoenix, 1993-96; dir. advanced mktg. Allmerican Fin., Phoenix, 1996—. Emergency rm. vol., centennial chair St. Joseph's Hosp., Phoenix, 1991—; mem. United Way Com.; treas., membership/auction chmn. Boys and Girls clubs of Met. Phoenix, 1991—. Fellow Life Underwriters Tng. Coun., Life Mgmt. Inst.; mem. Am. Soc. CLUs, Gen. agts. and Mgrs. Assn. (treas. cmty. svcs. 1995—), Phi Kappa Tau (bd. govs., chmn. 1996). Republican. Roman Catholic. Office: Allmerican Financial 2929 E Camelback Phoenix AZ 85016-4425

PFEIFFER, GERALD G., human resources specialist; b. Bowling Green, Ohio, Oct. 23, 1939; s. Harry A. and Velma C. (Morrow) P. BS, George Washington U., 1962; MBA, Wayne State U., Detroit, 1970. CLU. With FBI, Washington, Detroit, 1960-63, Am. Std. Corp., Detroit, 1963-70; labor rels. supr. to dir. personnel ITT Corp., various cities, 1970-76; labor rels. and safety advisor to sr. e.r. cons. various cities Mobil Oil Corp., 1976-85; exec. v.p., gen. mgr. HAP Ent., Inc., San Diego, 1985-90; human resources cons. Merit Resource Group, San Francisco, 1991-93; v.p. human resources Nat. Refractories and Minerals Corp., Livermore, Calif., 1993-96; v.p. human resources and adminstrv. svcs. Xing Tech. Corp., San Luis Obispo, Calif., 1996—. Contbr. articles to profl. jours. Advisor Jr. Achievement, 1967-84; human resources cons. Joan Kroc Homeless Ctr., San Diego, 1989-92, United Way, San Diego, 1989-92. Capt. USAF, 1962. W.I.N. grantee, 1968. Mem. Rotary. Home: 2673 Brentwood Circle Arroyo Grande CA 93420

PFEIFFER, JOHN WILLIAM, publisher, management consultant; b. Wallace, Idaho, July 10, 1937; s. John William and Mary Loretta (Schmidt) P.; children: Heidi Erika, Charles Wilson. BA, U. Md., 1962; PhD (fellow), U. Iowa, 1968; JD, Western State U., 1982; DABS (hon.), Calif. Am. U., Escondido, 1980. Instr. U. Md., 1965-67; dir. adult edn. Kirkwood (Iowa) Community Coll., 1967-69; dir. ednl. resources Ind. Higher Edn. Telecommunications Systems, Indpls., 1969-72; pres. Univ. Assocs., San Diego, 1972-90, Pfeiffer & Co., San Diego, 1991—; adj. tchr. Ind. U., 1969-72, Purdue U., 1971-72. Author: Instrumentation in Human Relations Training, 1973, 2d edit. 1976, Reference Guide to Handbooks and Annuals, 1975, 2d edit. 1977, 3d. edit. 1981, (With Goodstein and Nolan) Applied Strategic Planning, 1986, 2d edit. 1988, (with Judith A. Pfeiffer) LBP, 1990; editor: A Handbook of Structured Experiences for Human Relations Training, 10 vols., 1969-85, The Annual Handbook for Facilitators, 10 vols. 1972-81, Group and Orgns. Studies Internat. Jour. for Group Facilitators, 1976-79, The Annual for Facilitators, Trainers and Consultants, 1982-91, Strategic Planning: Selected Readings, 1986, The Instrumentation Kit, 1988, Shaping Strategic Planning, 1988, Training Technology, 7 vols., 1988, Theories and Models, 4 vols., 1992, Plan or Die, 1993, Pfeiffer Library, 28 vols., 1993. Served with U.S. Army, 1958-62. Office: Pfeiffer & Co 8517 Production Ave San Diego CA 92121-2204

PFEIFFER, ROBERT JOHN, business executive; b. Suva, Fiji Islands, Mar. 7, 1920; came to U.S., 1921, naturalized, 1927; s. William Albert and Nina (MacDonald) P.; m. Mary Elizabeth Worts, Nov. 29, 1945; children—Elizabeth Pfeiffer Tumbas, Margaret Pfeiffer Hughes, George, Kathleen. Grad. high sch., Honolulu, 1937; DSc (hon.), Maine Maritime Acad.; HHD (hon.), U. Hawaii; DHL (hon.), Hawaii Loa Coll. With Inter-Island Steam Navigation Co., Ltd., Honolulu, (re-organized to Overseas Terminal Ltd. 1950); with (merged into Oahu Ry. & Land Co 1954), 1937-55, v.p., gen. mgr., 1950-54, mgr. ship agy. dept., 1954-55; v.p., gen. mgr. Pacific Cut Stone & Granite Co., Inc., Alhambra, Calif., 1955-56, Matcinal Corp., Alameda, Calif., 1956-58; mgr. div. Pacific Far East Line, Inc., San Francisco, 1958-60; with Matson Nav. Co., San Francisco, 1960—, v.p., 1966-70, sr. v.p., 1970-71, exec. v.p., 1971-73, pres., 1973-79, 84-85, 89-90, CEO, 1973-92, chmn. bd., bd.dirs., 1978-95, chmn. emeritus, 1995—; v.p. The Matson Co., San Francisco, 1968-70; pres. The Matson Co., 1970-82; v.p., gen. mgr. Matson Terminals, Inc., San Francisco, 1960-62; pres. Matson Terminals, Inc., 1962-70, chmn. bd., 1970-79; chmn. bd. Matson Svcs. Co., 1973-79, Matson Agys., Inc., 1973-78; sr. v.p. Alexander & Baldwin, Inc., Honolulu, 1973-77; exec. v.p. Alexander & Baldwin, Inc., 1977-79, chmn. bd., 1980-95; chmn. emeritus Alexander & Baldwin, Inc., Honolulu, 1995—; CEO Alexander & Baldwin, Inc., 1980-92, pres., 1979-84, 89-91; chmn. bd., pres., dir. A&B-Hawaii, Inc., 1988-89, chmn. bd., 1989-95; chmn. emeritus A&B-Hawaii, Inc., Honolulu, 1995—; former mem. Gov.'s commn. on exec. salaries State of Hawaii, com. on jud. salaries. Past chmn. maritime transp. rsch. bd. NAS; former mem. select com. for Am. Mcht. Marine Seamanship Trophy Award; mem. commn. sociotech. systems NRC; mem. adv. com. Joint Maritime Congress; Pacific Aerospace Mus., also bd. dirs.; vice-chmn. Hawaii Maritime Ctr.; former chmn. A. Com. on Excellence (ACE), Hawaii; bd. govs. Japanese Cultural Ctr. Hawaii; hon. co-chmn. McKinley H.S. Found. Lt. USNR, WWII; comdr. Res. ret. Mem. VFW (life), Nat. Assn. Stevedores (past pres.), Internat. Cargo Handling Coord. Assn. (past pres. U.S. Com.), Propeller Club U.S. (past pres. Honolulu chpt.), Nat. Def. Transp. Assn., Containerization & Intermodal Inst. (hon. bd. advisors), 200 Club, Aircraft Owners and Pilots Assn., Pacific Club, Outrigger Club, Oahu Country Club, Maui Country Club, Pacific Union Club, Bohemian Club, World Trade Club (San Francisco), Masons, Shriners. Republican. Home: 535 Miner Rd Orinda CA 94563-1429 Office: Alexander & Baldwin Inc 822 Bishop St Honolulu HI 96813-3924

PFLOCK, KARL TOMLINSON, writer, researcher; b. San Jose, Calif., Jan. 6, 1943; s. Ernst Hugo and Eleanor Rose (Bracey) P.; div. 1983; children: Cynthia J. Newbury, Anna Y. Pflieger, Aaron B.; m. Mary Elizabeth Martinek, Feb. 7, 1986; 1 stepchild, Jennifer K. Martinek. BA cum laude in Philosophy, Polit. Sci., San Jose (Calif.) State U., 1964. Intelligence officer CIA, Washington, 1966-72; sr. editor Am Enterprise Inst., Washington, 1972-75; writer, rschr. pvt. practice Va., Colo., 1975-81; publs. dir., congrl. staff Jack Kemp., House Rep. Conf., Washington, 1981-83; spl. asst. for defense, space and sci. tech. Congrl. Staff U.S. Rep. Ken Kramer, Washington, 1983-85; dep. asst. sec. defense Office Operational Test Evaluation, Dept. Defense, Washington, 1985-89; sr. strategic planner BDM Internat., McLean, Va., 1989-92; writer, rschr. pvt. practice Annandale, Va., 1992-93, Placitas, N. Mex., 1993—; consulting sr. editor, Arlington House Publs., Washington, Colo., 1975-80; advisor U.S. Space Found., Colorado Springs, Colo., 1984-85; cons. TV feature, Unsolved Mysteries, 1994, (video documentary) Terra Nova TV, 1996. Author: (book) Roswell in Perspective, 1994; contbr. numerous short stories and articles to popular mags. and UFO jours, and other publs. Leader Boy Scouts Am., Arlington, Va., Colo. Springs, Colo., 1975-80. Recipient Superior Achievement award Dept. Def., 1988; recipient OutstandingPub. Svc. medal, Sec. Def., 1989; Fund for UFO Rsch. grantee, 1993. Mem. Am. Aviation Hist. Soc., San Jose State U. Alumni Assn. (life), Reagan Adminstrn. Alumni Assn., Soc. for Sci. Exploration (assoc.), Tau Delta Phi (pres. 1963). Libertarian. Office: PO Box 93338 Albuquerque NM 87199

PFLUG, ANDREW KNOX, aerospace company executive; b. Pontiac, Mich., Jan. 11, 1954; s. John Andrew and Marjorie Jean (Patterson) P.; m. Jeanne Miles, July 5, 1981 (div. Feb. 1994); children: Lindsay Brooke, Garrick Patterson; m. Julie Rushton, Aug. 23, 1996. Student, Albion (Mich.) Coll., 1972-74; BS in BA, U. Colo., 1976, MBA, 1977; DDiv (hon.), Am.

Fellowship Ch., Rolling Bay, Wash., 1987. Mgr. contract adminstrn. Thiokol Corp., Brigham City, Utah, 1986-88, mgr. material/procurement, 1988-90, dir. contracts materiel and estimating, 1990-92, bus. mgr., 1992-96, mgr. resource planning and estimating, 1996—; govt. contract cons., Utah, 1990—. Contbr. articles to profl. jours. Mem. Civil Air Patrol, Longmont, Colo., Citizen's Against Phys. and sexual abuse, Logan, Utah. Co-recipient Stratospheric Ozone Protection award U.S. EPA, 1994. Mem. Nat. Assn. Purchasing Mgrs., Nat. Contract Mgmt. Assn., Kiwanis, Lyle Richman Club. Republican. Office: Thiokol Corp Space Ops PO Box 707 MS T80 Brigham City UT 84302

PFLUGHAUPT, JANE RAMSEY, secondary school educator; b. Houston, Dec. 19, 1940; Sidney Clarence and Lillian Bess (Melton) Ramsey; m. Louis Elliott Pflughaupt, Aug. 11, 1962; children: Cheryl Diane, Russell Alan. BA, U. Tex., 1962; MA, Stanford U., 1971. Cert. life secondary tchr., Calif., Tex. Tchr. math. Austin (Tex.) Ind. Sch. Dist., 1962-65; tchr. math. San Jose (Calif.) Unified Sch. Dist., 1967—, mentor tchr., 1985-90, mem. dist. math task force, 1985—, mem. prin.'s cabinet, 1997; mem. dist. curriculum adv. com. San Jose (Calif.) United Sch. Dist., 1991-93; mem. textbook rev. com. State of Calif., Sacramento, 1988-89; writer of textbook correlations for State of Oreg., 1995; chmn. math. dept. Pioneer H.S., 1990—, mem. prin.'s cabinet, 1996—; cons. McDougal Littel-Houghton Mifflin, 1993—, D.C. Heath, 1993—. Author: Integrated Math Teacher's editions, 1, 2 and 3, 1993-95, Algebra I, 1995, Algebra II, 1996, Geometry, 1997, Heath Algebra I, 1997. Vol. Indian Guides, Girl Scouts U.S.A., Lyceum, Los Madres, San Jose and Los Gatos, Calif., 1974-88; participant Coll. Bds. Project Equity 2000, 1991, 92, 93, 94, 95, 96; demonstration tchr. NSF/Equity 2000, 1992. Named Tchr. of Yr. Pioneer H.S., 1990, 95; grantee Hewlett-Packard Co., 1989, 91, 92, Inst. Computer Aided Math., 1989, Tandy Co., 1994; fellow, grantee Semicondr. Rsch. Corp., 1990; Tandy Tech. Math. nat. scholar, 1994. Mem. NEA, Math. Assn. Am., Nat. Coun. Tchrs. Math., Calif. Math. Coun., Calif. Tchrs. Assn., Santa Clara Valley Math. Assn., San Jose Tchrs. Assn. Office: Pioneer High Sch 1290 Blossom Hill Rd San Jose CA 95118-3126

PFORZHEIMER, HARRY, JR., oil consultant; b. Manila, Nov. 19, 1915; s. Harry and Mary Ann (Horan) P.; BS in Chem. Engring., Purdue U., 1938; postgrad. Case Inst. Tech., Law Sch., George Washington U., Case Western Res. U.; m. Jean Lois Barnard, June 2, 1945; children: Harry, Thomas. with Standard Oil Co. (Ohio), various locations, 1938-80, pres. White River Shale Oil Corp., 1974-76, v.p. Sohio Natural Resources Co., 1971-80, program dir. Paraho oil shale demonstration, Grand Junction, 1974-80; pres., chmn. bd., chief exec. officer Paraho Devel. Corp., 1980-82, sr. mgmt. advisor and dir., 1982-85, cons., 1985—; pres. Harry Pforzheimer Jr. and Assocs., 1983—, Ind. Colo. West Fin., Inc.; dir. IntraWest Bank Grand Junction; adj. prof. chem. engring. Cleve. State U. Contbr. articles to tech. and trade jours. Mem. planning adv. bd. St. Mary's Hosp. and Med. Ctr.; long-range planning com. Immaculate Heart of Mary Ch.; bd. dirs. Colo. Sch. Mines Research Inst.; mem. Petroleum Adminstrn. for War, Washington, 1942-45, Purdue U. Pres.'s Coun.; chmn. Wayne N. Aspinall Found.; mem. long range planning com. Immaculate Heart Mary Ch. Mem. Am. Inst. Chem. Engrs. (chmn. Cleve. 1955, gen. chmn. internat. meeting, Cleve. 1961), Am. Petroleum Inst., Am. Mining Congress, Colo. Mining Assn., Rocky Mountain Oil and Gas Assn., Denver Petroleum Club, Purdue Alumni Assn., Sigma Alpha Epsilon. Clubs: Army and Navy (Washington), Bookcliff Country, Rio Verde Country. Lodge: Kiwanis. Home: 2700 G Rd # 1-c Grand Junction CO 81506-1408 Office: 743 Horizon Ct Grand Junction CO 81506-3938

PFUND, EDWARD THEODORE, JR., electronics company executive; b. Methuen, Mass., Dec. 10, 1923; s. Edward Theodore and Mary Elizabeth (Banning) P.; BS magna cum laude, Tufts Coll., 1950; postgrad U. So. Calif., 1950, Columbia U., 1953, U. Calif., L.A., 1956, 58; m. Marga Emmi Andre, Nov. 10, 1954 (div. 1978); children: Angela M., Gloria I., Edward Theodore III; m. Ann Lorenne Dille, Jan. 10, 1988 (div. 1990). Radio engr., WLAW, Lawrence-Boston, 1942-50; fgn. svc. staff officer Voice of Am., Tangier, Munich, 1950-54; project. engr. Crusade for Freedom, Munich, Ger., 1955; project mgr., materials specialist United Electrodynamics Inc., Pasadena, Calif., 1956-59; cons. H.I. Thompson Fiber Glass Co., L.A., Andrew Corp., Chgo., 1959, Satellite Broadcast Assocs., Encino, Calif., 1982; teaching staff Pasadena City Coll. (Calif.), 1959; dir. engring., chief engr. Electronics Specialty Co., L.A. and Thomaston, Conn., 1959-61; with Hughes Aircraft Co., various locations, 1955, 61-89, mgr. Middle East programs, also Far East, Latin Am. and African market devel., L.A., 1971-89, dir. internat. programs devel., Hughes Comm. Internat., 1985-89; mng. dir. E.T. Satellite Assocs. Internat., Rolling Hills Estates, Calif., 1989—; dir. programs devel. Asia-Pacific TRW Space and Tech. Group, Redondo Beach, Calif., 1990-93, Pacific Telecom. Coun., Honolulu, 1993—. With AUS, 1942-46. Mem. AIAA, Phi Beta Kappa, Sigma Pi Sigma. Contbr. articles to profl. jours. Home: 25 Silver Saddle Ln Palos Verdes Peninsula CA 90274-2437 *Edward Pfund served as chairman of the Sub-committee on Communications, Space Flight Operations group, and chief of Johannesburg Operations, 1961-63. He was director of Spacecraft Performance Analysis and Command, 1964-68, for which he directed the real-time commanding, control, and performance of all United States unmanned soft lunar landings and the world's first lunar lift-off and translation, 1966-68. He was also program manager for the Lunar Rover Ground Data System Design, 1969-70; chairman of the Technical Committee for International Consortium (Japan, France, United States, Jordan), 1974-78. He received an Award of Merit and a Congressional Commendation for materials in design engineering for design development of two unique kinds of coaxial cable having low losses over one thousand degrees Fahrenheit for Mach 3 aerospace vehicles.*

PFUNTNER, ALLAN ROBERT, entomologist; b. Buffalo, May 19, 1946; s. Robert James and Verna May (Colton) P.; m. Sri Hartini Hartono, Aug. 23, 1970; children: Nicolis Dean, Erin Tristina. BA in Biology, San Jose State U., 1969, MA in Biology, 1977. Cert. entomologist. Sanitarian Monterey County Health Dept., Salinas, Calif., 1972-73; vector control asst. Santa Clara County Health Dept., San Jose, Calif., 1973-75; entomologist Northwest Mosquito Abatement Dist., Riverside, Calif., 1975-84; asst. mgr. West Valley Vector Control Dist., Chino, Calif., 1984-89, mgr., 1989—. Contbr. articles to jours. Served with U.S. Army, 1969-72. Mem. Entomol. Soc. Am., Am. Mosquito Control Assn., Soc. for Vector Ecology. Office: West Valley Vector Control Dist 13355 Elliot Ave Chino CA 91710-5255

PHAM, KINH DINH, electrical engineer, educator, administrator; b. Saigon, Republic of Vietnam, Oct. 6, 1956; came to U.S., 1974; s. Nhuong D. and Phuong T. (Tran) P.; m. Ngan-Lien T. Nguyen, May 27, 1985; children: Larissa, Galen. BS with honors, Portland State U., 1979; MSEE, U. Portland, 1982; postgrad., Portland State U., 1988—. Registered profl. engr., Oreg., Calif., Ariz., Fla., Wash. Elec. engr. Irvington-Moore, Tigard, Oreg., 1979-80; elec. engr. Elcon Assocs., Inc., Beaverton, Oreg., 1980-87, from sr. elec. engr., assoc. ptnr., 1987-96, v.p., 1996—; adj. prof. Portland (Oreg.) Community Coll., 1982—; mem. adv. bd. Mass Transit System Compatibility, 1994. Contbr. articles to profl. jours. Recipient Cert. Appreciation Am. Pub. Transit Assn. and Transit Industry, 1987. Mem. IEEE, N.Y. Acad. Scis., Mass Transit Sys. Compatibility Adv. Bd, Eta Kappa Nu. Buddhist. Office: Elcon Assocs Inc 12670 NW Barnes Rd Portland OR 97229-6016

PHANES, MARGARET ASTRID, trainer, visual designer; b. San Francisco, May 11, 1949; d. John Hollister Hilton and Eleanor Elizabeth (Roe) Seymour. BA, Calif. State Coll., Sonoma, 1971; MA, Lone Mountain Coll., 1972; postgrad., Humanistic Psychology Inst., 1973-74, Calif. Inst. Integral Studies, 1980-81. Lic. marriage, family and child counselor. Image editing and graphic software trainer Santa Cruz (Calif.) Adult Edn., 1991-95; trainer U. Calif. Extension, Santa Cruz, 1994-95; counselor Solano C.C., Suisun, Calif., 1973-80; trainer U. Calif., Davis, 1975. Prin. works include Grace, Making Women Artists Visible Galeria Tonantzin. Mem. IEEE, NAFE, Women's Caucus for Art, Union Concerned Scientists, Artists Using Sci. and Tech. Office: 1112F Mission St Santa Cruz CA 95060-3501

PHELAN, JEFFREY PATRICK, obstetrician, gynecologist, lawyer; b. Boston, Apr. 7, 1946; m. Marilyn Marcy, May 3, 1969; children: Kelly Elizabeth, Shane Patrick, Shannon Leigh. MD, U. Miami, 1973; JD, Loyola Law Sch., 1988. Diplomate Am. Bd. Ob-Gyn. Intern, resident Naval Regional Med. Ctr., Portsmouth, Va., 1973-77; obstet. cons. Pregnant Cardiac Clinic U. So. Calif.-L.A. County Med. Ctr., 1981-83, dir. Normal Birth Ctr., 1981-88, dir. External Cephalic Version Clinic, 1982-85, obstet. cons. Post Date Clinic, 1984-86, assoc. dir. Women's ICU, 1984-88, dir. antepartum fetal surveillance, 1984-88; dir. maternal-fetal medicine Queen of the Valley Hosp., West Covina, Calif., 1987-91; co-dir. maternal-fetal medicine Pomona (Calif.) Valley Hosp. Med. Ctr., 1987—; dir. maternal-fetal medicine San Antonio Hosp., Upland, Calif., 1991—; co-dir. maternal-fetal medicine Garfield Med. Ctr., 1995—. Editor: Critical Care Obstetrics, 1987, Cesarean Delivery, 1988, Prevention in Prematurity, 1992; editor jour. Ob-Gyn. and the Law, 1989; perinatal editor Jour Perinatology, 1993; editor in chief OBG Mgmt., 1994; co-editor: Critical Care Obstetrics, 2d edit., 1991, Handbook of Critical Care Obstetrics, 1994. Named Best Doctor in Am., 1994. Fellow ACOG (1st award for sci. presentation 1989, dist. VIII/IX award 1996), Am. Coll. Legal Medicine; mem. ABA, Calif. Bar Assn., Soc. Perinatal Obstetricians (Soc. award 1989). Office: 959 E Walnut St Pasadena CA 91106

PHELPS, BARTON CHASE, architect, educator; b. Bklyn., June 27, 1946; s. Julian Orville and Elizabeth Willis (Faulk) P.; m. Karen Joy Simonson; 1 child, Charlotte Simonson Phelps. BA in Art with honors, Williams Coll., 1968; MArch, Yale U., 1973. Registered architect, Calif. With Colin St. John Wilson & Ptnrs., London, 1972-73, Frank O. Gehry and Assocs., Inc., Santa Monica, Calif., 1973-76, Charles Moore/Urban Innovations Group, L.A., 1976-78; dir. architecture Urban Innovations Group, L.A., 1980-84; prin. Barton Phelps & Assocs., L.A., 1984—; asst. prof. architecture Rice U. Sch. of Architecture, Houston, 1977-79; asst. dean Grad. Sch. Architecture and Urban Planning, UCLA, 1980-83; prof. architecture Sch. Arts and Architecture UCLA; faculty mem. Nat. Endowment Arts, Mayors Inst. for City Design, 1990, 92. Author, editor: Architecture California, 1988-92. Fellow Graham Found. for advanced Studies in Fine Art, 1989, Nat. Endowment for the Arts, 1988. Mem. AIA (Coll. of Fellows, chair nat. com. on design, recipient design awards for Arroyo House, Kranz House, North Range Clark Libr. UCLA, L.A. Dept. Water and Power Ctrl. Dist. Hdqrs., No. Hollywood Pump Sta., East Bldg. Seeds U. Elem. Sch., UCLA, Inst. Honor for Collaborative Design, Games XXIII Olympiad L.A. 1984). Democrat. Home: 10256 Lelia Ln Los Angeles CA 90077-3144 Office: Barton Phelps & Assocs 5514 Wilshire Blvd Los Angeles CA 90036-3829

PHELPS, BECKY JUNE, school library professional; b. Reno, Nev., Nov. 15, 1965; d. James Eugene and Loretta Ann (Owen) P. Forest fire fighter U.S. Forest Svc., Brookings, Oreg., 1984; presch. tchr. Discovery Time Presch., Brookings, 1984-87; staff mem. Salem (Oreg.) Boys & Girls Club, 1987-89; site dir. Salem Family YMCA, 1989-91; childcare dir. Salem-Keizer Sch. Dist., 1991-95, libr./media asst., 1995—. Republican. Office: McKay HS 2440 Lancaster Dr NE Salem OR 97305

PHELPS, KATHRYN ANNETTE, mental health counseling executive, consultant; b. Creswell, Oreg., Aug. 1, 1940; d. Henry Wilbur and Lake Ilene (Wall) M.; children: David Bryan (dec.), Derek Alan, Darla Ailene. BS in edn., Western Oreg. State Coll., 1962; MSW, Columbia State U., 1992, PhD, 1993. Tchr. Germany, Thailand, U.S., 1962-88; acct. exec. ins. industry; weight-loss counselor, alchohol/drug abuse prevention/intervention counselor teens, 1990-93; counselor Eugene, 1989-94; sr. exec. v.p., edn. dir. Light Streams, Inc., Eugene, 1993—; sr. exec. v.p., therapist Comprehensive Assessment Svcs./The Focus Inst., Inc., Eugene, 1994—; mental health counselor in pvt. practice; ednl. cons. specializing in learning disability testing Comprehensive Assessment Svcs., Eugene, 1996—; CEO Comprehensive Assessment Svcs., LLC, 1995—; cons. consumer edn.; mem. Am. Bd. Disability Analysts. Author: Easy Does It, books 1 & 2; hosted weekly TV cooking segment, Portland and U.S. Guardian Jobs Daughters, 1980-82; bd. dirs., den mother Cub Scouts, Boy Scouts, Kansas, Oreg., 1974-82; coach girls volleyball, 1974-80; vol. in orphanages, elderly nursing homes, Thailand, Germany, U.S., 1954-95; sunday sch. tchr., 1956-90; sponsored exchange student, 1984-88. Mem. Am. Bd. Disability Analysts, Eastern Star, Nat. Assn. Social Workers, Am. Counseling Assn., Columbia State U. Alumni Assn., Women's Internat. Bowling Conf. Home: 3838 Kendra St Eugene OR 97404 Office: Comprehensive Assessment Sv The Focus Inst Inc 400 E 2d St Ste 103 Eugene OR 97401

PHELPS, MICHAEL EVERETT JOSEPH, energy company executive; b. Montreal, Que., Can., June 27, 1947; s. Arthur A. and Hendrina (Von De Roer) P.; m. Joy Slimmon, Aug. 8, 1970; children: Erica, Julia, Lindsay. BA, U. Manitoba, 1967, LLB, 1970; LLM, London Sch. Econs., 1971. Crown atty. Province of Man., Winnipeg, 1971-73; ptnr. Christie, Degraves, Winnipeg, 1973-76; counsel Dept. Justice, Ottawa, Ont., 1976-78; exec. asst. Minister of Justice, Ottawa, 1978-79, Minister of Energy, Mines & Resources, Ottawa, 1980-82; sr. advisor to pres. & chief exec. officer Westcoast Transmission Co. Ltd., Vancouver, B.C., 1982-83; v.p. strategic planning Westcoast Transmission Co. Ltd., Vancouver, 1983-87, sr. v.p., 1987, exec. v.p., chief fin. officer, 1987-88; pres., chief exec. officer Westcoast Energy, Inc. (formerly Westcoast Transmission Co Ltd.), Vancouver, from 1988, now chmn., CEO, also bd. dirs.; bd. dirs. Saratoga Processing Co. Ltd.; chmn. bd. Westcoast Petroleum Co. Ltd., chmn. bd. dirs. Can. Roxy Petroleum Ltd., vice-chmn., bd. dirs. Foothills Pipe Lines (Yukon) Ltd. Mem. Interstate Natural Gas Assn. Am. (bd. dirs.), Can. Petroleum Assn. (bd. dirs.), Bus. coun. British Columbia, The Vancouver, Hollyburn Country, Terminal City (Vancouver), Vancouver Club, Hollyburn Golf & Country Club, Terminal City Ckub. Office: Westcoast Energy Inc, 3400-666 Burrard St, Vancouver, BC Canada V6C 3M8*

PHELPS, WILLARD, Canadian government official. Min. Edn., Health and Social Svcs., Can., 1993—. Office: Govt Yukon, PO Box 2703, Whitehorse, YK Canada Y1A 2C6

PHIBBS, HARRY ALBERT, interior designer, professional speaker, lecturer; b. Denver, Jan. 9, 1933; s. Harry Andrew and Mary May (Perriam) P.; m. Alice Conners Glynn, Oct. 23, 1957 (div. Jan. 1988); children: Kathleen Ann Phibbs Pierz, Paul Robert, Mary Alice Phibbs Hettle, Michael John, Peter James, Daniel Edward; m. Nevelle Haley Jones, Feb. 1988. B.A., U. Colo., 1954, B.F.A., 1957. Interior designer Howard Lorton, Inc., Denver, 1957-68; interior designer, v.p. Ronald Ansay Inc., Wheatridge, Colo., 1969-71; interior designer, pres. Phibbs Design Assos., Inc., Denver, 1972-78; interior designer, mgr. Howard Lorton, Inc., Colorado Springs, Colo., 1979-93; prin. Phibbs Design, Colorado Springs, 1993—; pres. Interior Designers Housing Devel. Corp., 1969-72. V.p. Arvada (Colo.) Hist. Soc., 1973; bd. dirs. Colo. Opera Festival, also pres., 1986; bd. dirs. Downtown Colorado Springs, Inc., also pres., 1984; chmn. bd. trustees Interior Design Inst. Denver, 1991-94. With U.S. Army, 1954-56. Fellow Am. Soc. Interior Designers (nat. pres. 1977); mem. Am. Arbitration Assn., Theta Xi (pres. Denver Area alumni club 1958-64). Democrat. Roman Catholic. Home: 91 W Boulder St Colorado Springs CO 80903-3371 Office: 10 Boulder Crescent St Colorado Springs CO 80903-3344 *Each of God's infinite creations was carefully placed on earth with the same responsibility....to grow. Man has the unique role in that plan in that he can help other things and the people around him to grow. This process is contingent upon "loving your neighbor as yourself." Transposing the equation therefore requires that you love yourself. I wish I had learned at an earlier age to take what you do seriously, but not to take yourself too seriously.*

PHILIPP, JOHN JOSEPH, family physician, managed care consultant; b. Chgo., Nov. 15, 1928; s. Guenther Max and Florence Marie (Doyle) P.; m. Mary Louise Grimmer, Mar. 15, 1949; children: Deborah, Melissa, Nancy, John, Christopher. BS, Loyola U., 1950; MS, Northwestern U., 1953, MD, 1957; MBA, U. Chgo., 1983. Intern Evanston (Ill.) Hosp. Assn., 1957-58; physician, med. dir. Field Med. Group, Chgo., 1958-83; chmn. dept. family medicine Ravenswood Hosp. Med. Ctr., Chgo., 1973-76; med. dir. Ctr. for Family Medicine Ill. Masonic Med. Ctr., Chgo., 1984-93, chmn. dept. family medicine, 1986-93; v.p. Metro-Med. Health System, Chgo., 1988-93; ret., 1993.

PHILIPPI, ERVIN WILLIAM, mortician; b. Lodi, Calif., June 4, 1922; s. William and Rebecca (Steinert) P.; m. Emma Grace Mosely, May 8, 1958 (div. Mar. 1979); m. Helen Jo Hunt, June 3, 1979. Grad., Calif. Coll. Motuary Sci., 1948. Embalmer, mortician, mgr. Salas Bros. Chapel, Modesto, Calif., 1946-92; dep. coroner Stanislaus County, Calif., 1955-75. With U.S. Army, 1942-46.

PHILIPSBORN, JOHN TIMOTHY, lawyer, author; b. Paris, Oct. 19, 1949; s. John David and Helen (Worth) P. AB, Bowdoin Coll., 1971; MEd, Antioch Coll., 1975; JD, U. Calif., Davis, 1978. Bar: Calif. 1978, U.S. Dist. Ct. (no. and ea. dists.) Calif. 1978, U.S. Ct. Appeals (9th cir.) 1985, U.S. Supreme Ct. 1985; cert-specialist in criminal law State of Calif., 1985. VISTA vol. Office of Gov. State of Mont., Helena, 1972-73; cons. U.S. Govt., Denver, 1974; lectr. Antioch New Eng. Grad. Sch., Keene, N.H., 1973-75, U. N.H., Durham, 1973-75; ptnr. Philipsborn & Cohn, San Jose, Calif., 1978-80; atty., supr. Defenders Inc., San Diego, 1980-83; assoc. Garry, Dreyfus & McTernan, San Francisco, 1983-87; pvt. practice, San Diego and San Francisco, 1987—; cons. Nicaraguan ct. evaluation projects, 1987—, UN Internat. Tribunal, 1995—; coord. Internat. Conf. Adversarial Sys., Lisbon, Portugal, 1990; mem. adj. faculty New Coll. Law, San Francisco, 1991—; legal asst. project refugee camps S.E. Asia, 1992—, legal edn. projects, Cambodia, 1995—; cons. on continuing edn. of bar, 1995—. Bd. editors Champion, Forum; contbr. articles to profl. jours., chpts. to book. Founder trial program San Francisco Schs., 1986; bd. dirs. Calif. Indian Legal Svcs., 1990—. Fulbright scholar, Portugal, 1989. Mem. Nat. Assn. Criminal Def. Lawyers (assoc., co-chmn. death penalty impact litigation group 1989, co-chmn. govtl. misconduct com. 1990-92, vice chmn. task force on emerging democracies 1990-91), Calif. State Bar (evaluation panel criminal law specialists 1986—, com. on continuing edn. of bar 1991-94, criminal law subcom. state bd. legal specialists 1995-96), Calif. Attys. for Criminal Justice (bd. govs. 1989-94, assoc. editor jour. 1987—, chmn. Amicus Curiae com. 1992—, co-chmn. govtl. misconduct com. 1989-92), World Affairs Coun. Office: 1231 Market St San Francisco CA 94103-1411

PHILL, DANIEL STOUFFER, artist; b. Tacoma, Oct. 1, 1955; s. Philip George and Martha Marie (Stouffer) P. Student, Wash. State U., 1974-77; BFA, San Francisco Art Inst., 1978; MFA, Stanford U., 1983. Tchg. asst. Stanford (Calif.) U., 1981-83, lectr. undergrad. studies, 1982; photographer, technician IBM Sci. Ctr., Palo Alto, Calif., 1981-84. One man shows Dana Reich Gallery, San Francisco, 1984, Wade Gallery, 1989, John Pence Gallery, San Francisco, 1986, 87, 89, 91, 94; group exhbn. San Diego Mus. Art, 1993; permanent collections include Jossey-Bass Inc., San Francisco, Kimberly Clark Inc., Dallas, KMS Corp., Seattle, Koret Found., San Francisco, Nordstrom, San Francisco and Skokie, Ill., Societe Generale Bank, Atlanta, SAP Am. Inc., Foster City, Calif., Sterling Software, Dallas, Tucson Mus. Art, Yuma (Ariz.) Art Ctr., 1st USA, Dallas, GTE, Dallas. Fellow Stanford U., 1981-83. Office: Daniel Phill Studio 1086 Folsom St San Francisco CA 94103-4022

PHILLIPS, ANNA, publisher, editor-in-chief newspaper; b. Oakalla, Tex., Nov. 19, 1936; d. Edward C. and Barbara W. (Roberts) Spinks; 1 child, Kenny E. Phillips. Asst. sales mgr. Am. Legion Newspaper, San Antonio, 1961-68; sales profl. Sta. KLRN-TV Ednl. Broadcasting, San Antonio, 1969-73; sales mgr. Victor Bloom Advt. Agy., L.A., 1973-77, Non-Commd. Officers Assn., Oceanside, Calif., 1977-80; asst. sales mgr. Marshals Assn., San Diego, 1978-81; editor-in-chief, founder World of Entertainment, 1981-90; founder, pub. Associated News of So. Calif., San Bernardino, 1985-93; pub. Sheriff & Police News Southern Calif., 1987—; news editor, publ. films, Hollywood and Las Vegas, Nev., 1980-94; pub. for Hollywood celebrities and major stage productions, 1984—. Mgr. pub. rels. dept. Student Coun., Trinity U. for world famous celebrities, jazz musicians, concert news and public relations; news and pub. rels. coord. for Native Am. Indians; fundraiser scholarships for American Indian students, 1989-94. Recipient Nat. Pub. award Nat. Fedn. of Fed. Employees, 1966, Golden Halo Trophy Motion Picture Coun. So. Calif., 1996, Star Sapphire award Motion Picture Coun. So. Calif., 1996. Mem. Associated Press (recipient Hon. Charter Mem. Plaque award, 1997, lifetime charter mem.). Office: Associated News PO Box 336 Yucaipa CA 92399

PHILLIPS, ARTHUR MORTON, II, botanist, consultant; b. Cortland, N.Y., Jan. 20, 1947; s. Arthur Morton Jr. and Ruth (Mason) P.; m. Diedre Weage, Sept. 3, 1988. BS, Cornell U., 1969; PhD, U. Ariz., 1977. Instr., dept. biol. sci. U. Ariz., Tucson, 1971-73, rsch. asst., dept. geosciences, 1973-76; rsch. botanist Mus. No. Ariz., Flagstaff, 1976-80, curator biology, 1980-89; environ. cons. Flagstaff, 1990—; mem. Ariz. plant recovery team U.S. Fish & Wildlife Svc. Endangered Species, Phoenix, 1981—, Natural Areas Adv. Coun. Ariz. State Pks., Phoenix, 1980-89, chmn. 1985-86; adj. prof. No. Ariz. U., Flagstaff, 1984—. Author: Grand Canyon Wildflowers, 2d edit., 1990; co-author: Checklist, Vascular Plants, Grand Canyon National Park, 1987, High Country Wildflowers, 1987, Expedition to San Francisco Peaks, 1989, 5 endangered plants recovery plans, 1984-95. Fellow Ariz.-Nev. Acad. Sci.; mem. Am. Quaternary Assn., Soc. for Conservation Biology, Flagstaff Rotary Club (sec. 1989-92, achievement 1990, pres. 1993-94). Home and Office: Bot & Environ Cons PO Box 201 Flagstaff AZ 86002-0201

PHILLIPS, B. KELLY L., sculptor; b. Calgary, Alta., Can., Oct. 23, 1957; d. James Bruce Ross and Elizabeth Phillips. A.O.C.A., Ont. Coll. Art, Toronto, 1978; MFA, U. Wash., 1995. Graphic artist B.C. TV, Vancouver, 1980-85, Can. Broadcasting corp., Vancouver, 1985-90. Art editor Signs Jour. of Women in Culture and Soc., seattle, 1995; artist sculpture entitled Dicks, 1996, Oral Harvest, 1995. Founding mem. The Women's Monument Project, Vancouver, 1990-97. Recipient 1st place, Left, right and Center, Orange County Ctr. for Contemporary Art's 16th Ann. Exhbn., Santa Ana, for Dicks, 1996, Oral Havest, 1996, Collector's award The N.Am. sculpture Exhbn., The Foothills Art Ctr., Golden, Colo., 1995, Juror's Merit award, Austin Mus. of Art at Laguna Gloria, Tex., 1996.

PHILLIPS, BETTY LOU (ELIZABETH LOUISE PHILLIPS), author, interior designer; b. Cleve.; d. Michael N. and Elizabeth D. (Materna) Suvak; m. John S. Phillips, Jan. 27, 1963 (div. Jan. 1981); children: Bruce, Bryce, Brian; m. John D.C. Roach, Aug. 28, 1982. BS, Syracuse U., 1960; postgrad. in English, Case Western Res. U., 1963-64. Cert. elem. and spl. edn. tchr., N.Y. Tchr. pub. schs. Shaker Heights, Ohio, 1960-66; sportswriter Cleve. Press, 1976-77; spl. features editor Pro Quarterback Mag., N.Y.C., 1976-79; freelance writer specializing in books for young people, 1976—; interior designer residential and comml.; bd. dirs. Cast Specialties Inc., Cleve. Author: Chris Evert: First Lady of Tennis, 1977; Picture Story of Dorothy Hamill (ALA Booklist selection), 1978; American Quarter Horse, 1979; Earl Campbell: Houston Oiler Superstar, 1979; Picture Story of Nancy Lopez, (ALA Notable book), 1980; Go! Fight! Win! The NCA Guide for Cheerleaders (ALA Booklist), 1981; Something for Nothing, 1981; Brush Up on Your Hair (ALA Booklist), 1981; Texas ... The Lone Star State, 1989, Who Needs Friends? We All Do!, 1989; also contbr. articles to young adult and sports mags. Bd. dirs. The Children's Mus., Denver; mem. Friends of Fine Arts Found., Denver Art Mus., Cen. City Opera Guild, Alameda County Cancer League. Mem. Soc. Children's Book Writers, Internat. Interior Design Assn. (profl. mem.), Am. Soc. Interior Designers (profl. mem., cert.),. Delta Delta Delta. Republican. Roman Catholic. Home: 4278 Bordeaux Ave Dallas TX 75205

PHILLIPS, BILLY SAXTON, artist, designer, painter; b. Louisville, Nebr., June 20, 1915; d. Charles William and Georgia Hazel (de le Zene) Tremblay; m. John Henry Phillips, Sept. 3, 1937; 1 dau., Terry. Grad., Art Ctr. Coll. of Design, 1950. Free-lance artist L.A., 1951—; package designer Wilson Paper-Disneyland, Anaheim, Calif., 1952-56; inventor Vernon (Calif.) Container Corp., 1952-56; instr. Clatsop C.C., Astoria, Oreg., 1990-92; painter Reva-Reva Gallery, Papeete, French Polynesia, 1972-92, Royal Gallery, Lahaina, Maui, Hawaii, 1993-94; artist P.M. Prodns., L.A., 1951-90; instr., motivator Maoridom, New Zealand, 1980—; instr. Art Ctr. Coll. Design, 1952-53. Designer, patentee Ukili, 1967, packages, 1960 (Zipper openings on cardboard containers); designer Disneyland's Tinkerbell; group shows include Royal Art Gallery, Met. Gallery, Lahanina, Maui, Hawaii, 1994, Kona, Hawaii, 1995. Developer Cultural Exchange Program First Ams.-Maori, S.W. Am. Indians and New Zealand Maoris, 1986. Mem. Art Ctr. Alumni (charter, life), Trail's End Art Assn., Lady Elk, Inventors and Scientists Am.

PHILLIPS, DARRELL, retail executive; b. Hamilton, Ohio, Oct. 7, 1956; s. Bill L. and Lois J. (Marcum) P. Student, Western State Coll., Gunnison, Colo., 1974-77; BSBA, U. No. Colo., Greeley, 1979. Sales rep. Econ. Lab.,

White Plains, N.Y., 1979, Color Tile, Inc., Denver, 1980-81; store mgr. Color Tile, Inc., Lake Charles, La., 1981-82; v.p. Phillips Stationers, Inc., Denver, 1982-87; pres. Pro-Dispatch Office Supply, Denver, 1988-95; pres., CEO BDLS & Assocs., Inc., 1994—. Mem. Family Firm Inst. Republican.

PHILLIPS, DAVID SPENCER, statistician, educator; b. Marion, Ind., Oct. 10, 1936; s. Harold F. and Catherine Ann (Spenser) P.; m. Sally Gregory, Aug. 16, 1958; children: Michael, Daniel, Beth. AB, Wabash Coll., 1958; MS, Purdue U., 1960, PhD, 1962. Asst. prof. stats. Oreg. Health Scis. U., Portland, 1965-67, assoc. prof., 1967-78, prof., 1978—. Author: Basic Statistics for Health Science Students, 1978; contbr. over 40 articles to profl. jours. NIMH postdoctoral fellow, 1963-65. Mem. APHA, APS, AAAS, Am. Statis. Assn., Psychonomic Soc., Sigma Xi. Home: 3155 SW Grace Ln Portland OR 97225-3354 Office: Oreg Health Scis Univ CB669 3181 SW Sam Jackson Park Rd Portland OR 97201

PHILLIPS, DEBORA R., psychotherapist; b. Bklyn.; d. Samuel and Iris (Weinstein) Rothman; William Phillips, Jan. 25, 1969 (div. Aug. 1988); children: Ron, Wendy; m. Dennis J. Mrujack, Sept. 2, 1989. BA, Barnard Coll., N.Y.; MEd, Chatham Coll., Pa.; ArtsD, Inst. Advanced Study Human Sexuality. Lic. clin. psychologist; cert. sch. psychologist, sex therapist, counselor. Dir. Princeton (N.J.) Ctr. Behavior Therapy, 1970-88; pvt. practice N.Y.C., Beverly Hills, 1988—; dir. SECH, Princeton, 1973-79; dir. clin. tng. Temple Univ., Phila., 1974-80, asst. clin. prof., 1976-86; cons. Wesley-Westminster Found., Princeton, 1979-81, NBC-TV, 1981, Mad at You, L.A., 1996, Broken Hearts, L.A., 1996; ; lectr. child psychiatry Columbia U., N.Y.C., 1980—; asst. clin. prof. U. So. Calif., L.A., 1984-90, 95-96. Author: How to Fall Out of Love, 1978, Sexual Confidence, 1980, How to Give Your Child a Great Self-Image, 1989. Dir. spl. projects Fund for Future of Our Children, L.A. Recipient Author citation N.J. Inst. Tech., 1981. Fellow Behavior Therapy Rsch. Soc.; mem. Assn. Advancement Behavior Therapy, Soc. Sex Therapy Rsch., Am. Assn. Sex Educators, Am. Assn. Counseling, Cou. Register Health Svc. Providers. Office: Beverly Hills Ctr Depression Anxiety 435 N Bedford Dr Ste 216 Beverly Hills CA 90210-4313

PHILLIPS, DEBORAH DELORES, adolescent therapist; b. Detroit, Oct. 22, 1967; d. John Wesley II and Mattie Jewel (Weddle) Morrow; m. Clayton Leonard Phillips, June 10, 1989; 1 child, Aliyah Danielle. BA in Sociology, Lane Coll., Jackson, Tenn., 1989; MS in Counseling Psychology, U. Ctrl. Tex., Killeen, 1995; postgrad., U. Hawaii, 1996—. Adolescent therapist Family In Crisis, Killeen, 1992-93; case mgr. Cmtys. in Schs., Killeen, 1993-95; adolescent therapist Child and Family Svcs., Honolulu, 1995-96; clinician III Waianae (Hawaii) Coast Cmty. Mental Health Ctr., Inc., 1996—. Mem. Parent Adv. Bd., Schofield, Hawaii, 1996. Mem. ACA. Democrat. Baptist.

PHILLIPS, DONNA ROSE, production artist, writer; b. Cheyenne, Wyo., June 16, 1961; d. Leyson Kirk and Leona Anna (Rasmussen) P.; m. Steven Gary Steinsapir, May 17, 1992; 1 child, Andrew Trevor Steinsapir. Student, Mt. San Antonio Coll., Walnut, Calif., 1982-83, Citrus Coll., Azusa, Calif., 1988. Prodn. artist Treasure Chest Advt., Pomona, Calif., 1986-89, Rutland Tool & Supply Co. Inc., Industry, Calif., 1989-92; freelance writer Baldwin Park, Calif., 1992—. Contbg. author: Book of Days, 1989; contbr. articles to mags. Recipient award for art Bank of Am., Covina, Calif., 1979. Mem. Sons of the Desert. Republican. Lutheran. Home: 3700 Baldwin Park Blvd Unit D Baldwin Park CA 91706-4101

PHILLIPS, FRANK SIGMUND, business executive; b. Anchorage, June 17, 1952; s. Charles W. and Kirsten H. (Alsos) P. BA, U. Calif., San Diego, 1973; JD, NYU, 1976; postgrad., U. Mo., 1977. Bar: Calif. 1977. Atty. Nat. Labor Rels. Bd., Washington, 1976-77; ptnr. Phillips and Phillips, San Diego, 1978-83; sr. atty. Namco of Am., Inc., Sunnyvale, Calif., 1983-85; v.p., gen. counsel Hang Ten Internat., San Diego, 1985-89; ptnr. Scenic Visuals Publs., San Diego, 1988—; exec. v.p. Licensing Enterprises, Inc., San Clemente, Calif., 1990-93; sr. cons. J. Bergman and Assocs., Inc., 1993-96; dir. Internat. Equity Mgmt., Inc., 1996—; instr. U. San Diego, 1979-83; gen. counsel San Diego Booksellers Assn., 1986—; bd. dirs. Green Found. for Earth Scis., La Jolla, Calif., 1986—. Bd. regents U. Calif., 1981-83; mem. chancellors assocs. U. Calif. San Diego, La Jolla, 1982—. Root-Tilden scholar NYU, 1973-76. Mem. Calif. State Bar, San Diego County Bar Assn., U. Calif. San Diego Alumni Assn. (pres. 1981-83). Democrat. Home: PO Box 633090 San Diego CA 92163-3090 Office: 4365 Executive Dr Ste 1000 San Diego CA 92121

PHILLIPS, GAIL, state legislator; b. Juneau, Alaska; m. Walt Phillips; children: Robin, Kim. BA in Bus. Edn., U. Alaska. Mem. Homer (Alaska) City Coun., 1981-84, Kenai Peninsula Borough Assembly, 1986-87; chmn. legis. com. Alaska Mcpl. League; mem. Alaska Ho. of Reps., 1990-92-94-96, house majority leader, 1993-94, speaker, 1995-97; owner, mgr. Quiet Sporting Goods; ptnr. Lindphil Mining Co.; pub. rels. cons. Active Homer United Meth. Ch., Rep. Ctrl. Com. Alaska, Kenai Peninsula Coll. Coun.; past mem. com. bd. and race coord. Iditarod Trail Dog Sled Race. Mem. Western States Legis. Coun. (exec. com.), Am. Legis Exch. Coun. (state chmn.), Resource Devel. Coun. Alaska, Western Legis. Conf. (exec. bd.), Western States Coalition (exec. bd.), The Energy Coun. Home: PO Box 3304 Homer AK 99603-3304 Office: 126 W Pioneer Ave Homer AK 99603-7564 also: Alaska House of Reps State Capitol Juneau AK 99801-1182

PHILLIPS, GENEVA FICKER, editor; b. Staunton, Ill., Aug. 1, 1920; d. Arthur Edwin and Lillian Agnes (Woods) Ficker; m. James Emerson Phillips, Jr., June 6, 1955 (dec. 1979). BS in Journalism, U. Ill., 1942; MA in English Lit., UCLA, 1953. Copy desk Chgo. Jour. Commerce, 1942-43; editl. asst. patents Radio Rsch. Lab., Harvard U., Cambridge, Mass., 1943-45; asst. editor adminstrv. publs. U. Ill., Urbana, 1946-47; editorial asst. Quar. of Film, Radio and TV, UCLA, 1952-53; mng. editor The Works of John Dryden, Dept. English, UCLA, 1964—. Bd. dirs. Univ. Religious Conf., L.A., 1979—. UCLA teaching fellow, 1950-53, grad. fellow 1954-55. Mem. Assn. Acad. Women UCLA, Dean's Coun., Coll. Letters and Scis. UCLA, Friends of Huntington Libr., Friends of UCLA Libr., Friends of Ctr. for Medieval and Renaissance Studies, Samuel Johnson Soc. of So. Calif., Assocs. of U. Calif. Press., Conf. Christianity and Lit., Soc. Mayflower Descs. Lutheran. Home: 213 1st Anita Dr Los Angeles CA 90049-3815 Office: UCLA Dept English 2225 Rolfe Hall Los Angeles CA 90024

PHILLIPS, JAMES ROBERT, psychologist; b. Wichita, Kans., Apr. 21, 1950; s. Earnest Delmar Phillips; m. Patti Jo Marie Marsh, Nov. 9, 1974; children: Jason Todd, Jill Elizabeth. BA, San Diego State U., 1972; MA, Pepperdine U., 1973; PhD, U. Idaho, 1994. Lic. psychologist, profl. counselor, Idaho; nat. cert. counselor. Asst. dir. psycho-ednl. program for emotionally disturbed children Harbor Area Retarded Children's Found., San Pedro, Calif., 1972-73, dir., 1973-74; continuing edn. instr. Boise (Idaho) State U., 1976-77; psychologist II Idaho State Sch. and Hosp., Nampa, 1975-77; psychologist III, program coord. Region II Mental Health Svcs., Grangeville, Idaho, 1977-80; community rehab. mgr. dept. health and welfare Region II State of Idaho, Lewiston, 1980-81; regional program mgr. dept. health and welfare Region II Mental Health Svcs., State of Idaho, Lewiston, 1981-89, psychologist specialist, 1989-92; adj. faculty Lewis-Clark State Coll., Lewiston, 1980—; pvt. practice Lewiston, 1989—; owner Phillips Agy. Inc., Lewiston, 1996—. Mem. Rotary. Office: 504 Main St Ste 460 Lewiston ID 83501-1869

PHILLIPS, JEFFREY RICHARD, magazine writer; b. San Francisco, Mar. 9, 1947; s. Robert and Dorothy Phillips; m. Rosalind Jill Phillips, Aug.4, 1973; children: Scott, Katherine. Student, Coll. San Mateo, 1967, Calif. State U., San Francisco, 1969; Pub. Program, Stanford U., 1981. Sr. writer, editor Sunset Mag., Menlo Park, Calif., 1969—; Pub. speaker Maui Writers Conf., 1994; writer various mags.; cons. films-pub. TV. Coach Am. Youth Soccer, Palo Alto, 1985-91, 92, Little League, Palo Alto, 1984-87; Calif. del. White House Conf. on Travel and Tourism, 1995; bd. dirs. Friends of Paly Choirs, 1996—. Recipient Maggie award Western Publs. Assn. Calif., 1991, 92, Lowell Thomas Travel Journalism award, 1985, 89, 92, 96. Mem. Soc. Am. Travel Writers, Soc. Profl. Journalists, Sierra Club, Calif. Trout (Disting. Svc. award 1987), Sierra Nev. Alliance. Office: Sunset Mag 80 Willow Rd Menlo Park CA 94025-3661

PHILLIPS, JILL META, novelist, critic, astrologer; b. Detroit, Oct. 22, 1952; d. Leyson Kirk and Leona Anna (Rasmussen) P. Student pub. schs., Calif. Lit. counselor Book Builders, Charter Oak, Calif., 1966-77; pres. Moon Dance Astro Graphics, Covina, Calif., 1994—. Author: (with Leona Phillips) A Directory of American Film Scholars, 1975, The Good Morning Cookbook, 1976, G.B. Shaw: A Review of the Literature, 1976, T.E. Lawrence: Portrait of the Artist as Hero, 1977, The Archaeology of the Collective East, 1977, The Occult, 1977, D.H. Lawrence: A Review of the Literature and Biographies, 1978, Film Appreciation: A College Guide Book, 1979, Annus Mirabilis: Europe in the Dark and Middle Centuries, 1979, (with Leona Rasmussen Phillips) The Dark Frame: Occult Cinema, 1979, Misfit: The Films of Montgomery Clift, 1979, Butterflies in the Mind: A Précis of Dreams and Dreamers, 1980; The Rain Maiden: A Novel of History, 1987, Walford's Oak: A Novel, 1990, The Fate Weaver: A Novel in Two Centuries, 1991, Saturn Falls: A Novel of the Apocalypse, 1993; columnist Horoscope Guide Monthly; contbr. book revs. to New Guard mag., 1974-76; contbr. numerous articles to profl. jours. including Dell Horoscope, Midnight Horoscope, Astrology-Your Daily Horoscope, Am. Astrology. Mem. Young Ams. for Freedom, Am. Conservative Union, Elmer Bernstein's Film Music Collection, Ghost Club London, Count Dracula Soc., Dracula Soc. London, Richard III Soc. Republican. Home: 515 E Claraday St Apt 8 Glendora CA 91740 Office: Moon Dancer Astro Graphics 1037 N Grand Ave Ste 202 Covina CA 91724-2048

PHILLIPS, JOHN GARDNER, educator, astrophysicist; b. New Haven, Jan. 9, 1917; s. Ray Edmund and Dora (Larson) P.; m. Margaret Ann Butler, June 11, 1944; children: Mary Jane, Cynthia Ann Hart, Gail Elizabeth. B.A., Carleton Coll., 1939; M.A., U. Ariz., 1942; Ph.D., U. Chgo., 1948. Instr. Yerkes Obs., U. Chgo., 1948-50; faculty U. Calif. at Berkeley, 1950—, prof. astrophysics, 1960-87, prof. emeritus, 1987—, chmn. dept. astronomy, 1964-67, 71-75; dir. Leuschner Obs., 1964-67, 71-75; Cons. NASA, Ames Lab. Author: (with S.P. Davis) The Red System of the CN Molecule, 1963, The Swam System of the C2 Molecule, The Spectrum of the HgH Molecule, (with Alter and Cleminshaw) Pictorial Astronomy, 1963, rev., 1969, 75, 82; assoc. editor: Ann. Revs. Astronomy and Astrophysics, 1966-89. Guggenheim fellow, 1956. Mem. AAAS, Am. Astron. Soc., Internat. Astron. Union (pres. commn. 14, 1979-82), Astron. Soc. Pacific (sec.-treas. 1968-88). Home: 1234 Lawrence St El Cerrito CA 94530-2437 Office: Dept Astronomy U Calif Berkeley CA 94720

PHILLIPS, JOHN RICHARD, engineering educator; b. Albany, Calif., Jan. 30, 1934; s. Eric Lester and Adele Catherine (Rengel) P.; m. Joan Elizabeth Soyster, Mar. 23, 1957; children: Elizabeth Huntley, Sarah Rengel, Catherine Hale. BS, U. Calif., Berkeley, 1956; M in Engring., Yale U., 1958, PhD in Engring., 1960. Registered profl. engr., Calif. Chem. engr. Stanford Rsch. Inst., Menlo Park, Calif., 1960; rsch. engr. Chevron Rsch. Co., Richmond, Calif., 1962-66; mem. faculty Harvey Mudd Coll., Claremont, Calif., 1966—, prof. engring., 1974—, James Howard Kindleberger prof. engring., 1991—, dir. engring. clinic, 1977-93, chmn. engring. dept., 1993—; vis. prof. U. Edinburgh, Scotland, 1975, Cambridge (Eng.) U., 1981, ESIEE, France, 1981, Naval Postgrad. Sch., 1984-85, Calif. Poly. U., San Luis Obispo, 1992; vis. scientist So. Calif. Edison Co., 1980; founder Claremont Engring., 1973; cons. in field. Contbr. articles to profl. jours. 1st lt. AUS, 1960-62. Mem. Am. Inst. Chem. Engrs., Sigma Xi, Alpha Delta Phi, Tau Beta Pi. Home: 911 W Maryhurst Dr Claremont CA 91711-3320

PHILLIPS, KATHRYN ANN, health services researcher; b. Austin, Tex., Nov. 22, 1957; d. Beeman Noal and Sarah Ann (Haworth) P.; m. Abram B. Rosenblatt, May 19, 1991. BA in Psychology, U. Tex., 1978; MPA in Policy Analysis, Harvard U., 1986; PhD in Health Svcs. Rsch., U. Calif., Berkeley, 1991. Rsch. agt., counselor Med. Rsch. Assn., San Antonio, 1979-80; pers. specialist Kelly AFB, San Antonio, 1980-83; asst. to pers. dir., analyst Office of Naval Rsch., Arlington, Va., 1983-86; strategic planner FAA, Washington, 1987; instr. U. Calif., Berkeley, 1987-90, rsch. asst., 1987-90; postdoctoral fellow U. Calif., San Francisco, 1991-93, asst. prof., 1993—. Reviewer Jour. of AMA, 1989—, Agy. for Health Care Policy and Rsch., 1993; contbr. articles to profl. jours. Grantee Am. Cancer Soc., 1989-90, Agy. for Health Care Policy and Rsch., 1990-91, NIAID, 1993—, CDC, 1994—. Mem. APHA, Am. Econs. Assn., Assn. Health Svcs. Rsch., Assn. Pub. Policy Analysis and Mgmt., Soc. Med. Decision Making, Soc. Advancement Socio-Econs. Office: U Calif 74 New Montgomery St Ste 600 San Francisco CA 94105-3444

PHILLIPS, LARRY DUANE, gemologist, appraiser; b. Silver City, N.Mex., Nov. 19, 1948; s. Fredric Duane and Bernice Larry (Dannelley) P.; m. Ellen Catherine Keaveny, May 6, 1972; 1 child, Tamara Lynn. Student, N.Mex. State U., 1966-70, Ind. U., 1986—; grad. in gemology, Gemological Inst. Am. Cert. gemologist and appraiser. Jeweler, designer Larry Phillips Studios, Albuquerque, 1971-73; jewelry mfr. The Cloud Gatherer, Albuquerque, 1973-78; custom jeweler, gemologist The Jewelry Works, Albuquerque, 1978-82; gemologist, appraiser Butterfield Jewelers, Albuquerque, 1982-90; owner Phillips & Assocs., Albuquerque, 1990—. Musician, entertainer Larry Phillips Studios, Albuquerque, 1971—; entertainment dir. Four Hills Country Club, Albuquerque, 1984-85. Mem. Am. Soc. Appraisers (v.p. N.Mex. chpt. 1987-88, treas. 1990-91, pres. 1991-92, nat. gem. and jewelry com. 1991—, chair internat. gems and jewelry com. 1993-95, profl. devel. com., regional gov. 1995—, internat. issues task force 1996), Internat. Soc. Appraisers (designated, Disting. Svc. award 1990), Nat. Jewelers Assn., N.Mex. Jewelers Assn. (arbitration bd., treas. 1984, bd. dirs. 1989—), Appraisal Found. (personal property stds. task force, jewelers vigilance com., appraisal task force, stds. chair), Accredited Gemologists Assn., Nat. Cert. Master Gemologist Com. (bd. govs. 1995—, chmn. 1992-93), Albuquerque Musicians Co-op (publicity chair 1977-78). Home: 801 Marie Park Dr NE Albuquerque NM 87123-1718

PHILLIPS, PETER MARTIN, sociologist, educator, media researcher; b. Sacramento, Calif., Dec. 9, 1947; s. Donald B. and Jeanne Marie (Perrin) P.; m. E. Susan Phillips,Nov. 19, 1967 (dec. Dec. 1979); 1 child, Jeff. BA, Santa Clara (Calif.) U., 1970; MA, Calif. State U., Sacramento, 1975, U. Calif., Davis, 1992; PhD, U. Calif., Davis, 1994. Prof. sociology Sacramento City Coll., 1975-94; asst. prof. sociology Sonoma State U., Rohnert Park, Calif., 1994—; instr. U. Calif. Davis Extension, 1990—; social welfare cons. various social welfare agys., 1979-94; dir. Project Censored, Rohnert Park, 1996—. Author: Censored 1997: The News That Didn't Make the News, 1997. Mem. Am. Sociol. Assn., Pacific Sociol. Assn. Office: Sonoma State U 1901 E Cotati Ave Rohnert Park CA 94928

PHILLIPS, ROBERT EAST, religious camps administrator; b. Denver, Dec. 25, 1940; s. Richard Ross and Evelyn (East) P.; m. Pamela Joy MacDonald, Nov. 28, 1964; children: Lisa Joy Phillips Ortman,Christy Lynne Phillips Anderson. BA in Christian Edn. and Bible, Biola U., Lamarida, Calif., 1964; MA in Counseling, Calif. State U., Fresno, 1979; PhD in Counseling, Trinity Sem., Newburg, Ind., 1986. Lic. marriage, family and child counselor. Asst. dir. Hume (Calif.) Lake Christian Camps, 1958-74, exec. dir., 1980—; assoc. pastor counseling ministries Northwest Ch., Fresno, Calif., 1974-78; dir. Fresno Counseling Ctr., 1979-80. Author: Anger is a Choice, 1982, The Delicate Art of Dancing with Porcupines, 1989, Encyclopedia of Good Clean Jokes, 1992, Friendship, Love, and Laughter, 1993, Phillips Book of Great Thoughts and Funny Sayings, 1993, What to Do Until the Psychiatrist Comes, 1995. Republican. Baptist. Home: 3224 W Tenaya Ave Fresno CA 93711-1665 Office: Hume Lake Christian Camps 64144 Hume Rd Hume CA 93628

PHILLIPS, ROBERT WARD, advertising executive; b. Spokane, Wash., June 5, 1956; s. Robert Henry and Yvonee E. (Carlsen) P.; m. Terry Lynne McDowell, Jan. 28, 1978; children: Robert Kyle, Kevin William. BA, Wash. State U., 1978. Advt. sales Yakima (Wash.) Herald Republic, 1978-80; acct. exec. Smith, Phillips Advt., Yakima, 1980-94; mktg. dir. Yakima Bait Co., Granger, Wash., 1994—; bd. dirs. Northwest Sportfishing Ind. Assn., Portland. Contbr. over 300 articles to outdoor mags. Pres. bd. dirs. Yakima Valley Visitors & Conv. Bur., 1987; bd. dirs. Salvation Army. Mem. Outdoor Writers Assn. Am., Northwest Outdoor Writers Assn. (Excellence in Craft award 1992, 93, 94, 95), Yakima Advt. Fedn. (pres. 1982-94). Office: Yakima Bait Co PO Box 310 Granger WA 98932

PHILLIPS, ROGER, steel company executive; b. Ottawa, Ont., Can., Dec. 17, 1939; s. Norman William Frederick and Elizabeth (Marshall) P.; m. Katherine Ann Wilson, June 9, 1962; 1 child, Andrée Claire. B.Sc., McGill U., Montreal, 1960. Vice pres. mill products Alcan Can. Products Ltd., Toronto, Ont., Can., 1969-70, exec. v.p., 1971-75; pres. Alcan Smelters and Chems. Ltd., Montreal, Que., Can., 1976-79; v.p. tech. Alcan Aluminium Ltd., Montreal, Que., Can., 1980-81; pres. Alcan Internat. Ltd., Montreal, Que., Can., 1980-81; pres., chief exec. officer IPSCO Inc., Regina, Sask., Can., 1982—; sr. mem. Conf. Bd. Inc., N.Y., 1987—; bd. dirs. Toronto Dominion Bank. Bd. govs. Coun. for Can. Unity, Montreal, 1987—; bd. dirs. Conf. Bd. of Can., 1984-87, Inst. for Polit. Involvement, Toronto, 1982-88. Mem. Can. Assn. Physicists, Bus. Coun. on Nat. Issues, Am. Iron and Steel Inst. (bd. dirs. 1984—), Inst. of Physics U.K. (chartered physicist), Sask. C. of C. (bd. dirs. 1984—), Que. C. of C. (pres. 1981), Pub. Policy Forum (bd. dirs.), Collegium of Work and Learning, Assiniboia Club (Regina), St. Denis Club, Univ. Club (Montreal). Home: 3220 Albert St, Regina, SK Canada S4S 3N9 Office: IPSCO Inc, Armour Rd, Regina, SK Canada S4P 3C7

PHILLIPS, TED RAY, advertising agency executive; b. American Falls, Idaho, Oct. 27, 1948; s. Virn E. and Jessie N. (Aldous) P.; m. Dianne Jacqulynne Walker, May 28, 1971; children: Scott, Russell, Stephen, Michael. BA, Brigham Young U., 1972, MA, 1975. Account exec. David W. Evans, Inc., Salt Lake City, 1972-75; dir. advt. Div. Continuing Edn., U. Utah, Salt Lake City, 1975-78; sr. v.p. Evans/Lowe & Stevens, Inc., Atlanta, 1978, exec. v.p., 1979; pres., CEO David W. Evans/Atlanta, Inc., 1979-80; dir. advt. O.C. Tanner Co., Salt Lake City, 1980-82; pres. Thomas/Phillips/Clawson Advt., Inc., Salt Lake City, 1982-86; pres. Hurst & Phillips, Salt Lake City, 1986-94; CEO, chmn. Phillips Twede & Spencer Advt., Salt Lake City, 1994—; advt. instr. div. continuing edn. Brigham Young U., 1983-85. Dir. publicity, promotion Western States Republican Con., 1976. Recipient Silver Beaver award Boy Scouts Am., 1994, Spurgeon award, 1995. Mem. Am. Advt. Fedn. (8 Best-in-West awards, 2 nat. Addy awards, Clio finalist 1984, Telly award 1991, 92), Utah Advt. Fedn. (bd. dirs. 1976-78, 80-87, pres. 1984-85). Mormon. Home: 1792 Cornwall Ct Sandy UT 84092-5436 Office: Phillips Twede Spencer Advt Inc 428 E 6400 S Salt Lake City UT 84107-7500

PHILLIPS, THOMAS EMBERT, artist; b. Chickasha, Okla., Apr. 7, 1927; s. William Ross and Bess Delia (Clark) P.; m. Marie Ellen McDivitt, Nov. 14, 1948 (div. Sept. 1981); children: Kathryn Marie, Thomas Richard, Stephen Ross, Donald Grayson. Student, Phillips U., 1939, Kansas City Art Inst., 1975. Comml. artist Arnold-Chezem Advt., Oklahoma City, 1948, 49, M and H Advt., Oklahoma City, 1950; illustrator Murray Collens Studio, N.Y.C., 1952-56; art dir. William Barber & Co., Advt., Colorado Springs, 1956-64; staff artist, illustrator Am. Hereford Assn., Kansas City, Mo., 1964-69; artist Am. Hereford Jour., Kansas City, Mo., 1969-72; ptnr. Philan Aural, Visual Enterprises, San Francisco, 1976—; art tchr. Army Spl. Svcs., Sapporo, Japan, 1951; demonstration painting Pikes Peak Art Assn., Colorado Springs, 1960-63, Assn. Fine Artists Greater Kansas City, Mo., 1972-74. Artist, author: (book) The Sketches of Tom Phillips, 1971, (paintings with essays) Dakota Mag., 1989; paintings for Am. Hereford Assn., 1967, 68, Western Horseman Mag., 1961-66, Am. Pork Prodr.'s Coun., 1970, Animal Science Textbook, 1990; cover design for 45th Divison History Book, 1951; painting of The Chase from Dances With Wolves for S.D. Hall of Fame, 1991, painting of Black Bear for ecology stamp, Mexico City, 1996; portraits included in Saddle and Sirloin Club Portrait Gallery, Louisville, 1971, 85, 88; mural included in Acta Lacota Mus., Chamberlain, 1991; represented in permanent collection Marion Eugene Ensminger and Audrey Helen Ensminger Internat. Rm., Iowa State U., Chickasaw Mus., Tishamingo, Okla., 1995-96; sculptor bronze model for Statue of Equality, Chamberlain, 1995; contbr. essays on Native Am. History, Dakota Hist. Conf., Ctr. for Western Studies, Augustana Coll., Sioux Falls, S.D., 1990. Tchr. drawing Liberty (Mo.) Christian Ch. Day Care Ctr., 1973-75, Rocky Mountain Participation Nursery Sch. affiliated with City Coll. San Francisco, 1980—; trustee, CFO The Anstendig Inst., San Francisco, 1978—; voting mem. Chickasaw Nation, Ada, Okla. Sgt. U.S. Army, 1950-52, Korea; cadet midshipman U.S. Merchant Marine Cadet Corps, USNR, 1945. Home and Office: Philan Aural-Visual Enterprises 915 Fulton St San Francisco CA 94117-1701

PHILLIPS, WANDA CHARITY, secondary education educator, writer; b. Gettysburg, Pa., Apr. 1, 1947; d. Roy Homer and Frances Marie (White) Kuykendall; m. James E. Phillips; children: Jenny, Peter, Micah. BS in Secondary Edn., Shippensburg U., 1968; elem. edn. cert., Grand Canyon Coll., 1973; MA in Adminstrn., No. Ariz. U., 1993. Tchr. Littlestown (Pa.) H.S., 1969, Phoenix (Ariz.) Indian Sch., 1971-72, Peoria (Ariz.) Sch. Dist., 1973—; author ISHA Enterprises, Inc., Scottsdale, Ariz., 1985—; ednl. seminar presenter ISHA Enterprises, Scottsdale, 1986—, Assn. Christian Schs. Internat., Calif., 1988—. Author: Easy Grammar, 1986, Daily Grams: Guided Review Aiding Mastery Skills, 1986, Daily Grams: Guided Review Aiding Mastery Skills for Grades 4-5, 1987, Grades 3-4, 1988, Grades 5-6, 1993, Easy Writing, 1991, Daily Grams: Guided Teaching and Review for Grades 2 and 3, 1992, Easy Grammar, Level 1, 1994 (children's book) My Mother Doesn't Like to Cook, 1993, Easy Grammar Plus, 1995, Easy Grammar: Grades 4 and 5, 1996. Active Concerned Women of Am., 1993—. Mem. Nat. Trust for Hist. Preservation, Paradise Valley Women's Club, Internat. Platform Assn., Phi Delta Kappa. Office: ISHA Enterprises Inc PO Box 12520 Scottsdale AZ 85255

PHILLIPS, WILLIAM GRANT, health physicist, nuclear emergency consultant; b. Boulder City, Nev., July 7, 1949; s. William Lewis and Shirley Jean (Bakerink) P.; m. Janice Kaye Lanuti, Dec. 24, 1987. BS in Physics, U. Nev., Las Vegas, 1971, MS in Nuclear Physics, 1973; MS in Radiol. Scis., U. Wash., 1990. Cert. radiation health physicist Am. Bd. Health Physics; diplomate Health Physics Soc. Physicist USPHS, Las Vegas, 1968-76; physicist/pilot U.S. EPA, Las Vegas, 1976-81; corp. pilot West Coast Holdings Inc., Las Vegas, 1981-82; physicist U.S. EPA, Las Vegas, 1982-88, health physicist, 1988-93; pvt. cons. Profl. Analysts Inc./U.S. Dept. Energy, Las Vegas, 1993—; cons., bd. dirs. Sci. and Aviation Cons. Inc., Las Vegas, 1981—; cons. JANAL Corp./Lockheed, Las Vegas, 1989—; corp. officer Brentwood Fin. Group Inc., Las Vegas, 1992-94, BID Investment and Devel. Inc., Las Vegas, 1992-94; internat. lectr. nuc. physics Nev. Tech. Assocs., 1993—. Author: (poem) A Tourist of the Earth, 1978; contbr. articles to physics publs. and other mags. Mem. U.S. Ultralight Assn., Soaring Soc. Am., Am. Nuclear Soc. Home and Office: 4755 N Grand Canyon Dr Las Vegas NV 89129

PHILLIPSON, DONALD E., lawyer; b. Denver, July 22, 1942. BS, Stanford U., 1964, JD, 1968; MS, U. Calif., Berkeley, 1965. Former mem. Davis, Graham & Stubbs, Denver. Mem. Nat. Soccer Hall of Fame (adminstr.). Office: PO Box 185 14325 Braun Rd Golden CO 80401-1431

PHILPOTT, LARRY LA FAYETTE, horn player; b. Alma, Ark., Apr. 5, 1937; s. Lester and Rena (Owens) P.; m. Elise Robichaud, Nov. 24, 1962 (div. June 1975); children: Daniel, Stacy; m. Anne Sokol, Feb. 14, 1984. B.S., Ga. So. Coll., 1962; Mus.M., Butler U., 1972. Instr. in horn Butler U., De Pauw U.; dir. music Cedarcrest Sch., Marysville, Wash., 1991—; instr. horn Western Wash. U., Dept Music, Bellingham, 1995—. Mem., N.C. Symphony, 1960, Savannah (Ga.) Symphony, L'Orchestre Symphonique de Quebec, Que., Can., 1962-64, prin. horn player, Indpls. Symphony Orch., 1964-89, Flagstaff Summer Festival, 1968—; artist in-residence Ind.-Purdue Indpls.; appeared with, Am. Shakespeare Theatre, summer 1965, Charlottetown Festival, summers 1967-68, Flagstaff Summer Festival, 1968-85, Marrowstone Music Festival, 1985—. Served with USN, 1956-60. Mem. Music Educators Nat. Conf., Am. Fedn. Musicians, Internat. Conf. Symphony and Opera Musicians, Internat. Horn Soc., Coll. Music Soc., Phi Mu Alpha Sinfonia. Home: 14925 63rd Ave SE Snohomish WA 98296-5277 Office: Cedarcrest Sch 6400 88th St NE Marysville WA 98270-2800 also: Western Wash U Dept Music Bellingham WA 98225-9107

PHILPOTT, LINDSEY, civil engineer, researcher, educator; b. Bridestowe, Devonshire, Eng., Aug. 2, 1948; came to U.S., 1983; s. George Anthony and Joyce Thirza (Teeling) P.; m. Christine May Pembury, Aug. 20, 1974 (div.); children: David, Elizabeth; m. Kathleen Linda Matson, Feb. 17, 1982 (div.); children: Nicholas, Benjamin; m. Kim Elaine Moore, Nov. 24, 1991. Higher

Nat. Cert. in Civil Engring., Bristol (Eng.) Poly., 1973; BSCE, U. Ariz., 1986, MSCE, 1987. Registered profl. engr., Calif. Area structural engr. Dept. Environment (Property Svcs. Agy.), Bristol, 1971-73; civil engr. Webco Civil Engring., Exeter, Eng., 1973-75; tech. mgr. Devon & Cornwall Housing Assn., Plymouth, Eng., 1975-79; prin., architect S.W. Design, Plymouth, 1979-81; archtl. engr. United Bldg. Factories, Bahrain, 1981-83; jr. engr. Cheyne Owen, Tucson, 1983-87; civil engr. Engring. Sci. Inc., Pasadena, Calif., 1987-89; project engr. Black & Veatch, Santa Ana, Calif., 1989-90; sr. engr. Brown & Caldwell, Irvine, Calif., 1990-91; environ. engr. Met. Water Dist. So. Calif., San Dimas, 1991—; adj. prof. hydraulics and instrumentation, San Antonio Coll., Walnut, Calif., 1995—. Foster parent Foster Parents Plan, Tucson, 1985-87; vol. reader tech. books Recording for the Blind, Hollywood, Calif., 1988-89, South Bay, Calif., 1990-91, Pomona, Calif., 1991—; vol. sailor/tchr. L.A. Maritime Inst. Topsail Youth Program, 1994—. Mem. ASCE, Am. Water Works Assn., Am. Water Resources Assn. (water quality com. 1990—), Water Environment Fedn., Engrs. Soc. (pres. 1985-96), Mensa, South Bay Yacht Racing Club (Marina del Rey, Calif., vice commodore 1995, commodore 1996), Marina Venice Yacht Club (Marina del Rey, fleet capt. 1997). Office: Met Water Dist Environ Compliance Divsn PO Box 54153 Los Angeles CA 90054-0153

PHIPPS, CLAUDE RAYMOND, research scientist; b. Ponca City, Okla., Mar. 15, 1940; s. Claude Raymond Louis and Deva Pauline (DeWitt) P.; m. Lynn Malarney, Dec. 1, 1962 (div. Feb. 1989); 1 child, David Andrew; life ptnr. Shanti E. Bannwart. BS, MIT, 1961, MS, 1963; PhD, Stanford U., 1972. Rsch. staff Lawrence Livermore (Calif.) Nat. Lab., 1972-74; rsch. staff Los Alamos (N.Mex.) Nat. Lab., 1974-95, project leader engine support sys. tech. program, 1993; assoc. dir. Alliance for Photonic Tech., Albuquerque, 1992-95; pres. Photonic Assocs., Santa Fe, 1995—; co-instr. (with Shanti E. Bannwart) "Pairs" Relationship Tng., Santa Fe, N.Mex., 1990—; dir. Santa Fe Investment Conf., 1987; mem. program com. MIT Workshop on High Temperature Superconductors, Cambridge, 1988; mem. Instl. R & D Com., Los Alamos Nat. Lab., 1990-92, project leader laser effects, 1982-87, mem. internat. rsch. tour, Australia, Japan, Scotland, 1988-89; invited discussion leader Gordon Conf. on Laser Particle Interactions, N.H., 1992; invited plenary spkr. Physics of Quantum Electronics meeting, Snowbird, Utah, 1997. Co-author: Laser Ionization Mass Analysis, 1993; author internat. lecture series on laser surface interactions, Berlin, Antwerp, Marseilles, Xiamen, Cape Town, Durban, 1987—; contbr. articles to profl. jours. Lt. USN, 1963-65. Grad. fellow W. Alton Jones Found., N.Y.C., 1962-63. Home and Office: Photonic Assocs 1621 Calle Torreon Santa Fe NM 87501

PHIPPS, DONALD WILLIAM, JR., microbiologist; b. Tacoma Park, Md., Apr. 3, 1955; s. Donald William, Sr. and Marian Teresa (Pugleisi) P.; m. Linda Jo Tarr, Sept. 12, 1987. BS, Univ. Calif., Irvine, 1977; MS, Univ. Nebr., 1982. Staff rsch. assoc. Univ. Calif., San Diego, 1982-85; sr. microbiologist Orange County Water Dist., Fountain Valley, Calif., 1985—. Author Avatar, 1991, Shalidar, 1994; contbr. articles to profl. jours. Office: Orange County Water Dist 10500 Ellis Ave Fountain Valley CA 92708-6921

PI, EDMOND HSIN-TUNG, psychiatry educator; b. China, June 1, 1948. MD, Cath. U. Coll. Medicine, 1972. Cert. Am. Bd. Psychiatry and Neurology. Chief resident U. Ky. Med. Ctr., Lexington, 1977-78; instr. psychiatry U. So. Calif. Sch. Medicine, L.A., 1978-80, asst. prof., 1980-83; assoc. prof. Med. Coll. Pa., Phila., 1983-85; assoc. prof. U. So. Calif. Sch. Medicine, 1985-88, prof. clin. psychiatry, 1988—; asst. dir. psychopharmacology U. So. Calif. Sch. Medicine, 1978-80; asst. dir. adult psychiat. clinic L.A. County and U. So. Calif. Med. Ctr., 1980-83; dir. adult psychiat. clinic Med. Coll. Pa., Phila., 1983-85; dir. Adult Psychiat. Inpatient Svcs., L.A. County and U. So. Calif. Med. Ctr., 1985-91, dir. Adult Psychiat. Outpatient Svcs., 1995—; dir. transcultural psychiatry U. So. Calif. Sch. Medicine, 1991—. Author: Reactions to Psychotropic Medications, 1987, (book chpts.) Transcultural Psychiatry, Clinical Psychopharmacology, 1985—; contbr. articles to profl. jours. Bd. dirs. Chinese Bus. Assn., L.A., 1990-92, Com. of 100, N.Y.C., 1993—, ARC, San Gabriel chpt., Calif., 1994—, Mental Health Assn. L.A. County, 1995—; mem. Calif. Gov.'s Com. Employment of Disabled Persons, Scaremento, 1993—. Vis. scholar Com. on Scholarly Comm. with People's Republic of China U.S. Nat. Acad. Scis., Washington, 1987-88; Treval fellow Am. Coll. Neuropsychopharmacology, 1982. Fellow Am. Psychiat. Assn., Am. Soc. Social Psychiatry, Pacific Rim Coll. Psychiatry (treas. 1991—); mem. Am. Coll. Psychiatrists, Soc. Study Psychiatry and Culture, Pacific Rim Assn. Clin. Pharmogenetics, Assn. Chinese Am. Psychiatrists (pres. 1995—). Office: U So Calif Sch Medicine Dept Psychiatry 1937 Hospital Pl Grad Hall Los Angeles CA 90033

PI, WEN-YI SHIH, aircraft company engineer, researcher; b. Peiping, People's Republic of China, Feb. 28, 1935; came to U.S., 1959; d. Chih-Chuan and Hsiu-Yun (Yang) Shih; m. William Shu-Jong Pi, July 2, 1961; 1 child, Wilfred. BS, Nat. Taiwan U., Taipei, Republic of China, 1956; MS, Stanford U., 1961, PhD, 1963. Research assoc. Stanford (Calif.) U., 1963-64; engring. specialist Northrop-Grumman Corp., Hawthorne, Calif., 1965-83, sr. tech. specialist, 1983—. Contbr. articles to profl. jours. Recipient Silver Achievement award Los Angeles YWCA, 1983; Amelia Earhart Scholar Zonta Internat., 1961-62. Fellow: AIAA (assoc.); mem. Sigma Xi. Office: Northrop Grumman Corp Aircraft Divsn Dept 7B91/63 One Northrop Ave Hawthorne CA 90250-3277

PIAZZA, DUANE EUGENE, biomedical researcher; b. San Jose, Calif., June 5, 1954; s. Salvador Richard and Mary Bernice (Mirassou) P.; m. Sandra Patrignani, Sept. 19, 1992. BS in Biology, U. San Francisco, 1976; MA in Biology, San Francisco State U., 1986. Staff rsch. assoc. I U. Calif., San Francisco, 1975-81; sr. rsch. technician XOMA Corp., San Francisco, 1981-82; biologist II Syntex USA Inc., Palo Alto, Calif., 1982-85; pres., cons. Ryte For You, Oakland, Calif., 1985—; rsch. assoc. I Cetus Corp., Emeryville, Calif., 1986-90; rsch. assoc. II John Muir Cancer and Aging Rsch. Inst., Walnut Creek, Calif., 1991-92; rsch. assoc. Pharmagenesis, Palo Alto, Calif., 1993—. CPR & first aid instr. ARC, 1980-92, vol. 1st aid sta. instr., Santa Cruz, 1985-86, vol. 1st aid sta. disaster action team, Oakland, 1986—, br. chmn. disaster action team, 1987-88; treas. Reganti Homeowner Assn., 1990-92. Mem. AAAS, Am. Soc. Microbiology, N.Y. Acad. Scis., Astron. Soc. Pacific, Planetary Soc., Mt. Diablo Astronomy Soc. Republican. Roman Catholic. Home: 1055 Rebecca Dr Boulder Creek CA 95006-9442

PIAZZA, MICHAEL JOSEPH, professional baseball player; b. Norristown, Pa., Sept. 4, 1968. Student, Miami (Fla.)-Dade C.C. Player L.A. Dodgers, 1988—; mem. Nat. League All-Star Team, 1993-96. Named Nat. League Rookie Player of Yr., Sporting News, 1993, Catcher on the Sporting News N.L. All-Star Team, 1993-96, N.L. Silver Slugger Team, 1993-94, named to Nat. League Slugger Team, 1993; named Nat. League Rookie of Yr., Baseball Writers Assn., 1993. Office: LA Dodgers Dodger Stadium 100 Elysian Park Ave Los Angeles CA 90012

PICCOLO, RICHARD ANDREW, artist, educator; b. Hartford, Conn., Sept. 17, 1943; S. John D. and Lenore (Pasqual) P. BID, Pratt Inst., 1966; MFA, Bklyn. Coll., 1968. Instr. Pratt Inst., Bklyn., 1966-68, Rome, 1969—; dir. Pratt Inst., 1980—; instr. U. Notre Dame Rome Program, 1984—. Artist: solo exhibitions include: Robert Schoelkopf Gallery, N.Y.C., 1975, 79, 83, 89, Suffolk C.C., Long Island, N.Y., 1976, Am. Acad. in Rome, 1977, Galleria Temple, Rome 1979, Galleria Il Gabbiano, Rome. 1985, Contemporary Realist Gallery, San Francisco, 1989, 95; exhibited in group shows Six Americans in Italy, 1973, Metaphor in Painting, Fed. Hall Meml., N.Y., 1978, Realism and Metaphor, U. S. Fla. (traveling), 1980, Contemporary Figure Drawings, Robert Schoelkopf Gallery, 1981, Contemporary Arcadian Painting, 1982, Moravian Coll. Invitational, Bethlehem, Pa., 1981, Art on Paper , Weatherspoon Gallery of Art, N.C., 1981, Out of N.Y., Hamilton Coll., Clinton, N.Y., 1981, Galleria Gabbiano, Rome, FIAC, Paris, 1982, Contemporary Arts Mus., Houston, 1984, Umbria: Americans Painting in Italy, Gallery North, Setauket, N.Y., 1985, Storytellers, Contemporary Realist Gallery, San Francisco, Painted from Life, Bayly Mus., Charlottesville, Va., 1987; work in permanent collections Crown Am. Corp., Johnstown, Pa., Grosvenor Internat., Sacramento, Calif., Mrs. Lillian Cole, Sherman Oaks, Calif., Mr and Mrs. Robert Emery, San Francisco, Mr. Graham Gund, Boston, Dr. Robert Gutterman, San Francisco, Mr and Mrs. Joseph Jennings, San Francisco, Dr. and Mrs. Donald Innes, Jr., Charlottesville, Va., Mr. and Mrs. Alan Ovson, San Francisco, Mr. Frank Pasquerilla, Johnstown, Pa., Mr. Jon Roberts and Mr. John Boccardo, L.A. Recipient E. A. Abbey Meml. scholarship for mural painting, 1973-75; grantee NEA, 1989; mural commn. Simplicity Inspiring Invention: An Allegory of the Arts, Crown Am. Corp., Johnstown, Pa., 1989, Aer, Ignis, Terra, Aqua, U.S. Bank Plaz., Sacramento, Calif., 1991-94. Home: Piazza S Apollonia 3, Rome 00153, Italy Office: Hacket-Freedman Gallery 250 Sutter St Fl 4 San Francisco CA 94108-4403

PICK, JAMES BLOCK, management and sociology educator; b. Chgo., July 29, 1943; s. Grant Julius and Helen (Block) P. BA, Northwestern U., 1966; MS in Edn., No. Ill. U., 1969; PhD, U. Calif., Irvine, 1974. Cert. computer profl. Asst. rsch. statistician, lectr. Grad. Sch. Mgmt. U. Calif., Riverside, 1975-91, dir. computing, 1984-91; co-dir. U.S.-Mex. Database Project, 1988-91; assoc. prof. mgmt. and bus., dir. info. mgmt. program U. Redlands, Calif., 1991-95, prof. mgmt. and bus., chair dept. mgmt. and bus., 1995-97; cons. U.S. Census Bur. Internat. Div., 1978; mem. Univ. Commons Bd., 1982-86; mem. bd. govs. PCCLAS, Assn. Borderlands Studies, 1989-92. Trustee Newport Harbor Art Mus., 1981-87, 88-96, chmn. permanent collection com., 1987-91, v.p., 1991-96; trustee Orange County Mus. Art, 1996—, chmn. collection com., 1996—. Recipient Thunderbird award Bus. Assn. Latin Am. Studies, 1993. Mem. AAAS, Assn. Computing Machinery, Assn. Systems Mgmt. (pres. Orange County chpt. 1978-79), Am. Statis. Assn., Population Assn. Am., Internat. Union for Sci. Study of Population, Soc. Info. Mgmt. Club, Standard (Chgo.). Author: Geothermal Energy Development, 1982, Computer Systems in Business, 1986, Atlas of Mexico, 1989, The Mexico Handbook, 1994, Mexico Megacity, 1997; condr. research in info. systems, population, environ. studies; contbr. sci. articles to publs. in fields.

PICKARD, DEAN, philosophy and humanities educator; b. Geneva, N.Y., Mar. 12, 1947; s. William Otis and Frances (Dean) P.; children: Justin Matthew, Christopher Dean. BA cum laude, U. Calif., Riverside, 1973; MA, Calif. State U., Long Beach, 1976-77; PhD, Claremont (Calif.) Grad. Sch., 1992. Instr. phys. edn. Pomona Coll., Claremont, 1975-82; instr. philosophy, humanities, and phys. edn. Moorpark (Calif.) Coll., 1978-82; assoc. prof. philosophy, humanities, and phys. edn. Mission Coll., Sylmar, Calif., 1979-83; instr. philosophy Calif. State U., Northridge, 1988-94; prof. philosophy and humanities Pierce Coll., Woodland Hills, Calif., 1983—. Author: Nietzsche, Transformation and Postmodernism; contbr. articles to profl. jours. Marious De Brabent & Henry Carter scholar, 1973; fellow Claremont Grad. Sch., 1988-89; grantee NEH, 1995. Mem. Am. Philos. Assn., Am. Fedn. Tchrs., N.Am. Nietzsche Soc., L.A. Area Nietzsche Soc. (bd. dirs. 1994-97), Phi Beta Kappa. Office: Pierce Coll 6201 Winnetka Ave Woodland Hills CA 91371-0001

PICKENS, ALEXANDER LEGRAND, education educator; b. Waco, Tex., Aug. 31, 1921; s. Alex LeGrand and Elma L. (Johnson) P.; m. Frances M. Jenkins, Aug. 20, 1955. B.A., So. Methodist U., 1950; M.A., North Tex. State U., Denton, 1952; Ed.D., Columbia U., 1959. Tchr. art public schs. Dallas, 1950-53, Elizabeth, N.J., 1953-54; instr. Coll. Architecture and Design U. Mich., 1954-59; assoc. prof. dept. art U. Ga., Athens, 1959-62; assoc. prof. Coll. Edn. U. Hawaii, Honolulu, 1962-68, prof. edn., 1968—; U. Hawaii; chmn. doctoral studies curriculum instrn. Coll. Edn. U. Hawaii, Honolulu, 1984-89, asst. to dean for coll. devel., 1989—; dir. children's classes Ft. Worth Children's Mus., 1951-53; head art Nat. Music Camp, Interlochen, Mich., summers, 1957-58, U. Oreg., Portland, summers 1959-60, 62; cons. youth art activities Foremost Dairies, 1964-74; cons. art films United World Films, 1970-75; art edn. cons. Honolulu Paper Co., 1970-76, Kamehameha Sch., Bishop Estate, 1978-95. Exhibited ceramics, Wichita Internat. Exhbn., Syracuse (N.Y.) Nat. Exhbn., St. Louis Mus., Dallas Mus., San Antonio Mus., Detroit Art Inst., Hawaii Craftsmen, also others; editorial bd.: Arts and Activities mag, 1955-82; editor: U. Hawaii Ednl. Perspectives, 1964—; contbr. articles to profl. jours. Memm. adult com. Dallas County chpt. Jr. ARC, 1951-53; exec. com. Dallas Crafts Guild, 1950-53; v.p., publicity chmn. U. Ga. Community Concert Assn., 1960-62, mem., program chmn. Gov.'s Commn. Observing 150 Yrs. Pub. Edn. in Hawaii, 1990-91. Served with USAAF. Recipient award merit, Tex. State Fair, 1957, All-Am. award, Ednl. Press Assn. Am., 1968, 70, 72, 75, 79, Regents' medal for excellence in teaching, U. Hawaii, 1989, Gov.'s Commn. Observance of 150 Yrs. Pub. Edn., 1990-91. Mem. AAUP, NEA, Internat. Soc. Edn., Nat. Art Edn. Assn., Coun. for Advancement and Support of Edn., Nat. Soc. Fundraising Execs., Hawaii Planned Giving Coun., Phi Delta Kappa, Kappa Delta Pi. Address: 1471 Kalaepohaku St Honolulu HI 96816-1804

PICKERING, AVAJANE, specialized education facility executive; b. New Castle, Ind., Nov. 5, 1951; d. George Willard and Elsie Jean (Wicker) P. BA, Purdue U., 1974; MS in Spl. Edn., U. Utah, 1983, PhD, 1991. Cert. spl. edn. Co-dir. presch. for gifted students, 1970-74; tchr. Granite Community Edn., Salt Lake City, 1974-79; tchr. coordinator Salt Lake City Schs., 1975-85; adminstrv. dir., owner Specialized Ednl. Programming Svc., Inc., Salt Lake City, 1976—; mem. Utah Profl. Adv. Bd.; adj. instr. U. Utah, Salt Lake City, 1985—; instr. Brigham Young U., 1993—. Rep. del. Utah State Conv., also county conv.; vol. tour guide, hostess Temple Square, Ch. Jesus Christ of Latter-Day Saints, 1983-88. Mem. Coun. for Exceptional Children, Coun. for Learning Disabilities, Learning Disability Assn., Ednl. Therapy Assn. Profl., Learning Disabilities Assn. Utah (profl. adv. bd.), Attention Deficit Coalition Utah (treas.), Hadassah, Delta Kappa Gamma, Phi Kappa Phi. Home: 1595 S 2100 E Salt Lake City UT 84108-2750 Office: Specialized Ednl Programming Svcs 1760 S 1100 E Salt Lake City UT 84105-3430

PICKETT, ANNA MARGARET, newspaper editor; b. Anchorage, Apr. 27, 1962; d. Peter and Beatrice Carol (Havercamp) P.; m. Carl D. Willis, Apr. 16, 1983 (div. 1986). Grad., Dimond H.S., Anchorage, 1980. Advt. salesperson, office mgr., prod./circulation mgr. Tundra Times, Anchorage, 1979-84; exec. editor Tundra Times, 1992-96; adminstrv. asst. Klukwan Forest Products, Anchorage, 1986-89; occupancy specialist Aleutian Housing Auth., Anchorage, 1989-90; editor Tanana Chiefs Conf., The Council, 1996—. Mem. Native Alaskan Profl. and Bus. Soc., Advt. Fedn., Women of the Moose. Home: PO Box 82354 Fairbanks AK 99708-2354

PICKETT, DONN PHILIP, lawyer; b. Chgo., May 3, 1952; s. Philip Gordon and Gloria Joan (Hansen) P.; m. Janet Benson, Aug. 25, 1973; children: Jessica Kelly, William Benson. BA, Carleton Coll., Minn., 1973; JD, Yale U., 1976. Bar: Calif. 1976, U.S. Dist. Ct. (no. dist.) Calif. 1976, (ctrl. dist.) Calif. 1980, (ea. dist.) Calif. 1983, U.S. Ct. Appeals (9th cir.) Calif. 1979, U.S. Ct. Appeals (5th cir.) Tex. 1994, U.S. Supreme Ct. 1991, Ariz. 1997, Colo. 1997. Assoc. McCutchen, Doyle, Brown & Enersen, San Francisco, 1976-83, ptnr., 1983—; mem. U.S. Dist. Ct. Civil Justice Reform Act adv. group, 1995—). Mem. State Bar Calif. (mem. com. on adminstrn. of justice 1988-91, vice chmn. 1992-93, chmn. 1993-94, legis. chmn. 1994-96), San Francisco Bar Assn. (mem. judiciary com. 1988-92, mem. exec. com. conf. of dels. 1993-96, bd. dirs. 1997—), Phi Beta Kappa. Home: 25 Meadow Hill Dr Tiburon CA 94920-1638 Office: McCutchen Doyle Brown & Enersen Three Embarcadero Ctr San Francisco CA 94111

PICKETT, HAL GENE, prosthodontist; b. Oakley, Idaho, Apr. 14, 1926; s. Eugene and Emma Adelaide (Mabey) P.; m. Patty Ann Monson, Jan. 18, 1957 (div. June 1981); children: Rex, Eric, Clarke, Sharon, Lynda. BS in Zoology, U. Idaho, 1950, MS in Zoology, 1952; DMD, U. Oreg., 1956; MS in Prosthodontics, U. Iowa, 1967. Pvt. practice Boise, Idaho, 1956-63, 67—. Capt. U.S. Army, 1944-46. Mem. ADA, Internat. Coll. Dentists, Rotary. Republican. Mem. LDS Ch. Home: 3204 Kootenai Boise ID 83705 Office: 909 Warren St Boise ID 83706-3825

PICKETT, MICHAEL D., computer hardware and software distributor; b. 1947. BSBA, U. So. Calif. With Deloitte Haskins & Sells, 1969-83; v.p. fin., chief fin. officer Merisel Internat. (formerly Softsel Computer Products), 1983-86, pres., chief oper. officer, 1986-88, now vice chmn., CEO. Office: Merisel Internat 200 Continental Blvd El Segundo CA 90245-4526*

PICKETT-TRUDELL, CATHERINE, family therapist; b. Winslow, Ariz., May 30, 1953; d. Jack Roderick and Mary McLaws (Turley) Pickett; children: Rachael Kristy Grogan, Ericka Edan Grogan. BA in Mgmt. of Human Resources, George Fox Coll., Newberg, Oreg., 1992; MA in Counseling Psychology, Western Evang. Sem., Tigard, Oreg., 1996. Tchr./trainer Children's World Learning Ctr., Beaverton, Oreg., 1989-96; family therapist in pvt. practice Portland, Oreg., 1994—; outpatient therapist Lake Powell Inst., Behavioral Health Svcs., Fredonia, Ariz., 1996—; cons. Dept. Health and Human Svcs., 1996—. Democrat. Roman Catholic. Home: 623 W Chamberlaine Kanab UT 84741 Office: 670 NW Saltzman Rd Apt 69 Portland OR 97229-6079

PICKLE, JOSEPH WESLEY, JR., religion educator; b. Denver, Apr. 8, 1935; s. Joseph Wesley and Wilhelmina (Blacketor) P.; m. Judith Ann Siebert, June 28, 1958; children: David E., Kathryn E., Steven J. BA, Carleton Coll., 1957; B.D., Chgo. Theol. Sem., 1961; MA, U. Chgo., 1962, PhD, 1969. Ordained to ministry Am. Bapt. Conv., 1962. Asst. pastor Judson Meml. Ch., N.Y.C., 1959-60; acting dean summer session Colo. Coll., Colorado Springs, 1969-70, from asst. prof. to prof. religion, 1964—, faculty dir. internat. studies, 1994—; vis. prof. theology Iliff Sch. Theology, Denver, 1984; vis. prof. religious studies U. Zimbabwe, Harare, 1989; cons. Colo. Humanities Program, Denver, 1975-89; coord. Sheffer Meml. Fund, Colo. Coll., Colorado Springs, 1983—. Co-editor Papers of the 19th Century Theology Group, 1978, 88, 93. Pres. bd. dirs. Pikes Peak Mental Health Ctr., Colorado Springs, 1975; chmn. Colo. Health Facilities Rev. Coun., Denver, 1979-84; mem. Colo. Health Facilities Rev. Coun., Denver, 1976-84, Colo. Bd. Health, Denver, 1986-91; bd. dirs. Marson Found., Colorado Springs, 1994—. Am. Bapt. Conv. scholar, 1953-59; Fulbright Hays Grad. fellow U. Tübingen, Fed. Republic Germany, 1963-64, Danforth fellow, 1957-63, Joseph Malone fellow, 1987. Fellow Soc. for Values in Higher Edn.; mem. Am. Theol. Soc. (pres. 1996-97), Am. Acad. Religion (regional pres. 1983-84, 92-93), Cath. Theol. Soc. Am., Fulbright Assn., Phi Beta Kappa. Democrat. Home: 20 W Caramillo St Colorado Springs CO 80907-7314 Office: Colo Coll 14 E Cache La Poudre St Colorado Springs CO 80903-3243

PICKMAN, PHILLIP, management consultant; b. Mpls., May 6, 1938; s. Sam and Rose G. (Chiat) P.; m. 1962; children: Michael, Kara, Todd. BS, U. Minn., 1960, MSME, 1962. Supr. oper. systems Bell Telephone Labs., Whippany, N.J., 1962-68; mgr. systems planning Dayton Hudson Corp., Mpls., 1968-73; dir. info. svcs. Red Owl Stores, Inc., Mpls., 1973-74; dir. systems and mgmt. info Cook United, Cleve., 1974-77; regional v.p. May Dept. Stores, L.A., 1977-79; sr. assoc., exec. recruiter Westlake Group, Westlake Village, Calif., 1980-81; pres. and founder Info. Resources Group, Westlake Village, Calif., 1981-87; dir. product mgmt. Cap Gemini Am., Canoga Park, Calif., 1987-93; account mgr. mgmt. devel. consulting and tng. Leadership Mgmt. Assocs. Calif., Agoura Hills, 1994-96; mgmt. cons. in info. systems project mgmt./systems devel., 1996—. Treas. Foxmoor Hills Homeowners Assn., Westlake Village, 1989-91, pres., 1991-92, 92-93; treas. Morris County (N.J.) Dem. County Com., 1965-68; vice chmn. Parsippany-Troy Hills (N.J.) Planning Bd., 1967-68; mem. adv. bd. B'nai Brith Hillel Found., U. Minn., 1972-73. Mem. Tau Beta Pi, Pi Tau Sigma. Jewish. Home and Office: 1815 Stonesgate St Westlake Village CA 91361-1612

PICRAUX, SAMUEL THOMAS, physics researcher; b. St. Charles, Mo., Mar. 3, 1943; s. Samuel F. and Jeannette D.; m. Danice R. Kent, July 12, 1970; children: Jeanine, Laura, Daryl. BS in Elec. Engring., U. Mo., 1965; postgrad. Cambridge U., Eng., 1965-66; MS in Engring. Sci., Calif. Inst. Tech., 1967, PhD in Engring. Scis. and Physics, 1969. Mem. tech. staff Sandia Nat. Labs., Albuquerque, 1969-72, div. supr., 1972-86, dept. mgr., 1986-96, dir., 1996—; mem. solid state scis. com. NRC; vis. scientist dept. physics Aarhus U., Denmark, 1975; NATO lectr., 1979, 81, 83, 86.; NSF lectr. 1976, 81. Author: Materials Analysis by Ion Channeling, 1982; editor: Applications of Ion Beams to Metals, 1974, Metastable Materials Formation by Ion Implantation, 1982, Nuclear Instruments and Methods International jour., 1983-91, Surface Alloying by Ion Electon and Laser Beams, 1986, Beam-Solid Interactions and Transient Processes, 1987; contbr. numerous articles to profl. jours. Fulbright fellow, 1965-66. Recipient Ernest Orlando Lawrence Meml. award, U.S. Dept. Energy, 1990, 3 Basic Energy Scis. Outstanding Rsch. awards, U.S. Dept. Energy. 1985, 92, 94. Fellow Am. Phys. Soc. (chmn. materials physics divsn., 1990); mem. IEEE, Am. Vacuum Soc., Materials Rsch. Soc. (pres. 1993). Office: Sandia Nat Labs POB 5800 Albuquerque NM 87185-1427

PIELSTICK, CLAYTON DEAN, academic administrator; b. McMinnville, Oreg., Apr. 4, 1947; m. Carol J. Pielstick; children: Benjamin, Jana, Molly. BS, Oreg. State U., 1970, MBA, 1987, EdD, 1996. Rsch. instr. Oreg. State Sys. Higher Edn., Monmouth, 1972; sr. planning analyst State of Oreg., Salem, 1973-75; contr. White Oaks, Salem, 1979-86; instr. Western Oreg. State Coll., Monmouth, 1986-89; bus. office mgr. Chemeketa C.C., Salem, 1989-91, registrar, 1991-95; exec. dean Yavapai Coll., Prescott, Ariz., 1995—; cons. in field, 1987-95. Contbr. articles, revs. to profl. publs. Fundraiser Big Bros./Big Sisters, Prescott, Ariz., 1996—; pres. bd. dirs. Salem Art Assn., 1983-91; mem. Leadership Salem, Salem C. of C., 1985-87. Recipient Toastmaster of Yr. award Toastmasters Club, 1984, Outstanding Mem. award Inst. Mgmt. Accts., 1994, Horizon award Phi Theta Kappa, 1994. Mem. Am. Assn. C.C.s, Nat. Assn. Coll. and Univ. Bus. Officers, Western Assn. Coll. and Univ. Bus. Officers, Rotary (chair com. 1995—), Phi Kappa Phi. Office: Yavapai Coll 1100 E Sheldon Prescott AZ 86301

PIEPER, DAROLD D., lawyer; b. Vallejo, Calif., Dec. 30, 1944; s. Walter A. H. and Vera Mae (Ellis) P.; m. Barbara Gillis, Dec. 20, 1969; 1 child, Christopher Radcliffe. AB, UCLA, 1967; JD, USC, 1970. Bar: Calif. 1971. Ops. rsch. analyst Naval Weapons Ctr., China Lake, Calif., 1966-69; assoc. Richards, Watson & Gershon, L.A., 1970-76, ptnr., 1976—; spl. counsel L.A. County Transp. Commn., 1984-93, L.A. County Met. Transp. Authority, 1993-94; commr. L.A. County Delinquency and Crime Commn., 1983-94, pres., 1987-94; chmn. L.A. County Delinquency Prevention Planning Com., 1987-90. Contbr. articles to profl. jours. Peace officer Pasadena (Calif.) Police Res. Unit, 1972-87, dep. comdr., 1979-81, comdr., 1982-84; chmn. pub. safety commn. City of La Canada Flintridge, Calif., 1977-82, commr. 1977-88; bd. dirs. La Canada Flintridge Coordinating Council, 1975-82, pres. 1977-78; exec. dir. Cityhood Action Com., 1975-76; active Calif. Rep. Party, Appellate Circle of Legion Lex U. So. Calif.; chmn. Youth Opportunities United, Inc., 1990-96, vice-chmn. 1988-89, bd. dirs. 1988-96; mem. L.A. County Justice Systems Adv. Group, 1987-92; trustee Lanterman Hist. Mus. Found., 1989-94, Calif. City Mgmt. Found., 1992—. Recipient commendation for Community Service, L.A. County Bd. Suprs., 1978, Commendation for Svc. to Youth, 1996. Mem. La Canada Flintridge C. of C. and Cmty. Assn. (pres. 1981, bd. dirs. 1976-83), Navy League U.S., Pacific Legal Found., Peace Officers Assn., L.A. County, UCLA Alumni Assn. (life), U. So. Calif. Alumni Assn. (life), L.A. County Bar Assn., Calif. Bar Assn., ABA, U. So. Calif. Law Alumni Assn. Office: Richards Watson & Gershon 333 S Hope St Fl 38 Los Angeles CA 90071-1406

PIERCE, DEBORAH MARY, educational administrator; b. Charleston, W. Va.; d. Edward Ernest and Elizabeth Anne (Trent) P.; m. Henry M. Armetta, Sept. 1, 1967 (div. 1981); children: Rosse Matthew Armetta, Stacey Elizabeth Pierce. Student, U. Tenn., 1956-59, Broward Jr. Coll., 1968-69; BA, San Francisco State U., 1977. Cert. elem. tchr., Calif. Pub. relations assoc. San Francisco Internat. Film Festival, 1965-66; account exec. Stover & Assocs., San Francisco, 1966-67; tchr. San Francisco Archdiocese Office of Cath. Schs., 1980-87; part-time tchr. The Calif. Study, Inc. (formerly Tchr's. Registry), Tiburon, Calif., 1988—; pvt. practice as paralegal San Francisco, 1989—; tchr. Jefferson Sch. Dist., Daly City, Calif., 1989-91. Author: (with Frances Spatz Leighton) I Prayed Myself Slim, 1960. Pres. Mothers Alone Working, San Francisco, 1966, PTA, San Francisco, 1979, Parent Tchr. Student Assn., San Francisco, 1984; apptd. Calif. State Bd. Welfare Cmty. Rels. Com., 1964-66; block organizer SAFE, 1996; active feminist movement. Named Model of the Yr. Modeling Assn. Am., 1962. Mem. People Med. Soc., Assn. for Rsch. and Enlightenment, A Course in Miracles, Commonwealth Club Calif, Angel Club San Francisco. Democrat. Mem. Unity Christ Ch. Home: 1479 48th Ave Apt 2 San Francisco CA 94122-2832 *Personal philosophy: We are living in the most exciting time on the planet. As rapidly as we have come to terms with world peace, we must realize we are all one and achieve the same peace one-to-one.*

PIERCE, DIANE JEAN, artist; b. Evanston, Ill., Apr. 9, 1952; d. Kenneth William and Marjorie J. (Hansen) P.; m. William Carry Reuling, Sept. 8, 1991 (div. July 1992). BFA in Drawing and Painting, U. Utah, 1976. Illustrator Ensign Mag., Salt Lake City, 1977-79, Scott Foresman & Co. Pubs., Glenview, Ill., 1980, Children's Press, Chgo., 1981-82; mansion artist Adnan-

Khoshagi's Devereaux Mansion, Salt Lake City, 1984-87; illustrator Friend Mag./Era Mag., Salt Lake City, 1978-80; artist-painter Lido Gallery, Park City, Utah, 1990-93, Thomas Charles Gallery, Las Vegas, Nev., 1994, Art Dimensions Gallery, Hollywood, Calif., 1994-96, Meyer Gallery, Park City, Utah, 1996—; apprentice photographer Reynel Salgado Mirando, 1980 Elections, Acapulco, Mexico, 1980; juror exhbn. com. Alliance Gallery, Salt Lake Art Ctr., 1984, 85. Exhibited in group shows New Genre, 1985, 5 Star Auction Invitational, 1985, Springville Nat. Salon, 1985, Utah Women Artists, 1985, Chase Mansion Guthrie Artists Show, 1986, Guthrie Artists, 1986, NAD, 1986, 95, Eccles Art Ctr., 1986, 87, Women's Show, 1987, 89, 91, 93, Park City Open Painting Competition, 1989-90, 93, Mus. Art, Alliance Gallery, Eccles Art Ctr., Chase Mansion, Salt Lake Art Ctr., Tivoli Gallery, Cliff Lodge Gallery, U. Utah Mus. Art, Devereaux Mansion, 1984-87, Utah divsn. Assn. Women Artists traveling show, 1989, 90, 100 Yrs.-100 Women traveling show, N.Y.C., 1989-91, Springville Mus. Art, 1992, Nat. Assn. Women ann. nat. competition, 1993, Janet Dumbar Interiors, Sun Valley, Idaho, 1991-93, Lido Gallery, 1990-93, Thomas Charles Gallery, 1994, Art Dimensions Gallery, 1994-96, Springville Mus. Art nat. competition, Art Space, 1995, Gallery Stroll, 1995, Nat. Assn. Women Artists ann., Soho, N.Y., 1995, Nat. Assn. Women Artists, Athens, Greece, 1996; represented in permanent collections Girl Scouts Hdqs., Salt Lake City, Profl. Figure Skaters Hdqs., Sun Valley, Springville Mus. Art, also pvt. collections; contbr. articles to profl. jours. Recipient Art Dirs. award Era Mag., 1979, Dirs. award U. Utah Statewide Women's Competition, Springville Mus. Fine Art, 1987, 1st pl. Best of Show, Eccles Statewide Competition, Ogden, Utah, 1987, Best Traditional Painting Nat. Assn. U. Women, Utah divsn., Ogden, 1989, Best of Show, Open Painting Exhbn., Kimball Art Ctr., Park City, Utah, 1989, 3rd pl. open painting competition Kimball Art Ctr., 1990, award Artists Fellowship Inc., N.Y.C., 1993, Best of Show open painting exhbn. Kimball Art Ctr., Park City, 1993, award of merit Springville Mus. Fine Art, 1995, grant Artists Fellowship, Inc., N.Y.C., 1993. Mem. Nat. Assn. Women Artists (Susan Kahn award 1987), Nat. Mus. Women in Arts, Salt Lake Art Ctr. Office: Meyer Gallery Park City UT 84060

PIERCE, GEORGE ADAMS, university administrator, educator; b. Carlsbad, N.Mex., May 21, 1943; s. Jack Colwell and Shirley (Adams) P.; m. Margaret Mary Brakel, Feb. 10, 1980; children: Christopher, Catherine Rose. BA in Polit. Sci., Fairleigh Dickinson U., 1969; MA in Polit. Sci., New Sch. Social Rsch., 1971; PhD in Higher Edn., Claremont Grad. Sch., 1976. Asst. dir. promotion Afco, N.Y.C., 1969-71; dir. spl. programs U. Calif., Riverside, 1971-73; asst. to pres. Claremont (Calif.) Grad. Sch., 1973-75; asst. to pres. Seattle U., 1975-78, dir. planning, 1978-83, v.p. adminstrn., 1983-87, v.p. planning, 1987-89; v.p. bus. and fin. affairs Western Wash. U., Bellingham, 1989—; chmn. regional rev. panel Truman Scholarship Found., 1977-90. Chmn. Seattle Ctr. Adv. Commn., 1977-83; bd. dirs. N.W. Kidney Found., Seattle, 1986—, YMCA, Bellingham, 1990—; chmn. pack 41 Boy Scouts Am., Bellingham, 1992-94, chmn. troop 7, 1995—. With USAF, 1963-65. Recipient Cert. Merit Riverside County Comprehensive Health Planning, 1972, Cert. Appreciation Office Mayor City of Seattle, 1983, Nat. Truman Scholarship Found., 1986. Mem. Am. Assn. Higher Edn., Assn. Instnl. Rsch. (regional pres. 1977), Nat. Assn. Coll. and Univ. Bus. Officers (chmn. pers. and benefits com. 1992-94), Rotary. Democrat. Roman Catholic. Home: 421 Morey Ave Bellingham WA 98225-6344 Office: Western Wash U Old Main 300 Bellingham WA 98225

PIERCE, HILDA (HILDA HERTA HARMEL), painter; b. Vienna, Austria; came to U.S., 1940; 1 child, Diana Rubin Daly. Student, Art Inst. of Chgo.; studied with Oskar Kokoschka, Salzburg, Austria. Art tchr. Highland Park (Ill.) Art Ctr., Sandburg Village Art Workshop, Chgo., Old Town Art Center, Chgo.; owner, operator Hilda Pierce Art Gallery, Laguna Beach, Calif., 1981-85; guest lectr. major art mus. and Art Tours in France, Switzerland, Austria, Italy; guest lectr. Russian river cruise and major art mus. St. Petersburg and Moscow, 1994. One-woman shows include Fairweather Hardin Gallery, Chgo., Sherman Art Gallery, Chgo., Marshall Field Gallery, Chgo.; exhibited in group shows at Old Orchard Art Festival, Skokie, Ill., Union League Club (awards), North Shore Art League (awards), ARS Gallery of Art Inst. of Chgo.; represented in numerous private and corporate collections; commissioned for all art work including monoprints, oils, and murals for Carnival Cruise Lines megaliner M.S. Fantasy, 1990, 17 murals for megaliner M.S. Imagination, 1995, 49 paintings for megaliner M.S. Imagination, 1995; contbr. articles to Chgo. Tribune Mag., American Artist Mag., Southwest Art Mag., SRA publs., others; featured in video Survivors of the Shoah (Holocaust) visual History Foundation, 1996. Recipient Outstanding Achievement award in Field of Art for Citizen Foreign Birth Chgo. Immigrant's Svc. League. Mem. Arts Club of Chgo. Studio: PO Box 7390 Laguna Niguel CA 92607-7390 *An artist's most precious quality is curiosity. It has kept me young for many years, kept me searching, experimenting and never being complacent, in my life and my work.*

PIERCE, LESTER LAURIN, aviation consultant; b. Merlin, Oreg., Sept. 26, 1907; s. Frank Arthur and Charlotte (Allen) P.; m. Helen Ramona Thomas, Mar. 22, 1937; children: Adrienne C. Freeman, Nancy E. Johnson. Grad. high sch., 1925. Theatre mgr. Redwood Theatres, Inc., Fortuna and Eureka, Calif., 1927-28; salesman, bookkeeper Thomas Furniture House, Eureka, 1930-39; pilot, mgr. Pierce Bros. Flying Svc., Eureka, 1934-41; aerial photographer Pierce Flying Svc., Eureka, 1934-75; chief flight instr. Govt. Approved Flight Sch., Eureka, 1947-60; aerial seeder, mgr., pres., salesman Pierce Flying Svc., Inc., Eureka, 1946-68; flight examiner FAA, Eureka, 1948-68, aircraft maintenance insp., 1950-68; mapping pilot Stand Aerial Surveys, Newark, 1938. Lt., flight tng., safety officer USNR, 1942, comdr., 1950. Mem. Soc. Aircraft Safety Investigators Aviation Cons., Elks. Home and Office: 3428 Jacoby Creek Rd Bayside CA 95524-9304

PIERCY, GORDON CLAYTON, bank executive; b. Takoma Park, Md., Nov. 23, 1944; s. Gordon Clayton and Dorothy Florence (Brummer) P.; m. Roberta Margaret Walton, 1985; children: Elizabeth Anne, Kenneth Charles, Virginia Walton, Zachary Taylor Walton. BS, Syracuse U., 1966; MBA, Pace U., 1973. Mgmt. trainee Suburban Bank, Bethesda, Md., 1962-66; mktg. planning assoc. Chem. Bank, N.Y.C., 1966-70; sr. market devel. officer Seattle-First Nat. Bank, 1970-74; product expansion adminstr., mktg. planning mgr. VISA, Inc., San Francisco, 1974-76; v.p., dir. mktg. Wash. Mut. Savs. Bank, Seattle, 1976-82; v.p., mktg. dir. First Interstate Bank of Wash. N.A., 1983-86; sr. v.p. mktg., dir. Puget Sound Nat. Bank, Tacoma, 1986-92; sr. v.p., dir. mktg. and sales Key Bank, 1993-94, dir. corp. sales Kiro Inc., 1994; dir. mktg. and sales InterWest Bancorp, Oak Harbor, Wash., 1994—. Mem. Am. Mktg. Assn., Bank Mktg. Assn., Mktg. Communications Execs. Internat., Seattle Advt. Fedn., Ctrl. Whidbey Lions (bd. dirs.), Island County United Way (allocations com.), Northwest Railcar (bd. dirs.), Sigma Nu, Alpha Kappa Psi, Delta Mu Delta. Episcopalian. Home: 750 Snowberry Ln Coupeville WA 98239 Office: InterWest Bancorp PO Box 1649 Oak Harbor WA 98277

PIERIK, MARILYN ANNE, librarian; b. Bellingham, Wash., Nov. 12, 1939; d. Estell Leslie and Anna Margarethe (Onigkeit) Bowers; m. Robert Vincent Pierik, July 25, 1964; children: David Vincent, Donald Lesley. AA, Chaffey Jr. Coll., Ontario, Calif., 1959; BA, Upland (Calif.) Coll., 1962; cert. in teaching, Claremont (Calif.) Coll., 1963; MSLS, U. So. Calif., L.A., 1973. Tchr. elem. Christ Episcopal Day Sch., Ontario, 1959-60; tchr. Bonita High Sch., La Verne, Calif., 1962-63; tchr., libr. Kettle Valley Sch. Dist. 14, Greenwood, Can., 1963-64; libr. asst. Monrovia (Calif.) Pub. Libr., 1964-67; with Mt. Hood C.C., Gresham, Oreg., 1972—, reference libr., 1983—, chair faculty scholarship com., 1987—; campus archivist Mt. Hood C.C., Gresham, 1994—; mem. site selection com. Multnomah County (Oreg.) Libr., New Gresham br., 1987, adv. com. Multnomah County Libr., Portland, Oreg., 1988-89; bd. dirs. Oreg. Episcopal Conf. of Deaf, 1985-92. Bd. dirs. East County Arts Alliance, Gresham, 1987-91; vestry person, jr. warden St. Luke's Episc. Ch., 1989-92; founding pres. Mt. Hood Pops, 1983-88, orch. mgr., 1983-91, 93—, bd. dirs., 1983-88, 91—. Recipient Jeanette Parkhill Meml. award Chaffey Jr. Coll., 1959, Svc. award St. Luke's Episcopal Ch., 1983, 87, Edn. Svc. award Soroptimists, 1989. Mem. AAUW, NEA, Oreg. Edn. Assn., Oreg. Libr. Assn., ALA, Gresham Hist. Soc. Office: Mt Hood CC Libr 26000 SE Stark St Gresham OR 97030-3300

PIERRE, JOSEPH HORACE, JR., commercial artist; b. Salem, Oreg., Oct. 3, 1929; s. Joseph Horace and Miriam Elisabeth (Holder) P.; m. June Anne Rice, Dec. 20, 1952; children: Joseph Horace III, Thomas E., Laurie E., Mark R., Ruth A. Grad., Advt. Art Sch., Portland, Oreg., 1954, Inst. Comml. Art, 1951-52. Lithographic printer Your Town Press, Inc., Salem, Oreg., 1955-58; correctional officer Oreg. State Correctional Instn., 1958-60; owner Illustrators Workshop, Inc., Salem, 1960-61; advt. mgr. North Pacific Lumber Co., Portland, 1961-63; vocat. instr. graphic arts Oreg. Correctional Instn., 1963-70; lithographic printer Lloyd's Printing, Monterey, Calif., 1971-72; illustrator McGraw Hill, 1972-73; owner Publishers Art Svc., Monterey, 1972-81; correctional officer Oreg. State Penitentiary, 1982-90; ret.; owner Northwest Syndicate, 1993—. Editor/publisher: The Pro Cartoonist & Gagwriter; author: The Road to Damascus, 1981, The Descendants of Thomas Pier, 1992, The Origin and History of the Callaway and Holder Families, 1992; author numerous OpEd cols. in Salem, Oreg. Statesman Jour., others; pub. cartoons nat. mags.; mural Mardi Gras Restaurant, Salem; cartoon strip Fabu, Oreg. Agr. mo. Mem. Rep. Nat. Com., Citizens Com. for Right to Keep and Bear Arms. Served with USN, 1946-51. Decorated victory medal WWII, China svc. medal, Korea medal, Navy occupation medal. Mem. U.S. Power Squadron, Nat. Rifle Assn., Acad. of Model Aeronautics, Oreg. Correctional Officers Assn. (co-founder, hon. mem.), Four Corners Rod and Gun Club. Republican. Home: 4822 Oak Park Dr NE Salem OR 97305-2931

PIERRE, PHIL, food products executive; b. 1944. With Ventura (Calif.) Coastal Corp., 1968-82; exec. v.p. S & J Ranch Inc., Madera, Calif., 1982—. Office: S & J Ranch Inc 39639 Ave 10 Madera CA 93638*

PIERSON, PETER O'MALLEY, history educator; b. Indpls., Oct. 4, 1932; s. Russell Frazier and Mary Emily (Bingham) P. Student, Denison U., 1950-52; BA in Polit. Sci., UCLA, 1954, MA in History, 1963, PhD, 1966. From asst. prof. to assoc. prof. dept. history Santa Clara (Calif.) U., 1966-89, prof., 1989—, chmn. history dept., 1988-92, Lee and Seymour Graff prof., 1993—; mem. adv. bd. Humanities West, San Francisco, 1982—. Author: Philip II of Spain, 1975, Commander of the Armada, 1989; contbr. articles to various pubs. Lt. j.g. USNR, 1954-58. Recipient Fulbright grant, Spain, 1964-66; named NEH fellow, Europe, 1974. Mem. Am. Hist. Assn., Soc. Spanish & Portugese Hist. Studies (exec. com. 1977-81), Bohemian Club (San Francisco), Phi Gamma Delta. Roman Catholic. Office: Santa Clara U History Dept Santa Clara CA 95053

PIERT, EDWYNA PATRICE, child care worker; b. L.A., Oct. 21, 1969; d. Edward Piert and Patricia Ann Benefield. BS, Calif. State U., L.A., 1992. Student asst. VA Outpatient Clinic, L.A., 1991-92; child care worker Stanford Home for Children, Sacramento, Calif., 1993—. Canvasser, NAACP, Hollywood, Calif., 1987-89. Democrat. Baptist. Home: PO Box 8734 Sacramento CA 95818 Office: Stanford Home for Children PO Box 418000 Sacramento CA 95841

PIERZCHALA, EDMUND, electronics engineer; b. Warsaw, Jan. 15, 1958; came to the U.S., 1989; s. Henryk and Wieslawa P.; m. Sarah Kirk Williams, May 1, 1993. MSEE, Warsaw (Poland) U. Tech., 1982. Rsch. asst. Inst. Biocybernetics & Biomed. Engrng., Polish Acad. Scis., Warsaw, 1982-84; rsch. asst., sr. rsch. asst. Inst. Atomic Energy, Swierk, Poland, 1984-89; cons. software engrng. Cypress Semiconductor, Beaverton, Oreg., 1990; tester Analogy, Inc., Beaverton, 1991-92; v.p. product devel., founder Analogix Corp., Portland, Oreg., 1993—; modeling engr. Analogy, Inc., 1996—; tchg. asst., adj. instr. Portland (Oreg.) State U., 1989—. Inventor in field. Officer grad. students in elec. engring. Portland (Oreg.) State U., 1991-94, pres., 1992-93. Co-recipient award Design Automation Conf., San Francisco, 1991. Mem. IEEE, Assn. Computing Machinery (student mem.), Polish Nat. Alliance, Eta Kappa Nu. Roman Catholic. Office: Portland State U Dept Elec Engring PO Box 751 Portland OR 97207-0751

PIES, RONALD E., city official; b. Rochester, N.Y., Mar. 21, 1940; s. Herman S. and Sylvia P.; m. Bernita Orloff, Aug. 27, 1964; children: Cara Jean Tracy, David Paul. BS, Ariz. State U., 1963. Recreation leader City of Phoenix, Ariz., 1962-64; head recreation div. City of Scottsdale (Ariz.) Parks and Recreation Dept., 1964-69; dir. parks and recreation, City of Tempe, Ariz., 1969-84, community services dir., 1984—; guest lectr. Ariz. State U. Mem., pres. Kyrene Sch. Dist. Governing Bd., 1979-82. Chmn., bd. regents Pacific Revenue Sources Mgmt. Sch. NRPA; gen. chmn. Fiesta Bowl Soccer Classic, 1982—; founding mem. Tempe YMCA bd. mgrs.; apptd. mem. Ariz. State Parks Bd., 1987-93, chair, 1991. Named Outstanding Young Man, Jaycees; recipient Superior Svc. Mgmt. award ASPA, Ariz. chpt., 1988; named to Hall of Fame, Ariz. State U. Alumni for Coll. Pub. Programs, 1996, Hall of Fame, Tempe Elem. Sch. Dist., 1996. Mem. Tempe C. of C., Ariz. Parks and Recreation Assn. (bd. dirs. 1986—, pres. adminstrs., Disting. Fellow award 1983), Nat. Recreation and Parks Assn. (Outstanding Profl. 1991), Cactus League Baseball Assn. (pres. 1993-94, appointed mem. of Ariz. baseball commn. by Gov. Symington, 1994—, chair 1995—), Sigma Alpha Epsilon. Club: Tempe Diablos. Office: Box 3500 Rural Road Tempe AZ 85282-5482

PIETSCH, JEFFREY GARETT, real estate consultant; b. Redwood City, Calif., Mar. 9, 1968; s. Charles Joseph and Margaret Jean (Hustace) P. BS, Cornell U., 1990. Cons. KPMG Peat Marwick, Honolulu, 1990—. Office: KPMG Peat Marwick Payahi Tower 10001 Bishop StSte 2100 Honolulu HI 96813-4124 Office: Sea Life Park Hawaii 41-202 Kalanianaole Hwy Waimanalo HI 96795*

PIGOTT, CHARLES MCGEE, transportation equipment manufacturing executive; b. Seattle, Apr. 21, 1929; s. Paul and Theiline (McGee) P.; m. Yvonne Flood, Apr. 18, 1953. B.S., Stanford U., 1951. With PACCAR Inc, Seattle, 1959—, exec. v.p., 1962-65, pres., 1965-86, chmn., pres., 1986-87, chmn., chief exec. officer, 1987-97, also bd. dirs., chmn. emeritus, 1997—; dir. The Seattle Times, Chevron Corp., The Boeing Co. Pres. Nat. Boy Scouts Am., 1986-88, mem. exec. bd. Mem. Bus. Council. Office: Paccar Inc 777 106th Ave NE Bellevue WA 98004-5001

PIGOTT, MARK C., automotive executive. CEO PACCAR, Bellevue, Wash. Office: 777 106th Ave NE Bellevue WA 98004*

PIIRTO, DOUGLAS DONALD, forester, educator; b. Reno, Nev., Sept. 25, 1948; s. Rueben Arvid and Martha Hilma (Giebel) P.; BS, U. Nev., 1970; MS, Colo. State U., 1971; PhD, U. Calif., Berkeley, 1977; m. Mary Louise Cruz, Oct. 28, 1978. Rsch. asst. Colo. State U., 1970-71, U. Calif., Berkeley, 1972-77; forester, silviculturist U.S. Dept. Agr., Forest Svc., Sierra Nat. Forest, Trimmer and Shaver Lake, Calif., 1977-85; assoc. prof. natural resources mgmt. dept. Calif. Poly. State U., San Luis Obispo, 1985-90, prof. 1990—; researcher in field; instr. part-time Kings River Community Coll., Reedley, Calif.; forestry cons., expert witness. Registered profl. forester, Calif.; cert. silviculturist USDA Forest Svc. Recipient Meritorious Performance and Profl. Promise award CalPoly, 1989, 96, 97, CalPoly Coll. Agr. Outstanding Tchg. award Dole Food Co., 1995. Mem. Soc. Am. Foresters, Am. Forestry Assn., Forest Products Rsch. Soc., Soc. Wood Sci. and Tech., Alpha Zeta, Xi Sigma Pi, Sigma Xi, Beta Beta Beta, Phi Sigma Kappa. Lutheran. Contbr. articles to sci. and forestry jours. Home: 7605 El Retiro Ave Atascadero CA 93422-3722 Office: Calif Poly State U Dept Natural Resources Mgmt San Luis Obispo CA 93407

PIJAWKA, K. DAVID, environmental educator, researcher; b. Baumberg, Germany, July 16, 1947; arrived in Can., 1957; came to U.S., 1974; s. Aaron and Ann Pijawka; m. Judith M. Dworkin, May 27, 1975; 1 child, Benjamin Michael. BA, Brock U., St. Catherines, Can., 1971; MA, Clark U., 1978, PhD, 1983. Rsch. mgr. Mountain West Rsch. Inc., Phoenix, 1979-82; prin. Mgmt. Strategies and Rsch., Inc., Phoenix, 1988-96; assoc. prof. Ariz. State U., Tempe, 1988-93, prof., 1994—; asst. dir. Ctr. Environ. Studies, Ariz. State U., Tempe, 1983-95, interim dir., 1995-97; mem. mgmt. com. Ctr. S.W. Rsch. and Policy, 1995-97. Author: Environment Comes Home, 1996 (Valley Forward award 1996); co-author: The Environment Comes Home: APS's Environmental Showcase Home, 1995, One Hundred Centuries of Solitude: Redefining America's High Level Nuclear Waste Policy, 1995, Nuclear Power: Assessing and Managing Hazardous Technology, 1996; editor Recycling Rev., 1992— (Gov.'s award 1996); contbr. articles to profl. jours. Office: Ariz State U Ctr Environ Studies Tempe AZ 85287

PIKE, NANCY ANN, pediatric cardiothoracic surgery nurse; b. Rome, N.Y., July 13, 1963; d. Bruce Martin and Marie (Parent) Pike. BS, Pa. State U., 1985; M in Nursing, UCLA, 1993. CCRN; cert. pediatric cardiothoracic surgery clin. nurse specialist; cert. BLS, ACLS, BLS instr. Staff nurse ICU/CCU Aliquippa (Pa.) Hosp., 1985-86; staff nurse IMC/ICU Pa. State U., Hershey, 1986-90; staff nurse ICU UCLA Med. Ctr., 1990-93; CNS cardiothoracic surgery Children's Hosp. at Stanford, Calif., 1993—; part-time transplant coord. Stanford U., 1993—; teaching asst. undergrad. nursing UCLA Sch. Nursing, 1993—. Author: RN jour., 1994; article reviewer: Am. Jour. Critical Care, 1993—; contbr. chpt. to book. Mem. AACN, Am. Heart Assn., Soc. Pediat. Cardiovasc. Nursing, Sigma Theta Tau (Gamma Tau chpt.). Roman Catholic. Home: 725 Roble Ave Apt 12 Menlo Park CA 94025-4829

PIKE, RICHARD JOSEPH, JR., geologist; b. Nantucket, Mass., June 28, 1937; s. Richard Joseph and Idolize Evelyn (Roderick) P.; m. Jane Ellen Nielson, Sept. 2, 1967 (div. 1982); children: Benjamin R., Owen S.; m. Linda Hutchinson Grossman, May 4, 1986. BS, Tufts Coll., 1959; MA, Clark U., 1963; PhD, U. Mich., 1968. Geographer U.S. Army, Natick, Mass., 1962-63; ops. analyst Cornell Aero Labs., Buffalo, 1964; geologist astrogeology br. U.S. Geol. Survey, Flagstaff, Ariz. and Menlo Park, Calif., 1968-86; geologist br. of regional geology U.S. Geol. Survey, Menlo Park, 1987—; mem. various NASA panels, Ariz., Calif., and Tex., 1968-70, 74-78; vis. prof. Instituto di Ricerce per la Protezione Idrogeologica nell Italia centrale del Consiglio Nazionale delle Ricerche, Perugia, Italy, 1988-89. Author: (with others) Impact Craters on Mercury, 1988, (with G.P. Thelin) Digital Shaded-Relief Map of the U.S., 1991 (in map exhibit Cooper-Hewitt Mus., N.Y.C., 1992-93 and Smithsonian Inst., Washington, 1993-94, 3rd printing 1997), Advances in Geomorphometry, 1995; contbr. articles to profl. jours. Recipient Apollo medallion NASA Hdqrs., 1971. Mem. AAAS, Am. Geophys. Union, Geol. Soc. Am., 356 Registry (essayist, editor 1978-93), Sigma Xi. Office: US Geol Survey M/S 975 345 Middlefield Rd Menlo Park CA 94025-3561

PIKE, STEVEN, occupational health physician. BS magna cum laude in Chemistry, Coll. Santa Fe, 1973, BS magna cum laude in Math., 1973; MD, U. N.Mex., 1979; MS in Toxicology, U. Ariz., 1990. Diplomate Am. Bd. Emergency Medicine, Am. Bd. Preventive Medicine/Occupl. Medicine, Am. Bd. Med. Toxicology, Am. Bd. Indsl. Hygiene, Nat. Bd. Med. Examiners; cert. indsl. hygienist, med. rev. officer. Intern Tucson Med. Ctr., 1979-80; resident Ariz. Ctr. for Occupational Safety & Health, Tucson, 1980-81; dir. emergency svcs. Miami (Ariz.) Inspiration Hosp., 1981-86; pres. EnviroMD, Tucson, 1986—; program chmn. 37th ann. Western Occupl. Health Conf., 1993; cons. Ariz. Poison Control Ctr., 1981—; emergency physician Tucson Med. Ctr., 1981—; med. dirs., pres. Cobre Valley Emergency Physicians, 1981-82, Anasazi Emergency Physicians, 1982-87; v.p. Tabershaw & Pike, Inc., Tucson, 1983-86; emergency physician El Dorado Med. Ctr., Tucson, 1987—; pres. TEManalytics, Inc., 1989-95; cons. Kingdom of Lesotho, Africa, 1992; adj. prof. dept. of pharmacology and toxicology U. Ariz. Health Scis. Ctr., 1986—. Chmn. Ariz. Comparative Environ. Risk Project, 1993-94; mem. Ariz. Corp. Commn. externalities prioritization working group, 1993-94; steering com. Tucson/Almaty (Kazakhstan) Health Care Coalition, 1992—; multi-profl. com. Pima County Bd. Health, 1991; chair occupl. and environ. health com. Ariz.-Mex. Commn. pub. health com.; med. dir. occupl. and environ. medicine health ptnrs. of So. Ariz., 1994-95; med. dir. emergency dept. Carondeley St. Jospeh's Hosp., 1996—. Fellow Am. Coll. Emergency Physicians (bd. dirs. Ariz. chpt. 1990—, editor 1990-92), Am. Coll. Occupl. and Environ. Med. Assn. (bd. dirs. 1992-94, newsletter editor 1994, treas. 1985, 2nd v.p. 1996, del. 1995); mem. Am. Acad. Clin. Toxicologists, Am. Coll. Preventive Medicine, Internat. Commn. Occupl. Health, Am. Acad. Cons. Toxicologists. Office: EnviroMD Ste 208 4400 E Broadway Blvd Tucson AZ 85711-3517

PILCHER, ELLEN LOUISE, rehabilitation counselor; b. Washington, Feb. 5, 1949; d. Donald Everett and Edna Lois (Walker) P.; m. Adam J. Buzon Jr., July 27, 1974 (div. Apr. 1991). BA in Psychology, So. Ill. U., 1971, MA in Rehab. Counseling, 1973. Social svcs. asst. Dept. Army, Ft. Huachuca, Ariz., 1973-74, New Ulm, Germany, 1974-75, Ft. Sill, Okla., 1977-87; counselor Goodwill Industries, Lawton, Okla., 1976-77; ind. living specialist Ariz. Bridge to Ind. Living, Phoenix, 1984-87; disability specialist Samaritan Rehab. Inst., Phoenix, 1987-89; disability cons. Peoria, Ariz., 1989—; founder Problems of Architecture and Transp. to Handicapped, Lawton, Okla., 1976-79; founder, past pres. Polio Echo Support Group, Phoenix, 1985—; co-founder, bd. mem. Disability Network of Ariz., Phoenix, 1986—; disability speaker Easter Seal Soc. and free lance, Phoenix, 1984—; producer, host Cable Community Svc. TV Show, Glendale, Ariz., 1987-91; mem. nat. adv. bd. Polio Support Groups, St. Louis, 1987. Named Ms. Wheelchair Ariz. Good Samaritan Med. Ctr., Phoenix, 1986, Second Runner-Up Ms. Wheelchair Am., Ms. Wheelchair Am. Assn., Richmond, Va., 1986, Outstanding Bus. Person Ariz. Parks/Recreation, 1987; recipient Celebration of Success award Impact for Enterprising Women, Phoenix, 1989, Extraordinary Personal Achievement award Lions Club Found., Phoenix, 1987. Mem. NOW (co-founder Lawton chpt. 1982, Glendale, Ariz. chpt. 1984), Nat. Rehab. Assn., Nat. Rehab. Counselors Assn., Ariz. Rehab. Assn., Ariz. Rehab. Counselors Assn. Democrat. Unitarian.

PILE, JAMES WILLIAM, artist educator; b. Pueblo, Colo., Nov. 7, 1943; s. William H. and Annabelle (Bryan) P.; m. Marcia E. Bell, Apr. 22, 1943 (dec.); m. Teresa de Jesus Espinosa, Feb. 5, 1945; children: Larissa, Taylor James. BFA in Edn., U. Nebr., 1965, MFA, 1971. Instr. art Ariz. State U., Tempe, 1971-74, asst. prof. art, 1974-78, assoc. prof. art, 1978-88, prof. art, 1988—. Represented in pub./corp. collections West Pub. Co., St. Paul, Ariz. State U. Art Mus., Tempe, Medley Distilling, Louisville, Federated Dept. Stores, Fla., IBM Collection, Tucson, Sioux City Art Ctr., U. S.D. Art Collection, Vermillion, Kalicow Corp., N.Y.C., Krasdale Foods Inc., Bronx, N.Y.; represented in numerous pvt. collections in N.Y.C., Scottsdale, Ariz., Beverly Hills, Calif., N.J., Houston, Huntingdon Valley, Pa., L.A., Nashville, Greenwich, Conn., Old Westbury, N.Y., Phila., Dallas. Recipient Purchase award First Ann. Upper Midwest Art Festival, 1970, Purchase award 32nd Ann. Fall Show Sioux City Art Ctr., 1970, Woods fellowship, 1971, Hon. diploma Univ. de Sonora, 1972, First prize New West Invitational '81, 1981, NEA Visual Artist fellowship, 1987. Home: 7347 E Navarro Ave Mesa AZ 85208 Office: Ariz State U Sch of Art Tempe AZ 85287-1505

PILLAR, CHARLES LITTLEFIELD, retired mining consultant; b. Denver, May 25, 1911; s. Charles and Alice May (Littlefield) P.; m. Elizabeth Reed Broadhead, Sept. 10, 1932 (div. May 1939); m. Gwendola Elizabeth Lotz, Sept. 16, 1939; children: Ann, Catherine, Pamela. Engr. mines, Colo. Sch. Mines, 1935. Registered profl. engr., B.C., Ariz. Various positions in field, 1935-75; mine cons. Pillar, Lowell & Assocs., Tucson, Ariz., 1976-83; cons. Bechtel Corp., San Francisco, 1976-79, Fluor Corp., Redwood City, Calif., 1979-83; mem. Colo. Sch. Mines Rsch. Inst., Golden, 1975-83, pvt. practice Tucson, 1985-89; bd. dir. Internat. Geosystems Corp., Vancouver, B.C.; mem. pres.'s coun. Colo. Sch. Mines. Contbr. articles to profl. jours. Mem. Nat. Rep. Senatorial com.; rep. Presdl. Task Force. Capt. USAF, 1942-45; maj. USAF Res. 1946-54. Recipient Achievement in the Mining Field award Colo. Sch. Mines, 1995, Medal of Merit award Am. Mining Hall of Fame, 1996. Mem. AIME (William Saunders Gold Medal award, Disting. mem. award), Can. Inst. Mining and Metallurgy, Profl. Engrs. B.C., Heritage Found., Smithsonian Assocs., Mining Found. S.W., Nat. Exch. Club, U.S. Senatorial Club (presdl. task force), Vancouver Club, Tucson Nat. Country Club. Republican. Episcopalian. Home: 8700 N La Cholla Blvd Apt 5109 Tucson AZ 85741-4430

PILLAY, GAUTAM, chemical engineer, electrochemist; b. Buffalo, Jan. 28, 1967; s. Sivasankara K.K. and Revathi (Krishnamurthy) P. BS, N.Mex. State U., Las Cruces, 1988; PhD, Tex. A&M U., 1993. Grad. rschr., staff mem. Los Alamos Nat. Lab., 1984-87; grad. rschr. Tex. A&M U., College Station, 1988-92; rsch. engr. Pacific N.W. Lab., Richland, Wash., 1992-95; sr. rsch. engr. Pacific N.W. Lab., Richland, 1995—; adj. faculty Wash. State U., Richland, 1993—. Contbr. articles to profl. jours. NSF grad. rsch. fellow, 1988-91; recipient Fed. Lab. Consortium award for excellence in tech. transfer, 1997. Mem. AIChE (symposium chair), The Electrochem. Soc. (symposium chair 1993—, exec. com. 1994—, pres. Pacific N.W. sect.

1996—), Am. Chem. Soc., Am. Nuclear Soc., Am. Electroplaters and Surface Finishers Soc., Tau Beta Pi, Omega Chi Epsilon, Alpha Chi, Phi Kappa Phi. Office: Pacific NW Lab PO Box 999 Richland WA 99352-0999

PILLAY, MICHAEL, botanist, researcher; b. Durban, Natal, South Africa, June 27, 1950; came to U.S., 1984; s. Dorasamy and Muniamma Pillay; m. Grace Veronica Michael, Oct. 10, 1981; children: Delicia, Anton, Alban. BSc, U. Durban Westville, 1973; BEd, U. South Africa, Pretoria, 1977, BA, 1980; MS, La. State U., 1986; PhD, Va. Tech., 1991. Tchr. sci. Durban, 1974-84; rsch. asst. Wash. State U., Prosser, 1991-94; rschr. dept. agronomy La. State U., Baton Rouge, 1994—. Scholar South African Edn. Program, 1984-86. Mem. Internat. Soc. Plant Molecular Biologists, Soc. for Systematic Biolgists, Crop Sci. Soc. Am. Baptist. Home: 11850 Wentling Ave Apt I-5 Baton Rouge LA 70816 Office: Louisiana State Univ 104 M B Surgis Hall Baton Rouge LA 70803

PILLER, CHARLES LEON, journalist; b. Chgo., Jan. 9, 1955; s. Jack H. and Alice (Shakow) P.; m. Surry Piller Bunnell, Aug. 21, 1984; 1 child, Nathan Bunnell Piller. BA, Lone Mountain Coll., 1977. Editor, writer U. Calif., San Francisco, 1982-89; sr. editor Macworld mag., San Francisco, 1990-96; columnist L.A. Times, 1996—; exec editor PC World Mag., San francisco, Calif., 1996—; sec. Ctr. for Pub. Integrity, Washington, 1988—, also bd. dirs.; cons. U.S. Senate, Washington, 1989-92. Author: Gene Wars, 1988, The Fail-Safe Society, 1991; contbr. numerous articles to newspapers and mags. Recipient of the John Swett Journalism award, 1993, Benjamin Fine Journalism award, 1995, Runner-Up Lincoln Steffens Journalism award, 1994, Am. Soc. of Business Press Editors (various awards).

PILTZ, ANTHONY ROBERT, accounting educator, consultant; b. Scottsdale, Ariz., Oct. 4, 1967; s. Robert Joe and Helen Lorraine (Shahan) P. BS in Bus., Grand Canyon U., Phoenix, 1988; M of Accountancy, Truman State U., Kirksville, Mo., 1990. Cert. mgmt. acct.; cert. fin. mgmt. Assoc. prof. acctg. Rocky Mountain Coll., Billings, Mont., 1990—. Baseball coach Am. Legion Baseball, Billings, 1991-96. Recipient Abrams award Rocky Mountain Coll., 1991-94. Mem. APICS, Inst. Mgmt. Accts. (Beyer Gold medal 1994). Home: 224 Burlington Ave Billings MT 59101 Office: Rocky Mountain Coll 1511 Poly Dr Billings MT 59102

PIMBLE, TONI, artistic director, choreographer, educator. Student, Elmhurst Sch. Ballet and Dramatic Arts, Royal Acad. Dancing, London. Resident choreographer Dance Aspen Co. Project; artistic dir., resident choreographer Eugene (Oreg.) Ballet Co., 1978—; past mem. faculty Dance Aspen Summer Dance Sch. Choreographer (festival) Carlisle Choreographer's Showcase, Pa. and Colo., (ballets) Two's Company, N.Y.C., Common Ground, Atlanta, 1994, Playing Field, Indlps., Borderline, Alice in Wonderland, Nebr., 1994, Wash., 1996, Quartet in Blue, Oreg., 1994, Petrushka, Nev., 1994, 95, Children of the Raven, India, Bangladesh, Sri Lanka, Syria, Jordan, Tunisia, 1995, 96, A Midsummer Night's Dream, Nev., 1997, numerous tours and sch. performances; choreographer, tchr. U. Iowa, Interlochen Sch. Arts; resident choreographer Dance On Tour Nat. Endowment Arts; artistic dir. Ballet Idaho. Active outreach programs Young Audiences Oreg., Wash. State Cultural Enrichment Program. Oreg. Arts Commn. artist fellow, Nat. Endowment Arts grantee; co-recipient Gov.'s Arts award, Oreg., 1996. *

PIMENTEL, BENJAMIN IMPELIDO, journalist; b. Manila, Philippines, June 20, 1964; s. Benjamin C. and Isabel (Impelido) P.; m. Maria Teresita Torres, Dec. 23, 1992. BA in Polit. Sci., U. The Philippines, 1985; M.Journalism, U. Calif., Berkeley, 1993. Staff writer Nat. Midweek mag., Manila, 1986-89; gen. assignment, Asian Am. affairs and transp. reporter San Francisco Chronicle, 1993—. Author: Rebolusyon: A Generation of Struggle in the Philippines, 1991; writer, prodr. Toxic Sunset: On the Trail of Hazardous Waste from Subic and Clark, Philippine Ctr. for Investigative Journalism, Manila, 1993. Mem. Asian Am. Journalists Assn. Office: San Francisco Chronicle 901 Mission St San Francisco CA 94103

PINCUS, HOWARD JONAH, geologist, engineer, educator; b. N.Y.C., June 24, 1922; s. Otto Max and Gertrude (Jankowsky) P.; m. Maud Lydia Roback, Sept. 6, 1953; children: Glenn David, Philip E. BS, CCNY, 1942; PhD, Columbia U., 1949. Mem. faculty Ohio State U., 1949-67, successively instr., asst. prof., assoc. prof., 1949-59, prof., 1959-67, chmn. dept. geology, 1960-65; rsch. geologist U. S. Bur. Mines, summers 1963-67; geologist, rsch. supr. U.S. Bur. Mines, 1967-68; prof. geol. sci. and civil engring. U. Wis., Milw., 1968-87, prof. emeritus, 1987—, dean Coll. Letters and Sci., 1969-72; rsch. assoc. Lamont Geol. Obs., Columbia, 1949, 50, 51; geologist Ohio Dept. Natural Resources, summers 1950-61; cons. geology and rock mechanics, 1954-67, 68—; mem. U.S. nat. com. on tunnelling tech. NAE, 1972-74, mem. U.S. nat. com. on rock mechanics NAS/NAE, 1975-78, 80-89, chmn., 1985-87; mem. U.S. com. Internat. Assn. Engring. Geology/NAS, chmn., 1987-90; sr. postdoctoral fellow NSF, 1962. Tech. editor: Geotech. Testing Jour., 1992-95; editl. bd. Geotech Testing Jour., 1996—. Served to 1st lt. C.E. AUS, 1942-46. Recipient award for teaching excellence U. Wis.-Milw. Alumni Assn., 1978. Fellow ASTM (Reinhart award 1987, Award of Merit 1989), AAAS, Geol. Soc. Am.; mem. NSPE, AAUP (pres. Ohio State U. chpt. 1955-56, mem. coun. 1965-67, pres. U. Wis.-Milw. chpt. 1976-77), Am. Geophys. Union, Geol. Soc. Am. (chmn. engring. geology divsn. 1973-74), Soc. Mining Engrs., Internat. Assn. Engring. Geology, Internat. Soc. Rock Mechanics, Assn. Engring. Geologists, Am. Inst. Profl. Geologists (pres. Ohio sect. 1965-66), Phi Beta Kappa (pres. Ohio State U. chpt. 1959-60, pres. U. Wis.-Milw. chpt. 1976-77), Sigma Xi. Home: 17523 Plaza Marlena San Diego CA 92128-1807 Office: PO Box 27598 San Diego CA 92198-1598

PINE, LOIS ANN HASENKAMP, nurse; b. Cheyenne, Wyo., Feb. 21, 1950; d. Clifford Norbert and Julie Adda (Younglund) Hasenkamp; m. Julius William Pine Jr., Feb. 16, 1974; children: Margaret Ann, Julius William III, Lawrence Michael. BS, U. Wyo., 1976, MS in Parent-Child Nursing, 1989. RN. From staff nurse to charge nurse Ivinson Meml. Hosp., Laramie, Wyo., 1976-86; maternal-child nurse cons. Perinatal and Prevention Program, Wyo. Dept. Health, Cheyenne, 1988-96; ind. maternal-child health nurse cons., 1996—. Mem. St. Lawrence Coun. of Cath. Women, Laramie, 1980—, St. Cecilia's Group, Laramie, 1980—, Albany County PTA, Laramie, 1985-91; mem. health profl. adv. com. March of Dimes Wyo. Chpt., 1988—. Mem. ANA, NAACOG (sect. vice chmn. 1980-86), Wyo. Nurses Assn., Am. Acad. Pediat. (perinatal pediat. dist. VIII sect.), Nat. Assn. Neonatal Nurses (charter), Sigma Theta Tau (Alpha Pi chpt. treas. 1990-94, corr. sec. 1983-84, sec. 1994—). Democrat. Home: 1062 Empinado St Laramie WY 82070-5019

PINE, WILLIAM CHARLES, foundation executive; b. Canton, Ill., Nov. 4, 1912; s. William Charles and Katherine Pauline (Prichard) P.; m. Virginia Rae Keeley, June 14, 1945; children: William Charles, Barry Scott, Nancy Katherine Pine McMahon. BS, Monmouth Coll., Ill., 1939; DHL (hon.), Southwestern at Memphis, 1961; Dr.Laws (hon.), Mercy Coll. Detroit, 1966. Asst. dir. admissions Monmouth Coll., 1939-42; spl. agt. FBI, 1942-45; assoc. dir. Am. City Bur., N.Y.C. and Chgo., 1945-47; dir. pub. relations Lake Forest (Ill.) Coll., 1947-48, v.p., 1948-51; dir. scholarship prog. Ford Motor Co. Fund., Dearborn, Mich., 1951-72; asst. dir. Ford Motor Co. Fund., 1972-75; prog. dir. The Collins Found., Portland, Oreg., 1976-79; exec. v.p. The Collins Found., 1979—. Contbr. articles to profl. jours. Mem. Historic Records Adv. Bd., Salem, Oreg., 1984-87. Mem. Soc. Former Spl. Agts. of FBI. Office: 1618 SW 1st Ave Ste 305 Portland OR 97201-5708

PINEDA, ANSELMO, neurosurgery educator; b. Lima, Peru, Apr. 3, 1923; s. Anselmo Vicente and Juana (Munayco)P.; m. Monique Yvonne Martin, Mar. 15, 1955; children: Patricia M., Richard A., Gilbert V., Katherine A. MD, San Marcos U., Lima, 1951; MS, Northwestern U., 1962. Diplomate Am. Bd. Neurol. Surgery. Rotating intern Loayza Hosp., Lima, 1950-51; head histology sect. Leprosy dept. Ministry Pub. Health, Lima, 1951; asst. pathologist Nat. Inst. Neoplastic Diseases, 1952; vol. asst. lab. normal and path. histology nervous system San Marcos U. Sch. Medicine, 1953; rotating intern Augustana Hosp., Chgo., 1954, resident in gen. surgery, 1955; jr. asst. resident in neurosurgery U. Chgo., 1955-56, sr. asst. resident in neurosurgery, 1956-57, chief resident in neurosurgery, 1957-58; assoc. instr. neurosurgery U. Tex., 1958-61; assoc. neurosurgeon John Sealy Hosp., Galveston, Tex., 1960-61, attending neurosurgeon, 1961; acting chief neurosurgery VA Hosp., Long Beach, Calif., 1962-63; assoc. clin. prof., mem. Brain Research Inst. UCLA, 1962—; cons. VA Hosp., Long Beach, 1966-67. NIH spl. fellow in Neuroanatomy Northwestern U., 1961-62. Fellow ACS, Am. Coll. Angiology, Royal Soc. Medicine; mem. AAUP, AAAS, AMA, Congress of Neurol. Surgeons, World Med. Assn., Am. Assn. Neurol. Surgeons, Calif. Med. Assn., Orange County Med. Assn., Am. Acad. Neurology, Am. Assn. Neuropathologists, Internat. Coll. Surgeons, Am. Assn. Anatomists, Am. Assn. Trauma, Am. Soc. Stereotaxic and Functional Neurosurgery, N.Y. Acad. Scis., Internat. Assn. Study Pain, Sigma Xi. Home: 16571 Carousel Ln Huntington Beach CA 92649-2115 Office: 2880 Atlantic Ave Ste 160 Long Beach CA 90806-1715

PINGS, ANTHONY CLAUDE, architect; b. Fresno, Calif., Dec. 16, 1951; s. Clarence Hubert and Mary (Murray) P.; m. Carole Clements, June 25, 1983; children, Adam Reed, Rebecca Mary. AA, Fresno City Coll., 1972; BArch, Calif. Poly. State U., San Luis Obispo, 1976. Lic. architect, Calif.; cert. Nat. Council Archtl. Registration Bds. Architect Aubrey Moore Jr., Fresno, 1976-81; architect, prin. Pings & Assocs., Fresno, 1981-83, 86—, Pings-Taylor Assocs., Fresno, 1983-85. Prin. works include Gollaher Profl. Office (Masonry Merit award 1985, Best Office Bldg. award 1986), Fresno Imaging Ctr. (Best Instnl. Project award 1986, Nat. Healthcare award Modern Health Care mag. 1986), Orthopedic Facility (award of honor Masonry Inst. 1987, award of merit San Joaquin chpt. AIA 1987), Modesto Imaging Ctr. (award of merit San Joaquin chpt. AIA 1991), Peachwood Med. Ctr. (award of merit San Joaquin chpt. AIA). Mem. Calif. Indsl. Tech. Edn. Consortium Calif. State Dept. Edn., 1983, 84. Mem. AIA (bd. dirs. Calif. chpt. 1983-84, v.p. San Joaquin chpt. 1982, pres. 1983, Calif. Coun. evaluation team 1983, team leader Coalinga Emergency Design Assistance team), Fresno Arts (bd. dirs., counsel 1989—, pres. 1990-93), Fig Gardens Home Owners Assn. (bd. dir. 1991—, pres. 1994—). Republican. Home: 4350 N Safford Ave Fresno CA 93704-3509 Office: 1640 W Shaw Ave Ste 107 Fresno CA 93711-3506

PINIELLA, LOUIS VICTOR, professional baseball team manager; b. Tampa, Fla., Aug. 28, 1943; m. Anita Garcia, Apr. 12, 1967; children: Lou, Kristi, Derrick. Student, U. Tampa. Baseball player various minor-league teams, 1962-68, Cleve. Indians, 1968, Kansas City Royals, 1969-73; baseball player N.Y. Yankees, 1974-84, coach, 1984-85, mgr., 1985-87, 1988, gen. mgr., 1987-88, spl. advisor, TV announcer, 1989; mgr. Cin. Reds, 1990-92, Seattle Mariners, 1992—. Named to Am. League All-Star Team, 1972; recipient Ellis Island Medal of Honor, 1990; Named A.L. Rookie of the Yr Baseball Writers Assoc of Amer, 1969, Named A.L. Manager of the Yr, 1995. Office: Seattle Mariners PO Box 4100 83 S King St Seattle WA 98104-2875*

PINKEL, SHEILA MAE, artist, photographer, educator; b. Newport News, Va., Aug. 21, 1941; d. Benjamin and Anne (Abel) P. B.A. in Art and Art History, U. Calif.-Berkeley, 1963; M.F.A. in Photography, UCLA, 1977. Instr. photography and silkscreen, UCLA Extension, 1976-78; instr. photography Otis Art Inst., Los Angeles, 1980-83, Calif. Poly. Inst., Pomona, 1980-81; instr. silkscreen Santa Monica (Calif.) Coll., 1980-83; instr. photography Sch. of Art Inst. Chgo., 1983-84; instr. Calif. Inst. Arts, 1984-85; assoc. prof. Pomona Coll. , 1986—; project dir. Multicultural Focus, Los Angeles, 1981, Los Angeles Portrait: Eleven Views, LACE Gallery, 1982, Bay Area Slide Library, Santa Monica Library, 1982. Coordinator Artists Against Proposition 13, City Hall and Los Angeles Mcpl. Gallery, 1978. NEA artist grantee in photography, 1979, 82, MTA book pub. grantee, 1994; recipient Hammer award Ctr. Study Polit. Graphics, 1996. Mem. Soc. for Photog. Edn., Los Angeles Center for Photog. Studies. Contbr. to Park La Brea Towers Mural Instllation, Los Angeles, 1976, books including: The Print (Time-Life Series) 1981, 1980 Time-Life Photo Annual, Innovative Printmaking, 1978, Darkroom Art, 1981, The New Photography, 1984, Naked to the Bone, 1997, Other Voices, Other Visions, 1995, Yesterday and Tomorrow, 1989; co-author Kou Chang's Story, 1992; co-editor: Leonardo. Office: Pomona Coll Lebus Ct/Art Dept Claremont CA 91711

PINKERTON, RICHARD LADOYT, management educator; b. Huron, S.D., Mar. 5, 1933; s. Abner Pyle and Orral Claudine (Arneson) P.; m. Sandra Louise Lee, Aug. 28, 1965 (div. 1992); children—Elizabeth, Patricia. B.A. (La Verne Noyes scholar 1952-55), U. Mich., 1955; M.B.A., Case Western Res. U., 1962; Ph.D. (Nat. Assn. Purchasing Mgmt. fellow 1967-68), U. Wis., 1969. Sr. market research analyst Harris-Intertype Corp., Cleve., 1957-61; mgr. sales devel. Triax Corp., Cleve., 1962-64; coordinator mktg. program Mgmt. Inst., U. Wis., 1964-67; dir. exec. programs Mgmt. Inst., U. Wis. (Grad. Sch. Bus.), also asst. prof. mktg., 1969-74; prof. mgmt., dean Grad. Sch. Adminstrn., Capital U., Columbus, Ohio, 1974-86; prof. mgmt., dir. Univ. Bus. Ctr., Craig Sch. of Bus. Calif. State U., Fresno, 1986-89, prof. mktg., 1989—, chair mktg. and logistics dept., 1996—; trustee Ohio Coun. Econ. Edn., 1976-87; bd. dirs. Univ. Bus. Ctr.; cons. to govt. and industry, 1960—. Co-author: The Purchasing Manager's Guide to Strategic Proactive Procurement, 1996; contbr. articles to profl. jours. Bd. dirs. The Fresno Townhouse Assn.; bd. govs. Hannah Neil Home for Children, Columbus, 1975-78. Served as officer USAF, 1955-57, lt. col. USAFR, 1957-78. Mem. Nat. Assn. Contract Mgmt. (chmn. validation cert. com. 1990), Nat. Assn. Purchasing Mgmt. (chmn. acad. planning 1979-84, rsch. symposium 1992), Am. Mktg. Assn. (chpt. pres. 1972-73), Res. Officers Assn., Air Forces Assn., Ft. Washington Golf and Country Club, Beta Gamma Sigma, Alpha Kappa Psi, Phi Gamma Delta, Rotary (Paul Harris fellow). Home: 4721 N Cedar Ave Apt 111 Fresno CA 93726-1007 Office: Calif State U Dept of Mktg Fresno CA 93740-0007

PINNEY, EDMUND, educator, mathematician; b. Seattle, Aug. 19, 1917; s. Henry Lewis and Alice (Joy) P.; m. Eleanor Russell, Mar. 10, 1945; children: Henry Russell, Gail Shiela. BS, Calif. Inst. Tech., 1939, PhD, 1942. Research asso. Radiation Lab., Mass. Inst. Tech., 1942-43; research analyst Consol.-Vultee Aircraft Corp., 1943-45; instr. Ore. State Coll., 1945-46; mem. faculty U. Calif., Berkeley, 1946—, prof., math., 1959—; cons. in field. Author: Ordinary Difference-Differential Equations, 1958. Fellow AAAS; mem. Am. Math. Soc., Am. Phys. Soc. Home: 66 Scenic Dr Orinda CA 94563-3412 Office: Univ Calif 839 Evans Hall Berkeley CA 94720

PINNOW, TIMOTHY DAYNE, theater educator, fight choreographer; b. Racine, Wis., Oct. 2, 1964; s. Larry Danye and Carolyn June (Kness) P.; m. Jennifer Alphonsine Jeffries, Aug. 1, 1992. BA, Luther Coll., Decorah, Iowa, 1987; MFA, U. Fla., 1990. Actor Hippodrome State Theatre, Gainesville, Fla., 1990, Old Creamery Theatre Co., Garrison, Iowa, 1990-91; asst. prof. theatre St. Olaf Coll., Northfield, Minn., 1990-95, N.Mex. State U., Las Cruces, 1995—; bd. dirs. Am. S.W. Theatre Co., Las Cruces, 1996—; dir. Am. S.W. Theatre, Las Cruces, 1995—, actor, 1995—. Grad. Coun. fellow U. Fla., 1988-89. Mem. AAUP, Actors Equity Assn., Voice and Speech Trainers Assn., Soc. Am. Fight Dirs. (regional rep. 1992—), Phi Beta Kappa, Phi Kappa Phi, Alpha Psi Omega. Lutheran. Home: 1867 Defiance Rd Las Cruces NM 88001 Office: N Mex State U Dept 3072 Box 30001 Las Cruces NM 88003

PINSKY, CHARLOTTE LEE (CHERIE PINSKY), academic administrator; b. Hartford, Conn., Aug. 12, 1946; d. David and Charlotte (Abrams) P. BFA, R.I. Sch. Design, 1968. Nutritionist, handicraft developer U.S. Peace Corps., Narino, Colombia, 1971-74; adminstr. dept. radiology U. Calif., San Francisco, 1987—. Mem. de Young Meml. Mus. (docent). Docent Fine Arts Mus., San Francisco. Home: 1925 Leavenworth St # 12 San Francisco CA 94133-2503

PINTER, JOSEPH KALMAN, mathematician; b. Janoshalma, Hungary, Jan. 12, 1953; arrived in Can., 1981; s. József and Teréz (Hoványi) P.; m. Mary Tan, Oct. 12, 1985; children: Kálmán Bonaventure, Elizabeth Anne. MS in Elec. Engring., Tech. U. Budapest, Hungary, 1976, PhD in Elec. Engring., 1979; MS in Pure Math., U. Calgary, Can., 1986, MS in Applied Math., 1996. Researcher Sefel Geophys., Calgary, Alta., Can., 1981-82; explroration geophysicist Sci. and Exploration Computer Applications, Dome Pete Ltd., Calgary, Alta., Can., 1982-87, sr. applied geophysicist, 1987-88; sr. staff geophysicist Amoco Can., Ltd., Calgary, Alta., 1988-92. Author: Propositions on the Geophysical Applications of the Radon Integral, 1990; inventor fully automated interpreter for refraction data, direct and inverse scattering in the Radon domain. Mem. Am. Math. Soc., Soc. for Indsl. and Applied Math., Assn. of Profl. Engrs. Geologists and Geophysicists of Alta. Roman Catholic. Home: # 864 Lake Lucerne Dr SE, Calgary, AB Canada T2J 3H4

PINTO, MICHAEL JACK, philanthropist, therapist, educator; b. London, Feb. 17, 1942; came to U.S., 1946; s. Maurice Pinto and Norma (Sherwin) Zimmer; m. Carol Brodovsky, July 21, 1968 (div. 1974); children: Rachel, Evan; m. Susan Deasy, Mar. 30, 1979. BA, Calif. State U., Long Beach, 1963; Holistic Health Practitioner, Mueller Coll., 1993; PhD, Calif. Inst. Integral Studies, 1996. Cert. secondary tchr., Calif. Secondary tchr. L.A. Schs., 1965-69; owner, pres. Platterpuss Records, 1968-83, Sound Music Sales, 1971-81; philanthropist Calif., N.Y., 1979—; pvt. practice cranio-sacral therapist Calif., 1992—; cons. numerous non-profit orgns., 1980—; bd. dirs. Ctr. for Study of Philanthropy. Author: How Much is Enough, 1987, Private Fundraising For Public Schools, 1996. Mem. fin. com. Pacific Oaks Coll., Pasadena, Calif., 1975-76; pres. United Jewish Appeal, Orange County, Calif., 1981-84, Laguna Beach (Calif.) Edn. Found., 1985, Laguna Canyon Found., 1991-96, The Men's Found. Mem. Arnova Assn. Rsch. Non-Profit and Voluntary Action. Home: PO Box 1809 Laguna Beach CA 92652-1809

PIOUS, DONALD A., medical educator; b. Bridgeport, Conn., Feb. 12, 1930; s. William and Rena (Milgram) P.; m. Constance Gayl Pious, Oct. 3, 1954; children: Lisa, Tony. BA, U. Pa., 1952, MD, 1956. Diplomate Am. Bd. Pediatrics; lic. physician Conn., Calif., Wash. Intern in medicine Cin. Gen. Hosp., 1956-57; resident in pediatrics Yale Med. Ctr., New Haven, 1957-59; postdoctoral fellow in genetics U. Calif.-San Diego, LaJolla, 1961-64; asst. prof. pediats. U. Wash., Seattle, 1964-69, assoc. prof., 1969-76, prof. pediats. and genetics, 1976—, prof. immunology, 1990—; vis. scientist Oxford (Eng.) U., 1972-73; vis. prof. Coll. de France, Paris, 1978; Phillips visitor Haverford (Pa.) Coll., 1993; mem. mammalian genetics and genetic basis of disease adv. group NIH, 1978-82, 83-87. Assoc. editor Exptl. and clin. Immunogenetics, 1985—; editl. bd. Mammalian Genome, 1990-92; contbr. over 100 articles to profl. jours., chpts. to books. Capt. U.S. Army, 1959-61. Recipient Rsch. Career Devel. award NIH, 1965-75, Merit award, 1990—; NIH grantee, 1964—. Mem. Am. Assn. Immunologists, Am. Soc. for Cell Biology, Am. Soc. Human Genetics, Soc. Pediat. Rsch. Home: 3602 E Schubert Pl Seattle WA 98122 Office: University of Washington Dept Pediatrics Box 356320 Seattle WA 98195-6328

PIPER, LLOYD LLEWELLYN, II, engineer, government and service industry executive; b. Wareham, Mass., Apr. 28, 1944; s. Lloyd Llewellyn and Mary Elizabeth (Brown) P.; BSEE, Tex. A&M U., 1966; MS in Indsl. Engring., U. Houston, 1973; m. Jane Melonie Scruggs, Apr. 30, 1965; 1 child, Michael Wayne. With Houston Lighting & Power Co., 1965-74; project mgr. Dow Chem. Engring. & Constrn. Svcs., Houston, 1974-78; project mgr. Ortloff Corp., Houston, 1978, mgr. engring., 1979-80, v.p., 1980-83; pres., chief exec. officer Plantech Engrs. & Constructors, Inc. subs. Dillingham Constrn. Corp., Houston, 1983-86; pres. The Delta Plantech Co., Houston, 1985-86; dir. on-site tech. devel. Chem. Waste Mgmt., Inc., Oak Brook, Ill., 1986-88; mgr. projects Chem. Waste Mgmt., Inc., Houston, 1988-94, dir. facility devel., 1994-95; asst. mgr. Richland (Wa.) Ops. U.S. Dept. Energy, 1995-96, dep. mgr., 1996—; bd. dirs., pres. Harris County Water Control and Improvement Dist., 1973-83; bd. dirs.Environ. Sci. and Tech. Found., 1997—; Ponderosa Joint Powers Agy. Harris County, 1977-83, pres., 1977-83; pres. bus. and industry adv. coun. North Harris Montgomery C. C. Dist., 1991-92. Recipient Disting. Svc. award Engrs. Coun. Houston, 1970, Outstanding Svc. award Houston sect. IEEE, 1974; named Tex. Young Engr. of Yr., 1976, Nat. Young Engr. of Yr., 1976; registered profl. engr., Tex, diplomate hazardous waste mgmt. Am. Acad. Environ. Engrs. Mem. IEEE, Nat. Soc. Profl. Engrs. (chpt. pres. 1978, nat. chmn. engrs. in industry div. 1977, nat. v.p. 1977, chmn. nat. polit. action com. 1979-82, vice chmn. nat. engrs. week 1988-92, nat. trustee edn. found. 1988-90), Project Mgmt. Inst., Phi Kappa Phi, Tau Beta Pi. Contbr. articles to profl. jours. Home: 129 Mountain View Ln Richland WA 99352 Office: Dept of Energy PO Box 550 (A7-50) Richland WA 99352

PIRAINO, ANN MAE, seminar trainer, leader, vocational counselor; b. Vancouver, Wash.; d. Elsworth Wallace Schmoeckel and Alice Marie (Blankenbickler) Avalos; m. Michael Salvatore, Nov. 19, 1983. BA in Edn., Seattle U., 1972; MA in Appl. Behavioral Sci., City U. Leadership Inst of Sea, 1987. Cert. rehab. counselor. Sec. to supt. Pasco (Wash.) Sch. Dist. No. 1, 1972-74; adminstrv. asst. Burns and Roe, Inc., Richland, Wash., 1974-81; exec. sec. UNC Nuclear Industries, Inc., Richland, Wash., 1981-83, Fairchild Semiconductor, Inc., Puyallup, Wash., 1984-87; instr. Eton Tech. Inst. (ETI), Federal Way, Wash., 1987-89; trainer, cons. Piraino Prodns., Wash., 1985—; seminar leader and cons. Profl. Sec. Internat., Wash., Alaska and Oreg. state chpts., 1985—; cons. Fed. Way Women's Network and Career Devel. Network, Wash., 1985-88; employment coord. Bus. Computer Tng. Inst., Tacoma, 1989-90; adj. faculty Office Automation Griffin Coll., Tacoma, 1990; vocat. rehab. counselor Total Care Svcs., 1990-92, 94-95, Favorite Cons., 1990-94, Genex Svcs. Inc., 1995-97, VRC, Iam Crest/Boeing, 1996—. Editor: (newsletter) The Circuit Writer, 1985-87, (pub. assn. newsletters) Hear Ye, Hear Ye, 1986-88, Training Wheels, 1987-90, Speak Up!, 1991-92, Reflections, 1991-94; role expert: (competency study) ASTD Competency and Standards Project, 1988. Co. rep. United Way/Fairchild Semiconductor, Wash., 1986; team co-leader March of Dimes/Fairchild Semiconductor, Wash., 1986; team leader March of Dimes/Town Criers Toastmasters, Wash., 1989, 90. Recipient Xi Alpha Epsilon and Beta Sigma Phi Woman of Yr. award, 1979-81; named Sec. of Yr. Pas-Ric-Ken/Sea Tac Chpts., Profl. Secs. Internat., Richland/Fed. Way, Wash., 1979, 90; Sec. of Yr. Wash.-Alaska Div. Profl. Secs. Internat., Spokane, 1980. Mem. NAFE, ASTD (chpt. v.p. 1988-89, pres. 1990), Profl. Secs. Internat. (chpt. pres. 1985-86, 91-92, pres.-elect Wash./Alaska divsn. 1986-87, pres. 1987-88), Internat. Platform Soc., Toastmasters (area gov. 1991-92, dean Leadership Inst. dist. 32 1992-94), Nat. Assn. Rehab. Profls. in Pvt. Sector, Wash. Women in Worker's Compensation, Internat. Case Mgmt. Assn., NRA-Nat. Rehab. Assn. Home: 38807 134th Pl SE Auburn WA 98092-8583

PIROFSKY, HARVEY, psychiatrist; b. N.Y.C., Nov. 13, 1920; s. Samuel and Esther (Wolpin) P.; m. Florence Pirofski, Mar. 30, 1950; children: Liise Anne, Kira. BS, CCNY; MD, U. Geneva. Diplomate Am. Bd. Psychiatry and Neurology. Intern Kings County Med. Ctr., Bklyn., 1955, resident in psychiatry, 1956-59; sr. psychiatrist Agnew (Calif.) State Hosp.; pvt. practice Calif. Mental Rsch., Palo Alto, 1961-94; assoc. clin. prof. Stanford (Calif.) Med. Ctr., 1964-94, assoc. prof. emeritus, 1994—. With USN, 1944-46. Fellow APA (life). Office: Mental Rsch Inst 555 Middlefield Rd Palo Alto CA 94301-2124

PIRONTI, LAVONNE DE LAERE, developer, fundraiser; b. L.A., Jan. 11, 1946; d. Emil Joseph and Pearl Mary (Vilmur) De Laere; m. Aldo Pironti, May 21, 1977. BA in Internat. Rels., U. So. Calif., L.A., 1967. Commd. ensign USN, 1968-91, advanced through grades to comdr., 1979; pers. officer Lemoore (Calif.) Naval Air Sta., 1972-74; human rels. mgmt. specialist Human Resource Mgmt. Detachment, Naples, Italy, 1975-78; comms. staff officer Supreme Hdqrs. Allied Powers Europe, Shape, Belgium, 1979-83; dir. Navy Family Svc. Ctr. Sigonella Naval Air Sta., Sicily, 1983-85; exec. officer Naval Sta. Guam, Apra Harbor, 1985-87; comms. staff officer NATO Comm. and Info. Sys. Agy., Brussels, Belgium, 1987-89; polit. officer for Guam, trust Territories Pacific Islands Comdr. Naval Forces Marianas, Agana, Guam, 1989-91; store mgr. Sandal Tree, Lihue, Hawaii, 1991-92; CEO, exec. dir. YWCA of Kauai, Lihue, 1992—. Mem. Kauai Children's Justice com., Lihue, 1993—; co-chair Kauai Human Svcs. Coun., Lihue; bd. dirs. Hawaii Health and Human Svcs. Alliance, Lihue, 1993—; chair Kauai County Family Self Sufficiency Program Adv. Bd., Lihue, 1993—. Decorated Navy Commendation medal, Meritorious Svc. Medal with 1 star, Def. Meritorious Svc. Medal with 2 stars, others; named Fed. Woman of the Yr. Comdr. Naval Forces Marianas, 1986-87. Roman Catholic. Office: YWCA of Kauai 3094 Elua St Lihue HI 96766-1209

PIROOZMANDI, FARID, mechanical engineer; b. Abadan, Iran, Mar. 27, 1958; came to U.S., 1979; s. Ruhollah Pirooz and Ghodsi (Roshana'i) P.; m. Neda Sayyah, Aug. 2, 1991; 1 child, Arezu Hope. BSME, U. Tex., 1981; MSME, Portland State U., 1985. Rsch. asst. U. Tex., Austin, 1979-81; engring. asst. Tex. Nuclear Div., Austin, 1981; rsch. engr. Portland (Oreg.) State U., 1983-83; prodn. mgr. Hy-Tek Industries, Beaverton, Oreg., 1983-84; gen. mgr. Electro Mech. Tech. Inc., West Linn, Oreg., 1984-91; mgr.

transducer design project Kistler-Morse Corp., Redmond, Wash., 1991-96; sr. specialist engr. SATCOM/Datalink Group, Boeing Co., Everett, Wash., 1996—. Author: Carbide Insert Crusher, 1981, Control System Computer Aided Design, 1983, Transient Flow Inverse Study Calculation of Unsaturated Permeability of Wood, 1985; patentee load cell for weighting contents of storage vessels, zero height load measuring system and method of installing. Chmn. local spiritual assembly Baha'i Faith, Bothell, Wash., 1993-96. Mem. Tau Beta Pi, Pi Tau Sigma. Home: 9005 NE 151st Pl Bothell WA 98011-4590

PISCIOTTA, SAMUEL JAMES, small business owner; b. Pueblo, Colo., Dec. 10, 1938; s. Sam Jr. and Eva May (Padula) P.; m. Cynthia Diane Garrett, Aug. 8, 1961; children: Samuel, Pamela, Richard, Michael. BA, Western State Coll., 1967. Pres., mgr. Pueblo (Colo.) Bus. Men's Club, Inc., DBA Capt. Sam's Family Athletic Club, Inc., 1961—. Composer symphonic music. Co-founder, v.p. Pueblo Performing Arts Guild, 1986—; founder, co-organizer Pueblo Office So. Colo. Better Bus. Bur., 1985—, chmn. bd. 1987-88). Recipient Order of Arrow, Boy Scouts Am., 1972; named Small Bus. Man of Yr., Colo. C. of C., 1988. Mem. Nat. Swim and Recreation Assn. (pres. 1976-77), Greater Pueblo Sports Assn. and Hall of Fame (co-founder 1972), Pueblo Jaycees (state bd. dirs. 1973-75), Pueblo Bus. Exch. (co-founder 1982, pres. 1984), Kiwanis (bd. dirs. 1986), Elks, Masons, Knight Templar, Jesters, Shriners (potentate 1992), Dante Alighieri Soc., Royal Order Scotland, Order of Quetzalcoatl (charter camaxtli 1992), Tau Kappa Epsilon. Republican. Home: 27 Pedregal Ln Pueblo CO 81005-2917 Office: Capt Sam's Family Athletic Club Inc 1500 W 4th St Pueblo CO 81004-1207 *Personal philosophy: Love is king.*

PISTER, KARL STARK, engineering educator; b. Stockton, Calif., June 27, 1925; s. Edwin LeRoy and Mary Kimball (Smith) P.; m. Rita Olsen, Nov. 18, 1950; children: Francis, Therese, Anita, Jacinta, Claire, Kristofer. BS with honors, U. Calif., Berkeley, 1945, MS, 1948; PhD, U. Ill., 1952. Instr. theoretical and applied mechanics U. Ill., 1949-52; mem. faculty U. Calif., Berkeley, 1952-91, prof. engrng. scis., 1962—, Roy W. Carlson prof. engrng., 1985-90, dean Coll. Engrng., 1980-90; chancellor U. Calif., Santa Cruz, 1991—, now pres., chancellor; Richard Merton guest prof. U. Stuttgart, W. Ger., 1978; cons. to govt. and industry; bd. dirs. Monterey Bay Aquarium Rsch. Inst.; bd. trustees Monterey Inst. Internat. Studies; chmn. bd. Calif. Coun. Sci. and Tech. Author research papers in field; assoc. editor: Computer Methods in Applied Mechanics and Engrng, 1972, Jour. Optimization Theory and Applications, 1982; editorial adv. bd. Encyclopedia Phys. Sci. and Tech. Served with USNR, World War II. Recipient Wason rsch. medal Am. Concrete Inst., 1960, Vincent Bendix Minorities in Engrng. award Am. Soc. for Engrng. Edn., 1988, Lamme medal, 1993, Alumni Honor award U. Ill. Coll. Engrng., 1982, Disting. Engrng. Alumnus award U. Calif. Coll. Engrng., 1992. Fellow ASME, AAAS, Am. Acad. Mechanics, Am. Acad. Arts and Scis., Calif. Acad. Scis. (hon.); mem. NAE, ASCE, Soc. Engrng. Sci. Office: U Calif Santa Cruz Office of Chancellor 1156 High St Santa Cruz CA 95064-1077

PITCHER, HELEN IONE, healthcare services administrator, retired; b. Colorado Springs, Colo., Aug. 6, 1931; d. William Forest Medlock and Frankie La Vone (Hamilton) Tweed; m. Richard Edwin Pitcher, Sept. 16, 1949; children: Dushka Myers, Suzanne, Marc. Student, U. Colo., 1962-64, Ariz. State U., 1966, Maricopa Tech. Coll., 1967, Scottsdale C.C., 1979-81. Design draftsman Sundstrand Aviation, Denver, 1962-65; tech. illustrator Sperry, Phoenix, 1966-68; art dir. Integrated Circuit Engrng., Scottsdale, Ariz., 1968-71, dir. advt., 1981-92; advt. artist Motorola Inc., Phoenix, 1971-74; pres. Pitcher Tech. Pubs., Scottsdale, 1974-81; nursing cons. Nursing Cons. Connection, Fountain Hills, Ariz., 1993-96; retired, 1996. Profl. advisor Paradise Valley Sch. Dist., Phoenix, 1984—; mem. bd. advisors graphic arts dept. Ariz. State U., Tempe. mem. Nat. Audio Visual Assn., Bus. Profl. Advt. Assn. (treas. 1982-86), Direct Mktg. Club. Democrat. Mem. Ch. Christ. Home: 13681 N Pima Rd Scottsdale AZ 85260-4105

PITNEY, JOHN JOSEPH, JR., political science educator; b. Saratoga Springs, N.Y., June 18, 1955; s. John Joseph and Mary Katherine (Furey) P.; m. Lisa Michelle Minshew, May 27, 1989. BA, Union Coll., Schenectady, N.Y., 1977; MA, Yale U., 1978, MPhil, 1981, PhD, 1985. Legis. asst. N.Y. State Senate, Albany, 1978-80; Congl. fellow Am. Polit. Sci. Assn., Washington, 1983-84; sr. domestic policy analyst Ho. Rep. Rsch., Washington, 1984-86; dep. rsch. dir. Rep. Nat. Com., Washington, 1989-91; asst. prof. Claremont McKenna Coll., Claremont, Calif., 1986-94; assoc. prof. Claremont McKenna Coll., Claremont, 1994—. Co-author: Congress' Permanent Minority?, 1994; contbr. articles to profl. jours. Dep. editor Rep. Nat. Conv. platform, Houston, 1992; rsch. advisor George Bush for Pres., Washington, 1988. Recipient rsch. grant Gould Humanities Ctr., Claremont, 1992, grad. fellowship Nat. Sci. Found., 1977, Danforth Found., St. Louis, 1977. Mem. Am. Polit. Sci. Assn. (rsch. grant 1987), Western Polit. Sci. Assn., Nat. Assn. Scholars, Phi Beta Kappa (chpt. sec. 1993-95), Pi Sigma Alpha. Republican. Office: Govt Dept Claremont McKenna Coll 850 Columbia Ave Claremont CA 91711-3901

PITT, WILLIAM ALEXANDER, cardiologist; b. Vancouver, B.C., Can., July 17, 1942; came to U.S., 1970; s. Reginald William and Una Sylvia (Alexander) P.; m. Judith Mae Wilson, May 21, 1965; children: William Matthew, Joanne Katharine. MD, U. B.C., Vancouver, 1967. Diplomate Royal Coll. Physicians Can. Intern, Mercy Hosp., San Diego, 1967-68, resident, 1970-71; resident Vancouver Gen. Hosp., 1968-70, U. Calif., San Diego, 1971-72; assoc. dir. cardiology Mercy Hosp., San Diego, 1972-92; with So. Calif. Cardiology Med. Group, San Diego, 1984—; pvt. practice Clin. Cons. Cardiology; bd. trustees San Diego Found. for Med. Care, 1983-89, 91—, pres., chmn. bd. trustees, 1986-88, med. dir., 1991-96; trustee Pacific Found. for Med. Care, 1996—, med. dir., 1996—; bd. dirs. Mut. Assn. for Profl. Services, Phila., 1984-92; pres. Alternet Med. Svcs., Inc., 1992-95, San Diego IPA, 1996—. Fellow Royal Coll. Physicians Can., Am. Coll. Cardiology (assoc.); mem. AMA, Am. Heart Assn., Calif. Med. Assn., San Diego County Med. Soc., San Diego County Heart Assn. (bd. dirs. 1982-88). Episcopalian. Office: So Calif Cardiology Med Group 6386 Alvarado Ct Ste 101 San Diego CA 92120-4906

PITTS, BARBARA TOWLE, accountant, painter; b. St. Paul, Minn., Nov. 8, 1944; d. James Francis and Helen (Gorman) Towle; m. E.R. Pitts, Oct. 19, 1965; 1 child, Paris Tucker Pitts. BSBA, U. Ala., 1980. CPA, Wash., Tenn. Prin. Barbara M. Pitts Assocs., Fayetteville, Tenn., 1982-90, Barbara M. Pitts CPA, Seattle, 1990—. Exhibited in group shows Midwest Watercolor Soc. 20th Ann. Nat. Open Show, 1996, Red River Watercolor Soc. 3d Ann. Nat. Juried Art Exhbn., 1996, Ea. Wash. Watercolor Soc. Ann. Nat. Competition, 1996 (Allied Arts award), Niagara Frontier Watercolor Soc. Nat. Exhbn., 1996 (Winsor and Newton award), City of Brea (Calif.) Gallery, 1996, Ariz. Aqueous '97 Nat. Competition, Tubac (Ariz.) Ctr. of Arts, 1997, Tex. Watercolor Soc. 48th Ann. Mus. of S.W., 1997. Bd. dirs. United Way Lincoln County, Fayetteville, 1989, Lincoln County Bd. Edn., Fayetteville, 1988-90; mem. planning com. Tenn. Hist. Soc., Nashville, 1989. Recipient Cert. of Recognition Tenn. Main St. Program, 1989, Best of Show award Juried Arts Ocean Shores, Wash., 1996, Best of Show awards Tex. Watercolor Soc. 48th Ann., Traveling Show Tex. Watercolor Soc. 48th Ann., 1996; named Woman of Yr., Fayetteville Bus. and Profl. Women, 1988. Mem. AICPA, Nat. Watercolor Soc., Midwest Watercolor Soc., Am. Watercolor Soc., Wash. Soc. CPA, N.W. Watercolor Soc. (treas.), Red River Watercolor Soc., Tex. Watercolor Soc., Group Health Coop. Puget Sound (cen. regional coun.), Women Painters Wash. Home: 3515 E Marion St Seattle WA 98122-5258

PITTS, FERRIS NEWCOMB, physician, psychiatry educator; b. St. Louis, Feb. 11, 1931; s. Ferris Newcomb and Florence A. (Morris) P.; m. Jocelyn Millner, May 14, 1955; children: Andrew Ferris, Jonathan Millner, Amy Pitts Buckner. BA, Washington U., St. Louis, 1952, MD, 1955. Diplomate Am. Bd. Pediats., Am. Bd. Psychology and Neurology. Intern Wash U., St Louis Children's Hosp, 1955-56; resident pediats. Washington U., St. Louis, 1955-56, resident psychiatry, 1959-62, assoc. prof. psychiatry, 1963-76; prof. psychiatry U. So. Calif., L.A., 1976—; pres. med. staffs several hosps., 1970—, Am. Assn. Advancement Electrotherapy, 1986. Editor-in-chief Jour. Clin. Psychiatry, 1980-88; patentee in field of hyperimmunization therapy for AIDS and other viral disorders; contbr. over 100 articles to profl. jours. Lt. comdr. USN, 1957-62. Career Rsch. Devel. award, NIMH. Fellow Am. Psychiat. Assn. (life); mem. Psychiat. Rsch. Soc. (founding mem.), Internat. Soc. Neurochemistry (founding mem.), Am. Soc. Neurochemistry (founding mem.), West Coast Coll. Psychiat. Rsch. (founding mem.). Home and Office: 3500 E California Blvd Pasadena CA 91107-5653

PITTS, MICHAEL DUANE, secondary education educator; b. Moultrie, Ga., July 3, 1947; s. M. J. and Emegene Patricia (Mulvihill) P.; m. Jonnie Elizabeth Reichert, Dec. 28, 1973; children: John-Michael Jeremy, Joshua Mulvihill, Daniel Lee. BA in German, Valdosta State Coll., 1971, MA in English, 1978; EdD in Literacy Edn., Wash. State U., 1992. Cert. secondary edn. Tchr. Valdosta (Ga.) Schs., 1971-78, Colfax (Wash.) Sch. Dist., 1979-81, Odessa (Wash.) Sch. Dist., 1981—; adj. prof. Heritage Coll., Toppenish, Wash., 1993—; mem. Parkside Day Care Adv. Com., Odessa, 1992—; cons. N.W. Inland Writing Project, Pullman, Wash., 1986—. Advisor: (mag.) The Wheatstalk, 1981—; editor N.W. Inland Writing Project Newsletter, 1986—. Deacon Heritage United Ch. of Christ, Odessa, 1996. Mem. Nat. Coun. Tchrs. English, Inland N.W. Coun. Tchrs. English (pres.-elect 1985—). Democrat. Home: PO Box 385 305 S 2d St Odessa WA 99159 Office: Odessa H S PO Box 248 Odessa WA 99159

PITTS, SADIE TURNER, retired educator; b. Tucson; d. Joe and Sadie (Osborne) Turner; m. William E. Pitts, July 4, 1956; children: William E. II, Allen B., Melissa A. BA in Elem. Edn., U. Ariz., 1955; MA in Elem. Edn., Calif. State Poly., Pomona, 1975. Elem. tchr. Tucson Unified Schs., 1955-62; elem. tchr. Pomona Unified Schs., 1964-72, 90-92, reading tchr., 1972-75, lang. arts specialist, 1975-90; mem. adv. bd. title I, Claremont (Calif.) Unified Sch. Dist., 1976-78; coord. tutorial reading program Alpha Kappa Alpha, Pomona, 1977-79. Author: (children's books) Sparkle, 1989(Lorraine Hansberry award 1990), The Tri Bros, 1995 (Pomona Alliance Black Sch. Educators award 1996), (poetry) Sons on the Wind, 1995. Spkr. Pomona Schs. Career Day, 1990—; vol. lang. arts activities Convalescent Care Nursing Home; mem. com. Inland Valley Coun. Chs.; vacation Bible sch. coord. South Hills Presbyn. Ch., Pomona. Mem. NAACP, Nat. Coun. Negro Women, Soc. Children's Book Writers and Illustrators, Internat. Soc. Poets, Calif. Ret. Tchrs. Assn., Delta Kappa Gamma (pres. 1982-84, Nat. Women's History Mo. award 1995), Alpha Kappa Alpha (treas. 1960—). Home: 395 Guilford Ave Claremont CA 91711

PITTS, WILLIAM CLARENCE, physicist; b. Seattle, Apr. 19, 1929; s. Clarence H. and Emily B. (Kepp) P.; m. Joanne R. Lawson, May 18, 1952 (dec. Jan. 1978); children: Starr R., Nancy H.; m. Patricia A. Kirkland, May 1, 1981. BS in Physics, U. Wash., 1951; postgrad., Stanford U., 1951-58. Rsch. scientist NACA/NASA, Moffett Field, Calif., 1951-86, Eloret Inst., Moffett Field, 1986-95; cons. Steve Miller and Assocs., Flagstaff, Ariz., 1995—. Contbr. numerous articles to profl. publs.; inventor two-force measuring balance for earth orbit application. Home and Office: 7753 Beltane Dr San Jose CA 95135-2138

PIVNICKA, BARBARA MILLIKEN, marketing executive; b. Fremont, Nebr., Apr. 24, 1953; d. James Dale and Jane (Little) Milliken; m. Richard J. Pivnicka, Sept. 24, 1977. BA in English and Art History magna cum laude, U. San Francisco, 1975. Dir. pub. rels. Schwabacher/Frey Inc., San Francisco, 1977-79; dir. investor rels. Servamatic Systems Inc., San Ramon, Calif., 1983-86; mgr. investor rels. Deloitte & Touche, San Francisco, 1986—. Dir. Sanctuary for the Homeless, San Francisco, 1986—; mem. Arthritis Found., San Francisco, 1986— ; co-chair Commonwealth Club Arts Sect., chmn. 1994; chmn. Transitional Housing Fund. Mem. Internat. Assn. Bus. Communicators, Am. Mgmt. Soc., Sales and Mktg. Execs. Assn., Commonwealth Club (gov., bd. govs.). Republican. Roman Catholic. Home: 2220 Stockbridge Ave Woodside CA 94062-1130 Office: Deloitte & Touche 50 Fremont St San Francisco CA 94105-2230

PIZZORNO, JOSEPH EGIDIO, JR., college president; b. San Gabriel, Calif., Dec. 7, 1947; s. Joseph Egidio Sr. and Mary (Carmela) P.; m. Mavis Bonnar (div. Oct. 1983); 1 child, Raven Muir; m. Lara Elise Udell, Sept. 28, 1985; 1 child, Galen Udell. BS with Distinction, Harvey Mudd Coll., Claremont, Calif., 1969; Naturopathic Doctor with honors, Nat. Coll. Naturopathic Medicine, Portland, Oreg., 1975. Rsch. asst. Lockheed Aircraft, Ontario, Calif., 1968; rsch. technologist U. Wash., Seattle, 1970-75; practice naturopathic medicine Seattle, 1975-82, practice midwifery, 1978-82; pres., researcher Bastyr U., Seattle, 1978—; pres. Coun. on Naturopathic Med. Edn., Portland, Oreg., 1985-87; apptd. adv. panel safety and efficacy of dietary supplements U.S. Office of Tech. Assessment, 1993-95; sr. med. advisor Alternative and Complementary Therapies, 1995—. Author: Total Wellness, 1996; co-author: A Textbook of Natural Medicine, 1985, Encyclopedia of Natural Medicine, 1990; contbg. editor Let's Live mag., Los Angeles, 1987—; contbr. articles to profl. jours. Mem. Seattle/King County Bd. Health, 1996—. Mem. Am. Assn. Naturopathic Physicians (bd. dirs. 1984-93), Wash. Assn. Naturopathic Physicians (edn. dir. 1976), Seattle Midwifery Sch. (edn. com. 1978-91), Northwest Sci. Fiction Soc. Libertarian. Home: 4220 NE 135th St Seattle WA 98125-3836 Office: Bastyr Univ 14500 Juanita Dr Bothell WA 98011

PIZZUTO, MICHAEL JULIAN, pianist, entertainer; b. Warner Robins, Ga., Mar. 12, 1943; s. Lee Anthony Pizzuto and Jeannine Helen (Wieza) Porter; children: Lee Michael, Jan Joseph. MusB in Piano, Chgo. Conservatory Coll., 1973, MusM in Piano, 1975. Ind. pianist entertainer, 1966—; pianist, entertainer Ambassador East, Chgo., 1966-68, Flame Restaurant, Countryside, Ill., 1968-73, Clocktower Inn, Rockford, Ill., 1983-87; owner, operator Off Broadway Restaurant, Rockford, 1985-87; pianist, entertainer Riverboat Restaurant, Rockford, 1987-88, Rockford Country Club, 1988-94; Atrium Restaurant, 1994—; faculty Rockford Coll., 1982; ann. guest artist Rockford Park Dist. Concert Band, 1978—; guest artist Kishwaukee Valley Band, Belvidere, Ill., 1983, 85; performer recent concerts Madison, Wis., San Diego. Composer (mus. arrangement) It's a Small World in the Style of 7 Famous Composers, 1977; rec. artist 4 albums, 1 cassette tape; producer, performer 3 generation concert featuring father and son., 1989. With USAR, 1967-73. Named Best Solo Entertainer Rockford mag., 1988. Mem. Mendelssohn Club. Home and Office: 8833 E Gray Rd Scottsdale AZ 85260-7079

PLAAS, KRISTINA MARIA, neonatal nurse specialist; b. Salt Lake City, June 6, 1959; d. Hyrum and Johanna Emilie Maria (Westerduin) P. BSN, U. Tenn., 1981; MSN, Vanderbilt U., 1990. APRN, Utah. Staff nurse intensive care nursery U. Tenn. Meml. Rsch. Ctr. and Hosp., Knoxville, 1981-84; staff nurse neonatal ICU Vanderbilt U. Hosp., Nashville, 1984-86; staff specialist newborn ICU U. Utah Hosp., Salt Lake City, 1986, staff nurse/clin. specialist newborn ICU, 1987—; mem. nursing purchasing coun. U. Hosp. Consortium, Oak Brook, Ill., 1993—; cons., product specialist Baxter Healthcare, Round Lake, Ill., 1994—. Author, editor: U. Utah Dept. Nursing Standards of Practice, 1986—, Nat. Assn. Neonatal Nurses Practice Guidelines, 1993-95; editor: Perspective newsletter, 1994-96. Mem. Nat. Assn. Neonatal Nurses (practice com. 1993-95, Robyn Main Excellence in Clinical Practice award 1990), Utah Perinatal Assn. (edn. bd. 1994-96), Utah Assn. Neonatal Nurses, Nat. Perinatal Assn., Sigma Theta Tau. Home: 2256 Foothill Dr # F 116 Salt Lake City UT 84109-3971 Office: U Utah Hosp Newborn ICU 50 N Medical Dr Salt Lake City UT 84132-0001

PLAMONDON, MAYNARD ALFRED, civil engineer; b. Hanover, N.H., Dec. 29, 1940; s. Maynard Albert and Lucille Norma (McNamara) P.; m. Mona Clare Peck, June 17, 1961; children: Michael A., Steven D. BS, U. N.H., 1962; MS, U. Ill., 1964, PhD, 1966. Registered profl. engr., N.Mex. Tech. advisor civil engrng. AFWL, Kirtland AFB, N.Mex., 1966-87; v.p. engrng. tech. BDM Internat., Albuquerque, 1987-88; prin. engr. Applied Rsch. Assocs., Inc., Albuquerque, 1988—. Fellow ASCE. Home: 3705 Tewa Dr NE Albuquerque NM 87111-4317 Office: Applied Rsch Assoc PO Box 3588 Albuquerque NM 87185-3588

PLANE, FREDRICK ALAN, county official; b. Eugene, Oreg., Dec. 25, 1955; s. Richard Alan Plane and Dorothy Elizabeth (Morris) Touchstone; m. Karen Maureen Dirksen Bryant, Aug. 1, 1976 (div. Sept. 1987); children: Alison Michelle, Breanna Renee; m. Sheila Kay Brown, Oct. 18, 1992. BS in Bus., Calif. State U., Bakersfield, 1978, MPA, 1994. Bus. mgr. Niles Med. Group, Bakersfield, 1978-80; sr. buyer County Kern, Bakersfield, 1980-87, dep. adminstrv. officer, 1988—. Sec., treas. So. Valley Toastmasters, Bakersfield, 1989, pres., 1990, v.p., 1991, 92; bd. dirs. Kern County Econ. Opportunity Corp., Bakersfield, 1992—, v.p., 1996, pres., 1997. Mem. Am. Soc. Pub. Adminstrn. (sec. 1991, pres. 1992, 93, past pres. 1994). Democrat. Home: 11901 April Ann Ave Bakersfield CA 93312-4601 Office: Kern County Adminstrv Office 5th Fl 1115 Truxtun Ave Fl 5 Bakersfield CA 93301-4617

PLANN, SUSAN JOAN, linguist, foreign language educator; b. Hollywood, Calif., Aug. 3, 1946; d. Paul I. and Paula Mae (Witaschek) P.; m. Gonzalo Navajas, Nov. 8, 1975 (div. May 1988); 1 child, Paul Navajas-Plann. BA in Spanish, UCLA, 1968, MA in Spanish, 1970, PhD in Romance Linguistics, 1975. Prof. Spanish and Portuguese UCLA, 1975—; cons. Projecto Educativo Comunitario, L.A. Author: Relative Clauses in Spanish, 1980, A Silent Minority, 1997; reviewer jours. Hispanic Linguistics, Issues in Applied Linguistics, Linguistic Inquiry; contbr. articles to profl. jours. Del Amo Faculty fellow UCLA, 1985; Com. Internat. Exch. of Scholars grantee Fulbright, 1987; named Powrie Doctor Chair Deaf Studies Gallaudet U., 1994. Mem. Linguistic Soc. Am., Deaf History Internat. Office: UCLA Dept Spanish & Portuguese 405 Hilgard Ave Los Angeles CA 90024-1301

PLATT, JAMES ROBERT, business executive; b. Batavia, N.Y., Oct. 23, 1948; s. Robert John and Mildred J. (Foote) P.; m. Shelly A. Tunis, May 24, 1980; children: Shane Christopher, Tristan Robert. BS, SUNY, Brockport, 1970; MA, Ariz. State U., 1982. Cert. tchr., N.Y. Inside sales supr. Mallco Distbrs., Phoenix, 1972-77; grad. teaching asst. Ariz. State U., Tempe, 1978-79; sales rep. Wisco Equipment Co., Inc., Phoenix, 1979-82, sales mgr., 1984-88; sales rep. Clyde Hardware Co., Tucson, 1982-84; v.p. Wistech Controls, Phoenix, 1988—. Mem. Ariz. Coun. Excellence. Regents scholar SUNY, 1966-70. Mem. Instrument Soc. Am., Young Execs.-Fluid Power Distbrs. Assn., Am. Soc. Environ. History, Soc. Mfg. Engrs., Phi Alpha Theta. Office: Wistech Controls 4810 S 36th St Phoenix AZ 85040-2905

PLATT, JOSEPH BEAVEN, former college president; b. Portland, Oreg., Aug. 12, 1915; s. William Bradbury and Mary (Beaven) P.; m. Jean Ferguson Rusk, Feb. 9, 1946; children: Ann Ferguson Walker, Elizabeth Beaven Garrow. BA, U. Rochester, 1937; PhD, Cornell U., 1942; LLD, U. So. Calif., 1969, Claremont McKenna Coll., 1982; DSc, Harvey Mudd Coll., 1981. Instr. physics U. Rochester, N.Y., 1941-43, from asst. prof. to prof., 1946-56, assoc. chmn. dept. physics, 1954-56; staff mem. radiation lab. MIT, Cambridge, 1943-46; pres. Harvey Mudd Coll., Claremont, Calif., 1956-76, now part-time sr. prof. physics; pres. Claremont U. Ctr., 1976-81; trustee Aerospace Corp., 1972-85, Consortium for Advancement of Pvt. Higher Edn., 1985-92; chief physics br. AEC, 1949-51; cons. U.S. Office Ordnance Rsch., NSF, 1953-56; mem. com. on sci. in UNESCO, NAS-NRC, 1960-62, mem. com. on internat. orgns. and programs, 1962-64, sci. advisor U.S. Del., UNESCO Gen. Conf., Paris, 1960, alt. del., 1962, chmn. Subcom. on Sino-Am. Sci. Cooperation, 1965-79; mem. panel on internat. sci. Pres.'s Sci. Adv. Com., 1961; trustee Analytic Svcs., Inc., 1958-89, chmn., 1961-89; mem. adv. com. on sci. edn. NSF, 1965-70, 72-76, chmn., 1969-70, 73-74, 74-75; bd. dirs. Lincoln Found., 1979-85, Bell & Howell Corp., 1978-88, Am. Mut. Fund, 1981-88, DeVry, Inc., 1984-87, Sigma Rsch., 1983-87, Jacobs Engring. Co., 1978-86. Author: Harvey Mudd College: The First Twenty YEars, 1994. Trustee China Found. for Promotion of Edn. and Culture, 1966—, Carnegie Found. for Advancement Tchg., 1970-78; chmn. select com. Master Plan for Higher Edn. Calif., 1971-73; mem. Carnegie Coun. for Policy Studies in Higher Edn., 1975-80. Fellow Am. Phys. Soc.; mem. IEEE, Automobile Club So. Calif. (bd. dirs. 1973-90, chmn. bd. dirs. 1986-87), Calif. Club, Sunset Club, Twilight Club, Cosmos Club, Bohemian Club, Phi Beta Kappa, Sigma Xi, Phi Kappa Phi. Home: 452 W 11th St Claremont CA 91711-3833

PLATT, LEWIS EMMETT, electronics company executive; b. Johnson City, N.Y., Apr. 11, 1941; s. Norval Lewis and Margaret Dora (Williams) P.; m. Joan Ellen Redmund, Jan. 15, 1983; children: Caryn, Laura, Amanda, Hillary. BME, Cornell U., 1964; MBA, U. Pa., 1966. With Hewlett Packard, Waltham, Mass., 1966-71, engrng. mgr., 1971-74, ops. mgr., 1976-77, div. gen. mgr., 1974-80, group gen. mgr., Palo Alto, Calif., 1980-84, v.p., 1983-85, exec. v.p., 1987-92, pres., CEO, chmn., 1993—; dir. Pacific Telesis. Trustee Waltham Hosp., 1978-80, Wharton Sch. Bd. Overseers, 1993; mem. Mid-Peninsula YMCA, 1980—, bd. couns. YMCA-USA, 1993—, Cornell U. Coun., 1992, Computer Sys. Policy Project, 1993, Calif. Bus. Roundtable, 1993, Bus. Coun., 1993, Bay Area Coun., 1993, Bus. Roundtable, 1993; vice chmn. Y Coun., 1989, mem. bd. dirs. Joint Venture, Silicon Valley, 1996. Recipient Red Triangle award Min-Peninsula YMCA, 1992, Internat. Citizens award World Forum Silicon Valley, San Jose, Calif., 1994, outstanding alumnus, Wharton Alumni Honor Roll, Wharton Schl. Business, Univ. Pa., 1994-95, award for bus. excellence U. Calif. Sch. Bus. Adminstrn., 1996, Tree of Life award Jewish Nat. Fund, 1996, Leadership and Vision award San Francisco Chpt. French-Am. C. of C., 1997. Mem. IEEE, Sci. Apparatus Mfg. Assn. (dir. 1978-80). Office: Hewlett Packard Co 3000 Hanover St Palo Alto CA 94304-1112

PLATT, WARREN E., lawyer; b. McNary, Ariz., Aug. 5, 1943. BA, Mich. State U., 1965; JD, U. Ariz., 1969. Bar: Ariz. 1969, Calif. 1991, Texas 1993. Atty. Snell & Wilmer, Phoenix. Mng. editor: Ariz. Law Rev., 1968-69. Fellow Am. Coll. Trial Lawyers; mem. Blue Key, Order of Coif, Phi Alpha Delta. Office: Snell & Wilmer One Arizona Ctr Phoenix AZ 85004-0001

PLAZAK, DEAN JAMES, physician, psychiatrist; b. Wisconsin Rapids, Wis., June 1, 1927; s. James Joseph and Amelia Elizabeth (Liska) Plzak; m. Carole Jane Marshall, Feb. 21, 1964; children: David, Deanna, Nancy, Elisabeth. BS in Med. Sci., U. Wis., 1949, MD, 1951. Diplomate Am. Bd. Psychiatry and Neurology, Am. Bd. Forensic Psychiatry. Intern Abington Meml. Hosp., 1951-52; resident U. Colo. Med. Ctr., 1952-53, Nat. Naval Med. Corps, 1954-56; pvt. practice forensic psychiatry Boulder, Colo., 1957—; Nat. Naval Med. Ctr.; forensic psychiatrist state, fed., and civil cts., Colo. and others, 1977—; nat. examiner Am. Bd. Psychiatry and Neurology, 1974—. Contbr. articles to profl. jours. Co-founder devel. disabilities program and various offices Boulder County Devel. Disabilities Ctr., 1968-91. Lt. M.C. USN, 1950-57. Fellow Am. Acad. Forensic Scis.; mem. Am. Psychiat. Assn. (life), Am. Acad. Psychiatry and The Law. Office: PO Box 3229 Boulder CO 80307-3229

PLEDGER, LELAND JAMES (LEE PLEDGER), publisher, travel writer; b. Black River Falls, Wis., June 14, 1943; s. Lyle James and Verna L. (Nelson) P.; m. Sharon Dell Mathews, Dec. 30, 1964; children: Troy Edward, Shawnna Patrice. Student, Kans. State U., 1961-63; BA, U. Alaska, 1966; grad., Columbia Sch. Broadcasting, 1971. Sales rep. Xerox Corp., Torrance, Calif., 1968-70, adminstrv. mgr., 1970-72; mgr., owner Marshall (Wis.) Lumber Co., Inc., Calif., 1972-77; radio broadcaster Sta. WTTN, Watertown, Wis., 1975-76; pub. Freighter Travel News, Roy, Wash., 1977—, tour leader, 1977—; piano tuner, Alaska, Wis., Oreg., Wash., 1964—; guide Pacific Trailways and Evergreen Stage Lines, Salem, Oreg., 1972-77. Contbr. numerous articles on travel and automotives to mags., newspapers, and periodicals; inventor air purification and fuel enhancement devices. Alderman Village of Marshall, 1973-75; bd. pres. Unity of Salem (Oreg.) Ch., 1985-86. 1st lt. U.S. Army, 1966-68. Named One of Outstanding Young Men in Am. 1975, Village of Marshall, Wis. and Farmers & Merchants Bank, Marshall. Fellow Am. Assn. Travel Editors, World Ship Soc. Home: 3524 Harts Lake Rd Roy WA 98580 Office: Freighter Travel Club Am 3524 Harts Lake Loop Rd S Roy WA 98580-9195

PLESSNER, GERALD MAURICE, business executive; b. St. Louis, Oct. 10, 1934; s. Herman and Rose (Goldstein) P.; m. Carole Renee Spirtas, May 25, 1959; children: Mitchell Scott, Janice Aurelia, Ellen Beth Bartell. BA, Missouri Valley Coll., Marshall, Mo., 1957. Cert. fund-raising exec. Exec. dir. Boy Scouts Am., various locations, 1957-75; mng. editor Consumer Newsletter, L.A., 1975-76; pres. Fundraiser, Inc., Arcadia, Calif., 1976—, Non-Profit Network, Arcadia, 1986-90, Am. Breathing Machines, Inc., Arcadia, 1992—; adj. faculty U. So. Calif., L.A., 1985-92, UCLA, 1992-94. Author: Ency. of Fundraising, 1980-90; pub. video tapes: Internat. Certification in Fund Raising, 1987. Mem. Nat. Soc. Fund Raising Exec. (vice chmn., treas. 1988-91, greater L.A. chpt. pres. 1984-86, Outstanding Profl. 1983). Office: American Breathing Machines PO Box 661148 Arcadia CA 91066-1148

PLETSCH, CARL ERICH, history educator; b. Boston, May 19, 1943; s. Erich Carl and Mary (Hart) P.; 1 child, Laura. BA in History, Philosophy, Brigham Young U., 1968; MA in European History, U. Chgo., 1971, PhD in History, Philosophy, 1977. Lectr. U. Chgo., 1972-74, Harper fellow, 1975-77; asst. prof. history U. N.C., Chapel Hill, 1978-85; Mellon fellow U. Pitts., 1985-86; vis. asst. prof. Appalachian State U., Boone, N.C., 1986-87, U. N.C., Wilmington, 1987-88; asst. prof. Miami U., Oxford, Ohio, 1988-92, assoc. prof., 1992—; vis. rsch. prof. USAF Acad., Colo., 1995-97. Author: Young Nietzsche, Becoming a Genius, 1991, (with others) Psychoanalytic Studies of Biography, 1987; co-editor: (with Samuel H. Baron) Introspection in Biography: Psychological Dimensions of the Biographic Process, 1985, (with Dwight Baldwin & Judith de Luce) Beyond Preservation, 1993; contbr. articles to profl. jours., revs. Mem. City Coun., Oxford, Ohio, 1991-95, vis. rsch. prof. United States Air Force Acad. Colo., 1995-97. Internat. Rsch. and Exch. Bd. fellow, Halle, Germany, 1981, Inst. for Advanced Study fellow, Princeton, 1977-78, German Acad. Exch. Svc. fellow, 1971-72, 74-75, Ferdinand Schevill fellow for grad. study U. Chgo., 1969-71; NEH Conf. grantee, 1981. Office: Miami U History Dept Oxford OH 45056 also: USAF Acad 2354 Fairchild Dr Ste 4K25 U S A F Academy CO 80840

PLETSCH, MARIE ELEANOR, plastic surgeon; b. Walkerton, Ont., Can., May 3, 1938; came to U.S. 1962; d. Ernest John and Olive Wilhemina (Hossfeld) P.; m. Ludwig Philip Breiling, Aug. 25, 1967; children: John, Michael, Anne. Dr. Med., U. Toronto, 1962. Diplomate Am. Bd. Plastic Surgery. Intern Cook County Hosp., Chgo., 1962-63, resident, gen. surgery, 1963-64; resident, gen. surgery St. Mary's Hosp., San Francisco, 1964-66; resident in plastic surgery St. Francis Hosp., San Francisco, 1966-69; practice med. specializing in plastic surgery Santa Cruz, Calif., 1969—; adminstr. Plasticenter, Inc., Santa Cruz, 1976-88, med. dir., 1987-88. Mem. AMA, Am. Soc. Plastic and Reconstructive Surgeons, Calif. Soc. Plastic Surgeons (mem. coun. 1986-89, sec. 1989-93, v.p. 1994-95, pres. elect 1995-96, pres. 1996-97), Calif. Med. Assn., Assn. Calif. Surgery Ctrs. (pres. 1988-92), Santa Cruz County Med. Soc. (bd. govs. 1983-88, 1992-94), Santa Cruz Surgery Ctr. (bd. dirs. 1988-93). Roman Catholic. Office: Santa Cruz Can-Am Med Group 1669 Dominican Way Santa Cruz CA 95065-1523

PLOMP, TEUNIS (TONY PLOMP), minister; b. Rotterdam, The Netherlands, Jan. 28, 1938; arrived in Can., 1951; s. Teunis and Cornelia (Pietersma) P.; m. Margaret Louise Bone, July 21, 1962; children: Jennifer Anne, Deborah Adele. BA, U. B.C. (Can.), Vancouver, 1960; BD, Knox Coll., Toronto, Ont., Can., 1963, DD (hon.), 1988. Ordained to ministry Presbyn. Ch., 1963. Minister Goforth Meml. Presbyn. Ch., Saskatoon, Sask., Can., 1963-68, Richmond (B.C.) Presbyn. Ch., 1968—; clerk Presbytery of Westminster, Vancouver, 1969—; moderator 113th Gen. Assembly Presbyn. Ch. Can., 1987-88, dep. clk., 1987—; chaplain New Haven Correctional Centre, Burnaby, B.C. Contbr. mag. column You Were Asking, 1982-89. Office: Richmond Presbyn Ch, 7111 #2 Rd, Richmond, BC Canada V7C 3L7*

PLONE, ALLEN L., media company executive, writer, game designer; b. Phila., Jan. 30, 1947; s. Herman Issac and Anne Anita (Stuart) P.; m. Carol A. Marcus, Nov. 11, 1978; children: Denise Ann Plone Sullivan, Brian Elliott. BA, San Francisco State U., 1968, MA; PhD, U. Calif., Santa Cruz, 1977. Dir. visual art films, San Francisco, 1977-83; CEO, Snow Lion Interactive Media, L.A., 1993—. Writer, dir. (television) Wow!, For the Common Good, Crocker's Dream, Simple Machines, (film) Sweet Justice; dir. (television) Shelly Berman: Getting a Laugh, (films) Phantom of the Ritz, Night Screams, (theater) The Hairy Ape, The Prisoner, King Lear, Zoo Story, R.U.R., The Birthday Party; writer, dir. (CD interactive media) Isis, Alphabet Adventure, Shyft, Bootleggers; contbr. short stories to mags.; dir. more than 500 TV commls., others. Recipient Clio award, 1982, Golden Eagle award Coun. for Internat. Non-theatrical Events, 1983, award Rosebud mag., 1995, Telly Golden award U.S. Film Festival Silver award, Cine Golden Eagle, IFPA Silver Cindy, others. Democrat. Jewish. Office: Snow Lion Interactive Media 1119 Colorado Ave Santa Monica CA 90401

PLORDE, JAMES JOSEPH, physician, educator; b. Brewster, Minn., Feb. 16, 1934; s. James Arthur and Mary Jeanette (Lutz) P.; m. Diane Sylvia Koenigs, Aug. 28, 1964 (div. July 1974); children: Lisa Marie, Michele Louise, James Joshua. BA, U. Minn., 1956, BS, 1957, MD, 1959. Diplomate Am. Bd. Internal Medicine, Am. Bd. Pathology. Vol. leader Peace Corps, Gondar, Ethiopia, 1964-66; intern King County Hosp., Seattle, 1959-60; resident U. Wash., Seattle, 1960-62, asst. prof. medicine, 1967-69, assoc. prof., 1971-78, prof. medicine, lab. medicine, 1978—; head clin. investigation U.S. Naval Med. Research, Addis Ababa, Ethiopia, 1968-71; chief infectious diseases, microbiology VA Hosp., Seattle, 1973—; cons. WHO, 1975, Suez Canal U. Faculty of Medicine, Ismailia, Arab Republic of Egypt, 1981-85. Contbr. numerous articles to profl. jours., chpts. to books. Fellow Infectious Disease Soc., ACP; mem. AAAS, Am. Soc. Microbiology, Acad. Clin. Lab. Physicians and Scientists. Home: 3134 W Laurelhurst Dr NE Seattle WA 98105-5346 Office: Vets Med Ctr 1660 S Columbian Way Seattle WA 98108-1532

PLOUGH, CHARLES TOBIAS, JR., retired electronics engineering executive; b. Oakland, Calif., Sept. 7, 1926; s. Charles Tobias Sr. and Miriam Lucille (Miller) P.; m. Jean Elizabeth Rose, June 13, 1950 (div. May 1969); children: Charles III, Cathleen, Mark, Barbara; m. Janet Mary Ansell Lumley, July 5, 1969; children: Mark Ansell Lumley, Simon John Lumley. AB with honors, Amherst Coll., 1950; BSEE with honors, U. Calif., Berkeley, 1953. Mgr. tech. devel. Fairchild Semiconductor, Palo Alto, Calif., 1958-71; v.p. Multi-State Devices, Montreal, Can., 1971-78; mgr. research and devel. Dale Electronics, Norfolk, Nebr., 1978-89, ret., 1989. Patentee in field. Mem. Lions (sec. Norfolk 1982-86); Leader Albuquerque Interfaith 1993—. Home: 2030 Quail Run Dr NE Albuquerque NM 87122-1100

PLUM, THOMAS SCHUNIOR, software company executive; b. Washington, Sept. 8, 1943; s. George E. and Ruby (Pritchett) S.; m. Joan Hall, Sept. 18, 1975 (dec. Aug. 1989); m. Lana Lee Eastman Plum, Oct. 1, 1990. BS, Rice U., 1965; PhD, U. Mich., 1972. Asst. prof. SUNY, Binghamton, 1972-76; instr. Yourdon Inc., N.Y.C., 1976-78; mgr. AGS Computers, Piscataway, N.J., 1978-79; chmn. Plum Hall, Inc., Cardiff, N.J., 1979-89; pres. Plum Hall, Inc., Kamuela, Hawaii, 1990—; vice-chair X3J11, Washington, 1984-94; internat. rep. X3J16, Washington, 1991-94; convenor JTC1/SC22/WG21 (C), 1996—. Author: Learning to Program in C, 1982, C Programming Guidelines, 1983, Reliable Data Structures in C, 1985; co-author: C Programming Guidelines, 1991 (Jolt award 1992). Mem. Rotary Club North Hawaii (club svc.). Office: Plum Hall Inc PO Box 44610 Kamuela HI 96743-4610

PLUMMER, ORA BEATRICE, nursing educator, trainer; b. Mexia, Tex., May 25, 1940; d. Macie Idella (Echols); B.S. in Nursing, U. N.Mex., 1961; M.S. in Nursing Edn., UCLA, 1966; children—Kimberly, Kevin, Cheryl. Nurses aide Bataan Meml. Meth. Hosp., Albuquerque, 1958-60, staff nurse, 1961-62, 67-68; staff nurse, charge nurse, relief supr. Hollywood (Calif.) Community Hosp., 1962-64; instr. U. N.Mex. Coll. of Nursing, Albuquerque, 1968-69; sr. instr. U. Colo. Sch. Nursing, Denver, 1971-74; asst. prof. U. Colo. Sch. Nursing, Denver, 1974-76; staff assoc. III Western Interstate Commn. for Higher Edn., Boulder, Colo., 1976-78; dir. nursing Garden Manor Nursing Home, Lakewood, Colo., 1978-79; ednl. coordination Colo. Dept. Health, Denver, 1987—. Active Colo. Cluster of Schs.-faculty devel.; mem. adv. bd. Affiliated Children's and Family Services, 1977; mem. state instl. child abuse and neglect adv. com., 1984—; mem. bd. trustee Colo. Acad., 1990—; mem. planning com. State Wide Conf. on Black Health Concerns, 1977; mem. staff devel. com. Western Interstate Commn. for Higher Edn., 1978, minority affairs com., 1978, coordinating com. for baccalaureate program, 1971-76; active minority affairs U. Colo. Med. Center, 1971-72; mem. ednl. resources com. public relations com., rev. com. for reappointment, promotion, and tenure U. Colo. Sch. Nursing, 1971-76; regulatory tng. com., 1989—, gerontol. adv. com., Met. State Coll., 1989-93; expert panel mem. Long Term Care Training Manual, HCFA, Balt., 1989; mem. EDAC com. Colo. Dept. of Health, 1989-96. Mem. NAFE, Am. Soc. Tng. and Devel., Am. Nurses Assn., Colo. Nurses Assn. (affirmative action comm. 1977, 78, 79, 93-96), bd. trusteesColo. Acad., 1990-96, Phi Delta Kappa. Avocation: pub. speaking, training. Contbr. articles in field to profl. jours. Office: 4300 Cherry Creek South Dr Denver CO 80222-1523

PLUMMER, STEVEN TSOSIE, bishop; b. Coalmine, N. Mex., Aug. 14, 1944; m. Catherine B. Tso; children: Brian Tso, Byron Tso, Steven, Jr., Cathlena. Student, San Juan Community Coll., Farmington, N. Mex., Phoenix (Ariz.) Jr. Coll., Ch. Divinity Sch. of the Pacific, San Francisco. Ordained deacon, The Episc. Ch., 1975, priest, 1976. Deacon, priest Good Shepherd Mission, Fort Defiance, Ariz., 1976-77; vicar St. John the Baptizer, Montezuma Creek, Utah, 1977-83; regional vicar for Utah Bluff, Utah, from 1983; consecrated bishop Episc. Ch. in Navajoland, Farmington, N. Mex., 1990; mem. Episc. Council of Indian Ministries. Office: The Episcopal Ch Navajoland Area Mission PO Box 720 Farmington NM 87499-0720 Address: The Episcopal Ch Navajoland Area Mission PO Box 40 Bluff UT 84512*

PLUNKETT, MARVIN WAYNE, data processing company executive; b. Roseburg, Oreg., Mar. 16, 1952; s. Kenneth V. and Minnie E. (Bible) P. Student, Umpqua C.C., 1978-79. Founder, owner Profit Systems Software, Roseburg, 1979—. Mem. Roseburg Optimist Club (bd. dirs. 1993-95). Office: Profit Systems Software 1641 NW Rutter Ln Roseburg OR 97470-1949

PLUNKETT, MICHAEL C., psychotherapist; b. Nyack, N.Y., Feb. 23, 1953; s. Stephen J. Jr. and Naomi M. (Davies) P.; m. Barbara E. Sellers, Sept. 2, 1983; 1 child, Joshua E. BSBA, St. Thomas Aquinas Coll., 1975; MA in Psychology, U. No. Colo., 1986. Lic. profl. counselor, Colo.; cert. addiction counselor, Colo., instr. in prevention of HIV disease among substance abusers, Nat. Inst. Drug Abuse, instr. in outreach and retention of methadone clients. Diagnostic coord. El Paso County Dept. Health and Environ./McMaster Ctr., Colorado Springs, 1987-95, prevention & outreach supr. Prevention HIV IHEPB among IDUs; instr. psychology Pikes Peak C.C., Colorado Springs, 1988-96, SCAP-Client Svcs. Com., 1996—; mem. Colorado Springs HIV Edn. and Prevention Consortium. Bd. dirs. So. Colo. AIDS Project, HIV Edn. and Prevention Consortium, Colorado Springs, 1995; mem. ad hoc com. HIV Prevention Cmty. Planning Com., 1994; bd. dirs. Pikes Peak region Nat. Coun. Alcoholism and Drug Dependency, 1988-91, vice-chmn., 1990; mem. subcom. on needle exch. Gov.'s AIDS Coun.; active Coloradans Working Together Core Planning Com., Parity, Inclusion, and Representation Com., Combined Intervention Com., 1995—, Safety Network Project, 1996; mem. subcom. needle exch. Govs. Aid Coun.; fetal alcohol syndrome coord. El Paso County Dept. Health and Edn., Safety Network. Mem. Hard Reduction Coalition, Nat. Assn. Preventions Profls. Office: El Paso County Health and Environ 301 S Union Blvd Colorado Springs CO 80910-3123

PLUTA, STANLEY JOHN, manufacturing project engineer; b. Ware, Mass., Feb. 5, 1966; s. John Henry and Josephine Ann (Wojnicki) Heupel; m. Sandra Akiko Ishizaka. AAS in Aero. Ground Equipment Tech., C.C. of USAF, 1987; BS in Indsl. Tech., So. Ill. U., 1988; MBA, Calif. State U., Long Beach, 1994. Registered profl. engr., Calif. Sort coord. Roadway Package System, L.A., 1989-90; assoc. indsl. engr. Northrop Corp., Hawthorne, Calif., 1990, indsl. engr., 1990-94, sr. indsl. engr., 1994-95; mfg. project engr. Packard-Hughes Interconnect, Irvine, Calif., 1995—. Staff sgt. USAF, 1985-89. Decorated Air Force Commendation medal. Mem. Am. Prodn. and Inventory Control Soc., Inst. Indsl. Engrs. Home: 24069 Chateney Ln Murrieta CA 92562 Office: Packard-Hughes Interconnect MS 111 17150 Von Karman Ave Irvine CA 92614-0901

POCKLINGTON, PETER H., business executive; b. Regina, Sask., Can., Nov. 18, 1941; s. Basil B. and Eileen (Dempsey) P.; m. Eva d. Jack McAvoy, June 2, 1974; 4 children. Pres. Westown Ford, Tilbury, Ont., Can., 1967-69; pres. Chatham, Ont., 1969-71, Edmonton, Alta., Can., 1971-82; chmn. Pocklington Fin. Corp., Edmonton, 1982—; owner, gov. Edmonton Oiler Hockey Club, 1976—; owner Edmonton Trapper Triple A Baseball Club, 1981—; formed Hartford Properties, Inc., 1985, Edmonton, Club Fit Inc., 1990; purchased Superior Furniture Systems Mfg., Inc., 1987, Canbra Foods Ltd., 1988, Green Acre Farms, Sabastool, Miss., 1988, Green Acre Foods Inc., Nacadoches, Tex., 1988. Mem. Mayfair Golf and Country Club, Edmonton Golf and Country Club, Vintage Golf Club, Indian Wells, Calif. Office: Pocklington Fin Corp Ltd, 2500 Sun Life Pl 10123-99 St, Edmonton, AB Canada T5J 3H1 also: Edmonton Oilers, Edmonton, AB Canada T5B 4M9*

POCKROS, PAUL JOSEPH, gastroenterologist; b. Cin., July 1, 1952; s. Marvin Ned Pockros and Sophia (Mansbach) Ralson; m. Ann Marie Whealen, July 6, 1980; children: Lara, Jacob, Alana. BA, U. Calif. San Diego, 1974; MD, U. So. Calif., 1978. Diplomate Am. Bd. Gastroenterology, Am. Bd. Internal Medicine. Intern in internal medicine U. So. Calif. Med. Ctr., L.A., 1978-79; resident in internal medicine USC Med. Ctr., L.A., 1979-81; from fellow in gastroenterology to gastroenterologist Scripps Clinic & Rsch. Found., La Jolla, Calif., 1981—; fellow hepatology USC/Rancho Los Amigos Hosp., 1984-85; head divsn. gastro/hepatology Scripps Clinic & Rsch. Ctr., 1996—; med. dir., liver transplantation co-dir. Liver Disease Ctr., Scripps Clinic & Rsch. Ctr. Founding mem. Am. Liver Found., 1989. Fellow ACP, Am. Coll. Gastroenterology (gov. So. Calif. region 1996—); mem. Am. Assn. Study of Liver Disease, Am. Gastroenterology Assn., Am. Soc. Transplant Physicians, Am. Liver Found. (bd. dirs. 1990—), S.D. Gastroenterol. Soc. (pres. 1992). Democrat. Jewish. Home: PO Box 9905 Rancho Santa Fe CA 92067-4905 Office: Scripps Clinic 10666 N Torrey Pines Rd La Jolla CA 92037-1027

PODBOY, JOHN WATTS, clinical, forensic psychologist; b. York, Pa., Sept. 27, 1943; s. August John and Harriett Virginia (Watts) P.; 1 son, Matthew John. B.A., Dickinson Coll., 1966; M.S., San Diego State Coll., 1971; Ph.D., U. Ariz., 1973. Dir., Vets. Counseling Center, U. Ariz., Tucson, 1972-73; project dir. San Mateo County (Calif.) Human Relations Dept., Redwood City, 1974; staff psychologist Sonoma State Hosp., Eldridge, Calif., 1975-81; cons. clin. psychologist Comprehensive Care Corp., Newport Beach, Calif., 1974-75, Sonoma County (Calif.) Probation Dept., 1976-88; pvt. practice, Kenwood, Calif., 1982—; cons. to No. Calif. Superior Cts., 1983-85; asst. prof. Sonoma State U., 1977-81; dir. Sonoma Diagnostic and Remedial Center, 1979-82. Chmn. San Mateo County Diabetes Assn., 1975. Served to lt. USNR, 1966-69. Fellow Am. Coll. Forensic Psychology, Am. Bd. Med. Psychotherapists (fellow); mem. APA, Western Psychol. Assn., Redwood Psychol. Assn. (pres. 1983), Nat. Council Alcoholism, Nat. Rehab. Assn. Home: PO Box 488 Kenwood CA 95452-0488

PODESTO, GARY, mayor. Mayor City of Stockton, Calif. Office: 425 N El Dorado St Stockton CA 95202

POE, LENORA MADISON, psychotherapist and author; b. New Bern, Ala., Jan. 3, 1934; d. Tommy and Carrie (Norfleet) Madison; m. Levi Mathis Poe, June 21, 1957; children: Michael DeWayne, Michelle DaNita Burke. BS, Stillman Coll., Tuscaloosa, Ala., 1956; MA, Calif. State U., Hayward, 1972, MS, 1980; PhD, Ctr. for Psychol. Studies, Albany, Calif., 1991. Lic. marriage, family and child therapist. Classroom tchr. Perry County Schs., Uniontown, Ala., 1956-59, Richmond (Calif.) Unified Schs., 1962-69; guidance counselor Berkeley (Calif.) Unified Schs., 1969-79; psychotherapist in pvt. practice Berkeley, 1982—, West Coast Children's Ctr., El Cerrito, Calif., 1982—; lectr. Grandparents as Parents, 1992—; part-time prof. J.F.K. U., Orinda, Calif., 1993; del. White House Conf. on Aging, Washington, 1995; cons. in field; staff cons. Cmty. Adult Day Health Svcs., Highland Gen. Hosp., Oakland. Author: Black Grandparents as Parents, 1992. Pres. nat. bd. dirs. Stillman Coll., 1992—; mentor cons. Black Women Organized for Ednl. Devel., Oakland, Calif., 1994—; mem. adv. bd. Nat. Black Aging Network, Oakland, 1992—; founding mem., advisor Realmindcas Civic Club, Richmond, 1976—; mem. Families United Against Crack Cocaine, Oakland; bd. dirs. Ctr. for Elders for Independence, Oakland; trustee Ctr. for Psychol. Studies, Albany; chairperson Grandparents Caregivers Advocacy Task Force, Oakland, Calif.; mem. bd. edn. Ministry of Ch. by Side of Road, Berkeley; also others. Recipient cert. of Appreciation African Am. Hist. and Cultural Soc., San Francisco, 1992, President's citation for Excellence Nat. Assn. for Equal Opportunity in Higher Edn., 1993, award Excellence in Edn. Nat. Coun. Negro Women, 1993, S award Stillman Coll., Appreciation award for Excellence Nystrom Elem. Sch., Richmond, 1994, Outstanding Alumna of the Yr. award Ctr. for Psychological Studies, 1995. Mem. Nat. Coalition Grandparents as Parents (adv. com. 1992—), No. Coalition Grandparents as Parents (co-chmn. 1991-93), Stillman Coll. Nat. Alumni Assn. (pres.), Calif. Coalition Grandparent/Relative Caregivers (co-chair), Nat. Coalition Grandparent/Relative Caregivers (advisor). Home: 940 Arlington Ave Berkeley CA 94707-1929 Office: 2034 Blake St Ste 1 Berkeley CA 94704-2604

POE, ROBERT ALAN, lawyer; b. Bracken County, Ky., Apr. 25, 1951. Student, U. Ky.; BA, Centre Coll., 1973; JD, U. Va., 1976. Bar: Colo. 1976. Mem. Holland & Hart, Denver; adj. prof. taxation U. Denver, 1986-88. Articles editor Va. Law Review, 1974-76. Mem. ABA, Order Coif, Phi Beta Kappa. Office: Holland & Hart Ste 200 8350 East Crescent Pkwy Englewood CO 80111

POEDTKE, CARL HENRY GEORGE, JR., management consultant; b. Chgo., Jan. 12, 1938; s. Carl H. Sr. and Irene F. (Eskilson) P.; m. Marie-Paule M. Thiriet, Mar. 10, 1962 (dec.); children: Gislaine Canavan, Carl Henry George III; m. Janice M. Barron, Aug. 26, 1991. BS, MIT, 1959. Mgr. value engring. Chgo. Rawhide Mfg. Co., Chgo., 1962-66; ptnr. Price Waterhouse, Chgo., Paris, N.Y.C., 1966-91; ret. Price Waterhouse, Chgo., 1991. Author: Managing and Accounting for Inventories, 1980; contbr. articles to profl. jours. Bd. dir. Guild Bd. Lyric Opera, Chgo., 1984-92; mem. vis. adv. com. sch. acctg. De Paul U., Chgo., 1986-91. 1st lt. U.S. Army, 1959-62. Fellow Am. Prodn. and Inventory Control Soc.; mem. AIIE (sr., cert.) Inst. Mgmt. Cons. (bd. dirs. 1987-90, life mem.), Coun. Cons. Orgns. (bd. dirs. 1989-90), Union League Club, Masons. Home: PO Box 677 Tesuque NM 87574-0677

POHL, JOHN HENNING, chemical engineer, consultant; b. Ft. Riley, Kans., May 29, 1944; s. Herbert Otto and Ellen Irene (Henning) P.; m. Judith Lynn Sykes, Aug. 10, 1968; children: J. Otto, Clint. AA, Sacramento City Coll., 1964; BS, U. Calif., Berkeley, 1966; SM, MIT, 1973, DSci, 1976. Inspector constrn. C.O. Henning Cons. Engrs., Sacramento, 1965; engr. E.I. du Pont Nemours, Wilmington, Del., 1966-70; rsch. asst. MIT, Cambridge, 1971-75, lectr., 1975-76; mem. tech. staff Sandia Nat. Labs., Livermore, Calif., 1976-81; dir. fossil fuels Energy and Environ. Rsch., Irvine, Calif., 1981-86; dir. R & D Energy Systems Assocs., Tustin, Calif., 1986-89; sr. scientist energy W.J. Schafer Assocs., Irvine, 1989-91; pres. Energy Internat., Laguna Hills, Calif., 1988—; sr. cons. ESA Engring., Laguna Hills, 1989—; v.p. Advanced Combustion Tech. Co., Hsinchu, Taiwan, 1993-95; v.p. tech. Energeo, Inc., San Mateo, Calif., 1995-96; black coal utilization prof. chem. engring., dir. Black Coal Utilization Rsch. Unit U. Queensland, Brisbane, Australia, 1996—. Contbr. articles to profl. jours.; patentee in field. Treas. Headstart, Cambridge, 1975-76. Recipient Sci. and Tech. Achievement award U.S. EPA, 1987, Best Energy Projects award Energy Commn., Taiwan, coal evaluation, 1989, Low NOx Burner, 1992. Fellow Australian Inst. Energy (bd. dirs. 1996—); mem. ASME (advisor corrosion and deposits com. 1989—, rsch. project subcom. 1994—), AIChE (combustion advisor 1988-92), Am. Flame Rsch. Com., Am. Chem. Soc., Combustion Inst. Western States (mem. exec. com. 1988-95), Combustion Inst. (mem. program subcom. 1976—), Engring. Found. (mem. steering com. on ash deposits 1989—). Home: 26632 Cortina Dr Mission Viejo CA 92691-5429

POHLMAN, DAVID LAWRENCE, training systems consultant; b. Detroit, May 17, 1944; s. Lawrence Luther and Lois Betty (Huffcut) P.; m. Diane Lee Ewing, Dec. 27, 1967 (div. 1980); children: Scott David, Anne Kiersten; m. Katherine Margaret Wattigney, Dec. 11, 1981; children: Ann Margaret Williams, David Joseph Williams. BS in Edn., Ohio U., 1967; MA in Psychology, U. No. Colo., 1977. Commd. officer USAF, 1967, advanced through grades to lt. col.; instr. pilot USAF, Chandler, Ariz., 1975-78, rsch. pilot, 1978-82; div. chief USAF, San Antonio, 1982-87; ret., 1987; tng. div. mgr. Gallegos Rsch. Group, Wheatridge, Colo., 1987-88; mgr. fed. systems div. Andersen Consulting, Denver, 1988-90; pres. Dave Pohlman Assocs., Aurora, 1990—; com. chmn. Dept. Def., Washington, 1982-87, subcom. chmn. industry panel, 1988-92; subcom. mem. Intersvc.-Industry Tng. Sys., Orlando, Fla., 1987; industry co-chmn. Computer-Aided Acquisition and Logistics Human Sys. Components Com., 1987-92; vice-chair Aurora Vets. Affairs Commn., 1993-96; mem. 6th Congrl. Dist. Vets. Adv. Coun., 1993. Contbr. articles to profl. publs. Mem. Am. Ednl. Rsch. Assn., Am. Def. Preparedness Assn., Nat. Security Indsl. Assn., Air Force Assn. Roman Catholic. Home: 2557 S Evanston St Aurora CO 80014-2519 Office: 15200 E Girard Ave Ste 4400 Aurora CO 80014-5040

POLAKOFF, KEITH IAN, historian, university administrator; b. N.Y.C., Dec. 12, 1941; s. Irwin L. and Edna (Sopkin) P.; m. Carol J. Gershuny, June 21, 1964; children: Amy Ellen, Adam Matthew. BA magna cum laude, Clark U., 1963; MA, Northwestern U., Evanston, Ill., 1966, PhD, 1968. Lectr. Herbert H. Lehman Coll., CUNY, 1967-69; asst. prof. history Calif. State U., Long Beach, 1969-73, assoc. prof. 1973-78, prof., 1978—, assoc. dean instrnl. support Sch. Social and Behavioral Scis., 1980-81, assoc. dean ednl. policy, 1981-84, dean, 1985-86; dean Sch. Fine Arts, 1984-85, asst. v.p. acad. affairs, dean grad. studies, 1986-90, assoc. v.p. acad. affairs, dean grad. studies, 1991-96, assoc. v.p. instrnl. programs & rsch., 1996—; co-chair Calif. Minority Grad. Edn. Forum, 1990—; mem. coun. Big West Conf. (formerly Pacific Coast Athletic Assn.), 1982-90, Western Collegiate Athletic Assn., 1982-85. Author: The Politics of Inertia, 1973, (with others) Generations of Americans, 1976, Political Parties in American History, 1981; contbg. author: The Presidents: A Reference History, 1984, 2d edit., 1996; editor: The History Tchr., 1972-77, prodn. mgr., 1977-80. Mem., clk. bd. trustees Los Alamitos Sch. Dist., 1980-81; mem. Los Alamitos Unified Sch. Dist. Bd. Edn., 1990-94, pres. 1992-93; chmn. adv. com. on facilities, Los Alamitos Sch. Dist., 1989, chair steering com. for measure K for kids, 1990; bd. dirs. Long Beach Opera Assn., 1981-89, pres. 1982-83, treas., 1987-88; bd. dirs. Los Alamitos Jr. Baseball, 1988-90, Los Alamitos Basball, 1990-92. Avocations: travel, photography. Home: 2971 Druid Ln Los Alamitos CA 90720-4948 Office: Calif State U 1250 N Bellflower Blvd Long Beach CA 90840-0006

POLANCO, ROSANA LIM, grant writer; b. Hong Kong, May 16, 1969; came to U.S., 1970.; d. Harrison B. and Margaret Lim; m. Jose Martin Polanco, Sept. 8, 1993; 1 child, Jonathan M. BA, U. Calif., Berkeley, 1991. Office mgr. Merrit Bakery, Oakland, Calif., 1986-95; program devel. dir. Charity Cultural Svcs. Ctr., San Francisco, 1994—. Office: Charity Cultural Svcs Ctr 827 Stockton St San Francisco CA 94108

POLDING, BRIAN EARL, assistant dean; b. New Castle, Pa., Feb. 3, 1962; s. Dana Ellis and Gaylene Su (Deiger) P.; m. Brenda Rae Conant, Oct. 1995. BA, Slippery Rock (Pa.) Univ., 1984, MA, 1986; MA, Univ. Fla., 1988, PhD, 1995. Dir. pub. rels. City Rescue Mission, New Castle, 1985; coord. student judicial affairs U. Fla., Gainesville, 1986-90, asst. dir. leadership ctr., 1990-91; asst. dean students Univ. N.M., Albuquerque, 1991—; teaching asst. philosophy dept. Univ. Fla., Gainesville, 1985-86. Mem. adv. bd. Albuquerque Rape Crisis Ctr., 1994—. Mem. Nat. Assn. Student Personnel Adminstrs. (program com. 1994, state coord. 1994-96, Outstanding New Profl. award 1992), Assn. Student Judicial Affairs (charter, chair nat. conf. program com. 1994, 95, 10th circuit rep. 1994-96, Young Profl. award 1995). Office: Univ NM 280 Student Svcs. Ctr. Albuquerque NM 97131

POLITES, DEMETRI JOHN, psychiatrist; b. New Orleans, Sept. 6, 1934. MD, La. State U., 1959. Diplomate Am. Bd. Psychiatry and Neurology. Intern S. Pacific Meml. Hosp., San Francisco, 1959-60; resident U. Va. Hosp., 1960-63; pvt. practice San Francisco, 1966—; mem. staff Calif. Pacific Med. Ctr., San Francisco, 1966—. Office: 1255 Post St Ste 1150 San Francisco CA 94109-6704

POLKINGHORNE, PATRICIA ANN, hotel executive; b. Galveston, Tex., Aug. 17, 1948; d. C.L. and Barbara Ann (Rathke) Hughes; children: Pamela, Christopher. Student, Sam Houston State Tchrs. Coll., Huntville, Tex. Catering mgr. Rodeway Inn, Denver; office mgr. sales dept. Hyatt Regency, Phoenix; asst. to v.p., treas., controller Continental Drilling, Okla. City; asst. to v.p. resort food and beverage The Pointe Resorts Inc., Phoenix; dir. adminstrn. S.W. Audio Visual, Inc.; asst. to dir. and mgr. catering Phoenician Resort, 1991-92, asst. to dir. of travel industry sales, 1992-93, exec. adminstrv. asst. to dir. of food and beverage divsn., 1993—. Mem. NAFE. Republican. Episcopalian. Office: 6000 E Camelback Rd Scottsdale AZ 85251-1949

POLLACK, ALAN MYRON, physician; b. N.Y.C., Feb. 16, 1958; s. Samuel and Jean Anna (Friedman) P. BS in Biochemistry, UCLA, 1979; MD, U. Tex., 1983. Diplomate Am. Bd. Internal Medicine. Intern Cedars Sinai Med. Ctr., L.A., 1983-84, resident, 1984-86; physician internal medicine Kaiser Permanente, Panorama City, Calif., 1986—. Mem. Phi Beta Kappa, Alpha Omega Alpha. Home: 24502 Skyridge Dr Newhall CA 91321 Office: Kaiser Permanente 13652 Cantara St Panorama City CA 91402-5423

POLLACK, BETTY GILLESPIE, health care executive; b. Oak Park, Ill., Apr. 4, 1940; d. Leon H. and Elta F. Gillespie; B.A., Whittier coll., 1962; M.S., Columbia U., 1964; m. David Pollack, Dec. 18, 1971; 1 son, Michael Alan. Community organizer, Boston, 1964-66; faculty mem. Grad. Sch. Social Welfare, U. Calif., Berkeley, 1967-71; exec. dir. Calif. chpt. Nat. Assn. Social Workers, Millbrae, 1971-81; pres., chief exec. officer Vis. Nurse Assn., Santa Clara County, Calif., 1981-94; exec. dir. San Francisco Med. Soc., 1994—; mem. exec. com. Assn. United Way Agencies, 1982-85, 91-93, chmn. Cert. Assn. Execs. Study Course, 1981; mem. home care com. of Santa Clara County Sr. Care Com., 1987-92; chmn. bylaws commn. of San Mateo County Jr. Hockey Club, 1988-89. Mem. No. Calif. Soc. Assn. Execs. (sec.-treas. 1980-82, pres.-elect 1982-83, pres. 1983-84, program chmn. 1984-85, chmn. nominating com. 1985-86, chmn. publs. com. 1995), Peninsula Profl. Women's Network (sec. 1981-82, chmn. networking conf. 1981, pres. ednl. fund 1981-82), No. Calif. Coalition Vis. Nurse Assns. (v.p. 1983-85, pres. 1985, v.p. reorganized VNA Network No. Calif. 1993-94), Bay Area Profl. Women's Network (mem. newsletter com. 1980-81), Am. Soc. Assn. Execs., Peninsula Forum West, Rotary (San Jose chpt., chmn. program com. 1993-94, youth leadership com., internat. com. 1991-92, chmn. health programs subcom. 1992-94; co-chair Acad. Decatholon San Francisco chpt. 1996, mem. membership com., program com.), Med. Underwriters Calif. (bd. mem.), Med. Execs. Conf. Democrat. Home: 316 Sycamore St San Carlos CA 94070-2020 Office: 1409 Sutter St San Francisco CA 94070-2020

POLLACK, JEFFREY LEE, restaurateur; b. San Francisco, May 1, 1945; s. Albert and Loretta (Popper) P.; m. Patricia Bowdle Connell, Feb. 20, 1983; children: Lizabeth Ann, Hilary Margaret, Nicholas Albert. BA, San Jose State U. Owner, surety underwriter North Beach Bonding Co., San Francisco, 1968-75; proprietor Old Waldorf, San Francisco, 1974-80, Punchline, 1978-80, Julius' Castle, San Francisco, 1980—, New Joe's, San Francisco, 1984—, Shadows, San Francisco, 1985-95, Iron Horse, 1986-92, Pollack Group, San Francisco, 1985—, Nick's Lighthouse Restaurant, San Francisco, 1991—, Original Joe's # 2, 1992-95, O'Connell's, 1994-96, Dalla Torre, 1996—. Mem. Downtown Assn. (bd. dirs. 1987—, v.p. 1992), Union Sq. Assn., North Beach C. of C. (bd. dirs. 1989, v.p. 1992), Port Tenants Assn., Fisherman Wharf Assn., Commonwealth Club. Democrat. Home: 302 Greenwich St San Francisco CA 94133-3210 Office: Pollack Group Ltd 347 Geary St San Francisco CA 94102-1801

POLLAK, ERICH WALTER, surgeon, educator; b. Steyr, Austria, July 16, 1930; came to U.S., 1968; s. Franz and Margit (Götzl) P.; m. Martha Pollak, Feb. 5, 1961; children: Adriana E. Pollak-Lazzaro, E. Susana Pollak-Chernila. MD, U. of the Republic, Montevideo, Uruguay, 1960. Resident, chief resident UCLA, 1974; asst. prof. surgery U. Calif., Davis, 1974-77; assoc. prof. U. Mo., Kansas City, 1977-82; dir. trauma svcs. Queen of Valley Hosp., West Covina, Calif., 1983; chief surgeon, dir. Mancy Med. Ctr. Med. Group, West Covina, 1983—; clin. assoc. prof. surgery Osteo. Med. Coll., Pomona, Calif., 1983—; dir. quality assurance West Covina Hosp., 1991—; chmn. governing bd. Covina Valley Cmty. Hosp., West Covina, 1990; mem. governing bd. Doctors Hosp., West Covina, 1991—, mem. exec. com., 1991—, co-chmn. dept. surgery, 1994—, dir. utilization rev., 1995—; med. cons. Glendale dist. Med. Bd. Calif. Author, editor: Thoracic Outlet Syndrome, 1987; contbr. articles to profl. jours. Fellow ACS, Internat. Coll. Surgeons, Am. Coll. Angiology (emeritus), Am. Coll. Sports Medicine (emeritus); mem. Internat. Soc. for Cardiovascular Surgery (sr.), Earl Wolfman's Surg. Soc. (sec. 1974). Office: Mancy Med Ctr Med Group 1038 S Glendora Ave West Covina CA 91790

POLLAK, NORMAN L., retired accountant; b. Chgo., Aug. 16, 1931; s. Emery and Helen P.; m. Barbara Zeff, Aug. 21, 1955 (div. 1980); children: Martin Joel, Elise Susan McNeal, Rhonda Louise Wilder; m. Sharon Levin, Nov. 12, 1995. BS Sch. Commerce, Northwestern U., 1955. CPA, Calif.; lic. real estate agt. Calif. Sr. acct., staff acct., 1952-58, pvt. practice, 1958-86; ret. acct., fin. and mgmt. cons., pres. Norman L. Pollak Accountancy Corp., Westlake Village, 1958-86; expert witness on domestic dissolution, 1984-86; lectr. profl. orgns.; bus. mgr. for Steven Martin, Nitty Gritty Dirt Band, 1967-77; acct. for Gregg and Howard Allman, 1967, Marion Ross, 1980s. Former pres. Ventura County Estate Planning Coun., 1975-78, 78-79); founder San Fernando Valley Estate Planning Coun., 1962, chpt. pres., 1964-65; founder Ventura Co. Estate Planning Coun.; chmn. Comm. Contest for Hearing Impaired Optimist Club, emergency com. Disaster Preparedness, Oak Forest Mobile Estates Assn.; compiled disaster preparedness plan; coach Braile Olympics for Blind; mem. Conejo Future Found.; bd. dirs. Oak Forest Homeowners Assn., Honokowai Palms Homeowners Assn.; bd. trustees Westlake Cultural Found.; active sponsor Code 3 for Homeless Children, 1993. Mem. AICPA, Calif. Soc. CPAs (former chmn. San Fernando tech. discussion group 1960-61, former mem. com. on cooperation with credit grantors), Nat. Assn. Accts., Westlake Village C. of C., Northwestern U. Alumni Club, Delta Mu Delta. Home and Office: 143 Sherwood Dr Lake Sherwood CA 91361-4814

POLLEY, HARVEY LEE, retired missionary and educator; b. Wapato, Wash., Aug. 14, 1924; s. Edward Prestley and Alda June Polley; m. Corinne Weber; children: Catherine, David, Corinne, Robert. BA, Whitworth Coll., Spokane, Wash., 1951; postgrad., East Wash. Coll., 1953, Berkeley Bapt. Div. Sch., 1958-59; MEd, Cen. Wash. Coll., 1958; postgrad., Ecole d'Adminstrn. des Affaires Africaines, Brussels, 1959-60. Tchr. Quincy (Wash.) Pub. Schs., 1953-57, N.W. Christian Schs., Spokane, 1958; missionary Am. Bapt. Fgn. Missionary Soc., Zaire, 1958-89; tchr. Evang. Pedagogical Inst., Kimpese, Zaire, 1961-69, asst. legal rep., dir., prin., supt., 1969-72; dir. BIM Hostel, Kinshasa, Zaire, 1972-73; mem. staff Ctr. for Agrl. Devel. Lusekele, Zaire, 1975-85, dir., 1976-79, 83-85; dir. Plateau Bateke Devel. Program, Kinshasa, 1985-89; ret., 1989. Author: Mpila Kele, a rural development guide written in the Kituba lang., 1989. Mem. Coun. Elders, Kimpese, 1969-72; pres. bd. adminstrn. Vanga (Zaire) Hosp., 1981-83; mem. exec. com. Nat. Human Nutrition Planning Coun. Govt. Zaire-USAID, Kikwit, 1983-85. Home: W2405 W Johansen Rd Spokane WA 99208-9616

POLLEY, TERRY LEE, lawyer; b. Long Beach, Calif., June 2, 1947; s. Frederick F. and Geraldine E. (Davis) P.; m. Patricia Yamanoha, Aug. 4, 1973; children: Todd, Matthew. AB, UCLA, 1970; JD, Coll. William and Mary, 1973. Bar: Calif. 1973, U.S. Tax Ct. 1974, U.S. Supreme Ct. 1987. Assoc. Loeb & Loeb, L.A., 1973-78; ptnr. Ajalat, Polley & Ayoob, L.A., 1978—; lectr. taxation law U. So.Calif., 1978-94. Author (with Charles R. Ajalat) California's Water's Edge Legislation, 1987; contbr. articles to profl. jours., legal jours.; editorial bd. William and Mary Law Rev. Chmn. bd. dirs. Greater Long Beach Christian Schs., 1988-92, sec., 1994—; elder Grace Brethren Ch., Long Beach, 1988—. Mem. ABA (state and local tax com. 1973-92), Calif. Bar Assn. (chmn. taxation sect. 1990-91, exec. com. 1987-92, state and local tax com. 1975—, taxation sect., recipient V. Judson Klein award 1993), L.A. County Bar Assn. (exec. com. 1980-87, chmn. exec. com. 1985-86, taxation sect.), Nat. Assn. State Bar Tax Sects. (exec. com. 1990—, chmn. 1995-96). Republican. Office: Ajalat Polley & Ayoob 643 S Olive St Bldg 200 Los Angeles CA 90014-1685

POLLIS, RICHARD P., orthopedic surgeon; b. Elizabeth, N.J., Nov. 7, 1943; s. Phidias L. and Catherine (Demos) P.; m. Victoria Elizabeth Romer, July 4, 1982; 1 child, R. Brendon. BS magna cum laude, Tufts U., 1965; MD, Yale U., 1969. Diplomate Am. Bd. Orthopaedic Surgery. Pvt. practice orthopaedic surgery L.A., 1975—. Fellow Am. Coll. Surgeons, Internat. Coll. Surgeons, Bay Surgical Soc., Am. Acad. of Neurol. and Orthopaedic Surgeons. Office: 2118 Wilshire Blvd Ste 776 Santa Monica CA 90403-5784

POLLOCK, JOHN PHLEGER, lawyer; b. Sacramento, Apr. 28, 1920; s. George Gordon and Irma (Phleger) P.; m. Juanita Irene Gossman, Oct. 26, 1945; children: Linda Pollock Harrison, Madeline Pollock Chiotti, John, Gordon. A.B., Stanford U., 1942; J.D., Harvard U., 1948. Bar: Calif. 1949, U.S. Supreme Ct. 1954. Ptnr. Musick, Peeler & Garrett, L.A., 1953-60, Pollock, Williams & Berwanger, L.A., 1960-80; ptnr. Rodi, Pollock, Pettker, Galbraith & Cahill, L.A., 1980-89, of counsel, 1989—. Contbr. articles to profl. publs. Active Boy Scouts Am.; trustee Pitzer Coll., Claremont, Calif., 1968-76, Pacific Legal Found., 1981-91, Fletcher Jones Found., 1969—, Good Hope Med. Found., 1980—. Fellow Am. Coll. Trial Lawyers; mem. ABA, L.A. County Bar Assn. (trustee 1964-66). Home: 30602 Paseo Del Valle Laguna Niguel CA 92677-2317 Office: 801 S Grand Ave Los Angeles CA 90017-4613

POLLOCK, KENT, editor. Editor Anchorage Daily News. Office: Anchorage Daily News 1001 Northway Dr Anchorage AK 99514-9001

POLLOCK, RICHARD EDWIN, former county administrator; b. Phila., Aug. 27, 1928; s. Ernest Edwin and Evelyn Marie (Scarlett) P. Student Armstrong Coll., 1947, U. Calif., Berkeley, 1949-51, 55; BA in Recreation, San Jose State U., 1961; postgrad. San Fernando Valley State U., 1969-70, U. Calif., Davis, 1963-77, UCLA, 1964, U. Calif., Santa Barbara, 1970, U. Redlands, 1979; m. Yvonne May Graves, Oct. 11, 1952 (div. Aug. 1989); children: Colleen May, Karen Marie, Richard Irvin, Annette Yvonne, Mary Ann. Swim pool mgr. and instr. Berkley Tennis Club, 1955-56; police officer City of Berkeley, 1956; recreation and aquatic supr. Pleasant Hill (Calif.) Recreation and Park Dist., 1956-62; gen. mgr. Pleasant Valley Recreation and Park Dist., Camarillo, Calif., 1962-68; bldg. insp. Ventura County (Calif.), 1969-71; adminstr. Sacramento County-Carmichael Recreation and Park Dist., 1971-73; dir. parks and recreation Imperial County (Calif.), 1973-81; ret.; mem. faculty Imperial Valley Jr. Coll., 1974-94, aquatic cons., 1957—; real estate investor, 1984—; chmn. San Francisco Bay Area Conf. for Cooperation in Aquatics, 1958-59. Adviser/scoutmaster Desert Trails council Boy Scouts Am.; bd. dirs., instr. ARC; work with devel. disabled and handicapped children and adults; res. dep. Sheriff, 1981— Served from pvt. to lt. U.S. Army, 1951-55; Korea. Recipient recognition for 52 years vol. service ARC, 1989; registered recreator and park mgr.; cert. elem., secondary and community coll. tchr., Calif.; reg. hypnotherapist. Mem. Nat. Recreation and Park Assn., AAHPER, Calif. Park and Recreation Soc., Calif. County Dirs. Parks and Recreation Assn., Calif. Boating Safety Officers Assn., Aircraft Owners and Pilots Assn., Nat. Assn. Emergency Med. Technicians. Democrat. Mormon. Author: Bibliography: A Pool of Aquatic Sources, 1960. Home: 961 S Sunshine Ave Apt 5 El Cajon CA 92020

POLLOCK, ROBERT A., author; b. London, Mar. 19, 1930; came to U.S., 1973; s. Louisa M. Pollock Taylor; children: Adam, Ben. Pub. rels. cons. BPW Assocs. Ltd., London, 1962-71; tchr., cons. Ind. U., Bloomington, 1973-74; dir. multimedia U. Calif., Berkeley, 1974-79. Author: The Persuader, 1970, Loophole or How to Rob a Bank, 1973, Soccer for Juniors, 1982, The Legend of John Dougan, 1994. Cpl. Brit. Army, 1948-50. Home and Office: 1517 N Main St #209 Walnut Creek CA 94596

POLON, LINDA BETH, elementary school educator, writer, illustrator; b. Balt., Oct. 7, 1943; d. Harold Bernard and Edith Judith Wolff; m. Marty I. Polon, Dec. 18, 1966 (div. Aug. 1983). BA in History, UCLA, 1966. Elem. tchr. L.A. Bd. Edn., 1967—; writer-illustrator Scott Foresman Pub. Co., Glenview, Ill., 1979—, Frank Schaffer Pub. Co., Torrance, Calif., 1981-82, Learning Works, Santa Barbara, Calif., 1981-82, Harper Row Co.; editorial reviewer Prentice Hall Pub. Co., Santa Monica, Calif., 1982-83. Author: (juvenile books) Creative Teaching Games, 1974, Teaching Games for Fun, 1976, Making Kids Click, 1979, Write up a Storm, 1979, Stir Up a Story, 1981, Paragraph Production, 1981, Using Words Correctly, 3d-4th grades, 1981, 5th-6th grades, 1981, Whole Earth Holiday Book, 1983, Writing Whirlwind, 1986, Magic Story Starters, 1987, (teacher's resource guides) Just Good Books, 1991, Kid's Choice/Libraries, 1991. Mem. Soc. Children's Book Writers. Democrat. Home: 1308 9th St Santa Monica CA 90401 Office: L A Bd of Edn 980 S Hobart Blvd Los Angeles CA 90006-1220

POLSON, DONALD ALLAN, surgeon; b. Gallup, N.Mex., May 12, 1911; s. Thomas Cress and Carrie Fern (Cantrall) P.; m. Cecily, Lady Avebury, Nov. 9, 1946; 1 child, Carolyn Kathleen. Student Stanford U.; MD, Northwestern U., 1936, MSc, 1947. Diplomate Am. Bd. Surgery. Intern, then resident in surgery St. Luke's Hosp., Chgo., 1936-38; practice medicine specializing in gen. surgery, Phoenix, 1947-83; formerly chmn. Drs. Polson, Berens & Petelin, Ltd.; chief staff Maricopa County Hosp., 1952-53, St. Joseph's Hosp., 1961; bd. dirs. Ariz. Blue Shield, 1950-55, pres., 1956. Served to col. M.C., AUS, World War II. Mem. AMA, ACS, Ariz. Med. Assn. (dir. 1955-60), Maricopa County Med. Soc. (pres. 1954), Phoenix Surg. Soc. (pres. 1959), White Mountain Country Club, Alpha Omega Alpha, Nu Sigma Nu. Republican. Episcopalian. Home: 7619 N Tatum Blvd Paradise Valley AZ 85253-3378

POLSTER, LEONARD H., investment company executive; b. Columbus, Ohio, June 24, 1921; s. Max and Henrietta Polster; m. Constance L. Buderus, Mar. 20, 1948 (dec. Aug. 1967); children: Leonard M., Lance E., Lewis E.; m. Edith Motridge, Nov. 19, 1968. BA, Ohio State U., 1942. Pres. Polster, Inc., 1952-68; pres. real estate and investments co. Polster, Inc., Rancho Santa Fe, 1968—; sr. v.p. PaineWebber Inc., L.A. and Rancho Santa Fe, Calif., 1971-91. Author: Pearls Before Swine, 1994. Pres. Polster Found., Rancho Santa Fe, 1988—; fin. officer, bd. dirs. San Dieguito Boys Club, Solana Beach, Calif., 1991—; bd. dirs. Fairbanks Ranch Cmty. Svcs. Dist., Rancho Santa Fe, 1987-92; pres. Fairbanks Ranch Assn., Rancho Santa Fe, 1985-86, bd. dirs., 1984-86. With USAF, 1942-46. Recipient Commitment to Youth award San Dieguito Boys and Girls Club, 1989; Olympic torch bearer, Apr. 28, 1996. Mem. Fairbanks Ranch Country Club, Phi Alpha Theta. Republican. Presbyterian. Home and Office: PO Box 8291 Rancho Santa Fe CA 92067-8291

POLUMBUS, GARY M., lawyer; b. Tulsa, 1941. BS, U. Colo., 1964; JD, U. Denver, 1967. Bar: Colo. 1967, D.C. 1968. Mem. Dorsey & Whitney, Denver. Mem. ABA, Am. Intellectual Property Law Assn. Office: Dorsey & Whitney Ste 3200 370 17th St Ste 4400 Denver CO 80202

POMBO, RICHARD, congressman, rancher, farmer; b. Tracy, Calif., 1961; m. Annette, 1983; children: Richard Jr., Rena, Rachael. Student, Calif. State U., Pomona, 1981-83. Councilman City of Tracy, 1991-92; mayor pro-tem Tracy City Coun., 1992; mem. 103rd-105th Congresses from 11th Calif. dist., 1993—, chmn. agrl. com., subcom. on livestock, dairy and poultry; mem. Agrl. Com., Resources Com.; chmn. Pvt. Property Rights Task Force, 1993-94, Endangered Species Act Task Force, 1995-96; co-chmn. Spkr.'s Environ. Task Force, 1996. Co-founder San Joaquin County Citizen's Land Alliance, Calif., 1986—; active San Joaquin County Econ. Devel. Assn., Tracy Bus. Improvement Dist., City Coun. (vice chmn. Cmty. Devel. Agy., Cmty. Parks Com., and Waste Mgmt. Com.), San Joaquin County Rep. Ctrl. Com. Mem. Rotary Club. Roman Catholic. Office: US Ho of Reps 1519 Longworth HOB Washington DC 20515-0511

POMERANTZ, MARVIN, thoracic surgeon; b. Suffern, N.Y., June 16, 1934; s. Julius and Sophie (Luksin) P.; m. Margaret Twigg, Feb. 26, 1966; children: Ben, Julie. AB, Colgate U., 1955; MD, U. Rochester, 1959. Diplomate Nat. Bd. Med. Examiners, Am. Bd. Surgery, Am. Bd. Thoracic Surgery (dir. 1989—). Intern Duke U. Med. Ctr., Durham, N.C., 1959-60, resident, 1960-61, 63-67, instr. surgery, 1966-67; asst. prof. surgery U. Colo. Med. Sch., Denver, 1967-71, assoc. prof. surgery, 1971-74, assoc. clin. prof. surgery, 1974-93, prof. surgery, chief gen. thoracic surgery, 1992—; chief thoracic and cardiovascular surgery Denver Gen. Hosp., 1967-73, asst. dir. surgery, 1967-70, assoc.dir. surgery, 1970-73; pvt. practice Arapahoe CV Assocs., Denver, 1974-92; clin. assoc. surgery br. Nat. Cancer Inst., 1961-63; mem.staff Univ. Hosp., Denver, Denver Gen. Hosp., Rose Med. Ctr., Denver, Denver VA Med. Ctr., Children's Hosp., Denver, U. Coll. Health Sci. Ctr., 1992—, bd. dirs., 1995-97, chmn., 1997, Am. Bd. Thoracic Surgery. Guest editor Chest Surgery Clinics N.Am., 1993; contbr. numerous articles to profl. publs., chpts. to books. Fellow ACS, Am. Coll. Chest Surgeons; mem. AMA, Western Thoracic Surg. Assn. (v.p. 1992, pres. 1993-94, counselor-at-large 1988-90), Am. Assn. Thoracic Surgeons (program com. 1991), Am. Heart Assn. (bd. dirs. Colo. chpt. 1993), Colo. Med. Soc., Denver Acad. Surgery (pres. 1980), Internat. Cardiovascular Soc., Rocky Mtn. Cardiac Surgery Soc., Rocky Mtn. Traumatologic Soc., Soc. Thoracic Surgeons (nomenclature/coding com. 1991-95, standards and ethics com., govt. rels. com., chmn. program com. 1994-95), Soc. Vascular Surgeons, Am. Bd. Thoracic Surgery (vice chmn. 1996—). Office: UCHSC Divsn CTS 4200 E 9th Ave # C310 Denver CO 80220-3706

POMEROY, KENT LYTLE, physical medicine and rehabilitation physician; b. Phoenix, Apr. 21, 1935; s. Benjamin Kent and LaVerne (Hamblin) P.; m. Karen Jodelle Thomas (dec. Dec. 1962); 1 child, Charlotte Ann; m. Margo Delilah Tuttle, Mar. 27, 1964 (div. Jan. 1990); children: Benjamin Kent II, Janel Elise, Jonathan Barrett, Kimberly Eve, Kathryn M.; m. Brenda Pauline North, Sept. 1, 1990. BS in Phys. Sci., Ariz. State U., 1960; MD, U. Utah, 1963. Diplomate Am. Bd. Phys. Medicine and Rehab., Am. Bd. Pain Medicine. Rotating intern Good Samaritan Hosp., Phoenix, 1963-64; resident in phys. medicine and rehab. Good Samaritan Hosp., 1966-69, asst. tng. dir. Inst. Rehab. Medicine, 1970-74, dir. residency tng., 1974-76, asst. med. dir., 1973-76; dir. Phoenix Phys. Medicine Ctr., 1980-85, Ariz. Found. on Study Pain, Phoenix, 1980-85; pvt. practice, Phoenix and Scottsdale, Ariz., 1985—; lectr. in field. Contbr. articles to med. jours. Leader Theodore Roosevelt coun. Boy Scouts Am.; mem. exec. posse Maricopa County Sheriff's Office, Phoenix, 1981—, posse comdr., 1992-94, qualified armed posseman; mem. med. adv. bd. Grand Canyon-Saguaro chpt. Nat. Found. March of Dimes, 1970-78; missionary, 1955-57. Recipient Scouter's Tng. award Theodore Roosevelt coun. Boy Scouts Am., 1984, Scouter's Woodbadge, 1985. Mem. AMA, Am. Acad. Phys. Medicine and Rehab., Internat. Rehab. Medicine Assn., Am. Assn. Orthopaedic Medicine (co-founder, sec.-treas. 1982-88, pres. 1988-90), Pan Am. Med. Assn. (diplomate), Prolotherapy Assn. (pres. 1981-83), Am. Pain Soc., Western Pain Soc., Am. Assn. for Study Headache, Am. Soc. Addiction Medicine (sec. Ariz. chpt.), Am. Acad. Pain Medicine, Nat. Eagle Scout Assn., Acad. Clin. Neurophysiology, Ariz. Soc. Phys. Medicine (pres. 1977-78), Ariz. Med. Assn., Maricopa County Med. Soc., others, Nat. Sheriff's Assn., Law Enforcement Alliance of Am., Ariz. Narcotic Officers Assn. Mem. LDS Ch.

POMEROY, LYNDON FAYNE, sculptor; b. Sidney, Mont., Mar. 9, 1925; s. Earl Bert and Brownie Pauline (Blue) P.; m. Lenore Anna Dolphay, Feb. 25, 1952; children: Decora, Deen, Dru, Derik. BS in Art, Mont. State U., 1952, M of Applied Art, 1960. Asst. prof. No. Mont. Coll., Havre, 1953-58, Ea. Mont. Coll., Billings, 1958-61; sculptor Billings, 1961—; visual arts chmn. Mont. Arts Coun., Helena, 1966-71; adv. coun. Pres. Mont. State U., Bozeman, 1972-84; exhibit com. Yellowstone Art Ctr., Billings, 1975-80. Sculptor: (steel mural) Phylogenic Continuum, 1965, (monumental sculptures) Loggers, 1980, Canal Builders, 1989, Bison Bull, 1994. Bd. dirs. Growth Thru Art, Billings, 1990-95. 2d lt. U.S. Air Corps, 1943-46. Recipient Mont. State Gov.'s Award for Visual Arts, 1991. Mem. Stillwater Soc., Exptl. Aircraft Assn. (pres. chpt. 57 1975-76). Home: # 6 5000 Rimrock Rd # 6 Billings MT 59106-1313

POMEROY, MARY BARNAS, artist, illustrator, writer; b. Frankfurt, Hessen, Germany, Mar. 3, 1921; came to U.S., 1946; d. Carl Franz Joseph and Elizabeth Jacoba Gertruida (Van Holk) Barnas; m. Frederick George Pomeroy, Dec. 20, 1953; children: Anne Pomeroy Hess, Flora Pomeroy Smith. Student, coll., Quito, Ecuador, 1936-38; studied with father/German-Ecuadorean, artist Carl Barnas, Quito, 1938-46; student, Pa. Acad. Fine Arts, Phila., 1946-48; studied with Daniel Garber, Roy Nuse,, Franklin Watkins and Henry, Pitz. Illustrator geology dept. U. Cen., Quito, 1939-42; illustrator paleontology dept. Internat. Petroleum Co., Guayaquil, Ecuador, 1943-44; scientific illustrator botany dept. U. Calif., Berkeley, 1948-53; free-lance artist, 1953—. Artwork pub. in numerous publs. including Américas mag., Mus. of Calif. mag., 1993, poster for Asilomar Operating Corp. and Calif. Dept. Parks and Recreation, Pacific Grove, 1990, cover of Fremontia mag./Native Plant Soc., 1988, others; exbhns. include Pacific Grove Art Ctr., 1992, Sangre de Cristo Art and Conf. Ctr., Pueblo, Colo., 1989, Marjorie Evans Gallery, Sunset Ctr., Carmel, Calif., 1986, Mus. of Art, Monterey, Calif., 1985, City Hall, Seaside, Calif., 1983, Hunt Inst. Botanical Documentation, Pitts., others; work in various pvt. collections; contbr. 300 botanical illustrations to textbook.

POND, BILL, museum executive, director. BS, Whitworth Coll., 1941; postgrad., Wash. State U., U. Wash., U. Oreg., U. Calif., Davis. Cert., registered pk. and recreation adminstr., Calif. Supt. pks. and recreation City of Renton, Wash., 1946-49; supr. recreation divsn. Wash. State Pks. and Recreation Commn., Olympia, 1949-55; supt. pks. and recreation Tualatin Hills Pk. and Recreation Dist., Beaverton, Oreg., 1955-59; dir. pks. and recreation Sacramento (Calif.) County, 1959-68; dir. dep. gen. svcs. Sacramento County, 1980-84; exec. officer Nat. Recreation and Pk. Assn., Washington, 1968-72; acting exec. dir. Sacramento City-County Housing Authority, 1972; adminstr. Sacramento County Cmty. Devel. and Environ. Protection Agy., 1973-80; acting exec. dir. North Highlands Recreation and Pk. Dist., 1984; exec. dir. Sacramento Sci. Ctr.-Jr. Mus., 1985-88; interim exec. dir. Sacramento Mus. History, Sci. and Tech.-Discover Mus., 1996—. Bd. dirs. Sacramento Symphony Assn.; bd. dirs., past pres. Sacramento Symphony Chorus, Sacramento Jr. Mus.; active inner city project Sacramento Campfire Girls; chmn. recreation and leisure svcs. com. Cmty. Planning Coun.; active United Crusade Allocations Com.; mem. Concerned Citizens for Conservation Edn., Save the Am. River Assn.; chmn. Sacramento Area Ridesharing Com. Recipient Disting. Svc. award Am. Inst. Pk. Execs., cert. of merit Nat. Recreation Assn., Calif. Assn. Pk. and Recreation Adminstrs., Nat. Assn. County Pk. and Recreation Ofcls.; recipient resolutions and citations from Nat. Assn. County Ofcls., Assembly of Calif. State Legislature, Sacramento County Bd. Suprs., Sacramento City Coun., Save the Am. River Assn., City Coun. of Renton, Bd. Dirs. of Tualatin Hills Pk. and Recreation Dist., Bd. Dirs. Union H.S. Dist., Beaverton. Mem. Nat. Recreation and Pk. Assn. (Pacific N.W. Dist. adv. com., Pacific S.W. Dist adv. com.), Am. Pk. and Recreation Soc., Nat. Conf. on State Pks., Calif. Pk. and Recreation Soc., Sacramento Horsemen's Assn. (citation), Sierra Club, Audubon Soc. Home: 5779 Gloria Dr Sacramento CA 95822 Office: Sacramento Mus History Sci & Technology 101 I St Sacramento CA 95815

POND, WALLACE KIMBALL, education educator; b. Montgomery, Ala., June 11, 1964; s. Wallace Kimball and Sharon Pond; m. Natalie Diane Townsend, July 21, 1990; children: Addison O'Neill, Annamae Katharine. BA, U. Utah, 1987; MEd, Boston U., 1992; PhD, Walden U., 1994. Lic. tchr. Spanish, English, ESL. Tchr. Realms of Inquiry, Salt Lake City, 1988-90, Dept. Def., Mannheim, Germany, 1990-92; prof., trainer Big Bend C.C., Bad Kreuznach, Germany, 1992-93; adminstr., dir. Blaine County Pub. Schs., Hailey, Idaho, 1993-95; prof. Coll. of Santa Fe, 1995—; mem. bd. advisors for policy devel. Big Bend C.C., 1992-93; cons. to sch. dists. State Depts. Edn., 1993-96. Author: Managing Organizational Change, 1993, Leadership and Motivation, 1993. Facilitator for profl. devel. Santa Fe Pub. Schs., 1995-96; pro bono cons. Pojonque (N.Mex.) Parent U., 1996. Mem. ASCD, TESOL, Nat. Assn. Bilingual Edn., Doctoral Assn. N.Y. Educators. Office: College of Santa Fe 1600 Saint Michaels Dr Santa Fe NM 87505-7615

PONTSLER, DONALD N., electrical engineer; b. Wenatchee, Wash., Jan. 18, 1943; s. Clement M. and Exer LaVern (Preston) P.; m. Kathy J. Johnson, June 12, 1965; children: Jon D., Steven W. BSEE, Washington StateU., 1966; M in Pub. Adminstrn., U. Puget Sound, 1981. registered profl. engr., Wash. Electrical engr. Tacoma (Wash.) Pub. Utilities, 1966, profl. electrical engr., 1972, prin. profl. electrical engr., 1975-96; prin. High Voltage Power Engring., Puyullup, Wash., 1996—. Mem. IEEE. Presbyterian. Home: 6806 86th St E Puyallup WA 98371-6450 Office: High Voltage Power Engring 6806 86th St E Puyallup WA 98371-6450

POOL, TIMOTHY KEVIN, facilities management consultant; b. Lyons, Kans., Sept. 25, 1954; s. Rubben Roy and Vera Maxine (Vinson) P. BS, Kans. State U., 1977. With F.G. Holl Oil Co., Wichita, Kans., 1972-77; project mgr. The Bunce Corp., St. Louis, 1978-82, Bartex, Inc., Dallas, 1982-84; v.p. corp. real estate Bank Am.-Tex., 1984-94; pres., CEO Facilities Advantage, Inc., Dallas, 1994-95; dir. devel. svcs. Equity Realty & Investment Co., Inc., Colorado Springs, 1995-97; project mgr. Chistofferson Comml. Builders, Inc., 1997—. Mem. Planning Commn., Town of Green Mountain Falls, Colo. Mem. Internat. Facility Mgmt. Assn. (fin. svcs. coun., cert. 1993). Democrat. Christian Ch. Office: Christofferson Comml Builders Inc 1014 N Weber Colorado Springs CO 80903

POOLE, CECIL F., circuit court judge; b. Birmingham, Ala., 1914; children: Gayle, Patricia. LL.B., U. Mich.; LL.M., Harvard U., 1939. Practice of law San Francisco, former asst. dist. atty., 1951-58; clemency sec. to Gov. Brown of Calif., 1958-61; U.S. atty. No. Dist. Calif., 1961-70; Regents prof. Law U. Calif., Berkeley, 1970; counsel firm Jacobs, Sills & Coblentz, San Francisco, 1970-76; judge U.S. Dist. Ct., No. Dist. Calif., 1976-79, U.S. Ct. of Appeals for 9th Circuit, 1979—; adj. prof. Golden Gate U. Sch. Law, 1953-58; mem. adv. com. Nat. Commn. for Reform Fed. Criminal Laws, 1968-70. Served to 2d lt. AUS, World War II. Mem. ABA (chmn. sect. individual rights 1971-72, ho. of dels. 1972-74), San Francisco Bar Assn. (dir. 1975-76). Office: US Ct Appeals 9th Cir PO Box 193939 San Francisco CA 94119-3939

POOLE, HENRY JOE, JR., business executive; b. Rocky Point, N.C., July 5, 1957; s. Henry Joe Sr. and Marjorie (Morse) P.; m. Loretta Lynn Scott, Sept. 12, 1981; children: Robert Howard, Amanda Lynn. AA, Cypress Coll., 1977; student, San Diego State U., 1978, Calif. State U., Fullerton, 1978-79. Pres. Poole Ventura Inc., Ventura, Calif., 1979-92; gen. mgr. W.I.C. PVI systems divsn., Ventura, Calif., 1992-94; pres. PVI, Oxnard, Calif., 1995—. Inventor in field. Mem. ASME, Soc. Mfg. Engrs., Am. Vacuum Soc., Am. Welding Soc., Soc. Vacuum Coaters. Office: PVI PO Box 5023 Oxnard CA 93031

POOLE, THOMAS RICHARD, endowment campaign director, fund raising counsel; b. Newark, July 15, 1947; s. Frank Baldwin and Edna Laura (Harper) Poole. BA, Ohio Wesleyan U., 1969; MEd, Wright State U., 1975. Cert. fund-raising exec., 1985. Assoc. program dir. Brakeley, John Price Jones Inc., Stamford, Conn., Newport Beach, Calif., 1976-79; program dir. Brakeley, John Price Jones Inc., Newport Beach, Calif., 1979-81, v.p., 1981-91, sr. v.p., 1991—; assoc. campaign dir. Columbia-Presbyn. Med. Ctr., N.Y.C., 1976-79; campaign dir. Manhattan Eye, Ear and Throat Hosp., N.Y.C., 1979-82; endowment/capital campaign dir., cons. Albany (N.Y.) Med. Ctr., 1984-89; endowment/capital campaign dir. Long Beach (Calif.) Meml. Med. Ctr., 1989-95; endowment campaign dir. Samaritan Health Sys., Phoenix, 1995—. Author various corporate reports and feasibility studies. Mem. Nat. Soc. Fund-Raising Execs., Assocs. Ohio Wesleyan U. Office: Brakeley John Price Jones Inc 366 San Miguel Dr Ste 300 Newport Beach CA 92660

POON, PETER TIN-YAU, engineer, physicist; b. Hengyang, Hunan, China, May 31, 1944; came to U.S., 1967; s. Sam. Chak-Kwong and Lai (Yiu) P.; m. Mable Tsang, Apr. 13, 1974; children: Amy Wei-Ling, Brian Wing-Yan. BS, U. Hong Kong, 1965, MA, Calif. State U., Long Beach, 1969; PhD, U. So. Calif., L.A., 1974. Sr. engr. gasdynamics, planetary probe heat shield design, sys. simulation Jet Propulsion Lab./Calif. Inst. Tech., Pasadena, 1974-77, tech. mgr. advanced solar receiver, task leader advanced solar concentrator, 1978-80, systems engr. mission control and computing ctr. devel., 1981-83; advisor Space Sta. Ada Task, staff mem, task leader software mgmt. and assurance program NASA, 1984-85; mission control ctr. devel. telemetry systems engr. software mgmt. stds., element mgr. NASA software info. sys. Jet Propulsion Lab./Calif. Inst. Tech., Pasadena, 1986-88, systems mgr. for missions to Mars, Comet/Asteroid/Saturn, flight projects interface office, 1988-91, multimission ground systems office mgr. Mission to Mars, 1991-93, telecomm. and mission svcs. mgr. Cassini Mission to Saturn, 1993—; U.S.A. chmn., program com. 2nd Internat. Software Engring. Stds. Symposium, Montreal, Can., 1994-95; program com. session chair Software Engring. Stds. Symposium, Brighton, Eng., 1992-93; chair panel, mem. program mgmt. com., panel chair 3rd Internat. Software Engring. Stds. Symposium, 1995-97; session chair, mem. program com. IEEE Internat. Conf. on Engring. of Complex Computer Systems, Montreal, 1995-96, Como, Italy, 1996-97; mem. Internat. Orgn. for Standardization/Internat. Electrotech. Com./Joint Tech. Com. in Info. Tech. Subcom. Working Group and U.S. Technical Adv. Group, 1995—; U.S. del., Prague, Czech Republic, 1996, Paris, 1996, Walnut Creek, Calif., 1997; program com. mem. 5th Ann. Conf. on Artificial Intelligence and Ada, 1989, 6th Ann. Conf. on Artificial Intelligence and Ada, 1990. Author numerous profl. publs. Recipient numerous group awards in field, NASA, 1977-93. Mem. IEEE Software Engring. Stds. (exec. com. 1993—, co-author long range plans and stds. survey 1993), Arcadia Music Club (pres. 1994-95, 1st v.p. 1993-94), Sigma Xi, Eta Kappa Nu, Phi Kappa Phi, Athenaeum. Office: Jet Propulsion Lab Calif Inst Tech Mail Stop 303-402 4800 Oak Grove Dr Pasadena CA 91109

POONJA, MOHAMED, business reorganization, financial and management consultant; b. Mombasa, Kenya, Nov. 8, 1948; came to U.S., 1984; s. Abdulrasul and Maleksultan (Dharsee) P.; m. Zaitun Virji, Feb. 24, 1979; children: Jamil Husayn, Karim Ali. Student, Inst. Chartered Accts., Eng., Wales; MS in Mgmt. and Organizational Behavior, U.S. Internat. U. CPA. Audit supr. Ernst & Young (formerly Ernst & Whinney), Dublin, Ireland, 1966-72, Coopers & Lybrand, Dublin, 1973-76; group controller Diamond Trust of Kenya, Nairobi, 1976-78; chief operating officer Kenya Uniforms, Ltd., Nairobi, 1978-81; sr. mgr. Coopers & Lybrand, Calgary, Alta., Can., 1981-84; ptnr. Coopers & Lybrand, San Jose, Calif., 1984-92; chpt. 7 panel bankruptcy trustee No. Dist. Calif., San Jose, Calif., 1991—; with Poonja & Co., 1992—; ptnr. Manzanita Capital Ptnrs. Ltd., 1993—; former pres. Bay Area Bankruptcy Forum; bd. dirs. Calif. Bankruptcy Forum, Los Altos Ednl. Found. Am. Youth Soccer Orgn. Mem. ABA, Am. Bankruptcy Inst., Assn. Insolvency Accts., Inst. Bus. Appraisers, Cert. Fraud Examiners, Rotary. Home: 630 Milverton Rd Los Altos CA 94022-3930 Office: Poonja & Co 150 Giffin Rd Los Altos CA 94022-3902

POOR, CLARENCE ALEXANDER, retired physician; b. Ashland, Oreg., Oct. 29, 1911; s. Lester Clarence and Matilda Ellen (Doty) P.; AB, Willamette U., 1932; MD, U. Oreg., 1936. Diplomate Am. Bd. Internal Medicine. Intern U. Wis., Madison, 1936-37, resident in internal medicine, 1937-40, instr. dept. pathology Med. Sch., 1940-41, clin. instr., clin. asst. dept. internal medicine, 1942-44; pvt. practice medicine specializing in internal medicine, Oakland, Calif., 1944-97; mem. emeritus staff Highland Alameda County Hosp., Oakland, 1949—; mem. staff Providence Hosp., Oakland, 1947-97, pres. staff, 1968-69; staff mem. Samuel Merritt Hosp., Oakland, 1958-97; staff mem. Summit Med. Ctr. (merger Providence Hosp. and Samuel Merritt Hosp.), 1991-97; retired, 1997—. Mem. Nat. Coun. on Alcoholism, 1974—, bd. dirs. Bay Area, 1977—. Mem. Am., Calif., Alameda-Contra Costa med. assns., Alameda County Heart Assn. (trustee 1955-62, 72-82, pres. 1960-61), Calif. Heart Assn. (dir. 1962-72), Soc. for Clin. and Exptl. Hypnosis, Am. Soc. Clin. Hypnosis, San Francisco Acad. Hypnosis (dir. 1966—, pres. 1973). Home: 1241 West View Dr Berkeley CA 94705-1650 *Personal philosophy: No matter how easy or how hard the task, the goal is that it be an enjoyment on final review.*

POPE, ALEXANDER H., lawyer, former county official; b. N.Y.C., June 4, 1929; s. Clifford H. and and Sarah H. (Davis) P.; m. Katherine Mackinlay, Sept. 14, 1985; children by previous marriage: Stephen C., Virginia L., Daniel M. A.B. with honors, U. Chgo., 1948, J.D., 1952. Bar: Ill. 1952, Republic of Korea 1953, Calif. 1955, U.S. Supreme Ct. 1970. Pvt. practice L.A., 1955-77, 87-96; assoc. David Ziskind, L.A., 1955; ptnr. Shadle, Kennedy & Pope, L.A., 1956, Fine & Pope, L.A., 1957-59, 61-77; legis. sec. to gov. State of Calif., 1959-61; county assessor Los Angeles County, L.A., 1978-86; ptnr. Mayer, Brown & Platt, L.A., 1987-88, Barash & Hill, L.A., 1989-92; of counsel Seyforth, Shaw, Fairweather & Geraldson, L.A., 1993-96; exec. dir. Calif. citizens budget commn. Ctr. Govtl. Studies, Los Angeles, 1997—. Pres. Westchester Mental Health Clinic, 1963; nat. bd. mem. Vols. for Stevenson, 1952; vice-chmn. L.A. County Dem. Cen. Com., 1958-59; mem. Calif. Hwy. Commn., 1966-70; mem. L.A. Bd. Airport Commrs., 1973-77, v.p., 1973-75, pres., 1975-76; trustee, sec. L.A. Theatre Ctr., 1984-89. With U.S. Army, 1952-54, Korea. Mem. ACLU, Calif. State Bar Assn. (state and local tax com. 1991—, chair 1993-94), L.A. County Bar Assn. (state and local tax com. 1987—, chair 1995-96), U. Chgo. Alumni Club Greater L.A. (pres. 1970-71), Zero Population Growth, Ams. United, Common Cause, Order of Coif, Phi Beta Kappa. Democrat. Unitarian. Home: Unit 2205 800 W 1st St Los Angeles CA 90012-2412 Office: Calif Citizens Budget Commn 10951 W Pico Blvd Ste 120 Los Angeles CA 90064

POPE, EDWARD JOHN ANDREW, corporate executive, consultant; b. N.Y.C., July 18, 1962; s. Thomas Andrew and Barbara (McInnes) P. BS, U. Calif., L.A., 1983, MS, 1985, PhD, 1989. Engring. asst. U. Calif., 1979-83, rsch. asst., 1984-89; pres. MATECH, Westlake Village, Calif., 1989—; cons. Orion Labs., Inc., Camarillo, Calif., 1988-89, Refractory Composites, Inc., Whittier, Calif., 1989-90, ENSCI, Inc., Woodland Hills, Calif., 1990—; bd. dirs. Ventura County World Affairs Coun. Contbr. numerous articles to profl. jours. Mem. State Ctrl. Com. of Rep. Party, Calif., 1981-83; pres. UCLA Bruin Reps., L.A., 1981-82; active UCLA Chem. Adv. Coun., 1993; apptd. Ventura County Coun. on Econ. Vitality, 1993. Regent's scholar U. Calif., 1979, Chancellor's scholar, 1979; IBM Corp. fellow Watson Rsch. Ctr., 1988. Mem. Am. Ceramic Soc. (chair edn. com. 1990—), Nat. Inst. Ceramic Engrs., Materials Rsch. Soc. (acad. affairs com. 1987-89), UCLA chpt. Materials Rsch. Soc. (pres. 1982-89). Office: MATECH 31304 Via Colinas Ste 102 Thousand Oaks CA 91362-3901

POPP, DALE D., orthopedic surgeon; b. Tama County, Iowa, July 6, 1923; s. Herbert John and Millie (Rayman) P.; m. Dorothy L. Higgins (div. July, 1970); children: Mark, Craig, Gordon, Brian, Nancy, James, Melissa; m. Carla Jean Drobny, Aug. 27, 1970; 1 child (stepson) Gary. BA, U. Iowa, 1944, MD, 1947. Am. Bd. Orthopedic Surgeons. Orthopedic surgeon Spokane (Wash.) Orthopedic Clinic, 1954-82, Inland Medic Evaluations, Spokane, 1986-87. Capt. USAF, 1951-53. Mem. Am. Acad. Orthopedic Surgeons, North Pacific Orthopedic Soc., Western Orthopedic Assn., Spokane Surg. Soc. Republican.

PORAD, FRANCINE JOY, poet, painter; b. Seattle, Sept. 3, 1929; d. Morris H. and Gertrude (Volchok) Harvitz; m. Bernard L. Porad, June 12, 1949; children: Laurie, Bruce, Ken, Constance, Marci, Jeffrey. BFA, U. Wash., 1976. Founder, coord. Haiku NW Poets/Readers, Mercer Isle, Wash., 1988—; editor Brussels Sprout, Mercer Isle, 1988-95; co-editor Haiku Northwest Anthology, Seattle, 1996, Red Moon Press, Berryville, Va., 1996—; workshop presenter Haiku Can., Toronto and Alymer, Que., Can., 1992, 95, Haiku N.Am., Calif., Toronto, 1993, 95, Haiku N.Am., Oreg., 1997, Haiku Internat., Tokyo, 1997; judge Internat. Haiku Contest New Zealand Poetry Soc., 1995, San Francisco Contest for Haiku Poets of North Calif., 1992, Hawaii Edn. Assn., Honolulu, 1995. Author: Connections, 1986, Pen and Inklings, 1986, After Autumn Rain, 1987, Blues on the Run, 1988, Free of Clouds, 1989, Without Haste, 1989 (Cicada Chapbook award 1990), Hundreds of Wishes, 1990, A Mural of Leaves, 1991, Joy is My Middle Name, 1993, The Patchwork Quilt, 1994 (Haiku Soc. Am. Merit Book 1994), Waterways, 1995 (Haiku Can. Sheet Book series 1995), All Eyes, 1995, Ladies and Jellyspoons, 1996, Extended Wings, 1996. Recipient 1st prize Internat. Tanka competition Poetry Soc. Japan, Tokyo, 1993. Mem. Nat. League Am. Penwomen (treas. 1992-94, Owl award 1982, 92, 1st prize state art exhbn. Frye Mus. 1993, 1st pl. Haiku, 1995), Haiku Soc. Am. (pres. 1993, 94, Merit book 1994), N.W. Watercolor Soc. (treas. 1980-85), Women Painters Wash. (v.p. 1987, bd. 1985-93). Home: 6944 SE 33rd St Mercer Island WA 98040-3324

PORAD, LAURIE JO, jewelry company official; b. Seattle, Dec. 19, 1951; d. Bernard L. and Francine J. (Harvitz) P. BA, U. Wash., 1974; postgrad., Seattle Pacific U., summers 1975-76. Cert. standard tchr., Wash. Substitute tchr. Issaquah (Wash.) Sch. Dist., 1974-77; with data processing dept. Ben Bridge Jeweler, Seattle, 1977-83, auditing mgr., 1983-87, systems mgr., 1987-92, MIS special project mgr., 1992—; mem. adv. bd. computer sci. dept. Highline C.C., Midway, Wash., 1985—; mem. tech. prep. leadership com., 1993-95. Tchr. religion sch. Temple de Hirsch Sinai, Seattle, 1972-76, 84—, coord. computerized Hebrew learning ctr., 1987-88, coord. of religion sch. city facility, 1988-93, coord. mentor tchr. program, 1993—; tutor Children's Home Soc. Wash., Seattle, 1976-77. Mem. Assn. for Women in Computing (life mem., chmn. chpt. workshop 1985-88, nat. chpts. v.p. 1985-88, nat. pres. 1988-90, nat. chpt. v.p., 1992-93, rep. ind. mems. 1993—). Home: 14616 NE 44th St Apt M-2 Bellevue WA 98007-3196 Office: Ben Bridge Jeweler PO Box 1908 Seattle WA 98111-1908

PORCARO, MICHAEL FRANCIS, advertising agency executive; b. N.Y.C., Apr. 3, 1948; s. Girolamo M. and Marianna (DePasquale) P.; m. Bonnie Kerr, Apr. 7, 1972; children: Sabrina, Jon. BA in English, Rockford (Ill.) Coll., 1969. Broadcaster Sta. KFQD-AM; KENI-AM/TV, Anchorage, 1970-71, Sta. KENI-AM/TV, Anchorage, 1972-73; v.p. ops. Cook Inlet Broadcasters, Anchorage, 1973-74; owner Audio Enterprises, Anchorage, 1974-75; asst. Alaska Pub. Broadcasting Commn., Anchorage, 1975-76; exec. dir. Alaska Pub. Broadcasting Commn., 1976-81; chief exec. officer, ptnr. Porcaro Blankenship Advt. Corp., Anchorage, 1981—; cons. Arco Alaska TV sta., Anchorage, 1981; expert witness U.S. Senate Subcom. on Telecom., Washington, 1978; chmn. citizens adv. com. dept. journalism U. Alaska, 1995-96. Chmn. Municipality of Anchorage Urban Design Commn., 1990-93; mem. mayor's transition team Municipality of Anchorage, 1987-88; bd. dirs. Anchorage Glacier Polits Baseball Club, 1987-88, Anchorage Mus. History and Art, Alaska Ctr. Internat. Bus., 1996, Commonwealth North, 1996, Friends of Alaska Children's Trust, 1996-97, Anchorage Symphony Orch.; chmn. bd. dirs. Brother Francis Shelter for the Homeless, Anchorage, 1993-96; mem. mktg. com. gov.'s transition team, 1995; mem. United Way Anchorage Cabinet, 1996. Recipient Silver Mike award Billboard mag., 1974, Bronze award N.Y. Film Critics, 1981, Best of North award Ad. Fedn. Alaska, 1982—, Addy award, 1985, 91, Grand Addy award 1990, Cable TV Mktg. award 1986; Paul Harris fellow. Mem. Advt. Fedn. Alaska, Anchorage C. of C. (bd. dirs.). Republican. Roman Catholic. Office: Porcaro Blankenship Advt 433 W 9th Ave Anchorage AK 99501-3519

PORFILIO, JOHN CARBONE, federal judge; b. Denver, Oct. 14, 1934; s. Edward Alphonso Porfilio and Caroline (Carbone) Moore; m. Joan West, Aug. 1, 1959 (div. 1983); children: Edward Miles, Joseph Arthur, Jeanne Kathrine; m. Theresa Louise Berger, Dec. 28, 1983; 1 stepchild, Katrina Ann Smith. Student, Stanford U., 1952-54; BA, U. Denver, 1956, LLB, 1959. Bar: Colo. 1959, U.S. Supreme Ct. 1965. Asst. atty. gen. State of Colo., Denver, 1962-68, dep. atty. gen., 1968-72, atty. gen., 1972-74; U.S. bankruptcy judge Dist. of Colo., Denver, 1975-82; judge U.S. Dist. Ct. Colo., Denver, 1982-85, U.S. Ct. Appeals (10th cir.), Denver, 1985—; instr. Colo. Law Enforcement Acad., Denver, 1965-70, State Patrol Acad., Denver, 1968-70; guest lectr. U. Denver Coll. Law, 1978. Committeeman Arapahoe County Republican Com., Aurora, Colo., 1968; mgr. Dunbar for Atty. Gen., Denver, 1970. Mem. ABA. Roman Catholic. Office: US Ct Appeals Byron White US Courthouse 1823 Stout St Denver CO 80257-1823

PORRERO, HENRY, JR., construction company executive; b. Upland, Calif., Aug. 16, 1945. AA, Chaffey Coll., 1970; BS, Calpoly Pomona U., 1973. Bus. mgr. Guy F. Atkinson Co., South San Francisco, 1973-83; controller Laird Constrn. Co., Inc., R. Cucamonga, Calif., 1983-85; pres., founder PLT Computer Systems, Inc., Upland, Calif., 1986-93; founder, mgr. Porrero Constrn. Co., Upland, Calif., 1993—; fin. cons. Parrott & Wright Constrn., Corona, Calif., 1987-93. With USN, 1966-69. Mem. Am. Legion, Friends Upland Library, Calif. Sheriffs Assn. Republican. Home: 854 Carson St Upland CA 91784-1828 Office: 902 W 9th St Ste B Upland CA 91786-4542

PORTENIER, WALTER JAMES, aerospace engineer; b. Davenport, Iowa, Oct. 9, 1927; s. Walter Cleveland and Doris Lucile (Williams) P.; m. Martha L. Dallam, Aug. 26, 1950 (dec. Apr. 1986); children: Andrea Ellen, Renee Suzanne; m. Patty Grosskopf Caldwell, Oct. 3, 1992. B in Aero Engring., U. Minn., 1950; MS in Aero Engring., U. So. Calif., 1958, Engr. in Aerospace Engring., 1969. Sr. engr. aerodynamics N. Am. Aviation, L.A., 1951-61; MTS project engr., mgr. The Aerospace Corp., El Segundo, Calif., 1961-85; instr. U. So. Calif., L.A., 1979; cons. L-Systems, Inc., El Segundo, 1985-89. Pres., bd. dirs. First United Meth. Ch., Santa Monica, Calif., 1988-90; judge, range officer Internat. Shooting Union, 1989—. Recipient Bronze Medal Internat. Shooting Union, 1990. Fellow Am. Inst. Aeronautics and Astronautics (assoc.). Republican. Home and Office: 2443 La Condessa Dr Los Angeles CA 90049-1221

PORTER, A. DUANE, mathematics educator; b. Detroit, Dec. 31, 1936; s. Alphonse Walter and Nelda (Hoffman) P.; m. Carol Burt, Aug. 12, 1960; children: Lisa Luane, Joshua Duane. BS, Mich. State U., 1960, MS, 1961; PhD, U. Colo., 1964. Statistician Gen. Motors, Flint, Mich., 1960; asst. prof. U. Wyo., Laramie, 1964-67, assoc. prof., 1967-69, prof., 1969—, acting head math. dept., 1976-79; vis. prof. Clemson (S.C.) U., 1977, Humboldt State U., Arcata, Calif., 1978; dir. Sci. & Math. Teaching Ctr., Laramie, 1979-83, RMMC Summer Sch., Laramie, 1982—, NSF Faculty Enhancement, Laramie, 1988—. Contbr. articles to profl. jours. Grantee NSF. Mem. Am. Math. Soc., Math. Assn. Am. (gov. 1978-81), Nat. Coun. Tchrs. Math., N.Y. Acad. Scis. Office: U Wyo Math Dept Laramie WY 82071

PORTER, BARBARA REIDHAAR, accounting executive; b. St. Maries, Idaho, Nov. 1, 1954; d. James Eugene and RoseMary (Norton) Reidhaar; m. David James Porter, Oct. 1, 1982; children: Jonathan Carl, Eric James. BS in Genetics, U. Utah, 1977. Rsch. analyst Idaho State Govt., Boise, 1978-85, fin. mgmt. analyst, 1985-91, adminstr., 1991-95, exec. dir., 1996—; cons., trainer Boise, 1995-96. Mem. Nat. Assn. State Bds. Accountancy, State Human Resource Assn., Fiscal Officers Assn., Assn. Governmental Accts. Office: Idaho Bd Accountancy PO Box 83720 Boise ID 83720-0002

PORTER, DIXIE LEE, insurance executive, consultant; b. Bountiful, Utah, June 7, 1931; d. John Lloyd and Ida May (Robinson) Mathis. BS, U. Calif. at Berkeley, 1956, MBA, 1957. Personnel aide City of Berkeley (Calif.), 1957-59; employment supr. Kaiser Health Found., L.A., 1959-60; personnel analyst UCLA, 1961-63; personnel mgr. Reuben H. Donnelley, Santa Monica, Calif., 1963-64; personnel officer Good Samaritan Hosp., San Jose, Calif., 1965-67; fgn. svc. officer AID, Saigon, Vietnam, 1967-71; gen. agt. Charter Life Ins. Co., L.A., 1972-77, Kennesaw Life Ins. Co., Atlanta, from 1978, Phila. Life Ins. Co., San Francisco, from 1978; now pres. Women's Ins. Enterprises, Ltd.; cons. in field. Co-chairperson Comprehensive Health Planning Commn. Santa Clara County, Calif., 1973-76; bd. dirs. Family Care, 1978-80, Aegis Health Corp., 1977-92, U. Calif. Sch. Bus. Adminstrn., Berkeley, 1974-76; mem. task force on equal access to econ. power U.S. Nat. Women's Agenda, 1977—. Served with USMC, 1950-52. C.L.U. Mem. C.L.U. Soc., U. Calif. Alumni Assn., U. Calif. Sch. Bus. Adminstrn. Alumni Assn., AAUW, Bus. and Profl. Women, Prytanean Alumni, The Animal Soc. Los Gatos/Saratoga (pres. 1987-90), Beta Gamma Sigma, Phi Chi Theta. Republican. Episcopalian.

PORTER, DONNA JEAN, genealogist; b. Monte Vista, Colo., Aug. 20, 1931; d. George W. and Alma R. (Kile) Bishop; m. Earl Edwin Carmack, Nov. 14, 1949 (div. 1955); m. Paul W. Porter, June 4, 1955; children: LeiLonia Virginia, Paul Benjamin, Rebecca Ann. Registered profl. genealogist. Genealogist Denver, 1969—; owner Stagecoach Libr. for Geneal. Rsch., Denver; instr., lectr. in field. Co-author: Welding Lind, An Introduction to Genealogy, 1968; editor Colo. Genealogist mag., 1970-75; contbr. articles to profl. jours. and mags. Asst. libr. Family History Ctr. Libr., LDS Ch., Denver, 1966-76, mem. acquisition com., instr. spl. geneal. instrn. com.; v.p. Colo. chpt. Palatines to Am., Denver, 1985-86, pres., 1986-87, exhibitor's chair Nat. Conf., 1988. Mem. West Palm Beach Geneal. Soc. (founder, pres. 1964-66), Colo. Geneal. Soc. (corr. sec. 1968-69, pres. 1969-70, 2nd v.p., program chairperson 1971-73, seminar chairperson 1974, chairperson, judge Black Sheep contest 1988), Foothills Geneal. Soc. (pres. 1996—, genealogist 1983-88, ednl. dir. 1992—, staff genealogist Foothills Inquirere mag. 1983—, Genie of Yr. award 1992), Colo. Coun. Geneal. Socs. (v.p. 1986-87, pres. 1987-90, chairperson Colo. State Archives Ednl. Gift Fund 1991—), Nat. Soc. DAR (Peace Pipe chpt. state lineage chairperson 1970-73, registrar 1971-77), Ind. Hist. Soc., Ind. Geneal. Soc., Nat. Geneal. Soc., Internat. Soc. for Brit. Genealogy and Family History, Ohio Geneal. Soc. (life, Colo. chpt., Champaign County chpt., Madison County chpt., Ross County chpt., Monroe County chpt.), Mo. Geneal. Soc. (life), Md. Geneal. Soc. (life), St. Andrew Soc. (life), Inst. Heraldic and Geneal. Studies, Assn. Profl. Genealogists, Assn. for Gravestone Studies, Palatines of Am. (Colo. chpt.), Lower Delmara Geneal. Soc., Baltimore County Geneal. Soc., Shockey Family Meml. Fellowship. Home: 1840 S Wolcott Ct Denver CO 80219-4309

PORTER, JAMES B., hieroglyphic specialist; b. Berkeley, Calif., June 11, 1954; s. Neil Robert and Mary Newcomb (Edwards) P. BA History of Sci., Antioch U., 1979; MA in Anthropology, U. Calif., Berkeley, 1983, PhD in Anthropology, 1989. Cert. adult tchr. Staff artist U. Calif. Berkeley Abaj Takalik Project, Guatemala, 1978-80; illustrator U Calif. Berkeley Archaeol. Rsch. Facility, 1980-88; tchng. asst. anthropology U. Calif., Berkeley, 1984, rsch. asst., 1988-89, instr. anthropology univ. ext. classes, 1989-96; tour lectr. Calif. Alumni Assn. Tours, Berkeley, 1988; instr. calligraphy Oakland (Calif.) Art Supply, 1992; instr. humanities Rose St. Sch., Berkeley, 1993; instr. anthropology Piedmont (Calif.) Adult Sch., 1993-96; instr. anthropology and archaeology Laney Coll., Oakland, Calif., 1995—; presenter, lectr. in field. Author: Exploring Maya Glyphs Vol. I Introduction, 1996; exhbns. include Escultura monumental de la costa sur; Nat. Mus., Guatemala, 1979, Berkeley Community Arts Ctr., 1989, Pro-Arts Gallery, Oakland, 1993; designer 25th anniversary artwork Berkeley Free Clinic, 1995; contbr. articles to numerous profl. jours. and publs. Recipient scholarship Studio Study Ctr., Yakima, Wash., 1972-73; Tinker Travel Fund grantee, Ctr. for Latin Am. Studies, U. Calif., Berkeley, 1983-84, Robert H. Lowie Fund grantee, 1985, Olsen scholar, 1986-89; recipient scholarship Mesoamerican Art Rsch. Inst., San Francisco, 1989. Manichaean.

PORTER, L(AWRENCE) B(ENJAMIN), artist; b. Friona, Tex., Mar. 3, 1929; s. Carter Clayton and Lilly Katherine (Patching) P.; m. Helen Duffy Burchell, Mar. 13, 1950 (div. 1986); children: Carter Burchell, Katherine Unity; m. Marcia Joan Orcutt, May 12, 1993. BS in Agriculture, N.Mex. Coll. Agriculture, 1955; MA, N.Mex. State U., 1959; PhD, London Inst. Applied Rsch., 1972. Tchr. Clovis & Las Cruces (N.Mex.) Pub. Schs., 1955-57; field man Western Cotton Oil Co., El Paso, 1957-60; visual info. specialist White Sands (N.Mex.) Missile Range, 1960-64; artist Anthony, N.Mex., 1964—. Author: Some Famous New Mexico Ranches, 1957. Staff sgt. USAF, 1948-53. Home: PO Box 2300 Anthony NM 88021-2300

PORTER, MARIE ANN, neonatal nurse, labor and delivery nurse; b. St. Paul, June 29, 1961; d. Theodore J. Morrison and Betty Ann Verdick; 1 child, Angela. ADN, Columbia Basin Coll., 1988. RN, Wash.; cert. neonatal resusitation, Neonatal Resuscitation Program instr. Staff RN Kennewick (Wash.) Gen. Hosp., 1988-95; legal nurse cons. Richland, Wash., 1995—; owner, pres. Porter Med. Cons.; owner, pres. Porter Med. Conss. Active March of Dimes. Mem. ANA, Nat. Assn. Neonatal Nurses, Tri-Cities Coun. Nursing, Richland C. of C.(amb.).

PORTER, MARSHA KAY, Language professional and educator, English; b. Sacramento, Feb. 7, 1954; d. Charles H. and Eileen J. (Miller) P. BA in English and Edn., Calif. State U., Sacramento, 1976, traffic safety credential, 1979, MA in Ednl. Adminstrn., 1982. Cert. lang. devel. specialist, Calif.; cert. first aid instr. ARC. Bookkeeper Chuck's Parts House, Sacramento, 1969-76; substitute tchr. Sacramento City Unified Sch. Dist., 1976-78; coord. Title I, Joaquin Miller Mid. Sch., Sacramento, 1978-81; tchr. ESL and driver's edn. Hiram Johnson H.S., Sacramento, 1981-85, C.K. McClatchy H.S., Sacramento, 1985—; freelance editor, 1981-87; guest lectr. Nat. U., Sacramento, 1992-93. Co-author film reference book Video Movie Guide, pub. annually; contbr. movie revs., short stories and articles to publs. Vol. instr. CPR and first aid ARC, Sacramento, 1986-92; guest writer United We Stand Calif., Sacramento, 1993-94. Gov.'s scholar State of Calif., 1972. Mem. NEA, Calif. Tchrs. Assn., Calif. Assn. Safety Educators, Calif. Writers, Calif. Writers Assn. (sec. 1987-94, pres. 1996-98), Delta Kappa Gamma. Roman Catholic.

PORTER, RICHARD ERNEST, speech educator, author; b. Long Beach, Calif., Dec. 7, 1933; s. Ernest Long and Arlene Mary (Dietz) P.; m. Rosemary Jean Macias, June 18, 1957; children: Tamre Lynn Cardozo, Gregory Richard. BA, Calif. State U., Long Beach, 1956; MA, San Diego State U., 1968; PhD, U. So. Calif., L.A., 1974. Commd. ensign USN, 1956, advanced through grades to lt. comdr., 1965, resigned, 1967; prof. Calif. State U., 1970-96, prof. emeritus, 1996—. Author: Understanding Intercultural Communication, 1981, Communication Between Cultures, 1990-97; editor: Intercultural Communication: A Reader, 1972-97 (Best Book awrd 1986). Mem. Speech Comm. Assn., Western Speech Comm.

PORTER, RICHARD KANE, audio engineer, consultant; b. Pitts., Apr. 26, 1953; s. James Albert and Dorothy Louise (Kane) P.; m. Pamela Jean Mongeon, July 6, 1990. Student, U. Pitts., 1971-74; BA, Muskingum Coll., 1977. Field engr. customer svc. divsn. Singer Bus. Machine/TRW, 1979-81; field specialist data comm. Internat. Computers Ltd., 1981-85; applications engr. Burr-Brown Corp., Tucson, 1985-88; sr. rsch. assoc. II optical scis. ctr., lunar & planetary lab. U. Ariz., Tucson, 1988-89; systems design engr. Math. Systems Design, L.A., 1989-90; field engr. Siemens Audio Inc., Hollywood, Calif., 1991-94; chief engr. Waves Sound Recorders, Hollywood, 1993-96; supervising engr. Todd-Ao Studios West, Santa Monica, Calif., 196—; composer, performer RavenWolf Music, Marina Del Rey, Calif., 1991—. Contbr. articles to profl. publs. Mem. Soc. Composers and Lyricists.

PORTER, ROBERTA ANN, counselor, educator, school system administrator; b. Oregon City, Oreg., May 28, 1949; d. Charles Paul and Verle Maxine (Zimmerman) Zacur; m. Vernon Louis Porter, Dec. 27, 1975. B in Bus. Edn., So. Oreg. Coll., 1971, M in Bus. Edn., 1977; cert. in counseling, Western Oreg. Coll., 1986; cert. adminstrn., Lewis and Clark Coll., 1995. Cert. in leadership Nat. Seminars, 1991. Tchr. Klamath Union H.S., Klamath Falls, Oreg., 1971-73, Mazama Mid./H.S., Klamath Falls, Oreg., 1973-83; instr. Oreg. Inst. Tech., Klamath Falls, Oreg., 1975-92; counselor Mazama H.S., Klamath Falls, 1983-93, mem. site based mgmt. steering com., 1991-95; vice prin. Bonanza (Oreg.) Schs., 1993-95; counselor Klamath County Sch. Dist., Oreg., 1995—; site com. chair Lost River Jr./Sr. H.S., 1995—; presenter Oreg. and Nat. Assn. Student Coun., 1989-92, Oreg. Sch. Bds. Assn., Sch. Counselor Assn., 1995, state mini workshops counselors/adminstrs.; mem. task force for ednl. reform in Oreg., 1993-94; trainer asst. Leadership Devel. Am. Sch. Counselor Assn.; bd. dirs. Turning Point, 1996—. Mem. editl. bd. dirs. Eldorado Wellness, 1996—. Trainer U.S. Army and Marines Recruiters, Portland and Medford, Oreg., 1988-89; master trainer Armed Svcs. Vocat. Aptitude Battery/Career Exploration Program, 1992—; candidate Klamath County Sch. Bd., Klamath Falls. Recipient Promising, Innovative Practices award Oreg. Sch. Counselors, 1990. Mem. NEA, ACA, COSA, ASCD, ASCA, Oreg. Sch. Counseling Assn. (presenter, v.p. h.s. 1988-91, mem. com. 1991-93, pres. 1992-95, pres.'s award), Oreg. Edn. Assn., Oreg. Counseling Assn. (pres. award 1995, parliamentarian 1994-95, area 8 rep. 1995—, pres.-elect 1997—), Oreg. Assn. Student Couns. (bd. dirs. activity advisors 1989-91), Nat. Assn. Student Couns., Klamath Falls Edn. Assn. (bldg. rep. 1990-93, sec. 1991-92, negotiations team 1992-93), Delta Kappa Gamma (exec. bd. Alpha chpt. 1985-94, pres. 1990-92, state conv. chmn. 1992, state legis. com. 1991-93, chmn. 1993-95, state expansion com.). Home: 3131 Derby St Klamath Falls OR 97603-7313 Office: Lost River Jr/Sr High Sch 23330 Highway 50 Merrill OR 97633-9706

PORTER, VERNA LOUISE, lawyer; b. L.A., May 31, 1941. B.A., Calif. State U., 1963; JD, Southwestern U., 1977. Bar: Calif. 1977, U.S. Dist. Ct. (cen. dist.) Calif. 1978, U.S. Ct. Appeals (9th cir.) 1978. Ptnr. Eisler & Porter, L.A., 1978-79, mng. ptnr., 1979-86, pvt. practice law, 1986—; judge pro-tempore L.A. Mcpl. Ct., 1983—, L.A. Superior Ct., 1989—, Beverly Hills Mcpl. Ct., 1992—; mem. state of Calif. subcom. on landlord tenant law, panelist conv., mem. real property law sect. Calif. State Bar, 1983; speaker on landlord-tenant law to real estate profls., including San Fernando Bd. Realtors; vol. atty. L.A. County Bar Dispute Resolution, mem. client rels. panel, fee arbitrator. Mem. adv. coun. Freddie Mac Vendor, 1995—. Editl. asst., contbr. Apt. Owner Builder; contbr. to Apt. Bus. Outlook, Real Property News, Apt. Age; mem. World Affairs Coun. Fre Mem. ABA, L.A. County Bar Assn. (client-rels. vol. dispute resolution and fee arbitration, 1981—), L.A. Trial Lawyers Assn., Wilshire Bar Assn., Women Lawyer's Assn., Landlord Trial Lawyers Assn. (founding mem., pres.), Freddie Mac Vendor Adv. Coun., da Camera Soc. Republican. Office: 2500 Wilshire Blvd Fl 1226 Los Angeles CA 90057-4317

PORTERFIELD, ANDREW MAURICE, journalist; b. Woodbury, N.J., Feb. 20, 1962; s. Richard Maurice and Janet Ann (Davidson) P. BA, U. Pa., 1984. Research asst. dept anthropology U. Pa., Phila., 1981-84; research technician Wistar Inst. Anatomy, Phila., 1984-85; reporter Bay City News Service, San Francisco, 1985-86; staff writer Ctr. Invesitgative Reporting, San Francisco, Washington, 1986-90; editor Fin. Newsletter, 1990-91; pub. affairs specialist FDIC, Washington, 1991-94, western U.S. media rep., 1994-96; asst. v.p. pub. rels. Union Bank Calif., L.A., 1996—. Contbr. articles on environ. govt. to profl. jours. Mem. Pub. Rels. Soc. Am., Internat. Assn. Bus. Communicators (v.p. L.A. chpt.), No. Calif. Sci. Writers Assn., Soc. Profl. Journalists, Surfrider Found. Democrat. Home: 9515 Via Venezia Burbank CA 91504-1250 Office: Union Bank Calif 445 S Figueroa St Los Angeles CA 90071

PORTNEY, JOSEPH NATHANIEL, aerospace executive; b. L.A., Aug. 15, 1927; s. Marcus and Sarah (Pilson) P.; m. Ina Mae Leibson, June 20, 1959; children: Philip, Jeffrey. BS, U.S. Naval Acad., 1952. Commd. 2d lt. USAF, 1952, advanced through grades to capt., 1956, resigned, 1960; with Litton Systems, Inc., Woodland Hills, Calif., 1960—; project engr. Litton Aero Products, 1967-68; program mgr. Litton Aero Products Litton Systems, Inc., Woodland Hills, 1968-72, advanced program mgr. Guidance and Control Sys., 1972-85, mgr. advanced programs Guidance and Control Sys., 1985—; navigator engr. on 3 historic inertial crossings of the North Pole. Creator solar compass, pilot and navigator calendar. Mem. Inst. of Navigation (v.p. 1988-89, pres. 1989-90), U.S. Naval Acad. Alumni Assn. (trustee 1980-83). Jewish. Home: 4981 Amigo Ave Tarzana CA 91356-4505 Office: Litton Systems Inc 5500 Canoga Ave Woodland Hills CA 91367-6621

PORTUESI, DONNA RAE, psychotherapist, consultant; b. Easton, Pa., Nov. 19, 1949; d. Peter and Alice Lorraine (Hull) Stagnito; m. Sebastian Portuesi, Jr., Nov. 22, 1972 (div. Sept. 1986); 1 child, Christi Noel Buck. AA, No. Seattle C.C., 1987; BA magna cum laude, Western Wash. U., 1989; MSW cum laude, U. Wash., 1992. Registered counselor, Wash. Sec. for Sen. Harry Byrd, Jr. U.S. Senate, Washington, 1970-72; founder Denver chpt. Nat. Found. for Crohn's and Colitis, 1975-79; counselor Mental Health Svcs., Everett, Wash., 1982-84; co-founder Adoption Search and Counseling Cons., Seattle, 1990-96; psychotherapist, cons. ASCC Svcs., Seattle, 1992—, press and speech asst. U.S. Senate, Washington, 1970-72, post adoption cons., Seattle, 1992-96; workshop developer, leader Adoption Search and Counseling, Seattle, 1992-96, exec. dir., 1990-96; ind. search cons. Reunite Adoptees and Birth Parents, 1991—. Contbr. articles to profl. jours. Mem. NASW, Am. Counseling Assn., Am. Adoption Congress. Democrat. Home and Office: 4109 3rd Ave NW Seattle WA 98107

PORZAK, GLENN E., lawyer; b. Ill., Aug. 22, 1948; m. Judy Lea McGinnis, Dec. 19, 1970; children: Lindsay and Austin. BA with distinction, U. Colo., 1970, JD, 1973. Bar: Colo. 1973. Assoc. Holme Roberts & Owen, Denver, 1973-80, ptnr., 1980-85, mng. ptnr. Boulder office, 1985-95; mng. ptnr. Porzak Browning & Johnson LLP, Boulder, 1996—; bd. dirs. Norwest Bank Boulder, 1993—. Contbr. articles to profl. jours. 1st Lt. U.S. Army, 1970-78. Named Disting. Alumnus U. Colo., 1991. Fellow Explorers Club (bd. dirs. 1995—); mem. Am. Alpine Club (pres. 1988-91), Colo. Mtn. Club (pres. 1983, hon. mem. 1983—), Colo. Outward Bound (trustee 1992—), Phi Beta Kappa. Home: 771 7th St Boulder CO 80302-7402 Office: Porzak Browning & Johnson 1300 Walnut St Ste 100 Boulder CO 80302-5248

POSERT, HARVEY PERES, public relations professional; b. Memphis, May 29, 1930; s. Hardwig Peres and Natlee Alice (Isenberg) P.; m. Myra Gail Gainsboro, June 28, 1958 (div. Apr. 1982); children: Harvey Peres III, Robert L., Peter D. BA, Yale U., 1951. Diplomate Acad. Wine Comm. Reporter Comml. Appeal, Memphis, 1944-54; account exec. Edelman Pub. Rels., Inc., Chgo., N.Y.C., and San Francisco, 1956-75; owner Harvey Posert & Assocs., Memphis, 1960-62; pub. rels. dir. Wine Inst., San Francisco, 1975-80; v.p. comm. Robert Mondavi Winery, Napa Valley, Calif., 1980-96; cons., 1997—; lectr. pub. rels. various profl. and ednl. instns. Author: Public Relations for Wineries, 1976; editor Alcohol in Moderation, 1992—. Sgt. CIC, U.S. Army, 1951-54, Germany. Recipient Consumer Program award Pub. Rels. News, N.Y.C., 1970, Golden Corkscrew award Order of Knights of the Vine, Sacramento, 1976. Mem. Am. Wine Alliance (bd. dirs. 1990—). Democrat. Jewish. Office: 1140 Victoria Ln Saint Helena CA 94574

POSEY, F. BRUCE, mortgage banker; b. Bozeman, Mont., Dec. 17, 1954; s. Frederick Lloyd and Frances Lucille (LeBlanc) P.; m. Janis Lee Matota, Feb. 10, 1989. BA in Fin., U. Mont., 1977; MS in Fin., Colo. State U., 1978. Cert. mortgage banker. Loan officer First Bank of Billings, Mont., 1979-84; mgr. Better Homes and Gardens Agy., Billings, 1984-86; v.p., CEO Streeter Bros. Mortgage, Billings, 1986—; instr, Eastern Mont. U., Billings, 1981-88. Treas., v.p., pres. Breakfast Exch. Club, Billings, 1980-85; bd. dirs. Metra Park, Billings, 1983-89, Metra Park Found., 1996—. Named Home Builders Assn. Assoc. of the Yr., 1983. Mem. Mortgage Bankers Assn. (mem. various coms.), Home Builders Assn. (dir. 1979-84), Elks, Billings Petroleum Club. Roman Catholic. Office: Streeter Bros Mortgage corp PO Box 1416 Billings MT 59103

POSEY, JAMES MADISON, commissioner; b. Beaumont, Tex., June 14, 1946; s. Herbert Miles and Albertha (Howard) P.; m. Cassandra Delois Holt, Nov. 20, 1976; children: Elizabeth, Cathryn, Joseph, David, Patricia. BA, Wichita State U., 1972; JD, U. Kans., 1975. Bar: Kans. 1975. Landman Atlantic Richfield Co., Dallas and Denver, 1975-77; sr. landman Atlantic Richfield Co., Anchorage, Alaska, 1979-82; oil and gas atty. Worldwide Energy Co., Denver, 1977-79; dist. landman Arco Alaska Inc., Denver, 1982-84, land mgr., 1984-85, issues advocacy mgr., 1985-91, mgr. fed. govt. rels., 1991-94, mgr. fed. & local govt. rels., 1994-95; mgr. bldg. safety divsn. Municipality of Anchorage, 1996; commr. Alaska Pub. Utilities, 1997—. Pres. Bayshore/Klatt Cmty. Coun., Anchorage, 1987-94; treas. Alaska Dem. Party, 1990-94; bd. dirs. Jr. Achievement of Alaska, Anchorage, 1986-92. Mem. ABA, Am. Assn. Blacks in Energy (bd. dirs. 1994-97), Rotary. Baptist.

POSIN, DANIEL Q., physics educator, television lecturer; b. Turkestan, Aug. 13, 1909; came to U.S., 1918, naturalized, 1927; s. Abram and Anna (Izritz) P.; m. Frances Schweitzer, 1934; children: Dan, Kathryn. A.B., U. Cal., 1932, A.M., 1934, Ph.D., 1935. Instr. U. Cal., 1932-37; prof. U. Panama, 1937-41; dean natural scis. U. Mont., prof., 1941-44, chmn. dept. physics and math., 1942-44; staff Mass. Inst. Tech., 1944-46; prof. physics, chmn. dept. N.D. State Coll., Fargo, 1946-55; prof. dept. physics DePaul U., 1956-67; prof. phys. sci. dept. Calif. State U., San Francisco, 1967—; chmn. dept. interdisciplinary scis. Calif. State U., 1969—; dir. Schwab Sci. Lecture Series, Atoms for Peace exhibit Mus. Sci. and Industry, Chgo.; Chief cons. Borg Warner Sci. Hall and Allied Chem. Sci. Hall, Times Square; scientific cons. CBS-TV. (Recipient 6 Emmy awards for best educator on TV in Chgo., and best ednl. TV programs). Author: Trigonometria, 1937-41, Fisica Experimental, Fisica, 1937-41, Mendeleyev—The Story of a Great Scientist, 1948, I Have Been to the Village, with Introduction by Einstein, 1948, rev. edit., 1974, Out of This World, 1959, What is a Star, 1961, What is Chemistry, 1961, What is a Dinosaur, 1961, The Marvels of Physics, 1961, Find Out, 1961, Chemistry for the Space Age, 1961, Experiments and Exercises in Chemistry, 1961, What is Matter, 1962, What is Electronic Communication, 1962, What is Energy, Dr. Posin's Giants, 1962, Life Beyond our Planet, 1962, Man and the Sea, 1962, Man and the Earth, 1962, Man and the Jungle, 1962, Man and the Desert, 1962, Science in the Age of Space, 1965, Rockets and Satellites, Our Solar System, The Next Billion Years, 1973; contbr. to: Today's Health; sci. cons.: Compton's Yearbook; contbr. to: feature articles Chgo. Tribune, (book) After Einstein-Remembering Einstein, 1981; co-contbr. to book The Courage to Grow Old, 1989; appearances, CBS Radio-TV, WTTW-WGN-TV, 1956-67, NET; ABC TV series Dr. Posin's Universe. Chmn. edn. com. Chgo. Heart Assn., 1963-67; Trustee Leukemia Soc. James T. Grady award Am. Chem. Soc., 1972. Fellow Am. Phys. Soc.; mem. A.A.A.S., Phi Beta Kappa, Sigma Xi.

POSKANZER, ARTHUR M., nuclear physicist and chemist; b. N.Y.C., June 28, 1931; s. Samuel I. and Adele (Kerman) P.; m. Lucille Block, June 12, 1954; children: Deborah, Jeffrey, Harold. AB, Harvard U., 1953; MA, Columbia U., 1954; PhD, MIT, 1957. Chemist Brookhaven Nat. Lab., Upton, N.Y., 1957-66; sr. scientist Lawrence Berkeley Nat. Lab., Berkeley, Calif., 1966-95, Bevalac sci. dir., 1978-79, disting. scientist, 1995—; head Relativistic Nuclear Collisions Program, 1990-95; chmn. nuclear chemistry Gordon Conf., 1970; sci. assoc. European Ctr. for Particle Physics, Geneva, 1979-80; mem. panel on future nuclear sci. Nat. Acad. Sci., 1976; organizer Quark Matter Conf., 1995. Fellow Guggenheim Found., 1970-71; recipient NATO sr. fellowship, 1975, Von Humboldt Sr. U.S. Scientist award, 1986, 95. Fellow AAAS, Am. Phys. Soc.; mem. Am. chem. Soc. (chmn. div. nuclear chemistry and tech. 1977, nuclear chemistry award 1980). Discovered isotopes of light elements at the limits of stability; co-discovered collective flow of nuclear matter.

POSNER, JUDITH LOIS, art dealer; b. Milw., Sept. 22, 1941; d. Sol J. and Miriam (Posner) K.; divorced; children: Wendy,. Daivd. BFA, U. Wis., 1963. Dir. Posner Fine Art, L.A., 1966—, Boritzer, Gray, Hamano. Bd. dirs. Mt. Sinai Hosp., Milw., 1991-94. Mem. Milw. Art Dealers Assn. (pres. 1993-94), L.A. Bus./Conv. Ctr., Santa Monica Art Dealers Assn. Office: c/o Posner Fine Art Boritzer/Gray/Hamano 2525 Michigan Ave D4 Santa Monica CA 90404

POST, GERALD STEVEN, veterinarian; b. Lake Success, N.Y., June 16, 1961; s. Stanley and Sandra Mae (Newman) P. BS with distinction, Cornell U., 1983; DVM, U. Minn., 1988. Diplomate Am. Coll. Veterinary Internal Medicine. Intern Animal Med. Ctr., N.Y.C., 1988-89, resident in oncology, 1990-92; staff oncologist Darien (Conn.) Animal Hosp., 1992-94, Companion Animal Hosp., Belmont, Calif., 1995—. Co-author: Tigers of the World, 1987. Recipient Excellence in Feline Medicine and Surgery award Assn. Feline Practioners, 1988. Mem. Am. Vet. Med. Assn., N.Y. Acad. Scis., Conn. Vet. Med. Assn., Phi Kappa Phi, Phi Zeta. Office: Companion Animal Hosp 1685 Old County Rd Belmont CA 94002-3936

POSTAER, LARRY, advertising executive; b. Chgo.. Grad., U. Mo. Sch. Journalism, 1959. Catalog copywriter Sears; with Stern, Walters & Simmons, Chgo., 1962-64, creative dir., 1964-76; sr. v.p., group creative dir. Needham Harper & Steers, Chgo., 1976-81; exec. v.p., dir. creative svcs. Needham Harper & Steers, L.A., 1981-86; co-founder, exec. v.p., dir. creative svcs. Rubin Postaer, Santa Monica, 1986—. Named Co-leader of Yr. for 1990, Western States Advt. Agys. Assn., 1991. Office: 1333 2nd St Santa Monica CA 90401

POSTEL, MITCHELL PAUL, association administrator; b. Chgo., May 27, 1952; s. Bernard and Rosalin P.; B.A., U. Calif.-Berkeley, 1974; M.A., U. Calif.-Santa Barbara, 1977; m. Kristie McCune, Mar. 29, 1981. Devel. officer San Mateo County Hist. Mus., San Mateo, Calif., 1977-81; exec. dir. Fort Point and Army Mus. Assn., San Francisco, 1981-84, San Mateo County Hist. Assn., 1984—; faculty Coll. of San Mateo. ; Author: History of the Burlingame Country Club, 1982, Peninsula Portrait: A Pictorial History of San Mateo County, San Mateo: A Centennial History; Seventy-five Years in San Francisco, History of Rotary Club No. 2. Mem. San Mateo County Historic Resources; bd. dirs. San Mateo C. of C.; pres., bd. dirs. Presidio Hist. Soc., Home: 120 Trinity Ct San Bruno CA 94066-2554 Office: San Mateo County Hist Assn 1700 W Hillside Blvd San Mateo CA 94402

POTASH, STEPHEN JON, public relations executive; b. Houston, Feb. 25, 1945; s. Melvin L. and Petrice (Edelstein) P.; m. Jeremy Warner, Oct. 19, 1969; 1 son, Aaron Warner. BA in Internat. Rels., Pomona Coll., 1967. Account exec. Charles von Loewenfeldt, Inc., San Francisco, 1969-74, v.p., 1974-80; founder, pres. Potash & Co., Pub. Rels., Oakland, Calif., 1980-87; cons. APL Ltd. (formerly Am. Pres. Lines, Ltd.), 1979-87, 90—, v.p. corp. comm., 1987-90; exec. dir. Calif. Coun. Internat. Trade, 1970-87; chmn. Potash & Co., Oakland, 1990—. Bd. dirs. Calif. Coun. Internat. Trade, 1987-94, Calif.-Southeast Asia Bus. Coun., 1992—, Temple Sinai, Oakland, 1979-81, mktg. com. United Way Bay Area. Mem. Pub. Rels. Soc. Am., Commonwealth Club of Calif., World Trade Club San Francisco. Office: Potash & Co Pub Rels 1946 Embarcadero Oakland CA 94606-5213

POTROVITZA, NICHOLAS POMPEI, mechanical engineer, solar energy researcher; b. Oradea, Romania, July 7, 1952; came to U.S., 1989; s. Valentin and Aurelia (Todor) P.; m. Victoria Cornelia Caproiu Potrovitza, July 9, 1974; children: Jessica, Tanissa. BA in Mech. Engring., Mech. Faculty Poly. Inst., Romania, 1977. Cert. quality engr., welding inspector, quality assurance mgmt. Mech. engr. Vulcan Boiler Mfg. Co., Bucharest, Romania, 1977-79, Crane Factory, Timishoara, Romania, 1979-81; researcher Dept. Tech. Mech. Faculty, Timishoara, Romania, 1981-86; solar power plant designer Luz Industries Ltd., Jerusalem, Israel, 1986-89, Borom, Calif., 1989-91; sr. mech. engr. KJC Oper. Co., Borom, Calif., 1991—. Contbr. articles to profl. jours. Mem. Am. Welding Soc., Am. Soc. Quality Control, Soc. Mfg. Engrs. Office: KJC Operating Co 41100 Us Highway 395 Boron CA 93516-2109

POTTENGER, MARK MCCLELLAND, computer programmer; b. Tucson, Feb. 9, 1955; s. Henry Farmer and Zipporah Herrick (Pottenger) Dobyns. BA, UCLA, 1976. Data entry operator Astro Computing, Pelham, N.Y., 1976-77; programmer/analyst LA-CCRS, L.A., 1977-80; programmer/analyst cons. L.A., 1977—, R. Gonzalez Mgmt., L.A., 1980—; rsch. dir. Internat. Soc. for Astrol. Rsch., L.A., 1985-95. Editor: Astrological Research Methods, 1995; co-author: Tables for Aspect Research, 1986; editor The Mutable Dilemma, 1977—; author: (computer programs) CCRS Horoscope program, 1977-92, Frequencies for Aspect Rsch., 1986-92. Recipient Jansky award Aquarius Workshops, L.A., 1989. Mem. Internat. Soc. for Astrol. Rsch., Nat. Coun. for Geocosmic Rsch. Democrat. Mem. Religious Sci. Ch. Home and Office: 838 5th Ave Los Angeles CA 90005-3522

POTTER, GEORGE KENNETH, artist; b. Bakersfield, Calif., Feb. 26, 1926; s. Howard Eugene and Edythe (Keast) P.; m. Heliodora Carneiro de Mendonca, July 30, 1954 (div. July 1956); 1 child, Helen Marcia Pessoa; m. Ruth Mary Griffen, Aug. 4, 1962; children: Katherine Anne Klein, Claire Lorraine, Cynthia Ann. Student, Acad. Art Coll., San Francisco, 1947-48; student Jean Metzinger, Academie Frochot, Paris, 1950-52; student, Istituto Statale dei Belli Arti, Florence, Italy, 1951; BA magna cum laude, San Francisco State U., 1974. tchr. pvt. art classes; lectr. San Francisco State U.; instr. Acad. Art Coll., San Francisco; judge Marin County Ann., 1963, Calif. State Fair Art Exhbn., 1968. One-man shows include U. Calif.-Berkeley, 1959, U. Santa Clara, Calif., 1958, Coll. Marin, Calif.,1958, Rosacrucian Mus., San Jose, Calif., 1959, Brazilian-Am. Inst., Rio de Janeiro, 1955, Frances Young Gallery, Ross, Calif., 1952, John A. Muir Gallery, Modesto, Calif., 1958, Gallerie 8, Paris, 1952, Maxwell Galleries, San Francisco, 1958, 62, Gallery 5, Santa Fe, 1960, Rotunda Gallery, San Francisco, 1949, 52, Marquoit Galleries, San Francisco, 1973, Palo Alto (Calif.) Cultural Ctr., 1977, Art Ovations Gallery, San Francisco, 1980, Kaiser Art Ctr. Gallery, Oakland, Calif., 1980, Marin County Civic Ctr., San Rafael, Calif., 1985, Northwind Gallery, Mill Valley, Calif., 1987, NutTree Gallery, Vacaville, Calif., 1987, numerous others; competitive exhibitions include Am. Watercolor Soc., 1961, 74, 76, 79, Phelan Awards Competition San Francisco Mus. Art, 1949, Calif. Palace Legion Honor, 1958, 60, San Francisco, 1958, 60, 63, 75 (San Francisco Art Festival Exhbn. award 1975), Springville (Utah) Invitational, 1963, Jack London Invitational (award 1958), Oakland, Calif., 1957-65, Calif. State Fair (awards 1958, 72) Sacramento, 1957-58, 61-68, 70-74, 76, 79, Oakland Watercolor Ann., 1948, 52, Mother Lode Ann., Sonora, Calif., 1957-58, 63, 65, Kingsley Ann., E.B. Crocker Art Mus. (award), Sacramento, 1958, 61, 62, 64, 65, Marin Soc. Artists Ann., 1948-49, 58, 61, 65-73, 75, 77, Marin County Ann. (awards 1966, 67), 1962, 65-67, 70, 71, 76, Western Assn. Mus. Shows, 1964, 67, 74, No. Calif. Arts Ann., 1961, 68, 88, Fukuoka (Japan) Invitational Exchange Show with Oakland, 1964, Soc. Western Artists Ann. at M.H. De Young Mus., San Francisco, 1956-64, Statewide Watercolor Show (award), Santa Cruz, 1958, Watercolor U.S.A., Springfield, Mo., 1973, 74, Royal Watercolor Soc. Invitational Exhbn., London, 1975, San Francisco Art Festival Award Exhbn., 1975, Palo Alto Cultural Ctr., 1977; executed murals Moore Bus. Forms, Inc., Oakland, Town Hall, Corte Madera, Calif., Macy's of Calif., Sacramento, San Mateo, Stockton, stained glass dome for Hale Meml., Soc. Calif. Pioneers, San Francisco, 1974, Calif. Dept. Motor Vehicles, Oakland, 1975; stained glass and resin triptych U. Calif. at San Francisco Moffitt Hosp., 1976; represented in permanent collections including HUD San Francisco regional office, San Francisco Art Commn.,; art dir. McCann-Erickson Advt. Inc., Rio de Janeiro, 1954-55, Johnson and Lewis Advt., San Francisco, 1957, Michelson Advt., Palo Alto, Calif., 1959-60; contbr. The Calif. Style-Watercolor Artists 1925-55 (McClelland and Last), 1985, The N.Y. Art Rev., 1988. Served with USMCR, 1944-46, PTO. Recipient Macy's Art award, San Francisco, 1958, 1st award Watercolor Delta Ann., Antioch, Calif., 1969, 1st award Alameda County Fair, 1974, 79, 85, Santa Rosa 12th Ann., 1975, Best of Show Calif. Arts League Open Exhibition, 1988, numerous other awards. Mem. West Coast Water Color Soc. (pres. 1968-69), Marin Soc. Artists. Address: 4824 Skyway Dr Fair Oaks CA 95628-6520

POTTER, J(EFFREY) STEWART, property manager; b. Ft. Worth, July 8, 1943; s. Gerald Robert Potter and Marion June (Mustain) Tombler; m. Dianne Eileen Roberb, Dec. 31, 1970 (div. Aug. 1983); 1 child, Christopher Stewart; m. Deborah Ann Blevins, Oct. 20, 1991. AA, San Diego Mesa Coll., 1967. Cert. apartment mgr., apartment property supr., housing adminstr. Sales mgr. Sta. KJLM, La Jolla, Calif., 1964-67; mgr. inflight catering Host Internat., San Diego, 1967-69; lead aircraft refueler Lockheed Co., San Diego, 1969-70; property mgr. Internat. Devel. and Fin Corp., La Jolla, 1970-72; mgr. bus. property BWY Constn. Co., San Diego, 1972-73; mgr. residents Coldwell Banker, San Diego, 1973-74; mgr. Grove Investments, Carlsbad, Calif., 1974-76, Villa Granada, Villa Seville Properties Ltd., Don Cohn, Chula Vista, Calif., 1976-83; gen. mgr. AFL-CIO Bldg. Trades Corp., National City, Calif., 1983—; instr., Cert. Apt. Mgmt. San Diego Apt. Assn. Bd. dirs. San Diego County Apt. Assn., 1995—. Fellow Internat. Platform Assn., Nat. City C. of C., Toastmasters, Founding Families San Diego Hist. Soc., Am. Assn. Retired Persons, San Diego County Apt. Assn. (bd. dirs.), La Jolla Monday Night Club (treas. 1984-89). Roman Catholic. Home: 2550 5th Ave Ste 401 San Diego CA 92103-6622 Office: AFL-CIO Bldg Trades Corp 2323 D Ave National City CA 91950-6730

POTTER, ROBERT ALONZO, dramatic art educator; b. N.Y.C., Dec. 28, 1934; s. Henry Codman and Lucilla Annie (Wylie) P.; m. Sally Alabaster (div.); m. Nancy Elizabeth Collinge (div.); m. Pamela Howard (div.); children: Lucilla Callander Potter Hoshor, Daniel Latimer Potter, Jane Wylie Thornquist, Maria Theresa Potter, Bryn Ann Potter. BA, Pomona Coll., 1956; MA, Claremont Grad. Sch., 1963, PhD, 1965. Lectr. in humanities Harvey Mudd Coll., Claremont, Calif., 1964-65; asst. prof. English U. Calif., Santa Barbara, 1965-72, lectr. in dramatic art, 1972-75, assoc. prof. of dramatic art, 1975-81, prof. dramatic art, 1981—; vis. prof. theatre studies U. Kent, Canterbury, Eng., 1984-85. Author: The English Morality Play, 1975 (plays) Where is Sicily, 1969, In A Pig's Eye, 1975, Fifteen Signs of the Apocalypse, 1978, Just Across the Border, 1980, The Vision of Children, 1980, The Sea Lion, 1983, The Wind Dancers, 1987, The Lady in the Labyrinth, 1987, (with Ellen Anderson) A Fine and Private Place, 1991, Bedtime Story, 1992, Saint Barbara in the Flesh, 1995. Mem. County Dem. Ctrl. Com., Santa Barbara, 1968-74. Cpl. U.S. Army, 1957. Fulbright scholar U. Bristol, Eng., 1963-64. Home: 1070 Miramonte Dr Apt 7 Santa Barbara CA 93109-1367 Office: U Calif Dept Dramatic Art Santa Barbara CA 93106

POTTER, STEPHEN ARNOLD, production designer; b. Glendale, Calif., July 11, 1937; s. Lorne Arnold and Mary Elizabeth (Bilheimer) P.; m. Cathleen Burt, July 11, 1957 (dec. 1987); m. Fumiko Morio, Oct. 8, 1992. Spl. studies, Am. Acad., Rome, 1957, Bishop Acad., Honolulu; AA, UCLA. Producer, dir. Gloria Swanson Film Festival, Orlando, Fla., 1980; prodn. designer, set decorator Zoetrope/Francis Ford Coppola, 20th Century Fox, Hollywood, Calif., 1990; prodn. designer Landmark Entertainment, North Hollywood, Calif., 1990-91, Concorde Pictures, West L.A., Calif., 1991-93; founder S.W. Props, Phoenix, 1978—; pres. Jupiter Prodns., Beverly Hills, Calif., 1968—. Author: The Nile Triangle, 1979, Dragonsong, 1980, Magicswan, 1997. Active Rep. Presdl. Task Force, Washington, 1986—; dir. S.E. campaign Youth Movement for Reagan, Orlando, 1986. Recipient Bronze Halo of Special Merit So. Calif. Motion Picture Coun., 1983. Mem. Acad. Motion Picture Arts and Scis. (fgn. film com. 1990—, Nichols scholar 1991—), Set Decorators Soc. Am. (v.p. 1993-94), SAR (v.p. 1964-68), Sons of Confederacy, Barons of Runnymede, Order of Crown. Office: PO Box 11416 Beverly Hills CA 90213-4416

POTTERAT, JOHN JAMES, public health officer, researcher; b. Geneva, Switzerland, July 5, 1942; came to U.S., 1956; s. Lucien Charles and Liliane Johanna (Jacot) P.; m. Susan Louise Block, Oct. 3, 1969; children: Nico Christopher, Anna Louise. BA, UCLA, 1965. Pub. health officer L.A. County Health Dept., 1968-72; dir. STD/HIV control El Paso County Health Dept., Colorado Springs, Colo., 1972—; cons. WHO, 1990; mem. editorial bd. jour. Sexually Transmitted Disease; presenter in field. Author: (with others) Strategies for Management of Sexual Partners, 1984, rev. edit., 1990, Prostitution, Intravenous Drug Use and HIV-1 in the U.S., 1990; contbr. numerous articles to profl. jours. With U.S. Army, 1965-67, Vietnam. Recipient Dr. Nathan Davis award AMA, Chgo., 1993, Dr. Cleere award Colo. Pub. Health Assn., Denver, 1992, P.W. Jacoe award, 1979; named Soldier of Month U.S. Army, 1966. Mem. Internat. AIDS Soc., Colo. Pub. Health Assn., Colo. Osteo. Found. (bd. dirs.). Home: 2901

Country Club Dr Colorado Springs CO 80909-1020 Office: El Paso County Health Dept 301 S Union Blvd Colorado Springs CO 80910-3123

POTTRUCK, DAVID STEVEN, brokerage house executive; b. 1948. BA, U. Pa., 1970, MBA, 1972. Now pres., CEO U.S. Govt., 1972-74; with Arthur Young & Co., 1974-76, sr. cons.; with Citibank N.Am., 1976-81, v.p.; with Shearson/Am. Express, 1981-84, sr. v.p. consumer mktg. and advt.; with Charles Schwab & Co., San Francisco, 1984—; exec. v.p. mktg., br. adminstr. Charles Schwab and Co., Inc.; pres., CEO The Charles Corp., Charles Schwab & Co.; pres., COO The Charles Schwab Corp. Office: Charles Schwab & Co Inc 101 Montgomery St San Francisco CA 94104-4122*

POTTS, CHARLES AARON, management executive, writer; b. Idaho Falls, Idaho, Aug. 28, 1943; s. Verl S. and Sarah (Gray) P.; m. Judith Samimi, 1977 (div. 1986); 1 child, Emily Karen; m. Ann Weatherill, June 19, 1988; 1 child, Natalie Larise. *Charles Potts is 14th generation North American and 5th generation out west. General Robert Caldwell from Warwickshire arrived in Rhode Island in 1653, the first of three generations of generals in the British Army in Potts' Colonial American lineage. Captain Dan Jones, great great grandfather, was with the prophet Joseph Smith when he was martyred. He converted and brought to Utah in 1849 the Welsh choral musicians who began the Mormon Tabernacle Choir. In 1926, Potts' great aunt Stella Gray Evans was the only licensed midwife in Idaho and delivered more than 600 children.* BA in English, Idaho State U., 1965. Lic. real estate broker, Wash. Owner Palouse Mgmt., Inc., Walla Walla, Wash.; founder, dir. Litmus Inc., 1967-77; founding editor COSMEP, Berkeley, Calif., 1968; host poetry radio program Oasis, NPR-KUER, Salt Lake City, 1976-77; N.W. rep. Chinese Computer Communications, Inc., Lansing, Mich., 1988; pres. Tsunami Inc. Author: Blues from Thurston County, 1966, Burning Snake, 1967, The Litmus Papers, 1969, Little Lord Shiva, 1969, Blue Up the Nile, 1972, Wating in Blood, 1973, The Trancemigracion of Menzu, 1973, The Golden Calf, 1975, Charlie Kiot, 1976, The Opium Must Go Thru, 1976, Valga Krusa, 1977, Rocky Mountain Man, 1978, A Rite to the Body, 1989, The Dictatorship of the Environment, 1991, Loading Las Vegas, 1991, How the South Finally Won the Civil War, 1995, One 100 Yrs. In Idaho, 1996; columnist (with Kyushu Gleaner) Japan's Polit. Choices, 1995—; pub., editor The Temple, 1997—. Rep. to exec. com. 5th Congl. Dist., Wash. State Dem. Party, 1993-95. Recipient First Place Novel award Manuscript's Internat., 1991, Disting. Profl. Achievement award Idaho State U., 1994. Mem. Italian Heritage Assn. (ice cream chair 1990, award 1993), Pacific N.W. Booksellers Assn., Walla Walla Area C. of C., Downtown W2 Found., Blue Mountain Arts Alliance, Fukuoka Internat. Forum, Chinese Lang. Computer Soc., Soc. Neurolinguistic Programming (master practitioner), Toastmasters. Avocations: tennis, raspberries. Office: Palouse Mgmt 34 S Colville St Walla Walla WA 99362-1920 *Charles Potts is called "An editor and publisher of acumen and flair who consistently showcases works of excellence," in The Selected Essays of Rich Mangelsdorff. Multiple Fulbright and OAS scholar, professor Hugh Fox of Michigan State University published the first full length study of Potts' work through Dustbooks in 1979, The Poetry of Charles Potts. Scott Preston reviewing The Dictatorship of the Environment in Western American Literature called his work "A determined attack on decadence...the real postmodern western American poetry," while Doug Marx, in Writers Northwest said, "In spirit, he is reminiscent of the late, great Thomas McGrath."*

POTTS, JAMES, mayor. Mayor Tustin, Calif. Address: 15222 Del Amo Ave Tustin CA 92680

POTTS, SANDRA DELL, elementary education educator; b. Lakeview, Oreg., Aug. 17, 1937; d. George A. and Maxine E. (Withers) Campbell; children: Alexander B. Potts, Casey C. Potts. BA, Chico (Calif.) State U., 1959; postgrad., San Jose State U., Santa Clara U. Elem. tchr. Cupertino (Calif.) Union Sch. Dist., 1959—; tchr. 1st grade parent edn. classes Smart Start and Megaskills Sedgwick Elem. Sch., Cupertino, 1994-97. Recipient Hon. Svc. award PTA; named Tchr. of Yr., Santa Clara County, 1991-92. Mem. NEA, ASCD, Calif. Tchrs. Assn., Cupertino Edn. Assn.

POULSON, LYNN HANSEN, home and family studies educator, writer; b. Roosevelt, Utah, Jan. 11, 1949; s. Kermit and Gertrude Ilean (Hansen) P.; m. Julie Karen Gividen, Nov. 2, 1972; children: Kermit Ty, Cory, Nickolas, Kimilyn, Kareena. AA, Snow Coll., Ephraim, Utah, 1972; BA, Utah State U., 1974; MEd, Brigham Young U., 1975. Counselor Snow Coll., 1975-80, prof. home and family studies, 1980—, chmn. div. social and behavioral scis., 1991-93. Author: Uncommon Common Sense: A Guide for Engaged and Married Couples, 1993. Sec., Sanpete Cmty. Theater, Ephraim, 1977, pres., 1978; asst. chmn. Scandinavian Festival, Ephraim, 1989-90. Named Tchr. of Yr., Snow Coll., 1991. Mem. Nat. Coun. on Family Rels. Republican. Mem. LDS Ch. Home: 110 N 460 E # 86 1 Ephraim UT 84627-1215 Office: Snow Coll 150 College Ave Ephraim UT 84627

POUNDS, ELTON WILLIAM, pastoral care educator; b. Smith Ctr., Kans., June 27, 1935; s. Elton Lee and Thelma (Wookey) P.; children: Jan, Mark, Kimberly, Andrew, Christopher, Kyra, Chandra. AB, Hastings Coll., 1957; MDiv, Seabury-Western Theol. Sem., 1960. Rector Grace Ch., Columbus, Nebr., 1965-69, Holy Trinity Parish, Gillette, Wyo., 1969-72; dir. Trinity Ranch Diocese of Colo., Wetmore, 1972-77; curate Grace Ch., Colorado Springs, Colo., 1977-85; dir. pastoral care and edn. P/SL Health Care System, Denver, 1985—; chmn. bd. examining Chaplains, Diocese of Colo., 1968-84. Editor: Large Print Book of Common Prayer, 1982. Judge Campbell County, Wyo., 1970-72; pres. Chaplaincy Corps Colorado Springs Police Dept., 1980-81; mem. Civil Rights Commn., 1965-67; del. Gov.'s Conf. on Aging, Colo., 1980; chmn. Neonatal Com. Colo. Collective Med. Disorders, 1993—. Fellow Seabury, 1971, 78. Mem. AAMS, Am. Assn. Clin. Pastoral Edn., Amnesty Internat., Episcopal Soc. Ministry on Aging (bd. dirs. 1980-82), N.Y. Acad. Scis. Republican. Episcopalian. Home: 1576 E Mineral Ave Littleton CO 80122 Office: Columbia Swedish Med Ctr 501 E Hampden Ave Englewood CO 80110

POWELL, JAMES LAWRENCE, museum director; b. Berea, Ky., July 17, 1936; s. Robert Lain and Lizena (Davis) P.; m. Joan Hartmann; children: Marla, Dirk, Joanna. AB, Berea Coll., 1958; PhD, MIT, 1962; DSc (hon.), Oberlin Coll., 1983; LHD (hon.), Tohoku Gakuin U., 1986; DSc (hon.), Beaver Coll., 1992. Mem. faculty Oberlin Coll., Ohio, 1962-83, also prof. geology, asso. dean, 1973-75, v.p., provost, 1976-83; pres. Franklin and Marshall Coll., Lancaster, Pa., 1983-88, Reed Coll., Portland, Oreg., 1988-91; pres., chief exec. officer The Franklin Inst., Phila., 1991-94; pres., dir. Los Angeles County Mus. Natural History, L.A., 1994—; mem. Nat. Sci. Bd., 1986—. Author: Strontium Isotope Geology, 1972, Pathways to Leadership: Achieving and Sustaining Success: A Guide for Nonprofit Executives, 1995. Fellow Geol. Soc. Am. Home: 150 S Muirfield Rd Los Angeles CA 90004-3729 Office: LA County Mus Natural Histo 900 Exposition Blvd Los Angeles CA 90007-4057

POWELL, JOSEPH EDWARD, English language educator; b. Ellensburg, Wash., Jan. 22, 1952; s. Arthur G. and Dorothy J. (Davis) P.; m. Judith A. Kleck, July 14, 1988; 1 child, Evan Ellis. BA, U. Wash., 1975; MA, Ctrl. Wash. U., 1978, BA, 1982; MFA, U. Ariz., 1981. Classroom tchr. Sequim (Wash.) H.S., 1982-83; instr. Ctrl. Wash. U., Ellensburg, 1983-88, asst. prof. English, 1989-90, assoc. prof. English, 1991-95, prof. English, 1995—. Author: Counting the Change, 1986, Winter Insomnia, 1993, Getting Here, 1996; contbr. poems and essays to publs. V.p. Ellensburg (Wash.) Arts Commn., 1988-90, 91-92, pres., 1989-90, 92-93. Mem. Associated Writing Programs, Alpine Lakes Protection Soc. Home: 221 Cross Creek Dr Ellensburg WA 98926-8531 Office: Dept English Ctrl Wash Univ Ellensburg WA 98926-7558

POWELL, KEITH PETER, marketing professional, small business owner; b. Patterson, N.J., Nov. 6, 1955; s. Marc Victor and Dorothy (Doyle) P.; m. Martha Ruiz, June 15, 1985. Cert. in alcohol counseling, U. Utah, 1975; AA in Bus. Mktg., Rio Hondo Coll., 1976; student, Whittier Coll., 1977-79. Cert. adult edn. tchr., Calif. Dir. student svcs. Rio Hondo Coll., Whittier, Calif., 1976-81; pres., chief exec. officer Attache Case Travel, Newport Beach, Calif., 1981-84; with sales and mktg. depts. Joint Venture Travel, 1985-86; instr. in travel mktg., mgmt. and sales Coastline Community Coll., Fountain Valley, Calif., 1982—, acad. senate pres., 1990—; profl. spkr. trends & mktg.; with mktg. dept. INternat. Travel Acad., 1987—; v.p. mktg. Travel Concepts, Brea, Calif., 1987—; pres. Powell and Assocs., Mktg. Cons., Brea, 1986—; owner Passage by Powell Cruise Only Travel Agy., 1990—; lectr. Rio Hondo Coll., 1987. Mem. Kiwanis (pres., bd. dirs. Whittier chpt. 1983). Mem. Christian Ch. Office: Powell & Assocs Mktg Cons 417 S Associated Rd # A-321 Brea CA 92821-5802

POWELL, LANE ALAN, editor; b. Alamogordo, N.Mex., Mar. 8, 1955; s. Cecil Lane Holmes and Janet Marie (LeRoux) Powell; m. Mari Catherine Priemesberger, July 15, 1989; children: Lane Cody, Sarah Blais. BS in Journalism, U. Fla., 1984. Info. specialist Engring. Coll. U. Fla., Gainesville, 1983-85; editor Windsor Publs., L.A., 1985-89; coord. publs. East Bay Regional Park Dist., Oakland, Calif., 1989—. Editor: Jacksonville and Florida's First Coast, 1989. Named Outstanding Hard Cover Pub. of Yr. Am. Chambers of Commerce Execs., 1989; recipient Best Spl. Facility Brochure in Calif. Calif. Park and Recreation Soc., 1990, Best Brochure Calif. Park and Recreation Soc., 1995. Home: 1882 N 5th St Concord CA 94519-2628 Office: East Bay Regional Park Dist 2950 Peralta Oaks Ct Oakland CA 94605-5320

POWELL, MARLYS KAYE, artist; b. L.A., May 17, 1942; d. Willys Gerald Stennes and Nanne Gloria Entner; m. Russell Lloyd Mallett, Nov. 24, 1961; children: Jeffrey Russell Mallet, Erik Lloyd Mallett; m. Allen Edward Powell, Aug. 17, 1984. Student, Cornish Sch. Allied Arts, 1962, John McCrady Art Sch., 1964. Freelance muralist New Orleans, 1964-65; tchr. fine art Westgate MIT, 1968; gallery dir. Pacific Art League, Palo Alto, Calif., 1975-80, tchr. calligraphy, 1982. Illustrator (book) Fun and Magic of Inventing, 1982; represented in various corp. collections including Scottsdale Ins. Co., Hewlett-Packard, Oracle Corp., Catalytica Asso, Inc., MIT; pvt. collections include A.L. Zeigler, Bechtel Internat. Ctr., Stanford Hosp., Burton Reiss, Newport Beach, Calif., Donald Horowitz, Arts Coun., Seattle; numerous other exhibits include Wilde-Meyer Gallery, Scottsdale, 1992-95, Casa Grande (N.Mex.) Mus., 1995, Casa de Artistas, Scottsdale, 1995-97, Courtyard Gallery, New Buffalo, Mich., 1995-97, Swansons Fine Art, San Francisco, 1994-97. Graphic artist Cancer Soc., New Orleans, 1964; chmn. art exhibit Stanford (Calif.) Hosp., 1975-78; pres. San Francisco Artist' Coop., 1979-80; participant Sedona (Ariz.) Forum, 1995. Recipient Painting award Casa Grande Mus., 1995. Mem. Asso. Pour La Promotion du Patrimoine Artistique Francais, Nat. Mus. Women in the Arts, Sedona Arts Ctr. (juror 1996-97, featured artist 1997). Office: PO Box 10039 Sedona AZ 86339

POWELL, MEL, composer; b. N.Y.C., Feb. 12, 1923. Studied piano from age 4; studied composition with Ernst Toch, L.A., 1946-48; with Paul Hindemith, Yale U., from 1948, MusB, 1952. Mem., chmn. faculty composition, Yale U., 1957-69; mem. staff, head faculty composition, formerly dean Calif. Inst. Arts, Valencia, provost, 1972-76, now Inst. fellow, Roy E. Disney chair in mus. composition. Albums include Six Recent Works, 1982-88, The Return of Mel Powell, 1989; composer: Duplicates: A Concerto for Two Pianos and Orchestra (premier L.A. Philharm. 1990, Pulitzer prize for music 1990), Modules for chamber orch. (recorded L.A. Philharm. 1991), Woodwind Quintet (recorded 1991), Setting for Two Pianos (recorded 1992), Settings for Small Orch., 1992 (commissioned by chamber orchs. of St. Paul, L.A., N.J.), Settings for Guitar (recorded 1993), numerous other compositions; subject of profile in New Yorker mag. Recipient Creative Arts medal Brandeis U., 1989; Pulitzer Prize for music, 1990; Guggenheim fellow; Nat. Inst. Arts and Letters grantee. Mem. Arnold Schoenburg Inst. (hon. life). Office: Calif Arts Inst Dept Composition 24700 Mcbean Pky Santa Clarita CA 91355-2340*

POWELL, ROBERT FRANCIS, manufacturing engineer; b. Chgo., May 17, 1936; s. John Joseph and Clara Mary (Brzczinski) Pawula. BS, Ill. Inst. of Tech., 1960; MS, MIT, 1961; Calif. Inst. of Tech., 1965. Prof. U. Calif., San Diego, 1965-75; cons. Random Applications, Inc., San Diego, 1981-91, comml. pilot, 1973—; vis. prof. chemistry U. Calif., San Diego, 1991-96, vis. lectr. physics, U. Barcelona, 1992—, vis. scholar math. U. Ariz., 1993—; pres. Tricel Corp., San Diego, 1994—, Debonair Press, San Diego, 1994—; cons. Cubic Corp., San Diego, 1975-92, JPL, Pasadena, Calif., 1985, Hughes Aircraft Co., Culver City, Calif., 1965-70. Author: Naked Strangers, 1993; contbr. articles to profl. jours.; inventor math. theory, 1965. Pilot, flight coord. Flying Samaritans, San Diego, 1974-76. With U.S. Army, 1974-76. Alfred Sloan Found. fellow, MIT, 1960-61, Howard Hughes Found. fellow, Calif. Inst. Tech., 1962-65. Mem. Experimental Aircraft Assn., Baja Bush Pilots, So. Ariz. Aerobatic Club, San Diego Flying Club (pres. 1973-74), Sigma Xi, Tau Beta Pi, Eta Kappa Nu, Phi Eta Sigma, Rho Epsilon. Home: 4611 Chateau Dr San Diego CA 92117-3003 Office: Tricel Corp San Diego CA 92117

POWELL, STEPHANIE, visual effects director, supervisor; b. Dayton, Ohio, Sept. 27, 1946; d. Harley Franklin and Evelyn Luella Pence. Pres., CEO Video Assist Systems, Inc., North Hollywood, Calif., 1979—, Out of the Blue Visual Effects, 1989. Cons.: (motion pictures) Jurassic Park, 1993, Flintstones, 1994, Waterworld, 1995, Get Shorty, 1995; visual effects supr.: Blown Away, 1994, My Brother's Keeper, 1994, Powder, 1995, Mrs. Santa Claus, 1996, Devil's Advocate, 1997, various commls.; co-visual effects supr. Quantum Leap (TV); developer using 3/4-inch videotape for broadcast. Mem. Acad. TV Arts and Scis., Acad. Magical Arts and Scis. Office: Video Assist Systems Inc 11030 Weddington St North Hollywood CA 91601-3212

POWER, DENNIS MICHAEL, museum director; b. Pasadena, Calif., Feb. 18, 1941; s. John Dennis and Ruth Augusta (Mott) P.; m. Kristine Moneva Fisher, Feb. 14, 1965 (div. Aug. 1984); children: Michael Lawrence, Matthew David; m. Leslie Gabrielle Baldwin, July 6, 1985; 1 stepchild, Katherine G. Petrosky. BA, Occidental Coll., 1962, MA, 1964; PhD, U. Kans., 1967. Asst. curator ornithology Royal Ont. Mus., Toronto, Can., assoc. curator, 1971-72; asst. prof. zoology U. Toronto, 1967-72; exec. dir. Santa Barbara (Calif.) Mus. Natural History, 1972-94, Oakland Mus. of Calif., 1994—; biol. rschr.; cons. ecology. Editor: The California Islands: Proceedings of a Multidisciplinary Symposium, 1980, Current Ornithology, vol. 6, 1989, vol. 7, 1990, vol. 8, 1991, vol. 9, 1992, vol. 10, 1993, vol. 11, 1993, vol. 12, 1995; contbr. articles to sci. jours. Bd. dirs. Univ. Club Santa Barbara, 1989-92, v.p., 1991-92; bd. dirs. Santa Barbara Chamber Orch., 1990-94, v.p., 1991-94; mem. adv. coun. Santa Cruz Island Found., 1989—; mem. discipline adv. com. for museology Coun. for Internat. Exch. of Scholars, 1991-95. NSF fellow U. Kans., 1967; NRC grantee, 1968-72, 74-78. Fellow Am. Ornithologists Union (life, sec. 1981-83, v.p. 1988-89), Am. Assn. Mus. (mem. coun. 1980-83), Calif. Acad. Scis.; mem. AAMS, Cooper Ornithol. Soc. (bd. dirs. 1976-79, pres. 1978-81, hon. mem. 1993), Calif. Assn. Mus. (bd. dirs. 1981-92, chmn. 1987-89), Western Mus. Conf. (bd. dirs. 1977-83, pres. 1981-83), Am. Soc. Naturalists, Assn. Sci. Mus. Dirs., Ecol. Soc., Am. Soc. Study of Evolution, Soc. Systematic Zoology, Bohemian Club, Sigma Xi. Office: Oakland Mus of California 1000 Oak St Oakland CA 94607-4820

POWER, MARGARET RAE (MARGO POWER), publisher; b. Missoula, Mont., Mar. 28, 1943; d. Lawrence Joseph Anthony and Lenore (Shrider) Schuck; m. Dale Lawrence Power Sr., Dec. 21, 1962; children: Stephanie, Stacy, Sylvia, Dale Jr., Kelly. ADN, Clark Coll., 1976. Owner Madison Pub. Co., Vancouver, Wash., 1994—; pub. Murderous Intent Mystery Mag., Vancouver, 1994—. Co-author: (with Margo Power and Dale Power) Wildlife Carving with Dale Power, Vol. I and II, 1995. Mem. Short Myster Fiction Soc. (founder, pres.), Mystery Writers of Am., Sisters in Crime. Office: Madison Pub Co PO Box 5947 Vancouver WA 98668-5947

POWERS, EDWIN MALVIN, consulting engineer; b. Denver, July 20, 1915; s. Emmett and Bertha Malvina (Guido) P.; m. Dorothy Lavane Debler, Jan. 18, 1941; children: Dennis M., Kenneth E., James M., Steven R. BS in Chem. Engring., U. Denver, 1939, MS, 1940. Registered profl. engr., N.J., Colo., Fall Out Analysts Engr., U.S. Fed. Emergency Mgmt. Agency, 1975-87. Prodn. supr. Nat. Aniline Div., Buffalo, 1940-45; engr., project supr. Merck & Co., Rahway, N.J., 1945-67, chief project coordinator, 1967-72, purchasing engr., 1972-82; ret., 1982; cons. engr., Conifer, Colo., 1982—. Capt. Air Raid Wardens, River dist., Buffalo, 1942-45. Mem., del. Conifer Home Owners Assns. Protect Our Single Homes, 1984-86, Regional Environ. Assn. Concerned Home Owners, 1985-86, task force area devel. Hwy. 285/Conifer Area County Planning Bd. Community, 1986-88. Mem. NSPE, Am. Chem. Soc. (emeritus), Am. Inst. Chem. Engrs. (emeritus, treas. N.J. 1960, exec. com. 1961-63), Nat. Soc. Profl. Engrs. Home and Office: 26106 Amy Cir Conifer CO 80433-6102

POWERS, J. D., III, marketing executive. Pres. J.D. Powers & Assocs., Calif. Office: J D Powers & Assocs 30401 Agoura Rd Agoura Hills CA 91301*

POWERS, JEFFREY, business executive, speaker; b. Milw., Nov. 25; s. Averill and Rose Powers. BA in Psychology, U. Wis., 1971. Pres. Powers Travel Svc. Inc., Milw., 1973-86; CEO Checkpoint World Team, Westlake Village, Calif., 1988—, Twin Vision, Westlake Village, 1989—, Checkpoint World Team, Inc., Carson City, Nev., Twin Vision Am., Las Vegas, Psychic Inst., Westlake Village, 1992—, Health Watch, Westlake Village, 1993—, Invisible Empire, Westlake Village, 1993—; creator Smart Universe, first virtual nation. Creator, pioneer Live, Interactive Pay-Per-Call Tech. for Bus. Applications, 1989. Recipient Phi Eta Sigma Nat. Scholastic Honors award U. Wis., 1968. Nominating Com. mem., 3rd Annual Screen Actors Guild award, 1997. Office: Checkpoint World Team Inc 251 Jeanell Dr Ste 3 Carson City NV 89703

POWERS, JUDITH KAY, educational administrator, English educator; b. Eau Claire, Wis., Sept. 23, 1942; d. Clifford Lyle and Marcille Leone (Bunce) P.; m. Rex Earl Gantenbein, May 13, 1983. BA in English, U. Wis., 1964; MA in English, U. Wyo., 1965; PhD in English, Rice U., 1971. Asst. prof. Iowa State U., Ames, 1973-79; test specialist Am. Coll. Testing, Iowa City, 1979-85; lectr., acad. profl. U. Wyo., Laramie, 1985-94; asst. dir. Wyo. Coun. for the Humanities, Laramie, 1994—; writer, rschr. Wyo. Territorial Prison, 1989-91. Assoc. editor: Iowa Woman mag., 1983-85; contbr. articles to profl. jours. Mem. Com. for Campus Access for the Disabled, Laramie, 1986-94. Wyo. Coun. for the Humanities scholar, 1991-94; grantee Ctr. for Tchg. Excellence, Laramie, 1991, 92, 93, 94. Mem. MLA, TESOL, Conf. Coll. Composition and Comm., Nat. Coun. Tchrs. English. Democrat. Home: 150 Butte Loop Laramie WY 82070-6825 Office: Wyoming Coun Humanities PO Box 3643 Laramie WY 82071-3643

POWERS, LINDA SUE, biophysicist, educator; b. Pitts., Feb. 8, 1948; d. Luther Thurston and Helen Grace (Currence) Powers. BS in Physics and Chemistry, Va. Poly. Inst. and State U., 1970; MA in Physics, Harvard U., 1972, PhD in Biophysics, 1976. Mem. tech. staff AT&T Bell Labs., Murray Hill, N.J., 1976-88; dir. bio catalysis sci. ctr., prof. chemistry & biochemistry Utah State U., Logan, 1988-91, prof. elec. engring., biol. & irrigation engring., 1991—; dir. Nat. Ctr. for the Design of Molecular Function, Logan, 1991—; adj. prof. U. Pa. Med. Sch., Phila., 1978—, organizer VII Internat. Biophysics Congress, 1981; vis. fellow Princeton U., 1981-82. Mem. editl. corr. Comments Molecular Cellular Biophysics, 1980-89; editl. bd. Biophysics Jour., 1989-96, Am. Inst. of Physics Internat. Basic and Applied Biol. Physics, 1993—; contbr. numerous articles to profl. jours. and books. Recipient 1st U.S. Bioenergetics award, 1982, State of Utah Gov.'s medal for sci. and tech., 1994. Fellow Am. Phys. Soc. (coun. divsn. biol. physics 1988-92, exec. bd. 1977-83, chmn. 1984-85), Am. Inst. Chemists; mem. IEEE, AAAS, Biophys. Soc., Soc. Applied Spectroscopy, Sigma Pi Sigma, Phi Lambda Upsilon. Office: Utah State U Nat Ctr for Design of Molecular Function 11 Engring Lab Bldg Logan UT 84322-4630

POWERS, STEPHEN, educational researcher, consultant; b. Bakersfield, Calif., June 10, 1936; s. Robert Boyd and Mildred (Irwin) P.; m. Gail Marguerite Allen, Dec. 28, 1968; children: Rick, Joseph, Rebecca. BS in Edn., No. Ariz. U., 1959; MA, U. Ariz., Tucson, 1970, MEd, 1972, PhD, 1978. Cert. tchr., Calif.; cert. tchr., adminstr., jr. coll. tchr., Ariz. Policeman, City of Bakersfield, 1967-69; tchr. Marana (Ariz.) Pub. Schs., 1969-72; dir. Am. Sch. Belo Horizonte, Brazil, 1972-73; tchr. Nogales (Ariz.) Pub. Schs., 1973-75; rsch. specialist Tucson Unified Sch. Dist., 1975-94; prof. Walden U., U. Ariz., 1981, U. Phoenix, 1990; founder Creative Rsch. Assocs., 1991—, now pres.; bd. dirs. Manchester Coll., Oxford U.; internat. evaluator USAID, 1991. Contbr. articles to profl. jours. Nat. Inst. Edn. grantee, 1980. Mem. Am. Ednl. Rsch. Assn., Royal Statis. Soc. (U.K. chpt.), Am. Statis. Assn. Bahai. Office: 2030 E Broadway Ste 9 Tucson AZ 85719-5813

POYNTER, DANIEL FRANK, publisher; b. N.Y.C., Sept. 17, 1938; s. William Frank and Josephine E. (Thompson) P. BA, Calif. State U., Chico, 1960; postgrad., San Francisco Law Sch., 1961-63. federally lic. master parachute rigger; lic. pilot. Pub., prin. Para Pub., Santa Barbara, Calif., 1969—; listed as expert witness Nat. Forensic Ctr., Tech. Adv. Service for Attys., Consultants and Consulting Organizations Directory, Lawyer's Guide to Legal Consultants, Expert Witnesses, Services, Books and Products. Author: The Parachute Manual, Parachuting, The Skydiver's Handbook, Parachuting Manual with Log, Hang Gliding, Manned Kiting, The Self-Publishing Manual, How to Write, Print & Sell Your Own Book, Publishing Short Run Books, Business Letters For Publishers, Computer Selection Guide, Word Processing and Information Processing, Publishing Forms, Parachuting Manual for Square/Piggyback Equipment, Frisbee Players' Handbook, Toobee Players' Handbook, 65 others, some translated in fgn. languages; past editor news mag. Spotter; monthly columnist Parachute mag., 1963—; contbr. over 500 tech. and popular articles and photographs to mags; patentee parachute pack, POP TOP. Recipient numerous certs. of appreciation for directing parachuting competitions. Mem. U.S. Parachute Assn. (life, chmn. bd., exec. com. 12 yrs., nat. and internat. del., achievement award, 1981, cert. 25 yr. mem., awarded Gold Parachute Wings, 1972), Parachute Industry Assn. (pres. 1985, 86), AIAA, Soc. Automotive Engrs., Nat. Aeronautic Assn., Aviation Space Writers Assn. (internat. conf. mem. 1978,79, 82), Calistoga Skydivers (past sec.), No. Calif. Parachute Council (past sec.), U.S. Hang Gliding Assn. (life, past dir., del.), Internat. Assn. Ind. Pubs. (past bd. dirs., pres. Santa Barbara chpt. 1979-82), Assn. Am. Pubs., Pub. Mktg. Assn. (bd. dirs., v.p.), Book Pubs. So. Calif., Am. Booksellers Assn., Commn. Internat de Vol Libre of Fedn. Aero. Internat. in Paris (U.S. del., past pres., lifetime Pres. d'Honneur award 1979, recipient Paul Tissander Diploma, 1984). Home: RR 1 Santa Barbara CA 93117-1047 Office: Para Publishing PO Box 8206 Santa Barbara CA 93118-8206

PRACKO, BERNARD FRANCIS, II, artist, business owner; b. Ada, Okla., Jan. 17, 1945; m. Patricia Fairmont Butterfield Stone, 1967 (div. 1971); 1 child, Genevieve Suydam Stone Davis; m. Elaine Jean Nisky, 1980 (div. 1981); m. Renee Ericson Whitman, 1982 (div. 1986). AA, N.Mex. Mil. Inst., 1965; BA, U. Colo., 1970; postgrad., Ariz. State U., 1991. With Fayber Assocs., Inc., Boulder, Colo., 1974—; ednl. rschr. Tomatis Ctr., Phoenix, 1991—. One-man shows include Grand Champions, Aspen, 1992, Scottsdale Culinary Inst., 1992; exhibited in group shows at Sena Galleries, Santa Fe, 1991, Sacred Spaces, L.I., N.Y., 1991, Cultural Exch. Gallery, Scottsdale, 1992, Nelson Fine Art Mus., Tempe, Ariz., 1992, Aspen Art Mus., 1992, Sun Cities Art Mus., Sun City, ARiz., 1992, San Diego Art Inst., 1993; represented in permanent collections Scottsdale Culinary Inst., Am. West Airlines, Tempe, U. Colo., Boulder, Ariz. State U., Tempe, Sun Cities Art Mus., Sun City, Amnesty Internat., Washington. Peace awareness trainer Egypt, Israel, South Africa, Kenya, Nigeria, 1986; vol., artist coord. Amnesty Internat., U.S.A. calendar, 1990. Office: Fayber Assocs Inc PO Box 740399 Arvada CO 80006-0399

PRASAD, JAYASIMHA SWAMY, electrical engineer; b. Pavagada, India, Oct. 18, 1948; came to U.S. 1978.; BE, Indian Inst. Sci., Bangalore, 1971; MTech, Indian Inst. Tech., Madras, 1973; MS, Oreg. State U., 1980, PhD, 1985. Sr. engr. Hindustan Aeronatucis Ltd., Hyderabad, India, 1973-74; asst. prof. Indian Inst. Tech., Madras, 1974-78; sr. engr. Nat. Semiconductor Corp., Santa Clara, Calif., 1980-82, sr. engring. mgr., 1995—; tech. fellow Tektronix Inc., Beaverton, Oreg., 1985-95; cons. Internat. Microelectronic Products, San Jose, 1982-83, Textronix, 1983-85; adj. prof. Oreg. State U., 1985—, Santa Clara U., 1996—; disting. lectr. IEEE Electron Devices Soc. Contbr. articles to profl. jours.; inventor in field. Chevron scholar, 1983-84. Mem. IEEE (sr.). Home: 5472 Livorno Ct San Jose CA 95138-2211

PRATHER, RICHARD SCOTT, author; b. Santa Ana, Calif., Sept. 9, 1921; s. Sydney Scott Prather and Effie Alberta Kuykendall Middleton; m. Alma Tina Hager, July 31, 1945. Student, Riverside (Calif.) Poly., 1936-39, Riverside Jr. Coll., 1940. Civilian clk. March AFB, Riverside, 1941, chief clk., surplus property disposal office, 1946-49; fireman, 2d engr. U.S. Merchant Marine, 1942-45. Author: Case of the Vanishing Beauty, 1950,

Bodies in Bedlam, 1951, Everybody Had a Gun, 1951, Find This Woman, 1951, Way of a Wanton, 1952, Lie Down, Killer, 1952, Dagger of Flesh, 1952, Darling, It's Death, 1952, Too Many Crooks (originally, Ride a High Horse), 1953, Always Leave 'Em Dying, 1954, Pattern for Panic, 1954, Strip for Murder, 1955, Dragnet: Case #561, 1956, The Wailing Frail, 1956, Have Gat - Will Travel, 1957, Three's a Shroud, 1957, Slab Happy, 1958, Take a Murder, Darling, 1958, The Scrambled Yeggs, 1958 (originally Pattern for Murder by David Knight, 1952), The Peddler, 1958 (originally by Douglas Ring, 1952), Over Her Dear Body, 1959, Double in Trouble (with Stephen Marlowe), 1959, Dance With the Dead, 1960, Shell Scott's Seven Slaughters, 1961, Dig That Crazy Grave, 1961, Kill the Clown, 1962, Joker in the Deck, 1964, The Cockeyed Corpse, 1964, Dead Heat, 1964, The Trojan Hearse, 1964, Kill Him Twice, 1965, Dead Man's Walk, 1965, The Meandering Corpse, 1965, The Kubla Khan Caper, 1966, Gat Heat, 1967, The Cheim Manuscript, 1969, The Shell Scott Sampler, 1969, Kill Me Tomorrow, 1969, Shell Scott's Murder Mix, 1970, Dead Bang, 1971, The Sweet Ride, 1972, The Sure Thing, 1975, The Amber Effect, 1986, Shellshock, 1987; editor: The Comfortable Coffin, 1960; stories in Manhunt, Cavalier, Thrilling Detective, Menace, Justice, Accused, Suspect, Murder!, Ed McBain's Mystery Book, Adam, Escapade, Man's World, Swank, For Men Only, Tiger, Shell Scott's Mystery Mag., several anthologies. Recipient Life Achievement award Pvt. Eye Writers of Am., 1986. Home: 810 E Saddlehorn Rd Sedona AZ 86351

PRATT, GEORGE JANES, JR., psychologist, author; b. Mpls., May 3, 1948; s. George Janes and Sally Elvina (Hanson) P.; married; 1 child, Whitney Beth. BA cum laude, U. Minn., 1970, MA, 1973; PhD with spl. commendation for overall excellence, Calif. Sch. Profl. Psychology, San Diego, 1976. Diplomate Am. Bd. Med. Psychotherapists, Am. Acad. Pain Mgmt.; lic. psychologist, Calif. Psychology trainee Ctr. for Behavior Modification, Mpls., 1971-72, U. Minn. Student Counseling Bur., 1972-73; predoctoral clin. psychology intern San Bernardino County (Calif.) Mental Health Svcs., 1973-74, San Diego County Mental Health Services, 1974-76; mem. staff San Luis Rey Hosp., 1977-78; postdoctoral clin. psychology intern Mesa Vista Hosp., San Diego, Calif., 1976; clin. psychologist, dir. Psychology and Cons. Assocs. of San Diego, 1976—; chmn. Psychology and Cons. Assocs. Press, 1977—; bd. dirs. Optimax, Inc., 1985—; pres. George Pratt Ph.D., Psychol. Corp., 1979—; chmn. Pratt, Korn & Assocs., Inc., 1984—; mem. staff Scripps Meml. Hosp., La Jolla, Calif., 1986—, chmn. psychology, 1993—; founder La Jolla Profl. Workshops, 1977; clin. psychologist El Camino Psychology Ctr., San Clemente, Calif., 1977-78; grad. teaching asst. U. Minn. Psychology and Family Studies div., 1971; teaching assoc. U. Minn. Psychology and Family Studies div., Mpls., 1972-73; instr. U. Minn. Extension div., Mpls., 1971-73; faculty Calif. Sch. Profl. Psychology, 1974-83, San Diego Evening Coll., 1975-77, Nat. U., 1978-79, Chapman Coll., 1978, San Diego State U., 1979-80; vis. prof. Pepperdine U., L.A., 1976-80; cons. U. Calif. at San Diego Med. Sch., 1976—, also instr. univ., 1978—; psychology chmn. Workshops in Clin. Hypnosis, 1980-84; cons. Calif. Health Dept., 1974, Naval Regional Med. Ctr., 1978-82, ABC-TV; also speaker. With USAR, 1970-76. Fellow Am. Soc. Clin. Hypnosis (cert., approved cons.); mem. APA, Internat. Soc. Hypnosis, San Diego Psychology Law Soc. (exec. com.), Am. Assn. Sex Educators, Counselors and Therapists (cert.), San Diego Soc. Sex Therapy and Edn. (past pres.), San Diego Soc. Clin. Hypnosis (past pres.), San Diego Psychol. Assn., Soc. Clin. and Exptl. Hypnosis., U. Minn. Alumni Assn., Nat. Speakers Assn., Beta Theta Pi. Author: Rx for Stress, 1994, HyperPerformance, 1987, A Clinical Hypnosis Primer, 1984, 88, Release Your Business Potential, 1988, Sensory/Progressive Relaxation, 1979, Effective Stress Management, 1979, Clinical Hypnosis: Techniques and Applications, 1985; contbr. chpts. to various books. Office: Scripps Hosp Med Bldg 9834 Genesee Ave Ste 321 La Jolla CA 92037-1216

PRATT, JOHN WILLIAM, sales representative; b. Spring Valley, N.Y., Apr. 6, 1955; s. John Lafayette and Elizabeth (Coccia) P.; m. Marianne Leonchuck, June 25, 1977; 1 child, James Michael. BS in Chemistry, Lehigh U., 1977. Chemist PPG Industries, New Martinsville, W.Va., 1977-78; sales support engr. Hewlett-Packard Co., Avondale, Pa., 1978-81; rsch. chemist Betz Labs., Trevose, Pa., 1982-84; sales rep. Finnigan Corp., San Jose, Calif., 1984-94, Perkin-Elmer Corp., Foster City, Calif., 1994—. Asst. coach Little League, Mt. Laurel, N.J., 1991, 92, Parks and Recreation, Newark, Del., 1993, 94. Mem. Am. Soc. for Mass Spectrometry, Am. Chem. Soc., U.S. Golf Assn., Golden Key. Home: 112 Amherst Dr Newark DE 19711 Office: Perkin-Elmer Applied Biosys Divsn 850 Lincoln Centre Dr Foster City CA 94404-1128

PRATT, PAUL BERNARD, financial services executive; b. Johnson City, Tenn., Aug. 7, 1946; s. Paul Bernard Pratt and Lois Kathern (Arnold) Thomas; m. Diann Margurite Scroggins, Apr. 2, 1971 (dec.); 1 child, Jennifer Elaine White; m. Patricia Lea Kell Alleman, June 21, 1992 (dec.). BA, Chapman Coll., 1975; MBA, Webster U., 1993; postgrad., Western State U., 1994—. Commd. 2d lt. USMC, 1966, advanced through grades to lt. col., 1983, svc. in RVN, 1969, 70, regimental air officer 2nd Marines, 1977-80, ops. officer MAWTS-1, 1980-83, ops. officer marine corps air sta. Iwakuni SA, 1984-87; asst. dean command and staff coll. USMC, Quantico, Va., 1987-90; dir. morale, welfare and recreation MCAS USMC, El Toro, Calif., 1991-93; ret. USMC, 1993; pres. Success Seminars, Irvine, Calif., 1993—; v.p. ERIC Equities Inc., Santa Ana, Calif., 1993—. Precinct inspector Orange County (Calif.) Voting Commn., 1994; pres. Cath. Parish Coun., Japan, 1986. Recipient Meritorious Svc. medal Pres. of the U.S., 1990, 93. Mem. Internat. Assn. of Fin. Planners. Office: ERIC Equities Inc 2021 E 4th St Santa Ana CA 92705-3912

PRATT, RONALD FRANKLIN, public relations executive; b. Savannah, Ga., July 15, 1948; s. Frank Tecumseh and Lila Elizabeth (Lee) P. BA, Washington U., St. Louis, 1972. Reporter Savannah News-Press, 1972; news dir. WSOK Radio, Savannah, 1973; editor Hilton Head News, Hilton Head Island, S.C., 1974-77; account exec. Russom & Leeper, San Francisco, 1978-80; sr. account exec. Russom & Leeper, 1981-83, v.p., 1983-85; sr. v.p., prin. The Leeper Grp., San Francisco, 1985-86; pres. Ronald Pratt Pub. Rels., San Francisco, 1987-90; sr. v.p., mgmt. supr. Porter/Novelli, L.A., 1990-92, sr. v.p., group exec., 1993-94, exec. v.p., gen. mgr., 1995—; cons. Coro Found., San Francisco, 1989-90. Bd. dirs. Hilton Head Jazz Festival, 1976-77; pres. Hilton Head Inst. for the Arts, 1976-77; dir., v.p. San Francisco Coun. on Entertainment, 1985-87. Recipient Enterprise award, AP, Ga., 1973. Mem. Internat. Assn. Bus. Communicators (Gold Quill 1983), Internat. Foodsvc. Editl. Coun., Agrl. Rels. Coun., Am. Inst. Wine and Food.

PRATT, ROSALIE REBOLLO, harpist, educator; b. N.Y.C., Dec. 4, 1933; d. Antonio Ernesto and Eleanor Gertrude (Gibney) Rebollo; Mus.B., Manhattanville Coll., 1954; Mus.M., Pius XII Inst. Fine Arts, Florence, Italy, 1955; Ed.D., Columbia U., 1976; m. George H. Mortimer, Esquire, Apr. 22, 1987; children: Francesca Christina Rebollo-Sborgi, Alessandra Maria Pratt Jones. Prin. harpist N.J. Symphony Orch., 1963-65; soloist Mozart Haydn Festival, Avery Fisher Hall, N.Y.C., 1968; tchr. music public schs., Bloomfield and Montclair, N.J., 1962-73; mem. faculty Montclair State Coll., 1973-79; prof. Brigham Young U., Provo, Utah, 1984—, coord. grad. studies dept. music, 1985-87.; biofeedback and neurofeedback rsch. specialist, 1993—. U.S. chair 1st internat. arts medicine leadership conf., Tokyo Med. Coll., 1993. Co-author: Elementary Music for All Learners, 1980; editor Internat. Jour. Arts Medicine, 1991—, (proceedings) 2d, 3d, 4th Internat. Symposia Music Edn. for Handicapped; contbr. articles to Am. Harp Jour., Music Educators Jour., others. Fulbright grantee, 1979; Myron Taylor scholar, 1954. Mem. Am. Harp Soc. (Outstanding Service award 1973), AAUP (co-chmn. legis. rels. com. N.J. 1978-79), Internat. Soc. Music Edn. (chair commn. music in spl. edn., music therapy, and medicine 1985—), Internat. Soc. Music in Medicine (v.p. 1993—), Internat. Assn. of Music for the Handicapped (co-founder, exec. dir., jour. editor), Coll. Music Soc., Music Educators Nat. Conf., Soc. for Study of Neuronal Regulation, Brigham Young U. Grad. Coun., Phi Kappa Phi, Sigma Alpha Iota. Office: Brigham Young U Harris Fine Arts Ctr Provo UT 84602 *Personal philosophy: I believe in offering my students what I have learned from the educational heroes in my life, the teachers whose example is the reason I prepare my classes carefully and thoughtfully. What I am and what I cherish most in life is also the result of a grandmother and father, neither of whose formal education went beyond the third grade, but whose wisdom was timeless.*

PRATT, WALDEN PENFIELD, research geologist; b. Columbus, Ohio, Mar. 22, 1928; s. Julius William and Louisa Gabriella (Williamson) P.; m. Janice May Eddy, Dec. 21, 1957; children: Julius William II, Susan Elizabeth, David Milton. AB, U. Rochester, 1948; postgrad. Yale U., 1948-49; MS, Stanford U., 1956, PhD, 1964. Geologist, U.S. Geol. Survey, Iron River, Mich., 1949-51, Claremont, Calif., 1953-55, research geologist, Lakewood, Colo., 1956-89, scientist emeritus, 1989—; geologist Pacific Coast Borax Co., Salta, Argentina, 1955. Co-editor: United States Mineral Resources, 1973 (U.S. Geol Survey monetary award), Proceedings, Internat. Conf. on Miss. Valley-type lead-zinc deposits, 1984; editor Soc. Econ. Geologists Newsletter, 1986-91; contbr. articles to U.S. Geol. Survey publs. Served with U.S. Army, 1951-53. Recipient Meritorious Service award Dept. Interior, 1983. Fellow Geol. Soc. Am., Soc. Econ. Geologists (hon., Marsden award 1994); mem. Am. Assn. Petroleum Geologists, Rocky Mountain Assn. Geologists, Colo. Sci. Soc. Republican. Presbyterian. Office: U S Geol Survey MS 905 Box 25046 Denver CO 80225-0046

PRAUSNITZ, JOHN MICHAEL, chemical engineer, educator; b. Berlin, Jan. 7, 1928; came to U.S., 1937, naturalized, 1944; s. Paul Georg and Susi Prausnitz; m. Susan Prausnitz, June 10, 1956; children: Stephanie, Mark Robert. B Chem. Engring., Cornell U., 1950; MS, U. Rochester, 1951; Ph.D., Princeton, 1955; Dr. Ing., U. L'Aquila, 1983, Tech. U. Berlin, 1989; DSc, Princeton U., 1995. Mem. faculty U. Calif., Berkeley, 1955—, prof. chem. engring., 1963—; cons. to cryogenic, polymer, petroleum and petrochem. industries. Author: (with others) Computer Calculations for Multicomponent Vapor-Liquid Equilibria, 1967, (with P.L. Chueh) Computer Calculations for High-Pressure Vapor-Liquid Equilibria, 1968, Molecular Thermodynamics of Fluid-Phase Equilibria, 1969, 2d edit., 1986, (with others) Regular and Related Solutions, 1970, Properties of Gases and Liquids, 3d edit., 1977, 4th edit., 1987, Computer Calculations for Multicomponent Vapor-Liquid and Liquid-Liquid Equilibria, 1980; contbr. to profl. jours. Recipient Alexander von Humboldt Sr. Scientist award, 1976, Carl von Linde Gold Meml. medal German Inst. for Cryogenics, 1987, Solvay prize Solvay Found. for Chem. Scis., 1990, Corcoran award Am. Soc. for Engring. Edn., 1991, D.L. Katz award Gas Processors Assn., 1992; named W.K. Lewis lectr. MIT, 1993; Guggenheim fellow, 1962, 73, fellow Inst. Advanced Study, Berlin, 1985; Miller rsch. prof., 1966, 78; Christensen fellow St. Catherine's Coll. Oxford U., 1994, Erskine fellow U. Canterbury Christchurch, New Zealand, 1996. Mem. AIChE (Colburn award 1962, Walker award 1967, Inst. Lectr. award 1994), Am. Chem. Soc. (E.V. Murphree award 1979, Petroleum Chemistry Rsch. award 1995), NAE, NAS, Am. Acad. Arts and Scis. Office: U Calif 308 Gilman Hall Berkeley CA 94720

PRAY, RALPH EMERSON, metallurgical engineer; b. Troy, N.Y., May 12, 1926; s. George Emerson and Jansje Cornelius (Owejan) P.; student N.Mex. Inst. of Mining and Tech., 1953-56, U. N.Mex., 1956; BSMetE, U. Alaska, 1961; DScMetE. (Ideal Cement fellowship, Rsch. grant), Colo. Sch. of Mines, 1966; m. Beverley Margaret Ramsey, May 10, 1959; children: Maxwell, Ross, Leslie, Marlene. Engr.-in-charge Dept. Mines and Minerals, Ketchikan, Alaska, 1957-61; asst. mgr. mfg. rsch. Universal Atlas Cement div. U.S. Steel Corp., Gary, Ind., 1965-66; rsch. metallurgist Inland Steel Co., Hammond, Ind., 1966-67; owner, dir. Mineral Rsch. Lab., Monrovia, Calif., 1968—; pres., Keystone Canyon Mining Co., Inc., Pasadena, Calif., 1972-79, U.S. Western Mines, 1973—, Silveroil Rsch. Inc., 1980-85; v.p. Mineral Drill Inc., 1981-90; pres., CEO Copper de Mex. S.A. de C.V.; prime contractor def. logistics agy. U.S. Dept. Def., 1989-92; designer, turn-key constructor Vanavara Electrolytic Gold Refinery, Krasnoyarsk, Russia, 1995; owner Precision Plastics, 1973-82; bd. dirs. Bagdad-Chase Inc., 1972-75; ptnr. Mineral R&D Co., 1981-86; lectr., Purdue U., Hammond, Ind., 1966-67, Nat. Mining Seminar, Barstow (Calif.) Coll., 1969-70; guest lectr. Calif. State Poly U., 1977-81, Western Placer Mining Conf., Reno, Nev., 1983, Dredging and Placer Mining Conf., Reno, 1985, others; v.p., dir. Wilbur Foote Plastics, Pasadena, 1968-72; strategic minerals del. People to People, Republic of South Africa, 1983; vol. Monrovia Police Dept.; city coord. Neighborhood Watch, 1990—. With U.S. Army, 1950-52. Fellow Geol. Mining and Metall. Soc. India (life), Am. Inst. Chemists, South African Inst. Mining and Metallurgy; mem. Soc. Mining Engrs., Am. Chem. Soc., Am. Inst. Mining, Metall. and Petroleum Engrs., NSPE, Can. Inst. Mining and Metallurgy, Geol. Soc. South Africa, Sigma Xi, Sigma Mu. Achievements include research on recovery of metals from refractory ores, benefication plant design, construction and operation, underground and surface mine development and operation, mine and process plant management; syndication of natural resource assets with finance sources; contbr. articles to sci. jours.; guest editor Calif. Mining Jour., 1978—; patentee chem. processing and steel manufacture. Office: 805 S Shamrock Ave Monrovia CA 91016-3651

PREBLE, LOU-ANN M., state legislator; m. Bill Preble. Grad., Tuomey Hosp. Sch. Nursing, 1950, Prima C.C., 1978. RN S.C., 1951-77; physical evaluator Medi-Quik, Tucson, 1978-82; co-owner, mgr. retail apparel store, 1972-75, ret.; mem. Ariz. Ho. of Reps., mem. assignments com. former precinct committeeman, dep. registr.; state committeeman, 1974-92; rep. at large State Exec. Com., 1991-92. Republican. Roman Catholic. Office: House of Representatives 1700 W Washington St Phoenix AZ 85007-2812*

PREBLE, PATRICIA JOAN, visual artist, writer; b. Great Lakes, Ill., Oct. 29, 1951. Cert. in broadcast announcing, Brown Inst., Mpls., 1972; BA in Philosophy and Art cum laude, U. Minn., 1978. asst. to dir. Real Art Ways, Hartford, Conn., 1982-83. Contbr. articles to profl. jours.; represented in permanent collections in pvt., corp. and mus., N.Y., Chgo., Miami, Houston, Mpls.-St. Paul, San Francisco, Boston, Oklahoma City, Hartford, Conn.; exhibited in group shows at U. Minn., 1978, Quinlan Art Ctr., Gainesville, Ga., 1979, Image South Gallery, Atlanta, 1980-84, Minnetonka (Minn.) Art Ctr., 1980, Studio 203 Fine Arts, Mpls., 1981, Gallery Bwana, Denver, 1985, Circle Works Visions Gallery, 1986, Artistic Visions: San Francisco, Haight Asbury Cmty. Cultural Ctr., 1987, Fall Group Showing: Weir Gallery, Berkeley, Calif., 1990, Earth Art: Art Resources, Internat. Mill Valley, 1990, Gallery Juno, N.Y.C., 1996; solo exhibits include Earth & Sky: L.E. Ross Fine Art, Mpls., 1979, Journey to the Light U. Storrs, Conn., 1984, Summer Colors M.S. Gallery, Hartford, Conn., 1984, Seven Colors: N.Y. Open Ctr., 1986, Drawings: Cornelia Street Cafe, West Village, N.Y., 1986, Mus. of the Nat. Arts Found., Oklahoma City, 1986, Colorado Skies N.Y. Open Ctr., 1987, Open Studio San Francisco Open Studio Program, 1988, Five Yr. Perspective: Studio 141, San Francisco, 1990, Biblical Themes in Modern Dress, San Francisco, 1995, Angels, Archangels and the Clear Light, San Francisco, 1995. Soul Passage, San Francisco, 1996. Chmn., bd. dirs. Mus. of Nat. Arts Found., Denver, 1985-86. Recipient Marathon Traveler award Ctr. for Rsch. and Enlightenment, 1984. Buddhism and comparative religion. Office: Preble Studios PO Box 22682 San Francisco CA 94122-0682

PREGERSON, HARRY, federal judge; b. L.A., Oct. 13, 1923; s. Abraham and Bessie (Rubin) P.; m. Bernardine Seyma Chapkis, June 28, 1947; children: Dean Douglas, Kathryn Ann. B.A., UCLA, 1947; LL.B., U. Calif.-Berkeley, 1950. Bar: Calif. 1951. Pvt. practice Los Angeles, 1951-52; Assoc. Morris D. Coppersmith, 1952; ptnr. Pregerson & Costley, Van Nuys, 1953-65; judge Los Angeles Mcpl. Ct., 1965-66, Los Angeles Superior Ct., 1966-67, U.S. Dist. Ct. Central Dist. Calif., 1967-79, U.S. Ct. Appeals for 9th Circuit, Woodland Hills, 1979—; faculty mem., seminar for newly appointed distr. Judges Fed. Jud. Center, Washington, 1970-72; mem. faculty Am. Soc. Pub. Adminstrn., Inst. for Ct. Mgmt., Denver, 1973—; panelist Fed. Bar Assn., L.A. chpt., 1989, Calif. Continuing Edn. of Bar, 9th Ann. Fed. Practice Inst., San Francisco, 1986, Internat. Acad. Trial Lawyers, L.A., 1983; lect. seminars for newly-appointed Fed. judges, 1970-71. Author over 450 published legal opinions. Mem. Community Rels. Com., Jewish Fedn. Coun., 1984—, Temple Judea, Encino, 1955—; bd. dirs. Marine Corps Res. Toys for Tots Program, 1965—, Greater Los Angeles Partnership for the Homeless, 1988—; bd. trustees Devil Pups Inc., 1988—; adv. bd. Internat. Orphans Inc., 1966—, Jewish Big Brothers Assn., 1970—, Salvation Army, Los Angeles Met. area, 1988—; worked with U.S. Govt. Gen. Svcs. to establish the Bell Shelter for the homeless, the Child Day Care Ctr., the Food Partnership and Westwood Transitional Village, 1988. 1st lt. USMCR, 1944-46. Decorated Purple Heart, Medal of Valor Apache Tribe, 1989; recipient Promotion of Justice Civic award, City of San Fernando, 1965, award San Fernando Valley Jewish Fedn. Coun., 1966, Profl. Achievement award Los Angeles Athletic Club, 1980, Profl. Achievement award UCLA Alumni Assn., 1985, Louis D. Brandeis award Am. Friends of Hebrew U., 1987, award of merit Inner City Law Ctr., 1987, Appreciation award Navajo Nation and USMC for Toys for Tots program, 1987, Humanitarian award Los Angeles Fed. Exec. Bd., 1987-88, Grateful Acknowledgement award Bet Tzedek Legal Svcs., 1988, Commendation award Bd. Suprs. Los Angeles County, 1988, Others award Salvation Army, 1988, numerous others. Mem. ABA (vice-chmn., com. on fed. rules of criminal procedure and evidence sect. of criminal 1972—, panelist Advocacy Inst., Phoenix, 1988), L.A. County Bar Assn., San Fernando Valley Bar Assn. (program chmn. 1964-65), State Bar Calif., Marines Corps Res. Officers Assn. (pres. San Fernando Valley 1966—), DAV (Birmingham chpt.), Am. Legion (Van Nuys Post),. Office: US Ct Appeals 9th Cir 21800 Oxnard St Ste 1140 Woodland Hills CA 91367-3657*

PRELL, JOEL JAMES, medical group administrator; b. L.A., Aug. 16, 1944; s. Samuel and Mary Devorah (Schwartz) P.; children: Vanessa S., Matthew. BA, U. So. Calif., L.A., 1967; cert. fin. mgmt., Ohio State U., 1979; M. Pub. Health, UCLA, 1981. Various positions, 1967-72; chief adminstrv. office sr. adminstrv. analyst L.A. County, 1972-73; dep. regional dir. for planning and community rels. L.A. County Dept. Health Svcs. Region, 1973-75; adminstr. ambulatory care L.A. County Harbro Gen. Hosp., 1975-76; assoc. dir. hosp. and clinics ambulatory care svcs. U. Calif.-Irvine Med. Ctr., 1976-78; asst. to the dir. rsch. and analysis unit U. Calif., Davis, 1978-80; v.p. profl. svcs. San Pedro Peninsula Hosp., 1981-84; sr. v.p. South Coast Med. Ctr., 1984-87; pres., CEO Harbor Health Systems, Inc., 1987-90; CEO Santa Monica (Calif.) Plz. Med. Group, Inc., 1990-93; administrator Pathology Cons. Med. Group, Torrance, Calif., 1993—; spl. asst. to the contr. UCLA Hosp. and Clinics, 1980-81, adminstr. emergency medicine ctr., 1981. Mem. Hosp. Coun .So. Calif. (polit. action steering com., chmn. legis. affairs com.), Calif. Hosp. Polit. Action Com. (bd. dirs.), Health Care Execs. So. Calif., UCLA Health Svcs. Adminstrs. Alumni Assn. (pres.), Med. Group Mgmt. Assn., Am. Coll. Health Care Adminstrs., Friends of Westwood. Office: Pathology Cons Med Group 20221 Hamilton Ave Torrance CA 90502-1321

PRENDERGAST, THOMAS JOHN, JR., physician, epidemiologist; b. St. Louis, June 17, 1940; s. Thomas John Sr. and Virginia (Hyatt) P.; m. Mary Lou Fairfield, Mar. 7, 1965 (div. Apr. 1981); children: Thomas John III, Allen David, Brian Lee; m. Carolyn Swatzel, Apr. 28, 1990; children: Paul Swatzel, David Swatzel. BA, Washington U., St. Louis, 1962, MD, 1966; MPH, U. N.C., 1972. Lic. physician, Mo., N.C., Calif.; Diplomate Am. Bd. Preventive Medicine. Intern St. Luke's Hosp., St. Louis, 1966-67, resident, 1967; assoc. Duke U. Med. Ctr., Durham, N.C., 1971-72; asst. prof. U. Mo., Columbia, 1972-77; dir. epidemiology and disease control Health Care Agy., Orange County, Calif., 1977-90; dep. dir. Dept. Pub. Health, San Bernardino County, Calif., 1990-93, health officer, dir., 1993—; assoc. clin. prof. U. Calif. Med. Ctr., Irvine, 1977-90, pub. health/preventive medicine Loma Linda U., 1990—; cons. Disease Control Com. Calif. Conf. Local Health Officials, Sacramento, 1977-93, chair, 1994-96, pres., 1996-97; lectr. in field. Contbr. articles to profl. jours. Served to maj. USAR, 1968-71. Recipient Community Service award Vietnamese Cultural Soc., Orange County, 1980, Disting. Service award, AIDS Response Program, Orange County, 1986, Vol. Service Recognition award, Am. Cancer Soc., 1981. Mem. Am. Pub. Health Assn., Soc. Tchrs. Preventive Medicine, Assn. Practitioners in Infection Control, Calif. Conf. Local Health Officers (pres. 1996-97), Health Officers Assn. Calif. (pres.-electr 1994-96, 96-97), So. Calif. Pub. Health Assn. (chmn. epidemiology sect. 1979—, Best Section 1982, pres. 1983-84), Sigma Xi, Delta Omega, Pi Tau Epsilon Pi. Home: Box 4939 950 Jungfrau Dr Crestline CA 92325 Office: San Bernardino Dept Pub Health 351 N Mountain View Ave San Bernardino CA 92415-0010

PRENDERGAST, WILLIAM JOHN, ophthalmologist; b. Portland, Oreg., June 12, 1942; s. William John and Marjorie (Scott) P.; m. Carolyn Grace Perkins, Aug. 17, 1963 (div. 1990); children: William John, Scott; m. Sherryl Irene Guenther, Aug. 25, 1991. BS, U. Oreg., Eugene, 1964; MD, U. Oreg., Portland, 1967. Diplomate Am. Bd. Ophthalmology. Resident in ophthalmology U. Oreg., Portland, 1970-73; pvt. practice specializing in ophthalmology Portland, 1973-82; physician, founder, ptnr. Oreg. Med. Eye Clinic, Portland, 1983—; founder, pres. (Focus Group) Inc. Focus Group Inc., Ophthalmic Clinic Networking Venture, Portland, 1992—; clin. asst. prof. ophthalmology Oreg. Health Sci. U., 1985—; pres. Focus Group. Vol. surgeon N.W. Med. Teams, Oaxaca, Mexico, 1989, 90. With USPHS, 1968-70. Fellow Am. Acad. Ophthalmology; mem. Met. Bus. Assn., Multnomah Athletic Club, Mazamas Mountaineering Club, Portland Yacht Club, Phi Beta Kappa, Alpha Omega Alpha. Office: Oregon Med Eye Clinic 1955 NW Northrup St Portland OR 97209-1614

PRENSNER, STEVEN R., nonprofit organization executive; b. Houston, Oct. 19, 1949; s. Steven and Selma I. (Berger) P.; m. Melanie Porter, July 23, 1977; children: David S., Jonathan D., Benjamin A., Matthew J. BA in Bus. and Math., Howard Payne Coll., 1972; MBA in Fin. and Mgmt., So. Ill. U., 1974. V.p. bus. affairs Trinity Coll., Chgo., 1974-79; v.p. adminstrn. The Navigators, Colo. Springs, 1979—; prin. Mgmt. Devel. Network, Colorado Springs, 1984-88. Home: PO Box 6000 Colorado Springs CO 80934 Office: The Navigators 3820 N 30th St Colorado Springs CO 80904-5001

PRESCOTT, LAWRENCE MALCOLM, medical and health writer; b. Boston, July 31, 1934; s. Benjamin and Lillian (Stein) P. BA, Harvard U., 1957; MSc, George Washington U., 1959, PhD, 1966; m. Ellen Gay Kober, Feb. 19, 1961 (dec. Sept. 1981); children: Jennifer Maya, Adam Barrett; m. Sharon Lynn Kirshen, May 16, 1982; children: Gary Leon Kirshen, Marc Paul Kirshen. Nat. Acad. Scis. postdoctoral fellow U.S. Army Rsch., Ft. Detrick, Md., 1965-66; microbiologist/scientist WHO, India, 1967-70, Indonesia, 1970-72, Thailand, 1972-78; with pub. rels. Ted Klein & Co., Hill & Knowlton, Interscience, , Smith, Kline, Beecham, others, 1984—; cons. health to internat. orgns., San Diego, 1978—; author manuals; contbr. articles in diarrheal diseases and lab. scis. to profl. jours., numerous articles, stories, poems to mags., newspapers, including Living in Thailand, Jack and Jill, Strawberry, Bangkok Times, Sprint, 1977-81; mng. editor Caduceus, 1981-82; pub., editor: Teenage Scene, 1982-83; pres. Prescott Pub. Co., 1982-83; med. writer numerous jours. including Modern Medicine, Dermatology Times, Internal Medicine World Report, Drugtherapy, P&T, Clinical Cancer Letter, Hospital Formulary, Female Patient, Australian Doctor, Inpharma Weekly, American Family Physician, Ophthalmology Times, Group Practice News, Newspaper of Cardiology, Paacnotes, Genetic Engineering News, Medical Week, Medical World News, Urology Times, Gastroenterology and Endoscopy News; author: Curry Every Sunday, 1984. Home and Office: 18264 Verano Dr San Diego CA 92128-1262

PRESCOTT, RICHARD CHAMBERS, writer; b. Houston, Apr. 1, 1952; s. Chambers Richard and Dorothy Mae (Bashara) P.; m. Sarah Elisabeth Grace, Oct. 13, 1980. Author: The Sage, 1975, Moonstar, 1975, Neuf Songes (Nine Dreams), 1976, 2nd edit., 1991, The Carouse of Soma, 1977, Lions and Kings, 1977, Allah Wake Up, 1978, 2nd edit., 1994, Night Reaper, 1979, Dragon Tales, 1983, Dragon Dreams, 1986, 2nd edit., 1990, Dragon Prayers, 1988, 2nd edit., 1990, Dragon Songs, 1988, 2nd edit., 1990, Dragon Maker, 1989, 2nd edit., 1990, Dragon Thoughts, 1990, Dragon Sight: A Cremation Poem, 1992, Kings and Sages, 1991, Three Waves, 1992, Disturbing Delights: Waves of The Great Goddess, 1993, Kalee Bhava: The Goddess and Her Moods, 1995, The Skills of Kalee, 1995, Because of Atma, 1995, Measuring Sky Without Ground, 1996, The Goddess And The God Man, 1996, Kalee: The Allayer of Sorrows, 1996, Living Sakti, 1997; contbr. articles and essays to profl. publs.

PRESECAN, NICHOLAS LEE, civil, environmental engineer, consultant; b. Indpls., Sept. 4, 1940; s. Nicholas Eli and Dorothy Lee (Moore) P.; m. Joan Westin, Nov. 11, 1940; children: Julie Marie, Mary Lee, Anne Westin. BSCE, Purdue U., 1963; MS in Engring., U. Calif., Berkeley, 1967. Cert. profl. engr., 31 states. Project engr. San Bernardino County (Calif.) Flood Control, 1963, Engring. Sci. Inc., Arcadia, Calif., 1968-70; office mgr. Engring. Sci. Inc., Cleve., 1970-72, v.p., chief engr., 1972-81; v.p. internat. divsn. Engring. Sci. Inc., Arcadia, 1981-84, group v.p., 1984-87; sr. v.p. Engring. Sci. Inc., Pasadena, Calif., 1987—; mem. industry adv. bd. Sch. Engring. and Tech. Calif. State U., L.A., 1986—. Contbr. articles to profl. jours. Commr. Archtl. Commn., Claremont, Calif., 1980-86; councilman Claremont City Coun., 1986-94; mayor City of Claremont, 1989-92; mem. Pasadena Tournament of Roses Assn., 1980—, L.A. 2000 Environ. Com.,

1987-88. With USMC, 1963-67. Recipient Disting. Engring. Achievement award Inst. for Advancement of Engring., 1993. Fellow ASCE (mem. internat. adv. com. 1987-90); mem. NSPE, Am. Acad. Environ. Engrs., Am. Water Works Assn. (life), Water Environ. Fedn., Soc. Am. Value Engrs., Rotary. Republican. Home: 727 E Alamosa Dr Claremont CA 91711-2008 Office: Parsons Engring Sci Inc 100 W Walnut St Pasadena CA 91124-0001

PRESLEY, MARSHA ANN, planetary scientist; b. Modesto, Calif., Oct. 9, 1958; d. Doreen (Gordon) Presley-Schmiedl. BS, U. Calif., Davis, 1981; MA, Wash. U., St. Louis, 1986; PhD, Ariz. State U., 1995. Lab. asst. U. Calif., 1978-80, undergrad. tchg. asst. astronomy, 1979-82; grad. tchg. asst. Wash. U., 1982-84, grad. rsch. asst., 1984-86; grad. rsch. asst. Ariz. State U., Tempe, 1987-95; postdoctoral rsch. asst. Ariz. State U., 1995; Nat. Rsch. Coun. assoc. NASA Ames Rsch. Ctr., Moffett Field, Calif., 1995—. Contbg. writer Am. Hydrogen Assn. newsletter, 1993-94; contbr. articles to profl. jours. Dist. organizer Ariz. Right to Choose, Phoenix, 1991-92. Grantee U. Calif., 1976-80, Pell grantee, 1980-81; Diablo scholar Diablo Scholarships, 1976-77. Mem. Am. Geophysical Union. Democrat. Office: NASA Ames Rsch Ctr M/S 239-14 Moffett Field CA 94035

PRESSLEY, JAMES RAY, electrical engineer; b. Ft. Worth, July 14, 1946; s. Loy Dale and Dorothy Helen (Foust) P.; m. Barbara Kay McMillin, Oct. 9, 1968 (div. 1981); children: James Foust Pressley, Kreg Milam Pressley; m. Susan Marie Straw, Apr. 27, 1985 (div.); children: Shaye Eugene Straw, Rebecca Alycen Straw, Rachel Leilani Straw. BSEE, U. Tex., Arlington, 1970. Registered profl. engr., Alaska, Hawaii, Oreg., Wash. Designer/draftsman Romine & Slaughter, Ft. Worth, 1967-71; engr. Crews MacInnes & Hoffman, Anchorage, 1971-73, O'Kelly & Schoenlank, Anchorage, 1973-75, Theodore G. Creedon, Anchorage, 1975-77; v.p. Fryer, Pressley Elliott, Anchorage, 1977-80, Fryer/Pressley Engring., 1980-91, FPE Roen Engrs., Inc., 1991—, also chmn. bd., 1991-95; mem. elec. constrn. and maintenance industry evaluation panel, 1982—. Mem. IEEE, Illuminating Engring. Soc. (sustaining), Internat. Assn. Elec. Inspectors, Nat. Fire Protection Assn., Nat. Assn. Corrosion Engrs., Am. Soc. Quality Control. Office: FPE/Roen Engrs Inc 560 E 34th Ave Ste 300 Anchorage AK 99503-4161 *Personal philosophy: Success through diligent attention addressed toward maintaining the highest standards of quality in my profession.*

PRESSMAN, SCOTT HUGHES, ophthalmologist; b. Eugene, Oreg., Aug. 6, 1950; s. E. Charles and Hope Hughes P.; m. Beverly Kay Glover, Mar. 29, 1975; children: Peter, Nicole, Andrew. BS, U. Oreg., 1974; MD, Oreg. Health Sci. U., 1976. Diplomate Am. Bd. Ophthalmology. Dir. emergency physicians St. Elizabeth Hosp., Baker, Oreg., 1977-80; ophthalmology resident Ea. Va. Med. Sch., Norfolk, Va., 1980-83; fellowship in pediatric ophthalmology U. iowa, Iowa City, 1983-84; fellow Am. Bd. Ophthalmology, 1984; asst. prof. ophthalmology U. Utah, Salt Lake City, 1986—. Author: (book) Common Ophthalmic Proceedures, 1986; contbr. articles to profl. jours. Fellow Am. Bd. Ophthalmology; mem. Idaho Ophthalmology Soc. (pres. 1993-95), Idaho Med. Soc., Am. Assn. Pediatric Ophthalmology, Am. Acad. Ophthalmology. Office: The Eye Assocs 901 N Curtis Rd Ste 302 Boise ID 83706-1341

PRESTI, JOSEPH CHARLES, JR., urologist; b. San Francisco, June 15, 1958; s. Joseph C. and Angelina A. (Alioto) P.; m. Micaela Thompson, Dec. 7, 1985. AB, U. Calif., Berkeley, 1980; MD, U. Calif., Irvine, 1984. Diplomate Am. Bd. Urology. Resident gen. surgery U. Calif., San Francisco, 1984-86, resident urology, 1986-89; fellow urologic oncology Meml. Sloan Kettering Cancer Ctr., N.Y.C., 1989-92; asst. prof. dept. urology U. Calif., San Francisco, 1992—; prin. investigator merit rev. VA Rsch. Office, 1993-95. Recipient Clin. Oncology fellowship, Am. Cancer Soc., 1989-92, Clin. Oncology Career Devel. award, 1993-96. Fellow Am. Coll. Surgeons; mem. Am. Urol. Assn. (western sect.), Am. Assn. Cancer Rsch. Democrat. Roman Catholic. Office: U Calif San Francisco Mt Zion Cancer Ctr Urol Onc 2356 Sutter St San Francisco CA 94115-3006

PRESTON, ASTRID, artist; b. Stockholm, Sept. 29, 1945; came to U.S., 1952; d. Stanley and Milda E. Borbals; m. Howard J. Preston, Sept. 1, 1943; 1 child, Max. BA, UCLA, 1967. One-woman shows include L.A. Inst. of Contemporary Art, 1982, Newspace, L.A., 1983, 84, 85, Patty Aande Gallery, San Diego, 1986, Krygier/Landau Contemporary Art, L.A., 1987, Laguna Art Mus., Laguna Beach, Calif., 1987, Jan Turner Gallery, L.A., 1989, 91, Peter Blake Gallery, Laguna Beach, 1994, 97. Bd. dirs. L.A. Contemporary Exhibits, 1984-89, Beyond Baroque, Venice, Calif., 1994-95. Grantee Nat. Endowment of the Arts, 1987.

PRESTON, DAVID RAYMOND, lawyer; b. Harlingen, Tex., Feb. 12, 1961; s. Raymond C., Jr. and Janet (Bowman) P. BS, Univ. Fla., 1983, MS, 1985, PhD, 1989; JD, George Mason Sch. Law, 1996. Bar: Calif., U.S. Patent and Tradmark Office. Postdoctoral rsch. U.S. Army, Frederick, Md., 1989-90; patent examiner U.S. Patent and Trademark Office, Washington, 1990-94; tech. devel. specialist Nat. Cancer Inst., NIH, Bethesda, Md., 1994-96; intern for Judge Rader U.S. Ct. Appeals for the Fed. Cir., Washington, 1995; patent attorney Campbell & Flores, San Diego, 1996—. Judge internat. sci. fair U.S. Patents and Trademark Office, Va., Tenn., 1991. NIH fellow, 1987, Pres.'s fellow Am. Soc. Microbiology, 1988. Mem. AAAS, ABA, Am. Intellectual Property Law Assn., Fed. Circuit Bar Assn., San Diego Intellectual Property Law Assn. Republican. Home: 7160 Shoreline Dr Apt 4304 San Diego CA 92122-4919 Office: Campbell & Flores Ste 700 4370 Sa Jolla Village Dr San Diego CA 92122

PRESTON, MARTHA SUE, pharmaceutical company executive; b. Cheverly, Md., Oct. 15, 1952; d. George Millard and Martha Lee Preston. BA in Biology cum laude, Lycoming Coll., 1974; postgrad., U. Md., 1981-85, Am. U. Lab. asst biology dept Lycoming Coll., Williamsport, Pa., 1973-74; biologist arthritis and rheumatism br. NIH, Bethesda, Md., 1974-75, biologist nutrition and endocrinology lab., 1975-80; biologist divsn. blood and blood products FDA, Bethesda, 1980-88; mgr. regulatory affairs Baxter Healthcare Corp., Glendale, Calif., 1988-90; mgr. quality and regulatory Trancel/Neocrin, Santa Ana, Calif., 1990-92; dir. quality and regulatory Medarex Corp., Princeton, N.J., 1992-93; v.p. quality and regulatory Alpha Therapeutic Care, L.A., 1993—; chmn. regulatory affairs Am. Blood Resources Assn., Anapolis, Md., 1993—. Author: (book chpt.) AIDS Safety of Blood and Blood Products, 1988; contbr. articles to profl. jours. FDA award 1984, 88. Office: Alpha Therapeutic Corp 2410 Lillyvale Ave Los Angeles CA 90032

PRESTON, ROBERT ARTHUR, astronomer; b. N.Y.C., June 29, 1944; s. Arthur Lloyd and Dorothy Elizabeth (Smith) P.; m. Ann Lee Archer, July 18, 1970; 1 child, Karen Ann. BS, Cornell U., 1966, MS, 1967; PhD, MIT, 1972. Rsch. scientist Lockheed Rsch. Lab., Palo Alto, Calif., 1972-73; astronomer Jet Propulsion Lab., Calif. Inst. Tech., Pasadena, 1973—, supr. astronomical measurements group, 1975—, mgr. astrophysics rsch. program, 1983-92, project scientist Space VLBI project, 1991—; leader U.S. Sci. teams for Vega Venus Balloon and Phobos Lander Missions, 1982-90. Recipient Exceptional Svc. award NASA, 1986; rsch. grantee NASA, 1975—, Nat. Park Svc., 1980—. Mem. Am. Astron. Soc., Internat. Astron. Union. Home: 24618 Golfview Dr Santa Clarita CA 91355-2301 Office: Calif Inst Tech Jet Propulsion Lab 4800 Oak Grove Dr Pasadena CA 91109-8001

PRESZLER, SHARON MARIE, psychiatric home health nurse; b. L.A.; d. Rudolph Edward Wirth and Bertha Marie (Thornton) Paddock; m. Alan Preszler, Aug. 31, 1966; children: Brent, Alison. BS in Nursing, Loma Linda (Calif.) U., 1963, MS in Marriage and Family Counseling, 1978. RN, Calif., Idaho; cert. pub. health nurse. Team leader med. fl. Loma Linda U. Hosp., 1963-64; office nurse Dr. Lowell Johnson, Redlands, Calif., 1964-65, Dr. H. Glenn Stevens, Loma Linda, 1965-72; team leader women's oncology Loma Linda U. Hosp., 1974-75; pub. health nurse Riverside County Pub. Health, Hemet, Calif., 1975-78; nurse, staff psychologist Dept. Health and Welfare, Idaho Falls, Idaho, 1989-91, Boise, Idaho, 1991-92; psychiat. nurse Cmty. Home Health, Boise, 1992-94, Mercy Home Health & Hospice, Nampa, Idaho, 1995—; hospice nurse, home health nurse Mercy Med. Ctr., 1995—, personal care supr. nurse for medicaid, 1996—; instr. YWCA, Bartlesville, Okla., 1984-88; tchr. Bartlesville Pub. Sch., 1984-88, Heritage Retirement, Boise, 1994. Contbr. to Focus, 1986. Mem. Am. Assn. Marriage and Family Therapy, Sigma Theta Tau.

PREUSS, CHARLES F., lawyer; b. Santa Barbara, Calif., Feb. 27, 1941. BA, Dartmouth Coll., 1962; JD, Stanford U., 1969. Bar: Calif. 1970. Ptnr. Preuss Walker & Shanagher, San Francisco. Mem. PLAC, ABOTA, IADC (pres.-elect), Def. Rsch. Inst., Mng. Counsel Group, Internat. Assn. Def. Counsel. Office: Preuss Walker & Shanagher 595 Market St Fl 16 San Francisco CA 94105-2802

PREUSS, GREGORY EDWARD, insurance association manager; b. West Union, Iowa, Dec. 24, 1946; s. Edward Arthur and Arlene Lucille (Otdoerfer) P.; m. Doreen Kay Williams, Aug. 29, 1969; children: Gretchen, Cara, Bryan, Amy. Student, Casper Coll., 1968; BS in Indsl. Mgmt., U. Wyoming, 1971; Chartered Fin. Cons., Am. Coll., Bryn Mawr, Pa., 1984. CLU; chartered fin. cons. Supr. Western Electric, Phoenix, 1971-75; dist. rep. Aid Assn. Lutherans, Phoenix, 1976-84; gen. agt. Aid Assn. for Luths., Mission Viejo, Calif., 1984-93; dist. reps. Aid Assn. for Luths. and Agy. Specialist, 1994—. Trustee Christ Coll. Irvine (Calif.) Found., 1985—. Mem. (life) Million Dolar Round Table (pres. 1984—), Nat. Assn. Life Underwriters, Am. Soc. CLU's, Nat. Assn. Fraternal Ins. Counselors. Republican.

PRICE, BETTY JEANNE, choirchime soloist, writer; b. Long Beach, Calif., June 12, 1942; d. Grant E. and Miriam A. (Francis) Sickles; m. Harvey H. price, Aug. 6, 1975; 1 child, Thomas Neil Gering. Degree in Acctg., Northland Pioneer Coll., Show Low, Ariz., 1977. Youth missionary Open Bible Standard Missions, Trinidad, 1958-59; typographer Joel H. Weldon & Assocs., Scottsdale, Ariz., 1980-89; exec. chief acct. Pubs. Devel. Corp., San Diego, 1991-93; coord. music and worship College Ave. Bapt. Ch., San Diego, 1994-95; ChoirChime soloist, 1986—; founder, owner Customized Funding Svcs., San Diego, 1996—. Author: 101 Ways to Fix Broccoli, 1994, ABC's of Abundant Living, 1995; co-author: God's Vitamin C for the Spirit, 1995, Bounce Back, 1997. Mem. Christian Writers Guild, Am. Cash Flow Assn., San Diego Cash Flow Assn. (founder, exec. bd. mem.), Nat. Entrepreneurs Assn., Bus. Incubator Alliance, Econ. Devel. Coun., Fin. Women Internat., Am. Soc. Notaries, Soroptimist Internat. Home: PO Box 151115 San Diego CA 92175-1115

PRICE, BONNIE BURNS, political science educator; b. San Diego, June 26, 1940; d. Jack and June (Chandonia) Burns, stepdau. Lois (Maus) Burns; m. John Paul Price, Sept. 2, 1961; 1 child, Jacqueline. Student, Am. U., 1961; BA in Polit. Sci., Albright Coll., 1962; MA in Polit. Sci., U. Pa., 1966; PhD in Polit. Sci., Temple U., 1979. Secondary tchr. Daniel Boone Sch. Dist., Athol, Pa., 1962-63, Muhlenberg Sch. Dist., Laureldale, Pa., 1963-66; instr. polit. sci. Albright Coll., Reading, Pa., 1966-67, adj. instr. history, 1969; asst. prof. history Kutztown (Pa.) U., 1970; prof. polit. sci. Reading Area Community Coll., 1971-87, 89-92, acting v.p. acad. affairs, 1987-88; v.p. adminstrn. Prof. Sch. Psychol. Studies, San Diego, 1991; founder, pres. Western Am. U., San Diego, 1992—; chief cons. Orgnl. Techs., Inc., Reading, 1980-87; chair divsn. behavioral sci. and human svcs. Reading Area C.C., 1975-87. Bd. dirs. Muhlenberg Sch. Dist., 1975-87, Planned Parenthood N.E. Pa., Trexlertown, 1987-90; mem. steering com. Pa. Choice Coalition, 1989-91. Lilly fellow U. Pa., Phila., 1983-85; grantee Pa. Pub. Commn. for Humanities, 1980, NSF grantee U. Pa., 1989-90. Mem. Am. Soc. Pub. Adminstrn., Pa. Polit. Sci. Assn., Am. Fedn. Tchrs., AAAS, ACLU (bd. dirs. Berks chpt. 1979-87). Democrat. Home: 2750 Wheatstone St Spc 160 San Diego CA 92111-5446 Office: Western Am U 3517 Camino Del Rio S Ste 215 San Diego CA 92108-4028

PRICE, CHARLES STEVEN, lawyer; b. Inglewood, Calif., June 10, 1955; s. Frank Dean Price and Ann (Rounds) Bolling; m. Sandra Helen Laney, Feb. 26, 1983; children: Katherine Laney, Courtney Ann, Diana Emily. BA, U. Calif., Santa Barbara, 1976; JD, U. Chgo., 1979. Bar: Ariz. 1980, U.S. Dist. Ariz. 1980, U.S. Ct. Appeals (9th cir.) 1982. Assoc. Brown & Bain P.A., Phoenix, Ariz., 1979-85, ptnr., 1985-96; ptnr. Allen & Price P.L.C., Phoenix, Ariz., 1996—. Office: Allen & Price PLC 2850 E Camelback Rd Ste 170 Phoenix AZ 85016-4380

PRICE, CLIFFORD WARREN, retired metallurgist, researcher; b. Denver, Apr. 22, 1935; s. Warren Wilson and Vivian Fredricka (Cady) P.; m. Carole Joyce Waterman, June 14, 1969; children: Carla Beth, Krista Lynn Kilton. MetE, Colo. Sch. Mines, 1957; MS, Ohio State U., 1970, PhD, 1975. Design engr. Sundstrand Aviation-Denver, 1957-60; materials specialist Denver Rsch. Inst., 1960-63; sr. metallurgist Rocky Flats div. Dow Chem. Co., Golden, Colo., 1963-66; staff metallurgist Battelle Columbus (Ohio) Labs., 1966-75; sr. scientist Owens-Corning Fiberglas, Granville, Ohio, 1975-80; metallurgist Lawrence Livermore (Calif.) Nat. Lab., 1980-93; retired, 1993. Contbr. articles to profl. jours. Battelle Columbus Labs. fellow, 1974-75. Mem. Metall. Soc. AIME, Microscopy Soc. Am. (treas. Denver 1961-62), Am. Soc. for Metals.

PRICE, HARVEY RAYMOND, safety, environmental health services administrator; b. Ochsenfurt, Germany, Apr. 27, 1947; s. Randall Dean and Annemarie (Biesecke) P.; m. Elizabeth Ann Panoske, May 29, 1974; 1 child, Joseph Raymond Dean. AAS, Cen. Tex. Coll., 1979; BS, U. Ctrl. Tex., 1981; MA, Webster U., 1991; MS, Regis U., 1995. Cert. protection officer; cert. fraud examiner, cert. healthcare protection adminstr., healthcare risk mgr. Enlisted USMC, 1966; transfered to U.S. Army, 1969; investigative supr., spl. agt. Criminal Investigative Divsn., 1979-82, spl. agt. supr., 1982-86, dir. exec. protection Europe, Mid. East, Africa, 1986-89; spl. agt. in charge Criminal Investigative Divsn., Denver, 1989-91; retired Criminal Investigative Divsn., 1991-94; dir. safety and risk mgmt. Regional West Med. Ctr., Scottsbluff, Nebr., 1991-94; environ. care cons. St. Joseph Hosp., Denver, 1994—; chmn. safety com., hazardous materials com., disaster com. Regional West Med. Ctr., 1991-94. Active Local Emergency Planning Commn., Scottsbluff, 1991, Hazardous Waste Planning Commn., Scottsbluff, 1991. Decorated Bronze Star with two bronze oak leaf clusters, Air medal with three bronze oak leaf clusters, 1970-72; Airborne badge (Germany); Cross of Gallantry (Vietnam). Mem. Internat. Assn. Healthcare Safety and Security, Assn. Cert. Fraud Examiners, Am. Soc. Indsl. Security, Am. Soc. Healthcare Risk Mgrs., Retired Officers Assn., Masons, Shriners, Alpha Phi Sigma. Episcopalian. Office: Hosp Shared Svcs 1395 S Platte River Dr Denver CO 80223-3467

PRICE, HUMPHREY WALLACE, aerospace engineer; b. San Antonio, Sept. 25, 1954; s. Humphrey Rodes and Ruth (Wallace) P. BS in Engring., U. Tex., 1976, MS in Engring., 1978. Rsch. asst. nuclear reactor lab. U. Tex., Austin, 1976; nuclear engr. EDS Nuclear, Inc., San Francisco, 1977-78; engr. Jet Propulsion Lab., Pasadena, Calif., 1978-82; rsch. engr. SW Rsch. Inst., San Antonio, 1982-84; tech. group leader Jet Propulsion Lab., Pasadena, Calif., 1984-89; configuration engr. Cassini spacecraft NASA, 1989-93; system engr. Pluto Spacecraft, 1994—; cons. Am. Rocket Co., Camarillo, Calif., 1986-87; tech. staff World Space Found., Pasadena, 1980—. Patentee in field; contbr. to tech. papers in field. Mem. AIAA (sr.), Brit. Interplanetary Soc. Office: HW Price Cons PO Box 454 La Canada Flintridge CA 91012-0454

PRICE, JOE (ALLEN), artist, former educator; b. Ferriday, La., Feb. 6, 1935; s. Edward Neill and Margaret (Hester) P. BS, Northwestern U., 1957; postgrad., Art Ctr. Coll., L.A., 1967-68; MA, Stanford U., 1970. Free-lance actor, artist N.Y.C., 1957-60; freelance illustrator, actor, L.A., 1960-68; freelance comml. artist, San Carlos, Calif., 1968-69; package designer Container Corp. Am., Santa Clara, Calif., 1969; prof. studio art and filmmaking, chmn. dept. art Coll. San Mateo, Calif., 1970-94. One-man shows include Richard Sumner Gallery, Palo Alto, Calif., 1975, San Mateo County Cultural Ctr., 1976, 82, Tahir Galleries, New Orleans, 1977, 82, Kerwin Galleries, Burlingame, Calif., 1977, Edits. Gallery, Melbourne, Australia, 1977, Ankrum Gallery, Los Angeles, 1978, 84, Edits. Ltd. West Gallery, San Francisco, 1981, Miriam Perlman Gallery, Chgo., 1982, San Mateo County Arts Council Gallery, 1982, Candy Stick Gallery, Ferndale, Calif., 1984, Assoc. Am. Artists, N.Y.C. and Phila., 1984, Gallery 30, Burlingame, 1991, San Mateo, 1984, Triton Mus. Art, Santa Clara, Calif., 1986, Huntsville (Ala.) Mus. Art, 1987, Gallery 30, San Mateo, 1988-91, Concept Art Gallery, Pitts., 1991, Eleonore Austerer Gallery, San Francisco, 1995; exhibited in groups shows at Berkeley Art Ctr., Calif., 1976, Burlingame Civic Art Gallery, 1976, Syntex Gallery, Palo Alto, Calif., 1977, Gump's Gallery, San Francisco, 1976, 77, Nat. Gallery of Australia, 1978, Sonoma County Gallery, 1979, Gov. Dummer Acad. Art, Byfield, Mass., 1979, Miss. Mus. Art, 1982, C.A.A. Galleries, Chautauqua, N.Y., 1982, Huntsville Mus. Art, 1983, Tahir Gallery, New Orleans, 1983, Hunterdon Art Ctr., N.J., 1984, Editions Galleries, Melbourne, Australia, 1988, Van Stratten Gallery, Chgo., 1988, 6th Internat. Exhbn., Carnegie-Mellon U., Pa., 1988, Forum Gallery, Jamestown, N.Y., 1988, 5th Internat. Biennale Petite Format de Papier, Belgium, 1989, 4th Internat. Biennial Print Exhibit, Taipei Fine Arts Mus., People's Republic China, 1990, Interprint, Lviv '90, USSR, 1990, New Orleans Mus. Art, 1990, Internat. Print Triennale, Cracow, Poland, 1991, 15th Ann. Nat. Invitational Drawing Exhbn. Emporia State U., Kans., 1991, Haggar U. Gallery, U. Dallas, 1991, Directions in Bay Area Printmaking: Three Decades Palo Alto Cultural Ctr., 1992, Am. Prints: Last Half 20th Century, Jane Haslem Gallery, Washington, 1992, Wenniger Graphics, Boston, 1993, Eleonore Austerer Gallery, San Francisco, 1994, Triton Mus. Art, Santa Clara, 1994, Mobile Mus. Art, 1995, Huntsville (Ala.) Mus. Art, 1995, J.J. Brookings Gallery, San Francisco, 1996, Grisham Cornell Gallery, Decatur, Ala., 1996; represented in permanent collections San Francisco Mus. Modern Art, Achenbach Found. Graphic Arts, San Francisco, Phila. Mus. Art, New Orleans Mus. Art, Portland Mus. Art, Maine, The Libr. of Congress, Washington. Huntsville Mus. Art, Midwest Mus. Am. Art, Ind., Cracow Nat. Mus., Poland, Cabo Frio Mus., Brazil, Nat. Mus. Am. Art, Smithsonian Inst., Washington. Recipient Kempshall Clark award Peoria Art Guild, 1981, Paul Lindsay Sample Meml. award 25th Chautauqua Nat. Exhbn. of Am. Art, 1982, 1st Ann. Creative Achievement award Calif. State Legislature/Arts Coun. San Mateo County, 1989. Mem. Am. Color Print Soc., Audubon Artists (Louis Lozowick Meml. award 1978, Silver medal of honor award 1991), Boston Printmakers (Ture Bengtz Meml. award 1987), Calif. Soc. Printmakers (mem. council 1979-81), Los Angeles Printmaking Soc., Phila. Print Club (Lessing J. Rosenwald prize 1979), Arts Council of San Mateo Count, Theta Chi. Democrat. Studio and Office: PO Box 3305 Sonora CA 95370-3305 *Personal philosophy: In being an artist, I do not wish to be just a "recorder" of my time, what I see, what I think. To me, the joy of art is in expressing the love of being an artist, for in loving without shame, without fear, and without doubt one transcends to the moment and speaks with integrity. For the rest of my life I wish to reflect on what life is, and to have the courage to create that which touches not only men's eyes, but their hearts and spirits. I seek the profound truth of what it is to be human and the universal truth of what is means to be creative in expressing the love of being.*

PRICE, JOHN JAMES, JR., retired orthopaedic surgeon, forensic reporter; b. Meridian, Miss., Sept. 10, 1920; s. John James Sr. and Maurice (DeLauncey) P.; m. Helen Hall, Oct. 24, 1943 (dec. Aug. 1975); children: Deborah Fay, Lee Hunter. BS in Biology, BA in Chemistry, U. Miss., 1941; MD, U. Louisville, 1943. Diplomate Am. Bd. Orthopaedic Surgery. Chief orthopaedics VA, Charleston, S.C., 1966-68; asst. prof. orthopaedics Med. Coll. S.C., Charleston, 1966-68; staff orthopaedist Dept. Mental Health Calif., Napa, 1968-81; forensic reporter Napa, 1981—. Capt. MC, USN, 1961-65. Fellow Am. Assn. Orthopaedic Surgeons (emeritus); mem. Calif. Med. Assn. Presbyterian. Home: 1033 Bell Ln Napa CA 94558-2104

PRICE, KATHLEEN MCCORMICK, book editor, writer; b. Topeka, Kans., Dec. 25, 1932; d. Raymond Chesley and Kathleen (Shoffner) McCormick; m. William Faulkner Black, Aug. 25, 1956 (div. 1961); 1 child, Kathleen Serena; m. William Hillard Price, Aug. 13, 1976. BA, U. Colo., Denver, 1971. Book reviewer Denver Post, 1971-78; book editor San Diego Mag., 1978-92; cons. editor St. John's Cathedral, Denver, 1985-95. Author: There's a Dactyl Under My Foot, 1986, The Lady and the Unicorn, 1994. Dir. Colo. Episcopal Vestment Guild. Mem. PEN, Denver Women's Press Club, Denver County Club, La Garita Club, Phi Beta Kappa. Episcopalian. Home: 27 Crestmoor Dr Denver CO 80220-5853

PRICE, KEITH GLENN, accountant; b. Ft. Morgan, Colo., Nov. 24, 1941; s. George Felt and Irene Lois (Gibbs) P.; m. Norma Helen Witt, Feb. 28, 1970; children: Diana, Michael, Troy, Aaron, Christopher. BS, BA, Colo. State U., 1968. CPA. Auditor IRS, Casper, Wyo., 1968-75; ptnr. Hines, Price and Co., Cheyenne, Wyo., 1975-76, Fisher, Hines and Price, Cheyenne, Wyo., 1976-80; sole practice Cheyenne, Wyo., 1980—; co-founder, pres. High Plains Mortgage Co., 1990-91; chmn. bd. dirs. Goodwill Industries of Wyo., 1980-87. Treas. North Christian Ch., 1986—, Salesman with a Purpose, 1980; mem. Heels, 1975—; founder Cheyenne Typing Svc. Served to sgt. USMCR, 1963-71. Mem. AICPA, Wyo. Soc. CPAs, Nat. Soc. Pub. Accts., Nat. Fedn. Ind. Bus., U.S. C. of C., Cheyenne C. of C., Nat. Soc. Tax Profls. Republican. Mem. Ind. Ch. of Christ. Home: 5333 Frederick Dr Cheyenne WY 82009 Office: 721 E 16th St Cheyenne WY 82001-4703

PRICE, LEIGH CHARLES, petroleum geologist and geochemist; b. Whittier, Calif., Feb. 27, 1944; s. Charles Stewart and Barbara Mary (Moyle) P.; m. Martha Sue Allen, Sept. 18, 1970 (div. June 1979); m. Gayl Anderson Baader, Feb. 28, 1983. BS in Chemistry, U. Calif., Riverside, 1966, BS in Geology, 1968, MS in Geology, 1970, PhD in Geology/Geochemistry, 1973. Rsch. scientist Exxon Prodn. Rsch., Houston, 1972-73, U.S. Geol. Survey, Denver, 1974—; lectr. in field. Editor Jour. Petroleum Geology, 1992—; reviewer Geochemica Cosmochimica Acta, Nature, Energy & Fuels, others; contbr. articles and abstracts to profl. jours. Active various civic orgns. NDEA fellow, 1968-72. Mem. Am. Assn. Petroleum Geologists (Matson award 1973, 75, Disting. lectr. 1974, 75), Assn. Petroleum Geochem. Explorations, Geochem. Soc. (Paper of Yr. 1993, best paper com. 1993—). Home: 1075 S Linda Ln Evergreen CO 80439-9528 Office: US Geol Survey Denver Fed Ctr MS 940 Denver CO 80225

PRICE, LEW PAXTON, writer, engineer; b. Takoma Park, Md., Dec. 19, 1938; s. Raymond Miller and Clarene Pearl (Morris) P.; m. Sherrie Darlene Sellers, June 25, 1960 (div. Apr. 1979); children: Terilyn Ann, Heather Rae, Crystal Alene. Student, U.S. Air Force Acad., Colorado Springs, Colo., 1956-60. Hon. Kyoshi 6th Dan Master. Electronics engr. Pacific Telephone, Sacramento, Calif., 1965-66, engring. coord., bldgs., 1966-85; pres., design engr. Condor Aeroplane Works, Ltd., Sacramento, 1983-85; engring. coord. Tuttle Engring. and Constrn. Consultants, El Dorado Hills, Calif., 1989-92; freelance rschr., writer, flutemaker Fair Oaks, Garden Valley, Calif., 1977—; internat. cons. flute design, 1990—. Author: The Cosmic Stradivarius, 1974, Aquarian Anastasis, 1975, The Music of Life, 1984, Dimensions in Astrology, 1985, Native North American Flutes, 1990, Secrets of the Flute (Math, Physics & Design), 1991, Creating & Using the Native American Love Flute, 1995, Creating & Using Grandfather's Flute, The Oldest Magic (Prehistory & Influence of Music), 1995, Creating & Using Older Native American Flutes, 1995, Creating & Using Smaller Native American Flutes, 1995, Creating & Using the Native American Concert Flute, 1996, More Secrets of the Flute, 1997; author, programmer: (computer program) Flute Design (Native American), 1996. Co-advisor Aviation Explorers, archery/space/sci. merit badge instr./examiner, Boy Scouts Am., North Highlands, Calif., 1968-70; panelist United Crusade, Sacramento, Calif., 1971; rifle/pistol/shotgun safety instr. NRA, Fair Oaks, Calif., 1970-72. Capt. USAF, 1960-65. Mem. No. Calif. Flute Circle (co-organizer 1996), Oreg. Native Am. Flute Circle (hon.).

PRICE, MARGARET RUTH, financial services company executive; b. Phoenix, Sept. 12, 1956; d. James John and Mavis Marie (Anderson) Knopp; m. Michael Reid Price, Sept. 15, 1979. BS in Instl. Food Svc. and Mgmt., Mont. State U., 1978. CFP. Dir. nutrition programs Human Resource Devel. Coun., Bozeman, Mont., 1979-82; investment cons. Shearson Lehman Bros., Anchorage, 1982-85; v.p., investment cons. Boettcher & Co.-Kemper Fin. Svcs., Anchorage, 1985-88; sr. v.p. investment cons., fin. planner Kemper Securities, Inc.-Kemper Fin. Svcs., Anchorage, 1988-95, Everen Securities, Anchorage, 1995—; mem. qualified plan adv. bd. Kemper Securities, mem. Chmns. Circle of Excellence. Chairperson Anchorage Employee Retirement Income Security Act, 1987—, Anchorage Estate Planning Coun., 1991—; bd. dirs. YWCA, 1995—. Mem. Amnesty Internat., Anchorage Nordic Ski Club. Home: 4620 Golden Spring Cir Anchorage AK 99507-4351 Office: Everen Securities 550 W 7th Ave Ste 1980 Anchorage AK 99501-3571

PRICE, PAUL BUFORD, physicist, educator; b. Memphis, Nov. 8, 1932; s. Paul Buford and Eva (Dupuy) P.; m. JoAnn Margaret Baum, June 28, 1958; children—Paul Buford III, Heather Alynn, Pamela Margaret, Alison Gaynor. BS summa cum laude, Davidson Coll., 1954, DSc, 1973; MS, U. Va.,

1956, PhD, 1958. Fulbright scholar U. (Eng.) Bristol, 1958-59; NSF postdoctoral fellow Cambridge (Eng.) U., 1959-60; physicist R&D Ctr. GE, Schenectady, 1960-69; vis. prof. Tata Inst. Fundamental Rsch., Bombay, India, 1965-66; adj. prof. physics Rensselaer Poly. Inst., 1967-68; prof. physics U. Calif., Berkeley, 1969—, chmn. dept. physics, 1987-91, McAdams prof. physics, 1990-92, dean phys. scis., 1992—, dir. Space Scis. Lab., 1979-85; vis. com. Bartol Rsch. Inst., 1991-94; adv. bd. Indian Inst. Astrophysics, Bangalore, 1993-95; cons. to lunar sample analysis planning team NASA; space sci. bd. Nat. Acad. Scis.; vis. prof. U. Rome, 1983, 92; sci. assoc. Ctr. d'Etude Rsch. Nuclear, 1984; Miller rsch. prof. U. Calif., Berkeley, 1972-73; researcher in space and astrophycs, nuclear physics. Author: (with others) Nuclear Tracks in Solids; Contbr. (with others) articles to profl. jours. Regional dir. Calif. Alliance for Minority Participation, 1993—. Recipient Disting. Svc. award Am. Nuclear Soc., 1964, Indsl. Rsch. awards, 1964, 65, E.O. Lawrence Meml. award AEC, 1971, medal for exceptional sci. achievement NASA, 1973; John Simon Guggenheim fellow, 1976-77. Fellow Am. Phys. Soc., Am. Geophys. Union; mem. Nat. Acad. Scis. (chmn. geophysics sect. 1981-84, sec. class phys.-math. scis. 1985-88, chmn. 1988-91).

PRICE, RICHARD TAFT, JR., manufacturing company executive; b. San Diego, June 7, 1954; s. Richard Taft and Murial Martha (Weinhold) T. Student, Brigham Young U., 1972-76; BS, Ariz. State U., 1978. Sales mgr. Imperial Metals, L.A., 1978-83; pres. Alumatone, Inc., No. Hollywood, Calif., 1983-88; acquisitions mgr. Calif. Custom Shapes Inc., L.A., 1988-90, pres., 1990—; bd. dirs. IMCOA, Inc., L.A., Calif. Window Corp., Walnut; pres., bd. dirs. Taft Holdings, Inc., Anaheim, Calif., 1995—. Republican. Office: Calif Custom Shapes Inc 1800 E Talbot Way Anaheim CA 92805-6727

PRICE, ROBERT O., mayor; b. Abilene, Kans., Jan. 4, 1932; s. Iru Paul and Irene Isabel (Parrish) P.; m. Dorothy Faye Price, Jan. 26, 1951; children: Fred Dennis, Donald Eugene. BA, U. Redlands, 1978. Patrolman, sgt., lt., capt. Bakersfield Police Dept., 1956-73, chief police, 1973-88; cons., troubleshooter, various cities, 1988-92; mayor City of Bakersfield, 1993—; pres. Secret Witness Bd., 1980-83. Mem. Calif. Coun. on Criminal Justice, Sacramento, 1983-93; chmn. State Adv. Group on Juvenile Justice, Sacramento, 1988-93, Citizens Adv. Com., Fresno, Calif., 1993—, Youth Devel. Coalition, Bakersfield, 1993—, Econ. Devel. Discussion Group, Bakersfield, 1993—; chmn. western region Nat. Coalition Juvenile Justice and Delinquency Prevention, 1988-93; founder, cons. Youth Adv. Coun., Bakersfield, 1993—; founder Bakersfield Action Team, 1994. Sgt. U.S. Army, 1952-54. Recipient John W. Doubenmier award Am. Soc. Pub. Admins., 1978, Califf Morris award Calif. Probation, Parole and Corrections Officers Assn., 1982. Mem. Internat. Assn. Chiefs Police, Calif. Police Chiefs Assn., Calif. Peace Officers Assn., Calif. Council Criminal Justice, Kern County Police Chiefs Assn. (pres. 1979), Kern County Law Enforcement Admin. Assn. (pres. 1974). Republican. Office: City of Bakersfield 1501 Truxtun Ave Bakersfield CA 93301-5201*

PRICE, ROBERT WILLIAM, school superintendent, consultant; b. Ogden, Utah, May 13, 1950; s. William Robert and Eileen Louise (Rabe) P.; m. Sally Sandman, Sept. 20, 1975; children: Geoffrey Thomas, Caitlin Elizabeth. BS in Child Devel., Calif. State U., Hayward, 1973, MS in Sch. Adminstrn., 1986; postgrad., U. Pacific, 1988—. Cert. elem. tchr., Calif. Tchr. Turlock (Calif.) Sch. Dist., 1974-81; asst. prin. Monte Vista Mid. Sch., Tracy, Calif., 1981-82, prin., 1982-87; asst. supt. instrn. Tracy Pub. Schs., 1987-90, 91-93, interim supt., 1990-91; supt. Empire Union Sch. Dist., Modesto, Calif., 1993—. Cons. Campfire, Tracy, 1983; founding mem. Tracy Exch. Club, 1985; co-founder Project Bus. & Edn. Together, Tracy, 1985; bd. dirs. Boys and Girls Club of Tracy, 1987-93. Recipient Adminstrv. Leadership award Calif. Media & Libr. Educators Assn., 1994. Mem. Assn. Calif. Sch. Adminstrs. (planning com. supts. symposium 1995—, v.p. programs Region 7 1994—), Calif. League Mid. Schs. (adv. panel Region 6 1993—, chair legis. action 1994-95, Region 6 Educator of Yr. 1991). Democrat. Office: Empire Union Sch Dist 116 N Mcclure Rd Modesto CA 95357-1329

PRICE, THOMAS MUNRO, computer consultant; b. Madison, Wis., Oct. 2, 1937; s. John Edward and Georgia Winifred (Day) P.; m. Judith Ann Holm, Aug. 8, 1959; children: Scott Michael, Andrea Lynn. BS, Carroll Coll., Waukesha, Wis., 1959; MS, U. Wis., 1961, PhD, 1964. Prof. math. U. Iowa, 1964-77, U. Wyo., Laramie, 1978-79; computer user cons. U. Wyo., 1979-85, MIS prof., 1985-89; computer cons. Laramie, 1989-93; home rebuilder Pecos, N.Mex., 1994—. Contbr. articles to profl. jours. Home: 17 Crazy Rabbit Dr Santa Fe NM 87505

PRICHARD, MERRILL E., business executive; b. Wheaton, Ill., July 13, 1925; s. Harold C. and Ann F. (Bailey) P.; B.S., U. Ill., 1948; postgrad. U. Chgo., Northwestern U.; m. Betty Ann Tibbits, Sept. 2, 1947 (div.); children—Ann (Mrs. David M. Considine), Sue (Mrs. James O. Hodges V); m. Bonnie S. Fortunato, May 14, 1984. Sports reporter Wheaton Daily Jour., Chgo. City News Bur., Lombard (Ill.) Spectator, 1940-42; sports editor Glen Ellyn (Ill.) News, summer 1942; asst. editor Mag. of Sigma Chi and Sigma Chi Bull., 1948-49, editor, 1949-55, also exec. dir. Sigma Chi Frat., 1953-55; asst. to pres. C.P. Clare & Co., mfrs., 1956-59, v.p., 1959-66, exec. v.p., 1966-71, also dir., 1961-71; vice chmn. C.P. Clare Internat. N.V., Tongren, Belgium, 1962-71; group v.p. Gen. Instrument Corp., 1968-71; dir. C.P. Clare Can., Ltd., 1957-71; v.p. ops. Cummins-Allison Corp., 1971-73; group v.p., dir. Powers Regulator Co., Skokie, Ill., 1973-77, pres., 1977-78; vice chmn., dir. v.p., dir. Powers Regulator Co., Can. Ltd., Toronto, Ont., 1974-78; v.p., gen. mgr. Pneutronics div. Gardner-Denver Co., Grand Haven, Mich., 1978-80; pres. Cooper Electronics div. Cooper Industries, Nashua, N.H., 1980-81, pres., bd. dirs. CTI Industries Corp., Barrington, Ill., 1981-86; v.p., exec. dir., Sigma Chi Found., 1986-88, pres. 1988-95, v.p., 1995—, bd. dirs., 1989—. Served as staff sgt. AUS, 1945-46; editor, pub. relations Camp McCoy, Wis. Mem. Sigma Chi (past pres. house corp.), Kappa Tau Alpha, Sigma Delta Chi. Clubs: Tucson Nat. Golf, Oro Valley Country (Tucson). Editor 1950, 52, 54 edits. The Norman Shield, also centennial commemorative issue The Mag. of Sigma Chi, 1955. Home and Office: 8444 Nob Hill Tucson AZ 85742

PRICKETT, DAVID CLINTON, physician; b. Fairmont, W.Va., Nov. 26, 1918; s. Clinton Evert and Mary Anna (Gottschalk) P.; m. Mary Ellen Holt, June 29, 1940; children: David C., Rebecca Ellen, William Radcliffe, Mary Anne, James Thomas, Sara Elizabeth; m. Pamela S. Blackstone, Nov. 17, 1991. Student Fairmont (W.Va.) State Coll., 1940-42, AB, W.Va. U., 1944; MD, U. Louisville, 1946; MPH, U. Pitts., 1955. pres. Prickett Chem. Co., 1938-43; acct. W.Va. Conservation Commn., Fed. Works Agy., 1941, 42; lab. asst., instr. chemistry, W.Va. U., 1943; intern, Louisville Gen. Hosp., 1947; surg. resident St. Joseph's Hosp., Parkersburg, W.Va., 1948-49, gen. practice, 1949-50, 55-61; physician USAF, N.Mex., 1961-62, U.S. Army, Calif., 1963-64, San Luis Obispo County Hosp., 1965-66, So. Calif. Edison Co., 1981-84; assoc. physician indsl. and gen. practice Los Angeles County, Calif., 1967—; med. dir. S. Gate plant GM, 1969-71; physician staff City of L.A., 1971-76; relief med. practice Appalachia summer seasons, 1977, 1986, 1988-96. Med. Officer USPHS, Navajo Indian Reservation, Tohatchi (N.Mex.) Health Ctr., 1953-55, surgeon, res. officer, 1957-59; pres. W.Va. Pub. Health Assn., 1951-52; local and dist. health officer, W.Va., 1951-53, sec. indsl. and pub. health sect. W.Va. Med. Assn., 1956; dist. health officer Allegheny County, Pa., 1957. Author: The Newer Epidemiology, 1962, rev., 1990, Public Health, A Science Resolvable by Mathematics, 1965. Served to 2d lt. AUS, 1943-46. Dr. Thomas Parran fellow U. Pitts. Sch. Pub. Health, 1955; named to Hon. Order Ky. Cols. Fellow Am. Pub. Health Assn.; mem. SAR, Am. Occupational Med. Assn., Western Occupational Med. Assn., Am. Med. Assn., Calif. Med. Assn., L.A. County Med. Assn., Am. Acad. Family Physicians, Am. Legion, Elks, Phi Chi. Address: PO Box 4032 Whittier CA 90607-4032

PRIEST, MARSHALL FRANKLIN, III, cardiologist; b. Rio de Janeiro, Feb. 27, 1943; came to the U.S., 1945; s. Marshall Franklin Jr. and Eleanor Margaret (Harris) P.; m. Martha Prather, June 11, 1966; children: Paula Carol, Molly McCall, Marshall Franklin IV. BS, U. Tenn., 1965, MS, 1969, MD, 1973. Bd. cert. internal medicine and cardiovascular disease. Intern U. Tenn. Affiliated Hosp., Memphis, 1973-74, resident, 1974-76; cardiology fellow U. Ala. Hosps., Birmingham, 1976-78, instr. medicine and cardiology, 1978-79; cardiologist Boise (Idaho) Heart Clinic, 1979-94, Idaho Cardiology Assocs., Boise, 1994—; clin. asst. prof. medicine U. Washington. Fellow Am. Coll. Cardiology, Am. Soc. Cardiac Angiography and Interventions; mem. Am. Heart Assn. (fellow coun. on clin. cardiology), Alpha Omega Alpha. Office: Idaho Cardiology Assocs 300 E Jefferson St Ste 201 Boise ID 83712-6221

PRIEST, TERRANCE LEE, logistics professional; b. Shoshone, Idaho, Jan. 20, 1942; s. Joseph Lyle Priest and Esther May (Jones) Brown; m. Pixie Ann Anderson, June 28, 1965 (dec. Mar. 1968); m. Mary Coco Koep, May 22, 1971; children: Victoria Leigh, Samantha Jayne. BS, BA, BBA, Boise State U., 1972; PhD honoris causa, Gustavus Adolphus Coll., 1986. Agt., telegrapher Union Pacific R.R., Pocatello, Idaho, 1961-69; corp. traffic mgr. J.R. Simplot Co., Boise, Idaho, 1969-82; corp. commerce mgr. logistics Coors Brewing Co., Golden, Colo., 1982—. Active Rep. Party, 1971—. With USNG, 1964-70. Mem. Am. Soc. Transp. and Logistics (pres. 1991-92, Award for Excellence 1994), Transp. Clubs Internat. (Person of Yr. 1991), Coun. Logistics Mgmt. (dir. 1991—), Delta Nu Alpha (award for excellence 1986). Mem. LDS Ch. Home: 302 S Carr St Lakewood CO 80226

PRIMAVERA, DIANNE L., customer service representative administrator; b. Denver, Jan. 28, 1950; d. Franck R. and Irene Inez (Nikkel) P.; children: Kelsey Celeste Magnuson, Darcie Kristin Magnuson. BS in Psychology, Regis U., 1972; MA, U. No. Colo., 1975. Supr. vocat. rehab. Dept. Social Svcs., Boulder, Colo., 1989-90; coord. edn., tng. Rocky Mtn. Regional Brain Injury Ctr., Denver, 1990-94; mgr. customer svc. Dept. Health Care Policy and Financing, Denver, 1996-97. Exec. prodr. (video) Think Twice, 1991 (Colo. Authors' League Top Hand 1991), When the Cheering Stops, 1992 (Colo. Authors' League Top Hand 1992). Bd. dirs. Family Healing Network, Denver, 1993—, N.W. Family YMCA, Arvada, Colo., 1994—; room mother St. Anne Sch., Arvada, 1994—; alumnae class rep. Regis U., 1993—. Mem. Alpha Sigma Nu. Democrat. Roman Catholic. Home: PO Box 865 Arvada CO 80001 Office: Health Care Policy and Financing 1575 Sherman St Denver CO 80203

PRINCE, DEBORAH ANN, academic counselor; b. Portland, Oreg., Dec. 8, 1948; d. Frank Robertson and Ann (Staples) P.; m. Douglas Fenner, Jan. 8, 1972 (div. July 1995). BA in Biology, Reed Coll., 1971; MEd in Counseling, U. Pa., 1974; MA in Sociology, U. Wash., 1993. Sch. counselor Carlisle (Pa.) Pub. Schs., 1978-81; team leader Planned Parenthood, Seattle, 1982-84; acad. counselor U. Wash., Seattle, 1984—; trustee Reed Coll., Portland, 1993-97/. Vol. Woodland Park Zoo, Seattle, 1991—. Named Advisor of Yr., Assn. Profl. Advisors and Counselors, U. Wash., 1992. Mem. Nat. Assn. Advisors in Health Professions (treas. 1996—), Western Assn. Advisors in the Health Professions (pres. 1995-97), Profl. Staff Assn. U. Washington (chair recognition com. 1993-95, chair selection com. 1995-96).

PRINDLE, ROBERT WILLIAM, geotechnical engineer; b. L.A., Nov. 19, 1950; s. Robert Edward and Margaret Elizabeth (Johnson) P.; m. Nancy K. Hayden, Apr. 5, 1986; children: William Robert, Amy Elizabeth. Student St. John's Coll., Camarillo, Calif., 1968-70; BSCE summa cum laude, Loyola U., L.A., 1974; MS, Calif. Inst. Tech., 1975; 40-hours hazardous waste ops. and emergency response tng.; 8-hours hazardous waste ops. supr./mgr. tng. Lic. geotechnical engr., Calif.; registered profl. civil engr., Ariz., Calif., Colo., N. Mex. Engring. aide L.A. County Sanitation Dists., 1973-74; student engr. L.A. Dept. Water and Power, 1974, 75; staff engr. Fugro, Inc., Long Beach, Calif., 1976-78; sr. staff engr. Woodward-Clyde Consultants, Orange, Calif., 1978-79; mem. tech. staff Sandia Nat. Labs., Albuquerque, 1980-89; v.p. engring. Deuel & Assocs, Inc., Albuquerque, 1989-90, pres., 1990-94; pres. Prindle-Hinds Environ., Inc., 1990-96; v.p. SVS Environ. Sys., Inc., 1996, exec. v.p., 1996-97. Regional referee Am. Youth Soccer Orgn., 1995—. Contbr. articles to profl. jours. Mem. N. Mex. Symphony Orch. Chorus, 1981-84. Office: SVS Environmental Systems Inc 11024 Montgomery NE Ste 259 Albuquerque NM 87111

PRINE, STEPHEN BRENT, publisher; b. Alton, Ill., Feb. 21, 1952; s. Virgil Earl and Isabelle (Antoinette) P.; m. Bonnie Lynn White; children: Stephen, Evan, Nicole, Jacqueline. AA with honors, Am. River Coll., Sacramento, Calif., 1971; BA, Washington U., 1973. Owner Vitrino's Pizza, St. Louis, 1972-73, S.B. Prine & Assocs., St. Louis, 1973-75, PM Petroleum, La Jolla, Calif., 1975-76, Pacific Western Imports, San Francisco, 1976-78, Prine & Assocs. Real Estate and Land Devel., Sacramento, Calif., 1978-83, Brent Oil & Gas, Houston, 1983-88, Ctrs. West Investments, Sacramento, 1987-88; pub. U.S. Realty Report, Sacramento, 1988-90, S.P. Publications, Sacramento, 1990—. Chmn. Big Hearts Internat., Sacramento, Calif. 1990—; founder, exec. dir. Missing Children Report, 1992—. Author: Foreign Investment in U.S. Real Estate, 1990. Roman Catholic. Address: 564 La Sierra Dr Ste 186 Sacramento CA 95864-7206

PRINGLE, EDWARD E., legal educator, former state supreme court chief justice; b. Chgo., Apr. 12, 1914; s. Abraham J. and Lena (Oher) P.; m. Pauline Judd, Aug. 17, 1941; children: Bruce, Eric. LL.B., U. Colo., 1936, LL.D., 1976; LL.D., U. Denver, 1979. Bar: Colo. Practiced in Denver, 1936-42, 47-57; with fed. govt. service Washington, 1943-47; dist. judge Colo. Dist. Ct., Denver, 1957-61; justice Supreme Ct. Colo., Denver, 1961-79; chief justice Supreme Ct. Colo., 1970-78; dir. research and writing program U. Denver Coll. Law, 1979-90, prof. emeritus, 1990—. Contbr. articles to profl. jours. Bd. dirs. Am. Med. Center, Denver; mem. Nat. Commn. for Establishment of Nat. Inst. Justice. Served with USAAF, 1942. Recipient William Lee Knous award U. Colo. Law Sch., 1975. Mem. Am., Colo., Denver bar assns., Conf. Chief Justices (chmn. 1973-74), Am. Judicature Soc. (Herbert Lincoln Harley award 1973, chmn. bd. 1974-76), Nat. Center State Cts. (pres. 1977-79). Jewish. Club: Masons (33 deg.). Office: U Denver Coll Law 1900 Olive St Denver CO 80220-1857

PRINGLE, THOMAS HIVICK, sales executive; b. Ardmore, Okla., Aug. 22, 1945; s. William Cuthbert and Pauline (Gill) P.; m. Donda Martinovich, Dec. 28, 1982 (div. 1984); 1 child, Thomas Anthony. Grad. high sch., Greensburg, Pa. Owner Mohawk Recreational Ctr., Latrobe, Pa., 1970-72; mgr. Courtesy R.V., Las Vegas, 1977-79, Ace Auto Sales, Las Vegas, 1980-85; salesman Norm Baker Motors, Las Vegas, 1986-90; sales mgr. Sterling Motors, Las Vegas, 1990-91; gen. mgr. Sys. Supply, Inc., Las Vegas, 1992—; owner Poorhouse Pizza, Youngwood, Pa., 1970-72. Author: Bar Table 9 Ball, 1994. With U.S. Army, 1963-66. Mem. Christian Coalition. Republican. Home: 1340 Challenge Ln Las Vegas NV 89110 Office: Sys Supply Inc 3325 Ali Baba Ln Ste 618 Las Vegas NV 89118-1775

PRINJA, ANIL KANT, nuclear engineering educator; b. Mombasa, Kenya, Apr. 9, 1955; came to U.S., 1980; s. Kapil Dev and Kushal (Dharney) P.; m. Renu Mohan, Sept. 18, 1983; children: Vivek Kapil, Akash Prinja. BSc in Nuclear Engring. with 1st class honors, London U., 1976, PhD in Nuclear Engring., 1980. Asst. rsch. engr. UCLA, 1980-87; asst. prof. nuclear engring. U. N.Mex., Albuquerque, 1987-89, assoc. prof., 1989-95, prof., 1995—; chmn., host Internat. Conf. Transport Theory, 1991, U.S. Edge Plasma Physics: Theory and Applications Workshop, 1993; cons. Sandia Nat. Labs., Albuquerque, 1987—, Sci. Applications Internat., Inc., Albuquerque, 1987—, Los Alamos Nat. Lab., 1989—; vis. prof. dept. reactor physics Chalmers U. Tech., Goteborg, Sweden, 1993, 95; vis. prof. UCLA, 1994. Assoc. editor: Annals of Nuclear Energy; contbr. chpts. to books and articles to profl. jours. Recipient Outstanding Acad. Achievement award Instn. Nuclear Engrs., 1976; grantee Dept. of Energy, Sandia Nat. Lab., Los Alamos Nat. Lab., Culham Labs., U.K., KFA Julich, Germany, 1989—, others. Mem. Am. Phys. Soc., Am. Nuc. Soc., Soc. Indsl. and Applied Math., N.Y. Acad. Scis. Hindu. Office: U New Mex 209 Farris Engring Ctr Albuquerque NM 87131

PRINZING, DANIEL LEE, secondary education educator; b. Portland, Oreg., Mar. 1, 1958; s. Raymond H. and Doris Mae P.; m. Belinda Ann Roden, Sept. 3, 1977 (div. Nov. 1982); 1 child, Leeann; m. Carol Jean Nelson, June 12, 1987; 1 child, Elise. BA in History and Secondary Edn., Boise State U., 1983, MA in Edn, 1987; postgrad. in edn. history/govt., U. Portland, 1996; postgrad. in edn., U. Idaho, 1997—. Tchr. English and history West Jr. H.S., Boise, 1985-93; history tchr. Les Bois Jr. H.S., Boise, 1993—; bd. examiners Nat. Coun. Accreditation of Tchr. Edn., Washington, 1992—; state coord. Ctr. for Civic Edn., Calabasas, Calif., 1995—. James Madison Found. Meml. fellow, Washington, 1995; named State Am. History Tchr. of Yr., DAR, 1996; recipient tchr. incentive grant Idaho Humanities Coun., 1994, 95. Mem. Journalism Edn. Assn. (state dirl. 1994-96), Idaho Coun. Social Studies (pres. 1995-96). Home: 3421 S Crosspoint Boise ID 83706 Office: Les Bois JHS 701 E Boise Ave Boise ID 83706-5119

PRISBREY, REX PRINCE, retired insurance agent, underwriter, consultant; b. Washington, Utah, Mar. 18, 1922; s. Hyrum William and Susan (Prince) P.; m. Pinka Julieta Lucero, Nov. 16, 1943; children: Karol Sue Prisbey Lewallen, Pamela Blanche Prisbrey Ebert, Michael Rex. BA in Acctg., Denver U., 1949. CLU. Ptnr. Allen Stamm & Assocs., home builders, Farmington, N.Mex., 1949-52; acct. Linder Burke & Stevenson, Santa Fe, N.Mex., 1949-52; agt. State Farm Ins. Cos., Farmington, 1952-56; mgr. State Farm Ins. Cos., Phoenix, 1956-60; contractor, agt. State Farm Ins. Cos., Scottsdale, Ariz., 1960—; v.p., treas. Original Curio Store Inc., Santa Fe. Pres. Farmington Jr. C. of C., 1952; v.p. N.Mex. Jr. C. of C., 1953. 1st lt. USAAF, 1941-46, CBI. Decorated DFC, Air medal with oak leaf cluster; recipient Disting. Life Underwriter award Cen. Ariz. Mgrs. Assn., 1979. Mem. Am. Soc. CLU's, Scottsdale Assn. Life Underwriters (pres. 1980-81), Airplane Owners and Pilots Assn., Hump Pilots Assn. (life, speaker at meml. of Hump Flyers, Kunming, China 1993), Pinewood Country Club (bd. dirs., treas., v.p. 1985—), Civitans (pres. Scottsdale 1962-63). Home: 4011 N 65th St Scottsdale AZ 85251-4235

PRISTUPA, DAVID WILLIAM, secondary education educator; b. Phila., June 17, 1953; s. William Donald and Doreen (Braithwaite) P.; children: Scott David, Jamie Amanda. BS, U. Idaho, 1980. Cert. secondary edn. tchr., Idaho. Instr. North Gem Sch. Dist., Bancroft, Idaho, 1980—; mem. adv. bd. ISU Sch. of Applied Tech Farm Mgmt., Pocatello, Idaho, 1994-96. With USN, 1971-77. Mem. Nat. Vocat. Tchrs. Assn., Am. Vocat. Assn., Idaho Vocat. Assn., Idaho Vocat. Agrl. Tchrs. Assn., Bancroft Lions Club (treas. 1989-96). Home: PO Box 4 Bancroft ID 83217 Office: North Gem Sch Dist PO Box 70 Bancroft ID 83217

PRITCHARD, JACKIE LEE, information center manager; b. Logan, W.Va., Feb. 12, 1948; s. Leondas Bell and Edna Lorene (Embry) P.; m. Patricia Louise Rose, Dec. 27, 1947; 1 child, Tracy Suzanne. BA, U. Oreg., 1969; MA, Ohio State U., 1972, PhD, 1980; MLS, U. Wash., 1984. Faculty Calif. State U., L.A., 1976-77; libr. U. Wash., Seattle, 1984-88, mgr. Primate Info. Ctr., 1988—. Editor: Current Promate References, 1988—. Mem. Am. Soc. Primatologists, Internat. Soc. Primatologists, Pacific Northwest chpt. Soc. Info. Sci. (chair 1990-91). Home: 14012 110th Pl NE Kirkland WA 98034-1003 Office: Primate Info Ctr 1101 Westlake Ave N Seattle WA 98109-3527

PRITCHARD, JOEL, state lieutenant governor; b. Seattle, May 5, 1925; children: Peggy, Frank, Anne, Jeanie. Student, Marietta Coll.; PhD (Hon.), Seattle U. Pres. Griffin Envelope Co., Seattle; mem. Wash. Ho. of Reps., Olympia, 1958-66, Wash. State Senate, 1966-70, U.S. Ho. of Reps., Washington, 1972-84; dir. govt. rels. Bogle & Gates, 1985-88; lt. gov. State of Wash., Olympia, 1989—; mem. Merchant Marine and Fisheries Com. U.S. Ho. of Reps., subcom. on Asia and the Pacific Fgn. Rels. Com., Panama Canal Consultative Commn., 1987-88; U.S. del. to UN Gen. Assembly, 1983. With U.S. Army, PTO, WWII. Office: Lt Gov's Office PO Box 40482 304 Legislative Bldg Olympia WA 98504-0482

PRITCHETT, JAMES W., orthopaedic surgeon, educator; b. Seattle, Aug. 8, 1953; s. James W. Pritchett Jr. BS, U. Wash., 1974, MD, 1979. Resident, surgery Phoenix VA Med. Ctr., 1979-80, resident, orthopaedic surgery, 1983-84; resident, surgery Phoenix Indian Med. Ctr., 1980-81; resident, orthopaedic surgery Maricopa County Hosp., Phoenix, 1981-82, Ariz. Children's Hosp., Tempe, Ariz., 1982-83; instr., orthopaedic surgery U. Wash. Med. Ctr., Seattle, 1985-88, asst. clin. prof. orthopaedic surgery, 1988-93, assoc. clin. prof., 1993—; chief, orthopaedic surgery Pacific Med. Ctr., Seattle, 1984—, Providence Med. Ctr., Seattle, 1993—. Author: Practical Bone Growth, 1993; contbr. articles to profl. jours. Inventor hip, shoulder, spine implants. Med. dir. Bone Reconstrn. Assn., Seattle, 1983—. Recipient Meyerding award for fracture rsch. Am. Fracture Assn., 1985. Fellow Am. Acad. Orthopaedic Surgeons, Am. Acad. Pediatrics (exec. com. 1990-93); mem. ACS, Assn. Bone and Joint Surgeons (membership com. 1992-95), North Pacific Orthopaedic Soc. Home and Office: 226 2nd Ave W Seattle WA 98119-4204

PRO, PHILIP MARTIN, judge; b. Richmond, Calif., Dec. 12, 1946; s. Leo Martin and Mildred Louise (Beck) P.; m. Dori Sue Hallas, Nov. 13, 1982; 1 child, Brenda Kay. BA, San Francisco State U., 1968; JD Golden Gate U., 1972. Bar: Calif. 1972, Nev. 1973, U.S. Ct. Appeals (9th cir.) 1973, U.S. Dist. Ct. Nev. 1973, U.S. Supreme Ct. 1976. Pub. defender, Las Vegas, 1973-75; asst. U.S. atty., Dist. Nev., Las Vegas, 1975-78; ptnr. Semenza, Murphy & Pro, Reno, 1978-79; dep. atty. gen. State of Nev., Carson City, 1979-80; U.S. magistrate U.S. Dist. Ct. Nev., Las Vegas, 1980-87; U.S. dist. judge, 1987—; instr. Atty. Gen.'s Advocacy Inst., Nat. Inst. Trial Advocacy, 1992; chmn. com. adminstrn. of magistrate judge system Jud. Conf. U.S., 1993—. Bd. dirs. NCCJ, Las Vegas, 1982—, mem. program com. and issues in justice com. Mem. ABA, Fed. Judges Assn. (bd. dirs. 1992—), Nev. State Bar Assn., Calif. State Bar Assn., Nev. Judges Assn. (instr.), Assn. Trial Lawyers Am., Nev. Am. Inn Ct. (pres. 1989—), Ninth Cir. Jury (instructions com.), Nat. Conf. U.S. Magistrates (sec.), Nev. Am. Inn of Ct. (pres. 1989-91). Republican. Episcopalian. Office: US Dist Ct 341 Fed Bldg 300 Las Vegas Bldv S Las Vegas NV 89101

PROBASCO, CALVIN HENRY CHARLES, clergyman, college administrator; b. Petaluma, Calif., Apr. 5, 1926; s. Calvin Warren and Ruth Charlene (Winans) P.; m. Nixie June Farnsworth, Feb. 14, 1947; children—Calvin, Carol, David, Ruth. B.A. cum laude, Biola Bible Coll., La Mirada, Calif., 1953; D.D. (hon.), Talbot Theol. Sem., La Mirada, 1983. Ordained to ministry, 1950. Pastor Sharon Baptist Ch., El Monte, Calif., 1951-58, Carmichael Bible Ch., Calif., 1958—; pres. Sacramento Bible Inst., Carmichael, 1968—. Mem. Ind. Fundamental Chs. Am. (rec. sec. 1978-81, pres. 1981-84, 1st v.p. 1987-88), Delta Epsilon Chi. Republican. Office: Carmichael Bible Ch 7100 Fair Oaks Blvd Carmichael CA 95608-6452

PROBASCO, DALE RICHARD, management consultant; b. Ogden, Utah, July 23, 1946; s. Robert Vere and Dorleen E. (Oppliger) P.; m. Joan Michele Takacs, Dec. 20, 1969; children: Todd Aaron, Brad Dillon. BS, Utah State U., 1975; MS, U. Phoenix, 1988. Inventory asst. Moore Bus. Form, Logan, Utah, 1973-75; systems engr. Electronic Data Systems, Dallas, 1975-76; start-up engr. Bechtel Corp., San Francisco, 1976-78; supr. project scheduling Toledo Edison Co., 1978-80; mgr. project controls Utah Power and Light Co., Salt Lake City, 1980-87, mgr. mktg. strategy, 1987-89; pres. Probasco Cons., Inc., West Jordan, Utah, 1989-90; mgr. Metzler & Assocs., Deerfield, Ill., 1990—. Contbr. articles to profl. publs. Pres. Emery County Little League, Castledale, Utah, 1981-84; coach Little League Baseball, West Jordan, Utah, 1985-86. With USN, 1965-72. Mem. Am. Econ. Devel. Conf., Nuclear Info. and Records Mgmt. Assn., Assn. for Info. and Image Mgmt., Assn. Energy Svcs. Profls., Am. Pub. Power Assn., Nat. Rural Electric Coop. Assn. Lutheran.

PROBERT, COLIN, advertising executive. Ptnr., pres. Goodby, Silverstein & Ptnrs., San Francisco. Office: Goodby Silverstein & Ptnrs 921 Front St San Francisco CA 94111

PROCCI, WARREN R., psychiatrist; b. S.I., N.Y., Jan. 19, 1947; s. Waddie R. and Anita M. (Veen) P.; m. Linda L. Kautza, June 4, 1972. BS, Wagner Coll., 1968; MD, U. Wis., 1972; PhD, So. Calif. Psychoanalytic Inst., 1984. Diplomate Am. Bd. Psychiatry and Neurology. Intern Univ. Hosps., Madison, Wis., 1972-73; resident Univ. Hosps., Madison, 1971-74; asst. prof., then assoc. prof. psychiatry Sch. Medicine U. So. Calif., L.A., 1975-82; assoc. prof., dir. residency edn. in psychiatry Harbor-UCLA Med. Ctr., Torrance, 1982-88, assoc. clin. prof., 1988—. Mem. Am. Psychoanalytic Assn. (councilor at large 1997—), So. Calif. Psychoanalytic Inst. (pres. 1994-96, tng./supervising psychoanalyst 1991—, dean tng. sch. 1996—). Office: 181 N Oak Knoll Ave Ste 1 Pasadena CA 91101-1817

PROCTOR, BETTINA REA, fish and wildlife organization administrator; b. Columbia, Mo., Oct. 29, 1946; d. Charles Johnson and Mary Elizabeth (Rea) P.; m. Dennis Stockdale Grogan, Apr. 21, 1973; children: Kelley Grogan, Tyler Grogan, Dylan Grogan. BA in Biology, U. Colo., 1968; MS in Wildlife Biology, Colo. State U., 1975. Ops. mgr. Boulder (Colo.) County Pks. and Open Space Dept., 1976-79; rsch. scientist Sci. Applications, Inc., Boulder, 1980-81; rsch. assoc. Resource Assocs., Denver, 1983-85; asst. dir. Colo. Natural Areas Program, Denver, 1985; pub. affairs dir. Planned Parenthood, Denver, 1985-92; partnerships coord. U.S. Fish and Wildlife Svc., Denver, 1992—; sec. nongame adv. coun. Colo. Div. Wildlife, Denver, 1979-80; v.p. Check-off for Wildlife, Lincoln, Nebr., 1981. Editor: (handbooks) Practices for Protecting and Enhancing, Fish and Wildlife in Coal Surface, Mined Land, 1983. Bd. dirs. Colo. Nat. Abortion Rights Action League, Denver, 1987, Colo. Open Space Coun., Denver, 1983-84, Colo. Wildlife Fedn. (treas. 1995); pres. Boulder Audubon Soc., 1975-76. Office: US Fish and Wildlife Svc PO Box 25486 Denver Federal Ctr Denver CO 80207

PROCTOR, VINCENT P., music educator; b. Rock Springs, Wyo., July 7, 1953; s. Edward G. and Georgia A. (Peterson) P.; m. Marlene R. Koscak, Aug. 2, 1975; 1 child, Linde T. MusB, U. Wyo., 1975, MA, 1991. Cert. music tchr. Band dir. Sch. Dist. #1, Rock Springs, Wyo., 1975—. Chmn. Rock Springs Planning and Zoning Commn., 1997—. Mem. NEA, Sweetwater Edn. Assn. (negotiator 1992-94, tchr. of the year, 1984), Wyo. Music Edn. Assn. (adjudicator 1996—), Assn. for Supervision, Nat. Assn. Jazz Educators. Home: 1912 Park View Ave Rock Springs WY 82901 Office: Sweetwater County Sch Dist #1 PO Box 1089 Rock Springs WY 82902

PROCUNIER, RICHARD WERNER, environmental scientist, administrator; b. Dallas, Tex., Oct. 27, 1936; s. Werner Richard and Dorothy (Koch) P.; m. Janet Mesing, Sept. 5, 1958 (div. Aug. 28, 1984); children: Nancy, Carol, Ellen; m. Carolyn Harris, June 25, 1988. BSEE, MIT, 1958; PhD, Univ. Coll. London, 1966. Prof. U. London, 1966-68; rsch. scientist Lockheed, Palo Alto, Calif., 1968-72; mgr. Hewlett Packard, Santa Clara, Calif., 1972-74; chief of noise control U.S. EPA, San Francisco, 1974-82, sci. advisor, 1982-83, environ. scientist, 1990—; prof. U. Calif., Davis, 1984-85; adminstr. County Health Svcs., Martinez, Calif., 1986-89; mem. Nat. Edn. Com., Nat. Environ. Health Assn., Denver, 1980-87; enforcement coord., U.S. EPA, San Francisco, 1990. Contbr. many articles to profl. jours. Proponent to incorporate Orinda, Calif., 1984. Recipient Presidential citation, Nat. Environmental Health Assn., 1981. Fellow Royal Soc. London; mem. World Affairs Coun., Commonwealth Club, Kappa Sigma (Leadership award 1958).

PROFAIZER, JOSEPHINE E., elementary education educator; b. Rock Springs, Wyo., Sept. 2, 1951; d. Joseph and Enrica (Filippi) P. BS, U. Wyo., 1973; MEd, Utah State U., 1983. Cert. tchr., Wyo. Tchr. 3d grade Sweetwater Sch. Dist. 1, Rock Springs, 1973-79, tchr. kindergarten, 1980, tchr. 2d grade, 1980-89, tchr. Title 1 reading and math., 1989—. Bd. dirs. Internat. Tirolean Trentino Orgns. N.Am., 1991-95. Recipient Outstanding Young Educator award Rock Springs Jaycees, 1980. Mem. NEA, Wyo. Edn. Assn., Sweetwater Edn. Assn. (Tchr. of Yr. 1994-95), Tyrloean Trentini Wyo. (sec. 1986-91, newsletter editor 1989-92, 94—, pres. 1991-95), Delta Kappa Gamma (sec. 1982-84, v.p. 1990-92, treas. 1994—), Beta Sigma Phi (sec. 1990-91, v.p. 1993-94, pres. 1996—). Roman Catholic.

PRONZINI, BILL JOHN (WILLIAM PRONZINI), author; b. Petaluma, Calif., Apr. 13, 1943; s. Joseph and Helene (Guder) P.; m. Marcia Muller. Coll. student, 2 years. Author: 50 novels (including under pseudonyms), 4 books of non-fiction, 6 collections of short stories, 1971—; first novel, The Stalker, 1971; editor 80 anthologies; contbr. numerous short stories to publs. Recipient Scroll award, Best First Novel, Mystery Writers Am., 1972, Life Achievement award Pvt. Eye Writers Am., 1987. Democrat. Office: PO Box 2536 Petaluma CA 94953-2536

PROPHET, TODD ELLIOTT, financial executive; b. Spokane, Wash., Sept. 23, 1965; s. Larry Don Prophet and Judith Marie (Smith) Gemmrig; children: Casey Brian, Katlyn Dianne. BA in Bus., U. Wash., 1989. CPA, Alaska. Audit and tax jr. acct. Hogan, Mecham, Richardson, Ketchikan, Alaska, 1989-90, audit and tax sr. acct., 1990-92, audit and tax mgr., 1992-93; fin. mgr. Campbell Towing Co., Wrangell, Alaska, 1993—; cons. Prophet Adv. Svcs., Wrangell, 1993—. Mem. AICPA, Alaska Soc. CPAs (mem. ethics com. 1994—, mem. industry com. 1994—), Nat. Mgmt. Acctg. Assn., Elks. Republican. Home: 238 Evergreen Wrangell AK 99929 Office: Campbell Towing Co PO Box 170 Wrangell AK 99929-0170

PROSSER, MICHAEL JOSEPH, community college staff member; b. Syracuse, N.Y., May 9, 1948; s. Palmer Adelbert and Viola Mary (Clairmont) P. AA, Riverside (Calif.) City Coll., 1971; BA in History, Calif. State Coll., San Bernardino, 1977; MSLS, U. So. Calif., L.A., 1981. Cert. cmty. coll. instr., librarian, Calif. Libr. clk. Riverside C.C., 1968-81, learning resources asst., 1981—. Author: California and the Pacific Plate: A Bibliography, 1979. Tutor, Queen of Angels Ch., Riverside, 1985—, facilitator/patrons, 1985—. With U.S. Army, 1969-71. Mem. ASCD, Internat. Soc. Poets, Calif. Media Libr. Educators Assn., Calif. Libr. Assn. Democrat. Roman Catholic. Home: 6800 Palos Dr Riverside CA 92503-1330 Office: Riverside Cmty Coll 4800 Magnolia Ave Riverside CA 92506-1242

PROTIGAL, STANLEY NATHAN, lawyer; b. Wilmington, Del., June 3, 1950; s. Bernard Protigal. BS in Aircraft Maintenance Engring., Northrop U., 1973; JD, Vt. Law Sch., 1978. Bar: U.S. Patent Office 1977, D.C. 1978. Assoc. Sixbey F. & L., Arlington, Va., 1978-79, atty., 1979-82; patent atty. Allied-Signal Bendix Aerospace, Teterboro, N.J., 1982-88; patent counsel Micron Tech., Inc., Boise, Idaho, 1988-94; pvt. practice Boise, Idaho, 1994-96, Seattle, 1996—. Mem. IEEE, MENSA. Avocations: pvt. pilot, bicycling, skiing.

PROTZMAN, GRANT DALE, university administrator, state legislator; b. Ogden, Utah, May 3, 1950; s. Paul L. and Maxine E. (Nelson) P.; m. Linda Sue Gerasta, Mar. 30, 1985; children: Heather Sue, Kristen Marie, Erin Elizabeth. BA, Utah State U., 1976; MS, Calif. Am. U., 1979; MA, U. No. Colo., 1987, EdD, 1988. Coord. student activities Weber State U., Ogden, 1976-81, coord. student govt., 1981-82, assoc. dir. student life, 1982-84, dir. co-curricular learning, 1984-87, planning and devel. officer, dir. drug and alcohol program, 1987-91, asst. to v.p., 1991—; mem., asst. minority whip Utah State Ho. of Reps., Salt Lake City, 1986—; sr. cons. Inst. for Leadership Devel., Ogden, 1978—. Author: An Examination of Select Motivational Variables of Members in Three Different Types of Volunteer Organizations in a Collegiate Setting, 1988, An Investigation of the State of Motivation Management and Assessment in Volunteer Organizations, 1988; contbr. articles to profl. jours. Mem. adv. bd. Wasatch Care Ctr., Ogden, 1986-93, Families in Edn., 1992, Weber Sch. Dist., 1992; mem. Weber Area Emergency Planning Com., Ogden, 1988-93, critical workplace skills adv. bd. Applied Tech. Ctr., 1991—, mem. adv. bd. Pvt. Industry Coun./Local Community Coun., 1994—, State of Utah Region II Dept. Corrections, 1992—; mem. bd. dirs. Hospice No. Utah, 1994—. Named Outstanding Young Man of the Year, Jay Cees; Recipient Ptnrs. in Edn. Recognition award Weber Sch. Dist., 1987, Appreciation award Utah Vocat. Leadership Orgns., 1987, Extended Svc. award Ogden Sch. Dist., 1988, Outstanding Legislator award Utah Democratic Party Chmn's. award, 1988, Utah Sch. Employees Assn. Scroll of Honor award as Outstanding legislator, 1990, Weber State U. Student Svcs. Soar award, 1991, Utah Edn. Assn. Honor Roll award as Outstanding legislator, 1991, Utah Ednl. Libr. Media Assn. award for Outstanding Dedication and Svc. to Utah Lib. Media programs, 1992, Utah Assn. of Rehabilitative Facilities award for Svc. to Persons with disabilities, 1992, U.B.A.T.C. award for Support of Vocational Edn., 1992, Golden Key award, 1993, Utah Govt. Coun. for People with Disabilities award State Legis. Coalition, 1994. Mem. Nat. Assn. Campus Activities (regional coord. 1982-85, conf. educator 1980-83, Nat. Outstanding Unit of Yr. 1986, Regional Outstanding Unit of Yr. 1985), Utah Edn. Assn. (honor roll award 1991), Rotary, Kappa Delta Pi, Phi Sigma Alpha, Phi Delta Kappa. Democrat. Mormon. Home: 3073 N 575 E Ogden UT 84414-2077 Office: Weber State U 3750 Harrison Blvd Ogden UT 84408-0001*

PROUT, CARL WESLEY, history educator; b. Bakersfield, Calif., Apr. 19, 1941; s. George Hecla and Ruth (King) P. BA, U. Calif., Santa Barbara, 1964, MA, 1965; postgrad., U. Tenn., Knoxville, 1968-71, Am. U., Cairo, 1974, U. So. Calif., 1981, Ain Shams U., Cairo, 1981. Instr. history Santa Barbara Coll., 1965-66, U. Tenn., Knoxville, 1968-71; instr. Orange Coast Coll., Costa Mesa, 1966-68, asst. prof., 1971-73, assoc. prof., 1973-75, prof., 1975—; treas. Willmore Corp., 1980-81, sec., 1984-85, v.p., 1985-86, pres., chmn., 1988-89, also bd. dirs.; group facilitator Coastview Meml. Hosp., Long Beach, 1986-89. Research and publs. in field. Pres., chmn. bd. Alamitos Heights Improvement Assn., 1979-80, bd. dirs., 1980-82; mem. East Long Beach Joint Council, 1979-80, Local Coastal Planning Adv. Com., 1979-80 mem. preservation bd. Palm Springs Historic Site, 1994—, mem. Palm Springs Hist. Soc. Recipient Salgo Outstanding Tchr. award, 1974-76. Mem. Am. Hist. Assn., Writers' Guild of Palm Springs (v.p. 1996—). Office: Orange Coast Coll 2701 Fairview Rd Costa Mesa CA 92626-5563 *Personal philosophy: Honesty, Openmindedness, Willingness = How to succeed in life!.*

PROUT, RALPH EUGENE, physician; b. Los Angeles, Feb. 27, 1933; s. Ralph Byron and Fern (Taylor) P.; m. Joanne Morris, Sept. 17, 1980; children: Michael, Michelle. BA, La Sierra Coll., 1953; MD, Loma Linda U., 1957; D of Nutri-Medicine (hon.), John F. Kennedy Coll., 1987. Diplomate: Nat. Bd. Med. Examiners. Intern Los Angeles County Hosp., 1957-58; resident internal medicine White Meml. Hosp., Los Angeles, 1958-60; resident psychiatry Harding Hosp., Worthington, Ohio, 1960-61; practice medicine specializing in internal medicine Napa, Calif., 1961-63; staff internist Calif. Med. Facility, Vacaville, 1963-68, chief med. officer, 1968-84; chief med. cons. Calif. Dept. Corrections, 1977-86, chief med. services, 1983; med. cons. Wellness Cons., Placerville, Calif., 1986—; pres. Addiction Medicine Treatment Ctr., Placerville, Calif., 1986-96; instr. Sch. Medicine, Loma Linda U., 1965-66; clin. assoc. U. Calif.-Davis Sch. Medicine, 1978-84; med. cons. Substance Abuse Pine Grove Camp, 1986—; expert witness alcoholism El Dorado (Calif.) Superior Ct., 1994—; pres. Union Am. Physicians and Dentists, Calif. State Employee chpt., 1970-72. Treas. Vacaville Republican Assembly, 1972-75; del. Republican Central Com. Solano County, 1975-78; Bd. dirs. Napa-Solano County United Crusade, Vallejo, Calif., 1969-71, v.p., 1970-71; bd. dirs., co-founder Project Clinic, Vacaville, 1974-77, Home Health Com. Inter-Community Hosp., Fairfield, 1978-80; pres. MotherLode Citizens for Drug-Free Youth, Amador County, 1985—. Named One of Outstanding Young Men of Am., 1968. Mem. AMA, Am. Assn. Sr. Physicians, Internat. Assn. New Sci., Union Concerned Scis., Mother Lode Citizens for Drug-Free Youth, Native Sons of Golden West, Alpha Omega Alpha. Republican. Home and Office: 24405 Shake Ridge Rd Volcano CA 95689-9728 *When we ask better questions, the answers will follow.*

PROUTY, ALAN LESLIE, environmental engineer; b. Weiser, Idaho, Dec. 3, 1960; s. Alton L. and Carole Jean Prouty; m. Shelley Joe Eyrand, June 7, 1986. BSc in Chemistry, Idaho State U., 1983; MSc in Forest Products, U. Idaho, 1987. Process analyst City of Pullman, Wash., 1986-87; assoc. chemist James River Corp., Camas, Wash., 1987-89, sr. environ. engr., 1989-93, mgr. air quality engring., 1993-95; environ. engring. mgr. Potlatch Corp., 1995—. Mem. TAPPI, Air and Waste Mgmt. Assn., Pacific Coast TAPPI (Shibley award 1992). Office: James River Corp 4th And Adams Camas WA 98607

PROVINCE, SHARON G., research and development executive; b. 1948. Staff counsel Madaf, Tex., 1972-73; staff atty. Fed. Power Commn., Washington, 1973-74; various positions Analytical Tech. Inc., San Diego, 1974—, now sr. v.p., sec. Office: Analytical Tech Inc 5550 Morehouse Dr San Diego CA 92121

PROWELL, ANNE DURFEE, marketing consultant, writer; b. Champaign, Ill., Dec. 5, 1948; d. Jack Prowell and Nancy (Dillavou) Gaillard; m. Jon Clark Ranney, Mar. 27, 1967 (div. Mar. 1983); children: Jeff Ranney, Travis Prowell; m. Robin Steele, July 22, 1990. BA in Internat. Rels., Calif. State U., San Francisco, 1978; MA in Creative Writing, and Lit., Calif. State U., Fresno, 1993. Reporter News-Gazette, Champaign, Ill., 1966-67; writer, editor Rossmoor News, Walnut Creek, Calif., 1974-78, Pacific Bell, San Francisco, 1983-84; dir. mktg. com. Pacific Telesis Internat., San Francisco, Madrid, 1984-86; v.p., creative dir. Torme & Co., San Francisco, 1986-87; instr. Calif. State U., Fresno, 1991-94; CEO, cons. Specific Gravity, Inc., San Rafael, Calif., 1995—. Author: (poems) Frontiers, 1996. Founder Working Women of Ariz., Phoenix, 1969, Lit. Arts of Marin, Colo., 1982; dir. youth svcs. Arabian Am. Oil Co., Saudi Arabia, 1972-74; press aide U.S. Congresswoman Boxer, San Rafael, 1982-83. Recipient Artist's Proof Poetry award Artist's Proof Bookshop, 1993. Office: Specific Gravity Inc 54 Mission San Rafael CA 94901

PRUNES-CARRILLO, FERNANDO, plastic surgeon, educator; b. Chihuahua, Mex.; m. Linda R. Underwood; children: Alexander, Ariadne, Anthony. MD, U. Chihuahua, Mex., 1968. Surg. intern Booth Meml. Med. Ctr., Flushing, N.Y., 1971-72; resident in gen. surgery Tucson Hosps. Med. Edn. Program, 1972-76; resident in plastic surgery Mayo Grad. Sch. Medicine, 1979-81; chief divsn. plastic surgery Kern Med. Ctr., Bakersfield, Calif., 1983—; asst. clin. prof. surgery U. Calif., San Diego, 1983—. Mem. Am. Soc. Plastic and Reconstructive Surgeons, Mayo Alumni Assn. Office: Kern Med Ctr 1830 Flower St Bakersfield CA 93305-4144

PRYOR, LOIS MARIE, management consultant; b. Oakland, Calif., Apr. 16, 1950; d. Arthur William and Lila Marie (Carlin) P. BA, U. Calif., Berkeley, 1971, postgrad., 1981. Instr. English and chem. engring. grad. sch. edn. U. Calif., Berkeley, 1974-83; pres., co-founder Echols & Pryor Tech. Comms., Inc., San Francisco, 1981-92; owner, pres. Pryor Comms., San Francisco, 1992—; cons., trainer Support Ctr., San Francisco, 1985—; cons., tchr., mem. steering com. Bay Area Writing Project, Berkeley, 1980-84. Co-editor: Borzoi College Reader, 1980; author manual Borzoi College Reader, 1980, also over 160 workshop manuals, 1981—. Vol., Marin Humane Soc., 1992—. U. Calif. regents fellow, 1976, 81; U. Calif. English dept. scholar, 1970. Mem. AAUW, NAFE, Inst. Mgmt. Cons. Office: Pryor Comms 116 New Montgomery St Ste 200 San Francisco CA 94105-3607

PRZYBYLA, LEON HUGH, JR., sales executive; b. Annapolis, Md., May 25, 1944; s. Leon Hugh and Doric Catherine (Wearwein) P.; m. Janice Lynn White, May 25, 1967; children: Leon II, Scott, Amy, Judy, Jay, David. Degree in microbiology, Brigham Young U., 1968. Registered profl. engr. Detailman Marion Labs., L.A., 1968-69; owner, pres. Priz-Co, Inc., Palo Alto, Calif., 1969-92; v.p. sales Computing Edge, Salt Lake City, 1995-96; dir. strategic alliances Teltrust Comm. Inc., Salt Lake City, 1997—; bd. dirs. Marich Confectionary, Watsonville, Calif., 1985—; cons. in field, Salt Lake City, 1992-95. Pres. Profl. Soc., 1974-75; scoutleader Stanford Area coun. Boy Scouts Am., 1969—. Recipient Silver Beaver BSA award, 1997. Mem. Instrument Soc. Am. (sr. mem., sect. pres. 1974-75, Level III Cert. Control Sys. Technician 1995). Republican. Mormon.

PTASYNSKI, HARRY, geologist, oil producer; b. Milw., May 26, 1926; s. Stanley S. and Frances V. (Stawicki) P.; m. Nola G. Whitestine, Sept. 15, 1951; children: Ross F., Lisa Joy. BS, Stanford U., 1950. Cert. profl. geologist; cert. petroleum geologist. Dist. geologist Pure Oil Co., Amarillo, Tex., 1951-55, Casper, Wyo., 1955-58; ind. geologist, Casper, 1958—. With USN, 1944-46, PTO. Mem. Am. Assn. Petroleum Geologists, Am. Inst. Profl. Geologists, Ind. Petroleum Assn. Am. (v.p., bd. dirs. 1976-85), Ind. Petroleum Assn. Mountain States (v.p., bd. dirs. 1976-80), Rocky Mountain Oil and Gas Assn. (bd. dirs., exec. com. 1980—). Republican. Episcopalian. Home: 1515 Brookview Dr Casper WY 82604-4895 Office: 123 W 1st St Ste 560 Casper WY 82601-2483

PUCK, THEODORE THOMAS, geneticist, biophysicist, educator; b. Chgo., Sept. 24, 1916; s. Joseph and Bessie (Shapiro) Puckowitz; m. Mary Hill, Apr. 17, 1946; children: Stirling, Jennifer, Laurel. B.S., U. Chgo., 1937, Ph.D., 1940. Mem. commn. airborne infections Office Surgeon Gen., Army Epidemiol. Bd., 1944-46; asst. prof. depts. medicine and biochemistry U. Chgo., 1945-47; sr. fellow Am. Cancer Soc., Calif. Inst. Tech., Pasadena, 1947-48; prof. biophysics U. Colo. Med. Sch., 1948—, chmn. dept., 1948-67, disting. prof., 1986—; founder, dir. Eleanor Roosevelt Inst. Cancer Research, 1962-95; Disting. research prof. Am. Cancer Soc., 1966—; nat. lectr. Sigma Xi, 1975-76. Author: The Mammalian Cell as a Microorganism: Genetic and Biochemical Studies in Vitro, 1972. Mem. Commn. on Physicians for the Future. Recipient Albert Lasker award, 1958, Borden award med. rsch., 1959, Louisa Gross Horwitz prize, 1973, Gordon Wilson medal Am. Clin. and Climatol. Assn., 1977, award Environ. Mutagen Soc., 1981, E.B. Wilson medal Am. Soc. Cell Biology, 1984, Bonfils-Stanton award in sci., 1984, U. Colo. Disting. Prof. award, 1987, Henry M. Porter medal, 1992; named to The Colo. 100, Historic Denver, 1992; Heritage Found. scholar, 1983; Phi Beta Kappa scholar, 1985; Fogarty Internat. scholar NIH, 1997. Fellow Am. Acad. Arts and Scis.; mem. Am. Soc. Human Genetics, Am. Chem. Soc., Soc. Exptl. Biology and Medicine, AAAS (Phi Beta Kappa award and lectr. 1983), Am. Assn. Immunologists, Radiation Research Soc., Biophys. Soc., Genetics Soc. Am., Nat. Acad. Sci., Tissue Culture Assn. (Hon. award 1987), Paideia Group, Santa Fe Inst. Sci. Bd., Phi Beta Kappa, Sigma Xi. Office: Eleanor Roosevelt Inst Cancer Rsch 1899 Gaylord St Denver CO 80206-1210 *Our age is threatened by distorted emphasis on power, material wealth, and competitiveness, and by an explosive increase in population which exceeds our traditional regulative capacities. But it also holds promise for new and profound understanding of ourselves - of our basic human biological intellectual and emotional needs. There is room for hope.*

PUCKETT, MARTHA LOUISE, publishing company executive; b. Alamance, N.C.; d. Clarence Edgar and Enzie J. (Allen) Councilman; m. Melvin Duane Puckett, Sept. 25, 1953; children: Cynthia Lynne Puckett Backus, Craig Duane Puckett, Melody Kae Puckett Grant, Tamara Sue Puckett Blackmore. BA, Owosso Bible Coll., 1952; BS, Pacific Christian Coll., 1980. Accredited record technician Am. Med. Record Assn. Gospel singer in trio in so. states, 1947-49; nurse aide Owosso (Mich.) Meml. Hosp., 1949-52; dir. med. records Garden Park Gen. Hosp., Anaheim, Calif., 1957-71, Humana West Anaheim Hosp., 1971-86; pres., CEO, Channel Pub., Ltd., Reno, 1987—, Reno Diamonds Baseball, 1993—, Crowne Emerald Pubs., Inc., Reno, 1995—. Chmn. bd. trustees Childrens' Outreach Ministries, 1990—. Home: 1800 Aquila Ave Reno NV 89509 Office: Channel Pub Ltd 4750 Longley Ln Ste 110 Reno NV 89502-5981

PUCKETT, PAUL DAVID, electronics company executive; b. Atlanta, July 31, 1941; s. Jonas Levi and Ovella (Juhan) P.; m. Margaret Ann Straetz, June 29, 1974, (div. Jan. 1984); m. Catherine Marie Ryan, Apr. 5, 1984; children: Shawn Michael, Glen David. BS in Edn., Nyack Coll., 1963; MBA in Mgmt., Pace U., 1988. Mgr. quality Rockland Systems Corp., Blauvelt, N.Y., 1971-75, Electronics for Medicine, Inc., White Plains, N.Y., 1975-77; mgr. ops. Tele-Resources, Inc., Armonk, N.Y., 1977-79; mgr. quality Materials Rsch. Corp., Orangeberg, N.Y., 1979-83; mgr. quality plasma systems div. Perkin-Elmer, Wilton, Conn., 1983-84, dir. ops. plasma systems div., 1984-86, mgr. spl. studies semiconductor group, 1986-87; mgr. quality programs instrument group Perkin-Elmer, Norwalk, Conn., 1987-90; dir. ops. applied sci. div. Perkin-Elmer (sold applied sci. div. to Orbital Scis. Corp.), Pomona, Calif., 1990-93; dir. ops. Pomona (Calif.) ops. Orbital Scis. Corp., 1993—; examiner Malcolm Baldrige Nat. Quality award, Gathersberg, Md., 1989-90, Conn. State Quality award, Stamford, 1988-90, cons., trainer, 1990. Contbr. articles to profl. jours. Mem. Young Reps., New City, N.Y., 1975-76; vol. police officer Rockland County Sheriff's Dept., New City, 1974-83; coach Am. Youth Soccer Orgn., Bethel, Conn., 1984-85. Recipient Conn. State Quality award, 1989. Mem. N.Y. Acad. Sci., Am. Soc. Quality Control, Assn. for Quality and Participation, Am. Electronics Assn. Republican. Episcopalian. Home: 1500 Mansfield Ct Upland CA 91784-7963 Office: Orbital Scis Corp Pomona Ops 2771 N Garey Ave Pomona CA 91767-1809

PUCKETT, RICHARD EDWARD, artist, consultant, retired recreation executive; b. Klamath Falls, Oreg., Sept. 9, 1932; s. Vernon Elijah and Leona Belle (Clevenger) P.; m. Velma Faye Hamrick, Apr. 14, 1957 (dec. 1985); children: Katherine Michelle Briggs, Deborah Alison Bolinger, Susan Lin Rowland, Gregory Richard. Student So. Oreg. Coll. Edn., 1951-56, Lake Forest Coll., 1957-58; Hartnell Jr. Coll., 1960-70; B.A., U. San Francisco, 1978. Acting arts and crafts dir., Fort Leonard Wood, Mo., 1956-57; arts and crafts dir., asst. spl. svcs. officer, mus. dir., Fort Sheridan, Ill., 1957-59; arts and crafts dir., Fort Irwin, Calif., 1959-60, Fort Ord, Calif., 1960-86; dir. arts and crafts br. Art Gallery, Arts and Crafts Center Materials Sales Store, 1960; opening dir. Presidio Monterey Army Mus., 1968; dir. Model Army Arts and Crafts Program. Recipient First Place, Dept. Army and U.S. Army Forces Command awards for programming and publicity, 1979-81, 83-85, 1st and 3d place sculpture awards Monterey County Fair Fine Arts Exhibit, 1979, Comdrs. medal civilian svcs., 1986, other awards, Golden Acad. award, Internat. Man of Yr. award, 1991-92. Mem. Monterey Peninsula Art Assn., Salinas Fine Arts Assn., Rogue Valley Art Assn., Fort Ord Alumni Assn. One-man shows: Seaside City Hall, 1975, Fort Ord Arts and Crafts Center Gallery, 1967, 73, 79, 81, 84, 86, Presidio of Monterey Art Gallery, 1979, Rogue Valley Art Assn., Salinas Valley Art Gallery; Glass on Holiday, Gatlinburg, Tenn., 1981, 82; exhbns. in Mo., Ill., and pvt. collections; designed and opened first Ft. Sheridan Army Mus., Presidio of Monterey Mus. Home: 110 Ashland Ave Medford OR 97504-7523 also: 1152 Jean Ave Salinas CA 93905-3321

PUCKLE, DONNE ERVING, priest; b. London, June 17, 1940; came to U.S., 1946; s. Raymond Donne Aufrere and Elizabeth (Price) P.; m. Lola Rose Avery, June 24, 1972; children: Donne Edward Christopher, Elizabeth Berry Rose. AA, Phoenix Coll., 1960; BA, Ariz. State U., 1962; MDiv, Bexley Hall, Rochester, N.Y., 1966; M in Counseling, U. Phoenix, 1994. Priest, rector St. John's Ch., Bisbee, Ariz., 1967-73; priest, vicar Grace Episcopal Ch., Lake Havasu City, Ariz., 1973-76; asst. priest Christ Episcopal Ch., Lacrosse, Wis., 1976-78; priest, rector Trinity Episcopal Ch., Mattoon, Ill., 1979-81, Christ Episcopal Ch., Chippewa Falls, Wis., 1981-90; priest St. John's Episcopal Ch., Bisbee, 1993—; asst. chaplain L.E. Phillips Treatment Ctr., Chippewa Falls, 1981-90; acad. dean, instr. Episcopal Sch. Ch. Studies, Eau Claire, Wis., 1987-90; counselor U.S. Salvation Army, Tucson, 1993-94; cons. Standing Liturgical Commn., N.Y.C., 1976-79; mem. Pub. Health Adv. Bd., Chippewa Falls, 1986-89, Diocesan Exec. coun., Eau Claire, 1982-90, Anglican/Roman Catholic Dialogue, Springfield, Ill., 1979-81; counselor single parent program Cochise C.C., Douglas, Ariz., 1995—. Author: Winter Sunday in Norway, Maine, 1990 (award 1992), Ceremonial Guide for Lent and Holy Week, 1980; editor: Prayers for Advent, Christmas and Epiphany, 1972. Coord. food pantry Chippewa Falls, 1984-90; mem. dist. com. Boy Scouts Am., Chippewa Falls, 1986-88; chmn. Red Cross County Bd., Chippewa Falls, 1985-90. Recipient award Am. Bible Soc., 1966. Mem. ACA, Nat. Assn. Alcohol and Drug Abuse Counselors, Soc. of Holy Cross, Mensa, Delta Psi Omega, Phi Theta Kappa. Democrat. Home: 125 Kayetan Dr NE Sierra Vista AZ 85635-1117

PUDER, JANICE, special education educator; b. Phila., Apr. 6, 1950; d. Allen Thrasher and Dorothy Ruth (Mathis) P.; foster child: Corienna Gallagher. AA, Pasadena (Calif.) City Coll., 1970; BA, U. Calif., Chico, 1973; postgrad., U. Calif./Chico and San Jose,, U. Pacific, 1973-74, 82; MA in Spl. Edn., Santa Clara U., 1996. Cert. elem./secondary edn. tchr., spl. edn., Calif.; cert. early childhood intervention. Tchr. New Covenant Christian H.S., Palo Alto, Calif., 1977-81; spl. edn. tchr. Sunnyvale (Calif.) Christian Jr. and Sr. H.S., 1981-82; adapted phys. edn. and cons. to spl. edn. local plan area 3 Santa Clara County Office Edn., 1983-92, adapted phys. edn. specialist, 1992—. Vol. Christian Counseling. Mem. PEO. Home: 575 Tyndall St # 6 Los Altos CA 94022

PUDNEY, GARY LAURENCE, television executive; b. Mpls., July 20, 1934; s. Lawrence D. and Agnes (Hansen) P. BA, UCLA, 1956. V.p. ABC, Inc., N.Y.C., 1968—; v.p., sr. exec. in charge of spls. and talent ABC Entertainment, 1979-89; pres. The Gary L. Pudney Co., Beverly Hills, Calif., 1988—; chief oper. officer Paradigm Entertainment, Beverly Hills, 1989-92; xec. producer World Music Awards, ABC-TV, 1993, World's Greatest Magic, NBC-TV, 1994—, Grand Illusions, 1994, Caesar's World Entertainment, 1994-95, Lance Burton and Houdini, NBC-TV, 1995, Champions of Magic, ABC-TV, 1996, Hidden Secrets of Magic, NBC-TV, 1996, 30th Anniversary, Ceasars Palace-ABC, Happy Birthday Elizabeth-A Celebration of Life. Exec. producer for United Cerebral Palsy Aspen and Lake Tahoe Pro-Celebrity Tennis Festivals, 4 yrs., AIDS Project L.A. Dinner, 1985, The 25th Anniversary of the L.A. Music Ctr. Bd. dirs. nat. Cerebral Palsy Found., Ctr. Theatre Group Ahmanson Theatre, L.A., Ctr. Theatre Group of L.A. Music Ctr.; mem. bd. La Quinta Arts Found., 1991—. Recipient Helena T. Deveraux Meml. award, 1985, Humanitarian award Nat. Jewish Ctr. for Immunology and Respiratory Medicine, 1986, Gift of Love award Nat. Ctr. Hyperactive Children, 1988, Winner award Excellence The L.A. Film Adv. Bd. Mem. Hollywood Radio and TV Soc. (bd. dirs.), Acad. TV Arts and Scis. (exec. com.), Met. Mus. Art, Mus. Modern Art. Democrat. Lutheran.

PUENTE, TITO ANTHONY, orchestra leader, composer, arranger; b. N.Y.C., Apr. 20, 1923; s. Ernest Anthony and Ercilia (Ortiz) P.; m. Margaret Asencio, Oct. 19, 1963; children: Ronald, Audrey, Tito Anthony. Student, Julliard Conservatory Music, N.Y. Sch. Music, Schillinger System; MusD (hon.), SUNY, Albany, 1987. Orch. leader appearing in numerous night clubs and ballrooms, throughout U.S., 1949—; appeared in Woody Allen's Radio Days, John Candy's Armed & Dangerous, 1986-87; recorded 96 albums; appeared in concert Red Sea Jazz Festival, Israel, all major jazz festivals, including Montreaux, Monterey, Munich, North Sea, others, Tribute in P.R., 1986, Los Angeles Ford Theatre Tribute, 1987; composer Para Los Rumberos, 1960, Oye Como Va, 1962, numerous other works recorded with Dizzy Gillespie, Lionel Hampton, George Shearing, Woody Herman, other major jazz artists; sold out performance Radio City Music Hall & Apollo Theatre, 1986; appeared Madison Square Garden, N.Y.C., 1986, Los Angeles Amphitheatre, 1986, on Bill Cosby Show, 1987, Regis Philbin, Bill Boggs shows, 1987; guest artist with Bklyn. Philharmonic Symphony Orch., N.Y. and Phila., 1987. Founder T. Puente Scholarship fund, 1980. Served with USN, 1942-45. Recipient Bronze medallion City of N.Y., 1969, Key to City Los Angeles, 1976, Key to City of Chgo., 1985, Key to City of Miami, 1986; named Musician of Month on several occasions by Downbeat, Metronome, Playboy and trade mags., 1950's; named King of Latin Music, La Prensa newspaper, 1955; his band named Best Latin Am. Orch. New York Daily News, 1977; recipient 6 Grammy nominations, Grammy award, 1978, 83, 85, 90; N.Y. Music award, 1986. Office: Thomas Cassidy Inc 11761 E Speedway Blvd Tucson AZ 85748*

PUGAY, JEFFREY IBANEZ, mechanical engineer; b. San Francisco, June 26, 1958; s. Herminio Salazar and Petronila (Ibanez) P. BSME, U. Calif., Berkeley, 1981, MSME, 1982; MBA, Pepperdine U., 1986, MS in Tech. Mgmt., 1991. Registered profl. engr., Calif. Engring. asst. Lawrence Berkeley Nat. Lab., 1978-80; assoc. tech. staff Aerospace Corp., L.A., 1981; tech. staff Hughes Space & Comm. Co., El Segundo, Calif., 1982-85, from project engr. to project mgr., 1985-95; mgr. spaceway program mktg. Hughes Comm. Inc., Long Beach, Calif., 1995-97, dir. bus. devel., 1997—. Active ARC Emergency Svcs. White House Fellow regional finalist, 1991, 92. Mem. ASME, Soc. Competitor Intelligence Profls., Am. Mgmt. Assn., L.A. World Affairs Coun., Make A Wish Found., Pi Tau Sigma, Delta Mu Delta. Republican. Roman Catholic. Home: 8180 Manitoba St Apt 120 Playa Del Rey CA 90293-8651 Office: Hughes Comms Inc PO Box 9712 Long Beach CA 90810-9928

PUGH, KYLE MITCHELL, JR., musician, retired music educator; b. Spokane, Wash., Jan. 6, 1937; s. Kyle Mitchel, Sr. and Lenore Fae (Johnson) P.; m. Susan Deane Waite, July 16, 1961; children: Jeffray, Kari. BA in Edu., East Wash. U., 1975. Cert. tchr., Wash. Tuba player Spokane Symphony Orch., 1958-63; rec. assoc. Century Records, Spokane, 1965-73; tuba player World's Fair Expo '74, Spokane, 1974; bass player Russ Carlyle Orch., Las Vegas, 1976, Many Sounds of Nine Orch., northwest area, 1969-81; band tchr. Garry Jr. High School, Spokane, 1976-79, Elementary Band Program, Spokane, 1979-96; bass player Doug Scott Cabaret Band, Spokane, 1982-91; dept. head Elem. Band Dept., Spokane, 1984-89. Editor (newsletter) The Repeater, 1987 (Amateur Radio News Svc. award 1987); extra in movie Always, 1989. Active in communications Lilac Bloomsday Assn., Spokane, 1977. Served to E-5 USNR, 1955-63. Recipient Disting. Service award Wash. State Commn., 1974, Nev. Hollerin' Champ Carl Hayden Scribe, 1979. Mem. Am. Fedn. Musicians (life), Spokane Edn. Assn. (rec. sec. 1987), Music Educator's Nat. Conf., Am. Radio Relay League (asst. dir. 1987), Ea. Wash. Music Educator's Assn. (pres. 1978-79), Dial Twisters Club (pres. 1979-80), VHF Radio Amateurs (dir. 1980-83), Elks, Moose. Home: 5006 W Houston Ave Spokane WA 99208-3728 Office: Elem Mus Office 503 W 4th Ave Spokane WA 99204-2603

PUGLIESE, JOHN DAVID, mechanical engineer, consultant, programmer; b. San Jose, Calif., Apr. 5, 1966; s. Joseph Anthony and Linda Jeanette (Hodgkins) P. BSME, Calif. Poly. State U., San Luis Obispo, 1990. Registered engr.-in-tng., Calif. Engring. aide NASA Ames Rsch. Ctr., Moffett Field, Calif., 1987-88, Treese & Assocs., Santa Barbara, Calif., 1990; field application engr. Minarik Electric Co., Portland, Oreg., 1990-93; engr., trainer, instr. Berkeley Process Control, Richmond, Calif., 1993-95; engr. Parker Compumotor, Rohnert Park, Calif., 1993—; cons. Computer Reporting Svc., San Jose, Calif., 1992—; instr. seminars on motion control topics, 1992. Mem. Order of Omega. Home: 655 Enterprise Dr # 21 Rohnert Park CA 94928 Office: Compumotor 5500 Business Park Dr Rohnert Park CA 94928

PUGLIESE, VINCENT JOSEPH ALFRED, manufacturing executive; b. Washington, Apr. 9, 1962; s. Vincent Augustus and Judith Ann (Excog) P.; m. Nancy Lynne Baker Pugliese, Jan. 9, 1987; children: Amanda Lynne, Andrea Gail. BS in Adminstrn., Mgmt. Sci., Carnegie Mellon U., Pitts., 1984; BS in Applied Math., Carnegie Mellon U., 1984; MBA, U. Balt., 1989. Indsl. engr. Westinghouse Electric Corp., Balt., 1984-87, mfg. engr., 1987-88, sr. mfg. engr., 1988-89, mfg. ops. program mgr., 1989-92; ops. mgr. Edge Emitter Tech., Inc., Fremont, Calif., 1992-94, project mgr. Hewlett Packard, Fremont, 1994-96; equipment enging. mgr. Hewlett Packard assignment Candescent Techs., Inc., San Jose, Calif., 1996—. Office: Hewlett Packard 2667 Torrey Ct Pleasanton CA 94588 also: Candescent Techs Inc 6500 Via Del Oro San Jose CA 95119

PUGMIRE, GREGG THOMAS, optical engineer; b. Montpelier, Idaho, Sept. 23, 1963; s. Vaughn Rich and Yvonne (Thomas) P.; m. Linda Lee Harris, July 17, 1987; children: Lindsay, Stephanie, Sydney. BS, MS, Brigham Young U., 1990. Summer rsch. engr. Nat. Security Agy., Ft. Meade, Md., 1988; rsch. asst. Brigham Young U., Provo, Utah, 1988-90; optical engr., scientist TRW Inc., Sunnyvale, Calif., 1990—; 1993 conf. presenter in field. Engring. scholar Brigham Young U., 1989-90. Mem. Optical Soc. Am., Golden Key, Eta Kappa Nu. Mem. LDS Ch. Home: 1765 Cunningham St Santa Clara CA 95050-4069 Office: TRW Inc 495 E Java Dr Sunnyvale CA 94089-1125

PUGSLEY, ROBERT ADRIAN, legal educator; b. Mineola, N.Y., Dec. 27, 1946; s. Irvin Harold and Mary Catherine (Brusselars) P. BA, SUNY-Stony Brook, 1968; JD, NYU, 1975, LLM in Criminal Justice, 1977. Instr. sociology New Sch. Social Rsch., N.Y.C., 1969-71; coordinator Peace Edn. programs The Christophers, N.Y.C., 1971-78; assoc. prof. law Southwestern U., L.A., 1978-81, prof., 1981—; adj. asst. prof. criminology and criminal justice Southampton Coll.-Long Island U., 1975-76; acting dep. dir. Criminal Law Edn. and Rsch. Ctr., NYU, 1983-86; bd. advisors Ctr. Legal Edn. CCNY-CUNY, 1978, Sta. KPFK-FM, 1985-86; founder, coordinator The Wednesday Evening Soc., L.A., 1979-86; vis. prof. Jacob D. Fuchsberg Law Ctr. Touro Coll., L.I., N.Y., summers 1988, 89; lectr. in criminal law and procedure Legal Edn. Conf. Ctr., L.A., 1982-96; lectr. legal profl. responsibility West Bar Rev. Faculty, Calif., 1996—; legal analyst/commentator for print and electronic media, 1992—. Creative advisor Christopher Closeup (nationally syndicated pub. svc. TV program), 1975-83; host Earth Alert, Cable TV, 1983-87; producer, moderator (pub. affairs discussion program) Inside L.A., Sta. KPFK-FM, 1979-86, Open Jour. program, Sta. KPFK-FM, 1991-94; contbr. articles to legal jours. Founding mem. Southwestern U. Pub. Interest Law com., 1992—; mem. L.A. County Bar Assn. Adv. Com. on Alcohol & Drug Abuse, 1991-95, co-chair, 1993-95; mem. exec. com. nongovtl. orgns. UN Office of Pub. Info., 1977; mem. issues task force L.A. Conservancy, 1980-81, seminar for law tchrs. NEH UCLA, 1979; co-convener So. Calif. Coalition Against Death Penalty, 1981-83, convener, 1983-84; mem. death penalty com. Lawyer's Support Group, Amnesty Internat. U.S.A.; founding mem. Ch.-State Coun., L.A., 1984-88. Robert Marshall fellow Criminal Law Edn. and Rsch. Ctr., NYU Sch. Law, 1976-78; bd. dirs. Equal Rights Sentencing Found., 1983-85, Earth Alert Inc., 1984-87; mem. adv. bd. First Amendment Info. Resources Ctr., Grad. Sch. of Libr. and Info. Sci., UCLA, 1990—; mem. coun. Friends UCLA Libr., 1993—, pres., 1996—. Mem. Am. Legal Studies Assn., Am. Soc. Polit. and Legal Philosophy, Assn. Am. Law Schs., Inst. Soc. Ethics and Life Scis., Soc. Am. Law Tchrs., Internat. Platform Assn., The Scribes. Democrat. Roman Catholic. Office: Southwestern U Sch Law 675 S Westmoreland Ave Rm 410 Los Angeles CA 90005-3905 Address: PO Box 440 East Hampton NY 11937

PULCRANO, DAN MICHAEL, newspaper and online services executive; b. New Brunswick, N.J., Oct. 1, 1958; s. Charles A. and Edith (Tanner) Ostern. BA in Journalism and Newspaper Mgmt., U. Calif., Santa Cruz, 1980. Reporter Santa Barbara (Calif.) News & Rev., 1978; asst. to pub. L.A. Weekly, 1978, 79; editor, pub. Santa Cruz (Calif.) Weekly, 1981, Los Gatos (Calif.) Weekly, 1982-84; editor Metro, San Jose, Calif., 1985-93, 95—; exec. editor Los Gatos Weekly-Times, Saratoga News, Willow Glen Resident, Cupertino Courier, Sunnvale Sun, Metro Santa Cruz, San Francisco Met., Sonoma County Independent, 1990—; pres., CEO Metro Pub., Inc., San Jose, 1992—, Virtual Valley, Inc., San Jose, 1993—; pres. Boulevards New Media Inc., 1996—. Founding pres., bd. mem. San Jose Downtown Assn., 1986-95. Recipient Disting. Svc. award Oakes Coll., 1980; named Dist. Honoree City of San Jose, Dist. 3, 1989. Mem. Calif. Free Press Assn. (pres. 1991-92), Assn. Alternative Newspapers (v.p. 1993-94, bd. dirs.s 1993-95), Rotary. Home: PO Box 7 San Jose CA 95103-0007 Office: Metro Newspapers 550 S 1st St San Jose CA 95113-2806

PULIDO, MARK A., pharmaceutical and cosmetics company executive; b. 1953. McKesson Drug Co., 1975-88; Exec. v.p. FoxMeyer Drug Co., 1988-89; chmn., pres., CEO Red Line Healthcare Corp., 1989-96; pres., CEO Sandoz Pharmaceuticals Corp., 1994-95; pres., CEO, dir. McKesson Corp., 1996—. Office: McKesson Corp 1 Post St San Francisco CA 94104

PULIDO, MIGUEL, mayor; b. Mexico City, 1956; m. Laura Pulido; 1 child, Miguel Robert. BSME, Calif. State U., Fullerton. Dir. computer program McCaughey & Smith Energy Assocs., v.p.; mem. Santa Ana (Calif.) City Coun., 1986—; mayor City of Santa Ana, 1994—; mem. Santa Ana Redevel. Agy., Downtown Santa Ana Bus. Assn.; mem. 1st dist. Orange County Transp. Authority. Office: 20 Civic Ctr Plz PO Box 1988 Santa Ana CA 92702

PULLEN, RICK DARWIN, dean; b. Bandon, Oreg., Apr. 23, 1945; s. Harold Darwin and Dorothy May (Stevens) P.; m. Jill Anne Gray, Sept. 23, 1967; children: Melinda Rose, Reid Victor, Erica Joy. BA, Linfield Coll., 1967, MEd, 1968; PhD, So. Ill. U., 1973. Sports editor McMinnville (Oreg.) News-Register, 1967-68; tchr. David Douglas H.S., Portland, Oreg., 1968-70; prof. Calif. State U., Fullerton, 1973-90, assoc. dean, 1991-95, acting dean, 1995-96, dean, 1996—. Author: Keeping It Legal, 1989, 91; co-author: Mass Media Law in California, 1979, 81, Major Principles of Media Law, 1982, 86. Named Outstanding Journalism Prof. in Calif., Calif. Newspaper Pubs. Assn., Sacramento, 1982; Sabbatical scholar Reporters Com. for Freedom of the Press, Washington, 1984. Mem. Assn. for Edn. in Journalism and Mass Comm., Soc. Profl. Journalists. Republican. Office: Calif State Univ Fullerton Sch Comm PO Box 34080 Fullerton CA 92834

PULLIAM, FRANCINE SARNO, real estate broker and developer; b. San Francisco, Sept. 14, 1937; d. Ralph C. Stevens and Frances I. (Wilson) Sarno; m. John Donald Pulliam, Aug. 14, 1957 (div. Mar. 1965); 1 child, Wendy; m. Terry Kent Graves, Dec. 14, 1974. Student, U. Ariz., 1955-56, U. Nev., Las Vegas, 1957. Airline stewardess Bonanza Airlines, Las Vegas, 1957; real estate agt. The Pulliam Co., Las Vegas, 1958-68, Levy Realty, Las Vegas, 1976-76; real estate broker, owner Prestige Properties, Las Vegas, 1976—; importer, exporter Exports Internat., Las Vegas, 1984—; bd. dirs. Citicorp Bank of Nev.; mem. adv. bd. to Amb. to Bahamas Chic Hect. Bd. dirs. Las Vegas Bd. Realtors, Fedn. Internat. Realtors, Nat. Kidney Found., Assistance League, Cancer Soc., Easter Seals, Econ. Rsch. Bd., Children's Discovery Mus., New Horizons Ctr. for Children with Learning Disabilities, Girl Scouts, Home of the Good Shepard, St. Jude's Ranch for Homeless Children; pres., bd. dirs. Better Bus. Bur.; chmn. Las Vegas Taxi Cab Authority; pres. Citizens for Pvt. Enterprises. Mem. Las Vegas C. of C. (bd. dirs., developer). Republican. Roman Catholic. Office: 2340 Paseo Del Prado Ste D202 Las Vegas NV 89102-4341

PURAT, JACEK, library director; b. Poznan, Poland, Nov. 8, 1957; came to U.S., 1981; s. Czeskaw and Boleskawa (Wizta) P.; m. Katie Mangotich, May 1, 1986; children: Nemo, Felix, Jan. BA, U. Poznan, 1981. Animal keeper Poznan Zoo, 1980, U. Calif. Amphibian Lab., Berkeley, 1985; exec. dir. Green Libr., Berkeley, 1986—; chmn. of bd. Ecol. Libr., Poznan, 1988—, Green Libr., Inc., Berkeley, 1988—; spl. advisor to minister of environment Min. Environ. Protection, Warsaw, Polan d, 1992; researcher dept. geography Ocean Initiative, U. Calif., Berkeley, 1993. Founder, publisher: Green Libr. Jour., 1991. Pres. N. Calif. div. Polish Am. Congress, San Francisco, 1991-92, chmn. Environ. Commn., Chgo., 1991-92. Recipient scholarship Kosciuszko Found.; named Honorary Citizen Poznan, 1990. Mem. Nature Protection League. Home: 1929 Fairview St Apt A Berkeley CA 94703-2718 Office: Green Libr PO Box 11284 Berkeley CA 94701

PURCELL, JOHN F., lawyer; b. Bellingham, Wash., Apr. 25, 1954. AB with honors, Stanford U., 1976; JD, Lewis and Clark Coll., 1980. Bar: Oreg. 1980. Ptnr. Miller, Nash, Wiener, Hager & Carlsen, Portland. Mem. Oreg. State Bar. Office: Miller Nash Wiener Hager & Carlsen 111 SW 5th Ave Portland OR 97204-3604

PURCELL, KEVIN BROWN, elementary school principal; b. Longview, Wash., Apr. 17, 1955; s. Wayne Donald and Joyce Elizabeth (Brown) P.; m. Carol Lynn Vincent, Mar. 29, 1980; children: Keelan Kathryn, Kelly Jean. BA, Western Wash. U., 1980; MS, Western Oreg. State Coll., Monmouth, 1986; degree in Ednl. Adminstrn., Portland (Oreg.) State U., 1989. Tchr. multiply handicapped Yamhill County Sch. Dist., McMinnville, Oreg., 1980-83; learning resource tchr. Newberg (Oreg.) Sch. Dist., 1983-89, asst. prin., 1989-91; prin. Dayton (Oreg.) Sch. Dist., 1991—. Mem. Nat. Assn. Elem. Prins., Assn. Supervision and Curriculum Devel., Oreg. Assn. Elem. Prins., Confedn. Oreg. Sch. Adminstrs. Democrat. Roman Catholic. Home: 2103 Haworth Ave Newberg OR 97132-1330 Office: Dayton Grade School 526 Ferry St Dayton OR 97114-9706

PURDY, KEVIN M., estate planner; b. Escondido, Calif., Jan. 26, 1952; s. Kenneth C. and Helen M. (Moore) P.; m. Janice M. Cook, May 12, 1982. BA in Philosophy, Psychology, U. Redlands, 1974. CFP. Pres. Timeline Pub., San Diego, Calif., 1980-90; estate planner CIGNA Fin. Advisors, San Diego, Calif., 1990—; pub. speaker. Author: A Brief History of the Earth and Mankind, 1986, A Brief History of Mankind, 1987. Fundraiser San Diego Hist. Soc., 1993-94. Office: CIGNA Fin Advisers 4275 Executive Sq Ste 400 La Jolla CA 92037-1476

PURDY, TEDDY GEORGE, JR., programmer, analyst, researcher, consultant; b. Leadville, Colo., May 11, 1954; s. Teddy George and Geneva Ruth Purdy; m. Karen Ann Puleo, May 28, 1977 (div. Dec. 19, 1983); children: Christopher, Sarah. Student, Colo. U., 1972-75. Free-lance programmer/analyst Boulder, Colo., 1975-84; pres., treas. IBEX Bus. Systems, Leadville, 1984—; cons. Carlson Promotions, Mpls., 1987-91, Unidata, Inc., Denver, 1992, Household Fin., Chesapeake, Va., 1992—, Focus Tech., Dallas, 1992—.

PURSEL, HAROLD MAX, SR., mining engineer, civil engineer, architectural engineer.; b. Fruita, Colo., Sept. 15, 1921; s. Harold Maurice and Viola Pearl (Wagner) P.; m. Virginia Anna Brady, May 6, 1950; children: Harold Max, Leo William, Dawn Allen, Helen Virginia, Viola Ruth. BS in Civil Engring., U. Wyo., 1950. Asst. univ. architect U. Wyo., 1948-50; with Sharrock & Pursel, Contractors, 1951-55; owner Max Pursel, Earthwork Constrn., 1955-59; project engr. Farson (Wyo.) Irrigation Project, 1960-61; owner Wyo. Builders Service, Casper, 1962-66; head dept. home improvement Gamble Stores, Rawlins, Wyo., 1967; resident work instr. Casper (Wyo.) Job Corps Conservation Center, 1968; P.M. coordinator Lucky Mc Uranium Mine, Riverton, Wyo., 1969-80; constrn. insp. U.S. Bur. Reclamation, 1983—; cons. freelance heavy and light constrn., 1984—. Served with U.S. Army, 1942-45. Mem. Nat. Rifle Assn., Internat. Platform Assn., Mensa. Lodges: Eagles, Masons, Shriners. Exptl. research with log, timber and frame constrn. in conjunction with residential applications.; expanded experimental research to develop methods to up-date and modernize early area residences while retaining period styles, materials and general construction methods. Home: PO Box 572 Riverton WY 82501-0572

PURSGLOVE, BETTY MERLE, small business owner, technical writer, quality assurance tester; b. Pitts., Sept. 15, 1923; d. Earle E. and Merle A. (Smith) Baer; m. Larry A. Pursglove, June 30, 1944; children: Diana, Kathleen, Merry, Tanya, Yvonne. BS in Physics, U. Pitts., 1944; postgrad., Minn. U., 1945-47, Carnegie-Mellon U., 1947-49, W.Va. U., 1949-51, Mich. State U., 1968-69. Micro-pilot plant operator Minn. Mining and Mfg., St. Paul, 1944-46; cons. rsch. chemist Food Mach Co., Pitts., 1947-49; computer coder Dow Chem. Co., Midland, Minn., 1954; asst. entomologist pvt. collections, Midland, 1955-56; instr. chemistry Cen. Mich. U., Midland, 1958; head chem. dept. Midland Hosp., 1958-64; tchr. chemistry and physics parochial schs., Bay City, Mich., 1964; prin., chief exec. officer Crypticlear, Inc., Applegate, Oreg., 1965—. Leader Midland troup Girl Scout U.S., 1953-63. Mem. AAUW, Sigma Xi, Sigma Pi Sigma. Home and Office: PO Box 3125 Applegate OR 97530-3125

PURSGLOVE, LAURENCE A., technical writer, computer quality tester; b. Monongahela, Pa., July 29, 1924; s. Laurence Edwards and Gladys Leona (Spencer) P.; m. Betty Merle Baer, June 30, 1944; children: Diana, Kathleen, Merry, Tanya, Yvonne. BSChE, Carnegie Inst. Tech., Pitts., 1944, MSChE, 1946, ScD in Organic Chemistry, 1949. Cert. U.S. patent agt. Designer of pilot plant Minn. Mining & Mfg. Co., St. Paul, 1944-46; asst. prof. chemistry W.Va. U., Morgantown, 1949-53; rsch. chemist Dow Chem. Co., Midland, Mich., 1953-58; asst. prof. dept. chemistry Delta Coll., University Center, Mich., 1958-63; tech. writer Am. Petroleum Inst., Dallas, 1964-74, Entelek, Newburyport, Mass., 1975-89, Mich. Nat. Bank, Lansing, 1970-89, IBM, Santa Clara, Calif., 1990-92; software quality assurance tester Aristacom Internat., Alameda, Calif., 1993-96; tech. writer Oreg. Dept. Transp., Salem, 1996-97; translator Chem. Abstracts, Ohio, 1950-63. Contbr. articles to profl. jours.; patentee chem. products. Mem. Am. Chem. Soc., Sigma Xi, Phi Lambda Upsilon. Libertarian. Unitarian. Home: Box 3125 Applegate OR 97530 Office: Crypticlear Inc Box 3125 Applegate OR 97530

PURTILL, RICHARD LAWRENCE, philosopher, writer; b. Chgo., May 12, 1931; s. Joseph T. Purtill; m. Elizabeth Banks, June 20, 1959; children: Mark, Timothy, Steven. BA, U. Chgo., 1958, MA, 1960, PhD, 1965. From asst. prof. to prof. philosophy Western Wash. U., Bellingham, 1962—. Author: Logic for Philosophers, 1971, Thinking About Ethics, 1976, C.S. Lewis's Case for the Christian Faith, 1981, Enchantment at Delphi, 1986, others. Pres. The Alexander Nevsky Fund, Bellingham. Sgt. U.S. Army, 1949-52. Mem. Am. Writers Union, Authors Guild, Sierra Club. Roman Catholic. Office: Western Wash U Philosphy Dept Bellingham WA 98225

PURVIS, JOHN ANDERSON, lawyer; b. Greeley, Colo., Aug. 31, 1942; s. Virgil J. and Emma Lou (Anderson) P.; m. Charlotte Johnson, Apr. 3, 1976; 1 child, Whitney; children by previous marriage: Jennifer, Matt. B.A. cum laude, Harvard U., 1965; J.D., U. Colo., 1968. Bar: Colo. 1968, U.S. Dist. Ct. Colo. 1968, U.S. Ct. Appeals (10th cir.) 1978, U.S. Ct. Claims, 1980. Dep. dist. atty. Boulder, Colo., 1968-69; asst. dir. and dir. legal aid U. Colo. Sch. Law, 1969; assoc. Williams, Taussig & Trine, Boulder, 1969; head Boulder office Colo. Pub. Defender System, 1970-72; assoc. and ptnr. Hutchinson, Black, Hill, Buchanan & Cook, Boulder, 1972-85; ptnr. Purvis, Gray, Schuetze and Gordon, 1985—; acting Colo. State Pub. Defender, 1978; adj. prof. law U. Colo., 1981, 84-88, 94, others; lectr. in field. Chmn., Colo. Pub. Defender Commn., 1979-89; mem. nominating commn. Colo. Supreme Ct., 1984-90; mem. com. on conduct U.S. Dist. Ct., 1993—, chmn., 1996—; chmn. Boulder County Criminal Justice Com., 1975-81, Boulder County Manpower Coun., 1977-78. Recipient Ames award Harvard U., 1964; Outstanding Young Lawyer award Colo. Bar Assn., 1978. Mem. Internat. Soc. Barristers, Am. Coll. of Trial Lawyers, Colo. Bar Assn. (chair litigation sect. 1994-95), Boulder County Bar Assn., Colo. Trial Lawyers Assn., Am. Trial Lawyers Assn., Trial Lawyers for Pub. Justice. Democrat. Address: 1050 Walnut St Ste 501 Boulder CO 80302-5144

PUSATERI, RICHARD ANTHONY, minister, naval chaplain; b. Albany, N.Y., Apr. 13, 1951; s. Frank Anthony and Alma Loreen (Swanson) P.; m. Sandra Lee Ambrose, Apr. 18, 1987; children: Dorothy, Thomas, John, Lydia. BA, Case Western Reserve U., 1973; MS, Syracuse U., 1974; MDiv, Vanderbilt U., 1979; MA, Salve Regina U., 1992. Ordained elder United Meth. Ch., 1981, full mem. Tenn. Ann. Conf. Libr. Scarritt Coll., Nashville, 1974-77; pastor Pegram (Tenn.) United Meth. Ch., 1977-81; campus minister Wesleyan Found., Cookeville, Tenn., 1981-83; infantry tng. chaplain Marine Corps Base, Camp Lejune, N.C., 1983-85; battalion chaplain Seabee Battalion (MCB) 74, Gulfport, Miss., 1985-88; group chaplain Marine Aircraft Group -13, Yuma, Ariz., 1988-91; command chaplain USS Hunley (AS-31), Norfolk, Va., 1992-94; ship chaplain USS Yellowstone (AD-41); Norfolk, 1994-95; regimental chaplain 1st Marine Divsn., Camp Pendleton, Calif., 1995—; sch. vol. coord. USS Yellowstone, Norfolk and Charleston, S.C., USS Hunley, Norfolk, Va., 1993-95. Author: (book) Upper Room Disciples, 1982; also contbr. mil. jours. Vol. youth worker St. Andrew's United Meth. Ch., Portsmouth, Va., 1992-95; vol. food kitchen Oasis Ministry, Portsmouth, Va., 1992-95; vol. and recruiter Habitat for Humanity, Norfolk, Va., 1994-95. Decorated Navy Commendation medal, Navy Achievement medal, 1987-95; recipient Recognition award Govt. Guam and various charitable orgns., 1983-96. Mem. U.S. Naval Inst., Tenn. Ann. Conf., United Meth. Ch., Zoolog. Soc. San Diego. Republican. Home: 173 Rupertus Dr San Clemente CA 92672-2564 Office: 1st Marines Box 555402 Camp Pendleton CA 92055

PUTMAN, ROBERT DEAN, golf course architect; b. Wallace, Idaho, Dec. 18, 1924; m. Sally Harmon, 1945; 3 children. Grad., Fresno State Coll. Art dir. Sta. KJEO-TV, Fresno, Calif. Prin. works include Arvin Mcpl. Golf Course, Wasco, Calif., Madera (Calif.) Mcpl. Golf Course, Rancho Canada Golf Course, Carmel Valley, Calif., La Manga Golf Course, Costa Blanca, Spain, Monterey (Calif.) Country Club Shore Course, San Joaquin Country Club, Fresno, Visalia (Calif.) Mcpl. Golf Course, River Island Golf Course, Poterville, Calif., Kings River Country Club, Kingsburg, Calif. Office: Robert Dean Putman GCA 5644 N Briarwood Ave Fresno CA 93711-2501*

PUTNAM, HOWARD DEAN, speaker, writer, former airline executive; b. Bedford, Iowa, Aug. 21, 1937; s. Virgil Glen and Mary Nancy (Livingston) P.; m. Krista Delight Moser, Oct. 20, 1957; children: Michael Dean, Susan Delight. M.B.A. in Mktg., U. Chgo., 1966; grad., Advanced Mgmt. Program, Harvard U., 1978. With Capital Airlines, Chgo., 1955-61; passenger service mgr. Capital Airlines, 1957-59, sales rep., 1959-61; with United Airlines, Chgo., 1961-78; regional v.p. United Airlines, San Francisco, 1971-74; group v.p. mktg. United Airlines, Chgo., 1974-78; pres., chief exec. officer S.W. Airlines, Dallas, 1978-81, also dir.; chmn., pres., chief exec. officer Braniff Internat. Corp., Dallas, 1981-83; chmn. The Diamond Mgmt. Group, Dallas. Presbyterian. Club: Bohemian (San Francisco). Office: Putnam Enterprises Inc 1125 Austrian Pine Rd Reno NV 89511-5705 Address: 1125 Austrian Pine Rd Reno NV 89511-5705

PUTNAM, J. O., construction executive; b. 1951. MBA, U. Alta., Can., 1975. With PCL Constrn. Group Inc., Edmonton, Alta., Can., 1975-86; v.p. PCL Constrn. Svcs., Bellevue, Wash., 1986—. *

PUTNEY, MARY ENGLER, federal auditor; b. Overland, Mo., May 1, 1933; d. Bernard J. and Marie (Kunkler) Engler; children: Glennon (dec.), Pat Michael, Michelle. Student Fontbonne Coll., 1951-52; AA, Sacramento City Coll., 1975; BS in Bus., Calif. State U., 1981; CPA, Calif; cert. fraud examiner; cert. govt. fin. mgr. From asst. to acct. Mo. Rsch. Labs., Inc., St. Louis, 1953-55, adminstrv. asst., 1955-60; sec. western region fin. office Gen. Electric Co., St. Louis, 1960-62; credit analyst Crocker Nat. Bank, Sacramento, 1962-72 ; student tchr. Sacramento County Dept. Edn., 1979-81; acctg. technician East Yolo Community Services Dist., 1983; mgmt. specialist USAF Logistics Command, 1984; auditor Office Insp. Gen., U.S. Dept. Transp., 1984-92; auditor Adminstrn. for Children and Families U.S. Dept Health and Human Svcs., 1992—. Mem. Sacramento Community Commn. for Women, 1978-81, bd. dirs., 1980—; mem. planning bd. Golden Empire Health Systems Agy. Mem. AARP (tax counselor for the elderly), AAUW (fin. officer 1983—), AICPA, Nat. Assn. Accts. (dir., newsletter editor), Fontbonne Coll. Alumni Assn., Calif. State Alumni Assn., Assn. Govt. Accts. (chpt. officer), Calif. Soc. CPAs, German Geneological Soc. (bd. dirs. 1990—, publicity dir. 1994—), Rio Del Oro Racquet Club, Beta Gamma Sigma, Beta Alpha Psi. Roman Catholic. Home: 2616 Point Reyes Way Sacramento CA 95826-2416 Office: US Dept Health & Human Svcs ACF/OCSE Div of Audits 801 I St Ste 214 Sacramento CA 95814

PUZDER, ANDREW F., lawyer; b. Cleve., July 11, 1950; s. Andrew F. and Winifried M. Puzder; m. Deanna L. Descher, Sept. 26, 1987. BA, Cleve.

State U., 1975; JD, Washington U., 1978. Gen. counsel, exec. v.p. Fidelity Nat. Fin., Inc., CKE Restaurants, Inc. Editor Washington U. Law Quarterly, 1977-78. Author of law upheld by U.S. Supreme Ct. in Webster v. Reproductive Health Svcs., 1989; founding dir. Common Ground Network for Life and Choice, 1993. Mem. State Bar Nev., The Mo. Bar, State Bar Calif., Phi Alpha Theta. Address: 17911 Von Karman Ave #300 Irvine CA 92714-6253

PYE, DAVID THOMAS, computer technology company executive; b. Darby, Pa., June 12, 1942; s. David and Grace Marie (Dale) P. BS, Widener U., 1964. CPA, Pa., Calif. Tax cons. Price Waterhouse & Co., Phila., 1964-70; dir. taxes Am. Instl. Devel., Inc., Phila., 1970-75; dir. tax adminstrn. Syntex Corp., Palo Alto, Calif., 1975-93; group tax mgr. Logitech Inc., Fremont, Calif., 1995-96; dir. taxes West Marine, Inc., Watsonville, Calif., 1996—. Mem. AICPAs, Calif. CPA Soc., Tax Execs. Inst. Home: 201 S 4th St Apt 704 San Jose CA 95112-3669 Office: 500 Westridge Dr Watsonville CA 95076

PYLE, ROBERT MICHAEL, naturalist, writer; b. Denver, July 19, 1947; s. Robert Harold Pyle and Helen Lee (Miller) Lemmon; m. JoAnne Clark Heron, Aug. 6, 1966 (div. Aug. 1973); m. Sarah Anne Hughes, June 7, 1974 (div. Feb. 1984); m. Thea Linnaea Peterson, Oct. 19, 1985; stepchildren: Thomas M. Hellyer, Dorothea A. Hellyer. BS, U. Wash., 1969, MS, 1973; MPhil, Yale U., 1976, PhD, 1976. N.W. land steward Nature Conservancy, Portland, Oreg., 1977-79; cons. biologist Dept. Wildlife, Govt. Papua New Guinea, 1977; editor, mgr. Conservation Monitoring Ctr., Cambridge, Eng., 1979-82; freelance writer, lectr. Gray's River, Wash., 1982—; guest prof. Evergreen State Coll., Olympia, Wash., Portland State U., Lewis and Clark Coll., Portland, 1983—. Author: Wintergreen (Govs. award Pacific N.W. Booksellers 1987, John Burroughs medal 1987), The Thunder Tree, 1993, Where Bigfoot Walks, 1995, also 6 books on butterflies; over 350 essays & papers, articles, stories, and poems. contbr. to profl. publs. Mem. Nat. Heritage Adv. Coun., Olympia, 1988-95; founder Xerces Soc., Portland, 1971; chair Monarch Project, Portland, 1983-89. Fulbright scholar, 1971-72; fellow Nat. Wildlife Fedn., 1973-76, John Simon Guggenheim Found., 1990. Mem. Nature Conservancy, Authors Guild, Lepidopterists' Soc. (exec. com. 1980-83), Patrons of Husbandry (Grange), Orion Soc. (adv. bd. 1995—), Willapa Alliance (adv. bd. 1995—). Democrat.

PYM, BRUCE MICHAEL, lawyer; b. Alameda, Calif., Sept. 29, 1942; s. Leonard A. and Willamay (Strandberg) P. B.B.A., U. Wash., 1964, J.D., 1967. Bar: Wash. 1967, U.S. Dist. Ct. (we. dist.) Wash. 1968, U.S. Ct. Appeals (9th cir.) 1968, U.S. Tax Ct. 1969, U.S. Supreme Ct. 1971. Law clk. Wash. State Supreme Ct., Olympia, 1967-68; assoc. Graham & Dunn, Seattle, 1968-73, shareholder, 1973-92; ptnr. Heller, Ehrman, White & McAuliffe, Seattle, 1992—; mng. ptnr. Northwest Offices, 1994—. Bd. dirs. United Way of King County, 1986-92, chmn., 1990. Mem. ABA, Wash. State Bar Assn., King County Bar Assn. (pres. 1984-85). Office: Heller Ehrman White & McAuliffe 701 5th Ave Ste 6100 Seattle WA 98104-7016

PYPER, JAMES WILLIAM, chemist; b. Wells, Nev., Sept. 5, 1934; s. William Jones and Wilma (Bjelke) P.; m. Phyllis Diane Henry, Aug. 30, 1957; children: Scott, Mark, Gregory, Heather, Melanie, Tara, Tammy, Wendy, Michael, Tanya, David. BS, Brigham Young U., 1958, MS, 1960; PhD, Cornell U., 1964. Ordained bishop Ch. Jesus Christ of Latter-day Saints, 1973. Research chemist Lawrence Livermore (Calif.) Nat. Lab., 1963-84, mass spectrometry group leader, 1973-75, tritium tech. group leader, 1977-78, applied phys. chemistry group leader, 1979-80, sect. leader for analytical chemistry, 1980-83, dep. sect. leader for analytical chemistry, 1983-87, assoc. div. leader condensed matter and analytical scis. div., 1987-89, quality assurance mgr., 1989-90, ret., 1990. Contbr. articles to sci. jours. Presided over local congrs., 1973-75, 87-91, 91-93; mem. stake high coun., 1976-87; missionary Ch. of Jesus Christ of Latter Saints, Thessaloniki, Greece, 1991-93, Scotland and Eng., 1994-95, Nauvoo, Ill., 1997—. Republican. *Personal philosophy: To love God and my fellow man and to assist in bringing souls in to Christ.*

QUACKENBUSH, CHUCK, insurance commissioner. Commr. of ins. State of Calif., Sacramento. Office: Dept Ins 300 Capitol Mall Ste 1500 Sacramento CA 95814

QUACKENBUSH, JUSTIN LOWE, federal judge; b. Spokane, Wash., Oct. 3, 1929; s. Carl Clifford and Marian Huldah (Lowe) Q.; m. Marie McAtee; children: Karl Justin, Kathleen Marie, Robert Craig. BA, U. Idaho, 1951; LLB, Gonzaga U., Spokane, 1957. Bar: Wash. 1957. Dep. pros. atty. Spokane County, 1957-59; ptnr. Quackenbush, Dean, Bailey & Henderson, Spokane, 1959-80; dist. judge U.S. Dist. Ct. (ea. dist.) Wash., Spokane, 1980—, now sr. judge; part-time instr. Gonzaga U. Law Sch., 1960-67. Chmn. Spokane County Planning Commn., 1969-73. Served with USN, 1951-54. Mem. ABA, Wash. Bar Assn., Spokane County Bar Assn. (trustee 1976-78), Internat. Footprint Assn. (nat. pres. 1967), Spokane C. of C. (trustee, exec. com. 1978-79). Episcopalian. Club: Spokane Country. Lodge: Shriners. Office: US Dist Ct PO Box 1432 Spokane WA 99210-1432

QUALLEY, CHARLES ALBERT, fine arts educator; b. Creston, Iowa, Mar. 19, 1930; s. Albert Olaf and Cleora (Dietrick) Q.; m. Betty Jean Griffith, Nov. 26, 1954; children: Janet Lynn, John Stuart. B.F.A., Drake U., 1952; M.A., U. Iowa, 1956, M.F.A., 1958; Ed.D., Ill. State U., 1967. Art tchr. Des Moines Pub. Schs., 1952,, 54-55; critic art tchr. U. Iowa, 1955-57; prof. fine arts U. Colo., Boulder, 1958-90, prof. emeritus, 1990—; chmn. dept. fine arts U. Colo., 1968-71, assoc. chmn., 1981-82; vis. prof. Inst. for Shipboard Edn., semester at sea, 1979, Ill. State U., 1985. Author: Safety in the Art Room, 1986; contbg. editor Sch. Arts, 1978-85, mem. editorial adv. bd., 1985-87; author column Safetypoint, 1981-85. Served with AUS, 1952-54, Korea. Mem. Nat. Art Edn. Assn. (v.p. 1980-82, pres. 1987-89, dir. conv. svcs. 1990—, fellow 1990—, Art Educator of Yr. 1993), Nat. Art Edn. Found. (trustee 1987—, chair bd. trustees 1996—), Colo. Art Edn. Assn. (editor 1965-67, 75, pres. 1976-78), Delta Phi Delta, Omicron Delta Kappa, Pi Kappa Delta. Home: 409 Fillmore Ct Louisville CO 80027-2273

QUICK, JOHN ANTONY, film and video producer; b. Avonwick, Devon, U.K., Jan. 28, 1941; came to U.S., 1962; s. Ken and Mary Stephanie (Weeks) Q.; m. Barbara Tritel, Aug. 1, 1988; 1 child, Julian Antony. BA in Motion Pictures with honors, UCLA, 1966. Freelance producer, cameraman and editor, 1966—; prodr., dir., photographer and editor U. Calif., Berkeley, 1967—; film cameraman and editor KQED TV, San Francisco, 1970-72. Prodr. films including: Don't Tell Me, I'll Find Out! (CINE Golden Eagle award), What Would Happen If...? (CINE Golden Eagle award), Discover: The LHS Approach (CINE Golden Eagle award), Natural Rubber Bearings for Earthquake Protection (Creative Excellence award U.S. Indsl. Film Festival); co-photographer and editor: Let's Speak English! (Gold Award for Excellence in Promotions, Nat. U. Continuing Edn. Assn.).

QUICK, WILLIAM THOMAS, author, consultant; b. Muncie, Ind., May 30, 1946; s. Clifford Willett and Della May (Ellis) Q. Student, Ind. U., 1964-66. Pres. Iceberg Prodns., San Francisco, 1986—. Author: Dreams of Flesh and Sand, 1988, Dreams of God and Men, 1989, Yesterday's Pawn, 1989, Systems, 1989, Singularities, 1990, (as Quentin Thomas) Chains of Light, 1992, Ascensions, 1997, (as Margaret Allan) The Mammoth Stone, 1993, Keeper of the Stone, 1994, The Last Mammoth, 1995, Spirits Walking Woman, 1997, (as W.T. Quick) Star Control: Interbellum, 1996, American Gothic: Family, 1996, (with William Shatner) Quest for Tomorrow: Delta Search, 1997, Quest for Tomorrow: In Alien Hands, 1997. Mem. Sci. Fiction and Fantasy Writers Am., The Authors Guild. Home and Office: 1558 Leavenworth St San Francisco CA 94109-3220

QUIGLEY, JEROME HAROLD, management consultant; b. Green Bay, Wis., Apr. 19, 1925; s. Harold D. and Mabel (Hansen) Q.; BS, St. Norbert Coll., 1951; m. Lorraine A. Rocheleau, May 3, 1947; children: Kathy, Ross, Michael, Daniel, Mary Beth, Andrew, Maureen. Personnel adminstr. Gen. Motors Corp., 1959-64; dir. indsl. rels. Raytheon Co., Santa Barbara, Calif., 1964-67; dir. personnel U. Calif., Santa Barbara, 1967-72; corp. dir. indsl. rels. Gen. Rsch. Corp., 1972-73; dir. indsl. rels. ISS Sperry Univac, 1973-75; corp. dir. indsl. rels. Four-Phase Systems, Inc., Cupertino, Calif., 1975; sr. v.p. human resources UNC, Annapolis, Md., 1975-86; pres. Profl. Guidance Assocs. Inc., 1986—. Aviator with U.S. Navy, 1943-47. Mem. Am. Electronics Assn., Assn. Former Intelligence Officers, Machinery and Allied Products Inst., Assn. Naval Aviation, Tailhook Assn., Ariz. County Atty.'s and Sheriff's Assn., Marines' Meml. Assn., Ret. Officers Assn., AVCAD/NAVCAD Assn., Navy Aviation Mus. Found., Navy League, Scottsdale Radisson Racquet Club. Republican. Roman Catholic. Office: Profl Guidance Assocs Inc 7789 E Joshua Tree Ln Scottsdale AZ 85250-7962

QUIGLEY, JOHN MICHAEL, economist, educator; b. N.Y.C., Feb. 12, 1942. B.S. with distinction, U.S. Air Force Acad., 1964; M.Sc. with honors, U. Stockholm, Sweden, 1965; A.M., Harvard U., 1971, Ph.D., 1972. Commd. 2d lt. USAF, 1964, advanced through grades to capt., 1968; asst. prof. econs. Yale U., 1972-74, assoc. prof., 1974-81; prof. pub. policy U. Calif., Berkeley, 1979—, prof. econs., 1981—, chmn, dept. econs., 1992-95; vis. prof. econs. and stats. U. Gothenberg, 1978; cons. numerous govt. agys. and pvt. firms; econometrician Hdqrs. U.S. Air Force, Pentagon, 1965-68; research assoc. Nat. Bur. Econ. Research, N.Y.C., 1968-78; mem. com. on nat. urban policy NAS, 1985-93. Author, editor, contbr. articles to profl. jours.; editor in chief Reg. Sci. and Urban Econs., 1987—; mem. editorial bd. Land Econs., 1974-81, Jour. Urban Econs., 1978-93, Coun. on Pub. Policy and Mgmt., 1979—, AREUEA Jour., 1985—, Property Tax Jour., 1990—, Jour. Housing Econs., 1990—. Fulbright scholar, 1964-65; fellow NSF, 1968-69, Woodrow Wilson, 1968-71, Harvard IBM, 1969-71, NDEA, 1969-71, Thord-Gray Am. Scandinavian Found. 1971-72, Social Sci. Research Council, 1971-72. Mem. Am. Econ. Assn., Econometric Soc., Regional Sci. Assn. (bd. dirs. 1986—), Nat. Tax Assn., Assn. for Pub. Policy and Mgmt. (bd. dirs. 1986-89, v.p. 1987-89), Am. Real Estate and Urban Econs. Assn. (bd. dirs. 1987—, pres. 1995—). Home: 875 Hilldale Ave Berkeley CA 94708-1319 Office: U Calif 2607 Hearst Ave Berkeley CA 94709-1005

QUIGLEY, KEVIN, state senator; b. Lake Stevens, Wash., Feb. 23, 1961; m. Suzanne Quigley; children: Mattie, Aidan. BA, The George Washington U.; JD, NYU; LLM, Harvard. Atty. Perkins Coie, Seattle, 1993—; mem. Wash. State Senate, 1993-96. Democrat. Office: 1510 Longworth Washington DC 20515

QUIGLEY, PHILIP J., telecommunications industry executive; b. 1943. With Advanced Mobile Phone Svc. Inc., 1982-84, v.p., gen. mgr., Pacific region; with Pac Tel Mobile Access, 1984-86, pres., chief exec. officer; with Pac Tel Personal Communications, 1986-87, pres., chief exec. officer; exec. v.p., chief oper. officer Pac Tel Corp., 1987; with Pacific Bell, San Francisco, 1987—; now chmn., pres., chief exec. officer Pacific Telesis Group, San Francisco; pres. Pacific Bell, 1987-94. Office: Pacific Telesis 130 Kearny St San Francisco CA 94108

QUIGLEY, RICHARD LAWRENCE, artist, educator; b. Spokane, Wash., June 13, 1951; s. Richard Eldrid and Barbara June (Frisk) Q.; m. Sandra Lee White, Aug. 26, 1972; children: Shasta Dawn, Sean Richard. AA, Lower Columbia Coll., 1970-72; BA, Western Washington Coll., 1974; BFA, Cornish Art Inst., 1976. Instr. oil and watercolor painting Dept. Parks and Recreation, City of Eugene, Oreg., 1976-77; instr. oil and acrylic painting, watercolor, multimedia, drawing, life drawing and graphics Lane C.C., Eugene, 1976—; instr. oil painting and drawing Maude I. Kerns Art Ctr., Eugene, 1977, dept. head painting and drawing, instr. oil, acrylic, watercolor and life drawing, 1978-79; juror and lectr. in field, art inst., lectr. One-person shows include Maude I. Kearns Art Ctr., Eugene, 1977, Lane C.C., Eugene, 1979, High Street Cafe Gallery, Eugene, 1980, U. Oreg., Eugene, 1986, Argus Fine Arts Gallery, Eugene, 1988, Hanson Howard Gallery, Ashland, Oreg., 1988, Jacobs Gallery, Eugene, 1990, Excelsior Gallery, Eugene, 1991, Maryhill Mus. Art, Goldendale, Wash., 1992, Artworks Gallery, Florence, Oreg., 1993, Alder Gallery, Eugene, 1994, others; selected group shows include Emily Thorpe Gallery, Sisters, Oreg., 1984, Oceanside Gallery, Lincoln City, Oreg., 1985, Green Earth Gallery, Eugene, 1986, Argus Gallery, Eugene, 1987-90, Vistra Gallery, Eugene, 1987, Whitebird Gallery, Cannon Beach, Oreg., 1988-89, Graystone Gallery, Portland, Oreg., 1989, Alder Gallery, 1991, 93, Augen Gallery, 1992, Artworks Gallery, Bandon, Oreg., 1994, Mindpower Gallery, Reedsport, Oreg., 1995, 96, others; numerous juried shows; permanent collection Maryhill Mus., Goldendale, Wash. Mem. Watercolor Soc. Oreg., Calif. Watercolor Assn., Colorpencil Soc. Am.

QUILLEN, EDWARD KENNETH, III, freelance writer, columnist; b. Greeley, Colo., Nov. 12, 1950; s. Edward Kenneth II and Dorothy May (Wollen) Q.; m. Martha Alice Patterson, June 26, 1969; children: Columbine Kay, Abigail Cynara. Student, U. No. Colo., 1968-74. Reporter Longmont (Colo.) Scene, 1972; editor Middle Park Times, Kremmling, Colo., 1974-77, Summit County Jour., Breckenridge, Colo., 1977-78; mng. editor Mountain Mail, Salida, Colo., 1978-83; freelance writer, Salida, 1983—; columnist Denver Post, 1986—. Author: The White Stuff, 1985, 11 westerns under pseudonym; pub. Colo. Cen. Mag., 1994—; contbr. numerous articles to mags. Recipient award for best personal column Colo. Press Assn., 1983, 88. Democrat. Office: PO Box 548 Salida CO 81201-0548

QUINCY, ALPHA ELLEN BEERS, school board executive; b. Olympia, Wash., Oct. 15, 1924; d. George Howard and Grace Florence (Penrose) Beers; m. John J. Quincy, Nov. 12, 1942 (dec. Feb. 1987); children: Cheri Sue, John Jay. BE in Edn., Calif. State U., Sacramento, 1960; MA in Edl. Adminstrn., U. Calif., Berkeley, 1966, postgrad., 1996—. Life cert. adminstrn., presch., K-12 and adult, elem. sch. adminstrn., elem. tchg. Tchr., resource tchr., vice prin., prin., dist. cons. Mt. Diablo Unified Sch. Dist., 1959-83; coord. Acad. Curriculum and Instrn. Leaders Assn. Calif. Sch. Adminstrs., 1985-89; cons. edn., spkr., writer, workshop leader, 1983—; exec. dir. San Ramon Valley Sch. Age Child Care Alliance, 1992-93; mem. Contra Costa County Bd. Edn., 1988—, pres., 1992, 96; mem. Calif. Curriculum Devel. and Supplemental Materials Commn., State Bd. Edn., 1971-74; chair com. for reading and lit. Calif. Curriculum Devel. and Supplemental Materials Commn., State Bd. Edn., 1971-74, mem. English lang. arts adv. Calif. Assessment Program, 1971—. Contbr. articles to profl. jours. Bd. dirs. U. Calif. Berkeley, Inst. Sch. Adminstrs., 1979-88, Diablo Internat. Resources Ctr. Recipient Adminstr. of Yr. ann. award Assn. Calif. Sch. Adminstrs., Region 7, 1983. Mem. LWV (leader Lafayette unit 1985, edn. chairperson Diablo Valley 1987, chair nominating com. 1991, edn. chair 1989—), ASCD, Nat. Coun. Tchrs. English (writing awards com. 1990-92, ency. entry team, emeritus assembly), Calif. Assn. Tchrs. English (past bd. dirs., program chair 1990 ann. conf.), Ctrl. Coun. Tchrs. English (past bd. mem., curriculum study com. 1970—, conf. chmn. 1991, 96), Assn. Calif. Sch. Adminstrs. (past mem. mid. sch. com., C&I acad. coord. 1984-88, area VI scholarship chmn. 1990-96), Calif. Sch. Bds. ASsn., Calif. County Bds. Edn., Contra Costa Sch. Bds. Assn., Calif. Retired Tchrs. Assn., East Contra Costa County Retired Tchrs. Assn. (program chair 1992-93, pres. 1995—), Nat. Women's Polit. Caucus, U. Calif. Berkeley Alumni Assn., Internat. Reading Assn., Calif. Reading Assn., Contra Costa Reading Assn., Commonwealth Club Calif., Concord Century Club, Home Group, Phi Delta Kappa, Delta Kappa Gamma. Home: 1529 Rancho View Dr Lafayette CA 94549-2231

QUINN, FRANCIS A., bishop; b. L.A., Sept. 11, 1921. Ed., St. Joseph's Coll., Mountain View, Calif., St. Patrick's Sem., Menlo Park, Calif., Cath. U., Washington, U. Calif., Berkeley. Ordained priest Roman Cath. Ch., 1946; ordained titular bishop of Numana and aux. bishop of San Francisco, 1978; bishop Diocese of Sacramento, 1979-94, bishop emeritus, 1994—. Office: 2110 Broadway Sacramento CA 95818-2518

QUINN, JOHN R., archbishop; b. Riverside, Calif., Mar. 28, 1929; s. Ralph J. and Elizabeth (Carroll) Q. Student, St. Francis Sem., Immaculate Heart Sem., San Diego, 1947-48; Ph.B., Gregorian U., Rome, 1950, Licentiate in Sacred Theology, 1954, S.T.L., 1954. Ordained priest Roman Cath. Ch., 1953, as bishop, 1967. Assoc. pastor St. George Ch., Ontario, Calif., 1954-55; prof. theology Immaculate Heart Sem., San Diego, 1955-62, vice rector, 1960-62; pres. St. Francis Coll. Sem., El Cajon, Calif., 1962-64; rector Immaculate Heart Sem., 1964-68; aux. bishop, vicar gen. San Diego, 1967-72; bishop Oklahoma City, 1972-73, archbishop, 1973-77; archbishop San Francisco, 1977-95; provost U. San Diego, 1968-72; pastor St. Therese Parish, San Diego, 1969; apptd. consultor to Sacred Congregation for the Clergy in Rome, 1971; pres. Nat. Conf. Cath. Bishops, 1977-80, chmn. Com. of Liturgy; chmn. com. on Family Life U.S. Cath. Conf.; chmn. Bishops' Com. on Pastoral Rsch. and Practices, Bishops' Com. on Doctrine; mem. Bishops' Com. on Sems., Pontifical Commn., Seattle, 1987-88, Bishops' Com. for Pro-Life Activies, 1989—; apptd. pontifical del. for religious in U.S., 1983; pres. Calif. Cath. Conf., 1985; mem. Synod of Bishops, Rome, 1994; chmn. Nat. Conf. Cath. Bishops Com. on Doctrine, 1994—; vis. fellow Campion Hall, U. Oxford, 1996. Trustee U. San Diego, 1991-93. Mem. Cath. Theol. Soc. Am., Canon Law Soc. Am., Am. Cath. Hist. Soc. Address: 445 Church St San Francisco CA 94114-1720

QUINN, MAURA KATHLEEN, television producer; b. Paris, July 17, 1961; d. Joseph Patrick and Margaret Patricia (Norton) Q. BA in Comm., U. Tulsa, 1994. Assoc. producer Entertainment Tonight Potomac News, Washington, 1986, news producer, 1987; assignments mgr. Potomac Comm., Washington, 1988-92; off air reporter Denny Trial ABC News TV, L.A., 1993, producer Simpson Trial, 1994-95, producer line and spot, 1995—. Author (short stories) Zonxy, 1984. Mem. NABET. Home: 2427 Silver Ridge Ave Los Angeles CA 90039-3321

QUINT, BERT, journalist; b. N.Y.C., Sept. 22, 1930; s. George and Sadye (Slonim) Q.; m. Diane Frances Schwab, Apr. 10, 1975; children: Lara Gabrielle, Amy Frances. BS, NYU, 1952. Reporter Worcester (Mass.) Telegram, 1952-53, AP, 1953-54, N.Y. Herald Tribune, 1956-58; mag. editor, free lance corr. N.Y. Herald Tribune, Wall Street Jour., CBS News, others, Mexico City, 1958-65; corr. CBS News, 1965-93; adj. prof. broadcast journalism U. Colo., Boulder, 1993—; journalist/anchor/writer TV Quint Colo. Inc. Recipient Radio Reporting award Overseas Press Club, 1971. Mem. Soc. Profl. Journalists, Fgn. Corr. Assn. Mex. (pres.). Home and Office: 539 Bari Ct Boulder CO 80303-4312

QUIRKE, TERENCE THOMAS, JR., genealogist, retired geologist; b. Mpls., Aug. 18, 1929; s. Terence Thomas and Anne Laura (McIlraith) Q.; m. Ruth Mary Carter, Jan. 18, 1958; 1 child, Grace Anne. BS, U. Ill., 1951; MS, U. Minn., 1953, PhD, 1958. Cert. genealogist Bd. for Cert. of Genealogists. Asst. prof. U. N.D., Grand Forks, 1958-60; rsch. geologist INCO Ltd., Thompson, MB, Can., 1970-75, regional mgr., 1970-75; supervisory staff geologist Am. Copper & Nickel Co., Milw., 1975-79; sr. supervisory staff geologist Am. Copper & Nickel Co., Wheat Ridge, Colo., 1979-90; rsch. cons. Quirke, Quirke & Assocs., Golden, Colo., 1990—. Contbr. articles to profl. jours., numerous others. Pres. Colo. Genealogical Soc. Computer Interest Group, Denver, 1991-93; sec.-treas., bd. dirs. Genesee Water and Sanitation Dist., Golden, Colo., 1994—. Mem. Soc. Genealogists (London), Irish Genealogical Soc. Internat., Irish Genealogical Rsch. Soc., Ontario Genealogical Soc., Sussex Family History Group, Kent Family History Soc., Irish Family History Soc. Home: 2310 Juniper Ct Golden CO 80401-8087

QUIRÓS-WINEMILLER, BEL, language educator; b. Panama City, Panama, Dec. 18; came to U.S., 1976; d. Afable and Bélgica (Ordónez) Q.; m. Mark D. Winemiller, Feb. 14, 1981; children: Cristina, Carolena. BA, Ariz. State U., 1979, MA, 1984, PhD, 1988; postgrad., Anhui U., China, 1989. Full-time faculty Glendale (Ariz.) C.C., 1988—; part-time faculty Rio Salado Coll., Phoenix, 1988—, Ariz. State U. West, Phoenix, 1994—; freelance writer McMurray Pub. Co., Phoenix, 1995—. Organizer Glendale Intercultural Festival, 1991—; active Martial Arts Inst., Phoenix; advisor Vietnamese Club, 1996. Mem. MLA, Ariz. Assn. Chicanos in Higher Edn., Asian and Pacific Islander Assn. (sec. 1994—). Office: Glendale C C 6000 W Olive Glendale AZ 85302-3006

QUIRÓZ, ALFRED JAMES, art educator, artist, lecturer; b. Tucson, May 9, 1944; s. Nicolas J. Segura and Hilda F. (Quiróz) Alvarado; m. Marcia Denis Duff, Sept. 15, 1977; children: Demian A., James A. BFA in Painting, San Francisco Art Inst., 1971; MAT in Art Edn., RISD, 1974; MFA in Studio Arts, U. Ariz., 1984. Visual arts and film specialist R.I. State Coun. on Arts, Providence, 1974-77; art coord. Sch. One, Providence, 1975-77; project dir. ESAA Spl. Arts, Central Falls, R.I., 1978-79; freelance artist Lisa Frank Inc., Tucson, 1981-84; instr. art Tucson Dept. Parks and Recreation, 1981-86; artist in residence Ariz. Commn. on Arts, Phoenix, 1985-89; asst. prof. U. Ariz., Tucson, 1989-93, assoc. prof., 1993—; adj. lectr. U. Ariz., Tucson, 1988; bd. dirs. Tucson Pima Arts Coun., Western States Arts Fedn., Santa Fe, visual arts com., 1993—; advisor Ariz. Arts Edn. Planning Partnership, Phoenix, 1993—. One-man shows include Scottsdale (Ariz.) Ctr. for Arts, 1994; exhibited in group shows at Walker Art Ctr., Minn., 1992, San Francisco Ctr. for Art, 1993, San Diego Mus. Contemporary Art, 1993. Cmty. mem. Tucson Vis. Artist's Consortium, 1989—; mem. Pub. Art Com., Tucson, 1989-93; juror at large WESTAF, Arts Midwest, others, 1993—; panelist Nat. Endowment of Arts, 1994, 95. With USN, 1963-67. Recipient Visual Arts fellowship Ariz. Commn. on Arts, Phoenix, 1989, 95, Ariz. Arts award Tucson Cmty. Found., 1989; New Forms Regional grantee Diverseworks, Houston, 1991; commd. work for San Francisco Ctr. for the Arts, 1993. Mem. AAUP, Nat. Arts and Arts Orgns., Coll. Art Assn., Am. Coun. for Arts. Office: Univ of Arizona Art Dept Tucson AZ 85721

QUISENBERRY, ROBERT MAX, architect, industrial designer; b. Eugene, Oreg., Nov. 18, 1956; s. Clifford Hale and Annemaria Gertrude (Frank) Q.; m. Dawnese Elaine Tarr, Sept. 18, 1982. BArch, U. Oreg., 1982. Registered architect, Wash., Calif. Project architect Merritt & Pardini, Tacoma, 1984-87; project mgr. Lorimer-Case, San Diego, 1987-89; project design architect The Austin Hansen Group, San Diego, 1989-91; prin. Studio Q Architecture, Chula Vista, Calif., 1991-93; design dir. Exponents, Inc., San Diego, 1993-94, Powerhouse Exhibits, San Diego, 1995—. Recipient Washington State Passive Solar Design and Bldg. award Western Solar Utilization Network, 1981, Gold and Bronze Summit Awards, 1996. Republican. Home: 644 Hartford St Chula Vista CA 91913-2456

RAAS, DANIEL ALAN, lawyer; b. Portland, Oreg., July 6, 1947; s. Alan Charles and Mitzi (Cooper) R.; m. Deborah Ann Becker, Aug. 5, 1973; children: Amanda Beth, Adam Louis. BA, Reed Coll., 1969; JD, NYU, 1972. Bar: Wash. 1973, Calif. 1973, U.S. Dist. Ct. (we. dist.) Wash. 1973, U.S. Ct. Appeals (9th cir.) 1975, U.S. Supreme Ct. 1977, U.S. Tax Ct. 1983, U.S. Ct. Claims 1984. Atty. Seattle Legal Svcs, VISTA, 1972-73; reservation atty. Quinault Indian Nation, Taholah, Wash., 1973-76, Lummi Indian Nation, Bellingham, Wash., 1976—; mem. Raas, Johnsen & Stuen, P.S., Bellingham, 1982—; cons. Falmouth Inst., Fairfax, Va., 1992—, Nat. Am. Ind. Ct. Judges Assn., McLean, Va., 1976-80. Rules chmn. Whatcom County Dem. Conv., Bellingham, 1988, 92, 94, 96; bd. dirs. Congregation Beth Israel, Bellingham, pres., 1990-92; mem. adv. com. legal asst. program Bellingham Vocat. Tech. Inst., 1985-91; trustee Whatcom County Law Libr., 1978—; pres. Vol. Lawyer Program, 1990-93, bd. dirs., 1988-94; pres. Cliffside Cmty. Assn., 1978-80, bd. dirs., 1977-89; bd. dirs. Friends Maritime Heritage Ctr., 1983-86, Samish Camp Fire Coun., 1988-94, pres. 1991-94, v.p., 1989-91, regional v.p. Union Am. Hebrew Congregations, 1986-93, nat. trustee, exec. com., 1995—, sec. Pacific N.W. region, 1993-95, pres., 1995—. John Ben Snow scholar, NYU, 1969-70, Root-Tilden scholar, NYU, 1970-72. Mem. Wash. State Bar Assn. (trustee Ind. law sect. 1989-95, Pro Bono award 1991), Whatcom County Bar Assn. (v.p. 1981, pres. 1982, Pro Bono award 1991), Grays Harbor Bar Assn. (v.p. 1976). Home: 1929 Lake Crest Dr Bellingham WA 98226-4510 Office: Raas Johnsen & Stuen PS 1503 E St Bellingham WA 98225-3007

RABE, ELIZABETH ROZINA, hair stylist, horse breeder; b. Granby, Quebec, Canada, Sept. 28, 1953; d. John J. and Christina Maria (De Vaal) Gluck; m. Oct. 21, 1972 (div. 1981); children: Diana Marie Claire, Michelle Diane. Diploma in hairstyling, Art Inst. Film hairstylist Internat. Alliance Theatrical, Stage Employees and Moving Pictures Machine Operators Local 706, L.A., 1977-94. Recipient Design Patent hock support horse brace U.S. Design Patent Office, Washington, 1994. Home: 522 W Stocker St Apt 1 Glendale CA 91202-2299

RABINOWITZ, HOWARD NEIL, history educator; b. Bklyn., June 19, 1942; s. Abe and Gertrude (Finkelman) R.; m. Anita Joyce Blau, Aug. 28, 1966 (div. Mar. 1981); children: Lori Karen, Deborah Michelle; m. Marsha Diane Wood, July 6, 1991. BA magna cum laude, Swarthmore Coll., 1964; MA, U. Chgo., 1967, PhD, 1973. Vis. instr. in history Grinnell (Iowa) Coll., 1970-71; instr. in history U. New Mex., Albuquerque, 1971-73, asst. prof. of history, 1973-77, assoc. prof. history, 1977-85, prof., 1985—; cons. Ednl.

Testing Svc., Princeton, N.J., 1971, 77-88, Albuquerque Mus., 1981, NEH, Washington, 1983—, Valentine Mus., Richmond, Va., 1988—. Author: Race Relations in the Urban South 1865-1890, 1978, 80, 96 (Pulitzer prize nominee 1978), The First New South, 1865-1920, 1992, Race, Ethnicity and Urbanization: Selected Essays, 1994 (Myers Ctr. award for the study of human rights in N.Am. 1994); editor and contbr. Southern Black Leaders of the Reconstruction Era, 1982; assoc. editor American National Biography, 1991—; contbr. numerous articles to hist. jours., anthologies and golf jours. Vice chmn. Albuquerque Landmark and Urban Conservation Commission, 1978-82, chmn. 1982-84; bd. dirs. Albuquerque Conservation Assn., 1986-89; mem. Good Government Com., Albuquerque, 1989-95; vice chmn. Albuquerque Mcpl. Golf Adv. Bd., 1995—. NEH fellow, 1978; Newberry Libr. fellow, 1978; Ctr. for Advanced Study in Behavioral Scis., Stanford, 1989-90; Am. Assn. State and Local History grantee, 1985. Mem. Am. Hist. Assn., Urban Hist. Assn. (bd. dirs. 1993-95), Orgn. Am. Historians (Frederick Jackson Turner prize com. 1989), So. Hist. Assn. (bd. editors Jour. So. History 1980-84, chmn. program com. 1992, exec. coun. 1995-98). Democrat. Jewish. Office: Univ New Mex Dept History Mesa Vista Hall Albuquerque NM 87131

RABINOWITZ, MARIO, physicist; b. Mexico City, Mex., Oct. 24, 1936; came to U.S., 1939; s. Laib and Rachel (Loschak) R.; m. Laverne Marcotte; children: Daniel L., Benjamin M., Lisa B. BS in Physics, U. Wash., 1959, MS in Physics, 1960; PhD in Physics, Washington State U., 1963. Electronics engr. Collins Radio Co., Burbank, Calif., 1957; rsch. engr. Boeing Co., Seattle, 1958-61; rsch. asst. physics dept. Wash. State U., Pullman, 1961-63; sr. physicist Westinghouse Rsch. Ctr., Pitts., 1963-66; mgr. gas discharges and vacuum physics Varian Assocs., Palo Alto, Calif., 1966-67; rsch. physicist Stanford (Calif.) Linear Accelerator Ctr., 1967-74; sr. scientist and mgr. Electric Power Rsch. Inst., Palo Alto, 1974-95; CEO, Armor Assocs., Redwood City, Calif., 1996—; adj. prof. Ga. Inst. Tech., Atlanta, 1987—, U. Houston, 1990—, Va. Commonwealth U., Richmond, 1990—, Case Western Res. U., Cleve., 1975-77, Boston U., 1975-77. Contbr. numerous articles to profl. jours.; patentee in field. Del., counselor Boys State, Ellensburg, Wash., 1953-55. Scholarship Baker Found., 1955-58; recipient Alumni Achievement award Wash. State U., 1992. Home: 715 Lakemead Way Redwood City CA 94062-3922

RABY, WILLIAM LOUIS, author; b. Chgo., July 16, 1927; s. Gustave E. and Helen (Burgess) R.; m. Norma Claire Schreiner, Sept. 8, 1956; children: Burgess, Marianne, Marlene. BSBA, Northwestern U., 1949; MBA, U. Ariz., 1961, PhD, 1971. Ptnr. VAR CPA Firms, 1950-76, Touche Ross & Co., N.Y.C., 1977-87; pres. Ariz. State Bd. Accountancy, 1993-94; mem. Ariz. State Bd. Tax Appeals, 1994—, chmn., 1997—; prof. acctg. emeritus Ariz. State U.; columnist Tax Notes mag., Arlington, Va., 1990—; cons. on video and audio tax edn. tapes Bisk Pub. Co., 1992—. Author: The Income Tax and Business Decisions, 1964, Building and Maintaining a Successful Tax Practice, 1964, The Reluctant Taxpayer, 1970, Tax Practice Management, 1974, Introduction to Federal Taxation, annually, 1980-91, Tax Practice Management: Client Servicing, 1986; editor: Raby Report on Tax Practice, 1986-96, PPC Guide To Successful Tax Practice, 1991; mem. editorial adv. bd. Taxation for Accountants, The Tax Adviser; contbr. articles to profl. jours. Mem. AICPA (chmn. fed. tax divsn. 1980-83, v.p. 1983-84, coun. 1983-90), Tax Ct. Bar. Presbyterian (elder, chmn. adv. coun. on ch. and soc. 1979-81). Office: PO Box 26846 Tempe AZ 85285-6846

RACHELEFSKY, GARY S., medical educator; b. N.Y.C., 1942. Intern Bellevue Hosp. Ctr., N.Y.C., 1967-68; resident in pediatrics Johns Hopkins Hosp., 1968-70, Ctr. Disease Control, 1970-72; fellow UCLA Med. Ctr., 1972-74; clin. prof., assoc. dir. A/I Tng. Program UCLA. Mem. Am. Acad. Allergy, Asthma and Immunology (bd. dirs., pres.-elect). Office: 11620 Wilshire Blvd Ste 200 Los Angeles CA 90025-1767

RACICOT, MARC F., governor; b. Thompson Falls, Mont., July 24, 1948; s. William E. and Patricia E. (Bentley) R.; m. Theresa J. Barber, July 25, 1970; children: Ann, Timothy, Mary Catherine, Theresa, Joseph. BA, Carroll Coll., Helena, Mont., 1970; JD, U. Mont., 1973; postgrad., U. Va., 1973, Cornell U., 1977. Bar: Mont. 1973. With U.S. Army, 1973-76; advanced through grades to capt., 1973; legal assistance officer U.S. Army, Ft. Lewis, Wash., 1973; chief trial counsel U.S. Army, Kaiserslautern, Fed. Republic of Germany, 1975-76; resigned, 1976; dep. county atty. Missoula (Mont.) County, 1976-77; bur. chief County Prosecutor Svcs. Bur., Helena, Mont., 1977-89; asst. atty. gen. State of Mont., Helena, 1977-89; spl. prosecutor for the Atty. Gen.'s Office State of Mont., atty. gen., 1989-93, gov., 1993—. Founder Missoula Drug Treatment Program, 1977; active United Way, Helena; bd. visitors U. Mont. Sch. Law. Inducted into Basketball Hall of Fame Carroll Coll., 1982. Mem. Mont. Bar Assn., Carroll Coll. Century Club. Republican. Roman Catholic. Office: State Capitol RM 204 Helena MT 59620

RACINA, THOM (THOMAS FRANK RAUCINA), television writer, editor; b. Kenosha, Wis., June 4, 1946; s. Frank G. and Esther May (Benko) Raucina. B.F.A., Goodman Sch. Drama, Art Inst. Chgo., 1970, M.F.A. in Theatre Arts and Directing with honors, 1971. TV writer Hanna-Barbera Co., Hollywood, Calif., 1973-74, MTM Enterprises, Inc., Hollywood, 1974-76; head writer General Hospital ABC-TV, Hollywood, 1981-84; head writer Days of Our Lives NBC-TV, 1984-86, head writer Another World, 1986-88, co-head writer Generations daytime series, 1988-91, head writer syndicated Dangerous Women night-time TV series, 1991-92; assoc. head writer daytime TV series Santa Barbara, 1992-93. Author: Lifeguard, 1976, The Great Los Angeles Blizzard, 1977, Quincy, M.E., 2 vols., 1977, Kodak in San Francisco, 1977, F.M., 1978, Sweet Revenge, 1978, The Gannon Girls, 1979, Nine to Five, 1980, Tomcat, 1981, Secret Sex: Male Erotic Fantasies (as Tom Anicar), 1976, Magda (as Lisa Wells), 1981, Snow Angel, 1995, Hidden Agenda, 1997; ghost writer: non-fiction The Happy Hustler (Grant Tracy Saxon), 1976, Marilyn Chambers: My Story (Marilyn Chambers), 1976, Xaviera Meets Marilyn (Xaviera Hollander and Marilyn Chambers), 1977; musical plays A Midsummer Night's Dream, music and lyrics, 1968, Allison Wonderland, music and lyrics, 1970, The Marvelous Misadventure of Sherlock Holmes, book, music and lyrics, 1971; TV scripts Sleeping Over segment of Family, ABC, 1978, Russian Pianist segment, ABC, 1979, 1 Child of the Owl, NBC After-Sch. Spl., 1979; contbr. articles to Playboy, Cosmopolitan, Penhouse, Oui, Los Angeles, Gentleman's Quar., Westways; West Coast editor: Grosset & Dunlap, Inc., N.Y.C., 1978—; lead writer for TV: Family Passions, 1993-94, Life's A Bitch!, 1994, Friends & Lovers, 1994; theatre dir., pianist, organist, composer. Recipient Emmy award nomination 1982, 83, 84, 85, 87; U.S. Nat. Student Assn. grantee, 1965. Mem. Authors Guild Am., Writers Guild Am. West. Democrat. Roman Catholic. Home: 2851 Calle Loreto Palm Springs CA 92264-6702 *Nearly losing my life to the disease pancreatitis at sixteen years of age certainly opened my eyes to how precious the future was—I had a second chance, and I knew I'd been given talent for a reason: to use. I've since lived wanting to do it all, know it all, feel and experience all that life has to offer. I've no desire to write literature, but rather to entertain, and everything I write has that motivation as a core. If my storytelling ability moves just one person to laughter—or tears—I've accomplished all I set out to do.*

RACITI, CHERIE, artist; b. Chgo., June 17, 1942; d. Russell J. and Jacque (Crimmins) R. Student, Memphis Coll. Art, 1963-65; B.A. in Art, San Francisco State U., 1968; M.F.A., Mills Coll., 1979. Assoc. prof. art San Francisco State U., 1984-89, prof., 1989—; lectr. Calif. State U., Hayward, 1974, San Francisco Art Inst., 1978; mem. artist com. San Francisco Art Inst., 1974-85, sec., 1980-81. One woman show U. Calif., Berkeley, 1972, Nicholas Wilder Gallery, Los Angeles, 1975, San Francisco Art Inst., 1977, Marianne Deson Gallery, Chgo., 1980, Site 375, San Francisco, 1989, Reese Bullen Gallery, Humboldt State U., Arcata, Calif., 1990; group shows include Whitney Mus. Art, 1975, San Francisco Sci. Fiction, The Clocktower, N.Y.C., Otis-Parsons Gallery, Los Angeles, 1984-85, San Francisco Art Inst., 1985, Artists Space, N.Y.C., 1988, Angles Gallery, Santa Monica, 1987, Terrain Gallery, San Francisco, 1992, Ctr. for the Arts, San Francisco, 1993. Bd. dirs. New Langton Arts, 1988-92. Eureka fellow Fleishhacker Found., San Francisco; recipient Adaline Kent award San Francisco Art Inst., 1976, Djerassi resident, 1994, Tyrone Guthrie Ctr. resident, Ireland, 1995. Office: San Francisco State U Art Dept 1600 Holloway Ave San Francisco CA 94132-1722

RACOWSKY, CATHERINE, reproductive physiologist, researcher; b. Oxford, Eng., May 30, 1951; came to U.S., 1976; d. Derek Gerald and Joan (Elsey) Wyatt; m. Marshall Lewis Racowsky, June 13, 1982; triplets: Adam, Lauren, Daniel. BA, U. Oxford, 1974; PhD, U. Cambridge, Eng., 1978. Postdoctoral fellow in ob-gyn. Harvard Med. Sch., Boston, 1976-78, Lalor fellow in reproduction, 1978-79; rsch. assoc. Ariz. State U., Tempe, 1979-83, rsch. asst. prof., 1983-89, rsch. assoc. prof., 1989-91; assoc. prof. ob-gyn. U. Ariz., Tucson, 1991—; in vitro fertilization cons. S.W. Fertility Ctr., Phoenix, 1989-91; dir. rsch. ob-gyn. U. Ariz., Tucson, 1991—, dir. In-Vitro Fertilization Lab., 1991—; interviewed for TV and mag. Guest editor: Jour. Microscopy Rsch. Tech., 1994; contbr. chpt. to book, articles to profl. jours. Lectr. Valley Presbyn. Ch., Green Valley, Ariz., 1994. NIH grantee, 1982-85, 85-89; recipient Career Advancement award NSF, 1992, Internat. Basic Sci. award Soc. Assisted Reproduction Tech. and Andrology, 1992. Mem. Soc. Study of Reproduction (mem. editorial bd. 1990-94), Am. Fertility Soc. Office: Univ of Ariz Coll Medicine Dept Ob-Gyn Tucson AZ 85724

RADA, ALEXANDER, university official; b. Kvasy, Czechoslovakia, Mar. 28, 1923; s. Frantisek and Anna (Tonnkova) R.; came to U.S., 1954, naturalized, 1959; M.S., U. Tech. Coll. of Prague, 1948; postgrad. Va. Poly. Inst., 1956-59, St. Clara U., 1966-67; Ed.D., U. Pacific, 1975; m. Ingeborg Solveig Blakstad, Aug. 8, 1953; children: Alexander Sverre, Frank Thore, David Harald. Head prodn. planning dept. Mine & Iron Corp., Kolin, Czechoslovakia, 1941-42; mgr. experimenting and testing dept. Avia Aircraft, Prague, 1943-45; sec.-gen. Central Bldg. Office, Prague, 1948; head metal courses dept. Internat. Tech. Sch. of UN, Grafenaschau, W.Ger., 1949-50; works mgr. Igref A/S, Oslo, 1950-51; cons. engr., chief sect. machines Steel Products Ltd., Oslo, 1951-54; chief engr., plant supr. Nelson J. Pepin & Co., Lowell, Mass., 1954-55; sr. project engr., mfg. supt. Celanese Corp. Am., Narrows, Va., 1955-60; mgr. mfg., facilities and maint. FMC Corp., San Jose, Calif., 1960-62; mgr. adminstrn. Sylvania Electronic Systems, Santa Cruz, Calif., 1962-72; asst. to pres., devel. officer Napa (Calif.) Coll., 1972-88; chief exec. officer NAVCO Pacific Devel. Corp., Napa, 1984-91; pres. NAVCO Calif. Co., 1991—; prof. indsl. mgmt. Cabrillo Coll., Aptos, Calif., 1963-72; mgmt. and engring. cons., 1972—. Pres. ARC, Santa Cruz, 1965-72, bd. dirs., pres., Napa, 1977-88; mem. Nat. Def. Exec. Res., U.S. Dept. Commerce, Washington, 1966—, chmn. No. Calif. region 9, 1981-88; mem. President's Export Council-DEC, San Francisco, 1982—. Recipient Meritorious Service citation ARC, 1972, Etoile Civique l'Ordre de l'Etoile Civique, French Acad., 1985; registered profl. engr., Calif. Mem. NSPE, Calif. Soc. Profl. Engrs., Am. Def. Preparedness Assn., Assn. Calif. Community Coll. Adminstrs., Nat. Assn. Corp. Dirs., World Affairs Council No. Calif., Phi Delta Kappa. Editor-in-chief Our Youth, 1945-48; co-editor (with P. Boulden) Innovative Management Concepts, 1967. Home and Office: 1019 Ross Cir Napa CA 94558-2118

RADANOVICH, GEORGE P., congressman. BS in Agr. Bus. Mgmt., Calif. State Polytechnic U., 1978. Pres. Radanovich Winery, Mariposa, Calif., 1982—; county supr., 1986-87; chair County Planning Commn., 1988-92; mem. U.S. Ho. of Reps., 104th Congress, Washington, 1995—; mem. Budget Com., Resources Com., subcoms. Water & Power Resources, Nat. Parks, Forests & Lands. U.S. Ho. of Reps., 104th Congress, mem. Resources Com. Task Force on Endangered Species. Mem. Calif. Agrl. Leadership Program Class XXI, Rotary (Paul Harris Fellowship). Office: US House Reps 213 Cannon Washington DC 20515

RADCLIFFE, ALBERT E., judge. BA in History, U. Oreg., 1969, JD, 1972. Bar: Oreg. 1972, U.S. Dist. Ct. Oreg. 1973, U.S. Ct. Appeals (9th cir.) 1983. Pvt. practice, 1973-86; judge U.S. Bankruptcy Ct. Oreg., Eugene, 1986—; vis. bankruptcy judge We. Dist. Wash., 1992; spkr. in field. Mem. Fed. Bar Assn. (hon.), N.W. Bankruptcy Inst. Planning Com., Lane County Bar Assn. (bankruptcy subcom. chmn. 1993-94), Tau Kappa Epsilon. Office: US Bankruptcy Ct Oreg PO Box 1335 151 W Seventh Ave Eugene OR 97440

RADER, DIANE CECILE, lawyer; b. San Francisco, Sept. 8, 1949; d. Dale A. and Genevieve A. (Couture) R. BA, Portland State U., 1987; JD, Lewis and Clark Coll., 1990. Bar: Oreg. 1990, Idaho 1992, U.S. Dist. Ct. Idaho 1992, U.S. Dist. Ct. Oreg. 1995. Founder, cons. D.C. Rader & Assocs., Portland, 1972-88; real estate broker Rader Realty, Portland, 1982—; pvt. practice law Boise, 1992—; with Rader and Rader, Ontario, Oreg., 1990—; bd. dirs. Criminal Justice Adv. Bd., Malheur County, Oreg. Asst. mng. editor: Internat. Legal Perspectives, 1989-90. Polit. cons. and fundraiser various parties and campaigns, Oreg., 1972-88; fundraiser, cons. charitable orgns., Oreg., 1972—, others. Mem. ABA, ATLA, Nat. Assn. Criminal Def. Lawyers, Oreg. Trial Lawyers Assn., Oreg. Criminal Def. Lawyers Assn., Oreg. State Bar (pub. svc. and info. com. 1994-97, chmn. pub. rels. subcom. 1994—), Phi Alpha Delta. Office: Rader & Rader 381 W Idaho Ave Ontario OR 97914-2344

RADER, PAUL ALEXANDER, minister, administrator; b. N.Y.C., Mar. 4, 1934; s. Lyell M. and Gladys Mina (Damon) R.; m. Kay Fuller, May 29, 1956; children: Edith Jeanne, James Paul, Jennifer Kay. BA, Asbury Coll., Wilmore, Ky., 1956; BD, Asbury Theol. Sem., 1959; LLD (hon.), Asbury Coll., Wilmore, Ky., 1984; ThM, So. Bapt. Theol. Sem., Louisville, 1961; D Missiology, Fuller Theol. Sem., 1973. Ordained to ministry Salvation Army, 1961. Tng. prin. The Salvation Army, Seoul, 1973-74, edn. sec., 1974-77, chief sec., 1979-83; tng. prin. The Salvation Army, Suffern, N.Y., 1983-86; divisional comdr. for Ea. Pa. and Del. The Salvation Army, Phila., 1986-88; chief sec. ea. ter. The Salvation Army, N.Y.C., 1988; territorial comdr. U.S.A. western ter. The Salvation Army, Rancho Palos Verdes, Calif., 1989—; adj. prof. Seoul Theol. Sem., 1980-82; trustee Asian Ctr. for Theol. Studies and Mission, 1980-83, Asbury Coll., 1988—; pres. The Salvation Army Calif. Corp., Rancho Palos Verdes, 1989—. Recipient Alumnus A award Asbury Coll., 1982, Disting. Alumni award Asbury Theol. Sem., 1989; Paul Harris fellow Rotary Internat., 1989. Mem. Am. Soc. Missiology, Internat. Assn. Mission Studies. Office: The Salvation Army 639 Sabrina Way Vista CA 92084-6264*

RADKE, LINDA FOSTER, publishing consultant; b. Gary, Ind., July 14, 1952; d. Marvin Bremmy and Ann (Weiss) Foster; m. Lowell Radke, Mar. 10, 1983; children: Gradey Benjamin, Daniel Spencer. BA, Ariz. state U., 1978. Cert. elem. spl. edn., edn. mentally handicapped and learning disabilities tchr. Instr. Ariz. State U., Tempe; instrnl. aid Coronado High Sch., Scottsdale, Ariz.; learning resource specialist Saguaro High Sch., Scottsdale; tchr. 6th grade Griffith Elem. Sch. Balsz Sch. Dist., Phoenix, 1981-83; owner, mgr. Domestic Cons. Inc., Scottsdale, 1983-88; publ., cons. Five Star Publs. Inc., Chandler, Ariz., 1988—. Author: (book directory) The Options Directory of Child and Senior Care, 1987, 89, (book) Nannies Maids and More, 1989, That Hungarian's in My Kitchen, 1990, 94, 95, Household Careers, 1993 (Citation 1994, Citation for Excellence 1994, 1st Pl. non-fiction book award Ariz. Pres Women, Inc. 1994, Citation for Career Edn. Initiatives, Am. Assn. Career Edn. Initiatives 1994); pub. Economical Guide to Self-Publishing, Kosher Kettle: International Adventures in Jewish Cooking, 1996, The Proper Pig's Guide to Mealtime Manners, Shakespeare for Children, 1989 (Named Best Toys Under $10 Ladies Home Jour. 1993), The Sixty-Minute Shakespeare, 1990, Shakespeare: To Teach or Not to Teach, 1992, 94, Profits of Death: An Insider Exposes the Death Care Industries, 1997. Mem. Ariz. Book Publ. Assn. (founding mem.), Ariz. Authors' Assn., Ariz. Press Women Inc. (recipient awards for non-fiction book, newsletter, news release, brochure, others), Internat. Assn. Ind. Pubs., Pubs. Mktg. Assn. Democrat.

RADLEY, GREGORY NORMAN, custom furniture maker, educator; b. Santa Monica, Calif., May 30, 1956; s. Norman Carlyle and Donna May (Ludlow) R.; m. Debra Kay Policky; children: Scott, Melissa, Matthew. BS in Indsl. Tech. Edn., Brigham Young U., 1989. Custom cabinet/furniture maker Radley Woodworks, Ventura, Calif., 1983-85; indsl. arts tchr. Buena High Sch., Ventura, 1990-91, Moorpark (Calif.) H.S., 1991-92; craftsman, owner Radley Fine Furniture, Ventura, 1992—; speaker at woodworking shows, 1992-93. Contbr. chpt. to book. Recipient 1st place nat. cabinetmaking competition Vocat. Indsl. Clubs Am., 1989, 2d place traditional furniture award Design in Wood, 1994, 3d place furniture award Art of Calif. mag., 1993, Best Craftsmen-Traditional Furniture award Early Am. Life mag., 1994. Mem. San Diego Fine Woodworkers. Office: Radley Fine Furniture 2745 Sherwin Ave Ste 12 Ventura CA 93003

RADOVSKY, FRANK JAY, zoologist, museum administrator; b. Fall River, Mass., Jan. 5, 1929; s. David Reuben and Minnie Esther (Simon) R. AB, U. Colo., 1951; MS, U. Calif., Berkeley, 1959, PhD, 1964. Asst. rsch. parasitologist U. Calif., San Francisco, 1963-69; acarologist Bishop Mus., Honolulu, 1969-85, chmn. dept. entomology, 1972-85, asst. dir., 1977-85, disting. chair of zoology, 1984-86; vis. prof. entomology Oreg. State U., Corvallis, 1987; dir. rsch. and collections N.C. State Mus. Natural Scis., Raleigh, 1987-91; prof. Oreg. State U., 1994—; faculty affiliate U. Hawaii, Honolulu, 1971-85, U. Okla., 1991; rsch. assoc. Bishop Mus., 1986—. Author: (book) Mites Parasitic on Bats, 1967, Pacific Tropical Biogeography, 1984; (with others) Life Histories and Reproductive Patterns of Mites, 1993; editor Ann. Rev. Entomology, 1978—, Jour. of Med. Entomology, 1969-85, 87; contbr. over 70 articles to profl. jours. Mem. Animal Species Adv. Commn., Hawaii, 1972-80. Lt. USNR, 1951-55. Fellow NIH, USPHS, 1959-62; grantee NIH, 1964-76, NSF, 1970-85. Mem. AAAS, Entomol. Soc. Am., Internat. Congress Acarology (exec. sec. 1971-78), Soc. Vector Ecologists, Assn. Systematics Collections (bd. dirs. 1982-85), Acarological Soc. Am. (bd. dirs. 1988-90), Sigma Xi. Democrat. Jewish. Office: Cordley Hall 2046 Dept Entomology Oreg State U Corvallis OR 97331-2907

RAE, MATTHEW SANDERSON, JR., lawyer; b. Pitts., Sept. 12, 1922; s. Matthew Sanderson and Olive (Waite) R.; m. Janet Hettman, May 2, 1953; children: Mary-Anna, Margaret Rae Mallory, Janet S. Rae Dupree. AB, Duke, 1946, LLB, 1947; postgrad., Stanford U., 1951. Bar: Md. 1948, Calif. 1951. Asst. to dean Duke Sch. Law, Durham, N.C., 1947-48; assoc. Karl F. Steinmann, Balt., 1948-49, Guthrie, Darling & Shattuck, L.A., 1953-54; nat. field rep. Phi Alpha Delta Law Frat., L.A., 1949-51; research atty. Calif. Supreme Ct., San Francisco, 1951-52; ptnr. Darling, Hall & Rae (and predecessor firms), L.A., 1955—; mem. Calif. Commn. Uniform State Laws, 1985—, chmn., 1993-94; chmn. drafting com. for revision Uniform Prin. and Income Act of Nat. Conf., 1991—, Probate and Mental Health Task Force, Jud. Coun. Calif., 1996—. Vice pres. L.A. County Rep. Assembly, 1959-64; mem. L.A. County Rep. Ctrl. Com., 1960-64, 77-90, exec. com., 1977-90; vice chmn. 17th Congl. Dist., 1960-62, 28th Congl. Dist., 1962-64; chmn. 46th Assy. Dist., 1962-64, 27th Senatorial Dist., 1977-85, 29th Senatorial Dist., 1985-90; mem. Calif. Rep. State Ctrl. Com., 1966—, exec. com., 1966-67; pres. Calif. Rep. League, 1966-67; trustee Rep. Assocs., 1979-94, pres., 1983-85, chmn. bd. dirs., 1985-87. 2d lt. USAAF, WWII. Fellow Am. Coll. Trust and Estate Counsel; academician Internat. Acad. Estate and Trust Law (exec. coun. 1974-78); mem. ABA, L.A. County Bar Assn. (chmn. probate and trust law com. 1964-66, chmn. legis. com. 1980-86, chmn. program com. 1981-82, chmn. membership retention com. 1982-83, trustee 1983-85, dir. Bar Found., 1987-93, Arthur K. Marshall award probate and trust law sect. 1984, Shattuck-Price Meml. award 1990), South Bay Bar Assn., State Bar of Calif. (chmn. state bar jour. com. 1970-71, probate com. 1974-75; exec. com. estate planning trust and probate law sect. 1977-83, chmn. legis. com. 1977-89; co-chmn. 1991-92; probate law cons. group Calif. Bd. Legal Specialization 1977-88; chmn. conf. dels. resolutions com. 1987, exec. com. conf. dels. 1987-90), Lawyers Club L.A. (bd. govs. 1981-87, 1st v.p. 1982-83), Am. Legion (comdr. Allied post 1969-70), Legion Lex (bd. dirs. 1964—, pres. 1969-71), Air Force Assn., Aircraft Owners and Pilots Assn., Town Hall (gov. 1970-78, pres. 1975), World Affairs Coun., Internat. Platform Assn., Breakfast Club (law, pres. 1989-90), Commonwealth Club, Chancery Club (pres. 1996-97), Rotary, Phi Beta Kappa (councilor Alpha Assn. 1983—, pres. 1996), Omicron Delta Kappa, Phi Alpha Delta (supreme justice 1972-74, elected to Disting. Svc. chpt. 1978), Sigma Nu. Presbyterian. Home: 600 John St Manhattan Beach CA 90266-5837 Office: Darling Hall & Rae 777 S Figueroa St Fl 37 Los Angeles CA 90017-5800

RAEBER, JOHN ARTHUR, architect, construction specifier consultant; b. St. Louis, Nov. 24, 1947; s. Arthur William and Marie (Laux) R. AA, Jefferson Coll., 1968; AB, Washington U., 1970, MArch, 1973. Registered architect, Calif., Mo.; cert. constrn. specifier; cert. Nat. Coun. Arch. Specification writer Hellmuth, Obata & Kassabaum, St. Louis, 1973-78, constrn. administr., 1978-79; mgr. of specifications Gensler & Assocs., San Francisco, 1979-82; ind. constrn. specifier San Francisco, 1982—; adj. prof. architecture Calif. Coll. Arts and Crafts, San Francisco, 1986—; access code advisor Constrn. Industry & Owners, 1982—; spkr., instr. seminars orgns., univs., 1982—; mem. Calif. State Bldg. Standards Commn. Accessibility Adv. Panel, Sacramento, 1981, Calif. Subcom. Rights of Disabled Adv. Panel, Sacramento, 1993; cons. Nat. Inst. Bldg. Scis., 1996—. Author: CAL/ABL: Interpretative Manual to California's Access Barriers Laws, 1982; co-author: (with Peter S. Hopf) Access for the Handicapped, 1984; columnist Constrn. Specifier Mag., 1988-95. Vol. Calif. Office Emergency Svcs. Safety Assessment, Sacramento, 1991—. Fellow AIA (San Francisco chpt. codes com., Calif. coun. codes and standards com., nat. masterspec rev. com. 1982-84, nat. codes com. corr.), Contrns. Specifications Inst. (cert., columnist newsletter San Francisco chpt. 1984-95, Ben John Small award for Outstanding Stature as practicing specifications writer 1994, pres. St. Louis chpt. 1978-79, pres. San Francisco chpt. 1993-94, tech. com., edn. com., publs. com., Specifications Proficiency award San Francisco chpt. 1989, Tech. Commendation award 1987); mem. Specifications Cons. in Ind. Practice (nat. pres. 1990-92, nat. sec./treas. 1988-90), Internat. Conf. Bldg. Officials, Phi Theta Kappa. Home and Office: 888 Farrell W 606 San Francisco CA 94109

RAECKER, JEFFREY SCOTT, aerospace engineer; b. Denver, Mar. 4, 1964; s. W. Ronald Raecker and Saundra Louise (Nicholls) Proctor; m. Kelli Maurene McClintock, Mar. 14, 1992; children: Taylor Ryan, Kendall Morgan. BS in Aeronautics, San Jose State Univ., 1987; MS in Aerospace Engring., Calif. State Univ., Long Beach, 1991. Cert. airframe and powerplant mechanic, FAA. Engr., scientist Douglas Aircraft Co., Long Beach, 1987-89, McDonnell Douglas Space Sys., Huntington Beach, Calif., 1989-93; sys. engr. Gen. Rsch. Corp., El Segundo, Calif., 1993-95; sr. engr. McDonnell Douglas Aerospace, Long Beach, 1995-96; sr. specialist engr. Boeing Co., Everett, Wash., 1996—. Mem. AIAA, Nat. Space Soc., SpacePac, Space Cause. Office: Boeing Comml Airplane Group PO Box 3707 M/S 04-EH Seattle WA 98124-2207

RAEDEKE, LINDA DISMORE, geologist; b. Great Falls, Mont., Aug. 20, 1950; d. Albert Browning and Madge (Hogan) Dismore; m. Kenneth John Raedeke, Dec. 26, 1971 (div. 1982); m. Charles Moore Swift, Jr., Mar. 14, 1992. BA in History, U. Wash., 1971, MS in Geology, 1979, PhD, 1982. Geomorphologist, park planner Corporacion Nacional Forestal and U.S. Peace Corps, Punta Arenas, Chile, 1972-74; glacial geologist Empresa Nacional del Petroleo, Punta Arenas, 1972-75; geologist FAO, UN, Punta Arenas, 1974; geologist Lamont-Doherty Geol. Obs., Columbia U., Tierra del Fuego, Chile, 1974-75; Wetlands evaluation project coord. Wash. Dept. Agr., U. Wash., Seattle, 1975-76; curator Remote Sensing Applications Lab., U. Wash., 1976-77; geol. rsch. asst. U. Wash., Seattle, 1977-81; exploration geologist Chevron Resources Co., Denver, 1981-84; rsch. geologist Chevron Oil Field Rsch. Co., La Habra, Calif., 1984-89; sr. compensation analyst Chevron Corp., San Francisco, 1989-90; staff geologist Chevron Overseas Petroleum, Inc., San Ramon, Calif. 1990-91, project leader, 1991-95, new ventures coord. for the far east, 1995-96, sr. staff analyst for planning, 1996—. Contbr. articles to profl. jours. Recipient Cert. of Achievement YWCA, 1988. Mem. Am. Geophys. Union, Geol. Soc. Am., Am. Assn. Petroleum Geologists (poster chmn. 1987, internat. chmn. 1996 meeting). Office: Chevron Overseas Petroleum Inc PO Box 5046 San Ramon CA 94583-0946

RAEL, HENRY SYLVESTER, retired health administrator, financial and management consultant; b. Pueblo, Colo., Oct. 2, 1928; s. Daniel and Grace (Abeyta) R.; m. Helen Warner Loring Brace, June 30, 1956 (dec. Aug. 1980); children: Henry Sylvester Jr., Loring Victoria. AB, U. So. Colo., 1955; BA in Bus Adminstrn., U. Denver, 1957, MBA, 1958. Sr. boys counselor Denver Juvenile Hall, 1955-58; adminstrv. asst. to pres. Stanley Aviation Corp., Denver, 1958-61; Titan III budget and fin. control supr. Martin Marietta Corp., Denver, 1961-65; mgmt. adv. services officer U. Colo. Med. Center, Denver, 1965-72; v.p. fin., treas. Loretto Heights Coll., Denver, 1972-73; dir. fin. and adminstrn. Colo. Found. for Med. Care, 1973-86, Tri-County Health Dept., Denver, 1986-96; fin. cons., Denver, 1996—; instr. fin. mgmt., mem. fin. com. Am. Assn. Profl. Standards Rev. Orgn., 1980-85; speaker systems devel., design assns., univs., 1967-71. Mem. budget lay adv. com. Park Hill Elem. Sch., Denver, 1967-68, chmn., 1968-69; vol. worker Boy and Girl Scouts, 1967-73; bd. dirs. Community Arts Symphony, 1981-83, 85-87; controller St. John's Episcopal Cathedral, 1982-83; charter mem.

Pueblo (Colo.) Coll. Young Democrats, 1954-55; block worker Republican party, Denver, 1965-68, precinct committeeman, 1978-84 ; trustee Van Nattan Scholarship Fund, 1974-96; bd. dirs. Vis. Nurse Assn., 1977-84, treas., 1982-84. Served with USAF, 1947-53; res. 1954-61. Recipient Disting. Service award Denver Astron. Soc., 1968, Citation Chamberlin Obs., 1985; Stanley Aviation masters scholar, 1957; Ballard scholar, 1956. Mem. Assn. Systems Mgmt. (pres. 1971-72), Hosp. Systems Mgmt. Soc., Budget Execs Inst. (v.p. chpt. 1964-65, sec. 1963-64), Colo. Pub. Employees Retirement Assn. (bd. dirs. 1993), Denver Astron. Soc. (pres. 1965-66, bd. dirs. 1982-94), Am. Assn. Founds. for Med. Care (fin. com. 1981-82), Nat. Astronomers Assn. (exec. bd. 1965—). Epsilon Xi, Delta Psi Omega. Episcopalian. Home: 7755 E Quincy Ave # 57 T-8 Denver CO 80237

RAESE, JOHN THOMAS, physiologist; b. West Chester, Pa., Apr. 3, 1930; s. John Curtis and Alice Nelson (McKelvey) R.; m. Joan Marie Keeney, Sept. 12, 1953; children: John Craig, David Senna, Carolyn Kendall, Mary Ann. BS in Agr., W.Va. U., 1952, MS in Agronomy, 1959; PhD in Agronomy, U. Md., 1963. Soil tester for state W.Va. U., Morgantown, 1956-59, instr., 1958-59; rsch. asst. U. Md., College Park, 1959-62; tchr. biology Wheaton (Md.) High Sch., 1962-63; rsch. plant physiologist USDA Agrl. Rsch. Svc., Bogalusa, La., 1963-68; plant physiologist USDA Agrl. Rsch. Svc., Monticello, Fla., 1968-71; rsch. plant physiologist USDA Agrl. Rsch. Svc., Wenatchee, Wash., 1971-89, collaborator, 1990—; rschr. Wash. State U., Wenatchee, 1990—; hon. prof. Wenatchee Valley Coll., 1994—; speaker and cons. in field. Author: (with others) Horticultural; Reviews, 1989; editor: Pear Production-Pacific Northwest, 1990; contbr. 150 articles to profl. jours. Scoutmaster Boy Scouts Am., Bogalusa, 1967-=68, chmn. bd. com., Tallahassee, Fla., 1969-71, com. mem., Wenatchee, 1972-73; coach girls softball Little League, Wenatchee, 1973-75; co-organizer pear meeting Internat. Horticulture, Corvallis, Oreg., 1981. With USN, 1952-56. Recipient Pear Growers award Wash. Pear Growers, 1990, Wash. State Hort. Assn. Silver Pear award, 1996; grantee Wash. State Horticulture, 1965-89, Comml. Cos., 1990—. Republican. Presbyterian. Office: US Tree Fruit Rsch Lab 1104 N Western Ave Wenatchee WA 98801-1230

RAFAEL, RUTH KELSON, archivist, librarian, consultant; b. Wilmington, N.C., Oct. 28, 1929; d. Benjamin and Jeanette (Spicer) Kelson; m. Richard Vernon Rafael, Aug. 26, 1951; children: Barbara Martinez Yates, Brenda Elaine. BA, San Francisco State U., 1953, MA, 1954; MLS, U. Calif.-Berkeley, 1968. Cert. archivist, 1989. Tchr. San Francisco Unified Sch. Dist., 1956-57; libr. Congregation Beth Sholom, San Francisco, 1965-83; archivist Western Jewish History Ctr. of Judah L. Magnes Mus., Berkeley, Calif., 1968, head archivist, libr., curator of exhibits, 1969-94; cons. NEH, Washington, NHPRC, Congregation Sherith Israel, San Francisco, Mount Zion Hosp., San Francisco, Benjamin Swig archives project, San Francisco, Koret Found., Camp Swig, Saratoga, Calif.; project dir. Ethnicity in Calif. Agriculture, 1989, San Francisco Jews of European Origin, 1880-1940, an oral history project, 1976; curator exhibits Western U.S. Jewry. Author: Continuum, San Francisco Jews of Eastern European Origin, 1880-1940, 1976, rev. edit., 1977; (with Davies and Woogmaster) poetry book Relatively Speaking, 1981; Western Jewish History Center: Archival and Oral History Collections, Judah L. Magnes Meml. Mus., 1987; contbg. editor Western States Jewish History, 1979—. Mem. exec. bd. Bay Area Library Info. Network, 1986-88. NEH grantee, 1985. Mem. Calif. Libr. Assn., Soc. Am. Archivists, Acad. Cert. Archivists.

RAFEEDIE, EDWARD, federal judge; b. Orange, N.J., Jan. 6, 1929; s. Fred and Nabeeha (Hishmeh) R.; m. Ruth Alice Horton, Oct. 8, 1961; children: Fredrick Alexander, Jennifer Ann. BS in Law, U. So. Calif., 1957, JD, 1959; LLD (hon.), Pepperdine U., 1978. Bar: Calif. 1960. Pvt. practice Santa Monica, Calif., 1960-69; mcpl. ct. judge Santa Monica Jud. Dist., Santa Monica, 1969-71; judge Superior Ct. State of Calif., L.A., 1971-82; dist. judge U.S. Dist. Court (cen. dist.) Calif., L.A., 1982—; bd. adv. Santa Monica UCLA Med. Ctr., 1982. With U.S. Army, 1950-52, Korea. Office: US Dist Ct RM 244P 312 N Spring St Los Angeles CA 90012-4701

RAFKIN, ALAN, television and film director; b. N.Y.C., July 23, 1928; s. Victor and Til (Bernstein) R.; children—Dru, Leigh Ann. B.S., Syracuse U., 1950. guest lectr. Bowling Green State U., 1975. Actor Robert Q. Lewis TV Show, 1955, daytime shows, CBS-TV; dir. Verdict is Yours, 1960, Mary Tyler Moore Show, 1970-71, Sanford and Son, 1972, Bob Newhart Show, 1972-73, Rhoda, 1973, Let's Switch, 1975, MASH, 1976-77, Love, American Style, 1970-71, Laverne & Shirley, 1977-83; TV movie: One Day at a Time: Barbara's Crisis, 1981-82; films include Ski Party, 1965, The Ghost and Mr. Chicken, 1966, The Ride to Hangman's Tree, 1967, Nobody's Perfect, 1968, The Shakiest Gun in the West, 1968, Angel in my Pocket, 1969, How to Frame a Figg, 1971. Served with U.S. Army, 1950-52. Democrat. Jewish. also: Grey Entertainment 9150 Wilshire Blvd Beverly Hills CA 90212*

RAFTERY, MIRIAM GENSER, writer, columnist; b. San Diego, Apr. 22, 1957; d. Philip and Mary Evelyn (Vick) Genser; m. Mark Raymond Raftery, July 21, 1979; children: Jason Michael, Kathleen Shannon. BA in Environ. Studies, U. Calif., Santa Barbara, 1979. Intern Planning & Conservation League, Sacramento, 1979; legis. aide Senator Bob Wilson, Sacramento, 1979-80, Assemblyman Elihu Harris, Sacramento, 1981-82; newsroom copy asst. Idaho Statesman, Boise, 1983-84; regional mktg. mgr. Con Am, San Diego, 1984-86; freelance writer La Mesa, Calif., 1986—; columnist San Diego Union-Tribune, 1992—; contracted feature writer San Diego Decorating Mag., 1994—; instr. The Writing Ctr., San Diego, 1994. Author: Apollo's Fault; contbr. articles to popular mags. Mem. Nat. Fedn. Press Women, Romance Writers Am. (workshop co-chair San Diego chpt. 1993-94), Calif. Press Women (pres. so. dist. 1993-95, v.p. membership 1993, Sweepstakes award 1992), Internat. Interior Designers Assn. (press mem.), San Diego Press Club, Phi Beta Kappa. Home and Office: 4438 Hideaway Pl La Mesa CA 91941-6800

RAGAN, SUSAN SWARTZ, art educator; b. Ft. Scott, Kans., Dec. 14, 1947; d. Daniel V. and Jean (Berry) Swartz; m. James Burton Ragan; children: Alison, John, Jennifer. BS in Edn., Mo. U., 1969; MEd, Colo. State U., Ft. Collins, 1974. Cert. tchr., Colo., Mo. Tchr. Colorado Springs (Colo.) Schs., 1970-72, Ft. Collins Schs., 1973-74; counselor St. Vrain Schs., Longmont, Colo., 1979-80; counselor, tchr. Sch. Dist. R32J, Salida, Colo., 1980—. Freelance artist for local and area agys., Salida, 1980—. Bd. dirs. Developmental Tng. Svcs., Salida, 1983-85; bd. trustees Salida Libr., 1992—. Recipient Excellence in Quilting award That Patchwork Pl., Bothell, Wash., 1991. Mem. NEA, PEO, Salida Edn. Assn., Colo. Quilt Coun. (Quilt Colo. 1st Pl. 1994), Delta Kappa Gamma. Democrat. Office: Salida Schs PO Box 70 Salida CO 81201

RAGEN, DOUGLAS M., lawyer; b. Oakland, Calif., May 1, 1942. BA, U. Oreg., 1964; LLB, Stanford U., 1967. Bar: Oreg. 1967. Ptnr. Miller, Nash, Wiener, Hager & Carlsen, Portland, Oreg. Mem. ABA (mem. securities, natural resources, utilities and environ. law sects., mem. litigation sect., chairperson environ. law, tort and ins. practice sect. com.), Oreg. State Bar. Office: Miller Nash Wiener Hager & Carlsen 111 SW 5th Ave Portland OR 97204-3604

RAGLAND, BOB, artist, educator; b. Cleve., Dec. 11, 1938; s. Carey and Violet (English) R. Cert. Completion, Rocky Mount Sch. Art, Denver, 1968. Instr. painting and drawing Denver Pub. Libr., 1969-71, Eastside Action Ctr., Denver, 1969-71; artist-in-residence Model Cities Cultural Arts Ctr. Workshop, 1971-73; artist/tchr. KRMA-TV; lectr. in field; vis. artist Denver Pub. Sch. for the Arts, 1993-96, Urban Peak Homeless Ctr., Denver, 1996; founding faculty mem. Auraria campus C.C. Denver, 1970-72; lectr. Afro-Am. art of the 60's and 70's; visual arts coord. City Spirit Project, Denver, 1978; instr. Gove Cmty. Sch., 1979—, Met. State Coll., Denver, Arapahoe C.C., Littleton, Colo. Exhibited in 16th Ann. Drawing Exhbn., Dallas Mus. Fine Art Traveling Exhbn., 1967, Tubman Gallery, Boston, 1981; one man shows at Cleve. State U., 1968, Denver Nat. Bank, 1980-81, Century Bank Cherry Creek, Denver, 1980-81; works in permanet collections at Denver Pub. Libr., Karamu House, Cleve., Irving St. Ctr. Cultural Arts Program, Denver; group exhibns. include Colo. History Mus., 1993, 94, 95, Savageau Art Gallery, 1995-96, Met. State Coll. Visual Arts Ctr., 1993; Author: The Artists Survival Handbook or What to do till You're Rich and Famous, 1980; pub.: Colo. Gallery Guide, 1978—; contbr. Black Umbrella/Black Artists Denver. Chmn. Arts and Humanities Com., 1968-69. Inducted in Colo. 100, Denver Post, Colo. Hist. Soc., 1993; recipient Excellence in Arts award Denver Black Arts Festival, 1993, Recognition award KCNC-TV and Denver Ctr. Performing Arts, 1986. Mem. Colo. Black Umbrella. Home and Studio: 1723 E 25th Ave Denver CO 80205

RAGLAND, CARROLL ANN, law educator, judicial officer; b. New Orleans, Nov. 28, 1946; d. Herbert Eugene Watson and Mary May (LeCompte) Leathers; children: Robert A. Sinex, Jr., Stacie Bateman, Joy Montgomery. JD, San Francisco Law Sch., 1980. Bar: Calif. 1980, U.S. Supreme Ct. 1993. Pvt. practice Santa Rosa, Calif., 1980-85; child custody mediator Sonoma County Superior Ct., Santa Rosa, 1985-86; chief dep. county counsel Butte County Counsel, Oroville, Calif., 1986-87; chief dep. dist. atty. Butte County Dist. Atty., Oroville, 1987-95; referee Shasta County Superior Ct., Redding, Calif., 1995-96; commr. Shasta County Superior Ct., Redding, 1996—; dean faculty, law prof. Calif. No. Sch. of Law, Chico, 1987—; instr. Shasta Coll., 1996—. Commr. Yuba County Juvenile Justice and Delinquency Prevention Commn., Marysville, Calif., 1993-94. Fellow Lawyers in Mensa. Office: Shasta County Superior Ct 1431 Market St Redding CA 96001

RAGLAND, SAMUEL CONNELLY, industrial engineer, management consultant; b. Nashville, July 12, 1946; s. Julian Potter and Stella (Thompson) R.; m. Marilyn Margaret Oppelt, July 15, 1967; children: Sherry Anne, David Michael. BSBA, Ariz. State U., 1974; MBA U. Phoenix, 1991. Indsl. engr. First Interstate Bank, Phoenix, 1966-76, Beckman Instruments, Scottsdale, Ariz., 1976-78; mgmt. analyst Ariz. Legislative Budget Com., Phoenix, 1978; indsl. engr. mgmt. systems ITT Courier Terminal Systems, Tempe, Ariz., 1978-81; project control adminstr. Gen. Host Corp., Phoenix, 1981; sr. cons. Arthur Young & Co., Phoenix, 1981-82; ops. analyst City of Phoenix, 1982-84; project leader Garrett Engine div. Allied-Signal Corp. (formerly Garrett Turbine Engine Co.), Phoenix, 1984-92, cons., program mgr., TRW, Mesa, 1992-93; prin., owner Ragland Assocs., 1994—; exec. mgmt. cons. Gov.'s Office Excellence in Govt., State of Ariz., 1995-96, mgr. quality assurance Coxreels, Inc., 1996—; dir. Mary Moppets of Highland Inc., 1977-81. Mem. Inst. Indsl. Engrs. (sr. mem. cen. Ariz. chpt., dir. cmty. rels. 1983-85, dir. chpt. devel. 1985-86, v.p., pres.-elect 1986-87, pres. 1987-88), Inst. Indsl. Engrs. (nat. chpt. devel. com. 1988-91, chmn.), Assn. Systems Mgmt. (div. dir. 1989-92, pres. 1992-93), Phoenix Philatelic Assn. Contbr. articles to profl. publs. Address: 11319 E Jenan Dr Scottsdale AZ 85259-3121 *Personal philosophy: Information and information resource management are the foundation to success and survival. Information must be timely, accurate and available and must be used effectively.*

RAHE, RICHARD HENRY, psychiatrist, educator; b. Seattle, May 28, 1936; s. Henry Joseph and Delora Lee (Laube) R.; m. Laurie Ann Davies, Nov. 24, 1960 (div. Dec. 1990); children: Richard Bradley, Annika Lee. Student, Princeton U., 1954-57; MD, U. Wash., 1961. Diplomate Am. Bd. Psychiatry and Neurology. Chief resident in psychiatry U. Wash. Sch. Medicine, Seattle, 1965; rsch. psychiatrist USN, San Diego, 1965-75; commdg. officer Naval Health Rsch. Ctr., San Diego, 1976-80; exec. officer Long Beach (Calif.) Naval Hosp., 1980-82; commdg. officer Guam Naval Hosp., Agana, 1982-84; prof. psychiatry U.S. Univ. Health Scis. Mil. Med. Sch., Bethesda, Md., 1984-86, U. Nev. Sch. Medicine, Reno, 1986—; dir. Mil. Stress Studies Ctr., Bethesda, 1984-86, Nev. Stress Ctr. Vets. Affairs Med. Ctr., Reno, 1986—. Contbr. numerous articles to sci. jours., chpts. to books; photographer prints and video. Dir. Nev. Mental Health Inst., Sparks, 1991-94. Capt. USN, 1965-86. Recipient Humanitarian award Vietnamese Refugee Com., 1974, Dept. of State award for treatment of Am. hostages held in Iran, 1981. Fellow Am. Psychiat. Assn.; mem. Am. Psychosomatic Soc. (past pres.), World Psychiat. Assn. (past pres. mil. sect.). Home: 638 Saint Lawrence Ave Reno NV 89509-1440 Office: VA Med Ctr Code 151-C 1000 Locust St Reno NV 89520-0102

RAIKLEN, HAROLD, aerospace engineering consultant; b. Boston, June 7, 1920; s. Michael Isaac and Jennie Zelda (Jaffee) R.; m. Shirley Gesetz, Nov. 24, 1954; children: David R., Margery Claire. B, MIT, 1947, M, 1949. Dir. electronics and electrics Rockwell, El Segundo, Calif.; v.p. program mgr. Saturn II Rockwell, Downey and Seal Beach, Calif., 1965-70; v.p. rsch. and engring. Rockwell, Downey, Calif., 1970-72; v.p. B-1 bomber engring. Rockwell, El Segundo, Calif., 1972-80, v.p. strategic aircraft, 1980-82; amateur anthropologist, Long Beach, Calif., 1982—. Contbr. articles to profl. jours.; co-patentee in anti-skid sys. Co-recipient Collier trophy USAF, 1976, Pub. Svc. award NASA, 1969. Fellow AIAA (assoc., Aircraft Design award 1979); mem. IEEE (life), Old Crows Assn., China Burma India Veterans Assn., Pi Tau Sigma, Tau Beta Pi, Phi Kappa Phi. Home and Office: 4300 Cerritos Ave Long Beach CA 90807-2462

RAILSBACK, SHERRIE L., adoption search and reunion consultant; b. Phila., Mar. 12, 1942; children: Ricky, Cindy. BBA, U. Ky., 1981. Sales mgr. Marjo Cosmetics, Ft. Wayne, Ind.; asst. dir. patient fin. svcs. Riverside Meth. Hosp., Columbus, Ohio; cons. Railsback and Assocs., Long Beach, Calif.; adoption search/reunion cons. Searchers Connection, L.A. Mem. NAFE, ASTD, Am. Adoption Congress, Book Publicists of So. Calif., Toastmasters.

RAIN, RHONDA L., performing arts executive, counselor, educator; b. Grinnell, Iowa, Feb. 28, 1952; d. Henry Garrett and Anne Lucille (Roberts) Rook. B in Univ. Studies, U. N.Mex., 1984, MA in Counseling, 1993. Lic. profl. counsel, N.Mex.; nat. cert. counselor. Tchr./counselor Rough Rock (Ariz.) Demo. Sch., 1973; acad. support staff U. N.Mex. Med. Sch., Albuquerque, 1974-84, U. N.Mex. Main Campus, Albuquerque, 1988-91; intern counselor Manzanita Ctr. U. N.Mex., Albuquerque, 1993; intern counselor Career Ctr. and Albuquerque Tech.-Vocat. Inst., 1993, career counselor, 1993—; acad. advisor and counselor, coord. advisement and testing U. N.Mex.-Valencia, Los Lunas, 1994-96, chief examiner GED, 1994-96; CEO Raindrops, 1996—; vocat. adv. com. New Futures H.S., Albuquerque, 1988-93; peer counselor U. N.Mex. Main Campus, Albuquerque, 1988-93; grad. asst. counseling dept. U. N.Mex., Albuquerque, 1991-92; vol. counselor Youth Diagnostic and Detention Ctr., Albuquerque, 1992. Neighborhood Watch capt. Crime Prevention Program, N.Mex., 1986-94; vol. musician Albuquerque Civic Light Opera Assn., 1978-83; mem. Valley cultural com. U. N.Mex.-Valencia, 1994-96. Recipient Fine Arts award Bank of Am., Huntington Beach, Calif., 1970; No. Ariz. U. music scholar, 1970-73. Mem. ACA, Nat. Acad. Advising Assn., Nat. Career Devel. Assn., N.Mex. Career Devel. Assn., Nat. Bd. Cert. Counselors (nat. cert. counselor), Internat. Platform Assn., Golden Key Internat. Honor Soc. (life), Pi Lambda Theta (v.p. 1986).

RAINEY, BARBARA ANN, sensory evaluation consultant; b. Fond du Lac, Wis., Nov. 11, 1949; d. Warren and Helen Eileen (Ginther) Bradley; m. Phillip Michael Rainey, Sept. 5, 1970; 1 child, Nicolette. BS, Kans. State U., 1975. Group leader Armour & Co. R&D Ctr., Scottsdale, Ariz., 1976-80; owner Barbara A. Rainey Cons., Manteca, Calif., 1980—. Contbr. articles to profl. jours. Kans. State Alumni fellow Kans. State U. Alumni Assn., 1990. Mem. ASTM, Inst. Food Technologists (prof. sensory divsn. sec. 1980-82, chmn. 1984-85, short course spkr. 1979-81, Ctrl. Valley subsect., treas. 1989-91, chmn.-elect./sec. 1991-92, chmn. 1992-93), Phi Kappa Phi. Office: PO Box 622 Manteca CA 95336-0622

RAISIAN, JOHN, university institute director, economist; b. Conneaut, Ohio, July 30, 1949; s. Ernest James and Ruby Lee (Owens) R.; m. Joyce Ann Klak, Aug. 17, 1984; children: Alison Kathleen, Sarah Elizabeth. BA, Ohio U., 1971; PhD, UCLA, 1978; LLD (hon.), Albertson Coll. Idaho, 1995. Rsch. assoc. Human Resources Rsch. Ctr., U. So. Calif., L.A., 1972-73; cons. Rand Corp., Santa Monica, Calif., 1974-75, 76; vis. asst. prof. econs. U. Wash., Seattle, 1975-76; asst. prof. econs. U. Houston, 1976-80; sr. economist Office Rsch. and Evaluation, U.S. Bur. Labor Stats., Washington, 1980-81; spl. asst. for econ. policy Office Asst. Sc. for Policy, U.S. Dept. Labor, Washington, 1981-83, dir. rsch. and tech. support, 1981-84; pres. Unicon Rsch. Corp., L.A., 1984-86; sr. fellow Hoover Instn., Stanford, Calif., 1986—, assoc. dir., dep. dir., 1986-90, dir., 1990—; exec. dir. Presdl. Task Force on Food Assistance, Washington, 1983-84. Mem. editorial bd. Jour. Labor Rsch., 1983—; contbr. articles to profl. jours. Advisor Nat. Coun. on Handicapped, Washington, 1985-86, Nat. Commn. on Employment Policy, Washington, 1987-88; chmn. minimum wage bd. Calif. Indsl. Welfare Commn., 1987; mem. nat. adv.com. Student Fin. Assistance, Washington, 1987-89; corp. mem. Blue Shield Calif., 1994-96; bd. dirs. Sentinel Groups Fund, Inc., 1997—; mem. Pacific Coun. Internat. Policy, nat. adv. bd. City Innovation. Recipient Best Publ. of Yr. award Econ. Inquiry, Western Econ. Assn., 1979, Disting. Teaching award U. Houston Coll. Social Scis., 1980, Disting. Svc. award U.S. Dept. Labor, 1983; predoctoral fellow Rand Corp., 1976. Mem. Am. Econs. Assn., Western Econ. Assn. (chmn. nominating com. 1992), Commonwealth Club of Calif., World Affairs Coun., Mont Pelerin Soc., Coun. on Fgn. Rels., Nat. Assn. Scholars, Phi Beta Kappa. Republican. Office: Stanford U Hoover Hoover Inst War-Revolution Stanford CA 94305-6010

RAJALA, KAREN RAE, economic and community development administrator; b. Richland, Wash., July 30, 1950; d. Raymond Edward and Georgia Marie (Dickson) Burns; m. Jacob August Rajala, Sept. 2, 1972; children: Matthew August, Andrew George. BA in Sociology with distinction, Wash. State U., 1972, BA in Polit. Sci. cum laude, 1974, MA in Polit. Sci., 1978. Adminstrv. asst. Whitman County Epton Soc., Pullman, Wash., 1973-78; cons., grantwriter, planner Ely, Nev., 1981-83; coord. White Pine County Econ. Diversification Program, Ely, 1983—, White Pine Power Project, Ely, 1988—; alt. Block Grant Adv. Bd., Carson City, Nev., 1994, adv. bd. 1995—; vol. cons. Little People's Hedstart, Ely, 1981-83; cons. White Pine C. of C., Ely, 1982-83; mem. Nev. State Comty. Devel., 1992. Project leader, mem. 4-H Parents and Leaders Coun., Ely, 1984—; active No. Nev. Comty. Coll. Adv. Bd., Ely, 1984—, White Pine Pub. Mus., Ely, 1992—, PEO Sisterhood, 1970—, v.p., 1981, pres., 1986. Recipient Meritorious Svc. award White Pine Dist. 4-H, 1993, Rural Nevadans Who Dare to Care award U. Nev. Med. Sch., 1994. Mem. Am. Soc. Pub. Adminstrn., Nev. Econ. Devel. Assn., Pi Sigma Alpha. Democrat. Methodist. Office: White Pine County Econ Div 953 Campton St Ely NV 89301-1973

RAKOWSKI, JOHN MICHAEL, geologist; b. Southampton, N.Y., June 25, 1946; s. John J. and Gertrude (Kuroski) R.; m. Alice D. Reiber, Dec. 20, 1968; children: Janet L., David A. BS in Geology, Fla. State U., 1968. Geologist Amoco Prodn. Co., New Orleans, 1968-73, 75-79, Denver, 1979-81; geologist Amoco Internat. Oil Co., Chgo., 1973-74; geologist Tesoro Petroleum, Jakarta, Indonesia, 1974-75, La Paz, Bolivia, 1975; v.p. exploration Striker Petroleum Corp., Denver, 1981-84; geol. cons. Rak-Energy, Lakewood, Colo., 1984—. Counselor, asst. cub scout troop Boy Scouts Am., Lakewood, Colo., 1983-86. Mem. Am. Assn. Petroleum Geologists (cert.), New Orleans Geol. Soc., Rocky Mountain Assn. Geologists, Soc. Ind. Profl. Earth Scientists (bd. dirs. 1993-95), Houston Geol. Soc., Nat. Fedn. Ind. Bus., Denver Gem and Mineral Guild (pres. 1995). Republican. Office: Rak-Energy 2357 S Devinney St Lakewood CO 80228-4807

RALEIGH, CECIL BARING, geophysicist; b. Little Rock, Aug. 11, 1934; s. Cecil Baring and Lucile Nell (Stewart) R.; m. Diane Lauster, July 17, 1982; children: Alison, Marianne, Lawrence, David. B.A., Pomona (Calif.) Coll., 1956; M.A., Claremont (Calif.) Grad. Sch., 1958; Ph.D., UCLA, 1963. Fellow Research Sch. Phys. Sci., Australian Nat. U., Canberra, 1963-66; geophysicist U.S. Geol. Survey, Menlo Park, Calif., 1966-80; program mgr. for earthquake prediction research program U.S. Geol. Survey, 1980-81; dir. Lamont-Doherty Geol. Obs. and prof. geol. scis. Columbia U., Palisades, N.Y., 1981-89; dean Sch. Ocean and Earth Sci. and Tech. U. Hawaii, Honolulu, 1989—; CEO Ctr. for a Sustainable Future, Inc., 1996—; mem. Gov.'s Task Force on Sci. Tech., 1996—; mem. NAS/NRC Ocean Studies Bd.; chmn. NAS/NRC Yucca Mountain Panel; bd. dirs. JOI, Inc., High Tech. Devel. Corp. Author papers control earthquakes, rheology of the mantle, mechanics of faulting, crystal plasticity. Recipient Interdisciplinary award U.S. Nat. Com. Rock Mechanics, 1969, 74; Meritorious Service award Dept. Interior, 1974; Barrows Dist. Alumnus award Pomona Coll. Fellow Am. Geophys. Union, Geol. Soc. Am. Democrat. Office: U Hawaii Sch Ocean Earth Sci & Tech Honolulu HI 96822

RALEY, WILLIAM GREENE, systems analyst; b. Pensacola, Fla., July 8, 1958; s. Nathaniel Greene and Virginia Phillips (Glass) R. BS magna cum laude, U. Ala., 1979, MA, 1980. FLMI; cert. in gen. ins. Programmer Shell Oil, Houston, 1981-82; staff cons. Am. Gen., Houston, 1982-85; host computer tech. specialist Avco Aerostructures, Nashville, Tenn., 1985-86; sr. programmer/analyst Auto Club So. Calif., Costa Mesa, 1986—. Editor, pub. After Hours mag., 1989-95; copy editor Huntington Beach News, 1991.Editor, pub., coord. Neon Vanilla newsletter. Active Mus. Neon Art, L.A., 1988—, Ctr. for Sci. in Pub. Interest, Washington, 1992—. Mem. Horror Writers Assn., Mensa, Phi Beta Kappa, Delta Phi Alpha, Pi Mu Epsilon. Home: PO Box 538 Sunset Beach CA 90742-0538

RALLISON, MARVIN L., pediatrician, educator; b. Coalville, Utah, Feb. 8, 1929; s. Robert Leo and Lucile (Peterson) R.; m. Beth West, June 21, 1957; children: Scott W., Mark W., Todd W., Lisa. BS in Chemistry, Utah State U., 1954; MD, U. Utah, 1957. Diplomate Am. Bd. Pediatrics, Am. Bd. Endocrinology. Intern Mpls. Gen. Hosp., 1957-58; resident in pediatrics U. Minn. Hosp., 1958-61; instr. U. Minn., Mpls., 1960-61; pediatrician Salt Lake Clinic, Salt Lake City, 1961-63; fellow in endocrinology U. Utah, Salt Lake City, 1963-65, asst. prof., 1968-73, assoc. prof. pediatrics, 1973-79, prof. pediatrics, 1979—. Author: Growth Problems in Children, 1986; contbr. numerous articles to profl. jours. Med. dir. Camp Utada for diabetic youth, Salt Lake City area, 1963-93. Maj. Med. Corps U.S. Army, 1957-68. Mem. Am. Thyroid Assn. (pub. health com.), Am. Diabetes Assn. (bd. dirs. 1987-89, chmn. com. on edn. 1981-83, mem. youth com. 1984-89, Outstanding Contbr. to Camping and Am. Diabetes Assn. award 1993), Lawson Wilkins Pediatric Endocrine Soc., Western Soc. Pediatric Rsch. Home: 1706 Oakridge Dr Salt Lake City UT 84106-3253 Office: U Utah Med Ctr Salt Lake City UT 84132

RALSTON, LENORE DALE, academic policy and program analyst; b. Oakland, Calif., Feb. 21, 1949; d. Leonard Earnest and Emily Allison (Hudnut) R. BA in Anthropology, U. Calif., Berkeley, 1971, MPH in Behavioral Sci., 1981; MA in Anthropology, Bryn Mawr Coll., 1973, PhD in Anthropology, 1980. Asst. rschr. anthropology inst. internat. studies U. Calif., Berkeley, 1979-82, rsch. assoc. Latin Am. Study Ctr., 1982-83, acad. asst. to dean Sch. of Optometry, 1990-95, prin. policy analyst, chancellor's office, 1995—; assoc. scientist, rsch. adminstr. Med. Rsch. Inst., San Francisco, 1982-85; cons. health sci. Berkeley, 1986-90; mem. fin. bd. Med. Rsch. Inst., 1983-84; speaker in field. Co-author: Voluntary Effects in Decentralized Management, 1983; contbr. articles to profl. jours. Commr. Cmty. Health Adv. Com., Berkeley, 1988-90; vice chair, commr. Cmty. Health Commn., Berkeley, 1990-93; mem. bd. safety com. Miles, Inc., Berkeley, 1992—. Grantee Nat. Rsch. Svc. Award, WHO, NIMH, NSF. Fellow Applied Anthropology Assn.; mem. APHA, Am. Anthropology Assn., Sigma Xi. Home: 1232 Carlotta Ave Berkeley CA 94707-2707

RAMALEY, JUDITH AITKEN, academic administrator, endocrinologist; b. Vincennes, Ind., Jan. 11, 1941; d. Robert Henry and Mary Krebs (McCullough) Aitken; m. Robert Folk Ramaley, Mar. 1966 (div. 1976); children: Alan Aitken, Andrew Folk. BA, Swarthmore Coll., 1963; PhD, UCLA, 1966; postgrad., Ind. U., 1967-69. Rsch. assoc., lectr. Ind. U., Bloomington, 1967-68, asst. prof. dept. anatomy and physiology, 1969-72; asst. prof. dept. physiology and biophysics U. Nebr. Med. Ctr., Omaha, 1972-74, assoc. prof., 1974-78, prof., 1978-82, assoc. dean for rsch. and devel., 1979-81; asst. v.p. for acad. affairs U. Nebr., Lincoln, 1980-82; prof. biol. scis. SUNY, Albany, N.Y., 1982-87, v.p. for acad. affairs, 1982-85, acting pres., 1984, exec. v.p. for acad. affairs, 1985-87; exec. vice chancellor U. Kans., Lawrence, 1987-90; pres. Portland (Oreg.) State U., 1990—; mem. endocrinology study sect. NIH, 1981-84; cons.-evaluator North Cen. Accreditation, 1978-82, 89-90; mem. regulatory panel NSF, 1979-82; mem. Ill. Commn. Scholars, 1980-90; adv. com. Bank of Am.; mem. ACE Commn. on Govt. Rels. Co-author: Progesterone Function: Molecular and Biochemical Aspects, 1972; Essentials of Histology, 8th edit., 1979; editor: Covert Discrimination, Women in the Sciences, 1978; contbr. articles to profl. jours. Bd. dirs. Family Svc. of Omaha, 1979-82, Albany Symphony Orch., 1984-87, mem. exec. com., 1986-87, 2d v.p., mem. exec. com., 1986-87, Capital Repertory Co., 1986-89, Assn. Portland Progress, 1990—, City Club of Portland, 1991-92, Metro Family Svcs., 1993—, Campbell Inst. for Children, Portland Met. Sports Authority, 1994; vice-chair Ore. Campus Compact (exec. com. 1996—), nat. adv. coun. Sch.-Work Opportunities, 1996—; bd. dirs. NCAA Pres. Commn., 1991, chair divsn. II subcom., 1994, mem. joint policy bd., 1994; chmn. bd. dirs. Albany Water Fin. Authority, 1987; mem.

exec. com. United Way Douglas County, 1989-90; mem. adv. bd. Emily Taylor Women's Resource Ctr., U. Kans., 1988-90; mem. Silicon Prairie Tech. Assn., 1989-90, Portland Opera Bd., 1991-92, Portland Leaders Roundtable, 1991—; mem. bd. devel. com. United Way of Columbia-Willamette, 1991—; active Ore. Women's Forum, 1991—, Portland Met. Sports Authority; progress bd. Portland-Multnomah County, 1993—. NSF grantee, 1969-71, 71-77, 75-82, 77-80, 80-83. Fellow AAAS; mem. Nat. Assn. State Univs. and Land Grant Colls. (exec. com., mem. senate 1986-88, vice chair commn. urban agenda 1992—), Assn. Am. Colls. and Univs. (bd. dirs. 1995—), ACE commn. govt. rels., Kellogg Commn. on future of state and land-grant univs.; mem. Endocrine Soc. (chmn. edn. com. 1980-85), Soc. Study Reprodn. (treas. 1983-85), Soc. for Neuroscis., Am. Physiol. Soc., Am. Coun. on Edn. (chmn. commn. on women in higher edn. 1987-88), Assn. Portland Progress (bd. dirs.), Portland C. of C. (bd. dirs. 1995), Western Assn. of Schs. and Colls. (commr. 1994). Office: Portland State U Office of the President PO Box 751 Portland OR 97207-0751

RAMASWAMY, PADMANABHAN, materials scientist; b. Ambattur, India, Mar. 5, 1953; came to U.S., 1977; s. Ramaswamy Iyer and Bhagavathy (Narayanan) Padmanabhan. BSc in Physics, Loyola Coll., Madras, India, 1972; B of Engring. in Metallurgy, Indian Inst. Sci., Bangalore, 1975; PhD in Materials Sci., Oreg. Grad. Ctr., 1982. Research and devel. engr. Bharat Electronics, Ltd., Bangalore, 1975-77; research scientist Oreg. Grad. Ctr., Beaverton, 1982-83; sr. staff engr. Motorola, Inc., Phoenix, 1984-86, prin. staff scientist, 1987-91, mem. tech. staff, mgr. materials and characterization lab., adv. pkg. deve. ctr., 1991-95, mgr. electron microscopy lab., materials rsch./strat. techs., 1995—. Contbr. articles to profl. jours. Mem. Electron Microscopy Soc. Am., Electrochem. Soc., Materials Rsch. Soc. Home: 1325 E Grandview St Mesa AZ 85203-4427

RAMBO, A. TERRY, anthropologist, research program director; b. San Francisco, Apr. 3, 1940; s. Arthur Ira Rambo and Dorothy V. (Miller) Schlee; m. Dawn Jean Bowman, Jan. 24, 1971 (dec. July 1987); children: Charmaine Malia, Claire Norani. AB in Anthropology with distinction, U. Mich., 1963; MA in Anthropology, Am. U., 1969; PhD in Anthropology, U. Hawaii, 1972. Rsch. scientist Human Scis. Rsch., Inc., McLean, Va., 1964-69; acting asst. prof. anthropology U. Hawaii, 1971-72; asst. prof. anthropology Wash. State U., 1972-73; vis. prof. social sci. Grad. Sch. Politics and Econs., Dalat U., Saigon, Vietnam, 1973-75; lectr. dept. anthropology and sociology U. Malaya, 1975-80; sr. fellow, coord. program on renewable resources mgmt. East-West Ctr. Environ. and Policy Inst., Honolulu, 1980-92; dir. program on environ., coord. Indochina initiative East-West Ctr., Honolulu, 1992-97, sr. fellow, program on environment, 1997—; bd. dirs. S.E. Asian Univs. Agroecosystem Network; cons. in field. Author: Primitive Polluters, 1985, Comparison of Peasant Social Systems of Northern and Southern Vietnam, 1973; co-editor: An Introduction to Human Ecology Research on Agricultural Systems in Southeast Asia, 1984, Cultural Values and Human Ecology in Southeast Asia, 1985, Ethnic Diversity and the Control of Natural Resources in Southeast Asia, 1988, Agroecosystems of the Midlands of Northern Vietnam: A Report on a Preliminary Human Ecology Field Study of Three Districts in Vinh Phu Province, 1990, Environment, Natural Resources, and the Future Development of Laos and Vietnam: Papers from a Seminar, 1991, Profiles in Cultural Evolution, 1991, The Challenges of Vietnam's Reconstruction, 1992, Too Many People, Too Little Land: The Human Ecology of a Wet Rice-Growing Village in the Red River Delta of Vietnam, 1993, The Challenges of Highland Development in Vietnam, 1995, Some Issues of Human Ecology in Vietnam (in Vietnamese), 1995, Red Books, Green Hills: The Impact of Economic Reform on Restoration Ecology in the Midlands of Northern Vietnam, 1996; also reports, papers, monographs, procs. in field; contbr. articles to profl. publs., chpts. to books. Grantee Asia Soc./SEADAG, 1969-70, U. Malaya, 1976-79, Ford Found., 1978-79, 84, 85-87, 87-89, 91-93, 95-96, 96—, U. Hawaii East-West Ctr., 1981-82, 84-85, Rockefeller Bros. Fund, 1988-89, 90-92, 94-95, 97—, MacArthur Found., 1990-91, 91-93, 93-95, 96—, Luce Found., 1995-96; Nat. Def. Fgn. Lang. fellow 1970-71, Ford Found. S.E. Asia rsch. fellow, 1972, 73-74, 75-76. Office: East-West Ctr Program on Environment 1601 East-West Rd Honolulu HI 96848-1601

RAMBO, ELIZABETH LOUISE, English literature educator; b. Phila., July 27, 1954; d. Victor Birch and Margaret (Gordon) R.; m. James Worth Pence III, May 20, 1989. BA in English, St. Andrews Presbyn. Coll., 1976; MA in English and Creative Writing, U. Mo., 1978; PhD in English, U. N.C., 1990. Asst. prof. English Biola U., La Mirada, Calif., 1990—, chair dept. English, 1993-96, assoc. prof. English, 1995—. Author: Colonial Ireland in Medieval English Literature, 1994. Mem. MLA, Nat. Coun. Tchrs. of English, Medieval Acad. Am., Conf. on Christianity and Lit., Medieval Assn. of Pacific. Presbyterian. Office: Biola U English Dept 13800 Biola Ave La Mirada CA 90639-0002

RAMER, BRUCE M., lawyer; b. Teaneck, N.J., Aug. 2, 1933; s. Sidney and Anne S. (Strassman) R.; children: Gregg B., Marc K., Neal I. BA, Princeton U., 1955; LLB, Harvard U., 1958. Bar: Calif. 1963, N.J. 1958. Assoc., Morrison, Lloyd & Griggs, Hackensack, N.J., 1959-60; ptnr. Gang, Tyre, Ramer & Brown, Inc., L.A., 1963—; bd. dirs. Home Shopping Network, Inc., Inc. Exec. dir. Entertainment Law Inst., Law Ctr. of U. So. Calif.; bd. of councilors Law Ctr. U. So. Calif.; past pres. L.A. chpt.; chmn., nat. bd. govs. Am. Jewish Com., nat. v.p., 1982-88, pres. L.A. chpt., 1980-83, chair Western region, 1984-86, comty. svc. award, 1987; chmn. Asia Pacific Rim Inst.; trustee Loyola Marymount U., L.A. Children's Mus., 1986-89; vice chair United Way, 1991-93, corp. bd. dirs., 1981-93, chair coun. pres. 1989-90, mem. cmty. issues coun., 1989-90, chair discretionary fund distbn. com., 1987-89; bd. dirs., chair Geffen Playhouse, bd. dirs. L.A. Urban League, 1987-93, 96—, Jewish Fedn. Coun. of Greater L.A. (mem. Cmty. Rels. com., bd. dirs., exec. com.), Jewish TV Network, Sta. KCET-TV; mem., bd. dirs. Rebuild L.A.; bd. govs. Calif. Cmty. Found.; recipient Ann. Brotherhood award NCCJs, 1990; mem. Fellows of Am. Bar Found. Pvt. U.S. Army, 1958-59, 2d lt., 1961-62. Mem. ABA, L.A. County Bar Assn., Calif. Bar Assn., Beverly Hills Bar Assn. (Exec. Dirs. award 1988, Entertainment Lawyer of Yr. award 1996), L.A. Copyright Soc. (pres. 1974-75), Calif. Copyright Conf. (pres. 1973-74), Princeton Club (pres. 1975-78). Office: Gang Tyre Ramer & Brown Inc 132 S Rodeo Dr Beverly Hills CA 90212-2403

RAMES, DOUGLAS DWIGHT, civil engineer; b. Colorado Springs, Colo., Apr. 14, 1942; s. Dwight S. and Eleanor A. (Roach) R.; m. Audrey Joan Satter, Nov. 26, 1963; children: Steven D., Wendy M., Eydee J. BSCE, S.D. Sch. Mines & Tech., 1965; postgrad., Ind./Purdue U., Harvard U. Registered profl. engr., Colo. Project engr. Colo. Dept. of Hwys., Eagle, 1970-72; resident engr. Colo. Dept. of Hwys., Grand Junction, 1972-78; preconstrn. engr. Colo. Dept. of Hwys., Greeley, 1978-84, asst. dist. engr., 1984-88; region dir. Colo. Dept. Transp., Greeley, 1988—. Commr. urban renewal City of Greeley, 1993—. Office: Colo Dept Transp 1420 2d St Greeley CO 80631

RAMESH, KALAHASTI SUBRAHMANYAM, materials scientist; b. Tiruchi, Madras, India, Mar. 22, 1949; s. Subrahmanyam Veeraragaviah and Kuntala (Chinnaswami) Kalahasti; m. Atsumi Yoshida Ramesh, Jan. 30, 1990; children: Siva, Arjun. MS in Ceramic Engring., Benaras Hindu U., India, 1973; D in Engring., Tokyo Inst. Tech., 1986. Asst. rsch. mgr. Steel Authority India Ltd., Ranchi, Bihar, 1979-80; lectr. dept. ceramic engring. Benaras U., Varanasi, India, 1980-82; tech. mgr. ceramics div. TYK Corp., Tokyo, 1986-89; mgr. rsch. and devel. Mer Corp., Tuscon, Ariz., 1989; prin. scientist Battelle meml. Inst., Columbus, Ohio, 1989-93; sr. sci. Pacific N.W. Lab., Richland, Wash., 1993—; adv. Internat. Bus. Svc., Tokyo, 1988-89; cons. HTP Inc., Sharon, Pa., 1989—, Pierce Leslie Cashew & Coffee Ltd., 1997—, Hi-Tech Internat. Cons., 1997—; mem. U.S. Dept. Energy Ceramics Adv. Com., Washington, 1991—; tech. dir. XTALONIX, Inc., Columbus, Ohio, 1993—; mem. Boreskov Meml. Conf. Catalyst and Catalysis Sci. and Engring., Russia, 1997. Panel mem. NSF on Materials and Mechanics, 1995. Mombusho rsch. fellow Ministry Edn. Japan, 1982-84, Max Planck Soc. fellow, 1989. Fellow Indian Inst. Ceramics, Inst. Ceramics U.K.; mem. Japan India Assn., Found. for Indsl. Rsch. (expert), N.Y. Acad. Scis. Hindu. Home: 100 Hillview Dr Richland WA 99352-9668 Office: Hi Tech Internat Cons 100 Hillview Dr Richland WA 99352-9668

RAMESH, UTPALA G., biochemist; b. Delhi, India, Oct. 12, 1956; came to U.S., 1982; d. Gopal Krishna and Prema Kamath; m. S.K. Ramesh, Jan. 21, 1987; 1 child, Arvind. BSc, Bombay U., 1976, MSc, 1978; PhD, So. Ill. U., 1987. Postdoctoral fellow U. Calif., Davis, 1987-90; scientist Baxter MicroScan, West Sacramento, Calif., 1990—; sr. scientist, supr. Dade Internat., West Sacramento, Calif., 1994—. Dakshina fellow Bombay U., 1976-78. Fellow Biophys. Soc.; mem. AAAS, Am. Chem. Soc., Am. Soc. Microbiologists. Office: Dade Internat 2040 Enterprise Blvd West Sacramento CA 95691-3427

RAMEY, FELICENNE HOUSTON, business educator; b. Phila.; m. Melvin R. Ramey, Sept. 5, 1964; 2 children. BS, Pa. State U., University Park, 1961; MS, Duquesne U., 1967; JD, U. Calif., Davis, 1972; MA, Calif. State U., Sacramento, 1978. Bar: Calif. Microbiologist Pa. Dept. Labs., Phila., Walter Reed Army Med. Ctr., Washington; chemist Calgon Corp., Pitts.; instr. Carnegie-Mellon U., Pitts.; dep. atty. gen. Calif. Dept. Justice, Sacramento; clk. U.S. Dist. Ct. Calif., Sacramento; asst. prof. Calif. State U. Sch. Bus. Adminstrn., Sacramento, assoc. prof., chmn. dept. behavior and environment, assoc. dean, prof.; exec. officer U. Calif., Davis; dir. litigation Human Rights Commn., Sacramento; bd. dirs. Legal Aid Soc., Sacramento mag.; vis. scholar Ga. Inst. Tech., 1981, Boston Coll., 1988. Mem. edn. com. Blacks for Effective Community Action, 1978—. ACE fellow U. Calif., Santa Cruz, 1992—. Mem. Calif. Agrl. Alumni Assn. (bd. dirs.), Western Bus. Law Assn. (pres., pres. elect, v.p., exec. sec. Calif. and Nev. chpts. 1983-89), Nat. Assn. Women Deans and Adminstrs., Sacramento Black C. of C. (edn. com. 1990—, bd. dirs. 1989—). Home: 612 Cleveland St Davis CA 95616-3128 Office: Calif State U Sch Bus Adminstrn Sacramento CA 95819-6088

RAMIL, MARIO R., judge; b. Quezon City, The Philippines, June 21, 1946; came to U.S., 1956; s. Quintin A. and Fausta M. (Reyes) R.; m. Judy E. Wong, Nov. 6, 1971; children: Jonathan, Bradley. BA in Polit. Sci., Calif. State U., Hayward, 1972; JD, U. Calif., San Francisco, 1975. Bar: Calif. 1976, Hawaii 1976, U.S. Dist. Ct. Hawaii, U.S. Dist. Ct. (no. dist.) Calif., U.S. Ct. Appeals (9th cir.). Law clk. San Francisco Neighborhood Legal Aid Found., 1973-75; legal counsel Sandigan-Newcomers Svcs., Inc., San Francisco, 1975-76; dep. atty. gen. Dept. Labor and Indsl. Rels., 1976-79; dep. atty. gen. cen. adminstrn. U. Hawaii, 1979-80; staff atty. house majority atty.'s office Hawaii Ho. of Reps., 1980; pvt. practice, 1980-82; dep. atty. gen. adminstrv. div. State of Hawaii, 1982-84, ins. commr., 1984-86; dir. Hawaii State Dept. Labor and Indsl. Rels., Honolulu, 1986-91; of counsel Lyons, Brandt, Cook and Hiramatsu, 1991-93; assoc. justice Hawaii Supreme Ct., Honolulu, 1993—. Bd. dirs. Hawaii Youth-At-Risk, 1989; co-chair state conv. Dem. Party State of Hawaii, 1984; mem. Adv. Coun. on Housing and Constrn., State of Hawaii, 1981; pres., bd. dirs. Hawaii Non-Profit Housing Corp.; exec. sec., chmn. adminstrv. budget com. Oahu Filipino Community Coun.; bd. dirs, legal advisor Oahu Filipino Jaycees, 1978-81. Office: Ali'iolani Hale 417 S King St Honolulu HI 96813-2902 Mailing Address: PO Box 2560 Honolulu HI 96804-2560*

RAMIREZ, CARLOS B., college administrator; b. Oakland, Calif., July 12, 1945; s. LeRoy and Belina R. Ramirez; m. Judy Dale Behrend, Feb. 1, 1969; children: Elizabeth Maria Brazil, Carlos Joaquin Behrend. BA, U. San Francisco, 1968; MA, U. N.ex., 1969; PhD in Polit. Sci., U. Calif., Santa Barbara, 1979. Coord. for Fillmore Santa Paula Ednl. Ctr., Ventura, Calif., 1975-76; divsn. dir. social sci. Moorpark (Calif.) Coll., 1976-79; assoc. dean instrn. Oxnard (Calif.) Coll., 1979-81; pres. City Coll. of San Francisco, 1983-88; campus dir. U. N.Mex., Los Alamos, 1989—; pres. Coun. of Two-Yr. Colls. of Four-Yr. Instns., Washington, 1995-96; vice chair Vocat. Opportunity State of N.Mex., Santa Fe, 1995—; treas. N.Mex. Assn. Cmty. Colls., 1995—; mem. No. N.Mex. Def. Adjustment Task Force, Santa Fe, 1993—. Author pamphlet series: Decolonizing the Interpretation of the Chicano Political Expereience, 1975. Recipient Image award Image de Los Alamos, 1992, Disting. Alumni award San Francisco U., 1988, 2d Ednl. award, 1983. Home: 189 La Cueva Los Alamos NM 87544 Office: U NMex-Los Alamos 4000 University Dr Los Alamos NM 87544

RAMIREZ, JANICE L., assistant school superintendent; b. Dodge City, Kans., July 16, 1947; d. Chris William and Lois (Moore) Langvardt; 1 child, Jessica. BS, Emporia State U., 1969, MA, 1970; PhD, Kans. State U., 1982. Div. prin. Highland Park High Sch./Topeka (Kans.) pub. schs.; prin. Topeka pub. schs.; prin. Mesa (Ariz.) pub. schs., asst. supt.; mem. mid. level task force Ariz. Dept. Edn. Contbr. articles to profl. jours. Recipient Kamelot award; named one of Top 100 Bus. Women in Ariz., Today's Ariz. Woman Success Mag., 1996-97. Mem. Am. Assn. Sch. Pers. Adminstrs., Ariz. Sch. Pers. Adminstrs. Assn., Nat. Assn. Ednl. Negotiators, Kans. Assn. for Middle Level Edn., Nat. Mid. Sch. Assn., Ariz. Hispanic Sch. Adminstrs. Assn., Pi Gamma Mu, Phi Delta Phi, Delta Kappa Gamma, Phi Delta Kappa. Office: 546 N Stapley Dr Mesa AZ 85203-7204

RAMIREZ, JOEL TITO, artist; b. Albuquerque, June 3, 1923; s. Fortunato and Juliana Armijo Ramirez; m. Carmen M. Varela, Dec. 7, 1946; children: Joel Robert, Eugene Peter, Jo Anne. Student, U. N.Mex. Illustrator (coloring book) Juan Diego and the Virgin of Guadalupe, 1975, St. Vincent de Paul, 1978; contbg. artist Across America, 1986, Art Studies, 1989; art dir. Quijotes de Am. Bibliography Jacinto Quiarte. Commissions include Ford Motor Co., 1973, Kennecott Copper Corp., 1974, Keep N.Mex. Beautiful Campaign, Tex. Internat. Airlines, Paramount Pictures, Universal Studios, Arthritis Found., Greek Cath. Melekite Ch., Albuquerque, Mrs. Mary Olin Harrell, Albuquerque; exhibited in group shows at Mus. N.Mex., Santa Fe, Galerie de Paris, 1965, Mus. Iberiano, Madrid, 1985—. With USAF, 1942-45. Winning artist for portrayal of discovery of Am. quincentenial competition Bur. Land Mgmt., 1992; recipient Insignia for 98th Bombardment Group, Freedom Force, 1988-94. Mem. China-Burma-India-Albuquerque Basher, VFW. Roman Catholic. Home: 10305 Santa Paula Ave NE Albuquerque NM 87111-3654 Office: Ramirez Art Signs 701 Aspen Ave NW Albuquerque NM 87102-1217

RAMIREZ, RALPH ROY, management consultant; b. L.A., Nov. 9, 1937; s. Jorge Williams and Eleanor (Reyes) R.; m. Margot Joyce Cote, Aug. 17, 1959; children: Aaron, Alvina, Belinda, Felicia. AA, East L.A. Coll., 1962; CLU degree, Am. Coll., 1970; tchg. cert., Pasadena City Coll., 1980; BA, Sierra U., 1987. Cert. community coll. tchr., Calif. Safety engr. spl. agt. mgmt. trainee Ins. Co. N.Am., L.A., 1961-64; owner Ramirez Fin. Svcs., San Gabriel, Calif., 1964—; field underwriter Mutual Life Ins. Co. N.Y., Pasadena, Calif., 1964-69; dist. mgr. Franklin Life Ins. Co., Pasadena, 1969-86; mgmt. cons. Ramirez Mgmt. Svcs., San Gabriel, 1985—; guest lectr. Whittier (Calif.) Coll., 1980-86, East L.A. Coll., Calif. Poly. U., Calif. State U., L.A., Northridge; adminstrv. dir. State Calif. Divsn. Indsl. Accidents, San Francisco, 1983-85; instr. ins. Pasadena City Coll., 1981-83; ins. broker Ramirez Ins. Svcs., Alhambra, Calif., 1964-80; bd. dirs. San Gabriel Valley Econ. Coun. contbr articles to profl. jours. Chmn. san Gabriel Valley March of Dimes, Calif. Coun. Calif. Mil. Mus., 1994—; past co-chmn. Covenant House of Calif.; bd. dirs. Calif. Consortium for Prevention Child Abuse, San Gabriel Valley Med. Ctr. Found.; probation monitor State Bar Ct. Calif.; mem. productivity/Quality Mgmt. Forum Indsl. Rels. Ctr. Calif. Inst. Tech., Soc. of Industrial Medicine and Surgery; spkr. Rep. Nat. Conv., New Orleans, 1988, Calif. Mfg. Assn., Calif. Self Ins. Assn., Calif. Assn. Rehab. Profls., Calif. Applicant Attys. Assn., Calif. Applicant Hearing Reps. Assn.; congrl. candidate, 1982, 88; voting mem. Calif. Rep. Ctrl. Com., 1968-90. Res. petty officer USN, 1955-61; maj. Calif. State Mil. Res., 1961—. Recipient Civitan of Yr. Civitan Internat., Gold Medallion award Boy Scouts Am., Cmty. Svc. award L.A. County Bd. Suprs., Hispanic Alumni of Yr. Whittier Coll. Mem. Nat. Assn. Life Underwriters (past pres. San Gabriel Valley chpt.), Latin Bus. Assn. (co-founder), Hispanic Leaders Coalition (founder, past pres.), Monterey Park Boys and Girls Club (founder, past pres.), Christian Svcs. for Blind Internat. (pres. 1996-98), L.A. Ctrs. for Prevention of Alcohol and Drug Abuse (v.p., past pres.), So. Calif. coun. Self Insurers (past pres.), L.A. County Pvt. Industry Coun. (chmn. fin. and budget com.), Calif. Mex.-Am. C. of C. (v.p. 1996-98), Calif. Nat. Guard Hist. Soc. (bd. dirs. 1995—). Office: 219 Segovia Ave San Gabriel CA 91775-2945

RAMIREZ, RICARDO, bishop; b. Bay City, Tex., Sept. 12, 1936; s. Natividad and Maria (Espinosa) R. B.A., U. St. Thomas, Houston, 1959; M.A., U. Detroit, 1968; Diploma in Pastoral Studies, East Asian Pastoral Inst., Manila, 1973-74. Ordained priest Roman Catholic Ch., 1966; missionary Basilian Fathers, Mex., 1968-76; exec. v.p. Mexican Am. Cultural Ctr., San Antonio, 1976-81; aux. bishop Archdiocese of San Antonio, 1981-82; bishop Diocese of Las Cruces, N.M., 1982—; cons. U.S. Bishop's Com. on Liturgy, from 1981; advisor U.S. Bishop's Com. on Hispanic Affairs, from 1981. Author: Fiesta, Worship and Family, 1981. Mem. N.Am. Acad. on Liturgy, Hispanic Liturgical Inst., Padres Asociada Derechos Religiosos Educativos y Sociales. Lodges: K.C; Holy Order Knights of Holy Sepulcher. Office: Diocese of Las Cruces 1280 Med Park Dr Las Cruces NM 88005-3239

RAMLER, SIEGFRIED, educator; b. Vienna, Austria, Oct. 30, 1924; s. Lazar and Eugenia Ramler; m. Piilani Andrietta Ahuna, Jan. 27, 1948; children: David K., Dita L., Laurence K., Malia R. Diplôme supérieur, U. Paris, 1958; MA, U. Hawaii, 1961. Interpreter Internat. Mil. Tribunal, Nuremberg, Germany, 1945-46, chief interpreting br., 1946-49; chair fgn. lang. dept. Punahou Sch., Honolulu, 1951-71, dir. instnl. svcs., 1971-91, dir. Wo Internat. Ctr., 1990-95; exec. dir. Found. for Study in Hawaii and Abroad, Honolulu, 1969-90; vis. fellow East-West Ctr., 1995—; chmn. adv. bd. Pacific Basin Consortium, Hawaii, 1997—. Contbr. articles to profl. publs. Sec., bd. dirs. crown Prince Akihito Scholarship Found., 1989—. Decorated medal Freedom Found., 1958, Order of the Palmes Académiques, French Govt., 1964, Order of the Sacred Treasure, Japanese Govt., 1992, Ordre National du Mérite, French Govt., 1993. Mem. ASCD, Internat./Global Edn. Com. (chair nat. adv. com. 1987-93), Japan-Am. Soc. Hawaii (pres. 1986-87, program chmn. 1975-94, Alliance Française of Hawaii (pres. and founder 1961, bd. dirs. 1992—). Home: 921 Maunawili Cir Kailua HI 96734-4620 Office: East West Ctr 1777 E West Rd Honolulu HI 96822-2323

RAMO, SIMON, engineering executive; b. Salt Lake City, May 7, 1913; s. Benjamin and Clara (Trestman) R.; m. Virginia Smith, July 25, 1937; children: James Brian, Alan Martin. BS, U. Utah, 1933, DSc (hon.), 1961; PhD, Calif. Inst. Tech., 1936; DEng (hon.), Case Western Res. U., 1960, U. Mich., 1966, Poly. Inst. N.Y., 1971; DSc (hon.), Union Coll., 1963, Worcester Polytechnic Inst., 1968, U. Akron, 1969, Cleve. State U., 1976; LLD (hon.), Carnegie-Mellon U., 1970, U. So. Calif., 1972, Gonzaga U., 1983, Occidental Coll., 1984, Claremont U., 1985. With Gen. Electric Co., 1936-46; v.p. ops. Hughes Aircraft Co., 1946-53; with Ramo-Woolridge Corp., 1953-58, Ramo-Wooldridge Corp., 1954-58; dir. TRW Inc., 1954-85, exec. v.p., 1958-61, vice chmn. bd., 1961-78, chmn. exec. com., 1969-78, cons., 1978—; pres. The Bunker-Ramo Corp., 1964-66; chmn. bd. TRW-Fujitsu Co., 1980-83; bd. dirs. Arco Power Techs.; vis. prof. mgmt. sci. Calif. Inst. Tech., 1978—; Regents lectr. UCLA, 1981-82, U. Calif. at Santa Cruz, 1978-79; chmn. Center for Study Am. Experience, U. So. Calif., 1978-80; Faculty fellow John F. Kennedy Sch. Govt., Harvard U., 1980-84; mem. White House Energy Research and Devel. Adv. Council, 1973-75; mem. adv. com. on sci. and fgn. affairs U.S. State Dept., 1973-75; chmn. Pres.'s Com. on Sci. and Tech., 1976-77; mem. adv. council to Sec. Commerce, 1976-77, Gen. Atomics Corp., 1988—, Aurora Capital Ptnrs., 1991—, Chartwell Investments, 1992—; co-chmn. Transition Task Force on Sci. and Tech. for Pres.-elect Reagan; mem. roster consultants to adminstr. ERDA, 1976-77; bd. advisors for sci. and tech. Republic of China, 1981-84; chmn. bd. Aetna, Jacobs & Ramo Venture Capital, 1987-90, Allenwood Ventures Inc., 1987—. Author: The Business of Science, 1988, other sci., engring. and mgmt. books. Bd. dirs. L.A. World Affairs Coun. 1973-85, Mus. Ctr. Found., L.A., L.A. Philharm. Assn., 1981-84; life trustee Calif. Inst. Tech., Nat. Symphony Orch. Assn., 1973-83; trustee emeritus Calif. State Univs.; bd. visitors UCLA Sch. Medicine, 1980—; bd. dirs. W.M. Keck Found., 1983—; bd. govs. Performing Arts Coun. Mus. Ctr. L.A., pres., 1976-77. Recipient award IAS, 1956; award Am. Inst. Elec. Engrs., 1959; award Arnold Air Soc., 1960; Am. Acad. Achievement award, 1964; award Am. Iron and Steel Inst., 1968; Disting. Svc. medal Armed Forces Communication and Electronics Assn., 1970; medal of achievement WEMA, 1970; awards U. So. Calif., 1971, 79; Kayan medal Columbia U., 1972; award Am. Cons. Engrs. Coun., 1974; medal Franklin Inst., 1978; award Harvard Bus. Sch. Assn., 1979; award Nat. Medal Sci., 1979; Disting. Alumnus award U. Utah, 1981; UCLA medal, 1982; Presdl. Medal of Freedom, 1983; named to Bus. Hall of Fame, 1984; recipient Aesculapian award UCLA, 1984, Durand medal AAIA, 1984, John Fritz medal, 1986, Henry Townley Heald award Ill. Inst. Tech., 1988, Nat. Engring. award Am. Assn. Engring. Socs., 1988, Franklin-Jefferson medal, 1988, Howard Hughes Meml. award, 1989. Fellow IEEE (Electronic Achievement award 1953, Golden Omega award 1975, Founders medal 1980, Centennial medal 1984), Am. Acad. Arts and Scis., Am. Acad. Polit. Sci.; mem. N.Y. Acad. Scis., Nat. Acad. Engring. (founder, coun. mem. Bueche award), Nat. Acad. Scis., Am. Phys. Soc., Am. Philos. Soc., Inst. Advancement Engring., Coun. Fgn. Rels., Pacific Coun. Internat. Policy, Internat. Acad. Astronautics, Eta Kappa Nu (eminent mem. award 1966), Theta Tau (Hall of Fame laureate). Office: 9200 W Sunset Blvd Ste 801 Los Angeles CA 90069-3603

RAMO, VIRGINIA M. SMITH, civic worker; b. Yonkers, N.Y.; d. Abraham Harold and Freda (Kasnetz) Smith; B.S. in Edn., U. So. Calif., DHL (hon.), 1978; m. Simon Ramo; children—James Brian, Alan Martin. Nat. co-chmn. ann. giving U. So. Calif., 1968-70, vice chmn., trustee, 1971—, co-chmn. bd. councilors Sch. Performing Arts, 1975-76, co-chmn. bd. councillors Schs. Med. and Engring.; vice-chmn. bd. overseers Hebrew Union Coll., 1972-75; bd. dirs. The Muses of Calif. Mus. Sci. and industry, UCLA Affiliates, Estelle Doheny Eye Found., U. So. Calif. Sch. Medicine; adv. council Los Angeles County Heart Assn., chmn. com. to endow Chair in cardiology at U. So. Calif.; vice-chmn., bd. dirs. Friends of Library U. So. Calif.; bd. dirs., nat. pres. Achievement Rewards for Coll. Scientists Found., 1975-77; bd. dirs. Les Dames Los Angeles, Community TV So. Calif.; bd. dirs., v.p. Founders Los Angeles Music Center; v.p. Los Angeles Music Center Opera Assn.; v.p. corp. bd. United Way; v.p. Blue Ribbon-400 Performing Arts Council; chmn. com. to endow chair in gerontology U. So. Calif.; vice chmn. campaign Doheny Eye Inst., 1986. Recipient Service award Friends of Libraries, 1974, Nat. Community Service award Alpha Epsilon Phi, 1975, Disting. Service award Am. Heart Assn. 1978, Service award U. So. Calif., Spl. award U. So. Calif. Music Alumni Assn., 1979, Life Achievement award Mannequins of Los Angeles Assistance League, 1979, Woman of Yr. award PanHellenic Assn., 1981, Disting. Service award U. So. Calif. Sch. Medicine, 1981, U. So. Calif. Town and Gown Recognition award, 1986, Asa V. Call Achievement award U. So. Calif., 1986, Phi Kappa Phi scholarship award U. So. Calif., 1986, Vision award Luminaires of Doheny Eye Inst., 1994. Mem. UCLA Med. Aux., U. So. Calif. Pres.'s Circle, Commerce Assos. U. So. Calif., Cedars of Lebanon Hosp. Women's Guild (dir. 1967-68), Blue Key, Skull and Dagger.

RAMOS, ALBERT A., electrical engineer; b. L.A., Feb. 28, 1927; s. Jesus D. and Carmen F. (Fontes) R.; B.S. in Elec. Engring., U. So. Calif., 1950, M.S. in Systems Mgmt., 1972; Ph.D., U.S. Internat. U., 1975; m. Joan C. Pailing, Sept. 23, 1950; children—Albert A., Richard R., James J., Katherine. With guided missile test group Hughes Aircraft Co., 1950-60; with TRW DSG, 1960-91, sr. staff engr. Norton AFB, San Bernardino, Calif., 1969-91, ret., 1991. Served with USNR, 1945-46. Registered profl. engr., Calif. Mem. IEEE, NSPE, Air Force Assn., Mexican-Am. Engring. Soc., Mexican-Am. Profl. Mgmt. Assn. (mem. administering commn. dept. community svcs.), Sigma Phi Delta, Eta Kappa Nu, Tau Beta Pi. Home: 8937 Napoli Dr Las Vegas NV 89117-1182

RAMOS, CHARLES JOSEPH (JOE RAMOS), financial consultant; b. Orinda, Calif., July 29, 1960; s. Charles Pimentel Ramos and Louise Antoinette Bianchi; m. Christine S. Schulz, Sept. 25, 1994. BS, U. Calif., Berkeley, 1982. CPA, Calif.; CFP. CPA Arthur Andersen, San Francisco, 1982-85; sr. analyst Montgomery Securities, San Francisco, 1985-87; fin. cons. Ramos Fin. Group, San Francisco, 1987—. Mem. Internat. Bd. CFP, Nat. Assn. Life Underwriters, Nat. Assn. Securities Dealers, Ct. of the Table, Olympic Club. Republican. Office: 475 Sansome St 18th Fl San Francisco CA 94111

RAMOS, CHRISTINA SIERRA, natural resource specialist; b. El Paso, Tex., Aug. 26, 1961; d. Albert Garcia and Emma Sierra Ramos; m. David L. Walker, June 11, 1988. BS in Range Sci., N.Mex. State U., 1984; MBA, U. Phoenix, 1991. Range conservationist Bur. Land Mgmt., U.S. Dept. Interior, Phoenix and Kingman, Ariz., 1981-92; range conservationist Bur. Land Mgmt., U.S. Dept. Interior, Phoenix, 1993—, ops. mgr. interagy. assignment Ariz. Conservation Corps., 1992-93. Am. Field Svc. scholar, 1979. Mem. Am. Bus. Women's Assn. (pres. 1992-93), Soc. for Range Mgmt., Image. Office: US Dept Interior Bur Land Mgmt 3707 N 7th St Phoenix AZ 85014-5059

RAMSAY, JANICE SUSAN, computer programmer, analyst; b. Nashville, Ark., Aug. 20, 1952; d. Reginald Carlyle and Jesse Evelyn (Hill) R. BA in English, Ariz. State U., 1977. With data ops. Maricopa County Govt., Phoenix, 1973-82, programmer analyst I, 1982-84, programmer analyst II, 1984-86; sr. programmer analyst Peralta Community Colls., Oakland, Calif., 1986-90; applications programmer analyst East Bay Mcp. Utilities Dist., Oakland, 1990—. Author: Recovery Techniques, 1984, User-Friendly FAMS, 1985. Active Sierra Club, World Wildlife. Mem. Assn. for Women in Computing, No. Calif. Profls., Assn. Systems Mgmt. Home: # 404 909 Marina Village Pky # 404 Alameda CA 94501-1048 Office: East Bay Mcpl Utilities Dist PO Box 24055 Oakland CA 94623-1055

RAMSAY, JOHN BARADA, research chemist, educator; b. Phoenix, Dec. 28, 1929; s. John A. and Helen G. Ramsay; m. Barbara Ann Hilsenhoff, Apr. 18, 1953; children: Bryan J., Kathleen L., Carol A., David A. BS in Chemistry, Tex. Western U., 1950; PhD in Analytical Chemistry, U. Wis., 1954. Mem. staff Los Alamos Nat. Lab., 1954-70, 73-95; assoc. prof. Coll. Petroleum and Minerals, Dhahran, Saudi Arabia, 1970-73; cons. U.S. Navy, USAF, 1980—; adj. prof. U. N.Mex., Los Alamos, 1980-85, Comforce 1995—. Author sci. articles. Recipient award of excellence U.S. Dept. Energy, 1984, 92. Mem. N.Mex. Acad. Sci. (pres. 1988), Am. Inst. Archeol. (chpt. pres. 1979, 96), Nat. Ski Patrol (appt. 7651), Westerners Internat. (chpt. pres. 1988-90), Sigma Xi. Democrat. Home: 6 Erie Ln Los Alamos NM 87544-3810

RAMSAY, MACKAY, food executive; b. 1953. Student, Calif. Polytechnic State U.; MBA, Calif. State U., Fullerton, 1984. With Sunkist Growers, L.A., 1976-78, Topco Assocs., Skokie, Ill., 1978-80; exec. v.p., gen. mgr. Calberti Inc., Santa Ana, Calif., 1981—. Office: Calberi Inc 3605 W Pendleton Ave Santa Ana CA 92704-3814

RAMSBY, MARK DELIVAN, lighting designer and consultant; b. Portland, Oreg., Nov. 20, 1947; s. Marshall Delivan and Verna Pansy (Culver) R.; divorced; children: Aaron Delivan, Venessa Mercedes. Student, Portland (Oreg.) State U., 1966-67. With C.E.D., Portland, 1970-75; minority ptnr. The Light Source, Portland, 1975-78, pres., 1978-87; prin. Illume Lighting Design, Portland, 1987-90; ptnr. Ramsby, Dupuy & Seats, Inc., Portland, 1990-91; dir. lighting design PAE Cons. Engrs., Inc., Portland, 1991—; pvt. practice cons. Portland, 1979—. Recipient Top 100 Outstanding Achievement award Metalux Lighting, 1981-85, 100% award, 1985, Edwin F. Guth award of merit, 1990, Edison award of excellence, 1990, Edwin F. Guth award of excellence, 1993, 94, Paul Waterbury award of Merit, 1995. Mem. Illuminating Engring. Soc. Am. (sec.-treas. Oreg. sect. 1978-79, Oreg. Section and Regional and Internat. awards 1989, 90, 93, 94, Lighting Design awards), Internat. Assn. Lighting Designers. Republican. Lutheran. Office: PAE Cons Engrs 808 SW 3rd Ave Ste 300 Portland OR 97204-2426

RAMSDELL, KRISTIN ROMEIS, librarian, researcher; b. Fresno, Calif., June 3, 1940; d. Robert S. and L. Haldene (Oller) Romeis; m. Jerald R. Ramsdell, Aug. 21, 1965 (dec. Sept. 1992); children: Jennifer Haldene, Jacob Brooks, Jonathan Richard. BA, Carthage Coll., 1962; MA, Calif. State U., Sacramento, 1969; MLS, UCLA, 1983. H.s. tchr. various subjects L.A., 1978-83; libr. L.A. County Pub. Libr., Claremont (Calif.) Pub. Libr., 1983-84; undergrad. reference libr. Meyer Libr. Stanford (Calif.) U., 1984-87; reference and bibliographic instrn. libr. Calif. State U., Hayward, 1987—; mem. libr. adv. bd. Simon & Schuster, 1989-91. Author: Happily Ever After: A Guide to Reading Interests in Romance Fiction, 1987; editor romance sect.: What Do I Read Next?, 1990—; columnist Libr. Jour., 1994—; mem. editl. bd. Rsch. Strategies jour., 1990—. Mem. ALA, Am. Coll. and Rsch. Librs., Romance Writers of Am. (Libr. of Yr. 1996), Libr. Instrn. Round Table, Calif. Libr. Assn., Calif. Clearinghouse on Libr. Instrn., Calif. Acad. and Rsch. Librs. Home: 16611 Rolando Ave San Leandro CA 94578 Office: Calif State U Univ Libr Hayward CA 94542

RAMSDEN, NORMA LA VONNE HUBER, nurse; b. Lewiston, Idaho, Aug. 1, 1921; d. Lawrence Henry and Gertrude Melissa (Ryder) Huber; m. John Burton Wormell, Nov. 18, 1942 (div. 1950); m. Everett Glenn Ramsden, Dec. 25, 1957; 1 child, Valerie Ann Ramsden Brooks. Diploma in nursing, St. Joseph's Hosp., Lewiston, 1952. Psychiatric nurse Oreg. State Hosp., Salem, 1952-57; clin. instr. Idaho State Hosp., Orofino, Idaho, 1957-58; night nurse ICU Tri State Hosp., Clarkston, Wash., 1969-94; ret., 1994, Rogers Counseling Ctr., Clarkston, 1994; adv. bd. Rogers Counseling Ctr., Clarkston, 1969—. Leader Camp Fire Girls Am., 1958-61, 69-71; Episcopalian vestry, 1992—, fellowship chmn., 1994—; vol. Interlink, 1994—. Recipient Woman Achievement award Altrusa Club, 1985. Mem. Am. Nurses Assn., Anatone Grange, Pollyette (pres., sec., treas.). Home: 817 Highland Ave Clarkston WA 99403-2760

RAMSEY, DOUGLAS ARTHUR, foundation executive; b. Choteau, Mont., Oct. 3, 1934; s. Arthur Bailey and Edith Mae (Tash) R.; m. Charlene Rae Lindberg, July 29, 1961; children: Paul Douglas, Miles Damon (dec.). BA in Journalism, U. Wash., 1956. Reporter, copy editor Seattle Times, 1956; mgr. Far East Network, Iwakuni, Japan, 1958-60; anchor, news dir. KIMA-TV, Yakima, Wash., 1960-61; documentary prodr. KYW-TV, Cleve., 1962; anchor, reporter KOIN-TV, Portland, Oreg., 1963; anchor KATU-TV, Portland, Oreg., 1963-66; instr. broadcast journalism Loyola U., New Orleans, 1968-70; anchor WDSU-TV, New Orleans, 1966-70, WPIX-TV, N.Y.C., 1970-73; chief corr. UP Internat. TV News, N.Y.C., 1973-74; news dir. KSAT-TV, San Antonio, 1975-77, WDSU-TV, New Orleans, 1977-81, KGO-TV, San Francisco, 1981-83; v.p. Found. for Am. Comm., L.A., 1983-84, sr. v.p., 1984—; lectr. Ea. Europe and Germany, 1992—. Author: Jazz Matters: Reflections on the Music and Some of its Makers, 1989; editor: (with Dale Ellen Shaps) Journalism Ethics: Why Change?, 1986; contbg. editor Tex. Monthly, 1974-96; columnist Dallas Morning News, 1988-90; contbr. articles to books and profl. jours. Capt. USMC, 1957-60. Recipient Emmy award Acad. TV Arts and Scis., 1981. Mem. Soc. Profl. Journalists, Soc. Environ. Journalists, Nat. Acad. Rec. Arts and Scis., Jazz Journalists Assn., Nat. Assn. Sci. Writers, Investigative Reporters and Editors, Radio TV New Dirs. Assn., Am. Soc. Newspaper Editors (ethics com.), Assn. Edn. in Journalism and Mass Comm., AP Mng. Editors (2000 com.), UN Corr. Assn., Nat. Acad. Rec. Arts and Scis., Delta Upsilon.

RAMSEY, JERRY VIRGIL, educator, financial planner, radio broadcaster; b. Tacoma, July 24, 1940; s. Virgil Emory and Winifred Victoria (Carothers) R.; m. Elaine Sigrid Perdue, June 24, 1967; 1 child, Jason Perdue. BA in Elem. Edn., U. Puget Sound, 1967; MEd in Tchr. Tng. and Curriculum Devel., U. Wash., 1971; PhD in Econ. Geography, Columbia Pacific U., 1995. Tchr. Tacoma Pub. Schs., 1967-95; fin. planner Primerica Corp., Tacoma, 1986-90, Waddell & Reed, Inc., Tacoma, 1990-93; N.Am. Mgmt., 1993-96; real estate investor, CEO Ramsey Properties, Gig Harbor, Wash., 1970—; radio broadcaster KGHP, KJUN/The Country Club Network, KMAS, 1990-96, KGY, 1996—; study skills specialist Sylvan Learning Ctr., 1995—; lectr. Pacific Luth. U., Tacoma, 1972-86. Precinct committeeman Pierce County Rep. Com., Tacoma, 1968-78, 95—; mem. steering com. Peninsula Neighborhood Assn., Gig Harbor, Wash., 1991-92; mem. Fort Nisqually Hist. Stie Adv. Coun., 1996—. With USAF, 1959-62. Recipient Golden Acorn award PTA, 1975, Meritorious Teaching award Nat. Coun. Geog. Edn., 1978, achievement award Rep. Nat. Com., 1985; grantee U.S. Office Edn., 1971. Mem. NEA (life), Knife and Fork Club (pres. 1983), Kiwanis (pres. Tacoma 1976), Phi Delta Kappa. Methodist. Office: Ramsey Properties Gig Harbor Fin Svcs PO Box 1311 Gig Harbor WA 98335-3311

RAN, XIAONONG, research and development engineer; b. Chengdu, Sichuan, China, Jan. 25, 1958; s. Yinhua and Minzhen (Wang) R.; m. Minmin Qin, Mar. 13, 1985; children: Mengchen, Chungchen. BSEE, Chongqing (China) U., 1982, MSEE, 1984; PhD, U. Md., 1992. Scientific rschr., lectr. Chongqing U., 1984-86; staff engr. Nat. Semiconductor Corp., Santa Clara, Calif., 1992—. Contbr. articles to profl. jours. Scholarship The L.I. Found., 1986, SRC fellowship Sys. Rsch. Ctr. U. Md., 1987, Grad. Sch. Dissertation fellowship U. Md., 1991. Mem. IEEE. Home: 10980 Barranca Dr Cupertino CA 95014-0102 Office: Nat Semiconductor Corp M/S D3-969 2900 Semiconductor Dr Santa Clara CA 95051-0606

RANCE, QUENTIN E., interior designer; b. St. Albans, Eng., Mar. 22, 1935; came to U.S., 1981; s. Herbert Leonard and Irene Ann (Haynes) R.; m. India Adams, May 17, 1974. Grad., Eastbourne (Eng.) Sch. Art, 1960. Soft furnishings buyer Dickeson & French Ltd., Eastbourne, 1960-61, outside sales mgr., 1961-62; design dir. Laszlo Hoenig, Ltd., London, 1962-73; mng. dir. Quentin Rance Interiors Ltd., London, 1973-81; pres. Quentin Rance Enterprises, Inc., Encino, Calif., 1981—. Works featured in Designers West, 1983, Design House Rev., 1983, Profiles mag., 1987, Nat. Assn. Mirror Mfrs. Jour., 1988, Designer Specifier, 1990. Mem. Founders for Diabetic Research/City of Hope. Served with RAF, 1953-55. Recipient Hon. Mention award Nat. Assn. Mirror Mfrs., 1987, 1st Pl. Nat. Pub. Svc. award, Designer Specifier, 1990. Fellow Chartered Soc. Designers (Eng.); mem. Am. Soc. Interior Designers (profl., chpt. bd. dirs. 1983-87, 89-91, chmn. Avanti 1983-85, admissions chmn. 1985—, Presdl. citations 1984, 87, 91, 95), Knights of Vine. Home and Office: 18005 Rancho St Encino CA 91316-4214 *Personal philosophy: Good design is always there to be seen, there to be appreciated, and there for expanding one's own boundaries of creativity.*

RANCK, JOHN STEVENS, human resources executive, consultant; b. Warren, Ohio, Sept. 14, 1945; s. Charles Thomas and Helen Marie (Weir) R.; m. Bibbie-Ann Rose Robertson, Dec. 25, 1975; children: James L., Edward L. BS, USAF Acad., 1971; MS in Human Resources, Gonzaga U., 1979, MBA, 1984. Cert. adminstrv. mgr.; sr. profl. in human resources mgmt. Salesman Neal's Family Shoes, Warren, 1964-65; prodn. staff Packard Elec. div. GMC, Warren, 1965-66; personnel mgr. United Paint Mfg., Inc., Greenacres, Wash., 1981-82; personnel dir. Sheraton-Spokane Hotel, 1982-83; personnel mgr. Students Book Corp., Pullman, Wash., 1984-87; personnel analyst Spokane Co., 1988-90; pres. Top Ranck Mgmt., Spokane and Loon Lake, Wash., 1990—; v.p., sec.-treas. TONGA Coffee, Co., 1993; pres. ArabiCafe, Inc., 1993-94. Active Stevens County Rep. Com. Capt. USAF, 1966-80. Paul Harris fellow, 1992. Mem. Am. Compensation Assn., Internat. Pers. Mgmt. Assn., N.W. Human Recourse Mgmt. Assn. (exec. bd. 1989-93, treas. 1993, legis. liaison 1991-92, v.p. programs 1990, coll. rels. com. 1989), Soc. Human Resource Mgmt., Mensa, Masons (Knight York Grand Cross of Honor, Order of Purple Cross, Knight Comdr. Ct. of Honor), K.T. (grand comdr. 1987-88), Red Cross Constantine, Royal Order Scotland, Shriners, Grotto, Loon Lake Health Assn. (bd. dirs. 1997—). Lutheran. Home: 40151 Morgan Rd PO Box 297 Loon Lake WA 99148-0297 Office: Top Ranck Mgmt PO Box 501 Loon Lake WA 99148-0501

RANDALL, EARL VANCE, educational leadership educator, consultant; b. Monticello, Utah, June 14, 1951; s. Earl Larson and Dorothy Rae (Frost) R.; m. Vickie Heaton, Oct. 10, 1974; children: Melissa, Curtis, Matthew, Marilee, April, Jonathan. BS, Brigham Young U., 1975, M of Ednl. Adminstrn., 1978; PhD, Cornell U., 1989. Cert. secondary tchr. Asst. prof. ednl. leadership Brigham Young U., Provo, Utah, 1992—. Author: Private Schools and Public Power, 1994; contbr. articles to profl. jours. Instr., prin. ch. ednl. system LDS Ch., Phoenix, 1975-79, Farmington, Minn., 1979-82, Ithaca, N.Y., 1982-92; sec., pres. adv. com. Dryden (N.Y.) Sch. Dist., 1985-86; v.p. Cornell United Religious Work, Ithaca, N.Y., 1987-88. Recipient Marvin Glock award Cornell U., 1990. Mem. Am. Ednl. Fin. Assn., Assocs. for Rsch. on Pvt. Edn., Am. Ednl. Rsch. Assn. Office: Brigham Young Univ 310C Mckb Provo UT 84602-1038

RANDAU, KAREN LYNETTE, public relations executive; b. Grand Junction, Colo., Feb. 13, 1953; d. George Irvin Gray and Phyllis Joanita (Knaak) Helton; m. James V. Arp, 1979 (div. 1988); 1 child, Joanna; m. Eric E. Randau, Jan. 21, 1989; 1 child, Nathan. BA in Journalism, U. Tex., 1979. Merchandising mgr. Tex. Instruments, Austin, Tex., 1979-82; mktg. comms. mgr. Intel, Chandler, Ariz., 1982-86; self-employed writer Chandler, Ariz., 1986-87; mktg.dir. Charter Hosp., Chandler, Ariz., 1987-88, Hope Comty., Scottsdale, Ariz., 1988-90; dir. pub. rels. Food for the Hungry, Scottsdale, 1990—. Author: (books) Conquering Fear, 1990, Life Doesn't Have to Hurt, 1991; (booklet) Panic Attacks, 1991, Teaching Your Child God's Love for the World, 1996, Jesus Loves You and Me: A Vacation Bible School Curriculum, 1997. Mem. Pub. Rels. Soc. Am. (accredited pub. rels. profl.), Christian Bus. Women (newsletter editor Phoenix 1992-93). Office: Food for the Hungry Inc 7729 E Greenway Rd Scottsdale AZ 85260-1705

RANDEL, WILLIAM JOHN, physicist; b. Cleve., May 13, 1956; s. Marvin William and Virginia Mary (Pettit) R.; m. Sharon Lea Gutche, Aug. 20, 1983; children: Matthew William, Katherine Grace. BS in Physics, U. Cin., 1978; PhD, Iowa State U., 1984. Postdoctoral rsch. fellow Nat. Ctr. for Atmospheric Rsch., Boulder, Colo., 1986-87, rsch. scientist, 1988—; mem. ozone trends panel UN Environ. Program World Meterol. Orgn., Geneva, 1993-94, mem. temperature trends panel, chair stratospheric climatology panel, 1995—. Contbr. articles to profl. jours. and chpts. to books. Pres. Mt. Hope Luth. Ch., Boulder, 1994—. Rsch. grantee NASA, 1990-97; fellow Nat. Ctr. for Atmospheric Rsch., 1985-87. Mem. Am. Meterol. Soc. (com. chair 1994—), Am. Geophys. Union, Sigma Pi Sigma. Home: 4458 Wellington Rd Boulder CO 80301-3144 Office: Nat Ctr Atmospheric Rsch PO Box 3000 Boulder CO 80307

RANDHAWA, BIKKAR SINGH, psychologist, educator; b. Jullundur, India, June 14, 1933; came to Can., 1961, naturalized, 1966; s. Pritam S. and Sawaran K. (Basakhi) R.; m. Leona Emily Bujnowski, Oct. 8, 1966; children—Jason, Lisa. BA in Math., Panjab U., 1954, BT in Edn., 1955, MA in History, 1959; BEd, U. Alta., Can., 1963; MEd in Measurement and Evaluation, U Toronto, 1967, PhD, 1969. Registered psychologist. Tchr. secondary sch. math. Panjab, 1955-61; asst. headmaster, then headmaster, 1955-61; tchr. high sch. math. and sci. Beaver County, Riley, Alta., 1964-65, Camrose County, Alta., 1961-64; tchr. high sch. math. and sci. Edmonton (Alta.) Public Schs., 1965-67; tutor in math. for social sci. Ont. Inst. Studies in Edn., Toronto, 1968-69; mem. faculty U. Sask., Saskatoon, 1969-76, 77—; prof. ednl. psychology U. Sask., 1977—, asst. dean research and field services, 1982-87; prof., coord. Visual Scholars' Program, U. Iowa, 1976-77; cons. in field. Contbr. articles profl. jours. Fellow APA, Am. Psychol. Soc. (charter), Can. Psychol. Assn.; mem. Am. Ednl. Rsch. Assn., Can. Ednl. Rsch. Assn. (pres. 1997—), Can. Soc. Study Edn., Sask. Psychol. Assn., Phi Delta Kappa (pres. Saskatoon chpt. 1971, 85). Home: 510 Forsyth Crescent, Saskatoon, SK Canada S7N 4H8 Office: U Sask, 3117 Edn Bldg 28 Campus Dr, Saskatoon, SK Canada S7N OX1

RANDISI, ELAINE MARIE, law corporation executive, educator; b. Racine, Wis., Dec 19, 1926; d. John Dewey and Alveta Irene (Raffety) Fehd; AA, Pasadena Jr. Coll., 1946; BS cum laude (Giannini scholar), Golden Gate U., 1978; m. John Paul Randisi, Oct. 12, 1946 (div. July 1972); children: Jeanine Randisi Manson, Martha Randisi Chaney (dec.), Joseph, Paula, Catherine Randisi Carvalho, George, Anthony (dec.); m. John R. Woodfin, June 18, 1994. With Raymond Kaiser Engrs., Inc., Oakland, Calif., 1969-75, 77-86, corp. acct., 1978-79, sr. corp. acct., 1979-82, sr. payroll acct., 1983-86, acctg. mgr., Lilli Ann Corp., San Francisco, 1986-89, Crosby, Heafey, Roach & May, Oakland, Calif., 1990—; corp. buyer Kaiser Industries Corp., Oakland, 1975-77; lectr. on astrology Theosophical Soc., San Francisco, 1979—; mem. faculty Am. Fedn. Astrologers Internat. Conv., Chgo., 1982, 84. Mem. Speakers Bur., Calif. Assn. for Neurologically Handicapped Children, 1964-70, v.p. 1969; bd. dirs. Ravenwood Homeowners Assn., 1979-82, v.p., 1979-80, sec., 1980-81; mem. organizing com. Minority Bus. Fair, San Francisco, 1976; pres., bd. dirs. Lakewood Condominium Assn., 1984-87; mem., trustee Ch. of Religious Sci., 1992-95; treas. First Ch. Religious Sci., 1994—. Mem. Am. Fedn. Astrologers, Nat. Assn. Female Execs., Calif. Scholarship Fedn. (life), Alpha Gamma Sigma (life). Mem. Ch. of Religious Science (lic. practioner pres. 1990-91, sec. 1989-90). Initiated Minority Vendor Purchasing Program for Kaiser Engrs., Inc., 1975-76. Home: 742 Wesley Way Apt 1C Oakland CA 94610-2339 Office: Crosby Heafey Roach & May 1999 Harrison St Oakland CA 94612-3517

RANDLE, ELLEN EUGENIA FOSTER, opera and classical singer, educator; b. New Haven, Conn., Oct. 2, 1948; d. Richard A.G. and Thelma Lousie (Brooks) Foster; m. Ira James William, 1967 (div. 1972); m. John Willis Randle. Student, Calif. State Coll., Sonoma, 1970; studied with Boris Goldovsky, 1970; student, Grad. Sch. Fine Arts, Florence, Italy, 1974; studied with Tito Gobbi, Florence, 1974; student, U. Calif., Berkeley, 1977; BA in World History, Lone Mountain Coll., 1976, MA in Performing Arts, 1978; studied with Madam Eleanor Steber, Graz, Austria, 1979; studied with Patricia Goehl, Munich, Fed. Republic Germany, 1979; MA in Counseling and Psychology, U. San Francisco, 1990, MA in Marital Family Therapy, 1994. asst. artistic dir. Opera Piccola, Oakland, Calif., 1990-92; instr. East Bay Performing Art Ctr., Richmond, Calif., 1986, Chapman Coll., 1986; pres. grad. student coun. U. San Francisco, 1996-97. Singer opera prodns. Porgy & Bess, Oakland, Calif., 1980-81, LaTraviata, Oakland, Calif., 1981-82, Aida, Oakland, 1981-82, Madame Butterfly, Oakland, 1982-83, The Magic Flute, Oakland, 1984, numerous others; performances include TV specials, religious concerts, musicals; music dir. Natural Man, Berkeley, 1986; asst. artistic dir. Opera Piccola, Oakland, Calif., 1990—. Art commr. City of Richmond, Calif. Recipient Bk. Am. Achievement award. Mem. Music Tchrs. Assn., Internat. Black Writers and Artists Inc. (life mem., local #5), Nat. Coun. Negro Women, Nat. Assn. Negro Musicians, Calif. Arts Fedn., Calif. Assn. for Counseling and Devel. (mem. black caucus), Nat. Black Child Devel. Inst., The Calif.-Nebraskan Orgn., Inc., Calif. Marital & Family Therapist Assn. (San Francisco chpt.), Black Psychotherpist of San Francisco and East Bay Area, San Francisco Commonwealth Club, Gamma Phi Delta. Democrat. Mem. A.M.E. Zion Ch. Home: 5314 Boyd Ave Oakland CA 94618-1112

RANDOLPH, HARRY FRANKLIN, III, health facility administrator, physician assistant; b. Vallejo, Calif., Nov. 5, 1946; s. Harry Franklin Jr. and Viola Vinnie (Snyder) R.; m. Candice Patricia Garrison, Dec. 30, 1970; 1 child, Brandon Todd. BS in Zoology, San Diego State U., 1969; BS, Baylor Coll. Med., 1977. Cert. physician asst., Nat. Commn. Cert. Physician Assts. Staff rsch. assoc. U. Calif. San Diego, La Jolla, 1969-72; med. mach. Technitian VA Hosp., San Diego, 1972-75; physician asst. So. Calif. Permenente Med. Group, San Diego, 1977-79, Mt. Health Ctr., Boulevard, Calif., 1979-81, So. Calif. HMO, San Diego, 1981-82, Scripps Clin. Med. Group, La Jolla, 1982—; chief physician extender sect. Scripps Clin. Med. Group, La Jolla, 1991—, expert witness/pysician asst. practice, 1992—, chief physician assts. Green Hosp., 1994—; med. legal cons. Contbr. articles to profl. jours.; editor Surg. Physician Asst., 1994-97. Mem. Health Sys. Agency Sub-area Coun. VI, El Cajon, Calif., 1980-81, San Diego Zool. Soc., 1985—. Fellow Am. Acad Physician Assts., Am. Assn. Surgeon Assts. (treas. 1994-97), Calif. Acad. Physician Assts. (dir. at large 1984, chmn. continuing med. edn. com. 1984-86, v.p. 1985, chmn. prof. practice com. 1996, 97, Outstanding Achievement award 1985, Outstanding Svc. award, 1994). Democrat. Office: Scripps Clin Med Group Mail Drop MS 213 10666 N Torrey Pines Rd La Jolla CA 92037

RANDOLPH, KEVIN H., marketing executive; b. Seattle, July 6, 1949; s. Howard Amos and Betty Elaine (Leahy) R.; m. Deborah Lou Newell, Sept. 18, 1976; children: Heather, Lyndsay. BA, Wash. State U., 1972. Mgr. Computers for Mktg., L.A., 1972-74; data processing mgr. Parker Rsch., Pasadena, Calif., 1974-77; prin. Randolph & Assocs., L.A., 1977-79; v.p. Bank Am. Corp., San Francisco, 1979-87, Interactive Network, Mountain View, Calif., 1987-91; sr. v.p. ICTV, Santa Clara, Calif., 1991-93; pres. Interactive Enterprises, San Ramon, Calif., 1993—; v.p. U.S. West Mrg., Inc., Benicia, Calif., 1993-94; exec. v.p., COO Interactive Video Enterprises, Inc., San Ramon, 1994-95; cons. Randolph Home Ctr., Ephrata, Wash., 1972—. Mem. Am. Mktg. Assn., Am. Mgmt. Assn. Home: 170 Edinburgh Cir Danville CA 94526-2906

RANDOLPH, LINDA MARIE, geneticist; b. Bakersfield, Calif., Nov. 12, 1953; d. Clinton Elwood and Dorothy Jane (Swanson) R.; m. Jonathan Bole Eddison, Nov. 30, 1985; children: Marie Randolph, Elizabeth Jane. BS, U. Redlands, 1975; MA, U. Calif., Irvine, 1980; MD, George Washington U., 1982. Diplomate Am. Bd. Pediatrics, Am. Bd. Med. Genetics. Pediatric resident Children's Nat. Med. Ctr., Washington, 1982-85; clin. and rsch. fellow Harbor-UCLA Med. Ctr., L.A., 1985-88; rsch. scientist Cedars Sinai Med. Ctr., L.A., 1988-89; clin. geneticist, cytogeneticist Alfigen/The Genetics Inst., Pasadena, Calif., 1989-92, med. dir. prenatal genetics, 1993—; assoc. med. dir. Integrated Genetics, Long Beach, Calif., 1992-93. Rsch. fellowship Blinder Found., 1988, Nat. Found. for Iletis and Colitis, 1988. Mem. AMA, Am. Acad. Pediat., Am. Soc. Human Genetics, Alpha Omega Alpha. Office: Alfigen/The Genetics Inst 11 W Del Mar Blvd Pasadena CA 91105-2505

RANDOLPH, STEVEN, insurance and estate planner; b. Nebr., Oct. 14, 1946; m. Sherri Hamrick, 1980 (div. 1989); children: David, John, Michelle; m. Kathleen Riley, 1991. BS, U. Nebr., 1971. Registered rep. Nat. Assn. Securities Dealers, SEC; lic. in variable annuities, ins. and disabilities. Rep. Real Estate Consulting Svcs., Inc., Newport Beach, Calif., 1971-86; fin. svcs. advisor Prudential Fin. Svcs., Laguna Hills, Calif., 1986—. With USMC, 1964-68, Vietnam. Mem. Nat. Assn. Securities Dealers, Nat. Assn. Life Underwriters (Nat. Sales Achievement award, Nat. Quality award), Million Dollar Round Table Club, Pres.'s Club (awards). Home and Office: PO Box 9612 Newport Beach CA 92658-9612

RANFTL, ROBERT MATTHEW, management consulting company executive; b. Milw., May 31, 1925; s. Joseph Sebastian and Leona Elaine (Goetz) R.; m. Marion Smith Goodman, Oct. 12, 1946. BSEE, U. Mich., 1946; postgrad. UCLA, 1953-55. Product engr. Russell Electric Co., Chgo., 1946-47; head engring. dept. Radio Inst. Chgo., 1947-50; sr. project engr. Webster Chgo. Corp., 1950-51, product design engr., 1951-53, head equipment design group, 1953-54, head electronic equipment sect., 1954-55, mgr. product engring. dept., 1955-58, mgr. reliability and quality control, 1958-59, mgr. adminstrn. 1959-61, mgr. product effectiveness lab., 1961-74; corp. dir. engring./design mgmt., 1974-84, corp. dir. managerial productivity Hughes Aircraft Co., Los Angeles, 1984-86; pres. Ranftl Enterprises Inc., Mgmt. Cons., Los Angeles, 1981—; guest lectr. Calif. Inst. Tech., Cornell U., U. Calif.; mem. White House Conf. on Productivity, 1983; mem. human resources productivity task force Dept. of Def., 1985-86. Author: R&D Productivity, 1974, 78; (with others) Productivity: Prospects for Growth, 1981; contbr. articles to profl. jours. Mem. AAAS, AIAA, Am. Soc. Engring. Edn., Am. Soc. Tng. and Devel., IEEE, Inst. Mgmt. Scis., Acad. Mgmt., N.Y. Acad. Scis., U. Mich. Alumni Assn., UCLA Alumni Assn. Office: Ranftl Enterprises Inc PO Box 49892 Los Angeles CA 90049-0892

RANKIN, JIMMIE R., neuroscience nurse; b. Auburn, Calif., May 22, 1941; s. Gilbert O. and Wilma E. (Robertson) R. MSN, U. Calif., San Francisco, 1989; BSN, USNY, 1983; BA, U. Calif., Berkeley, 1969; BS in Psychology, ASN, USNY, Albany, 1977. Staff nurse Neurol. Inst., N.Y.C.; ind. nurse, prin. Dry Bones Nursing BBS, Dry Bones Press, San Francisco; dir. nursing Pacific Coast Hosp., San Francisco. Mem. AANN. Office: Dry Bones Press 655 Sutter St Ste 401 San Francisco CA 94102-1032

RANKIN, WILLIAM PARKMAN, educator, former publishing company executive; b. Boston, Feb. 6, 1917; s. George William and Bertha W. (Clowe) R.; m. Ruth E. Gerard, Sept. 12, 1942; children: Douglas W., Joan W. BS, Syracuse U., 1941; MBA, NYU, 1949, PhD, 1979. Sales exec. Redbook mag., N.Y.C., 1945-49; sales exec. This Week mag., N.Y.C., 1949-55, adminstrv. exec., 1955-60, v.p., 1957-60, v.p., dir. advt. sales, sales devel. dir., 1960-63, exec. v.p., 1963-69; gen. exec. newspaper div. Time Inc., N.Y.C., 1969-70; gen. mgr. feature svc. Newsweek, Inc., N.Y.C., 1970-74, fin. and ins. advt. mgr., 1974-81; prof., asst. to the dir. Walter Cronkite Sch. Journalism and Telecommunication, Ariz. State U., Tempe, 1981—; lectr. Syracuse U., NYU, Berkeley Sch. Author: Selling Retail Advertising, 1944; The Technique of Selling Magazine Advertising, 1949; Business Management of Consumer Magazines, 1980, 2 ed. 1984, The Practice of Newspaper Management, 1986. Mem. Dutch Treat Club. Home: 1220 E Krista Way Tempe AZ 85284-1545 also: Rustics Rd Bomoseen VT 05732 Office: Ariz State U Walter Cronkite Sch Journalism/Telecom Tempe AZ 85287-1305

RANSEL, SANDRA LEE, academic administrator; b. Mil., Mar. 15, 1949; d. Gordon Virgil and Virginia Hanna (Meyers) Wells; m. Alfred Dennison Ransel, July 10, 1976; children: Christopher Jonathan, Hugh Franklin. BS, Colo. State U., 1969, MEd, 1970; PhD, U. Okla., 1991. Cert. tchr. Tchr. social studies Pondre R-1, Ft. Collins, Colo., 1969-74, Ft. Valley (Ga.) Sch. Dist., 1975-76; instr., adminstr. City Colls. Chgo., Aviano, Italy, 1976-80; tchr. gifted and talented Sch. Dist. 193, Mountain Home, Idaho, 1980-85; instr. Boise State U., Mountain Home AFB, Idaho, 1980-85; tchr. English Internat. Sch. Naples, Bagnolia, Italy, 1985-86, Dept. Def., Naples, Italy,

1986-88; tchr. reading Choctaw (Okla.) Sch. Dist., 1988-92; instr. U. Okla., Norman, 1991-92; tchr., then adminstr. secondary sch. Garside Mid. Sch. Clark County Sch. Dist., Las Vegas, Nev., 1992—; tchr. NOVA Grad. Program, Las Vegas, 1993—. Chair Mountain Home Centennial, 1983-85, Elmore County (Idaho) Legacy Project, 1983-85, City-Schs. Partnership, Choctaw, 1988-91, Fine Arts Com., Choctaw, 1989-91. Assn. for Humanities History grantee, 1983. Mem. Clark County Sch. Dist. Adminstrs., Phi Delta Kappa.

RANSOM, EVELYN NAILL, language educator, linguist; b. Memphis, Apr. 20, 1938; d. Charles Rhea and Evelyn (Goodlander) Naill Ransom; m. Gunter Heinz Hiller, June 7, 1960 (div. Mar. 1964). AA, Mt. Vernon Jr. Coll., 1958; BA, Newcomb Coll., 1960; MA, N.Mex. Highlands U., 1965; PhD, U. Ill., 1974. Cert. secondary tchr., N.Mex. Instr. Berlitz Sch. Langs., New Orleans, 1961; tchr. MillerWall Elem. Sch., Harvey, L.A., 1961-62; teaching asst. N.Mex. Highlands U., Las Vegas, 1963-64; instr. U. Wyo., Laramie, 1965-66; teaching asst. U. Ill., Urbana, 1966-70; prof. English lang. Ea. Ill. U., Charleston, 1970-93; vis. prof. in linguistics No. Ariz. U., Flagstaff, 1990-91, adj. faculty, 1993-94; adj. faculty Ariz. State U., Tempe, 1995—; referee Pretext: Jour. of Lang. and Lit., Ill., 1981; co-chair roundtable Internat. Congress of Linguistics, 1987; linguistics del. People to People, Moscow, St. Petersburg, Prague, 1993; dissertation reader SUNY, Buffalo, 1982; vis. scholar UCLA, 1977; conductor workshop LSA summer inst. Author: Complementation: Its Meanings and Forms, 1986; contbr. articles to profl. publs. Organizer Prairie Women's Cir., Champaign, 1981-83. Nat. Def. Fgn. Lang. fellow, 1969; grantee Ea. Ill. U., 1982, 87, 88, NSF, 1988. Mem. Linguistic Soc. Am., Linguistic Assn. S.W. Home: 201 E Southern Ave # 135 Apache Junction AZ 85219-3740

RANSOM, RICHARD EDWARD, retired state supreme court justice; b. Hampton, Iowa, Dec. 9, 1932. BA, U. N.Mex., 1954; LLB, Georgetown U., 1959. Bar: N.Mex. 1959, D.C. 1959. Trial lawyer Albuquerque, 1959-86; justice N.Mex. Supreme Ct., Santa Fe, 1987-97; chief justice N. Mex. Supreme Ct., 1992-94, sr. justice, 1994-97. 1st lt. USMC, 1954-56. Fellow Am. Coll. Trial Lawyers, Internat. Soc. Barristers, Internat. Acad. Trial Lawyers. Office: PO Drawer D Albuquerque NM 87103*

RANSONS, ELLEN FRANCES, high school administrator; b. Orange, Calif., Oct. 2, 1954; d. Kenneth London and Billie Margaret (Jenson) Keith; m. Silvio Theodore Ransons, Apr. 1, 1978; children: Paul, Keith, Amy. BA, Calif. State U., Fullerton, 1977; MEd, Whittier (Calif.) Coll., 1988. Cert. tchr. English, social sci., Calif., Wash.; adminstrv. cert., Calif., Wash. Tchr. Mission H.S., San Gabriel, Calif., 1977-86, Suzanne Mid. Sch., Walnut, Calif., 1986-95; asst. prin. student svcs. Lynnwood (Wash.) H.S., 1995—; mentor tchr. Walnut Valley Unified Sch. Dist., 1994-95. Editor student lit. publs.; author newsletter. Mem. SPARK, Walnut, 1992-94. Mem. NEA, ASCD, Am. Assn. of Sch. Adminstrs., Washington Assn. Sch. Adminstrs., Nat. Assn. Secondary Sch. Prins. Democrat. Roman Catholic. Home: 18801 215th Way NE Woodinville WA 98072-7151 Office: Lynnwood HS 3001 184th St Lynnwood WA 98037

RAPHAEL, MARTIN GEORGE, research wildlife biologist; b. Denver, Oct. 5, 1946; s. Jerome Maurice and Alys (Salmonson) R.; m. Susan Williams, August 4, 1967; 1 child, Samantha Marie. BA, Sacramento State U., 1968; BS, U. Calif., Berkeley, 1972, MS, 1976, PhD, 1980. Staff research assoc. U. Calif., Berkeley, 1974-80, assoc. specialist, 1980-84; project leader USDA Forest Svc., Laramie, 1984-89, Olympia, Wash., 1989—; adj. prof. U. Wyo., Laramie, 1986-89; cons. ecologist Pacific Gas and Electric Co., San Ramon, Calif., 1981-84. Contbr. articles to sci. jours. Mem. Ecol. Soc. Am. (editl. bd. Ecol. Applications), Soc. for Conservation Biology, Am. Ornithologists' Union, Cooper Ornithol. Soc. (chmn. membership com. 1985-90, asst. sec. 1986—, bd. dirs. 1989-92), The Wildlife Soc. (local pres. publs. com. 1983-84, assoc. editor Wildlife Soc. Bull. 1987-90), Phi Beta Kappa, Sigma Xi, Xi Sigma Pi. Home: 3224 Biscay Ct NW Olympia WA 98502-3558 Office: Pacific NW Rsch Sta 3625 93rd Ave SW Olympia WA 98512-9145

RAPHAEL, TAMAR AMITA, development director; b. L.A., Mar. 14, 1962; d. Eli and Judith Raphael. BA, Smith Coll., 1983; student, Inst. Polit. & Econ. Studies, Eng. Legis. aide Sen. John Garamendi Calif. State Legis., Sacramento, 1984-86; nat. press asst. NOW, Washington, 1986-87; nat. comms. dir. Feminist Majority, Washington, 1987-91; devel. dir. Feminist Majority, San Rafael, Calif., 1991-95; owner Eco Express, Novato, Calif., 1996—. Editor Feminist Majority Report, 1988-91. Bd. dirs. Family Law Ctr., San Rafael, 1993-95, Marin Abuse Women's Svcs., San Rafael, 1994-96. Office: Eco Express 28 Pamaron Way Ste F Novato CA 94949

RAPIER, PASCAL MORAN, chemical engineer, physicist; b. Atlanta, Jan. 11, 1914; s. Paul Edward and Mary Clare (Moran) R.; m. Martha Elizabeth Doyle, May 19, 1945; children: Caroline Elizabeth, Paul Doyle, Mollie Clare, John Lawrence, James Andrew. BSChemE, Ga. Inst. Tech., 1939; MS in Theoretical Physics, U. Nev., 1959; postgrad., U. Calif., Berkeley, 1961. Registered profl. engr., Calif., N.J. Plant engr. Archer-Daniels-Midland, Pensacola, Fla., 1940-42; group supr. Dicalite div. Grefco, Los Angeles, 1943-54; process engr. Celatom div. Eagle Picher, Reno, Nev., 1955-57; project mgr., assoc. research engr. U. Calif. Field Sta., Richmond, 1959-62; project mgr. sea water conversion Bechtel Corp., San Francisco, 1962-66; sr. supervising chem. engr. Burns & Roe, Oradell, N.J., 1966-74; cons. engr. Kenite Corp., Scarsdale, N.Y., Rees Blowpipe, Berkeley, 1960-66; sr. cons. engr. Sanderson & Porter, N.Y.C., 1975-77; staff scientist III Lawrence Berkeley Lab., 1977-84; bd. dirs. Newtonian Sci. Found.; v.p. Calif. Rep. Assembly, 1964-65; discoverer phenomena faster than light, origin of cosmic rays and galactic red shifts. Contbr. articles to profl. jours.; patentee agts. to render non-polar solvents electrically conductive, direct-contact geothermal energy recovery devices; contbr. Marks' Standard Handbook for Mechanical Engineers, 10th edit., 1996. Mem. Am. Inst. Chem. Engrs., Gideons Internat., Lions Internat., Corvallis, Sigma Pi Sigma. Home: 8015 NW Ridgewood Dr Corvallis OR 97330-3026 *Personal philosophy: Adopt a primary causal principle in your life and your work will not go unrewarded. Seek a guiding principle for your life, and find your efforts well rewarded.*

RAPIER, STEPHEN MICHAEL, marketing executive; b. Inglewood, Calif., Apr. 8, 1957; s. Oliver C. III and Helen (Bilsn) R. BSBA, Calif. State U., Long Beach, 1981. Sales rep. Dieterich-Post Co., Monterey Park, Calif., 1981-82; pres. S.M. Rapier Corp./Sebring Hard Disc Sys., Carson, Calif., 1982-87; v.p. J.B. Schultz & Assocs., L.A., 1987-88; v.p., pres. Concept Data Corp./Quality Rsch. Inst., L.A., 1988-95; dir. mktg. Power Lift SCMH, Pico Rivera, Calif., 1995—; guest lectr. U. So. Calif., 1984, Calif. State U., Long Beach, 1985, Calif. State U., L.A., 1990. Mem. Am. Mktg. Assn. (So. Calif.) chpt.). Republican. Roman Catholic. Office: 8314 Slauson Ave Pico Rivera CA 90660-4323

RAPOZA, GLENN ROBERTS, vocational rehabilitation counselor, teacher; b. Honolulu, May 16, 1948; s. Frank Gordon and Geraldine Evelyn (Souza) R.; m. Cathy Louise Bristow Iriarte, SEpt. 6, 1980 (div. Oct. 1982); 1 child, Heather. BS suma cum laude, Calif. State U., Fresno, 1973, MA, 1975. Cert. C.C. tchr. adult edn., cert. C.C. counselor, Calif. Group counselor I Solano County Juvenile Hall, Fairfield, Calif., 1975-76; vocat. specialist for handicapped Office Solano County Supt. Schs., Fairfield, Calif., 1976-79; case mgr., program coord. Westcom Rehab Ctr., Richmond, Calif., 1979-81; mgr. rehab. svcs. Westcom Rehab Ctr., El Ceritto, Calif., 1981-86; employment svc. specialist SETA, Sacramento, Calif., 1989-94; vocat. rehab. counselor Dept. of Vet. Affairs, Sacramento, 1994; mem. adv. bd. North Bay Regional Ctr., Napa, Calif., 1976-77; bd. dirs. Solano Workshop Svcs., 1977-78; guidance counselor Youth for Christ, Sacramento, 1989-91; group co-facilitator Kaiser Alcohol & Drug Program, Sacramento, 1989-91. Vol. Com. to Elect Dr. Dan Muller, Vallejo, Calif., 1977-78; local bd. dirs., Am Fedn. State-County Mcpl. Employees, Sacramento, 1994. Democrat. Roman Catholic. Home: 2649 River Plaza Dr Apt 243 B Sacramento CA 95833-3279 Office: Dept VA 1825 Bell St Ste 202 Sacramento CA 95825-1020

RAPP, NINA BEATRICE, financial company executive; b. Copenhagen, Denmark, Sept. 3, 1958; came to the U.S., 1984; d. Sven Ove Lars Larsen and Kirsten Rung Mechik; m. Steven Douglas Rapp, July 14, 1984; 1 child, Stepanie Beatrice. BA in Econs. and Polit. Sci., Danish Royal Mil. Acad., 1982; MBA in Fin., Harvard U., 1990. Cert. explosives expert; lic. ins. and securites rep. Cons. Mei & Assocs., Waltham, Mass., 1987-88; leasing mgr. Wright Runstad & Co., Seattle, 1990-92; regional v.p. Primerica Fin. Svcs., Seattle, 1992—; ptnr. R & R Assocs., Seattle, 1990-93. Author: International Terrorism, 1982. Capt. Danish Army, 1977-82, lt., 1982-84. Mem. NAFE. Home: 6516 163rd St SW Lynnwood WA 98037-2717 Office: Primerica Fin Svcs 21911 64th Ave W # C Mountlake Terrace WA 98043-2278

RASCO, BARBARA A., food chemistry educator. BS in Engring & Chem. Engring., U. Pa., 1979; PhD in Food Sci. & Nutrition, U. Mass., 1983; JD, Seattle U., 1995. Biochem. engr. Cargill, Inc., Mpls., 1982-83; quality control mgmt. Cargill, Inc., Memphis, 1983-84; asst. prof. U. Wash., Seattle, 1984-89, assoc. prof., 1989—; advisor Northwest Food Safety Coun., 1992—. Contbr. chpts. to books and articles to profl. jours.; inventor in field. Mem. ABA, Am. Chem. Soc., Inst. Food Technologists. Office: Univ Washington Inst Food Sci & Tech Box 355680 Seattle WA 98195

RASCÓN, ARMANDO, artist; b. Calexico, Calif., Dec. 9, 1956; s. Reynoldo and Maria (Herrera) R. BFA Coll. Creative Studies, U. Calif., Santa Barbara, 1979. Owner Terrain Gallery, San Francisco, 1988—; mem. artist's com. San Francisco Art Inst., 1988-90; guest faculty dept. art U. Calif., Davis, 1988, Calif. Coll. Arts and Crafts, Oakland, 1991, dept. art practice U. Calif., Berkeley, 1995; co-juror McMilan award, San Francisco Art Inst., 1993; Intersection for the Arts, San Francisco, 1993; juror, panelist Artist Trust Fellowship Grants, Visual Arts, Seattle, 1994; lectr. N.Y. Mus. Modern Art, 1995; panelist LEF Found. Orgn. Grants, Cambridge, Mass., 1996, Nev. State Coun. on the Arts Grants, Carson City, 1996, 97, San Diego Mus. Contemporary Art, 1997; presenter various lectrs., panels, workshops, confs. Bd. dirs. New Langton Arts, San Francisco, 1988-92; vice-chair Art Commn. City of San Francisco, 1997. Recipient Hazel S. Lagerson scholarship U. Calif., Santa Barbara, 1975, fellowship grant in painting Nat. Endowment for Arts, Washington, 1987, Adaline Kent award San Francisco Art Inst., 1994, Goldie award in visual art San Francisco Bay Guardian, 1994. Home & Office: 165 Jessie St Ste 2 San Francisco CA 94105-4008

RASGON, BARRY MITCHELL, otolaryngologist; b. L.A., Dec. 18, 1958; s. Irving and Ethel R. BA magna cum laude, U. Calif., Riverside, 1981; MD, U. So. Calif., 1985. Diplomate Am. Bd. Otolaryngology. Intern Kaiser Permanente, 1986, resident in gen. surgery, 1987, resident in head and neck surgery, 1987-90; staff otolaryngologist, head and neck surgeon Oakland Kaiser Head and Neck Surgery Residency Tng. Program, 1990—; mem. East Bay Head and Neck Pretreatment Tumor Bd., 1990—. Contbr. articles to profl. jours. Recipient Golden Adam's Apple award, 1993; grantee in field. Mem. Pacific Coast Oto-Ophthalmic Soc. (coun. 1994—), Phi Beta Kappa.

RASHBA, EMMANUEL IOSIF, physicist, educator; b. Kiev, Ukraine, Oct. 30, 1927; came to U.S., 1991; s. Iosif Ovsei and Rosalia (Mirkine) R.; m. Erna Kelman, July 13, 1957; 1 child, Julia. Diploma with Honor, U. Kiev, Ukraine, 1949; PhD, Ukrainian Acad. Scis., 1956; DSc, Ioffe Inst. Physics and Tech., Leningrad, 1963. Jr. and sr. scientist Inst. of Physics Ukrainian Acad. of Scis., Kiev, Ukraine, 1954-60; head theoretical divsn. Inst. of Semiconductors Ukrainian Acad. of Scis., Kiev, 1960-66; head divsn. of theory of semiconductors, prin. scientist Landau Inst. for Theoretical Physics, Acad. Sci. of Russia, Moscow, 1966—; prof. Moscow Inst. for Physics and Tech., 1967-82; rsch. prof. dept. physics U. Utah, Salt Lake City, 1992—; vis. scholar CNRS, Grenoble, France, 1987, U. Stuttgart, Germany, 1988, U. Warsaw, Poland, 1989, Inst. for Sci. Interchange, Torino, Italy, 1990, Internat. Ctr. for Theoretical Physics, Trieste, Italy, 1990, Racah Inst. for Physics, Hebrew U., Jerusalem, 1991, CUNY, 1991-92, Dartmouth Coll., N.H., 1997. Co-author: Collection of Problems in Physics, 1978, 2d edit., 1987, English edit., 1986, Japanese edit., 1989; Spectroscopy of Molecular Excitons, Russian edit. 1981, English edit. 1985; assoc. editor Jour. Luminescence, 1985—; editl. bd. Letters to the Jour. of Exptl. and Theoretical Physics, 1967-88; contbr. numerous sci. and rev. articles to profl. jours. Recipient Lenin prize Sci. Govt. of USSR, 1966, A.F. Ioffe prize Acad. of Scis. of the USSR, 1987. Fellow Am. Phys. Soc. Office: U Utah Dept of Physics 201 J Fletcher Bldg Salt Lake City UT 84112

RASMUSON, BRENT (JACOBSEN), photographer, graphic artist; b. Logan, Utah, Nov. 28, 1950; s. Eleroy West and Fae (Jacobsen) R.; m. Tess Bullen, Sept. 30, 1981; children: John, Mark, Lisa. Grad. auto repair and painting sch., Utah State U. Pre-press supr. Herald Printing Co., Logan, 1969-79; profl. drummer, 1971-75; owner Valley Automotive Specialties, 1971-76; exec. sec. Herald Printing Co., 1979-89; owner Brent Rasmuson Photography, Smithfield, Utah, 1986—, Brent Rasmuson Temple Photographs, Smithfield, 1996—. Author photo prints of LDS temples: Logan, 1987, 96, Manti, 1989, Jordan River, 1989, 96, Provo, 1990, Mesa, Ariz., 1990, 96, Boise, Idaho, 1990, 96, Salt Lake LDS Temple, 1990, 96, Idaho Falls, 1991, 96, St. George, 1991, 96, Portland, Oreg., 1991, 96, L.A., 1991, 96, Las Vegas, Nev., 1991, Seattle, 1992, Oakland, Calif., 1993, 96, Ogden, 1996; author photo print: Statue of Angel Moroni, 1994; author photos used to make neckties and watch dials of LDS temples: Salt Lake, Manti, Logan, L.A., Oakland, Seattle, Las Vegas, Mesa, Portland, St. George, Jordan River, scenic tie Mammoth Hot Springs in Yellowstone Park, 1995; landscape scenic photographs featured in Best of Photography Ann., 1987, 88, 89, also in calendars and book covers. Mem. Internat. Platform Assn., Assoc. Photographers Internat., Internat. Freelance Photographers Orgn., Nat. Trust Hist. Preservation. Republican. Mem. LDS Ch. Home and Office: 40 N 200 E Smithfield UT 84335-1543

RASMUSON, ELMER EDWIN, banker, former mayor; b. Yakutat, Alaska, Feb. 15, 1909; s. Edward Anton and Jenny (Olson) R.; m. Lile Vivian Bernard, Oct. 27, 1939 (dec. 1960); children: Edward Bernard, Lile Muchmore (Mrs. John Gibbons, Jr.), Judy Ann; m. Col. Mary Louise Milligan, Nov. 4, 1961. BS magna cum laude, Harvard U., 1930, AM, 1935; student, U. Grenoble, 1930; LLD, U. Alaska, 1970, Alaska Pacific U., 1993. C.P.A., N.Y., Tex., Alaska. Chief accountant Nat. Investors Corp., N.Y.C., 1933-35; prin. Arthur Andersen & Co., N.Y.C., 1935-43; pres. Nat. Bank of Alaska, 1943-65, chmn. bd., 1966-74, chmn. exec. com., 1975-82, now chmn. emeritus; mayor City of Anchorage, 1964-67, dir., emeritus and cons., 1989; civilian aide from Alaska to sec. army, 1959-67; Swedish consul Alaska, 1955-77; Chmn. Rasmuson Found.; Rep. nominee U.S. Senate from Alaska, 1968; U.S. commr. Internat. N. Pacific Fisheries Commn., 1969-84; mem. Nat. Marine Fisheries Adv. Com., 1974-77, North Pacific Fishery Mgmt. Council, 1976-77, U.S. Arctic Research Commn., 1984-92. Mem. City Coun. Anchorage, 1945, chmn. city planning commn., 1950-53; pres. Alaska coun. Boy Scouts Am., 1953; regent U. Alaska, 1950-69; trustee King's Lake Camp, Inc., 1944—, Alaska Permanent Fund Corp., 1980-82; bd. dirs. Nat. Mus. Natural History Smithsonian Inst. 1994-97. Decorated knight first class Order of Vasa, comdr. Sweden; recipient silver Antelope award Boy Scouts Am., Japanese citation Order of the Sacred Treasure, Gold and Silver Star, 1988; outstanding civilian service medal U.S. Army; Alaskan of Year award, 1976. Mem. Pioneers Alaska, Alaska Bankers Assn. (past pres.), Defense Orientation Conf. Assn., NAACP, Alaska Native Brotherhood, Explorers Club, Phi Beta Kappa. Republican. Presbyn. Clubs: Masons, Elks, Anchorage Rotary (past pres.); Harvard (N.Y.C.; Boston); Wash. Athletic (Seattle), Seattle Yacht (Seattle), Rainier (Seattle); Thunderbird Country (Palm Desert, Calif.); Bohemian (San Francisco); Eldorado Country (Indian Wells, Calif.); Boone & Crockett. Home: PO Box 100600 Anchorage AK 99510-0600

RASMUSSEN, ELLEN L., secondary school educator; b. Clark, S.D., Nov. 25, 1936; d. Lloyd R. and Zella Dollie (Fisk) Acker; m. Donald M. Rasmussen, Aug. 6, 1960; children: LaDonna, Diann, Curtis. BS, S.D. State U., 1963. Cert. secondary edn. tchr., S.D. Educator Strandburg (S.D.) Sch. Dist., 1956-61, Brookings (S.D.) Pub. Sch., 1963, Hurley (S.D.) Sch. Dist., 1963-64, Bridgewater (S.D.) Sch. Dist., 1964-65, Lakeview (Oreg.) High Sch., 1965-66; educator South Lane Sch. Dist. 45J3, Cottage Grove, Oreg., 1966-95, ret., 1995. Mem. NEA, Nat. Coun. Tchrs. Math., Oreg. Coun. Tchrs. Math., Oreg. Edn. Assn., Lane Unified Bargaining Coun. (sec.-treas. 1988-91), Three Rivers Edn. Coun. (treas. 1991-95), South Lane Edn. Assn. (treas. 1982-95). Lutheran. Home: 1218 W D St Springfield OR 97477-8111 Office: Lincoln Mid Sch 1565 S 4th St Cottage Grove OR 97424-2955

RASMUSSEN, MIKE JOSEPH, academic administrator; b. Avalon, Calif., Aug. 1, 1947; s. Herman Joseph and Nina (Walker) R.; m. Jo Anne Eckhardt; children: Dawn Michelle, Stephen Michael. AA, West Valley Coll., 1967; AA (two), Butte Coll., 1980, 83; BA, San Jose State Coll., 1969; MA, San Jose State Univ., 1976. Cert. community coll. counselor, instr., chief adminstrv. officer, super., Calif. Vets. counselor San Jose (Calif.) State Univ., Office of Vets. Affairs, 1976-77; vets. counselor, program coord. Butte Coll., Office of Vets. Affairs, Oroville, Calif., 1977-80; dir. fin. aid and vets. affairs Butte Coll., Oroville, 1980-92, dir. spl. programs and svcs., 1992-94, interim asst. dean of student svcs., 1994-95; asst. dean of EOPS and spl. programs and svcs., 1995—; bd. dirs. Chico (Calif.) Community Hosp. Found. With USN, 1970-74, Vietnam. Recipient Cert. Appreciation Butte-Glenn County Vets. Employment Com., 1979, Boy Scouts Am. Troop 770, Paradise, Calif., 1985, Paradise (Calif.) Lioness Club, 1986, Pub. Svc. award State of Calif. Oroville Employment Devel. Dept., 1980. Mem. Calif. Community Coll. Student Fin. Aid Adminstrs. Assn. (treas. 1984-86, coord. region I, 1985-87, bd. dirs. No. Calif. 1986-87, pres.-elect 1988-89, pres. 1989-90, immediate past pres. 1990-91, Outstanding Svc. award 1985, 87, cert. of appreciation 1985, 86, 89, 90). Home: 2209 Mariposa Ave Chico CA 95926-1539 Office: Butte Coll 3536 Butte Campus Dr Oroville CA 95965-8303

RASMUSSEN, NEIL WOODLAND, insurance agent; b. Portland, Oreg., Sept. 14, 1926; s. Ernest Roy and Lulu Mildred (Woodland) R.; m. Mary Ann Cannon, Aug. 10, 1957; children: Kirk, Sally, P. Cannon, Eric (dec.). BA, Stanford U., 1949. Registered mut. funds rep. Warehouseman Consol. Supply Co., Portland, Oreg., 1949-50, sales rep., 1955-56; sales rep. Consol. Supply Co., Eugene, Oreg., 1950-52; sales rep. Consol. Supply Co., Salem, Oreg., 1956-64, br. mgr., 1964-82; agt. life and health ins. N.Y. Life Ins. Co., Salem, 1982—. Lt. Cmdr. USN, 1952-55; officer U.S. Army Res., 1969-73. Recipient Nat. Quality award Nat. Assn. Life Underwriters, 1986-88. Mem. Salem Assn. Life Underwriters, Res. Officers Assn. (bd. dirs. 1988-91, v.p. 1988-91), Rotary (bd. dirs. East Salem 1980-83, sr. active mem. 1990-92, Paul Harris fellow). Republican. Episcopalian. Office: NY Life Ins Co 530 Center St NE Salem OR 97301-3744

RASMUSSEN, R. KENT, writer; b. Albany, Calif., Oct. 11, 1943; s. Clyde L. and Marian (Bambrough) R.; m. Nancy Carpenter, July 2, 1966 (div. Mar. 1985); children: Christopher, Erik; m. Kathleen Nancy Patrick, June 18, 1988; stepchildren: Erin Heenan Moreno, Noelle Heenan, Heather Heenan. BA in Econs., U. Calif., Berkeley, 1966; MA in History, UCLA, 1969, PhD, 1975. Mng. editor FourWay Comms., L.A., 1983-86; assoc. editor Marcus Garvey Papers Project UCLA, 1986-91; editl. assoc. Ctr. Civic Edn., Calabasas, Calif., 1992-93; editor Salem Press, Pasadena, Calif., 1994—. Author: Mzilikazi of the Ndebele, 1977, Migrant Kingdom: Mzilikazi's Ndebele in South Africa, 1978, Historical Dictionary of Rhodesia/Zimbabwe, 1979, On This Day in History, 1991, 92, 93, 94, Mark Twain A to Z, 1995, Farewell to Jim Crow: The Rise and Fall of Segregation in America, 1997; co-author: Dictionary of African Historical Biography, 1978, revised and expanded edit., 1986, Historical Dictionary of Zimbabwe 2d edit., 1990; editor: Tournament of Roses, 1988, Mark Twain's Book for Bad Boys and Girls, 1995; co-editor: Black Empire, 1991; contbg. editor: Africa for the Africans: The Marcus Garvey and Universal Negro Improvement Association Papers, 1995; contbr. articles to profl. jours. Office: Salem Press 131 N El Molino Ave Ste 350 Pasadena CA 91101-1878

RASMUSSEN, THOMAS VAL, JR., lawyer, small business owner; b. Salt Lake City, Aug. 11, 1954; s. Thomas Val and Georgia (Smedley) R.; m. Donita Gubler, Aug. 15, 1978; children: James, Katherine, Kristin. BA magna cum laude, U. Utah, 1978, JD, 1981. Bar: Utah 1981, U.S. Dist. Ct. Utah 1981, U.S. Supreme Ct. 1985. Atty. Salt Lake Legal Defender Assn., Salt Lake City, 1981-83, Utah Power and Light Co., Salt Lake City, 1983-89, Hatch, Morton & Skeen, Salt Lake City, 1989-90; ptnr. Morton, Skeen & Rasmussen, Salt Lake City, 1991-94, Skeen & Rasmussen, Salt Lake City, 1994—; co-owner, developer Handi Self-Storage, Kaysville, Utah, 1984-93; instr. bus. law Brigham Young U., Salt Lake City, 1988-90. Adminstrv. editor Jour. Contemporary Law, 1980-81, Jour. Energy Law and Policy, 1980-81. Missionary Ch. of Jesus Christ of Latter-Day Sts., Brazil, 1973-75. Mem. Utah, Salt Lake County Bar Assn., Intermountain Miniature Horse Club (pres. 1989, 2d v.p. 1990), Phi Eta Sigma, Phi Kappa Phi, Beta Gamma Sigma. Home: 3094 Whitewater Dr Salt Lake City UT 84121-1561 Office: Skeen & Rasmussen 4659 Highland Dr Salt Lake City UT 84117-5137

RATH, STEPHEN CHARLES, controller; b. Port Angeles, Wash., Apr. 14, 1959; s. Dennis Doane and Dorothy Anne (Sargent) R. B in Bus. Adminstrn., Wash. State U., 1981. CPA, Calif., Wash. Staff acct. Deloitte Haskins & Sells, Seattle, 1981-83; sr. acct. Marynov Madsen Garden & Campbell, Palm Springs, Calif., 1983-86; v.p., asst. contr. Metro-Goldwyn-Mayer Inc., Santa Monica, Calif., 1986—. Mem. Am. Inst. CPAs, Calif. Soc. CPAs. Home: 753 Pier Ave # C Santa Monica CA 90405-4515

RATHE, KAREN MARIE, editor; b. Eugene, Oreg., May 18, 1954; d. Hjalmar Jacob and Janet Roberta (Johnson) R.; m. Kevin Smith Donnelly, June 28, 1992; 1 child, Liam Rathe Donnelly; stepchildren: Amanda Moon Donnelly, Sara Logan Donnelly. B in Interior Arch., U. Oreg., 1979, MS in Journalism, 1986. Reporter, editor, photographer The Headlight-Herald, Tillamook, Oreg., 1981-84; news desk copy editor The Oregonian, Portland, 1985; news desk copy editor The Seattle Times, 1987, letters editor, columnist, 1987-91, news features copy editor, layout editor, 1991—. Co-founder, v.p. bd. Tillamook Crisis and Resource Ctr., 1982-84; bd. dirs. Columbia County Women's Resource Ctr., St. Helens, Oreg., 1980-81. Recipient 1st pl. award Wash. Press Assn., 1994, and other awards; grad. teaching fellow U. Oreg., 1984-86, Poynter Inst. fellow, 1986. mem. Soc. Profl. Journalists (sec. Western Wash. chpt. 1989-90, pres. 1990-91), Kappa Tau Alpha. Democrat. Presbyterian. Office: The Seattle Times PO Box 70 Seattle WA 98111-0070

RATHMELL, SANDRA LEE, women's health nurse; b. St. Louis, Apr. 3, 1944; d. Charles Chester and Estelle Lucille (Simon) Dunham; m. Thomas S. Rathmell, Sept. 17, 1965 (div. May 1990); children: John Thomas, Tamara Lynn. Diploma, St. Luke's Hosp., 1965. RN, Ariz., Mo., Del. Staff nurse Dover (Del.) AFB Hosp., 1966-68, Luth. Med. Ctr., St. Louis, 1975-82, Maricopa Med. Ctr., Phoenix, 1982-84, Chandler (Ariz.) Regional Hosp., 1984-96; instr. hosp. postpartum classes, St. Luke's Hosp., Phoenix. Mem. St. Luke's Alumni Assn.

RATLIFF, GERALD LEE, dean, speech and theater educator; b. Middletown, Ohio, Oct. 23, 1944; s. Ray and Peggy (Donisi) R. BA magna cum laude, Georgetown (Ky.) Coll., 1967; MA, U. Cin., 1970; PhD, Bowling Green (Ohio) State U., 1975. Area head English theatre Glenville State Coll., 1970-72; prof., chair theatre Montclair State Coll., Upper Montclair, N.J., 1975-92; dean Sch. Fine and Performing Arts Ind.-Purdue U., Ft. Wayne, Ind., 1993-95; dean Coll. Arts and Architecture Mont. State U., Bozeman, Mont., 1995—; feature writer Lexington (Ky.) Herald-News, 1967-68. Author: Beginning Scene Study: Aristophanes to Albee, 1980, Speech and Drama Club Activities, 1982, Oedipus Trilogy, 1984, Combating Stagefright, 1985, Playscript Interpretation and Production, 1985, (Machiavelli's) The Prince, 1986, (with Suzanne Trauth) Introduction to Musical Theatre, 1986, Playing Scenes: A Sourcebook for Performance, 1993, Playing Contemporary Scenes: A Sourcebook for Performance, 1996; contbr. articles and revs. to profl. jours. Exec. coun. mem. Assn. for Commn. Adminstrn., 1995—; bd. dirs. Am. Conf. Acad. Deans. Fulbright scholar, 1989; recipient Nat. Medallion of Honor award Theta Alpha Phi, 1989; Alumni Assn. faculty rsch. grantee, 1980, 83, 86. Mem. Speech Communication Assn. (legis. coun. 1987-88, chair theatre div. 1986-87), Am. Assn. Theatre in Secondary Edn. (nat. bd. dirs. 1986-87), Secondary Sch. Theatre Assn. (nat. bd. dirs. 1983-86), Internat. Arts Assn. (v.p. 1975-76), Eastern Communication Assn. (exec. sec. 1986-89, 1st v.p. elect 1989, exec. com. 1986—, pres. 1991, Disting. Svc. award 1993), Theta Alpha Phi (nat. pres. 1984-87, nat. coun. 1979-82, 84-87). Home: 317 S 16th Ave Apt C Bozeman MT 59715-4179 Office: Mont State U Theatre Dept Bozeman MT 59717

RATLIFF, JAMES CONWAY, hotel executive; b. Evanston, Ill., Mar. 28, 1940; s. Harold Sugart and Marjorie (Elmore) R. BA, Mich. State U., 1967. Dir. food & beverage ops. Detroit Hilton, 1970-71; dir. food & beverage purchasing Hilton Hotels Corp., N.Y.C., 1972-77; corp. dir. procurement

Hilton Hotels Corp., Beverly Hills, Calif., 1977—; bd. dirs. Am. Inst. Food Distbn., Fair Lawn, N.J., 1985-96, treas., 1989-90, vice chmn., 1991-92, chmn., 1994-95; instr. Calif. State Poly. U., Pomona, 1987, 88. With U.S. Army, 1963-65. Mem. Food Svc. Purchasing Assn. Can. (hon.), Produce Mktg. Assn. (bd. dirs. 1986-88, v.p. 1989-90, sec.-treas. 1991, chmn. elect 1992, chmn. 1993, chmn. exec. com. 1994), Product Mktg. Assn. (chmn. foodsvc. divsn. 1989-90, bd. dirs. foodsvc. divsn. 1985-88), Nat. Restaurant Assn. Foodsvc. Purchasing Mgrs. (bd. dirs. 1977-81, chmn. 1981-83), Pacific Corinthian Yacht Club. Republican. Methodist. Office: Hilton Hotels Corp 9336 Civic Center Dr Beverly Hills CA 90210-3604

RATLIFF, LEIGH ANN, pharmacist; b. Long Beach, Calif., May 20, 1961; d. Harry Warren and Verna Lee (Zwink) R. D in Pharmacy, U. Pacific, 1984. Registered pharmacist, Calif., Nev. Pharmacist intern Green Bros. Inc., Stockton, Calif., 1982-84, staff pharmacist Thrifty Corp., Long Beach, Calif., 1984-85, head pharmacist, 1986-87, pharm. buyer, 1987-92; pharmacy. mgr. Kmart Pharmacy, Long Beach, Calif., 1992-97; staff pharmacist Egyptian Pharmacy, Long Beach, Calif., 1997—; mem. joint mktg. com. Calif. Pharmicist's Assn. Mem. Pacific Alumni Assocs., Nat. Trust for Hist. Preservation, Friends of Rancho Los Cerritos; treas. Bixby Knolls Ter. Homeowners Assn., 1988-92, pres. 1992-96; vol. Docent Rancho Los Cerritos Hist. Site, 1988—; vol. preceptor U. So. Calif. Sch. Pharmacy; vol. Fairfield YMCA, Long Beach. Mem. Am. Pharm. Assn., Am. Inst. History Pharmacy, Calif. Pharmacist Assn., Lambda Kappa Sigma. Republican. Methodist. Avocations: raising African cichlids, growing herbs, collecting Hull pottery, antiquing. Home: 3913 N Virginia Rd Unit 301 Long Beach CA 90807-2670 Office: Egyptian Pharmacy 5128 E 2nd St Long Beach CA 90803

RATLIFF, WILLIAM ELMORE, curator, researcher; b. Evanston, Ill., Feb. 11, 1937; s. Harold Shugart and Marjorie (Elmore) R.; m. Lynn Louise Robbins, June 1959; children: Sharon, Paul, Susan, David, John. BA, Oberlin Coll., 1959; MA, U. Wash., 1968, PhD, 1974. Rsch. fellow Hoover Instn., Stanford, Calif., 1968-79; cons., dir. rsch. Rsch. Internat., San Francisco, 1976-82; critic, chief editorial writer Times Tribune, Palo Alto, Calif., 1979-86; sr. rsch. fellow Hoover Instn., Stanford, 1986—; music stringer L.A. Times, 1975-95, Opera News, 1978-93; cons., lectr. U.S. Info. Agy., Washington, 1986, 88, 89, 90; lectr. U.S. Dept. Def. confs./seminars, Washington, 1984—. Author: Castroism in Latin America, 1978; author, editor: Media and Cuban Revolution, 1987; co-author, co-editor: The Law and Economics of Development, 1997; Judicial Reform in Latin America, 1996; co-author: Capitalist Revolution in Argentina, 1990, The Civil War in Nicaragua, 1993, Argentina's Capitalist Revolution Revisited, 1993, Inside the Cuban Interior Ministry, 1994; co-editor: Juan Peron Cartas del exilio, 1991; area editor: Yearbook on Internat. Communist Affairs, 1968-91; contbr. articles to profl. jours. Office: Hoover Inst Stanford U Stanford CA 94305

RATTO, CAROLYN ELIZABETH, educator; b. Oakland, Calif., July 16, 1951; d. Frederick McLean and Elizabeth Ellen (Geers) Cranston; m. Michael Peter Ratto, June 24, 1973; children: Rebecca, Luke, Jessica. BA in English cum laude, Holy Names Coll., 1973. Cert. tchr., Calif. Tchr. Our Lady of the Rosary Sch., Union City, Calif., 1973, St. Brendan's Sch., San Francisco, 1973-75, Turlock (Calif.) Unified Sch. Dist., 1986-88. Commr. Parks and Recreation, City of Turlock, 1984-88, planning commr., 1988-90 Office mgr., Dr. Michael Rattto, 1993—; mem. Turlock City Coun., 1990—; chair leadership tng. coun. Nat. League of Cities, 1996, mem. adv. coun. 1995—, mem. bd. dirs. 1993-95; mem. bd. dirs. Emmanuel Hosp., 1996—, League of Calif. Cities, 1993, 95, pres., League of Calif. Cities, 2nd v.p.,1996, 1st v.p., 1997, mayor's and coun. mems. dept. 1994-95. Named Tchr. of the Year Julien PTA, 1988. Mem. Statesman Club (past bd. dirs., pres. 1984-88). Roman Catholic. Office: 315 Crane Ave Turlock CA 95380-4543

RATZLAFF, VERNON PAUL, elementary education educator, consultant; b. Mt. Lake, Minn., May 16, 1925; s. Peter Benjamin and Helen (Dick) R.; m. Bonnie Lou Sommers, Dec. 17, 1955; children: Paul, Gwen, Jay, Peter. BA in Elem. Edn., German, Goshen Coll., 1954; MA, U. N.D., 1971; student, U. Minn., 1956-57, U. Oreg., 1965, U. No. Ariz., 1968. Cert. tchr. Elem. tchr. Richfield (Minn.) Pub. Schs., 1954-74; tchr. Tuba City (Ariz.) Pub. Sch., 1975—; resource person to tchrs., Grand Forks, N.C., 1970-72, resource person to upper elem. tchrs. and children, Richfield, 1967-70; administr. of Christian Sch. Hopi Mission, Oraibi, Ariz., 1971-75; math tchr. Nortland Pioneer Coll.; established "Look Folks-No Fail" classrooms. Author: Side by Side " Up from the Pit to Become a Shining Star" (Where Students Take Responsibility for Learning), 1990; contbr. articles to numerous jours. Mem. NEA, Ariz. Edn. Assn., Am. Assn. Retired People. Republican. Home: 5743 Smoke Rise Dr Flagstaff AZ 86004-2746 *Personal philosophy: Tell me, I forget, Show me, I remember, Involve me, I understand.*

RAUCINA, THOMAS FRANK See RACINA, THOM

RAUGH, MICHAEL RANDOLPH, mathematician; b. Altoona, Pa., Sept. 26, 1938. BS, UCLA, 1962; MS, Stanford U., 1978, PhD, 1979. Programmer Lawrence Berkeley (Calif.) Lab., 1967-71, Inst. for Math Studies in Social Scis./Stanford U., Stanford, Calif., 1971-74; mathematician, computer sci. profl. U.S. Geol. Survey, Menlo Park, Calif., 1978-82; mem. tech. staff Hewlett-Packard Labs., Palo Alto, Calif., 1982-85; chief scientist, sr. scientist Rsch. Inst. for Advanced Computer Sci., Mountain View, Calif., 1985-94; co-founder, v.p. Interconnect Tech. Corp., Mountain View, Calif., 1993—; adj. prof. dept. mech. engring. and engring. sci., U. N.C., 1992-95. Inventor, patentee of X-Y stage calibration of mathematically rigorous techniques for lithographic imaging equipment. Recipient certs. of appreciation for creation of innovative rsch. programs NASA, Ames Rsch. Ctr., Mountain View; NSF fellow; Fulbright-Hayes fellow in math. at Manchester U., 1963-64; internship at design studio of Charles and Ray Eames, Venice, Calif. Mem. SPIE, Geol. Soc. Am., Calif. Botanical Soc., Soc. Indsl. and Applied Math., Calif. Native Plant Soc., Sigma Xi. Office: Interconnect Tech Corp PO Box 4158 Mountain View CA 94040-0158

RAUGHTON, JIMMIE LEONARD, educational foundation administrator, urban planner; b. Knoxville, Tenn., Oct. 9, 1943; s. George L. and Ann (Simotes) R. BA in Urban and Regional Planning, U. No. Colo., 1974, MA, 1976, PhD, U. Colo., 1993. Mgr., Flexitran div. Gathers, De Vilbliss Architects and Planners, 1966-68; asst. dir. planning City of Aurora, Colo., 1970-71; planner City of Lakewood, Colo., 1971-73; planner City of Boulder, Colo., 1973-74; instr. urban planning C.C. of Denver, 1974-76, div. dir. human resources and svcs., 1976-81, div. dir. sci. and tech., 1981-85; v.p. State of Colo. C.Cs., 1985—; exec. dir. Edn. Found. Colo., 1989—; coord. devel. Rocky Mountain Energy and Environ. Tech. Center, 1980. cons. Denver Regional Council of Govts. for Model Sign Code, 1973, City of Boulder Transp. Dept., 1975—; chmn. profl. advisory com. to Colo. Gov.'s Land Use Adviser, 1973; also public speaker. Mem. exec. bd. Civic Center Assn., Denver, 1973-75; supervisory com. Colo. State Employees Credit Union, 1986—;mem. bd. Support Systems Consol., 1984, Bridge Industry, 1984-85; candidate Denver City Council, 1975; bd. dirs. Plan Metro Denver, 1975-76, Four Corner Art Collection, 1973—. Recipient Citizen Award of Honor, Assn. of Beautiful Colo. Roads, 1972. Mem. Am. Inst. of Planners (mem. exec. bd. Colo. 1970-75, treas. 1972-73), Colo. City Mgrs. Assn., Am. Soc. Planning Ofcls., Am. Vocat. Assn., Am. Soc. for Tng. and Devel., Pi Alpha Alpha. Methodist. Contbr. articles to local newspapers. Home: 2501 High St Denver CO 80205-5565 Office: State of Colo CCs 1391 Speer Blvd Denver CO 80204-2508

RAUH, J. RANDALL, physician; b. Hardtner, Kans., June 30, 1947; s. John Harry and Dorothy Mae (Dimmick) R.; m. Janice Yvonne Weigand, July 1, 1967 (div. Jan. 1989); children: Heather Elaine, Sarah Elaine, Travis Randall, Joshua Blaine. BS in Chemistry and Biology, Northwestern Okla. State U., 1969; MD, U. Okla., 1973. Diplomate Am. Bd. Ob-Gyn. Resident Tulsa Med. Coll. U. Okla., 1973-76; pvt. practice Okmulgee, Okla., 1976-80; pvt. group practice Stillwater Women's Clinic, Okla., 1980; pvt. practice. Miles City, Mont., 1981—; clin. instr. U. N.D. Sch. Medicine; chief of staff Holy Rosary Hosp., Miles City, 1981-82, 88-89, trustee, 1983-89; mem. ethics com. Presentation Health System, Aberdeen, S.D., 1986-90. Contbr. articles to profl. jours. Pres. Little League com. Miles City Youth Baseball Assn., 1988-90, pres. Am. Legion baseball com., 1991—. Recipient Excellence in Clin. Tchg. award Am. Acad. Fam. Practice, 1977. Fellow ACOG, ACS, mem. AMA, Am. Fertility Soc., Mont. Med. Assn., U. Okla. Coll. Med. Alumni Assn. (life), Miles City Area C. of C. Republican. Lutheran. Office: 219 N Merriam Ave Miles City MT 59301-2700

RAUTENBERG, ROBERT FRANK, consulting research statistician; b. Milw., Sept. 14, 1943; s. Raymond Clarence and Anna Josephine (Winter) R.; m. Meredith Taylor, June 2, 1965 (div. Feb. 1975); 1 child, Matthew Carl. PhD in Bus. Adminstrn., Pacific Western U., 1983; postgrad., Sorbonne U., Paris. Pvt. practice Kansas City, Mo., 1975-76; pres. Seven Diamond Enterprises, San Francisco, 1976-78; CEO Assurance Sys., San Francisco, 1984-96, Honolulu, 1997—. Author: The Analytical Management Handbook, 1985, Supplement to the Analytical Management Handbook, 1991, London edit., 1996, A Bayesian Approach to Management, 1996; contbr. articles to profl. jours. and conf. proceedings. Fellow Royal Statis. Soc.; mem. Internat. Soc. Bayesian Analysis (charter). Episcopalian. Office: Ste 124 Box 210 1164 Bishop St Honolulu HI 96813-2810 *Personal philosophy: I am always surprised at the willingness of the human spirit to face new challenges.*

RAVAL, RUCHIKA, regulatory affairs specialist; b. New Delhi, July 4, 1960; came to U.S., 1983; d. Raman and Rohini (Bhatt) R. MS in Microbiology, Wagner Coll., 1984. Med. technologist Jaslok Hosp., Bombay, 1980-82; rsch. scientist R & D Baxter Biotech, L.A., 1990-93, rsch. scientist quality control, 1993-94, rsch. scientist virology, 1994-96, regulatory affairs scientist, 1996—. Vol. educator M.S. U., Baroda, India, 1988-90. Mem. Am. Assn. Pharm. Scientists, Regulatory Affairs Profl. Soc., Toastmasters Club (sec. Diamond Bar chpt. 1996-97). Office: Baxter Healthcare Hyland Divsn 550 N Brand Blvd Glendale CA 91203

RAVEN, ROBERT DUNBAR, lawyer; b. Cadillac, Mich., Sept. 26, 1923; s. Christian and Gladys L. (Dunbar) R.; m. Leslie Kay Erickson, June 21, 1947; children: Marta Ellen, Matt Robert, Brett Lincoln. AB with honors, Mich. State U., 1949; LLB, U. Calif., Berkeley, 1952. Bar: Calif. 1953. Assoc. Morrison & Foerster and predecessor, San Francisco, 1952-56, ptnr., 1956-94, sr. of counsel, 1994—; chmn. Morrison & Foerster (and predecessor), San Francisco, 1974-82; mem. Jud. Coun. of Calif., 1983-87. Bd. dirs. Bay Area USO, 1964-73, pres., 1968-70; mem. San Francisco Mayor's Criminal Justice Coun., 1971-72; co-chmn. San Francisco Lawyer's Com. for Urban Affairs, 1976-78; bd. dirs. Lawyers Com. for Civil Rights Under Law, 1976-96. With USAAF, 1942-45. Decorated Air medal with oak leaf cluster. Mem. ABA (pres. 1989, mem. standing com. fed. judiciary 1975-80, chmn. 1978-80, chmn. standing com. on legal aid and indigent defendants 1981-83, chair standing com. dispute resolution 1991-93, chair sect. dispute resolution 1993-94), FBA, Am. Arbitration Assn. (bd. dirs. 1988-96), CPR Inst. for Dispute Resolution (mem. exec. com.), Internat. Acad. Trial Lawyers, State Bar Calif. (gov. 1978-81, pres. 1981), Bar Assn. San Francisco (pres. 1971), Am. Law Inst., Am. Bar Found., Am. Judicature Soc., Boalt Hall Alumni Assn. (pres. 1972-73), World Trade Club (San Francisco), Order of Coif. Democrat. Home: 1064 Via Alta Lafayette CA 94549-2916 Office: Morrison & Foerster 425 Market St San Francisco CA 94105-2482

RAWLINGS, JAMES SCOTT, neonatologist; b. Ft. Oglethorpe, Ga., Feb. 17, 1943; s. James Garland and Mary Katherine (Coffey) R.; m. Virginia Buess, June 14, 1969; children: Mary Margaret Anderson, Scott Kirkpatrick. BS in Engring., Va. Polytech Inst., 1965; MD, Vanderbilt U., 1973. Commd. 2d lt. U.S. Army, 1965, advanced through grades to col., 1993; assoc. prof. F. edward Herbert Sch. Medicine, Uniformed Svcs. of Health Scis., Bethesda, Md., 1980—. Contbr. rsch. papers to profl. jours. Mem. March of Dimes Task Force on Infant Mortality, Pierce County, Wash., 1987-89. Neonatal-Perinatal Medicine fellow, Honolulu, 1980-86. Fellow Am. Acad. Pediatrics (Andrew M. Margileth award, 1985, 88, 91, 94); mem. AMA, Western Soc. Pediatric Rsch., So. Soc. PEdiatric Rsch. Episcopalian. Home: 1107 Sequalish St Steilacoom WA 98388-2412 Office: Neonatal Assocs Inc PC Tacoma WA 98405

RAWLINGS, ROBERT HOAG, newspaper publisher; b. Pueblo, Colo., Aug. 3, 1924; s. John W. and Dorothy (Hoag) R. Student Colo. U., 1943-44; BA, Colo. Coll., 1947; m. Mary Alexandra Graham, Oct. 18, 1947; children: Jane Louise, John Graham, Carolyn Anne, Robert Hoag II. Reporter Pueblo Chieftain and Pueblo Star-Jour., 1947-51, advt. rep. 1951-62, gen. mgr., 1962-79, pub. and editor, 1980—; sec. Star-Jour. Pub. Corp., 1962-84, pres., 1984—; Past chmn. bd. dir. Colo. Nat. Bank-Pueblo; bd. dir. U.S. Air Force Acad. Found., U. So. Colo. Found., Colo. Water Edn. Found.; pres. Robert Hoag Rawlings Found. Served with USNR, 1942-46. Named Colo. Newspaper Person of the Year, 1989, Disting. Univ. Fellow Pres. Club U. So. Colo., 1993, Outstanding Citizen of Yr. Pueblo C. of C., 1994, Colo. Bus. Leader of the Yr. Colo. Assn. of Commerce and Industry, 1994; recipient Outstanding Svc. to Univ. award U. So. Colo. Alumni Assn., 1993, Colo. Corp. Philanthropy award Nat. Philanthropy Assoc., 1993, Louis T. Benezet award Colo. Coll. Alumni Assn., 1996, Outstanding Am. Achievement award U. So. Colo., 1997; named Donor of Yr. Nat. Assn. Univ. Athletic Devel. Dirs., 1995. Mem. Colo. Press Assn., (dir. 1963-66, 76-78, pres. 1985, chmn. bd. dirs. 1986), Rocky Mountain Ad Mgrs. (past pres.), Colo. AP (past pres.), Elks, Rotary. Presbyterian. Home: 27 Calle del Sol Pueblo CO 81008 Office: Star-Jour Pub Corp PO Box 4040 Pueblo CO 81003-0040

RAWLINS, JAN, educator; b. Salt Lake City, July 2, 1961; d. Robert E. and Carol Anne (Boss) R. BS in Home Econs. Edn., Brigham Young U., 1985. Tchr. family and consumer sci. Clearfield (Utah) High Sch., 1985-92; tchr. consumer sci., student govt. advisor Northridge High Sch., Layton, Utah, 1992-97. Mem. Am. Vocat. Assn., Nat. Assn. Vocat. Home Econs. Tchrs., Nat. Assn. Secondary Sch. Prins., Utah Assn. Vocat. Tchrs., Utah Edn. Assn., Utah Assn. Student Couns., Davis Edn. Assn. Office: Northridge High Sch 2430 Hill Field Rd Layton UT 84041-4747

RAWLINSON, DENNIS PATRICK, lawyer; b. Portland, Oreg., Mar. 1, 1947; s. Thomas F. and Betty (Price) R.; m. M. Diane Schatz, Apr. 26, 1980. BA, U. Notre Dame, 1969; MBA, Cornell U., 1976, JD, 1976. Bar: Oreg. 1976, U.S. Dist. Ct. Oreg. 1976. Assoc. Miller, Nash, Wiener, Hager & Carlsen, Portland, Oreg., 1976-82, ptnr., 1982—. Contbr. articles to profl. jours. Pres., bd. dirs. Portland Opera Assn., 1990—. 1st lt. Army Med. Svc. Corps, 1970-72, Korea. Mem. Oreg. State Bar Assn. (mem. exec. com. debtor/creditor sect. 1988-91, mem. exec. com. litigation sect. 1992—, mng. editor litigation jour. 1992—, mng. editor Oreg. Comml. Practice manual 1988—), Arlington Club Toastmasters (pres.), Rotary Club Portland (bd. dirs.), Multnomah Athletic Club (pres., trustee). Office: Miller Nash Wiener Hager & Carlsen 111 SW 5th Ave Ste 3500 Portland OR 97204-3638

RAWLS, JAMES JABUS, history educator; b. Washington, Nov. 10, 1945; s. Jabus W. and Jane Kathleen (Brumfield) R.; m. Linda Joyce Higdon, Dec. 29, 1967; children: Benjamin Jabus, Elizabeth Jane Kathleen. BA with honors in History, Stanford U., 1967; MA, U. Calif., Berkeley, 1969, PhD, 1975. Instr. history San Francisco State U., 1971-75, Diablo Valley Coll., Pleasant Hill, Calif., 1975—; vis. lectr. U. Calif., 1977-81, vis. assoc. prof., 1989; scholar-in-residence Calif. State U., Sacramento, 1987; moderator Chautauqua progrma NEH, Calif., Oreg., 1992; radio pseronality Dr. History, Sta. KNBR, San Francisco, 1990-94; cons. Walt Disney Imagineering, 1995—. Co-author: Land of Liberty: A United States History, 1985; author: Indians of California, 1986, Dr. History's Whizz-Bang, 1992, Dame Shirley and the Gold Rush, 1993, Never Turn Back: Father Serra's Mission, 1993, Dr. History's Sampler, 1994, California Dreaming, 1995, Chief Red Fox Is Dead: A History of Native Americans Since 1945, 1996; editor: Dan De Quille of the Big Bonanza, 1980, New Directions in California History, 1989; co-editor: California: A Place, A People, A Dream, 1986; contbr. Worldmark Ency. of the States, 1981; World Book Ency., 1993, Ency. of the Am. West, 1995, Am. Nat. Biography, 1995, Dictionary of Am. History, 1995, Microsoft Encarta and Encyclopedia, 1996; cons. editor Us Kids History Series, 1990—, California Missions Series, 1994-96. Recipient faculty lectr. award Diablo Valley Coll., 1988, Nat. Teaching Excellence award of Yr., 1989. Fellow Calif. Hist. Soc. (book rev. editor Calif. History 1983—); mem. Am. Hist. Assn. Democrat. Office: Diablo Valley Coll Dept History Pleasant Hill CA 94523

RAY, MARIANNE YURASKO, social services administrator; b. Mpls., Sept. 25, 1934; d. Andrew George and Ann (Rusinko) Yurasko; m. Raymond Robert Ray, Nov. 22, 1962 (div. July 1980); children: Joel Christopher, Angela Christine. BA, U. Utah, 1956; student, U. Wash., 1975; MA, Pacific Lutheran U., 1978. Case worker, vol. agy. liaison State of Wash. Dept. Social and Health Services, Tacoma, Wash., 1963-65, 1971-79, 1983; child placement project dir. State of Wash. Dept. Social and Health Services, Olympia, Wash., 1979-80; casework supr. Child Protective Service State of Wash. Dept. Social and Health Services, Tacoma, Wash., 1980-81, foster home recruiter and licenser, 1981-83; owner, cons. Myray Focuses, Seattle, 1983—; pres. Delta Dynamics Inc., Seattle, 1984-86; mental health therapist Children's Indsl. Home, Tacoma, 1985-86, Good Samaritan Mental Health, Puyallup, Wash., 1986-87; part-time faculty Cen. Wash. U., Ellensburg, 1985—, Highline Community Coll., Midway, Wash., 1985-87, Renton (Wash.) Vocational Tech. Inst., 1985—, Lake Washington Vocational Tech. Inst., Kirkland, Wash., 1985-96; dir. child abuse treatment Cath. Community Services, Seattle, 1987-96; cons. Tacoma Sch. Dist., 1985-86; presenter nat. conferences and workshops. Creator workshops: Humor Techniques for Stress Management in the Classroom, 1985, Humor in Stress Management: Applications in Helping Professions, 1987, Kicking the Holiday Blues, 1986, Humor for the Health of It, 1987, Laughing Matters--It Really Does!, 1984—, Relocation: What it means for the Employee and Family, 1984—, Humor in the Workplace for Higher Productivity and Team Building, 1984—, Laughter and Liberation in the Classroom to Promote Learning, 1987—, Creative Imagery in Relaxation Techniques, 1987—. Mem. Am. Psychol. Assn. (assoc.), Pacific Northwest Orgn. Devel. Network, Pacific Northwest Speakers Assn. Office: Myray Focuses Counseling/Consulting PO Box 98570 Seattle WA 98198-0570

RAY, PAULA DICKERSON, elementary education educator; b. Paterson, N.J., Apr. 24, 1941; d. Paul J. and Rose (Labowsky) Baron; m. Gene Wells Ray, Nov. 8, 1980 (div. July 1992); children: Donald Dickerson III, Katherine Dickerson Pratt, Nancy Dickerson Solomon. BA, San Diego State U., 1964, MA, 1981. Tchr. 6th grade San Diego City Schs., 1968—, resource tchr. Mem. San Dieguito Planning Group, Rancho Santa Fe, 1988-90. Mem. Achievement Rewards Coll. Scientists (pres. 1986-96), Honors Seminar (bd. dirs., v.p. 1988-97).

RAY, RICHARD STANLEY, accountant; b. Miami, Ariz., June 12, 1937; s. Milton Sevier and Anne Elizabeth (Mickelson) R.; m. Laura Ann Young, Apr. 11, 1963; children: Denise, Mark, Melanie, Laura, Jordon. AA, Ea. Ariz. Jr. Coll., 1957; BS in Acctg., Ariz. State U., 1962, MS in Acctg., 1964. CPA, Ariz. Staff acct. Deloitte, Haskins & Sells, Phoenix, 1963-65; controller AMECO, Phoenix, 1965-70, U-Haul Co., Phoenix, 1970-76; dir. audit svcs. Ariz. Pub. Service Co., Phoenix, 1976—; advisor to bd. Credit Data of Ariz., Phoenix, 1981—, chmn. bd., 1980-81; dir. Arcoa Internat., Phoenix, 1973-76. Treas., bd. mem. Big Sisters of Ariz., Phoenix, 1972-78; dist. coun. Boy Scouts Am., Phoenix, 1982-84; stake pres. Mormon Ch., Tempe, Ariz. 1987—. Grad. rsch. fellowship, Ariz. Bankers Assn., Phoenix, 1962. Mem. Am. Inst. CPA's, Ariz. Soc. CPA's (Acctg. Achievement award 1962), Ariz. State Bd. Accountancy (continuing profl. edn. com. 1986—), Edison Electric Inst. (com. mem. 1976—), Rotary. Republican.

RAY, ROBERT DONALD, artist; b. Denver, Oct. 2, 1924; s. Carl James and Irene (Wilt) R. B.F.A. cum laude, U. So. Calif., 1950; M.A. magna cum laude, Mex. City Coll., 1952. Represented in permanent collections Denver Art Mus., Balt. Mus. Art, Joslyn Art Mus., Omaha, Roswell Mus., N.Mex., Columbia Mus. Art, S.C., Colorado Springs Fine Arts Ctr, Aspen Inst. Exec. Ctr., Utah State U., U. Tex., Austin, U. N.Mex., Albuquerque, Bklyn. Mus., Mus. N.Mex., Santa Fe, Sheldon Mus, U. Nebr., others. Pres., adv. bd. Harwood Found. U. N.Mex., Taos, 1983; bd. dirs. Taos Sch. Music, 1980—, 1st v.p., 1980-83. Served with USNR, 1943-46; PTO. Home: HC 68 Box 4B Taos NM 87571-9408

RAY, SANKAR, opto-electric device and communication network research and development administrator; b. Calcutta, India, Dec. 30, 1953; came to U.S., 1976; s. Asok Kumar and Sumitra (Dey) R.; m. Diana Konaszewski, June 8, 1985; children: Krishanu, Monisha. BSc in Physics with honors, U. Calcutta, 1974; MSc in Physics, Indian Inst. Tech., Kanpur, 1976; PhD in Physics, Brown U., 1981. Prin. rsch. scientist Honeywell Corp. Tech. ctr., Bloomington, Minn., 1981-87; lead rsch. scientist Boeing High Tech. Ctr., Bellevue, Wash., 1987-90, mgr. advanced components for fiber optic networks, 1990-93, mgr. comm. sys., 1993—; evaluator rsch. proposals Jet Propulsion Lab., Pasadena, Calif., U. Wash., Seattle, Simon Fraser U., Vancouver, B.C., Can., 1990; chmn. organizing com. Boeing Photonics Symposium, Seattle, 1991; mem. Compound Semiconductor Adv. Com., Wash. Tech. Ctr., U. Wash., 1992; mem. exec. com. Internat. Comm. Conf., 1995. Contbr. articles to Phys. Rev. Letters, Applied Physics Letters, IEEE Electron devices; author, co-author over 25 jour. articles, conf. procs. Mem. IEEE, Am. Phys. Soc., Comm. Soc. Office: Boeing Def & Space Group MS 3W-51 PO Box 3999 Seattle WA 98124-2499

RAYMOND, C. ELIZABETH, history educator; b. Kansas City, Mo., Feb. 9, 1953; m. James R. Pagliarini. AB cum laude, Princeton (N.J.) U., 1974; MA, U. Pa., 1975, PhD, 1979. Rsch. assoc. Nev. Hist. Soc., Reno, 1981-84; asst. prof. history U. Nev., Reno, 1984-91, assoc. prof. history, 1991—; chair univ. accreditation com., 1996-97; acting asst. dean Coll. of Arts and Scis., U. Nev., 1994, faculty senate chair, 1991-92. Author: George Wingfield: Owner and Operator of Nevada, 1992 (Shepperson Humanities award 1993), (with others) Shopping Time: A Re-photographic Survey of Lake Tahoe, 1992; contbr. articles to profl. jours. Rsch. grantee Nev. Humanities Com., 1993, Newberry Libr. Fellowship, 1993. Mem. Am. Studies Assn., Orgn. of Am. Historians, Western History Assn.

RAYMOND, EUGENE THOMAS, technical writer, consultant, retired aircraft engineer; b. Seattle, Apr. 17, 1923; s. Evan James and Katheryn Dorothy (Kranick) R.; m. Bette Mae Bergeson, Mar. 1, 1948; children: Joan Kay Hibbs, Patricia Lynn Adams, Robin Louise Flashman. BSME, U. Wash., 1944; postgrad., 1953-55; registered profl. engr., Tex. Rsch. engr. The Boeing Co., Seattle, 1946-59, sr. group engr., 1959-63, 66-71, sr. specialist engr., 1971-81, prin. engr. flight control tech., 1982-88; project design engr. Gen. Dynamics, Ft. Worth, 1963-66. Lt., USNR, 1943-46, 49-52; PTO. Author (book) Aircraft Flight Control Actuation System Design, 1993. Recipient prize Hydraulics and Pneumatics mag., 1958. Mem. Soc. Automotive Engrs. (cert. of appreciation, chmn. adv. bd. com. A-6 nat. com. for aerospace fluid power and control tech. 1983-88, vice-chmn. com. 1986-88, cons.), Fluid Power Soc. (dir. northwest region 1973-74), Puget Sound Fluid Power Assn., AIAA, Beta Theta Pi, Meridian Valley Country Club, Masons, Shriners. Lutheran. Aircraft editorial adv. bd. Hydraulics and Pneumatics mag., 1960-70; achievements include 5 patents in Fluid Sealing Arrangements, Quasi-Open-Loop Hydraulic Ram Incremental Actuator with Power Conserving Properties, Rotary Digital Electrohydraulic Actuator, Two-Fluid Nonflammable Hydraulic System and Load-Adaptive Hydraulic Actuator System and Method for Actuating Control Surfaces; designed and developed mechanical systems for the XB-47 and B-52 jet bombers, 707 airliner and many other aircraft, including the X-20 Dyna-Soar hypersonic space plane, the American SST, the rewinged Navy A-6 attack plane the B-2 Stealth Bomber and the Chinese XAC Y-7 commuter; contbr. over 20 technical papers and articles to profl. jours. Home and Office: 25301 144th Ave SE Kent WA 98042-3401 *Personal philosophy: I have always tried to act correctly, fairly, and truthfully and to set a good example for my children and my peers.*

RAYMOND, GREGORY ALAN, political science educator; b. Irvington, N.J., Jan. 5, 1947; s. Andrew and Irene (Skalicky) R.; m. Christine Lawton, June 12, 1971. BA, Park Coll., 1968; MA, U. S.C., 1973, PhD, 1975. Asst. prof. Boise (Idaho) State U., 1975-79, assoc. prof., 1979-83, prof. polit. sci., 1983—; cons. State Exec. Inst., Idaho, 1985, Human Rights Commn., Idaho, 1988, Office of the Gov., Idaho, 1988; bd. dirs. Univ. Survey Rsch. Ctr., Boise, 1986-89, chair dept. polit. sci., 1990—. Author: Conflict Resolution and the Structures of the State System, 1980, The Other Western Europe, 1983, When Trust Breaks Down, 1990, A Multipolar Peace?, 1994. Mem. State Higher Edn. Resource Coun., Idaho, 1988—. With U.S. Army, 1969-71. Recipient Outstanding Tchg. award Boise State U. Alumni Assn., 1985, Outstanding Rsch. award Boise State U Found., 1994; named Idaho Prof. of Yr., Carnegie Found. for Advancement of Tchg., 1994. Mem. Internat.

Studies Assn., Internat. Polit. Sci. Assn. Office: Boise State U 1910 University Dr Boise ID 83725-0001

RAYMOND, LLOYD WILSON, machinery company executive; b. Middleboro, Mass., Jan. 4, 1922; s. Millard Edgar and Ethel (Morrison) R.; m. Joyce Elaine Cox, Nov. 10, 1972. ThB, Christian Bible Coll., Rocky Mount, N.C., 1995, ThM, 1996, PhD in Religion, 1996, DD (hon.), 1995; postgrad., S.W. Bible Coll. & Sem., Sulphur, La., 1996—. Clk. Pub. Housing Adminstrn., Washington, 1941-42; adminstrv. asst. devel. dept. Pub. Housing Adminstrn., N.Y.C., 1946-55; machinery data mgr. Nat. Machinery Exch., Inc., Newark, 1955-76, Pico Rivera, Calif., 1976—. Designer computerized info. mgmt. and quote generating sys., 1991. Founder Living Pictures Programs, 1965, Living Word Ministries/Heal Our Nation Crusade, 1995. Mem. Soc. Profl. Journalists, Christian Writers Guild, Am. Christian Writers, Am. Legion, Nat. Assn. Evangelicals, Profl. Photographers Calif. Office: Heal our Nation Crusade PO Box 188 Upland CA 91785

RAYNER, STEVEN ROBERT, management consultant; b. Portland, Dec. 8, 1959. Student, U. Birmingham, Eng., 1980; BA with distinction of honors, Lewis and Clark Coll., 1982; MS in Orgn. Devel. with honors, Pepperdine U., 1986. Historian Tektronix Corp., Forest Grove, Oreg., 1982-83; orgn. devel. specialist Tektronix Corp., Vancouver, Wash., 1983-85, sr. orgn. devel. cons., 1985-89; mgr. thin film fabrication Tektronix Corp., Beaverton, Oreg., 1988; co-founder, co-chmn. Belgard Fisher Rayner, Inc., Beaverton and Freeland, Wash., 1989—; founder Rayner & Assocs., Inc., Freeland, 1994—; presenter in field. Author: New Excellence: The Forest Grove Project, 1984, Re-Creating the Workplace: The Pathway to High Performance Work Systems, 1993, Team Traps: Survival Stories and Lessons from Team Disasters, Near-Misses, Mishaps and Other Near-Death Experiences, 1996; co-author: (with K. Kimball Fisher and William Belgard) Tips for Teams: A Ready Reference for Solving Common Team Problems Packed with 100s of Solutions, 1994; (with P. Murray, J. Manuel and J. Whittinghill) Team Innovations: Best Practice Tools and Resources for Team-Based Management, 1996; author essays and guides in field.

RAYNOLDS, DAVID ROBERT, buffalo breeder, author; b. N.Y., Feb. 15, 1928; s. Robert Frederick and Marguerite Evelyn (Gerdau) R.; m. May (Kean) Raynolds, May 12, 1951; children: Robert, Linda, Martha, Laura, David A.F. AB, Dartmouth Coll., 1949; MA, Wesleyan U., Middletown, Conn., 1955; predoctoral, Johns Hopkins Sch. Advanced Internat. Studies, Washington, 1956; grad., Nat. War Coll., Washington, 1973. Account exec. R.H. Morris Assoc., Newtown, Conn., 1949-50; fgn. svc. officer Dept. of State, Washington, 1956-76; pres. Ranch Rangers, Inc., Lander, Wyo., 1976—; pres. Nat. Buffalo Assn., Ft. Pierre, S.D., 1987-88. Author: Rapid Development in Small Economies (Praeger); contbr. articles to profl. jours. Mem. mgmt. com. Wyo. Heritage Soc.; bd. dirs. Liberty Hall Found., Wyo. Community Found. With U.S. Army, 1950-53. Recipient Meritorious Svc. Award, Dept. of State, Washington, 1966. Mem. The Explorers Club, Fremont County Farm Bur., Fgn. Svc. Assn., Am. Legion, Rotary, Elks. Republican. Episcopalian. Office: Table Mountain Group PO Box 1310 Lander WY 82520-1310

RAY-SIMS, DEBORAH, marketing analyst; b. Detroit, May 5, 1953; d. June Louis and Irma Waldine (Prentice) Ray; 1 child, Aishah Nicole. BA in TV, Radio and Film, Mich. State U., 1975; postgrad. in telecom. mgmt., NYU, 1984-85; MA in Telecomm., Golden Gate U., 1996. TV producer WTVS, Detroit, 1978-83; tng. instr. Jacaranda Internat., Lagos, Nigeria, 1983-84; account exec. US Sprint Comm., Sacto., 1986-88; mktg. rep. Employment Devel. Dept. State of Calif., Sacto., 1989-93; mktg. programs analyst Dept. Gen. Svcs. State of Calif., Sacramento, 1993—; mem. adv. bd. Sacramento Valley Black United Fund; pres. Diasporic Comms., Sacramento, 1989—. Summit scholar, Golden Gate U., 1993, Minority Bus. scholar, 1993; recipient Mayor's award of merit, City of Detroit, 1983. Mem. Internat. TV Assn., Internat. Teleconferencing Assn. (Merit award 1994), Sacramento Black Journalists Assn., NAFE, Assn. Black Women Entrepreneurs. Home: 8551 Summit Brook Ct Elk Grove CA 95624

RAYSON, GARY DONN, chemistry educator; b. Oklahoma City, Okla., Apr. 27, 1957; s. Ralph LeRoy and Muriel Rayson; m. Jenny Ruth Moorer, June 18, 1988. BS, Baker U., 1979; PhD, U. Tex., Austin, 1983. Teaching asst. U. Tex., Austin, 1979-80, rsch. asst., 1980-83; rsch. assoc. Ind. U., Bloomington, 1983-86; asst. prof. N.Mex. State U., Las Cruces, 1986-93, assoc. prof., 1993—. Inventor in field. Mem. Am. Chem. Soc., Soc. Applied Spectroscopy, Optical Soc. Am. Republican. Methodist. Office: NM State U PO Box 30001 # 3C Las Cruces NM 88003-8001

RAZOR, BEATRICE RAMIREZ (BETTY RAZOR), enterostomal therapy nurse, educator, consultant; b. Miami, Ariz., Oct. 18, 1931; d. Jorge William and Eleanor (Reyes) Ramirez; m. James Howard Razor, Sept. 5, 1953; children: James Steven, Susan Marie, Jorge William, Edward Thomas. AA, East L.A. City Coll., 1953; RN, L.A. County Sch. Nursing, 1953; cert. enterstomal therapy, U. So. Calif., 1979, 95; BS in Health Scis., Chapman U., 1979. RN, Calif., Alaska. Staff nurse Providence Hosp., Anchorage, 1953-54; svc. coord. Native Svc. Hosp., Anchorage, 1954-56; staff nurse, head nurse to enterstomal therapy nurse coord. Meth. Hosp. of So. Calif., Arcadia, 1973-83; clin. instr. Pasadena (Calif.) City Coll., 1983-93; enterstomal nursing instr. Azusa (Calif.) Pacific U., 1983-93; enterstomal nursing coord. City of Hope Nat. Med. Ctr., Duarte, Calif., 1983-93; enterstomal nursing instr. U. So. Calif., L.A., 1990—; enterstomal nursing cons. Arcadia, 1993—; cons. San Gabriel Valley Ostomy Ctr., Covina, Calif., 1982-94; lectr. Am. Cancer Assn., 1983—, San Gabriel Valley Ostomy Assn., 1979—, Citrus Coll. Sch. Nursing, 1982-85, Pasadena City Coll. Sch. Nursing, 1981-93, Pharmacy Tech. Assn. Conf., 1982-93, Arroyo H.S., 1980, 81, 83, 90, Congress for World Coun. Enterstomal Therapists, Perth, Australia, 1990, Lyon, France, 1992, Guttenberg, Sweden, 1994, Jerusalem, 1996, Symposium on Advanced Wound Care, 1989, 91, City of Hope Planned Giving Program, 1989-93, Oncology Nursing Soc., 1987, 89, also others. Author: Seminars in Oncology Nursing, 1993, other publs. Merit badge cons. San Gabriel Valley coun. Boy Scouts Am., 1965-94; chmn. Byron-Thompson Cmty. Svcs., El Monte, 1983—; mem., chmn. nursing edn. com. Am. Cancer Soc., Pasadena, 1980-90; mem. chronic disease prevention adv. com. State of Calif., Sacramento, 1982-90; sec. El Monte Rep. Women. Recipient Silver Beaver award Boy Scouts Am., 1978, cmty. svc. award City of El Monte, 1983, Svc. award Calif. PTA, Nurse of Yr. award City of Hope, 1992. Mem. Oncology Nursing Soc., World Coun. Enterstomal Therapy (editl. bd. 1990—), United Ostomy Assn. (med. advisor San Gabriel Valley chpt. 1980-95), Wound, Ostomy and Continence Nursing Soc. (pub. rels. coord. Pacific Coast region 1992—, bd. dirs. 1992—, pres. 1988-92), Sigma Theta Tau. Republican. Lutheran. Office: Enterstomal Nursing Cons Ste 404 701 S 1st Ave Arcadia CA 91732

REA, WILLIAM J., district judge; b. 1950; BA, Loyola U., 1942, LLB, U. Colo., 1949. With U.S. Census Bur., Denver, 1949-50; adjuster Farmers Ins. Group, L.A., 1950; pvt. practice law, L.A., 1950-64, Santa Ana, Calif., 1964-68; judge Superior Ct., L.A., 1968-84; judge U.S. Dist. Ct. (cen. dist.) Calif., L.A., 1984—. Past pres. L.A. chpt. Nat. Exec. Com.; chmn. Constn. and By-Laws Com. With USN, WWII. Mem. L.A. County Bar Assn. (Outstanding Jurist award 1985), So. Calif. Def. Counsel Assn. Disting. Svc. award 1982), Internat. Acad. Trial Lawyers (Trial Judge of Yr. 1982), L.A. Trial Lawyers Assn., Am. Bd. Trial Advs. (nat. pres.). Office: US Dist Ct 312 N Spring St Rm 128 Los Angeles CA 90012-4701*

READ, CHARLES RAYMOND, SR., business executive; b. Clovis, N.Mex., Apr. 21, 1915; s. Charles Edward and Mary Ellen (Elder) R.; m. Elenore Littlefield, Oct. 10, 1936 (dec. July 1985); children: Charles Raymond Jr., Nancy Ann Walsh; m. Debra Rae Stutzman, Mar. 30, 1989. Baker, candymaker Peter-Paul's Candy, Clovis, 1932-34; baker Holsum Bakery, Boise, Idaho, 1934-35, Elsner's Bakery, Everett, Wash., 1935-37; head baker United Bakery, Ellensburg, Wash., 1937-40; owner, baker Read's Royal Bakery, Ellensburg, 1940-42; mgr., baker Clark's Bakery, Seattle, 1945-57; owner, baker Read's Bakery, Seattle, 1957-62; pres. Read Products, Inc., Seattle, 1962—; ptnr. Peasley-Read, Seattle, 1968—; guest TV programs KING-5, Seattle, 1950-62; distbr. Richlite, 1962—. With USN, 1942-45. Seattle Pacific U. fellow; recipient trophies, plaques for cake decorating Pacific N.W. Clinary Arts Exhibit, 1950-62. Mem. United Comml. Travelers, Smithsonian Inst., Masons (3d degree). Office: Read Products Inc 3615 15th Ave W Seattle WA 98119-1303

READ, STEPHEN L., physician, psychiatrist; b. Denver, Jan. 10, 1948; s. Warren Arthur and Elizabeth Ann (Gutel) R.; m. Diana Kos, Sept. 14, 1979; children: Jonathan Kos-Read, Isaac Kos-Read. BS, U. Calif., 1971; MD, U. B.C., 1978. Diplomate Am. Bd. Psychiatry and Neurology with added qualifications in geriatric psychiatry; cert. in geriatric psychiatry. Intern in internal medicine Presbyn. Med. Ctr., Denver, 1978-79; resident in psychiatry Harbor-UCLA Med. Ctr., Torrance, 1979-81, chief resident in psychiatry, 1981-82; fellow in geriatric psychiatry, neurobehavior UCLA, L.A., 1982-84; assoc. clin. prof., 1994—; asst. prof. UCLA/VAMC W. L.A., 1984-87; med. dir. John Douglas French Ctr., Los Alamitos, Calif., 1987-94; pvt. practice L.A., 1987—; asst. clin. prof. UCLA/VAMC, W. L.A., 1987-94. Mem. scientific adv. bd. John Douglas French Alzheimer's Found., L.A., 1987—. Mem. AMA, Am. Psychiat. Assn., Am. Assn. Geriatric Psychiatry, Am. Med. Dir.'s Assn. Office: 760 Westwood Plz Rm 37-425 Los Angeles CA 90024

READ, THOMAS A., editor, retired. Assoc. editor Seattle Post-Intelligence; ret., 1995. Home: 101 Elliot Ave W Seattle WA 98111

REAGAN, GARY DON, state legislator, lawyer; b. Amarillo, Tex., Aug. 23, 1941; s. Hester and Lois Irene (Marcum) R.; m. Nedra Ann Nash, Sept. 12, 1964; children: Marc, Kristi, Kari, Brent. AB, Stanford U., 1963, JD, 1965. Bar: N.Mex. 1965, U.S. Dist. Ct. N.Mex., 1965, U.S. Supreme Ct. 1986. Assoc. Smith & Ransom, Albuquerque, 1965-67; ptnr. Smith, Ransom, Deaton & Reagan, Albuquerque, 1967-68, Williams, Johnson, Houston, Reagan & Porter, Hobbs, N.Mex., 1968-77, Williams, Johnson, Reagan, Porter & Love, Hobbs, 1977-82; sole practice, Hobbs, 1982—; city atty. City of Hobbs, 1978-80, City of Eunice, N.M., 1980—; mem. N.Mex. State Senate, 1993-96; instr. N.Mex. Jr. Coll. and Coll. of S.W., Hobbs, 1978-84; N.Mex. commr. Nat. Conf. Commrs. Uniform State Laws, 1993-96; mem. adv. mem. N.Mex. Constl. Revision Commn., 1993-95. Mayor, City of Hobbs, 1972-73, 76-77, city commr., 1970-78; pres., dir. Jr. Achievement of Hobbs, 1974-85; pres., trustee Landsun Homes, Inc., Carlsbad, N.Mex., 1972-84; trustee Lydia Patterson Inst., El Paso, Tex., 1972-84, N.Mex. Conf. United Meth. Ch., 1988—, Coll. of S.W., Hobbs, 1989—; chmn. County Democratic Com., 1983-85. Mem. ABA, State Bar N.Mex. (coms. 1989-96, v.p. 1992-93, pres. 1994-95), Lea County Bar Assn. (pres. 1976-77), Hobbs C. of C. (pres. 1989-90), Rotary (pres. Hobbs 1985-86), Hobbs Tennis (pres. 1974-75). Home: 200 E Eagle Dr Hobbs NM 88240-5323 Office: 501 N Linam St Hobbs NM 88240-5715

REAGAN, JANET THOMPSON, psychologist, educator; b. Monticello, Ken., Sept. 15, 1945; d. Virgil Joe and Carrie Mae (Alexander) Thompson; m. Robert Barry Reagan, Jr., Aug. 7, 1977; children: Natalia Alexandria, Robert Barry. B.A. in Psychology, Berea Coll., 1967; Ph.D. in Psychology, Vanderbilt U., 1972. Mgr. research and eval. Nashville Mental Health Center, 1971-72; mgr. eval. Family Health Found., New Orleans, 1973-74; asst. prof. dept. health systems mgmt. Tulane U., New Orleans, 1974-77; dir. eval. Project Heavy West, Los Angeles, 1977-78; asst. prof. health adminstrn. Calif. State U.-Northridge, 1978-83, assoc. prof., director health adminstrn., 1983-87, prof., dir. health adminstrn., 1987—; cons. in field. Mem. Am. Pub. Health Assn., Am. Coll. Health Care Adminstrn., Assn. Health Svcs. Rsch., Am. Coll. Health Care Execs. (com. on higher edn. 1987, chmn. 1991), Assn. Univ. Programs in Health Adminstrn. (task force on undergrad. edn. 1985-90, chmn. 1988-90, mem. bd. dirs. 1995), Psi Chi, Phi Kappa Phi. Mem. editorial adv. bd. Jour. of Long Term Care Administrn.; contbr. to books, articles to profl. jours., papers to profl. assns. Home: 9354 Encino Ave Northridge CA 91325-2414 Office: Calif State U Dept Health Sci Northridge CA 91330

REAGAN, NANCY DAVIS (ANNE FRANCIS ROBBINS), volunteer, wife of former President of United States; b. N.Y.C., July 6, 1923; d. Kenneth and Edith (Luckett) Robbins; step dau. Loyal Davis; m. Ronald Reagan, Mar. 4, 1952; children: Patricia Ann, Ronald Prescott; stepchildren: Maureen, Michael. BA, Smith Coll.; LLD (hon.), Pepperdine U., 1983; LHD (hon.), Georgetown U., 1987. Contract actress, MGM, 1949-56; films include The Next Voice You Hear, 1950, Donovan's Brain, 1953, Hellcats of the Navy, 1957; Author: Nancy, 1980; formerly author syndicated column on prisoner-of-war and missing-in-action soldiers and their families; author: (with Jane Wilkie) To Love a Child, (with William Novak) My Turn: The Memoirs of Nancy Reagan, 1989. Civic worker, visited wounded Viet Nam vets., sr. citizens, hosps. and schs. for physically and emotionally handicapped children, active in furthering foster grandparents for handicapped children program; hon. nat. chmn. Aid to Adoption of Spl. Kids, 1977; spl. interest in fighting alcohol and drug abuse among youth: hosted first ladies from around the world for 2d Internat. Drug Conf., 1985; hon. chmn. Just Say No Found., Nat. Fedn. of Parents for Drug-Free Youth, Nat. Child Watch Campaign, President's Com. on the Arts and Humanities, Wolf Trap Found. bd. of trustees, Nat. Trust for Historic Preservation, Cystic Fibrosis Found., Nat. Republican Women's Club; hon. pres. Girl Scouts of Am. Named one of Ten Most Admired Am. Women, Good Housekeeping mag., ranking #1 in poll, 1984, 85, 86; Woman of Yr. Los Angeles Times, 1977; permanent mem. Hall of Fame of Ten Best Dressed Women in U.S.; recipient humanitarian awards from Am. Camping Assn., Nat. Council on Alcoholism, United Cerebral Palsy Assn., Internat. Ctr. for Disabled; Boys Town Father Flanagan award; 1986 Kiwanis World Service medal; Variety Clubs Internat. Lifeline award; numerous awards for her role in fight against drug abuse. Address: Century City Fox Plaza 2121 Ave Of Stars Fl 34 Los Angeles CA 90067-5010*

REAGAN, RONALD WILSON, former President of United States; b. Tampico, Ill., Feb. 6, 1911; s. John Edward and Nelle (Wilson) R.; m. Jane Wyman, Jan. 25, 1940 (div. 1948); children: Maureen E., Michael E.; m. Nancy Davis, Mar. 4, 1952; children: Patricia, Ronald. AB, Eureka Coll., 1932, MA (hon.), 1957. Actor GE Theatre, 1954-62; host TV series Death Valley Days, 1962-66; gov. State of Calif., 1967-74; businessman, rancher, commentator on public policy, 1975-80, Pres. of U.S., 1981-89. Sports announcer, motion picture and TV actor, 1932-66. Author: Where's The Rest of Me?, Speaking My Mind: Selected Speeches, 1989, An American Life: The Autobiography, 1990. Mem. Calif. State Rep. Ctrl. Com., 1964-66; del. Rep. Nat. Conv., 1968, 72; chmn. Rep. Gov. Assn., 1968-73; mem. presdl. Commn. CIA Activities Within U.S., 1975; bd. dirs. Com. Present Danger, Washington, 1977—; cand. for Rep. nomination for Pres., 1976. Served as capt. USAAF, 1942-45. Recipient Great Am. of Decade award, Va. Young Am. for Freedom, Man of Yr. Free Enterprise award, San Fernando Valley Bus. & Profl. award, 1964, Am. Legion award, 1965, Horation Alger award, 1969, George Washington Honor medal, Freedoms Found. Valley Forge award, 1971, Disting. Am. award; inducted into Nat. Football Found. Hall of Fame, Am. Patriots Hall of Fame. Mem. SAG (pres. 1947-52, 59), Am. Fedn. Radio & TV Artists, Lions, Friars, Tau Kappa Epsilon. Republican. Address: Century City Fox Plaza 2121 Avenue Of The Stars Fl 34 Los Angeles CA 90067-5010*

REAL, MANUEL LAWRENCE, federal judge; b. San Pedro, Calif., Jan. 27, 1924; s. Francisco Jose and Maria (Mansano) R.; m. Stella Emilia Michalik, Oct. 15, 1955; children: Michael, Melanie Marie, Timothy, John Robert. B.S., U. So. Calif., 1944, student fgn. trade, 1946-48; LL.B., Loyola Sch. Law, Los Angeles, 1951. Bar: Calif. 1952. Asst. U.S. Atty.'s Office, Los Angeles, 1952-55; pvt. practice law San Pedro, Calif., 1955-64; U.S. atty. So. Dist. Calif., 1964-66; judge U.S. Dist. Ct. (cen. dist.) Calif., L.A., 1966—. Served to ensign USNR, 1943-46. Mem. Am., Fed., Los Angeles County bar assns., State Bar Calif., Am. Judicature Soc., Chief Spl. Agts. Assn., Phi Delta Phi, Sigma Chi. Roman Catholic. Club: Anchor (Los Angeles). Office: US Dist Ct 312 N Spring St Rm 217P Los Angeles CA 90012-4701*

REALE, PAUL VINCENT, composer, music educator; b. New Brunswick, N.J., Mar. 2, 1943; s. Frank Paul and Lena Adele (Kowalski) R. BA, Columbia Coll., 1963; MA, Columbia U., 1967; PhD, U. Pa., 1970. Prof. UCLA, 1969—. Created ednl. website as project in interacting learning; Composer 7 piano sonatas, 9 concertos (NEA grantee 1976-91), 2 piano trios, others. Mem. NARAS (mem. exec. vote 1989—). Office: UCLA 405 Hilgard Los Angeles CA 90095

REAM, LLOYD WALTER, JR., molecular biology educator; b. Chester, Pa., Mar. 20, 1953; s. Lloyd Walter Sr. and Mary Elizabeth (Alexander) R.; m. Nancy Jane Smith, May 17, 1975. BA in Molecular Biology cum laude, Vanderbilt U., 1975; PhD in Molecular Biology, U. Calif., Berkeley, 1980. Am. Cancer Soc. sr. rsch. fellow dept. microbiology U. Wash., Seattle, 1980-83; asst. prof. biology Ind. U., Bloomington, 1983-88; assoc. prof. dept. agrl. chemistry Oreg. State U., Corvallis, 1988-97, assoc. prof. dept. microbiology, 1997—, co-dir. genetics program, 1994—; sci. advisor Midwest Plant Biotechnology Consortium, West Lafayette, Ind., 1989—; sci. adv. panel mem. Am. Cancer Soc., Atlanta, 1989-96. Editor Plant Molecular Biology/ Kluwer, Dordrecht, Netherlands, 1984-94, Molecular Plant Microbe Interactions, 1996—; contbr. chpt. to book and articles to profl. jours. Active Calvin Presbyn. Ch.; classroom instr. curriculum devel. Scientist/Educator Partnerships, Corvallis, 1993—. Recipient Jr. Faculty Rsch. award Am. Cancer Soc., 1987, Rsch. Career Devel. award NIH, 1987-92; Regents fellow U. Calif., Berkeley, 1977-78; rsch. grantee USDA, 1993—. Mem. AAAS, Am. Soc. for Microbiology, Genetics Soc. Am., NRA, Albany Rifle and Pistol Club (small bore rifle team, marksman award 1994), Delta Kappa Epsilon. Republican. Home: 6005 NW Vineyard Dr Corvallis OR 97330-9737 Office: Oreg State Univ Dept Microbiology Corvallis OR 97331

REARDEN, CAROLE ANN, clinical pathologist, educator; b. Belleville, Ont., Can., June 11, 1946; d. Joseph Brady and Honora Patricia (O'Halloran) R. BSc, McGill U., 1969, MSc, MDCM, 1971. Diplomate Am. Bd. Pathology, Am. Bd. Immunohematology and Blood Banking, Am. Bd. HIstocompatibility and Immunogenetics. Resident and fellow Children's Meml. Hosp., Chgo., 1971-73; resident in pediatrics U. Calif., San Diego, 1974, resident then fellow, 1975-79, asst. prof. pathology, 1979-86, dir. histocompatability and immunogenetics lab., 1979-94, assoc. prof., 1986-92, prof., 1992—, head divsn. lab. medicine, 1989-94; dir. med. ctr. U. Calif. Thornton Hosp. Clin. Labs., San Diego, 1993—; prin. investigator devel. monoclonal antibodies to erythroid antigens, recombinant autoantigens; dir. lab. exam. com. Am. Bd. Histocompatibility and Immunogenetics. Contbr. articles to profl. jours.; patentee autoantigen pinch. Mem. Mayor's Task Force on AIDS, San Diego, 1983. Recipient Young Investigator Rsch. award NIH, 1979; grantee U. Calif. Cancer Rsch. Coordinating Com., 1982, NIH, 1983; scholar Nat. Blood Found. Mem. Am. Soc. Investigative Pathology, Am. Soc. Hematology, Am. Assn. Blood Banks (com. organ transplantation and tissue typing 1982-87, tech. com. 13 edit. tech. manual 1996—), Am. Soc. Histocompatibility and Immunogenetics. Office: U Calif San Diego Dept Pathology 0612 9500 Gilman Dr La Jolla CA 92093-5003

REARDON, JAMES LOUIS, education educator, consultant; b. Vinton, Iowa, June 29, 1943; s. James Harold and Hazel Alice (Pieper) R.; m. Antonia Anita Boni, July 3, 1971. BSBA, U. Iowa, 1966, MA in Edn., 1966; EdD, U. LaVerne, 1985. Cert. tchr., Calif. Supr. tchr. edn. U. Calif., Riverside, 1971—, coord. intern credential program, 1994; co-dir. Inland Area History-Social Sci. Project, Riverside, 1990-94; cons. We. Assn. Schs. and Colls., State Dept. Edn. Expanded Accreditation, Sacramento, 1990-92; reviewer Charles Merrill Pubs., Columbus, Ohio, 1988-91; convenor Tch. Edn. Program Area Com., Riverside, 1990; edn. specialist Nat. Assn. Trade and Tech. Schs., Washington, 1983—. Recipient People Who Make a Difference award, Riverside Press, 1989. Mem. Inland Empire Coun. for the Social Studies (treas. 1986—, Leadership in Social Studies Edn. award 1993), Calif. Coun. for the Social Studies (mem. editl. bd. 1985—), Nat. Coun. for the Social Studies, Network for Secondary Edn. Profs. (pres. 1985-86). Home: 1513 Lynne Ct Redlands CA 92373-7143 Office: U Calif 2105 Sproul Hall Riverside CA 92521

REBER, MICK, artist, educator; b. St. George, Utah, June 6, 1942; s. Ernest Glen and Elsie (Turner) R.; m. Melanie Conditt, Jan. 14, 1964; children: Sherise, Shahn, Rachele. AS, So. Utah U., 1964; BFAs, Brigham Young U., 1966, MFA, 1968. Dir. gallery ops. Ft. Lewis Coll., Durango, Colo., 1968-76; owner Reber Advt., Durango, Colo., 1969-74; illustrator Las Vegan Mag., Las Vegas, Nev., 1978-80; artist Donrey Advt., Las Vegas, Nev., 1980-81; owner Reber Studio-Gallery, Durango, 1981-96; From instr. to full prof. Ft. Lewis Coll., Durango, 1969—; judge All Utah Jam Show, Salt Lake City, 1991, Nat. Small Painting Exhbn., 1972. One-man shows include Elaine Sternberg Gallery, Chgo., 1991, Byne-Getz Gallery, Aspen, Colo., 1991, Presden Gallery, Santa Fe, 1991, Gomes Gallery, St. Louis, 1992; executed mural Hilton Hotel Corp. 1988; appeared in PBS documentary Mick Reber, Wild Bill, 1983; exhibited sculpture Nat. Sculpture Traveling Exhbn., Colo. Biennial Exhibition; contbr. articles to mags. Recipient Painting award Springfield Mus., 1968, Sculpture award H. Lester Cooke, 1976, award Academia Italia Delle Arti E Del Lavord, 1980; subject in numerous mags. Home and Studio: 846 CR 207 Durango CO 81301

REBER, WILLIAM FRANCIS, music educator, conductor; b. Oakland, Calif., Dec. 3, 1940; s. Otto Francis and Garna (Wiman) R.; m. Donna Lee Knight, Oct. 18, 1965 (div.); children: Arianna Lynnette, William Daniel; m. Margaret Susan Moffatt, June 24, 1986. MusB magna cum laude, U. Utah, 1964, MusM, 1966; D of Mus. Arts, U. Tex., 1977; student, Wesley Balk Opera/Mus. Theatre Inst., 1976. Condr., vocal coach Minn. Opera Co., St. Paul, 1976-77; asst. prof., lectr. music U. Tex., Austin, 1978-90; condr. Corpus Christi (Tex.) Ballet, 1986—; assoc. prof. Calif. State U., Fullerton, 1990-91; assoc. prof. Ariz. State U., Tempe, 1991-96, prof., 1996—; mem. music staff Minn. Dance Theatre; condr. U. Tex., 1978-90, founder, mus. dir. chamber orch., condr. opera theatre, assoc. condr. symphony, music dir. mus. theatre; coach, condr. Am. Inst. Mus. Studies, Graz, Austria, 1985, 86, 93—; guest condr. Corpus Christi Symphony, 1986-91; music dir. symphony, condr. opera theatre Calif. State U., 1990-91; dir., prin. condr. lyric opera theatre, Ariz. State U., Tempe, 1991—; music advisor Staatsoperette Dresden, Germany, 1993; condr., vocal coach Altenburger Musiktheater Akademie, Altenburg, Germany; jury chair Corpus Christi Young Artists' Competition, Kingsville Internat. Young Performers' Competition, flute/ piano recital Ohrid Internat. Festival, Skopje Summer Festival, 1994, Macedonian Am. Music Festival, 1995; accompanist various instrumental and vocal recitals. Author: Operas of Ralph Vaughan Williams, 1977; translator: Das Christelflein, 1977. Selection panelist Ariz. Commn. Arts, Phoenix, 1993. Capt. USAF, 1966-72. Recipient B. Iden Payne award Austin Circle Theatres, 1990, Arizoni award Ariz. Prodn. Assn., 1995, 96; Cultural travel grantee U.S. Info. Svc., 1992, 95. Mem. Opera Am., Nat. Opera Assn., Am. Symphony Orch. League, Condrs.' Guild, Coll. Music Soc. Office: Ariz State U Lyric Opera Theatre Box 870405 Tempe AZ 85287-0405

REBERT, CHARLES SIDNEY, research neuroscientist, educator; b. Detroit, Feb. 8, 1938; s. Ivan R. and Gertrude C. (Murdoch) R.; m. Lana L. Jolley, Jan. 6, 1962 (div. Aug. 1989); children: Alison L., Andrea L. BA, San Diego State Coll., 1962, MA, 1964; PhD, U. Iowa, 1968. Cert. jr. coll. tchr.; lic. psychologist, Calif. Assoc. dir. dept. neurosci. SRI Internat., Menlo Park, Calif., 1968-94; prof. Calif. Sch. Profl. Psychology, San Francisco, 1975-76, Coll. of San Mateo, 1996—; vis. scholar Hoover Inst., Stanford (Calif.) U., 1994; vis. prof. Inst. for Psychology, U. Vienna, Austria, 1990; mem. animal care ad hoc com. SRI Internat., 1992-94, mktg. com., 1994. Contbr. sci. articles to profl. jours.; mem. editl. bd. Internat. Jour. Psychophysiology, 1991-95. Rsch. grantee NIH, EPA, Nat. Bur. Standards, Jet Propulsion Lab., Nat. Inst. on Drug Abuse, Air Force Office of Sci. Rsch., Styrene Info. and Rsch. Ctr., Advanced Rsch. Projects Adminstrn., 1969-93. Mem. Internat. Orgn. Psychophysiology (bd. dirs. 1987—). Libertarian. Home: 3015 E Bayshore Rd Redwood City CA 94063-4136 Office: SRI Internat 333 Ravenswood Ave Menlo Park CA 94025-3453

REBHUN, JOSEPH, allergist, immunologist, medical educator; b. Przemysl, Poland, Oct. 7, 1921; came to U.S., 1950; s. Baruch and Serel R.; m. Maria Birkenhejm, Aug. 10, 1945; children: Lillian Friedland, Richard B.R., Donald. MD, U. Innsbruck, Austria, 1950; MS in Medicine, Northwestern U., 1954. Diplomate Am. Bd. Allergy and Immunology. Intern Barnert Meml. Hosp., Patterson, N.J.; resident in internal medicine Tompkins County Meml. Hosp. and Cornell U.; L.A., 1951-52; fellow in allergy Northwestern U. Med. Sch./Chidlren's Meml. Hosp., Chgo., 1952-54; fellow instr. Northwestern U. Med. Sch., 1954; asst. clin. prof. medicine Loma Linda U., 1957-93; clin. prof. medicine U. So. Calif., L.A., 1965-91; chief allergy Chgo. Eye, Ear, Nose and Throat Hosp., 1953-55; cons. Pacific State Hosp., Spadra Pomona Valley Cmty. Hosp., Pomona Casa Colina Hosp. Contbr. over 50 articles to med. jours.; author: SOS, 1946, The Cry of

Democracy for Help, God and Man in Two Worlds, 1985, The Embers of Michael, 1993. Pres. Am. Congress Jews from Poland, 1969-70. Capt., U.S. Mil., San Francisco. Recipient honors City and County of L.A., L.A. Office Dist. Atty., Senate of State of Calif., all 1985. Fellow Am. Acad. Allergy (rsch. coun. 1960-65), Am. Coll. Allergy, Assn. Clin. Allergy and Immunology; mem. West Coast Allergy Soc., Calif. Allergy Assn., L.A. Soc. Allergy, L.A. Med. Assn., Calif. Med. Assn. Office: 1850 N Garey Ave Pomona CA 91767

RECORDS, RAYMOND EDWIN, ophthalmologist, medical educator; b. Ft. Morgan, Colo., May 30, 1930; s. George Harvey and Sara Barbara (Louden) R.; 1 child, Lisa Rae. BS in Chemistry, U. Denver, 1956; MD, St. Louis U., 1961. Diplomate Am. Bd. Ophthalmology. Intern St. Louis U. Hosp. Group, 1961-62; resident in ophthalmology U. Colo. Med. Ctr., Denver, 1962-65; instr. ophthalmology, 1965-67, asst. prof., 1967-70; prof. ophthalmology U. Nebr. Coll. Medicine, Omaha, 1970-93, prof. emeritus, 1993, dept. chmn., 1970-89. Author: Physiology of Human Eye (Med. Writers award 1980), 1979. Author, editor: Biomedical Foundations of Ophthalmology, 1982. Med. dir. Nebr. Lions Eye Bank, 1970-81. Fellow Am. Acad. of Ophthalmology (outstanding contbn. award 1978, lifelong edn. award 1995); mem. AMA, Nev. Med. Assn., Clark County Med. Soc., Omaha Ophthal. Soc. (pres. 1981-82), Assn. Rsch. in Vision and Ophthalmology. Home: 21919 Riverside Cir Elkhorn NE 68022-1708 Office: 1640 Alta Dr Ste 1 Las Vegas NV 89106-4165

REDDAN, JOHN GORDON, III, computer scientist; b. Joliet, Ill., July 9, 1955; s. John Gordon and Dorothy Ollana (Jordan) R.; m. Stacy Layne Wilson, June 12, 1976; children: Patricia Lynette, Jerel Evan. BS in Math., U. Redlands, 1976; MS in Computer Sci., West Coast U., 1981. Software analyst Cubic Corp., 1977-78, Johnson Controls, Inc., 1978-81, Bolt, Beranek, and Newman, 1981; software devel. mgr. SYSCON Corp., San Diego, 1981-84; program unit mgr. Logicon Syscon, San Diego, 1995—. Contbr. articles to profl. jours. Mem. IEEE, IEEE Computer Soc., Assn. for Computing Machinery. Home: 1885 Sefton Pl San Diego CA 92107-3646

REDDECLIFFE, KARIN LINNAE ELLIS, educator; b. Moscow, Idaho, Dec. 16, 1948; d. Everett Lincoln and Eva Lillian (Johnson) Ellis; m. Terance Frederick Diaper, Aug. 15, 1976 (div. 1980); m. Owen Andrew Reddecliffe, Aug. 8, 1981; children: Aaron Linnae, Irene Asha; stepchildren: Sean David, Andrew Mark, David John. BS, Oreg. State U., 1971; MSc, U. London, 1973; postgrad., U. Sydney, Australia, 1979-81, United Theol. Coll., Sydney, 1979-81, 86. Programmer Oreg. State U., Corvallis, 1970-72; systems analyst Burroughs Ltd., London, 1973-74, Wellington, New Zealand, 1974-76; systems rep. Burroughs Ltd., Canberra, Australia, 1976-77; sr. systems rep. Burroughs Ltd., Canberra, Sydney, 1977-78; project mgr. Burroughs Ltd., Sydney, 1978-79, customer and support tng. mgr., 1979-81; cons., dir. Reddecliffe and Assocs., Sydney, 1981-87; water safety instr., lifeguard City of Montlake Ter., Wash., 1989-92, 96; instr. info. sci. Edmonds C.C., 1991-92; instr. North Seattle C.C., 1991-94, 97—; dir. Granny's Sch. Needles, 1996—; instr. Friday Forum, Kellog Mid. Sch., Seattle; dir. KO Devel., Seattle. Author: Training Patrol Leaders, 1989, (manual) Data Association Compiler, 1977, DMSII Description Table, 1977; contbr. articles to profl. jours. Leader Girl Guide Assn., New Zealand, Wellington, 1974-75, Boy Scout Assn., Australia, Canberra, Sydney, 1976-83; leader, cert. trainer Girl Guide Assn., of NSW, Sydney, 1976-87; master trainer, program dir., Daisy cons., del., leader Totem coun. Girl Scouts U.S.A., Seattle, 1987—; trainer ARC, Everett, Seattle, 1987—; team leader ACT Emergency Svcs., Canberra, 1974-75; leader Boy Scouts Am., Seattle, 1990—; founder Shoreline ADD/ADHD Parent Support Group, Seattle; active PTA Wash. Mem. NAFE, AAUW, Woodland Park Zoo Soc., Nature Conservancy, Peace Action of Washington, World Wildlife Fund, Wilderness Soc., U. Wash. Faculty Aux., Alpha Delta Phi (alumni chpt.). Mem. United Ch. Christ. Home and Office: 129 NW 182nd St Shoreline WA 98177-3437

REDDEN, JAMES ANTHONY, federal judge; b. Springfield, Mass., Mar. 13, 1929; s. James A. and Alma (Cheek) R.; m. Joan Ida Johnson, July 13, 1950; children: James A., William F. Student, Boston U., 1951; LL.B., Boston Coll., 1954. Bar: Mass., 1954, Oreg., 1955. Pvt. practice Mass., 1954-55; title examiner Title & Trust Ins. Co., Oreg., 1955; claims adjuster Allstate Ins. Co., 1956; mem. firm Collins, Redden, Ferris & Velure, Medford, Oreg., 1957-73; treas. State of Oreg., 1973-77; atty. gen., 1977-80; U.S. dist. judge, now sr. judge U.S. Dist. Ct. Oreg., Portland, 1980—. Chmn. Oreg. Pub. Employee Relations Bd.; mem. Oreg. Ho. of Reps., 1963-69, minority leader, 1967-69. With AUS, 1946-48. Mem. ABA, Mass. Bar Assn., Oreg. State Bar. Office: US Dist Ct 612 US Courthouse 620 SW Main St Portland OR 97205-3037

REDDING-LOWDER, CHRISTINE ARNITA, elementary education educator; b. Terrell County, Ga., Mar. 14, 1938; d. Otis Sr. and Fannie Mae (Roseman) Redding; m. Billy Earl Lowder, Feb. 5, 1961; children: Charles DeWayne, Penelope Darcel, Trevor Demetrius. AA, West L.A. Jr. Coll., 1970; BA in Psychology, Calif. State U.-Dominguez Hill, Carson, 1972; MS in Edn., U. So. Calif., 1975. Cert. tchr. K-8, adult edn., Calif. Telephone operator L.A. County Probation Dept., 1964-66; clk. L.A. County Assessor Dept., 1966; clk.-typist Dept. Pub. Social Svcs., L.A., 1966-67; intern L.A. Unified Sch. Dist., 1972-73, tchr., 1973—. Contbr. articles to profl. jours. Pres. Nat. Coun. Negro Women, L.A., 1994—; chair polit. subcom. 110th Anniversary 2d Bapt. Ch., L.A., 1995, mem. recruiters league, rec. sec. 1992-96; treas., v.p. Marvin Ave. Sch. PTA, L.A., 1967-69. Recipient Negotiation award Pres. United Tchrs. of L.A., 1984, Dedication/Svc. plaque United Tchrs. L.A./Black Educators, 1988, WHO award United Tchrs. L.A./NEA, 1995. Mem. AAUW, NEA (del. rep. assembly 1977—, mem. Black Caucus), Calif. Tchrs. Assn. (del. state coun. 1977-89, 90—, vice chair credentials and profl. devel. com. 1983-85, Assn. Better Citizenship com. Dist. J, United Tchrs.- LA 1994—), Nat. Assn. Univ. Women (regional by-laws chair 1991), Delta Sigma Theta (journalist Century City Alumnae chpt.). Democrat. Office: Ralph Waldo Emerson Middle School 1650 Selby Ave Los Angeles CA 90024-5716

REDDING-STEWART, DEBORAH LYNN, psychologist; b. Miami, Fla., Feb. 16, 1953; d. Sidney Douglas and Lois May (Tily) R.; m. John Thomas Stewart, Aug. 19, 1978; children: Garrett Lorne, Tyler Douglas, Kelly Lynn. BA in Psychology, San Diego State U., 1975; MA in Psychology, U. Calif., Santa Barbara, 1980. Instr. Allan Hancock Coll., Lompoc, Calif., 1980-86; adminstr., dir. clin. svcs. Mary Lou Stewart Learning Ctr., Lompoc, Calif., 1982—; prin. Pacific Health and Fitness, Lompoc, 1994—; owner Pacific Health and Fitness. Author: The Soft Voice of the Rain, 1993. State Coun. Devel. Disabilities PDF grantee, 1990, Instructional Deve. grantee U. Calif., 1979. Home: 1019 Onstott Rd Lompoc CA 93436-2342

REDDY, A. S. N., plant molecular biology educator; b. India, July 8, 1956; came to U.S., 1985; s. Anireddy Kantha and Julakanti (Kanthamma) R.; m. Katt Padma Latha, May 29, 1987; children: A. Rashmi, A. Sudhira. MS in Botany, Kakatiya U., India, 1979; PhD in Plant Molecular Biology, Jawaharlal Nehru U., New Delhi, 1984. Rsch. assoc. molecular biology unit Jawaharlal Nehru U. Sch. Life Scis., 1980-84, postdoctoral rsch. assoc., 1984-85; postdoctoral rsch. assoc. Lab. Plant Molecular Biology Wash. State U., Pullman, 1985-89, staff scientist, 1989-92; asst. prof. dept. biology Colo. State U., Ft. Collins, 1992—; rsch. presenter profl. confs., lectr. in field; reviewer grant proposals U.S.-Israel Binat. Agrl. R & D Fund, Australian Rsch. Coun., USDA, NSF, NASA. Contbr. numerous articles and abstracts to profl. jours. Jr. rsch. fellow Coun. Sci. and Indsl. Rsch., 1980-82, sr. rsch. fellow, 1982-84; computer analysis tng. fellow Molecular Biology Computer Resource Ctr., Dana Farber Cancer Inst., Harvard Sch. Pub. Health, Harvard Med. Sch., 1990; scholar Cold Spring Harbor Lab., 1991; rsch. grantee Colo. State U., 1992-94, San Luis Valley Rsch. Ctr., 1993-95, Colo. RNA Ctr., 1993-94, USDA, 1994-96, NASA, 1995, NSF, 1996—. Mem. AAAS, Am. Soc. Plant Physiologists, Colo.-Wyo. Acad. Sci., Soc. Plant Biochemistry and Biotech. (life), Am. Soc. Cell Biology, Sigma Xi. Office: Colo State U Dept Biology Fort Collins CO 80523

REDFIELD, DAVID ALLEN, chemistry educator; b. Grand Junction, Colo., Aug. 26, 1948; s. Donald Lee and Wilda Mae (Bean) R.; m. Sandra Kay Trandem, Dec. 13, 1969; children: Daniel, John, Jessica. BA, Point Loma Nazarene Coll., 1970; PhD, U. Nevada, Reno, 1974. Postdoctoral fellow U. Ill., Urbana, 1974-75; sr. rsch. chemist Olin Corp., New Haven, 1975-80; prof. and chair dept. chemistry N.W. Nazarene Coll., Nampa, Idaho, 1980—; cons. Nyssa (Oreg.)-Nampa Sugar Beet Growers, 1982—. Participant Valli Vue Band Parents, Caldwell, Idaho, 1991—; participant Vallivue Sch. Mission Setting Team, Caldwell, 1994-95. Recipient tchr. recognition program Nampa C. of C., 1989. Mem. Am. Chem. Soc., Idaho Acad. Sci. (treas. and pres. 1980—). Nazarene. Office: N W Nazarene Coll 623 Holly St Nampa ID 83686

REDFIELD, JOHN DUNCAN, computer programmer, artist; b. Hackensack, N.J., Sept. 27, 1947; s. Daniel Smith and Shirley Carolyn (Gray) R. AA, San Bernardino Valley Jr. Coll., Colton, Calif., 1971, Westark C.C., Ft. Smith, Ark., 1984. Free-lance programmer Phoenix, 1975-78, San Bernardino, 1978-80, Ft. Smith, Ark., 1980-90, Las Vegas, Nev., 1990—. With USN, 1966-70, Vietnam. Mem. DAV (life), Mobile Riverine Forces Assn. Moravian/Presbyterian.

REDICK, KEVIN JAMES, cultural organization administrator; b. L.A., July 25, 1964; s. James Dallas and Mary Louise (Strong) R.; m. Megan Beryl Pritchard, May 29, 1993; 1 child, Emma Claire. BA, Westmont Coll., Santa Barbara, Calif., 1986. Profl. baseball player Giants, San Francisco, 1986-88; group counselor Kern County Probation Dept., Bakersfield, Calif., 1989-90; dir. Santa Barbara Boys and Girls Club, 1990—. Mem. adv. multicultural adv. com. Westmont Coll., Santa Barbara, 1994-96; mem. multicultural task force City of Santa Barbara, 1994-96; mem. bd. dirs. Kids Passport to Arts, Santa Barbara, 1994-95; mem. pro-youth coalition Fighting Back, Santa Barbara, 1994-96. Mem. Boys and Girls Club Profl. Orgn. Democrat. Office: Santa Barbara Boys and Girls Club PO Box 1485 Santa Barbara CA 93111

REDING, JOHN A., lawyer; b. Orange, Calif., May 26, 1944. AB, U. Calif., Berkeley, 1966, JD, 1969. Bar: Calif. 1970, U.S. Dist. Ct. (no., ctrl. ea. and so. dists.) Calif., U.S. Claims Ct., U.S. Supreme Ct. Formerly mem. Crosby, Heafey, Roach & May P.C., Oakland, Calif.; now ptnr. Paul, Hastings, Janofsky & Walter LLP, San Francisco. Mem. ABA (sects. on litigation, intellectual property, and natural resources, energy and eviron. law, coms. on bus. torts, internat. law, trial practice and torts and insurance), Am. Intellectual Property Law Assn., State Bar Calif. (sect. on litigation), Alameda County Bar Assn., Bar Assn. San Francisco, Assn. Bus. Trial Lawyers. Office: Paul Hastings et al 345 California St San Francisco CA 94104-2635

REDMON, BOB GLEN, insurance company executive; b. Snyder, Okla., July 30, 1931; s. Ed Ray and Gertrude (Lett) R.; m. Harriet Ann Nicholas, Mar. 12, 1953; children: Patricia, Pamela, Susanne. Student, Phoenix Coll., 1949-51. Ins. adjuster various ins. cos. L.A., 1952-62, Phoenix, 1952-62; branch claims mgr. Western Ins. Cos., Phoenix, 1962-71; pres. B.G. Redmon & Assocs., Inc., Phoenix, 1971—; risk mgmt. cons. Bashas' Markets, Chandler, Ariz., 1976—. Sgt. USAF, 1951-52. Recipient Robert Charles Meml. award Ariz. Pond Blue Goose Internat., 1972. Mem. Ariz. Ins. Claims Assn. (pres. 1961), Self-Insurers Inst. Am., Early V8 Ford Club Am. Home: 8655 N Farview Dr Scottsdale AZ 85258-2040 Office: B G Redmon & Assocs Inc SRT Corp 2255 N 44th St Ste 220 Phoenix AZ 85008-3278

REDO, DAVID LUCIEN, investment company executive; b. Lakewood, Ohio, Sept. 1, 1937; s. Joseph L. and Florence M. (Morse) R.; m. Judy L. Ijams, Aug. 4, 1962; children: Jenny, Mark. BSEE, U. Calif., Berkeley, 1961; MBA, U. Santa Clara, 1967. Registered investment advisor. Asst. engring. mgr. AT&T, N.Y.C., 1968-71; pension fund mgr. Pacific Telephone, San Francisco, 1971-77; mng. dir. The Fremont Group (formerly Bechtel Investments Inc.), San Francisco, 1977—; pres., CEO Fremont Investment Advisors, Inc., San Francisco, 1986—; chmn., CEO Fremont Mutual Funds, 1986—; bd. dirs. The Fremont Group (formerly Bechtel Investments, Inc.) San Francisco, Fremont Investors, Inc., J.P. Morgan Securities Asia, Singapore, Sequoia Ventures Inc., San Francisco, Fremont Investment Advisors, Sit/Kim Internat. Investments; chmn., CEO Fremont Mutual Funds. Bd. trustees U. Calif., Berkeley, 1988—; chmn. investment com. U. Calif. Found., 1988—. Mem. Sentinel Pension Inst. (bd. advisors), Treas. Club of San Francisco, Internat. Assn. of Fin. Planners. Office: Fremont Investment Advisors 333 Market St Ste 2600 San Francisco CA 94105

REECE, THOMAS HOWARD, physician; b. Takoma Park, Mo., July 25, 1955; s. Howard C. and Elaine Florence (Ross) R. BS in Chemistry, Tulane U., 1977; BS in Human Biology, Kans. Newman Coll., Wichita, 1980; D in Natoropathic, Nat. Coll. Natoropathic Med., Portland, Oreg., 1982; DO, Kirksville Coll. Osteo. Med., Mo., 1990. Intern Mesa (Ariz.) Gen. Hosp., 1990-91; resident Cmty. Hosp., Mesa, Ariz.; pvt. practice specializing in natoropathic medicine Phoenix, 1982-86, pvt. practice specializing in osteo. medicine, 1990—; clin. tchr. S.W. Coll. Natoropathic Medicine, 1995; med. dir. Southwest Naturopathic Med. Ctr. Mem. Am. Osteo. Med. Assn., Am. Coll. Osteo. Family Practitioners, Am. Osteo. Acad. Sports Medicine, Am. Assn. Naturopathic Physicians, Ariz. Osteo. Medicine Assn., Nat. Hon. Osteo. Fraternity. Home: 6818 E Fanfol Paradise Valley AZ 85253 Office: SW Natoropathic Med Ctr 8010 E Mcdowell Rd Scottsdale AZ 85257-3867

REED, ALAN BARRY, university executive, consultant, investor; b. Leavenworth, Kans., June 28, 1940; s. Warren Lillard and Violet Florence (Seichepine) R.; m. Shari Laine Waetzig, Oct. 5, 1962; 1 child, Selena Eden. PhD, U. Tex., 1971. Dir. U. N.Mex., Santa Fe, 1989—; sr. assoc. N.Mex. Engring. Rsch. Inst., Albuquerque, 1988-95; advisor Navajo Nation, Window Rock, Ariz., 1988—; dir. Western Infrastructure Leadership Inst., Albuquerque, 1993. Contbr. articles to profl. jours. Councilman City of Albuquerque, 1975-79; chmn. Vols. for the Outdoors, N.Mex., 1982-83. Grantee Kellogg Found., 1992, U.S. Dept. Energy, 1994. Office: U NMex Sch Pub Adminstrn Social Sci Bldg 3014 Albuquerque NM 87131

REED, CAROL LOUISE, designer; b. Pontiac, Ill., Apr. 16, 1938; d. Rollin Kenneth and Lucille Hortence (Myer) Snethen; m. Richard Willis Reed, Feb. 13, 1960; children: Rena Louise Davis, Ronda Lee Howle. BBA in Mktg. and Advt., Tex. Tech. U., 1959. Office mgr. Sappington Devel., Inc., Rociada, N.Mex., 1990-91; owner Designs by Carol, Rociada, 1988—. Elected state officer Tierra y Montes Soil and Water Conservation Dist., Las Vegas, 1990—; mem. Mora-San Miguel Water Planning Bd., 1991-94; treas. 1st Meth. Ch., Las Vegas, 1989-90; sec. Calvary Bapt. Ch., Las Vegas, 1991-92; treas. 1st Bapt. Ch., 1996. Recipient award of merit Goodyear Tire and Rubber Co., 1991; named Outstanding Supr. of Tierra y Montes Soil and Conservation Dist., 1992, 94, 95. Mem. N.Mex. Assn. Soil and Water Conservation Dists. (chair region IV 1994-96, nat. coun., 1995-96, 1st v.p. state 1996—), Phi Kappa Phi. Republican. Home and Office: PO Box 853 Rociada NM 87742-0853

REED, DAVID GEORGE, entrepreneur; b. Alameda, Calif., July 19, 1945; s. David Francis and Anna Amelia Vangeline (Paulson) R.; m. Marianne Louise Watson, Apr. 7, 1971 (div. June 1975); m. Michele Ann Hock, June 28, 1989; 1 child, Casey Christine Michele. AA in Bus. Adminstrn., Diablo Valley Coll., Pleasant Hill, Calif., 1965; BA in Design and Industry, San Francisco State U., 1967, MBA in Mktg., 1969; cert. res. police officer, Los Medanos Coll., Pittsburg, Calif., 1977. Owner Western Furs, Ltd., Walnut Creek, Calif., 1963-72; mgmt. cons. Controlled Interval Scheduling, Rolling Hills Estates, Calif., 1972-73; owner Dave Reed's Texaco, Concord, Calif., 1973-76; mgmt. cons. Mgmt. Scheduling Systems, Houston, 1974-76, Thomas-Ross Assocs., Mercer Island, Wash., 1972-82; plant mgr. Bonner Packing, Morgan Hill, Calif., 1981; mfg. engr. Systron Donner, Concord, 1982-84, Beckman Instruments, San Ramon, Calif., 1984-90; owner Dave Reed & Co. Water Ski Sch., White Water Rafting, Chiloquin, Oreg., 1987—, Dave Reed & Co., design, market, mfg. Contender boats, Chiloquin, Oreg., 1976—; lectr. wildlife mgmt. Dave Reed & Co., Chiloquin, 1965—, lectr. mgmt. seminars, 1982—; coach Japanese Water Ski Team, Bluff Water Ski Club, Tokyo, 1984; fin. mgr. Japanese investors Dave Reed & Co., Chiloquin, 1986—, design and supply solar electric power sys., 1994—. Res. dep. sheriff Contra Costa County Sheriff's Dept., Martinez, Calif., 1977-80. With U.S. Army, 1969-71, Vietnam. Recipient Gold medal internat. freestyle wrestling Sr. Olympics, Fullerton, Calif., 1983. Mem. Am. Water Ski Assn. (Calif. state water ski champion 1977, 86, western region water ski champion 1977, silver medal nat. water ski championships 1977), Bay Area Tournament Assn. (chmn. 1968—), Diablo Water Ski Club (bd. dirs. 1968—). Republican. Home: PO Box 336 Chiloquin OR 97624-0336

REED, EDWARD CORNELIUS, JR., federal judge; b. Mason, Nev., July 8, 1924; s. Edward Cornelius Sr. and Evelyn (Walker) R.; m. Sally Torrance, June 14, 1952; children: Edward T., William W., John A., Mary E. BA, U. Nev., 1949; JD, Harvard U., 1952. Bar: Nev. 1952, U.S. Dist Ct. Nev. 1957, U.S. Supreme Ct. 1974. Atty. Arthur Andersen & Co., 1952-53; spl. dep. atty. gen. State of Nev., 1967-79; judge U.S. Dist. Ct. Nev., Reno, 1979—, chief judge, now sr. judge. Former vol. atty. Girl Scouts Am., Sierra Nevada Council, U. Nev., Nev. Agrl. Found., Nev. State Sch. Adminstrs. Assn., Nev. Congress of Parents and Teachers; mem. Washoe County Sch. Bd., 1956-72, pres. 1959, 63, 69; chmn. Gov.'s Sch. Survey Com., 1958-61; mem. Washoe County Bd. Tax Equalization, 1957-58, Washoe County Annexation Commn., 1968-72, Washoe County Personnel Com., 1973-77, chmn. 1973; mem. citizens adv. com. Washoe County Sch. Bond Issue, 1977-78, Sun Valley, Nev., Swimming Pool Com., 1978, Washoe County Blue Ribbon Task Force Com. on Growth, Nev. PTA (life); chmn. profl. div. United Way, 1978; bd. dirs. Reno Siver Sox, 1962-65. Served as staff sgt. U.S. Army, 1943-46, ETO, PTO. Mem. ABA (jud. adminstrn. sect.), Nev. State Bar Assn. (adminstrv. com. dist. 5, 1967-79, lien law com. 1965-78, chmn. 1965-72, probate law com. 1963-66, tax law com. 1962-65), Am. Judicature Soc. Democrat. Baptist. Office: US Dist Ct 400 S Virginia St Ste 606 Reno NV 89501

REED, ENID, neuropsychologist; b. N.Y.C., June 10, 1939; d. Edward and Laura (Gale) Janssen; m. Benjamin Halper, 1956 (dec. Nov. 1962); m. Lewis Reed, Dec. 24, 1963 (dec. Feb. 1970). Grad., UCLA, 1960, PhD in Comm., 1973; PhD in Psychology, U.S. Internat. U., San Diego, 1976. Buyer Sears, Roebuck, L.A., 1958-62; psychologist L.A. City Schs., 1962-73; psychologist Psychologics, Inc., Beverly Hills, Calif., 1976—, neuropsychologist, 1978—. Fellow Am. Psychol. Soc.; mem. AAAS, APA, Nat. Acad. Neuropsychologists (diplomate Fellow). Home: PO Box 1060 Beverly Hills CA 90213-1060 Office: 337 S Beverly Dr Ste 107 Beverly Hills CA 90212-4307

REED, EVA SILVER STAR, chieftain; b. Vinita, Okla., Nov. 29, 1929; d. Robert Elbert Jones and Anna Mae (Campfield) Reed; m. Johnnie Silver Eagle Reed, June 10, 1946 (dec. Sept. 1982); children: Patty Deeanne, Lorrie Ann, Billy John. Sec. United Lumbee Nation of N.C. and Am., Fall River Mills, Calif., 1979-82; nat. head chieftain United Lumbee Nation of N.C. and Am., Fall River Mills, 1982—, also bd. dirs.; bd. dirs., sec. Chapel of Our Lord Jesus, Exeter, Calif., 1974—, Native Am. Wolf Clan, Calif., 1977—; tchr. Indian beading and crafts, Calif., 1977—. Author, compiler: Over the Cooking Fires, 1982, Lumbee Indian Ceremonies, 1982, United Lumbee Deer Clan Cook Book, 1988; editor: (newspaper) United Lumbee Nation Times, 1981—. Mem. parent com. Title IV & Johnson O'Malley Indian Edn. Program, Tulare/Kings County, 1976-80, Shasta County, Calif., 1982-84. Recipient United Lumbee Nation of N.C. and Am.'s Silver Eagle award, 1991, also various awards for beadwork Intermountain Fair, Shasta County, 1982-96. Office: United Lumbee Nation of NC & Am PO Box 512 Fall River Mills CA 96028

REED, FRANK FREMONT, II, retired lawyer; b. Chgo., June 15, 1928; s. Allen Martin and Frances (Faurot) R.; m. Jaquelin Silverthorne Cox, Apr. 27, 1963; children: Elizabeth Matthiessen Mason, Laurie Matthiessen Stern, Mark Matthiessen, Jeffrey, Nancy, Sarah. Student Chgo. Latin Sch.; grad. St. Paul's Sch., 1946; A.B., U. Mich., 1952, J.D., 1957. Bar: Ill., 1958. Assoc. Byron, Hume, Groen & Clement, 1958-61, Marks & Clerk, 1961-63; pvt. practice law, Chgo., 1963-78; dir. Western Acadia (Western Felt Works), 1960-75, chmn. exec. com., 1969-71. Rep. precinct capt. 1972-78; candidate for 43d ward alderman, 1975; bd. dirs., sec. Chgo. Found. Theater Arts, 1959-64; vestryman St. Chrysostom's Ch., 1975-79, mem. ushers guild, 1964-79, chmn., 1976-78; bd. dirs. North State, Astor, Lake Shore Dr. Assn., 1975-78, pres. 1977-78; bd. dirs. Community Arts Music Assn. of Santa Barbara, 1984-93, treas. 1988-93; bd. dirs. Santa Barbara Arts Coun., 1987-89. Cpl. AUS, 1952-54. Mem. ABA, Ill. Bar Assn., Phi Alpha Delta, Racquet Club, Wausaukee Club (sec., dir. 1968-71, 92-94) (Chgo.); Birnam Wood Golf Club (Santa Barbara, Calif.). Episcopalian. Author: History of the Silverthorn Family, 4 vols., 1982, Allen Family of Allen's Grove, 1983, Goddard and Ware Ancestors, 1987, Faurot Family, 1988. Contbr. articles to The Am. Genealogist, 1972-73, 76-77. Home: 1944 E Valley Rd Santa Barbara CA 93108-1428

REED, FRANK METCALF, bank executive; b. Seattle, Dec. 22, 1912; s. Frank Ivan and Pauline B. (Hovey) R.; student U. Alaska, 1931-32; BA, U. Wash., 1937; m. Maxine Vivian McGary, June 11, 1937; children: Pauline Reed Mackay, Frank Metcalf. V.p. Anchorage Light & Power Co., 1937-42; pres. Alaska Electric & Equipment Co., Anchorage, 1946-50; sec., mgr. Turnagain, Inc., Anchorage, 1950-56; mgr. Gen. Credit Corp., Anchorage, 1957; br. mgr. Alaska SBA, Anchorage, 1958-60; sr. v.p. First Interstate Bank of Alaska, Anchorage, 1960-87, also dir., corp. sec.; dir. First Interstate Corp. of Alaska, First Nat. Bank of Fairbanks; pres., dir. Anchorage Broadcasters, Inc.; past pres., chmn. Microfast Software Corp.; dir., treas. R.M.R. Inc.; dir. Anchorage Light & Power Co., Turnagain, Inc., Alaska Fish and Farm, Inc., Life Ins. Co. Alaska. Pres., Anchorage Federated Charities, Inc., 1953-54; mem. advisory bd. Salvation Army, 1948-58; mem. Alaska adv. bd. Hugh O'Brian Youth Found., 1987-91; trustee Anchor Age Endowment Fund, 1988-96, chmn., 1991; mem. City of Anchorage Planning Commn., 1956; mem. City of Anchorage Coun., 1956-57; police commr. Ter. of Alaska, 1957-58; chmn. City Charter Commn., 1958; mem. exec. com. Greater Anchorage, Inc., 1955-65; pres. Sch. Bd., 1961-64; mem. Gov.'s Investment adv. com., 1970-72; mem. Alaska State Bd. Edn.; mem. citizens adv. com. Alaska Meth. U.; chmn. Anchorage Charter Commn., 1975; chmn. bldg. fund dr. Cmty. YMCA, 1976-96; sec.-treas. Breakthrough, 1976-78 ; bd. dirs Alaska Treatment Ctr., 1980-87, pres. 1985-86; trustee Marston Found., Inc., 1978, exec. dir. 1988. Served as lt. USNR, 1942-46. Elected to Hall Fame, Alaska Press Club, 1969; named Outstanding Alaskan of Year Alaska C. of C., 1976, Alaskan of Yr., 1990, Outstanding Vol. in Philanthropy Alaska chpt. Nat. Soc. Fundraising Execs, 1991. Mem. Am. Inst. Banking, Am. (exec. council 1971-72) Alaska (pres. 1970-71) bankers assns., Nat. Assn. State Bds. Edn. (sec.-treas. 1969-70) , Anchorage C. of C. (pres. 1966-67, dir.), Pioneers of Alaska, Navy League (pres. Anchorage council 1961-62). Clubs: Tower (life), San Francisco Tennis. Lodges: Lions (sec. Anchorage, 1953-54, dir. 1988, pres., 1962-63, life), Elks (life). Home: 1361 W 12th Ave Anchorage AK 99501-4252

REED, FRANK VERN, principal; b. Basin, Wyo., Sept. 20, 1951; s. Frank Junior and Irene (McKim) R.; m. Kristine Malcolm; children: Tania, Frank. BS, U. Wyo., 1976; MA, Nova U., 1985; EdD, No. Ariz. U., 1997; BA, Ariz. State U. Cert. supt., prin., tchr., Ariz. Tchr. Apache Junction (Ariz.) Sch. Dist., 1982-85, prin., 1985-89; prin. Somerton (Ariz.) Sch. Dist., 1989—. Mem. ASCD, Ariz. Sch. Adminstrn., Phi Delta Kappa. Democrat. Methodist. Home: 1481 Michelle Ln Yuma AZ 85365 Office: Somerton Sch Dist PO Box Bin E Somerton AZ 85350

REED, HAROLD ERVIN, artist, educator; b. Frederick, Okla., Feb. 22, 1921; s. Perry and Eva (Ervin) R.; m. Gladys Lorraine Oulman, Dec. 7, 1968. Founder, CEO Art Video Prodns., Inc., Woodland Hills, Calif., 1987—. Prin. works include Ofcl. Bicentennial medals USN and USMC, 1975, Statue of Liberty coin medal, 1986, Am. Cup Race coin medal, 1986, U.S. Constn. Bicentennial medal, 1987, Walking Liberty coin, 1987, Uriah Levi medal, 1988, Summer Olympics coin, 1988, 10 Olympic coins, 1988, 45 coins Desert Storm, 1993, 45 coins World War II, 1993. With U.S. Army. Decorated Bronze star, 5 Battle stars, Unit citation, Battlefield commn. Home: PO Box 5018 Woodland Hills CA 91365-5018

REED, JAMES ANTHONY, hotel industry executive, consultant; b. Marion, Ohio, June 12, 1939; s. James E. and Sue (McCurdy) R. Student, Fla. State U., 1956-59, U. N.H., 1978. Food and beverage mgr. Caneel Bay Plantation, St. John, Virgin Islands, 1960-64; mgr. Mauna Kea Beach Hotel, Kamuela, Hawaii, 1964-72; v.p. C. Brewer & Co., Ltd., Honolulu, 1972-77, Dunfey Hotel Corp., Hampton, N.H., 1977-80, Marriott Hotels & Resorts, Calif., Hawaii and Asia, 1980-89; pres. The Reed Group, Irvine, Calif., 1989; gen. mgr. La Posada de Santa Fe, 1990-91, Hotel Santa Fe, 1991-93; asst. to pres. LaJolla (Calif) Beach and Tennis Club, Inc., 1993-95; pres. The Reed Group, Santa Fe, N.M., LaJolla, 1993—; pres. Kilauea Volcano House Inc., Mackensie Hawaii Ltd., Augustine's Decor Spain; vice-chmn., bd. dirs. Picuris Pueblo Enterprises, cons. to Native Am. Tribes. Named Outstanding Young Men of Am., 1969. Mem. Calif. Thoroughbred Breeders Assn., Calif.

Hotel Assn., Sch. Am. Rsch., Community Leaders of Am., Appaloosa Horse Club. Home and Office: 7550 Eads Ave La Jolla CA 92037-3104

REED, JAMES EARL, fire department commander; b. San Francisco, Mar. 21, 1957; s. Arlen Earl and Louise (Gibbs) R.; m. Jody Lynn Bales, Feb. 14, 1976 (div. Aug. 1978); 1 child, Darci Lynn; m. Donna Kaye Lewis, June 25, 1994. A in fire sci., Casper Coll., 1995. State cert. fire fighter I, II, III, state cert. fire svc. instr. I, state cert. fire prevention officer I. Shop worker, shop foreman, salesman Becker Fire Equipment, Casper, Wyo., 1975-78; safety equipment maintance Bell H2S Safety and Oilind Safety Engring., Casper, 1978-80; tchr. outreach program Casper Coll., 1988-90; owner operator J.R.'s Custom Hand Planted Signs, 1980-93; capt. Casper (Wyo.) Fire Dept., 1978-93, comdr., 1993—; artist Images Studio, Casper, 1991—; instr. CPR courses Am. Heart Soc., ARC, 1980—; instr. SCBA courses, 1983-85. Active fund raisers City/County Fire Fighters Burn Fund, 1982, 84—, fund raisers Muscular Dystrophy Assn., 1981, 82, 85-89, fund raisers March of Dimes, 1984, 85, 87, fund raisers Casper Mountain Racers Youth Olympics, 1985-87, Casper Event Ctr.'s "Spl. Christmas for Spl. Kids," 1984-87. Named Firefighter of Yr. Casper Fire Dept., Casper Ladies Auxiliary, Am. Legion Regional and Post 2, 1984, Man in Blue, Casper Fire Dept., 1994. Mem. Casper Fire Fighters Assn. (entertainment com. 1980—, exec. com. 1988-90), City County Fire Fighters Burn Fund (trustee 1985-86, treas. 1986-89, sec. 1989-91, pres. 1992—). Republican. Seventh-day Adventist. Home: 1847 Jim Bridger Ave Casper WY 82604-3118

REED, JANICE LYNN (JANICE LYNN DENNIE), systems analyst, writer, publisher; b. Denver, July 1, 1953; d. Lawrence Herman and Wilma Jean (Jackson) Dennie; m. Gregory Darrel Reed; children: Gregory Jr., Sharita, James. BS, Calif. State U., Hayward, 1990. Publ. asst. U. Calif., Berkeley, 1980-86; sys. adminstr. Spectrum Bus. Svcs., Emeryville, Calif., 1986-89; sys. analyst GSA, San Francisco, 1989—; pres. Kente Computer Consulting, Graphics and Pub., Richmond, Calif., 1995—. Author: (romance novel) Lion of Judah, 1997. Mem. Black Data Processing Assn., Zeta Phi Beta, Xi Lambda Zeta. Democrat. Home: 119 Lakeshore Ct Richmond CA 94804

REED, JOAN-MARIE, special education educator; b. St. Paul, Sept. 8, 1960; d. William Martin Reed and Diana-Marie (Miller) Reed Moss. BA, U. Minn., 1982, BS, 1983; MEd, Tex. Woman's U., 1986. Cert. tchr., Tex. Tchr. emotionally disturbed Birdville Ind. Sch. Dist., Ft. Worth, 1984-86; tchr. emotionally disturbed Goose Creek Ind. Sch. Dist., Baytown, Tex., 1986-92, ctr. leader, 1992-93, dept. chairperson, 1987-91; tchr. emotionally disturbed Conroe (Tex.) Ind. Sch. Dist., 1993-94, Willis (Tex.) Ind. Sch. Dist., 1994-95, Jefferson County Pub. Schs., 1995—; Co-editor: New Teacher Handbook, 1986-87, Behavior Improvement Program Handbook, 1987-88. Mem. NEA, Coun. for Exceptional Children. Congregationalist. Office: Ctrl Lakewood Adolescent Day Treatment Program 1005 Wadsworth Blvd Lakewood CO 80215-5101

REED, JOHN E., producer, consultant; b. Torrance, Calif., Aug. 18, 1954; s. J.E. and Dorothy Charlene (Bitner) R.; m. Christine Elaine Haddon, Aug. 10, 1975 (div. Aug. 1980); m. Beth Walker, Sept. 16, 1988; 1 child, Kelly Kristen. AA, El Camino, Torrance, Calif.; cert. in bus., UCLA. Sr. customer engr. Datapoint, Sherman Oaks, Calif., 1977-81; sr. sales engr. United Techs., L.A., 1981-86, U.S. West Info. Sys., Torrance, Calif., 1986-88; prodr. Music Room Pub., Redondo Beach, Calif., 1987-88; sr. sales engr. NEC Am., Gardenia, Calif., 1988-93; v.p. ops. Elixir Entertainment, Culver City, Calif., 1991-93; pres., prodr. Music Room Prodns., Redondo Beach, 1993—; S.W. regional supr. Internat. Computer Equipment, L.A., 1973-77. Prodr.: (video) Comedy at Warped Speed, 1992, (feature film) Shadow Warriors, 1996; co-prodr.: (TV series) Adventures of Virgil Badd, 1994 (Golden Halo award 1994), Universal Cops, 1996. Mem. ASCAP, BMI, Harry Fox, Am. Cinematech. Office: Music Room Prodns PO Box 219 Redondo Beach CA 90277-0219

REED, KRISTEN KING, broadcast sales manager; b. Evanston, Ill., Mar. 24, 1962; d. Robert Bruce and Diane (Buchholz) King; m. Edward Cloy Reed, Oct. 30, 1987; children: Taylor Cloy, Zachary Edward, Dillon Robert. BA in Communications, U. Ariz., 1984. Sales asst. Avery Knodel TV, Chgo., 1984-85, account exec., 1985; account exec. WPWR-TV, Chgo., 1986-87, WZRC-FM, Chgo., 1987, KQIL-AM/KQIX-FM, Grand Junction, Colo., 1987-88; account exec. KJCT-TV, Grand Junction, 1988-91, sales mgr., 1991-96; gen. sales mgr. KRDO-TV, Colorado Springs, 1996—. Co-chmn. leadership div. Mesa County Econ. Devel. Coun., Grand Junction, 1994. Mem. Rotary. Office: KJCT-TV 8 Foresight Cir Grand Junction CO 81505-1014

REED, LEONARD NEWTON, secondary school educator; b. Alva, Okla., Feb. 27, 1952; s. Leonard S. and Vevian M. (Chew) R. BA, Northwestern Okla. State U., 1970, MA, 1980; postgrad., No. Ariz. U., 1982-89; cert. ESL, U. Phoenix, 1992. Cert. social sci. tchr., Ariz., Okla., ESL, Ariz. Social sci. tchr. Chinle (Ariz.) Unified Sch. Dist., 1974—; night staff Navajo C.C., 1988—; student coun. advisor Chinle Unified Sch. Dist., 1975-76, 78-83, 84-93. Mem. com. Apache County (Ariz.) Dem. Party, 1980-88, 93-96; state del. Ariz. Dem. Party, 1980; mem. Nat. Gay and Lesbian Task Force, 1976—. 20868551 (gay and lesbian caucus 1988—, rural and small caucus, 1986—, Ariz. Edn. Assn. (bd. dirs. 1984-88, 89-90, human rels. com. 1987-94, 95—, chair, human rels. com. 1992-94, treas. N.E. adv. coun., Bill Hodge award 1989, first male co-chair gay, lesbian caucus 1995-97, founder 1995—), Ariz. Student Coun. Advisors Assn., Chinle Edn. Assn. (past pres. 1979, 81, treas.), CHS (social sci. dept. chair 1981-84, 85-93). Home: PO Box 1678 Chinle AZ 86503-1678 Office: Chinle Unified Sch Dist # 24 PO Box 587 Chinle AZ 86503-0587

REED, LYNDA BERNAL, video producer, writer; b. Detroit, July 9, 1959; d. Bernard and Joyce Lydia (Gunnett) Harris; m. Ronald Daniel Bernal, June 21, 1980 (div. Oct. 1985); m. Jack Milton Reed, Nov. 4, 1993. BS in Health Sci., Ariz. State U., 1982. Audiovisual coord. Salt River Project, Phoenix, 1985-93; ind. writer/prodr. Phoenix, 1993-96; writer, prodr. Ednl. Mgmt. Group, Scottsdale, 1996—. Writer, dir.: (videotape) Montezuma Castle: Home of the Prehistoric Sinagua, 1994 (Southwest Book award 1995), Lake Powell: Heart of the Grand Circle, 1986 (Rocky Mountain Emmy award 1987, ITVA award 1986), The Wolf: A Howling in America's Parks, 1989 (CINDY award 1989), 1993 Page Promo (TELLY award 1994). Media cons. YWCA of Maricopa County, Phoenix, 1986-90. Mem. NATAS, Internat. TV Assn. Office: 16423 N 54th Ave Glendale AZ 85306-1911

REED, MARY LOU, state legislator; m. Scott Reed; children: Tara, Bruce. BA, Mills Coll. Mem. Idaho State Senate, 1985—; Senate Minority Leader; coord. Com. for Fair Rates. Democrat. Office: 10 Giesa Rd Coeur D Alene ID 83814-9489 Office: State Capitol PO Box 83720 Boise ID 83720-0081*

REED, MICHAEL RAYBREN, government affairs consulting executive; b. Reno, June 21, 1947; s. Jack Raybren and Mary Elizabeth (Williams) R.; m. Betty Joan Banta, July 29, 1967; children: Alicia L., Brian R., Kipp T. BA in Journalism, U. Nev., 1972; MA in Human Resources Mgmt., Troy State U., 1992; student, USAF Air War Coll., 1991-92. Printer Nev. Bell Tel. Co., Reno, 1966-67, 69-72; reporter Reno Evening Gazette, 1973-75; supr., mgr. corp. comm. Sierra Pacific Power Co., Reno, 1975-90, mgr. govtl. affairs, 1992-93, dir. govtl. affairs, 1993-95; owner Pub. Affairs Strategies, 1995—. Bd. dirs. Washoe County K-16 Coun.; mem. Washoe County Fiscal Adv. Group. Lt. col. USAF, 1968-69, 90-92; state exec. officer Nev. Air NG, 1972—. Named Outstanding Young Journalist Nev. State Press Assn., 1974. Mem. Pub. Rels. Soc. Am. (treas. 1989-90, Silver Spike award 1989), Greater Reno-Sparks C. of C. (chmn. legis. affairs task force), Soc. Profl. Journalists, Air Force Assn., Sparks Rotary Club, Reno South Kiwanis Club (pres. 1979-80, 84-85). Roman Catholic. Office: 14315 Riata Cir Reno NV 89511-9018

REED, NANCY BOYD, English language and elementary education educator; b. Lodi, Calif., Oct. 10, 1946; d. Leo H. and Anna Gwen (Coombes) Boyd; m. Maurice Allen Reed, Dec. 22, 1966; 1 child, Scot Alastair. AA Recreational Adminstrn. with honors, Delta Coll., 1974; BA Recreational Adminstrn. with honors, Calif. State U., Sacramento, 1976, MA in Edn., English Lang. Devel., 1988; cert. computers in edn., U. Calif., Davis, 1984. Cert. multiple subject, phys. edn., computers in edn. teaching. Tchr. 4th grade Hagginwood Sch., Sacramento, 1980-81; tchr. 4th/5th grade impacted lang. Noralto Sch., Sacramento, 1981-88, bilingual resource tchr., 1988-91, tchr. English lang. devel., 1991-96, bilingual resource tchr., 1996—; mentor tchr. North Sacramento Sch. Dist., Sacramento, 1992-95, bilingual resource tchr., 1996—; fellow, tchr./cons. No. Calif. Math. Project, U. Calif., Davis, 1985—. Dir. Jasmine Flower Dancers, Sacramento, 1984-96; comty. rep. Am. Host Found., Sacramento, 1976—. Named Outstanding Educator Capitol Svc. Ctr., 1992, Tchr. of Yr., Noralto Sch., North Sacramento Sch., 1996; scholar Fridtjof-Nansen-Akademie, Ingleheim, Germany, 1993, Adenauer Found., Berlin, 1982, 93. Mem. NEA, Nat. Vis. Tchrs. Assn. (bd. dirs. 1994—), Nat. Assn. Bilingual Edn., Nat. Coun. Tchrs. Math., Calif. Tchrs. Assn. (state coun. rep. 1995-96), North Sacramento Edn. Assn. (sec. 1986-88, v.p. 1988-90, pres. 1990-92, outstanding educator 1992). Home: 3665 Halter Ct Sacramento CA 95821-3266 Office: Noralto Sch North Sacramento Sch Dist 477 Las Palmas Ave Sacramento CA 95815-1605

REED, NANCY ELLEN, computer science educator; b. Mpls., Aug. 11, 1955; d. Jacob Allen and Mary Emeline (Howser) Lundgren; m. Todd Randall Reed, June 18, 1977. BS in Biology, U. Minn., 1977, MS in Computer Sci., 1988, PhD in Computer Sci., 1995. Rsch. lab. technician gastroenterology rsch. unit Mayo Clinic, Rochester, Minn., 1978-81; phys. sci. technician U.S. Environ. Hygiene Agy., Fitzsimmons Army Med. Ctr., Aurora, Colo., 1982-83; profl. rsch. asst. molecular, cellular, devel. biology dept. U. Colo., Boulder, 1983-84; tchg. asst. U. Minn., 1985-86, rsch. asst., 1985-88; computer programmer Control Data Corp., Arden Hills, Minn., 1986; asst. Artificial Intelligence Lab. Swiss Fed. Inst. Tech., Lausanne, 1989-91; lectr. computer and info. sci. dept. Sonoma State U., Rohnert Park, Calif., 1993-94; lectr. U. Calif., Davis, 1994-95, 96, rschr., 1995, asst. adj. prof. computer sci. dept., 1996—. Contbr. articles to profl. jours.; spkr. in field; reviewer for Artificial Intelligence in Medicine, Internat. Jour. of Man-Machine Studies, Integrated Computer-Aided Engring. Microelectronic and Info. Scis. Fellowship, 1984-85, Am. Electronics Assn. Fellowship, 1985-89. Mem. IEEE, Am. Assn. for Artificial Intelligence (scholarship for travel nat. conf. on artificial intelligence 1992, 94, session chair for spring syposium 1994), Assn. for Computing Machinery. Office: U Calif Computer Sci Dept Davis CA 95616-8562

REED, RAY PAUL, engineering mechanics measurement consultant; b. Abilene, Tex., May 26, 1927; s. Raymond Roseman and Gladys Daisy (Reddell) R.; m. Mary Antoinette Wied, Oct. 7, 1950; children: Mary Kathryn, Patricia Lynn. BSME, Tex. A&M U., 1950; MS in Engring. Mechanics, U. Tex., 1958, PhD, 1966. Registered profl. engr., N.Mex., Tex. Rsch. engr. S.W. Rsch. Inst., San Antonio, 1950-54; rsch. scientist U. Tex., Austin, 1954-56; mem. tech. staff Sandia Nat. Labs., Albuquerque, 1956-61, rsch. fellow, 1961-66, disting. mem. tech. staff, 1966-94. Author: manual on the use of thermocouples; contbr. numerous reports and articles on shock measurement and thermometry to profl. jours. With USNR, 1945-46, PTO. NIH grantee U. Tex., 1962-66. Mem. ASTM (chmn. com. 1985—), ASME, Instrument Soc. Am., Am. Physics Soc., Sigma Xi. Home and Office: Proteun Svcs 6640 Casa Loma NE Albuquerque NM 87109-3962

REED, ROBERT WILLIAM, city planner, educator; b. Cambridge, Mass., June 10, 1946; m. Diane C. Drigot, June 23, 1977 (div. Dec. 1989). BS in Econs., Cornell U., 1969; MS in Urban Planning, Wayne State U., 1973; PhD in Econs./Planning, U. Mich., 1979. Rsch. assoc. Johns Hopkins U., 1972-73; regional dir. Nat. Water Assessment, Washington, 1974-77; city planner City/County Honolulu, 1978-94; prof. econs. Hawaii Pacific U., Honolulu, 1994—; adj. prof. econs. Chaminade U., Honolulu, 1984—; adj. prof. bus. U. Hawaii, Manoa, 1986—; pres. R. W. Reed & Assocs., Honolulu, 1984—; cons. editor Irwin Pubs., Burr Ridge, Ill., 1994; advisor Internat. Joint Commn., Toronto, Can., 1974-77; cons. economist World Bank, Hong Kong, 1994. McVoy scholar Cornell U., 1966, Knickerbocker scholar, 1967. Mem. Sierra Club (exec. com. 1990-92), English Speaking Union, Honolulu Arts Acad., Honolulu Club, Waikiki Yacht Club. Republican. Home: 101 Ohana St Kailua HI 96734-2351

REED, WILLIAM GLEN, retired insurance agency executive; b. Burr Oak, Kans., Jan. 15, 1917; s. Alva Allen and Adina Rosina (Decker) R.; m. Lillie Evelyn Matthews, Sept. 4, 1943; children: Glenda Rae, Donald Eugene. AB in Secondary Edn., N.W. Nazarene Coll., 1943, BA in Secondary Edn.; student, Hartford Ins./Prudential Ins., 1946, 53. Owner, mgr. Glen Reed Ins. Agy., Nampa, Idaho, 1946-82. With USN, 1943-46. Mem. Nampa Exch. Club (charter mem., various offices), Good Samaritan Club (King's Traveler's chapt., treas.). Nazarene. Home: 604 E Hawaii Ave Nampa ID 83686-7426

REEDER, SAMUEL KENNETH, analytical laboratory executive; b. Vinita, Okla., July 25, 1938; s. Dwight Cecil and Melba Mae (Mattox) R.; m. Camille Augusta Goepfert, Aug. 17, 1959; children: Jerold, Jeanne, Jodi. BA, La Sierra Coll., Riverside, Calif., 1960; PhD, Mont. State U., 1971. Tchr. Seventh-day Adventist Schs., San Diego and Springfield, Org., 1961-66; chief scientist R&D Sunkist Growers, Inc., Ontario, Calif., 1971-79; lab. mgr. R&D Beatrice/Hunt-Wesson, Inc., Fullerton, Calif., 1979-90; v.p. tech. svcs. C.L. Tech., Inc., Corona, Calif., 1990-94; lab. dir. C.L. tech. divsn. Microbac Analytic Svcs., Inc., Corona, Calif., 1994-96; cons. Reeder & Assocs., Riverside, Calif., 1996; with Coulton Chem. Co., Toledo, 1996—. Contbr. sci. papers to profl. jours. Trustee Ontario City Libr., 1976-80, pres. bd. trustees, 1978-80. Recipient Bank of Am. award, 1956. Mem. Am. Chem. Soc., Inst. Food Technologists, Assn. Ofcl. Analytical Chemists (assoc.). Seventh-day Adventist. Home and Office: 4790 Jackson St # 206 Riverside CA 91720-7943 Office: Coulton Chem Co Toledo OH 43650

REED-GRAHAM, LOIS L., administrator, secondary education educator; b. Muscogee, Okla., Jan. 19, 1933; d. Louis G. and Bonnie (Hill) Reed; children: Harold Gibson, Kathryn Ann Graham. RN, San Diego County Hosp., 1957; BA, Calif. State U., Sacramento, 1972, MPA, 1978; postgrad., Calif. State U., Sacremento; EdD, U. Laverne. Tchr., adminstr., job developer CETA, Sacramento, 1972-78; bus. instr. Los Rios Community Coll., Sacramento, 1978-84; tchr. grade 6 Mark Hopkins Sch., Sacramento, 1984-89; acting adminstr. Fern Bacon Sch., Sacramento; adminstr. Sacramento City Schs.; tchr. grades 7,8, mentor tchr. Fern Bacon Sch., Sacramento; asst. prin. secondary edn. Sacramento City Schs., 1989-93; elem. sch. prin. Theodore Judah Elem. Sch., Sacramento, 1993—; asst. supt. secondary, middle and K-8 schs. Sacramento City Unified Sch.; cons. Prentice Hall Pub. Co. Contbr. articles to profl. publs. Mem. Calif. State Fair Employment and Housing Commn. Mem. AAUW (bd. dirs., pres. Sacramento chpt. 1990), Nat. Assn. Univ. Women (pres.). Home: 7408 Toulon Ln Sacramento CA 95828-4641

REED-JACKSON, LEONA MAE, educational administrator; b. Crosby, Tex., Sept. 9, 1945; d. Elton Phillip and Ora Lee (Jones) Reed; m. Aaron B. Mounds Jr., Aug. 21, 1965 (div.); 1 child, Lisa Nichelle; m. Emanuel Jackson, Mar. 8, 1997. BS in Elem. Edn., Bridgewater State Coll., 1973; MA in Mental Retardation, U. Alaska, 1980. Cert. tchr. Alaska, Colo., Tex., Mass., cert. adminstrv. prin. Tchr., Sch. Dist. # 11, Colorado Springs, Colo., 1973-75; tchr. Anchorage Sch. Dist., 1976-78, 80—, mem. maths. curriculum com., reading contact tchr., mem. talent bank. Tchr. Del Valle (Tex.) Sch. Dist., 1979-80; adminstrv. prin. intern Anchorage Sch. Dist., 1989-90; asst. prin. Spring Hill Elem. Sch., Anchorage, 1990-91; elem. prin. intern.; asst. prin. Ptarmigan Elem. Sch., Anchorage, 1991-93, prin., 1993-94; with Child in Transition Homeless Project Title I Anchorage Sch. Dist., Anchorage, Alaska, 1994—. Bd. dirs. Urban League, 1974; 1st v.p. PTA, Crosby, Tex.; del. Tex. Dem. Conv., 1980; chmn. dist. 13 Dem. Party; mem. Alaska Women Polit. Caucus; bd. dirs. C.R.I.S.I.S. Inc.; tchr. religious edn., lay Eucharist minister St. Martin De Pores Roman Cath. Ch., St. Patrick's Roman Cath. Ch.; pres. Black Educators of Pike Peak Region, 1974; mem. social concerns commn. Archidiocese of Anchorage, Coun. for Exceptional Children. With USAF, 1964-66. Alaska State Tchr. Incentive grantee, 1981, Ivy Lutz scholar, 1972. Mem. NEA (human rels. coord. Alaska chpt., region 6 bd. dirs., bd. dirs Alaska chpt., vice-chmn. women's caucus), NAACP, LWV, Nat. Coun. Negro Women, Anchorage Edn. Assn. (minority chmn. 1982—, mem. black caucus polit. action com., v.p. programs 1986-88), Anchorage Edn. Assn. (v.p. programs com. 1986-87, women's caucus), Assn. Supervision and Curriculum Devel., Alaska Women in Adminstrn., Prins. Assn., Alaska Women's Polit. Caucus, Alpha Kapp Alpha, Phi Delta Kappa.

REEDY, PENELOPE MICHAL, publisher, writer; b. Everett, Wash., June 5, 1947; d. Ralph Warner Croner and Patricia Ann (Elzea) Leek; m. Jim Reedy, Oct. 2, 1971 (div. Feb. 1989); children: Patricia Louise, Katherine Lena, James Joseph, Edward Thomas Elzea. AA in English, Coll. So. Idaho, 1991; BA in English, Marquette U., 1993; postgrad., Idaho State U., 1995—. Comms. cert., Idaho Law Enforcement. Pub. Redneck Rev. Lit., Pocatello, Idaho, 1975—; dispatcher Idaho State Police, Pocatello, 1994-95; tchg. asst. Idaho State U., Pocatello, 1995—; exec. com. Idaho Humanities Coun., Boise, 1982-86. Author: (poetry) The Last Fairfield Rodeo, 1993. Pres. Camas County Hist. Soc., Fairfield, Idaho, 1975-80. Recipient Lit. award Phi Theta Kappa, 1991; winner Mae Gales Essay Contest Marquette U., 1992, Mae Gales Fiction Contest, 1993. Mem. Western Lit. Assn., Sigma Tau Delta. Office: Redneck Rev Lit PO Box 0654 Pocatello ID 83204

REEL, JAMES, music critic, writer; b. Yuma, Ariz., May 2, 1958; s. Robert James Burton and Shirley Ray (Brown) Burton Hightower. BA, U. Ariz., 1979, MLS, 1980. Announcer arts producer KUAT Radio, Tucson, 1976-83, music dir., arts producer, 1983-88; classical music critic, feature writer Ariz. Daily Star, Tucson, 1988-95; arts and entertainment editor Ariz. Daily Star, 1995—. Author: The Timid Soul's Guide to Classical Music, 1992; program annotator: Ensemble 21, 1990-92; columnist, contbr. FanFare, 1991—; online columnist The Whole Wired Word, 1997—. Recipient Project Reporting award Ariz. Press Club, 1991. Democrat. Office: Arizona Daily Star PO Box 26807 Tucson AZ 85726

REENSTJERNA, FREDERICK ROBERTS, librarian, writer; b. Lexington, S.C., Sept. 30, 1948; s. Otto Frederick and Miriam Swann (Roberts) R.; m. Hope Shields, June 3, 1971; 1 child, Elisabeth Shields. BA in Am. History, Coll. of Charleston, 1969; MLS, U. Md., 1971; M Adminstrn. in Human Resources, Lynchburg Coll., 1981; EdD, W.Va. U., 1991. Reference specialist congl. rsch. svc. Libr. of Congress, Washington, 1972-75; dir. Franklin County Libr., Rocky Mount, Va., 1975-77; br. libr. Hollins Br. Libr. Roanoke County (Va.) Pub. Libr., 1977-82, head reference main libr., 1982-84; bus. mgr. autism tng. ctr. Marshall U., Huntington, W.Va., 1984-86, asst. mgr. housing, 1986-88, head pub. svcs. Morrow Libr., 1989, asst. prof. instrnl. tech. Coll. Edn., 1989-90; freelance writer, Roseburg, Oreg., 1990-91; rsch. libr. Douglas County Mus., Roseburg, 1991—. Author: Library Survival Skills: A Guide to the Resources of the James Morrow Library, 1990, (with Jena Mitchell) Life in Douglas County, Oregon: The Western Experience, 1993; contbr. articles to various publs. Mem. needs task force Douglas County United Way, 1994. Mem. Soc. Am. Archivists. Home: 964 SE Terrace Dr Roseburg OR 97470-4330 Office: Douglas County Mus 123 Museum Dr Roseburg OR 97470

REES, NORMA S., academic administrator; b. N.Y.C., Dec. 27, 1929; d. Benjamin and Lottie (Schwartz) D.; m. Raymond R. Rees, Mar. 19, 1960; children—Evan Lloyd, Raymond Arthur. B.A., Queens Coll., 1952; M.A., Bklyn. Coll., 1954; Ph.D., NYU, 1959. Cert. speech-language pathology, audiology. Prof. communicative disorders Hunter Coll., N.Y.C., 1967-72; exec. officer, speech and hearing scis. grad. sch. CUNY, N.Y.C., 1972-74, assoc. dean for grad. studies, 1974-76, dean grad. studies, 1976-82; vice chancellor for acad. affairs U. Wis., Milw., 1982-85, from 1986, acting chancellor, 1985-86; vice chancellor for acad. policy and planning Mass. Bd. Regents for Higher Edn., Boston, 1987-90; pres. Calif. State U., Hayward, 1990—; bd. dirs. Am. Assn. State Colls. and Univs., 1995—, Coun. of Postsecondary Accreditation, Washington, 1985-94; chmn. Commn. Recognition of Postsecondary Accreditation, 1994-96. Contbr. articles to profl. jours. Trustee Citizens Govtl. Rsch. Bur., Milw., 1985-87; active Task Force on Wis. World Trade Ctr., 1985-87; bd. dirs. Greater Boston YWCA, 1987-90; mem. Mayor's Cabinet Ednl. Excellence, Oakland, Calif.; mem. steering com. Econ. Devel. Adv. Bd. Alameda County, 1995—. Fellow Am. Speech-Lang-Hearing Assn. (honors); mem. Am. Coun. Edn. (com. internat. edn. 1991-93), Am. Assn. Colls. and Univs. (chair task force on quality assessment 1991-92, mem. steering com. of coun. of urban met. colls. & univs. 1992—), Nat. Assn. State Univs. and Land Grant Colls. (exec. com. divsn. urban affairs 1985-87, com. accreditation 1987-90). Office: Calif State Univ-Hayward 25800 Carlos Bee Blvd Hayward CA 94542-3001

REESE, JOHN ROBERT, lawyer; b. Salt Lake City, Nov. 3, 1939; s. Robert McCann and Glade (Stauffer) R.; m. Francesca Marroquin Gardner, Sept. 5, 1964 (div.); children—Jennifer Marie, Justine Francesca; m. Robin Ann Gunsul, June 18, 1988. AB cum laude, Harvard U., 1962; LLB, Stanford U., 1965. Bar: Calif. 1966, U.S. Dist. Ct. (no. dist.) Calif. 1966, U.S. Ct. Appeals (9th cir.) 1966, U.S. Dist. Ct. (cen. dist.) Calif. 1974, U.S. Supreme Ct. 1976, U.S. Dist. Ct. (ea. dist.) Calif. 1977, U.S. Ct. Appeals (6th cir.) 1982, U.S. Ct. Appeals (8th cir.) 1985, U.S. Ct. Appeals (10th cir.) 1992, U.S. Ct. Appeals (Fed. cir.) 1994. Assoc. McCutchen, Doyle, Brown & Enersen, San Francisco, 1965-74, ptnr., 1974—; adj. asst. prof. law Hastings Coll. of Law, 1991; lectr. U. Calif., Berkeley, 1987, 92. Mem. editorial, adv. bds. Antitrust Bull., Jour. Reprints for Antitrust Law and Econs. Bd. dirs. Friends of San Francisco Pub. Libr., 1981-87; bd. vis. Stanford U., 1983-86. Capt. U.S. Army, 1966-68. Decorated Bronze Star. Mem. ABA, State Bar Calif., San Francisco Bar Assn., U.S. Supreme Ct. Hist. Soc., Ninth Jud. Cir. Hist. Soc., Calif. Acad. Appellate Lawyers, Order of the Coif. Home: 9 Morning Sun Dr Petaluma CA 94952-4780 Office: McCutchen Doyle Brown & Enersen 3 Embarcadero Ctr San Francisco CA 94111-4003

REESE, MONTE NELSON, agricultural association executive; b. Mooreland, Okla., Mar. 31, 1947; s. James Nelson and Ruby Edith (Bond) R.; m. Treisa Lou Bartow, May 25, 1968; children: Bartow Allan, Monica Lynnelle. BS in Agrl. Econs., Okla. State U., 1969. Staff asst. Wilson Cert. Foods, Oklahoma City, 1969-71; asst. farm dir. Sta. WKY Radio and TV, Oklahoma City, 1971-73; radio-TV specialist Tex. A&M U., College Station, 1973; dir. agrl. devel. Oklahoma City C. of C., 1973-76; asst. exec. dir. Am. Morgan Horse Assn., Westmoreland, N.Y., 1976-77; v.p. pub. affairs Farm Credit Banks of Wichita, Kans., 1977-87; exec. dir. Coffey County Econ. Devel., Burlington, Kans., 1987-88; farm dir. Mid-Am. Ag Network, Wichita, 1988-89; CEO Cattlemen's Beef Promotion and Rsch. Bd., Englewood, Colo., 1989-96; exec. dir. Cattlemen's Beef Promotion & Rsch. Bd., Englewood, CO, 1996—. Lt. col. USAR, 1969—. Home: 982 S Dearborn Way Apt 2 Aurora CO 80012-3878 Office: Cattlemen's Beef Promotion and Rsch Bd 5420 S Quebec St Englewood CO 80111*

REESE, WILLIAM ALBERT, III, psychologist; b. Tabor, Iowa, Nov. 23, 1932; s. William Albert and Mary-Evelyn Hope (Lundeen) R.; B.A., U. Washington Reed Coll., 1955; M.Ed., U. Ariz., 1964, Ph.D., 1981; m. Barbara Diane Windermere, Dec. 22, 1954 (dec. Jan. 1995); children: Judy, Diane, William IV, Sandra-Siobhan, Debra-Anne, Robert-Gregory, Barbara-Joanne; m. Ruth Alice Moller, Sept. 12, 1996. Diplomate Am. Bd. Christian Psychology. Clin. Psychology cons. Nogales Pub. Schs., Nogales-Tucson, Ariz., 1971-79; clin. psychologist Astra Found., N.Y.C., 1979-86, chief psychology svc., neuropsychiatry, 1980-89; chief psychologist Family Support Ctr. Community-Family Exceptional Mem. Svcs., Sonoita, Ariz., 1986-89, Psychol. Svc. Ctr., Mount Tabor, Iowa, 1989-95, Calif. Ctr., 1995—; dir. religious Marriage and Family Life Wilderness Ctr., Berchtesgaden, W.Ger., summer 1981-82; exec. sec. Astra Ednl. Found., 1975-79, bd. dirs., 1979—, EEO officer, 1978—. Served with USAF, 1967-71: Vietnam. Decorated Bronze Star. Fellow in cons. psychology and holistic medicine Clin. Services Found., Ariz., 1979—. Fellow Am. Psychol. Soc.; mem. APA, Calif. Psychol. Assn., Am. Counseling Assn., Iowa Psychol. Assn. Clubs: Los Padres Wilderness Center, Outdoor, Sierra, Skyline Estates Golf and Country (Tucson), K.C. Author: Developing a Scale of Human Values for Adults of Diverse Cultural Backgrounds, 1981, rev. edit., 1988. Office: Psychol Service Ctr Integrated Med Ctr-Wellness Clin 225 Crossroads Blvd Ste 274 Carmel CA 93923-8649 also: PO Box 1089 Bellevue NE 68005-1089

REEVES, BRUCE, social worker; b. Centerville, Utah, Jan. 8, 1955; s. Leon W. and Maxine (Hodson) R. BA, U. Utah, 1979, MSW, 1983. Mental health caseworker Traveler's Aid Soc. Salt Lake, Salt Lake City, 1983-86; socialwork cons. Home Health of Utah, Bountiful, 1985-86; victim svcs. counselor Salt Lake County Atty's. Office, Salt Lake City, 1986-87; mgr., cons. AIDS and employee assistance program Aetna and Human Affairs Internat., Salt Lake City, 1987-96; dir. social work and therapies Paracelsus

Home Care & Hospice, Salt Lake City, 1996—; health educator Health Horizons, L.C., 1996—; presenter in field. Bd. dirs. Walk-ons, Inc., Salt Lake City, 1989—; mem. appropriations com. United Way Greater Salt Lake, Salt Lake City, 1990—, bd. assocs. Ririe-Woodbury Dance Co., Salt Lake City, 1991-95, human svcs. com. Utah Stonewall Ctr., Salt Lake City, 1992-95. Mem. NASW, APHA, NLGHA. Democrat. Office: Paracelsus Home Care Ste 101 1002 E So Temple Salt Lake City UT 84102

REEVES, CARLA MARIANNE, women's health, nurse midwife; b. San Francisco, June 25, 1949; d. Robert Dwight and Irma Marianne (Nelson) R. BS in Nursing, U. Md., Balt., 1971; MS in Nursing, U. Ky., 1975. RN, Ariz., Calif.; cert. nurse midwife, Ariz., Calif. Commd. officer U.S. Army, 1967-77; commd. officer USAF, 1978, advanced through grades to maj., 1971-83; nurse, midwife USAF Hosp. Luke, Luke AFB, Ariz., 1978-84, sr. nurse, midwife, 1985-88; sr. nurse, midwife Regional Med. Ctr., Clark Air Base, The Philippines, 1984-85; ret., 1988; nurse midwife S.W. Women's Health Svcs., Phoenix, 1988-94, Loma Vista Med. Group, San Jose, Calif., 1994-96, Palo Alto Med. Found., Fremont, Calif., 1996—; pvt. duty-clinic nurse Homemakers Upjohn, Santa Maria, Calif., 1978; ob-gyn nurse practitioner Planned Parenthood Santa Barbara (Calif.), Inc., 1978. Decorated Meritorious Svc. medal with oak leaf cluster; named Ariz. Outstanding Achievement-PMH Physician Office Nurse of Yr., 1992. Mem. Am. Coll. Nurse Midwifes (cert.), Assn. of Women's Health, Obstetric and Neonatal Nurses, Soc. of Retired Air Force Nurses, World Wildlife Fund, Ariz. Humane Soc., Doris Day Animal League, Cousteau Soc. Home: 882 Bedford St Fremont CA 94539-4704 Office: Palo Alto Med Found 39500 Liberty St Fremont CA 94538-2211

REEVES, JAMES N., lawyer; b. Albert Lea, Minn., Oct. 14, 1945. AB, Dartmouth Coll., 1967; student, George Washington U.; JD, U. Minn., 1970. Bar: Minn. 1970, Alaska 1972, U.S. Ct. Appeals (9th cir.), U.S. Supreme Ct. Law clk. U.S. Dist. Ct. Minn., 1970-71; asst. atty. gen. State of Alaska, 1971-78; mem. Bogle & Gates, Anchorage. Sr. fellow East-West Ctr., Honolulu, 1977. Mem. ABA, Alaska Bar Assn. Office: Bogle & Gates 1031 W 4th Ave Ste 600 Anchorage AK 99501-5907

REGALIA, GWEN, mayor. Mayor Walnut Creek, Calif. Address: 1666 N Main St Walnut Creek CA 94596

REGGIO, GODFREY, film director; b. New Orleans, 1940. Dir. (films) Koyaanisqatsi, 1983, Powaqqatsi, 1988 (Best Film, Sao Paolo Film festival), Anima Mundi, 1992, Evidence, 1995. Mem. Christian Bros., 1954-68; founder Inst. for Regional Edn., Santa Fe, N.Mex., 1972. Home: care Inst for Regional Edn PO Box 2404 Santa Fe NM 87504*

REGNIER, JAMES, state supreme court justice; b. Aurora, Ill.; m. Linda Regnier; 3 children. BS, Marquette U., 1966; JD, U. Ill., 1973. Judicial Fellow ACTL, Internat. Soc. Barristers; completed atty. mediator tng., Atty.-Mediator Tng. Inst., Dallas, 1993. Lawyer pvt. practice, Rochelle, Ill., 1973-78; co-founder, ptnr. Regnier, Lewis and Boland, Great Falls, Mont., 1979-91; lawyer pvt. practice, Missoula, Mont., 1991-97; justice Mont. Supreme Ct., Helena, 1997—; appt. Mont. Supreme Ct. Commn. on Civil Jury Instrn.; appt. lawyer-rep. to 9th Cir. Judicial Confs., 1987, 88, 89, chair Mont. lawyer delegation, 1989; lectr. U. Mont. Sch. Law, numerous continuing legal edn. seminars. Contbr. Mont. Pattern Jury Instrns. for Civil Cases, 1985. Co-founder Mont. chpt. Am. Bd. Trial Advocates, 1989—, pres. Officer USN, Vietnam. Office: Montana Supreme Ct Justice Bldg 215 N Sanders PO 203001 Helena MT 59620-3001

REGOLI, ROBERT MICHAEL, sociologist, researcher; b. Pitts., Aug. 25, 1950; s. Arthur Adolph and Meta Hellen (Callan) R.; m. Deborah Kay White, June 10, 1972; children: Andrea Kay, Adam Michael. AA, Diablo Valley Coll., Concord, Calif., 1970; BS, Wash. State U., 1971, MA, 1972, PhD, 1975. Asst. prof. Ind. State U., Terre Haute, 1975-77, Tex. Christian U., Ft. Worth, 1977-81; assoc. prof. U. Colo., Boulder, 1981—; pres. Acad. Criminal Justice Scis. Mem. Western Social Sci. Assn. (editor 1985-87), Acad. Criminal Justice Scis. (bd. trustees 1982-84, 2d v.p. 1984-85, 1st v.p. 1985-86, pres. 1986-87), Phi Beta Kappa. Democrat. Home: 577 Flying Jib Ct Lafayette CO 80026 Office: U Colo Dept Sociology CB 327 Boulder CO 80309

REHART, BURTON SCHYLER, journalism educator, freelance writer; b. Pacific Grove, Calif., July 24, 1934; s. Burton Schyler Sr. and Ruth Evelyn (Whitaker) R.; m. Catherine Loverne Morison, Apr. 14, 1962 (div. Aug. 1983); children: William, Anne Marie, Catherine Evelyn; m. Felicia Rose Cousart, June 30, 1984 (div. Aug. 1995); m. Shirlee Jan Mynatt, July 20, 1996. BA in Journalism, Fresno (Calif.) State Coll., 1957; MA in History, Calif. State U., Fresno, 1966; cert., Coro found., 1961, Stanford U., summer 1975. Cert. adult edn. tchr., Calif. Reporter Bakersfield Californian, 1955; reporter, photographer Fresno Bee, 1957, Madera (Calif.) Daily Tribune, 1960-61, Ventura (Calif.) Free Press, 1961-62; from instr. to prof. journalism Calif. State U., Fresno, 1963—, prof. journalism, 1979—, chmn. dept. journalism, 1992-94. Author: M. Theo. Kearney-Prince of Fresno, 1988, (with others) Fresno in the 20th Century, 1986; editor, chmn. editorial bd. Fresno City, County Hist. Soc. Jour.; contbr. articles to profl. jours. Asst. foreman Fresno County Grand Jury, 1969. With U.S. Army, 1958-60. Mem. Soc. Profl. Journalists (pres. 1987-89), World Future Soc. (writer), Phi Kappa Phi (pres. 1977-78, Calif. State U. Fresno chpt.), Kappa Tau Alpha. Democrat. Episcopalian. Home: 1557 E Roberts Ave Fresno CA 93710-6433 Office: Calif State U Dept Journalism Shaw and Cedar Avenues Fresno CA 93740-0010

REHORN, LOIS M(ARIE), nursing administrator; b. Larned, Kans., Apr. 15, 1919; d. Charles and Ethel L. (Canaday) Williamson; m. C. Howard Smith, Feb. 15, 1946 (dec. Aug. 1980); 1 child, Cynthia A. Huddleston; m. Harlan W. Rehorn, Aug. 25, 1981. RN, Bethany Hosp. Sch. Nursing, Kansas City, Kans., 1943; BS, Ft. Hays Kans. State U., Hays, 1968, MS, 1970. RN, N.Mex. Office nurse, surg. asst. Dr. John H. Luke, Kansas City, Kans., 1943-47; supr. nursing unit Larned (Kans.) State Hosp., 1949-68, dir. nursing edn., 1968-71, dir. nursing, 1972-81, ret., 1981. Named Nurse of Yr. DNA-4, 1986. Mem. Am. Nurses Assn., Kans. Nurses Assn. (dist. treas.), N.Mex. Nurses Assn. (dist. pres. 1982-86, dist. bd. dirs. 1992-94). Home: 1436 Brentwood Dr Clovis NM 88101-4602 *Keep within you a place where dreams may grow. The fountain of understanding is the willingness to listen.*

REHR, JOHN JACOB, physicist, educator; b. Carlisle, Pa., May 6, 1945. BSE, U. Mich., 1967; PhD, Cornell U., 1972. Prof. physics U. Washington, Seattle, 1975—; cons. prof. Stanford Synchrotron Radiation Lab., Calif., 1993—; affiliate staff scientist Pacific N.W. Nat. Lab., Wash., 1995—. Office: U Washington Physics Box 351560 Seattle WA 98195

REIBER, GREGORY DUANE, forensic pathologist; b. Loma Linda, Calif., May 25, 1955; s. Clifford D. and Anna M. (Field) R.; m. Faustina Mae Davis, Feb. 10, 1980; children: Jenessa Anne, Zachary Duane. BS magna cum laude, Andrews U., Berrien Springs, Mich., 1977; MD, Loma Linda (Calif.) U., 1981. Diplomate Am. Bd. Pathology. Resident in pathology Loma Linda U. Med. Ctr., 1981-85; fellow in forensic pathology Root Pathology Lab., San Bernardino, Calif., 1985-86; assoc. pathologist Root Pathology Lab., 1986-90, No. Calif. Forensic Pathology, Sacramento, 1990—; asst. clin. prof. pathology Loma Linda U. Sch. Medicine, 1987-90, U. Calif., Davis, 1990—; program dir., forensic pathology fellowship NCFP/U. Calif. Davis, 1994—; apptd. Calif. SIDS Autopsy Protocol Com. Contbr. articles to profl. jours. Fellow Am. Soc. Clin. Pathologists, Am. Coll. Forensic Examiners; mem. Am. Bd. Forensic Examiners, AMA, Internat. Wound Ballistics Assn., Nat. Assn. Med. Examiners, Am. Acad. Forensic Scis., Calif. Med. Assn., Sacramento-El Dorado Med. Soc., Alpha Omega Alpha. Republican. Seventh-day Adventist. Office: No Calif Forensic Pathology 2443 Fair Oaks Blvd Ste 311 Sacramento CA 95825-7684

REICHARD, GARY WARREN, university administrator, history educator; b. Phila., Nov. 23, 1943; s. David Carl and Gabrielle Rosalind (Doane) R.; m. Marcia Ann King, Aug. 7, 1965 (div. 1978); children: Jennifer D., James J. BA, Coll. of Wooster (Ohio), 1965; MA, Vanderbilt U., Nashville, 1966; postgrad., Ohio U., 1966-67; PhD, Cornell U., 1971. Instr. history Coll. of Wooster, 1967-69; asst. prof. to assoc. prof. history, chmn. dept. Ohio State U., Columbus, 1971-82; assoc. prof. history and dir. univ. honors program U. Del., Newark, 1983-85; assoc. vice chancellor for acad. affairs, assoc. prof. hist. U. Md., College Park, 1985-89; prof. history and dean undergrad. studies Fla. Atlantic U., Boca Raton, Fla., 1989-92; chmn. dept. history Fla. Atlantic U., Boca Raton, 1992-94; assoc. vice pres. acad. affairs, prof. history Calif. State U., Long Beach, 1994—. Assoc. editor Ency. of Am. Legislative System; reviewer numerous comml. and univ. presses; author: The Reaffirmation of Republicanism, 1975, Politics as Usual, 1988; co-author: America: Changing Times, 1979, 2d edit., 1982; co-editor: Reshaping America, 1982, American Choices, 1986, American Issues, 1988, 2d edit., 1994; contbr. articles to profl. jours. Moody rsch. grantee Lyndon B. Johnson found., 1977, Harry S. Truman Libr. Inst. rsch. grantee, 1979, Congl. Leadership rsch. grantee, 1981, Carl Albert Congl. rsch. grantee, 1993, Minn. Hist. Soc. grantee, 1993. Mem. Am. Assn. Higher Edn., Am. Hist. Assn., Orgn. Am. Historians, Immigration Hist. Soc., Phi Beta Kappa, Phi Kappa Phi. Office: Calif State U Long Beach Divsn Acad Affairs 1250 N Bellflower Blvd Long Beach CA 90840-0006

REICHEL, JOHN KENTO, small business owner, writer; b. Oakland, Calif., Dec. 28, 1959; s. David and Hisae (Kawashima) R. BA, U. Calif., Berkeley, 1982. Lab. asst. Kaiser Permanente Med. Care Program, Berkeley, 1978-84; editor Kaiser Permanente, Oakland, Calif., 1984-91; standards analyst, contbr. to corp. mag. Kaiser Permanente, Walnut Creek, Calif., 1991-95; hobby shop propr., 1996—. Contbr. music revs. and articles to various publs. Named Pivot Pin, Teen Assn. Model Railroaders, 1990. Democrat.

REICHEL, PHILIP LEE, sociology educator; b. Bakersfield, Calif., Oct. 8, 1946; s. Joseph J. and Virginia (Spry) R.; m. Paula Jean Hauschild, June 1969 (div. 1980); children: Scott Andrew, Matthew Jason; m. Eva Maria Jewell, Dec. 15, 1983. BS, Nebr. Wesleyan U., 1969; MA, Kans. State U., 1972, PhD, 1979. Classification officer Nebr. Penal and Correctional Complex, Lincoln, 1970-71; assoc. prof. Augusta (Ga.) Coll., 1972-83, U. No. Colo., Greeley, 1983-91; full prof. U. No. Colo., 1991—; dir. criminal justice studies U. No. Colo., Greeley, 1983-93. Author: Comparative Criminal Justice Systems: A Topical Approach, 1994, Corrections, 1997; contbr. articles to profl. jours. Advisor United Way Greeley, 1989, 93; bd. dirs. Planned Parenthood, Augusta, 1982, Legal Aid Soc., Greeley, 1993—. Named Favorite Prof., Mortar Bd., U. No. Colo., 1985, 87, 89, 90, 92, 94, 95. Mem. Acad. Criminal Justice Scis. (program com. mem. 1995). Democrat. Home: 2506 57th Ave Greeley CO 80634-4506 Office: U No Colo Sociology Dept Greeley CO 80639

REICHMAN, HENRY FREDERICK, history educator; b. N.Y.C., Feb. 10, 1947; s. Charles and Vera (Stein) R.; m. Susan Alyne Hutcher, June 27, 1976; children: Daniel, Alice. AB, Columbia Coll., 1969; PhD, U. Calif., Berkeley, 1977. Instr. U. Calif., Berkeley, 1975-76; lectr. history U. Calif., San Diego, 1978; asst. prof. history Northwestern U., Evanston, Ill., 1979-80; asst. dir. office for intellectual freedom Am. Libr. Assn., Chgo., 1980-81; asst. prof. history Memphis State U., 1983-89; asst. prof. history Calif. State U., Hayward, 1989-91, assoc. prof. history, 1991-96, prof. history, 1996—; vis. asst. prof. history U. Calif., Davis, 1989; chair dept. history Calif. State U., 1994—; assoc. editor newsletter on intellectual freedom Am. Libr. Assn., 1982—. Author: Railwaymen and Revolution: Russia, 1905, 1987, Censorship and Selection, 1988, rev. edit., 1993; contbr. articles to profl. jours. Mem. Am. Hist. Assn., Am. Assn. for Advancement of Slavic Studies, Freedom to Read Found., Phi Beta Kappa. Democrat. Jewish. Office: Calif State U Dept History Hayward CA 94542

REICHMAN, RONALD PETER, medical educator; b. Chgo., Jan. 18, 1951; s. Heinz Charles and Margot Reichman; m. Carolyn Elizabeth Kean, May 27, 1984. BA in Psychology, UCLA, 1973, MD, 1977. Diplomate Nat. Bd. Med. Examiners, Am. Bd. Internal Medicine, Am. Bd. Rheumatology. Lab. asst., technician dept. biochemistry UCLA, 1971-73, teaching asst. dept. psychology, 1972-73, rsch. asst. dept. psychology, 1973, lab. technician hemodialysis unit med. ctr., 1973-74, med. curriculum evaluation com., 1973-75, lab. technician cardiopulmonmary procedure rm. med. ctr., 1974-75; jr. resident Cedars-Sinai Med. Ctr., Fresno, 1978-79; sr. resident internal medicine Cedars-Sinai Med. Ctr., 1979-80; fellow in Rheumatology Cedars Sinai Med. Ctr./ UCLA, 1981-82, sr. fellow in Rheumatology, 1982-83, asst. clin. prof. Medicine, 1983—; housestaff liaison nursing recruitment and retainment com. Valley Med. Ctr. Fresno, Calif., 1977-78, intern in internal medicine, 1977-78, jr. resident in internal medicine, 1978; cons. Calif. State Office Emergency Svcs., 1980—; pvt. cons., med. tech. advisor TV and motion pictures, 1980—; guest speaker Am. Medicine Writers Assn. Conv., 1982; med. advisor Antelope Valley chpt. Am. Lupus Soc., 1983—; pres. San Vicente Rehab., Inc., 1985-89; med. adv. bd. Ankylosing Spondylitis Assn., 1985—; media contact physician Am. Coll. Rheumatology, 1992—; qualified med. evaluator Indsl. Med. Coun., State of Calif., 1992—. Author: (with others) Progress in Clinical Rheumatology, 1984; contbr. articles to profl. jours. Bd. dirs. Good Beginnings Charitable Found., 1985—. Fellow Am. Rheumatism Assn.; mem. AMA (physician adv. panel to TV, motion pictures and radio 1980—), Am. Coll. Physicians, Calif. Med. Assn., So. Calif. Rheumatism Assn., L.A. County Med. Assn., Medicus Assn., Phi Beta Kappa, Pi Gamma Mu, Phi Eta Sigma, Pi Lambda Phi, Phi Delta Epsilon.

REID, BELMONT MERVYN, brokerage house executive; b. San Jose, Calif., May 17, 1927; s. C. Belmont and Mary Irene (Kilfoyl) R. BS in Engring., San Jose State U., 1950, postgrad.; m. Evangeline Joan Rogers, June 1, 1952. Pres., Lifetime Realty Corp., San Jose, 1969-77, Lifetime Fin. Planning Corp., San Jose, 1967-77; founder, chmn. bd. Belmont Reid & Co., Inc., San Jose, 1960-77; pres., registered investment advisor JOBEL Fin. Inc., Carson City, Nev., 1980—; pres., chmn. bd. Data-West Systems, Inc., 1984-85. County chmn. 1982-85, Carson City Rep. Cen. Com., treas., 1979-81; chmn. Carson City Gen. Obligation Bond Commn., 1986—; rural county chmn. Nev. Rep. Cen. Com., 1984-88; mem. Carson City Charter Rev. Com., 1986-91, chmn., 1988-91. With USN, 1945-46, 51-55. Decorated Air medals. Mem. Nat. Assn. Securities Dealers, Mcpl. Securities Rulemaking Bd., Carson City C. of C. (pres. 1986-87, bd. dir. 1982-88), Capital Club of Carson City, Rotary (chpt. sec. 1983-84, 86-87, pres. 1988-89, Paul Harris fellow). Home: 610 Bonanza Dr Carson City NV 89706-0201 Office: 711 E Washington St Carson City NV 89701-4063

REID, CHRISTOPHER ERVIN, mathematician, software engineer; b. Indpls., Oct. 22, 1950; s. Marshall George and Marian (Ossman) R.; m. Jane Ellen Gallup, Sept. 16, 1972; children: Tobias, Alexander, Hannah, Obadiah. Student, U. Mo., Rolla, 1969-71; BS in Physics, Ohio State U., 1973, postgrad. in physics, 1973-74, MS in Math., 1977. Instr.physics Ohio State U., 1973-75, instr. math., 1975-81; with MITRE Corp., 1981-91, team leader Adaptive High Frequency Comm. Network, 1981-84, software engr. dept. automatic speech recognition, 1984-87, software engr., 1987-91; with Cadence Design Systems, 1991-95; owner Reid Assocs., 1992—; with Interconnectix Inc., 1995—. Author: (with Thomas B. Passin) Signal Processing in C, 1992; (software) DSP Environment, DSP Source Code Library. Methodist. Home: 9315 SW Lake St Portland OR 97223-6034

REID, HARRY, senator; b. Searchlight, Nev., Dec. 2, 1939; s. Harry and Inez Reid; m. Landra Joy Gould; children—Lana, Rory, Leif, Josh, Key. AS, Southern Utah State U., 1959; LLD (hon.), U. So. Utah, 1984; BA, Utah State U., 1961; JD, George Washington U., 1964. Senator, chmn. dem. policy com. 104th Congress U.S. Senate, Washington; mem. appropriations, ethics/environment & pub. works, Indian affairs coms. *

REID, MEGAN BETH, museum administrator; b. Durango, Colo., May 1, 1954; d. Charles Henry Jr. and Jean Phyllis (Siegfried) R. BA in Studio Art, Ft. Lewis Coll., 1975; postgrad., U. Minn., 1977-79. Intern U. Minn. Gallery, Mpls., 1978-79; curator Dacotah Prairie Mus., Aberdeen, S.D., 1980, dir., 1981-82; exhibit technician Fulton (Tex.) Mansion State Hist. Structure, Tex. State Pks., 1983-84, pk. supt./mus. dir., 1985; dir. Rio Colo. div. Ariz. Hist. Soc., Yuma, 1985—; exhibit designer and constuctor, 1980—. Living history researcher and performer, 1985—; contbr. articles to profl. publs., 1985—. Bd. dirs. cultural coun. and hist. designation rev. com. City of Yuma, 1985—; bd.dirs. Main St. Com., 1988-94; cons. S.D. Arts Coun., 1982, Ariz. Arts Coun.-Tribal Mus. Assessment Program, 1990. Art pruchase grantee NEA, 1981-82, gen. operating grantee Inst. Mus. Svcs., 1981-82, grantee Ariz. Humanities Coun., 1987—, various bldg. preservation grantee Ariz. State Hist. Preservation Office, 1985—. Mem. Am. Assn. Mus., Nat. Trust for Hist. Preservation, Assn. State and Local History, Western Assn. Mus., Ariz. Mus. Assn. (cons. 1990, bd. dirs. 1993—), Mt. Plains Mus. Assn. Office: Ariz Hist Soc 240 S Madison Ave Yuma AZ 85364-1421

REID, ROBERT TILDEN, medical association administrator, internist; b. Dallas, Feb. 20, 1931; s. Robert Tilden and Gldays Tressy (King) R.; divorced; children: Robert Tilden, Richard Thomas, Annette Marie, Randolph Young. BS, So. Meth. U., Dallas, 1957; MD, U. Tex.-Southwestern, Dallas, 1959. Diplomate Am. Bd. Internal Medicine, Am. Bd. Rheumatology, Am. Bd. Allergy and Immunology. Intern Parkland Meml. Hosp., Dallas, 1959-60, resident, 1960-63; with Scripps Clinic and Rsch., La Jollla, Calif., 1963-70; pvt. practice La Jollla, Calif., 1970—; chief staff Scripps Meml. Hosp., La Jollla, Calif., 1976-78; scientific dir. Erik and Ese Banck Clinical Rsch. Ctr., San Diego, 1994—. Mem. San Diego County Med. Soc. (pres. 1991), Calif. Med. Assn. (trustee 1992-95). Office: 9850 Genesee Ave Ste 860 La Jolla CA 92037-1219 also: Erik & Ese Banck Clinical Rsch 12395 El Camino Real Ste 117 San Diego CA 92130-3083

REID, WALLACE LEO, manufacturing executive; b. Indpls., Dec. 30, 1924; s. Norman Oscar and Margaret (Quinn) R.; m. Jean Marie Berry, May 21, 1942; children: Kelly, Tim, Denise. Chmn. Fur Wardrobe, 1978; CEO Holiday Furs, 1969; pres. Hall Reid Fur Co., 1949; fur cutter Furrier Ind. Fur Co., 1949. Designer: Luster Life Cleaning Process, 1949, TVRC Garment Weather Vane, 1959. Served with USMC, 1941-45. Roman Catholic. Home: 45 E 56th St Long Beach CA 90805

REIDY, RICHARD ROBERT, publishing company executive; b. Patchogue, N.Y., May 9, 1947; s. Joseph Robert and Irene (Jennings) R.; m. Carolyn Alyce Armstrong, Mar. 21, 1970; children: Dawn Patricia, Shawn Patrick, Christopher Keith. Student, Suffolk County Community Coll., 1966-68, L.I. Tech. Sch., 1969-70, Scottsdale Community Coll., 1983-84, 85-86. Lic. real estate agt., Ariz. Restaurant owner Reidy's, Patchogue, 1973-77; design draftsman Sverdrop & Parcel, Tempe, Ariz., 1978-79, Sullivan & Masson, Phoenix, 1979-81; pres. Success Pub. Co., Scottsdale, Ariz., 1983—; with U.S. Postal Dept., 1980—. Editor, owner, pub.: Who's Who in Arizona, 1984-85, 89-90. Chief Scottsdale YMCA, 1983-84; eucharistic minister St. Daniel the Prophet Cath. Ch., Scottsdale, 1985—; mem. World Wide Marriage Encounter, 1986—; pres. Coronado High Sch. Band Boosters, 1988-89. Mem. Scottsdale C. of C., Phoenix Better Bus. Bur. Office: Success Pub Co PO Box 3431 Scottsdale AZ 85271-3431

REIERSON, LAWRENCE EDWARD, organizational development consultant, executive; b. Astoria, Oreg., Feb. 27, 1934; s. Lawrence Engvold and Edith Fay (Raymond) R.; m. Gail Lorene Gronnel, Apr. 23, 1954 (div. June 1967); children: Careen Jump, Lorrie; m. Star Ellis Van Valkenburgh, Dec. 13,1969; stepchildren: Candalee Olstedt, Lonnie Foster. Student, Portland State U., 1957-59; MS in Orgn. Devel., Pepperdine U., 1977. With Tektronix, Inc., Beaverton, Oreg., 1959-79, mgr. mgmt. devel., 1974-77, mgr. employee devel., 1977-79; dir. mgmt. devel. Weyerhaeuser Co., Tacoma, 1979-82; mgr. adminstrn. Pro-Log Cos., Monterey, Calif., 1982-85; chmn., CEO, bd. dirs. Saltwater Inst., Monterey, 1986—; cons. U. Oreg. Med. Sch., Portland, 1967-70, Oreg. State System Higher Edn., Portland, 1966-70; sr. faculty mem. Mahler Assocs. Advanced Mgmt. Skills Program, Fair Lawn, N.J., 1986—. Contbr. articles to profl. publs. Mem. Oreg. Sci. Edn. Coun., Portland, 1966-72. Mem. Monterey C. of C. (bd. dirs. 1986). Office: Saltwater Inst Ste 210 411 Pacific St Monterey CA 93940

REIF, (FRANK) DAVID, artist, educator; b. Cin., Dec. 14, 1941; s. Carl A. and Rachel L. (Clifton) R.; m. Ilona Jekabsons, July 30, 1966; 1 child, Megan Elizabeth. BFA, Art Inst. Chgo., 1968; MFA, Yale U., 1970. Asst. prof. art U. Wyo., Laramie, 1970-74, assoc. prof., 1974-81, prof., 1981—; assoc. prof. U. Mich., Ann Arbor, 1980-81; acting head dept. art U. Wyo., Laramie, 1986-87; selection cons. Ucross Found. Residency Program, Wyo., 1983—; exhibit juror Artwest Nat., Jackson, Wyo., 1986; panelist Colo. State U., Ft. Collins, 1981; lectr. U. Mich., 1980; apptd. Wyo. Arts Coun., 1993—; vis. artist lectr. Colo. State U., 1996; vis. artist Colo. State U., Ft. Collins, 1996. One-man shows include U. Wyo. Art Mus., 1993, Dorsky Galleries, N.Y.C., 1980, No. Ariz. U., 1977, 87, U. Mich., 1980, 81, One West Ctr. Contemporary Art, Ft. Collins, 1991; exhibited in group shows at First, Second and Third Who. Biennial Tour, 1984-88, U.S. Olympics Art Exhbn., L.A., 1984, Miss. Mus. Art and NEA Tour, 1981-83, L.A. Invitational Sculpture Tour Exhbn., 1991-92, Nicolaysen Art Mus., Casper, Wyo., 1994. Apptd. chair Wyo. Arts Coun., 1995-96. With USAR, 1963-69. Recipient F.D. Pardee award Yale U., 1970; Best Sculpture award Joslyn Art Mus. Omaha, 1978; Nat. Endowment Arts grantee, 1978-79, Wyo. Basic Rsch. grantee, 1983-84, 86-87. Mem. Coll. Art Assn., Internat. Sculpture Ctr. Democrat. Home: 3340 Aspen Ln Laramie WY 82070-5702 Office: U Wyo Dept Art PO Box 3138 Laramie WY 82071-3138

REIF, MARY ELLEN, neurologist; b. Rock Island, Ill., Oct. 10, 1953; m. H.B. Edwards, Oct. 31, 1988; children: Conner, Lauren. BS, U. Iowa, 1975, MD, 1978. Intern U. Utah, 1978-79; intern U. Wash., Seattle, 1978-79, resident in neurology, 1979-82; pvt. practice Seattle, 1982—. Mem. Am. Acad. Neurology. Office: 1229 Madison Ste 1110 Seattle WA 98104-1357

REIFF, THEODORE CURTIS, construction executive; b. Cleve., Aug. 6, 1942; s. William Fred and Dorothy Louise (Knauer) R.; m. Janis Lynn Brunk, May 6, 1966 (div. Aug. 1980); m. Theresa Dolores Baranello, Oct. 30, 1982 (div. Dec. 1992). BS, Ohio State U., 1969. Lic. real estate broker, demolition contractor. Dir. adminstrv. svcs. Mgmt. Horizons, Inc., Columbus, Ohio, 1969-73; v.p. Danco Mgmt. Co., Lancaster, Ohio, 1973-74; sr. v.p. Anchor Lighting Corp., Columbus, 1974-75; ptnr. Curtis-Lee & Assocs., Delaware, Ohio, 1974-77; pres. Cartunes Corp., San Diego, Calif., 1977-91; also bd. dirs. Cartunes Corp., San Diego; facilities coord. Raytheon Co., Burlington, Mass., 1979-82; ptnr. Greenstone & Reiff, San Diego, 1982-86; pres. Creative Bus. Strategies, Inc., San Diego, 1986—, pres., bd. dirs.; pres. Bus. Pubs. Inc., San Diego, 1989-91, also bd. dirs.; mng. dir. PM Co., Tijuana, B.C., Mex., 1991-94; co-founder, pres. Bldg. Materials Distbrs., San Diego, 1994—, also bd. trustees; co-founder, treas. Materiales de Construccion de Baja California, Tijuana, Mex., 1995-97, also bd. dirs.; co-founder, ptnr. Las Mas Barata, Tijuana, Mex.; bd. dirs. Integrated Ceramic Tech., San Marcos, Calif., 1986-88, Pacific Rim Interface Mems. Enterprises Inc., 1988-90, Distributed Comm. Corp., San Diego, 1990-91, Phoenix Systems & Techs., Chula Vista, Calif., 1990-91; instr. Miramar Coll., San Diego, 1984-90. Mem. Friends of San Diego Zoo, 1980—; chmn. bus. adv. com. San Diego State U. Coll. of Bus., 1979-82; mem. adv. com. Coll. Bus. Calif. State U., 1992-94. With Ohio N.G., 1966-72. Named Outstanding Businessman City of Columbus, Ohio, 1974; recipient Recognition award San Diego State U. Coll. of Bus., 1983, Appreciation award Am. Mktg. Assn., 1984, IEEE, 1986. Mem. Am. Electronics Assn. (chmn. small bus. com. 1988-89, chmn. fin. com. 1989-91.). Home: 3946 Murray Hill Rd La Mesa CA 91941-7649

REIHEL, RONALD ERNEST, pilot; b. Berwyn, Ill., Aug. 16, 1941; s. Elmer and Ella Reihel; m. Mary Kathleen Pellicer, June 30, 1963; children: Ronald E. Jr., Margaret Jennifer. BS in Math., U.S. Naval Acad., 1963; MS in Indsl. Engring., Stanford (Calif.) U., 1964. Pilot Ea. Airlines, Miami, Fla., 1970-89; B747 pilot, instr. pilot United Airlines, Denver, 1992-97, B-747-400 pilot, 1997—; master coord. Shaklee Corp., San Francisco, 1972—. Airport Commn. mem. Ocean Reef Club, Key Largo, Fla., 1981-86. Col. USAF, 1963-71, USAFR, 1971-93. Selected Outstanding Dep. Comdr. for Resource Mgmt., USAFR, 1989, IMA Chief of Programs, 1990-93. Mem. U.S. Naval Acad. Alumni Assn., U.S. Naval Acad. Athletic Assn. (baseball most valuable player 1963), Ocean Reef Club, Silver Falcons.

REILLEY, KATHLEEN PATRICIA, lawyer; b. Pitts., Oct. 31, 1948; d. Edward Michael and Mary Elizabeth (Davidson) R. BA, U. Calif., Berkeley, 1976; JD, Golden Gate U., 1979. Bar: Calif. Staff atty. Fresno County Legal Svcs., Calif., 1979-85, Santa Monica (Calif.) Rent Control Bd., 1985-89; asst. city atty. City of Berkeley, 1990-91; atty. Linda DeBene Inc., Danville, Calif., 1991-94. Co-founder Calif. Housing Action & Info. Network, 1976. Mem. Calif. State Bar Assn. (real property and litigation sect.). Democrat. Episcopalian. Office: 1563 Solano Ave # 528 Berkeley CA 94707-2116

REILLY, ROBERT JOSEPH, counselor; b. Spokane, Wash., Mar. 7, 1936; s. John Francis and Vivian Helen (White) R.; m. Joan Steiner, June 20, 1960; children: Sean Michael, Patrick Joseph, Bridget Colleen. BA in Psychology, Seattle U., 1985; postgrad., Infantry Officer Candidate Sch, Ft. Benning, 1960, EOAC, Ft. Belvoir, 1968, Leadership Inst. Seattle/City U., 1991-92. Ordained Congl. Ch. Practical Theology, 1992. Enlisted U.S. Army, 1953, advanced through grades to maj., 1981, ret., 1981; with U.S. Army, Korea, 1961-62, Vietnam, 1966-69; counseling supr. Schick Shadel Hosp., Seattle, 1984-89; dir. Canyon Counseling, Puyallup, Wash., 1987-92, 95—; social worker Wash. State Employee Adv. Svc., Olympia, 1992—; v.p. Nat. Bd. for Hypnotherapy and Hypnotic Anaesthesiology, 1991-97, pres. Wash. chpt. 1991-94; exec. v.p. Coll. Therapeutic Hypnosis, Puyallup, 1989-94; mem. adj. faculty Pierce Coll., Tacoma, 1991-92. Pres. Irish Cultural Club, Tacoma, 1983-85, 93-94; sec. Tacoma chpt. Ret. Officers Assn., 1983-87, pres., 1993-96, bd. dirs., 1992-97. Decorated Vietnamese Cross of Gallantry with silver star, Bronze Star with oak leaf cluster, Army Commendation medal with 2 oak leaf clusters; named Profl. of Yr. Chem. Dependency Profls. Wash., 1994. Mem. Nat. Bd. Hypnotherapy and Hypnotic Anesthesiology (v.p. 1991-97, Mem of Yr. 1994, pres. Wash. chpt. 1991-94), Nat. Guild Hypnotists, Nat. Assn. Alcohol and Drug Abuse Counselors (mem. del. Russia & Czech Rep. 1996), Am. Congress Hypnotist Examiners, Army Engr. Assn., Nat. 4th Inf. Divsn. Assn. (sec.-treas. N.W. chpt. 1993—), Employee Assistance Profls. Assn. Office: Wash State Employee Adv Svc PO Box 47540 Olympia WA 98504-7540

REILLY, WILLIAM KANE, former government official, educator, lawyer, conservationist; b. Decatur, Ill., Jan. 26, 1940; s. George P. and Margaret (Kane) M.; m. Elizabeth Buxton; children: Katherine, Megan. B.A. in History, Yale U., 1962; J.D., Harvard U., 1965; M.S. in Urban Planning, Columbia U., 1971. Bar: Ill., Mass. 1965. Atty. firm Ross & Hardies, Chgo., 1965; asso. dir. Urban Policy Center, Urban Am., Inc., also Nat. Urban Coalition, Washington, 1969-70; sr. staff mem. Pres.'s Council Environ. Quality, 1970-72; exec. dir. Task Force Land Use and Urban Growth, 1972-73; pres. Conservation Found., Washington, 1973-89, World Wildlife Fund, Washington, 1985-89; adminstr. U.S. EPA, Washington, 1989-93; chmn. Natural Resources Coun. Am., 1982-83; head U.S. del. Earth Summit, 1992; head U.S. del. to negotiate Amendments to Montreal Protocol on the Ozone Layer, 1990, 92; Payne vis. prof. Stanford U., 1993-94, vis. prof. 1994—; assoc. Tex. Pacific Group, San Francisco, 1994—; chmn. bd. dirs. Clean Sites, Inc.; bd. dirs. Allied Waste Industries, Inc., Am. Farmland Trust, E.I. DuPont de Nemours and Co., Evergreen Holdings, Inc., German Marshall Fund of the U.S., Nat. Geog. Soc., Ptnrs. for Livable Communities, World Wildlife Fund, Yale U.; mem. sci. adv. bd. The Nature Conservancy. Editor: The Use of Land, 1973, Environment Strategy America, 1994-96; author articles in field, chpts. in books. Served to capt., CIC U.S. Army, 1966-67. Clubs: University (Washington), Univ. (N.Y.C.). Office: care World Wildlife Fund 1250 24th St NW Washington DC 20037-1175

REIM, RUTHANN, career and personal counselor, corporate trainer; b. Fresno, Calif., Oct. 4, 1943; d. F. Wayne and Charlene Marie (Young) Howd; m. Terry D., Nov. 29, 1963; children: Tracey, Brandon. BA in Sociology, San Jose State U., 1966; MA Guidance & Counseling, Pacific Luth. U., 1984. Cert. counselor, nat. Tchr., elem. sch. Dupont Sch. Dist., Tacoma, 1966-67, Prince Georges Sch. Dist., Lanham, Md., 1967-68, Franklin Pierce sch. Dist., Tacoma, 1968-70; owner Rainbow Glassworks, Tacoma, 1973-76, Creative Womanlife, Tacoma, 1976-78; dir., counselor Individual Devel. Ctr., Tacoma, 1984-88; pres. Career Mgmt. Inst., Tacoma, 1989—; adj. faculty mem. dept. edn. Pacific Luth. U., 1980-84. Author: (career booklet) Career Change Made Easy, 1990; artist 5' round stained glass window "Dogwood", 1980. Trainer Jr. League Tacoma, 1977-79. Mem. Rotary (1st woman pres. 1991-92, bd. dirs. 1988—), Phi Kappa Phi. Office: Career Mgmt Inst 8404 27th St W Tacoma WA 98466-2723

REIMNITZ, ELROI, minister; b. Porto Alegre, Brazil, June 20, 1948; s. Elmer and Kordula Luise (Schelp) R.; m. Ruth Weimer, June 16, 1973; children: Patrick, Kristeen, Nicholas. Diploma, Seminario Concordia, Porto Alegre, 1966; postgrad., Faculdade Porto-Alegrense E.C.L., 1968; MDiv, Concordia Sem., St. Louis, 1971, ThD, 1975; postdoctoral studies, Faculdade de Direito I.R.R., Canoas, Brazil, 1976-77, Faith Luth. Sem., Tacoma, 1990-92. Ordained to ministry Luth. Ch.-Mo. Synod, 1975. Vicar Immanuel Luth. Ch., Bristol, Conn., 1969-70; asst. to pastor Our Savior's 1st Luth. Ch., Granada Hills, Calif., 1974-75; pastor Zion Luth. Ch., Alamo, Tex., 1975, St. John's Luth. Ch., Canoas, 1976-78; pastor, dir. ministries Trinity Luth. Ch., Grand Island, Nebr., 1978-86; pastor Redeemer Luth. Ch., Thousand Oaks, Calif., 1986—; 1990-93; instr. U. Luterana do Brasil, Canoas, 1976-78; adminstrv. dir. Cultural Lang. Inst., Canoas, 1976-78; supt. Trinity Luth. Sch., Grand Island, 1978-86; treas. Grand Island cir. Nebr. dist. Luth. Ch.-Mo. Synod, 1984-86; chaplain police, sheriff and fire depts. City of Grand Island, 1985-86; counselor campus ministry Calif. Luth. U., Thousand Oaks, 1986—; adj. faculty mem. Trinity Theol. Sem., Newburgh, Ind., 1993—. Contbr. articles to religious jours. Adv. mem. Grand Island Luth. Family and Social Svcs., 1985-86; mem. programs com. Cen. Platte Natural Resources Dist., 1985-86; site coun. Cypress Elem. Sch., Newbury Park, Calif., 1987-88, Community Devel. Allocation Com., Thousand Oaks, 1991-92; bd. dirs. Casas De La Senda Homeowners Assn., Newbury Park, 1986—, Citizens Quality of Life Action Alliance, Thousand Oaks, 1992-93; alt. mem. ad hoc com. Newbury Park Libr., 1987-90, Newbury Park High Sch. Site Coun., 1992-93; treas. circ. one pacific s.w. dist. Luth. Ch. Mo., Synod, 1991—, mem. social svcs. funding com., Thousand Oaks, 1993-94; bd. dirs. AYSO, 1993-95; commr. Traffic and Transp. Adv. Commn., Thousand Oaks, 1993-95; vol. World Cup USA, 1994, L.A. Venue, 1994; assoc. mem. Rep. State Ctrl. Com. Calif., 1995—. Home: 3883 San Marcos Ct Newbury Park CA 91320-3725 Office: Redeemer Luth Ch 667 Camino Dos Rios Thousand Oaks CA 91360-2354

REINER, ANNIE, writer, psychotherapist; b. May 11, 1949. BA, UCLA, 1973; MSW, U. So. Calif., 1975. Self employed psychotherapist Beverly Hills, Calif., 1991-96; lectr. in psychoanalysis. Author: (poetry) The Naked I, 1994, (short stories) This Nervous Breakdown Is Driving Me Crazy, 1996, (essay) Infancy and the Essential Nature of Work included in anthology Work and Its Inhibitions, 1996; author 4 children's books, Winner of Golden award for Best Audio of 1996, from Parents Choice for Dancing In the Park, 1996. Mem. Nat. Assn. Social Workers, Soc. Clin. Social Work. Office: 436 N Roxbury Dr Ste 208 Beverly Hills CA 90210-5017

REINER, JAMES ANTHONY, marketing executive; b. Orange, Calif., Sept. 12, 1958; s. Earl Arthur and Mary Ann (Cuff) R. BBA in Acctg., U. Mo., 1983, MBA in Mktg., 1984. Mktg. intern Seven-UP Co., St. Louis, 1984-85; mktg. analyst Rawlings Sporting Goods, St. Louis, 1992-94; mktg. mgr. Rawlings Sporting Goods Co., St. Louis, 1986-88; product mgr. Con Agra Consumer Frozen Food Co., St. Louis, 1988-89, sr. product mgr., 1989-90, group product mgr., 1990-91, dir. mktg., 1991-92; dir. diversification Samsonite Corp., Denver, 1992-94; pres. Global Voyager Corp., Denver, 1994-95; v.p. sales and mktg. Outdoor Recreation Group, L.A., 1995—. Mem. Am. Mktg. Assn., Alpha Mu Alpha (hon.). Republican. Home: 3608 Barham Blvd Apt U229 Los Angeles CA 90068-1106

REINERS, WILLIAM ARNOLD, botany educator; b. Chgo., June 10, 1937; s. Bernard Martin and Catharine Louise (Amidon) R.; m. Norma Marilyn Miller, Apr. 21, 1962; children: Peter William, Derek Seth. BA, Knox Coll., 1959; MS, Rutgers U., 1962, PhD, 1964. From instr. to asst. prof. U. Minn., Mpls., 1964-67; from asst. prof. to prof. Dartmouth Coll., Hanover, N.H., 1967-83; dept. chmn. Dartmouth Coll., Hanover, 1982-83; prof. U. Wyo., Laramie, 1983—, dept. head, 1983-96, J.E. Warren prof. energy and environment, 1996—; program dir. NSF, Washington, 1976-77; fellow Wissenschaftskolleg zu Berlin, Germany, 1989-90. Contbr. articles to profl. jours. 2d lt. U.S. Army, 1959-60. Named H.J. Oosting lectr. Dept. Botany, Duke U., Durham, N.C., 1981; recipient U. Wyo. Presdl. award for scholarly work. Mem. AAAS, Am. Geophys. Union, Ecol. Soc. Am. (treas. 1981-84), Internat. Assn. Landscape Ecology, Soil Sci. Soc. Am. Unitarian-Universalist. Office: Univ Wyo Dept Botany PO Box 3165 Laramie WY 82071

REINESS, C(ECIL) GARY, biology educator; b. Pitts., Aug. 20, 1945; s. Meyer Reiness and Esther Lee (Butler) Black; 1 child, Daniel Evan. BA in Chemistry, Johns Hopkins U., 1967; MPhil, Columbia U., 1974, PhD in Biol. Scis., 1975. Rsch. fellow dept. neurobiology Harvard Med. Sch., 1975-76; postdoctoral scholar dept. physiology U. Calif., San Francisco, 1976-81; from asst. prof. to assoc. prof. biology Pomona Coll., Claremont, Calif., 1981-93, prof., 1993, chair dept. biology, 1988-90; assoc. dean of the coll. Pomona Coll., Claremont, 1990-93; prof., chair biology Lewis and Clark Coll., Portland, Oreg., 1994—; vis. assoc. prof. anatomy and neurobiology Washington U. Med. Sch., St. Louis, 1987-88. Contbr. numerous articles to profl. jours. Gen. Motors scholar, 1963-67; NIH fellow, 1970-73, Muscular Dystrophy Assn. fellow, 1976-78, NIH postdoctoral fellow, 1978-80, Calif. Cancer Soc. postdoctoral fellow, 1980-81; grantee NSF, Am. Heart Assn., others. Mem. AAAS, Am. Soc. for Cell Biology, N.Y. Acad. Scis., Soc. for Neurosci. Coun. on Undergrad. Rsch., Phi Beta Kappa, Sigma Xi, Phi Lambda Upsilon. Office: Lewis and Clark Coll Biology Dept 0615 SW Palatine Hill Rd Portland OR 97219-7879

REINFELDS, JURIS, computer science educator; b. Riga, Latvia, Apr. 1, 1936; came to U.S., 1989; s. Nikolais Janis and Irma (Kaulins) R.; m. Lauma Petersons, Sept. 15, 1962; children: Peteris Maris, Ivars Valdis, Martins Nikolais. BSc, U. Adelaide, Australia, 1959; PhD, U. Adelaide, 1963; postdoctoral work, ICI. Postdoctoral fellow U. Edinburgh, Scotland, 1961-64; postdoctoral rsch. fellow U. Adelaide, Australia, 1964-65; NSF postdoctoral rsch. assoc. NASA, Huntsville, Ala., 1965-66; asst. prof. computer sci. U. Ga., Athens, 1966-72; vis. scientist CERN, Geneva, 1972-75; found. prof. computer sci. U. Wollongong NSW, Australia, 1975-89; prof. computer sci. N.Mex. State U., Las Cruces, 1989—; cons. Australian Internat. Devel. Program, Hat Yai, Thailand, 1983-91, Los Banos, Philippines, 1983-90. Mem. IEEE Computer Soc., Assn. for Computer Machinery, Australian Computer Soc., Las Cruces Rotary Club. Office: NMex State U Klipsch Sch Elec & Computer Engring Dept 3-0 Las Cruces NM 88003-8001 also: 445 E Cheyenne Mtn Blvd # C-368 Colorado Springs CO 80906-4570

REINHARD, RAYMOND MILLER, public policy analyst, consultant; b. Mt. Kisco, N.Y., Aug. 3, 1953; s. T. Joseph Brant and Doris M. (Bruning) Reinhard; m. Catherine Marion Genetti, July 11, 1987; children: Michael Christopher, Jeremy Matthew. AB in Econs., Dartmouth Coll., 1974; M in Pub. Policy, U. Calif., Berkeley, 1978. Rsch. assoc. The Urban Inst., Washington, 1978-79; program analyst Legis. Analyst's Office, Sacramento, 1979-83, K-12 edn. supr., 1983-91; dep. sec. child devel. and edn. Gov.'s Office, Sacramento, 1991-96; dir. Rsch. Inst. Sch. Svcs. Calif., Inc., Sacramento, 1996—. Pub. Svc. Edn. scholar U.S. Dept. HEW, 1976-78. Mem. Phi Beta Kappa. Office: Sch Svcs Calif 1121 L St # 1060 Sacramento CA 95814

REINHARDT, LINDA LOU, medical and surgical nurse; b. Meadville, Pa., July 15, 1950; d. Kenneth A. and Dorothy M. (Hartman) Beers; m. John F. Reinhardt, May 15, 1979 (div. Sept. 1995); 1 child, Moses A. ADN, Clarion U., 1982, BSN, 1993. RN, Calif.; Cert. BLS, ACLS. Staff nurse Oil City (Pa.) Health Ctr., 1982-84; nursing supr. Beverly Enterprises, Oil City, 1984-88, 92-93, Snyder Meml. Hosp. Ctr., Marianville, Pa., 1988-90; staff nurse Titusville (Pa.) Hosp., 1990-92; commd. 1st lt. USAF, 1993, advanced through grades to capt., 1994; asst. officer in charge med.-surg. Vandenberg AFB 30 Med. Group, Lompoc, Calif., 1993—; tutor Lompoc Lit. Counsel (pub. svc. award), 1994. Author: (original care plan) Nursing Plan of Care for Homeless of Venango County According to Roy's Model of Nursing, 1992. Mem. Sigma Theta Tau. Home: 1002 Hazelnut St Vandenberg AFB CA 93437-1127 Office: 30 Med Group South Dakota St Vandenberg AFB CA 93437

REINHARDT, RICHARD WARREN, writer; b. Oakland, Calif., Mar. 25, 1927; s. Emil Charles Henry and Eloise (Rathbone) R.; m. Joan Maxwell, Dec. 15, 1951; children: Kurt, Paul, Andrew. BA, Stanford U., 1949; MS, Columbia U., 1950; postgrad., Princeton U., 1958. Reporter San Francisco (Calif.) Chronicle, 1951-57; campaign mgr. various local, state and nat. campaigns, 1960-67; lectr. Grad. Sch. Journalism, U. Calif., Berkeley, 1971-93. Author: The Ashes of Smyrna, 1971, Treasure Island, 1973, San Francisco's Chinatown, 1982; prin. author: California 2000: The Next Frontier, 1982; assoc. editor San Francisco Mag., 1964-67; contbg. editor Am. West Mag., 1965-75, World's Fair, 1981-95. Trustee Calif. Hist. Soc., 1978-85; bd. dirs. Calif. Tomorrow, 1984-94; bd. mem., chair, pres. San Francisco Archtl. Heritage, 1980—. Ensign USNR, 1945-46. Pulitzer Traveling scholar Columbia U., N.Y.C., 1951; Near East Studies fellow Ford Found., 1957-60. Mem. Squaw Valley Cmty. Writers (adv. com., non-fiction dir. 1982—), Authors Guild, Delta Tau Delta. Office: 712 Lake St San Francisco CA 94118-1227

REINHARDT, STEPHEN ROY, federal judge; b. N.Y.C., Mar. 27, 1931; s. Gottfried and Silvia (Hanlon) R.; children: Mark, Justin, Dana. B.A. cum laude, Pomona Coll., 1951; LL.B., Yale, 1954. Bar: Calif. 1958. Law clk. to U.S. Dist. Judge Luther W. Youngdahl, Washington, 1956-57; atty. O'Melveny & Myers, L.A., 1957-59; partner Fogel Julber Reinhardt Rothschild & Feldman (L.C.), L.A., 1959-80; judge U.S. Ct. Appeals (9th cir.), L.A., 1980—; Mem. exec. com. Dem. Nat. Com., 1969-72, nat. Dem. committeeman for Calif., 1976-80; pres. L.A. Recreation an dParks Commn., 1974-75; mem. Coliseum Commn., 1974-75; mem. L.A. Police Commn., 1974-78, pres., 1978-80; sec., mem. exec. com. L.A. Olympic Organizing com., 1980-84; bd. dirs. Amateur Athletic Found. of L.A., 1984-92; adj. prof. Loyola Law Sch., L.A., 1988-90. Served to 1st lt. USAF, 1954-56. Mem. ABA (labor law coun. 1975-77). *

REINHARDT, WILLIAM PARKER, chemical physicist, educator; b. San Francisco, May 22, 1942; s. William Oscar and Elizabeth Ellen (Parker) R.; m. Katrina Hawley Currens, Mar. 14, 1979; children: James William, Alexander Hawley. BS in Basic Chemistry, U. Calif., Berkeley, 1964; AM in Chemistry, Harvard U., 1966, PhD in Chem. Physics, 1968; MA (hon.), U. Pa., 1985. Instr. chemistry Harvard U., 1967-69, asst. prof. chemistry, 1969-72, assoc. prof., 1972-74; prof. U. Colo., Boulder, 1974-84, chmn. dept. chemistry, 1977-80; prof. chemistry U. Pa., Phila., 1984-91, chmn. dept., 1985-88, D. Michael Crow prof., 1987-91; prof. chemistry U.Wash., Seattle, 1991—, assoc. chmn. undergrad. program, 1993-96; vis. fellow Joint Inst. for Lab. Astrophysics of Nat. Bur. Stds. and U. Colo., 1972, 74, fellow, 1974-84; dir. Telluride Summer Rsch. Ctr., 1986-89, treas., 1989-93; com. on atomic, molecular and optical scis. NRC, 1988-90; vis. scientist Nat. Inst. Stds. and Tech., summers 1993, 94, 96, 97; vis. prof. chemistry U. Melbourne, Australia, 1997, Harvard U., 1998. Mem. editl. bd. Phys. Rev. A., 1979-81, Chem. Physics, 1985-94, Jour. Chem. Physics, 1987-89, Jour. Physics B (U.K.), 1992—, Internat. Jour. Quantum Chemistry, 1994—; rschr. theoretical chem. physics, theoretical atomic and molecular physics for numerous publs. Recipient Camille and Henry Dreyfus Tchr. Scholar award, 1972; Alfred P. Sloan fellow, 1972; J.S. Guggenheim Meml. fellow, 1978; Coun. on Rsch. and Creative Work faculty fellow, 1978; Wilsmore fellow U. Melbourne (Australia), 1997; J.W. Fulbright sr. scholar, Australia, 1997. Fellow AAAS, Am. Phys. Soc.; mem. Am. Chem. Soc., Phi Beta Kappa, Sigma Xi (nat. lectr. 1980-82), Phi Lambda Upsilon (Fresenius award 1977). Office: U Wash Dept Chemistry Box 351700 Seattle WA 98195-1700

REINISCH, NANCY RAE, therapist, consultant; b. Chgo., Mar. 31, 1953; d. Charles Richard and Marianne (Gross) R.; m. Paul A. Salmen, June 14, 1980; children: Chas, Marcus. BA in Sociology cum laude, Colo. Coll., 1975; cert. drug and alcohol counseling, U. Minn., 1980; MSW, U. Denver, 1982. Cert. relationship therapist; lic. clin. social worker. Counselor Rampart Boys' Home, Colorado Springs, Colo., 1975; advocate bilinqual community Migrants in Action, St. Paul, 1976; therapist Chrysalis Ctr. for Women, Mpls., 1979; team leader and prevention specialist Project Charlie, Edina, Minn., 1977-80, also trainer, cons., 1985—; mental health worker Bethesda Mental Health Ctr. and Hosp., Denver, 1980-83; therapist Gateway Alcohol Recovery Ctr., Aurora, Colo., 1983-84; pvt. practice therapy, also dir. Family Practice Counseling Service, Glenwood Springs, Colo., 1984—; co-dir. Valley Sexual Abuse Ctr.; bd. dirs. Adv./Safehouse Project, Glenwood Springs; mem. Valley View Hosp. Ethics com., Glenwood Springs, 1986—. Mem. sch. accountability com. Glenwood Springs, Human Svcs. Commn., Garfield County. Recipient Countywide Humanitarian Svc. award Glenwood Post and Garfield County Human Svcs. Commn., 1995. Mem. Nat. Assn. Social Workers, NOW, Nat. Abortion Rights Action League, ACLU, Colo. Pub. Interest Research Group. Democrat. Office: Family Practice Counseling Svc 1905 Blake Ave Glenwood Springs CO 81601-4250

REINKE, STEFAN MICHAEL, lawyer; b. Concord, Calif., May 7, 1958; s. Albert Richard and Patricia Eleanor (Stefan) R. AA, Bakersfield Coll., 1978; AB, U. So. Calif., 1981; JD, U. Calif., Davis, 1984. Bar: Hawaii 1984, U.S. Dist. Ct. Hawaii 1984, U.S. Ct. Appeals (9th and Fed. cirs.) 1985. Assoc. Carlsmith, Wichman, Case, Mukai & Ichiki, Honolulu, 1984-86; dir. Lyons, Brandt, Cook & Hiramatsu, Honolulu, 1986—; lectr. Windward C.C.; lawyer rep. 9th Cir. Jud. Conf., 1995; lawyer rep. Jud. Conf. for the U.S. Dist. Ct. Hawaii, 1996—. Bd. dirs. Hawaii Ctrs. for Ind. Living, Honolulu, 1985-91, Prevent Child Abuse Hawaii, 1995—. Mem. ABA, FBA (pres. Hawaii chpt. 1994-96), Hawaii Bar Assn., Am. Arbitration Assn. (arbitrator and mediator), Def. Rsch. Inst., Nat. Employment Law Assn., Phi Beta Kappa, Phi Alpha Delta. Office: Lyons Brandt Cook & Hiramatsu 841 Bishop St Ste 1800 Honolulu HI 96813-3918

REINKOESTER, ROBERT WILLIAM, JR., critical care nurse; b. Port Clinton, Ohio, Feb. 27, 1951; s. Robert W. and Betty C. (Wightman) R.; m. Pamela C. Ertel, Mar. 16, 1973 (div. 1995); children: Andrew, Erin. BA cum laude, U. Utah, 1978, BSN cum laude, 1985. RN, Utah; cert. critical care nurse. With McKesson Drug Co., 1973-82; staff nurse, charge nurse intermountain burn ctr. U. Utah Med. Ctr., 1985-88, asst. head nurse, 1988-89; cardiac catheterization lab. nurse U. Utah Health Sci. Ctr., 1989-91, supr. catheterization lab., nurse cardiac catheterization lab., 1991—, co-coord. catheterization lab., 1993-95, clin. nurse, coord. cardiac catheterization lab., 1995-97; sr. rsch. nurse dept. cardiology U. Utah Sch. Medicine, 1997—; instr. advanced cardiac life support, advanced burn life support, basic cardiac life support; counselor HIV testing program; community lectr. intermountain burn unit U. Utah, 1986-89, tutorial staff, 1984-85. Michael Found. scholar, 1983, Clara Hansen Jensen scholar, 1985. Mem. Am. Assn. Critical Care Nurses, Intercollegiate Knights (life), Delta Tau Delta. Home: 2241 E Laney Ave H Holladay UT 84117

REISBERG, LEON ELTON, education educator; b. Dallas, Sept. 1, 1949; s. Morris Abraham and Gertrude (Turner) R.; m. Iris Fudell, July 3, 1973 (div. 1986); children: Joshua Fudell, Leah Fudell; m. Donna Brodigan, July 11, 1993. BS in Edn., U. Tex., Austin, 1971; MEd, U. Ark., Fayetteville, 1972; EdD, U. Kans., Lawrence, 1981. Tchr. Oklahoma City Sch. Dist., 1972-75, Putnam City Sch. Dist., Oklahoma City, 1975-78, U. Kans. Med. Ctr., Kansas City, 1978-79; asst. prof. Pacific Luth. U., Tacoma, 1981-88; tchr. Tacoma (Wash.) Sch. Dist., 1989-90; assoc. prof. edn. Pacific Luth. U., 1988-94; chmn. dept. spl. edn. Pacific Luth. U., Tacoma, 1986-93, chmn. profl. edn. adv. bd., 1992-94, assoc. dean sch. edn., 1993—, prof., 1995—; project dir., Consulting Spl. Edn. Personnel Tng. Project, Tacoma, 1983-86; chmn. Profl. Edn. Adv. Bd. Cons. editor Learning Disability Quar., 1981-89, Acad. Therapy, 1988-90, Intervention, 1990—; contbr. articles to profl. publs. Mem. Coun. Exceptional Children, Coun. Learning Disabilities (Pacific Rim region rep. 1993-96), Assn. Trainer Spl. Edn. Pers. (chmn. 1991), Phi Kappa Phi. Democrat. Jewish. Office: Pacific Luth U Sch Edn Tacoma WA 98447 *Personal philosophy: Research and professional interests in promoting the inclusion of students with disabilities in regular classrooms.*

REISCH, MICHAEL STEWART, social work educator; b. N.Y.C., Mar. 4, 1948; s. Joseph and Charlotte (Rosenberg) R.; m. Amy Jane Lewis, May 21, 1972; children: Jennifer, Nikki. BA in History with highest honors, NYU, 1968; PhD in History with distinction, SUNY, Binghamton, 1975; MSW with honors, CUNY, 1979. Youth worker Washington-Heights-Inwood YM-YWHA, N.Y.C., 1965-66; editor, columnist Heights Daily News, Bronx, N.Y., 1966-68; rsch./teaching asst. SUNY, Binghamton, 1970-72; unit dir., program cons. Child Study Assn.-Wel Met, Inc., N.Y.C., 1970-72; asst. dir. youth div. Mosholu-Montefiore Community Ctr., Bronx, 1972-73; project dir. Silberman Found./N.Y. Assn. Deans, N.Y.C., 1973-74; asst. dean Sch. Social Welfare, asst. prof. SUNY, Stony Brook, 1974-79; asst. prof., then assoc. prof. Sch. Social Work U. Md., Balt., 1979-86; dir. Sch. Social Work, prof. social work/pub. adminstrn. San Francisco State U., 1986-95; prof. social work U. Pa., Phila., 1995—; cons. and spkr. in field. Co-author: From Charity to Enterprise, 1989 (Social Sci. Book of Month), Social Work in the 21st Century, 1997; editor, author various books in field; contbr. articles to profl. publs., chpts. to books. Cons. to numerous local, state, and fed. polit. campaigns, 1971—; mem. Gov.'s Adv. Coun. Human Resources, Md., 1983-86; pres. Welfare Advs., Md., 1983-86; campaign mgr. Rep. Barbara Mikulski, Balt., 1982; bd. dirs. Coleman Advs. for Children and Youth, 1987-95, San Francisco Internat. Program, 1987-95, Calif. Social Work Edn. Ctr., 1991-95, Ctr. for S.E. Asian Refugee Resettlement, 1992-95, Am. Jewish Congress, N. Calif., 1994-95, Coun. Internat. Programs, 1995; chair Children's Budget Task Force City of San Francisco, 1989-92; mem. Mayor's Adv. Coun. on Drug Abuse, San Francisco, 1988-91; mem. steering com. Poverty Action Alliance, 1993-95. Woodrow Wilson Found. fellow, 1972-73. Mem. NASW (del. 1990-92, 94-96, chair peace and justice com. 1992—), Coun. on Social Work Edn. (com. on status of women 1989-92, bd. dirs. 1993—, chair commn. on ednl. policy 1994—), Am. Hist. Assn., Bertha Capen Reynolds Soc., Soc. for Social Work Rsch., Assn. for Advancement of Social Work with Groups, Assn. Cmty. Orgns. and Social Adminstrn.

REISINGER, GEORGE LAMBERT, management consultant; b. Pitts., Aug. 28, 1930; s. Eugene Merle and Pauline Jane (Lambert) R.; m. Judith Ann Brush, Nov. 24, 1967; children—Douglas Lambert, Christine Elizabeth. B.S. in Bus. Adminstrn., Central Coll., 1953; postgrad., Cleveland-Marshall Law Sch., 1962-67. Asst. personnel mgr. Continental Can Co., Houston, 1958-60; mgr. labor relations The Glidden Co., Cleve., 1960-67; dir. employee relations Mobil Oil Corp., N.Y.C., Caracas, Dallas, Denver, 1967-78; sr. v.p. Minton & Assocs., Denver, 1978-82; v.p., ptnr. Korn-Ferry Internat., Denver, 1982-86; pres. The Sigma Group, Inc., Denver, 1986—. Bd. dirs. Ponderosa Hills Civic Assn., 1977-80, Arapahoe County Youth League, Parker Action Team for Drug Free Colo.; pres. Douglas County Youth League; bd. dirs., steering com. Rocky Mountain Lions Eye Inst. With USAF, 1953-58. Mem. Am. Soc. Pers. Adminstrs., N.Y. Pers. Mgmt. Soc., Colo. Soc. Pers. Adminstrn., Am. Soc. Profl. Cons., Rocky Mountain Inst. Fgn. Trade and Fin., Employment Mgmt. Assn. Republican. Methodist. Clubs: Denver Petroleum, Pinery Country, Republican 1200. Home: 7924 Deertrail Dr Parker CO 80134-8262 Office: Sigma Group Internat 6551 S Revere Pkwy Ste 125 Englewood CO 80111-6410

REISLER, RAYMOND FRANK, foundation administrator; b. N.Y.C., Apr. 27, 1946; s. Raymond and Harriet (Spitzer) R. B.S., Cornell U., 1968, M.A., 1971; Ed.D., U. Mass., 1976. Tchr. pub. jr. high sch., N.Y.C., 1970-71; asst. prof. mgmt. U. Calgary, Alta., 1976-77; spl. asst. for exec. ops. Office U.S. Commr. Edn., Washington, 1978-79; sr. policy, mgmt. analyst President's Commn. for Nat. Agenda for Eighties, Washington, 1980-81; asst. commr. N.J. Dept. Labor, Trenton, 1982-83; corp. dir. policy, planning and pub. responsibility, exec. dir., mgr. Am. Can Co. Found., Greenwich, Conn., 1983-86; pres. RFR Assocs., Greenwich, 1987-88; exec. dir. S. Mark Taper Found., L.A., 1989—; instr., trainer U. Mass., Amherst, 1972-74; research assoc. Yale U., New Haven, 1974-75. Community worker VISTA, N.Y.C., 1968-70. Author: Discussing Death, 1975; jour. Educational Theory, 1978; Phi Delta Kappan, 1981. Mem. Gov.'s Commn. on Conn.'s Future. Edn. Policy fellow Inst. for Ednl. Leadership, Washington, 1978-79; chmn. bd. dirs. Inst. Responsive Edn., Boston, 1984-89; bd. dirs. Nat. Com. Citizens in Edn., Washington, 1990-93. Recipient Cosby award for Dist. Nat. Service, U. Mass. Grad. Sch. Edn., 1981. Mem. Am. Soc. Tng. and Devel., N.Y. Area Pub. Affairs Profls., Nat. Network Grantmakers, Phi Delta Kappa. Democrat. Home: 10525 Cushdon Ave Los Angeles CA 90064 Office: S Mark Taper Found 12011 San Vicente Blvd # 400 Los Angeles CA 90049

REISMAN, RICHARD S., publisher; b. Spring Valley, N.Y., Nov. 6, 1953; s. Herbert and Phyllis Sharon (Hendler) R.; children: Marisa, Kimberly. BA, SUNY, Binghamton, 1975; JD, George Washington U., 1978; MBA, UCLA, 1985. Assoc. McCandless & Barrett, Washington, 1978-80, Donahue, Gallagher, Thomas & Woods, Oakland, Calif., 1980-83; mgr. corp. strategy Times Mirror, L.A., 1985-87; dir. mktg. L.A. Times/Orange County Edit., Costa Mesa, Calif., 1987-90; pub. Orange County Bus. Jour., Newport Beach, Calif., 1990—. Adv. bd. Orange County Com. for the Arts, 1993—; sr. adv. bd. Chapman U. Bus. Sch., 1993; bd. dirs. Orange County Bus. Coun., 1995—. R.C. Baker Found. fellow UCLA Sch. Mgmt., 1984. Mem. Jr. Achievement Assn. (bd. govs. 1992—), World Trade Ctr. Assn. (bd. dirs. 1992—), Partnership 2010 (bd. dirs. 1992—). Office: Orange County Bus Jour 4590 Macarthur Blvd Ste 100 Newport Beach CA 92660-2024

REISTROFFER, JEFF PAUL, fire management supervisor, electronics technician; b. Sioux Falls, S.D., June 26, 1957; s. Dennis E. and Carol L. (Capen) R.; m. Marla J. Treece, June 25, 1982; children: Tom, Brett, Steven. AA in Gen. Edn., Lassen Coll., 1980; BS in Wildlife Mgmt., U. Alaska, 1983. Cert. electronics technician. Firefighter U.S. Forest Svc., Ojai, Calif., 1975-77; fire specialist U.S. Bur. Land Mgmt., Fairbanks, Alaska, 1978-83; forester Alaska Divsn. Forestry, Fairbanks, 1983-86; owner, woodworker Birch Hill Woodworks, Fairbanks, 1985-90; rschr. Arctos Rsch., Plains, Mont., 1989—; owner, electronics technician Arctos Repair, Plains, 1993—; planning bd. mem. Plains Planning Bd., 1994—. Asst. fire chief Plains Fire Dept., 1991—.

REITAN, HAROLD THEODORE, management consultant; b. Max, N.D., Nov. 3, 1928; s. Walter Rudolph and Anna Helga (Glesne) R.; m. Margaret Lucille Bonsac, Dec. 29, 1954 (div.); children: Eric, Karen, Chris, Jon. BA, St. Olaf Coll., 1950; MA in Social Psychology, U. Fla., 1962, PhD, 1967. Commd. officer U.S. Air Force, 1951, advanced through grades to col.; comdr., U.S. Air Force Spl. Treatment Ctr., Lackland, Tex., 1971-74, U.S. Air Force Corrections and Rehab. Group, Lowry, Colo., 1974-76, Tech. Tng. Wing, 1976-78, ret., 1978; mgr. health svcs. Coors Industries, Golden, Colo., 1978-84, mgr. tng. and organizational devel., 1984-89, cons. mgmt. asseessment, tng. and devel., 1989—. Decorated Legion of Merit with oak leaf cluster, D.F.C. with oak leaf cluster, Bronze Star, Meritorious Svc. medal, Air medal with five oak leaf clusters. Mem. Am. Psychol. Assn., Phi Kappa Phi. Republican. Lutheran. Contbr. articles to profl. jours. Office: 116 S Nome St Aurora CO 80012-1242 *Personal philosophy: Sucess is not acclaim or affluence. Sucess is very personal and in the heart. Regardless of your background, race, color, creed or vocation, if you maximize your innate gifts, and actively, openly and continually focus your energies to assist and uplift your fellow man, and under all circumstances live the vow that you will not lie, cheat or steal, you will be a magnificent success. And you are the only one who can make it happen.*

REITEN, RICHARD G., natural gas industry executive; b. 1939. BA, U. Wash., 1962. With Simpson Timber Co., Seattle, 1962-64, St. Regis Paper Co., Tacoma, 1964-66, Hearin Products, Inc., Portland, Oreg., 1966-71; with Di Giorgio Corp., San Francisco, 1971-79, pres. bldg. material group; with Nicoli Co., Portland, 1979-87; dir. Oreg. Econ. Devel. Dept., Salem, 1987-89; pres. Portland Gen. Corp., 1989-92; pres. Portland Gen. Electric Co., 1992-95, pres., COO, 1996—. Office: Northwest Natural Gas Co One Pacific Square 13th Fl 220 NW 2nd Ave Portland OR 97209-3991

REITER, MICHAEL JAY, cardiologist educator; b. N.Y.C., May 28, 1942; s. Arthur and Sally (Schneider) R.; m. Catherine Morton, Feb. 6, 1983. BS, Rensselaer Polytech. Inst., 1964; PhD, U. Rochester, 1969; MD, SUNY, Stony Brook, 1975. Diplomate Am. Bd. Internal Medicine, Nat. Bd. Med. Examiners; lic. MD, Colo., N.C., Tex., Calif. Intern and resident Parkland Meml. Hosp., Dallas, 1975-78; dir. Physicians Assoc. Sch. Duke U., Durham, N.C., 1979-82; asst. prof. U. Colo. Health Scis. Ctr., Denver, 1982-88, assoc. prof., 1988-94, prof., 1994—. Editl. reviewer Am. Jour. Cardiology, 1983—, Archives Internal Medicine, 1984—, Jour. Am. Coll. Cardiology, 1984—, Jour. Electrophysiology, 1987—, Chest, 1985—, Jour. Electrocardiology, 1988—, Circulation, 1989—, Am. Jour. Physiology, 1990; contbr. numerous articles to profl. jours. Rsch. fellow NIMH, 1969-71, Duke U., 1978-82, Mark C. Lidwill, 1991-92; staff physician VA Hosp., Denver, 1987—, Fitzsimons Army Med. Ctr., Denver, 1987—, Univ. Hosp., Denver, 1982—. Mem. Fellow Am. Coll. Cardiology (gov., pres. Colo. chpt. 1992-95, bd. govs. ad hoc task force for tort reform 1993—); mem. Am. Heart Assn. (Clin. Cardiology Coun.), Am. Fedn. Clin. Rsch. (sr.), N.Am. Soc. Pacing and Electrophysiology, Cardiac Electrophysiology Soc., Colo. Soc. Cardiovascular Medicine. Home: 8101 E Dartmouth Ave Apt 77 Denver CO 80231-4260 Office: Univ Colo Health Scis Ctr 4200 E 9th Ave Box B-130 Denver CO 80262

REITZ, BRUCE ARNOLD, cardiac surgeon, educator; b. Seattle, Sept. 14, 1944; s. Arnold B. and Ruth (Stillings) R.; m. Nan Norton, Oct. 3, 1970; children: Megan, Jay. BS, Stanford U., 1966; MD, Yale U., 1970. Diplomate: Am. Bd. Surgery, Am. Bd. Thoracic Surgery. Intern Johns Hopkins Hosp., Balt., 1970-71, cardiac surgeon-in-charge, 1982-92; resident Stanford U. Hosp., (Calif.), 1971-72, 74-78; clin. assoc. Nat. Heart Lung Blood Inst., NIH, Bethesda, Md., 1972-74; asst. prof. Stanford U. Sch. Medicine, 1977-81, assoc. prof., 1981-82; prof. surgery Johns Hopkins U. Sch. Medicine, Balt., 1982-92; prof., chmn. Sch Medicine Stanford (Calif.) U., 1992—. Developer heart-lung transplant technique, 1981. Office: Stanford U Sch Medicine Dept Cardiothoracic Surgery Stanford CA 94305

REITZ, RONALD CHARLES, biochemist, educator; b. Dallas, Feb. 27, 1939; s. Percy Allison and Hazel Alberta (Thomison) R.; m. Jeanne, Jan. 23, 1965; children: Erica, Brett. BS in Chemistry, Tex. A&M U., 1961; PhD in Biochemistry, Tulane U., 1966. Lab. instr., rsch. asst. Tulane U., New Orleans, 1962-66; rsch. assoc., NIH postdoc. fellow U. Mich., Ann Arbor, 1966-69; asst. prof. biochemistry U. N.C., Chapel Hill, 1969-75; assoc. prof. U. Nev., Reno, 1978-80, prof., 1980—, interim chmn. biochemistry, 1988-90, dir. undergrad. studies in biochemistry, 1996—; vis. scientist Unilever Rsch. Lab. The Frythe, Welwyn Herts., England, 1968, E.I. DuPont de Nemours, 1984; vis. prof. Nagoya City (Japan) U., 1990, Max-Planck Inst. fur Biophys. Chemie, Gottingen, Germany, 1990-91; vis. scientist lectr. idaho State U., Pocatello, 1987. Contbr. numerous papers and articles to profl. jours. Mem. AAAS, Am. Soc. Biol. Chemists, Am. Soc. Pharmacology and Exptl. Therapeutics, Am. Oil Chemists' Soc., Western Pharm. Soc., Rsch. Soc. Alcoholism, Sigma Xi. Republican. Methodist. Office: U Nev Sch of Medicine Dept Biochemistry Reno NV 89557

REJMAN, DIANE LOUISE, industry analyst; b. Hartford, Conn., Jan. 14, 1956; d. Louis P. and Genevieve (Walukevich) R. BS in Aviation Adminstrn., Embry Riddle Aero. U., 1980; M in Internat. Mgmt., Am. Grad. Sch. Internat. Mgmt., 1991; cert. in cross cultural negotiation, Western Internat. Univ., 1994. Indsl. engr./planner Hamilton Aviation, Tucson, 1980-82; indsl. engr. assoc. Gates Learjet, Tucson, 1984; tech. writer, FAA coord. Dee Howard Co., San Antonio, 1984-86; indsl. engr. McDonnell Douglas Helicopter Systems, Mesa, Ariz., 1986-88; systems analyst McDonnell Douglas Helicopter Sys., Mesa, Ariz., 1988-95; sr. aerospace industry analyst Frost & Sullivan, Mountain View, Calif., 1995—; bd. dirs. McDonnell Douglas Helicopter Sys. Employee Community Fund., adminstr. 1992-95. Author: (reports) World Commercial Avionics Market, 1996, World Airport Ground Equipment Markets, 1996. Mem. City of Mesa Leadership Tng. Class of 1995. With U.S. Army, 1977-80. Home: 25 Newell Rd Apt 8 Palo Alto CA 94303

REMER, DONALD SHERWOOD, engineering economist, cost estimator, educator; b. Detroit, Mich., Feb. 16, 1943; s. Nathan and Harriet R.; m. Louise Collen, Dec. 21, 1969; children: Tanya, Candace, Miles. BS, U. Mich., 1965; MS, Calif. Inst. Tech., 1966, PhD, 1970. Registered profl. engr., Calif., Mich., La. Tech. service engr., chem. raw materials div. coordinator, sr. running plan coordinator, task team mgr. Exxon, Baton Rouge, 1970-75; assoc. prof. engring. Harvey Mudd Coll., Claremont, Calif., 1975-79, prof., 1980—, Oliver C. Field prof. engring., dir. Energy Inst., 1981-83; cons., mem. tech. staff, mgr. planning analysis Jet Propulsion Lab., Calif. Inst. Tech., 1976—; co-founder, ptnr. Claremont Cons. Group, 1979—; mem. adv. council Nat. Energy Found., N.Y.C., 1981-85; mem. Inst. Mgmt. Cons., 1988-89; presenter short courses Caltech's Indsl. Rels. Ctr. and UCLA's Engring. and Mgmt. Program, 1994—, also to industry and vogt. on cost estimation of projects, econ. evaluation of projects, software devel., schedule estimation. Case study editor Am. Soc. Engring. Edn., Inst. Indsl. Engrs., Engring. Economist, 1977-89; mem. editorial bd. Jour. Engring. Costs and Prodn. Econs., 1985-91, Internat. Jour. Prodn. Econs., 1992—; contbr. articles to profl. jours. Shelter mgr. ARC, Baton Rouge, 1965-70. Recipient Outstanding Chem. Engr. award U. Mich., 1965, First Place Pub. Relations award Am. Inst. Chem. Engring., 1975, Outstanding Alumni Fund Achievement award Calif. Inst. Tech., 1976, Outstanding Young Man of Am. award, 1976, NASA award, 1983, Best Paper of the Year in Jour. Parametrics, Internat. Soc. Parametric Analysts, 1991-92, Centennial award certificate Am. Soc. Engring. Edn., 1993; named Outstanding Research Seminar Speaker Occidental Research Corp., 1976. Mem. Am. Soc. Engring. Mgmt. (bd. dirs. 1981-83), Toastmasters Club (pres. Claremont-Pomona chpt. 1978).

RENARD, RONALD LEE, allergist; b. Chgo., July 31, 1949; s. Robert James and Dorothy Mae (Fruik) R.; m. Maureen Ann Gilmore, Aug. 5, 1972 (div. Mar. 1992); children: Jeffrey, Stephen, Justin, Leigh Ellen; m. Catherine L. Walker, Apr. 1, 1992; children: Morgan, Michal, Luke. 1 & 2 Degre de la Langue, U. de Montpelier, France, 1970; BS in French, U. San Francisco, 1971; MD, Creighton U., 1976. Dir. med. ICU, lt. U.S. Army Hosp., Ft. Leonard Wood, Md., 1980-81; dir. respiratory therapy, asst. chief allergy svc. Walter Reed Med. Ctr., Washington, 1981-84; staff allergist Chico (Calif.) Med. Group, 1984-86; allergist pvt. practice Redding, Calif., 1986—; dir. ACLS program Enloe Hosp., Chico, 1988-91; bd. dirs. Am. Lung Assn. Calif., 1989-91, med. dir. asthma camp, Chico, Redding, 1986-95; asst. prof. medicine USPHS, Bethesda, Md., 1982-84; asst. prof. family medicine U. Calif. Davis Med. Sch., Redding, 1990-94; Shasta County Planning Commr., 1994-95. Contbr. articles to profl. jours. Fellow Am. Acad. Allergy & Immunology, Am. Coll. Allergists; mem. Alpha Omega Alpha Nat. Honor Med. Soc., Assn. Mil. Allergists, Calif. Thoracic Soc. Republican. Roman Catholic. Office: 1950 Rosaline Ave Ste A Redding CA 96001-2543

RENAUD, ROBERT (EDWIN), librarian; b. Westmount, Que., Can., Dec. 31, 1952; came to the U.S., 1994; s. Lawrence Joseph and Caroline (Elie) R.; m. Martha Jane Carnegie, Sept. 12, 1987 (div. Jan. 1990); m. Jennifer Stairs, Aug 7, 1993. AB, Vassar Coll., 1976; MLS, U. Toronto, Ont., Can., 1980. Cataloger McGill U., Montreal, Que., 1976-78; sys. analyst U. Toronto, 1980-84; mgr. sys. Met. Toronto Libr., 1984-90; dep. CEO Markham (Can.) Pub. Libr., 1990-94; team leader U. Ariz. Libr., Tucson, 1994—; mem. rep. Nat. Libr., Ottawa, Ont., 1991-93; chmn. tech. com. Multinet Consortium, Markham, 1991-93; mem. bd. exec. com. Lib. Svcs. Ctr., Inc., Waterloo, Can., 1991-93; pres. Can. Serials Industry Sys. Adv. Com., Toronto, 1993-94. Contbr. chpt. to book and articles to profl. jours. Scholar Vassar Coll., Poughkeepsie, N.Y., 1973-76; Grad. fellow U. Toronto, 1978-80; Resident fellow Massey Coll.-U. Toronto, 1978-80. Mem. Assn. Coll. and Rsch. Librs. (steering com. nat. conf. 1997). Roman Catholic. Office: U Ariz Libr PO Box 210055 Tucson AZ 85721

RENEKER, MAXINE HOHMAN, librarian; b. Chgo., Dec. 2, 1942; d. Roy Max and Helen Anna Christina (Anacker) Hohman; m. David Lee Reneker, June 20, 1964 (dec. Dec. 1979); children: Sarah Roeder, Amy Johannah, Benjamin Congdon. BA, Carleton Coll., 1964; MA, U. Chgo., 1970; DLS, Columbia U., 1992. Asst. reference libr. U. Chgo. Libraries, 1965-66; classics libr. U. Chgo. Libr., 1967-70, asst. head acquisitions, 1970-71, personnel libr., 1971-73; personnel/bus. libr. U. Colo. Libr., Boulder, 1978-80; asst. dir. sci. and engring. div. Columbia U., N.Y.C., 1981-85; assoc. dean of univ. librs. for pub. svcs. Ariz. State U. Libr., Tempe, 1985-89; dir. instrnl. and rsch. svcs. Stanford (Calif.) Univ. Librs., 1989-90; dir. info. svcs., dir. Dudley Knox Libr. Naval Postgrad. Sch., Monterey, Calif., 1993—; acad. libr. mgmt. intern Coun. on Libr. Resources, 1980-81; chmn. univ. librs. sect. Assn. Coll. and Rsch. Librs., 1989-90. Contbr. articles to profl. jours. Rsch. grantee Coun. on Library Resources, Columbia U., 1970-71, fellow, 1990-92. Mem. ALA, Am. Soc. Info. Sci., Sherlockian Scion Soc., Phi Beta Kappa, Beta Phi Mu. Home: 740 Dry Creek Rd Monterey CA 93940-4208 Office: Naval Postgrad Sch Dudley Knox Libr 411 Dyer Rd Monterey CA 93943-5198

RENETZKY, ALVIN, publisher; b. Bklyn., Aug. 2, 1940; s. Sam and Anna (Preiser) R.; m. Phyllis Ann (div.); 1 child, Davida; m. Cheryl Linden. PhD, U. Southern Calif., 1966. Publisher Academic Media, Los Angeles, 1967-70, Ready Reference Press, Santa Monica, Calif., 1974—. Editor: Directory of Career Resources for Women, 1980, Directory of Career Resources for Minorities, 1981, Career Employment Opportunities Directory, 1985, Directory of Internships; exec. prodr.: (video series) Guidance Club for Kids, 1992, Guidance Club for Teens, 1993, 94, Guidance Club for Women, 1994, Guidance Club for Parents, 1994, Career Club, 1994. Office: Ready Reference Press PO Box 5879 Santa Monica CA 90409-5879

RENFRO, LEONARD EARL, II, retired protective services professional; b. Ventura, Calif., July 18, 1937; s. Leonard Earl and Mary Frances (Gillette) R.; m. Mavis Helen Whitten, Jan. 27, 1956; children: Marjorie Lynne, Teresa Lea, Julie Eileen, Karen Jean. AA, Ventura Coll., 1957; BS, Calif. Luth. U., 1975. Advanced cert. law enforcement, Calif. Farm laborer Valley Ranch Assocs., Oxnard, Calif., 1955-57; roustabout oil field Texaco, Inc., Santa Paula, Calif., 1957-60; dep. sheriff Ventura (Calif.) County Sheriff's Dept., 1960-87; field rep. Calif. Bd. Corrections, Sacramento, 1987-95; ret., 1995. Cpl. USMC, 1954-62. Mem. Calif. State Sheriff's Assn., Ventura County Dep. Sheriff's Assn. (pres. 1968-69), Al Malakiah Shrine, York Rite (Ventura Valley), Scottish Rite (Ventura Valley), Masons (master 1980-81). Republican. Baptist. Home: 102 Rawlings Ct Folsom CA 95630-4846

RENFRO, MICHAEL, human services administrator. Dir. Alaska Divsn. Mental Health, Juneau. Office: Alaska Dept Health & Social Svcs Pouch H-04 Juneau AK 99811

RENGARAJAN, SEMBIAM RAJAGOPAL, electrical engineering educator, researcher, consultant; b. Mannargudi, Tamil Nadu, India, Dec. 12, 1948; came to U.S., 1980; s. Srinivasan and Rajalakshmi (Renganathan) Rajagopalan; m. Kalyani Srinivasan, June 24, 1982; children: Michelle, Sophie. BE with honors, U. Madras, India, 1971; MTech, Indian Inst. Tech., Kharagpur, 1974; PhD in Elec. Engring., U. N.B., Fredericton, Can., 1980. Mem. tech. staff Jet Propulsion Lab., Pasadena, Calif., 1983-84; asst. prof. elec. engring. Calif. State U., Northridge, 1980-83, assoc. prof., 1984-87, prof., 1987—; vis. rschr. UCLA, 1984-93, vis. prof., 1987-88; vis. prof. U. de Santiago de Compastela, Spain, 1996; cons. Hughes Aircraft Co., Canoga Park, Calif., 1982-87, NASA-Jet Propulsion Lab., Pasadena, 1987-90, 92-94, 96—, Ericsson Radar Electronics, Sweden, 1990-92, Martin Mariette, 1995; guest rschr. Chalmers U., Sweden, 1990, UN Devel. Program, 1993, Rome Lab., USAF, summer 1995. Contbr. sci. papers to profl. publs. recipient Outstanding Faculty award Calif. State U., Northridge, 1985, Disting. Engring. Educator or Yr. award Engrs. Coun., L.A., 1995, Meritorious Performance and profl. Promise award, 1986, 88, Merit award San Fernando Valley Engrs., Coun., 1989, cert. of recognition NASA, 1991, 92; Nat. Merit scholar Govt. India, 1965-71. Fellow Inst. Advancement Engrs., IEEE (L.A. chpt. sec., treas. antennas and propagation soc. 1981-82, vice chmn. 1982-83, chmn. 1983-84), Internat. Union Radio Sci. (U.S. nat. com.), The Electromagnetics Acad. Office: Calif State U 18111 Nordhoff St Northridge CA 91330-0001 *Personal philosophy: I wish to contribute to the society through my work in science and technology.*

RENNE, JANICE LYNN, interior designer; b. Los Angeles, July 16, 1952; d. George Joseph and Dolly Minni (Neubaurer) R.; m. William Lee Kile, Dec. 6, 1975 (div. Sept. 1983). BA, Sweet Briar Coll., 1974; AA, Interior Designers Inst., 1985. Lic. gen. contractor, Calif.; cert. interior designer, Calif. Coun. for Interior Design Certification. Exec. trainee Bullock's, Santa Ana, Calif., 1974, Pub. Fin., Inc., Huntington Beach, Calif., 1975; bookkeeper William L. Kile DDS, Inc., Santa Barbara, Calif., 1979-81, Nelson & Hamilton, Inc., Santa Barbara, 1981-82; interior designer Ultimate Designs, Irvine, Calif., 1984-85, sr. designer, 1985-86; draftsperson JBI Inc., Long Beach, Calif., 1984-85; prin. designer Janice Renne Interior Designs, Newport Beach, Calif., 1986-92, Costa Mesa, Calif., 1992—; space planner Design Pak II, Newport Beach, 1987-88; State of Calif. rep. task force for developing self-cert. process for Calif. interior designers, Internat. Soc. Interior Design, 1991. Created utility room design for Easter Seals Design House, 1985; weekly radio show host on restaurant design, 1986; work published in Orange County mag. and L.A. Times., 1988. Recipient scholarship Calif. Inst. Applied Design, Newport Beach, 1984. Mem. Am. Inst. Archs. (assoc.), Internat. Soc. Interior Designers (grad. assoc. designer butler's pantry, assoc. designer Design House powder room 1988, asst. editor Orange County chpt. 1988-89, chpt. Quar. Newsletter, chpt. gen. bd. 1991-92, chmn. licensing com. 1991-92, bd. dirs. 1991-92), Color Assn. U.S., Constrn. Specifications Inst., Nat. Exec. Women in Hospitality, Calif. Legis. Conf. in Interior Design (gen. bd. 1991-92, v.p. comm. 1992-93), Orange County and Newport Beach Letip Internat. (sec. 1987, 89-90, treas. 1991, pres. 1993), Internat. Interior Design Assn., Tall Club Orange County (exec. v.p. 1995, co-editor High Life 1995-96, editor 1995-97, Miss Congeniality award 1994, rec. sec. 1996-97, del. t conv. 1996, del. Tall Club Internat. Conv. 1996). Republican. Lutheran. Office: 2915 Red Hill Ave Ste E100 Costa Mesa CA 92626-5932

RENNEBOHM FRANZ, KRISTI, primary education educator; b. Seattle, Sept. 3, 1946; d. William Edwin and Elizabeth Ruth (Mickey) Rennebohm; m. Eldon Henry Franz, June 17, 1967; children: Wendy Elizabeth Franz, Benjamin Robert Franz, Matthew Zachary Franz. BS in Speech Correction, U. Ill., 1968; B in Music, U. Ga., 1987; MEd, Wash. State U., 1989. Speech correctionist Champaign (Ill.) Pub. Schs., 1968-71; speech and lang. tchr. Headstart/Clarke County Sch. Dist., Athens, Ga., 1972; staff cello tchr., dept. music U. Ga., Athens, 1977; pvt. cello tchr. Pullman, Wash., 1981-87; grad. teaching asst. Coll. Edn. Wash. State U., Pullman, 1988-89; kindergarten tchr. Internat. Sch. of Kenya, Nairobi, 1989-90; primary tchr. Sunnyside Elem. Sch., Pullman, 1990—, bdlg. tech. coord., 1993—; lead tchr. Internat. Edn. and Resource Network, 1994—; vis. scholar Harvard U. Grad. Sch. of Edn., Program in Profl. Edn., Cambridge, Mass., 1997. Recipient award of merit AT&T/Time, 1995; Wash. State Assn. Sch. Dirs. Found. profl. devel. scholar, 1996; N.W. Coun. on Computer Edn. grantee, 1994. Office: Sunnyside Elem Sch SW 425 Shirley St Pullman WA 99163

RENNER, JEANNETTE IRENE (JAY RENNER), publishing executive; b. Omaha, Feb. 28, 1930; d. Arthur Thomas and Agnes Irene (Miller) R.; m. Edward Francis Witucki, June 11, 1949 (div. June 1967); children: Lynn Witucki Rolston, Daniel Oren. BA in Anthropology summa cum laude, UCLA, 1960, PhD in Anthropology, 1966. Instr. anthropology Calif. State U., L.A., 1967-69, asst. prof., 1970-75, assoc. prof., 1976-82, prof., 1983-86, prof. emeritus, 1986—; owner, pub. Condor Book Co., Auburn, Calif., 1983—. Author: (textbooks) Introducing Linguistic Analysis: The Comprehensive Course, 1984, Introducing Linguistic Analysis: Phonemics, 1984, Introducing Linguistic Analysis: Morphology and Syntax, 1984; contbr. articles and rev. to profl. publs. Mem. Am. Anthropol. Assn. (presenter, past mem. panel on future cultures), West Coast Assn. Women Historians (presenter), Sigma Xi (field work grantee 1971), Phi Beta Kappa. Office: Condor Book Co 3037 Grass Valley Hwy Auburn CA 95602-2501

RENO, HARLEY WAYNE, environmental scientist; b. Oakland, Calif., Feb. 13, 1939; s. Dorris Gaylin and Margaret Eileen (Moffitt) R.; m. Claire Lamar Danielson, Aug. 30, 1968 (div. Aug. 26, 1988); children: Robin Virginia, Katy Carolyn. AS, Connors State Coll., 1959; BS, MS, Okla. State U., 1963, PhD, 1967. Prof. Baylor U., Waco, Tex., 1967-74; resident Scott & White Hosp., Temple, Tex., 1968-74; vis. prof. Pan Am. U., Edinburg, Tex., 1974-75; mgr. environ. sci. Williams Bros. Engring. Co., Tulsa, 1975-78; mgr. EG&G Idaho Inc., Idaho Falls, 1978-94; prof. U. Idaho, Idaho Falls, 1979-96; mgr. Lockheed Martin Co., Idaho Falls, 1994—; postdoctoral fellow U. Okla., Norman, 1974. Author (with others), Pocket Guide to Target/Field Archery, 1996, A Pocket Guide to Lure Fishing for Trout in a Stream, 1996, Pocket Guide to Walleye Fishing in Lakes, 1996; Contbr. articles to profl. jours. Fellow Tex. Acad. of Scis.; mem. Eagle Rock Numismatic Soc. Office: Lockheed Martin Idaho Techs Box 1625 Idaho Falls ID 83415

RENSE, PAIGE, editor, publishing company executive; b. Iowa, May 4, 1929; m. Kenneth Noland, Apr. 10, 1994. Student, Calif. State U., L.A. Editor-in-chief Architectural Digest, L.A., 1970—. Recipient Nat. Headliner award Women in Communications, 1983, pacifica award So. Calif. Resources Coun., 1978, editl. award Dallas Market Ctr., 1978, golden award Chgo. Design Resources Svc., 12982, Agora award, 1982, outstanding profl. in comms. award, 1982, trailblazers award, 1983, disting. svcs. award Resources Coun., Inc., 1988; named woman of yr. L.A. Times, 1986, Muses, 1986, woman of internat. accomplishment, 1991; named to Interior Design Hall of Fame. Office: Architectural Digest 6300 Wilshire Blvd Fl 11 Los Angeles CA 90048-5202

RENSON, JEAN FELIX, psychiatry educator; b. Liège, Belgium, Nov. 9, 1930; came to U.S., 1960; s. Louis and Laurence (Crahai) R.; m. Gisèle Bouillenne, Sept. 8, 1956; children: Marc, Dominique, Jean-Luc. MD, U. Liege, 1959; PhD in Biochemistry, George Washington U., 1971. Diplomate Am. Bd. Psychiatry. Asst. prof. U. Liège, 1957-60; rsch. fellow U. Liege, 1966-72; clin. assoc. prof. dept. psychiatry U. Calif., San Francisco, 1978—; vis. asst. prof. Stanford U., Palo Alto, Calif., 1972-77. Assoc. editor: Fundamentals of Biochemical Pharmacology, 1971. NIH fellow, 1960-66. Democrat.

RENTELN, ALISON DUNDES, political science educator; b. Bloomington, Ind., Jan. 9, 1960; d. Alan and Carolyn (Browne) Dundes; m. Paul Alexander Renteln, June 9, 1985; children: David Alexander, Michael Alan. BA in History and Lit. cum laude, Harvard U., 1981; postgrad., London Sch. Econs., 1981-82; M of Jurisprudence, U. Calif., Berkeley, 1985, PhD in Jurisprudence and Social Policy, 1987; JD, U. So. Calif., 1991. Acting dir., vis. lectr. law and soc. U. Calif., Santa Barbara, 1986-87; asst. prof. polit. sci. U. So. Calif., L.A., 1987-93, assoc. prof. polit. sci., 1993—, acting dir. Unruh Inst. Pol., 1995-96, vice-chair dept. polit. sci., 1995—; lectr. Calif. State Judges Assn., Nat. Assn. Women Judges, UN Assn., Nat. Assn. Fgn. Student Affairs, L.A. Refugee Forum, Calif. Assn. of Adminstrn. of Justice Educators Delinquency Control Inst.; others; coord. Contemporary Issues in Law and Pub. Policy lectr. series Pasadena Sr. Citizens Ctr.; participant Hearing of U.S. Adv. Bd. on Child Abuse and Neglect; vis. prof. Sch. Law U. Calif., Berkeley, 1996-97; vis. prof. dept. polit. sci. Stanford U., 1997. Author: International Human Rights: Universalism Versus Relativism, 1990; co-editor: (with Alan Dundes) Folk Law: Essays on the Theory and Practice of Lex Non Scripta, 1994; reviewer: Am. Anthropologist, Am. Jour. Comparative Law, Am. Jour. Polit. Sci., Human Rights Quar., Jour. of Peace Rsch., others; contbr. numerous articles to profl. publs. Named Mentor of Distinction, Women's Caucus for Polit. Sci., 1993; Soroptomist Internat. Founder fellow, 1986; grantee Mark De Wolfe Howe Fund for rsch. in civil rights civil rights, civil liberties, and legal history Harvard U., 1985, Faculty Rsch. and Innovation Fund, 1988, Irvine Found. for diversity course devel., 1991, Faculty Fund for innovative tchg., 1993, Zumberge Faculty Rsch. and Innovation Fund, 1994. Mem. Am. Polit. Sci. Assn., Law and Soc. Assn., Commn. on Folk Law and Legal Pluralism, Am. Soc. Internat. Law, Internat. Law Assn. Office: U So Calif Dept Polit Sci VKC 327 Los Angeles CA 90089-0044

RENWICK, EDWARD S., lawyer; b. L.A., May 10, 1934. AB, Stanford U., 1956, LLB, 1958. Bar: Calif. 1959, U.S. Dist. Ct. (cen. dist.) Calif. 1959, U.S. Ct. Appeals (9th cir.) 1963, U.S. Dist. Ct. (so. dist.) Calif. 1973, U.S. Dist. Ct. (no. dist.) Calif. 1977, U.S. Dist. Ct. (ea. dist.) Calif. 1981, U.S. Supreme Ct. 1985. Ptnr. Hanna and Morton, L.A.; mem., bd. vis. Stanford Law Sch., 1967-69; mem. environ. and natural resources adv. bd. Stanford Law Sch. Bd. dirs. Calif. Supreme Ct. Hist. Soc. Fellow Am. Coll. Trial Lawyers, Am. Bar Found.; mem. ABA (mem. sect. on litigation, antitrust law, bus. law, chmn. sect. of nat. resources, energy and environ. law 1987-88, mem. at large coord. group energy law 1989-92, sect. rep. coord. group energy law 1995—, Calif. del. legal com., interstate oil compact com.), Calif. Arboretum Assn. (trustee 1986-92), L.A. County Bar Assn. (chmn. natural resources law sect. 1974-75), The State Bar of Calif., Assn. Atty.- Mediators, Chancery Club (pres. 1992-93), Phi Delta Phi. Office: Hanna & Morton 600 Wilshire Blvd Fl 17 Los Angeles CA 90017-3212

REPLOGLE, STEPHEN PATRICK, osteopath, health facility administrator; b. L.I., Apr. 29, 1957; s. Fred W. and Wilma E. (Fuhrman) R.; m. Jan A. Smith, May 12, 1979; children: Joy S., Benjamin D. BA with honors, Temple U., 1984; DO, Kirksville Coll. Osteo. Med., 1990. Intern Philips County Regional Med. Ctr., Rolla, Mo.; physician Indian Health Svc., Yuma, Ariz., 1991-92, 16th St. Med. Clinic, Yuma, 1992-94; med. dir., physician Yuma (Ariz.) Urgent Care, 1994-96, Replogle Osteo. Med. Clinic, Yuma, 1996—. Founder, dir. Manna Ministries, Phila., 1982-86. Lt. Indian Health Svc. Commn. Corps, 1991-92. Republican. Home: 8300 Shannon Way Yuma AZ 85365 Office: Replogle Osteo Med Clinic 475 W 16th St Yuma AZ 85364

RESCH, CHARLOTTE SUSANNA, plastic surgeon; b. Charlottesville, Va., Sept. 24, 1957; d. Johann Heinrich and Eleonore Susanne (Stenzel) R.; m. John Arthur Niero, Jan. 31, 1990. Student, Dalhousie U., Halifax, Nova Scotia, Can., 1974-76; MD with distinction, Dalhousie U. Med. Sch., Halifax, Nova Scotia, Can., 1980. Diplomate Dalhousie U., Am. Bd. Plastic Surgery; licentiate Med. Coun. Can.; cert. Bd. Med. Quality Assurance Calif. Intern Ottawa Gen. Hosp., Ont., Can., 1980-81; gen. surgery resident Dalhousie U., Halifax, Nova Scotia, Can., 1981-85; plastic surgery resident Wayne State U., Detroit, 1985-87; pvt. practice San Francisco, 1988-89; preptnr. Southern Calif. Permanente Physicians Group, Fontana, 1989-92, ptnr., 1992—. Contbr. articles to profl. jours. Fellow ACS; mem. Am. Soc. Plastic and Reconstructive Surgeons, Calif. Med. Soc., San Bernardino Med. Soc., Alpha Omega Alpha. Office: Kaiser Found Hosp Dept Plastic Surgery 9985 Sierra Ave Fontana CA 92335-6720

RESCIGNO, THOMAS NICOLA, theoretical physicist; b. N.Y.C., Sept. 10, 1947; s. Joseph Aiello and Leona Rees (Llewellyn) R.; m. Erie Ann Mills, May 24, 1986. BA, Columbia U., 1969; MA, Harvard U., 1971, PhD, 1973. Rsch. fellow Calif. Inst. Tech., Pasadena, 1973; staff scientist Lawrence Livermore Lab., Livermore, Calif., 1975-79, group leader, 1979-86, sr. scientist, 1986—; lectr. atomic and molecular physics U. N.Mex., Albuquerque, summers 1993, 94. Editor 2 sci. monographs; mem. editl. staff Phys. Rev. A, 1996-99; contbr. more than 100 articles to profl. jours., chpts. to books. Recipient Am. Inst. Chemists medal, 1969; Nat. Energy fellow NSF, 1975. Fellow Am. Phys. Soc. (local chair 1990). Office: Lawrence Livermore Nat Lab PO Box 808 Livermore CA 94551-0808

RESNICK, JEFFREY I., plastic surgeon; b. Jersey City, Mar. 2, 1954; s. Victor and Regina (Bistritz) R.; m. Michele Gail Zinger, July 12, 1981; children: Andrew Gregory, Daniel Zachary. BS, Yale U., 1975; MD, U. Pa., 1980. Diplomate Am. Bd. Surgery, Am. Bd. Plastic Surgery. Resident in surgery Mass. Gen. Hosp., Boston, 1980-85, resident in plastic surgery, 1985-87; fellow in craniofacial surgery UCLA, 1987-88; pvt. practice plastic surgery Santa Monica, Calif., 1989—; asst. clin. prof. plastic surgery UCLA, 1987—. Contbr. articles to profl. jours. Surgeon Indochina Surg. Ednl. Exch., Vietnam. Mem. Am. Soc. Plastic and Reconstructive Surgeons, Am. Soc. Maxillofacial Surgeons, Am. Cleft Palate-Craniofacial Assn., Plastic Surgery Ednl. Found., Sigma Xi, Alpha Omega Alpha. Office: 1301 20th St Ste 470 Santa Monica CA 90404-2054

RESS, DAVID BRUCE, physicist, electrical engineer; b. Camden, N.J., Nov. 17, 1958; s. Thomas Ignaz and Edith (Heyer) R.; m. Lucille Mitrovich, Jan. 22, 1985. Student, U. Calif., Irvine, 1975-78; BSEE, U. Calif., Davis, 1980; MSEE, Stanford U., 1984, PhD in Elec. Engring., 1988. Tutor U. Calif., Davis, 1979-80; electronics engr. Pacific Measurements Inc., 1980-82; rsch. asst. Stanford U., Calif., 1982-84; exptl. physicist Lawrence Livermore (Calif.) Nat. Lab., 1984, physicist, 1985—. Inventor laser fusion diagnostic techniques, 1989; contbr. numerous articles to profl. jours. Mem. Am. Phys. Soc., IEEE, Sierra Club, Commonwealth Club, Tau Beta Pi. Home: 30 Rishell Dr Oakland CA 94619-2332 Office: Lawrence Livermore Nat Lab 7000 East Ave L-473 Livermore CA 94551-5508

RETHERFORD, ROBERT DENNIS, demographer; b. N.Y.C., July 17, 1941; s. Robert Curtis and Ruth (Shere) R.; m. Ursula Cadalbert, Jan. 30, 1965; children: Tania, My-Hanh, Leah. BA in Phys. Sci., U. Calif., Berkeley, 1964, MA in Sociology, 1966, PhD of Sociology, 1970. Sr. fellow program on population East-West Ctr., Honolulu, 1970—; lectr. dept. demography U. Calif., Berkeley, 1970; grad. faculty dept. sociology U. Hawaii, Honolulu, 1973—; asst. specialist Internat. Population and Urban Rsch. Ctr. U. Calif., Berkeley, 1969-70; cons. UN Econ. Commn. for Asia and Far East, 1971-72, UN Fund for Population Activities, 1980, Nat. Inst. Child Health and Human Devel., 1984, UN Econ. and Social Commn. for Asia and Pacific, 1984. Author: Statistical Models for Causal Analysis, 1993; editor: Asian and Pacific Population Forum, 1980-85, assoc. editor 1985-91; contbr. articles to profl. jours. Grantee Commn. on Population and the Hawaiian Future, 1982, Nat. Inst. Child Health and Human Devel., 1983, 84-85, 85-86, 86-88, Ford Found., Pioneer Fund, Inc., 1984-85, U.S. Agy. for Internat. Devel., 1989-93. Mem. AAAS, Internat. Union of Sci. Study of Population, Population Assn. Am., Soc. for Study of Social Biology (pres. 1991-93, bd. dirs.). Home: 42 N Kainalu Dr Kailua HI 96734-2302 Office: Program on Population East-West Center Honolulu HI 96848

REUS, VICTOR I., psychiatry educator, hospital administrator; b. Bordeaux, France, Oct. 18, 1947; came to U.S., 1949; BA, Cornell U., 1969; MD, U. Md., Balt., 1973; postgrad., U. Wis., 1973-76. Diplomate Nat. Bd. Med. Examiners, Am. Bd. Psychiatry and Neurology (sr. examiner 1996—), Am. Bd. Geriatric Psychiatry. Clin. assoc. Inst. Psychiatry Maudsley Hosp., London, 1973; consulting physician Mendota Mental Health Inst., Madison, Wis., 1974-76; fellow in adminstrv. psychiatry, psychiatry edn. br., divsn. manpower tng. NIMH, Rockville, Md., 1975; clin. assoc., ward adminstr. sect. psychobiology, biol. psychiatry br. NIMH, Bethesda, Md., 1976-78; chief resident adult inpatient svc. U. Wis. Hosp., Madison, 1976; instr. George Washington Sch. Medicine, Washington, 1976-78; instr. sch. medicine Georgetown U., Washington, 1977-78; dir. behavioral neuroscience svc. Langley Porter Neuropsychiatric Hosp., U. Calif., San Francisco, 1978-87, med. dir., 1986—; from asst. prof. to assoc. prof. dept. psychiatry sch. medicine U. Calif., San Francisco, 1978-89, prof., 1989—; mem. behavioral scis. com. Nat. Bd. Med. Examiners; mem. various coms. sch. medicine U. Calif., 1978—; grant reviewer, site visitor NIMH, 1977, 1984—, mem. initial rev. group, small grant rev. com., biol. and neurosciences subcom., 1989-91, mem. initial rev. group, individual faculty scholar award, 1990, mem. initial rev. group, biol. psychopathology rev. com., 1991-93, mem. reviewers res., 1993—, reviewer behavioral sci. track award for rapid transition, 1994; mem. ad hoc com. on psychotropic drugs City of San Francisco Mental Health Adv. Coun., 1979-80; grant reviewer, site visitor Nat. Inst. Drug Abuse, 1979, 87, Nat. Inst. Aging, 1985, 92; cons., examining psychiatrist Superior Ct., City and County of San Francisco, 1979—, U.S. Dist. Ct. (no. dist.) Calif., 1980—, Juvenile Ct., Dept. Social Svcs., City and County of San Francisco, 1987-90; cons. Pfizer Pharms., 1984-85, Abbott Diagnostic Labs., 1987-88, Abbott Pharms. Product Devel., 1993; cons. to subcom. mental health Calif. State Legislature, Sacramento, 1984; grant reviewer NSF, 1985, others; mem. Scientist's Inst. Pub. Info., N.Y.C., 1985—; mem. grant rev. com. Dept. Mental Health, State of Calif., 1986; mem. San Francisco Peer Rev. Com., Pacific Peer Rev., 1986-89; mem. profl. adv. bd. No. Calif. chpt. Epilepsy Found. Am., 1989—; presenter in field. Mem. editl. bd. Western Jour. Medicine, 1991-93; editl. reviewer Internat. Jour. of Psychiatry in Medicine, Western Jour. Medicine, Archives of Gen. Psychiatry, Am. Jour. Physiology, Gordon and Breach, Sci. Pubs., Inc., others; contbr. chpts. to books and articles and book revs. to profl. jours. Lt. comdr. USPHS, 1976-78. Co-investigator Nat. Inst. Drug Abuse, 1980-94, NIMH, 1991—, Scottish Rite Schizophrenia Rsch. Program, 1993-95, Upjohn Pharms., 1993—. Fellow Am. Psychiat. Assn. (cons. consultation svc., rsch. program devel. 1991—), West Coast Coll. Biol. Psychiatry (charter, mem. edn. and tng. com. 1983-87, mem. and chmn. credentials com. 1983-87, pres. 1989); mem. AAAS, Am. Soc. Clin. Psychopharmacology (mem. membership com. 1994—), Am. Coll. Psychiatrists, No. Calif. Psychiat. Soc. (mem. and chmn. pub. info. com. 1978-82, chmn. psychobiology com. 1982-84, mem. hosp. com. 1987-91, councilor 1993—, sec. 1996-97), Calif. Acad. Medicine, Calif. Psychiat. Assn. (mem. ann. meeting planning com. 1995), Soc. Biol. Psychiatry (sec. program com. 1982-83, 83-84, mem. and chair Ziskind-Somerfeld rsch. award com. 1991-94), Psychiat. Rsch. Soc., Internat. Soc. Psychoneuroendocrinology, Academia, Medicinae & Psychiatriae Found., Inc., Collegium Internationale Neuro-Psychopharmacologicum, Psi Chi. Office: U Calif Box F-0984 401 Parnassus Ave San Francisco CA 94143-0984

REUSS, GARRETT MICHAEL, real estate broker; b. Smithtown, N.Y., Nov. 5, 1969; s. Edward George and Jill Stephanie (Hargrave) R.; m. Doretta Angela Icolari, June 3, 1970. BA, St. Bonaventure U., Olean, N.Y., 1992. Gen. mgr. Booba Ptnrs., Aspen, Colo., 1992-94; mgr., rental Snowmass (Colo.) Real Estate Co., 1994—. Democrat. Office: Snowmass Real Estate 50 Snowmass Village Snowmass CO 81615

REUTHER, RONALD THEODORE, museum director; b. Dec. 29, 1929; s. Frederick and Grace (Roehl) R.; m. Mary B. Howard, 1956; children: Catherine, Virginia, Paul, Douglas, Jon Frederick, Victoria Grace. BA, U. Calif., 1951, postgrad., 1953; postgrad., U. Ariz., 1952. Mgr. Micke Grove Zoo, 1957-62; gen. curator Cleve. Zoo, 1958-62; asst. dir., 1964-66; dir. Indpls. Zoo, 1962-64, San Francisco Zoo, 1966-73; pres., exec. dir. Phila. Zoo, 1973-78; dir. corp. devel., exploration San Francisco, 1980-81; founder We. Aerospace Mus., Oakland, Calif., 1980, exec. dir., 1995—; field rep. Bell & Howell Edn. Corp./DeVry Inst. Tech., 1983-88; exec. dir. Whale Ctr., Oakland, Calif., 1988-89; edn. cons. Sierra Acad. Aeronautics, Oakland, Calif., 1989-92; lectr. Golden State U., San Francisco, 1992; co-founder Pt. Reyes Bird Observatory, Calif., 1968-70; v.p. Del. Valley Mus. Coun., 1976-78. Author zoo guidebooks, Wings Over San Francisco Bay, 1997,. Mgr. exec. com. Greater Phila. Cultural Alliance, 1976-78. 2nd lt. USAF, 1953-57; with USNG, 1958-66; USAR, 1966-81. Mem. The Explorers Club (chmn. Calif. chpt. 1990-95), Tamalpais Conservation Club (sec. 1988-91), Ox-5 Pioneers (bd. govs. Golden Gate chpt. 1996—). Office: We Aerospace Mus Oakland Airport 8260 Boeing St Oakland CA 94614

RE VELLE, JACK B(OYER), statistician, consultant; b. Rochester, N.Y., Aug. 2, 1935; s. Mark A. and Myril (Bubes) Re V.; m. Brenda Lorraine Newcombe, Aug. 2, 1968; 1 child, Karen Alyssa. BS in Chem. Engring., Purdue U., 1957; MS in Indsl. Engring. and Mgmt., Okla. State U., 1965, PhD in Indsl. Engring. and Mgmt., 1970. Commd. 2d lt. USAF, 1957, advanced through grades to major, 1968, resigned, 1968; adminstrv. asst. Gen. Dynamics, Ft. Worth, 1970-71; cons. engr. Denver, 1971-72; chmn. decision scis. U. Nebr., Omaha, 1972-77; dean Sch. Bus. and Mgmt. Chapman U., Orange, Calif., 1977-79; sr. staff engr. McDonnell Douglas Space Systems, Huntington Beach, Calif., 1979-81; head mfg. tng. and devel. Hughes Aircraft Co., Fullerton, Calif., 1981-82, sr. statistician, 1982-86; corp. mgr. R & D Hughes Aircraft Co., L.A., 1986-88, corp. chief statistician, 1988-93; leader continuous improvement Hughes Missile Systems Co., Tucson, Ariz., 1994—; mem. bd. examiners Malcolm Baldridge nat. quality award Nat. Inst. Stds. and Tech., U.S. Dept. Commerce, Washington, 1990, 93; judge Ariz. Quality Alliance, Phoenix, 1994-96, Rochester Inst. Tech.-USA Today Quality Cup Competition, 1994—, Def. Contract Mgmt. Command-Commdrs. Cup, 1995—; cons. to various pub. and pvt. orgns.; presenter, lectr. in field. Author: Safety Training Methods, 1980, The Two-Day Statistician, 1986, The New Quality Technology, 1988, Policy Deployment, 1993, (with others) Quest for Quality, 1986, Mechanical Engineers Handbook, 1986, Production Handbook, 1987, Handbook of Occupational Safety and Health, 1987, A Quality Revolution in Manufacturing, 1989, Quality Engineering Handbook, 1991; co-author: Quantitative Methods for Managerial Decisions, 1978, The Executive's Handbook on Quality Function Deployment, 1994, From Concept to Customer, 1995, The Quality Function Deployment Handbook, 1997, (software packages) TQM ToolSchool, 1995, QFD/Pathway, 1997. Bd. dirs. Assn. for Quality and Participation, Cin., 1985-86. Fellow Inst. for the Advancement Engring., 1986; recipient Disting. Econs. Devel. award Soc. Mfg. Engrs., 1990. Fellow Am. Soc. for Quality Control (co-chair total quality mgmt. com. 1990-92), Am. Soc. Safety Engrs. (nat. accreditation project dir. 1978-80), Inst. Indsl. Engrs. (regional v.p. 1982-84, treas. 1992-93, sr. v.p. 1993-94), Aerospace and Defense Soc. (pres. 1997—). Office: Hughes Missile Systems Co Old Nogales Hwy Tucson AZ 85734

REVIER, CHARLES FRANKLIN, economics educator; b. Lubbock, Tex., Sept. 1, 1944; s. Frank Fancher and Dorothy Charlene (Lawson) R.; m. Susan Ann Nethaway, Aug. 7, 1971; children: Emily Ann, Lauren Ann. BA in Physics, U. Colo., 1966, MA in Econs., 1968; PhD in Econs., MIT, 1978. Teaching asst. U. Colo., Boulder, 1968; rsch. asst. MIT, Cambridge, Mass., summer 1969; intern Coun. of Econ. Advisors, Washington, summer 1970; cons. intern Adv. Commn. on Intergovernmental Rels., Washington, 1971-72; teaching asst. MIT, Cambridge, Mass., 1972-73; rsch. asst. Nat. Bur. Econ. Rsch., Cambridge, Mass., 1973; instr. Colo. State U., Ft. Collins, 1974-78, asst. prof., 1978-87, assoc. prof., 1987—; chmn. dept. econs. Colo. State U., Ft. Collins, 1988-96. Contbr. articles to profl. jours. NSF fellow, 1968-71, Charles Abrams Joint Ctr. for Urban Studies, MIT and Harvard U., 1973-74. Mem. Am. Econ. Assn. Democrat. Methodist. Office: Colo State U Dept Econs Fort Collins CO 80523-1771

REVOYR, JACK RONALD, trademark licensing consultant, writer; b. LaCrosse, Wis., Dec. 14, 1935; s. Ronald John and Mildred Alice (Giles) R.; 1 child, Nina. BS with high honors, U. Wis., 1957; postgrad., Stanford U., 1962. Japan rep. Hong Kong Tourist Assn., Tokyo, 1966-74; mgr. Am. Express, N.Y.C., 1974-75; dir. tourism State of Wis., Madison, 1976-78; mng. dir. Far East Uni-Mgrs. Internat., L.A., 1978-79; mgr. Torizen Restaurant, Gardena, Calif., 1980-81; licensing dir. UCLA, 1981-94; owner Intelic, Oak View, Calif., 1994—; mgr. Furushima Pub. Rels., Tokyo, 1965-66; staff announcer Japan Broadcasting Corp., Tokyo, 1963-65; editor Asahi Evening News, Tokyo, 1962-63; news editor Sta. KERN, Bakersfield, Calif., 1960-61; presenter in field. Author: How To Guide to Collegiate Licensing, 1985, 2d edit., 1994, A Primer on Licensing, 1994, 2d edit., 1995, Licensee Survival Guide, 1995. Mem. Assn. Collegiate Licensing Adminstrs. (founder, regional dir., mem. steering com., original mem. West Coast anti-counterfeiting coalition), Phi Beta Kappa. Office: PO Box 1617 Oak View CA 93022-1617

REXNER, ROMULUS, publishing executive; b. Odessa, Russia, July 16, 1920; came to U.S., 1956; s. Richard Rexner and Nina Norvid; m. Elisabeth Unger, Aug. 22, 1964. BS in Econs. with hons., Univ. London, 1951. Founder, mgr. Pantheon Press, Gen. Enterprises, L.A., 1951-86, Honolulu, 1986—. Author: Planetary Legion, 1961, 2nd edit., 1987; pub., editor Cosmopolitan Contact, 1962—; patentee in field. Founder Planetary Legion for Peace, 1955. With Brit. Forces WWII. Office: Pantheon Press Gen Enterprises Planetary Legion PO Box 89300 Honolulu HI 96830

REYES, ARTHUR ALEXANDER, software engineer, researcher, business manager; b. New Rochelle, N.Y., Feb. 16, 1964; s. Richard Ortleib R. and Janice Hall; m. Colette Esther Nicolas, Apr. 2, 1988; children: Naomi Janice, Gabrielle Victoria. BS suma cum laude, Poly. U., 1987; MS, U. Calif., 1995, postgrad., 1997—. Asst. produce mgr. Shopwell, Inc., New Rochelle, N.Y., 1981-83; machinist Photographic Equipment Svcs., Inc., New Rochelle, N.Y., 1984, Reyes Engring. & Mfg., Haltom City, Tex., 1984-87; engr. B-2 divsn. Northrop, Pico Rivera, Calif., 1987-92; researcher U. Calif., Irvine, 1992—, tchg. asst., 1996; new bus. devel. mgr. Formal Devel., Oceanside, Calif., 1995—. Campaign activist Alan Keyes for Pres. '96, Oceanside, Calif., 1996; block co-capt. Neighborhood Watch, Oceanside, 1991-92; area dir. A Place for Us, Torrance, Calif., 1991. Grad. fellow NASA, 1993-96. Mem. IEEE (reviewer trans software engring. tech. com. software engring. 1996), AIAA, NRA (grassroots activist Oceanside 1994—), Assn. Computing Machinery, Automobile Club So. Calif., Sigma Gamma Tau. Home: PO Box 3081 Oceanside CA 92051-3081 Office: Dept Info and Computer Sci 277 ICS2 Bldg 304 Irvine CA 92697-3425

REYES, EDWARD, pharmacology educator; b. Albuquerque, May 5, 1944; s. Salvador and Faustina (Gabaldon) R.; m. Shirley Ann Trott, Aug. 15, 1970; children: David Joshua, Elizabeth Ann, Steven Mark. BS in Pharmacy, U. N.Mex., 1968; MS in Pharmacology, U. Colo., 1970, PhD in Pharmacology, 1974. Asst. prof. pharmacy U. Wyo. Sch. of Pharmacy, Laramie, 1974-75; asst. prof. pharmacology Dept. Pharmacology, U. N.Mex., Albuquerque, 1976-85, assoc. prof. pharmacology, 1985—; dir. minority biomed. rsch. support program U. N.Mex. Sch. of Medicine, Albuquerque, 1994—; referee Pharmacology Biochemistry Behavior, San Antonio, 1986—; adv. com. mem. NIMH Minority Neuro Sci. Fellowship, Washington, 1991—. Author: (with others) Alcohol and Drug Abuse Review, 1991; contbr. articles to profl. jours. Scoutmaster Boy Scouts Am., Albuquerque, 1986-94, dist. camping com. chair, 1994—, Silver Beaver, 1996; vis. scientist N.Mex. Acad. Sci., Las Vegas, 1988—; youth preacher Rio Grande Bapt. Ch., Albuquerque, 1980—. Grantee Nat. Inst. of Alcohol Abuse and Alcoholism, NSF. Mem. Rsch. Soc. on Alcoholism, Western Pharmacology Soc., Soc. for Neurosci. (chair minority edn. tng. and profl. adv. 1987-94), Soc. for Advancement of Chicanos and Native Ams. in Sci. Office: Univ NMex Sch Medicine 915 Camino de Salud NE Albuquerque NM 87131

REYHNER, JON ALLAN, education educator; b. Fountain Hill, Pa., Apr. 29, 1944; s. Theodore O. and Alice Elizabeth (Cornish) R.; m. Helen Marie Bennett, July 15, 1972; children: Deborah Dawn, Tsosie Dean. BA, U. Calif., Davis, 1966, MA, 1967; MEd, No. Ariz. U., 1973, EdS, 1977; EdD, Mont. State U., 1984. Asst. prin. Navajo (N.Mex.) Pub. Sch., 1975-77; prin. Wallace Sch., Parker, Ariz., 1977-78, Rocky Boy (Mont.) Sch., 1978-80, Heart Butte (Mont.) Sch., 1982-84; chief adminstr. Havasupai Sch., Supai, Ariz., 1984-85; assoc. prof. Mont. State U., Billings, 1986-95; assoc. prof. and coord. bilingual multicultural edn. program No. Ariz. U., Flagstaff, 1995—; coord. Indian tchr. tng. program Ea. Mont. Coll., Billings, 1986. Editor: Teaching American Indian Studies, 1992; co-author: A History of Indian Education, 1989. Mem. Am. Edn. Rsch. Assn., Phi Alpha Theta, Phi Delta Kappa. Home: 1719 W Sunshine Dr Flagstaff AZ 86001 Office: No Ariz U PO Box 5774 Flagstaff AZ 86011

REYNALDS, JEREMY GRAHAM, rescue mission administrator; b. Bath, Eng., Oct. 19, 1957; came to U.S., 1978; s. Graham John and Ruth (Bowden) R.; m. Sylvia Ellen Page, Apr. 14, 1979; children: Ben, Joshua, Jeremiah, Joel, Josiah. B Univ. Studies, U. N.Mex., 1996, postgrad., 1996—. Founder, exec. dir. His Place, Santa Fe, 1982-86, Joy Junction, Albuquerque, 1986—. Author: Homeless in America, 1994, The Walking Wounded, 1996. Recipient Jefferson award Am. Inst. for Pub. Svc., 1994. Mem. Internat. Union Gospel Missions. Mem. Calvary Chapel. Office: Joy Junction PO Box 27693 4500 2d St SW Albuquerque NM 87125

REYNOLDS, BRIAN ARTHUR, library director; b. Visalia, Calif., June 28, 1950; s. William Arthur and Marilyn (Hart) R.; m. Diane Leigh MacVeagh, June 20, 1977; children: Nathaniel Arthur, Matthew Wayne. BA, U. Calif., Berkeley, 1972; MLS, U. Calif., L.A., 1974; MPA, Calif. State U., Chico, 1984. Asst. libr. dir. Universidad Centroamericana, Managua, Nicaragua, 1975; pub. svcs. libr. Bensenville (Ill.) Pub. Libr., 1976; ref. libr. Shasta County Pub. Libr., Redding, Calif., 1977-82; libr. dir. Siskiyou County Pub. Libr., Yreka, Calif., 1982-93, San Luis Obispo (Calif.) City County Libr., 1993—. Producer (adult literacy radio series) READ Radio Series I, II, 1988-89. Mem. ALA, Calif. Libr. Assn., Calif. Soc. Librs. (pres. 1991), Rotary (San Luis Obispo). Democrat. Office: San Luis Obispo City Co Lib PO Box 8107 995 Palm St San Luis Obispo CA 93403-8107

REYNOLDS, CHARLES PATRICK, pediatric oncologist, researcher; b. El Paso, Tex., Aug. 8, 1952; s. Charles Albert and Lallah Elizabeth (Munro) R.; m. Debra Dawn Adams, Feb. 3, 1979; children: Amy Elizabeth, Jennifer Ann. BA in Biology, U. Tex., 1974; MD, U. Tex. Southwestern Med. Sch., Dallas, 1979; PhD, U. Tex., 1979. Lic. Tex., Calif. Postdoctoral fellow U. Tex. Southwestern Med. Sch., Dallas, 1979-80; pediatric intern Nat. Naval Med. Ctr., Bethesda, Md., 1980-81; battalion surg. Third Marine Div., Okinawa, Japan, 1981-82; rsch. med. officer Naval Med. Rsch. Inst., Bethesda, 1982-87; asst. prof. UCLA, 1987-89; assoc. prof. U. So. Calif., L.A., 1989—; head devel. therapeutics sect. divsn. hematology-oncology Children's Hosp. L.A., 1993—; dir. Neuroblastoma Marrow Purging Lab. Childrens Cancer Group, L.A., 1988—; team physician U.S. Shooting Team, 1991—. Patentee in field; contbr. articles to profl. jours. Mem. 1992 USA Olympic Shooting Team, Barcelona, Spain. Grantee Nat. Cancer Inst., Am. Inst. Cancer Rsch., Am. Cancer Soc. Mem. Am. Soc. Clin. Oncology, Am. Assn. Cancer Rsch., Soc. Analytical Cytology. Roman Catholic. Office: Childrens Hosp LA Div Hematology Oncology PO Box 54700 Los Angeles CA 90054-0700

REYNOLDS, DAVID KENT, writer, educator; b. Dayton, Ohio, Sept. 28, 1940; s. Charles K. and Frances M. (Worrell) R.; m. Lynn Sanae Tamashiro, May 6, 1978. BA, UCLA, 1964, MA, 1965, PhD, 1969. Asst. prof. Sch. Pub. Health, Divsn. Behavioral Scis. UCLA, 1970-71; asst. prof. Sch. Medicine, Dept. Psychiatry U. So. Calif., 1974-79; assoc. prof. anthropology U. Houston, 1979-80; dir. ToDo Inst., L.A., 1980-89, Constructive Living Ctr., Coos Bay, Oreg., 1989—; temporary adviser WHO, People's Rep. of China; papers presented at Am. Anthropol. Assn., Am. Acad. Psychoanalysis, Am. Psychiat. Assn., VI World Congress of Psychiatry, Internat. Assn. for Suicide Prevention, Am. Assn. of Suicidology, Western Psychol. Assn., Western Gerontol. Soc., Soc. for Applied Anthropology, and others in the U.S. and Japan. Author: (in English and Japanese) Suicide: Inside and Out, 1976, Constructive Living, 1984, The Heart of the Japanese People, 1980, Morita Psychotherapy, 1976, (in English) Reflections on the Tao te Ching, 1993, Plunging Through the Clouds, 1993, Naikan Psychotherapy, 1991, The Quiet Therapies, 1980; author: (with others) Current Psychiatric Therapies, 1973, Suicide in Different Cultures, 1975, Emergency and Disaster Management, 1976, Modern Morita Therapy, 1977, Handbook of Innovative Psychotherapies, 1981, Living and Dying with Cancer, 1981, Coping with Aging, 1982, Encyclopedia of Japan, 1987, Encyclopedia of Psychology, 1987, Health, Illness, and Medical Care in Japan, 1987; contbr. to profl. jours. Mem. adv. bd. Okamoto Found., Japan, 1990—, Hakkenkai Orgn., 1978—. Fulbright-Hays scholar 1973, 78; grantee Tokyo Met. Inst. of Gerontology, 1979, NIMH, 1972, 73, 75-78, Japanese NIMH 1967, 68, NDEA, 1967, NSF, 1967, and others. Mem. Am. Anthropol. Assn., Japan Assn. Morita Therapy (Kora prize 1992). Office: Constructive Living PO Box 85 Coos Bay OR 97420-0007

REYNOLDS, EDWARD EVAN, JR., information systems consultant; b. N.Y.C., Aug. 5, 1935; s. Edward Evan Reynolds and Evelyn Abagail (Kight) Kimball; m. Judy Lookanoff, May 18, 1963; children: Wendy, Robin. BS in Mgmt., Bellevue U., 1969; BA in Adminstrn., N.H. Coll., 1970; MA in Mgmt., U. Nebr., 1973. Commd. 2nd lt. USAF, 1957, advanced through ranks to lt. col., ret., 1979; mgr. applications maintenance United Airlines, San Francisco, 1979-82; sr. info. sys. cons. SRI Internat., Menlo Park, Calif., 1982-86; European site mgr. ERC, Spangdalham AFB, Germany, 1986-87; dir. customer svcs. Nucleus Internat. Corp., Culver City, Calif., 1987-92; pres. Client Server Solutions Corp., Woodland Hills, Calif., 1992—; chief scientist tech. network MCI Systemhouse, Woodland Hills, 1992—. Mem. Air Force Assn. (prres. Tennessee Ernie Ford chpt. 1985-86, Gen. Doolittle chpt. 1990-92). Home and Office: 23368 Burbank Blvd Woodland Hills CA 91367

REYNOLDS, HALLIE BELLAH, elementary education educator; b. L.A., May 12, 1930; d. Luther Hutton and Lillian (Neely) Bellah; m. Jack C. Reynolds (div.); children: Ann Luce, Reede, Susan Todd. BA, U. So. Calif., 1952; teaching credential, U.S. Internat. U., San Diego, 1973, MA in Edn., 1979. Tchr. math. Poway (Calif.) Unified Sch. Dist., 1973—; mem. San Diego County Math. Leaders Com., 1988—, San Diego County Math. Staff Developers Com., 1988—. Mem. Jr. League San Diego, Trojan League, San Diego. Recipient hon. svc. award Los Penasquitos PTA, 1987. Mem. Nat. Coun. Tchrs. Math. (reader's adv. panel for Arithmetic Tchr. mag. 1989), Calif. Math. Coun., Greater San Diego Math. Coun. Republican. Episcopalian. Home: 6290 Caminito Del Oeste San Diego CA 92111-6829 Office: Los Penasquitos Sch 14125 Cuca St San Diego CA 92129-1852

REYNOLDS, JAMES FRANCIS, JR., physician; b. St. Albans, Vt., June 20, 1947; s. James F. Sr. and Eleanor (Paquette) R.; married; children: Matthew, Katelyn, Aaron. BS, U.S. Mil. Acad., West Point, N.Y., 1969; MD, U. Louisville, 1978. Diplomate Am. Bd. Pediatrics, Am. Bd. Med. Genetics. Commd. U.S. Army, 1969, advanced through grades to col., 1974; pediatrics resident U. Va., Charlottesville, 1978-81, genetics fellow, 1981-83; clin. geneticist dept. med. genetics Shodair Hosp., Helena, Mont., 1983—. Assoc. editor Am. Jour. Med. Genetics, 1983-95; editor various books on med. genetics; contbr. articles to profl. jours. Mem. health profl. adv. com. Mont. March of Dimes, 1987—; mem. Mont. Coun. for Maternal and Child Health, 1987—. Fellow Am. Acad. Pediatrics, Am. Coll. Med. Genetics; mem. Am. Soc. Human Genetics. Office: Shodair Hosp PO Box 5539 Helena MT 59604-5539

REYNOLDS, JOHN CURBY, sales representative; b. San Jose, Calif., Aug. 15, 1948; s. Ivan Randolph and Lillie Murrel (McBrown) R.; m. Sharon Taylor, June 12, 1982; children: Brian James, Chris John. AA, Cabrillo Jr. Coll., Aptos, Calif., 1969; student, Calif. Polytechnic U., 1969-71. Sales rep. Equitable of Iowa Ins. Co., Sacramento, 1973-79, Grand Auto Inc., Sacramento, 1979-82, Princess House, Sacramento, 1982-84; sales telemktg. Montgomery Ward, Sacramento, 1984-85; sales rep. Sanitary Supply Co., Tucson, 1986—; mem. SVEA Bus. Group, Sierra Vista, Ariz., 1986—. Mem. First So. Bapt. Ch., Sierra Vista, 1989—. Mem. Sierra Vista C. of C. (mil. affairs com.). Republican. Office: Sanitary Supply Co Inc 360 S 7th St Sierra Vista AZ 85635-2506

REYNOLDS, KATHLEEN DIANE FOY (K.D.F. REYNOLDS), transportation executive; b. Chgo., Dec. 9, 1946; d. David Chancy Foy and Vivian Anne (Schwartz) R. Student, San Francisco State U., 1964-68. Studio coord. KTVU-TV, Oakland, Calif., 1968-70; assoc. prodr. KPIX-TV, San Francisco, 1970-72; music publicist Oakland, 1966-78; writer PLEXUS, West Coast Women's Press, Oakland, 1974-82, gen. mgr., 1984-86; screen writer Oakland, 1970—; gen. ptnr. Designated Driver Group, Oakland, 1990-97; mng. ptnr. Foy Scribes (divsn. Tallahassee Group), 1997—; coun. mem. West Coast Women's Press, Oakland, 1975-86; founding assoc. Women's Inst. for Freedom of the Press, Washington, 1977—; assoc. owner DeSoto Cab, San Francisco, 1995—; medallion permit owner City & County San Francisco, 1995—. Author of periodical news, reviews, features, 1974-82; author of six documentaries for comml. and PBS-TV, 1968-73. Mem. Soc. Mayflower Descendants, Casper, Wyo., 1967—. Mem. San Francisco Film Soc. Home: PO Box 2742 Oakland CA 94602-0042

REYNOLDS, RAY THOMAS, planetary scientist; b. Lexington, Ky., Sept. 2, 1933; s. Oscar Ray and Margaret Louise (Gudgel) R.; m. Yolanda Maria de la Luz Gallegos, Oct. 15, 1962; children: Mark Andrew, Daniel Alan. BS in Chemistry, U. Ky., 1954, MS in Physics, 1960. Rsch. scientist Am. Geog. Soc., Thule, Greenland, 1960-61, U. Calif., Los Alamos, N.Mex., 1961; chief theoretical studies br. NASA Ames Rsch. Ctr., Moffett Field, Calif., 1969-78, rsch. scientist, 1962-69, 78-88, Ames assoc., 1988—. Recipient Exceptional Sci. Achievement award NASA, 1980, Exceptional Svc. medal, 1996. Fellow Am. Geophys. Union, Meteoritical Soc.; mem. Am. Astron. Soc., AAAS (Newcombe prize 1979). Contbr. over 170 sci. reports on planetary formation structure and evolution, articles to profl. publs. Home: 1650 Shasta Ave San Jose CA 95128-5213 Office: NASA Ames Rsch Ctr Moffett Field CA 94035

REYNOLDS, ROBERT HARRISON, retired export company executive; b. Mpls., Sept. 6, 1913; s. Clarence H. and Helen (Doyle) R.; m. Gladys Marie Gaster, Apr. 7, 1934; 1 child, Shirley Anne (Mrs. Frank S. Potestio); m. Viola E. Shimel, June 26, 1982. Export sales mgr., rolled products sales mgr. Colo. Fuel & Iron Corp., Denver, 1938-46; pres. Rocky Mountain Export Co., Inc., Denver, 1941-93. Mem. Denver Club (life). Home: 13850 E Marina Dr Aurora CO 80014-5509 Office: 12331 E Cornell Ave Aurora CO 80014-3323

REYNOLDS, ROGER LEE, composer; b. Detroit, July 18, 1934; s. George Arthur and Katherine Adelaide (Butler) R.; m. Karen Jeanne Hill, Apr. 11, 1964; children: Erika Lynn, Wendy Claire. BSE in Physics, U. Mich., 1957, MusB in Music Lit., 1960, MusM in Composition, 1961. Assoc. prof. U. Calif. San Diego, La Jolla, 1969-73, founding dir. Ctr. Music Expt. and Related Rsch., 1972-77, prof., 1973—; George Miller prof. U. Ill., 1971—; Valentine prof. Amherst Coll., Mass., 1988; George Miller prof. U. Ill., 1971; vis. prof. Yale U., New Haven, 1981; sr. rsch. fellow ISAM, Bklyn. Coll., 1985; Valentine prof. Amherst (Mass.) Coll., 1988; Rothschild composer in residence Peabody Conservatory of Music, 1992-93. Author: MIND MODELS: New Forms of Musical Experience, 1975, A Searcher's Path: A Composer's Ways, 1987, A Jostled Silence: Contemporary Japanese Musical Thought, 1992-93; contbr. numerous articles and revs. to profl. jours. Bd. dirs. Am. Music. Ctr., Meet the Composer, Fromm Found. Harvard U.; mem. bd. govs. Inst. Current World Affairs. Recipient citation Nat. Inst. Arts and Letters, 1971, Koussevitzky Internat. Rec. award 1971, NEA awards, 1975, 78, 79, 86, Pulitzer prize for music, 1989; sr. fellow Inst. Studies in Am. Music, 1985, fellow Inst. Current World Affairs, Rockefeller Found., Guggenheim Found.; Fulbright scholar. Office: U Calif San Diego Dept Music 0326 La Jolla CA 92093

REYNOLDS, RON L., foundation administrator, fundraising consultant; b. Bonners Ferry, Idaho, Sept. 11, 1956; s. Harry LeRoy and Alice Maxine (Clark) R.; m. Sherri Lynn Reynolds, Apr. 11, 1975 (div. Aug. 1979); 1 child, Cory Lee; m. Jacqueline Reynolds, May 8, 1992; children: Lori, Ann Browning, Ginger Adele Ferguson, Deanna Dawn Anderst. AS in Bus., U. So. Calif., Northridge, 1980; BS, Lewis-Clark State Coll., Lewiston, Idaho, 1994. Warehouse mgr. Delta Pacific Distbrs., L.A., 1979-83; mgr. E.T. Industries, Vancouver, Wash., 1983-86; self-employed Bus. Svcs., Lewiston, Idaho, 1987-91; plant supr. Goodwill Industries, Lewiston, Idaho, 1993-95; exec. dir. Clearwater Valley Hosp. Found., Orofino, Idaho, 1995—; pres. Banana Belt Cruisers, Lewiston, 1994-96; mem. LC Fundraisers, Inc., Lewiston, 1995-96. Mem. Clearwater Valley Hosp. Aux., Orofino. Grantee GTE Found., Spokane, Wash., 1996, Donna Bauer Found., Orofino, 1996, Steele Reece Found., Berklund Found., 1996. Mem. Orofino C. of C., Eagles. Democrat. Southern Baptist. Home: 836 Pine St Lewiston ID 83501 Office: Clearwater Valley Hosp Found PO Box 2169 1075 Michigan Ave Orofino ID 83544

REYNOLDS, STUART ARNOLD, surgeon; b. Berkeley, Calif., Oct. 16, 1936; s. Zen Vestal and Gladys Buellah (Rook) R.; m. Virginia A. Sterm-Reynolds; children: Karen E. Hanson, Julia E. Reynolds. BS in Med. Sci., Stanford U., 1959, MD, 1962. Cert. am. bd. surgery, 1970, 80, 91. Pvt. practice Havre, Mont., 1969-96; cons. emergency medicine and trauma Havre, 1996—. Recipient Physicians Recognition award AMA, 1986, Trauma Achievement award, Am. Coll. Surgeons, 1986, 89, 92, Outstanding Svc. award Emergency Med. Svcs., 1988, Meritorious Svc. award Advanced trauma Life Support, 1991. Fellow ACS, Mont. Med. Assn. Home: Star Rt 36 Box 56 Havre MT 59501

REYNOLDS-SAKOWSKI, DANA RENEE, science educator; b. Centralia, Ill., June 28, 1968; d. David Lavern and Betty Lou (Shelton) Reynolds; m. Jason Bielas Sakowski, Oct. 8, 1994. BS in Edn., U. No. Colo., 1991, MEd in Middle Sch. Edn., 1996. Tchr. life sci. and math. Ken Caryl Mid. Sch., Littleton, Colo., 1991-92; tchr. sci. Moore Mid. Sch., Arvada, Colo., 1992-93; tchr. life sci. Moore Mid. Sch., Arvada, 1993—. Mem. Nat. Wildlife Fedn., Colo. Assn. Sci. Tchrs., Colo. Biology Tchrs. Assn., Sierra Club, World Wildlife Fund, Nat. Parks and Conservation Assn., Natural Resources Def. Coun., Audubon Soc., Nature Conservancy. Office: Moore Mid Sch 8455 W 88th Ave Arvada CO 80005-1620

REZA, JACQUELYN VALERIE, counselor, consultant; b. San Francisco, Sept. 12, 1953; d. Armando Rosalio Reza and Jacquelyn Joan Jordan; 1 child, Antonio Vincent Reza-James. BS in Zoology with honors, Ahmadu Bello U., Zaria, Nigeria, 1978; BA, San Francisco State U., 1979, MS in Rehab. Counseling, 1981; EdD in Internat. and Multicultural Edn., U. San Francisco, 1995. Lic. marriage family child counselor, nat. cert. counselor, cert. hypnotherapist. Counselor San Francisco State U., 1980-82, Calif. State U. Stanislaus, Turlock, 1982-84; marriage family child counselor pvt. practice therapist, workshop cons. San Francisco, Sacramento and San Jose, Calif., 1982—; counselor Gavilan C.C., Gilroy, Calif., 1984-85, De Anza C.C., Cupertino, Calif., 1985—; cons. Driver Performance Inst., San Francisco, 1984-91, Extended Opportunities and Svcs. Program Student Leadership Inst., Calif., 1987—; cons., examiner Bd. Behavioral Scis., Sacramento, 1986-92; pres. faculty senate De Anza C.C., 1989-90. Editor: (booklet) A Guide for I.D. and Referral of Students in Stress, 1985; contbr. articles to newsletters. Recipient Women Leaders in Edn. of Santa Clara County award, 1990, Golden Torch award San Francisco State U. Alumni, 1993; honoree Chicana Found. No. Calif., 1994; Title 7 fellow Office Bilingual & Minority Affairs, 1993-94, 94-95. Mem. Am. Assn. Women Community & Jr. Colls., Am. Counselor Assn., Am. Minority Counseling Assn., Latina Leadership Network Calif. C.C. (v.p. 1991-93, pres. 1993-94), Acad. Senate Calif. C.C. (mem. exec. bd. 1990-92), Minority Staff Assn., Third World Counselors Assn., De Anza Faculty Assn. (mem. exec. bd. 1987-89). Home: 6262 Thomas Ave Newark CA 94560-4042 Office: De Anza Coll 21250 Stevens Creek Blvd Cupertino CA 95014-5702

REZLER, JULIUS, labor arbitrator; b. Miskolc, Hungary, May 31, 1911; came to U.S., 1952; s. Gyula and Ilona (Kozma) R.; m. Agnes Graig, Aug. 16, 1954. PhD summa cum laude, U. Szeged, 1938; Dr.pol.sc. cum laude, U. Pecs, 1941, docent, 1948. Rapporteur, econ. rsch. sec. Hungarian Prime Ministry, 1938-41; dir. Hungarian Inst. Labor Studies, Budapest, 1943-45; econ. policy advisor to Min. of Reconstruction, Budapest, 1945-48; assoc. prof. econs. St. Francis Coll., Bklyn., 1954-57; prof. indsl. rels. Loyola U., Chgo., 1957-76, dir. inst. indsl. rels., 1965-69; labor arbitrator pvt. practice, Albuquerque, 1976—. Author: Automation and Industrial Labor, 1969, Arbitration and Health Care, 1981; contbr. articles to profl. jours. Recipient Cross of Distinction Hungarian Govt., 1993. Mem. Nat. Acad. Arbitrators, Indsl. Rels. Rsch. Assn. Home and Office: 2321 Ada Pl NE Albuquerque NM 87106-2501

REZNIK, BENJAMIN MENACHEM, lawyer; b. Haifa, Israel, June 18, 1951; came to the U.S., 1961; s. David and Helen (Kupferman) R.; m. Janice Kamenir, June 1, 1974; children: Jonathan, Devorah, Samson. BA in Polit. Sci., U. Calif., L.A., 1973; JD, U. So. Calif., 1976. Bar: Calif. 1976. Founder Law Offices of Benjamin M. Reznik, Beverly Hills, Calif., 1977-82; founding ptnr. Reznik & Reznik, Sherman Oaks, Calif., 1982—; trustee San Fernando Valley Bar, Van Nuys, Calif., 1991-93. Bd. dirs. Greater L.A. Bldg. Industry Assn., 1990-91, The Cultural Found., 1990—; chmn. Valley Industry and Commerce Assn., Encino, Calif., 1992-93, Econ. Alliance San Fernando Valley, L.A., 1994—; mem. Mayor Richard Riordan Devel. Reform Com., L.A., 1994—; pres. Valley Job Recovery Corp., L.A., 1994—. Recipient award Jewish Nat. Fund, 1994, Parents award March of Dimes, 1994, commendations Ho. of Reps., U.S. Congress, Calif. State Assembly, Calif. Lt. Gov., Calif. Atty. Gen., L.A. County Bd. Suprs., others. Mem. L.A. County Bar Assn., Valley Devel. Forum, 2000 Partnership (com. chair 1991-92, bd. dirs. 1993—), Encino C. of C. (bd. dirs. 1985-91, pres. 1989). Democrat. Jewish. Office: Reznik & Reznik 5th Fl 15456 Ventura Blvd Sherman Oaks CA 91403

RHEINISH, ROBERT KENT, university administrator; b. Mt. Vernon, N.Y., Oct. 27, 1934; s. Walter Washington and Doris Elizabeth (Standard) R.; m. Dorothy Ellen Steadman, May 3, 1957 (div. 1976); children: Robert Scott, Joel Nelson; m. Shirley Marie Suter, Aug. 1, 1976. BA, U. South Fla., 1963; MS, Ind. U., 1969, EdD, 1971. Staff engr. Armed Forces Radio & TV Svc., Anchorage, 1960-61; trainee Nat. Park Svc. Tng. Ctr., Grand Canyon, Ariz., 1965; historian Home of F.D.R., Nat. Historic Site, Hyde Park, N.Y., 1964-65, Sagamore Hill Nat. Hist. Site, Oyster Bay, N.Y., 1965-66; asst. coord. nat. environ. edn. devel. program Dept. of Interior, Washington, 1968; supervisory historian Lincoln Boyhood Nat. Meml., Lincoln City, Ind., 1966-68; dir. learning resources ctr. Whittier (Calif.) Coll., 1971-73; dir. media and learning resources Calif. State U., Long Beach, 1973-88; chmn. media dirs. The Calif. State Univs., Long Beach, 1975-76; radio announcer Sta. WTCX-FM, St. Petersburg, Fla., 1961-63; co-host with David Horowitz (2 broadcasts) On Campus, Sta. KNBC-TV, L.A., 1972-73; guest lectr. 6th Army Intelligence Sch., Los Alamitos Armed Forces Res. Ctr., 1987; founder Rheino Ltd., 1997. Coord. multi-media program: In Search of Yourself, 1975 (Silver award Internat. Film and TV Festival of N.Y.), The House that Memory Built, 1981 (Cindy award Info. Film Producers of Am.), The Indochinese and Their Cultures, 1985 (Silver award Internat. Film & TV Festival of N.Y.). With RCAF, 1954-55, USAF, 1957-61. U.S. Office of Edn. grad. fellow, 1969-71; recipient Learning Resources Ctr. Fund Devel. award Pepsico, Sears, Prentice-Hall, et al, 1973; Nat. Def. Edn. Act grantee, 1974-76. Mem. NRA, Am. Legion. Republican. Home: 1975 Gold Dust Dr Lake Havasu City AZ 86404-1011

RHINE, MARK WOODFORDE, psychiatrist, psychoanalyst; b. Wellfleet, Mass., Nov. 10, 1934; s. Raymond Otto and Margaret Dorothy Mount (Woodforde) R.; m. Clare Williams, June 18, 1961; children: Kate, Michael, Maria. BA, Harvard U., 1957, MD, 1961; postgrad., Denver Psychoanalytic Inst., 1972-77. Diplomate Am. Bd. Psychiatry and Neurology; qualifications in addiction psychiatry, geriatric psychiatry. Inst. U. Colo. Med. Sch., Denver, 1968-74, 87200, 1968-74, asst. clin. prof., 1974-92, clin. prof., 1992—; pvt. practice Denver, 1974—; clin. dir. adult svcs. Columbine Psychiat. Ctr., Denver, 1990-96; clin. dir. Sr. Behavior Health Svcs., Rose Med. Ctr., 1996—. Lt. comdr. USPHS, 1962-64. Fellow Am. Psychiat. Assn.; mem. Denver Psychoanalytic Soc., Colo. Psychiat. Soc., Am. Assn. Psychiatrists in Alcohol and Addictions, Am. Geriatric Psychiat. Assn., Am. Soc. clin. Psychopharmacology. Office: 3545 S Tamarac Dr Ste 370 Denver CO 80237-1432

RHINELANDER, ESTHER RICHARD, secondary school educator; b. Honolulu, Aug. 31, 1940; d. William Wise and Elizabeth (Chilton) Richard; m. Harvey James Rhinelander, July 24, 1965; 1 child, Lori. BEd, U. Hawaii, 1963, profl. cert., 1964. Tchr. music Kamehameha Sch., Honolulu, 1965—, Kamehameha Sch. for Girls, Honolulu, 1964, Waianae High and Intermediate Sch., Honolulu, 1965; dir. Waiokeola Ch. Choir, Honolulu, 1964-67, Kawaiahao Ch. Choir, Honolulu, 1980-87; judge song contest Kamehameha Schs., 1972, 88; judge choral composition contest Hawaii Found. on Culture and Arts, Honolulu, 1984, 85; pianist Kahikuonalani Ch., Honolulu, 1987—, Ch. Choral Ensemble, 1987—; tchr. Sunday Sch., 1988—. Mem., asst. accompanist Honolulu Opera Guild, 1955-59. Mem. Am. Choral Dirs. Assn., Soc. Gen. Music Tchrs. (sec. 1989-90), Music Educators Nat. Conf., Hawaii Music Educators Assn. Democrat. Mem. United Ch. of Christ. Office: Highlands Child Care Ctr 757 Hoomalu St Pearl City HI 96782-2711

RHOADS, RICK, writer, editor; b. N.Y.C., Jan. 19, 1944; s. Lester and Doris (Geldzahler) R.; m. Margaret Cooke, June 6, 1979; children: Linden, Bonita, Maya. BA, CCNY, 1970. Writer, editor Expert Connections, N.Y.C., 1980-85; sr. editor Rick Rhoads & Assocs., L.A., 1985—. Pres. Westside Dem. Club, L.A., 1992-94. Mem. PNG, Assn. for Bus. Comm., L.A. MacIntosh Group. Home and Office: 3520 Tilden Ave Los Angeles CA 90034-6109

RHODES, DAISY CHUN, writer, researcher; b. Kahuku, Hawaii, Nov. 16, 1933; d. Pyung Chan Chun and Shin Ai Park; children: Joseph, Carmella, Thomas Francese. BA in Creative Writing, Eckerd Coll., 1995. Info. specialist Reconstrn. Devel. Corp., Washington, 1970; specialist indigent funding George Washington U. Hosp., Washington, 1971-74; mgr. hosp. assistance Alexandria (Va.) Hosp., 1975-79; asst. editor Employee Futures Rsch., Luray, Va., 1980-84; editor Inside Negotiations, Rochester, N.Y., 1985-87, Educators Negotiating Svc., New Port Richey, Fla., 1987-89; novelist, writer New Port Richey, 1989-95; rschr., oral historian Honolulu, 1994; writer Colorado Springs, 1995; rschr., cons. Donna Ladd, Writer, Colorado Springs, 1996. Author: (nonfiction) Forever Long-Never End, 1990, Wahiawa Red Dirt, 1991, At Crossroads of Inspiration, 1993, Shirley Temple Feet, 1993, Remembering the Fallen, 1994, (play) I Know About Olympus, 1993, (novel) Eye of the Dragon (finalist Hemingway 1st Novel Competition), 1994, (scholarly and abstract) How Oral History of the First Koreans in America Advances Archival Research, 1996. Del. Kiwanis Internat., Anaheim, Calif., 1989. Mem. Assn. for Asian Studies, Korea Soc., Korean Am. Women's Soc. Greater Washington (pres. 1983-84, bd. dirs. 1984—, Commendation), West Pasco Kiwanis (pres. 1990-92). Home: 1994 Copper Creek Dr Colorado Springs CO 80910

RHODES, DALLAS D., geologist and educator; b. El Dorado, Kans., Aug. 8, 1947; s. Earl and Peggy Lee (White) R.; m. Lisa Ann Rossbacher. BS with honors, U. Mo., 1969; MA, PhD, Syracuse U., 1973. Instr. Syracuse (N.Y.) U., 1972-73; asst. prof. geology U. Vt., Burlington, 1973-77; cons. geologist N.Y. State Geol. Survey, Albany, summers 1975-77; vis. rschr. U. Uppsala, Sweden, 1983-84; cons. geologist Jet Propulsion Lab., Pasadena, Calif., 1980-85; prof. geology Whittier (Calif.) Coll., 1977—, dir. Fairchild Aerial Photography Collection, 1981—; dir. Image Processing Lab. W.M. Keck Found., 1990—. Editor: Adjustments of the Fluvial System, 1979. NASA Summer Faculty fellow, 1980, 81. Mem. Am. Geophys. Union, Geol. Soc. Am., Nat. Assn. Geology Tchrs., Sigma Xi. Democrat. Office: Whittier College Dept Geology Whittier CA 90608

RHODES, GERALD LEE, writer; b. Redding, Calif., June 18, 1954; s. Howard Gordon and Rosalie (Lowell) R.; m. Sue Ann Williams, April 28, 1990; 1 child, Erin Nicole Fossum. BA in Journalism and Native Am. Ethnic Studies, Calif. State U., Sacramento, 1976; MS in Interdisciplinary Studies, U. Oregon, 1984. Reporter The Springfield (Oreg.) News, 1984-90; writer bus. and sci. The Columbian, Vancouver, Wash., 1990-93; freelance writer, 1993—; comm. rep. Kaiser Permanente N.W. Divsn., 1996—; fire fighter U.S. Forest Svc., Redding, 1971-73, U.S. Bur. Land Mgmt., Anchorage, 1975-78; fire mgmt. tng. instr., adminstr. U.S. Bur. Land Mgmt., Alaska Fire Svc., Fairbanks, 1979-84; freelance writer Comm. Works, Springfield, 1989-90; v.p. Lane Press Club, Eugene, 1990. Reporter, photographer: (newspaper series) Future Forests, 1987 (Bus. Reporting Award for Non-Daily Newspapers, Associated Oregon Industries, 1988). Vol. Forward Edge Internat., Vancouver, 1994—. Fellow Sci. Writers Workshop, Am. Chem. Soc., Washington, 1991; New Horizons fellow, Coun. for the Advancement of Sci. Writing, 1992; recipient 1st Gen. Column Writing award Soc. Profl. Journalists, Oreg., 1988, 1st Sci. and Environ. Reporting award, Pacific N.W., 1993. Mem. Nat. Assn. Sci. Writers. Lutheran.

RHODES, JESS LYNN, counselor; b. Houston, Apr. 18, 1942; s. Jess Lynn and Eunice Pauline (Moser) R.; m. Martha Camille McNeill; children: Robert Lynn, Rhonda Cheri. BA, BS, Harding U., 1964; postgrad., Tex. Tech. U., 1964-66; MA, U. No. Colo., 1992. Lic. profl. counselor. Instr. Lubbock (Tex.) Christian Coll., 1964-65; min. Church of Christ, Abernathy, Tex., 1965-68, Tulia, Tex., 1969-73, Wichita Falls, Tex., 1973-82, Greeley, Colo., 1983-92; profl. counselor Luth. Family Svcs., Greeley, 1992-93, Pathways, Greeley, 1993—. Author: Sermons for the Seventies, 1973; contbr. articles to profl. jours.; mem. editorial bd. (jour.) Power for Today, 1967-94; guest editor (jour.) 20th Century Christian, 1966, 67. Mem. bd. devel. Lubbock Christian U., 1970-80; trustee Texhoma Christian Care Ctr., Wichita Falls, 1980-82, Christian Camp of the Rockies, Greeley, 1983-91, Wichita Christian Sch., Wichita Falls, 1975-82; mem. adv. bd. Tulia Satellite Sch. for Retarded, 1970-73. Mem. ACA, Internat. Assn. Marriage & Family Counselors. Home: 1964 28th Ave Greeley CO 80631-5719

RHYNE, DENNIS ALFRED, orthopedic surgeon; b. N.Y.C., Mar. 21, 1943; s. Elbert Alfred and Florence Ann (Klein) R.; m. Linda Lee Forsey; children: Cheryl, Laura, Mathew, Dennis Jr., Pegeen. BS, Fordham U., 1964; MD, N.J. Coll. Medicine, 1968. Diplomate Am. Bd. Orthopaedic Surgery; cert. qualified med. evaluator. Intern U.S. Naval Hosp., St. Albans, N.Y., 1969-72; resident U.S. Naval Hosp., Oakland, Calif., 1969-72, A.I. duPont Inst., Wilmington, Del., 1972-73; staff orthopaedic surgeon U.S. Naval Regional Med. Ctr., Long Beach, Calif., 1974-76; pvt. practice orthopaedic surgery Laguna Hills, Calif., 1976—; chief orthopedics Mission Hosp., 1982-83; sec.-treas. med. staff Saddleback Hosp. 1981-82, vice chief of staff, 1982-84, chief of staff, 1985-86, bd. dirs., 1985-87; mem. staff Mission Regional Med. Ctr., Mission Viejo, Calif., 1976—, Saddleback Meml. Ctr., Laguna Hills, 1976—, Irvine (Calif.) Med. Ctr., 1990-92; bd. dirs. Orange County PSRO, 1981-82. V.p. Calif. Dept. Res. Officers Assn., 1989-90. Capt. USN, 1967-76, res., 1990-91, Operation Desert Shield/Storm. Fellow ACS, Am. Acad. Orthopaedic Surgeons; mem. AMA, Calif. Med. Assn. (alternate del. 1988-91, 91-92, del. 1992—), Soc. Mil. Orthopaedic Surgeons, Western Orthopaedic Assn., Soc. Mil. Orthopaedic Surgeons. Office: 24411 Health Center Dr Ste 420 Laguna Hills CA 92653-3633

RIACH, DOUGLAS ALEXANDER, marketing and sales executive, retired military officer; b. Victoria, B.C., Can., Oct. 8, 1919; s. Alex and Gladys (Provis) R.; came to U.S., 1925, naturalized, 1942; BA, UCLA, 1948; postgrad. in mktg. Fenn Coll., 1959, Grad. Sch. Sales Mgmt. and Mktg., 1960, U.S. Army Command and Gen. Staff Coll., 1966, Armed Forces Staff Coll., 1968, Indsl. Coll. of the Armed Forces, 1970-71; m. Eleanor Montague, Mar. 28, 1942; 1 child, Sandra Jean. With Gen. Foods Corp., 1948-80, terr. sales mgr., San Francisco, 1962-80; with Food Brokers, San Francisco Bay area, 1980-90; exec. v.p. Visual Market Plans Inc., Novato, Calif., 1984-87; ter. mgr. Ibbotson, Berri, DeNola Brokerage, Inc., Emeryville, Calif., 1990-96; account exec. Sales Max Inc., Richmond, Calif., 1996—. Served to capt. inf. AUS, 1941-46, ETO; to col. inf. USAR, 1946-79, from comdr. 2d inf. brigade Calif. State mil. res., 1984-87 to brigadier gen. (ret.) 1990. Decorated Legion of Merit, Bronze Star with V device and oak leaf cluster, Purple Heart, Combat Infantry Badge, Croix de Guerre avec Palme (France and Belgium), Fouragerre (Belgium), Combattant Cross-Voluntaire (France), Combattant Cross-Soldier (France), Medaille-Commemorative de la Liberee (France), Medaille-Commemorative Francais (France), Medaille-War Wounded (France), Medaille-Commemorative Belgique (Belgium), Medaille-de la Reconnaissance (Belgium), Medaille du Voluntaire (Belgium), Cross of Freedom (Poland), Virtuti Militari-Silver Cross (Poland), Royal Commemorative War Cross (Yugoslavia); named knight Order of the Compassionate Heart (internat.), knight Magnus Officialis (GOTJ), Sovereign Mil. Order, Temple of Jerusalem (knights templar), CDR Commandery of Calif. (knights templar 1992-94), comdr. Commandery of St. Francis (knights templar); knight commdr. sovereign Order of St. John of Jerusalem (knights hospitaller), knight commdr. Cross with Star Polonia Restituta, knight comdr. Cross with Star Order of St. Stanislaus; named to U.S. Army Inf. Hall of Fame, 1982; recipient Calif. Medal of Merit and cluster, Commendation medal. Mem. Long Beach Food Sales Assn. (pres. 1950), Assn. Grocers Mfrs. Reps. (dir. 1955), Am. Security Coun. (nat. adv. bd. 1975—), Res. Officers Assn. (San Francisco Presidio pres. 1974-76, v.p. 1977-82, v.p. dept. Calif. 1979, exec. v.p. 1980, pres. 1981, nat. councilman 1981-82), Nat. Assn. Uniformed Svcs., Exchange Club (v.p. Long Beach 1955), St. Andrews Soc. Queens Club San Francisco, Combat Infantry Assn., Assn. U.S. Army, Am. Legion, Assn. Former Intelligence Officers, Presidio Soc., Navy League, Ret. Officers Assn., Mil. Order Purple Heart, DAV, Psychol. Ops. Assn., Nat. Guard Assn. Calif., State Def. Force Assn. Calif., Internat. Diplomacy Coun. San Francisco, Nat. Assn. Uniformed Svcs., Merchandising Execs. San Francisco (dir. 1970-75, sec. 1976-77, v.p. 1978-79, pres. 1980, bd. dirs. 1981-89), Commonwealth of Club Calif. (nat. def. sect. vice chmn. 1964-66, chmn. 1967-72), Elks, Masons (master, lodge 400, Shrine, Islam Temple, 32d degree Scottish Rite, sojouner chpt. #277). Republican. Episcopalian. Home: 2609 Trousdale Dr Burlingame CA 94010-5706

RIANDA, DAVID NOEL, medical foundation administrator; b. Salinas, Calif., Dec. 25, 1938; s. Lee F. and Dorothy M. L. (Hoertkorn) R.; m. Janice Evelyn Kautto, Sept. 7, 1963; children: Christopher Paul, Jill Noelle. BA, U. Oreg., 1960, MA, 1965. Program dir. U. Mont., Missoula, 1960-62; asst. dir. edn. activities Portland (Oreg.) State U., 1962-63; dir. union publicity U. Wis., Milw., 1965-68; dir. pub. affairs Reed Coll., Portland, 1968-73; dir. fund devel. Providence Med. Ctr., Portland, 1974-76; pres. Providence Child Ctr. Found., Portland, 1976-86; exec. dir. N.W. Osteo. Med. Found., Portland, 1986—; fund raising cons. to numerous non-profit orgns., 1974—; journalism arts adv. bd. Mt. Hood C.C., 1970-76, chmn. 1973-74; mem. Gov.'s Commn. on Youth, 1978-81; advancement coun. U. Oreg. Sch. Journalism and Comm., 1993—. Bd. dirs. Firehouse Theater, 1984-87, pres., 1984-86; mem. cmty. adv. bd. Providence Child Ctr., 1995—; bd. dirs. Women's Intercmty. AIDS Resource, 1995-96. Named Man of the Yr., Assn. Retarded Citizens, Multnomah County, Oreg., 1986; recipient Award of Excellence, Pacific Indsl. Communicators Assn., 1970. Mem. Nat. Assn. Osteo. Founds. (pres. 1991), Grantmakers of Oreg. and S.W. Wash. (steering com. 1991-95, sec. 1991), Willamette Valley Devel. Officers (pres. 1987, Award of Merit 1993), Assn. Healthcare Philanthropy (cert. 1977, accredited 1981, v.p. Region 12, nat. bd. dirs. 1979-81), Oregon Internat. Assn. Bus. Communicators (pres. 1972-73, Awards of Merit/Excellence 1970, 71, 72, 74, 76, 79, Presdl. Citation for Outstanding Svc. 1974, Rodney Adair Meml. award 1975), U. Oreg. Friars, Phi Kappa Signa. Home: 4140 NE Alameda St Portland OR 97212-2909

RIASANOVSKY, NICHOLAS VALENTINE, historian, educator; b. Harbin, China, Dec. 21, 1923; came to U.S., 1938, naturalized, 1943; m. Arlene Ruth Schlegel, Feb. 15, 1955; children—John, Nicholas, Maria. B.A., U. Oreg., 1942; A.M., Harvard U., 1947; D.Phil., Oxford (Eng.) U., 1949. Mem. faculty U. Iowa, 1949-57; mem. faculty U. Calif., Berkeley, 1957—, prof. history, 1961—, Sidney Hellman Ehrman prof. European history, 1969—; trustee Nat. Council Soviet and E. European Research, 1978-82; mem. Kennan Inst. Acad. Council, 1986-89; vis. research prof. USSR Acad. Scis., Moscow, 1969, Moscow and Leningrad, 1974, 79. Author: Russia and the West in Teaching of the Slavophiles: A Study of Romantic Ideology, 1952, Nicholas I and Official Nationality in Russia, 1825-1855, 1959, A History of Russia, 1963, 5th edit., 1993, The Teaching of Charles Fourier, 1969, A Parting of Ways: Government and the Educated Public in Russia, 1801-1855, 1976, The Image of Peter the Great in Russian History and Thought, 1985, The Emergence of Romanticism, 1992, Collected Writings 1947-94, 1993; co-editor: California Slavic Studies, 1960—; editl. bd. Russian rev., Zarubezhnaia Periodicheskaia Pechat' Na Russkom Iazyke, Simvol; contbr. articles to profl. jours. Served to 2d lt. AUS, 1943-46. Decorated Bronze Star; recipient Silver medal Commonwealth Club Calif., 1964; Rhodes scholar, 1947-49; Fulbright grantee, 1954-55, 74, 79; Guggenheim fellow, 1969; sr. fellow Nat. Endowment Humanities, 1975; Fulbright sr. scholar, sr. fellow Ctr. Advanced Studies in Behavioral Scis., 1984-85; sr. fellow Woodrow Wilson Internat. Ctr. for Scholars, 1989-90. Mem. AAAS, Am. Assn. Advancement Slavic Studies (pres. 1973-76, Disting. Contbr. award 1993), Am. Hist. Assn. (award for Scholarly Distinction 1995).

RICARDO-CAMPBELL, RITA, economist, educator; b. Boston, Mar. 16, 1920; d. David and Elizabeth (Jones) Ricardo; m. Wesley Glenn Campbell, Sept. 15, 1946; children: Barbara Lee, Diane Rita, Nancy Elizabeth. BS, Simmons Coll., 1941; MA, Harvard U., 1945, PhD, 1946. Instr. Harvard U., Cambridge, Mass., 1946-48; asst. prof. Tufts U., Medford, Mass., 1948-51; labor economist U.S. Wage Stabilization Bd., 1951-53; economist Ways and Means Com. U.S. Ho. of Reps., 1953; cons. economist, 1957-60; vis. prof. San Jose State Coll., 1960-61; sr. fellow Hoover Instn. on War, Revolution, and Peace, Stanford, Calif., 1968-95, sr. fellow emerita, 1995—; lectr. health svc. adminstrn. Stanford U. Med. Sch., 1973-78; bd. dirs.

Watkins-Johnson Co., Palo Alto, Calif., Gillette Co., Boston; mgmt. bd. Samaritan Med. Ctr., San Jose, Calif. Author: Voluntary Health Insurance in the U.S., 1960, Economics of Health and Public Policy, 1971, Food Safety Regulation: Use and Limitations of Cost-Benefit Analysis, 1974, Drug Lag: Federal Government Decision Making, 1976, Social Security: Promise and Reality, 1977, The Economics and Politics of Health, 1982, 2d edit., 1985; co-editor: Below-Replacement Fertility in Industrial Societies, 1987, Issues in Contemporary Retirement, 1988, Resisting Hostile Takeovers: The Gillette Company, 1997; contbr. articles to profl. jours. Commr. Western Interstate Commn. for Higher Edn. Calif., 1967-75, chmn., 1970-71; mem. Pres. Nixon's Adv. Coun. on Status Women, 1969-76; mem. task force on taxation Pres.'s Coun. on Environ. Quality, 1970-72; mem. Pres.'s Com. Health Services Industry, 1971-73, FDA Nat. Adv. Drug Com., 1972-75; mem. Econ. Policy Adv. Bd., 1981-90, Pres. Reagan's Nat. Coun. on Humanities, 1982-89, Pres. Nat. Medal of Sci. com., 1988-94; bd. dirs. Ind. Colls. No. Calif., 1971-87; mem. com. assessment of safety, benefits, risks Citizens Commn. Sci., Law and Food Supply, Rockefeller U., 1973-75; mem. adv. com. Ctr. Health Policy Rsch., Am. Enterprise Inst. Pub. Policy Rsch., Washington, 1974-80; mem. adv. coun. on social security Social Security Adminstrn., 1974-75; bd. dirs. Simmons Coll. Corp., Boston, 1975-80; mem. adv. coun. bd. assocs. Stanford Librs., 1975-78; mem. coun. SRI Internat., Menlo Park, Calif., 1977-90. Mem. Am. Econ. Assn., Mont Pelerin Soc. (bd. dirs. 1988-92, v.p. 1992-94), Harvard Grad. Soc. (coun. 1991), Phi Beta Kappa. Home: 26915 Alejandro Dr Los Altos Hills CA 94022-1932 Office: Stanford U Hoover Instn Stanford CA 94305-6010

RICCARDI, VINCENT MICHAEL, pediatrician, researcher, educator, entrepreneur; b. Bklyn., Oct. 14, 1940; s. Gabriel John and Frances Mary (Novak) R.; m. Susan Leona Bogda, July 27, 1967; children: Angela M., Ursula M., Mikah F. AB, UCLA, 1962; MD, Georgetown U., 1966; MBA, U. LaVerne, 1993. Intern, resident in medicine U. Pitts., 1966-68; fellow in genetics Harvard Med. Sch., Boston, 1968-70, 72; asst. prof. medicine U. Colo. Med. Ctr., Denver, 1973-75; assoc. prof. medicine, pediatrics Med. Coll. Wis., Milw., 1975-77; prof. medicine, pediatrics Baylor Coll. Medicine, Houston, 1977-90; med. dir. The Genetics Inst., Pasadena, Calif., 1990-92; clin. prof. pediatrics UCLA, 1991—; founder, CEO Am. Med. Consumers, La Crescenta, 1992; dir. The Neurofibromatosis Inst., La Crescenta, Calif., 1985—. Author: Genetic Approach to Human Disease, 1977, Communication and Counseling in Health Care, 1983, Neurofibromatosis, 1986, rev. edit., 1992. Maj. U.S. Army, 1970-71. Fellow ACP, AAAS, Am. Coll. Med. Genetics; mem. Am. Soc. Human Genetics, Am. Coll. Physician Execs. Home: 5415 Briggs Ave La Crescenta CA 91214-2205 Office: Am Med Consumers Inc 5415 Briggs Ave La Crescenta CA 91214-2205

RICE, BARBARA POLLAK, advertising and marketing executive; b. Ft. Scott, Kans., Nov. 11, 1937; d. Olin N. and Jeanette E. (Essen) Brigman; m. Stanley Rice, Apr. 28, 1978; 1 child, Beverly Johnson. Student N. Central Coll., 1955, Elmhurst Coll., 1956; BA in Communications, Calif. State U., Fullerton, 1982. Art dir. Gonterman & Assos., St. Louis, 1968-71; advt. mgr. Passpoint Corp., St. Louis, 1971-73; advt., pub. relations mgr. Permaneer Corp., St. Louis, 1973-74; advt. cons., advt. mgr. Hydro-Air Engring., Inc., St. Louis, 1974-76; mgr. mktg. services Hollytex Carpet Mills subs. U.S. Gypsum Co., City of Industry, Calif., 1976-79; pres. B.P. Rice & Co., Inc., Cerittos, Calif., 1979—; press affiliate Inst. Bus. Designers. Recipient Designer Best Exhibit award Nat. Farm Builders Trade Show, Creative Challenge Mead Top 60 award L.A. Bus. Profl. Advt. Assn., Top 100 L.A. Women-Owned Bus. Mem. Am. Advt. Fedn. (past nat. bd. dirs., region chmn., Silver medal), L.A. Advt. Women (pres., dir., LULU award), Bus. Profl. Advt. Assn., Calif. State U.-Fullerton Sch. Comm. Alumni Assn., Beta Sigma Phi (past pres., outstanding mem.). Author: Truss Construction Manual, 1975. Office: 16330 Marquardt Ave Cerritos CA 90703-2350

RICE, DONALD BLESSING, business executive, former secretary of air force; b. Frederick, Md., June 4, 1939; s. Donald Blessing and Mary Celia (Santangelo) R.; m. Susan Fitzgerald, Aug. 25, 1962; children: Donald Blessing III, Joseph John, Matthew Fitzgerald. BSChemE, U. Notre Dame, 1961, DEng (hon.), 1975; MS in Indsl. Adminstrn., Purdue U., 1962, PhD in Mgmt. and Econs., 1965, D. Mgmt. (hon.), 1985; LLD (hon.), Pepperdine U., 1989; LHD (hon.), West Coast U., 1993; D in Pub. Policy (hon.), Rand Grad. Sch., 1995. Dir. cost analysis Office Sec. Def., Washington, 1967-69, dep. asst. sec. def. resource analysis, 1969-70; asst. dir. Office Mgmt. and Budget, Exec. Office Pres., 1970-72; pres., CEO The Rand Corp., Calif., 1972-89; sec. USAF, 1989-93; pres., COO Teledyne, Inc., L.A., 1993-96; pres., CEO Urogenesys., Santa Monica, Calif., 1996—; bd. dirs. Vulcan Materials Co., Wells Fargo Bank, Wells Fargo & Co.; mem. Nat. Sci. Bd., 1974-86; chmn. Nat. Commn. Supplies and Shortages, 1975-77; mem. Nat. Commn. on U.S.-China Relations; mem. nat. adv. com. oceans and atmosphere Dept. Commerce, 1972-75; mem. adv. panel Office Tech. Assessment, 1976-79; adv. council Coll. Engring., U. Notre Dame, 1974-88; mem. Def. Sci. Bd., 1977-83, sr. cons., 1984-88; U.S. mem. Trilateral Commn.; dir. for sec. def. and Pres. Def. Resource Mgmt. Study, 1977-79. Author articles. Served to capt. AUS, 1965-67. Recipient Sec. Def. Meritorious Civilian Service medal, 1970, Def. Exceptional Civilian Svc. medal, 1993, Forrestal award, 1992; Ford Found. fellow, 1962-65. Fellow AAAS; mem. Council Fgn. Relations, Inst. Mgmt. Scis. (past pres.), Tau Beta Pi. Office: Urogenesys 1701 Colorado Ave Santa Monica CA 90404*

RICE, FRANCES MAE, pediatrician; b. Oakland, Calif., Apr. 19, 1931; d. George Henry and Clare Evelyn (Youngman) Rice. AB cum laude, U. Calif., Berkeley, 1953, MPH in Epidemiology, 1964; MD, U. Calif., San Francisco, 1957. Intern U. Calif. Hosp., San Francisco, 1957-58; pediatric resident U. Calif., San Francisco, 1959-61; pediatric and family physician HMO, Hanford, Calif., 1974-75; clin. pediatrician Kern County Health Dept., Bakersfield, Calif., 1975-76; physician Kern Med. Group, Inc., Bakersfield, 1976-83; pvt. practice Shafter, Calif., 1983-89; physician Kern County Health Dept., Bakersfield, 1989, Mercy Medicenter, Bakersfield, 1990-91, K.C.E.O.C. Family Clinic, Bakersfield, 1993—. USPHS fellow, 1963-64. Fellow Royal Soc. Medicine; mem. AMA, N.Y. Acad. Sci., Calif. Med. Assn., Kern County Med. Soc. Home: 5909 Lindbrook Way Bakersfield CA 93309 Office: KCEOC Family Health Clinic 1611 1st St Bakersfield CA 93304-2901

RICE, JERRY LEE, professional football player; b. Starkville, Miss., Oct. 13, 1962; m. Jackie Rice; 1 child, Jaqui. Student, Miss. State Valley U. Football player San Francisco 49ers, 1985—. Named MVP, Super Bowl XXIII, 1989, Sporting News NFL Player of Yr., 1987, 90; named to Sporting News Coll. All-Am. team, 1984, Sporting News All-Pro team, 1986-92, Pro Bowl team, 1986-93, 95, Pro Bowl MVP, 1995. Office: care San Francisco 49ers 4949 Centennial Blvd Santa Clara CA 95054-1229*

RICE, JONATHAN C., retired educational television executive; b. St. Louis, Feb. 19, 1916; s. Charles M. and May R. (Goldman) R.; m. Kathleen Feibelman, Aug. 6, 1946 (dec. June 1964); children: Jefferson Charles, Kit (dec.), May Nanette. AB, Stanford U., 1938. War photographer, reporter Acme Newspix/NEA Svc., PTO of WWII, 1941-43; picture book editor Look Mag., N.Y.C., 1947-48; news/spl. events dir. Sta. KTLA-TV, L.A., 1948-53; program mgr. Sta. KQED-TV, San Francisco, 1953-67, dir. program ops., 1967-78, asst. to pres., 1978-90, bd. dirs., 1990-96, spl. advisor to the bd., 1997—, bd. dirs., 1990-96; cons. NET, PBS, Corp. for Pub. Broadcasting, Ford Found., TV Lima Peru, Sta. WGBH-TV, Boston, Sta. WNET-TV, N.Y.C., French TV, Europe Eastern Edn. TV, Dept. Justice, 1955-90; lectr. Stanford U., 1958-77. Editor: Look at America, The South, Official Picture Story of the FBI, 1947. Bd. dirs. NATAS, San Francisco, Planned Parenthood, San Francisco and Marin County, Calif. Maj. USMC, 1943-47, PTO. Recipient George Foster Peabody award, 1956, Thomas Alva Edison award for best station, N.Y.C., 1960, Gov.'s award NATAS, 1972-73, Ralph Lowell award Corp. for Pub. Broadcasting, 1972; Jonathan Rice Studio named in his honor, 1986. Home: 1 Russian Hill Pl San Francisco CA 94133-3605

RICE, JULIAN CASAVANT, lawyer; b. Miami, Fla., Dec. 31, 1923; s. Sylvan J. and Maybelle (Casavant) R.; m. Dorothy Mae Haynes, Feb. 14, 1958; children—Scott B., Craig M. (dec.), Julianne C., Linda D., Janette M. Student, U. San Francisco, 1941-43; JD cum laude, Gonzaga U., 1950. Bar: Wash. 1950, Alaska 1959, U.S. Tax Ct. 1988. Pvt. practice law Spokane, 1950-56, Fairbanks, Alaska, 1959—; prin. Law Office Julian C. Rice (and predecessor firms), Fairbanks, 1959; bd. dirs. Key Bank of Alaska, Anchorage; founder, gen. counsel Mt. McKinley Mut. Savs. Bank, Fairbanks, 1965—, chmn. bd., 1979-80; v.p., bd. dirs., gen. counsel Skimmers, Inc., Anchorage, 1966-67; gen. counsel Alaska Carriers Assn., Anchorage, 1960-71, Alaska Transp. Conf., 1960-67. Mayor City of Fairbanks, 1970-72. Served to maj. USNG and USAR, 1943-58. Decorated Bronze Star, Combat Infantryman's Badge. Fellow Am. Bar Found. (life); mem. ABA, Wash. Bar Assn., Alaska Bar Assn., Transp. Lawyers Assn., Spokane Exchange Club (pres. 1956). Office: 1008 16th Ave Ste 102 Fairbanks AK 99701-6038 Office: PO Box 70516 Fairbanks AK 99707-0516

RICE, KAY DIANE, elementary education educator, consultant; b. Redding, Calif., Mar. 21, 1952; d. Ray H. and Patricia Barton (Stabler) Quibell; m. 1976 (div. 1982); 1 child, Brooke Elise; m. F. Scott Rice. AA in Gen. Edn., Shasta Coll., Redding, 1972; BA in Liberal Studies, Calif. State U., Chico, 1975; EdM in Policy and Govt., U. Wash., 1991. Cert. tchr., Calif., Wash., cert. prin., Wash. Tchr. grade 3 Anderson (Calif.) Schs., 1976-79; tchr. grades 1, 2, and 3 Redding (Calif.) Elem. Schs., 1979-81, tchr. grade 1, 1981-83, tchr. grade 5, 1986-87; tchr. grade 2 Bellevue (Wash.) Pub. Schs., 1987-88; tchr. grade 4 Lake Wash. Sch. Dist., Kirkland, Wash., 1988-89; tchr. grades 3-4 Bellevue (Wash.) Pub. Schs., 1989-90; prin. intern Bellevue (Wash.) and Mercer Island (Wash.) Schs., 1990-91; tchr. grades K-1 Bellevue (Wash.) Pub. Schs., 1991-93, tchr. grades 1-2, 1993—; mem. adv. com. Ednl. Program Com., Bellevue Pub. Schs., 1992-94, mem. Early Childhood Assessment Project, 1993—; presenter in field. Vol. ZEST Sch. Dist. Vol. Program, Bellevue, 1991-93. Recipient Pres.'s Merit award Parent Student Tchr. Assn., 1988, U.S. Presdl. EPA award, 1987; Bellevue Schs. Found. grantee, 1987, 95-96, 96-97, Danforth Edn. Leadership grantee Bellevue Pub. Schs., 1990-91, Ednl. Travel Study grantee Shunju Club, Japanese Bus. People Wash., 1994. Mem. ASCD, NEA, AAUW (hospitality com. 1982), PTSA, Wash. Orgn. for Reading Devel., PEO. Home: 6818 205th Ave NE Redmond WA 98053-4721 Office: Somerset Elem Sch 14100 Somerset Blvd SE Bellevue WA 98006

RICE, LINDA JOHNSON, publishing executive; b. Chgo., Mar. 22, 1958; d. John J. and Eunice Johnson; m. Andre Rice, 1984. BA Journalism, Univ. Southern California, Los angeles, 1980; MBA, Northwestern Univ., Evanston, 1988. With Johnson Pub. Co., 1980—, past v.p. and asst. to pub., pres., 1987—, also chief oper. officer. Office: 820 S Michigan Ave Chicago IL 60605*

RICE, MICHAEL JOHN, psychiatric mental health nurse; b. Neligh, Nebr., Jan. 12, 1953; s. Arlo and Mary Madeline (Conger) R.; children: Erin Marie, Michael John Jr., Colleen Kay. BSN, Mt. Marty Coll., 1974; MSN, U. Nebr., 1976; PhD, U. Ariz., 1988. Student health nurse Mt. Marty Coll., Yankton, S.D., 1973-74; nurse trainee adolescent svcs. Nebr. Psychiat. Inst.-U. Nebr. Med. Ctr., Omaha, 1975, staff nurse adult acute care svcs., 1976; clin. nurse specialist, sr. staff Crisis Svcs. Langley Porter Neuro-Psychiat. Inst., U. Calif. Med. Ctr., San Francisco, 1977-80; asst. clin. prof. Sch. Nursing U. Calif. Med. Ctr., San Francisco, 1979-80; grad. rsch. assoc., psychiat. nurse liaison U. Ariz., Tucson, 1980-84; staff nurse Rincon Nurses Profl. Registry, Tucson, 1984-85; dir. acute care treatment teams, asst. to chmn. psychiatry Kino Community Hosp., Tucson, 1985-89; founder, mgr. Omega Care Nursing Svcs., Tucson, 1987-91; assoc. prof. psychiat. nursing Intercollegiate Ctr. Nursing Edn., Spokane, Wash., 1989—; mem. mental health awareness planning com. So. Ariz. Mental Health Coun., 1986-87; mem. dist. community task force on alcoholism Community Mental Health Ctr., San Francisco, 1978; cons., therapist Ogden Hall Shelter for Women and Children, Spokane, 1990—; rsch. cons., head trauma force Sacred Heart Med. Ctr., Spokane, 1992-93; founder, dir. Spokane Therapy and Art Resource Svcs., 1991—; therapist YWCA Sch. for Homeless Children, Spokane, 1992—; presenter at profl. confs. Contbr. chpts. to nursing textbooks, articles to profl. jours.; author conf. procs. Mem. tech. adv. com. on community needs assessment, Pima County, Ariz., 1984-85, data collection com. Human Svcs. Coordinating Coun., Pima County, 1984-85. Nursing rsch. emphasis rsch. assoc. and div. nursing fellow HHS, 1981-84. Mem. ANA (coun. nurse rschrs. 1982-86, 90—), Western Inst. Nursing (membership and fin. com. 1992-93, chmn. 1994-95, bd. govs. 1993—), Western Soc. Nursing Rsch., Wash. States Nurses Assn., Inland Empire Nurses Assn., Sigma Xi, Sigma Theta Tau. Home: 9610 N Wickiup Ct Spokane WA 99208 Office: Intercollegiate Ctr Nursing 2917 W Fort George Wright Dr Spokane WA 99224-5202

RICE, NORMAN B., mayor; b. 1943. With govt. City of Seattle, 1978—, city councilman, 1978-89, mayor, 1990—; pres. U.S. Conf. of Mayors, 1995. Office: Office of the Mayor Municipal Bldg 12th Fl 600 4th Ave Seattle WA 98104-1826

RICE, RICHARD LEE, JR., minister, office manager; b. Hillsboro, Oreg., Mar. 29, 1967; s. Richard Lee Rice and Nanci Carol (Losli) Skriiko. AA in Biblical Studies, Multnomah Sch. of the Bible, Portland, 1988; LittD, Abilene (Kans.) Bible Coll. and Seminary, 1988. Youth dir. Rock Creek Foursquare Ch., Portland, 1984-86; assoc. pastor Valley Full Gospel Ch., Hillsboro, 1986-88; min. Congl. Bible Chs., Inc., Hillsboro, 1988—, bishop, 1988-90; office mgr. Alliance Properties, Inc., Aloha, Oreg., 1990-96; founder, pres. Pentecostal-Fire Evangelistic Assn., Hillsboro, 1986—; chmn. Gen. Presbytery, Congl. Bible Chs., Inc., 1988-90; bible tchr. Portland Foursquare Ch., 1993-96; founder, sr. pastor Crtl. Bible Ch., Hillsboro, 1996—. Author: Our Pentecostal Heritage: A Study in Pentecostal Precursors, Promotion, Personalities and Principle, 1995, A Study in Acts, 1986, Systematic Theology, 1988, A Study in the Word: Ephesians, 1993, A Study in the Word: Minor Prophets of the Old Testament, 1994, A Study in the Word: Matthew, 1994, The Bible: How Did It Come to Us and Is It Reliable, 1995, Water Baptism: Its Meaning and History in the Christian Church, 1996, A Brief Examination of the History and Theology of the Lord's Supper, 1996, Hermeneutics: The Artful Science of Biblical Interpretation, 1996, A Commentary on Paul's Epistle to the Church in Rome, 1996; editor (newsletter) Pentecostal Fire Crusader. Committeeperson Rep. Cen. Com., Hillsboro, 1992—; mem. Oreg. Right to Life Com., Hillsboro, 1990—, Portland City Club, 1995—. Mem. NRA, Nat. Rep. Senatorial Com., Rep. Nat. Com., Rep. Presdl. Task Force, Nat. Congl. Club, Federalist Soc. Home: 23585 NW Jacobson Rd Unit 51 Hillsboro OR 97124-9389 Office: 349 SE 4th Ave Hillsboro OR 97123

RICE, ROBERT ARNOT, school administrator; b. San Francisco, Apr. 4, 1911; s. Abraham Lincoln and Mary Eugenia (Arnot) R.; m. Frances Von Dorsten, Aug. 15, 1936 (dec. sept. 1986); m. Esther Pauline Railton, July 11, 1989. BA, U. Calif., Berkeley, 1934, MA, 1947; postgrad., Columbia U., 1948. Various ednl. positions, 1935-61; supr. sci. and math. Berkeley Unified Sch. Dist., 1961-64; adminstr. NSF Summer Insts. for Sci. Tchr., U. Calif., Berkeley, 1957-65; dir. On Target Sch., Berkeley Unified Sch. Dist., 1971-73; coord. pub. programs Lawrence Hall of Sci., 1964-70; work experience edn. coord. Berkeley Unified Sch. Dist., 1973-75; exec. dir. Calif. Sci. Tchr. Assn., 1964-90; dir. No. Calif.-Western Nev. Jr. Sci. and Humanities Symposium, 1962-93; cons. Berkeley Unified Sch. Dist., 1964-70; bd. dirs. San Francisco Bay Area Sci. Fair, 1960—; mem. steering com. Chem. Study, 1960-75; coord. Industry Initiatives for Sci. and Math. Edn. Program, 1985-86; dir. Industry Initiatives for Sci. and Math. Edn. Acad., 1987; mem. Internat. Sci. and Engring. Fair Coun., Sci. Svc., Inc., 1959-68; dir. 18th Internat. Sci. and Engring. Fair, San Francisco, 1967; exec. dir. San Francisco Bay Area Sci. Fair, 1954-59; resource cons. Calif. Farm Bur. Fedn.-Youth Power Conf., Asilomar, 1966; judging chair Nat. Jr. Sci. and Humanities Symposium, 1993—. Contbr. articles to profl. publs. Bd. dirs. Calif. Heart Assn., 1966-71, Alameda County Heart Assn., 1966-71; mem. Cen. Calif. Sci. Com., 1965-70; mem. rsch. com. Alameda County TB and Health Assn., 1965-69, mem. adv. com., 1965-69. Recipient Benjamin Ide Wheeler medal, 1985, San Francisco Bay Area Sci. Fair award of honor Calif. Acad. Sci., 1970, Armed Forces Chem. Assn. award for outstanding chemistry tchr. in San Francisco Bay Area, 1965; named to Berkeley H.S. Hall of Fame, 1994. Mem. NEA, Nat. Sci. Tchrs. Assn. (region VIII dir. 1955-57, Calif. state dir. 1949-56, mem. chemistry com. 1956-60, pres. 1960-61, Disting. Svc. to Sci. Edn. award 1986), No. Calif. Com. on Problem Solving in Sci., Calif. Sci. Tchrs. Assn. (pres. no. sect. 1949-50, Disting. Svc. to Sci. Teaching award 1981), Calif. Tchrs. Assn., Bay Area Curriculum Coords. (N.C. Sci. Specialists), Berkeley Kiwanis Club, Phi Delta Kappa (pres. Lambda chpt. 1942-43). Office: U Calif Berkeley Lawrence Hall of Sci Berkeley CA 94720-5200

RICE, SHARON MARGARET, clinical psychologist; b. Detroit, Sept. 4, 1943; d. William Christopher and Sylvia Lucille (Lawecki) R.; m. John Robert Speer, Aug. 14, 1977 (dec. Mar. 1994). AB, Oberlin Coll., 1965; MA, Boston U., 1968, PhD, 1977. Clin. psychologist Los Angeles County Juvenile Probation, L.A., 1969-75, Las Vegas (Nev.) Mental Health Ctr., 1976-81, Foothills Psychol. Assn., Upland, Calif., 1981—; pvt. cons., Claremont, Calif., 1984—. NIMH grantee, 1967-69; recipient Good Apple award Las Vegas Tchrs. Ctr., 1978-80. Mem. APA, Calif. Psychol. Assn., Internat. Soc. for Study of Dissociation, Inst. Noetic Scis., Sigma Xi. Office: Foothills Psychol Assn 715 N Mountain Ave # G Upland CA 91786-4364

RICE, STEVEN DALE, electronics educator; b. Valparaiso, Ind., Aug. 11, 1947; s. Lloyd Dale and Mary Helen (Breen) R.; m. Reyanna Danti, Mar. 4, 1972; children: Joshua, Breanna. AAS, Valparaiso Tech. Inst., 1969; BS Health Sci., Ball State U., 1973; BSEE, Valparaiso Tech. Inst., 1973; MS in Vocat. Edn., No. Mont. Coll., 1991. Electronics technician Heavy Mil. Electronic Systems GE, Syracuse, N.Y., 1969-70; electronics technician Ball State U., Muncie, Ind., 1974-75; with electronic sales Tandy Corp., Valparaiso, 1976-77; electronics technician Missoula (Mont.) Community Hosp., 1977-84; instr. electronics Missoula Coll. Tech. U. Montana-Missoula, 1984-88; chmn. dept. electronics Coll. of Tech. U. Mont., Missoula, 1988—. Book reviewer Merrill Pub., 1988—, Delmar, McGraw Hill. Bd. dirs. Victor (Mont.) Sch. Bd., 1989—, chmn. bd., 1992-95. Mem. IEEE, Instrument Soc. Am., Mont. Fedn. Tchrs. Office: Coll Tech U Montana Missoula 909 South Ave W Missoula MT 59801-7910

RICE, STUART EVAN, music educator; b. Bakersfield, Calif., Dec. 28, 1964; s. Stephen Lee Rice and Shirley (Gray) Lacy; m. Nolana Lord, July 1991; 1 child, Emily Jean. Student, Juilliard Sch. Music, 1983; BMus, U. Utah, 1996. Libr. Juilliard Sch., N.Y.C., 1983; libr. music dept. U. Utah, Salt Lake City, 1986-88, 90-96; support specialist Centennial Devel. Svcs., Greeley, Utah, 1989-90; music tchr. Duchesne (Utah) Sch. Dist., 1996—. Editor Flatland Press, 1993—; editl. writer Drum Corps World Mag., 1996—; editor slide compilation Works for Band-Messiaen, Bukvitch, 1988, 89; marching band choreographer; founder method of functional marching, method of choreography analysis. Co-founder, chmn. steering com. RAMD Virtual Symposium, 1995; presenter in field. Juilliard Sch. of Music scholar, 1983. Mem. LDS Ch. Home: 9958 Bardum Ln Sandy UT 84094

RICE, WALLACE WILLIAM, secondary education educator; b. Basin, Wyo., May 3, 1936; s. William Peace Jr. and Emma Anne (Wahl) R.; m. Rozella Peterson, June 23, 1962; children: Steven C., Kevin E. BS in Geology, U. Wyo., 1959, MS in Natural Sci., 1967. Oil well logger Anders Well Logging, Fort Collins, Colo., 1959-61; office mgr. Wyo. Hwy Dept., Cheyenne, Wyo., 1962; adminstrv. asst. Sch. Dist. #1, Cheyenne, 1962-63; sci. tchr. Johnson High Sch., Cheyenne, 1963-65; earth sci. tchr. Ctrl. H.S., Cheyenne, 1966-96; ret.; athletic ticket mgr. Ctrl. H.S., Cheyenne, 1968-96, asst. wrestling coach, 1962, 63, 67—. Sec., treas. Laramie County Rheumatic Fever Prevention Soc., Cheyenne, 1962—; leader Boy Scouts Am.; v.p. Trinity Luth. Ch., 1978, 79, King of Glory Luth. Ch., 1989, 90, 91. With USNG, 1954-62. Recipient Silver Beaver award Boy Scouts Am., 1985, Commr. award, 1988, Dist. award of Merit, 1994, Founder's award Order of Awrow, 1996. Mem. Nat. Sci. Tchr. Assn. (regional meeting dir. 1972), Wyo. Math. Sci. Assn., Am. Fedn. Tchrs. (pres. 1978, 79, 82, sec. 1982-96). Home: 815 1/2 W 24th St Cheyenne WY 82001

RICE-DIETRICH, THERESE ANN, elementary education educator; b. Washington, June 27, 1954; d. Harry Woodrow and Catherine Frances (Hefinger) Rice; m. Robert Lynn Dietrich, Aug. 21, 1979; children: Tasha Marie, Robin Michael, Christopher Lee, Dana Jeffrey. BS in Music Edn., U. Ala., Tuscaloosa, 1976; M. Music in Music Therapy, Fla. State U., 1978. Cert. tchr., Nev. Music therapist Washoe County Sch. Dist., Reno, Nev., 1978-86, spl. edn. tchr., 1986-89, elem. edn. tchr., 1989—. Mem. Nat. Assn. Tchrs. of Math., Nat. Coun. Tchrs. of English, Washoe County Tchrs.' Assn. (Disting. Performance award 1988), Nev. State Edn. Assn., Phi Kappa Phi.

RICH, ANDREA LOUISE, museum executive. BA, UCLA, 1965, MA, 1966, PhD, 1968. Asst. prof. comms. studies UCLA, L.A., 1976; asst. dir. office learning resources UCLA, 1976, acting dir. Media Ctr., 1977, dir. office of instructional devel., 1978-80, asst. vice chancellor office of instructional devel., 1980-86, asst. exec. vice chancellor, 1986-87, vice chancellor acad. adminstrn., 1987-91, exec. vice chancellor, 1991-95; pres., CEO L.A. County Mus. of Art, L.A., 1995—. Office: L A County Mus Art 5905 Wilshire Blvd Los Angeles CA 90036

RICH, BEN ARTHUR, lawyer, educator; b. Springfield, Ill., Mar. 27, 1947; s. Ben Morris and Betty Lorraine (Ingalls) R.; m. Caroline Rose Castle, Oct. 4, 1984 (div. Nov. 1988); m. Kathleen Mills, Aug. 17, 1991. Student, U. St. Andrews, Scotland, 1967-68; BA, DePauw U., 1969; JD, Washington U., 1973; postgrad., U. Colo. Bar: Ill. 1973, N.C. 1975, Colo. 1984. Rsch. assoc. U. Ill. Coll. Law, Urbana, 1973-74; staff atty. Nat. Assn. Attys. Gen., Raleigh, N.C., 1974-76; prin. Hollowell, Silverstein, Rich & Brady, Raleigh, 1976-80; dep. commr. N.C. Indsl. Commn., Raleigh, 1980-81; counsel N.C. Meml. Hosp., Chapel Hill, 1981-84; assoc. univ. counsel U. Colo. Health Scis. Ctr., Denver, 1984-86; gen. counsel U. Colo., Boulder, 1986-89, spl. counsel to the regents, 1989-90; asst. clin. prof. U. Colo. Sch. Medicine, 1992-94; asst. prof. U. Colo. Health Scis. Ctr., 1995—, asst. dir. program in healthcare ethics, humanities and law, 1995—; asst. prof. attendent U. Colo. Sch. Medicine, 1996-91, adj. instr. Sch. Law, 1988—, vis. assoc. prof., 1990-91; lectr. U. Denver Coll. Law. Contbr. articles to jours., chpt. to book. Mem. Am. Coll. Legal Medicine (assoc.-in-law 1987), Am. Philos. Assn., Soc. for Health and Human Values, Am. Soc. Medicine and Ethics (health law tchrs. sect.), Toastmasters Internat. (pres. Raleigh chpt. 1978). Unitarian. Home: 222 S Elm St Denver CO 80222-1133 Office: Univ Colo Health Scis Ctr Box B137 4200 E 9th Ave Denver CO 80262

RICH, DAVID BARRY, city official, auditor, accountant, entertainer; b. Bronx, N.Y., July 3, 1952; s. Steven and Gizella (Kornfeld) R.; m. Biverly Hayag, Dec. 6, 1995; 1 child, Suzanne Stephanie. BS in Health Adminstrn., Ithaca Coll., 1976; postgrad. in acctg., Bryant and Stratton Coll., Buffalo, 1977. Office mgr. Rubin Gorewitz, CPA, N.Y.C., 1977-78; auditor State of Ariz., Phoenix, 1979-83; internal auditor City of Phoenix, 1983-84; sales use tax auditor City of Mesa (Ariz.), 1984—; pres. Clovis Acctg. Inc., Mesa, 1980-94; rep. H.D. Vest Investment Inc., Irving, Tex., 1984-94; owner D.B. Rich Enterprises Import/Export, Mesa, 1992—; stage name Barry Rich, Stand-up Comedy, 1994—. Treas., bd. dirs. Missing Mutts Inc., Tempe, Ariz., 1986-88. With USAF, 1971-76. Fellow Nat. Assn. Tax Preparers; mem. Toastmasters (treas. Mesa 1986-87), Phi Beta Kappa. *The world is one big neighborhood and we are all neighbors. If we will survive as a planet we must work together as friends. We must treat all people as our equals.*

RICH, GARETH EDWARD, financial planner; b. Gainesville, Fla., Feb. 28, 1961. Assoc. in Bus. Adminstrn., Gainesville Coll., 1981; BBA, U. Ga., 1983; postgrad., Coll. for Fin. Planning, Denver, 1986-88. CFP; registered prin. Acct. exec. Gallo Wine Co., L.A., 1983-84; ins. and investment broker Fin. Design Group, Inc., Woodland Hills, Calif., 1984-92; ins. and investment broker, dir. equities and investments Calif. Fin. Advisors and Lincoln Nat Life/LNC Equities, Sherman Oaks, Calif., 1992—. Vol. City of Hope, L.A.; referee Am. Youth Soccer Orgn., Conejo Valley, Calif.; umpire Little League Baseball, Conejo Valley. Mem. San Fernando Valley Underwriters Assn., Internat. Assn. Fin. Planning, Gen. Agents and Mgrs. Assn. Republican. Home: 5626 Fairview Pl Agoura Hills CA 91301-2228 Office: 15260 Ventura Blvd Ste 200 Sherman Oaks CA 91403-5325

RICH, JOSEPH DAVID, psychiatrist; b. Springfield, Mo., Apr. 22, 1939; s. William Daniel and Madge Lucile (Clark) R.; m. Judith Ann Briggs, Aug. 19, 1961; children: Joseph Curtis, David William, Scott Thomas. BA in Chemistry, S.W. Mo. State Coll., 1961; MD, U. Minn., 1965. Diplomate Am. Bd. Psychiatry and Neurology, Am. Bd. Forensic Examiners, Am. Bd. Forensic Medicine; lic. physician, Mont. Intern San Diego County (Calif.) Gen. Hosp., 1965-66; lt., gen. med. officer USN, Guam, 1966-68; resident in gen. psychiatry U. Kans. Med. Ctr., Kansas City, 1968-71; pvt. practice Billings, Mont., 1971—; med. dir. psychiatric unit Deaconess Med. Ctr., Billings, 1974-79, 85-88; med. dir. Deaconess Psychiat. Ctr., Billings, 1988—, Deaconess Behavioral Health Clinic, Billings, 1992—; med. dir. psychiat. svcs. Deaconess Billings Clinic Health Sys., 1995—; chief resident dept.

psychiatry U. Kans., 1970-71; pres. med. staff Deaconess Med. Ctr., 1982; psychiat. cons. South Ctrl. Mont. Regional Mental Health Ctr., Billings, 1976-87, Indian Health Svc. PHS Hosp., Crow Agy., Mont., 1984-87, dept. spl. edn. Billings Pub. Schs., 1985-87. Mem. med. exec. com. No. Rockies Cancer Ctr., Billings, 1993—; med. dir. Yellowstone Boys and Girls Ranch, Billings, 1977-87. Fellow am. Psychiat. Assn.; mem. AMA, Mont. Psychiat. Assn. (pres. 1985, 96, sec. 1987, 88, legis. rep. 1986-96, Gladys V. Holmes award 1994), Mont. Med. Assn., Yellowstone Valley Med. Soc., Am. Acad. Psychiatry and the Law, Am. Coll. Forensic Examiners. Office: Deaconess Billings Clinic Health Sys PO Box 37000 Billings MT 59107

RICH, LESLEY MOSHER, artist; b. Chgo., May 12, 1944; d. Robert Gollnick and Lillian Schmelzle; m. Keith Rich, July 6, 1995. Student, U. Ill., 1962-66, Inst. Allende, San Miguel de Allende, Mex., 1976-78. Cons., artist Med. Imaging Sys., Chgo., 1990-93; art instr., 1993—. One-woman shows include Palette & Chisel, Chgo., 1995 (Best Show of Yr. 1995), Gallery North, New Buffalo, Mich., 1995, Birchstone, Egg Harbor, Wis., 1996, 1997; exhibited in group show at China Art Mus., Beijing, 1996. Artist Art for Inner City, Chgo., 1988-89, Arusha (Tanzania) Women's Devel. Ctr., 1996. Recipient award of excellence Oil Painters of Am., 1994, Wichita Art Mus., 1994, Arts for the Pks., 1996. Mem. Palette & Chisel (Harriet Bitterly award 1994, award of excellence 1994), Am. Artists Profl. League, Knickerbocker Soc., Allied Artists. Home: 4225 Park Blvd Palo Alto CA 94306

RICH, RAY, human behavior educator; b. Oklahoma City, Dec. 10, 1940; s. Jack and Myrtle (Grantland) Bowen; m. Julie Bennett Rich, Oct. 26, 1970. AA, Clark County C.C., Las Vegas, 1976; BA, U. Nev., Las Vegas, 1978; MS, U. Nev., 1980. Mem. adj. faculty C.C. Southern Nev., Las Vegas, 1978-81; prof. dept. human behavior C.C. Southern Nev., 1981—. Recipient Outstanding Svc. to Humanity award Phi Theta Kappa, 1988. Home: 3332 Calle De Corrida Las Vegas NV 89102 Office: CC Southern Nev 6375 W Charleston Blvd WIA Las Vegas NV 89102-1124

RICH, ROBERT STEPHEN, lawyer; b. N.Y.C., Apr. 30, 1938; s. Maurice H. and Natalie (Priess) R.; m. Myra N. Lakoff, May 31, 1964; children: David, Rebecca, Sarah. AB, Cornell U., 1959; JD, Yale U., 1963. Bar: N.Y. 1964, Colo. 1973, U.S. Tax Ct. 1966, U.S. Supreme Ct. 1967, U.S. Ct. Claims 1968, U.S. Dist. Ct. (so. dist.) N.Y. 1965, U.S. Dist. Ct. (ea. dist.) N.Y. 1965, U.S. Dist. Ct. Colo. 1980, U.S. Ct. Appeals (2d cir.) 1964, U.S. Ct. Appeals (10th cir.) 1978; conseil juridique, Paris, 1968. Assoc. Shearman & Sterling, N.Y.C., Paris, London, 1963-72; ptnr. Davis, Graham & Stubbs, Denver, 1973—; adj. faculty U. Denver Law Sch., 1977—; adv. bd. U. Denver Ann. Tax Inst., 1985—; adv. bd. global bus. and culture divsn. U. Denver, 1992—, Denver World Affairs Coun., 1993—; bd. dirs. Clos du Val Wine Co. Ltd., Danskin Cattle Co., Areti Wines , Ltd., Taltarni Vineyards, Christy Sports, Copper Valley Assn., pres.; bd. dirs. several other corps.; mem. Colo. Internat. Trade Adv. Coun., 1985—, tax adv. com. U.S. Senator Hank Brown; mem. Rocky Mountain Dist. Export Coun. U.S. Dept. Commerce, 1993—. Author treatises on internat. taxation; contbr. articles to profl. jours. Bd. dirs. Denver Internat. Film Festival, 1978-79, Alliance Française, 1977—; actor, musician N.Y. Shakespeare Festival, 1960; sponsor Am. Tax Policy inst., 1991—; trustee, sec. Denver Art Mus., 1982—; mem. adv. bd. Denver World Affairs Coun., 1993—. Capt., AUS, 1959-60. Fellow Am. Coll. Tax Counsel (bd. regents 10th cir. 1992—); mem. ABA, Internat. Bar Assn., Colo. Bar Assn., N.Y. State Bar Assn., Assn. of Bar of City of N.Y., Asia-Pacific Lawyers Assn., Union Internationale des Avocats, Internat. Fiscal Assn. (pres. Rocky Mt. br. 1992—, U.S. regional v.p. 1988—), Japan-Am. Soc. Colo. (bd. dirs., 1989—, pres. 1991-93), Confrerie des Chevaliers du Tastevin, Meadowood Club, Denver Club, Mile High Club, Cactus Club Denver, Yale Club, Denver Tennis Club. Office: Cherry Creek Sta PO Box 61429 Denver CO 80206-8429 also: Antelope Co 555 Seventeenth St Ste 2400 Denver CO 80202

RICH, SUSAN ABBY, efficiency consultant; b. Bklyn., Apr. 11, 1946; d. Milton and Jeanette (Merns) Rich. BA, Bklyn. Coll., 1967, MA, 1976, advanced cert. in administrn. and supervision, 1977; cert. indsl. rels. UCLA, 1981. Tchr. speech, theater N.Y.C. Bd. Edn., 1967-77; employee rels. supr. Crocker Nat. Bank, 1977-81; plant personnel mgr. Boise Cascade Corp., 1981-82; speaker, cons., writer office efficiency and productivity Get Organized, Get Rich!, Playa del Rey, Calif. Bd. dirs. Barlow Respiratory Hosp.; bd. trustees South Bay Master Chorale. Mem. Women's Referral Svc. (Mem. of Year award 1985, Humanitarian award 1993), Nat. Speakers Assn. (Greater L.A. chpt., Bronze award 1987, Silver award 1990). Office: Get Organized Get Rich! 7777 W 91st St Ste 1154B Playa Del Rey CA 90293-8352

RICHARD, BRENDA G., administrative professional; b. New Orleans, Apr. 11, 1951; Honora Joseph and Mary Alice (Turner) Richard; children: Tyra Latrell, Tyron DeShon Thomas. Paraprofl. Riverside County Office of Edn., Riverside, Calif., 1989—. Home: PO Box 1174 Palm Springs CA 92263-1174

RICHARD, CAMILLE ELIZABETH, ecologist, consultant; b. Lawton, Okla., Mar. 21, 1962; d. Joseph C. and Sarah Elizabeth (Adams) R. BA, Trinity U., 1984; MS, Colo. State U., 1990. Lab technician USDA-Agrl. Rsch. Sta., Ft. Collins, Colo., 1986-87; vegetation analyst Colo. State U., Ft. Collins, 1987-90; range/watershed mgmt. specialist Inst. Forestry Peace Corps, Pokhara, Nepal, 1990-92; natural resource specialist Annapunna Conservation Area Peace Corps, Pokhara, 1993; rsch. coord. Ctr. Ecol. Rish Assessment Colo State U., 1994-95; ecologist Colo. natural heritage program The Nature Conservancy, Ft. Collins, 1995-96; ecol. cons. and prin. Stony Ridge Environ. Cons., Lake City, Colo., 1995—; reclamation technician Trapper Mine, Craig, Colo., summer 1987, 88; reclamation planner Summitville Mine Superfund Site, Del Norte, Colo., 1994—; wetlands consultant Southway Constrn., Alamosa, Colo., 1996—; cons. Winrock Internat., Himachal Predesh, India, 1997. Mem. Lake City (Colo.) Planning Commn., 1995—; bd. dirs. Greater San Juan Partnership, Pagosa Springs, Colo., 1995—. Hill Meml. fellow Colo. State U., 1988. Mem. Nat. Peace Corps Assn., Colo. Native Plant Soc., Soc. Ecol. Restoration, Soc. Range Mgmt., Soc. Wetland Scientists. Home: PO Box 188 881 Primrose Ln Lake City CO 81235

RICHARD, CAROLYN LEE, curator, park ranger, fire fighter; b. LaPorte, Ind., June 2, 1958; d. Arthur Stephen and Mary Lou (Boyd) Crowley; m. Ellis Edward Richard Jr., June 21, 1989. AA in natural scis., Cottey Coll., Nevada, Mo., 1978; BS in leisure studies, Ariz. State U., 1980. Fee collection pk. technician Assateague Island Nat. Seashore Pk., Berlin, Md., 1981; interpretation pk. technician Lincoln Home Nat. Hist. Site/Martin Van Buren Nat. Hist. Site, Ill., N.Y., 1982; fee collection and interpretation pk. technician Death Valley (Calif.) Nat. Monument, 1983; patrol pk. ranger Quachita River C.E., Columbia, La., 1983-84; fee collection, interpretation and mgmt. pk. ranger Death Valley Nat. Monument, 1984-85; supervisory pk. ranger Old Post Office Tower, Washington, 1985-87; curator, pk. ranger Sequoia Nat. Pk./Kings Nat. Pk., Three Rivers, Calif., 1987-88; mus. curator Grand Canyon (Ariz.) Nat. Pk., 1988—. Stain Glass Work artist, 1980—; sect. writer Nat. Pk. Svc. Manual Nat. Pk. Svc. Curator's Office, Washington, 1991; contbr. articles to profl. jours. Vol. Big Bend (Tex.) Nat. Pk., fall 1980, Recycling Drop-off Point, Grand Canyon, 1990—, Grand Canyon Community Libr., Grand Canyon, 1990—; mem. Planned Parenthood, Nature Conservancy, Western Pa. Conservancy, Philanthropic and Ednl. Organ. Mem. Pub. Broadcasting TV. Home: PO Box 2025 Grand Canyon AZ 86023-2025 Office: Grand Canyon Nat Pk PO Box 129 Grand Canyon AZ 86023-0129*

RICHARD, GERALD LAWRENCE, soil scientist; b. Brush, Colo., Oct. 26, 1931; s. Donald Lehman and Gladys Lucile (Eikenbary) R.; m. Phyllis Darlene Hansen, Dec. 28, 1952; children: Donald Lawrence, Dale Kendall, Lori Ann Fosmire, Julie Lynn Young. BS in Agronomy, Colo. State U., 1956. Soil scientist Soil Conservation Svc., Wheatland, Wyo., 1957, Torrington and Cheyenne, Wyo., 1959-65; work unit conservationist Soil Conservation Svc., Laramie, Wyo., 1965; area soil scientist Soil Conservation Svc., Bellefonte, Pa., 1965-71; asst. state soil scientist Soil Conservation Svc., Spokane, Wash., 1971-78; sr. soil scientist Soil Conservation Svc./U.S. Agy. for Internat. Devel., Lashkar Gah, Afghanistan, 1978-79; soil scientist/land use interpreter Soil Conservation Svc./U.S. Agy. for Internat. Devel., Kathmandu, Nepal, 1979-80; dep. co-mgr./soil scientist Soil Conservation Svc./Western Carolina U., Kathmandu, 1980-82, team leader resource conservation project, 1982-85; state soil scientist Soil Conservation Svc., Boise, Idaho, 1985-89; cons. soil scientist Spokane, 1989—; Contbr. articles to profl. publs. 1st lt. U.S. Army, 1957-59. Mem. Am. Soc. of Agronomy, Soil Sci. Soc. Am., Soil and Water Conservation Soc. (pres. keystone chpt. Pa. 1971), Washington Soc. of Profl. Soil Scientists. Methodist. Home: 2709 S Post St Spokane WA 99203-1877

RICHARD, ROBERT CARTER, psychologist; b. Waterloo, Iowa, Apr. 4, 1938; s. Quentin Leroy and Adeline Pauline (Halverson) R.; student Pomona Coll., 1956-57, Westmont Coll., 1957; BA, Wheaton (Ill.) Coll., 1960; BD, Fuller Theol. Sem., 1963, PhD, 1973; STM, Andover Newton Theol. Sch., 1964; m. Shirley Ruth Jones, Aug. 25, 1962; children: David, John. Ordained to ministry Am. Bapt. Conv., 1963; pastor Peninsula Bapt. Ch., Gig Harbor, Wash., 1965-68; marriage and family counselor Glendale (Calif.) Family Service, 1970-71; psychol. asst., Oakland and Pleasant Hill, Calif., 1972-74; clin. psychologist Rafa Counseling Assos., Pleasant Hill, 1974—; mem. faculty John F. Kennedy U., Orinda, Calif., 1975-78; adj. faculty mem. New Coll., Berkeley, Calif., 1986. Co-founder, bd. dirs. New Directions Counseling Center, 1974-81. Recipient Integration of Psychology and Theology award, 1973; lic. psychologist, marriage, family and child counselor, Calif. Mem. Am., Calif., Contra Costa (past pres.) psychol. assns., Christian Assn. Psychol. Studies. Republican. Am. Baptist. Author: (with Deacon Anderson) The Way Back: A Christian's Journey to Mental Wholeness, 1989; contbr. articles to profl. publs. Researcher assertiveness tng., long-term marriage, lay counselor tng., psychotherapy and religious experience, treatment of adults abused as children. Office: Rafa Counseling Assocs 101 Gregory Ln Ste 33 Pleasant Hill CA 94523-4915

RICHARDS, BENNESS MELVIN, airline pilot; b. Denver, May 24, 1921; s. Benness and Carrie Beatrice (Hayes) R.; m. Mary Jane Chrysler, May 24, 1942; 1 child, Chrysler Steven. Student, U. Colo., 1939-41. Lic. comml. airline transport pilot. Capt. Continental Airlines, L.A., 1946-81; sr. flight tng. device instr. McDonnell Douglas, Long Beach, Calif., 1989-93, contractor, 1993-96. Lt. comdr. USNR, 1941-56. Decorated Air medal. Mem. Masons. Home: 5801 Lockhurst Dr Woodland Hills CA 91367-2932

RICHARDS, CHARLES FRANKLIN, JR., lawyer; b. Evergreen Park, Ill., Jan. 30, 1949; s. Charles Franklin and Mary Corinne (Joyce) R.; m. Maureen Patricia Duffy, June 17, 1972 (div. Mar. 1989); m. Deborah Ann Murphy, May 20, 1991; children: Patrick, Corrine, Meghan, Shannon. BA, St. Mary's of Minn., 1971; JD, U. Ill., 1974. Bar: Minn. 1974, U.S. Dist. Ct. Minn. 1974, Ariz. 1985, U.S. Dist. Ct. Ariz. 1985, U.S. Ct. Appeals (9th cir.) 1985; cert. civil trial adv. Nat. Bd. Trial Advocacy. Asst. city atty. City of Rochester, Minn., 1974-76; assoc., then ptnr. O'Brien, Ehrick, Wolf, Deaner & Downing, Rochester, 1976-85; assoc., shareholder Gallagher & Kennedy, PA, Phoenix, 1985-94; pvt. practice, Phoenix, 1994—; judge pro tem Ariz. Ct. Appeals, 1994. Contbr. articles to legal pubs. Bd. dirs. St. Mary's Hosp., Rochester, 1983-85; del. Dem. Nat. Conv., San Francisco, 1984. Mem. ABA, ATLA, State Bar Ariz. (mem. trial practice sect. exec. coun. 1994—, mem. civil jury instrns. com. 1994—, co-editor Trial Practice Newsletter 1990—), Ariz. Assn. Def. Counsel, Ariz. Trial Lawyers Assn., Maricopa County Bar Assn. (mem. CLE com. 1988-91), Minn. Bar Assn. Roman Catholic. Office: 5308 N 12th St Ste 401 Phoenix AZ 85014-2903

RICHARDS, EVELYN JEAN, journalist; b. Lake Forest, Ill., Mar. 2, 1952; d. Richard K. and Erika (Nord) R.; m. Greg L. Pickrell, 1982. BS in Journalism, Northwestern U., 1974, MS in Journalism, 1975. City hall reporter Elyria (Ohio) Chronicle-Telegram, 1975-76; reporter Palo Alto (Calif.) Times, 1976-79; bus. editor Peninsula Times Tribune, Palo Alto, 1979-81; tech. reporter San Jose (Calif.) Mercury News, 1981-84, tech. editor, 1984-88, asst. bus. editor, 1996—; staff writer The Washington Post, Washington, 1988-91; reporter, editor Waterman & Assocs., San Francisco, 1992; contbg. editor The Nikkei Weekly, Tokyo, 1993-96; freelance writer Tokyo, 1993-96. Recipient Davenport fellowship in Bus. & Econ. Reporting, U. Mo., 1980, Interant. Press Inst. fellowship Japan, 1983, John S. Knight fellowship for Profl. Journalists, Stanford U., 1986-87, First Pl. Reporting award World Affairs Coun. of No. Calif., 1986, Overseas Press Club 1st Pl. Reporting award, 1987. Mem. Soc. for Profl. Journalists, Investigative Reporters and Editors, Coll. Women Assn. Home: PO Box 4179 Mountain View CA 94040-0179 Office: San Jose Mercury News Bus News Dept 750 Ridder Park Dr San Jose CA 95190

RICHARDS, GERALD THOMAS, lawyer, consultant; b. Monrovia, Calif., Mar. 17, 1933; s. Louis Jacquelyn Richards and Inez Vivian (Richardson) Hall; children: Patricia M. Richards Grauf, Laura J., Dag Hammarskjold; m. Mary Lou Richards, Dec. 27, 1986. BS magna cum laude, Lafayette Coll., 1957; MS, Purdue U., 1963; JD, Golden Gate U., 1976. Bar: Calif. 1976, U.S. Dist. Ct. (no. dist.) Calif. 1977, U.S. Patent Office 1981, U.S. Ct. Appeals (9th cir.) 1984, U.S. Supreme Ct. 1984. Computational physicist Lawrence Livermore (Calif.) Nat. Lab., 1967-73, planning staff lawyer, 1979, mgr. tech. transfer office, 1980-83, asst. lab. counsel, 1984-93; sole practice, Livermore, 1976-78, Oceanside, Calif., 1994—; mem. exec. com., policy advisor Fed. Lab. Consortium for Tech. Transfer, 1980-88; panelist, del. White House Conf. on Productivity, Washington, 1983; del. Nat. Conf. on Tech. and Aging, Wingspread, Wis., 1981. Commr. Housing Authority, City of Livermore, 1977, vice chairperson, 1978, chairperson, 1979; pres. Housing Choices, Inc., Livermore, 1980-84; bd. dirs. Valley Vol. Ctr., Pleasanton, Calif., 1983, pres., 1984-86. Recipient Engring. award Gen. Electric Co., 1956. Maj. U.S. Army, 1959-67. Mem. ABA, Calif. State Bar (conv. alt. del. 1990-92), Alameda County Bar Assn., Eastern Alameda County Bar Assn. (sec. 1978, bd. dirs. 1991-92, chair lawyers referral com. 1992-93), Santa Barbara County Bar Assn., San Diego County Bar Assn., Bar Assn. of Northern San Diego County, Phi Beta Kappa, Tau Beta Pi, Sigma Pi Sigma. Home: 3747 Vista Campana S Apt 59 Oceanside CA 92057-8228

RICHARDS, GLENICE DEBIQUE, education educator; b. Chateaubelair, St. Vincent, Apr. 25, 1958; came to U.S., 1990; d. Ambrose Reddock and Iris DeBique; m. Aug. 1, 1982; children: Tamar, Cliff. BS in Edn., Fla. A&M U., Tallahassee, 1993, MS in Edn., 1994; PhD Candidate in Edn., Wash. State U., 1994—. Qualified tchr. 4th grade tchr. Chateaubelair Meth. Sch., 1976-77; secondary sch. tchr. Petit Bordel Secondary Sch., St. Vincent, 1977-78; mid. sch. tchr. Richmond Govt. Sch., St. Vincent, 1980-81, Lodge Village Govt. Sch., St. Vincent, 1981-85; multiple grades tchr. Liberty Lodge Tng. Sch., St. Vincent, 1985-90; presch. tchr. Fla. A&M U., Tallahassee, 1991-93, rsch. asst., 1992-93; grad. asst. Sch. Grad. Studies, Tallahassee, 1993-94, Coll. Edn., Tallahassee, 1993-94; instr. Coll. Edn. Wash. State U., Pullman, 1994—. Asst. sec., sec. Tchrs. Union Coll. Br., St. Vincent, 1977-80; tchr. Seventh Day Adventist Ch., 1991-96, supt. Sabbath Sch. Troy, Idaho, 1996-97. Mem. ASCD, Internat. Reading Assn., Am. Ednl. Rsch. Assn., Golden Key. Home: 1630 NE Valley Rd Apt F102 Pullman WA 99163-4459 Office: Wash State U Coll Edn Pullman WA 99164

RICHARDS, HERBERT EAST, minister emeritus, commentator; b. Hazleton, Pa., Dec. 30, 1919; s. Herbert E. and Mabel (Vannaucker) R.; m. Lois Marcey, Jan. 1, 1942; children: Herbert Charles, Marcey Lynn, Robyn Lois, Fredrick East, Mark Allen. AB, Dickinson Coll., 1941; BD, Drew U., 1944; MA, Columbia, 1944; DD, Coll. of Idaho, 1953; postgrad., Union Theol. Sem., 1941-48, Bucknell U., 1943-44. Accredited news reporter Nat. Assn. Broadcasters. Ordained to ministry Methodist Ch., 1944; pastor in Boiling Springs, Pa., 1937-40, West Chester, Pa., 1940-41, Basking Ridge, N.J., 1941-47; mem. faculty Drew U. and Theol. Sem., 1944-51, assoc. prof. homiletics and Christian criticism, chmn. dept., asst. dean, 1947-51; spl. lectr. religion Howard U., 1947; minister 1st Meth. Cathedral, Boise, Idaho, 1951-69, 1st United Meth. Ch., Eugene, Oreg., 1969-78; minister Tabor Heights United Meth. Ch., Portland, Oreg., 1978-86, minister emeritus, 1986—; weekly radio broadcaster Sta. KBOI, Sta. KIDO, 1941—; weekly TV broadcaster CBS, 1945—, ABC, 1969—, NBC, 1973; pres. Inspiration, Inc., TV Found., 1965—, TV Ecology, 1973; producer Life TV series ABC, 1974-85, also BBC, Eng., Suise Romande, Geneva; chmn. Idaho bd. ministerial tng. Meth. Conf., 1954-60, TV, Radio and Film Commn., 1954-62, Oreg. Coun. Public Broadcasting, 1973; del. Idaho Conf. Meth. Gen. Conf., 1956, Jurisdictional Conf., 1956, World Meth. Coun., 1957, 81, World Meth. Conf., 1981, mem. Gen. Conf., 1956-60, Jurisdictional Conf., 1956, 60; meml. chaplain Idaho Supreme Ct., 1960; chaplain Idaho Senate, 1960-68; mem. Task Force on TV and Ch., 1983. Author: In Time of Need, 1986, Faith and the Pursuit of Healing, 1996; contbr. articles to religious publs.; composer: oratorios Prophet Unwilling, 1966, Meet Martin Luther, 1968, Dear Jesus Boy, 1973. Mem. Commn. on Centennial Celebration for Idaho, 1962-63; committeeman Boy Scouts Am.; bd. dirs. Eugene chpt. ARC, 1954-73; trustee Willamette U., Cascade Manor Homes; adv. bd. Medic-Alert Found. Recipient Alumni citation in religious edn. Dickinson Coll., 1948, Golden Plate award Am. Acad. Achievement, 1965, Jason Lee Mass Media TV award, 1983; named Clergyman of Yr., Religious Heritage Am., 1964. Mem. AAUP, CAP (chaplain Idaho wing, lt. col.), Am. Acad. Achievement (bd. govs. 1967—), Am. Found. Religion and Psychiatry (charter gov.), Greater Boise Ministerial Assn. (pres.), Eugene Ministerial Assn. (pres. 1978), Masons (33 degree, editor Pike's Peak Albert That Is), Shriners, Elks, Rotary (editor Key and Cog, pres. dist. 510 Pioneer Club), Kappa Sigma (Grand Master of Beta Pi). Home: 10172 SE 99th Dr Portland OR 97266-7227 Office: Tabor Heights United Meth Ch 6161 SE Stark St Portland OR 97215-1935 *When a person presses his face against the window pane of life, he becomes as a child waiting for his father's return; simple, trusting and infinitely wiser. In our present time of growth/conflict, such a face-pressing is essential to get us safely from where we are to where we ought to be.*

RICHARDS, JAMES WILLIAM, electromechanical engineer; b. Portland, Oreg., Oct. 24, 1921; s. Jarvis William and Thelma Helen (Eoff) R.; m. Violet Victor Ray, Oct. 9, 1946; children: Betty, Sandra, Diane, William. Student, Nat. Tech. Sch., 1942, Nat. Radio Inst., 1948, Internat. Corr. Sch., 1955; AA, Pierce Coll., 1968. Mgr. Western Design, Santa Barbara, Calif., 1948-55; sr. engr. Bendix Corp., North Hollywood, Calif., 1955-66; v.p. Talley Corp., Newbury Park, Calif., 1966-75, dir. engring., 1982-87; pvt. practice electromech. engr., Eugene, Oreg., 1975-82, 87-89; pres. Western Design, Eugene, Oreg., 1990—. Mem. Masons. Republican. Baptist. Home: PO Box 5498 Eugene OR 97405-0498 Office: Western Design 28983 Fox Hollow Rd PO Box 5549 Eugene OR 97405

RICHARDS, JOE MCCALL, chemical company executive; b. Eugene, Oreg., May 3, 1937; s. Joseph Albert and Bertha (McCall) R.; m. Katherine Mary Enright, June 30, 1961 (div. 1966); m. Ann F. Potter, Jan. 2, 1981; children: Dean A., Ann L. BSChE, Oreg. State U., 1959. Tech. asst. pulp mgr. Pubs. Paper Co., Oregon City, 1960-66; chem. engr. Boise Cascade, Vancouver, Wash., 1966-68; area mgr. Nalco Chem. Co., Milwaukie, Oreg., 1968-82; mgr. RPS, Milwaukie, 1982-86; Western regional mgr. Eka Nobel Paper Chems., Clackamas, Oreg., 1986—. With USAF, 1960-64. AIChE scholar, 1958. Mem. Am. Mgmt. Assn., Tech. Assn. Pulp and Paper Industry (v.p. 1982). Republican. Episcopalian. Home: 12027 SE 115th Ave Clackamas OR 97015-9605 Office: Eka Nobel Paper Chems Divsn 2211 New Market Pky Marietta GA 30067-9310

RICHARDS, KENNETH EDWIN, management consultant; b. N.J., Oct. 9, 1917; s. Kenneth G. and Laura (Benson) R.; m. Evelyn Henderson, Dec. 12, 1942 (div. June 1963); children: Kenneth A., Grant B., Kyle E. Umansky, Diane L. Parmley, Kathleen E. Hilton, Kim E. Richards-Davis, Cynthia G. Burger, Cheri O. Greer, Steven E. Benedict; m. Sylvia Marie Benedict, Nov. 1979. BA, Wesleyan U., 1939. Asst. buyer J.C. Penney Co., 1945-48, buyer, 1948-55, dept. head women's & girl's sportswear apparel, 1955-58; from v.p., mdse. mgr. to dir. S.H. Kress Co., 1958-60; v.p. mdse. and sales Firth Carpet Co., 1960-62, dir., 1961-62; spl. cons. to pres. Mohasco Industries Inc., 1962-63; v.p., dir. Yorkshire Terrace Motel Corp., 1963-66; ptnr. Roxbury Hollow Farm, Claverack, N.Y., 1955-66; sr. ptnr. Mgmt. Assocs., 1963-95; pres. Western Dept. Stores, L.A., 1968-70; v.p. merchandising Rapid Merchandising, Costa Mesa, Calif., 1970-72; exec. v.p., gen. mgr. Skor-Mor Products, Santa Barbara, Calif., 1972-75; pres., CEO Resort to Life, Inc., Calabasas, Calif., 1980-84; exec. dir. Retirement Jobs of Idaho, Boise, 1985-87; pres. Seniors, Inc., Boise, 1987-94; CEO Compunet, Boise, 1995—. Mem. adv. editorial bd. Surgeon Gen. U.S. Army, 1948-55; co-developer noiron cotton; developer women's wear "skort"; pioneer use of mix and match sportswear. Lt. col. AUS, 1940-45. Decorated for action against enemy in Normandy, France, 1944. Mem. Chi Psi. Methodist.

RICHARDS, KENT HAROLD, religion educator; b. Midland, Tex., July 6, 1939; s. Eva E. Richards; children: Lisken Lynn, Lisanne Elizabeth. BA, Calif. State U., 1961; MTh., Claremont Sch. Theology, 1964; PhD, Claremont Grad. Sch., 1969. Rsch. assoc. Inst. for Antiquities & Christianity, Claremont, Calif., 1967-68; asst. prof. Old Testament U. Dayton (Ohio), 1968-72; prof. Old Testament Iliff Sch. Theology, Denver, 1972—; vis. prof. Sch. of Theology/Grad. Sch., Claremont, 1969; mem. bd. of ordained ministry UMC, Rocky Mt. Conf., Denver, 1976-82, bd. of diaconal ministry, 1976-78. Editor: Biblical Scholarship in North America, 16 vols., 1981—, Writings in the Ancient World, (with David Peterson) Interpreting Hebrew Poetry, 1992, (with Tamara C. Eskenazi) Second Temple Studies 2, Temple Community in the Persian Period, 1994. Chmn. Colo. Gov.'s award in Edn. Com., Denver, 1989-91, Vision 2020: A Study of the Colo. Cts.; jud. adv. coun. Colo. Supreme Ct., 1993—; bd. dirs. Colo. Jud. Inst., 1991—. Rsch. grantee NEH, 1985-91, Lilly Found., 1985-86. Mem. Internat. Meeting Program (chair 1973-92), Cath. Bibl. Assn. (program com. 1976-80), Soc. Bibl. Lit. (exec. sec. 1981-87), Am. Coun. Learned Socs. (coun. sec. 1981-87), Profl. Ski Instrs. Am. Office: Iliff Sch of Theology 2201 S University Blvd Denver CO 80210-4707

RICHARDS, MORRIS DICK, social work administrator, educator; b. L.A., Aug. 20, 1939; s. Morris Dick Richards and Annette (Fox) Briggs; m. Leslie Sondra Lefkowitz, Mar. 22, 1975. BA cum laude, Claremont Men's Coll., 1962; MA, U. Chgo., 1964; MPA, U. So. Calif., 1965; LLB, La Salle Ext. U., 1971; MS in Hygiene, PhD in Social Work, U. Pitts., 1973; MBA, Chapman Coll., 1987. Cert. social worker. Asst. dep. dir. children and youth services Orange County (Calif.) Dept. Mental Health, 1973-77; gen. mgr., indsl. therapist Paragon West, Anaheim, Calif., 1977-83; acting dir. alcohol and drug program Horizon Health Corp., Newport Beach, Calif., 1983-84; editor, pub. relations rep., sr. social worker Orange County Social Services Agy., 1983-85; staff analyst Environ. Mgmt. Agy., Orange County, 1985-90; exec. asst. to dir. planning Orange County, 1990-92; staff analyst Orange County Social Svc. Agy., 1992-95; ret., 1995, part-time contract adminstr. for health care agy., 1996—; adj. clin. prof. Chapman Coll., Orange, Calif., 1974-85; instr. Calif. Grad. Inst., 1988-93; instr. U. Phoenix, 1992-95; supervising child welfare worker, program analyst, head child welfare worker, exec. asst. L.A. County Pub. Social Svcs., 1967-71; psychiat. clin. specialist Jewish Big Bros., L.A. County, 1964-67; med. social work cons. Whittier (Calif.) Presbyn. Hosp., 1973-76; pvt. practice psychotherapy, Tustin, Calif., 1975-77; lectr. Calif. State U., Fullerton. Editor newsletter Orange County Adv., 1984-85, Planning Perspective, 1990-91, Broadmoor Cmty. News, 1992-93; contbr. articles to profl. jours. Past bd. dirs. Orange County chpt. Am. Jewish Com., 1982-88, Broadmore Cmty. Assn., Anaheim Hills, Calif., 1981-83, sec., 1990-94; mem. Orange County Mental Health Adv. Bd., 1981-88, sec., bd. dirs.; mem. bd. dirs. Orange County Mental Health Assn., 1988-91; mem. Juvenile Diversion Task Force of Orange County, 1977. Served with USAR, 1958-64. Fellow U. Chgo., 1962, NIMH, 1962, 72; Haynes scholar U. So. Calif. Sch. Pub. Adminstrn., 1964; grantee Faulk Program in Urban Mental Health, U. Pitts., 1973. Mem. NASW (mental health liaison, v.p. local chpt. 1975-88, Social Worker of Yr. award Orange County chpt. 1987), ACLU, Acad. Cert. Social Workers (lic. clin. social worker and marriage, family, child counselor), Registry Clin. Social Workers (diplomate in clin. social work), Orange County Mental Health Assn. (past sec.).

RICHARDS, PAUL A., lawyer; b. Oakland, Calif., May 27, 1927; s. Donnell C. and Theresa (Pasquale) R.; m. Ann Morgans, Nov 20, 1948 (dec. 1984); 1 child, Paul M. Office: 248 S Sierra St Reno NV 89501-1908

RICHARDS, PAUL H., II, mayor; m. Dorothy Richards, 1982; children: Genevieve, Alicia. BBA in Econ. with honors, U. So. Calif.; JD with honors, UCLA. Bar: Calif. Adminstr. City of Carson, Calif.; exec. adminstr., legal counsel City of Compton, Calif., 1995; mayor City of Lynwood, Calif., 1986—. Pres. Ind. Cities Assn., 1992-93; pres. League Calif. Cities, L.A., 1994-95; bd. dirs. Dominguez Hills Found.; vice-chmn. Alameda Corridor Transp. Authority; pres.-elect Nat. Black Caucus Local Elected Officials. Recipient Outstanding Achievement award U.S. Conf. Mayors, 1994, Nat. League of Cities Urban Enrichment award. Office: City of Lynwood Office of Mayor 11330 Bullis Rd Lynwood CA 90262

RICHARDS, RICHARD, lawyer, political consultant; b. Ogden, Utah, May 14, 1932; s. Blaine Boyden and Violet Geneva (Williams) R.; m. Frances

Annette Bott, Jan. 15, 1954; children: Julie R. Dockter, Richard Albert, Jan R. Stevenson, Amy R. Hartvigsen, Brian Lee. AS, Weber Jr. Coll., Ogden, Utah, 1959; JD, U. Utah, 1962; DHum (hon.), Coll. Boca Raton, Fla., 1982. Journeyman sign painter Richards Sign Co., Ogden, 1958-62; legis. asst. Congressman from Utah, Washington, 1962-63, adminstrv. asst., 1963-64; lawyer Froerer, Parker, Richards, Ogden, 1964-69; polit. dir. Rep. Nat. Com., Washington, 1969-70, dep. chmn., 1971; lawyer Mecham & Richards & Self, Ogden, 1972-80; pres. Commerce Cons. Internat., Washington, also Utah, 1984—; we. Presdl. coord. for Nixon, Rep. Party, Washington, 1972; we. coord. Reagan Campaign, Washington, 1980; headed transition team for Reagan Adminstrn. at Dept. Interior, 1980; Rep. nat. chmn. Rep. Nat. Com., Washington, 1981-83. Utah state chmn. Rep. Party, Salt Lake City, 1965-67, 75-77; mem. Ogden ARts Coun., 1961. 2d lt. U.S. Army, 1952-55. Named Outstanding Young Man, Ogden Jaycees, 1967, State of Utah Jaycees, 1968. Mem. Ogden Rotary Club. Republican. Mormon. Home: 4612 Jefferson Ave Ogden UT 84403

RICHARDS, ROBERT CHARLES, management consultant; b. Portland, Oreg., Jan. 18, 1939; s. Charles Robert and Mildred Marie (Merrill) R.; m. Marilyn Cornelia Poole, Sept. 1, 1961 (dec.); children: Kristin Elizabeth (dec.), Jeffrey Robert. BA, Lewis and Clark Coll., 1961. Tng. officer, mgr. edn. dept. U.S. Bancorp, Portland, Oreg., 1965-74; mgr. orgn. devel. Coors Container Co., Golden, Colo., 1974-77; mgmt. cons., mgr. western office Cons. Assocs. Internat., Inc., Lakewood, Colo., 1977-84; mgmt cons., pres. Cons. Network, Lakewood, 1985—; pres., CEO Epoch Prodns., 1986—; exec. v.p., sec.-treas. A Pretty Woman, Inc., Lakewood, Colo., 1994—; instr. Portland State U., 1972-73, U. Oreg., Portland Extension, 1973-74, Portland C.C., 1971-74; adj. faculty Bryant Coll. Ctr. for Mgmt. Devel., Smithfield, R.I., 1979—; mgmt. cons.; seminar leader; devel. cons. Martin Marietta Space Systems Co., 1989-91, Martin Marietta Astronautics Group, 1991-92, Inst. Integrated Product/Process Design and Devel., 1993—, founder, chmn.; bd. dir., sec. Sr. Mgmt. Programs, Inc., 1971-73, pres., 1973-74. Author tng. materials; contbr. articles to profl. publs. Mem. adv. com. C.C. of Denver, scholarship and employment com. Portland State U. Found.; adj. faculty USMC Svc. Support Schs., Camp Lejeune, N.C. With USMCR, 1961-64; col. Res., 1966-92, Persian Gulf, 1990-91. Mem. Am. Soc. Tng. and Devel. (bd. dirs. chpt. 1976, v.p. 1977, bd. dirs. Oreg. chpt. 1972, pres. 1971, bd. dirs. Western region 1971-72), World Futures Soc., Planning Execs. Inst., Rocky Mountain Orgn. Devel. Network, Marine Corps Res. Officers Assn. (pres. Mile High chpt.), Marine Corps Meml. Assn. (sec.). Home and Office: 13362 W Montana Ave Lakewood CO 80228-3726

RICHARDS, ROSALIE ANNE, community college administrator; b. Peoria, Ill., Jan. 21, 1959; d. Fred Vernon and Julia Elizabeth (Morgenthaler) Corbett; m. J. Mark Richards, Dec. 12, 1987; 1 child, Michele D. Corbett. BS, Ea. N.Mex. U., 1980, MA, 1996. Waitress, asst. mgr. Pizza Hut, Portales, N.Mex., 1984-85, 85-87; activity/social svc. dir. Golden Age Nursing Ctr., Clovis, N.Mex., 1985; employment interviewer N.Mex. Dept. Labor, Tucumcari, 1985; employment counselor N.Mex. Dept. Labor, Clovis, 1988-89; coord. Clovis C.C., 1989—, part-time instr., 1992—; grad. intern Clovis Counseling Ctr., 1995-96; part-time instr. Ea. N.Mex. U., 1996-97; apptd. to gov.'s devel. disabilities planning coun., 1996. Mem. adv. bd. Mental Health Resources Juvenile Cmty. Corrections, Clovis, 1994-96, Regional Alliance in Sci., Engring. and Math., Las Cruces, N.Mex., 1994—; leader Girl Scouts U.S., Portales, 1986-92. Recipient Award of Excellence, Ea. N.Mex. U., 1996. Mem. ACA (profl.), APA (student affiliate), Am. Vocat. Assn., N.Mex. Vocat. Assn. (bd. dirs. 1990—), N.Mex. Vocat. Spl. Needs Assn. (pres., sec.-treas., Vocat. Educator of the Yr. 1994). Presbyterian. Office: Clovis Community College 417 Schepps Blvd Clovis NM 88101-8345

RICHARDSON, ALFRED, food service executive, consultant; b. Red Bluff, Calif.. D in Food Svc., Nat. Mfrs. Assn., New Orleans, 1979; D in Food Svc. Adminstrn., Dallas, Tex., 1983. Asst. food svc. dir. Folsom State Prison, Represса. Calif., 1945-48; food adminstr. Univ. Portland, Oreg., 1948-53; food svc. dir. Oreg. State Penitentiary, Salem, 1953-57, Utah State Prison, Draper, 1957-80, Utah Tech. Coll., Salt Lake C. C., 1980-90; cons. Am. Instns. Food Svc. Assn., Salt Lake City, 1990—; tchr. Weber State Coll., Ogden, Utah, 1971; pres. Utah State Prison Employees Assn.; mem. evaluation team Am. Correctional Assn., Colo. State Prison, Canon City, 1973; founder Honor Camp One and Two, Utah State Prison, Salt Lake City; cons. Salvation Army Food Svc.; presenter in field. Author standards/goals sect. Food Svc. Accreditation Manual; compiler, pub. Am. Correctional Food Svc. Assn. Nat. Dir., 7 edit.; author, pub. Food Svc. Control Manual, 1981. Vol. Svc. Corps. Retired Execs., Cottonwood Hosp., Meals-on-Wheels. Named Boss of Yr., Beehive State Chpt. Am. Bus. Women's Assn., 1980-81, Outstanding Male Employee, Utah Pub. Employees Assn., 1983; recipient Silver Plate award Internat. Food Svc. Mfrs. Assn., 1980, Gov.'s citation, others. Mem. Am. Correctional Food Svc. Assn. (founder, past pres., past exec. dir.). Home: 7420 S 100 West Midvale UT 84047

RICHARDSON, A(RTHUR) LESLIE, former medical group consultant; b. Ramsgate, Kent, Eng., Feb. 21, 1910; s. John William and Emily Lilian (Wilkins) R.; came to U.S., 1930, naturalized, 1937; student spl. courses U. So. Calif., 1933-35; m. B. Kathleen Sargent, Oct. 15, 1937. Mgr., Tower Theater, Los Angeles, 1931-33; accountant Felix-Krueper Co., Los Angeles, 1933-35; indsl. engr. Pettengill, Inc., Los Angeles, 1935-37; purchasing agt. Gen. Petroleum Corp. Los Angeles, 1937-46; adminstr. Beaver Med. Clinic, Redlands, Calif., 1946-72, exec. cons. 1972-75, 95; sec.-treas. Fern Properties, Inc., Redlands, 1955-75, Redelco, Inc., Redlands, 1960-67; pres. Buinco, Inc., Redlands, 1956-65; vice chmn. Redlands adv. bd. Bank of Am., 1973-80; exec. cons. Med. Adminstrs. Calif., 1975-83. Pres., Redlands Area Community Chest, 1953; volunteer exec. Internat. Exec. Service Corps; mem. San Bernardino County (Calif.) Grand Jury, 1952-53. Bd. dirs. Beaver Med. Clinic Found., Redlands, 1961—, sec.-treas., 1961-74, pres., 1974-75, chmn. bd. dirs. 1992—. Served to lt. Med. Adminstrv. Corps., AUS, 1942-45. Recipient Redlands Civic award Elks, 1953. Fellow Am. Coll. Med. Practice Execs. (life, disting. fellow 1980, pres. 1965-66, dir.); mem. Med. Group Mgmt. Assn. (hon. life; mem. nat. long range planning com. 1963-68, pres. western sect. 1960), Kiwanis (pres. 1951), Masons. Episcopalian. Home: 1 Verlie Dr Redlands CA 92373-6943 *Personal philosophy: Do unto others as you would have them do unto you.*

RICHARDSON, ARTHUR WILHELM, lawyer; b. Glendale, Calif., Apr. 3, 1963; s. Douglas Fielding and Leni (Tempelaar-Lietz) R. AB, Occidental Coll., 1985; student, London Sch. Econs., 1983; JD, Harvard U., 1988. Bar: Calif. 1989. Assoc. Morgan, Lewis and Bockius, L.A., 1988-90; staff lawyer U.S. SEC, L.A., 1990-92, br. chief, 1992-96, sr. counsel, 1996—. Mem. ABA, Calif. Bar Assn., L.A. County Bar Assn., Harvard/Radcliffe Club So. Calif., Town Hall Calif., L.A. World Affairs Coun., Sierra Club, Phi Beta Kappa. Presbyterian. Home: 2615 Canada Blvd Apt 208 Glendale CA 91208-2077 Office: US SEC 11th Fl 5670 Wilshire Blvd Los Angeles CA 90036-3648

RICHARDSON, BETTY H., prosecutor; b. Oct. 3, 1953. BA, U. Idaho, 1976; JD, Hastings Coll. Law, 1982. Jud. law clk. Chamber of Idaho Supreme Ct. Justice Robert C. Huntley, Jr., 1984-86; legal rsch. asst. Criminal divsn. San Francisco Superior Ct., 1982-84; teaching asst. Hastings Coll. Law, 1980-82; atty. U.S. Dept. Justice, Boise, Idaho, 1993—; instr. Boise State U., 1987, 89; mem. U.S. Atty. Gen.'s Adv. Com. subcoms. on environ. juvenile justice issues; mem. hon. adv. bd. fro Crime Victims Amendment in Idaho, 1994; mem. Dist. of Idaho Judges and Lawyer Reps. com. and gender fairness com. Mem. Idaho Indsl. Commn., 1991-93, chmn., 1993—; bd. dirs. Parents and Youth Against Drug Abuse; adv. bd. of the Family and Workplace Consortium. Tony Patino fellow Hastings Coll. Law, 1982. Mem. Idaho State Bar Assn. (Pro Bono Svc. award 1988—), Idaho State Prosecuting Attys. Assn. Office: US Attys Office PO Box 32 Boise ID 83707-0032

RICHARDSON, DANIEL RALPH, lawyer; b. Pasadena, Calif., Jan. 18, 1945; s. Ralph Claude and Rosemary Clare (Lowery) R.; m. Virginia Ann Lorton, Sept. 4, 1965; children: Brian Daniel, Neil Ryan. BS, Colo. State U., 1969; MBA, St. Mary's Coll. of Calif., 1977; JD, JFK U., 1992. Bar: Calif. Systems engr. Electronic Data Systems, San Francisco, 1972-73; programmer/analyst Wells Fargo Bank, San Francisco, 1973-74; systems analyst Crown-Zellerbach Corp., San Francisco, 1974; programming mgr. Calif. Dental Svc., San Francisco, 1974-75, Fairchild Camera and Inst., Mountain View, Calif., 1975-77; sr. systems analyst Bechtel Corp., San Francisco, 1977; pres. Richardson Software Cons., Inc., San Francisco, 1977—; pvt. practice San Francisco, 1993—; instr. data processing Diablo Valley Coll., Concord, Calif., 1979-80. Author: (book) System Development Life Cycle, 1976, (computer software) The Richardson Automated Agent, 1985. Asst. scoutmaster Boy Scouts Am., Clayton, Calif., 1983-91; soccer coach Am. Youth Soccer League, Clayton, 1978-83. 1st lt. USAF, 1966-72. Mem. ABA, State Bar Calif., Computer Law Assn., Acad. Profl. Cons. and Advisers (cert. profl. cons.), Assn. Systems Mgrs. Office: 870 Market St Ste 400 San Francisco CA 94102-3010

RICHARDSON, DONN CHARLES, business and marketing educator; b. Indpls., Mar. 3, 1940; s. George Covey and Edythe Francis (Chesterfield) R.; m. Carolyn Jean Hassan, Nov. 8, 1969; children: Bradley George, Jason Arthur, Christopher Charles. BA in Journalism and Polit. Sci., Butler U., 1962; MA in Mass Comm., Ohio State U., 1969. Staff editor Cin. Bell Mag. Cin. (Ohio) Bell, 1969-73; mgmt. newsletter editor, spl. projects mgr. US West Comms., Denver, 1973-76; Colo. pub. rels. and outreach dir. US West Comms., Boulder, 1976-84, Colo. employee comm. mgr., 1984-85, market mgr. market planning, 1986-88; fed. govt. market mgr. US West Comms., Englewood, Colo., 1989-94; pres. Richardson Info. Resources, Boulder, Colo., 1994—; cons. Northglenn (Colo.) Recreation Ctr., 1982; presenter in field. Author, pub.: The Quick Consultant's Guide to Public Speaking; contbr. articles to profl. jours. Pres. Shannon Estates Homeowners Assn., Boulder, 1978-80; pub. rels. dir. Boulder (Colo.) Mental Health Ctr. Benefit, 1980; publicity dir. FC Boulder (Colo.) Soccer Club, 1991-94. Capt. USAF, 1963-69. Mem. Internat. Assn. Bus. Communicators (dist. profl. devel. chair 1982-84, chpt. v.p. 1985, internat. pub. rels. chair 1985-86, accredited bus. communicator), Pub. Rels. Soc. Am. (dist. conf. program chair 1996, accredition judge 1989, accredited pub. rels. profl.). Home: 1212 Cavan St Boulder CO 80303-1602

RICHARDSON, EARL WILSON, elementary education educator; b. Emporia, Kans., June 4, 1942; s. Clarence Earl and Dorothy Ann (Draper) R.; m. Mariann Hirsig, July 31, 1965; 1 child, Rachelle Ranae. BS in Elem. Edn., Emporia (Kans.) State U., 1964; MED in Elem. Edn., U. Wyo., 1971. Tchr. 5th-6th grades Alta Vista Elem. Sch., Cheyenne, Wyo., 1964-68, ecolab. and sci. tchr. 5th-6th grades, 1972-74, 83-84; tchr. 5th-6th grades Bain Elem. Sch., Cheyenne, 1968—. Recipient Presdl. award NSF, 1990. Mem. NEA, Wyo. Edn. Assn., Wyo. Sci. Tchrs. Assn. (Excellence in Sci. Teaching award 1984), Phi Delta Kappa. Home: 708 Arapaho St Cheyenne WY 82009-4216 Office: Laramie County Sch Dist #1 2810 House Ave Cheyenne WY 82001-2860 also: Bain Elem Sch 903 Adams Ave Cheyenne WY 82001-6672

RICHARDSON, ELAINE, state legislator. State senator Ariz. Dist. 11, Tucson, 1996—. Office: S Bldg Rm 201 400 W Congress Tucson AZ 85701

RICHARDSON, ELSIE HELEN, retired elementary education educator; b. Vancouver, Wash., Feb. 1, 1918; d. Anthony William and Marie Julia (Dušek) Podhora-Clark; m. Clyde Stanley Richardson, Oct. 16, 1944 (dec. 1989). BA, Cen. Washington Coll. Edn., 1939. Cert. jr. high sch. prin.; cert. life elem. tchr., Calif., life spl. secondary to teach mentally retarded; cert. psychometrist, Calif. Tchr. 2d and 3d grades Randle (Wash.) Sch. Dist., 1939-40; remedial tchr. Randle, 1940-41; 2d grade tchr. Seattle Sch. Dist., 1941-44; remedial tchr., mental testing specialist Vancouver, Wash., 1944-45; tchr. 3rd grade Lancaster (Calif.) Sch. Dist., 1946-48; tchr. spl. edn. Bakersfield (Calif.) Sch. Dist., 1948-49; tchr. 2d grade Norco (Calif.) Sch. Dist., 1950-51; tchr. 4th grade Chino (Calif.) Sch. Dist., 1951-55, tchr. spl. edn., 1955-79, ret., 1979. Leader Girl Res., Camp Rimrock, Wash., summer 1939; leader Bluebird Club, 1939. Recipient Cert. of Appreciaiton, State Assembly of Calif., 1979. Mem. NEA, AAUW, Am. Assn. Ret. Persons, Calif. Tchrs. Assn. (rep.), Calif. Ret. Tchrs. Assn., Vancouver Edn. Assn., Chino Tchrs. Assn. (past v.p., sec.), Wash. State Tchrs. Assn. (rep.), PTA (life), Fun After Fifty Club, Delta Kappa Gamma.

RICHARDSON, ERNEST RAY (ROCKY RICHARDSON), housing program supervisor; b. Dermott, Ark., Sept. 5, 1932; s. Louis Jr. and Leila Mae (Purdom) R.; m. Deloris Cobb, Mar. 25, 1955 (div. Apr. 1964); children: Victor Ray, Rodney Lynn, Regenia Ann; stepchildren, Denise Nelson, Darrin Hicks; m. Doretha Tolbert, Apr. 1964 (div. June 1978); m. Shirley Ann Johnson, June 8, 1978; 1 child, Kimberly Ann; stepchildren: Janet, Kay, and Jerome Pate. BA in Bus. Adminstrn., Franklin U., 1975; AA in Real Estate, Parkland Coll., 1980; postgrad., Lewis U., 1980-83; grad., Intergovtl. Mgmt. Tng., 1993, Leadership Modesto, 1996. Cert. real estate broker, Ill. Dir. edn. & tng. Champaign County Opportunities Industrialization Ctr., Champaign, Ill., 1968-70, exec. dir., pers. dir., 1970-73; fin. specialist City of Urbana, Ill., 1975-79; fin. specialist City of Joliet, Ill., 1979-82, dir. neighborhood svcs. divsn., 1982-87; exec. pers. dir. Aurora (Ill.) Housing Authority, 1987-89; housing program supr. City of Modesto, Calif., 1989—; mem. adv. bd. Ctrl. Valley Opportunities Ctr., Inc. Modesto, 1992-96; vice chmn. mgmt. devel. com., City of Modesto, 1993-94, mem. mgmts. continuous improvement com., 1995, 96; alt. Stanislaus County Civil Grand Jury, 1996-97; mem. nat. funds allocation rev. com. Opportunities Industrialization Ctr., 1971-72. Sgt. USAF, 1951-67. Mem. nat. Assn. Real Estate Appraisers (pres.-elect Ill. chpt. 1984-85, pres. Ill. chpt. 1985-86, Ill. chpt. Mem. of the Yr., 1988), Am. Legion, Modesto Kiwanis Club. Home: 309 Yuba Ridge Ln Modesto CA 95354-3369 Office: City of Modesto Ofc Housing/Neighborhoods 940 11th St Modesto CA 95354-2319

RICHARDSON, GLENN EARL, health education educator; b. La Mesa, Calif., Dec. 20, 1946; s. Glenwood Leigh and Ruth Elaine (Rugg) R.; m. Kathleen Reading, Mar. 26, 1974; children: Brannon, Tavan, Jordan, Lauren. BS, So. Utah U., 1971; MS, Utah State U., 1973; PhD, U. Utah, 1976. Cert. health edn. specialist, biofeedback therapist, Utah. Tchr. Murtaugh (Idaho) Sch. Dist., 1973-75; asst. prof. U. Ky., Lexington, 1976-80; coord. allied health Tex. A&M U., College Station, 1980-85; prof. health edn. U. Utah, Salt Lake City, 1985—, chmn. dept., 1985-89, exec. dir. The Human Experience Inst., 1995—; v.p. edn. TWI Corp., College Station, 1986—; v.p. R & D Life Enrichment Internat., The Bahamas, 1990—; chair, bd. assoc. editors Journal of Health Education, 1989—. Author: Educational Imagery, 1982, Decisions on Health, 1989, Resiliency Training Manual, 1995, Resilient Youth Curriculum, 1996, Health Enrichment Training Handbook; contbr. articles to profl. jours.; chair bd. of assoc. editors Jour. of Health Edn., 1989-91. Chmn. Salt Lake County Alcohol and Drug Allocation Coun., 1987-90; chmn. Davis County Bd. Health, Bountiful, Utah, 1988—. Mem. Am. Sch. Health Assn. (life, governing coun.), Health Edn. Assn. Utah (pres. 1987-88, Disting. Svc. award 1988). Mem. LDS Ch. Office: U Utah Dept Health Edn HPRN 213 Hper # 215 Salt Lake City UT 84112-1184

RICHARDSON, JANE, librarian; b. Sept. 16, 1946; d. Robert Clark and Evagene (Davis) Richardson; m. Frank Velasques Martinez Jr., May 28, 1966 (div. July 1970); 1 child, Robert Louis Martinez; m. William John Lorance, Feb. 14, 1983 (div. 1996). BA in History, U. Wyo., 1971; MLibr, U. Wash., 1972. Reference and fine arts libr. Clark County Libr., 1973; dept. head Clark County Libr. Dist., 1974-77; br. supr./adminstr. Newport Beach (Calif.) Pub. Libr., 1978-82; on-call libr. Santa Ana and Newport Beach Pub. Librs., Calif. State U., Fullerton, 1984; br. adminstr. Las Vegas-Clark County Libr. Dist., 1985—. Mem. Freedom to Read Found. Mem. ALA, Popular Culture Assn., Nev. Libr. Assn., Mountain Plains Libr. Assn., So. Calif. On-Line Users Group, Newport Beach Profl. and Tech. Employees Assn. Office: Las Vegas-Clark County Libr 833 Las Vegas Blvd N Las Vegas NV 89101-2030

RICHARDSON, JEAN MCGLENN, retired civil engineer; b. Everett, Wash., Nov. 15, 1927; d. Clayton Charles and Marie Elizabeth (Mellish) McGlenn; BSCE, Oreg. State U., 1949; registered profl. engr., Ala., Oreg.; m. William York Richardson, II, June 11, 1949; children: William York III, Paul Kress II, Clayton McGlenn. Engr., Walter Schoel Engring. Co., Birmingham, Ala., 1950-54; office engr. G.C. McKinney Engring. Co., San Jose, Calif., 1972-74; civil design leader Harland Bartholomew & Assocs., Birmingham, 1974-78, Rust Engring. Co., Birmingham, 1978-82; owner, prin. Jean Richardson and Assocs. Inc., 1983-88; cons. engr. Rust Internat. Corp., 1988-90, Fed. Emergency Mgmt. Agy.; sr. engr. City of Portland, Oreg., 1991-94; ret., 1994; women's engring. del. to China and USSR, 1984; counselor to female students on engring. as a career; state chmn. Mathcounts, Ala., 1986-88, Oreg., 1995—; mem. Girl Scout Coun., Portland, math. vol. pub. schs. Named Woman of Distinction in Engring., 1993. Fellow Soc. Women Engrs.; mem. NSPE, Soc. Women Engrs. (sr. sect. rep. to nat. bd.), Ala. Soc. Profl. Engrs. (pres. Birmingham chpt., state dir., state chmn. Mathcounts, Oreg. 1991-94), Women's Golf Assn. Club, Sunriver Golf Club, Alpha Phi. Republican. Episcopalian.

RICHARDSON, JOHN EDMON, marketing educator; b. Whittier, Calif., Oct. 22, 1942; s. John Edmon and Mildred Alice (Miller) R.; m. Dianne Elaine Ewald, July 15, 1967; 1 child, Sara Beth. BS, Calif. State U., Long Beach, 1964; MBA, U. So. Calif., 1966; MDiv, Fuller Theol. Sem., 1969, D of Ministry, 1981. Assoc. prof. mgmt. Sch. Bus. and Mgmt. Pepperdine U., Malibu, Calif., 1969—. Author: (leader's guides) Caring Enough to Confront, 1984, The Measure of a Man, 1985; editor: Ann. Editions: Marketing, 1987—, Bus. Ethics, 1990—. Lay counselor La Canada (Calif.) Presbyn. Ch., 1978-84, mem. lay counseling task force, 1982-84. Mem. Am. Mgmt. Assn., Soc. Bus. Ethics, Christian Writers Guild, Fuller Sem. Alumni Cabinet (pres. 1982-85), Am. Mktg. Assn., Beta Gamma Sigma. Office: Pepperdine U Sch Bus and Mgmt 400 Corporate Pt Culver City CA 90230-7615

RICHARDSON, JUDY MCEWEN, education administrator, consultant, cartoonist; b. Appleton, Wis., June 3, 1947; d. John Mitchell and Isabel Annette (Ruble) McEwen; m. Larry Leroy Richardson, Mar. 19, 1972 (div. Oct. 1983). BA in English, Stanford U., 1968, MA in Edn., 1969; PhD in Higher Edn., U. Wash., 1975. Dir. ednl. rsch. St. Olaf Coll., Northfield, Minn., 1975-79; evaluation specialist Northwest Regional Ednl. Laboratory, Portland, 1980-82; legis. rsch. analyst Ariz. State Sen., Phoenix, 1982-87; dir. sch. fin. Ariz. Dept. Edn., Phoenix, 1987-92, assoc. superintendent, 1992-94; ednl. cons. Scottsdale, Ariz., 1994-96; exec. dir. Ariz. State Bd. for Sch. Capital Facilities, Phoenix, 1996—. Cartoonist for the Ariz. Capitol Times, 1995-96. Office: Ariz State Bd for Sch Capital Facilities 1700 W Washington Ste 308 Phoenix AZ 85007

RICHARDSON, KATHLEEN, microbiologist, educator; b. Balt., Aug. 24, 1950; d. Wilbur Andeen and Elouise (Bidwell) R. BA, UCLA, 1972, PhD, 1981; MS, Calif. State U., San Diego, 1976. Tchg. asst. dept. microbiology Calif. State U., 1973-76; predoctoral fellowship UCLA, 1976-81; postdoctoral fellowship dept. microbiology/immunology U. Mo., Columbia, 1981-83; postdoctoral fellow Ctr. for Vaccine Devel. U. Md., Balt., 1983-85; asst. prof. dept. microbiology and immunology Oreg. Health Scis. U., Portland, 1985-93; staff scientist Gen. Atomics, San Diego, 1993-96; rsch. assoc. prof. dept. biology Portland State U., 1995—; lectr. biotech. San Diego City Coll., 1994-95; rschs. on bioremediation of chlorinated solvents, 1993-95, cons., 1996—. Author rsch. publs. in bacterial pathogenesis of Vibrio cholerae and bioremediation of chlorinated solvents. Rsch. grantee Oreg. Med. Rsch. Found., 1985-86, 89-90, NIH-NIAID, 1986-89, 91-96. Mem. Am. Soc. Microbiology, AAAS, Iota Sigma Pi. Office: Portland State U Dept Biology Portland OR 97207

RICHARDSON, KENNETH T., JR., psychotherapist, consultant, educator, author; b. Santa Monica, Calif., Sept. 16, 1948; s. Kenneth T. Richardson and Florence (Wheeler) Neal; m. Mary L. Nutter, Dec. 31, 1983; children: Kenneth T. III, Russell A., Shad Martin, Cheralyn Martin. BA, Prescott (Ariz.) Coll., 1985; postgrad., Antioch (Ohio) Coll., 1987-88. Cert. addictions counselor, Ariz.; nat. cert. NCRC/ADOA. Program dir. Calvary Rehab. Ctr., Phoenix, 1979-82; clin. dir. Friendship House Comprehensive Recovery Ctr., San Francisco, 1982-84; dir. treatment The Meadows, Wickenburg, Ariz., 1984-87; co-founder, dir. The Orion Found., Phoenix, 1989—; owner, dir. Phoenix Cons. and Counseling Assocs., 1987—; cons. Addictions Svcs., The Hopi Tribe, Kykotsmoni, Ariz., 1989—, Baywood Hosp., Houston, 1988-89; advisor Nat. Coun. on Co-Dependence, Phoenix, 1990—, Recourse Found., Phoenix, 1989-93; faculty instr. Rio Salado C.C., Phoenix, 1987-90, The Recovery Source, Houston, 1989-90; co-chair Nat. Conv. of Men., Relationships and Recovery, Phoenix, 1990, 91. Creator, presenter audiotape series: Codependence and the Development of Addictions, 1991, Your Spiritual Self: The Child Within, 1991, Relationship Recovery, 1992, Men's Sexuality and Relationships, 1993-96, Body Mind and Spirit, 1994-96; creator edn. and support materials related to addictions, relationships and family sys., 1987—. Mem. Nat. Assn. Alcoholism and Drug Counselors, Am. Counseling Assn., Internat. Certification Reciprocity Consortium. Office: Phoenix Cons and Counseling 5333 N 7th St Ste A202 Phoenix AZ 85014-2821

RICHARDSON, MARY LOU, psychotherapist; b. Topeka, Oct. 4, 1953; d. Darrell and Beverly Nutter; m. Kenneth T Richardson Jr. children: Shad Martin, Cheralyn Pasbrig, Kenneth T Richardson III, Russ Richardson. Cert. behavioral health examiner, addictions counselor, Ariz.; cert. Nat. Assn. of Alcolism and Drug Abuse Counselors. Counselor Compcare Alcoholism Ctr. The Meadows Treatment Ctr., Phoenix, 1986-88; co-dir. Phoenix Cons. & Counseling Assocs., Ariz., 1989—; founder and adminstr. The Orion Found., Ariz.; project mem. The Hutoomkhum Com. and Support Program, Hopi Reservation, Ariz.; cons. Baywood Hosp., 1988-89; faculty instr. The Recovery Source, 1989-90; chair Nat. Conv. Women, 1992. Author: Women's Acts of Power, 1991-93, Relationship Recover, 1992—, Women's Empowerment, 1992—, Body, Mind & Spirit, 1994—. Mem. Am. Mental Health Counselors, Am. Counseling Assn., Nat. Assn. Alcoholism & Drug Abuse Counselors, Nat. Reciprocity Consortium. Office: Phoenix Cons & Counseling Assocs 5333 N 7th St Ste A202 Phoenix AZ 85014-2821

RICHARDSON, RICHARD COLBY, JR., leadership and policy studies educator, researcher; b. Burlington, Vt., Sept. 10, 1933; s. Richard Colby and Florence May (Barlow) R.; m. Patricia Ann Barnhart, Dec. 21, 1954; children—Richard Colby III, Michael Donald, Christopher Robin. BS, Castleton State Coll., 1954; MA, Mich. State U., 1958; PhD, U. Tex., 1963; Litt.D. (hon.), Lafayette Coll., 1973. Instr., counselor Vt. Coll., Montpelier, 1958-61; dean instrn. Forest Park Community Coll., St. Louis, 1963-67; pres. Northampton County Area Community Coll., Bethelehem, Pa., 1967-77; chmn. dept. higher edn. and adult edn. Ariz. State U., Tempe, 1977-84, prof. edn. leadership and policy studies, 1984—. Jr. author: The Two Year College: A Social Synthesis, 1965; sr. author: Governance for the Two-Year College, 1972, Functional Literacy in the College Setting, 1981, Literacy in the Open Access College, 1983, Fostering Minority Acess and Achievement in Higher Education, 1987, Achieving Quality and Diversity, 1991. Bd. dirs. Easton Hosp., 1973-77, v.p., 1975-77; exec. council Minsi Trails council Boy Scouts Am., Bethelehem, 1973-77. Named Disting. Grad., Coll. Edn., U. Tex., Austin, 1982; recipient Outstanding Research Publ. award Council Univ. and Colls.-Am. Assn. Community and Jr. Colls., 1983, Disting. Service award, 1984. Mem. Am. Assn. Higher Edn. (charter life, dir. 1970-73), AAUP, Assn. for Study of Higher Edn. (bd. dirs. 1984), Am. Assn. Community and Jr. Colls. (dir. 1980-83). Democrat. Home: 5654 E Wilshire Dr Scottsdale AZ 85257-1950 Office: Ariz State U Dept Higher Edn Tempe AZ 85287

RICHARDSON, ROBERT CARLETON, engineering consultant; b. Grand Junction, Colo., Mar. 17, 1925; s. Carleton O. and Mabel Grace (Davy) R.; m. Ruby Lucille Morrison, Jan. 11, 1947 (dec.); children: Robert James, Lori Dianne Richardson Dismont. Student, U. Colo., Boulder, 1943-44, U. Calif., Berkeley, 1946-47, I.C.S., Scranton, Pa., 1947-50, Calif. State U., Long Beach, 1983, John F. Kennedy U., Martinez, Calif., 1967. Chief engr./gen. mgr. Gilmore Fabricators, Oakland, Calif., 1948-56; nat. sales mgr. Gilmore Steel Contrs., Oakland, 1957-72; v.p. engring. R&D Davis Walker Corp., L.A., 1972-86; tech. dir. Ivy Steel divsn. MMI, Houston, 1986-93; engring. cons. R.C. Richardson & Assocs., Sun Lakes, Ariz., 1993—; engring. instr. Calif. State U., Long Beach, 1983-85; pres. Nat. Concrete Industry Bd., San Francisco, 1984; chmn. bd. Wire Reinforcement Inst., Findlay, Ohio, 1978, 82; bd. dirs. ASCC, 1982-84. Chpt. author: Manual of Standard Practice, 1988-90, Structural Detailing Manual, 1990-94. With USMC, 1943-45. Recipient Outstanding Achievement award Wire Reinforcement Inst., 1993; named Boss of the Yr., Women in Constrn., Oakland, 1964, 65. Fellow Am. Concrete Inst. Internat. (chair 439-A 1991—); mem. ASTM, ASCE/Fed. Emergency Mgmt. Agy., Structural Engrs. Assn. of Calif., Marines Meml. Assn., Earthquake Engring. Rsch. Inst. Republican. Home and Office: 10930 E San Tan Blvd Sun Lakes AZ 85248

RICHARDSON, THOMAS ANDREW, business executive, educator; b. Providence, Aug. 31, 1955; s. Edward Ferris and Olive Elizabeth (Lynaugh) R.; m. Patricia Ann Mundie, Dec. 30, 1982; children: Michael Edward, Lauren Elizabeth, Kristen Mundie. AS in Oceanography, Fla. Inst. Tech., 1977, BS in Environ. Sci., 1979, MBA, 1985. Asst. prof., div. head sch. marine and environ. tech. Fla. Inst. Tech., Jensen Beach, 1979-85; tng. mgr. PADI Internat., Santa Ana, Calif., 1985-88, dir. tng. and edn., 1988-90, v.p., 1991—; v.p. Capital Investment Ventures Corp., 1991—; dir. lakefront City of Evanston, Ill., 1980-82; bd. dirs. CIVCO, Project AWARE Found., Santa Ana; pres. DSAT Inc., Santa Ana, 1989—; guest faculty Duke Med. Sch. continuing edn., Durham, N.C., 1992. Editor in chief: Open Water Diver Manual, 1988, Rescue Diver Manual, 1988, Divemaster Manual, 1990, Undersea Journal, 1987, Adventures in Diving; Open Water Diving video, Adventures in Diving video, Peak Performance video; contbr. articles to profl. jours. CPR and first aid instr. Martin County Sch. Dist., Stuart, Fla., 1982-83. Recipient Diver of Yr. award Divers Alert Network/Rolex, Inc., 1992. Mem. Am. Mgmt. Assn., Am. Soc. Training and Devel., Am. Soc. Assn. Exec., Undersea and Hyperbaric Med. Soc., South Pacific Undersea Med. Soc., Sierra Club, Nat. Audubon Soc., Emergency Med. Planning Inc., Am. Acad. Underwater Scis., Nat. Assn. Search and Rescue.

RICHARDSON, WILLIAM BLAINE, former congressman; b. Pasadena, Calif., Nov. 15, 1947; m. Barbara Flavin, 1972. BA, Tufts U., Medford, Mass., 1970; MA, Fletcher Sch. Law and Diplomacy, 1971. Mem. staff U.S. Ho. of Reps., 1971-72, Dept. State, 1973-75; mem. staff fgn. relations com. U.S. Senate, 1975-78; exec. dir. N. Mex. State Democratic Com., 1978, Bernalillo County Democratic Com., 1978; businessman Santa Fe, N. Mex., 1978-82; mem. 98th-103rd Congresses from 3rd N.Mex. dist., Washington, 1982-97; democratic chief dep. majority whip 103d Congress; U.S. amb. to U.N., 1997—; ranking minority mem. Resources Com. on Nat. Pks., Forests and Lands; mem. Select Com. on intelligence, Helsinki Commn. Vice chair Dem. Nat. Com.; active Big Bros.-Big Sisters, Santa Fe. Mem. Santa Fe Hispanic C. of C., Santa Fe C. of C., Council Fgn. Relations, NATO 2000 Bd., Congl. Hispanic Caucus, Am. G.I. Forum. Office: US Mission to UN 799 UN Plz New York NY 10017*

RICHENS, MURIEL WHITTAKER, AIDS therapist, counselor and educator; b. Prineville, Oreg.; d. John Reginald and Victoria Cecilia (Pascale) Whittaker; children: Karen, John, Candice, Stephanie, Rebecca. BS, Oreg. State U.; MA, San Francisco State U., 1962; postgrad., U. Calif., Berkeley, 1967-69, U. Birmingham, Eng., 1973, U. Soria, Spain, 1981. Lic. sch. adminstr., tchr. 7-12, pupil personnel specialist, Calif., marriage, child and family counselor, Calif. Instr. Springfield (Oreg.) High Sch., San Francisco State U.; instr., counselor Coll. San Mateo, Calif., San Mateo High Sch. Dist., 1963-86; therapist AIDS Health Project U. Calif., San Francisco, 1988—; pvt. practice MFCC San Mateo; guest West German-European Acad. seminar, Berlin, 1975. Lifeguard, ARC. postgrad. student Ctr. for Human Communications, Los Gatos, Calif., 1974, U. P.R., 1977, U. Guadalajara (Mex.), 1978, U. Durango (Mex.), 1980, U. Guanajuato (Mex.) 1982. Mem. U. Calif. Berkeley Alumni Assn., Am. Contract Bridge League (Diamond Life Master, cert. instr., tournament dir.), Women in Comm., Computer-Using Educators, Commonwealth Club, Pi Lambda Theta, Delta Pi Epsilon. Republican. Roman Catholic. Home and Office: 847 N Humboldt St Apt 309 San Mateo CA 94401-1451

RICHEY, EVERETT ELDON, religion educator; b. Claremont, Ill., Nov. 1, 1923; s. Hugh Arthur and Elosia Emma (Longnecker) R.; m. Mary Elizabeth Reynolds, Apr. 9, 1944; children: Eldon Arthur, Clive Everett, Loretta Arlene, Charles Estel. ThB, Anderson U., 1946; MDiv, Sch. Theology, Anderson, Ind., 1956; ThD, Iliff Sch. of Theology, Denver, 1960. Pastor Ch. of God, Bremen, Ind., 1946-47, Laurel, Miss., 1947-48; pastor First Ch. of God, Fordyce, Ark., 1948-52; prof. Arlington Coll., Long Beach, Calif., 1961-68; pastor Cherry Ave. Ch. of God, Long Beach, 1964-68; prof. Azusa (Calif.) Pacific U., 1968-93; mem. Christian Ministries Tng. Assn., 1968; mem., chmn. Commn. on Christian Higher Edn./Ch. of God, 1982-93; pres. Ch. Growth Investors, Inc., 1981—. Author: ednl. manual Church Periodical--Curriculum, 1971-83. Mem. Assn. Profs. and Rschrs. Religious Edn., Christian Ministries Tng. Assn. Republican. Home and Office: 413 N Valencia St Glendora CA 91741-2418

RICHEY, MARVIN E(LDEN), electrical engineer, administrator; b. Wichita, Kans., Nov. 21, 1946; s, Marvin Elden Sr. and Barbara Jean (Carterette) R.; m. Linda Louise Wheeler, Oct. 15, 1966 (div. Sept. 1977); m. Janice Ellen Doyle, Nov. 21, 1990; children: Brittany, Sean, Amy, Rachel. BBA, Nat. U., San Diego, 1991, MBA, 1992. Registered profl. elec. engr., Nev., Ariz. Elec. project mgr. Intercontinental Engring., Riverside, Mo., 1971-78; engr. IV Princeton (N.J.) U., 1980-89; engr. specialist I EG&G, Morgantown, W.Va., 1978-80; sr. engr. EG&G, Las Vegas, Nev., 1989-94; dir. elec. engring. Design Engring. Assocs., Las Vegas, 1994-96; pres. Argus Engring., 1995-96; dir. R & D U-Products, Internat., Las Vegas, 1989—. Cons. Aid for Aids Nev., Las Vegas, 1990-92. Recipient Nuclear Weapons award for Excellence, U.S. Dept. Energy and U.S. Dept. Def., Las Vegas, 1991, 94. Mem. Assn. Energy Engrs. (sr.). Home: 7324 Atwood Ave Las Vegas NV 89129

RICHMAN, ANTHONY E., textile rental industry association executive; b. Los Angeles, Dec. 13, 1941; s. Irving M. and Helen V. (Muchnic) R.; m. Judy Harriet Richman, Dec. 19, 1964; children: Lisa Michele, Jennifer Beth. BS, U. So. Calif., 1964. With Reliable Textile Rental Svcs., L.A., 1964—, svc. mgr., 1969, sales and svc. mgr., 1970-73, plant mgr., 1973-75, gen. mgr., bd. dirs., 1975-78, v.p., sec.-treas., 1975-82, exec. v.p., CEO, 1982-84, pres., CEO, 1984—. Bd. dirs. Guild for Children, 1979—, Valley Guild for Cystic Fibrosis, 1974—, Cystic Fibrosis Found. of L.A. and Orange Counties, 1989—; pres. Textile Rental/Svc. Assoc. Am., 1993-95; exec. dir.Western Textile Svcs. Assn., Studio City, Calif., 1996—. Office: Western Textile Svcs Assn 12444 Ventura Blvd Ste 204 Studio City CA 91604-2409

RICHMAN, DAVID BRUCE, entomologist, educator; b. Dunkirk, N.Y., Nov. 6, 1942; s. Melvin Stanley and Florence Irene (Nottis) R.; m. Olive Lynda Goin, June 18, 1977; children: Julia Anne, Rebecca Leonna. AA, Ariz. Western Coll., 1968; BS, U. Ariz., 1970, MS, 1973; PhD, U. Fla., 1977. Grad. asst., then asst. curator U. Ariz., Tucson, 1970-73; grad. asst., then rsch. assoc. U. Fla., Gainesville, 1973-78, 81-82; rsch. assoc./asst. prof. N.Mex. State U., Las Cruces, 1978-81, rsch. assoc., 1983-85, coll. asst. prof., 1985-90, sci. specialist dept. entomology-plant pathology-weed sci., 1990—; rsch. assoc. Fla. State Collection Arthropods, Gainesville, 1978—. Contbr. articles to sci. jours. Mem. Am. Arachological Soc., Brit. Arachological Soc., Entomol. Soc. Am. (chmn. resolutions com. southwestern br. 1990-91), Assn. Systematic Collections, Ctr. Internat. Documentation Arachologique, Entomol. Collections Network, Southwestern Entomol. Soc., Sigma Xi. Democrat. Mem. Soc. of Friends. Office: N Mex State U Dept Entomology Plant Las Cruces NM 88003

RICHMAN, DAVID WILLIAM, aerospace executive; b. LaPorte, Ind., Aug. 3, 1940; s. Milfred William and Ethelyn Belle (Morton) R.; m. Carolyn Jean Nicholson, Oct. 24, 1964 (div. Aug. 1971); children: Keith William, Michael David; m. Jean Shutts Dunn, June 2, 1990. BSME, Purdue U., 1962; MSME, U. Mo., 1968, MS in Engring. Mgmt., 1974. Thermodynamicist Gemini McDonnell Aircraft, St. Louis, 1962-65; thermodynamicist Skylab McDonnell Douglas Corp., St. Louis, 1965-69, subcontract mgr. Skylab, 1968-70, advanced designer Shuttle, 1970-71, aerodynamicist missiles, 1971-75, mgr. space commercialization, 1975-78; chief engr. electrophoresis McDonnell Douglas Corp., Huntington Beach, Calif., 1978-87, dir. integration, 1987-92, centrifuge program mgr., 1992—; mem. adv. bd. Univ. Space Rsch. Assn., Washington, 1984; cons. Ctr. for Cell Rsch., State College, Pa., 1990-94. Patentee electrophoresis chamber, sys. for hydrodynamic compensation, electrophoresis apparatus, continuous flow electrophoresis. Mem. AIAA (adv. bd. space processing com. 1982-84, tech. achievement award 1982), Am. Soc. Engring. Mgmt., Electrophoresis Soc., Am. Soc. Gravitational and Space Biology. Home: 20802 Hunter Ln Huntington Beach CA 92646-6414 Office: McDonnell Douglas Aerospace 5301 Bolsa Ave Huntington Beach CA 92647-2048

RICHMAN, JOEL ESER, lawyer, mediator, arbitrator; b. Brockton, Mass., Feb. 17, 1947; s. Nathan and Ruth Miriam (Bick) R.; m. Elaine R. Thompson, Aug. 21, 1987; children: Shawn Jonah, Jesse Ray, Eva Rose. BA in Psychology, Grinnell Coll., 1969; JD, Boston U., 1975. Bar: Mass. 1975, U.S. Dist. Ct. MAss. 1977, U.S. Supreme Ct. 1980, U.S. Ct. Appeals (1st cir.) 1982, Hawaii 1985, U.S. Dist. Ct. Hawaii 1987. Law clk. Richman & Perenyi, Brockton, Mass., 1973-75, atty., 1975-77; atty. pvt. practice, Provincetown, Mass., 1977-82, Paia, Hawaii, 1985—; arbitrator Am. Arbitration Assn., Paia, 1992—, mediator, 1994—. Pres. Jewish Congregation Maui (Hawaii), 1989-97, bd. dirs., 1984-89; bd. dirs. Pacific Primate Ctr., 1991—, pres., 1994—. Office: PO Box 46 Paia HI 96779-0046

RICHMAN, MARVIN JORDAN, real estate developer, investor, educator; b. N.Y.C., July 13, 1939; s. Morris and Minnie (Graubart) R.; m. Amy Paula Rubin, July 31, 1966; children: Mark Jason, Keith Hayden, Susanne Elizabeth, Jessica Paige. BArch, MIT, 1962; M Urban Planning, NYU, 1966, postgrad., 1967-69; MBA, U. Chgo., 1977; U.S. Dept. State fellow U. Chile, 1960. Architect, planner Skidmore, Owings & Merrill, N.Y.C., 1964, Conklin & Rossant, N.Y.C., 1965-67; ptnr. Vizbaras & Ptnrs., N.Y.C., 1968-69; v.p. Urban Investment & Devel. Co., Chgo., 1969-79, sr. v.p., 1979; pres. bd. dirs. First City Devels. Corp., Beverly Hills, Calif., 1979-80; pres. Olympia & York (U.S.) Devel. (West), 1987-89, Olympia & York Calif. Equities Corp., L.A., 1981-87, Olympia & York Calif. Devel. Corp., 1981-87, Olympia & York Hope St. Mgmt. Corp., 1982-87, Olympia & York Homes Corp., 1983-89, Olympia & York Calif. Constrn. Corp., 1986-89, The Richman Co., L.A., 1989-96, pres. Richman Real Estate Group, Salt Lake City, 1995—; dean Sch. Bus. and Mgmt. Woodbury U., Burbank, Calif., 1993—; pres. Millennium Holdings, Beverly Hills, Calif., 1996—; lectr. NYU, 1967-69, UCLA, 1989-90, Nat. Humanities Inst., other univs. Adv. NEA. Bd. advisors UCLA Ctr. Fin. and Real Estate. With USAF, 1963-64. Registered architect; lic. real estate broker. Mem. AIA, Am Planning Assn., Internat. Coun. Shopping Ctrs., L.A. World Affairs Coun., Urban Land Inst., Nat. Assn. Office and Indsl. Parks, Chief Exec.'s Round Table, Air Force Assn., Lambda Alpha.

RICHMOND, HUGH MACRAE, English language educator; b. Burton-upon-Trent, Eng., Mar. 20, 1932; came to U.S., 1957; s. Ronald Jackson and Isabella (MacRae) R.; m. Velma Elizabeth Bourgeois, Aug. 9, 1958; children: Elizabeth Merle, Claire Isabel. Diploma, U. Florence, Italy, 1952, U. Munich, 1956; BA in English with honors, Cambridge (Eng.) U., 1954; DPhil in English, Oxford (Eng.) U., 1957. Asst. d'Anglais Lycée Jean Perrin, Lyon, France, 1954-55; prof. English U. Calif., Berkeley, 1957—, dir. Shakespeare Program, 1974—, dir. Shakespeare Forum, 1981-95; edn. dir. Shakespeare Globe Centre, 1995—. Author: The School of Love, 1964, Shakespeare's Political Plays, 1967, Renaissance Landscapes, 1973, Shakespeare's Sexual Comedy, 1971, The Christian Revolutionary: John Milton, 1974, Puritans and Libertines, 1981, Shakespeare in Performance: King Richard III, 1990, Shakespearean Performance King Henry VIII, 1994; prodr. videos Shakespeare and the Globe, 1985, Shakespeare's Globe Restored, 1997; dir., prodr. stage and videos for NEH, 1984—. Bd. dirs. Calif. Shakespeare Festival, Berkeley, 1980-90; chair adv. coun. Shakespeare Globe Ctr., 1988—, dir. edn., 1995—. 2d lt. Royal Arty., U.K., 1950-51. Fellow Am. Coun. Learned Socs., 1964-65, NEH, 1977, 88; NEH grantee, 1984-86. Mem. MLA, Shakespeare Assn. Am. Roman Catholic. Office: U Calif English Dept Berkeley CA 94720

RICHMOND, MITCHELL JAMES, professional basketball player; b. Ft. Lauderdale, Fla., June 30, 1965; M. Juli Richmond; children: Phillip Mitchell, Jerin Mikell. Bachelor in Social Sci., Kansas State U., 1988. Guard Golden State Warriors, 1988-91, Sacramento Kings, 1991—. Hon. bd. dirs. NCPCA (Spl. Friend award); established Solid As A Rock Scholarship Found., Ft. Lauderdale, 1992. Selected Rookie of the Yr., 1989, Rookie of the Month 3 times, Dec., Jan., March; named NBA Player of the Week, Mar. 25, 1991; selected to NBA All-Star Team, 1993, 94, 95. Office: Sacramento Kings One Sports Parkway Sacramento CA 95834*

RICHMOND, RAY S(AM), journalist; b. Whittier, Calif., Oct. 19, 1957; s. Henry and Terri C. (Epstein) R.; m. Beth Lyn Trachman, Oct. 2, 1983 (div. Feb. 1993); children: Joshua Adam, Gabrielle Reneé; m. Heidi Merle Lieberman, May 28, 1994; 1 child, Dylan Jake. B, Calif. State U., Northridge, 1980. Feature writer L.A. Daily News, Woodland Hills, Calif., 1978-85; segment prodr. Merv Griffin Show, Hollywood, Calif., 1985-86; television writer L.A. Herald Examiner, 1986-87; television critic Orange County Reigster, Santa Ana, Calif., 1987-92, L.A. Daily News, 1992-96; television reporter Daily Variety, L.A., 1996—. Co-author: Unofficial Olympic Guide, 1984; editor: The Simpsons Companion, 1997. Vol. AIDS Project L.A., 1993-94. Mem. Television Critics Assn. Democrat. Jewish. Home: 1010 Hammond St Apt 302 West Hollywood CA 90069-3852 Office: Daily Variety 5700 Wilshire Blvd # 120 Los Angeles CA 90036

RICHMOND, ROCSAN, television and video producer, director, publicist, actress, inventor; b. Chgo., Jan. 30; d. Alphonso and Annie Lou (Combest) R.; divorced; 1 child, Tina S. Student, Wilson Jr. Coll., 1963, 2d City Theatre, Chgo., 1969, Alice Liddel Theatre, Chgo., 1970, L.A. City Coll., 1996. Lic. 3d class radio/tel. operator FCC. Vegetarian editor Aware mag., Chgo., 1977-78; investigative reporter, film critic Chgo. Metro News, 1975-81; producer, talk show host Sta. WSSD Radio, Chgo., 1980-81; dir. pub. rels. IRMCO Corp., Chgo., 1981-82; pub. rels. agt., newsletter editor Hollywood (Calif.) Reporter newspaper, 1985-86; exec. producer Donald Descendent's Prodns., Hollywood, 1983—, (TV show) Future News, 1983-86; pres. Richmond Estates; fingerprint identification classifier. Inventor invisible drapery tieback. Jehovah's Witness. Office: PO Box 665 Los Angeles CA 90078-0665

RICHTER, BURTON, physicist, educator; b. N.Y.C., Mar. 22, 1931; s. Abraham and Fanny (Pollack) R.; m. Laurose Becker, July 1, 1960; children: Elizabeth, Matthew. B.S., MIT, 1952, Ph.D., 1956. Research assoc. Stanford U., 1956-60, asst. prof. physics, 1960-63, assoc. prof., 1963-67, prof., 1967—, Paul Pigott prof. phys. sci., 1980—, tech. dir. Linear Accelerator Ctr., 1982-84, dir. Linear Accelerator Ctr., 1984—; cons. NSF, Dept. Energy; bd. dirs. Varian Corp., Litel Instruments; Loeb lectr. Harvard U., 1974; DeShalit lectr. Weizmann Inst., 1975; pres. Internat. Union of Pure and Applied Physics. Contbr. over 300 articles to profl. publs. Recipient E.O. Lawrence medal Dept. Energy, 1975; Nobel prize in physics, 1976. Fellow Am. Phys. Soc. (pres. 1994), AAAS; mem. NAS, Am. Acad. Arts and Scis. Office: Stanford Linear Accel Ctr PO Box 4349 Stanford CA 94309-4349

RICKABAUGH, MICHAEL PAUL, city official; b. Altoona, Pa., Feb. 24, 1951; s. Lawrence E. and Esther M. (Schirf) R.; m. Dianna Moriates, SEpt. 19, 1970; children: Julie, Lauren. Assoc. in Engring., Pa. State U., Mont Alto, 1971. Chief of surveys Nassavy-Hemsley Inc., Chambersburg, Pa., 1972-76; pres. Nassavy-Hemsley-Rickabaugh, Inc., Hazelton, Pa., 1976-78; br. mgr. Christian Spring, Seilbach & Assocs., Gillette, Wyo., 1978-79; chief bldg. insp. Cityo f Gillette, 1979-89; chief bldg. ofcl. City of Ormond Beach, Gla., 1989-90, City of Rock Springs, Wyo., 1990—; mem. coun. Con. on Fire Prevention and Elec. Safety, Cheyenne, 1994—; chmn. edn. com. Internat. Conf. Bldg. Ofcls., Whittier, Calif., 1994-95, mem. edn. com., 1987-94. Named Employe of the Yr., City of Gillette, 1986. Mem. Wyo. Conf. Bldg. Ofcls. (pres. 1984-85), Internat. Assn. Elec. Insps. (pres. 1985), Nat. Fire Protection Assn., Internat. Conf. Bldg. Ofcls., Internat. Fir Code Inst. (charter). Office: City of Rock Springs 212 D St Rock Springs WY 82901

RICKE, P. SCOTT, obstetrician, gynecologist; b. Indpls., June 28, 1948; s. Joseph and Betty (Rae) R.; divorced; 1 child. BA, Ind. U., 1970; MD, Ind. U. Sch. of Medicine, 1974. Bd. cert. ob-gyn., 1981. Intern St. Lukes Hosp., Denver, 1975; resident U. Calif. at Irvine, Orange, 1977-79; pvt. practice ob-gyn. Tucson, 1981-96; founder, dir. Inst. for Med. Weight Loss. Inventor (med. instrument) Vaginal Retractor, 1989. Bd. dirs. City of Hope, Tucson, 1981-85, Am. Cancer Soc., Tucson, 1981-83. Fellow Am. Bd. Ob-Gyn.; mem. Am. Bariatric Soc. Home: 3755 N Tanuri Dr Tucson AZ 85750-1939 Office: 3972 N Campbell Ave Tucson AZ 85719-1460

RICKELS, LAURENCE ARTHUR, foreign language educator; b. Cherokee, Iowa, Dec. 2, 1954; s. Karl and Christa (Loessin) R. BA in English Lit., U. Pa., 1975; Hauptseminaraufnahmeprufung, Freie U. Berlin, Germany, 1975; MA, PhD in German Lit., Princeton U., 1978, 80; MA in Clin. Psychology, Antioch U., Santa Barbara, Calif., 1994. Lectr. U. Dusseldorf, Germany, 1980-81; asst. prof. U. Calif., Santa Barbara, 1981-86, assoc. prof., 1986-90, prof., 1990—, chair dept. Germanic, Slavic and semitic studies, 1989-95; cons. Psychiat. Rsch. Group, 1982—; mem. Film Studies Adv. Bd., U. Calif. Santa Barbara, 1987—; regular contbr. Artforum Internat., 1992—. Author: Aberrations of Mourning, 1988, Der Unbetrauerbare Tod, 1989, The Case of California, 1991; editor: Looking After Nietzsche, 1990. Recipient Rsch. Assistance awards Ctr. for German and European Studies, Berkeley, 1991, 93, 94; rsch. fellow Alexander Von Humboldt-Stiftung, Berlin, 1985-86, 88, 89. Mem. MLA (del. assembly mem. 1988-90), Internat. Initiative on Tech. and the Unconscious-U. Calif. Humanities Rsch. Inst. (founding). Home: 959 Medio Rd Santa Barbara CA 93103-2445 Office: Univ Calif Dept Germanic Slavic & Semitic Studies Santa Barbara CA 93106

RICKERSON, JEAN MARIE, video producer, journalist, photographer; b. Takoma Park, Md., Dec. 29, 1956; d. Charles Marvin and Rita Ann (Smith) Blackburn; m. Ronald Wayne Rickerson, Oct. 18, 1989; children: Drew Elliott, Ella Celine. BS, U. Md., 1978. Pres. Videofax Inc., Bethesda, Md., 1982-90; founder, dir. Found. for Acad. Excellence Inc., Bethesda, 1985-90; video prodr. Applied Measurement Systems Inc., Bremerton, Wash., 1990—; pres. Photo Graphics Inc., Bremerton, 1992—; video coord. 2nd Internat. Submarine Races, Ft. Lauderdale, Fla., 1991. Contbr. articles and photographs to profl. jours; writer, prodr., dir. videotape SEAFAC, 1992, USNS Hayes, 1993, High Gain Array Test Module, 1993, Advanced Mine Detection Sonar, 1995, BQH-9 Signal Data Recording Set, 1996, Submarine Acoustic Maintenance Program, 1996, Intermediate Scale Measurement System, 1996; creator, editor (newsletter) Oceaneer, 1990; editor (newsletter) Crosstalk, 1990—. Office: Applied Measurement Sys Inc 645 4th St Ste 202 Bremerton WA 98337-1402

RICKLER, MARTIN, human services agency administrator; b. Bronx, N.Y., June 25, 1944; s. Charles Evraykes and Kate (Matilsky) R.; m. Marsha Widawski, Mar. 14, 1965 (div. 1981); children: Monica Lynn, Eileen Michelle. BA in Psychology, Calif. State U., L.A., 1975, MA in Psychology, 1977; PhD in Edn., U. Calif., Santa Barbara, 1983. Dir. rsch. Eclectic Comms., Inc., Ojai, Calif., 1982-85; comty. projects coord. S. B. Alcohol and Drug Program, Santa Barbara County, Calif., 1985-89; project coord. Fighting Back, Santa Barbara, 1989-93; dir. The Paladin Group, Santa Barbara, 1993-97; v.p. Correctional Systems, Inc., San Diego, 1996—; mem. adv. bd. U. Calif.-Santa Barbara Alcohol and Drug Cert. Program, 1987-96; mem. nat. adv. bd. Earth Comms. Office, L.A., 1996. Co-founder Men Against Domestic Violence, Santa Barbara, 1995-96; comty. organizer Santa Barbara County, 1985-89. Recipient Robert W. Wetzel award Calif. Adv. Bd. on Alcohol Problems, 1988, IRIS award Nat. Assn. TV Programming Execs., 1991, Emmy award nomination NATAS, 1991. Office: Correctional Sys Inc 1666 Garnet Ave # 1026 San Diego CA 92109

RICKS, DAVID ARTEL, business educator, editor; b. Washington, July 21, 1942; s. Artel and Focha (Black) R. BS, Brigham Young U., 1966; MBA, Ind. U., 1968, PhD, 1970. Asst. prof. Ohio State U., 1970-75, assoc. prof., 1975-81; prof. internat. bus. U. S.C., Columbia, 1981-92; v.p. acad. affairs Thunderbird-the Am. Grad. Sch. Internat. Mgmt., 1992-94, disting. prof., 1992—; editor Kent Pub. Co., Boston, 1978—. Author books, articles in field, including Directory of Foreign Manufactures in the U.S. (Best Reference Book 1974 ALA, 1975); editor-in-chief Jour. of Internat. Business Studies, 1984-92, Jour. Internat. Mgmt., 1994—. Mem. Acad. Internat. Bus. (treas. 1981-82), Acad. Mgmt. (chmn. internat. divsn. 1988-89). Home: 14815 N 15th Ave Phoenix AZ 85023-5174 Office: 15249 N 59th Ave Glendale AZ 85306-3236

RICKS, MARY F(RANCES), academic administrator, anthropologist; b. Portland, Oreg., July 6, 1939; d. Leo and Frances Helen (Corcoran) Samuel; m. Robert Stanley Ricks, Jan. 7, 1961; children: Michael Stanley, Allen Gilbert. BA, Whitman Coll., 1961; MA, Portland State U., 1977, MPA, 1981, PhD, 1995. Asst. to dir. auxiliary services Portland State U., 1975-79, instnl. researcher, 1979-85, dir. instnl. research and planning, 1985—, rsch. assoc. prof., 1994—. Contbr. articles and presentations to profl. socs. Vol. archeologist BLM-USDI, Lakeview, Oreg., 1983—. Fellow Soc. Applied Anthropology; mem. Soc. Am. Archaeology, Soc. Coll. and U. Planning, Pacific N.W. Assn. Instnl. Rsch. and Planning (pres. 1990-91), Assn. Oreg. Archaeologists (v.p. 1988-90), Assn. Instl. Rsch., City Club of Portland, Sigma Xi. Home: 5466 SW Dover Loop Portland OR 97225-1033 Office: Portland State U Office Instnl Rsch/Planning PO Box 751 Portland OR 97207-0751

RIDDELL, JACQUELINE ANNE, computer company executive; b. Galesburg, Ill., Apr. 9, 1965; d. Danny Earl and Diane Claire (Shull) R.; m. Paul Joseph Stolarczuk, Mar. 31, 1990; children: John Paul Riddell Stolarczuk, Mitchell Joseph Riddell Stolarczuk, Troy Michael Riddell Stolarczuk. BS in Journalism, U. Ill., 1987; MBA, City U., Seattle, 1989. Tech. editor Microsoft Corp. Hdqrs., Redmond, Wash., 1987-90, localization mgr., 1991-95; group program mgr. MS Ireland, 1995; group localization mgr. Microsoft Corp., 1996—. Editor: Microsoft Works Reference, 1987, Microsoft Works Appendices, 1987, Microsoft Project View Book, 1989, Microsoft Project Class-In-A-Box, 1990, Microsoft Project Reference, 1991. Vo. pub. TV telethons, Seattle, 1988, 89. Mem. Soc. Tech Communication (award of excellence 1990), Am. Translators Assn., Profl. Assn. Diving Instrs., Scuba Diving Assn. (cert.), Puget Sound U. Ill. Alumni Club (sec. 1987-91, newsletter editor). Republican. Presbyterian. Office: Microsoft Corp 16011 NE 36th Way Redmond WA 98052-6301

RIDDOCH, HILDA JOHNSON, accountant; b. Salt Lake City, July 25, 1923; d. John and Ivy Alma (Wallis) Johnson; m. Leland Asa Riddoch, Nov. 22, 1942; children: Ivy Lee (dec.), Leland Mark. Vocal student, Ben Henry Smith, Seattle; student, Art Instrn. Schs. Sales clk, marking room and dist. office Sears, Roebuck & Co., Seattle, 1940-42; with billing dept., receptionist C.M. Lovsted & Co., Inc., Seattle, 1942-51; acct., exec. sec. Viking Equipment Co., Inc., Seattle, 1951-54; acct., office mgr. Charles Waynor Collection Agy., Seattle, 1955-57; pvt. practice, 1957-96; acct., office mgr. Argus Mag., Seattle, 1962-67; acct. Law Offices Krutch, Lindell, Donnelly, Dempsey & Lageschulte, Seattle, 1967-72, Law Offices Sindell, Haley, Estep, et al, Seattle, 1972-77; co-founder, acct. Bus. Svc., Inc. and Diversified Design & Mktg., Fed. Way, Auburn & Orting, Wash., 1975-96; co-founder L & H Advt. and Distbg. Co., Wash., 1992—; sec.-treas., dir. Jim Evans Realty, Inc., Seattle, 1973-87; agt. Wise Island Water Co., P.U.D., Victoria, B.C., 1973-88, Estate Executrix, Seattle, 1987-95. Author: Ticking Time on a Metronome, 1989-90; writer, dir. hist. play Presidents of Relief Society Thru Ages; writer epic poetry; writer, dir. teenager activation video, 1984; pub., editor Extended Family Newsletter, 1983—. Dir. speech and drama LDS Ch., 1938-88, ward pres. young women's orgn., mem. ward and stake choirs, 1963-85, stake genealogy libr., Federal Way, 1983-85, ward and stake newsletter editors various areas, West Seattle, Seattle, Renton, Auburn, 1950-90, 1st counselor in presidency, tchr. various courses Ladies' Relief Soc. Orgn., 1965—; co-dir., organizer 1st Silver Saints Group, 1990-92; interviewer LDS Ch. Emplyment Svcs., 1992-93; founder WE CARE, 1993; co-resident mgr. Mountain View Estates, Orting. Recipient Letter of Recognition Howard W. Hunter, Pres. LDS Ch. Fellow Am. Biographical Assn. (life). Home: care 803 S Skyline Dr Idaho Falls ID 83402

RIDER, FAE B., writer; b. Summit Point, Utah, Mar. 1, 1932; d. Lee Collingwood and Jessie (Hammond) Blackett; m. David N. Rider, Jan. 26, 1952; children: David Lee, Lawrence Eugene. BS, No. Ariz. U., 1971, MA, 1974; postgrad., U. Nev., Las Vegas, 1985-88. Lic. tchr. in elem., reading, spl. edn. Learning specialist Las Vegas, summers 1974-76; tchr. kindergarten Indian Springs (Nev.) Pub. Schs., 1971-76; reading tchr. Las Vegas Pub. Schs., 1976-80; curriculum coord. Indian Springs Pub. Schs., 1980-91; tchr. 1st grade Las Vegas Pub. Schs., 1991-92, reading specialist, 1992-93; pvt. edn./reading cons. Las Vegas, 1993—. Author booklet: Door to Learning - A Non-Graded Approach, 1978. Bd. dirs. Jade Park, Las Vegas, 1988. Recipient Excellence in Edn. award, 1988, Outstanding Sch.and Cmty. Svc. award, 1990. Mem. Internat. Reading Assn., Ret. Tchrs. Assn., Am. Legion Aux., A.R.E study group, Delta Kappa Gamma (pres., Rose of Recognition), Kappa Delta Phi.

RIDER, JANE LOUISE, artist, educator; b. Brownfield, Tex., Sept. 11, 1919; d. Oscar Thomas and Florence Myrtle (Bliss) Halley; m. Rolla Wilson Rider Jr., Mar. 26, 1944 (dec. July 1992); 1 child, Dorothy Jo Neil. BA,

UCLA, Westwood, 1943, tchg. diploma in secondary art; postgrad., Chgo. Art Inst., 1945, Chouniards, L.A., U. Oreg., Scripps, Claremont, Calif. Art supr., elem. and jr. high art tchr. Tulare (Calif.) City Schs. Dist., 1943-44, 44-45; art tchr. Beverly Hills (Calif.) High Sch., 1946-47; art tchr. jr. high gen. art and ceramics Santa Barbara City Schs., Goleta, Calif., 1964-66; head art dept., tchr. Morro Bay (Calif.) Jr.-Sr. High Sch. Dist., 1967-70; pvt. practice studio potter Cambria, Calif., 1961-85; artist, Santa Rosa, Calif., 1985—; founder, dir., tech. La Canada (Calif.) Youth House Art Program, 1953-60; dir. Pinedorado Art Show, Allied Arts Assn., Cambria, 1970-80. Exhibited in group shows Wine Country Artist's Spring Show, 1991, 92, 93, 94, 95, 97, Gualala Art in Redwoods, 1986, 87, 88, 96, Rodney Strong Vineyards Art Guild, 1994; revolving exhibits Berger Ctr. and Chalais-Oakmont, Santa Rosa, 1985-97, Oakmont Art Assn., Santa Rosa, 1985-97, Santa Rosa Art Guild, 1986-97; statewide art shows Spring Palettes Mumm Cuvee Winery, Napa, Calif., 1985-95, Women Creating, Luther Burbank Ctr., 1995, Summer House Gallery, Healdsberg, 1995, Armida Winery Show, 1995, Coddington Mall Show, 1995-96, Audubon-Bouverie Preserve Show, Glen Ellen, Calif., 1996, Pedroncelli Winery Show, 1996, Wasco Invitational Show Marin Art Assn., 1996, others. Mem. WASCO, Nat. League Am. Pen Woman, Inc. (artist 1994-97), Santa Rosa Art Guild (exhibits 1986-95, rec. sec. 1989), Ctrl. Coast Watercolor Soc. (charter 1977), Watercolor Artist Sonoma. Republican. Home: 7019 Overlook Dr Santa Rosa CA 95409-6376

RIEDER, RICHARD WALTER, federal government official; b. Mpls., Feb. 18, 1940; s. Walter and Virginia (Lincoln) R.; m. Edelgard Lestin, May 12, 1966; children: Stephanie, Arnold. BA, Yale U., 1961; MPA, George Washington U., 1970, U. So. Calif., 1976. Budget and program analyst NASA, Washington, 1967-69, 71-81, adminstrv. officer, 1969-71, mgmt. analyst, 1982—. Elder Good Shepherd Luth. Ch., 1979-81. Served to lt. USN, 1961-66. Mem. AIAA, Am. Assn. Budget and Program Analysis, Am. Soc. Pub. Adminstrn. Club: Swiss.

RIEGEL, BARBARA J., nursing educator, clinical researcher, editor; b. St. Louis, Apr. 3, 1950; d. Lawrence Virgil and Shirley Jean (Weil) R.; m. m. Thomas A. Gillespie, May 23, 1978. Diploma, Jewish Hosp. Sch. Nursing, 1974; B in Nursing, San Diego State U., 1981; M in Nursing, UCLA, 1983; DNSc in Nursing, 1991. Staff nurse intensive care/coronary care unit Mo. Baptist Hosp., St. Louis, 1974-75; staff nurse coronary care unit Barnes Hosp., St. Louis, 1975-76; organizer U.S. Army Cmty. Health Orgn., Frankfurt, Fed. Republic of Germany, 1977-78; cardiovascular nurse specialist collaborative practice, San Diego, 1983-84, Scripps Clinic, La Jolla, Calif., 1984-85; faculty San Diego State U., 1984-87; adv. coun. San Diego State U. Sch. Nursing, 1983-85, mem. strategic planning comm., 1995-96; clin. rschr. Sharp HealthCare, San Diego, 1990—; assoc. prof. San Diego State U., 1995—. Editor: Dreifus' Pacemaker Therapy: An Interprofessional Approach, 1986, Psychol. Aspects of Critical Care Nursing, 1989; editor Jour. Cardiovascular Nursing, 1986—; mem. editl. rev. bd. Heart and Lung, 1985—, Critical Care Nursing Quar., 1986—, Jour. of Advanced Med.-Surg. Nursing, 1988-89, Am. Jour. Critical Care, 1992—; contbr. articles to profl. jours. Fellow Am. Acad. Nursing; mem. ANA (cert.), AACN (mem. task force ethics in critical care rsch. 1983-84, rsch. com. 1990-92), Am. Heart Assn. (coun. on cardiovascular nursing, So. Calif. rep. 1993-95, automatic external defibrillator task force, co-chair rsch. sub task force 1994-97, Am. Coll. Cardiology/Am. Heart Assn. acute myocardial infarction guideline com. 1994-96), Sigma Theta Tau (chpt. pres. Gamma Gamma 1992-93). Republican. Home: 15578 Raptor Rd Poway CA 92064-6906 Office: San Diego State U Sch of Nursing San Diego CA 92182-4158

RIEGEL, BYRON WILLIAM, ophthalmologist; b. Evanston, Ill., Jan. 19, 1938; s. Byron and Belle Mae (Huot) R.; BS, Stanford U., 1960; MD, Cornell U., 1964; m. Marilyn Hills, May 18, 1968; children—Marc William, Ryan Marie, Andrea Elizabeth. Intern, King County Hosp., Seattle, 1964-65; asst. resident in surgery U. Wash., Seattle, 1965; resident in ophthalmology U. Fla., 1968-71; pvt. practice medicine specializing in ophthalmology, Sierra Eye Med. Group, Inc., Visalia, Calif., 1972—; mem. staff Kaweah Delta Dist. Hosp., chief of staff, 1978-79. Bd. dirs., asst. sec. Kaweah Delta Dist. Hosp., 1983-90. Served as flight surgeon USN, 1966-68. Co-recipient Fight-for-Sight citation for research in retinal dystrophy, 1970. Diplomate Am. Bd. Ophthalmology, Nat. Bd. Med. Examiners. Fellow ACS, Am. Acad. Ophthalmology; mem. Calif. Med. Assn. (del. 1978-79), Tulare County Med. Assns., Calif. Assn. Ophthalmology (v.p. 3d party liaison 1994-96, dir. 1996—), Am. Soc. Cataract and Refractive Surgery, Internat. Phacoemulsification and Cataract Methodology Soc. Roman Catholic. Club: Rotary (Visalia). Home: 3027 W Keogh Ct Visalia CA 93291-4228 Office: 2830 W Main St Visalia CA 93291-4300

RIEGER, ELAINE JUNE, nursing administrator; b. Lebanon, Pa., June 7, 1937; d. Frank and Florence (Hitz) Plasterer; m. Jere LeFever Longenecker, Sept. 13, 1958 (div. 1968); children: Julie Lyn Porto, Jere Lee Longenecker; m. Bernhard Rieger, Oct. 12, 1971. Nursing diploma, Coatesville (Pa.) Hosp. Sch. of Nursing, 1958; BA, U. Redlands, 1976; MS in Healthcare Mgmt., Calif. State U., L.A., 1984. Cert. nursing adminstr., gerontol. nurse. From staff nurse to clin. supr. to dir. of nurses St. Johns Regional Med. Ctr., Oxnard, Calif., 1966-86; dir. of nurses Motion Picture and TV Hosp., Woodland Hills, Calif., 1987-89; with Care West, Nothridge-Reseda, Calif., 1989-90; dist. nurse mgr. Hillhaven Corp., Newbury Park, Calif., 1990-91; quality mgmt. nursing cons. Beverly Enterprises, Memphis, 1991-95; DON Beverly Manor Rehab. and Nursing Ctr., Van Nuys, Calif., 1996—. Home: 1817 Shady Brook Dr Thousand Oaks CA 91362-1335 Office: Beverly Manor Rehab and Nursing Ctr 6700 Sepulveda Blvd Van Nuys CA 91411-1248

RIEPE, DALE MAURICE, philosopher, writer, illustrator, educator, Asian art dealer; b. Tacoma, June 22, 1918; s. Rol and Martha (Johnson) R.; m. Charleine Williams, 1948; children: Kathrine Leigh Riepe Herschlag, Dorothy Lorraine. BA, U. Wash., 1944; MA, U. Mich., 1946, PhD, 1954; postgrad. (Rockefeller-Watamull-McInerny fellow), U. Hawaii, Banaras and Madras, India, Tokyo and Waseda, Japan, 1949. Instr. philosophy Carleton Coll., 1948-51; asst. prof. U. S.D., 1952-54; assoc. prof. U. N.D., 1954-59, prof., 1959-62, chmn. dept., 1954-62; prof., chmn. C.W. Post Coll., 1962-63; prof. philosophy SUNY, Buffalo, 1963—; chmn. dept. social scis., assoc. dean SUNY Grad. Sch., 1964—; instr. marine electricity Naval Tng. Program, Seattle, 1943-45; mem. nat. screening bd. South Asia, Fulbright Selection, 1968-70, Asia, 1970-72; chmn. Fulbright Selection Com. for Asia, 1972, 82; vis. Fulbright lectr. Tokyo U., 1957-58; vis. lectr. Western Wash. U., 1961, Delhi U., 1967; exchange lectr. U. Man., 1955, Moscow State U., 1979, Beijing Higher Edn. Inst., 1984; docent Albright-Knox Art Gallery; cons. Ctr. for Sci., Tech. and Devel., Council of Sci. adn Indsl. Rsch., Govt. India, 1978—, Inst. Fang Studies, 1987—; del. Cuban-N.Am. Philosophy Conf., Cuban Inst. Social Sci., 1982, Fang Centennial, Taiwan Nat. U., Taipeh, 1987, Hungarian-Am. Philos. Conf., Budapest, 1988; sports columnist The Town Crier; vis. scholar Andhra U., 1996. Author: The Naturalistic Tradition in Indian Thought, 1961, The Philosophy of India and its Impact on American Thought, 1970, Indian Philosophy Since Independence, 1979, The Owl Flies by Day, 1979, Asian Philosophy Today, 1981, Objectivity and Subjectivism in the Philosophy of Science, 1985, Philosophy and Revolutionary Theory, 1986, also articles in field.; editor: Phenomenology and Natural Existence, 1973, Philosophy and Political Economy; co-editor: The Structure of Philosophy, 1966, Contributions of American Sankritists in the Spread of Indian Philosophy in the United States, 1967, Radical Currents in Contemporary Philosophy, 1970, Reflections on Revolution, 1971, Philosophy at the Barricade, 1971, Contemporary East European Philosophy, 1971, Essays in East-West Dialogue, 1973, Explorations in Philosophy and Society, 1978; illustrator The Quick and the Dead, 1948; editorial com. Chinese Studies in History, 1970—, Chinese Studies in Philosophy, 1970—; publs. bd. Conf. for Asian Affairs; Editor various series.; editl. bd. Philos. Currents and Revolutionary World, 1972-86, Soviet Studies in Philosophy, 1979-87, Marxist Dimensions, 1987—. Active ACLU; mem. com. overseers Chung-an U., Korea; bd. dirs. Evergreen Coll. Cmty. Orgn., 1988—; bd. dirs. Friends of Evergreen Coll. Libr., 1992—; active Henry Gallery, Frye Gallery, Palm Springs Desert Mus., Seattle Art Mus., Phila. Mus. Art; mem. Capital Mus. and Art Soc., Wash. State Hist. Soc. Fulbright scholar India, 1951-52; Fulbright lectr. U. Tokyo, 1957-58; U. Mich. fellow, 1945-48, Carnegie Corp. fellow Asian Studies, 1960-61, Am. Inst. Indian Studies Rsch. fellow, 1966-67; grantee 4th East-West Philosophers Conf., 1964, Penrose fund Am. Philos. Soc., 1963; SUNY Research Found., 1965-67, 69, 72-73, Bulgarian Acad. Sci., 1975, London Sch. Oriental and African Studies, 1971. Fellow Royal Asiatic Soc., Far Eastern Inst. (Tokyo); mem. AAAS, Internat. Hegel-Vereinigung, Conf. Asian Affairs (sec. 1995), Am. Oriental Soc., Am. Philos. Soc., Indian Inst. Psychology, Philosophy and Psychical Rsch. (hon. adviser), Soc. for Am. Philosophy (chmn. 1960), Am. Inst. Indian Studies (trustee 1965-66), Soc. for Creative Ethics (sec.), Am. Archaeol. Soc., Am. Assn. Asian Studies, Am. Math. Soc., Am. Aesthetics Soc., Internat. Soc. Aesthetics, Am. Soc. Comparative and Asian Philosophy, Asiatic Soc. (Calcutta), Soc. for Philos. Study Dialectical Materialism (founding sec.-treas. 1962—), Soc. for Philos. Study Marxism (publs. sec. 1973-86), Union Am. and Japanese Profls. Against Nuclear Omnicide (treas. U.S. sec. 1978—), Internat. House of Japan, Internat. Philosophers for Prevention Nuclear Omnicide, United Univ. Profs. of SUNY-Buffalo (v.p.), Kokusai Bunka Shinkokai, Union Concerned Scientists, Alpha Pi Zeta. Office: SUNY 605 Baldy Hall Buffalo NY 14261

RIES, RICHARD KIRKLAND, psychiatrist; b. Seattle, Dec. 6, 1947; s. Lincoln and Lorna (Kirkland) R.; m. Sarah Bledsoe, Aug. 6, 1977; 1 child, Stephanie. BA, Stanford U., 1970; MD, Northwestern U., 1975; postgrad. in Psychiatry, U. Wash., 1978. Diplomate Am. Bd. Psychiatry and Neurology. Asst. prof. psychiatry U. Wash. Med. Sch., Seattle, 1978-84, assoc. prof. psychiatry, 1984—; dir. in-patient psychiatry Harborview Med. Ctr., Seattle, 1987-92, dir. out-patient psychiatry, 1992—, dir. Harborview Mental Health Ctr., 1992—; dir. addictions edn. U. Wash. Med. Ctr., 1983—. Editor: Treatment Improvement Protocal Dual Diagnosis, 1994; contbr. articles to profl. jours. Bd. dirs. Wash. Physician Health Program, Seattle, 1990—. Fellow Am. Psychiat. Assn. (Teach of Psychiatry award 1992); mem. Am. Acad. Psychiats. Alcoholism and Addictions, Assn. Med. Educators Rsch. in Substance Abuse, Am. Soc. Addiction Medicine. Office: Harborview Med Ctr Dept Psychiatry Seattle WA 98104

RIESE, ARTHUR CARL, environmental engineering company executive, consultant; b. St. Albans, N.Y., Jan. 2, 1955; s. Walter Herman and Katherine Ellen (Moore) R. BS in Geology, N.Mex. Inst. Mining and Tech., 1976, MS in Chemistry, 1978; PhD in Geochemistry, Colo. Sch. Mines, 1982. Lic. geologist, N.C.; registered profl. geologist, N.C., S.C., Ark., Fla., Tenn., Wyo. Asst. petroleum geologist N.Mex. Bur. Mines and Mineral Resources, Socorro, 1973-76; geologist Nord Resources, Inc., Albuquerque, 1975; rsch. asst. N.Mex. Inst. Mining and Tech., Socorro, 1976-78; vis. faculty Colo. Sch. Mines, 1978-81; rsch. geochemist Gulf R & D Co., Houston, 1982-84; sr. planning analyst/mgr. tech. planning Atlantic Richfield Co., L.A., 1984-87; sr. v.p. Harding Assocs. and Harding Lawson Assocs., Denver, 1987—; mem. affiliate faculty U. Tex., Austin, 1983—; speaker, conf. chmn. in field. Numerous patents in field. Panel participant N.Mex. First, Gallup, 1990. Recipinet Engrng. Excellence award Cons. Engrs. Coun. Colo., 1991, 95. Mem. Am. Inst. Hydrology (cert. profl. hydrogeologist 1988), Am. Inst. Profl. Geologists (cert. geol. scientist 1988). Office: Harding Lawson Assocs 2400 MCI Tower 707 17th St Denver CO 80202-3404

RIFE, MARY LOU, school counselor; b. Denver, Sept. 28, 1939; d. Paul Darlington and Marion Ambrose; m. David Bruce Rife, Sept. 1, 1961; children: Robin Lee, Renee Lou. BS, U. Colo., 1962; MA, U. No. Colo., 1965. Tchr. Brighton (Colo.) H.S., 1962, Bishop (Calif.) Union H.S., 1962-64; counselor Pioneer Elem. Sch., Quincy, Calif., 1965-66; counselor for disabled Plumas County, Calif., 1977-84; counselor/tchr. Portola (Calif.) Schs., 1984—; child custody investigator Plumas County Probation, 1994; home health social worker Ea. Plumas Dist. Hosp., Portola, 1994; pvt. counselor, Portola, 1993-94; juvenile justice commn. Plumas County, 1993—; chairperson impact team Portola Schs., 1985—. Mem. Beta Sigma Phi (citizen of yr. 1980).

RIFFENBURGH, RALPH SIDNEY, ophthalmologist; b. Washington, Feb. 27, 1923; s. Harry Buchholz and Ada Ernestine (Swallow) R.; m. Angelyn Faith Kelley, July 13, 1946; children: Roger R., Stephen K., Bruce A. Student, Calif. Inst. Tech., 1941-42; BS, Va. Polytech. Inst., 1943; MD, Med. Coll. of Va., 1947; MA, U. So. Calif., 1966. Diplomate Am. Bd. Ophthalmology; lic. med. bd. Calif. Instr. Washington U. Med. Sch., St. Louis, 1952-54; pvt. practice specializing in ophthalmology Pasadena, Calif., 1954—; from instr. to prof. U. So. Calif. Med. Sch., L.A., 1954—; eye pathologist, Doheny Eye Found., L.A., 1954—; mem. med. adv. bd. Planned Parenthood, Pasadena, 1984—, Young and Healthy, Pasadena, 1990—. Contbr. numerous articles to profl. jours. Mem. Tournament of Roses Com., 1968—; vice chmn. Sister City Com., Pasadena, 1972-84; res. comdr. S. Pasadena Police, 1975-88; pilot-lt. San Bernardino County Sheriff, Rialto, Calif., 1988—. Lt. comdr. USNR, 1950-52. Recipient 50 Yr. award Silver Wings, Cin., 1994; honoree Doheny Eye Inst., 1995. Fellow Am. Acad. Ophthalmology, Current Anthropology; mem. AMA, Calif. Med. Assn., L.A. County Med. Assn., Am. Anthropol. Assn. Office: Pasadena Eye Med Group 595 E Colorado Blvd Pasadena CA 91101

RIGAS, ANTHONY LEON, univerity department director; b. Andros, Greece, May 3, 1931; s. Leon Anthony and Katina (Sarris) R.; m. Harriett B. Rigas, Feb. 14, 1959 (dec. 1989); 1 child, Marc Leonard; m. Mary Dunham, Dec. 29, 1990. BSEE, U. Kans., 1958, MSEE, 1962; postgrad., Stanford U., 1965; PhD in Engrng., U. Beverly Hills, 1978. Elec. engr. Naval Missile Ctr., Point Mugu, Calif., 1958-61; engrng. analyst Mpls. Honeywell Co., 1962; instr. elec. engrng. U. Kans., Lawrence, 1962-63; sr. rsch. engr. aerospace systems Lockheed Missile and Space Co., Sunnyvale, Calif., 1963-65, Dalmo-Victor Co., Belmont, Calif., 1965-66; asst. prof. elec. engrng. San Jose (Calif.) State U., 1963-65; asst. prof., assoc. prof., then prof. elec. engrng. U. Idaho, Moscow, 1966-84, dir. instrnl. media svcs., 1983-84; prof. elec. and computer engrng. Naval Postgrad. Sch., Monterey, Calif., 1984-87; dir. engrng. lifelong edn. Mich. State U., East Lansing, 1987-92; prof. elec. engrng., dir. engrng outreach emeritus U. Idaho, 1994—; presenter at profl. confs.; prof. elec. engrng., dir. engrng. outreach emeritus U. Idaho, 1994—. Contbr. to profl. publs. Grantee NSF, 1971-75, 71-76, 1979-82, HEW, 1979-80, Kellogg Found., 1977-80. Fellow IEEE; mem. Am. Soc. Engrng. Edn., Nat. Soc. Profl. Engrs., Nat. Univ. Continuing Edn. Assn., Sigma Xi, Sigma Tau, Tau Beta Pi. Home: 4000 Highway 200 E Sandpoint ID 83864-9436

RIGBY, AMANDA YOUNG, paralegal firm executive; b. Yokosuka, Japan, Nov. 15, 1961; came to U.S., 1961; d. James Linton Young and Serena Margaret (Murray) Poisson; m. D'Arcy A. Rigby, Apr. 6, 1991; children: Ian A., Helen E. Cert. paralegal, U. San Diego, 1989; AA in Social Sci., Miramar Coll., 1990; student in bus. mgmt., Pepperdine U. Cert. domestic violence counselor, Calif. Sec. Martin & Branfman, Solana Beach, Calif., 1988-89; sr. paralegal DiGennaro & Davis, San Diego, 1989-91; owner, pres. paralegal firm AR & Co., San Diego, 1989—. Author poetry in Taking Chances mag., 1992. Vol. clinic coord. San Diego Vol. Lawyer Program, 1989-96; vol. asst. to abuse victims San Diego Police Dept., 1992—; parliamentarian Mira Mesa Town Coun., San Diego, 1992-95; founding mem. Scripps Ranch High Found., San Diego, 1992-95; sec., nat. and state rep. Pamerado Hosp. Mothers of Twins, Poway, Calif., 1994—; mem. Vista (Calif.) Unified Sch. Dist. Common Ground Task Force, 1995—; staff paralegal San Diego Vol. Lawyer Program, 1994-95. Mem. ABA, San Diego Assn. Legal Assts. Republican. Methodist. Office: AR & Co 615 Cabezon Pl Fl 2 Vista CA 92083-6309 *Amanda Young Rigby has been honored with two Special Commendations from the San Diego City Council; the Distinguished Service Award from the San Diego Volunteer Lawyer Program (SDVLP); three Wiley W. Manuel Awards for Pro Bono Legal Services from the California State Bar; Volunteer of the Month award from the Mira Mesa Town Council (MMTC); Certificate of Appreciation from the San Diego Police Department; was a finalist for SDVLP's Community Service Award; and was nominated for the MMTC's Volunteer of the Year award three times. She was featured in the Sorrento Times newspaper as a community leader and was on the Dean's List in college.*

RIGDON, JUDY ANNE, business administrator; b. Orange, Calif., Dec. 7, 1946; d. Marion David and Daisy E. (Carr) R. Student, Orange Coast Coll., Costa Mesa, Calif., 1971-74. Clk. Knott's Berry Farm, Buena Park, Calif., 1964-67; head dept. Bank of Am., El Toro, Calif., 1967-85; office mgr., sec. Richmond Law Offices, Laguna Hills, Calif., 1985-94, W.R. Mills & Co., Tustin, Calif., 1995—; owner Rigdon Bookeeping, Laguna Hills, 1994—. Mem. Philanthropic Ednl. Orgn. (treas. 1995—). Republican. Office: W.R. Mills & Co. 17671 Irvine Blvd Ste 207 Tustin CA 92780-3129

RIGGS, FRANCIS PORTER, sculptor; b. N.Y.C., May 1, 1922; s. Francis Porter and Margery (Cummings) R.; m. June Rosemary Clarke, Sept. 13, 1945; children: John Prescott, Gillian Anne Brown, Jacqueline June Wahlstrom. Student, Pratt Inst., Bklyn., 1946-48. Indsl. designer Michael Hallward, Boston, 1948-50; sculptor with Alfred Duca, Boston, 1964-66; furniture designer Milo Baughman Design, Wellesley, Mass., 1967-72; instr. Brigham Young U., Provo, Utah, 1969-88; sculptor Ivins, Utah, 1975—. Mem. planning bd. Highland City, Utah, 1985-86. 1st lt. USAF, 1942-45, ETO. Recipient Purchase award Utah Arts Coun., Salt Lake City, 1976, Springville (Utah) Mus., 1989. Home and Studio: 654 Wisteria Way Ivins UT 84738-6316

RIGGS, FRANK, congressman; b. Louisville, Ky., Sept. 5, 1950; m. Cathy Anne Maillard; three children: Ryan, Matthew, Sarah Anne. BA, Golden Gate U. With Veale Investment Properties, until 1987; co-founder (with wife) Duncan Enterprises; mem. 102nd Congress 1st Calif. Dist., 1991-92, mem. 104th and 105th Congresses, 1995—. With U.S. Army, 1972-75. Republican. Office: US House Reps 1714 Longworth Office Bldg Washington DC 20515-0501

RIGGS, FRED WARREN, political science educator; b. Kuling, China, July 3, 1917; (parents Am. citizens); s. Charles H. and Grace (Frederick) R.; m. Clara-Louise Mather, June 5, 1943; children: Gwendolyn, Ronald (dec.). Student, U. Nanking, China, 1934-35; BA, U. Ill., 1938; MA, Fletcher Sch. Law and Diplomacy, 1941; PhD, Columbia U., 1948. Lectr. CUNY, 1947-48; rsch. assoc. Fgn. Policy Assn., 1948-51; asst. dir. Pub. Adminstrn. Clearing House, N.Y.C., 1951-55; Arthur F. Bentley prof. govt. Ind. U., 1956-67; dir. Social Sci. Rsch. Inst. U. Hawaii, 1970-73, prof. polit. sci., 1967-87, prof. emeritus, 1987—; vis. asst. prof. Yale U., 1955-56; vis. lectr. Nat. Officials Tng. Inst., Korea, 1956; vis. prof. U. Philippines, 1958-59, MIT, 1965-66, CUNY, 1974-75; vis. scholar Inst. Soc. Studies, The Hague, 1972; sr. specialist East-West Ctr. U. Hawaii, 1962-63. Author: Pressures on Congress: A Study of the Repeal of Chinese Exclusion, 1950, reprinted, 1973, Formosa under Chinese Nationalist Rule, 1952, reprinted, 1972, The Ecology of Public Administration, 1961 (pub. in Portuguese, 1964), Administration in Developing Countries: The Theory of Prismatic Society, 1964 (pub. in Korean, 1966, Portuguese, 1968), Thailand: The Modernization of a Bureaucratic Polity, 1966, Organization Theory and International Development, 1969, Administrative Reform and Political Responsiveness: A Theory of Dynamic Balancing, 1971, Prismatic Society Revisited, 1973 (pub. in Korean, 1987), Applied Prismatics, 1978, (with Daya Krishna) Development Debate, 1987; author: (with others) Contemporary Political Systems: Classifications and Typologies, 1990, Handbook of Comparative and Development Public Administration, 1991, Terminology: Applications in Interdisciplinary Communication, 1993, Parliamentary vs. Presidential Government, 1993, Public Administration in the Global Village, 1994, Comparing Nations: Concepts, Strategies, Substance, 1994, Handbook of Bureaucracy, 1994, Standardizing and Harmonizing Terminology, 1995, Korea in the Era of Post-Development and Globalization, 1996, Viable Constitutionalism and Bureaucracy, 1996, Onomantics and Terminology, 1996, Designs for Democratic Stability, 1997; co-author, editor: Frontiers of Development Administration, 1971, Tower of Babel: On the Definition and Analysis of Concepts in the Social Sciences, 1975, Viable Constitutional and Bureaucracy, 1996, Onomantics and Terminology, 1996. Dir. INTERCOCTA project Internat. Social Sci. Coun., 1970-93; chair UNESCO com. INTERCONCEPT project, 1977-79; chair Comm. on Conceptual and Terminological Analysis (COCTA), Internat. Polit. Sci. Assn., Internat. Sociol. Assn. and Internat. Social Sci. Coun., 1973-79; co-chair N.AM. roundtable on cooperation Social Sci. Info. Mpls., 1979; chair lexicographic terminology com. Dictionary Soc. N.Am., 1983-86; co-chair Com. on Viable Constitutionalism (COVICO), 1993—. Decorated Order of White Elephant, King of Thailand, 1986; fellow com. comparative politics Social Sci. Rsch. Coun., 1957-58, Ctr. Advanced Study in Behavioral Scis., 1966-67; honoree Eastern Regional Orgn. Pub. Adminstrn. Conf., 1983. Mem. ASPA (chair comparative adminstrn. group 1960-71, Dwight Waldo award 1991), Am. Polit. Sci. Assn., Internat. Studies Assn. (chair comparative interdisciplinary studies sect. 1970-74, v.p. 1970-71, co-chair ethnicity, nationalism and migration sect. 1994-95), Internat. Polit. Sci. Assn., Internat. Sociol. Assn., Assn. Asian Studies (chair com. rsch. materials S.E. Asia 1969-73). Home: 3920 Lurline Dr Honolulu HI 96816-4006 Office: U Hawaii Political Science Dept 2424 Maile Way Honolulu HI 96822-2223

RIGGS, GEORGE E., newspaper publishing executive. Pub., CEO Contra Costa (Calif.) Times.

RIGGS, HENRY EARLE, academic administrator, engineering management educator; b. Chgo., Feb. 25, 1935; s. Joseph Agnew and Gretchen (Walser) R.; m. Gayle Carson, May 17, 1958; children: Elizabeth, Peter, Catharine. BS, Stanford U., 1957; MBA, Harvard U., 1960. Indsl. economist SRI Internat., Menlo Park, Calif., 1960-63; v.p. Icore Industries, Sunnyvale, Calif., 1963-67, pres., 1967-70; v.p. fin. Measurex Corp., Cupertino, Calif., 1970-74; prof. engrng. mgmt. Stanford U., Calif., 1974-88, Ford prof., 1986-88, Ford prof. emeritus, 1990—, v.p. for devel., 1983-88; pres. Harvey Mudd Coll., Claremont, Calif., 1988-97, pres. emeritus, 1997—; pres. Grad. Inst. Applied Life Scis., Claremont, 1997—; bd. dirs. Mutual Funds of capital Rsch. Group. Author: Accounting: A Survey, 1981, Managing High-Tech Companies, 1983, Financial and Cost Analysis, 1994; contbr. articles to Harvard Bus. Rev. Bd. dirs. Mt. Baldy Coun. Boy Scouts Am., 1993—. Baker scholar Harvard Bus. Sch., Boston, 1959; recipient Gores Teaching award Stanford U., 1980. Mem. Stanford U. Alumni Assn. (bd. dirs. 1990-94, chmn. 1993), Calif. Club, Sunset Club, Phi Beta Kappa, Tau Beta Pi. Congregationalist. Office: Grad Inst Applied Life Scis 1263 N Dartmouth St Claremont CA 91711

RIGGS, ROBERT EDWON, law and political science educator; b. Mesa, Ariz, June 24, 1927; s. Lyle Alton and Goldie Esther (Motzkus) R.; m. Hazel Dawn Macdonald, Sept. 1, 1949; children: Robert, Richard, Russel, Rodney, Raymond, Reisa, Preston. BA, U. Ariz., 1952, MA, 1953, LLB, 1963; PhD in Polit. Sci., U. Ill., 1955. Bar: Ariz. 1963. Instr., then asst. prof. polit. sci. Brigham Young U., Provo, Utah, 1955-60, prof. J. Reuben Clark Law Sch., 1975-91, Guy Anderson prof. law, 1991-92; rsch. specialist Bur. Bus. and Pub. Rsch., U. Ariz., 1960-63; assoc. Riggs & Riggs, Tempe, Ariz., 1963-64; mem. faculty U. Minn., 1964-75, prof. polit. sci., 1968-75, dir. Harold Scott Quigley Center Internat. Studies, 1968-70; of counsel Law Offices of Russel O. Riggs, PLC, 1995—. Author: Politics in the United Nations, 1958, reprinted 1984, The Movement for Administrative Reorganization in Arizona, rev. edit, 1964, (with Jack C. Plano) Forging World Order, 1967, Dictionary of Political Analysis, 1973, 2d edit. (with Jack C. Plano and Helenan S. Robin), 1982, US/UN: Foreign Policy and International Organization, 1971, (with Plano and others) Political Science Dictionary, 1973, (with I. J. Mykletun) Beyond Functionalism: Attitudes toward International Organization in Norway and the U.S, 1979, (with Jack C. Plano) The United Nations, 1988, 2d edit. 1994. Dem. precinct chmn., 1970-72, 76-80, 84-86; mem. Utah Dem. State Ctrl. Com., 1978-82; mayor Golden Valley, Minn., 1972-75; Dem. candidate for U.S. Congress from Minn. 3d dist., 1974; bd. dirs. Minn. UN Assn., 1967-74, Utah Legal Svcs. Corp., 1978-81; chmn. Utah State Adv. Com. to U.S. Commn. on Civil Rights, 1988-92. With AUS, 1945-47. Rotary Found. fellow Oxford (Eng.) U., 1952-53; James W. Garner fellow U. Ill., 1953-55; Rockefeller rsch. fellow Columbia U., 1957-58; NEH rsch. grantee, U. Minn., Brigham Young U. Mem. Phi Beta Kappa, Order of Coif, Phi Kappa Phi, Delta Sigma Rho, Phi Alpha Delta. Mem. Ch. of Jesus Christ of Latter-day Saints (missionary in Eng. 1947-49, in Ariz. 1993-94). Home: 2540 E Camino Mesa AZ 85213-9999

RIGGS, WILLIAM G(ERRY), art gallery director, museum studies educator; b. Frankfurt am Main, Germany, Dec. 12, 1950; (parents Am. citizens); s. William G. and Billie Jean (Johnson) R. BFA in Art, U. Okla., 1979, MLS in Museum Studies, 1987. Preparator U. Okla. Mus. Art, Norman, 1978-79; mgr. collections, preparator Okla. Art Ctr., Oklahoma City, 1979-81, asst. curator, registrar, 1982-84, curator collections, 1985-87; dir. Goddard Ctr. for Performing and Visual Arts, Ardmore, Okla., 1987-90; exhbn. coord. Colorado Springs (Colo.) Art Ctr., 1990, curator fine art, 1991; dir., curator Gallery Contemporary Art, U. Colo., Colorado Springs, 1991—, asst. prof. mus. studies, 1991—; lectr. in field. Author: (essay) Facets of Modern Art from the Oklahoma Art Centr, 1987, (catalog) The Rug Route: From Istanbul to Bokhara, 1990; contbr. articles to profl. publs.;

curator Contemporary Abstraction, 1986, Westheimer Mus. Acquisitions, 1988, Okla. Artists, A Centennial Exhbn., 1990, Art of New West, 1990-91, Colo. Photographers: 10 X 10, 1992, Front Range Revisited, 1992, Tom Wesselmann and Larry Rivers: Graphics and Multiples, 1965-92, also others. Mem. Colorado Springs Arts Commn., 1992—; mem. art and architecture com. USAF Acad., Colorado Springs, 1993-96; mem. adv. com. Save Outdoor Sculpture, Colorado Springs Parks and Recreation Dept., 1992-93; mem. art com. Colorado Springs Airport. Mem. Am. Assn. Mus. (surveyor mus. assessment program II 1986-87), Assn. Coll. and Univ. Mus. and Galleries, Colo.-Wyo. Assn. Mus., Nat. Assn. for Mus. Exhbns. (regional rep. 1991-93). Home: 318 Locust Dr Colorado Springs CO 80907-4348 Office: U Colo Gallery Contemporary Art 1420 Austin Bluffs Pky Colorado Springs CO 80918-3733

RIGHTS, CLYDE SIEWERS, obstetrician and gynecologist; b. Tampa, Fla., Oct. 31, 1923; s. Clyde Seiwers and Anna Louise (Ormsby); m. Charlene Montee Greene; children: Lisa, Bill, Kristen, Scott. MD, Wake Forest U., 1947; BS, Emory U., 1945. Diplomate Am. Bd. Ob-Gyn. Intern Grace-New Haven Hosp., 1948; asst. resident Grace-New Haven Hosp./Yale U., 1949-50; fellow Parkland Hosp/U. Tex. Southwestern Br., Dallas, 1950-51; mem. staff San Diego County Hosp., 1955; pvt. practice ob-gyn. Pacific Beach, Calif., 1955-90; locum tenens, 1990—. Fellow Am. Coll. Ob-Gyn.; mem. San Diego Gynecology Soc., San Diego Cunty med. Soc., La. Jolla Acad. Medicine. Moravian. Home: 5780 Rutgers Rd La Jolla CA 92037-7830

RILES, WILSON CAMANZA, educational consultant; b. Alexandria, La., June 27, 1917; m. Mary Louise Phillips, Nov. 13, 1941; children: Michael, Narvia Riles Bostick, Wilson, Phillip. B.A., No. Ariz. U., 1940; M.A., 1947, LL.D., 1976; LL.D., Pepperdine Coll., 1965, Claremont Grad. Sch., 1972, U. So. Calif., 1975, U. Akron, 1976, Golden Gate U., 1981; L.H.D., St. Mary's Coll., 1971, U. Pacific, 1971, U. Judaism, 1972. Tchr. elem. schs., adminstr. pub. schs. Ariz., 1940-54; exec. sec. Pacific Coast region Fellowship of Reconciliation, Los Angeles, 1954-58; with Calif. Dept. Edn., 1958-83, dep. supt. pub. instrn., 1965-70, supt. pub. instruction, 1971-83; pres. Wilson Riles & Assocs., Inc., 1983—; dir. emeritus Wells Fargo Bank, Wells Fargo Co. Past mem. editorial adv. bd.: Early Years mag. Ex-officio mem. bd. regents U. Calif., 1971-82; ex-officio trustee Calif. State Univs. and Colls., 1971-82; nat. adv. council Nat. Schs. Vol. Program; former mem. council Stanford Research Inst.; former mem. adv. council Stanford U. Sch. Bus.; former mem. adv. bd. Calif. Congress Parents and Tchrs.; former trustee Am. Coll. Testing Program; former mem. Edn. Commn. of States; past 2d v.p. Nat. PTA.; former trustee Found. Teaching Econs.; former mem. Joint Council Econ. Edn.; former mem. Nat. Council for Children and TV. With USAF, 1943-46. Recipient Spingarn medal NAACP, 1973. Mem. Assn. Calif. Sch. Adminstrs., Cleve. Conf., NAACP (Spingarn medal 1973), Nat. Acad. Pub. Adminstrn., Phi Beta Kappa. Office: 400 Capitol Mall Ste 1540 Sacramento CA 95814-4408 *Is growing up in rural Louisiana during the depression as an orphan, poor and black, attending a segregated school, a handicap? I have never thought so. Maybe it's because of the superb teachers who never let me feel sorry for myself. As I recall, some did not even have college degrees, but they believed I could learn. Because they did, it never occurred to me that I couldn't. Forrest Paul Augustine, the principal, admonished us to get as much education as we could because, "that is one thing no one can ever take away from you". I chose education as a career because those humble public schools gave me a chance. I want all boys and girls to have a chance, too.*

RILEY, ANN J., state legislator, technology specialist; b. Memphis, Oct. 27, 1940; m. Ray T. Riley, Apr. 28, 1962. BSBA, U. Albuquerque, 1985; MBA, Webster U., 1988; cert. in pub. policy, Harvard U., 1994. Loan officer Ravenswood Bank, Chgo., 1970-74; mgr. dist. sales Security Lockout, Chgo., 1974-77; owner AR Fasteners, Albuquerque, 1977-82; tech. transfer agt. Sandia Nat. Labs., Albuquerque, 1983—; mem. N.Mex. Senate, Santa Fe, 1993—; resolutions chair energy com. Nat. Order of Women Legis. Nat. Conf. State Legislators. Bd. dirs. All Faiths Receiving Home. Albuquerque, 1989-92, Law Enforcement Acad., Santa Fe, 1991-92; active Leadership Albuquerque, 1991, state federal task force U.S. Office Sci. & Tech., 1995. Flemming fellow Am. U. Ctr. for Policy Alternatives, 1996. Democrat. Home: 10301 Karen Ave NE Albuquerque NM 87111-3633

RILEY, BRIAN M., banker; b. Upland, Calif., Feb. 1, 1965; s. Lewis Monroe and Catherine Ann (Smith) R.; m. Maureen Hurley, Oct. 6, 1996. BS in Fin., Calif. State Poly. U., 1990. Acctg. asst. Chino Valley Bank, Ontario, Calif., 1984-85, investment officer, 1986-88, asst. vp., asst. controller, 1988-91, v.p. fin., 1991-92; exec. v.p., CFO Metro Commerce Bank, San Rafael, Calif., 1992—; organizer SofTec, Novato; v.p. edn. Banker's Exec. Coun., 1995—. Treas., bd. dirs. Crossroads, Fontana, Calif., 1986-91, West Colony Cmty. Assn., San Bernardino, Calif., 1991-92, Drucker Ctr. Fin. Assn., Claremont, Calif., 1991-92. Mem. Bank Adminstrn. Inst. Office: Metro Commerce Bank 1248 5th Ave San Rafael CA 94901-2918

RILEY, CARROLL LAVERN, anthropology educator; b. Summersville, Mo., Apr. 18, 1923; s. Benjamin F. and Minnie B. (Smith) R.; m. Brent Robinson Locke, Mar. 25, 1948; children: Benjamin Locke, Victoria Smith Evans, Cynthia Winningham. A.B., U. N.Mex., 1948, Ph.D., 1952; M.A., UCLA, 1950. Instr. U. Colo., Boulder, 1953-54; asst. prof. U. N.C., Chapel Hill, 1954-55; asst. prof. So. Ill. U., Carbondale, 1955-60, assoc. prof., 1960-67, prof., 1967-86, Disting. prof., 1986-87, Disting. prof. emeritus, 1987—, chmn. dept., 1979-82, dir. mus., 1972-74; rsch. assoc. lab. anthropology Mus. N.Mex., 1987—; rsch. collaborator Smithsonian Instn., 1988—; adj. prof. N.Mex. Highlands U., 1989—. Author: The Origins of Civilization, 1969, The Frontier People, 1982, expanded edit., 1987, Rio del Norte, 1995, Bandelier, 1996; editor: Man Across the Sea, 1971, Southwestern Journals of Adolph F. Bandelier, 4 vols., 1966, 70, 75, 84, Across the Chichimec Sea, 1978, others; contbr. numerous articles to profl. jours. Served in USAAF, 1942-45. Decorated 4 battle stars; grantee Social Sci. Research Council, NIH, Am. Philos. Soc., Am. Council Learned Socs., NEH, others. Home and Office: 1106 6th St Las Vegas NM 87701-4311

RILEY, DOROTHY ELAINE, nursing executive; b. Boston, July 4; d. Daniel Thomas and Josephine Marie (Durken) Horgan; m. Timothy John Riley; children: Timothy John Jr., Christopher John, Shannon Marie. BS in Nursing, Boston Coll., 1966; MS in Nursing, U. Wis., Milw., 1977. Cert. advanced nursing adminstr. Staff nurse various hosps., 1969-75; dir. nursing Samaritan Home, West Bend, Wis., 1975-76; mem. nursing faculty Marquette U., Milw., 1977-79; asst. dir. nursing Outagamie County Health Care Ctr., Appleton, Wis., 1979-80; mem. nursing faculty U. Wis., Oshkosh, 1980-83; nursing svc. adminstr. Brown County Mental Health Ctr., Green Bay, Wis., 1983-88, nursing home adminstr., 1988-93; nursing home adminstrn. Washoe Care Ctr., Sparks, Nev., 1994; DON Nev. Mental Health Inst., Sparks, 1994—. Mem. NOW, LWV, Planned Parenthood, The Feminist Majority. Lt. Nurses Corps USN, 1966-69. Named Nurse of Yr., Appleton Dist. Nurses Assn., 1984. Mem. Wis. Nurses Assn. (bd. dirs. 1984-86, sec. 1986-88, pres. 1993—), Green Bay Nurses Assn. (bd. dirs. 1986-89, pres. 1990-92), Green Bay Dist. Nurses Assn. (Svc. award 1992), Nev. Nurses Assn., Sigma Theta Tau.

RILEY, ERIN LEE, biology educator, forensic scientist; b. Loveland, Colo., June 3, 1963; d. Merlin Blaine Jr. and Lynn Claudette (Hart) R. BS, Colo. State U., 1987; MS, U. Strathclyde, Glasgow, Scotland, 1988. Forensic DNA analysis researcher U.S. Army Criminal Investigation Lab.-Europe, Frankfurt, Fed. Republic of Germany, 1988; instr. biology Merced (Calif.) Coll., 1990; criminalist L.A. Police Dept. Scientific Investigation Div., L.A., 1990—; cons. U.S. Army Criminal Investigation-Europe, Frankfurt, 1988-89; DNA rsch. scientist FBI Acad., Quantico, Va., 1991-92; lectr. forensic serology/DNA analysis Calif. State U., L.A., 1997. Fellow Am. Bd. Criminalistics (cert. in criminalistics and molecular biology); mem. AAAS, Am. Acad. Forensic Scis., Forensic Sci. Soc., Internat. Soc. Forensic Scis., Internat. Soc. Haemogenetics, Internat. Assn. Identifications (mem. innovative and gen. techniques com. 1994-96), Calif. Assn. Criminalists, So. Calif. DNA Study Group (co-chmn. 1993—), Phi Theta Kappa.

RILEY, GRANNAN, performing company executive. Studied with Doreen gilday, Eugene, Oreg.; BFA, U.S. Internat. U., San Diego; postgrad., Academie des Grand Ballets Canadiens, Montreal. Co-founder Eugene (Oreg.) Ballet Co, 1978—, mng. dir., 1984—; mem. dance touring panel Western States Arts Found.; mem. selection panel Arts N.W., Individual Artist Fellowship, Oreg. and Idaho. Dancer (ballets) Petrushka, the Firebird, Coppelia, others, worldwide tours. Active outreach programs Young Audiences Oreg., Wash. State Cultural Enrichment Program. co-recipient Gov.'s Arts award, 1996. Office: Eugene Ballet Co PO Box 11200 Eugene OR 97440*

RILEY, JOHN ECKEL, retired academic administrator; b. Haverhill, Mass., Jan. 23, 1909; s. George Duncan and Mary Jane (Oliver) R.; m. Dorcas Mine Tarr, June 1, 1932; children: Jane Noel, Lynn Roberta, Gail Katherine. BA, Ea. Nazarene Coll., 1930, DD, 1950; MA, Boston U., 1931. Ordained Church of the Nazarene, 1933. Pastor Ch. of the Nazarene, Auburn, Maine, 1931-32, Livermore Falls, Maine, 1932-35, New Haven, 1935-38, South Portland, Maine, 1938-42, Toronto, Ont., 1942-44, Nampa, Idaho, 1944-52; faculty N.W. Nazarene Coll., Nampa, 1944-52, pres., 1952-73, pres. emeritus, 1973—; mem. higher commn. N.W. Assn. Secondary and Higher Schs., Seattle, 1954-60; mem. State Commn. on the Arts, Boise, Idaho, 1960-62; ednl. cons. Schs. and Colls. of the Dept. World Missions, Kansas City, Mo., 1973-82. Author: The Golden Stairs, 1947, This Holy Estate, 1957, From Sagebrush to Ivy: Story of NNC, 1988, R & R: Recollections and Reflections, 1992; co-author: The Wind Runs Free, 1981. Recipient Disting. Citizen's award Idaho Statesman, Boise. Mem. Nampa (Idaho) Athletic Club, Lions Club, Nampa (Idaho) Indsl. Corp., Nampa C. of C. (life mem.), Nampa Kiwanis Club (hon. mem.). Republican. Home: 207 Mountain View Dr Nampa ID 83686-8867

RILEY, LARRY WILLIAM, agency executive, insurance agent; b. Anaconda, Mont., May 5, 1953; s. Lawrence William and Mary Ann (Frankovich) R.; m. Colleen Mary McCarthy, Aug. 20, 1983; children: Katy Erin, Britni Nicole. Grad., Western Mont. Coll., 1977. Agy. mgr. Aetna Ins.; dir. agys. Farm Bur., St. Paul, Minn., 1993-95; agy. v.p. Farm Bur., Salt Lake City, 1995—. Home: 109 Country Club Dr Stansbury Park UT 84074 Office: Farm Bur Fin Svc 5300 S 360 W #210 Salt Lake City UT 84123-4600

RILEY, MARILYN GLEDHILL, communications executive; b. Pitts., Pa., July 17, 1954; d. John Edward and Mary Elizabeth (Ogden) Gledhill; m. John F. Riley Jr. AS with high honors, C.C. of Allegheny County, 1981; BS in Bus. Adminstrn. cum laude, Robert Morris Coll., 1985. With MODCOM Assocs., Pitts., 1977-79, asst. account exec., 1979-82, account exec., 1982-84; gen. mgr. MODCOM Advt., Pitts., 1984-90, v.p., gen. mgr., 1989-90; dir. comms. Allegheny County Med. Soc., Pitts., 1990-93; advt. mgr. Intergroup Healthcare Corp., Phoenix, Ariz., 1994; mgr. advt. and media rels. Health Ptnrs. Health Plans, Inc., Phoenix, 1995-97; mktg. svcs. mgr. Sun Health, Sun City, Ariz., 1997—; guest spkr. Pa. State U., Robert Morris Coll., Allegheny C.C., 1987; mem. pub. issues and info. com. adolescent resource network adv. bd. Hosp. Coun. of West Pa., 1990-93; counselor Small Bus. Devel. Ctr., 1995. Mem. editl. bd. Nursing News, 1991; editor: Valley of the Sun Gardener, 1994. Communications vol. North Hills Art Festival, McCandless, Pa., 1986-87; judge Jefferson (Pa.) Hosp. Poster Contest, 1987; bd. mgrs. YMCA North Boroughs; reading tutor Greater Pitts. Literacy Coun., 1988-89; bd. dirs. Rachel Carson Homestead Assn. Recipient Communications Mgmt. Honors award Robert Morris Coll. Mem. Bus. and Profl. Advt. Assn. (bd. dirs., v.p. edn.), North Hills C. of C., SMC Pa. Small Bus. Coun., Pitts. Advt. Club, Phoenix Advt. Club, Greater Phoenix Pond Soc. (co-founder), WebMaster Guild, Alpha Tau Sigma. Office: Sun Health 13101 N 103d Ave Sun City AZ 85372

RILEY, PETER CHRISTOPHER, aeronautics company official; b. Oak Park, Ill., May 12, 1958; s. Peter Eugene and Patrice Edith (Lindahl) R.; m. Kelley Kay Proctor, June 5, 1976 (div. Feb. 1978); m. Denise Marie Burkard, May 16, 1980; 1 child, Chance Robert. AAS in Flight Engring., C.C. of Air Force, 1993; BS in Workforce Edn., So. Ill. U., Carbondale, 1994, MS in Edn., 1995. Cert. tchr., Calif. Enlisted man USAF, 1978; flight engr. USAF, Ft. Walton Beach, Fla., 1978-88; resigned, 1988; instrnl. designer McDonnell Douglas, Aurora, Colo., 1988-92; multimedia dir., dir. multimedia prodn. Lockheed Martin Corp., Albuquerque, 1992-97; mem. instrnl. tech. adv. bd. Lockheed Martin Corp., Ft. Worth, 1995-96; asst. prof. Coll. Mass Comm. and Media Arts, So. Ill. U., Carbondale, 1997—; cons. Mediatech, Inc., Ormond Beach, Fla., 1992—; vis. instr. So. Ill. U., 1996—. Contbr. articles to profl. procs. Mem. Internat. Soc. for Performance Improvement (exec. bd. 1996—), Soc. for Applied Learning Tech., Interactive TV Assn. Republican. Roman Catholic. Home: 12024 Gazelle Pl NE Albuquerque NM 87111 Office: Lockheed Martin Corp 4250 Aberdeen Ave Albuquerque NM 87117

RILEY, RICHARD LEON, psychiatrist, consultant; b. Omak, Wash., Jan. 31, 1932; s. George Maurer and Lounettie Grace (Chapman) R.; m. Carol Ann Franklin (div. Dec. 1971); children: Kevin, Erin, Brian, Patrick, Michael; m. Renata Karolina Roeber, Dec. 28, 1972; 1 child, Alexandra Elizabeth. Student, El Camino Coll., 1954-56, U. Calif., L.A., 1956-57; BS in Medicine, Duke U., 1960; MD, U. So. Calif., L.A., 1961. Bd. cert. pediatrics; cert. psychiat. examiner, Calif. Pediatric intern L.A. (Calif.) Children's Hosp., 1961-62, pediatric resident, 1962-64, attending physician, 1964-69; pediatric cons. Gen. Hosp., Peace Corp. APIA, Western Samoa, 1969-70; child psychiatry fellowship Pasadena (Calif.) Guidance Clinic, 1971-73, clin. supr., 1973-75; med. dir., acting exec. dir. San Luis Valley Comp. Cmty. Mental Health Ctr., Alamosa, Colo., 1975-77; chief outpatient dept., cons. Humboldt County Dept. Mental Health, 1977-79; pvt. practice psychotherapy and pharmacotherapy, 1979-86; behavioral pediatrician U.S. Army Exceptional Family Member Program, Stuttgart, Germany, 1986-87; chief EFMP U.S. Army Exceptional Family Member Program, Shape, Belgium, 1987-88, evaluator William Beaumont Army Med. Ctr., 1988-91; cons. Indian Health Svc., Portland, 1991—; staff Kaiser-Permanente Med. Group, 1964-69, psychiatrist, supr., 1973-75; asst. clin. prof. pediatrics U. Calif., Irvine, 1967-69; pediatric cons. and lectr. Hope Ship Ceylon, Sri Lanka, 1968; presenter in field. Contbr. articles to profl. jours. With USN, 1950-54. Mem. Am. Psychiat. Assn., Am. Acad. Pediatrics, Am. Acad. Child and Adolescent psychiatry, Wash. State Psychiat. Soc. Home: 7132 W Greenwood Rd Spokane WA 99224-9160 Office: Indian Health Svc PO Box 357 Wellpinit WA 99040-0357

RILEY, WILLIAM L., lawyer; b. Bay Shore, N.Y., 1942. BA, Williams Coll., 1964; JD, Duke U., 1967. Bar: N.Y. 1967, Calif. 1970. Mem. Orrick, Herrington & Sutcliffe, San Francisco. Contbr. to profl. jours. Office: Orrick Herrington & Sutcliffe Fed Reserve Bank Bldg 400 Sansome St San Francisco CA 94111-3308

RIMEL, LINDA JUNE, writer; b. Seattle, June 4, 1952; d. Ira Wesley Rimel and Mary MacKinlay (Weir) R. BA in Gen. Humanities, U. Oreg., 1977; postgrad., Willamette U., 1977-79. English instr. U. Great Falls, Mont., 1988-90; asst. libr., acting libr. dir. Columbus Health Scis. Libr., Great Falls, 1990-92; writer, rschr., editor, tchr. Great Falls, 1979—. Exhibited quilts in Gallery 16, Great Falls, 1985; workshop instr. D.A. Davidson & Co., Great Falls, 1990; staff writer Merit System Index and Digest, 1979; author: Quicker Quilts, 1985, (play) Treasure This House, 1989; contbr. books revs., humor to profl. publs.; lyricist, librettist The Ms. Seattle Skyline Contest, 1990, Anybody but Liza, 1996; librettist Thumbelina, 1996. Costume builder, wardrobe mistress Eugene (Oreg.) Ballet, Eugene Opera, 1980-82; machine quilting instr. Paris Gibson Sq. Mus. of Art, Great Falls, 1984-86; tutor Native Am. Program, Great Falls, 1987-89; pubicity chair Cascade County chpt. '89ers Mont. Statehood Centennial, 1988; program annotator, performer mus. theater U. Great Falls, 1992-93; active Urgent Action Network of Amnesty Internat., 1987—. Mem. Dramatists Guild, Falls Quilt Guild (bd. dirs., program chair 1992-94, publicity chair 1992-93). Home: 104 16th St North Great Falls MT 59401

RIMOIN, DAVID LAWRENCE, physician, geneticist; b. Montreal, Nov. 9, 1936; s. Michael and Fay (Lecker) R.; m. Mary Ann Singleton, 1962 (div. 1979); 1 child, Anne; m. Ann Pilani Garber, July 27, 1980; children: Michael, Lauren. BSc, McGill U., Montreal, 1957, MSc, MD, CM, 1961; PhD, Johns Hopkins U., 1967. Asst. prof. medicine, pediatrics Washington U., St. Louis, 1967-70; assoc. prof. medicine, pediatrics UCLA, 1970-73, prof., 1973—, chief med. genetics, Harbor-UCLA Med. Ctr., 1970-86; dir. dept. pediatrics, dir. Med. Genetics and Birth Defects Ctr., 1986—; Steven Spielberg chmn. pediatrics Cedars-Sinai Med. Ctr., L.A., 1989—; chmn. coun. Med. Genetics Orgn., 1993. Co-author: Principles and Practice of Medical Genetics, 1983, 90, 96; contbr. articles to profl. jours., chpts. to books. Recipient Ross Outstanding Young Investigator award Western Soc. Pediatric Research, 1976, E. Mead Johnson award Am. Acad. Pediatrics, 1976, Col. Harland Saunders award March of Dimes, 1997. Fellow ACP, AAAS, Am. Coll. Med. Genetics (pres. 1991—); mem. Am. Fedn. Clin. Rsch. (sec.-treas. 1972-75), Western Soc. Clin. Rsch. (pres. 1978), Western Soc. Pediatric Rsch. (pres. 1995), Am. Bd. Med. Genetics (pres. 1979-83), Am. Soc. Human Genetics (pres. 1984), Am. Pediatric Soc., Soc. Pediatric Rsch., Am. Soc. Clin. Investigation, Assn. Am. Physicians, Johns Hopkins Soc. Scholars, Inst. Medicine. Office: Cedars-Sinai Med Ctr 8700 Beverly Blvd Los Angeles CA 90048-1804

RIMSZA, SKIP, mayor; b. Chgo.; m. Kim Gill; children: Brian, Jenny, Alexander, Taylor, Nicole. Mem. Phoenix City Coun., 1990-94; vice mayor City of Phoenix, 1993, mayor, 1994—; former pres. Bd. Realtors. Mem. several cmty. bds. Office: Office of the Mayor 200 W Washington St Phoenix AZ 85003-1611

RINEHART, CHARLES R., savings and loan association executive; b. San Francisco, Jan. 31, 1947; s. Robert Eugene and Rita Mary Rinehart; married; children: Joseph B., Kimberly D., Michael P., Scott. BS, U. San Francisco, 1968. Exec. v.p. Fireman's Fund Ins. Cos., Novato, Calif., 1969-83; pres., CEO Avco Fin. Services, Irvine, Calif., 1983-89, H.F. Ahmanson & Co., Irwindale, Calif., 1989—; chmn., CEO Home Savs. of Am., Irwindale; mem. Fannie Mae Nat. Adv. Coun., Thrift Instn. Adv. Coun.; bd. dirs. Fed. Home Loan Bank San Francisco, L.A. Bus. Advisors, Kaufman and Broad Home Corp. Mem. adv. com. Drug Use is Life Abuse; mem. Tustin Pub. Sch. Found. Camp com. Served to 2d lt. U.S. Army, 1968-69. Fellow Casualty Actuarial Soc.; mem. Am. Mgmt. Assn., Am. Acad. Actuaries. Republican. Roman Catholic. Office: Ho Savs Am/H F Ahmanson & Co 4900 Rivergrade Rd Irwindale CA 91706-1404

RINEY, HAL PATRICK, advertising executive; b. Seattle, July 17, 1932; s. Hal Patrick and Inez Marie R.; m. Elizabeth Kennedy; children: Benjamin Kennedy, Samantha Elizabeth. BA, U. Wash., Seattle, 1954. From art dir./writer to v.p., creative dir. BBDO, Inc., San Francisco, 1956-72; exec. v.p., creative dir. Botsford Ketchum, San Francisco, 1972-76; sr. v.p., mng. dir., creative dir. Ogilvy & Mather, San Francisco, 1976-81; exec. v.p. Ogilvy & Mather West, 1981-86; chmn. Hal Riney & Ptnrs., Inc., San Francisco, 1986—. Recipient 5 Lion d'Or du Cannes awards, 17 Clio awards, 15 Addy awards, Grand Prix du Cannes; named to Creative Hall of Fame. Mem. Am. Assn. Advt. Agys., San Francisco Advt. Club, San Francisco Soc. Communicating Arts, Wild Goose Club, Meadow Club, St. Francis Yacht Club. Home: 1 Los Pinos Nicasio CA 94946-9701 Office: Hal Riney & Ptnrs Inc 735 Battery St San Francisco CA 94111-1501*

RINGEL, STEVEN PETER, neurology educator; b. Hamilton, Ohio, Feb. 17, 1943; s. Edward and Hedy (Fried) R.; m. Joan Deutsch, May 29, 1969; children: Andrew, Timothy. MD, U. Mich., 1968. Diplomate Am. Bd. Neurology and Psychiatry. Intern in medicine Rush Presbyn. St. Luke's Hosp., Chgo., 1968-69, resident in neurology, 1969-72; rsch. fellow NIH, NINDS, Bethesda, Md., 1974-76; from asst. to prof. U. Colo., Denver, 1976—; vis. prof. U. Padua, Italy, 1983; dir. Office of Clin. Practice, U. Hosp., Denver, 1994—. Author 4 books; contbr. over 240 articles to profl. jours. Maj. U.S. Army Med. Corps, 1972-74. Robert Wood Johnson Health Policy fellow U.S. Senate, 1991-92; resident scholar Inst. Medicine, 1991-92; recipient Postdoctoral Rsch. fellowship NIH, 1974-76, Rsch. fellowship NATO, 1982-84. Mem. Am. Acad. Neurology (treas. 1989-91, pres. 1997—).

RINGLER, JEROME LAWRENCE, lawyer; b. Detroit, Dec. 26, 1948. BA, Mich. State U., 1970; JD, U. San Francisco, 1974. Bar: Calif. 1974, U.S. Ct. Appeals (9th cir.) 1974, U.S. Dist. Ct. (no. dist.) Calif. 1974, U.S. Dist. Ct. (ctrl. dist.) Calif. 1975, U.S. Dist. Ct. (so. dist.) Calif. 1981. Assoc. Parker, Stansbury et al, L.A., 1974-76; assoc. Fogel, Feldman, Ostrov, Ringler & Klevens, Santa Monica, Calif., 1976-80, ptnr., 1980—; arbitrator L.A. Superior Ct. Arbitration Program, 1980-85. Named O'Brien's Evaluator 1996 Trial Lawyer of the Yr. Mem. ATLA, ABA, State Bar Calif., L.A. County Bar Assn. (litigation sect., exec. com. 1994—), L.A. Trial Lawyers Assn. (bd. govs. 1981—, treas. 1988, sec. 1989, v.p. 1990, pres.-elect 1991, pres. 1992, Trial Lawyer of the Yr. 1987), Calif. Trial Lawyers Assn., Am. Bd. Trial Advs. (assoc. 1988, adv. 1991), Inns of Ct. (master). Office: Fogel Feldman Ostrov et al 1620 26th St #100 S Santa Monica CA 90404-4040

RINGLER, ROBERT LLOYD, JR., family practice physician, naval officer; b. Raleigh, N.C., Feb. 1, 1957; s. Robert Lloyd and Virginia Marie (Morrow) R.; m. Marie Celeste Crom, Aug. 18, 1979; children: Kimberly Heather, Kristin Nicole, Thomas Robert, Alana Danielle. AB in Chemistry, Duke U., 1978; MD, Uniformed Svcs. U. Health Sci., 1982. Commd. ensign USN, advanced through grades to comdr., 1993; family practice intern Naval Hosp., Charleston, S.C., 1982-83, family practice resident, 1983-85; family practice staff physician, quality assurance physician advisor Naval Hosp., Newport, R.I., 1985-88; asst. dept. head family practice, chair pharmacy and therapeutics com. Naval Hosp., Agana, Guam, 1988-90; family practice teaching staff Naval Hosp., Bremerton, Wash., 1990-93; sr. med. officer USN Support Facility, Diego Garcia, British Indian Ocean Territory, 1993-94; family practice teaching staff Naval Hosp., Bremerton, Wash., 1994—; asst. program dir. Puget Sound Family Medicine Residency, 1996. Lector, lay eucharistic min. Navy Base Chapel, Newport, 1986-88, Agana, 1988-90, Diego Garcia, British Indian Ocean Territory, 1993-94, Naval Hosp. Chapel, Brenerton, 1994—. Mem. AMA, Assn. Mil. Surgeons U.S., Am. Acad. Family Physicians, Uniformed Svcs. Acad. Family Physicians (bd. dirs. 1990-93, chair membership and svcs. com. 1991-93, 95-96), Am. Soc. Colposcopists and Cervical Pathologists. Roman Catholic. Office: Naval Hosp Code 035 Boone Rd Bremerton WA 98312-1898

RINGWALD, LYDIA ELAINE, artist, poet; b. L.A., Oct. 8, 1949; d. Siegfried Carl Ringwald and Eva M. (Macksoud) Mack; m. Hal von Hofe, July 31, 1972 (div. 1978). BA, Scripps Coll., 1970; student, Ruprecht-Karl Univ., Heidelberg, Germany, 1971; MA in Comparative Lit., U. Calif., Irvine, 1972; studied with William Bailey, Yale Art Sch., 1972-74; postgrad., U. Conn., 1976. Instr. English and German Cerritos (Calif.) Coll., 1975-83; instr. German Golden West Coll., Huntington Beach, Calif., 1976-83; instr. English Saddleback Coll., Mission Viejo, Calif., 1976-81, Long Beach (Calif.) City Coll., 1976-83; curator exhbns. Cultural Affairs Satellite Dept., L.A., 1994; cons., lectr. in field. Solo exhbns. include Great Western Bank, 1989, Atlantis Gallery, 1992, L.A. Pub. Libr., Sherman Oaks, Calif., 1993, Sumitomo Bank, 1993, Phoenix Gallery, 1994; group exhbns. include Long Beach (Calif.) Arts, 1988-89, Installations One, 1989, 90, Heidelberger Kunstverein, Heidelberg, Germany, 1990, Barbara Mendes Gallery, L.A., 1991, Folktree Gallery, 1991-92, Armand Hammer Mus., 1992, Jansen-Perez Gallery, L.A., 1993; author: Blessings in Disguise: Life is a Gift; Accept it with Both Hands, 1990, Blau: Kaleidescope einer Farbe, 1992. Mem. Internat. Friends Transformative Arts, Humanistic Arts Alliance, Nat. Mus. Women in Arts, L.A. Mcpl. Art Gallery, Mus. Contemporary Art, L.A. County Mus., U. Calif. Irvine Alumni Assn., Scripps Coll. Alumni Assn., Inst. Noetic Scis., Philosophical Rsch. Soc. Home and Office: Creative Realities 2801 Coldwater Canyon Dr Beverly Hills CA 90210-1305

RINSCH, CHARLES EMIL, insurance company executive; b. Vincennes, Ind., June 28, 1932; s. Emil and Vera Pearl (White) R.; m. Maryann Elizabeth Hitchcock, June 18, 1964; children: Christopher, Daniel, Carl. BS in Stats., Ind. U., 1953; MS in Bus., Butler U., 1959; MBA, Stanford U., 1960. Budget analyst Chrysler Corp., Indpls., 1955-57; sr. fin. analyst Ford Motor Co., Indpls., 1957-59; budget dir. Nat. Forge Co., Warren, Pa., 1960-61; div. controller and asst. to v.p., fin. Norris Industries, L.A., 1961-65; v.p., treas., sec. Teledyne Inc, L.A., 1965-88; pres., chief exec. officer Argonaut Group Inc., L.A., 1988—. Cubmaster Pack 721, Boy Scouts Am., L.A., 1987-88, treas. 1981-87; mem. dean's adv. coun. Ind. U. Sch. Bus. 1st lt. U.S. Army, 1953-55. Mem. Acad. Alumni Fellows Ind. U. Sch. Bus., L.A. Treas.'s Club. Home: 19849 Greenbriar Dr Tarzana CA 91356-5428

Office: Argonaut Group Inc Ste 1175 1800 Avenue Of The Stars Los Angeles CA 90067-4213

RINSCH, MARYANN ELIZABETH, occupational therapist; b. L.A., Aug. 8, 1939; d. Harry William and Thora Analine (Langlie) Hitchcock; m. Charles Emil Rinsch, June 18, 1964; children: Christopher, Daniel, Carl. BS, U. Minn., 1961. Registered occupational therapist, Calif. Staff occupational therapist Hastings (Minn.) State Hosp., 1961-62, Neuropsychiat. Inst., L.A., 1962-64; staff and sr. occupational therapist Calif. Children's Svcs., L.A., 1964-66, head occupational therapist, 1966-68; researcher A. Jean Ayres, U. So. Calif., L.A., 1968-69; pvt. practice neurodevel. and sensory integraton Tarzana, Calif., 1969-74; pediat. occupational therapist neurodevel. & sensory integration St. Johns Hosp., Santa Monica, Calif., 1991-95; pvt. practice, cons. Santa Monica-Malibu Unified Sch. Dist., 1994—. Mem. alliance bd. Natural History Mus., L.A. County, 1983—; cub scouts den mother Boy Souts Am., Sherman Oaks, Calif., 1986-88, advancement chair Boy Scout Troop 474, 1989-92; mem. vol. League San Fernando Valley, Van Nuys, Calif., 1985-93; trustee Viewpoint Sch., Calabasas, Calif., 1987-90, Valley Women's Ctr., 1990-91. Mem. Am. Occupational Therapy Assn., Calif. Occupational Therapy Assn. Home: 19849 Greenbriar Dr Tarzana CA 91356-5428

RINSKY, ARTHUR C., lawyer; b. Cin., July 10, 1944. AB with honors, U. Cin., 1966; JD cum laude, U. Mich., 1969; LLM in Taxation, NYU, 1974. Bar: Fla. 1969, Calif. 1975, U.S. Tax Ct. 1974; cert. tax specialist. Atty. Gray, Cary, Ware & Freidenrich, P.C., Palo Alto, Calif. Mem. ABA, State Bar Calif., Phi Beta Kappa, Phi Eta Sigma. Office: Gray Cary Ware & FreidenrichPC 400 Hamilton Ave Palo Alto CA 94301-1809

RIORDAN, GEORGE NICKERSON, investment banker; b. Patchogue, N.Y., May 16, 1933; s. E. Arthur and Constance E. (Whelden) R.; m. Ann Wiggins, Jan. 4, 1958; children—Susan M., Peter G. B.S., Cornell U., 1955; M.B.A., Harvard U., 1960. Vice-pres. Lehman Bros., N.Y.C., 1960-71; mng. dir. Blyth Eastman Paine Webber, Los Angeles and N.Y.C., 1971-81, Prudential-Bache Securities, Los Angeles, 1981-88, Bear Stearns & Co., Inc., L.A., 1988-89, Dean Witter Reynolds Inc., 1989-91; bd. dirs. MacNeal Schwnedler Corp., L.A., chmn. bd. 1997—; bd. dirs. Pancho's Mexican Buffet, Inc., Ft. Worth. Served to capt. USAF, 1955-57. Mem. Calif. Club, Quoque Field Club (L.I., N.Y.), Athenaeum Club, Valley Hunt Club (Pasadena, Calif.). Office: Ste 104 815 Colorado Blvd Los Angeles CA 90041

RIORDAN, MICHAEL, author, scientist; b. Springfield, Mass., Dec. 3, 1946; s. Edward John and Evelyn Anna (Hnizdo) R.; m. Linda Michele Goodman, Apr. 10, 1979 (div. Aug. 1988); m. Sandra Lee Foster, Sept. 10, 1988 (div. July 1990). BS in Physics, MIT, 1968, PhD in Physics, 1973. Rsch. assoc. MIT, Cambridge, Mass., 1973-75; editor, publisher Cheshire Books, Inc., Palo Alto, Calif., 1976-85; rsch. scientist U. Rochester, N.Y., 1985-87; sci. info. officer Stanford (Calif.) Linear Accelerator Ctr., 1988-90, asst. to dir., 1992—; asst. to pres. and staff scientist Univs. Rsch. Assn., Inc., Washington, 1990-91; rsch. physicist U. Calif., Santa Cruz, 1995—; treas., dir. Contemporary Physics Edn. Project, Inc., Portola Valley, Calif., 1991-94. Author: The Hunting of the Quark, 1987 (Sci. Writing award Am. Inst. Physics 1988); co-author: The Solar Home Book, 1977, The Shadows of Creation, 1991, Crystal Fire, 1997; editor: The Day After Midnight, 1982. Treas., v.p. Cuesta La Honda (Calif.) Guild, 1986, 87. Mem. Am. Phys. Soc., Nat. Assn. Sci. Writers. Democrat. Home: 4532 Cherryvale Ave Soquel CA 95073-9748 Office: Stanford Linear Accelerator Mail Stop 80 Stanford CA 94309

RIORDAN, RICHARD J., mayor; b. Flushing, N.Y., 1930; m. Eugenia Riordan; 6 children (2 dec.); m. Jill Riordan. Attended, U. Calif., Santa Clara; grad., Princeton U., 1952; JD, U. Mich., 1956. With O'Melveny & Myers, L.A.; owner, operator Original Pantry Cafe; founder Total Pharmaceutical Care, Tetra Tech; mayor L.A., 1993—. Co-founder LEARN, 1991; sponsor Writing to Read computer labs Riordan Found.; active Eastside Boys and Girls Club. Lt. U.S. Army, Korea. Office: Los Angeles City Hall 200 N Spring St Rm 305 Los Angeles CA 90012-4801*

RIPLEY, ROBERT ELLIOTT, author, psychologist, training film producer; b. Mpls., Aug. 2, 1930; s. Richard Rolland Elliott and Irma May (Strait) Hanson; m. Lois Johanna Colbiornsen, Oct. 10, 1953 (div. 1968); children: Robert Vincent, Richard Allen, Erika Louise; m. Marie June Schert, Dec. 7, 1968; children: Briana May, Rodrick Elliott. BA, U. Minn., 1957, BS, 1967; M.A., Ariz. State U, 1968-69; PhD, U. Minn., 1967. Cert. psychologist, Minn., S.D., Iowa, Ariz. Stockbroker IDS, Houston, 1958-59; grad. rsch. asst. U. Minn., Mpls., 1959-61, instr., 1965-67; prof. No. State Coll., Aberdeen, S.D., 1961-62, Iowa State U., Ames, 1962-65, Ariz. State U., Tempe, 1967-79; mgmt. trainer, cons. Behavior Tech. Inst., Scottsdale, Ariz., 1979-84; stockbroker, fin. planner Raymond-James, Boca Raton, Fla., 1984-88; freelance author, cons. Carefree, Ariz., 1988—; cons. U.S. Labor Dept., Washington, 1969-72, U.S. Dept. Edn., Washington, 1970-73, cons. dept. Navy-TQC tng., 1996—, Tng. Film Prodn., 1992—, TV. radio personality, 1995—; sr. mgmt. cons., trainer Motorola, Honeywell, 1974-85,. Author: Manage it All! Yourself, Your Company and Others, 1989, Your Child's Age and Stages, 1994, Training your Child to Succeed as an Adult, 1996, Understanding and Training Adults, 1997, Woman Power, 1997; contbr. articles to numerous publs.U. Sgt. USAF, 1949-55, Europe. Named Outstanding Man of Phoenix, City of Phoenix, 1973. Mem. ACA (life), Assn. Counselor Educators and Suprs. (life), Iowa Pers. and Guidance Assn. (life), Brit. Literati Club. Republican. Home: PO Box 6105 Carefree AZ 85377-6105

RIPLEY, STUART MCKINNON, real estate consultant; b. St. Louis, July 28, 1930; s. Rob Roy and Nina Pearl (Young) R.; B.A., U. Redlands, 1952; M.B.A., U. Calif., Berkeley, 1959; m. Marilyn Haerr MacDiarmid, Dec. 28, 1964; children—Jill, Bruce, Kent. Vice pres., dir. J.H. Hedrick & Co., Santa Barbara and San Diego, 1958-63; v.p. mktg. Cavanaugh Devel. Co., San Gabriel, Calif., 1963-65; v.p. mktg. dir. Calabasas Park, Bechtel Corp., Calabasas, Calif., 1967-69; v.p. mktg. Avco Community Developers, Inc., La Jolla, Calif., 1969-74; mktg. dir. U.S. Home Corp., Fla. Div., Clearwater, 1974-75; pres., dir. Howard's Camper Country, Inc., National City, Calif., 1975-77; v.p., mktg. dir. Valcas Internat. Corp., San Diego, 1976-77, pres., 1977-79; pres. Stuart M. Ripley, Inc., 1977—, Sunview Realty, Inc., a Watt Industries Co., Santa Monica, Calif., 1979-80; owner Everett Stunz Co., Ltd., La Jolla, 1981—; exec. v.p. Harriman-Ripley Co., Fallbrook, Calif.; avocado/floraculture rancher, subdivider, Fallbrook, 1978—; lectr. UCLA, 1961; pres. Century 21 Coastal, Century 21 Bajamar, Baja California, Mex., 1994—. Served with USN, 1952-55. U. Redlands fellow, 1960—. Mem. Nat. Assn. Homebuilders, Sales and Mktg. Council, Sales and Mktg. Execs., Pi Chi. Republican. Episcopalian. Club: Elks. Home: 13180 Portofino Dr Del Mar CA 92014-3828 Office: 7624 Girard Ave La Jolla CA 92037-4420

RIPPE, LYNN E., contract administrator; b. Superior, Nebr., Dec. 27, 1947; children: Douglas E., Christopher C. BA in Econs., Kansas State U., 1969; MBA, So. Ill. U., Edwardsville, 1977. Contract specialist, contracting officer Naval Constrn. Battalion Ctr., Port Hueneme, Calif., 1989-93; sr. contract adminstr. U. Calif. Lawrence Livermore (Calif.) Nat. Lab., 1993—. Mem. Nat. Contract Mgmt. Assn. (v.p. Tri Valley chpt. 1995-96, pres. 1996—). Republican. Roman Catholic. Home: PO Box 5142 Modesto CA 95352 Office: U Calif Lawrence Livermore Nat Lab L-650 PO Box 5012 Livermore CA 94551

RIPPER, RITA JO (JODY RIPPER), strategic planner, researcher; b. Goldfield, Iowa, May 8, 1950; d. Carl Phillip and Lucille Mae (Stewart) Ripper; BA, U. Iowa, 1972; MBA, NYU, 1978. Contracts and fin. staff Control Data Corp., Mpls., 1974-78; regional mgr. Raytheon Corp., Irvine, Calif., 1978-83; v.p. Caljo Corp., Des Moines, Iowa, 1980-84; asst. v.p. Bank of Am., San Francisco, 1984-88; pres. The Northhaven Co., 1988—, The Boardroom Adv. Group, 1990-93. Am. United; vol. Cancer, Heart, Lung Assns., Edina, N.Y.C., Calif., 1974-78, 84—. Mem. Amnesty Internat., Internat. Mktg. Assn., World Trade Ctr. Assn., Acctg. Soc. (pres. 1975-76), World Trade Club, Intertel, Mensa, Beta Alpha Psi (chmn. 1977-78), Phi Gamma Nu (v.p. 1971-72) Presbyterian. Club: Corinthian Yacht. Home and Office: 1730 Marguerite Ave Corona Del Mar CA 92625-1121

RIPPLE, WILLIAM JOHN, forestry researcher, educator; b. Yankton, S.D., Mar. 10, 1952; s. John Franklin and Margaret (Sondergroth) R. BS, S.D. State U., 1974; MS, U. Idaho, 1978; PhD, Oreg. State U., 1984. Geographer S.D. State Planning Bur., Pierre, 1977-81; rsch. assoc. Oreg. State U., Corvallis, 1984-88; asst. prof. Forest Resources Dept. Oreg. State U., Corvallis, 1988-92; assoc. prof. forest resources dept. Oreg. State U., Corvallis, 1992—; dir. Environ. Remote Sensing Applications Lab. Oreg. State U., Corvallis, 1988—; cons. U.S. GAO, Washington, 1989. Editor: GIS for Resource Management, 1987, Fundamentals of GIS, 1989, The GIS Applications Book, 1994; contbr. articles to profl. jour. Active Corvallis Folklore Soc., treas., 1988-91. Fellow Am. Soc. for Photogrammetry and Remote Sensing (Presdl. Citation for Meritorious Svc. 1987, 88, 90), Columbia River Region (treas. 1987-88, v.p. 1988-89, pres. 1989-90). Home: 1228 NW Dixon St Corvallis OR 97330-4645 Office: Oreg State U Dept Forest Resources Corvallis OR 97331

RIPPON, THOMAS MICHAEL, art educator, artist; b. Sacramento, Apr. 1, 1954; s. Samuel Joseph Jr. and June Evelyn (Garnet) R.; m. Sarah Sterrett, Dec. 22, 1980; children: Adam Michael, Peter Thomas. MFA, Art Inst. Chgo., 1979. Instr. Columbia Coll., Chgo., 1978-79; asst. prof. Montana State U., Bozeman, 1980, Calif. State U., Sacramento, 1981; assoc. prof. Tenn. Tech. U., Cookeville, 1982-87; asst. prof. U. Nev., Reno, 1987-89; assoc. prof. U. Montana, Missoula, 1989—, chair dept. art, 1990—; artist in residence U. Nevada, Reno, 1988; vis. prof. U. Calif., Davis, 1989; lectr. in field, 1973—. Solo exhbns. include Quay Gallery, San Francisco, 1975, 77, 81, 85, Rochester (Minn.) Art Ctr., 1979, Betsy Rosenfield Gallery, Chgo., 1980, 82, 84, Drake U., Des Moine, Iowa, 1985, Cross Creek Gallery, Malibu, Calif., 1987, 88, Judith Weintraub Gallery, Sacramento, 1990, 91, Huntington (W.Va.) Mus. Art, 1991, Kohler Art Ctr., Sheboygan, Wis., 1992, Yellowstone Art Ctr., Billings, Mont., 1993, Missoula Mus. Arts, 1994, Holter Mus. Art, Helena, Mont., 1995, John Natsovlas Gallery, 1995, 97, others; group exhbns. include San Francisco Mus. Modern Art, 1972, Davis (Calif.) Art Ctr., 1973, Oakland Mus., 1974, Evanston (Ill.) Art Ctr., 1974, Fendrick Gallery, Washington, 1975, Campbell Mus., Camden, N.J., 1976, Montana State U., Bozeman, 1976, De Young Mus., San Francisco, 1978, Am. Craft Mus., N.Y.C., 1978, 81, Phila. Mus. Modern Art, 1980, Craft and Folk Mus., L.A., 1980, Indpls. Mus. Art, 1982, Impressions Today Gallery, Boston, 1982, Elements Gallery, N.Y.C., 1983, Tampa (Fla.) Mus., 1983, Hyde Park Art Ctr., Chgo., 1983, 85, Traver-Sutton Gallery, Seattle, 1984, Erie (Pa.) Art Mus., 1985, Fay Gold Gallery, Atlanta, 1986, Seattle Art Mus., 1987, Candy Store Art Gallery, Folsom, Calif., 1987, Crocker Art Mus., Sacramento, 1988, Lang Gallery Scripps Coll., Claremont, Calif., 1988, Sherley Koteen & Assoc., Washington, 1989, 90, Eve Mannes Gallery, Atlanta, 1989, Art Gallery Western Australia, 1989, Joanne Rapp Gallery, Scottsdale, 1990, Missoula Mus. of Arts, 1991, 92, Sutton West Gallery, Missoula, 1992, Yellowstone Art Ctr., 1992, Natsoulas Gallery, Davis, Calif., 1993, many others; represented in pvt. collections; pub. collections include San Francisco Mus. Art, L.A. County Mus. Art, Sheldon Meml. Collection U. Nebr., Mus. Fine Arts, Salt Lake City, Ch. Fine Arts Collection U. Nev., Reno, Kanzawa-Shi, Hokkoku Shinbun, Kyoto, Japan, Renwick Gallery Smithsonian Institution, Contemporary Art Mus., Honolulu, J.B. Speed Art Mus., Louisville, Ky., U. Iowa, Ames, Missoula Mus. Arts, others. Recipient Kingsley Art Club award Crocker Art Mus., Sacramento, 1971, Crocker-Kingsley award, 1972; NEA fellow, 1974, 81, Nelson Raymond fellow Art Inst. Chgo., 1979. Office: Univ of Montana Dept Of Art Missoula MT 59812

RIRIE, CRAIG MARTIN, periodontist; b. Lewiston, Utah, Apr. 17, 1943; s. Martin Clarence and VaLera (Dixon) R.; m. Becky Ann Ririe, Sept. 17, 1982; children: Paige, Seth, Theron, Kendall, Nathan, Derek, Brian, Amber, Kristen. AA, San Bernadino Valley Coll., 1966; DDS, Creighton U., 1972; MSD, Loma Linda U., 1978. Staff mem. Flagstaff (Ariz.) Med. Ctr., 1974—; pvt. practice dentistry specializing in periodontics Flagstaff, 1974—; assoc. prof. periodontics No. Ariz. U., Flagstaff, 1979—, chmn. dept. dental hygiene, 1980-81; med. research cons. W.L. Gore, Flagstaff, 1983—. Contbr. articles to profl. jours. Vice pres. bd. dirs. Grand Canyon coun. Boy Scouts Am., 1991—. Lt. col. USAFR. Health professions scholarship Creighton U., Omaha, 1969-71; recipient Mosby award Mosby Pub. Co., 1972; research fellowship U. Bergen, Norway, 1978-79. Mem. ADA, Am. Acad. Periodontology (cert.), Western Soc. Periodontology (chmn. com. on rsch. 1982—, bd. dirs. 1983—), No. Ariz. Dental Soc. (pres. 1994-96), Am. Acad. Oral Implantologists, Internat. Congress Oral Implantologists, Ariz. Dental Assn., Am. Cancer Soc. (bd. dirs.), Flagstaff C. of C., Rotary. Republican. Mem. LDS Ch. Home: 1320 N Aztec St Flagstaff AZ 86001-3004 Office: 1050 N San Francisco St Flagstaff AZ 86001-3259

RISBECK, PHILIP EDWARD, graphic designer; b. Kansas City, Mo., July 25, 1939; s. Clair O. and Lillian T. (Reverger) R.; m. Marie Vescial, Mar. 14, 1970; 1 child, Heather Lynn. BFA, U. Kans., 1961, MFA, 1965. Prof. graphic design Colo. State U., Ft. Collins, 1965—; chmn. dept Art Colo. State U., 1993—. Exhibited in group shows in U.S. (50 poster awards including Bronze medal Czechoslova Exhibition 1982); one-man shows include, Moscow, Paris, Oporto, Kiev. Co-dir. Colo. Internat. Poster Exhibition Biennale, Ft. Collins, 1979-90. Mem. Art Dirs. Club Denver (pres. 1982-83, bd. dirs. 1983-87). Home: 3521 Canadian Pky Fort Collins CO 80524-1368 Office: Colo State U Dept Art Fort Collins CO 80523

RISCH, JAMES E., lawyer; b. Milw., May 3, 1943; s. Elroy A. and Helen B. (Levi) R.; m. Vicki L. Choborda, June 8, 1968; children—James E., Jason S., Jordan D. B.S. in Forestry, U. Idaho, 1965, J.D., 1968. Dep. pros. atty. Ada County, Idaho, 1968-69, chief dep. pros. atty., 1969-70, pros. atty., 1971-75; mem. Idaho Senate, 1974-88, 95—, majority leader, 1977-82, 97—, pres. pro tem, 1983-88, asst. majority leader, 1996; ptnr. Risch Goss & Insinger, Boise, Idaho, 1975—; prof. law Boise State U., 1972-75. Chmn. George Bush Presdl. Campaign, Idaho, 1988; mem. Gen. Coun. Idaho Rep. Party, 1991-95. Mem. ABA, Idaho Bar Assn., Boise Bar Assn., Am. Judicature Soc., Nat. Dist. Attys. Assn. (bd. dirs. 1977), Idaho Pros. Attys. Assn. (pres. 1976), Ducks Unlimited, Nat. Rifle Assn., Nat. Cattlemans Assn., Idaho Cattlemans Assn., Am. Angus Assn., Idaho Angus Assn., Am. Legis. Exch. Coun., Boise Valley Angus Assn., Phi Delta Theta, Xi Sigma Pi. Republican. Roman Catholic. Home: 5400 S Cole Rd Boise ID 83709-6401 Office: Risch Goss & Insinger 407 W Jefferson St Boise ID 83702-6049

RISEBROUGH, DOUG, professional hockey team executive; b. 1954; m. Marilyn Risenbrough; children: Allison, Lindsay. Former player Montreal (Que.) Canadiens, for 8 years; former player Calgary (Alta., Can.) Flames, for 5 years, former asst. coach, 1987-89, asst. gen. mgr., 1989-90, head coach, 1990-92; General Manager Calgary (Alt., Can.) Flames, 1992—. Office: Calgary Flames, PO Box 1540 Sta M, Calgary, AB Canada T2P 3B9*

RISIN, JACK See BUTCHER, JACK ROBERT

RISING, CATHARINE CLARKE, author; b. Berkeley, Calif., Jan. 7, 1929; d. Philip Seymour and Helen Katharine (Davis) Clarke; m. Boardman Rising, Sept. 16, 1950. BS, U. Calif., Berkeley, 1950, PhD, 1987; MA, San Francisco State U., 1979. Cert. cmty. coll. instr., Calif. Author: Darkness at Heart: Fathers and Sons in Conrad, 1990; contbr. articles to profl. jours. Mem. MLA, Joseph Conrad Soc. Am., Phi Beta Kappa.

RISLEY, TODD ROBERT, psychologist, educator; b. Palmer, Alaska, Sept. 8, 1937; s. Robert and Eva Lou (Todd) R.; 1 child, Todd Michael. A.B. with distinction in Psychology, San Diego State Coll., 1960; M.S., U. Wash., 1963, Ph.D., 1966. Asst. prof. psychology Fla. State U., Tallahassee, 1964-65; research assoc. Bur. Child Research, U. Kans., Lawrence, 1965-77, sr. scientist, 1977—, asst. prof. dept. human devel., 1967-69, assoc. prof., 1969-73, prof., 1973-84; prof. psychology U. Alaska, Anchorage, 1982—; pres. Ctr. for Applied Behavior Analysis, 1970-82; dir. Johnny Cake Child Study Ctr., Mansfield, Ark., 1973-74; vis. prof. U. Auckland (N.Z.), 1978; acting dir. Western Carolina Ctr., Morgantown, N.C., 1981; dir. Alaska Div. Mental Health and Devel. Disabilities, 1988-91; cons. in field to numerous orgns. and instns. Co-author: The Infant Center, 1977, Shopping with Children: Advice for parents, 1978, The Toddler Center, 1979, Meaningful Differences, 1995; editor: Jour. Applied Behavior Analysis, 1971-74; mng. editor: Behavior Therapy, The Behavior Therapist, Behavioral Asessment, 1977-80; mem. editl. bds. of numerous profl. jours.; contbr. revs. and numerous articles. Co-chmn. Fla. task force on use of behavioral procedures in state programs for retarded, 1974—; mem. resident abuse investigating com. div. retardation Fla. Dept. Health and Rehab. Services, 1972—; mem. adv. com. Social Research Inst., U. Utah, 1977—; mem. Alaska Gov.'s Council on Handicapped and Gifted, 1983-88, NIH Mental Retardation Research Com., 1987-88, Alaska Mental Health Bd., 1988. Grantee NIMH, 1971-72, 72-73; research grantee Nat. Ctr. Health Services, 1976-79; grantee Nat. Inst. Edn., 1973, NIH, 1967—. Fellow Am. Psychol. Assn. (coun. of reps. 1982-85, pres. div. 25, 1989); mem. AAAS, Am. Psychol. Soc., Am. Assn. Mental Deficiency, Assn. Advancement of Behavior Therapy (dir. 1975-80, pres. 1976-77, chmn. profl. rev. com. 1977—, series editor Readings in Behavior Therapy 1977—), Soc. Behavioral Medicine, Assn. Behavior Analysis, Sigma Xi. Office: U Alaska-Anchorage Dept Psychology 3211 Providence Dr Anchorage AK 99508-4614

RISLEY-CURTISS, CHRISTINA, social worker, educator; b. Torrington, Conn., Jan. 3, 1948; d. Henry B. and Marjorie Louise (Utz) Risley. BA, U. Conn., 1969; MSSW, U. Tenn., 1980; cert., Cen. Conn. State Coll., 1970; PhD, U. Md. At Balt. Staff devel./tng. cons. Tenn. Dept. Human Svcs., Nashville; cons., social svc. worker, supr. rural an durban Dept. Social Svcs., Laurens, S.C.; dist. dir. social worker S.C. Dept. Health and Environ. Control, Greenwood; rsch. cons. Westat, Rockville, Md.; asst. rsch. U. Md. at Balt.; instr. U. Md. at Balt. Sch. Social Work; asst. prof. Sch. Social Work Ariz. State U., 1993—, co-dir. child welfare tng. project; mem. S.C. Gov.'s Juvenile Justice Adv. Coun.; presenter workshops; rsch. cons. Health Start Program Evaluation and Interagy. Case Mgmt. Project. Contbr. articles to profl. publs. Mem. NASW, Am. Profl. Soc. on the Abuse of Children, Coun. on Social Work Edn.

RISSER, ARTHUR CRANE, JR., zoo administrator; b. Blackwell, Okla., July 8, 1938; s. Arthur Crane and Mary Winn (Stevenson) R.; children: Michelle W., Stephen C., Michael R. BA, Grinnell Coll., Iowa, 1960; MA, U. Ariz., Tucson, 1963; PhD, U. Calif., Davis, 1970. Mus. technician, Smithsonian Instn., Washington, 1963-64; research assoc. Sch. Medicine U. Md., Balt., 1964-65; grad. teaching asst. U. Calif., Davis, 1965-70; asst. prof. biology U. Nev.-Reno, 1970-74; asst. curator birds Zool. Soc. San Diego, 1974-76, curator birds, 1976-81, gen. curator birds, 1981-86; gen. mgr. San Diego Zoo, 1986—; co-chmn. Calif. Condor Working Group on Captive Breeding and Reintroduction, 1983-85; mem. Calif. Condor Recovery Team, 1984-86. Treas., Planned Parenthood, Reno, 1972; bd. dirs. Internat. Found. Conservation Birds, 1979-88, Conservation Rsch. Found. of Papua New Guinea, 1991—. Fellow Am. Assn. Zool. Parks and Aquariums. Office: San Diego Zoo PO Box 551 San Diego CA 92112-0551

RISSER, JAMES VAULX, JR., journalist, educator; b. Lincoln, Nebr., May 8, 1938; s. James Vaulx and Ella Caroline (Schacht) R.; m. Sandra Elizabeth Laaker, June 10, 1961; children: David James, John Daniel. BA, U. Nebr., 1959, cert. in journalism, 1964; JD, U. San Francisco, 1962. Bar: Nebr. 1962. Pvt. practice law Lincoln, 1962-64; reporter Des Moines Register and Tribune, 1964-85, Washington corr., 1969-85, bur. chief, 1976-85; dir. John S. Knight fellowships for profl. journalists, prof. communication Stanford U., 1985—; lectr. Wells Coll., 1981; mem. com. on agrl. edn. in secondary schs. Nat. Acad. Scis., 1985-88. Trustee Reuter Found., 1989—; mem. Pulitzer Prize Bd., 1990—. Profl. Journalism fellow Stanford U., 1973-74; recipient award for disting. reporting public affairs Am. Polit. Sci. Assn., 1969; Thomas L. Stokes award for environ. reporting Washington Journalism Center, 1971, 79; Pulitzer prize for nat. reporting, 1976, 79; Worth Bingham Found. prize for investigative reporting, 1976; Raymond Clapper Meml. Assn. award for Washington reporting, 1976, 78; Edward J. Meeman award for Conservation Reporting, 1985. Mem. Nebr. Bar Assn., Soc. Environ. Journalists, Soc. Profl. Journalists (Disting. Svc. award 1976), Investigative Reporters and Editors Assn. Club: Gridiron. Home: 394 Diamond St San Francisco CA 94114-2821 Office: Stanford U Communication Dept Stanford CA 94305-2050

RISTER, GENE ARNOLD, humanities educator; b. Merkel, Tex., Apr. 18, 1943; s. Jettie William and Mary Evelyn (Scott) R.; m. Janet Kathleen Ledermann, Jan. 21, 1967. BA summa cum laude, McMurry U., 1965; MA, Tex. Christian U., 1966; PhD, U. Wis., 1972; postgrad., U. Ariz., 1990, No. Ariz. U., 1990. Prof., divsn. chmn. McMurry U., Abilene, Tex., 1970-81, East Ctrl. U., Ada, Okla., 1981-83; prof. dept. humanities, divsn. chmn. Maricopa C.C., Phoenix, 1983—; adj. prof. No. Ariz. U., Phoenix, 1994—; del. Nat. Inst. Higher Edn. for Mex.-Ams., Albuquerque, 1975. Book reviewer Tex. Rev., 1985; illustrator Tex. Rev. and Tex. Anthology, 1979-82; contbr. articles to profl. jours.; contbr. poetry to Galleon, Originals, Quetzal, Rectangle, Sam Houston Lit. Rev., Tex. Anthology, Tex. Rev., Works by Abilene Writers. Regional cons. Human Rels. Coun., Midland; moderator, dir. West Tex. Coun. Govts.; mem. Tex. Com. for Humanities and Pub. Policy, 1975-81; ECU rep. Intertribal Coun., Five Nations, Sulphur, Okla., 1981; co-sponsor Tex. Reading Cir. Consortium of Univs., 1977-79. Recipient Faculty Recognition award Consortium for C.C. Devel., 1996; named Innovator of the Yr. Maricopa CCD/League for Innovation, 1988, Outstanding Faculty Employee award Maricopa C.C. Dist., 1985, 89, 92, 95; NDEA Title VI fellow, 1965-67, Am. Grad. Sch. Internat. Mgmt. fellow, 1995, East-West Ctr. fellow, 1994, Japan Found. fellow, 1995; U.S. Dept. Edn. Title VIA grantee, 1996—. Mem. Ariz. State Bd. Dirs. for Cmty. Colls. (cert.), C.C. Humanities Assn. (Ariz. state rep. to nat. bd. 1992). Democrat. Baptist. Home: 14407 N 60th St Scottsdale AZ 85254 Office: Paradise Valley Community Coll 18401 N 32d St Phoenix AZ 85032

RISTINE, JEFFREY ALAN, reporter; b. Ann Arbor, Mich., Apr. 21, 1955; s. Harold G. and Amelita (Schmidt) R.; m. Karen Lin Clark, Oct. 27, 1996. BA, U. Mich., 1977. Reporter The Midland (Mich) Times, 1978-79, Johnstown (Pa.) Tribune Dem., 1979-80, San Diego Tribune, 1980-92, San Diego Union-Tribune, 1992—. Recipient Appreciation award Am. Planning Assn., San Diego sect., 1988; named Best polit./govt. reporter San Diego Press Club, 1986. Office: San Diego Union-Tribune 350 Camino De La Reina San Diego CA 92108-3003

RISTOW, BRUNNO, plastic surgeon; b. Brusque, Brazil, Oct. 18, 1940; came to U.S., 1967, naturalized, 1981; s. Arno and Ally Odette (von Buettner) R.; student Coll. Sinodal, Brazil, 1956-57, Coll. Julio de Castilhos, Brazil, 1957-58; M.D. magna cum laude, U. Brazil, 1966; m. Urannia Carrasquilla Gutierrez, Nov. 10, 1979; children by previous marriage: Christian Kilian, Trevor Roland. Intern in surgery Hosp. dos Estrangeiros, Rio de Janeiro, Brazil, 1965, Hospital Estadual Miguel Couto, Brazil, 1965-66, Instituto Aposentadoria Pensão Comerciarios Hosp. for Gen. Surgery, 1966; resident in plastic and reconstructive surgery, Dr. Ivo Pitanguy Hosp. Santa Casa de Misericordia, Rio de Janeiro, 1967; fellow Inst. of Reconstructive Plastic Surgery, N.Y. U. Med. Center, N.Y.C., 1967-68, jr. resident, 1971-72, sr. and chief resident, 1972-73; practice medicine specializing in plastic surgery, Rio de Janeiro, 1967, N.Y.C., 1968-73, San Francisco, 1973—; asst. surgeon N.Y. Hosp., Cornell Med. Center, N.Y.C., 1968-71; clin. instr. surgery N.Y. U. Sch. of Medicine, 1972-73; chmn. plastic and reconstructive surgery div. Presbyn. Hosp., Pacific Med. Center, San Francisco, 1974-92, chmn. emeritus, 1992—. Served with M.C., Brazilian Army Res., 1959-60. Decorated knight Venerable Order of St. Hubertus; Knight Order St. John of Jerusalem; fellow in surgery Cornell Med. Sch., 1968-71; diplomate Am. Bd. Plastic and Reconstructive Surgery. Fellow A.C.S., Internat. Coll. Surgeons; mem. Am. Soc. Aesthetic Plastic Surgery (chmn. edn.), Am. Soc. Plastic and Reconstructive Surgeons, Internat. Soc. Aesthetic Plastic Surgeons, Calif. Soc. Plastic Surgeons, AMA (Physician's Recognition award 1971-83), Calif. Med. Assn., San Francisco Med. Assn. Republican. Mem. Evang. Lutheran Ch. Club: San Francisco Olympic. Contbg. author: Cancer of the Hand, 1975, Current Therapy in Plastic and Reconstructive Surgery, 1988, Male Aesthetic Surgery, 1989, How They Do It: Procedures in Plastic and Reconstructive Surgery, 1990, Middle Crus: The Missing Link in Alar Cartilage Anatomy, 1991, Surgical Technology International, 1992, Aesthetic Plastic Surgery, 1993, Mastery of Surgery: Plastic and Reconstructive Surgery, 1993; Reoperative Aesthetic Plastic Surgery of the Face and Breast, 1994, 95; contbr. articles on plastic surgery to profl. publs. Office: Calif Pacific Med Ctr Pacific Profl Bldg Ste 501 2100 Webster St San Francisco CA 94115-2381

RITCHEY, HAROLD W., retired chemical engineer; b. Kokomo, Ind., Oct. 5, 1912; s. Glen Robert and Mabel Ann (Wilson) R.; m. Helen Hively, Aug. 29, 1941; children: Stephen, David. BSChemE, Purdue U., 1934, MS in

Chemistry, 1936, PhD in Chemistry, 1938; MSChemE, Cornell U., 1945. Rsch. chemist Union Oil Corp., Calif., 1938-41, 46-47; nuclear reactor engr. GE Co., Richland, Wash., 1947-49; tech. dir. rocket divsn. Thiokol Corp., Huntsville, Ala., 1949-60; v.p. rocket divsn. Thiokol Corp., Ogden, Utah, 1960-64; pres. Thiokol Corp., Bristol, Pa., 1964-70; CEO, chmn. bd. dir. Thiokol Corp., Newtown, Pa., 1970-77. Mem. Rotary Club, Ogden, 1974—. Lt. comdr. USN, 1941-46. Named Outstanding Chem. Engr., Purdue U., 1994. Mem. AIAA, ADPA, AUSA, AIA, AFA, Purdue Rsch. Found., Am. Rocket Soc. (bd. dirs. 1956-60, v.p. 1960, pres. 1961, C.N. Hickman award 1954), Sigma Xi, Phi Lambda Upsilon. Home: 1756 Doxey St Ogden UT 84403-0524

RITCHEY, SAMUEL DONLEY, JR., retired retail store executive; b. Derry Twp., Pa., July 16, 1933; s. Samuel Donley and Florence Catherine (Litsch) R.; m. Sharon Marie Anderson, Apr. 6, 1956; children: Michael Donley, Tamara Louise, Shawn Christopher. BS, San Diego State U., 1955, MS, 1963; postgrad., Stanford U., 1964. With Lucky Stores Inc., 1951-61, 64-86, pres., chief operating officer, 1978-80, pres., chief exec. officer, 1980-81, chmn., chief exec. officer, 1981-85, chmn. bd., 1981-86; bd. dirs. SBC Comms. McClatchey Newspapers, De La Salle Inst., Rosenberg, FDT; grad. mgr. San Diego State U., 1961-63; lectr. in field; past mem. adv. coun. Grad. Sch. Bus., Stanford U. Sloan Found. fellow. Mem. Mex. Am. Legal Def. and Edn. Fund, Western Assn. Food Chains (bd. dirs., pres.), Food Mktg. Inst. (bd. dirs., vice chmn.), Sloan Alumni Assn. (adv. bd., pres.). Office: 485 Hartz Ave Ste 105 Danville CA 94526-3803

RITCHIE, ANNE, educational administrator; b. Grants Pass, Oreg., July 1, 1944; d. William Riley Jr. and Allie Brown (Clark) R.; m. Charles James Cooper, Sept. 4, 1968 (div. 1985); children: Holly Anne, Wendy Nicole. BA in Edn. with honors, Calif. State U., Sacramento, 1981. Cert. elem. tchr., Calif. CEO El Rancho Schs., Inc., Carmichael, Calif., 1981—; citizen amb. del. People to People Internat., Russia, Lithuania, Hungary, 1993, China, 1994. Active Crocker Art Mus.; mem. Rep. Senatorial Inner Circle, Washington, 1997. Mem. AAUW, Nat. Assn. Edn. for Young Children, Profl. Assn. Childhood Educators, Nat. Child Care Assn. Episcopalian.

RITCHIE, CATHERINE D., correctional officer, deputy marshal; b. Lynwood, Calif., Aug. 22, 1954; d. Harold Francis and Betty J. (Matlock) R.; m. Walter B. Ritchie Jr., July 21, 1977; children: Jeffrey, Bradley. Bookkeeper, sec. Severy Dental Labs., Orange, Calif., 1972-74, Shell Oil Co., Santa Ana, Calif., 1974-77; owner, ptnr. Vista (Calif.) Chevron Co., 1977-78; sec.-treas. Am. Battery Corp., Escondido, Calif., 1978-85; owner, operator Sophisticated 2ds, Vista, 1983-85, Bridal Elegance, Escondido, 1984-87; sr. correctional officer Humboldt County Sheriff's Dept., Eureka, Calif., 1988—; dep. marshal North Humboldt Jud. Dist., Arcata, Calif., 1991—; sgt. correction divsn. Humboldt County Sheriff's Dept., Arcata, 1991—, jail compliance sgt., vice chmn. jail population mgmt. team, 1995—; Co-pub. How to Avoid Auto Repair Rip-offs, 1981. Mem. Nat. Bridal Service (cert., cons.), Nat. Assn. Female Execs., Escondido C. of C., Calif. Farm Bur. Republican.

RITCHIE, C(LAUDE) ALEN, secondary education educator, tax preparer; b. Loma Linda, Calif., June 13, 1939; s. Claude Callahan and Alena Lee (Sease) R.; m. Marian Ruth Phillips, Sept. 6, 1960 (div. Sept. 1980); children: Robert Alen, Catherine Elizabeth Ritchie Lynch; m. Jerlynn S. Smith, Feb. 17, 1981 (div. Aug. 20, 1991); m. Carolyn Elliot Hart, June 20, 1992. MusB, U. Redlands, 1961; MA, Calif. State Coll., San Bernardino, 1982. Cert. jr. high tchr., Calif. Tchr. Redlands (Calif.) Unified Sch. Dist., 1961—; choir dir. Presbyn. Ch., Redlands; chair San Gorgonio Svc. Ctr., San Bernardino, 1995—; treas. Citrus Belt Uniserv, Redlands, 1991-93. Treas. Redlands Yucaipa Guidance Clinic, 1971. Recipient Disting. Svc. award Redlands Jaycees, 1972. Mem. NEA (rep. 1988—), Calif. Tchrs. Assn. (state coun. rep. 1992—), Redlands Tchrs. Assn. (pres. 1990-93), Phi Delta Kappa. Democrat. Presbyterian. Home: 938 Nottingham Dr Redlands CA 92373-6663 Office: Orangewood High Sch 515 Texas St Redlands CA 92374-5518

RITCHIE, DANIEL LEE, academic administrator; b. Springfield, Ill., Sept. 19, 1931; s. Daniel Felix and Jessie Dee (Binney) R. B.A., Harvard U., 1954, M.B.A., 1956. Exec. v.p. MCA, Inc., Los Angeles, 1967-70; pres. Archon Pure Products Co., Los Angeles, 1970-73; exec. v.p. Westinghouse Electric Corp., Pitts., 1975-78; pres. corp. staff and strategic planning Westinghouse Broadcasting Co., 1978-79, pres., chief exec. officer, 1979-81, chmn., chief exec. officer; chmn., chief exec. officer Westinghouse Broadcasting & Cable, Inc., 1981-87; owner Grand River Ranch, Kremmling, Colo., 1977—, Rancho Cielo, Montecito, Calif., 1977—; chancellor U. Denver, 1989—. With U.S. Army, 1956-58. Office: U Denver Office of the Chancellor University Park Denver CO 80208*

RITCHIE, ERIC ROBERT DAVID, manufacturing executive; b. Belfast, No. Ireland, Jan. 11, 1942; came to U.S., 1968; BME, Gen. Motors Inst., 1967; MSME, Union Coll., 1972. Registered profl. engr. Iowa, N.Y., Oreg. Process engr. GM of Can. Ltd., 1964-68; mgr. plant engring. GE, Schenectady, N.Y., 1968-73, mgr. internat. facilities, 1973-78; mgr. plant engring. services John Deere Waterloo Works, Waterloo, Iowa, 1978-85; mgr. materials engring. John Deere Component Works, Waterloo, 1985-89; ops. mgr. Garrett Productos Automotrices, Mexicali, Mexico, 1989-90; corp. mfg. engring. mgr. Sulzer Bingham Pumps Inc., Portland, Oreg., 1990-93, corp. materials mgr., 1993-95; v.p. ops. Christensen Shipyards Ltd., Vancouver, Wash., 1996—. Active planning and allocation com. Cedar Valley United Way, Waterloo, 1986-89; elder, session leader, State St. Presbyn. Ch., Schenectady, 1972-78, Immanuel Presbyn. Ch., Waterloo, 1979-82, First Presbyn. Ch., Portland, Oreg., 1993—; mem. Mayors Commn. Mcpl. Power, Waterloo, 1987-88. Mem. ASHRAE, Soc. Automotive Engrs., Am. Soc. Metals. Republican. Office: Christensen Shipyards Ltd 4400 SE Columbia Way Vancouver WA 98661

RITCHIE, STEVEN JOHN, foundation administrator, fundraising consultant; b. Salem, Oreg., Aug. 23, 1951; s. John Allen and Hilda Rose (Speasl) R.; m. Susan Katherine Murray, Nov. 17, 1979; children: Shea, Emma, Steven. BS, Western Oreg. State U., 1974. Dir. Lents Edn. Ctr., Portland, Oreg., 1978-83; devel. dir. Portland Art Mus., 1983-86; exec. dir. Benedictine Found. of Oreg., Mt. Angel, 1986—; co-owner Inquiry Consulting, Silverton, Oreg., 1993—. Editor (jour.) Developments, 1993-95. Mem. budget com. Silverton Elem. Sch. Dist., 1993—. Recipient Willamette Valley Devel. Officers Leadership award, Portland, 1994. Mem. Lions Club (pres. 1990-91), C. of C. (bd. mem. 1988-91). Democrat. Roman Catholic.

RITSEMA, FREDRIC A., lawyer; b. Kansas City, Mo., Feb. 12, 1951. AB, Calvin Coll., 1973; JD, U. Colo., 1976. Bar: Colo. 1976. Mem. Hall & Evans, Denver; mem. subcoms. Workers' Compensation. Mem. Denver Bar Assn., Colo. Def. Lawyers Assn. Office: Hall & Evans 1200 17th St Ste 1700 Denver CO 80202-5835

RITTER, HENRY, JR., physician; b. N.Y.C., Apr. 14, 1920; s. Henry and Beatrice Victoria R.; m. Mary Loewe, June 10, 1949; children: Mark, Caroline. BA, Lafayette Coll., 1941; MD, NYU, 1945. Physician pvt. practice, N.Y.C., 1954-55, Redwood, Calif., 1955-94, Palo Alto, Calif., 1955-72, Menlo Park, Calif., 1972-94, Atherton, Calif., 1994—; treas. Sequia Hosp., Redwood, 1983—, chmn. urology, 1975—, chmn. credit com., 1988. Author: From Man to Man, 1979. Mem. AMA, Am. Coll. Surgeons, Am. Urological Assn. (western sect.), Northwest Med. Assn. (pres. elect 1996, bd. dirs. 1993-96), Calif. Med. Assn. (communication commn.), No. Calif. Urological Soc., N.Y.C. Med. Soc., Rotary. Office: Peninsula Urology Clinic 3351 El Camino Real # 101 Atherton CA 94027-3802

RITTER, RUSSELL JOSEPH, mayor, college official; b. Helena, Mont., July 22, 1932; s. Walter A. and SallyC. (Mellen) R.; m. Linaire Wells, Aug. 4, 1956; children—Michael, Leslie, Teresa, Gregory, Daniel. Student Carroll Coll., Helena, 1950-53; A.B. in History, U. Mont.-Missoula, 1957, M.A. in History and Polit. Sci., 1962, postgrad. in History, 1963. Salesman, Capital Ford, 1953-54, 56-57; tchr., coach Billings (Mont.) Central High Sch., 1957-58, Loyola High Sch., Missoula, 1958-62, Flathead High Sch., Kalispell, Mont., 1962-69; dir. devel. and community relations Carroll Coll., Helena, 1969-76, v.p. for coll. relations, 1976-91; dir. corp. & govt. rels. Washington Corp., 1991—; pres. Dennis & Phyllis Washington Found., Helena; commr. City of Helena, 1977-80, mayor pro-tem, 1980, mayor, 1981—; exec. sec.-treas. Carroll Coll. Found., Inc.; owner Danny's Drive In, Kalispell, 1965-69; ptnr. R-B Enterprises, Inc., Kalispell, 1967-71; bd. dirs. Brubaker & Assos., Inc., Kalispell, 1971-74; v.p. Capital Investment, Inc. (KMTX Radio), Helena, 1973-80; pres. Swinging Door Art Gallery, Inc., Helena, 1973—; bd. dirs. Norwest Bank of Helena. Bd. dirs. All Am. Indian Hall of Fame, 1972-78, Jr. Achievement, 1975-79, Mont. Physicians Service, 1984-86, Blue Cross/Blue Shield Mont., 1986—, Mont. C. of C., chmn., Mont. Community Fin. Corp., 1986; bd. govs. Mont. Spl. Olympics, 1984-86; mem. Citizen's Adv. Council, 1975-76; chmn. City-County Bldg., Inc., 1978; mem. Mont. Friendship Force; co-chmn. Mont. Centenial Celebration. Served with USMC, 1953-56. Mem. Helena C. of C. (dir. 1972-75, v.p. 1973, pres. 1974, Ambassador's Club 1976—, chmn. 1978), Mont. Ofcls. Assn., Mont. Ambassadors (Ambassador of Yr. 1986, bd. dirs. 1989, 2d v.p. 1989, pres. 1991). Club: Montana. Lodge: K.C. (4th degree).

RITTER, SALLIE, painter, sculptor; b. Las Cruces, N.Mex., May 9, 1947; d. John Barnes Ritter and Billie Ruth (Carter) Simpson; m. Kent Frederick Jacobs, Apr. 13, 1971. Student, U. Rome Coll. Art History, 1965, Edinburgh (Scotland) Coll. Art, 1967-68; BA, Colo. Coll., 1969. One-woman shows include Lubbock (Tex.) Art Ctr., 1970, N.Mex. Arts Commn., Santa Fe, 1974, Las Cruces Cmty. Ctr., 1975, Aldridge Fine Arts, Albuquerque, 1980, Woodrow Wilson Fine Arts, Santa Fe, 1989, Adobe Patio Gallery, Mesilla, N.Mex., 1991, 93, Contemporary Southwest Galleries, Santa Fe, 1996, Adair Margo Gallery, 1997; exhibited in group shows at El Paso (Tex.) Mus. Art, 1988, Colorado Springs (Colo.) Fine Arts Ctr., 1995, Laguna Gloria Mus., Austin, Tex., 1979, Santa Fe Festival of the Arts, 1979, 83, The Governor's Gallery, Santa Fe, 1987, 94, Pioneer's Mus., Colo. Springs, 1985, 86, 88, N.Mex. State U., Las Cruces, 1988, 89, Dona Ana Arts Coun., Las Cruces, 1992, Tex. Commn. Arts, Austin, 1987, Tucson Mus. Art, 1995, Nat. Cowboy Hall of Fame, Oklahoma City, 1996, Autry Mus. Western Art, L.A., 1996, Albuquerque Mus. Art, 1996; represented in permanent collections U. Tex. Sch. of Law, Phelps Dodge Corp., Sunwest Bank, Albuquerque, N.Mex. State U., Mus. N.Mex., Santa Fe, Nat. Mus. Women in Arts, Washington; featured in Contemporary Women Artists, 1984, Contemporary Western Artists, 1985. Bd. dirs. Women's Bd., Mus. N.Mex., Santa Fe, 1987—, Dona Ana Arts Coun., Las Cruces, 1990—. Mem. Nat. Mus. of Women in the Arts. Episcopalian. Home and Studio: 3610 Southwind Rd Las Cruces NM 88005-5556 also: 1114 Main Rd Ruidoso NM 88345

RITZ, RICHARD ELLISON, architect, architectural historian, writer; b. Colfax, Wash., Dec. 8, 1919; s. Henry Clay and Katharine Fredericka (Failing) R.; m. Evelyn R. Robinson, Sept. 21, 1940; children: Margaret Karen Ritz Barss, Susan Elizabeth Ritz Williams. Student, Whitman Coll., 1936-37. Registered architect, Oreg. Draftsman, job capt. Pietro Belluschi, Architect, Portland, Oreg., 1946-51; project mgr., chief prodn. Belluschi and Skidmore, Owings & Merrill, Portland, 1951-56; project mgr., then gen. mgr. Skidmore, Owings & Merrill, Portland, 1956-82; pvt. practice architecture Portland, 1982—; founder Greenhills Press, 1991. Author: A History of the Reed College Campus, 1990, An Architect Looks at Downtown Portland, 1991, The Central Library Portland's Crown Jewel, 1997; editor: A Guide to Portland Architecture, 1968; contbr. articles to profl. jours. Bd. dirs. Architecture Found., Portland, 1982-85; mem. Portland Hist. Landmarks Commn., 1987—. Sgt. USAF, 1942-45. Fellow AIA (bd. dirs. Portland chpt. 1975-79, pres. 1978, mem. handbook com. Fin. Mgmt. for Architects 1980); mem. Soc. Archtl. Historians, Oreg. Coun. Architects (del. 1975-79), Portland Art Mus., Oreg. Hist. Soc., Lang Syne Soc., City Club Portland, Univ. Club (Portland), Multnomah Athletic Club. Republican. Presbyterian. Home and Office: 4550 SW Greenhills Way Portland OR 97221-3214

RIVARA, FREDERICK PETER, pediatrician, educator; b. Far Rockaway, N.Y., May 17, 1949; s. Frederick P. and Mary Lillian (Caparelli) R.; m. J'May Bertrand, May 17, 1975; children: Matthew, Maggie. BA, Holy Cross Coll., 1970; MD, U. Pa., 1974; MPH, U. Wash., 1980. Diplomate Am. Bd. Pediatrics. Intern Children's Hosp. and Med. Ctr., Boston, 1974-75, resident, 1975-76; resident Children's Hosp. and Med. Ctr., Seattle, 1978-80; RWJ clin. scholar U. Wash., Seattle, 1978-80, assoc. prof. pediatrics, 1984-89, prof. pediatrics, head divsn. gen. pediatrics, 1990—; mem. staff Nat. Health Svc. Corps, Hazard, Ky., 1976-78; asst. prof. pediatrics U. Tenn., Memphis, 1981-84; dir. Harborview Injury Prevention Ctr., Seattle, 1987—. Fellow Am. Acad. Pediatrics; mem. Ambulatory Pediatrics Assn., Internat. Assn. Child, Adolescent and Injury Prevention (pres. 1993—). Office: Harborview Med Ctr 325 9th Ave Box 359960 Seattle WA 98122

RIVERA, GEORGE, private investigator, consultant; b. N.Y.C., Nov. 29, 1959; s. George Franco Rivera and Sara (Diaz) Perez; m. Linda Marie Donnelly, Apr. 12, 1986. AS, Mt. San Antonio Coll., 1994; BS, U. La Verne, 1996. Cert. in risk mgmt., Calif.; cert. fraud examiner. EMT Arcadia-Monrovia Amb. Svc., Monrovia, Calif., 1979-81; dep. sheriff Los Angeles County Sheriff's Dept., L.A., 1981-94; legal investigator Miramar Rsch. Group, Alta Loma, Calif., 1994—; cons. Rex Gutierrez for Congress Com., Rancho Cucamonga, Calif., 1995-96; labor rep. Assn. L.A. Dep. Sheriff's, L.A., 1982-94. Mem. Nat. Puerto Rican Coalition, Washington, 1989—. Mem. Calif. Assn. Lic. Investigators, Assn. Cert. Fraud Examiners. Republican. Roman Catholic. Home: 11750 Mount Cambridge Ct Rancho Cucamonga CA 91737-7916 Office: Miramar Rsch Group 8780 19th St Alta Loma CA 91730

RIVERA, JAIME ARTURO, secondary education educator; b. San Luis, Sonora, Mexico, Oct. 11, 1968; came to U.S., 1969; s. Daniel Gerardo and Marie Esther (Valencia) R. AS, Ariz. Western Coll., Yuma, 1992; BS, No. Ariz. U., 1994, MEd, 1995. Cert. secondary sch. tchr. and sec. sch. prin., Ariz. Resident asst. Ariz. Western Coll., Yuma, 1990-92; advisor, peer No. Ariz. U., Yuma, 1992-94; social studies tchr. Cibola H.S., Yuma, 1993—; textbook adoption com. mem., Yuma Union H.S. Dist., 1994, Ariz. Ednl. Assn. Sch. Dist. rep., 1994. Rsch. mem. Yuman Town Hall Youth rsch. report, 1994 (recognition award). Polit. cons. Jr. Jaycees, Yuma, 1995—. Named Tchr. of Yr. Yuman Ednl. Found., 1994. Mem. NEA, Nat. Assn. Secondary Prins., Nat. Criminal Justice Assn., Ariz. Ednl. Assn., Lambda Alpha Epsilon (v.p. 1994-95, recognition 1995). Home: PO Box 4501 Yuma AZ 85366 Office: Cibola High Sch 4100 W 20th St Yuma AZ 85364-4800

RIZZA, JOSEPH PADULA, naval officer, former president maritime academy; b. Johnstown, Pa., Jan. 30, 1915; s. Paul and Concetta Rizza; m. Marie Follin, Aug. 30, 1947 (dec. Mar. 1992). Diploma, Pa. Maritime Acad., 1936; BA, U. Wash., 1950; MA, Boston U., 1958. Lic. master mariner USCG. Mcht. marine officer U.S. Lines Co., 1936-42; commd. ensign USN, 1942, advanced through grades to capt., 1972; chief staff U.S. Naval Forces, Vietnam, 1968-69; dir. instrn. and curriculum devel. Nat. War Coll., Washington, 1969-72; rear adm. U.S. Maritime Svc., 1972—; pres. Calif. Maritime Acad., 1972-84, pres. emeritus, 1984—. Mem. Civil Svc. Commn. San Diego County, 1986-93, pres., 1988; mem. Silverado coun. Boy Scouts Am., v.p., 1979-82); mem. steering com. Coronado Roundtable, 1984—; bd. dirs. World Affairs Coun. San Diego, 1994-96, Coronado Hosp., 1995—. Decorated Legion of Merit (2), Meritorious Svc. medal; recipient commendations Calif. Senate and Assembly, 1983, others. Mem. Am. Soc. Internat. Law, Nat. Assn. for Indsl. Tech., Coun. Am. Master Mariners, Rotary Internat. (pres. Vallejo Club 1981-82, named Coronado Rotarian of Yr. 1993), Vallejo C. of C. (bd. dirs. 1980-83), Propeller Club U.S. (pres. San Diego, recipient Brass Hat award Golden Gate 1981, named Man of Yr. 1987), Navy League (bd. dirs. 1984—), Phi Beta Kappa. Home: 1830 Avenida Del Mundo Apt 1605 Coronado CA 92118-3022

RIZZI, TERESA MARIE, bilingual speech and language pathologist; b. Denver, Aug. 8, 1964; d. Theophilus Marcus and Maudie Marie (Pitts) R. BA in Speech Pathology, U. Denver, 1986, BA in Spanish, 1986; MS in Speech Pathology, Vanderbilt U., 1988. Pediatric speech-lang. pathologist Rose Med. Ctr., Denver, 1988-90; pvt. practice Denver, 1990—; Spanish tchr. Temple Emanual, Denver, 1992-95; owner, operator Niños De Colo., Denver, Talk of The Town Speech-Lang. Pathologists; Spanish tutor and interpreter, Denver, 1988—; bilingual pediatric speech-lang. pathologist The Children's Hosp., Denver, 1994—; presenter in field. G'arin grantee Ctrl. Agy. Jewish Edn., 1993, grantee U. No. Colo. Grad. Sch., 1994. Mem. Am. Speech-Lang.-Hearing Assn. (Continuing Edn. award 1991), Colo. Speech-Lang.-Hearing Assn., Internat. Assn. Orofacial Myology, Phi Sigma Iota. Office: Talk of the Town Speech-Lang Pathologists 695 S Colorado Blvd Ste 410 Denver CO 80222-8008

RIZZO, MICHAEL ANTHONY, contract manager, baseball coach; b. Pittsfield, Mass., Aug. 27, 1964; s. Anthony Joseph and Margaret Mary (Lavelle) R. BA in Polit. Sci., Whittier Coll., 1986. Contracts mgr. Pacific-Sierra Rsch. Corp., Santa Monica, Calif., 1986—; asst. head baseball coach Whittier (Calif.) Coll., 1987—. Mem. Nat. Contract Mgmt. Assn., Purple Gold Booster Club (sec., treas. 1992—). Republican. Roman Catholic. Home: 14353 E Mar Vista St Whittier CA 90602 Office: Pacific-Sierra Rsch Corp 2901 28th St Santa Monica CA 90405

RIZZO, TERRY LEE, physical education educator; b. Chgo., July 2, 1951; s. Albert Ross and Charlene R.; m. Judy L., Jan. 5, 1974; children: Colin Ross, Kyle Ryan. BA with honors, Northeastern Ill. U., 1973; MEd, U. Ariz., 1974; PhD, U. Ill., 1983. Grad. tchg. asst. U. Ariz., Tucson, 1973-74, lectr., 1974-77; phys. edn. tchr. Schubert Elem. Sch., Chgo., 1977-78; rsch. asst. U. Ill., Champaign, 1978-80, lectr., 1980-83, vis. asst. prof., 1983-85; asst. prof. SUNY, Cortland, 1985-88, coord. undergrad. studies, 1987-88; asst. prof. Calif. State U., San Bernardino, 1988-91, assoc. prof., 1991-95, prof., chair dept. kinesiology and phys. edn., 1995—; part-time phys. edn. tchr. Fenster Coll. Prep. Sch., Tucson, 1974-75; vis. lectr. Northeastern Ill. U., Chgo., 1978; cons. Urbana Pub. Schs., 1982-85, Devel. Svcs. Ctr. Champaign County, Ill., 1982-83, Marriott Motor Hotel, Chgo.; tech. advisor various attys. Contbr. over 20 articles to profl. jours., presenter and reviewer in field; mem . editorial bd. Adapted Phys. Activity Quar., 1993—. Bd. dirs. Easter Seals Soc. Inland Counties, San Bernardino, 1990-93. Mem. AAHPERD (Assn. for Rsch., Adminstrn., Profl. Couns. & Socs.; Nat. Assn. for Sport & Phys. Edn.), Calif. Assn. Health, Phys. Edn., Recreation and Dance, Phi Delta Kappa. Home: 1481 W Cypress Ave Redlands CA 92373-5660 Office: CSU San Bernardino 5500 University Pky San Bernardino CA 92407-2318

RIZZOLO, ROBERT STEVEN, small business owner; b. San Jose, Calif., Sept. 27, 1951; s. Nicholas Salvador and Fannie Rose (Formosa) R. AA in History, West Valley C.C., 1971; BA in History, San Jose State U., 1974. Pvt. investigator John Pearne Investigations, San Jose, 1973-74; ind. rschr. San Jose, 1974-76; mgr. Books Inc., San Jose, 1975-76; dept. mgr. McWhorter's Stationery, Cupertino, Calif., 1976-79; mgr./sales rep. Campbell Stationery, Campbell, Calif., 1980-93; owner EuroData Resources, San Jose, 1991-94, OSCAN Press, San Jose, 1995—. Gen. editor/writer Italian-Am. Heritage News, 1985-88; author/pub.: Office Supply Buyer's Guide, 1996; compiler/editor: Encyclopedia of Southern Italy, 1996—. Mem. Planetary Soc., Archeol. Inst. Am.

ROACH, JOHN D. C., manufacturing company executive; b. West Palm Beach, Fla., Dec. 3, 1943; s. Benjamin Browning and Margaret (York) R.; m. Pam Flebbe, Dec. 29, 1967 (div. Aug. 1981); children: Vanessa, Alexandra; m. Elizabeth Louise Phillips, Aug. 28, 1982; children: Bruce Phillips, Bryce Phillips, Brian Phillips. BS in Indsl. Mgmt., MIT, 1965; MBA, Stanford U., 1967. Dir. mgmt. acctg. and info. systems Ventura div. Northrop Corp., Thousand Oaks, Calif., 1967-70; co-founder, mgr. Northrop Venture Capital, Century City, Calif., 1970-71; v.p., dir. Boston Consulting Group, Boston and Menlo Park, Calif., 1971-80; v.p., world-wide strategic mgmt. practice mng. officer Booz, Allen, Hamilton, San Francisco, 1980-82; Houston, 1982-83; vice chmn., mng. dir. Braxton Assocs., Houston, 1983-87; sr. v.p., chief fin. officer Manville Corp., Denver, 1987-88, exec. v.p. ops., 1988-91; pres. Manville Sales Corp., Denver, 1988-90, Manville Mining and Minerals Group, Denver, 1990-91, Celite Corp., Denver, 1990-91; chmn., pres., chief exec. officer Fibreboard Corp., Dallas, Calif., 1991—; bd. dirs. Thompson PBE, Morrison Knudsen. Author: Strategic Management Handbook, 1983. Bd. dirs. Cystic Fibrosis, Houston, 1986-87, Am. Leukemia Soc., Houston, 1986, Opera Colo., Denver, 1987-91, Bay Area Coun., San Francisco; bd. trustees Alta Bates Med. Ctr.; mem. exec. com. San Francisco Opera Assn. Mem. N.Am. Soc. Strategy Planners, Greater Denver C. of C. (bd. dirs.), Geol. Energy and Minerals Assn. (bd. dirs.), Colo. Forum, Soc. Corp. Planners (charter), Fin. Execs. Inst., Stanford Grad. Sch. Bus. Club, MIT Alumni Club, Cherry Hills Country Club (Englewood, Colo.), Beaver Creek (Colo.) Country Club, TPC Sports Club (Dallas). Home: 4278 Bordeaux Dallas TX 75205

ROADARMEL, STANLEY BRUCE, federal government official; b. Albion, N.Y., May 5, 1937; s. Kenneth A. and Catherine Louise (Bobel) R.; m. Carole Ann Hayes, Nov. 26, 1959; children: Karen Marie, Oscar Pacific, Ann Catherine, William Hayes. Student, Purdue U., 1956-58; BA, Syracuse U., 1962; postgrad., Golden Gate U., 1976-78; grad., Squadron Officer Sch., 1965, Air Command Staff Coll., 1974-76, Indsl. Coll. Armed Forces, 1976. Commd. 2d lt. USAF, 1962, advanced through grades to maj.; adminstrv., security and recruiting ops. officer Air Tng. Command, Tex. and W.Va., 1962-69; chief field maintenance Titan II ICBM Strategic Air Command, Davis Monthan AFB, Ariz., 1969-71; chief meintenance evaluation team Strategic Air Command, Vandenberg AFB, Calif., 1971-74, logistics staff officer, 1974-77, contract specialist, 1977-82; contract specialist U.S. Air Forces Europe, Adana, Turkey, 1980-81; launch complex constrn. contract negotiator, adminstr. NASA/USAF Space Shuttle Program, Lompoc, Calif., 1983-89; launch complex constrn. contract negotiator, adminstr. USAF Titan IV Space Booster, Vandenberg AFB, 1991-92; ret. USAF, 1982; constrn. and maj. svcs. contract negotiator, adminstr. 30th Contracting Squadron USAF Space Command, Vandenberg AFB, 1992—; pres. Ctrl. Coast Profls., Mut. Profl. Counseling/Placement, Santa Maria, Calif., 1990-91. Author manual: Man Lifting Crane Operations, 1976 (Air Force Commendation award 1977); revision officer Air Force Manual 66-1 Maintenance Management, 1976 (Air Force Commendation award 1977); contbr. Strategic Air Command Manual. Spkr. World Orgn. Ovulation Method, Calif., 1987—; pro life advocate, activist Am. Life League, Nat. Right to Life, 1980—; vol. Rep. Party, 1992—; marriage preparation instr. Cath. Archdiocese of L.A., Santa Maria, Calif., 1995—. Mem. Nat. Contract Mgmt. Assn., Air Force Assn. (life), Ret. Officers Assn. (life), Assn. Air Force Missileers, Am. Legion, Couple to Couple League. Home: 4532 Glines Ave Santa Maria CA 93455

ROARK, SUSAN PAMELA, advertising executive, publisher; b. La Mesa, Calif., May 10, 1958; d. Robert Cameron and Lois Joan (Maynard) R. Student, U. Calif., Santa Barbara, U. Calif., Berkeley, 1976-81. A/R mgr. Levi Strauss, San Francisco, 1980-83; sales mgr. Eagle Computer, Orange County, Calif., 1983-85; dir. ops. Thomson Consumer Products, L.A., 1985-89; account exec. Nynex, L.A., 1990-91; area dir. Harmon Pub., Orange County, 1991-96; pub., owner The Prodn. Dept., Anaheim, Calif., 1996—. Pub., The Home Gallery Mag., 1996-97; contbr. articles to profl. jours. Mem. AAUW, Women's Coun. of Realtors (sec. 1994-96, governing bd. 1994—, editor newsletter 1994—, chair mktg. com., pub. rels. com., mem. of Yr. 1995), Pacific West Assn. Realtors. Home: 10610 Lakeside # F Garden Grove CA 92640 Office: The Prodn Dept 1240 N Jefferson Anaheim CA 92807

ROARK, TERRY PAUL, academic administrator, physicist; b. Okeene, Okla., June 11, 1938; s. Paul J. and Erma K. (Morrison) R.; m. Beverly Brown, Sept. 7, 1963; 1 child, David. C. BA in Physics, Oklahoma City U., 1960; MS in Astronomy, Rensselaer Poly. Inst., 1962, PhD in Astronomy, 1966. Asst. provost for curricula Ohio State U., Columbus, 1977-79, assoc. provost for instrn., 1979-83; prof. physics Kent (Ohio) State U., 1983-87, v.p. acad. and student affairs, 1983-87, pres., 1987-97, pres. U. Wyo., Laramie, 1987-97, prof. physics and astronomy, 1997—; bd. dirs. Rocky Mountain Fed. Savs. Bank, chmn. audit com., 1989-93; commr. Western Interstate Commn. for Higher Edn., 1987-97, chmn., 1991; bd. dirs. Associated Western Univs., 1987-94, chmn., 1991, bd. trustees, 1994-97, chmn. 1996; adv. bd. Wyo. Geol. Survey, 1987-97; mem. Warren AFB Civilian Adv. Coun., 1987-97; bd. dirs. First Interstate Bank of Wyo. Mem., treas. Ctr. for Pub. Edn., Columbus, 1980-83; mem. fin. adv. com. LWV, Kent, 1986; mem. long range planning com. Cleve. Urban League, 1985-86; mem. adv. com. Battelle youth sci. program Columbus and Ohio Pub. Schs., 1982; bd. dirs. Ivinson Hosp. Found., 1987—. Mem. Am. Astron. Soc., Internat. Astron. Union, Nat. Assn. State Univs. and Land Grant Colls. (bd. dirs. 1994-96, chair commn. on intenat. affairs 1995), Sigma Xi, Phi Kappa Phi, Omicron Delta Kappa. Home: 1752 Edward Dr Laramie WY 82070-2331 Office: U Wyo Dept Physics and Astronomy PO Box 3905 Laramie WY 82071-3434*

ROBARDS, TIMOTHY ALAN, forester; b. Gary, Ind., July 8, 1963; s. Charles Edwin and Francis Kathleen (Kipling) R.; children: Sarah Robards Sheaks, Corrine Robards Sheaks. BS, Purdue U., 1985; MS, U. Calif., 1988. Researcher U. Calif., Berkeley, 1988-89; programmer/analyst Calif. Dept. Forestry, Sacramento, Calif., 1989-94, forest biometrician, 1994—. Contbr. articles to profl. jours. Mem. Soc. Am. Foresters, Toastmasters Internat. Office: Calif Dept Forestry PO Box 944246 Sacramento CA 94244-2460

ROBB, CANDACE, novelist; b. Taylorsville, N.C., Sept. 15, 1950; s. Benjamin A. and Genevieve J. (Wojtaszek) Chestocholoski; m. Charles L. Robb, Dec. 13, 1974. BA, U. Cin., 1972, MA, 1976. Reservation sales agt. Am. Airlines, Cin., 1973-74; instr. freshman composition U. Cin., 1974-78; tech. writer Pan Am Base Svcs., Bangor, Wash., 1979-80; editor rsch. publs. Applied Physics Lab., U. Wash., Seattle, 1980-93; novelist Seattle, 1993—; creative writing instr. U. Wash. Extension, Seattle, 1996—. Author: (novels) The Apothecary Rose, 1993, The Lady Chapel, 1994, The Nun's Tale, 1995, The King's Bishop, 1996, The Riddle of St. Leonard, 1997, (short story) The Bone Jar, 1995. Mem. Authors Guild, Mystery Writers Am. (bd. dirs.), Medieval Acad. Am., Crime Writers Assn., Internat. Assn. Crime Writers, Am. Crime Writers League. Office: PO Box 15902 Seattle WA 98115

ROBB, PEGGY HIGHT, artist, educator; b. Gallup, N.Mex., Sept. 14, 1924; d. John George and Beatrice Allen (Colton) Hight; m. John Donald Robb, Feb. 8, 1946; children: John Donald III, Celeste Robb Nicholson, Ellen Bea, Bradford Hight, George Geoffrey, David MacGregor. BFA, U. N.Mex., 1946, MA, 1960. Juror for varied art exhbns., 1987-91; instr. drawing continuing edn. U. N.Mex., 1987—. Works have been exhibited at N.Mex. State Fair, Albuquerque, 1951-90, Jonson Gallery-U. N.Mex., Albuquerque, 1970-81, Guangzhuo (China) Art Inst., 1984, Christians in the Visual Arts, Washington, 1987, Five States Biennial, Los Alamos, N.Mex., 1987, Graham Mus., Wheaton, Ill., 1987-89, Expressions of Faith, Scottsdale, 1988, Civic Ctr. Mus., Phila., 1989, Magnifico Festival Arts, Albuquerque, 1991-93, Peoria (Ill.) Art Guild, 1993, Nat. Christian Fine Arts Exhibit, Farmington, N.Mex., 1994, 95, 96, 97. Mem. Albuquerque United Artists (dir. 1983-84), Fellowship Artists for Cultural Exch., Christians in the Visual Arts, Coll. Fine Arts Alumni (dir. 1989—). Home: 7200 Rio Grande Blvd NW Albuquerque NM 87107-6428

ROBBINS, ANNE FRANCIS See REAGAN, NANCY DAVIS

ROBBINS, CHARLES DUDLEY, III, manufacturing executive; b. Montclair, N.J., Sept. 21, 1943; s. Charles Dudley Robbins Jr. and Elaine (Siebert) Stark; m. Rebecca Lucille Bender; children: Seth A., Evan F., Gwendolyn M., Catherine E., Christopher W. BS in Bus. Adminstrn., U. Phoenix, Irvine, Calif., 1982; MBA, U. Phoenix, Salt Lake City, 1986. Cert. mfg. engr., robotics. Project engr. Mead Paper Corp., Atlanta, 1969-73; engr. McGaw Labs., Glendale, Calif., 1973-75; mgr. tool engring. Weiser Lock Co., South Gate, Calif., 1975-77; chief engr. Bivans Corp., L.A., 1977-79; sr. project engr. Charls Wyle Engring. Corp., Torrance, Calif., 1979-80; automation specialist Mattel Toys Inc., Hawthorne, Calif., 1980-83; dir. automation engring. Deseret Med., Warner Lambert, Sandy, Utah, 1983-86, Becton Dickinson, Sandy, 1986-91; dir. Worldwide Mfg., Becton Dickinson Vascular Access, 1991—; chmn. program adv. com. Salt Lake City Cmty. Coll., 1994. Patentee in field. Mem. Sandy C. of C. (bd. dirs. 1990-92). Democrat. Episcopalian. Office: 9450 State St Sandy UT 84070-3213

ROBBINS, CONRAD W., naval architect; b. N.Y.C., Oct. 11, 1921; s. Girard David and Ethyl Rae (Bergman) R.; m. Danae Gray McCartney, Jan. 8, 1923 (dec. Jan. 1971); children: Lorraine, Linton, Jennifer; m. Melissa Jahn, Apr. 15, 1971 (dec. Mar. 1992). BSE, U. Mich., 1942. Estimator Pacific Electric Co., Seattle, 1946-47; pres. Straus-Duparquet, Lyons-Alpha, Albert Pick, N.Y.C. and Chgo., 1947-67, C.W. Robbins, Inc., Carefree, Ariz., 1967—; cons. in field. Capt. floating drydock USN, 1942-46. Home: 4401 E Mountainview Rd Phoenix AZ 85028 Office: CW Robbins Inc 7500 Stevens Rd Carefree AZ 85377

ROBBINS, DANIEL CHARLES, music educator; b. New Orleans, Nov. 4, 1947; s. Charles Daniel and Doris (Simeon) R. MusB, Calif. State U. Long Beach, 1970; MusM, U. So. Calif., 1976; PhD of Music, UCLA, 1997. Lectr. music theory and piano Long Beach City Coll., 1976-78; lectr. music theory and composition Calif. State U., Long Beach, 1978-84; lectr. music theory Cerritos Coll., Norwalk, Calif., 1980-86; lectr. piano L.A. Pierce Coll., 1995—; lectr. music theory and piano Golden West Coll., Huntington Beach, Calif., 1980-83; lectr. music theory UCLA, 1995-96. Orchestrator, arranger Intrada CDs, San Francisco, 1994—, Varese Srabande CDs, Studio City, Calif., 1996, Miklos Rozsa Estate, Corte Madera, Calif., 1994—, Alfred Newman Estate, L.A., 1996; orchestrator (film score recording) Ivanhoe, 1994, Julius Caesar, 1995; composer original music. Recipient 1st Pl. Composition prize Southwestern Youth Music Festival, 1964, 65, 1st Pl. Piano Performance prize, 1964, 67, Nat. Winner award Nat. Guild Piano Tchrs. Auditions, 1965-67, Dist. Winner award, 1964, 69. Mem. ASCAP, Nat. Assn. Composers. Home and Office: 5250 Hayter Ave #5 Lakewood CA 90712-2332

ROBBINS, HEATHER LEE, special education educator; b. Frankfurt, Germany, Oct. 17, 1962; (parents Am. citizens); d. Jack Earl and Ruth Arlene (Flathman) Dimond; m. James Thomas Robbins, Dec. 28, 1991. BA in Elem. Edn., Trinity U., San Antonio, 1984; MA in Curriculum & Instrn., U. Tex., San Antonio, 1993. Tchr. spl. edn. San Antonio Ind. Sch. Dist., 1985-92; itinerant tchr. spl. edn. Bur. Indian Affairs Shiprock (N.M.) Agy.-Navajo, 1993—. Mem. Internat. Reading Assn., Coun. for Exceptional Children, Kappa Delta Pi. Home: #3 Rd 6285 Kirtland NM 87417

ROBBINS, JAMES EDWARD, electrical engineer; b. Renovo, Pa., May 11, 1931; s. James Edward and Marguerite Neva (Cleary) R.; m. Elizabeth Anne Caton, 1959 (div. July 1971); children: James, Katherine, Ellen; m. Dorothy Raye Bell, July 23, 1971; stepchildren: Mark, Lori. BEE, Pa. State U., 1958; MS in Math., San Diego State U., 1961. Registered profl. engr., Calif., Ariz. Rsch. engr. Astronautics div. Gen. Dynamics Co., San Diego, 1961-62; sr. engr. Kearfott div. Gen. Precision Co., San Marcos, Calif., 1962-65; systems engring. specialist Teledyne Ryan Aerospace Co., San Diego, 1965-76; mgr. tech. ops. Electronics divsn. Gen. Dynamics Co., Yuma, Ariz., 1965-76; v.p. Cibola Info. Systems, Yuma, 1982-84; cons. engr. Robbins Engring. Co., Yuma, 1984-85; sr. engring. specialist Gen. Dynamics Svcs. Co., Yuma, Ariz., 1985-90; systems engr. Trimble Navigation, Sunnyvale, Calif., 1990—. Contbr. articles to profl. jours. With USN, 1951-55, Korea. Mem. Inst. Navigation, Nat. Soc. Profl. Engrs., Ariz. Soc. Profl. Engrs. (pres. western div. 1986), Am. Legion, VFW (post comdr. 1963-65), Tau Beta Pi. Home: PO Box 1728 430 Ave Portola El Granada CA 94018-1728 Office: Trimble Navigation 585 N Mary Ave Sunnyvale CA 94086-2905

ROBBINS, JEANETTE LEE, sales and manufacturing executive; b. Portland, Oreg., July 21, 1956; d. Robert Lee and Norma Yvonne (Smith) Rassi; m. Michael Keith Robbins, May 22, 1981. A in Gen. Sci., Portland C.C., 1982. Cert. engring. aide, Oreg. With prodn. thrift Salvation Army, Portland, 1979, Goodwill Industries, Denver, 1983-87, St. Vincent De Paul, Portland, 1987-88; owner Job Devel. Rsch. Ctr., Portland, 1985—, Eye-Dea Devel. Sales & Mfg., Portland, 1988—. Author: (textbook) Prime Factor Pattern, 1991, Prime Pattern of (Square) Root Ends, 1994; contbr. articles and book revs. to profl. publs. and books; artist, author: (visual aid) Arithmetic, 1982, Patricia Mae, U.S. White House, 1996. Corr., advisor, World Gov., Nat. Gov., State Gov., Local Gov., Private Citizen, Bus. owners, Dem. Nat. Com., Washington, 1993—. With USAF, 1977. Mem. Pub. Libr. Sys. (rschr. 1978—), Nat. Geographic Soc. (corr. 1993). Office: Eye-Dea Delev Sales & Mfg PO Box 66221 Portland OR 97290-6221

ROBBINS, JOHN, foundation executive, writer. Founder EarthSave, Santa Cruz, Calif.; speaker in field for major confs. for Physicians for Social Responsibility, Beyond War, Oxfam, Sierra Club, Humane Soc. U.S., UNICEF, UN Environ. program, also others; guest on Oprah Winfrey, Phil Donahue, Geraldo Rivera shows. Author: Diet for a New America (Pulitzer Prize nominated), May All Be Fed--Diet for a New World, Reclaiming Our Health..

ROBBINS, NANCY LOUISE See MANN, NANCY LOUISE

ROBBINS, STEPHEN J. M., lawyer; b. Seattle, Apr. 13, 1942; s. Robert Mads and Aneita Elberta (West) R.; children: Sarah E.T., Alicia S.T. AB, UCLA, 1964; JD, Yale U., 1971. Bar: D.C. 1973, U.S. Dist. Ct. D.C. 1973, U.S. Ct. Appeals (D.C. cir.) 1973, U.S. Ct. Appeals (3d cir.) 1973, U.S. Dist. Ct. (ea. and no. dists.) Calif. 1982, U.S. Dist. Ct. (cen. dist.) Calif. 1983, Supreme Ct. of Republic of Palau, 1994. Pres. U.S. Nat. Student Assn., Washington, 1964-65; assoc. Steptoe & Johnson, Washington, 1972-75; chief counsel spl. inquiry on food prices, com. on nutrition and human needs U.S. Senate, Washington, 1975; v.p., gen. counsel Straight Arrow Pubs., San Francisco, 1975-77; dep. dist. atty. City and County of San Francisco, 1977-78; regional counsel U.S. SBA, San Francisco, 1978-80; spl. counsel Warner-Amex Cable Communications, Sacramento, 1981-82; ptnr. McDonough, Holland and Allen, Sacramento, 1982-84; v.p. Straight Arrow Pubs., N.Y.C., 1984-86; gen. legal counsel Govt. State of Koror, Rep. of Palau, Western Caroline Islands, 1994-95; pvt. practice law, 1986—. Staff sgt. U.S. Army, 1966-68. Mem. ABA (sect. urban, state and local govt. law-land use, planning and zoning com., sect. real property, probate and trust law, sect. natural resources energy, environ. law, forum com. on affordable housing and cmty. devel.), Internat. Mcpl. Lawyers Assn., D.C. Bar, State Bar of Calif., Urban Land Inst. (assoc.), Am. Planning Assn. (planning and law divsn., internat. divsn.), Internat. Urban Devel., Law Assn. for Asia and the Pacific (Law Asia), Chamber Music Soc. of Sacramento, Oreg. Shakespeare Festival, Shaw Island Hist. Soc. Unitarian. Office: 3300 Douglas Blvd Ste 365 Roseville CA 95661-3829

ROBECK, CECIL MELVIN, JR., religious studies educator; b. San Jose, Calif., Mar. 16, 1945; s. Cecil Melvin and Berdetta Mae (Manley) R.; m. Patsy Jolene Gibbs, June 14, 1969; children: Jason Lloyd, John Mark, Peter Scott, Nathan Eric. AA, San Jose City Coll., 1967; BS, Bethany Bible Coll., Santa Cruz, Calif., 1970; MDiv, Fuller Theol. Seminary, Pasadena, Calif., 1973, PhD, 1985. Ordained to ministry Assemblies of God, 1973. Instr. religion So. Calif. Coll., Costa Mesa, 1973-74; adminstrv. asst. to dean Fuller Theol. Sem., 1974-77, acting dir. admissions, 1975-77, dir. admissions and records, 1977-79, dir. student svcs., 1979-83, dir. acad. svcs., 1983-85, asst. dean, asst. prof. ch. history, 1985-88, assoc. dean, assoc. prof. ch. history, 1988-92, adj. instr. hist. theology, 1981-85, prof. ch. history ecumenics, 1992—; dir. David J. DuPlessis Ctr. for Christian Spirituality, Pasadena, 1996—; trustee Bethany Bible Coll., 1985-88, exec. com. 1986-88; exec. com. Internat. Roman Cath. and Pentecostal Dialogue, 1986—, co-chair, 1992—; active Commn. on Faith and Order, Nat. Coun. Chs., 1984—, Sec. Christian World Communions, 1993—; Pentecostal advisor World Coun. Chs., 1989, mem. commn. on faith and order, 1991—; co-chair Nat. Coun. of Chs. and Pentecostal Dialogue, 1988-91, 95—, L.A. Evang. and Roman Cath. Com., 1992—, World Alliance of Reformed Chs. and Pentecostal Dialogue, 1996—. Author: Prophecy in Carthage, Perpetua, Tertullian and Cyprian, 1992; editor: Charismatic Experiences in History, 1985; contbr. articles to profl. jours. Joseph L. Gerhart scholar, 1969; Assn. Theol. Schs. grantee, 1977. Fellow Wesleyan Holiness Studies Ctr.; mem. Soc. for Pentecostal Studies (1st v.p. 1981-82, pres. 1982-83, editor Pneuma 1984-92), N.Am. Acad. Ecumenists (exec. com. 1989—, v.p. 1995—) N.Am. Patristics Soc. Republican. Home: 1140 N Catalina Ave Pasadena CA 91104-3807 Office: Fuller Theol Sem 135 N Oakland Ave Pasadena CA 91182-0001

ROBECK, MILDRED COEN, educator, writer; b. Walum, N.D., July 29, 1915; d. Archie Blain and Mary Henrietta (Hoffman) Coen; m. Martin Julius Robeck, Jr., June 2, 1936; children: Martin Jay Robeck, Donna Jayne Robeck Thompson, Bruce Wayne Robeck. BS, U. Wash., 1950, MEd, 1954, PhD, 1958. Ordnance foreman Sherman Williams, U.S. Navy, Bremerton, Wash., 1942-45; demonstration tchr. Seattle Pub. Schs., 1946-57; reading clinic dir. U. Calif., Santa Barbara, 1957-64; vis. prof. Victoria Coll., B.C., Can., summer 1958, Dalhousie U., Halifax, summer 1964; rsch. cons. State Dept. Edn., Sacramento, Calif., 1964-67; prof., head early childhood edn. U. Oreg., Eugene, Oreg., 1967-86; vis. scholar West Australia Inst. Tech., Perth, 1985; v.p. acad. affairs U. Santa Barbara, Calif., 1987-92, 92-95; trainer evaluator U.S. Office of Edn. Head Start, Follow Thru, 1967-72; cons., evaluator Native Am. Edn. Programs, Sioux, Navajo, 1967-81; cons. on gifted Oreg. Task Force on Talented and Gifted, Salem, 1974-76; evaluator Early Childhood Edn., Bi-Ling. program, Petroleum and Minerology, Dhahran, Saudi Arabia, 1985. Author: Materials KELP: Kgn. Evaluation Learning Pot, 1967, Infants and Children, 1978, Psychology of Reading, 1990, Oscar: His Story, 1997; contbr. articles to profl. jours. Evaluation cons. Rosenburg Found. Project, Santa Barbara, 1966-67; faculty advisor Pi Lambda Theta, Eugene, Oreg, 1969-74; guest columnist Oreg. Assn. Gifted and Talented, Salem, Oreg., 1979-81; editorial review bd. ERQ, U.S. Calif., L.A., 1981-91. Recipient Nat. Dairy award 4-H Clubs, Wis., 1934, scholarships NYA and U. Wis., Madison, 1934-35, faculty rsch. grants U. Calif., Santa barbara, 1958-64, NDEA Fellowship Retraining U.S. Office Edn., U. Oreg., 1967-70. Mem. APA, Am. Ednl. Rsch. Assn., Internat. Reading Assn., Phi Beta Kappa, Pi Lambda Theta. Democrat. Home: 95999 Highway 101 S Yachats OR 97498-9714

ROBENSON, JAMES MELFORD, protective services official; b. Brookhaven, Miss., Oct. 28, 1941; m. Susan Burt. BA in Sociology, Calif. State U., Los Angeles, 1972; M in Pub. Adminstrn., U. So. Calif., 1976; postgrad., Pub. Exec. Inst., Lyndon B. Johnson Sch. Pub. Affairs, 1986. Police officer Pasadena (Calif.) Police Dept., 1964, police agt., 1969, police sgt., 1971, police lt., 1974, police commdr., 1979, police chief, 1985—. Contbr. articles to profl. jours. Mem. Pasadena Hispanic Scholarship Com., Pasadena Edn. Found.; mem. exec. bd. San Grand Valley council Boy Scouts Am.; bd. dirs. United Way. Recipient Law Enforcement award Crown City Optimist Club, 1975, Community Svc. award Pasadena Alliance of Substance Abuse Agys., 1982, Respect for Law commendation Altadena Optimist Club, 1986, Outstanding Svc. award Just Say No Found. Mem. Nat. Orgn. Black Law Enforcement Execs., San Gabriel Valley Police Chiefs, Internat. Assn. Chief's of Police, Calif. Police Chiefs' Assn., San Gabriel Valley Mental Health Edn. Found., Alpha Kappa Delta. Club: University (Pasadena). Home: 1014 FM 775 Floresville TX 78114

ROBERSON, KELLEY CLEVE, army officer; b. McAlester, Okla., July 11, 1950; s. Cleo Connie and Helen Frances (Sewell) R.; m. Georgia Lee Brown, Jan. 15, 1970; children: Kevin Christopher, Matthew Guy. BBA, Tex. Christian U., 1973; postgrad., U. Md., 1983-88, U. So. Calif., 1991-93. Cert. govt. fin. mgr. Commd. 2d lt. U.S. Army, 1973, advanced through grades to lt. col., 1992; exec. officer Med. Co., Ft. Carson, Colo., 1974; aviation sect. leader 377th Med. Co., Republic of Korea, 1975-76; ops. officer Aeromed. Evacuation Unit, Ft. Stewart, Ga., 1976-79; exec. officer Aeromed. Evacuation Unit, Grafenwoehr, Germany, 1980-81; comdr. Med. Co. 2nd Armored Div., Garlstedt, Germany, 1981-83; compt. Walter Reed Army Inst. Rsch., Washington, 1983-88; comdr. Aeromed. Evacuation Unit, Hickam AFB, Hawaii, 1988-90; chief manpower Tripler Army Med. Ctr., Honolulu, 1990-92; chief resource mgmt., dep. comdr. adminstrn. Letterman U.S. Army Hosp. and Health Clinic, San Francisco, 1992-94; chief resource mgmt. Tripler Army Med. Ctr., Honolulu, 1994—. Pres. Parents Club Damien Meml. High Sch., Honolulu, 1990-91. Mem. Assn. Govt. Accts. (cert. govt. fin. mgr.), Am. Acad. of Med. Admintrs., Order Mil. Med. Merit, Am. Soc. Mil. Comptrs., Assn. U.S. Army, Retired Officers Assn., Phi Delta Kappa. United Methodist. Home: 1212 Hase Dr Honolulu HI 96819-2180 Office: Resource Mgmt Divsn Tripler Army Med Ctr Honolulu HI 96859-6414

ROBERTS, ALAN SILVERMAN, orthopedic surgeon; b. N.Y.C., Apr. 20, 1939; s. Joseph William and Fannie (Margolies) S.; BA, Conn. Wesleyan U., 1960; MD, Jefferson Med. Coll., 1966; children: Michael Eric, Daniel Ian. Rotating intern, Lankenau Hosp., Phila., 1966-67; resident orthopaedics Tulane U. Med. Coll., 1967-71; pvt. practice medicine, specializing in orthopedics and hand surgery, Los Angeles, 1971—; mem. clin. faculty UCLA Med. Coll., 1971-76. Served with AUS, 1961. Recipient Riordan Hand fellowship, 1969; Boyes Hand fellowship, 1971. Mem. Riordan Hand Soc., Western Orthopaedic Assn., A.C.S., AMA, Calif., Los Angeles County Med. Assns., Am. Acad. Orthopaedic Surgeons. Republican. Jewish. Contbr. articles to profl. jours.

ROBERTS, ANNA RUTH, financial consultant; b. Sweetwater, Tex., Apr. 10, 1942; d. Charles Heddington and Ethel Dorothy (Harris) Elliott; m. David Ira Roberts, Apr. 10, 1960; children: Craig Spencer, Edward Aaron. BA in Edn., Ariz. State U., 1976. CFP. Acct. Miller-Wagner & Co. Ltd., Phoenix, 1982-87; asst. v.p., sr. fin. cons. Merrill Lynch, Sun City, Ariz., 1987—; organizer, presenter seminars Pres.'s Club. Recipient Dist. Merit award Boy Scouts Am., Flagstaff, Ariz., 1975. Mem. Am. Bus. Women Assn., B'nai B'rith Women (Edith K. Baum chpt., Woman of Yr. 1976), Kiwanis (Disting. Svc. award 1991). Home: 6090 W Lone Cactus Dr Glendale AZ 85308-6280 Office: Merrill Lynch 9744 W Bell Rd Sun City AZ 85351-1343

ROBERTS, ANNE CHRISTINE, interventional radiologist, educator; b. Boston, Feb. 20, 1951; d. John D. and Edith Mary (Johnson) R.; m. John Edward Arnold, Feb. 25, 1989. BA, UCLA, 1972, MA, 1973; MD, U. Calif. San Diego, La Jolla, 1982. Diplomate Am. Bd. Radiology, cert. of added qualification interventional radiology, 1994. Clin. fellow radiology Harvard Med. Sch., Boston, 1983-87; asst. prof. radiology U. Calif. San Diego, La Jolla, 1987-93, assoc. prof. radiology, 1993—; chief vascular radiology VA Med. Ctr., La Jolla, 1990-93, acting chief of radiology, 1992-93; chief of radiology Thornton Hosp., 1993-96; chief vascular and interventional radiology U. Calif. San Diego Med. Ctr., La Jolla, 1996—. Author: (with others) Current Practice of Interventional Radiology, 1991, Vascular Diseases: Surgical and Interventional Therapy, 1994, Abram's Angiography, 1996; contbr. articles to profl. jours. Fellow Am. Heart Assn. (mem. exec. coun. cardiovascular coun.), Am. Coll. Radiology, Soc. Cardiovasc. and Interventional Radiology (sec.-treas. 1994-95, program dir. 1994, coun. chair exec. com. 1995-96, pres. 1996-97); mem. Western Angiographic and Interventional Radiology Soc. (sec.-treas. 1994-95, program dir. 1994, pres. 1995-96), Radiol. Soc. N.Am., Roentgen Ray Soc. Office: Thornton Hosp/ UCSD Med Ctr 9300 Campus Point Dr La Jolla CA 92037-1300

ROBERTS, ARCHIBALD EDWARD, retired army officer, author; b. Cheboygan, Mich., Mar. 21, 1915; s. Archibald Lancaster and Madeline Ruth (Smith) R.; grad. Command and Gen. Staff Coll., 1952; student U.S. Armed Forces Inst., 1953, U. Md., 1958; m. Florence Snure, Sept. 25, 1940 (div. Feb. 1950); children—Michael James, John Douglas; m. 2d, Doris Elfriede White, June 23, 1951; children—Guy Archer, Charles Lancaster, Christopher Corwin. Enlisted U.S. Army, 1939, advanced through grades to lt. col., 1960; served in Far East Command, 1942, 1953-55, ETO, 1943-45, 57-60; tech. info. officer Office Surgeon Gen., Dept. Army, Washington, 1950, Ft. Campbell, Ky., 1952-53, info. officer, Camp Chicamauga, Japan, Ft. Bragg, N.C., Ft. Campbell, Ky., 1953-56, Ft. Campbell, 1956-57, Ft. Benning, Ga., Wurzburg, Germany, 1957-58, spl. projects officer Augsburg, Germany, 1959-60, U.S. Army Info. Office, N.Y.C., 1960-61; writer program precipitating Senate Armed Services Hearings, 1962; ret., 1965; mgr., salesman Nu-Enamel Stores, Ashville, N.C., 1937-38; co-owner, dir. Roberts & Roberts Advt. Agy., Denver, 1946-49; pres. Found. for Edn., Scholarship, Patriotism and Americanism, Inc.; founder, nat. bd. dirs. Com. to Restore Constn., Inc., 1965—. Recipient award of merit Am. Acad. Pub. Affairs, 1967; Good Citizenship medal SAR, 1968; Liberty award Congress of Freedom, 1969; Man of Yr. awards Women for Constl. Govt., 1970, Wis. Legislative and Research Com., 1971; medal of merit Am. Legion, 1972; Speaker of Year award We, The People, 1973; Col. Arch Roberts Week named for him City of Danville, Ill., 1974; recipient Spl. Tribute State of Mich., 1979. Mem. Res. Officers Assn., Airborne Assn., SAR, Sons Am. Colonists. Author: Rakkasan, 1955; Screaming Eagles, 1956; The Marne Division, 1957; Victory Denied, 1966; The Anatomy of a Revolution, 1968; Peace: By the Wonderful People Who Brought You Korea and Viet Nam, 1972; The Republic: Decline and Future Promise, 1975; The Crisis of Federal Regionalism: A Solution, 1976; Emerging Struggle for State Sovereignty, 1979; How to Organize for Survival, 1982; The Most Secret Science, 1984; also numerous pamphlets and articles. Home: 2218 W Prospect PO Box 986 Fort Collins CO 80522-0986

ROBERTS, CHARLES S., software engineer; b. Newark, Sept. 25, 1937; s. Ben and Sara (Fasten) R.; m. Wendy Shadlen, June 8, 1959; children: Lauren Roberts Gold, Tamara G. Roberts. BS in Chemistry, Carnegie-Mellon U., 1959; PhD in Physics, MIT, 1963. MTS, radiation physics rsch. AT&T Bell Labs., Murray Hill, N.J., 1963-68, head info. processing rsch., 1968-73, head interactive computer systems rsch., 1973-82; head, advanced systems dept. AT&T Bell Labs., Denver, 1982-87; head software architecture planning dept. AT&T Bell Labs., Holmdel, N.J., 1987-88; R&D mgr., system architecture lab. Hewlett-Packard Co., Cupertino, Calif., 1988-90, R&D mgr. univ. rsch. grants, 1990-92; prin. lab. scientist Hewlett-Packard Labs., Palo Alto, Calif., 1992—. Contbr. articles to profl. jours. Westinghouse scholar Carnegie Mellon U., 1955-59; NSF fellow MIT, 1959-63. Mem. IEEE, Assn. for Computing Machinery, Am. Phys. Soc., Sigma Xi, Tau Beta Pi, Phi Kappa Phi. Home: 210 Manresa Ct Los Altos CA 94022-4623 Office: Hewlett-Packard Labs PO Box 10490 1501 Page Mill Rd Palo Alto CA 94303-0969

ROBERTS, DAVID LOWELL, journalist; b. Lusk, Wyo., Jan. 12, 1954; s. Leslie James and LaVerne Elizabeth (Johns) R. BA, U. Ariz., 1979; postgrad., U. Nebr., 1992—. Founder, editor, publisher Medicine Bow (Wyo.) Post, 1977-88; journalism instr. U. Wyo., Laramie, 1987-92; adviser U. Wyo. Student Publs., Laramie, 1987-92; gen. mgr. Student Media Corp U No. Colo., Greeley, 1995—; founder, publisher Hanna Herald, Wyo., 1979-80; exch. reporter The Washington Post, 1982; freelance reporter Casper (Wyo.) Star-Tribune, 1978-83, various publs.; founder, The Hanna Herald, 1979-80. Co-author: (book) The Wyoming Almanac, 1988, 90, 94, 96; author: (book) Sage Street, 1991; columnist Sage Street, 1989-92. Chmn. Medicine Bow Film Commn., 1984; treas. Friends of the Medicine Bow Mus., 1984-88; pres. Medicine Bow Area C. of C., 1984; dir. Habitat for Humanity of Albany County, Laramie, 1991-92. Recipient Nat. Newspaper Assn. awards, over 40 Wyo. Press. Assn. awards, Five Editorial awards U. Wyo., Citizen of Yr. award People of Medicine Bow, 1986, Student Publs. awards U. Wyo., 1990, 92. Mem. Friends of Medicine Bow Mus., Habitat for Humanity of Albany County. Democrat. Methodist. Home: 4966 W 8th St Greeley CO 80631

ROBERTS, DENNIS WILLIAM, association executive; b. Chgo., Jan. 7, 1943; s. William Owen and Florence Harriet (Denman) R. BA in Journalism, U. N.Mex., 1968; MA in Legal Studies, Antioch U., 1982; MA, St. John's Coll., 1984. Cert. assn. exec. Gen. assignment reporter Albuquerque Pub. Co., 1964, sports writer, 1960-64, advt. and display salesman, 1967-68; dir. info. N.Mex. bldg. br. Assoc. Gen. Contractors Am., Albuquerque, 1968-79, asst. exec. dir., 1979-82, dir., 1982—. Active United Way, Albuquerque, 1969-78; chmn. Albuquerque Crime Prevention Council, 1982; bd. dir. ARC (Rio Grande chpt., 1992—). Recipient Pub. Relations Achievement award Assoc. Gen. Contractors Am., 1975, 78. Mem. N.Mex. Pub. Relations Conf. (chmn. 1975, 82-83), Pub. Relations Soc. Am. (accredited, pres. N.Mex. chpt. 1981, chmn. S.W. dist. 1984, chmn. sect. 1988), Am. Soc. Assn. Execs. (cert.), Contrn. Specifications Inst. (Outstanding Industry Mem. 1974, Outstanding Com. Chmn. 1978), Sigma Delta Chi (pres. N.Mex. chpt. 1969). Republican. Lutheran. Clubs: Toastmasters (dist. gov. 1977-78, Disting. dist. award 1978, Toastmaster of Year 1979-80), Masons, Shriners, Elks. Home: #210 1520 University Blvd NE Albuquerque NM 87102 Office: Assn Gen Contractors 1615 University Blvd NE Albuquerque NM 87102-1717 *Personal philosophy: Set your priorities in life, then your goals. In pursuing your goals, visualize their accomplishment. Be persistent, and you will accomplish what you set out to accomplish. Learn to be fair to others and empathetic.*

ROBERTS, DWIGHT LOREN, engineering consultant, novelist; b. San Diego, June 3, 1949; s. James Albert and Cleva Lorraine (Conn) R.; B.A., U. San Diego, 1976, M.A., 1979; m. Phyllis Ann Adair, Mar. 29, 1969; children: Aimee Renee, Michael Loren, Daniel Alexandr. Engring. aide Benton Engring. Inc., San Diego, 1968-73; pres. Robert's Tech. Research Co., also subs. Marine Technique Ltd., San Diego, 1973-76; pres. Research Technique Internat., 1978—; freelance writer, 1979—; owner Agrl. Analysis, 1985-88; constrn. mgr. Homestead Land Devel. Corp., 1988-92; sr. engr. cons. Morrison Knudson, 1992-95; sr. soils analyst Geotechnics, Inc., 1995—. Served with U.S. Army, 1969-71. Mem. ASTM, AAAS, Nat. Inst. Sci., N.Y. Acad. Scis., Nat. Inst. Cert. in Engring. Techs., Soil and Found. Engr. Assn., Phi Alpha Theta. Baptist. Author: Geological Exploration of Alaska, 1898-1924, Alfred Hulse Brooks, Alaskan Trailblazer, Papaveraceae of the World, Demarchism, Arid Regions Gardening, Visions of Dame Kind: Dreams, Imagination and Reality, Antal's Theory of the Solar System, Science Fair-A Teacher's Manual, Common Ground: Similarities of the World Religions, Black Sheep-Scientific Discoveries From the Fringe, After Manhattan, The Christofilos Effect; and others; contbr. articles to profl. jours. Office: 3111 E

Victoria Dr Alpine CA 91901-3679 *Personal philosophy: Honesty and ethical behavior at all times. Trueness of being throughout my life. Love of my wife and children makes my life worth living and is always a light when there is darkness. God watches over my shoulder.*

ROBERTS, GEORGE CHRISTOPHER, manufacturing executive; b. Ridley Park, Pa., May 27, 1936; s. George H. and Marion C. (Smullen) R.; m. Adriana Toribio, July 19, 1966; children: Tupac A., Capac Y. PhD, Frederico Villareal Nat. U., Lima, Peru, 1989, Inca Garcilosa de la Vega U., Lima, 1992. Sr. engr. ITT, Paramus, N.J., 1960-65; program mgr. Arde Rsch., Mawah, N.J., 1965-67; Space-Life Sci. program mgr., rsch. div. GATX, 1967-69; dir. rsch. and devel. Monogram Industries, L.A., 1969-71; chmn. Inca Mfg. Corp, 1970-72; pres. Inca-One Corp., Hawthorne, Calif., 1972—; pres. Environ. Protection Ctr., Inc., L.A., 1970-76. Bd. dirs., trustee Fairborn Obs.; founder Culver Nat. Bank, 1983; trustee Calif. Mus. Sci. and Industry, 1988-92; trustee Internat. Am. Profl. Photoelectric Photometrists, 1983—, Buckley Sch., 1984-92, Belair Prep Sch., 1992-93; chmn. solar and stellar physics Mt. Wilson Rsch. Corp., 1984-87; bd. dirs. Peruvian Found. 1981, pres. 1986-89, chmn. 1989-91, appt. rep. govt. of Peru in L.A., 1988-91; chmn. Santa Monica Coll. Astronomy Ctr. Found., 1993—; chair adv. coun. Ctr. Internat. Bus. Edn. & Studies Santa Monica Coll., 1994, Peruvian Gov. Cultural Commn. for L.A, Peruvian Calif. C. of C. (advisor); mem. adv. coun. dept. mech. engrng. Calif. Poly. State U., San Luis Obispo, 1997—. Decorated Grade of Amauta Govt. Peru, 1989. Mem. Am. Astron. Soc., Astron. Soc. Pacific. Patentee advanced waste treatment systems, automotive safety systems. Office: 13030 Cerise Ave Hawthorne CA 90250-5523

ROBERTS, GEORGE R., investment banking company executive; married; 3 children. JD, U. Calif., San Francisco. With Bears, Stearns, New York, until 1976; founding ptnr. Kohlberg, Kravis, Roberts, San Francisco; dir. Beatrice Co., Chgo., Houdaille Industries Inc., Northbrook, Ill., Malone and Hyde, Memphis, Union Tex. Petroleum Holdings Inc., Houston. Office: Kohlberg Kravis Roberts & Co 2800 Sand Hill Rd Ste 200 Menlo Park CA 94025-7022*

ROBERTS, HOLLY LYNN, artist; b. Boulder, Colo., Dec. 22, 1951; d. Harold Albert Roberts and Emma Jane (Holmes) Evangelos; m. Robert H. Wilson, Dec. 1, 1989; children: Ramey Wilson, Teal Wilson. Student, Bellas Artes de Mex., San Miguel de Allende, Mex., 1971, U. N.Mex., Quito, Ecuador, 1971-72; BA with spl. distinction, U. N.Mex., 1973; MFA, Ariz. State U., 1981. One woman shows include Roth Art Series, Hobbs, N.Mex., 1980, Harry Wood Gallery, Ariz. State U., Tempe, 1981, Etherton Gallery, Tucson, 1983, 85, 87, Linda Durham Contemporary Art Gallery, Santa Fe, 1986, 87, 89, 91, 95, Jayne H. Baum Gallery, N.Y.C., 1989, 91, Baker Gallery, Kansas City, 1990, Friends of Photography, San Francisco, 1990, Etherton-Stern Gallery, N.Y.C., 1991, 95, Benteler-Morgan Gallery, Houston, 1991, Gallery 210, U. Mo., St. Louis, 1992, Ehlers/Caudill Gallery, Chgo., 1992, 95, Ctr. Photographic Art, Carmel, Calif., 1993, Robert Koch Gallery, San Francisco, 1994, others; group exhbns. include Hunterdon Art Ctr., Clinton, N.J., 1978, U. N.Mex. Art Mus., Albuquerque, 1979, 83, Am. Consulate Gen., Hermosillo, Mex., 1982, Phoenix Art Mus., 1982, 83, 84, Houston Ctr. for Photography, 1983, Robert Freidus Gallery, N.Y.C., 1984, Santa Fe Ctr. for Photography, 1984, John Michael Kohler Arts Ctr., Sheboygan, Wis., 1984, 89, Laurence Miller Gallery, N.Y.C., 1984, Ctr. for Contemporary Arts, Santa Fe, 1985, Mus. Fine Arts, Santa Fe, 1985, 86, 94, Robert Koch Gallery, San Francisco, 1986, Mus. Photographic Art, San Diego, 1987, Mus. Contemporary Photography, Chgo., 1988, Blue Sky Gallery, Portland, Oreg., 1989, Graham Modern, N.Y.C., 1990, Palm Springs (Calif.) Desert Mus., 1990, Pratt-Manhattan Gallery, N.Y.C., 1991, Art Inst. Chgo., 1991. L.A. County Art Mus., 1992, The Light Factory, Charlotte, N.C., 1993, Spectrum Gallery, Rochester, N.Y., 1995, U. Galleries, Coll. Fine Arts, U. Fla., Gainesville, 1996, Atrium Gallery, Sch. Fine Arts, U. Conn., Storrs, 1996, Soros Ctr. Contemporary Art, Kyiv, Ukraine, 1996; represented in permanent collections Mus. Photographic Art, San Diego, Phoenix Mus. Art, Prudential Ins., Ctr. for Creative Photography, Tuscon, San Francisco Mus. Modern Art, Mus. Fine Arts, Santa Fe, Mus. Fine Arts, Houston, Albuquerque Mus. Art, Monterey (Calif.) Peninsula Mus. Art, Calif. Mus. Photography, Riverside, L.A. Mus. Contemporary Art, Art Inst. Chgo., Green Libr. Stanford U., others. Ferguson grantee Friends of Photography, 1986, grantee Nat. Endowment for Arts, 1986, 88.

ROBERTS, JAMES DONZIL, lawyer; b. St. Louis, Mo., Apr. 4, 1957; s. Donzil D. and Barbara V. Malona; m. Jody A. Garcia, Dec. 7, 1985; children: James D. Jr., Jessica E. Student, Calif. State U., Northridge, 1976-79, Calif. State U., Dominguez Hills, 1981; JD, U. LaVerne, 1985. Bar: Calif. 1985, U.S. Dist. Ct. (ctrl. dist.) Calif. 1986. Staff and supr. atty. Bollington Stilz & Bloeser, Woodland Hills, Calif., 1985-90; mng. atty. Bollington and Roberts, Long Beach, Calif., 1990—; judge pro tem Long beach Mcpl. Ct., Long Beach, 1992—; lectr. extension program UCLA, 1994—. Trustee U. LaVerne San Fernando Valley Coll. Law, Encino, 1984-85; active West L.A. County Coun., Boy Scouts Am., West Hills, Calif., 1995. Mem. Assn. Calif. House Counsel (founding mem.); mem. L.A. County Bar Assn., Long Beach Bar Assn., Assn. So. Calif. Def. Counsel, Long Beach Barristers Assn., Am. Inn Ct. (Long Beach, barrister). Office: Bollington & Roberts 3780 Kilroy Airport Way Ste 540 Long Beach CA 90806-2459

ROBERTS, JAMES LEWIS, JR., insurance executive; b. Toledo, Ohio, Nov. 26, 1942; s. James Lewis Sr. and Mary Margaret (Steele) R.; m. Leslie Knutson, Dec. 16, 1967 (div. 1979); children: James III, David Earl. BA, U. Toledo, 1964. CPCU. Spl. agt. Northwestern Mut. Ins. Co., L.A., 1967-68; underwriter Unigard Ins. Group, Huntington Beach, Calif., 1968-70; underwriting mgr. Unigard Ins. Group, Van Nuys, Calif., 1970-72; mktg. mgr. Unigard Ins. Group, Huntington Beach, 1972-75; sales mgr. Am. States Ins. Co., Santa Ana, Calif., 1975-77; ins. agt., v.p. Don Kiger & Assocs., Torrance, Calif., 1977-90; ins. agt., ptnr. Bettis Ins. Svcs., San Pedro, Calif., 1990—. Chpt. pres. Amnesty Internat. USA, Long Beach, Calif., 1985-86, area coord. Los Angeles County, 1992-96, case coord. for prisoner of conscience and 1991 Nobelist Aung San Suu Kyi of Myanmar, 1993-95, dist. refugee coord., 1994—, coord. S.E. Asia Country (Burma) Group, 1996—; mem. United We Stand America. Lt. USN, 1964-67, Viet Nam. Mem. Soc. CPCU, Sigma Phi Epsilon (alumnus). Home: 2215 E 1st St Apt 8 Long Beach CA 90803-2412 Office: Bettis Ins Svcs 1891 N Gaffey St Ste 221 San Pedro CA 90731-1270

ROBERTS, JERRY (GERALD KEITH ROBERTS), film critic, writer; b. Kittanning, Pa., Oct. 1, 1956; s. Alexander and Ann Louise (Grabowski) R. BA in Journalism, Indiana U. of Pa., 1978. Sports editor Leader-Vindicator, New Bethlehem, Pa., 1978-79, Leader-Times, Kittanning, 1979-80; staff writer Pitts. Post-Gazette, 1980-83; film critic Copley L.A. Newspapers, Torrance, Calif., 1984-95; freelance mag. writer, 1995—. Author: Robert Mitchum: A Bio-Bibliography, 1992, Reading the Rainforest, 1997; co-editor: Movie Talk from the Front Lines, 1994; columnist Video Rewind for Microsoft Word's Cinemania mag., 1996—; contbr. to Daily Variety, The Holly Reporter. Recipient honorable mention awrd Copley Ring of Truth award, 1985, 3d place, 1992. Mem. L.A. Film Critics Assn. (sec. 1989-91, v.p. 1993-95), S.Am. Explorers Club.

ROBERTS, JERRY BILL, publishing company executive; b. Topeka, Jan. 22, 1937; s. William Carlton and Valera Irene (Duncan) R.; m. Judy Ann Roberts, Aug. 20, 1956; children: Jay Brent, Juli Ann Roberts Smith. B Physics, U. Calif., Riverside, 1961; MBA, U. Redlands, Calif., 1988; PhD in Bus. Adminstrn., Calif. Coast U., Santa Ana, 1990. Physicist Naval Labs., Corona and Oxnard, Calif., 1961-66, NASA, Houston, 66-72; pres. Automated Med. Inc., Houston, 1972-76; sci. adminstr. Naval Lab., Bay St. Louis, Miss., 1976-81; founder, chmn. bd. J. Melvin Storm Co., Inc., Ridgecrest, Calif., 1988—; sec. bd. dirs. San Bernardino Steel and Machine Corp., 1962-72. Author: A Generic Central Computer Facility Operations and Maintenance Manual, 1977, The Art of Winning Contracts; inventor world's first computerized birth process monitor, 1972, velocity ind. info. sys., 1973 (Navy patent award 1976). Recipient invention award Lockheed Electronics Co., Houston, 1967. Office: J Melvin Storm Co 1467 W Felspar Ave Ridgecrest CA 93555-8629

ROBERTS, KENNETH MELVIN, investment advisor; b. Lewiston, Idaho, Aug. 7, 1946; s. Merle Virgil and Ethel Viola (Gooch) R.; m. Sharon Kay Wilson, June 17, 1967; children: Lisa Marie, Michael Lowell. BA in Econs., Whitworth Coll., Spokane, 1968; MBA in Fin., Harvard U., 1971. Security analyst Murphey-Favre, Spokane, 1968-69, security analyst/portfolio mgr., 1971-73; security analyst/stockbroker Foster & Marshall, Spokane, 1973-81; v.p., portfolio mgr. Shearson Asset Mgmt., Spokane, 1981-90; pres., chief investment officer Ken Roberts Adv. Group, Spokane, 1990-94, Ken Roberts Investment Mgmt., 1994—; pres., dir. Ken Roberts Fin. Svcs., 1994——; cons. in investments Whitworth Found., Spokane, 1977—; v.p., dir., Roberts Ranch, Inc., Lewiston, 1974-94; pres., dir. N.W. Asset Mgmt., Spokane, 1991—; bd. dirs. Flow Internat., Kent, Wash., 1991—. Bd. dirs. Whitworth Found., Spokane, 1977-81. Mem. Assn. for Investment Mgmt. and Rsch. Christian.

ROBERTS, KENNETH RICHARD, artist, educator; b. Galashiels, Scotland, July 2, 1951; came to U.S., 1985; s. David and Alana (Guthrie) R.; m. Ruth Dickson, Aug. 3, 1985; children: Andrew Kenneth, Peter Richard. BA, Manchester (Eng.) Poly., 1973; MA, Birmingham (Eng.) Poly., 1974; Postgrad. Cert. in Edn., U. Reading, 1976; MFA, U. N.Mex., 1989. Lectr. Southport (Eng.) Coll. Art, 1976-85; asst. prof. U. N.Mex., Gallup, 1993—; mem. adv. coun. ACT N.Mex., 1993—; adv. panel mem. N.Mex. Arts Divsn., Santa Fe, 1996—. Exhibited in numerous shows in Eng. and U.S. including Grundy Pub. Art Gallery, Blackpool, Eng., 1981, Atkinson Pub. Gallery, Southport, Eng., 1984, Art Zone, Denver, 1996, Art Prospect, La Jolla, Calif., 1996, Painting in General, Winston-Salem, N.C., 1996, Artist Selects, Santa Fe, 1996. Office: U NMex 200 College Rd Gallup NM 87301-5603

ROBERTS, NORMAN FRANK, English composition and linguistics educator; b. Guilford, Maine, Aug. 18, 1931; s. John Francis and Pearl Estelle (Crozier) R.; m. Shoko Kawasaki, Sept. 18, 1959; children: Norman F. Jr., Kenneth K., Kathryn M. BA, U. Hawaii, 1960, MA, 1963, cert. in linguistics, 1972. Instr. ESL, U. Hawaii, Honolulu, 1962-68; prof. English, linguistics Leeward C.C., Pearl City, Hawaii, 1968-95, prof. emeritus, 1995, chmn. divsn. lang. arts, 1975-81, 92-95; cons. Nat. Coun. Tchrs. English, 1972-94. Author: Model Essay Booklet, 1989; co-author: Community College Library Instruction, 1979; contbr. articles to profl. jours. V.p. Pacific Palisades Community Assn., Pearl City, pres., 1973-74; mem. Aloha coun. Boy Scouts Am., Honolulu, 1972—, dir wood badge course, 1985, chmn. camping promotions, 1989-92. Recipient Dist. award of Merit Boy Scouts Am., 1986. Mem. Hawaii Coun. Tchrs. English (program chmn. 1974), Am. Dialect Soc. (program chmn. Honolulu conf. 1977). Office: Leeward Community Coll Lang Arts Div 96-045 Ala Ike St Pearl City HI 96782-3366 *Personal philosophy: My personal philosophy of life derives from the lessons learned as I was growing up in the Maine woods: the value of work, pride of workmanship, respect for others (especially when they've earned it), the essential goodness of people, and to consider the effect of my actions on others. In spite of all, people matter (some more than others, it seems), often times to get along, one must go along, and most times it is as important to look good as to be good. After a life of curing ignorance, I now accept that a lot of people find their ignorance more comfort than the cure.*

ROBERTS, PATRICIA LEE, education educator; b. Coffeyville, Kans.; d. Philip Lee Brighton and Lois Ethel Wortham; m. James E. Roberts, Oct. 5, 1953; children: James Michael, Jill Frances. BA, Calif. State U., Fresno, 1953, MA, 1964; EdD, U. Pacific, 1975. Lifetime tchg. diploma; sch. adminstrn. cert. Prof. edn. Calif. State U., Sacramento, 1969—; cons. in field. Author: (textbook) A Resource Guide for Elementary School Teaching, 4th edit., 1996, Literature-Based History Activities, 1996. Named Disting. Alumnae of Yr., U. Pacific, 1975-76. Mem. Internat. Reading Assn., Nat. Coun. Rsch. on English.

ROBERTS, PAUL DALE, health services administrator; b. Fresno, Calif., Jan. 17, 1955; s. Paul Marceau and Rosemarie Roberts; m. Patricia Mary Mitchell, Mar. 24, 1964; 1 child, Jason Randall Porter. AA, Sacramento City Coll., 1977; diploma in pvt. investigations, Ctrl. Investigation & Security, 1984. Office asst. I Dept. Benefit Payments, Sacramento, Calif., 1976-77; firefighter Calif. Divsn. Forestry, Colfax, 1977; key data operator Dept. Justice, Sacramento, 1977-78; intelligence analyst, spl. forces instr. U.S. Army Mil. Intelligence, Seoul, Korea, 1979-84; law libr. Employment Devel. Dept., Sacramento, 1989-92; office asst. II Dept. Health Svcs., Sacramento, 1992—; disaster courier dept. social svcs. Gov.'s Office of Emergency Svcs., L.A., 1994; chief cert. support Dept. Health Svcs., Sacramento, 1992—. Author: Organization of D.E.A.T.H. (Destroy Evildoers and Teach Harmony), 1984, The Cosmic Bleeder, 1991, Madam Zara, Vampiress, 1993, People's Comic Book Newsletter, 1996, The Legendary Dark Silhouette, 1997, Vacationing in Dublin, Ireland and Newry, Northern Ireland, 1997; (jour.) Memoirs of Paul Roberts, 1991; prodr.: (book) Villalobos Family, 1993. Sgt. U.S. Army Mil. Police, 1973-76. Democrat. Roman Catholic. Home: 60 Parkshore Cir Sacramento CA 95831-3061 Office: Dept Health Svcs Radiologic Health Br 601 N 7th St Sacramento CA 95814-0208

ROBERTS, PETER CHRISTOPHER TUDOR, engineering executive; b. Georgetown, Demerara, Brit. Guiana, Oct. 12, 1945; came to U.S., 1979; s. Albert Edward and Dorothy Jean (Innis) R.; m. Julia Elizabeth Warner, Nov. 10, 1984; children: Kirsta Anne, Serena Amanda, Angelee Julia, Zephanie Elizabeth, Fiona Ann, Emrys Tudor, Peter Christopher Tudor Roberts II. BSc with honors, Southampton (Eng.) U., 1969, PhD in Microelectronics, 1975. Rsch. fellow dept. electronics Southampton U., 1974-77; prof. microcircuit dept. electronics INAOE, Tonantzintla, Mexico, 1977-79; staff scientist Honeywell Systems & Rsch. Ctr., Mpls., 1979-84; dir. advanced tech. Q-Dot Inc. R&D, Colorado Springs, Colo., 1984-86; program mgr. Honeywell Opto-Electronics, Richardson, Tex., 1986; vis. prof. U. N.Mex. CHTM, Albuquerque, 1987; supr. engring. Loral Inc. (formerly Honeywell), Lexington, Mass., 1988-90; mgr. engring. Litton Systems Inc., Tempe, Ariz., 1990-96; staff engr. Motorola Space and Systems Tech. Group, Scottsdale, Ariz., 1996—; dir. Pi-Rho Technics Internat., Inc., Gilbert, Ariz., 1996—; cons. engr. Q-Dot, Inc. R&D, Colorado Springs, 1982—, pvt. stockholder, 1984—. Author: (with P.C.T. Roberts) Charge-Coupled Devices and Their Applications, 1980; contbr. articles to Boletin del INAGE, IEEE Transactions on Electron Devices, Procs. of the IEE (UK), Procs. of the INTERNEPCON, Internat. Jour. Electronics,IEEE Electron Device Letters, Electronics Letters, Solid State and Electron Devices, IEEE Jour. Solid State Circuits, others. Republican. Home: 1418 N Cliffside Dr Gilbert AZ 85234-2659 Office: Motorola Space and Systems Tech Grp 8201 E McDowell Rd Scottsdale AZ 85252

ROBERTS, PHILIP JOHN, history educator, editor; b. Lusk, Wyo., July 8, 1948; s. Leslie J. and LaVerne Elizabeth (Johns) R. BA, U. Wyo., 1973, JD, 1977; PhD, U. Wash., 1990. Bar: Wyo. 1977. Editor Lake Powell Chronicle, Page, Ariz., 1972-73; co-founder, co-pub. Medicine Bow (Wyo.) Post, 1977; pvt. practice in law Carbon and Laramie County, Wyo., 1977-84; historian Wyo. State Hist. Dept., Cheyenne, 1979-84; editor Annals of Wyo., Cheyenne, 1980-84, 95—; owner, pub. Capitol Times, Cheyenne, 1982-84; co-editor Wyo. History Jour., 1995-96; editor, 1996—; owner, pub. Skyline West Press, Seattle, 1985-90; asst. prof. history U. Wyo., Laramie, 1990—; indexer Osborne-McGraw-Hill, Berkeley, 1988—; guest lectr. media law, Dubai, United Arab Emirates, 1996; mem. editl. bd. Annals of Wyo., 1990-95. Author: Wyoming Almanac, 1989 (pub. annually), Buffalo Bones: Stories from Wyoming's Past, 1979, 82, 84, Readings in Wyoming History, 1994-96; contbr. articles to profl. jours. Mem. Wyo. State Hist. Soc. (life), Wyo. State Bar, Pacific N.W. Historians' Guild, 9th Judicial Cir. Hist. Soc., Western History Assn., Am. Hist. Assn., Orgn. of Am. Historians. Office: U Wyo Univ Sta PO Box 4286 Laramie WY 82071

ROBERTS, RON, county board supervisor; b. 1942. BA, San Diego State U.; MA, U. Calif., Berkeley, 1968. Chmn. county dist. 4 Office of Bd. of Suprs., San Diego, 1994—. Office: Office Bd Suprs County Adminstrn Ctr 1600 Pacific Hwy Rm 335 San Diego CA 92101

ROBERTS, TIMOTHY WYNELL, journalist; b. French Camp, Calif., Nov. 1, 1957; s. Loron Sr. and Garnola Marie (Wilson) R.; m. Vella Kee Black, July 26, 1986; children: Alaina Elizabeth, Rachel Marie. BA in Mass Comm., Calif. State U., Hayward, 1979; MS, Northwestern U., 1982. Gen. assignment reporter Hayward Daily Rev., 1979-80; prodr., program coord. Hayward Cable TV 3, 1980-81; TV/radio reporter Medill News Svc., Washington, 1982; gen. assignment reporter, photographer, prodr. KERO TV 23, NBC affiliate, Bakersfield, Calif., 1983; pub. affairs dir. Kaiser Permanente Med. Care Program, Oakland, Calif., 1984-89; cons. pub. rels., video prodr., freelance journalist TWR Enterprises, San Leandro, Calif., 1989—; comm./media specialist Alameda County Social Svcs./Pub. Health Agys., Oakland, Calif., 1993—. Video prodr: Health Care: Antioch Pre-Natal Program, 1989. Mem. adv. bd. Judie Davis African Am. Bone Marrow Donor Recruitment Program, Oakland, Calif., 1993—; treas., past pres., v.p. Hesperian Villas Homeowners Assn., San Leandro, Calif., 1989—. Mem. Soc. Profl. Journalists, Sigma Delta Chi. Home and Office: 24316 Machado Ct Hayward CA 94541-4559

ROBERTS, VERN EDWARD, sport association executive; b. Cin., July 14, 1954; s. Vernon E. and Marion Roberts; m. Gina V. Roberts, Jan. 2, 1982; children: Adam V., Samantha V. BA, Lake Forest (Ill.) Coll., 1972-76. Exec. dir. U.S. Handball, Tucson, 1980—. Mem. Am. Soc. Assn. Execs. Office: US Handball 2333 N Tucson Blvd Tucson AZ 85716-2726

ROBERTS, WILLIAM LAWRENCE, JR., education researcher, statistician; b. Oakland, Calif., June 11, 1949; s. William Lawrence and Helen Haller (Stotts) R.; m. Fern Lee Labuhn; 1 child, Adre Lee. BA in Psychology, San Francisco State U., 1987, MA in Psychology Rsch., 1991; postgrad. in Edn., U. San Francisco, 1996—. Rsch. asst. City Coll. of San Francisco, 1988-89; pvt. private San Franciso, 1989-92; rsch. assoc. Devel. Studies Ctr., Oakland, 1992—; cons. San Francisco State U., 1989-92, Kaiser Permeente, Oakland, 1989-92, St. Mary's Coll., Moraga, Calif., 1996. Author: Cultural Influences on Nonverbal Behavior, 1992; presenter (poster-paper) Am. Ednl. Assn., 1995, Orton Soc., 1996. Mem. Am. Ednl. Rsch. Assn., Am. Statis. Assn., Am. Psychol. Assn. Office: Develop Studies Ctr Ste 305 2000 Embarcadero Oakland CA 94606-5300

ROBERTSON, CAREY JANE, musician, educator; b. Culver City, Calif., Apr. 18, 1955; d. Robert Bruce and Marjorie Ellen (Greenleaf) Coker;l m. Brian Collins Robertson, June 28, 1975 (div. July 1985); 1 child, Sean Kalen. BMus, Calif. State U., Northridge, 1977; MMus, U. So. Calif., L.A., 1979, PhD of Mus. Arts, 1987. Organist/choir dir. Village Meth. Ch., North Hollywood, Calif., 1972-75, St. Bede's Episcopal Ch., Mar Vista, Calif., 1975-79; organist interim St. Alban's Episcopal Ch., Westwood, Calif., 1985; organist Covenant Presbyn. Ch., Westchester, Calif., 1985-90; organist/choir dir. St. David's United Ch., West Vancouver, B.C., Can., 1990-91; prin. organist Claremont (Calif.) United Ch. of Christ, 1991—; prof. organ Claremont Grad. Sch., 1991—; concert organist Am. Guild of Organists, throughout U.S. and Can., 1974—; cons. Sch. Theology, U. B.C., 1990. Bd. dirs. Ruth and Clarence Mader Found., Pasadena, Calif., 1993—. Recipient Music Tchrs. Nat. Assn. Wurlitzer Collegiate Artist award, 1980; Irene Robertson scholar, 1977, 78. Mem. Am. Guild Organists (historian, sec. 1985-92, exec. com. 1983-85), Pi Kappa Lambda (Scholastic award 1987). Home: 7514 Pepper St Rancho Cucamonga CA 91730-2125

ROBERTSON, ERIC EUGENE, state trooper; b. Washington, Dec. 6, 1963; s. Eugene E. and Lois I. (Matthews) R.; m. Carolyn M. Hosford, Aug. 6, 1989; children: Zachary Andrew, Evan, Katherine. Student, Green River Coll., 1982-83; grad., Wash. State Patrol Acad., 1985. Trooper Wash. State Patrol, Olympia, 1983—. Precinct com. officer Wash. State Rep. Party, 1990-92, 93-96; asst. majority whip Wash. State Ho. of Reps., 1995, 96, majority caucus chmn., 1996—; mem. PTA, 1992—. Mem. Sons of Am. Legion, C. of C., Lions Club. Methodist. Home: PO Box 1309 Buckley WA 98321 Office: Ho of Reps 407 Legislative Bldg Olympia WA 98504

ROBERTSON, HUGH DUFF, lawyer; b. Grosse Pointe, Mich., Mar. 14, 1957; s. Hugh Robertson and Louise (Grey) Bollinger. BBA in Fin., U. Wis., Whitewater, 1978; JD, Whittier Coll., 1982. Bar: Calif. 1983, U.S. Tax Ct. 1984. Pres., CEO, A. Morgan Maree Jr. & Assocs., Inc., L.A., 1979—. Mem. ABA (forum com. on entertainment 1982—), State Calif., L.A. County Bar Assn., Beverly Hills Bar Assn., Acad. TV Arts and Scis., Am. Film Inst., Phi Alpha Delta. Republican. Episcopalian. Office: A Morgan Maree Jr & Assocs 4727 Wilshire Blvd Ste 600 Los Angeles CA 90010-3875

ROBERTSON, JACQUELINE LEE, entomologist; b. Petaluma, Calif., July 9, 1947; d. John Lyman and Nina Pauline (Klemenok) Schwartz; m. Joseph Alexander, Sept. 12, 1970 (div. Jan. 1978). BA, U. Calif., Berkeley, 1969, PhD, 1973. Registered profl. entomologist. Research entomologist USDA Forest Service, Berkeley, 1970—. Editor: Jour. Econ. Entomology, 1982-96, Can. Entomologist, 1992—; author: Pesticide Bioassays with Arthropods, 1992; contbr. articles to profl. jours.; patentee lab. device, 1982. Mem. Entomol. Soc. Am., Entomol. Soc. Can., AAAS. Democrat. Office: US Forest Svc PSW Sta PO Box 245 Berkeley CA 94701-0245

ROBERTSON, MARIAN ELLA (MARIAN ELLA HALL), small business owner, handwriting analyst; b. Edmonton, Alta., Can., Mar. 3, 1920; d. Orville Arthur and Lucy Hon (Osborn) Hall; m. Howard Chester Robertson, Feb. 7, 1942; children: Elaine, Richard. Student, Willamette U., 1937-39; BS, Western Oreg. State U., 1955. Cert. elem., jr. high. tchr., supt. (life) Oreg.; cert. graphoanalyst. Tchr. pub. schs. Mill City, Albany, Scio and Hillsboro, Oreg., 1940-72; cons. Zaner-Bloser Inc., Columbus, Ohio, 1972-85, assoc. cons., 1985-89; pres. Write-Keys, Scio, 1980-90; owner Lifelines, Jefferson, Oreg., 1991-94; tchr. Internat. Graphoanalysis Soc., Chgo., 1979; instr. Linn-Benton Community Coll., 1985-89. Sr. intern 5th Congl. Dist. Oreg., Washington, 1984, mem. sr. adv. coun.; precinct com. mem. Rep. Cen. Com., Linn County, 1986, alt. vice-chair, 1986, parliamentarian, 1988—; candidate Oreg. State Legis., Salem, 1986; del. Northwest Friends Yearly Meeting, Newberg, Oreg., 1990, 91, 92; master gardener vol. Marion County, Oreg. State U. Extension Svc., 1992; floriculture judge Marion County Fair, 1992; master gardener clinic Oreg. State Fair, 1992; clerk Marion Friends Monthly Meeting, 1992-93. Mem. Altrusa Internat. (internat. chmn. 1985-86, chmn. pub. rels. 1989—, corr. sec. 1990-91), Internat. Platform Assn. Republican. Mem. Soc. of Friends. Home: 2757 Pheasant Ave SE Salem OR 97302-3170 *Personal philosophy: Keep on learning and keep on working to make the world a better place.*

ROBERTSON, MERLE GREENE, art historian, academic administrator; b. Miles City, Mont., Aug. 30, 1919; d. Darrel Irving and Ada Emma (Foote) McCann; m. Wallace McNeill Greene, Dec. 2, 1936 (div. Sept. 1950); children: Barbara Merle Greene Metzler, David Wallace Greene; m. Lawrence William Robertson, Dec. 19, 1966 (dec. May 1981). Student, U. Washington, 1933-35; BA, U. San Francisco, 1952; MFA, U. Guana Guato, Mex., 1963; PhD, Tulane U., 1987. Cert. tchr., Calif. Camp dir. Camp Tapawingo, Sequim, Wash., 1951-53; tchr. San Rafael Mil. Acad., 1952-64; camp dir. Marin County Camp Fire Girls, San Rafael, Calif., 1954-56; expedition dir. Tulane U., New Orleans, 1962—; tchr. Monterey (Calif.) Peninsula Coll., 1974-76, Robert Louis Stevenson Sch., Pebble Beach, Calif., 1967-76; exec. dir. Pre-Columbian Art Rsch. Inst., San Francisco, 1971—; adj. curator H.M. de Young Meml. Art Mus., San Francisco, 1991—, com. mem. pre-Columbian art, 1990—; rsch. assoc. Middle Am. Rsch. Inst./Tulane U., New Orleans, 1976—, U. Calif. Archaeol. Rsch. Facility, Berkeley, 1982—, Calif. Acad. Scis., San Francisco, 1985—; dir. Archaeol. Recording Maya Art in Mex., Gualemala, Belize, Honduras, 1962—. Author: Sculpture of Palenque, 4 vols., 1983-91, Ancient Maya Relief Sculpture, 1967 (Best Design 1967), (CD-ROMS) Merle Greene Robertson's Rubbings of Maya Sculpture; editor: Palenque Round Table, 10 vols., 1973-95; prin. works include over 3000 rubbings of Maya Sculpture. Merle Greene Robertson Sch. named in her honor, Chiapas, Mex., 1981; recipient Order of the Aztec Eagle award Mexican Govt., 1994. Fellow AAAS, The Explorers Club, Soc. for Am. Archaeology; mem. 47th Internat. Cong. Americanists (hon. v.p. 1992), Am. Anthropol. Assn., Assn. de Artistes Mougins. Home and Office: 1100 Sacramento St San Francisco CA 94108-1918

ROBERTSON, SUSAN JOYCE COE, special education educator; b. Pinedale, Wyo., May 22, 1954; d. Cecil James and Geraldine Ada (Greene) Coe; children: Jamie Michelle, Mark David. BS in Edn., Chadron (Nebr.) State Coll., 1976, MS in Counseling and Guidance, 1977; specialist in emotionally disturbed, U. No. Colo., 1982. Cert. crisis prevention intervention master trainer, peer mediation facilitator. Elem. tchr. pub. schs., Alliance, Nebr., 1976-77; social worker Community Action, Cheyenne, Wyo., 1978-79; Chpt. 1 tchr. Laramie County Sch. Dist. 1, Cheyenne, 1979-81, elem. tchr., 1981-84, tchr. severely emotionally disturbed, 1984-89, cons., specialist for severely emotionally disturbed, 1989-92, behavior intervention team specialist, 1992-95, tchr. learning disabled, 1995—; mem. Dist. Placement Com., 1981-92. Mem. Cmty. Commn., Cheyenne, 1981-92; basketball coach YMCA, 1994; deacon Presbyn. Ch. Mem. NEA, Am. Guidance and Counseling Assn., Coun. for Exceptional Children (faculty adviser 1991), Wyo. Edn. Assn., Cheyenne Tchr. Edn. Assn., Trailblazer Parent Assn., PEO. Presbyterian. Home: 5425 Gateway Dr Cheyenne WY 82009-4035 Office: 6000 Education Dr Cheyenne WY 82009

ROBINETT, RUSH DALETH, III, robotics research manager; b. Albuquerque, July 14, 1960; s. Rush Daleth Jr. and Dorothy (Sohl) R.; m. Laurie Ellen Bowman, Dec. 28, 1993; 1 child Rush Daleth IV. Student, U. Notre Dame, 1978-80; BS magna cum laude, Tex. A&M U., 1982, PhD, 1987; MS, U. Tex., 1984. Teaching asst. U. Notre Dame, South Bend, Ind., 1979-80; rsch. asst. Tex. A&M U., College Station, 1981-82, U. Tex., Austin, 1983-84; rsch. assoc. Ctr. for Strategic Tech., College Station, 1984-87; rsch. mgr. Sandia Nat. Lab., Albuquerque, 1988—, disting. mem. tech. staff, 1995; student intern NASA Hdqs. Washington, 1981; rsch. engr. Northrop Aircraft Divsn., Hawthorne, Calif., summer, 1983; adj. prof. U. N.Mex., Albuquerque, 1994—; cons. Corning, Elmira, N.Y., 1993-95, Albuquerque Pub. Schs. Budget Rev. Bd., 1990; sci. advisor Albuquerque Pub. Schs., 1990-94, sci. instr., summer, 1988-90; presenter, cons. Explora, Albuquerque, 1992. Inventor: two axis hydraulic joint, sway suppressed crane control, moving mass spacecraft attitude control system; contbr. articles to profl. jours. Mentor Valley Acad., Albuquerque, 1989-92. Mem. AIAA (assoc. fellow, tech. com. 1991-93, student v.p. 1981-82, Best Presentation award 1992), N.Y. Acad. Scis., Am. Helicopter Soc., Phi Kappa Phi, Sigma Gamma Tau. Home: PO Box 1661 Tijeras NM 87059-1661 Office: Sandia Nat Lab MS 1003 PO Box 5800 Albuquerque NM 87185

ROBINS, MORRIS JOSEPH, chemistry educator; b. Nephi, Utah, Sept. 28, 1939; s. Waldo George and Mary Erda (Anderson) R.; m. Jerri Johnson, June 11, 1960 (div. July 1972); children: Dayne M., Diane, Douglas W., Debra, Dale C.; m. Jackie Alene Robinson, Aug. 24, 1973; children: Mark K., Janetta A., Tiffany A. BA, U. Utah, 1961; PhD, Ariz. State U., 1965. Cancer rsch. scientist Roswell Park Meml. Inst., Buffalo, 1965-66; rsch. assoc. U. Utah, Salt Lake City, 1966-69; from asst. prof. to prof. chemistry U. Alberta, Edmonton, Can., 1969-86; prof. chemistry Brigham Young U., Provo, Utah, 1987—; vis. prof. medicinal chemistry U. Utah, Salt Lake City, 1981-82; adj. prof. medicine U. Alberta, Edmonton, 1988—; grant evaluation panel Am. Cancer Soc., N.Y.C., 1977-80, Nat. Cancer Inst. Can., Toronto, 1983-86; mem. AIDS & Related Rsch. Study Sect. 4, NIH, Washington, 1995—; cons. in field. Mem. editl. bd. Nucleic Acids Rsch., 1980-83; contbr. articles to profl. jours., chpts. to books; patentee in field. NSF fellow, 1963-64; Rsch. grantee Nat. Cancer Inst. Can., Natural Scis. and Engring. Rsch. Coun. Can., 1969-87, Am. Cancer Soc., NIH, 1987—; named J. Rex Goates prof. Brigham Young U., 1989—; recipient medal for sci. and tech. award Gov. Utah, 1996. Mem. Am. Assn. for Cancer Rsch., Am. Chem. Soc., Internat. Soc. for Antiviral Rsch., Internat. Soc. Nucleic Acids Chemistry (mem. adv. bd. 1995—). Mem. LDS Ch. Office: Brigham Young Univ Dept Chemistry/Biochemistry Provo UT 84602-5700

ROBINS, ROBERT EDWARD, research scientist; b. Miami, Fla., Aug. 4, 1942; s. Harold Robins and Mildred Arnette Connolly; m. Carol Lynn Belkind Robins, June 12, 1965; 1 child, Joshua Benjamin. BS summa cum laude, Poly. U., Brooklyn, 1964; MS, NYU (Courant Inst.), 1966, U. Wash., 1967-69. Rsch. engr. Boeing Aerospace, Seattle, 1967-68; programmer analyst King County, Seattle, 1970-72; system analyst Puget Sound Govtl. Coun., Seattle, 1972; rsch. scientist Flow Rsch., Inc., Kent, Wash., 1972-80; system analyst Boeing Computer Svcs., Seattle, 1980-81; rsch. scientist Physical Dynamics, Bellevue, Wash., 1981-86, N.W. Rsch. Assocs., Inc., Bellevue, Wash., 1986—. Contbr. articles to profl. jours. Bd. dirs., treas. Seattle Youth Soccer Assn., 1989-93. Grad. fellow NSF, 1964-67. Mem. AIAA, Am. Geophys. Union, Assn. Computing Machinery, Soc. Indsl. and Applied Math. Office: N W Rsch Assocs Inc 14508 NE 20th St Bellevue WA 98007

ROBINSON, ANNETTMARIE, entrepreneur; b. Fayetteville, Ark., Jan. 31, 1940; d. Christopher Jacy and Lorena (Johnson) Simmons; m. Roy Robinson, June 17, 1966; children: Steven, Sammy, Doug, Pamela, Olen. BA, Edison Tech. U., 1958; BA in Bus., Seattle Community Coll., 1959. Dir. perss. Country Kitchen Restaurants, Inc., Anchorage, 1966-71; investor Anchorage, 1971—; cons. Pioneer Investments, Anchorage, 1983—, M'RAL, Inc. Retail Dry Goods, Anchorage, 1985. Mem. Rep. Presdl. Task Force, Washington, 1984—, Reps. of Alaska, Anchorage, 1987; mem. chmn. round table YMCA, Anchorage, 1986—; active Sta. KWN2, KQLO, Reno, Nev.; active in child abuse issues and prosecution; dir., sec. Hunter Lake Townhouse Assn., Revno, Nev., Sta. KSRU and KHWG-Radio, KIHM Cath. Radio, Revno, 1996—. Named Woman of Yr. Lions, Anchorage, 1989, marksman first class Nat. Rifle Assn., 1953. Mem. Rep. Presdl. Task Force, Washington, 1984—, Reps. of Alaska, Anchorage, 1987; mem. chmn. round table YMCA, Anchorage, 19866; active Sta. KWN2, KQLO, KSRN, KHW6, Reno, Nev.; bd. dirs., sec. Hunter Lake Townhouses Assn., Reno, 1995—, active in child abuse issues and prosecution.

ROBINSON, ARTHUR BROUHARD, scientist, educator; b. Chgo., Mar. 24, 1942; s. Edward Hill and Zelma A. (Brouhard) R.; widowed; children: Zachary, Naoh, Aryanne, Joshua, Bethany, Matthew. BS, Calif. Inst. Tech., 1963; PhD, U. Calif., San Diego, 1967. Faculty mem. U. Calif., San Diego, 1968-73; pres. Linus Pauling Inst. Sci. & Medicine, Menlo Park, Calif., 1973-78, Oreg. Inst. Sci. & Medicine, Cave Junction, 1981—. Home and Office: 2251 Dick George Rd Cave Junction OR 97523-9622

ROBINSON, BERNARD LEO, retired lawyer; b. Kalamazoo, Feb. 13, 1924; s. Louis Harvey and Sue Mary (Starr) R.; m. Betsy Nadell, May 30, 1947; children: Robert Bruce, Patricia Anne, Jean Carol. BS, U. Ill., 1947, MS, 1958, postgrad. in structural dynamics, 1959; JD, U. N.Mex., 1973. Rsch. engr. Assn. Am. Railroads, 1947-49; instr. architecture Rensselaer Poly. Inst., 1949-51; commd. 2d lt. Corps Engrs., U.S. Army, 1945, advanced through grades to lt. col., 1965, ret., 1968; engr. Nuclear Def. Rsch. Corp., Albuquerque, 1968-71; admitted to N.Mex. bar, 1973, U.S. Supreme Ct. bar, 1976; practiced in Albuquerque, 1973-85, Silver City, N.Mex., 1985-89, Green Valley, Ariz., 1989-90, Sierra Vista, Ariz., 1990-91; pres. Robinson Fin. Svcs., 1993-95. Dist. commr. Boy Scouts Am., 1960-62; vice chmn. Rep. Dist. Com., 1968-70. Decorated Air medal, Combat Infantry badge. Mem. ASCE, ABA, Ret. Officers Assn., DAV, Assn. U.S. Army, VFW. Home: 1037 W Eagle Look Ln Tucson AZ 85737-6986

ROBINSON, BEULAH LOBDELL, educator; b. Chico, Calif., Dec. 19, 1928; d. James Britton and Beulah May (Shirley) L.; m. Gordon Sidney Taylor, Aug. 9, 1953; (div. Jan., 1964) 1 child, Allis Rosemary; m. Charles Dwayne Robinson, July 15, 1967 (dec.). BA, U. Calif., Berkeley, 1950. Cert. tchr., adminstr., Calif. Supt., prin. Manzanita Sch. Dist., Gridley, Calif., 1974-81; elem., middle sch. prin. Williams (Calif.) Unified Sch. Dist., 1981-84; dir., elem. sch. prin. Chico (Calif.) Unified Sch. Dist., cons., 1994—. Named Adminstr. of Yr. Butte County Adminstrs. Assn., 1995. Mem. ASCD, LWV, AAUW, (mem. juvenile justice study com. 1994—), Assn. of Calif. Sch. Adminstrs. (pres. region 2, 1981-82, del. state assembly, 1981-86, Adminst. of Yr. 1980), Bidwell Mansion Assn., Chico Mus. Home: 938 W 12th Ave Chico CA 95926

ROBINSON, CARMEN DELORES, educator; b. Kingston, Jamaica, Jan. 15, 1954; came to the U.S., 1973; d. Alphonso Constantine and Lena Maud (Ellis) R.; 1 child, Chrystle Khalya Robinson-White. BA, Calif. State U., L.A., 1978, MS, 1981. Profl. clear multiple subject credential. Tchr., instr. Hacienda La Puenta Unified Sch. Dist., L.A., 1986-88; tchr. L.A. Unified Schs., 1985-86, 88-90, SDC tchr., 1990-92, 92-94, bilingual coord., 1994-95; bilingual and curriculum resource tchr. Pasadena (Calif.) Unified Sch. Dist., 1995—. Republican.

ROBINSON, CHARLES PAUL, nuclear physicist, diplomat, business executive; b. Detroit, Oct. 9, 1941; s. Edward Leonard and Mary Opal (Edmondson) R.; m. Barbara Thomas Woodard; children by previous marriage: Paula S., Colin C. BS in Physics, Christian Bros. U., 1963; PhD in Physics, Fla. State U., 1967. Mem. nuclear test staff Los Alamos (N.Mex.) Nat. Lab., 1967-69, chief test operator, 1969-70, mem. advanced concepts staff, 1971-72, assoc. div. leader, lasers, 1972-76, div. leader, 1976-79, assoc. dir., 1980-85; sr. v.p., bd. dirs. Ebasco Services Inc. subs. Enserch Corp., N.Y.C., 1985-88; ambass. to nuclear testing talks U.S. Dept. State, Geneva, 1988-90; v.p. Sandia Nat. Labs., Albuquerque, 1990-95, pres., 1995—; mem. sci. adv. group Def. Nuclear Agy., Washington, 1981-86; mem. nat. security bd. Los Alamos Nat. Lab., 1985-88; chmn. Presdl. Tech. Adv. Bd., 1991; mem. U.S. Strategic Command Adv. Bd. Pres. Student Concerts Inc., Los Alamos, 1972-74; instr. U. N.Mex., Los Alamos, 1974-76; exec. bd. Boy Scouts of N.Mex. Recipient Outstanding Pub. Svc. medal Joint Chiefs of Staff, 1996. Mem. Am. Phys. Soc., Am. Nuclear Soc. Office: Sandia Nat Labs Albuquerque NM 87185-0101

ROBINSON, CHARLES WESLEY, energy company executive; b. Long Beach, Calif., Sept. 7, 1919; s. Franklin Willard and Anna Hope (Gould) R.; m. Tamara Lindovna, Mar. 8, 1957; children: Heather Lynne, Lisa Anne, Wendy Paige. AB cum laude in Econs., U. Calif., Berkeley, 1941; MBA, Stanford U., 1947. Asst. mgr. mfg. Golden State Dairy Products Co., San Francisco, 1947-49; v.p., then pres. Marcona Corp., San Francisco, 1952-74; undersec. of state for econ. affairs Dept. State, Washington, 1974-75, dep. sec. of state, 1976-77; sr. mng. partner Kuhn Loeb & Co., N.Y.C., 1977-78; vice chmn. Blyth Eastman Dillon & Co., N.Y.C., 1978-79; chmn. Energy Transition Corp., Santa Fe and Washington, 1979-82; pres. Robinson & Assocs., Inc., Santa Fe, 1982—; pres. Dyna-Yacht, Inc., San Diego, 1982—; bd. dirs. The Allen Group, NIKE, Inc. Patentee slurry transport., Brookings Instn., Washington, 1977—. Served to lt. USN, 1941-46. Recipient Disting. Honor award Dept. State, 1977. Republican. Methodist. Office: Robinson & Assocs Inc PO Box 2224 Santa Fe NM 87504-2224

ROBINSON, CLEO PARKER, artistic director. Degree in Dance Edn. Psychology, Denver U., DFA (hon.), 1991. Founder, exec. artistic dir., choreographer Cleo Parker Robinson Dance Ensemble, Denver; mem. dance, expansion arts and inter-arts panels NEA; bd. dirs. Denver Ctr. Performing Arts; tchr. in workshops. Co-creator (documentary) African-Americans at Festae, Run Sister Run, (film) Black Women in the Arts, (music video) Borderline. Recipient Thelma Hill Ctr. for the Performing Arts award, 1986; Choreography fellow NEA; named one of Colo. 100, 1992; named to Blacks in Colo. Hall of Fame, 1994. Mem. Internat. Assn. Blacks in Dance (2nd v.p.). Office: Cleo Parker Robinson Dance Ensemble 119 Parker Ave W Denver CO 80205

ROBINSON, DAVID B., psychiatrist; b. N.Y.C., Dec. 4, 1959; s. Clyde O'Dell and Jane Hayes (Vick) R. BA in Biology, Oberlin Coll., 1983; MD, U. N.C., 1987, MPH, 1989. Diplomate Am. Bd. Psychiatry and Neurology. Resident in psychiatry U. N.C. Hosps., Chapel Hill, 1988-92, fellow in child psychiatry, 1991-93; psychiatrist Bartlett Meml. Hosp. Counseling Ctr., Juneau, AK, 1993-95; pvt. practice Juneau, 1995—; presenter in field. Contbr. articles to profl. publs. Oberlin Coll. scholar, 1979-80, Oberlin Coll. Class of 1928 scholar, 1980-83, Sarah Graham Kenan scholar, 1984-87; U. N.C. fellow Princess Mary Maternity Hosp., Newcastle-Upon-Tyne, England, 1986. Mem. APA (Burroughs-Wellcome fellow 1991-93, corr. mem. com. managed care 1994-95), Physicians Social Responsibility (Broad Street Pump award 1990), Am. Acad. Child Adolescent Psychiatry, Ctrl. Con. Conscientious Objectors, Internat. Physicians Prevention Nuclear War, Delta Omega Theta (Student Svc. award 1989). Office: Alaska Psychiatric Concepts 8800 Glacier Hwy Ste 216 Juneau AK 99801-8080

ROBINSON, DAVID BROOKS, retired naval officer; b. Alexandria, La., Oct. 26, 1939; s. Donald and Marion (Holloman) R.; m. Gene Kirkpatrick, Aug. 1, 1964; children: Kirk, David. Student, Tex. A&M U., 1958-59; BS, U.S. Naval Acad., 1963; MS in Physics, Naval Postgrad. Sch., Monterey, Calif., 1969. Commd. ensign USN, 1963, advanced through grades to vice admiral, 1993; comdg. officer USS Canon and USS Ready, Guam, 1969-71; adminstrv. aide to Chmn. Joint Chiefs Staff, Washington, 1971-74; comdg. officer USS Luce, Mayport, Fla., 1976-78; surface comdr. assignment officer, and dir. fiscal mgt. and procedural control divsn. Naval Mil. Pers. Cmd., 1979-81; mem. Fgn. Service Inst. Exec. Seminar, Washington, 1982; comdg. officer USS Richmond K. Turner, Charleston, S.C., 1983-84; chief of staff, comdr. Naval Surface Force, Atlantic Fleet, Norfolk, Va., 1984; exec. asst. and sr. aide to vice chief Naval Ops., Washington, 1985, dir. Manpower and Tng. div., 1986, dir. Surface Warfare div., 1987-88; cmdr. cruiser destroyer group 8, 1988-89; vice dir. and subsequently dir. operational plans and interoperability directorate Joint Staff, Washington, 1989-91; dep., chief of staff to comdr. U.S. Pacific Fleet, 1991-93, comdr. naval surface force, 1993-96; ret. USN, 1996. Decorated Navy Cross, Def. D.S.M., D.S.M., Legion of Merit with 4 gold stars, Bronze Star, Purple Heart. Mem. Optimists (pres. Oakton, Va. 1986-87). Methodist. Office: 1001 B Ave Ste 200 Coronado CA 92118

ROBINSON, DONALD WALLACE, journalist; b. Burns, Oreg., Dec. 30, 1937; s. Wallace Reginald and Esther Berliot (Rognan) R.; m. Deanna Mae Campbell, Mar. 29, 1958; children: Bruce Campbell, Jennifer Jean Robinson Radlet. BS in Journalism, U. Oreg., 1959. Reporter Medford (Oreg.) Mail Tribune, summer 1955-58, Leader-Post, Regina, Sask., Can., 1959, La Grande (Oreg.) Observer, 1960, Washington Post, 1966-68; reporter The Register-Guard, Eugene, Oreg., 1960-65, assoc. editor, 1969-77, editorial page editor, 1977—. Recipient Outstanding Reporting of Pub. Affairs award Am. Polit. Sci. Assn.; Congl. fellow Am. Polit. Sci. Assn., 1965-66; Knight fellow Stanford U., 1973-74. Home: 2890 Emerald St Eugene OR 97403-1636 Office: The Register-Guard 975 High St Eugene OR 97401-3204

ROBINSON, FRANK ROBERT, radio station executive; b. Hollywood, Calif., Sept. 17, 1938; s. Frank Robert and Helen Macdonnel (James) R.; m. Ann Katherine Carman, Apr. 24, 1965 (div. 1984); children: Geoffrey Scott, Hilary Ann; m. Dian Winget, July 19, 1991. BS, Westminster Coll., 1967. Gen. mgr. Sta. KLUB and Sta. KISN, Salt Lake City, 1970-85; sta. mgr. KUER, 1986-90; western sales mgr. Custom Bus. Systems, Inc.

ROBINSON, HERBERT HENRY, III, educator, psychotherapist; b. Leavenworth, Wash., Mar. 31, 1933; s. Herbert Henry II and Alberta (Sperber) R.; m. Georgia Murial Jones, Nov. 24, 1954 (div. 1974); children: Cheri Dean Asbury, David Keith, Peri Elizabeth Layton, Tanda Rene Graff, Gaila Daire. Grad. of Theology, Bapt. Bible Coll., 1959; BA in Philosophy/Greek, Whitworth Coll., 1968; MA in Coll. Teaching, Ea. Wash. U., 1976; postgrad., Gonzaga U., 1980—. Cert. psychotherapist, perpetrator treatment program supervision. Choir dir. Twin City Bapt. Temple, Mishawaka, Ind., 1959-61; min. Inland Empire Bapt. Ch., Spokane, 1961-73; tchr. philosophy Spokane (Wash.) C.C., 1969-72; dir. Alternatives to Violence, Women in Crisis, Fairbanks, Alaska, 1985-87; tchr. pub. rels. U. Alaska, Fairbanks, 1986-87; dir. Alternatives to Violence Men Inc., Juneau, 1988-89; tchr. leadership mgmt. U. Alaska S.E., Juneau, 1988-89; min. Sci. of Mind Ctr., Sandpoint, Idaho, 1989-92; dir., therapist Tapio Counseling Ctr., Spokane, 1991—; cert. psychotherapist, supr. perpetrator treatment program Wash.; cons. Lilac Blind/Alpha Inc./Marshall Coll., Spokane, 1975-85, Alaska Placer Mining Co., Fairbanks, 1987; tchr. Spokane Falls C.C., Spokane, 1979-85; seminar, presenter Human Resource Devel., Spokane and Seattle, Wash., Pa., 1980; guest trainer United Way/Kellogg Found. Inst. for Volunteerism, Spokane, 1983. 1st trombone San Diego Marine Band, 1953-56, Spokane Symphony, 1961; bd. dirs. Tanani Learning Ctr., Fairbanks, 1987; mem. consensus bldg. team Sci. of Mind Ctr., Sandpoint, 1989-92. Cpl. USMC, 1953-56. Mem. ACA, Assn. for Humanistic Edn. and Devel., Assn. for Religious Values in Counseling, Internat. Assn. Addictions and Offender Counselors, Internat. Assn. Marriage and Family Counselors, Am. Assn. Profl. Hypnotherapists, Masterson Inst. Home: 11611 E Maxwell Ave Spokane WA 99206-4867 Office: Tapio Counseling Svcs Red Flag Bldg # 101A 104 S Freya Tapio Ctr Spokane WA 99202

ROBINSON, HERBERT WILLIAM, corporate executive, economist; b. Hull, Yorkshire, Eng., Jan. 2, 1914; came to U.S., 1943, naturalized, 1948; s. Herbert and Mary Elizabeth (Ellis) R.; m. Elsie Caroline Roenfeldt, May 8, 1948; children—Denise Patricia, Keith Brian. BS in Econs. with 1st class hons., U. Coll. Hull (London/ext.), Eng., 1935; PhD, London Sch. Econs., 1937; DPhil, Oxford U., 1939; DSc in Econs. (hon.), U. Hull, 1992. Sr. lectr. math. statistics, econ. theory, trade cycle theory, indsl. orgn. U. Coll., Hull, 1939; asst. to Lord Cherwell, Prime Minister's Pvt. Office, 1939-42; asst. to Lord Layton, Ministry Prodn., 1942-43; Brit. staff mem. Combined Prodn. and Resources Bd., U.S., U.K., Can., 1943-44; dep. dir. statistics, econ. and statistics div. Ministry Agr. and Fisheries, 1945; chief econ. trends VA, 1946; chief operational analysis div. UNRRA Mission to Poland, 1946-47; loan and econs. depts. World Bank, 1947-51; dep. div. dir. Office Program and Requirements, Def. Prodn. Administrn., 1951-53; pres. Council Econ. and Industry Research, Inc., Washington, 1954-57; pres. renamed corp. C-E-I-R, Inc., 1958-67, chmn. bd., 1954-67; v.p. Control Data Corp., 1968-70; chmn. Internat. Mgmt. Systems Corp., 1970—. Author: Economics of Building, 1939, Election Issues, 1976, Challenge to Government: Management of a Capitalist Economy, 1991, In on the Ground Floor of the Twentieth Century Automation Revolution: An Autobiography, 1997; author articles and reports on econ. subjects. Fellow Royal Statis. Soc. (mem. coun. 1943-44, chartered statistician); mem. Am. Soc. Cybernetics (dir. 1967-75), Am. Econ. Assn., Inst. Mgmt. Scis., Am. Statis. Assn., Royal Econ. Soc., Ops. Rsch. Soc., Econometric Soc., Cosmos Club (Washington), Fountain Hills (Ariz.) Club, Lambda Alpha, Alpha Kappa Psi. *Hard work, intense concentration, planning based on discerning future trends, plus a deep interest in and love for people means success even if combined only with common sense.*

ROBINSON, HURLEY, surgeon; b. L.A., Feb. 25, 1925; s. Edgar Ray and Nina Madge (Hurley) R.; m. Mary Anne Rusche, Mar. 14, 1953; children: Kathleen Ann Robinson Petschke, Mary Elizabeth, Lynda Jean Robinson Lamb, William Hurley, Patricia Kay Robinson Hardy, Paul Edgar. Student, U. Calif., Berkeley, 1943, U. Calif., Santa Barbara, 1946-48; BS, Northwestern U., 1950, MD, 1952. Diplomate Am. Bd. Surgery. Intern Wesley Meml. Hosp., Chgo., 1952-53; resident Milw. County Hosp., 1953-57; surgeon Abbott Med. Group, Ontario, Calif., 1957-59; pvt. practice Upland, Calif., 1959-64; ptnr. Robinson & Schechter Surg. Med. Group, Upland, 1964-92; sr. surg. staff San Antonio Cmty. Hosp., Upland, 1958—, trustee, 1979-81, pres. med. staff, 1980; mem. staff Pomona (Calif.) Valley Med. Ctr., U.S. Family Care Ctr., Montclair, Calif.; exec. com. San Bernardino (Calif.) County Med. Ctr., 1974, adv. bd., 1974; clin. asst. vascular surgery London Hosp., 1973; cons. in field. Co-contbr. articles to Wis. Med. Jour. Chmn. troop com., camp dr. Boy Scouts Am., Upland, 1970-72. With U.S. Army, 1943-46. Fellow ACS, Am. Coll. Chest Physicians, Am. Coll. Angiology; mem. AMA, Am. Med. Soc. Vienna, Calif. Med. Assn., San Bernardino County Med. Soc., Tri-County Surg. Soc. So. Calif. (pres.), Pan-Pacific Surgical Assn., Soc. Clin. Vascular Surgery. Republican. Presbyterian. Office: 415 W 16th St Upland CA 91784-1971

ROBINSON, LAURA ANN, elementary education educator; b. Ridgecrest, Calif., May 8, 1958; d. Robert Louis and Marvel Adeline (Farr) Mick; m. Stephen David Robinson, May 28, 1977 (div. Dec. 1994); children: Nicole Lynne, David James. BS, No. Ariz. U., Flagstaff, 1986, MA, 1991. Elem. tchr. Yuma (Ariz.) Sch. Dist. 1, 1987—. Organizer, editor Youth Authors' Conf. and Book (Dist. Recognition 1989-93). Named Intermediate Tchr. of Yr. Edn. Found., Yuma, 1991. Mem. Yuma Elem. Edn. Assn. (instrn. and profl. devel. 1988-90, treas. 1990-92, pres. elect 1992-93, pres. 1993-94, past pres. 1994-95, bd. liason 1995). Office: Gwyneth Ham Sch 840 E 22nd St Yuma AZ 85365-2425

ROBINSON, LISA HERTZ, public relations consultant; b. Kansas City, Mo., Nov. 13, 1964; d. Frederick Hertz and Judith Tucker; m. John David Robinson, Nov. 16, 1993; 1 child, Rachel Leigh. Student, Phillips Exeter Acad., 1980-83; BA in English Lit. and Composition, Smith Coll., 1987; postgrad., Harvard U. Ext., 1988-90. Devel. and pub. affairs dept. chair Children's Hosp., Boston, 1987-90; mgr. pub. rels. Children's Hosp., Denver, 1990; dir. devel. Women's Found. Colo., Denver, 1991-93; pres. Lisa Robinson Cons., Denver, 1994-96; assoc. dir. Rose Cmty. Found., Denver, 1996—. Mem. Leadership Denver, 1992-93. Jewish. Home: 10 Belleview Way Greenwood Village CO 80121 Office: Rose Cmty Found 4495 Hale Pky Ste 150 Denver CO 80220

ROBINSON, MARK LEIGHTON, oil company executive, petroleum geologist, horse farm owner; b. San Bernadino, Calif., Aug. 4, 1927; s. Ernest Guy and Florence Iola (Lemmon) R.; m. Jean Marie Ries, Feb. 8, 1954; children: Francis Willis, Mark Ries, Paul Leighton. AB cum laude in Geology, Princeton U., 1950; postgrad. Stanford U., 1950-51. Geologist Shell Oil Co., Billings, Mont., Rapid City, S.D., Denver, Midland, Tex., 1951-56, dist. geologist, Roswell, N.Mex., 1957-60, div. mgr., Roswell, N.Mex., 1961-63, Jackson, Miss., 1964-65, Bakersfield, Calif., 1967-68, mgr. exploration econs., N.Y.C., 1969; mgmt. advisor BIPM (Royal Dutch Shell Oil Co.), The Hague, The Netherlands, 1966; pres., chmn. bd. dirs. Robinson Resource Devel. Co., Inc., Roswell, 1970—; chmn., pres. Como Petroleum Corp., Roswell, 1994—. Campaign chmn. Chaves County Rep. Com., Roswell, 1962; mem. alumni schs. com. Princeton U., 1980—. Served with USNR, 1945-46. Mem. Roswell Geol. Soc. (trustee 1972), Am. Assn. Petroleum Geologists, Stanford U. Earth Scientists Assn., Yellowstone Bighorn Research Assn., Am. Horse Shows Assn., SAR, Sigma Xi. Episcopalian. Discovered Lake Como oil field, Miss., 1971, McNeal oil field, Miss., 1973, North Deer Creek Gas Field, Mont., 1983, Bloomfield East Oil Field, Mont., 1986. Home: 1508 Oljato Rd Roswell NM 88201-9300 Office: Robinson Resource Devel Co Inc PO Box 1227 Roswell NM 88202-1227

ROBINSON, MARY SUSAN, nurse administrator; b. San Luis Obispo, Calif., July 3, 1951; d. Allen Marion Diamond and Ella Geraldine (Eidson) Oatman; m. Richard Eugene Robinson, Apr. 21, 1991. AAS in Nursing, Casper Coll., 1982. RN, Colo. Staff nurse, charge nurse Meml. Hosp., Colorado Springs, Colo., 1983-88; staff nurse Colonial Columns Health Care Ctr., Colorado Springs, 1988, coord. staff devel., 1989, DON, 1990; supr. night shift Laurel Manor Care Ctr., Colorado Springs, 1990-91; staff nurse Lincoln Community Hosp. and Nursing Home, Hugo, Colo., 1991, nursing svc. adminstr., 1991-94, 95—. Mem. Am. Soc. Long-Term Care Nurses. Republican. Lutheran. Office: Lincoln Community Hosp and Nursing Home 111 6th St Hugo CO 80821

ROBINSON, RICHARD ALLEN, JR., human resources development trainer, consultant; b. Ellensburg, Wash., Aug. 21, 1936; s. Richard Allen and Rosa Adele (Oswald) R.; m. R. Elaine Whitham, Sept. 8, 1956; children: Sharon E. Robinson Losey, Richard Allen, René L. Rivera. BA, U. Wash., 1958; postgrad. U.S. Army Command and Gen. Staff Coll., 1969-70; MA , U. Mo., 1971. Commd. 2d lt. U.S. Army, 1958, advanced through grades to lt. col., 1972, various infantry assignments including command, 1958-72, research and devel. assignments including dep. dir. test of behavioral sci., dep. commandant U.S.A. Organizational Effectiveness, 1975-77, ret., 1979; chief office orgn. and employee devel. Wash. Dept. Social and Health Services, Olympia, 1979—; pvt. practice orgn. and mgmt. devel. cons./trainer, 1979—. Decorated Legion of Merit with oak leaf cluster, Bronze Star. Mem. Am. Soc. Tng. and Devel., Organizational Devel. Network. Contbg. author: Games Trainers Play, vol. II, 1983. Office: DSHS Mail 8425 27th St W Tacoma WA 98466-2722

ROBINSON, RICHARD GARY, management consultant, accountant; b. Oakland, Calif., Aug. 17, 1931; s. William Albert and Inez Wilhelmina (Zetterblad) R.; BBA, U. Minn., 1955; grad. Indsl. Coll. Armed Forces, 1972; M. Internat. Mgmt., Am. Grad. Sch. Internat. Mgmt., 1980; ABD Internat. Econs., U. Denver; m. Lorraine Mary Deshaies, Nov. 13, 1965 (dec.); children: Elisabeth Claudine (dec.), Christopher Paul. CPA, Colo., N.Mex.; cert. mgmt. cons. Commd. 2d lt. U.S. Air Force, 1955, advanced through grades to maj.; dir. radar ops. tactical air warfare, comdr. strategic missile operation and maintenance functions, project mgr., dir. mgmt. info. systems Dept. Def. activities, S.E. Asia; ret., 1976; mgmt. cons., Colorado Springs, Colo., 1976—; mng. ptnr. A-Action Acctg. & Tax Profls., Colorado Springs, 1994-96; pres. Bus. Devel. Specialists, 1980—; cons. People to People Project Assist to Baltic States Govts. on Trade and Econ. Legis.; dir. CFO Unique Equipment Co.; bd. dirs. United Air Freight Ltd.; CFO, bd. dirs. U.S. Gaming Finance Corp.; mem. adv. bd. Pegasus Learning Co., Inc.; mem. adj. faculty Embry Riddle Aero. U., Luke AFB, Ariz.; mem. faculty U. Phoenix; adj. prof. econs. and internat. bus. Colorado Springs br. Regis U.; U. So. Colo. Mem. bus. adv. council Colo. Internat. Trade Office. Decorated Meritorious Service medal with oak leaf cluster, AF Commendation medal with 2 oak leaf clusters. Mem. Internat. Bus. Assn. of the Rockies (past pres.), Colo. Springs World Affairs Council (bd. dirs.), Am. Mktg. Assn., Armed Forces Communications and Electronics Assn., Am. Mgmt. Assn., Nat. Assn. Accts., Inst. Mgmt. Cons., Assn. Profl. Risk Analysts, N.Am. Soc. Corp. Planning. Lutheran. Home: HC 75 Box 315 13 Camino Potrillo Lamy NM 87540 Office: PO Box 2714 1624 S 21st St Colorado Springs CO 80901

ROBINSON, RONALD ALAN, manufacturing executive; b. Louisville, Mar. 23, 1952; s. J. Kenneth and Juanita M. (Crosier) R.; m. Joan Parker, 1986; children: Rex., Jay. BS, Ga. Inst. Tech., 1974; MBA, Harvard U., 1978. Staff engr., asst. to exec. v.p. ops. Dual Drilling Co., Wichita Falls, Tex., 1978-80; v.p. Dreco, Inc., Houston, 1980-84, pres., dir. subs. Triflo Industries Internat. Inc.; pres., COO Ramteck Systems, Inc., 1984-87; chmn. and CEO Denver Techs. Inc., 1988-95; pres. Svedala Industries, Inc., 1996—; bd. dirs. Dreco Energy Svcs., Ltd., Edmonton, 1984—. Recipient Optimist Internat. Citizenship award, 1970; Gardiner Symonds fellow, 1977. Mem. Harvard Alumni Assn. Home: 4815 Newstead Pl Colorado Springs CO 80906-5935 Office: Denver Equipment Co 621 S Sierra Madre St Colorado Springs CO 80903-4021

ROBINSON, RONALD HOWARD, aeronautical engineer; b. Boise, Idaho, Oct. 21, 1945; s. Jesse Dwite Robinson and Annie Belle (Baxter) Robinson Bruner; m. Linda Anne Kibble, June 17, 1967; children: James Edward, Kristine Marie. AS, Boise State U., 1966; BSAeroE, U. Wash, 1968; MBA with honors, City U., Seattle, 1980. Registered profl. engr., Wash.; lic. pilot, FAA. Various engrng. duties Gen. Electric Corp., Evendale, Ohio, 1969-73; various engrng. duties Boeing Co., Seattle, 1966-69, with comml. airplane div., 1973—, aerodynamics tech. engr., 1973-78, flight ops. engr., jet transport ops. cons., 1978-82, spl. projects mgr., 1982-84, tech. requirements mgr., 1984-85, mgr. airline support 7J7 div., 1986-87, mgr. maintenance and reliability advanced programs, 1987-88, mgr. reliability data acquisition and reporting, 1988-89, chief engr. 777 reliability and maintainability, 1990-93, chief engr. 777 test integration, 1993-95, chief engr. 777 test and cert., 1995-96, dep. chief project engr. 777 design, 1996, chief engr. 747-600/500 test, validation and cert., 1996—, dir. airplane safety, 1997—. Patentee in field. Mem. No. Assn. Retarded Citizens, Seattle, 1978—, Northwest Gifted Child Assn., 1980, Port of Seattle Joint Com. on Aircraft Overflights, 1983-86; com. mem. Boy Scouts Am., Seattle, 1984-88, chmn. 1988-89. Mem. AIAA (sr.), Aircraft Owners and Pilots Assn., Boeing Mgmt. Assn. Republican. Home: 16813 NE 33rd St Bellevue WA 98008-2017 Office: Boeing Comml Airplane Group PO Box 3707 MS 67-XK Seattle WA 98124-2207

ROBINSON, THEODORE GOULD, golf course architect; b. Long Beach, Calif., May 17, 1923; s. Franklin Willard and Hope (Gould) R.; m. Barbara Henderson, Oct. 28, 1949; children: Theodore G. Jr., Kristine Robinson Monroe, Leigha Robinson Ramsey. BA, U. Calif., Berkeley, 1944; MS, U. So. Calif., 1948. With Gordon Whitnall & Assocs., L.A., 1941-51; prin. Robinson Golf Design, Dana Point, Calif., 1951—. Designer 150 golf courses throughout world. Ensign USN, 1943-46. Recipient awards for best new courses Golf Digest. Mem. Am Soc. Golf Course Architects (pres. 1983). Office: Robinson Golf Designs Inc 30131 Town Center Dr # 268 Laguna Niguel CA 92677-2040

ROBISON, WILLIAM THOMAS, retired trade association executive; b. Knoxville, Tenn., Oct. 9, 1924; s. Charles Wilson and Elizabeth Pauline (McGinley) R.; m. Eliza Edwards Lide, Sept. 11, 1948; children: Charlotte Elizabeth, Mary Margaret, Eliza Ann, William Thomas Jr. BS, U. Tenn., 1948; MS, Iowa State Coll., 1949. Asst. extension architect U. Tenn., Knoxville, 1950-51; field rep. Am. Plywood Assn., Atlanta, 1951-63; asst. dir. field services Am. Plywood Assn., Tacoma, 1963-65, dir. field services, 1965-72, v.p. mktg., 1972-81, gen. mgr., 1981-84, pres., 1984-92; ret., 1992. Served to sgt. USAAF, 1943-46, Natousa. Mem. Oakbrook Golf Club (Tacoma). Presbyterian.

ROBKIN, MAURICE ABRAHAM, nuclear engineer, educator; b. N.Y.C., Apr. 25, 1931; s. Simon and Sylvia (Grauer) R.; m. Anne Lou Hawkins, Dec. 30, 1962; children: Matthew Holmes, Jeremy Alexander, Susan Ruth. B.S., Calif. Inst. Tech., 1953; cert., Oak Ridge Reactor Tech. Sch., 1954; Ph.D., M.I.T., 1961. Registered profl. engr., Wash. Scientist Bettis Atomic Power Lab., Pitts., 1954-56; sr. scientist Vallecitos Atomic Lab., Pleasanton, Calif., 1961-67; mem. faculty U. Wash., Seattle, 1967—; prof. nuclear engrng. U. Wash., 1979-91, prof. environ. health, 1981—, dir. Nuclear Reactor Lab., 1983-91; mem. tech. steering panel for Hanford Environ. Dose Reconstrn. Project. Author papers in field. Mem. Am. Nuclear Soc., Health Physics Soc.

ROCCA, JAMES VICTOR, political science educator; b. Spokane, Wash., Mar. 22, 1930; s. Victer Joseph and Pierina (Balzaretti) R.; m. Hilda Kalchhauser, Jan. 16, 1966. BBA, Gonzaga U., 1952; Absolutorium, U. Vienna, Austria, 1962; Doctorate, U. Vienna, 1964. Claims mgr. Gen. Electric, Oakland, Calif., 1956-58; prof. polit. sci. and polit. econ. N.Mex. Highlands Univ., Las Vegas, N.Mex., 1965—; pres. AAUP, Las Vegas, N.Mex., 1968-70. Author: Imunitaet Von Lokaler Strafgerichtsbarkeit, 1965, Ius Humanitas, 1980; contbr. articles to profl. jours. With U.S. Army, 1952-55. Mem. AAUP (pres. N.Mex. state chpt.), VFW, Benevolent Order of Elks.

ROCHA, MARILYN EVA, clinical psychologist; b. San Bernardino, Calif., Oct. 23, 1928; d. Howard Ray Gonding and Laura Anne (Johanson) Walker; m. Hilario Ursala Rocha, Mar. 25, 1948 (dec. Feb. 1971); children: Michael, Sherry, Teri, Denise. AA, Solano Jr. Coll., 1970. BA, Sacramento State U., 1973, MA, 1974; PhD, U.S. Internat. U., 1981. Psychologist, Naval Drug Rehab. Ctr., U.S. Navy, San Diego, 1975-85, chief psychologist, 1983-84; staff clin. psychologist Calif. Youth Authority No. Reception Ctr. Clinic, 1985-92, El Paso de Robles Sch., 1992—; dir. Self-Help Agys., San Diego. Author short story. Vol. counselor Hamonium, San Diego, 1976-77; SMRC Planning Group Scripps/Miramar Ranch, 1982-85; leader Vacaville council Cub Scouts Am., Calif., 1957-62, 4-H, also Brownie's. Recipient Outstanding Svc. award CYA, 1993, Woman of the Yr. award CYA, 1995. Mem. APA, PTA (hon., life), Calif. Scholastic Fedn., Am. Assn. Suicidology, Friends of the Libr. (sec.), Bus. and Profl. Women, Kiwanis Internat., Delta Zeta. Democrat. Unitarian. Home: Morning Glory Ranch 4625 Ross Dr Paso Robles CA 93446-9379

ROCHE, CATHERINE MARY, music educator; b. Salt Lake City, Nov. 27, 1922; d. Maurice Augustine and Marie Joanna (Osborne) R. Student, Royal Conservatory Music, Toronto, Can., 1940-43; BA, U. Man., Winnipeg, Can., 1944; B of Sacred Music, Manhattanville Coll., 1965, B of Music Edn., 1967; MA in Edn., U. San Francisco, 1967; postgrad., Ind. U., 1979-85, U. Pacific, 1990-97; cert. in kodaly, Holy Name Coll., 1992. Cert. tchr., Que., Ind., Calif. Tchr. Soc. of Sacred Heart, Montreal, Halifax, Vancouver, and Winnipeg, Can., 1946-68; tchr. music, art Coll. Sophie Barat, Montreal, Que., 1968-70; tchr. music Acad. Sacred Heart, Montreal, Que., 1970-71; tchr. music, art St. Paul's Sch., Montreal, Que., 1971-79; tchr. music Ind. U., Bloomington, 1979-82, Sir Wilfrid Laurier H.S. and Sir William Hingston H.S., Montreal, 1982-84; pvt. practice Montreal, 1984-89; supr. sch. edn. U. Pacific, Stockton, Calif., 1990-93; Kodaly specialist St. George Sch., Stockton, 1991-97; comml. actor and model, 1996-97; lectr. in field. Recorded Year in Song, 1966; appeared in numerous theatrical prodns. including starring role in (film) Strangers in Good Company, 1988. Organizer, sec. Liturgical Soc., Halifax, Vancouver, 1956-57; organizer edn. projects Filmore Dist., San Francisco, 1966-67; active prison programs Stoney Mountain Prison, Winnipeg, 1967-68. Mem. Am. Assn. Kodaly Educators, Music Educators Nat. Conf., Coll. Music Soc., Internat. Soc. Music Edn., Met. Opera Guild, Pi Kappa Lambda, Phi Delta Kappa. Democrat. Roman Catholic. Home and Studio: CMR Studio 819 Bedford Rd Stockton CA 95204-5215

ROCK, JAMES MARTIN, economics educator, administrator; b. Plymouth, Wis., Aug. 17, 1935; s. Carroll George and Lillian Augusta (Leverenz) R.; m. Bonnie Kirkland Brown, Aug. 20, 1962; children: Jennifer, Peter, James, Sara. BS in Geography, U. Wis., 1957, MS in Rural Sociology, 1960; PhD in Econs., Northwestern U., 1966. Statistician State of Wis., Madison, 1957-58, U.S. Dept. Agrl., Madison, 1958-60, Purdue U., West Lafayette, Ind., 1960-61; econ. analyst CIA, 1964-66; asst. prof. U. Wis., Oshkosh, 1966-67; prof. U. Utah, Salt Lake City, 1967—, univ. prof., 1990—, dept. chairperson, 1992—; founder Econ. Forum, Salt Lake City, 1969-86; dir. Am. Assn. for Advancement of Core Curriculum, Denver, 1989-94. Author: Wisconsin Aluminum Cookware Industry, 1967, Money, Banking and Macroeconomics, 1977, Keynes on Paradox, Rationality and Common Sense, 1997; editor, author: Debt and the Twin Deficits Debate, 1991; contbr. articles to profl. jours. Active ACLU, 1968, Juvenile Justice Coun., Salt Lake City, 1983-85; chairperson Sch. Cmty. Coun., Salt Lake City, 1973-75; life mem. PTA, Salt Lake City, 1983—; founder minority scholarship U. Utah, 1986. Recipient Students' Choice award Assoc. Students, U. Utah, 1992, Svc. award Delta Epsilon, U. Wisc., 1957. Mem. Nat. Assn. Colored People (life, treas. 1980, pres. award 1991), Am. Econs. Assn., Alberta Henry Edn. Found. (co-founder, treas. 1967, pres. award 1973), Utah Assn. Acad. Profls. (vice chair 1977), Omicron Delta Epsilon (organizer, advisor 1971, pres. award 1981), Phi Kappa Phi (faculty award 1971). Office: U Utah Dept Economics Salt Lake City UT 84112

ROCKOFF, SHEILA G., nursing and health facility administrator, nursing and health occupations educator; b. Chgo., Mar. 15, 1945; d. Herbert Irwin and Marilyn (Victor) R.; divorced. ADN, Long Beach City Coll., 1966; BSN, San Francisco State U., 1970; MSN, Calif. State U., L.A., 1976; EDD, South Ea. Nova U., 1993. RN, pub. health nurse, nursing instr., prof., health facility supr., Calif. Staff nurse Meml. Hosp., Long Beach, Calif., 1966-67, Mt. Zion Med. Ctr., San Francisco, 1967-69; instr. nursing Hollywood Presbyn. Med. Ctr., L.A., 1970-74; nursing supr. Orthop. Hosp., L.A., 1974-76; instr. nursing Ariz. State U., Tempe, 1976-78; nurse supr. Hoag Meml. Hosp., Newport Beach, Calif., 1977-78; nurse educator U. Calif., Irvine and Orange, 1978-80; nursing prof. Rancho Santiago Coll., Calif., 1980-89, dir. health svcs., 1989-95, dir., chair Health Occupations, 1995—; nursing prof. Rancho Santiago C.C., Santa Ana Campus; nurse cons. Home Health Care Agy., Irvine, 1983; educator, cons. Parenting Resources, Tustin, Calif., 1985-89. Contbr. articles to profl. jours. Mem. Nat. Assn. Student Personal Administrs., Am. Coll. Health Assn., Calif. Nurses Assn. (chmn. com. 1970-73), Assoc. of Calif. C.C. Administr., Calif C.C. Health Occpl. Educators, Assn. (bd. dirs.), Pacific Coast Coll. Health Assn., Soroptimist Internat., Phi Kappa Phi. Democrat. Jewish. Office: Rancho Santiago CC 1530 W 17th St Santa Ana CA 92706-3315

ROCKRISE, GEORGE THOMAS, architect; b. N.Y.C., Nov. 25, 1916; s. Thomas S. and Agnes M. (Asbury) R.; m. Margaret Lund Paulson, June 12, 1948 (dec. Aug. 1957); children: Christina, Peter; m. Sally S. Griffin, Dec. 1959 (div.); 1 child, Celia; m. Anneliese Warner, Nov. 27, 1985. B.Arch., Syracuse U., 1938; M.S. in Architecture, Columbia U., 1941. Fellow architecture Columbia U., 1940-41; architect Army and Navy, Panama, 1941-45; designer Edward D. Stone, N.Y.C., 1945-46, UN Hdqrs. Planning Commn., 1946-47; archtl. assoc. Thomas D. Church, San Francisco, 1948-49; pvt. practice architecture San Francisco, 1949-86, Glen Ellen, Calif., 1986-87; chmn. bd. Rockrise, Odermatt, Mountjoy Assocs. (architects and planners); lectr. Sch. Architecture, U. Calif., 1949-53; adviser to faculty com. Sch. Architecture, U. Venezuela, Caracas, 1954; mem. San Francisco Art Commn., 1952-56; cons. architect U.S. Dept. State, Japan, 1957-58, Fed. Republic Germany, Venezuela, Brazil, 1978-80, Bahrain, Brazil, Venezuela, Fed. Republic of Germany, 1981; architect U.S. embassy, Bahrain; vis. lectr. Cornell U., Clemson Coll., 1961, Syracuse U., U. Utah, Stanford U., 1962-65, Nat. U. Mex.; lectr. urban design Spanish Ministry Housing and Devel., Madrid, 1978; mem. San Francisco Planning Commn., 1961-62; adviser to Sec. for design HUD, 1966-67; participant State Dept. AID Urban Seminars Latin Am., 1971; mem. U.S. del. Pan Am. Congress Architects, Caracas, 1980; vis. prof. Universidad Central, Mex., 1985. Mem. pres.'s adv. com. U. Mass., 1971; mem. adv. council San Francisco Planning Urban Renewal Assn.; bd. dirs. Telegraph Hill Dwellers Assn., 1985-86, v.p.; pres. Archtl. Found. No. Calif., 1986; apptd. San Francisco Art Commn., 1986-87. Recipient AIA nat. award for residential work, 1953, 59, prog. architecture award citation, 1956, award of honor and award of merit AIA Homes for Better Living Program, 1956, regional awards for residential architecture AIA, 1957, Silver Spur award for Cmty. Svc. to San Francisco, 1996, others; Fulbright fellow in urban design U. Rome, 1978-79. Fellow AIA (pres. No. Calif. chpt. 1961, nat. v.p. 1969-72, mem. nat honor awards jury, mem. nat. commn. urban design and planning 1978); mem. Am. Soc. Planning and Housing Ofcls., Am. Inst. Cert. Planners, Am. Soc. Landscape Architects, Nat. Assn. Housing and Redevel. Ofcls., Glen Ellen (Calif.) Hist. Soc. (housing coord., dir. com. migrant housing workers), Delta Kappa Epsilon, Tau Sigma Delta, Lambda Alpha. Home and Studio: 1280 Hill Rd Glen Ellen CA 95442-9658 *My adult life as architect and planner has been devoted to the construction and improvement of the man-made environment. I have come to believe through this endeavor, that it is the concern and responsibility of all thinking persons, whether professional or lay person to comprehend the forces for change in the environment and to work for the protection and enhancement of our cities and the natural environment.*

ROCKSTROH, DENNIS JOHN, journalist; b. Hermosa Beach, Calif., Feb. 1, 1942; s. Philip Herman and Alicia (Rubio) R.; m. Le Thi Que Huong, May 2, 1970; children: Bryan Benjamin, Paula Kim-Mai. Student, San Luis Rey Coll., 1960-61, El Camino Coll., 1961-62, San Fernando Valley State Coll., 1965-67. Reporter Thousand Oaks (Calif.) News Chronicle, 1966-67; tchr. Girls' High Sch., Qui Nhon, Vietnam, 1967-70; instr. Dalat U./Vietnamese Mil. Acad., 1970-71, Ohlone Coll., Fremont, Calif., 1984—; freelance war corr. Dispatch News Svc., Vietnam, 1967-71; city editor Santa Paula (Calif.) Daily Chronicle, 1972-73; reporter San Jose (Calif.) Mercury News, 1973-90, columnist, 1990—; guest lectr. U. Calif., Berkeley, 1987-91. Vol. Internat. Vol. Svcs., Vietnam, 1967-71; bd. dirs. San Jose unit ARC, 1978, Hope Rehab., San Jose, 1976-77. With U.S. Army, 1962-65, Vietnam. Co-recipient Pulitzer prize for Loma Prieta earthquake coverage, 1989; decorated Army Commendation Medal for Valor, 1965. Mem. Soc. Profl. Journalists, St. Anthony's Sem. Alumni Assn., Nat. Soc. Newspaper Columnists. Roman Catholic. Home: 3573 Tankerland Ct San Jose CA 95121-1244 Office: San Jose Mercury News 39355 California St Ste 305 Fremont CA 94538-1447

ROCKWELL, BURTON LOWE, architect; b. Utica, N.Y., June 3, 1920; s. Burton Lowe and Blanch Louise (Taylor) R.; m. Ruth Aldrich, May 19, 1949; children: Peter Grant, Abbie. BArch, MIT, 1946, MArch, 1947. Registered architect, Calif., N.Y., Vt., Mich., Ind. Project architect John Lyon Reid, Architect, San Francisco, 1947-53; ptnr. John Lyon Reid & Ptnrs., San Francisco, 1953-60, Reid Rockwell Banwell & Tarics, San Francisco, 1960-62, Rockwell & Banwell, San Francisco, 1962-70; pvt. practice Burton Rockwell, FAIA, San Francisco, 1970-88; ptnr. Rockwell, Chatham, Marshall, San Francisco, 1977-88, Rockwell & Rockwell, Architects, San Francisco, 1987—; faculty mem. U. Calif. Berkeley, Coll. Environ. Design, 1962-71; guest prof. MIT, 1969-70; juror Calif. Coalition for Adequate Sch. Housing, Archtl. Competition, 1991; chmn. Calif. Coun. Architects and Engrs., 1965. Architect-designer: Med. Rsch. Facilities, U. Calif., San Francisco, 1968 (AIA honor 1968), ch. sanctuary Lafayette Orinda Presbyn. Ch., 1968 (AIA Bay Area Honor 1974), Ct. House, Govt. Ct., Santa Cruz County, 1967 (Progressive Architecture award); contbr. articles to profl. jours. Bd. dirs. Community Music Ctr., San Francisco, 1972-74, Eastshore Pk. Project, San Francisco, 1975-80, Friends of Recreation and Parks, San Francisco, 1993—; mem. citizens' adv. com. San Francisco Bay Conservation and Devel. Commn., 1966—; mem. archtl. edn. com. Calif. Coun. Higher Edn., Sacramento, 1968-70; mem. bd. examiners Dept. Pub. Works, San Francisco, 1977-78; choir Golden Gate Pk. Master Plan Task Force, 1994—. Served to capt. U.S. Army, 1942-46. Recipient 22 nat. awards for archtl. excellence San Francisco Art Commn., 1953—. Fellow AIA (pres. San Francisco chpt. 1965, bd. dirs., other officers); mem. ASTM, Calif. Coun. Architects (pres. 1968, bd. dirs., other offices 1965—), Constrn. Specification Inst., Am. Soc. Testing and Materials, Internat. Coun. Bldg. Officials. Home: 150 Edgewood Ave San Francisco CA 94117-3713 Office: Rockwell & Rockwell Architects 888 Post St San Francisco CA 94109-6013

ROCKWELL, DON ARTHUR, psychiatrist; b. Wheatland, Wyo., Apr. 24, 1938; s. Orson Arthur and Kathleen Emily (Richards) R.; m. Frances Pepitone-Arreola, Dec. 23, 1965; children: Grant, Chad. BA, Wash. U., 1959; MD, U. Okla., 1963; MA in Sociology, U. Calif., Berkeley, 1967. Diplomate Am. Bd. Psychiatry and Neurology. Intern in surgery San Francisco Gen. Hosp., 1963-64; resident in psychiatry Langley-Porter Neuropsychiatric Inst. U. Calif. Med. Ctr., San Francisco, 1964-67; instr. dept. psychiatry U. Calif. Sch. Medicine, Davis, 1969-70, asst. prof., 1970-74, assoc. prof., 1974-80, acting. assoc., dean curricular affairs, 1979-80, acting assoc. dean student affairs, 1980, assoc. dean student affairs, 1980-82, prof., 1980-84; career tchr. NIMH, 1970-72; assoc. psychiatrist Sacramento Med. Ctr.; med. dir. U. Calif. Med. Ctr., Davis, 1982-84; prof., vice chmn. dept. psychiatry and biobehavioral scis. UCLA, 1984-96, dir. of ops. svcs., 1996—, chief profl. staff Neuropsychiat. Inst.,, 1984-85, also dir. outpatient svcs.; chmn. U. Calif. Hosp. Dirs. Council, 1988-89; cons. Nat. Commn. on Marijuana, Washington, 1971-73. Co-author: Psychiatric Disorders, 1982; contbr. chpts. to books; articles to profl. jours. Bd. dirs. Bereavement Outreach, Sacramento, 1974-84, Suicide Prevention, Yolo County, 1969-84; bd. visitors U. Okla. Sch. Medicine; chmn. hosp. dirs. coun. U. Calif. Hosp.; governing coun. AHA Psychiat. Hosp. Fellow Am. Psychiat. Assn., Am. Coll. Psychiatrists, Am. Coll. Mental Health Adminstrs.; mem. AMA (gov. coun. psych. hosp.), Am. Sociologic Assn., Calif. Med. Assn. (med. staff survey com.), Cen. Calif. Psychiat. Assn. (sec.-pres. 1977-78), U. Okla. Alumni Assn. (trustee 1981-86), Alpha Omega Alpha. Home: 1816 E Las Tunas Rd Santa Barbara CA 93103-1744

ROCKWOOD, LINN ROY, retired recreation executive, educator; b. Salt Lake City, July 26, 1920; s. Franklin Perry and Elizabeth (Riedlebaugh) R.; m. Elsie Morin, Jan. 23, 1946; children: Alan L., Scott C., Kathy, Mary Carol (dec.), Franlin J. BS, Brigham Young U., 1947, MS, 1952; EdD, U. Utah, 1967. Supt. recreation Provo (Utah) City Corp., 1950-60, dir. parks and recreation, 1960-64; pro-mgr. Salt Lake Swim and Tennis Club, Salt Lake City, 1964-66; chmn. recreation dept., tennis coach U. Wis., LaCrosse, 1966-68; chmn. recreation divsn., health/phys. edn./recreation U. Utah, Salt Lake City, 1968-73, grad. coord., 1973-84, prof. emeritus, 1984. Contbr. articles to profl. jours. 1st lt. USMC, 1943-46. Named to Nat. Pub. Parks Tennis Hall of Fame, 1964; named Athlete of Yr. in Utah, Deseret News, 1952; inducted into Utah Sports Hall of Fame, 1974, Brigham Young U. Athletic Hall of Fame, 1976, Utah Tennis Hall of FAme, 1994. Republican. Mormon. Home: 2066 E Rolling Knolls Way Salt Lake City UT 84121

RODDICK, DAVID BRUCE, construction company executive; b. Oakland, Calif., Oct. 31, 1948; s. Bruce Ergo and Hortensia Cabo (Castedo) R.; m. Sharon Ann Belan, May 25, 1975; children: Heather Marie, Christina Dee-Ann. BSCE, U. Calif., Davis, 1971. Engr. Bechtel Corp., San Francisco, 1971-77, contract specialist, 1977-78; subcontract adminstr. Boecon Corp., Richland, Wash., 1978-79; constrn. mgr. BE&C Engrs., Inc., Vancouver, Wash., 1979-81; contracts mgr. Boecon Corp., Tukwila, Wash., 1981-83; sr. constrn. mgr. BE&C Engrs., Inc., Wichita, Kans., 1983-84; v.p. ops. Carl Holvick Co., Sunnyvale, Calif., 1984-88, also sec. bd. dirs.; v.p., gen. mgr. Brookman Co. div. B.T. Mancini Co., Inc., Milpitas, Calif., 1988-92; v.p., sec., CFO B.T. Mancini Co., Inc., 1992—. Mem. devel. com. San Jose (Calif.) Mus. Assn., 1993-95; mem., dir. Constrn. Fin. Mgmt. Assn., 1995—, v.p. Silicon Valley chpt., 1997-98; pres. Reed Sch. PTA, San Jose, 1986-88, San Jose Coun. PTA's, 1988-89; trustee Heart of Valley Bapt. Ch.; bd. dirs. Vinehill Homeowners Assn., 1975-77. Lt. col. USAR, 1969—. Decorated Army Achievement medal, 1988, Commendation medal, 1991, 96; recipient Calif. State PTA Hon. Svc. award, 1988. Mem. ASCE, OCTA, Res. Officers Assn., Am. Arbitration Assn. (mem. panel arbitrators), Engr. Regimental Assn., Calif. Aggie Alumni Assn., Ill. State Geneal. Soc., Santa Maria Valley Geneal. Soc., Army Engr. Assn., U. Calif.-Davis Century Club, Elks, Sigma Nu. Republican. Office: B T Mancini Co Inc 876 S Milpitas Blvd Milpitas CA 95035-6311

RODDY, DAVID BRUCE, college program director; b. Bozeman, Mont., May 18, 1960; s. Robert Bruce and Joanne (Dorn) R.; m. Elizabeth Ann Mittman, Sept. 10, 1994. BA, Mesa State Coll., 1985. Ops. mgr. radio sta. Rodmar Inc., Pagosa Springs, Colo., 1985-87; staff writer Leader Publ., Delta, Colo., 1987-90, News West Publ., Bullhead City, Ariz., 1990; dir. pub. info. Mohave C.C., Kingman, Ariz., 1990—. Dir. Good Shepherd Luth. Ch. Youth Group, Kingman, 1995-96. Recipient amateur photography awards, 1987-88. Mem. Ariz. C.C. Pub. Rels. Coun. (pres. 1993-94), Nat. Coun. for Mktg. and Pub. Rels. Coun. (bd. dirs. 1993-95), Tri-State Press Club (treas. 1995—). Mem. Independent Party. Office: Mohave CC 1971 Jagerson Ave Kingman AZ 86401-1238

RODEFER, JEFFREY ROBERT, lawyer, prosecutor; b. Santa Fe, Mar. 29, 1963; s. Robert Jacob and Joanne D. (Thomas) R. BS, U. Nev., 1985; JD, Willamette U., 1988, cert. dispute resolution, 1988. Bar: Calif. 1990, Nev. 1990, U.S. Dist. Ct. Nev. 1990, U.S. Dist. Ct. (ea. dist.) Calif. 1990, U.S. Ct. Appeals (9th cir.) 1990, Colo. 1991, Oreg. 1997, U.S. Supreme Ct. 1997; cert. arbitrator, Nev. Legal intern Willamette U. Legal Aid Clinic, Salem, Oreg., 1987-88; legal rschr. transp. divsn. Nev. Atty. Gen. Office, Carson City, 1989-90, dep. atty. gen. taxation divsn., 1990-93, dep. atty. gen. gaming divsn., 1993—. Author: Nevada Property Tax Manual, 1993; contbr. articles to Nev. Lawyer. Contbg. mem. U. Nev. Coll. Bus. Adminstrn. and Athletic Dept., Reno, 1992, Willamette U. Coll. Law, Ann. Law Fund, Salem, 1992; active Nat. Parks and Recreation Assn., Washington, 1991; mem. First Christian Ch. Mem. Internat. Assn. Gaming Attys., U. Nev. Coll. Bus. Alumni Assn., Am. Inns of Ct. (Bruce R. Thompson chpt.), State Bar Nev. (functional equivalency com. 1994—), Phi Delta Phi. Republican. Office: Nev Atty Gen Office Capitol Complex Carson City NV 89710

RODEFFER, STEPHANIE LYNN HOLSCHLAG, archaeologist, government official; b. Newark, Ohio, Oct. 5, 1947; d. Jerry Bernard and Joan Elizabeth (Dasher) Holschlag; m. Michael Joe Rodeffer, Sept. 11, 1971. BA, U. Ky., 1969; PhD, Wash. State U., 1975. Instr., then asst. prof. anthropology Lander Coll., Greenwood, S.C., 1974-77; archaeologist interagy. archaeol. svcs. Nat. Park Svc./Heritage Conservation and Recreation Svc., Atlanta, 1977-80; archaeologist divsn. cultural programs Heritage Conservation and Recreation Svc./Nat. Park Svc., Albuquerque, 1980-81; archaeologist div. cultural programs Nat. Park Svc., Santa Fe, N.Mex., 1981-82; archaeologist, acting chief preservation planning br. Nat. Park Svc., Phila., 1982-86; chief interagy. archaeol. svcs. br. div. nat. register programs Nat. Park Svc., San Francisco, 1986-90; chief mus. collections repository Western Archaeol. and Conservation Ctr. Nat. Park Svc., Tucson, 1990—. Muster Chmn. Star Ft. Hist. Com., Ninety Six, S.C., 1975. Recipient spl. achievement award Nat. Park Svc., 1980, 82, mgmt. award So. Ariz. Fed. Execs. Assn., 1992; Woodrow Wilson fellow, 1969. Mem. Soc. for Hist. Archeology (membership chmn. 1976-78, sec.-treas. 1978—, Carol Ruppé Disting. Svc. award 1994), Soc. for Am. Archaeology, Soc. Profl. Archaeologists, Phi Beta Kappa, Zeta Tau Alpha (pres. 1995-97, historian 1994). Roman Catholic. Office: Nat Park Svc Western-Archaeol Cons Ctr 1415 N 6th Ave Tucson AZ 85705-6643

RODES, DAVID STUART, college program director; b. 1939. BA in Comparative Lit. summa cum laude, So. Meth. U., 1961; PhD in English, Stanford U., 1968. Asst. prof. English UCLA, 1966-74, lectr., 1974-79, sr. lectr. in English, 1980—, acting dir. Grunwald Ctr. for the Graphic Arts, 1989-92, dir. Grunwald Ctr. for the Graphic Arts, 1992—; founder chancellor's adv. com. Office of Instrnl. Devel., 1974, chair, 1980-89; acad. advisor BBC-TV Shakespeare series, 1978-84; artistic dir. Shakespeare Santa Cruz, 1981—. Gen. editor Augustan Reprint Soc. Clark Libr., 1969-91; contbr. articles to profl. jours. Mem. Phi Beta Kappa (sec. 1979-72, treas. 1978-80). Office: Armand Hammer Mus Art Culture Ctr Grunwald Ctr Graphic Arts UCLA 10899 Wilshire Blvd Los Angeles CA 90024-4201

RODGERS, FREDERIC BARKER, judge; b. Albany, N.Y., Sept. 29, 1940; s. Prentice Johnson and Jane (Weed) R.; m. Valerie McNaughton, Oct. 8, 1988; 1 child: Gabriel Moore. AB, Amherst Coll., 1963; JD, Union U., 1966. Bar: N.Y. 1966, U.S. Ct. Mil. Appeals 1968, Colo. 1972, U.S. Supreme Ct. 1974, U.S. Ct. Appeals (10th cir.) 1981. Chief dep. dist. atty., Denver, 1972-73; commr. Denver Juvenile Ct., 1973-79; mem. Mulligan Reeves Teasley & Joyce, P.C., Denver, 1979-80; pres. Frederic B. Rodgers, P.C., Breckenridge, Colo., 1980-89; ptnr. McNaughton & Rodgers, Central City, Colo., 1989-91; county ct. judge County of Gilpin, 1987—; presiding mcpl. judge cities of Breckenridge, Blue River, Black Hawk, Central City, Edgewater, Empire, Idaho Springs, Silver Plume and Westminster, Colo., 1978-96; chmn. com. on mcpl. ct. rules of procedure Colo. Supreme Ct., 1984—; mem. gen. faculty Nat. Jud. Coll. U. Nev., Reno, 1990—, elected to faculty coun., 1994—. Author: (with Dilweg, Fretz, Murphy and Wicker) Modern Judicial Ethics, 1992; contbr. articles to profl. jours. Mem. Colo. Commn. on Children, 1982-85, Colo. Youth Devel. Coun., 1989—, Colo. Family Peace Task Force, 1994—. Served with JAGC, U.S. Army, 1967-72; to maj. USAR, 1972-88. Decorated Bronze Star with oak leaf cluster, Air medal. Recipient Outstanding County Judge award Colo. 17th Judicial Dist. Victim Adv. Coalition, 1991; Spl. Community Service award Colo. Am. Legion, 1979. Fellow Colo. Bar Found.; mem. ABA (jud. div. exec. coun. 1989—, vice-chair 1996—, ho. dels. 1993—), Colo. Bar Assn. (bd. govs. 1986-88, 90-92, 93—), Continental Divide Bar Assn., Denver Bar Assn. (bd. trustees 1979-82), First Jud. Dist. Bar Assn., Nat. Conf. Spl. Ct. Judges (chmn. 1989-90), Colo. County Judges Assn. (sec. 1995-96), Colo. Mcpl.

Judges Assn. (pres. 1986-87), Colo. Trial Judges Coun. (v.p. 1994-95, sec. 1996—), Denver Law Club (pres. 1981-82), Colo. Women's Bar Assn., Am. Judicature Soc., Nat. Coun. Juvenile and Family Ct. Judges, Univ. Club (Denver), Arlberg Club (Winter Park), Marines Meml. Club (San Francisco), Westminster Rotary Club (Paul Harris fellow 1996). Episcopalian. Office: Gilpin County Justice Ctr 2960 Dory Hill Rd Golden CO 80403-8768

RODGERS, MARILYN CAROL, special education educator; b. Derby, Conn., May 20, 1951; d. Stanley and Mary Irene (Wojiski) Slowik; m. Billy John Rodgers, Oct. 25, 1940; children: David Warner, Merlinna, Jai, Daniel. BA in Psychology, U. Conn., 1973; AMS Cert., Montessori Western Tchr. Prog., Los Alamitos, Calif., 1975; MA in Spl. Edn., U. Hawaii, Manoa, 1996. Tchr. Hans Christian Anderson Montessori Sch., Tolland, Conn., 1974-76; breathing therapist Rebirth America, San Francisco, 1977-80; singer Allright Family Band, 1980—; spl. edn. tchr. Pahoa Elem. Sch., 1994—; cameraperson Buck Rodgers Hawaiian Beat TV Show and Public Access; founder Hawaii Island for Inclusive Vocat. Experiences, 1996—; lectr. in field. Contbr. articles to profl. jours. Sec. Hawaii Island Theatre, Pahoa. Jehovah's Witness. Home and Office: PO Box 1653 Pahoa HI 96778-1653

RODGERS, STEVEN EDWARD, tax practitioner, educator; b. Pierre, S.D., Feb. 8, 1947; s. Thomas Edward and Dorothy Zoe (Barker) R.; m. Donna Lynn Joyner, June 10, 1984; 1 child, Michelle Ann. Student, State U. S.D., 1964-65, U. Calif., Berkeley, 1968-72; cert., Coll. for Fin. Planning, 1986-87; fellow, Nat. Tax Practice Inst., 1988-89. CFP, Enrolled Agent. Collection mgr. Cenval Leasing-Ctrl. Bank, Long Beach, Calif., 1972-77; tax preparer Rodgers Tax Svc., Las Vegas, 1977-78; CEO Rainbow Tax Svc. Inc., Las Vegas, 1978—; pres. Rainbow Tax Svc., Inc., Las Vegas, 1978-90. Author: Marketing To Build Your Tax Practice, 1994. Active Amnesty Internat., Mensa; chmn. Best in the West Edn. Found., Las Vegas, 1994—, Nat. Assn. Enrolled Agents Edn. Found., 1995-96. With U.S. Army, 1965-68, Vietnam. Mem. Nat. Assn. Enrolled Agts. (nat. sec. 1989-90, nat. treas. 1991-92, nat. edn. chair 1994-95, named Tax Educator of the Yr., 1995), Nat. Assn. Enrolled Agents Edn. Found. (chair 1995-96), Nev. Soc. Enrolled Agts. (charter pres. 1985-86, fellow edn. found.), So. Nev. Assn. Tax Cons. (pres. 1981-82), Nat. Soc. Pub. Accts., Vietnam Vets. Am. Home: 1101 Cahill Ave Las Vegas NV 89128-3335 Office: Rainbow Tax Svc Inc 6129 Clarice Ave Las Vegas NV 89107-1401

RODMAN, ALPINE CLARENCE, arts and crafts company executive; b. Roswell, N.Mex., June 23, 1952; s. Robert Elsworth and Verna Mae (Means) R.; m. Sue Arlene Lawson, Dec. 13, 1970; 1 child, Connie Lynn. Student, Colo. State U., 1970-71, U. No. Colo. Ptnr. Pinel Silver Shop, Loveland, Colo., 1965-68, salesman, 1968-71; real estate salesman Loveland, 1971-73; mgr. Traveling Traders, Phoenix, 1974-75; co-owner Deer Track Traders, Loveland, 1975-85; pres. Deer Track Traders, Ltd., 1985—. Author: The Vanishing Indian: Fact or Fiction?, 1985. Mem. Civil Air Patrol, 1965-72, 87-92, dep. comdr. for cadets, 1988-90; cadet comdr. Ft. Collins, Colo., 1968, 70, Colo. rep. to youth tng. program, 1969, U.S. youth rep. to Japan, 1970. Mem. Bur. Wholesale Sales Reps., Western and English Salesmen's Assn. (bd. dirs. 1990), Internat. Platform Assn., Indian Arts and Crafts Assn. (bd. dirs. 1988-94, exec. com. 1989-92, v.p. 1990, pres. 1991, market chmn. 1992), Crazy Horse Grass Roots Club. Republican. Office: Deer Track Traders Ltd PO Box 448 Loveland CO 80539-0448 *Personal philosophy: I believe that most good and bad in the world comes out of respect or lack of respect for one's self, fellow man, environment and creator.*

RODMAN, FRANCIS ROBERT, psychoanalyst, writer; b. Boston, Feb. 3, 1934; s. Wilfred and Sarah Frieda (Kraus) R.; m. Inger Marianne Andersson, Aug. 17, 1961 (dec. Sept. 1974); children: Ingrid, Simone; m. Katharine Newton; children: Sarah, Nicholas. AB cum laude, Harvard U., 1955; MD, Boston U., 1959. Diplomate Am. Bd. Psychiatry and Neurology. Intern San Francisco Hosp., 1959-60; resident in psychiatry UCLA, 1960-63; staff psychiatrist children's divsn. Camarillo (Calif.) State Hosp., 1963-64; pvt. practice psychiatry, Encino, Calif., 1964-66; tng. in psychoanalysis L.A. Psychoanalytic Soc. and Inst., 1965-71; pvt. practice psychoanalysis, Beverly Hills, Calif., 1968—; mem. Ctr. for Advanced Psychoanalytic Studies, Princeton, N.J., 1978—. Author: Not Dying: A Memoir, 1977, Keeping Hope Alive, 1986; editor: The Spontaneous Gesture-Selected Letters of D.W. Winnicott, 1987. Capt. M.C., U.S. Army, 1966-68. Mem. Am. Psychiat. Assn., Am. Psychoanalytic Assn., So. Calif. Psychiat. Soc., L.A. Psychoanalytic Soc. and Inst., Am. PEN, PEN West. Office: 450 N Bedford Dr Ste 211 Beverly Hills CA 90272

RODMAN, SUE ARLENE, wholesale Indian crafts company executive, artist; b. Fort Collins, Colo., Oct. 1, 1951; d. Marvin F. Lawson and Barbara I. (Miller) Lawson Shue; m. Alpine C. Rodman, Dec. 13, 1970; 1 child, Connie Lynn. Student Colo. State U., 1970-73. Silversmith Pinel Silver Shop, Loveland, Colo., 1970-71; asst. mgr. Traveling Traders, Phoenix, 1974-75; co-owner, co-mgr. Deer Track Traders, Loveland, 1975-85, v.p. Deer Track Traders, Ltd., 1985—. Author: The Book of Contemporary Indian Arts and Crafts, 1985. Mem. U.S. Senatorial Club, 1982-87, Rep. Presdl. Task Force, 1984-90; mem. Civil Air Patrol, 1969-73, 87-90, pers. officer, 1988-90. Mem. Internat. Platform Assn., Indian Arts and Crafts Assn., Western and English Sales Assn., Crazy Horse Grass Roots Club. Mem. Am. Baptist Ch. Avocations: museums, piano, recreation research, fashion design, writing. Office: Deer Track Traders Ltd PO Box 448 Loveland CO 80539-0448

RODNUNSKY, SIDNEY, lawyer, educator; b. Edmonton, Alta., Can., Feb. 3, 1946; s. H. and I. Rodnunsky; m. Teresita Asuncion; children: Naomi, Shawna, Rachel, Tevie, Claire, Donna, Sidney Jr. BEd, U. Alberta, 1966, LLB, 1973; MEd, U. Calgary, 1969, grad. diploma, 1990; BS, U. of State of N.Y., 1988; MBA, Greenwich U., 1990. Served as regional counsel to Her Majesty the Queen in Right of the Dominion of Can.; former gov. Grande Prairie Regional Coll.; now prin. legal counsel Can.; Alta. coord. for gifted children Mensa Can., nat. exec.; past pres. Grande Prairie and Dist. Bar Assn. Author: Breathalyzer Casebook; editor: The Children Speak. Decorated knight Grand Cross Sovereign and Royal Order of Piast, knight Grand Cross Order of St. John the Baptist; knight Hospitaller Order St. John of Jerusalem; Prince of Kiev, Prince of Trabzon, Prince and Duke of Rodori, Duke of Chernigov, Count of Riga, County of St. John of Alexandria; named to Honorable Order of Ky. Colonels; named adm. State of Tex.; recipient Presdl. Legion of Merit. Mem. Law Soc. Alta., Law Soc. Sask., Can. Bar Assn., Inst. Can. Mgmt., Phi Delta Kappa. Home: 3 Grandview Garden Ct, 4802-46A Ave, Athabasca, AB Canada T9S 1H9

RODOLFF, DALE WARD, sales executive, consultant; b. Casa Grande, Ariz., Aug. 5, 1938; s. Norval Ward and Mary Louise (Grasty) Rodolff; m. Kathleen Pennington, Sept. 3, 1960 (div. July 1983); children: David Ward (dec.), Julia Ann. BS in Mining Engring., U. Ariz.; PMD, U. Cape Town; postgrad., Denver Sem. Registered profl. engr., Republic of South Africa. Supt. smelting and fabricating Inspiration Consol. Copper Co., Claypool, Ariz., 1960-72; smelter and refinery supt. Palabora Mining Co, Phalaborwa, Republic of South Africa, 1972-74; asst. mgr. Empress Nickel Mining Co., Gatooma, Zimbabwe, 1974-77; smelter supt. Magma Copper Co., San Manuel, Ariz., 1977-81; v.p., gen. mgr. Sentinel Mgmt. Corp., Tucson, 1981-82; dir., mgr. metallurgy Outokumpu Engring. Inc., Denver, 1982-86, mgr. N.Am., 1986-96, also bd. dirs.; supt. flash smelting and flash converting Kennecott Utah Copper, 1996-97; cons., pres. Dale W. Rodolff Cons., 1986—; pres. Bus. Performance Svcs., Inc., 1986-90; dir. Grace Ministries. Contbr. articles to tech. jours.; inventor scrap rod feed system, 1970. Pres. Y Men's Club, Miami, Ariz., 1969. Kennecott scholar U. Ariz., 1959. Mem. AIME (metall. soc., soc. mining engrs., chmn. smelter div. 1970, 71, pyro metall. com. 1973-77). Lodge: Elks. Home and Office: 6527 S Jungfrau Way Evergreen CO 80439-5308

RODRIGUE, CHRISTINE M(ARY), geography educator, business consultant; b. L.A., Oct. 27, 1952; d. John-Paul and Josephine Genevieve (Gorsky) R. AA in French, German, L.A. Pierce Coll., 1972; BA in Geography summa cum laude, Calif. State U., Northridge, 1973, MA in Geography, 1976; PhD in Geography, Clark U., 1987. Computer analyst Jet Propulsion Labs., Pasadena, Calif., 1977; teaching asst. Clark U., Worcester, Mass., 1976-79, rsch. asst., 1977-78; instr. geography L.A. Pierce Coll., Woodland Hills, Calif., 1981—; cons. Area Location Systems, Northridge, 1984—, tech. writer, 1990—; asst. prof. urban studies and geography Calif. State U., Northridge, 1980-89; asst. prof. geography and planning Calif. State U., Chico, 1989-94, assoc. prof., 1994—; co-dir. Ctr. for Hazards Rsch., 1994—; faculty senator Calif. State U., Chico, 1990-92, grad. geog. adviser, 1992-93, 96—, dir. rural and town planning program, grad. advisor, 1996—; ptnr. Carmel Poster Gallery and Framing, Carmel, Calif., 1989-96; owner Nomad Arabians. Exhibited in L.A. Mcpl. Art Show, 1996, Faculty-Staff Art Show, Chico, 1994, 97; contbr. numerous articles to refereed profl. publs. Mem. bd. advisers So. Calif. Environment and History Conf., 1995—; founder, mem. bd. advisers No. Calif. Environment and History Conf., 1996—. Recipient Meritorious Performance and Profl. Promise award Calif. State U., 1987, 88, 89, Calif. State U. summer scholar grant, 1990, 92, 94. Mem. NOW, Am. Statis. Assn., Assn. Am. Geographers (chmn. splty. group 1983-84, councillor splty. group 1994—), Capitalism Nature Socialism (mem. editl. bd. 1991—), L.A. Geog. Soc. (v.p. 1987, pres. 1988, editor 1981-84), Planetary Soc., Internat. Arabian Horse Assn., Arabian Horse Registry. Democrat. Office: Calif State U Dept Geography & Planning Chico CA 95929-0425

RODRIGUES, ALFRED BENJAMIN KAMEEIAMOKU, marketing consultant; b. Honolulu, Jan. 23, 1947; s. Alfred Benjamin Kameeiamoku and Ruth Shiegeko (Kameda) R. BA, U. San Francisco, 1969; postgrad. U. Wis., 1977. Pub. info. mgr. Hawaiian Tel.-GTE, Honolulu, 1979-80, pub. affairs program mgr., 1980-84, dir. pub. affairs, 1984-85, dir. mktg. communications, 1986-87, dir. mktg. communications and svcs., 1987-89 sr. v.p., Milici, Valenti and Gabriel Advt., Inc., 1989-91, exec. v.p., 1991-92; pres. Al Rodrigues & Assocs., 1992—. Bd. dirs., pub. rels. chmn. Am. Lung Assn., 1981-88; trustee, v.p. Hawaii Army Mus. Soc., 1982—; bd. dirs. ARC Hawaii, 1983-85; budget com. Aloha United Way. Maj. USAR, 1969-89. Decorated Bronze Star with three oak leaf clusters, Meritorious Svc. medal with oak leaf cluster, Army Commendation medal with 2 oak leaf clusters, Purple Heart with oak leaf cluster, Air medal with oak leaf cluster. Mem. Am. Mktg. Assn. (bd. dirs. Hawaii chpt.), Am. Advt. Fedn., Hawaii Advt. Fedn. (bd. dirs., pres., Advt. Man of Yr., 1989), Pub. Rels. Soc. Am. (pres. Hawaii), Res. Officers Assn., Hawaii C. of C., Rotary. Republican. Roman Catholic.

RODRIGUES, MARK, financial executive, manpower consultant; b. Jhansi, India, Oct. 7, 1948; came to U.S., 1983; s. Basil and Monica (Dasgupta) R.; m. Sandra Williams, Mar. 27, 1976; children: Sarah, Daniel. BTech, Loughborough U., Leicester, Eng., 1970; MBA, Strathclyde U., Glasgow, Scotland, 1971. Cert. Acct., Eng. Fin. analyst Ford Europe, Inc., London, 1971-73; mgmt. cons., London mgr. Mann Judd Mgmt. Cons., 1973-78; pres. Bur. and Industry Svcs. Ltd., London, 1978-81; mng. dir. Indsl. Engring. Svcs., London, 1981-83; v.p. Internat. Staffing Cons., Newport Beach, Calif., 1983-88; pres. Brit. Workforce, Inc., Mission Viejo, Calif., 1988—; chmn. Euro Precision Inc., Mission Viejo, Calif., 1992—; pres. Computer Workforce, 1997—. Fellow Assn. Cert. Accts.; mem. Royal Oriental Club. Office: Brit Workforce Inc Ste 234 26012 Marguerite Pkwy Mission Viejo CA 92692-3262

RODRIGUES, MICHELLE BEACHLY, association executive; b. Denver, Oct. 21, 1954; d. Ramey Edward and Nancy Jean (Lund) Beachly; m. Edward Daniel Rodriguez, Aug. 8, 1982. BS in Edn., U. Kans., 1976, MS in Journalism, 1981. Cert. assn. exec. Mng. editor San Francisco Med. Soc., 1984-86, dir. comm., 1986-91, dir. pub./legis. affairs, 1991-92; dir. Calif. Acad. Family Physicians Found., San Francisco, 1994—; asst. exec. dir. Calif. Acad. Family Physicians, San Francisco, 1992—. Contbr. articles to profl. jours. Vol. Feinstein for Gov., San Francisco, 1992, Achtenberg for Mayor, San Francisco, 1995, Habitat for Humanity, 1995—; vol., fundraiser Feinstein for Senate, San Francisco, 1994; vol., designer Mathews for Ctrl. comm. San Francisco, 1996; mem. pub. affairs com. Planned Parenthood of Bay Area, 1991—, abortion providers task force, 1993—; mem. pub. edn./image work group Calif. Primary Care Consortium, 1992—; Haight Ashbury neighborhood vol. San Francisco Neighborhood Emergency Response Team, 1996. Mem. Am. Assn. Med. Execs. Soc. (bd. dirs. 1992—, exec. com., 1996—), Am. Soc. Assn. Execs. (assns. advance Am. com. 1993-94), No. Calif. Soc. Assn. Execs. (Assn. Exec. of Yr. 1996), Nat. Hispanic Bar Assn. (editor, nat. press advisor 1984). Democrat. Presbyterian. Office: Calif Acad Family Physicians 114 Sansome St Ste 1305 San Francisco CA 94104-3824

RODRIGUEZ, ANGELINA, primary school educator; b. Selma, Calif., July 7, 1953; d. John C. and Carmen (Tovar) Martinez; m. Henry Rodriguez, Mar. 9, 1973; children: Michael, Eric-John, Gabriel. AA, Reedley (Calif.) Coll., 1977; BA, Calif. State U., Fresno, 1985; MS, Nat. U., 1996. Multiple subjects tchg. credential. Tchrs. aide Parlier (Calif.) Unified Sch., 1975-77, tchr., 1987—; prin.'s sec. Sanger (Calif.) Unified Sch., 1977-83; tchr. Cutler/Orosi Schs., Orosi, Calif., 1986-87; chairperson Curriculum Coun., Parlier Unified Sch. Dist., 1994-96. Mem. Parlier Women for Action, 1996—. Mem. Am. Assn. Mexican Edn. (pres. 1996—), San Joaquin Valley Math. Project. Office: Parlier Unified Sch Dist 900 Newmark Ave Parlier CA 93648

RODRIGUEZ, CARLOS, fire chief; b. San Jose, Jan. 31, 1953; s. Oscar and Zoila Esther (Juarez) R.; m. Carol Elaine Zajac, Oct. 8, 1996. BS in Fire Sci., Cogswell Coll., 1990. Cert. state fire officer, HazMat technician, paramedic, fire instr. II, fire sci. tchg. credential. Paramedic, paramedic supr. L.A. County, 1972-76; paramedic supr. Medevac, San Mateo County, Calif., 1976-77; firefighter, fire engr. Redwood City (Calif.) Fire, 1977-84, fire capt., 1984-95; fire chief City of Hollister Fire, Calif., 1995—; cons. Real World Enterprises, Hollister, 1996—; chmn. San Benito County Comms. Com., Hollister, 1996—. Participant Calif. Chief's Polit. Action Group, Sacramento, 1996. Sgt. USMC, 1969-72. Decorated Bronze Star, Silver Star, Purple Heart. Mem. Internat. Assn. Fire Chiefs, Calif. Fire Chief's Assn., League of Calif. Cities, Calif. Fire Instrs. Democrat. Roman Catholic. Office: Hollister Fire Dept 110 5th St Hollister CA 95023-3926

RODRIGUEZ, EDWARD JOHN, educational software developer; b. San Antonio, Mar. 27, 1959; s. Robert Benedict and Maria Alicia Rodriguez. BA in Journalism, U. N.Mex., 1981; MBA, Pepperdine U., 1997. Sports reporter, photographer KOAT-TV, Albuquerque, 1978; news announcer KUNM Radio, Albuquerque, 1978-79; news reporter, photographer KOB-TV, Albuquerque, 1979-83; pres. Kismet Prodn. Corp., Albuquerque, 1983-87; asst. coord. Columbia Pictures TV, L.A., 1988-93; adminstr. UCLA Med. Ctr., 1994-95; pres. Evening Star Prodns., L.A., 1996—. Recipient 1st pl. N.Mex. State Wrestling Championship, 1976, 1st pl. award S.W. Creative Writing Assn., 1977, 1st pl. TV comml. award ADDY, Albuquerque, 1985. Home and Office: 3741 S Benley Ave Apt 2 Los Angeles CA 90034

RODRIGUEZ, LEONARD, foundation administrator; b. Phoenix, Jan. 27, 1944; s. Jesus H. and Manuela (Razo) R.; m. Jo Ann Gama, Jan. 16, 1965 ; 1 child, Lena Teresa. BS in Mktg., Ariz. State U., 1981, MPA, 1995. Cert. tchr., Ariz. Adminstrv. svcs. officer Title XX Adminstrn., Phoenix, 1979-81, Block Grants Adminstrn., Phoenix, 1981-84; property mgmt. mgr. State of Ariz., Phoenix, 1984-86; pres. LTR Mgmt. Svcs., Phoenix, 1986-93; dir. PALS computer literacy program N.W. Resources and Learning Ctr., 1989-91; program cons. City of El Mirage, 1989-91; master tchr. Rio Salado C.C., 1989-91; project dir., exec. dir. Westside Coalition for Substance Abuse Prevention, 1990-91; mem. chpt. svcs. Make-A-Wish Found. of Am., 1993—; adj. clin. instr., faculty assoc. Ariz. State U., 1979-89; cons. Applied Econs. Curriculum, Jr. Achievement of Cen. Ariz., Inc., 1987; nat. tng. cons. Ctr. Substance Abuse Prevention, Housing & Urban Devel., Macro Internat., Washington, 1992-93. Chmn. community rels. minority recruitment program Ariz. State U., Tempe, 1985-86; bd. dirs. Concilio Latino de Salud, Inc., pres. 1993-94, Friendly House, Inc., Phoenix, 1985-87, pres., 1987; mem. community problem solving coordinating com. Valley of the Sun United Way, 1988; alliance chmn. Gov.'s Office of Drug Policy, mem. statewide exec. com., 1991; program cons. Cada Uno, Inc., 1990-91; adult literacy coord. Chandler Pub. Libr., 1992-93; tng. cons. Phoenix Fight Back Program, 1992-93; outreach coord. Hemophilia Assn., Ariz., 1992-93. Mem. Ariz. Adminstrs. Assn., Counterparts (founder 1986), Hispanic C. of C., Vesta Club (chmn. scholarship com. 1983), Rotary (pres. 1987-88, voting del. internat. conv. 1987). Home: 6225 N 30th Way Phoenix AZ 85016-2212

RODRIGUEZ, MARGARET LOUISE, crisis intervention counselor, community debriefer and trainer; b. San Diego, Aug. 6, 1962; d. John Francis and Justine Margaret (Deggelman) Wurzel; m. Michael Vincent Rodriguez, Sept. 28, 1962. AA in Social Svcs., Pima C.C., Tucson, Ariz., 1992; BA in Psychology, Prescott Coll., Tucson, 1993; MA in Counseling, Chapman U., Tucson, 1994. Lic. domestic violence, critical incident stress debriefing, Ariz. Asst. mgr. TMC Theatres, Tucson, 1978-82; accounts payable clk. P.F. West, Inc., Tucson, 1982-84; dir. accounts payable E.C. Garcia & Co. Inc., Tucson, 1984-87; mediator Our Town Family Ctr., Tucson, 1993—; crisis interventionist Victim Witness, Tucson, 1990—; dir. support program Tucson Fire Dept. F.L.A.M.E.S., Tucson, 1993, 94; trainer crisis intervention Victim Witness, New Zealand, 1994, vol. coord.; debriefer in pub. schs. after fed. bldg. explosion, Oklahoma City, 1995. Mem. ACA, ASTD, Internat. Assn. Trauma Counselors, Nat. Orgn. Victim Assistance.

RODRIGUEZ, RICK, newspaper managing editor; b. Salinas, Calif.. Grad., Stanford U., 1976; postgrad., Guadalajara, Mex. Newspaper intern Salinas Californian; reporter Fresno (Calif.) Bee; reporter Sacramento (Calif.) Bee, asst. mng. editor, mng. editor, 1993—; mem. Pulitzer Prize juries 1994, 95. Mem. Calif. Chicano News Media Assn. (co-founder Sacramento chpt., past bd. dirs.). Office: Sacramento Bee 2100 Q St Sacramento CA 95852

RODRIGUEZ, WILLIAM JOSEPH, vocational counselor, mental health professional; b. Albuquerque, June 21, 1965; s. Willie Joseph and Bessie (Sedillo) R.; m. Linda G. Rodriguez, Nov 3, 1990; 1 child, William Andrew. Bachelor of Univ. Studies, U. N.Mex., 1990; MA, Webster U., Albuquerque, 1995. Psychol. tech. N.Mex. Dept. of Health, Albuquerque, 1993-94; employment counselor N.Mex. Dept. of Human Svcs., Belen, 1994-95; vocat. counselor divsn. vocat. rehab. N.Mex. Dept. of Human Svcs., Albuquerque, 1995—; mental health worker child-adolescent unit Charter Heights Hosp., Albuquerque, 1996; case mgr. U. N.Mex. Hosp., 1996—; dir. job placement DVR Employer Svcs., Albuquerque, 1995—. Mem. Am. Counseling Assn., Multicultural Counseling and Devel. Assn. Republican. Roman Catholic. Home: 5704 Valle Vista NW Albuquerque NM 87120

ROE, BENSON BERTHEAU, surgeon, educator; b. L.A., July 7, 1918; s. Hall and Helene Louise (Bertheau) R.; m. Jane Faulkner St. John, Jan. 20, 1945; children: David B., Virginia St. John. AB, U. Calif., Berkeley, 1939; MD cum laude, Harvard U., 1943. Diplomate Am. Bd. Surgery, Am. Bd. Thoracic Surgery (dir. 1971-83, chmn. bd. 1981-83, chmn. exam. com. 1978, chmn. long-range planning com. 1980, chmn. program com. 1977). Intern Mass. Gen. Hosp., Boston, 1943-44, resident, 1946-50; nat. rsch. fellow dept. physiology Med. Sch., Harvard U., Boston, Mass., 1947, instr. surgery, 1950; Moseley Traveling fellow Harvard. U. at U. Edinburgh, Scotland, 1951; asst. clin. prof. surgery U. Calif., San Francisco, 1951-58, chief cardiothoracic surgery, 1958-76, prof. surgery, 1966-89, emeritus prof., 1989—; pvt. practice medicine specializing in cardiothoracic surgery San Francisco, 1952-85; cons. thoracic surgery VA Hosp., San Francisco Gen. Hosp., Letterman Army Hosp., St. Lukes Hosp., Blue Shield of Calif., Baxter Labs., Ethicon, Inc.; bd. dirs. Control Laser Corp.; vis. prof. U. Utah, U. Ky., U. Gdansk, Poland, Nat. Heart Hosp., London, U. Ibadan, Nigeria, Sanger Clinic, Charlotte, Rush-Presbyn. Hosp., Chgo., Penrose Hosp., Colorado Springs. Mem. editl. bd. Annals of Thoracic Surgery, 1969-82, Pharos; editor 2 med. texts; author 21 textbook chpts.; contbr. 174 articles to profl. jours. Bd. dirs. United Bay Area Crusade, 1958-70, mem. exec. com., 1964-65; bd. dirs. chmn. exec. com. San Francisco chpt. Am. Cancer Soc., 1955-57; bd. dirs. San Francisco Heart Assn., 1964-72, pres., 1964-65, chmn. rsch. com., 1966-71; mem. various coms. Am. Heart Assn., 1967-70; pres. Miranda Lux Found., 1982-94; trustee Avery Fuller Found.; bd. dirs. Internat. Bioethics Inst., Point Reyes Bird Observatory. Served with Med. Svc. Corps, USNR, 1944-46. Fellow Am. Coll. Cardiology, ACS (chmn. adv. coun. thoracic surgery, program chmn. thoracic surgery, cardiovascular com.), Polish Surg. Assn. (hon.); mem. Am. Assn. Thoracic Surgery (chmn. membership com. 1974-75), AMA (residency rev. com. for thoracic surgery), Am. Surg. Assn., Pacific Coast Surg. Assn., Calif. Acad. Medicine (pres. 1974), Calif. Med. Assn., Soc. Univ. Surgeons, Soc. Throacic Surgerons (pres. 1972, chmn. standards and ethics com.), Soc. Vascular Surgery (v.p.). Clubs: Cruising of Am, Pacific Union, St. Francis Yacht, Calif. Tennis. Office: U Calif Div Cardiothoracic Surgery U Calif M593 San Francisco CA 94143-0118

ROE, CHARLES RICHARD, baritone; b. Cleve., May 24, 1940; s. Andrews Rogers and Margaret (Dalton) R.; children by previous marriage—Charles Andrews, Richard Nevins, Robert Arthur; m. Jo Ann Marie Belli, May 21, 1988. B.Mus., Baldwin-Wallace Coll., 1963; M.Mus., U. Ill., 1964. Instr. in music Tex. Tech. U., 1964-68; asst. prof. music Eastern Mich. U., 1968-74; vis. assoc. prof. U. So. Calif., L.A., 1976-77, assoc. prof., 1979-84, prof., 1984-89; prof. U. Ariz., Tucson, 1989—; vis. prof. and artist in residence Western Mich. U., 1978-79; faculty Music Acad. of the West, 1981, 82. Leading singer, N.Y.C. Opera, 1974-81; appeared in leading roles with, Mich. Opera Theater, Sacramento Opera, San Antonio Opera, Ft. Worth Opera, Ky. Opera, Conn. Opera, Utah Opera, Cleve. Opera, Miss. Opera, Lake George Opera, Shreveport Opera, Toledo Opera; appeared with, symphonies: Phila., Cleve., Detroit, Toledo, Wichita, Duluth. Mem. Am. Guild Musical Artists, Actors Equity, Nat. Assn. Tchrs. Singing (S.W. region Singer of Year 1966), AAUP. Office: U Ariz Sch Music Tucson AZ 85721

ROE, WILLIAM THOMAS, behaviorial engineer, educator, researcher; b. N.Y.C., July 7, 1944; s. William T. and Harriet E. (Higgins) R.; m. Susan C. Kane, Aug. 30, 1972. BA in Engining./Indsl. Psychology, Calif. State U.-Northridge, 1971, MA in Human Factors and Applied Exptl. Psychology, 1978; postgrad., Walden U.; Rsch. asst. XYZYX Info. Corp., Canoga Park, Calif., 1973-74; mem. psychol. staff Manned Systems Scis. Inc., Northridge, 1974-75; rsch. psychologist Inst. Safety and Systems Mgmt., U. So. Calif., L.A., 1975-76; mgr., acct. exec. systems and data processing Mgmt. Recruiters So. Calif., Encino, 1976-79; resource evaluation analyst Samaritan Health Svc., Phoenix, 1979; sr. methods analyst Valley Nat. Bank, Phoenix, 1979-81; indsl. engr. City of Scottsdale, Ariz., 1981-84; prof. psychology Phoenix Coll., 1984—; editorial reviewer numerous major text publs. Author: Ergonomic Models of Human Performance: Source Materials for the Analyst, 1975, Behavioral Engineering:Paradigm for Human Transformation, 1988, Mind-Body Psychology: Source Materialsfor Medical Education, 1995; contbr. articles to profl. jours. With USN, 1961-67, Vietnam. Recipient Recognition certs. San Fernando Valley chpt. Data Data Processing Mgmt. Assn., 1978, Phoenix chpt. 1983, NISOD Teaching Excellence award, 1996. Mem. APA (divsns. 2, 21, 24, 27, 30, 46), AACD, Am. Inst. Indsl. Engrs., Human Factors Soc., World Future Soc., Western Psychol. Assn., Ariz. Counselors Assn., Ariz. Mental Health Counselors Assn. Office: Phoenix Coll 1202 W Thomas Rd Phoenix AZ 85013-4208

ROELKE, ADA (KNOCK-LEVEEN), psychotherapist; b. Cumberland, Md., Aug. 24, 1928; d. George William Knock and Mary Emma (Roelke) Eichelberger; children: Karen Bahnsen, Steven Leveen. BA, Syracuse U., 1950; MSW, San Diego State U., 1967; PhD, Profl. Sch. of Psychol. Studies, 1986. Diplomate Am. Bd. Psychotherapy; bd. cert. social worker; lic. clin. social worker, Calif. Tchr. pub. schs., Syracuse, N.Y., 1960-61; social worker Dept. Pub. Welfare, San Diego, 1964-66; psychiat. social worker State of Calif., Bakersfield, 1967-68; child protection worker Dept. Social Svc., San Diego, 1968-77; pvt. practice psychotherapy La Mesa, Calif., 1969-93; field supr. Sch. of Social Wk. San Diego U., 1969-88; coord., psychotherapist chronic program Grantville Day Treatment Ctr., San Diego, 1977-81; chief social svcs. Edgemoor Geriatric Hosp., Santee, Calif., 1981-88; field supr. Grad. Sch. U. Nev., Reno, 1993-94. Columnist The Nev. Appeal, 1996, 97. Fellow NASW. Unitarian. Home: 919 Arrowhead Dr Carson City NV 89706-0620

ROEMER, EDWARD PIER, neurologist; b. Milw., Feb. 10, 1908; s. John Henry and Caroline Hamilton (Pier) R.; m. Helen Ann Fraser, Mar. 28, 1935 (dec.); children: Kate Pier, Caroline Pier; m. Marion Clare Zimmer, May 24, 1980. BA, U. Wis., 1930; MD, Cornell U., 1934. Diplomate Am. Bd. Neurology. Intern Yale-New Haven Hosp., 1934-36; resident internal medicine N.Y. Hosp., 1936; resident neurology Bellevue Hosp., N.Y.C., 1936-38; instr. Med. Sch. Yale U., New Haven, 1935-36; asst. prof. neurology Cornell U., N.Y.C., 1936-41; prof. neurology U. Wis., Madison, 1946-64; chief of neurology Huntington Meml. Hosp., Pasadena, Calif., 1964-78; pvt. practice Capistrano Beach, Calif., 1978—; founder, dir. Wis. Neurol.

Found., Madison, 1946-64; dir. Wis. Multiple Sclerosis Clinic, Madison, 1946-64; adv. bd. Inst. Antiquities and Christianity, Claremont Grad. Sch., 1970—; dir. found. Univ Good Hope, S.Africa. Contbr. rsch. articles on multiple sclerosis, neuropathies to profl. jours. Lt. col. med. corps U.S. Army, 1941-46, ETO. Fellow ACP, Royal Coll. Medicine, L.S.B. Leakey Found.; mem. Rotary Internat., Annandale Golf Club, El Niguel Country Club, Nu Sigma Nu, Phi Delta Theta. Republican. Home: 35651 Beach Rd Capo Beach CA 92624-1710

ROEMMELE, BRIAN KARL, internet and electronics and publishing and financial and real estate executive; b. Newark, Oct. 4, 1961; s. Bernard Joseph and Paula M. Roemmele. Grad. high sch., Flemington, N.J. Registered profl. engr., N.J. Design engr. BKR Techs., Flemington, N.J., 1980-81; acoustical engr. Open Reel Studios, Flemington, 1980-82; pres. Ariel Corp., Flemington, 1983-84, Ariel Computer Corp., Flemington, 1984-89; pres., chief exec. officer Ariel Fin. Devel. Corp., N.Y.C., 1987-91; pres., CEO Avalon Am. Corp., Temecula, Calif., 1990—; CEO United Credit Card Acceptance Corp., Beverly Hills, 1992—, United ATM Card Acceptance Corp., Beverly Hills, 1992—; pres. Multiplex Media Corp., Beverly Hills, 1993—; pres., CEO Coupon Book Ltd., 1987-89, Value Hunter Mags., Ltd., AEON Cons. Group, Beverly Hills; bd. dirs. The Emporium Network, 1995, Beverly Hills, Waterman Internat., Whitehouse Station, N.J.; electronic design and software cons., L.A., 1980—. Pub., editor-in-chief: Computer Importer News, 1987—. Organizer Internat. Space Week or Day, 1978-83, Internet Engrs. Soc., 1993, Internet Soc., Geneva, 1993—; lectr. Trenton (N.J.) State Mus., 1983; chmn. Internet tech. com. Safe Water Internat., Paris; assoc. dir. World Payment Assn., Geneva. Mem. AAAS, AIAA, ABA, IEEE, World Wide Web Assn. (founder), Am. Bankers Assn., Bankcard Svcs. Assn., Boston Computer Soc., Ford/Hall Forum, Am. Soc. Notaries, Planetary Soc. Office: Avalon Am Corp PO Box 1615 Temecula CA 92593-1615

ROESCHLAUB, JEAN MARIAN CLINTON, restaurant chain executive; b. Berkeley, Calif., June 12, 1923; d. Clifford E. and Nelda M. (Patterson) Clinton; m. David J. Davis III, June 26, 1946 (dec. 1963); children: David J. Davis IV, Diane Davis, Burce Clinton Davis.; m. Ronald Curtis Roeschlaub, Jan. 9, 1965; 1 child, Ronald W. AA, Stephens Coll., 1944. Civilian cons. on loan Q.M. Gen., 1944-45; co-owner, exec. v.p. Clinton's Restaurants, Inc., operators Clinton's Cafeterias, Los Angeles, 1944—. Bd. dirs. Assistance League of So. Calif.; mem. aux. bd. Braille Inst. Am., Los Angeles. Mem. Nat. Restaurant Assn., Calif. State Restaurant Assn., Los Angeles Country Club. Republican. Presbyterian. Home: 222 Monterey Rd Unit 1606 Glendale CA 91206-2071 Office: 515 W 7th St Los Angeles CA 90014-2505

ROFER, CHERYL KATHRINE, chemist; b. Hackensack, N.J., May 7, 1943; d. Christian and Evelyn Friedericke (Grapatin) R. AB, Ripon Coll., 1963; MS, U. Calif., Berkeley, 1964. Project leader Los Alamos (N.Mex.) Nat. Lab., 1965—. Contbr. articles to profl. jours.; patentee in field. Trustee Ripon Coll., 1992—. Recipient Disting. Alumni citation, Ripon Coll., 1991, Disting. Performance award Los Alamos Nat. Lab., 1990; named to Women of Sci. Hall of Fame, Nat. Atomic Mus, 1995. Fellow Am. Inst. Chemists; mem. AAAS, Am. Chem. Soc., N.Y. Acad. Scis., Assn. Women in Sci. Office: Los Alamos Nat Lab PO Box 1663 MS E510 Los Alamos NM 87545

ROGALSKI, CHESTER HARRY, JR., English language and literature educator; b. Grand Rapids, Mich., Mar. 25, 1953; s. Chester Harry and Clara (Sokowolski) R.; m. Jane Elizabeth Bontekoe, Mar. 16, 1958; children: Margaret Sarah, Micah Bryant. BS, Ctrl. Mich. U., 1975, MA, 1977; D of Arts, Idaho State U., 1991. Prof. English, chair Humanities, Fine Arts Ctrl. Wyo. Coll., Riverton, Wyo., 1983—; coord. Ctrl. Wyo. Coll. Title III project, 1983—; faculty cons., reader, Ednl. Testing Ctr., Princeton, N.J., 1992—; presenter We. Regional Honors Conf. Texts of Exploration and Exploitation, 1993. Wyo. Ctrl. Coll. English Conf., Multculturism in the English Classroom, 1993. Recipient Doctoral fellowship and assistantship Idaho State U., Pocatello, 1987, 89; Named Tchr. of Yr., Phi Theta Kappa (Ctrl. Wyo. Coll. chpt.), 1988-89. Office: Ctrl Wyo Coll 2669 Peck St Riverton WY 82501-2216

ROGAN, RICHARD A., lawyer; b. L.A., Sept. 6, 1950. AB with honors, Hamilton Coll., 1972; JD, U. Calif., 1975. Bar: Calif. 1975. Ptnr. Broad, Schulz, Larson & Wineberg, 1978-94, chmn., 1991-93; mem. Jeffer, Mangels, Butler & Marmaro, San Francisco, 1994—. Editorial assoc. Hastings Law Jour., 1974-75. Trustee Bentley Sch., 1989-92. Mem. ABA (mem. corp., banking, and bus. sect.), Bar Assn. of San Francisco (mem. comml. law and bankruptcy sect.), Delta Sigma Rho. Office: Jeffer Mangels Butler et al 12th Fl One Sansome St San Francisco CA 94104

ROGEL, STEVEN R., paper company executive. CEO Willamette Industries, Portland, Oreg. Office: 1300 SW Fifth Ave Portland OR 97201*

ROGERS, ANDREA MARIA, medical administrator; b. Sao Paulo, Brazil, Oct. 7, 1953; came to U.S., 1956; d. Andreas and Erna Josefa (Bihler) Strasser; m. Jerome Edward Rogers, Jan. 10, 1976; 1 child, Shane Jerome. BSN, Loretto Hts. Coll., 1976; MS in Health Svc. Adminstrn., Coll. St. Francis, 1988. RN, Colo., Wash.; cert. rehab. nurse; cert. nursing home adminstr., Colo. Staff nurse ortho/med.-surg. Beth Israel Hosp., Denver, 1976-77; nurse, patient and staff educator rehab. Julia Temple North Rehab., Denver, 1977-79; staff developer Christopher House, Wheat Ridge, Colo., 1979-80; charge nurse, med.-surg. staff nurse Provenant St. Anthony No. Hosp., Denver, 1980-83, charge nurse, med.-surg./oncol. nurse, 1983-87; staff developer Provenant Sr. Life Ctr., Denver, 1987-89, program mgr. Subacute/Extended Care Facility, 1989-92; medicare nurse specialist Denver dist. Hillhaven Corp., Aurora, Colo., 1992-94; medicare compliance case mgr. corp. office Hillhaven Corp., Tacoma, Wash., 1994-96; clin. reimbursement specialist Unison Healthcare, Scottsdale, Ariz., 1996; dir. patient mgmt. Sunquest Consulting, 1996—; cons. Hillhaven Corp., Aurora, 1992-94. Mem. Assn. Rehab. Nurses, Colo. Trout Unltd. Roman Catholic. Home: 3160 Wright St Denver CO 80215 Office: Sunquest Consulting 440 Marshall St Wheat Ridge CO 80033

ROGERS, DONNA ARLENE, counselor; b. L.A., Nov. 14, 1947; d. Glenn M. and Bernice M. Rogers. BS, Calif. State U., 1971; tchg. cert., Oreg. State U., 1979; MS in Counseling Psychology, U. Oreg., 1984. Sales rep. JP Stevens, L.A., 1971-79; tchr. Ashland (Oreg.) Mid. Sch., 1980-87; counselor South Umpqua H.S., Myrtle Creek, Oreg., 1987-89, Forest Grove (Oreg.) H.S., 1989—; on site chair Portland Nat. Coll. Fair, 1995—. Mem. Oreg. Sch. Counseling Assn. (pres. 1996—), Oreg. Counseling Assn. (pres. 1994-97). Office: Forest Grove HS 1401 Nichols Ln Forest Grove OR 97116-3207

ROGERS, DWANE LESLIE, management consultant; b. Maywood, Calif., Oct. 6, 1943; s. Lloyd Donald and Della (McAlister) R.; B.S., Ariz. State U., 1967; M.S., Bucknell U., 1968; m. Doris L. Fantel, Aug. 22, 1970; 1 dau., Valerie Lynn. Successively mktg. research coordinator, customer service analyst, merchandising mgr., product planning mgr., order processing mgr. Samsonite Corp., Denver, 1968-74; dir. adminstrn. WISCO Equipment Co., Inc., Phoenix, 1974-75; dir. discontinued ops. Bowmar Instrument Corp., Phoenix, 1975-77; mgmt. cons., dir. Ariz. ops. Mariscal & Co., Phoenix, 1977-80; mgmt. cons. Ariz. Small Bus. Devel. Center, 1980-81; dir. accounts payable, accounts receivable, crude and finished product acctg. Giant Industries, Phoenix, 1981-92; instr. Maricopa County Community Coll., 1979-83; controller Hawaii Pacific Air, 1993-94; ptnr. Pacific Palms Gift World, 1994—. Mem. Am. Mktg. Assn., Mass Retailing Inst. Republican. Episcopalian. Home: 441 Lewers St Apt 502 Honolulu HI 96815-2449

ROGERS, EARL LESLIE, artist, educator; b. Oakland, Calif., July 8, 1918; s. Robert Ray and Addie Myrtle (Dice) R.; m. Eileen Estelle MacKenzie, Apr. 9, 1945; children: Leslie Eileen, Brian Donald (dec.). Student, L.A. Valley Coll., 1949-52, Northridge State U., 1958-59, UCLA Extension, 1967, Sergei Bongart Sch. Art, 1967-68; AA, Pierce Coll., 1958. Cert. tchr., Calif. Various positions City of L.A., Van Nuys, Calif., 1948-55, Reseda, Calif., 1955-68; pvt. practice Canoga Park, Calif., 1948-68; art tchr. Mariposa (Calif.) County High Sch., 1969-70; art instr. Merced (Calif.) County Coll., 1970—; instr. Earl Rogers Studio Workshop, Mariposa, Calif., 1969—; art dir. Yosemite Nat. Park, Calif., 1973; instr. art Asilomar Conf. Grounds, Pacific Grove, Calif., 1980; juror various art orgns., 1971-95; demonstrator Clovis (Calif.) Art Guild, 1971, 89, Sierra Artists, Mariposa, 1972, 81, 82, 84, 91, Merced Art League, 1976, Yosemite Western Artists, Oakhurst, Calif., 1973, Madera (Calif.) Art Assn., 1978, Chowchilla (Calif.) Art Guild, 1983, 86, 87, 89, 91, Soc. Western Artists, 1981, 89, 93. One-man shows include L.A. City Hall, 1968, Merced Coll., 1969, 95, Mariposa Title Co. Bldg., 1969, Coffee's Gallery, 1970, others; exhibited in group shows including West Valley Artists Assn., 1966-68, L.A. City Hall, 1967, Yosemite Nat. Park, 1973, Soc. Western Artists, 1977-78, Cannon Bldg. Rotunda, Washington, 1982, Mother Lode Gallery, Columbia, Calif., 1977, 78, Arbor Gallery, Merced, 1988, 96, Gold Country Gallery, 1990, 91, Merced Coll., 1969-92, 96, others; represented in permanent collections including John C. Freemont Hosp., Mariposa, Mariposa County Arts Coun., Mariposa Mus. and History Ctr. Asst. scout master Boy Scouts of Am., Canoga Park, Calif., 1956-58; art instr. L.A. Recreation Corps, L.A. Parks and Recreation Dept., 1967. Mem. Soc. Western Artists (Neva Rall Meml. award 1978), Mariposa Mus. and Hist. Ctr. (life), Pastel Soc. West Coast, Oil Painters of Am. Home and Office: 5323 State Highway 49 N Mariposa CA 95338-9503

ROGERS, FRANKLIN ROBERT, former language educator, writer; b. N.Y.C., July 25, 1921; s. Verner Brownell and Anna Elizabeth (Willard) R.; m. Mary Ann Cate, May 26, 1946; 1 child, Bruce David. BA, Fresno State Coll., 1950, MA, 1952; PhD, U. Calif., Berkeley, 1958. Instr. U. Wis.-Milw., 1958-60, asst. prof., 1960-63; asst. prof. U. Calif., Davis, 1963-64; assoc. prof. San Jose State Coll., 1964-68, prof., 1968-86; assoc. prof. U. Lyon, France, 1969-71, U. Paris Sorbonne, 1975-76; seminar lectr. Inst. des Hautes Etudes Sci., Burres-sur-Yvette, France, 1976, Kyoto Am. Studies summer seminar, Kyoto, Japan, 1986; ret., 1986; Fulbright prof. Lyon, 1966-67. Editor: Simon Wheeler, Detective by Mark Twain, 1963, Mark Twain's Satires and Burlesques, 1967, Roughing It by Mark Twain, 1972; author: Mark Twain's Burlesque Patterns, 1960, The Pattern for Mark Twain's Roughing It, 1961, Painting and Poetry (with Mary Rogers), 1985, Occidental Ideographs (with Mary Rogers), 1991; contbr. articles to profl. jours. Mem. MLA. Home: 19205 Skyline Blvd Los Gatos CA 95030-9565

ROGERS, GARTH WINFIELD, lawyer; b. Fort Collins, Colo., Nov. 4, 1938; s. Harlan Winfield and Helen Marie (Orr) R.; m. Joanne Kathleen Rapp, June 16, 1962; children: Todd Winfield, Christopher Jay, Gregory Lynn, Clay Charles. BS, U. Colo., 1958, LLB, 1962. Bar: Colo. 1962; U.S. Dist. Ct. Colo. 1962. Law clk. to presiding justice U.S. Dist. Ct., Denver, 1962-63; assoc. Allen, Stover & Mitchell, Ft. Collins, 1963-68; ptnr. Allen, Rogers & Vahrenwald, Ft. Collins, 1968—. Articles editor Rocky Mountain Law Rev., 1961-62. Bd. advs. Salvation Army, Ft. Collins; past bd. dirs. United Way of Ft. Collins, Trinity Luth. Ch., Ft. Collins, others. Mem. Ft. Collins C. of C. (past bd. dirs.), ABA, Colo. Bar Assn., Larimer County Bar Assn. Office: Allen Rogers & Varenwald 125 S Howes St Fort Collins CO 80521-2737

ROGERS, MICHAEL ALAN, writer; b. Santa Monica, Calif., Nov. 29, 1950; s. Don Easterday and Mary Othilda (Gilbertson) R.; m. Suzanne Elaine Lavoie, May 21, 1995. BA in Creative Writing, Stanford U., 1972. Assoc. editor Rolling Stone Mag., San Francisco, 1972-76; editor-at-large Outside mag., San Francisco, 1976-78; sr. writer Newsweek mag., San Francisco, 1983—; mng. editor Newsweek InterActive, San Francisco, 1993—; exec. prodr. broadband divsn. The Wash. Post Co., 1995-96; v.p. Post-Newsweek New Media, 1996—; vis. lectr. fiction U. Calif., Davis, 1980. Author: Mindfogger, 1973, Biohazard, 1977, Do Not Worry About The Bear, 1979, Silicon Valley, 1982, Forbidden Sequence, 1988; contbr. articles to mags., newspapers. Recipient Disting. Sci. Writing award AAAS, 1976, Best Feature Articles award Computer Press Assn., 1987. Mem. Author Guild, Sierra Club.

ROGERS, PHILO ALAN, osteopath; b. Kirksville, Mo., July 30, 1957; s. Edward A. and Ada (Scott) R.; m. Marla K. Lowe, May 26, 1979; children: Michelle, Joshua, Jessica, Sean. BS, NE Mo. State U., 1979; DO, Kirksville Coll., 1992. Diplomate Am. Bd. Osteo. Medicine; cert. ACLS, Pediat. Advanced Life Support, Am. Heart Assn., Advanced Trauma Life Support, ACS. Intern Mesa (Ariz.) Gen. Hosp., 1992-93, resident in family practice, 1993-95; physician, owner Patients' Choice, Mesa, 1995—. team physician soccer league; coach little league. mem. Am. Osteo. Assn., Christian Med. and Dental Assn., Ariz. Osteo. Med. Assn., Am. Cranial Acad. Office: Patients Choice 6336 E Brown Rd # 101 Mesa AZ 85205-4842

ROGERS, RICHARD GREGORY, sociology educator; b. Albuquerque, Sept. 14, 1955; s. Calvin B. and Eloise (Wood) R.; m. Cynthia P. Raglin, June 14, 1980; children: Mary, Molly, Stacy. BA, U. N.Mex., 1978; MA, U. Tex., 1982, PhD, 1985. Programmer Cancer Rsch. and Treatment Ctr., Albuquerque, 1979-80; NIH population trainee NIH, Austin, 1981-84; asst. dir. tng. Population Prog., U. Colo., Boulder, 1985—, asst. prof. sociology, 1985-92, assoc. prof., 1992—, assoc. chair, 1996-97. Contbr. articles to profl. jours.; assoc. editor Jour. Health & Social Behavior, 1989-92. Mem. Am. Pub. Health Assn., Am. Sociol. Assn., Pacific Sociol. Assn., Population Assn. Am., Soc. for Study of Social Biology (v.p. 1997), So. Demographic Assn. (bd. dirs. 1989-91, v.p. 1991-92, pres.-elect 1996, pres. 1997). Office: Univ Colo Dept Sociology Campus Box 327 Boulder CO 80309-0327

ROGERS, ROBERT REED, manufacturing company executive; b. Oak Park, Ill., Feb. 22, 1929; s. Glen Charles and Lucile (Reed) R.; m. Barbara June Fain, Feb. 22, 1951 (div.); children: Robin, Janeen, Kevin; m. Celeste Sim, Sept. 29, 1993. BS in Chemistry, Berea Coll., 1951; MBA, Ill. Inst. Tech., 1958, postgrad., 1959-62. Asst. mgr. metallurgy research dept. Armour Research Found., Ill. Inst. Tech., 1955-56, mem. faculty, econs. dept., 1956-62; cons. McKinsey & Co., Inc., 1962-64; mgr. devel. planning, profl. group Litton Industries, Inc., 1964-67; pres. N.Am. subs. Muirhead & Co., Ltd., 1967-68; group v.p. Am. Electric Inc. subs. City Investing Co., 1968-70; pres. Cleartight Corp., 1971-73; pres. Newport Internat. Metals Corp., 1973-76; pres. Kensington Assocs., Inc., Newport Beach, Calif., 1976-83; pres., chmn. bd. Proteus Group, Inc., Newport Beach, 1981-83, pres., chmn. bd. Comparator Systems Corp., Newport Beach, Calif., 1983—. Officer USN, 1951-55. Decorated Knight of Grace Sovereign Order St. John; Machinery and Allied Products Inst. fellow, 1956-62; Berea Coll. grantee, 1947-51. Mem. Navy League, Mensa, Intertel, Ferrari Owners Club, Lido Isle Yacht Club. Republican. Mem. Ch. of Religious Sci. Home: 621 Lido Park Dr Ste F1 Newport Beach CA 92663-4409 Office: Comparator Systems Corp 4350 Von Karman Ave Ste 180 Newport Beach CA 92660-2041

ROGERS, STEVEN RAY, physicist; b. Tachikawa, Honshu, Japan, Dec. 6, 1952; came to U.S., 1953; s. Culis Doyle Martin and Mary Lu (Bowles) Rogers; m. Robina Rae Behel, Dec. 27, 1975; children: Miranda Rae, Kellina Gail. BA in Math./Physics magna cum laude, U. No. Colo., 1975; MS in Physics, Kans. State U., 1977. Rschr., instr. Kans. State U., Manhattan, 1975-79; tech. staff ElectroMagnetic Applications, Lakewood, Colo., 1979-82; lead engr. MITRE Corp., Colorado Springs, Colo., 1982—; cons., advisor on system survivability and hardening North Am. Aerospace Def. Command * U.S. Space Command, Colorado Springs, 1982—; adj. prof. Webster U., Colorado Springs, 1994. Contbr. articles to Jour. Physics: Atomic & Molecular, IEEE Transactions on Nuclear Sci. and other profl. jours. Mentor for gifted students Colorado Springs Schs. #20, 1992-93; host family for cadet USAF Acad., Colorado Springs, 1994—. Recipient Program Recognition award MITRE Corp., 1988, 1996. Mem. IEEE (sr., chmn. Pikes Peak sect. 1993-94), Sigma Pi Sigma, Lambda Sigma Tau. Home: 5510 Broadmoor Bluffs Dr Colorado Springs CO 80906-7971 Office: MITRE Corp 1150 Academy Park Loop Ste 212 Colorado Springs CO 80910-3716

ROGERS, STUART EAMES, aerospace engineer; b. Seattle, Aug. 27, 1961; s. Kent Raymond and Anne (Streeter) R.; m. Tamara Ann Eastep, May 26, 1984; 1 child, Zachary James. BS in Aerospace Engring., U. Colo., 1983, MS in Aerospace Engring., 1985; PhD, Stanford U., 1989. Rsch. asst. U. Colo., Boulder, 1983-85; rsch. scientist Sterling Fed. Systems, Palo Alto, Calif., 1985-89; aerospace engr. NASA Ames Rsch. Ctr., Moffett Field, Calif., 1989—. Contbr. articles to profl. jours. mem. AIAA (sr.), Tau Beta Pi. Office: NASA Ames Rsch Ctr Mail Stop 227-2 Moffett Field CA 94035-1000

ROGERS, WILLIAM CORDELL, financial executive; b. Louisville, Apr. 16, 1943; s. Delbert Clifton and Nelle Frances (Grimsley) R.; m. Elaine Elizabeth Nicolay, Apr. 10, 1966; children: William C. II, Erin D., Nicole M., Shannon D. AA, Lincoln Coll., 1969; BS, Ill. State U., 1971; MBA, U. Phoenix, 1993. Exec. Ill. Dept. Revenue, Springfield, 1972-74; fin. dir. Old Heritage Life Ins. Co., Lincoln, Ill., 1974-77; corp. fin. cons. DEN, Inc. CPAs, Tempe, Ariz., 1977-83; v.p., treas. Dahlberg Industries, Scottsdale, Ariz., 1983-91; cons. Act II Printed Cirs. Inc., Tempe, Ariz., 1991-93; self-employed fin. analyst Scottsdale; cons., Scottsdale, 1977—; instr. econ. Lincoln Coll., 1972-77, real estate taxation, 1978-80. With U.S. Army, 1964-67, Vietnam. Recipient Dow Jones award Dow Jones-Wall St. Jour., 1969. Mem. Nat. Assn. Pub. Accts., Ariz. Soc. Pub. Accts., Rotary (bd. dirs. Scottsdale club 1986—, pres., Paul Harris fellow 1985—). Republican. Home and Office: 8549 E Turney Ave Scottsdale AZ 85251-2831

ROGERS, WILLIAM DARROW, history educator; b. Columbia, Mo., Aug. 1, 1944; s. William Eugene and Aurelia Adreon (Gutman) R.; m. Jean Roberts, Dec. 30, 1978. AB in Govt., Cornell U., 1966; AM in History, U. Mo., 1967, postgrad., 1970-73, 79-85. Tchr. Nova H.S., Redding, Calif., 1967-70; claims rep. U.S. Social Security, San Jose, Calif., 1974-76; self-employed banjo tchr. Palo Alto, Calif., 1976-79; news ops. mgr. KOPN-FM, Columbia, Mo., 1981-83; lectr. U. Mo., Columbia, 1984; reporter Columbia Daily Tribune, 1984-86; tchr. Franklin H.S., Stockton, Calif., 1986—. Mem. Orgn. Am. Historians. Democrat. Office: Franklin H S 300 N Gertrude Ave Stockton CA 95215-4820

ROGGE, RICHARD DANIEL, former government executive, security consultant, investigator; b. N.Y.C., July 5, 1926; s. Daniel Richard and Bertha (Sarner) R.; m. Josephine Mary Kowalewska, June 6, 1948 (dec. June 1995); children: Veronica Leigh Rogge-Erbeznik, Richard Daniel, Christopher Ames, Meredith Ann Rogge-Pierce. BS in Bus. Adminstrn., NYU, 1952. Cert. profl. investigator. Clerical worker FBI, N.Y.C., 1947-52, spl. agt., Phila., 1952-54, Washington, 1954-58, supr., 1958-65, asst. spl. agt. in charge, Richmond, Va., 1965-66, Phila., 1966-67, L.A., 1967-69, inspector, 1969, spl. agt. in charge, Honolulu, 1969-72, Richmond, 1972-74, Buffalo, 1974-77, now security cons., investigator, Calif.; police tng. instr.; writer, lectr. in field. With USMC, 1944-46; PTO. Recipient Order of Arrow award Boy Scouts Am., 1943, Svc. to Law Enforcement awards Va. Assn. Chiefs Police, 1975, N.Y. State Assn. Chiefs Police, 1977, others. Mem. Calif. Assn. Lic. Investigators, Calif. Peace Officers Assn., Peace Officers Assn. of Los Angeles County, World Assn. Detectives, Inc., Soc. Former Agts. FBI, Inc., FBI Agents Assn., Am. Legion, K.C., Elks. Republican. Roman Catholic. Home and Office: 32010 Watergate Ct Westlake Village CA 91361

ROGOFF, ALICE ELIZABETH, writer, editor; b. New Rochelle, N.Y., Aug. 10, 1949; d. Julian Rogoff and Gladys Charlotte (Pollak) Rogoff-Sternberg; m. David Henry Williams, Mar. 2, 1989. BA in Anthropology, Grinnell Coll., 1971; MA in English/Creative Writing, San Francisco State U., 1980, MA in Drama, 1990. Co-editor Noe Valley Poets Workshop, San Francisco, 1974; tchr. Rural Inst., Ukiah, Calif., 1993-95; co-editor Haight Ashbury Lit. Jour., San Francisco, 1984—; co-dir. Sr. Reading Theatre, San Francisco, 1996—; bd. dirs. Bay Area Ctr. for Art and Tech., San Francisco, 1994-96, Rural Inst., Ukiah, 1992. Co-editor: (anthologies) Noe Valley: An Anthology of Poetry, 1974, This Far Together, 1996. Mem. newsletter com. San Franciscans for Tax Justice, 1995-96; mem. working com.. War Resisters League, West San Francisco, 1979. Zellerbach Family Fund grantee, 1992, 93, 96. Mem. Coun. Lit. Mags. and Presses, Nat. Writers Union. Home: 558 Joost Ave San Francisco CA 94127-2408

ROHDE, JAMES VINCENT, software systems company executive; b. O'Neill, Nebr., Jan. 25, 1939; s. Ambrose Vincent and Loretta Cecilia R.; children: Maria, Sonja, Daniele. BCS, Seattle U., 1962. Chmn. bd. dirs., pres., Applied Telephone Tech., Oakland, 1974; v.p. sales and mktg. Automation Electronics Corp., Oakland, 1975-82; pres., chief exec. officer, chmn. bd. dirs. Am. Telecorp, Inc., 1982—; bd. dirs. Enerlogica, Inc., 1989-91. Chmn. exec. com., chmn. emeritus Pres.'s Coun. Heritage Coll., Toppenish, Wash., 1985—; chmn. No. Calif. chpt. Coun. of Growing Cos., 1990-93; bd. dirs. Ind. Colls. No. Calif., 1991-93. Named Export U.S. Dept. Commerce Exec. Yr. No. Calif., 1993. Mem. Am. Electronics Assn. (bd. dirs. 1992-94, vice chmn. No. Calif. coun. 1992-93, chmn. 1993-94). Republican. Roman Catholic. Office: Am Telecorp Inc 100 Marine Pky Redwood City CA 94065-1031

ROHLFING, FREDERICK WILLIAM, travel company executive, political consultant, retired judge; b. Honolulu, Nov. 2, 1928; s. Romayne Raymond and Kathryn (Coe) R.; m. Joan Halford, July 15, 1952 (div. Sept. 1982); children: Frederick W., Karl A., Brad (dec.); m. Patricia Ann Santos, Aug. 23, 1983. BA, Yale U., 1950; JD, George Washington U., 1955. Bar: Hawaii 1955, Am. Samoa 1978. Assoc. Moore, Torkildson & Rice, Honolulu, 1955-60; ptnr. Rohlfing, Nakamura & Low, Honolulu, 1963-68, Hughes, Steiner & Rohlfing, Honolulu, 1968-71, Rohlfing, Smith & Coates, Honolulu, 1981-84; sole practice Honolulu, 1960-63, 71-81, Maui County, 1988—; dep. corp. counsel County of Maui, Wailuku, Hawaii, 1984-87, corp. counsel, 1987-88; land and legal counsel Maui Open Space Trust, 1992—; pres. Rohlfing Consulting & Travel, Inc., 1985—; magistrate judge U.S. Dist. Ct. Hawaii, 1991-96; polit. cons., cruise travel adv. Mem. Hawaii Ho. Reps., 1959-65, 80-84; Hawaii State Senate, 1966-75; U.S. alt. rep. So. Pacific Commn., Noumea, New Caledonia, 1975-77, 1982-84. Capt. USNR, 1951-87. Mem. Hawaii Bar Assn., Maui Country Club, Outrigger Canoe Club. Home and Office: RR 1 Box 398 Kekaulike Ave Kula HI 96790

ROHRABACHER, DANA, congressman; b. June 21, 1947; s. Donald and Doris Rohrabacher. Student, L.A. Harbor Coll., 1965-67; BA in History, Long Beach State Coll., 1969; MA in Am. Studies, U. So. Calif., 1976. Reporter City News Svc./Radio West, L.A., 4 yrs.; editorial writer Orange County Register, 1979-80; asst. press sec. Reagan for Pres. Campaign, 1976, 80; speechwriter, spl. asst. to Pres. Reagan White House, Washington, 1981-88; mem. 101st-102nd Congresses from Calif. dist., 1989-93, 103d-105th Congress from 45th dist. Calif., 1993—; U.S. del. Young Polit. Leaders Conf., USSR; disting. lectr. Internat. Terrorism Conf., Paris, 1985; mem. Internat. Rels. com.; chmn. sci. subcom. on space and aeronautics. Recipient Disting. Alumnus award L.A. Harbor Coll., 1987. Office: US House of Reps Rayburn Bldg 2338 Washington DC 20515-0545

ROHRER, DAVID ARNOLD, surgeon; b. Great Falls, Mont., Apr. 6, 1960; s. Arnold M. and Robert B. (Busby) R.; m. Stephanie A. Arnot, Aug. 14, 1982; children: Allison, Kyle, Benjamin. BA in Biology, Carroll Coll., 1982; MD, Creighton U., 1986. Diplomate Am. Bd. Surgery, Nat. Bd. Med. Examiners. Resident in surgery Rush-Presbyn. St. Lukes, Chgo., 1986-91; pvt. practice Gen. and Vascular Surgery, Great Falls, Mont., 1995—. Author: (chpt.) Adjuncts to Cancer Surgery, 1991. Maj. U.S. Army Med. Corps, 1991-95. Fellow Am. Coll. Surgeons; mem. Am. Soc. Gen. Surgeons (charter mem.), Mont. Med. Assn., Cascade County Med. Soc., Alpha Omega Alpha. Office: David A Rohrer MD FACS 400 15th Ave S Ste 107 Great Falls MT 59405-4375

ROHRER, JANE CAROLYN, gifted education specialist, administrator, consultant; b. Faribault, Minn., July 17, 1940; d. Christian A. and Lydia G. (Hilleboe) R.; children: Paula Eisenrich, Lisa Eisenrich, Peter Eisenrich. BS in English, U. Minn., 1962, MA in English, 1964; MA in Edn., Boise (Idaho) State U., 1976; PhD in Spl. Edn./Gifted, Kent State U., 1992. Tchr. English Lompoc (Calif.) High Sch., 1962-63; gifted and talented facilitator Boise Sch. Dist., 1976-84, spl. edn. cons. tchr., 1984-89, spl. edn. adminstrv. intern, 1989-90; faculty Kent (Ohio) State U., 1991-92; dir. Tchr. Edn. Program Sierra Nev. Coll., Incline Village, Nev., 1993—, dean acad. programs, 1995—; mem. Nev. Statewide Task Force on Tchr. Edn., Nev. State English Framework Commn.; numerous publs. and conf. presentations. Choir dir., La., Japan, Idaho, Ohio, Nev., 1966-95. Whittenberger fellow Boise State U., 1975-76. Mem. ASCD, Coun. Exceptional Children (state bd. dirs. 1987-88), Nat. Assn. Gifted Children, S.W. Regional Spl. Edn. Adv. Bd., Idaho Talented and Gifted Assn. (state pres. 1988-89), Nev. Assn. Colls. of Tchr. Edn. (sec.-treas.), Mortar Bd., Phi Beta Kappa, Eta Sigma Upsilon, Pi Lambda Theta, Phi Delta Kappa.

ROITMAN, JAMES NATHANIEL, chemist; b. Providence, R.I., June 29, 1941; s. Aaron H. and Rose B. R.; m. Esther Thommen, June 8, 1972; 1

child, Thomas B. BA, Brown U., 1963; PhD, UCLA, 1969. Rsch. chemist U.S. Dept. Agr., Albany, Calif., 1969—. Mem. Am. Chem. Soc., Am. Soc. Pharmacognosy, N.Y. Acad. Scis. Home: 796 Grizzly Peak Blvd Berkeley CA 94708-1337 Office: USDA WRRC 800 Buchanan St Berkeley CA 94710-1105

ROIZ, MYRIAM, foreign trade marketing executive; b. Managua, Nicaragua, Jan. 21, 1938; came to U.S., 1949; d. Francisco Octavio and Maria Herminia (Briones) R.; m. Nicholas M. Orphanopoulos, Jan. 21, 1957 (div.); children: Jacqueline Doggwiler, Gene E. Orphanopoulos, George A. Orphanopoulos. BA in Interdisciplinary Social Sci. cum laude, San Francisco State U., 1980. Lic. ins. agt. Sales rep. Met. Life Ins. Co., San Francisco, 1977-79; mktg. dir. Europe/Latin Am., Allied Canners & Packers, San Francisco, 1979-83, M-C Internat., San Francisco, 1983-88; v.p. mktg. Atlantic Brokers, Inc., Bayamon, P.R., 1988-92; owner Aquarius Enterprises Internat., San Ramon, Calif., 1992—. Coord. Robert F. Kennedy Presdl. campaign, Millbrae, San Mateo County, local mayoral campaign, Millbrae, 1975; bd. dir., organizer fund-raising campaign for earthquake-devastated Nicaragua; active World Hunger Program Brown U., Childhelp USA. Named Outstanding Employee of Yr. Hillsborough City Sch. Dist., 1973; recipient Sales award Met. Life Ins. Co., 1977. Mem. NAFE, World Affairs Coun. Democrat. Roman Catholic.

ROKKE, DONALD LEIF, aerospace engineer, mechanical engineer; b. Pendleton, Oreg., June 9, 1924; s. Leif R. and Edith Marjorie (Mack) Kraft; divorced; children: Jonathan Leif, Lynn A. BS in Mathematic, U. Wash., 1945; BS in Aerospace Engring., U.S.N.R Midshipman Sch., 1947; BSME, U. Wash., 1948; postgrad., La Salle U., 1996—. Lic. profl. aerospace and mech. engr. Sr. project engr. The Boeing Co., Seattle, 1949-72; sr. engr. Comarco, Ridgecrest, Calif., 1973-74; strategy planner Chemsult A.G., Zug, Switzerland, 1975-79; staff engr. Martin Marietta, Denver, 1980-87; pres., CEO Major Spector Corp., Seattle, 1983—. Contbr. articles to profl. jours. Mem. VFW., received 2 presidential Commendations, 1977, 87, Declared to be Nat. Treas., U.S. Central Intelligence Agy., 1979.Founder & Pres., The Celibacy Found. Seattle, 1991—, pres.,The Endorphn Press, 1995—.

ROKOSZ, RICHARD EUGENE, aerospace manager; b. Evergreen Park, Ill., July 23, 1946; s. Eugene Anthony and Stephanie Bernice (Bedus) R.; m. Darlene Anne Dabney, May 19, 1973; children: Jeffrey Tyler, Bradley Alan. BSBA, Regis Coll., 1968; MS in Mgmt., Regis U., 1991. Chief adminstrv. ops. Martin Marietta, El Segundo, Calif., 1977-80; mgr. bus. ops. Martin Marietta, Houston, 1980-85, Sunnyvale, Calif., 1985-86; mgr. bus. ops. Martin Marietta, Denver, 1986-87, mgr. engring. adminstrn., 1987-92; mgr. info. sys. Lockheed Martin, Denver, 1992—; educator Regis U., Denver, 1992—, chairperson devel. com., 1992, mem. regents bd., 1996. Chairperson Douglas County (Colo.) Sch. adv. bd. Douglas County Schs., 1988-90. Decorated Bronze star. Republican. Roman Catholic. Home: 7968 Chaparral Rd Littleton CO 80124 Office: Lockheed Martin care R E Rokosz DC 1055 PO Box 179 Denver CO 80201

ROLIN, CHRISTOPHER E(RNEST), lawyer; b. Santa Monica, Calif., Feb. 15, 1940; s. Carl A. and Kate (Northcote) R.; m. Debbie Best, April, 1994; children: Whitney, Brett. BA, U. Calif.-Berkeley, 1961; JD, U. So. Calif., 1965. Bar: Calif. 1966. Assoc. Meserve, Mumper & Hughes, L.A., 1966-71, ptnr., 1972; ptnr. Haight, Dickson, Brown & Bonesteel, Santa Monica, Calif., 1974-88; ptnr. Rodi Pollock, L.A., 1990-96, Newkirk, Newkirk & Rolin, 1996—. Bd. dirs. Legion Lex, 1991—, sec., 1995, v.p., 1996, pres. 1997—. Mem. So. Calif. Def. Counsel (bd. dirs. 1981-85), Am. Bd. Trial Advs. (bd. dirs. 1994), L.A. County Bar Assn. (bd. dirs. and vice chmn. law mgmt. sect. 1994, chmn. 1995-96), Am. Arbitration Assn. (arbitrator 1977—). Republican. Club: Optimists (pres. 1989). Home: 2993 Haddington Dr Los Angeles CA 90064-4441 Office: # 460 11620 Wilshire Blvd Los Angeles CA 90025

ROLL, JOHN MCCARTHY, judge; b. Pitts., Feb. 8, 1947; s. Paul Herbert and Esther Marie (McCarthy) R.; m. Maureen O'Connor, Jan. 24, 1970; children: Robert McCarthy, Patrick Michael, Christopher John. B.A., U. Ariz., 1969, J.D., 1972, LLM U. Va., 1990. Bar: Ariz. 1972, U.S. Dist. Ct. Ariz. 1974, U.S. Ct. Appeals (9th cir.) 1980, U.S. Supreme Ct. 1977. Asst. pros. atty. City of Tucson, 1973; dep. county atty. Pima County (Ariz.), 1973-80; asst. U.S. atty. U.S. Atty.'s Office, Tucson, 1980-87; judge Ariz. Ct. Appeals, 1987-91, U.S. Dist. Ct. Ariz., 1991—; lectr. Nat. Coll. Dist. Attys. U. Houston, 1976-87; mem. criminal justice mental health standards project ABA, 1980-83. Contbr. to Trial Techniques Compendium, 1978, 82, 84, Merit Selection: The Arizona Experience, Arizona State Law Journal, 1991, The Rules Have Changed: Amendments to the Rules of Civil Procedure, Defense Law Journal, 1994. Coach, Frontier Baseball Little League, Tucson, 1979-84; mem. parish coun. Sts. Peter and Paul Roman Catholic Ch., Tucson, 1983-91, chmn., 1986-91; mem. Roman Cath. Diocese of Tucson Sch. Bd., 1986-90. Recipient Disting. Faculty award Nat. Coll. Dist. Attys., U. Houston, 1979, Outstanding Alumnus award U. Ariz. Coll. Law, 1992. Mem. Am. Judicature Soc., Fed. Judges Assn., Pima County Bar Assn. Republican. Lodge: K.C. (adv. coun. 10441). Office: US Dist Ct 55 E Broadway Blvd Tucson AZ 85701-1719

ROLLE, MYRA MOSS (MYRA E. MOSS), philosophy educator, author, translator; b. L.A., Mar. 22, 1937; d. Roscoe and Edith (Wheeler) Moss; m. Andrew Rolle, Nov. 5, 1983. BA, Pomona Coll., 1958; PhD, John Hopkins U., 1965. Asst. prof. U. Santa Clara, Calif., 1970-74; tutor philosophy Claremont (Calif.) McKenna Coll., 1975-82, adj. assoc. prof., 1982-88, adj. prof., 1988-89, prof., 1990—, chairperson, 1993-95, assoc. dir. Gould Ctr. for Humanities, 1992-94. Author: Benedetto Croce Reconsidered, 1987; transl.: Benedetto Croce's Essays on Literature, 1990; contbr. articles, essays, book revs. to profl. jours. and books. Mem. adv. coun. Milton Eisenhower Libr., Johns Hopkins U., 1994-96. Mem. Am. Philos. Assn., Am. Soc. for Aesthetics, Am. Soc. for Social Philosophy (bd. dirs. 1983-90, asst. edit. 1988), Am. Soc. for Value Inquiry (assoc. editor jour. 1990-95, assoc. editor book series 1990-96), Phi Beta Kappa. Office: Claremont McKenna Coll Dept Philosophy Claremont CA 91711

ROLLER, DAVID ISAAC, financial services company executive; b. Bklyn., Jan. 13, 1949; s. Morton and Helen (Deligtisch) R.; m. Susan Firtle, June 3, 1973; children: Aviva Natanya, Yael Elisheva. BA, L.I. U., 1971; MA, NYU, 1980, PhD, 1983; PhD, Cleo Soc., Oakland, Mich., 1991; DD, N.W. Ecumenical Inst., Petaluma, Calif., 1992. Ordained rabbi, 1980; cert. religious counselor. Rabbi North Rockland Jewish Cmty. Ctr., Pomona, N.Y., 1980-81; educator, asst. rabbi Old Westbury (N.Y.) Hebrew Congregation, 1982-83; rabbi Beth Emek Congregation, Livermore, Calif., 1983-85; pres., founder Roller Fin. Assocs., Livermore, 1985—; guest rabbi High Holidays, East Bay Chavuarah, Danville, Calif., 1990-93; chaplain Masonic Home for Adults, Union City, Pa., 1992—; mem. Sys Op AOL-Jew Comm Bd., 1995—. Mem. Internat. Assn. Fin. Planners, Am. Coun. Life Underwriters, Am. Assn. Rabbis, East Bay Bd. Rabbis, Masons (chaplain 1985-86), Mensa, Rotary. Republican. Jewish.

ROLLER, SUSAN LORRAYNE, industrial communications specialist, consultant; b. Portsmouth, Va., Sept. 13, 1954; d. Gilbert John Roller and Lois Carolyn (Moore) Logan. BS in Med. Scis., U. Wash., 1976, BA, 1980. Dir. med. programming Omnia Corp., Mpls., 1980-82; program developer Golle & Holmes, Mpls., 1982-83; dir. mktg. Santal Corp., St. Louis, 1983; pres. Fine Line, Ltd., Reno, Nev., 1984—; ind. film prodr., writer. Mem. Reno C. of C., Kappa Kappa Gamma. Republican. Episcopalian.

ROLLINS, LOUIS ARTHUR, editor; b. Cody, Wyo., Sept. 4, 1948; s. George Anthony Rollins and Leslie Vivian (Billings) Lay. BA, Calif. State Coll., 1970. Asst. editor Inst. for Hist. Rev., Torrance, Calif., 1985; editor Loompanics Unltd. (book pub.), Port Townsend, Wash., 1986-96. Author: The Myth of Natural Rights, 1983, Lucifer's Lexicon, 1987. Office: Loompanics Unltd PO Box 1197 Port Townsend WA 98368-0997

ROLLOSSON, MATTHEW PAUL, neuroscience nurse; b. Fayetteville, Ark., July 27, 1962; s. John Paul and Margaret Joan (Lemon) R. AS in Nursing, Highline Comty. Coll., 1992. RN, Wash.; cert. neurosci. RN. Patient care asst. Valley Med. Ctr., Renton, Wash., 1991-92; nurse technician Harborview Med. Ctr., Seattle, 1991-92, registered nurse, 1992-96; registered nurse Thomas Jefferson U. Hosp., Philadelphia, Pa., 1996—. Mem. Am. Assn. Neurosci. Nurses (chmn. recruitment com N.W. chpt. 1996—). Home: 327 Central Ave North Hills PA 19038

ROLLSTIN, GARY RAYMOND, electrical engineer; b. Ephrata, Wash., Jan. 11, 1945; s. Raymond E. and Marie (Danielson) R.; m. Catherine A. Reikofski, June 10, 1971; 1 child, Andrew. BSEE, Colo. State U., 1967, BSBA, 1969. Registered profl. engr., Colo., Ariz., N.Mex. From jr. transmission engr. to substation engr. Tucson Electric Power, Tucson, 1969-74; elec. engr. III City of Grand Island (Nebr.) Utilities, 1974-86; from sr. prodn. engr., chief engr., to asst. elec. dir. City of Farmington (N.Mex.), 1986—. Judge Dist. Sci. Fair, Farmington, 1990, 91, 92, 93, 94, 96; pres. Trinity Evang. Luth. Ch. in Am., 1989, 92, 95, 96, v.p. 1988, 93. Mem. IEEE. Office: Farmington Elec Utility Sys 101 Browning Pky Farmington NM 87401-7995

ROLOFF, JOHN SCOTT, artist, art educator; b. Portland, Oreg., Sept. 20, 1947; s. Harvey John and Eileen (Lyons) R. BA in Art, U. Calif., Davis, 1970; MA in Art, CSUH, Arcata, Calif., 1973. Asst. prof. U. Ky., Lexington, 1974-78; assoc. prof. San Francisco Art Inst., 1978-87, prof., 1988—; asst. prof. U. So. Calif., L.A., 1987-88; artist trustee Djerassi Resident Artists Program, Woodside, Calif., 1995—. Exhibited in group shows at Whitney Mus. Biennial, 1975, Newport Biennial, 1986, Fragile Ecologies, 1992, Internat. Photoscene Cologne, 1996; commd. pub. work Deep Gradient, Yerba Buena Gardens, San Francisco, 1993. Recipient Visual Arts award NEA, 1977, 80, 86; fellow J.S. Guggenheim Found., 1983. Home: 2020 Livingston St Oakland CA 94606 Office: San Francisco Art Inst 800 Chestnut St San Francisco CA 94133-2206

ROLSTON, HOLMES, III, theologian, educator, philosopher; b. Staunton, Va., Nov. 19, 1932; s. Holmes and Mary Winifred (Long) R.; m. Jane Irving Wilson, June 1, 1956; children: Shonny Hunter, Giles Campbell. BS, Davidson Coll., 1953; BD, Union Theol. Sem., Richmond, Va., 1956; MA in Philosophy of Sci., U. Pitts., 1968; PhD in Theology, U. Edinburgh, Scotland, 1958. Ordained to ministry Presbyn. Ch. (USA), 1956. Asst. prof. philosophy Colo. State U., Ft. Collins, 1968-71, assoc. prof., 1971-76, prof., 1976—; vis. scholar Ctr. Study of World Religions, Harvard U., 1974-75; lectr. Yale U., Vanderbilt U., others; official observer UNCED, Rio de Janiero, 1992. Author: Religious Inquiry: Participation and Detachment, 1985, Philosophy Gone Wild, 1986, Science and Religion: A Critical Survey, 1987, Environmental Ethics, 1988, Conserving Natural Value, 1994; assoc. editor Environ. Ethics, 1979—; mem. editorial bd. Oxford Series in Environ. Philosophy and Pub. Policy, Zygon: Jour. of Religion and Sci.; contbr. chpts. to books, articles to profl. jours. Recipient Oliver P. Penock Disting. Svc. award Colo. State U., 1983, Coll. award for Excellence, 1991, Univ. Disting. Prof., 1992; Disting. Russell fellow Grad. Theol. Union, 1991, Disting. Lectr., Chinese Acad. of Social Scis., 1991, Disting. Lectr., Nobel Conf. XXVII, Gifford Lectr., U. Edinburgh, 1997. Mem. AAAS, Am. Acad. Religion, Soc. Bibl. Lit. (pres. Rocky Mountain-Gt. Plains region), Am. Philos. Assn., Internat. Soc. for Environ. Ethics (pres. 1989-94), Phi Beta Kappa. Home: 1712 Concord Dr Fort Collins CO 80526-1602 Office: Colo State U Dept Philosophy Fort Collins CO 80523

ROMAN, STAN G., lawyer; b. Athens, Ga., Dec. 31, 1954; s. Costic and Marilyn (Gracey) R.; m. Elizabeth Ann Whelan, Sept. 18, 1982; children: John, Matthew, Nicholas. BA, U. N.C., 1976; JD with honors, U. Tex., 1979. Bar: Calif. 1979, U.S. Dist. Ct. Calif., U.S. Ct. Appeals (9th cir.). Congl. intern Honorable John Buchanan, Washington, 1977; summer assoc. Bradley, Arant, Rose & White, Birmingham, Ala., 1978; assoc. Bronson, Bronson & McKinnon, San Francisco, 1979-85, ptnr., 1985—; arbitrator, mediator Calif. Superior Ct., San Francisco, 1989—. Mem. ABA, Assn. Bus. Trial Lawyers, Def. Rsch. Inst., Calif. Bar Assn., San Francisco Bar Assn. San Francisco Com. Urban Affairs, Phi Beta Kappa, Phi Eta Sigma. Office: Bronson Bronson & McKinnon 505 Montgomery St San Francisco CA 94111-2552

ROMANO, ALBERT, retired educator, statistical consultant; b. N.Y.C., Feb. 2, 1927. BA, Bklyn. Coll., 1950; MA, Washington U., St. Louis, 1954; PhD, Va. Poly. Inst., 1960. Cert. in mathematical stats. Asst. prof. Ariz. State U., Tempe, 1958-60; staff statistician Motorola Semicondr., Phoenix, 1960-62; postdoctoral fellow Bur. of Standards, Washington, 1962-63; prof. stats. San Diego State U., 1963-90; statis. cons. San Diego, 1990—. Author: Applied Statistics for Science and Industry, 1977; co-author: Business Statistics: Elements and Applications, 1993. Home: 5697 Amaro Dr San Diego CA 92124

ROMANOS, NABIL ELIAS, business development manager; b. Roumie, Metn, Lebanon, June 3, 1965; came to U.S., 1982; s. Elias Rachid and Kamale (Salame) R. BA in Econs. and History magna cum laude, Georgetown U., 1986; postgrad., Hautes Etudes Commerciales, France, 1989; MBA, U. Calif., Berkeley, 1989. Rsch. assoc. Am. Fin. Svcs. Assn., Washington, 1986-87; fin. analyst Varian Assocs., Palo Alto, Calif., 1988, sr. fin. analyst, 1989-91; mgr. fin. mkt. analysis Varian Oncology Systems, Palo Alto, 1991-92; mgr. bus. devel. Varian Health Care Systems, Palo Alto, 1992-94, Zug, Switzerland, 1994-95, São Paulo, Brazil, 1996—. Author: Finance Facts Yearbook, 1987. Vol. tutor for refugees Community Action Coalition, Washington, 1985-86; vol. interpreter emergency room Georgetown U., Washington, 1984-86; internat. vol. Internat. House U. Calif., Berkeley, 1987-89. Scholar Georgetown U., 1985-86, U. Calif., Berkeley, 1987-89. Mem. Phi Alpha Theta. Maronite Catholic.

ROMANOW, ROY JOHN, provincial government official, barrister, solicitor; b. 1939; s. Michael and Tekla R.; m. Eleanore Boykowich, 1967. Arts and Laws degrees, U. Sask. Mem. Sask. Legislative Assembly, 1967-82, 1986—, provincial sec., 1971-72, atty. gen. of province, 1971-82, minister of intergovernmental affairs, 1979-82, leader, Sask. New Dem. Party, 1987—, leader of the opposition, 1987-91, leader of the majority, 1991—, premier, 1991—; opposition house leader for New Dem. Party Caucus, 1986. Co-author: Canada Notwithstanding, 1984. Office: Legislative Bldg, Rm 226, Regina, SK Canada S4S 0B3

ROMANS, ELIZABETH ANNE, writer, artist; b. San Carlos, Calif., May 2, 1961; d. Claude Neal and Patricia Anne (Joynson) R. BA in Econs., San Francisco State U., 1984. Program devel. specialist Am.-Israel C. of C., L.A., 1986-88; pub. rels. exec. Hope Inst., L.A., 1988-89; dir. devel. Sierra Madre coun. Girl Scouts U.S., Pasadena, Calif., 1989-91, Pasadena YWCA, 1991; asst. dir. devel. Rand, Santa Monica, Calif., 1992-94; ptnr. Intrinsic Entertainment, L.A., 1994; freelance writer, cons. L.A., 1993—. Contbr. articles, poems to profl. publs. Grantee Cultural Affairs Divsn. City of Pasadena, 1994, 96; artist resident Armory Ctr. for the Arts, Pasadena, 1994-95, Barnsdall Art Park, L.A., 1995. Mem. Women in Film, Internat. Interactive Comms. Soc., Calif. Poets in the Schs. (asst. area coord. 1995). Democrat.

ROMER, ANN ELIZABETH, school psychologist; b. Jamestown, N.Y., June 21, 1940; d. Andrew Martin and Ellen Jean (Chiverton) Gunnarson; m. Paul A. Romer, July 14, 1962; children: Kirsten, Daniel, Erika. BA, Alfred U., 1962; MEd, Kent State U., 1979, Ednl. Specialist, 1980. Lic. sch. psychologist, Ohio, N.Mex.; assoc. psychologist, Tex. Sch. psychologist Astabual County Bd. Edn., Jefferson, Ohio, 1980-85, Trumbull County Bd. Edn., Warren, Ohio, 1985-90; ednl. diagnostician Gadsden Ind. Sch. Dist., Anthony, N.Mex., 1992-93; level I sch. psychologist Gadsden Ind. Sch. Dist., Anthony, 1993-94, level II sch. psychologist, 1994—; cons. sch. psychologist. Listener Trumbull Contact, Warren, 1972-74; co-leader Girl Scouts U.S., 1971-74. Mem. Nat. Assn. Sch. Psychologists, N.Mex. Assn. Sch. Psychologists (So. state rep. 1993-95, pres.-elect 1995-96, pres. 1996—). Mem. Christian Ch. Office: Gadsden Ind Sch Dist Curriculum & Instrn Dept PO Box Drawer 70 Anthony NM 88021

ROMER, ROY R., governor; b. Garden City, Kans., Oct. 31, 1928; s. Irving Rudolph and Margaret Elizabeth (Snyder) R.; m. Beatrice Miller, June 10, 1952; children: Paul, Mark, Mary, Christopher, Timothy, Thomas, Elizabeth. B.S. in Agrl. Econs., Colo. State U., 1950; LL.B., U. Colo., 1952; postgrad., Yale U. Bar: Colo. 1952. Engaged in farming in Colo., 1942-52; ind. practice law Denver, 1955-66; mem. Colo. Ho. of Reps., 1958-62, Colo. Senate, 1962-66; owner, operator Arapahoe Aviation Co., Colo. Flying Acad., Geneva Basin Ski Area; engaged in home site devel.; owner chain farm implement and indsl. equipment stores Colo.; commr. agr. State of Colo., 1975, chief staff, exec. asst. to gov., 1975-77, 83-84, state treas., 1977-86, gov., 1987—; chmn. Gov. Colo. Blue Ribbon Panel, Gov. Colo. Small Bus. Council; mem. agrl. adv. com. Colo. Bd. Agr. Bd. editors Colo. U. Law Rev., 1960-62. Past trustee Iliff Sch. Theology, Denver; mem., past chmn. Nat. Edn. Goals Panel; co-chmn. Nat. Coun. on Standards and Testing. With USAF, 1952-53. Mem. Dem. Gov.'s Assn. (chmn.), Nat. Gov.'s Assn. (former chmn.), Colo. Bar Assn., Order of the Coif. Democrat. Presbyterian. Office: Office of Gov State Capitol Bldg Rm 136 Denver CO 80203*

ROMERO, OLIVIA DOLORES, counselor; b. Albuquerque, Dec. 10, 1969; d. Alfonso Lincoln and Celsa Josephine Romero. BA in Psychology, U. N.Mex., 1991, MA in Counseling, 1993. Cert. counselor, N.Mex. Fashions clerk K-Mart, Albuquerque, 1990-1993, cashier, 1993-1994; family counseling intern Youth & Family Counseling, Albuquerque, 1993; outreach counselor Martineztown House of Neighborly Svc., Albuquerque, 1994; counselor Peanut Butter & Jelly Therapeutic Presch., Albuquerque, 1994—. Mem. ACA, Am. Assn. Aging & Devel. Democrat. Roman Catholic. Home: 1304 Delamar NW Albuquerque NM 87107 Office: 1101 Lopez SW Albuquerque NM 87105

ROMERO, PHILIP JOSEPH, economic and policy advisor; b. Abington, Pa., Mar. 22, 1957; s. Joseph John and Mildred Edith (Laundis) R.; m. Lita Grace Flores, Oct. 6, 1984. BA in Econs. and Polit. Sci., Cornell U., 1979; PhD in Policy Analysts, Rand Grad. Sch., 1988. Asst. to mayor Twp. of East Brunswick, N.J., 1977-78; policy analyst Sci. Applications Internat. Corp., Washington, 1980-83; rsch. assoc. RAND Corp., Santa Monica, Calif., 1983-88, assoc. economist, 1988-90; dir. strategic planning United Technologies/Carrier, Hartford, Conn., 1990-91; chief economist Gov.'s Office, Sacramento, Calif., 1991—, dep. cabinet sec., 1995—; exec. dir. Calif. Managed Health Care Improvement Task Force, 1996—; cons. Office of Tech. Assessment, Washington, 1989-90, RAND Corp., Washington, 1990-91, Sec. of Air Forces Sci. Adv. Bd., Washington, 1980-83, Undersec. of Def., Washington, 1985-86; adj. prof. U. So. Calif. and Calif. State U., 1994—; mem. Coun. on Fgn. Rels., 1994—; mem. econ. adv. coun. Calif. Congl. Delegation, 1993—. Co-author: (book) The Deescalation of Nuclear Crises, 1992; contbr. numerous reports and papers to profl. publs. Pres. RAND Grad. Sch. Alumni Assn., Santa Monica, 1989—; founder Adopt-A-School Honors Program, Pacific Palisades, Calif., 1986. Recipient Internat. Affairs fellowship Coun. on Fgn. Rels., N.Y.C., 1989. Mem. The Planning Forum, Am. Econ. Assn., Ops. Rsch. Soc. of Am., Pacific Coun. on Internat. Policy (founding), Acad. Pub. Policy Analysts and Mgmt., Inst. Mgmt. Sci. Home: 1587 Barnett Cir Carmichael CA 95608-5852 Office: Gov's Office State Capitol Sacramento CA 95814-4906

ROMESBURG, KERRY D., state education administrator; b. Akron, Ohio, Mar. 12, 1945; s. Bert Lewis and Edna (Bartlett) R.; m. Judy Kaye Land, July 2, 1965; children—Rod A., Donald A. B.A., Ariz. State U., 1967, M.A., 1968, Ph.D., 1972. Tchr. math. East High Sch., Phoenix, 1969-70; asst. dir. instl. research Ariz. State U., Tempe, 1972-73; planning analyst Ariz. Bd. Regents, Phoenix, 1973-74; exec. dir. Ariz. Commn. Post Secondary Edn., Phoenix, 1974-75; exec. dir. Alaska Commn. Postsecondary Edn., Juneau, 1975—. Mem. Western Insterstate Commn. on Higher Edn., Boulder, Colo., 1977—, chmn., 1981-82; mem. Western Tech. Manpower Council, 1982—; mem. Nat. Adv. Council for United Student Aid Funds, N.Y.C., 1978—. Recipient Outstanding Alumnus award Ariz. State U., 1982; NDEA fellow, 1972. Mem. State Higher Edn. Exec. Officers, Nat. Adv. Council State Postsecondary Planning Commns., Am. Assn. Higher Edn., NEA. Home: 308 Distin Ave Juneau AK 99801-1669 Office: Alaska Commn Postsecondary Edn Pough FP Juneau AK 99811 also: Utah Valley Community Coll 800 W 1200 N Provo UT 84604-3222

RONALD, ANN, English literature educator; b. Seattle, Oct. 9, 1939; d. James Quintin and Cleo Elizabeth (Keller) R. BA, Whitman Coll., 1961; MA, U. Colo., 1966; PhD, Northwestern U., 1970. Prof. English lit. U. Nev., Reno, 1970—, acting dean grad. sch., 1988-89, dean Coll. of Arts and Sci., 1989-96. Author: The New West of Edward Abbey, 1982, reprint, 1988, Functions of Setting in the Novel, 1980, Earthtones: A Nevada Album, 1995; editor: Words for the Wild, 1987; mem. editl. bd. Western Am. Lit., 1982—, U. Nev. Press, 1985-94, Studies in Short Fiction, 1988—, I.S.L.E., 1996—. Office: U Nev Reno Dept 098 English Reno NV 89557

RONCI, CURTIS LEE, marketing professional; b. Dayton, Ohio, Sept. 21, 1955; s. William Lionel and Deyne (Fox) R.; 1 child, Maxwell Lee Ronci. AAS in Comml. Arts, Ferris U., 1975. Freelance graphic artist Curtis Ronci & Assocs., Chgo., 1975-78; account exec. Phase II, Inc., Chgo., 1978-80; ind. talent rep. John Ball & Assocs., Chgo., 1980-83; account exec. Phase II, Inc., Chgo., 1983-90; dir. sales and mktg. Clonetics Corp., San Diego, 1991-94; dir. mktg. comms. Clonetics Corp., 1995; pres., CEO DMD Communications, San Diego, 1995—; dir. mktg. Coast Sci., San Diego, 1995—; academic advisor U. Calif. San Diego International Rels. Pacific Studies, La Jolla, Calif., 1993-94. Mem. AAAS. Office: Coast Sci Ste 101 6310 Nancy Ridge Dr San Diego CA 92121

RONDELL, THOMAS, public relations consultant, marketing communications consultant; b. N.Y.C., Sept. 16, 1933; s. Lester and Florence (Robinson) R.; div.; children: Alexis Sonya, Gabrielle Lee. AB in Sociology, Bard Coll., 1958; postgrad., NYU, 1960. V.p. corp. comm. Citizen Savs. and Loan, San Francisco, 1976-80; pub. rels. cons. Bell Savs., San Mateo, Calif., 1985-88; investor rels. cons. San Francisco Fed. Savs., 1986-88; pub. rels. cons. Cornish and Carey Residential Real Estate, Palo Alto, Calif., 1989 95, The Benham Group, Mountain View, Calif., 1992-95. V.p., dir. Mental Health Assn. San Francisco, 1982-86, trustee, 1982-86, 94—. With U.S. Army, 1954-56. Mem. Pub. Rels. Soc. Am. (accredited), Nat. Investor Rels. Inst. Home: 217 Ada Ave Condo 21 Mountain View CA 94043-4958

RONDORF-KLYM, LOUANN M., clinical investigator, nurse; b. Thief River Falls, Minn., Oct. 27, 1953; d. Eugene LeRoy and Edna Lila (Iverson) Rondorf; m. Michael Allyn Klym, May 16, 1976; children: Trevor William, Matthew Robert. BSN, U. N.D., 1976, MSN, 1990; postgrad., Oreg. Health Scis. U., 1993—. RN, Oreg. Cmty. health nurse Stark County Comty. Health, Dickinson, N.D., 1977-80; DON Dickinson Nursing Ctr., 1980-88; charge nurse St. Luke's Nursing Home, Dickinson, 1988-90; cardiac rehab. nurse St. Joseph's Hosp., Dickinson, 1988-90; DON Oak Villa Care Ctr., Hillsboro, Oreg., 1990-91; clin. investigator Laerdal Mfg. Corp., Tualatin, Oreg., 1991-95; grad. rsch. asst. Oreg. Health Scis. U. Sch. Nursing, 1995—; clin. study coord. Hilltop Rsch., Inc., 1996—; mem. ad-hoc com. case-mix sys. N.D. State Human Svcs., 1987-89; mem. ad-hoc com. entry into practice N.D. Assoc. Degree LPN, 1985-86, forum faculty, 1987; team mem. Midwest Alliance in Nursing, 1986; cons. Treasure Valley Living Ctr., Boise, 1989, Laerdal Med. Corp., 1995, Diagnostic Cardiology divsn. Hewlett-Packard, 1995-96. Author: (video) Med. Center One, 1990; contbr. articles to med. jours. Mem. BLS subcom. Am. Heart Assn., Portland, 1992—, instr. BLS, Calif., N.D. and Oreg., 1976—; vol. Adopt-a-Grandparent King City (Oreg.) Convalescent & Rehab. Ctr., 1992—; mem. govtl. rels. com. N.D. Nurses Assn., Bismarck, 1986-90; vol. Hopkins Elem. Sch., Sherwood, Oreg., 1991—; vol. gardener St. Paul Luth. Ch., Sherwood, 1991—; sec. Badlands Nurses Assn., 1983-85, dir.-at-large, 1985-87, legis. com., 1990, mem. program com., 1990. Instl. Nat. Rsch. scholar, 1995. Mem. ANA (cabinet on edn. N.D. chpt 1987-90), Am. Assn. Med. Instrumentation, Internat. Soc. Quality of Life Studies, Soc. Urol. Nurses and Assocs., Regulatory Affairs Profls. Soc., Gerontol. Assn. Am. Home: 20730 SW Houston Dr Sherwood OR 97140-8723 Office: Hill Top Rsch Inc 5331 SW Macadam Ave Ste 210 Portland OR 97201

RONEY, JOHN HARVEY, lawyer, consultant; b. L.A., June 12, 1932; s. Harvey and Mildred Puckett (Cargill) R.; m. Joan Ruth Allen, Dec. 27, 1954; children: Pam Roney Peterson, J. Harvey, Karen Louise Hanke, Cynthia Allen Harmon. Student, Pomona Coll., 1950-51; B.A., Occidental Coll., 1954; LL.B., UCLA, 1959. Bar: Calif. 1960, D.C. 1976. Assoc. O'Melveny & Myers, L.A., 1959-67, ptnr., 1967-94, of counsel, 1994—; gen. counsel Pa. Co., 1970-78, Baldwin United Corp., 1983-84; dir. Coldwell Banker & Co., 1969-81, Brentwood Savs. & Loan Assn., 1968-80; spl. advisor to dep. Rehab. of Mut. Benefit Life Ins. Co., 1991-94; cons., advisor to Rehab. of Confederation Life Ins. Co., 1994-95; mem. policy adv. bd. Calif.

Ins. Commn., 1991-95. Served to 1st lt. USMCR, 1954-56. Mem. ABA, Calif. Bar Assn. (ins. law com. 1991-95, chmn. 1993-94), Los Angeles County Bar Assn., D.C. Bar Assn., N.Y. Coun. Fgn. Rels., Pacific Coun. on Internat. Policy, Conf. Ins. Counsel, Calif. Club, Sky Club (N.Y.), Gainey Ranch Golf Club (Scottsdale). Republican. Home: The Strand Hermosa Beach CA 90254 Office: 400 S Hope St Ste 1600 Los Angeles CA 90071-2801

RONNING, CHARLOTTE JEAN, foreign language educator; b. Billings, Mont., Dec. 19, 1953; d. Charles and Ruth Alice (Johnson) R. BA, Mont. State U., Billings, 1978, BS, 1980; MA, U. Colo., 1995. Nat. cert. counselor. Sales/office mgr. Clint Faubions, Denver, 1980-81; office mgr. Virginia Horn Travel, Denver, 1981-82; sales, instr. R.B. Bonar & Assocs., Denver, 1982-86; fgn. lang. educator Cherry Creek Schs., Denver, 1987—; student Fgn. Study League, Europe, 1970; Dale Carnegie course instr., N.Y.C., 1982-87; sponsor Cherry Creek in Costa Rica, 1988. Mem. Fgn. Lang. Proficiency Com., Denver, 1993—; treas. Bromley Commons, Denver, 1994—. Mem. ACA, Colo. Counseling Assn., Chi Sigma Iota, Alpha Lambda Delta, Alpha Mu Gamma, Kappa Alpha Theta. Republican. Presbyterian. Home: 350 Detroit St # 207 Denver CO 80206

RONSMAN, WAYNE JOHN, insurance company executive; b. Milw., Jan. 21, 1938; s. Harry Martin and Martha Elizabeth (Popp) R.; m. Joan P. Murphy-Mays, Nov. 30, 1974; children: Allison, Alanna; children by previous marriage: Rosemary, Harry, Martha. Student Marquette U., 1955-58, U. San Francisco, 1960-66. CLU, CFP, chartered fin. cons. Acct. Otis McAllister & Co., 1960-62; acct., salesman of data processing Statis. Tabulation Corp., San Francisco, 1962-66; chief acct., gen. mgr. Dillingham Bros. Ltd., Honolulu, 1966-67; ins. salesman Mut. Benefit Life Ins. Co., 1968-91, mgr. Met Life Honolulu, 1991-93, gen. agt., Hawaii, Alaska, 1991; v.p. Brenno Assos., Honolulu, 1972-80; prin. Ronsman-Brenno, Anchorage, Alaska, 1980-90; owner Ronsman, Hammond & Assocs., 1991—; bd. dirs. Aloha Nat. Bank, Kihei, Maui, 1989-90; guest lectr. Chaminade U. Law Sch., Honolulu. Mem. Gov.'s Task Force to Program Correctional Facilities Land, 1970-72; mem. State Bd. Paroles and Pardons, 1972-75; treas. Spl. Edn. Ctr. Oahu, 1969-78; pres. Ballet Alaska, 1986-87, Maui Ballet Co. Ltd., 1992-93; v.p. devel. Make A Wish Hawaii, 1992—; chmn. Maui County Salary Commn., 1996—. Served with USMCR, 1958-60. Mem. Inst. Mgmt. Acct. (pres. Anchorage chpt. 1989-90), Am. Soc. CLUs, Hawaii Estate Planning Coun. (dir. 1994), Honolulu Assn. Life Underwriters (million dollar round table 1973—), Inst. Mgmt. Accts. (pres. Honolulu 1994-95, 95-96), Hawaii (state editor 1970-71, nat. dir. 1972-73), Kailua (pres. 1968-69) Jaycees, Hawaii C. of C., Nat. Assn. Securities Dealers, Kailua C. of C. (pres. 1977-78). Roman Catholic. Home: Ronsman-Hammond & Assocs 1099 Alakea St Ste 1500 Honolulu HI 96813-4500 Office: PO Box 336 Honolulu HI 96809-0336

ROOKS, CHARLES S., foundation administrator; b. Whiteville, N.C., June 29, 1937. BA in English, Wake Forest Coll., 1959; Rockefeller Brothers fellow, Harvard U., 1959-60; MA in Polit. Sci., Duke U., 1964, PhD in Polit. Sci., 1968. Rsch. assoc. Voter Edn. Project, Atlanta, 1969-70, dir. tech. assistance programs, 1970-71, dep. dir., 1971-72; exec. dir. Southeastern Coun. of Founds., Atlanta, 1972-78; dir. mem. svcs. Coun. on Founds., Washington, 1979-80, v.p., 1981-82, acting CEO, 1981-82; exec. dir. Meyer Meml. Trust, Portland, Oreg., 1982—; instr. polit. sci. Duke U., Durham, N.C., 1963, 65-67; asst. prof. of govt. Lake Forest Coll., Ill., 1967-69; asst. prof. polit. sci. Clark Coll., Atlanta, 1969-71; bd. dirs. Pacific Northwest Grantmakers Forum; mem. adv. bd. Neighborhood Partnership Fund (Oreg. Cmty. Found.). Contbr. articles to profl. jours. Home: 2706 SW English Ct Portland OR 97201-1622 Office: Meyer Memorial Trust 1515 SW 5th Ave Ste 500 Portland OR 97201-5450

ROOP, JOSEPH MCLEOD, economist; b. Montgomery, Ala., Sept. 29, 1941; s. Joseph Ezra and Mae Elizabeth (McLeod) R.; B.S., Central Mo. State U., Warrensburg, 1963; Ph.D., Wash. State U., Pullman, 1973; m. Betty Jane Reed, Sept. 4, 1965; 1 dau., Elizabeth Rachael. Economist, Econ. Research Service, U.S. Dept. Agr., Washington, 1975-79; sr. economist Evans Econs., Inc., Washington, 1979-81; staff scientist Battelle Pacific N.W. Nat. Lab., Richland, Wash., 1981—; instr. dept. econs. Wash. State U., 1969-71; with Internat. Energy Agy., Paris, 1990-91. Contbr. tech. articles to profl. jours. Served with U.S. Army, 1966-68. Dept. Agr. Coop. State Research Service research grantee, 1971-73. Mem. Am. Econ. Assn., Econometric Soc., Internat. Assn. Energy Economics. Home: 715 S Taft St Kennewick WA 99336-9587 Office: PO Box 999 MSIN K8-17 Richland WA 99352-0999

ROOS, GEORGE WILLIAM, physicist; b. Yonkers, N.Y., July 1, 1932; s. George William Jr. and Corinne Elizabeth (Kelly) R.; m. Grace Lennon, Oct. 4, 1958; children: George, John, Edward, Daniel. BS in Physics, Iona Coll., 1953. Physicist Naval Rsch. Lab., Washington, 1953-54; program mgr. electric boat divsn. Gen. Dynamics Co., Groton, Conn., 1957-68, mgr. chg. control, 1968-72, dir. indsl. rels. and mgmt. engring., 1972-77; dir. resource mgmt. Gen. Dynamics Co., Ft. Worth, 1977-79; dir. integrated logistic support Convair divsn. Gen. Dynamics Co., San Diego, 1979-86, v.p. human resources Convair divsn., 1986-92; gen. mgr. Hughes Unmanned Strike Sys., San Diego, 1992-93; chmn. Sandarc, Inc., 1994—. Bd. dirs. ARC, San Diego, 1987-93. Lt. USNR, 1953-57, Korea. Recipient A.A. Loftus award Iona Coll., 1974. Mem. Calif. Mgrs. Assn. (bd. dirs. 1988-93, vice chmn. exec. com. 1990-92), Corp. Assn. Univ. San Diego (chmn. exec. com. 1995—), U.S. Naval Inst., Escondido Country Club. Republican. Roman Catholic. Home: 10726 Vista Valle Dr San Diego CA 92131-1232

ROOS, NESTOR ROBERT, consultant; b. St. Louis, Aug. 19, 1925; s. Maurice and Fannie (Friedman) R.; m. Fay Weil, July 8, 1951; children: Marilyn Roos Hall, Eileen Roos Ruddell, Robert F. BBA, Washington U., St. Louis, 1948; MSBA, Washington U., 1949; D of Bus. Adminstrn., Ind. U., 1959. Instr. bus. La. State U., Baton Rouge, 1949-51; teaching fellow Ind. U., Bloomington, 1951-53; asst. prof. Ga. State U., Atlanta, 1953-55; prof. U. Ariz., Tucson, 1955-86, prof. emeritus, 1986; pres. Risk Mgmt. Pub. Co., Tucson, 1976-90, cons. editor, 1990—; cons., expert witness in field; bd. dirs. Blue Cross-Blue Shield Ariz., sec., 1993-95, vice chair, 1995—; mem. Ins. Dirs. Adv. Com., Phoenix, 1987—, Reverse Mortgage Adv. Com., Tucson, 1988-90. Author: (with others) Multiple Line Insurers, 1970, Governmental Risk Management Manual, 1976, Industrial Accident Prevention, 1980. Bd. dirs. Handmaker Geriatric Ctr., Tucson, 1987-92; pres. Temple Emanu-El, Tucson, 1981-83. With U.S. Army, 1943-45, ETO. Grantee Nat. Inst. Occupational Safety and Health, 1975. Mem. Risk and Ins. Mgmt. Soc., Western Risk and Ins. Assn. (pres. 1972-73), Public Risk and Ins. Mgmt. Assn. (dir. edn. and tng. 1982-89). Democrat. Jewish. Home: 7311 E Camino De Cima Tucson AZ 85715-2212 Office: Risk Mgmt Pub Co 2030 E Broadway Blvd Ste 106 Tucson AZ 85719-5908

ROOSEVELT, MICHAEL A., lawyer; b. L.A., Dec. 7, 1946. BA, Harvard U., 1969; JD, Columbia U., 1972. Bar: Calif. 1973. With Friedman, Olive, mcCabbin, Spalding, Bilter Roosevelt et al, San Franciso. Mem. ABA. Office: Friedman Olive McCabbin Spalding et al Ste 2200 425 California St San Francisco CA 94104

ROOT, CHARLES JOSEPH, JR., finance executive, consultant; b. Pierre, S.D., July 26, 1940; s. Charles Joseph and Hazel Ann (Messenger) R.; 1 child from previous marriage, Roseann Marie; m. Sharon Lee, June 24, 1995; stepchildren: Nichole Marie Marcillac, Monique Marie Marcillac. Student, San Francisco Jr. Coll., 1963-65, La Salle Extension U., 1970-71, Coll. of Marin, 1971-72, Am. Coll. Life Underwriters, 1978-82. Registered investment advisor; charter fin. cons.; cert. fin. planner. Estate planner Bankers Life Co., San Francisco, 1966-78; fin. planner Planned Estates Assocs., Corte Madera, Calif., 1978-81; mng. dir. Double Eagle Fin. Corp., Santa Rosa, Calif., 1981—, investment advisor, 1983—; personal bus. mgr., 1987—. V.p. Big Bros. of Am., San Rafael, Calif., 1976-80; treas. com. to elect William Filante, San Rafael, 1978, Cmty. Health Ctrs. of Marin, Fairfax, Calif., 1982-83, Wellspring Found., Philo, Calif., 1981-85; treas., bd. dirs. Ctr. for Attitudinal Healing, Tiburon, Calif., 1989-92; bd. dirs. Pickle Family Circus, San Francisco, 1988, United Way Sonoma Lake, Mendocino Counties, 1993—; bd. dirs. Redwood Empire Estate Planning Coun., Santa Rosa, Calif., 1992—, v.p. programs, 1993, pres. 1995-96). Mem. Internat. Assn. Fin. Planners, Coll. Fin. Planning (cert. fin. planner 1988), Registry of fin. Planning, Nat. Assn. Life Underwriters, Marin County Assn. Life Underwriters (v.p. 1971-76, editor newsletter 1976-80), Rotary (Paul Harris Fellow 1980). Republican. Office: Double Eagle Fin Corp 2300 Bethards Dr Ste R PO Box 2790 Santa Rosa CA 95405

ROOT, DORIS SMILEY, portrait artist; b. Ann Arbor, Mich., June 28, 1924; d. George O. and Hazel (Smith) Smiley. Student, Art Inst. of Chgo., 1943-45, N.Y. Sch. Design, 1976-77, Calif. Art Inst., 1984-85. Creative dir. All May Co.'s, L.A., 1962-63; advt. sales pro. dir. Seibu, L.A., 1963-64; v.p. Walgers & Assoc., L.A., 1964-70; owner, designer At The Root of Things, L.A., 1970-73; adv. sales pro. dir. Hs. of Nine, L.A., 1973-74; asst. designer MGM Grand, Reno, Nev., 1974-76; designer, office mgr. Von Hausen Studio, L.A., 1976-82; ABC libr. ABC/Cap Cities, L.A., 1982-89; portrait artist (also known as Dorian), AKA Dorian, art studio, L.A., 1982—. One-man shows include Cookeville, Tenn., 1989, Beverly Hills, Calif., 1991; artist in residence, Cookeville, 1989-90. Republican. Presbyterian. *I'm one of the luckiest women alive. I love fun and found a little of it the best space to create in, in my career and in my personal life. People feel free to try things in a fun place to work. And I must admit, I'm still having fun with painting people's portraits!.*

ROOT, GEORGE L., JR., lawyer; b. 1947. BA, Syracuse U.; JD cum laude, U. San Diego. Ptnr. Foley, Lardner Weissburg & Aronson, San Diego; guest lectr. Nat. U., U. Calif., San Diego; adj. prof. San Diego State U. Mem. San Diego County Bar Assn. (chmn. mental health com. 1983, task force on children at risk 1995), Assn. Calif. Hosp. Dists. (legis. com. 1995), Calif. Soc. Healthcare Attys., Healthcare Fin. Mgmt. Assn., Nat. Health Lawyers Assn. Office: Foley Lardner Weissburg & Aronson 402 W Broadway Fl 23 San Diego CA 92101-3542

ROOT, GERALD EDWARD, courts resource manager; b. Gridley, Calif., May 5, 1948; s. Loris Leo Root and Mary Helen (Wheeler) Murrell; m. Tricia Ann Caywood, Feb. 13, 1981; children: Jason Alexander, Melinda Ann. AA in Bus., Yuba C.C., Marysville, Calif., 1968; BA in Psychology, Calif. State U., Sonoma, 1974; MA in Social Sci., Calif. State U., Chico, 1977; EdD candidate orgn. and leadership, U. San Francisco, 1997. Gen. mgr. Do-It Leisure Therapeutic Recreation, Chico, 1977-79; CETA projects coord. City of Chico, 1980-81; exec. dir. Voluntary Action Ctr., Inc., South Lake Tahoe, Calif., 1981-83; devel. dir. Work Tng. Ctr., Inc., Chico, 1983-92; exec. dir. North Valley Rehab. Found., Chico, 1986-92; resource adminstrn. and devel. mgr. Sacramento Superior and Mcpl. Cts., 1992—; planning, resource devel. and project mgr. Juvenile Detention Alternatives Initiative, 1992-97, Feather River Industries Vocat. Tng., 1991, Creative Learning Ctr. Constrn., 1988, Correctional Options-Drug Ct., 1994, Violence Prevention Resource Ctr., 1995, Juvenile Delinquency Prevention Initiative, 1995, Securing the Health and Safety of Urban Children Initiative, 1995-97, Joint Cabinets Youth Work Group/Child Welfare League Am., 1996, Task Force on Fairness-The Juvenile Justice Initiative, 1994-97, SacraMentor, Inc., CA Wellness Found., 1994-97, Violent Injury Prevention Coalition/Calif. Dept. Health and Human Svcs., 1995-97, Domestic Violence Coordinating Coun., Sacramento County, 1995-97, Multicultural Perspectives on Family Violence Conf., 1997, Family Violence Summit, 1997, Healthy Teen Mothers Program, 1997. Bd. dirs. Cmty. Action Agy., Butte County, Calif., 1990, ARC, Butte County, 1989, Sunrise Recreation and Park Dist., 1996—; adv. bds. Butte C.C. Dist., 1987-92, Cmty. Svcs. Planning Coun., 1994-96. Grantee Annie E. Casey Found., USDA, U.S. Bur. Justice, Robert Wood Johnson Found., Calif. Office Criminal Justice Planning, Office of Juvenile Justice & Delinquency Prevention. Phi Delta Kappa. Office: Sacramento Supr & Mcpl Cts Ct Resources 9555 Kiefer Blvd Sacramento CA 95827-3816

ROOT, NILE, photographer, educator; b. Denver, Dec. 11, 1926; s. Victor Nile and Ella May (Holaway) R.; student U. Denver, 1968; MS in Instructional Tech., Rochester Inst. Tech., 1978; m. Abigail Barton Brown, Feb. 5, 1960; 1 child, James Michael. Microphotographer, U.S. Dept. Commerce, Field Info. Agy. Tech., Fed. Republic Germany, 1946-48; free-lance photographer, 1949-51; pres. Photography Workshop, Inc., Denver, 1952-60; dir. dept. biophotography and med. illustration Rose Meml. Med. Ctr., Denver, 1960-70; dir. med. illustration dept. Children's Hosp., Denver, 1970-71; dir. Photography for Sci., Denver, 1971-72; prof. biomed. photog. communications Rochester Inst. Tech. (N.Y.), 1972-86 , chmn. dept., 1974-86, prof. emeritus Coll. Imaging Arts and Scis., 1986—; travel writer, photographer, Japan, China, S.E. Asia, 1986-89; writer, photographer, Tucson, 1989—. dir. HEW project for devel. of field, 1974-77. Served with USN, 1945-46. Recipient numerous awards for sci. photographs; Eisenhart Outstanding Tchr. award Rochester Inst. Tech., 1986; 1st Ann. Faculty fellow Sch. Photog. Arts and Scis., Rochester Inst. Tech., 1979. Fellow Biol. Photog. Assn. (registered, emeritus, bd. govs. 1977-79, Louis Schmidt award 1986); mem. Ctr. Creative Photography. Democrat. Contbr. illustrations to med. textbooks; represented in numerous mus. photog. exhibits and numerous pvt. collections. Home and Office: 314 N Banff Ave Tucson AZ 85748-3311

ROOT, ROBERT ALAN, ecologist, project manager; b. Erie, Pa., Mar. 29, 1940; s. Kenneth Melvin and Anne Dorothy (Smith) R.; m. Jill Brainerd, June 25, 1966; children: Michael Shepard, Cynthia Anne. BS, U. Maine, 1963; MS, U. Mont., 1968; PhD, Miami U., Oxford, Ohio, 1971. Rsch. assoc. U. Ill., Urbana, 1971-73; sr. ecologist, project mgr. Dames and Moore, Park Ridge, Ill., 1973-80; project coord. Dames and Moore, Sydney, Australia, 1981-83; lectr. U. Mass., Amherst, 1984; sr. environ. mgr. Battelle Meml. Inst., Columbus, Ohio, 1985-87; dep. program mgr. Battelle Meml. Inst., Springfield, Ill., 1988-92; sr. rsch. scientist Battelle Meml. Inst., Albuquerque, 1993—; adj. asst. prof. botany dept. Ohio State U., Columbus, 1987-92. Co-author: (travel guide) Interstate 90: A Guide to Points You Can See-Without Stopping, 1984. Pres., mem. Dist. 21 Sch. Bd., Wheeling-Buffalo Grove, Ill., 1979-81. Recipient Cert. of Appreciation, U.S. Dept. Energy, 1987. Office: Battelle Meml Inst 2000 Randolph Rd SE Ste 105 Albuquerque NM 87106-4267

ROOT, WILLIAM DIXON, construction company executive; b. Medford, Oreg., July 27, 1951; s. Earl Merrit and Helen Edith (Dixon) R.; m. Catherine Jeanine Smiraglia, July 10, 1981; children: Stacie Marie, Shawn Dixon. BSBA, U. Nev., Reno, 1978. Contr., sec.-treas. Jensen Elec., Inc., Reno, 1977-82; v.p., sec.-treas. Clark & Sullivan, Inc., Reno, 1982—; v.p., asst. sec. G & S Gen. Inc., Reno, 1986—; v.p., sec., treas. Westech Devel., Reno, 1986—, also bd. dirs.; cons. Micro-Tech., Reno, 1984-93. Mem. Am. Coun. for Constrn. Edn., Assn. Sysm. Mgrs. Constrn. Fin. Mgrs. Assn. (v.p. 1986-88, exec. com. 1997—, com. chair 1997—, pres. 1988-90, chmn. 1990—, nat. bd. dirs., nat. chmn. chpt. formation com., exec. com., vice chmn. conf. planning com., chmn. liaison com. 1995—), Assn. Gen. Contractors, Sierra Nevada IBM Users, Sertoma Club (treas. 1983-88, Centurian award 1986, Tribune award 1989, Disting. Svc. award 1989), Rotary (sgt.-at-arms, treas. 1995—), Sierra Challenge Athletics Assn. (pres., past treas., bd. dirs.). Republican. Home: 2505 Homeland Dr Reno NV 89511-9269 Office: Clark & Sullivan Inc 905 Industrial Way Sparks NV 89431-6009

ROPCHAN, REBECCA G., nursing administrator; b. Decatur, Ill., Apr. 6, 1950; d. Jack R. and Mildred E. (Mecum) Hathaway; m. Jim. R. Ropchan, June 13, 1987. Diploma, St. Lukes Hosp. Sch. Nursing, St. Louis, 1971; BS in Nursing, St. Louis U., 1974, MS in Nursing, 1976. Cardiovascular clin. nurse specialist UCLA Med. Ctr., asst. dir. nursing, assoc. dir. nursing, 1976-91; v.p. City Hope Nat. Med. Ctr., 1991-95; asst. adminstr. ops. Scripps Meml., Encinitas, Calif., 1995—; editorial bd. J.B. Lippencott, Dimensions in Critical Care Nursing, 1982-89, Aspen Systems, Critical Care Quarterly, 1981—; nat. adv. com. Nursing Profl. Seminar Consultants, Inc., Albuquerque, 1980-88; lectr., cons. in field. Contbr. numerous articles to profl. jours. Recipient Mgmt. & Profl. Staff Incentive award UCLA Med. Ctr., 1989, UCLA Med. Ctr. Spl. Performance award, 1984, Rufus D. Putney Meml. award, 1971, Excellence award Am. Acad. Nurse Practitioners, State of Calif., 1995. Mem. AACN, Am. Orgn. Nurse Execs., Orgn. Nurse Execs. Calif., Oncology Nurse Soc., Am. Acad. Med. Adminstrs., Am. Coll. Healthcare Execs., Sigma Theta Tau.

RORABAUGH, WILLIAM JOSEPH, historian; b. Louisville, Dec. 11, 1945; s. Matthew Irvin and Agnes Cecilia (Graf) R. AB in History, Stanford U., 1968; MA in History, U. Calif., Berkeley, 1970, PhD in History, 1976. Asst. prof. history U. Wash., Seattle, 1976-82, assoc. prof., 1982-87, prof., 1987—. Author: The Alcoholic Republic, 1979, The Craft Apprentice, 1986, Berkeley at War: The 1960s, 1989; co-author: America! A Concise History, 1994. NEH fellow, 1981, Nat. Humanities Ctr. fellow, Research Triangle Park, N.C., 1983-84, Sorensen fellow John F. Kennedy Presdl. Libr., Boston, 1992; recipient Book prize Old Sturbridge Village, Sturbridge, Mass., 1987. Mem. Am. Hist. Assn., Orgn. Am. Historians, Soc. for Historians of Early Am. Republic (pres. 1993-94), Alcohol and Temperance History Group. Office: Univ Wash History Box 353560 Seattle WA 98195-3560

ROSA, EUGENE ANTHONY, sociologist, environmental scientist, educator; b. Canandaigua, N.Y., Sept. 20, 1941; s. Louis Gastaldo and Flora Louise (Brevette) R.; m. Jody Ross, Sept. 7, 1985 (div. 1993). BS, Rochester Inst. Tech., 1967; MA, Syracuse U., 1975, PhD, 1976. Research assoc., instr. Stanford U., 1976-78; from asst. to prof. Wash. State U., Pullman, 1978—, prof., 1993—; cons. Brookhaven Nat. Lab., Upton, N.Y., 1978—, Nuclear Regulatory Commn., Washington, 1978—; vis. prof. London Sch. Econs., 1988; chmn. dept., Edward R. Meyer Disting. prof. natural resources and environ. policy Wash. State Univ., Pullman, 1978—. Editor: Public Reactions to Nuclear Power, 1984, Pub. Reactions to Nuclear Waste, 1993; contbr. articles to profl. jours. Mem. nuclear waste adv. coun. Wash. State, 1987-92. Mem. Am. Sociol. Assn., AAAS, Am. Acad. Polit. and Social Scis., N.Y. Acad. Scis., Internat. Soc. Assn., Soc. for Human Ecology, Soc. Risk Analysis, Sigma Xi. Home: 1007 NE Alfred Ln Pullman WA 99163-3950 Office: Wash State U Dept Sociology Pullman WA 99164

ROSA, FREDRIC DAVID, construction company executive; b. Monroe, Wis., Oct. 31, 1946; s. Fredric Carl Rosa and Irene (Sommers) Rosa Figi; m. Melanie A. Downs, May 31, 1986; children: Mark, Katherine. BBA in Mktg., U. Wis., 1968. Dir. mktg. Swiss Colony Stores, Inc., Monroe, 1968-80; pres. Videotape Indsl. Prodns., Inc., Madison, Wis., 1980-82; agt. VR Bus. Brokers, Colorado Springs, Colo., 1982-83; sales rep. NCR Corp., Denver, 1983-85; prin. F. D. Rosa & Assocs., Denver, Aspen and Eagle, Colo., 1985-89; pres. Peak Benefit Cons., Colorado Springs, 1989-95; registered prin. Nexus Fin. Programs, Inc., Colorado Springs, Colo., 1990-92, Nutmeg Securities Ltd., Colorado Springs, 1992-94; sales staff Am. Airlines, Colorado Springs, Colo., 1993-95; cons. Kolb-Lena Cheese Co., Lena, Ill., 1983-85; instr. The Am. Coll., Bryn Mawr, Pa., 1990-91, A.D. Banker & Co., Overland Park, Kans., 1995—; owner Rosa Constrn., Colorado Springs, 1990-94, Lakewood, Colo., 1995—. Contbr. articles to trade publs. and newspapers. Mem. Am. Soc. CLU and Chartered Fin. Cons., Mensa, Internat. Legion of Intelligence, Delta Sigma Pi (life). Methodist. Home and Office: Fred Rosa Constrn 1270 Cody St Lakewood CO 80215-4897

ROSALES, SUZANNE MARIE, hospital coordinator; b. Merced, Calif., July 23, 1946; d. Walter Marshall and Ellen Marie (Earl) Potter; children: Anita Carol, Michelle Suzanne. AA, City Coll., San Francisco, 1966. Diplomate Am. Coll. Utilization Review Physicians. Utilization review coord. San Francisco Gen. Hosp., 1967-74; mgr. utilization review/discharge planning UCLA Hosp. and Clinics, 1974-79; nurse III Hawaii State Hosp., Kaneohe, 1979-80; review coord. Pacific Profl. Std. Review Orgn., Honolulu, 1980-81; coord. admission and utilization reviewq The Rehab. Hosp. of the Pacific, Honolulu, 1981-85; coord. Pacific Med. Referral Project, Honolulu, 1985-87; dir. profl. svcs. The Queen's Healthcare Plan, Honolulu, 1987-88; utilization mgmt. coord. Vista Psychiat. Physician Assocs., San Diego, 1989; admission coord. utilization review San Francisco Gen. Hosp., 1989-91, quality improvement coordinator, 1991—; cons. Am. Med. Records Assn. Contbr. articles to profl. jours. Mem. Nat. Assn. Utilization Review Profls. Home: 138 Alta Vista Way Daly City CA 94014 Office: San Francisco Gen Hosp 1001 Potrero Ave San Francisco CA 94110-3518

ROSANDER, ARLYN CUSTER, mathematical statistician, management consultant; b. Mason County, Mich., Oct. 7, 1903; s. John Carl and Nellie May (Palmer) R.; m. Beatrice White, Aug. 26, 1933 (div.); children: Nancy Rosander Peck, Robert Richard Roger (dec.); m. Margaret Ruth Guest, Aug. 15, 1964. BS, U. Mich. 1925; MA, U. Wis., 1928; PhD, U. Chgo., 1933; postgrad. Dept. Agr., 1937-39. Rsch. asst. U. Chgo., 1933-34; rsch. fellow Gen. Edn. Bd. Tech. dir. Am. Youth Commn., Balt. and Washington, 1935-37; chief statistician urban study U.S. Bur. Labor Stats., Washington, 1937-39; sect. and br. chief War Prodn. Bd., Washington, 1940-45; chief statistician IRS, Washington, 1945-61; chief math. and stats. sect. ICC, Washington, 1961-69; cons. Pres.'s Commn. on Fed. Stats., Washington, 1970-71; cons., Loveland, Colo.; lectr. stats. George Washington U., 1946-52. Recipient Civilian War Service award War Prodn. Bd., 1945; Spl. Performance award Dept. Treasury, 1961. Fellow AAAS, Am. Soc. Quality Control (25 yr. honor award 1980, Howard Jones Meml. award 1984, chmn. emeritus svc. industries divsn. 1991, A.C. Rosander award Svc. Industries divsn. 1991); mem. Am. Statis. Assn. Author: Elementary Principles of Statistics, 1951; Statistical Quality Control in Tax Operations, IRS, 1958; Case Studies in Sample Design, 1977; Application of Quality Control to Service Industries, 1985, Washington Story 1985, The Quest for Quality in Services, 1989 (translated into Spanish, 1993, Italian, 1994), Deming's 14 Points Applied to Services, 1991 (translated into Spanish, 1994). Home and Office: 4330 Franklin Ave Loveland CO 80538-1715

ROSAS, LOU, mayor. Mayor City of Concord, Calif. Office: 1950 Parkside Dr Concord CA 94519

ROSCH, JOHN THOMAS, lawyer; b. Council Bluffs, Iowa, Oct. 4, 1939; s. H.P. and Phebe Florence (Jamison) R.; m. Carolyn Lee, Aug. 18, 1961; children: Thomas Lee, Laura Lee. BA, Harvard U., 1961, LLB, 1965. Bar: Calif. 1966, U.S. Dist. Ct. (no. dist.) Calif. 1966, U.S. Dist. Ct. (ea. dist.) Calif. 1967, U.S. Ct. Appeals (9th cir.) 1966. Assoc. McCutchen, Doyle, Brown & Enersen, San Francisco, 1965-72, ptnr., 1972-73, 75-93; office mng. ptnr. Latham & Watkins, San Francisco, 1994—; dir. Bur. Consumer Protection, FTC, Washington, 1973-75. Contbr. articles profl. jours. Fellow Am. Bar Found., Am. Coll. Trial Lawyers; mem. ABA (past chmn. antitrust sect.), State Bar Calif., San Francisco Bar Assn., Calif. State Antitrust and Trade Regulation Sect. (past chair). Republican. Episcopalian. Office: Latham & Watkins 505 Montgomery St San Francisco CA 94111-2552

ROSE, CYNTHIA, psychiatrist; b. Boston, Apr. 26, 1936; came to U.S., 1936; d. Irving and Eleanor Lillian (Fox) R.; m. Cameron E. Berry, June 6, 1964 (div. Oct. 1979); children: Scott David,Daniel Irving. AB, Tufts U., 1959; MD, Boston U., 1963. Diplomate Am. Bd. Psychiatry and Neurology. Intern U. Calif. Hosps., San Francisco, 1963-64; resident U. Colo. Health Scis. Ctr., Denver, 1964-67; med. dir. Pikes Peak Mental Health Ctr., Colorado Springs, Colo., 1970-84; psychiat. staff cons. Colo. Coll., Colorado Springs, 1970-77; asst. clin. prof. psychiatry U. Colo. Health Scis. Ctr., Denver, 1975-81, assoc. clin. prof., 1981—; pvt. practice Colorado Springs, 1981—; bd. mem. Psychiatrist's Mut. Ins., Barbados, 1993—. Mem. adv. bd. Head Start, Colorado Springs, 1969-72; mem. Citizens Goals, Colorado Springs, 1978-80. U. Colo. Health Scis. Ctr. child psychiatry fellow, 1967-69. Fellow Am. Psychiat. Assn. (area rep. to assembly 1983-90, exec. com. assembly 1984-90); mem. AMA, Colo. Psychiat. Soc. (sec. 1979-80, pres. 81-82, Spokesperson of Yr. 1991), Colo. Psychiat. Assn., Airplane Owners and Pilots Assn.,Colo. Internat. Women's Forum, Am. Acad. Child and Adolescent Psychiatry, Am. Psychoanalytic Assn. (affiliate). Office: 730 N Cascade Ave Ste 2 Colorado Springs CO 80903-3258

ROSE, DAVID ALLAN, investment manager; b. N.Y.C., Feb. 15, 1937; s. Edward William and Marion (Nadelstein) R.; m. Frances Helaine Dushman, Aug. 16, 1959; children: Evan Denali, Mitchell Franklin. BS in Acctg., Queens Coll., 1958; MBA, Syracuse U., 1968. Fin. mgr. U.S. Army, Fort Richardson, Alaska, 1961-75; comptroller U.S. Army, Fort Richardson, 1975; exec. dir. Alaska Mcpl. Bond Bank Authority, Anchorage, 1975-82, Alaska Indsl. Devel. Authority, Anchorage, 1980; co-owner Downtown Investment Co., Anchorage, 1980—, Downtown Delicatessen, Inc., Anchorage, 1976—; CEO, Alaska Permanent Fund Corp., Juneau, 1982-92; chmn., CEO, Alaska Permanent Capital Mgmt. Co., Inc., Anchorage, 1992—; ptnr. Russian Alaska Export/Import Co., Anchorage, 1993—; fin. advisor Fin. Green Lake Dam, Sitka, Alaska, 1977, Fin. Dutch Harbor Port, Unalaska, Alaska, 1979-80, Fin. Kenai-Anchorage Pipeline, Anchorage, 1979-80, Fin. Pulp Mill Pollution Control, Ketchikan, Alaska, 1979-80. Mem. City Coun., Anchorage, 1971-75, Borough Assembly, Anchorage, 1971-75, Mcpl. Assembly, Anchorage, 1975-80; pres. Alaska Mcpl. League, 1975, Mcpl. Assembly, Anchorage, 1975-77; vice chmn. endowment fund Alaska Pacific U., 1994—. Recipient Golden Man award Boys Club Alaska, Anchorage, 1974, Decoration for Meritorious Civilian Service, U.S. Army, 1975, Pub. Service award City and Borough, Juneau, 1986, Lions Internat. awards, awards for fundraising Am. Diabetes Assn.; named Pub. Adminstr. Yr. Am. Soc. Pub. Adminstrn., Alaska chpt., 1986. Mem. Rotary (awards). Republican. Jewish. Office: Alaska Permanent Capital 900 W 5th Ave Ste 601 Anchorage AK 99501-2029

ROSE, FAYE SCHUMAN, retired university department director communications; b. Mt. Vernon, Ill.; m. Seymour J. Rose, June 21, 1953 (div. Dec. 1979); children: Lawrence Jay, Susan Alison Rose Verner. BSBA, Washington U., St. Louis, 1952. Pub. affairs asst. San Diego C.C. Dist., 1975-77; pub. affairs writer San Diego State U., 1977-79; dir. comms. San Diego State U. Coll. of Extended Studies, 1979-96; ret., 1996. Candidate Bd. Edn., San Diego, 1972. Recipient Best Audio/Visual Program award, Internat. Assn. Bus. Comms., 1987. Mem. Pub. Rels. Soc. Am., Pub. Rels. Club San Diego (Best Publicity Program 1989, Best Brochure 1990), San Diego Mus. Art, City Club San Diego, Coun. for Advancement and Support of Edn., San Diego Press Club.

ROSE, GREGORY MANCEL, neurobiologist; b. Eugene, Oreg., Feb. 3, 1953; s. Mancel Lee and Ilione (Schenk) R.; m. Kathleen Ann Frye, June 30, 1979; 1 child, Julian Mancel. BS cum laude, U. Calif., Irvine, 1975, PhD, 1980. Research fellow M.P.I. for Psychiatry, Munich, 1976; rsch. assoc. Miescher Labor, M.P.I., Tuebingen, Republic of Germany, 1980-81; regular fellow dept. pharmacology U. Colo. Health Sci. Ctr., Denver, 1981-84, asst. prof., 1984-89, assoc. prof., 1989—; rsch. biologist VA Med. Ctr., Denver, 1981—, co-dir. neurosci. tng. program, 1986-89, assoc. rsch. career scientist, 1989—. Achievements include discovery of importance of stimulus patterning for induction of hippocampal synaptic plasticity. Bd. dirs. Greater Park Hill Community, 1987-90. VA Rsch. Svc. grantee, 1984, 86, 89, 93, NSF grantee, 1988, 90, NIMH grantee, 1989, 94, NIA grantee, 1991. Mem. AAAS, Am. Aging Assn., Soc. Neurosci., Internat. Brain Rsch. Orgn., N.Y. Acad. Sci. Democrat. Episcopalian. Office: VA Med Ctr Med Rsch 151 1055 Clermont St Denver CO 80220-3808

ROSE, HUGH, management consultant; b. Evanston, Ill., Sept. 10, 1926; s. Howard Gray and Catherine (Wilcox) R.; m. Mary Moore Austin, Oct. 25, 1952; children: Susan, Nancy, Gregory, Matthew, Mary. BS in Physics, U. Mich., 1951, MS in Geophysics, 1952; MBA with highest distinction, Pepperdine U., 1982. Mgr. Caterpillar, Inc., Peoria, Ill., 1952-66; v.p., mktg. mgr. Cummins Engine Co., Columbus, Ind., 1966-69; pres., CEO Cummins Northeastern, Inc., Boston, 1969-77; pres. Power Systems Assocs., L.A., 1980-83, C.D. High Tech., Inc., Austin, Tex., 1984-87; mgmt. cons. Rose and Assocs., Tucson, 1984, 87—. Contbr. paleontol. articles to various publs. Bd. dirs. Raymond Alf Mus., Claremont, Calif., 1975—, Comstock Found., Tucson, 1988, Environ. Edn. Exch., 1991, Heart Ctr. U. Ariz., Tucson, 1992. With USAAF, WWII. Fellow AAAS; mem. Acacia, Soc. Vertebrate Paleontology, Beacon Soc. Boston (pres. 1979-80), Algonquin Club Boston (v.p., bd. dirs. 1974-80), Duxbury Yacht Club, Longwood Cricket Club, Cum Laude Soc., Phi Beta Kappa, Delta Mu Delta, Sigma Gamma Epsilon, Beta Beta Beta. Republican. Presbyterian. Office: Rose & Assocs 5320 N Camino Sumo Tucson AZ 85718-5132

ROSE, JOAN MARIE, medical-surgical nurse; b. Fresno, Calif., Aug. 12, 1952; d. Hobert Lee and Ila Marie (Jacobson) Hamilton; m. Steven Arthur Westenrider, May 1, 1976 (div. Dec., 1984); m. Richard Lee Rose, Aug. 6, 1994; children: John Rose, Dan Rose, Denise Haight. AS in Nursing, Fresno City Coll., 1987. RN, ANCC. Nurse Valley Med Ctr., Fresno, Calif., 1988-95. Author: (book) Dreams Come True, 1996; also poetry.

ROSE, MASON H., IV, psychoanalyst; b. Charlevoix, Mich., July 4, 1915; s. Mason III and Catharine (DIebel) R.; m. Marlene Alexander, 1990. Student, Philips Exeter, 1932, U. Fla., 1933, Duke U., 1934, U. So. Calif., 1935; B.A., Inst. Religious Sci., 1939; MS, Calif. Inst. Advanced Studies, 1941, PhD, 1944; LL.D. (hon.), Asso. Univs., Hong Kong, 1959. Tennis profl. The Inn, Charlevoix, Mich., 1932-35; lectr. Inst. Religious Sci., 1937-43; pvt. practice psychoanalysis Los Angeles, 1941-81; exec. dir. Nat. Found. Psychol. Research, 1940-60; feature writer L.A. Herald Express, 1945-55; psychol. cons. Med. Found. Am., 1948-62; leader Humanist Ch. of Religious Sci., 1957—; v.p., dean undergrad. sch. Calif. Inst. Advanced Study, 1959-65; chancellor Cape Pacific Inst. Advanced Studies, 1965—; pres. Mason Rose; chmn. Gt. Books of Modern World, 1959—; exec dir. Olympic League Am., 1967—; bd. dirs. Ctr. Organic Ecology, 1968—, Everywoman's Village, 1960-70, Disease Prevention and Life Extension Ctr., World Environ. Systems, 1970-73. Author: You and Your Personality, 1944, Community Plan for the Returning Serviceman, 1945, Sex Education from Birth to Maturity, 1948, Creative Education, 1953, Humanism as Religion, 1959, The Nutra-Bio-Zyme Soil Management, 1969, The Nutra Nutra-Bio-Zyme Manutrol system, 1970, Bio-N-Gest Sewage Treatment and Water Reclamation System, 1970, Bio-N-Gest Waste Recycling System, 1970, Bio-Dynamics, 1970, The Island Tribe, 1971, New Hopes for the Emotionally Disturbed Child, 2nd 1974, Humanics Health System, 1975, Nutrition for Pregnancy and Lactation, 1976, How to Provide Optimum Nutrition for You and Your Child, 1978, Suntanning, The World's Most Dangerous Sport, 1979, How to Scare Your Teenager Straight, 1980, Radiant Living, 1986, Multimodal System for the Management of Pain and Stress, 1987, Glasscrete System of Construction, 1987, Macho Manifesto, How to Avoid Rape, 1995, Glamorous Hollywood-Fabulous Hollywood, 1996, syndicated newspaper column You and Your Child, 1950-54; TV programs, 1951-52. Mem. AAAS, NAACP, ACLU, Fedn. Am. Scientists, Social Responsibility in Sci., Aircraft Owners and Pilots Assn., Helms Athletic Found., So. Calif. Olympic Games Com., Philips Exeter Acad. Alumni Assn., PEN, So. Calif. Publicists, Trojan Football Alumni, Athletic Club (L.A.), Press Club (L.A., adv. bd. 1952-75). *During forty years of clinical psychoanalysis my constant preoccupation has been to develop a wholistic treatment individualized to the human person. This has resulted in the concept of human ecology which utilizes biopsyen, i.e. biological-psychological-environmental therapy.*

ROSE, RAY VINCENT, surgeon; b. St. Paul, May 5, 1921; s. Raymond Charles and Vinnie Kathryn (Falk) R.; m. Elsa Marie Janda, June 25, 1948; children: Steven, Anita, Richard, Laura, Lynnette. BS, U. Minn., 1943, MB, 1946, MD, 1946. Diplomate Am. Bd. Surgery. Intern U. Colo. Med. Ctr., Denver, 1946-47, resident internal medicine, 1949-51, resident in surgery, 1951-54; pvt. practice Pasco, Wash., 1954—; bd. dirs. Our Lady of Lourdes Hosp., Pasco, 1972-80. Bd. dirs. Wash. divsn. Am. Cancer Soc., Seattle, 1993-95, Tri-City Cancer Ctr., Wash., 1993—. Capt. USAF, 1947-49. Fellow ACS (past pres. Wash. chpt. 1973-74); mem. Wash. State Med. Assn. (past trustee), AMA, Benton Franklin County Med. Soc. (past pres. 1965). Home: 4508 W Riverhaven Blvd Pasco WA 99301-3015

ROSE, RAYMOND ALLEN, computer scientist; b. Alhambra, Calif., Aug. 20, 1951; s. David Bernard and Gerri (Swiryn) R.; m. Elue Maria Adams, Aug. 18, 1975 (div. 1981); children: James Michael, Brian Seth, Joshua Aaron, Jeffrey Steven, Kyle Christopher. AS in Computer Sci., Grossmont Coll., El Cajon, Calif., 1975; BS in Computer Engring., San Diego State U., 1977, BS in Computer Sci. Programming, 1978; M in Computer Engring., Stanford U., 1979. Chief program design W.P.S., Houston, 1977-79, v.p. program design, 1980-83; v.p. software design Computer Tape, Houston, 1983-88; pres., chief exec. officer C.A.R.D., San Diego, 1988—; Netware LANs adminstr. Grossmont Coll. Dist., 1991—; software devel. cons. U.S. Govt., Houston, 1983-88; hiring bd. adv. San Diego State U., 1990-91; instr. computer sci. Grossmont Coll. Contbr. articles to profl. jours. Lt. col. U.S. Army, 1968-75. NASA software devel. grantee, 1984; named Coach of the Yr., El Cajon Little League Assn., 1989. Office: CARD 294 Orlando St Apt 9 El Cajon CA 92021-7011

ROSE, ROBERT E(DGAR), state supreme court justice; b. Orange, N.J., Oct. 7, 1939. B.A., Juniata Coll., Huntingdon, Pa., 1961; LL.B., NYU, 1964. Bar: Nev. 1965. Dist. atty. Washoe County, 1971-75; lt. gov. State of Nev., 1975-79; judge Nev. Dist. Ct., 8th Jud. Dist., Las Vegas, 1986-88; justice Nev. Supreme Ct., Carson City, 1989—, chief justice, 1993-94. Office: Nev Supreme Ct 201 S Carson St Carson City NV 89710

ROSE, SCOTT A., lawyer; b. Flint, Mich., Feb. 10, 1953. BS with distinction, Ariz. State U., 1975, JD cum laude, 1979. Bar: Ariz. 1979. Chmn. bd. O'Connor, Cavanagh, Anderson, Killingsworth & Beshears, Phoenix, Ariz. Articles editor Ariz. State Law Jour., 1978-79. Ariz. Govt. Affairs chmn. Internat. Coun. Shopping Ctrs. Mem. ABA, State Bar Ariz., Maricopa County Bar Assn., Downtown Phoenix Rotary Club 100 (bd. dirs.). Office: O'Connor Cavanagh Anderson Killingsworth & Beshears Ste 1100 1 E Camelback Rd Phoenix AZ 85012-1656

ROSEBERRY, EDWIN SOUTHALL, state agency administrator; b. Roanoke, Va., July 4, 1925; s. Edwin Alexander and Gladys Edmonia (Southall) R.; m. Mary Louise Sprengel, Sept. 2, 1949 (dec. 1978); children: Edwin Jr., David, Kevin; m. Alice Proffit Boger, Dec. 27, 1980; 1 stepdaughter, Elizabeth Leigh Boger. BS in Commerce, U. Va., 1949. Registered sanitarian, Hawaii, Va. Store mgr. Allied Arts, Charlottesville, Va., 1949-51; retail credit sales mgr. B.F. Goodrich Co., Charlottesville, 1951-53; environ. health specialist Dept. of Health, Charlottesville, 1953-84, Dept. of Labor, Honolulu, 1987—; self-employed photographer, Charlottesville, 1949-85, Honolulu, 1985—. Contbr. photographs: The Inward Eye, 1986. Election ofcl. State of Hawaii, Honolulu, 1988—. With USN, 1944-46. Recipient numerous nat. awards Eastman Kodak Co., nat. newspapers, and photography mags., 1951-69. Mem. VFW (life), Am. Indsl. Hygiene Assn., Austrian Hawaiian Club (v.p., bd. dirs. 1985), Antique Auto Assn. (pres. Piedmont region 1964), Hawaii Photo Soc. (v.p. 1989), Elks (tiler and inner guard 1985), Am. Legion, Masonic Lodge, Pi Delta Epsilon. Episcopalian. Home: 1101E Kumukumu St Honolulu HI 96825-2602 Office: State of Hawaii DLIR/DOSH 830 Punchbowl St Honolulu HI 96813-5045

ROSEHNAL, MARY ANN, educational administrator; b. Bklyn., July 25, 1943; d. Frank Joseph and Mary Anna (Corso) R.; 1 child, Scott Stoddart. BA in Sociology, San Francisco State U., 1968; M in Sch. Bus. Adminstrn., No. Ariz. U., 1985. Lic. substitute tchr., Ariz.; lic. vocat. nurse, Calif.; cert. sch. bus. mgr., Ariz. Deliquency counselor, Calif., 1969-73; office mgr. Nurses Central Registry, Sun City, Ariz., 1973-75; bus. mgr. Nadaburg sch. dist., Wittmann, Ariz., 1975-78, Morristown (Ariz.) sch. dist., 1978—; served on 1st Assessment Handbook editing task force, Fair Employment Practices Handbook Task Force, 1979-80; mem. tech. adv. com. Ariz. Dept. Tech. adv. com. Ariz. Dept. Edn., 1993-94; mem. adv. com. Ariz. Auditor Gen. Uniform Sys. Fin. Records, Auditor, 1993—. Columnist Wickenburg Sun, 1975—. Clk. Morristown sch. bd., 1974-76; pres. Morristown PTA, 1977-78; sec. Wickenburg area bd., 1979; bd. dirs. Future Frontiers, 1979-81; rep. HUD block grant adv. com., 1979-85; active Wickenburg Friends of Music, 1984—, bd. dirs., 1986—, sec. bd. dirs., 1986-92, 96; sec. Wickenburg Regional Health Care Found., 1989-92, trustee, 1988-94; mem. com. Wickenburg Scenic Corridor, 1990-92. Named to Ariz. Sch. Bd. Assn. Honor Roll, 1976; named Morristown Area Vol. of Yr., 1988. Mem. AAUW, Ariz. Assn. Sch. Bus. Ofcls. (fin. dir., bd. dirs. 1985-91, v.p. 1991, pres. elect 1992-93, pres. 1993-94, immediate past pres. 1994-95, Gold award 1986-88, 90-95, 96, Silver award 1989), Assn. Sch. Bus. Ofcls. Internat. (mem. pres.'s adv. coun. 1993-94, election com. 1994-95), Morristown Federated Women's Club (edn. chmn. com. 1990—),Theatre Guild, Wickenberg C. of C. (assoc. 1993-95). Roman Catholic. Office: PO Box 98 Morristown AZ 85342-0098 *Personal philosophy: Always Look at your "glass" as 1/2 full rather than 1/2 empty and with this positive approach, anything can be achieved.*

ROSELL, SHARON LYNN, physics and chemistry educator, researcher; b. Wichita, Kans., Jan. 6, 1948; d. John E. and Mildred C. (Binder) R. BA, Loretto Heights Coll., 1970; postgrad., Marshall U., 1973; MS in Edn., Ind. U., 1977; MS, U. Wash., 1988. Cert. profl. educator, Wash. Assoc. instr. Ind. U., Bloomington, 1973-74; instr. Pierce Coll. (name formerly Ft. Steilacoom (Wash.) Community Coll.), 1976-79, 82, Olympic Coll., Bremerton, Wash., 1977-78; instr. physics, math. and chemistry Tacoma (Wash.) Community Coll., 1979-89; instr. physics and chemistry Green River Community Coll., Auburn, Wash., 1983-86; researcher Nuclear Physics Lab., U. Wash., Seattle, 1986-88; asst. prof. physics Cen. Wash. U., Ellensburg, 1989—. Lector and dir. Rite of Christian Initiation of Adults, St. Andrew's Ch., Ellensburg, Wash., 1993—, mem. parish coun., 1995—. Mem. Am. Phys. Soc., Am. Assn. Physics Tchrs. (rep. com. on physics for 2-yr. colls. Wash. chpt. 1986-87, v.p. 1987-88, 94-95, pres. 1988-89, 95-96, past pres. 1996-97), Am. Chem. Soc., Internat. Union Pure and Applied Chemistry (affiliate), Pacific Northwest Assn. Coll. Physics (bd. dirs. 1997—). Democrat. Roman Catholic. Home: 1100 N B St Apt 2 Ellensburg WA 98926-2570 Office: Cen Wash U Physics Dept Ellensburg WA 98926 *Personal philosophy: Every human being is born with a unique set of talents and gifts with which to serve the Lord and other people; the greater the gift, the greater the obligation to serve.*

ROSEME, SHARON DAY, lawyer; b. Sacramento, Aug. 6, 1953; d. George Roseme and Alice Diane Day; m. Daniel George Glenn, June 26, 1982 (div. Nov. 1989); 1 child, Hilary. Student, San Francisco State U., 1971-72; BA, U. Calif., Santa Cruz, 1975; JD, Boalt Hall Sch. of Law, 1978. Jud. staff atty. Calif. State Ct. of Appeal, San Francisco, 1978-80; assoc. Feldman, Waldman & Kline, San Francisco, 1980-82, McDonough, Holland & Allen, Sacramento, 1982—; speaker to profl. and cmty. orgns. Contbr. articles to profl. jours. Mem. Leadership Calif. Class of 1996. Mem. ABA, State Bar Calif., County Bar Sacramento, County Bar Placer, Am. Arbitration Assn. (arbitrator, Sacramento adv. com.), Sacramento Area Commerce and Trade Orgn. (devel. com. 1994-96, chmn. 1996-97), Comml. Real Estate Women Sacramento (pres. 1997, chmn. cmty. svc. com. 1994-95, Mem. of Yr. award 1993), Order of Coif. Office: McDonough Holland & Allen 555 Capitol Mall Ste 950 Sacramento CA 95814-4601

ROSEMIRE, ADELINE LOUISE, writer, publisher; b. Modesto, Calif., Sept. 5, 1951; d. Henry Machado and Theresa Constance (Silveira) Azevedo; m. Michael Edward Rosemire, Dec. 17, 1971. AA, Modesto Coll., 1971. Mktg. profl. Blue Cross, San Jose, Calif., 1971-74; newsletter editor No. Telecom, Santa Clara, Calif., 1974-77; editor Bryan Pubs., Santa Clara, 1978-81; owner, writer The Write Stuff, San Jose, 1981—, Rosemire/Bedford-White, Santa Clara, 1983-92; owner, author Meridian Pub., Inc., San Jose, 1993—. Author: The Other Mid-Life Crisis, 1994, The 2-Ingredient Cookbook, 1996. Dir. Bay Area Lupus Found., San Jose, 1994—, Crippled Children's Soc., Santa Clara, 1990-96, Bldg. Industry Assn., Dublin, Calif., 1981-89. Recipient Pres.' award Bldg. Industry Assn. Ednl. Coun., 1989. Mem. Pubs. Mktg. Assn. Office: Meridian Pub Inc 2431 Tulip Rd San Jose CA 95128-1143

ROSEN, DAVID ALLEN, manufacturing executive; b. Anchorage, Aug. 4, 1955; s. Harold E. and Marlene (Allen) R.; m. Phyllis A. Romans, Aug. 19, 1980; children: Stephanie, Kevin, Stanford, Alex, Samuel, Kimberly. BS in Bus., Brigham Young U., 1980; MBA, U. Utah, 1990. Coord. Youth Devel. Enterprises, Salt Lake City, 1978-79; instr. Brigham Young U., Provo, 1980; v.p., loan officer Key Bank of Utah, Salt Lake City, 1980-92; dir. of mfg. Larson-Davis Labs., Provo, 1992—; chmn. applied tech. adv. com. Mountainland Region Applied Tech. Edn., 1994-96. Mem. fin. com. Greater Salt Lake City Area, YMCA, 1987-91. Mem. Brigham Young Univ. Mgmt. Soc. (Utah County chpt. 1989—), Kiwanis (pres. 1990-91). Mem. LDS Ch. Home: 124 E 3800 N Provo UT 84604-4510 Office: Larson Davis Labs 1681 W 820 N Provo UT 84601-1341

ROSEN, JON HOWARD, lawyer; b. Bklyn., May 20, 1943; s. Eli and Vera (Horowitz) R.; m. Georgeanne Evans, 1993; children of a previous marriage: Jason Marc, Hope Terry. BA, Hobart Coll., 1965; JD, St. John's U., 1968; postgrad. Bernard Baruch Sch. Bus., CCNY, 1969-71. Bar: N.Y. 1969, Calif. 1975, Wash. 1977. Atty. FAA, N.Y.C., 1968-71; regional atty., contract adminstr. Air Line Pilots Assn., N.Y.C., Chgo., L.A., San Francisco, 1971-77; pvt. practice Seattle, 1977-80; ptnr. Frank and Rosen, Seattle, 1981—; instr. labor studies Shoreline Community Coll., 1978-90. Trustee Temple DeHirsch Sinai, 1992—. Mem. ABA (union co-chmn. com. on Employee Rights and Responsibilities 1992-96, co- regional EEOC liaison), Seattle-King County Bar Assn. (past chmn. aviation and space law sect., past chmn. Pacific Coast Labor Law Conf., past chmn. labor law sect.), Nat. Employment Lawyers Assn. (state steering com., chair 1990-95), Wash. State Trial Lawyer's Assn. (past chair employment law com.). Office: Frank & Rosen 705 2nd Ave Ste 1200 Seattle WA 98104-1711

ROSEN, MARTIN JACK, lawyer; b. L.A., Sept. 9, 1931; s. Irving and Sylvia (Savad) R.; B.A., UCLA, 1953; J.D., U. Calif.-Berkeley, 1956; m. Joan D. Meyersieck, Oct. 22, 1954; children—Dirk Rosen, Marika. Bar: Calif. 1957. Pvt. practice, Merced, Calif., 1960-62, San Francisco, 1962-82; mem. Silver, Rosen, Fischer & Stecher, P.C., San Francisco, 1964-79. Pres. Trust for Pub. Land, 1979—. Served with USAF, 1958-60. Fellow internat. legal studies U. Calif. Law Sch./Inst. Social Studies, The Hag ue, 1956-57.

ROSEN, MOISHE, religious organization administrator; b. Kansas City, Mo., Apr. 12, 1932; s. Ben and Rose (Baker) R.; m. Ceil Starr, Aug. 18, 1950; children: Lyn Rosen Bond, Ruth. Diploma, Northeastern Bible Coll., 1957; DD, Western Conservative Bapt. Sem., 1986. Ordained to ministry Bapt. Ch., 1957. Missionary Am. Bd. Missions to the Jews, N.Y.C., 1956; minister in charge Beth Sar Shalom Am. Bd. Missions to the Jews, Los Angeles, 1957-67; dir. recruiting and tng. Am. Bd. Missions to the Jews, N.Y.C., 1967-70; leader Jews for Jesus Movement, San Francisco, 1970-73, exec. dir., 1973-96, founder, 1973—; speaker in field. Author: Saying of Chairman Moishe, 1972, Jews for Jesus, 1974, Share the New Life with a Jew, 1976, Christ in the Passover, 1977, Y'shua, The Jewish Way to Say Jesus, 1982, Overture to Armageddon, 1991, The Universe is Broken: Who on Earth Can Fix It?, 1991, Demystifying Personal Evangelism, 1992. Trustee Western Conservative Bapt. Sem., Portland, Oreg., 1979-85, 86-91, Bibl. Internat. Coun. on Bibl. Inerrancy, Oakland, Calif., 1979-89; bd. dirs. Christian Advs. Serving Evangelism, 1987-91. Office: Jews for Jesus 90 Miraloma San Francisco CA 94127

ROSEN, STEVEN O., lawyer; b. N.Y.C., Jan. 11, 1949; s. Albert I. and Yvette (Sterenbuch) R.; m. Martha M., July 10, 1983; 1 child, Melissa L. BS Aerospace Engring., SUNY, 1970; MS System and Control Engring., Case Western Reserve, 1975; JD, Lewis & Clark Coll., 1977. Bar: Ill. 1977, Oreg. 1978. Assoc. Lord, Bissell & Brook, Chgo., 1977-79; assoc. Miller, Nash, Wiener, Hager & Carlsen, Portland, Oreg., 1979-84, ptnr., 1984—; disting. adj. prof. Lewis & Clark Law Sch., 1986. Mem. ABA (dir. divsns. sect. of litigation 1996-97, chair aviation litigation com. 1990-93), Oreg. State Bar Assn. (exec. com. aviation sect. 1984—, chair 1994-95). Office: Miller Nash Wiener Hager & Carlsen 111 SW 5th Ave Ste 3500 Portland OR 97204-3638

ROSENBAUM, LAWRENCE ALAN, evangelist; b. Camp Kilmer, N.J., Jan. 18, 1946; s. Irving and Dorothy Berger Rosenbaum. BA, Yale U., 1967; MA, Brandeis U., 1970. Dir. SOS Ministries, Oakland, Calif., 1980—; adminstrv. dir. Internat. St. and Evangelism Ministries Assn., Oakland, 1985—. Author: You Shall Be My Witnesses, 1986. Office: PO Box 27358 Oakland CA 94602-0358

ROSENBAUM, MICHAEL FRANCIS, securities dealer; b. N.Y.C., Feb. 9, 1959; s. Francis Fels Jr. and Joyce (Keefer) R.; m. Elika Sosnick, Mar. 8, 1986; children: Erin Sosnick, Sarah Greer, Kira Keefer. AB, Princeton U., 1981. Cert. Nat. Assn. Securities Dealers. Product mgr. Sutro & Co., Inc., San Francisco, 1981-84; v.p. sales Pacific Securities, San Francisco, 1984-89; v.p., br. mgr. Rauscher Pierce Resfnes, San Francisco, 1989-92; v.p. sales Smith Mitchell Investment Group, San Francisco, 1992-93; sr. v.p. sales Gruntal & Co., Inc., San Francisco, 1993-94; sr. v.p. taxable fixed income Coast Ptnrs. Securities, San Francisco, 1994—; bd. dirs. S.G. Rosenbaum Found., N.Y.C. Patroller Nat. Ski Patrol, Northstar, Calif., 1988; trustee Princeton U. Democrat. Jewish. Home: PO Box 1104 Ross CA 94957-1104

ROSENBAUM, RICHARD BARRY, neurologist; b. Rochester, Minn., Aug. 17, 1946; s. Edward E. and Davida (Naftalin) R.; m. Lois Peretz Omenn, Apr. 4, 1971; children: Steven, Laura. AB cum laude, Harvard U., 1967, MD cum laude, 1971. Diplomate Am. Bd. Psychiatry and Neurology, Am. Bd. Internal Medicine, Am. Bd. Electrodiagnostic Medicine; lic. MD, Oreg., Calif. Neurologist The Oreg. Clinic, Portland, Oreg., 1977—; clin. prof. neurology Oreg. Health Scis. U., Portland, Oreg., 1992—. Co-author: Carpal Tunnel Syndrome and Other Disorders of the Median Nerve, 1992, Clinical Neurology of Rheumatic Diseases, 1996. With USPHS, 1973-75. Recipient Meritorious Achievement award Oreg. Health Scis. U., 1993. Mem. Am. Acad. Neurology, Am. Assn. Electrodiagnostic Medicine, Alpha Omega Alpha. Office: 5050 NE Hoyt St Ste 314 Portland OR 97213-2982

ROSENBERG, ALEX, mathematician, educator; b. Berlin, Germany, Dec. 5, 1926; came to U.S., 1949, naturalized, 1959; s. Theodore and Rela (Banet) R.; m. Beatrice Gershenson, Aug. 24, 1952 (div. Apr. 1985); children: Theodore Joseph, David Michael, Daniel Alex; m. Brunhilde Angun, June 14, 1985. B.A., U. Toronto, 1948, M.A., 1949; Ph.D., U. Chgo., 1951. From instr. to assoc. prof. math. Northwestern U., 1952-61; prof. math. Cornell U., Ithaca, N.Y., 1961-88, prof. emeritus, 1988—, chmn. dept., 1966-69; prof. U. Calif., Santa Barbara, 1986-94, chmn. dept., 1986-87, prof. emeritus, 1994—; mem. com. undergrad. program math. Math Assn. Am., 1966-76; mem. Inst. Advanced Study, 1955-57; vis. prof. U. Calif., Berkely, 1961, 1979, U. Calif., Los Angeles, 1969-70, 82, U. London, Queen Mary Coll., 1963-64, U. Munich, 1975-76, E.T.H Zurich, 1976, U. Dortmund, 1984-85; trustee Am. Math Soc., 1973-83. Editor: Proc. Am. Math. Soc., 1960-66, Am. Math. Monthly, 1974-77; Contbr. articles to profl. jours. Recipient Humboldt Stiftung Sr. U.S. Scientist award U. Munich, 1975-76, U. Dortmund, 1981. Home: 1225 Plaza Del Monte Santa Barbara CA 93101-4819

ROSENBERG, DAN YALE, retired plant pathologist; b. Stockton, Calif., Jan. 8, 1922; s. Meyer and Bertha (Naliboff) R.; AA, Stockton Jr. Coll., 1942; AB, Coll. Pacific, 1949; MS, U. Calif. at Davis, 1952; m. Marilyn Kohn, Dec. 5, 1954; 1 son, Morton Karl. Jr. plant pathologist Calif. Dept. Agr., Riverside, 1952-55, asst. plant pathologist, 1955-59, assoc. plant pathologist, 1959-60, pathologist IV, 1960-63, program supr., 1963-71, chief exclusion and detection, div. plant industry, 1971-76, chief nursery and seed svcs. div. plant industry, 1976-82, spl. asst. div. plant industry, 1982-87; pres. Health, Inc., 1972-73; agrl. cons., 1988—; mem. Citrus Rsch. Adv. com. U. Calif., Riverside, 1992—; mem. Gov.'s Interagy. Task Force on Biotech., 1986—; bd. dirs. Health Inc., Sacramento, 1967, pres., 1971-72, 79-81, 81-83. Contbr. articles to profl. jours. Served with AUS, 1942-46; ETO. Mem. Am. Phytopath. Soc. (fgn. and regulatory com. 1975—, grape diseases sect. 1977-79, grape pests sect. 1979—), Calif. State Employees Assn. (pres. 1967-69), Sacramento Met. C. of C. (internat. trade com. 1993—). Home and Office: 2328 Swarthmore Dr Sacramento CA 95825-6867

ROSENBERG, DONALD LEE, magazine publisher; b. Atlantic City, N.J., Feb. 22, 1953; s. Sidney J. and Lois Rosenberg; m. Ellen Steiger, Apr. 9, 1979; children: Drew, Evan, Amanda. BS in Bus. Adminstrn. and Mktg., U. Md., 1976. Gen. mgr. Schwartz Bros., Inc. (SBI Video), Lanham, Md., 1980-86; dir. sales HBO Video, N.Y.C., 1986-87, FOX Home Video, Palatine, Ill., 1987-89; pres. Epic Home Video, L.A., 1989-90, DLR Assocs., Westlake Village, Calif., 1990-91; exec. v.p. Video Software Dealers Assn., Encino, Calif., 1991-94; publ. Video Store Mag., Santa Ana, Calif., 1994—. Office: Video Store Mag 201 Sandpointe Ave Ste 600 Santa Ana CA 92707-8700

ROSENBERG, JANE, author, illustrator; b. N.Y.C., Dec. 7, 1949; d. Abner Emmanuel and Lily (Quittman) R.; m. Robert F. Porter, May 30, 1982; children: Melo Ann Porter, Ava Hermine Porter, Eloise Pearl Porter. BFA, Beaver Coll., 1971; MA in Painting, NYU, 1973. Painter, freelance illustrator N.Y.C., 1974-82; art tchr. Ethical Culture Sch., N.Y.C., 1974-75; art dir. N.Y. News for Kids, N.Y.C., 1979-80; children's book author, illustrator N.Y.C., L.A., 1982—. Author, illustrator: Dance Me a Story: Twelve Tales from the Classic Ballets, 1985, Sing Me a Story: The Metropolitan Opera's Book of Opera Stories, 1989, Play Me a Story: A Child's Introduction to Classical Music through Stories and Poems, 1994; one-woman shows include Every Picture Tells a Story Gallery, L.A., 1991, Summerlin Libr. and Performing Arts Ctr., Las Vegas, Nev., 1995. Mem. Authors' Guild.

ROSENBERG, JEANETTE L., personal business advisor, speaker; b. Bklyn., July 5, 1960; d. Nathan and Kathy (Frank) R. AA in Acctg., Pierce Coll., 1981; BS in Fin., Calif. State U., 1983. Fin. analyst Warner Bros., Electra, Asylum Internat., Burbank, Calif., 1983-85; fin. mgr., sales asst. Ron Dufault Lapidary, Denver; sales cons. Comprehensive Acctg., Arvada, Colo.; tng. cons., sales trainer Dale Carnegie Inst., Denver, Bellevue, Wash.; owner, writer, trainer, orgnl. devel. specialist Jeanette L. Rosenberg-An Enterprise Devel. Co., Kirkland, Wash., 1985—; cons. Revlon, IRS. Author: Secrets to Running a Successful Business (How to Have Fun Getting More Business), 1993, (cassette) 15 Minute Revitalization, 1995, (software) Inspirations by Jeanette, 1996. Mem. Bus. Profl. Women, Kirkland C. of C., Woodenville C. of C. Office: PO Box 8392 Kirkland WA 98034-0392

ROSENBERG, JILL, realtor, civic leader; b. Shreveport, La., Feb. 17, 1940; d. Morris H. and Sallye (Abramson) Schuster; m. Lewis Rosenberg, Dec. 23, 1962; children: Craig, Paige. BA in Philosophy, Tulane U., 1961, MSW, 1965; grad., Realtor Inst., 1994. Cert. residential specialist Residential Sales Coun.; grad. Realtor Inst. 1993. Social worker La. Dept. Pub. Welfare, 1961-62, 63-64; genetics counselor Sinai Hosp., Balt., 1967-69; ptnr. Parties Extraordinaire, cons., 1973-77; realtor assoc. Robert Weil Assocs., Long Beach, Calif., 1982—. Pres. western region Brandeis U. Nat. Women's Com., 1972-73; bd. dirs. Long Beach Symphony Assn., 1984-85; v.p. Jewish Cmty. Fedn. Long Beach and West Orange County, 1983-86, bd. dirs., 1982-86; pres. Long Beach Cancer League, 1987-88, exec. bd. dirs., 1984—; pres. Long Beach Jewish Cmty. Sr. Housing Corp., 1989-91; v.p. fundraising S.E. unit Long Beach Harbor chpt. Am. Cancer Soc., 1989-90; bd. dirs. Westerly Sch. Assoc., 1991—; bd. trustees St. Mary Med. Ctr. Found., 1991—; fund chair St. Mary Med. Ctr., 1992-94; pres. nat. conf. NCCJ, 1994-96; pres. Leadership Long Beach, 1994-95, Phoenix Long Beach Mus. Art, 1995—, Rotary Club of Long Beach, 1996—; bd. dirs. Am. Diabetes Assn., Long Beach, Calif., 1997—; numerous others. Recipient Young Leadership award Jewish Community Fedn. Long Beach and West Orange County, 1981, Jerusalem award State of Israel, 1989, Hannah G. Solomon award Nat. Coun. Jewish Women, 1992, Alumnus of Yr. award Leadership Long Beach, 1995, Humanitarian award The Nat. Conf., 1997; scholar La. Dept. Pub. Welfare, 1962, NIMH, 1964. Office: Robert Weil Assocs 5220 E Los Altos Plz Long Beach CA 90815-4251

ROSENBERG, RICHARD MORRIS, banker; b. Fall River, Mass., Apr. 21, 1930; s. Charles and Betty (Peck) R.; m. Barbara K. Cohen, Oct. 21, 1956; children: Michael, Peter. BS, Suffolk U., 1952; MBA, Golden Gate U., 1962; LLB, Golden Gate Coll., 1966. Publicity asst. Crocker-Anglo Bank, San Francisco, 1959-62; banking services officer Wells Fargo Bank, N.A., San Francisco, 1962-65; asst. v.p. Wells Fargo Bank, N.A., 1965-68, v.p. mktg. dept., 1968, v.p., dir. mktg., 1969, sr. v.p. mktg. and advt. div., 1970-75, exec. v.p., from 1975, vice chmn., 1980-83; vice chmn. Crocker Nat. Corp., 1983-85; pres., chief operating officer Seafirst Corp., 1986-87, also dir.; pres., chief operating officer Seattle First Nat. Bank, 1985-87; vice chmn. bd. BankAm. Corp., San Francisco, 1987-90, chmn., CEO, 1990-96; dir. Airborne Express, Potlatch Corp., Northrop Cor., SBC Comms., Pacific Mut.; past chmn. Mastercard Internat. Bd. dirs. San Francisco Symphony, United Way; trustee Calif. Inst. Tech. Jewish. Office: BankAm Corp Dept 3001-B PO Box 37000 San Francisco CA 94137-0002

ROSENBLATT, ALLAN D., psychiatrist; b. St. Louis, June 18, 1926. PhB and BS in Physiology, U. Chgo., 1945, MD, MS in Neurophysiology, 1948. Diplomate Am. Bd. Psychiatry and Neurology in Psychiatry. Intern L.A. (Calif.) County Gen. Hosp., 1948-49; resident in psychiatry Bellevue Hosp., 1949-50; USPH fellow, resident in psychiatry N.Y. State Psychiat. Inst., 1950-51; psychoanalytic tng. Columbia U. Psychoanalytic Ctr., 1950-53; clin. asst. Child Guidance Clinic Mt. Sinai Hosp., N.Y.C., 1951-52; adj. psychiatrist Child Guidance Clinic Hosp. for Joint Disease, N.Y.C., 1952-53; pvt. practice N.Y.C., 1951-53, San Diego, 1955—; pres. San Diego Soc. Psychiatry and Neurology, 1956-59, San Diego Assn. Psychiatry and Psychology, 1958-60, San Diego Psychoanalytic Found., 1966-71; chmn. governing coun. San Diego Acad. Behavioral Scis., 1960-63; chmn. bd. dirs. San Diego Psychoanalytic Inst., 1980-83, dir. and chmn. edn. com., 1977-80, 83-86, tng. and supervising analyst, sr. instr.; clin. prof. psychiatry U. Calif., Sch. Medicine, San Diego; cons. in field. Editor: Am. Psychoanalytic Assn. Newsletter, 1982-84; consulting editor Psychoanalytic Inquiry; contbr. articles to profl. jours. Lt. USNR, 1951-53. Fellow Am. Psychiat. Assn. (life, cons. quality assurance com.), Am. Coll. Psychoanalysts; mem. Am. Psychoanalytic Assn. (life, fellow bd. profl. standards 1974-80, 83-86, exec. councilor 1980-83, 91—, exec. councilor-at-large 1987-91, mem. task force on certification 1991-92, chair com. on appts., chair external credentialing com., co-chair com. on socs.), San Diego Psychoanalytic Soc., San Diego Psychiat. Soc., San Diego County Med. Soc. Home: 1689 Los Altos Rd San Diego CA 92109-1357 Office: 3252 Holiday Ct Ste 205 La Jolla CA 92037-1808

ROSENBLATT, MURRAY, mathematics educator; b. N.Y.C., Sept. 7, 1926; s. Hyman and Esther R.; m. Adylin Lipson, 1949; children—Karin, Daniel. B.S., CCNY, 1946; M.S., Cornell U., 1947, Ph.D. in Math., 1949. Asst. prof. statistics U. Chgo., 1950-55; assoc. prof. math. Ind. U., 1956-59; prof. probability and statistics Brown U., 1959-64; prof. math. U. Calif., San Diego, 1964—; vis. fellow U. Stockholm, 1953; vis. asst. prof. Columbia U., 1955; guest scientist Brookhaven Nat. Lab., 1959; vis. fellow U. Coll., London, 1965-66, Imperial Coll. and Univ. Coll., London, 1972-73, Australian Nat. U., 1976, 79; overseas fellow Churchill Coll., Cambridge U., Eng., 1979; Wald lectr., 1970; vis. scholar Stanford U., 1982. Author: (with U. Grenander) Statistical Analysis of Stationary Time Series, 1957, Random Processes, 1962, (2d edit), 1974, Markov Processes, Structure and Asymptotic Behavior, 1971, Studies in Probability Theory, 1978, Stationary Sequences and Random Fields, 1985, Stochastic Curve Estimation, 1991; editor: The North Holland Series in Probability and Statistics, 1980; mem. editorial bd. Jour. Theoretical Probability. Recipient Bronze medal U. Helsinki, 1978; Guggenheim fellow, 1965-66, 71-72. Fellow Inst. Math Statistics, AAAS; mem. Internat. Statis. Inst., Nat. Acad. Scis. Office: U Calif Dept Math La Jolla CA 92093 also: PO Box 2066 La Jolla CA 92038-2066

ROSENBLATT, PAUL GERHARDT, federal judge. AB, U. Ariz., 1958, JD, 1963. Asst. atty. gen. State of Ariz., 1963-66; adminstrv. asst. to U.S. Rep., 1967-72; sole practice, Prescott, 1971-73; judge Yavapai County Superior Ct., Prescott, 1973-84; judge, U.S. Dist. Ct. Ariz., Phoenix, 1984—. Office: US Dist Ct US Courthouse & Fed Bldg 230 N 1st Ave Ste 7012 Phoenix AZ 85025-0007*

ROSENBLUM, RICHARD MARK, utility executive; b. N.Y.C., Apr. 28, 1950; s. Victor Sigmund and Julia (Kessler) R.; m. Michele E. Cartier, Aug. 30, 1979; children: Gialisa, Jeremy Scott. BS, MS, Rensselaer Poly. Inst., 1973. Registered profl. engr., Calif. Startup engr. Combustion Engring. Inc., Windsor, Conn., 1973-76; engr. So. Calif. Edison Co., Rosemead, 1976-82, project mgr. San Onofre Nuclear Generating Sta., 1982-83, tech. mgr., 1983-84, nuclear safety mgr., 1984-86, mgr. quality assurance, 1986-89, mgr. nuclear regulatory affairs, 1989-93, v.p. Engring. and Tech. Svcs., 1993-95, v.p. distribution, 1996—. N.Y. State Regents scholar, 1968-73. Office: 2244 Walnut Grove Ave Rosemead CA 91770-3714

ROSENBLUTH, MURRAY JOSEPH, chemical engineer; b. Phila., June 6, 1931; s. Louis and Fannie S. (Pinkowitz) R.; m. Adele E. Goldman, June 28, 1953; children: Harry J., Ellen P., Joshua H. BSChemE, Drexel U., 1953, MSChemE, 1959. Registered profl. engr., Calif., Pa. Tech. engr. to sect. project Procter and Gamble Co., 1960-90; sr. tech. project engr., project mgr. IPC Sys. Engring., Inc., Oxnard, Calif., 1990—. Dir. Cancer Share, Cin., 1989; mem. Port Hueneme (Calif.) City Coun., 1996—. 1st Lt. U.S. Army, 1953-55. Jewish. Home: 2591 Northstar Cv Port Hueneme CA 93041-1568

ROSENBURG, JEFFREY MICHAEL, cardiovascular and thoracic surgeon; b. L.A., Jan. 6, 1955; s. Marvin Joseph and Janis Faye (Moss) R.; m. Jeanette Renee Lewey, May 29, 1988; children: Mathew, Michael. BS, U. So. Calif., 1979, MD, 1983. Diplomate Am. Bd. Surgery, Am. Bd. Thoracic Surgery. Resident in gen. surgery Harbor-UCLA Med. Ctr., Torrance, 1983-85, Kaiser Permanente Med. Ctr., Oakland, Calif., 1985-89; fellow in cardiothoracic surgery Kaiser Permanente Med. Ctr., San Francisco, 1989-90; resident in cardiopulmonary surgery SUNY, Syracuse, 1990-92; pvt. practice, San Diego, 1992-95, Chula Vista, Calif., 1995—; asst. chief surgery Sharp Chula Vista Med. Ctr., 1996—. Fellow ACS, Am. Coll. Chest Physicians, Am. Coll. Cardiology; mem. AMA, Am. Heart Assn. (bd. dirs. Chula Vista 1996—), Calif. Med. Assn. (alt. del. 1995—), San Diego County Med. Assn. Office: 450 4th Ave Ste 200 Chula Vista CA 91910-4428

ROSENDAHL, ROGER WAYNE, lawyer. B, U. So. Calif., 1965; JD, Georgetown U., 1969, LLM, 1971. Bar: N.Y. 1973, Calif. 1975. Mng. ptnr. Cadwalader, Wickersham & Taft, L.A.; lectr. law U. Frankfurt, Germany. Mng. editor Law and Policy in Internat. Bus. Mem. fgn. svc. adv. com. U.S. Trade Rep. Schulte zur Hausen fellow. Mem. ABA (past officer, coun.), Asia-Pacific Lawyers Assn. (founding coun. 1991-92), L.A. County Bar Assn. (bd. advisors, exec. com.), Am. Arbitration Assn. Office: Cadwalader Wickersham & Taft 660 S Figueroa St 23d Fl Los Angeles CA 90017

ROSENDAL, HANS ERIK, meteorologist; b. Lyngby, Denmark, July 19, 1931; s. Kaj and Anna Katrine (Hansen) R.; m. Angela Karlos, Dec. 20, 1958; children: Erik P., Dana G., Paul A. BS, U. Wis., 1960; MS, U. Mich., 1965. Meteorologist U.S. Weather Bur., Washington, 1960-65; state climatologist Nat. Weather Svc., Madison, Wis., 1965-73; meteorologist Nat. Weather Svc., Milw., Wis., 1973-74, Phoenix, 1974-76, Honolulu, 1976—. Editor Mariners Weather Log, 1962-64. Recipient Gold medal U.S. Dept. Commerce, Honolulu, 1992. Fellow Am. Meteorol. Soc. (spl. award 1992). Lutheran. Home: 1242 Mokapu Blvd Kailua HI 96734-1847 Office: Nat Weather Svc U Hawaii at Manoa Manoa HI 96734

ROSENFELD, RON GERSHON, pediatrics educator; b. N.Y.C., June 22, 1946; s. Stanley I. and Deborah (Levin) R.; m. Valerie Rae Spitz, June 16, 1968; children: Amy, Jeffrey. BA, Columbia U., 1968; MD, Stanford U., 1973. Intern Stanford (Calif.) U. Med. Ctr., 1973-74, resident in pediatrics, 1974-75, chief resident pediatrics, 1975-76; pvt. practice Santa Barbara, Calif., 1976-77; postdoctoral fellow Stanford U. Sch. Medicine, 1977-80, from asst. to assoc. prof. pediatrics, 1980-89, prof. pediatrics, 1989-93; chmn., prof. pediatrics Oreg. Health Scis. U., 1993—; physician-in-chief Doernbecher Children's Hosp., 1993—; cons. Genentech Inc., South San Francisco, 1980—, Pharmacia-Upjohn, Inc., Stockholm, 1990—, Novo Nordisk, Inc., Copenhagen, 1991—, Diagnostic Systems Labs., Webster, Tex., 1991—, Serono, Norwell, Mass., 1992—; prof. Cell and Devel. Biology Oreg. Health Scis. U. Editor: Growth Abnormalities, 1985, Turner Syndrome, 1987, Turner Syndrome: Growth, 1990, Growth Regulation; mem. editl. bd.: Jour. Clin. Endocrinology and Metabolism, Growth Factors, Clin. Pediatric Endocrinology, Growth and Growth Factors, Growth Regulation, Hormone Rsch. Recipient Ross Rsch. award Ross Laboratories, 1985. Mem. Endocrine Soc., Soc. for Pediat. Rsch., Lawson Wilkins Pediat. Endocrine Soc. (pres. 1996-97), European Soc. for Pediat. Endocrinology, Diabetes Soc. Office: Oreg Health Scis Univ Dept Pediatrics 3181 SW Sam Jackson Park Rd Portland OR 97201-3011

ROSENFELD, SARENA MARGARET, artist; b. Elmira, N.Y., Oct. 17, 1940; d. Thomas Edward and Rosalie Ereny (Fedor) Rooney; m. Robert Steven Bach, June 1958 (div. 1963); children: Robert Steven, Daniel Thomas; m. Samson Rosenfeld III, June 5, 1976. Student, Otis/Parson Art Inst., L.A., 1994—, Idyllwild Sch. Music and Arts, 1994—. One-woman shows and group exhbns. include Robert Dana Gallery, San Francisco, Gordon Gallery, Santa Monica, Calif., Hespe Gallery, San Francisco, Gallery 444, San Francisco, Art Expressions, San Diego, Ergane Gallery, N.Y.C., Nat. Mus. of Women in the Arts, Washington, also in L.A., La Jolla, Calif., Aspen, Colo., New Orleans, Soho, N.Y.C., Santa Barbara, Calif., Tanglewood, Mass., Honolulu, Johannesburg, South Africa, La Sierra U., Riverside, Calif. Mem., vol., animal handler Wildlife Waysta., Angeles Nat. Forest, Calif. Recipient Best of Show award Glendale Regional Arts Coun., 1984-85, 1st pl. awards Santa Monica Art Festival, 1982, 83, 84, 85, 86, Sweepstakes award and 1st pl., 1986, Purchase prize awards L.A. West C. of C., 1986-87, Tapestry in Talent Invitational San Jose Arts Coun., 1986, 1st pl. awards Studio City and Century City Arts Couns., 1976-84. Mem. Nat. Mus. of Women in the Arts. Republican. Home: 6570 Kelvin Ave Canoga Park CA 91306-4021

ROSENHEIM, DANIEL EDWARD, journalist, television news director; b. Chgo., Aug. 12, 1949; s. Edward W. and Margaret Morton (Keeney) R.; m. Christina J. Adachi, May 10, 1976 (div. 1979); m. Cindy Catherine Salans, June 20, 1980; children: Joseph Michael, James Salans, Nicholas Edward. BA, Wesleyan U., 1971. Factory worker Pitts. and Chgo., 1972-77; reporter Sun-Jour., Lansing, Ill., 1977; bus./labor editor Hammond (Ind.) Times, 1977-80; bus. writer Chgo. Sun Times, 1980-82, spl. writer, 1982-84; bus. writer Chgo. Tribune, 1984-85; econs. editor San Francisco Chronicle, 1985-87, city editor, 1987-94, mng. editor, 1994-96; news dir. KRON-TV, San Francisco, 1996—. Mem. Radio and TV News Dirs. Assn., San Francisco Tennis Club. Office: KRON-TV 1001 Van Ness Ave San Francisco CA 94109*

ROSENKILDE, CARL EDWARD, physicist; b. Yakima, Wash., Mar. 16, 1937; s. Elmer Edward and Doris Edith (Fitzgerald) R.; m. Bernadine Doris Blumenstine, June 22, 1963 (div. Apr. 1991); children: Karen Louise, Paul Eric; m. Wendy Maureen Ellison, May 24, 1992. BS in Physics, Wash. State Coll., 1959; MS in Physics, U. Chgo., 1960, PhD in Physics, 1966. Postdoctoral fellow Argonne (Ill.) Nat. Lab., 1966-68; asst. prof. math. NYU, 1968-70; asst. prof. physics Kans. State U., Manhattan, 1970-76, assoc. prof., 1976-79; physicist Lawrence Livermore (Calif.) Nat. Lab., 1979-93, lab. assoc., 1994-95, participating guest, 1995-97, cons., 1974-79; chief scientist C.R. Sci., 1993—. Contbr. articles on physics to profl. jours. Woodrow Wilson fellow, 1959, 60. Mem. Am. Phys. Soc., Am. Assn. Physics Tchrs., Calif. Math. Coun. C.C., Am. Coll. Forensic Examiners, Am. Astron. Soc., Soc. for Indsl. and Applied Math., Am. Geophys. Union, Acoustical Soc. Am., Math. Assn. Am., Phi Beta Kappa, Phi Kappa Phi, Phi Eta Sigma, Sigma Xi. Republican. Presbyterian. Club: Tubists Universal Brotherhood Assn. (TUBA). Research includes nonlinear wave propagation in complex media; subspecialties: theoretical physics, fluid dynamics.

ROSENMEYER, THOMAS GUSTAV, retired classics educator, researcher; b. Hamburg, Germany, Apr. 3, 1920; came to U.S., 1946; s. Kurt and Kate (Weiss) R.; children: Kathy G. Frenchman, Patricia A. BA in Classics, McMaster U., Hamilton, Ont., Can., 1944; MA in Classics, U. Toronto, 1945; PhD in Classics, Harvard U., 1949. Asst. prof. classics U. Iowa, Iowa City, 1947-52, Smith Coll., Northampton, Mass., 1952-55; asst. prof. to prof. classics U. Wash., Seattle, 1955-66; prof. Greek and comparative lit. U. Calif., Berkeley, 1966-90, prof. emeritus, 1990—; vis. prof. Am. Sch. Classical Studies, Athens, Greece, 1961-62, Princeton (N.J.) U., 1975, Harvard U., Cambridge, Mass., 1985. Author: The Masks of Tragedy, 1963, The Green Cabinet, 1970, The Art of Aeschylus, 1982, Senecan Tragedy, 1989, and other books; contbr. articles to profl. jours.; former editor Calif. Studies in Classical Antiquity, U. Calif. Press, Berkeley; former editor EIDOS: Studies in Classical Kinds, U. Calif. Press, Berkeley. Guggenheim fellow 1967-68, 82-83, NEH sr. fellow, Paris, 1972-73.. Mem. Am. Philol. Assn. Democrat. Home: 76 Eucalyptus Rd Berkeley CA 94705-2802

ROSENTHAL, ALAN JAY, psychiatry educator; b. Detroit, Sept. 4, 1938; married; 3 children. AB magna cum laude, Wayne State U., 1960; MD, U. Mich., 1963. Diplomate Am. Bd. Psychiatry and Neurology in Psychiatry, Am. Bd. Child Psychiatry. Intern Kaiser Found. Hosp., San Francisco, 1963-64; resident in psychiatry U. Mich. Med. Ctr., Ann Arbor, 1964-65; resident in child psychiatry Stanford (Calif.) U. Med. Ctr., 1967-68, instr., chief resident in child psychiatry, 1968-69, asst. prof. dept. psychiatry, 1969-75, dir. child psychiatry, 1970-73, dir. child psychiatry resident tng. program, 1970-75, clin. assoc. prof. dept. psychiatry, 1975-88, clin. prof. dept. psychiatry, 1988—; dir. Children's Health Coun. Mid-Peninsula, Palo Alto, Calif., 1973-95; med. dir. Children's Health Coun., Palo Alto, 1995—; bd. dirs. Children's Health Coun., Palo Alto Adolescent Svcs. Corp.; cons. in field; presenter, lectr. in field. Mem. Am. Psychiat. Assn., Am. Acad. Child Psychiatry, Assn. Mid-Peninsula (bd. dirs. family svc.), Victor Vaughn Soc., Delta Sigma Rho, Phi Beta Kappa. Office: 700 Sand Hill Rd Palo Alto CA 94304-2003

ROSENTHAL, CHARLES LOUIS, artist, educator; b. Chgo., Apr. 9, 1917; s. Henry Ditmar and Fredericka (Hoff) R.; m. Joyce Mary La Rocca, Aug. 5, 1944; children: John, James. Student, Central Coll., Chgo., 1937, Art Inst. of Chgo., 1936, Northwestern U., Chgo., 1939, Ariz. State U., 1972, Am. Acad. Art, 1937. Ptnr. Hobbs Rosenthal Studios, Chgo., 1935-40, Metcalf Engravers, Chgo., 1940-53; owner Metcalf Printers, Inc., Itasca, Ill., 1954-68, Pro/Ad Inc., Itasca, 1960-68; pvt. artist/tchr. of papermaking Scottsdale, Ariz., 1968—; tchr. Shemer Art Ctr., Phoenix, 1980—, Guild Sch. of Art, Phoenix, 1980—; condr. seminars and workshops in field. Writer/artist: The Art World at Your Fingertips, 1991. Founder Inner City Art Program, Phoenix, 1989, Guild Sch. of Art, Phoenix, 1988. Named to Ariz. Artists Guild Hall of Fame, 1995. Mem. Ariz. Artists Guild, Ariz. Watercolor Assn., No. Ariz. Watercolor Assn., Scottsdale Artists League. Republican. Home: 8125 E Gail Rd Scottsdale AZ 85260

ROSENTHAL, JOHN DAVID, dentist; b. Portland, Oreg., Feb. 26, 1950; s. Lawrence A. and H. Bertha (Klein) R.; m. Barbara J. Loomis, Apr. 1, 1977; children: Kristin, Benjamin. BS, U. Oreg., 1973; DMD, U. Oreg. Health Sci. U., 1976. Dentist Rosenthal & Rosenthal, DMD, Portland, 1976-79; pvt. practice Portland, 1979—; ptnr. Downtown Dental Assocs., 1995—. Dental chmn. United Way of Oreg., Portland, 1985; mem. membership com. Temple Beth Israel, Portland, 1984-87; mem. adv. com. Robison Retirement Home, Portland, 1986—. Fellow Am. Coll. Dentists, Acad. Gen. Dentistry, Acad. Dentistry Internat.; mem. Oreg. Soc. Dentistry for Children, Western Soc. Periodontology, Multnomah Dental Soc. (b.d dirs. 1979-81, pres. 1986), Oreg. Dental Assn. (membership chmn. 1984-88, chmn. mem. svcs. coun. 1988-91, Svc. award 1991), Oreg. Acad. Gen. Dentistry (bd. dirs. 1986-90, sec.-treas. 1990-91, pres. 1991-92, regional dir. 1995—), Oreg. Health Sci. U. Sch. Dentistry Alumni Assn. (bd. dirs. 1987-90), Theta Chi. Home: 6565 SW 88th Pl Portland OR 97223-7273 Office: 1221 SW Yamhill St # 310 Portland OR 97205-2009

ROSENTHAL, PHILIP, gastroenterologist; b. Bayshore, N.Y., Oct. 18, 1949; m. Sherrin Jean Packer; children: Seth, Aaron. BS, SUNY, Albany, 1971; MD, SUNY, Bklyn., 1975. Asst. prof. pediatrics Coll. of Physicians and Surgeons Columbia U., N.Y.C., 1981-83; asst. prof. pediatrics U. So. Calif., L.A., 1983-89, tenured assoc. prof. pediatrics, 1989; dir. pediatrics and nutrition, med. dir. pediatric liver transplant program Cedars-Sinai Med. Ctr., L.A., 1989-95; assoc. prof. UCLA, 1989-95; prof. pediat. and surg. U. Calif. San Francisco Med. Ctr., 1995—; asst. attending physician Presbyn. Hosp./Vanderbilt Clinic, N.Y.C., 1981-83, Babies Hosp./Columbia U., 1981-83, Children's Hosp. of L.A., 1983-89; with Vanderbilt Clinic/Columbia U., 1981-83; attending physician Harlem Hosp. and Med. Ctr., N.Y.C., 1981-83, L.A. County/U. So. Calif. Med. Ctr., 1988-89. Vol. City of L.A. Marathon, 1989-90; v.p. Westside Jewish Community Ctr., L.A., 1989-92, bd. dirs. program com., 1987, Children's Liver Found., 1986; mem adv. bd. Jewish Activities Mus., 1990-95. Nat. Inst. Arthritis grantee, 1978-81, Children's Hosp. of L.A. grantee, 1984-86, 86-87, Abbott Labs. grantee, 1984-85, Children's Liver Found. grantee, 1985-86. Mem. Am. Acad. Pediatrics, N.Am. Soc. Pediatric Gastroenterology and Nutrition. Office: U Calif San Francisco Med Ctr MU4 East 500 Parnassus Ave San Francisco CA 94143-0136

ROSENTHAL, SETH ALLAN, radiologist, oncologist; b. Bucks County, Pa., July 9, 1961; s. Isadore and Corinne Rosenthal; children: Ruth, Eli. BA in Chemistry and History, Wesleyan U., Middletown, Conn., 1982; MD, Yale U., 1987. Diplomate Nat. Bd. Med. Examiners, Am. Bd. Radiology. Medicinal chemist Merck Sharp & Dohme, West Point, Pa., 1982-83; intern Yale New Haven (Conn.) Hosp., 1987-88; resident in radiation oncology U. Pa., Phila., 1988-90, chief resident in radiation oncology, 1990-91; asst. prof. in residence in radiation oncology U. Calif. San Francisco, 1991-93; asst. clin. prof. surgery U. Calif. Davis, Sacramento, 1993—; asst. clin. prof. radiation oncology U. Calif., San Francisco, 1993—; attending physician Radiation Oncology Ctrs., Sacramento, 1993—. Recipient Young Oncologist award Am. Radium Soc., 1982. Mem. Phi Beta Kappa. Office: Sutter Radiation Oncology Ctr 2800 "L" St Ste 10 Sacramento CA 95816

ROSENTHAL, SOL, lawyer; b. Balt., Oct. 17, 1934; s. Louis and Hattie (Getz) R.; m. Diane Myra Sackler, June 11, 1961; children: Karen Abby, Pamela Margaret, Robert Joel. AB, Princeton U., 1956; JD, Harvard U., 1959. Bar: Md. 1959, Calif. 1961. Law clk. to chief judge U.S. Ct. Appeals, 4th cir., Balt., 1959-60; assoc. Kaplan, Livingston, Goodwin, Berkowitz & Selvin, Beverly Hills, Calif., 1960-66, ptnr., 1966-74; ptnr. Buchalter, Nemer, Fields & Younger, L.A., 1974-96; of counsel Blanc, Williams, Johnston & Kronstadt, L.A., 1996—; bd. dirs. Playboy Enterprises, Inc., Chgo.; arbitrator Dirs. Guild Am., L.A., 1976—, Writers Guild Am., L.A., 1976—, Am. Film Mktg. Assn., 1989—; negotiator Writers Guild-Assn. Talent Agts., L.A., 1978—. Founder Camp Ronald McDonald for Good Times, L.A., 1985; charter founder Mus. Contemporary Art, L.A., 1988. Mem. ABA, Calif. Bar Assn., L.A. County Bar Assn. (trustee 1981-82), L.A. Copyright Soc. (pres. 1973-74), Acad. TV Arts and Scis. (bd. govs. 1990-92), Beverly Hills Bar Assn. (pres. 1982-83), Phi Beta Kappa. Office: Blanc Williams Johnston & Kronstadt 1900 Ave of the Stars Ste 1700 Los Angeles CA 90067-4403

ROSENZWEIG, HERBERT STEPHEN, stockbroker; b. Phila., Aug. 5, 1943; s. Morton and Helen (Katzen) R.; m. Myra Pauline Saltzburg, June 7, 1964; children: Helene, Michael, Elisa, Jeffrey. BS in Fin., Temple U., 1965. CFP. Stockbroker Walston & Co., Phila., 1967-73, Reynolds Securities, Phila., 1974, Merrill Lynch, Riverside, Calif., 1974—. Vol. Spl. Olympics, 1980—; chmn. Pomona Valley Coun. Chs. Hunger Walk; pres. Upland Youth Accountability Bd. Mem. Kiwanis (past pres., lt. gov. Divsn. 15 1992-93, Club Kiwanian of Yr., Divsn. Kiwanian of Yr. 1992). Republican. Jewish. Office: Merrill Lynch PO Box 472 Riverside CA 92502-0472

ROSENZWEIG, MARK RICHARD, psychology educator; b. Rochester, N.Y., Sept. 12, 1922; s. Jacob and Pearl (Grossman) R.; m. Janine S.A. Chappat, Aug. 1, 1947; children: Anne Janine, Suzanne Jacqueline, Philip Mark. BA, U. Rochester, 1943, MA, 1944; PhD, Harvard U., 1949; hon. doctorate, U. René Descartes, Sorbonne, 1980. Postdoctoral rsch. fellow Harvard U., 1949-51; asst. prof. U. Calif., Berkeley, 1951-56, assoc. prof., 1956-60, prof. psychology, 1960-91, assoc. rsch. prof., 1958-59, rsch. prof., 1965-66, prof. emeritus, 1991—, prof. grad. sch., 1994—; vis. prof. biology U. Sorbonne, Paris, 1973-74. Author: Biologie de la Mémoire, 1976, (with A.L. Leiman) Physiological Psychology, 1982, 2nd edit., 1989, (with M.J. Renner) Enriched and Impoverished Environments: Effects on Brain and Behavior, 1987, (with D. Sinha) La Recherche en Psychologie Scientifique, 1988; editor: (with P. Mussen) Psychology: An Introduction, 1973, 2nd edit., 1977, (with E.L. Bennett) Neural Mechanisms of Learning and Memory, 1976, International Psychological Science: Progress, Problems, and Prospects, 1992, (with A.L. Leiman and S.M. Breedlove) Biological Psychology, 1996; co-editor: (with L. Porter) Ann. Rev. of Psychology, 1968-94; contbr. articles to profl. jours. Served with USN, 1944-46. Recipient Disting. Alumnus award U. Rochester; Fulbright rsch. fellow; faculty rsch. fellow Social Sci. Rsch. Coun., 1960-61; rsch. grantee NSF, USPHS, Easter Seal Found., Nat. Inst. Drug Abuse. Fellow AAAS, APA (Disting. Sci. Contbn. award 1982, Disting. Contbn. award for Advancement of Psychology 1997), Am. Psychol. Soc.; mem. NAS, NAACP (life), Am. Physiol. Soc., Am. Psychol. Soc., Internat. Union Psychol. Sci. (hon. life, mem. exec. com. 1972-96, v.p. 1980-84, pres. 1988-92, past pres. 1992-96, mem. U.S. nat. com. with Internat. Union Psychol. Sci., NRC and NAS 1984-96), Internat. Brain Rsch. Orgn., Soc. Exptl. Psychologists, Soc. for Neurosci., Société Française de Psychologie, Sierra Club (life), Common Cause, Fulbright Assn. (life), Phi Beta Kappa, Sigma Xi. Office: U Calif Dept Psychology 3210 Tolman Hall Berkeley CA 94720-1650

ROSHONG, DEE ANN DANIELS, dean, educator; b. Kansas City, Mo., Nov. 22, 1936; d. Vernon Edmund and Doradell (Kellogg) Daniels; m. Richard Lee Roshong, Aug. 27, 1960 (div.). BMusEd., U. Kans., 1958; MA in Counseling and Guidance, Stanford U., 1960; postgrad. Fresno State U., U. Calif.; EdD, U. San Francisco, 1980. Counselor, psychometrist Fresno City Coll., 1961-65; counselor, instr. psychology Chabot Coll., Hayward, Calif., 1965-75; coord. counseling services Chabot Coll., Valley Campus, Livermore, Calif., 1975-81, asst. dir. student pers. svcs., 1981-89, Las Positas Coll., Livermore, Calif., 1989-91, assoc. dean student svcs., 1991-94, dean student svcs., 1994—; writer, coord. I, A Woman Symposium, 1974, Feeling Free to Be You and Me Symposium, 1975, All for the Family Symposium, 1976, I Celebrate Myself Symposium, 1977, Person to Person in Love and Work Symposium, 1978; The Healthy Person in Body, Mind and Spirit Symposium, 1979, Feelin' Good Symposium, 1980, Change Symposium, 1981, Sources of Strength Symposium, 1982, Love and Friendship Symposium, 1983, Self Esteem Symposium, 1984, Trust Symposium, 1985, Prime Time: Making the Most of This Time in Your Life Symposium, 1986, Symposium on Healing, 1987, How to Live in the World and Still Be Happy Symposium, 1988, Student Success is a Team Effort, Sound Mind, Sound

Body Symposium, 1989, Creating Life's Best Symposium, 1990, Choices Symposium, 1991, Minding the Body, Mending the Mind Symposium, 1992, Healing through Love and Laughter Symposium, 1993, Healing Ourselves Changing the World Symposium, 1994, Finding Your Path Symposium, 1995, Build the Life You Want Symposium, 1996, Making Peace With Yourself and Your Relationships Symposium, 1997; mem. cast TV prodns. Eve and Co., Best of Our Times, Cowboy; chmn. Calif. C.C. Chancellor's Task Force on Counseling, Statewide Regional Counseling Facilitators, 1993-95, Statewide Conf. on Emotionally Disturbed Students in Calif. C.C.s, 1982—, Conf. on the Under Represented Student in California C.C.s, 1986, Conf. on High Risk Students, 1989; bd. dirs. Teleios Sinetar Ctr., Tri-Valley Unity Ch.; choir dir., 1996; title III activity dir. Las Positas Coll., 1995—. Mem. Assn. Humanistic Psychologists, Western Psychol. Assn., Nat. Assn. Women Deans and Counselors, Assn. for Counseling and Devel., Calif. Assn. Community Colls. (chmn. commn. on student services 1979-84), Calif. Community Colls. Counselors Assn. (Svc. award 1986, 87, award for Outstanding and Disting. Service, 1986, 87, Spl. Svc. award for outstanding svc Calif. advocated for re-entry edn., 1991), Alpha Phi. Author: Counseling Needs of Community Coll. Students, 1980. Home: 1856 Harvest Rd Pleasanton CA 94566-5456 Office: 3033 Collier Canyon Rd Livermore CA 94550-9797

ROSICH, RAYNER KARL, physicist; b. Joliet, Ill., Aug. 28, 1940; s. Joseph F. and Gretchen (Cox) R.; BS in Physics cum laude with distinction and honors, U. Mich., 1962, MS in Physics, 1963; PhD, U. Colo., 1977; MBA, U. Denver, 1982; m. Judy Louise Jackson, Aug. 20, 1966; children: Heidi Ann, Kimberly Ann, Dawn Ann. Teaching fellow and rsch. asst. U. Mich., Ann Arbor, 1962-67; staff, Argonne (Ill.) Nat. Lab. Applied Math. Div., summers 1961-63; physicist, project leader Inst. for Telecommunication Sci., U.S. Dept. Commerce, Boulder, Colo., 1967-80; sr. scientist and program mgr. Electro Magnetic Applications, Inc., Denver, 1980-82; applications mgr. Energy Systems Tech., Inc., Denver, 1982-83, mgr. R&D, 1983; prin. scientist, program mgr. Contel Info. Systems, Inc., Denver, 1983-84, dir. tech. audits, 1985, dir. basic and applied R&D, 1986; lab. scientist for systems engring. lab. Hughes Aircraft Co., Denver, 1986, lab. scientist for data systems lab, 1986-90, lab. scientist for systems lab., 1990-92; prin. engr., Advanced System Techs., Inc., Denver, 1992-95; project mgr. Evolving Systems, Inc., 1995; network planning engr., project mgr. Apollo Travel Svcs., 1996—. instr. math. Arapahoe Cmty. Coll., 1987-97. Vol. judo instr., county recreation dist., 1976-77. Recipient Spl. Achievement award U.S. Dept. Commerce, 1974, Outstanding Performance award, 1978, Sustained Superior Performance award, 1979; Libbey-Owens-Ford Glass Co./U. Mich. Phoenix Meml. fellow, 1964-66; NSF Summer fellow, 1965. Mem. Am. Phys. Soc., AAAS, IEEE, Assn. Computing Machinery, Applied Computational Electromagnetics Soc., Soc. Computer Stimulation, Sigma Xi, Phi Kappa Phi. Home: 7932 W Nichols Ave Littleton CO 80123-5558 Office: Apollo Travel Svcs 5347 S Valentia Way Englewood CO 80111

ROSIER, DAVID LEWIS, investment banker; b. Sioux City, Iowa, Mar. 22, 1937; s. Orel Lewis and Jewell May (Palmer) R.; m. Jackie Dodd, July 1965 (div. 1973); 1 child, Michele, m. Carol Mary Byre, Nov. 25, 1982. BSBA, U. Denver, 1960. V.p., mgr. mktg. Hertz Internat., Ltd., N.Y., 1970-71; regional v.p. Amtrak, N.Y., 1971-73; mng. ptnr. Rosier & Assocs., Ltd., San Diego, 1969—; sr. v.p. for strategic mktg. Am. Prins. Holdings, Inc., San Diego, 1979-84; v.p., registered prin. Am. Diversified Equity Corp., Costa Mesa, Calif., 1984-85; pres. Glen Eagle, Inc., 1986-87; sr. v.p. Western Region Cozad Investment Svcs. Inc., San Diego, 1987-88; dir. corp. fin.-spl. products Brookstreet Securities Corp., Irvine, Calif., 1993—. Appeared as speaker on nat. TV and at various industry conferences. Bd. dirs. Nautical Heritage Soc. (Hamburg award 1988). Mem. Oceanside Rotary (Paul Harris fellow, benefactor, pres., founder Rotary Club of Oceanside Found.), Regional Investment Bankers Assn. (govt. rels. com.), Kona Kai Internat. Yacht Club (commodore 1987), Internat. Order of the Blue Gavel (founder, past chmn. bd. trustees Humanities Found.), Phone Charities Internat. (founder, mng. mem. 1996—). Home: 5114 Bella Collina St Oceanside CA 92056-1903

ROSKY, BURTON SEYMOUR, lawyer; b. Chgo., May 28, 1927; s. David T. and Mary W. (Zelkin) R.; m. Leatrice J. Darrow, June 16, 1951; children: David Scott, Bruce Alan. Student, Ill. Inst. Tech., 1944-45; BS, UCLA, 1948; JD, Loyola U., L.A., 1953. Bar: Calif. 1954, U.S. Supreme Ct 1964, U.S. Tax Ct 1964; C.P.A., Calif. Auditor City of L.A., 1948- 51; with Beidner, Temkin & Ziskin (C.P.A.s), L.A., 1951-52; supervising auditor Army Audit Agy., 1952-53; practiced law L.A., Beverly Hills, 1954—; ptnr. Duskin & Rosky, 1972-82; s Rosky, Landau & Fox, 1982-93; ptnr. Rosky, Landau, Stahl & Sheehy, Beverly Hills, 1993; lectr. on tax and bus. problems; judge pro tem Beverly Hills Mcpl. Ct., L.A. Superior Ct.; mem. L.A. Mayor's Community Adv. Council. Contbr. profl. publs. Charter supporting mem. Los Angeles County Mus. Arts; contbg. mem. Assocs. of Smithsonian Instn.; charter mem. Air and Space Mus; mem. Am. Mus. Natural History, L.A. Zoo; supporting mem. L.A. Mus. Natural History; mem. exec. bd. So. Calif. coun. Nat. Fedn. Temple Brotherhoods, mem. nat. exec. bd.; mem. bd. govs. Loyola Sch. Law, L.A. With USNR, 1945-46. Walter Henry Cook fellow Loyola Law Sch. Bd. Govs. Fellow Jewish Chautauqua Soc. (life mem.); mem. Am. Arbitration Assn. (nat. panel arbitrators), Am. Assn. Attys.-CPAs (charter mem. pres. 1968), Calif. Assn. Attys.-CPAs (charter mem., pres. 1963), Calif. Soc. CPAs, Calif., Beverly Hills, Century City, Los Angeles County bar assns., Am. Judicature Soc., Chancellors Assocs. UCLA, Tau Delta Phi, Phi Alpha Delta; mem. B'nai B'rith. Jewish (mem. exec. bd., pres. temple, pres. brotherhood). Club: Mason. Office: Rosky Landau Stahl & Sheehy 8383 Wilshire Blvd Beverly Hills CA 90211-2410

ROSNER, ROBERT ALLAN, advocate; b. Lincoln Park, N.J., Nov. 2, 1956; s. Henry and Katherine (Kravitt) R.; m. Robin Simons, May 20, 1989. BS, U. Puget Sound, 1980; MBA, U. Wash., 1992. Restaurant mgr. Eatery, Phila., 1976-78; pub. rels. mgr. Big Brothers/Sisters, Tacoma, Wash., 1979; pub. affairs dir. Sta. KNBQ, Tacoma, 1980; exec. dir. Safety Assistance from the Elderly, Seattle, 1981-82, Smoking Policy Inst., Seattle, 1982-93; dep. campaign chair United Way of King County, 1993-94; COO The Sci. Club, 1995; United Features syndicated columnist Working Wounded, 1995; chmn., shop steward Working Wounded.Com; cons. Seattle Sch. Dist., 1996; bd. dirs., chmn. bd. Giraffe Project, Langley, Wash., 1989, Coming of Age in Am., Seattle, 1989; adj. prof. Heritage Inst./Antioch, Seattle, 1988, Seattle Pacific U. Grad. Sch. Bus., 1993; radio program host KOMO radio; reporter Sta. KOMO-TV, Seattle, 1996. Author: U.S. Environmental Protection, 1990, Guide to Workplace Smoking Policies, 1990; contbr. articles to profl. jours. Bd. dirs. Salvation Army, Seattle, 1992. Recipient Gen. News Reporting award, Soc. Profl. Journalists, 1980, Emerald award Internat. TV and Video Assn., Seattle, 1986, Surgeon Gen.'s medallion, 1988. Mem. Seattle Downtown Rotary. Office: 9187 Mandus Olson Rd NE Bainbridge Island WA 98110-1529

ROSNER, ROBERT MENDEL, securities analyst; b. Newark; s. Martin Max and Judith (Miller) R.; m. Julie Lynn Goldman, Mar. 26, 1988; children: Jacob Gabriel Maxwell, Seth Aaron. AB in Econs., U. Calif., Santa Cruz, 1978; MBA, Stanford U., 1984. Assoc. Goldman Sachs & Co., N.Y.C., 1984-87; with Pacific Equity Mgmt., Oakland, Calif., 1988-92; dir. Sofaer Capital Inc., Hong Kong, 1992-93; ptnr. SRCI, San Francisco, 1993—. Mem. Concordia Argonaut Club. Home and Office: 79 Divisadero St San Francisco CA 94117-3210

ROSS, ALVIN, manufacturing executive; b. Minot, N.D., Apr. 4, 1922; s. Samuel and Goldie (Perlin) R.; m. Barbie Wechsler, Apr. 14, 1946; children: Talby W., Gelb, Elyse M. Piper, Mark W. Ross. BA, U. Wash., 1946, Master degree, 1958. Sales mgr. midwest H.D. Lee Co., Mission, Kans., 1963-72; v.p. Wrangler Boys div. Midwest Blue Bell Corp. (Wrangler Co.), Greensboro, N.C., 1972-85; v.p. mktg. Lavon Sportswear, 1985-92, 96-97; pres. Opportunity Mktg., City of Industry, Calif., 1990—; pres. Opportunity Mktg. Co. consulting Apparel Industry, Kirland, Wash., 1991; v.p. mktg. Jaime L'amour Sportswear divsn. Summit Ridge Corp., 1994-96. Office: Opportunity Mktg Co 11110 NE 41st Dr # 44 Kirkland WA 98033-7729

ROSS, AMY ANN, experimental pathologist; b. Glendale, Calif., Apr. 28, 1953; d. William F. Ross and Joyce V. (Stuart) Ruygrok. BA, Calif. State U., Northridge, 1981; PhD, U. So. Calif., 1986. Assoc. dir. rsch. Inst. Cancer and Blood Rsch., Beverly Hills, Calif., 1986-89; dir. R & D Biologic and Immunologic Sci. Labs., Reseda, Calif., 1989-94; dir. diagnostic applications Cell Pro Inc., Bothell, Wash., 1995—; rsch. asst. Sch. Medicine U. So. Calif., L.A., 1975-80, rsch. assoc., 1982-86. Mem. AAAS, Am. Soc. Clin. Pathology, Assn. of Women in Sci. (pres. L.A. chpt. 1979-80). Office: Cell Pro Inc 22215 26th Ave SE Bothell WA 98021

ROSS, BERNARD, engineering consultant, educator. BME, Cornell U., 1957; MSc in Aero. Engring., Stanford U., 1959, PhD in Aero. and Aerospace Engring., 1965; Diploma, Ecole Nat. Superieure L'Aero., France, 1960; cert., U. Edinburgh, Scotland, 1961. Registered profl. engr., Calif. Structural test engr. Gen. Dynamics Corp., Montreal, Quebec, Can., 1956; servomechanism and control sys. design engr. Marquardt Corp., Van Nuys, Calif., 1957; stress analyst Douglas Aircraft Co., Santa Monica, Calif., 1959; vibration and dynamics engr. ONERA, Paris, 1960; rsch. asst. Stanford U., 1961-63, rsch. assoc., 1963-65; sr. rsch. engr., program mgr. Stanford Rsch. Inst., Menlo Park, Calif., 1965-70; founder, chmn. emeritus Failure Analysis Assocs., San Francisco, 1967—; vis. prof. U. Santa Clara, Calif., 1970-79; adv. coun. Stanford U., 1991—, cons. prof., 1992—; pres. internat. adv. bd. structural failure, product liability and tech. ins. confs. U. Vienna, 1986—; mem. univ. coun. Cornell U., 1995; speaker and lectr. in field. Contbr. articles to Exptl. Mechanics, AIAA Jour., Israel Jour. Tech., Profl. Safeyt, others. Cons. U.S. Consumer Product Safety Commn., Washington. NATO scholar, 1960. Mem. ASME, NSPE, AIAA, AAAS, Am. Soc. Safety Engrs., Am. Soc. Agrl. Engrs., Calif. Soc. Profl. Engrs., Soc. Automotive Engrs., Soc. Exptl. Mechanics, Internat. Soc. for Law, Technology and Ins. Office: Failure Analysis Assocs PO Box 3015 149 Commonwealth Dr Menlo Park CA 94025

ROSS, DAVID EDWARD, software engineer; b. L.A., Aug. 5, 1941; s. Sydney Harold and Lillian (Weiss) R.; m. Evelyn Rita Rappaport, Oct. 25, 1964; children: Allen Michel, Heather Michelle. BA in Math., UCLA, 1964, cert. in numerical analysis, 1965. Computer programmer UCLA, 1962-66, Computer Applications, Inc., L.A., 1966-69; software engr. Unisys Corp., Santa Monica, Camarillo, Calif., 1969-93; computer software engr. Sci. Applicatoins Internat. Corp., Camarillo, 1993-95; software quality assurance cons. Omnikron Sys., Inc., Calabasas, Calif., 1996—. Reviewer Computing Revs., 1981—. Mem. Mcpl. Adv. Coun., Oak Park, Calif., 1974-81; mem. sch. bd. Oak Park Unified Sch. Dist., 1981-89; mem. Parks and Recreation Planning Com., Oak Park, 1978-79, 85-86, 90-92, 94—; trustee, pres. Cmty. Found. Oak Park, 1980—. Mem. Assn. Computing Machinery. Jewish. Home: 6477 Bayberry St Oak Park CA 91301-1204 Office: Omnikron Sys Inc 5016 N Pky Calabasas Calabasas CA 91302

ROSS, FRANCES MARGARET, medical technologist, artist; b. Brockport, N.Y., Nov. 20, 1950; d. Benjamin Berlin and Marjorie Lou (Wilder) R. BA in Bacteriology, U. Calif., L.A., 1976. Cert. med. technologist. Med. technologist Oreg. Med. Labs, Eugene, 1978—. Artist numerous watercolor paintings, 1991—; exhbns. include 152nd Ann. Exhibit and travelling exhbn. Am. Watercolor Soc., 1994, Watercolor West Ann. Exhbn., 1994-95. Recipient Grumbacher Bronze medal N.W. Watercolor Soc., 1992, Award of Excellence, Sacramento Fine Arts Ctr. Nat. Open Exhibit, 1991, People's Choice award Beaverton Arts Commn., 1991, Best in Show and Judge's Choice award Lane County Fair, 1990, 92. Mem. Watercolor Soc. Oreg. (Bronze Merit award 1992, Silver Merit award 1993, Gold Merit award 1994), Eugene Concert Choir (graphic artist, Spl. Recognition award 1991, 92). Home: 8830 SW Woodside Dr Portland OR 97225

ROSS, GERALDINE YVONNE, biologist, educator; b. Avonmore, Pa., Nov. 18, 1934; d. Peter Louis and Marian Faye (Prusack) DeGrazia; m. Peter Anthony Ross, June 21, 1958; children: Eric Peter, Christopher Allan, Bryan Mitchell. BA, Seton Hill Coll., 1956; MS, Northwestern U., 1957; postgrad., U. Wis., 1957-60, U. Wash., 1974-77. Teaching asst. Northwestern U., Evanston, Ill., 1956-57; rsch. fellow U. Wis., Madison, 1957-60; instr. Bellevue (Wash.) C.C., 1968-89; prof. Highline C.C., Des Moines, Wash., 1980-89; sec. faculty senate Highland C.C., Des Moines, Wash., 1990-94; co-organizer critical thinking workshops; textbook reviewer. Author: Study Guide to Accompany Microbiology by Cano and Colome, 1985; co-author: Instructor's Resource Manual for Starr and Taggart's Biology, 1989, 92, 95, Instructor's Resource Manual for Starr's Biology, 1991, 94; contbr. revs to profl. jours. Active Directions for the '70's Bellevue Sch. Dist., 1969, sci. adv. com., 1970-73. Recipient Excellence in Teaching award Nat. Instn. for Staff and Orgnl. Devel., 1992, Sullivan Class prize Seton Hill Coll., 1954, 56, Disting. Teaching award Phi Theta Kappa, 1990. Mem. Human Anatomy and Physiology Soc., N.W. Biology Instrs. Orgn., Puget Sound Microbiologists, N.Am. Biology Tchrs. Assn., Sigma Xi, Alpha Lambda Delta, Kappa Gamma Pi. Office: Highline CC PO Box 98000 Des Moines WA 98198-9800

ROSS, JANINE, elementary education educator; b. Detroit, June 5, 1945; d. Peter J. and Evelyn (Stowell) Jensen; m. Michael F. Ross, Apr. 7, 1973; children: Neil, Daniel. BSEd, U. Nebr., 1967; MSEd, Wayne State U., Detroit, 1973; postgrad., U. Nev., Las Vegas. Tchr. 2nd and 4th grades Cherry Hill Sch., Inkster, Mich.; reading specialist R. E. Tobler Elem., Las Vegas, Nev.; Project Life facilitator Clark County Sch. Dist. Mem. RIP Coun. of Clark County (v.p.), Las Vegas Coun. of Internat. Reading Assn., Delta Omicron, Sigma Kappa (advisor to v.p. of alumnae rels. for Theta Eta chpt.).

ROSS, JONATHAN, director, writer, producer; b. N.Y.C., July 17, 1961; s. Peter and Carol Angela (Barnes) R. BA, Columbia U., 1983. Investment banker Paine Webber Inc., N.Y.C., 1983-86; creative exec. 20th Century Fox Film Corp., L.A., 1986-87; pres. JR Prodns., L.A., 1987—. Prodr.: (short film) ...And Then I Woke Up, 1994, (play) Unbeatable Harold, 1991, Terry Neal's Future, 1988; prodr. TV commls., 1987—; dir.: (film) The Valiant, 1995. Coord. Achilles Track Club for People with Disabilities, So. Calif., 1988—; advisor Crippled Children's Soc., L.A., 1992. 1994 L.A. Marathon honoree, KCOP-TV. Mem. Krav Maga Assn.

ROSS, KATHLEEN ANNE, college president; b. Palo Alto, Calif., July 1, 1941; d. William Andrew and Mary Alberta (Wilburn) R. BA, Ft. Wright Coll., 1964; MA, Georgetown U., 1971; PhD, Claremont Grad. Sch., 1979; LLD (hon.) Alverno Coll. Milw., 1990, Dartmouth Coll., 1991, Seattle U., 1992; LHD (hon.) Whitworth Coll., 1992, LLD (hon.) Pomona Coll., 1993. Cert. tchr., Wash. Secondary tchr. Holy Names Acad., Spokane, Wash., 1964-70; dir. rsch. and planning Province Holy Names, Wash. State, 1972-73; v.p. acads. Ft. Wright Coll., Spokane, 1973-81; rsch. asst. to dean Claremont Grad. Sch., Calif., 1977-78; assoc. faculty mem. Harvard U., Cambridge, Mass., 1981; pres. Heritage Coll., Toppenish, Wash., 1981—; cons. Wash. State Holy Names Schs., 1971-73; coll. accrediting assn. evaluator N.W. Assn. Schs. and Colls., Seattle, 1975—; dir. Holy Names Coll., Oakland, Calif., 1979—; cons. Yakama Indian Nation, Toppenish, 1975—; speaker, cons. in field. Author: (with others) Multicultural Pre-School Curriculum, 1977, A Crucial Agenda: Improving Minority Student Success, 1989; Cultural Factors in Success of American Indian Students in Higher Education, 1978. Chmn. Internat. 5-Yr. Convocation of Sisters of Holy Names, Montreal, Que., Can., 1981, 96; TV Talk show host Spokane Council of Chs., 1974-76. Recipient E.K. and Lillian F. Bishop Founds. Youth Leader of Yr. award, 1986, Disting. Citizenship Alumna award Claremont Grad. Sch., 1986, Golden Aztec award Washington Human Devel., 1989, Harold W. McGraw Edn. prize, 1989, John Carroll award Georgetown U., 1991, Holy Names medal Ft. Wright Coll., 1981, Pres. medal Eastern Washington U., 1994; named Yakima Herald Rep. Person of Yr. 1987, First Annual Leadership award Region VIII Coun. Advancement and Support Edn., 1993; Wash. State Medal of Merit, 1995; numerous grants for projects in multicultural higher edn., 1974—. Mem. Nat. Assn. Ind. Colls. and Univs., Am. Assn. Higher Edn., Soc. Intercultural Edn., Tng. and Rsch., Sisters of Holy Names of Jesus and Mary-SNJM. Roman Catholic. Office: Heritage Coll Office of Pres 3240 Fort Rd Toppenish WA 98948-9562

ROSS, KELLEY LEE, II, philosophy educator, politician; b. Hollywood, Calif., Oct. 4, 1949; s. Kelley Lee and Frances Caroline (Wilson) R.; m. Gaye Haunani Rathburn, Sept. 25, 1973 (div. Aug. 15, 1978); m. Jacqueline Ilyse Ehrlich Stone, June 22, 1991. BA magna cum laude, UCLA, 1971; MA in Philosophy, U. Hawaii, 1974; PhD in Philosophy, U. Tex., 1985. Instr. L.A. Valley Coll., 1987—. Pub., editor: The Proceedings of the Friesian School, Fourth Series, 1996—. Mem. ctrl. com. 40th assembly dist. Libertarian Party, L.A., 1994, 96. Recipient NDEA fellowship U. Hawaii, 1972-74. Mem. Am. Philos. Assn., Cato Inst., Naturist Soc., U. N.Mex. Alumn. Assn., Am. U. Beirut Alumni Assn., UCLA Alumni Assn., U. Tex. Alumni Assn., Phi Beta Kappa. Office: LA Valley Coll 5800 Fulton Ave Van Nuys CA 91401-4062

ROSS, LANSON CLIFFORD, JR., religion educator, pastor, author; b. Killdeer, N.D., June 23, 1936; s. Lanson Charles and Mabel (Smith) R.; children: David F., Lanson III. BA in Biblical Studies, Seattle Pacific U., 1960; M. Sacred Theology, Internat. Coll., 1984; D of Ministries, 1986. founder Planned Living Seminars; pastor Quilcene Bible Ch.; pres. Viet/Aid; pres. Barnabas Ministries. Club: Seattle Yacht. Author: Total Life Prosperity, 1983; Give Your Children a Target, 1985, Take Charge of Your Life, 1986, The Bubble Burst, 1987; producer 5 vol. video seminar A Planned Life Style, 1986, and film A Time to Grow (J.C. Mc Pheeters award 1988). Office: PO Box 546 Quilcene WA 98376-0546

ROSS, MARK L., mortgage broker; b. Tucson, Feb. 13, 1948; s. Boyd N. and Helen M. (Brown) R.; m. Bari Ross, Apr. 17, 1983; children: A. David, Jordan; 1 stepchild, Jacob Weber. BS in Bus. Adminstrn., U. Ariz., 1970. Lic. mortgage broker; lic. real estate broker and agt. Gen. mgr. Pueblo Equity Loans, Tucson, 1976-85; ind. mortgage broker Tucson, 1985-86; pres. Prime Capital, Inc., Tucson, 1986—; instr. Ariz. Dept. Real Estate; bd. dirs. Consumer Credit Counseling Svcs. Ariz., 1971-90, pres., 1978. Active United Way, Jewish Cmty. Rels. Coun., Miramonte Neighborhood Assn.; mem. fund-raising com. Temple Emanu-El, 1993—. Mem. Nat. Assn. Mortgage Brokers (bd. dirs. 1987-91, chair ethics and bylaws com. 1989-91, chair broker agreements com. 1994-95, mem. edn. com. 1993-96), Ariz. Assn. Mortgage Brokers (state pres. 1988, Broker of Yr., so. chpt. 1991), Tucson Assn. Realtors, Tucson Met. C. of C. Republican. Office: Prime Capital Inc 5397 E Pima Tucson AZ 85712

ROSS, MARY CASLIN, educational/academic administrator; b. N.Y.C., Oct. 15, 1953; d. Michael John and Mary Rose (Harkins) Caslin; m. Alexander Barker Ross, Mar. 21, 1992. BA, St. John's U., 1975; MA, Manhattanville Coll., 1986; Doctorate (hon.), Marymount U., 1990. Exec. dir. The Fund for Am. Studies, Washington, 1976-77; library researcher Interbank Card Assn., N.Y.C., 1977-78; devel. cons. Martin J. Moran Co., N.Y.C., 1978-80; dir. devel. Internat. Ctr. for Disabled, N.Y.C., 1980-83; trustee, v.p. bd. ICD Internat. Ctr. for the Disabled, N.Y.C., 1984—; exec. dir. The Bodman/Achelis Found., N.Y.C., 1983-94; dir. programs Econ. Sci. Lab. U. Ariz., Tucson, 1994—; rsch. fellow Claremont Inst., 1994—; mem. grants com. Barker Welfare Found., 1996—; cons. Nat. Ctr. for Policy Analysis, 1995—; mem. grants com. Barker Welfare Found., 1996—; trustee JM Found., N.Y.C., 1984—, Goldwater Inst., 1996—; bd. dirs. Philanthropy Roundtable, Indpls., N.Y.C., 1988—; mem. adv. bd. A Different September Found., 1992. Recipient Pres. medal St. John's U., Jamaica, N.Y., 1975, Human Resources Ctr., Albertson, N.Y., 1991. Mem. Cold Spring Harbor Fish Hatchery. Republican. Roman Catholic. Office: Univ Arizona 116 McClelland Hall Econ Sci Lab Tucson AZ 85721

ROSS, MOLLY OWINGS, gold and silversmith, jewelry designer, small business owner; b. Ft. Worth, Feb. 5, 1954; d. James Robertson and Lucy (Owings) R. BFA, Colo. State U., 1976; postgrad., U. Denver, 1978-79. Graphic designer Amber Sky Illustrators and Sta. KCNC TV-Channel 4, Denver, 1977-79; art dir. Mercy Med. Ctr., Denver, 1979-83, Molly Ross Design, Denver, 1983-84; co-owner Deltex Royalty Co., Inc., Colorado Springs, Colo., 1981—, LMA Royalties, Ltd., Colorado Springs, 1993—; art dir., account mgr. Schwing/Walsh Advt., Mktg. and Pub. Rels., Denver, 1984-87, prodn. mgr., 1987-88; jewelry designer Molly O. Ross, Gold and Silversmith, Denver, 1988—. Pres. Four Mile Hist. Park Vol. Bd., Denver, 1985-87; bd. dirs. Four Mile Hist. Park Assn., 1985-86, Hist. Denver, Inc., 1986-87, Denver Emergency Housing Coalition, 1989-90; coun. mem. feminization of poverty critical needs area coun. Jr. League Denver, 1989-90, chmn. children in crisis/edn. critical needs area, 1990-91, chmn. project devel., 1991-92, co-chmn. Done in a Day Comty. Project 75th Anniversary Celebration, 1991-93; mem. bd. dirs., 1993-94, v.p. comty. projects, 1993-94; co-chmn. Project IMPACT, 1994-95; exec. v.p. external affairs Jr. League of Denver, 1995-96; co-chmn. Comty. Coalitions Com., 1996-97; bd. dirs. Rocky Mountain PREP, 1994—, pres. bd. dirs., 1997—; mem. steering com. Denver Urban Resources Partnership, 1995—. Named Vol. of Month (March), Jr. League Denver, 1990, Vol. of Yr., Four Mile Hist. Pk., 1988; recipient Gold Peak Mktg. award-team design Am. Mktg. Assn., 1986, Silver Peak Mktg. award-team design Am. Mktg. Assn., 1986, Gold Pick award-art dir. Pub. Rels. Soc. Am., 1980-81. Mem. Natural Resources Def. Coun., Physicians for Social Responsibility, Am. Farmland Trust, Nat. Trust for Hist. Preservation, Sierra Club, Environ. Def. Fund.

ROSS, MURIEL DOROTHY, research scientist; b. Grand Rapids, Mich., Jan. 22, 1927; d. Theophilus Joseph and Marie Rose (Bonk) Karp; m. Bernard Alfred Ross, Mar. 31, 1951; children: Mary Katherine, Carol Anne, Patricia Lynn, Sharon Marie. BA in Biology, Aquinas Coll., 1948; MS in Anatomy, U. Mich., 1950, PhD in Anatomy, 1953. Instr. biology Wayne State U., Detroit, 1951-53; instr. anatomy U. Mich., Ann Arbor, 1966-67, assoc. prof., 1971-79, prof., 1979-86; chief space biology NASA Ames Rsch. Ctr., Moffett Field, Calif., 1986-88; dir., sr. rsch. scientist NASA Biocomputation Ctr., Moffett Field, Calif., 1988—; founder NASA Biocomputation Ctr. NASA Biocomputation Ctr., Moffett Field, 1991; vis. prof. UCLA, 1987—. Author: (with others) Auditory Physiology, 1981, rev. edit. 1987, Basic and Applied Aspects of Vestibular Function, 1988; contbr. articles to profl. jours. Troop leader Girl Scouts U.S., Dearborn, Mich., 1962-64; chmn. Acad. Women's Caucus, U. Mich., Ann Arbor, 1982-84. Recipient Disting. Svc. award Women's Acad. Caucus, 1986, Excellence in Rsch. award NASA, Washington, 1990. Mem. IEEE, Barany Soc. (Sweden, rsch. award 1987), Am. Soc. Gravitational and Space Biology (adv. group, bd. dirs. 1986-89). Office: NASA Ames Rsch Ctr Ms 261 # 2 Moffett Field CA 94035

ROSS, RENAE LYNN, marketing professional; b. Conneaut, Ohio, June 5, 1962; d. Richard Edward and Patricia Ann (Sanford) R. BS, Ohio State U., 1985; MBA, U. So. Calif., 1996. Programmer E I du Pont de NeMours, Circleville, Ohio, 1984-85, IBM Corp., Lexington, Ky., 1985-86; software engr. Rolm Corp., Santa Clara, Calif., 1986-87; software team leader IBM Corp., Boca Raton, Fla., 1987-88; product planner IBM Corp., Boca Raton, 1988-89; mktg. rep. IBM Corp., L.A., 1989-93; sr. sales rep. Worldtalk, Corp., Los Gatos, Calif., 1993-94; vendor rels. mgr. 4th Dimension Software, Irvine, Calif., 1994-95; cons. Mission Viejo, Calif., 1995-96; mgr. market devel. Earthlink Network, Pasadena, Calif., 1996—. Mem. Profl. Assn. Diving Instrs. (master scuba diver trainer), Nat. Ski Patrol (Alpine patrol), Mensa. Office: Ste 160 27758 Santa Margarita Pkwy Mission Viejo CA 92691-6709

ROSS, ROBERT JOSEPH, head professional football coach; b. Richmond, Va., Dec. 23, 1936; s. Leonard Aloysius and Martha Isabelle (MMiller) R.; m. Alice Louise Bucker, June 13, 1959; children: Chris, Mary Catherine, Teresa, Kevin, Robbie. BA, Va. Mil. Inst., 1959. Tchr., head football coach Benedictine High Sch., Richmond, 1959-60; tchr., coach Colonial Heights (Va.) High Sch., 1962-65; asst. football coach Va. Mil. Inst., Lexington, 1965-67, Coll. William and Mary, Williamsburg, Va., 1967-71, Rice U., Houston, 1971-72, U. Md., College Park, 1972-73; head football coach The Citadel, Charleston, S.C., 1973-77; head coach U. Md., College Park, 1982-87; head football coach Ga. Inst. Tech., Atlanta, 1987-91; asst. coach Kansas City (Mo.) Chiefs, 1978-82; head coach San Diego Chargers, 1992-96, Detroit Lions, 1997—. 1st lt. U.S. Army, 1960-62. Named Coach of Yr., Washington Touchdown Club, 1982, Kodak Coach of Yr., 1990, Bobby Dodd Coach of Yr., 1990, Bear Bryant Coach of Yr., 1990, Scripps-Howard Coach of Yr., 1990, Nat. Coach of Yr., CBS Sports, 1990, Coach of Yr., Walter Camp Football Found., 1990, NFL Coach of Yr. UPI, 1992, Pro Football Weekly, 1992, Pro Football Writers' Assn., 1992, Football News, 1992, Football Digest, 1992, Maxwell Football Club, 1992, AFC Coach of Yr. Kansas City 101 Banquet. Mem. Am. Football Coaches Assn., Coll. Football Assn. (coaching com. 1988-92). Roman Catholic. *

ROSS, SANDRA K., critical care nurse; b. Ellensburg, Wash., Mar. 18, 1951; d. Charles Vernon and Thalia Kathleen (Collias) La Due; m. Leon T. Ross, Nov. 21, 1982; 1 child, Traci Kathleen. ADN, San Joaquin Delta

Coll., Stockton, Calif., 1985; BS, Wash. State U., Pullman, 1973. Cert. critical care nurse. Sr. staff nurse San Joaquin Gen. Hosp., Stockton; staff nurse St. Joseph's Med. Ctr., Stockton; staff nurse ICU St. Dominic's Hosp., Manteca, Calif. With U.S. Army, 1974-76. Mem. AACN, Alpha Xi Delta, River City Quilters Guild. Home: 4867 Bridgewater Cir Stockton CA 95219-2014

ROSS, SHERMAN EDWARD, biochemist; b. Ft. Benning, Ga., Sept. 24, 1957; s. Charles Edward and Wilhelmina Alexandria (Sherman) R. BA in Biology with distinction, U. Colo., 1980; MA in Biochemistry, U. Tex. Health Sci. Ctr., 1983. Biochemist U. Colo. Sch. Medicine, Denver, 1984-89, Cortech Inc., Denver, 1989—. Author: Juggernaut, 1996; contbr. articles to profl. jours.; inventor, patentee in field. O'Hara Competitive fellow U. Tex. Health Sci. Ctr., 1980. Home: 540 S Forest # 5-203 Denver CO 80222 Office: 6850 N Broadway Denver CO 80221

ROSS, STAN, accounting firm executive; b. 1939. With Kenneth Leventhal & Co., L.A., 1964—, now mng. ptnr.; now vice chmn., mng. ptnr. real estate Ernst & Young, LLP, L.A., 1995—. Office: Kenneth Leventhal & Co 2049 Century Park E Ste 1700 Los Angeles CA 90067-3119*

ROSS, STEVEN CHARLES, business administration educator, consultant; b. Salem, Oreg., Jan. 14, 1947; s. Charles Reed and Edythe Marie (Calvin) R.; m. Meredith Lynn Buholts, June 15, 1969; children: Kelly Lynn, Shannon Marie. BS, Oreg. State U., 1969; MS, U. Utah, 1976, PhD, 1980. Cons. IRS Tng. Staff, Ogden, Utah, 1977-80; asst. prof. Marquette U., Milw., 1980-88; assoc. prof. Mont. State U., Bozeman, 1988-89; assoc. prof. bus. adminstrn. Western Wash. U., Bellingham, 1989—; govt. and industry cons.; cons. editor microcomputing series West Pub. Co. Author 30 books and several articles in computer systems field. Mem. adv. com. Milwaukee County Mgmt., 1981-85, Port of Bellingham, 1990—. Capt. U.S. Army, 1969-75. Recipient rsch. fellowship, U. Utah, 1977-79, Marquette U., 1981-84. Mem. Acad. Mgmt., Decision Scis. Inst., Inst. Mgmt. Scis., Assn. for Computing Machinery, Assn. Computer Educators, Bellingham Yacht Club (trustee 1992-93, sec. 1993-94, rear commodore, 1994-95, vice commodore 1995-96, commodore 1996—). Office: Western Wash U Coll Bus and Econs Bellingham WA 98225

ROSS, SUEELLEN, artist; b. Oakland, Calif., July 12, 1941; d. Eugene Paul Burton and Edith Ellen (Metcalf) Burille; m. Paul Louis Ross, Oct. 20, 1976 (div. 1989); m. Richard A. Lyon, Nov. 7, 1993. BA in Speech Arts, U. Calif., Berkeley, 1969, postgrad., 1978-79. Educator various jr. and sr. high schs. Calif., N.Y. and P.R., Calif., 1966-71; publicist and publicity dir. N.Y.C., Seattle, 1971-80; artist, 1980—; judge painting and drawing Anacortes Art Fair, Wash., 1989, Edmonds Art Fair, 1994; judge painting, drawing and sculpture Pacific Rim Wildlife Art Show, 1987-89, 91-94, 97. Exhibited works in numerous shows including Leigh Yawkey Woodson Art Mus., Wausau, Wis., 1987, 89, 91, 92, 93, 94, 95, 96, Nat. Park Found., Jackson Hole, Wyo., 1991, 92, N.W. Watercolor Soc. Ann. Show, Kirkland, Wash., 1991, 92, 94, Howard/Manville Gallery, Kirkland, 1993-97, others; works represented in numerous pub. collections including Leigh Yawkey Woodson Art Mus., Mpls. Savs. and Loan, Safeco Ins. Co., Seattle, SeaFirst Bank, Seattle, Shell Oil Co., Houston, Signature; works included in numerous publs. including Painting Birds Step by Step, 1996, Atlas of North American Birds, 1997, The Best of Wildlife Painting, 1997. Recipient Region I award Arts for the Parks, 1991. Mem. N.W. Watercolor Soc. (signature mem.). Home and Office: 1909 SW Myrtle St Seattle WA 98106-1646

ROSS, TERRY D., lawyer; b. Glendale, Calif., Aug. 12, 1943. BA, U. Calif., Santa Barbara, 1965; JD, U. Calif., San Francisco, 1968. Bar: Calif. 1969. Ptnr. Gray, Cary, Ware & Freidenrich, San Diego; mem. panel arbitrators Am. Arbitration Assn. Note and comment editor Hastings Law Jour., 1967-68. Bd. dirs. Davis Grossmont YMCA. Mem. ABA (sect. litigation), State Bar Calif., San Diego County Bar Assn. (mem. arbitration panel, superior ct. com.), S.D. Marlin Club, SDMB Boat and Ski Club, Phi Delta Phi. Office: Gray Cary Ware & Freidenrich 401 B St Ste 1700 San Diego CA 92101-4240

ROSS, TIMOTHY MICHAEL, geologist; b. Bakersfield, Calif., Aug. 18, 1961; s. James Douglas and Zannie Lynn (Dixon) R.; m. Joan Esther Fryxell, Sept. 5, 1992; children: Paul Griffin, Daniel Hamish. BS in Geology, Calif. State U., Fresno, 1986; MA in Geology, U. Calif., Santa Barbara, 1988; PhD, La. State U., 1994. Vis. scholar, lectr. Calif. State U., San Bernardino, Calif., 1994—. Contbr. article to profl. jour. Regent fellow La. State U., Baton Rouge, 1988.

ROSS, WAYNE ANTHONY, lawyer; b. Milw., Feb. 25, 1943; s. Ray E. and Lillian (Steiner) R.; m. Barbara L. Ross, June 22, 1968; children: Gregory, Brian, Timothy, Amy. BA, Marquette U., 1965, JD, 1968. Bar: Wis. 1968, Alaska 1969. Asst. atty. gen. State Alaska, 1968-69; trustee, standing master Superior Ct. Alaska, 1969-73; assoc. Edward J. Reasor & Assocs., Anchorage, 1973-77; prin. Wayne Anthony Ross & Assocs., 1977-83; ptnr. Ross, Gingras & Frenz, Anchorage and Cordova, Alaska, 1983-84, Ross & Gingras, Anchorage and Cordova, 1985; pres. Ross, Gingras and Miner, P.C., Anchorage, 1986-93; pres. Ross and Miner P.C., Anchorage, 1993—; inactive col. Alaska State Def. Force; pres. Tyone Mountain Syndicate, Inc. Alaska Rep. Nat. Committeeman. Named Knight Comdr. Order of Polonia Restituta (Poland), Knight Equestrian Order of the Holy Sepulchure of Jerusalem (Vatican). Mem. NRA (bd. dirs. 1980-92, 94—, benefactor), Alaska Bar Assn. (Stanley award), Anchorage Bar Assn., Alaska Gun Collectors Assn. (pres. emeritus), Ohio Gun Collectors Assn. (hon. life), Smith and Wesson Collectors Assn., 49th Territorial Guard Regiment (pres. 1987-94, 95-96), Alaska Territorial Cavalry (sec.), State Guard Assn., Military Vehicle Preservation Assn. (v.p. 1994-96), Alaska Peace Officers Assn. Roman Catholic. Home: PO Box 101522 Anchorage AK 99510-1522 Office: Ross & Miner 327 E Fireweed Ln Ste 201 Anchorage AK 99503-2110

ROSSER, JAMES MILTON, academic administrator; b. East St. Louis, Ill., Apr. 16, 1939; s. William M. and Mary E. (Bass) R.; 1 child, Terence. B.A., So. Ill. U., 1962, M.A., 1963, Ph.D., 1969. Diagnostic bacteriologist Holden Hosp., Carbondale, Ill., 1961-63; research bacteriologist Eli Lilly & Co., Indpls., 1963-66; coordinator Black Am. studies, instr. health edn. So. Ill. U., Carbondale, 1966-69; asst. prof. Black Am. studies dir. So. Ill. U., 1969-70, asst. to chancellor, 1970; asso. vice chancellor for acad. affairs U. Kans., Lawrence, 1970-74; assoc. prof. edn., pharmacology and toxicology U. Kans., 1971-74; vice chancellor dept. higher edn. State of N.J., Trenton, 1974-79; acting chancellor State of N.J., 1977; pres., prof. health care mgmt. Calif. State U., Los Angeles, 1979—; mem. tech. resource panel Ctr. for Research and Devel. in Higher Edn., U. Calif., Berkeley, 1974-76; mem. health maintenance orgn. com. Health Planning Coun., State of N.J., 1975-79; mem. standing com. on research and devel. bd. trustees Ednl. Testing Service, 1976-77; mem. steering com. and task force on retention of minorities in engring. Assembly of Engring. NRC, 1975-78; mem. Bd. Med. Examiners, State of N.J., 1978-79; vis. faculty mem. Inst. Mgmt. of Lifelong Edn., Grad. Sch. Edn., Harvard U., 1979; mem. Calif. State U. Trustees Spl. Long Range Fin. Planning Com., 1982-87; mem. Am. Coun. on Edn., 1979—, AFL/CIO Labor Higher Edn. Coun., 1983—, Nat. Commn. Higher Edn. Issues, 1981-82; mem. The Calif. Achievement Coun., 1983-89, strategic adv. counc. Coll. and Univs. Systems Exchange, 1988-91; bd. dirs. Am. Humanities Coun., So. Calif. Am. Humanics, Inc. Coun., Sanwa Bank Calif., 1993—, Edison Internat., 1985—, Fedco, Inc., 1987—. Author: An Analysis of Health Care Delivery, 1977. Mem. exec. bd., chmn. varisty scouting program L.A. area coun. Boy Scouts Am., 1980—; bd. dirs. Hispanic Urban Ctr., L.A., 1979—, L.A. Urban League, 1982-95, Cmty. TV of So. Calif., Sta. KCET, 1980-89, United Way, L.A., 1980-91, Orthopaedic Hosp., 1983-86, L.A. Philharm. Assn., 1986—, Nat. Health Found., 1990—, Calif. C. of C., 1993—; mem. Citizen's Adv. Coun. Congl. Caucus Sci. and Tech., 1983—; mem. performing arts coun./edn. coun. Music Ctr., 1984—; mem. minority bus. task force Pacific Bell, 1985-86; mem. bd. govs. Nat. ARC, 1986-91, Mayor's Blue Ribbon Task Force on Drugs, City of L.A., 1988, L.A. Annenberg Met. Project, 1994—; Nat. Adv. Coun. on Aging, 1989-93; bd. trustees Woodrow Wilson Nat. Fellowship Found., 1993—; mem. bd. advisors Historically Black Colls. and Univs. and Minority Insts., Dept. Air Force, 1997—. NSF fellow, 1961; NDEA fellow, 1967-68; recipient award of recognition in Edn. Involvement for Young Achievers, 1981, Pioneer of Black Hist. Achievement award Brotherhood Crusade, 1981, Alumni Achievement award So. Ill. U., 1982, Friend of Youth award Am. Humanics, Inc., 1985, Leadership award Dept. Higher Edn. Ednl. Equal Opportunity Fund Program, 1989, Medal of Excellence Gold State Minority Found., 1990, Take Charge of Learning Success award Inst. for Redesign of Learning. Mem. Calif. C. of C. (bd. dirs. 1993—), Alhambra C. of C. (bd. dirs. 1979—), Los Angeles C. of C. (bd. dirs. 1985-90), Am. Assn. State Colls. and Univs., Kappa Delta Pi, Phi Kappa Phi. Roman Catholic. Office: Calif State Univ Office of the Pres 5151 State University Dr Los Angeles CA 90032-8500

ROSSI, AMADEO JOSEPH, chemist; b. Seattle, Sept. 23, 1954; s. Amadeo Joseph and Maria Asilia (Chinella) R.; m. Frances Marie Stotts, Sept. 19, 1981; children: Anthony Joseph, Matthew Christopher, Brian Michael. BS in Wood and Fiber Sci., U. Wash., 1979, MS in wood chemistry, 1987. Research aide U. Wash., Seattle, 1978-79; environ. engr. Georgia-Pacific Corp., Eugene, Oreg., 1980; v.p. hazardous waste remediation projects Foster Wheeler Environ. Corp., Seattle, 1981—. Contbr. articles to profl. jours. Mem. Am. Chem. Soc., Air Pollution Control Assn., Forest Products Rsch. Soc., Xi Sigma Pi, Sigma Xi. Office: Foster Wheeler Environ Corp 10900 NE 8th St Bellevue WA 98004-4405

ROSSIN, HERBERT YALE, television producer; b. Phila., May 15, 1936; s. Jack Rossin and Edna Wolinsky; m. Meryl Ann Barsky, Nov. 15, 1965; children: Abby Rae, Shane J.P. Degree in journalism, Temple U., 1958. Gen. mgr. KIKU TV/13, Honolulu, 1968-70; br. mgr. Columbia Pictures, Las Vegas, 1970-74; pres. Internat. TV Concepts, Las Vegas, 1974-78; sta. mgr. KUAM AM/FM/TV, Agana, Guam, 1978-80; v.p. Tag Mktg. and Advt., Cherry Hill, N.J., 1981-83; gen. mgr. WLXI-TV/61, Greensboro, N.C., 1983-85; v.p., gen. mgr. WHLL-TV/27, Boston, 1986-87; v.p. Home Shopping Network, L.A., 1987-88; owner A.S.A.P. Multi-Corp., Las Vegas, 1988—; broadcast cons. Fashion Channel-Video Mall, L.A., 1987-88, Las Vegas TV Network, 1987-88; script writer Four Star Pictures, L.A., 1988-89; pres. Video Music TV Stas. Am., 1984-88; network cons.; mem. Guam Gaming Commn., 1979. Prodr. motion picture Miss Conduct, 1957; creator TV shows New Millionaires, Slim Scents, Big Bucks Bingo, Football Weekly, Wireless Wonder, Las Vegas at Nite; editor Israel Mag., 1960. Prodr. telethon Heart Fund Am., Las Vegas, 1972. With Pa. Air Nat. Guard, 1954-59. Named Broadcaster of Yr., Video Music TV Stas. Am., 1985; recipient Edn. award Albert Einstein Acad., 1974, People Law Sch. award Nev. Trial Lawyers, 1992, others. Mem. Nat. Assn. TV Program Execs. Home and Office: ASAP Multi Corp 7704 Musical Ln Las Vegas NV 89128-4082

ROSSMANN, ANTONIO, lawyer, educator; b. San Francisco, Apr. 25, 1941; s. Herbert Edward and Yolanda (Sonsini) R.; m. Kathryn A. Burns, Oct. 6, 1991; children: Alice Sousini, Maria McHale. Grad. Harvard U., 1963; JD, 1971. Bar: Calif. 1972, D.C. 1979, U.S. Supreme Ct. 1979, N.Y. 1980. Law clk., Calif. Supreme Ct., 1971-72; assoc. Tuttle & Taylor, Los Angeles, 1972-75; pub. advisor Calif. Energy Commn., 1975-76; sole practice, San Francisco, 1976-82, 85—; exec. dir. Nat. Center for Preservation Law, 1979-80; mem. McCutchen, Doyle, Brown & Enersen, San Francisco, 1982-85; adj. prof. law Hastings Coll. Law, 1981-84; vis. prof. UCLA Sch. Law, 1985-88; adj. prof. Stanford Law Sch., 1989-90, U. Calif. Sch. Law, 1991—. Bd. dirs. Planning and Conservation League, 1984—, Calif. Water Protection Council, 1982-83, San Francisco Marathon, 1982-90; pres. Western State Endurance Run, 1986-96, counselor, 1996—; pres., bd. dirs. Toward Utility Rate Normalization, 1976-79. Served to lt. comdr. USN, 1963-68. Fulbright lectr., U. Tokyo, 1987-88. Mem. Calif. State Bar (chmn. com. on environment 1978-82), Assn. Bar City of N.Y., U.S. Rowing Assn., U.S. Soccer Fed. (state referee), L.A. Athletic Club, Harvard Club (San Francisco, N.Y.C.). Contbr. articles to legal jours.; editor Harvard U. Law Rev., 1969-71. Office: 380 Hayes St San Francisco CA 94102-4421

ROSTEN, DAVID BRUCE, international investment advisor; b. Long Branch, N.J., July 28, 1953; s. Philip Rosten and Leila June Freeman; m. Kristin Brigetta West, Jan. 10, 1993. BA, U. Calif., Irvine, 1982; student, U. Copenhagen; JD, Oxford (Eng.) U., 1984; JD in Internat. Law and Politics, U. San Diego, 1984. Dir. Wilshire Savs. and Loan, L.A., 1986-88; owner Rosten Realty, Newport Beach, Calif., 1986-93; owner, pres. Rosten Capital, Newport Beach, 1994—. Office: Rosten Capital 1009 W Balboa Blvd Newport Beach CA 92661-1003

ROSVALL, PATRICIA LYNN, biology educator; b. Salt Lake City, Feb. 20, 1944; d. William Mack and La Veta (Mangum) Harvey; m. Gene Howard Rosvall, Apr. 3, 1970; children: Robert, Todd, Jennifer. ADN, Weber State Coll., 1983; BS, Westminster Coll., 1986. RN, Utah; cert. biology educator, Utah. Flight attendant United Airlines, San Francisco, 1965-70; biology tchr. Granite Sch. Dist., West Valley City, Utah, 1987—; implementor new sci. course for sch. dist., 1994-95. Author: Legacy of Love. Docent Hogle Zoo, Salt Lake City, 1981-83; state conv. rep. Rep. Party, Salt Lake City, 1988, county conv. rep., 1988; rep. Utah Edn. Assn. House of Dels., 1988-93; com. mem. Ptnrs. in Edn., 1990-91; mem. Centennial Sch. Com., West Valley, 1993-94. Mem. Granite Edn. Assn. (rep. 1988-93), People to People Internat. (student amb. program), Utah Speaker Assn. LDS. Office: John F Kennedy Jr High Sch 4495 S 4800 W West Valley City UT 84120-5927

ROTEN, ROBERT CHARLES, newspaper reporter, movie critic, columnist; b. Salem, Oreg., Apr. 22, 1947; s. Edwin Milton and Florene Ellen (Shepherd) R.; m. Martha Jane Hanscom, Dec. 12, 1979. BS in Journalism, U. Oreg., 1970. Newspaper reporter Ironwood (Mich.) Daily Globe, 1972-75; freelance writer Cmty. Press, Tigard, Oreg., 1976; reporter, editorial writer Laramie (Qyo.) Daily Boomerang, 1979—. Author/webmaster Internet Web Page, 1996—. Recipient Hist. award Wyo. State Hist. Soc., 1990, 95, Pacemaker award Wyo. Press Assn., 1980, 89. Mem. Laramie Astron. Soc. (bd. dirs., publicity chair), Laramie Internet Access and Telecomms. (asst. adminstr.), Soc. Profl. Journalists, Soc. Environ. Journalists. Democrat. Christian Fundamentalist. Home: 3019 Pope Springs Rd Laramie WY 82070 Office: Laramie Daily Boomerang 320 Grand Ave Laramie WY 82070

ROTH, EVELYN AUSTIN, elementary school educator; b. Coronado, Calif., May 31, 1942; d. Robert Emmett and Marjorie Eastman (Rice) Austin; m. John King Roth, June 25, 1964; children: Andrew Lee, Sarah Austin. BA, San Diego State U., 1964; MA, U. of LaVerne, Calif., 1984; postgrad., U. Calif., Riverside, 1985. Cert. elem. tchr., Calif. Elem. tchr. Poway (Calif.) Unified Schs., 1964, Wallingford (Conn.) Unified Schs., 1964-66, Ontario (Calif.) Montclair Sch. Dist., 1982-88, Claremont (Calif.) Unified Schs., 1966-67, 83-93, Foothill Country Day Sch., Claremont, 1993—. Pres., bd. trustees Friends of Stone Libr., Claremont, 1993-94. Mem. AAUW, NEA, Calif. Tchrs. Assn., Internat. Reading Assn. (treas. Foothill Reading Coun. 1985-86), Delta Kappa Gamma (v.p. 1991-92). Republican. Presbyterian.

ROTH, FREDERIC HULL, JR., secondary education educator; b. Cleve., July 27, 1941; s. Frederic Hull and Emmy Alice (Braun) R.; m. Kathleen Marie Keady, Nov. 15, 1962; children: Frederic Hull III, Kimberley Adrienne, Lara Hilary. BA, Yale U., 1963; MA, Columbia U., 1967; PhD, U. Va., 1973. English instr. Robert Louis Stevenson Sch., Pebble Beach, Calif., 1963-65, chmn. dept. English, 1991—; English instr. Landon Sch., Bethesda, Md., 1966-68; coord. pres.'s youth opportunity program Walter Reed Army Med. Ctr., Washington, summer 1968; asst. prof. English Hamilton Coll., Clinton, N.Y., 1971-77; chmn. dept. English Cranbrook Kingswood Sch., Bloomfield Hills, Mich., 1977-91; chmn., co-founder, bd. dirs. Clinton (N.Y.) ABC Program, 1974-76. Keynote lectr. Cranbrook Elderhostel, Bloomfield Hills, Mich., summers 1980-90; bd. dirs. Detroit Film Soc., 1986-91. Travel/rsch. grantee NEH, 1974. Mem. MLA, SAR, Nat. Coun. Tchrs. of English, World Affairs Coun., Founders & Patriots, Union Club Cleve., Detroit Econ. Club. Episcopalian. Home: 135 Littlefield Rd Monterey CA 93940-4917 Office: Robert Louis Stevenson Sch PO Box 657 Pebble Beach CA 93953

ROTH, GARY NEAL, accountant; b. Santa Monica, Calif., Nov. 30, 1961; s. Lewis David and Beverly Sue (Steel) R. BS in Bus. Adminstrn., Calif. State U., Northridge, 1983. CPA, Calif.; cert. tax profl. Clk., field rep. Equifax Svcs., Inc., Santa Monica, Calif., 1979-86; acctg. mgr., contr. One-Card Systems Corp., L.A., 1983-88; sr. tax acct., auditor Pannell Kerr Forster, CPAs, L.A., 1989-91; sr. acct., auditor Getz, Krycler & Jakubovits, CPAs, Sherman Oaks, Calif., 1992-96; sr. acct. London & Co, CPAs, L.A., 1996&; cons. U.S. Resolution Trust Corp., Denver, 1991. Auditor Stop Cancer, L.A., 1992-96; acct. Fair-Taste of L.A., Santa Monica, Calif., 1989-90; venue acct. L.A. Summer Olympics, 1984; tax preparer Vol. Income Tax Assn., L.A., 1983. Mem. AICPA, Calif. Soc. CPAs, Nat. Soc. Tax Profls., Zeta Beta Tau. Home: 19728 Lull St Winnetka CA 91306-2675 Office: London & Co CPAs Ste 2040 11601 Wilshire Blvd Los Angeles CA 90025

ROTH, HADDEN WING, lawyer; b. Oakland, Calif., Feb. 10, 1930; s. Mark and Jane (Haley) R.; m. Alice Becker, Aug., 1987; 1 child, Elizabeth Wing. AA, Coll. Marin, 1949; BA, U. Calif., Berkeley, 1951; JD, U. Calif., San Francisco, 1957. Bar: Calif. 1958, U.S. Dist. Ct. (no. dist.) Calif. 1958, U.S. Ct. Appeals (9th cir.) 1958, U.S. Supreme Ct. 1966. Pvt. practice San Rafael, 1970—; judge Marin County Mcpl. Ct., 1966-70; spl. cons. Marin Muni Water Dist., Corte Madera, Calif., County of Marin; atty. Bolinas Pub. Utility Dist., Ross Valley Fire Svc., Town of Ross and San Anselmo, Calif.; hearing officer dist. hosps., 1981—; lectr. law Golden Gate Coll. Law, San Francisco, 1971-73. Chmn. Marin County prison task force, 1973; bd. dirs. Marin Gen. Hosp., 1964-66. Named Outstanding Citizen of Yr., Coll. Marin, 1972. Mem. ABA, Am. Trial Lawyers Assn., Calif. Bar Assn., Marin County Bar Assn., San Francisco Trial Lawyers Assn., Am. Assn. Ind. Investors, Assn. Bus. Trial Lawyers. Home: 343 Fairhills Dr San Rafael CA 94901-1110 Office: 1050 Northgate Dr San Rafael CA 94903-2544

ROTH, JOHN KING, philosopher, educator; b. Grand Haven, Mich., Sept. 3, 1940; s. Josiah V. and Doris Irene (King) R.; m. Evelyn Lillian Austin, June 25, 1964; children: Andrew Lee, Sarah Austin. BA, Pomona Coll., 1962; student, Yale U. Div. Sch., 1962-63; MA, Yale U., 1965, PhD, 1966; LHD, Ind. U., 1990. Asst. prof. philosophy Claremont McKenna Coll., Calif., 1966-71, assoc. prof., 1971-76, Russell K. Pitzer prof. philosophy, 1976—; vis. prof. philosophy Franklin Coll., Lugano, Switzerland, 1973; Fulbright lectr. Am. studies U. Innsbruck, Austria, 1973-74; vis. prof. philosophy Doshisha U., Kyoto, Japan, 1981-82; vis. prof. Holocaust studies U. Haifa, Israel, 1982; Fulbright lectr. in Am. studies Royal Norwegian Ministry of Edn., Oslo, Norway, 1995-96. Author: Freedom and the Moral Life, 1969, Problems of the Philosophy of Religion, 1971, American Dreams, 1976, A Consuming Fire, 1979, (with Richard L. Rubenstein) Approaches to Auschwitz, 1987, (with Frederick Sontag) The American Religious Experience, 1972, (with Frederick Sontag) The Questions of Philosophy, 1988, (with Robert H. Fossum) The American Dream, 1981, (with Fossum) American Ground, 1988, (with Rubenstein) The Politics of Latin American Liberation Theology, 1988, (with Michael Berenbaum) Holocaust: Religious and Philosophical Implications, 1989, Ethics, 1991, (with Carol Rittner) Memory Offended, 1991, (with Creighton Peden) Rights, Justice, and Community, 1992, (with Carol Rittner) Different Voices, 1993, American Diversity, American Identity, 1995, Inspiring Teaching, 1997. (with Carol Rittner) From the Unthinkable to the Unavoidable, 1997. Spl. advisor U.S. Holocaust Meml. Coun., Washington, 1980-85, mem., 1995—. Danforth grad. fellow, 1962-66; Graves fellow, 1970-71; NEH fellow, 1976-77; Faculty Pairing grantee Japan-U.S. Friendship Commn., 1981-83; named U.S. Prof. of Yr. Coun. Advancement and Support of Edn. and Carnegie Found. Advancement of Tchg., 1988. Mem Am. Philos. Assn., Am. Acad. Religion, Am. Studies Assn., Calif. Coun. for Humanities, Phi Beta Kappa. Presbyterian. Home: 1648 N Kenyon Pl Claremont CA 91711-2905 Office: Claremont McKenna Coll 850 Columbia Ave Claremont CA 91711-3901

ROTH, LELAND MARTIN, art and architecture educator; b. Harbor Beach, Mich., Mar. 22, 1943; s. Leland Monroe and Margaret Hannah (Martin) R.; m. Carol Lynn Mangold, June 25, 1965; 1 child, Amanda Catherine. BArch, U. Ill., 1966; M of Philosophy, Yale U., 1971, PhD, 1973. Instr. U. Ill., Urbana, 1966-67, Ohio State U., Columbus, 1971-73; asst. prof. Northwestern U., Evanston, Ill., 1973-78; assoc. prof. archtl. history, art history U. Oreg., Eugene, 1978-82, assoc. prof., 1982-90; prof., 1990—; cons. historian Boston Pub. Libr., 1985—, The N.Y. Hosp., N.Y.C., 1985-86. Author: Architecture of McKim, Mead & White, 1978, Concise History of American Architecture, 1979, McKim, Mead & White, Architects, 1983, Understanding Architecture, 1993; editor: Monograph of McKim, Mead & White, 1974, America Builds, 1983. NEH fellow, 1982-83; Kamphoefner Found. grantee, Raleigh, N.C., 1985. Mem. Coll. Art Assn., Soc. Archtl. Historians (bd. dirs. 1977-80, founder's award 1979). Office: U Oreg Dept Art History Eugene OR 97403-5229

ROTH, MICHAEL JAMES, magazine publisher; b. Burbank, Calif., Feb. 24, 1952; s. Murray M. and Frances (Ackerman) R. BS, Calif. State U., Northridge, 1978; MBA, Calif. State U., San Francisco, 1983. Regional mgr. Cass Advt., San Francisco, 1979-82, Media Networks, Inc., San Francisco, 1982-83; pub. Golden State Mag., San Francisco, 1983-89; assoc. pub. Aloha Mag., Honolulu, 1990-92; pres. Roth Comms., Honolulu, 1992—; founder Wailea (Hawaii) Mag., 1991-94, Golden State Mag., 1984—. Pub.: (vis. guide) Discover the Californias, 1988 (Belding award 1988); mktg. dir.: (vis. guides) Islands of Aloha, 1992 (Pele award 1992), Golf Hawaii, The Complete Guide, 1994 (Pele award 1994); project mgr. (vis. guide) Wailea Mag., 1993 (Belding award 1993). Haul-out mgr. Waikiki Yacht Club, Honolulu, 1992-94; skipper Trans Pacific Yacht Race, San Francisco-Honolulu, 1990; mem. U.S. Sailing race com., 1993-94; commr. of Yachting Aloha State Games, 1994. 1st place trimmer, St. Francis Yacht Club Big Boat Series, 1990. Mem. St. Francis Yacht Club, Waikiki Yacht Club. Home: 960 Prospect St Apt 11 Honolulu HI 96822-3438

ROTH, RICHARD WAYNE, media consultant; b. Amarillo, Tex., Jan. 5, 1932; s. Mattison Hargrove and Marie Almond (Tidwell) R.; m. Roberta Louise Kolmus, Sept. 4, 1954; children: Rick Wayne, John David. BS in Engring., Ariz. State U., 1958, postgrad., 1962-63. Chief application engr. Motorola Controls, Phoenix, 1966-68, mgr. digital sys. market, 1968-71; co-founder, pres., CEO Engineered Sys. Inc., Tempe, Ariz., 1971-96; prin. Tech. Bus. Cons., Phoenix, 1997—; bd. dirs. Meteor Optics, Phoenix, 1996—; mgmt. tchg. facilitator Ariz. State U., Tempe, 1996—. Inventor: Digital Control. Zoning activist, 1996; bd. dirs. Phoenix Christian H.S., 1984-96, Ariz. Home Bible League, Phoenix, 1996—; prin. ptnr. Help Now, Inc. With USAF, 1951-52. Recipient Internat. Market award U.S. Dept. Commerce; named Hall of Fame World Trade Mag., 1992. Mem. Ind. Liquid Terms Assn., Petro Equipment Inst., Western Petro Marketers. Republican. Office: Tech Bus Cons 4040 E McDowell # 209A Phoenix AZ 85008

ROTH, STEVEN D., mental health counselor; b. Sandusky, Ohio, Feb. 10, 1952; s. Charles A. and Betty J. Roth; m. Gerilyn F. Sekela, Oct. 25, 1975; 1 child, Linsday M. BA, Bowling Green State U., 1974, MA, 1979. Case mgr. Erie County Welfare Dept., Sandusky, Ohio, 1974-78; job placement/procurement specialist Double S Industries, Sandusky, 1978-80; coord. resident svcs., staff devel. Luther Home of Mercy, Williston, Ohio, 1980-86; coord. psychosocial devel. Ruth Ide Mental Health Ctr., Toledo, Ohio, 1986-89; dir. program evaluation Wood County Mental Health Bd., Bowling Green, Ohio, 1989-90; behavior mgmt. specialist Wood County Bd. of Mental Retardation, Bowling Green, 1991-92; instr. U. Toledo, 1992; quality assurance mgr. Charter Hosp., Toledo, 1992; coord., therapist No. Wyo. Mental Health Ctr., Sheridan, Wyo., 1992—; statis. cons. St. Vincent's Hosp., Toledo, 1984; instr. psychology Sheridan Coll., 1993—. Mem. APA (student affiliate), ACA, Am. Mental Health Counselors Assn., Nat. Coun. Self-Esteem, Masons, Elks. Episcopal. Home: 81 Davis Tee Sheridan WY 82801-6024 Office: Supported Independence Project 101 W Brundage St Sheridan WY 82801-4217

ROTHBLATT, DONALD NOAH, urban and regional planner, educator; b. N.Y.C., Apr. 28, 1935; s. Harry and Sophie (Chernofsky) R.; m. Ann S. Vogel, June 16, 1957; children: Joel Michael, Steven Saul. BCE, CUNY, 1957; MS in Urban Planning, Columbia U., 1963; Diploma in Comprehensive Planning, Inst. Social Studies, The Hague, 1964; PhD in City and Regional Planning, Harvard U., 1969. Registered profl. engr. N.Y. Planner N.Y.C. Planning Commn., 1960-62, N.Y. Housing and Redevel. Bd., 1963-66; research fellow Ctr. for Environ. Design Studies, Harvard U., Cambridge, Mass., 1965-71; teaching fellow, instr., then asst. prof. city and regional planning Harvard U., 1967-71; prof. urban and regional planning, chmn. dept. San Jose State U., Calif., 1971—; Lady Davis vis. prof. urban and regional planning Hebrew U., Jerusalem and Tel Aviv U., 1978; vis. scholar Indian Inst. Architects, 1979, Shandong Province, China, 1996; vis. scholar, rsch. assoc. Inst. Govtl. Studies, U. Calif., Berkeley, 1980—; cons. to pvt.

industry and govt. agys. Author: Human Needs and Public Housing, 1964, Thailand's Northeast, 1967, Regional Planning: The Appalachian Experience, 1971, Allocation of Resources for Regional Planning, 1972, The Suburban Environment and Women, 1979, Regional-Local Development Policy Making, 1981, Planning the Metropolis: The Multiple Advocacy Approach, 1982, Comparative Suburban Data, 1983, Suburbia: An International Assessment, 1986, Metropolitan Dispute Resolution in Silicon Valley, 1989, Good Practices for the Congestion Management Program, 1994, Activity-Based Travel Survey and Analysis of Responses to Increased Congestion, 1995, An Experiment in Sub-Regional Planning: California's Congestion Management Policy, 1995, Estimating the Origins and Destinations of Transit Passengers from On/Off Counts, 1995, Changes in Property Values Induced by Light Transit, 1996, Models of Statewide Transportation Planning Under ISTEA, 1996; editor: National policy for Urban and Regional Development, 1974, Regional Advocacy Planning: Expanding Air Transport Facilities for the San Jose Metropolitan Area, 1975, Metropolitan-wide Advocacy Planning; Dispersion of Low and Moderate Cost Housing in the San Jose Metropolitan Area, 1976, Multiple Advocacy Planning: Public Surface Transportation in the San Jose Metropolitan Area, 1977, A Multiple Advocacy Approach to Regional Planning: Open Space and Recreational Facilities for the San Jose Metropolitan Area, 1979, Regional Transpotation Planning for the San Jose Metropolitan Area, 1981, Planning for Open Space and Recreational Facilities in the San Jose Metropolitan Area, 1982, Regional Economic Development Planning for the San Jose Metropolitan Area, 1984, Planning for Surface Transportation in the San Jose Metropolitan Area, 1986, Expansion of Air Transportation Facilities in the San Jose Metropolitan Area, 1987, Provision of Economic Development in the San Jose Met. Area, 1988, Metropolitan Governance: American/Canadian Intergovernmental Perspectives, 1993; contbr. numerous articles to profl. jours.; dir.: Pub. TV series Sta. KTEH, 1976. Mem. adv. coun. Bay Area Met. Transp. Commn., 1995—. Served to 1st lt. C.E., U.S. Army, 1957-59. Rsch. fellow John F. Kennedy Sch. Govt. Harvard U., 1967-69; William F. Milton rsch. fellow, 1970-71; faculty rsch. grantee, NSF, 1972-82, Calif. State U., 1977-78; grantee Nat. Inst. Dispute Resolution, 1987-88, Can. Studies Enrichment Program, 1989-90, Can. Studies Rsch. Program, 1992-93, Univ. Rsch. and Tng. Program grantee Calif. Dept. Transp., 1993-97; recipient Innovative Teaching award Calif. State U. and Coll., 1975-79; co-recipient Best of West award Western Ednl. Soc. for Tele-communication, 1976; recipient award Internat. Festival of Films on Architecture and Planning, 1983, Meritorious Performance award San Jose State U., 1986, 88, 90. Mem. Assn. Collegiate Schs. of Planning (pres. 1975-76), Am. Inst. Cert. Planners, Am. Planning Assn., Planners for Equal Opportunity, Internat. Fedn. Housing and Planning, AAUP, Calif. Edn. Com. on Architecture and Landscape, Architecture and Urban and Regional Planning (chmn. 1973-75). Office: San Jose State U Dept Urban & Regional Planning San Jose CA 95192-0185 *My basic view is that we should try to develop ourselves fully and help others do the same, so that we will be able to live in harmony with, and contribute to, our world community.*

ROTHENBERG, HARVEY DAVID, educational administrator; b. Fort Madison, Iowa, May 31, 1937; s. Max and Cecelia Rothenberg; AA, Wentworth Mil. Acad., 1957; BBA, State U. Iowa, 1960; M.A, U. No. Colo., 1961; postgrad. Harris Tchrs. Coll., 1962-63, St. Louis U., 1962-63; PhD, Colo. State U., 1972; m. Audrey Darlynne Roseman, July 5, 1964; children: David Michael, Mark Daniel. Distributive edn. tchr. Roosevelt H.S., St. Louis, 1961-63, Proviso West High Sch., Hillside, Ill., 1963-64, Longmont (Colo.) Sr. High Sch., 1964-69, 70-71; supr. research and spl. programs St. Vrain Valley Sch. Dist., Longmont, Colo., 1971-72; chmn. bus. div. Arapahoe C.C., Littleton, Colo., 1972-75; dir. vocat., career and adult edn. Arapahoe County Sch. Dist. 6, Littleton, 1975-96; part-time instr. Met. State Coll., Denver, 1975-85, Arapahoe C.C., Littleton, 1975—, Regis U., 1996—; dir. faculty, curriculum Sch. Profl. Studies, Regis U., 1996—; vis. prof. U. Ala., Tuscaloosa, summer 1972; dir. Chatfield Bank, Littleton, 1974-83, Yaak River Mines Ltd., Amusement Personified Inc.; pres. Kuytia Inc., Littleton, 1975—; co-owner Albuquerque Lasers, profl. volleyball team. Author: Conducting Successful Business Research, 1996 . Mem. City of Longmont Long-Range Planning Commn., 1971-72, pres. Homeowners Bd., 1978-80. Recipient Outstanding Young Educator award St. Vrain Valley Sch. Dist., 1967, Outstanding Vocational Educator, Colo. 1992, We. Region U.S., 1993. Mem. Am., Colo. (mem. exec. com. 1966-68, treas. 1972-73) vocat. assns., Littleton C. of C., Colo. Assn. Vocat. Adminstrs, Colo. Educators For and About Bus., Delta Sigma Pi, Delta Pi Epsilon, Nat. Assn. Local Sch. Adminstrs., Colo. Council Local Sch. Adminstrs. Clubs: Elks, Masons, Shriners. Home: 7461 S Sheridan Ct Littleton CO 80123-7084 Office: Regis U Sch Profl Studies 3333 Regis Blvd Denver CO 80221-1154

ROTHENBERG, MARCY MIROFF, public relations consultant; b. Hollywood, Calif., Dec. 23, 1950; d. Victor and Eugenie Alice (Wankel) Miroff; m. Peter Jay Rothenberg, June 22; 1 child, Valerie Jill. AB, UCLA, 1973; MA, U. So. Calif., 1977. Publicity coord. Ruben for Assembly Com., Van Nuys, Calif., 1971-72; staff writer dept. pub. rels. Prudential Ins. Co. Am., L.A., 1973-74; pub. rels. cons. to econ. devel. program Mayor's Office, City of L.A., 1974-75; staff writer dept. pub. affairs ARCO, L.A., 1975-78; comm. rep. divsn. pub. affairs So. Calif. Gas Co., L.A., 1978-79; dir. bus. devel. Meserve, Mumper & Hughes, L.A., 1979-80; account supr. Hill and Knowlton, Inc., L.A., 1980-82; asst. prof. Sch. Journalism U. So. Calif., L.A., 1986-89; owner Rothenberg Comm., Porter Ranch, Calif., 1982—; mktg. and pub. rels. dir. Jewish Vocat. Svc., 1996—. Author: (study guides) Something Ventured, 1991, The Sales Connection, 1992. Pub. rels. cons. PRIDE (Porter Ranch is Developed Enough!), 1989-91; mem. shared decision making coun. Castlebay Lane Elem. Sch., Porter Ranch, 1990-92, Frost Mid. Sch., Granada Hills, Calif., 1992-94. Recipient Bronze Quill award of Merit (2nd pl.), L.A. chpt. Internat. Assn. Bus. Communicators, Bronze Quill award of Excellence (1st pl.), 1985, ACE award of Excellence, 1989, 1st pl. award of Excellence, Med. Mktg. Assn., 1985, 86. Mem. Pub. Rels. Soc. Am. (accredited, bd. dirs. L.A. chpt. 1989, mem. nat. profl. devel. com. 1978-79, mem. nat. social responsibility com. 1980-81), Publicity Club L.A., UCLA Alumni Assn., U. So. Calif. Journalism Alumni Assn., Phi Beta Kappa. Democrat. Jewish. Office: Rothenberg Comm 19041 Braemore Rd Porter Ranch CA 91326-1202

ROTHERHAM, LARRY CHARLES, insurance executive; b. Council Bluffs, Iowa, Oct. 22, 1940; s. Charles Sylvester and Edna Mary (Sylvanus) R.; m. Florene F. Black, May 29, 1965; children: Christopher Charles, Phillip Larry, Kathleen Florene. Student, Creighton U., 1959-61; BSBA, U. Nebr., 1965; postgrad., Am. Coll., Bryn Mawr, Pa., 1985, 87. CPCU, CLU, ARM. Claims rep. and underwriter Safeco Ins. Co., Albuquerque, New Mex., 1965-69; br. mgr. Ohio Casualty Group, Albuquerque, 1969—; assoc. in risk mgmt. Ins. Inst. Am., 1976—. Mem. PTA Collet Park Elem. Sch., Albuquerque, 1963-82, Freedom H.S., Albuquerque, 1982-86; bd. chmn. N.Mex. Property Ins. Program; mem. N.Mex. Workers compensation Appeals Bd. Mem. New Mex. Soc. Chartered Property & Casualty Underwriters (charter mem., pres. 1975-77), New Mex. Soc. Chartered Life Underwriters, New Mex. Ins. Assn. Democrat. Roman Catholic. Home: 2112 Gretta St NE Albuquerque NM 87112-3238 Office: Ohio Casualty Group 10400 Academy Rd NE Ste 200 Albuquerque NM 87111-7365

ROTHHAMMER, CRAIG ROBERT, social worker, consultant; b. San Francisco, May 17, 1954; s. Robert Charles and Gloria Lee (Molloy) R.; m. Dawn Alicia Alvarez, 1988. BA, U. Calif., Santa Barbara, 1976; MSW, San Diego State U., 1979. Lic. clin. social worker, Calif. Social work asst. Mercy Hosp., San Diego, 1977; psychiat. social worker Lanterman State Hosp., Pomona, Calif., 1979-83, Sonoma State Hosp., Eldridge, Calif., 1983-84; children's social worker County Adoption Service, San Bernardino, Calif., 1984-86; psychiat. social worker Patton State Hosp., 1987-88; psychiat. soc. worker II Crisis Outpatient Svcs. Riverside (Calif.) County Mental Health, 1988-90; mental health svcs. supr. Interagy. Svcs. for Families, Riverside County Mental Health, 1990-95; mgr. inpatient psychiatry west bay sub-region Kaiser Permanente, Redwood City, Calif., 1995—; expert examiner Behavioral Sci. Examiners, Calif.; pvt. practice (part time) social work Redlands, Calif., 1986-89; field instr. MSW program Calif. State U., San Bernardino, 1989-95, marriage, family & child counselor program Loma Linda (Calif.) U., 1993. Vol. Social Advs. for Youth, Santa Barbara, Calif., 1974-76, Am. Diabetes Assn., San Diego, 1978-79, San Diego Assn. For Retarded, 1978-80; liason Adoptive Family Assn., San Bernardino, 1986. Mem. NASW, Acad. Cert. Social Workers (diplomate in clin. social work). Democrat. Office: Kaiser Permanente Dept Inpatient Psychiarty 1150 Veterans Blvd Redwood City CA 94061

ROTHLISBERG, ALLEN PETER, librarian, educator, deacon; b. Jamaica, N.Y., Nov. 15, 1941; s. Allen Greenway and Agnes Clare (Donohoe) R.; m. Linda Lee Lillie, Oct. 17, 1964; children: Bethanie Lynn, Craig Allen. AB, San Diego State U., 1963; MLS, Our Lady of the Lake U., 1970. Cert. tchr., Ariz.; ordained deacon Episcopal Ch., 1989. Libr. dir. Prescott (Ariz.) Pub. Libr., 1963-75; dir. learning resources, head libr. Northland Pioneer Coll., Holbrook, Ariz., 1975-92; libr. dir. Chino Valley (Ariz.) Pub. Libr., 1992—; libr. media instr. Northland Pioneer Coll., Holbrook, Ariz., 1978—. Author: Dance to the Music of Time: Second Movement, 1972; contbr. articles to profl. publs. Recreation dir. Town of Chino Valley, 1993—, pub. access TV dir., 1993—; Episcopal deacon St. George's Ch., Holbrook, 1989-92, St. Luke's, Prescott, 1992—. Recipient Libr. of Yr. Ariz. State Libr. Assn., 1966. Mem. Elks, Masons. Democrat. Episcopalian. Office: Chino Valley Pub Libr PO Box 1188 Chino Valley AZ 86323-1188

ROTHMAN, MICHAEL JUDAH, lawyer; b. Mpls., June 7, 1962; s. Harvey Michael and Elaine Louise (London) R.; m. Shari Latz, Aug. 1, 1993. BA, Carleton Coll., 1984; JD, U. Minn., 1988. Bar: Minn. 1988, U.S. Dist. Ct. Minn. 1988, Calif. 1993, U.S. Dist. Ct. (ctrl. dist.) Calif. 1993, U.S. Ct. Appeals (9th cir.) 1995, U.S. Supreme Ct. 1995. Law clk. to J. Gary Crippen Minn. Ct. of Appeals, St. Paul, 1988-89; adminstrv. asst. Minn. State Senate, St. Paul, 1989-92; atty. Rubenstein & Perry, L.A., 1993-95, Loeb & Loeb, L.A., 1995-96; assoc. Barger & Wolen, LLP, L.A., 1996—. Vol. atty. F.A.M.E. Ch. and Temple Isaiah Legal Project, L.A., 1994-96. Recipient Best Brief award Regional Internat. Moot Ct. Competition, Colo., 1988. Mem. ABA, Calif. Bar Assn., L.A. County Bar Assn. Democrat. Office: Barger & Wolen 515 S Flower St 34th Fl Los Angeles CA 90071-2205

ROTHMAN, PAUL ALAN, publisher; b. Bklyn., June 26, 1940; s. Fred B. and Dorothy (Regosin) R.; m. Mary Ann Dalson, July 28, 1966 (div. 1992); children: Deborah, Diana. BA, Swarthmore Coll., 1962; JD, U. Mich., 1965; LLM in Taxation, NYU, 1967. Bar: N.Y. 1965. Assoc. Dewey, Ballentine, Busby, Palmer & Wood, N.Y.C., 1965-67; v.p. Fred B. Rothman & Co., Littleton, Colo., 1967-85, pres., 1985—; chmn. bd. Colo. Plasticard, Littleton, 1983-95. Editor Mich. Law Rev., 1963-65. Home: 25437 Stanley Park Rd Evergreen CO 80439-5512 Office: Fred B Rothman & Co 10368 W Centennial Rd Littleton CO 80127-4205

ROTH-NELSON, STEPHANIE FAYE, technical writer, trainer; b. Cleve., July 24, 1949; d. William Allan and Lillian Annette (Greenfeld) Roth; m. William Hartnell Pence, Nov. 6, 1971 (div. June 1981); m. R. Wayne Nelson, Feb. 14, 1988; children: Jason Allan, Jasmine Nichole. BS in Tech. Writing, Carnegie-Mellon U., 1971; M Criminal Justice, U. Colo., Denver, 1993. Sec. Boulder (Colo.) Valley Schs., 1975-78; adminstrv. svcs. coord. Hanson Industries, Boulder, 1978-82; tech. writer T.P. Clark, Boulder, 1982-84; prin. Bus. Plans Plus, Boulder, 1984-89; tech. writer Spectrum Human Resource Corp., Denver, 1989-92; dir. Ctr. Adolescent Self-Esteem, Louisville, 1993—; trainer, cons. various juvenile justice agys. Co-author: Empowering Vision, 1987, SEEK Facilitators Guide, 1994; author: SEEK (Self-Esteem Enhancement Kit), 1993 (Athena Hon. Mention award 1996). Active Cmty. Corrections Bd., Boulder County, 1993—, chair, 1995—. Mem. Juvenile Justice Trainers Assn. Office: Ctr for Adolescent Self-Esteem PO Box 104 Louisville CO 80027

ROTHSCHILD, HELENE, marriage/family therapist and author; b. Bklyn., Oct. 11, 1940. BS in Health Edn., Bklyn. Coll., 1962, MS in Health Edn., 1965; MA in Marriage/Family/Child Counseling, U. Santa Clara, Calif., 1980. Lic. marriage, family and child counselor; lic. tchr., Calif., N.Y. Founder, dir. Inst. for Creative Therapy, Sedona, Ariz., 1982-86, dir. tng., 1982—; pvt. practice marriage, family therapy, Sedona, 1980—; health edn. tchr. Lafayette High Sch., Bklyn., 1961-65, 73-76; part-time health edn. tchr. in pvt. elem. schs., Bklyn., 1966-73. Host TV show Creative Therapy with Helene Rothschild, radio show Hello Helene, KEST, San Francisco; author 10 tapes, 2 books, 5 booklets, 10 posters, 5 cards, 48 articles; lectr. in field; facilitator hundreds of seminars and workshops; appeared numerous times on TV, radio; addressed numerous mags., newspapers, convs., corps. Author: Free to Fly-Dare to be a Success; prodr. tapes: Free to Fly-Dare to be a Success, Dare to be Thin, Raise Self Esteem-Heal the Inner Child, Successful Parenting, Fantastic Relationships, Dare to be Prosperous, Healing Your Body, Enjoying Your Sexuality; contbr. articles to profl. jours. Home and Office: PO Box 10419 Sedona AZ 86339-8419

ROTHSTEIN, BARBARA JACOBS, federal judge; b. Bklyn., Feb. 3, 1939; d. Solomon and Pauline Jacobs; m. Ted L. Rothstein, Dec. 28, 1968; 1 child, Daniel. B.A., Cornell U., 1960; LL.B., Harvard U., 1966. Bar: Mass. 1966, Wash. 1969, U.S. Ct. Appeals (9th cir.) 1977, U.S. Dist. Ct. (we. dist.) Wash. 1971, U.S. Supreme Ct. 1975. Pvt. practice law Boston, 1966-68; asst. atty. gen. State of Wash., 1968-77; judge Superior Ct., Seattle, 1977-80; judge Fed. Dist. Ct. Western Wash., Seattle, 1980—, chief judge, 1987-94; faculty Law Sch. U. Wash., 1975-77, Hastings Inst. Trial Advocacy, 1977, N.W. Inst. Trial Advocacy, 1979—; mem. state-fed. com. U.S. Jud. Conf., chair subcom. on health reform. Recipient Matrix Table Women of Yr. award Women in Communication, Judge of the Yr. award Fed. Bar Assn., 1989; King County Wash. Women Lawyers Vanguard Honor, 1995. Mem. ABA (jud. sect.), Am. Judicature Soc., Nat. Assn. Women Judges, Fellows of the Am. Bar, Wash. State Bar Assn., U.S. Jud. Conf. (state-fed. com., health reform subcom.), Phi Beta Kappa, Phi Kappa Phi. Office: US Dist Ct 705 US Courthouse 1010 5th Ave Seattle WA 98104-1130

ROTHWELL, GEOFFREY SCOTT, economics educator; b. Longview, Wash., July 20, 1953; s. Michael Olin and Dona B. (Adams) R. BA, The Evergreen State Coll., Olympia, Wash., 1975; MA in Econs., U. Calif., Berkeley, 1981, MA in Jurisprudence, 1984, PhD, 1985. Postdoctoral fellow Calif. Inst. Tech., Pasadena, 1985-86; instr. dept. econs. U. Calif., Berkeley, 1984-85; rsch. assoc. Ctr. Econ. Policy Rsch. Stanford (Calif.) U., 1986-89, sr. rsch. assoc. Ctr. Econ. Policy Rsch., 1991—, lectr. dept. econs., 1986—. Contbr. articles to profl. jours. Mem. Am. Econs. Assn., Econometrics Soc., Western Econs. Assn. (assoc. editor Contemporary Econ. Policy, Resources and Energy Econs.). Office: Stanford U Dept Econs Stanford CA 94305

ROTTER, JEROME ISRAEL, medical geneticist; b. L.A., Feb. 24, 1949; s. Leonard L. and Jeanette (Kronenfeld) R.; m. Deborah Tofield, July 14, 1970; children: Jonathan Moshe, Amy Esther, Samuel Alexander. BS, UCLA, 1969, MD, 1973. Intern Harbor-UCLA Med. Ctr., Torrance, Calif., 1973-74; fellow in med. genetics Harbor-UCLA Med. Ctr., Torrance, 1975-78, asst. research pediatrician, 1978-79, faculty div. med. genetics, 1978-86; resident in medicine Wadsworth VA Hosp., Los Angeles, 1974-75; asst. prof. medicine and pediatrics Sch. Medicine UCLA, 1979-83, assoc. prof. Sch. Medicine, 1983-87, prof. Sch. Medicine, 1987—; dir. divsn. med. genetics and co. dir. med. genetics birth defect ctr. Cedars-Sinai Med. Ctr., 1986—; key investigator Ctr. for Ulcer Rsch. and Edn., L.A., 1980-89; dir. genetic epidemiology core Ctr. for Study of Inflammatory Bowel Disease, Torrance, 1985-91; assoc. dir. Cedars-Sinai Inflammatory Bowel Disease Ctr., L.A., 1992—; dir. Stuart Found. CSMC Common Disease Risk Assessment Ctr., 1986—; dir. genetic epidemiology core project molecular biology of arteriosclerosis UCLA, 1987—. Mem. bd. govs. Cedars-Sinai, chair med. genetics, 1990—. Recipient Regents scholarship UCLA, 1966-73; recipient Richard Weitzman award Harbor-UCLA, 1983, Ross award Western Soc. for Pediatric Rsch., 1985. Mem. Am. Heart Assn., Am. Soc. Human Genetics, Am. Gastroent. Assn., Am. Diabetes Assn., Soc. for Pediatric Research, Western Soc. for Clin. Investigation (mem. council 1985-88), Am. Fedn. for Clin. Rsch., Western Assn. Physicians, Am. Soc. for Clin. Investigation. Jewish. Office: Cedars-Sinai Med Ctr Div Med Genetics 8700 Beverly Blvd Los Angeles CA 90048-1804

ROTTER, PAUL TALBOTT, retired insurance executive; b. Parsons, Kans., Feb. 21, 1918; s. J. and LaNora (Talbott) R.; m. Virginia Sutherlin Barksdale, July 17, 1943; children—Carolyn Sutherlin, Diane Talbott. BS summa cum laude, Harvard U., 1937. Asst. mathematician Prudential Ins. Co. of Am., Newark, 1938-46; with Mut. Benefit Life Ins. Co., Newark, 1946—; successively asst. mathematician, asso. mathematician, mathematician Mut. Benefit Life Ins. Co., 1946-59, from v.p. to exec. v.p., 1959-80, ret., 1980. Mem. Madison Bd. Edn., 1958-64, pres., 1959-64; Trustee, mem. budget com. United Campaign of Madison, 1951-55; mem. bd., chmn. advancement com. Robert Treat council Boy Scouts Am., 1959-64. Fellow Soc. Actuaries (bd. govs. 1965-68, gen. chmn. edn. and exam. com. 1963-66, chmn. adv. com. edn. and exam. 1969-72); mem. Brit. Inst. Actuaries (asso.), Am. Acad. Actuaries (v.p. 1968-70, bd. dirs., chmn. edn. and exam. com. 1965-66, chmn. rev. and evaluation com. 1968-74), Asso. Harvard Alumni (regional dir. 1965-69), Actuaries Club N.Y. (pres. 1967-68), Harvard Alumni Assn. (v.p. 1964-66),Am. Lawn Bowls Assn. (pres. SW div.), Phi Beta Kappa Assos., Phi Beta Kappa. Clubs: Harvard N.J. (pres. 1956-57); Harvard (N.Y.C.); Morris County Golf (Convent, N.J.); Joslyn-Lake Hodges Lawn Bowling (pres. 1989-90). Home: 18278 Canfield Pl San Diego CA 92128-1002

ROTZIEN, FREDERICK WILLIAM, III, marketing executive; b. Portland, Oreg., Aug. 9, 1944; s. Frederick William Jr. and Vilma E. (Brandon) R.; m. Yvonne Miller, June 12, 1975 (div. Aug. 1979). Student, Clark Coll. Mktg. pres. Rotzien and Assocs., Portland, 1970-85; mktg. exec. Heartland Farms, Portland, 1985-88; mfg./mktg. pres. Blue Ribbon Market, Portland, 1985-90; mfg. pres. Probe Electronics, Portland, 1985-90; mktg. exec. Adventure Mktg., Portland, 1990-94, Am. Elec. Motorcycle, Portland, 1994—. Author, editor: World Chart of History, 1988; author: Step by Step Tobacco Guide, 1988. Pres. Oreg. chpt. Young Am. Freedom Portland, 1962, Portland Young Reps., 1968, Oreg. Young Reps., Portland, 1969. Mem. Am. Mktg. Assn. Lutheran. Home: 13005 NE Broadway Portland OR 97230

ROUDA, ROBERT E., dentist; b. San Francisco, Feb. 26, 1933; s. Harry David and Marguerite Beatrice (Klein) R.; m. Frances Anne Freistadt, June 16, 1957; children: Robin, Gail, David. DDS, U. Calif., San Francisco, 1957. Cert. dentist, Calif. Practice gen. dentistry San Francisco, 1960—; asst. clin. prof. U. Calif. San Francisco Sch. Dentistry, 1996—. Mem. Marin County Dem. Coun., 1976. Capt. USAF, 1957-59, France. Fellow Am. Coll. Dentists, Acad. Dentistry Internat.; mem. San Francisco Dental Soc. (pres. 1973), U. Calif. San Francisco Dental Assn. (pres. 1985, Medal of Honor 1996), Alumni Assn. of U. Calif. San Francisco (pres. 1994-95), Marin Rowing Assn., U. Calif. San Francisco Dental Alumni Assn. Home: 237 N Almenar Dr Greenbrae CA 94904 Office: 490 Post St San Francisco CA 94102

ROUNDS, DONALD MICHAEL, public relations executive; b. Centralia, Ill., May 9, 1941; s. Donald Merritt and Alice Josephine (Soulsby) R.; m. Alma Genevieve Beyer, Dec. 13, 1975. BS in History, Polit. Sci., Colo. State U., 1963. Police reporter, night city editor The Rocky Mountain News, Denver, 1960-70; mgr. Don M. Rounds Co., Denver, 1970-75; sr. editor Western Oil Reporter, Denver, 1975-80; energy writer The Rocky Mountain News, Denver, 1980-87; sr. media rels. advisor Cyprus Minerals Co., Englewood, Colo., 1987-92, media and community rels. mgr., 1992-93; media and community rels. mgr. Cyprus Amax Minerals Co., Englewood, 1994-95, dir. coms., 1995—; adv. bd Colo. State Minerals, Energy, and Geology (appointed by gov.), 1992—. Contbr. articles to mags. and newspapers. Mem. covenant com. Ken Caryl Ranch Master Assn., Littleton, Colo., 1996—; vol. naturalist Roxborough State Park, Colo., 1997—. Recipient MerComm Mercury Gold award, 1995, MerComm Silver award (Denver Post), 1995, 1996, 1st pl. spl. news series AP, 1987, 1st pl. news sweepstakes, 1987, Margolin award U. Denver Coll. Bus., 1986, Betty McWhorter Commendation of Honor Desk & Derrick Club of Denver, 1987, Journalism award Rocky Mountain Assn. Geologists, 1985, Citizen Svc. award Denver Police Dept., 1969, Pub. Svc. award Englewood Police Dept., 1967, finalist awd. Cyprus Amax corp. brochure Elements of Growth. Mem. Nat. Mining Assn. (pub. rels. com.), Soc. Profl. Journalists, Sigma Delta Chi, Denver Press Club (bd. dirs. 1987). Republican. Methodist. Home: 8220 S San Juan Range Rd Littleton CO 80127-4011 Office: Cyprus Amax Minerals Co 9100 E Mineral Cir Englewood CO 80112-3401

ROUSSEAU, DAVID, agricultural products executive; b. 1961. Ptnr. Rousseau Farming Co. I, Litchfield Park, Ariz., 1979—; with Rousseau Farming Co., 1979—. Office: Rousseau Farming Co II PO Box 100th Ave Tolleson AZ 85353-9217*

ROUSSEAU, WILL, agricultural products executive; b. 1958. Ptnr. Rousseau Farming Co. I, Litchfield Park, Ariz., 1979—; with Rousseau Farming Co., 1979—. Office: Rousseau Farming Co II PO Box 100 Tolleson AZ 85353-9217*

ROUTMAN, BURTON NORMAN, medical educator; b. Youngstown, Ohio, Apr. 21, 1941; s. Samuel Leonard and Beatrice Roberta (Epstein) R.; children: Stephanie Lynn Routman Leverage, Leslie Gail. BA, Johns Hopkins U., 1963; DO, U. Osteo. Med. & Health Sci., 1968. Intern Cuyahoga Falls (Ohio) Gen. Hosp., 1968-69; asst. prof. clin. scis. U. Osteo. Med. & Health Sci., Des Moines, 1972-76; asst. chief primary care unit Ben Gurion U., Beer Sheva, Israel, 1980-81; assoc. prof. clin. scis. U. Osteo. Medicine & Health Sci., Des Moines, 1981-82, assoc. prof. family practice, 1990-94; assoc. prof. family practice Western U. Health Scis., Pomona, Calif., 1995—. Capt. USAFMC, 1969-71. Mem. Am. Osteo. Assn., Am. Coll. Osteo. Family Physicians, Calif. Soc. Osteo. Physicians, Nat. Alumni Assn. Coll. Osteo. Medicine & Surgery, Israel-Am. Physicians Fellowship Assn., Sigma Sigma Phi, Lambda Omicron Gamma. Jewish. Office: Coll Osteo Medicine Pacific 309 E 2nd St Pomona CA 91766-1854

ROUTSON, CLELL DENNIS, manufacturing company executive; b. Elkhart, Ind., Oct. 8, 1946; s. Clell Dean and Olene Maize (Replogle) R.; m. Paula Leone McLallin, Sept. 2, 1967 (div. June 1988); children: Clell Dustin, Courtney Trevor; m. Suzann Kay Bron, 1995. BSBA, Ball State U., Muncie, Ind., 1971. With Proctor & Gamble, Cin., 1971-74; nat. sales mgr. Palmer Instruments, Inc., Cin., 1974-76; with Nordson Corp., Amherst, Ohio, 1976-81, MCC Powers, Cleve., Chgo., Singapore, 1981-86; sales mgr., v.p., pres. Burgess, Inc., Freeport, Ill., 1986-89; mgr. mktg. and sales, v.p. sales and mktg. Kloppenberg & Co., Englewood, Colo., 1990-92; v.p. ops., gen. mgr. T.E.I. Engineered Products, Englewood, 1992-96; pres. (one-yr. contract) Bailco Svc. Corp., Englewood, 1996—; mng. dir. Resource Dynamics, Singapore, Chgo., 1985-86; bd. dirs. TEI Engineered Products, Englewood. Contbr. articles to profl. jours. Mem. Met. Club (Denver). Republican. Baptist. Office: Bailco Svc Corp 6790 S Dawson Cir Englewood CO 80112

ROVEN, ALFRED NATHAN, surgeon; b. Czechoslovakia, Apr. 6, 1947; came to the U.S., 1949.; BA in Psychology, Calif. State U., Northridge, 1969; MD, U. So. Calif., 1977. Diplomate Am. Bd. Plastic and Reconstructive Surgery, Am. Bd. Otolaryngology. Resident in otolaryngology U. So. Calif., 1977-82; clin. chief plastic surgery Cedars Sinai Med. Ctr., L.A., 1989-91; resident in plastic and reconstructive surgery U. N.C., 1982-84; clin. chief burns Cedars Sinai Med. Ctr., L.A., 1990-92; clin. chief hands Cedars Sinai Med. Ctr., 1990-92; qualified med. examiner State of Calif., 1985. Contbr. articles to profl. jours. Physician L.A. Free Clinic, 1995—. Mem. Am. Soc. Head and Neck Surgery, L.A. County Med. Assn. (com. environ. health), Calif. Med. Assn., Am. Pain Soc., Am. Burn Assn., Am. Soc. Plastic and Reconstructive Surgeons, Internat. Confedn. Plastic Surgery, Fed. Issues Emergency Task Force, Nathan A. Womack Surg. Soc. Office: 444 S San Vicente Blvd # 600 Los Angeles CA 90048-4165

ROVIRA, LUIS DARIO, state supreme court justice; b. San Juan, P.R., Sept. 8, 1923; s. Peter S. and Mae (Morris) R.; m. Lois Ann Thau, June 25, 1966; children—Douglas, Merilyn. B.A., U. Colo., 1948, LL.B., 1950. Bar: Colo. 1950. Chief justice Colo. Supreme Ct., Denver., 1990-95; ret., 1995; mem. Pres.'s Com. on Mental Retardation, 1970-71; chmn. State Health Facilities Council, 1967-76. Bd. dirs Children's Hosp.; trustee Temple Buell Found., Denver Found., Harry S. Truman Scholarship Found. With AUS, 1943-46. Mem. ABA, Colo. Bar Assn., Denver Bar Assn. (pres. 1970-71), Colo. Assn. Retarded Children (pres. 1968-70), Alpha Tau Omega, Phi Alpha Delta. Clubs: Athletic (Denver), Country (Denver). Home: 4810 E 6th Ave Denver CO 80220-5137

ROWAN, RONALD THOMAS, lawyer; b. Bozeman, Mont., Nov. 6, 1941; s. Lawrence Eugene and Florence M.; m. Katherine Terrell Sponenberg, Sept. 4, 1964; children: Heather, Nicholaus, Matthew. BA, Wichita U., 1964; JD, U. Denver, 1969. Bar: Colo. 1969, U.S. Dist. Ct. Colo. 1969. Asst. city atty. City of Colorado Springs, Colo., 1969-71; asst. dist. atty. 4th Jud. Dist., Colorado Springs, 1971-79; gen. counsel U.S. Olympic Com., Colorado Springs, 1979—, dir. legal affairs, 1986—. Chmn. CSC, Colorado Springs, 1975—; chmn. Criminal Justice Adv. Bd., 1983—; chmn. El Paso Criminal Justice Adv. Com.; bd. dirs. Crimestoppers, 1982-87, past pres. 1985-87, Internat. Anti-counterfeiting Coalition; chmn. Community Corrections Bd., 1981, 86, 87. Mem. ABA, Colo. Bar Assn., El Paso County Trial Lawyers (pres. 1972), El Paso County Bar Assn., U. Denver Law Alumni (chmn.), Colo. Trial Lawyers Assn., Pikes Peak or Bust Rodeo Assn. (Ramrod 1989). Republican. Roman Catholic. Home: 215 Ridge Rd Colorado Springs CO 90804 Office: US Olympic Com One Olympic Plz Colorado Springs CO 80909

ROWE, CARL OSBORN, business consultant; b. Colorado Springs, Colo., Feb. 3, 1944; s. Prentiss Eldon and Jo Ann (Osborn) R.; m. Dale Robin Oren, Apr. 12, 1984; 1 child, Stefanie Osborn. BA in Govt. cum laude, George Mason U., 1972; M Urban Affairs, Va. Poly. Inst. and State U., 1976. Cert. pub. housing mgr. Spl. clk. FBI, Washington, 1968-71; mgmt. analyst ICC, Washington, 1972-75; dir. policy and mgmt. U.S. Bur. Reclamation, Washington, 1975-82; exec. dir. City of Las Vegas Housing Authority, 1990-94; pres. Rowe Bus. Consulting, Las Vegas, Nev., 1982-90, 94—; exec. dir. So. Nev. Housing Corp., 1994-95; assoc. Success Strategies, Las Vegas, 1995-96, Fair, Anderson and Langerman, CPAs, Las Vegas, 1996—; bd. dirs. Flowtronics, Inc., Phoenix, Sportstech, Inc., Scottsdale, Ariz., MSP Sys., Inc., Scottsdale. Columnist Las Vegas Bus. Press, 1989-90, 94—. Exec. dir. So. Nev. Housing Corp., So. Nev. Reinvestment and Affordable Housing Com.; founding bd. dirs., CEO Family Cabinet of So. Nev., Affordable Housing Inst. So. Nev.; bd. dirs. Opportunity Village, LLV Alumni Found.; active So. Nev. Homeless Coalition; mem. exec. bd. Pacific S.W. Regional Conf., Oasis So. Nev. Cmty. Svc. Guild, Las Vegas Cmty. Empowerment Commn.; mem. adv. bd. Comty. Food Bank Clark County. Decorated USAF Commendation medal; named one of Top 50 over 50 in Las Vegas, Prime Mag. Mem. Am. Soc. Pub. Adminstrn. (mem. governing coun.), Nat. Assn. Housing and Redevel. Ofcls. (mem. exec. bd.), Pub. Housing Authorities Dirs. Assn. (mem. exec. bd.), No. Calif./Nev. Exec. Dirs. Assn. (mem. exec. bd.), Leadership Las Vegas, Las Vegas C. of C., LLV Alumni Found. (pres.), Phi Theta Kappa. Office: Fair Anderson and Langerman CPAs Ste 110 3811 W Charleston Blvd Las Vegas NV 89102

ROWE, DAVID ALAN, magazine publisher; b. La Jolla, Calif., Feb. 8, 1956; s. Harold Derwood and Carmen Alida (Chenier) R.; m. Danette Leslee Nordick, July 31, 1982; 1 child, Evan Christopher. BA, U. Calif. San Diego, La Jolla, 1979. Dir. pub. rels. Cath. Cmty. Svc., San Diego, 1979-80; editor Hare Publs. Inc., Carlsbad, Calif., 1980-82; pub., editor-in-chief Harcourt Brace Jovanovich, Inc., Irvine, Calif., 1982-87; pub., pres. Video Software Mag./VSD Publs., Inc., L.A., 1987-91; pub., pres., CEO Oreg. Bus. Mag./ Mediamerica, Inc., Portland, 1991—; mktg. rsch. cons. Mem. mktg. com. United Way, Portland, 1992-94; dir. Associated Oreg. Industries, Salem, 1992-93; chmn. Oreg. Enterprise Forum, Portland, 1994; dir. Portland C. of C., 1993-95. Recipient Maggie award for best entertainment publ., L.A., 1990, 91, 92; named Media Adv. of Yr., U.S. Small Bus. Adminstrn., Oreg., 1993, Pacific N.W. region, 1993, Maggie award for Best Managerial and Profl. Pub., 1995. Mem. Am. Bus. Press, Western Publs. Assn., Portland Met. C. of C. (dir. 1994—). Roman Catholic. Office: Oreg Bus Media 610 SW Broadway Ste 200 Portland OR 97205-3403

ROWE, HENRY THEODORE, JR. (TED ROWE), industrial video producer, director; b. Englewood, N.J., Oct. 8, 1932; s. Henry Theodore and Florence Jane (Bivins) R.; m. Judith Lyttelton Waddell, June 8, 1957 (div. Apr. 1982); children: Henry Theodore III, Lyttelton Waddell, Eliza Ritnour, Virginia Bivins; m. Phyllis Arlene Prevosto, Dec. 26, 1983. Student, Cornell U., 1951-53; BS, St. Lawrence U., 1956; postgrad., Columbia U., 1956-57. Pub. affairs fellow Brookings Instn., Washington, 1961; with IBM Corp., 1957-88; sr. requirements adminstr. IBM Corp., White Plains, N.Y., 1970-76; sr. bus. programs adminstrn. IBM Corp., White Plains, also Irving, Tex., 1976-86; cons. mktg. support rep. IBM Corp., Roanoke, Tex., 1986-88; owner Ted Rowe Assocs., Dallas, El Jebel, Colo., 1989—; v.p., bd. dirs. West End Post, Dallas. Co-writer, editor weekly food column Food for Thought. 1st lt. U.S. Army, 1956-57. Mem. Am. Film Inst., Am. Fedn. Musicians, Aspen Chamber Resort Assn. Republican. Office: Ted Rowe Assocs PO Box 28327 El Jebel CO 81628

ROWE, MARJORIE DOUGLAS, retired social services administrator; b. Bklyn., July 29, 1912; d. Herbert Lynn and Mary Manson (Hall) Douglas; m. Richard Daniel Rowe, July 29, 1937 (dec.); 1 child, Richard Douglas. AB cum laude, Whitman Coll., 1933; MS in Social Adminstrn., Case Western Res. U., 1936. Caseworker Children's Svcs., Cleve., 1933-36, supr., 1937-39; dir. Adoption Svc. Bur., Cleve., 1940-41; social work supr., psychiat. social work cons. Ea. State Hosp., Medical Lake, Wash., 1962-67; dir. social svcs. Interlake Sch.for Developmentally Disabled, Medical Lake, 1967-74, supt., 1975-82; retired, 1982. Pres. chpt. R.P.E.O., Spokane, Wash., 1949, Spokane Alumnae chpt. Delta Delta Delta, 1955-57; chpt. mem. ARC, Orofino, Idaho, 1941-45, Orofino chpt. chmn., 1945-46; sec. Idaho state chpt. AAUW, 1945-46. Mem. Am. Assn. for Mental Deficiency (region I chmn. 1976-77, social work chmn. 1971-73), NASW (gold card mem.), P.E.O. (pres. Spokane Reciprocity 1950), Acad. Cert. Social Workers, Spokane Women of Rotary (pres. 1960-61), Phi Beta Kappa, Delta Sigma Rho, Mortar Bd. Episcopalian. Home: 946 E Thurston Ave Spokane WA 99203-2948

ROWE, MARY SUE, accounting executive; b. Melrose, Kans., Aug. 31, 1940; d. Gene and Carmen (Glidewell) Woffard; m. Edward Rowe, Nov. 27, 1985; children from previous marriage: Denise, Dynell, Dalene, Denette. Student, MTI Bus. Coll., 1968, Calif. State U., Fullerton, 1969, Broome (N.Y.) Community Coll., 1974-76; cert. Sch. Bus. Mgmt., Calif. State U., San Bernardino, 1986. Variou bookkeeping and secretarial, 1968-76; asst. mgr., acct. RM Dean Contracting, Chenango Forks, N.Y., 1976-80; acctg. asst. Hemet (Calif.) Unified Sch. Dist., 1981-86; dir. acctg. Desert Sands Unified Sch. Dist., Indio, Calif., 1986-91; bus. svcs. cons. ednl. div. Vicenti, Lloyd & Stutzman, CPA, La Verne, Calif., 1991-97; sch. bus. cons., computer trainer Hemet, Calif., 1997—. Bd. dirs. Family Svcs. Assn., Hemet, 1982-83, PTA Officer, 1993-95. Mem. NAFE, Calif. Assn. Sch. Bus. Ofcls. (acctg. com., R*D com., vice chmn. 1988-90, chmn. 1990-91, state acctg. adv. com. 1990-92), Riverside Assn. Chief Accts. (co-chmn. 1986-88), Coalition for Adequate Sch. Housing. Republican. Home and Office: 4981 Vailwood Dr Hemet CA 92544-7819 *Personal philosophy: Something good can come of any event no matter how bad it first appears.*

ROWE, RANDY ROLAND, nonprofit organization executive, consultant; b. Redmond, Oreg., Aug. 23, 1955; s. Melvin Charles and Myrna Louise (Carlson) R.; m. Dana Fawn Nimmons, Apr. 26, 1980; children: Jered Randall, Jeremy James. BA, Northwest Coll., 1979; MA, U. No. Colo., 1982; PhD, Internat. Sem., 1992. Ordained to ministry Assemblies of God, 1982. Asst. farm mgr. Carlson Farms, Boardman, Oreg., 1974-75; farm prodn. mgr. Rowe Farms, Mesa, Wash., 1975-79; dir. Teen Challenge of the Rocky Mountains, Denver, 1979-84; adminstr. Teen Challenge of the Rocky Mountains, Sundance, Wyo., 1984-91; exec. dir. Teen Challenge of Wyo., Inc., Sundance, Wyo., 1991—; charter bd. mem. Life Challenge, Inc., Ramona, Calif., 1988-92; treas. Happy Trails Unltd., Inc., Cripple Creek, Colo., 1991-94; tng. com. mem. Teen Challenge Nat., Inc., Springfield, Mo., 1994. Author: The Nature of Life-Controlling Sin Among Christians, 1992. Elected officer Vista West Improvement and Svcs. Dist., Crook County, Wyo., 1984-94. Recipient Most Ednl. Presentations award Crook County Family Violence, Sundance, 1986. Mem. ACA (profl. mem.), Am. Assn. Christian Counselors (charter mem.), Christian Mgmt. Assn. (regional dir. 1990-94), Assn. Christian Schs. Internat., Kiwanis Internat. Office: Teen Challenge of Bay Area 16735 Lark Ave Los Gatos CA 95030

ROWE, SANDRA MIMS, newspaper editor; b. Charlotte, N.C., May 26, 1948; d. David Lathan and Shirley (Stovall) Mims; m. Gerard Paul Rowe, June 5, 1971; children: Mims Elizabeth, Sarah Stovall. BA, East Carolina U., Greenville, N.C., 1970; postgrad., Harvard U., 1991. Reporter to asst. mng. editor The Ledger-Star, Norfolk, Va., 1971-80, mng. editor, 1980-82; mng. editor The Virginian-Pilot and The Ledger Star, Norfolk, Va., 1982-84, exec. editor, 1984-86, v.p., exec. editor, 1986-93; editor The Oregonian, Portland, 1993—; mem. Pulitzer Prize Bd., 1994—. Bd. visitors James Madison U., Harrisonburg, VA., 1991-95. Named Woman of Yr. Outstanding Profl. Women of Hampton Rds., 1987. Mem. Am. Soc. Newspaper Editors (pres., bd. dirs. 1992—), Va. Press Assn. (bd. dirs. 1985-93). Episcopalian. Office: The Oregonian 1320 SW Broadway Portland OR 97201-3411

ROWEN, MARSHALL, radiologist; b. Chgo.; s. Harry and Dorothy (Kasnow) R.; m. Helen Lee Friedman, Apr. 5, 1952; children: Eric, Scott, Mark. AB in Chemistry with highest honors, U. Ill., Urbana, 1951; MD with honors, U. Ill., Chgo., 1954, MS in Internal Medicine, 1954. Diplomate Am. Bd. Radiology. Intern Long Beach (Calif.) VA Hosp., 1955; resident in radiology Los Angeles VA Hosp., 1955-58; practice medicine specializing in radiology Orange, Calif., 1960—; chmn. bd. dirs. Moran, Rowen and Dorsey, Inc., Radiologists, 1969—; asst. radiologist L.A. Children's Hosp., 1958; assoc. radiologist Valley Presbyn. Hosp., Van Nuys, Calif., 1960; dir. dept. radiology St. Joseph Hosp., Orange, 1961—, v.p. staff, 1972; dir. dept. radiology Children's Hosp. Orange County, 1964—, chief staff, 1977-78, v.p., 1978-83, v.p., trustee, 1990-91, 92-95; asst. clin. prof. radiology U. Calif., Irvine, 1967-70, assoc. clin. prof., 1979-72, clin. prof. radiology and pediatrics, 1976-97, pres. clin. faculty assn., 1980-81; trustee Choc. Padrinos; sec. Choco Health Svcs., 1987-89, v.p., 1990-93, trustee, 1995—; trustee Found. Med. Care Orange County, 1972-76, Calif. Commn. Adminstrn. Svcs. Hosp., 1975-79, Profl. Practice Systems, 1990-92, Med. Specialty Mgrs., 1990—, St. Joseph Med. Corp., 1993—; v.p. Found. Med. Care Children's Hosp., 1988-89; v.p., sr. v.p., bd. dirs. St. Joseph Med. Corp. IPA, 1995-97; bd. dirs. Orange Coast Managed Care Svcs., 1995-97, sr. v.p., 1995-97, Paragon Med. Imaging, 1993—, Calif. Managed Imaging, 1994—, Alliance Premier Hosps., 1995-96; chmn. bd. dirs. Children's Healthcare of Calif., 1995-97; corp. mem. Blue Shield Calif., 1995-97; mem. physician's rev. com. Blue Cross Calif., 1996-97. Mem. editorial bd. Western Jour. Medicine; contbr. articles to med. jours. Founder Orange County Performing Arts Ctr., mem. Laguna Art Mus., Laguna Festival of Arts, Opera Pacific, S. Coast Reportory, Am. Ballet Theater, World Affairs Council. Served to capt. M.C., U.S. Army, 1958-60. Recipient Rea sr. med. prize U. Ill, 1953; William Cook scholar U. Ill., 1951, Friend of Children award, 1995, Charley award Children's Hosp., 1996. Fellow Am. Coll. Radiology; mem. AMA, Am. Heart Assn., Soc. Nuclear Medicine (trustee 1961-62), Orange County Radiol. Soc. (pres. 1968-69), Calif. Radiol. Soc. (pres. 1978-79), Radiol. Soc. So. Calif. (pres. 1976), Pacific Coast Pediatric Radiologists Assn. (pres. 1971), Soc. Pediatric Radiology, Calif. Med. Assn. (chmn. sect. on radiology 1978-79), Orange County Med. Assn. (chmn. UCI liaison com. 1976-78), Cardioradiology Soc. So. Calif., Radiol. Soc. N.Am., Am. Roentgen Ray Soc., Am. Coll. Physician Execs., Soc. Chmn. Radiologists Children Hosp., Center Club, Phi Beta Kappa, Phi Eta Sigma, Omega Beta Phi, Alpha Omega Alpha. Office: 1201 W La Veta Ave Orange CA 92868-4213

ROWLAND, FRANK SHERWOOD, chemistry educator; b. Delaware, Ohio, June 28, 1927; m. Joan Lundberg, 1952; children: Ingrid Drake, Jeffrey Sherwood. AB, Ohio Wesleyan U., 1948; MS, U. Chgo., 1951, PhD, 1952, DSc (hon.), 1989; DSc (hon.), Duke U., 1989, Whittier Coll., 1989, Princeton U., 1990, Haverford Coll., 1992, Clark U., 1996, U. East Anglia, 1996; LLD (hon.), Ohio Wesleyan U., 1989, Simon Fraser U., 1991. Instr. chemistry Princeton (N.J.) U., 1952-56; asst. prof. chemistry U. Kans., 1956-58, assoc. prof. chemistry, 1958-63, prof. chemistry, 1963-64; prof. chemistry U. Calif., Irvine, 1964—, dept. chmn., 1964-70, Aldrich prof. chemistry, 1985-89, Bren prof. chemistry, 1989-94, Bren rsch. prof., 1994—; Humboldt sr. scientist, Fed. Republic of Germany, 1981; chmn. Dahlem (Fed. Republic of Germany) Conf. on Changing Atmosphere, 1987; vis. scientist Japan Soc. for Promotion Sci., 1980; co-dir. western region Nat. Inst. Global Environ. Changes, 1989-93; del. Internat. Coun. Sci. Unions, 1993—; fgn. sec. NAS, 1994—; lectr., cons. in field. Contbr. numerous articles to profl. jours. Mem. ozone commn. Internat. Assn. Meteorology and Atmospheric Physics, 1980-88, mem. commn. on atmospheric chemistry and global pollution, 1979-91; mem. acid rain peer rev. panel U.S. Office of Sci. and Tech., Exec. Office of White House, 1982-84; mem. vis. com. Max Planck Insts., Heidelberg and Mainz, Fed. Republic Germany, 1982-96; ozone trends panel mem. NASA, 1986-88; chmn. Gordon Conf. Environ. Scis.-Air, 1987; mem. Calif. Coun. Sci. Tech., 1989-95, Exec. Com. Tyler Prize, 1992—. Recipient numerous awards including John Wiley Jones award Rochester Inst. of Tech., 1975, Disting. Faculty Rsch. award U. Calif., Irvine, 1976, Profl. Achievement award U. Chgo., 1977, Billard award N.Y. Acad. Sci., 1977, Tyler World Prize in Environment Achievement, 1983, Global 500 Roll of Honor for Environ. Achievement UN Environment Program, 1988, Dana award for Pioneering Achievements in Health, 1987, Silver medal Royal Inst. Chemistry, U.K., 1989, Wadsworth award N.Y. State Dept. Health, 1989, medal U. Calif., Irvine, 1989, Japan prize in Environ. Sci., 1989, Dickson prize Carnegie-Mellon U., 1991; Guggenheim fellow, 1962, 74, Albert Einstein prize of World Cultural Coun., 1994, Nobel Prize in Chemistry, 1995. Fellow AAAS (pres. elect 1991, pres. 1992, chmn. bd. dirs. 1993), Am. Phys. Soc. (Leo Szilard award for Physics in Pub. Interest 1979), Am. Geophys. Union (Roger Revelle medal 1994); mem. NAS (bd. environ. studies and toxicology 1986-91, com. on atmospheric chemistry 1987-89, com. atmospheric scis., solar-terrestial com. 1979-83, co-DATA com. 1977-82, sci. com. on problems environment 1986-89, Infinite Voyage film com. 1988-92, Robertson Meml. lectr. 1993, chmn. com. on internat. orgns. and programs 1993—, chmn. office of internat. affairs 1994—, co-chmn. interacad. panel 1995—), Am. Acad. Arts and Scis., Am. Chem. Soc. (chmn. divsn. nuclear sci. and tech. 1973-74, chmn. divsn. phys. chemistry 1974-75, Tolman medal 1976, Zimmerman award 1980, E.F. Smith lectureship 1980, Environ. Sci. and Tech. award 1983, Esselen award 1987, Peter Debye Phys. Chem. award 1993), Am. Philos. Soc., Inst. Medicine. Home: 4807 Dorchester Rd Corona Del Mar CA 92625-2718 Office: U Calif Irvine Dept of Chemistry 571 PS1 Irvine CA 92697-2025

ROWLAND, RUTH GAILEY, retired hospital official; b. Salt Lake City, Dec. 7, 1922; d. Frederick George and Lucy Jane (Hill) N.; m. Joseph David Gailey, Apr. 9, 1942 (dec. July 1984); children: Sherylynne Harris-Roth, Joseph David Jr., Robert Nelson; m. Joseph Brigham Rowland, Oct. 14, 1986. Student, Felt-Tarrant Community Coll., Salt Lake City, 1941-42, U. Utah. Dir. vol. svcs., pub. rels. dir. Lakeview Hosp., Bountiful, Utah, 1961-92. Mem. com. Women's State Legis. Coun., Salt Lake City, 1970-92; mem. legis. com. Utah Comprehensive Planning Agy., Salt Lake City; mem. Farmington (Utah) Bd. Health, 1979-85; mem. Davis County Adv. Bd. Volunteerism; mem. social svcs. com. LDS Ch. Recipient Total Citizen award Utah C. of C., 1992. Mem. Assn. Dirs. Vol. Svcs. of Am. Hosp. Assn., Utah Assn. Vol. Auxs. (pres.), Utah Dirs. Vol. Svcs. (pres.), Salt Lake Dental Aux. (pres.), Bountiful C. of C. (bd. dirs. 1975-80), Soromipimists. Republican. Home: 871 S 750 E Bountiful UT 84010-3824

ROWLEY, MAXINE LEWIS, home economics educator, writer; b. Provo, Utah, Sept. 23, 1938; d. Max Thomas Lewis and Illa Lewis Sanford; BA (Ford Found. scholar), Brigham Young U., 1960; BS, U. Utah, 1974; MA, Utah State U., 1980; PhD in Edn. Adminstrn. Brigham Young U., 1989; m. Arthur William Rowley, Sept. 23, 1960; children: Anne, Jenefer. Promotion writer sta. KCPX-TV, 1960; extension home economist USDA, 1961; mgmt. trainee Deseret Book Co., Salt Lake City, 1969; chmn. dept. Patricia Stevens Career Coll., Salt Lake City, 1970; chmn. consumer and homemaking dept. Weber Sch. Dist., Roy, Utah, 1975, learning experience designer, 1976-78; mem. consumer and homemaking faculty Utah State U., Logan, 1978-79, spl. appointee to Utah State U. by Utah State Bd. Edn., 1978-86, cons. Utah Vocat. Bd. Edn., instrumental writer Utah State U. Found., 1979; mem. Faculty Brigham Young U., 1979; intern Gladys Chalkley/Brannegan Chalkley Am. Home Econs. Assn., 1993. Author filmstrips, texts and teachers guide CHECS, 1979; author curriculum guide Operation: Free Enterprise, 1982; author curriculum on food sci., nutrition, 1990, 92, 93. Active ward, stake and region positions Ch. of Jesus Christ of Latter-day Saints; leader 4-H Club, mem. councils and adv. bds.; leader Girl Scouts U.S.A., Young Homemakers; mem. State Text Book Evaluation Com., 1978-86, U. Utah Evaluation Com., 1979; mem. edn. and rsch. com. Am. Cancer Soc., State of Utah, 1993, 94. Named Outstanding Leader Am. Edn., 1976, Nat. Tchr. of Yr., 1977, Outstanding Tchr. in Dept., Brigham Young U., 1984-94, Outstanding Vocat. Edn. Leader State of Utah, 1996. Mem. Nat. Assn. Vocat. Home Econs. Tchrs., Am. Home Econs. Assn. (contbr., author yearbook 1984, Nat. Leadership award 1993), Am. Assn. Family and Consumer Scis. (nat. v.p. 1995-97, nat. bd. dirs. 1995-97, nat. chair ann. meeting 1995-97, bd. liason publs. 1995-97), Am. Vocat. Assn., NEA, Utah Home Econs. Assn., Utah Vocat. Assn., Utah Council for Improvement of Edn., Utah Nutrition Coun. (chair 1995), Utah Edn. Assn. (award for womens' awareness task force project 1976), County Welfare Com., Home Econs. Edn. Assn., Vocat. Home Econs. Tchrs. (nat. chmn. public rels. and legis. coms. 1978), White Key (pres. 1960), Kappa Omicron Nu, Omicron Nu (nat. endowment honoree 1989), Phi Kappa Phi, Spurs, Gamma Phi Omicron. Home: PO Box 839 West Jordan UT 84084-0839

ROY, LISA RAI, education program administrator; b. Balt., Aug. 31, 1963; d. STephen Eugene Smith, Sr. and Brenda Ann (Harris) Sagee; m. James Wibur Roy, Sr., Dec. 22, 1984; children: James Wilbur, II, Amanda Brianne, Jason Wesley. AA, C.C. Aurora, Colo., 1992; BA, Met. State Coll., Denver, 1994; MA, Univ. Colo., 1996. Pre-sch. tchr. Denver Pub. Schs., 1991-92; customer svc. rep. Columbia Savings, Denver, 1992-93, First Interstate Bank, Denver, 1993-94; student tour rep., admissions rep. Met. State Coll., Denver, 1994; facilitator children's group Family Cmty. Edn. Support, Denver, 1994; coord. early childhood program AmeriCorps, Clayton Found., Denver, 1994—; panel mem. Paretn Edn. Support Programs: a Closer Look, 1995. Mem. bd. dirs. New Beginnings Statewide Adv., Denver, 1994—, Colo. Office Resource Referral, Englewood, 1995—, Met. State Coll. Psychology Cmty. Adv. Bd., Denver, 1995—, Colo. Parent Info. Resource Ctr., Denver, 1994—, Colo. Juvenile Firesetter Prevention Program, Denver, 1995—; participant Denver Cmty. Leadership Forum, 1996. Recipient Gov.'s citation State Colo., 1995, Barbara Jordan Inspirational award African Am. Affairs Coun., Met. State Coll., 1995; grantee Univ. Colo., 1995-96. Mem. Am. Counseling Assn. Democrat. Office: Clayton Found 3801 Martin Luther King Blvd Denver CO 80205-4972

ROY, RAYMOND, bishop; b. Man., Can., May 3, 1919; s. Charles-Borromé e and Zephirina (Milette) R. B.A. in Philosophy and Theology, U. Man., 1942; student, Philos. Sem., Montreal, 1942-43, Major Sem., Montreal, 1943-46, Major Sem. St. Boniface, 1946-47. Ordained priest Roman Catholic Ch. 1947. Asst. pastor, then pastor chs. in Man., 1947-50, 53-66; chaplain St. Boniface (Man.) Hosp., 1950-53; superior Minor Sem., St. Boniface, 1966-69; pastor Cathedral Parish, St. Boniface, 1969-72; ordained bishop, 1972; bishop of St. Paul, Alta., Can., 1972—. Club: K.C. Address: 4410 51st Ave Box 339, Saint Paul, AB Canada T0A 3A0*

ROY, RAYMOND ALBERT, JR., pharmacist; b. Matewan, W.Va., Mar. 3, 1954; s. Raymond Albert and Mary (Howerton) R. B.S. in Pharmacy, W.Va. U., 1977. Registered pharmacist, Va., W.Va., N.C., S.C., Nev. Pharmacist Strosnider Drug Co., Williamson, W.Va., 1977-78; pharmacy mgr. Rite Aid Pharmacy, Morgantown, W.Va., 1978-80; pharmacist in charge, pharmacy mgr. K Mart Pharmacy, Lynchburg, Va., 1980-88, Las Vegas, 1988—; elder care and child care pharmacist Park-Davis Pharms., Morris Plains, N.J., 1985—. Recipient Pharmacy Edn. Program award Burroughs Wellcome Co., 1982. Mem. Am. Pharm. Assn., Nev. Pharmacist Assn. Roman Catholic. Home: 2713 Saint Clair Dr Las Vegas NV 89128-7296 Office: K Mart Pharmacy 3680 3760 E Sunset Rd Las Vegas NV 89120-3233

ROY, WILLIAM GLENN, sociology educator; b. Rochester, N.Y., Mar. 22, 1946; s. James Rider and Nona Alice (Monks) R.; m. Alice Madeleine Royer, Apr. 3, 1976; children: Margaret Alice, Joseph Edward. BA, Emory U., 1968; PhD, U. Mich., 1977. Prof. UCLA, 1976—. Author: Socializing Capital: The Rise of the Large Industrial Corporation in America, 1997. Woodrow Wilson fellow, 1968; rsch. grantee NSF, 1987. Mem. Phi Beta Kappa. Office: UCLA Dept Sociology Los Angeles CA 90024

ROYBAL-ALLARD, LUCILLE, congresswoman; b. Boyle Heights, Calif., June 12, 1941; d. Edward Roybal; m. Edward T. Allard; 4 children. BA, Calif. State U., L.A. Former mem. Calif. State Assembly; mem. 103rd Congress from 33rd Calif. dist., 1993—; mem. Banking and Fin. Svcs., Budget Com. Office: Ho of Reps 2435 Rayburn Washington DC 20515

ROYCE, EDWARD R. (ED ROYCE), congressman; b. Los Angeles, Oct. 12, 1951; m. Marie Porter. BA, Calif. State U., Fullerton. Tax mgr. Southwestern Portland Cement Co.; mem. Calif. Senate, 1983-93, 103rd Congress from 39th dist. Calif., 1993—; vice chmn. Public Employment and Retirement Com.; mem. Bus. and Profs. com., Indsl. Rels. com.; legis. author, campaign co-chmn. Proposition 15 Crime Victims/Speedy Trial Initiative; author nation's 1st felony stalking law, bill creating Foster Family Home Ins. Fund, legis. creating foster parent recruitment and tng. program; mem. Banking and Fin. Svcs. Com., Internat. Rels. Com. Named Legis. of Yr. Orange County Rep. Com., 1986, Child Adv. of Yr. Calif. Assn. Svc. for Children, 1987. Mem. Anaheim C. of C. Republican. Office: US Ho of Reps 1113 Longworth Ho Office Bldg Washington DC 20515-0539*

ROYER, VICTOR HENRY, marketing consultant, author; b. Prague, Czech Republic, June 6, 1955; s. Georgina Sidonia Lukas Royer. BA in Philosophy, U. Melbourne, Australia, 1978; MA in Philosophy, U. Wollongong, Australia, 1982. Advt. asst. Melbourne, Australia, 1972-73; sales exec., 1974; writer/prodr./personality ABC Radio, 1975-76; writer/prodr./ presenter radio show, 1978; advt. cons., writer/designer Fairfax Press, Australia, 1981-83, Olympic Games fgn. corres., 1984; staff writer Sta. KCOP-13 TV, L.A., 1984; art dir. L.A. Songwriters Showcase, 1984; mgr. creative svcs., writer promotional material Beverly Hills, Calif., 1985-86; prodn. coord. and buyer Ridesharing Orgn., L.A., 1986-89; pres., ptnr. Premier Gaming, Las Vegas, Nev., 1994—; pres. Exec. Data Info. Svcs., Las Vegas, 1993—; pres. MRM Entertainment, Inc., Hollywood, Calif., 1989-90; creative and mktg. cons. Weddle/Caldwell Advt. Agy., Las Vegas, Nev., 1990; comml. mktg. cons. and writer/prodr./dir. TV commls., comml. video, Las Vegas, 1990—; gaming corr., nat. gaming mags., 1985—; gaming cons. and spkr., Las Vegas, 1993—; judge prime time Emmy awards Acad. TV Arts and Scis., Hollywood, 1987-94. Author: Play Smart and Win, 1994; contbr. numerous articles to profl. jours. Home: 257 El Camino Verde Henderson NV 89014 Office: MRM Entertainment Inc 269 S Beverly Dr Ste 146 Beverly Hills CA 90212

ROYLE, ANTHONY WILLIAM, accountant; b. Corona, Calif., Dec. 22, 1956; s. William Lloyd Royle and Patricia Rae (McGahan) Magda; m. Patricia Jean Blaylcok, Aug. 13, 1977 (div. Nov. 1983); children: Nicholas Anthony, Elizabeth Marie. BS in Acctg., Weber State U., 1979. CPA, N.Mex. Sr. tax acct. Fox & Co. CPA, Farmington, N.Mex., 1981-83; tax mgr. Cox & Co. CPA, Farmington, 1983-85; tax supr. Arthur Young, Albuquerque, 1985-87; tax supr., tax mgr. Neff & Co., Albuquerque, 1987-95, tax ptnr., 1995—; advisor for Sound Advice C. of C., Albuquerque, 1996—. With U.S. Army, 1974-76. Mem. AICPA (tax divsn.), N.Mex. Soc. CPA, Constrn. Fin. Mgmt. Assn. (Albuquerque chpt.). Office: Neff & Co LLP 7001 Prospect Pl NE Albuquerque NM 87110

ROZARIO, GWENDOLYN MICHELLE, educator; b. San Francisco, Dec. 14, 1954; children: Alicia, Alexander Jr. BA, U. San Francisco, 1976; Master's degree, Coll. Notre Dame, 1991; Doctorate, U. San Francisco, 1995. Lifetime tchg. credential. Tchr. San Francisco Unified Sch. Dist., 1977-81, Hanford (Calif.) Elem., 1981-85, Ravenswood Sch. Dist., East Palo Alto, 1985-89, San Lorenzo (Calif.) Unified Sch. Dist., 1989-92, Madera (Calif.) Unified Sch. Dist., 1992—; instr. Merced (Calif.) C.C., 1994—; grant-writing cons. Gwen's Consulting Firm, Madera. Author: (handbook) An Analysis of the Madera Unified School District New Teacher Induction Program, 1995. Recipient Comty. Svc. award Martin Luther King Found., 1992. Mem. USN Sea Cadet Corp. (ednl. svc. officer 1995—), Phi Delta Kappa. Home: 2340 W Cleveland Ave # 143 Madera CA 93637-8710

ROZEN, LELAND ALLEN, newspaper publishing executive; b. Aberdeen, Wash., Dec. 26, 1948; s. William Henry and Esther Alice (Argent) R.; m. Sydney Lee Craft, Nov. 27, 1971; children: Geoffrey Lee, Amanda Colette. BA in Comm., U. Wash., 1975. Reporter, copy editor, copy desk chief The Columbian, Vancouver, Wash., 1971-84; from copy editor, sr. news editor, asst. mng. editor Seattle Post-Intelligencer, 1984-96, mgr. of new media, 1996—; mem. U. Wash. Bd. Student Publs., Seattle, 1991-95; coll rev. team Pacific N.W. Newspaper Assn. Editor: (book) A Magic Season, 1995; editor (periodical) P-I News for Kids, 1988-94. Mem. Soc. Profl. Journalists, NAA New Media Fedn. Office: Seattle Post Intelligencer 101 Elliott Ave W Seattle WA 98119-4220

ROZENFELD, KIM DAVID, television company executive and producer; b. L.A., Dec. 19, 1964; s. Louis Leon and Evelyn (Fine) R. BA, UCLA, 1986. Asst. to mgrs. current comedy NBC, Burbank, Calif., 1986-87; assoc.

prodr. Columbia TV, Hollywood, Calif., 1990-91, Warner Bros. TV, Burbank, 1994-95; prodr. Walt Disney TV, Burbank, 1992-94; dir. series devel. Columbia Tristar TV, Culver City, Calif., 1995—; prodn. cons. Activision, Inc., L.A., 1993, Rysher Entertainment, Burbank, 1995. Author teleplays My Two Dads, 1989, Press Box, 1993; dir. TV series Dinosaurs, 1991-94. Mem. SAG, Acad. TV Arts and Scis., UCLA Alumni Assn. Democrat. Jewish. Home: 632 Ocean Park Blvd Apt 6 Santa Monica CA 90405

RUBALD, TERRY ELLEN, state official; b. Riverton, Wyo., Nov. 12, 1953; d. Dale Brice Trubey and Elizabeth Frances (Sheldon) Knapp; m. Timothy Mark Rubald, July 1, 1978; 1 child, Lawrence Sheldon. BSBA with honor, U. Wyo., 1976. Cert. permanent property tax appraiser, Wyo. Adminstr. lease records Am. Nuclear Corp., Casper, Wyo., 1977-79; land agt. Gulf Mineral Resources, Denver, 1979-80; owner, operator Mateo Village, Sundance, Wyo., 1980-89; county assessor Crook County, Sundance, 1987-91; mem. Wyo. Bd. Equalization, Cheyenne, 1991-97, chmn., 1995-97. Past pres. Crook County Rep. Women; current pres. Laramie County Rep. Women; former chmn. Crook County Rep. Ctrl. Com., 1991; bd. dirs., treas., past pres. Devils Tower Tourism Assn., 1984-91; treas. troop 116 Boy Scouts Am., Cheyenne, 1994-97; pub. rels. com. Cheyenne Frontier Days, 1994-97. Recipient Honor Book for excellence in field mgmt. bus. adminstrn. dept. U. Wyo.; scholar Wyo. H.H., Bugas law scholar. Mem. Internat. Assn. Assessing Officers, Wyo. County Assessors Assn. (pres. 1990-91), U. Wyo. Alumnae Assn. (bd. dirs. 1985-89), Cheyenne Lions (3rd v.p.). Methodist. Office: Wyo Bd Equalization Herschler Bldg Cheyenne WY 82003

RUBENDALL, RICHARD ARTHUR, civil engineer; b. Pierre, S.D., Sept. 24, 1957; s. Quentin Theodore and Doris (Noe) R. BSCE, S.D. Sch. Mines & Tech., 1979; postgrad., U. N. Mex. Registered profl. engr., Mont., Ariz. Field engr. USPHS/Indian Health Svc., Lame Deer, Mont., 1979-86; sr. field engr. USPHS/Indian Health Svc., Many Farms, Ariz., 1986-89; sr. field engr. USPHS/Indian Health Svc., Sells, Ariz., 1989-90, dist. engr., 1990-93; dist. engr. USPHS/Indian Health Svc., Tucson, Ariz., 1993—. Comdr. USPHS, 1979—. Recipient USPHS Isolated Hardship award, 1980, 84, 88, 91, USPHS Hazardous Duty award 1984, USPHS Citation with plaque, 1990, USPHS Achievement medal, 1985; named Indian Health Svc. Engr. of Yr., Tucson area, 1990. Mem. ASCE, Am. Water Works Assn., Water Environment Fedn., USPHS Commd. Officers Assn. (pres. Tucson chpt. 1993-95, nat. recorder 1995-96, pres.-elect 1996-97), Res. Officers Assn., Assn. Mil. Surgeons U.S. Home: 6944 E 42nd St Tucson AZ 85730-1626 Office: USPHS 7900 South J Stock Rd Tucson AZ 85746-9352

RUBENSTEIN, LEONARD SAMUEL, communications executive, ceramist, painter, sculptor, photographer; b. Rochester, N.Y., Sept. 22, 1918; s. Jacob S. and Zelda H. (Gordon) R.; m. (dec. 1983); children: Carolinda, Eric, Harley. BFA cum laude, Alfred U., 1939; student Case Western Res. U., 1938; postgrad. U. Rochester, 1940-41. Creative dir. Henry Hempstead Advt. Agy., Chgo., 1949-55; v.p., exec. art dir. Clinton E. Frank Advt. Agy., Chgo., 1955-63; v.p., nat. creative dir. Foster & Kleiser divsn. Metromedia, Inc., L.A., 1967-73, v.p. corp. creative cons., Metromedia, Inc., L.A., 1973-88; guest lectr. U. Chgo.; instr. Columbia Coll., Chgo.; past. pres. Art Dirs. Club Chgo. (spl. citation); instr. Fashion Inst., L.A.; lectr. in field. Mem. Soc. Typog. Arts (past dir.), Am. Ceramic Soc. (design chpt.), Am. Craft Coun., Inst. Outdoor Advt. (mem. past plans bd.), L.A. County Mus. Art, Mus. Contemporary Art of L.A. (charter), Palos Verdes (Calif.) Art Ctr., B'nai B'rith, Phi Epsilon Pi. Author: (with Charles Hardison) Outdoor Advertising; contbr. articles to profl. publs.; one-man show at Calif. Mus. Sci. and Industry, 1970; two-person exhibition of porcelains, Palos Verdes Art Ctr., 1987; participant nat. and regional group shows; creator concept for Smithsonian exhibition Images of China: East and West, 1982; writer-prodr. (ednl. video) Paul Soldner, Thoughts on Creativity, 1989, (video documentary) High-Tech/Low-Tech: The Science and Art of Ceramics, 1994; porcelains in permanent collections. Home and Office: 30616 Ganado Dr Rancho Palos Verdes CA 90275 *Personal philosophy: I have a disdain for the trendy, the superficial and the transient.*

RUBIN, BRUCE I., newspaper editor, geologist; b. Bklyn., Oct. 14, 1942; s. Lazarus and Lillian (Zadikow) R.; m. Leona Molotch, Sept. 6, 1965 (div. July 1985); children: Jefferson Scott, Melissa Pam. BS in Geology, Bklyn. Coll., 1964; postgrad., Rutgers U., 1964-65. Geologist Teton Exploration Drilling Co., Casper, Wyo., 1968-76, GPU Svc. Corp., Albuquerque, 1976-79, C&K Petroleum, Denver, 1980-83; geol. cons. Pine Mountain Resources, Evergreen, Colo., 1983-92; editor Limon (Colo.) Leader, 1992, Winter Park (Colo.) Manifest, 1992-94, Sheridan (Wyo.) County Roundup, 1995-97; editor, pub. Cavalier County Rep., Langdon, N.D., 1995; editor Pay Dirt Mag., Bisbee, Ariz., 1997—. Author: Uranium Foll Front Zonation in the Southern Powder River Basin, Wyoming, 1970, The Contessa's Legacy, 1992, (novel) The Contessa's Legacy, 1992, (screenplays) The Ides of October, 1993, Marmalade Chameleon, 1994; editor Pay Dirt Mag., Bisbee, Ariz., 1997—; contbr. articles to profl. publs. Chmn. Wyo. Young Ams. for Freedom, Casper, 1970-72. Home: Box 756 Bisbee AZ 85603

RUBIN, JONATHAN, government relations consultant; b. Topeka, Kans., Feb. 19, 1949; s. Sidney and Claire (Bodian) R.; m. Diane Kefauver, Dec. 27, 1981; children: Benjamin Estes, David Bodian. BA, Syracuse U., 1971. Mem. nat. field staff McGovern for Pres., 1972; pvt. cons. Calif., 1972-76; field staff dir. Carter for Pres., Calif., 1976, 80; polit. dir. Calif. Dem. Party, 1978-81; pres. Rubin/Kefauver Assocs., San Francisco, 1981-87; chief of staff State Senator Quentin Kopp, Sacramento, 1988-91; ptnr. Bay Rels., San Francisco, 1991—; bd. dirs. CalTrain/Joint Powers Bd., 1992—, commr. Met. Transp. Commn., 1995—; exec. dir. Coalition Colena Cemeteries. Creator, commentator TV for San Francisco Giants It Came From Left Field mag. show, 1988, 89; film and theater reviewer San Francisco Bus. Times, 1977-78. Bd. dirs. Bread and Roses, Mill Valley, Calif., 1989-93; founding bd. dirs. Bay Area Transportation Alliance; mem. Bay Bridge Design Task Force, 1997—. Mem. Masons (3 deg.). Office: Bay Rels 2171 Junipero Serra Blvd Daly City CA 94014-1980

RUBIN, KENNETH HOWARD, geochemistry educator, artist; b. Sherman Oaks, Calif., July 11, 1962; s. Sheldon and Ann Rene (Lustgarten) R. BA in Chemistry, U. Calif., San Diego, 1984, MS in Oceanography, 1985, PhD in Earth Sci., 1991. Rsch. asst. Scripps Inst. Oceanography U. Calif.-San Diego, La Jolla, 1984-91, postdoctoral rschr. Scripps Inst. Oceanography, 1991-92; asst. rschr. Sch. Ocean and Earth Sci. and Tech. U. Hawaii, Honolulu, 1992-94, asst. prof. Sch. Ocean and Earth Sci. and Tech., 1994—; vis. scientist Lawrence Livermore (Calif.) Nat. Lab., 1988-90; rschr. Hawaii Ctr. for Volcanology, Honolulu, 1992—; mem. NSF-RIDGE program, 1991—; presentor sci. papers in field. Two person show Mandeville Gallery, U. Calif., San Diego, 1984, group show, 1984; contbr. sci. publs. to profl. jours. Mem. numerous environ. orgns., 1984—. Rsch. grantee NSF, 1993, 94, 96, State of Hawaii, 1993, 94. mem. Am. Geophys. Union, Geol. Soc. Am., Am. Chem. Soc. Office: U Hawaii Sch Ocean & Earth Sci & Tech 2525 Correa Rd Honolulu HI 96822-2219

RUBINFIEN, ELISABETH SEPORA, journalist; b. Chgo., Mar. 29, 1957; d. David and Shulamith (Schultz) R.; m. Daniel Charles Sneider, Oct. 25, 1987; children: Noah Richard, Benjamin Julian. BA, Pomona Coll., 1978; MS, Columbia U., 1984. Rschr. City of Hope, Duarte, Calif., 1978-79; v.p. Daruma, Inc., Palo Alto, Calif., 1979-90; assoc. prodr./dir. Constance Marks Films, N.Y.C., 1980-83; corr., Tokyo Reuters, 1984-87, Wall St. Jour., 1987-90; freelancer/journalist Tokyo & Moscow, 1985—; corr., Moscow Wall St. Jour. Europe, Russia, 1990-94; lectr. Stanford (Calif.) U., 1995; asst. bus. editor San Jose (Calif.) Mercury News, 1995—; consulting/speaking engagements, 1987—. Co-rschr. Final Biochem. Genetics, 1979. Sec. Fgn. Correspondents Club of Japan, Tokyo, 1989. Fellow John S. Knight Fellowships, Stanford, Calif., 1994-95, U.S.-Japan Friendship Comm., N.Y.C. and Tokyo, 1983-85. Mem. Internat. House of Japan. Jewish. Office: San Jose Mercury News 750 Ridder Park Dr. San Jose CA 95131

RUBY, ALLEN JOEL, lawyer; b. Detroit, July 3, 1945; s. Bert and Irene (Feder) R.; m. Cynthia, Dec. 30, 1972; children: Sarah, Daniel. BA, Mich. State U., 1965; JD, Stanford U., 1969. Ptnr. Morgan, Ruby, Schofield, Franich & Fredkin, San Jose, Calif., 1970-95, Ruby & Schofield, San Jose, Calif., 1995—; judge pro tem Santa Clara Superior Ct., San Jose, 1987-91; presenter in field. Mem. Am. Bd. Trial Advocates, Trial Lawyers for Pub. Justice. Office: Ruby & Schofield 60 S Market St Ste 1500 San Jose CA 95113

RUBY, CHARLES LEROY, law educator, lawyer, civic leader; b. Carthage, Ind., Dec. 28, 1900; s. Edgar Valentine and Mary Emma (Butler) R.; certificate Ball State U., 1921-22; AB, Cen. Normal Coll., 1924, LLB, 1926, BS, 1931, BPE, 1932; MA, Stanford, 1929; JD, Pacific Coll. of Law, 1931; PhD, Olympic U., 1933; m. Rachael Elizabeth Martindale, Aug. 30, 1925; children: Phyllis Arline (Mrs. Norman Braskat), Charles L., Martin Dale. Prin., Pine Village (Ind.) High Sch., 1923-25; Glenwood (Ind.) Pub. Schs., 1925-26; tchr. El Centro (Calif.) Pub. Sch., 1926-27, Fresno Cen. (Calif.) Union High Sch., 1927-29; prof. law Fullerton Coll., 1929-66; prof. edn. Armstrong Coll., summer 1935, Cen. Normal Coll., summers 1929-33; admitted to Ind. bar, 1926, U.S. Supreme Ct. bar, 1970; pres. Ret. Service Vol. Program, North Orange County, Calif., 1973-76, 83-84; dir. North Orange County Vol. Bur., Fullerton Sr. Citizens Task Force. Life trustee, co-founder Continuing Learning Experiences program Calif. State U., Fullerton, hon. chmn. fund com. Gerontology Bldg; founder, dir. Fullerton Pub. Forum, 1929-39; founder Elks Nat. Found.; co-founder, benefactor Gerontology Ctr. Calif. State U., Fullerton; pres. Fullerton Rotary, 1939-40, hon. mem., 1983—; mem. U.S. Assay Commn., 1968—; mem. Orange County Dem. Cen. Com., 1962-78; bd. dirs. Fullerton Sr. Multi-purpose Ctr., 1981—; bd. dirs. Orange County Sr. Citizens Adv. Council; mem. pres.'s com. Calif. State U., Fullerton. Recipient Medal of Merit, Am. Numis. Assn., 1954, Spl. Commendation Calif. State Assembly, 1966, 88, Calif. State Senate, 1978, 86, Commendation Ind. Sec. of State, 1984, Commendation Bd. Suprs. Orange County, 1985, Commendation Fullerton City Council, 1986, 88, Commendation Orange County Bd. Supervisors, 1986, Commendation Calif. State Senate, 1986, Commendation Exec. Com. Pres. Calif. State U., Fullerton, 1986, Commendation Calif. gov., 1988; Charles L. and Rachael E. Ruby Gerontology Ctr. named in his and late wife's honor, Calif. State U., Fullerton. Fellow Ind. Bar Found.; mem. Pres. Assocs. Calif. State U. Fullerton, Fullerton Coll. Assocs. (named Spl. Retiree of Yr. 1986, Commendation 1986), Calif. (life, pres. So. sect. 1962-63, treas. 1964-65, pres. 1960-61, dir. 1956-65), pres. Fullerton Secondary Tchrs. Assn., Orange County Tchrs. Assn. (pres. 1953-55), Fullerton Coll. (pres. 1958-60) Tchrs. Assn., NEA (life), Ind. Bar Assn., Stanford U. Law Soc., Calif. State Council Edn., Am. Numismatic Assn. (gov. 1951-53, life adv. bd.), Ind. Bar Assn. (hon. life, Golden Career award 1983), Calif. Bus. Educators Assn. (hon. life), Calif. Assn. Univ. Profs., Pacific S.W. Bus. Law Assn. (pres. 1969-70, life), Numismatic Assn. So. Calif. (life, pres. 1961), Calif. Numis. Assn., Indpls. Coin Club (hon. life), Los Angeles Coin Club (hon. life), U.S. Supreme Ct. Hist. Soc., Calif. Town Hall, North Orange County Mus. Assn. (life, benefactor dir.), Stanford U. Alumni Assn. (life), Old Timers Assay Commn. (life), Fullerton Archeology (hon. life, benefactor dir.). Methodist. Clubs: Elks, Fullerton Coll. Vets. (hon. life). Contbr. articles in field to profl. jours. Home: 308 Marwood Ave Fullerton CA 92832-1139

RUCH, CHARLES P., academic administrator; b. Longbranch, N.J., Mar. 25, 1938; s. Claud C. and Marcella (Pierce) R.; m. Sally Joan Brandenburg, June 18, 1960; children: Cheryl, Charles, Christopher, Cathleen. BA, Coll. of Wooster, 1959; MA, Northwestern U., 1960, PhD, 1966. Counselor, tchr. Evanston (Ill.) Twp. High Sch., 1960-66; asst. prof. U. Pitts., 1966-70, assoc. prof., dept. chmn., 1970-74; assoc. dean sch. edn. Va. Commonwealth U., Richmond, 1974-76, dean sch. edn., 1976-85, interim provost, v.p., 1985-86, provost, v.p., 1986-93; pres. Boise (Idaho) State U., 1993—; cons. various univs., govtl. agys., ednl. founds. Author or co-author over 50 articles, revs., tech. reports. Mem. Am. Psychol. Assn., Am. Ednl. Research Assn., Phi Delta Kappa. Office: Boise State U 1910 University Dr Boise ID 83725-0001

RUCKER, THOMAS DOUGLAS, purchasing executive; b. Ottumwa, Iowa, Aug. 30, 1926; s. Everett Henry and Harriett Mary (Evans) R.; A.B., Loyola U., 1951; postgrad. St. Patrick's Coll., 1950-52; m. Rita Mary Rommelfanger, Apr. 18, 1953; children—David, Theresa, Martin, Paul. Asst. purchasing agt. Radio TV Supply, Los Angeles, 1952-53; buyer Consol. Western Steel div. U.S. Steel, Commerce, Calif., 1953-64, S.W. Welding & Mfg. Co., Alhambra, Calif., 1964-70; dir. purchasing Sr. Engring. (formerly Southwestern Engring.), Commerce, Calif., 1970-87, ret. Served with USAAF, 1945-46. Home: 330 W Central Ave Brea CA 92821-3029 Office: Sr Engring 5701 S Eastern Ave Ste 300 Los Angeles CA 90040-2934

RUDE, MAUREEN JOY, state agency administrator; b. East Lansing, Mich., Apr. 26, 1962; d. William Raymond Lassey and Marion Hogarty (Lassey) Rosa; m. Mathew Charles Rude, Aug. 11, 1959. BSBA, U. Mont., 1985. CPA, Mont. Resident asst. U. Mont., Missoula, 1982-83; clk. UPS, Missoula, 1983-86; fin. compliance auditor Legis. Auditor, Helena, Mont., 1986-87, performance auditor, sr. performance auditor, 1987-92; multifamily program mgr. Bd. of Housing, Helena, 1992-95; adminstr. housing divsn., exec. dir. Bd. of Housing Dept. Commerce, Helena, 1995—. tutor, mentor Helena Pub. Schs./Hosts, 1992—; mem. Helena Jaycees, 1991-92; vol. Helena Jazz Festivals/Rocky Mountain Elk Found., Helena, 1990—. Named Outstanding New Jaycee of Quar., Helena Jaycees, 1991. Mem. Nat. Coun. State Housing Agys. Office: Mont Bd Housing Housing Divsn 836 Front St Helena MT 59620-0528

RUDER, MELVIN HARVEY, retired newspaper editor; b. Manning, N.D., Jan. 19, 1915; s. Moris M. and Rebecca (Friedman) R.; m. Ruth Bergan, Feb. 10, 1950; 1 dau., Patricia E. Morton. B.A., U. N.D., 1937, M.A., 1941; grad. student, Northwestern U., 1940. Asst. prof. journalism U. N.D., 1940; indsl. relations specialist Westinghouse Electric Co., Sharon, Pa., 1940-41; pub. relations with Am. Machine & Foundry Co., N.Y.C., 1946; founder, editor Hungry Horse News, Columbia Falls, Mont., 1946-78; editor emeritus Hungry Horse News, 1978—. Chmn. adv. coun. Flathead Nat. Forest, Dist. 6 Sch. Bd., 1967-70; pres. Buffalo Hill Terr. Resident Coun., 1997. Served to lt. (s.g.) USNR, 1942-45. Recipient Pulitzer prize for gen. local reporting, 1965. Mem. Mont. Press Assn. (pres. 1957), Flathead Associated C. of C. (pres. 1971), Glacier Natural History Assn. (pres. 1983). Home: Buffalo Hill Terr 40 Claremont Kalispell MT 59901

RUDIBAUGH, MELINDA CAMPBELL, mathematics educator; b. Indiana, Pa., Feb. 25, 1948; d. Steele Evans and Kathryn Norine (Grater) C.; m. Jerry Rudibaugh, Dec. 5, 1970; children: Amy, Evan. BS in Edn., Indiana (Pa.) U., 1970; M Natural Sci., Arizona State U., 1981, postgrad.; postgrad., No. Arizona U., Ariz. State U. Tchr. sci., math. Western Christian High, Phoenix, Ariz., 1979-80, Phoenix Hebrew Sch., 1980-81; instr. math. Arizona State U., Tempe, 1980-84, Maricopa C.C., Phoenix, 1981-89, Chandler-Gilbert C.C., Chandler, Ariz., 1989—; instr. Ottawa U. Vol. March of Dimes, 1988—, Am. Cancer Soc., 1989—; advisor Phi Theta Kappa, Chandler-Gilbert C.C., 1993. 2d lt. USAF, 1970-71. Mem. ASCD, Nat. Coun. Tchrs. Math., Math. Assn. Am., Am. Math. Assn. Two-Yr. Colls., Am. Assn. Higher Edn., Ariz. Assn. Supervision and Curriculum Devel., Phi Delta Kappa, Phi Kappa Phi. Republican. Home: 10417 S 46th Way Phoenix AZ 85044-1112 Office: Chandler Gilbert C C 2626 E Pecos Rd Chandler AZ 85225-2413

RUDIN, ANNE NOTO, former mayor, nurse; b. Passaic, N.J., Jan. 27, 1924; m. Edward Rudin, June 6, 1948; 4 children. BS in Edn., Temple U., 1945, RN, 1946; MPA, U. So. Calif., 1983; LLD (hon.), Golden Gate U., 1990. RN, Calif. Mem. faculty Temple U. Sch. Nursing, Phila., 1946-48; mem. nursing faculty Mt. Zion Hosp., San Francisco, 1948-49; mem. Sacramento City Council, 1971-83; mayor City of Sacramento, 1983-92; ind. pub. policy cons. Pres. LWV, Riverside, 1957, Sacramento, 1961, Calif., 1969-71, Calif. Elected Women's Assn., 1973—; trustee Golden Gate U., 1993-96; mem. adv. bd. U. So. Calif., Army Depot Reuse Commn., 1992-94; bd. dirs. Sacramento Theatre Co., Sacramento Symphony, 1003-96, Calif. Common Cause, 1993-96, Japan Soc. No. Calif., Sacramento Edn. Found.; v.p. Sacramento Traditional Jazz Soc. Found. Recipient Women in Govt. award U.S. Jaycee Women, 1984, Woman of Distinction award Sacramento Area Soroptimist Clubs, 1985, Civic Contbn. award LWV Sacramento, 1989, Woman of Courage award Sacramento History Ctr., 1989, Peacemaker of Yr. award Sacramento Mediation Ctr., 1992, Regional Pride award Sacramento Mag., 1993, Humanitarian award Japanese Am. Citizen's League, 1993, Outstanding Pub. Svc. award Am. Soc. Pub. Adminstrn., 1994; named Girl Scouts Am. Role model, 1989.

RUDIN, NORAH, forensic genetic consultant, science writer; b. N.Y.C., Nov. 10, 1957; d. Benjamin and Jenny (Sadovsky) R. BA, Pomona Coll., 1979; PhD, Brandeis U., 1987. Postdoctoral fellow Lawrence Berkeley Lab., Berkeley, Calif., 1987-90; cons. Calif. Dept. Justice DNA Lab., Berkeley, 1990-93; freelance sci. writer and forensic DNA cons. Richmond, Calif., 1994—. Co-author: DNA Demystified, 1994, An Introduction to Forensic DNA Analysis, 1997, Dictionary of Modern Biology, 1997; contbr. articles to profl. jours. Goldwyn fellow, 1981-85; NIH grantee, 1983-85. Mem. AFTRA, No. Calif. Sci. Writers Assn. Home and Office: 452 Key Blvd Richmond CA 94805-2428

RUDINSKY, NORMA LEIGH, English language educator, translator; b. Cedar City, Utah, Oct. 23, 1928; d. Wilford Webster and Anna Mae (Langford) Leigh; m. Julius A. Rudinsky, June 12, 1954 (dec. 1980); children: Helen Ann, Alexander John, Stephen Anthony, Paul Joseph, Michael Francis, Mary Louise. AB in English, Stanford (Calif.) U., 1950, AM in English, 1953; certs. in Slovak lang., Comenius U., Bratislava, Slovakia, 1981, 82, 84, 90. Sr. instr. English Oreg. State U., Corvallis, 1966—; lectr. in field. Author: Incipient Feminists, 1991; translator: Seven Slovak Stories by Martin Kukucin, 1980, That Alluring Land: Slovak Stories By Timrava, 1992 (Heldt Prize for Transl. 1993). Internat. Rsch. & Exch. Bd. fellow, 1982, 84, 86-87, Humanities Ctr. fellow, 1988. Mem. Am. Assn. Advancement Slavic Studies, Czechoslovak History Conf., Slovak Studies Assn. (v.p. 1984-86), Slovak Inst. Roman Catholic. Office: Oreg State U Dept Of English Corvallis OR 97331

RUDKIN, GEORGE HENRY, plastic surgeon; b. Wilmington, Del., July 29, 1964; s. George Osborne and Helene Rita (De Sanctis) R.; m. Jill Christine Brittenham, Sept. 30, 1995. BA, Johns Hopkins U., 1986; MD, Columbia U., 1990. Resident in gen. surgery UCLA Med. Ctr., 1990-96, resident in plastic surgery, 1996—. Mem. Alpha Omega Alpha, Phi Beta Kappa. Office: UCLA Med Ctr 10833 Le Conte Ave Los Angeles CA 90024-1602

RUDNICK, REBECCA SOPHIE, lawyer, educator; b. Bakersfield, Calif., Nov. 26, 1952; d. Oscar and Sophie Mary (Loven) R.; m. Robert Anthoine, Dec. 2, 1990. BA, Willamette U., Salem, Oreg., 1974; JD, U. Tex., 1978; LLM, NYU, 1984. Bar: Tex. 1978, La. 1979, N.Y. 1980, Calif. 1980. Law clk. to Hon. Charles Schwartz, Jr. U.S. Dist. Ct., New Orleans, 1978-79; assoc. Winthrop, Stimson, Putnam & Roberts, N.Y.C., 1979-85; spl. counsel N.Y. Legis. Tax Study Commn., N.Y.C., 1983-84; asst. prof. law Ind. U., Bloomington, 1985-90; assoc. prof. of law Ind. U. Sch. of Law, Bloomington, 1990-94; assoc. prof. law London Law Consortium, Eng., 1994; vis. assoc. prof. law U. Conn., Hartford, 1984-85; vis. asst. prof. law U. Tex., Austin, 1988; vis. assoc. prof. law U. N.C., Chapel Hill, 1991, Boston U., 1994-95, U. Pa., Phila., 1995-96; prof.-in-residence, IRS, 1991-92; vis. scholar NSW, Australia, 1994, U. Sydney, Australia, 1994; vis. prof. law Seattle U., 1996—. Contbr. articles to various profl. jours. and publs. Dir., gen. counsel Project GreenHope: Svcs. for Women, N.Y.C., 1980-83; advisor, tech. asst. Internat. Monetary Fund, Washington, 1994. Mem. ABA (tax sect. 1982—, sec. tax sect. passthrough entities task force 1986-88, subcom. chairs for incorps. and CLE/important devel. tax sect., 1989—, corp. tax com. 1989—, tax sect. task force on integration 1990—), Am. Assn. Law Schs. (editor tax sect. newsletter 1987—), Assn. Bar of City of N.Y. (admiralty com. 1982-85), Internat. Fiscal Assn., Internat. Bar Assn. Office: Seattle U Sch Law 950 Broadway Tacoma WA 98402-4405

RUDO, NEIL DENNIS, surgeon; b. White Plains, N.Y., Mar. 15, 1947; s. Milton and Roslind (Mandel) R.; m. Sandra Sandberg, Jan. 19, 1974; children: Kimber, Abraham. BA, Stanford U., 1969; MD, U. Chgo., 1975, PhD, 1975. Intern and residency in surgery U. Calif., San Francisco, 1975-80; fellow in vascular surgery Northwestern U., Chgo., 1980-81; attending surgeon Sequoia Hosp., Redwood City, Calif., 1981-88; clin. surgeon Stanford VA Hosp., Palo Alto, Calif., 1981-88; attending surgeon Salinas (Calif.) Valley Meml. Hosp., 1988—. Mem. Alpha Omega Alpha. Office: 110 John St Salinas CA 93901-3321

RUDOLPH, JEFFREY N., museum director. Exec. dir. California Museum of Science and Industry, Los Angeles, Calif. Office: Calif Mus Sci & Industry 700 State Dr Los Angeles CA 90037-1237*

RUDOLPH, RONALD ALVIN, human resources executive; b. Berwyn, Ill., May 12, 1949; s. Alvin J. and Gloria S. (Nicoletti) R. BA, U. Calif., Santa Cruz, 1971. Sr. cons. De Anza Assocs., San Jose, Calif., 1971-73; pers. adminstr. McDonnell Douglas Corp., Cupertino, Calif., 1974-75; employment rep. Fairchild Semiconductor, Mountain View, Calif., 1973-74, 75; compensation analyst Sperry Univac, Santa Clara, Calif., 1975-78; mgr. exempt compensation div. Intel Corp., Santa Clara, 1978-79, compensation mgr., 1979-82; dir. corp. compensation Intel Corp., 1982-85; v.p. human resources UNISYS Corp., San Jose, 1985-91, ASK Group Inc., Mountain View, Calif., 1991—; cons. Rudolph Assocs., Cupertino, 1982—; bd. dirs. Dynamic Temp. Svcs., Sunnyvale, Calif. Mem. Spl. Com. for Parolee Employment, Sacramento, 1973-75; bd. dirs. Jr. Achievement, San Jose, 1987-88. Mem. Am. Soc. Pers. Adminstrs., Am. Compensation Assn., No. Calif. Human Resources Coun. Office: ASK Computer Systems Inc PO Box 58013 2880 Scott Blvd Santa Clara CA 95050-2554

RUDOLPH, ROSS, surgeon, researcher, educator; b. Reading, Pa., Nov. 25, 1940; m. Nancy Taylor; children: Daniel, Rebecca, David, Susan. BA in Philosophy, Yale U., 1962; MD, Columbia U., 1966. Cert. Am. Bd. Plastic Surgery, Am. Bd. Surgery, Nat. Bd. Med. Examiners. Intern Hosp. of the U. of Pa., Phila., 1966-67; resident plastic and gen. surgery U. Hosp. of Cleve. and Case Western Res. U., 1969-74; asst. prof. plastic surgery Med. Coll. Wis., Milw., 1974-75; asst. prof. plastic surgery in residence U. Calif., San Diego, 1975-79, assoc. prof. plastic surgery in residence, 1979-80, assoc. adj. prof. plastic surgery, 1980-84, assoc. clin. prof. plastic surgery, 1984—; chief divsn. plastic surgery VA Hosp., San Diego, 1975-80; operating rm. com., pharmacy com. VA Hosp., La Jolla, 1976-79, tissue com., 1978-80; electives com., com. on edn. policy U. Calif. San Diego Sch. Medicine, 1976-79; cons. plastic surgery San Diego (Calif.) Zoo, 1977-79; med. risk mgmt. com. Univ. Hosp., 1977-79; rehab. com. Sharp Meml. Hosp., 1983-84; edn. com. Childrens Hosp., 1985-88; vis. prof. com. Plastic Surgery Ednl. Found., 1987-88; operating rm. com. Green Hosp. Scripps Clinic, 1987; reviewer various jours.; others. Contbr. articles to profl. jours. Chmn. health and scis. com. Torrey Pines dist. Boy Scouts Am., 1977-79; trustee San Diego (Calif.) Opera, 1990-92. With USPHS, 1967-69. Grantee Adria Labs., 1975—, Ednl. Found. Am. Soc. Plastic and Reconstructive Surgeons, 1975-76, 84-85, 90, VA, 1976-78, 77-80, 81-83, McGhan Corp., 1977—, Dow-Corning Corp., 1977-79, NIH, 1978-80, Orthopedic Rsch. and Edn. Found., 1981-82, M. Larry Lawrence Found., 1990. Fellow ACS; mem. AAAS, Am. Assn. Plastic Surgeons (local arrangements com. 1984-85, audit com. 1986-87, program com. 1987-88, 90-91, 93-94, program chmn. 1994—), Am. Cleft Palate Assn. (time and place com. 1978-79), Am. Soc. for Aesthetic Plastic Surgery (sci. rsch. com. 1989—, vice chmn. silicone implant rsch. com. 1992, candidate group, symposium com. 1992), Am. Soc. Plastic and Reconstructive Surgeons (program com. 1979-80), Calif. Soc. Plastic Surgeons (mem. com. 1980-82, 89-90), Plastic Surgery Rsch. Coun., San Diego Plastic Surgery Assn., Soc. Univ. Surgeons, Wis. Soc. Plastic Surgeons, Phi Gamma Delta, Phi Beta Kappa, Alpha Omega Alpha, others. Office: Scripps Clinic & Rsch Found 10666 N Torrey Pines Rd La Jolla CA 92037-1027

RUDOLPH, THOMAS KEITH, aerospace engineer; b. Jamestown, N.D., Oct. 4, 1961; s. Arthur John and Melinda Magdelina (Nehlich) R. BS in Aerospace Engring., Iowa State U., 1983. Registered profl. engr., Wash. Engr. Boeing Mil. Airplanes, Seattle, 1984-88, sr. engr., 1988-90; sr. engr. Boeing Comml. Airplanes, Seattle, 1990-91, specialist engr., 1991-94; specialist engr. Boeing Mil. Airplanes, Seattle, 1994—; chmn. weight improvement program Boeing B-2 Program, Seattle, 1986-88. Mem. AIAA (sr.), Soc. Allied Weight Engrs. (sr., chmn. activities com. 1985-86, treas. 1986-87, facilities chmn. internat. conf. 1987, v.p. 1987-88, pres. 1991-92), Iowa State U. Alumni Assn. (life), Marston Club (life). Republican. Methodist. Office: Boeing Mil Airplanes M/S 4C-42 PO Box 3707 Seattle WA 98124

RUDOLPH, WALTER PAUL, engineering research company executive; b. Binghamton, N.Y., Aug. 17, 1937; s. Walter Paul and Frieda Lena (Hennemann) R.; m. Leila Ortencia Romero, Dec. 18, 1960; children: Jonathan, Jana, Catherine. BEE, Rensselaer Poly. Inst., 1959; MSBA, San Diego State U., 1964. Elec. engr. Gen. Dynamics/Astronautics, San Diego, 1959-62; ops. research analyst Navy Electronics Lab., San Diego, 1962-64; mem. profl. staff Gen. Electric Tempo, Honolulu, 1964-70, Ctr. for Naval Analysis, Arlington, Va., 1970-77; pres. La Jolla (Calif.) Research Corp., 1977—. Served to Capt. USNR, 1959-92. Republican. Presbyterian. Home: 1559 El Paso Real La Jolla CA 92037-6303 Office: La Jolla Rsch Corp PO Box 1207 La Jolla CA 92038-1207

RUEBE, BAMBI LYNN, interior, environmental designer; b. Huntington Park, Calif., Nov. 13, 1957; d. Leonard John Ruebe and Vaudis Marie Powell. BS, UCLA, 1988. Millwright asst. Kaiser Steel Corp., Fontana, Calif., 1976-79; electrician Fleetwood Enterprises, Riverside, Calif., 1977; fashion model internat., 1977-85; free-lance draftsman, 1982-83; project coord. Philip J. Sicola Inc., Culver City, Calif., 1982-83; prin. designer Ruebe Inclusive Design, Highland, Calif., 1983-89, Ventura, Calif., 1990—; cons. mfg. design Burlington Homes New Eng. Inc., Oxford, Maine, 1987-90, DeRose Industries, Chambersburg, Pa., 1984, Skyline Corp., Redlands, Calif., 1982-84; cons. lighting Lightways Corp., L.A., 1984-87; mem. design rev. bd. San Bernardino (Calif.) Downtown Main St. Redevel. Com., 1987-89. Motion picture project designer, lighting design, archtl. design for the movie Deceptions, 1990. Mem. World Affairs Coun., Inland So. Calif., 1986—; mem. Citizens adv. com. Highland Calif. Gen. Plan, 1988-90; co-chmn. civil rights com. AFL-CIO, Fontana, 1978-79. Recipient Cert. Merit Scholastic Art award Scholastic Mags. Inc., Southeastern Calif., 1974, Dirs. Incentive award for Archtl. Design City of Ventura, Calif., 1990. Mem. Nat. Trust for Hist. Preservation. Democrat. Office: Ruebe Inclusive Design 50 N Oak St Ventura CA 93001

RUECKERT, RONALD FRANK, engineering executive; b. Shawano, Wis., Aug. 19, 1947; s. Frank William and Meta Marie (Karstedt) R.; m. Annette Marion Mulay; children: Douglas, Stacy, Nicholas, Amanda. BSEE, Devry Inst. Tech., 1967. Calibration technician Lockheed Missiles & Space Co., Sunnyvale, Calif., 1967-70; sr. test technician Burroughs Bus. Machines, Mission Niejo, Calif., 1970-71; sr. technician Telex Direct Access Divsn., Santa Clara, Calif., 1971-73; staff engr. Storage Tech., Louisville, Colo., 1973-76, Memorex, Santa Clara, 1976-78; program mgr. Priam, Inc., San Jose, Calif., 1978-82, Seagate Tech., Scotts Valley, Calif., 1991-93, Mini Scribe, Longmont, Colo., 1982-91; dir. engring. Maxtor, Longmont, Colo., 1993—. Home: 2621 Danbury Dr Longmont CO 80503

RUETTIGER, DANIEL EUGENE (RUDY RUETTIGER), author, speaker; b. Joliet, Ill., Aug. 22, 1948; s. Daniel Oscar and Elizabeth (Mandella) R. AA, Holy Cross Coll., South Bend, Ind., 1974; BA, Notre Dame U., 1976; LittD (hon.), Our Lady of Holy Cross, New Orleans, 1996. Ins. agt. Pat Ryan & Assoc., Chgo., 1978-82; pres. Wellington Corp., South Bend, 1982-84; sales mgr. Gurlex Leep, South Bend, 1986-91; tech. advisor Tri-Star Pictures, Culver City, Calif., 1991-93; spkr. Rudy Internat. Ltd., Las Vegas, Nev., 1993—. Author: Rudy's Insights & Rudy Rules, Rudy's Lesson for Young Champions; actor and author (film) Rudy, 1993 (Crystal award 1993). With USN, 1968-70. Recipient Walter Camp award Walter Camp Found., 1994; named Hon. Citizen City of Abilene, Tex., 1994, Oil City, Pa., 1994. Home and Office: 109 Weatherwood Ct Henderson NV 89014

RUFF, LORRAINE MARIE, public relations executive; b. Washington, Feb. 13, 1947; d. William Stanley and Jeanne Ann (Murray) Charlton; m. R. Eugene Ruff, July 17, 1968; 1 child, David Michael. BS in Liberal Arts, Oreg. State U., 1976. Reporter The Oregonian, Corvallis, Oreg., 1976-79, Union-Bull., Walla Walla, Wash., 1979-80; dir. pub. rels. Strategic Mktg., Corvallis, 1980-82; gen. mgr. Campaigns Northwest, Corvallis, 1982-84; account supr. Arthur D. Little, Inc., Cambridge, Mass., 1985-87, mgr. corp. ID, 1988-89; dir. biotechnology New Eng. Hill and Knowlton, Waltham, Mass., 1989, v.p., dir. biotechnology, 1990, sr. v.p., mng. dir. internat. biotechnology practice, 1990-91, sr. v.p., gen. mgr., 1991-93; sr. v.p., mng. dir. divsn. biosci. comm. Stoorza, Ziegaus & Metzger, San Diego, 1993-94, dir. life scis. practice, 1993-94; owner Charlton Ruff Comm., Puyallup, Wash., 1994—; mem. bd. dirs. Coll. Liberal Arts Devel. Coun., Oreg. State U. Bd. dirs. Wash. State Biotech. & Biomed Assn., Oreg. State U. Coll. Liberal Arts Devel. Coun. Mem. Pub. Rels. Soc. Am., Nat. Investor Rels. Inst., Oreg. Biotech. Assn., Wash. State Biotech. and Biomed. Assn. (bd. dirs.), B.C. Biotech. Alliance, Coll. Club Seattle, Rotary (univ. dist. chpt.). Republican. Office: Charlton Ruff Comm 12124 138th Ave E Puyallup WA 98374-4536

RUGENSTEIN, ROBERT WAYNE, clothing designer; b. Indpls., Dec. 4, 1921; s. August Carl and Dorothy Jane (Wuellner) R.; m. Ida May Vazzano; children: Mark, Dominick, Warren, Connie, Kathryn. Leader Civilian Conservation Corps, Oreg., 1939-40; lineman Alaska Hwy. telephone line Miller Constrn. Co., 1942-43; designer Ft. Wayne (Ind.) Tailors Co., 1946-63, Craddock Uniform Co., Kansas City, Mo., 1963-67, Hayes Garment Co., Nashville, 1967-69, Fechheimer Co., Cin., 1969-70, Campus Sweater and Sportswear, Paramus, N.Y., 1970-78; v.p. prodn., design Cherokee Apparel Corp., Venice, Calif., 1978-82; internat. clothing cons. Rugida Apparel Svc., Orovilla, Calif., 1982—. Patentee adjustable die cutter, solar energy home, solar energy builders; author: Revelation House, 1992, Executive Peace Corps, 1996. With U.S. Army, 1943-46, India. Recipient award Nat. Inventor's Soc., 1962, David Rockefeller Spirit of Svc. award Internat. Exec. Svc. Corp., 1992. Mem. Internat. Exec. Svc. Corp. (vol. exec.), Vols. in Tech. Assistance' Mensa, Shriners. Republican. Home and Office: 3229 Rugida Rd Oroville CA 95965-9762

RUGGERI, ZAVERIO MARCELLO, medical researcher; b. Bergamo, Italy, Jan. 7, 1945; came to U.S., 1978; s. Giovanni and Anna (Dolci) R.; m. Rosamaria Carrara, June 12, 1971. MD magna cum laude, U. Milan, 1970; degree in Clin. and Exptl. Hematology magna cum laude, U. Pavia, Italy, 1973, degree in Internal Medicine magna cum laude, 1981. Asst. clin. prof. hematology U. Milan, 1972-80; assoc. dir. hemophilia ctr. Policlinico Hosp., Milan, 1980-82; vis. investigator Scripps Clinic and Research Found., La Jolla, Calif., 1978-80, asst. mem., 1982-89; assoc. mem. Scripps Clinic and Rsch. Found., La Jolla, Calif., 1989-93; mem. Scripps Rsch. Inst., 1993—; dir. Roon Ctr. for Arteriosclerosis and Thrombosis, 1989—; head div. Exptl. Thrombosis and Hemostasis, 1989—; vis. investigator St. Thomas/St. Bartholomews Hosps., London, 1974-76. Editor: Clinics in Haematology, 1985; mem. editl. bds. Blood, 1988-92, Peptide Rsch., 1988—, Haematologica, 1990—, Jour. Biol. Chemistry, 1993—; assoc. editor: Jour. Clin. Investigation, 1993-96; contbr. articles to profl. jours., chpts. to books. Research scholar Italian Ministry of Edn., 1970, Italian Hemophilia Found., 1970-72. Mem. AAAS, Assn. Am. Physicians, Italian Hemophilia Found., Am. Soc. Clin. Investigation, Italian Soc. Thrombosis and Hemostasis, Internat. Soc. Thrombosis and Hemostasis, Am. Heart Assn. (council on thrombosis), World Fedn. Hemophilia, Am. Fedn. Clin. Research, N.Y. Acad. Scis., Am. Soc. Hematology. Office: Scripps Rsch Inst 10550 N Torrey Pines Rd La Jolla CA 92037-1000

RUGGLES, JAMES AUSTIN, biochemist; b. Albuquerque, Nov. 22, 1964; s. Joseph Austin and Nancy Sue (Edgerly) R. BS in Biology, N.Mex. State U., 1986, BA in Chemistry, 1986; PhD in Chemistry, U. Colo., 1991. Postdoctoral fellow U. Colo., Boulder, 1991-95; asst. prof. chemistry Angelo State U., 1995—. Postdoctoral fellow Merck Chem. Co., 1992, Damon Runyon-Walter Winchell Cancer Rsch. Fund, 1992-95. Mem. AAAS. Office: Angelo State U Dept Chemistry San Angelo TX 76909

RUIZ, ANTHONY, organizational development consultant, educator; b. L.A., Apr. 15, 1943; s. Gustavo and Rafaela (Loya) R.; m. Irene Pardo, June 1, 1968; 1 child, Michael Anthony. BSBA, Calif. State U., L.A., 1970; MPA, U. So. Calif., L.A., 1976; EdD, Seattle U., 1990. Asst. exec. dir. Eastland Cmty. Youth Ctrs., L.A., 1967-70; asst. dir. Epic program Calif. State U., L.A., 1970-72, dir. Epic program, 1972-75; dir. manpower programs Maravilla Found., L.A., 1975-77; asst. dir. continuing edn. Western Washington U., Bellingham, Wash., 1977-81; exec. asst. to pres. South Seattle C.C., 1981-84, assoc. dean instrn., 1984-92; asst. to vice chancellor Seattle C.Cs., 1992-94; pres., CEO Ruiz & Assocs., Bellevue, Wash., 1994—; mem. occupl. edn. adv. com. Seattle Pub. Schs., 1984-90; mem. adv. bd. King 5 TV, Seattle, 1990—. Bd. dirs. Se. Ctr. West Seattle, 1983-87, Ch. Coun. Greater Seattle, 1986-91, Consejo Mental Health Ctr., 1986-90, Seattle Sister City Program, 1988—, Vols. of Am., Seattle, 1990—, United Way King County, Seattle, 1994—, also chair project lead, 1988-93; mem. adv. bd. Seattle Housing Authority, 1988-92. Mem. Kiwanis Club (bd. dirs. West Seattle 1981-92, bd. dirs. Stadium Way 1993—). Democrat. Roman Catholic. Home: 13604 SE 54th Pl Bellevue WA 98006-4218

RUIZ, LUIS RAFAEL, investment and financial planning consultant; b. Mayaguez, P.R., Jan. 18, 1946; s. Louis Rafael and Aida Luz (Reteguis) R.; m. P. Eneida Sanchez, Aug. 26, 1967; children: Kristina M., Michael L. AA, Bronx C.C., 1976; BA cum laude, CCNY, 1978; postgrad, U. Phoenix, Brea, Calif., 1982-84. Registered prin. NASD; registered investment advisor SEC. Supr. Thomson McKinnon, N.Y.C., 1968-69, Reynolds and Co., N.Y.C., 1969-70; mgr./supr. Weiss Voison, N.Y.C., 1970-72; mgr. W.E. Hutton, N.Y.C., 1972-74; investment cons. in pvt. practice Orange, Calif., 1969—; ops. mgr., v.p. Paine Webber, N.Y.C. and Calif., 1974-84; ops. mgr., v.p., asst. mgr. Shearson Lehman, Beverly Hills, Calif., 1984-86; compliance officer, v.p. Assoc. Securities Co., L.A., 1987-96; pres. Lou R. Ruiz & Assocs., Orange, Calif., 1985—; exec. v.p., dir. of compliance Quest Capital Strategies, Inc., Laguna Hills, Calif., 1996—; dir., v.p. Assoc. Securities Corp. of Nev., Reno, 1992-95; registered investment advisor Assoc. Planners, L.A., 1987-96; arbitrator, panelist, expert witness SEC, NASD, PSE, NYSE, NFA, Washington, 1987—, notary pub., Calif., 1982—. Troop leader Boy Scouts Am., Orange, 1987-92; bd. dirs., coach Little League, Orange, 1985-92; fin. planner, counsel La Purisima Ch. and Sch., Orange, 1985-92, St. Jeanne's Sch., Tustin, Calif., 1983-87; bd. dirs. Cowan Hills Assn., 1996—. Sgt. USAF, 1964-68. Democrat. Roman Catholic. Home: 7412 E White Oak Rdg Orange CA 92869-4519 Office: Ste 101 7412 E White Oak Ridge Orange CA 92669-4519

RULE, ROGER COLLINS, builder, developer, publisher; b. Kansas City, Mo., Dec. 31, 1944; s. Forrest and Margaret Evelyn (Thompson) H.; m. Joyce Eileen Kindred, Dec. 26, 1965 (div. Nov. 1987); children: Robin Sean, Ryan Major; m. Eileen Frances Lacerte, Aug. 31, 1991. BS in Math., U. Mo., 1966. Tchr. math. North Kansas City Pub. Schs., Mo., 1966-69; gen. contractor Rule Devel., Modesto, Calif., 1973-76, pres. Rule Enterprises, Modesto, 1977-90 , Alliance Books, Inc., Northridge, Calif., 1982-92, Freemark Devel., Modesto, 1990—, Etre-Cal, Inc., Modesto, 1994—. Author: The Riflemans Rifle, 1982, 20th Century Winchester, 1984, Buying a Franchise, 1994, Forming a Franchise System, 1994, Financing for Franchising, 1995, The Franchise Redbook, 1995, The Synoptikos, 1995. Contbr. articles to profl. jours. Former mem. North Kansas City Prin.'s Adv. Com. Served to capt. U.S. Army, 1969-72. Recipient Pvt. Bus. award Assn. Retarded Citizens, Stanislaus County, Calif., 1983, also others. Mem. NEA, North Coast Builders Assn., Nat. Home Builders Assn., Modesto Home Builders Assn., Nat. Rifle Assn., Modesto Rifle Assn., U. Mo. Alumni Assn., Winchester Collector Arms Assn. (news editor 1982). Republican. Methodist. Club: Winchester of Am. (charter dir. 1984). Home: 77-6452 Alii Dr Kailua Kona HI 96740-2499 Office: KMS 75-166 Kalani Ste 104 Kailua Kona HI 96740

RULEY, STANLEY EUGENE, cost analyst; b. Akron, Ohio, Jan. 24, 1934; s. Royal Lovell and Opal Lenora (McDougall) R.; m. Annie Adam Patterson, Dec. 15, 1962; children: Cheryl Ann, Janice Lynn. Student, Kent State U., 1951-53; BSBA, Ohio State U., 1955. Registered profl. engr., Calif. Indsl. engr. Gaffers & Satler Inc., Hawthorne, Calif., 1961-62; mfg. engr. data systems div. Litton Industries Inc., Van Nuys, Calif., 1962-65; contract price analyst Naval Plant Rep. Office Lockheed, Burbank, Calif., 1966-72; contract negotiator Naval Regional Procurement, Long Beach, Calif., 1972-75; cost/price analyst Def. Contract Adminstrn. Services, Van Nuys, 1975-82; chief of contract pricing, dir. contracting Air Force Flight Test Ctr., Edwards AFB, Calif., 1982-89; cons. engr., Northridge, Calif., 1971—. Served as sgt. U.S. Army, 1956-59. Recipient Sustained Superior Performance award Air Force Flight Test Ctr., 1984, Excellent Performance award Air Force Flight Test Ctr., 1982-83, Outstanding Performance award NAVPRO Lockheed, 1970. Mem. Am. Inst. Indsl. Engrs., IBM Computer User Group (Madison, Wis., Conn., San Fernando Valley), Air Force Assn. (life), Nat. Contract Mgmt. Assn. Republican. Presbyterian. Clubs: Lockheed Employee Recreation (treas. Gem and Mineral 1976, pres. 1976), Camper (Burbank) (pres. 1974). Lodge: Masons (past master, 1992). Home: 18751 Vintage St Northridge CA 91324-1529 Office: Indsl Engring Svcs 18751 Vintage St Northridge CA 91324-1529

RULIFSON, JOHNS FREDERICK, computer company executive, computer scientist; b. Bellefontaine, Ohio, Aug. 20, 1941; s. Erwin Charles and Virginia Helen (Johns) R.; m. Janet Irving, June 8, 1963; children: Eric Johns, Ingrid Catharine. BS in Math., U. Wash., 1966; PhD in Computer Sci., Stanford U., 1973. Mathematician SRI, Internat., Menlo Park, Calif., 1966-73; scientist Xerox Rsch., Palo Alto, Calif., 1973-80; mgr. ROLM, Santa Clara, Calif., 1980-85; scientist Syntelligence, Sunnyvale, Calif., 1985-87; exec. Sun Microsystems, Mountain View, Calif., 1987—. Fellow Assn. for Computing Machinery (System Software award 1990); mem. IEEE. Home: 3785 El Centro Ave Palo Alto CA 94306-2642 Office: Sun Microsystems 2550 Garcia Ave Mountain View CA 94043-1109

RUMBAUGH, CHARLES EARL, lawyer, arbitrator/mediator; b. San Bernardino, Calif., Mar. 11, 1943; s. Max Elden and Gertrude Maude (Gulker) R.; m. Christina Carol Pinder, Mar. 2, 1968; children: Eckwood, Cynthia, Aaron, Heather. BS, UCLA, 1966; JD, Calif. Western Sch. Law, 1971; cert. in Advanced Mgmt., U. So. Calif., 1993. Bar: Calif. 1972, U.S. Dist. Ct. (cen. dist.) Calif. 1972, U.S. Ct. Appeals (9th cir.) 1972. Engr. Westinghouse Electric Corp., Balt., 1966-68; legal counsel Calif. Dept. of Corps., L.A., 1971-77; legal counsel Hughes Aircraft Co., L.A., 1977-84, asst. to corp. dir. contracts, 1984-89, asst. to corp. v.p. contracts, 1989-95; corp. dir. contracts/pricing Lear Astronics Corp., 1995-97; arbitrator, mediator, 1997—; arbitrator/mediator comml., franchise, securities, real estate and constrn. panels Am. Arbitration Assn., L.A., 1989—; mem. arbitration and mediation panels Franchise Arbitration and Mediation, Inc., 1994—, Arbitration and Mediation Internat., 1994—, Ctr. for Conflict Resolution, L.A., 1990—, L.A. County Superior Ct., 1993; spkr. to profl. and trade assns. Mem. editl. bd. Nat. Contract Mgmt. Jour.; contbr. articles to profl. jours. Counselor Boy Scouts Am., L.A., 1976—; mem. City of Palos Verdes Estates (Calif.) Citizen's Planning Com., 1986-90; judge pro tem Los Angeles County Superior Ct., L.A., 1991—. Fellow Nat. Contract Mgmt. Assn. (founder, chmn. alt. dispute resolution com., cert. profl. contracts mgr., nat. bd. advisors, nat. v.p. southwestern region 1993-95, nat. dir. 1992-93, pres. L.A./South Bay chpt. 1991-92, Outstanding Fellow award 1994); mem. ABA (alt. dispute resolution sect., forum on franchising, forum on constrn. industry), Nat. Security Indsl. Assn. (vice-chmn. west coast legal subcom. 1994—), Fed. Bar Assn. (pres. Beverly Hills chpt. 1992-93), State Bar Calif. (franchise law com. 1992-95, Wiley W. Manual award 1992), LA County Bar Assn., South Bay Bar Assn., Soc. Profls. in Dispute Resolution (co-chmn. internat. sector), Aerospace Industries Assn. (chmn. procurement techniques com. 1987-88, 93-94), Christian Legal Soc. Office: PO Box 2636 Rolling Hills CA 90274

RUML, TREADWELL, English language educator; b. N.Y.C., Mar. 22, 1952; s. Alvin and Zona Ruml; m. Laura Susan Funkhouser, Dec. 30, 1990; children: James Alvin Treadwell, John Jordan Beardsley. AB, Harvard Coll., 1974, JD, 1977; PhD, U. Va., 1989. Assoc. Nutter, McClennan & Fish, Boston, 1977-80; lectr. in English U. Va., Charlottesville, 1989-90; asst. prof. Calif. State U., San Bernardino, 1990-94, assoc. prof., 1994—. Contbr. articles to profl. jours. Chair adv. com. Calif. Reading & Literacy Project, Riverside, Inyo, Mono and San Bernardino County, 1995-96. Mem. Am. Soc. for Eighteenth Century Studies, Western Soc. for Eighteenth Century Studies, Samuel Johnson Soc. So. Calif. Office: Calif State U Dept English 5500 University Pky San Bernardino CA 92407

RUMLER, DIANA GALE, geriatrics nurse; b. Manchester, Tenn., Feb. 23, 1943; d. Donald Yale and Thelma Irene (Beach) Miller; m. Herschel Hinkle, Aug. 1961 (div. Jan. 1978); children: David, John, Jody Hinkle West; m. Lester Rumler, Jr. (div. June 1984). AA in Nursing, Ind. U.-Purdue U., Indpls., 1974; BS in Pub. Health-Journalism-Psychology, Ball State U., Muncie, 1983. RN; cert. ACLS, BLS. Psychiat. nurse Meth. Hosp., Indpls., 1974-78; women's infant and children's coord. Cmty. & Family Svcs. Inc., Portland, Ind., 1978-81, Ball Meml. Hosp., Muncie, Ind., 1981-84; pub. health nurse Health & Rehab. Svcs., Ft. Lauderdale, Fla., 1984; med.-surg. nurse Holy Cross Hosp., Ft. Lauderdale, 1985; pre-op/post-op nurse VA Med. Ctr., Nashville, 1986-89; nurse vascular, orthopedics, intensive care, telemetry, tchg VA Med. Ctr., Tucson, 1990—; WIC advocate hearings/radio show, Ind., 1978-81; health vol. outreach clinic St. Mary's Hosp., Tucson, 1993-94; vol. Hospice Family Care, Tucson. Contbr. articles to profl. jours. Mem. Nurses of Vet. Affairs, Am. Fedn. Govt. Employees, Ladies' Hermitage Assn. Democrat. Roman Catholic. Home: PO Box 17764 Tucson AZ 85731-7764 Office: VA Med Ctr S 6th Ave Tucson AZ 85723

RUMMERFIELD, PHILIP SHERIDAN, medical physicist; b. Raton, N. Mex., Feb. 27, 1922; s. Lawrence Lewis and Helen Antoinette (Roper) R.; m. Mary Evelyn Kubick, Dec. 29, 1978; children: Casey Regan, Dana Jay. BSME, Healds Coll., 1954; MSc, U. Cin., 1964, DSc, 1965. Registered profl. engr., safety, nuclear, Calif. Piping engr. Morrison Knudsen Co., Surabaja, E. Java, 1956-57; civil engr. State of Calif., San Francisco, 1957-59, constn. and radiation engr., 1959-63; hosp. physicist and radiation safety officer U. Calif., San Diego, 1966-73; prin. Applied Radiation Protection Svc., Encinitas, Calif., 1973—. Contbr. articles to Science, Bull. Atomic Scientists, Occupational Health Nursing, Health Physics Jour., Internat. Jour. Applied Radiation & Isotopes. Cpl. C.E. U.S. Army, 1943-46. Grantee Teaching grant NSF, 1969-71. Mem. Am. Nuclear Soc., Calif. Soc. Profl. Engrs., Am. Indsl. Hygiene Assn., Am. Assn. Physicists in Medicine (pres. So. Calif. chpt. 1971-72), Calif. Soc. Profl. Engrs., Health Physics Soc. (pres. So. Calif. chpt. 1973-74). Democrat. Home: 3303 Dorado Pl Carlsbad CA 92009-7706 Office: Applied Radiation Protection Svcs 700 2nd St Ste C Encinitas CA 92024-4459

RUNCK, ROGER JOHN, editor; b. Dolores, Colo., May 24, 1912; s. Philip and Annie Elizabeth (Marsh) R.; m. Theadora May Ridgway, Oct. 16, 1934; children: Robert, Rogene, Rhonda, Robin. Student, Union Coll., Lincoln, Nebr., 1929-33; BSChemE, U. Colo., 1943; MS in Metallurgy, Stevens Inst. Tech., Hoboken, N.J., 1947. Process engr. Metal & Thermit Corp., Rahway, N.J., 1943-47; asst. div. chief Battelle Meml. Inst., Columbus, Ohio, 1947-57, mgr. def. metals info. ctr., 1957-62, dir. def. metals info. ctr., 1962-69; cons., 1970-76; govt. agt. Dept. of Energy, Laramie, Wyo., 1977-83; editor Precious Metals News Internat. Precious Metals Inst., Allentown, Pa., 1977—; pres. Inst. Precious Metals Inst., Allentown, 1976-78. Home and Office: 1117 Firethorn Ct Rifle CO 81650

RUNICE, ROBERT E., retired corporate executive; b. Fargo, N.D., Aug. 20, 1929; s. E.M. and Ruth (Soule) R.; m. Geraldine Kharas, June 26, 1954; children: Michael, Christopher, Paul, Karen. B.S., N.D. State U., 1951. Sr. v.p. Northwestern Bell Tel. Co., Omaha, Nebr., 1945-81; v.p. Am. Tel. & Tel. Co.-Info. Systems, Morristown, N.J., 1981-83; v.p., pres. comml. devel. div. US West, Inc., Englewood, Colo., 1983-91; bd. dirs. Bombay Co., Ft. Worth, Tandy Brands Accessories, Arlington, Tex., Utilx Corp., Kent, Wash. Trustee Colo. Symphony Assn. Republican. Episcopalian. Home: Box 503 10940 S Parker Rd Parker CO 80134-7440 Office: 9785 S Maroon Cir Ste 332 Englewood CO 80112-5922

RUNNER, GEORGE CYRIL, JR., minister, educational administrator; b. Scotia, N.Y., Mar. 25, 1952; s. George Cyril and Kay Carol (Cooper) R.; m. Sharon Yvonne Oden, Jan. 13, 1973; children: Micah Stephen, Rebekah Kay. Student, Antelope Valley Coll., Lancaster, Calif., 1970-88; grad. mgmt. cert., Azusa Pacific U., 1988; student, U. Redlands. Lic. to ministry Am. Bapt. Chs. in USA, 1977. Exec. pastor 1st Bapt. Ch. Lancaster, 1973—; founder, exec. dir. Desert Christian Schs., Lancaster, 1977—; founder, internat. dir. Supporting Ptnrs. in Christian Edn., Lancaster, Guatemala City, Guatemala, 1989—; seminar leader Internat. Ctr. for Learning, Ventura, Calif., 1972-82; curriculum cons. Gospel Light Publs., Glendale, Calif., 1974-80; bd. dirs. Greater L.A. Sunday Sch. Assn., 1978-79. Assemblyman State of Calif., 36th Dist., Lancaster, 1996; bd. dirs. Lancaster Econ. Devel. Corp.; mem. Salvation Army, Lancaster. Mem. Internat. Fellowship Ch. Sch. Adminstrs., Assn. Christian Schs. Internat., Christian Mgmt. Assn., Lancaster Ministerial Assn. Republican. Office: Desert Christian Schs 1st Bapt Ch 44648 15th St W Lancaster CA 93534-2806*

RUNYON, STEVEN CROWELL, university administrator, communications educator; b. San Rafael, Calif., June 20, 1946; s. Charles A. and Katherine C. (Pease) R.; m. Lynna Lim, Mar. 9, 1974; 1 child, Wendy Victoria. BA in Econs., U. San Francisco, 1971, postgrad., 1978—; MA in Radio and TV, San Francisco State U., 1976. Radio producer Sta. KGO, San Francisco, 1965-68; engr., announcer Stas. KSFR, KSAN, San Francisco, 1966-68; publicist Kolmar Assocs./Chuck Barris Prodns., San Francisco, 1970; instructional media technician U. San Francisco, 1968-72; technician, archivist, mgr. Wurster, Bernardi & Emmons, San Francisco, 1972-73; projectionist So. Pacific R.R., San Francisco, 1974; broadcast ops. engr. Stas. KPEN, KIOI, KIQI, San Francisco, 1968-74, public and community affairs program producer, 1971-74, AM transmitter engr., 1974; lectr. communication arts, U. San Francisco, 1974—, gen. mgr. Sta. KUSF-FM, 1974—, dir. mass media studies program, 1975—, acting chmn. communication arts dept., 1976; TV historian; producer, engr., cons. radio and TV programs; communications and audiovisual cons. Author: A Study of the Don Lee Broadcasting Systems' Television Activities, 1930-41, 1976, Educational Broadcast Management Bibliography, 1974, (with others) Television in America, 1996, The Encyclopedia of Television, 1997, Historical Dictionary of American Radio, 1997; contbr. articles to profl. jours. Grantee Calif. Coun. Humanities in Public Policy, Rockefeller Found., Father Spieler Meml. Trust, NSF; recipient cert. of merit for documentary radio series Peninsula Press Club, 1979, Diploma of Honor, Internat. Robert Stolz Soc., 1981, Fr. Dunne award U. San Francisco, 1986, Coll. Svc. award Coll. Arts and Scis. U. San Francisco, 1988; lic. gen. class radiotelephone operator FCC. Mem. Soc. Broadcast Engrs., Broadcast Edn. Assn. (Divsnl. First Place award Refereed Paper Competition 1996), Assn. Communication Adminstrs., Assn. for Edn. in Journalism and Mass Communication, Assn. Recorded Sound Collections, Pres.'s Ambassadors of U. San Francisco, Internat. Communication Assn. Office: U San Francisco 2130 Fulton St San Francisco CA 94117-1080

RUOTOLO, LUCIO PETER, English language educator; b. N.Y.C., Mar. 14, 1927; s. Onorio and Lucia (Sperling) R.; m. Marcia Mauney, June 11, 1960; children: Cristina, Vanessa, Peter. BA, Colgate U., 1951; MA, Columbia U., 1954, PhD, 1960. Part-time lectr. Hofstra Coll., Hempstead, N.Y., 1956-57; lectr. New Sch. for Social Rsch., N.Y.C., 1957; acting instr., prof. English Stanford (Calif.) U., 1957—, prof. emeritus English, 1994—; cons. panelist NEH, Washington, 1974-75; reader Nat. Humanities Ctr., N.C., 1986; film editor Christianity and Crisis, N.Y.C., 1965-66. Author: Six Existential Heroes, 1973 (Wilson prize 1972), The Interrupted Moment: A View of Virginia Woolf's Novels, 1986; editor: Virginia Woolf's Freshwater, 1976; founding editor Virginia Woolf Miscellany, 1973—. Co-chmn. Stanford/Palo Alto (Calif.) Dem. Club, 1968; co-pres. bd. Palo Alto Chamber Orch., 1980; bd. dirs. Peninsula Drama Guild, Palo Alto, 1964-67. Rsch. grantee NEH, 1973. Mem. MLA, Virginia Woolf Soc. (pres. 1983-87). Presbyterian. Home: 951 Mears Ct Stanford CA 94305-1041 Office: Stanford U Dept English Stanford CA 94305

RUOTSALA, JAMES ALFRED, historian, writer; b. Juneau, Alaska, Feb. 17, 1934; s. Bert Alfred and Eva (Karppi) E.; m. Janet Ann Whelan, July 31, 1987; stepchildren: Theresa Cowden, Douglas Whelan, Peggy MacInnis, Michael Whelan, Bruce Whelan. Student, U. Md., 1960-61, Basic Officers Sch., Maxwell AFB, 1964, Air U., Maxwell AFB, 1985; AA, U. Alaska, Kenai, 1990. Asst. div. mgr. Macmillan Pub. Co., 1964-80; mgr. Denny's Restaurants, 1980-82; dir. mktg. and sales Air Alaska, 1982-89; state security supr., lt. Knightwatch Security, Juneau, Alaska, 1990-96; ret., 1996; archival dir. Alaska Aviation Heritage Mus., 1987-90. Author: Lockheed Vegas in Southeast Alaska, 1980, We Stand Ready, 1986, Eielson, Father of Alaskan Aviation, 1986, Pilots of the Panhandle, The Early Years 1920-1935, 1997; Alaska's Aviation Heritage Air Alaska newspaper; contbr. articles to profl. jours. Journalist 1st cl. USN, 1951-56; sgt. U.S. Army, 1958-64; 1st sgt. USAR, 1983-94; ret. USAR, 1994; lt. col. ASDF, 1985—. Decorated Korean Svc. medal with 2 combat stars, Korean Presdl. unit citation, UN Svc. medal, Nat. Def. Svc. medal, Vietnam Svc. medal, Meritorious Svc. medal with 2 oak leaf clusters, Army Commendation medal with 4 oak leaf clusters; recipient USAF Brewer Aerospace award, Grover Leoning award, Paul E. Garber award, 1984-85, State of Alaska Gov.'s Cert. Appreciation,

1983, Mayor's Pub. Svc. award, Anchorage, 1985, Commendation from Gov. of Alaska, 1993, 94, 18th Session Alaska Legis. Cert. Recognition, 1993, 94. Mem. VFW (sr. vice comdr. 1995, post quartermaster 1996-97), Res. Officers Assn. (pub. affairs officer 1985—), U.S. Naval Inst., Aviation and Space Writers Assn., Am. Aviation Hist. Soc., Am. Legion (historian), Pioneers of Alaska (sec. 1988, v.p. 1989, pres. 1990, Igloo 33, treas. 1994-95, Igloo 6, Cert. Appreciation 1988). Lutheran. Home: 2723 John St Juneau AK 99801-2020

RUPE, DALLAS GORDON, III, real estate property manager, securities arbitrator; b. Dallas, Dec. 10, 1934; s. Dallas Gordon and Ruby Lee (Landers) R.; m. Ann Walker Caldwell, Mar. 12, 1983; children: Robin, Sean, Amy, Dallas IV. BA, So. Meth. U., 1957; student, Northwestern U., 1959. V.p., dir. Rupe Investment Corp., Dallas, 1955—; v.p. Quinn & Co., Inc., Albuquerque, 1981-86, Underwood Neuhause, Inc., Houston, 1986-87; pres. The Market, Inc., Taos, N.Mex., 1987-89, The Rupe Cos., Inc., Ontario, Oreg., 1989—; bd. dirs. Big D. Prodns., Inc., Dallas, Rupe Capital Corp., Dallas, Moore Investment Co., Dallas, Moore Royalty Co., Dallas. Bd. dirs. Ontario Devel. Corp.; trustee Rupe Found., Dallas, 1955—. Mem. Ontario C. of C. (bd. dirs.), Treasure Valley Rental Assn., Kappa Sigma. Office: The Rupe Cos Inc 93 SW 4th Ave Ontario OR 97914-2757

RUPP, JEAN LOUISE, communications executive, author; b. Portland, Oreg., Aug. 29, 1943; d. Edward Howard and Dorothy Eugenia (Ross) Brown; m. Herbert Gustav Rupp, July 4, 1987. BA in English, Portland State U., 1965. Cert. tchr., Oreg. Tchr., dept. head Beaverton (Oreg.) Sch. Dist., 1967-88; pres., founder Write Communications, Portland, 1988—; adj. faculty Portland C.C., Concordia U., Portland State U.; nat. trainer, cons.State of Oreg., City of Portland, Nike, Inc., Oreg. Health Scis. U., Oreg. Mil. Acad., Oreg. Fin. Instns. Assn., Freightliner, Automated Data Processing, others, 1988—; spkr. Tektronix, Fred Meyer, Pacific Power, Am. Inst. of Banking, Utah Power, Pacific Telecom, Inc., other; writing dir. U.S. Army C.E., USDA Forest Svcs., PacifiCare, others, 1989-90. Author: Grammar Gremlin: An Instant Guide to Perfect Grammar for Everybody in Business, 1994; TV appearances include Stas. KATU-TV and KGW-TV. Vol. Dove Lewis Emergency Vet. Clinic, Portland, 1989—, Doerbecher Children's Hosp., Oreg. Humane Soc. Mem. ASTD, Oreg. Speakers Assn. (pres. bd. dirs. 1997—), Nat. Speakers Assn., Ctr. for Marine Conservation. Republican. Office: Write Comm 14657 SW Teal Blvd # 200 Beaverton OR 97007

RUPPENTHAL, KARL M., author, educator; b. Russell, Kans., Oct. 5, 1917; s. John P. and Viola (Whitaker) R.; m. Irja Alice Autio, May 30, 1942; children: Sara (Mrs. Michael Katz), Stephen, Brian. A.B., U. Kans., 1939, LL.B., 1941, J.D., 1968; M.B.A., U. Calif.-Berkeley, 1950; Ph.D., Stanford U., 1959. Bar: D.C., Kans., U.S. Tax Ct., U.S. Ct. Appeals (9th cir.), U.S. Supreme Ct. Reporter Russell County News, 1934-35; owner bookstore and restaurant, 1940-41; pilot TWA, 1942-68; UPS Found. prof., dir. Centre Transp. Studies U. B.C., Vancouver, 1971-84; mem. TWA/ALPA System Bd. Adjustment, 1947-49; exec. v.p. Airline Pilots Assn., 1950; prof., dir. transp. mgmt. program Stanford, 1958-69, dir. European logistics mgmt. program, summers, 1969-71; Ryder prof. transp. U. Miami (Fla.), 1970; founder, editor Farwest Press Ltd.; dir. Aero Air, Inc., Hazleton Labs., Hazleton Nuclear Sci., Karloid Corp.; cons. Can. Ministry Transport, Am. Airlines, Alltalia, C.P. Air, Saudi Arabian Airlines, VASP, TWA, Air Transport Assn., Ethiopian Air Lines, Pacific Western Airlines, NASA, Boeing Co., World Bank, Govts. of Alta. and B.C. Author: Regulation, Competition and the Public Interest, Case Problems in Air Transportation, Canada's Ports and Waterborne Trade; founder, editor: Logistics and Transp. Rev.; cons. editor New Can. Ency.; contbg. editor The Nation, Ency of Mgmt. Pres. Palo Alto Friends of Library, 1952-58; mem. Palo Alto (Calif.) City Council, 1953-59; mem. 1st Unitarian Ch. Berkeley; pres. Karl and Alice Ruppenthal Found. Arts. Stanford Sloan fellow; recipient Nathan Burkham award in copywright law; Wilton Park fellow. Fellow Chartered Inst. Transport; mem. NAS (com. mem.), Acad. Logistics (founding), Am. Econ. Assn., Indsl. Relations Research Assn., Transp. Research Forum, Canadian Transp. Research Forum, Am. Judicature Soc., Am. Arbitration Assn. (nat. panel), Peninsula Funeral Soc. (founding bd. dirs.), Univ. Club, Masons, Phi Beta Kappa, Sigma Phi Epsilon, Beta Gamma Sigma. Home: 2016 Pine Knoll Dr # 1 Walnut Creek CA 94595-2108

RUPPERT, JOHN LAWRENCE, lawyer; b. Chgo., Oct. 7, 1953; s. Merle Arvin and Loretta Marie (Ford) R.; m. Katharine Marie Tarbox, June 5, 1976. BA, Northwestern U., 1975; JD, U. Denver, 1978; LLM in Taxation, NYU, 1979. Bar: Colo. 1978, U.S. Dist. Ct. Colo. 1978, Ill. 1979, U.S. Tax Ct. 1981. Assoc. Kirkland & Ellis, Denver, 1979-84, ptnr., 1984-88; ptnr. Ballard, Spahr, Andrews & Ingersoll, Denver, 1988-96; shareholder Brownstein Hyatt Farber & Strickland, P.C., Denver, 1996—; lectr. U. Denver Coll. Law, fall 1984-92; adj. prof. law grad. tax program, 1993-94; sec. Capital Assocs., Inc., 1989-96, acting gen. counsel, 1989-90; sec. and spl. counsel to the bd. dirs. Bros. Gourmet Coffees, Inc., 1995—; asst. sec. Renaissance Cosmetics, Inc., 1996—. Contbr. articles to profl. jours. Mem. ABA, Colo. Bar Assn. (mem. exec. coun. tax sect. 1985-89), Denver Bar Assn., Equipment Leasing Assn. Am. Office: Brownstein Hyatt et al Ste 2200 410 17th St 22d Fl Denver CO 80202-4437

RUPPERT, SIEGFRIED, scientist; b. Langenschwarz, Germany, Oct. 2, 1958; came to U.S., 1991; s. Roland and Lina (Krug) R. Diploma degree in Biology, U. Heidelberg, Germany, 1984, PhD, 1989. Postdoctoral fellow U. Heidelberg, 1989-91, U. Calif., Berkeley, 1991-94; scientist Genentech, Inc., South San Francisco, Calif., 1994—; cons. Biopharm, GmbH, Heidelberg, Germany, 1988-91. Contbr. articles to profl. jours. Rsch. fellow German Cancer Rsch. Ctr., 1988, 90; hon. fellow Boehringer Ingelheim, 1991-93; long-term fellow EMBO, 1991-93; fellow Howard Hughes Med. Inst., 1993-94. Home: 4150 17th St Apt 7 San Francisco CA 94114-1995 Office: Genentech Inc 460 Point San Bruno Blvd South San Francisco CA 94080-4918

RUSCH, PAMELA JEAN, middle school educator; b. Berwyn, Ill., Mar. 1, 1949; d. James M. and Arlene A. (Meyer) Sanders; m. Steven Paul Rusch, Dec. 23, 1973; children: Matthew, Christiana. BFA with honors, U. Denver, 1971; MA, Lesley Coll., Cambridge, Mass., 1983. Art tchr. Jefferson County Pub. Schs., Lakewood, Colo., 1971—; area coord. Lesley Coll. Outreach Program, Denver, 1981-84; cons. Standard Based Edn., Jefferson County, 1993—; writing team mem. Jefferson County Art Stds., 1995—; cons. Middle Sch. Resource Team, 1990—. Author curricula. Mem. ASCD, Nat. Mid. Sch. Assn., Colo. Art Edn. Assn. Lutheran. Home: 7746 Orion St Arvada CO 80007

RUSCH, PATRICIA HULL, dietitian; b. Long Beach, Calif., Oct. 27, 1946; d. Donald Benjamin and Jeanne Marie (Cullin) Hull; m. Dale Allen Williamson, July 21, 1969 (div. Mar. 1983); children: Cary Lynn, Sandra Lee; m. Robin Alan Rusch, June 27, 1987. BS in Dietetics, Calif. State U., L.A., 1969; MPH Nutrition, U. Calif., L.A., 1970. Registered dietitian. Metabolic dietitian City of Hope Med. Ctr., Duarte, Calif., 1971-73; clin. dietitian St. Agnes Med. Ctr., Fresno, Calif., 1974; food svc. dir. Bel Haven Conv. Hosp., Fresno, 1974-76; pvt. practice cons. dietitian Fresno, 1976-79; pres., bd. dirs. Dietary Directions, Inc., Fresno, 1979—; keynote spkr. Spring Meeting Calif. Dietetic Assn., L.A., 1973. Author: Diet Manual for Long-term, 1980, 85, 90. Recipient Kitchen Layout and Design award So. Calif. Gas Co., L.A., 1970. Mem. Am. Dietetic Assn., Cons. Dietitians of Calif. (chmn., editor 1986—), Ctrl. Valley Dietetic Assn. (sec., chmn. various coms. 1973—), Dietitians in Psychology/Diabilities), Sea Knights Dive Club (pres. editor 1986—). Republican. Office: Dietary Directions Inc 2350 N Chestnut Ave Ste 111 Fresno CA 93703-2899

RUSCONI, LOUIS JOSEPH, marine engineer; b. San Diego, Calif., Oct. 10, 1926; s. Louis Edward and Laura Ethelyn (Salazar) R.; m. Virginia Caroline Bruce, Jan. 1, 1972. BA in Engring. Tech., Pacific Western U., 1981, MA in Marine Engring. Tech., 1982; PhD in Marine Engring. Mgmt., Clayton U., 1986. Cert. nuclear ship propulsion plant operator, surface and submarine. Enlisted USN, 1944, electrician's mate chief, 1944-65, retired, 1965; marine electrician planner U.S. Naval Shipyard, Vallejo, Calif., 1965-72; marine elec. technician Imperial Iranian Navy, Bandar Abbas, Iran, 1974-79; marine shipyard planner Royal Saudi Navy, Al-Jubail, Saudi Arabia, 1980-86; cons. in marine engring., 1986—. Author: Shipyards Operations manual, 1980, poetry (Golden Poet award 1989, Silver Poet award 1990). Mem. Rep. Presdl. Task Force, Washington, 1989-90, trustee, 1991. Mem. IEEE, U.S. Naval Inst., Soc. of Naval Architects and Marine Engrs. (assoc. mem.), Fleet Res., Nat. Geographic Soc. Home: 949 Myra Ave Chula Vista CA 91911-2315

RUSH, DOMENICA MARIE, health facilities administrator; b. Gallup, N.Mex., Apr. 10, 1937; d. Bernardo G. and Guadalupe (Milan) Iorio; m. W. E. Rush, Jan. 5, 1967. Diploma, Regina Sch. Nursing, Albuquerque, 1958. RN N.Mex.; lic. nursing home adminstr. Charge nurse, house supr. St. Joseph Hosp., Albuquerque, 1958-63; dir. nursing Cibola Hosp., Grants, 1960-64; supr. operating room, dir. med. seminars Carrie Tingley Crippled Children's Hosp., Truth or Consequences, N.Mex., 1964-73; adminstr. Sierra Vista Hosp., Truth or Consequences, 1974-88, pres., 1980-89; clin. nursing mgr. U. N.Mex. Hosp., 1989-90; adminstr. Nor-Lea Hosp., Lovington, N.Mex., 1990-94; with regional ops. divsn. Presbyn. Healthcare Svcs., Albuquerque, 1994—, regional ops., 1994—; adminstr. Sierra Vista Hosp., Truth or Consequences, N.Mex., 1995—; bd. dirs. N.Mex. Blue Cross/Blue Shield, 1977-88, chmn. hosp. relations com., 1983-85, exec. com. 1983—; bd. dirs. Region II Emergency Med. Svcs. Originating bd. SW Mental Health Ctr., Sierra County, N.Mex., 1975; chmn. Sierra County Personnel Bd., 1983—. Named Lea County Outstanding Woman, N.Mex. Commn. on Status of Women; Woman of Yr. for Lea County, N.Mex., 1993. Mem. Am. Coll. Health Care Adminstrs., Sierra County C. of C. (bd. dirs. 1972, 75-76, svc. award 1973, Businesswoman of the Yr. 1973-74), N.Mex. Hosp. Assn. (bd. dirs., sec.-treas., pres.-elect, com. chmn., 1977-88, pres. 1980-81, exec. com., 1980-83, 84-85, recipient meritorius svc. award 1988), N.Mex. So. Hosp. Coun. (sec. 1980-81, pres. 1981-82), Am. Hosp. Assn. (N.Mex. del. 1984-88, regional adv. bd. 1984-88). Republican. Roman Catholic. Home: 1100 N Riverside Truth Or Consequences NM 87901 Office: 800 E 9th Ave Truth Or Consequences NM 87901-1954

RUSK, LAUREN, editor, educator; b. Boston, Oct. 22, 1948; d. Henry G. and Olga (Wester) Russell. BA, Reed Coll., 1980; PhD, Stanford U., 1995. English instr. Stanford (Calif.) U., 1981-82, 84-85, writing cons. Engring. Sch., 1985—, instr. western culture, 1987-88, editor geophysics dept., 1990—, lectr. continuing studies program, 1996—; devel. editor Addison-Wesley Pub. Co., Reading, Mass., 1993—; contract editor Ctr. for the Future of Children, Packard Found., Palo Alto, Calif., 1994-96. Contbr. articles, poems to profl. publs., chpts. to books. Stanford fellow, 1980-84. Mem. MLA, Soc. for Study of Multi-Ethnic Lits. of U.S. Democrat. $D. Home and Office: 2256 Bowdoin St Palo Alto CA 94306-1214

RUSSEL, RICHARD ALLEN, telecommunications consultant, aerospace engineer, nuclear engineer, electrical engineer, retired naval officer; b. Shreveport, La., Jan. 24, 1958; s. Robert Lee and Gloria Jeanette (Gile) R.; m. Kathryn Joy Koehler, Dec. 30, 1983; children: Richard Allen Russel Jr., Kammie Joyce Jeanette, Jonathan Mark, Katie Jacqueline Keala, Stephen Sungmin. BSEE, U. N.Mex., 1980; Engrs. Degree in Aeros. and Astronautics, Naval Postgrad. Sch., Monterey, Calif., 1994, MSc in Astron. Engring., 1994. Commd. ensign, nuclear submarine officer USN, 1980, advanced through grades to lt. comdr., 1990; main propulsion analyst USS Puffer, Pearl Harbor, Hawaii, 1981-85; antisubmarine analyst, nuclear engr., comdr. 3d fleet USN, Pearl Harbor, 1985-87; combat systems officer USS TAUTUG, Pearl Harbor, 1987-89; navigator, ops. officer USS Indpls., Pearl Harbor, 1989-92; UHF/EHF satellite navy rep. PEO-SCS USN, El Segundo, Calif., 1994-96; project mgr. for spacecraft comms. Booz-Allen and Hamilton, Inc., San Diego, 1996—. Contbr. articles to profl. jours. Sch. bd. mem. Our Savior Luth. Sch., Aiea, Hawaii, 1986; den leader webelos Boy Scouts Am., 1995—. Fellow Inst. for the Advancement of Engring.; assoc. fellow AIAA (vice-chair edn. L.A. sect. 1991—, dep. dir. edn. region VI 1994—); mem. Space Nuclear Thermal Propulsion, Eta Kappa Nu. Republican. Lutheran. Home: 7405 Andasol St San Diego CA 92126-1014

RUSSELL, CARINA BOEHM, interior designer; b. Livingston, Mont., Dec. 21, 1954; d. Edward and Pia Maria (Fondelli) Boehm; m. John N. Russell, Dec. 14, 1978; children: Cara, Evan. BS, Mont. State U., 1977. Pvt. practice Rocky Mountain Design-Interiors, Livingston, 1978—. Active com. Livingston Comprehensive Plan, 1993-94; v.p. Livingston Youth Soccer League, 1993—; sec. Livingston Meml. Hosp. League, 1995—. Mem. Am. Soc. Interior Designers (profl.), Soroptimists (pres. 1992—), Livingston C. of C. (bd. dirs. 1993—). Episcopalian. Office: Rocky Mountain Design 601 W Park St Livingston MT 59047-2531

RUSSELL, CARL LLOYD, technical writer; b. Hayward, Calif., Oct. 12, 1950; s. Carl John Russell and Janet Modenia (Schaeffer) Martin; m. Ronda Lynn Neu; children: Kristina Yvonne, Kathleen Marie, Billie Lin Jensen. BA, Northwest Nazarene Coll., Nampa, Idaho, 1976. Computer operator Meredian Wood Products, Nampa, 1978-80; computer programmer Latah, Inc., Boise, Idaho, 1980-82; computer programmer Cougar Mountain Software, Boise, 1982-86, mgr. of rsch. and devel., 1986-97; tech. writer, multi-media developer Sykes Enterprises, Boise, 1997—. Author computer software, 1978. With USN, 1968-69. Republican. Nazarene. Home: 2054 N Hampton Rd Boise ID 83704 Office: Cougar Mountain Software 9180 Potomac Dr Boise ID 83704

RUSSELL, CAROL ANN, personnel service company executive; b. Detroit, Dec. 14, 1943; d. Billy and Iris Koud; m. Victor Rojas (div.). BA in English, CUNY-Hunter Coll., 1993. Registered employment cons. Various positions in temp. help cos. N.Y.C., 1964-74; v.p. Wollborg-Michelson, San Francisco, 1974-82; co-owner, pres. Russell Staffing Resources, Inc., San Francisco and Sonoma, 1983—; media guest, spkr., workshop and seminar leader in field; host/cmty. prodr. Job Net program for TCI Cable T.V. Pub. Checkpoint Newsletter; contbr. articles to profl. publs. Named to the Inc. 500, 1989, 90. Mem. Am. Women in Radio and TV, Soc. to Preserve and Encourage Radio Drama Variety and Comedy, No. Calif. Human Resources Coun., Soc. Human Resource Mgmt., Calif. Assn. Pers. Cons. (pres. Golden State chpt. 1984-85), Calif. Assn. Temp. Svcs., Bay Area Pers. Assn. (pres. 1983-84), Pers. Assn. Sonoma County, Profl. Resume Writers Am., Am. Jewish Congress. Office: Russell Staffing Resources Inc 351 California St Fl 8 San Francisco CA 94104

RUSSELL, FRANCIA, ballet director, educator; b. Los Angeles, Jan. 10, 1938; d. W. Frank and Marion (Whitney) R.; m. Kent Stowell, Nov. 19, 1965; children: Christopher, Darren, Ethan. Studies with, George Balanchine, Vera Volkova, Felia Doubrouska, Antonina Tumkovsky, Benjamin Harkarvy; student, NYU, Columbia U. Dancer, soloist N.Y.C. Ballet, 1956-62, ballet mistress, 1965-70; dancer Ballets USA/Jerome Robbins, N.Y.C., 1962; tchr. ballet Sch. Am. Ballet, N.Y.C., 1963-64; co-dir. Frankfurt (Fed. Republic Germany) Opera Ballet, 1976-77; dir., co-artistic dir. Pacific N.W. Ballet, Seattle, 1977—; dir. Pacific N.W. Ballet Sch., Seattle; affiliate prof. of dance U. Wash. Dir. staging over 100 George Balanchine ballet prodns. throughout world, including the Soviet Union and People's Republic of China, 1964—. Named Woman of Achievement, Matrix Table, Women in Comm., Seattle, 1987, Gov.'s Arts award, 1989, Dance Mag. award, 1996. Mem. Internat. Women's Forum. Home: 2833 Broadway E Seattle WA 98102-3935 Office: Pacific NW Ballet 301 Mercer St Seattle WA 98109-4600

RUSSELL, JAMES T., physicist and inventor; b. Bremerton, Wash., Feb. 23, 1931; m. Barbara Ann Giblett, Sept. 12, 1953; children: Janet, James C., Kristen. BA, Reed Coll., Portland, Oreg., 1953. Physicist GE Co., Richland, Wash., 1953-65; sr. scientist Battelle Meml. Inst./Pacific N.W. Labs., Richland, 1965-80; v.p. Digital Recording Corp., Salt Lake City, 1981-85; pres. Russell Assocs., Inc., Bellevue, Wash., 1985—; v.p. Info. Optics Corp., Issaquah, Wash., 1989—. Patentee (45) in field. Recipient IR-100 award Internat. Rsch. Mag., 1974. Mem. IEEE, Am. Phys. Soc., Optical Soc. Am., Soc. Photographic and Instrumentation Engrs. Home: 14589 SE 51st St Bellevue WA 98006-3509

RUSSELL, JAY D., marketing executive; b. Milw., Dec. 20, 1950; s. John Frank and Veronica Cecilia (Jones) R.; m. Carol Jean Croft, Feb. 14, 1976 (div. 1980); 1 stepchild, Kirsten Jean. BS, Ariz. State U., 1984, MBA, 1987. Prin. Southwest Casting Corp., Albuquerque, 1973-77; exec. v.p. Creative Constrn. Inc., Albuquerque, 1977-78; ops. supt. Demas Constrn. Inc., Alameda, N.M., 1978-81; adminstrv. mgr. Investment and Retirement Systems Inc., Phoenix, 1984-85; research asst. dept. communications Ariz. State U., Tempe, Ariz., 1985-86; grad. asst. Ariz. State U., 1986-87; project coordinator CHR Interiors, Scottsdale, Ariz., 1987-88; assoc. CHR Equipment and Space Planning, Scottsdale, 1988-89; prin. AJR Equipment Co., Scottsdale, 1985-90; pres., CEO AJR Equipment Co., Inc., Scottsdale, 1991—; research intern Gov's Office State of Ariz., Phoenix, 1986; mktg. intern Chase Bank Ariz., cons. 1988—, Fin. Ctr., Scottsdale, 1987; grad. liaison Econ. Club of Phoenix, Tempe, 1986-87. Named Outstanding Grad. Student Fin., Wall St. Jour., 1987; Exxon Ednl. Found. scholar, 1986. Mem. Ariz. State U. Alumni Assn., Sigma Iota Epsilon, Phi Kappa Phi, Beta Gamma Sigma. Roman Catholic. Club: Econ. (Phoenix). Office: AJR Equipment Co Inc 8010 E Mcdowell Rd Ste 114 Scottsdale AZ 85257-3868

RUSSELL, MARJORIE ROSE, manufacturing company executive; b. Welcome, Minn., Sept. 3, 1925; d. Emil Frederick and Ella Magdalene (Sothman) Wohlenhaus; m. Kenneth Kollmann Russell, Sept. 15, 1947 (div. May 1973); children: Jennie Rose, Richard Lowell, Laura Eloise, James Wesley. Student, Northwestern Sch., Mpls., 1944-45, St. Paul Bible Inst., 1946-47. Cook U. Minn., Mpls., 1943-45; maintenance person U. Farm Campus/N.W. Schs., St. Paul, 1945-46; clk. Kresge Corp., Mpls., 1945; cook, waitress, mgr. Union City Mission Bible Camp, Mpls., 1944-47; caterer for v.p. Gt. No. R.R., St. Paul, 1947; custodian Old Soldiers Home, St. Paul, 1946; nurse Sister Elizabeth Kenney Polio Hosp., St. Paul, 1946; seamstress Hirsch, Weis, White Stag, Pendleton, Mayfair, Portland, Oreg., 1960-72; owner, operator, contract mgr., creative designer The Brass Needle, Portland, 1972—; contractor Forrester's Sanderson Safety, Scotsco, Nero & Assocs., Gara Gear, Portland, 1972—, Columbia Sportswear; tchr. Indo Chinese Cultural Ctr., Portland, 1982; mfr. of protective chaps and vests for the Pacific Northwest hogging industry. Designer, producer Kisn Bridal Fair, 1969; composer: He Liveth in Me, 1968; prodr. Safety Chaps for Loggers. Sec. Model Cities Com., Portland, 1969; com. mem. Neighborhood Black Christmas Parade, Portland, 1970; custume designer Local Miss Jr. Black Beauty Contest, Portland, 1973; nominating com. Nat. Contract Mgmt. Assn., Portland, 1978; mem. nominating com. Multi-Cultural Sr. Adv. Com., 1988-91. Mem. NAFE, Urban League, Urban League Guild (historian 1991-92), Am. Assn. Ret. Persons, Nat. Contract Mgmt. Assn. Democrat. Mem. United Ch. of Christ. Home and Office: The Brass Needle 2809 NE 12th Ave Portland OR 97212-3219

RUSSELL, MARLOU, psychologist; b. Tucson, June 2, 1956; d. William Herman and Carole Eleanor (Musgrove) McBratney; m. Jan Christopher Russell, Sept. 9, 1989. BA U. Ariz., 1981; MA Calif. Grad. Inst., 1983, PhD, 1987. Lic. psychologist, marriage, family and child counselor. Asst. to pres. Western Psychol. Svcs., L.A., 1978-81; crisis counselor Cedars-Sinai Med. Ctr., L.A., 1980-84; counselor South Bay Therapeutic Clinic, Hawthorne, Calif., 1982-84; psychotherapist PMC Treatment Systems, L.A., 1984-85, Beverly Hills Counseling Ctr., 1984-85, Comprehensive Care Corp., L.A., 1985-86; pvt. practice, L.A., 1986—; counselor Brotman Med. Ctr., L.A., 1982-83, Julia Ann Singer Ctr., L.A., 1984; bd. dirs. Los Angeles Commn. Assualts Against Women, 1987-89. Author: Adoption Wisdom: A Guide to the Issues and Feelings of Adoption, 1996. Mem. Internat. Assn. Eating Disorders Profls., Women in Health (bd. dirs. 1993-94), Women's Referral Svc., Calif. State Psychol. Assn., Calif. Assn. Marriage & Family Therapists (bd. dirs. 1993-94), Am. Adoption Congress, Westside Bus. Womens Assn. (bd. dirs. 1993-94). Democrat. Office: 1452 26th St Ste 103 Santa Monica CA 90404-3042

RUSSELL, PATRICK JAMES, priest; b. Boise, Idaho, May 10, 1959; s. Glenn Edward and Doralea (Trumble) R. BA, Boise U., 1982; MDiv, St. Patrick's Sem., 1986. Ordained priest Roman Catholic Ch., 1986. Assoc. pastor St. Marks Cath. Ch., Boise, 1986-91; chaplain Chateau de Boise, 1991—, Bishop Kelly H.S., 1993—. Active Nat. Cath. Office for Persons With Disabilities, 1991—, Idaho Vocations Bd., 1992-95; founder, dir. Father Russell Charity Golf Scramble for Persons with Chronic Illnesses, 1986—; apptd. tribunal advocate Office of Canonical Affairs, Idaho, 1996—. Named Idaho Handicapped Student of Yr., 1974, Best Actor, Boise Little Theatre, 1979-80, Outstanding Young Man of Am., 1983, 84, 86, 87, Outstanding Youth in Achievement, Cambridge, U.K., Internat. Man of Yr., Cambridge, 1995. Mem. Am. Film Inst., Amnesty Internat., Nat. Theatre Comm. Group (charter), Internat. Soc. Poets (life, award), Internat. Biog. Ctr., Right to Life/Spl. Olympics, Sigma Phi Epsilon. Democrat.

RUSSELL, THOMAS ARTHUR, lawyer; b. Corona, Calif., Aug. 2, 1953; s. Larry Arthur Russell and Patricia Helena (Collins) Heath; m. Mary Ellen Leach, June 20, 1992; children: James Trevor, Elizabeth Mary. BS, U. Calif., Berkeley, 1976; JD, U. So. Calif., 1982. Bar: Calif. 1983, U.S. Dist. Ct. (cen. dist.) Calif. 1983, U.S. Ct. Appeals (9th cir.) 1986, U.S. Supreme Ct. 1988. Law clk. Calif. Ct. Appeal, L.A., 1981; assoc. Graham & James, Long Beach, Calif., 1982-88; ptnr. Cogswell Woolley Nakazawa & Russell, Long Beach, 1988—; spkr., panelist Nat. Marine Bankers Assn., Chgo., 1987—; bd. dirs. Ctr. Internat. Comml. Arbitration, 1991—; bd. dirs. Internat. Bus. Assn. So. Calif., 1989—, pres., 1994-95. Author: (with others) Benedict on Admiralty, 1995, Recreational Boating Law, 1992, Moore's Federal Practice, Admiralty Vol., 1997; editor Boating Briefs, 1991-96. Bd. dirs. Greater L.A. World Trade Ctr. Assn., L.A.-Long Beach, 1996—, Long Beach Area C. of C., 1994—; hon. mem. Am. Vessel Documentation Assn., 1995. Mem. ABA (Bronze Key award 1982, maritime fin. subcom., chmn. 1994—), Maritime Law Assn. U.S. (proctor, fin. and recreational boating coms., chmn. subcom. on recreational boating edn. 1991—), Calif. Bar Assn., L.A. County Bar Assn., Long Beach Bar Assn., Legion of Lex. Am. Inn of Ct. (barrister). Republican. Roman Catholic. Home: 7 Mustang Rd Rancho Palos Verdes CA 90275-5250 Office: Cogswell Woolley Nakazawa & Russell 111 W Ocean Blvd Ste 2000 Long Beach CA 90802-4646

RUSSIN, ROBERT ISAIAH, sculptor, educator; b. N.Y.C., Aug. 26, 1914; s. Uriel and Olga (Winnett) R.; m. Adele Mutchnick, May 21, 1937; children: Joseph Mark, Lincoln David, Uriel Robin. BA, CCNY, 1933, MS, 1935; postgrad. (Inst. fellow), Beaux Arts Inst. Design, 1935-36. Tchr. sculpture Copper Union Art Inst., N.Y.C., 1944-47; prof. art U. Wyo., Laramie, 1947-86; prof., artist-in-residence U. Wyo., 1976-85, Disting. prof. emeritus, 1985—. One-man shows Tucson Fine Arts Ctr., 1966, Colorado Springs (Colo.) Fine Arts Ctr., 1967, Palm Springs (Calif.) Desert Mus., Chas. G. Bowers Meml. Mus., Judah L. Magnes Meml. Mus., Berkeley, Calif.; retrospective one-man exhbn. Nat. Gallery Modern Art, Santo Domingo, Dominican Republic, 1976, Tubac Ctr. of the Arts, Ariz., 1987, Old Town Gallery-Park City, Ut., Riggins Gallery, Scottsdale, Ariz., 1989, Fine Arts Mus., U. Wyo., 1991; sculpture commns. include 2 8-foot metal figures, Evanston (Ill.) Post Office, 1939, three life-size carved figures, Conshohocken (Pa.) Post Office, 1940, Benjamin Franklin Monument, U. Wyo., 1957, Bust of Lincoln, Lincoln Mus., Washington, (now in Gettysburg Mus.), 1959, Lincoln Monument atop summit Lincoln Hwy., (now U.S. Interstate 80), Wyo, 1959, monumental bas-relief bronze Cheyenne (Wyo.) Fed. Bldg, 1966, two carved wood walls, Denver Fed. Bldg., 1966, monumental fountain, City of Hope Med. Ctr., Los Angeles, 1966-67, statue, Brookhaven (N.Y.) Nat. Lab., 1968, life-size bronze sculpture fountain, Pomona Coll., 1969, monumental bronze sculpture Prometheus Natrona County (Wyo.) Pub. Library, 1974, Man and Energy, Casper (Wyo.) C. of C., 1974, 12-foot marble carving Menorah Med. Ctr., Kansas City, Mo., 1975, Einstein and Gershwin medals Magnes Meml. Mus, Berkeley, Nat. Mus. Art, Santo Domingo, Dominican Republic, 1975, monumental fountain, Galleria d'Arte Moderna, Santo Domingo, 1977, Duarte Monument, Santo Domingo, 1977, 30 foot steel and water fountain monument City Hall, Casper, 1980, marble and bronze monument, Lincoln Centre, Dallas, 1982, acrylic steel and bronze monument, Herschler State Office Bldg., Cheyenne, 1984, marble monument, U. Wyo., Laramie, 1985, portrait head Charles Bluhdorn, chmn. Gulf & Western, 1975, portrait bust Pres. J. Balaguer of Dominican Republic, 1975, portrait head G. Wilson Knight, Shakespearean actor and scholar, 1975, 2 12-foot bronze figures The Greeting and the Gift for Bicentennial Commn., Cheyenne, 1976, monumental marble head of Juan Pablo Duarte liberator Dominican Republic, Santo Domingo, 1976, marble sculpture Trio, U. Wyo., 1985, Isaac B. Singer medal for Magnes Mus., 1983, monumental Holocaust Figure Tucson Jewish Community Ctr., 1989, granite monument Chthonodynamis, Dept. Energy Bldg., Washington, 1992, bust Hon. Milward Simpson, 1993, bust James Forest U. Wyo., 1993, bronze statue Univ. Med. Ctr., Tuscon, Head, Gov. Stanley Hathway, Cheyenne, Wy. 1995; contbr. articles to profl. jours.Head, Pres. Franklin D. Roosevelt, Rotunda (pres.hosp. Bethsda, Md.). Recipient awards sec. fine arts U.S. Treasury, 1939, 40, Lincoln medal U.S. Congress, 1959, Alfred G.B. Steel award Pa.

Acad. Fine Arts, 1961, medal of Order of Duarte Sanchez y Mella, Dominican Republic, 1977; Ford Found. fellow, 1953. Mem. Nat. Sculpture Conf. (exec. bd.), Sculptors Guild, Nat. Sculpture Soc., AIA, AAUP, Coll. Art Internat. Inst. Arts and Letters, Phi Beta Kappa (hon.). Home: 61 N Fork Rd Centennial WY 82055 also: 1160 Placita Salubre Green Valley AZ 85614

RUSSO, LAURA, gallery director; b. Waterbury, Conn., Mar. 7, 1943; d. Lawrence and Lillian A. (Russo) Kaplan; m. John I. Lawrence, May 6, 1962 (div. 1974); children: Maia Giosi, Dylan Russo. Cert., Pacific N.W. Coll. Art, 1975. Art instr. Tucker Maxon Oral Sch., Portland, Oreg., 1970-74, Pacific N.W. Coll. Art, Portland, 1977-78; assoc. dir. Fountain Fine Arts, Seattle, 1981-82; asst. dir. Fountain Gallery of Art, Portland, 1975-86; owner, dir. Laura Russo Gallery, Portland, 1986—; lectr. Portland State Coll., 1992; juror Oreg. Sch. Design, Portland, 1988, Western Oreg. State Coll. 1992, Beaverton Arts Commn., 1992, Oreg. Hist. Soc., 1990; com. mem. Oreg. Com. for Nat. Mus. Women in Arts, 1988; guest interviewer art dept. Oreg. State Coll., 1996; advisor art dept. Portland State U., 1997. Mem. com. awards and grants Met. Arts Commn., Portland, 1988, 89; mem. P.N.C.A.; juror Art in Pub. Schs. Program, 1990; juror ArtQuake, Portland, 1994; juror Corvallis (Oreg.) Art Ctr., 1995. Mem. Alumni Friends, Contemporary Arts Coun. (program chmn., v.p. 1989-91), Portland Art Mus. (search com. 1993-94), Oreg. Art Inst., Friends Print Soc., Oreg. Art Inst., L.A. Mus. Contemporary Art, Seattle Art Mus. (lectr. 1987), Art Table (West Coast br.). Democrat. Office: Laura Russo Gallery 805 NW 21st Ave Portland OR 97209-1408

RUSSO, VINCENT BARNEY, music educator; b. Carmel, Calif., Oct. 19, 1944; s. Salvatore Dody and Betty Lou (Posey) R. BA, San Francisco State U., 1967, MA, 1969; lic. de concert, Ecole Normale de Musique, Paris, 1973; PhD, U. Calif., San Diego, 1978. Assoc. in voice U.S. Internat. U., San Diego, 1976-83; assoc. in music Internat. U., London, 1979-80; adj. prof. Tex. Christian U., Ft. Worth, 1986-88, asst. prof. vocal performance pedagogy, 1988-95; faculty Coll of the Redwoods, Mendocino, Calif., 1996—; apprentice artist Santa Fe Opera Co., 1971; tching. asst., rsch. asst. U. Calif., San Diego, 1974-78; baritone San Diego Opera Co., 1976-82; asst. editor, editor Jour. Rsch. in Singing, Ft. Worth, 1978-95; music coach, dir. Inst. Vocal Studies, Ft. Worth, 1981-88. Baritone soloist French Radio TV, 1971; performer The Merry Widow, PBS, 1977; editor: Jour. Rsch. in Singing and Applied Vocal Pedagog, 1987-95. Recipient Alexander Saunderson award Met. Opera San Francisco, 1969, Young Artist award Nat. Fedn. Music Clubs, 1969, 77, Harriet H. Wooley and Frank Huntington Beebe award, 1972, 73, William M. Sullivan Music Found. award for European audition, 1974. Mem. Internat. Assn. Rsch. in Singing (gen. sec. 1987-95), Nat. Assn. Tchrs. Singing (Singing Artist award 1971), Coll. Music Soc.

RUSSON, LEONARD H., judge; b. Salt Lake City, May 15, 1933. JD, Utah Coll., 1962. Pvt. practice Salt Lake City, 1962-84; judge Utah Dist. Ct. (3d dist.), Utah Ct. Appeals; now assoc. justice Utah Supreme Ct., Salt Lake City; vice chair Utah Bd. Dist. Ct. Judges; mem. Jud. Conduct Commn., Utah Supreme Ct. Adv. Com. on Code of Profl. Conduct. Office: Utah Supreme Ct 332 State Capitol Building Salt Lake City UT 84114-1202*

RUSUNEN, ROBERT LEE, purchasing manager; b. Missoula, Mont., Mar. 16, 1946. BS in Bus., U. Mont., 1971; MBA in Bus., Wash. State U., 1977. Cert. purchasing mgr.; cert. prodn. inventory mgmt. Buyer, merchandise mgr. Hart-Aldin Co., Billings, Mont., 1971-75; region materials mgr. GE Supply, Seattle, 1976-79; dir. purchasing Riedel International, Portland, Oreg., 1979-82, v.p. purchasing and pers., 1982-84; mgr. corp. purchasing Pacific Telecom, Inc., Vancouver, Wash., 1985—. V.p. Wishing Wells Home Owners Assn., Ridgefield, Wash., 1996-97. Staff sgt., USAF, 1964-68. Mem. Nat. Assn. Purchasing Mgmt., Am. Prodn. and Inventory Control Soc., Constrn. Owners Assn. Am., Nat. Contract Mgmt. Assn. Home: 2730 S Cornett Dr Ridgefield WA 98642

RUTAN, DOUGLAS EDWIN, administrator; b. Boise, Idaho, Apr. 24, 1949; s. Leonard Lyle and nancy (Etta) R.; m. Nancy Elizabeth Cooksey, June 9, 1973; children: Jessica, Sarah, Kathryn. BS in Edn., Northern Az. U., 1971; MS in Edn., U. Az., 1975; Ednl. Specialist, U. Idaho, 1990. Tchr. Yuma (Az.) Sch. Dist., 1971-76; tchr. Meridian (Idaho) Sch. Dist., 1976-77, sch. prin., 1977-91, dir. spl. svcs., 1991—. Sec. Meridian (Idaho) Rotary Club, 1988-93, pres. elect, 1993; mem. Idaho State Centennial Commn., 1990, Meridian Centennial Commn., 1992-93. Recipient Idaho Gem award Idaho Assn. Elem. Prin., Boise, 1986, Excellence in Edn. award nat. Assn. Elem. Prin., Washington, 1991; named Adminstr. of Yr., Ada County Edn. Office Personnel, Boise, 1991. Mem. Coun. for Exceptional Children, Idaho Assn. Sch. Adminstrs., Meridian C. of C. Republican. Presbyterian. Home: 11211 W Hickory Dale Dr Boise ID 83713-1029 Office: Meridian Sch Dist 911 N Meridian Rd Meridian ID 83642-2241

RUTES, WALTER ALAN, architect; b. N.Y.C., Sept. 21, 1928; s. Jack and Sarah (Ogur) R.; m. Helene Darville, Apr. 2, 1952; children: Daniel J., Linda Lee. B.Arch. (Sands Meml. medal 1950), Cornell U., 1950; fellow city planning, MIT, 1951; postgrad., Harvard U. Grad. Sch. Design, 1978. Cert. Nat. Council Archtl. Registration Bds. Assoc. ptnr. Skidmore, Owings & Merrill, N.Y.C., 1951-72; v.p. John Carl Warnecke & Assocs., N.Y.C., 1972-74; staff v.p. Intercontinental Hotels Corp., N.Y.C., 1974-80; dir. architecture Holiday Inns, Inc., Memphis, 1980-83; dir. design The Sheraton Corp., Boston, 1983-85; chmn 9 Tek Ltd. Hotel Cons., 1985—; chmn. adv. bd. Hult Fellowships for Constrn. Industry, 1968-75, Architects and Engrs. Com. New Bldg. Code, 1968; mem. zoning adv. com. N.Y.C. Planning Commn., 1970; lectr. in field, 1968—; mem. steering com. UNESCO Council Tall Bldgs. and Urban Habitat, 1980—; vis. prof. Cornell-Essec Grad. Program; vis. prof. Nova U. Author: Hotel Planning and Design, New Trends in Resort Design and Development; (software system) SHAPE, Megatrends and Marketecture; contbr. articles to profl. jours.; prin. works include Lincoln Center Library for Performing Arts, N.Y.C., 1967, Am. Republic Ins. Co. Nat. Hdqrs., Des Moines, 1967, HUD Apts., Jersey City, 1972, Merrill Lynch Bldg., N.Y.C., 1973, Tour Fiat, Paris, 1974, Aid Assn. for Luths. Nat. Hdqrs., Appleton, Wis., 1976, Semiramis Intercontinental Hotel, Cairo, 1985, Intercontinental, Jeddah, 1983, Embassy Suites Internat., 1985, Universal City Hotel Complex, L.A., 1986, TechWorld Conv. Hotel, Washington, 1986, Sheraton Fairplex Conv. Ctr., L.A., 1992, Orlando Conv. Ctr. Hotel, 1993, Winter Olympiad Media Complex, Norway, 1993, Ephesus Resort Complex, Turkey, 1986, Royal Christiania Hotel, Oslo, Norway, 1991, EuroFrance Leisure Park Complex, Cannes, 1993, Kuna Hills Multi Resort, Guam, 1994. Recipient Platinum Circle award Hotel Design Industry, 1988. Fellow AIA; mem. Ethical Culture Soc. Office: 8501 N 84th Pl Scottsdale AZ 85258-2419 also: 25 Richbell Rd White Plains NY 10605-4110

RUTHER, CHRISTINE L., biomedical engineer; b. Dayton, Ohio, May 17, 1963; d. Frank J. and Nancy L. (Patten) R.; m. Gregory R. Adams, Sept. 1992. BS in Physics, Xavier U., Cin., 1985; MS in Biomed. Engring., Ohio State U., 1990. Physics and math tchr. Chaminade-Julienne High Sch., Dayton, 1985-86, chmn. dept. sci., 1986-87; teaching assoc. Ohio State U., Columbus, 1987-90; rsch. asst. Bionetics for NASA, Kennedy Space Ctr., Fla., 1991; clin. engr. William Beaumont Hosp., Royal Oak, Mich., 1991-92, Biomed. Cons. Svcs., Irvine, Calif., 1993-95; dir. product devel. and regulatory affairs AirBed Corp., Anaheim, Calif., 1995-96; med. product safety engr. TÜV Product Svcs., San Diego, 1996—. Mem. IEEE, Assn. for Women in Sci. Office: TÜV Product Svcs Med Divsn 10040 Mesa Rim Rd San Diego CA 92121

RUTHERFORD, GEORGE WILLIAMS, III, preventive medicine physician; b. San Diego, Apr. 6, 1952; s. G. Williams and Anna Gwyn (Dearing) R.; m. Lisa Anderson, Aug. 24, 1974 (div. 1984); children: Alicia Gwyn, George Williams IV; m. Mary Workman, Feb. 23, 1985; children: Alexandra Catherine, Anne Elizabeth Martha, Hugh Thomas Gwyn, Amanda Frances Julia. AB in Classics, Stanford U., 1974, BS in Chemistry, 1975, AM in History, 1975; MD, Duke U., 1978. Diplomate Am. Bd. Pediat., Am. Bd. Preventive Medicine, Nat. Bd. Med. Examiners. Intern in pediat. U. Calif. Med. Ctr., San Diego, 1978-79; resident in pediat. U. Calif. Med. Ctr., Hosp. for Children, San Diego, 1979-80; resident Hosp. for Sick Children, Toronto, 1980-81; chief resident Children's Hosp. and Health Ctr., San Diego, 1981-82; EIS officer divsn. viral diseases, divsn. field svcs Epidemology Office Ctrs. for Disease Control, Atlanta, 1982-84; dir. divsn. immunization, acting dir. divsn. tropical disease N.Y.C. Dept. Health, 1983-85; med. epidemologist AIDS program Ctrs. for Disease Control, San Francisco Dept. Pub. Health, 1985-87; from med. dir. to dir. AIDS office San Francisco Dept. Pub. Health, 1986-90; chief, infectious disease br. and state epidemologist Calif. Dept Health, Berkeley, 1990-92, dep. dir. prevention svcs. and state epidemologist, 1992-95, state health officer, 1993-95; assoc. dean adminstrn., prof. epidemiology/health adminstrn. Sch. Pub. Health, U. Calif., Berkeley, 1995—; transport physician Children's Hosp. and Health Ctr., San Diego, 1981; clin. asst. prof. pediatrics Emory U., Atlanta, 1982-83, Cornell U., N.Y.C., 1984-85, U. Calif., San Francisco, 1986-92, asst. clin. prof. epidemiology and biostats., 1987-92, family and cmty. medicine, 1988-90; assoc. adj. prof. epidemiology, biostats. and pediatrics, 1992-95, adj. prof., 1996—; assoc. clin. prof. cmty. health u. Calif., Davis, 1991-95; cons. Pan-Am. Health Orgn., S.Am., 1986-89, Ctrs. Disease Control, Atlanta, 1987—, WHO, 1988-90. Contbr. numerous articles to profl. jours., chpts. to books; co-translator cardiology teaching manual, other Spanish med. articles; editor in chief Calif. Morbidity, 1990-92; mem. editl. bd. Calif. AIDS Update, 1988—, Current Issues in Pub. Health, 1993—; referee: AIDS, 1988—, Am. Jour. Pub. Health, 1989—, Brit. Med. Jour., 1994—, Internat. Jour. Epidemology, 1991—, Jour. Acquired Immune Deficiency Syndrome, 1989—, New Eng. Jour. Medicine, 1989—, Western Jour. Medicine, 1989—. Mem. numerous profl. adv. coms., task forces, etc. which aid govt. and charitable orgns. in work against infectious disease, especially AIDS. Commdr. USPHSR, 1982—. Fellow Am. Acad. Pediatrics; mem. APHA, Am. Assn. for History of Medicine, Am. Soc. Tropical Medicine and Hygiene, Bay Area Communicable Disease Exch., Calif. Med. Assn., Infectious Diseases Soc. Am., No. Calif. Pub. Health Assn., Internat. AIDS Soc., Soc. for Epidemiol. Rsch., Soc. for Pediatric Epidemiol. Rsch., Assn. State and Territorial Health Ofcls. Republican. Episcopalian. Office: U Calif Sch Pub Health 140 Warren Hall Berkeley CA 94720-7360

RUTHERFORD, REID, finance company executive; b. Morristown, N.J., Dec. 30, 1952; s. Clinton Homer and Bonnie Beth (Bergner) R.; m. Beth Ann Husak, Apr. 3, 1977; children: Ian Michael, Laurel Bryce, Corinne Leigh, Alyse Allyne. BA, Pepperdine U., 1975; MBA, Stanford U., 1981. Exec. v.p. Analytics, Inc., N.Y.C., 1976-79; pres. Softlink Corp., Santa Clara, Calif., 1981-83, Rsch. Applications for Mgmt., Menlo Park, Calif., 1984-85; pres., CEO Concord Growth Corp., San Jose, Calif., 1985—, with, 1985—. Contbr. articles to profl. jours. Office: Concord Growth Corp 3590 N First St Ste 200 San Jose CA 95134

RUTHERFORD, ROBERT BARRY, surgeon; b. Edmonton, Alta., Can., July 29, 1931; s. Robert Lyon and Kathleen Emily (Gunn) R.; m. Beulah Kay Folk, Aug. 20, 1955; children: Robert Scott, Lori Jayne, Holly Anne, Trudy Kaye, Jay Wilson. BA in Biology, Johns Hopkins U., 1952, MD, 1956. Surgeon U. Colo. Health Sci. Ctr., Denver; emeritus prof. surgery U. Colo., Denver, 1996—. Editor: (texts) Management of Trauma, 1968, 4 edits., Vascular Surgery, 1978, 4 edits., An Atlas of Vascular Surgery, 1993; editor quar. rev. Seminars in Vascular Surgery; sr. editor Jour. Vascular Surgery. Mem. Internat. Soc. for Cardiovascular Surgery, Phi Beta Kappa, Alpha Omega Alpha. Republican. Unitarian. Office: 0146 Spring Beauty Dr Box 23159 Silverthorne CO 80498

RUTHERFORD, WILLIAM DRAKE, investment executive, lawyer; b. Marshalltown, Iowa, Jan. 14, 1939; s. William Donald and Lois Esther (Drake) R.; m. Janice W. Rutherford, Feb. 4, 1965 (div. Mar. 1982); children: Wayne Donald, Melissa Drake; m. Karen Anderegg, Jan. 2, 1994. BS, U. Oreg., 1961; LLB, Harvard U., 1964. Bar: Oreg. 1964, U.S. Dist. Ct. Oreg. 1966. Assoc. Maguire, Kester & Cosgrave, Portland, Oreg., 1966-69; house counsel May & Co., Portland, 1969-70, pvt. practice, 1970-71; pvt. practice McMinnville, Oreg., 1971-84; mem. Oreg. Ho. of Reps., Salem, 1977-84; state treas. State of Oreg., Salem, 1984-87; chmn. Oreg. Investment Coun., Salem, 1986-87; exec. v.p., dir. U.S. and Australia ops. ABD Internat. Mgmt. Corp., N.Y.C., 1987-88, pres., chief exec. officer, bd. dirs., 1988-89; pres., bd. dirs. Societé Gen. Touche Remnant, 1990-93; dir. spl. projects Metallgesellschaft Corp., N.Y.C., 1994-95; mng. dir. Macadam Capital Ptnrs., Portland, 1995-96; CEO Fiberboard Asbestos Compensation Trust, Portland, 1996—; bd. dirs. Metro One Telecomms. Bd. dirs. Portland Opera Assn. 1st lt. U.S. Army, 1964-66. Recipient Contbn. to Individual Freedom award ACLU, 1981. Mem. Internat. Bar Assn., Nat. Assn. State Treas. (exec. v.p. 1985, 86, pres. western region 1985, 86), Nat. Assn. State Auditors, Comptr. and Treas. (exec. com. 1987). Republican. Home and Office: 6978 SW Foxfield Ct Portland OR 97225-6054

RUTLEDGE, JOE, pathologist, scientist; b. Lewisburg, Tenn., Aug. 18, 1950; s. Edward and Geraldine Rutledge; m. Ellen Armistead, May 15, 1976; children: Jack, Rosemary. BS, Rhodes Coll., 1972; MD, Vanderbilt U., 1976. Diplomate Am. Bd. Pediatric Pathology, Am. Bd. Anatomic and Clin. Pathology. Asst. prof. pathology Univ. Tex. Southwestern Medical Sch., Dallas, 1980-88; assoc. prof. lab. medicine U. Washington, Seattle, 1988—; mem. adv. bd. Human Developmental Anatomy Ctr., Washington, 1992—; collaborative rschr. Oak Ridge (Tenn.) Nat. Lab., 1982—. Contbr. chpts. to books; contbr. articles to profl. jours. Adv. bd. Healthcare Profl. West Washington, Seattle, 1992-96, March of Dimes. Fellow Coll. Am. Pathology (practice com. 1990-95); mem. Soc. for Pediatric Pathology (coun. 1988-94), Am. Assn. Clin. Chemistry (pediatric com. 1980-94), Am. Soc. Clin. Pathology, Am. Soc. Human Genetics. Office: Childrens Hosp & Med Ctr Lab Ch 37 4800 Sand Point Way NE Seattle WA 98105-3901

RUTTENCUTTER, BRIAN BOYLE, manufacturing company executive; b. Long Beach, Calif., June 15, 1953; s. Wayne Andrew and Florence Mae (Heckman) F.; m. Marilyn Ruth Grubb, Sept. 9, 1978; children: Christi Anne (dec.), Melissa Lyn. BS in Bus. Adminstrn. and Acctg., Biola U., 1976; MBA, Calif. State U., Long Beach, 1983. Cert. mgmt. acct. Controller Fuller Theol. Sem., Pasadena, Calif., 1976-80; dir. gen. acctg. Air Calif., Newport Beach, 1980-84; corp. controller PBS Bldg. Systems, Inc., Anaheim, Calif., 1984-88, v.p. fin. and adminstrn., 1988-93; CFO, v.p. fin. For Better Living, Inc., and The Quikset Orgn., Auburn and Irvine, Calif., 1993-95; v.p. fin., CFO Phillips Industries Inc., Commerce, Calif., 1996—; chmn., vice chmn., fin. commn. City of Irvine (Calif.), Calif., 1990-94, cmty. svcs. commn., 1996—. Mem. Drivers for Hwy. Safety, Irvine, Calif., 1986; bd. dirs. Grace Brethren Ch., Long Beach, 1978-80; bd. dirs. Woodbridge Cmty. Ch., Irvine, 1986-88, 91-92, vice chmn., 1991, chmn., 1992; v.p. Greater Irvine Rep. Assembly, 1990, treas., 1991. Mem. Inst. Cert. Mgmt. Accts., Inst. Mgmt. Accts., Fin. Execs. Inst. (dir. Orange County chpt.). Republican. Home: 14262 Wyeth Ave Irvine CA 92606-1838

RUTTER, DEBORAH FRANCES, orchestra administrator; b. Pottstown, Pa., Sept. 30, 1956; d. Marshall Anthony and Winifred (Hitz) R. BA, Stanford U., 1978; MBA, U. So. Calif., 1985. Orch. mgr. L.A. Philharm., 1978-86; exec. dir. L.A. Chamber Orch., 1986-92, Seattle Symphony, 1992—. Bd. dirs. AIDS project L.A., 1985-92; active Jr. League L.A., 1982-92. Mem. Am. Symphony Orch. League, Assn. Calif. Symphony Orchs. (pres. 1988-91), Assn. N.W. Symphony Orchs. (bd. dirs. 1993—), Chamber Music Soc. L.A. (bd. dirs. 1987-92), Ojai Festival (pres.'s coun.). Democrat. Episcopalian. Office: Seattle Symphony Ctr House 305 Harrison St Fl 4 Seattle WA 98109-4623*

RUTTER, GEORGE B., JR., career officer; b. El Dorado, Ill., Jan. 22, 1949; s. George B. Sr. and Margaret (Wilson) R.; m. Betty J. Leyland, May 15, 1971; 1 child, Melinda. Student, U. Ariz., 1968-69. Enlisted Ariz. Air N.G., Tucson, 1967, advanced through grades to maj.; phys. therapy asst. Tucson Med. Ctr., 1968-69, asst. mgr. transp. com., 1969; phys. therapy asst. J.J. Villano RPT, Tucson, 1970; fuels technician Ariz. Air N.G., Tucson, 1971-74, transp., maintenance analyst, 1974-82, disaster preparedness officer, 1982-88, fgn. tng. officer internat. protocol, 1989-94, support group comdr., 1995—. Mem. Air Transport Airport, Tucson, 1994—. Mem. Ariz. Nat. Guard Assn. (v.p. 1994-95, pres. 1995-96). Roman Catholic. Office: 162 Fighter Wing 1650 E Perimeter Way Tucson AZ 85706-6079

RUTTER, MARSHALL ANTHONY, lawyer; b. Pottstown, Pa., Oct. 18, 1931; s. Carroll Lennox and Dorothy (Tagert) R.; m. Winifred Hitz, June 6, 1953 (div. 1970); m. Virginia Ann Hardy, Jan. 30, 1971 (div. 1992); children: Deborah Frances, Gregory Russell, Theodore Thomas; m. Terry Susan Knowles, Dec. 19, 1992. BA, Amherst (Mass.) Coll., 1954; JD, U. Pa., 1959. Bar: Calif 1960. Assoc. O'Melveny & Myers, Los Angeles, 1959-64; assoc. Flint & MacKay, Los Angeles, 1964-67, ptnr., 1967-72; ptnr. Rutter, Hobbs & Davidoff, Los Angeles, 1973—. Gov. The Music Ctr. of L.A. County, 1978-86, 89-92; dir. Music Ctr. Operating Co., 1992-96; bd. dirs. Chorus Am., Phila., 1987-96, pres., 1993-95; bd. dirs., pres. L.A. Master Chorale Assn., 1963-92, chmn. 1992-96; vestryman All Saints Ch., Beverly Hills, Calif., 1983-86, 88-90; bd. dirs. Music Ctr. Operating Co., 1992-96. Mem. ABA, Assn. Bus. Trial Lawyers (bd. dirs. 1980-82), L.A. County Bar Assn., Beverly Hills Bar Assn., Century City Bar Assn., English-Speaking Union (various offices L.A. chpt. 1963-91), L.A. Jr. C. of C. (bd. dirs. 1964-67). Democrat. Episcopalian. Home: 1045 S Orange Grove Blvd # 10 Pasadena CA 91105 Office: Rutter Hobbs & Davidoff Ste 2700 1900 Avenue Of The Stars Los Angeles CA 90067-4508

RUYBALID, LOUIS ARTHUR, social worker, community development consultant; b. Allison, Colo., Apr. 6, 1925; s. Mike Joseph and Helen Mary (Rodriguez) R.; m. Seraphima Alexander, June 12, 1949; children: Mariana, John. BA, U. Denver, 1946-49, MSW, 1951; PhD, U. Calif., Berkeley, 1970; Professor Ad-Honorem (hon.), Nat. U., Caracas, Venezuela, 1964. Social worker Ariz., Calif., Colo., 1951-62; advisor community devel. Unitarian Service Com., Caracas, 1962-64, U.S. Agy. for Internat. Devel., Rio de Janeiro, Brazil, 1964-66; area coordinator U.S. Office Econ. Opportunity, San Francisco, 1966-68; prof., dept. head U. So. Colo., Pueblo, 1974-80; licensing analyst State of Calif., Campbell, 1984—; prof. sch. of social work Highlands U., Las Vegas, N.Mex., 1988-89; cons. UN, Caracas, 1978, Brazilian Govt., Brazilia, 1964-66, Venezuelan Govt., Caracas, 1962-64. Author: (books) Favela, 1970, Glossary for Hominology, 1978, (research instrument) The Conglomerate Hom., 1976. Mem. exec. com. Pueblo (Colo.) Regional Planning Com., 1974-79, Nat. Advisory com. The Program Agy. United Presbyn. Ch., 1978-79. Served with USN, 1944-46. Recipient Pro Mundo Beneficio medal Brazilian Acad. Human Sci., Sao Paulo, 1976; United Def. Fund fellow U. Calif., Berkeley, 1961-62, Cert. World Leadership Internat. Leaders of Achievement, 1988-89. Mem. NASW (cert.), Ethnic Minority Commn., IMAGE (nat. edn. chair), Am. Hominol. Assn. (nat. pres. 1975-79), U. Calif. Alumni Assn., AARP (minority spokesperson), Phi Beta Kappa, Phi Sigma Iota. Democrat. Home and Office: Ruybalid Assoc Inc 129 Calle Don Jose Santa Fe NM 87501-2364 *Personal philosophy: As a personal credo, I have adopted the philosophy of the Pueblo Indians of New Mexico which is: Amity, not conquest, stability, not strife, conservation, not waste, restraint, not aggression, I embrace the conviction that human energy should be used to care for the primal needs of people!.*

RUYTER, NANCY LEE CHALFA, dance educator; b. Phila., May 23, 1933; d. Andrew Benedict Chalfa and Lois Elizabeth (Strode) McClary; m. Ralph Markson (div.); m. Hans C. Ruyter, Dec. 7, 1968. BA in History, U. Calif., Riverside, 1964; PhD in History, Claremont Grad. Sch., 1970. Tchr. theater dept. Pomona Coll., 1965-72; instr. dance program U. Calif., Riverside, 1972-76, acting chair dance program, 1974-75; instr. dance dept. UCLA, 1976; instr. phys. edn. dept. Orange Coast Coll., 1976-77; asst. prof. dept. phys. edn. and dance Tufts U., 1977-78; asst. prof. phys. edn. dept. Calif. State U., Northridge, 1978-82; asst. prof., then assoc. prof. dance dept. U. Calif., Irvine, 1982—, assoc. dean Sch. Fine Arts, 1984-88, 95-96, chair dept. dance, 1989-91; presenter in field. Appeared with Jasna Planina Folk Ensemble, 1972-77, 78-79, Di Falco and Co., 1955-57; choreographer, dir. numerous coll. dance prodns.; contbr. articles, revs. to profl. publs.; author: Reformers and Visionaries: The Americanization of the Art of Dance, 1979. Mem. Am. Soc. Theatre Rsch., Bulgarian Studies Assn., Congress on Rsch. in Dance (bd. dirs. 1977-80, pres. 1981-85), Folk Dance Fedn., Internat. Fedn. Theatre Rsch., Soc. Dance Rsch., Soc. Ethnomusicology, Soc. Dance History Scholars (steering com. 1980-81), Spanish Dance Soc., Theatre Libr. Assn. Office: U Calif-Irvine Dept Dance Irvine CA 92697

RYAN, ALLYN CAUAGAS, author, educator; b. Larena, The Philippines, June 2, 1938; came to U.S., 1957; d. Ignacio Fallorina Cauagas and Ignacia (Prudencia) Padayhag; m. James Edward Ryan, June 13, 1964; children: Monica Lynn Ryan-Border, Colleen Marie. BA in English, UCLA, 1959, MFA in Theater, 1964. Cert. tchr. lang. arts, lit., comm. arts, theater arts, basic edn., Calif. Adj. faculty Saddleback Coll., Mission Viejo, Calif., 1983-90, Orange Coast Coll., Costa Mesa, Calif., 1986-87, Chapman U., Orange, Calif., 1987-88, Rancho Santiago Coll., Santa Ana, Calif., 1986—. Contbr. poetry, short stories to profl. jours. Mem. legis. adv. com. Rancho Santiago Coll., 1996—, instructional calendar group mem., 1996—. UCI Writing Project fellow, 1989. Mem. NEA, Calif. Tchrs. Assn., C.C. Assn. (WHO award 1997), Continuing Edn. Faculty Assn. (Rancho Santiago Coll. chpt. pres. 1996—, negotiations chmn. 1995-96), Romance Writers of Am. Home: 45 Grant Irvine CA 92620-3355

RYAN, CATHRINE SMITH, publisher; b. Calif.; d. Owen W. and Margarette D. Griffin; A.A., Bellevue Jr. Coll., Denver, 1948; grad. Barnes Sch. Commerce, Denver, 1950; student N.Y. Ballet Acad., 1954. Dir. Ballet Workshop, Enumclaw, Wash., 1958-64; dir. confs. and seminars San Francisco Theol. Sem., 1977-80; pres., dir. Cathi, Ltd., pub. and cons. office orgn. and mgmt., San Francisco, 1980—; freelance travel photographer, 1968-80; guest instr. in field; guest lectr. on German rsch. Recipient various certs. of recognition. Republican. Mormon. Author: Face Lifting Exercises, 1980, Sullivan's Chain, 1986; author visitor guide books; contbr. articles to procedure and policy manuals, geneal. rsch., family histories; translator old German script. Avocation: scuba diving. *Personal philosophy: Learn everything about everything you can. Exercise every opportunity that comes your way. You never know who you will grow up to be!.*

RYAN, CHARLOTTE MURIEL, oncology nurse; b. Beedeville, Ark., Sept. 2, 1939; d. Eugene Sanford and Edith Elizabeth (Goforth) Breckenridge; children: Russell Kent, Cary Randall, Molly Renee. BSN cum laude, Calif. State U., Fresno, 1991, MSN, 1997. OCN cert. nurse. Psychiat. technician Porterville (Calif.) State Hosp., 1959-67; tchr. developmentally disabled Ariz. Tng. Ctr., Coolidge, 1967-71; Montessori tchr. Tucson, 1972-77; tchr. developmentally disabled Heartland Opportunity Ctr., Madera, Calif., 1977-79; med. office mgr. office of orthopedic surgeon, Madera, 1979-83, office mgr., x-ray technician, 1983-87; staff nurse in oncology St. Agnes Med. Ctr., Fresno, 1991—; instr. nursing dept. Calif. State U., Fresno, 1992, 93, 95. Treas. Hospice of Madera County, 1990-92, bd. dirs., 1992; peer counselor Calif. State U., Fresno, 1989-91; pres. bd. dirs. Easter Seals Soc., Madera, 1981. Mem. Oncology Nursing Soc., Nightingale Soc., Golden Key, Sigma Theta Tau (chair pub. com., editor MUNEWS newsletter 1994-95). Republican. Home: 4544 N Barton Ave Fresno CA 93726-2621 Office: Saint Agnes Med Ctr 1303 E Herndon Ave Fresno CA 93720-3309

RYAN, CLARENCE AUGUSTINE, JR., biochemistry educator; b. Butte, Mont., Sept. 29, 1931; s. Clarence A. Sr. and Agnes L. (Duckham) R.; m. Patricia Louise Meunier, Feb. 8, 1936; children: Jamie Arlette, Steven Michael (dec.), Janice Marie, Joseph Patrick (dec.). BA in Chemistry, Carroll Coll., 1953; MS in Chemistry, Mont. State U., 1956, PhD in Chemistry, 1959. Postdoctoral fellow in biochemistry Oreg. State U., Corvallis, 1959-61, U.S. Western Regional Lab., Albany, Calif., 1961-63; chemist U.S. Western Regional Lab., Berkeley, Calif., 1963-64; asst. prof. biochemistry Wash. State U., Pullman, 1964-68, assoc. prof., 1968-72, prof., 1972—, Charlotte Y. Martin disting. prof., 1991—, chmn. dept. agrl. chemistry, 1977-80, fellow Inst. Biol. Chemistry, 1980—; faculty athletics rep. to PAC-10 & NCAA Wash. State U., 1991-94, 96-97; vis. scientist dept. biochemistry U. Wash., 1981, Harvard U. Med. Sch., 1982, Bert and Natalie Vallee vis. prof., 1997; res. adv. bd. Kemin Industries, Des Moines, 1981—, Plant Genetics, Davis, Calif., 1987-89; research adv. bd. Frito-Lay, Inc., Dallas, 1982, Plant Genetic Engring. Lab., N.M. State U., Las Cruces, 1986-89, Noble Found., 1996—; mem. NRC rev. bd. Plant Gene Exptl. Ctr., Albany, Calif., 1990-93; mgr. biol. stress program USDA Competitve Grants Program, Washington, 1983-84; former mem. adv. panels for H. McKnight Found., Internat. Potato Ctr., Lima, Peru, Internat. Ctr. Genetic Engring. and Biotech., New Delhi, Internat. Ctr. Tropical Agr., Cali, Columbia, Internat. Tropical Agr., Ibandan, Africa; mem. grant rev. panels NSF, USDA, DOE, NIH; co-organizer Internat. Telecommunications Symposium on Plant Biotech.; mem. adv. bd. Bert and Natalie Vallee Found., Harvard Med. Sch., 1997—. Mem. edit. bd. several biochem. and plant physiology jours.; contbr. articles to profl. publs., chpts. to books; co-editor 2 books. Grantee USDA, NSF, NIH, Rockefeller Found., McKnight Found.; recipient Merck award for grad. rsch. Mont. State U., 1959, career devel. awards NIH, 1964-74, Alumni Achievement award Carroll Coll., 1986, Pres.'s Faculty Excellence award in rsch. Wash.

State U., 1986; named to Carroll Coll. Alumni Hall of Fame, 1981, Carroll Coll. Basketball Hall of Fame, 1982; non-resident fellow Noble Found., 1996—. Mem. AAAS, Nat. Acad. Scis. (elected 1986), Am. Chem. Soc. (Kenneth A. Spencer award 1992), Am. Soc. Plant Physiologists (Steven Hales Prize 1992), Am. Soc. Exptl. Biology, Biochem. Soc., Internat. Soc. Chem. Ecology (Silverstein-Simione award 1997), Internat. Soc. Plant Molecular Biology (bd. dirs.), Phytochem. Soc. N.Am., Nat. U. Continuing Assn. (Creative Programming award 1991), Phi Kappa Phi (Recognition award 1976, selected 1 of 100 centennial disting. alumni Mont. State U. 1993). Democrat. Office: Wash State Univ Inst Biol Chemistry Pullman WA 99164

RYAN, FREDERICK JOSEPH, JR., lawyer, public official; b. Tampa, Fla., Apr. 12, 1955; s. Frederick Joseph and Cordelia Beth (Hartman) R.; m. Genevieve Ann McSweeney, Dec. 28, 1985; children: Genevieve Madeline, Madeline Elizabeth. BA, U. So. Calif., 1977, JD, 1980. Bar: Calif. 1980, D.C. 1986. Assoc. Hill, Farrer and Burrill, Los Angeles, 1980-82; dep. dir. then dir. presdl. appointments and scheduling The White House, Washington, 1982-87, dir. pvt. sector initiatives, 1985-87, asst. to the Pres., 1987-89; chief of staff Office of Ronald Reagan, L.A., 1989-95; vice chmn. Allbritton Comm. Co., Washington, 1995—; bd. cons. Riggs Bank Washington, 1995—; mem. staff Reagan-Bush Campaign, Los Angeles, 1980; dir. Internat. Conf. on Pvt. Sector Initiatives, Paris, 1986, Italian-Am. Conf. on Pvt. Sector Initiatives, 1987, Brit.-Am. Conf. on Pvt. Sector Initiatives, 1988; bd. dirs. Riggs Bank Europe Ltd., London. Author (column) Legal Briefs, 1980-82; editor: Ronald Reagan: The Wisdom and Humor of the Great Communicator, 1995. Chmn. Monterey Park (Calif.) Cmty. Rels. Commn., 1977-78; bd. dirs. Ford's Theater, Washington, Town Hall of Calif., L.A., Nancy Reagan Found.; trustee Ronald Reagan Presdl. Found.; mem. bd. advisors Ronald Reagan Inst. for Emergency Medicine, George Washington U. Med. Ctr. Recipient Presdl. Commendation for pvt. sector initiatives Pres. Ronald Reagan, 1986, Medal of Arts and Letters, Govt. of France, 1986, Golden Ambrosiana medal of Milan, Italy, 1987, The Lion of Venice medal, Italy, 1987, comdr. Order of Merit of Republic of Italy, 1992, comdr. Ouissam Alaouite of Morocco, 1995. Mem. ABA, Jonathan Club (L.A.), Metro. Club (Washington). Presbyterian. Office: Allbritton Comm Co 808 17th St NW Washington DC 20006-3903

RYAN, JANE FRANCES, corporate communications executive; b. Bronxville, N.Y., Nov. 1, 1950; d. Bernard M. and Margaret M. (Griffith) R.; m. Kevin Horan, Dec. 26, 1982; 1 child, Kevin. BS in Journalism, Ohio U., 1972; MBA in Mktg., Golden Gate U., 1990. Asst. promotion mgr. Fawcett Publs., Greenwich, Conn., 1972-75; mktg. coordinator Fawcett Mktg. Services div. CBS, Greenwich, Conn., 1975-78; dist. sales mgr. CBS Publs., San Francisco, 1978; prodn. mgr. Cato Inst., San Francisco, 1979-81; account supr. Bus. Media Resources, Mill Valley, Calif., 1981-90, dir. mktg. svcs., 1990-93; assoc. dir. publs. RAND Corp., Santa Monica, Calif., 1993—; bd. dirs. Daybreak, Santa Monica, Calif. Office: RAND 1700 Main St Santa Monica CA 90401-3208

RYAN, JODELL, fine artist; b. Fresno, Calif., Oct. 13, 1932. Student with various artists. Exhibited Fresno Art Mus., Hall of Flowers, San Francisco, Don Price Gallery, Commonwealth Club, San Francisco, Fresno Art Ctr., Fresno Dist. Fair Fine Art Show, others. Recipient Best of Show award S.W.A. Spring Show, Best of Show award Clovis Old West Show, 1st Pl. award 53rd Ann. Statewide Exhbn., Santa Cruz, Judges Choice award 24th Ann. Open Representational Art Show, 1995, more than 50 other awards. Mem. Soc. Western Artists (signature mem.), Pastel Soc. of West Coast, Pastel Soc. of Am. (assoc.), Knickerbocker Artists.

RYAN, JULIE MAE, optometrist, educator, researcher; b. Des Moines, Sept. 3, 1951; d. Albert Boyd and A. Gretchen (Manderscheid) Berg; m. Patrick D. Ryan, June 27, 1976. AA, Southwestern C.C., Creston, Iowa, 1971; BS in Visual Sci., Ill. Coll. Optometry, Chgo., 1975, OD, 1975; MS, Calif. State U., Fullerton, 1986. Diplomate Am. Acad. Optometry. Pvt. practice assoc. Champaign, Ill., 1976-77; instr. So. Calif. Coll. Optometry, Fullerton, 1977-81, asst. prof., 1981-86, assoc. prof., 1986—, chief pediatric vision svcs., 1986-88; co-owner, ptnr. Irvine (Calif.) Optometric Group, 1988—; bd. dirs. Irvine Child Devel. Ctr., 1991-93. Contbr. chpt. to book, articles to profl. jours. Named to Outstanding Young Women of Am., 1979. Fellow Am. Acad. Optometry (vice chair binocular vision and perception sect. 1986-88, coord. written exam. 1991-96), Coll. Optometrists in Vision Devel.; mem. Am. Optometric Assn. (primary care com. 1988-90, long range planning com. 1990-92, mem. membership com. 1992-94, mem. binocular vision com. 1994—), Orton Dyslexia Soc. (bd. dirs. 1994-96), Orange County Optometric Soc. (trustee 1995-96). Home: 5510 Avenida Del Tren Yorba Linda CA 92887-4901 Office: Irvine Optometric Group 4950 Barranca Pkwy Ste 310 Irvine CA 92604

RYAN, MARY GENE, military officer, occupational health nurse; b. Corona, Calif., Sept. 11, 1953; d. Robert James and Genevieve Louise (Kubilis) Guzinski; m. Robert Eldon Ryan III, June 9, 1979; children: Michael Warren, Jessica Gene, Matthew James. BSN, So. Conn. State Coll., 1975; MPH, U. Tex., 1980. Commd. 2d lt. USAF, 1976, advanced through grades to lt. col., 1995; staff nurse obstetrics U. Conn. Med. Ctr., Farmington, 1975-76; med.-surgical staff nurse Williams AFB (Ariz.) Hosp., 1976-77; flight nurse instr. 2d Aeromed. Evacuation Squadron, Rhein Main, Fed. Republic of Germany, 1977-79; officer in charge environ. health Wilford Hall Med. Ctr., Lackland AFB, Tex., 1980-84; chief environ. health AFSC Hosp., Edwards AFB, Calif., 1984-88; dir. occupational health Peterson Med. Clinic, Oxnard, Calif., 1988-89; mgr. health and safety County of Ventura (Calif.)/Gen. Svcs. Agy., 1989—; cons. environ. health L.A. AFB, 1984-88; chief nurse Calif. Air Nat. Guard 146 Med. Sqd., 1992—. Contbr. articles to profl. jours. Mem. choir, soloist, lay eucharistic min. Edwards AFB Cath. Chapel, 1984-88, mem. religious edn. com., 1984-85, lectr., commentator, 1986-87, marriage encounter counselor, 1991—; team mom for various sports, 1989—; AIDS educator, Edwards AFB, 1986-88. Recipient Meritorious Svc. medals USAF, Clin. award Am. Assn. Occupational Health Nurses, 1991. Mem. APHA (occupational health sect.), Am. Assn. Occupational Health Nurses, Calif. Assn. Occupational Health Nurses, Calif. Ctrl. Coast Occupational Health Nurses Assn. (pres. 1993—), Ventura County Med. Aux.

RYAN, MICHAEL LOUIS, controller; b. Corning, Iowa, Feb. 22, 1945; s. Leo Vincent and Elda May (Lawrence) R. AAS in Constrn. Tech., Iowa State U., 1965; BS in Acctg., Drake U., 1972. CPA, Iowa, Wyo. Acct. Ernst & Ernst, Des Moines, 1972-75, Becker, Herrick & Co., Pueblo, Colo., 1975-78; pvt. practice acctg. Gillette, Wyo., 1978-81; acct. Karen M. Moody, CPAs, Sheridan, Wyo., 1981-85; contr. T-C Investments, Inc., Sheridan, 1985—; ptnr. WHG Partnership, Sheridan, 1991—; v.p. Bosley-Ryan Constrn., Inc., Sheridan, 1993—. With spl. forces U.S. Army, 1966-68, Vietnam. Mem. AICPA (tax div.), Wyo. Soc. CPAs, Am. Legion (fin. officer 1977-81), Lodge (sec. Sheridan club 1982-90, pres. 1989), Phi Kappa Phi, Beta Alpha Psi, Beta Gamma Sigma. Democrat. Roman Catholic. Home: 735 Canby St Sheridan WY 82801-4907 Office: T-C Investments Inc 856 Coffeen Ave Sheridan WY 82801-5318

RYAN, SYLVESTER D., bishop; b. Catalina Island, Calif., Sept. 3, 1930. Grad., St. John's Sem., Camarillo, Calif. Ordained priest Roman Cath. Ch., 1957, titular bishop of Remesiana. Aux. bishop L.A., 1990-92; bishop Monterey, Calif., 1992—. Office: Chancery Office PO Box 2048 580 Fremont St Monterey CA 93942

RYBAK, JAMES PATRICK, engineering educator; b. Cleve., Mar. 16, 1941; s. John Anthony and Irene Marcella (Kovar) R.; m. Linda Louise Watkins, Oct. 12, 1968. BSEE, Case Western Res. U., 1963; MS, U. N.Mex., 1965; PhD, Colo. State U., 1970. Registered profl. engr., Colo. Mem. tech. staff Sandia Nat. Labs., Albuquerque, 1963-66; rsch. asst., NDEA fellow Colo. State U., Ft. Collins, 1966-70, postdoctoral fellow, 1970-72; prof. engring. and math. Mesa State Coll., Grand Junction, Colo., 1972—, asst. v.p. acad. affairs, 1986-88, v.p. acad. affairs, 1988—. Contbr. articles to profl. publs. including IEEE Transactions, Engring. Edn., Popular Electronics, Elektrosvyaz (Russia), Radio (Russia). Mem. adv. bd. Grand Mesa Youth Svcs., Grand Junction, 1986-88; bd. dirs. Hilltop Rehab. Hosp., Grand Junction, 1989-93, Salvation Army, Grand Junction, 1993—. NEDA fellow, 1968-70, THEMIS fellow, 1970-72. Mem. IEEE, Am. Soc. Engring. Edn. (vice chmn. Rocky Mountain sect. 1974-75, chmn. 1975-76). Home: 314 Quail Dr Grand Junction CO 81503 Office: Mesa State Coll 1175 Texas Ave Grand Junction CO 81501-7605

RYCHETSKY, STEVE, civil and environmental engineer, consultant; b. Phoenix, Oct. 9, 1951; s. Edward and Maria (Zabroni) R.; m. Dawna Marie Strunk, June 10, 1972 (div. Oct. 1985); children: Brian, Melissa; m. Michaele Ann Turner, Dec. 28, 1986; children: Mike, Kristi, Jaye, Karly. AA in Engring., Oreg. Inst. Tech., 1972, BTech, 1976. Registered profl. civil engr., Oreg., Calif. Mgr. sales engring. Varcopruden, Turlock, Calif., 1976-79, AMCA Internat., Winston-Salem, N.C., 1979-82; civil engr. USDA Natural Resources Conservation Svc., Klamath Falls, Oreg., 1983-85; tech. advisor USDA Soil Conservation Service, Klamath Falls, Oreg., 1983-88; civil engr., tech. advisor USDA Natural Resources Conservation Svc., Tillamook, Oreg., 1985—; private cons. engr. Tillamook, Oreg., 1985—. Active vol. cons. svcs. for environ. handicapped and children projects; bd. dirs. Tillamook Anglers, Inc., 1990-94. Democrat. Roman Catholic. Home: PO Box 1457 Redmond OR 97756 Office: Rychetsky Turner & Assocs Inc PO Box 1457 Redmond OR 97756

RYDELL, AMNELL ROY, artist, landscape architect; b. Mpls., Sept. 17, 1915; s. John S. and Josephine Henrietta (King) R.; m. Frances Cooksey, Jan. 24, 1942. BFA, U. So. Calif., 1937; postgrad., Atelier 17, Paris, 1938, U. Calif., Berkeley, 1939-40, U. Calif., Santa Cruz, 1988. Instr. engring. Douglas Aircraft, El Segundo, Calif., 1940-46; ind. artist, designer San Francisco, 1946-48; ind. artist, designer Santa Cruz, 1948—, ind. landscape architect, 1958-91. Author, cons.: Low Maintenance Gardening, 1974; restoration design Sesnon House Garden Cabrillo Coll., 1995. Pres. Santa Cruz Hist. Soc., 1978-79, Rural Bonny Doon Assn., 1955-56, Santa Cruz Orgn. for Progress and Euthenics, 1977-78; mem. vision bd. City of Santa Cruz, 1991-92; mem. task force Ctr. for Art and History, 1986-94; bd. dirs. Santa Cruz Hist. Trust, 1978-94, Art Mus. Santa Cruz County, 1982-94; donor advisor Roy and Frances Rydell Visual Arts Fund, Greater Santa Cruz County Cmty. Found.; archivist pers. hist. archives, spl. collections Libr. U. Calif., Santa Cruz. Recipient Eloise Pickard Smith award, 1997. Mem. Am. Soc. Landscape Architects (emeritus), William James Assn. (vice chair bd. 1979-95, chair 1995-96), Art Forum (chair 1983-90), Art League (Disting. Artist 1996, Eloise Pickard Smith award 1997), Friends of Sesnon Gallery U. Calif., Santa Cruz. Home: 201 Pine Flat Rd Santa Cruz CA 95060-9708

RYDER, HAL, theater educator, director; b. Evanston, Ill., Aug. 21, 1950; s. Lee Sigmund and Katherine (Philipsborn) Rosenblatt; m. Caroline Margaret Ogden, Nov. 17, 1976 (div. 1991). Student, U. Ariz., 1968-72, U. Miami, summer 1971; cert. in drama, Drama Studio London, 1973; BA in Drama, U. Wash., 1987. Drama specialist Rough Rock (Ariz.) Demonstration Sch., 1971-72; artistic dir. Mercury Theatre, London, 1973-75, Fringe Theatre, Orlando, Fla., 1976-79; dir. Drama Studio London, 1980-82, interim adminstrv. dir., 1985; artistic dir. Alaska Arts Fine Arts Camp, Sitka, 1987, Shakespeare Plus, Seattle, 1983-92; instr. Cornish Coll. Arts, Seattle, 1982—, producer theatre, 1987-97, acting-chmn. theatre dept., 1990; artistic dir., exec. dir. Open Door Theatre, 1992—; artistic dir. Snoqualmie Falls Forest Theatre, 1992-94; founder, v.p. Ednl. Arts Resource Svcs., Inc., 1996—; creative cons. Sea World Fla., Orlando, 1979; lit. mgr. Pioneer Square Theatre, Seattle, 1983; space mgr. Seattle Mime Theatre, 1986-87. Author: Carmilla, 1976, (with others) Marvelous Christmas Mystery, 1978; editor: Will Noble BLood Die, 1987, The New Emperor's Premier, 1990, Hamlet & Juliet, 1997; dir. over 125 stage plays; appeared in over 40 prodns. Recipient Faculty Excellence award Seafirst Bank, Seattle, 1988. Mem. SAG, AFTRA, Am. Fedn. Tchrs. (Cornish chpt.), Alpha Kappa Lamda. Democrat. Jewish. Home: 1012 NE 62nd St Seattle WA 98115-6604 Office: Cornish Coll Arts 710 E Roy St Seattle WA 98102-4604

RYGIEWICZ, PAUL THADDEUS, plant ecologist; b. Chgo., Feb. 19, 1952; s. Sigismund Thaddeus and Regina (Korpalski) R. BS in Forestry, U. Ill., 1974; MS in Wood Sci., U. Calif., Berkeley, 1976; PhD in Forest Resources, U. Wash., 1983. Research wood technologist ITT Rayonier, Inc., Shelton, Wash., 1977; research assoc. Centre National de Recherches Forestières, Nancy, France, 1983-84; research soil microbiologist U. Calif., Berkeley, 1984-85; rsch. ecologist, global climate change project leader EPA, Corvallis, Oreg., 1985—; asst. prof. dept. forest sci. Oreg. State U., 1987—. Contbr. articles to profl. jours.; rsch. on reforestation of tropical forests in Brazil, global climate changes on forests. Vol. Big Bros. of Am., Urbana, Ill., 1972-74. Fellow Regents U. Calif., Berkeley, 1973-74, Weyerhaeuser U. Calif., Berkeley, 1978-79, Inst. Nat. de la Recherche Agronomique, France, 1983-84, French Ministry of Fgn. Affairs, 1983-84. Mem. Ecol. Soc. Am., Soil Ecology Soc., Forestry Club, Sigma Xi, Gamma Sigma Delta, Xi Sigma Pi (officer 1973-74). Office: EPA 200 SW 35th St Corvallis OR 97333-4902

RYLAARSDAM, WILLIAM F., judge; b. Haarlemmemeer, The Netherlands, Feb. 13, 1937; came to U.S., 1953; s. Daniel D. and Mary (Van Andel) R.; m. Janice E. Veneman, Sept. 7, 1957; children: Mary Jane Pike, Jennifer Vischer, Alice Jean, Daniel. BS, U. Calif., 1957; JD cum laude, Loyola U., 1964. Bar: Calif. 1964, U.S. Supreme Ct. 1969. Ptnr. Breidenbach, Swaninston, Yokaitis & Crispo, L.A., 1964-73, 78-80, Pasadena, Calif., 1974-78; mng. ptnr. Breidenbach, Swaninston, Yokaitis & Crispo, Newport Beach, Calif., 1980-85; judge Superior Ct., L.A., 1985-86; judge (family law) Superior Ct., Orange County, Calif., 1986-88, supervising judge law and motion, 1988-89, supervising judge complex litigation, civil, 1990-95, presiding judge appellate panel, 1990-92; on assignment Calif. Ct. Appeals, 1994, assoc. justice, 1995—; adj. prof. ins. law Sch. Law Loyola U., 1973-79; lectr. bus. law Grad. Sch. Mgmt. U.C.I., 1990-94; lectr., panelist civil procedure and ins. law The Rutter Group, Calif. Cont. Edn. of the Bar, civil procedure, courtroom behavior Rutter Group; arbitrator L.A. Superior Ct., 1970-80. Mem. planning com. City of Pasadena, 1973-80, chmn., 1976-78. Named Judge of the Yr. litigation sect. Orange County Bar Assn. Mem. Am. Bd. Trial Advs. (Judge of the Yr. 1992), Am. Inns of Ct. (pres. Robert A. Banyard Inn 1990-92), Calif. State Bar (mem. com. maintenance profl. competence 1976-81, chmn. 1978-81, bd. legal specialization 1978-81, disciplinary com. 1973-76, bd. govs. litigation sect., jud. adv. 1991—), Calif. Judges Assn. (mem. com. civil procedure 1985-92, chair 1990-91, 94-95, jud. ethics com. 1995—), Orange County women Lawyers Assn., Loyola Law Sch. Alumni Assn. (bd. govs. 1983-90), Pasadena Tournament of Roses Assn. Republican. Presbyterian. Office: Calif Ct Appeals 925 N Spurgeon Santa Ana CA 92701

RYLANDER, ROBERT ALLAN, financial service executive; b. Bremerton, Wash., Apr. 8, 1947; s. Richard Algot and Marian Ethelyn (Peterson) R.; m. Donna Jean Marks, June 28, 1984; children: Kate, Josh, Erik, Meagan. BA in Fin., U. Wash., 1969; postgrad., U. Alaska, 1972-74. Controller Alaska USA Fed. Credit Union, Anchorage, 1974-77, mgr. ops., 1977-80, asst. gen. mgr., 1980-83, exec. v.p., chief operating officer, 1983—; chmn. Alaska Home Mortgage, Inc., Anchorage, 1992—, Alaska Option Svcs. Corp., Anchorage, 1983—, Alaska USA Trust Co., Anchorage, 1997—; bd. dirs. Alaska USA Ins., Inc., Anchorage. Served to capt. USAF, 1969-74. Mem. Credit Union Execs. Soc. Home: PO Box 220587 Anchorage AK 99522-0587 Office: Alaska USA Fed Credit Union PO Box 196613 Anchorage AK 99519-6613

RYLES, GERALD FAY, private investor, business executive; b. Walla Walla, Wash., Apr. 3, 1936; s. L. F. and Janie Geraldine (Bassett) R.; m. Ann Jane Birkenmeyer, June 12, 1959; children—Grant, Mark, Kelly. B.A., U. Wash., 1958; M.B.A., Harvard U., 1962. With Gen. Foods Corp., White Plains, N.Y., 1962-65, Purex Corp., Ltd., Lakewood, Calif., 1966-68; cons. McKinsey & Co., Inc., Los Angeles, 1968-71; with Fibreboard Corp., San Francisco, 1971-79, v.p., 1973-75, group v.p., 1975-79; with Consol. Fibres, Inc., San Francisco, 1979-88, exec. v.p., 1979-81, pres., dir., 1981-86, chief exec. officer, 1986-88; cons. Orinda, Calif., 1988-90; with Interchecks Inc., 1990-92, pres., CEO, 1990-92; bus. exec., pvt. investor, 1992-94; chmn. bd., CEO Microserv, Inc., Kirkland, Wash., 1994—; bd. dirs. Morning Sun, Inc., Tacoma, Sitewerks Inc., Seattle. Mem. adv. com. entrepreneur and innovation program U. Wash. Bus. Sch. Served to capt. U.S. Army, 1958-66. Mem. Harvard Bus. Sch. Assn., Univ. Wash. Alumni Assn., World Trade Club (San Francisco), Wash. Athletic Club. Republican. Episcopalian. Home: 2625 90th Ave NE Bellevue WA 98004-1601

RYMAN, RUTH (STACIE) MARIE, primary education educator; b. Moline, Ill., July 22, 1952; d. Henry Joseph and Gladys Julia (Campbell) DeKeyzer; m. Phillip DeForrest Ryman, Aug. 14, 1976; children: Michelle, Daniel, Jennifer. BA, Augustana Coll., 1974; MA, U. Denver, 1988. Cert. tchr. Resource tchr. Notre Dame Sch., Denver, 1986-91, 2nd grade tchr., 1991—; cons. Notre Dame Sch., Denver, 1991—. mem. Nat. Cath. Edn. Assn., Nat. Coun. Tchrs. Math. Office: Notre Dame Sch 2165 S Zenobia St Denver CO 80219-5058

RYMAR, JULIAN W., manufacturing company executive; b. Grand Rapids, Mich., June 29, 1919; student Grand Rapids Jr. Coll., 1937-39, U. Mich., 1939-41, Am. Sch. Dramatic Arts, 1946-47, Wayne U., 1948-52, Rockhurst Coll., 1952-53; Naval War Coll., 1954-58; m. Margaret Macon Van Brunt, Dec. 11, 1954; children: Margaret Gibson, Gracen Macon, Ann Mackall. Entered USN as aviation cadet, 1942, advanced through grades to capt., 1964; chmn. bd., chief exec. officer, dir. Grace Co., Belton, Mo., 1955-90; chmn. bd. dirs. Shock & Vibration Research, Inc., 1956-66; chmn. bd., CEO Bedtime Story Fashions; bd. dirs. Am. Bank & Trust; comdg. officer Naval Air Res. Squadron, 1957-60, staff air bn. comdr., 1960-64. Mem. Kansas City Hist. Soc.; bd. dirs. Bros. of Mercy, St. Lukes Hosp.; adv. bd. dirs. St. Joseph Hosp.; trustee Missouri Valley Coll., 1969-74; pres. Rymar Found. Active Sch. Am. Rsch., Inst. Am. Arts, Mus. N.Mex. Found., Spanish Colonial Art Soc. Mem. Mil. Order World Wars, Navy League U.S. (pres. 1959-60, dir. 1960-70), Rockhill Homes Assn. (v.p.) Friends of Art (pres., chmn. bd. govs. 1969-70, exec. bd. 1971-74), Soc. of Fellows of Nelson Gallery Found. (exec. bd. 1972-77), Soc. Profl. Journalists, Press Club, Univ. of Mich. Club, Arts Club of Washington, Sch. of Am. Rsch., Santa Fe Symphony, Inst. Am. Indian Art, Mus. NMex. Found., Mus. Indian Arts & Culture, Mus. Internat. Folk Art, Mus. Fine Arts, Spanish Colonial Arts Soc., Quiet Birdman Club, Sigma Delta Chi. Episcopalian (dir., lay reader, lay chalice, vestryman, jr. warden, sr. warden, diocesan fin. bd., parish investment bd.).

RYMER, PAMELA ANN, federal judge; b. Knoxville, Tenn., Jan. 6, 1941. AB, Vassar Coll., 1961; LLB, Stanford U., 1964; LLD (hon.), Pepperdine U., 1988. Bar: Calif. 1966, U.S. Ct. Appeals (9th cir.) 1966, U.S. Ct. Appeals (10th cir.), U.S. Supreme Ct. V.p. Rus Walton & Assoc., Los Altos, Calif., 1965-66; Assoc. Lillick McHose & Charles, L.A., 1966-72, ptnr., 1973-75; ptnr. Toy and Rymer, L.A., 1975-83; judge U.S. Dist. Ct. (cen. dist.) Calif., L.A., 1983-89, U.S. Ct. Appeals (9th cir.), L.A., 1989—; faculty The Nat. Jud. Coll., 1986-88; mem. com. summer ednl. programs Fed. Jud. Ctr., 1987-88; chair exec. com. 9th Cir. Jud. Conf., 1990; mem. com. criminal law Jud. Conf. U.S., 1988-93, Ad Hoc com. gender-based violence, 1991-94, fed.-state jurisdiction com., 1993—. Mem. editorial bd. The Judges' jour., 1989-91; contbr. articles to profl. jours. and newsletters. Mem. Calif. Post-secondary Edn. Commn., 1974-84, chmn., 1980-84; mem. L.A. Olympic Citizens Adv. Commn.; bd. visitors Stanford U. Law Sch., 1986—, chair, 1993-96, exec. com.; bd. visitors Pepperdine U. Law Sch., 1987—; mem. Edn. Commn. of States Task Force on State Policy and Ind. Higher Edn., 1987-89; bd. dirs. Constnl. Rights Found., 1985; Jud. Conf. U.S. Com. Fed.-State Jurisdiction, 1993, Com. Criminal Law, 1988-93, ad hoc com. gender based violence, 1991-94; chair exec. com. 9th cir. jud. conf., 1990-94. Recipient Outstanding Trial Jurist award L.A. County Bar Assn., 1988. Mem. ABA (task force on civil justice reform 1991—), State Bar Calif. (antitrust and trade regulation sect., exec. com. 1990-92), L.A. County Bar Assn. (chmn. antitrust sect. 1981-82), Assn. of Bus. Trial Lawyers (bd. govs. 1990-92), Stanford Alumni Assn., Stanford Law Soc. Soc. Calif., Vassar Club So. Calif. (past pres.). Office: US Ct Appeals 9th Cir US Court of Appeals Bldg 125 S Grand Ave Box 91510 Pasadena CA 91109-1510*

RYMER DAVIS, CAROL ANN, radiologist; b. Denver, Nov. 28, 1944; d. Charles Albert and Marion (Reinhart) Rymer; m. John Charles Davis IV, May 10, 1969; children: Heather Mead, Marne Anne. BS, Colo. Coll., 1965; MD, U. Colo., 1969. Bd. cert. radiology and nuclear medicine. Intern U. N.Mex., Albuquerque, 1969-70, resident radiology, 1971-74, fellow nuclear medicine, 1974; resident gen. surgery Lovelace Med. Ctr., Albuquerque, 1970-71, staff physician, chief nuclear medicine, 1974-91; staff physician Fitzsimmons Med. Ctr., Denver, 1991; staff physician, chief nuclear medicine St. Joseph Hosp., Denver, 1991—, chief breast imaging, 1992—. Safety officer, chief safety officer Albuquerque Internat. Balloon Fiesta, Albuquerque, 1990-91. Col. USAR. Recipient Pres. Recognition award Greater Albuquerque Med. Assn., 1988; named Woman of Yr. Zonta Club Albuquerque, 1989; set 14 world records in hot air ballooning and 20 world records in gas ballooning. Mem. Internat. Women's Forum (Woman That Makes a Difference 1991). Episcopalian. Home: 1158 S Vine St Denver CO 80210-1831

RYNIKER, BRUCE WALTER DURLAND, industrial designer, manufacturing executive; b. Billings, Mont., Mar. 23, 1940; s. Walter Henry and Alice Margaret (Durland) R.; B. Profl. Arts in Transp. Design (Ford scholar), Art Ctr. Coll. Design, Los Angeles, 1963; grad. specialized tech. engring. program Gen. Motors Inst., 1964; m. Marilee Ann Vincent, July 8, 1961; children: Kevin Walter, Steven Durland. Automotive designer Gen. Motors Corp., Warren, Mich., 1963-66; mgmt. staff automotive designer Chrysler Corp., Highland Park, Mich., 1966-72; pres., dir. design Transform Corp., Birmingham, Mich., 1969-72; indsl. designer, art dir. James R. Powers and Assocs., Los Angeles, 1972-75; sr. design products mgr. Mattel Inc., El Segundo, Calif., 1975-95; pres., CEO Durland Prodns. and Product Devel. Co., Torrance, Calif., 1996—; dir. design and devel. Microword Industries, Inc., Los Angeles, 1977-80, also dir.; exec. mem. Modern Plastics Adv. Council, 1976-80; elegance judge LeCercle Concours D'Elegance, 1976-77; mem. nat. adv. bd. Am. Security Council, 1980; cons. automotive design, 1972— . Served with USMC, 1957-60. Mem. Soc. Art Ctr. Alumni (life), Mattel Mgmt. Assn., Second Amendment Found., Am. Def. Preparedness Assn., Nat. Rifle Assn. Designer numerous exptl. automobiles, electric powered vehicles, sports and racing cars, also med. equipment, electronic teaching machines, ride-on toys. Home: 21329 Marjorie Ave Torrance CA 90503-5443 Office: Durland Prodns Inc 21213 B Hawthorne Blvd Torrance CA 90503

RYPKA, EUGENE WESTON, microbiologist; b. Owatonna, Minn., May 6, 1925; s. Charles Frederick and Ethel Marie (Ellerman) R.; m. Rosemary Speeker, June 1, 1967. Student, Carleton Coll., 1946-47; BA, Stanford U., 1950, PhD, 1958. Prof. microbiology, systems, cybernetics U. N.Mex., Albuquerque, 1957-62; bacteriologist Leonard Wood Meml. Lab. Johns Hopkins U., Balt., 1962-63; sr. scientist Lovelace Med. Ctr., Albuquerque, 1963-71, chief microbiologist, 1971-93; adj. prof. U. N.Mex., 1973—; cons. Hoffmann-LaRoche Inc., 1974—, Airline Pilots Assn., Washington, 1976, Pasco Lab., Denver, 1983—; advisor Nat. Com. Clinic Lab. Standards, Pa., 1980-84. Contbr. articles to profl. jours. and chpts. in books. Served with USNR, USMC 1943-46. Fellow AAAS; mem. IEEE, Internat. Soc. Systems Sci. Republican. Presbyterian. Home: PO Box 8345 Highland Sta Albuquerque NM 87198

SA, JULIE, restaurant chain owner, former mayor; b. Korea, Dec. 15, 1950; came to US, 1970:; married;. Degree in Polit. Sci., Dong-A U., Korea. Owner restaurant chain; councilwoman City of Fullerton, Calif., 1992-94, mayor, 1994-95; rep. bd. Orange County Sanitation Dists. Mem. Fullerton C. of C., Orange County Korean C. of C., Orange County Chinese C. of C. Office: Office of the Mayor 303 W Commonwealth Ave Fullerton CA 92832-1710*

SA, LUIZ AUGUSTO DISCHER, physicist; b. Lages, Brazil, Sept. 28, 1944; came to U.S., 1983; s. Catulo J.C. and Maria (Discher) S. MSc in Physics, Carnegie Mellon U., 1969; PhD in Elec. Engring., Stanford U., 1989. Asst. prof. Cath. U. of Rio, Rio de Janeiro, 1969-72, Fed. U. of Rio, Rio de Janeiro, 1973-83; post-doctoral scholar Stanford (Calif.) U., 1990-91, rsch. scientist, 1991—; rsch. scientist SOI/MDI project The MDI instrument is on board the SOHO spacecraft launched by NASA, 1995. Contbr. articles to Jour. of Applied Physics, Jour. Geophys. Rsch., Proc. of 4th SOHO Workshop on Helioseismology, ESA, 1995. Recipient of Recognition award NASA, 1994. Mem. Am. Astronomical Soc., Am. Geophysical Union, Sigma Xi. Roman Catholic. Office: CSSA HEPL Annex A207 Stanford CA 94305

SAAD, MOHAMMED FATHY, medical educator; b. Kom Hamada, Behaira, Egypt, Jan. 23, 1952; came to the U.S., 1981; s. Hassaneen Hilmy and Faiza S. (Younis) S. MBBCh with honors, U. Alexandria, Egypt, 1975, M of Medicine, 1979, MD, 1986; MS in Biomedical Scis., U. Tex., Houston, 1984. Intern Alexandria U. Hosp., 1976-77, resident dept. medicine, 1977-80; asst. lectr. Alexandria U., 1980-81, instr., 1984-86, asst. prof. medicine and endocrinology, 1986-87; fellow sect. endocrinology, dept. medicine U. Tex., Anderson Hosp. and Tumor Inst., Houston, 1981-84; staff physician Sacaton (Ariz.) Indian Hosp., 1987-91, Phoenix Indian Med. Ctr., 1988-91; attending physician dept. medicine Rancho Los Amigos Med. Ctr., L.A., 1991—; attending physician dept. medicine U. So. Calif.-Los Angeles County Med. Ctr., 1991—, assoc. prof. medicine, 1991—, dir. diabetes inpatient svc.; vis. assoc. Phoenix epidemiology and clin. rsch. br. Nat. Inst. Diabetes and Digestive and Kidney Diseases, NIH, 1987-91; vis. endocrinologist Maricopa Med. Ctr., Phoenix, 1988-91. Author: (with others) Fundamentals of Surgical Oncology, 1986, Cardiology and Coexisting Diseases, 1994; subeditor sect. endocrine tumors Year Book Cancer, 1985-88; reviewer Am. Jour. Physiology, Diabetes, Diabetes Care, European Jour. Clin. Investigations, Jour. Lipid Rsch., Obesity Rsch., Ethnicity and Disease; contbr. articles to profl. jours. Recipient Egyptian State prize and medal of honor Nat. Acad. Sci., 1985; grantee Ariz. Kidney Found., 1989-90, Nat. Heart, Lung and Blood Inst., 1991—, Genentech, Inc., 1992-93, 94—, Nat. Inst. Diabetes and Digestive and Kidney Diseases, 1994—. Mem. Am. Diabetes Assn. (grantee 1989-90, 93—), Am. Fedn. Clin. Rsch., Royal Coll. Physicians U.K., Am. Heart Assn. (mem. high blood pressure coun.), Egyptian Med. Assn., European Assn. Study Diabetes, Endocrine Soc. Office: U So Calif Med Sch Divsn Endocrinology 1200 N State St Rm 8250 Los Angeles CA 90033-4525

SAARI, ALBIN TOIVO, electronics engineer; b. Rochester, Wash., Mar. 16, 1930; s. Toivo Nickoli and Gertrude Johanna (Hill) S.; m. Patricia Ramona Rudig, Feb. 1, 1958; children: Kenneth, Katherine, Steven, Marlene, Bruce. Student, Centralia Community Coll., Wash., 1950-51; AS in Electronic Tech., Wash. Tech. Inst., Seattle, 1958; BA in Communications, Evergreen State Coll., Olympia, Wash., 1977. Electronic technician Boeing Co., Seattle, 1956-59; field engr. RCA, Van Nuys, Calif., 1959-61; tv engr. Gen. Dynamics, San Diego, 1961-65, Boeing Co., Seattle, 1965-70; mgr. electronic maintenance and engring. Evergreen State Coll., Olympia, Wash., 1970—; mem. adv. bd. KAOS-FM Radio, Olympia, 1979-82, New Market Vocat. Skills Ctr., Tumwater, Wash., 1985—, South Puget Sound Cmty. Coll., Olympia. Soccer coach King County Boys Club, Federal Way, Wash., 1968-70, Thurston County Youth Soccer, Olympia, 1973-78. With USAF, 1951-55. Recipient Merit award for electronic systems design Evergreen State Coll., 1978. Mem. Soc. Broadcast Engrs. (chmn. 1975-77), Soc. of Motion Picture and TV Engrs., IEEE, Audio Engring. Soc., Tele-Communications Assn., Assoc. Pub. Safety Communications Officers. Lutheran. Home: 6617 Husky Way SE Olympia WA 98503-1433 Office: Evergreen State Coll Media Engring # L1309 Olympia WA 98505

SABALIUS, ROMEY, foreign language and literature educator; b. Lubeck, Germany, Mar. 9, 1963; came to U.S., 1984; m. Atscaux Kagami. BA, U. Mainz, Germany, 1984; MA, U. So. Calif., L.A., 1986, PhD, 1992; Magister, U. Munich, Germany, 1989. Vis. prof. Vassar Coll., Poughkeepsie, N.Y., 1992; asst. prof. German lit. Utah State U., Logan, 1992-95; asst. prof., German coord. San Jose (Calif.) State U., 1995—. Author: The Dream Never Becomes Reality, 1994, Die Romane Hugo Loetschers, 1995; editor: Neue Perspektiven zur deutschsprachigen Literatur der Schweiz, 1997; contbr. articles to profl. jours. San Jose State U. grantee, 1997, Utah State U. grantee, 1993-95; Quadrille Ball Found. scholar, 1986-87, Friedrich-Ebert Found. scholar, 1983-89. Mem. MLA, Am. Assn. Tchrs. German, German Studies Assn., Pacific Ancient and Modern Lang. Assn., Internat. Vereinigung der Germanisten. Office: San Jose State U Dept Fgn Langs 1 Washington Sq San Jose CA 95112-0091

SABATELLA, ELIZABETH MARIA, clinical therapist, educator, mental health facility administrator; b. Mineola, N.Y., Nov. 9, 1940; d. D. F. and Blanche M. (Schmetzle) S; 1 child, Kevin Woog. BS, SUNY, Brockport, 1961; MA, SUNY, Stony Brook, 1971, MSW, 1983. Lic. social worker, N.Y., N.Mex., tchr., N.Y., N.Mex.; registered clin. social worker, Calif. Tchr. physical edn. Comseqogue Sch. Dist., Port Jefferson, N.Y., 1968-73, 84-87, 88-91; clin. therapist Cibola Counseling Svcs., Grants, N.Mex., 1991-95, regional dir., 1993-95; clin. therapist Family Growth Counseling Ctr., Encinitos, Calif., 1995-96; clin. social worker Family Advocacy, San Diego, 1995—; therapist for abused children Farmingville Mental Health Clinic; therapist for adolescents Comsewogue Sch. Dist.; therapist for alcoholics Lighthouse Ctr.; mem. Family Systems Network for Continuing Edn., Calif., Colo., 1978-80; mem. biofeedback and mediation com. McLean Hosp., Boston, 1978; mem. therapeutic touch team East and West Ctr., N.Y.C., 1980-84, sexual abuse treatment coord., 1992-95. Art and photographs exhibited at group show N.Mex. Art League, 1991; contbr. poetry and children's story to various publs. Recipient Editor's Choice award and Best New Poet award Nat. Libr. Poetry, 1988, Merit award and Place Winner for Poetry, Iliad Press, 1993. Mem. NASW, N.Y. State United Tchrs., Writers Assn., Sierra Club. Home: 3852 Jewell St Apt 208 San Diego CA 92109-6417

SABATINI, JOSEPH DAVID, librarian; b. Bronx, N.Y., Oct. 25, 1942; s. Amadeo Sabatini and Victoria (Azriel) Curry; m. Mary Helena Budinger, Nov. 11, 1972; 1 child, Robert Amadeo. BA, UCLA, 1964, MLS, 1965. Vol. in Svc. to Am., various locations, 1965-67; asst. libr. Sch. Law Libr., U. N.Mex., Albuquerque, 1968-72; head info. svcs. Albuquerque Pub. Libr., 1973-76, cmty. resources specialist, 1977-80, head main libr., 1980—. Mem. N.Mex. Libr. Assn. (chair various coms., chair legis. com., pres. 1980-81). Home: 3514 6th St NW Albuquerque NM 87107-2419 Office: Albuquerque Pub Libr 501 Copper Ave NW Albuquerque NM 87102-3129

SABATINI, LAWRENCE, bishop; b. Chgo., May 15, 1930; s. Dominic and Ada (Piloi) S. Ph.L., Gregorian U., Rome, 1953, S.T.L., 1957, J.C.D., 1960; M.S. in Edn., Iona Coll., 1968. Ordained priest, Roman Catholic Ch., 1957, bishop, 1978. Prof. canon law St. Charles Sem., S.I., N.Y., 1960-71; pastor St. Stephen's Parish, North Vancouver, B.C., Canada, 1970-78; provincial superior Missionaries of St. Charles, Oak Park, Ill., 1978; aux. bishop Archdiocese Vancouver, B.C., Can., 1978-82; bishop Diocese Kamloops, B.C., Can., 1982—; procurator, adviser Matrimonial Tribunal, N.Y.C., 1964-71; founder, dir. RAP Youth Counseling Service, S.I., N.Y., 1969-71; vice ofcl. Regional Matrimonial tribunal of Diocese Kamloops, 1978-82; chmn. Kamloops Cath. Pub. Schs., 1982—. Named Man of Yr. Confratellanza Italo-Canadese, 1979. Mem. Can. Canon Law Soc., Canon Law Soc. Am., Can. Conf. Cath. Bishops. Office: Diocese of Kamloops, 635A Tranquille Rd, Kamloops, BC Canada V2B 3H5*

SABATINI, WILLIAM QUINN, architect; b. Pitts.; s. William L. and Lydia M. (Contento) S.; m. Carol Anne Christoffel, Feb. 26, 1972; children: Quinn, Jay, Jillian. BA, Franklin & Marshall Coll., 1971; MArch, U. N.Mex., 1978. Registered arch., N.Mex., Nev.; cert. Nat. Coun. Archtl. Registration Bds. Intern Jess Holmes, Arch., Albuquerque, 1974-78; project mgr. Jack Miller & Assocs., Las Vegas, 1978-81; sr. design arch. HNTB, Kansas City, Mo., 1981-84; prin. Holmes Sabatini Assocs. Arch., Albuquerque, 1984—. Prin. works include Ctrl. Campus Bookstore U. N.Mex. (Merit award N.Mex. Soc. Archs. 1977), Luna County Courthouse, Deming, N.Mex. (Honor award N.Mex. Hist. Preservation Soc. 1978), James R. Dickinson Libr. U. Nev., Las Vegas (Merit award AIA 1981, Honor award Nev. Soc. Arch. 1981), Reno Conv. Ctr. (Merit award Nev. Soc. Archs. 1983), Corp. Hdqs. Nev. Power Co., Las Vegas (Honor award Nev. Soc. Archs. 1983), YMCA, Las Vegas (Honor award Nev. Soc. Archs. 1983), Sanctuary Remodel St. Johns United Meth. Ch., Albuquerque (Best Interiors award N.Mex. Bus. Jour. 1986), The Presidio Office Bldg., Albuquerque (Best Bldgs. award and Best Interiors award N.Mex. Bus. Jour. 1987, Project of Yr. award Assoc. Gen. Contractors N.Mex. 1987), Suarez Residence, Albuquerque (Merit award N.Mex. Soc. Am. 1988), Fire Sta. Number 13 and Fire Marshall's Office, Albuquerque (Merit award Albuquerque Conservation Soc. 1987, Best Bldgs. award N.Mex. Bus. Jour. 1988), Santa Fe Imaging Ctr. (Citation of Excellence, Modern Health Care Mag., AIA com. on healthcare 1989, Best Bldgs. award N.Mex. Bus. Jour. 1989), Health Scis. Bldg. U. N.Mex. (Best Bldgs. award N.Mex. Bus. Jour. 1989), U.S. Port of Entry, Columbus, N.Mex. (Best Bldgs. award N.Mex. Bus. Jour. 1989, Honor award N.Mex. Soc. Archs. 1990, GSA Design award U.S. Gen. Svcs. Adminstrn. 1990), Student Svcs. Bldg., Albuquerque TVI (Best Bldgs. award N.Mex. Bus. Jour. 1989, Merit award Albuquerque Conservation Soc. 1990), Expansion and Renovation Albuquerque Conv. Ctr. (Best Bldgs. award N.Mex. Bus. Jour. 1990), Lovelace Multi-Specialty Clinic Facility, Albuquerque (Merit award N.Mex. Soc. Archs. 1991), Pete's Playground U. N.Mex. Hosp. (Honor award N.Mex. Soc. Archs. 1992, Best Bldgs. Spl. award N.Mex. Bus. Jour. 1993), Nursing Unit Remodel U. N.Mex. Hosp. (Excellence award Am. Soc. Interior Designers 1992), 3.5 Meter Telescope Kirtland AFB, N.Mex. (Honor award AIA 1993). Bd. dirs. Albuquerque Chamber Orch., 1988, Hospice Rio Grande, 1992—; mem. adv. bd. Balloon Mus., 1989—; v.p., mem. adv. bd. St. Pius High Sch., 1993—. With USAR, 1971-78. Mem. AIA (bd. dirs. Albuquerque chpt. 1986-87). Roman Catholic. Office: Holmes Sabatini Assocs Archs West Courtyard 202 Central Ave SE Albuquerque NM 87102-3459*

SABEY, J(OHN) WAYNE, academic administrator, consultant; b. Murray, Utah, Dec. 10, 1939; s. Alfred John and Bertha (Lind) S.; m. Marie Bringhurst, Sept. 10, 1964; children: Clark Wayne, Colleen, Carolyn, Natasha Lynne. BA in Asian Studies, Brigham Young U., 1964, MA in Asian History, 1965; PhD in East Asian History, U. Mich., 1972. Teaching asst. Brigham Young U., Provo, 1964-65, rsch. asst., 1965, adj. prof. history, 1988-89; rsch. asst. U. Mich., Ann Arbor, 1966; from instr. to asst. prof. history U. Utah, Salt Lake City, 1970-80; v.p. Western Am. Lang. Inst., Salt Lake City, 1980-84, dir., 1984-86, pres., 1986—; exec. v.p. Pacific Rim Bus. Coords., Salt Lake City, 1993—, also bd. dirs., 1993—; dir. Japan Ops. E'OLA Products, Inc., St. George, Utah, 1996—; assoc. dir. exch. program between U. Utah and Nagoya Broadcasting Network of Japan, 1973-79; lectr. in field, Superior award in extemporaneous speaking, 1956. Author essay, contbr. articles to ency. Chmn. bd. trustees Western Am. Lang. Inst., 1986—, sec. to bd. trustees, 1980-86; chmn. bd. trustees Found. for Internat. Understanding, 1982—; mem. internat. adv. coun. Salt Lake C.C., 1988-94; mem. bd. advisors Consortium for Internat. Edn., 1972-77. Horace H. Rackham Sch. grad. studies fellow, 1969-70, Fulbright-Hays rsch. fellow (Japan), 1968-69, U.S. Nat. Def. fgn. lang. fellow, 1965-68. Mem. Assn. for Asian Studies (gen. chairperson, chairperson local arrangements western conf. 1970-72), Phi Kappa Phi. Home: 8710 Oakwood Park Cir Sandy UT 84094

SABHARWAL, RANJIT SINGH, mathematician; b. Dhudial, India, Dec. 11, 1925; came to U.S., 1958, naturalized, 1981; s. Krishan Ch and Devti (An) S.; m. Pritam Kaur Chadha, Mar. 5, 1948; children—Rajinderpal, Amarjit, Jasbir. B.A. with honors, Punjab U., 1944, M.A., 1948; M.A. U. Calif, Berkeley, 1962; Ph.D., Wash. State U., 1966. Lectr. math. Khalsa Coll., Bombay, India, 1951-58; teaching asst. U. Calif., Berkeley, 1958-62; instr. math. Portland (Oreg.) State U., 1962-62, Wash. State U., 1963-66; asst. prof. Kans. State U., 1966-68; mem. faculty Calif. State Hayward, 1968—, prof. math., 1974—. Author papers on non-Desarguesian planes. Mem. Am. Math. Soc., Math. Assn. Am., Sigma Xi. Address: 27892 Adobe Ct Hayward CA 94542-2102

SABIN, JACK CHARLES, engineering and construction firm executive; b. Phoenix, June 29, 1921; s. Jack Byron and Rena (Lewis) S.; B.S., U. Ariz., 1943; B in Chem. Engring., U. Minn., 1947; m. Frances Jane McIntyre, Mar. 27, 1950; children—Karen Lee, Robert William, Dorothy Ann, Tracy Ellen. With Standard Oil Co. of Calif., 1947-66, sr. engr., 1966—; pres., dir. Indsl. Control & Engring., Inc., Redondo Beach, Calif., 1966—; owner/mgr. Jack C. Sabin, Engr.-Contractor, Redondo Beach, 1968—; staff engr. Pacific Molasses Co., San Francisco, 1975-77; project mgr. E & L Assocs., Long Beach, Calif., 1977-79; dir. Alaska Pacific Petroleum, Inc., 1968—, Marlex Petroleum, Inc., 1970, 71—, Served with U.S. Army, 1942-46; capt. Chem. Corps, Res., 1949-56. Registered profl. engr., Calif., Alaska; lic. gen. engring. contractor, Ariz., Calif. Mem. Nat. Soc. Profl. Engrs., Ind. Liquid Terminals Assn., Conservative Caucus, Calif. Tax Reduction Com., Tau Beta Pi, Phi Lambda Upsilon, Phi Sigma Kappa. Republican. Clubs: Elks; Town Hall of Calif. Address: 151 Camino De Las Colinas Redondo Beach CA 90277-5828

SABOE, LAVERNE ALDEN, JR., chiropractor, author, educator; b. Vancouver, Wash., Oct. 3, 1954; s. LaVerne Alden and Patricia May (Hammer) S.; m. Denise Michelle Anderson, Dec. 3, 1991; 1 child, Jackson Tayler. Degree, Western States C.C., Portland, 1979. Cert. in neurology Tex. Coll. Chiropractic, Am. Acad. Pain Mgmt.; Diplomate Am. Bd. Disability Analysts. Pvt. practice, Albany, 1979—; Mem. select exam. com. Oreg. Bd. Chiropractic Examiners, Salem, 1992-93, chmn. IME com., 1996, mem. peer rev. com. 1993—, mem. com. P & U practice guidelines, 1996; mem. postgrad. faculty Tex. Coll. Chiropractic, Houston, 1992—, Western States Chiropractic Coll., Portland, 1996. Contbr. articles to profl. jours.; inventor chart note sys. Mem. FISH Emergency Svcs., Albany, 1994. Recipient cert. of recognition Am. Soc. Safety Engrs., 1982. Fellow Internat. Coll. Chiropractors, Am. Back Soc. (cert. of appreciation 1987); mem. Am. Chiropractic Assn. (alt. del. 1993—), Am. Coll. Orthopedic Medicine (founding), Am. Coll. Orthopedists, Am. Chiropractic Acad. Neurologists, Am. Med. Writers Assn., Nat. Assn. Disability Evaluation Profls., Chiropractic Assn. Oreg. (chmn. hosp. staff mem. 1988, com. on ethics 1990, appreciation award 1992, svc. award 1993), Albany Area Chiropractors (pres. 1991-92). Republican. Roman Catholic. Home: 915 SE 19th Ave Albany OR 97321

SABSAY, DAVID, library consultant; b. Waltham, Mass., Sept. 12, 1931; s. Wiegard Isaac and Ruth (Weinstein) S.; m. Helen Glenna Tolliver, Sept. 24,1 966. AB, Harvard U., 1953; BLS, U. Calif., Berkeley, 1955. Circulation dept. supr. Richmond (Calif.) Pub. Library, 1955-56; city libr. Santa Rosa (Calif.) Pub. Library, 1956-65; dir. Sonoma County Library, Santa Rosa, 1965-92; libr. cons., 1992—; coordinator North Bay Coop. Library System, Santa Rosa, 1960-64; cons. in field, Sebastopol, Calif., 1968—. Contbr. articles to profl. jours. Commendation, Calif. Assn. Library Trustees and Commrs., 1984. Mem. Calif. Library Assn. (pres. 1971, cert. appreciation 1971, 80), ALA. Club: Harvard (San Francisco). Home and Office: 667 Montgomery Rd Sebastopol CA 95472-3020

SACHS, ROBERT MICHAEL, author; b. Cleve., July 13, 1952; s. Sherman David and Thelma (Bordo) S.; m. Melanie Anne Brown, July 28, 1976; children: Kai Ling, Harriet Christina, Jabeth David-Francis. BA, U. Lancaster, Eng., 1974; Dipl. in Human Rels., Richmond Fellowship Coll., London, 1975; MSW, U. Ky., 1987. Lic. ind. social worker. Dep. dir. Richmond Fellowship, London, 1974-76; primary therapist Holistic Med. Ctr., Lexington, Ky., 1981-86; social worker Presbyn. Hosp., Albuquerque, 1987-88; preventive health care educator self-employed, Albuquerque, also San Luis Obispo, Calif., 1988—; social worker Homecare Hospice, Albuquerque, 1993-96; state examiner N.Mex. Bd. of Massage, 1994—. Author: The Complete Guide to 9-Star Ki, 1992, Rebirth Into Pure Land, 1993, Health for Life: Secrets of Tibetan Ayurveda, 1995; editor: Ayurvedic Beauty Care, 1994. Vol. Hosp. of San Luis Obispo, 1996—; health educator various chs., civic ctrs., 1987—. Mem. Am. Massage Therapy Assn., Alpha Delta Mu. Office: Diamond Way Ayurveda PO Box 13753-3753 San Luis Obispo CA 93406

SACKETT, TIMOTHY DAVID, information systems specialist; b. Portland, OR, Sept. 1, 1955; s. Stanley McKennon and Lurah Louise (Slocum) S.; m. Leslie Elizabeth Porterfield, July 21, 1979; children: Stewart McKennon, Andrey Elizabeth. Student, Portland State U., 1973-76, Linfield Coll., 1993—. Mgmt. trainee U.S. Bank Oreg., 1973-77, br. officer ops./loans, 1977-80, liaison analyst info. processing divsn., 1980-83, info. resource mgmt. specialist III, 1983-84; sr. software specialist Info. Ctr. Nike, Inc., 1984-85, office systems adminstr., 1986-87; sr. info. ctr. analyst Info. Ctr. Fred Meyer, Inc., Portland, Oreg., 1987-89, decision support supr., 1989, project coord., 1989-91, project mgr. tech. svcs., 1991-94; network mgr. Columbia Mgmt. Co., Portland, 1994—; instr. Portland C.C., 1989-91; mem. adv. bd. continuing edn. program Linfield Coll., Portland, 1990; ind. bus. cons., 1991-94. Mem. vestry St. Michael & All Angels Ch., Portland, 1991-94. Mem. Data Processing Mgmt. Assn. (pres. Portland chpt. 1989-90), Portland Personal Computer Club. Democrat. Episcopalian. Office: Columbia Mgmt Co 1301 SW 5th Ave Portland OR 97201-5601

SACKHEIM, ROBERT LEWIS, aerospace engineer, educator; b. N.Y.C., N.Y., May 16, 1937; s. A. Frederick and Lillian L. (Emmer) S.; m. Babette Freund, Jan. 12, 1964; children: Karen Holly, Andrew Frederick. BSChemE, U. Va., 1959; MSChemE, Columbia U., 1961; postgrad., UCLA, 1966-72. Project engr. Comsat Corp., El Segundo, Calif., 1969-72; project mgr. TRW, Redondo Beach, Calif., 1964-69, sect. head, 1972-76, dept. mgr., 1976-81, mgr. new bus., 1981-86, lab. mgr., 1986-90, dep. ctr. dir., 1990-93, ctr. dir., 1993—; instr. UCLA engring. ext., 1986; mem. adv. bds. NASA, Washington, 1989—; mem. peer rev. bd. various univs. and govtl. agys., 1990—; mem. Nat. Rsch. Coun./Aeronautics and Space Engring. Bd., 1994—; guest lectr. various univs. and AIAA short courses. Author: Space Mission Analysis and Design, 1991, Space Propulsion Analysis and Design, 1995; contbr. over 90 articles to profl. jours., confs. Mem. adv. bd. L.A. Bd. Edn., 1990-92; fund raiser March of Dimes, L.A., 1970-90, YMCA, San Pedro, Calif., 1974-86. Capt. USAF, 1960-63. Recipient Group Achievement award NASA, 1970, 78, 86. Fellow AIAA (chmn. com. 1980-83, chmn. L.A. sect. 1997, J.H. Wyld Propulsion award 1992, Shuttle Flag award 1984). Office: TRW Space & Elects Group Bldg 01/RM 2010 1 Space Park Blvd Rm 2010 Redondo Beach CA 90278-1001

SACKMAN, DAVE, marketing executive; married; 3 children. BA in Anthropology, U. Calif. Pres., CEO Lieberman Rsch. Worldwide, L.A.; dir. rsch. Columbia Pictures; dir. mktg. Winchell's; dir. mktg. dept. group health svcs. Am. Med. Internat. Active Young Pres. Orgn. Mem. Mktg. Rsch. Assn. (mem. strategic planning com., mem. exec. forum on rsch. quality, mem. exec. com. nat. bd. dirs.). Office: Liberman Rsch Worldwide 1900 Ave of the Stars Los Angeles CA 90067*

SACKS, ARTHUR BRUCE, environmental and liberal arts educator; b. N.Y.C., Apr. 21, 1946; s. Fred and Lillian Pearl (Levy) S.; m. Normandy Roden, May 17, 1987; children: Rachel, Erica. BA, Bklyn. Coll., 1967; MA, U. Wis., 1968, PhD, 1975. Teaching asst. dept. English, U. Wis., Madison, 1968-72, asst. to assoc. dean for student acad. affairs, 1972-76, lectr. dept. English, 1975, sr. lectr. Inst. for Environ. Studies, 1976-90, coord. acad. programs, 1976-78, asst. to dir., asst. dir., then assoc. dir., 1983-85, acting dir., then dir., 1985-90, assoc. mem. dept. urban and regional planning, 1985-93, adminstr. acad. programs, 1978-85; sr. spl. asst. to dean grad. sch. U. Wis., 1990-93; assoc. mem. Russian and East European studies U. Wis., Madison, 1992-93, acting dir. internat. faculty and staff svcs., 1993; dir., prof. liberal arts and internat. studies Colo. Sch. Mines, Golden, 1993—; mem. adj. faculty Ohio State U., Columbus, 1992-94; prof. environ. sci. Internat. U., Moscow, 1992—. Bd. dirs. Friends of Waisman Ctr. on Mental Retardation and Human Devel., 1991-93; mem. Emergency Med. Svcs. Commn., 1992-93. Recipient blue ribbon for poetry Am. Assn. Interpretive Naturalists, 1983. Mem. AAAS, Am. Assn. Higher Edn., N.Am. Assn. Environ. Edn. (adv. group internat. rels. com. 1991-94, rep. to jour. 1988—, nominating com. 1989-90, pres. 1984-85, pres.-elect 1983-84, sec. 1982-83, exec. com. 1982-86, chmn. devel. com. 1986-94, liaison to Friends of the UN Environ. Programme, chmn. participation World Decade of the Environ., 1982-92, bd. dirs., 1980-84, chmn. environ. studies sect. 1980-82, program com. confs., publs. com. 1978-83, chmn. 1981-83, polit. strategies com. 1982-83, sec.-treas. environ. studies sect. 1978-80, chmn. com. on establishing jour. environ. studies 1978, mem. spl. task force on mission, membership and orgnl. structure 1977-78, mem. planning group nat. com. environ. edn. rsch. 1979-80), Internat. Soc. Environ. Edn., World Conservation Union, Russian Acad. Edn. (fgn.). Office: Colo Sch Mines 301 Stratton Hall Golden CO 80401

SACKS, DAVID HARRIS, historian, humanities educator; b. Bklyn., Dec. 14, 1942; s. Fred and Lillian Pearl (Levy) S.; m. Eleanor Darby Woodward, July 25, 1971. BA magna cum laude, Bklyn. Coll., 1963; AM in History, Harvard U., 1965, PhD in History, 1977. Lectr. history U. Mass., Boston, 1977-79; preceptor in expository writing Harvard U., Cambridge, Mass., 1979-80, lectr. in history and lit., 1980-83, rsch. affiliate Ctr. for European Studies, 1983-86; asst. prof. history and humaniteis Reed Coll., Portland, Oreg., 1986-89, assoc. prof., 1989-93, prof., 1993—. Author: Trade Society and Politics in Bristol, 1500-1640, 1985, The Widening Gate: Bristol and the Atlantic Economy, 1450-1700, 1991; contbr. articles to profl. jours. Recipient fellowships Folger Shakespeare Libr., Washington, 1989-90, Woodrow Wilson Internat. Ctr. for Scholars, 1992-93, John Simon Guggenheim Meml. Found., 1992-93. Fellow Royal Hist. Soc.; mem. N.Am. Conf. Brit. Studies (chair nominating com. 1993-95, exec. sec. 1995—), Am. Hist. Assn. (program com. 1993-95, Leo Gershey prize com. 1992-95). Office: Reed Coll 3203 SE Woodstock Blvd Portland OR 97202-8138

SACKS, ROBERT NEIL, lawyer; b. Oberlin, Ohio, Oct. 29, 1960; s. Norman and Miriam Sacks; m. Gabrielle Gopin, July 18, 1992. BA, U. Wis., 1981; JD, UCLA, 1986. Bar: Calif. 1986. Assoc. Morrison & Foerster, L.A., 1986-91; ptnr. Ross, Sacks & Glazier, L.A., 1991—; arbitrator L.A. Superior Ct., 1993—; judge pro tem L.A. Mcpl. Ct., 1993—; speaker on estate and trust litigation topics, L.A., 1994—. Mem. ABA, L.A. County Bar Assn., Beverly Hills Bar Assn. Office: Ross Sacks & Glazier 300 S Grand Ave Ste 3900 Los Angeles CA 90071-3149

SACKTON, FRANK JOSEPH, public affairs educator; b. Chgo., Aug. 11, 1912; m. June Dorothy Raymond, Sept. 21, 1940. Student, Northwestern U., 1936, Yale, 1946, U. Md., 1951-52; BS, U. Md., 1970; grad., Army Inf. Sch., 1941, Command and Gen. Staff Coll., 1942, Armed Forces Staff Coll., 1949, Nat. War Coll., 1954; MPA, Ariz. State U., 1976, DHL (hon.), 1996. Mem. 131st Inf. Regt., Ill. N.G., 1929-40; commd. 2d lt. U.S. Army, 1934, advanced through grades to lt. gen., 1967; brigade plans and ops. officer (33d Inf. Div.), 1941, PTO, 1943-45; div. signal officer, 1942-43, div. intelligence officer, 1944, div. plans and ops. officer, 1945; sec. to gen. staff for Gen. MacArthur Tokyo, 1947-48; bn. comdr. 30th Inf. Regt., 1949-50; mem. spl. staff Dept. Army, 1951; plans and ops. officer Joint Task Force 132, PTO, 1952; comdr. Joint Task Force 7, Marshall Islands, 1953; mem. gen. staff Dept. Army, 1954-55; with Office Sec. Def., 1956; comdr. 18th Inf. Regt., 1957-58; chief staff 1st Inf. Div., 1959; chief army Mil. Mission to Turkey, 1960-62; comdr. XIV Army Corps, 1963; dep. dir. plans Joint Chiefs Staff, 1964-66; army general staff mil. ops., 1966-67, comptroller of the army, 1967-70, ret., 1970; spl. asst. for fed./state relations Gov. Ariz., 1971-75; chmn. Ariz. Programming and Coordinating Com. for Fed. Programs, 1971-75; lectr. Am. Grad. Sch. Internat. Mgmt., 1973-77; vis. asst. prof., lectr. public affairs Ariz. State U., Tempe, 1976-78; founding dean Ariz. State U. Coll. Public Programs, 1979-80; prof. public affairs Ariz. State U., 1980—, finance educator, v.p. bus. affairs, 1981-83, dep. dir. intercollegiate athletics, 1984-85, dir. strategic planning, 1987-88. Contbr. articles to public affairs and mil. jours. Mem. Ariz. Steering Com. for Restoration of the State Capitol, 1974-75, Ariz. State Personnel Bd., 1978-83, Ariz. Regulatory Coun., 1981-93. Decorated D.S.M., Silver Star, also Legion of Merit with 4 oak leaf clusters, Bronze Star with 2 oak leaf clusters, Air medal, Army Commendation medal with 1 oak leaf cluster, Combat Inf. badge. Mem. Ariz. Acad. Public Adminstrn., Pi Alpha Alpha (pres. chpt. 1976-82). Clubs: Army-Navy (Washington); Arizona (Phoenix). Home: 12000 N 90th St Apt 3072 Scottsdale AZ 85260-8635 Office: Ariz State U Sch Pub Affairs Tempe AZ 85287-0603

SADILEK, VLADIMIR, architect; b. Czechoslovakia, June 27, 1933; came to U.S., 1967, naturalized, 1973; s. Oldrich and Antoine (Zlamal) S.; Ph.D. summa cum laude in City Planning and Architecture, Tech. U. Prague, 1957; m. Jana Kadlec, Mar. 25, 1960; 1 son, Vladimir, Jr. Chief architect State Office for City Planning, Prague, 1958-67; architect, designer Bank Bldg. Corp., St. Louis, 1967-70, assoc. architect, San Francisco, 1970-74; owner, chief exec. officer Bank Design Cons., San Mateo, Calif., 1974-81, West Coast Development Co., San Mateo, 1975—; pres., chief exec. officer Orbis Devel. Corp., San Mateo, 1981—. Served with Inf. of Czechoslovakia, 1958. Recipient awards of excellence from Bank Building Corp. and AIA for planning and design of fin. instns. in Hawaii, Calif. (1971), Ariz., N.Mex., Tex. (1972), Colo., Wyo. (1973), Idaho, Oreg., Washington (1974); lic. architect, 28 states. Republican. Roman Catholic. Home: 80 Orange Ct Burlingame CA 94010-6516 Office: 1777 Borel Pl San Mateo CA 94402-3509

SADLER, NORMA J., educator, writer; b. Youngstown, Ohio, June 13, 1944; d. Anthony James and Ann (Hlasta) Narky; m. Jeffrey A. Sadler, Aug. 20, 1966. BA, UCLA, 1966; MA, Calif. State U., Long Beach, 1967; PhD, U. Wis., 1973. Tchr. 3d grade Sacred Hearts Parish, Sun Prairie, Wis., 1967-68; tchr. 4th and 5th grades Middleton (Wis.) Sch. Dist., 1968-69, tchr., 1969-70; prof. Boise (Idaho) State U., 1973—; cons. to sch. dists. on literacy,

1991—. Author: (poetry) Mirabelle's Country Club for Cats and Other Poems, 1986; contbr. poetry to mags. Active in planning and fundraising Boise Chamber Music Soc., 1985—; mem. com. internat. bd. U.S. sect. Books for Young People, 1997—. Recipient Outstanding Tchr. award Boise State Alumni Assn., 1978. Mem. Internat. Reading Assn. (presenter), Am. Assn. for Colls. of Tchr. Edn. (presenter). Office: Boise State U 1910 University Dr Boise ID 83725

SADOWSKI, RICHARD J., publishing executive. Publ. Press-Telegram, Long Beach, Calif. Office: 604 Pine St Long Beach CA 90844

SADRUDDIN, MOE, oil company executive, consultant; b. Hyderabad, India, Mar. 3, 1943; came to U.S., 1964; m. Azmath Oureshi, 1964; 3 children. BSME, Osmania U., Hyderabad, 1964; MS in Indsl. Engring., NYU, 1966; MBA, Columbia U., 1970. Cons. project engr. Ford, Bacon & Davis, N.Y.C., 1966; staff indsl. engr. J.C. Penney, N.Y.C., 1966-68; sr. cons. Drake, Sheahan, Stewart & Dougall, N.Y.C., 1968-70, Beech-Nut Inc. subs. Squibb Corp., N.Y.C., 1970-72; founder, pres. Azmath Constrn. Co., Englewood, N.J., 1972-77; crude oil cons., fgn. govt. rep., 1977—; pres. A-One Petroleum Co., Fullerton, Calif., 1985—; govt. advisor Puerto Rico, 1980-82, Dominica, 1983-84, St. Vincent, 1981-82, Kenya, 1983-84, Belize 1984-85, Costa Rica 1983-86, Paraguay 1984-87. Chmn. Azhar Found., 1989—; bldg. 6 charitable hosps. in India; mem. L.A. World Affairs Coun. Mem. Internat. Platform Assn. Address: A-One Petroleum Co 2656 Camino Del Sol Fullerton CA 92833-4806 *Personal philosophy: I learned from a young age that acquisition of knowledge, developing honesty and integrity and service to humanity in the form of charity, love and struggle to help the poor and needy, are the main foundation stones of a successful life. I believe that acquisition of wealth is only a means to an end and not an end in itself. With accumulation of wealth, one has to care for the underprivileged and try to improve their lot.*

SADUN, ALFREDO ARRIGO, neuro-ophthalmologist, scientist, educator; b. New Orleans, Oct. 23, 1950; s. Elvio H. and Lina (Ottoleghi) S.; m. Debra Leigh Rice, Mar. 18, 1978; children: Rebecca Eli, Elvio Aaron, Benjamin Maxwell. BS, MIT, 1972; PhD, Albert Einstein Med. Sch., Bronx, N.Y., 1976, MD, 1978. Intern Huntington Meml. Hosp. U. So. Calif., Pasadena, 1978-79; resident Harvard U. Med. Sch., Boston, 1979-82, HEED Found. fellow in neuro-ophthalmology Mass. Eye and Ear Inst., 1982-83, instr. ophthalmology, 1983, asst. prof. ophthalmology, 1984; dir. residential tng. U. So. Calif. Dept. Ophthalmology, L.A., 1984-85, 90—; asst. prof. ophthalmology and neurosurgery U. So. Calif., L.A., 1984-87, assoc. prof., 1987-90; full prof. U. So. Calif., 1990—, mem. internal review bd.; prin. investigator Howe Lab. Harvard U., Boston, 1981-84, E. Doheny Eye Inst., L.A., 1984—; examiner Am. Bd. Ophthalmology; mem. internal rev. bd. U. So. Calif.; mem. sci. exec. bd. K. Rasmussen Found.; mem. sci. adv. bd. Internat. Found. for Optic Nerve Diseases. Author: Optics for Opthalmologists, 1988, New Methods of Sensory Visual Testing, 1989; contbr. articles to profl. jours. and chpts. to books. James Adams scholar, 1990-91; recipient Pecan D. award, 1988-92, Rsch. to Prevent Blindness Sr. Investigator award, 1996-97, Rsch. to Prevent Blindness Sr. Investigator award, 1996. Fellow Am. Acad. Ophthalmology Neuro-Ophthalmologists; mem. NIH (Med. Scientists Tng. award 1972-78), Am. Assn. Anatomists, Assn. Univ. Prof. Ophthalmology (assoc.), Am. Bd. Ophthalmology (rep. to residency rev. com. 1994—), Soc. to Prevent Blindness, Nat. Eye Inst. (New Investigator Rsch. award 1983-86, rsch. grants 1988-91, 93—), Soc. Neuroscis., Assn. Rsch. in Vision and Ophthalmology, N.Am. Neuro-Ophthal. Soc. (chmn. membership com. 1990—, v.p. 1994—). Home: 2478 Adair St San Marino CA 91108-2610 Office: U So Calif E Doheny Eye Inst 1450 San Pablo St Los Angeles CA 90033-4615

SAFERITE, LINDA LEE, library director; b. Santa Barbara, Calif., Mar. 25, 1947; d. Elwyn C. and Polly (Frazer) S.; m. Andre Doyon, July 16, 1985. BA, Calif. State U., Chico, 1969; MS in Library Sci., U. So. Calif., 1970; cert. in Indsl. Relations, UCLA, 1976; MBA, Pepperdine U., 1979. Librarian-in-charge, reference librarian Los Angeles County Pub. Libr. System, 1970-73, regional reference librarian, 1973-75, sr. librarian-in-charge, 1975-78, regional adminstr., 1978-80; libr. dir. Scottsdale (Ariz.) Pub. Libr. System, 1980-93, Fort Collins (Colo.) Pub. Libr., 1993-96; exec. dir. Tulsa (Okla.) City County Libr., 1996—; task force del. White House Conf. on Libr. and Info. Svcs., 1992—, rep. Region V, 1992-94. Bd. dirs. Scottsdale-Paradise Valley YMCA, 1981-86, Ariz. Libr. Friends, 1990-92; bd. dirs. AMIGOS, 1990, chmn., 1992-93; mem. Class 5, Scottsdale Leavership, 1991. Recipient Cert. Recognition for efforts in civil rights Ariz. Atty. Gen.'s Office, 1985, Libr. award Ariz. Libr. Friends, 1988, Women of Distinction award for Edn., 1989, State Project of Yr. award, 1995, Ariz. Disting. Svc. award, 1993; named State Libr. of Yr., 1990. Mem. ALA, Ariz. State Libr. Assn. (pres. 1987-88), Ariz. Women's Town Hall AlumniAssn., Met. Bus. and Profl. Women (Scottsdale, pres. 1986-87), Soroptimist (pres. 1981-83). Republican. Office: Tulsa City County Libr 400 Civic Ctr Tulsa OK 74103

SAGAR, MAHENDRAKUMAR PITAMBER, pharmaceutical company executive; b. Mangrol, Gujarat, India, Oct. 24, 1962; came to U.S. 1988; s. Pitamber Khimji and Hemlata P. (Soni) S.; m. Sejal Ranjit Dhanak, July 17, 1990. BSChemE, M.S. U., Baroda, India, 1986, MBA, 1988; MBA, Rutgers U., 1992; MS in CIS, N.J. Inst. Tech., 1993. Rsch. asst. N.J. Inst. Tech., Newark, 1988-91; SAS programmer Schering-Plough Corp., Kenilworth, N.J., 1991-92; sr. SAS programmer Parexel Internat. Corp., Waltham, Mass., 1992-94; clin. data sys. adminstr. Seragen, Inc., Hopkinton, Mass., 1994; tech. coord. Genentech, Inc., South San Francisco, 1994-96; pres. The Sagar Group, Redwood City, Calif., 1996—; cons. N.J. Inst. Tech., 1992—. Contbr. articles to profl. jours. Univ. Grant Com. of India nat. merit scholar, 1981-85, 86-87; N.J. Inst. Tech. rsch. fellow, 1988-90; recipient Best Contributed Paper award, Western Users SAS Software, 1996. Mem. ACM, Inst. Mgmt. Sci., SAS Users Group Internat., Pharma SAS Users Group, Am. Philatelic Soc., India Study Circle, Royal Philatelic Soc. London. Democrat. Hindu. Home: 35 Queens Way Ste 7 Framingham MA 01701 Office: The Sagar Group 15 Atherwood Ave # 12 Redwood City CA 94061

SAGER, DONALD ALLEN, insurance company executive; b. Cleve., Sept. 13, 1930; s. Albert Allen and Dolores Vera (Stone) S.; m. Shirley T. Sager, Dec. 23, 1951; children: Donald A. II, David Allen. BA, U. Md., 1958; postgrad., U. Md. Law Sch., 1958-60. Sr. underwriter Monumental Life Ins. Co., Balt., 1958-64; v.p. Am. Health & Life Ins. Co., Balt., 1964-77; asst. v.p. Univ. Life Ins. Co., Indpls., 1977-81; v.p. Vulcan Life Ins. Co., Birmingham, Ala., 1981-84, Modern Pioneers' Life Ins. Co., Phoenix, 1984-87, Old Reliance Ins. Co., Phoenix, 1987-96; pres. Imaginative Solutions, Inc., 1996—. Dir. Hearing and Speech Agy., Balt., 1974-77; treas. Essex Recreational Coun., Balt., 1966-73; bd. dirs. Arthritis Found., Phoenix, 1988-91; precinct capt. Rep. Party, Phoenix, 1990—; dir. City of Phoenix Pacific Rim adv. coun., mem. Abraham Lincoln Soc.; bd. dirs. Ariz. Dept. Ins. Small Group Reinsurance Bd., mem. examination com. Ariz. Dept. Ins. License; bd. advisors Ariz. Korean Assn. With U.S. Army, 1951-53, Korea. Decorated Bronze Star. Mem. Assn. Health Underwriters (legis. com. 1992—), Masons, Shriners, Moose, Elks, Order of De Molay (cert., N.D. gov. 1988-90). Lutheran. Home: 5429 E Charter Oak Rd Scottsdale AZ 85254-4217 Office: Imaginative Solutions Inc 5429 E Charter Oak Rd Scottsdale AZ 85254-4217

SAGMEISTER, EDWARD FRANK, business owner, hospitality industry executive, civic official, retired consultant, fund raiser, career officer; b. N.Y.C., Dec. 10, 1939; s. Frank and Anna (Unger) S.; m. Anne Marie Ducker, Aug. 18, 1962; children: Cynthia Anne, Laura Marie, Cheryl Suzanne, Eric Edward. BS, U. San Francisco, 1962; MBA, Syracuse U., 1968; postgrad., Air Command and Staff Coll., 1977, Air War Coll., 1981. Commd. 2d lt. USAF, 1963, advanced through grades to lt. col., pers. officer, 1963, aide-de-camp, 1965; dir. pers. sys. Alaskan Air Command, 1968; sys. design program analysis officer HQ USAF, The Pentagon, 1971; spl. asst. sec. Air Force Pers. Coun., USAF, 1975; dir. pers. programs and assignments HQUSAF Europe, 1979; Air Force dep. asst. inspector gen., 1982; ret. USAF, 1984; dir. devel. Am. Cancer Soc., Riverside, Calif., 1984-87; cons. Redlands, Calif., 1987-92; chmn. of bd., pres., CEO Hospitality Pub and Grub, Inc., San Bernardino, Calif., 1992—; instr. Am. Internat. U., L.A., 1987; program dir. Am. Radio Network, L.A., 1987; ptnr., owner Midway Med. Ctr., San Bernardino, 1990-91. Foreman pro-tem San Bernardino County Grand Jury, 1990-91; mem. Redlands 2000 Com., 1988; campaign cabinet mem. Arrowhead United Way, San Bernardino, 1986-87, loaned exec., 1985; exec. dir. Crafton hills Coll. Found., Yucaipa, Calif., 1988; vol. San Bernardino County Dept. Probation, 1985-88; mem. Redlands Cmty., Chorus, 1988-90; vice-chmn., charter mem. Redlands Human Rels. Commn., 1994—, chmn., 1996; mem. Redlands Youth Accountability Bd., San Bernardino County, 1994—, treas. 1996; mem. supt.'s human rels. adv. com., Redlands Unified Sch. Dist., 1996—. Mem. San Bernardino C. of C., Redlands C. of C., Ret. Officers Assn., Nat. Soc. Fundraising Execs., (dir., charter mem. Inland Empire chpt. 1987-88), Empire Singers (v.p. 1987). Republican. Roman Catholic. Home: 503 Sunnyside Ave Redlands CA 92373-5629 Office: Hospitality Pub and Grub Inc 1987 Diners Ct San Bernardino CA 92408-3330

SAHATJIAN, MANIK, nurse, psychologist; b. Tabris, Iran, July 24, 1921; came to U.S., 1951; d. Dicran and Shushanig (Der-Galustian) Mnatzaganian; m. George Sahatjian, Jan. 21, 1954; children: Robert, Edwin. Nursing Cert., Am. Mission Hosps.-Boston U., 1954; BA in Psychology, San Jose State U., 1974, MA in Psychology, 1979. RN, Calif., Mass. Head nurse Am. Mission Hosp., Tabris, 1945-46; charge nurse Banke-Melli Hosp., Tehran, 1946-51; vis. nurse Vis. Nurse Assn., Oakland, Calif., 1956-57; research asst. Stanford U., 1979-81, Palo Alto (Calif.) Med. Research Found., 1981-84; documentation supr. Bethesda Convalescent Ctr., Los Gatos, Calif., 1985-86; sr. outreach worker City of Fremont (Calif.) Human Svcs., 1987-90, case mgr., 1990—; guest rsch. asst. NASA Ames Lab., Mountain View, Calif., summers 1978, 79. Author (with others) psychol. research reports. Fulbright scholar, 1951; Iran Found. scholar, 1953. Mem. AAUW, Western Psychol. Assn. Democrat. Mem. St. Andrew Armenian Church. Home: 339 Starlite Way Fremont CA 94539-7642

SAHS, MAJORIE JANE, art educator; b. Altadena, Calif., Aug. 27, 1926; d. Grayson Michael and Janie Belle (Aaron) McCarty; m. Eugene Otto Sahs, July 21, 1949; children: Victoria, Stephen, Jeffry. Student, Art Ctr. of L.A., 1943-45, Emerson Coll., Boston, 1945; BA, Sacramento State U., 1970; MA in Art Edn., Calif. State U., Sacramento, 1972, postgrad., 1973-79. Cert. secondary tchr., Calif. Tchr. art Sacramento County Schs., 1971-80; cons. Whole Brain Learning Modes, Sacramento, 1980-84; tng. specialist Art Media, Sacramento, Calif., 1983—; instr. Found. for Continuing Med. Edn., Calif., 1985; presenter Nat. Art Edn. Conf., Chgo., 1992, 93, Asian Pacific Conf. on Arts Edn., Franklin, Australia, Internat. Conf., Montreal, Can., 1993; cons., lectr. in field; judge U.S. Treas., 1994, 95, 96, 97; Dept. of Calif. Student Art. Prodr., writer guide and video Gesture Painting Through T'ai Chi, 1992; editor, pub. Calif.'s state newspaper for art edn., 1987-90; editor: Crocker Mus. Docent Guide, 1990; mem. editl. bd. Jour. for Nat. Art Edn. Assn., 1990—; editor: (newsletter) U.S. Soc. for Edn. Through Art, 1994-97; designer of ltd. edits. scarves and cards for Nat. Breast Cancer Rsch. Fund, Exploration Inspiration '95; works publ. in The Best in Silk Painting, 1997. Del. Calif. Arts Leadership Symposium for Arts Edn., 1979, Legis. Coalition Through The Arts, Calif., 1989, 95; judge Calif. State Fair Art Show, 1989, 95, Fed. Treasury Poster Contest, 1994, 95, 96, 97; organizer and host art show and fundraiser for women candidates, 1992. Recipient Patriotic Svc. award Fed. Treasury Dept., 1996, 97, State award of Merit. Mem. Internat. Assn. Edn. through Art, U.S. Soc. Edn. through Art (editor newsletter 1994-97), Nat. Art Edn. Assn. (mem. editl. bd. jour. 1990—, Nat. Outstanding Newspaper Editor award 1988, 89), Calif. Art Edn. Assn. (mem. state coun., mem. area coun., editor state paper, State Award of Merit), Calif. Children's Homes Soc. (pres. Camellia chpt. 1990-91), Asian Pacific Arts Educators Assn., Creative Arts League Sacramento, Emerson Coll. Alumni, Art Ctr. L.A. Alumni. Home and Office: 1836 Walnut Ave Carmichael CA 95608-5417

SAIF, MEHRDAD, electrical engineering educator; b. Tehran, Iran, Dec. 7, 1960; came to U.S. 1978; s. Jahangir and Shahrebanou (Jamshidi) S.; m. Maira De los Angeles Alvarez, May 20, 1989; children: Cyrus Anthony, Darius Alexander. MSEE, Cleve. State U., 1984, DEng, 1987. Rsch. asst. Cleve. State U./NASA Lewis, 1984; rsch. assoc. Cleve. Adv. Mfg. Program (CAMP)/Adv. Mfg. Ctr. (AMC), 1985-87; instr. Cleve. State U., 1987; assoc. prof. elec. engring. Simon Fraser U., Burnaby, B.C., 1987-93, 1993—; assoc. fellow Inst. for Computational and Applied Math., Burnaby, 1990—; internat. com. 4th Internat. Symposium on Robotics and Mfg., Albuquerque, 1991; vis. scholar to N.Am. Operation (NAO) R&D Ctr. of GM, 1993-94. Co-editor: Robotics and Manufacturing, 1991; contbr. articles to profl. jours. Grantee, NSERC of Can., 1988-90, 91—; Adv. Systems Inst. grantee, 1990. Mem. IEEE, AIAA, Assn. Profl. Engrs. and Geoscientists B.C. (registered), Internat. Fedn. Automatic Control, Eta Kappa Nu. Office: Simon Fraser Univ, Sch Engring Sci, Burnaby, BC Canada V5A 1S6

SAILOR, J. DOUGLAS, engineering consultant; b. Elkhart, Ind., Nov. 14, 1927; s. Clifford Earl and Mildred Marie (Scholl) S.; m. Florence Margaret Magee, Aug. 30, 1960; children: Brian Scott, Craig Randall. BSEE, Purdue U., 1950, MSEE, 1951. Project engr. Wright Air Devel. Ctr., Dayton, Ohio, 1951-55, U.S. Army White Sands (N.Mex.) Signal Corp., 1955-56; mgr. systems engring. Lockheed Missiles & Space Co., Sunnyvale, Calif., 1957-92; pvt. cons. Morgan Hill, Calif., 1993—. Author: Space System Engineering, 1962, System Engineering Management Guide, 1983, System Engineering Manual, 1985. Pfc. U.S. Army, 1955-56. Fellow AIAA (assoc., chmn. San Francisco Bay area, Engr. of Yr. award 1986), Am. Astro. Soc. (chmn. San Francisco Bay area 1964), Nat. Coun. System Engrs. Home: 14125 Sycamore Dr Morgan Hill CA 95037-9405

ST. AMAND, PIERRE, geophysicist; b. Tacoma, Wash., Feb. 4, 1920; s. Cyrias Z. and Mable (Berg) St. A.; m. Marie Pöss, Dec. 5, 1945; children: Gene, Barbara, Denali, David. BS in Physics, U. Alaska, 1948; MS in Geophysics, Calif. Inst. Tech., 1951, PhD in Geophysics and Geology, 1953; Dr. honoris causa, U. De Los Altos, Tepatitlan, Mex., 1992. Asst. dir. Geophys. Lab., U. Alaska, also head ionospheric and seismologic investigations, 1946-49; physicist U.S. Naval Ordnance Test Sta., China Lake, Calif., 1950-54; head optics br. U.S. Naval Ordnance Test Sta., 1955-58; head earth and planetary sci. div. U.S. Ordnance Test Sta., 1961-78, now cons. to tech. dir., head spl. projects office, 1978-88; fgn. service with ICA as prof. geol. and geophys. Sch. Earth Scis., U. Chile, 1958-60; originator theory rotational displacement Pacific Ocean Basin; pres. Saint-Amand Sci. Services; adj. prof. McKay Sch. Mines, U. Nev., U. N.D.; v.p., dir. Covillea Corp.; v.p., dir. tech. Muetal Corp.; cons. World Bank, Calif. Div. Water Resources, Am. Potash & Chem. Co., OAS; mem. U.S. Army airways communications system, Alaska and Can., 1942-46; cons. Mexican, Chilean, Argentine, Philipines, Can. govts.; mem. Calif. Gov.'s Com. Geol. Hazards; mem. com. magnetic instruments Internat. Union Geodesy and Geophys., 1954-59, Disaster Preparation Commn. for Los Angeles; charter mem. Sr. Exec. Service. Adv. bd. GeoScience News; contbr. 100 articles to scientific jours. Chmn. bd. dirs. Ridgecrest Comty. Hosp.; chmn. bd. dirs. Indian Wells Valley Airport Dist.; dir. Indian Wells Valley Water Dist.; v.p. bd. dirs. Kern County Acad. Decathlon. Decorated knight Mark Twain, Mark Twain Jour.; recipient cert. of merit OSRD, 1945, cert. of merit USAAF, 1946, letter of commendation USAAF, 1948, Spl. award Philippine Air Force, 1969, Diploma de Honor Sociedad Geologica de Chile, Disting. Civilian Svc. medal USN, 1968, L.T.E. Thompson medal, 1973, Thunderbird award Weather Modification Assn., 1974, Disting. Pub. Svc. award Fed. Exec. Inst., 1976, Meritorious Svc. medal USN, 1988, Disting. Alumnus award U. Alaska, 1990; Fulbright rsch. fellow France, 1954-55. Fellow AAAS, Geol. Soc. Am., Earthquake Engr. Rsch. Inst.; mem. Am. Geophys. Union, Weather Modification Assn., Am. Seismol. Soc., Sister Cities (Ridgecrest-Tepatitlan) Assn. (pres.), Rotary (past pres., Paul Harris fellow), Footprinters Internat. (mem. grand bd., pres.), Sigma Xi. Home: 1748 W Las Flores Ave Ridgecrest CA 93555-8635

ST. CLAIR, BARBARA LOUISE, healthcare facility administrator; b. Green Bay, Wis., Sept. 14, 1947; d. Francis Joseph and Esther (Morris) Bergeron; m. John Frederick St. Clair, June 28, 1969; children: Thomas William, Elizabeth Grace, Maria Bethany. Liberal arts, U. Wis., 1969; postgrad., Western Internat. U., 1996—. Social worker AZ Physicians IPA, Phoenix, 1987-90; quality assurance supr. Thunderbird Health Care Ctr., Phoenix, 1990-92, dir. admissions, 1992-93; dir. mktg. Phoenix Mtn. Nursing Ctr., Phoenix, 1993-94; dir. admissions and mktg. Grancare Med. Ctr., Phoenix, 1994-95; adminstr. Mimosa Springs Plaza Health Care, Scottsdale, Ariz., 1995—; programs co-chair Human Svcs. Profls., Phoenix, 1994-95. Participant Alzheimers Walk Alzheimer's Assn., 1994, 96. Mem. Am. Coll. Health Care Adminstrs., Delta Mu Delta. Office: Plaza Health Care Mimosa Springs 8435 E Mcdowell Rd Scottsdale AZ 85257-3903

ST. CLAIR, CARL, conductor, music director. Music dir. Pacific Symphony Orch., Santa Ana, Calif., 1990—. Office: Pacific Symphony Orch 1231 E Dyer Rd Santa Ana CA 92705-5606

ST. CLAIR, SHANE SCOTT, communications and international health specialist; b. Salem, Oreg., Feb. 27, 1965; s. Leo Christian and Cecelia Loraine (Hall) St. C.; m. Carol Lynn Stewart, Apr. 4, 1993. Student, La Sierra U., 1983, Crafton Hills Coll., 1987-89, Sierra Coll., 1990. Dir. Sale Away, Grand Terrace, Calif., 1986-90; capt. Canvasback Mission Inc., Benicia, Calif., 1991-94, devel. dir., 1993-94; exec. dir. Search for One, Inc., 1994—. Contbr. articles to profl. jours. Charter pres. Jr. C. of C., Benicia, 1993-94. Capt. U.S. Merchant Marine. Mem. Toastmasters Internat. (1st pl. Internat. Speech award 1994). Home: PO Box 752 Gladstone OR 97027 Office: PO Box 624 Gladstone OR 97027

ST. GEORGE, LAURA M., middle school educator; b. Yakima, Wash., Apr. 4, 1935; d. Clarence C. and Bertha E. (Roy) S. BA, Cen. Wash. Coll., 1957; MEd, Seattle U., 1969. Tchr., staff devel. Bellevue (Wash.) Sch. Dist., 1958-90; adj. faculty Seattle Pacific U., 1981-90; teaching assoc., instr. edn. U. Wash., Seattle, 1989-91; tchr. Forest Ridge Mid. Sch., Bellevue, Wash., 1990—; mem. Nat. Bd. for Profl. Teaching Standards. Mem. NEA, ASCD, Nat. Mid. Sch. Assn., Wash. Edn. Assn. Home: 9004 132nd Ave NE Redmond WA 98052-1936 Office: Forest Ridge Mid Sch 4800 139th Ave SE Bellevue WA 98006-3015

SAINT-MARIE, MARY SHEILA, artist, writer, educator; b. Nevada, Iowa, Apr. 16, 1942; d. Merlyn Gilford and Sidney Eugene (McKim) Smalldridge; m. David Earl Piper (div.); 1 child, Kimberly Paige Piper; m. Michael Robert Allen, 1975 (div. 1977); 1 child, Rebecca Rachael Allen. BA in Edn., U. No. Iowa, 1964; postgrad., U. Wis., 1967-70, Oreg. Coll. Edn., 1972, U. Va., 1982, Coll. of Siskiyou, 1983. Cert. tchr., Iowa. Tchr. English Monoma Grove (Wis. H.S., 1964-67; asst. coord. WHA TV, U. Wis., Madison, 1968-69; instrnl. TV svcs. comm. skills instr. Chemeketa C.C., Salem, Oreg., fall 1972; master tutor English Coll. of Siskiyou, Weed, Calif., 1980-81; writer Universal Child Newsletter, Mt. Shasta, Calif., 1980-84; writer, artist Mount Shasta, Calif., 1973—; curriculum writer Monona Grove H.S., summer 1965-66; guest presenter, artist, performer Crone Counsel III, Scottsdale, Ariz., 1995—. Author: Galactic Shamanism, 1995; writer, narrator (cassettes) She..it is..Who Remembers, 1994, Soul Sounds of World Birth, 1995; writer Mt. Shasta Directions mag., 1995-97; art illustrator The Quest of Theosophical Soc., 1995-96; artist Dream Network Jour., 1994-96, Crone Chronicles, 1995—; prodr., dir., performer Sacred Enactments of Ancient Remembering, 1990—; exhibited in group shows Chemeketa Coll., Salem, Oreg., 1973, Bush Barn, Salem, 1973, Light Works, Mt. Shasta, 1979, Crystal Unicorn, Mt. Shasta, 1979, Blue Star Gallery, Ashland, Oreg., 1980, Great Western Savs. and Loan, Mt. Shasta, 1985, Orchid Gallery, Ashland, Oreg., 1989, Shasta Song, Mt. Shasta, 1989, Crystal Reflections, Mt. Shasta, 1989, Whole Life Expn., L.A., San Francisco, 1989, Asilomar Conf. Ctr., Monterey Peninsula, Calif., 1990, Whole Self Festival, Medford, Oreg., 1990, Bentley's, Ashland, 1990, The Gathering, Joshua Tree, Calif., 1990, Ashland Hills Inn, 1990, Crystal Shaman Gallery, Mt. Shasta, 1990, Delphinium Gallery, Sedona, Ariz., 1990, Sacred Spaces Gallery, Santa Fe, 1990, Mark Anthony Hotel, Ashland, 1991, Whole Life Expn., Seattle, 1991, 5th Dimension Gallery, Ashland, 1991, 92, Horizons Unltd. Gallery, Mt. Shasta, 1991, Stoney Brook Inn, McCloud, Calif., 1991, Unitarian Fellowship, Redwood City, Calif., 1991, Whole Life Expn., San Francisco, 1991, Horizons Unlimited Gallery, Mt. Shasta, Calif., 1991, Atlanta Trade Show, Ga., 1991, Monterey Peninsula Coll., Monterey, Calif., 1991, Mountain Mist Gallery, Jacksonville, Oregon, 1992, Follow Your Heart Gallery, Santa Barbara Calif., 1992, Hilton Hotel, L.A., Calif., 1992, U. Sci. and Philosophy, Waynesboro, Va., 1992, Whole Life Exposition, Seattle Wash., 4th St. Garden Gallery, Ashland, Oreg., 1993, BMSE Exposition, Ashland Hills Inn, 1993, Kirsten Gallery, Seattle, Wash., 1993, In Her Image Gallery, Portland Oreg., 1993, Visionary Gallery, 1993, New Age Renaissance Fair, San Jose Convention Ctr., Calif., 1993, Fifth Dimension Nature Galley, Ashland Oreg., 1993, Firedworks Gallery, Alamosa, Colo., 1993, Golden Lotus Gallery, Mt. Shasta Calif., 1994, Ani Lea, Belgium, 1993, Awara Color & Design, Gent, Belgium, 1995, Wings Gallery, Mt. Shasta, Calif., 1995, Oreg. Country Fair, 1995, Crone Counsel III, Scotsdale, Ariz., 1995, The Glass Onion, Ashland, Oreg., 1995, Lifeways Expo., Ashland, Calif., 1996, Colombiere, Idyllwild, Calif., 1996.New Age Retailer Trade Show, San Diego, Calif., 1996, NAPRA Trade Show, Denver, Colo., 1996. Featured artist KPIX-TV, Channel 5, 1990; interview as artist/author Star Comm./TV, Ashland, Oreg., 1995; recipient Hon. mention award Renaissance Faire, San Jose Conv. Ctr., 1993. Home: PO Box 704 Mount Shasta CA 96067-0704

ST. PETER, JEFFREY F., publishing executive, consultant; b. Phoenix, July 22, 1956; s. Sylvester Earl and Pearl Rose (Bovee) St. P.; m. Jowell J. Holtz, Jan. 2, 1992; children: Leslie E., Lindsay J., Sean D. BS in Polit. Sci., U. Mont., 1993. Asst. supr. Acts Christian Sch., Lewiston, Idaho, 1986-89; announcer, chief engr. KMCM Radio, Miles City, Mont., 1989-91; asst. publ. UC Bookstore, Missoula, Mont., 1991-93; staff writer Idaho County Free Press, Grangeville, 1994; editor The Clearwater Progress, Kamiah, Idaho, 1994-96; cons., publ. Aletheia Publ., Kamiah, Idaho, 1996—. Lobbyist Missoula County Commn., Missoula, Mont., 1993-94. Mem. Golden Key, Idaho Press Club. Mem. U.S. Taxpayer Party. Mem. Full Gospel Ch. Home: 520 Bryan Dr Kamiah ID 83536 Office: Aletheia Publ & Cons PO Box 308 Kamiah ID 83536

SAITO, FRANK KIYOJI, import-export firm executive; b. Tokyo, Feb. 28, 1945; s. Kaoru and Chiyoko S.; LL.B., Kokugakuin U., 1967; m. Elaine Tamami Karasawa, Feb. 22, 1975; children—Roderic Kouki, Lorine Erika. With import dept. Trois Co. Ltd., Tokyo, Japan, 1967-68; founder import/export dept. Three Bond Co., Ltd., Tokyo, 1968-71; sales mgr. Kobe Mercantile, Inc., San Diego, 1971-76; pres. K & S Internat. Corp., San Diego, 1976—. Office: K & S Internat Corp K & S Bldg 8015 Silverton Ave San Diego CA 92126-6383

SAIZ, BERNARD R., principal; b. Albuquerque, Apr. 21, 1962; s. Jose Eduardo Leon and Mildred (Sanchez) S.; m. Deanna Lee Neel, July 12, 1986. BA in Edn., Univ. N.Mex., 1984, MA in Secondary Edn., 1988. Tchr. art, English Socorro (N.M.) Middle Sch., 1984-88, asst. prin., 1988-89; asst. prin. Socorro H.S., 1989-92, prin., 1992—; artist. Mem. Assn. Supervision Curriculum Devel., Nat. Assn. Secondary Sch. Prins., N.M. Sch. Adminstrs., Kappa Sigma. Republican. Roman Catholic. Office: Socorro HS 1200 Michigan Ave Socorro NM 87031

SAKAMOTO, KATSUYUKI, college chancellor, psychology educator; b. L.A., Oct. 24, 1938; m. Edna Christine Sakamoto; children: David Katsu, Bryce Yoshio. BA in Psychology, Calif. State U., Fresno, 1961, MA in Psychology, 1968; PhD in Exptl. Social Psychology, So. Ill. U., Carbondale, 1971; postgrad., Carnegie Mellon U., 1984. Acting dir. Army Edn. Ctr., Munich, 1962-63; dir. social svcs. Salvation Army, Fresno, Calif., 1964-66; assoc. prof. psychology Keuka Coll., Keyka Park, N.Y., 1971-78; prof. social psychology Ea. Oreg. State Coll., La Grande, 1978-85, assoc. dean, then acting dean, 1980-82, 84, assoc. dean acad. affairs, 1982-85; prof. psychology Ind. U. East, Richmond, 1985-91, vice chancellor for acad. affairs, 1985-90, spl. asst. to chancellor, 1990-91; prof., chancellor Calif. Sch. Profl. Psychology, Alameda, 1991—; lectr. So. Ill. U., 1970-71; vis. prof. SUNY, Binghamton, 1973; adj. prof. Alfred (N.Y.) U., 1972-76, Nazareth Coll. Rochester, N.Y., 1975-78, Eisenhower Coll., Seneca Falls, N.Y., 1975-77; evaluator Western Assn. Schs. and Colls., 1991—; commr.-at-large North Ctrl. Assn. Colls. and Schs., 1989-91, educator, cons., 1986-91; mem. exec. bd. for study ctrs. in Japan, China and Korea, campus dir. Oreg. Sys. Higher Edn., 1980-85; bd. visitors Newark (N.Y.) Devel. Ctr., 1975-77; presenter in field. Contbr. articles to profl. jours. Bd. dirs. troop 119 Boy Scouts Am., Richmond, 1986-91, Project 100001, Townsend Cmty. Ctr., Richmond, 1987-89, Alameda Girls Club, Inc., 1992—, Asian Cmty. Mental Health Svcs., 1991—, Found. for Ednl. Excellence, Alameda, 1993—; pres., bd. dirs. Whitewater Opera Co., Richmond, 1987-91, Leadership Wayne County, Richmond, 1988-91; cons. teaching mini-grant program Richmond Cmty. Schs., 1988-91; mem. citizens adv. bd. Wayne County Sheriff's Dept., 1989-

91. Mem. APA, Am. Assn. for Higher Edn., Am. Assn. State Colls. and Univs., Am. Assn. Univ. Adminstrs. (nat. v.p. 1990-92, bd. dirs. Found. 1991—), Am. Assn. for Higher Edn. (founding mem. Asian Am. caucus), Asian Am. Psychol. Assn. (treas., membership officer 1983-91, pres. 1988-91), Calif. Psychol. Assn., Nat. Assn. Acad. Affairs Adminstrs., Nat. Coun. Schs. Profl. Psychology, Rotary (bd. dirs. Alameda 1993—). Home: 2837 Brown St Alameda CA 94502-7949 Office: Calif Sch Profl Psychology 1005 Atlantic Ave Alameda CA 94501-1148*

SAKAMOTO, NORMAN LLOYD, civil engineer; b. Honolulu, May 22, 1947; s. Shuichi and Fusa (Hayashi) S.; m. Penelope A. Hayasaka, July 12, 1970; children: David H., Gregory F., Katherine E. BSCE, U. Hawaii, 1969; MSCE, U. Ill., 1970. Registered profl. engr., Calif., Hawaii; lic. spl. inspector, Hawaii; lic. contractor, Hawaii. Engr. storm drain City of L.A., 1970-71, engr. streets and frwys., 1972-73; engr. hydrology C.E., 1971-72; v.p. S & M Sakamoto, Inc., Honolulu, 1973-85; pres. SC Pacific Corp., Kapolei, Hawaii, 1985—; bd. dirs. Bldg. Industry Assn., Honolulu, spl. appointee, 1991-92, pres.-elect, 1993, pres., 1994; bd. dirs. City Contractors Assn., Honolulu; trustee Home Builders Inst., 1993-96; del. White House Conf. on Small Bus., 1995; co-chair Hawaii Congress on Small Bus. Scoutmaster Honolulu area Boy Scouts Am., 1989-92; elected to Hawaii State Senate, Dist. 16, 1996—. Named Remodeler of Month Bldg. Industry Assn., 1990, 91, 96, Remodeler of Yr., 1991. Mem. ASCE, Nat. Assn. Home Builders (dir. 1992—), Internat. Fellowship Christian Businessmen, Constrn. Industry Legis. Assn., C. of C. Evangelical. Office: SC Pacific Corp 91-178 Kalaeloa Blvd Kapolei HI 96707-1819

SAKKAL, MAMOUN, architect, interior designer; b. Damascus, Syria, Dec. 31, 1950; came to U.S., 1978; s. Lutfi Sakkal and Dourieh Khatib; m. Seta K. Sakkal, Mar. 13, 1980; children: Aida, Kindah. BArch with honors, U. Aleppo, Syria, 1974; MArch, U. Wash., 1982, cert. urban design, 1982. Registered architect, Wash., Syria; lic. interior designer, U.S. Archtl. designer MCE, Damascus, 1974-75; dir. design MCE, Aleppo, 1975-76; prin. Sakkal & Assocs., Aleppo, 1976-78; archtl. designer Arch. Assocs., Seattle, 1978-82; sr. designer RD&S, Bellevue, Wash., 1982-84; prin. Restaurant/Hotel Design, Seattle, 1984—, Sakkal Design, Bothell, 1991—; lectr. U. Aleppo, 1974-75, Applied Arts Inst., 1977-78, affiliate instr. U. Wash., 1990—. Author: Geometry of Muqarnas in Islamic Architecture, 1981; designer Oct. Mus., Damascus, Syria, 1977 (1st prize Syrian Ministry Dev.); one man shows include Nat. Mus. Aleppo, Syria, 1969, U. Aleppo, 1984, U. Wash., 1979, 80, 90, 91, U. Cambridge, Eng., 1990, Islamic Soc. N.Am. Conv., Chgo., 1994; contbr. articles to profl. jours. Recipient Best Logo Design award Arab Union Sports, 1976, Best Project Design award Aleppo Ministry of Culture, 1975, Best Modernization Project award Holiday Inns System, 1986, Best Lounge Renovation award Bowlers Jour. Ann. Design Contest, 1987, 1st award in Kufi style 3d Internat. Calligraphy Competition, Rsch. Ctr. for Islamic History, Art and Culture, Istanbul, Turkey, 1993. Office: Sakkal Design 1523 175th Pl SE Bothell WA 98012-6460

SAKOGUCHI, BEN, artist, art educator; b. San Bernardino, Calif., 1938. Student, San Bernardino Valley Coll., 1956-58; BA, UCLA, 1960, MFA, 1964; postgrad., Calif. State U., L.A., 1982-83. Prof. art Pasadena (Calif.) City Coll., 1964—. Solo exhbns. include Ceeje Gallery, L.A., 1964, 65, 67, La Jolla (Calif.) Mus., 1965, U. Calif. Santa Cruz, 1967, L.A. City Coll., 1968, 81, Santa Barbara (Calif.) Mus. Art, 1968, Brand Art Ctr., Glendale, Calif., 1971, Zara Gallery, San Francisco, 1973, Compton (Calif.) Coll., 1977, Works, San Jose, Calif., 1978, Mira Costa Coll., Oceanside, Calif., 1983, Roberts Gallery, Santa Monica, Calif., 1985, Mount St. Mary's Coll., L.A., 1988, Aljira Ctr. Contemporary Art, Newark, 1992, Alternative Mus., N.Y.C., Rancho Santiago Coll., Santa Ana, 1995, Space, U. Redlands (Calif.), 1995; 2 person exhbns. Santa Ana Coll., 1978, Aarnum Gallery, Pasadena, 1980, San Francisco Fine Arts Mus., 1980, Gorman Mus. U. Calif. Davis, 1984, Rancho Santiago Coll., Santa Ana, 1995; group exhbns. include Alternative Mus., 1982, 89, 91, 92, 95, NYU Stony Brook, 1983, Triton Mus., Santa Clara, 1984, ARCO Ctr. Visual Arts, L.A., 1984, L.A. Mcpl. Art Gallery, 1985, Watts Towers Art Ctr., L.A., 1986, Whatcom Mus. History and Art, Bellingham, Wash., 1989 (circulated various museums nationwide, 1992), New Mus. Contemporary Art, N.Y.C., 1990, Peace Mus., Chgo., 1995, Fort Mason Ctr., San Francisco, 1995, Mus. Modern Art, N.Y.C., 1995, others; represented permanent collections Am. Express Co., N.Y.C., Atlantic Richfield Corp., L.A., Bklyn. Mus., Chgo. Art Inst., Mus. Modern Art, N.Y.C., Phila. Mus. Art, Nat. Mus. Am. Art, Smithsonian Instn., Fogg Art Mus., Harvard U., numerous others; subject numerous articles, publs., exhbn. catalogs and revs., 1965—. NEA fellow 1980, 95; Pasadena Arts Commn. fellow 1991, Calif. Cmty. Found. J. Paul Getty Trust Fund for Visual Arts fellow, 1997. Home: 1183 Avoca Ave Pasadena CA 91105 Office: Pasadena City Coll Dept Art 1570 E Colorado Blvd Pasadena CA 91106

SALAITA, GEORGE NICOLA, physicist; b. Madaba, Jordan, Apr. 22, 1931; came to U.S., 1954; s. Nicola J. and Azizeh (Shamas) S.; m. Linda Masou, July 30, 1959; children: Nicholas, John, Nadya. BS in Physics, Millikin U., 1957; MS in Physics, Tex. A&M, 1959; PhD, Va. Polytech. Inst. & State U., 1966. Rsch. tech. Mobil Rsch., Dallas, 1959-62; asst. prof., assoc. prof., prof. So. Meth. U., Dallas, 1966-81; sr. staff rsch. scientist Chevron Petroleum Tech. Co., LaHabra, Calif., 1981—; cons. Gearhart Inc., Ft. Worth, 1970-80; chmn. numerous IEEE, Soc. Petroleum Engrs. and Soc. Profl. Well Log Analysts symposia. Editor: The Log Analyst, 1988-89; contbr. tech. articles to profl. jours. Mem. Soc. Petroleum Engrs., Soc. Profl. Well Log Analysts, Am. Nuclear Soc., Sigma Xi. Office: Chevron Pet Tech Co 1300 S Beach Blvd La Habra CA 90631-6374

SALAMON, MIKLOS DEZSO GYORGY, mining engineer, educator; b. Balkany, Hungary, May 20, 1933; came to U.S., 1986; s. Miklos and Sarolta (Obetko) S.; m. Agota Maria Meszaros, July 11, 1953; children: Miklos, Gabor. Diploma in Engring., Polytech U., Sopron, Hungary, 1956; PhD, U. Durham, Newcastle, England, 1962; doctorem honoris causa, U. Miskolc, Hungary, 1990. Research asst. dept. mining engring. U. Durham, 1959-63; dir. research Coal Mining Research Controlling Council, Johannesburg, South Africa, 1963-66; dir. collieries research lab Chamber of Mines of South Africa, Johannesburg, 1966-74, dir. gen. research org., 1974-86; disting. prof. Colo. Sch. Mines, Golden, 1986—, dir. Colo. Mining and Mineral Resources Rsch. Inst., 1990-94; pres. Salamon Cons. Inc., Golden, 1995—; 22d Sir Julius Wernher Meml. lectr., 1988; hon. prof. U. Witwatersrand, Johannesburg, 1979-86; vis. prof. U. Minn., Mpls., 1981, U. Tex., Austin, 1982, U. NSW, Sydney, Australia, 1990, 91-96; mem. Presdl. Commn. of Inquiry into Safety and Health in South African Mining Industry, 1994-95. Co-author: Rock Mechanics Applied to the Study of Rockbursts, 1966, Rock Mechanics in Coal Mining, 1976; contbr. articles to profl. jours. Mem. Pres.'s Sci. Adv. Council, Cape Town, South Africa, 1984-86, Nat. Sci. Priorities Com., Pretoria, South Africa, 1984-86. Recipient Nat. award Assn. Scis. and Tech. Socs., South Africa, 1971. Fellow South African Inst. Mining and Metallurgy (hon. life, v.p. 1974-76, pres. 1976-77, gold medal 1964, 85, Stokes award 1986, silver medal 1991), Inst. Mining and Metallurgy (London); mem. AIME, Internat. Soc. Rock Mechanics. Roman Catholic. Office: Colo Sch of Mines Dept Of Mining Engring Golden CO 80401

SALAND, LINDA CAROL, anatomy educator, researcher; b. N.Y.C., Oct. 24, 1942; d. Charles and Esther (Weingarten) Gewirtz; m. Joel S. Saland, Aug. 16, 1964; children—Kenneth, Jeffrey. B.S., CCNY, 1963, Ph.D. in Biology, 1968; M.A. in Zoology, Columbia U., 1965. Research assoc. dept. anatomy Columbia U. Coll. Physicians and Surgeons, N.Y.C., 1968-69; sr. research assoc. dept. anatomy Sch. Medicine, U. N.Mex., Albuquerque, 1971-78, asst. prof., 1978-83, assoc. prof., 1983-89, prof., 1989—, prof. dept. neurosics., 1997—. Ad hoc reviewer NIH study sect., 1994, 95, site visit team. Mem. editorial bd. Anat. Record, 1980—; contbr. articles to profl. jours. Predoctoral fellow NDEA, 1966-68; research grantee Nat. Inst. on Drug Abuse, 1979-83, NIH Minority Biomed. Research Support Program, 1980—; NIH research grantee, 1986-95. Mem. AAAS, Am. Assn. Anatomists, Soc. for Neurosci., Women in Neuroscience (chair steering comm. 1991-93), Am. Soc. Cell Biology, Sigma Xi. Office: U NMex Sch Medicine Dept Neuroscis Basic Med Sci Bldg Albuquerque NM 87131

SALAZAR, KIMBERLY D'NAE, secondary educator; b. Hayden, Colo., Mar. 20, 1967; d. Demetrio and Sonya Jean (Updike) S. Student, San Juan Coll., 1985-87; BS, N.Mex. State U., 1990, MA, 1996. English tchr. Tibbetts Jr. H.S., Farmington, N.Mex., 1990-96; asst. prin. Farmington High Sch., 1996—; cons. Ednl. Testing Svc., Princeton, N.J., 1991. Mem. Nat. Assn. Secondary Sch. Prin., Nat. Coun. Tchrs. English, Phi Delta Kappa, Kappa Kappa Iota. United Methodist. Home: 2703 Cliffside Dr #2 Farmington NM 87402 Office: Farmington HS 2200 Sunset Ave Farmington NM 87401

SALAZAR, LUIS ADOLFO, architect; b. New Orleans, Sept. 17, 1944; s. Gustavo Adolfo and Luz Maria (Florez) S.; m. Sandra Kay Bucklew, May 30, 1969 (div. Jan. 1984); 1 child, Staci Dahnal. AA, Harbor Coll., 1966; BArch, Ariz. State U., 1971. Registered architect, Ariz., Calif., N.Mex. Area architect Peace Corps, Sierra Leone, 1971-73; project architect Van Sittert Assocs., Phoenix, 1973-77; pres., owner Salazar Assoc. Architects, Ltd., Phoenix, Inc., Inc., 1977—; Prin. works include bldg. design Kenema Cathedral, Kenema, Sierra Leone, West Africa, 1980, U.S. West Foothills Switching Ctr., Phoenix, Celebration Luth. Ch., Phoenix. Bd. dirs. Community Behavioral Services, Phoenix, 1983-85; Phoenix Meml. Hosp., 1984-94, Terraco Properties. mem. Subcom. on Bond Election, Phoenix, 1984; mem. Visual Improvement Awards Com., City of Phoenix, 1985-88. Mem. AIA (chmn. program com., honor award Ariz. chpt. 1984, visual improvement awards coms. 1985, 86), Inst. Architects. Roman Catholic.

SALAZAR, WAYNE HARDY, arts and social services administrator; b. N.Y.C., May 17, 1960; s. Oscar René and Barbara Sloan (Hardy) S. Student, Cornell U., 1978-80; BFA, Sch. Visual Arts, N.Y.C., 1984. Prodn. designer Mirror on the Moon Prodns., N.Y.C., 1983; non-theatrical sales mgr. First Run Features, N.Y.C., 1983-85; graphic designer Forty Acres and a Mule Filmworks, Bklyn., 1984-87; mgr. spl. projects Cinecom Entertainment Group, N.Y.C., 1985-90; producer, dir. Wayne Salazar Video, Bklyn., 1987-91; dir. Latino Collaborative, Bklyn., 1988-91; film coord. Hawaii Internat. Film Festival, Honolulu, 1990-92; exec. dir. Visual Aid, San Francisco, 1992-95; devel. mgr. Shanti, San Francisco, 1996—; panelist N.Y. State Coun. on Arts, N.Y.C., 1990-91; prodn. asst. Character Generators Video, N.Y.C., 1986-90; lectr. U. Hawaii/Manoa, Honolulu, 1990; festival programmer Adam Baran Honolulu Gay and Lesbian Film Festival, 1991-93, cons., 1994—; cons. EBS Prodns., San Francisco, 1992—. Contbr. film revs., essays to profl. publs. Recipient Bd. Dirs. award Cable Car Awards, 1993. Mem. Artist's Equity. Home: 787A Castro St San Francisco CA 94114-2849

SALDAÑA, JOHNNY, theater educator, researcher; b. Austin, Tex., Aug. 20, 1954; s. Isabel Martinez and Dominga (Olivo) S. BFA, U. Tex., 1976, MFA, 1979. Cert. K-12 theatre tchr., Ariz. Asst. prof. Wash. State U., Pullman, 1979-81; prof. theatre Ariz. State U., Tempe, 1981—; cons. New Orleans Pub. Schs., 1989, 91; instr. Northwestern U., Evanston, Ill., 1990, Ariz. Artist-Tchr. Inst., Phoenix, 1993-97. Author: Drama of Color; co-author: (plays) I Didn't Know That!, 1978, Flashback!, 1979; contbr. articles to profl. jours. Recipient Burlington Resources Found. Faculty Achievement award Ariz. State U., 1991, Coll. of FIne Arts Disting. Faculty award, 1995. Mem. Am. Alliance for Theatre and Edn. (conf. chmn. 1993-94, Creative Drama award 1989, Rsch. award 1996), Ednl. Theatre Assn., Nat. Assn. for Multicultural Edn. Democrat. Office: Ariz State U Dept Theatre PO Box 872002 Tempe AZ 85287-2002

SALDAÑA, MATTHEW ARNOLD, principal, academic administrator; b. Avalon, Calif., June 17, 1959; s. Herman Mesa and Gayle Dee (Brodehl) S.; m. Valerie Jean Abdallah, July 8, 1995; children: Yannick Walker, Cherizar Walker, Elton Barker, Alexa. AA, Golden West Coll., 1980; BA, Long Beach State Coll., 1982; MEd, U. LaVerne, 1990. Lic. ocean operator; cert. tchr., adminstr., Calif. Harbor patrolman City of Avalon, 1977-91; tchr. Long Beach (Calif.) Unified Schs., 1985-89, activities dir., 1989-91, asst. prin., 1991-95, lead administr., 1995-96; prin Avalon Sch., 1996—. Mem. NAACP, Assn. Hispanic Educators, bd. dirs., Family Svcs. of Long Beach, Lions Club of Avalon. Roman Catholic. Home: 339 Whitley Ave Bellflower CA 90707

SALDICH, ANNE RAWLEY, counseling psychologist; b. Orange, N.J., Nov. 20, 1933; d. William and Mary (Burke) Rawley; divorced; 1 child, Alan George. BA in English Lit. cum laude, U. Detroit, 1956; postgrad., U. Calif., Berkeley, 1961-62; MA in Polit. Sci. magna cum laude, Wayne State U., 1962; PhD in Sociology with honors, U. Paris, Sorbonne, 1971; MA Counseling Psychology magna cum laude, U. Calif., San Francisco, 1990. Lic. marriage and family counselor, Calif. Lectr. San Jose (Calif.) State U., 1972, U. Santa Clara, Calif., 1973; freelance writer, 1971-84; lectr. U. Calif., Berkeley, 1972-77; instr. govt. French Press Inst., Paris, 1984; asst. editor Stanford U. Jour. Econ. Lit., 1980-85; intern in counseling Miramonte Mental Health Ctr., Palo Alto, 1988-89, New Day Residential Treatment Ctr., East Palo Alto, 1989, Family Svc. Agy., Burlingame, Calif., 1989-90, Growth and Leadership Ctr., Mountainview, 1991-92, Palo Alto Psychol. Svcs., Palo Alto, 1992. Author: Electronic Democracy: Television's Impact on The American Political Process, 1979; contbr. articles to profl. jours. Chmn., mediator Palo Alto Rental Housing Mediation Task Force, 1978-79; co-chmn. com. on environ., Palo Alto Futurecast Com. for the Yr. 2001, 1986; mem. publicity and fundraising com. Career Action Ctr., 1987-88; founder, mgr. internat. visitors com. Hospitality Ctr., 1988-89, co-founder mentoring program for girls St. Elizabeth Seton Sch., Palo Alto; bd. dirs. Neighbors Abroad, 1994. Woodrow Wilson fellow, 1962. Mem. AAUW (chmn. bus. and profls. group), Internat. Inst. Comm., Calif. Assn. Marriage and Family Therapists, Experience Corps, Chi Sigma Iota. Home and Office: 2585 Park Blvd # Z-100 Palo Alto CA 94306-1944

SALDICH, ROBERT JOSEPH, electronics company executive; b. N.Y.C., June 7, 1933; s. Alexander and Bertha (Kasakove) S.; m. Anne Rawley, July 21, 1963 (div. Nov. 1979); 1 child, Alan; m. Virginia Vaughan, Sept. 4, 1983; stepchildren: Tad Thomas, Stan Thomas, Melinda Thomas, Margaret Thomas Dudley. BSChemE, Rice U., 1956; MBA, Harvard U., 1961. Mfg. mgr. Procter & Gamble Mfg. Co., Dallas, Kansas City, Kans., 1956-59; rsch. asst. Harvard Bus. Sch., Boston, 1961-62; asst. to pres. Kaiser Aluminum & Chem. Corp., Oakland, Calif., 1962-64; mgr. fin. and pers., then gen. mgr. various divs. Raychem Corp., Menlo Park, Calif., 1964-83, with office of pres., 1983-87, sr. v.p. telecommunications and tech., 1988-90, pres., CEO, 1990—; pres. Raynet Corp. subs. Raychem Corp., 1987-88, ret., 1995. Chair mfg. com. adv. bd. Leavy Sch. Bus. and Administrn., Santa Clara U. Mem. Calif. Roundtable (dir. Bay Area Coun.), San Francisco Com. on Fgn. Rels. Jewish. Office: 635 Bryant St Palo Alto CA 94301

SALDIN, THOMAS R., consumer products company executive, corporate lawyer; b. 1946. BA, Carleton Coll., 1968; JD, Cin. Coll. Law, 1974. Law clk. to presiding justice U.S. Dist. Ct. (so. dist.) Ohio, 1974-76; assoc. Benjamin, Faulkner & Tepe & Sach, Cin., 1976-78; asst. gen. counsel Albertson's Inc., Boise, Idaho, 1978-81, v.p., gen. counsel, 1981-83, sr. v.p. gen. counsel, 1983—. Office: Albertson's Inc 250 E Parkcenter Blvd Boise ID 83706-3940*

SALE, GEORGE EDGAR, physician; b. Missoula, Mont., Apr. 18, 1941; s. George Goble and Ruth Edna (Polleys) S.; m. Joan M. Sutliff, 1989; children: George Gregory Colby, Teo Marie Jonsson. AB, Harvard U., 1963; MD, Stanford U., 1968. Intern U. Oreg., Portland, 1968-69; sr. asst. surgeon USPHS, Albuquerque, 1969-71; resident in pathology U. Wash., Seattle, 1971-75, instr. pathology, 1975-78, asst. prof., 1978-81, assoc. prof., 1981-88, prof., 1988—; asst. mem. faculty, dept. oncology Hutchinson Cancer Ctr., Seattle, 1975-88, assoc. mem., 1988-91, mem., 1991—. Author, editor: Pathology of Bone Marrow Transplantation, 1984, Pathology of Transplantation, 1990. Mem. AAAS, Internat. Acad. Pathology, Coll. Am. Pathologists, Am. Assn. Investigative Pathologists, Physicians for Social Responsibility. Home: 12146 Sunrise Dr NE Bainbridge Island WA 98110-4304 Office: Fred Hutchinson Cancer Rsh Ctr 1100 Fairview Ave N Seattle WA 98109

SALEEM, MOHAMMAD, mathematics educator; b. Sept. 25, 1953. BSc with high honors, Punjab U., 1974, MSc in Applied Math., 1976; MA in Math., U. Calif., Berkeley, 1982; PhD in Applied Math., U. Calif., Davis, 1988. Lectr. Multan U. and Bahawalpur U., Pakistan, 1976-80; teaching asst. U. Calif., Davis, 1982-86, assoc. instr., 1985-86; postgrad. researcher U. Calif. and Ames Rsch. Ctr. NASA, 1987-88; asst. prof. U. Mo., St. Louis, 1988-90; assoc. prof. Calif. State U., San Jose, 1990—; speaker U. Calif., Davis, Ames Rsch Ctr. NASA, Calif. Contbr. articles to profl. jours. Mem. Am. Math. Soc., Math. Assn. Am., Soc. for Indsl. and Applied Math. Office: Calif State U Dept Math and Computer Sci San Jose CA 95192

SALERNO, CHRISTOPHER, air quality specialist; b. Lincoln, Nebr., Dec. 22, 1957; s. Joseph F. and Joan C. (Bradfield) S. BS in Biology, U. Nebr., 1982; M of Environ. Sci., U. Alaska, 1992. Air quality specialist Municipality of Anchorage, 1992—. Asst. campaign mgr., Anchorage, 1988, 90, 92, 96. Mem. Air and Waste Mgmt. Assn. Home: 5400 W Dimond Blvd Anchorage AK 99515-1014 Office: Anchorage Air Pollution Control Agy 825 L St Anchorage AK 99501-3337

SALESKY, WILLIAM JEFFREY, manufacturing company executive; b. Boston, June 12, 1957; s. Harry Michael Salesky and Eleanor Faith (Stutman) Spater; m. Cherri Lynne DeGreek, Nov. 27, 1982; 1 child, Joshua Steven. BS, U. Calif., Davis, 1978; MS, U. Calif., Berkeley, 1980, PhD, 1982. Co-op engr. Bechtel Corp. Inc., San Francisco, 1977-78; engr. U. Calif., Davis, 1978-79; rsch. assoc. Lawrence Berkeley Lab., 1979-82; project mgr. Smith Internat., Irvine, Calif., 1982-89; dir. engring. & quality assurance Mark Controls, Long Beach, Calif., 1989-94; v.p. engring. Stamet Inc., Gardena, Calif., 1994—; cons. Printnonix Corp., Irvine, Calif., 1988, Metal Alloys Inc., Irvine, 1986-88, Ceracon Inc., Irvine, 1984-86; chmn. L.A. Conf. on Fugitive Emissions from Valves, 1993. Patentee in field. Mgr. Irvine Baseball Assn., 1990; grad. asssembly rep. U. Calif., Berkeley, 1980-81; mem. race com. Internat. Am.'s Cup Class World Championship; mem. San Diego Crew Classic Race Com., 1992-95; mem. Am.'s Cup Race Com., 1992, 95. Recipient Meritorious award Petroleum Engr. mag., 1988, award for outstanding contbns. Valve Mfrs. Assn. Am., 1993. Mem. ASTM, Am. Soc. Metals Internat. (bd. dirs. 1988-90, Earl Parker fellow 1981), Soc. Petroleum Engrs., Am. Petroleum Inst., South Shore Yacht Club (CFO 1989-91, bd. dirs. 1991-93). Office: Stamet Inc 17244 S Main St Gardena CA 90248-3101

SALINGER, JOAN ADAH, computer graphics, photography and art educator; b. Detroit, 1951. Student, U. Wis., 1969-71; BFA in Art magna cum laude, U. Mich., 1973; MFA in Photography, Cranbrook Acad. Art, 1976. Calif. cmty. coll. instr. credential. Resident artist Artist in Schs., Flint, Mich., 1976-77; assoc. prof. computer graphics, photography, art Orange Coast Coll., Costa Mesa, Calif., 1980—; part time instr. Cerritos Coll., Art Inst. So. Calif., Santa Ana Coll., Saddleback Coll., Chapman Coll., East L.A. Coll., Otis Art Inst. Parsons Sch. Design, L.A. Valley Coll., Pasadena City Coll., C.S. Mott Coll., Andover H.S. Works exhibited at Joslyn Ctr. of the Arts, Torrance, Calif., Moreau Gallery-St. Mary's Coll., Notre Dame, Ind., Orange Coast Coll., Costa Mesa, Otis Art Inst. Parsons Sch. Design, L.A., Laguna Beach (Calif.) Sch. Art, Cerritos Coll., Norwalk, Calif., GMB Gallery, Birmingham, Mich., B.C. Space Gallery, Laguna Beach, Assn. Internat. Photo Art Dealers Exposition, N.Y.C., Ikono Photo Gallery, Venice, Italy, others; represented in numerous pub. collections. Grantee Nat. Endowment for the Arts, Mich. Coun. of the Arts, C.S. Mott Found. Mem. Assn. Computing Machinery, SIGGRAPH Interest Group Graphics (nat. and L.A. chpt.), NCGA, L.A. Ctr. for Photographic Studies, Phi Delta Kappa, Sigma Epsilon Sigma. Office: Orange Coast Coll 2701 Fairview Rd Costa Mesa CA 92626-5563

SALISBURY, DAVID FRANCIS, newspaper, television science writer; b. Seattle, Feb. 24, 1947; s. Vernon H. and Lurabelle (Kline) S. BS, U. Wash., 1969. Sci. editor Christian Sci. Monitor, Boston, 1972-76; correspondent Christian Sci. Monitor, Los Angeles, Boulder (Colo.) and San Francisco, 1976-85; sci. and tech. writer U. Calif., Santa Barbara, 1985-93, Stanford (Calif.) U., 1993—; mem. research adv. com. Pub. Service Electric and Gas Co., Newark, N.J., 1979-83. Author: Money Matters, 1982. contbr. many articles to popular mags. and tech. jours. Recipient sci. writing awards, NSPE, 1978, Aviation Space Writers Assn., 1981, Grand Gold medal and Bronze medal Coun. for Advancement and Support of Edn., 1988. Mem. AAAS (sci. writing award 1976), Nat. Assn. Sci. Writers (Sci-in-Soc. award 1974). Christian Scientist. Office: Stanford U News Svc Press Courtyard Santa Teresa St Stanford CA 94305

SALL, JENI P., marketing executive; b. Wilmington, Del., Jan. 28, 1949; d. Bernard and Esther (Wien) Sall; m. Fritz Bettjer, Sept. 21, 1985. BA, Hofstra U., 1971; MA, U. Hawaii, 1974. Brand supr. Procter & Gamble, Cin., 1974-76; brand asst. Clorox Co., Oakland, Calif., 1976-77; acct. exec. M/A/R/C, Burlingame, Calif., 1978-81; mgr. mktg. rsch. and planning Apple Computers, Cupertino, Calif., 1982-84; gen. mgr. Western ops. Decision Rsch. Corp., Palo Alto, Calif., 1984-86; pres. Genesis Rsch. Assocs., Palo Alto, 1986—. Bd. dirs. Santa Clara Valley Vis. Nurses Assn. Mem. Am. Mktg. Assn. (v.p. Santa Clara Valley chpt. 1985, exec.), Am. Psychol. Assn. Home: 2005 Rocky Ridge Rd Morgan Hill CA 95037-9443

SALLEE, WESLEY W(ILLIAM), nuclear chemist; b. Perry, Okla., June 5, 1951; s. Jimmie Richard and Nadine A. (Barnes) S.; m. Exine Mamie Clark, Mar. 21, 1979; children: Rachel Nadine, Daniel Mason. BS in Chemistry, Okla. State U., 1974; PhD in Chemistry, U. Ark., 1983. Commd. 1st lt. USAF, 1976, advanced through grades to capt., 1978, resigned, 1979; nuclear physicist U.S. Army White Sands Missile Range, 1983—. Author technical reports and symposium papers; contbr. articles to profl. jours. Mem. ASTM. Republican. Home: 1515 Dorothy Cir Las Cruces NM 88001-1625 Office: DATTS-R White Sands Missile Range NM 88002

SALLEY, GEORGE HENRY, III, lawyer; b. Miami, Fla., Oct. 9, 1954; s. George H. Salley and Audrey L. Stone; m. Jean Welch Salley, Dec. 28, 1979; children: Paul Ryan, Adam Keith. BS, Brigham Young U., 1977; JD, Pepperdine U., 1980. Bar: Colo. 1981, U.S. Dist. Ct. Colo. 1981. Pvt. practice Colorado Springs, Colo., 1981—. Office: 104 S Cascade Ave Ste 207 Colorado Springs CO 80903-5102

SALLQUIST, GARY ARDIN, minister, planned giving administrator; b. Sioux City, Iowa, July 7, 1938; s. Hal Thurston and Rosemary (Daggett) S.; m. Joyce Darleen Casey, June 10, 1960; children: Susan L. Rail, Steven P. BA, U. Nebr., Omaha, 1960; MDiv, Princeton Theol. Sem., 1993; D of Ministry, La. Bapt. U., 1997. ChFC, CLU. Ptnr. Sallquist-Wilkinson Inc., Omaha, 1976-80, Lee-Sallquist Group, Cin., 1981-83, The Fin. Edge, Cin., 1984-86; pres. Planned Giving Sys., Cin., 1987-90; min. adult edn. Coll. Hill Presbyn. Ch., Cin., 1993-95; dir. planned giving Promise Keepers, Denver, 1995—. Author: A Seminary Journey, 1995. Pres. Omaha Jaycees, 1966-67, Ednl. Found., Memphis, 1976; dirs. Creighton-St. Joseph Hosp., Omaha, 1975-81, Cin. Assn. CLUs, 1982-84, Leadership Cin. Alumni Assn., 1987-89. Recipient Golden Key award Nebr. Jaycees, 1975, Friar's Club award, N.Y.C., 1993. Mem. U. Nebr. Omaha Alumni Assn. (pres. 1968-70, Outstanding Alumnus award 1977), Pi Kappa Alpha (nat. pres. 1970-72). Home: 500 W 123d Ave # 3221 Westminster CO 80234 Office: Promise Keepers PO Box 103001 Denver CO 80250-3001

SALLS, JENNIFER JO, secondary school educator; b. Reno, May 8, 1952; d. Edmund Allenby and Georgia Theresa (Mullison) Naphan; m. Mitchell Aaron Marshall, Dec. 18, 1971; children: Kevin Alexander, Christopher Allen, Brian Andrew. BS, U. Nev., 1974, MEd, 1985. Cert. math., lang. and computer tchr., Nev. Tchr. Reno High sch., 1977-82; chair math. dept., tchr. McQueen High Sch., Reno, 1982-90; edn. cons. Nev. Dept. of Edn., Carson City, 1990-91; secondary math./computer coord. Washoe County Sch. Dist., Reno, 1991-94, K-12 math. coord., 1994—; in-svc. instr. Washoe County Sch. Dist., Reno, 1980—; cons. U. Nev., Reno, 1986-87; referee Math. Tchr., Reston, Va., 1988—, mem. editl. bd., 1990-94. Co-author: Turtle Geometry, 1986; contbr.: (video course) Teaching Mathematics with Manipulatives Grades 7-12, 1995. NSF grantee, 1984. Mem. Nat. Coun. Tchrs. Math., Nat. Coun. Suprs. Math., Assn. State Suprs. Math., Calif. Math. Coun., Oreg. Coun. Tchrs. Math., No. Nev. Math. Coun. (pres. 1984-85, 87-88), So. Nev. Math. Coun., Nat. State Tchrs. Yr., Coun. Presdl. Awardees of Math. Democrat. Mem. LDS Ch. Office: Washoe County Sch Dist Bullis Curriculum Ctr 14101 Old Virginia Rd Reno NV 89511-8912

SALMAN, JENAN AL-YAZDI, pharmacist, small business owner; b. Basrah, Iraq, May 3, 1948; came to U.S., 1973; d. Mahmood M. Al-Yazdi and Sadeeka Sh. Ridha; m. Kadhim N. Salman, Feb. 21, 1969; children: Ayser, Zaid, Lameace. BA in Pharmacy, Bagdad, Iraq, 1969; PharmD, U. Ky., 1990. Pharmacist pvt. drug store, Bagdad, 1970-73; research technician

Ohio State U. Sch. Pharmacy, Columbus, 1974-75; research asst. Ohio State U. Vet. Sci., Columbus, 1975-77; rsch. analyst Coll. Pharmacy U. Ky., Lexington, 1977-78, Agriculture Sta. U. Ky., Lexington, 1978-79; sci. demonstrator Coll. Medicine King Saud U., Saudi Arabia, 1980-85; pres., owner J.J. Gazelle Ltd., Lexington, 1985-88; clin. coord. Merrillville, Ind., 1990-92; clin. pharmacy mgr. Valley Hosp. Med. Ctr., Las Vegas, 1992—. Contbr. articles to profl. jours. Home: 9720 Trail Rider Dr Las Vegas NV 89117-6624 Office: Valley Hosp Med Ctr 620 Shadow Ln Las Vegas NV 89106-4119

SALMON, MATT, congressman; b. Salt Lake City, Jan. 21, 1958; s. Robert James and Gloria (Aagard) S.; m. Nancy Huish, June, 1979; children: Lara, Jacob, Katie, Matthew. BA in English Lit., Ariz. State U., 1981; MA in Pub. Adminstrn., Brigham Young U., 1986. Mgr. pub. affairs U.S. West, Phoenix, 1988-94; mem. Ariz. Senate, Mesa, 1990-94; congressman, Ariz. U.S. House of Reps., Washington, D.C., 1995—, 1995—. Bd. dirs. Mesa United Way, 1990—, Ariz. Sci. Mus., 1992—. Recipient Outstanding Svc. award Ariz. Citizens with Disabilities, 1991, Excellence in Govt. award Tempe Ctr. for Handicapped, 1992; named Outstanding Young Phoenician, Phelps Dodge/Phoenix Jaycees, 1990, Outstanding Legislator, Mesa United Way, 1991. Republican. Mormon. Office: 105th Congress Cannon 115 House Office Bldg Washington DC 20515

SALMON, MERLYN LEIGH, laboratory executive; b. Macksville, Kans., June 24, 1924; s. Kenneth Elbert and Inez Melba (Prose) S.; student U. Kans., 1943-44; BS, U. Denver, 1951, MS, 1952; m. Flora Charlotte Sievers, Mar. 20, 1948; children: Charla Lee, Merlyn Leigh. Rsch. engr. Denver Rsch. Inst., U. Denver, 1951-56; owner-operator Fluo-X-Spec Lab., Denver, 1956-92; ret. 1992; cons. in field. With AUS, 1943-45, 45-47. Mem. Am. Chem. Soc., Am. Soc. Metals, Sigma Xi, Tau Beta Pi, Phi Lambda Upsilon. Omicron Delta Kappa. Democrat. Contbr. articles to profl. jours. Address: 718 Sherman St Denver CO 80203

SALMON, SYDNEY ELIAS, medical educator, director; b. S.I., N.Y., May 8, 1936; m. Joan; children: Howard, Julia, Laura, Stewart, Russell. BA cum laude, U. Ariz., 1958; MD, Washington U., St. Louis, 1962. Intern, then resident in medicine Strong Meml. Hosp., Rochester, N.Y., 1962-64; rsch. fellow in immunology dept. pediats. Harvard U. Med. Sch., Boston, 1965-66; rsch. fellow dept. medicine Medicine and Cancer Rsch. Inst. U. Calif., San Francisco, 1966-68, asst. prof. medicine dept. medicine, 1968-72; assoc. prof. medicine U. Ariz., Tucson, 1972-74, head sect. hematology and oncology, 1972-81, prof. medicine, 1974-89, founding dir. Ariz. Cancer Ctr., 1976—, regents prof. medicine, 1989—; NIH spl. fellow Cancer Rsch. Inst., U. Calif., San Francisco, 1966-68, rsch. assoc., 1968-72; mem. nat. cancer adv. bd. Nat. Cancer Inst., 1990—; founding sci. Selectide Corp., 1990; mem. sci. adv. bds. Amplimed Corp., SUGEN Corp.; bd. dirs. Synergen Devel. Corp., Repligen Devel. Corp. Editor: Cloning of Human Tumor Cells, Human Tumor Cloning, Adjuvant Therapies of Cancer, 1982, Clinics of Haematology, 1982; mem. adv. bd. Cancer Treatment Reports, 1979-82; mem. editl. bd. Stell Cells, Jour. Clin. Oncology; patentee in field; contbr. articles to profl. jours. Surgeon USPHS, 1964-66. Recipient Lectureship award Gold Headed Cane Soc., 1979, Alumni Achievement award U. Ariz., 1986. Mem. AAAS, Am. Soc. Hematology, Am. Soc. Clin. Investigation, Am. Soc. Clin. Oncology (pres. 1984-85), Am. Cancer Soc. (bd. dirs. Ariz. divsn.), Leukemia Soc. Am., Am. Assn. Cancer Rsch., Assn. Am. Cancer Insts. (pres. 1988-89). Office: U Ariz Cancer Ctr 1515 N Campbell Ave Tucson AZ 85724-0001*

SALMONSON, MARTY LEE, stockbroker, consulting engineer; b. Wellsville, N.Y., Sept. 23, 1946; s. John William and Alice May (Olson) S.; Gail White, Sept. 17, 1971; children: René, Marci. AS in Engring. Sci., SUNY, Alfred, 1970; postgrad., SUNY, Buffalo, 1971; BS in Sci. and Bus. Mgmt., Empire State Coll., 1979. Engr. Dresser-Rand, Olean, N.Y., 1974-90, Petro-Marine, Gretna, La., 1990-91; stockbroker Franklin Lord, Scottsdale, Ariz., 1992, Charles Schwab, Phoenix, Ariz., 1993—; cons. engr., Phoenix, 1994—. With U.S. Army, 1967-69, Vietnam. Mem. NSPE, ASME, VFW, Moose, Elks. Episcopalian. Home: PO Box 26601 Phoenix AZ 85068

SALONEN, ESA-PEKKA, conductor; b. Helsinki, Finland, June 30, 1958. Student, Sibelius Acad., Helsinki; studies with, Rautavaara and Panula. Guest condr. orchs., London, Berlin, Paris, L.A., Phila.; prin. condr. Swedish Radio Symphony Orch., 1985-95; prin guest condr. Philharmonia Orch., London, 1985-94, Oslo Philharm. Orch., 1985-90; artistic advisor Stockholm Chamber Orch., 1986—; music dir. L.A. Philharm. Orch., 1992—. Office: VanWalsum Mgmt, 4 Addison Bridge Pl, London W14 8XP, England also: Los Angeles Philharm Orch 135 N Grand Ave Los Angeles CA 90012-3013

SALSIG, DOYEN, photographer, photography studio owner; b. San Diego, Jan. 17, 1923; d. Felix and Fay (Doyen) Johnson; m. Budd Salsig, June 11, 1943; children: Winter, Kristin, Fay, Ben. AA, San Diego City Coll., 1965; BA in Biology, U. Calif., San Diego, 1970. Owner West Wind Studio, Flagstaff, Ariz., 1972—; photo workshop leader Mus. of No. Ariz., Flagstaff, 1978-93. Author: Parole: Quebec; Counter-sign: Ticonderoga, 1980 (grand prize Coconino County Women of the Arts 1985); contbr., photos and photographic essays to profl. jours. Bd. dirs., v.p. Grand Canyon (Ariz.) Natural History Assn., 1988—; vice chmn. Coconino County Rep. Com., Flagstaff, 1990—; pres. Rep. Women's Club, Flagstaff, 1989-91; docent Mus. No. Ariz., Flagstaff, 1975-82; mem. Ariz. Humanities Coun., 1991-94; del. Rep. Nat. Conv., 1992, 96. Home and Office: 428 E Birch Ave Flagstaff AZ 86001-5226

SALSKI, ANDRZEJ M., journalist, editor; b. Warsaw, Poland, Jan. 16, 1948; came to U.S., 1987; s. Zbigniew and Kazimiera (Muszynski) S.; m. Elzbieta Piwowarczyk, Sept. 23, 1975 (div. Jan. 1990); children: Alicja, Andrzej J.; m. Izabella Staroscinska, June 29, 1991. BA, U. Warsaw, 1977, MA in Journalism, 1982. Adminstrv. asst. PAX, pub. house, Warsaw, 1965-71, Polish Press Agy., Warsaw, 1971-74; asst. mgr. R & D Inst., Warsaw, 1974-76; journalist Polish Press Agy. (PAP), Warsaw, 1976-82; editor-in-chief Cen. Union of Coops. of Folk Art and Fine Arts, Warsaw, 1982-85; dir. pub. rels. Dem. Party, Warsaw, 1985-88; asst. editor Monitor, Silicon Valley Polish Am. Assn., San Jose, Calif., 1990-92; editor-in-chief Nasze Wiadomosci, Polish Am. Congress, San Francisco, 1992-93; pub., editor-in-chief The Summit Times, Calif., 1993—. Contbr. numerous articles to various publs.; translator in field. Recipient Golden Siren, Coun. of Warsaw, 1987, Silver Cross of Merit, State Coun. of Poland, Warsaw, 1987. Mem. Polish Inst. Arts and Scis. Am., Am. Coun. for Polish Culture, Polish Am. Hist. Assn., Inst. of J. Pilsudski. Home: 1116 The Alameda Berkeley CA 94707-2502

SALTARELLI, THOMAS RICHARD, lawyer; b. Beaver, Pa., Apr. 22, 1947; s. Dominic J. and Lena M. (Setting) S.; m. Donna Perry, Oct. 20, 1979; children: Grant, Anna. BS, Pa. State U., 1969; MBA, U. So. Calif., 1975; JD, Western State U. Coll., 1978. Bar: Calif. 1981, D.C. 1992, U.S. Dist. Ct., U.S. Mil. Ct. Appeals, U.S. Supreme Ct. With Am. Hosp. Supply Corp., Irvine, Calif., 1972-76; sales rep. Cenco Med., L.A., 1976-78; pres. Dacion Corp., Irvine, 1978-81; pvt. practice lawyer Newport Beach, Calif., 1981-85; ptnr. Wildish, Boehmer & Saltarelli, Orange, Calif., 1985-87, King & Saltarelli, Irvine, 1987-89, Saltarelli & Steponovich,, Irvine, 1989-94, Saltarelli Law Corp., Newport Beach, 1994—; dir. AEI Corp., Irvine, 1989—. Mayor, city coun. City of Tustin, Calif., 1992—. Lt. USN, 1969-72, Vietnam. Republican. Roman Catholic. Home: 2212 Palermo Tustin CA 92782-8707 Office: Saltarelli Law Corp PO Box 10367 4400 MacArthur Blvd Ste 900 Newport Beach CA 92658-0367

SALTER, JAMES, writer; b. Passaic, N.J., June 10, 1925; m. Ann Altemus, June 6, 1951 (div. 1976); children: Allan Conard, Nina Tobe, Claude Cray, James Owen; m. Kay Eldredge; 1 child, Theo Shaw. BS, USMA, 1945; M in Internat. Affairs, Georgetown U., 1950. Author: The Hunters, 1957, The Arm of Flesh, 1961, A Sport and a Pastime, 1967, Light Years, 1976, Solo Faces, 1981, Dusk and Other Stories, 1989 (Pen, Faulkner prize 1989). Lt. Col. USAF, 1960. Home: 500 N St Aspen CO 81611-1253 Office: Sterling Lord Literistic 65 Bleecker St New York NY 10012

SALTZ, LORI HODGSON, plastic surgeon; b. Portland; d. Richard Arthur and Pebble (Desart) Hodgson; m. Steven Allen Saltz, APril 21, 1985; children: Jonathan, Gillian. BS, Standford U., Palo Alto, Calif., 1976; MD, U. Oreg., Portland, 1980. Diplomate Am. Bd. Plastic Surgery. Resident surgery Mt. Sinai Med. Ctr., Miami Beach, Fla., 1980-83; plastic surgery resident Loyola U., Maywood, Ill., 1983-86; pvt. practice La Jolla (Calif.) Cosmetic Surgery Ctr., 1990—. Mem. Am. Soc. Plastic & Reconstructive Surgery, Am. Soc. Aesthetic Plastic Surgery. Office: 9850 Genesee Ave # 130 La Jolla CA 92037

SALTZMAN, BETH MELANIE, medical librarian; b. Washington, Jan. 14, 1963; life ptnr. Patricia Sue Levey, June 25, 1995. BA in Integral Studies, Calif. Inst. Integral Studies, San Francisco, 1995. Rschr. Planetree Health Resource Ctr., San Francisco, 1987-92; audio-visual technician, libr. asst. St. Mary's Med. Ctr., San Francisco, 1989-95; med. libr. St. vincent Hosp. Libr., Santa Fe, N.Mex., 1996—. Mem. Med. Libr. Assn., City Different Bus. and Profl. Assn., Consortium of Biosci. and Hosp. Librs. of N.Mex. Office: St Vincent Hospital PO Box 2107 455 St Michaels Dr Santa Fe NM 87505-7601

SALTZMAN, JOANNE ELLEN, cooking school administrator; b. Rochester, Minn., Sept. 14, 1948; d. William and Muriel Saltzman; m. Bill Cunningham, Oct. 8, 1972 (div. June 1983); children: Maia, Joseph, Jacob, Ryan. Grad., Guild of Performing Arts, 1970. Profl. dancer Guild of Performing Arts, Mpls., 1970-73; founder, dir. Sch. Natural Cookery, Boulder, Colo., 1983—. Author: Amazing Grains, 1990, Romancing the Bean, 1993; developer vegetarian cooking curriculum, 1989. Office: Sch Natural Cookery PO Box 19466 Boulder CO 80308-2466

SALVATORE, RICHARD JOHN, cinematographer, company executive; b. Bklyn., May 25, 1950; s. Peter Louis and Julia (Stampano) S. AA, Los Angeles Valley Coll., 1972. Artist George Whiteman & Assocs., Hollywood, Calif., 1968-72; ind. cinematographer Hollywood, 1976—; founder RJS Motion Picture and TV, Northridge, 1991—; co-founder HJS Promotions, 1993—; tchr. Prodrs. Assn., Hollywood, 1975—, Am. Film Inst., Beverly Hills, Calif., 1984—; CEO Omnicom Sys., Canoga Park, Calif., 1981—; co-owner Norman Borines World Bruce Lee Mus., Northridge, 1992—; founder RJS Comms., 1995—; bd. dirs., cinematographer Davidson Design Prodns., San Diego; cons. entertainment mktg. and advt. spl. projects (tie-ins and global exposure), 1991—. Photographer: Solace, 1968 (Memorable mention Los Angeles County Fair 1968), Night Wind Dragon, 1972. Pres. Robert F. Kennedy campaign com., Los Angeles, 1967, Gun Control Act of 1968, Los Angeles; dist. leader/area leader Muscular Dystrophy Assn., Los Angeles County, 1966-70. Recipient fin. grant U. Calif., 1972. Mem. Soc. Operating Cameramen (assoc.), Acad. TV Arts and Scis. (assoc.).

SALWASSER, HAL, forest ecologist; b. Fresno, Calif., Aug. 4, 1945; s. Mervin James and Elizabeth Jean (Thonen) S.; m. Susan Louise Fite, July 12, 1969 (div. 1993); 1 child, James Barrett; m. Linda White Smith, May 28, 1994 (div. 1996); children: Ryan James Smith, Paul Gordon Smith. BA in Biology, Calif. State U., Fresno, 1971; PhD in Wildland Resource Sci., U. Calif., Berkeley, 1979. Cert. wildlife biologist. Rsch. assoc. U. Calif., Berkeley, 1976-79; regional wildlife ecologist Forest Svc., USDA, San Francisco, 1979-82; nat. wildlife ecologist Forest Svc., USDA, Washington, 1982-85, dep. dir. wildlife and fisheries, 1985-90, dir. new perspectives, 1990-92; prof. U. Mont., 1992-95; regional forester no. region USDA Forest Svc., Missoula, Mont., 1995—. Contbr. articles to profl. jours. With U.S. Army, 1965-68. Mem. Soc. Am. Foresters, Wildlife Soc. (v.p. 1991-92, pres.-elect 1992-93, pres. 1993-94), Ecol. Soc. Am. (bd. editors Ecol. Applications 1993-95), Soc. for Conservation Biology (bd. govs. 1985-91). Republican. Office: USDA Forest Svc No Region Fed Bldg Missoula MT 59807

SALZMAN, DAVID ELLIOT, entertainment industry executive; b. Bklyn., Dec. 1, 1943; s. Benjamin and Rose Harriet (Touby) S.; m. Sonia Camelia Gonsalves, Oct. 19, 1968; children: Daniel Mark, Andrea Jessica, Adam Gabriel. B.A., Bklyn. Coll., 1965; M.A., Wayne State U., 1967. Dir. TV ops. Wayne State U., 1966-67; producer Lou Gordon Program, 1967-70; program mgr. Sta. WKBD-TV, Detroit, 1970-71; program mgr. Sta. KDKA-TV, Pitts., 1971-72, gen. mgr., 1973-75; program mgr. Sta. KYW-TV, Phila., 1972-73; chmn. bd. Group W Prodns., N.Y.C and Los Angeles, 1975—; founder, pres. United Software Assocs., 1980-81; creator News Info. Weekly Service, 1981; exec. v.p. Telepictures Corp., 1980-84, vice chmn., 1984; pres. Lorimar Telepictures Corp. (merger Telepictures and Lorimar, Inc.), 1985-90, Lorimar TV, 1986-90; creator Newscope: Nat. TV News Cooperative, 1983; pres., CEO David Salzman Entertainment, Burbank, Calif., 1990-93; co-CEO Quincy Jones-David Salzman Entertainment (QDE), 1993—; exec. prodr. Jenny Jones Show, 1991—; exec. prodr. Mad-TV, In the House, 68th Ann. Acad. awards; co-owner QD7 Interactive, 1994; bd. dirs. Premiere Radio, 1994, 7th Level; guest lectr. at schs.; bd. govs. Films of Coll. and Univ. Students. Contbr. articles to Variety and numerous communications trade publs. Bd. dirs. Pitts. Civic Light Opera, Am. Blood Bank, Pitts., Hebrew Inst., Jewish Community Ctr., Harrison, N.Y., Temple Etz Chaim, USC Sch. Cinema-TV, Emory U. Ctr. for Leadership, Emory Bus. Sch., Bklyn. Coll. Found. Recipient award Detroit chpt. Am. Women in Radio and TV, 1969, award Golden Quill, 1971, award Golden Gavel, 1971, local Emmy award, 1972, award AP, 1974, Gold medal Broadcast Promotion Assn., 1983, Lifetime Achievement award Bklyn. Coll., 1990, Disting. Alumnus award, Golden Plate award Am. Acad. Achievement, 1995; BPME Gold medal San Francisco Film Festival, 1984, N.Y., 1985, Chgo., 1986, Tree of Life award Jewish Nat. Fund, 1988. Mem. Acad. TV Arts and Scis., Nat. Assn. TV Program Execs., Radio-TV News Dirs. Assn., Am. Mgmt. Assn., Am. Film Inst., Brooklyn Coll. Found. Office: QDE Entertainment 3800 Barham Blvd Ste 503 Los Angeles CA 90068-1042 *"Courage is the first of human qualities because it is the quality which guarantees all the others."**

SALZMAN, KEITH LAWRENCE, family practice physician, military officer; b. Tachikawa, Honshu, Japan, Aug. 2, 1955; s. Kenneth Maxwell and Juanita Mae (Riley) S.; m. Margaret Ruth Richards, June 18, 1983; children: Heath Alexandr, Rachelle Marie. BA in Philosophy, U. Minn., 1984; MD, Mayo Med. Sch., Rochester, Minn., 1989; grad., Officer Basic Course U.S. Army, 1989, Combat Casualty Care Course, U.S. Army, 1990; AMEDD Officer's Advanced Course, U.S. Army, 1995. Diplomate Am. Bd. Family Physicians; cert. ACLS instr., ATLS provider, instr. Commd. capt. U.S. Army, 1989, advanced through grades to maj., 1995; intern, resident in family practice Eisenhower Army Med. Ctr., Ft. Gordon, GA., 1989-92; clinic comdr., sr. physician 536th Gen. Dispensary, Katterbach, Germany, 1992-95; team leader family practice residency tng. program Tripler Army Med. Ctr, Honolulu, 1995—, mem. tchg. staff, 1995—. Contbr. articles to profl. jours. Recipient Woodridge scholarship U. Minn., 1984, Lucy B. Gooding scholarship Mayo Med. Sch., 1985-89, Harry Hoffman 3d World Externship, Derbe, Australia, 1989; grantee Rsch. Stimulation award. Mem. Am. Acad. Family Physicians, Uniformed Svcs. Acad. of Family Physicians. Home: 1330 Ala Amoamo St Honolulu HI 96819-1705

SALZMAN, WILLIAM RONALD, chemistry educator; b. Cut Bank, Mont., Feb. 27, 1936; s. Ralph Irwin and Oleta Fern (Owens) S.; m. Virginia Ann Harbin; children: Suzanne R. Barnes, Sandra R. Kavanaugh. BS in Chemistry, UCLA, 1959, MS in Physics, 1964, PhD in Chemistry, 1967. Asst. prof. chemistry U. Ariz., Tucson, 1967-72, assoc. prof., 1972-79, prof., 1979—; head dept. chem., U. Ariz., 1977-83. Contbr. numerous articles to profl. jours. Elder Christ Community Ch., 1970-1995; With U.S. Army, 1959-61. Mem. AAAS, Am. Chem. Soc., Am. Physical Soc., Am. Assn. Univ. Profs., Sigma Xi. Republican. Home: 6736 E Rosewood Cir Tucson AZ 85710-1214 Office: U Ariz Dept Chemistry Tucson AZ 85721

SAM, DAVID, federal judge; b. Hobart, Ind., Aug. 12, 1933; s. Andrew and Flora (Toma) S.; m. Betty Jean Brennan, Feb. 1, 1957; children: Betty Jean, David Dwight, Daniel Scott, Tamara Lynn, Pamela Rae, Daryl Paul, Angie, Sheyla. BS, Brigham Young U., 1957; JD, Utah U., 1960. Bar: Utah 1960, U.S. Dist. Ct. Utah 1966. Sole practice and ptnr. Duchesne, Utah, 1963-76; dist. judge State of Utah, 1976-85; judge U.S. Dist. Ct. Utah, Salt Lake City, 1985—; atty. City of Duchesne, 1963-72; Duchesne County atty., 1966-72; commr. Duchesne, 1972-74; mem. adv. com. Codes of Conduct of Jud. Conf. U.S., 1987-91, Jud. Coun. of 10th Cir., 1991-93; mem. U.S. Del. to Romania, Aug. 1991. Chmn. Jud. Nomination Com. for Cir. Ct. Judge, Provo, Utah, 1983; bd. dirs. Water Resources, Salt Lake City, 1973-76. Served to capt. JAGC, USAF, 1961-63. Mem. Utah Bar Assn., Am. Judicature Soc., Supreme Ct. Hist. Soc., Am. Inns of Ct. VII (counselor 1986-89), A. Sherman Christensen Am. Inn of Ct. I (counselor 1989—), Utah Jud. Conf. (chmn. 1982), Utah Dist. Judges Assn. (pres. 1982-83), Order of Coif (hon. Brigham Young U. chpt.). Mem. LDS Ch. Office: US Dist Ct 148 US Courthouse 350 S Main St Salt Lake City UT 84101-2106

SAMANIEGO, PAMELA SUSAN, organization administrator; b. San Mateo, Calif., Nov. 29, 1952; d. Armando C. and Harriott Susan (Croot) S. Student, UCLA, 1972, Los Angeles Valley Coll., 1970-72. Asst. new accts. supr. Beverly Hills Fed. Savings, 1970-72; asst. controller Bio-Science Enterprises, Van Nuys, Calif., 1972-74; adminstr. asst. Avery/Tirce Prodns., Hollywood, Calif., 1974-78; sr. estimator N. Lee Lacy and Assocs., Hollywood, 1978-81; head of prodn. Film Consortium, Hollywood, 1981-82; exec. producer EUE/Screen Gems Ltd., Burbank, Calif., 1982-88; advt. agency dir. Barrett & Assocs., Las Vegas, Nev., 1988-90; exec. producer Laguna/Take One, Las Vegas, 1990-93; dir. Sta. KXLY-4 ABC, Spokane, Wash., 1993-94; dir. advt. and mktg. Appaloosa Horse Club, Moscow, Idaho, 1994—. Author: Millimeter & Backstage, 1982-88. Emergency room vol. San Mateo (Calif.) County Hosp., 1968-70; Sunday sch. tchr. Hillsdale Meth. Ch., San Mateo, 1968-70; vol. worker Hillsdale Meth. Ch. Outreach, San Francisco, 1967-70. Recipient CLIO award CLIO Awards, Inc., 1985, ADDY award Las Vegas Advt. Fedn., 1988. Mem. Dirs. Guild Am. (2nd asst. dir. 1987-88), Assn. Ind. Comml. Producers, Am. Horse Show Assn., Internat. Arabian Horse Assn., AHASFV (sec. 1978-79), AHASC (sec. 1978-88). Democrat. Methodist. Home: 323 E First St Moscow ID 83843 Office: Appaloosa Horse Club 5070 Highway 8 W Moscow ID 83843-4000

SAMARAS, THOMAS THEODORE, management system specialist, author, researcher; b. N.Y.C., Mar. 1, 1932; s. Theodore and Garifalia (Toutounou) S.; m. Mary Stenning Jones, June 19, 1960 (div. Mar. 1981); children: Danny, William. AAS, N.Y. State U., Bklyn., 1951; BS in Engring., Calif. State U., L.A., 1959; MBA, Pepperdine U., L.A., 1976. Engr. Hughes Aircraft Co., Fullerton, Calif., 1959-63; staff engr. Electro-Optical Systems, Pasadena, Calif., 1963-69; engring. specialist Universal Monitor Corp., Pasadena, 1969-71; mgr. design support Hoffman Electronics, El Monte, Calif., 1971-73; systems adminstr. GA Industries, San Diego, 1973-79; configuration mgmt. specialist Gen. Dynamics, San Diego, 1979-92; owner Reventropy Assocs., San Diego, 1993—. Author: Engineering Graphics Desk Book, 1975, Industrial Documentation Handbook, 1978, Industrial Manager's Deskbook, 1988, Configuration Management Deskbook, 1991, Truth About Your Height, 1994; co-author: Fundamentals of Configuration Management, 1971, Computerized Project Management, 1979; contbr. articles to profl. jours. Served to cpl. U.S. Army, 1951-53. Home: 11487 Madera Rosa Way San Diego CA 92124-2877 Office: Reventropy Assocs 11487 Madera Rosa Way San Diego CA 92124-2877

SAMPLE, JOSEPH SCANLON, foundation executive; b. Chgo., Mar. 15, 1923; s. John Glen and Helen (Scanlon) S.; m. Patricia M. Law, Dec. 22, 1942 (div.); children: Michael Scanlon, David Forrest, Patrick Glen; m. Miriam Tyler Willing, Nov. 19, 1965. B.A., Yale U., 1947. Trainee, media analyst, media dir. Dancer-Fitzgerald-Sample, Inc., advt. agy., Chgo., 1947-50; v.p., media dir. Dancer-Fitzgerald-Sample, Inc., advt. agy., 1952-53; pres. Mont. Television Network KTVQ, Billings, KXLF-AM-TV, Butte, Mont., KRTV, Great Falls, Mont., KPAX-TV, Missoula, Mont., 1955-84. Pres. Greater Mont. Found., 1986—; chmn. Wheeler Ctr. Mont State U., 1988—. Served with AUS, 1943-46. With U.S. Army, 1950-52. Mem. Rotary, Yellowstone Country Club, Port Royal Club, Hole in The Wall Golf Club, Hilands Golf Club, Naples Yacht Club. Home: 606 Highland Park Dr Billings MT 59102-1909 Office: 14 N 24th St Billings MT 59101-2422

SAMPLE, STEVEN BROWNING, university executive; b. St. Louis, Nov. 29, 1940; s. Howard and Dorothy (Cunningham) S.; m. Kathryn Brunkow, Jan. 28, 1961; children: Michelle Sample Smith, Melissa Ann. BS, U. Ill., 1962, MS, 1963; DHULL (hon.), Canisius Coll., 1989; PhD, U. Ill., 1965; LLD (hon.), U. Sheffield, Eng., 1991; EdD (hon.), Purdue U., 1994; DHL (hon.), Hebrew Union Coll., 1994; DL (hon.), U. Nebr., 1995. Sr. scientist Melpar Inc., Falls Church, Va., 1965-66; assoc. prof. elec. engring. Purdue U., Lafayette, Ind., 1966-73; dep. dir. Ill. Bd. Higher Edn., Springfield, 1971-74; exec. v.p. acad. affairs, dean Grad. Coll., prof. elec. eng. U. Nebr., Lincoln, 1974-82; prof. elec. and computer engring. SUNY, Buffalo, 1982-91, pres., 1982-91; pres. U. So. Calif., L.A., 1991—, prof. elec. engring., 1991—; bd. dirs. Ind., First Interstate Bancorp, L.A., Presley Cos., Newport Beach, Calif., Western Atlas Inc., Beverly Hills, Calif.; vice chmn., bd. dirs. Western N.Y. Tech. Devel. Ctr., Buffalo, 1982-91; chmn. bd. dirs. Calspan-UB Rsch. Ctr., Inc., Buffalo, 1983-91; mem. Calif. Coun. Sci. and Tech., Irvine, Calif.; cons. in field. Contbr. articles to profl. jours.; patentee in field. Timpanist St. Louis Philharm. Orch., 1955-58; chmn. Western N.Y. Regional Econ. Devel. Coun., 1984-91; trustee U. at Buffalo Found., 1982-91, Studio Arena Theatre, Buffalo, 1983-91, Western N.Y. Pub. Broadcasting Assn., 1985-91; bd. dirs. Buffalo Philharm. Orch., 1982-91, Regenstrief Med. Found., Indpls., 1982—, Rsch. Found. SUNY, 1987-91; chmn. Gov.'s Conf. on Sci. and Engring. Edn., Rsch. and Devel., 1989-91; chair Calif. Bus.-Higher Edn. Forum; bd. dirs. L.A. chpt. World Affairs Coun., Hughes Galaxy Inst. Edn., L.A., 1991-94, Rebuild L.A. Com., L.A., Annenberg Metro Project, Coalition of 100 Club of L.A.; trustee L.A. Ednl. Alliance for Restructuring Now. Recipient Disting. Alumnus award Dept. Elec. Engring. U. Ill., 1980, citation award Buffalo Coun. on World Affairs, 1986, Engr. of Yr. award N.Y. State Soc. Profl. Engrs., 1985, Alumni Honor award Coll. Engring., U. Ill., 1985, Outstanding Elec. Engr. award Purdue U., 1993, Humanitarian award Nat. Conf. Christians and Jews, L.A., 1994, Hollzer Meml. award Jewish Fedn. Coun. Greater L.A., 1994; Sloan Found. fellow, 1962-63, NSF grad. fellow, 1963-65, Am. Coun. Edn. fellow Purdue U., 1970-71, NSF. Mem. AAU (chmn. com. on postdoctoral edn. 1994—), IEEE (Outstanding Paper award 1976), Nat. Assn. State Univs. and Land-Grant Colls. (ednl. telecommunications com., 1982-83, chmn. coun. of pres. 1985-86, edn. and tech. com. 1986-87, exec. com. 1987-89), Coun. on Fgn. Rels., Sigma Xi. Episcopalian. Home: 1550 Oak Grove Ave San Marino CA 91108-1108 Office: U So Calif Office of the Pres University Park ADM 110 Los Angeles CA 90089-0012*

SAMPLINER, LINDA HODES, psychologist, consultant; b. Cleve., Sept. 25, 1945; d. Walter J. and Caroline Jean (Klein) Hodes; m. Richard Evan Sampliner, July 31, 1966; children: Robert David, Steven Jay. BS, Western Res. U., Cleve., 1967; EdM, Boston U., 1972, EdD, 1975. Lic. psychologist, Ariz; cert. grief counselor, cons. in clin. hypnosis. Counselor The Family Life Ctr., Columbia, Md., 1976-80; psychologist Psychology & Rehab. Assocs., Tucson, 1981-85; pvt. practice Tucson, 1985—; cons., psychologist div. econ. security Child and Family Svcs., Tucson, 1985—; psychologist Sonora Behavioral Health Assn., 1994—; cons. SHARE, Tucson, 1985—; trainer comm. skills for police Balt. County Dept. Mental Health, 1975-80, drub abuse adminstrn. trainer for counselors, 1975-80. Bd. dirs. Adapt Inc., Tucson, 1985-93, pres., 1990-91; bd. dirs. Mental Health Resources, 1993-95; bd. dirs. Tucson Symphony Soc., 1984-89, v.p., 1987-89; pres. bd. dirs. Tucson Mus. of Art League, 1985-86; mem. adv. bd. dept. art U. Ariz., 1993—. Mem. APA, Assn. Death Edn. and Counseling, Ariz. Psychol. Assn., So. Ariz. Psychol. Assn. Office: Sonora Behavioral Health Network 2001 W Orange Grove Rd #410 Tucson AZ 85704

SAMPLINER, RICHARD EVAN, physician; b. Cleve., Apr. 14, 1941; m. Linda Sampliner. BA, Yale U., 1963; MD, Case Western Res. U., 1967. Diplomate Am. Bd. Internal Medicine, Am. Bd. Gastroenterology. Intern Univ. Hosps., Cleve., 1967-68; resident New England Med. Ctr., Boston, 1970-71; sr. resident Boston City Hosp., 1971-72; chief of gastroenterology divsn. U. Ariz. and VA Med. Ctr., Tucson, 1987—; prof. medicine U. Ariz., Tucson, 1990—. Contbr. articles to profl. jours. With USPHS, 1968-70. Fellow ACP, Am. Coll. Gastroenterology. Office: Univ Med Ctr 1501 N Campbell Ave Tucson AZ 85724-0001

SAMPSON, RICHARD ARNIM, security professional; b. New Haven, June 9, 1927; s. Richard Arnim Sampson and Ora Viola (Reese) Jackson; m. Marilyn Jo Gardner, June 10, 1950 (div. 1962); children: Gary, Susan; m. Janet Margaret Battaglia, Jan. 26, 1963 (div. 1987); children: Cynthia, David; m. Alice Annette Whitfield, July 23, 1988; stepchildren: Shareasa, Anthony, Erika. BS, Mich. State U., 1951; MPA, Auburn U., 1972; grad., Air War Coll., 1972. Exec. CIA, Washington, 1951-76; mgr. spl. projects Hughes Aircraft Co., El Segundo, Calif., 1976-80; mgr. security Advanced Systems div. Northrop Aircraft Co., Pico Rivera, Calif., 1980-83, Electronics div.

Gen. Dynamics Corp., San Diego, 1983-92; dir. security GDE Systems, Inc., San Diego, 1992-96; adj. prof. Webster U., San Diego, 1991—, Calif. State U., San Marcos, 1994; v.p. Pexis Corp., 1996—. Author: The Police of Taiwan, 1960, Excessive Bureaucracy-Causes and Cures, 1972, Advanced Ocean Mining and Energy Program, 1975, The Hughes Glomar Explorer Project, 1994, The Business Side of Security, 1994; author spl. projects indsl. security manual, 1965. Active Boy Scouts Am., McLean, Va., 1974, Palos Verdes, Calif., 1978; trustee 1st Congl. Ch. of Escondido, Calif., 1990-93; mem. Escondido Citizens Patrol, 1995—; mem. security mgmt. adv. com. Grossmont Coll., 1996—; mem. adv. com. to leadership and mgmt. program in security Sch. of Criminal Justice, Mich. State U., 1991—; bd. dirs. San Diego County Crime Commn., 1995—. Mem. Am. Soc. Indsl. Security (life, chmn. 1958-59, 97—, vice chmn. 1993-94, bd. dirs. 1994—), Signa Soc., CIA Retirees Assn. (treas. 1986-87, pres. 1996-97), Assn. Former Intelligence Officers (bd. dirs. San Diego chpt. 1995, vice-pres. 1995—), Ops. Security Profls. Soc. (cert. profl., sec. San Diego region 1995—), Calif. Crime Prevention Officer's Assn. (1995—), Internat. Hist. Aviation Search Inc. (bd. dirs. 1995), Am. Biographical Inst. (mem. rsch. bd. advisors 1992—). Republican. Home: 1408 Westwood Pl Escondido CA 92026-1752

SAMS, H. LEON, principal; b. Chgo., July 19, 1941; s. Lafayette J. and Mary Kathryn (McDearmon) S.; m. Marylee Severson, June 13, 1964; children: Christopher, Jennifer, Marybeth. BA in Bus. and Mgmt., Whitworth U., 1964, BA in Edn., 1968, MA in Edn., 1976. Tchr. Spokane (Wash.) Sch. Dist. #81, 1968-86; asst. prin. Stanwood (Wash.) Dist. #401, 1986-90; prin. Stanwood (Wash.) Elem., 1990—. Prodr. (16 mm film/video) Landforms of Washington, 1976, Tidelands, 1980. Sgt. U.S. Army, 1966-68. Recipient Golden Acorn, PTA, Spokane, 1986; named Tchr. of Yr., Spokane Wilson Sch., 1985. Mem. Assn. Wash. Sch. Prins. Home: 20028 Beach Dr Stanwood WA 98292-7818 Office: Stanwood Elem Sch 10227 273rd Pl NW Stanwood WA 98292-8043

SAMSON, STEN OTTO, x-ray crystallographer, consultant, researcher; b. Stockholm, Mar. 25, 1916; came to U.S., 1953; m. Lage and Wilhelmine (Lode) S.; m. Lalli Sandström, July 3, 1948; children: Karl-Otto, Karin. FilKand, U. Stockholm, 1953, FilLic, 1956, Fil. Dr, 1968. Rsch. fellow U. Stockholm, 1947-53; rsch. fellow Calif. Inst. Tech., Pasadena, 1953-61, sr. rsch. fellow, 1961-73, rsch. assoc., 1973-80, sr. rsch. assoc., 1980-86, sr. rsch. assoc. emeritus, 1986—. Sect. editor Crystallog. Data DeterminationTables, 1973. Mem. U.S. panel U.S.-Brazil Study Group on Grad. Tng. and Rsch. in Brazil, 1974-76. Mem. Am. Crystallog. Assn. Evangelical Lutheran. Home: 351 S Parkwood Ave Pasadena CA 91107 Office: Calif Inst Tech Pasadena CA 91125

SAMUEL, CHARLES E., virologist, educator; b. Portland, Oreg., 1945; married; 2 sons. BS in Chemistry, Mont. State U., 1968; PhD in Biochemistry, U. Calif., Berkeley, 1972. USPHS trainee U. Calif., Berkeley, 1968-72; postdoctoral tng. in virology Duke Med. Sch., Durham, N.C., 1974; asst. prof. U. Calif., Santa Barbara, 1974-79, assoc. prof., 1979-83, prof., 1983—, chmn. interdept. program biochem. and molecular biology, 1987-95; mem. Materials Rsch. Lab., 1992—; chmn. dept. molecular, cellular, and devel. biology U. Calif., Santa Barbara, 1995—; guest prof. U. Zurich, 1986-87; prin. investigator NIAID, NIH, 1975—. Mem. editl. bd. Virology, 1980—, Jour. Virology, 1984-95, Jour. Biol. Chemistry, 1989-93, 95—, Jour. Interferon and Cytokine Rsch., 1980—; contbr. over 125 articles to profl. jours. Recipient Damon Runyon postdoctoral award, 1972, Career Devel. award NIH, 1979, Merit award NIH, 1989, Wellcome award, 1994. Mem. AAAS, Am. Soc. Biochemistry-Molecular Biology, Am. Soc. for Virology, Internat. Soc. for Interferon Rsch. Office: U Calif Dept Biology Santa Barbara CA 93106

SAMUELS, BARBARA ANN, university administrator, planner, educator, information architect; b. Montreal, Oct. 20, 1949; d. Louis and Frances Kalb; m. Keith Michael Samuels, Aug. 23, 1970; 1 child, Sumerlee Eden. BSc, U. Calgary, Alta., Can., 1969; MEd, U. Oreg., 1973, PhD, 1978. Cert. profl. tchr., Alta. Tchr., asst. prin. Calgary Bd. Edn., 1971-79, planning specialist, 1980-83; asst. v.p. svcs. U. Calgary, 1983-84, dir. planning, 1986—; exec. dir. Can. Ctr. for Learning Sys., Calgary, 1984-86; pres. B.A. Samuels & Assocs., Calgary, 1985—; treas. Knowledge & Work Project, 1995—. Author: Understanding Culture, 1985, Multiculturalism in Canada: Images and Issues, 1996; developer, writer (video) New Faculty Recruitment, 1991; author, rschr. rsch. studies; author mag. and CD-ROM articles. Trustee Calgary Zoo, 1996—, Vision of the Future Com., Jr. Achievement, Can., 1995, Akiva Acad. Sch. Bd., Calgary, 1986-87; dir. Banff-Cochrane Progressive Conservative Constituency Assn., 1989-91. F.J.C. Seymour fellow Alta. Tchrs'. Assn., 1977; recipient Women & Coop. Edn. grant Sec. of State, 1989, Centres of Excellence citation, 1984. Mem. Internat. Soc. for Planning and Strategic Mgmt., Can. Soc. for Study in Higher Edn., Kappa Delta Pi. Office: U Calgary Office of VP, 103C Administration Bldg, Calgary, AB Canada T2N 1N4

SAMUELS, JOSEPH, JR., police chief; b. 1949; m. Sabrina Samuels; 1 child, Joseph. BA in Psychology, Lincoln U.; MPA, Calif. State U., Hayward, 1988; student, Nat. Exec. Inst. Br. mgr. Household Fin. Corp.; with Oakland (Calif.) Police Dept., 1974-91, capt. patrol divsn., chief police, 1993—; police chief Fresno (Calif.) Police Dept., 1991-93; chair regional citizens adv. com. Calif. Youth Authority, 1986-91; former mem. Calif. State Commn. Crime, Juvenile Justice and Delinquency Prevention. Active YMCA, Oakland, East Oakland Youth Devel. Ctr., Oakland Citizens Com. Urban Renewal. Mem. Nat. Orgn. Black Law Enforcement Execs., Calif. Peace Officers Assn., Calif. Police Chiefs Assn., Internat. Assn. Chiefs Police, Police Exec. Rsch. Forum. Office: Police Headquarters 455 7th St Oakland CA 94607-3940

SANBORN, DOROTHY CHAPPELL, librarian; b. Nashville, Apr. 26, 1920; d. William S. and Sammie Maude (Drake) Chappell. BA, U. Tex., 1941; MA, George Peabody Coll., 1947; MPA, Golden Gate U., 1982; m. Richard Donald Sanborn, Dec. 1, 1943; children: Richard Donald, William Chappell. Asst. cataloger El Paso (Tex.) Pub. Libr., 1947-52, Libr. of Hawaii, Honolulu, 1953; cataloger Redwood (Calif.) City Pub. Libr., 1954-55, 57-59, Stanford Rsch. Inst., Menlo Park, Calif., 1955-57; libr. Auburn (Calif.) Pub. Libr., 1959-62; cataloger Sierra Coll., Rocklin, Calif., 1962-64; reference libr. Sacramento City Libr., 1964-66; county libr. Placer County (Calif.), Auburn, 1966-89, ret., 1989; chmn. Mountain Valley Libr. Sys., 1970-71, 75-76, 1984-85; cons. county libr. Alpine County Libr., Markleeville, Calif., 1973-80. Peace corps vol., Thailand, 1991-93; pres. Auburn Friends of Libr., 1995—. With WAVES, 1944-46. Mem. AAUW (pres. chpt. 1982-84), Calif. Libr. Assn., Soroptimists. Democrat. Mem. United Ch. Christ. Home: 135 Midway Ave Auburn CA 95603-5415 *Personal philosophy: To strive to make a continuing contribution.*

SANCHEZ, GILBERT, retired academic administrator, microbiologist, researcher; b. Belen, N.Mex., May 7, 1938; s. Macedonio C. and Josephine H. Sanchez; m. Lorena T. Tabet, Aug. 26, 1961; children—Elizabeth, Phillip, Katherine. B.S. in Biology, N.Mex. State U., 1961; Ph.D. in Microbiology, U. Kans., 1967. Research asst. U. Kans., Lawrence, 1963-67; research assoc., postdoctoral fellow Rice U., Houston, 1967-68; prof. N.Mex. Inst. Tech., Socorro, 1968-79; dean grad. studies Eastern N.Mex. U., Portales, 1979-83; v.p. acad. affairs U. So. Colo., Pueblo, 1983-85; pres. N.Mex. Highlands U., Las Vegas, 1985-95; cons. NIH, NSF, Solvex Corp., Albuquerque, 1979-83; bd. dirs. Fed. Res. Bank, Denver. Contbr. numerous articles to profl. jours. Patentee in field. Pres. Socorro Sch. Bd., 1974-79, Presbyn. Hosp. Bd., Socorro, 1977-79. Research grantee Dept. Army, 1976-79, N.Mex. Dept. Energy, 1979-83, NSF, 1979. Mem. Am. Soc. Microbiology, Am. Soc. Indsl. Microbiology, AAAS, Am. Assn. Univs. and Colls. (bd. dirs. 1988-90), Hispanic Assn. Univs. and Colls. (pres. 1986-89). Roman Catholic. Lodge: Rotary.

SANCHEZ, LEONEDES MONARRIZE WORTHINGTON (DUKE DE LEONEDES), fashion designer; b. Flagstaff, Ariz., Mar. 15, 1951; s. Rafael Leonedes and Margaret (Monarrize) S. BS, No. Ariz. U., 1974; studied, Fashion Inst. Tech., N.Y.C., 1974-75; AA, Fashion Inst. D&M, L.A., 1975; lic., La Ecole de la Chambre Syndical de la Couture Parisian, Paris, 1976-78. Lic. in designing. Contract designer/asst. to head designer House of Bonnet, Paris, 1976—; dress designer-in-residence Flagstaff, 1978—; mem. faculty No. Ariz. U., Flagstaff, 1978-80; designer Ambiance, Inc., L.A., 1985—; designer Interiors by Leonedes subs. Studio of Leonedes Couturier, Ariz., 1977, Calif., 1978, London, Paris, 1978, Rome, 1987, Milan, Spain, 1989; designer Liturgical Vesture subs. Studio of Leonedes Couturier; CEO Leonedes Internat.; owner, CEO, designer Leonedes Internat., Ltd., London, Milan, Paris, Spain, Ambian Ariz, Calif., Appolonian Costuming, Ariz., London, Milan, Paris, El Castillo de Leonedes, Sevilla, Spain, Villa Appolonian de Leonedes, Mykonos, Greece; cns. House of Bonnet, Paris, 1976—, Bob Mackie, Studio City, Calif., 1974-75; CEO, designer artistical dir., Leonedes internat. Bd. dirs. Roman Cath. Social Svcs., 1985-86, Northland Crisis Nursery, 1985—; bd. dirs., chmn. Pine Country Transit, 1986-88; pres. Chicanos for Edn.; active master's swim program ARC, Ariz., 1979—; eucharistic min., mem. art and environ. com., designer liturgical vesture St. Pius X Cath. Ch.; vol. art tchr., instr. St. Mary's Regional Sch., Flagstaff, 1987-90, vol. art dir.; mem. Flagstaff Parks and Recreation Commn., 1994-96, citizens' adv. com. master plan, 1994-96; mem. cmty. bd. adv. com. Flagstaff Unified Sch. Dist., 1995; active Duke de Leonedes Found. de Nuevo Espana, Santa Fe. Decorated Duke de Leonedes (Spain), 1994; recipient Camellian Design award 1988, Atlanta. Mem. AAU (life, chairperson swiimming Ariz. 1995, vice chairperson physique, mem. citizen adv. bd. parks and recreation), Am. Film Inst., Am. Assn. Hist. Preservation, Costume Soc., Am. Nat. Physique Com., Internat. Consortium Fashion Designers, Nat. Cath. Ednl. Assn., La Legion de Honour de la Mode Parisienne, Social Register Assn., Phi Alpha Theta (historian 1972-73, pres. 1973-74), Pi Kappa Delta (pres. 1972-73, historian 1973-74). Republican. Office: El Castillo de Leonedes, Seville Spain Also: El Castillo de Nuevo Espana, Santa Fe Greece

SANCHEZ, LORETTA, congresswoman; b. Anaheim, Calif., Jan. 7, 1960. BA, Chapman U., 1982; MBA, Am. U., 1984. With Orange County Transp. Authority, 1984-87, Fieldman Rolapp & Assocs., 1987-90; strategic mgmt. cons. Booz Allen & Hamilton, 1993—; owner, operator AMIGA Advisors Inc., 1993—; mem. 105th Congress from 46th Calif. dist., 1997—. Mem. Anaheim Rotary Club. Democrat. Office: House Office Bldg 116 Cannon Washington DC 20518

SANCHEZ, MARLA RENA, finance director; b. Espanola, N.Mex., Mar. 3, 1956; d. Tomas Guillermo and Rose (Trujillo) S.; m. Bradley D. Gaiser, Mar. 5, 1979. BS, Stanford U., 1979, MS, 1979; MBA, Santa Clara U., 1983. Rsch. biologist Syntex, Palo Alto, Calif., 1980-81; fin. analyst Advanced Micro Devices, Sunnyvale, Calif., 1983-85; fin. mgr. ultrasound divsn. Diasonics, Inc., Milpitas, Calif., 1985-86, contr. therapeutic products divsn., 1989-93, contr. internat. divsn., 1992-93; contr. Ridge Computers, Santa Clara, Calif., 1986-88; dir. fin. VLSI Tech., Inc., San Jose, Calif., 1993—. Home: 1234 Russell Ave Los Altos CA 94024-5541

SANCHEZ, RUBEN DARIO, minister, family counselor, parochial school educator, writer; b. Buenos Aires, Feb. 13, 1943; s. Ramon Jose and Maria Concepcion (Pardino) S.; m. Lina Alcira Tabuenca, Feb. 7, 1966; children: Adrian Nelson, Vivian Ethel. BA, River Plate Coll., Puiggari, Argentina, 1969; postgrad., Andrews U., 1971-72, MA, 1975; PhD, Calif. Sch. Theology, 1979; MA in counseling psychology, Nat. U., 1996. Ordained to ministry Seventh-day Adventist Ch., 1976. Pastor, tchr. River Plate Coll., Puiggari, 1969; min. lit. So. Calif. Conf., Glendale, 1970-71, Ill. Conf., Brookfield, 1972-77, Oreg. Conf., Portland, 1977-80; dir. Bible sch., assoc. speaker Voice of Prophecy, Thousand Oaks, Calif., 1980-84; dir. devel. Written Telecast, 1985—; founder Pacific N.W. Christian Sch., Woodburn, Oreg., 1979; founder, dir. Instituto Biblico Christiano, 1979-80; dir. Escuela Radiopostal (corr. Bible sch.), 1980-84; pres. ADVI Internat., 1990—; founder Asociacion Latino Americana para el Bienstar Familiar, 1995; dir.-spkr. daily internat. radio program Learning to Live; mem. Religious Broadcasters. Editor: Antologia Poetica, 1976; author: (textbook) Apasionante Exploration de la Biblia, 1977, Introduction to the Old Testament, 1979, (book) Back to Our Beginnings, 1996, (doctrinal devotionals) Hungary Heart, 1984, The Danger of Loving Money, 1997, Take Care of Your Self-Esteem, 1997; contbr. articles to publs. Recipient Outstanding Service to Spanish Community in Oreg. award Sta. KROW, 1980; Andrews U. scholar, 1972. Mem. Assn. Christian Counselors, Christian Mgmt. Assn. Home: 24978 Ave 208 Lindsay CA 93247 Office: Lindsa Adventist Comty Ch 588 E Honolulu St Lindsay CA 93247-2144

SANCHEZ, SHEILA LEONOR, journalist; b. Van Nuys, Calif., July 1, 1963; d. James William Van Camp and Maria Elena (Santos) Palacios; m. Mario Miguel Sanchez, Nov. 25, 1989; children: Mackenzie, Cassidy. BA, Brigham Young U., 1990. Staff writer La Opinion Newspaper, L.A., 1987-89, Deseret News, Salt Lake City, 1989-90, The Daily Herald, Provo, Utah, 1990—. Journalist, Jedi Women, Salt Lake City, 1995—. Recipient Award for Investigative Reporting, AP (Intermountain region), 1992, Award for Best News Series, Utah Press Assn., 1995, Award for Spot News Reporting, AP, 1995, Sharing the Vision award Utah Valley State Coll., 1995. Mem. Soc. Profl. Journalists (bd. dirs. 1994-96), Religion Newswriters Assn. Office: The Daily Herald 1555 N Freedom Blvd Provo UT 84603

SANCHEZ-H., JOSE, fine arts educator, producer, director, media consultant; b. Cochabamba, Bolivia, June 28, 1951; s. Victor Sanchez and Margarita Hermoso. MA, U. Mich., 1977, PhD, 1983. Camera operator NBC, WDIV/TV 4, Detroit, 1980-81; assoc. prof. Univ. del Sagrado Corazon, P.R., 1984-88, Calif. State U., Long Beach, 1988—; actor Ninon Davalos Co., Cochabamba, 1969, Dept. of Fine Arts, Guadalajara, Mex., 1970-72; rsch. cons. U. Mich., Ann Arbor, 1984, media engr., 1982-83; photographer Mus. of Contemporary Art, L.A., 1989—; cons. Loyola Marymount U., L.A., 1989. Cinematographer (film) Chautauqua: Famous American Voices of 1914, 1984; still photography (film) Secret Honor, 1984; dir. (video) Pope John Paul II, 1984; producer/dir. (videos) The Carillon Concert, 1979, Yo No Entiendo a la Gente Grande, 1986, Platinotipo, 1988, Artificial Intelligence, 1989, Partners for Success, 1990, The L.A. Mexican Dance Co., 1990, Rudolf Arnheim: A Life in Art, 1994, Ca/Rep 1995, Themes in Bicultural Education, 1991, Fue Cosa de Un Dia, 1992, (films) You and I, 1976, Who Cares About the Time?, 1977, Inside Cuba: The Next Generation, 1990; writer, producer, dir. (film) La Paz, 1994, The Delirium of Simon Bolivar, 1997; writer (play) La Paz, 1989. Mem. The Long Beach Mus. of Art, Hispanic Acad. of Arts, 1987-89. Recipient Exceptional Achievement award Coun. Advancement and Support of Edn., 1982, Rackham Dissertation award U. Mich., 1982, Rackham scholarship, 1980-83. Mem. NEA, Latin Am. Found., Am. Film Inst., Profl. Photographers, Ptnrs. of the Ams., Ind. Feature Project/West. Office: Calif State U Film & Elec Arts Dept 1250 N Bellflower Blvd Long Beach CA 90840-2801

SAND, FAITH ANNETTE, writer, publisher religious material; b. Mpls., May 13, 1939; d. Maurice Harry and Verna Annette (Huseboe) Sand; divorced; children: Heather Faith Pidcoke, Heidi Annette Pidcoke; m. Albert Gleaves Cohen, May 29, 1982. BA in History, Wheaton Coll., 1961; MA in Missiology, Fuller Theological Seminary, Pasadena, Calif., 1982. Missionary Co-Laboradores do Brasil, Umuarama, Brazil, 1962-72; publisher Edições Esperança, Paraná, Brazil, 1972-77; freelance editor, writer Pasadena, Calif., 1977-78; asst. editor Missiology Quarterly Review, Pasadena, Calif., 1977-83; pub. Hope Publishing House, Pasadena, Calif., 1983—; cons., writer World Vision Internat., Monrovia, Calif., 1977-80; bd. dir. Jian Hua Foun., Hong Kong, Internat. Christian Scholarship Found.;. Author: Travels of Faith, Prayers of Faith; contbr. numerous articles to profl. jours. Participant Women & Men in Ch. Community, Sheffield, England, 1981, One Earth, One Community, Bossey, Switzerland, 1991, Earth Summit, Rio De Janeiro, Brazil, 1992. Mem. Soc. Women Geographers, Zonta Internat. Democrat. Episcopalian. Office: Hope Publishing House PO Box 60008 Pasadena CA 91116-6008

SANDAHL, BONNIE BEARDSLEY, pediatric nurse practitioner, clinical nurse specialist, nurse manager; b. Washington, Jan. 17, 1939; d. Erwin Leonard and Carol Myrtle (Collis) B.; m. Glen Emil Sandahl, Aug 17, 1963; children: Cara Lynne, Cory Glen. BSN, U. Wash., 1962, MN, 1974, cert. pediatric nurse practitioner, 1972. Dir. Wash. State Joint Practice Commn., Seattle, 1974-76; instr. pediatric nurse practitioner program U. Wash., Seattle, 1976, course coord. quality assurance, 1977-78; pediatric nurse practitioner/health coord. Snohomish County Head Start, Everett, Wash., 1975-77; clin. nurse educator (specialist), nurse manager Harborview Med. Ctr., Seattle, 1978-97, dir. child abuse prevention project, 1986-97; mgr. Children's Ctr., Providence Health Sys. Northwest, 1997—; spkr. legis. focus on children, 1987; clin. assoc. Dept. of Pediatrics, U. Wash. Sch. medicine, 1987—, clin. faculty Sch. Nursing, nurse mgr. Providence Gen. Children's Ctr., Everett, 1997—. Mem. Task Force on Pharmacotherapeutic Courses, Wash. State Bd. Nursing, 1985-86; Puget Sound Health Sys. Agy., 1975-88, pres., 1980-82; mem. child devel. project adv. bd. Mukilteo Sch. Dist., 1984-85; mem. parenting adv. com. Edmonds Sch. Dist., 1985—; chmn. hospice-home health task force Snohomish County Hospice Program, Everett, 1984-85, bd. dirs. hospice, 1985-87, adv. com. 1986-88; mem. Wash. State Health Coordinating, Coun., 1977-82, chmn. nursing home bed projection methodology task force, 1986-87; mem., interim chair Nat. Coun. Health Planning and Devel., HHS, 1980-87; mem. adv. com. on uncompensated care Wash. State Legislature, 1983-84; mem. Joint Select Com., Tech. Adv. Com. on Managed Health Care Sys., 1984-85. Pres., Alderwood Manor Cmty. Coun., 1983-85; treas. Wash. St. Women's Polit. Caucus, 1983-84; mem. com. to examine changes in Wash. State Criminal Sex Law, 1987; appointee county needs assessment com. Snohomish County Govt. United Way, 1989, 94; chair human svcs. adv. coun. Snohomish County Human Svcs. Dept., chair adv. com., 1992-96; gubernatorial appointee Western Form Health Svcs. Adv. Com. for Wash. State, 1995—. Recipient Golden Acorn award Seattle-King County PTA, 1973, Katherine Rickey Vol. Participation award, 1987. Mem. Am. Nurses Assn. (chmn. pediatric nurse practitioner subcom. Com. Examiners Maternal-Child Nursing Practice, 1986-92, chair Com. Examiners Maternal-Child Nursing Practice 1988-90), Wash. State Nurses Assn. (hon. leadership award 1981, chair healthcare reform task force 1992—), King County Nurses Assn. (Nurse of Yr. 1985, 1st v.p. 1992—, pres. 1996—), Wash. State Soc. Pediatrics, Sigma Theta Tau. Methodist. Home: 1814 201st Pl SW Lynnwood WA 98036-7060 Office: Providence Children's Ctr Everett WA 98204

SANDDAL, NELS DODGE, foundation executive, consultant; b. Salt Lake City, Feb. 17, 1949; s. James Wesley and Charlotte Jean (Ewer) S.; m. Brenda Kay Lille Griffin, Sept. 27, 1970 (div. June 1990); m. Theresa Louise Knipe, Oct. 12, 1992; 1 child, Jami. BA in English, Carroll Coll., 1966-70; MS in Psychology, Mont. State U., 1996. In-svc. trainer Boulder (Mont.) River Sch. and Hosp., 1974-75; group home mgr. REACH, Inc., Bozeman, Mont., 1975-76; community home trainer Devel. Disabilities Tng. Inst., Helena, Mont., 1976-77; tng. coord. emergency med. svcs. bureau State Dept. Health and Environ. Scis., Helena, 1977-82; cons., lead staff Nat. Coun. State Emergency Med. Svcs. Tng. Coords., Inc., Lexington, Ky., 1981-86; account exec., lead staff Nat. Assn. Emergency Med. Techs., Clinton, Miss., 1986-87; pres., CEO Assn. Mgmt. and Cons., Inc., Boulder, 1983-89; writer, prodr., dir. North Country Media Group, Great Falls, Mont., 1990-91; chief conf. planner S.O.S. Conf. Planning Consortium, Great Falls, 1991-92; exec. dir. Critical Illness & Trauma Found., Bozeman, Mont., 1986-91; pres., CEO Critical Illness & Trauma Found., Bozeman, 1991—; season course leader Nat. Outdoor Leadership Sch., Lander, Wyo., 1966-74; mem. exec. com. Nat. Coun. State EMS Tng. Coords., 1977-82, chmn., Lexington, Ky., 1979-81; mem. adv. com. pediatric emergency med. svcs. tng. project Children's Hosp. Nat. Med. Ctr., Washington, 1985-88, pediatrics emergency instr., 1986-90; mem. grant peer rev. com. divsn. injury epidemiology Ctrs. for Disease Control, Atlanta, 1986-87; cons. Emergency Med. Svcs. Bureau, Helena, 1977, Devel. Disabilities Tng. Inst., Helena, 1977-78; mem. injury prevention profls. New Eng. Network to Prevent Childhood Injuries, Newton, Mass., 1988-95; mem. core faculty devel. trauma sys. tng. program U.S. Dept. Transp., Washington, 1989—, tech. assistance team mem. EMS, 1991-93; EMS instr. and program coord. Great Falls Vocat. Tng. Ctr., 1991-93; rsch. asst. inst. for cmty. studies U. Mo., Kansas City, 1983-95; pres. exec. com. Intermountain Regional EMS Children Coord. Coun., Salt Lake City, 1994—. Editor and tech. cons.: Workbook for Prehospital Care and Crisis Interventions, 4th edit., 1992, 5th edit., 1993, Instructor Resource Manual for Prehospital Care and Crisis Intervention, 4th edit., 1992, Workbook for First Responder, 1990; contbg. editor Jour. of Prehospital Care, 1984-85, The EMT Jour., 1980-81; editl. cons. Am. Acad. Orthopaedic Surgeons, 1980-81; contbr. numerous articles to profl. jours.; video prodr. and presenter in field. Mem. Park County DUI Task Force, Livingson, 1993-96; inaugural coord. Mont. Safe Kids Coalition, Big Timber, 1988-90; adv. com. Nat. Significance Project for Respite Care, 1977-78; mem. basic life support com. of Mont., Mont. Heart Assn., 1977-82. Recipient Golden award for humanity ARC, 1976, 500 Hour award, 1976, Outstanding Svc. award Nat. Coun. State EMS Tng. Coords., 1979, Leadership award, 1981, Charter Membership award, 1984, J.D. Farrington award for excellence Nat. Assn. Emergency Med. Technicians, 1981, Jeffrey S. Harris award, 1985, Outstanding Svc. award Am. Heart Assn., 1982, Appreciation cert. for paramedic emergency care U.S. Dept. Transp., 1984. Mem. Nat. Registry EMTs, Mont. Bd. Med. Examiners. Democrat. Home: 20 Arrowhead Trail Bozeman MT 59718 Office: Critical Illness Trauma Found 300 N Willson Ave Ste 3002 Bozeman MT 59715-3551

SANDE, BARBARA, interior decorating consultant; b. Twin Falls, Idaho, May 5, 1939; d. Einar and Pearl M. (Olson) Sande; m. Ernest Reinhardt Hohener, Sept. 3, 1961 (div. Sept. 1971); children: Heidi Catherine, Eric Christian; m. Peter H. Forsham, Apr. 1990. BA, U. Idaho, 1961. Lic. designer, Calif. Asst. mgr., buyer Home Yardage Inc., Oakland, Calif., 1972-76; cons. in antiques and antique valuation, Lafayette, Calif., 1977-78; interior designer Neighborhood Antiques and Interiors, Oakland, Calif., 1978-86; owner, Claremont Antiques and Interiors, Lafayette, Calif., 1987-94; assoc. Neiman-Marcus, San Francisco, 1994—; cons. Benefit Boutique Inc., Lafayette, 1995; cons., participant antique and art fair exhibits, Orinda and Piedmont, Calif., 1977—. Decorator Piedmont Christmas House Tour, 1983, 88, 89, Oakland Mus. Table Setting, 1984, 85, 86, Piedmont Showcase Family Room, 1986, Piedmont Showcase Music Room, 1986, Piedmont Kitchen House Tour, 1985, Santa Rosa Symphony Holiday Walk Benefit, 1986, Piedmont Benefit Guild Showcase Young Persons Room, 1987, Piedmont Showcase Library, 1988, Piedmont Showcase Solarium, 1989, Jr. League Table Setting, Oakland-East Bay, 1989, 90. Bd. dirs. San Leandro Coop. Nursery Sch., 1967; health coord. parent-faculty bd., Miramonte High Sch., Orinda, 1978, Acalanes Sch. Dist., Lafayette, Calif., 1978; bd. dirs. Orinda Community Ctr. Vols., 1979; originator Concerts in the Park, Orinda, 1979; cons. not-for-profit Benefit Boutique, Inc., Lafayette, Calif, 1991. Mem. Am. Soc. Interior Design (assoc.), Am. Soc. Appraisers (assoc.), Am. Decorative Arts Forum, De Young Mus., Nat. Trust Historic Preservation, San Francisco Opera Guild, San Francisco Symphony Guild. Democrat. Avocations: travel, hiking.

SANDEL, RANDYE NOREEN, artist; b. L.A., June 2, 1942; d. Alexander and Sara Lisa (Cohen) Newman. BA in Latin, U.C.L.A., 1965, MFA in Painting and Print Making, 1969. Art instr. L.A. Valley Coll., Van Nuys, 1970-87, L.A. Harbor Coll., Wilmington, 1969-82. One-woman shows include Stanislaus State Coll., Turlock, Calif., 1971, L.A. Mcpl. Art Gallery, 1979, Calif. State Art Gallery, Northridge, 1988, Sherry Frumkin Gallery, Santa Monica, Calif., 1990, 92, 94, 96, Riverside (Calif.) Art Mus., 1989, Stella Polaris Gallery, Beverly Hills, Calif., 1985, Space Gallery, L.A., 1977, 83, others; group exhbns. include Occidental Coll., L.A., 1996, Danville Fine arts Ctr., Calif., 1996, Irvine (Calif.) Med. Ctr., 1991, Mt. Saint Mary's Coll., Brentwood, Calif., 1989, L.A. Inst. Contemporary Art, 1976-78, Laguna Beach (Calif.) Art Mus., 1975, Market St Project, 1973, others; represented in permanent collections BankAmerica: Corporate Art Collection, Devon Industries, River Forest (Ill.) State Bank, others. Home and Studio: 14301 Martha St Van Nuys CA 91401-4619

SANDER, EUGENE GEORGE, vice provost, dean; b. Fargo, N.D., Sept. 17, 1935; s. Victor and Kathryn S.; m. Louise Canfield; children: Kathy, Jay. BS in Animal Sci., U. Minn., 1957; MS in Animal Nutrition, Cornell Univ., 1959, PhD in Biochemistry, 1965. From asst. prof. to prof. Coll. Medicine, Univ. Fla., Gainesville, 1967-75, prof., 1975-76; prof., chair dept. biochemistry W.Va. Univ. Med. Ctr., Morgantown, 1976-80; prof., head dept. biochemistry and biophysics Tex. A&M, College Station, 1980-86, dep. chancellor biotech. devel., 1986-87; vice provost, dean coll. agr. Univ. Ariz., Tucson, 1987—; vice chair exec. com. Consortium Internat. Devel., 1995; chair bd. dirs. Agrl. Distance Edn. Consortium, 1996—; chair-elect Nat. Agr. Biotech. Coun., 1996—. Contbr. over 70 articles to profl. publs. Capt. USAF, 1959-62. Mem. AAAS, Ariz. Farm Bur. Fedn. (bd. dirs.), Am. Soc. Biochemistry and Molecular Biology, Am. Chem. Soc. Office: Univ Ariz Forbes 306 PO Box 210036 Tucson AZ 85721

SANDER, SUSAN BERRY, environmental planning engineering corporation executive; b. Walla Walla, Wash., Aug. 26, 1953; d. Alan Robert and

Elizabeth Ann (Davenport) Berry; m. Dean Edward Sander, June 3, 1978. BS in Biology with honors, Western Wash. U., 1975; MBA with honors, U. Puget Sound, 1984. Biologist, graphic artist Shapiro & Assocs., Inc., Seattle, 1975-77, office mgr., 1977-79, v.p., 1979-84, pres., owner 1984—, also bd. dirs. Merit scholar Overlake Service League, Bellevue, Wash., 1971, Western Wash. U. scholar, Bellingham, 1974-75, U. Puget Sound scholar, 1984; named Employer of Yr. Soc. Mktg. Profl. Svcs. 1988, Small Bus. of Yr. City of Seattle, Environ. Cons. of Yr., King County, Entrepreneur of Yr., Inc. Mag. Founding mem. Bellevue Children's Mus.; ; bd. dirs. Seattle Aquarium. Recipient PEMA Corp. Identity award, 1996. Mem. Seattle C. of C. , Student Conservation Assn. (dir.). Club. Avocations: swimming, hiking, traveling, painting. Office: Shapiro & Assocs Inc 101 Yester Ste 400 Seattle WA 98104

SANDERLIN, TERRY KEITH, counselor; b. Ashland, Oreg., Aug. 5, 1950; s. Calvin Carney and Myrtle Estell (Cope) S.; m. Theresa Emma Garcia, Jan. 19, 1969 (div. Feb. 1976); 1 child, Sean Eric; m. Margaret Lillian Lutz, Dec. 26, 1987. B in Bus., U. N.Mex., 1982, M in Counseling, 1983, EdD, 1993. Lic. clin. mental health, N.Mex.; cert. hypnotherapist Internat. Assn. Counselors and Therapists. Unit supr. Bernalillo County Juvenile Detention Ctr., Albuquerque, 1978-80; counselor Independence Halfway House, Albuquerque, 1980-81; mental health worker Bernalillo County Mental Health Ctr., Albuquerque, 1981-82; probation parole officer N.Mex. Probation/Parole, Albuquerque, 1982-87; dist. supr. N.Mex. Probation/Parole, Gallup, 1987-88; vocat. counselor Internat. Rehab. Assn., Albuquerque, 1989-91; counseling psychologist VA, Albuquerque, 1991—; owner, dir. Counseling and Tng. Specialist, Albuquerque, 1988—; counselor Albuquerque (N.Mex.) Counseling Specialist, 1983-86; guest lectr. sociology dept. U. N.Mex., Albuquerque, 1992; presenter 5th Annual S.W. Substance Abuse Conf., Albuquerque, 1992; presenter N.Mex. Corrections Dept., Santa Fe, 1993. Author: (video tapes) Breathing Free & Good, 1991, Understanding Adolescent Satanism, 1991, (manual) Social Skills and Anger Management, 1993. Vol. counselor Adult Misdemeanor Probation, Albuquerque, 1974-76; panel mem. Cmty. Corrections Selection Panel, Albuquerque, 1987-90. With U.S. Army, 1969-72, Vietnam. Recipient Outstanding Citizenship, Albuquerque Police Dept., 1974; N.Mex. Dept. Pub. Safety rsch. grantee, 1995. Mem. ACA, Am. Corrections Assn., Am. Legion. Democrat. Office: Counseling & Tng Specialist 8016 Zuni SE Ste G Albuquerque NM 87108

SANDERS, ADRIAN LIONEL, educational consultant; b. Paragould, Ark., Aug. 3, 1938; s. Herbert Charles and Florence Theresa (Becherer) S.; m. Molly Jean Zecher, Dec. 20, 1961. AA, Bakersfield Coll., 1959; BA, San Francisco State U., 1961; MA, San Jose State U., 1967. 7th grade tchr. Sharp Park Sch., Pacifica, Calif., 1961-62; 5th grade tchr. Mowry Sch., Fremont, Calif., 1962-64; sci. tchr. Blacow Sch., Fremont, Calif., 1964-76; 5th grade tchr. Warm Springs Sch., Fremont, 1977-87, 5th grade gifted and talented edn. tchr., 1987-94; edn. cons., 1994—. Mem. History Mus. of San Jose, 1980—, Nat. Geog. Soc., Washington, 1976—, Alzheimer's Family Relief Program, Rockville, Md., 1986; vol. 7 km. Race for Alzheimer's Disease Willow Glen Founders Day, San Jose, 1988-92. Named Outstanding Young Educator, Jr. C. of C., Fremont, Calif., 1965. Mem. Smithsonian Assocs., U.S. Golf Assn. Home and Office: 15791 Rica Vista Way San Jose CA 95127-2735

SANDERS, AUGUSTA SWANN, retired nurse; b. Alexandria, La., July 22, 1932; d. James and Elizabeth (Thompson) Swann; m. James Robert Sanders, Jan. 12, 1962 (div. 1969). Student, Morgan State U., 1956. Pub. health nurse USPHS, Washington, 1963-64; mental health counselor Los Angeles County Sheriff's Dept., 1972-79; program coordinator Los Angeles County Dept. Mental Health, 1979-88; program dir. L.A. County Dept. Health Svcs., 1989-92; ret., 1992; apptd. by Calif. Gov. Jerry Brown to 11th Dist. Bd. Med. Quality Assurance, 1979-85; health cons., legal, 1994—; motivational spkr. Mem. Assemblyman Mike Roo's Commn. on Women's Issues, 1981—, Senator Diane Watson's Commn. on Health Issues, 1979—; chmn. Commn. Sex. Equity Los Angeles Unified Sch. Dist., 1984-90; pres. Victor Valley Bus. and Profl. Women Adminstrn.; mem. edn. com. Victor Valley African Am. C. of C. Named Woman of Yr., Crenshaw-Latijera Local Orgn., 1988, Victor Valley Local Orgn., 1994. Mem. NAFE, L.A. County Employees Assn. (v.p. 1971-72), So. Calif. Black Nurses Assn. (founding mem.), Internat. Fedn. Bus. and Profl. Women (pres. L.A. Sunset dist. 1988-89, dist. officer 1982-89, Calif. v.p. membership and mktg. 1995-96), Internat. Assn. Chemical Dependency Nurses (treas. 1990-92), Victor Valley Bus. and Profl. Women (pres. 1997—), High Desert LWV (founder), High Desert Intercoun. of Women's Orgns., Am. C. of C. (adminstrn.-ednl. chmn.), Chi Eta Phi. Democrat. Methodist.

SANDERS, DAVID CLYDE, management and marketing consultant; b. Lubbock, Tex., Oct. 8, 1946; s. Jasper Clyde and Mary Jo (Baber) S.; m. Barbara Ann Huck 1976 (div. July 1983); m. Marcia Lynn Fik, Nov. 20, 1983; children: Ashton Harrison, Geoffrey Davidson. Student, U. Tex., 1964; BA, Tex. Tech. U., 1969; postgrad., So. Meth. U., 1969-70, U. Tex., 1970-71. Exec., auditor Ch. Scientology Tex., Austin, 1971-75; exec., cons. Expansion Consultants, L.A., 1975-77; cons. pub. relations Exec. Mgmt. Specialists, L.A., 1977-80; exec. dir. Inst. for Fin. Independence, Glendale, Calif., 1980-83; mktg. dir. Michael Baybak & Co., Beverly Hills, Calif., 1983-85; sr. cons., ptnr. Mgmt. Tech. Consultants, L.A., 1985-86; sr. cons. Sterling Mgmt. Systems, Glendale, 1986-93, sr. v.p., 1988-89, exec. coun. mem., exec. establishment officer, 1988-89, advanced cons., 1989-93; workshop instr., exec. mgmt. and mktg. cons. Mgmt. Success!, Glendale, Calif., 1992-96; ptnr., sr. cons. Expansion Cons., Montrose, Calif., 1996—; spkr., ptnr. JPR & Assocs., L.A., 1985-88; pres. Prosperity Assocs., 1990—; direct distbr. 1991-93; Ruby Direct Distbn. Amway Corp., 1993—. Author, Sanders Newsletter, 1983-88. Co-founder, pres. Bus. Adv. Bur. So. Calif., Huntington Beach, 1977-79; founder, exec. dir. Bus. Adv. Bur. Internat., 1995; mem., contbr. Citizen's Commn. on Human Rights, L.A., 1976—; cofounder Vol. Ministers L.A., 1977-78. Mem. World Inst. Scientology Enterprises (charter), Internat. Hubbard Ecclesiastical League of Pastors, Citizens for Alternative Tax Sys. (sustaining), Friends of Narconon Chilocco New Life Ctr., Internat. Assn. Scientologists (founding mem.), Alpha Phi Omega (sec. Tex. Tech U. chpt. 1965-69). Republican. Home: 4648 Lasheart Dr La Canada CA 91011-2125 Office: Expansion Cons 2609 Honolulu Ave Ste 203 Montrose CA 91020

SANDERS, JERRY, protective services official; b. San Pedro, Calif., July 14, 1950; m. Rana Sampson; children: Jamie, Lisa. AA, Long Beach City Coll., 1970; BA in Pub. Adminstrn., Nat. U., 1988; postgrad., San Diego State U. Cert. P.O.S.T mgmt. Police officer San Diego Police Dept., 1973-93, chief of police, 1993—. Bd. dirs. NCCJ, San Diego State U. Cmty. Adv. Bd., Children's Initiative, Youth Econ. Enterprise Zones; mem. cmty. leaders adv. bd. ElderHelp of San Diego. Recipient Headliner of Yr. award San Diego Press Club, 1984, 93, Exceptional Performance citation for SWAT leadership, 1986. Office: San Diego Police Dept 1401 Broadway San Diego CA 92101-5710

SANDERS, NANCY IDA, writer; b. Everett, Pa., May 17, 1960; d. Richard J. and Phyllis (Harden) Hershberger; m. Jeffrey L. Sanders, May 23, 1982; children: Daniel M., Benjamin L. Freelance writer, 1985—; editor TCC Manuscript Svc.; contbg. editor The Christian Communicator; leader Chino Hills Writers Critique Group. Author: Favorite Bible Heroes: Activities for Ages 4 and 5, 1993, Bible Crafts on a Shoestring Budget for Grades 3 and 4, 1993, Amazing Bible Puzzles: Old Testament, 1993, Amazing Bible Puzzles: New Testament, 1993, Jumbo Bible Bulletin Boards: More Bible Stories for Preschool and Primary, 1994, Jumbo Bible Bulleton Boards: Fall and Winter, Preschool and Primary, 1994, Jonah: Six Fun Surprises, 1994, Moses: Six Fun Surprises, 1994, My Book About Ben and Me, 1994, My Book About Sara and Me, 1994, Cents-ible Bible Crafts, 1995, The Fall into Sin, 1995, Jesus Walks on the Water, 1995, WA-A-A-AY COOL Bible Puzzles, 1996, Red Hot Bible Puzzles, 1996, Marshal Matt and the Slippery Snacks Mystery, 1996, Marshal Matt and the Case of the Secret Code, 1996, Marshal Matt and the Topsy-Turvy Trail Mystery, 1996, Marshal Matt and the Puzzling Prints Mystery. Mem. Soc. Children's Book Writers and Illustrators. Home: 15212 Mariposa Ave Chino Hills CA 91709

SANDERS, RICHARD BROWNING, state supreme court justice; b. Tacoma; m. Kathleen Sanders; children: Amy, Brien, Laura. BA, U. Wash., 1966, JD, 1969. Assoc. Murray, Scott, McGavrils & Graves, Tacoma, Wash., 1969, Caplinger & Munn, Seattle, 1971; hearing examiner State Wash., Olympia, 1970; pvt. practice Wash., 1971-95; justice Wash. Supreme Ct., Olympia, 1995—; lectr. in field. Contbr. articles to profl. jours. Office: Temple of Justice PO Box 40929 Olympia WA 98504

SANDERS, RICHARD JEREMIAH, vascular surgeon, medical educator; b. Detroit, Jan. 26, 1931; s. Alexander and Rebecca Sanders; m. Joanne Phillips, Sept. 7, 1952; children: Debbie Carlton, David. BS, U. Mich., 1950, MS, 1954. Intern U. Colo., Denver, 1954-55, clin. prof. surgery, 1960—; resident in surgery U. Mich., Ann Arbor, 1955-56, 58-60; fellow in surgery Nat. Heart Inst., Bethesda, Md., 1956-58. Author: Anatomy of Skiing, 1979, Thoracic Outlet Syndrome, 1991. Mem. Soc. Vascular Surgery, Rocky Mountain Vascular Soc. (past pres.). Office: 4545 E 9th Ave Ste 240 Denver CO 80220-3909

SANDERS, WALTER JEREMIAH, III, electronics company executive; b. Chgo., Sept. 12, 1936. BEE, U. Ill., 1958. Design engr. Douglas Aircraft Co., Santa Monica, Calif., 1958-59; applications engr. Motorola, Inc., Phoenix, 1959-60; sales engr. Motorola, Inc., 1960-61; with Fairchild Camera & Instrument Co., 1961-69; dir. mktg. Fairchild Camera & Instrument Co., Mountain View, Calif., 1961-68, group dir. mktg. worldwide, 1968-69; pres. Advanced Micro Devices Inc., Sunnyvale, Calif., until 1987, chmn. bd., chief exec. officer, 1969—; dir. Donaldson, Lufkin & Jenrette. Mem. Semicondr. Industry Assn. (co-founder, dir.), Santa Clara County Mfg. Group (co-founder, dir.). Office: Advanced Micro Devices Inc PO Box 3453 One AMD Pl Sunnyvale CA 94086-3453*

SANDERS, WILLIAM JOHN, research scientist; b. Detroit, July 10, 1940; s. John William and Charlotte Barbara (Linsday) Steele; m. Gary Roberts, Sept. 12, 1961; children: Scott David, Susan Deborah. BS, U. Mich., 1962; MSEE, U. Calif., Berkeley, 1964. Sr. rsch. scientist Stanford (Calif.) U., 1967—; pres. Sanders Data Systems, 1991—; pres. Computers in Cardiology, 1990-93. Inventor cardiac probe; contbr. articles to profl. jours. Mem. IEEE Computer Soc., Assn. Computing Machinery. Home: 3980 Bibbits Dr Palo Alto CA 94303-4531 Office: Stanford U Med Ctr Cardiovasc Medicine Stanford CA 94305

SANDERSON, CATHY ANN, histotechnician, researcher; b. Key West, Fla., Apr. 12, 1954; d. Robert Gary and Cheri Dae (Colin) S.; 1 child, Nichole Renee. Grad. h.s., Phoenix, Ariz., 1972. Histology trainee St. Luke's Medical Ctr., Phoenix, 1972-73, histotechnician, 1973-83; histotechnician/rsch. Harrington Arthritis Rsch. Ctr., Phoenix, 1983-87, Emory U., Atlanta, 1987-88, VA Medical Ctr, Salt Lake City, 1988—; founder, chair hard tissue com. Nat. Soc. Histotech., Bowie, Md., 1989—, editor, 1992—, vet. indsl. rsch. com., 1989—, health and safety com., 1988—, mem. ednl. com., 1989-91; owner Wasatch Histo Cons., 1988—. Mem. editl. bd. Jour. Histotechnology, 1993—; contbr. articles to numerous profl. jours. Organizer Neighborhood Watch, West Valley City, Utah, 1993—. Named Histotechnologist of Yr., Nat. Soc. Histotechnology, 1992; recipient Hacker Instruments; Membership Incentive award, 1991-92, Superior Performance award, 1989-92, 95-96, William J. Hacker award, 1988, Rsch. Technician of Yr. award, 1989. Mem. Nat. Wildlife Fedn., Nat. Arbor Day Found., Utah Soc. Histotechnology, Am. Assn. Lab Animal Sci. (bd. dirs. 1989-91), The Cousteau Soc., Inc., Nat. Soc. Histotechnology. Office: VA Medical Ctr 500 Foothill Blvd 151F Salt Lake City UT 84148

SANDFORD, PAUL ALLAN, biomedical laboratory director, biochemist; b. Milford, Mich., Nov. 24, 1939; s. Federick Tom and Alice Ruth (Howland) S.; m. Caryl Ann Needham, Aug. 26, 1961; children: Thad Arthur, Amy Kathleen Sandford. AB in Chemistry and Math., Albion Coll., 1962; PhD in Biochemistry, U. Ill., 1967. Sr. rsch. scientist Ag. Rsch. Svc. NRRC, Peoria, 1967-77; rsch. fellow, mgr. new ventures Kelco (divsn. of Merck & Co.), San Diego, 1977-86; dir. bioapplications Protan, Inc., Woodinville, Wash., 1986-90; v.p., tech. devel. VivoRx, Inc., Santa Monica, 1990—; pres. P. A. Sandford & Affiliates, Del Mar, Calif., 1985—; chmn. Gordon Rsch. Conf. Chemistry Carbohydrates, 1979-81. Editor: Excocellular Microbial Polysaccharides, 1978, Fungal Polysaccharides, 1980, Chitin and Chitosan, 1989, Advances in Chitin and Chitosan, 1992, Internat. Jour. Carbohydrate Polymers, 1982—; contbr. numerous articles to sci. jours.; co-patentee in field. NIH fellow, 1962-67. Mem. Am. Chem. Soc. (chmn. Peoria sect. 1977-78, chmn. carbohybrate divsn. 1978-79, chmn. San Diego sect. 1981-82), Am. Chitosci. Soc. (co-founder). Home: 2822 Overland Ave Los Angeles CA 90064-4218 Office: VivoRx Inc 2825 Santa Monica Blvd Santa Monica CA 90404-4214

SANDHU, GURTEJ SINGH, engineer, researcher; b. London, Eng., Oct. 24, 1960; came to U.S., 1985; s. Sarjit S. and Gurmit K. (Minhas) S.; m. Sukesh Guleria, June 21, 1987; children: Gureet, Suntej. MS, Indian Inst. Tech., Delhi, 1985; PhD, U. N.C., Chapel Hill, 1989. Process devel. engr. Micron Semiconductor Inc., Boise, Idaho, 1989-91, sr. engr., 1991-93, sect. head, 1993—. Contbr. more than 40 articles to profl. jours.; patentee in field. Mem. IEEE, Electrochem. Soc., Am. Phys. Soc., Materials Rsch. Soc. Office: Micron Technology Inc 8000 S Federal Way Boise ID 83716-9624

SANDLER, HERBERT M., savings and loan association executive; b. N.Y.C., Nov. 16, 1931; s. William B. and Hilda (Schattan) S.; m. Marion Osher, Mar. 26, 1961. BSS, CCNY, 1951; JD, Columbia U., 1954. Bar: N.Y. 1956. Asst. counsel Waterfront Commn. N.Y. Harbor, 1956-59; partner firm Sandler & Sandler, N.Y.C., 1960-62; pres., dir., mem. exec. com. Golden West Savs. & Loan Assn. and Golden West Fin. Corp., Oakland, Calif., 1963-75; chmn. bd., co-chief exec. officer, dir., mem. exec. com. World Savs. & Loan Assn. and Golden West Fin. Corp., Oakland, 1975—; charter mem. Thrift Instns. Adv. Coun., to Fed. Res. Bd., 1980-81; former chmn. Legis. and Regulation Com. Calif. Savs. and Loan League; former mem. bd. dirs. Fed. Home Loan Bank, San Francisco. Pres., trustee Calif. Neighborhood Services Found.; chmn. Urban Housing Inst.; mem. policy adv. bd. Ctr. for Real Estate and Urban Econs. U. Calif., Berkeley. With U.S. Army, 1954-56. Office: Golden W Fin Corp 1901 Harrison St Oakland CA 94612-3574*

SANDLER, MARION OSHER, savings and loan association executive; b. Biddeford, Maine, Oct. 17, 1930; d. Samuel and Leah (Lowe) Osher; m. Herbert M. Sandler, Mar. 26, 1961. BA, Wellesley Coll., 1952; postgrad., Harvard U.-Radcliffe Coll., 1953; MBA, NYU, 1958; LLD (hon.), Golden Gate U., 1987. Asst. buyer Bloomingdale's (dept. store), N.Y.C., 1953-55; security analyst Dominick & Dominick, N.Y.C., 1955-61; sr. fin. analyst Oppenheimer & Co., N.Y.C., 1961-63; sr. v.p., dir. Golden West Fin. Corp. and World Savs. & Loan Assn., Oakland, Calif., 1963-75, vice chmn. bd. dirs., CEO, mem. exec. com., dir., 1975-80, pres., co- chief exec. officer, dir., mem. exec. com., 1980-93, chmn. bd. dirs., CEO, mem. exec. com., 1993—; pres., chmn. bd. dirs., CEO Atlas Assets, Inc., Oakland, 1987—, Atlas Advisers, Inc., Oakland, 1987—, Atlas Securities, Inc., Oakland, 1987—; mem. adv. com. Fed. Nat. Mortgage Assn., 1983-84. Mem. Pres.'s Mgmt. Improvement Coun., 1980, Thrift Insts. Adv. Coun. to Fed. Res. Bd., 1989-91, v.p., 1990, pres., 1991; mem. policy adv. bd. Ctr. for Real Estate and Urban Econs. U. Calif., Berkeley, 1981—, mem. exec. com. policy adv. bd., 1985—; mem. ad hoc com. to rev. Schs. Bus. Adminstrn. U. Calif., 1984-85; vice chmn. industry adv. com. Fed. Savs. and Loan Ins. Corp., 1987-88, Ins. Corp., 1987-88; bd. overseers NYU Schs. Bus., 1987-89; mem. Glass Ceiling Commn., 1992-93. Mem. Phi Beta Kappa, Beta Gamma Sigma. Office: Golden W Fin Corp 1901 Harrison St Oakland CA 94612-3574*

SANDOVAL, ISABELLE MEDINA, human resources specialist; b. Laramie, Wyo., Sept. 30, 1948; d. John Ben and Ida Medina Sandoval; 1 child, Tomas Andres Duran. BA, U. N.Mex., 1970; MA, U. Mo., 1976; EdD, U. Wyo., 1982. Cert. Spanish, reading, English, adminstrn. Tchr. Spanish and English Menaul Sch., Albuquerque, 1971-73; tchr. bilingual edn. and reading Kansas City, Mo., 1973-78; tchr. title I Sch. Dist. #60, Pueblo, Colo., 1978-83; adminstr. Sch. Dist. #60, Pueblo, 1983-88, Acad. Dist. 20, Colorado Springs, Colo., 1988-95; human resources coord. Harrison Dist. 2, Colorado Springs, 1995—; v.p. Hispano Crypto Jewish Resource Ctr., Denver. Author of poetry. Mem. Geneal. Soc. Hispanic Am., Colo. Assn. Sch. Pers. Assn., Soc. for Crypto Judaic Studies, Hispano Luncheon Club, Phi Kappa Phi, Kappa Delta Phi, Phi Delta Kappa. Jewish. Home: 4005 Thundercloud Colorado Springs CO 80920 Office: Harrison Sch Dist 1060 Harrison Rd Colorado Springs CO 80906

SANDRICH, JAY H., television director; b. L.A., Feb. 24, 1932; s. Mark R. and Freda (Wirtschafter) S.; m. Nina Kramer, Feb. 11, 1952 (div.); children: Eric, Tony, Wendy; m. Linda Green Silverstein, Oct. 4, 1984. BA, UCLA, 1953. Producer (TV show) Get Smart, 1965; dir. (TV shows) He and She, 1967, Mary Tyler Moore Show, 1970-88, Soap, 1977-79, Cosby Show, 1984-92; dir. (films) Seems Like Old Times, 1980, For Richer, For Poorer (HBO), 1992, Neil Simon's London Suite (NBC), 1996. Served to 1st lt. Signal Corps U.S. Army, 1952-55. Mem. Dirs. Guild Am. (award 1975, 85, 86), TV Acad. Arts and Scis. (Emmy award 1971, 73, 85, 86).

SANDS, SHARON LOUISE, graphic design executive, art publisher, artist; b. Jacksonville, Fla., July 4, 1944; d. Clifford Harding Sands and Ruby May (Ray) MacDonald; m. Jonathan Michael Langford, Feb. 14, 1988. BFA, Cen. Washington U., 1968; postgrad, UCLA, 1968. Art dir. East West Network, Inc., L.A., 1973-78, Daisy Pub., L.A., 1978; prodn. dir. L.A. mag., 1979-80; owner, creative dir. Carmel Graphic Design, Carmel Valley, Calif., 1981-85; creative dir., v.p. The Video Sch. House, Monterey, Calif., 1985-88; graphic designer ConAgra, ConAgra, Nebr., 1988; owner, creative dir. Esprit de Fleurs, Ltd., Carmel, Calif., 1988—; lectr. Pub. Expo, L.A., 1979, panelist Women in Mgmt., L.A., 1979; redesign of local newspaper, Carmel, Calif., 1982. Contbr. articles to profl. mags. Designer corp. ID for Carmel Valey C. of C., 1981, 90. Recipient 7 design awards Soc. Pub. Designers, 1977, 78, Maggie award, L.A., 1977, 5 design awards The Ad Club of Monterey Peninsula, 1983, 85, 87, Design awards Print Mag. N.Y., 1986, Desi awards, N.Y., 1986, 88. Mem. NAFE, Soc. for Prevention of Cruelty to Animals, Greenpeace. Democrat. Home and Office: 15489 Via La Gitana Carmel Valley CA 93924-9669

SANDSTROM, ROBERT EDWARD, physician, pathologist; b. Hull, Yorkshire, Eng., Apr. 4, 1946; came to U.S., 1946; s. Edward Joseph and Ena Joyce (Rilatt) S.; m. Regina Lois Charlebois (dec. May 1987); children: Karin, Ingrid, Erica. BSc, McGill U., Montreal, 1968; MD, U. Wash., 1971. Diplomate Am. Bd. Pathology, Am. Bd. Dermatopathology. Internship Toronto (Can.) Gen. Hosp., 1971-72; resident pathologist Mass. Gen. Hosp., Boston, 1974-78; clin. fellow Harvard U. Med. Sch., Boston, 1976-78; cons. King Faisel Hosp., Riyadh, Saudi Arabia, 1978; pathologist, v.p. St. John's Med. Ctr., Longview, Wash., 1996—; v.p. Intersect Systems Inc., Longview, Wash., 1990—; chmn. bd. Cowlitz Med. Svc., Longview, 1988; participant congl. sponsored seminar on AIDS, Wash., 1987. Script writer movie Blood Donation in Saudi Arabia, 1978; contbr. articles to profl. jours. Surgeon USPHS, 1972-74. Fellow Coll. Am. Pathologists, Royal Coll. Physicians; mem. Cowlitz-Wahkiakum County Med. Soc. (past pres.). Roman Catholic. Home: 49 View Ridge Ln Longview WA 98632-5556 Office: Lower Columbia Pathologists 1606 E Kessler Blvd Ste 100 Longview WA 98632-1841

SANFORD, ALLAN ROBERT, research seismologist, educator; b. Pasadena, Calif., Apr. 25, 1927; s. Roscoe Frank and Mabel Aline (Dyer) S.; m. Alice Elaine Carlson, Aug. 31, 1956; children: Robert Allan, Colleen Ann. BA, Pomona, 1949; MS, Caltech, 1954, PhD, 1958. Asst. prof. NMex. Tech. U., Socorro, N.M., 1957-64; assoc. prof. N.Mex. Tech. U., Socorro, 1964-68, coord. geophysics program, 1978—, prof., 1968-97, prof. emeritus, 1997—. Contbr. articles to profl. jours. With USN, 1945-46. Recipient Disting. Rsch. award New Mex. Tech., 1985. Mem. Am. Geophyscial Union, Am. Assn. Advancement Sci. (fellow 1964), Soc. Exploration Geophysicists, Seismological Soc. Am., Sigma Xi. Home: 1302 North Dr Socorro NM 87801-4442 Office: NMex Tech U Earth and Environ Sci Dept Socorro NM 87801

SANFORD, DAVID ROY, journalist, educator; b. Seattle, Apr. 6, 1959; s. Roy Arnold and Venetta Maxine (Johnson) S.; m. Renée Shawn Hord, Sept. 11, 1982; children: Elizabeth, Shawna, Jonathan, Benjamin. BS in Religious Edn. with hons., Multnomah Bible Coll., Portland, Oreg., 1982. Dir. print media Luis Palau Evangelistic Assn., Portland, 1983—; adj. prof. Western Bapt. Coll., Salem, Oreg., 1995—; lectr. in field, literary agent. Contbg. author: More Than Conquerors, 1992 (Gold Medallion 1993); co-author: Calling America & the Nations to Christ, 1994, God Is Relevant, 1997; editor over 30 books; contbr. articles to profl. jours.; editl. cons., 1990—; freelance writer, editor, 1982— . Spkr. Portland Pub. Schs., 1990—; lay pastor Spring Mountain Bible Ch., 1991—; dir., v.p. alumni bd. Multnomah Bible Coll, 1993—. Mem. Evang. Press Assn. (Merit award 1991, 92, Excellence award 1996), Delta Epsilon Chi. Home: 6406 NE Pacific St Portland OR 97213-4930 Office: Luis Palau Evang Assn 1500 NW 167th Pl Beaverton OR 97006-4885

SANFORD, LEROY LEONARD, rancher; b. Sanford Ranch, Wyo., June 24, 1934; s. Claude Leonard and Herminnie May (Brockmeyer) S.; m. Barbara Jo Shackleford, June 15, 1965 (dec. Oct. 1965); stepchildren: Christina Pedley, Marlena McCollum, Diana Sumners; 1 foster child, Catherine Frost. Cert. satellite geodesy, Johns Hopkins U., 1971; cert. astron. geodecy, U.S. Geol. Survey-Branch R & D, 1971. Cert. Geodesic Surveyor. Rancher Sanford Ranch, Douglas, Wyo., 1952-57; topographer, photogrametrist U.S. Geol. Survey-Topog. Divsn.-Hdqs., Denver, 1957-81; rancher Sanford Ranch, Douglas, 1981—; speaker various schs. and community orgns. Congl. Svc. medal U.S. Congress, 1972. Mem. NRA (patron), Am. Solar Energy Soc., Antarctican Soc., Wyo. Farm Bur. Republican. Home: 400 Windy Ridge Rd Douglas WY 82633-0145 *Early on I ran across this saying; author unknown to me, "Why is there never enough time to do it right, but always enough time to do it over?" I feel that anyone's time spent"doing it over" is wasted unless it is to do something better in light of new knowledge. Anything I build now will last longer than me and I want it to survive until the next technological leap forward.*

SANFORD, ROBERT STANLEY, physician, urologist; b. N.Y.C., July 5, 1938; s. Emanuel and Ruth (Rosen) S.; children: Michael, Meredith, Melissa. BS, Bklyn. Coll., 1959; MD, N.Y. Med. Coll., 1964. Diplomate Am. Bd. Urology. Commd. 2d lt. U.S. Army, 1966, advanced through grades to capt., 1968; intern Cedars of Lebanon, L.A., 1964-65; resident Jewish Hosp. & Med. Ctr., Bklyn., 1965-71; urologist Beverly Hills, Calif., 1971—; chief urology Cedars Sinai Med. Ctr., L.A., 1983-87; clin. asst., prof. urology U. So. Calif. Sch. of Medicine, 1993—; attending staff mem. Cedars Sinai. Fellow Am. Coll. Surgeons. Office: 414 N Camden Dr Ste 650 Beverly Hills CA 90210-4532

SANGUINETTI, EUGENE FRANK, art museum administrator, educator; b. Yuma, Ariz., May 12, 1917; s. Eugene F. and Lilah (Balsz) S.; children: Leslie, Gregory. BA, U. Santa Clara, 1939; postgrad., U. Ariz., 1960-62. Instr. art history U. Ariz., Tucson, 1960-64; dir. Tucson Mus. and Art Ctr., 1964-67, Utah Mus. Fine Arts, Salt Lake City, 1967—; adj. prof. art history U. Utah, Salt Lake City, 1967—. Contbr. articles to profl. jours. Served with USAAF, 1942-44, to capt. M.I., U.S. Army, 1944-46. Mem. Am. Assn. Museums, Am. Assn. Mus. Dirs., Am. Fedn. of Arts, Coll. Art Assn., Western Assn. Art Museums, Salt Lake City C. of C. Home: 30 S St Salt Lake City UT 84103-4133

SANKAR, SUBRAMANIAN VAIDYA, aerospace engineer; b. New Delhi, India, June 22, 1959; came to U.S. 1982; s. V.S.S. and Bala (Sankar) Narayanan; m. Asha Govindarajan, July 31, 1988; children: Sitara, Ankita. B.Tech., Indian Inst. Tech., Madras, 1982; MSAE, Ga. Inst. Tech., Atlanta, 1983; PhD, Ga. Inst. Tech., 1987. R & D dir. Aerometrics, Inc., Sunnyvale, Calif., 1987—. Contbr. articles to profl. jours. J.N. Tata scholar, India. Mem. AIAA, AAAS, Nat. Geog. Soc., ILASS. Home: 34211 Petard Ter Fremont CA 94555-2611 Office: Aerometrics Inc 755 N Mary Ave Sunnyvale CA 94086-2909

SANKOVICH, JOSEPH BERNARD, cemetery management consultant; b. Johnstown, Pa., Feb. 6, 1944; s. Joseph George and Helen Mary (Kasprzyk) S. Student, St. Francis Sem., 1964-68; BA, St. Francis Coll., 1966; postgrad., St. John Provincial Sem., 1968-69; MA, U. Detroit, 1973. Cert. cemetery exec., cath. cemetery exec., profl. cons. Assoc. pastor St. Mary's Ch., Nanty Glo, Pa., 1970-71, Sacred Heart Ch., Dearborn, Mich., 1971-74; dir. Mt. Kelly Cemetery, Dearborn, 1972-84; admissions counselor U. Detroit, 1974-81; dir. religious edn. St. James Ch., Ferndale, Mich., 1981-84; exec. Diocesan Cemetery Cons., Wyoming, Pa., 1984-86; dir. cemeteries Archdiocese of Seattle, 1986-91; mgmt. cons., owner Joseph B. Sankovich & Assocs., Edmonds, Wash., 1991—; cons. Archdiocese St. Paul and Mpls., 1990—, Diocese San Diego, 1991—, Archdiocese Santa Fe, 1991—, Diocese Tucson, 1991—, Diocese Toledo, 1992—, Diocese Saginaw, 1992—, Archdiocese Edmonton, Alta., Can., 1993—, Diocese Monterrey, 1993—, Diocese Fresno, Calif., 1994—, Archdiocese Anchorage, 1995, Diocese Gaylord, Mich., 1996; interim dir. cemeteries Diocese Saginaw, 1995-96; mem. Task Force on Cremation of Bishops Com. on Liturgy Nat. Conf. Cath. Bishops, 1990-92; instr. A. Cemetery Assn. Univ. Ops./Maintenance, 1994. Author, editor: Directory of Western Catholic Cemeteries, 1992, 94; author mgmt. assessments, sales programs, market analyses, 1986—; contbr. articles to profl. jours. Trustee St. Patrick's Cathedral Archdiocese N.Y., 1997. Mem. Internat. Cemetery and Funeral Assn., Nat. Cath. Cemetery Conf., Wash. Interment Assn. (bd. dirs. 1990-91), Cath. Cemeteries of the West (founder 1987, governancy com. 1987-90). Address: Joseph B Sankovich & Assocs 9216 240th St SW Edmonds WA 98020-5600

SANNWALD, WILLIAM WALTER, librarian; b. Chgo., Sept. 12, 1940; s. William Frederick and Irene Virginia (Stanish) S.; children: Sara Ann, William Howard. B.A., Beloit Coll., 1963; M.A.L.S., Rosary Coll., River Forest, Ill., 1966; M.B.A., Loyola U., Chgo., 1974. Mktg. mgr. Xerox Univ. Microfilms, 1972-75; assoc. dir. Detroit Public Library, 1975-77; dir. Ventura (Calif.) County Library, 1977-79; city libr. San Diego Public Libr., 1979—; vis. instr. mktg. San Diego State U. Author: Checklist of Library Building Design Considerations, 3d edit., 1997; chairperson editorial adv. bd. Pub. Librs. Pres. Met. Libraries Sect., 1989. Recipient Outstanding Prof. award and Outstanding Mktg. Prof. award, 1985; Award of Merit AIA San Diego chpt., 1988, Irving Gill award for Architecture and Mgmt., 1995. Mem. ALA, Online Computer Libr. Ctr. (mem. users coun. 1996), Calif. Library Authority for Systems and Services (pres. congress of mems. 1980), Calif. Library Assn., Libr. Admintrn. and Mgmt. Assn. (pres. 1995—). Roman Catholic. Home: 3538 Paseo Salamoner La Mesa CA 91941-7329 Office: San Diego Pub Libr 820 E St San Diego CA 92101-6416

SANO, EMILY J., museum director; b. Santa Ana, Calif., Feb. 17, 1942; d. Masao and Lois Kikue (Inokuchi) S. BA, Ind. U., 1967; MA, Columbia U., 1970, MPhil, 1976, PhD, 1983. Lectr. Oriental Art Vassar Coll., Poughkeepsie, N.Y., 1974-79; curator Asian Art, asst. dir. programs Kimbell Art Mus., Ft. Worth, 1979-89; dep. dir. collections and exhbns. Dallas Mus. Art, 1989-92; dep. dir., chief curator Asian Art Mus., San Francisco, 1993-95, dir., 1995—. Author: Great Age of Japanese Buddhist Sculpture, 1982; editor: The Blood of Kings, 1986, Weavers, Merchants and Kings, 1984, Painters of the Great Ming, 1993. Bd. dirs. Coll. Art Assn., N.Y.C., 1990-94. Woodrow Wilson Fellow, 1966-67; grantee Carnegie, 1963-64, Fulbright-Hays, 1977-78. Office: Asian Art Mus Golden Gate Park San Francisco CA 94118•

SANO, ROY I., bishop. Ordained to ministry United Meth. Ch., later consecrated bishop; appointed Bishop Rocky Mountain Conf., United Meth. Ch., Denver. Office: PO Box 6006 Pasadena CA 91102-6006

SANSWEET, STEPHEN JAY, journalist, author, marketing executive; b. Phila., June 14, 1945; s. Jack Morris and Fannie (Axelrod) S. BS, Temple U., 1966. Reporter Phila. Inquirer, 1966-69; reporter Wall Street Jour., Phila., 1969-71, Montreal, Que, Can., 1971-73; reporter Wall Street Jour., L.A., 1973-84, dep. bur. chief, 1984-87, bur. chief, 1987-96; dir. speciality mktg. Lucasfilm Ltd., San Rafael, Calif., 1996—; sr. editor Star Wars Galaxy Mag., 1996—; lectr. bus. journalism U. So. Calif., L.A., 1984-87. Author: The Punishment Cure, 1976, Science Fiction Toys and Models, 1981, Star Wars: From Concept to Screen to Collectible, 1992, Tomart's Guide to Worldwide Star Wars Collectibles, 1994, The Quotable Star Wars, 1996; cons. editor: Star Wars Galaxy, 1993, 2d series, 1994, 3d series, 1995; editor: Star Wars Trilogy Spl. Edn. card sets, 1997. Recipient award for best fire story Phila. Fire Dept., 1968, Pub. Svc.-Team Mem. award Sigma Delta Chi, 1977; finalist Loeb award, 1990. Mem. Soc. Profl. Journalists. Office: Lucasfilm Ltd PO Box 2009 San Rafael CA 94912-2009

SANTAVICCA, EDMUND FRANK, information scientist; b. Detroit, Jan. 4, 1947. BA in Comparative Lit., French, Wayne State U., 1968, MA in French, 1972; AMLS, U. Mich., 1971, PhD of Libr. and Info. Sci., 1977. Cert. hypnotherapist, Atwood Inst., 1996. Bibliographer U. Va., Charlottesville, 1971-74; asst. prof. libr. sci. Vanderbilt U., Nashville, 1979-81; bibliographer, head collection mgmt. svcs. Cleve. State U., 1983-89; head reference svcs. Ariz. State U., Tempe, 1990-94; faculty info. access Estrella Mountain C.C., Avondale, Ariz., 1994-95; dir. info. resources Estrella Mountain C.C., Avondale, 1995—. Author: Reference Work in the Humanities, 1980, Four French Dramatists, 1974, (play) Maximum Tumescence, 1989, Faux Sexe, 1992. Concurrence de poesie French Govt., 1969; recipient Pres.'s Program award Libr. Adminstn. and Mgmt. Assn., 1986; named Writer-in-Residence Found. Karolyi, 1989. Mem. ALA, Nat. Assn. Transpersonal Psych. Office: Estrella Mountain CC 3000 N Dysart Rd Avondale AZ 85323

SANTEE, DALE WILLIAM, lawyer, air force officer; b. Washington, Pa., Mar. 28, 1953; s. Robert Erwin and Elsbeth Emma (Bantleon) S.; married; 1 child, Enri De'Von; m. Junko Mori, June 2, 1992. BA, Washington & Jefferson Coll., 1975; MA, U. No. Ariz., 1982; JD, U. Pitts., 1978. Bar: Pa. 1978, U.S. Ct. Mil. Appeals 1979, Calif. 1989. Floor mgr., commn. salesman J.C. Penney Co., Washington, Pa., 1971-76; asst. mgr. Rach Enterprises, Charleroi, Pa., 1977-78; legal intern Washington County Pub. Defender; commd. 2d lt. USAF, 1979, advanced through grades to lt. col., 1996; from asst. staff judge advocate to area def. counsel Luke Air Force Base, Ariz., 1979-81; claims officer 343 Combat Support Group/Judge Advocate, Eielson AFB, Alaska, 1981-83; sr. staff legal adviser Dept. Vet. Affairs, Washington, 1983-89; asst. staff judge advocate Mil. Justice div. Air Force Judge Advocate Gen.'s Office, Washington, 1986-89, 63CSG/Judge Advocate, Norton Air Force Base, Calif., 1989-91; dep. pub. defender Juvenile div. San Diego County, 1990-93, dep. alt. pub. defender, 1993—; dep. staff judge advocate 452 AMW/Judge Advocate, March Air Res. Base, Calif., 1991—; v.p. Neuer Enterprises, Nanjemoy, Md., 1983-89; participant Mgmt. Devel. Seminar, 1988. Mem. San Diego County Rep. Party; pres., co-chmn. legis. com. PTA Zamorano Elem. Sch., San Diego, chmn. SITE com.; mem. San Diego County Child Abuse Coord. Coun., San Diego County Commn. on Children and Youth, San Diego County Juvenile Ct. Mental Health Task Force, San Diego County Unified Sch. Dist. Parent Adv. Coun., San Diego County Youth Ct., program bd. dirs.; bd. dirs. Pub. Defenders Assn., Train Ct. Apptd. Spl. Advocates for Voices for Children. Decorated Air Force Commendation medal, 1981, 89, Air Force Meritorious Svc. medal, 1991, 96; named Outstanding Young Man of Am., U.S. Jaycees, Montgomery, Ala., 1981; acad. scholar Washington & Jefferson Coll., 1971-75, Beta scholar Washington & Jefferson Coll., 1974, Pa. Senatorial scholar Pa. Senate, 1975, 76, 77, 78. Mem. Pa. Bar Assn., Calif. Bar Assn., San Diego County Bar Assn., San Diego County Psych-Law Soc. Home: 1156 Corrales Ln Chula Vista CA 91910-7956

SANTILLAN, ANTONIO, financial company executive; b. Buenos Aires, May 8, 1936; naturalized, 1966; s. Guillermo Spika and Raphaella C. (Abaladejo) S.; children: Andrea, Miguel, Marcos. Grad., Morgan Park Mil. Acad., Chgo., 1954; BS in Psychology, Coll. of William and Mary, 1958. Cert. real estate broker. Asst. in charge of prodn. Wilding Studios, Chgo., 1964; pres. Adams Fin. Services, Los Angeles, 1965—. Writer, producer, dir. (motion pictures) The Glass Cage, co-writer Dirty Mary/Crazy Harry, Viva Knievel; contbg. writer Once Upon a Time in America; TV panelist Window on Wall Street; contbr. articles to profl. fin. and real estate jours. Served with USNR, 1959. Recipient Am. Rep. award San Francisco Film Festival, Cork Ireland Film Fest, 1961. Mem. Writer's Guild Am., L.A. Bd. Realtors, Beverly Hills Bd. Realtors (income/investment divsn. steering com.), Westside Realty Bd. (bd. dirs.), L.A. Ventures Assn. (bd. dirs.), Jonathan Club (L.A.), Rotary, Roundtable, Toastmasters Internat. Office: Adams Fin Svcs Inc 425 N Alfred St West Hollywood CA 90048-2504

SANTOS, BARBARA ANN, writer, public relations executive; b. Montclair, N.J., May 11, 1951; d. Raymond Kocher and Anne (Foran) Yoder; m. Richard J. Santos, Oct. 3, 1970; children: Damien, James, Elizabeth. AA, Chabot Coll., 1983. Owner Santos! Pub. Rels., Kihei, Hawaii, 1991—; exec. dir. Maui (Hawaii) Writers Guild, 1991—; co-dir. Maui Writers Conf., 1992—; publicist Maui County Fair, Wailuku, Hawaii, 1993—; pub. rels. dir. Kihei Destination Assn., Maui, 1994—; mem. adv. bd. Maui Writers Conf., 1992-96; coord. Maui Onion Festival, Kaanapali, Hawaii, 1993—; sec. bd. dirs. Made In Maui Trade Coun., 1994—. Author: The Maui Onion Cookbook, 1996; author numerous poems. Pub. rels. dir. Senator Avery Chumbley Campaign, Hawaii, 1994. Scholar Bank of Am., 1982. Office: Santos! Pub Rels PO Box 537 Puunene HI 96784

SANTUCCI, SELENE MARIE, artist, educator; b. Seattle, 1950. BA with distinction, Wash. State U., 1972, MS, 1975, MFA, 1983; BFA with distinction, Mass. Coll. Art, 1981. Exhbns. include Mia Gallery, Seattle, Wash., 1997, 95, Gallery 500 Elkins Park, Pa., 1997, River Run Gallery, Ketchum, Idaho, 1995, Pacific Arts Ctr., Seattle, 1994, Gango Gallery, Portland, Oreg., 1994, Holter Art Mus., Helena, Mont., 1994, Prichard Gallery, Moscow, Idaho, 1994, Tacoma (Wash.) Art Mus., 1993, Boise State U. Gallery of Art, Idaho, 1993, Bellevue (Wash.) Art Mus., 1993, Gallery 500, Elkins Park, Pa., 1996, numerous others; work collected at Continental Mortgage Bank, Seattle, Wash. State Arts Commn./Wash. State U., Vancouver, Creston (Wash.) Sch., others; articles. Office: Mia Gallery 512 1st Ave S Seattle WA 98104-2804

SANWICK, JAMES ARTHUR, mining executive; b. Balt., Feb. 15, 1951; s. Alfred George and Catherine Anne (von Sas) S.; m. Brenda Julia Tietz, Sept. 20, 1980; children: Luke Graham, Sierra Catherine. AS, Catonsville (Md.) C.C., 1975; BS, U. No. Colo., 1976; M in Pub. Administn., U. Alaska S.E., 1985. Recreation therapist Md. Sch. for the Blind, Balt., 1974; dir. camp New Horizon United Cerebral Palsy Md., Balt., 1975; sub-dist. mgr. Nat. Park Svc., various, 1976-82; freelance mgmt. cons. Juneau, Alaska, 1982-84; regional mgr. div. labor standards Alaska Dept. Labor, Juneau, 1983-88; adj. faculty sch. bus. and pub. administrn. U. Alaska S.E., Juneau, 1985-93; mgr. Alaska Productivity Improvement Ctr., Juneau, 1989-93; mgr. human resources and pub. affairs Greens Creek Mining Co., Juneau, 1989-93; mgr. human resources, securities and pub. affairs Rawhide Mining Co., Fallon, Nev., 1993—; owner Sierra Bldg. Alternatives, 1995—; bd. dirs. Gov.'s Com. on Employment Disabled Persons, Alaska Acad. Decathalon Inc.; chmn. Job Svc. Employer Com., Alaska, 1989-93; bd. advisors Inst. Mine Tng. U. Alaska S.E., 1989-93. Co-author: (info. phamphlet) Blue Water Paddling in Alaska, 1980; editor: (film) Green's Creek Project, 1990; photographic editor: Inside Passage Mag., 1982, 83; photographer: (book) Death Valley, 1977. Patrolman Nat. Ski Patrol System, Juneau, 1978-83; instr., trainer ARC, Alaska, Utah, Ariz., 1979-82; v.p. bd. dirs. Alaska Acad. Decathlon; mem. Reno Exec. Roundtable, 1995—. Sgt. USMC, 1970-73. Recipient Nat. New Svc. award United Cerebral Palsey, 1975; named Candidate of Yr. Nat. Ski Patrol System, 1979. Mem. Nev. Mining Assn. (human resources com. 1993—), Soc. Human Resources Mgmt., Juneau Ski Club. Office: Rawhide Mining Co PO Box 2070 Fallon NV 89407-2070

SAPHIER, PETER F., film producer; b. L.A., Aug. 5, 1940; s. James L. and Arna (Finston) S.; m. Liliane Moreau, Oct. 2, 1964; children: Nathalie, Peter. BA, Antioch Coll., 1963. Exec. MCA/Universal Studios, Universal City, Calif., 1965-81; prodr. Martin bregman Prodns., Universal City, 1981-83; exec. Taft Entertainment, Inc., L.A., 1984-86, Ted Mann Prodns./Paramount Pictures, Hollywood, Calif., 1987-91, Tricor Entertainment, Hollywood, 1991-94; exec. prodr. Peter Saphier Prodns., Hollywood, 1994-96, Prelude Pictures, L.A., 1996—. Mem. Hollywood C. of C. (dir. 1991—), Entertainment Coun. (chmn. 1994—). Office: Prelude Pictures c/o Newline Prodns 9060 Santa Monica Blvd #202 Los Angeles CA 90069

SAPP, DONALD GENE, minister; b. Phoenix, Feb. 27, 1927; s. Guerry Byron and Lydia Elmeda (Snyder) S.; m. Anna Maydean Nevitt, July 10, 1952 (dec.); m. Joann Herrin Mountz, May 1, 1976; children: Gregory, Paula, Jeffrey, Mark, Melody, Cristine. AB in Edn., Ariz. State U., 1949; MDiv, Boston U., 1952, STM, 1960; D Ministry, Calif. Grad. Sch. Theology, 1975. Ordained to ministry Meth. Ch., 1950. Dir. youth activities Hyde Park (Mass.) Meth. Ch., 1950-52; minister 1st Meth. Ch., Peabody, Mass., 1952-54, Balboa Island (Calif.) Community Meth. Ch., 1954-57, Ch. of the Foothills Meth., Duarte, Calif., 1957-63; sr. minister Aldersgate United Meth. Ch., Tustin, Calif., 1963-70, Paradise Valley (Ariz.) United Meth. Ch., 1970-83; dist. supt. Cen. West Dist. of Desert S.W. Conf. United Meth. Ctr., Phoenix, 1983-89. Editor Wide Horizons, 1983-89; contbr. articles to profl. jours. Chaplain City of Hope Med. Ctr., Duarte, 1957-63; trustee Plaza Community Ctr., L.A., 1967-70; corp. mem. Sch. Theology at Claremont, Calif., 1972-80; pres. Met. Phoenix Commn., 1983-85; del. Western Jurisdictional Conf. United Meth. Ch., 1984, 88; bd. dirs. Coun. Chs., L.A., 1963-67, Orange County (Calif.) Human Rels. Coun., 1967-70, Interfaith Counseling Svc. Found., 1982-89, Wesley Community Ctr., Phoenix, 1983-89; mem. gen. conf. United Meth. Ch., 1988. With USN, 1945-46. Mem. Ariz. Ecumenical Coun., Bishops and Exec. Roundtable, Rotary (pres.), Kappa Delta Pi, Tau Kappa Epsilon. Democrat. Home: 5225 E Road Runner Rd Paradise Valley AZ 85253

SAPSOWITZ, SIDNEY H., entertainment and media company executive; b. N.Y.C., June 29, 1936; s. Max and Annette (Rothstein) Sapsowitz; m. Phyllis Skopp, Nov. 27, 1957; children: Donna Dawn Chazen, Gloria Lynn Aaron, Marsha Helene Gleit. BBA summa cum laude, Paterson (N.J.) State Coll., 1980. Various fin. and oper. systems positions Metro Goldwyn Mayer, Inc., N.Y.C., 1957-68; exec. v.p., dir. Penta Computer Assoc. Inc., N.Y.C., 1968-70, Cons. Actuaries Inc., Clifton, N.J., 1970-73; exec. v.p., CFO Am. Film. Theatre, N.Y.C., 1973-76, Cinema Shares Internat Dristb. Corp., N.Y.C., 1976-79; sr. cons. Solomon, Finger & Newman, N.Y.C., 1979-80; exec. v.p., chief fin. officer Metro Goldwyn Mayer, Inc., L.A., 1980-85; various positions leading to exec. v.p. fin. and adminstrn., CFO MGM/UA Entertainment Co., Culver City, Calif., 1985-86; also bd. dirs. MGM/UA Entertainment Co., L.A.; fin. v.p.; chief bus. and ops. officer, Office of Pres., dir. United Artists Corp., Beverly Hills, Calif., 1986-87; chmn. bd., CEO MGA/UA Telecommunications Corp., Beverly Hills, 1986-89; sr. exec. v.p., dir., mem. exec. com. MGA/UA Communications Co., 1986-89; chmn., CEO Sid Sapsowitz & Assocs., Inc., 1989—. Pres., Wayne Conservative Congregation, N.J., 1970-77. Mem. Am. Mgmt. Assn., Am. Film Inst., Acad. Motion Picture Arts and Scis., Fin. Exec. Inst., TV Acad. Arts and Scis., KP (chancellor comdr.).

SARANA, SHIREE, writer; b. L.A., Dec. 15, 1965; d. Annette (Lang) Rockey. Student, U. So. Calif., 1984-85, Santa Monica Jr. Coll., 1985-87. Featured poet Anansi Writers Workshop, 1993, Watts Summer Festival, 1994, Santa Monica Jr. Coll., 1995, Eso Won Bookstore, 1996, No Holds Barred Writer's Series, 1996, Jazz Speak, 1996. Author: Essence of Life, 1993, Mighty Is the Blackness, 1993; contbr. poems to profl. publs. Recipient 1st Pl. Short Story award U. Calif., Santa Barbara, 1983, Hon. Mention award U. Calif., Santa Barbara, 1984, Tommy award U.So. Calif., 1985, Best New Poet award Am. Poetry Anthology, 1985-87.

SARASOHN, LISA TUNICK, history educator; b. N.Y.C., Sept. 19, 1950; d. Irve Enoch and Adele Beatrice (Lehnstul) Tunick; m. David Sarasohn, June 23, 1974; children: Alex, Peter. BA, NYU, 1971; MA, UCLA, 1973, PhD; 1979. Asst. prof. Oreg. State U., Corvallis, 1979-84, assoc. prof., 1984-95, prof. history, 1995—. Author: Gassendi's Ethics, 1996. Recipient Meehan Tchg. award Oreg. State U., 1989, Ritchie Disting. Prof. award, 1992. Mem. Am. Hist. Assn., History of Sci. Soc. Office: Oregon State Univ Dept of History Corvallis OR 97331

SARAVO, ANNE COBBLE, clinical psychologist, mental health consultant; b. Atlanta, Feb. 23, 1938; d. William Edwin and Iris Benny (Norman) Cobble; m. James Vincent Saravo, June 13, 1958; children: Stacy Anne, Lisa Ames Furmanek. BA, Tex. Tech. U., 1959; MS, U. Mass., 1964, PhD, 1965; postgrad., Regional Health Authority, London, 1978-79, U. So. Calif., 1980-81. Lic. psychologist, Calif. Assoc. prof. psychology Antioch Coll., Yellow Springs, Ohio, 1966-69; cons. Winchester (Eng.) Day Treatment Nursery Sch., 1971-73; sch. psychologist Muroc Unified Sch. Dist., Edwards AFB, Calif., 1974-75; clinical psychologist Antelope Valley Hosp., Lancaster, Calif., 1975-76, Farnborough Hosp., Kent, Eng., 1978-80, Orange County (Calif.) Mental Health Svc., 1981-84; pvt. practice clin. psychology Seal Beach, Calif., 1981—; chief adult out-patient svc. Orange County (Calif.) Mental Health Svc., 1984-87, chief adult inpatient svcs., 1987-95; program mgr. Medi-Cal Inpatient Managed Care, 1995-97; bd. dirs. High Hopes Neurol. Recover Group, Costa Mesa, Calif., chair profl. adv. bd., 1988—; oral examination commr. Calif. Bd. Psychology, 1989—; geriatric coord. Orange County Mental Health Svcs., 1985-87; profl. adv. bd. Orange County Caregiver Resource Ctr., 1989—; mem. Alzheimers Disease rev. panel Calif. Dept. Mental Health, 1990—. Contbr. articles to profl. jours. Chairperson Conf. Geriatric Mental Health, Asilomar, Calif., 1986, So. Calif. Geriatric Mental Health Coordinators, 1985-87. U.S. Pub. Health fellow Fels Research Inst., 1966-67. Mem. APA, Calif. Psychol. Assn. (chair medicare/pub. sector subcom. 1990—, co-chair reimbursement and managed care com. 1996—), Nat. Acad. Neuropsychology (grad.), Brit. Psychol. Soc. Office: 550 Pacific Coast Hwy Ste 203 Seal Beach CA 90740-6601

SARGEANT, ROY, state agency administrator. Bur. chief Bur. Mental Health, Boise, Idaho. Office: Dept Health and Welfare PO Box 83720 Boise ID 83720-0036

SARGENT, DIANA RHEA, corporate executive; b. Cheyenne, Wyo., Feb. 20, 1939; d. Clarence and Edith (de Castro) Hayes; grad. high sch.; m. Charles Sargent, Apr. 17, 1975 (div. 1991); children: Rene A. Coburn, Rochelle A. Rollins, Clayton R. Weldy, Christopher J. IBM proof operator Bank Am., Stockton, Calif., 1956-58, gen. ledger bookkeeper, Modesto, Calif., 1963-66; office mgr., head bookkeeper Cen. Drug Store, Modesto, 1966-76; pres. Sargent & Coburn, Inc., Modesto, 1976—, sec.-treas., v.p. Mem. Stanislaus Women's Ctr., NOW, San Francisco Mus. Soc., Modesto Women's Network, Stanislaus County Commn. for Women, Yerba Buena Art Ctr. Office: 1101 Standiford Ave Ste D-2 Modesto CA 95350-0982

SARGENT, J. MCNEIL, artist, art educator; b. North Wilkesboro, N.C., Nov. 15, 1929; s. Sargent Dehaven and Agnes (Absher) Duffield; m. William Braley, May 1947 (div. Sept. 1955) 1 child, Robin Bradley Gomez. Student, Sch. Profl. Art, N.Y.c., 1944-47; BA, U. Calif., San Diego, 1977; printmaking student, Atelier 17, Paris, 1980, 81, 83, NYU, 1982. Docent San Diego Mus. Art, 1978-84; instr. art Mira Costa Coll., Oceanside, Calif., 1975—, Cochran Mus. Art, Washington, 1970-72, San Diego C.C., 1972—; art cons. Calif. Art Commn., 1980; juror So. Calif. Art Expo, Del Mar, 1990. Narrator film Process of Printmaking, 1980; exhibited in solo shows at Riverside (Calif.) Mus., 1978, Foxhall Gallery, Washington, 1984, Prestige Gallery, Boston, 1986, Gallery 35, Nice, France, 1987, Tarbox Gallery, San Diego, 1980, 85, 88, Musée l'Histoire, Biot, France, 1990, Galerie Antiboulanc, Antibes, France, 1995. Recipient awards for art. Mem. Artist Equity Assn. (prs. 1972-76), Printmakers Atelier (dir. 1984-95). Republican. Home: 1003 Woodgrove Dr San Diego CA 92007

SARGENT, J. MCNEIL See BRALEY, JEAN

SARICH, VINCENT M., anthropologist, educator; b. Chicago, Ill., Dec. 13, 1934; s. Matt and Manda Saric; m. Jorjan Snyder; children: Kevin, Tamsin. BS, Ill. Inst. Tech., 1955; PhD, U. Calif., Berkeley, 1967. Instr. anthropology Stanford U., Berkeley, Calif., 1965; from asst. prof. to assoc. prof. anthropology U. Calif., Berkeley, 1967-81, prof., 1981-94, prof. emeritus, 1994—. Office: U Calif Dept of Anthropology 232 Kroeber Hall Berkeley CA 94720-3711•

SARKAR, DIPAK KUMAR, physiologist, educator; b. Calcutta, India, Aug. 25, 1950; came to U.S., 1980; s. Joydeb Chandra and Aruna (Mondal) S.; m. Shirley Ann Sanderson, May 4, 1984; children: Abby Joya, Sophie Dipti. BSc, Calcutta U., 1970, MSc, 1973, PhD, 1975; DPhil, Oxford (Eng.) U., 1979. Vis. postdoctoral assoc. Sch. of Medicine Yale U., New Haven, 1979; rsch. assoc. Mich. State U., East Lansing, 1980-83; asst. prof. U. Calif., San Diego, 1983-88; assoc. prof. Wash. State U., Pullman, 1988-96, adj. prof. pharmacology and toxicology, 1989—, adj. prof. genetics and cell biology, 1989—, prof., 1996—; ad hoc grant reviewer NSF, Washington, 1987, 91; mem. rsch. rev. com. NIAAA/Pub. Health Svcs., Bethesda, Md., 1991—; invited speaker at nat. and internat. confs., various insts. Editor: Reproductive Neuroendocrinology of Aging and Drug Abuse; mem. editl. bd. Endocrinology, 1989—, Neuroendocrinology, 1987-90; contbr. chpt. to Neuroendocrinology of Aging, 1983; contbr. articles, abstracts to profl. publs. Ad hoc grant reviewer Dept. Vet. Affairs, 1995, NSF, Washington, 1987-96. Grantee Andrew Mellon Found., 1983-86, San Diego Reproductive Medicine Rsch. and Edn. Found., 1985-87, March of Dimes, 1985-87, NIH/NIA, 1985-89, NIH/NICHD, 1986-89, Wash. State U., 1988-91, NIH/NIAAA, 1991—, NIH/NCI, 1994-96. Fellow AAAS; mem. Soc. for Neurosci. (pres. No. Rocky Mountain chpt. 1996), Internat. Soc. Neuroendocrinology, Internat. Brain Rsch. Orgn., Soc. Endocrinology (U.K.), Endocrine Soc. (membership com. 1996—), Rsch. Soc. on Alcoholism. Office: Wash State Univ 215 Wegner Pullman WA 99164

SARKISIAN, PAMELA OUTLAW, artist; b. Spokane, Sept. 26, 1941; d. Willard Clinton and Frances (Montieth) Outlaw; m. Ronald Edward Sarkisian, Nov. 11, 1960; children: Ronald Abraham, Michelle Suzanne. Grad. high sch., Stockton, Calif. Art student Oceanside, Calif., 1972-80; founder Palette 'N Easel Studio, Oceanside, Calif., 1980—, operator, mgr., 1980-85; art tchr. in residence Palette 'N Easel Studio, Oceanside, 1985-96; publisher greeting cards Polytint, Ltd., England, 1995, 96; fine art prints pub. by Bentley House, Ltd., Walnut Creek, Calif., 1994-97. Designer floral collector plate series Danbury Mint/MBI, Inc.; represented by Casay Gallery, Kailau, Kona, Hawaii, 1991, Galeria Jean Lammelin, Paris, 1991, 2d St. Gallery, Encinitas, Calif., 1991, Blondes Gallery, San Diego, 1992, Valentine-Owens Gallery, Santa Monica, Calif., 1992, Sodarco Gallery, Montreal, 1993, Surtex, 1993, Jacob G. Javity Conv. Ctr., N.Y.C., 1993, Laura Larkin Gallery, Del Mar, Calif., 1993-94, Charles Hecht Galleries, Tarzana and Palm Desert, Calif., 1993-94, 95-96, Lou Martin Gallery, Laguna Beach, Calif., 1994, Charles Hecht Gallery, La Jolla, Calif., 1995-96, Calif. Art Gallery, Laguna Beach, 1996, Hunter Gallery, Tucson, 1996, Cottage Gallery at Carmel, Calif., 1996. Pres. Zonta Internat., Oceanside, 1980-81; mem. Emblem Club #177, Oceanside, 1971-96; princess Daughters of the Nile, San Diego, 1974; bd. dirs. Oceanside Girls Club, 1980. Recipient 1st Pl. award San Dieguito Art Guild, 1978, 85, 2nd Pl. award, 1983, 89, 3rd Pl. award, 1983, 1990; winner People's Choice award Internat. Show of Women Artists of the West, Las Vegas, 1992. Mem. North County Art Assn. (founder), Carlsbad Oceanside Art League, 1978, San Dieguito Art Guild, Fallbrook Art Assn., San Diego Art Inst., Assn. pour Promotion Artiste Français, ARTISPHERE. Office: Palette 'N Easel Studio 1021 S Coast Hwy Oceanside CA 92054-5004

SARLAT, GLADYS, public relations consultant; b. Elizabeth, N.J., July 22, 1923; d. Max and Dora (Levin) S. BS, U. Wash., 1946. Asst., Kay Sullivan Assocs. N.Y.C., 1949-50; fashion dir. Warsaw & Co., N.Y.C., 1950-54; asst. fashion coord. Emporium Dept. Store, San Francisco, 1955-56; asst. prodn. mgr. Cunningham & Walsh Advt., San Francisco, 1958-59; v.p., pub. rels. dir. Harwood Advt. Inc., Tucson and Phoenix, 1959-68; v.p., dir. Waller & Sarlat Advt. Inc., Tucson, 1968-69; pres. Godwin & Sarlat Pub. Rels., Inc., Tucson, 1970-87; counsel, Godwin Sarlat Pub. Rels., 1987-88, cons., 1988—; of counsel Liess Peck & Godwin, LP&G, Tucson, 1993—; cons. in field. Mem. adv. com. Downtown Devel. Corp., 1979-85, Festival in the Sun; bd. dirs. Tucson Conv. and Visitors Bur., 1993-95. Named Woman of Yr. for Bus., Ariz. Daily Star, 1963; recipient Lulu award L.A. Woman in Advt., 1962. Mem. Pub. Rels. Soc. Am. (past bd. mem., counselors acad.), Fashion Group, Tucson Met. C. of C. (v.p., dir. 1976-85, chmn bd. 1986-87). Republican. Jewish. Home: 5530 N Camino Arenosa Tucson AZ 85718-5417 Office: 177 N Church Ave Ste 315 Tucson AZ 85701-1118

SARLEY, JOHN G., broadcast executive, writer; b. Cleve., Mar. 1, 1954; s. Edward James and Ann Sarley. BA, Cleve. State U., 1977. Writer, producer Marschalk Co. Advt., Cleve., 1977-80, DOCSI Corp., Hollywood, Calif., 1980—; pres. Sarley, Bigg & Bedder Inc., Hollywood, 1981—. Recipient Clio awards, 1980, 84, 87, 90, 92, 93, 94. Mem. Broadcast Promotion and Mktg. Execs., Hollywood C. of C. Office: Sarley Bigg & Bedder Inc 1644 N Stanley Ave Hollywood CA 90046-2713

SARNAT, HARVEY BARRY, pediatric neurology educator; b. Chgo., Dec. 19, 1941; s. Bernard David and Sylvia Joan (Deitsch) S.; m. Margaret Ione Strom, Dec. 27, 1967; children: Naomi Beth, Daryl Jacob. BS, U. Ill., 1962; MS, U. Ill., Chgo., 1965, MD, 1966. Intern, resident in pediatrics U. Ill.

Hosp., Chgo., 1966-68; resident in neurology, fellow in neuropathology U. Va., Charlottesville, 1970-73; Asst. prof. St. Louis U., 1973-76; cons. U. Western Australia, Perth, 1976-77; assoc. prof. St. Louis U., 1977-78, U. Ark., Little Rock, 1978-81; assoc. prof. U. Calgary (Can.), 1981-86, prof., 1986-92; prof., head divsn. pediatric neurology U. Washington, Seattle, 1992—. Author: 3 med. textbooks; editor: 3 med. textbooks; contbr. 150 rsch. articles to various med. jours. Mem. WHO com. for revision of internat. classification of diseases UN, 1989-92. Capt. M.C., USAF, 1968-70. Recipient Carrell-Krusen award for neuromuscular rsch. U. Tex. S.W., 1994; Sarkowsky prof. of child neurology (endowed chair) U. Washington, 1993—. Mem. Child Neurology Soc., Am. Assn. Neuropathologists, Am. Neurol. Assn., Internat. Child Neurol. Assn. (exec. com. 1976—), Canadian Assn. Pediatric Neurology. Office: Children's Hosp CH-49 4800 Sand Point Way NE Seattle WA 98105-3901

SARNER, HARVEY, lawyer; b. N.Y.C., Feb. 13, 1934; s. Michael and Lillian (Greenblatt) S.; m. Lorisanne C. Jelle, June 9, 1956; children: Kyra, Surah. BS, U. Minn., 1958, LLB, 1959. Atty., advisor Fed. Communications Commn., Washington, 1959-61; assoc. ho. counsel Am. Dental Assn., Chgo., 1961-71; atty. Sarner and Assocs., Chgo., 1971-87. Author: Dental Jurisprudence, 1968, Herman Wouk Checklist, 1994; editor SAA Dr.'s newsletter, 1972-87. Bd. dirs. Jewish Found. for Christian Rescuers, 1985—, Temple Isiah, Palm Springs, 1994—. With USN, 1951-55. Recipient Polish Pres. medal Polish Govt., 1994, Humanitarian award Am. Soc. Oral Surgeons, San Diego, 1993. Jewish. Home: 701 W Panorama Rd Palm Springs CA 92262-2743

SARRACINO, MARGARET C., artist; b. South Bend, Ind., Dec. 8, 1950; d. James Robert and Mary M. (Fiedler) Crawford; m. John S. Sarracino, June 20, 1987; 1 child, John Terry. Student, U. Denver, 1968-70; BA, Fort Lewis Coll., 1978. Potter Bayfield, Colo., 1977-80, 83-85; shopowner, artist Pottery of Durango, Colo., 1980-83, Mud-Dauber Pottery, Los Alamos, N.Mex., 1985-92; artist Gaithersburg, Md., 1992-93, Germantown, Md., 1993-94, Los Alamos, 1994—; chairperson Los Alamos County Art in Pub. Places Bd., 1992, vice-chairperson, 1991. Exhibited in group shows at N.Mex. State Fair, 1995, N.Mex. Watercolor Soc., 1995, 96, Pastel Soc. N.Mex., 1996, Fuller Lodge Art Ctr., 1997. Mem. Pastel Soc. N.Mex., N.Mex. Watercolor Soc., Los Alamos Studio Tour (sec.-treas. 1990, juror, 1996). Home and Office: 1855 Camino Uva Los Alamos NM 87544

SARRIS, GREG, Native American educator; b. Santa rosa, Calif., Feb. 12, 1952; s. Emilio Arthur Hilario and Mary Bernadette Hartman. BA, UCLA, 1978; MA, Stanford U., 1981, 88, PhD, 1989. Adj. lectr. Am. studies U. Calif., Santa Cruz, 1982-86; writer HBO, L.A., 1995-96; prof. English UCLA, 1989—; cons. Sundance Writers, Salt Lake City, 1994, 96, Calif. Lit. Project, UCLA, 1993-96; lectr. Calif. Tchrs. Assn., Asilomar, 1995. Author: (book of critical essays) Keeping Slug Woman Alive, 1993, (biography) Mabel McKay Weaving the Dream, 1994 (award 1994), (novel) Grand Avenue, 1994 (award 1996), (screenplay) Grand Avenue, 1996 (8 awards 1996). Chief, Federated Coast Miwok Indian Tribe, Santa Rosa, Calif., 1993-94, 94-95; chmn. Word for Word Theatre Co., 1995—; mem. First Ams. in the Arts, 1995—. Recipient Award for best screenplay Santa Fe Film Festival, 1996, Am. Indian Film Festival, 1996, Best Reads award Calif. Ind. Booksellers, 1996, Work of Lit. Merit, Santa Rosa Jr. Coll., 1996. Mem. Screenwriters Guild, PEN, PEN-West, Authors Guild. Democrat. Home: 2062 N Sycamore Ave Los Angeles CA 90068 Office: UCLA Dept English 405 Hilgard Ave Los Angeles CA 90024

SARSAM, MUMTAZ BASHIR, bridge engineer; b. Mosul, Iraq, Jan. 18, 1933; came to the U.S., 1956; s. Bashir H. and Naima A. (Hafez) S.; m. Vivian Miller, July 29, 1961; children: Mark C., Samir M. BSc in Civil Engring., S.D. State U., 1960, MSc in Civil & Structural Engring., 1972. Registered profl. engr., Ariz. Bridge design squad leader S.D. Dept. Transp., Pierre, 1960-68; asst. instr. civil engring. S.D. State U., Brookings, 1968-72; bridge maintenance engr. S.D. Dept. Transp., Pierre, 1972-83; transp. rsch. engr. Ariz. Transp. Rsch. Ctr., Tempe, Ariz., 1984-85; transp. maintenance engr. Ariz. Dept. Transp., Phoenix, 1986, transp. bridge maintenance engr., 1986-93, bridge design leader, 1994-95; bridge maintenance engr., 1995—. Mem. ASCE. Republican. Mem. Orthodox Ch. Office: Ariz Dept Transp 261 E 205 S 17th Ave Phoenix AZ 85007-3212

SARSON, JOHN CHRISTOPHER, television producer, director, writer; b. London, Jan. 19, 1935; s. Arnold Wilfred and Annie Elizabeth (Wright) S.; m. Evelyn Patricia Kaye, Mar. 25, 1963; children: Katrina May, David Arnold. BA with honors, Trinity Coll., Cambridge, Eng., 1960, MA, 1963. Dir. Granada TV, Manchester, Eng., 1960-63; producer, dir. Sta. WGBH-TV, Boston, 1963-73; pres. Blue Penguin, Inc., Boulder, Colo., 1974—; v.p. TV programming Sta. WYNC-TV, N.Y.C., 1989-90; dir. Pub. Broadcasting Assocs., Newton, Mass.; cons. to numerous pub. TV stations. Creator, producer MAsterpiece Theatre, PBS, 1970-73, Zoom, PBS, 1971-73; producer Live From the Met, PBS, 1977-79, Kid's Writes, Nickelodeon, 1982-83, American Treasure, a Smithsonian Journey, 1986, Spotlight Colorado, 1991, PArenting Works, 1993, Club 303, 1994. Served with Royal Navy, 1956-57. Recipient Emmy award, 1973, 74, Peabody award Ohio State U., 1978, Internat. Emmy award, 1983, Nat. Acad. TV Arts and Scis. Gov.'s award, 1991. Mem. Dirs. Guild Am., Nat. acad. TV Arts and Scis. (gov. Heartland chpt.). Home and Office: 3031 5th St Boulder CO 80304-2501

SARTINI, RICHARD LEE, retired internist; b. Meriden, Conn., June 23, 1946; s. Silvio Joseph and Lena Josephine Sartini. AB in French, Coll. Holy Cross, 1968; MD, Tufts U., 1972. Intern and resident Cin. Gen. Hosp., 1972-75; intern Alexian Bros. Hosp., San Jose, Calif., 1976-78; pulmonary fellow U. Calif., Irvine, 1978-80; staff physician, chief respiratory medicine San Clemente (Calif.) Hosp., 1980-88; staff physician Mission Community Hosp., Mission Viejo, Calif., 1980-88, Saddleback Hosp., Laguna Hills, Calif., 1980-88, South Coast Hosp., Laguna Beach, Calif., 1980-88. Fellow Am. Coll. Chest Physicians; mem. ACP, Orange County Med. Assn., AMA, Calif. Med. Assn., Nat. Assn. Med. Dirs. Respiratory Care. Roman Catholic. Home and Office: PO Box 790 Los Angeles CA 90078-0790

SARTORIS, DAVID JOHN, radiologist; b. Chgo., Nov. 25, 1955; s. Cornelius Ugo and Helen Louise (Lesjak); m. Cyd Clariza Grepo. BS in Biol. Scis., Stanford U., 1976, MD, 1980. Diplomate Am. Bd. Radiology. Intern, diagnostic radiology Stanford (Calif.) Univ. Med. Ctr., 1980-81; resident, diagnostic radiology Stanford U. and Affil. Hosps., 1981-84; fellow, musculoskeletal radiology U. Calif. and Affil. Hosps., San Diego, 1984-85; asst. prof. radiology U. Calif., San Diego, 1985-87, assoc. prof. radiology, 1987-94, prof. radiology, 1994—; chief, musculoskeletal IMG U. Calif. San Diego Med. Ctr., 1985-91, chief, quantitative bone densitometry, 1985-94; lectr. in field; cons. Rsch. and Edn. Fund/Radiol. Soc. North Am.; vis. prof. numerous univs. including Creighton U. Med. Ctr., Omaha, 1993, U. Pitts., 1990, VA Med. Ctr., Long Beach, Calif., 1990, U. Ottawa/Ottawa Gen. Hosp., Ont., Can., 1987, others; served on numerous coms. in field. Contbr. over 400 articles to profl. jours., numerous chpts. to books in field; editorial adv. bd. Chem. Rubber Co. Pres., Inc., Boca Raton, Fla., Diagnostic Imaging mag., 1987, Thieme Med. Pubs., Inc., N.Y.C., Year Book Med. Pubs., Chgo., Applied Radiology Jour.; asst. editor: AJR/musculoskeletal sect., 1987-88; reviewer jours. Rsch. grantee The Arthritis Soc., Toronto, Ont.; recipient Silver Spoon awards from residents at U. Calif., San Diego, 1986, 93, 94, others. Mem. Am. Coll. Radiology, Am. Roentgen Ray Soc., Assn. U. Radiologists, Radiol. Soc. N. Am., Calif. Radiol. Soc., Physicians for Social Responsibility, Internat. Skeletal Soc. (Youngest-Ever New Mem. award 1987, Pres.'s medal 1989), So. Calif. Bone and Mineral Club, New Bone Densitometry Soc., Bone Dysplasia Soc., Phi Beta Kappa. Office: UCSD Med Ctr Dept Radiology 350 Dickinson St San Diego CA 92103-1913

SARVER, LINDA, mayor. Mayor City of Covina, Calif. Office: 125 E College St Covina CA 91723

SASAKI, DARRYL YOSHIO, research chemist; b. Honolulu, July 9, 1962; s. Charles Daigaku and Grace Hisako (Fujinaka) S.; m. Yukiko Takada, Mar. 22, 1991; 1 child, Dayne. BS, UH Manoa, 1984; MS in Organic Chemistry, U. Calif., Irvine, 1986, PhD in Organic Chemistry, 1989. Sr. mem. tech. staff Sandia Nat. Labs Org. 1811, Albuquerque, 1994—. Contbr. articles to profl. jours.; patentee in field. Mem. AAAS, Am. Chem. Soc., Soc. of Polymer Sci. Office: Sandia Nat Labs MS 1407 Albuquerque NM 87185

SASAKI, TSUTOMU (TOM SASAKI), real estate company executive, international trading company executive, consultant; b. Tokyo, July 28, 1945; came to U.S., 1979; s. Tsuneshiro and Kimiko (Fujiwara) S.; m. Yoko Katsura, Feb. 21, 1971; children: Mari, Tomoko. BA, Sophia U., Tokyo, 1969. Plant export adminstrn. Ataka & Co., Ltd., Osaka, Japan, 1969-76; officer Seattle-First Nat. Bank, Tokyo, 1976-79, AVP bus. mgr., 1982-84; AVP Japan mgr. Seattle-First Nat. Bank, Seattle, 1979-82, v.p. Japan mgr., 1984-90; owner BBS Internat., Inc., Seattle, 1990—; bd. dirs. Java Trading Internat., Co., Ltd., Seattle, Wired, Inc., Seattle, InterPac Devel. Inc. V.p. Adopt-a-Stream Found., Everett, Wash., 1987—. Am. Field Svc. scholar, 1963-64. Mem. Japan Am. Soc. Wash. (chmn. membership com. 1988), British Am. Bus. Coun., Fairwood Golf & Country Club. Home: 4761 149th Ave SE Bellevue WA 98006-3127 Office: BBS Internat Inc 720 Olive Way Ste 1025 Seattle WA 98101-1853

SASAKI, Y. TITO, business services company executive; b. Tokyo, Feb. 6, 1938; came to U.S., 1967, naturalized, 1983; s. Yoshinaga and Chiyoko (Imada) S.; m. Janet Louise Cline, June 27, 1963; 1 child, Heather N. BS, Chiba U., 1959; postgrad. Royal Coll. Art, London, 1961, U. Oslo, 1962; MS, Athens Tech. Inst., Greece, 1964; postgrad. U. Calif., Berkeley, 1969. Chief designer Aires Camera Industries Co., Tokyo, 1958-59; tech. officer London County Council, 1961-62; researcher Athens Ctr. Ekistics, 1964-66; sr. researcher Battelle Inst., Geneva, 1966-68; project engr. Marin County Transit Dist., San Rafael, Calif., 1968-69; chief planning, research Golden Gate Bridge Dist., San Francisco, 1969-74; pres. Visio Internat. Inc., Somona, Calif., 1973—; chmn. steering com. Kawada Industries Inc., Tokyo, 1974-82; chief exec. officer Quantum Mechanics Corp., Somona, 1981—; bd. dirs., v.p. Sonoma Skypark, Inc., 1986-89. Mem. ASME, AIAA, Am. Soc. Testing and Materials, Am. Welding Soc., Am. Inst. Cert. Planners, World Soc. Ekistics, Am. Vacuum Soc., Aircraft Owners and Pilots Assn. Roman Catholic. Office: Visio Internat Inc PO Box 1888 Sonoma CA 95476-1888

SASENICK, JOSEPH ANTHONY, health care company executive; b. Chgo., May 18, 1940; s. Anthony E. and Caroline E. (Smicklas) S.; m. Barbara Ellen Barr, Aug. 18, 1962; children: Richard Allen, Susan Marie, Michael Joseph. BA, DePaul U., 1962; MA, U. Okla., 1966. With Miles Labs., Inc., Elkhart, Ind., 1963-70; product mgr. Alka-Seltzer, 1966-68, dir. mktg. grocery products div., 1968-70; with Gillette Corp., Boston, 1970-79; dir. new products/new ventures, personal care div. Gillette Corp., 1977; v.p. diversified cos. and pres. Jafra Cosmetics Worldwide, 1977-79; mktg. dir. Braun AG, Kronberg, W. Ger., 1970-73; chmn. mng. dir. Braun U.K. Ltd., 1973-77; with Abbott Labs., North Chicago, 1979-84; corp. v.p., pres. consumer products div. Abbott Labs., 1979-84; pres., chief exec. officer Moxie Industries, 1984-87, Personal Monitoring Technologies, Rochester, N.Y., 1987; pres. Bioline Labs., Ft. Lauderdale, Fla., 1988; mng. dir., ptnr. Vista Resource Group, Newport Beach, Calif., 1988-90; pres., CEO, Alcide Corp., Redmond, Wash., 1991-92, CEO, 1992—. Mem. Columbia Tower Club, El Niguel Club, Wash. Athletic Club. Home: 1301 Spring St Seattle WA 98104-3533 Office: Alcide Corp 8561 154th Ave NE Redmond WA 98052-3557

SASMOR, JAMES CECIL, publishing representative, educator; b. N.Y.C., July 29, 1920; s. Louis and Cecilia (Mockler) S.; 1 child from previous marriage: Elizabeth Lynn; m. Jeannette L. Fuchs, May 30, 1965. BS, Columbia U., 1942; MBA, Calif. Western U., 1977, PhD, 1979. Cert. Am. Bd. Med. Psychotherapists, sex educator Am. Assn. Sex Educators, Counselors and Therapists, Healthcare Risk Mgr. Am. Inst. Med. Law, diplomate Am. Bd. Sexology, Am. Bd. Disability Analysts (sr. analyst). Advt. sales exec. 1946-59; registered rep. Nat. Assn. Security Dealers, 1956-57; founder, owner J.C. Sasmor Assocs. Publishers' Reps., N.Y.C., 1959-89; co-founder, pres., dir. adminstrn. Continuing Edn. Cons., Inc., 1976—; pub. cons., 1959—; clin assoc., U. So. Fla. Coll. of Medicine, 1987-89; adj. faculty Coll. Nursing, 1980-89, dir. Ednl. Counseling Comprehensive Breast Cancer Ctr., U. So. Fla. Med. Ctr., 1984-89, client librn. mental health inst., 1979-89. Team tchr. childbirth edn. Am. Soc. Childbirth Educators; bd. dirs. Tampa chpt. ARC; pres. Am. Cancer Soc. Sedona, Ariz. Unit, 1995—, co-chmn. adult edn. com.; bd. dirs. Ariz. State Divsn., mem. pub. edn. com.; county nursing ednl. cons. ARC, chmn. instrnl. com. on nursing and health, 1979-85. With USN, 1942-58, PTO; lt. USNR ret. Recipient cert. appreciation ARC, 1979, Dept. Health and Rehab. Svcs. award for Fla. Mental Health Inst. Svc., 1980, Cert. of Appreciation Am. Fgn. Svc. Assn., 1988. Internat. Coun. of Sex Edn. and Parenthood Am. U. fellow, 1981—. Mem. NAACOG (bd. dirs. Tampa chpt.), Nat. Assn. Pubs. Reps. (pres. 1965-66), Am. Soc. Psychoprophylaxis in Obstetrics (dir. 1970-71), Am. Soc. Childbirth Educators (co-founder, dir. 1972—), Internat. Coun. Women's Health Issues (chmn. resources com.), Health Edn. Media Assn., Nursing Educators Assn. Tampa, Lions (bd. dirs. Found. Ariz., pres. Sedona club). Author: Economics of Structured Continuing Education in Selected Professional Journals'; contbr. chpts. to Childbirth Education: A Nursing Perspective; contbr. articles to profl. jours. Home: 235 Arrowhead Dr Sedona AZ 86351-8900 Office: PO Box 2282 Sedona AZ 86339-2282

SASSO, GIUSEPPE, systems analyst; b. Capri, Italy, July 6, 1952; came to U.S., 1982; s. Paolo and Flora Scotto (Di Santolo) Sasso; m. Eliane Siqueira, June 6, 1976; 1 child, Chiara Francesca Perin Di Santolo. Student, Caracciolo Inst., Napoli, Italy, 1972, Salerno (Italy) U., 1973-75, Catholic Pontiff U., Rio de Janeiro, 1977; BS in Maths., St. Ursula U., Rio de Janeiro, 1981. Systems analyst UN, Rio de Janeiro, 1977-79, Getulio Vargas Found., Rio de Janeiro, 1978-82, Union Carbide, Rio de Janeiro, 1982, Software System Installations, L.A., 1984-85; sr. staff cons. Mmgt. Info. Sys. Internat., L.A., 1985-90; system analyst Farmers Ins. Group, L.A., 1990-91; sr. program analyst L.A. County, L.A., 1991-95, 1996—; mgmt. cons., sr. tech. staff Kaiser Permanente, 1995-96. Home: 102 Via Sevilla Redondo Beach CA 90277-6749 Office: Los Angeles County 9150 Imperial Hwy Downey CA 90242-2835

SASSONE, MARCO MASSIMO, artist; b. Florence, Italy, July 27, 1942; came to U.S., 1967; s. Nicola and Anna Maria (Freschi) S.; m. Diane Nelson, Jan. 25, 1972 (div. 1983); 1 child, Nicola. Student, Inst. Galileo Galilei, Florence, 1959-62, Fine Arts Acad., Florence, 1963. One-man shows include Galleria Arte Internat., Florence, 1973, Laguna Art Mus., Laguna Beach, Calif., 1979, L.A. Mcpl. Art Gallery, 1988, Mus. Italo Am., San Francisco, 1994, Italian Cultural Inst., L.A., 1996; exhibited in group shows Nat. Acad. Design, N.Y.C., 1977, Orange Coast Coll., Costa Mesa, Calif., 1978, Univ. Calif., San Francisco, 1987, L.A. Contemporary Exhibitions, 1992, Mus. Italian Am., San Francisco, 1994; subject of film, book, video documentary; TV guest. Recipient Gold medal Italian Acad., 1978, Mayor's commendation, L.A., 1987, Marco Sassone Day declared in his honor, San Francisco, 1994; knighted by Sandro Pertini, Pres. of Italy, 1982. Studio: Marco Sassone Studio 2140 Bush St Apt 8 San Francisco CA 94115-3166

SATCHER, CLEMENT MICHAEL, special education educator; b. L.A., Aug. 21, 1939; s. Dexter Getzwiller Satcher and Vera Janette (Laney) Long; m. Brenda Susan McMonigle, Oct. 1972 (div. Dec. 1980); children: Monica Blackhurst, Catherine Spechtenhauser. AA, Santa Monica Coll., 1972; BA, Calif. State U., Northridge, 1975; student, Calif. State U., San Bernardino, 1994—. Cert. tchr. Illustrator, film and sound operator U.S. Army Engr. Sch., Fort Belvoir, Va., 1961-63; lighting design engr. Walt E. Disney Enterprises, Glendale, Calif., 1981-82; elec. designer Walt E. Disney Enterprises, Anaheim, Calif., 1987-88; lighting technician Theater Vision Inc., North Hollywood, Calif., 1984; elec. engr. Tippetts-Abbett-McCarty-Stratton, L.A., 1984-85; architect Azarak Corp., Westlake Village, Calif., 1985-87, Ward Investment Co., Costa Mesa, Calif., 1988; portrait photographer DeSpain Portrait Svc., Milford, Iowa, 1989-90; checker Looking Glass Enterprises, Yucca Valley, Calif., 1990-92; caretaker Dusty Rose Ranch, Desert Hot Springs, Calif., 1992-94; chem. dependency technician Betty Ford Ctr., Rancho Mirage, Calif., 1994; sr. elec. draftsman Hughes Telecomm., El Segundo, Calif., 1969-73, elec. designer, 1973-76; architect Dept. Water Resources, State Calif., Santa Barbara, 1990; poet, painter, cartoonist. Author: Out of the Flock, 1965, 72; poetry included in anthologies; paintings represented in permanent collections ACLU Headquarters, L.A., Archbishop Office, L.A. With U.S. Army, 1961-63. Recipient Golden Poet award World of Poetry, 1989-90, Best Poets award Nat. Libr. Poetry, 1995-96. Mem. Internat. Soc. Poets, Poetry Soc. Am., 521 Studio Washington. Home: 2400 Junipero Ave #14 Palm Springs CA 92262-2874

SATCHWELL, CHRIS ALBERT, dental group executive; b. Burley, Idaho, Oct. 6, 1964; s. William Ernest and Twila Nancy (Prescott) S.; m. April Larsen, June 10, 1989; children: Keili, Spencer, Kamill. Electronic engring. technician, Ricks Coll., 1984; D of Dental Medicine, Oreg. Health Sci. U., 1993. Lab. technician Rollins, Brown & Gunnel, Provo, Utah, 1986-87, Gary Booth PhD, Provo, 1987-88; rschr. Environ. Toxicology, Provo, 1988-89; property mgr. Glenbourgh Corp., Beaverton, Oreg., 1989-90; painter Wilsonville, Oreg., 1990-93; assoc. dr. Wilsonville Dental Group P.C., 1993-95; pres., CEO Emmett (Idaho) Dental Group P.A., 1995—; mem. children's health bd. Tri-County Clackamas County, Oreg., 1994. Scoutmaster Boy Scouts Am., Wilsonville, 1994-95, asst. scoutmaster, Emmett, 1996—. Mem. ADA, Idaho State Dental Assn., Oreg. Dental Assn., Southwestern Idaho Dental Soc., Acad. Gen. Practitioners Orthodontics, Silverdale Study Club Orthodontics. Mormon. Office: Emmett Dental Group PA 119 N Wardwell Emmett ID 83617

SATER, WILLIAM FREDERICK, history educator, writer; b. N.Y.C., Nov. 17, 1937; 1 child, Rachel Mayen. AB in History, Stanford U., 1959; MA, UCLA, 1964, PhD, 1968. Prof. history Calif. State U., Long Beach, 1967—; cons. Rand Corp., Calif., 1977-90, Mellon Fellowship Found., 1982-88, NEH, 1983, ABC Cilo, 1985—, Libr. Congress, 1988—; book rev. editor The New World, 1984-90; guest lectr. Peace Corps, L.A., 1967, U. Chile, Santiago, 1968, UCLA, 1972, U. Concepcion, Chile, 1975, Cath. U., Santiago, 1980, U. Calgary, 1983, 87, 96, Western Can. Mil. Soc., 1983, 96; papers presented at Am. Hist. Assn., 1972, 76, Pacific Coast Conf. L.Am. History, 1972, Nat. Assn. Pvt. Schs., 1983, Conf. on Independence of Mex., U. Calif., Irvine, 1987, Can. Hist. Assn., 1990, 94, Rocky Mountain Conf. L.Am. History, Soc. for Mil. History, Ont., 1993. Editor, assoc. editor, book rev. editor The History Tchr., 1972-85; mng. editor TVI Report, 1984—; author: The Revolutionary Left and Terrorist Violence in Chile, 1986, Puerto Rican Terrorists: A Possible Threat to U.S. Energy Installations?, 1981, The Heroic Image in Chile, 1973, The History Teacher, 1981, The Research Guide to Andean History, 1981, The Southern Cone Nations, 1984, Chile and the War of the Pacific, 1986, Chile and the United States, 1990, A General History of Chile, 1996; contbr. articles to profl. jours. 1st lt. U.S. Army, 1959-60. Fellow U. Calif.-U. Chile, 1965-66, Orgn. Am. States, 1974-75; recipient Barros Arana Internat. Contest on Chilean History, Chilean Hist. Assn., 1984. Mem. Chilean Acad. History (corr.), Pacific Coast of L.Am. Studies (bd. govs., Hubert Herring award), Conf. on L.Am. History (chmn. com. teaching and teaching materials, chmn. andean studies com., acting chmn. Rio de la Plata com.), Am. Hist. Assn. Office: Calif State U Dept History Long Beach CA 90840

SATEREN, TERRY, theater technical production; b. Madison, Wis., Dec. 5, 1943; s. Leland Bernhard and Eldora (Johnson) S. BA, Augsburg Coll., 1968. Tech. prodn. dir. Guthrie Theatre, Mpls., 1974-78, dir. prodn., 1985-87; dir. exhibits Sci. Mus. Minn., St. Paul, 1978-85; tech. prodn. dir. Seattle Repertory Theatre, 1987—; cons. acad. and community theaters and museums, 1974—, U. Minn., 1992; Master class lectr. U. Wash., Seattle, 1989-91; adj. prof. U. Wash., 1991-92. Designer: (operas) Three Penny Opera, 1972, Newest Opera in the World, 1972, Don Giovanni, 1973; commd. sculptor numerous inds., chs. and acad. instns., 1966—. Pres.'s scholar Valparaiso (Ind.) U., 1967. Mem. U.S. Inst. Theatre Tech. Home: 7341 23rd Ave NW Seattle WA 98117-5661 Office: Seattle Repertory Theatre 155 Mercer St Seattle WA 98109-4639

SATHER, GLEN CAMERON, professional hockey team executive, coach; b. High River, Alta., Canada, Sept. 2, 1943. Former professional hockey player; pres., gen. mgr. Edmonton Oilers, Nat. Hockey League, Alta., Can., coach, 1977-89, now alt. gov.; coach winning team in Stanley Cup competition, 1987. Recipient Jack Adams Award for NHL Coach of the Yr., 1986. Office: care Edmonton Oilers, Edmonton Coliseum, Edmonton, AB Canada T5B 4M9*

SATO, IRVING SHIGEO, education consultant; b. Honolulu, Sept. 4, 1933; s. Jusaku and Matsuyo (Uchida) S.; m. Helen Hatsuko, Aug. 18, 1956. B.Ed. with honors, U. Hawaii, 1955; M.S., U. So. Calif., 1962. Tchr. high sch., Honolulu, 1957-58; tchr., chmn. English and history Pasadena High Sch., Calif., 1958-66; cons. gifted and creative student programs Colo. Dept. Edn., Denver, 1966-68; cons. edn. mentally gifted Calif. Dept. Edn., Los Angeles, 1968-72; dir. Nat. State Leadership Tng. Inst. on Gifted and Talented, Los Angeles, 1972-93; instr. U. Denver, 1966-67, U. Colo., 1967-68, U. So. Calif., 1970-75, U. Hawaii, 1976—, Widener U., Pa., 1981-91; cons. on gifted programs to numerous sch. dists., states, fgn. countries, 1966—; conf. speaker. Editor: (with James A. Gallagher and Sandra N. Kaplan) Promoting the Education of the Gifted/Talented: Strategies for Advocacy, 1983; co-editor (newsletter) The Gifted Pupil, 1968-72. Contbr. articles to profl. jours. Served to 1st lt. U.S. Army, 1955-57. Recipient cert. of recognition Office Gifted and Talented, U.S. Office Edn., 1974. Mem. Coun. State Dirs. Programs for Gifted (pres. 1969-71), Assn. for Gifted (exec. bd. 1972-79, pres. 1977-78), Nat. Assn. for Gifted Children (bd. govs. 1977-88, cert. of merit 1973, disting service award 1982), Calif. Assn. Gifted (Educator of Yr. award 1976), Assn. Supervision and Curriculum Devel., Phi Delta Kappa, Phi Kappa Phi. Home: 1744 Via Del Rey South Pasadena CA 91030-4128

SATO, MILES MASAKAZE, computer programmer, systems analyst; b. Honolulu, May 14, 1950; s. Seigi and Michie Sato; m. Miriam H. Nitta, Aug. 12, 1978; children: Matthew, Michael. AB in Exptl. Psychology, Grinnell Coll., 1972; MSPH in Biostats., U. Hawaii, 1976, MPH in Health Svcs. Adminstrn., 1978. Rsch. assoc. Pacific Biomed. Rsch. Ctr., Honolulu, 1973-75; sr. data reduction analyst U.S. Army Strategic Def. Command (tech. support contractors), Kwajalein Missile Range, Honolulu, 1978-92; programmer/analyst, LAN adminstr. Hawaii Employers Coun., Honolulu, 1992—. Contbr. articles to profl. jours. Mem. IEEE, APHA, Am. Statis. Assn., Assn. for Computing Machinery, Nat. Systems Programmers Assn., The Math. Assn. of Am. Lutheran. Office: Hawaii Employers Coun 2682 Waiwai Loop Honolulu HI 96819-1938

SATO, TADASHI, artist; b. Maui, Hawaii, Feb. 6, 1923. Student, Honolulu Sch. Art, Bklyn. Mus. Art Sch., New Sch. Soc. Rsch. Exhbns. include Guggenheim Mus., N.Y.C., 1954, Honolulu Acad. Arts, 1957, Pacific Heritage Exhibit, L.A., 1963, McRoberts and Tunnard Ltd., London, 1964, White House Festival Arts, Washington, 1965, Berlin Art Festival, 1967, Japanese C. of C., Honolulu, 1993-94, Maui Cmty. and Cultural Assn., 1994; represented in permanent collections Albright-Knox Art Gallery, Buffalo, Guggenheim Mus., Whitney Mus. Am. Art, N.Y.C., Honolulu Acad. Arts, U. Art Gallery, Tucson, (mosaic) Hawaii State Capitol Bldg., State Libr. Aina Haina, Oahu, State Hosp., Kea-lakekua, Hawaii, Wailulu War Meml. Gymnasium, Maui, Krannert Art Mus., Ill., U. Nebr.; executed murals Halekulani Hotel, Honolulu, (mosaic) West Maui Recreation Ctr., (oil) Bay Club, Kapalua, Maui; retrospective Hui No Eau, Makawao, Maui, 1992. Office: PO Box 476 Lahaina HI 96767-0476

SATO-VIACRUCIS, KIYO, nurse, inventor, entrepreneur, consultant; b. Sacramento, May 8, 1923; d. John Shinji and Mary Tomomi (Watanabe) Sato; m. Gene Viacrucis, Aug. 9, 1958 (div. May 1976); adopted children: Cia, Jon, Paul, Tanya. BS, Hillsdale Coll., 1944; M in Nursing in Grad. Studies/Pub. Health Nursing, Western Res. U., 1951. Cert. health and devel. specialist, Calif., pub. health nurse, Calif., audiologist. Nursery sch. attendant Poston (Ariz.) II Concentration Camp, 1942; staff nurse U. Hosps., Cleve., 1948; pub. health nurse Sacramento County Health Dept., 1948-50, 52-53; sch. nurse U. Oslo, 1953, Sacramento County Schs., 1954-58; presch. nurse Sacramento City Unified Sch. Dist., 1973-85; pvt. practice cons. Blackbird Vision Screening System, Sacramento, 1985—; cons., speaker Blackbird Vision Screening System, 1973—; cons. state task force Vision Screening Guidelines, 1981. Inventor Blackbird presch. vision screening method; cons. vision screening; contbr. articles to profl. jours. Served to capt. USAF, 1951-52. Recipient Excellence in Nursing award RN Mag. Found., 1983. Mem. Nat. Sch. Nurses Assn., Calif. Sch. Nurses Orgn., Japanese Am. Citizens League (pres. 1950), Am. Assn. Ret. Persons, VFW (pub. rels., post surgeon 1985—, cmty. activities 1986—, speaker's bur. Internment of Am. of Japanese Descent and the U.S. Constn.). Democrat. Home: PO Box 277424 Sacramento CA 95827 Office: Blackbird Vision Screening PO Box 277424 Sacramento CA 95827-7424

SATRE, RODRICK IVERSON, environmental consultant, business developer; b. Geneseo, N.Y., July 14, 1951; s. Roy Ingvold Jr. and Patricia Ruth (Holder) S.; m. Bonita Daley, Sept. 30, 1978. BS in Chem. Engring., Clarkson U., 1973; MBA in Internat. Bus., John F. Kennedy U., 1989. Plant engr., then operating asst. Chevron Chem. Co., Richmond, Calif., 1974-78, area supr., 1978-80; sr. analyst Chevron Chem. Co., San Francisco, 1980-85; group leader, then sr. rsch. engr. Chevron Chem. Co., Richmond, 1985-89; mgr. Internat. Tech. Corp., Martinez, Calif., 1990—; prin. SSD Consulting, Point Richmond, Calif., 1990-92; gen. mgr. Internat. Tech. Corp., Houston, 1992-93; mng. prin. engr. Harding Lawson Assocs., Novato, Calif., 1993-95; project dir. TRC/Environ. Solutions, Inc., Walnut Creek, Calif., 1995-96; assoc. Blasland, Bouck & Lee Inc., Novato, Calif., 1996-97; engring. mgr. ATI Engring. Svcs., San Francisco, 1997—; prin. assoc. Kertesz Internat., Inc., San Francisco, 1990—. Patentee in field. Sci. judge Richmond Unified Sch. Dist., 1985—. Mem. AIChE, PEMA, PRNC (pres. 1996—), Contra Costa Coun. (co-chair environ. task force), Hazardous Waste Assn. Calif., Berkeley Ski Club (v.p. 1978-79, pres. 1981-82). Republican. Office: ATI Engring Svcs Inc 944 Market St Ste 700 San Francisco CA 94102

SATTER, RAYMOND NATHAN, judge; b. Denver, Oct. 19, 1948; s. Charles Herbert and Muriel Vera (Tuller); m. Suzanne Elizabeth Ehlers, May 28, 1977. BA, U. Denver, 1970; JD, Cath. U., 1973. Bar: Colo. 1973, U.S. Dist. Ct. Colo. 1973, U.S. Ct. Appeals (10th cir.) 1973, U.S. Supreme Ct. 1976, U.S. Tax Ct. 1981. Assoc. Wallace, Armatas & Hahn, Denver, 1973-75; ptnr. Tallmadge, Wallace & Hahn, Denver, 1975-77; pvt. practice Denver, 1978-87; Denver County judge, 1987—; gen. counsel Satter Dist., Denver, 1977-78; assoc. mcpl. judge City of Englewood, Colo., 1985-86; mem. Colo. Supreme Ct. Com. on Civil Rules. Pres. Young Artists Orch. Denver, 1985-87; sec. Denver Symphony Assn., 1985-86. Mem. Colo. Bar Assn. (ethics com.), Denver Bar Assn. (Jud. Excellence award 1992, 95). Office: Denver County Ct 108 City & County Bldg 1437 Bannock St Denver CO 80202-5308

SATTERLEE, T(HOMAS) MICHAEL, mortgage broker; b. Seattle, Mar. 26, 1968; s. Thomas Michael and Evelyn Gwen (Foss) S. Grad. in pub. adminstrn. and humanities, Seattle U., 1993. Loan officer Foss & Assocs., Kirkland, Wash., 1993—. Mem. Nat. Assn. Mortgage Brokers, Wash. Assn. Mortgage Brokers, Ballard C. of C., Lions (pres. Ballard 1993-94). Democrat. Lutheran. Home: 109 N 51st St Seattle WA 98103 Office: Foss & Assocs Inc 5715 20th Ave NW Seattle WA 98107

SATTIN, ALBERT, psychiatry and neuropharmacology educator; b. Cleve., Oct. 5, 1931; s. Sam and Edith (Stolarsky) S.; m. Renee Schnider, Dec. 16, 1962; children—Rebecca Lee, Michael M. B.S., Western Reserve U., 1953, M.D., 1957. Diplomate Am. Bd. Psychiatry and Neurology. Intern Washington U., St. Louis, 1957-58; resident in psychiatry Case-Western Reserve U., Cleve., 1958-62; fellow Dept. Biochemistry, U. London, 1965-66; instr., sr. instr. Case-Western Res. U. Sch. Medicine, 1965-1970, asst. prof. psychiatry and pharmacology, 1970-77; assoc. prof. psychiatry Ind. U. Sch. Medicine, Indpls., 1977-84, assoc. prof. psychiatry and neurobiology, Ind. U. Grad. Sch., 1984-91; assoc. prof. psychiatry and biobehavioral scis. UCLA, 1991—; chief Antidepressant Neuropharmacology Lab, West L.A. and Sepulved VA Med. Ctrs., 1991—; mem. Brain Rsch. Inst., UCLA, 1997—. Contbr. articles to profl. jours. Grantee NIMH, NSF, VA; mem. Am. Psychiat. Assn. (life); mem. Am. Psychiat. Assn., Soc. for Neurosci. Soc. Biol. Psychiatry, Internat. Soc. Neurochemistry. Office: West LA VA Med Ctr 2N-BC 11301 Wilshire Blvd Los Angeles CA 90073

SATTLER, BRUCE WEIMER, lawyer; b. South Gate, Calif., July 30, 1944; s. LeRoy Edward and Mary Beth (Weimer) S.; m. Earle Martha Ross, July 22, 1972. BA, Stanford U., 1966, JD, 1969. Bar: Colo. 1969, U.S. Dist. Ct. Colo. 1969, U.S. Dist. Ct. Mont. 1982, U.S. Dist. Ct. (no. dist.) Tex. 1989, U.S. Ct. Appeals (10th cir.) 1969, U.S. Ct. Appeals (9th cir.) 1984, U.S. Ct. Appeals (5th cir.) 1972. Assoc. Holland & Hart, Denver, 1969-75, ptnr., 1975-87; assoc. Equal Employment Opportunity Commn., Denver, 1973, Morris, Lower & Sattler, Denver, 1987-90; ptnr. Faegre & Benson, Denver, 1990—. Bd. dirs. ACLU of Colo., Denver, 1975-80, 88-94, Legal Aid Soc. of Metro Denver, 1976—, Colo. Lawyers Com., Denver, 1990-94, Children's Legal Clinic, Denver, 1989-91, Colo. Women's Employment and Edn., Denver, 1986-89. Mem. ABA, Denver Bar Assn., Colo. Bar Assn. Office: Faegre & Benson 370 17th St Denver CO 80202

SAUER, ANNE KATHERINE, glass blower, artist, educator; b. Madison, Wis., Sept. 2, 1958; d. Collin Harold and Margaret (Isabell (Roberts) S. BS, U. Wis., 1982; MFA, Mass. Coll. Art, Boston, 1987. Owner, mgr. Brick House Glass, Madison, 1989; lectr., demonstrator Madison Art Ctr., 1992, Madison East H.S., 1992, Univ. League, 1993. Exhibited in group shows Valperine Gallery, Madison, 1992, City-County Arts, Madison, 1993, Newell Gallery, Waunakee, Wis., 1993, 94, Blue Bird Gallery, Prairie du Sac, Wis., 1994; work represented in various mags. Home: 3860 N River Hills Dr Tucson AZ 85720 Office: Brick House Glass 3860 N River Hills Dr Tucson AZ 85750-2070

SAUER, DAVID ANDREW, writer, computer consultant; b. Urbana, Ill., Feb. 25, 1948; s. Elmer Louis and Frances (Hill) S. BA, Northwestern U., 1970; MS, Simmons Coll., 1975. Reference libr. Boston U., 1976-78, bibliographer, 1978-84, sci. bibliographer, 1984-88, head Stone Sci. Libr., 1988-94; v.p. info. svcs. CyberHelp, Inc., 1995—. Co-author: Internet for Windows, 1994, WinComm Pro: The Visual Learning Guide, 1995, ProComm Plus V2 for Windows: The Visual Learning Guide, 1995, Access for Windows 95: The Visual Learning Guide, 1995, Cruising America Online 2.5, 1995, Internet for Windows: The America Online 2.5 Edition, 1995, Internet for Windows: The Microsoft Network Edition, 1995, Cruising the Microsoft Network, 1996, Cruising CompuServe, 1996, WinFax Pro 7 for Windows: The Visual Learning Guide, 1996, Windows NT 4.0 Visual Desk Reference, 1997. Mem. S.W. Corridor Project, Boston, 1977-87, Forest Hills Neighborhood Improvement Assn., Boston, 1977-90, Forest Hills/Woodbourne Neighborhood Group, 1991-94. Mem. ALA, Spl. Librs. Assn., San Diego Computer Soc., Highland Casitas Homeowners Assn. (chmn. 1996—). Democrat. Home and Office: 1034 La Tierra Dr San Marcos CA 92069-4617

SAUERS, WILLIAM DALE, lawyer, playwright; b. Santa Cruz, Calif., June 18, 1926; s. Myrl Melvin and Helen (Fightmaster) S.; m. Barbara Jean Cole, May 9, 1945; children: Kathleen McCarthy, Deborah Nelson, Susan Reeves. AB, Fresno State U., 1949; JD, Stanford U., 1952. Bar: Calif. 1953, U.S. Supreme Ct. 1964. Asst. sec. State Bar of Calif., San Francisco, 1952-55; dep. dist. atty. County of Santa Clara, San Jose, Calif., 1955-58; ptnr. Finch, Sauers et al., Palo Alto, Calif., 1958-88; pvt. practice law Palo Alto, Calif., 1988—. Playwright: A Rainbow on Mt. Olympus, 1993, Did Not I Dance with You?, 1994, A Fork in the Road, 1995, What'll We Do With Mame, 1996. Sec. Urban Coaliton of Palo Alto, 1969-72; chmn. ARC chpt. Palo Alto, Calif., 1973-76, Family Svc. Assn., 1973-76, Sr. Coun. Affiliates, Palo Alto, 1981-85; chmn. bd. trustees Menlo Coll., Atherton, Calif., 1984-88;, dir. Oreg. Shakespeare estival, Ashland, 1989-95; pres. San Jose Repertory Theatre, 1989-91; chmn. San Francisco Shakespeare Festival, 1994—. Mem. ABA, Calif. State Bar Assn., Phi Delta Phi. Republican. Episcopalian. Office: Hamilton, Dalton & Sauers 90 Middlefield Rd Menlo Park CA 94025

SAULT, NICOLE LANDRY, anthropologist and educator; b. St. Paul, 1952; m. Peter C. Reynolds. BA in Anthropology and English, U. Calif., Santa Barbara, 1970; MA in Anthropology, UCLA, 1975, PhD in Anthropology, 1985. Vis. asst. prof. anthropology Santa Clara (Calif.) U., 1977—. Author and editor: Many Mirrors: Body Image and Social Relations, 1994; contbr. articles to profl. jours. Recipient Sisterhood is Powerful award Santa Clara U., 1994; Irvine Found. grantee, 1992; Fulbright-Hays scholar, 1989. Mem. Am. Anthropol. Assn., Amnesty Internat., Greenpeace, Phi Beta Kappa. Roman Catholic. Office: Santa Clara Univ Dept Anthropology Santa Clara CA 95053

SAUNDERS, BRIAN KEITH, consulting company executive; b. Columbus, Ohio, June 4, 1961. BSEE, Purdue U., 1983; MBA, Dartmouth U., 1988. Asst. mgr. engring. New Eng. Telephone, Boston, 1983-85, asst. product mgr., 1985-86; assoc. Booz Allen & Hamilton, N.Y.C., 1987-90; dir. strategy and planning Pacific Bell, San Ramon, Calif., 1991-92; gen. mgr. Compus Svcs. Corp., Pleasanton, Calif., 1993-94; prin. cons., designer BKS Design, San Ramon, Calif., 1994—; sr. prin. The McKenna Group, Palo Alto, Calif., 1995—; bd. dirs. Children's Media Lab., Berkeley, Calif., 1993—, Family Stress Ctr., Concord, Calif., 1995—; mem. industry coun. Mt. Diablo Coll., Pleasant Hill, Calif., 1993-95; mem. exec. coun. Tuck MBEP Alumni Assn. Dartmouth Coll., Hanover, N.H., 1994—. Mem. Computer Game Developers Assn., Joint Ctr. for Polit. and Econ. Studies (assoc.), The Internet Soc., World Future Soc., Armed Forces Comms. and Electronics Assn.

SAUNDERS, DEBRA J., columnist; b. Newton, Mass., Dec. 8, 1954. BA in Latin and Greek, U. Mass., Boston, 1980. Asst. dir. Arnold Zenker Assocs., 1982-83; writer/rschr., account exec. Todd Domke Assocs., Sacramento, 1983-84, Russo Watts & Rollins, Sacramento, 1985-86; asst. to Rep. Leader Calif. Legislature, Sacramento, 1987-88; columnist, editl. writer L.A. Daily News, 1988-92; columnist San Francisco Chronicle, 1992—; leader study group on polit. speechmaking Harvard U., Cambridge, Mass., 1984; tchr. editl. and column writing UCLA Ext., 1992. Published in Wall St. Jour., Nat. Review, Weekly Std.; syndicated nationally via Creators Syndicate. Office: San Francisco Chronicle 901 Mission St San Francisco CA 94103-2905

SAUNDERS, JAMES, management and training consultant; b. Chgo., Sept. 22, 1924; s. James Windam and Carrie Evelyn (Cox) S.; m. Gwendolyn Haithcox, Oct. 21, 1945 (dec. May 1971); children: Patricia Ann, Kathryn Lynn; m. Anita Joanne Laster, Sept. 16, 1972 (div. Oct. 1977); m. Bettye Jean Ricks, Apr. 18, 1981. BS in Math., Roosevelt U., 1953. Quality assurance rep. Dept. Army and Signal Corps., Chgo., 1945-63; dep. dir. quality assurance U.S. Naval Ordnance Plant, Forest Park, Ill., 1963-70; quality systems mgr. Gen. Foods Corp., Chgo., 1970-82; pres. Saunders and Assocs., Peoria, Ariz., 1982-91; councilman, vice mayor City of Peoria, 1985-91; examiner Ariz. Govs. Alliance for Quality, 1995. Bd. dirs., sec. Ariz. Retirement Ctrs., Peoria, 1984-85; pres., chmn., bd. dirs., founder Peoria Econ. Devel. Group, 1987-91, dir. emeritus, 1991—; mem. Peoria Personnel Bd., 1984-85, Maricopa County Pvt. Industry Coun., 1984-89, chmn., 1988-89, exec. com. Westside Transp. Coalition, Peoria, 1988-89. Recipient Black Achiever of Industry award Chgo. YMCA, 1977, Image Govt. award NAACP, 1989, also various other awards. Mem. Peoria C. of C. (v.p., bd. dirs. 1985), Westside Coalition Chambers Commerce, Lions (sec., v.p. Peoria chpt. 1983-86), Kiwanis, Masons, Alpha Phi Alpha. Home: 18847 N 88th Dr Peoria AZ 85382-8528

SAUNDERS, JAMES HARWOOD, accountant; b. Carlsbad, N.Mex., Apr. 2, 1948; s. Eugene C. and Ruth (Powelson)S.; m. Kathleen Sue Matson, Jan. 26, 1974 (div. Apr. 1982); m. Bette Kim McCutcheon, Sept. 4, 1982; children: James C., Carl J., William K. AA in Adminstrn. Justice, Glendale Coll., Glendale, Ariz., 1975; BSBA, Ariz. State U., 1978. CPA, N.M., Ariz., Colo., Nev., Utah; lic. funeral dir. and embalmer; cert. fraud examiner. Embalmer Denton Funeral Home, Carlsbad, 1964-69; clk., trainee Sears & Roebuck Co., Dallas and Albuquerque, 1969-71, Phoenix, 1971-73; police sgt. spl. ops. Phoenix Police Dept., 1973-80; staff acct. various CPA firms, Carlsbad, 1980-83; owner James H. Saunders Acctg., Carlsbad, 1983-86; pvt. practice acctg. Eagar, Ariz., 1987—; auditor, mgmt. advisor to several Ariz. municipalities, 1987—; bd. dirs. Ariz. Lion Eye Bank. Vol. fireman Carlsbad Fire Dept., 1965-68; reserve dep. Bermallio County Sheriff Dept., Albuquerque, 1969-70. Mem. AICPA, Ariz. Soc. CPAs, N.Mex. Soc. CPAs, N.Mex. Assn. Funeral Dirs., Lions (sec. Carlsbad chpt. 1985-87, pres. Springerville, Ariz. chpt. 1987-91). Office: PO Box 1270 74 N Main Eagar AZ 85925

SAUNDERS, KAREN ESTELLE, secondary school educator; b. San Carlos, Ariz., June 13, 1941; d. Walter Carl and Irma Marie (Gallmeyer) Sorgatz; m. John Richard Saunders, Dec. 27, 1962 (div. Nov. 1981). BA, Ariz. State U., 1964, MA, 1968, postgrad., 1982—. Tchr., chair fine arts dept. McClintock High Sch., Tempe, Ariz., 1964-77; tchr., chair art dept. Corona del Sol High Sch., Tempe, 1977—, chair fine arts dept., 1987—; tchr., chair art dept. McClintock High Sch., Tempe, 1964-77; coord. artists-in-schs. program Tempe Union H.S., 1975-80, program adminstr. travel/study program, 1976-78, 80, Corona del Sol H.S., 1994-95; program chair Four Corners Art Educators Conf., Scottsdale, Ariz., 1982; co-chair S.W. Indian Art Collectibles Exhbn., Carefree, Ariz., 1982, also editor, designer catalogue; adv. editorial bd. Sch. Arts Mag., 1989-96; artist-in-schs. coord. Corona del Sol High Sch., 1994-95; strategic planning team Tempe Union H.S. Dist., 1994-95; mem. occupational edn. adv. com. Tempe Union H.S. Dist., 1995—; mem. East Valley Sch. To Work Equity Team, 1996—, Corona Del Sol H.S., 1996—. Editorial bd. Jour. Art Edn., 1982-85; dir. mural project Corona Del Sol H.S., 994-95. Mem. State Art Guide Com., Tempe, 1975-77; mem. planning com. Sheldon Lab. Systems Facilities, 1980-83; chmn. Tempe Sculpture Competition, Fine Arts Ctr., 1983; mem. Ariz. Scholastic Art Adv. Bd., Phoenix, 1983-87; judge Mill Ave. Arts Festival, Tempe, 1989, 1991-94. Recipient Vincent Van Gogh award Colo. Alliance for Arts Edn., 1978, Ariz. Art Educator of Yr. award Ariz. Art Edn. Assn., 1979, Leadership award Four Corners Art Educators Conf., 1982, Lehrer Mel. award Ariz. State U. Sch. Art, 1986, Tempe Diablos Ednl. Excellence awards, 1991; Ariz. State U. fellow, 1967-68. Mem. NEA, Nat. Art Edn. Assn. (v.p., bd. dirs. 1980-82, chmn. leadership workshop 1979, Pacific Secondary Art Educator of Yr. award 1985, co-chair Pres.' Day 1992-95 Conv.), Assn. Secondary Curriculum Devel., Ariz. Alliance for Arts Edn. (bd. dirs. 1976-81, co-chmn. western regional conf. 1978), Tempe Secondary Edn. Assn., Ariz. Art Edn. Assn. (pres. 1976-78), Tempe Sister Cities Orgn. (exch. tchr. Regensburg, Germany 1992, coord.), Women's Image Now Club, Mortar Bd., Phi Delta Kappa, Alpha Phi. Home: 930 S Dobson Rd Unit 22 Mesa AZ 85202-2912 Office: Corona del Sol High Sch 1001 E Knox Rd Tempe AZ 85284-3204

SAUNDERS, SHARON, media director; b. Provo, Utah, Apr. 17, 1946; d. Lynn Furlong and Beulah (Hatch) Olsen; m. Kevin Forrest Saunders, Aug. 9, 1986; 1 child, Kelsey. AA, BYU, 1966. Media buyer, planner Tracy-Locke, Denver, 1977-80; sr. media buyer The Gap, San Francisco, 1983; media dir. Dakis Concern, Orinda, Calif., 1985-86; pres., owner Media Mentor, San Francisco, 1984—. Sponsor advt. team softball league, 1993—. Office: Media Mentor 642 Chenery St San Francisco CA 94131-3000

SAURMAN, ANDREW (SKIP SAURMAN), state agency executive; b. Abington, Pa., Feb. 11, 1951; s. Andrew Charles and Doris (Margerum) S.; m. April Diane Young, Aug. 15, 1973 (div. June 1982); 1 child, Wendy Dawn; m. Susan Lynne MacMillan, July 30, 1988; children: Shelly Lloyd, Aaron Lloyd. BS in Vocat. Edn., So. Ill. U., 1993. Cert. master automotive technician. Automotive and truck technician various dealerships, Albuquerque and Belen, N.Mex., 1972-83; automotive instr. Santa Fe H.S. and Santa Fe C.C., 1984-95; state supr. for trade, indsl. and tech. edn. N.Mex. State Dept. Edn., Santa Fe, 1995—; tech. cons. N.Mex. Better Bus. Bur., Albuquerque, 1987—, Megatech Corp., Tewksbury, Mass., 1989—, N.Mex. Atty. Gen.'s Office, Santa Fe, 1994—; facilitator N.Mex. Automotive Adv. Com., Santa Fe, 1995—. Served with U.S. Army, 1969-72, Vietnam. Decorated Bronze Star medal; recipient Gold Wrench award Snap-on Tools, 1990, Gt. Tchr. award Century Savs. and Loan, Santa Fe, 1993. Mem. N.Am. Coun. Automotive Tchrs., Vocat. Indsl. Clubs Am., Am. Vocat. Assn., N.Mex. Vocat. Assn. Home: 1803 San Felipe Circle Santa Fe NM 87505 Office: NMex State Dept Edn 300 Don Gaspar Ave Santa Fe NM 87501-2752

SAUSE, HELEN, redevelopment executive; b. Reedsport, Oreg., June 13, 1934; d. Howard Forrest and Blanche Irene (Cope) Perkins; m. Samuel Hunter Sause, Feb. 29, 1964; children: David, Paula, Carole. BA, U. Calif., Hayward, 1976. Loan officer, office mgr. Scott Built Homes, Eugene, Oreg., 1957-60; dep. dir. Eugene (Oreg.) Urban Renewal, 1960-62, Seaside (Calif.) Urban Renewal, 1962-64; assoc. Whisler/Patri Assoc., Planning and Archtl. Firm, San Francisco, 1964-68; asst. to dir., corp. sec. San Francisco (Calif.) Redevel. Agy., 1968-80, project dir. for Yerba Buena Ctr., 1980—. Chair econ. devel. commn. City of Alameda, Calif., 1990—; active Devel. Fund, 1990—; vestry mem., stewardship chair Christ Ch. Episcopal, 1992—; treas. Citizens Housing Corp., 1993—. Recipient award Mayors Fiscal Adv. Com., San Francisco, 1993, 94. Mem. Nat. Assn. Housing and Redevel. Ofcls. (pres. 1987-89, chair internat. com. 1989—, Lange award 1994), Lambda Alpha (exec. com. 1992). Democrat. Office: San Francisco Redevel Agy 770 Golden Gate Ave San Francisco CA 94102-3120

SAUSSER, GAIL DIANNE, insurance broker; b. Richland, Wash., May 8, 1952; d. Lenard Merl and Julia Esther (Saxerud) Oathes; m. Harvey Wilson Sausser II, 1979 (div. 1984). BA in Humanities, Heritage Coll., Spokane, Wash., 1974; MA in Psychology, Antioch West, Vancouver, B.C., Can., 1977; postgrad., Seattle U., 1996—. Cert. assoc. risk mgmt., Ins. Inst. Am. Counselor Chem. Dependency Program, Seattle, 1982-84; acctg. asst. Newdata Corp., Seattle, 1986-87; adminstrv. broker Johnson & Higgins, Seattle, 1987-96. ral. counselor Cmty. Mental Health Inst., Spokane, Wash., 1972-75, Seattle Mental Health Inst., 1975-77; pres. Acupuncture Rsch. Treatment Assn., Seattle, 1992-96; mem. rsch. roundtable King County Natural Health Clinic, Seattle, 1995, mem. adv. bd., 1996-97; mem., co-chmn. evaluation com., managed care com. King County HIV/AIDS Planning Coun., Seattle, 1996; mem. adv. bd. N.W. Inst. Acupuncture and Oriental Medicine, Seattle, 1996. Mem. N.W. Environ. Claims Assn. Home & Office: Acupuncture Rsch Treatment Assn PO Box 1009 Seattle WA 98111

SAUTER, GAIL LOUISE, speech pathologist; b. Williamsport, Pa., Mar. 14, 1951; d. Irvin Lamont and Mary Christine (Gephart) Guthrie; m. Gary Lee Sauter, Apr. 1974; children: Amberlynn Marie, Steven James. BS in Edn., Calif. State Coll., 1974; M of Communicative Disorders, Brigham Young U., 1985. Cert. clin. speech/lang. pathologist, resource tchr.; lic. speech pathologist. Asst. dir., dir. rehab. Summer Camp for Handicapped Children, Amherst, Ohio, 1976-77; speech/lang. pathologist Easter Seal Summer Clinic, Lorain, Ohio, 1978, Vermilion (Ohio) Sch. System, 1975-80; speech/lang. pathologist Alpine Sch. Dist., Orem, Utah, 1980-86, spl. edn. tchr., 1986—; ednl. cons. Accelerated Learning Ctr., also mem. adv. bd. Pres. No. Ohio Speech & Lang. Assn., 1978-79. Mem. Am. Speech/Lang., Hearing Assn. Republican. Home: 632 S 600 W Orem UT 84058-6017 Office: Orchard Elem Sch 1035 N 800 E Orem UT 84097-3430

SAVAGE, TERRY RICHARD, information systems executive; b. St. Louis, Oct. 21, 1930; s. Terry Barco and Ada Vanetta (Cochran) S.; m. Gretchen Susan Wood, Sept. 26, 1964; children: Terry Curtis, Christopher William, Richard Theodore. AB, Washington U., St. Louis, 1951, MA, 1952; PhD, U. Pa., 1954. Mgr. system software IBM Rsch., Yorktown Heights, N.Y., 1956-63; dir. data processing Documentation Inc., Bethesda, Md., 1963-64; mgr. info. systems Control Data Corp., Rockville, Md., 1964-67; dir. rsch. Share Rsch. Corp., Santa Barbara, Calif., 1967-68; computer-aided acquisition and logistic support program mgr. TRW, Redondo Beach, Calif., 1968-92; ret., ind. cons. pvt. practice, 1992—; expert witness for various coms. U.S. Congress, 1981, 84, 88, 89. Contbr. articles to profl. jours. Bd. dirs. ABC-Clio Press, Santa Barbara, 1970-75, Help the Homeless Help Themselves, Rancho Palos Verdes, Calif., 1988-94, ChorusLiners, Rancho Palos Verdes, 1983—, Savage Info. Svcs., Inc., Torrance, Calif., 1992—. Mem. Cosmos Club. Home and Office: 30000 Cachan Pl Rancho Palos Verdes CA 90275-5412

SAVAGE, THOMAS WARREN, engineering manager; b. Morgantown, W.Va., Feb. 6, 1959; s. Thomas Louis Savage and Sandra Mabel (Ferguson) Crawford; m. Cydney Ellen Fry, May 8, 1981; children: Jessica Louise, Kristin Anne, Thomas Dylan. BS in Computer Engring., Santa Clara U., 1993. Electronic technician ITT North, Galion, Ohio, 1977-79; electronic test engr. Fairchild Test Systems, San Jose, Calif., 1979-82; design engr. Tandem Computers, Cupertino, Calif., 1982-94; engring. mgr. Tandem Computers, Cupertino, 1994-95, Synopsys Inc., Mountain View, Calif., 1995—. Patentee in field. Mem. Order of the Engr. Home: 1648 Capitancillos Pl San Jose CA 95120-5701 Office: Synopsys Inc 700 E Middlefield Rd Mountain View CA 94043

SAVEDRA, JEANNINE EVANGELINE, art educator, artist; b. L.A., Dec. 21, 1965; d. Robert Anthony Savedra and April Elizabeth (Sanchez) Baroth. Student, Otis Coll. Art and Design, 1987-88; BFA, Calif. State U., L.A., 1991; postgrad., Calif. State U., Dominguez Hills, 1995—, UCLA Extn., 1997. Cert. art tchr., Calif. Children's counselor Salvation Army, Pasadena, Calif., 1987-88; graphic artist Calif. State U., L.A., 1989; pvt. investigator Larry J. Larsen Investigations and Trial Preparations, L.A., 1990-93; substitute art instr. Pasadena Unified Sch. Dist., 1994-95; studio art instr. Visual Arts and Design Acad., Pasadena, 1995—; upr. mural project Pasadena Playhouse Improvement Assn., 1995-96; high sch. men tor Puente program U. Calif., Berkeley, 1995—; educator Nat. Conf. Human Rels., Temescal Canyon, Calif., 1996; apptd. to ednl. adv. com. Jack Scott, mem. Assembly, Calif. State Legislature, 1997—. Exhibited in group shows at John F. Kennedy Libr., 1989, Calif. Fine Arts Gallery, 1990-92, Calif. State U., 1992 (Jurors' award), So. Calif. Juried Grad. Exhbn., 1995. Calif. Partnership Acad. grantee, 1996-97; recipient Excellence in Visual Arts award Calif. State U., 1990. Mem. L.A. County Mus. Art, Mus. Contemporary Art, Nat. Soc. Women Artists, Mus. Tolerance, Pasadena Armory Ctr. for Arts. Office: Visual Arts and Design Acad 2925 E Sierra Madre Blvd Pasadena CA 91107

SAVERY, MATTHEW, music conductor, director, educator; b. Berkshire County, Mass.. MusB, New Eng. Conservatory Music; MusM, U. Mich.; studied with Gustav Meier, Pascal Verrot, Frank Battisti. Music dir., conductor Symphonic Choir, 1994—, Butte Symphony Orch., 1994—, Bozeman (Mont.) Symphony Orch., 1994—; lectr. schs. Mont.; clincian Music Ekucators N.W. Conf., 1997; chmn. young artist competition Mont. Assn. Symphony Orch., 1997—. Music dir., conductor (theater) Damn Yankees, Guys and Dolls, Annie; past music dir. Comic Opera Guild, Ann Arbor, Mich., Stockbridge (Mass.) Sinfonia, Tecumseh (Mich.) Orch.; past conductor orch. festivals Mont. AA H.S.; appeared in , conductor Tchaikovsky's Nutcracker, 1995, 96, Tchaikovsky's Sleeping Beauty, The Magic Toy Shop. U. Mich. fellow; recipient Eugene and Sadie Power award for performing arts. Office: Bozeman Symphony Orch PO Box 1174 Bozeman MT 59771-1174*

SAVITRIPRIYA, SWAMI, religious leader, author; b. Apr. 1, 1930; divorced; three children. Ordained Hindu nun, Holy Order of Sannyas, 1975. Psychotherapist, 1970-75; founder, spiritual dir. Shiva-Shakti Kashmir Shaivite Hindu Ch., Ashram, Marin County, Calif., 1975-77, Shiva-Shakti Ashram, Oakland, Calif., 1978, Convent of the Divine Mother, Kona, Hawaii, 1979-80, Holy Mountain Monastery and Retreat Ctr., Groveland, Calif., 1984-92, Holy Mountain U., Groveland, Calif., 1985-92; founder, spiritual dir. Inst. for New Life, Groveland, Calif., 1990-92, Santa Cruz, Calif., 1993-95; founder, spiritual dir. Shiva-Shakti Ashram, Lake Chapala-Ajijic, Jalisco, Mexico, 1995—. Author (books) Kundalini-Shakti: From Awakening to Enlightenment, 1980, The Psychology of Mystical Awakening: The Yoga Sutras, 1991, The Cloud of the Universe, 1986, The Worlds of the Chakras, 1987, Arising Woman, 1988, Arising Man, 1988, Tantras of Personal and Spiritual Unfoldment, 1989, New World Hinduism, 1990, others; translator: Bhagavad Gita, 1974, Narada Bhakti Sutras, 1976, Upanishads, 1981, Shiva Sutras, 1984, Pratyabhijnahridayam, 1987, Vijnana Bhairava, 1989, others. Office: Shiva-Shakti Ananda Ashram 9297 Siempre Viva Rd # 71-270 San Diego CA 92173

SAVONA, MICHAEL RICHARD, physician; b. N.Y.C., Oct. 21, 1947; s. Salvatore Joseph and Diana Grace (Menditto) S.; m. Dorothy O'Neill, Oct. 18, 1975. BS summa cum laude, Siena Coll., 1969; MD, SUNY, Buffalo, 1973. Diplomate Am. Bd. Internal Medicine. Intern in internal medicine Presbyn. Hosp. Columbia U., N.Y.C., 1973-74, resident in internal medicine, 1974-76; vis. fellow internal medicine Delafield Hosp./Columbia U. Coll. Physicians and Surgeons, N.Y.C., 1974-76; practice medicine specializing in internal medicine Maui Med. Group, Wailuku, Hawaii, 1976-87, gen. practice medicine, 1987—; dir. ICU, Maui Meml. Hosp., also dir. respiratory therapy, CCU., chmn. dept. medicine, 1980—; clin. faculty John A. Burns Sch. Medicine, U. Hawaii, asst. prof. medicine, 1985—, asst. rsch. prof., 1989—. Bd. dirs. Maui Heart Assn.; dir. profl. edn. Maui chpt. Am. Cancer Soc.; mem. Maui County Hosp. Adv. Commn.; mem. coun. Community Cancer Program of Hawaii. Recipient James A. Gibson Wayne J. Atwell award, 1970, physiology award, 1970, Ernest Whitebsky award, 1971, Roche Lab. award, 1972, Pfiser Lab. award, 1973, Phillip Sang award, 1973, Hans Lowenstein M.D. Meml. award, 1973. Mem. AMA, Am. Thoracic Soc., Hawaii Thoracic Soc., Maui County Med. Assn. (past pres.), Hawaii Med. Assn., Hawaii Oncology Group, ACP, SW Oncology Coop. Group, Alpha Omega Alpha, Delta Epsilon Sigma. Office: 1830 Wells St Wailuku HI 96793-2365

SAVRUN, ENDER, engineering executive, researcher, engineer; b. Adana, Turkey, July 29, 1953; came to U.S., 1978; s. Yusuf and Nemide Savrun; m. Canan Erdamar, Oct. 23, 1979; 1 child, Altay. BS, Istanbul (Turkey) Tech. U., 1976, MS, 1978; PhD, U. Wash., 1986. Rsch. engr. Charlton Industries, Redmond, Wash., 1984-85; rsch. scientist Flow Industries, Kent, Wash., 1985-87, Photon Scis., Bothell, Wash., 1987-88; mgr. rsch. Keramont Rsch. Corp., Tucson, 1988-89; v.p. R & D Keramont Corp., Tucson, 1989-92; founder, pres. Sienna Rsch., Inc., Tucson, 1992—. Contbr. articles to profl. jours.; patentee in field. Turkish Govt. scholar, 1979. Mem. ASME, Am. Soc. for Metals, Am. Ceramic Soc. Office: Sienna Techs Inc 9004 Inverness Dr NE Seattle WA 98115-3980

SAWYER, GERALD, interior designer; b. L.A., Nov. 7, 1938; s. W. L. and Hazel Elizabeth (Duncan) S.; m. Mary L. Long, Feb. 18, 1966. BA, Northeastern State Coll., 1960; MA, Calif. State U., Fullerton, 1972. Tchr. Tulsa (Okla.) Unified Sch. Dist., 1960-64, Garden Grove (Calif.) Unified Sch. Dist., 1964-81; freelance artist Sunriver, Oreg., 1981-84; designer Village Interiors, Sunriver, 1985-87; designer, ptnr. Sawyer & Sawyer Interior Design, Sunriver, 1987—. Bd. dirs. Sunriver (Oreg.) Music Festival, 1983-87, Sunriver (Oreg.) Art Assn., 1984-85, Ctrl. Oreg. Arts Assn., Bend, Oreg., 1985-86, Regional Arts Coun. Ctrl. Oreg., 1987-88. Named Most Outstanding Speech Tchr., State of Okla., 1961. Mem. Am. Soc. Interior Designers (allied mem.). Home and Office: Sawyer & Sawyer Interior Design PO Box 3282 15 Camas Ln Sunriver OR 97707

SAWYER, JOY ROULIER, counselor; b. Schenectady, N.Y., July 7, 1960; d. Leon Eldon and Barbara Adele (Hauck) Roulier; m. Scott Sawyer, Aug. 20, 1988. BS, Evangel Coll., 1983; MA, NYU, 1993, Colo. Christian U., 1994. Writer, editor New Life Mag., Denver, 1983-85; tv prodr. KMGH-TV, Denver, 1984-85; sr. writer Christian Broadcasting Network, Virginia Beach, Va., 1985-88; editor, pastoral counselor Times Square Ch., N.Y.C., 1988-93; pvt. practice counselor Denver, 1994—; instr. of counseling. Colo. Christian U., 1997—; freelance writer and editor. Columnist, contbg. editor Inklings mag., 1994—; poetry editor, contbg. editor Mars Hill Rev., 1995—; contbr. articles to profl. jours. Mem. ACA, Am. Assn. Pastoral Counselors, Nat. Assn. Poetry Therapists, Evangelicals for Social Action. Democrat. Presbyterian. Office: 7114 W Jefferson Ave Ste 100 Denver CO 80235-2309

SAWYER, NELSON BALDWIN, JR., credit union executive; b. Jacksonville, Fla., Nov. 11, 1948; s. Nelson Baldwin and Nancy (Watson) S.; m. Carla Lee Dowden, Aug. 9, 1986. BA, U. North Fla., 1974. Program cons. State of Fla., Jacksonville, 1974-81; product mgr. Qualified Plan Designs, Inc., Jacksonville, 1981-83, Associated Gen. Contractors, Jacksonville, 1983-86; membership mgr. Calif. Credit Union League, Pomona, 1986-87, comm. mgr., 1987-90; sr. v.p., COO Calif. League Svcs. Corp., Pomona, 1990-93; sr. v.p. Wescorp, San Dimas, Calif., 1994—; chmn. bd. dirs. Calif. Ctr. Credit Union, Product Rsch. Orgn. for Credit Unions. Bd. dirs. Jacksonville C. of C., 1984-85. Mem. U.S. Jaycees (pres. Jacksonville 1983-84, chmn. bd. '84-85, senator, U.S., 1984—, Outstanding Young Man Am. 1983), Am. Soc. Assn. Execs., Fla. Yacht Club. Republican. Episcopalian. Office: WesCorp 924 Overland Ct San Dimas CA 91773-1742

SAWYER, THOMAS EDGAR, management consultant; b. Homer, La., July 7, 1932; s. Sidney Edgar and Ruth (Bickham) S.; BS, UCLA, 1959; MA, Occidental Coll., 1969; PhD, Walden U., 1990; m. Joyce Mezzanatto, Aug. 22, 1954; children—Jeffrey T., Scott A., Robert J., Julie Anne. Project engr. Garrett Corp., L.A., 1954-60; mgr. devel. ops. TRW Systems, Redondo Beach, Calif., 1960-66; spl. asst. to gov. State of Calif., Sacramento, 1967-69; prin., gen. mgr. Planning Rsch. Corp., McLean, Va., 1969-72; dep. dir. OEO, Washington, 1972-74; assoc. prof. bus. mgmt. Brigham Young U., 1974-78; pres. Mesa Corp., Provo, 1978-82, chmn. bd., 1978-82; pres. and dir. Sage Inst. Internat., Inc., Provo, Utah, 1982-88; chmn. bd., CEO Pvt. Telecom Networks, Inc. (name changed to Nat. Applied Computer Techs., Inc.), Orem, Utah, 1988—; chief tech. officer GST Telecommunications (formerly Greenstar Telecomm., Inc.), San Francisco, 1993—; also bd. dirs., Vancouver, Wash., 1995—; dir. Intechna Corp., HighTech Corp., Indian Affiliates, Inc., Greenstar USA, Inc., San Francisco, 1994—. Chmn. Nat. Adv. Council Indian Affairs; chmn. Utah State Bd. Indian Affairs; mem. Utah Dist. Export Coun.; mem. Utah dist. SBA Council; chmn. So. Paiute Restoration Com.; mem. adv. coun. Nat. Bus. Assn.; mem. Utah Job Tng. Coordinating Coun. Served with USMC, 1950-53. Mem. Am. Mgmt. Assn., Am. Soc. Public Adminstrn., Utah Coun. Small Bus. (dir.), Utah State Hist. Soc. (bd. dirs. 1993—). Republican. Mormon. Club: Masons. Author: Assimilation Versus Self-Indentity: A Modern Native American Perspective, 1976, Computer Assisted Instruction: An Inevitable Breakthrough, Current Challenges of Welfare: A Review of Public Assistance As Distributive Justice, 1989, Impact of Failure By Senior Executives to Receive Accurate Critical Feedback on Pervasive Change, 1990, The Promise of Funding a New Educational Initiative Using the Microcomputer, 1988, New Software Models for training and Education delivery, 1989, New Organizations: How They Deviate from Classical Models, 1989, Increasing Productivity in Organizations: The Paradox, 1989, An Introduction and Assessment of Strategic Decision Making Paradigms in Complex Organizations, 1989, The Influence of Critical Feedback and Organizational Climate on Managerial Decision Making, 1990, Future of Technology in Education, 1989. Home: 548 W 630 S Orem UT 84058-6154 Office: 382 E 720 S Orem UT 84058

SAXE, MARK IAN, artist; b. Boston, Oct. 30, 1946; s. Milton and Beatrice (Berman) S.; m. Laura Gibson Hendrie, Mar. 17, 1988. BA, Inst. Allende, Mex., 1974, MA, 1976. Tchr. Inst. Allende, San Miguel de Allende, Mex., 1977-78; owner Southwest Stoneworks, Dixon, N.Mex., 1980—. Fire chief Ojo Sarco (N.Mex.) Vol. Fire Dept., 1991-96. With U.S. Army, 1966-68, Vietnam. Mem. Internat. Sculpture Assn., Bldg. Stone Inst. Office: Southwest Stoneworks PO Box 248 Dixon NM 87527

SAXE, STEVEN LOUIS, lawyer; b. San Francisco, May 28, 1942; s. Jules Irving and Marian (Adams) S.; m. Joanne Saxe, July 12, 1964; children: Julie Ann, Jeffrey Scott. BS, U. Calif., Berkeley, 1964; JD, U. San Francisco, 1967. Bar: Calif. 1967, U.S. Dist. Ct. (no. and ea. dist.) Calif. 1967. Clk. Calif. Ct. Appeals, San Francisco, 1967-68; assoc. Farella, Brown & Martel, San Francisco, 1968-69; sr. counsel Bank Am., San Francisco, 1969-80; ptnr. Boyden, Cooluris, Hauser & Saxe, San Francisco, 1980-91, Pillsbury, Madison & Sutro, San Francisco, 1991—. Dir. Ecumenical Assn. Housing, San Rafael, Calif., 1985-92; pres. Congregation Rodef Sholom, San Rafael, 1992-94; dir. Fair Housing Marin, San Rafael, 1995—. Mem. ABA, Consumer Bankers Assn., Coll. Am. Coll. Fin. Svcs. Lawyers. Office: Pillsbury Madison & Sutro 235 Montgomery St San Francisco CA 94104-2902

SAXENA, NARENDRA K., marine research educator; b. Agra, India, Oct. 15, 1936; came to U.S., 1969; s. Brijbasi Lal and Sarbati Saxena; m. Cecilia H. Hsi, Mar. 21, 1970; Sarah Vasanti, Lorelle Sarita. Diploma Geodetic Engring., Tech. U., Hanover, Fed. Republic Germany, 1966; D in Tech Scis., Tech. U., Graz, Austria, 1972. Research assoc. geodetic sci. Ohio State U., Columbus, 1969-74; asst. prof. U. Ill., Urbana, 1974-78; asst. prof. U. Hawaii, Honolulu, 1978-81, assoc. prof., 1981-86, prof., 1986—, dept. chmn., 1994—; adj. research prof. Naval Postgrad. Sch., Monterey, Calif., 1984—; co-chmn. Pacific Congresses on Marine Tech., Honolulu, 1984, 86, 88; pres. Pacon Internat. Inc., 1987—. Editor Jour. Marine Geodesy, 1976—. Mem. Neighborhood Bd., Honolulu, 1984. Fellow Marine Tech. Soc. (various offices 1974—); mem. ASCE, Am. Geophys. Union, The Tsunami Soc. (sec. 1985—). Office: U Hawaii Dept Civil Engring Honolulu HI 96822

SAXENA, PARICHAY, software development executive; b. Allahabad, India, Feb. 26, 1965; came to the U.S., 1986; s. Baldev and Pushpa Saxena; m. Amrita Ballabh, Jan. 16, 1992. BS, Birla Inst. Tech., 1986; MS, SUNY, Albany, 1988. Grad. asst. SUNY, Albany, 1986-88; software engr. GE Power Generation, Schenectady, N.Y., 1988-92; computer scientist GE Corp. R&D, Schenectady, 1992-95; mgr. Andersen Cons., San Francisco, 1995-96, Sony Electronics Inc., San Jose, Calif., 1996—. Contbr. articles to profl. jours. Govt. of India scholar, 1982-86. Mem. IEEE (chmn. edn. Schenectady sect. 1990-92). IEEE Computer Soc. (chmn. Schenectady sect. 1992-93), Assn. Computing Machinery. Home: 625 Clyde Ct Milpitas CA 95035 Office: Sony Electronics Inc 3300 Zanker Rd San Jose CA 95134

SAXTON, LLOYD, psychologist, author; b. Loveland, Colo., Sept. 28, 1929; s. Oliver George and Alice Augusta (Andersen) S.; m. Nancy Alison Roberts, Dec. 17, 1955; children: Perry Brent, Jay Ronald, Barbara Jean. AB in English, U. Calif., Berkeley, 1950, BS in Psychology, 1954; MS in Psychology, San Francisco State U., 1955; PhD in Psychology, U. of the Pacific, Stockton, Calif., 1957. Diplomate Am. Bd. Forensic Examiners (cert. 1996); lic. psychologist, Calif. Intern in clin. psychology Chilldren's Hosp., San Francisco, 1955-56; teaching fellow U. Pacific, San Francisco, 1955-57, instr. psychology, 1957-58, asst. prof. psychology, 1958-60; assoc. prof. psychology Am. Acad. of Asian Studies, San Francisco, 1960-62, prof. psychology, 1962-65; chmn. dept. psychology Coll. of San Mateo, Calif., 1965-75, prof. psychology, 1975-92; pvt. practice San Francisco/Larkspur, 1958—; emeritus, 1995. Author: Individual, Marriage and the Family, 1968, Individual, 9th edit., 1996; author/editor: A Marriage Reader, 1970, The American Scene, 1970. Mem. APA, AAAS, AAUP, Am. Assn. Marriage and Family Therapists, Western Psychol. Assn., Am. Coll. Forensic Examiners, Mensa, Am. Chess Fedn. Democrat. Home and Office: 57 Hatzic Ct Larkspur CA 94939-1971

SAYANO, REIZO RAY, electrochemical engineer; b. Los Angeles, Dec. 15, 1937; s. George Keiichiro and Miyo (Nakao) S.; m. Tamiko Shintani, May 28, 1967; children—Kiyomi Coleen, Naomi Jennifer. A.A., Los Angeles Community Coll., 1958; B.S., UCLA, 1960, M.S., 1962, Ph.D., 1967. Research asst. electrochem. and shock tube research dept. engring. UCLA, 1961-66; mem. staff TRW Systems, corrosion and advanced battery research and devel. Redondo Beach, Calif., 1966-78; dir. engring. Intermedics Intraocular Inc., Pasadena, Calif., 1978-80, dir. research and devel., 1980-82, v.p. engring. devel. and research, 1982-84; v.p. research and devel. Interpore Internat. Inc., 1984-85; dir. research and devel., product process devel. IOLAB Corp. subs. Johnson & Johnson Co., Claremont, Calif., 1985-87, dir. new tech., research and devel., 1987-88; v.p., gen. mgr. Nidek Techs., Inc., Pasadena, Calif., 1988—. NASA predoctoral trainee, 1964-65. Mem. Electrochem. Soc., Nat. Assn. Corrosion Engrs., AAAS, Am. Mgmt. Assn., Sigma Xi. Office: 675 S Arroyo Pky Ste 330 Pasadena CA 91105-3264

SAYRE, EDWARD CHARLES, librarian; b. Longview, Wash., Aug. 15, 1923; s. Kenneth C. Sayre and Clare (Davis) Clingan; m. Virginia A. Hoy, June 9, 1951; children: Steven Anthony, Sabrina Karen. BA, Coll. of Gt. Falls, 1955; MA, U. Idaho, 1961; MLS, U. Md., 1968. Coordinator library services Thomas Nelson Community Coll., Hampton, Va., 1968-69; dir. Roswell Pub. Library, N.Mex., 1969-70; cons. N.Mex. State Library, Santa Fe, 1970-72; dir. Central Colo. Library System, Denver, 1972-78, Serra Coop. Library System, San Diego, 1978-79, Los Alamos County (N.Mex.) Library System, 1979-88; county adminstr. Los Alamos County, 1988-89; cons., 1976—, ret., 1989. Contbr. articles to profl. jours. Mem. state governing coun. Common Cause N.Mex. Maj. USAF, 1951-67. HEA Title II fellow, 1968. Mem. ALA, N.Mex. Library Assn. (pres.-elect 1972), Beta Phi Mu (dir. 1973-74). Democrat. Unitarian. Home: 3 Timber Ridge Rd Los Alamos NM 87544-2317

SAYRE, JOHN MARSHALL, lawyer, former government official; b. Boulder, Colo., Nov. 9, 1921; s. Henry Marshall and Lulu M. (Cooper) S.; m. Jean Miller, Aug. 22, 1943; children: Henry M., Charles Franklin, John Marshall Jr., Ann Elizabeth Sayre Taggart (dec.). BA, U. Colo., 1943, JD, 1948. Bar: Colo. 1948, U.S. Dist. Ct. Colo. 1952, U.S. Ct. Appeals (10th cir.) 1964. Law clk. trust dept. Denver Nat. Bank, 1948-49; asst. cashier, trust officer Nat. State Bank of Boulder, 1949-50; ptnr. Ryan, Sayre, Martin, Brotzman, Boulder, 1950-66, Davis, Graham & Stubbs, Denver, 1966-89, of counsel, 1993—; asst. sec. of the Interior for Water and Sci., 1989-93. Bd. dirs. Boulder Sch. Dist. 3, 1951-57; city atty. City of Boulder, 1952-55; gen. counsel Colo. Mcpl. League, 1956-63; prin. counsel No. Colo. Water Conservancy Dist. and mcpl. subdist., 1964-87, spl. counsel, 1987, bd. dirs. dist., 1960-64; former legal counsel Colo. Assn. Commerce and Industry. Lt. (j.g.) USNR, 1943-46, ret. Decorated Purple Heart. Fellow Am. Bar. Found. (life), Colo. Bar Found. (life); mem. ABA, Colo. Bar Assn., Boulder County Bar Assn. (pres. 1959), Denver Bar Assn., Nat. Water Resources Assn. (Colo. dir. 1980-89, 93-95, pres. 1984-86), Denver Country Club, Univ. Club, Mile High Club, Phi Beta Kappa, Phi Gamma Delta, Phi Delta Phi. Republican. Episcopalian. Home: Davis Graham & Stubbs 355 Ivanhoe St Denver CO 80220-5841 Office: Davis Graham & Stubbs PO Box 185 Denver CO 80201-0185

SAYSETTE, JANICE ELAINE, vertebrate paleontologist, zoo archaeologist; b. San Francisco, Feb. 27, 1949; d. James Monroe and Isabel Christine (Saysette) Heffern; m. Thomas Arthur Haygood, Aug. 6, 1978 (div. June 1991); children: Grant Thomas, Ian James. AA in Nursing, Ohlone Coll., 1974; BSN, Metro State, 1981; MSN, U. Colo., 1982; MA in Anthropology, Colo. State U., 1990, postgrad., 1991—. Staff nurse Palo Alto (Calif.) VA Hosp., 1974-75, San Jose (Calif.) Hosp., 1975-78, O'Connor Hosp., San Jose, 1978-80; clin. nursing instr. U. No. Colo., Greeley, 1982-87; nursing supr. Poudre Valley Hosp., Ft. Collins, Colo., 1988-89; grad. teaching asst. Colo. State U., Ft. Collins, 1988-90, ind. contractor-zooarchaeology, 1990—; crew mem. U. Wyo. Lookingbill Archaeological Site, 1991; crew chief Denver Mus. Natural History Porqupine Cave Paleontological Site, 1993; lectr., presenter in field. Mem. Am. Soc. Mammalogists, Internat. Coun. Archaeozoology, Soc. Am. Archaeology, Soc. Vertebrate Paleontology. Democrat. Office: Colo State U Dept of Biology Fort Collins CO 80523

SAYWARD, JENNY, cultural organization executive; b. Kennewick, Wash., Sept. 5, 1952; d. Russell Elwood and Elizabeth (Wilson) Nelson. BA in History, Conn. Coll., 1974; AA in Interpreting for the Deaf, Seattle Ctrl. C.C., 1988; cert. elem. teaching, Antioch U., 1991. Cert. elem. tchr. Family planning educator Family Planning of N.H., Dover, 1975-77; owner Open Arms Child Care, Seattle, 1981-87; interpreter Riverview Sch. Dist., Carnation, Wash., 1988-90; support group facilitator Lesbian Resource Ctr., Seattle, 1989-90; exec. dir. Lesbian Mothers Nat. Def. Fund, Seattle, 1991—. Author: (pamphlet series) Information for Lesbian Families, 1994; editor: (newsletter) Mom's Apple Pie, 1991—. Mem. NOW, Mensa. Office: Lesbian Mothers Nat Def Fnd PO Box 21567 Seattle WA 98111-3567

SAYWELL, WILLIAM GEORGE GABRIEL, foundation administrator; b. Regina, Sask., Can., Dec. 1, 1936; s. John Ferdinand Tupper and Vera Marguerite S.; m. Helen Jane Larmer; children: Shelley Jayne, William James Tupper, Patricia Lynn. BA, U. Toronto, 1960, MA, 1961, PhD, 1968; LLD (hon.), U. BC, 1994. Asst. prof. dept. East Asian studies U. Toronto, Ont., Ont., Can., 1963-69; asst. prof. U. Toronto, Ont., Can., 1969-71, assoc. prof., 1971-82, prof., 1982-83, chmn. dept., 1971-76; prof. dept. history, pres. Simon Fraser U., Burnaby, B.C., Can., 1983-93; pres., chief exec. officer Asia Pacific Found. of Can., Vancouver, B.C., 1993—; sinologist and 1st sec. Can. Embassy, Beijing, 1972-73; dir. U. Toronto-York U. Ctr. Modern East Asia, 1974-75; prin. Innis Coll., 1976-79; vice provost U. Toronto, 1979-83; dir. Westcoast Energy, Spar Aerospace, Western Garnet Internat. Author articles and revs. on Chinese affairs to profl. jours. Decorated Order B.C. Office: Asia Pacific Found Can, 666-999 Canada Pl, Vancouver, BC Canada V6C 3E1

SBRAGIA, GARY W., communications company executive; b. Chgo., Aug. 25, 1941; s. Gertrude Harriet (Legge) S.; m. Sharyn Lee Simpson, Aug. 26, 1961; children: Marci Lee Filyk, Melissa Ann. Student, Waldorf Jr. Coll., 1959-60, 61-62, Colo. State U., 1962-65. Supr. Woodward Gen. Gov. Co., Rockford, Ill. and Ft. Collins, Colo., 1985-65; v.p. Lift Trucks, Inc., Denver, 1972-74; mgr. Levenworth (Kans.) Cable TV, 1974-75; gen. mgr., then div. mgr. Athena Cablevision of Corpus Christi (Tex.), Inc., 1976-81; regional mgr., then asst. dir. ops. Telecommunications, Inc., Corpus Christi and Denver, 1981-84; v.p. Wegener Corp., Denver, 1984-91; pres. Telecrafter Services Corp., Denver, 1987-91; with Sbragia Trading Co., 1991—. Home: PO Box 8176 Breckenridge CO 80424-8176

SCAFE, LINCOLN ROBERT, JR., sales executive; b. Cleve., July 28, 1922; s. Lincoln Robert and Charlotte (Hawkins) S.; student Cornell U., 1940-41; m. Mary Anne Wilkinson, Nov. 14, 1945; children—Amanda Katharine, Lincoln Robert III. Service mgr. Avery Engring. Co., Cleve., 1946-51; nat. service mgr. Trane Co., LaCrosse, Wis., 1951-57; service and installation mgr. Mech. Equipment Supply Co., Honolulu, 1957-58; chief engr. Sam P. Wallace of Pacific, Honolulu, 1958-62; pres. Air Conditioning Service Co., Inc., Honolulu, 1962-84; sales engr. G.J. Campbell & Assocs., Seattle, 1984-89. Served with USNR, 1942-45; PTO. Mem. ASHRAE, Alpha Delta Phi. Clubs: Cornell Hawaii (past pres.); Outrigger Canoe. Republican. Author tech. service lit. and parts manuals; contbr. articles to trade publs. Home: 10721 SW 112th St Vashon WA 98070-3044 Office: GJ Campbell and Assocs 11613 Rainier Ave S Seattle WA 98178-3945

SCAGLIONE, CECIL FRANK, marketing executive, publisher; b. North Bay, Ont., Can., Dec. 2, 1934; came to U.S., 1967, naturalized, 1982; s. Frank and Rose (Aubin) S.; m. Mary Margaret Stewart, Nov. 11, 1954 (div. 1982); children: Cris Ann, Michael Andrew, Patrick Andrew; m. Beverly Louise Rahn, Mar. 25, 1983; student North Bay Coll., 1947-52, Ryerson Tech. Inst., Toronto, Ont., 1955-56, San Diego State U. Inst. World Affairs, 1979. Fin. writer Toronto Telegram, 1955; reporter Sarnia (Ont.) Observer, 1956-57; reporter, editor Kitchener-Waterloo (Ont.) Record, 1957-61; reporter, editor, analyst Windsor (Ont.) Star, 1961-67; writer, editor, photo editor Detroit News, 1967-71; reporter, assoc. bus. editor San Diego Union, 1971-80; mgr. corp. communications Pacific Southwest Airlines, San Diego, 1981-83; sr. v.p. media rels. Berkman & Daniels, Inc., San Diego, 1984-87, prin. Scaglione Mktg. Comm., 1987—; pres., CEO Mature Life Features, 1990—. Mem. adv. coun. SBA, Accredited Pub. Rels. Soc. Am.; mem. San Diego County Crime Commn. Recipient award B.F. Goodrich Can., Ltd., 1962, 66, San Diego Pub. Rels. Profl. of the Yr., 1995, Spl. Achievement award Nat. Assn. Recycling Industries, 1978, award SBA, 1980; Herbert J. Davenport fellow, 1977 U. Mo.; Can. Centennial grantee, 1966. Mem. San Diego Press Club (hon. life, past pres.) awards 1978, 80, 84, Airline Editors Forum awards 1982, 83, Soc. Profl. Journalists, Internat. Food, Wine & Travel Writers Assn. Roman Catholic. Founding editor-in-chief Aeromexico mag., 1973; contbr. articles, columns and photographs to various publs.

SCANLON, DERALEE ROSE, dietitian, educator, author; b. Santa Monica, Calif., Aug. 16, 1950; d. Stanley Ralph and Demba (Runkle) S.; m. Alex Spataru, July 20, 1970 (div. 1974). AA, Santa Monica Coll., 1968; accred. med. record tech., East L.A. Coll., 1980; BS, U. Calif., L.A., 1984. Registered dietitian. V.p. corp. sales, nutrition dir. LIfeTrends Corp., Carlsbad, Calif., 1984-86; dir. media, nutrition Irvine Ranch Farmers Markets, L.A., 1987-88; spokesperson for media Calif. Milk Adv. Bd., San. Diego, 1986; nutrition reporter Med-NIWS, L.A., 1990-91; dietitian Sta. ABC-TV The Home Show, L.A., 1991-92, Sta. NBC-TV David Horowitz Fight Back, L.A., 1991-92; dietitian, nutrition reporter Sta. KTTV-TV Good Day L.A., 1994-95; nutritionist Sta. KABC-TV Kids View, 1994—; co-host talk radio show Light and Lively, KABC, 1994—; mgr. Nutrition Svcs. Vitex Foods, Inc., 1995-96; spokesperson Sandoz Nutrition, 1995-96; host nat. cable TV health show To Your Health, 1996-97; media spokesperson Lifetime Food Co., Seaside, Calif., 1992—, Interior Design Nutritionals, Provo, Utah, 1993—, Weight Watchers, 1993-94; contbr. writer L.A. Parent Mag., Burbank, Calif., 1991—; syndicated nutrition reporter Live N'Well TV Series, Utah, 1992-93; nutrition educator Emeritus Coll. Sr. Health, Santa Monica, 1990-92; nutrition lectr. Princess Cruises, L.A., 1987; nutrition video host AMA Campaign Against Cholesterol, 1989; lectr. on nutrition and health to various orgns., 1993—; leader seminar series on I.B.S. UCLA Med. Ctr., 1994-95, others. Author: The Wellness Book of IBS, 1989, Diets That Work, 1991, rev. edit., 1992, 93; newspaper columnist: Ask the Dietitian, 1990-94; columnist Natural Way Mag.; Ask the Dietitian column in The Natural Way Mag., 1995; contbr. articles to profl. jours. Mem. AFTRA, Dietitians in Bus./Comms. (regional rep. 1990-92, So. Calif. chairperson 1991-92, editor nat. newsletter 1994-96), Am. Dietetic Assn. (pub. rels. chair 1985-87), Calif. Dietetic Assn. (Dietitian of Yr. in Pvt. Practice, Bus. and Comm. 1993), Soc. for Nutrition Edn., Nat. Speakers Assn. Home and Office: 10613 Eastborne Ave Los Angeles CA 90024-5920

SCANNELL, WILLIAM EDWARD, aerospace company executive, consultant, psychologist; b. Muscatine, Iowa, Nov. 11, 1934; s. Mark Edward and Catharine Pearson (Fowler) S.; m. Barbara Ann Hoemann, Nov. 23, 1957; children: Cynthia Kay, Mark Edward, David Jerome, Terri Lynn, Stephen Patrick. BA in Gen. Edn., U. Nebr., 1961; BS in Engring., Ariz. State U., 1966; MS in Systems Engring., So. Meth. U., 1969; PhD, U.S. Internat. U., 1991. Commd. 2d lt. USAF, 1956, advanced through grades to lt. col., 1972; B-47 navigator-bombardier 98th Bomb Wing, Lincoln Air Force Base, Nebr., 1956-63; with Air Force Inst. of Tech., 1963-65, 68-69; chief mgmt. engring. team RAF Bentwaters, England, 1965-68; forward air contr. 20th Tactical Air Support Squadron USAF, Danang, Vietnam, 1970-71; program mgr. Hdqrs. USAF, Washington, 1971-74, staff asst. Office of Sec. Def., 1974-75, ret., 1975; account exec. Merrill Lynch, San Diego, 1975-77; program engring. chief Gen. Dynamics, San Diego, 1977-79, engring. chief, 1979-80, program mgr., 1980-83; mgr. integrated logistics support Northrop Corp., Hawthorne, Calif., 1984-88; mgr. B-2 program planning and scheduling Northrop Corp., Pico Rivera, Calif., 1988-91; pres. Scannell and Assocs., Borrego Springs, Calif., 1991-97; mem. adj. faculty U.S. Internat. U., San Diego. Decorated DFC with three oak leaf clusters, Air medal with 11 oak leaf clusters. Mem. APA, Calif. Psychol. Assn., Soc. Indsl. and Orgnl. Psychology, Inst. Indsl. Engrs., Coronado Cays Yacht Club, De Anza Country Club, Psi Chi. Republican. Roman Catholic. Home: PO Box 2392 717 Anza Park Trail Borrego Springs CA 92004-2392 Office: Scannell & Assocs PO Box 2392 Borrego Springs CA 92004-2392

SCARBROUGH, ERNEST EARL, stockbroker, financial planner; b. Memphis, Jan. 7, 1947; s. Earl Carson and Mary Lillian (Keileber) S.; m. Cindy Cowley, Sept. 22, 1973; children: Michael E., William E. AA, Phoenix Coll., 1974; BA, Ottawa U., 1993; MBA, U. Phoenix, 1995; postgrad., Nova So. U., 1995—. Cert. fin. planner. Profl. pilot, airline transport rating, flight instr. various gen. aviation cos., Memphis and Phoenix, 1968-72; transp. analyst leasing and sales Rollins Leasing Co., Phoenix, 1971-73; cost analyst Ariz. Pub. Service Co., Phoenix, 1973-75; air traffic contr. FAA, Ariz. and Calif., 1975-81; account exec. E.F. Hutton & Co., Phoenix, 1982-83, asst. v.p., 1984-86, v.p., 1987; v.p., portfolio mgr. Prudential-Bache Securities, Inc., Phoenix, 1988-90; v.p. Esplanade Office Dean Witter Reynolds, Phoenix, 1990-95; mng. dir. investments, asst. br. mgr. Piper Jaffray, Phoenix, 1995—; adj. faculty Keller Grad. Sch. Mgmt., Phoenix and Mesa, 1995—. Corp. chmn. Phoenix chpt. climb-the-mountain campaign Am. Cancer Soc., 1986; chmn. stewardship, vice-chmn. fin. Cross in Desert United Meth. Ch., Phoenix, 1987-88; bd. dirs. Sojourner Ctr., 1988—, pres. bd., 1989-91, chmn. adv. bd., 1991-94; jr. achievement tchr. cons., 1992—. With USAF, 1966-70. Mem. Am. Mgmt. Assn., Fin. Mgmt. Assn., Internat. Assn. for Fin. Planning, Internat. Assn. CFPs, Profl. Air Traffic Contrs. Orgn. (local pres. 1975-81), Ctrl. Ariz. Estate Planning Coun., Rotary (v.p. Phoenix chpt. 1987, pres.-elect 1988). Republican. Home: 9409 N 17th Way Phoenix AZ 85020-2344 Office: Piper Jaffray 2525 E Camelback Rd Ste 900 Phoenix AZ 85016-4231

SCATENA, LORRAINE BORBA, rancher, women's rights advocate; b. San Rafael, Calif., Feb. 18, 1924; d. Joseph and Eugenia (Simas) de Borba; m. Louis G. Scatena, Feb. 14, 1960; children: Louis Vincent, Eugenia Gayle. BA, Dominican Coll., San Rafael, 1945; postgrad., Calif. Sch. Fine Arts, 1948, U. Calif., Berkeley, 1956-57. Cert. elem. tchr., Calif. Tchr. Dominican Coll., 1946; tchr. of mentally handicapped San Anselmo (Calif.) Sch. Dist., 1946; tchr. Fairfax (Calif.) Pub. Elem. Sch., 1946-53; asst. to mayor Fairfax City Recreation, 1948-53; tchr., libr. U.S. Dependent Schs., Mainz am Rhine, Fed. Republic Germany, 1953-56; translator Portugal Travel Tours, Lisbon, 1954; bonding sec. Am. Fore Ins. Group, San Francisco, 1956-60; rancher, farmer Yerington, Nev., 1960—; hostess com. Caldecott and Newbury Authors' Awards, San Francisco, 1959; mem. Nev. State Legis. Commn., 1975; coord. Nevadans for Equal Rights Amendment, 1975-78, rural areas rep., 1976-78; testifier Nev. State Senate and Assembly, 1975, 77; mem. adv. com. Fleischmann Coll. Agr. U. Nev., 1977-80, 81-84; speaker Grants and Rsch. Projects, Bishop, Calif., 1977, Choices for Tomorrow's Women, Fallon, Nev., 1989. Trustee Wassuk Coll., Hawthorne, Nev., 1984-87; mem. Lyon County Friends of Libr., Yerington, 1971—, Lyon County Mus. Soc., 1978; sec., pub. info. chmn. Lyon County Rep. Women, 1968-73, v.p. programs, 1973-75; mem. Lyon County Rep. Ctrl. Com., 1973-74; mem. Marin County Soc. Artists, San Anselmo, Calif., 1948-53; charter mem. Eleanor Roosevelt Fund Women and Girls, 1990, sustaining mem.,

1992—; Nev. rep. 1st White House Conf. Rural Am. Women, Washington, 1980; participant internat. reception, Washington, 1980; mem. pub. panel individual presentation Shakespeare's Treatment of Women Characters, Nev. Theatre for the Arts, Ashland, Oreg. Shakespearean Actors local performance, 1977; mem. Nev. Women's History Project, U. Nev., 1996—. Recipient Outstanding Conservation Farmer award Mason Valley Conservation Dist., 1992, Soroptimist Internat. Women Helping women award 1983, invitation to first all-women delegation to U.S.A. from People's Republic china, U.S. House Reps., 1979; Public Forum Travel grantee Edn. Title IX, Oakland, Calif., 1977; fellow World Lit. Acad., 1993. Mem. Lyon County Ret. Tchrs. Assn. (unit pres. 1979-80, 84-86, v.p. 1986-88, Nev. State Outstanding Svc. award 1981, state conv. gen. chmn. 1985), Rural Am. Women Inc., AAUW (br. pres. 1972-74, 74-76, chair edn. found. programs, 1983—, state convention gen. chmn. 1976, 87, state sec. 1970-72, state legis. program chmn. 1976-77, state chmn. internat. rels. 1979-81, state pres. 1981-83, br. travelship, discovering women in U.S. history Radcliffe Coll. State Humanities award 1975, Future Fund Nat. award 1983), Mason Valley Country Club, Italian Cath. Fedn. Club (pres. 1986-88), Uniao Portuguesa Estado da Calif. Roman Catholic. Home: PO Box 247 Yerington NV 89447-0247

SCAVEN, GREGORY JOSEPH, chemical engineer; b. Phila., Apr. 9, 1963; s. Joseph Charles and Josephine Marie (Rocco) S.; m. Lorraine Robbins Gilmore, Sept. 29, 1990; 1 child, Victoria Leigh Scaven. BS in Engring., Lehigh U., 1985; MS in Engring., U. Pa., 1987. Sr. engr. Talley Def. Systems, Mesa, Ariz., 1991—. Contbr. articles to profl. jours. Capt. U.S. Army, 1985-91. Mem. AICE, Am. Chem. Soc., Am. Def. Preparedness Assn., Internat. Pyrotechnics Soc. Home: 2037 E Hermosa Vista Dr Mesa AZ 85213-2211 Office: Talley Def Systems 3500 N Greenfield Rd Mesa AZ 85215-9117

SCHAAFSMA, POLLY DIX, archaeologist, researcher; b. Springfield, Vt., Oct. 24, 1935; d. Raymond Arthur and Mildred Elizabeth (Gafvert) Dix; m. Curtis Forrest Schaafsma, Sept. 28, 1958; children: Hoskinini Scott, Pieter Dix. BA, Mount Holyoke Coll., 1957; MA, U. Colo., 1962. Archaeologist Mus. N.Mex., Sante Fe, 1962-63, 94-96, project dir., 1966-67, rsch. assoc., 1985—; project dir. Utah State Pk. Commn. and Gov.'s Commn. on Historic Sites, Salt Lake City, 1970, N.Mex. State Planning Office, Santa Fe, 1971; project dir. Nat. Pk. Svc., Grand Canyon National Park, Ariz., 1987; mem. blue ribbon panel adv. bd. Petroglyph Nat. Monument, Albuquerque, 1992-96; mem. adv. coun. Four Corners Sch. Outdoor Edn., Monticello, Utah, 1996—; mem. rev. com. The Rock Art Archive, Inst. Archaeology, UCLA, 1997—. Author: The Rock Art of Utah, 1971, 2d edit., 1994, The Rock Art in New Mexico, 1972, 2d edit., 1994, Indian Rock Art of the Southwest, 1980, Images in Stone, 1995; editor: Kachinas in the Pueblo World, 1994. Mem. Am. Rock Art Rsch. Assn. (mem. adv. bd. 1985—), Soc. Am. Archaeology. Office: Mus N Mex Mus Indian Arts and Culture PO Box 2087 Santa Fe NM 87504

SCHABOW, JOHN WILLIAM, accountant; b. Chgo., Mar. 30, 1937; s. William John and Mary V. (Brink) S.; m. Gail P. Ekren, Oct. 17, 1959; children: Robin, John R. Student, Davis Elkins Coll., 1955-58, Ariz. State U., 1972-74. Accredited tax advisor Accreditation Coun. for Accountancy & Taxation. Cost clk. G.D. Searle, Skokie, Ill., 1958-60; acct. Sugarcreek Foods, Chgo., 1960-63, Arlington Park Rack Track, Chgo., 1963-65, G. Heiss & Assocs., Chgo., 1965-69, Murray & Murray CPA's, Phoenix, 1969-70, Wm. R. Schulz & Assocs., Phoenix, 1970-73; pres., owner John W. Schabow, Ltd., Phoenix, 1973—; registered rep. H.D. Vest Investment Securities, Inc., Phoenix, 1985—, adv. bd. dirs. Mem. editorial adv. bd. Accounting Today, 1993—. Bd. dirs. Inst. for Partially Sighted, Phoenix, 1986-87, Phoenix Girl's Choir, 1995—. With U.S. Army, 1961-62. Mem. Ariz. Soc. Practicing Accts. (pres. 1987-88, co-founder, co-chair legis. com. 1994—), Nat. Soc. Pub. Accts. (state dir. 1983-87, bd. govs. 1988-92, chmn. nat. affairs com. 1995—). Republican. Lutheran. Home: 4440 W Bluefield Ave Glendale AZ 85308-1613 Office: 11725 N 19th Ave Phoenix AZ 85029-3500

SCHACH, BARBARA JEAN, elementary education educator; b. Bakersfield, Calif., Dec. 3, 1945; d. James Fleming and Ann (Sanderson) Meeks; m. Henry Edward, June 20, 1970; children: David Henry, Natalie Ann. Student, U. Nev., 1967, UCLA, 1973, Calif. State U., Dominguez Hills, 1974. Tchr. Redondo Beach, Calif., 1967-73; tchr. 5th grade L.A. Unified Sch. Dist., 1981—; bd. dirs. Carson (Calif.) Coord. Coun.; com. mem. Carson 2000, 1995—. Prodr.: (TV prodns.) Education Connection Quiz Kids, 1994 (Educator of Yr. award 1994), Children's News, 1995 (Educator of Yr. award 1995); coord. (TV prodn.) The Learning Hour, 1996 (Educator of Yr. award 1996). Bd. dirs. Carson Family Ctr., 1993-96; mem. Rep. Women, L.A., 1990. Healthy Start grantee State of Calif., 1993, L.A. Ednl. Partnership grantee, 1991, 92, 94, Polaroid grantee Polaroid Corp., 1990, Early Literacy grantee L.A. Unified Sch. Dist., 1996. Mem. AAUW, ASCD, Women in Ednl. Leadership (v.p. programs 1994—, pres. 1994—), Video Using Educators, Phi Delta Kappa, Phi Kappa Phi. Home: 6917 Hartcrest Dr Rancho Palos Verdes CA 90275

SCHAEFER, DAN L., congressman; b. Gutenberg, Iowa, Jan. 25, 1936; s. Alvin L. and Evelyn (Everson) S.; m. Mary Margaret Lenney, 1959; children: Danny, Darren, Joel, Jennifer. BA, Niagara U., 1961, LLD (hon.), 1986; postgrad., Potsdam State U., 1961-64. Pub. rels. cons., 1967-83; mem. Colo. Gen. Assembly, 1977-78; mem. Colo. Senate, 1979-83, pres. pro tem, 1981-82, majority whip, 1983; mem. 98th-103rd Congresses from 6th dist. Colo., Washington, 1983—; mem. house small bus. com., 1983, govt. ops. com., 1983, energy and commerce com., 1984-86 (subcom. on fossil and synthetic fuels; commerce, transp. and tourism; oversight/investigations), environ. and energy study com., 1987— (subcoms. on Transp. and Hazardous materials, Telecom. and Fin.), Energy and Commerce ranking Rep Oversight and Investigations, 1993—, Rep. study com.; mem. house sci. and high tech. task force, mil. reforms caucus, congl. grace caucus; mem. adv. com., com. of concern for Soviet Jewry; mem. exec. bd. Environ. and Energy Study Conf., 1995; chmn. Subcom. on Energy and Power House Commerce Com.; mem. Subcom. on Telecom. and Fin., House Vet. Affairs Com., Subcom. on Edn., Training, Employment and Housing, 1995—; co-chmn. The Mainstream Conservative Alliance. Co-chair Nat. Retail Sales Tax Caucus, Congl. Oil and Gas Forum; mem. Spkrs. Task Force on Environ.; founder House Renewable Energy Caucus; pres. Foothills Recreation Bd., 1973-76; sec. Jefferson County Rep. Party, Colo., 1975-76. With USMCR, 1955-57. Recipient Colo. Park and Recreation citation, 1976; named Elected Ofcl. of Yr., Lakewood/South Jeffco C. of C., 1986, 88, 90, Leadership award U.S. Congl. Adv. Bd., Am. Security Coun. Found., Taxpayers Friend award Nat. Taxpayer's Union, 1985-86, 88, 90, 91, 92, 93, 94, 95, Golden Bulldog award Watchdog of Treasury, 1985-86, 87-88, 88-89, 89-90, 91-92, 93-94, 95-96, Spirit of Enterprise award U.S. C. of C., 1995, Nat. Health award Am. Assn. Nurse Anesthetists, 1996, Nat. Security Scorecare Perfect 100 award Ctr. for Security Policy, 1995, Friend of Taxpayer Perfect 100% award Ams. for Tax Reform, 1996; named Guardian of Small Bus., Nat. Fedn. Ind. Bus., 1996. Mem. C. of C., Rotary, Beta Theta Pi. Roman Catholic. Office: House of Representatives 2353 Rayburn House Office B Washington DC 20515

SCHAEFER, MICHAEL JUDE, industrial control systems engineer; b. Glen Ridge, N.J., Oct. 4, 1954; s. Hubert Emil and Agnes Alice (Boehmer) S.; m. Terry Lynn Vezerian, Jan. 28, 1988; m. Terri Lyn Armitage, July 10, 1993; children: Stephanie, Jessica, Nicole. Student, Grossmont C.C., 1976-78, U. Calif., San Diego, 1978-81; postgrad., U. Calif., San Diego, 1992. Gen. contractor Oakwood Constrn., San Diego, 1981-86; controls specialist Burke Engring., San Diego, 1986-90; control sys. engr. Omega Controls, San Diego, 1990-92, Centaurus Sys., San Diego, 1992-95, Medland Controls, Chula Vista, Calif., 1995—; cons. in field, 1995—. Mem. Instrument Soc. Am., Assn. Profl. Energy Mgrs. Home: 9375 E Heaney Cir Santee CA 92071-2926 Office: 2363 Newton Ave # B San Diego CA 92113-3648

SCHAEFER, SAUL, cardiologist; b. Tel Aviv, Israel, Dec. 6, 1947; came to U.S., 1952; s. Rudi and Gertrude S.; m. Sylvia Lopez, July 14, 1985; children: Jonathan, Adam. B of Engring., The Cooper Union, 1968; postgrad., U. So. Calif., 1968-69, UCLA, 1970-76; MD, U. Calif., Davis, 1981. Diplomate Am. Bd. Internal Medicine, Am. Bd. Internal Medicine (Cardiovasc. Disease), Nat. Bd. Med. Examiners; lic. physician, Calif.; profl. cert. in bioengring.; Calif. State teaching credential. Tchr. secondary level L.A. Unified Sch. Dist., 1970-76; residency internal medicine U. Calif., San Francisco, 1981-84; fellow cardiology U. Tex. Southwestern Med. Ctr., Dallas, 1984-87; asst. dir. echocardiography VA Med. Ctr., San Francisco, 1987-90; asst. prof. medicine and radiology in residence U. Calif., San Francisco, 1987-91; dir. interventional cardiology VA Med. Ctr., San Francisco, 1990-91; dir. interventional cardiology U. Calif., Davis, 1991-94, assoc. prof. medicine, 1991-97, prof., 1997—; co-chair cardiology dept. of vets. affairs No. Calif. Health Care Sys. Contbr. numerous articles to profl. jours. and chpts. to books. Recipient award for excellence in diagnostic radiology, 1981, clin. investigator award NIH, 1987, Hibbard E. Williams rsch. award, 1992; N.Y. State Regents scholar, 1964, Mosby scholar, 1981; grantee Calif. affiliate Am. Heart Assn., 1988, 90, 93, 96, dean's grantee U. Calif., Davis, 1993. Fellow Am. Coll. Cardiology; mem. AAAS, Am. Coll. Cardiology (mem. editl. bd. jour.), Am. Fedn. Clin. Rsch., Soc. Magnetic Resonance in Medicine, Am. Physiologic Soc., Am. Heart Assn. Office: U Calif Cardiovascular Medicine TB 172 Bioletti Way Davis CA 95616

SCHAEFFER, REINER HORST, air force officer, retired librarian, foreign language professional; b. Berlin, Lichterfelde, Fed. Republic Germany, Jan. 13, 1938; came to U.S., 1958; s. Immanuel Emil and Wilhelmine (Fahrni) Frei-S.; m. Cathy Anne Cormack, Apr. 6, 1966; 1 child, Brian Reiner. Nat. Cert., Bus. Sch., Thun, Switzerland, 1957; B.G.S. in Bus., U. Nebr., 1970; M.P.A. in Orgnl. Behavior, U. Mo., 1972; Ph.D. in Fgn. Lang. Edn., Ohio State U., 1979. Commd. officer USAF, 1958, advanced through grades to lt. col.; instr. German, French USAF Acad., Colorado Springs, Colo., 1975-77, assoc. prof., 1979-81, chmn. German, 1981, dir. librs., 1982-86, prof., 1986-92, dir. Acad. Librs., 1986—. Mem. People to People, Colorado Springs; bd. dirs. Friends of AF Acad. Librs. Named Disting. Grad. Air Force Inst. Tech, Wright-Patterson AFB, Ohio, 1979; recipient 5 Meritorious Service medals, 5 Air Force Commendation medals. Mem. Am. Assn. Tchrs. of German, Swiss Club (pres. Colorado Springs chpt. 1990-96, chmn.), Pi Alpha Alpha, Alpha Sigma Alpha. Republican. Home: 515 Celtic Ct Colorado Springs CO 80921-1807 Office: Fgn Lang Ctr LLC 315 E Willamette Ave Colorado Springs CO 80903-1115

SCHAFER, GERALD LEWIS, librarian; b. El Paso, Tex., Apr. 20, 1949; s. Norman Oscar and Clarice S. BA, U. Tex., El Paso, 1971; MLS, U. Denver, 1973. Info. specialist Denver Rsch. Inst., 1973-75; area mgr. Denver Pub. Libr., 1975-80; dir. profl. communications Skidmore, Owings & Merrill, Denver, 1981-84; coord. collection devel. svcs. Auraria Libr., Denver, 1984—. Editor: Master Plan-U.S. Air Force Academy, 1984. Chair collections task force Colo. State Libr., Denver, 1993-94, Access Colo. Libr. and Info. Network Collection Devel. Com., 1996—. Mem. ALA, Colo. Libr. Assn. Home: 2054 Clarkson St Denver CO 80205-5117 Office: Auraria Libr Lawrence At 11th St Denver CO 80204

SCHAFFER, JAMES RICHARD, aerospace company executive; b. Newburgh, N.Y., Dec. 15, 1956; s. William S. and Susan E. Schaffer; m. Elaine Ann Robbins, June 19, 1982; 1 child, Kathryn Ann. BS in Engring. and Mgmt., Clarkson Coll. Tech., 1978; MBA, Clarkson U., 1988. Mktg. rep. Allied Signal Aerospace, Jacksonville, Fla., 1978-84, contracts mgr., 1984-86; program mgr. Allied Signal Aerospace, South Bend, Ind., 1986-88, customer support mgr., 1988-93; corp. mktg. mgr. Allied Signal Aerospace, Phoenix, 1993-94, dir. programs, 1994—. Republican. Home: 14208 S 14th St Phoenix AZ 85048

SCHAFFER, JEFFREY L., lawyer; b. L.A., Aug. 21, 1952. AB, U. Calif., Berkeley, 1974; JD, U. Calif., 1979. Bar: Calif. 1979, U.S. Dist. Ct. (no. dist.) Calif., U.S. Ct. Appeals (9th cir.) 1985. Mem. Howard, Rice, Nemerovski, Canady, Falk & Rabkin, San Francisco; panelist Continuing Edn. Bar, 1983-92, computer law inst. U. So. Calif., 1986. Assoc. editor Calif. Law REv., 1977-79. Mem. ABA (bus. law sect.), Am. Bankruptcy Inst., State Bar Calif. (bus. law sect., mem. debtor/creditor and bankruptcy com. 1987-90, 96—), Bar Assn. San Francisco (comml. law and bankruptcy sect., co-chair barristers club's bankruptcy and comml. law com. 1984-85), Berkeley Law Found., Order of Coif, Phi Beta Kappa. Office: Howard Rice Nemerovski Canady Falk & Rabkin 3 Embarcadero Ctr Ste 7 San Francisco CA 94111-4003

SCHAFFER, JEFFREY LEE, nonprofit organization executive; b. L.A., Oct. 28, 1958; s. Mervin Bernard and Zena Harriet (Lindsay) S.; m. Reina Maria Alonso, Sept. 9, 1989, children: Philip Santos, Jacob José. BA, U. Calif., Berkeley, 1980; MPA, U. So. Calif., 1987. Field rep. Office Congressman A.C. Beilenson, Washington, L.A., 1980-82; mcpl. devel. advisor Peace Corps, Kosrae, Ea. Caroline Islands, 1982-84; staff asst. CARE, Washington, 1985; rsch. asst. Office Treasurer, State of Calif., Sacramento, 1986; account exec. Braun & Co., L.A., 1986-89; assoc. dir. Shelter Partnership, L.A., 1989-96; dir. L.A. Youth at Work, 1996-97; assoc. dir. Beyond Shelter, L.A., 1997—; instr. Sch. Pub. Adminstrn., U. So. Calif., 1995—. Editor Homeless Reporter newsletter, 1989-90; exec. prodr. video Neighbors in Need, 1990. Group leader Operation Crossroads Africa, Kithumula Kenya, 1986; bd. dirs. Friends of Coro, L.A., 1990-91, Los Angeles Countywide Coalition for Homeless, L.A., 1991-93; pres., bd. dirs. Peace Corps Svc. Coun., L.A., 1990-91; mem. met. bd. Jewish Fedn. Coun., L.A., 1990-92; active New Leaders Project, L.A., 1992; chmn. Ams. with Disabilities Act com. L.A. Emergency Food and Shelter Local Bd., 1992-96; sec. Asian Pacific Islander Planning Coun., San Fernando Valley, 1994-96; trainer Kellogg Tng. Ctr., 1994—; mem. steering com. L.A. Non-Profit Policy Coun.; mem. Peace Corps L.A. Mem. U. Calif. Alumni Assn., Sigma Delta Pi (life). Democrat. Office: Beyond Shelter Ste 902 3255 Wilshire Blvd Los Angeles CA 90010

SCHAFFER, JOEL LANCE, dentist; b. Bklyn., Oct. 18, 1945; s. Martin Alter and Irene Natalie (Shore) S.; m. Susan Anne Swearingen, Feb. 14, 1980 (div.); 1 child, Jericho Katherine. BS, L.I. U., 1967; DDS, Howard U., 1971. Dental intern Eastman Dental Ctr., Rochester, N.Y., 1971-72; gen. practice dentistry, Boulder, Colo., 1973—; evaluator Clin. Rsch. Assocs.; lectr. in field, 1972—. Contbr. articles to dental jours; patentee in field. Advisor Boulder Meals on Wheels; mem. Boulder County Com. for Persons with Disabilities. Named outstanding clinician Boulder County Dental Forum, 1979. Fellow Am. Soc. Dental Aesthetics; mem. ADA, Am. Acad. Oral Implantology, Boulder County Dental Soc., Tau Epsilon Phi, Alpha Omega. Jewish. Home: 4171 S Hampton Cir Boulder CO 80301-1793 Office: 2880 Folsom St Boulder CO 80304-3739 *Personal philosophy: Life is brief, enjoy it!.*

SCHAFFER, RICHARD ENOS, artist, registrar; b. Tucson, Nov. 25, 1955; s. Enos P. and Garnett (Jones) S.; m. Barbara Bottari, Feb. 24, 1979; children: Sara Nicole, Julie Ann. BFA, No. Ariz. U., 1979; MFA, U. Ariz., 1990. Gallery asst. Kay Bonfoey Art Gallery, Tucson, 1979-80; curatorial specialist U. Ariz. Mus. Art, Tucson, 1979-96, registrar, 1996—; exhibits cons. Etherton-Stern Gallery, Tucson, 1990-92; treas. Dinnerware Artist Coop Gallery, Tucson, 1993-94; mus. rep. Tucson Assn. Mus., 1989-96; cons. GASP Gallery Learning Project, Tucson, 1991-96; adj. prof. dept. fine art U. Ariz., 1996. One person shows include Dinnerware Gallery, 1993, Pima Coll. East Campus, 1994; exhibited in group shows Newton Art Ctr., Cambridge, Mass., 1993, Flandrau Sci. Ctr. and Cen. Arts, Tucson, 1996. Recipient 3d pl. award in printmaking Artquest 86 Internat., 1986. Mem. Nat. Assn. Mus. Exhbn., Profl. Exhibits Staffs of Tucson (founder, organizer), Mus. Computer Network. Home: PO Box 17694 Tucson AZ 85731 Office: U Ariz Mus Art PO Box 210002 Tucson AZ 85721

SCHAFFER, ROBERT, congressman; b. Cin., July 24, 1962; s. Robert James and Florence Ann (Bednar) S.; m. Maureen Elizabeth Menke, Feb. 8, 1986; children: Jenniffer, Emily, Justin, Sarah. BA in Polit. Sci., U. Dayton, 1984. Speechwriter republican caucus Ohio Gen. Assembly, 1984-85; legis. asst. State of Ohio, Columbus, 1985; majority adminstrv. asst. Colo. Senate, Denver, 1985-87, mem., 1987-96; mem. from Colo. 4th dist. 105th Congress, U.S. Ho. of Reps., Washington, 1997—; commr. Colo. Advanced Tech. Inst., 1988—; proprietor No. Front Range Mktg. and Distbn., Inc. Mem. Mental Health Bd. Larimer County, 1986-87; mem. com. on human svcs. Nat. Conf. State Legislatures; campaing co-chair Arnold for Lt. Gov.; Republican candidate for Lt. Gov. of Colo., 1994. Named Nat. Legislator of Yr., Rep. Nat. Legislators Assn., 1995, Taxpayer Champion, Colo. Union of Taxpayers, 1995. Mem. Jaycees (Mover and Shaker award 1989), KC. Roman Catholic. Home: 3284 Silverthorne Dr Fort Collins CO 80526-2766 Office: US Ho of Reps 2121 Cannon Washington DC 20515

SCHAFFER, THOMAS RAY, water and wastewater management executive; b. Inglewood, Calif., Apr. 7, 1955; s. Charles T. and Marilyn L. (Yost) S.; m. Lynitta M. Gerbert, Oct. 12, 1982; 1 child, Christopher. BS, UCLA, 1977; MS, Loyola Marymount, 1980. Registered profl. civil engineer, Calif., Ariz.; cert. class A wastewater operator, Colo. Water resource control engineer Calif. Regional Water Quality Control, L.A., 1977-80; sr. environ. engr. Jacobs Engring., Pasadena, Calif., 1980-84, Lee and Ro Consulting Engrs., Pasadena, 1984; sr. civil engr. County Sanitation Dists. L.A. County, Whittier, Calif., 1984-90; wastewater mgr. City of Sedona, Ariz., 1990-94; constrn. mgr., engr. Town of Silverthorne, Colo., 1995—. Fellow U.S. Govt., 1978. Mem. Water Environ. Fedn., Rocky Mountain Water Environment Assn. Home: PO Box 23384 Silverthorne CO 80498 Office: Town of Silverthorne PO Box 1309 Silverthorne CO 80498

SCHALLER, MATTHEW FITE, architect; b. Denver, Nov. 28, 1953; s. Frank Henry and Jane (Fite) S.; m. Lavrette DeMandel, Nov. 23, 1991. Student, U. Colo., 1972-76; BS, U. Idaho, 1981, M in Engring., 1985. Registered arch.; real estate salesperson. Foreman Inter-Island Builders, Honolulu, 1978-80; custom home designer Idaho, Montana, Hawaii, 1980-85; rsch. engr. U. Idaho, Moscow, 1982-85; design assoc. Design Assocs., Hanalei, Hawaii, 1985-89; arch. Custom Home Designs, Hanalei, 1987; project mgr. Princeville Corp., Princeville, Hawaii, 1989-96. Pres. Princeville II Cmty. Assn., 1995—. Mem. ASCE, Tau Beta Phi. Home and Office: PO Box 120 Hanalei HI 96714

SCHANDER, MARY LEA, police official; b. Bakersfield, Calif., June 11, 1947; d. Gerald John Lea and Marian Lea Coffman; BA (Augustana fellow) Calif. Luth. Coll., 1969; MA, UCLA, 1970; m. Edwin Schander, July 3, 1971. Staff aide City of Anaheim (Calif.) Police Dept., 1970-72, staff asst., 1972-78, sr. staff asst., 1978-80; with Resource Mgmt. Dept., City of Anaheim, 1980-82; asst. to dir. Pub. Safety Agy., City of Pasadena Police Dept., 1982-85, spl. asst. to police chief, 1985-88, adminstrv. comdr., 1988-92, police comdr., 1992—; freelance musician; publisher Australian Traditional Songs, 1985, Songs in the Air of Early California, 1994; lectr. Calif. Luth. Coll.; instr. Calif. State U., Northridge; cons. City of Lodz, Poland, Internat. Assn. Chiefs of Police; speaker, panelist League of Calif. Cities, Pasadena Commn. on Status of Women; mcpl. mgmt. asst. CLEARS; instr. Calif. State U., Northridge. Producer (cable TV program) Traditional Music Showcase. Contbr. articles in field to profl. jours. Bd. dirs. Women At Work, Step Up Adv. Program; mem. Inst. Bd. Corrections. Recipient Police Chief's Spl. award City of Pasadena, 1987, Women at Work Medal of Excellence, 1988. Mem. Nat. Womens Political Caucus, Nat. Ctr. for Women in Policing, Pasadena Arts Coun., L.A. County Peace Officers, Internat. Assn. Chiefs of Police, Rotary. Home: PO Box 50151 Pasadena CA 91115-0151 Office: Pasadena Police Dept 207 N Garfield Ave Pasadena CA 91101-1748

SCHANFIELD, MOSES SAMUEL, geneticist, educator; b. Mpls., Sept. 7, 1944; s. Abraham and Fanny (Schwartz) S. BA in Anthropology, U. Minn., 1966; AM in Anthropology, Harvard U., 1969; PhD in Human Genetics, U. Mich., 1971. Postdoctoral fellow in immunology U. Calif. Med. Ctr., San Francisco, 1971-74, rsch. geneticist, 1974-75; head of blood bank Milw. Blood Ctr., 1975-78; asst. dir. ARC, Washington, 1978-83; exec. dir. Genetic Testing Inst., Atlanta, 1983-85; lab. dir. Analytical Genetic Testing Ctr., Atlanta and Denver, 1985—; adj. asst. prof. Med. Coll. Wis., Milw., 1976-78; adj. assoc. prof. George Washington U., Washington, 1979-83, Emory U., Atlanta, 1984-89; adj. assoc. prof. Univ. Kans., 1992—; affiliated faculty Colo. State Univ., Fort Collins, 1992—; mem. Nat. Forensic DNA Rev. Panel for the Blind DNA Proficiency Testing, 1996. Author, editor: Immunobiology of the Erythrocyte, 1980, International Methods of Forensic DNA Analysis, 1996; contbg. author: Immunogenetic Factors and Thalassaemia of Hepatitis, 1975; contbr. articles to profl. publs. Recipient Gold medal Latin Am. Congress Hemotherapy and Immunohematology, 1979, R&D 100 award, 1993. Fellow Am. Acad. Forensic Sci.; mem. Am. Soc. Crime Lab. Dirs., Am. Soc. Human Genetics, Human Biology Coun., Phi Kappa Phi. Office: Analytical Genetic Testing Ctr Ste 201 7808 Cherry Creek South Dr Denver CO 80231-3218

SCHAPP, REBECCA MARIA, museum director; b. Stuttgart, Fed. Republic Germany, Dec. 12, 1956; came to U.S., 1957; d. Randall Todd and Elfriede Carolina (Scheppan) Spradlin; m. Thomas James Schapp, May 29, 1979. AA, DeAnza Coll., 1977; BA in Art, San Jose State U., 1979, MA in Art Adminstrn., 1985. Adminstrv. dir. Union Gallery, San Jose, Calif., 1979-82; from mus. coordinator to dep. dir. de Saisset Mus. Santa Clara (Calif.) U., 1982-92, dir., 1993—. Mem. San Francisco Mus. Modern Art; bd. dirs. Works of San Jose, v.p. 1983-85. Mem. Non-Profit Gallery Assn. (bd. dirs.). Democrat. Office: De Saisset Museum Santa Clara Univ 500 El Camino Real Santa Clara CA 95053-4345

SCHARF, BARRY W., artist, educator. BFA, East Carolina U., 1973; MFA, Otis Art Inst., L.A., 1975; postgrad., Advt. Ctr. Painter, sculptor; art instr., instr. computer graphics and photo imaging Art Inst. of Seattle, 1996—; art instr. Citurs Coll., Azusa, Calif., 1978, Studio 2034, 1984-93; founding dir. L.A. Contemporary Exhbns., 1977; evaluator King County Arts Commn, Wash., 1995. Solo shows include Ivey Gallery, L.A., Linda's on Melrose Ave., L.A., Baker Gallery, Mission Viejo, Calif., The Greenpeace Gallery, L.A., Ron Segal Gallery, Seattle, 1994, Waterworks Gallery, San Juan Island, Wash., 1996, Nelson/Rovzar Gallery, Kirkland, Wash., 1997; exhibited in group shows Mus. Sci. and Industry, L.A., The Experience Ctr. Gallery, Costa Mesa, Calif., DOR Gallery, Venice, Calif., L.A. Mcpl. Art Gallery, Ojai (Calif.) Arts Ctr.; represented in collections at East Carolina U., Robert Fox Enterprises, Netherlands Bank of Calif., others; subject of articles. Mem. Coll. Art Assn., Internat. Sculpture Ctr., Soc. Illustrators, Graphic Artists Guild, North Western Sculptors Assn. Address: 2810 233rd Pl NE Redmond WA 98053-5430

SCHARLACH, BERNICE SHERMAN, writer, lecturer; b. Bklyn., Nov. 3, 1919; d. Max and Gertrude Helen (Berger) Sherman; m. Arthur Gustav Scharlach, May 19, 1946; children: David, Alan, Gary. BA, U. Calif., Berkeley, 1941. Reporter, columnist C.C. Times, Walnut Creek, Calif., 1960-70; lectr. on San Francisco history, book reviewer, 1983—, freelance writer, contbr. to mags.., 1971—; v.p., bd.d irs. Am. Jewish Com., San Francisco, 1976—. Author: House of Harmony, 1983, Big Alma (Spreckels), 1990, Ben Swig; editor Jewish Cmty. Fedn. Greater East Bay, Oakland, Calif., 1971-78; author monographs. Bd. dirs. Evergreen Dem. Party, San Jose, Calif., 1994—. Mem. Women in Comms. (bd. dirs. 1971-80). Jewish. Home: 8702 Lomas Azules Pl San Jose CA 95135-2129

SCHATT, PAUL, newspaper editor; b. N.Y.C., Aug. 31, 1945; divorced; children: Suzannah, Andrew. BA with distinction Polit. Sci., English, Ariz. State U., 1967. Editor Ariz. Republic, 1964-66, reporter, 1965-74, urban affairs editor, 1974-75, asst. city editor, 1975-79, chief asst. city editor, 1979-82, asst. met. editor, 1985-86, met. editor, 1986-88, editor edit. pages, 1993—; asst. editor Ariz. Mag., 1981-82, editor, 1982-85; editor edit. pages Phoenix Gazette, 1988-93, The Ariz. Republic, 1993—; vis. lectr. Pub. Affairs Journalism, Ariz. State U., 1976—, instr. Mass. Comm. Dept., 1974-76; dir. Eugene C. Pulliam Fellowship. Phoenix program, 1990—; writing coach, 1989; del. Pre White House Conf. Librs., 1991. v.p. Crisis Nursery, 1984-87, bd. dirs. 1980-87; exec. bd. Hospice of the Valley, 1980-87; pres. Friends of Phoenix Pub. Libr., 1985-86, bd. dirs. 1986—; bd. trustees 1st Amendment Congress, 1989—; bd. dirs. Camelback Hosps. 1982-89, chmn. bd. dirs. 1986-87, Cactus Pine Coun. Girl Scouts Am., 1988-89, Sun Sounds Inc., 1982-89, Valley Leadership Inc., 1991—, alum. assn., 1985-89, Ariz. Zool. Soc., 1991—, Barrow Neurol. Found., 1991—, Kids Voting, 1991-93, Barry Goldwater Inst., 1991-93, Ariz. Club, 1991—. With Ariz. Nat. Guard, 1966-79. Recipient Montgomery award Outstanding Svc. to Community Friends of Phoenix Pub. Libr., 1989; profl. Journalism fellow Stanford U., 1970-71. Mem. Am. Soc. Newspaper Editors, Soc. Profl. Journalists (pres. Valley of Sun chpt. 1974-75, 83-84, exec. bd. 1988-92), Sigma Delta Chi (co-chair nat. convention 1974). Office: The Ariz Republic Editorial Dept 200 E Van Buren St Phoenix AZ 85004

SCHATZ, HOWARD, ophthalmologist; b. Chgo.; s. Lawrence and Beatrice Schatz; m. Beverly Ornstein; children: Jacqueline, Jessica. MD, U. Ill., Chgo. Diplomate Am. Bd. Ophthalmology, Nat. Bd. Med. Examiners. Intern Cook County Hosp., Chgo.; resident ophthalmology Ill. Eye and Ear Infirmary, U. Ill., Chgo.; fellowship med. retina Wilmer Eye Inst., Johns

Hopkins U. Sch. Medicine, Balt., fellowship surg. retina; dir., staff mem. Retina Rsch. Fund, St. Mary's Hosp. and Med. Ctr., San Francisco; clin. prof. ophthalmology U. Calif., San Francisco; presenter and lectr. in field. Editor: Retina-Am. Jour. Retinal and Vitreal Diseases, (with others) Laser Photocoagulation of Retinal Disease, 1988; author: Fundus Fluorescein Angiography: A Composite Slide Collection, 1975, 2d edit., 1976, (with T.C. Burton, L.A. Yannuzzi, M.F. Rabb) Intrepretation of Fundus Fluorescein Angiography, 1978, (with L.A. Yannuzzi, K.A. Gitter) The Macula, 1979, Laser Treatment of Fundus Disease: A Comprehensive Text and Composite Slide Collection, 1980, Essential Fluorescein Angiography: A Compendium of 100 Classic Cases, 1983, California Resource Directory for the Blind and Visually Impaired, 1991; contbr. articles to jours. With USAF, 1969-71. Recipient Honor award Am. Acad. Ophthalmology and Otolaryngology, 1977, Arlo A. Morrison Lectr. award Calif. Assn. Ophthalmology, 1988, Second Annual Vallotton Lectr. award Med. U. S.C., Charleston, 1990, Paul Chandler Professorship Lectr. award Harvard Med. Sch., Boston, 1991. Mem. AMA (Physicians Recognition awards 1974, 81, 84, 88, Dr. William Beaumont award 1981), Calif. Med. Assn., San Francisco Med. Soc., Retina Soc., Am. Macula Soc. (Paul Henkind Lectr. award 1994), Am. Fluorescein Angiography Club, Western Retina Study Club. Home: PO Box 640385 San Francisco CA 94164-0385 Office: 1 Daniel Burnham Ct Ste 210C San Francisco CA 94109-5460

SCHATZ, MONA CLAIRE STRUHSAKER, social worker, educator, consultant, researcher; b. Phila., Jan. 4, 1950; d. Milton and Josephine (Kivo) S.; m. James Fredrick Struhsaker, Dec. 31, 1979 (div.); 1 child, Thain Mackenzie. BA, Metro State Coll., 1976; postgrad., U. Minn., 1976; MSW, U. Denver, 1979; D in Social Work/Social Welfare, U. Pa., 1986. Teaching fellow U. Pa., Phila., 1981-82; asst. prof. S.W. Mo. State U., Springfield, 1982-85; assoc. prof. Colo. State U., Ft. Collins, 1985—, field coord., 1986-88, dir. non-profit agy. adminstrn. program, 1995—, project dir. Edn. and Rsch. Inst. for Fostering Families, 1987—, dir. youth agy. adminstrn. program Am. Humanics, 1988-90; cons. Mgmt. and Behavioral Sci. Ctr., The Wharton Sch. U. Pa., 1981-82; resource specialist So. N.J. Health Sys. Agy., 1982; adj. faculty mem. U. Mo., Springfield, 1994; med. social worker Rehab. and Vis. Nurse Assn., 1985-90; mem. Colo. Child Welfare Adv. Com., Family Conservation Initiative; internat. cons. and trainer Inst. for Internat. Connections, Russia, Latvia, Albania, U.S., Hungary, Ukraine, Romania, 1992—. Contbr. articles to profl. jours. Cons., field rep. Big Bros./Big Sisters of Am., Phila., 1979-83; acting dir., asst. dir. Big Sisters of Colo., 1971-78; owner Polit. Cons. in Colo., Denver, 1978-79; active Food Co-op, Ft. Collins, Foster Parent, Denver, Capital Hill United Neighbors, Adams County (Denver) Social Planning Coun., Co., Colo. Justice Coun., Denver, Regional Girls Shelter, Springfield; bd. dirs. Crisis Helpline and Info. Svc. Scholar Lilly Endowment, Inc., 1976, Piton Found., 1978; recipient Spl. Recognition award Big Bros./Big Sisters of Am., 1983, Recognition award Am. Humanics Mgmt. Inst., 1990. Mem. Inst. Internat. Connections (bd. dirs.), Coun. Social Work Edn., Group for Study of Generalist Social Work, Social Welfare History Group, Nat. Assn. Social Workers (nominating com. Springfield chpt., state bd. dirs., No. Colo. rep.), Student Social Work Assn. Colo. State U. (adv. 1986-89), Permanency Planning Coun. for Children and Youth, NOW (treas. Springfield chpt. 1984-85), Student Nuclear Awareness Group (advisor), Student Social Work Assn. (advisor), Har Shalom, Alpha Delta Mu. Democrat. Office: Colo State U Social Work Dept Fort Collins CO 80523

SCHATZMAN, SUSAN, adult education educator; b. Bridgeport, Conn., Nov. 21, 1946; d. George Schatzman and Edna (Scott) Capen; children: Cynthia, Jennifer, Elizabeth, Travis. BA, So. Conn. State U., 1968; MA, Calif. State U., Fullerton, 1976; PhD, Brigham Young U., 1986. Cert. tchr., Calif. Instr. Brigham Young U., Provo, Utah, 1984-91, Weber State U., 1991, Univ. Calif., Berkeley, 1992-95, San Lorenzo Sch. Dist., 1996-97, Univ. Phoenix, 1996—. Chair Math. and Sci. Network Conf., 1978—; mem. NSF, 1991, Calif. Sci. Project, 1992—, Ctr. Tchg. and Learning, 1996—. Distance Edn. grantee Toyota USA, 1994; Environ. Edn. grantee EPA, 1995. Mem. LDS Ch. Home: 16 Skylark Dr Larkspur CA 94939

SCHAUFEL, SHIRLEY, museum director, curator. Dir., curator Marin County Mus. Am. Indian. Office: Marin County Mus Am Indian 2200 Novato Blvd Novato CA 94947 also: PO Box 864 Novato CA 94948

SCHAUMBURG, DONALD ROLAND, art educator, ceramic artist; b. Oakland, Calif., Aug. 23, 1919; s. John J. and Ethel Florence (Gurney) S.; m. Darleen Jackson, Nov. 22, 1945; 1 child: Rhoda Jane Pertuit. BA in Art Edn., Calif. Coll. Arts and Crafts, 1941; MFA, Clare Coll., 1951; postgrad. advanced study, Pond Farm, Guerniville, Calif., 1957-59. Instr. Palamar Coll., San Marcos, Calif., 1946-49, Fine Arts Gallery, San Diego, 1952; tchr. La Jolla (Calif.) H.S., 1952-53; instr. San Diego State U., 1953; prof. art Ariz. State U., Tempe, 1953-88; dir. Payson (Ariz.) Art Ctr., summers 1967-70. Exhibited in group shows at 15th Nat. Syracuse (N.Y.) Bienniel, 1950, Mus. of Contemporary Crafts, N.Y., 1964, Mus. of Internat. Folk Art, Santa Fe, N.Mex., 1965, The U. Art Collections, Ariz. State U., Tempe, 1973, Nelson Art Ctr. Ariz. State U., Tempe. With USN, 1942-45. Recipient 1st price clay exhibn., Heard Mus., Phoenix, 1975; awards of merit Ariz. Crafts, Tucson, 1955-59. Mem. Ariz. Designer Craftsmen (life, Mary Soule award 1975). Home: 5410 E Vernon Ave Phoenix AZ 85008

SCHAUSS, ALEXANDER GEORGE, psychologist, researcher; b. Hamburg, Fed. Republic Germany, July 20, 1948; came to U.S., 1953; s. Frank and Alla S.; m. Laura Babin; children: Nova, Evan. BA, U. N.Mex., 1970, MA, 1972; PhD, Calif. Coast U., 1992. State probation/parole officer 2nd Judicial Dist. Ct., Albuquerque, 1969-73; criminal justice planner Albuquerque/Bernalillo County Criminal Justice Planning Com., 1973-75; state asst. adminstr. dept. corrections State of S.D., Pierre, 1975-77; dir. Pierce County Probation Dept., Tacoma, Wash., 1977-78; tng. officer IV Wash. State Criminal Justice Tng. Commn., Olympia, 1978-79; dir. Inst. Biosocial Rsch. City Univ. Grad. Sch., Seattle, 1979-80; exec. dir. Am. Inst. Biosocial Rsch. Inc., Tacoma, 1980-97, Am. Preventive Med. Assn., 1992-94, Citizens for Health, 1992-95; dir. Citizens for Health Edn., 1994-96; assoc. prof. behavioral scis. Nat. Coll. Naturopathic Medicine, Portland, program coord. for profl. studies and continuing edn., 1995—; assoc. prof. rsch. S.W. Coll. Naturopathic Medicine & Health Scis., Tempe, Ariz., 1995-96; rsch. dir. S.W. Coll. Naturopathic Medicine & Health Scis., Scottsdale, Ariz., 1995-96, sr. dir. rsch., 1996—; mem. WHO Study Group on Health Promotion, Copenhagen, 1985; vis. lectr. pediats. The John Radcliffe Hosp., Oxford U., Eng., summer 1985; sec. coun. on food policy Nat. Assn. Pub. Health Policy, 1990-94, chmn., 1994-96; vis. scholar Kans. C.C. Consortium, 1982; vis. lectr. McCarrison Soc. Conf. at Oxford U., 1983; presdl. adv. bd. Bastyr U., 1979—, S.W. Coll. Naturopathic Medicine, 1993—; mem. developmental planning com., Office of Dietary Supplements, Office of Disease Prevention NIH, Bethesda, 1996—. Author: Orthomolecular Treatment of Criminal Offenders, 1978, Diet, Crime and Delinquency, 1980, rev., 1995, Nutrition and Behavior, 1986, Nutrition and Criminal Behavior, 1990; co-author: Zinc and Eating Disorders, 1989, Eating for A's, 1991, Minerals, Trace Elements and Human Health, 1995, rev. 1996, Anorexia and Bulimia: Nutritional Therapies, 1996, Cat's Claw (Una de Gato) Uncaria Tormentosa, 1996, Silver and Other Mineral Colloids, 1997; editor-in-chief Internat. Jour. Biosocial and Med. Rsch., 1979—; mem. editl. bd. 18 jours. Master arbitrator Tacoma/Pierce County Better Bus. Bur., Tacoma, 1986-94; mem. Pierce County N. Area Transp. Adv. Coun., Tacoma, 1991-92; trustee mem. Pierce County Pub. Safety Task Team, 1993; trustee Nat. Inst. for Naturopathic Medicine, 1993—. Recipient Rsch. award Wacker Found., 1983-85, 88; fellow Am. Coll. Nutrition, 1986-87, Am. Orthopsychiat. Assn., 1980-95. Fellow N.Y. Acad. of Sci.; mem. Am. Nutritionists Assn., Assn. Chemoreception Scis., Internat. Assn. Eating Disorders Profls., Am. Assn. Correctional Psychologists (pres. Citizens For Health 1995-97), Am. Found. Preventative Medicine (treas. 1992-93), Acad. Criminal Justice Scis., Am. Soc. Criminology, N.Y. Acad. Scis. (emeritus), Rotary (chmn. cmty. svcs. com. Tacoma chpt. 1989-90, chmn. civic affairs com. 1989-90, mem. Vladivostok com. 1991-93, mem. internat. exch. com. 1994-95, world cmty. svcs. com. 1996-97). Office: Am Inst for Biosocial Rsch PO Box 1174 Tacoma WA 98401

SCHAWLOW, ARTHUR LEONARD, physicist, educator; b. Mt. Vernon, N.Y., May 5, 1921; s. Arthur and Helen (Mason) S.; m. Aurelia Keith Townes, May 19, 1951; children: Arthur Keith, Helen Aurelia, Edith Ellen. BA, U. Toronto, Ont., Can., 1941, MA, 1942, PhD, 1949, LLD (hon.), 1970; DSc (hon.), U. Ghent, Belgium, 1968, U. Bradford, Eng., 1970, U. Ala., 1984, Trinity Coll., Dublin, Ireland, 1986; DTech (hon.), U. Lund, Sweden, 1987; DSL (hon.), Victoria U., Toronto, 1993. Postdoctoral fellow, rsch. assoc. Columbia U., 1949-51, vis. assoc. prof., 1960; rsch. physicist Bell Tel. Labs., 1951-61, cons., 1961-62; prof. physics Stanford (Calif.) U., 1961-91, also J.G. Jackson-C.J. Wood prof. physics, 1978, prof. emeritus, 1991—, exec. head dept. physics, 1966-70, acting chmn. dept., 1973-74. Author: (with C.H. Townes) Microwave Spectroscopy, 1955; Co-inventor (with C.H. Townes), optical maser or laser, 1958. Recipient Ballantine medal Franklin Inst., 1962, Thomas Young medal and prize Inst. Physics and Phys. Soc., London, 1963, Schawlow medal Laser Inst. Am., 1982, Nobel prize in physics, 1981, Nat. Medal of Sci., NSF, 1991, Arata award High Temperature Soc. Japan, 1994, Ronald H. Brown Am. Innovator award U.S. Dept. Commerce, 1996; named Calif. Scientist of Yr., 1973, Marconi Internat. fellow, 1977; named to Am. Inventors Hall of Fame, 1996. Fellow Am. Acad. Arts and Scis., Am. Phys. Soc. (coun. 1966-70, chmn. div. electron and atomic physics 1974, pres. 1981), Optical Soc. Am. (hon. mem. 1983, dir.-at-large 1966-68, pres. 1975, Frederick Ives medal 1976); mem. NAS, IEEE (Liebmann prize 1964), AAAS (chmn. physics sect. 1979), Am. Philos. Soc., Royal Irish Acad. (hon.). Office: Stanford U Dept Physics Stanford CA 94305

SCHECHTER, CLIFFORD, financial executive, lawyer; b. N.Y.C., Feb. 14, 1958; s. Howard and Diana D. (Eiss) S.; m. Niely Okonsky, June 17, 1979; children: Dana Ann, Adam Hillel, Talia Beth. BS summa cum laude, U. R.I., 1979; JD, Fordham U. Sch. Law, 1982; MBA, L.I. U., 1988. Bar: N.Y. 1983, U.S. Tax Ct. 1983, U.S. Supreme Ct. 1986, D.C. 1990, U.S. Dist. Ct. (so. and ea. dists.) N.Y. 1983; lic. gen. securities prin., fin. and ops. prin. Nat. Assn. Securities Dealers; CFP; registered investment advisor. Tax supr. Touche Ross & Co., Jericho, N.Y., 1982-86; sr. v.p., dir. taxes L.F. Rothschild & Co. Inc., N.Y.C., 1986-91, chief fin. officer, dir. adminstrn. and taxes, 1991-93; pres. Royal Fin. Svcs. Inc., San Diego, 1993-96; personal fin. counseling mgr. Ernst & Young, San Diego, 1996—; adj. prof. Adelphi U., Garden City, N.Y., 1983-91, Pace U., N.Y.C., 1991-93. Bd. dirs. P.A.D. Pub. Svc. Ctr., Washington, 1986—, Congregation Chabad of Rancho Bernardo and Poway. Recipient Uniroyal Found. Fellowship award, 1978, Am. Jurisprudence award Scholastic Excellence in Estate Planning, 1982. Mem. ABA, N.Y. State Bar Assn., D.C. Bar Assn., Bar Assn. Nassau County, Internt. Assn. Fin. Planning, Fin. Mgmt. Assn., Securities Industry Assn., Wall St. Tax Assn., Profl. Fraternity Assn. (bd. dirs. 1994-95, treas. 1995-96, pres.-elect 1996—), Phi Alpha Delta (internt. proctor 1986-88, marshal 1988-90, historian 1990-92, treas. 1992-94, internat. vice justice 1994-96, internat. justice 1996—, dist. XV justice 1984-86, Outstanding Active mem. award 1982, Stan P. Jonse Meml. award 1985, Outstanding Alumnus mem. Wormser chpt. 1982-85), Beta Gamma Sigma, Phi Kappa Phi. Republican. Jewish. Home: 16334 Avenida Florencia Poway CA 92064 Office: Ernst & Young 501 W Broadway Ste 1100 San Diego CA 92101

SCHECHTER, JOEL, magazine editor, writer, educator; b. Washington, June 21, 1947; s. Henry Bear and Ruth (Lindauer) S. BA, Antioch Coll., 1969; DFA, Yale U., 1973. Lit. advisor Am. Place Theater, N.Y.C., 1973-77; asst. prof. SUNY, Stony Brook, 1974-77; prof. Sch. Drama Yale U., New Haven, 1977-91; editor Theater Mag., New Haven, 1977-91; prof., chair theatre arts dept. San Francisco State U., 1992—; polit. satire columnist New Haven Independent, 1988-90. Author: (Book) Satiric Impersonations, 1994, Durov's Pig, 1985, (play) The Complete Aristophanes, 1988. State senate candidate New Haven Green Party, 1988, 90. Fox fellow Yale U., Moscow, 1991. Mem. Lit. Mgrs. & Dramaturgs Am. (v.p. 1989—). Office: San Francisco State U Dept Theatre Arts 1600 Holloway Ave San Francisco CA 94132

SCHECHTER, ROBERTA LYNNE, English educator; b. Escondido, Calif., May 6, 1952; d. Raymond Lucas and Marlene (Ruppel) Howard; m. Paul Schechter, Dec. 3, 1982; children: Amy Lynne Serafin, Josiah Ray Serafin. BA, U. Ariz., 1979, M of English and Edn., 1981. Owner Med.-Dental Cons., San Diego, 1974-78; instr., adminstr. Sunnyside Unified, Tucson, 1979—; owner P.S. Enterprises, Tucson, 1981—; dir. Lamplight Reading Series, Tucson, 1988—; Cons. youth violence Mayors Task Force, Tucson, wellness cons. Contbr. articles to profl. jours.; author numerous poems. Active Pima County Inter-faith Coun., Tucson, 1996, Inter-Tribal Grad. Coun., Tucson, 1990-96; founder Southside Action Com., Tucson, 1995-96, Southside Coalition, Tucson, 1985-96. Mem. Nat. Coun. English Tchr. (presenter 1990), Nat. Sci. Tchr. Assn., Ariz. English Tchr. Assn. (presenter), Internat. Reading Assn. (presenter 1992), Inter-Tribal Red Nets. Home: 2572 W Mossman Rd Tucson AZ 85746 Office: 2602 W Mossman Rd Tucson AZ 85746-5105

SCHEER, JANET KATHY, mathematics educator; b. Bklyn., Apr. 22, 1947; d. Seymour and Hilda (Shoer) S. BA, Bklyn. Coll., 1968; MS, Syracuse (N.Y.) U., 1969; PhD, Ariz. State U., 1977. Cert. tchr., N.Y., Ariz.; cert. prin., Ariz. Math. tchr. Jamesville (N.Y.) DeWitt Middle Sch., 1969-72; math. tchr., middle sch. coordinator Am. Internat. Sch., Kfar Shmaryahu, Israel, 1972-74; from asst. prof. to assoc. prof. So. Ill. U., Carbondale, 1977-88; nat. product devel. specialist Scott, Foresman and Co., Glenview, Ill., 1989-90; dir. field svcs. for math. Scott, Foresman and Co., 1991; exec. dir. Create A Vision, Mountain View, Calif., 1992—; cons. in field, 1977—; sr. nat. math. cons. Holt, Rinehart & Winston, N.Y.C., 1986-89, Harcourt Brace-Jovanovich/Holt, 1989. Editor Ill. Math. Tchr. jour., 1980-83; author: Manipulatives in Mathematics Unlimited, 1987; columnist Learning Mag., 1996—; contbr. to textbooks and profl. jours. Named one of Outstanding Young Women Am., 1978, 81-85, Outstanding Tchr. Yr. So. Ill. U., 1978-79; recipient numerous grants. Mem. Nat. Council Tchrs. Math., Research Council for Diagnostic and Prescriptive Math. (charter mem., v.p. 1984-86), Ill. Council Tchrs. Math. (various offices), Phi Delta Kappa, Kappa Delta Pi. Office: Create A Vision 1300 Villa St Mountain View CA 94041-1197

SCHEFCIK, JERRY ALLEN, art gallery administrator, university official; b. Alliance, Nebr., Sept. 15, 1952; s. Robert and Verna Mae (Woodworth) S.; m. Tamara Dawn Forsyth, Apr. 24, 1979; children: Annie, David, Catherine. BA in Art and Design, Brigham Young U., 1979; MA in Art History, U. Denver, 1982. Instr. Spanish, Brigham Young U., Provo, Utah, 1979-80; mus. asst. Springville (Utah) Mus. Art, 1979-80; asst. curator Sch. Art Slide Libr., then grad. tchg. asst. U. Denver, 1981-82; curator Francis King Collection Western Art, Sangre de Cristo Arts and Conf. Ctr., Pueblo, Colo., 1982, curator visual arts, 1982-84; curator art Amarillo (Tex.) Art Ctr., 1984-89; curator Donna Beam Fine Art Gallery, U. Nev., Las Vegas, 1989-90, dir., 1991—, curator Metcalf Gallery, Tam Alumni Ctr., 1989—; curator Nev. Inst. for Contemporary Art, 1991—, interim dir., 1990-91; lectr. in field, 1983; cons. S.E. Colo. Arts Coun., Lamar, 1984, Marsh Media, Inc., Amarillo, 1986-87; book reviewer Harcourt Brace Jovanovich, Inc., San Diego, 1989; grant evaluator Nev. Coun. on Arts, 1989-90; mem. adv. panel Las Vegas Neon Mus., 1993; mem. arts adv. subcom. for Nev. artists for McCarran Art Gallery, McCarran Internat. Airport, 1990-94. Curator over 150 exhbns., including Julian Onderdonk: A Texas Tradition traveling exhbn., 1984, Georgia O'Keefe and Her Contemporaries, 1985, Divine Images and Magic Carpets: The Asian Art Collection of Dr. and Mrs. William T. Price, 1987, John Marin Watercolors, 1988, Figuratively Speaking: Art of the Human Form, 1991, ZOOID, 1993, Art—In, On and Out of the Bag, 1993, From New York: Recent Thinking in Comtemporary Photography, 1993; editor exhbn. catalogues and brochures. Bd. dirs. Area Arts Found., Amarillo, 1988-89; mem. adv. panel visual arts curriculum Las Vegas Acad., 1993. Mem. Am. Assn. Mus., Western Mus. Conf. (ann. meeting local arrangements com. 1991). Democrat. Mem. LDS Ch. Office: U Nev Las Vegas Donna Beam Fine Art Gallery Box 5002 4505 S Maryland Pky Las Vegas NV 89154

SCHEIB, GERALD PAUL, fine art educator, jeweler, metalsmith; b. L.A., Dec. 26, 1937; s. Harry William and Olive Bauer (Cartwright) S.; m. Elizabeth Ann Galligan, Dec. 27, 1965 (div. 1978); children: Gregory Paul, Geoffrey Paul; m. Dedra Lynn True, Oct. 1, 1983; 1 child, Adam True. AA, East L.A. Jr. Coll., 1959; BA, Calif. State U., L.A., 1962, MFA, 1968. Cert. life teaching credential in fine arts, secondary and coll. tchr., Calif. Secondary tchr. art L.A. Unified Sch. Dist., 1963-77; prof. fine art L.A. Community Coll. Dist., 1977—; pres. faculty senate L.A. Mission Coll., San Fernando, Calif., 1983-84; bargaining unit rep., AFT Coll. Guild Local 1521; elected Arts and Letters chair L.A. Mission Coll., 1993; owner, mgr. Artificers Bench, Sylmar, Calif., 1976—. Policy bd. mem. The Calif. Arts Project, 1995-97. With USNR, 1955—. Recipient of tribute City of L.A., 1983, Citizen of Month award, Los Angeles County, 1983. Mem. Calif. Art Edn. Assn. (membership chmn. 1985-87, pres.-elect 1989-91, pres. 1991-93, Calif.'s Outstanding Art Educator in Higher Edn. 1994-95), San Fernando Active 20-30 Club (pres. 1981-82), Nat. Assn. Scholars, Sons of Union Vets of Civil War, U.S. Naval Cryptologic Vets. Assn. Republican. Office: 13356 Eldridge Ave Sylmar CA 91342-3200

SCHEIBER, HARRY N., law educator; b. N.Y.C., 1935. BA, Columbia U., 1955; MA, Cornell U., 1957, PhD, 1961; MA (hon.), Dartmouth Coll., 1965. instr. to assoc. prof. history Dartmouth Coll., 1960-68, prof., 1968-71; prof. Am. history U. Calif., San Diego, 1971-80; prof. law Boalt Hall, U. Calif., Berkeley, 1980—, chmn. jurisprudence and social policy program, 1982-84, 90-93, assoc. dean, 1990-93, 96—; The Stefan Riesenfeld Prof., 1991—; vice chair Univ. Academic Senate, 1993-94. chair, 1994-95; Fulbright disting. sr. lectr., Australia, 1983, marine affairs coord. Calif. Sea Grant Coll. Program, 1989—; vis. rsch. prof. Law Inst. U. Uppsala, Sweden, 1995. Chmn. Littleton Griswold Prize Legal History, 1985-88; pres. N.H. Civil Liberties Union, 1969-70; chmn. Project '87 Task Force on Pub. Programs, Washington, 1982-85; dir. Berkeley Seminar on Federalism, 1986—; cons. judiciary study U.S. Adv. Commn. Intergovernmental Rels., 1985-88; dir. NEH Inst. on Constitutionalism, U. Calif., Berkeley, 1986-87, 88-91. Recipient Sea Grant Colls. award, 1981-83, 84-85, 86-96; fellow Ctr. Advanced Study in Behavioral Scis., Stanford Calif., 1967, 71; Guggenheim fellow, 1971, 88; Rockefeller Found. humanities fellow, 1979, NEH fellow, 1985-86; NSF grantee, 1979, 80, 88-89; Fellow U. Calif. Humanities Rsch. Inst., 1989. Mem. Am. Hist. Assn., Orgn. Am. Historians, Am. Soc. Intl. Law, Agrl. History Soc. (pres. 1978), Econ. History Assn. (trustee 1978-80), Law and Soc. Assn. (trustee 1979-81, 1996—), Am. Soc. Legal History (dir. 1982-86, 90-93, 96—), Nat. Assessment History and Citizenship Edn. (chmn. nat. acad. bd. 1986-87), Marine Affairs and Policy Assn. (bd. dirs. 1991-96), Ocean Governance Study Group (steering com. 1991—), Internat. Coun. Environ. Law. Author numerous books including: (with L. Friedman) American Law and the Constitutional Order, 1978, 2d edit. 1988; contbr. articles to law revs.and social sci. jours., 1963—. Office: U Calif Berkeley Law Sch Boalt Hall Berkeley CA 94720-2150

SCHEIDE, KATHLEEN ELLEN, music educator, musician; b. Milw., Jan. 12, 1962; d. Norman P. Scheide and Martha M. (Knuteson) Bartholomew. MusB, New Eng. Conservatory, Boston, 1983; MusM, New Eng. Conservatory, 1985; D Mus. Arts, U. So. Calif., 1992. Instr. organ, harpsichord and piano Cmty. Music Sch. San Diego State U., 1994—; instr. Cuyamaca Coll., El Cajon, Calif., 1996—; dir. music St. John the Evangelist Cath. Ch., San Diego, 1993—. Composer: The Organists' Companion, 1995, 96; composer, performer Liszt and Scheide, 1995; concert organist, harpsichordist Artist Recitals, L.A., 1993—. Mem. Am. Guild Organists (dean San Diego 1992-94), Organ Hist. Soc., Early Music Am., Music Tchrs.' Nat. Assn. (sec. Dist. I 1995—), Internat. League Women Composers. Roman Catholic. Office: PO Box 601364 San Diego CA 92160-1364

SCHEIDENHELM, RICHARD JOY, lawyer, legal historian, writer; b. Erie, Pa., Sept. 13, 1942; s. Edward and Jean (Monrad) S.; m. Lynn L. Whitaker, Aug. 30, 1969; children: Colan, Galen, Nathan. BA, Kenyon Coll., 1964; MA, U. Wis., 1966, PhD, 1970; JD, U. Colo., 1976. Bar: Colo. 1977, U.S. Dist. Ct. Colo. 1977. Editorial cons. Conn. Commn. on the Arts, Hartford, 1972; instr. Afro-Am. history evening sch. Rockford Coll., Ill., 1969-70; asst. city atty., Boulder, Colo., 1977-80; sole practice, Boulder, 1980—; lectr. history and govt. U. Wis., Menomonie, 1989-91; hearing officer, settlement officer Colo. State Personnel Bd., 1984; asst. prof. dept. history and govt., U. No. Colo., Greeley, 1987-89, instr. dept. history Colo. State U., Ft. Collins, 1994—. Author, editor: Artists in the Classroom, 1973; editor: The Response to John Brown, 1972. Town atty., Superior, Colo., 1986-87. Mem. Am. Soc. for Legal History, Am. Jour. Historians Assn. (treas.). Democrat.

SCHEID-RAYMOND, LINDA ANNE, property management professional; b. Rochester, N.Y., Aug. 13, 1953; d. Arthur F. and Anna M. Scheid; m. Dan Raymond, June 27, 1987. BFA, U. Colo., 1975. Leasing agt. Richard E. Rudolph, Boulder, Colo., 1975-77; adminstrv. asst., co-mgr. Harsh Investment Corp., Denver, 1977-83; property mgr. A.G. Spanos Mgmt., Colorado Springs, Colo., 1984-85, Carmel Devel. and Mgmt., Denver, 1985-88, Property Asset Mgmt., Denver, 1989-96, Gt. West Mgmt. & Realty, Denver, 1996—; with All Video Prodn., Boulder, 1994—. Contbr. photographs to profl. mags.

SCHELAR, VIRGINIA MAE, chemistry consultant; b. Kenosha, Wis., Nov. 26, 1924; d. William and Blanche M. (Williams) S. BS, U. Wis., 1947, MS, 1953; MEd, Harvard U., 1962; PhD, U. Wis., 1969. Instr. U. Wis., Milw., 1947-51; info. specialist Abbott Labs., North Chgo., Ill., 1953-56; instr. Wright Jr. Coll., Chgo., 1957-58; asst. prof. No. Ill. U., DeKalb, 1958-63; prof. St. Petersburg (Fla.) Jr. Coll., 1965-67; asst. prof. Chgo. State Coll., 1967-68; prof. Grossmont Coll., El Cajon, Calif., 1968-80; cons. Calif., 1981—. Author: Kekule Centennial, 1965; contbr. articles to profl. jours. Active citizens adv. coun. DeKalb Consol. Sch. Bd.; voters svc. chair League Women Voters, del. to state and nat. convs., judicial chair, election laws chair. Standard Oil fellow, NSF grantee; recipient Lewis prize U. Wis. Fellow Am. Inst. Chemists; mem. Am. Chem. Soc. (membership affairs com., chmn. western councilor's caucus, exec. com., councilor, legis. counselor, chmn. edn. com., editor state and local bulletins)

SCHELL, FARREL LOY, transportation engineer; b. Amarillo, Tex., Dec. 14, 1931; s. Thomas Phillip and Lillian Agnes (McKee) S.; m. Shirley Anne Samuelson, Feb. 6, 1955; children: James Christopher, Maria Leslyn Schell Peter. BS, U. Kans., 1954; postgrad., Carnegie-Mellon U., 1974. Registered profl. engr., Calif., Colo. Resident engr. Sverdrup & Parcel, Denver, 1957-61; project engr. Bechtel Corp., San Francisco, 1961-62, Parsons, Brinckerhoff-Tudor-Bechtel, San Francisco, 1962-67; mgr. urban transp. dept. Kaiser Engrs., Oakland, Calif., 1967-78; program dir. San Francisco Mcpl. Rwy I.C., 1978-80; project mgr. Houston Transit Cons., 1980-83, Kaiser Transit Group, Miami, 1983-85; mgr. program devel. Kaiser Engrs., Oakland, 1985-87; project mgr. O'Brien-Kreitzberg & Assocs., San Francisco, 1987-89; sr. project mgr. Bay Area Rapid Transit Dist., Oakland, Calif., 1989-96; dir. Schelter Devel. Corp., Piedmont, Calif., 1982—. Contbr. articles to profl. jours. Dir. Achenbach Graphic Arts Coun. Lt. (j.g.) USN, 1954-57, PTO. Mem. ASCE, ASME, Nat. Soc. Profl. Engrs., Nat. Coun. Engrng. Examiners, Am. Planners Assn., Am. Pub. Transit Assn., Lakeview Club, Scarab Club, Pachacamac Club, Sigma Tau, Tau Beta Pi. Home: 24 York Dr Piedmont CA 94611-4123

SCHELLER, ERIN LINN, publishing company executive; b. Port Arthur, Tex., Dec. 25, 1942; d. Truman Edward Jr. and Margaret Jane (Imhoff) Linn; m. Herman Scheller, Oct. 19, 1983; 1 child, Christopher Wayne Levy. Student, Barat Coll., 1960-61; BS, U. Tex., 1964. Tchr. Cath. Sch. Dist., Houston, 1965-67; owner, pres. The Pub.'s Mark, Incline Village, Nev., 1982—; pres., chmn. bd. EduVision Inc., computer software co., Incline Village, 1994—; guest lectr. death edn. related orgns., U.S., 1982—. Author: Children Are Not Paper Dolls, 1982, I Know Just How You Feel, 1986, Dear Teacher, 1988, 150 Facts About Grieving Children, 1990, Premonitions, Visitations and Dreams, 1991. Advisor Mo. Bapt. Children's Group, St. Louis, 1980-81; chpt. leader The Compassionate Friends, Denver, 1980-81, Greeley, Colo., 1981-83; 2nd v.p. Republican Women's Club, Incline Village, 1987-90; mem. AAUW, Incline Village, 1987-89; pres. Teester's Ladies Golf Assn., Incline Village, 1987-90; mem. Assn. for Death. Edn. and Counseling, 1985—, Grief Edn. Inst., 1981—, The Compassionate Friends, 1980—. Named Honored Author, Ill. Libr. Exposition, 1985. Republican. Lutheran. Home and Office: The Publishers Mark PO Box 6300 Incline Village NV 89450-6300

SCHENDEL, WINFRIED GEORGE, insurance company executive; b. Harpstedt, Germany, June 19, 1931; s. Willi Rudolf Max and Anna Margarete (Sassen) S.; came to U.S., 1952, naturalized, 1956; B.S. in Elect. and Indsl. Engring., Hannover-Stadthagen U., Hannover, W. Germany, 1952; m.

Joanne Wiiest, Aug. 24, 1953; children—Victor Winfried, Bruce Lawrence, Rachelle Laureen. Elec. draftsman Houston Lighting & Power Co., 1954-57; elec. draftsman, corrosion technician Transcontinental Gas Pipeline Co., Houston, 1957-59; elec. engr. Ken R. White Cons. Engrs., Denver, 1959-61; sales engr. Weco div. Food Machinery & Chem. Corp., various locations, 1961-64; ins. field underwriter N.Y. Life Ins. Co., Denver, 1964-66, asst. mgr., 1966-70, mgmt. asst., 1970-71, gen. mgr., 1971-77, mgr., 1979-85, field underwriter, 1985—; ind. gen. agt., Denver, 1978-79. Instl. rep., advancement chmn. Denver Area council Boy Scouts Am., Lakewood, Colo., 1968-72; precinct chmn. Republican Party, Jefferson County, Colo., 1976, 78; founder, mem. (life) Sister City Program, Lakewood, Colo.; chmn. adv. bd. ARC, Jefferson County, Colo., 1986-88. Recipient Centurion award, 1966; Northwestern Region Leader Manpower Devel. award N.Y. Life Ins. Co., 1968, Salesman of Yr. award Jefferson County Salesman with a Purpose Club, 1983, Top awards ARC, 1988-89. Mem. Nat. Assn. Life Underwriters, Gen. Agents and Mgrs. Assn. (recipient Conf. Nat. Mgmt. award, 1975), Colo. Life Underwriters Assn. (reg. v.p. Denver Metro area 1989-90), Mile High Assn. Life Underwriters (pres. 1986-87, nat. com. 1988, 91), Lakewood C. of C. (pres. people-to-people, Trailblazer of Yr. award 1982, 83, Trail Boss of Yr. 1983). Presbyterian (elder). Clubs: Lions, Edelweiss, Internat. Order Rocky Mountain Goats, N.Y. Life Star (leading asst. mgr. Continental region 1980), Masons, Rotary (Paul Harris award, 1995, Golden Rotary), Shriners. Home: 925 Deerhurst Cir Fort Collins CO 80525 Office: Woodman Accident and Life Ins Co Ste 200 300 E Horsetooth Fort Collins CO 80525

SCHENK, SUSAN KIRKPATRICK, geriatric psychiatry nurse, educator, consultant; b. New Richmond, Ind., Nov. 29, 1938; d. William Marcius and Frances (Kirkpatrick) Gaither; m. Richard Dee Brown, Aug. 13, 1960 (div. Feb. 1972); children: Christopher Lee, David Michael, Lisa Catherine; m. John Francis Schenk, July 24, 1975 (widowed Apr. 1995). BSN, Ind. U., 1962; postgrad., U. Del., 1973-75. RN, PHN, BCLS; cert. community coll. tchr., Calif. Staff nurse, then asst. dir. nursing Bloomington (Ind.) Hosp., 1962-66; charge nurse Newark (Del.) Manor, 1967-69; charge nurse GU Union Hosp., Terre Haute, Ind., 1971-72; clin. instr. nursing Ind. State U., Terre Haute, 1972-73; clin. instr. psychiatric nursing U. Del., Newark, 1974-75; psychiatric nursing care coord. VA Med. Ctr., Perry Point, Md., 1975-78; nurse educator Grossmont Hosp., La Mesa, Calif., 1978-90, cmty. rels. coord., 1990-91; dir. psychiat. svcs. Scripps Hosp. East County, El Cajon, Calif., 1991—; tech. advisor San Diego County Bd. Supervisors, 1987; tech. cons. Remedy Home and Health Care, San Diego, 1988; expert panelist Srs. Speak Out, KPBS-TV, San Diego, 1988; guest lectr. San Diego State U., 1987. Editor: Teaching Basic Caregiver Skills, 1988; author, performer tng. videotape Basic Caregiver Skills, 1988. Mem. patient svcs. com. Nat. Multiple Sclerosis Soc., San Diego, 1986-89; bd. dirs. Assn. for Quality and Participation, 1989. Adminstrn. on Aging/DHHS grantee, 1988. Mem. Am. Psychiat. Nurses Assn., Ind. U. Alumni Assn. (life), Mensa, Sigma Theta Tau. Home: 9435 Carlton Oaks Dr Apt D Santee CA 92071-2582 Office: Scripps Hosp East County 1688 E Main St El Cajon CA 92021-5204

SCHENKKAN, ROBERT FREDERIC, writer, actor; b. Chapel Hill, N.C., Mar. 19, 1953; s. Robert Frederic Sr. and Jean (McKenzie) S.; m. Mary Anne Dorward, Dec. 1, 1984; children: Sarah Victoria, Joshua McHenry. BA in Theatre Arts, U. Tex., 1975; MFA in Acting, Cornell U., 1977. Author: (plays) Final Passages, 1981, The Survivalist, 1982 (best of the fringe award Edinburgh Festival 1984), Tachinoki, 1987, Tall Tales, 1988 (Playwrights Forum award 1988, Best One Act Plays 1993), Heaven on Earth, 1989 (Julie Harris Playwright award Beverly Hills Theatre Guild 1989), The Kentucky Cycle, 1991 (Pulitzer prize for drama 1992, L.A. Drama Critics Circle Best Play award 1992, Penn Ctr. West award 1993, Best Play Tony award nominee 1993, Best Play Drama Desk award nominee 1993), Conversations with the Spanish Lady and Other One-Act Plays, 1993, (films) The Quiet American, 1997, Crazy Horse, 1996, The Long Ride Home, 1995. Grantee Vogelstein Found., 1982, Arthur Found., 1988, Fund for New Am. Plays grantee 1990, Calif. Arts Coun. grantee, 1991. Mem. Writers Guild, Dramatists Guild, Actors Equity, SAG, Ensemble Studio Theatre.

SCHERER, BONNIE LOU, writer; b. Aberdeen, S.D., Mar. 22, 1941; d. Lew Henry and Lillian Martha Erichsen; m. James J. Musso Jr., Jan. 9, 1964 (div. July 1969); 1 child, James J. Musso III; m. Jered H. Scherer, Nov. 2, 1970; 1 child, Lew H. Diploma in nursing, Mounds Midway, St. Paul, 1962. RN. RN Mounds Hosp., St. Paul, 1962-63; RN dept. pediat. Lakeland (Fla.) Gen. Hosp., 1963-69; RN dept. surgery Deaconess Hosp., Billings, Mont., 1969-70. Author: Benjy's New Home, 1990, Rescue of Rusty Rabbit, 1992, Cooking Cousins, 1994; co-author: Women at the Well: Meditations on Healing and Wholeness, 1997. Bd. dirs. Spl. K Ranch, Columbus, Mont., 1993-96; fellowship chair 1st Bapt. Ch.Billings, 1963—. Republican. Home: 1021 Alderson Billings MT 59102 Office: Bonnie Scherer Publs 1021 Alderson Billings MT 59102

SCHERER, PHIL, airport terminal executive; b. 1941. Dir. acctg. and adminstrn. All Trans Express, San Francisco, 1965-73; dir. acctg. Pacific Intermountain Express Co., Walnut Creek, Calif., 1973-82; CFO, COO Three Way Corp., Sunnyvale, Calif., 1982-90; with MCN Enterprises Inc., 1990—. Office: M C N Enterprises Inc 270 Lawrence Ave South San Francisco CA 94080-6817

SCHERICH, ERWIN THOMAS, civil engineer, consultant; b. Inland, Nebr., Dec. 6, 1918; s. Harry Erwin and Ella (Peterson) S.; student Hastings Coll., 1937-39, N.C. State Coll., 1943-44; B.S., U. Nebr., 1946-48; M.S., U. Colo., 1948-51; m. Jessie Mae Funk, Jan. 1, 1947; children—Janna Rae Scherich Thornton, Jerilyn Mae Scherich Dobson, Mark Thomas. Civil and design engr. U.S. Bur. Reclamation, Denver, 1948-84, chief spillways and outlets sect., 1974-75, chief dams br., div. design, 1975-78, chief tech. rev. staff, 1978-79, chief div. tech. rev. Office of Asst. Commr. Engring. and Rsch. Ctr., 1980-84; cons. civil engr., 1984—. Mem. U.S. Com. Internat. Commn. on Large Dams. Served with AUS, 1941-45. Registered profl. engr., Colo. Fellow ASCE; mem. NSPE (nat. dir. 1981-87, v.p. southwestern region 1991-93), Profl. Engrs. Colo. (pres. 1977-78), Jefferson County West C. of C. Republican. Methodist. Home and Office: 3915 Balsam St Wheat Ridge CO 80033

SCHEUER, PAUL JOSEF, chemistry educator; b. Heilbronn, Germany, May 25, 1915; came to U.S., 1938; s. Albert and Emma (Neu) S.; m. Alice Elizabeth Dash, Sept. 5, 1950; children: Elizabeth E., Deborah A., David A., Jonathan L.L. BS with high honors, Northeastern U., Boston, 1943; MA, Harvard U., 1947, PhD, 1950. Asst. prof. chemistry U. Hawaii, Honolulu, 1950-55, assoc. prof. chemistry, 1956-61, prof. chemistry, 1961-85, prof. chemistry emeritus, 1985—; vis. prof. Orsted Inst., U. Copenhagen, 1977, 89; Toyo Suisan vis. prof. U. Tokyo, 1992. Author: Chemistry of Marine Natural Products, 1973, editor 12 series, 1978-93; contbr. more than 265 articles to profl. jours. Spl. agt. U.S. Army, 1944-46, ETO. Recipient Rsch. Achievement award Am. Soc. Pharmacognosy, 1994, Regents award for rsch. excellence U. Hawaii, 1972; named P.J. Scheuer award Marine Chemists, 1992; NATO fellow, 1975. Fellow AAAS, Royal Soc. Chemistry; mem. Am. Chem. Soc. (sect. chair 1956, 87, Hawaii sect. award 1996, Ernest Guenther award 1994), Northeastern U. Alumni Assn. (Disting. Alumni award 1984). Office: U Hawaii Chemistry Dept 2545 The Mall Honolulu HI 96822-2275

SCHEURING, RICHARD ANTHONY, physician; b. Chgo., Aug. 30, 1964; s. Robert Norman and Judith Marie (Puttin) S.; m. Michelle C. Scheuring, Sept. 24, 1994; children: Joshua, Caitlin Marie, Emily. BA, Ea. Ill. U., 1987; DO, Chgo. Coll. Osteo. Medicine, 1993. Intern in family medicine Presbyn./St. Luke's Med. Ctr., Denver, 1993-94, resident in family medicine, 1994-96; pvt. practice, Galena, Ill., 1996—. Amb. Promise Keepers, Aurora, Colo., 1994—. Rsch. scholar NIH, 1993. Mem. AMA, Am. Acad. Family Physicians, Am. Osteo. Assn., Am. Coll. Sports Medicine, Aerospace Med. Assn., Ill. Acad. Family Physicians, Aircraft Owners and Pilost Assn., Colo. Med. Soc., Sigma Sigma Phi. Republican. Baptist. Home: 36 Shorewood Dr Galena IL 61036 Office: 219 Summit St Galena IL 61036

SCHIELE, PAUL ELLSWORTH, JR., educational business owner, writer; b. Phila., Nov. 20, 1924; s. Paul Ellsworth Sr. and Maud (Barclay) S.; m. Sarah Irene Knauss, Aug. 20, 1946; children: Patricia Schiele Tiemann, Sandra Schiele Kicklighter, Deborah Schiele Hartigan. AT, Temple U., 1949; BA, LaVerne U., 1955; MA, Claremont Associated Colls., 1961; PhD, U.S. Internat. U., San Diego, 1970. Cert. sec. tchr., Calif. 1961. Tchr. sci. and math. Lincoln High Sch., Phila., 1956-57, Ontario (Calif.) Sch. Dist., 1957-65; math. and sci. cons. Hacienda La Puente U. Sch. Dist., Calif., 1965-75; asst. prof. Calif. State U., Fullerton, 1975-83; pres., owner Creative Learning Environments and Resources, Glendora, Calif., 1983—, cons. sci. curriculum, 1985—; dir. title III project ESEA, 1974-75, cons. for project, 1975-77; cons. in field. Author: Primary Science, 1972, 2d edit., 1976, (novel) Under Cover of Night, 1995, Chasing the Wild Geese, 1996; editor: A Living World, 1974, 2d edit., 1986; writer 9 sound filmstrips, model units for sci. and math. activity books, 10 sci. activities for L.A. Outdoor Edn. Program, 1980; editor 21 sci. and math. activity books, 1975-76; writer, co-dir. (TV) Marine Biology Series, 1970-71; contbr. munerous articles to profl. mags., 1960-85; writer and designer of 2 sci. ednl. games; designer in field. Apptd. adv. com. Sci. and Humanities Symposium Calif. Mus. Sci. and Industry, 1974; mem. State Sci. Permit Com., Tide Pools of Calif. Coast, 1974-75; active Playhouse 90, Pasadena (Calif.) Playhouse; mem. Friends of Libr., Friends Libr. Found. Mem. Internat. Platform Assn., ABI Rsch. Assn. (bd. govs.), Calif. Elem. Edn. Assn. (hon.), Nat. PTA (hon.), Calif. Inter-Sci. Coun. (pres., chmn. 1971, 72), Elem Sch. Scis. Assn. (past pres., bd. dirs.), Phi Delta Kappa (chartered). Republican. Lutheran. Home: 231 Catherine Park Dr Glendora CA 91741-3018

SCHIFF, GUNTHER HANS, lawyer; b. Cologne, Germany, Aug. 19, 1927; came to U.S., 1936; s. Hans and Alice (Goldstein) S.; m. Katharine MacMillan, Jan. 27, 1950 (div. 1957); children: Eric Alan, Mary Alice; m. JoAnn R. Schiff; children: Jage, Hans Judson. B.S.F.S., Georgetown U., 1949, J.D., 1952. Bar: D.C. 1952, Calif. 1953. Assoc., ptnr., of counsel various firms, Beverly Hills, Calif., 1954-94; pvt. practice Beverly Hills, Calif., 1994—; sec. Los Angeles Copyright Soc., Beverly Hills, 1975-76. Contbr. articles to profl. jours. Pres. Beverly Hills Civil Svc. Commn., 1984-85, 88-89; pres. Free Arts for Abused Children, 1993-94, dir.; chmn. Rent Control Rev. Bd., Beverly Hills, 1980-84; trustee Young Musicians Found. With USNR, 1945-46. Mem. Beverly Hills Bar Assn. (chmn. Resolutions Com. 1977-78), Los Angeles County Bar Assn., ABA, U.S. Copyright Soc., Los Angeles Copyright Soc. Clubs: Lake Arrowhead Country, Calif. Yacht. Home: 612 N Foothill Rd Beverly Hills CA 90210-3404 Office: Law Office Gunther H Schiff 9430 W Olympic Blvd Beverly Hills CA 90212-4552

SCHIFF, LAURIE, lawyer; b. Newark, Apr. 24, 1960; d. Norman Nathan and Claire Jane (Schott) S.; m. Ralph Conrad Shelton II, 1992. BS in Law, We. State U., Fullerton, Calif., 1987, JD, 1988. Bar: Calif. 1989. Ptnr. Schiff Mgmt., Newport Beach, Calif., 1983-89; pvt. practice Schiff & Assocs., Irvine, Calif., 1989-91; ptnr. Schiff & Shelton, 1991—; probation monitor State Bar Ct. Calif., 1991—. Producer: (record album) Boys Just Want to Have Sex, 1984. Bd. dirs. Jewish Family Svcs. of Orange County, 1994—. Mem. Orange County Bar Assn. (arbitrator 1995—), Am. Mensa, Am. Polocrosse Assn., Saddlebrook Polocrosse (treas. 1991), Am. Quarterhorse Assn., Internat. Cat Assn. (chair legis. com. 1995—), Tonks West (v.p. 1994-96, pres. 1996—), Tonkinese Breed Assn., Online Feline Fanciers (v.p. 1995-97, bd. dirs. 1997—), Intern. Politically Incorrect Cat Club (v.p. 1996—). Democrat. Jewish. Office: Schiff & Shelton 3 Hutton Centre Dr Ste 620 Santa Ana CA 92707-8704

SCHIFF, STEVEN HARVEY, congressman, lawyer; b. Chicago, Ill., Mar. 18, 1947; s. Alan Jerome and Helen M. (Ripper) S.; m. Marcia Lewis, Nov. 8, 1968; children: Jaimi, Daniel. BA, U. Ill., Chgo., 1968; JD, U. N.Mex., 1972. Bar: N.Mex. 1972, U.S. Dist. Ct. N.Mex. 1972, U.S. Ct. Appeals (10th cir.) 1980. Asst. dist. atty. Dist. Atty.'s Office, Albuquerque, 1972-77, sole practice, 1977-79; asst. city atty. City of Albuquerque, 1979-81; dist. atty. State of N.Mex., Albuquerque, 1981-89; mem. 101st-104th Congresses from 1st N.Mex. dist., Washington, D.C., 1989—; mem. govt. reform & oversight com. U.S. House of Reps., mem. judiciary com. and standards of ofcl. conduct com., chmn. sci. subcom. on basic rsch.; lectr. U. N.Mex., Albuquerque, 1981—. Chmn. Bernalillo County Rep. Party Conv., Albuquerque, 1984, 87, staff judge adv. N.Mex. Air N.G. Col. JAGC, USAFR. Recipient Law Enforcement Commendation medal SR, 1984. Mem. ABA, Albuquerque Bar Assn., N.Mex. Bar Assn. Republican. Jewish. Club: Civitan. Lodge: B'nai Brith (pres. 1976-78). Home: 804 Summit Ave NE Albuquerque NM 87106-2045 Office: House of Reps 2404 Rayburn Washington DC 20515-3101 also: 625 Silver Ave SW Ste 140 Albuquerque NM 87102

SCHIFF BERNARD, ELLIE, political and nonprofit fundraiser; b. Saginaw, Mich.; d. William Clifford and Margaret (Adolfino) Bragg; children: David S., Andrew L.; m. George W. Bernard, Aug. 24, 1986. BA, Calif. State U. Exec. dir. Jimmy Stewart Marathon St. John's Hosp., Santa Monica, Calif., 1985-86; fundraiser Barbara Boxer (candidate U.S. Senate), L.A., 1991-92; west coast coord. The Woman's Legal Defense Fund, Washington, 1992-93; fin. dir. so. Calif. Delaine Eastin Com., L.A., 1994; assoc. dir. Women Vote Project, L.A., 1994; dir. corp. and found. giving City of Hope, L.A., La., 1994—. Mem. Nat. Soc. Fund Raising Execs. Democrat.

SCHIFFNER, CHARLES ROBERT, architect; b. Reno, Sept. 2, 1948; Robert Charles and Evelyn (Keck) S.; m. Iovanna Lloyd Wright, Nov. 1971 (div. Sept. 1981); m. Adrienne Anita McAndrews, Jan. 22, 1983. Student, Sacramento Jr. Coll., 1967-68, Frank Lloyd Wright Sch. Architecture, 1968-77. Registered architect, Ariz., Nev., Wis. Architect Taliesin Associated Architects, Scottsdale, Ariz., 1977-83; pvt. practice architecture Phoenix, 1983—; lectr. The Frank Lloyd Wright Sch. of Architecture, 1994, 95. Named one of 25 Most Promising Young Americans Under 35, U.S. mag., 1979; recipient AIA Honor award Western Mountain Region, 1993, Western Home awards Sunset Mag., 1989, 91, AIA Ariz. Merit award, 1993 and numerous others. Home: 5202 E Osborn Rd Phoenix AZ 85018-6137 Office: Camelhead Office Ctr 2600 N 44th St Ste 208 Phoenix AZ 85008-1565

SCHIFFNER, JOAN LESSING, consultant; b. Hollywood, Calif., Nov. 26, 1944; d. Lessing Robert and Ruth Isabel (Chamberlain) Sattler; children: Robert Garrett, Gregory Garrett, Laura Garrett. BA, San Jose State U., 1970; postgrad., U. Calif. Cert. in non-profit orgn.mgmt., mktg. comm., human resources adminstr. and tng. Cons. to health and human svc. govtl. and non-profit orgns. Civilian Pers. Office, Fort Ord, Calif., 1993-94; ptnr. Millson, Schiffner and Assocs.; bd. dirs. Growth and Opportunity, Inc, Am. Red Cross, 1990-94; cons. Saving Our Libr.'s Excellence Com. 1992-93. Pub. info. officer San Benito County (Calif.) United Way, bd. dirs., 1988-90; founding mem. San Benito County Vol. Ctr. Task Force, San Benito County Cable Access Commn., 1987-90; co-founder San Benito County Action Team; vice chair San Benito County Voluntary Orgns. Active in Disasters, 1990-91; appointed to cen. com. ARC No. Calif. Earthquake Relief and Preparedness Project, 1991; pres. Network of San Benito, 1988-90; mem. San Benito County Econ. Group, Mex. Am. Com. on Edn., 1970—, Hollister Sister Cities Assn., 1989—; sec. bd. dirs., overall econ. devel. plan com. Econ. Devel. Corp.; exec. dir. San Benito County Interfaith, 1990-91; chmn. adv. com. San Benito Health Found., 1991—; pub. rels. chair San Benito County AIDS Project, 1992-94; active numerous non-profit and civic orgns.; bd. dirs ARC. Mem. AAUW, San Benito County C. of C., Phi Alpha Theta, Psi Chi, Alpha Kappa Delta. Democrat. Roman Catholic. Home: 845 Helen Dr Hollister CA 95023-6613

SCHILBRACK, KAREN GAIL, system analyst; b. Tomahawk, Wis., Sept. 28; d. Edward Richard and Irene Angeline (Ligman) S. Student U. Calif.-Santa Barbara, 1967-69; BA in Anthropology, U. Calif.-Davis, 1971; postgrad. in Edn. and Archeology, Calif. State Poly. U., San Luis Obispo, 1971-72. Cert. tchr., computer specialist, data processing; lic. cosmetologist. Computer specialist Facilities Systems Office, Port Hueneme, Calif., 1975-78, sr. computer specialist, 1978-80, project mgr. U.S. Naval Constrn. Bn. Ctr., 1980-89, imaging systems computer specialist Comptr. Office, 1989-92; fiscal quality specialist Dept. Def. Finance and Acctg. Svc., DAO, Port Hueneme, 1992-95; fund adminstr. Naval Constrn. Tng. Ctr., Port Hueneme, 1995—; tng. cons. FACSO, 1981, 82; curriculum cons. Ventura Community Coll., Calif., 1981-89; instr. U.S. Navy, Port Hueneme, 1983, 91, Civil Service Commn., Port Hueneme, 1978-80. Author: AMALGAMAN Run Procedures, 1976; Cobol Programming Efficiencies, 1978, Imaging System UserManual, 1991; co-author, editor: Training Manual for Direct Data Entry System, 1983. Mem. Vols. for Camarillo State Hosp., Camarillo, 1978-88, coord. Ventura County, 1981; chmn. scholarship fund drive Ventura, Santa Barbara, Los Angeles, Counties, 1980. Named Young Career Woman of Yr., Calif. Bus. and Profl. Women, 1979. Mem. Young Ladies Inst. (pres. Santa Paula, dist. dep. Ventura/Santa Barbara Counties), Am. Biog. Inst. Research Assn. (lifetime dep. gov.). Lodge: Toastmistress. Home: 6993 Wheeler Canyon Rd Santa Paula CA 93060-9759 Office: Compt Office Code 243-A USNCBC Port Hueneme CA 93042

SCHILD, RAYMOND DOUGLAS, lawyer; b. Chgo., Dec. 20, 1952; s. Stanley Martin and Cassoundra Lee (McArdle) S.; m. Ellen Arthea Carstensen, Oct. 24, 1987; children: Brian Christopher, Melissa Nicole. Student, U.S. Mil. Acad., 1970; BA summa cum laude, De Paul U., 1974, JD magna cum laude, 1982; M in Life Scis., Order of Essenes, 1996. Bar: Ill. 1982, U.S. Dist. Ct. (no. dist.) Ill. 1982, U.S. Ct. Appeals (7th cir.) 1982, Idaho 1989, U.S. Dist. Ct. Idaho 1989, U.S. Ct. Appeals (9th cir.) 1989, U.S. Supreme Ct. 1990. Assoc. Clausen, Miller, Gorman, Caffrey & Witous, Chgo., 1982-84; law clk. to chief judge law divsn. Cir. Ct. Cook County, Chgo., 1984-85; assoc. John G. Phillips & Assocs., Chgo., 1985-87, Martin, Chapman, Park & Burkett, Boise, Idaho, 1988-89; pvt. practice Boise, 1989-90; pres. Martin, Chapman, Schild & Lassaw, Chartered, Boise, 1990-96; bd. dirs. Image Concepts Internat., Inc., Boise; lectr. on legal edn. ICLE and NBI, 1993—. Co-host legal radio talk show KFXD, 1994; legal columnist Idaho Bus. Rev., 1988-96. Mem. adv. bd. Alliance for the Mentally Ill, Boise, 1991—, Parents and Youth Against Drug Abuse, Boise, 1991-92; fair housing adminstr. Sauk Village (Ill.) Govt., 1987-88; instr. Ada County Youth Ct., Boise, 1992—. Schmitt fellow DePaul U., 1974; recipient award of merit Chgo. Law Coalition, 1987. Mem. ATLA, Idaho Trial Lawyers' Assn., Ill. State Bar Assn., Idaho State Bar Assn., Boise Estate Planning Counsel, Shriners (temple atty. 1994—), Masons (jr. steward 1992).

SCHILE, WAYNE, newspaper publishing executive. Pub. Billings (Mont.) Gazette, 1984—. Office: 401 N Broadway Billings MT 59107

SCHILLER, NELSON BENJAMIN, physician, cardiologist; b. Buffalo, Apr. 20, 1940; s. Arthur and Belle (Shroder) S.; m. Ellen Jane Wile, Aug. 29, 1964; children: Laura, Emily. BS, Union Coll., Schenectady, N.Y., 1962; MD, SUNY, Buffalo, 1966. Diplomate Am. Bd. Internal Medicine, sub-bd. Cardiology. Intern Ochsner Med. Found., 1966-67; resident in internal medicine U. Calif., San Diego, 1969-71; USPHS fellow in cardiology U. Calif., San Francisco, 1971-73, prof. medicine and radiology, 1988-92, prof. medicine, radiology and anesthesiology, 1992—, dir. echocardiography lab., 1973—. Assoc. editor Jour. Am. Coll. Cardiology, 1992—; author more than 200 sci. papers and book chpts. Lt. comdr. USPHS, 1967-69. NIH grantee. Fellow Am. Coll. Cardiology. Office: U Calif Med Ctr Box 0214 San Francisco CA 94143-0214

SCHILLING, DEAN WILLIAM, manufacturing executive; b. Waverly, Iowa, Apr. 25, 1944; s. Alvin Louis and Etta Christine (Poppe) S.; m. Betty Ann (Homeister), Aug. 5, 1962; children: Angela Marie, Christine Ann. AS, Iowa State U., 1964, BS, 1969. Engr. Systems Genetics, Clarksville, Iowa, 1970-81; sr. tech. support Hewlett Packard, Sunnyvale, Calif., 1983-85; pres. Cryo Genetic Technology, Soquel, Calif., 1985—. Inventor biol. devices and methods to remedy human infertility; holder 3 patents. Mem. Am. Fertility Soc., Soc. Cryobiology, Iowa State Alumni Assn., Douglas Electric Coop. (bd. dirs. 1995), Order of Knoll (founders club 1988). Lutheran.

SCHILLING, FREDERICK AUGUSTUS, JR., geologist, consultant; b. Phila., Apr. 12, 1931; s. Frederick Augustus and Emma Hope (Christoffer) S.; m. Ardis Ione Dovre, June 12, 1957 (div. 1987); children: Frederick Christopher, Jennifer Dovre. BS in Geology, Wash. State U., 1953; PhD in Geology, Stanford U., 1962. Computer geophysicist United Geophys. Corp., Pasadena, Calif., 1955-56; geologist various orgns., 1956-61, U.S. Geol. Survey, 1961-64; underground engr. Climax (Colo.) Molybdenum Co., 1966-68; geologist Keradamex Inc., Anaconda Co., M.P. Grace, Ranchers Exploration & Devel. Corp., Albuquerque and Grants, N.Mex., 1968-84, Hecla Mining Co., Coeur d'Alene, Idaho, 1984-86, various engring. and environ. firms, Calif., 1986-91; prin. F. Schilling Cons., Canyon Lake, Calif., 1991—. Author: Bibliography of Uranium, 1976. Del. citizen amb. program People to People Internat., USSR, 1990-91. With U.S. Army, 1953-55. Fellow Explorers Club; mem. Geol. Soc. Am., Am. Assn. Petroleum Geologists, Soc. Mining Engrs., Internat. Platform Assn., Adventurers' Club Inc. L.A., Masons, Kiwanis, Sigma Xi, Sigma Gamma Epsilon. Republican. Presbyterian. Office: F Schilling Cons 30037 Steel Head Dr Canyon Lake CA 92587-7460

SCHILLING, JANET NAOMI, nutritionist, consultant; b. North Platte, Neb., Mar. 1, 1939; d. Jens Harold and Naomi Frances (Meyer) Hansen; children: Allan Edward III, Karl Jens. BS, U. Neb., 1961; MS, Ohio State U., 1965; MPH, U. Calif., Berkeley, 1991. Registered dietitian. Tchr. home econs. Peace Corps., Dimbokro, Ivory Coast, 1962-64; cons. nutrition Wis. Divsn. Health, La Crosse, 1966-67, 69; dietary cons. Cozad (Neb.) Community Hosp., 1968; instr. Viterbo Coll., La Crosse, 1974-81; lectr. U. Wis., La Crosse, 1982-84; teaching asst. ESL Sch. Dist. La Crosse, 1984-87; nutrition educator Women, Infant, and Children Program, 1988-89; nutrition cons. Vis. Nurses, LaCrosse, 1987-89; dietitian Merrithew Meml. Hosp., Martinez, Calif., 1992; pub. health nutrition cons. Women Infant & Childrens Program Policy and Compliance Unit, Sacramento, 1995; nutrition cons. Wis. Winnebago Nation, 1991; pediatric dietitian in Romanian Orphanges thru World Vision, 1993; nutritionist Contra Costa Head Start & Child Devel., 1994. Author: Life in the Nutrition Community, 1980, Life in the Nutrition Cycle II, 1980; co-author: Nutrition Activities, 1984, Recipe Book of Nutritious Snacks, 1985. Mem. LaCrosse Sch. Dist. Nutrition Task Force, 1976-88; Sunday sch. tchr., supr. Our Savior's Luth. Ch., 1975-86, chmn. Mobile Meals, 1982-86; v.p. membership booster club Ctrl. H.S. LaCrosse, 1985-87, pres., 1987-88; bd. dirs. YMCA, LaCrosse, 1982-88; mem. No. Calif. Returned Peace Corps vols., 1990—; mem. Glide Ch. Housing Task Force, 1995—; trustee East Bay Habitat for Humanity, 1995—. Mem. AAUW (pres. 1978-80, Named Grant scholar 1981), APHA, LaCrosse Area Dietetic Assn. (1st pres. 1968-69, Outstanding Dietitian Yr. 1985), Wis. Dietetic Assn. (chmn. educators 1983-85), No. Wis. Dietetic Assn. (pres. 1982), Am. Dietetic Assn. (educators practice group 1978-90), LaCrosse Jaycees (Carol award 1973), Calif. Dietetic Assn. (pediat. practice group chmn. 1997-98). Democrat. Home: 1604 Roger Ct El Cerrito CA 94530-2028

SCHILLING, JOLYON DAVID, vascular and general surgeon; b. Oklahoma City, Oct. 10, 1958; s. John Albert and Lucille Olive (West) S.; m. Diane Helina Schilling, Apr. 2, 1994. BS, U. Wash., 1981, MD, 1986. Resident gen. surgery U. Tex. S.W. Med. Sch., Dallas, 1986-91; fellow vascular surgery U. Ariz. Sch. Medicine, Tucson, 1991-93; pvt. practice Southwestern Surgery Assocs., Tucson, 1993—; clin. asst. prof. dept. surgery U. Ariz., Tucson, 1994—; flight surgeon 162d F.G. Ariz. Air Nat. Guard, Tucson, 1993—. Fellow ACS, S.W. Surg. Assn., Rocky Mountain Vascular Surgery Soc., Soc. Clin. Vascular Surgery. Office: Southwestern Surg Assocs 5300 E Erickson Dr Ste 108 Tucson AZ 85712-2809

SCHILLING, VIVIAN, novelist, screenwriter and actress; b. Wichita, Kans.; d. Donald A. and Lou (Nichols) Schilling; m. Eric Parkinson. Student in theatre arts, Wichita State U., 1982. Actress with leading roles in Germans, Soultaker, The Legend of Wolf Mountain, In A Moment of Passion, Future Shock, Savage Land, others. Screenwriter, co-prodr. films: Terror-Eyes, 1990, Soultaker, 1991, Future Shock, 1993; author: Sacred Prey, 1994 (Golden Scroll award for outstanding achievement in lit. 1994). Recipient Saturn award Acad. Sci. Fiction, 1992. Mem. Women in Film (hon.), Screen Actors Guild, Authors Guild. Office: Truman Press Inc 15445 Ventura Blvd Ste 905 Sherman Oaks CA 91403-3005

SCHILTZ, KAREN LORAINE, neuopsychologist, educator, consultant; b. Marshfield, Wis., May 12, 1957; d. Fred and Loraine (Kath) S.; m. Scott Monroe Mellor, Oct. 7, 1995. BA in Psychology and Sociology, St. Olaf Coll., Northfield, Minn., 1979; MA in Psychology, Calif. Sch. Profl. Psychology, 1982, PhD in Psychology, 1984. Lic. psychologist, Calif.; registered Nat. Register Health Svc. Providers in Psychology. Psychol. asst. St. John's Hosp. Child Study Ctr., Santa Monica, Calif., 1981-82, intern, 1983-84; cons. Xavier Mental Health Clinic, L.A., 1984-87; pvt. practice, L.A., 1984-87, Thousand Oaks, Calif., 1988—; asst. clin. prof. dept. psychiatry and biobehavioral scis. UCLA Sch. Medicine, 1989—, clin. supr. psychophysiol.

program dept. neurology Brain Rsch. Inst., 1990-91, clin. supr. neuropsychology dept. Neuropsychiat. Inst., 1993—, clin. neuropsychologist, 1986-91; staff privileges UCLA Sch. Medicine, L.A., St. John's Pleasant Valley Hosp., St. John's Regional Med. Ctr.; mem. courtesy staff Los Robles Regional Med. Ctr.; presenter in field. Contbr. articles to profl. jours. Vol. Head Start, Ventura County, Califl; mem. Ventura County Panel Experts for Diagnosis and Treatment Head Injured Children. Fellow Stanford U., 1978; postdoctoral fellow UCLA, 1985-87. Mem. APA, Internat. Neuropsychol. Soc., Nat. Acad. Neuropsychologists, Nat. Head Injury Found. (mild head injury task force 1990), Undersea and Hyperbaric Med. Soc., Am. Coll. Forensic Examiners, Calif. Neuropsychol. Soc., Calif. Psychol. Assn., Ventura County Psychol. Assn., Psi Chi. Office: 516 Pennsfield Pl Ste 106 Thousand Oaks CA 91360-5576

SCHIMMEL, WALTER P., aerospace engineer, educator; b. Chgo.; s. Walter P. Sr. and Ruth Ann-Margaret (Herzan) S.; m. Jacqueline Pica, Dec. 29, 1962; children: Lisa N., Stephen P., Nadja A. BSME, Purdue U., 1965; MSME, U. Notre Dame, 1966, PhD, 1969. Mem. profl. staff Sandia Nat. Labs., Albuquerque, 1969-82; chief of svc. Hydro-Que. Rsch. Inst., Montreal, 1982-85; dept. chmn., prof. aerospace engring. Embry-Riddle U., Daytona Beach, Fla., 1985-93; tech. transfer mgr. Sandia Nat. Labs., Albuquerque, 1993—; pres. Performances Assocs., 1970—. Contbr. articles to profl. jours. Served with U.S. Army, 1954-62. Fellow ASME; mem. AIAA, Am. Bd. Engring./Tech. Accreditation, Sigma Xi, Tau Beta Pi, Pi Tau Sigma.

SCHIMMELBUSCH, WERNER HELMUT, psychiatrist; b. Vienna, Austria, Nov. 16, 1937; came to U.S., 1954; s. Hans Mowgli and Anneliese Martha (Koeppe) S.; m. Faye Karina Wrangel, Dec. 29, 1958 (div. Mar. 1967); m. Jeanette Ramona Dyal, Mar. 26, 1971; children: Andre Curt, Anne Ramona. *Wife Jeanette Ramona Schimmelbusch is an advanced registered nurse practitioner, board certified in psychiatric treatment of adults, adolescents and children, and a private consultant and psychotherapist. Son Andre Curt Schimmelbusch obtained his bachelor's degree in economics at the University of Washington, is currently a bank officer at Wells Fargo Bank in Seattle, and maintains his flight instructor rating for single engine airplanes. Daughter Anne Ramona Schimmelbusch is graduating from the honors program in psychology at USC, has been accepted into the PhD program of developmental psychology at Clairmont University. She has performed as an actress in commercial theatre in Seattle, including a leading role in Seattle Childrens Theatre.* MD, U. Wash., Seattle, 1962; psychiatrist, Yale U., 1968; adult psychoanalyst, Seattle Inst. Psychoanalysis, 1977, child psychoanalyst, 1992. Instr. Dept. Psychiatry and Behavioral Sci. U. Wash., Seattle, 1968-69; pvt. practice Seattle, 1969—; clin. prof. U. Wash., Seattle, 1984—; tng. and supervising psychoanalyst Seattle Inst. Psychoanalysis, 1990—. Capt. U.S. Army, 1963-65. Mem. AMA, Am. Psychiatric Assn., Am. Psychoanalytic Assn., Seattle Psychoanalytic Soc. (pres. 1979-80, 94-96). Office: 4033 E Madison Seattle WA 98112 *Werner Helmut Schimmelbusch is a member of the Center for Advancement of Psychoanalytic Studies in Princeton, New Jersey. He is involved with furthering the understanding of all aspects of the psychoanalytic treatment process for children and adults suffering from trauma anxiety and depressive problems. He has a particular interest in research that demonstrates how the psychoanalytic treatment experience alters physical brain structure in a corrective way.*

SCHIMMELFENNIG, LADONA BETH, special education educator; b. Tulsa, Apr. 29, 1948; d. James Wyatt and Ladona Babe (Robertson) Holder; m. Bryan Anapuni Schimmelfennig, July 4, 1988; 1 child, Malia M. BS in Spl. Edn., U. Tulsa, 1969; MA in Edn., Pepperdine U., Malibu, Calif., 1976. Tchr. asst. Sarasota (Fla.) Head Start, 1968; spl. edn. tchr. S.E.C.O., Honolulu, 1969-70, Monroe Jr. High Sch., Tulsa, 1970-73, Honolulu Community Action prog., Project Head Start, 1973-76; spl. edn. coord. Oahu Head Start, Honolulu, 1976-77; dir. spl. edn. Govt. of Am. Samoa, Pago Pago, 1977-79; ednl. specialist II for emotionally handicapped Dept. Edn., Oahu, Hawaii, 1984; dist. edn. specialist II for spl. edn. Windward Oahu Dept. Edn., Hawaii, 1979—; dir. 1st Am. Samoa Spl. Olympics, 1978, 79. Contbr. articles to profl. jours. Bd. dirs., pub. rels. chmn. Hawaii Spl. Olympics, 1980-84; bd. dirs. Spl. Parent Info. Network, Wai Nani Way Hoeke; sec.-treas. Pacific Basin Consortium, 1977-79; adv. panel on edn. handicapped children Southwestern Reg. Deaf-Blind Ctr., 1977-79, others in past. Mem. Coun. for Exceptional Children (chpt. pres. 1969), Nat. Assn. State Dirs. Spl. Edn., Nat. Info. for Spl. Edn. Mgmt., S.W. Deaf/Blind Assn. Democrat. Home: 739 W Hind Dr Honolulu HI 96821-1805 Office: Dept Edn 46-169 Kamehameha Hwy Kaneohe HI 96744-3651

SCHINE, WENDY WACHTELL, foundation administrator; b. White Plains, N.Y., May 5, 1961; d. Thomas and Esther Carole (Pickard) Wachtell; m. Jonathan Mark Schine, Sept. 2, 1990; children: Jameson Myer, Bradley Thomas. BA, Wellesley Coll., 1983; MA in Journalism, U. So. Calif., L.A., 1987. Legis. asst. U.S. House Reps., Washington, 1983-85; varied positions KCBS-TV, L.A., 1986-88; v.p. Joseph Drown Found., L.A., 1988—; bd. dirs. L.A. Urban Funders, So. Calif. Assn. Philanthropy; advisor Psychol. Trauma Ctr., L.A., 1988—, Ctr. for Talented Youth, Glendale, Calif., 1989—. Mem. oversight com. Pathways Project, Big Sisters, L.A. Office: Joseph Drown Found Ste 1930 1999 Avenue Of The Stars Los Angeles CA 90067-6051

SCHIPPER, MERLE, art historian and critic, exhibition curator; b. Toronto, Ont., Can.; came to U.S., 1943; d. Leon J. and Libby (Genesove) Solway; m. Bernard Schipper, May 22, 1943 (div. Jan. 1980); children: Lee, Amy Schipper Howe. BA, U. Toronto, 1943; MA, UCLA, 1970, PhD, 1974. Instr. extension UCLA, 1974-78, 83-84, lectr. summer session, 1977-79, 84; vis. artist grad. sch. Claremont (Calif.) U., 1979; lectr. U. So. Calif., L.A., 1985; corr. L.A. ARTNews, N.Y.C., 1985-87; columnist ARTScene, L.A., 1987—; project dir. Santa Monica (Calif.) Arts Found., 1987-89; art book reviewer L.A. Daily News, 1990-91; organizer Congress Internat. Assn. Art Critics, 1991; mem. pub. art panel Santa Monica Arts Commn., 1966—; mem. artist selection panel Met. Transp. Assn., Chinatown Sta., 1993. Panelist, mem. grants com. Art Orgn. Dept. Cultural Affairs, L.A., 1984-85; mem. selection com. of sculpture installation Calif. Med. Ctr., L.A., 1986; mem. Rev. Com. Hist. Resources Survey Project, L.A., 1978-85, So. Calif. Com. for Contemporary Art Documentation, L.A., 1985-89. Rsch. fellow Indo-U.S. Subcommn., 1988; travel grantee Ptnrs. of Ams., 1989. Mem. Coll. Art Assn., Internat. Assn. Art Critics. Home and Office: # 6 10650 Eastborn Ave Santa Monica CA 90405-1328

SCHIRRA, WALTER MARTY, JR., business consultant, former astronaut; b. Hackensack, N.J., Mar. 12, 1923; s. Walter Marty and Florence (Leach) S.; m. Josephine Cook Fraser, Feb. 23, 1946; children: Walter Marty III, Suzanne Karen. Student, Newark Coll. Engring., 1940-42; B.S., U.S. Naval Acad., 1945; D. Astronautics (hon.), Lafayette Coll., U. So. Calif., N.J. Inst. Tech. Commd. ensign U.S. Navy, 1945, advanced through grades to capt., 1965; designated naval aviator, 1948; service aboard battle cruiser Alaska, 1945-46; service with 7th Fleet, 1946; assigned Fighter Squadron 71, 1948-51; exchange pilot 154th USAF Fighter Bomber Squadron, 1951; engaged in devel. Sidewinder missile China Lake, Calif., 1952-54; project pilot F7U-3 Cutlass; also instr. pilot F7U-3 Cutlass and FJ3 Fury, 1954-56; ops. officer Fighter Squadron 124, U.S.S. Lexington, 1956-57; assigned Naval Air Safety Officer Sch., 1957, Naval Air Test Ctr., 1958-59; engaged in suitability devel. work F4H, 1958-59; joined Project Mercury, man-in-space, NASA, 1959; pilot spacecraft Sigma 7 in 6 orbital flight, Oct. 1962; in charge operations and tng. Astronaut Office, 1964-69; command pilot Gemini 6 which made rendezvous with target, Gemini 7, Dec. 1965; comdr. 11 day flight Apollo 7, 1968; ret., 1969; pres. Regency Investors, Inc., Denver, 1969-70; chmn., chief exec. officer ECCO Corp., Englewood, Colo., 1970-73; chmn. Sernco, Inc., 1973-74; with Johns-Manville Corp., Denver, 1974-77; v.p. devel. Goodwin Cos., Inc., Littleton, Colo., 1978-79; ind. cons., 1979-80; dir. Kimberly Clark, 1983-91. Decorated D.F.C.(3), Air medal (2), Navy D.S.M.; recipient Distinguished Service medal (2) NASA, Exceptional Service medal. Fellow Am. Astronautical Soc., Soc. Exptl. Test Pilots. Home and Office: PO Box 73 Rancho Santa Fe CA 92067-0073*

SCHLADOR, PAUL RAYMOND, JR., insurance agent; b. Riverside, Calif., Oct. 16, 1934; s. Paul Raymond Sr. Schlador and Lois Geraldine (Burrus) Kaeding; m. Evangeline Kathern, Aug. 19, 1955; children: Debora Lynn TeSam, Cheryl Jean Bastian, Bonnie Kay Tucker. Student, San Diego City Jr. Coll., 1954-55, Ins. Industry, San Diego, 1960-62, Am. Coll., San Diego, 1970-74. CLU. Agt. Bankers Life of Nebr., San Diego, 1959-63; agt./ mgr. Southwestern Life Ins. Co., San Diego, 1959—; ind. agt. State Farm Ins. Co., San Diego, 1978—. With USNG, 1952-60. Mem. San Diego Assn. Life Underwriters (pres. 1989-90, legis. v.p. 1988), Kiwanis Club El Cajon Valley. Republican. Methodist. Home: 1267 Oakdale Ave # C El Cajon CA 92021-6454 Office: State Farm Ins 7800 University Ave # 1A La Mesa CA 91941-4928 also: BPOE Lodge # 1812 El Cajon CA 92021

SCHLATTER, O. EDWARD, judge; m. Patricia Schlatter; 2 children. BA, So. Ill. U., 1964; JD, U. Denver, 1970. Dist. and chief judge 11th jud. dist. U.S. Dist. Ct. State of Colo., Denver, 1981-92, magistrate judge, 1992—. Mem. Colo. Bar Assn. (exec. coun. criminal law sect 1984-86, bd. govs. 1987-92, sr. v.p. 1991-92), 11th Jud. Dist. Bar Assn. (v.p. 1985-87, pres. 1987-89). Office: US Dist Ct State of Colo 1929 Stout St Rm C-162 Denver CO 80294

SCHLEGEL, JAMES M., educational administrator; b. Kansas City, Mo., Jan. 10, 1946; s. Jack Howard and V. Irene (Hall) S.; m. Janice Ann Taylor, Sept. 2, 1965; children: Shana R. Irish, Shan S. BS in Edn., Emporia State U., 1970, MS in Edn., 1972. Cert. tchr., counselor, adminstr., Alaska. Mktg. tchr./coord. Fremont County Sch. Dist. #1, Lander, Wyo., 1972-76, pupil svcs./vocat. edn. dir., 1976-79; vocat. leadership coord. Oreg. State U., Corvallis, 1979-82; vocat. edn. adminstr. Fairbanks North Sch. Dist., 1982-91; asst. v.p. U. Alaska Sys., Fairbanks, 1991-94; edn. program mgr. Ilisagvik Coll., Barrow, Alaska, 1994-95; vocat. edn. adminstr. Lower Kuskokwim Sch. Dist., Bethel, Alaska, 1995—; owner/mgr. (JS)2 Svcs., Fairbanks, 1982—; presenter to numerous confs.; evaluator Vocat. Edn. adminstrv. Assessment Team, Lebanon, S.D., Career and Vocat. Edn. Assessment Team, Reedsport, S.D., career guidance program Edn. divsn. Singer Corp., comprehensive coop. career edn. project Windsor (Colo.) Pub. Schs., Cheyenne Ctrl. H.S.; cons. in field. Contbr. articles to profl. jours. Mem. alaska Sch.-to-Work Implementation task Force, Gov.'s Human Resources Devel. Policy Adv. Com., Alaska Sch.-to-Work Rural Delivery Strategies Com., Alaska State Tech.-Prep Initative Planning Com., Alaska Vocat. Edn. Com. of Practitioners, Alaska Workforce Preparation Conf. Exec. Planning Com., Alaska Edn. Coord. Com., Alaska Vocat. Edn. Program Stds. Task Force, Alaska Sch. Found. Formula Fin. Adv. Com., Fairbanks Pvt. Industry Coun., North Star Ctr. Adv. Coun., others; bd. dirs. Alaska Crippled Children and Adults; mem. adminstrv. mgmt. team Fairbanks North Star Borough Sch. dist., numerous coms. U.S. Congl. fellow, 1975-76. Mem. Nat. Coun. of Local Adminstrs. for Vocat. Edn., Alaska State Vocat. Assn., Am. vocat. Assn., Phi Delta Kappa. Home: 180 Humboldt Way Fairbanks AK 99709-2958

SCHLEGEL, JOHN PETER, academic administrator; b. Dubuque, Iowa, July 31, 1943; s. Aaron Joseph and Irma Joan (Hingtgen) S. BA, St. Louis U., 1969, MA, 1970; BDiv, U. London, 1973; DPhil, Oxford U., 1977. Joined Soc. of Jesus, 1963, ordained priest Roman Cath. Ch., 1973. From asst. prof. to assoc. prof. Creighton U., Omaha, 1976-79, asst. acad. v.p., 1978-82; dean Coll. Arts and Scis. Rockhurst Coll., Kansas City, Mo., 1982-84, Marquette U., Milw., 1984-88; exec. and acad. v.p. John Carroll U., Cleve., 1988-91; pres. U. San Francisco, 1991—; cons. Orgn. for Econ. Devel. and Cooperation, Paris, 1975-76. Author: Bilingualism and Canadian Policy in Africa, 1979; editor: Towards a Redefinition of Development, 1976; contbr. articles to profl. jours. Mem. Milwaukee County Arts Coun., 1986-88, Mo. Coun. on Humanities, Kansas City, 1984; trustee St. Louis U., 1985-91, Loyola U. Chgo., 1988-95, Loyola U. New Orleans, 1995—, St. Ignatius H.S., Cleve., 1990-91, Loyola Coll. in Md., 1992—; bd. dirs. Coro Found., Commonwealth Club Calif. Oxford U. grantee, 1974-76; Govt. of Can. grantee, 1977-78. Mem. Am. Coun. on Edn., Can. Studies in U.S., Olympic Club, Univ. Club, Bohemian Club. Office: U San Francisco Office of Pres 2130 Fulton St San Francisco CA 94117-1080

SCHLEH, EDWARD CARL, business analyst; b. St. Paul, Nov. 2, 1915; s. Edward G. and Augusta (Seltz) S.; m. Myra Adelle Oberschulte, June 7, 1941; children: Jeanne, John, Richard, Elizabeth, Robert. BBA, U. Minn., 1937. Placement officer U. Minn. Employment Office, Mpls., 1937-39, Ells Employment Svc., Mpls., 1939-40; mgr. personnel rsch. 3-M Co., St. Paul, 1940-48; pres. Schleh Assocs., Inc., Mpls. and Palo Alto, Calif., 1948-95; U.S. del. to internat. mgmt. confs. in Chile, France, Germany, Australia, Japan; bd. Exec. Svc. Corps., San Francisco; adv. bd. Santa Clara U. Bus. Sch.; bd. dirs. Coun. Internat. Progress in Mgmt.; presenter seminars, speeches for profit orgns. U.S. and abroad. Author: Successful Executive Action, Management by Results, Effective Management of Personnel, The Management Tactician, How to Boost Your Return on Management; contbr. articles to profl. publs. Mem. Soc. Advancement of Mgmt. (Frederick Taylor Key award), Am. Mgmt. Assn. (wall of fame). Home: 368 Selby Ln Menlo Park CA 94027-3933

SCHLEI, NORBERT ANTHONY, lawyer; b. Dayton, Ohio, June 14, 1929; s. William Frank and Norma (Lindsley) S.; m. Jane Moore, Aug. 26, 1950 (div. 1963); children: Anne C. Buczynski, William K., Andrew M.; m. Barbara Lindemann, Mar. 7, 1965 (div. 1981); m. Joan Masson, Dec. 29, 1995; children: Bradford L., Graham L., Norbert L., Blake Lindsley, Elizabeth Eldridge. BA, Ohio State U., 1950; LLB magna cum laude, Yale U., 1956. Bar: Ohio 1956, Calif. 1958, D.C. 1963, U.S. Supreme Ct. 1963. Law clk. to Justice Harlan U.S. Supreme Ct., 1956-57; assoc. atty. O'Melveny & Myers, L.A., 1957-59; ptnr. Greenberg, Shafton & Schlei, L.A., 1959-62; asst. atty. gen. U.S. Dept. Justice, Washington, 1962-66; ptnr. Munger, Tolles, Hills & Rickershauser, 1968-70, Kane, Shulman & Schlei, Washington, 1968-70; ptnr.-in-charge Hughes Hubbard & Reed, L.A., 1972-89; pres., CEO Kahala Capital Corp., Santa Monica, Calif., 1983 ; spl. counsel Clinicorp Inc., L.A., 1991-93. Author: (with M.S. McDougal and others) Studies in World Public Order, 1961 (Am. Soc. Internat. Law ann. book award); State Regulation of Corporate Financial Practices, 1962; editor-in-chief Yale Law Jour., 1955-56. Dem. nominee for Calif. Assembly, 1962, for sec. of state Calif., 1966. Mem. Calif. Bar Assn., Ohio Bar Assn., D.C. Bar Assn., Riviera Country Club (Pacific Palisades, Calif.).

SCHLEICHER, ROBERT EARL, economist; b. Livingston, Mont., Dec. 16, 1960. BS in Bus., Mont. State U., 1984, MPA, 1986. Grad. teaching asst. Mont. State U., Bozeman, 1985-86; aide, adminstrv. asst. Gov.'s Office, Helena, Mont., 1987-89; rsch. specialist Mont. Dept. Labor and Industry, Helena, Mont., 1989—. Budget chair, treas. Helena Citizens' Coun., Helena, 1993, chair, 1994; mem. Helena Tax Increment Fin. Bd., Helena Cmty. Oriented Policing Leadership Coun. Mem. Am. Soc. Pub. Adminstrn., Internat. Assn. Pers. Employment Svcs. Home: 1823 E Broadway St Helena MT 59601-4711 Office: Mont Dept Labor & Industry 1301 Lockey Ave Helena MT 59601-5137

SCHLESINGER, DEBORAH LEE, librarian; b. Cambridge, Mass., Sept. 13, 1937; d. Edward M. and Edith D. (Schneider) Hershoff; divorced; children: Suzanne, Richard. BA, U. Mass., 1961; MS, Simmons Coll., 1974; postgrad., U. Pitts., 1983. Reference librarian Bently Coll., Waltham, Mass., 1964-65; dir. Carnegie Library, Swissvale, Pa., 1973-77, South Park Twp. Library, Library, Pa., 1977-81, Monessen (Pa.) Library, 1981-82, Lewis & Clark Library, Helena, Mont., 1983-88, 89—; state librarian Mont. State Library, Helena, Mont., 1988-89; vis. scholar Pitts. Regional Library Ctr., 1982-83. Editor Pa. Union List, 1982-83. Mem. exec. bd. Mont. Cultural Advocacy, 1983—. Mem. Mont. Library Assn. (chmn. legis. com. 1984-92, MLA lobbyist 1992—), Mont. Assn. Female Execs. (fin. com. 1986—), AAUW (exec. com. 1985-86). Democrat. Club: Montana (Helena). Home: 2 Washington Pl Helena MT 59601-4359 Office: Lewis & Clark Libr 120 S Last Chance Mall Helena MT 59601

SCHLESINGER, NORMA H., art historian, writer; b. N.Y.C., Mar. 29, 1931; d. Jack L. and Estelle (Wieder) Honig; m. Mathias Spiegel, Oct. 19, 1952 (div. 1965); children: Paul Spiegel, Andrew Spiegel; m. Elmer Schlesinger, Apr. 10, 1969 (dec.). BA, Vassar Coll., 1952; MA, NYU, 1969. Art cons. San Francisco, 1970—; asst. prof. Sonoma State U., Rohnert Park, Calif., 1972-78; art editor Rev. West, San Francisco, 1978-81; rsch. asst. Fine Arts Mus., San Francisco, 1981-89; lectr. Acad. Art Coll., San Francisco, 1992-95. Journalist Nob Hill Gazzette, 1995—. Trustee San Francisco Art Inst., 1975-81, L.S.B. Leakey Found., San Francisco, 1978-94, Univ. Art Mus., Berkeley, 1982-95, Calif. Coll. Arts and Crafts, 1990—; advisor Am. Art Study Ctr., San Francisco, 1997—. Mem. AAUP, Met. Club, St. Francis Yacht Club. Home: 3525 Pacific Ave San Francisco CA 94118

SCHLESINGER, ROBERT JACKSON, business administration educator; b. N.Y., Dec. 5, 1927; s. Robert B. and Corrine Marie (Jackson) S.; m. Sylvia Barbara Tiersten, Dec. 24, 1980; children: Lisa Roberta, Karen Ann. BSEE, U. Conn., 1953; MS in Ops. Rsch., West Coast U., 1972; PhD, Brunel U., Eng., 1984. Registered profl. engr., Calif. Design engr. GE Co., Syracuse, N.Y., 1953-55; mem. tech. staff Ramo-Wooldridge, L.A., 1955-58; mem. corp. staff Gen. Dynamics Corp., San Diego, 1958-61; v.p. mktg. and systems ITT, Calif. and N.J., 1961-65; dir. R&D Packard Bell divsn. Teledyne, Newbury Park, Calif., 1965-68; mem. tech. staff Cal-Tech.'s JPL, Pasadena, Calif., 1968-70; pres., CEO Rho Sigma Inc., L.A., 1970-80; prof. info. and decision systems dept. San Diego State U., 1984-97, prof. emeritus, 1997—; lectr. in field. Author: Principles of Electronic Warfare, 1961; contbr. articles to profl. publs., chpts. to books. Mem. IEEE, Sigma Xi. Home: 9291 Wister Dr La Mesa CA 91941-4137 Office: San Diego State U College Ave San Diego CA 92182-0127

SCHLISKE, ROSALIND ROUTT, journalism educator, journalist; b. Ft. Worth, Jan. 30, 1950; d. Glenn Calvin and Ruth (Warth) Routt; m. Robert P. Schliske, Aug. 14, 1980. BA, Tex. Christian U., 1972; MA, U. Wyo., 1980, MPA in Coursework, 1984. Asst. news editor Wyo. Eagle, Cheyenne, 1972-73; news editor Wyo. Eagle, 1973-76; dir. pub. info., prof. journalism Laramie County C.C., Cheyenne, 1976-84; prof. journalism Laramie County C.C., 1984—. Advisor Wingspan student newspaper, 1976— (Associated Collegiate Press Pacemaker award 1993, 94). Wyo. Ednl. Trust Fund grantee Wyo. C.C. Commn., 1991-92; recipient Keith L. Ware award U.S. Army, 1988, Excellence in Tchg. award Nat. Inst. Staff and Organal. Devel., Austin, Tex., 1995. Mem. Soc. Profl. Journalists (state pres. 1981-84, Spl. Achievement award 1982), Nat. Fedn. Press Women (prof. devel. com. 1993, various editing awards), Women in Comm., Phi Kappa Pi. Democrat. Mem. Disciples of Christ. Home: 5101 Yellowstone Rd Cheyenne WY 82009 Office: Laramie County C C 1400 E College Dr Cheyenne WY 82007

SCHLOSE, WILLIAM TIMOTHY, health care executive; b. West Lafayette, Ind., May 16, 1948; s. William Fredrick and Dora Irene (Chitwood) S.; m. Linda Lee Fletcher, June 29, 1968 (div. 1978); children: Vanessa Janine Schlose Hubert, Stephanie Lynn; m. Kelly Marie Martin, June 6, 1987; 1 child, Taylor Jean Martin-Schlose. Student, Bowling Green State U., 1966-68, Long Beach City Coll., 1972-75; teaching credential, UCLA, 1975. Staff respiratory therapist St. Vincent's Med. Ctr., L.A., 1972-75; cardio-pulmonary chief Temple Community Hosp., L.A., 1975-76; adminstrv. dir. spl. svcs. Santa Fe Meml. Hosp., L.A., 1976-79; mem. mktg. and pub. rels. staff Nat. Med. Homecare Corp., Orange, Calif., 1979-81, Medtech of Calif., Inc., Burbank, Calif., 1981-84; regional mgr. Mediq Health Care Group Svcs., Inc., Chatsworth, Calif., 1984-88; pres. Baby Watch Homecare, Whittier, Calif., 1988-90, Tim Schlose and Assocs., Orange, Calif., 1990—; staff instr., Montebello (Calif.) Adult Schs. Author: Fundamental Respiratory Therapy Equipment, 1977. With USN, 1968-72. Mem. Am. Assn. Respiratory Care, Calif. Soc. Respiratory Care (past officer), Nat. Bd. Respiratory Care, Nat. Assn. Apnea Profls., Am. Assn. Physicians Assts., L.A. Pediatric Soc., Calif. Perinatal Assn., Saleen Owners Enthusiasts Club, SVT Cobra Owner's Club So. Calif. Republican. Methodist. Office: Tim Schlose and Assocs 910 E Chapman Ave Orange CA 92866-2109

SCHLOSSER, THEA SUSSANNE, advocate, association executive; b. Hasenfeld, Germany, June 1, 1937; d. Theodor and Anna (Poppe) Hermesmeyer; divorced; children: Ingrid, Evelyn. Ed. in home econs., Austria; attended, N.Y. Inst. Photography, Modern Sch. Photography; postgrad., Am. Coll. Nutrition. Prin. World Wide Slides, Santa Barbara; founder Chronic Fatigue and Immune Dysfunction Media Awareness Assn., Santa Barbara; assoc. TV show Growing Younger; promotional dir. Kuhnan MD Xenotransplant Ctr.; advt. and bus. cons.; speaker, lectr. on chronic fatigue immune dysfunction of TV, radio, others. Author, publisher: Beyond the Dark Cloud, Road to Recovery from Chronic Fatigue and Immune Dysfunction after 25 Years, 1996; founder-pres., publisher-editor CFID Health Update Internat. Newsletter; inventor game show Challenge Your IQ. Recipient numerous gold medals in photography; swimming champion Austria, 1950. Mem. AMa, Internat. Platform Assn. Office: Chronic Fatigue Media Awareness Assn PO Box 41028 Santa Barbara CA 93140

SCHLUETER, ERIKA MANRIQUEZ, civil engineer research scientist; b. Santiago, Chile; came to U.S., 1980; d. Javier Bustos Manriquez and Constantina Vilos Anso; m. Ross Donald Schlueter, May, 1981; children: Dietrich, Kurt. B of Civil Constrn., Cath. U., Santiago, 1980; postgrad., MIT, 1980-81, San Jose State U., 1983; MS in Civil Engring., U. Wash., 1986; PhD in Engring. Sci., U. Calif., Berkeley, 1995. Instr. continuing edn. Cath. U., Santiago, 1975-77, tchg. asst., 1976-77; hydrogeologist Celzac Co., Santiago, 1978; med. asst. Stanford (Calif.) U. Med. Ctr., 1981, fin. aids analyst, 1981-82; homemaker Pleasanton, 1986-88; rsch. asst. Lawrence Berkeley Nat. Lab. U. Calif., Berkeley, 1988-95; rsch. scientist Lawrence Berkeley Nat. Lab. U. Calif., Berkeley, 1995—. Contbr. numerous articles to profl. jours. Fulbright fellow, 1980-81, Jane Lewis fellow, 1990-91. Mem. ASCE, Soc. Petroleum Engrs., Am. Geophys. Union, Soc. Exploration Geophysicists (Award of Merit 1994-95). Republican. Roman Catholic. Home: 780 Cragmont Ave Berkeley CA 94708-1345 Office: Lawrence Berkeley Nat Lab MS 90-1116 1 Cyclotron Rd Berkeley CA 94720

SCHMALENBERGER, JERRY LEW, pastor, seminary educator; b. Greenville, Ohio, Jan. 23, 1934; s. Harry Henry and Lima Marie (Hormel) S.; m. Carol Ann Walthall, June 8, 1956; children: Stephen, Bethany Allison, Sarah Layton. BA, Wittenberg U., 1956, DDiv (hon.), 1984; MDiv, Hamma Sch. Theology, Springfield, Ohio, 1959, D of Ministry, 1976. Ordained to ministry Luth. Ch., 1959. Dir. Camp Mowana, Mansfield, Ohio, 1958-59; pastor 3d Luth. Ch., Springfield, 1959-61, 1st Luth. Ch., Bellefontaine, Ohio, 1961-66; sr. pastor 1st Luth. Ch., Tiffin, Ohio, 1966-70, Mansfield, 1970-79; sr. pastor St. John's Luth. Ch., Des Moines, 1979-88; pres. Pacific Luth. Theol. Sem., Berkeley, Calif., 1988-96, prof. parish ministry, 1988—; co-dir. Iowa Luth. Hosp. Min. of Health Program, Des Moines, 1986-88; Roland Payne lectr. Gbarnga (Liberia) Sch. Theology, 1987; lectr. Luth. Theol. Sem., Hong Kong, 1994, The United Theol. Coll., Kingston, Jamaica, 1994; guest prof. The Augustana Hochschule, Germany, 1996. Author: Lutheran Christians' Beliefs Book One, 1984, Book Two, 1987, Iowa Parables and Iowa Psalms, 1984, Saints Who Shaped the Church, 1986, Stewards of Creation, 1987, Nights Worth Remembering, 1989, The Vine and the Branches, 1992, Call to Witness, 1993, Plane Thoughts on Parish Ministry, 1994, Invitation to Discipleship, 1995, The Preacher's Edge, 1996, Preparation for Discipleship, 1997; columnist Rite Ideas, 1987-88. Bd. dirs. Grand View Coll., Des Moines, 1980-88, Wittenberg U., Springfield, Ohio, 1974-87, Luth. Social Services of Iowa, 1980-87, chmn. pre fund drive, 1988; bd. dirs. Planned Parenthood of Mid-Iowa, Des Moines, 1987-88; dir. Evang. Outreach/Luth. Ch. Am., 1983-85; mem. Iowa Luth. Hosp. Charitable Trust, 1986-88; chair Com. for Homeless Fund, Des Moines, 1986. Named Outstanding Alumni Wittenberg U., 1965, Young Man of Yr. Tiffin Jaycees, 1965, Man of Yr. Bellefontaine Jaycees, Disting. Alumni award Trinty Sem., Columbus, 1989. Mem. NAACP, Acad. Preachers, Acad. Evangelists (organizer 1986—), Kiwanis, Rotary. Home & Office: 162 Pelican Loop Pittsburg CA 94565-2004 *Personal philosophy: Not perfect, but forgiven, we find real life in living ours for others.*

SCHMALTZ, ROY EDGAR, JR., artist, art educator; b. Belfield, N.D., Feb. 23, 1937; s. Roy and Mercedes (Martin) S.; m. Julia Mabel Swan, Feb. 1, 1958; children: Liese Marlene, Jennifer Lynn, Gregory Jason. Student Otis Art Inst., Los Angeles, 1959-60, U. Wash., 1960-61, Akademie der Bildenden Kunste, Munich, W. Ger., 1965-66; B.F.A., San Francisco Art Inst., 1963, M.F.A., 1965. Lectr. art Coll. of Notre Dame, Belmont, Calif., 1968-70, M. H. De Young Meml. Art Mus., San Francisco, 1968-70; prof. art St. Mary's Coll. of Calif., Moraga, 1969—, chmn. dept. art; mem. artists' bd. San Francisco Art Inst., 1989-92; exhbns. include: Seattle Art Mus., 1959, M. H. De Young Meml. Art Mus., 1969, Frye Art Mus., Seattle, 1957, San Francisco Mus. Modern Art, 1971, U. Calif.-Santa Cruz, 1977, Fine Arts Mus. of San Francisco, 1978, Oakland Art Mus., 1979, Rutgers U., Camden, N.J., 1979, Springfield (Mo.) Art Mus., 1980, Butler Inst. Am. Art, Youngstown, Ohio, 1981, Huntsville (Ala.) Mus. Art, 1982, Haggin Mus.,

Stockton, Calif., 1982, U. Hawaii-Hilo, 1983, Alaska State Mus., Juneau, 1981, Tex. State U., San Marcos, 1980, Crocker Art Mus., Sacramento, 1982, Hearst Art Gallery, 1986; group exhbns. include San Francisco Internat. Airport Gallery, 1987, Solano Coll., Fairfield, Calif., 1988, U. Del., Newark, 1988, San Francisco Art Inst., 1989, Natsoulas Gallery, Davis, Calif., 1989, Bedford Regional Ctr. Arts, Walnut Creek, Calif., 1989, Contemporary Realist Gallery, San Francisco, 1994, Hearst Art Gallery, Moraba, Calif., 1995; represented in permanent collections: Richmond Art Ctr. (Calif.), U. Hawaii-Hilo, Las Vegas Art Mus. (Nev.), Hoyt Mus. and Inst. Fine Arts, New Castle, Pa., Frye Art Mus., San Francisco Art Inst., M. H. De Young Meml. Art Mus., Mills Coll., Oakland, Amerika-Haus, Munich, Contra Costa County Art Collection, Walnut Creek, Calif., Western Wash. U., Bellingham, Clemson U., S.C.; dir. Hearst Art Gallery, St. Mary's Coll.; vis. artist lectr. Academie Art Coll., San Francisco, 1971, grad. program Lone Mountain Coll., San Francisco, 1973-74. Coach Little League Baseball Team, Concord, Calif., 1982; mem. artist's bd. San Francisco Art Inst., 1989-93. Fulbright fellow, 1965-66; Frye Art Mus. traveling fellow, 1957; recipient Painting award All Calif. Ann., 1965; Nat. Watercolor award Chautauqua Inst., 1980; Seattle Art Assn. Painting award, 1957; San Francisco Art Inst. award, 1961; Otis Art Inst. award, 1959; Walnut Creek Civic Art Ctr. award, 1982, San Francisco Art Commn. award, 1985, Calif. State Fair Art award, 1985, Sears award for excellence in leadership, 1989-90. Mem. Coll. Art Assn., Fine Arts Mus. of San Francisco, AAUP, San Francisco Art Inst. Alumni Assn. Home: 1020 Whistler Dr Suisun City CA 94585-2929 Office: Saint Marys Coll Dept Art Moraga CA 94575

SCHMALZ, CHARLES JOSEPH, artist, photographer, creative consultant; b. Indpls., Nov. 3, 1947; s. Charles Joseph and Mary Ann (Eberle) S. BFA Visual Comm., Advt. Design cum laude, Pratt Inst., Bklyn., 1971. Tchr. Sacred Heart Elem. Sch., Indpls., 1964-65; spl. projects art dir. Random House, Knopf, Inc., N.Y.C., 1970-73; art dir. Klemtner Advt., N.Y.C., 1973-76; v.p. group art dir. Medigraphics, Wm. D. McAdams, N.Y.C., 1976-79; exec. art dir. Vicom Assocs., San Francisco, 1980-81; creative dir. Rainoldi, Kerzner & Radcliffe, San Francisco, 1981-87; author, tchr. basic layout Acad. of Art Coll., San Francisco, 1989-90; prin. Charles Schmalz Creative Svcs., San Francisco, 1990—. Photographer: solo exhibitions include Galleria U. Calif. Extension, San Francisco, 1992, Davis Art Ctr. The Hallway Gallery Davis, Calif., 1993, LCR Gallery, Weed, Calif., 1994, Palos Verdes Art Ctr., Ranchos Palos Verdes, Calif., 1995, Merced (Calif.) Coll. Art Gallery, 1995, So. Vt. Art Ctr., Manchester, 1996, Cerro Coso Cmty. Fine Arts Gallery, Ridgecrest, Calif., 1996; group exhibitions include Lilian Paley Ctr. for Visual Arts, Oakland, 1992, Orange County Ctr. for Contemporary Art, Santa Ana, Calif., 1993, Paris Gibson Sq. Mus. of Art, Gt. Falls, Mont., 1993, Hoyt Nat. Art Show, 1993, Univ. of Toledo Ctr. for the Visual Arts, Nat. Juried Exhibit, 1993, Alexandria (La.) Mus. of Art, 1994, Dadian Gallery, The Ctr. for Arts and Religion, Washington, 1995, Colombia (Mo.) Coll., 1996, Mus. of N.W. Colo., Craig, 1996, Downey (Calif.) Mus. of Art, 1996, San Bernadino County Mus., Redlands, Calif., 1996, Barrett House Galleries, DCAA, Poughkeepsie, N.Y., 1997, 1078 Gallery, Chico, Calif., 1997, 750 Gallery, Sacramento, Calif., 1997. Exec. dir., founder Fresh Start reintegration process for the homeless, 1989-90. Recipient Merit award 15th Ann. N.D. Nat. Juried Exhibition U. N.D., 1992, 1st Pl. award 89th Open Juried Exhibit, Long Beach Arts, Calif., 1993, People's Choice award, 9th Ann. Photo Show, Mus. Anthropology Calif. State U., Chico, 1993, Gallery Choice award, Gallery 57, Fullerton, Calif., 1993, Purchase award S.W. Tex. State U., San Marcos, 1994, Univ. Gallery, U. Del., 1994; 1st pl. award Mus. N.W., Craig, 1995, Merit award, The Dishman Competition, Lamar U. Art Gallery, Beaumont, Tex., 1995, 2d pl. award Farm and Metaphor, E. New Mex. U., Portales, 1995; also numerous awards for work in advertising and design., 1969—. Mem. Amnesty Internat., Greenpeace, Artists Equity. Home and Studio: 271 Santa Rosa Ave San Francisco CA 94112-1906

SCHMID, INGRID, medical researcher; b. Treibach, Austria, Oct. 24, 1952; came to U.S., 1982, permanent resident, 1982; d. Ernst and Anny (Navratil) Dobrovolny; m. Peter Schmid, Dec. 23, 1981; 1 child, Ernst Walter. M in Pharmacy, U. Vienna, Austria, 1976. Lic. pharmacist, Austria. Intern pharmacist Pub. Pharmacy, Vienna, 1977-79; quality control mgr., head drug registration dept. Co. Substantia (Parke Davis Austria), Vienna, 1979-81; vol. lab. of Dr. George Fareed UCLA Molecular Biology Inst., 1982; staff rsch. assoc. lab. of Dr. John Fahey UCLA Dept. Microbiology and Immunology, 1983-87; staff rsch. assoc. lab. of Dr. Janis Giorgi UCLA Sch. Medicine, 1987-93, supr. flow cytometry core facility Jonsson Cancer Ctr., 1989—, acad. staff rsch. specialist, 1993—, flow cytometry instr., 1991—; nat. tech. cons. for flow cytometry on the Multictr. AIDS Cohort Study, 1989-90; presenter UCLA, 1988, 7th Ann. Clin. Applications of Cytometry meeting, Charleston, S.C., 1992; lectr. in field. Author: (with others) Vaccines, 1990; contbr. articles to profl. jours. Mem. Internat. Soc. for Analytical Cytology, UCLA Adminstrs. and Suprs. Assn., Clin. Cytometry Soc. (charter). Office: UCLA Sch Medicine Dept Medicine/CIA/CIC 12-236 Factor Bldg Los Angeles CA 90024-1745

SCHMID, RUDI (RUDOLF SCHMID), internist, educator, academic administrator; b. Switzerland, May 2, 1922; came to U.S., 1948, naturalized, 1954; s. Rudolf and Bertha (Schiesser) S.; m. Sonja D. Wild, Sept. 17, 1949; children: Isabelle S., Peter R. BS, Gymnasium Zurich, 1941; MD, U. Zurich, 1947; PhD, U. Minn., 1954. Intern U. Calif. Med. Center, San Francisco, 1948-49; resident medicine U. Minn., 1949-52, instr., 1952-54; research fellow biochemistry Columbia U., 1954-55; investigator NIH, Bethesda, Md., 1955-57; assoc. medicine Harvard U., 1957-59, asst. prof., 1959-62; prof. medicine U. Chgo., 1962-66; prof. medicine U. Calif., San Francisco, 1966-91, prof. emeritus, 1991—, dean Sch. Medicine, 1983-89, assoc. dean internat. rels., 1989-95; Cons. U.S. Army Surgeon Gen., USPHS, VA. Mem. editorial bd. Jour. Clin. Investigation, 1965-70, Blood, 1962-75, Gastroenterology, 1965-70, Jour. Investigative Dermatology, 1968-72, Annals Internal Medicine, 1975-79, Proceedings Soc. Exptl. Biology and Medicine, 1974-84, Chinese Jour. Clin. Scis., Jour. Lab. Clin. Medicine, 1991—, Hepatology Comm. Internat. (Japan), 1993—; cons. editor Gastroenterology, 1981-86. Served with Swiss Army, 1943-48. Master ACP; fellow AAAS, N.Y. Acad. Scis., Royal Coll. Physicians; mem. NAS, Am. Acad. Arts and Scis., Assn. Am. Physicians (pres. 1986), Am. Soc. Clin. Investigation, Am. Soc. Biol. Chemistry and Molecular Biology, Am. Soc. Hematology, Am. Gastroenterol. Assn., Am. Assn. Study Liver Disease (pres. 1965), Internat. Assn. Study Liver (pres. 1980), Swiss Acad. Med. Scis. (mem. senate), Leopoldina, German-Am. Acad. Coun. (exec. com.). Home: 211 Woodland Rd Kentfield CA 94904-2631 Office: U Calif Med Sch Office of Dean PO Box 0410 San Francisco CA 94143-0410

SCHMID-SCHOENBEIN, GEERT WILFRIED, biomedical engineer, educator; b. Albstadt, Baden-Wurttemberg, Germany, Jan. 1, 1948; came to U.S., 1971; s. Ernst and Ursula Schmid; m. Renate Schmid-Schoenbein, July 3, 1976; children: Philip, Mark, Peter. Vordiplom, Liebig U., Giessen, Germany, 1971; PhD in Bioengring., U. Calif., San Diego, 1976. Staff assoc. dept. physiology Columbia U., N.Y.C., 1976-77, sr. assoc., 1977-79; asst. prof. dept. applied mechs. & engring. scis. U. Calif., San Diego, 1979-84, assoc. prof., 1984-89, prof., 1989-94, prof. dept. bioengring., 1994—. Editor: Frontiers in Biomechanics, 1986, Physiology and Pathophysiology of Leukocyte Adhesion, 1994. Recipient Melville medal ASME, 1990. Fellow Am. Inst. for Med. & Biol. Engring., Am. Heart Assn.; mem. Biomed. Engring. Soc. (pres. 1991-92), Am. Microcirculatory Soc., European Microcirculatory Soc., Am. Physiol. Soc. Office: U Calif San Diego Dept Bioengineering La Jolla CA 92093-0412

SCHMIDT, ARNOLD ANTHONY, writer; b. N.Y.C., Sept. 21, 1954; s. Arnold Alfred and Anita (Venetion) S. BA in English, SUNY, New Paltz, 1987, MA, 1990; PhD, Vanderbilt U., 1994. Asst. editor Back Stage, N.Y.C., 1977-79; reporter The Hollywood Reporter, Los Angeles, 1982; playwright Group Repertory Theatre, North Hollywood, Calif., 1985-86; feature writer Dutchess mag., Millbrook, N.Y., 1987-88; writer, reporter Times Herald Record, Middletown, 1987-90; writer Shirley Jones Prodns., Cin., 1988-89; asst. prof. CSU/S, 1995—. Asst. producer (film) The Silence, 1982 (Acad. award nomination 1983); writer: (screenplay) Deja Vu, 1985, The Junkie Priest, 1988, (story for sitcom Alice) Tommy's Lost Weekend (Emmy award nomination 1985, Letter of Commendation County Los Angeles 1986); contbr. feature stories to Adweek, American Cinematographer, Emmy, Millimeter, Poughkeepsie Jour.; conbr. articles to profl. jours. SUNY New Paltz fellow, 1988-89, Mellon fellow, 1993-94. Mem. Writers Guild Am., Dramatists Guild (assoc.). Democrat. Office: Calif State Univ English Dept 801 West Monte Vista Turlock CA 95382

SCHMIDT, CAROL SUZANNE, hospital administrator; b. River Rouge, Mich., Aug. 8, 1936; d. J. T. Grant Vaden and Virginia Jean (Senker) Vaden Webster; m. Ronald Lee Schmidt, Aug. 18, 1957; children: Karen Suzanne Author, Linda Martin, Ronald Lee. RN diploma Hinsdale Hosp. Sch. Nursing, Ill., 1958; BS in Nursing cum laude, Met. State Coll., Denver, 1981; M.A. cum laude, Webster U.-Denver, 1984. RN, Colo. Operating room nurse Porter Meml. Hosp., Denver, 1961-69, charge relief nurse, 1975-76, adminstrv. supr., 1976-77, head nurse ortho/neuro unit, 1977-82; disease control nurse Vis. Nurse Assn., Denver, 1961-63; nurse Denver Gen. Hosp., 1966-67; office mgr., bookkeeper Timber Ridge Constrn., Evergreen, Colo., 1967-79; asst. dir. nursing Boulder Meml. Hosp., Colo., 1982-83, dir. nursing, 1984-89; v.p., chief clin. officer Avista Hosp., 1989-96, v.p. ops. Porter Care Hosp., Avista, 1996—. Tchr. Seventh Day Adventist Ch., Boulder and Denver, 1958-85; vol. Colo. Health Fair, Denver, 1979, 80; tchr. basic life support Am. Heart Assn., Denver, 1980-82; mem. Colo. Women's Forum Health Adminstrn., 1990—. Recipient Dist. Nurse of Yr. award Colo. Nurse Assn., 1975. Mem. Am. Coll. Hosp. Execs. of Am. Hosp. Assn., Am. Orgn. Nurse Execs., Assn. Seventh Day Adventist Nurses (bd. dirs. 1984-86), Colo. Soc. Nurse Execs. (active image of nursing 1985, Cir. of Excellence award 1996), Bus. and Profl. Women (legis. com. 1985), Colo. Fedn. Nursing Orgns. Avocations: needlework; travel. Office: Avista Hosp 100 Health Park Dr Louisville CO 80027-9583

SCHMIDT, CHRISTOPHER VAN ALST, systems programmer; b. Burlingame, Calif., Apr. 18, 1960; s. Werner F. and Mary Jane (Lodge) S.; m. Margret Buckley, Dec. 28, 1990. BS in Computer Sci., Yale U., 1982. Sys. programmer SUMEX Computer Project, 1982-90; developer Petaluma, Calif., 1991-93; editor San Mateo Libertarian, 1993-96, webmaster, 1996—. Congl. candidate 12th Dist. Calif., 1996. Mem. Nat. Space Soc., Nat. Wildlife Fedn., Nat. Taxpayers Union, Nature Conservancy, Greenpeace, Space Studies Inst., ACLU Peninsula Humane Soc., Internat. Fund for Family Planning, Natural Resources Def. Coun., Computer Profls. for Social Responsibility, Assn. for Computing Machinery, Drug Policy Found., Zero Population Growth, Assn. for Vol. Surg. and Safe Contraception. Libertarian.

SCHMIDT, DIANA GAIL, paralegal; b. Olney, Tex., Dec. 5, 1946; d. Ernest B. and Helen N. (Wright) Perkins; m. Lail William Schmidt, Jr., Aug. 14, 1974 (div. 1986); 1 child, Andrea. Student, U. Okla., 1965-67; mktg. cert., U. Phoenix, 1992, BA in Mgmt., 1993. Real estate lic., Colo. Owner DG Ventures, Lakewood, Colo., 1984-85; realtor Century 21 Profls., Lakewood, 1987-89; paralegal Attys. Svc. Ctr., Denver, 1987-92; paralegal specialist Resolution Trust Corp., Denver, 1992—. Dir. 6th Ave. Townhome Assn., Golden, Colo., 1993—; pres. Union Sq. Community Assn., Lakewood, 1988; chair mentor program Toastmasters Internat., Lakewood, 1990; speaker MADD, Denver, 1990, The Jungle Lady, Denver, 1994. Recipient Take Pride in Am. award U.S. Dept. of Interior, Washington, 1989, Community award City Coun., Lakewood, 1989. Republican. Home: 444 Gladiola St Golden CO 80401-5250 Office: Paralegal Resource Ctr 1050 17th St Denver CO 80203

SCHMIDT, FRANK BROAKER, executive recruiter; b. Shamokin, Pa., Aug. 8, 1939; s. Frank Wilhelm and Doris (Maurer) S.; children by previous marrage: Susan E., Tracie A.; m. Elizabeth Mallen, Mar. 18, 1989; children: Alexandra M., Frank W.M. BS, U. Pa., 1962; MBA, Case Western Res. U., 1969; cert. brewmaster, Siebel Inst. Brewing Tech., Chgo., 1964. With Carling Brewing Co., Cleve., 1964-69, mgr. sales and advt. div., brand mgr., 1969-70; advt. and merchandising mgr. The Pepsi-Cola Co., Purchase, N.Y., 1970-73, dir. mktg. programs, then dir. mgmt. devel., 1973-74; dir. sales and mktg. The Olga Co., Van Nuys, Calif., 1974-75; pres. F.B. Schmidt, Internat., L.A., 1975—; chmn. Mediterranean Properties, 1994—. Author: Draft Beer Manual, 1967, Assn. Nat. Advertisers Computerized Media System, 1970. Chmn. Morrison Ranch Estates Homeowners Assn., 1993-96. Mem. Calif. Exec. Recruiters Assn., Wharton Alumni Assn., Personnel Cons. Am. (region chmn. 1981-83, chmn. 92-95), Am. Mktg. Assn. Republican. Office: 30423 Canwood St Ste 239 Agoura Hills CA 91301-4318

SCHMIDT, JOANNE (JOSEPHINE ANNE SCHMIDT), language educator; b. N.Y.C., June 7, 1950; d. Joseph William and Maria Esther (Morazzani) S. BA, Chestnut Hill Coll., Phila., 1972; MA, U. Va., 1974, PhD, 1980. Tchg. asst. U. Va., Charlottesville, 1973-76, Lycée Marie Curie, Sceaux, France, 1976-77; lectr. U. Va., Charlottesville, 1977-79; asst. prof. Cedar Crest Coll., Allentown, Pa., 1981-84; asst. prof. Calif. State U., Bakersfield, 1984-88, assoc. prof., 1988-94, prof., 1994—; freelance translator, Bklyn., 1979-81, Allentown, Pa., 1981-84, Bakersfield, Calif., 1984—. Author: (book) If There Are No More Heroes There Are Heroines: A Feminist Critique of Corneille's Heroines, 1987, (jour.) San Jose Studies, 1987, (poetry book) (author as Teresita Bosch) Portraits, 1991; assoc. editor: (jour.) Coll. Tchg., 1985-89. V.p. Women, Inc., Allentown, 1983-84; pub. spkr. Alliance Against Family Violence, Bakersfield, Calif., 1985-90. Fulbright Hays grantee Fed. Govt., 1976-77, Affirmative Action grantee Calif. State U., 1985, 87, 91. Mem. MLA, NOW, Am. Assn. Tchrs. of French, Nat. Women's Studies Assn., Calif. Lang. Tchrs. Assn., Delta Kappa Gamma. Democrat. Office: Calif State U Fgn Langs Dept 9001 Stockdale Hwy Bakersfield CA 93311

SCHMIDT, JOHN WESLEY, engineer, environmental scientist; b. Pendleton, Oreg., Aug. 26, 1954; s. Earl B. and Mary C. (Eaton) S.; m. Julia Anne Hampton, Nov. 23, 1988. AA, Columbia Basin Coll., 1985, AAS in Nuclear Technology, 1985; BSME, Wash. State U., 1991. Health physics technician Rockwell Hanford Co., Richland, Wash., 1985-87; health physics technician Westinghouse Hanford Co., Richland, Wash., 1987-90, sr. engr., 1990-96; sr. engr. Rust Fed. Svcs., Inc., Richland, 1996-97; health physicist Wash. State Dept. Health, Olympia, 1997—. Mem. Assn. N.W. Environ. Profls., Health Physics Soc., Tri Cities Enological Soc., Columbia Basin Health Physics Soc., Richland Rod and Gun Club. Office: Wash State Dept Health PO Box 47901 1300 SE Quince St Olympia WA 98504-7901

SCHMIDT, JOSEPH DAVID, urologist; b. Chgo., July 29, 1937; s. Louis and Marian (Fleigel) S.; m. Andrea Maxine Herman, Oct. 28, 1962. BS in Medicine, U. Ill., 1959, MD, 1961. Diplomate Am. Bd. Urology. Rotating intern Presbyn. St. Luke's Hosp., Chgo., 1961-62, resident in surgery, 1962-63; resident in urology The Johns Hopkins Hosp., Balt., 1963-67; faculty U. Iowa Coll. Medicine, Iowa City, 1969-76; faculty U. Calif., San Diego, 1976—, prof., head div. urology, 1976—, vice-chmn. dept. surgery, 1985—; cons. U.S. Dept. Navy, San Diego, 1976—; attending urologist Vets. Affairs Dept., San Diego, 1976—. Author, editor: Gynecological and Obstetric Urology, 1978, 82, 93. Capt. USAF, 1967-69. Recipient Francis Senear award. U. Ill., 1961. Fellow Am. Coll. of Surgeons; mem. AMA, Am. Urol. Assn. Inc., Alpha Omega Alpha. Office: U Calif Med Ctr Divsn Urology 200 W Arbor Dr San Diego CA 92103-1911

SCHMIDT, KARL A., lawyer; b. Stockton, Calif., Sept. 18, 1947. BS, U. Calif., Berkeley, 1969, JD, 1974. Bar: Calif. 1974. Mem. Pillsbury Madison & Sutro, L.A. Mem. ABA. Office: Pillsbury Madison & Sutro Citicorp Plz 725 S Figueroa St Ste 1200 Los Angeles CA 90017-5443

SCHMIDT, L(AIL) WILLIAM, JR., lawyer; b. Thomas, Okla., Nov. 22, 1936; s. Lail William and Violet Kathleen (Kuper) S.; m. Diana Gail (div. May 1986); children: Kimberly Ann, Andrea Michelle; m. Marilyn Sue, Aug. 11, 1990; stepchildren: Leland Darrell Mosby, Jr., Crystal Rachelle Mosby. BA in Psychology, U. Colo., 1959; JD, U. Mich., 1962. Bar: Colo. 1962, U.S. Dist. Ct. Colo. 1964, U.S. Tax Ct. 1971, U.S. Ct. Appeals (10th cir.) 1964. Ptnr. Holland & Hart, Denver, 1962-77, Schmidt, Elrod & Wills, Denver, 1977-85, Moye, Giles, O'Keefe, Vermeire & Gorrell, Denver, 1985-90; of counsel Hill, Held, Metzger, Lofgren & Peele, Dallas, 1989—; pvt. practice law Denver, 1990—; lectr. profl. orgns. Author: How To Live-and Die-with Colorado Probate, 1985, A Practical Guide to the Revocable Living Trust, 1990; contbr. articles to legal jours. Pres. Luth. Med. Ctr. Found., Wheat Ridge, Colo., 1985-89; pres. Rocky Mountain Prison and Drug Found., Denver, 1986—; bd. dirs. Luth. Hosp., Wheat Ridge, 1988-92; bd. dirs. Denver Planned Giving Roundtable, Bonfils Blood Ctr. Found., Planned Giving Adv. Group of Nat. Jewish Hosp. Fellow Am. Coll. Trust and Estate Counsel (Colo. chmn. 1981-86); mem. ABA, Am. Judicature Soc., Rocky Mtn. Estate Planning Coun. (founder, pres. 1970-71), Greater Denver Tax Counsel Assn., Am. Soc. Magicians, Denver Athletic Club, Phi Delta Phi. Republican. Baptist. Office: 1050 17th St Ste 1700 Denver CO 80265-1050 also: Law Offices of Gregory J Morris 300 S 4th St Las Vegas NV 89101-6014

SCHMIDT, MARGRET BUCKLEY, real estate broker; b. Walnut Creek, Calif., June 3, 1971; d. Michael John and Barbara Caryl (Eltzroth) Buckley; m. Christopher Van Alst Schmidt, Dec. 28, 1990. BSEE, U. Calif., Berkeley, 1992. Cert. relocation profl.; cert. residential specialist. Real estate broker Coldwell Banker, Menlo Park, Calif., 1992—; bd. dirs. MLS Ops. Bd.- RE InfoLink, San Jose, Calif., 1996—. Libertarian. Office: Coldwell Banker 1377 El Camino Real Menlo Park CA 94025-4210

SCHMIDT, MARK DAVID, military officer; b. Schnectady, N.Y., Sept. 22, 1964; s. David P. and Gladys E. (Matasovsky) S.; m. Michele A. Quinn, Nov. 7, 1992; 1 stepchild, Anderson P. Quinn. BS in Aerospace Engring., Iowa State U., 1988. Facility survey engr. Iowa Office of Disaster Svcs., Des Moines, 1986-89; mil. officer USAF, Dyess AFB, Tex., 1989-95, Wyo. Air Nat. Guard, Cheyenne, 1995—. Usher St. John's Luth. Ch., Ft. Collins, Colo., 1995—; campaign vol. Gale Norton for U.S. Senate, Ft. Collins, 1996. Mem. Air Nat. Guard Officers Assn., Air Force Assn., Exptl. Aircraft Assn., Aircraft Owners and Pilots Assn., Aviation Internat., Am. Legion, Iowa State U. Alumni Assn., Strategic Air Command Soc., Sigma Iota Epsilon. Home: 1109 Sycamore St Fort Collins CO 80521

SCHMIDT, STANLEY EUGENE, retired speech educator; b. Harrington, Wash., Dec. 14, 1927; s. Otto Jacob and Ella Genevieve (Wilson) S.; m. Randall Lee, Stephen Douglas. BS in Edn., U. Idaho, 1956; MEd in Adminstrn., U. Oreg., 1958; MA in Speech, Wash. State U., 1975. Supt., tchr., coach Rose Lake (Idaho) Sch. Dist. # 35, 1949-55; forensics coach, speech tchr. Jefferson H.S., Portland, Oreg., 1955-65; dir. forensics Portland C.C., 1965-93, lead speech instr., 1979-82, subject area chmn., 1986-90; adj. prof. speech U. Portland, 1987-93; parliamentarian faculty senate, 1975-80. Coauthor anthology: The Literature of the Oral Tradition, 1963. Chmn., precinct committeeman Rep. Party, Kootenai County, Idaho, 1951-53; mem. Easter Seal Soc., Portland, 1980—; pres. Kootenai County Tchrs. Assn., 1953-54, North Idaho Edn. Assn., 1954-55, Oreg. Speech Assn., 1960-61, Oreg. C.C. Speech Assn., 1971-72. Recipient Excellence award U.S. Bank, Portland, 1993, Merit award N.W. Forensic Assn., 1992. Mem. Portland Rose Soc., Royal Rosarian, Masons (jr. grand deacon 1990-91, jr. grand steward 1991-92, grand orator, 1992-93, dist. dep. 1986-90, 32d deg. Scottish Rite, comdr. 1989-90), Cryptic Masons of Oreg. (grand orator 1994-95), Tualitin Valley Shrine Club, Shriners (pres. 1991, bd. dirs. 1989—), Red Cross of Constantine (St. Laurence Conclave, recorder 1993—, dir. of the work 1989—). Baptist. Home: 5460 SW Palatine St Portland OR 97219-7259

SCHMIDT, WALDEMAR ADRIAN, pathologist, educator; b. L.A., Aug. 22, 1941; s. Waldemar Adrian and Mary Charlotte (Parker) S.; m. Karmen LaVer Bingham, Feb. 1, 1963; children: Rebecca, Sarah, Waldemar, Diedrich. BS, Oreg. State U., 1965; PhD, U. Oreg., 1969, MD, 1969. Intern U. Oreg. Hosps. and Clinics, Portland, 1969-70, resident, 1970-73; pathologist LDS Hosp., Salt Lake City, 1973-77; prof. pathology U. Tex. Med. Sch., Houston, 1977-91, Oreg. Health Sci. U. and VA Med. Ctr., Portland, 1991—. Author: Principles and Techniques of Surgical Pathology, 1982; editor Cytopathology Annual, 1991—. Asst. scoutmaster Boy Scouts Am., Houston, 1982-91. Maj. U.S. Army, 1970-76. Mem. Coll. Am. Pathologists (program com.), Sigma Xi, Alpha Omega Alpha. Office: VA Med Ctr 3710 SW Us Veterans Hospital Rd Portland OR 97201-2964

SCHMIEDER, CARL, jeweler; b. Phoenix, Apr. 27, 1938; s. Otto and Ruby Mable (Harkey) S.; m. Carole Ann Roberts, June 13, 1959; children: Gail, Susan, Nancy, Amy. Student Bradley Horological Sch., Peoria, Ill., 1959-61; BA, Pomona Coll., 1961; Owner timepiece repair svc., Peoria, 1959-61; clock repairman Otto Schmieder & Son, Phoenix, 1961-65, v.p., 1965-70, pres., 1970—, chief exec. officer, 1970—. Mem. subcom. Leap Commn., 1966; area rep. Pomona Coll., 1972-76. Cert. jeweler; cert. gemologist, gemologist appraiser; recipient Design award Diamonds Internat., 1965, Cultured Pearl Design award, 1967, 68, Diamonds for Christmas award, 1970; winner Am. Diamond Jewelry Competition, 1973; bd. dirs. Lincoln Hosp., 1983—, Ariz. Mus., 1984-88; delegate White House Conf. on Small Bus., 1986, 95; chmn. Gov.'s Conf. on Small Bus., 1988-91; col. Confederate Air Force. Mem. Am. Gem. Soc. (dir. 1973-86, nat. chmn. nomenclature com. 1975-77, chmn. membership com. 1977-81, officer 1981-86), Ariz. Jewelers Assn. (Man of Yr. 1974), Jewelers Security Alliance (dir. 1974-78), Jewelers Vigilance Com. (dir. 1981-87), Jewelry Industry Council (dir. 1982-88), 24 Karat Club So. Calif., Exptl. Aircraft Assn., Warbirds of Am. (dir. 1990—), Deer Valley (Ariz.) Airport Tenants Assn. (dir. 1980-90, pres. 1983-90), Ariz. C. of C. (bd. dirs. 1985-89), Small Bus. Council (bd. dirs. 1985-89, chmn. 1988, del. to White House Conf., 1986, 95, chmn. Govs. Conf. on small bus. 1988-89), Nat. Small Bus. United (bd. dirs. 1990-94), Kiwanis (pres. Valley of Sun chpt. 1975-76), Friends of Iberia, Rotary. Republican. Methodist. Home: 1016 W Rovey Phoenix AZ 85013 Office: Park Ctrl Phoenix AZ 85013

SCHMITT, CATHERINE LAURA, academic career counselor; b. Santa Barbara, Calif., May 5, 1967; d. David R. and Harriet L. (Holland) S. Student, Santa Barbara C.C., 1987; BA in Social Ecology, U. Calif., Irvine, 1990; MS in Counseling, Calif. State U., Fullerton, 1993. Team facilitator knowledge and social responsibilty program U. Calif., Irvine, summer 1989, assoc. students commr., career paraprofl. counselor, 1989-90; peer counselor Ednl. Opportunity Program Irvine Valley C.C., 1991, specialist aide Cmty. Outreach, 1991-92, counseling intern Disabled Students Program and Svcs., 1991-93; career and workability program coord. Career Ctr. Calif. State Polytechnic U., Pomona, 1993-96, mem. univ. diversity com., 1994-96, interim coord. Univ. Advising Ctr., 1996—. Pres. Nat. Alliance for Blind Students, Washington, 1991-93; mem. bd. publs., membership com. Claif. Coun. of the Blind, Burbank, 1992—; treas., bd. dirs. Nat. Issues Forum of Orange County, 1992-93; mem. adv. bd. spl. needs in transit com. Orange County Transp. Authority, Garden Grove, Calif., 1992-93; conf. program selection com. AHEAD, 1994—. Recipient Vol.-in-People (VIP) award Vol. Ctr. of Greater Orange County, 1993. Mem. NAFE, Am. Counseling Assn., Toastmasters Internat. (pres. chpt. 1996—). Office: Calif Polytechnic U U Adv Ctr Bldg 66 3801 W Temple Ave Pomona CA 91768-2557

SCHMITT, DIANA MAE, elementary education educator; b. Dubuque, Iowa, Jan. 19, 1950; d. Raymond J. and Marie Arlen Schmitt. BA, U. Iowa, 1972; MA, Clarke Coll., Dubuque, 1981; postgrad., U. Wyo. 6th grade tchr. Shelby County Sch. Dist., Shelby, Iowa, 1972-73; 4th and 5th grade tchr. Dist. 200, Woodstock, Ill., 1973-76; rural sch. tchr. Albany County Sch. Dist., Laramie, Wyo., 1976-83; 1st, 3d, 5th and 6th grade tchr. Albany County Sch. Dist., 1983-92; chmn. outdoor classrm. devel. Indian Paintbrush Elem., 1992—; mem. rev. com. for excellence in sci. edn., adv. com. Western Edn. Adv. Com. for Wyo., 1989; tchr. sci. methods for elem. sch. U. Wyo., 1990-91; mem. Higher Edn. Grant Reading State Com., 1994; participant Sci. Grasp, 1990, Inst. Chemical Edn. Fundamental, 1992; presenter 1st Soviet-Am. Sci. Conv., Moscow, 1991; mem. workshop on water, Nat. Geog. Soc., 1993; presenter NSTA nat. and regional convs., state Wyo. Interdisciplinary Conf. convs., No. Iowa Beginning Reading conf. Named Dist. Exemplary Sci. Tchr., 1986-87; recipient Delta award, 1993. Mem. NEA, Internat. Reading Assn., Nat. Sci. Tchrs. Assn., Wyo. Sci. Tchrs. Assn. (sec.), Alpha Delta Kappa (pres.). Home: 5737 Southview Rd Laramie WY 82070-6801 Office: Indian Paintbrush 1653 N 28th St Laramie WY 82070-7340

SCHMITT, GARY A., energy company director; b. Idaho Falls, May 29, 1952; s. Bernard Frank and Betty Fay (Brown) S.; m. Nancy Panos, June 15, 1974; 1 child, Kyle Christopher. BS, U. Utah, 1974; MS, Va. Tech., 1976. Registered profl. engr., Utah. Indsl. engr. Mountain Fuel Supply, Salt Lake City, 1976-80, ops. mgr., 1980-85, sales mgr., 1985-90; dir. Questar Corp., Salt Lake City, 1990—; adj. prof. Westminster Coll., Salt Lake City, 1980-84; cons. Mktg./Mgmt. Inc., Salt Lake City, 1984-88; pres. Inst. Indsl. Engring., Salt Lake City, 1980-81. Contbr. articles to profl. jours. Participant Gov.'s Clean Air Task Force, Salt Lake City, 1991. Recipient Gold medal Pacific Coast Gas Assn., 1984, Silver medal 1982, Bronze medal, 1988, Mktg. Program award Am. Gass Assn., 1989. Mem. Assn. Energy Engrs., Rotary. Democrat. Episcopalian. Home: 1428 Canterbury Dr Salt Lake City UT 84108-2831 Office: Questar Corp 180 1st Ave Salt Lake City UT 84103-2301

SCHMITT, NANCY CAIN, public and corporate relations executive, writer; b. Fayetteville, N.C., June 12, 1942; d. Carlton White and Cleo Margaret (Parnell) Cain; m. Louis Dennis Schmitt, July 13, 1974 (div.). BA, Wake Forest U., 1960-64. Intern Winston-Salem (N.C.) Jour.-Sentinel, 1963-64; reporter Gastonia (N.C.) Gazette, 1964-66; copy editor, reporter Twin City Sentinel, Winston-Salem, 1966-67; entertainment editor Fayetteville Observer, 1967-78; lifestyle editor Anchorage Times, 1978-83; pub. rels. specialist Multivisions Cable TV Co., Anchorage, 1983-84; editor Alaska Jour. of Commerce, Anchorage, 1984-85; sr. comms. specialist U.S. Postal Svc., 1985—. Author: How to Care for Your Car: A Women's Guide to Car Care in Alaska, 1978 (nat. award 1979); mem. editl. bd. Episc. Diocean of Alaska, Fairbanks, 1983-86; contbr. articles to profl. jours. and nat. publs. Recipient Asst. Postmaster Gen.'s award for excellence, USPS Legis. Affairs Corp. Rel. Sr. VP Opportunity award, Sr. Op-Ed Writing award. Mem. Nat. Fedn. Press Women (nat. bd. dirs. 1990-91, pres. 1997—), Pub. Rels. Soc. Am., Alaska Press Women (pres. treas., sec., communicator of achievement, recipient numerous awards), Alaska Press Club (recipient 3 awards), Rotary Internat. (bd. dirs. 1991-92). Home: 6716 E 16th Ave Apt A Anchorage AK 99504-2513 Office: U S Postal Svc Corp Rels 3720 Barrow St Anchorage AK 99599-9998

SCHMITT, PAUL JOHN, history and geography educator; b. Pitts., Jan. 25, 1951; s. Phillip John and Adeline Marie (Barnhart) S.; m. Ruth Margaret Glass, June 20, 1987. BS, Ariz. State U., 1976, BA in Edn., 1978; MA, U. Nev., Las Vegas, 1994. Registration clk. Hermosa Inn Resort, Scottsdale, Ariz., 1978-79, asst. mgr., 1979-82; convention svc. mgr. Carefree (Ariz.) Inn Resort, 1982-84; tchr. Tonopah (Nev.) High Sch., 1984-85; reservation clk. Desert Inn Country Club and Spa, Las Vegas, Nev., 1985-92; prof. history C.C. of So. Nev., Las Vegas, 1992—. Mem. Assn. Am. Geographers, Orgn. Am. Historians, Am. Western History Assn., Orgn. Am. Historians, Phi Alpha Theta, Gamma Theta Upsilon. Office: CC So Nev Cheyenne Campus Dept Regional Studies 3200 E Cheyenne Ave S2C North Las Vegas NV 89030

SCHMITT, RICHARD GEORGE, industrial engineer; b. St. Cloud, Minn., June 18, 1948; s. George William and Viola Theresa (Mechenich) S.; m. Ligia Marie Pereira, Aug. 29, 1970; children: Christopher Michael, Scott Andrew. B in Indsl. Engring. with honors, Gen. Motors Inst., 1971. Indsl. engr. Gen. Motors, Fremont, Calif., 1966-78; sr. indsl. engr. Gen. Motors, Oklahoma City, 1978-80; indsl. engring. mgr. Shugart Assocs., Sunnyvale, Calif., 1980-81; mfg. tech. mgr. Magnex Corp., San Jose, Calif., 1981-82, prodn. mgr., 1982-83; facilities mgr. Apple Computer, Fremont, 1983, indsl. engring. mgr., 1984-85, robotics mgr., 1985-86, new product ops. mgr., 1987, Pacific logistics ops. mgr., 1988-93; Pacific phys. logistics mgr. Apple Computer, Cupertino, Calif., 1987—, Pacific ops. dir., 1993, Pacific supply chain design mgr., 1994-96, worldwide logistics strategy mgr., 1996—. Transp. chmn. Mt. Hamilton dist. Boy Scouts Am., 1984, asst. scoutmaster, 1986-92; chief YMCA Indian Guides, San Jose, 1977-83. Mem. Am. Assn. Indsl. Engrs. (sr.), Soc. Mfg. Engrs. (sr.), Coun. Logistics Mgmt., Am. Prodn. Inventory Control Soc., Lions (scholar 1966). Republican. Roman Catholic. Home: 1963 Wave Pl San Jose CA 95133-1127 Office: Apple Computer 900 E Hamilton Ave MS 72-RP Campbell CA 95008-0613

SCHMITZ, CHARLES EDISON, evangelist; b. Mendota, Ill., July 18, 1919; s. Charles Francis Schmitz and Lucetta Margaret (Foulk) Schmitz Kaufmann; m. Eunice Magdalene Ewy, June 1, 1942; children: Charles Elwood, Jon Lee. Student, Wheaton Coll., 1936-37, 38, 39; BA, Wartburg Coll., Waverly, Iowa, 1940; BD, Wartburg Theol. Sem., Dubuque, Iowa, 1942, MDiv, 1977. Ordained to ministry Luth. Ch., 1942. Founding pastor Ascension Luth. Ch., L.A., 1942-48, Am. Evang. Luth. Ch., Phoenix, 1948-65; dir. intermountain missions, founding pastor 14 Evang. Luth. Parishes, Calif., Ariz., N.Mex., Fla., 1948-65; evangelist Am. Luth. Ch., Mpls., 1965-73; sr. pastor Peace Luth. Ch., Palm Bay, Fla., 1973-89; pastor-at-large Am. Evang. Luth. Ch., Phoenix, 1989—; charter mem. Navajo Luth. Mission, Rock Point, Ariz., 1960—; pastoral advisor Ariz. Luth. Outdoor Ministry Assn., Prescott, 1958-65, 89—; Kogudus Internat. Retreat master and chaplain, Fla., Berlin and Marbach, Germany, 1990; mem. transition team Fla. Synod, Evang. Luth. Ch. Am., 1985-89. Author: Evangelism for the Seventies, 1970; co-author: ABC's of Life, 1968; assoc. editor Good News mag., 1965-71. Founder, chmn. Ariz. Ch. Conf. on Adult and Youth Problems, 1956-65; vice chmn. synod worship & ch. music com. Am. Luth. Ch., Mpls., 1960-66; chmn. Space Coast Luth. Retirement Ctr., Palm Bay, Fla., 1985-89; chaplain Ariz. chpt. Luth. Brotherhood, 1991—. Named Citizen of Yr., Palm Bay C. of C., 1979. Mem. Nat. Assn. Evangelicals, German Am. Nat. Congress (nat. chaplain), Lions (officer Phoenix and Palm Bay clubs 1952—, Ariz. Dist. 21A chaplain 1994-95), Kiwanis (bd. dirs. L.A. chpt. 1942-48). Republican. Home: 12444 W Toreador Dr Sun City West AZ 85375-1926 *The truly modern person today who, like the scribes of old, would aspire to fulfillment in leadership would do well to remember Jesus' words: "Therefore every scribe who has been trained for the Kingdom of Heaven is like the master of a household who brings out of his treasure what is new and what is old." (Matt. 13:52).*

SCHMITZ, DONNA JEAN, critical care nurse, nurse administrator; b. Des Moines, Sept. 16, 1949; d. William Edgar and Henrietta Genieve (Burch) Bishop; m. Stephen Paul McCarville, Mar. 31, 1976 (div. 1983); 1 child, Christopher Brian; m. Merle Joseph Schmitz, Nov. 19, 1993. ADN, Phoenix Coll., 1971; BSN, Grand Canyon U., Phoenix, 1993. CCRN, BLS, ACLS, RN, Ariz. Staff nurse med. ICU Maricopa Med. Ctr., Phoenix, 1971-73, asst. nurse mgr. med. ICU, 1973-78, asst. nurse mgr. CICU, 1978-87, nurse mgr. CICU, 1987-93, nurse mgr. CICU/med. ICU, 1993-94; program coord. CHF Home Program, Home Health, 1996—. Capt. USAR. Democrat. Roman Catholic. Home: 4541 W Bobbie Ter Glendale AZ 85306-1505

SCHMITZ, JOHN ANTHONY, systems analyst; b. Louisville, July 26, 1955; s. Melvin Anthony and Elizabeth Ann (Jonas) S.; m. Reina Aguila, Apr. 30, 1985; children: Elizabeth, Christopher. BA, Marquette U., 1978. Gen. clk. Fed. Res. Bank of Chgo., Milwaukee Branch, Wis., 1978, check processor, 1979, printer ops., 1979; check processor Fed. Res. Bank L.A., 1979-80, clk. files and old records, 1980-82, cash vault custodian, 1982-86, mail supr., 1986-87, computer analyst, 1988-91, supervising system analyst, 1991—. Home: 1305 N Aileron Valinda CA 91784 Office: Federal Res Bank San Fransisco L A Branch 950 S Grand Ave Los Angeles CA 90015-1422

SCHMOKER, MICHAEL JAMES, educator, writer, journalist; b. Ann Arbor, Mich., Sept. 23, 1954; s. Bartlett James and Mary L. (Daoust) S.; m. Cheryl Raymond, March 22, 1985; children: Michelle, Megan. EdD, U. Ariz., 1996; BS in Edn., No. Ariz. U., 1976, MA in English, 1983. Rsch. analyst Amphitheater Pub. Schs., Tucson, 1988-96; coord. state and fed. projects/continuous improvement Lake Havasu (Ariz.) Public Schs., 1996—; cons. various sch. dists., 1992—; spkr: Forbes Mag. Edn. Seminar, Washington, 1992, W. Edward Deming Seminar, San Jose, Calif., 1993; spl. cons. Phi Delta Kappa, Bloomington, Ind., 1994—. Author: Results: The Key to Continuous School Improvement, 1996; co-Author(with Richard Wilson), Total Quality Education, 1993; contr. articles to profl. jours. Mem. ASCD (yearbook com., 1995). Office: Lake Havasu Pub. Schs 2200 Havasupai Blvd Lake Havasu AZ 86403

SCHNACK, GAYLE HEMINGWAY JEPSON (MRS. HAROLD CLIFFORD SCHNACK), corporate executive; b. Mpls., Aug. 14, 1926; d. Jasper Jay and Ursula (Hemingway) Jepson; student U. Hawaii, 1946; m. Harold Clifford Schnack, Mar. 22, 1947; children: Jerrald Jay, Georgina, Roberta, Michael Clifford. Skater, Shipstad & Johnson Ice Follies, 1944-46; v.p. Harcliff Corp., Honolulu, 1964—, Schnack Indsl. Corp., Honolulu, 1969—, Nutmeg Corp., Cedar Corp.; ltd. ptnr. Koa Corp. Mem. Internat. Platform Assn., Beta Sigma Phi (chpt. pres. 1955-56, pres. city council 1956-57). Established Ursula Hemingway Jepson art award, Carlton Coll., Ernest Hemingway creative writing award, U. Hawaii. Office: PO Box 3077 Honolulu HI 96802-3077 also: 1200 Riverside Dr Reno NV 89503-5459

SCHNAPP, ROGER HERBERT, lawyer; b. N.Y.C., Mar. 17, 1946; s. Michael Jay and Beatrice Joan (Becker) S.; m. Candice Jacqueline Larson, Sept. 15, 1979; 1 child, Monica Alexis. *Father Michael Jay Schnapp was a respected entrepreneur and businessman on the East Coast until his retirement. He introduced innovative approaches in each of the industries in which he held leadership positions. Daughter Monica Alexis Schnapp attends the Pegasus School, a school which specializes in the education of intellectually gifted children* BS, Cornell U., 1966; JD, Harvard U., 1969; postgrad. Pub. Utility Mgmt. Program, U. Mich., 1978. Bar: N.Y. 1970, U.S. Ct. Appeals (2d cir.) 1970, U.S. Supreme, 1974, U.S. Dist. Ct. (so. dist.) N.Y. 1975, U.S. Ct. Appeals (4th and 6th cirs.) 1976, U.S. Ct. Appeals (7th cir.) 1977, U.S. Dist. Ct. (so. dist.) N.Y. 1975, U.S. Dist. Ct. (no. dist.) Calif. 1980, U.S. Ct. Appeals (8th cir.) 1980, Calif., 1982, U.S. Dist. Ct. (cen. dist.) Calif. 1982, U.S. Ct. Dist. (ea. dist.) Calif., 1984. Atty. CAB, Washington, 1969-70; labor atty. Western Electric Co., N.Y.C., 1970-71; mgr. employee rels. Am. Airlines, N.Y.C., 1971-74; labor counsel Am. Electric Power Svc. Corp., N.Y.C., 1974-78, sr. labor counsel, 1978-80; indsl. rels. counsel Trans World Airlines, N.Y.C., 1980-81; sr. assoc. Parker, Milliken, Clark & O'Hara, L.A., 1981-82; ptnr. Rutan & Tucker, Costa Mesa, Calif., 1983-84, Memel, Jacobs, Pierno, Gersh & Ellsworth, Newport Beach, Calif., 1985-86, Memel, Jacobs & Ellsworth, Newport Beach, 1986-87; pvt. practice, Newport Beach, 1987—; AV rated by Martindale Hubbell; bd. dirs. Dynamic Constrn., Inc., Laguna Hills, Calif., 1986—; commentator labor rels. Fin. News Network; commentator Sta. KOCN Radio, 1990-91; lectr. Calif. Western Law Sch., Calif. State U.-Fullerton, Calif. State Conf. Small Bus.; lectr. collective bargaining Pace U., N.Y.C.; lectr. on labor law Coun. on Edn. in Mgmt.; Nat. Vice Chmn., Finance Committee, National Republican Senatorial Committee, N.E. regional coord. Pressler for Pres., 1979-80. Mem. Bus. Rsch. Adv. Coun. U.S. Dept. Labor, Labor Law Consulting Group; bd. dirs. Legal Specialization; trustee Chapman U., 1991-95. Mem. Calif. Bar Assn., Labor Law Consulting Group, Calif. Bd. of Legal Specialization, Balboa Bay Club, The Ctr. Club. Republican. Jewish. Author: Arbitration Issues for the 1980s, 1981, A Look at Three Companies, 1982; editor-in-chief Indsl. and Labor Rels. Forum, 1964-66; columnist Orange County Bus. Jour., 1989-91; contbr. articles to profl. publs. Office: PO Box 9049 Newport Beach CA 92658-1049 *During a 28-year career in employment law, Roger Schnapp has been highly successful in assisting international, nationwide and California employers (including nonprofit organizations) with union avoidance and decertification of existing union representatives, with collective bargaining negotiations providing significant relief from limitations on management's ability to manage, with the development of individualized personnel policies and procedures which permitted these employers to manage in the most cost effective manner and in litigation before courts (including the Supreme Court of the United States), administrative agencies and arbitrators.*

SCHNEBLY, F(RANCIS) DAVID, aerospace and electronics company executive; b. San Francisco, May 1, 1926; s. Frederick Dorsey and Mary Florence (Blake) S.; m. Miriam Louise Ford, Aug. 27, 1949; children: Mary Diane, Linda Marie, Anne Louise, David Albert, Kathleen Marie. BE in Areo. Engring., U. So. Calif., 1950; cert. advanced mgmt., Harvard U., 1970. Project engr. Hiller Aircraft Corp., Palo Alto, Calif., 1950-55, mgr. ops. rsch., 1955-58; mgr. ops. analysis Lockheed Missiles & Space Co., Sunnyvale, Calif., 1958-63, mgr. mil. programs, 1963-65, asst. dir. advanced programs, 1965-67, project mgr. advanced aircraft, 1967-70, dir. airborne systems, 1970-76, dir. remotely piloted vehicles, 1976-83; pres. F. David Assocs., Inc., Santa Rosa, Calif., 1983—; v.p. devel., bd. dirs. Command Systems Group, Inc., Torrance, Calif.; mem. panel U.S. Army Sci. Adv. Bd., Washington, 1965-66; presenter seminars in field. Author: Helicopter Performance Analysis Method, 1955. Pres. Hiller Mgmt. Club, Palo Alto, 1957; capt. Mounted Patrol San Mateo County, Woodside, Calif., 1976. Recipient award U.S. Army Aviation Rsch. and Tech. Labs. Mem. Am. Unmanned Systems Orgn., Am. Assn. Profl. Mgrs., Shack Riders (bd. dirs. 1983-87), Alpha Eta Rho (pres. Iota chpt. 1949). Republican. Home and Office: 1160 Pine St # B Menlo Park CA 94025-3407

SCHNECK, STUART AUSTIN, retired neurologist, educator; b. N.Y.C., Apr. 1, 1929; s. Maurice and Sara Ruth (Knapp) S.; m. Ida I. Nakashima, Mar. 2, 1956; children—Lisa, Christopher. B.S. magna cum laude, Franklin and Marshall Coll., 1949; M.D., U. Pa., 1953. Diplomate Am. Bd. Psychiatry and Neurology (bd. dirs., sec. 1990-91, v.p. 1991-92, pres. 1992-93). Intern Hosp. U. Pa., Phila., 1953-54; resident in medicine U. Colo. Med. Center, Denver, 1954-55, 57-58, resident in neurology, 1958-61; instr. neurology U. Colo. Sch. Medicine, 1959-61; instr. neuropathology Columbia U., N.Y.C., 1961-63; vis. fellow in neurology Vanderbilt Clinic, Columbia-Presbyn. Med. Center, N.Y.C., 1961-63; asst. prof. neurology and pathology U. Colo., 1963-67, assoc. prof., 1967-70, prof., 1970-95, assoc. dean clin. affairs Sch. Medicine, 1984-89, emeritus prof., 1996—; cons. Fitzsimons Army Hosp., VA, Nat. Jewish Hosp.; pres. med. bd. Univ. Hosp., Denver, 1983-89, bd. dirs., 1989-90. Contbr. articles to profl. jours. Served with USAF, 1955-57. USPHS fellow, 1961-63. Mem. AAAS, Am. Acad. Neurology, Am. Assn. Neuropathologists, Am. Neurol. Assn., Alpha Omega Alpha (bd. dirs. 1989-93, treas., pres. 1990-93).

SCHNEIBEL, VICKI DARLENE, public relations administrator; b. Astoria, Oreg., Mar. 11, 1946; d. Howard Stanley and Sally (Thompson) Brandt; m. Lawrence Walter Schneibel, Mar. 18, 1967. AAS, Anchorage Community Coll., 1986; BA, Alaska Pacific U., 1991, MAT, 1994. Cert. profl. sec. Clk. typist The Oregonian, Portland, Oreg., 1964-67; statis. typist Rader Pneumatics, Inc., Portland, Oreg., 1967-71; sec., bookkeeper Larry's Custom Remodeling, Portland, Oreg., 1971-73; bookkeeper Tualatin Hills Pk. & Recreation Dist., Portland, Oreg., 1973-74; pvt. sec. Aloha (Oreg.) Community Bapt. Ch., 1974-79; exec. sec. Hyster Sales Co., Tigard, Oreg., 1979-83, 1st Nat. Bank of Anchorage, 1983-84; office mgr. Control Data Alaska, Anchorage, 1984-86; human resource adminstr. Westmark Hotels, Inc., Anchorage, 1986—; cmty. adv. bd. mgr. Holland Am. Line (parent co. Westmark Hotels, Inc.), 1996—; Cmty. Advisory Bd. Mgr. for Holland America Line (parent co. of Westmark Hotels, Inc.). Author: Let Sleeping Moose Lie, Good Dog!, 1994. Active Anchorage Women's Commn., 1995—, Alaska Worksite Wellness Alliance. Mem. ASTD, Am. Mgmt. Assn., Soc. For Human Resource Mgmt. Lutheran. Home: 6646 Cimarron Cir Anchorage AK 99504-3945 Office: Holland Am Lines 510 L St Ste 400 Anchorage AK 99501

SCHNEIDER, BRENDA LAUREEN, town official; b. Superior, Mont., Sept. 25, 1961; d. Glenn Harvey and Sharron Regina (Montang) Boyes; m. William C. Schneider, Mar. 7, 1981; 1 child, Sheila Rae. Student in bus. acctg., Gt. Falls (Mont.) Comml. Coll., 1980. Cert. mcpl. clk., mcpl. fin. adminstr. Dep. town clk. Town of Superior (Mont.), 1984, town clk., treas., 1984—. Mem. Mont. Clks. Treas.'s and Fin. Officers Assn., Internat. Inst. of Mcpl. Clks., Mcpl. Treas.'s Assn. of the U.S. and Can., Internat. Inst. of Mcpl. Clks. Office: Town of Superior 301 2d Ave E Superior MT 59872

SCHNEIDER, CALVIN, physician; b. N.Y.C., Oct. 23, 1924; s. Harry and Bertha (Green) S.; A.B., U. So. Calif., 1951, M.D., 1955; J.D., LaVerne (Calif.) Coll., 1973; m. Elizabeth Gayle Thomas, Dec. 27, 1967. Intern Los Angeles County Gen. Hosp., 1955-56, staff physician, 1956-57; practice medicine West Covina, Calif., 1957—; staff Inter-Community Med. Ctr., Covina, Calif. Cons. physician Charter Oak Hosp., Covina, 1960—. With USNR, 1943-47. Mem. AMA, Calif., L.A. County med. assns. Republican. Lutheran. Office: 224 W College St Covina CA 91723-1902

SCHNEIDER, CHARLES I., newspaper executive; b. Chgo., Apr. 6, 1923; s. Samuel Hiram and Eva (Smith) S.; m. Barbara Anne Krause, Oct. 27, 1963; children: Susan, Charles I. Jr., Kim, Karen, Traci. BS, Northwestern U., 1944. Indsl. engr., sales mgr., v.p. mktg. and sales Curtis-Electro Lighting Corp., Chgo., 1945-54, pres., 1954-62; pres. Jefferson Electronics, Inc., Santa Barbara, Calif., 1962-64; pres. 3 sub., v.p., asst. to pres. Am. Bldg. Maintenance Industries, Los Angeles, 1964-66; group v.p. Times Mirror Co., Los Angeles, 1966-88, ret.; pvt. investor and cons., 1988—; bd. dirs. Jeppesen Sanderson, Inc., Denver, Graphic Controls Corp., Buffalo, Regional Airports Improvement Corp. Bd. regents Northwestern U., Evanston, Ill.; trustee, past pres. Reiss-Davis Child Study Center, L.A.; bd. govs., past pres. The Music Ctr.; trustee the Menninger Found.; pres. St. John's Hosp. and Health Ctr. Found., Santa Monica, Calif. Served with AUS, 1942-44. Mem. Chief Execs. Orgn. (past pres., bd. dirs.). Clubs: Standard (Chgo.); Beverly Hills Tennis (Calif.); Big. Ten of So. Calif. Home: 522 N Beverly Dr Beverly Hills CA 90210-3318 *An individual's growth and success as a manager are in direct proportion to his or her ability to develop, motivate and lead able, capable people.*

SCHNEIDER, EDWARD LEE, botanic garden administrator; b. Portland, Oreg., Sept. 14, 1947; s. Edward John and Elizabeth (Mathews) S.; m. Sandra Lee Alfarone, Aug. 2, 1968; children: Kenneth L., Cassandra L. BA, Ctrl. Wash. U., 1969, MS, 1971; PhD, U. Calif., Santa Barbara, 1974. From asst. to assoc. prof. botany S.W. Tex. State U., San Marcos, 1974-84, prof., 1984-94, chmn. biology dept., 1984-89, dean sci., 1989-92; exec. dir. Santa Barbara (Calif.) Botanic Garden, 1992—. Author: The Botanical World; contbr. articles to profl. jours. Recipient Presdl. Rsch. award S.W. Tex. State U., 1986, Disting. Alumnus award Ctrl. Wash. U., 1996; grantee NSF, 1980, 90. Fellow Tex. Acad. Sci. (pres. 1992-93); mem. Internat. Water Lily Soc. (bd. dirs., sec. 1989-96, inducted into Hall of Fame), Internat. Pollination Congress, Nat. Coun. Deans, Tex. Assn. Deans. Home: 1140 Tunnel Rd Santa Barbara CA 93105-2134 Office: Santa Barbara Botanic Garden 1212 Mission Canyon Rd Santa Barbara CA 93105-2126

SCHNEIDER, EDWARD LEWIS, medicine educator, research administrator; b. N.Y.C., June 22, 1940; s. Samuel and Ann (Soskin) S. BS, Rensselaer Poly. Inst., 1961; MD, Boston U., 1966. Intern and resident N.Y. Hosp.-Cornell U., N.Y.C., 1966-68; staff fellow Nat. Inst. Allergy and Infectious Diseases, Bethesda, Md., 1968-70; research fellow U. Calif., San Francisco, 1970-73; chief, sect. on cell aging Nat. Inst. Aging, Balt., 1973-79, assoc. dir., 1980-84, dep. dir., 1984-87; prof. medicine, dir. Davis Inst. on Aging U. Colo., Denver, 1979-80; dean Leonard Davis Sch. Gerontology U. So. Calif., L.A., 1986—, exec. dir. Ethel Percy Andrus Gerontology Ctr., 1986—, prof. medicine, 1987—, William and Sylvia Kugel prof. gerontology, 1989—; sci. dir. Buck Ctr. for Rsch. in Aging, 1989—; cons. MacArthur Found., Chgo., 1985-93, R.W. Johnson Found., Princeton, N.J., 1982-87, Brookdale Found., N.Y.C., 1985-89. Editor: The Genetics of Aging, 1978, The Aging Reproductive System, 1978, Biological Markers of Aging, 1982, Handbook of the Biology of Aging, 1985, 95, Interrelationship Among Aging Cancer and Differentiation, 1985, Teaching Nursing Home, 1985, Modern Biological Theories of Aging, 1987, The Black American Elderly, 1988, Elder Care and the Work Force, 1990. Med. dir. USPHS, 1968—. Recipient Roche award, 1964. Fellow Gerontology Soc., Am. Soc. Clin. Investigation; mem. Am. Assn. Retired Persons, U.S. Naval Acad. Sailing Squadron (coach 1980-86). Office: U So Calif Andrus Gerontology Ctr Los Angeles CA 90089-0191

SCHNEIDER, ELAINE FOGEL, special education educator, consultant; b. Bklyn., Mar. 6, 1947; d. Maurice Seymour and Lillian (Marowitz) F.; m. Jack Schneider, June 12, 1977; 1 child, Karli. BA, Hunter Coll., 1967; MA, Queens Coll., 1969, NYU, 1977; PhD, Calif. Coast U., 1985. Cert. tchr.; registered dance/movement therapist; infant massage instr. Speech-lang. pathologist N.Y. Dept. Edn., 1969-72; dir. Dance Theatre, Coconut Grove, Fla., 1972-75; chairperson dept. lang.and speech Lancaster (Calif.) Sch. Dist., 1978-81; exec. dir. Antelope Valley Lang. Movement Therapy, Lancaster, 1981—; exec. dir. Baby Step 1 Antelope Valley Infant Devel., Lancaster, 1983—, exec. dir. First Touch, 1995—, exec. dir. Santa Clarita Baby Steps, scv. therapies, 1996—. Author: Pictures Please! Adult Language Supplement, 1990, The Power of Touch: Infant Message, 1995, In Infants and Young Children, 1996; contbr. articles to profl. jours.. Bd. dirs. Families for Families Resource Ctr., Lancaster, 1993—, United Way, Lancaster, 1988-96; mem. adv. bd. L.A. County Child Care, 1991—; mem. L.A. County teen pregnancy program State of Calif. Interagy. Coord. Coun., 1988—, state coun. appointee, 1988—; mem. Assistance League of Antelope Valley, 1992-94. Recipient L.A. County award Bd. Suprs., 1993, 1994, People Who Make a Difference award Antelope Valley Press, 1994; grantee March of Dimes, 1993. Mem. Am. Speech-Lang.-Hearing Assn. (dir.-elect dist. 7), Am. Dancer Therapy Assn., Am. Speech-Lang. Pathologists in Pvt. Practice, Infant Devel. Assn., Internat. Assocs. Infant Message, Nat. Assn. for Edn. Young Children, So. Calif. Assn. Edn. of Young Children, Calif. Speech Lang. Assn. Office: Antelope Valley Therapies Inc First Touch 540 W Lancaster Blvd Ste 106 Lancaster CA 93534

SCHNEIDER, EUGENE SAUL, microbiologist, laboratory administrator; b. N.Y.C., Apr. 28, 1920; s. Isreal and Gertrude (Mendelsohn) S.; m. Bertha Gollan, Feb. 18, 1945; 1 child, Myles Gordon. BS in Microbiology, Cornell U., 1942. Cert. med. technologist, microbiologist. Microbiologist 50th Gen. Hosp., 1942-45, Morrisania City Hosp., Bronx, N.Y., 1946; rsch. microbiologist Coll. Phys. and Surg., N.Y.C., 1946; microbiologist Tacoma Gen. Hosp., 1946-48; lab. dir. Pierce County Hosp., Tacoma, 1948-52, St. Helens Med. Labs., Tacoma, 1952-68, Nat. Health Labs., Kent, Wash., 1985-92, Meridian Valley Lab., Kent, 1992—; founding pres. Wash. State Soc. Med. Tch., 1947-48, Wash. Soc. AMTs, 1963-66; mem. Stae Commn. on Alcoholism. Contbr. articles to profl. jours.; presenter in field. Mem. Tacoma Coun. on Alcoholism, 1961-75. 1st lt. U.S. Army, 1949-52. Recipient Disting. Citizen award, Olympia, Wash., 1972, Order of Golden Microscope, AMT, 1963. Mem. Anaerobic Soc. of the Ams. Democrat. Jewish. Home: 6810 Opal Ln SW Tacoma WA 98498 Office: Meridian Valley Clin Lab 515 W Harrison Kent WA 98032

SCHNEIDER, GERALD L., plastic surgeon; b. Mechanicsburg, Pa., Oct. 25, 1945; s. Gordon Henry and Pauline Emma (Rife) S.; m. Patricia Davis, July 15, 1978; 1 child, Ross Roberts. BS, No. Ariz. U., 1968; MD, U. Ariz., 1973. Intern Naval Regional Med. Ctr., San Diego, 1973-74; resident in gen. surgery U.S. Naval Hosp., San Diego, 1974-78; resident in plastic surgery U.S. Naval Hosp., Portsmouth, Va., 1978-80; staff surgeon divsn. plastic surgery U.S. Naval Hosp., San Diego, 1981-83, chief divsn. plastic surgery, 1983-84; pvt. practice Flagstaff, Ariz., 1984-90; staff surgeon La Jolla (Calif.) Cosmetic Surgery Ctr., 1990-91; surgeon Scripps Clinic & Rsch. Found., La Jolla, 1991—. Capt. USNR. Fellow ACS; mem. Am. Soc. Plastic and Reconstructive Surgeons, Lipoplasty Soc. North Am. Avocation: golf. Office: Scripps Clinic & Rsch Found 10666 N Torrey Pines Rd La Jolla CA 92037-1027

SCHNEIDER, HARRY H., JR., lawyer; b. San Antonio, Jan. 12, 1954. AB, U. Calif., Berkeley, 1976; JD, U. Chgo., 1979. Bar: Wash. 1979. Mem. Perkins Coie, Seattle. Office: Perkins Coie 40th Flr 1201 3rd Ave Fl 40 Seattle WA 98101-3099

SCHNEIDER, PAUL, writer, retired; b. Passaic, N.J., Aug. 4, 1923; s. Solomon Peter and Rose (Levine) S.; m. Margaret Flood Perrin, Apr. 10, 1951; children: Peggy Lee, Peter Lincoln, Ann. BA, Harvard U., 1945. Writer N.Y.C., Hollywood, Calif., 1954-91; staff writer Universal City Studios, North Hollywood, Calif., 1967-74; head writer Love of Life CBS Studios, N.Y.C., 1974-76. Writer: (TV) Star Trek, 1954-85, Bonanza, 1954-85, Marcus Welby, M.D., 1954-85, (movies) The Looters, 1957, Ride the Wind, 1966, (plays) Effigy, 1983, Acrimonious, 1962. Mem. Writers Guild Am. (chmn. violence com. 1980-81), Harvard Alumni Assn., Dems. for Action. Home: PO Box 65 Idyllwild CA 92549-0065

SCHNEIDER, TAMMI JOY, archaeology educator; b. Detroit, Dec. 28, 1962; d. Edward Schnedier and Ruth Helene (Litwak) Aaron. BA, U. Minn., 1984; PhD in Ancient History, U. Pa., 1991. Coord. Middle East Ctr. U. Pa., Phila., 1991-93; asst. prof. The Claremont (Calif.) Grad. Sch., 1993—; asst. field dir. The Miqne/Ekron Archaeol. Execs., Jeruselem, 1986-94, dir. Tel Safi Excavation, 1994—; project dir. Instity for Antiquity Christianity, Calremont, Calif., 1993—; rsch. asst. Sumerian Dictionary Project, Phila., 1989-91; co-curator Temple Mus. Keneseth Israel, Elkins Park, Pa., 1990. Contbr. articles to profl. jours. Ancient History fellowship U. Pa., 1988-91, grantee, 1989-90; Dorot Travel grantee Dorot Found., 1986, Fletcher Jones grantee, 1995, grantee Claremont Colls. Mellon Tech., 1996-97. Mem. ASOR (trustee 1996—), Israel Exploration Soc., Am. Oriental Soc., Corp. of Am. Schs. of Oriental Rsch. (sec. 1994), Ancient Biblical Manuscript Ctr. (adv. bd.), Assn. of Ancient Historians. Office: The Claremont Grad Sch Harper Hall Rm 22 Claremont CA 91711

SCHNEITER, GEORGE MALAN, golfer, development company executive; b. Ogden, Utah, Aug. 12, 1931; s. George Henery and Bernice Slade (Malan) S.; B. Banking and Fin., U. Utah, 1955; m. JoAnn Deakin, Jan. 19, 1954; children: George, Gary, Dan, Steve, Elizabeth Ann, Michael. With 5th Army Championship Golf Team U.S. Army, 1955-56; assoc. golf pro Hidden

Valley Golf Club, Salt Lake City, 1957; golf pro Lake Hills Golf Club, Billings, Mont., 1957-61, sec., 1957-61, pres., 1964—; pres. Schneiter Enterprises, Sandy, Utah, 1974—; developer Schneiter's golf course, 1973—, and subdiv., 1961—; player PGA tour 1958-78; sr. player PGA tour, 1981—. With U.S. Army, 1955-56. Winner Utah sect. Sr. Championship, Wyo. Open Super Sr. Championship, Salt Lake City Parks Tournament, Vernal Brigham Payson Open, Yuma Open, Ariz.; named U.S. Army Ft. Carson Post Golf Champ, 5th Army Championship Golf Team, 1955-56. Mem. PGA, Am. Mormon, Salt Lake City C. of C., Internat. Golf Course Supertaints Assn. Office: 2009 Brassy Dr Las Vegas NV 89122 *Personal philosophy: I think everyone should try to make the world a better place to live than it was when we entered it and we should try to help each other and live in peace.*

SCHNELL, ROGER THOMAS, retired military officer, state official; b. Wabasha, Minn., Dec. 11, 1936; s. Donald William and Eva Louise (Barton) S.; m. Barbara Ann McDonald, Dec. 18, 1959 (div. Mar. 1968); children: Thomas Allen, Scott Douglas. A in Mil. Sci., Command and Gen. Staff Coll., 1975; A in Bus. Adminstrn., Wayland Bapt. U., 1987. Commd. 2d lt. Alaska N.G., 1959, advanced through grades to col., 1975; shop supt. Alaska N.G., Anchorage, 1965-71, personnel mgr., 1972-74, chief of staff, 1974-87, dir. logistics, 1987; electrician Alaska R.R., Anchorage, 1955-61, elec. foreman, 1962-64; dir. support personnel mgmt. Joint Staff Alaska N.G., 1988-92, ret.; personnel mgr. State of Alaska, 1992; asst. commr. dept. mil. and vets. affairs State of Alaska, Ft. Richardson, 1992-95, dep. commr. dept. mil. and vets. affairs, 1995—. Bd. dirs. Meth. Trust Fund. Mem. Fed. Profl. Labor Relations Execs. (sec. 1974-75), Alaska N.G. Officers Assn. (pres. 1976-78, bd. dirs. 1988—), Am. Legion, Amvets. Republican. Methodist. Lodge: Elks. Home: 6911 Hunt Ave Anchorage AK 99504-1891 Office: Dept Mil and Vets Affairs State of Alaska PO Box 5800 Camp Denali Bldg # 4900 Anchorage AK 99505-5800 *Personal philosophy: Success is built on honesty, hard work, determination, committment and the ability to make personal sacrifices to strive for high professional goals. Always keep a positive attitude and treat each person as you would like to be treated.*

SCHNELL, RUSSELL CLIFFORD, atmospheric scientist, researcher; b. Castor, Alta., Can., Dec. 12, 1944; s. Henry Emmanuel and Anna (Traudt) S.; m. Suan Neo Tan, May 25, 1974; children: Alicia, Ryan. BSc with distinction, U. Alta. (Can.), Edmonton, 1967; BSc, Meml. U., St. John's, Nfld., Can., 1968; MSc, U. Wyo., 1971, PhD, 1974. Research scientist U. Wyo., Laramie, 1971-74, Nat. Ctr. Atmospheric Research and NOAA, Boulder, Colo., 1974-76; dir. Mt. Kenya study World Meteorol. Orgn. div. UN, Nairobi, Kenya, 1976-78; research scientist U. Colo., Boulder, 1979-82, dir. Arctic Gas and Aerosol Sampling Program, 1982-92, fellow Coop. Inst. Research in Environ. Scis., 1985-92; dir. Mauna Loa Observatory, Hilo, Hawaii, 1992—; mem. aerobiology com. Nat. Acad. Sci., 1976-79; cons. UN, Geneva, 1977-80, Shell Devel., Modesto, Calif., 1978-79, Holme, Roberts & Owen, 1990-92; mem. adv. bd. Frost Tech., Norwalk, Conn., 1983-85; bd. dirs. TRI-S Inc., Louisville, Colo., Magee Sci.,. Editor Geophys. Research Letters, Arctic Haze Edit., 1983-84; discovered bacteria ice nuclei, 1969; patentee in field; contbr. articles to profl. jours. Bd. dirs. Boulder Valley Christian Ch., 1978-91; chmn. Boulder Council Internat. Visitors, 1983-85. Rotary Internat. fellow, 1968-69. Mem. Am. Geophys. Union, AAAS, Am. Meteorol. Soc. (cert. cons. meteorologist), Internat. Assn. Aerobiology, Soc. Cryobiology, Sigma Xi, Sigma Tau. Office: Mauna Loa Observatory PO Box 275 Hilo HI 96721-0275

SCHNELLER, EUGENE S., sociology educator; b. Cornwall, N.Y., Apr. 9, 1943; s. Michael Nicholas and Anne Ruth (Gruner) S.; m. Ellen Stauber, Mar. 24, 1968; children: Andrew Jon, Lee Stauber. BA, L.I. U., 1967; AA, SUNY, Buffalo, 1965; PhD, NYU, 1973. Rsch. asst. dept. sociology NYU, N.Y.C., 1968-70; project dir. Montefiore Hosp. and Med. Ctr., Bronx, N.Y., 1970-72; asst. prof. Med. Ctr. and sociology Duke U., Durham, N.C., 1973-75; assoc. prof., chmn. dept. Union Coll., Schenectady, 1975-79, assoc. prof., dir. Health Studies Ctr., 1979-85; prof., dir. Sch. Health Adminstrn. and Policy, Ariz. State U., Tempe, 1985-91, assoc. dean rsch. and adminstrn. Coll. Bus., 1992-94; dir. L. William Seidman Rsch. Ctr., Tempe, 1992-94, counselor to pres. for health profl. edn., 1994-96; clin. prof. cmty. and family medicine U. Ariz., 1995—; prof., dir. Sch. Health Adminstrn. and Policy Ariz. State U., 1996—; vis. rsch. scholar Columbia U., N.Y.C., 1983-84; chmn. Western Network for Edn. in Health Adminstrn., Berkeley, Calif., 1987-92; mem. Ariz. Medicaid Adv. Bd., 1990-92, Ariz. Data Adv. Bd., 1989-91, Ariz. Health Care Group Adv. Bd., 1989; mem. health rsch. coun. N.Y. State Dept. Health, 1977-85; fellow Accrediting Commn. on Edn. for Health Svcs. Adminstrn., 1983-84. Author: The Physician's Assistant, 1980; mem. editorial bd. Work and Occupations, 1975-93, Hosps. and Health Svcs. Adminstrn., 1989-92, Health Adminstrn. Press, 1991-94; Health Mgmt. Review, 1996; contbr. articles to profl. jours., chpt. to book. Trustee Barrow Neurol. Inst., Phoenix, 1989-95; chair nat. adv. com. Nat. Adv. Com. of the Investigator Awards in Health Svcs. Rsch. Robert Wood Johnson Found., 1993-96. Mem. APHA, Am. Sociol. Assn., Assn. Univ. Health Programs Health Adminstrn. (bd. dirs. 1990-96, chmn. bd. dirs. 1994-95). Home: 11843 N 114th Way Scottsdale AZ 85259 Office: Ariz State U Sch Health Admin & Policy Tempe AZ 85287

SCHNITZER, ARLENE DIRECTOR, art dealer; b. Salem, Oreg., Jan. 10, 1929; d. Simon M. and Helen (Holtzman) Director; m. Harold J. Schnitzer, Sept. 11, 1949; 1 child, Jordan. Student, U. Wash., 1947-48; BFA (hon.) Pacific NW Coll. Art., 1988. Founder, pres. Fountain Gallery of Art, Portland, Oreg., 1951-86; exec. v.p. Harsch Investment Corp., 1951—. Apptd. to Oreg. State Bd. Higher Edn., 1987-88; former bd. dirs. Oreg. Symphony Assn., v.p. Oreg. Symphony; former bd. dirs. U.S. Dist. Ct. Hist. Soc.; former bd. dirs. Boys and Girls Club, 1988—; mem. Gov.'s Expo '86 Commn., Oreg.; mem. exec. com., former bd. dirs. Artquake; former mem. adv. bd. Our New Beginnings; past bd. dirs. Artists Initiative for a Contemporary Art Collection; former trustee Reed Coll., 1982-88; mem. exec. com. bd. dirs. N.W. Bus. Com. for Arts.; trustee, mem. exec. com. Oreg. Health Scis. Univ. Found.; mem. arts acquisition and collections com. Portland Art Mus.; mem. Nat. Com. for the Performing Arts, Kennedy Ctr., 1995—; adv. bd. Svcs. to Children and Families, Orgn.; bd. trustees Oreg. Jewish Cmty. Found., 1996—; mem. Nat. Coun. Fine Arts Mus. San Francisco, 1995—. Recipient Aubrey Watzek award Lewis and Clark Coll., 1981, Pioneer award U. Oreg., 1985, Met. Arts Commn. award, 1985, White Rose award March of Dimes, 1987, Disting. Svc. award Western Oreg. State Coll. 1988, Oreg. Urban League Equal Opportunity award 1988, Gov.'s award for Arts, 1987, Woman of Achievement award YWCA, 1987, Disting. Svc. award U. Oreg., 1991, SAFECO Art Leadership award ArtFair/Seattle, 1994, Portland First Citizen award Portland Met. Assn. Realtors, 1995; honored by Portland Art Assn., 1979. Mem. Univ. Club, Multnomah Athletic Club, Portland Golf Club. Office: Harsch Investment Corp 1121 SW Salmon St Portland OR 97205-2000

SCHOBER, ROBERT CHARLES, electrical engineer; b. Phila., Sept. 20, 1940; s. Rudolph Ernst and Kathryn Elizabeth (Ehrisman) S.; m. Mary Eve Kanuika, Jan. 14, 1961; children: Robert Charles, Stephen Scott, Susan Marya. BS in Engring. (Scott Award scholar), Widner U., 1965; postgrad., Bklyn. Poly. Extension at Gen. Electric Co., Valley Forge, Pa., 1965-67, U. Colo., 1968-69, Calif. State U.-Long Beach, 1969-75, U. So. Calif., 1983-84. Engr. Gen. Electric Co., Valley Forge, 1965-68, Martin Marietta Corp., Denver, 1968-69; sr. engr. Jet Propulsion Lab., Pasadena, Calif., 1969-73, sr. staff, 1986—; mem. tech. staff Hughes Semiconductor Co., Newport Beach, Calif., 1973-75; prin. engr. Am. Hosp. Supply Corp., Irvine, Calif., 1975-83; sr. staff engr. TRW Systems, Redondo Beach, Calif., 1983-84; cons. Biomed. LSI, Huntington Beach, Calif. Mem. IEEE (student br. pres. 1963-65), Soc. for Indsl. and Applied Maths., Assn. for computing Machinery, Tau Beta Pi. Republican. Patentee cardiac pacemakers. Current Work: Develop large scale integrated circuits for computer, spacecraft, and military, as well as commercial applications; design high speed signal processing integrated circuits; instrumental in starting the quest for low power integrated circuits; actively persuing the advancment of ultra low power technology; provides dissemination through public domain distribution of a low power MOSIS cell library, workshops and publications. Subspecialties: application specific microprocessor architecture design; ultra low power analog and digital systems and integrated circuits; integrated circuit design; focal plane electronic signal processing arrays, neural networks; synchro converter electronics; sigma-delta analog to digital converters and signal processing electronics; implantable medical devices including cardiac pacemakers, defibulators and hearing aids. Office: Jet Propulsion Lab 4800 Oak Grove Dr Pasadena CA 91109-8001

SCHOCH, DAVID HENRY, real estate executive; b. N.Y.C., May 21, 1947; s. Theodore W. and Carol (Malmquist) S. AB, Syracuse U., 1968; MBA, UCLA, 1971. Cost analyst So. Pacific, San Francisco, 1971-72; acct. Peat Marwick Mitchell & Co., San Francisco, 1972-76; fin. analyst Rocor Internat., Palo Alto, Calif., 1976-77; v.p. property sales McNeil Corp., San Mateo, Calif., 1977-84; v.p. real estate fin. Metric Realty, San Francisco, 1984—. Mem. Am. Fin. Assn., Nat. Assn. Bus. Economists, Bay Area Mortgage Assn. Republican. Lutheran. Office: Metric Realty 1 California St San Francisco CA 94111

SCHOCK, ANTHONY, entertainment executive; b. Eugene, Oreg., Feb. 3, 1959; s. Kaley Cactus and Naida Lou (Casey) S. AA in Hotel Adminstrn., Sawyer Coll., Ventura, Calif., 1992. Writer Sand and Prodns., Ventura, 1992-93; prodr., writer Boss Prodns., Ventura, 1993-95; writer Ojai (Calif.) Voice Newspaper, 1996-97; creative dir. Polar Sport Enterprise, L.A., 1996—; adv. bd. Ojai Voice Newspaper, 1996-97, Polar Sport Enterprise, 1996—. Author intertainment interviews Ojai Voice, 1996; author: (children's book and characters) Surf Tacos Beach Patrol, 1996; author: (comedy TV game show) Comedy Theatre, 1993, (bus. TV game show) You're the Boss, 1995. Home: 2523 #4 Harbor Blvd Ventura CA 90025 Office: Polar Sport Enterprise Ste 421 12335 Santa Monica Blvd Los Angeles CA 90025

SCHOEN, EDGAR JACOB, pediatrician, pediatric endocrinologist; b. Bklyn., Aug. 10, 1925; s. Irving I. and Mathilda (Jacobs) S.; m. Fritzi M. Puehringer, May 15, 1960; children: Melissa, Eric. BS, U. Ill., 1946; MD, NYU, 1948. Intern Lincoln Hosp., N.Y.C., 1948-49; pediatric resident Mass. Gen. Hosp., Boston, 1949-50, 52-54, endocrinology fellow, 1949-50; pediatric and endocrine staff Kaiser Permanente, Oakland, Calif., 1954—; clin. prof. pediatrics U. Calif. Med. Ctr., San Francisco, 1960—; chief pediatrics Kaiser Permanente, Oakland, Calif., 1966-90; sr. cons. in pediatrics, 1990—, med. dir. regional prenatal screening Dept. of Genetics, 1990—; Contbr. over 100 articles to profl. jours. Lt. USNR, 1952-54. Home: 2309 Bywood Dr Oakland CA 94602-2012 Office: Kaiser Permanente Med Ctr 280 W Macarthur Blvd Oakland CA 94611-5642

SCHOEN, STEVAN JAY, lawyer; b. N.Y.C., May 19, 1944; s. Al and Ann (Spevack) S.; m. Cynthia Lukens; children: Andrew Adams, Anna Kim. BS, U. Pa., 1966; JD, Cornell U., 1969; MPhil in Internat. Law, Cambridge U. (Eng.), 1980. Bar: N.Mex. 1970, N.Y. 1970, U.S. Supreme Ct. 1976, U.S. Tax Ct. 1973, U.S. Ct. Internat. Trade 1982. Nat. dir. Vista law recruitment U.S. OEO, Washington, 1970-71; atty. Legal Aid Soc. of Albuquerque, 1971-73; chief atty., spl. asst. atty. gen. N.Mex. Dept. Health and Social Svcs., Albuquerque, 1973-77; ptnr. Brennan, Schoen & Eisenstadt, 1979—, Stevan J. Schoen P.A., 1989—; probate judge, Sandoval County, 1990—; arbitrator, NYSE. mem. N.Mex. Supreme Ct. Appellate Rules Com., 1982-92; chmn. rules com. Com. on Fgn. Legal Cons., 1993, Jud. Edn. Planning Com.; mem. Children's Code Rules Com., 1976-78; bd. edn. Bernalillo Pub. Sch. Dist., 1996-97. Mem. Mayor's Albuquerque Adv. Com. on Fgn. Trade Zone. Recipient Cert. for Outstanding Svc. to Judiciary N.Mex. Supreme Ct., 1982, cert. of Appreciation, N.Mex. Supreme Ct., 1992, Cert. of Appreciation, N.Mex. Sec. of State, 1980, Cert. of Appreciation, U.S. OEO, 1971, Pro Bono Pub. Svc. award 1989, cert. Recognition Legal Aid, 1994, award Las Placitas Assn., 1996. Mem. Am. Judges Assn., Nat. Coll. Probate Judges, State Bar N.Mex. (past chmn. real property, probate and trust sect. 1989, Outstanding Contbn. award 1989, task force on regulation of advt. 1990-91, past chmn. appellate practice sect. 1991, past chmn. internat. law sect. 1991-92, commn. on professionalism 1992-95, organizing com. U.S.-Mex. law inst. 1992), N.Mex. Probate Judges Assn. (chmn. 1993—), Oxford-Cambridge Soc. N.Mex. (sec.), N.Mex. Assn. Counties (adv. bd.). Home: 14 Rainbow Valley Rd Placitas NM 87043-8801 Office: 5700 Harper Dr NE Ste 430 Albuquerque NM 87109-3573

SCHOENBORN, BENNO P., biophysicist, educator; b. Basel, Switzerland, May 2, 1936; came to U.S., 1955; s. Wilhelm and Maria (Dobler) S.; m. Catherine Cowie Kay, Oct. 26, 1962. BA, UCLA, 1958; PhD, U. New South Wales, Australia, 1962; DSc (hon.), N.J. Inst. Tech., 1982. Teaching fellow U. New South Wales, Sydney, 1958-61; postdoctoral fellow U. Calif. Med. Coll., San Francisco, 1962-63; vis. scientist Molecular Biology Lab., Cambridge, Eng., 1966-67; asst. prof. dept. pharmacology U. Calif. Med. Ctr., San Francisco, 1966-67; assoc. prof. dept. pharmacology and biochemistry, 1966-67; biophysicist dept. biology Brookhaven Lab., Upton, N.Y., 1968-74, sr. biophysicist dept. biology, 1974-92, assoc. chmn. dept. biology, 1984-90; head ctr. structural biology, 1984-91; sr. fellow Los Alamos (N.Mex.) Nat. Lab., 1992—; adj. prof. biochemistry Columbia U., N.Y.C., 1978-93; adj. scientist biophysics SUNY, Stony Brook, 1988-92; mem. editorial bd. Biophys. Jour., 1977-80; mem. Reactor Safety Com., 1972-79. Editor: Neutrons in Biology, 1976, 84, 96; contbr. articles to profl. jours.; patent in multilager monochromator, 1975. Recipient E.O. Lawrence award Dept. of Energy, 1980. Mem. Nat. Com. for Crystallography, Biophys. Soc. (coun. mem. 1976-79). Republican. Office: Life Sci Divsn Los Alamos Nat Lab Los Alamos NM 87545

SCHOENDORF, JUDSON RAYMOND, allergist; b. New Orleans, Jan. 13, 1942; s. John Adam and Thelma Elizabeth (Verges) S. BA, Tulane U., 1962; MD, La. State U., 1966; MBA, Pepperdine U., 1992. Lic. physician, La., Calif.; cert. Am. Bd. Med. Mgmt. Intern Charity Hosp. of La., New Orleans, 1966-67; resident in pediatrics L.A. County/U. So. Calif. Med. Ctr., 1969-70; fellow UCLA/Harbor Gen. Hosp., 1970-72; allergist Russell T. Spears, M.D., Long Beach, 1972-76, The Harriman Jones Med. Group, Long Beach, 1976—; chief exec. officer The Harriman Jones Med. Group, 1989-91; pres., CEO, The Harriman Jones Med. Found., 1992-94; staff Kaiser Hosp, Bellflower, 1970-72, Children's Hosp., Long Beach, 1972—, Bauer/St. Mary's Hosp., Long Beach, 1972—, UCLA Hosp., 1972—, Community Hosp., Long Beach, 1977—; faculty UCLA, 1972—, Harbor Gen. Hosp., 1972—, others. Contbr. articles to profl. jours. Bd. dirs. Long Beach Children's Clinic, 1976-81, pres., 1978-81; bd. dirs. Long Beach Symphony Orch., 1985-89; bd. dirs. Am. Lung Assn. Calif., 1985—, exec. com., 1988—; adv. coun. phys. edn. dept. Calif. State U., Long Beach, 1985—; mem. Civil Svc. Commn., City of Long Beach, 1981-89, pres., 1982-83, 85-86; bd. dirs. Long Beach Civic Light Opera, 1986-88; mem. Redevel. Agy., City of Long Beach, 1989—; chair, RDA, 1993—; mem. cultural steering com. Pub. Corp. Arts, Long Beach; bd dirs. Adv. Com. Pub. Art, 1992—; mem. Mayor's Econ. Coun., 1994—, Joint Powers Authority Spring St. Corridor-Long Beach/Singal Hill, 1994—. Lt. USN, 1967-69, capt. USNR, 1985—. Decorated Navy Commendation medal, also others; recipient Katherine White Humanitarian award Long Beach Kiwanis Club, 1995. Mem. Calif. Med. Assn., L.A. County Med. Assn., Long Beach Med. Assn., Acad. Allergy, L.A. Soc. Allergy and Immunology, Am. Coll. Physician Execs. Office: Harriman Jones Med Group 2600 Redondo Ave Long Beach CA 90806-2325

SCHOENFELD, LAWRENCE JON, jewelry manufacturing company executive, travel industry consultant; b. Los Angeles, Nov. 30, 1945; s. Donald and Trudy (Libizer) S.; Carol Sue Gard, Aug. 24, 1969. AA, Los Angeles Valley Coll., Van Nuys, Calif., 1963; BBA, Wichita State U., 1969, MSBA, 1970; grad., US Army Command/Gen Staff Sch., Ft. Leavenworth, Kans., 1988. Cert. tchr., Calif.; lic. real estate broker, Calif. Asst. treas. Advance Mortgage, Los Angeles, 1970-72; v.p. ops. Unigem Internat., Los Angeles, 1972—; pres., L & C Schoenfeld Corp.; bd. dirs. The Schoenfeld Constrn. Co., South Star Wours, Uniorr Corp., Execucentre-West, Schoenfeld & Co., Customer Ground Handling Svc. Corp.; co-developer Los-Osos Mini Storage Co., San Luis Obispo, Calif., El Mercadero World Trade Show, Guatemala, 1986, Snatiago, 1987, Bahai, 1988, Paraguay, 1989, El Mercado, Costa Rica, 1990, Panama City, 1995, Manaus, 1996, Los Osos Mini Storage Co., Quito, 1991, Santa Cruz, 1993; pres. Accents on Beverly Hills, Accents at the Biltmore, Santa Barbara, 1995, Accents on Newport Beach, 1996. Mem. Improvement Commn., Hermosa Beach, Calif. 1976-78. Served to maj. US Army Med. Service Corps, 1970-72, lt. col. with res. 1972—. Mem. South Am. Travel Assn., World Trade Assn. (assoc.), Town Hall, Wichita State U. Alumni Assn. (nat. dist. rep., mem. coun. 1992—), Res. Officers Assn., Brit. Am. C. of C. Jewish. Office: Unigem Internat 350 S Beverly Dr Ste 350 Beverly Hills CA 90212-4817

SCHOENGARTH, R(OBERT) SCOTT, life insurance company executive; b. L.A., June 27, 1949; s. Bruce William and Barbara Agnes (Wiggins) S.; m. Margaret Kathleen Maguire, Nov. 29, 1986; children: Tobey, Mandy. Student, Glendale (Calif.) Coll., 1970; BA in Journalism, Calif. State U., Northridge, 1973. News and sports writer Sta. KFWB, Hollywood, Calif., 1971-72; sports writer Sta. KMPC, L.A., 1973-74; sr. writer, rsch. analyst, asst. dir. sales promotion Transam./Occidental Life Ins. Co., L.A., 1974-79; dir. mktg. svcs. Gt. Am. Life Ins. Co., Beverly Hills, Calif., 1979-81; asst. v.p., dir. mktg. communications Sunset Life Ins. Co., Olympia, Wash., 1981—; workshop host, meeting planner Olympia Visitors and Conv. Bur., 1989, 1st v.p., 1988. Pres. parish coun. Sacred Heart Ch., Lacey, Wash., 1980-85; chmn. credit com. Essell Credit Union, Olympia, 1987-95; lector, eucharistic min., choir leader St. Michael's Ch., Olympia, 1990—, cantor music com.; chmn. Sunset Life's United Way Campaign; bd. dirs., chmn. family svcs. allocations com. United Way Thurston County. Recipient Advt. Excellence award Nat. Underwriter Mag., 1992. Mem. Life Communicators Assn. (exec. com. 1989-90, chmn. ann. meeting 1989, media chmn. 1990-91, award of excellence 1986, 90, 94, Best of Show award 1988, 96, Morgan Crockford award 1989, Spl. Recognition award 1992, ann. meeting arrangements chmn. 1992), Ins. Conf. Planners Assn. Republican. Office: Sunset Life Ins Co 3200 Capitol Blvd S Olympia WA 98501-3304

SCHOENKE, MARILYN LEILANI, foundation administrator; b. Wahiawa, Hawaii; m. Donald N. Basham; children: Neil, Steven, Leilani. BB, Corpus Christi State U. Exec. dir. Moanalua Gardens Found., Hawaii, 1994—. Exec. dir. Lawyer's Care; vol. Am. Cancer Soc. Mem. Alzheimer's Assn. (support svcs. coord., vol.), Manu O Ke Kai Canoe Club, Native Hawaiian C. of C., U.S. Tennis Assn., Hawaii Pacific Tennis Assn. Office: Moanalua Gardens Found 1352 Pineapple Pl Honolulu HI 96819

SCHOENROCK, CHERI MICHELLE, elementary education educator; b. Renton, Wash., Mar. 10, 1961; d. Bruce A.E. and Roberta M. Schoenrock. AA, Bellevue (Wash.) C.C., 1981; BA, N.W. Coll., 1985; MEd, Seattle Pacific U., 1989. Lic. tchr. Wash. Tchr. Spanaway Christian Sch., Tacoma, 1985-92, Neighborhood Christian Sch., Bellevue, 1992-94, Renton Christian Sch., 1994—. Author: (bible curriculum) Assn. Christian Schs. Internat., 1993-94. Rep. precinct com. officer, Issaquah, Wash., 1991-93. Mem. Delta Epsilon Chi. Mem. Assembly of God Church. Home: 8230 Renton-Issaquah Rd SE Issaquah WA 98027 Office: Renton Christian Sch 15717 152nd Ave SE Renton WA 98058

SCHOEPPEL, CYNTHIA LOUISE, human resource executive; b. Wichita, Kans.; d. Robert C. and Rita L. Schoeppel. BA, Kans. State U., 1970; MS, Drake U., 1980. Dist. dir. Camp Fire, Des Moines, 1972-81; tng. specialist Norwest Fin., Des Moines, 1981-87, pers. mgr., 1987-92; pres. The Human Resource Connection, Highlands Ranch, Colo., 1992—. Tng. cons. United Way, Des Moines, 1987-88. Mem. ASTD (pres. Iowa chpt. 1989-92), Soc. Human Resource Mgmt. Office: The Human Resource Connection 3625 W Seramonte Dr Littleton CO 80126-4626

SCHOEPPEL, JOHN FREDERICK, mechanical and electrical engineer, consultant; b. South Bend, Ind., Oct. 25, 1917; s. Frederick Otto and Helen S.; m. Jacqueline Mae Gall, Apr. 17, 1949; children: Pamela Jo, Sonja Lou. BSc, Northwestern U., Evanston, Ill., 1939. Devel. engr. Honeywell, Inc., Mpls., 1939-47; mgr. flight references Lear, Inc., Grand Rapids, Mich., 1947-60; gen. mgr. instrn. and control divsn. Pneumo, Grand Rapids, Mich., 1960-66; dir. new products NWL Corp., Kalamazoo, 1966-71; v.p., gen. mgr. Sundstrand Data Control, Redmond, Wash., 1971-73; exec.. v.p. Verifio Corp., Richmond, Calif., 1974-90, cons. R & D, 1990—. Contbr. articles to profl. jours. Mem. ASTM, Semiconductor Equipment Mfrs. Inst. (com. 1990-92), SEMATECH Standards (com. 1991-93). Republican.

SCHOESLER, MARK GERALD, state legislator, farmer; b. Ritzville, Wash., Feb. 16, 1957; s. Gerald E. and Dorothy (Heinemann) S.; m. Ginger J. Van Aelst, Apr. 8, 1978; children: Veronica, Cody. AA, Spokane (Wash.) C.C., 1977. Mem. Wash. Ho. of Reps., Olympia, 1992—; vice chair agr. ecology, mem. rules, agr. and ecology, fin. chair joint adminstrv. rules rev. coms., 1995-96. Pres. Wash. Friends Farms and Forests, 1991-92; mem. Cmty. Econ. Revitalization Bd. Mem. Wash. Assn. Wheat Growers (dir. 1990-92). Republican. Mem. United. Ch. Christ. Home: Rte 1 Box 151 Ritzville WA 99169

SCHOETTLER, GAIL SINTON, state official; b. Los Angeles, Oct. 21, 1943; d. James and Norma (McLellan) Sinton; children: Lee, Thomas, James; m. Donald L. Stevens, June 23, 1990. BA in Econs., Stanford U., 1965; MA in History, U. Calif., Santa Barbara, 1969, PhD in History, 1975. Businesswoman Denver, 1975-83; exec. dir. Colo. Dept. of Personnel, Denver, 1983-86; treas. State of Colo., Denver, 1987-94, lt. govern., 1995—; bd. dirs. Nat. Jewish Hosp., Nat. Taxpayers' Union; past bd. dirs. Pub. Employees Retirement Assn., Mi Casa Resource Ctr., Women's Bank, Denver, Equitable Bankshares of Colo., Equitable Bank, Littleton; chair Colo. Commn. Indian Affairs, Aerospace States Assn.; mem. bd. trustees U. No. Colo., 1981-87. Mem. Douglas County Bd. Edn., Colo., 1979-87, pres., 1983-87; trustee U. No. Colo., Greeley, 1981-87; pres. Denver Children's Mus., 1975-85. Recipient Disting. Alumna award U. Calif. at Santa Barbara, 1987, Trailblazer award AAUW, 1997. Mem. Nat. Women's Forum (bd. dirs. 1981-89, pres. 1983-85), Internat. Women's Forum (mem. bd. dirs. 1981-89, pres. 83-85), Women Execs. in State Govt. (bd. dirs. 1981-87, chmn. 1988), Leadership Denver Assn. (bd. dirs. 1987, named Outstanding Alumna 1985), Nat. Congress Lt. Govs., Stanford Alumni Assn., Denver Rotary. Democrat.

SCHOFIELD, JAMES ROY, computer programmer; b. Reedsburg, Wis., Aug. 16, 1953; s. G. C. Schofield and Margaret (Collies) Tverberg. BA, Carleton Coll., 1976. Programmer Brandon Applied Systems, San Francisco, 1977-78, Rand Info. Systems, San Francisco, 1979-83; systems programmer IBM, San Jose, Calif., 1983-91; programmer Office of Instnl. Rsch./U. Calif., Berkeley, 1991-94, Datis Corp., San Mateo, Calif., 1994-95, Compuware Corp., Los Gatos, Calif., 1995-96, Pacific Bell, San Ramon, Calif., 1996—. Mem. Assn. for Computing Machinery, Assn. for Computing Machinery Spl. Interest Group in Computers and Soc., Phi Beta Kappa. Home: PO Box 25143 San Mateo CA 94402-5143 Office: Pacific Bell 2600 Camino Ramon San Ramon CA 94583

SCHOLER, DAVID MILTON, religion educator; b. Rochester, Minn., July 24, 1938; s. Milton Norris and Bernice Gladys (Anderson) S.; m. Jeannette Faith Mudgett, Aug. 16, 1960; children: Emily Hancock, Abigail Anne. BA, Wheaton Coll., 1960, MA, 1964; BD, Gordon Div. Sch., 1964; ThD, Harvard U., 1980. Ordained to ministry Am. Bapt. Chs. U.S.A., 1966. Asst. prof., then assoc. prof. N.T. Gordon-Conwell Theol. Sem., South Hamilton, Mass., 1969-81; dean of sem., Julius R. Mantey prof. N.T. No. Bapt. Theol. Sem., Lombard, Ill., 1981-88; Disting. prof. N.T. and early ch. history North Park Coll. and Theol. Sem., Chgo., 1988-94; prof. N.T. Fuller Theol. Sem., Pasadena, Calif., 1994—; mem. gen. bd. Am. Bapt. Chs. U.S.A., Valley Forge, Pa., 1989-92; mem. Bapt. World Alliance-Mennonite World Conf. Dialogue, McLean, Va., 1989-92; vis. scholar, theologian Am. Bapt. Chs. U.S.A., 1985-86. Author: Nag Hammadi Bibliography, 1948-69, 1971, A Basic Bibliographic Guide for New Testament Exegesis, 1973, The Caring God, 1989; assoc. editor N.T. book revs. Jour. Bibl. Lit., 1991-94; contbr. articles, book revs. to profl. publs. Mem. Assn. Theol. Schs. (chair com. on standards 1988-90), Nat. Assn. Bapt. Profs. of Religion (pres. 1986-87), Am. Acad. Religion, Chgo. Soc. Bibl. Rsch. (pres. 1991-92), Inst. for Bibl. Rsch., N.Am. Patristic Soc., Soc. Bibl. Lit., Studiorum Novi Testamentum Soc. Office: Fuller Theol Sem Pasadena CA 91182

SCHOLES, ROBERT THORNTON, physician, research administrator; b. Bushnell, Ill., June 24, 1919; s. Harlan Lawrence and Lura Zolene (Camp) S.; m. Kathryn Ada Tew, Sept. 3, 1948; 1 child, Delia. Student Knox Coll., 1937-38; BS, Mich. State U., 1941; MD, U. Rochester, 1950; postgrad. U. London, 1951-52, U. Chgo., 1953. Intern, Gorgas Hosp., Ancon, C.Z., 1950-51; lab. asst. dept. entomology Mich. State U., 1940-41; rsch. asst. Roselake Wildlife Exptl. Sta., 1941; rsch. assoc. Harvard U., 1953-57; served to med. dir. USPHS, 1954-71, med. officer, dep. chief health and sanitation div. U.S. Ops. Mission, Bolivia, 1954-57, chief health and sanitation div., Paraguay, 1957-60, internat. health rep. Office of Surgeon Gen., 1960-62; br. chief, research grants officer, acting assoc. dir. Nat. Inst. Allergy and Infectious

Diseases, NIH, Bethesda, Md., 1962-71; co-founder, pres. The Bioresearch Ranch, Inc., Rodeo, N.Mex., 1977—; cons. Peace Corps, 1961, Hidalgo County Med. Services, Inc., 1979-93, N.Mex. Health Systems Agy., 1980-86, N.Mex. Health Resources, Inc., 1981-93; Hidalgo County Health Coun., 1993—, Luna County Charitable Found., 1993—. Served to capt. USAAF, 1942-45. Commonwealth Fund fellow, 1953. Mem. AAAS, AMA, N.Y. Acad. Sci., Am. Pub. Health Assn., Am. Ornithologists Union, Sembot Hon. Soc. Contbr. papers to profl. publs. Achievements include research, writing and field test of first health survey indices detailing anthropological parameters; institution of first country wide malaria control project in Paraguay. Home and Office: PO Box 117 Rodeo NM 88056-0117

SCHOLICK, GARY P., lawyer; b. Bronx, N.Y., Apr. 28, 1948. AB cum laude, CUNY, 1968; JD magna cum laude, U. San Francisco, 1974. Bar: Calif. 1974. Extern clerk to Hon. R. L. Sullivan Calif. Supreme Ct., 1974; mem. Littler, Mendelson, Fastiff, Tichy & Mathiason, San Francisco, 1978—; adj. prof. coll. law U. San Francisco., 1987-95. Articles editor U. San Francisco Law Rev., 1973-74. Mem. ABA (EEO com.), State Bar Calif., Bar Assn. San Francisco, McAuliffe Honor Soc., Phi Beta Kappa, Pi Sigma Alpha. Office: Littler Mendelson Fastiff Tichy & Mathiason 650 California St Fl 20 San Francisco CA 94108-2702

SCHOLL, ALLAN HENRY, retired school system administrator, education consultant; b. Bklyn., May 6, 1935; s. Joseph Arnold and Edith (Epstein) S.; m. Marina Alexandra Mihailovich, July 3, 1960. BA, UCLA, 1957; MA, U. So. Calif., 1959, PhD in History, 1973. Lic. gen. secondary tchr. (life), administrv. svcs. (life), jr. coll. tchr. (life) Calif. Tchr. social studies L.A. Unified Sch. Dist., 1960-82, adviser social studies sr. high schs. div., 1982-84, dir. secondary history, social scis. Office Instrn., 1984-91; instr. history L.A. City Coll., 1966-69, U. So. Calif., L.A., 1968-69, Community Coll., Rio Hondo, Calif., 1972-74, Cerritos (Calif.) Coll., 1973-74; dir. ALMAR Ednl. Cons., Pasadena, Calif., 1991—; curriculum developer, writer history tchg. and resource guides; cons. Pasadena Unified Sch. Dist., 1987-88, Coll. Bd., 1980-88, Autry Mus. Western Heritage, 1992—, L.A. Unified Sch. Dist. Office Gifted Programs, 1995—; edn. cons. Am. Odyssey, 1991; cons. H.S. govt. and U.S. history textbooks, 1987; lectr. in history and art history. Author: United States History and Art, 1992; co-author: 20th Century World History: The Modern Era, 1993, History of the World: The Modern Era, 1994, History of the World, 1995; co-developer, contbr.: The Treatment of People of African Descent in Nazi Occupied Europe, 1995, The Holocaust Timeline, 1995, Those Who Dared: Rescuers and Rescued, 1995; cons. Anne Frank in Historical Perspective, 1995; contbr. articles to profl. jours. Bd. dirs. Pasadena Chamber Orch., 1977-78, Pasadena Symphony Orch., 1984-85, Pasadena Centennial Com., 1985; mem. exec. bd., chmn. edn. com. Martyrs Meml. and Mus. of Holocaust of L.A., 1992—; mem. Ednl. adv. bd. Autry Mus. of Western Heritage, 1992—. With U.S. Army, 1958-59. NDEA fellow Russian lang. studies, 1962; Chouinard Art Inst. scholar, 1952. Mem. Am. Hist. Assn., Nat. Coun. Social Studies, Calif. Coun. Social Studies, Soc. Calif. Social Studies Assn. (bd. dirs. 1982-84), Assoc. Adminstrs. L.A. (legis. coun. 1983-85), Crohn's and Colitis Found. Am., Phi Alpha Theta. *Personal philosophy: I have always believed that to achieve in life one should work hard and never give up. That is the only way we can ever hope to make a lasting contribution to society.*

SCHOLL, GLEN, principal; b. Newhall, Calif., Nov. 5, 1946; s. Thomas and Charlotte Avis (Levey) S.; m. Judith Anne Jones, Sept. 10, 1965; children: Marilee, Glena, Douglas, Arlen, Wesley, Laura, Keith. BS, U. Utah, 1969; MA in Edn., No. Ariz. U., 1972. specialist in ednl. adminstrn. Tchr. Fredonia (Ariz.) Pub. Schs., 1969-72; acting prin. Bullhead City (Ariz.) Sch. #15, 1974-75; prin. Bullhead Primary Sch., 1975-78, Bullhead City Intermediate Sch., 1978-89, Copper Rim Elem. Sch., Globe, Ariz., 1989—; pres., v.p. Bullhead City PTA, 1975-76; pres. Bullhead City Roadrunner Bobbysox, 1976-77, Mohave County Sch. Adminstrn., Kingman, Ariz., 1979-80. Dist. commr. Gila Dist. Boy Scouts Am., Globe, 1994 (Silver Beaver award 1987), dist. River Valley Dist., Bullhead City, 1979 (Dist. award Merit 1980). Mem. Nat. Assn. Elem. Sch. Prins., Ariz. Sch. Adminstrs. Assn., Rotary (pres. 1994). Republican. Mem. LDS Ch. Home: 185 Amarillo Dr Globe AZ 85501-1501 Office: Copper Rim Elem Sch 501 E Ash St Globe AZ 85501-2206

SCHOLNICK, JOSEPH B., public relations executive, journalist; b. Bklyn, Dec. 28, 1921; s. Philip and Esther (Kemper) S.; m. Lynne Okon, Aug. 22, 1948; children—Tina M., Eric Nils, Nadia Franzeska. AB, U. Miami, 1950; MS, Northwestern U., 1951; postgrad. in gen. mgmt. Am. Mgmt. Assn., 1958-59. Mem. staff Buffalo Evening News, 1951-56; dir. pub. relations Brown-Forman Distillers Corp., Louisville, 1956-62; contbg. editor Argosy Mag., 1962-65; v.p. pub. relations and communications Calif. World's Fair, Long Beach, 1963-65; gen. mgr. internat. expositions div. Am. Express Co., N.Y.C., 1965-69; pres. Communications Workshop, Long Beach, Internat. Group, Long Beach, 1969—, Creative Travel Svcs. Corp., Long Beach, 1973-89; mng. dir. admissions mktg. Pacific 21 Council, Century City, Los Angeles, 1974-75; dir. advance admissions mktg. Expo 74, Spokane, Wash., 1973-74; dir. mktg. Lion Country Safari, Inc., 1975-77; exec. v.p., chief exec. officer LA 200 Corp., 1977-82; pub. relations liaison U.S. and Can., Mex. Nat. Tourist Council, 1978-84; columnist, travel editor Capitol News Service of Sacramento, 1983—. Served with USAAF, 1942-45. Mem. Internat. Pub. Relations Assn., Pub. Relations Soc. Am., Sigma Delta Chi. Clubs: Nat. Press, Overseas Press, Greater Los Angeles Press. Home: 412 N Bellflower Blvd Unit 121 Long Beach CA 90814-2002

SCHOLTEN, PAUL, obstetrician, gynecologist, educator; b. San Francisco, Oct. 14, 1921; s. Henry Francis and Gladys (Lamborn) S.; m. Marion Lucy O'Neil, Feb. 7, 1948; children: Catherine Mary (dec.), Anne Marie, Pauline Marie, Joseph, Stephen, John. AB, San Francisco State U., 1943; postgrad., Stanford U., 1946-47; MD, U. Calif., San Francisco, 1951. Diplomate Am. Bd. Ob-Gyn. Intern San Francisco Gen. Hosp., 1951-52; resident in ob-gyn U. Calif., San Francisco, 1952-55; pvt. practice specializing in ob-gyn San Francisco, 1955-80; coll. physician Student Health Svc. San Francisco State U., 1956-80, dir. women's svcs. Student Health Svc., 1980-91; pvt. practice San Francisco, 1991—; part-time ship's surgeon Delta Lines, 1980-84; assoc. clin. prof. Med. Sch., U. Calif., San Francisco, 1955—, assoc. clin. prof. Nursing Sch., 1987—; preceptor Med. Sch., Stanford U., 1989-91; lectr. on health and wine at numerous univs., profl. groups. Contbr. articles to profl. publs., chpts. to books. Cons. U.S. Wine Inst.; sci. advisor Calif. State Adv. Bd. on Alcohol-Related Problems, 1980-86; bd. dirs. A.W.A.R.E., Century Coun. Sgt. U.S. Army, 1944-46. Mem. AMA, Calif. Med. Assn., Pan Am. Med. Assn., San Francisco Med. Soc. (editor 1971—, historian, past pres.), San Francisco Gynecol. Soc., Am. Coll. Ob-Gyn., Soc. Med. Friends of Wine (bd. dirs. 1955—, past pres.), San Francisco Wine and Food Soc. (bd. dirs. 1960—, past pres.), Internat. Wine and Food Soc. (gov. 1989—, Bronze medal 1989), San Francisco State U. Alumni Assn. (bd. dirs. 1962—), German Wine Soc., Sierra Club. Republican. Roman Catholic. Home and Office: 121 Granville Way San Francisco CA 94127-1133

SCHOMER, HOWARD, retired clergyman, educator, social policy consultant; b. Chgo., June 9, 1915; s. Frank Michael and Daisy (Aline) S.; m. Elsie Pauline Swenson, Mar. 23, 1942 (dec. Nov. 1996); children: Karine, Mark, Paul, Ellen. B.S. summa cum laude, Harvard U., 1937, postgrad., 1939-40; student, Chgo. Theol. Sem., 1938-39, 40-41, D.D., 1954; LL.D., Olivet Coll., 1966. Ordained to ministry Congl. Ch., 1941. Student pastor Fitzwilliam, N.H., Oak Park, Ill.; asst. dean U. Chgo. Chapel., 1940-41; counsellor Am. history Harvard U., 1939-40; civilian pub. service Am. Friends Service Com., 1941-45; Am. Bd. Mission fellow to chs. of Europe Chambon-sur-Lignon, France, 1946-55; history tchr., work camp dir. Coll. Cevenol; founder internat. conf. center Accueil Fraternel, Permanent Conf. Protestant Chs. in Latin Countries of Europe; asst. to rapporteur UN Commn. on Human Rights, UN Econ. and Social Council, 1947-48; inter-church aid sec. for Europe World Council Chs., Geneva, 1955-58; pres., prof. ch. history Chgo. Theol. Sem., 1959-66; exec. dir. dept. specialized ministries Div. Overseas Ministries, Nat. Council Chs., N.Y.C., 1967-70; participant integration demonstrations in Ala., Ga., Washington, Chgo., SCLC, 1960-66; world issues sec. United Ch. Bd. World Ministries, 1971-80; Indochina liaison officer World Council of Chs., 1970-71; United Ch. of Christ officer for social responsibility in investments, 1972-81; founder, dir. Corp. Adv. Services, 1980-90; founder, mem. United Ch. Christ Working Group with United Ch. in German Democratic Rep. and Fed. Rep. of Germany, 1977-86; vis. prof. religion and society Andover Newton Theol. Sch., 1981; vis. lectr. Manchester Coll., St. John's U.; Woodrow Wilson vis. fellow Drew U., 1981; pres. Internat. Fellowship of Reconciliation, 1959-63, v.p., 1963-65; participant 1st-3d assemblies World Council Chs., Amsterdam, 1948, Evanston, 1954, New Delhi, 1961; rep. UN non-govt. orgn. UNIAPAC, 1979-85; pastoral assoc. First Congl. Ch. (United Ch. Christ), Montclair, N.J., 1983-89; delegated observer Vatican Council II, 1963; v.p. Am. Friends Coll. Cevenol., 1981-89; bd. dirs. Interfaith Center for Corp. Responsibility, 1973-81; chmn. exec. com. Freedom of Faith - A Christian Com. for Religious Rights, 1978-81; mem. nat. adv. bd. N.Y. State Martin Luther King Jr. Inst. for Nonviolence, 1989-92. Translator: The Prayer of the Church Universal (Marc Boegner), 1954; editor: The Oppression of Protestants in Spain, 1955, the Role of Transnational Business in Mass Economic Development, 1975; editor-at-large Christian Century, 1959-70; contbr.; Business, Religion and Ethics-Inquiry and Encounter, 1982, Aspects of Hope, 1993; articles to religious and interdisciplinary publs.; corr. in U.S. for Évangile et Liberté, 1988—. Past co-chmn. Chgo. Com. for Sane Nuclear Policy; bd. dirs. World Conf. on Religion and Peace, 1974-84, sec. for Kampuchea issues, 1979-81; former trustee Am. Waldensian Aid Soc.; mem. internat. council Internat. Ctr. Integrative Studies, 1984-91, bd. dirs., 1987-91; trustee Internat. Inst. for Effective Communication, 1987-93; bd. dirs. Alternative Lifelong Learning, 1992—, Cambodian Found. for Justice, Peace and Devel., 1993—. Mem. ACLU, Wider Quaker Fellowship, Fellowship Reconciliation, Ctr. for Theology and the Natural Scis., Outlook Club (Berkeley), Harvard Club San Francisco, Phi Beta Kappa. Home: 110 41st St Apt 512 Oakland CA 94611-5240 *The human capacity to hope and the power of hope to achieve either good or evil are astonishing. Reasonable hope for the better calls simply for dedicated effort. Mystical hope for the perfect demands consecrated surrender.*

SCHONER, STEVEN RONALD, park ranger; b. L.A., Jan. 28, 1951; s. Eugene Harry and Nancy Ann (Truscello) S.; m. Diane Herman, July 30, 1978; 1 child, Anna Rachel. BS in Philosophy, No. Ariz. U., 1975. Lectr., tour guide Lowell Obs., Flagstaff, Ariz., 1971-74; machinist Mack Corp., Flagstaff, 1978-82, W. L. Gore and Assocs., Flagstaff, 1982-86; park svc. ranger Nat. Park Svc., Flagstaff, 1988—; dir., founder Am. Meteorite Survey, Flagstaff, 1978—. Dir. Right to Vote Com., Flagstaff, 1981-84. Mem. Gold Prospectors Assn. Am., Internat. Platform Assn. Republican. Home: 3 N Bonito St Flagstaff AZ 86001-5333 Office: Nat Park Svc 2717 N Steves Blvd Ste 3 Flagstaff AZ 86004-3959

SCHOOLEY, O. B., commercial airport executive. Airport dir. John Wayne Airport, Costa Mesa, Calif. Office: John Wayne Airport 3151 Airway Ave K101 Costa Mesa CA 92626

SCHOOLEY, ROBERT T., medical educator; b. Denver, Nov. 10, 1949; s. Robert Enoch and Lelia Francis (Barnhill) S.; m. Pamela Owen Cook, Mar. 29, 1972; children: Kimberly Dana, Elizabeth Kendall. BS, Washington and Lee U., 1970; MD, Johns Hopkins U., 1974. Diplomate Am. Bd. Internal Medicine. Intern Johns Hopkins Hosp., Balt., 1974-75, resident, 1975-76; clin. assoc. lab. clin. investigation Nat. Inst. Allergy & Infectious Disease, NIH, Bethesda, Md., 1976-77, chief clin. assoc. lab. clin. investigation, 1977-78, med. officer lab. clin. investigation, 1978-79; from instr. to assoc. prof. medicine Harvard Med. Sch., Boston, 1979-90; prof. medicine U. Colo., Denver, 1990—; cons. internal medicine Mass. Eye and Ear Infirmary, Boston, 1980-85, cons. infectious diseases Harvard U. Health Svcs., Cambridge, Mass., 1982-90. mem. editorial bd. Anrimicrobial Agts. and Chemotherapy, 1987—, Biotherapy, 1987-95, Jour. Acquired Immune Deficiency Syndromes, 1988—, Clin. and Diagnostic Lab. Immunology, 1992; contbr. articles to profl. jours. Clin. and rsch. fellow Infectious Disease Unit, Mass. Gen. Hosp., Boston, 1979-81; rsch. fellow Medicine Harvard Med. Sch., 1979-81. Fellow Infectious Disease Soc. Am.; mem. AAAS, Am. Assn. Immunologists, Am. Soc. Clin. Investigation, Assn. Am. Physicians, Omicron Delta Kappa. Office: U Colo Health Sci Ctr 4200 E 9th Ave B-168 Denver CO 80262

SCHOONOVER, MARGARET See LEFRANC, MARGARET

SCHOPF, JAMES WILLIAM, paleobiologist; b. Urbana, Ill., Sept. 27, 1941; s. James Morton and Esther Julie (Nissen) S.; m. Julie Morgan, Aug. 7, 1965 (div. 1979); 1 child, James Christopher; m. Jane Shen, Jan. 16, 1980. A.B. with high honors, Oberlin Coll., 1963; A.M., Harvard U., 1965, Ph.D. (Harvard fellow, NSF fellow), 1968. Research chemist NASA, Ames Research Center, Calif., 1967; mem. lunar sample preliminary exam. team Manned Spacecraft Center, Tex., 1968-71; asst. prof. dept. earth and space scis. UCLA, 1968-70, assoc. prof., 1970-73, prof., 1973—, mem. Inst. Evolutionary and Environ. Biology, 1970-76, mem. Inst. Geophysics and Planetary Physics, 1973—, dean honors div. Coll. Letters and Sci., 1983-85, dir. Ctr. for Study Evolution and Origin of Life, 1985—, Sigma Xi Disting. lectr., 1976, Rubey lectr., 1976, Golden Yr. Disting. lectr., 1980, Faculty Research lectr., 1984; Sigma Xi Disting. lectr. U. Cin., 1980; Disting. lectr. Buffalo Mus. Sci., 1982; J.A. Bownocker lectr. Ohio State U., 1982; vis. lectr. Am. Inst. Biol. Scis. Vis. Biologists Program, 1969-72; M.W. Haas vis. disting. prof. geology U. Kans., 1979; extraordinary vis. prof. exobiology U. Nijmegen, Netherlands, 1980-81; C. O'Neal lectr. Ohio Wesleyan U., 1982; Sandia disting. lectr. U. N.Mex., 1985; Sigma Xi disting. lectr. U. Oreg., 1985; Du Pont disting. lectr. U. Ill., 1985; R. Stanier disting. lectr. U. Calif.-Berkeley, 1987; H.P. Mangelsdorf disting. lectr. U. N.C., 1987; mem. Bot. Soc. Am. del., People's Republic China, 1978; Academia Sinica vis. research scientist, People's Republic China, 1981, 82; mem. NASA Terrestrial Bodies Sci. Working Group, 1975-76, space program adv. council NASA Life Scis. Com., 1976-78, NASA Working Group on Origins of Life, 1978-79, NASA Space Sci. Adv. Com., 1979-82, mem. NASA Life Scis. Strategic Planning Study Com., 1985—; Alan T. Waterman Award com. NSF, 1978-81; mem. working group on precambrian biostratigraphy Internat. Geol. Correlation Program, UNESCO, 1975—; mem. Working Group on Cambrian-Precambrian Boundary, 1976—; mem. adv. com. USSR and Eastern Europe, Commn. Internat. Relations NRC, 1981-85, mem. bd. earth sci. Commn. Phys. Scis., Math. and Resources, 1982-85, mem. space sci. bd., 1983-86; mem . com. on guidelines for paleontol. collecting, 1984-86, sub.-com. on evolution and diversity Commn. on Life Scis., 1986; mem. com. space research Internat. Council Sci. Unions. Mem. editorial bd.: Origins of Life, 1973—, Precambrian Research, 1973—, Evolutionary Theory, 1973—, U. Calif. Press, 1973-82, Paleobiology, 1974-83, Geomicrobiology Jour., 1977—, Evolutionary Monographs, 1977—; contbr. articles to profl. jours. Bd. dirs. Brentwood Glen (Calif.) Assn., 1972-75; trustee UCLA Found., 1983-85. Recipient N.Y. Bot. Garden award Bot. Soc. Am., 1966; Group Achievement award NASA, 1969; Outstanding Paper award Jour. Paleontology, 1971; Charles Schuchert award Paleontol. Soc., 1974; Disting. Teaching award UCLA, 1977; Alan T. Waterman award NSF, 1977; G. Hawk award U. Kans., 1979; spl. recognition diploma NASA, 1979; Outstanding Vol. in Phys. Scis. award Am. Assn. Pubs., 1983; Mark Clark Thompson medal Nat. Acad. Scis., 1986; Guggenheim fellow, 1973; U.S. Nat. Acad. Scis. exchange scientist USSR, 1975. Fellow Geol. Soc. Am. (vice-chmn. Cordilleran sect. 1983-84, chmn. 1984-85); mem. Bot. Soc. Am. (com. on sci. liaison with People's Republic China 1978—), Paleontol. Soc. (mem. Schuchert Award com. 1978-82), Internat. Soc. Study of Origin of Life (treas. 1977-83, nat. meeting adv. com. 1980, 83, 86, councilor, 1983—), Geochem. Soc. (nominating com. 1980-82), Soc. Study of Evolution (edn. com. 1980-83), Am. Philos. Soc., Sigma Xi (treas. UCLA chpt. 1972-74, chpt. v.p. 1984-84, pres. 1984-85). Office: U Calif Dept Earth And Scis Los Angeles CA 90024*

SCHOPPA, ELROY, accountant, financial planner; b. Vernon, Tex., Aug. 25, 1922; s. Eddie A. and Ida (Foerster) S.; m. Juanita C. Young, Aug. 11, 1956 (div.); children: Karen Marie, Vickie Sue; m. Gail O. Evans, May 12, 1984; stepchildren: Veronica, Vanessa. BBA, Tex. Tech U., 1943; postgrad. Law Sch., U. Tex., 1964-47; M.S., Mich. State U., 1950. CPA, Tex., Calif.; cert. real estate broker; cert. ins. agt. Mem. faculty Tex. Tech U., Lubbock, 1943, U. Tex., Austin, 1946-47, Mich. State U., East Lansing, 1947-50; auditor Gen. Motors Corp., 1950-56; dir. systems and procedures Fansteel Metall. Corp., 1956-59; gen. auditor Consol. Electro Dynamics Corp., 1959-60; auditor, sr. tax acct. Beckman Inst. Inc., Fullerton, Calif., 1960-70; pres. Elroy Schoppa Acctg. Corp., La Habra, Calif., 1960—; fin. planner Nat. Assn. Stock Dealers; cons. to bus. Treas. La Habra Devel. Corp.; organizer, pres. 4-H Club, Vernon; adviser Jr. Achievement, Waukegan, Ill.; bd. dirs. Klein Ctr. for Prevention of Domestic Violence; asst. football and basketball coach, Manzanola, Colo.; coach Am. Girls Sport Assn., La Habra. Served with USN, 1942-46; USNR, 1946-62. Mem. Calif. Soc. CPA's, Alpha Phi Omega, Theta Xi. Republican. Lutheran. Club: Phoenix (Anaheim, Calif.). Avocations: hunting, fishing, camping, traveling. Office: 801 E La Habra Blvd La Habra CA 90631-5531

SCHOPPE, JAMES HENRY, printing company executive, retired; b. Des Moines, Feb. 27, 1936; s. John Everett Sr. and Mary Lucile (Heizer) S. Grad. high sch., Gresham, Oreg. Founder, proprietor Schoppe Printing Co., Portland, Oreg., 1960—; pub. Schoppe Bookcrafters, Portland, 1992-95, retired, 1995. Editor: Hope Chimes, 1951-67; author: The Supreme Peacemakers, 1991; news writer The Vanguard (USAF Air Base newspaper), 1957; news editor: The Vanguard (Portland State U.), 1959. Precinct committeeman Rep. party, 1960-69. Presbyterian. Office: Schoppe Printing Co 2317 S E 146th Ave Portland OR 97233-2715

SCHOR, SUZI, lawyer; b. Chgo., Feb. 1, 1947; d. Samuel S. and Dorothy Helen (Hineline); 1 child, Kate. BABA, Ind. U., 1964; MBA Mktg., Northwestern U., 1967, JD, 1970; PhD in Fine Arts (hon.), U. Nev., PhD in Clin. Psychology, 1989. Bar: Ill., 1971. Pvt. practice L.A., 1971-80; v.p. legal affairs Little Gypzy Mgmt., Inc., Beverly Hills, Calif., 1980—; mem. Pres.'s Coun. on Alcoholism. Author: 13th Step to Death, 1995; contbg. author Wine and Dine Mag.; contbr. articles to profl. jours. Bd. dirs. Nat. Ctr. for Hyperactive Children, L.A., 1989-91, sec. Rainbow Guild Cancer Charity, L.A., 1985-89, ind. cons. Jewish Legal Aid, L.A., 1988—; campaign coord. advisor Dem. Nat. Campaign, L.A., 1990, 94; active L.A. Coun. on World Affairs. Recipient Poet of Yr. award Nat. Libr. and Assn. of Poetry, 1995. Mem. ABA (criminal justice com. 1994), AAUW, NAADAC, CAADAC, L.A. Breakfast Club (chmn. entertainment 1988-90), Rotary, Mensa. Jewish.

SCHORR, MARTIN MARK, forensic psychologist, educator, writer; b. Sept. 16, 1923; m. Dolores Gene Tyson, June 14, 1952; 1 child, Jeanne Ann. Student Balliol Coll., Oxford (Eng.) U., 1945-46; AB cum laude, Adelphi U., 1949; postgrad., U. Tex., 1949-50; MS, Purdue U., 1953; PhD, U. Denver, 1960; postgrad., U. Tex. Diplomate in psychology; diplomate Am. Bd. Profl. Disability Cons., Am. Bd. Forensic Examiners, Am. Bd. Forensic Medicine; lic. clin. psychologist. Chief clin. psychol. svcs. San Diego County Mental Hosp., 1963-67; clin. dir. human services San Diego County, 1963-76; pvt. practice, forensic specialist San Diego, 1962—; forensic examiner superior, fed. and mil. cts., San Diego, 1962—; prof. abnormal psychology San Diego State U., 1965-68; chief dept. psychology Center City (Calif.) Hosp., 1976-79; cons. Dept. Corrections State of Calif., Minnewawa, 1970-73, Disability Evaluation Dept. Health, 1972-75, Calif. State Indsl. Accident Commn., 1972-78, Calif. Criminal Justice Adminstrn., 1975-77, Vista Hill Found., Mercy Hosp. Mental Health, Foodmaker Corp., Convent Sacred Heart, El Cajon, FAA Examiner. Author: Death by Prescription, 1988, Betrayal, 1997; dir. Alpha Centauri Prodns. Recipient award for aid in developing Whistle Blower Law Calif. Assembly, 1986. Fellow Internat. Assn. Social Psychiatry, Internat. Biog. Assn. (life: Great Britain), Am. Coll. Forensic Examiners (life), Am. Bd. Forensic Med.; mem. AAAS, PEN, APA, Am. Acad. Forensic Scis. (qualified med. evaluator), Internat. Platform Assn., World Mental Health Assn., Mystery Writers Am., Nat. Writers Club, Mensa. Home: University City 2970 Arnoldson Ave San Diego CA 92122-2114 Office: 275 F St Chula Vista CA 91910-2820 *Personal philosophy: Some wag once said that the hardest thing one learns in life is which bridge to cross and which to burn!.*

SCHOVILLE, DENNIS A(RNOLD), lawyer; b. Richland Ctr., Wis., May 31, 1945. BS, U. Wis., 1967; JD with Distinction, Ill. Inst. Tech., 1973; LLM, Northwestern U., 1974. Bar: Wis. 1973, Ill. 1973, U.S. Dist. Ct. (no. dist.) Ill. 1973, Calif. 1974, U.S. Dist. Ct. (so. dist.) Calif. 1974, U.S. Ct. Appeals (9th cir.) 1985, U.S. Ct. Claims. Ptnr. Schoville & Arnell, San Diego. Capt. U.S. Army, 1968-73. Recipient Broderick award for professionalism, integrity and ethics, 1996; named Consumer Attys. San Diego Trial Lawyer of the Yr., 1995. Mem. ABA, ATLA, Am. Bd. Trial Advocates, Ill. State Bar Assn., State Bar Wis., State Bar Calif., San Diego County Bar Assn., San Diego Trial Lawyers Assn. (Outstanding Trial Advocacy award-civil 1984, 89, 94). Office: Schoville & Arnell 600 W Broadway Ste 2800 San Diego CA 92101

SCHOW, TERRY D., state official; b. Ogden, Utah, Dec. 14, 1948; s. Hugh Stuart Sloan and Minnie Aurelia (Ellis) Mohler; m. June Hansen, Feb. 14, 1973; children: Amy, Jason. AD, Honolulu C.C., 1975; BA, Chaminade U., 1975. Cert. in mgmt., Utah. Spl. and criminal investigator State of Utah, Ogden, 1976-83, lead investigator, 1984-92; investigator Fed. Govt., Salt Lake City, Denver, 1983-84; mgr. State of Utah, Ogden, 1992—. Mem. Gov.'s Coun. on Vets. Issues, 1989—, chmn., 1990—; mem. State of Utah Privatization Policy Bd., 1989-92; chmn. 1st Congressional Dist. Utah Rep. Party, 1982-83, mem. state exec. com., 1982-83; chmn. legis. dist. Weber County Rep. Party, Ogden, 1987-91, 93—; trustee Utah's Vietnam Meml., Salt Lake City, 1988—; leader Boy Scouts Am., Ogden, 1985—. Sgt. U.S. Army, 1967-70, 72-76; Vietnam. Decorated Bronze Star, 1970, Combat Inf. Badge, 1970; recipient Championship Team Trophy Pistol U.S. Army, 1975. Mem. DAV (life Weber chpt. 4, comdr. 1993—, state 3d jr. vice comdr. 1992, state 2d jr. vice comdr. 1993—, state sr. vice comdr. 1994, state comdr. 1995—), NRA (life), VFW, AL (comdr. Ogden post 9 1996-97, dist. vice comdr. 1996-97), Utah Peace Officers Assn., Utah Pub. Employees Assn. (bd. dirs. 1988-89, v.p. 1989-92, pres. 1992-93, chmn. Ogden Valley dist.), Kiwanis (Ogden chpt. pres. 1992-93, pres. Layton chpt. 1985-86, named Kiwanian of Yr. 1982-83, lt. gov. divsn. 3 ut/ld dist. Kiwanis internat. bd. dirs., 1995—, homeless vets. fellow Ogden 1992—, Weber County vets. meml. com. 1994—). Republican. Mormon. Home: 4045 Bona Villa Dr Ogden UT 84403-3203 Office: State of Utah Office Recoveries 2540 Washington Blvd Fl 4 Ogden UT 84401-3112

SCHRADER, HARRY CHRISTIAN, JR., retired naval officer; b. Sheboygan, Wis., Aug. 4, 1932; s. Harry Christian and Edna Flora (Stubbe) S.; m. Carol Joan Gossman, June 23, 1956; 1 child, Mary Clare. BS, U.S. Naval Acad., 1955; MS, U.S. Naval Postgrad. Sch., 1963. Commd. ensign USN, 1955, advanced through grades to vice adm., 1982; comdr. U.S.S. Tawasa, 1963-64, U.S.S. A. Hamilton, 1970-72, U.S.S. Jackson, 1972-73, U.S.S. Gilmore, 1973-75, U.S.S. Long Beach, 1975-78; dir. MLSF Amphibious, Mine Warfare and Advanced Vehicles div. Office Naval Ops., Washington, 1978-80; comdr. Cruiser Destroyer Group One, San Diego, 1980-82, Naval Surface Forces, U.S. Pacific Fleet, San Diego, 1982-85; ret. USN, 1985; mgr. Middle East/NATO programs, autonetics div. Rockwell Internat., Anaheim, Calif., 1985-87; pres. Coronado (Calif.) Tech. Internat., 1987; bd. dirs. Continental Maritime Industries, Inc.; adv. bd. Levine-Fricks, Recco, Inc. Mem. Am. Def. Preparedness Assn., San Diego Oceans Found. (mem. adv. bd.), Sigma Xi.

SCHRADER, LAWRENCE EDWIN, plant physiologist, educator; b. Atchison, Kans., Oct. 22, 1941; s. Edwin Carl and Jenna Kathryn (Tobiason) S.; m. Elfriede J. Massier, Mar. 14, 1981. BS, Kans. State U., 1963; PhD, U. Ill., 1967; grad., Inst. Ednl. Mgmt., Harvard U., 1991. Asst. prof. dept. agronomy U. Wis., Madison, 1969-72; assoc. prof. U. Wis., 1972-76, prof., 1976-84; prof., head dept. agronomy U. Ill., Urbana, 1985-89; dean Coll. Agr. and Home Econs. Wash. State U., Pullman, 1989-94, prof. dept. horticulture, 1994—; chief competitive rsch. grants office Dept. Agr., Washington, 1980-81; trustee, treas. Agrl. Satellite Corp., 1991-94. Contbr. chpts. to books, articles to profl. jours. Active Consortium for Internat. Devel., 1989-94, chair fin. com., vice chair exec. com., 1990-92, trustee 1989-94; mem. exec. com. Coun. Agrl. Heads of Agr., 1992-94. Capt. U.S. Army, 1967-69. Recipient Soybean Researchers Recognition award 1983, Disting. Service award in Agriculture Kansas State U., 1987; Romnes Faculty fellow U. Wis., 1979. Fellow AAAS (steering group sect. agr. 1991-95, chair-elect sect. on agr., food and renewable resources 1995-96, chmn. 1996-97, past chmn. 1997-98), Am. Soc. Agronomy, Crop Sci. Soc. Am.; mem. Am. Soc. Plant Physiologists (sec. 1983-85, pres.-elect 1986, pres. 1987), Am. Chem. Soc., Blue Key, Sigma Xi, Gamma Sigma Delta, Phi Kappa Phi, Phi Eta Sigma, Alpha Zeta. Methodist. Home: 3504 Crestview Rd Wenatchee WA 98801-9668 Office: Wash State U Tree Fruit Rsch & Extension Ctr 1100 N Western Ave Wenatchee WA 98801-1299

SCHRADER, ROBERT WESLEY, judge; b. Cheyenne, Wyo., Feb. 3, 1944; s. Marvin Glen and Bertha Lorene (Winingar) S.; m. Betty Ann Pruter, June 14, 1964; children: Christina Lynn, Tashana Dee. AA in Mortuary Sci., San Francisco Mortuary Sci., 1965; BSBA, U. Wyo., 1967, JD, 1979. Bar: Wyo., 1978, U.S. Dist. Ct. Wyo., 1978 U.S. Ct. Appeals (10th cir.), 1979, U.S. Supreme Ct., 1991. Assoc. Omohundro & O'Brien, Buffalo, Wyo., 1978-80; pvt. practice Schrader Law Office, Buffalo, 1980-84; ins. commr. State Wyo., Cheyenne, 1984-86; pvt. practice Schrader Law Office, Cheyenne, 1986-92; dist. ct. commr. 1st Jud. Dist., Cheyenne, 1987—; justice of the peace, Johnson County, Wyo., 1980-84; dist. ct. commr. 4th Jud. Dist., Johnson County, 1981-84; pres., bd. mem. Attention Homes, Inc., Cheyenne, 1983—; pres. Scottish Rite Found., Cheyenne, 1992—. Heels, Cheyenne Frontier Days, 1979—; Wyo. races officer Wyo. Emergency Mgmt. Agy., Cheyenne, 1991—. Capt. U.S. Army, 1967-70, Vietnam, lt. col. USAFR ret. 1994. Decorated three Meritorious Svc. medals USAF, Combat Med. badge U.S. Army, Vietnam, 1968. Mem. VFW Post 11454 (adv.), Burns Lodge 41 AF&AM (past master), Scottish Rite Bodies, York Rite Bodies, Korein Shrine (chief clown), Phi Epsilon Phi. Republican. Episcopalian. Home: 607 Monte Carlo Dr Cheyenne WY 82009 Office: First Jud Dist Dist Ct 309 W 20th St Cheyenne WY 82001-3601

SCHRADER, WILLIAM P., organization executive, farmer; b. Phoenix; m. Bondena; children: Alissa Schrader Urshel, William P. Jr., Larry, Travis. Student, Ariz. State U. Bd. dirs. Salt River Project, Phoenix, 1964-90, v.p. bd., 1990-94, pres., 1994—; pres. Schrader Farms, Inc. Bd. dirs. Greater Phoenix Econ. Coun., Groundwater Users Adv. Coun.; mem. Maricopa C.C.'s Found., East Valley Partnership, Scottsdale (Ariz.) Mcpl. Corp.; former mayor and mem. city coun. City of Scottsdale; 1st chmn. Parada del Sol, Scottsdale Rodeo. Named to Scottsdale Hall of Fame; named Citizen of Yr., City of Scottsdale. Mem. Am. Pub. Power Assn., Am. Mgmt. Assn., Nat. Water Resources Assn., Colorado River Water Users Assn., Scottsdale C. of C., Scottsdale Jr. C. of C. (life, Disting. Svc. award), Scottsdale Charros (life), White Mountain Country Club, Ariz. Club, Mesa Country Club (Ariz.). Methodist. Home: 5611 Calle Camelia Phoenix AZ 85018-4617 Office: Salt River Project PO Box 52025 Phoenix AZ 85072-2025*

SCHRAMM, WILLFRIED, biochemist; b. Koenigsberg, Germany, Jan. 22, 1944; came to U.S., 1979; s. Gerhard and Elsa (Gasenzer) S.; m. Gudrun Huebener, Sept. 21, 1968; children: Frauke, Antje. MS, U. Rostock (Germany), 1970; PhD, U. Hamburg (Germany), 1977. Rsch. assoc. U. Rostock, 1970-76; sr. rsch. assoc. Med. Sch., Luebeck, Germany, 1977-79, Worcester Found. Exptl. Biology, Shrewsbury, Mass., 1979-82; rsch. scientist U. Mich., Ann Arbor, 1982-90; v.p. rsch. and devel. BioQuant, Inc., Ann Arbor, 1985-93, Saliva Diagnostic Systems, Vancouver, Wash., 1993—; cons. for numerous biotechnology cos., 1984-86; mem. adv. bd. Inst. Biochemistry and Biotech., Oakland (Mich.) U., 1989-91; mem. faculty U. Mich., 1982-93; bd. dirs. BioQuant, 1991-93. Contbr. articles to profl. jours. Recipient Career Devel. award Deutsche Forschungsgemeinschaft, Germany, 1979; rsch. grantee NIH, 1985-93, NIDA, 1989-93, pvt. founds., U.S. Army, 1982-90. Mem. AAAS, Am. Chem. Soc., Am. Assn. Clin. Chemists, N.Y. Acad. Scis., Soc. for Study of Reprodn. Office: Saliva Diagnostic Systems 11719 NE 95th St Vancouver WA 98682-2444

SCHREIBER, ANDREW, psychotherapist; b. Budapest, Hungary, Aug. 1, 1918; s. Alexander and Bella (Gruen) S.; m. Mona Schreiber, Aug. 6, 1950; children: Julie, Brad, Robin. BA, CCNY, 1941, MEd, 1943; MSW, Columbia U., 1949; PhD, Heed U., 1972. Diplomate Am. Bd. Sexology; lic. psychotherapist, Calif. Pvt. practice Belmont, Calif., 1970—; sales mgr. vibro ceramics dir. Gulton Industries, Metuchen, N.J., 1949-57; mktg. mgr. Weldotron Corp., Newark, 1957-63; head dept. spl. edn. San Mateo (Calif.) High Sch. Dist., 1964-70; mem. faculty Heed U., 1970-71, advisor to doctoral candidates on West Coast, 1971; lectr. spl. edn. U. Calif.-Berkeley, 1973; cons. on hypnotherapy Psoriasis Rsch. Inst., Palo Alto, Calif., 1993—. Art Students League of N.Y. scholar, 1933-35, San Francisco State U. grantee. Fellow Am. Acad. Clin. Sexology; mem. NEA, AACD, Learning Disabilities Assn., Am. Assn. Sex Educators, Counselors and Therapists, Calif. Assn. Marriage and Family Therapists, Calif. Tchrs. Assn. Home: 2817 San Ardo Way Belmont CA 94002-1341

SCHREIBER, CARL WILLIAM, financial analyst; b. Abington, Pa., May 1, 1949; s. Carl Henry and Dorothy E. (Hughes) S.; m. Marsha Hillard, Nov. 25, 1970; children: Amy Jo, Jill Ann. BSBA, Pa. State U., 1971; MEd, Liberty U., 1985. Cert. mgmt. acctg. Asst. mgr. fin. studies, ctrl. fin. officer Pa. State U., State College, 1974-79; fin. planning and budget mgmt. officer, v.p. planning/rsch. Liberty U., Lynchburg, Va., 1979-87; dir. finance and info. sys. Biola U., LaMirada, Calif., 1987-93; v.p. fin. affairs and info. technology Biola U., LaMirada, 1993—. Treas. Reps. of Campbell County, Rustburg, Va., 1984—. Mem. Inst. Cert. Mgmt. Accts., Nat. Assn. Accts., Nat. Assn. Coll. and Univ. Bus. Officers, Transnat. Assn. Christian Colls. and Sch. Accreditation Commn. (vice-chmn. 1993—). Home: 14422 Valley View Ave La Mirada CA 90638 Office: Biola Univ 13800 Biola Ave La Mirada CA 90639

SCHREIER, CARL ALAN, writer, publisher; b. Lewistown, Mont., June 2, 1956; s. John Ambrose and Goldie (Thomas) S. BS, U. Mont., 1979; post-grad., U. Wyo., 1980, U. Utah, 1981. Mgr. Yellowstone Nat. Park, 1976-80, naturalist, 1979-81, 87-89; dir. Wyo. Waterfowl Trust, Cody, 1985-87; pub. Homestead Publishing, Moose, Wyo., 1981—; leader African Wildlife, Nairobi, Kenya, 1980-81. Author: Yellowstone Explorers Guide, 1982, A Field Guide to Yellowstone's Geysers, 1992, A Field Guide to Wildflowers, 1996. Office: Homestead Pub Box 193 Moose WY 83012

SCHREIMAN, HOWARD LESLIE, special education educator; b. L.A., Oct. 11, 1954; s. R. Robert Schreiman and Janet Ellen (Noble) Mondry. AA, L.A. City Coll., 1974; BA, UCLA, 1977, MEd, 1984; resource specialist cert., U. Calif., Riverside, 1990. Learning handicapped and severely handicapped credential, secondary social studies credential. Pres., CEO Mar-Tel Industries Inc., L.A., 1984-86; spl. day class instr. Palm Springs (Calif.) H.S., 1986-89, resource specialist, 1989—, dept. chair spl. edn., 1994-96; pres. faculty senate Palm Springs H.S., 1990-91; mem. Comm. Task Force, Palm Springs, 1988-89; mentor tchr. Palm Springs Unified Sch. Dist., 1989-90, workability job coach developer, 1989-93; mentor teacher selection com., 1995—. Mem. UCLA Alumni Scholarship Com., Coachella Valley, 1992—, dist. chair, 1989-91; mem. steering com. Young Leadership of the Desert, Jewish Fedn., Palm Springs, 1994-96; bd. dirs. Desert Synagogue, 1996—, Bikur Cholim, 1996—. Mem. Palm Springs Tchrs. Assn. (mem. budget com. 1993, mem. by-laws com. 1994, bldg. rep. 1988-90, 92-95, parliamentarian 1993-95), UCLA Club of the Desert, Phi Delta Kappa, Alpha Kappa Delta, Pi Gamma Mu. Democrat. Jewish. Office: Palm Springs HS 2248 E Ramon Rd Palm Springs CA 92264-7917

SCHREMPF, DETLEF, professional basketball player; b. Leverkusen, Germany, Jan. 21, 1963. Student, U. Washington. Forward Dallas Mavericks, 1985-89, Indiana Pacers, 1989-93, Seattle Supersonics, 1993—; player West German Olympic Team, 1984, 92. Recipient Sixth Man award NBA, 1991, 92; mem. NBA All-Star team, 1993. •

SCHRENK, GARY DALE, foundation executive; b. San Jose, Calif., Apr. 29, 1949; s. Robert Shepard and Katherine Mildred (Grant) S.; m. Rhonda Lynn King, Oct. 9, 1981 (div. Jan. 1989); children: Stephen, Kristen, James. BA in Communication, Am. U., 1970; postgrad., Regis U., 1990—. TV dir. WTOP (now WUSA), Washington, 1971-73, KBTV (now KUSA), Denver, 1973-75; with Denver Area Boy Scouts Am., 1975-80; regional dir. St. Jude Children's Rsch. Hosp., Memphis, 1980-83; dir. devel. Denver Art Mus., 1983-85; asst. dir. devel. The Children's Hosp., Denver, 1985-87; pres. North Colo. Med. Ctr. Found., Greeley, 1987—; dir., instr. Fast Start Course, 1985—; pres. Monfort Children's Clinic, Greeley, 1994—. Pres. Vision Together, Weld County, Colo., 1994-95; chair, founding dir. Weld Citizen Action Network, 1995—; founding dir., sec. First Steps Weld County, 1993—; chair Weld Cmty. Health Coalition, 1992—. Recipient Disting. Citizen award Highlanders, Denver, 1974; named Eagle Scout. Mem. Nat. Soc. Fund Raising Execs. (bd. dirs. Colo. chpt. 1979—, pres. 1984), Colo. Assn. Nonprofit Orgns. (founding dir. 1987-92), Greeley Rotary, Greeley Country Club, Tahosa Alumni Assn. (past pres., past chair). Methodist. Home: 4956 W 13th St Greeley CO 80634 Office: North Colo Med Ctr Found 1801 16th St Greeley CO 80631-5154

SCHRICKER, J. LOUIS, JR., neurosurgeon; b. Salt Lake City; m. Anna Lou Chinn; three children. AB, U. Utah, 1939; MD, Washington U. Sch. Medicine, 1943. Diplomate Am. Bd. Neurol. Surgery. Intern, resident gen. surgery Latter Day Saints Hosp., Salt Lake City, 1944-46; intern neurosurgery Letterman Army Hosp., San Francisco, 1948-49; intern neurosurgery Barnes Hosp., St. Louis, 1948-49, fellow in neurology, 1951-52; assoc. clin. prof. neurology U. Utah Coll. Medicine, Salt Lake City, 1952—. Fellow Am. Coll. Surgeons; mem. AMA, Am. Med. Peer Review Assn., Utah State Med. Assn., Salt Lake County Med. Soc., Salt Lake Surgical Soc., Am. Assn. Neurol. Surgeons, Neurosurg. Soc. Am., Utah Neurosurg. Soc., Congress Neurol. Surgeons. Mormon. Office: 324 10th Ave Ste 189 Salt Lake City UT 84103-2853

SCHROEDER, ARNOLD LEON, mathematics educator; b. Honolulu, May 27, 1935; s. Arnold Leon and Wynelle (Russell) S.; BS in Math., Oreg. State U., 1960, MS in Stats., 1962; NSF Insts. at UCLA, 1964, U. So. Calif., 1965; m. Maybelle Ruth Walker, Nov. 9, 1956; children: Steven, Michael, Wendy. Assoc. prof. math. Long Beach (Calif.) C.C., 1962—; computer cons. McDonnell-Douglas Corp., 1966-74, statis. researcher in med. and social sci., 1976-80; cons. statis. software including SPSS, BMDP, and Fortran, 1980—; dir. Schroeder's Statis. Svcs. Author: Statistics/Math Note's for Colleges, 1986—. Chmn. bd. elders Grace Bible Ch., South Gate, Calif., 1985-92. Served with USAF, 1953-57. Mem. Faculty Assn. Calif. C.C., C.C. Assn., Am. Bowlers Tour (life). Home: 5481 E Hill St Long Beach CA 90815-1923 Office: 4901 E Carson St Long Beach CA 90808-1706

SCHROEDER, CHERYL ANN, health and educational consultant; b. Cheyenne, Wyo., June 3, 1955; d. Milan and Clare (Gleason) Finley; m. David Paul Schroeder, July 14, 1979; children: Stacy, Stephanie. BA, U. Wyo., 1977, MEd, 1982, EdD, 1986. Cert. tchr., ednl. adminstr., Wyo., Nebr. Tchr. Lincoln (Nebr.) Pub. Schs., 1977-81; rsch. asst. U. Wyo., Laramie, 1982-83, 85, instr. reading and math. Lab. Sch., 1983-84, dir. Early Childhood Spl. Edn. Projects, 1986-87, project coord. Sch. Nursing, 1988-90, prin. investigator, chmn. Wyo. Task Force Infant Mortality, 1990-92, instr., 1990-92, dir. Wyo. Perinatal Substance Abuse Prevention Program, 1990-93, faculty Sch. Phys. and Health Edn., 1993; pres. Creative Cons., Inc., Laramie, 1993—; civer The Learning Ctr., Laramie; instr. Laramie County C.C., 1984, 85, 86, 96; dir. The A.D.A.M. Project, Laramie, 1986-88, co-facilitator parent group, 1988; presenter numerous workshops, seminars for univs., pub. schs., confs. and civic assns. Author: Modern Concepts in Fetal Alcohol Syndrome and Fetal Alcohol Effects, 1994; contbr. numerous articles to profl. jours. Chmn. Albany County Sch. Bd., Laramie, 1993—; chmn. Well Aware, 1994-95, chmn. Women's Health Month, 1993, 94; mem. Coun. Regional Networks for Genetic Svcs., 1993—; exec. com. Wyo. chpt., March of Dimes, 1989-91. Grantee Office Rural Health, Licensed Beverage Info. Coun., 1992, Office Substance Abuse Prevention, 1990, Union Pacific Railroad Found., 1986-87, 87-88, 89-90, Criminal Justice, 1987-88, Cmty. Svcs., 1986, 88, City of Laramie, 1988, Mountain States Regional Genetic Svcs. Network, 1987-88, March of Dimes, 1986; recipient Outstanding Prevention Demonstration Program award Ctr. Substance Abuse Prevention, 1993. Mem. Nat. Sch. Bd. Assn., Wyo. Sch. Bd. Assn., Mountain States Regional Genetic Svcs. Network (chmn. edn. com. 1993—, chmn. confs. and spl. projects grants 1989—, mem. steering and planning com. 1993—, mem. edn. com. 1987—), Nat. Perinatal Assn. (edn. com. 1992-95), Zontas Internat. (exec. bd. 1992-94), Kappa Delta Pi, Phi Delta Kappa, Alpha Epsilon Delta. Roman Catholic. Home: 1154 Frontera Dr Laramie WY 82070-5024 Office: Creative Consultants Inc The Learning Ctr 1526 Grand Ave Ste 2 Laramie WY 82070

SCHROEDER, DONALD J., orthopedic surgeon; b. Omaha, Nebr., Nov. 5, 1938; s. Frances A. and Maire L. (Schlueter) S.; m. Patricia A. Speer, Feb. 11, 1962 (div. June 1980); children: Cynthia, Douglas; m. Carol E. Schaan, Aug. 20, 1983. BS, Creighton U., 1960, MD, 1964. Diplomate Am. Bd. Orthopedic Surgery. Intern Detroit Receiving Hosp., 1964-65; resident in orthopedic surgery Wayne State U., Detroit, 1964-71; resident with affiliate hosp. Shriners Hosp., St. Louis, 1969-70; attending surgeon Sacred Heart Gen. Hosp., Eugene, Oreg., 1971—; resident orth. surgery Wayne State U.; attending surgeon Sacred Heart Gen. Hosp., Eugene, Oreg., 1971—. Pres. Marist Found., Eugene, 1993. Smith Kline fellow, 1964. Fellow Am. Acad. Orthopedic Surgeons; mem. AMA (alt. del. 1993—), Oreg. Med. Assn. (pres. 1993-94), Lane County Med. Soc. (pres. 1987-88), Western Orthopedic Assn., Alpha Omega Alpha. Republican. Roman Catholic. Office: 1180 Paterson Eugene OR 97401

SCHROEDER, GERALD F., judge; b. Boise, Idaho, Sept. 13, 1939; s. Frank Frederick and Josephine Ivy (Lucas) S.; m. Carole Ann McKenna, 1967; children: Karl Casteel, Erich Frank. BA magna cum laude, Coll. of Idaho (now Albertson Coll. of Idaho), 1961; JD, Harvard U., 1964. Bar: Idaho 1965. Assoc. Moffett, Thomas, Parret & Blanton, Boise, 1965-66; pvt. practice Boise, 1966-67; asst. U.S. atty. Dept. Justice, Boise, 1967-69; judge Ada County Probate Ct., Boise, 1969-71; magistrate State of Idaho, Boise, 1971-75; dist. judge U.S. Dist. Ct. (4th dist.) Idaho, 1975-95; justice Idaho Supreme Ct., 1995—; instr. Boise Bar Rev., 1973—; adj. faculty law Boise State U., 1986-95; former mem. Gov. Coun. on Crime and Delinquency. Author: Idaho Probate Procedure, 1971; (novel) Trianle of the Sons-Phenomena, 1983; contbr. chpt. to history text. Bd. dirs. Boise Philharm. Assn., 1978-81; adminstrv. and dist. judge 4th dist. State of Idaho, 1985-95. Tell fellow Nat. Coun. State Govt., 1990. Mem. Idaho Bar Assn., Boise Racquet and Swim Club (pres. bd. dirs. 1991-93). •

SCHROEDER, MARY MURPHY, federal judge; b. Boulder, Colo., Dec. 4, 1940; d. Richard and Theresa (Kahn) Murphy; m. Milton R. Schroeder, Oct. 15, 1965; children: Caroline Theresa, Katherine Emily. B.A., Swarthmore Coll., 1962; J.D., U. Chgo., 1965. Bar: Ill. 1966, D.C. 1966, Ariz. 1970. Trial atty. Dept. Justice, Washington, 1965-69; law clk. Hon. Jesse Udall, Ariz. Supreme Ct., 1970; mem. firm Lewis and Roca, Phoenix, 1971-75; judge Ariz. Ct. Appeals, Phoenix, 1975-79, U.S. Ct. Appeals (9th cir.), Phoenix, 1979—; vis. instr. Ariz. State U. Coll. Law, 1976, 77, 78. Contbr. articles to profl. jours. Mem. ABA, Ariz. Bar Assn., Fed. Bar Assn., Am. Law Inst. (coun. mem.), Am. Judicature Soc., Soroptimists. Office: US Ct Appeals 9th Cir 6421 Courthouse-Fed Bldg 230 N 1st Ave Phoenix AZ 85025-0230

SCHROEDER, MERRIE JO, law librarian; b. Detroit, Dec. 4, 1950; d. Albert Elmer Warren and Betty Jane (Kyser) Warren-Smith; m. Patrick Paul McNally, June 15, 1974 (div. June 30, 1990); 1 child, Sean Paul; m. Theodore Robert Schroeder, Jan. 2, 1996. BA in Elem. Edn., Mich. State U., 1972; MA in Libr. Media, U. Colo., Denver, 1990. Elem. sch. tchr. Fraser (Mich.) Pub. Schs., 1972-75; circulation clk. Adams County (Colo.) Libr., 1975-76; sub. tchr. Jefferson County Sch. Dist., Lakewood, Colo., 1976-77; health scis. libr. tech. St. Anthony Hosps., Denver, 1977-84; tech. svcs. libr. Holland & Hart, Denver, 1984-88, mgr. libr. and file svc., 1988—; mem. adv. bd. West Pub. Co., Eagan, Minn., 1995—. Author: (chpt.) Winning with Computers, 1991. Recipient Excellence in Pvt. Law Librarianship award West Pub. Co., 1996. Mem. Am. Assn. Law Librs., Colo. Assn. Law Librs. (editor jour./newsletter 1992-95). Home: 2576 Vivian Lakewood CO 80215 Office: Holland and Hart 555 17th St Ste 2900 Denver CO 80202-5555

SCHROEDER, PATRICIA SCOTT (MRS. JAMES WHITE SCHROEDER), congresswoman; b. Portland, Oreg., July 30, 1940; d. Lee Combs and Bernice (Lemoin) Scott; m. James White Schroeder, Aug. 18, 1962; children: Scott William, Jamie Christine. B.A. magna cum laude, U. Minn., 1961; J.D., Harvard U., 1964. Bar: Colo. 1964. Field atty. NLRB, Denver, 1964-66; practiced in Denver, 1966-72; hearing officer Colo. Dept. Personnel, 1971-72; mem. faculty U. Colo., 1969-72, Community Coll., Denver, 1969-70, Regis Coll., Denver, 1970-72; mem. 93d-104th Congresses from 1st Colo. dist., 1973-96; co-chmn. Congl. Caucus for Women's Issues, 1976-96; dir. New Solutions for a New Century, Inst. for a Civil Soc.; prof. Princeton U.; pres., CEO Assn. Am. Pubs., Washington, 1997—; mem. Ho. of Reps., ranking minority mem. judiciary subcom. on the Constitution, mem. Nat. Security Com. Inducted, National Women's Hall of Fame, 1995. Congregationalist. Office: Assn Am Pubs # 700 1718 Connecticut Ave NW Washington DC 20009-1148

SCHROEDER, RITA MOLTHEN, retired chiropractor; b. Savanna, Ill., Oct. 25, 1922; d. Frank J. and Ruth J. (McKenzie) Molthen; m. Richard H. Schroeder, Apr. 23, 1948 (div.); children—Richard, Andrew, Barbara, Thomas, Paul, Madeline. Student, Chem. Engring., Immaculate Heart Coll., 1940-41, UCLA, 1941, Palmer Sch. of Chiropractic, 1947-49; D. Chiropractic, Cleve. Coll. of Chiropractic, 1961. Engring.-tooling design data coordinator Douglas Aircraft Co., El Segundo, Santa Monica and Long Beach, Calif., 1941-47; pres. Schroeder Chiropractic, Inc., 1982-93; dir. Pacific States Chiropractic Coll., 1978-80, pres. 1980-81. Recipient Palmer Coll. Ambassador award, 1973. Parker Chiropractic Research Found. Ambassador award, 1976, Coll. Ambassador award Life West Chiropractic Coll. Mem. Internat. Chiropractic Assn., Calif. Chiropractic Assn., Internat. Chiropractic Assn. Calif., Assn. Am. Chiropractic Coll. Presidents, Council Chiropractic Edn. (Pacific State Coll. rep.), Am. Pub. Health Assn., Royal Chiropractic Knights of the Round Table. Home: 8701 N State Highway 41 Spc 18 Fresno CA 93720-1010 Office: Schroeder Chiropractic Inc 2535 N Fresno St Fresno CA 93703-1831

SCHROEDER, WILLIAM JOHN, electronics executive; b. Havre de Grace, Md., June 9, 1944; s. William Martin and Dorothy Jeanne (McLaughlin) S.; m. Marilee Jane Alne, May 28, 1966; children: Kristen, Kari Britt, Kimberley. BSEE, Marquette U., 1967, MSEE, 1968; MBA, Harvard U., 1972. Devel. engr. Honeywell Inc., Mpls., 1968-70; mgmt. cons. McKinsey & Co., Los Angeles, 1972-76; mgr. product planning Memorex Corp., Santa Clara, Calif., 1976-78; pres. Priam Corp., San Jose, Calif., 1978-85, chmn., 1985-86; pres. Conner Peripherals, Inc., San Jose, 1986-89, vice chmn., 1989-94; CEO Arcada Software Inc., a Conner Co., 1993-94; pres., CEO Diamond Multimedia Systems, Inc., San Jose, Calif., 1994—; bd. dirs. Xircom Corp., Thousand Oaks, Calif., MetaTools Inc., Carpenteria, Calif., CNF Transp., Inc., Palo Alto, Calif. Office: Diamond Multimedia Systems Inc 2880 Junction Ave San Jose CA 95134-1922

SCHROEDER, WILLIAM ROBERT, actor, graphic designer, linguist; b. L.A., July 9, 1941; s. Robert Manville and Miriam Ruth (Sloop) S.; m. Marie Paule Fautrel, Sept. 7, 1963. BA, UCLA, 1964; BFA, Art Ctr. Coll. Design, Pasadena, Calif., 1971. Mailman U.S. Post Office, Santa Monica, Calif., 1967-71; art dir., producer N.W. Ayer/West, Los Angeles, 1971-75; pres., gen. mgr. Advt. Ctr., Los Angeles, 1976-77, Alouette Internat., Santa Monica, Calif., 1972—; free-lance woodcarver, Santa Monica, 1981—; free-lance actor, Hollywood, Calif., 1983—; appeared in feature films King of the Streets, 1983, The Forbidden Tome, 1984, The End of Innocence, 1985, Poltergeist II, 1986. Producer TV commercials, 1972-75; author, creator computerized lang. courses Mattel Intellivision, 1980-82; real estate developer, 1989—. Publicity mgr. Concerned Homeowners of Santa Monica, 1981-82. Recipient 1st Pl. award Belding award for Excellence in Advt., Los Angeles, 1974; Cert. of Merit, Art Dirs. Club Los Angeles, 1972. Mem. Am. Fedn. Radio and TV Artists, Santa Monica C. of C., Mensa (Los Angeles), Combat Pilots Assn., Orange County Squadron, Internat. Plastic Modelers Soc., The Planetary Soc., The Found. Brain Rsch., Astronomical Soc. Pacific, Internat. Soc. Philosophical Inquiry, Internat. Legion of Intelligence, Santa Monica Theatre Guild, The Air Mus. Libertarian. Office: Alouette Internat 1626 Montana Ave Santa Monica CA 90403-1808

SCHROETER, VERNON WALTER, chiropractor; b. New London, Conn., July 16, 1956; s. Walter George Jr. and Marilyn Helen (Beatrice) S. AA, Moheagan C.C., 1979; D of Chiropractic, Palmer Coll. Chiropractic, 1984. Chiropractor All Chiropractic Care, Mesa, Ariz., 1983—. Author: From Conception to Birth and Beyond, 1994, Textbook of Self Defense Using Human Biomechanics, 1993; producer (videotape) Dr. Schroeter's Ultimate Self-Defense, 1990. Office: All Chiropractic Care 54 S Sirrine Mesa AZ 85210-1431

SCHRYVER, BRUCE JOHN, safety engineer; b. Newark, Aug. 14, 1944; s. Francis Henry and Ann Laura (Hart) S.; m. Lorraine Patricia Simodis, Oct. 8, 1966; children: Holly Lynn, Wendy Marie. BA in Occupational Safety and Health, Western States U., 1984, MS in Safety Mgmt., 1989, PhD in Safety Mgmt., 1989. Cert. safety profl.; cert. products safety mgr.; cert. hazard control mgr.; cert. hazardous materials mgr.; cert. healthcare safety profl. Inspector Lansing B. Warner Inc., Chgo., 1968-69; engring. rep. Glens Falls Ins. Co., Newark, 1969; safety dir. Hillside Metal Products, Newark, 1969-70; loss prevention specialist Warner Ins. Group, Chgo., 1970-79, regional loss control mgr., 1979-82, nat. loss control coordinator, 1982-85; mgr., asst. v.p. loss control svcs. Ins. Co. of the West, San Diego, 1985-90; v.p. loss control svcs. Ins. Co. of the West, 1990—; v.p. mcpl. law enforcement svcs. Ins. Co. of the West, San Diego, 1992—. Inventor Emergency Light Mount, 1971. Mem. Town of Clay (N.Y.) Pub. Safety Com., 1976-78, Beacon Woods East Homeowners Assn., Hudson, Fla., 1979-85, Meadowridge Homeowners Assn., La Costa, Calif., 1986—; cons. Town of Clay Police Dept., 1975-78. With USCG, 1964-68. Recipient lettter of appreciation Town of Clay, 1977, cert. of appreciation DAV, 1968, Golden State award, 1990. Mem. Am. Soc. Safety Engrs., Soc. Fire Protection Engrs., Nat. Safety Mgmt. Soc., Vets. Safety, Nat. Fire Protection Assn., San Diego Safety Coun., Calif. Conf. Arson Investigators. Republican. Roman Catholic. Home: 3047 Camino Limero Carlsbad CA 92009-4525 Office: Ins Co of the West 11455 El Camino Real San Diego CA 92130

SCHUBERT, RONALD HAYWARD, retired aerospace engineer; b. Bklyn., Aug. 25, 1932; s. John and Joan Sarah (Hayward) S.; m. Dorothy May Smith, Mar. 5, 1953 (div. 1961); children: Marcus H., Malcolm F., Ronald J. (dec.), Ann E.; m. Linda Jane van der Ploeg, Mar. 6, 1961 (div. 1988). BA cum laude, Ohio State U., 1956. Assoc. engr. Hughes Aircraft Co., Fullerton, Calif., 1957-61; physicist Nat. Cash Register Co., Dayton, Ohio, 1962-63; sr. research engr. Lockheed Missiles and Space Co., Sunnyvale, Calif., 1963-90. Served as staff sgt. USMC, 1951-54. Recipient Hon. mention Woodrow Wilson Fellowship Com. Mem. Phi Beta Kappa. Democrat. Roman Catholic. Home: 201 W California Ave Apt 1023 Sunnyvale CA 94086-5035

SCHUCK, JOYCE HABER, author; b. N.Y.C., Dec. 9, 1937; d. Frank F. and Florence (Smith) H.; m. Stephen Martin Schuck, June 15, 1958; children: William David, Thomas Allen, Ann Elizabeth. BA in Human Svcs. and Counseling, Loretto Hts. Coll., Denver, 1982. Counselor, tchr. Vision Quest, Colorado Springs, 1979-82; cons., program designer for govt. agys. Colorado Springs, 1982-85; author, 1987—; asst. to cons. Volusia County Dept. Corrections, Daytona Beach, Fla., 1982; cons. student svcs. program Pikes Peak C.C., Colorado Springs, 1982; cons., designer Juvenile Probation of El Paso County, Colorado Springs, 1982, 4th Jud. Dist./Dist. Atty.'s Office, Colorado Springs, 1984. Author: Political Wives, Veiled Lives, 1991. Cofounder Community Transitions, Colorado Springs, 1984; coord. El. Paso County Shape Up Program, 1982; v.p. Community Coun. of Pikes Peak Region, Colorado Springs, 1983, Women's Found. of Colo., Denver, 1987. Recipient Mayor's award for civic leadership City of Colorado Springs, 1983. Mem. Jr. League of Colorado Springs (sustaining), Salon de Femme (founding).

SCHUDSON, MICHAEL STEVEN, communications educator; b. Milw., Nov. 3, 1946; s. Howard M. and Lorraine (Spira) S.; m. Sue R. Leibovitz, 1982; m. Daniel, Jenna, Zachary. BA, Swarthmore Coll., Phila., 1969; MA, Harvard U., 1970, PhD, 1976. Asst. prof. sociology U. Chgo., 1976-80; assoc. prof., prof. sociology and comm. U. Calif. San Diego, La Jolla, 1980-85, prof., 1985—. Author: Discovering the News, 1978, Advertising the Uneasy Persuasion, 1984, Watergate in American Memory, 1992, The Power of News, 1995; mem. editl. bd. History of the Book in America, Am. Antiquarian Soc., 1995—. MacArthur Found. fellow, 1990-94, Guggenheim Found. fellow, 1990-91. Mem. Am. Sociol. Assn., Internat. Comm. Assn. Office: U Calif San Diego Dept Comm La Jolla CA 92093-0503

SCHUELE, DONNA CLARE, lawyer, educator; b. June 26, 1957; d. Donald Edward and Clare Ann (Kirchner) S.; m. Charles L. Valdez. BA, Case Western Res. U., 1979; JD, U. Calif., Berkeley, 1985; postgrad., U. Calif., 1985—. Bar: Calif. 1985, U.S. Dist. Ct. (no. dist.) Calif. 1985. Tchr. math. Beachwood (Ohio) High Sch., 1979, De La Salle High Sch., Concord, Calif., 1981-85; systems engr. IBM Corp., San Francisco, 1979-81; atty. Bowles & Verna, Walnut Creek, Calif., 1986-87; prof. law Whittier Coll., L.A., 1988-90; mem. Calif. State Bar Com. on History of Law in Calif., 1990-91; lectr. history polit. sci. law & soc. U. Calif., Santa Barbara, Calif., 1993-96; lectr. law U. Calif., Berkeley, 1997. Democrat. Roman Catholic.

SCHUETT, STACEY LYNN, writer, illustrator; b. Elmhurst, Ill., Oct. 9, 1960; d. Marvin Donald Schuett and Rita Cecile (Hassenhauer) Kimball; 1 child, Clare Adrienne. AA, Sierra Coll., 1981; BA, U. Calif., Davis, 1983. Illustrator: Lights Around the Palm, 1987, The Moon Comes Home, 1989, Watch Me, 1990, Is It Dark? Is It Light?, 1991, I'll See You in My Dreams, 1993, If You Want to Find Golden, 1993, When Spring Comes, 1993, Beginnings, 1994, Outside the Window, 1994, The Feather-Bed Journey, 1995; author, illustrator: Somewhere in the World, Right Now, 1995, Christina Katerina and Fats and the Great Neighborhood War, 1997. Mem. Graphic Artists Guild, Soc. Children's Writers and Illustrators. Home and Office: PO Box 15 Duncans Mills CA 95430

SCHUETZ, JOHN MICHAEL, sales executive; b. Chgo., Apr. 16, 1947; s. Henry Albert and Ann Delores (Kunst) S.; m. Jacqueline Claire Furneaux, Apr. 22, 1972; children: Michael Richard, Sean David. BS in Advt., Marquette U., Milw., 1969. Gen. field mgr. Ford Motor Co., San Jose, 1972-85; v.p. we. region IVECO Trucks of N.Am., Huntington Beach, Calif., 1985-91; nat. dealer mgr. Wynnoil Co., 1992-94; v.p., CEO Ben's Oil, Inc., Toro, Calif., 1994-95; nat. sales ops. mgr. KIA Motors America, Inc., 1995—; bd. dirs. Forsyte Rsch. Group, Santa Rosa, Calif., 1988-94. Leader Boy Scouts Am., El Toro, Calif., 1988—; coach Am. Youth Soccer Orgn., Saddleback Valley. Lt. USN, 1969-72. Mem. Sun and Sail Club, Phi Theta Psi. Republican. Roman Catholic. Home: 2 Cromwell Irvine CA 92618-1816

SCHUFLE, JOSEPH ALBERT, retired chemistry educator, writer; b. Akron, Ohio, Dec. 21, 1917; s. Albert Bernard and Daisy Susanna (Frick) S.; m. Lois Carolyn Mytholar, May 31, 1942; children: Joseph A. Jr., Jean Ann Fagerstrom. BS, U. Akron, 1938, MS, 1942; PhD, Case Western Res. U., 1948. Prof. chemistry N.Mex. Tech. U., Socorro, 1948-64, N.Mex. Highlands U., Las Vegas, 1964; vis. prof. U. Coll. Dublin, Ireland, 1961-62, Uppsala U., Sweden, 1977. Author: Bergman's Dissertation on Elective Attractions, 1968, D'Elhuyar Discoverer of Tungsten, 1981, Torbern Bergman, 1985, Vicinal Water, 1987, Ion Exchange, 1988, Scheffer's Lectures, 1992. Lt. col. U.S. Army, 1942-46. Recipient Disting. Service award N.Mex. Inst. Chemistry, 1982. Fellow N.Mex. Acad. Sci. (pres. 1960, named outstanding scientist 1972), AAAS (regional pres. 1973); mem. Am. Chem. Soc. (chmn. 1960, 64, recipient John Dustin Clark medal 1981), History of Sci. Soc., Rotary (pres. Las Vegas chpt. 1972-73). Home: 1301 8th St Las Vegas NM 87701-4221

SCHULER, ALISON KAY, lawyer; b. West Point, N.Y., Oct. 1, 1948; d. Richard Hamilton and Irma (Sanken) S.; m. Lyman Gage Sandy, Mar. 30, 1974; 1 child, Theodore. AB cum laude, Radcliffe Coll., 1969; JD Harvard U., 1972. Bar: Va. 1973, D.C. 1974, N.Mex. 1975. Assoc. Hunton & Williams, Richmond, Va., 1972-75; asst. U.S. atty. U.S. Atty's. Office, Albuquerque, 1975-78; adj. prof. law U. N.Mex., 1983-85, 90; ptnr. Sutin, Thayer & Browne, Albuquerque, 1978-85, Montgomery & Andrews, P.A., Albuquerque, 1985-88; sole practice, Albuquerque, 1988—. Bd. dirs. Am. Diabetes Assn., Albuquerque, 1980-85, chmn. bd. dirs., 1984-85; bd. dirs. June Music Festival, 1980-95, pres., 1983-85, 93-94; bd. dirs. Albuquerque Conservation Trust, 1986-90, N.Mex. Osteo. Found., 1993—; chairperson Albuquerque Com. Fgn. Rels., 1984-85; mem. N.Mex. Internat. Trade and Investment Coun., Inc., 1986—; mem. coun. and v.p. St. Lukes Luth. Ch., 1992, pres. 1993-96. Mem. Fed. Bar Assn. (coord.), ABA, D.C. Bar, Va. Bar Assn., N.Mex. State Bar Assn. (chmn. corp., banking and bus. law 1982-83, bd. dirs. internat. and immigration law sect. 1987—, chmn. 1993-94), Harvard U. Alumni Assn. (mem. fund campaign, regional dir. 1984-86, v.p. 1986-89, chmn. clubs com. 1985-88, chmn. communications com. 1988-91), Radcliffe Coll. Alumnae Assn. Bd. Mgmt. (regional dir. 1984-87, chmn. comms. com. 1988-91, Harvard-Radcliffe Club (pres. 1980-84). Home: 632 Cougar Loop NE Albuquerque NM 87122-1808 Office: 5700 Harper Dr NE Ste 430 Albuquerque NM 87109-3573

SCHULLERY, PAUL DAVID, editor, writer, consultant; b. Middletown, Pa., July 4, 1948; s. Stephen Emil and Judith Catherine (Murphy) S.; m. Dianne Patricia Russell, June 11, 1983 (div. Dec. 1988); m. Marsha Karle, June 22, 1996. BA in Am. History, Wittenberg U., 1970; MA in Am. History, Ohio U., 1977. Ranger, naturalist Nat. Park Service, Yellowstone Park, Wyo., 1972-77 (summers); historian, archivist Nat. Park Service, Yellowstone Park, 1974-77 (winters); exec. dir. Am. Mus. Fly Fishing, Manchester, Vt., 1977-82; freelance writer Livingston, Mont., 1982-86; assoc. editor Country Jour., Harrisburg, Pa., 1986—; v.p. comm. Fedn. Fly Fishers, West Yellowstone, Mont., 1983-84, sr. advisor, 1982-85; mem. coun. advisors Nat. Parks and Conservation Assn., Washington, 1987—; environ. protection specialist rsch. divsn. Yellowstone Nat. Park, 1988-90, resource naturalist, 1990-92, acting chief cultural resources, 1992-94; adj. prof. Am. Studies U. Wyo., 1991—; affiliate prof. History Mont. State U., 1991—. Author: The Bears of Yellowstone, 1980, 3d edit., 1992 (named one of Best Books of 1986 Mont. mag.), Mountain Time, 1984, American Fly Fishing: A History, 1987 (named one of Best Books of Last 30 Yrs. Trout mag.), The Bear Hunter's Century, 1988, Pregnant Bears and Crawdad Eyes, 1991, Yellowstone's Ski Pioneers, 1995, Yellowstone's Ski Pioneers: Peril and Heroism on the Winter Trail, 1995, Waterton/Glacier: Land of Hanging Valleys, 1996, Shupton's Fancy: A Tale of the Fly-Fishing Obsession, 1996; co-author: (with Austin Hogan) The Orvis Story, 1981, (with John D. Varley) Freshwater Wilderness: Yellowstone Fishes and Their World, 1983 (1st pl. award Competition of Conf. Nat. Park Coop. Assns. 1984, Overall Award for Excellence in Interpretive Pubs. Nat. Park Svc. 1984), (with Conger Beasley Jr., C.W. Buchholtz and Stephen Trimble) The Sierra Club Guides to the National Parks of the Rocky Mountains and the Great Plains, 1984, (with Don Despain, Douglas Houston and Mary Meagher) Wildlife in Transition: Man and Nature on Yellowstone's Northern Range, 1986, (with Bud Lilly) Bud Lilly's Guide to Western Fly Fishing, 1987, A Trout's Best Friend, 1988, (with William Sontag and Linda Griffin) The National Parks: A Seventy-Fifty Anniversary Album, 1991; contbg. author to 14 other books; editor: Old Yellowstone Days, 1979, The Grand Canyon: Early Impressions, 1981, American Bears: Selections from the Writings of Theodore Roosevelt, 1983, The National Parks, 1986, Theodore Roosevelt: Wilderness Writings, 1986, Island in the Sky: Pioneering Accounts of Mt. Rainier, 1986, Yellowstone Bear Tales, 1991; co-editor: (with J. Claar) Bears-Their Biology and Management, 1996, Echoes From the Summit, 1996, Mark of the Bear, Legend and Lore of an American Icon, 1996, The Yellowstone Wolf: A Guide and Sourcebook, 1996; contbr. articles to profl. jours. and mag. Trustee Am. Mus. Fly Fishing,. 1982-91, emeritus, 1991—. Recipient Design Excellence awards Printing Industries Am. Assn., 1981, 83, Award of Recognition Consol. Papers Inc., 1981. Mem. AAAS, Am. Inst. Biol. Scis., Theodore Roosevelt Assn. Greater Yellowstone Coalition, Trout Unltd., Yellowstone Grizzly Found., Internat. Assn. for Bear Rsch. and Mgmt., Gt. Bear Found., Phi Alpha Theta. Lutheran. Office: PO Box 168 Yellowstone National Park WY 82190-0168

SCHULMAN, ELIZABETH WEINER, financial consultant; b. Tucson, Nov. 17, 1950; d. Leonard and Doris (Goldman) Weiner; m. Steven Andrew Schulman, Aug. 15, 1981. BA, Brandeis U., 1972; postgrad., U. Ariz., 1976-78. Office mgr. Assocs. in Periodontics and Endodontics, Tucson, 1973-78; campaign cons. various polit. campaigns Tucson, 1978-79; asst. v.p. Merrill Lynch Pvt. Client Group, Tucson, 1979—. Bd. dirs. Catalina coun. Boy Scouts of Am., Tucson, 1987-90, adv. coun., 1990-92; bd. dirs. Jewish Community Found., Tucson, 1989-91; mem. alumni admissions coun. Brandeis U., 1990-95. Mem. Investment Mgmt. Cons. Assn. (bd. dirs. 1991—, chmn. cert. com. 1989—, treas. 1993-94, v.p. 1994-96, pres. 1997), Jr. League of Tucson (coun. sec. 1989-90), Hadassah (spl. gifts. chmn. 1989-91). Office: Merrill Lynch 5460 E Broadway Blvd Ste 350 Tucson AZ 85711-3728

SCHULMAN, PAUL STUART, radiologist; b. Buffalo, Mar. 1, 1943; s. Nathan Charles and Beatrice Estelle (Steinberg) S.; m. Suzanne Karen Cherry, Aug. 15, 1965; children: Jennifer Amy, Todd William. BA, SUNY, 1964, MD, 1968. Diplomate Am. Bd. Radiology, Am. Bd. Nuclear Medicine. Intern Rochester (N.Y.) Gen. Hosp., 1968-69; resident in radiology U. Colo., Denver, 1971-74; med. officer Brooke Army Med. Ctr., San Antonio, 1969-71; radiologist Scripps Clinic, La Jolla, Calif., 1974-75; pvt. practice radiology Chula Vista, Calif., 1975-94, San Diego, 1995—; v.p. San Diego Diagnostic Radiology Med. Group Inc. Fellow Am. Coll. Radiology; mem. Calif. Radiol. Soc., Alpha Omega Alpha. Office: San Diego Radiology Group 7930 Frost St Ste 301 San Diego CA 92123-2740

SCHULTE, HENRY GUSTAVE, college administrator; b. Seattle, Oct. 14, 1920; s. John Henry and Alma (Winter) S.; m. Joan Noel Burton, Aug. 20, 1949; children—Steven Craig, Scott John, Jane Martha. B.A. in Econs. and Bus., U. Wash., 1948. With D.K. MacDonald & Co., Seattle, 1952-67, asst. treas., 1957-60, treas., 1960-67; bus. mgr. legal firm Bogle, Gates, Dobrin, Wakefield & Long, Seattle, 1967; adminstr. Child Devel. and Mental Retardation Ctr. U. Wash., Seattle, 1968-86; mem. steering com. mental retardation research ctrs. group Nat. Inst. Child Health and Human Devel., 1971-85. Mem. exec. bd., treas. Assn. Univ. Affiliated Facilities, 1974-77. Served with AUS, 1940-45. Mem. Soc. Research Adminstrs. (mem. exec. com. 1971-72), Am. Assn. Mental Deficiency. Office: U Wash Box 357920 Seattle WA 98195-7920

SCHULTE, MARY ANN, finance executive; b. Phoenix, Feb. 6, 1953; d. Walter Barry and Norma Gladys (Caffey) S. BSBA, U. So. Calif., 1975, MBA, 1989. Mgr. acctg. Coldwell Banker, Los Angeles, 1975-78; controller Adams, Ray and Rosenberg, Inc. (now The William Morris Agy.), Century City, Calif., 1978-81; co-owner Marwal, Inc., Los Angeles, 1976-82; controller, chief fin. officer DNA Group, Inc., Pasadena, Calif., 1982-86; chief fin. officer Sukut Constrn., Inc., Santa Ana, Calif., 1986—; cons. Mikeselle DeKorff, L.A., 1981-82, Hollywood (Calif.) H.S., 1986-87; cons., bd. dirs. Inner Ear Prodns., L.A., 1983-85; guest speaker Am. Soc. Women Accts., Inland Empire Women in Bus. Conf., 1994, Associated Gen. Contractors, L.A., Riverside, San Bernardino, San Diego and Orange Counties. Assoc. producer (documentary film) Echoes of The Ozarks, 1989; speaker in field. Staff leader drop-out prevention program Hollywood H.S., 1986; bd. dirs., chair fin. com. STOP GAP; mem. joint budget task force City of Santa Ana, 1991-92; mem. adv. bd. Orange County Acad. Decathlon; chair vendor subcom. to master creditors com. Orange County Bankruptcy; chair County of Orange Govt. Practices Oversight Com. Named Bus. Woman of Yr. Orange County, 1996. Mem. U. So. Calif. Commerce Assocs., Alpha Chi Omega. Republican. Roman Catholic. Office: Sukut Constrn Inc 4010 W Chandler Ave Santa Ana CA 92704-5202

SCHULTZ, FREDERIK EMIL, academic administrator; b. Joplin, Mo., Oct. 25, 1944; s. Frederik Snelling and Elizabeth Jean (Canfield) S.; m. Rita I. Harrington, Aug. 28, 1984. BA in English, Athens (Ala.) Coll., 1970; student, N.C. State Univ., 1970-73. Freelance writer Raleigh, N.C., 1973-75; cons. cmty. arts devel. N.C. Arts Coun., Raleigh, 1975-82; cons. spl. events, mktg. Oakland, Calif., 1982-86; dir. instl. advancement Life Chiropractic Coll. West, San Lorenzo, Calif., 1986—; grad. tchg. asst. N.C. State Univ., Raleigh, 1970-73. With U.S. Army, 1965-67, Vietnam. Mem. Coun. Advancement Support Edn. Office: Life Chiropractic Coll West 2005 Via Barrett San Lorenzo CA 94580-1315

SCHULTZ, JAMES MICHAEL, nonprofit marketing administrator; b. Mt. Pleasant, Mich., Dec. 9, 1953; s. James Henery and Lorraine Helen (Conklin) S.; m. Shirley Jean Loesch, Nov. 25, 1988; 1 child, Luke Ruman. AA, Grand Rapids Jr. Coll., 1977; BS in Sociology, Grand Valley State Colls., 1977; MS in Urban Policy Analysis, So. Ill. State U., 1982; profl. devel. cert., Portland State U., 1991. Edn. coord. Utah Navajo Devel. Coun., Blanding, 1979-81; dir. of ops. Careco, Inc., Ft. Myers, Fla., 1983-85; exec. dir. S.E. Asian Refugee Ctr., Vancouver, Wash., 1986; sr. assoc. United Way Columbia-Willamette, Portland, Oreg., 1987-91, dir. mktg., 1991—. Coauthor: Portland Community Profile Report, 1989. Mem. Multnomah County Citizen Involvement Com., Portland, 1989-93, chmn., 1991-93; mem. Multnomah County Cen. Citizen Budget Adv. Com., Portland, 1991; VISTA vol. Dept. Action, Ute Indian Reservation, 1978-79; mem. Willamette Valley Devel. Officers, Portland, 1991—. Mem. Am. Mktg. Assn. (bd. dirs. Oregn. chpt. 1992—, sec. Oreg. chpt. 1992—, pres. 1995—, R. G. Ru Lund award Oreg. chtp. 1993), Oreg. Peace Inst. (bd. dirs., chair resource devel. com. 1994—), Nat. Soc. Fundraising Execs. (Oregon chpt. 1994—). Democrat. Roman Catholic. Home: 2714 NE Bryce St Portland OR 97212-1638 Office: United Way Columbia-Willame 619 SW 11th Ave Portland OR 97205-2646

SCHULTZ, JARED C., vocational counselor, therapist; b. Eugene, Oreg., Aug. 27, 1970; s. R. Conrad and Carolyn (Lake) S.; m. Deeann R. McCoy, April 16, 1994; 1 child, McKenzie Kathryn. BS in Psychology, Brigham Young Univ., Utah, 1993; MA in Counseling Psychology, George Fox Univ., Oreg., 1996. Psychiat. technician Charter Canyon Treatment Ctr., Provo, Utah, 1991-93; vocational counselor Abacus program Yamhill County, McMinnville, Oreg., 1994—. Mem. Am. Counselng Assn.

SCHULTZ, KENNETH W., engineering executive. B in Aeronautics, N.Y.U., 1950; MBA, George Washington U., 1960. Exec. v.p. Xonics Inc., Van Nuys, Calif., 1975-80; with Xantech, Inc., 1980—, now pres. Office: Xontech Inc 6862 Hayvenhurst Ave Van Nuys CA 91406-4717*

SCHULTZ, RICHARD DALE, national athletic organizations executive; b. Grinnell, Iowa, Sept. 5, 1929; s. August Henry and Marjorie Ruth (Turner) S.; m. Jacquilyn Lu Duistermars, June 26, 1949; children: Robert Dale, William Joel, Kim Marie. BS, Cen. Coll., Pella, Iowa, 1950; EdD Honoris Causa, Cen. Coll., 1987; LLD (hon.), Wartburg Coll., 1988, Alma Coll., 1989, Luther Coll., 1991; Phd, U.S. Sports Acad., 1993; LLD, Daniel Webster Coll., 1997. Head basketball coach, athletic dir. Humboldt (Iowa) High Sch., 1950-60; freshman basketball coach U. Iowa, Iowa City, 1960-62; head baseball coach, assoc. basketball coach U. Iowa, 1962-70, head basketball coach, 1970-74, asst. v.p., 1974-76; dir. athletics and phys. edn. Cornell U., Ithaca, N.Y., 1976-81; dir. athletics U. Va., Charlottesville, 1981-87; exec. dir. NCAA, Mission, Kans., 1987-94; pres. Global Sports Enterprises, 1994-95; exec. dir. U.S. Olympic Com., Colorado Springs, Colo., 1995—; mem. honors ct. Nat. Football Found. and Hall of Fame, Nat. Basketball Hall of Fame, 1992; chmn. bd. NCAA Found., 1989; organizer Iowa Steel Mill, Inc.; bd. trustees Gettysburg Coll., 1996—. Author: A Course of Study for the Coaching of Baseball, 1964, The Theory and Techniques of Coaching Basketball, 1970; Contbr. articles to mags. Bd. dirs. Fellowship of Christian Athletes, 1986, chmn., 1990; chmn. Multiple Sclerosis, 1974-75; mem. Knight Found. Commn. on Intercollegiate Athletics, 1990—; mem. adv. com. on svc. acad. athletic programs Def. Dept. Recipient Disting. Alumni award Ctrl. Coll., Pella, 1970, Lifetime Svc. award U. Iowa, 1994, Corbett award Nat. Assn. Collegiate Dirs. Athletics, 1994, medal of honor Ellis Island, 1997; mem. Basketball Hall of Fame Honor Ct., 1992, Sportsman of Yr. award Marine Corp., 1997; inducted into Iowa Baseball Hall of Fame, 1993. Mem. Nat. Assn. Coll. Basketball Coaches, Ea. Coll. Athletic Assn. (mem. exec. com. 1980-81), Am. Basketball Coaches Assn. (Award of Honor 1994), Am. Football Coaches Assn. (lifetime membership award 1995). Home: 3670 Twisted Oak Cir Colorado Springs CO 80904-2138 Office: US Olympic Com One Olympic Plz Colorado Springs CO 80909

SCHULTZ, THOMAS ROBERT, hydrogeologist; b. Van Wert, Ohio, July 2, 1946; s. Robert Roland and Mary Avanell (Davies) S.; m. Sandra Lee Pound, Aug. 29, 1968; children: Lindsay D., Zachary T. BS in Geology, Ohio State U., 1969, MS in Geology, 1972; Phd in Hydrology, U. Ariz., 1979. Cert. profl. hydrogeologist Am. Inst. Hydrology. Hydrologist Ariz. State Land Dept., Phoenix, 1977-79, U.S. Office Surface Mining, Denver, 1979-80; sr. hydrogeologist Wahler Assocs., Denver, 1980-82, Kaman Scis. Tempo, Denver, 1983-84; sr. project hydrogeologist Woodward Clyde Cons., Denver, 1984-87; sr. assoc. hydrogeologist Harding Lawson Assocs., Denver, 1987-92, Haley & Aldrich, 1992-96; sr. project mgr. Dames & Moore, Tucson, Ariz., 1996—; advisor Environ. Tech. Program, Colo. Mountain Coll., Leadville, 1985—, chmn. adv. bd., 1992-93. Contbr. articles to profl. jours. 2d lt. Ohio Nat. Guard, 1969-75. Mem. Nat. Ground Water Assn., Colo. Ground Water Assn. (bd. dirs. 1995-96), Arix. Hydrol. Soc. Office: Dames & Moore 1790 E River Rd Ste E-300 Tucson AZ 85718

SCHULTZE, ERNST EUGENE, marketing communications executive; b. Columbia, Mo., Jan. 20, 1944; s. Andrew Byron and Jeanne V. (Homsley) S.; m. Marlene Diane Finke, June 7, 1964 (div. 1981); 1 child, Nicole Johanna Dove. BA, Nebr. Wesleyan U., 1968; MBA, San Diego State U., 1975; lifetime teaching credential, Calif. Community Colls. Mktg. coord. Ektelon Corp., San Diego, 1976-79, ops. project mgr., 1979-80; exec. v.p. Mktg. Group, San Diego, 1980-83; v.p. Jack Lewis Agy., San Diego, 1983-84; mktg. strategist Gable Agy., San Diego, 1984-85; pres. Schultze & Wilson, San Diego, 1985-97; sr. v.p. mktg. IWC, Carlsbad, Calif.,, 1997—; investor, pres. Nat. Mgmt. Assn., 1979; mktg. com. Gaslamp Quarter Coun., San Diego, 1988-98; bd. dirs. MedEquip Ams., Inc. Author: Carry That Weight; contbr. articles to profl. jours. Counsel Schulze City Coun. campaign, San Diego, 1975, Killea City Coun. campagin, San Diego, 1981. Recipient Golden State award, 1989; named Big Hitter in Bus. City San Diego. Mem. Am. Mktg. Assn., Phi Kappa Tau. Republican. *Personal philosophy: Hard work, honesty and integrity coupled with good timing and background knowledge are keys to a full life.*

SCHULZ, JUSTIN WILLIAM, psychologist, management consultant; b. Dallas, Feb. 28, 1948; s. Julius Herman and Juanita Lee Schulz; m. Patricia Ann Barton, Aug. 9, 1984; children: David, Eric, Cara, Brenna. BS in Psychology, U. Tex., Arlington, 1970; PhD in Psychology, SUNY, Buffalo, 1976. Lic. psychologist. Cons. Buffalo Orgn. for Social and Tech. Innovation, Inc., 1973-75; psychology intern mental health programs Denver Dept. Health and Hosps., 1975-76; asst. prof. dept. psychology Wright State U., Dayton, Ohio, 1976-78; clin. psychologist mental health programs Denver Dept. Health and Hosps., 1978-82, acting dir. cons. and edn. mental health programs, 1980-81; pvt. practice Denver, 1979-84; regional dir. Human Affairs Internat., Denver, 1984-88; pvt. practice Englewood, Colo., 1988-89; pres. Applied Behavioral Scis., Greenwood Village, Colo., 1989—; advisor MCC Behavioral Care Choice Health, Sloans Lake Managed Care, Denver, 1993—; bd. dirs. Western Health Benefits, Aspen, Colo., 1993—, nat. mental health dir., 1993—; med. staff chair adolescent svcs. Oakview Hosp., Denver, 1988-89. Contbg. author planning sys. Planning Aid Kit, 1973-75; author Orgnl. Assessment Survey, 1991; author: (with B.B. Bunker and H.A. Pearlson) Student's Guide to Social Research, 1975; Psychological Approach to Interpersonal and Intergroup Conflict, 1975, Responding to Work Trauma: A Psychological First Aid Kit for the Workplace, 1994; contbr. articles to profl. jours. Advisor Colo. Coalition for the Homeless, Denver, 1990-94, Urban Peak, Denver, 1996—; fund raising com. Pro Bono Mental Health Project, Denver, 1989-95; cons. Colo. Bd. Dental Examiners, 1991-94. Recipient Nat. Svc. award DAV, Washington, 1981, Svc. award Colo. chpt., Denver, 1981. Mem. APA, Am. Soc. Clin. Hypnosis, Am. Nuclear Soc. Office: Applied Behavioral Scis 5200 Dtc Pkwy Ste 340 Greenwood Village CO 80111-2718

SCHULZ, LAURA JANET, retired writer, secretary; b. Alba, Tex., Aug. 12, 1931; d. Joseph Clifton and Laura Oza (Carruth) English; m. Gordon Robert Schulz, Dec. 4, 1953; children: LeAnn Clarinda Schulz Barclay, Peggy Gaynell Schulz Lingbloom. Grad. high sch., Denison, Tex. Sec. history dept. Tex. Christian U., Ft. Worth, 1948-49; continuity editor Sta. KDSX, Denison, 1949-51; clk., typist Perrin AFB, Sherman, Tex., 1951-55; acctg. clk. England AFB, Alexandria, La., 1955; sec. Emile R. Jardine, CPA, Stockton, Calif., 1957-59, Heather, Sanguinetti, Caminata & Sakai, CPAs, Stockton, 1983-92; sec., feature writer Lodi (Calif.) Dist. C. of C., 1993-97; ret., 1997. Author: Katy's Children, 1990, Little Rocky's True Adventures, 1991. Hon. life mem. Wesleyan svc. guild Meth. Ch., Denison, 1955—, Calif. Congress of PTA, 1984—; pres. PTA Needham Sch., Lodi, 1968-69, 69-70; leader Camp Fire, Lodi, 1974-82; vol. advisor, tchr. Grapevine Newspaper Vinewood Sch., Lodi, 1974-82; mem. First United Meth. Ch. Recipient Appreciation award Vinewood Sch., Lodi Unified Sch. Dist., 1974-82. Mem. Sierra Club. Democrat. Methodist. Home: 1910 W Tokay St Lodi CA 95242 Office: Lodi Dist C of C 35 S School St Lodi CA 95240

SCHULZ, MARIANNE, accountant; b. East Orange, N.J.; d. Clifford W. Schulz; m. James A. Willits, Dec. 29, 1991; children: Lukas James, Laura Christine. BA in Bus., U. Wash., 1979. Cert. mgmt. acct. Contr. Farwest Spl. Products, Bellevue, Wash., 1974-88; acct. Lakeside Industries, Bellevue, Wash., 1988—. Mem. Inst. Mgmt. Accts. (bd. dirs. 1990-92, v.p. 1992-93).

SCHULZ, RAYMOND ALEXANDER, medical marketing professional, consultant; b. Paris, June 2, 1946; s. Helmut W. and Colette (Prieur) S.; m. Dixie Lee Suzanne Specht, Apr. 9, 1977 (div. Dec. 1990); children: Christopher, William. BA in Physics, W.Va. U., 1970; MS in Computer Sci., Columbia U., N.Y.C., 1975. Sr. programmer Meml. Sloan Kettering Cancer Ctr., N.Y.C., 1972-74; program coord. Neurol. Inst. Columbia Presbyn. Hosp., N.Y.C., 1974-76; engring. mgr. EMI Med. Systems, Northbrook, Ill., 1976-78; product mgr. Johnson & Johnson (Technicare), Solon, Ohio, 1978-80; group product mgr. Siemens Corp., Iselin, N.J., 1980-82; mktg. mgr. Toshiba Am. Med. Systems (formerly Diasonics MRI), South San Francisco, 1983-92; dir. mktg. Voxel, Laguna Hills, Calif., 1992—. Contbr. over 70 papers on the application of holography to a variety of med. specialties to profl. publs. Recipient first prize Roentgen Centenary Congress, 1995. Mem. Am. Assn. Physicists in Medicine, N.Y. Acad. Scis., Internat. Soc. Magnetic Rsch. in Medicine, Larchmont Yacht Club, Commonwealth Club Calif., Eta Kappa Nu. Office: Voxel 26081 Merit Cir Ste 117 Laguna Hills CA 92653-7017

SCHULZ, RENATE ADELE, German studies and second language acquisition educator; b. Lohr am Main, Germany, Feb. 24, 1940; came to U.S., 1958; 1 child, Sigrid Diane. BS, Mankato State Coll., 1962; MA, U. Colo., 1967; PhD, Ohio State U., 1974. Edn. officer U.S. Peace Corps, Ife Ezinihitte, Nigeria, 1963-65; asst. prof. Otterbein Coll., Westerville, Ohio, 1974-76, State U. Coll. N.Y., Buffalo, 1976-77; from asst. to assoc. prof. U. Ark., Fayetteville, 1977-81; from assoc. to prof. U. Ariz., Tucson, 1981—, chair PhD program in second lang. acquisition and teaching, 1994—; disting. vis. prof. USAF Acad., Colorado Springs, Colo., 1990-91. Author: Options for Undergraduate Foreign Language Programs, 1979, Lesen, Lachen, Lernen, 1983, Aktuelle Themen, 1987, Im Kontext: Lesebuch zur Landeskunde, 1990; mem. editorial bd. Modern Lang. Jour., 1985—. Recipient Creative Tchg. award U. Ariz. Found., Tucson, 1984, Stephen A. Freeman award N.W. Conf. Tchg. Fgn. Langs., 1984, Bundesverdienstkreuz, Fed. Govt. Germany, 1990. Mem. Am. Coun. Tchg. Fgn. Langs. (exec. coun. 1979-81, Florence Steiner award 1993), Am. Assn. Tchrs. German (v.p. 1988-90, pres. 1990-91, editor Die Unterrichtspraxis 1980-85), MLA (del. 1989-91), Tchrs. of ESL, Am. Assn. Applied Linguistics, Am. Assn. Tchrs. French. Office: Univ of Ariz Dept German Studies Tucson AZ 85721

SCHULZKE, MARGOT SEYMOUR, artist, educator; b. San Francisco; d. Charles R. and Helen (Spande) Seymour; m. Ernest F. Schulzke, 1959; children: Kurt, Kristen, Eric, Kari, Stuart. BA in Art, Brigham Young U., 1959; studied with, Albert Handell and others. Tchr. art and English Washington Sch., Chicago Heights, Ill., 1960-62; instr. Maude I. Kerns Art Ctr., Eugene, Oreg., 1963-64; lectr. Brigham Young U. Edn. Weeks., Provo, Utah, 1966-68; instr. Roseville (Calif.) Art Ctr., 1985—; instr. painting workshops. Exhibited in shows at Nat. Art Club, N.Y.C., New Orleans, San Francisco, Colo., Oreg., Nev., Calif., others; at Mus. Ill., N.J., Utah (numerous awards); featured artist in Pastel Interpretations, Northlight, 1993, Best of Pastel, Rockport, Mass. Pubs., 1996; contbr. articles to profl. jours. Bd. dirs. Friends of Moldova Relief, Sacramento, 1992-93. Mem. Pastel Soc. Am., Pastel Soc. West Coast (bd. dirs. 1985—, adv. bd. 1988—, founding pres. 1985-88, ways and means chmn. 1985-94, pres. 1995-97), Degas Pastel Soc. New Orleans, Knickerbocker Artists of Am., Degas Pastel Soc. Mem. LDS Ch. Studio: 1840 Little Creek Rd Auburn CA 95602-9604

SCHUMACHER, HENRY JEROLD, former career officer, business executive; b. Torrance, Calif., June 17, 1934; s. Henry John and Rene (Wilcox) S.; m. Barbara Howell, Aug. 24, 1958; children: Sheri Lynn, Henry Jerold II. Student, Stanford U., 1953; B.S., U.S. Mil. Acad., 1957; M.S., Northeastern U., Boston, 1965; M.B.A., Auburn U., 1977. Commd. lt. U.S. Army, 1958, advanced through grades to maj. gen., 1982; army attaché Moscow, 1969-71; chief communications ops. Vietnam, 1971-72; exec. officer Office Chief of Staff, 1972-75; comdr. U.S. Army Communications Command, Panama, 1977-79; dir. network integration, Office Asst. Chief of Staff Automation and Communications, Dept. Army, 1979-81; comdr. The White House Communications Agy., Washington, 1981-82; chief U.S. Army Signal Corps, 1981-83; ret., 1983; sr. v.p. Visa Internat., 1983-86; chief oper. officer Fuel Tech., Inc., Stamford, Conn., 1986-87; pres. IMM Systems, Phila., 1987-89; exec. v.p. Cylink Corp., Sunnyvale, Calif., 1990-95; exec. dir. Hiller Mus. of No. Calif. Aviation History, Redwood City, 1995—. Decorated Def. D.S.M., D.S.M., Legion of Merit. Home: 156 Normandy Ct San Carlos CA 94070-1519 Office: Hiller No Calif Aviation Mus 601 Skyway Rd San Carlos CA 94070

SCHUMACHER, JON WALTER, accountant, educator; b. Quincy, Ill., Jan. 11, 1955; s. Harold Herman and Mina Ruth (Zierk) S.; m. Diana Irene Andrews, Sept. 6, 1980; children: Lisa, Roberta. BS in Bus. Adminstrn.,

Calif. Poly. State U., San Luis Obispo, 1977. Tax/cost acct. Guy F. Atkinson Co., South San Francisco, Calif., 1977-79; mine acct. Pathfinder Mines, Inc., Jeffrey City, Wyo., 1979-80; cost engr. Stauffer Chem. Co. Wyo., Green River, Wyo., 1980-84; mine acct. Summitville Cons. Mining Co., Del Norte, Colo., 1984-86; sr. acct. Kenneth Leventhal & Co., L.A., 1986-87; CFO Southwest Wyo. Rehab. Ctr., Rock Springs, 1987—. Asst. Vol. Income Tax Assistance Program, San Luis Obispo, 1976; v.p. Luth. Ch. Mission, Jeffrey City, 1980-81; helper Rock Springs (Wyo.) Food Bank, 1989. Recipient Disting. Leadership award Am. Biog. Inst.; named to Outstanding Young Men of Am., 1989. Mem. Assn. Retarded Citizens. Office: Southwest Wyo Rehab Ctr 4509 Foothill Blvd Rm 107 Rock Springs WY 82901

SCHUMACHER, MARK ALLEN, accountant; b. Sioux City, Iowa; s. Martin and Margaret (Stoeber) S.; m. Mary Elizabeth Toth, July 17, 1982; children: Justin, Lauren. BS in Acctg., U. Iowa, 1980; MS in Mktg., U. Colo., 1996. CPA, Colo. Sr. acct. Coopers & Lybrand, Denver, 1980-83; acctg. mgr. U.S. West Mktg. Resources, Denver, 1984-89, dir. fin., 1989-93; CFO Interactive Transaction Ptnrs., Denver, 1993-95, U.S. West Interactive Svcs., Denver, 1995—; pres. bd. dirs. The Trip Inc., Englewood, Colo., 1996—. Mem. AICPA, Colo. Soc. CPA. Republican. Roman Catholic. Home: 7946 S Eudora Circle Littleton CO 80122 Office: 9000 E Nichols Englewood CO 80112

SCHUNKE, HILDEGARD HEIDEL, accountant; b. Indpls., Nov. 24, 1948; d. Edwin Carl and Hildegard Adelheid (Baumbach) S. BA, Ball State U., Muncie, Ind., 1971, MA in German/English, 1973, MA in Acctg., 1975. CPA, Ind., Calif. Exch. teaching grad. asst. Padagogische Hochschule, Germany, 1971-72; teaching grad. asst. German/acctg. Ball State U., Muncie, 1972, 74-75, asst. prof. acctg., 1975-78; investing rschr. Family Partnership, Muncie, 1977-83; staff acct. Am. Lawn Mower Co., Muncie, 1984-88, G&J Seiberlich, CPAs, St. Helena, Calif., 1988-89, R.A. Gullotta, MBA, CPA, Sonoma, Calif., 1989-90; plant acct. Napa Pipe Corp., Napa, Calif., 1990—; continuing edn. instr. Calif. Soc. CPAs, Redwood City, 1990. ESOL instr. Napa County Project Upgrade, 1988-92; ticketing and refreshments com. North Ba Philharmonic Orch., Napa, 1988—, North Bay Wind Ensemble, Napa, 1988—. Mem. AICPAs, Calif. Soc. CPAs, Ind. Soc. CPAs, Inst. Internal Auditors, Environ. Auditing Roundtable, Am. Soc. Quality Control. Home: 1117 Devonshire Ct Suisun City CA 94585-3343 Office: Napa Pipe Corp 1025 Kaiser Rd Napa CA 94558-6257

SCHUSSEL, ALAN LEWIS, rehabilitation counselor; b. Bklyn., Oct. 27, 1963; s. Erwin Marvin and Suellen (Kleppel) S.; m. Clarice Ann West, June 9, 1991; children: Zachary Terence, Marni Amber. BA, Gallaudet U., 1989; MA, U. Ariz., 1994. Cert. rehab. counselor, cmty. coll. tchr., Ariz. Resident advisor Rochester (N.Y.) Inst. Tech., 1983-87; resident advisor Gallaudet U., Washington, 1987-89, tutor, 1987-92; residential counselor Family Svcs. Found., Landover, Md., 1989; case mgr. People Encouraging People, Balt., 1990-92; rehab. counselor dept. econ. security State of Ariz., Tucson, 1993-96; project assoc. Pima Prevention Partnership, Tucson, 1996—; adj. faculty Am. sign lang. Pima C.C., Tucson, 1995—; bd. dirs. Cmty. Outreach Program for Deaf, Rehab. Counselor Dir. Search, Ariz. Coun. for Hearing Impaired, 1994—, mem. rules writing com. 1996; mem. preconf. com. Am. Deafness and Rehab. Assn., San Francisco, 1992-93; mem. Statewide Interpreter Planning Com., Phoenix, 1993—, chair subcom. interpreter preparation planning, 1994—; mem. Com. on Real Time Captioning Project, 1995—; dir. New Agy. Planning Project, 1995—; rep. to bd. Ariz. Assn. of the Deaf, 1995-96, v.p., 1996—; panelist on deaf culture, 1992—. Active Silent Protest, U. Ariz., 1993, Deaf Pres. Now, Gallaudet U., Washington, 1988, Empowerment for the Deaf, Phoenix, 1994, Project Pride Cmty. Outreach, Tucson, 1992-93; com. mem. Christopher City Elections, Tucson, 1992. Recipient Pres. Recognition award Ariz. Assn. of Deaf, 1996, Proclamation Pima County Bd. Suprs., 1996. Mem. ACA, Nat. Rehab. Assn., Ariz. Rehab. Assn., Am. Sign Lang. Club (treas. 1992-93), Ariz. Assn. of the Dear (v.p. 1996—), Kappa Sigma. Democrat. Jewish. Home: 16960 W Falcon Ln Marana AZ 85653-9199 Office: Pima Prevention Partnership 345 E Toole Ave Tucson AZ 85701-1823

SCHUSTER, PHILIP FREDERICK, II, lawyer, writer; b. Denver, Aug. 26, 1945; s. Philip Frederick and Ruth Elizabeth (Robar) S.; m. Barbara Lynn Nordquist, June 7, 1975; children: Philip Christian, Matthew Dale. BA, U. Wash., 1967; JD, Willamette U., 1972. Bar: Oreg. 1972, U.S. Dist. Ct. Oreg. 1974, U.S. Ct. Appeals (9th cir.) 1986, U.S. Supreme Ct. 1986. Dep. dist. atty. Multnomah County, Portland, Oreg., 1972; title examiner Pioneer Nat. Title Co., Portland, 1973-74; assoc. Buss, Leichner et al, Portland, 1975-76; from assoc. to ptnr. Kitson & Bond, Portland, 1976-77; pvt. practice Portland, 1977-95; ptnr. Dierking and Schuster, Portland, 1996—; arbitrator Multnomah County Arbitration Program, 1985—; student mentor Portland Pub. Schs., 1988—. Contbg. author OSB LE Publ., Family Law; contbr. articles to profl. jours. Student mentor Portland Pub. Schs., 1988—; organizer Legal Aid Svcs. for Community Clinics, Salem, Oreg. and Seattle, 1969-73; Dem. committeeman, Seattle, 1965-70. Mem. ABA, ATLA, NAACP (exec. bd. Portland, Oreg. chpt. 1979—), ACLU, Multnomah Bar Assn. (Vol. Lawyers Project), Internat. Platform Assn., Alpha Phi Alpha. Office: 1500 NE Irving St Ste 540 Portland OR 97232-4209 *Hard work and perseverence are the keys to accomplishing any goal. Protecting and nurturing our children and our environment are life's most noble goals. Success is the pursuit of these goals.*

SCHUSTER, ROBERT PARKS, lawyer; b. St. Louis, Oct. 25, 1945; s. William Thomas Schuster and Carolyn Cornforth (Daugherty) Hathaway; 1 child, Susan Michele. AB, Yale U., 1967; JD with honors, U. of Wyo., 1970; LLM, Harvard U., 1971. Bar: Wyo. 1971, U.S. Ct. Appeals (10th cir.) 1979, U.S. Supreme Ct. 1984, Utah 1990. Dep. county atty. County of Natrona, Casper, Wyo., 1971-73; pvt. practice law, Casper, 1973-76; assoc. Spence & Moriarty, Casper, 1976-78; ptnr. Spence, Moriarty & Schuster, Jackson, Wyo., 1978—. Trustee U. Wyo., 1985-89; Wyo. Dem. nominee for U.S. House of Reps., 1994; polit. columnist Casper Star Tribune, 1987-94. Ford Found. Urban Law fellow, 1970-71; pres. United Way of Natrona County, 1974; bd. dirs. Dancers Workshop, 1981-83; chair Wyo. selection com. Rhodes Scholarship, 1989—; mem. bd. visitors Coll. Arts and Scis., U. Wyo., 1991—; mem. Dem. Nat. Com., 1992—; mem. Wyo. Public Policy Forum, 1992—. Mem. ABA, ATLA, Wyo. Trial Lawyers Assn. Home: PO Box 548 Jackson WY 83001-0548 Office: Spence Moriarity & Schuster 15 S Jackson St Jackson WY 83001

SCHÜTRUMPF, ECKART ERNST, classical languages and philosophy educator; b. Marburg, Hesse, Germany, Feb. 3, 1939; came to U.S., 1987; s. Hans Justus and Margarethe (Wetz) S.; m. MaryAnne Leaver, Dec. 21, 1971; children: Fleming, Caroline, Helen, Justin. PhD, Philipps U., Marburg, 1966, Habilitation, 1976. Lectr. Philipps U., Marburg, 1966-81; pvt. docent Philips U., Marburg, 1979-83; sr. lectr. U. Cape Town, 1983-85, prof., 1985-87; prof. classics U. Colo., Boulder, 1987—. Author: Die Bedeutung des Wortes ethos in der Poetik des Aristoteles, 1970, Die Analyse der polis durch Aristoteles, 1980, Xenophon Poroi, Vorschläge zur Beschaffung von Geldmitteln, 1982, Aristoteles Politik Buch I-III (2 vols.), 1991, (with H.J. Gehlke) vol. 3, 1995; contbr. 40 articles to profl. jours. Rsch. scholar Deutsche Forschungsgemeinschaft, 1973-75, Exch. scholar British Coun., 1979, Rsch. scholar Volkswagenwerk Found., 1981-83. Mem. APA, Classical Assn. Mid West and South, Mommsen Gesellschaft. Office: U Colo Classics Dept Campus Box 348 Boulder CO 80309

SCHUTTE, DOROTHY ANNE, art educator; b. Hays, Kans., Aug. 16, 1954; d. James Hewett and Harriett Elaine (Gugler) Rice; m. Jerry Lynn Schutte, Mar. 20, 1975. BA, Ariz. State U., 1976, MFA, 1981. Faculty Mesa (Ariz.) C.C., 1982-90; part-time faculty Ariz. State U. Sch. of Art, Tempe, 1990—; mem. adv. bd. Elizabeth Found. for the Art, N.Y., 1996—. One-man shows include Midwestern St. U., Wichita Falls, Tex., 1996, U. Ariz., 1997; represented in permanent collections Bradley U., Peoria, Ill., 1991, McAllen Internat. Mus., Tex., 1996, Yerseau Musee Internat. Art, Can. Recipient award of excellence Harper Coll. Art Dept., Palatine, Ill., 1990; artist grantee Nat. Ludwig Vojelstein Found, Bklyn., 1991, Internat. Elizabeth Found. for the Arts, N.Y., 1996.

SCHUTZ, JOHN ADOLPH, historian, educator, former university dean; b. L.A., Apr. 10, 1919; s. Adolph J. and Augusta K. (Gluecker) S. AA, Bakersfield Coll., 1940; BA, UCLA, 1942, MA, 1943, PhD, 1945. Asst. prof. history Calif. Inst. Tech., Pasadena, 1945-53; assoc. prof. history Whittier (Calif.) Coll., 1953-56, prof., 1956-65; prof. Am. history U. So. Calif., L.A., 1965-91; chmn. dept. history U. So. Calif., 1974-76, dean social scis. and communication, 1976-82. Author: William Shirley: King's Governor of Massachusetts, 1961, Peter Oliver's Origin and Progress of the American Rebellion, 1967, The Promise of America, 1970, The American Republic, 1978, Dawning of America, 1981, Spur of Fame: Dialogues of John Adams and Benjamin Rush, 1980, A Noble Pursuit: A Sesquicentennial History of the New England Historic Genealogical Society, 1995, Legislators of the Massachusetts General Court, 1691-1780, 1997; joint editor: Golden State Series; contbg. author: Spain's Colonial Outpost, 1985, Generations and Change: Genealogical Perspectives in Social History, 1986, Making of America: Society and Culture of the United States, 1990, rev. edit., 1992. Trustee Citizens Rsch. Found., 1985—. NEH grantee, 1971; Sr. Faculty grantee, 1971-74. Mem. Am. Hist. Assn. (pres. Pacific Coast br. 1972-73, sec.-treas. 1995-96), Am. Studies Assn. (pres. 1974-75), Mass. Hist. Soc. (corr.), New Eng. Hist. Geneal. Soc. (trustee 1988—, editor, author intro. book Boston Merchant Census of 1789, 1989, rec. sec. 1995—), Colonial Soc. Mass. (corr.). Home and Office: 1100 White Knoll Dr Los Angeles CA 90012-1353 *The excitement of collegiate activities makes each year an adventure in learning and a renewal of one's youth.*

SCHUYLER, ROBERT LEN, investment company executive; b. Burwell, Nebr., Mar. 4, 1936; s. Norman S. and Ilva M. (Hoppes) S.; m. Mary Carol Huston, June 13, 1958; children: Kylie Anne, Nina Leigh, Melynn Kae, Gwyer Lenn. BS, U. Nebr., 1958; MBA, Harvard U., 1960. Asst. to treas. Potlatch Forests, Inc., Lewiston, Idaho, 1962-64; dir. corp. planning Potlatch Forests, Inc., San Francisco, 1964-66; mgr. fin. analysis Weyerhaeuser Co., Tacoma, 1966-68; mgr. investment evaluation dept. Weyerhaeuser Co., 1968-70, v.p. fin. and planning, 1970-72, sr. v.p. fin. and planning, 1972-85, exec. v.p., chief fin. officer, 1985-91; mng. ptnr. Nisqually Ptnrs., Tacoma, 1991-95; chief exec. officer, bd. dirs. Grande Alberta Paper, Ltd., 1992—; past mem. nat. adv. bd. Chem. Bank, U. Wash. MBA program, coun. fin. exec. Conf. Bd., Pvt. Sector Coun., exec. com. Am. Paper Inst.; bd. dirs. Multicare Health Sys., Paragon Trade Brands Inc., One Sport, Inc. Vice chmn. Santa Fe County Bd. Econ. Advirs.; vice chmn. Santa Fe Bus. Incubators. Mem. Anglers Club, Sangre de Cristo Flyfishers, Las Campanas Golf & Country Club,. Home and Office: 46 Hollyhock Cir Santa Fe NM 87501-8595

SCHWAB, CHARLES R., brokerage house executive; b. Sacramento, 1937; m. Helen O'Neill; 5 children. Stanford U., 1959, Postgrad., 1961. Formerly mut. fund mgr. Marin County, Calif.; founder brokerage San Francisco, 1971; now chmn., CEO Charles Schwab & Co., Inc. Author: How to be Your Own Stockbroker, 1984. Republican. Office: Charles Schwab & Co Inc 101 Montgomery St San Francisco CA 94104-4122*

SCHWABE, MARCUS CHRISTOPHER, alumni affairs director; b. Winnipeg, Man., Can., Dec. 20, 1960; s. Lothar and Hanna (Ludwinski) S.; m. Lorie Ann Bustard, Aug. 16, 1986; children: Adam, Noah, Kayleigh. BS, U. Alta., 1982, BEd, 1984. High sch. tchr. Strathcona County, Sherwood Park, Alta., Can., 1985-87; real estate sales Re/Max Real Estate, Edmonton, Alta., Can., 1987-88; dir. alumni and ch. rels. Augusta Univ. Coll. (formerly Camrose Luth. U. Coll.), Camrose, Alta., 1988-92, dir. alumni, 1992-95; sr. devel. officer U. Alta., Edmonton, 1995—; owner Lifecare, 1985—; cons., presenter Lifecare, 1985—; owner Kidz-Own, 1993-96. Editor Kaluko mag., 1988-90, 94-95. Mem. coms. Evang. Luth. Ch. Can., chairperson synod youth com., 1982-88, mem. Alta. and the Ters. synod stewardship com., chairperson Office for Resource Devel., mgr. convs., coach slow pitch baseball team. Mem. Assn. Univs. and Colls. Can., Assn. Can. Alumni Adminstrn., Can. Coun. for Advancement of Edn., Coun. for Advancement and Support of Edn., Nat. Soc. Fund Raising Execs. (treas. 1996—), Assn. Alta. Fund-Raising Execs. (program chair), Augustana U. Coll. Alumni Assn. (exec. dir., bd. dirs. 1995). Home: 4504 13th Ave, Edmonton, AB Canada T6L 4A3 Office: U Alberta Devel Office, 4th Fl Athabasca Hall, Edmonton AB, AB Canada T6G 2E8

SCHWABE, PETER ALEXANDER, JR., judge; b. Portland, Oreg., July 23, 1935; s. Peter Alexander and Evelyn (Zingleman) S.; A.B., Stanford, 1958; J.D., Willamette U., 1960; m. Bonnie Jean LeBaron, June 21, 1958; children: Mark, Karen, Diane, Patricia, Kurt. Admitted to Oreg. bar, 1960; pvt. practice, Portland, 1960-76; fed. adminstrv. law judge, 1976—. Mem. ABA, Oreg. State Bar Assn., Beta Theta Pi, Phi Delta Phi. Home: 4366 Dorking Ct Sacramento CA 95864-6150 Office: 2031 Howe Ave Sacramento CA 95825-0176

SCHWALLER, JOHN FREDERICK, historian; b. Hays, Kans., July 2, 1948; s. Henry and Juliette (Trembly) S.; m. Anne Cardot Taylor, Aug. 15, 1970; children: Robert Clemens, William Henry. AB, Grinnell (Ia.) Coll., 1969; MA, U. Kans., 1971; PhD, Ind. U., 1978. Asst. prof. Fort Hays State U., Hays, Kans., 1978-79; asst. prof. Fla. Atlantic U., Boca Raton, 1979-82, assoc. prof., 1982-86, prof. history, 1986—, asst. dean, 1989-90, assoc. dean, 1990-93; dir. Acad. Am. Franciscan History Franciscan Sch. Theology, Berkeley, Calif., 1993—; assoc. provost, prof. history U. Mont., Missoula, 1995—. Author: A Kansan Looks at the Mexican Highway Association, 1971, Partidos y parrocos bajo la real corona en la Nueva Espana, sigio XVI, 1981, Origins of Church Wealth in Mexico: Ecclesiastical Finances and Church Revenues, 1523-1600, 1985, The Church and Clergy in Sixteenth-Century Mexico, 1987; contbr. articles to profl. jours. Grantee Fla. Atlantic U., 1980, 81, 82, 83, 88, Am. Philos. Soc., 1982, NEH, 1989-90; fellow Newberry Library Assocs., 1982, Fulbright-Hays, 1982-83, Tulane U., 1983, Tinker Found., 1984-86. Mem. Am. Hist. Assn., Conf. Latin Am. History, Latin Am. Studies Assn., Rocky Mountain Conf. Latin Am. Studies, Phi Alpha Theta, Sigma Delta Pi. Democrat. Episcopalian. Office: Univ Montana Office of Provost Missoula MT 59812-1340

SCHWANTES, CARLOS ARNALDO, history educator, consultant; b. Wilmington, N.C., Mar. 7, 1945; s. Arnaldo and Frances (Casteen) S.; m. Mary Alice Dassenko, Sept. 4, 1966; children: Benjamin, Matthew. BA, Andrews U., 1967; MA, U. Mich., 1968, PhD, 1976. From instr. to prof. Walla Walla Coll., College Place, Wash., 1969-85; prof. history U. Idaho, Moscow, 1984—; cons. TV History of Idaho, 1988. Author: Coxey's Army: An American Odyssey, 1985, The Pacific Northwest: An Interpretive History, 1989, In Mountain Shadows: A History of Idaho, 1991, Railroad Signatures Across the Pacific Northwest, 1993; also author or editor 7 other books; mem. editl. bd. Pacific N.W. Quar., 1982-97, Idaho Yesterdays, 1987—, Forest and Conservation History, 1988-95, Pacific Hist. Rev., 1991-95; contbr. articles to profl. jours. NEH fellow, 1982-83, rsch. fellow Idaho Humanities Coun., 1989-90; Idaho State Bd. Edn. rsch. grantee, 1990-91. Mem. Orgn. Am. Historians, Western History Assn., Mining History Assn. (coun. 1990-94), Lexington Soc., Idaho State Hist. Soc. Republican. Seventh-day Adventist. Office: U Idaho Dept History Moscow ID 83844

SCHWANTES, ROBERT SIDNEY, international relations executive; b. Beetown Township, Wis., July 11, 1922; s. Kurt John and Lillian Ellen (Walker) S.; m. Marion Laura Miles, July 15, 1943; children: Virginia, Janet, Ingrid. AB summa cum laude, Harvard U., 1943; MA, U. Colo., 1947; PhD, Harvard U., 1950. Instr. in history Harvard U., Cambridge, Mass., 1950-52; Carnegie rsch. fellow Coun. on Foreign Rels., N.Y.C., 1952-54; various positions The Asia Found., San Francisco and Tokyo, 1954-66; dir. of programs The Asia Found., San Francisco, 1966-69, v.p. for programs, 1969-84, exec. v.p., 1984-88; vis. rsch. scholar Hoover Inst., Stanford, 1988—; mem. Am. adv. com. Japan Found., Tokyo, 1984-86. Author: Japanese and Americans, 1955; contbr. articles to profl. jours. Vestryman St. Paul's Episcopal Ch., Burlingame, Calif., 1993-95. Lt. (j.g.), US NR, 1942-46, PTO. Assn. Asian Studies, World Affairs Coun. No. Calif. Democrat. Home: 1432 Benito Ave Burlingame CA 94010-5550

SCHWANZ, JUDITH ANN, seminary educator; b. Cleve., Apr. 19, 1955; d. Roger Alan and Jane Marie (Forsberg) Munson; m. Keith Duane Schwanz, June 28, 1975; children: Karla Kimberlee, Jason Andrew. MA in Counseling, Western Evang. Sem., 1987; MS in Psychology, Portland State U., 1994, PhD in Systems Sci. Psychology, 1996. Ordained min. Ch. of the Nazarene, 1989. In-patient staff counselor Christian Therapy Program, Portland, Oreg., 1987-89; counselor Christian Counseling Inst., Portland, 1987-90; adj. faculty mem. Western Evang. Sem., Portland, 1987-89, prof., 1989—; chair grad. dept. counseling Western Evang. Sem./George Fox U., Portland, 1995—. Dir. women's ministry Ch. of the Nazarene, 1979-88, 92—. Mem. APA, ACA, Assn. Counseling Edn. Supervision. Home: 7700 SE Strawberry Ln Portland OR 97267-5469

SCHWARTZ, ARTHUR ALAN, surgeon; b. N.Y.C., Sept. 16, 1945; s. Philip and Selma (Galen) S.; m. Ann Mass, June 14, 1969 (div. Mar. 1986); 1 child, Chelsea Lara; m. Lorie Jane Lybeck, Mar. 26, 1988; 1 child, Spencer Loren. BA, Columbia Coll., 1965; MD, NYU, 1969. Diplomate Am. Bd. Surgery. Surg. intern N.Y. Hosp.-Cornell Med. Ctr., N.Y.C., 1969-70; surg. resident Peter Bent Brigham Hosp., Children's Hosp., Harvard Med. Sch., Boston, 1970-73; surg. chief resident UCLA Harbor Gen. Hosp., Torrance, Calif., 1973-75, asst. prof. surgery, 1975-78; pvt. practice surgery Aspen (Colo.) Valley Hosp., 1978-92; surgeon No. Calif. Trauma Group, San Jose, Calif., 1992-93; pvt. practice surgery Mid-County Surg. Group, Capitola, Calif., 1993—. Fellow ACS; mem. Santa Cruz Med. Soc. Home: 2520 N Rodeo Gulch Rd Soquel CA 95073-9713 Office: Mid County Surg Group 1505 Soquel Dr Santa Cruz CA 95065

SCHWARTZ, ARTHUR ALLEN, trade show producer; b. Far Rockaway, N.Y., Mar. 11, 1931; s. Henry and Esther (Aronson) S.; children: Ellen, Steven. Student, U. Okla., 1949-51; BA, U. Conn., 1953. Account exec. Alfred Auerbach Assn., N.Y.C., 1952-55; sales rep, mgr. Aetna Life and Other Ins. Cos., N.Y.C., Phoenix, 1955-62; assoc. dir. Elec. League of Ariz., Phoenix, 1963-65; account exec. KTAR-TV, Phoenix, 1965-68; producer Ariz. Home Beautiful Show, Phoenix, 1966-68; exec. dir. Elec. Industries Assn., L.A., 1968-72; pres. Mktg., Assn. Svcs., L.A., 1972—. Contbr. over 100 articles on assn. mgt. to jours. in field, 1980-96. Mem. Mayor's City Audit Com., Phoenix, Ariz. Acad. Created promotion listed among top 60 Advertising Age, 1974. Mem. Western Assn. Equipment Lessors (life), Am. Soc. Assn. Execs. (Mgmt. Achievement award 1972), Internat. Assn. Exhibit Mgrs., Nat. Speakers Assn. Home: 5100 Via Dolce Marina Dl Rey CA 90292-7253 Office: 11110 Ohio Ave Los Angeles CA 90025-3329

SCHWARTZ, ARTHUR SOLOMON, research psychologist; b. N.Y.C., June 12, 1924; s. Aaron and Elsie (Silverstein) S.; m. Eileen Hannigan, June 2, 1951; children—Amy, Andrew, Jainah, Beth, Nancy. B.A., NYU, 1950; Ph.D., U. Buffalo, 1957, postdoctoral fellow, UCLA, 1956-58. Research psychologist NIH, Washington, 1958-62, Barrow Neurol. Inst., Phoenix, 1962-96; faculty assoc. prof. Ariz. State U. West, Phoenix, 1962—; cons. in field. Contbr. articles to profl. jours. Served with U.S. Army, 1943-46. Grantee NIH, NSF. Mem. Soc. Neurosci. Democrat. Jewish. Office: Barrow Neurol Inst 350 W Thomas Rd Phoenix AZ 85013-4409

SCHWARTZ, BETTY BARSHA, secondary education educator, writer, artist; b. Bklyn., Dec. 3, 1932; d. John Barsha and Daisy (Lack) Ferrari; m. Arthur Nathaniel Schwartz, Jan. 13, 1968 (div. Feb. 1980); 1 child, Jonathan Matthew. BA, Syracuse U., 1954; MPA, Calif. State U., Northridge, 1994. Ind. researcher, writer L.A., 1980-85; acct. exec. AT&T, L.A., 1985-92; policy analyst L.A. County Met. Transp. Authority, L.A., 1993; spl. events coord. Taiwan program Ctr. for Internat. Tng. and Devel., USC Sch. Pub. Adminstrn., 1994; mem. tchg. staff William S. Hart H.S., Santa Clarita, Calif., 1994—; project cons., guest lectr. Pasadena City Coll.; mem. scholar and adv. com. MTA Red Line Project, Ea. ext., 1994. Author: Tracking Transit Art, 1994, Art on Track, 1994; one-woman shows include Paideia Gallery, L.A., 1964, 1966, Orange County Art Assn., Fullerton, Calif., 1964; exhibited in group shows at Paideia Gallery, L.A., 1963, 64, 65, L.A. Art Assn., 1964, 65, Calif. State Coll., Long Beach, 1965, Bakersfield (Calif.) Coll., 1966, Long Beach Mus. Art, 1967, Fine Arts Fedn., Burbank, Calif., 1982, Orange County Art Assn., Brea, Calif., 1983, 86, Riverside (Calif.) Art Mus., 1987; represented in pvt. collections. Media relations vol. Stevenson Ranch (Calif.) Town Coun., 1992; campaign vol. Clinton campaign, Santa Clarita Valley Dem. Club, 1992, Senator Roberti's No on Recall, N. Hollywood, 1994. Recipient Second award modern oil All Calif. Art Exhibit, Riverside, 1966, Honorable Mention award Joslyn Ctr. of Arts, Torrance, Calif., 1984. Mem. Am. Soc. Pub. Adminstrn. Home: 25124 Steinbeck Ave Unit G Santa Clarita CA 91381-1293

SCHWARTZ, CHERIE ANNE KARO, storyteller, writer; b. Miami, Fla., Feb. 24, 1951; d. William Howard and Dorothy (Olesh) Karo; m. Lawrence Schwartz, Aug. 12, 1979. BA in Lit., The Colo. Coll., 1973; MA in Devel. Theater, U. Colo., 1977. Tchr. English, drame, mime, creative writing, speech coach South High Sch., Pueblo, Colo., 1973-76; tchr. English and drama Rocky Mountain Hebrew Acad., Denver, 1981-83; full-time profl. storyteller throughout N.Am., 1982—; storyteller, docent, tchr. tng., mus. outreach Denver Mus. Natural History, 1982—; trainer, cons., performer, lectr, keynote speaker various orgns., synagogues, instns., agys., confs. throughout the country, 1982—; co-founder, chairperson Omanim b'Yachad: Artists Together, Nat. Conf. Celebrating Storytelling, Drama, Music and Dance in Jewish Edn., Denver, 1993. Storyteller: (audio cassette tapes) Cherie Karo Schwartz Tells Stories of Hanukkah from Kar-Ben Books, 1986, Cherie Karo Schwartz Tells Stories of Passover From Kar-Ben Books, 1986, Miriam's Trambourine, 1988, Worldwide Jewish Stories of Wishes and Wisdom, 1988; storyteller, actor: (video tape) The Wonderful World of Recycle, 1989; author: (book) My Lucky Dreidel: Hanukkah Stories, Songs, Crafts, Recipes and Fun for Kids, 1994; author numerous stories in anthologies of Jewish literature. Title III grantee State of Colo. Edn., Pueblo, 1975-76. Mem. Coalition for Advancement of Jewish Edn. (coord. Jewish Storytelling Conf. 1989—, coord. Nat. Jewish Storytelling Network), Nat. Assn. for Preservation and Perpetuation of Storytelling, Nat. Storytelling Assn. (Colo. state rep. and liaison), Rocky Mountain Storytelling Guild, Rocky Mountain Storyteller's Conf. (bd. mem., performer, tchr.). Democrat. Jewish. Home: 996 S Florence St Denver CO 80231-1952

SCHWARTZ, DALE LEWIS, physician; b. Manhattan, Kans., June 25, 1932; s. Willard C. and Oma Grace (Lemon) S.; m. Mary Maxinoski, Jan. 11, 1958 (div. Sept. 1, 1977); children: Margaret, Deanna; m. Sharon D. Glasgow, Aug. 31, 1985. BS, Kans. State U., 1954; MD, Northwestern U., 1958. Diplomate Am. Bd. Internal Medicine. Intern Cook County Hosp., Chgo., 1958-59; resident in internal medicine VA Rsch. Hosp., Chgo., 1959-62, fellow in hematology, 1962-63; trainee USPHS, 1963-64; pvt. practice Manhattan, 1964-71, Rancho Mirage, Calif., 1971-87, Prescott, Ariz., 1987—; locum tenens physician Consol. Troop Med. Med. Clinic, Ft. Leonard Wood, Mo., 1995; physician Prescott VA Med. Ctr., 1987-95; mem. staff St. Mary Hosp, Kans., 1964-71, Meml. Hosp., Kans., 1964-71, Eisenhower Meml. Hosp., Rancho Mirage, 1971-87, Desert Hosp., Palm Springs, Calif., 1971-81, VA Med. Ctr., Prescott, 1987-95; mem. staff Keystone Rural Health Consortia, Cameron County Health Care, Emporium, Pa., 1995-96, Geisinger Health Care Assocs., Dallas, Pa., 1996, 97. Contbr. articles to profl. publs. Named Physician of Yr. Mil. Order Purple Heart, 1992. Mem. Phi Kappa Phi. Home and Office: 438 Fox Hollow Prescott AZ 86303

SCHWARTZ, HARRIETTE JEANNE, television operations company executive; b. N.Y.C., Aug. 26, 1950; d. Max Alan and Gussie (Chasan) S.; m. Jay Gary Sanderson, Nov. 22, 1978 (div. July 1990, dec. June 1993); 1 child, Merelle Ellen. Student Announcer Tng. Studios, 1972. 3rd Class license FCC. Reporter special events dept. Radio Free Europe, N.Y.C., 1972-74; traffic, production mgr. Broadcasting Div., Inc., N.Y.C., 1974-76; post production, traffic supr. Video Prodns., Inc., N.Y.C., 1976-77; v.p. TV ops. Fremantle Internat., Inc./Fremantle Corp., N.Y.C., 1977-85, v.p. global ops., 1985-87; dir. sales service, King Features Entertainment, 1987-88, ACI, L.A., 1991-94, Twentieth TV Internat., Hollywood, Calif., 1995—. Contbr. articles to profl. jours. Avocations: writing poetry and articles, keeping active, reading, photography, roller blading. Office: Twentieth TV Internat. 1546 N Argyle Ave Hollywood CA

SCHWARTZ, JOHN BENJAMIN, telecommunications and real estate executive; b. N.Y.C., July 19, 1950; s. Jerome Stephen and Anne (Simmons) S.; m. Diane Roberta Markrow, Jan. 12, 1985; children: Brendan, Jonathan. Student, Stanford U., 1969-70. Co-founder, gen. mgr. WYEP-FM, Pitts., 1972-75; founder, pres. KBDI-TV, Broomfield, Colo., 1976-80; telecom. cons. Boulder, Colo., 1980—; pres. Instrnl. Telecom. Found., Boulder, 1983—; gen. ptnr. J-K Realty Ptnrs., Boulder, 1983—; pres. The 90's Channel, Boulder, 1989-95; chief bureaucrat The 90's, Chgo., 1989-92; pres. Free Speech TV, 1995—; mgr. REM Investments, LLC, Boulder, Colo.,

1997—; bd. dirs. Inst. for Alternative Journalism, Sta. WYBE-TV, Phila.; pres., dir. Sta. KRZA-FM, Alamosa, Colo., 1982-84, hon. dir., 1984—. Contbr. articles to profl. jours. Mem. adv. bd. Ctr. for Media Edn., Washington, 1993—. English Spkg. Union scholar, 1969. Democrat. Office: Instrnl Telecom Found PO Box 6060 Boulder CO 80306-6060

SCHWARTZ, JOHN CHARLES, chemical engineer; b. Seattle, Apr. 30, 1939; s. Charles and Elizabeth Mercy (Dougherty) S.; m. Sandra Helene Waroff, Aug. 20, 1960 (div. Sept. 1982); children: Barry, Allan, Craig. BS in Chemistry, U. Okla., 1960; MS in Chemistry, Rutgers U., 1968. Research chemist FMC Corp., Carteret and Princeton, N.J., 1962-74; sr. process engr. FMC Corp., Green River, Wyo., 1974-94; ret., 1994; technologist phosphorous chem. divsn. FMC Corp., Green River, Wyo., 1989-94; lab. stockroom operator U. Okla., Norman, 1956-60. Contbr. articles to prof. jours.; patentee in field. Co-founder Cong. Beth Israel of Sweetwater County, Wyo., Wyo. chpt. Nat. Alliance for Mentally Ill, pres. Sweetwater County, Wyo. chpt.; facilitator Post Polio Support Group, Rock Springs, Wyo.; mem. adv. bd. Wyo. Easter Seal. Capt. Chem. Corps, U.S. Army, 1960-66. Mem. VFW, Am. Inst. Chem. Engr., Am. Legion, Am. Chem. Soc. (pres. U. Okla. chpt. 1957), Nat. Mental Health Consumer's Assn., Alpha Epsilon Pi, Alpha Chi Sigma, Phi Lambda Upsilon, Phi Eta Sigma. Democrat. Jewish. Lodge: Eagles. Home: PO Box 648 Green River WY 82935-0648 *Personal philosophy: We are all God's children--Above all else, I follow the Golden Rule.*

SCHWARTZ, LAWRENCE, aeronautical engineer; b. N.Y.C., Nov. 30, 1935; s. Harry and Fanny (Steiner) S.; m. Cherie Anne Karo, Aug. 12, 1979; children: Ronda, Daran. SB in Aero. Engring., MIT, 1958, SM in Aero. Engring., 1958; postgrad. Ohio State U., 1960, U. Dayton, 1962-63; PhD in Engring., UCLA, 1966. Electronics design engr. MIT. Instrumentation Lab., Cambridge, 1959; aerospace engr., Wright-Patterson AFB, Ohio, 1962-63; mem. tech. staff Hughes Aircraft Co., Culver City, Calif., 1963-65, staff engr., 1965-67, sr. staff engr., 1967-72, sr. scientist, 1972-79, chief scientist lab., 1979-93, tech. mgr. 1985-87; chmn., tech. adv. bd., 1987-88, prin. scientist/engr. 1993—; cons., tchr. in field. With USAF, 1959-62. Registered profl. engr., Colo., Calif. Mem. IEEE, AAAS, Sigma Xi, Sigma Gamma Tau, Tau Beta Pi. Contbr. articles to profl. jours. Home: 996 S Florence St Denver CO 80231-1952 Office: 16800 E Centretech Pky Aurora CO 80011-9046

SCHWARTZ, LAWRENCE JAY, ophthalmologist; b. Bklyn., May 24, 1943; s. Nathan and Rita Joan (Smolensky) S.; m. Sandra Berlin, Dec. 21, 1969; children: Andria, Richard, Marla. BA, Cornell U., 1964; MD, SUNY, Buffalo, 1968. Diplomate Am. Bd. Ophthalmology. Intern L.A. County-U. So. Calif. Med. Ctr., L.A., 1968-69, resident in internal medicine, 1969; resident in ophthalmology Pacific Med. Ctr., San Francisco, 1970-72; ophthalmologist in pvt. practice, L.A., 1974—; ophthalmology cons. L.A. Olympics, 1984; assoc. dir. Ellis Eye Ctr., L.A., 1983—; mem. med. exec. com. Cedars-Sinai Med. Ctr., L.A., 1990-93. Co-author textbook chpt. Bd. dirs. Crittenton Ctr., L.A., 1984-88. Served to maj. U.S. Army, 1973-74. Fellow Am. Acad. Ophthalmology, Phi Delta Epsilon (pres. 1986-87). Republican. Jewish. Office: 8635 W 3rd St Ste 390W Los Angeles CA 90048-6101

SCHWARTZ, LOUIS, radiologist; b. N.Y.C., Sept. 19, 1940; s. Abraham and Paula (Hojmon) S.; m. Marilyn Carole Altman, Aug. 28, 1965; children: Debra, Steven, Susan. BS magna cum laude, Adelphi Coll., 1961; MD, Albert Einstein Coll. Medicine, 1965. Radiologist Riverside (Calif.) Gen. Hosp., 1971-96; radiologist Parkview Community Hosp., Riverside, 1972-96, chief radiology, 1979-96; retired, 1996; pres. Arlington Radiol. Med. Group Inc., Riverside, 1982-96; chief of staff Parkview Community Hosp., Riverside, 1990-91. Mem. AMA, Am. Coll. Radiology, Calif. Radiol. Soc., Inland Radiol. Soc. (pres. 1979), Riverside County Med. Assn. Office: Arlington Radiol Med Group Inc 3900 Sherman Dr Riverside CA 92503-4005

SCHWARTZ, MICHAEL WARREN, physician investigator; b. Durham, N.C., Oct. 3, 1954; s. Theodore B. and Mrs. Schwartz; m. Patricia Shannon, June 30, 1984; children: Jay Wesley, Anne Shannon. BA in Biology, U. Colo., 1978; MD, Rush Med. Coll., 1983. Intern U. Wash. Sch. Medicine, Seattle, 1983-84, resident, 1984-86; acting instr. divsn. metabolism, endocrinology & nutrition U. Wash. Dept. Medicine & VA Med. Ctr., Seattle, 1990-92, acting ass.t prof., 1992-93, asst. prof., 1993—. Contbr. articles to profl. jours. Sr. Rsch. fellow in endocrinology and nutrition U. Wash. Sch. Medicine and VA Med. Ctr., 1987-89; recipient Nathan M. Freer award, 1983, NIH Rsch. Svc. award, 1987-90, Dept. Vets. Affairs Assoc. Investigator award, 1989, Pilot and Feasibility award, U. Wash., 1991, NIH Physician Scientist award, 1992, others. Mem. AMA, Am. Coll. Physicians, Am. Diabetes Assn., Am. Fedn. Clin. Rsch., N.Am. Assn. Study Obesity, Endocrine Soc., Alpha Omega Alpha, Sigma Xi. Office: VA Med Ctr Dept Medicine 1660 S Columbian Way Seattle WA 98108-1532

SCHWARTZ, MODEST EUPHEMIA, real estate company executive; b. Chgo., Dec. 14, 1915; d. Giles E. and Evelyn (Tomczak) Ratkowski; m. Edward Joseph Schwartz, Feb. 9, 1946 (dec. July 1979); children: Kathryn Ann, Edward Thomas. BA, UCLA, 1936, MA, 1938; libr. credential, Immaculate Heart Coll., L.A., 1958. Cert. tchr., libr., Calif. Tchr. Alhambra (Calif.) City Schs., 1938-58, libr., 1958-72; v.p. Fremont Svc., Alhambra, 1959-83, pres., 1983-86; v.p. Moulding Supply Co., Alhambra, 1967-83, pres., 1983-85; v.p., bd. dirs. Sequoia Mgmt. Co., Alhambra, 1969-86; mng. ptnr. SRSH Realty Ptnrs., Alhambra, 1986-89. Bd. dirs. Found. for Cardiovasc. Rsch., Pasadena, Calif., 1973-85, Progressive Savs., Alhambra, 1979-85; mem. Ret. Sr. Vol. Program, Alhambra, 1979—; mem. Alhambra Hosps. Aux., 1987—, med. libr., 1990—; mem. Friends of Alhambra Pub. Libr., 1981—, treas., 1993—; pres. bd. trustees Alhambra Pub. Libr., 1981-83, 89-91, mem., 1976-83, 85-93; pres. Alhambra Pub. Libr. Found., 1990-96; mem. Los Angeles County Art Mus., Met. Mus., N.Y.C. Mem. ALA, NEA, AAUW (life, Edn. Found. grant in her name 1988, br. treas. 1986-88, 89-91, corr. and rec. sec. 1992-93, co-chair ways-and means com. 1993—, auditor 1995-96), Calif. Ret. Tchrs. Assn. (co-chair hospitality 1991-93, membership chmn., 2d v.p. membership Pasadena-Foothill divsn. 1993-95, chmn. neighborhood group Pasadena-Foothill divsn. 1995—), UCLA Alumni Assn. Home: 30400 San Franciquito Canyon Rd Saugus CA 91350

SCHWARTZ, STEPHEN WAYNE, critical care, emergency and recovery room nurse; b. Alva, Okla., July 4, 1957; s. Arthur Gregory and Fern Marie (Burns) S. Cert. EMT, Phoenix Community Coll., 1982; LPN, Maricopa Tech. Community Coll., 1986, ADN, 1987; AAS in Electro-neuro Diagnostics, Phoenix Coll., 1992. RN, Ariz. EMT Ariz. Ambulance & Rescue, Mesa; LPN orthopedic and psychiatry Maricopa Med. Ctr., Phoenix; RN John C. Lincoln Hosp., Phoenix, Med Pro, Inc., Phoenix, Phoenix Bapt. Hosp., Health Temp, Inc., Phoenix. Mem. The Cousteau Soc.

SCHWARTZ, STEVEN MICHAEL, cardiothoracic surgeon; b. L.A., Oct. 14, 1955; s. Gary Howard and Ethel (Feiler) S.; m. Debra Charlen Durbin, Feb. 20, 1983; children: Rachel, Elise, Amanda. BS, U. Calif., Irvine, 1977, MD, 1981. Diplomate Am. Bd. Surgery, Am. Bd. Thoracic Surgery. Intern U. Calif. Med. Ctr., Irvine, 1981-82; resident surgery U. Hawaii, Honolulu, 1983-87, chief resident surgery, 1986-87, asst. prof. surgery, 1987-89; chief resident cardiac surgery U. Calif. San Diego Med. Ctr., 1989-91; pvt. practice San Jose (Calif.) Cardiac Surgery Group, 1991—. Contbr. articles to profl. jours. Grantee NSF, Irvine, 1975; Hawaii Heart Assn. fellow, Honolulu, 1987-89. Fellow ACS, Am. Coll. Cardiology, Am. Coll. Chest Physicians; mem. Soc. Thoracic Surgeons, Calif. Med. Assn. Office: San Jose Cardiac Surgery Group 3803 S Bascom Ave Ste 100 Campbell CA 95008-7317

SCHWARTZMAN, ARNOLD MARTIN, film director, graphic designer; b. London, England, Jan. 6, 1936; came to U.S., 1978; s. David and Rose S.; m. Isolde, Oct. 17, 1980; 1 child, Hannah. Student, Canterbury Coll. Art, 1953, Nat. Diploma in Design, 1955. Sr. designer Associated Rediffusion TV, London, England, 1959-65; concept planning exec. Erwin-Wasey Advt., London, England, 1965-68; dir. Conran Design Group, London, England, 1968-69; prin. Designers Film Unit, London, England, 1969-78; film dir. The Directors Studio, London, England, 1969-78; design dir. Saul Bass and Assoc. Inc., L.A., 1978-79; pres. Arnold Schwartzman Prod., L.A., 1979—; dir. design Olympic Games, L.A., 1982-83. Author, photographer: Graven Images, 1993; author: Phono-Graphics, 1993; co-author: Airshipwreck, 1978, Code Name: The Long Sobbing, 1994, Anglafile: The Best of British in Los Angeles, 1994; designer 69th Acad. Awards Poster. Recipient Oscar Acad. award, Acad. Motion Picture Arts and Scis., 1982, Silver award, Designers and Art Dirs. Assn. London, 1969, 71, 75. Mem. Acad. Motion Picture Arts and Scis. (documentary exec. com.), Alliance Graphique Internationale, Brit. Acad. Film and TV Arts (co-chmn.). Home: 317 1/2 N Sycamore Ave Los Angeles CA 90036-2689

SCHWARZ, GERARD, conductor, musician; b. Weehawken, N.J., Aug. 19, 1947; s. John and Gerta (Weiss) S.; m. Jody Greitzer, June 23, 1984; children: Alysandra, Daniel, Gabriella, Julian. BS, Juilliard Sch., 1972, MA, 1972; DFA (hon.), Fairleigh Dickinson U., Seattle U.; DMus (hon.), U. Puget Sound. Trumpet player Am. Symphony Orch., 1965-72, Am. Brass Quintet, 1965-73, N.Y. Philharm., 1973-77; trumpet player, guest condr. Aspen Music Festival, 1969-75, bd. dirs., 1973-75; music dir. Erick Hawkins Dance Co., 1967-72, SoHo Ensemble, 1969-75, Eliot Feld Ballet Co., N.Y.C., 1972-78; prin. condr. Waterloo Festival, 1975-93, Music Sch. Princeton (N.J.) U.; music dir. N.Y. Chamber Symphony, 1977—, L.A. Chamber Orch., 1978-86, White Mountains (N.H.) Music Festival, 1978-80, Music Today at Merkin Concert Hall, N.Y.C., 1988-89; music advisor Mostly Mozart Festival, Lincoln Ctr., N.Y.C., 1982-84, music dir., 1984—; music advisor Seattle Symphony, 1983-84, prin. condr., 1984-85, music dir., 1985—; artistic advisor Tokyu Bunkamura's Orchard Hall, Japan, 1994—; mem. faculty Juilliard Sch., N.Y.C., 1975-83, Mannes Coll. Music, 1973-79, Montclair (N.J.) State Coll., 1975-80; guest condr. various orchs. including Phila. Orch., L.A. Philharmonic, St. Louis, Buffalo, Detroit, San Francisco, Atlanta, Houston, Pitts., Minn., Jerusalem Symphony, Israel Chamber Orch., Moscow Philharmonic, Moscow Radio Orch., Orch. Nat. de France, Paris, London Symphony Orch., Frankfurt Radio, Stockholm Radio, Helsinki Philharm., Ensemble InterContemporain, Monte Carlo Philharm., Nat. Orch. Spain, English Chamber Orch., London Symphony, Scottish Chamber Orch., City of Birmingham (Eng.) Symphony, Nouvel Orchestre Philharmonique, Sydney (Australia) Symphony, Melbourne (Australia) Symphony, Orchestre National de Lyon, France, Orchestre Philharm. de Montpellier, France, Washington Opera, Da Capo Chamber Players, 20th Century Chamber Orch., Chamber Music Soc. Lincoln Ctr., San Francisco Opera, Seattle Opera, Tokyu Bunkamura, Japan, Residentie Orch. of The Hague, The Netherlands, St. Louis Symphony, London Mozart Players, Kirov Orch., St. Petersburg, Russia, Tokyo Philharm., Royal Liverpool (Eng.) Philharm., Vancouver (Can.) Symphony Orch., City of London Symphonia, Evian Festival in France, 1994; also numerous appearances on TV; rec. artist Columbia, Nonesuch, Vox, MMO, Desto, Angel, Delos records; record: Seattle Symphony 1994-95 Season, 1995. Bd. dirs. Naumburg Found., 1975—. Recipient award for concert artists Ford Found., 1973, Grammy award nominee, Mumms Ovation award, Record of Yr. awards, Ditson Condrs. award Columbia U., 1989; named Condr. of Yr., Musical Am. Internat. Directory of Performing Arts, 1994.*

SCHWARZ, GLENN VERNON, editor; b. Chgo., Nov. 24, 1947; s. Vernon Edward and LaVerne Louise (Schuster) S.; m. Cynthia Frances Meisenhoelder, June 17, 1984; 1 child, Chloe. BA, San Francisco State U., 1970. Sports writer San Francisco Examiner, 1970-87, sports editor, 1988—. Fundraiser San Francisco Zoological Soc., 1987—. Mem. AP Sports Editors, Baseball Writers Assn. Am. (bd. dirs. 1986-87). Office: San Francisco Examiner 110 5th St San Francisco CA 94103-2918

SCHWARZ, I. GENE, psychiatry educator; b. N.Y.C., Nov. 20, 1930; married; 3 children. BS, Wagner Coll., 1951, MA, 1953; MD, Med. Coll. Ga., 1960. Diplomate Am. Bd. Pschiatry and Neurology; cert. psychoanalyst. Instr. psychiatry U. Cin. Coll. Medicine, 1964-68; pvt. practice psychiatry, 1964—, pvt. practice psychoanalysis, 1965—; asst. prof. psychiatry U. Cin. Coll. Medicine, 1968-70; asst. dir. psychiatry Cin. Gen. Hosp., 1968-70; instr. Denver Inst. Psychoanalysis U. Colo. Sch. Medicine, 1970-71, asst. clin. prof. dept. psychiatry, 1970-84, assoc. clin. prof., 1984-92, clin. prof., 1992—; psychology specialist U.S. Army, 1953-55; sch. psychologist Richmond County Bd. Edn., Augusta, Ga., 1955-56; staff mem. Colo. Gen. Hosp., U. Colo. Health Scis. Ctr., Denver, 1970—; inst. assoc. Denver Inst. Psychoanalysis, U. Colo. Sch. Medicine, 1971-73, faculty mem., 1973—, assoc. tng. and supervising analyst, 1974-76, tng. analyst, 1976—, supervising analyst, 1979—; treas., 1983-86, assoc. dir., 1986-89, dir., 1989-92; cons. in field. Contbr. articles to profl. jours. Recipient Commendation, Chief Justice Pringle, Supreme Ct. of State of Colo., 1978, Svc. award Supreme Ct. Grievance Com. of State of Colo., 1978. Fellow Am. Psychiat. Assn., Colo. Psychiat. Assn.; mem. Internat. Psychoanalytic Assn., Am. Psychoanalytic Assn. (membership com. 1983-86, fellow to bd. of profl. standards 1984-92, com. for non-med. clin. tng. 1988), Denver Psychoanalytic Soc. (sec. 1973-75, chmn. membership com. 1982-85, v.p. 1985-87). Office: 4900 Cherry Creek South Dr Denver CO 80222-2283

SCHWARZ, JOSEPH RICHARD, engineering manager; b. Pomona, Calif., Dec. 7, 1954; s. Robert Joseph and Edith M. (Varian) S.; m. Pamela Anne Galligan, Apr. 8, 1978 (div. June 1983); m. Kathleen Linda Varder, Aug. 23, 1996. BSEE magna cum laude, Calif. State Polytech. U., Pomona, 1977. Digital systems engr. Metron Corp., Upland, Calif., 1977-78; installation mgr. Hughes Aircraft, Denmark, Hawaii and Fed. Republic Germany, 1978-88; co-owner Penrose Gallery, Big Bear Lake, Calif., 1988-90; system engr. Gen. Dynamics, Pomona, Calif., 1989-91; ops. mgr. Amacron/Cycad Corp., Rancho Cucamonga, Calif., 1991-94; sr. system engr. Sysecca Inc., Marina del Rey, Calif., 1995—; installation mgr. Chgo. Transit Authority Supervisory Control Sys., Balt. Transit Authority. Telephone counselor Garden Grove (Calif.) Community Ch., 1984-90. Mem. ACLU, L.A. Music Ctr., Sierra Club, Toastmasters, Eta Kappa Nu, Tau Beta Pi. Republican. Home: 611 Opal Ct Upland CA 91786-6525

SCHWARZ, MICHAEL, lawyer; b. Brookline, Mass., Oct. 19, 1952; s. Jules Lewis and Estelle (Kosberg) S. BA magna cum laude, U. No. Colo., 1975; postgrad. U. N.Mex., 1977, JD, 1980; Rsch. reader in Negligence Law, Oxford U., 1978; diploma in Legal Studies, Cambridge U., 1981. Bar: N.Mex. 1980, U.S. Dist. Ct. N.Mex. 1980, U.S. Ct. Appeals (10th, D.C., and Fed. cirs.) 1982, U.S. Ct. Internat. Trade, 1982, U.S. Tax Ct. 1982, U.S. Supreme Ct. 1983, N.Y. 1987. VISTA vol., Albuquerque, 1975-77; rsch. fellow N.Mex. Legal Support Project, Albuquerque, 1978-79; supr. law Cambridge (Eng.) U., 1980-81; law clk. to chief justice Supreme Ct. N.Mex., Santa Fe, 1981-82; pvt. practice law, Santa Fe, 1982—; spl. prosecutor City of Santa Fe, 1985; spl. asst. atty. gen., 1986-88; mem. editorial adv. com. Social Security Reporting Svc., 1983-95. Author: New Mexico Appellate Manual, 1990, 2nd. edit., 1996; contbr. articles to profl. jours. Vice dir. Colo. Pub. Interest Rsch. Group, 1974; scoutmaster Great S.W. Area coun. Boy Scouts Am., 1977-79; mem. N.Mex. Acupuncture Licensing Bd., 1983. Recipient Cert. of Appreciation Cambridge U., 1981, Nathan Burkan Meml. award, 1980, N.Mex. Supreme Ct. Recognition, 1992, 93, 95. Mem. ABA (litigation com. on profl. responsibility, litigation com. on pretrial practice and discovery), ATLA, Am. Arbit. Assn., Bar Assn. U.S. Dist. Ct. Dist. N.Mex., State Bar N.Y., N.Mex. State Bar (bd. dirs. employment law sect. 1990-96, chair employment law sect. 1991-92), N.Y. Bar Assn., First Jud. Dist. Bar Assn. (treas. 1987-88, sec. 1988-89, v.p. 1989-1990, pres. 1990-91, local rules com. mem. 1989-92), N.Mex. Supreme Ct. (standing com. on profl. conduct 1990—, hearing officer, reviewing officer disciplinary com. 1993—), Am. Inns. of Ct. N.Mex. (barrister), Nat. Employment Lawyers Assn. (Nat. chpt., N.Mex. chpt.), Sierra Club, Amnesty Internat., Internat Wolf Ctr. Home and Office: PO Box 1656 Santa Fe NM 87504-1656

SCHWARZER, WILLIAM W, federal judge; b. Berlin, Apr. 30, 1925; came to U.S., 1938, naturalized, 1944; s. John F. and Edith M. (Daniel) S.; m. Anne Halbersleben, Feb. 2, 1951; children: Jane Elizabeth, Andrew William. AB cum laude, U. So. Calif., 1948; LLB cum laude, Harvard U., 1951. Bar: Calif. 1953, U.S. Supreme Ct. 1967. Teaching fellow Harvard U. Law Sch., 1951-52; asso. firm McCutchen, Doyle, Brown & Enersen, San Francisco, 1952-60; ptnr. McCutchen, Doyle, Brown & Enersen, 1960-76; judge U.S. Dist. Ct (no. dist.) Calif., San Francisco, 1976—; dir. Fed. Jud. Ctr., Washington, 1990-95; sr. counsel Pres.'s Commn. on CIA Activities Within the U.S., 1975; chmn. U.S. Jud. Conf. Com. Fed.-State Jurisdiction, 1987-90; mem. faculty Nat. Inst. Trial Advocacy, Fed. Jud. Ctr., All-ABA, U.S.-Can. Legal Exch., 1987, Anglo-U.S. Jud. Exch., 1994-95, Salzburg Seminar on Am. Studies; disting. prof. Hastings Coll. Law U. Calif. Author: Managing Antitrust and Other Complex Litigation, 1982, Civil Discovery and Manadatory Disclosure, 1994, Federal Civil Procedure Before Trial, 1994; contbr. articles to legal publs., aviation jours. Trustee World Affairs Coun. No. Calif., 1961-88; chmn. bd. trustees Marin Country Day Sch., 1963-66; mem. Marin County Aviation Commn., 1969-76; mem. vis. com. Harvard Law Sch., 1981-86. Served with Intelligence, U.S. Army, 1943-46. Fellow Am. Coll. Trial Lawyers (S. Gates award 1992), Am. Bar Found.; mem. ABA (Meador Rosenberg award 1995), Am. Law Inst., San Francisco Bar Assn., State Bar Calif., Coun. Fgn. Rels. Office: 450 Golden Gate Ave San Francisco CA 94102

SCHWEBACH, GERHARD HERMANN, microbiologist; b. Asch, Czechoslovakia, Feb. 27, 1944; came to U.S., 1957; s. Leonard Valentine and Gertrude Margareta (Rogler) S.; m. Janet Elaine Peterson, July 1, 1966; children: Derek, Heidi, Daniel, Adam, Nathan, Elisabeth. MS, Brigham Young U., Provo, Utah, 1967; Cert. in Med. Tech., Malcolm grow Med. Ctr., Andrews AFB, Md., 1976. Cert. med. technologist. Honorarium prof. U. Colo., Colorado Springs, 1976-82; sci. instr. Pikes Peak C.C., Colorado Springs, 1988-92, Nat. Coll., Colorado Springs, 1992—; sr. microbiologist Water Resources divsn. City of Colorado Springs, 1982—; cons./rschs. Schwebach Environ. and Pub. Health Svcs., Colorado Springs, 1994—. Author: Practical Guide to Microbial and Parasitic Diseases, 1980; contbr. articles to profl. jours. Cub master Boy Scouts Am., Colo., 1977-79, explorer advisor, Utah, 1972-74; cmty. soccer coach Parks and Recreation, Colorado Springs, 1986-88. Capt. USAF, 1969-79. Decorated Air Force commendation medal with oak leaf cluster, meritorious svc. medal. Mem. AAAS, Coll. Allied Health Profls. of Am. (pres. 1979-97), Am. Soc. Microbiology, Am. Soc. Clin. Pathologists, Soc. Risk Analysis. Republican. LDS. Home: 3160 Meander Cir Colorado Springs CO 80917 Office: City of Colorado Springs PO Box 1103 Colorado Springs CO 80947

SCHWEINFURTH, SCOTT DAVID, accountant; b. Cleve., Mar. 2, 1954; s. George Jacob and Martha Jean (Stubbs) S.; m. Margaret Mary English, May 28, 1983; children: Carolyn Marie, Andrew David, Thomas Jacob, Patricia Ann. BS in Acctg., Miami U., 1976. CPA, Ill., Nev. Audit staff Ernst & Young, Chgo., 1976-81, mgr., 1981-88, ptnr., 1988-94; sr. v.p., CFO, treas. Bally Gaming Internat., Inc., Las Vegas, 1995-96, Alliance Gaming Corp., Las Vegas, 1996—. Pres. Omni Youth Svcs., Buffalo Grove, Ill., 1992-95, treas., 1987-92; v.p. City Club of Chgo., 1992-95. Mem. AICPAs, Nev. CPA Soc., Union League Club, Beta Gamma Sigma, Beta Alpha Psi. Episcopalian. Home: 1604 Bayonne Dr Las Vegas NV 89134-6185 Office: Alliance Gaming Corp 6601 Bermuda Rd Las Vegas NV 89119-3605

SCHWERIN, KARL HENRY, anthropology educator, researcher; b. Bertha, Minn., Feb. 21, 1936; s. Henry William and Audrey Merle (Jahn) S.; m. Judith Drewanne Altermatt, Sept. 1, 1958 (div. May 1975); children: Karl Frederic, Marguerite DelValle; m. Partha Louise Hake Buell, Jan. 25, 1979; stepchildren: Tamara, Brent, Taryn. BA, U. Calif., Berkeley, 1958; PhD, UCLA, 1965. Instr. Los Angeles State Coll., 1963; asst. prof. anthropology U. N.Mex., Albuquerque, 1963-68, assoc. prof., 1968-72, prof., 1972—, asst. chmn. dept. anthropology, 1983-85, chmn. dept. anthropology, 1987-93; prof. invitado Inst. Venezolano de Investigaciones Cientificas, Caracas, 1979. Author: Oil and Steel Processes of Karinya Culture Change, 1966, Antropologia Social, 1969, Winds Across the Atlantic, 1970; editor: Food Energy in Tropical Ecosystems, 1985; contbr. articles to profl. jours. V.p. Parents without Ptnr., Albuquerque, 1976-77. Grantee Cordell Hull Found., Venezuela, 1961-62, N.Y. Zool. Soc., Honduras, 1981; Fulbright scholar Cañar, Ecuador, 1969-70, Paris, 1986. Fellow Am. Anthropol. Assn.; mem. Am. Ethnol. Soc., Am. Soc. Ethnohistory (pres. 1975), Southwestern Anthropol. Assn. (co-editor Southwestern Jour. Anthropology 1972-75), N.Mex. Cactus and Succulent Soc. (v.p. 1970-71), Maxwell Mus. Assn. (bd. dirs. 1984-85), Internat. Congress of Americanists (35th-40th, 43d, 46th, 48th, 49th), Sigma Xi (chpt. pres. 1980-81). Office: U NMex Dept Anthropology Albuquerque NM 87131

SCHWERTLY, HARVEY KENNETH, JR., computer electronics educator; b. Camden, N.J., Dec. 26, 1941; s. Harvey Kenneth Sr. and Marjorie Anna (Younghanns) S.; m. Barbara Ann Sills, Nov. 18, 1961; children: Barbara Anne, Catherine Anna, Mary Theresa. AS, SUNY, Albany, 1982, BS, 1987; MS, Nat. U., 1988. Cert. instr., Calif.; cert. electronics technician. Enlisted USN, 1960, advanced througth grades to chief petty officer, 1980, ret., 1980; instr. Telemedia, Inc., Alkhobar, Saudia Arabia, 1980-83, San Diego OIC, 1984, ITT Ednl. Svcs., La Mesa, Calif., 1985-86, San Diego Community Coll. Dist., 1986—; computer cons. 6PT Micro Maintenance, Lemon Grove, Calif., 1990—. Mem. Internat. Soc. Cert. Electronics Technicians (computer option com.), Calif. Coun. Electronic Instrs., Inc., Nat. U. Alumni Assn., Calif. State Electronics Assn., VFW (post comdr. 1992-94), Fleet Res. Assn., Amvets, Am. Legion. Home: 3226 Harris St Lemon Grove CA 91945-2221 Office: San Diego CC 1400 Park Blvd San Diego CA 92101-4721

SCHWICHTENBERG, DARYL ROBERT, drilling engineer; b. nr. Tulare, S.D., Nov. 8, 1929; s. Robert Carl and Lillian Rose (Hardie) S.; m. Helen M. Spencer, 1955 (div. Jan. 1971); children: Helayne, Randall, Hyalyn, Halcyon, Rustan; m. Helen Elizabeth Doehring, Nov. 11, 1971 (div. May 1982); 1 child, Suzanne. Student, U. Wyo., 1954-55; BSME, S.D. Sch. Mines and Tech., 1957; postgrad., Alexander Hamilton Inst., N.Y.C., 1962-63. Lic. pilot, rated AMEL. Office engr. Ingersoll-Rand Co., Mpls., 1957-58; sub br. mgr. Ingersoll-Rand Co., Duluth, Minn., 1959-60; product engr. Ingersoll-Rand Co., N.Y.C., 1960-63, devel. engr., 1964; sales mgr. Ingersoll-Rand Co., Phillipsburg, N.J., 1965; pres., founder Daryl Drilling Co., Inc., Flagstaff, Ariz., 1965-82; pres. Silent Rose Mining Co., Fallon, Nev., 1982-85; sr. design engr. Nev. Test Site Fenix & Scisson, 1985-90; prin. project engr. Raytheon Svcs. Nev., 1990-95; project mgr. Raytheon Svcs. Nev., Nev. Test Site, 1995-96; asst.project mgr. Bechtel Nev., Las Vegas, 1996—; co-owner, mgr. Dead Shot Ranch, Bondurant, Wyo., 1977-82. Inventor electronic subtitling for opera patrons. 1st lt. U.S. Army, 1950-54, Korea. Decorated Bronze Star. Mem. ASME, NRA, VFW, Inst. Shaft Drilling Tech. (speaker, instr. 1986-96), Am. Legion, Mensa. Republican. Office: Bechtel Nev M/S NTS-330 PO Box 98521 Las Vegas NV 89193-8521

SCHWIER, EDWARD GEORGE, company executive; b. Cin., Oct. 3, 1947; s. George Walter and Alma Catherine (Lubbe) S.; m. Donna Marie Hesselbrook, June 7, 1969 (div.); children: Michael Edward, Andrew George, Melissa Marie; m. Lois Jean Faulkner, Dec. 24, 1994; stepchildren: Lisa Marie Arnold, Tricia Diane Arnold. BS in Aeronautical Engring., Naval Academy, 1969; MS in Weapons Systems Tech., Naval Postgrad. Sch., 1980. Commd. ensign USN, 1969, advanced through grades to capt., 1989; main propulsion asst. USS Eugene A. Greene, 1970-72; engr. officer USS Reasoner, 1973-75; staff commdr. Destroyer Squadron 15 USN, Yokosuka, Japan, 1975-78; exec. officer USS Estocin, 1980-82; flag sec. and aide Commander Naval Surface Force Atlantic Fleet, 1982-84; dir. ops. staff of Commander Joint Task Force Middle East, 1989-90; from comptroller to comptroller, bus. officer Naval Shipyard, Norfolk & Charleston, 1990-93; commanding officer Naval Welfare Assessment Divsn., Corona, Calif., 1993-95; mgr. Fluor-Daniel Hanford, Richland, Wash., 1996—. Mem. KC, Am. Soc. Military Comptrollers (pres. 1992-93. Comptroller of Yr. 1993), Am. Soc. Naval Engrs., Toastmasters, Mensa. Roman Catholic. Home: 1200 Knollwood Ct Richland WA 99352-5707 Address: Apt 320 1650 Mowry Sq Richland WA 99352-5707 Office: Fluor-Daniel Hanford PO Box 1000 MSIN H8-66 Richland WA 99352-1000

SCHWINDEN, TED, former governor of Montana; b. Wolf Point, Mont., Aug. 31, 1925; s. Michael James and Mary (Preble) S.; m. B. Jean Christianson, Dec. 21, 1946; children: Mike, Chrys, Dore. Student, Mont. Sch. Mines, 1946-47; B.A., U. Mont., 1949, M.A., 1950; postgrad., U. Minn., 1950-54. Owner grain farm Roosevelt County, Mont., 1954—; land commr. State of Mont., 1969-76, lt. gov., 1977-80, gov., 1981-89; disting. prof. pub. affairs, 1989—; mem. U.S. Wheat Trade Mission to Asia, 1968; dir. Stillwater Mining Co. Chmn. Mont. Bicentennial Adv. Council, 1973-76; mem. Mont. Ho. of Reps., 1959, 61, Legis. Council, 1959-61, Wolf Point Sch. Bd., 1966-69, Pub. Employees Retirement System Bd., 1969-74. Served with inf. AUS, 1943-46. Decorated Combat Inf. badge. Mem. Mont. Grain Growers (pres. 1965-67), Western Wheat Assos. (dir.). Democrat. Lutheran. Clubs: Masons, Elks. Home: 1335 Highland St Helena MT 59601-5242

SCHWINKENDORF, KEVIN NEIL, nuclear engineer; b. Newberg, Oreg., Mar. 11, 1959; s. Waldemar Adolf and Hattie Bertha (Baumgarten) S. BS,

Oreg. State U., 1981, MS, 1983; PhD, U. Wash., 1996. Reg. profl. engr., Wash. Advanced engr. UNC Nuclear Industries, Richland, Wash., 1983-84, engr., 1986-87; sr. engr. Westinghouse Hanford Co., Richland, 1987-96, Fluor Daniel Northwest, Richland, 1996—; v.p. numerical methods, Analyst Devel. Corp., Scappoose, Oreg., 1990—. Designer: (ballistics software) PC-Bullet-ADCs, 1990 (Best Paper award 1992); author tech. publ. in field. Participant March of Dimes Walk-a-Thon, Richland, 1989, 90. Mem. Am. Nuclear Soc., NSPE, NRA, Soc. Computer Simulation, Safari Club Internat., Tau Beta Pi. Republican. Home: 1121 Pine St Richland WA 99352-2135 Office: FDNW Criticality & Shielding MSIN HO-35 Engring Dept PO Box 1050 Richland WA 99352

SCHWYN, CHARLES EDWARD, accountant; b. Muncie, Ind., Oct. 12, 1932; s. John and Lela Mae (Oliver) S.; m. Mary Helen Nickey, May 25, 1952 (dec.); children: Douglas, Craig, Beth; m. Madelyn Steinmetz. BS, Ball State U., 1957. CPA, Calif., D.C. With Haskins, Sells & Orlando, Chgo., Orlando, Fla., 1958-67; mgr. Deloitte, Haskins & Sells, Milan, Italy, 1967-70, San Francisco, 1970-80; with Deloitte, Haskins & Sells (now Deloitte & Touche), Oakland, Calif., ptnr. in charge, 1980-92, ret., 1992. Bd. dirs. Jr. Ctr. Art and Sci., 1982-89, pres., 1987-88; bd. dirs., trustee Oakland Symphony, 1982-86, 89-91; bd. dirs. Oakland Met. YMCA, 1984-89, Oakland Police Activities League, 1981-91, Joe Morgan Youth Found., 1982-91, Summit Med. Ctr., 1989-94, 96—, Marcus A. Foster Ednl. Inst., 1986-95, pres., 1991-93; bd. dirs. Greater Oakland Internat. Trade Ctr., 1996, mem. adv. bd. Festival of Lake, 1984-89, U. Oakland Met. Forum, 1992—; co-chmn. Commn. for Positive Change in Oakland Pub. Schs.; mem. campaign cabinet United Way Bay Area, 1989; bd. regents Samuel Merritt Coll., 1994—; chmn., bd. regents, 1996—; chief of protocol, City of Oakland, 1996—; bd. dirs. Greater Oakland Internat. Trade Ctr., 1996—. With USN, 1952-56. Recipient Cert. Recognition Calif. Legis. Assembly, 1988, Ctr. for Ind. Living award, Oakland Bus. Arts award for outstanding bus. leader Oakland C. of C., 1992; date of job retirement honored in his name by Oakland mayor. Mem. AICPA (coun. 1987-90), Oakland C. of C. (chmn. bd. dirs. 1987-88, exec. com. 1982-89), Oakland Met. C. of C., pres., 1996, Calif. Soc. CPAs (bd. dirs. 1979-81, 83-84, 85-87, pres. San Francisco chpt. 1983-84), Nat. Assn. Accts. (pres. Fla. chpt. 1967), Claremont Country Club (treas., bd. dirs. 1989—), Lakeview Club (bd. govs. 1987-92), Oakland 100 Club (pres. 1994), Rotary (bd. dirs. Oakland club 1986-88, 91-92, treas. 1984-86, pres. 1991-92). Office: Office of Protocol City of Oakland 530 Water St Oakland CA 94607

SCHY, GAY, artist, investor; b. Greenwich, Conn., July 10, 1937; d. Ralph Morrel and Dorothy (Abrams) Griswold; m. John Craver (div. 1974); 1 child, Linda Craver; m. Charles W. Torrey, July 22, 1979. BS, U. Chgo., 1959, MSW, 1964; MA, San Jose State U., 1989, MFA, 1990. Social worker Santa Clara County, San Jose, Calif., 1970-80, pvt. practice, Los Gatos, Calif., 1980-86; artist Santa Cruz, Calif., 1986—; represented by Fredrick Spratt Gallery, San Jose, Calif.; bd. dirs. San Jose State Sch. Art and Design, 1988-92; advisor, bd. dirs. San Jose Inst. for Contemporary Art, 1990—. Vol. Habitat for Humanities, Santa Cruz, 1991—, U. Calif. Santa Cruze Arboraton, 1996—. Home: 3040 Pleasant Valley Rd Aptos CA 95003

SCIAME, DONALD RICHARD, computer systems analyst, dentist, magician, locksmith; b. Bklyn., Sept. 10, 1945; s. Mario and Ruth Marie (Kozell) S.; m. Kathy Ann Thamann, Mar. 17, 1987. AB, Rutgers U., 1967; DMD, N.J. Coll. Medicine & Dentistry, 1971; MAPA, U. N.Mex., 1984; cert. locksmith, electronic security, NRI Schs., 1988. Dep. chief svc. unit dental program USPHS Indian Hosp., Whiteriver, Ariz., 1971-73; chief svc. unit dental program USPHS Indian Hosp., Sacaton, Ariz., 1973-76, Santa Fe, 1976-88; systems analyst USPHS Area Office, Albuquerque, 1988-90; dir. div. info. mgmt. svcs. USPHS-IHS Area Office, Albuquerque, 1990—. Contbr. articles to profl. jours. Mem. IHS Dental Profl. Specialty Group, IHS Dental Computer Users Group, ADA, Internat. Coll. Dentists, Psi Omega Dental Fraternity, N.J. Dental Sch. Alumni Assn., USPHS Commn. Officers Assn., Albuquerque Area Dental Soc. Indian Health Svcs., M Tech. Assoc., Soc. Am. Magicians. Home: 1914 Conejo Dr Santa Fe NM 87505-6108 Office: IHS Area Office 505 Marquette Ave NW Ste 1506 Albuquerque NM 87102-2158 *Personal philosophy: Moving from bites to bytes.*

SCIAMMAS, JACQUES DANIEL, financial services executive, controller; b. Cairo, Jan. 9, 1956; came to U.S., 1968; s. Ben and Jenny (Massuda) Shammas. BA, Bowdoin Coll., 1975; MBA, Rutgers U., 1979. Fin. analyst TransWorld Airlines, Inc., N.Y.C., 1979-81, sr. fin. analyst, 1981-82, mgr., 1982-84, dir., 1985-86; group contr. McGraw-Hill, Inc., N.Y.C., 1987-88, contr., 1988-91; v.p. fin. Charles Schwab & Co. Inc., San Francisco, 1991—. V.p., bd. dirs., CFO retail brokerage Fin. Exec. Inst., San Francisco; chmn. CFO Coun. No. Calif. Recipient Book prize Harvard U., 1970, Man of Future citation Mayor Kevin White, Boston, 1970, full academic scholarship Bowdoin Coll., 1971-75. Mem. Rutgers U. Alumni Assn. (chmn. class of 1970s). Home: 2530 Fillmore St Apt 6 San Francisco CA 94115-1349 Office: Charles Schwab & Co Inc 101 Montgomery St San Francisco CA 94104-4122

SCIARONI, LINDA GILLINGHAM, high school educator; b. Torrance, Calif., Feb. 15, 1962; d. Robert Edward and Dorathea Ellenor (Dixon) Gillingham; m. Daniel Martin Sciaroni, Feb. 14, 1987. BA, Whitworth Coll., Spokane, Wash., 1983; MA in Spl. Edn.: Gifted, Calif. State U., L.A., 1996. Tchr. Franklin H.S. L.A. Unified Sch. Dist., 1984—, chair dept. sci., 1992-94, gifted coord., 1986-94, Title IX coord., 1993-94, sci. advisor LAUSD divsn. instrn., 1995-96. Named Outstanding Tchr., Rotary Club L.A., 1995; Sci-Mat fellow Coun. Basic Edn., 1993, Eleanor Roosevelt fellow AAUW, 1990, May V. Seagoe scholar Calif. Assn. for Gifted, 1993. Mem. AAUW, AAAS, Nat. Sci. Tchr. Assn., Calif. Sci. Tchr. Assn., Greater L.A. Sci. Tchrs. Assn., Calif. Assn. for the Gifted, Phi Delta Kappa.

SCIOTTO, COSIMO GINO, pathologist, hematopathologist; b. Veszprem, Hungary, Aug. 2, 1945; came to U.S., 1956; s. Vincent and Camilla (Udvary) S.; m. Susan E. Skinner, July 20, 1968; children: Carina Marie Sciotto-Kelly, Elisabeth Ann. BS, Case Inst. Tech., Cleve., 1968; MS, Cleve. State U., 1969; PhD, Case Western Res. U., 1976, MD, 1976. Dir. hematology Denver VA Hosp., 1979-81; staff pathologist Penrose Hosp., Colorado Springs, Colo., 1981—, dir. pathology, 1993—. Trustee Colo. Assn. for Continuing Med. Lab. Edn., Denver, 1981-92. Fellow Coll. Am. Pathologists, Hematopathology Soc., Am. Assn. Clin. Chemists; mem. Colo. Soc. Clin. Pathologists (pres. 1986), El Paso Med. Soc., Colo. Med. Soc. Office: Penrose Hosp Dept Pathology 2215 N Cascade Ave Colorado Springs CO 80907-6736

SCLAR, DAVID ALEXANDER, medical policy educator; b. Columbus, Ohio, Dec. 31, 1954. B Pharmacy cum laude, Wash. State U., 1985; PhD in Pharmacy and Bus. Adminstrn., U. S.C., 1988. Assoc. prof. health policy and adminstrn./Ingelheim Scholar Wash. State U. Coll. Pharmacy; advisor U.K. Dept. Health and Social Svcs., China Bur. of Drugs and Biologicals, U.S. Senate Select Com. on Aging; mem. FDA Rev. Com. on pharm. mktg. practice. Mem. editl. bd. Hosp. Formulary; editor: Clin. Therapeutics; contbr. articles to profl. jours. Grantee in field. Mem. Am. Assn. Pharm. Scientists, Am. Pharm. Assn., Am. Soc. Hosp. Pharmacists, Am. Pub. Health Assn., Am. Assn. Colls. of Pharmacy, Assn. Health Svcs. Rsch. Home: SE 1005 Spring St Pullman WA 99163 Office: Coll of Pharmacy Wash State Univ Pullman WA 99164

SCOBEY, JAN (JEANNETTE MARIE SCOBEY), jazz musician, store owner, author; b. Chgo., Feb. 9, 1935; d. Leo Dona and Sophie (Bochenska) Dona van Castile; m. Bob Scobey, Dec. 26, 1961 (dec. June 1963). Student pvt. sch., Chgo. Owner Jan Scobey's Hot Jazz, Upper Lake, Calif., 1958—. Author: (book) He Rambled, 1976, (mag.) Jan Scobey's Hot Jazz, 1958—; prodr. (recordings) Jan Scobey and Bob Scobey's Frisco Band, 1960—; band leader Jan Scobey and Her Dixie Cats, 1964—; prodr. (festival) Jan Scobey's Hot Jazz, Santa Rosa, Calif., 1991. Office: Jan Scobeys Hot Jazz PO Box 6 Upper Lake CA 95485

SCOLEDES, ARISTOTLE GEORGIUS MICHALE, retired science and technology educator, research consultant; b. N.Y.C., Feb. 22, 1929; s. Michael George and Soultanitsa (Hadtzifoca) S.; m. Anne-Marie Furchtenicht, Sept. 7, 1957 (dec. Nov. 1970); children: Alexander Michael, Alexandra Anne; m. Barbara Lynn Sterling, Aug. 14, 1977; 1 child, Dylan. AB, Syracuse U., 1951; MSE, Johns Hopkins U., 1953; ScD, MIT, 1957; PhD, Stanford U., 1965. Rsch. assoc. Johns Hopkins U., Balt., 1951-53; rsch. fellow U. Chgo., 1953-54, MIT, Cambridge, Mass., 1955-59; exec. engr., project coord. Philco Western Devel. Labs./Ford-Aerospace, Sunnyvale, Calif., 1960-62; asst. prof. philosophy of sci. Alfred (N.Y.) U., 1962-63; assoc. prof. philosophy of sci. and theoretical biology SUNY, Buffalo, 1963-68; prof. philosophy sci. and tech. Ga. Inst. Tech., 1968-72; sr. cons. sponsored minorities program Econ. Opportunity Atlanta/CETA, U.S. Govt., Atlanta, 1972-77; project mgr., dir. Consulting Consortium U.S./Stanford/MIT, Stanford, 1977-95. Contbr. articles to profl. jours. Recipient Rsch. Svcs. Recognition award Offices of Naval Rsch. and Chief of Naval Ops., 1984; hon. fellow Am. Inst. Aeronautics and Astronautics, 1971. Mem. Nat. Space Soc., Air Force Assn., Philosophy of Sci. Assn., Am. Philos. Assn., Tau Beta Pi. Home: 3609 S Court Palo Alto CA 94306-4258

SCOLES, EUGENE FRANCIS, law educator, lawyer; b. Shelby, Iowa, June 12, 1921; s. Sam and Nola E. (Leslie) S.; m. R. Helen Glawson, Sept. 6, 1942; children—Kathleen Elizabeth, Janene Helen. A.B., U. Iowa, 1943, J.D., 1945; LL.M., Harvard U., 1949; J.S.D., Columbia U., 1955. Bar: Iowa 1945, Ill. 1946. Assoc. Seyfarth-Shaw & Fairweather, Chgo., 1945-46; asst. prof. law Northeastern U., 1946-48, assoc. prof., 1948-49; assoc. prof. U. Fla., 1949-51, prof., 1951-56; prof. U. Ill., Champaign, 1956-68; Max Rowe prof. law U. Ill., 1982-89, prof. emeritus, 1989—; vis. prof. McGeorge Law Sch. U. Pacific, Sacramento, 1989-92; prof. U. Oreg., 1968-82, dean Sch. Law, 1968-74, disting. prof. emeritus, 1982—; vis. prof. Khartoum U., Sudan, 1964-65. Author: (with H.F. Goodrich) Conflict of Laws, 4th edit., 1964, (with R.J. Weintraub) Cases and Materials on Conflict of Laws, 2d edit., 1972, (with E.C. Halbach, Jr.) Problems and Materials on Decedents' Estates and Trusts, 5th edit., 1993, Problems and Materials on Future Interests, 1977, (with P. Hay) Conflict of Laws, 2d edit., 1992; contbr. articles to profl. jours.; notes and legislation editor Iowa Law Rev., 1945; reporter Uniform Probate Code Project, 1966-70; mem. joint editorial bd. Uniform Probate Code, 1972—. Mem. ABA, Soc. Pub. Tchrs. Law, Am. Law Inst., Ill. Bar Assn., Assn. Am. Law Schs. (pres. 1978), Order of Coif. Home: 1931 Kimberly Dr Eugene OR 97405-5849 Office: U Oreg Sch of Law 11th And Kincaid Eugene OR 97403-1221

SCORA, RAINER WALTER, botanist; b. Mokre, Silesia, Poland, Dec. 5, 1928; came to U.S., 1951; s. Paul Wendelin and Helene (Nester) S.; m. Christa Maria Fiala, June 24, 1971; children: George Alexander, Katharina Monarda, Peter Evan. BS, DePaul U., 1955; MS, U. Mich., 1958, PhD, 1964. From asst. prof. to prof. botany U. Calif., Riverside, 1964—. Author over 100 sci. publs. With U.S. Army, 2d Div., Signal Corps, 1955-57. Alfred P. Sloan fellow, 1959; recipient Cooley award Am. Inst. Biological Scis., 1968; grantee NSF, FAO-Rome. Mem. Am. Inst. Biol. Scis., Botanical Soc. Am., Phytochem. Soc. N.Am., Internat. Assn. Plant Taxonomists, Internat. Orgn. Plant Biosystematists, Gamma Sigma Delta, Sigma Xi. Republican. Roman Catholic. Office: Univ Calif Dept Botany Plant Scis Riverside CA 92521

SCORSINE, JOHN MAGNUS, lawyer; b. Rochester, N.Y., Dec. 3, 1957; s. Frank and Karin (Frennby) S.; m. Susan Nauss, May 31, 1980 (div.); m. Theresa A. Burke, Dec. 17, 1988; 1 child, Jennifer E. BS, Rochester Inst. Tech., 1980; JD, U. Wyo., 1984. Bar: Wyo. 1984, U.S. Dist. Ct. Wyo. 1984, U.S. Ct. Appeals (10th cir.) 1989, U.S. Army Ct. Criminal Appeals 1995. Part-time deputy sheriff Monroe County (N.Y.), 1978-80; police officer Casper (Wyo.) Police Dept., 1980-81; intern U.S. Atty. Office, Cheyenne, Wyo., 1983-84; sole practice Rock Springs, Wyo., 1984-85; ptnr. Scorsine and Flynn, Rock Springs, 1986; prin. Scorsine Law Office, Rock Springs, 1986-95; commr. Dist. and County Court, 1986-95; plans, ops. and mil. sup. officer Wyo. Nat. Guard, 1995—; ptnr. Sunset Advt., 1987-89; chmn. bd. dirs. Youth Home Inc., Rock Springs, 1987-88; treas. Sweetwater County Cmty. Corrections Bd., 1990-95; mem. Nat. Ski Patrol, 1976—. Leader Medicine Bow Ski Patrol, Laramie, Wyo., 1983; legal advisor Rocky Mountain divsn. Nat. Ski Patrol, 1984; asst. patrol leader White Pine Ski Area, Pinedale, Wyo., 1986; avalanche advisor Jackson Hole Snow King Ski Patrol, 1987-96, avalanche instr. 1993—; sect. chief Teton sect. nat. Ski Patrol, 1991-94, mem. Eldore Ski Patrol, 1996—; mem. Sweetwater County Search and Rescue, 1989-95, tng. officer, 1993-95; mem. Sweetwater County Emergency Dive Team, 1990-95, mem. Sweetwater County Fire Dept., 1992-94, Reliance Vol. Fire Dept., 1994-95; mem. Laramie Cmty. Fire Dist. #6 and Burns Ambulance Svc., 1995—, Am. N. Peary Land expdn., 1989; scoutmaster Boy Scouts Am., 1987-93, 96—; pres. Sweetwater County Vol. Fire Assn., 1993-94; mem. Laramie County Sch. Dist. #2 accreditation panel. Capt. JAG, USAR, 1991—. Recipient Yellow Merit star Nat. Ski Patrol, 1993, Fritch Volunteerism award, 1993, Armed Forces Outstanding Vol. Svc. medal. Mem. ABA, Wyo. State Bar, Wyo. Trial Lawyers Assn., Assn. Am. Trial Lawyers, Rock Springs C. of C., Res. Officers Assn. (nat. councilman 1993—, state pres. 1994). Democrat. Lutheran. Lodge: Rotary. Home: 1090 State Highway 214 Burns WY 82093 Office: Wyo Nat Guard 5500 Bishop Blvd Cheyenne WY 82009-3320

SCOTT, AURÉLIA CARMELITA, non-profit organization executive, writer; b. Madison, Wis., Feb. 21, 1956; d. Walter Hilton and Carmalita Foster (Benson) S.; m. Robert Edward Krug Jr., Feb. 21, 1987. BA, Simon's Rock Coll., Great Barrington, Mass., 1977; EdM, Harvard U., 1978. Program evaluator Mass. Dept. Mental Health, Northampton, 1978-79; sr. rsch. asst. McFann, Gray and Assocs., Monterey, Calif., 1979-81; rsch. scientist Am. Inst. Rsch., Palo Alto, Calif., Washington, 1981-86; project dir. Cosmos Corp., Washington, 1986-89; exec. dir. Habitat for Humanity, Taos, N.Mex., 1995—; freelance writer, Taos, 1992—. Contbr. articles to mags. Bd. dirs. Taos Inst. Arts, 1993, 94, 95, adv. bd., 1996—; bd. dirs. Taos Pub. Libr., 1996—; master gardener N.Mex. Coop. Ext. Svc., 1995—; founding mem. children's edn. program Millicent Rogers Mus., Taos, 1990-93. Recipient Grand prize Writer's Digest Mag., 1995. Mem. Taos Garden Club (pres. 1994, 95), Taos Investment Club (founding, presiding ptnr. 1997—). Home: PO Box 514 Arroyo Seco NM 87514 Office: Habitat for Humanity PO Box 1888 Taos NM 87571

SCOTT, BRUCE LAURENCE, physics educator; b. Waco, Tex., Oct. 8, 1932; s. Raymond Orben and Judith Lillian (Landers) Wilson; m. Betty Marie Moore, Dec. 30, 1954; children: Gregory Wilson, Susan Lynn Scott Bacina, Bradley Allen. BS, Calif. Inst. Tech., 1953; MS, U. Ill., 1955; PhD, UCLA, 1960. Rsch. assoc. U. So. Calif., L.A., 1960, asst. prof., 1960-65; from assoc. prof. to prof. Calif. State U., Long Beach, 1965-96, prof. emeritus, 1996—; cons. Atomics Internat., Canoga Park, Calif., 1957-60, TRW, Inc., Hawthorne, Calif., 1960-69. Co-author: 100AB Lab Manual, 1980. Mem. Am. Assn. Physics Tchrs. Home: 18388 Santa Veronica Cir Fountain Valley CA 92708 Office: Calif State U Physics Dept 1250 Bellflower Blvd Long Beach CA 90840-3901

SCOTT, DAVID CLINTON, research scientist; b. Brighton, Colo., Sept. 5, 1960; s. Robert Glenn and Janice Elizabeth (Smith) S.; m. Dana Jungschaffer, Aug. 7, 1988; children: Clinton P., Alexander. BA, U. Colo., 1986; PhD, U. So. Calif., 1993. R & D chemist ICI, Hawthorn, Calif., 1987-88; rsch. asst. chemistry dept. U. So. Calif., L.A., 1988-93; rsch. scientist Jet Propulsion Lab, Pasadena, Calif., 1993—. Contbr. articles to profl. jours. Mem. Am. Chem. Soc., Am. Meteorol. Soc., Phi Beta Kappa. Avocations: mountain biking, running, swimming, skiing, hiking.

SCOTT, DONALD MICHAEL, educational association administrator, educator; b. L.A., Sept. 26, 1943; s. Bernard Hendry and Barbara (Lannin) S.; m. Patricia Ilene Pancoast, Oct. 24, 1964 (div. June 1971); children: William Bernard, Kenneth George. BA, San Francisco State U., 1965, MA, 1986. Cert. tchr. Calif. Tchr. Mercy High Sch., San Francisco, 1968-71; park ranger Calif. State Park System, Half Moon Bay, 1968-77; tchr. adult div. Jefferson Union High Sch. Dist., Daly City, Calif., 1973-87; dir. NASA-NPS Project Wider Focus, Daly City, 1983-90; dir. Geo.S. Spl. Projects Wider Focus, San Francisco, 1990—; also bd. dirs. Wider Focus, Daly City; nat. park ranger/naturalist Grant-Kohrs Ranch Nat. Hist. Site, Deer Lodge, Mont., 1987-88; nat. park ranger pub. affairs fire team Yellowstone Nat. Park, 1988; nat. park ranger Golden Gate Recreation Area, 1988-92; rsch. subject NASA, Mountain View, Calif., 1986-90; guest artist Yosemite (Calif.) Nat. Park, 1986; nat. park ranger Golden Gate Nat. Recreation Area, Nat. Park Svc., San Francisco, 1986, nat. park svc. history cons. to Bay Dist., 1988-94; adj. asst. prof. Skyline Coll., 1989-94, Coll. San Mateo, 1992-94; aerospace edn. specialist NASA/OSU/AESP, 1994—. Contbr. articles, photographs to profl. jours., mags. Pres. Youth for Kennedy, Lafayette, calif., 1960; panelist Community Bds. of San Francisco, 1978-87; city chair Yes on A com., So. San Francisco, San Mateo County, Calif., 1986; active CONTACT Orgn., 1991—, bd. dirs. 1995—. Mem. Yosemite Assn. (life), Wider Focus, Friends of George R. Stewart, Nat. Sci. Tchrs. Assn., Nat. Coun. of Tchrs. of Math., Internat. Tech. Edn. Assn., Smithsonian Air and Space (charter mem.), Planetary Soc. (charter mem.), Indep. Scholar, 1982—. Democrat. Home and Office: MS 253-2 NASA Ames Rsch Ctr Moffett Field CA 94035-1000

SCOTT, DOUG, sculptor; b. Hillsboro, Oreg., Mar. 26, 1951; s. Cletis LeeRoy and Lorraine Ella (Trussell) M.; m. Vivian Sue Henderson, Aug. 22, 1980; children Rorke, Creede, Lichen, Talus, Echo. Diploma, Manzano H.S., Albuquerque, 1969. Part-time artist N. Mex. and Colo., 1970-82; sculptor Doug Scott Studio, Pleasant View, Colo., 1982-87, Pagosa Springs, Colo., 1987-91, Taos, N. Mex., 1991—; colleague mem. Nat. Sculpture Soc., N.Y.C., 1992—. One-mans show (Gallery) Roy Rogers and Dale Evans, Life size in white marble, Roy Rogers Mus., Victorville, Calif.,. Mem. N. Mex. Wildlife Assn. (v.p. 1994—). Home: Rt 1 Box 26 Taos NM 87571 Studio: Doug Scott Studio 26317 E Hwy 64 Taos NM 87571

SCOTT, G. JUDSON, JR., lawyer; b. Phila., Nov. 16, 1945; s. Gerald Judson and Jean Louise (Evans) S.; m. Ildiko Kalman, Mar. 21, 1971; children: Nathan Emory, Lauren Jean. AA, Foothill Jr. Coll., Los Altos, Calif., 1965; BA, U. Calif.-Santa Barbara, 1968; JD cum laude, U. Santa Clara, 1975. Bar: Calif. 1975, U.S. Dist. Ct. (no. dist.) Calif. 1975, U.S. Ct. Appeals (9th cir.) 1975, U.S. Supreme Ct. 1981. Assoc. Feldman, Waldman & Kline, San Francisco, 1975-76, Law Offices John Wynne Herron, San Francisco, 1976-80; of counsel firm Haines & Walker, Livermore, Calif., 1980; ptnr. Haines Walker & Scott, Livermore, 1980-84; officer, dir., shareholder firm Smith, Etnire, Polson and Scott, Pleasanton, Calif., 1984-88; pvt. practice, 1988—; judge pro tem Livermore-Pleasanton Mcpl. Ct., 1981—; lectr. Calif. Continuing Edn. of Bar. Contbg. author: Attorneys' Guide to Restitution, 1976; editor: The Bottom Line, 1989-91. Pres. Walnut Creek Open Space Found., Calif., 1981-83. Capt. USNR, 1968—. Mem. Assn. Trial Lawyers Am. (sustaining), Consumer Attys. Calif., Ea. Alameda County Bar Assn. (v.p. 1981-82), Calif. State Bar (standing com. on lawyer referral svcs. 1985-88, exec. com. law practice mgmt. sect. 1988-93, chair-elect 1991-92, chair 1992-93), Alameda County Bar Assn. (chmn. law office econs. com. 1986-87, jud. nomination evaluation com. 1996—, bd. dirs. 1997—), Alameda-Contra Costa County Trial Lawyers Assn., Livermore C. of C. (past chmn. growth study 1983), Pleasanton C. of C. Republican. Episcopalian. Office: Ste 125 6140 Stoneridge Mall Rd Pleasanton CA 94588-3232

SCOTT, GEORGE LARKHAM, IV, architect; b. Bloomington, Ill., Aug. 11, 1947; s. George Larkham III and Marilyn Louise (Bouseman) S.; m. Patricia Jean Gregurich, Aug. 1, 1969; 1 child, Matthew Larkham. B in Archtl. Studies, Wash. State U., 1973, BArch, 1974. Dir. facilities planning County of Spokane, Wash., 1978-79; project architect Skidmore, Owings & Merrill, Portland, Oreg., 1981-82; owner George L. Scott, Architect and Planner, Portland, Oreg., 1982—. Prin. works include masterplan Rancho Seco Nuclear Power Sta., Sacramento, Calif., masterplan Boeing Comml. Airplane Co., Portland, high tech. clean room facilities for nat. and internat. clients, helistop atop 42 story U.S. Bancorp Tower, U.S. Bancorp Office Bldg., Portland, Oreg., on-base family housing complex Trident Submarine Base, Bangor, Wash., interior archtl. design and space plan of Bonneville Power Adminstrn. 550,000 S.F. hdqrs. bldg., Portland; designer 2 130 foot ocean going motor yachts; lectr., contbr. articles on clean room tech. to profl. jours. Chmn. Task Force on Community Devel., Spokane, 1977; active Committee to Elect Gov. Ray, Wash., 1977-78, City of Spokane Planning Commn., 1977-78. Home and Office: 11445 SW Lanewood St Portland OR 97225-5301

SCOTT, GREGORY KELLAM, state supreme court justice; b. San Francisco, July 30, 1943; s. Robert and Althea Delores Scott; m. Carolyn Weatherly, Apr. 10, 1971; children: Joshua Weatherly, Elijah Kellam. BS in Environ. Sci., Rutgers U., 1970, EdM in Urban Studies, 1971; JD cum laude, Ind. U., Indpls., 1977. Asst. dean resident instrn. Cook Coll. Rutgers U., 1972-75; trial atty. U.S. SEC, Denver, 1977-79; gen. counsel Blinder, Robinson & Co., Inc., Denver, 1979-80; asst. prof. coll. law U. Denver, 1980-85, assoc. prof., 1985-93, prof. emeritus, 1993—, chair bus. planning program, 1986-89, 92-93; justice Colo. Supreme Ct., Denver, 1993—; of counsel Moore, Smith & Bryant, Indpls., 1987-90; v.p., gen. counsel Comml. Energies, Inc., 1990-91; presenter in field. Author: (with others) Structuring Mergers and Acquisitions in Colorado, 1985, Airport Law and Regulation, 1991, Racism and Underclass in America, 1991; contbr. articles to profl. jours. Mem. ABA, Nat. Bar Assn., Nat. Assn. Securities Dealers, Inc., Nat. Arbitration Panel (arbitrator), Colo. Bar Found., Sam Cary Bar Assn., Am. Inn Ct. (founding mem. Judge Alfred A. Arraj inn).

SCOTT, HOWARD WINFIELD, JR., temporary help services company executive; b. Greenwich, Conn., Feb. 24, 1935; s. Howard Winfield and Janet (Lewis) S.; B.S., Northwestern U., 1957; m. Joan Ann MacDonald, Aug. 12, 1961; children: Howard Winfield III, Thomas MacDonald, Ann Elizabeth. With R.H. Donnelly Corp., Chgo., 1958-59; sales rep. Masonite Corp., Chgo. also Madison, Wis., 1959-61; sales rep. Manpower Inc., Chgo., 1961-63, br. mgr., Kansas City, Mo., 1963-65, area mgr., Mo. and Kans., 1964-65, regional mgr. Salespower div., Phila., 1965-66; asst. advt. mgr. soups Campbell Soup Co., Camden, N.J., 1966-68; pres. PARTIME, Inc., Paoli, Pa., 1968-74; dir. marketing Kelly Services Inc., Southfield, Mich., 1974-78; pres. CDI Temporary Services, Inc., 1978-91; pres. Dunhill Pers. System, Inc., Woodbury, N.Y., 1991-94; v.p. SOS Temporary Svcs., Salt Lake City, 1994; pres., chief operating officer SOS Staffing Svcs., Salt Lake City, 1995—. Served with AUS, 1957-58. Mem. Nat. Assn. Temporary Services (sec. 1970-71, pres. 1971-73, bd. dirs. 1982-91), Kappa Sigma. Republican. Home: 4030 Saddleback Rd Park City UT 84098-4809 also: 1204 Annapolis Sea Colony E Bethany Beach DE 19930 Office: SOS Staffing Svcs 1415 S Main St Salt Lake City UT 84115-5313

SCOTT, JAMES MICHAEL, artist, filmmaker; b. Wells, England, July 9, 1941; came to U.S., 1989; s. William George and Hilda Mary Scott; m. Anna Katherine Partridge, Feb. 19, 1966 (div. 1976); children: Alexander, Rosie; m. Yolanda Orozco, 1995; 1 child, Paloma. Art scholar, Bryanston Sch., Sorbonne, Paris, 1959; student painting and theatre design, Slade Sch. Fine Art, London, 1960-61, Slade Sch. Fine Art, Berlin, 1964. Ind. filmmaker Maya Film Prodns., London, 1964-70; film prodr. and dir. Flamingo Pictures, London, 1980-88; artist Santa Monica, 1989—; tchr., lectr. cinema Bath Acad. Art, U.K., Maidstone Coll. Art, U.K., Royal Coll. Art, London, Nat. Film Sch., U.K., U. So. Calif. Writer, dir.: (feature films) The Sea, 1962, Adult Fun, 1972, Coilin and Platonida, 1976, Loser Takes All, 1989, (films about artists) Love's Presentation, 1966, R.B. Kitaj, 1967, Richard Hamilton, 1969, The Great Ice Cream Robbery, 1970, Antoni Tapies, 1974, Chance, History, Art..., 1979; dir.: (TV films) Every Picture Tells a Story, 1984, Getting Even, 1985, Inspector Morse - The Last Enemy, 1988, (documentaries) Night Cleaners, 1974, Hajj 75, 1975, '36 to '77, 1978, (shorts) The Rocking Horse, 1962, In Separation, 1965, A Shocking Accident (Acad. award best short film 1983, Brit. Acad. award nominee best live action short film 1983), People Are the Same the Universe Over, 1987, Crime in the City, 1987, (info. films and commls.) Ejectoret, Stamp Exhibition - Olympia, Patrick McGrath; writer: (screenplays) Circle of Fear, Darkroom Window, Dibs, Someone, Somewhere. Recipient Silver Boomerang award Melbourne, Australia, 1979. Mem. Am. Acad. Motion Picture Arts, Dirs. Guild Am., Dirs. Guild Great Britain, Brit. Acad. Film and TV Arts, Assn. Cinematograph and Allied Techs. Home and Office: 4217 Tracy St Los Angeles CA 90027

SCOTT, JOHN CARLYLE, gynecologist, oncologist; b. Mpls., Sept. 24, 1933; s. Horace Golden and Grace (Melges) S.; m. Beth Krause, 1958 (div. 1977); m. Paola Maria Martini, Feb. 8, 1986; children: Jeff, David, Suzanne, Danielle. AB, Princeton U., 1956; BS, MD, U. Minn., 1961. Diplomate Am. Coll. Ob-gyn., Pan Am. Ob-gyn. Soc. Intern Sch. Medicine Marquette U., Milw., 1961-62, resident Sch. Medicine, 1962-66; resident Harvard Med. Sch., Boston, 1965; Am. Cancer fellow Marquette Med. Sch., Milw., 1966-67, instr. ob-gyn., 1966-67; clin. instr. ob-gyn. U. Wash. Med. Sch., Seattle,

1968-75, clin. asst. prof., 1975-85, clin. assoc. prof., 1985—; mem. faculty adv. com. dept. ob-gyn. U. Wash., Seattle, 1973—. Author: First Aid for N.W. Boaters, 1977; author Am. Jour. Ob-Gyn., 1970, 75, 77. Bd. dirs. Renton (Wash.) Handicapped Ctr., 1968-70, March of Dimes, 1974-79; bd. dirs. enabling sys. U. Hawaii, Honolulu, 1977-80. Capt. U.S. Army, 1950-52, Korea. Decorated U.S. Senate Medal of Freedom, Bronze and Silver Stars, Pres. Ronald Reagan's Task Force Medal of Merit and Eternal Flame of Freedom. Fellow Royal Soc. Medicine (gynecology and oncology sects.), Am. Coll. Ob-Gyn, Internat. Coll. Surgeons (pres. elec. 1997—, v.p., N.Am. Fedn. sec. 1997—); mem. Pan Am. Ob-Gyn Soc., S.W. Oncology Group, N.W. Oncology Group, Puget Sound Oncology Group, Seattle Gynecol. Soc. (pres. 1978), Baker Channing Soc., Sigma Xi. Home: 726 16th Ave E Seattle WA 98112-3916 Office: 9730 4th Ave NE Ste 202 Seattle WA 98115-2143

SCOTT, KELLY, newspaper editor. Mng. editor sunday calendar The L.A. Times. Office: LA Times Times Mirror Sq Los Angeles CA 90012-3816

SCOTT, KENNETH CRAIG, artist; b. L.A., Mar. 19, 1955; s. Carl E. and Lois C. Scott. instr. stained glass U. Hawaii, Honolulu, 1985-90. One-man shows include The Croisanterie, Honolulu, 1987, Live Art Gallery, San Francisco, 1992, Caffe Valentino, Waikiki, Honolulu, 1993-94; group exhbns. include The Stained Glass Assn. Hawaii, Honolulu, 1985, 86, 87, Honolulu Acad. Arts, 1990, Live Art Gallery, San Francisco, 1992, 93, Ala Moana Ctr. Exhibit Hall, Honolulu, 1993, Linekona Ctr., Acad. Arts, Honolulu, 1993, Waikiki Gallery, Honolulu, 1994. Mem. Hawaiian Craftsmen Assn. (adminstrv. v.p. 1993-94). Home: # 102 1427 Alexander St Honolulu HI 96822

SCOTT, LINDA BYRNE, artist; b. San Francisco, Apr. 14, 1947; d. Daniel Thomas and Ellen Almeda (Flesher) Byrne; m. Darrel Scott, July 16, 1972 (div. 1982); children: Sarah Byrne, Tina Corrine; m. Edward Joseph Baldus, May 2, 1983. AA, City Coll. San Francisco, 1968; BA, Calif. State U. Sonoma, 1970; MFA, U. Idaho, 1995. Artist Taylor Agy., San Rafael, Calif., 1970-71, Holiday Magic, San Rafael, 1971-72; tchr. art Sch. Dist. 1, Lewiston, Idaho, 1982—; co-owner, treas. Holbrook Gallery, Lewiston, 1987-91; artist Diversified Art and Design, Lewiston, 1987—. Exhibited in group shows at Valley Art Ctr., Clarkston, Wash., Lewis-Clark Art Assn., Clarkston, 1988, 92, 96. Mem. Nat. Watercolor Soc., Northwest Watercolor Soc., Women's Caucus for Art (v.p. Idaho chpt. 1996). Democrat. Home: 1926 6th St Lewiston ID 83501 Office: Sch Dist 1 1926 6th St Lewiston ID 83501

SCOTT, MARY LOUISE, educator, writer; b. Ft. Worth, Tex., Oct. 15, 1932; d. Edward Hughes and Gertrude Elizabeth (Wiltshire) S. AB, U. San Diego, 1955; MA, San Diego State U., 1961; JD, U. San Diego, 1970. Bar: Calif. Tchr. San Diego Unified Sch. Dist., 1955-89; rsch. assoc. San Diego Aerospace Mus., 1989-94, edn. specialist, 1994-96; freelance writer, 1996—; curriculum writer San Diego City Schs., 1972, 73, 80-89. Author: San Diego: Air Capital of the West, 1991; co-author: Young Adults in the Marketplace (2 vols.), 1979; contbr. articles to profl. jours. Recipient Citation of Honor Diocese of San Diego, 1955, cert. of appreciation San Diego State U., 1985, recognition Calif. State Assembly, 1991; ednl. mentor Old Globe Theatre, San Diego, 1987, 88, 89. Mem. U.S. Naval Inst., Navy League U.S., Zool. Soc. San Diego, Amnesty Internat., Call to Action, Women's Ordination Conf. Democrat. Roman Catholic. Home: 4702 Norma Dr San Diego CA 92115-3136

SCOTT, OTTO, writer; b. N.Y.C., May 26, 1918; s. Otto Felix and Katherine (McGivney) S.; m. Rose Massing (div. 1952); 1 child, Katherine; m. Nellie Mouradian (div. 1963); children: Mary, Philipa; m. Anna Barney Scott, Apr. 29, 1963; 1 child, Ann Elizabeth. MA in Polit. Sci., Valley Christian U., Fresno, Calif., 1985. Mem. staff United Features Syndicate, N.Y.C., 1939-40; v.p. Globaltronix de Venezuela, Caracas, 1954-56, Mohr Assocs., N.Y.C., 1957-59, Becker, Scott & Assocs., N.Y.C., 1960-63; editor Bill Bros., N.Y.C., 1964-67; asst. to chmn. Ashland (Ky.) Oil, Inc., 1968, 69; edn. writer, reviewer San Diego Union Tribune, 1970; sr. writer Chalcedon Found., Vallecito, Calif., 1982-94; cons. Ashland Oil, Inc., 1972—; editor, pub. Otto Scott's Compass, Seattle, 1990—. Author: History Ashland Oil (The Exception) 1968, Robespierre: Voice of Virtue (History French Revolution), 1974, The Professional: Biography of J.B. Saunders, 1976, The Creative Ordeal: History of Raytheon Corporation, 1976, James I: The Fool as King, 1976, 86, Other End of the Lifeboat (History of South Africa), 1985, Buried Treasure: The Story of Arch Mineral, 1987, The Secret Six: The Fool as Martyr, 1987, The Great Christian Revolution, 1991, The Powered Hand, History of Black and Decker, 1994. With U.S. Merchant Marine, 1941-47. Mem. Author's Guild, Overseas Press Club, Com. for Nat. Policy, Com. for Monetary Rsch. and Edn. Presbyterian. Office: Otto Scotts Compass Uncommon Books 828 S 299th Pl Federal Way WA 98003-3749

SCOTT, PATRICIA JEAN, educational telecommunications administrator; b. Tacoma, Wash., Oct. 30, 1946; d. Donald Matthew and Gladys Myrtle (Olson) Gregurich; m. George Larkham Scott IV, Aug. 1, 1969; 1 child, Matthew Larkham. BA, Wash. State U., 1968; MA in Instrl. TV, Gonzaga U., 1975; PhD in Ednl. Policy and Mgmt., U. Oreg., 1994. Cert. secondary tchr., Wash. Tchr. secondary Moses Lake (Wash.) Schs., 1968-70; project dir. Wash. Commn. for Humanities, Spokane, 1975-77; adminstrv. asst. for telecourses Spokane Falls C.C., 1977; office mgr. Oreg. C.C. Telecom. Consortium, Portland, 1983-89; intern to dir. of edn. policy and planning, govs. office State Oreg.; intern to commr. for cmty. colls. State Dept. of Edn., Salem, 1988; ednl. cons. pvt. practice, 1997—; grant writer Riggs Inst., Beaverton, Oreg., 1986-88, tchr. adult literacy, Portland, 1986—. Fundraiser St. Mary of the Valley Cath. Sch., Beaverton, 1982-83; precinct com. person Spokane County, 1976-80; mem. Catlin Gabel Sch. Auction com., Portland, 1983-86. Mem. AAUW, NAFE, Women in Comms. Internat. Home: 11445 SW Lanewood St Portland OR 97225-5301

SCOTT, PETER, JR., vintner; b. 1952. Grad., U. Calif., Berkeley, 1976. With Touche Ross, San Francisco, 1976-84, Edgar Dunn & Conover, San Francisco, 1984-90, Kendall Jackson Winery, 1990—. Office: Kendall-Jackson Winery LTD 421 Aviation Blvd Santa Rosa CA 95403-1069

SCOTT, PETER BRYAN, lawyer; b. St. Louis, Nov. 11, 1947; s. Gilbert Franklin and Besse Jean (Fudge) S.; m. Suzanne Rosalee Wallace, Oct. 19, 1974; children: Lindsay W., Sarah W., Peter B. Jr. A.B., Drury Coll., 1969; J.D., Washington U., St. Louis, 1972, LL.M., 1980. Bar: Mo. 1972, Colo. 1980; diplomate Ct. Practice Inst. Sole practice, St. Louis, 1972-80; assoc. firm McKie and Assocs., Denver, 1980-81; ptnr. firm Scott and Chesteen, P.C., Denver, 1981-84, Veto & Scott, Denver, 1984-92; pvt. practice atty., Denver, 1992—; tchr. Denver Paralegal Inst., Red Rocks Community Coll. Mem. Evergreen Christian Ch., Disciples of Christ. Capt. USAR, 1971-79. Mem. ABA, Mo. Bar Assn., Colo. Bar Assn., Denver Bar Assn. Republican. Home: 26262 Wolverine Trl Evergreen CO 80439-6203 Office: Peter B Scott PC 6595 W 14th Ave Denver CO 80214-1998

SCOTT, ROBERT KEITH, economic development executive; b. Tegucigalpa, Honduras, Nov. 1, 1947; came to U.S., 1956; s. Virgil Everett and Olive (Halldorson) S.; m. Nancy Jean Moore Scott, July 4, 1970; children: Tracy, Leslie, Ann. BS in Electrical Engring., Colo. State U., 1969. cert. Econ. Developer Am. Econ. Devel. Coun. Engring. project mgr. U.S. Army, Ft. Meade, Md., 1970-74, Nat. Security Agency, Ft. Meade, Md., 1975-79; real estate sales, mgmt. various, 1980-88; CEO Colo. Springs (Colo.) Econ. Devel., 1989—. Former mem. adv. bds. Colo. Commn. on Higher Edn., U. Colo. Coll. of Engring., U. Colo. Coll. of Bus.; bd. dirs. Am. Econ. Devel. Coun., Japan Am. Soc. of Colo., Colo. Inst. of Tech. Transfer, Colo. Springs Sports Corp., Pub. Edn. Coalition, Tradition of Excellence Fdn., Fdn. for Colo. Springs Future; past bd. dirs. Econ. Developers Coun. of Colo. Capt. U.S. Army, 1970-74. Mem. Colorado Springs C. of C. (bd. dirs.), Country Club of Colo., Broadmoor Golf Club. Office: Colorado Springs Econ Devel Corp 90 S Cascade Ave Ste 1050 Colorado Springs CO 80903-1676

SCOTT, SHIRLEY, city council; married; four children. BA, Drew U., 1965; MA Germanic Langs., U. Cin., 1968. Operator Scott Supply Svc. Inc.; city coun., 1995—; bd. dirs. Tucson Clean and Beautiful. Office: 7575 E Speedway Tucson AZ 85710

SCOTT, WILLIAM CORYELL, medical executive; b. Sterling, Colo., Nov. 22, 1920; s. James Franklin and Edna Ann (Schillig) S.; m. Jean Marie English, Dec. 23, 1944 (div. 1975); children: Kathryn, James, Margaret; m. Carolyn Florence Hill, June 21, 1975; children: Scott, Amy Jo, Robert. AB, Dartmouth Coll., 1942; MD, U. Colo., 1944, MS in OB/GYN, 1951. Cert. Am. Bd. Ob-Gyn., 1956, 79, Am. Bd. Med. Mgmt., 1991. Intern USN Hosp., Great Lakes, Ill., 1945-46, Denver Gen. Hosp., 1946-47; resident Ob-Gyn St. Joseph's Hosp., Colo. Gen. Hosp., Denver, 1946-51; practice medicine specializing in Ob-Gyn Tucson, 1951-71; assoc. prof. emeritus U. Ariz. Med. Sch., Tucson, 1971-94, 1994; v.p. med. affairs U. Med. Ctr., Tucson, 1984-94. Contbr. articles to med. jours. and chpt. to book. Pres. United Way, Tucson, 1979-80, HSA of Southeastern Ariz., Tucson, 1985-87; chmn. Ariz. Health Facilities Authority, Phoenix, 1974-83. Served to capt. USNR, 1956-58. Recipient Man of Yr. award, Tucson, 1975. Fellow ACS, Am. Coll. Ob-Gyn, Pacific Coast Ob-Gyn Soc., Ctrl. Assn. of Ob-Gyn; mem. AMA (coun. on sci. affairs 1984-93, chmn. 1989-91), Am. Coll. Physician Execs., Am. Coll. Health Care Execs., Ariz. Med. Assn., La Paloma Country Club. Republican. Episcopalian. Home: PO Box 805 Sonoita AZ 85637-0805

SCOTTON, BRUCE WARREN, psychiatrist, educator; b. Champaign, Ill., Nov. 7, 1947; s. Donald W. and Beverly J. (Warren) S.; m. June Yokell, July 19, 1981; children: David, Lauren. BS in Zoology magna cum laude, U. Ill., 1964-68; MD, Columbia U., 1972; analytic tng., C.G. Jung Inst., 1978-87. lic. DEA; lic. surgeon and physician, Calif.; cert. Jungian analyst; cert. forensic examiner Nat. Bd. Forensic Examiners, 1994; bd. cert. in forensic medicine. Internal medicine intern Kaiser Found. Hosp., San Francisco, 1972-73; psychiatric resident U. Calif., San Francisco, 1973-75, 76-77; emergency room physician and surgeon Calif. Emergency Physicians, Oakland, 1974-78; interdisciplinary team leader inpatient treatment and rsch. Langley Porter Psychiatric Inst., U. Calif., San Francisco, 1970-80; pvt. practice San Francisco, 1977—; researcher in field, Liberia, India, Nepal, Zurich, and others, 1972—;. Sr. editor: Textbook of Transpersonal Psychiatry and Psychology, 1996; mem. editorial bd. Transpersonal Review, 1993—; contbr. articles to profl. jours. Bd. govs. C.G. Jung Inst. San Francisco, 1980-81. Office: 322 Clement St San Francisco CA 94118-2316

SCOZZARI, ALBERT, portfolio manager; b. Chgo., Mar. 1, 1942. BA, Northeastern Ill. U., 1973; MPA, Ill. Inst. Tech., 1974; PhD, Columbia Pacific U., 1986. Cons. World Bank Group. Author: Mass Communications in Politics, 1978, Managing for Effectiveness, 1986, Management in the 90s, 1990, First Love, 1994, Vietnam Faces, 1995, Field Cross, 1996, The Mountain, 1997, The Trail, 1997. Pres. Homeowners Assn., Phoenix, 1992-96, Scozzari Meml. Scholarship Found., 1991—. Lt. USNR, 1961-66. Mem. Am. Mensa Assn., Vietnam Vets. of Am. (life). Home: PO Box 8237 Phoenix AZ 85066

SCRIMSHAW, GEORGE CURRIE, retired plastic surgeon; b. Canajoharie, N.Y., Nov. 10, 1925; s. George and Margaret Eleanor (Salkeld) S.; m. Erna Christine Adam, Sept. 20, 1957 (div. 1982); m. Helen Irene Mott, Dec. 4, 1982; children: Katherine, Kristen, Kirby, Tracy. BA, Harvard U., 1948; MD cum laude, Tufts U., 1952. Diplomate Am. Bd. Plastic Surgery. Intern N.Y. Hosp./Cornell Med. Ctr., N.Y.C., 1952-53, resident in surgery, 1953-54; resident in surgery New England Med. Ctr., Boston, 1954-55; resident in plastic surgery Franklin Hosp./U. Calif., San Francisco, 1955-57; pvt. practice Fresno, Calif., 1957-58, Quincy, Mass., 1958-62; chief dept. plastic surgery Permanente Med. Group, Oakland, Calif., 1962-88, ret., 1988; cons., attending plastic surgeon Faulkner Hosp., Southshore Hosp., Quincy Hosp., 1959-62. Contbr. articles to profl. jours. With U.S. Army, 1944-46. Mem. ACS (life), Am. Cleft Palate Assn. (life), Am. Soc. of Plastics and Reconstructive Surgery (life), Calif. Soc. of Plastic Surgeons (life), Am. Soc. of Aesthetic Surgery (life), Alpha Omega Alpha (life).

SCRITSMIER, JEROME LORENZO, manufacturing company executive; b. Eau Claire, Wis., July 1, 1925; s. Fredrick Lorenzo and Alvera Mary (Schwab) S.; B.S., Northwestern U., 1950; m. Mildred Joan Lloyd, June 27, 1947; children—Dawn, Lloyd, Janet. Salesman, Sylvania Elec. Products, Los Angeles, 1951-69; chmn. Cameron Properties Inc.; chief fin. officer Environ. Lighting for Architecture Co., Los Angeles, 1973—. Served with USAAF, 1943-46. Mem. Apt. Assn. (pres., dir. Los Angeles County). Republican. Club: Jonathan (Los Angeles). Home: 2454 Cameron Ave Covina CA 91724-3921 Office: 17891 Arenth Ave City Of Industry CA 91748

SCRIVER, ROBERT MACFIE, sculptor; b. Browning, Mont., Aug. 15, 1914; s. Thaddeus Emery and Ellison Scriver; m. Mary Helen Strachan, Nov. 27, 1966 (div. Nov. 1970); m. Lorraine, Aug. 15, 1972. Student, Dickinson State Tchr's Coll., N.D., 2 years; Bachelor's degree, Vandercook Sch. Music, Chgo., 1935, Master's degree, 1941; postgrad., Northwestern Univ., summer 1937, U. Wash., summer 1938; D.Arts hon., Carroll Coll. mem. C.M. Russell Adv. Bd., Great Falls, Mont., 1983—. Group of works includes No More Buffalo, 1983 (gold medals 1983), An Honest Try (gold medals), Bob Scriver Hall of Bronze Mus. Mont. Wildlife, 1989; author: No More Buffalo, 1983 (pub. awards 1983), An Honest Try (pub. awards), The Blackfeet, Artists of the Northern Plains, 1990 (pub. awards). Justice of the peace Glacer County, Mont.; city magistrate City of Browning. Served to sgt. USAAF, 1940. Recipient Gold and Silver medals Cowboy Artists Am., Phoenix, Gold and Silver medals Nat. Acad. Western Arts, Oklahoma City, Mont. State Gov.'s award, 1990; honoree Bob Scriver Day State Mont., Helena. Mem. Nat. Sculpture Soc., Nat. Acad. Western Art, Soc. Animal Artists, Browning C. of C. (pres.); mem. emeritus Cowboy Artists Am. Republican. Native American. Lodge: Masons. Office: Museum Mont Wildlife Junction Hwys 2 & 89 Browning MT 59417*

SCRUGGS, ELAINE M., mayor; m. Larry Scruggs; 1 child, Jenny. Former mgmt. specialist various cos., various cities; elected mem. Glendale (Ariz.) City Coun., 1990-93; apptd., then elected mayor City of Glendale, 1993-96, re-elected, 1996—; chmn. Maricopa (Ariz.) Assn. Govts., chair youth policy adv. com., immediate past chmn. Regional Pub. Transp. Authority, vice chmn. Ariz. Mcpl. Water Users Assn., chair Maricopa Assn. Govt. Regional Aviation Systems policy com. Dir. Glendale Leadership Program, 1984-89; mem. Ariz. Coalition for Tomorrow, Ariz. Women in Mcpl. Govt.; mem. youth adv. commn., Mayor's Alliance Against Drugs and Gangs. Mem. Glendale C. of C. Office: Office of Mayor 5850 W Glendale Ave Glendale AZ 85301

SCUDERO, LESLIE JEANNINE, preschool teacher; b. Walnut Creek, Calif., May 26, 1955; d. Erasmo John and Betty Rose (Marchetti) Inzerillo; m. Robert Charles Scudero, Oct. 12, 1974; children: Natalie Jeannine, Nicole Christina. AS in Child Devel., Los Medanos Coll., 1995. Cert. in child devel., Calif. Head teller Homestead Savs., Antioch, Calif., 1974-79; gift buyer, store mgr. Crown Hallmark Shop, Antioch, 1983-91; presch. tchr. Child Day Sch., Antioch, 1994, Covenant Christian Presch., Antioch, 1994, Little Sprouts Presch., Antioch, 1994-96; presch. tchr., instrnl. asst. Prospects H.S., Antioch, 1996—; office asst. Child Devel. Consortium, Pittsburg, Calif., 1994—. V.p. Antioch Band Backers Assn., 1995—. Mem. Nat. Assn. for Edn. of Young Children. Roman Catholic.

SEABOLT, RICHARD L., lawyer; b. Chgo., Aug. 28, 1949; *Wife, Kathleen Hallissy, also graduated with a Juris Doctor from Hastings College of the Law, University of California, in 1975, and was a Contra Costa County district attorney from 1975 to 1993. Sons, Jack Seabolt, 9, and Will Seabolt, 7, are students at Wildwood Elementary School, Piedmont, California. Father, Lee Seabolt, before retirement was President and Chairman of Selz Seabolt Associates, a public relations firm located in Chicago, Illinois.* BGS with distinction, U. Mich., 1971; JD, U. Calif., Hastings, 1975. Bar: Calif. 1975. Ptnr. Hancock, Rothert & Bunshoft, San Francisco. Author: (with others) Insuring Real Property, 1988, Construction Litigation: Representing the Contractor, 1992; editorial adv. Construction and Environmental Insurance Case Digests, 1991; contbr. articles to profl. jours. Mem. ABA, State Bar Calif., Bar Assn. San Francisco. Office: Hancock Rothert & Bunshoft 10th Flr 4 Embarcadero Ctr San Francisco CA 94111-4106 *Hancock Rothert & Bunshoft has offices in San Francisco, Los Angeles, Tahoe City, and London, England, and focuses its practice on complex business and insurance litigation. Lead defense lawyer, representing certain Underwriters' at Lloyd's, London in an environmental insurance coverage trial between Aerojet-General Corporation and approximately forty of its liability insurers. After approximately ten months of trial, the jury rendered a verdict for the defendants. The defense verdict in that case was featured in 1992 articles in California Law Business and the National Law Journal as among the largest cases tried to a defense verdict in California and in the United States for that year.*

SEABORG, GLENN THEODORE, chemistry educator; b. Ishpeming, Mich., Apr. 19, 1912; s. H. Theodore and Selma (Erickson) S.; m. Helen Griggs, June 6, 1942; children: Peter, Lynne Seaborg Cobb, David, Stephen, John Eric, Dianne. AB, UCLA, 1934; PhD, U. Calif.-Berkeley, 1937; numerous hon. degrees; LLD, U. Mich., 1958, Rutgers U., 1970; DSc, Northwestern U., 1954, U. Notre Dame, 1961, John Carroll U., Duquesne U., 1968, Ind. State U., 1969, U. Utah, 1970, Rockford Coll., 1975, Kent State U., 1975; LHD, No. Mich. Coll., 1962; DPS, George Washington U., 1962; DPA, U. Puget Sound, 1963; LittD, Lafayette Coll., 1966; DEng, Mich. Technol. U., 1970; ScD, U. Bucharest, 1971, Manhattan Coll., 1976, U. Pa., 1983; PhD, U. Paris, 1996. Rsch. chemist U. Calif., Berkeley, 1937-39, instr. dept. chemistry, 1939-41, asst. prof., 1941-45, prof., 1945-71, univ. prof., 1971—, leave of absence, 1942-46, 61-71, dir. nuclear chem. research, 1946-58, 72-75, asso. dir. Lawrence Berkeley Lab., 1954-61, 71—; chancellor Univ. (U. Calif.-Berkeley), Berkeley, 1958-61; dir. Lawrence Hall of Sci. U. Calif., Berkeley, 1982-84, chmn. Lawrence Hall of Sci., 1984—; sect. chief metall. lab. U. Chgo., 1942-46; chmn. AEC, 1961-71, gen. adv. com., 1946-50; research nuclear chemistry and physics, transuranium elements.; chmn. bd. Kevex Corp., Burlingame, Calif., 1972-87, Advanced Physics Corp., Irvine, Calif., 1988-94; mem. Pres.'s Sci. Adv. Com., 1959-61; mem. nat. sci. bd. NSF, 1960-61; mem. Pres.'s Com. on Equal Employment Opportunity, 1961-65, Fed. Radiation Council, 1961-69, Nat. Aeros. and Space Council, 1961-71, Fed. Council Sci. and Tech., 1961-71, Nat. Com. Am.'s Goals and Resources, 1962-64, Pres.'s Com. Manpower, 1964-69, Nat. Council Marine Resources and Engring. Devel., 1966-71; chmn. Chem. Edn. Material Study, 1959-74, Nat. Programming Council for Pub. TV, 1970-72; dir. Ednl. TV and Radio Center, Ann Arbor, Mich., 1958-64, 67-70; pres. 4th UN Internat. Conf. Peaceful Uses Atomic Energy, Geneva, 1971, also chmn. U.S. del., 1964, 71; U.S. rep. 5th-15th gen. confs. IAEA, chmn., 1961-71; chmn. U.S. del. to USSR for signing Memorandum Cooperation Field Utilization Atomic Energy Peaceful Purposes, 1963; mem. U.S. del. for signing Limited Test Ban Treaty, 1963; mem. commn. on humanities Am. Council Learned Socs., 1962-65; mem. sci. adv. bd. Robert A. Welch Found., 1957—; mem. Internat. Orgn. for Chem. Scis. in Devel., UNESCO, 1981-92, pres., 1981-92, pres. emeritus, 1992—; mem. Nat. Commn. on Excellence in Edn., Dept. Edn., 1981-83; co-discoverer elements 94-102 and 106: plutonium, 1940, americium, 1944-45, curium, 1944, berkelium, 1949, californium, 1950, einsteinium, 1952, fermium, 1953, mendelevium, 1955, nobelium, 1958, seaborgium, 1974; co-discoverer nuclear energy isotopes Pu-239, U-233, Np-237, other isotopes including I-131, Fe-59, Te-99m, Co-60; originator actinide concept for placing heaviest elements in periodic system. Author: (with Joseph J. Katz) The Actinide Elements, 1954, The Chemistry of the Actinide Elements, 1957, (with Joseph J. Katz and Lester R. Morse) 2d ed. Vols. I & II, 1986, The Transuranium Elements, 1958, (with E.G. Valens) Elements of the Universe, 1958 (winner Thomas Alva Edison Found. award), Man-Made Transuranium Elements, 1963, (with D.M. Wilkes) Education and the Atom, 1964, (with E.K. Hyde, I. Perlman) Nuclear Properties of the Heavy Elements, 1964, (with others) Oppenheimer, 1969, (with Ben Loeb) Stemming the Tide, 1987, (with W.R. Corliss) Man and Atom, 1971, Nuclear Milestones, 1972, (with Ben Loeb) Kennedy, Khruschev and the Test Ban, 1981, (with Walt Loveland) Elements beyond Uranium, 1990, (with Ben Loeb) The Atomic Energy Commission Under Nixon, 1992, (with Ray C. Colvig) Chancellor at Berkeley, 1994, (with Ronald L. Kathren, Jerry B. Gough, Gary T. Benefiel) The Plutonium Story: The Journals of Professor Glenn T. Seaborg 1939-1946, 1994; editor: Transuranium Elements: Products of Modern Alchemy, 1978, (with W. Loveland) Nuclear Chemistry, 1982, Modern Alchemy: The Selected Papers of Glenn T. Seaborg, 1994, A Scientist Speaks Out: A Personal Perspective on Science and Society, 1996; assoc. editor Jour. Chem. Physics, 1948-50; mem. editorial adv. bd. Jour. Inorganic and Nuclear Chemistry, 1954-82, Indsl. Rsch., Inc, 1967-75; mem. adv. bd. Chem. and Engring. News, 1957-59; mem. editorial bd. Jour. Am. Chem. Soc, 1950-59, Ency. Chem. Tech., 1975—, Revs. in Inorganic Chemistry, 1977—; mem. hon. editorial adv. bd. Internat. Ency. Phys. Chemistry and Chem. Physics, 1957—, Nuclear Sci. and Techniques, Chinese Nuclear Soc., 1989—; mem. panel Golden Picture Ency. for Children, 1957-61; mem. cons. and adv. bd. Funk and Wagnalls Universal Standard Ency, 1957-61; mem. Am. Heritage Dictionary Panel Usage Cons., 1964-80; contbr. articles to profl. jours. Trustee Pacific Sci. Ctr. Found., 1962-77, Sci. Svc., 1965, pres., 1966-88, chmn., 1988-95; trustee Am.-Scandinavian Found., 1968—, Ednl. Broadcasting Corp., 1970-72; bd. dirs. Swedish Coun. Am., 1976—, chmn. bd. dirs., 1978-82; bd. dirs. World Future Soc., 1969—, Calif. Coun. for Environ. and Econ. Balance, 1974-83; bd. govs. Am. Swedish Hist. Found., 1972—; sr. tech. rev. group Amarillo Nat. Resource Ctr. for Plutonium, 1995—. Decorated officer Legion of Honor (France); recipient John Ericsson Gold medal Am. Soc. Swedish Engrs., 1948; Nobel prize for Chemistry (with E.M. McMillan), 1951, John Scott award and medal City of Phila., 1953, Perkin medal Am. sect. Soc. Chem. Industry, 1957, U.S. AEC Enrico Fermi award, 1959, Joseph Priestley Meml. award Dickinson Coll., 1960, Sci. and Engring. award Fedn. Engring. Socs., Drexel Inst. Tech., Phila., 1962; named Swedish Am. of Year, Vasa Order of Am., 1962; Franklin medal Franklin Inst., 1963; 1st Spirit of St. Louis award, 1964; Leif Erikson Found. award, 1964; Washington award Western Soc. Engrs., 1965; Arches of Sci. award Pacific Sci. Center, 1968; Internat. Platform Assn. award, 1969; Prometheus award Nat. Elec. Mfrs. Assn., 1969; Nuclear Pioneer award Soc. Nuclear Medicine, 1971; Oliver Townsend award Atomic Indsl. Forum, 1971; Disting. Honor award U.S. Dept. State, 1971; Golden Plate award Am. Acad. Achievement, 1972, Daniel Webster medal, 1976, John R. Kuebler award Alpha Chi Sigma, 1978; Founders medal Hebrew U. Jerusalem, 1981; Great Swedish Heritage award, Swedish Coun. Am., 1984, Ellis Island Medal of Honor, 1986, Seaborg medal UCLA, 1987, Vannevar Bush award NSF, 1988, Nat. Medal of Sci. NSF, 1991, Royal Order of the Polar Star Sweden, 1992, Profl. Fraternity Assn. Career Achievement award, 1993; Minor Planet 4856-Asteroid Seaborg named in his honor, 1995. Fellow Am. Phys. Soc., Am. Inst. Chemists (Pioneer award 1968, Gold medal award 1973), Chem. Soc. London (hon.), Royal Soc. Edinburgh (hon.), Am. Nuclear Soc. (hon. chair Spl. Panel on Protection and Mgmt. of Plutonium 1994—, Henry DeWolf-Smyth award 1982, Seaborg award 1984, 85, Am. Nuclear Soc., Calif. Acad. Scis., N.Y. Acad. Scis., Washington Acad. Scis., AAAS (pres. 1972, chmn. bd. 1973), Royal Soc. Arts (Eng.); mem. Am. Chem. Soc. (award in pure chemistry 1947, William H. Nichols medal N.Y. sect. 1948, Charles L. Parsons award 1964, Gibbs medal Chgo. sect. 1966, Madison Marshall award No. Ala. sect. 1972, Priestley medal 1979, pres. 1976, George C. Pimentel award in chem. edn., 1994), Am. Philos. Soc., Royal Swedish Acad. Engring. Scis. (adv. council 1980), Am. Nat., Argentine Nat., Bavarian, Polish, Royal Swedish, USSR acads. scis., Royal Acad. Exact, Phys. and Natural Scis. Spain (acad. fgn. corr.), Soc. Nuclear Medicine (hon.), World Assn. World Federalists (v.p. 1980), Fedn. Am. Scis. (bd. sponsors 1980—), Deutsche Akademie der Naturforscher Leopoldina (East Germany), Nat. Acad. Pub. Adminstrn., Internat. Platform Assn. (pres. 1981-86), Am. Hiking Soc. (bd. dirs. 1979-84, v.p. 1980, adv. com. 1984—), Royal Soc. of Edinburgh, Phi Beta Kappa, Sigma Xi, Pi Mu Epsilon, Alpha Chi Sigma (John R. Kuebler award 1978), Phi Lambda Upsilon (hon.); fgn. mem. Royal Soc. London, Chem. Soc. Japan, Serbian Acad. Sci. and Arts. Clubs: Bohemian (San Francisco); Chemists (N.Y.C.); Cosmos (Washington), University (Washington); Faculty (Berkeley). Office: Mailstop 70A-3307 1 Cyclotron Rd Berkeley CA 94720

SEAHORN, JANET JANE, educational researcher; b. Pueblo, Colo., Sept. 19, 1947; d. Charles and Ruth Isabelle (Tearpak) DiCiacco; m. Tony Seahorn, Oct. 3, 1970; children: Chad Anthony, Christopher Charles. BA, U. So. Colo., 1969; MA, U. No. Colo., 1988; PhD, Fielding Inst., Santa Barbara, Calif., 1993. Elem. tchr. Jefferson County Schs., Golden, Colo., 1969-87, mid. sch. tchr., 1992-94, ednl. rschr., 1994—; adj. prof. U. Colo., Denver, Met. State Coll., 1988-92, Regis U., Denver, 1989-92; cons. in field; mem. Nat. Bd. of Computers in English, Colo., 1994-96. Author: (workbooks) Self-Diagnostic Reading Scales, 1994, Performance Assessments..., 1995. Cons. Big Sisters of Colo., 1993; vol. soup kitchen, Westminster, Colo., 1992—. Mem. ASCD, Colo. Lang. Arts Assn., Jefferson County Coun. Adminstrs., Jefferson County Coun. Tchrs., Colo. Coun. Reading Tchrs., Colo. Assn. Gifted and Talented, Am. Ednl. Rsch. Assn. (reviewer 1996). Home: 14781 Tejon Broomfield CO 80020 Office:

Jefferson County Schools 4645 Independence St Wheat Ridge CO 80033-2952

SEALE, ROBERT L., state treasurer; b. Inglewood, Calif., Oct. 4, 1941; m. Judy Seale (dec.). BSA, Calif. Poly. U. Former contr. and sr. fin. officer Rockwell Internat.; sr. accountant Ernst & Ernst, L.A.; mng. ptnr. Pangborn & Co., Ltd. CPA's, 1985-88; now state treas. State of Nev. Former treas. Nev. Rep. Com. Mem. Nat. Assn. State Treas. (past pres.). Office: Office of State Treas Capital Bldg Carson City NV 89710

SEALE, ROBERT MCMILLAN, office services company executive; b. Birmingham, Ala., Feb. 1, 1938; s. Robert McMillan and Margaret Sutherland (Miller) S.; B.A., Emory U., 1959. With N.Y. Life Ins. Co., San Francisco, 1960-67; with Dictaphone Office Services div. Dictaphone Corp., San Francisco, 1967-69; pres. Am. Profl. Service, Inc., Dictation West, Miss Jones' Word Processing, San Francisco, Pleasant Hill, South San Francisco, Calif., Los Angeles, Beverly Hills, Riverside, Portland, Phoenix, Las Vegas, Orange County, Calif. and Denver, 1969-93, Environments West, 1980-86, Los Arcos Properties, 1980—; founder Seale Orgn., 1993; bd. dirs. The Rose Resnic Ctr. for Blind and Handicapped, Computer Based Patient Record Inst.; med. word processing cons. to hosps., health care insts., office equipment mfrs.; lectr. in field to profl. jours. Contbr. articles in field to profl. jours. Chmn. San Francisco Mayor's Com. for Employment of Handicapped, 1971-73; mem. Calif. Gov.'s Planning and Adv. Com. for Vocat. Rehab. Planning, 1968-69; pres. Calif. League for Handicapped, 1968-70, bd. dirs., 1966-73, 84-89, adv. council, 1973-77; v.p. Stebbins Found., 1980—89; pres Stebbins Housing Corp., 1980-89; assoc. St. Francis Hosp. Found., 1990—. Recipient Spoke and Spark award U.S. Jr. C. of C., 1967; KABL Outstanding Citizen's award, 1965, 71. Mem. Am. Health Info. Mgmt. Assn., Adminstrv. Mgmt. Soc., Sales and Mktg. Execs. Assn., Am. Assn. Med. Transcription (Disting. Service award 1985), Med. Transcription Industry Alliance, Emory U. Alumni Assn., Emory Lamplighters Soc., U.S. C. of C., Delta Tau Delta. Republican. Office: 280 W Camino Sur Palm Springs CA 92262-4303

SEAMAN, ARLENE ANNA, musician, educator; b. Pontiac, Mich., Jan. 21, 1918; d. Roy Russell and Mabel Louise (Heffron) S. BS, life cert., Ea. Mich. U., 1939; MMus, Wayne State U., 1951; postgrad., Colo. Coll., 1951-52, Acad. Music, Zermatt Switzerland, 1954, 58, U. Mich. guest conductor Shepherds and Angels, Symphonie Concertante, 1951; asst. conductor Detroit Women's Symphony, 1960-68; adjudicator Mich. State Band and Orch. Festivals, Solo and Ensemble Festivals, 1950-70, Detroit Fiddler's Band Auditions, 1948-52, Mich. Fedn. Music Clubs, 1948-55; tchr. Ea. Mich. U., 1939-42, Hartland Sch. Music, 1939-42, Pontiac (Mich.) Pub. Schs., 1942-45, Detroit Pub. Schs., 1945-73, pvt. studio, 1973-90. Performer cello South Oakland Symphony, 1958-65, Detroit Women's Symphony, 1951-68, Riviera Theatre Orch., 1959, 60, Masonic Auditorium Opera, Ballet Seasons, 1959-65, Toledo Ohio Symphony, 1963-70, others; performer trumpet Detroit Brass Quartet, 1974-78; piano accompanist various auditions, recitals, solo and ensemble festivals; composer: Let There Be Music, 1949, Fantasy for French Horn and Symphonic Band, 1951. Mem. Quota Internat., Delta Omicron. Home: 14650 N Alamo Canyon Dr Tucson AZ 85737-8812

SEARIGHT, MARY DELL (MRS. PAUL JAMES SEARIGHT), nursing educator; b. Cordell, Okla., Jan. 4, 1918; d. John Quitman and Grace Jewel (Giles) Williams; diploma St. Francis Hosp. Sch. Nursing, 1940; B.S. with honors, U. Calif. at Berkeley, 1960; M.S., U. Calif. at San Francisco, 1961; Ed.D., U. San Francisco, 1980; m. Paul James Searight, June 12, 1953; children—Gregory Newton, Sara Ann. Clin. nursing in various hosps., clinics, industries, drs. offices, 1940-59; instr. nursing Merritt Coll., Oakland, Calif., 1961-66; lectr. U. Calif. at San Francisco Sch. Nursing, 1966-68; nursing cons. regional med. programs, lectr. U. Minn., Mpls., 1968-71; chmn. dept. Sonoma State U., 1971-77, prof. nursing, 1971-87, prof. emeritus, 1987—; mem. acad. senate, 1972-75, cons. nursing edn., 1972-77; project dir. Nat. 2d Step Project, 1978-81; cons. Bur. Health Resources Devel., San Francisco, 1973-75; mem. chancellor's liaison com. nursing edn. Calif. State U. and Colls. Office of Chancellor, Los Angeles, 1973-76; chmn. Sonoma County Health Facilities Planning Com., Santa Rosa, Calif., 1970-72; mem. planning com. Sonoma Health Services/Edn. Activities, Santa Rosa, 1972; mem. exec. com., bd. dirs. Sonoma County Comprehensive Health Planning Com., 1970-72. Mem. Nat. League Nursing, Am. Assn. Colls. Nursing, Am., Calif. (Lulu Hassenplug award 1975) Nurses Assns., Santa Rosa Symphony League, Sigma Theta Tau. Author: Your Career in Nursing, 1970, 2d edit., 1977; editor, contbg. author: The Second Step, Baccalaureate Education for Registered Nurses (Book of Year, Am. Jour. Nursing), 1976; contbr. articles to profl. jours. Address: 5555 Montgomery Dr Apt C-1 Santa Rosa CA 95409-8844

SEARS, ALAN EDWARD, lawyer; b. Chattanooga, Oct. 31, 1951; s. Edward Lee and Anna Maria (Shepperd) S.; m. Paula Scott Lebeau, Nov. 11, 1988; children: Kelley, Shelby, Anna Marie, Rebecca, Isaiah, Isabella. BA, U. Ky., 1974; JD, U. Louisville, 1977. Bar: Ky. 1977, U.S. Supreme Ct. 1980, Ariz. 1987, D.C. 1989, Calif. 1990, U.S. Dist. Ct. (we. and ea. dists.) Ky., U.S. Dist. Ct. Ariz., U.S. Dist. Ct. D.C., U.S. Ct. Appeals (D.C., 4th, 5th, 6th, 7th, 9th, 11th and D.C. cirs.), U.S. Tax Ct., U.S. Dist. Ct. (ctrl. & so. dists.) Calif. Asst. corp. counsel City of Ashland, Ky., 1977-78; assoc. Johnson, Dunnagan & Martin, Ashland, 1977-79, Amshoff & Amshoff, Louisville, 1979-81; chief criminal div., asst. U.S. atty. U.S. Dept. Justice, Louisville, 1981-85; exec. dir. atty. gens. commn. on pornography U.S. Dept. Justice, Washington, 1985-86; assoc. solicitor U.S. Dept. Interior, Washington, 1986-87; exec. dir. Children's Legal Found., Phoenix, 1987-90; assoc. Snell & Wilmer, Phoenix, 1990; exec. dir., gen. counsel Nat. Family Legal Found., Phoenix, 1990-91; asst. U.S. atty. U.S. Dept. Justice, 1991-93; pres., gen. counsel Alliance Def. Fund, 1993—; cons. and pub. speaker to numerous organizations. Co-author: Time, Place & Manner Regulation, 1989, Prosecution & Trial of Obscenity Case, 1988; contbr. chpts. to books. Bd. dirs. Ariz. Family Rsch. Inst. Phoenix, 1988-92, Lincoln Caucus Ednl. Corp., Phoenix, 1990—, Nat. Family Legal Found., Phoenix, 1991—; precinct capt. Rep. Party, 1979-81, legis. dist. chmn., 1980-81; mem. campaign staff Gov. Louie Nunn, 1979, and Senator Cook for U.S. Senate, 1974, other party activities. Mem. ABA, Ariz. Lawyers Div. Federalist Soc. (dir. 1988—), Calif. Bar Assn., Ariz. Bar Assn., Ky. Bar Assn., D.C. Bar Assn. Office: Alliance Def Fund 7819 E Greenway Rd Ste 8 Scottsdale AZ 85260

SEARS, STEVEN LEE, screenwriter, consultant; b. Ft. Gordon, Ga., Dec. 23, 1957; s. Richard Bruce Sr. and Marian (Dean) S. AA, U. Fla., 1976; BA in Theater cum laude, Fla. State U., 1980. Writer Stephen J. Cannell Prodns., Hollywood, Calif., 1984-88, story editor, 1987-88; story editor VI-ACOM/Hargrove/Silverman Prodns., 1988; writer A. Shane Prodns., Superboy Prodns., 1989; exec. story cons. Highwayman Glen Larson/New West Prodns., Universal City, Calif., 1988; writer TV pilots Columbia Pictures TV, 1990. Writer (TV shows) Riptide, 1984-86, Hadcastle & McCormick, 1985, The A-Team, 1986-87, Stingray, 1987, Jesse Hawkes, 1989, Superboy, 1989, Grand Slam, 1989, Hardball, 1989, Who Gets Harry?, 1989, Robin's Hoods, 1994, Walker, Texas Ranger, 1994, (TV pilots) Harry O'Fell-Detective from Hell, 1990, The Inquisitor, 1990, (screenplay) Endangered Species, (interactive movie) Dreadnought, 1995, (TV show) Itsy Bitsy Spider, 1995; story editor TV shows J.T. Starbuck, 1987-88, The Father Dowling Mysteries, 1988; co-producer (TV show) Swamp Thing, 1991; producer (TV show) Raven, 1992-93; supervising prodr. (TV show) Xena Warrior Princess, 1995-97; exec. prodr. (feature) The Last Perfect Wave, 1995. Mem. AFTRA, SAG, Writers Guild Am. Democrat.

SEASTRAND, ANDREA H., former congresswoman; b. Chgo., Aug. 5, 1941; m. Eric Seastrand (dec.); children: Kurt, Heidi. BA in Edn., DePaul U., 1963. Prof. religion U. Santa Barbara; mem. Calif. Assembly, 1990-94, U.S. Ho. of Reps., 1995-96; asst. Rep. leader; mem. Rep. caucus; mem. edn. com., agr. com., consumer protection com., new tech. com., govtl. efficiency com., and ways and means com.; mem. rural caucus and select com. on marine resources. Mem. Calif. Fedn. Rep. Women (past pres.). *

SEASTRAND, JAMES KENT, mayor; m. Rosel Ruesch; 4 children. BS in Mktg., Acctg., Bus. Adminstrn., Brigham Young U., 1954; PhD (hon.), Nat. U., 1987; AA (hon.), C.C. So. Nev., 1991. Mgr. Vegas Village Shopping Corp., 1960-82; councilman City of North Las Vegas, Nev., 1973-81, mayor, 1981-97. Bishop, stake pres., regional rep. LDS Ch.; vol. Boy Scouts Am. Capt. USAF, 1955-58. Named Publ. Official of Yr., Nev. League Cities, 1990. Office: 2121 Reynolds Ave North Las Vegas NV 89030

SEAU, JUNIOR (TIANA SEAU, JR.), professional football player; b. Samoa, Jan. 19, 1969. Student, U. So. Calif. Linebacker San Diego Chargers, 1990—; player Super Bowl XXVIV, 1994. Named to Sporting News Coll. All-Am. Team, 1989, to Pro Bowl Team, 1991, 92, 93, to Sporting News NFL All Pro Team, 1992, 93. Office: San Diego Chargers PO Box 609609 San Diego CA 92160-9609*

SEAVEY, WILLIAM ARTHUR, lawyer, vintner; b. Los Angeles, Aug. 28, 1930; s. Arthur Jones and Dorothy (Keyes) S.; m. Mary van Beuren, June 25, 1955; children: Dorothy K., Arthur V.B., William G., Frederic A., Charles K. AB, Princeton U., 1952; LLB, Harvard U., 1955; grad. Inst. Internat. Studies, U. Geneva, Switzerland, 1956, D in Polit. Sci., 1970. Bar: Calif. 1957, U.S. Dist. Ct. (so. and no. dist.) Calif. 1957, U.S. Ct. Appeals (9th cir.) 1957. Assoc. Luce, Forward, Kunzel & Scripps, San Diego, 1956-57; asst. U.S. atty. U.S. Dist. Ct. (so. dist.) Calif., 1957-59; with Noon & Seavey, San Diego, 1959-65; lectr. in internat. law and econ., asst. to pres. Mills Coll., Oakland, Calif., 1968-74; ptnr. Richards & Seavey, San Francisco, 1974-76, Davis, Stafford, Kellman & Fenwick, San Francisco, 1976-78; of counsel Friedman, Olive, McCubbin, Spalding, Bilter, Roosevelt etal, San Francisco, 1987—; proprietor Seavey Vineyard, Napa County, 1981—. Author: Dumping Since the War: The Gatt and National Laws, 1970. Councilman City of Coronado, Calif., 1960-62, mayor 1962-64; trustee French-Am. Internat. Sch., San Francisco, 1968-96; pres. English Speaking Union, San Francisco, 1982-85, Alliance Francaise, San Francisco, 1979-81; chair Javits Fellowship Bd., Washington, 1989-92; mem. Columbus Fellowship Found. Bd., Washington, 1993—; dir. San Francisco Com. on Fgn. Rels., 1995—. Mem. ABA, Calif. Bar Assn., San Francisco Bar Assn., Am. Soc. Internat. Law. Republican. Clubs: Pacific Union, Cercle de l'Union, World Trade (San Francisco), The Met. (Washington). Home: 303 Pacific Ave Piedmont CA 94611-3432 Office: 425 California St 22nd Fl San Francisco CA 94104-2102 also: 1310 Conn Valley Rd Saint Helena CA 94574

SEBASCO, SALVADOR MONASTRA, safety engineer; b. Phila., Mar. 13, 1961; s. Sal Monastra and Elizabeth Sebasco Bauer; m. Berta J. Monastra, Oct. 13, 1983 (div. July 1994); children: Anthony, Samantha. BS in Occupl. Safety and Health, Mont. Tech., 1984. Registered profl. engr., Mass.; bd. cert. safety profl. Sr. safety engr. Lockheed Idaho Inc., Idaho Falls, 1991-95, Sci. Applications Internat. Corp., Pleasanton, Calif., 1995-97, Sebasco & Assocs., Livermore, Calif., 1997—; engring. adv. bd. N.Mex. Highlands U., Las Vegas, 1994—. Co-author: Bloodbourne Pathogens (booklet), 1993. Bd. dirs. Bonneville County Crime Stoppers, Idaho Falls, 1992-95. Mem. ASME (nat. nominating com.), Am. Soc. Safety Engrs. (pub. rels. chair 1992—), Soc. Hispanic Profl. Engrs. (bd. dirs. 1993-95), Internat. Conf. Bldg. Code Ofcls. Ch. of the Nazarene. Office: Sebasco & Assocs PO Box 725 Livermore CA 94551

SEBRIS, ROBERT, JR., lawyer; b. N.Y.C., May 20, 1950; s. Robert and Ruth (Kagis) S.; m. S. Lawson Hollweg, Sept. 8, 1973; children: Jared Matthew, Bryan Taylor. BS in Indsl. Labor Rels., Cornell U., 1972; JD, George Washington U., 1978. Bar: D.C. 1978, Wash. 1980. Labor rels. specialist Onondaya County Office labor rels., Syracuse, N.Y., 1973-74, U.S. Dept. Labor, Washington, 1972-75; labor rels. mgr. U.S. Treasury Dept., Washington, 1975-78; employee rels. mgr. Washington, 1978-80; assoc. Davis, Wright, Todd, Riese & Jones, Seattle, 1980-84; ptnr. Davis, Wright, Tremain, Bellevue, Wash., 1985-92, Sebris Busto, P.S., Bellevue, Wash., 1992—; expert witness T.E.A.M. Acd. Amendments NLRA hearing, 1997. Co-Author: Employer's Guide to Strike Planning, 1985; contbr. articles to profl. jours. Pres. Bellevue C.C. Found., 1988-95; co-chair employment law cert. program U. Wash. Law Sch., 1996. Mem. ABA (health law forum, labor and employment law sect., com. on employee rights), Wash. Bar Assn., D.C. Bar Assn., Seattle/King County Bar Assn. (chmn. 1991-92), Pacific Coast Labor Law Conf. (planning com. 1980-93, chmn. 1991-92), Nat. Acad. Hosp. Attys., Soc. Human Resource Mgmt. Home: 16301 Mink Rd NE Woodinville WA 98072-9463 Office: Sebris Busto PS 1500 Plaza Center 10900 NE 8th St Bellevue WA 98004-4405

SECUNDA, DAVID ABRAHAM, trade association executive director; b. L.A., May 27, 1963; s. Arthur and Gladys (Bullis) S.; m. Carmela Weber, July 31, 1993. BA in Psychology, U. Colo., 1985, BS in Outdoor Edn., 1985. Course dir. Outdoor Leadership Tng. Seminars, Denver, 1983-86; instr. Colo. Outward Bound, Denver, 1984-85; program dir. U. Colo. Outdoor Edn. Program, Boulder, Colo., 1986-89; founder, publisher Outdoor Network, Boulder, 1989-93; assoc. publisher Trilogy Mag., Boulder, 1990-91; instr. Wilderness Medicine Inst., Boulder, 1992-93; exec. dir. Outdoor Recreation Coalition of Am., Boulder, 1992—; mem. resource adv. coun. Bur. Land Mgmt., Colo., 1996. Mem. Am. Soc. Assn. Execs. (cert. assn. exec.), Am. Hiking Soc. (bd. dirs. 1995—), Student Conservation Assn. (bd. dirs. 1993—), Leave No Trace (bd. dirs. 1995—). Office: Recreation Coalition Am PO Box 1319 Boulder CO 80306

SEDARES, JAMES L., conductor; b. Chgo., Jan. 15, 1956. BMusEd, Webster U., 1977; MMusEd, Washington U., St. Louis, 1979. Assoc. condr. San Antonio Symphony, 1979-89; music dir. Phoenix Symphony Orch., 1989-96, also prin. condr. Office: Herbert Barrett Mgmt 1776 Broadway Ste 1610 New York NY 10019-3530*

SEDLANDER, JOHN WINGATE, controller; b. Detroit, July 26, 1946; s. E.J. and Mary Elizabeth (Wingate) S.; m. Jean Marie Whiteside, Aug. 17, 1968 (div. 1979); 1 child, Nathan John; m. Ellen Flanagan, Nov. 17, 1979; children: Mark, Erica. BA, U. Mich., 1968, MBA, 1970. Compensation analyst Jos. Schlitz Brewing Co., Milw., 1970-72, fin. analyst, 1972-73; mgr. purchasing and distbn. Geyser Peak Winery, Geyserville, Calif., 1973-78; dir. fin. planning CBS Specialty Stores, Emeryville, Calif., 1978-80; mgr. fin. planning Harris Corp., San Carlos, Calif., 1980-86, mgr. gen. acctg., 1986-87, credit mgr., 1987-88; mgr. fin. planning Sola Optical, Petaluma, Calif., 1988-92, contr., 1992—. Bd. dirs. The Endowment Bd., Oakland, Calif., 1980-93, Com. on the Shelterless, Petaluma, 1992—. Democrat. Lutheran. Home: 1629 Cerro Sonoma Cir Petaluma CA 94954-5768 Office: Sola Optical 1500 Cader Ln Petaluma CA 94954-6905

SEDLOCK, JOY, psychiatric social worker; b. Memphis, Jan. 23, 1958; d. George Rudolph Sedlock and Mary Robson; m. Thomas Robert Jones, Aug. 8, 1983. AA, Ventura (Calif.) Jr. Coll., 1978; BS in Psychology, Calif. Luth. U., 1980; MS in Counseling and Psychology, U. LaVerne, 1983; MSW, Calif. State U., Sacramento, 1986. Research asst. Camarillo (Calif.) State Hosp., 1981, tchr.'s aide, 1982; sub. tchr. asst. Vertura County Sch. Dist., 1981; teaching asst. Ventura Jr. Coll., 1980-82, tchr. adult edn., 1980-84; psychiatric social worker Yolo County Day Treatment Ctr., Broderick, Calif., 1986, Napa (Calif.) State Hosp., 1986—. Bd. dirs. Napa County Humane Soc. Home: PO Box 1095 Yountville CA 94599-1095 Office: Napa State Hosp Napa/Vallejo Hgwy Napa CA 49558

SEE, CAROLYN, English language educator, novelist, book critic; b. Pasadena, Calif., Jan. 13, 1934; d. George Newton Laws and Kate Louise (Sullivan) Daly; m. Richard Edward See, Feb. 18, 1955 (div. June 1959); 1 child, Lisa Lenine; m. Tom Sturak, June 11, 1959; 1 child, Clara Elizabeth Marya. BA, Calif. State U., L.A., 1958; PhD, UCLA, 1963. Prof. English, Loyola Marymount Coll., L.A., 1970-85, UCLA, L.A., 1985—; book critic L.A. Times, 1981-93, Washington Post, 1993—. Author: (novels) Rhine Maidens, 1980, Golden Days, 1986, Making History, 1991, Dreaming: Hard Luck and Good Times In America, 1995, The Handyman, 1998, also 3 others. Bd. dirs. Calif. Arts Coun., L.A., 1987-91, Day Break, for homeless, Santa Monica, Calif., 1989—, Friends of English, UCLA, 1990—; buddy for life AIDS Project Los Angeles, AIDS relief, L.A., 1990—. Recipient award Sidney Hillman Found., 1972, Robert Kirsch award L.A. Times, 1994; grantee Nat. Endowment for Arts, 1980, Guggenheim fellow, 1990-91. Mem. Writers Guild Am., Libr. Found. Calif., PEN Ctr. USA West (pres. 1990-91), Nat. Book Critics Cir. (bd. dirs. 1986-90). Democrat. Home: PO Box 107 Topanga CA 90290-0107 Office: UCLA Dept English 405 Hilgard Ave Los Angeles CA 90024-1301

SEEBACH, LYDIA MARIE, physician; b. Red Wing, Minn., Nov. 9, 1920; d. John Henry and Marie (Gleusen) S.; m. Keith Edward Wentz, Oct. 16, 1959; children: Brooke Marie, Scott. BS, U. Minn., 1942, MB, 1943, MD, 1944, MS in Medicine, 1951. Diplomate Am. Bd. Internal Medicine. Intern Kings County Hosp., Bklyn., 1944; fellow Mayo Found., Rochester, Minn., 1945-51; pvt. practice Oakland, Calif., 1952-60, San Francisco, 1961—; asst. clin. prof. U. Calif., San Francisco, 1981—; mem., vice chmn. Arthritis Clinic, Presbyn. Hosp., San Francisco, 1961-88, pharmacy com., 1963-78; chief St. Mary's Hosp. Arthritis Clinic, San Francisco, 1968-72; exec. bd. Pacific Med. Ctr., San Francisco, 1974-76. Contbr. articles to med. jours. Fellow ACP; mem. AMA, Am. Med. Womens Assn. (pres. Calif. chpt. 1968-70), Am. Rheumatism Assn., Am. Soc. Internal Medicine, Pan Am. Med. Womens Assn. (treas.), Calif. Acad. Medicine, Calif. Soc. Internal Medicine, Calif. Med. Assn., San Francisco Med. Soc., San Francisco Med. Assn., San Francisco Soc. Internal Medicine, No. Calif. Rheumatism Assn., Internat. Med. Women's Assn., Mayo Alumni (bd. dirs. 1983-89), Iota Sigma Pi. Republican. Lutheran. Office: 490 Post St Ste 939 San Francisco CA 94102-1410

SEEBER, JAMES J., sociology educator; b. Sigourney, Iowa, Nov. 1, 1940; s. John Ferdinand and Mable G. (Tracy) S.; m. Jeanne Marie Bennett, July 31, 1960 (div. Jan. 1977); children: Stephen James, Jennifer Marie; m. Lois June Allen, June 27, 1987. BA, Simpson Coll., 1963; D of Ministry, Sch. of Theology at Claremont, 1972; MA, Kans. State U., 1979, PhD, 1984. Exec. dir. North Cen./Flint Hills Area Agy. on Aging, Manhattan, Kans., 1973-77; tchg. asst. sociology dept. Kans. State U., Manhattan, 1977-83; adminstr. Inst. for Religion and Wholeness Sch. Theology at Claremont, Calif., 1984-87; assoc. prof. sociology Calif. Bapt. Coll., Riverside, 1987—; assoc. dir. Ctr. for Aging, Religion and Spirituality, Luther Sem., St. Paul, 1994—; founding mem. Inter-Facility Ethics Com., Claremont, 1992—; invited participant to nat. conf. Nat. Inst. Aging and Fetzer Inst., Bethesda, Md., 1995. Editor: Spiritual Maturity in Later Years, 1990; co-editor: Aging, Spirituality and Religion, 1995; contbr. articles to profl. jours. Elder Iowa United Meth. Conf.; pastor United Meth. Chs., Iowa and Kans., 1967-73, 81-84; chaplain Claremont Manor Retirement Home, 1986—; mem. Louis Ronfeldt Chorale, Claremont, 1985-87, Claremont Camerata Singers, 1987—. Mem. Am. Soc. on Aging (founding mem. and chmn. governing bd. forum on religion, spirituality and aging 1991-96, Outstanding Leadership award 1992), Assn. for Gerontology in Higher Edn. (religion and aging com. 1988-89), Gerontol. Soc. Am. (mem. R&A task force 1994—), Am. Sociol. Assn., Calif. Coun. Gerontology and Geriatrics. Democrat. United Methodist. Home: 1342 Briarcroft Rd Claremont CA 91711-3001 Office: Calif Bapt Coll 8432 Magnolia Ave Riverside CA 92504-3206

SEEDMAN, SUSAN ANN, surgeon; b. Miami Beach, Fla., Feb. 25, 1952; d. Philip and Dorothy S.; 1 child, Ian Bjorn Greenfield. BS, U. Fla., 1973, MD, 1978. Diplomate Am. Bd. Surgery. Resident in gen. surgery U. Okla., Oklahoma City, 1978-83; pvt. practice gen. surgery Santa Fe, N.Mex., 1983—; chmn. gen., vascular and thoracic sect. dept. of surgery St. Vincent Hosp., Santa Fe, 1988-96, med. dir. surg., women and children's svcs., 1996—. Fellow ACS (cancer liaison physician 1992—); mem. AMA, Southwestern Surg. Congress, Assn. Women Surgeons, Am. Med. Women's Assn. Office: Santa Fe Surg Assocs 435 Saint Michaels Dr Ste B-202 Santa Fe NM 87505-7672

SEEGALL, MANFRED ISMAR LUDWIG, retired physicist, educator, real estate executive; b. Berlin, Germany, Dec. 23, 1929; s. Leonhard and Vera Antonie (Vodackova) S.; came to U.S., 1952, naturalized, 1957; m. Alma R. Sterner Clarke; 2 stepchildren: James, Mark. BS magna cum laude, Loyola Coll., 1957; MS, Brown U., 1960; PhD, Stuttgart (Germany) Tech. U., 1965. Research engr. Autonetics Corp. div. N.Am. Aviation, Downey, Calif., 1959-61; physicist Astronautics div. Gen. Dynamics, Inc., San Diego, 1961-62; research scientist Max Planck Inst., Stuttgart, 1962-65; instr. stats. and algebra San Diego City Coll., 1966; sr. research engr. Solar div. Internat. Harvester Co., San Diego, 1967-73; research cons. in energy and pollution, San Diego, 1974-83; part-time evening instr. Mesa Coll., San Diego, 1980-81; instr. Grossmont Coll., El Cajon, Calif., 1981; sr. scientist Evaluation Research Corp., San Diego, 1981-82, RCS analyst Teledyne Micronetics, San Diego, 1983-84, sr. design specialist Alcoa Defense Systems, San Diego, 1984-87, cons. phys scis., 1987-89; ind. contractor in tech. writing, engring. rsch. and real estate, 1990-92, freelance writer, 1993—. Mem. IEEE (sr.), Internat. Platform Assn., Calif. Parapsychology Found. (pres. 1994-96), Cottage of Czechoslovakia of House of Pacific Rels., Rosicrucian Order, Loyola Coll., Brown U. alumni assns. Republican. Club: San Diego Lodge AMORC. Contbr. articles on acoustics, pollution and temp. measurement methods to tech. jours.; patentee in field. Address: 8735 Blue Lake Dr San Diego CA 92119-3512

SEEGER, SONDRA JOAN, artist; b. L.A., May 27, 1942; d. Reinhold Josheph and Bertha Catherine (Monese) S.; m. Richard John Pahl, Aug. 18, 1961 (div. 1974); children: Catherine Marie, Douglas Richard, Angela Gay, Susan Joan; m. David Ernest Matteson, Apr. 25, 1990. Student, Marylhurst Coll., 1960. Pvt. practice musician various locations, 1973-81; security guard MGM Hotel, Las Vegas, 1981-82; real estate salesperson Century 21, Kent, Wash., 1983-85; mgr. Viera Land & Cattle, Inc., La Grande, Oreg., 1984-92; freelance artist, Casper, Wyo., 1991—; ptnr. Old West Saddle Shop, Casper, 1989-93, Casper, Wyo., 1993—; com. mem. Oreg. State Forest Practices Com., N.E. Region, 1990-91. Named Union Co. Tree Farmer of Yr., Am. Tree Farm System, 1987. Mem. NRA, Nat. Soc. Artists, Women Artists of the West, Allied Artists, Cider Painters of Am., Australian Soc. of Miniature Art, Small Woodlands Assn., Knickerbocker Artists (assoc.), United Pastelists of Am. (signature), Nat. Soc. Artists (signature), Women Artists of the West, Pacific Art League, The Art League of Alexandria, Va., Miniature Art Soc. Fla., Oil Painters Am., Wyo. Artists Assn., Cody Country Art Guild, Am. Soc. Classical Realism, Gen. Artist Mem., Internat. Platform Assn., Oreg. Forest Resources Inst., Am. Artists' Profl. League. Republican. Home and Office: Old West Saddle Shop PO Box 4300 Casper WY 82604-0300

SEELENFREUND, ALAN, distribution company executive; b. N.Y.C., Oct. 22, 1936; s. Max and Gertrude (Roth) S.; m. Ellyn Bolt; 1 child, Eric. BME, Cornell U., 1959, M. in Indsl. Engring., 1960; PhD in Mgmt. Sci., Stanford U., 1967. Asst. prof. bus. adminstrn. Grad. Sch. Bus. Stanford U., Palo Alto, Calif., 1966-71; mgmt. cons. Strong, Wishart and Assocs., San Francisco, 1971-75; various mgmt. positions McKesson Corp., San Francisco, 1975-84, v.p., chief fin. officer, 1984-86, exec. v.p., chief fin. officer, 1986-89, chmn., CEO, 1989-97, chmn., 1997—, also bd. dirs., chmn., 1997—; bd. dirs. Pacific Gas and Electric Co. Bd. dir. Golden Gate Nat. Park Assn. Mem. World Affairs Coun. No. Calif., Bay Area Coun., Calif. Bus. Roundtable, Bankers Club, St. Francis Yacht Club, Villa Taverna Club, Pacific Union Club. Office: McKesson Corp 1 Post St San Francisco CA 94104-5203

SEELY, DONA MARLENE, orthodontist; b. Vancouver, Wash., Dec. 13, 1953; d. William Stanley and Marlys Elaine (Spicer) S.; m. Curtis Eugene Carlson, Feb. 14, 1982; children: Gina Christine Carlson, Erik Alan Carlson. DDS, U. Wash., 1978, MSD, 1980. Dentist Bellevue, Wash., 1978-80; orthodontist Bellevue, Seattle, 1980—. Mem. Am. Assn. Orthodontists, Pacific Coast Soc. Orthodontists, Wash. State Soc. Orthodontists, Wash. State Soc. Dentists, Seattle King County Dental Soc., Omicron Kappa Upsilon. Home: 16730 Shore Dr NE Seattle WA 98155-5634

SEELY, MARILYN RUTH, state agency administrator; b. Oklahoma City, Jan. 24, 1942; d. Dale Willard and Virginia Lea (Crosby) Thompson; m. John Bradley Seely, June 3, 1961; children: Teresa Maria Seely Wozniak, Jeffrey Bradley. BS, SUNY, New Paltz, 1974; MPH, U. Hawaii, 1978. Tchr. adult divsn. St. Louis High Sch., Honolulu, 1976-77; cmty. svcs. planner Health and Cmty. Svcs. Coun. Hawaii, Honolulu, 1979-80; sr. planner Atlanta Regional Commn., 1981-84; long term care planner Exec. Office Aging, Honolulu, 1986-95; dir. Exec. Office Aging, 1994—; mme. assoc. clin. faculty sch. pub. health U. Hawaii, Honolulu, 1994-96. Author: (with others) A Guide For People Who Care, 1993, The Unfinished Health Agenda, 1994. Active Town & Gown Com. sch. pub. health U. Hawaii, 1994—; mem. staff Gov.'s Blue Ribbon Panel on Death & Dying, 1996-97. Mem. Am. Soc. Quality Control, Am. Soc. Aging, Honolulu Acad. Arts, Soc. Pub. Health Edn. Democrat. Home: 46-402 Haiku Plantations Dr

Kaneohe HI 96744 Office: Exec Office Aging 250 South Hotel St # 107 Honolulu HI 96813

SEEMAN, BRIAN, actor, writer, comedian; b. Bronx, Nov. 17, 1962; s. Robert and Sheila Seeman; m. Marilyn Martin, Aug. 6, 1994. BFA, U. Conn., 1984. Actor in film, TV and commls.; appeared on The Tonight Show with Jay Leno; performer comedy for various colls., clubs, corps., and orgns. throughout the country; author: Being Homeless for Fun and Profit. Mem. SAG, AFTRA, Am. Guild Variety Artists. Home: 950 N Kings Rd Apt 129 West Hollywood CA 90069-4322

SEEMANN, CHARLES HENRY, JR., folklorist, cultural organization administrator; b. Globe, Ariz., Oct. 21, 1946; s. Charles Henry and Alice (Bashaw) S. BA, Calif. State U., San Francisco, 1970; MA, UCLA, 1974. Folklore, music prof. Moorpark (Calif.) Coll., 1972-78; folklorist Nat. Pk. Svc., San Francisco, 1978-81; curator of collections Country Music Found., Inc., Nashville, 1981-83, dep. dir., 1983-92; folk cultural specialist, program dir. Fund for Folk Culture, Santa Fe, N.Mex., 1993—. Co-editor: (book) Folklife and Museums, 1987; performer: (album) The Last Straw String Band, 1976; producer: (reissue hist. album) Back in the Saddle Again, 1983 (Grammy nominee 1983); annotater (reissue hist. albums) The Maddox Bros. and Rose, 1985, Bob Wills Fiddle, 1987, Le Gran Memou: A Cajun Anthology, 1990, Sons of the Pioneers, 1991, Tex Ritter, 1991, Uncle Dave Macon, 1992, Le Gran Prairie: A Cajun Anthology, vol. 2, 1992. Recipient Wrangler award Cowboy Hall of Fame, Oklahoma City, 1983. Mem. Tenn. Folklore Soc. (pres. 1989-90), Am. Folklore Soc., Am. Assn. Mus. Office: Fund for Folk Culture PO Box 1566 Santa Fe NM 87504-1566

SEETHALER, WILLIAM CHARLES, international business executive, consultant; b. N.Y.C., Dec. 4, 1937; s. William Charles and Catherine Frances (Flaherty) S. Student, Quinnipiac Coll., Conn., 1955-56, Ohio State U., 1956-58; BSBA, U. San Francisco, 1977; MBA, Pepperdine U., 1982. Asst. to v.p. sales T. Sendzimir, Inc., Waterbury, Conn. and Paris, 1960-66; mgr. internat. ops. Dempsey Indsl. Furnace Co., East Longmeadow, Mass., 1966-67; mgr. internat. sales Yoder Co., Cleve., 1967-74; mng. dir., owner Seethaler & Assocs., Palo Alto, Calif.; owner, chief exec. officer Seethaler Internat. Ltd., Palo Alto, Calif., 1974—; ptnr. DFS Computer Assocs., San Jose, Calif., 1976-87. Bd. dirs. Palo Alto Fund, 1979-93, chmn., 1986-88; comty. rels. advisor Stanford U., 1986—. Mem. Inst. Indsl. Engrs. (sr., v.p. profl. rels. Peninsula chpt. 1988-90, del. to Silicon Valley Engring. Coun. 1991—, bd. dirs.), Joint Venture: Silicon Valley (bd. dirs. 1992—), Assn. Iron and Steel Engrs., Assn. MBA Execs., Palo Alto C. of C. (v.p. orgn. affairs 1976-77, pres. 1977-78, bd. dirs. 1975-79), U. San Francisco Alumni Assn., Stanford U. Alumni Assn., Pepperdine U. Alumni Assn., Stanford Diamond Club. Office: Ste A-1117 701 Welch Rd Palo Alto CA 94304-1709

SEFF, KARL, chemistry educator; b. Chgo., Jan. 23, 1938; s. Joseph and Rose (Hauser) S. BS, U. Calif., Berkeley, 1959; PhD, MIT, 1964. Rsch. assoc. UCLA, 1965-67; asst. prof. chemistry U. Hawaii, Honolulu, 1968-73, assoc. prof. chemistry, 1973-75, prof. chemistry, 1975—; cons. Filtrol Corp., L.A., 1966-73, Mitsubishi Heavy Industry, Nagasaki, Japan, 1992-94; vis. scholar Princeton (N.J.) U., 1974-75, Oxford (Eng.) U., 1988, 89, Pusan and Kyungpook Nat. Univs., Korea, 1996; assoc. rschr. U. Mex., 1981-82; vis. prof. Dartmouth U., 1989; lectr. Tokyo Inst. Tech., 1980, 91, U. Salford, Eng., 1983, U. N.Mex., 1985, U. P.R., 1985, U. Bristol, 1988, ETH, Zurich, Switzerland, 1988, Goethe U., Frankfort, Germany, 1988, Imperial Coll., London, 1989, Cambridge U., 1989, Kyungpook Nat. U., Korea, 1990, Acad. Sci. Leningrad, 1990, Pusan Nat. U., Korea, 1990, Northwestern U., 1994, others. Contbr. numerous articles to profl. jours. NATO sr. fellow, NSF, 1975, Rsch. Travel award, 1988-90; grantee Army Rsch. Office, 1969-72, NIH, 1972-75, 75-78, NSF, 1973-76, 75, 77, 78-81, Petroleum Rsch. Fund, 1974-76, 95—, Gordon Conf., 1976, U.S.-Korea Coop. Rsch., NSF, 1982, 84-86, Mitsubishi Industries, 1992-93. Mem. Am. Chem. Soc. (local sect. chair, award 1983, councilor 1992-94), Am. Crystallographic Assn., Vegetarian Soc. Honolulu (exec. com. 1993—), Sigma Xi. Democrat. Office: U Hawaii Dept Chemistry 2545 The Mall Honolulu HI 96822-2233

SEGAL, D. ROBERT, publishing and broadcast company executive; b. Oshkosh, Wis., Oct. 30, 1920; s. Morris Henry and Ida (Belond) S.; m. Kathryn McKenzie; children: Jonathan McKenzie, Janet Elizabeth Crane. Currently pres., chief exec. officer, dir. Freedom Newspapers, Inc., Irvine, Calif.; pres. Freedom Communications, Inc., Orange County Cable News, Kinston (N.C.) Free-Press, New Bern (N.C.) Sun Jour., Burlington (N.C.) Times-News, Jacksonville (N.C.) Daily News, WLNE-TV, New Bedford, Mass. and Providence, KFDM-TV, Beaumont, Tex., WTVC-TV, Chattanooga, WRGB-TV, Schenectady, Freedom Newspapers of Fla., Inc., Crawfordsville Jour.-Rev. (Ind.), Greenville (Miss.) Delta Dem. Pub. Co., Dothan (Ala.) Progress.; mng. ptnr. Clovis News-Jour. (N.Mex.), Rio Grande Valley Newspaper Group (Tex.), Gastonia Gazette (N.C.), Lima News (Ohio), Odessa Am. (Tex.), Pampa Daily News (Tex.), Orange County Cablenews Network. Trustee Children's Hosp of Orange County, Calif., Boy Scout Council of Orange County. Served with USAAF, 1942-45. Office: Freedom Newspapers Inc 17666 Fitch Irvine CA 92614-6022*

SEGAL, STEVEN PAUL, social work educator; b. Bklyn., Jan. 13, 1943; married, 2 children. BA, Hunter Coll., Bronx, 1965; MSW, U. Mich., 1967; PhD, U. Wis., 1972. Caseworker N.Y. Bur. Child Welfare, N.Y.C., 1965; social group worker Windsor Group Therapy Project, Ont., 1965-66; unit supr. Fresh Air Soc., Detroit, 1966; caseworkr Lansing (Mich.) Cons. Ctr., 1966-67, Jewish Family & Children's Svcs., Detroit, 1967; asst. to assoc. prof. and rsch. social worker U. Calif., Berkeley, 1972-88; prin. investigator Inst. Sci. Analysis, Berkeley, 1982-94; assoc. dir. Ctr. for Rsch. on Orgn. and Financing, Western Consortium, Berkeley, 1988-92; dir. Mental Health and Social Welfare Rsch. Group U. Calif., Berkeley, 1973—; prof. sch. social welfare and pub. health U. Calif., 1988—; dir. Ctr. Self Help Rsch., 1990—; lectr. in field; conductor workshops in field. Contbr. numerous articles to profl. jours. Recipient Medal of Brescia, Italy, 1987, Western European Regional Rsch. Fulbright award, 1986-87; NIMH traineeships, 1965, 66, 67, 68, 69, 70-72; N.Y. State Rsch. fellow in psychiat. epidemiology, 1969-71, others. Mem. NASW, APHA, Am. Sociol. Assn., Am. Psychol. Assn. Home: 733 Santa Barbara Rd Berkeley CA 94707-2045 Office: U Calif Sch Social Welfare 120 Haviland Hall Berkeley CA 94720

SEGAN, KENNETH AKIVA, artist, educator; b. N.Y.C., 1950; s. Meyer S. and Barbara (Graff) S. BA in Art, So. Ill. U., 1977; MFA, U. Mo., 1980; postgrad., Acad. Fine Arts, Crakow, Poland, 1984, Jagiellonian U., Crakow, 1985. Owner Tsigana Art Studio, Seattle, 1980—; internat. artist-in-residence Aberdeen (Scotland) Art Gallery, 1987; founder, nat. and overseas programming dir. Under the Wings of G-D Found. for Holocaust Edn. Thru Art, Seattle, 1995—; liaison from printmakers in Scotland and Poland to Gilkey Ctr. for Graphics Arts Portland Art Mus., 1985-87; lectr. on teaching the Holocaust through art, 1994—. Creator: Under the Wings of G-D drawings, 1991—; represented in permanent collections: Albertina Graphic Arts Collection, Vienna, Austria, Bibliotheque Nationale, Paris, First Interstate Bank, Seattle, Musée d'Art Juif de Paris, Musée des Beaux-Arts, Budapest, Hungary, Mus. of Modern Art, Haifa, Israel, Portland Art Mus., Smithsonian Instn., Washington, Warner-Lambert Corp., Morris Plains, N.J., numerous others; pub. The West Collection: Art and the Law Book, 1986. Office: Under the Wings of G-D Found PO Box 114 Seattle WA 98111-0114 Studio: 540 First Ave 5 3rd Fl Seattle WA 93104

SEGEL, KAREN LYNN JOSEPH, accountant, taxation specialist, lawyer; b. Youngstown, Ohio, Jan. 15, 1947; d. Samuel Dennis and Helen Anita Joseph; m. Alvin Gerald Segel, June 9, 1968 (div. Sept. 1976); 1 child, Adam James. BA in Soviet and East European Studies, Boston U., 1968; JD, Southwestern U., 1975. Bar: Calif., 1996, U.S. Tax Ct., 1996, U.S. Dist. Ct. (cen. dist.) Calif., 1996, U.S. Supreme Ct., 1996, U.S. Ct. Appeals (9th cir.), 1997. Adminstrv. asst. Olds Brunel & Co., N.Y.C., 1968-69, U.S. Banknote Corp., N.Y.C., 1969-70; tax acct. S.N. Chilkov & Co. CPA's, Beverly Hills, Calif., 1971-74; intern Calif. Corps. Commr., 1975; tax. sr. Oppenheim Appel & Dixon CPA's, L.A., 1978, Fox, Westheimer & Co. CPA's, L.A., 1978, Zebrak, Levine & Mepos CPA's, L.A., 1979; ind. cons. acctg., taxation specialist Beverly Hills, 1980—; bd. dirs. World Wide Motion Pictures Corp., L.A.; law student mentor Southwestern U., 1996, tax moot ct. judge, 1997. Editorial adv. bd. Am. Biog. Inst. High sch. amb. to Europe People-to-People Orgn., 1963. Named 1991, 93 Woman of Yr., Am. Biog. Inst. Mem. Nat. Soc. Tax Profls., Nat. Assn. Tax Practitioners, Nat. Trust for Hist. Preservation, Am. Mus. Natural History, Calif. State Bar, Winterthur Guild, Women's Inner Circle of Achievement, Consumer Lawyers of L.A., Calif. Young Lawyers Assn., Beverly Hills Bar Assn., Santa Monica Bar Assn., Complex Litigation Inns of Ct., L.A. County Bar Assn.

SEGRE, EUGENE JOSEPH, drug development consultant, physician; b. Torino, Italy, Sept. 12, 1932; came to U.S., 1940; s. Ernesto and Anna (Jona) S.; m. Zina Cecilia Camarda, June 8, 1956; children: David, Paul, Lisa. BA, Cornell U., 1953, MD, 1956. Diplomate Am. Bd. Internal Medicine, Nat. Bd. Med. Examiners. Staff scientist Worcester Found., Shrewsbury, Mass., 1962-64; assoc. med. dir. Syntex Corp., Palo Alto, Calif., 1964-66; dir. clin. pharmacology Syntex Corp., Palo Alto, 1966-67; assoc. dir. Inst. of Medicine Syntex Corp., Palo Alto, 5, 1967-77, v.p., dir. Inst. of Medicine, 1977-80, sr. v.p. devel. rsch., mem. corp. mgmt. com., 1980-90; cons. Palo Alto, 1990—; mem., chair sci. adv. bds. Hana Biologics, Berkeley, Calif., 1990-92, Pharmagenesis, 1991-95, Acea Pharms., 1991—, Calydon, 1991—; asst. clin. prof. Stanford U. Med. Sch., Palo Alto, 1965-84, emeritus, 1993—. Author: Androgens, Virilization and the Hirsute Female, 1967; contbr. chpts. to books, more than 50 articles to profl. jours.; patentee in field. Capt. USAF, 1957-59, 61-62. Fellow ACP; mem. Am. Soc. for Clin. Pharmacology and Therapeutics, Phi Beta Kappa, Alpha Omega Alpha. Home and Office: 470 Santa Rita Ave Palo Alto CA 94301-3943

SEIBEL, ERWIN, oceanographer, educator; BS, CCNY, 1965; MS, U. Mich., 1966, PhD, 1972. Asst. research oceanographer U. Mich., Ann Arbor, 1972-75, assoc. research oceanographer, 1975-78, asst. dir. sea grant, 1975-78; environ. lab dir. San Francisco State U., 1978-81, chmn. dept. geoscis., 1981-88, dean undergraduate studies, 1988—. commr. Calif. Commn. on Tchr. Credentialing; sr. scientist cruises U. Mich., 1971-78; mem. sea grant site rev. teams Nat. Sea Grant Program, Washington, 1978—; bd. govs. Moss Landing Marine Labs., Calif., 1981—; mem. adv. com. Ctr. Advancement Mercantile Spacefaring; coord. Biology Forum Calif. Acad. Scis., 1988-89; exec. sec. Oceans 83 Marine Tech. Soc., IEEE, San Francisco, 1982-83; coord. Symposium for Pacific AAAS El Nino Effect, 1983-84; dir. environ. monitoring nuclear power plant, 1972-78; mem. sci. adv. panel Calif. Commn. Tchr. Credentialing, 1988-93; mem. steering com. Pacific Basin Studies Ctr., 1990-93; commr. Calif. Commn. on Teaching Credentialing, 1993—, fiscal planning & policy com., 1994—, performance stds. com., 1995—, appeals & waivers com., 1996—. Contbr. articles to profl. jours.; developer photogrammetric technique for continuous shoreline monitoring. Advisor MESA program for Minority Students, San Francisco area, 1981-88; vol. San Francisco Bay Area council Girl Scouts U.S., 1982-86. Served to capt. U.S. Army, 1967-71, Vietnam. Grantee Am. Electric Power Co., 1972-78, Gt. Lakes Basin Commn., 1975-76, Calif. Div. Mines and Geology, 1986-88, Am. Coun. Edn. and Ford Found., 1990-94. Recipient Exceptional Merit Service award San Francisco State U., 1984. Fellow AAAS, Calif. Acad. Scis., Geol. Soc. Am.; mem. N.Y. Acad. Scis., Am. Geophys. Union, Marine Tech. Soc. (pres. San Francisco Bay chpt. 1982-83), Western Assn. Schs. and Colls. (mem. student learning and teaching effectiveness task force 1994-95), U. Mich. Alumni Assn., Gold Key (hon.), Sigma XI (pres. San Francisco State U. chpt. 1982-84, 90-92, Chautauqua coord, 1989-96, faculty athletic rep. NCAA, NCAC, 1991-93). Office: San Francisco State U Dean of Undergrad Studies 1600 Holloway Ave San Francisco CA 94132-1722

SEID, MELINDA JOY, health and safety studies educator; b. San Francisco, May 29, 1952. BA in Bacteriology, Chemistry, U. Calif., Berkeley, 1974; MS in Biolog. Sci., Microbiology, U. Pacific, Stockton, 1978; MSA in Health Care Mgmt., Calif. State U., Bakersfield, 1986; PhD in Health Svcs. Adminstrn., U. So. Calif., 1991. Cert. secondary sch. tchr. Biol. Sci., Chemistry, Life Sci., Calif.; instr. Calif. C.Cs. Health and Physical Care Svcs. and Related Techs., Biolog. Sci. (life); cert. Health Edn. Specialist, Nat. Commn. Health Edn. Credentialing; lic. med. technologist, Am. Soc. Clin. Pathology, lic. clin. lab. technologist, Calif. Med. technologist trainee dept. pathology U. So. Calif. Med. Ctr., L.A., 1979-80, med. technologist, 1980; edn. coord., lectr., med. technologist Pioneers Meml. Hosp., Brawley, Calif., 1980-82; program dir. med.-technology program Kern Med. Ctr., Bakersfield, 1982-87; clin. supr. and instr. Family Medicine Ctr. Lab. Sch. of Medicine U. Nev., Reno, 1987-88; clin. intern PhD rsch. employee assistance program Dept. Health, San Francisco, 1988-90; from project investigator to coord., evaluator Regional Tobacco Prevention Ctr., Sacramento, 1991-93; project dir., evaluator Gold Country Tobacco Prevention Coalition, Sacramento, 1993; grad. tchg. asst. U. Pacific, Stockton, Calif., 1976-78; substitute health sci. instr. City Coll. San Francisco, 1990; lectr. dept. health and phys. edn. Calif. State U., Sacramento, 1990-91, program coord. dept. health and phys. edn., 1991—, asst. prof. dept. health and phys. edn., 1992—; med. technologist part time Pathology Lab., Inc. Los Gatos, Calif.; evaluation cons. Calif. Wellness Found.'s Violence Prevention Initiative The Johns Hopkins U. Injury Prevention Ctr., Stanford Ctr. for Rsch. in Disease Prevention and RAND Corp. Joint Evaluation partnership, Stanford, Calif., 1993-95;. Presenter at numerous workshops and confs. Vol. for comty. outreach program Californians Against Waste Found., Sacramento, 1991, vol. and tng. coord. for conf. facilitatior Multi-Ethnic Health Promotion Conf., Sacramento, 1991; Am. Lung Assn. Gold County Coalition prevention com. mem., Sacramento, 1992-95, rep. 1992-94; bd. dirs. Am. Lung Assn. of Sacramento Emigrant Trails, 1993—; proposal reviewer for Dept. of Health Svcs. Hypertension Control Program and Health Edn.-Risk Reduction Program, Sacramento, 1993; program co-chair Profl. Devel. Day, No. Calif. Soc. for Pub. Health Edn., Nat. U., Sacramento; mem. adv. panel Commn. Tchr. Credentialing Health Sci. Tchr. Preparation and Assessment, Sacramento, 1995—; and other civic and community involvements. Recipient Calif. State U. Doctoral Incentive Forgivable Loan, 1987-1990; Sacramento Ednl. Cable Consortium award, 1993, 94, 95. Mem. State of Calif. Wellness Info. Network, Soc. for Pub. Health Edn., Am. Soc. Pub. Adminstrn., Calif. Assn. Med. Lab. Tech., Am. Soc. Clin. Pathologists, Pi Alpha Alpha. Office: Calif State U Dept Health Phys Edn 6000 J St Sacramento CA 95819-2605

SEIDEL, GEORGE ELIAS, JR., animal scientist, educator; b. Reading, Pa., July 13, 1943; s. George E. Sr. and Grace Esther (Heinly) S.; m. Sarah Beth Moore, May 28, 1970; 1 child, Andrew. BS, Pa. State U., 1965; MS, Cornell U., 1968, PhD, 1970; postgrad., Harvard U. Med. Sch., Boston, 1970-71. Asst. prof. physiology Colo. State U., Ft. Collins, 1971-75, assoc. prof., 1975-83, prof., 1983—; vis. scientist Yale U., 1978-79, MIT, 1986-87; mem. bd. on agr. NRC. Co-editor: New Technologies in Animal Breeding, 1981; contbr. articles to profl. jours. Recipient Alexander Von Humboldt award, N.Y.C., 1983, Animal Breeding Research award Nat. Assn. Animal Breeders, Columbia, Mo., 1983, Clark award Colo. State U., 1982, Upjohn Physiology award, 1986; Gov's. award for Sci. and Tech., Colo., 1986. Mem. AAAS, NAS, Am. Dairy Sci. Assn., Am. Soc. Animal Sci. (Young Animal Scientist award 1983), Soc. for Study of Reprodn., Internat. Embryo Transfer Soc. (pres. 1979). Home: 3101 Arrowhead Rd Laporte CO 80535-9374 Office: Colo State U Biotechnol Lab Animal Reproduction Fort Collins CO 80523

SEIDEL, JAMES STEPHEN, pediatrician, educator; b. N.Y.C., June 24, 1943; s. Leo and Esther (Mellman) S. BS, Mich. State U., 1964; MSPH, U. N.C., 1967; MD, UCLA, 1973, PhD, 1976. Diplomate Am. Bd. Pediatrics. Chief gen. and emergency pediatrics Harbor/UCLA Med. Ctr., Torrance, Calif., 1977—; asst. prof. UCLA Sch. of Medicine, L.A., 1977-82, assoc. prof., 1982-91, prof. pediatrics, 1991—. Contbr. articles to profl. jours. Recipient Emil Bogen Rsch. prize, 1973. Mem. Am. Acad. Pediatrics (mem. com. on pediatric emergency medicine 1985-92, cons. 1992—), Am. Heart Assn. (chmn. various coms.), Am. Acad. Pediatrics, Ambulatory Pediatric Assn., Nat. Acad. Scis., L.A. Pediatric Soc. (exec. bd. 1990—, pres. 1993-94, Joseph W. St. Geme Meml. award 1987), Western Soc. Pediatric Rsch., Am. Soc. Tropical Medicine and Hygiene, Am. Soc. Parasitologists, So. Calif. Parasitologists (pres. 1987), Soc. for Pediatric Emergency Medicine (bd. dirs. 1990—), Brazilian Soc. of Tropical Medicine, Hawaiian Pediatric Soc. (hon.), AAAS, others.

SEIDEL, TAMMY SUE, secondary education educator; b. Roswell, N.Mex., Feb. 19, 1959; d. Harold C. and Nina Sarah (Nelson) Miller; m. David J. Seidel, Apr. 18, 1987; 1 child, Sarah Brianna. BBA, Ea. N.Mex. U., 1981; MA in Tng. and Learning Tech., U. N.Mex., 1992. Customer svc. rep. First Interstate Bank, Hobbs, N.Mex., 1983; sys. sales cons. Moore Bus. Forms, Hobbs, 1983-85; mktg. tchr. Los Alamos (N.Mex.) H.S., 1985—. Finalist Golden Apple Found. award 1996. Mem. Am. Vocat. Assn., Mktg. Edn. Assn., N.Mex. DECA (chmn. bd. govs. 1994-96, mem. bd. govs. 1996—, state officer/advisor 1996-97), N.Mex. Mktg. Edn. Assn. (10-Yr. award 1995), Los Alamos Schs. Credit Union, Phi Kappa Phi. Office: Los Alamos High Sch 1300 Diamond Dr Los Alamos NM 87544-2209

SEIERSTAD, ALBERTA JUNE, chemist; b. Cumberland, Wis., June 21, 1949; d. Albert Martin and Violette Anna (Peterson) S. BS in Chemistry and Math., U. Wis., River Falls, 1971; postgrad., Iowa State U., 1971-72, U. Nebr., 1972-74. Lab. asst. U. Wis., River Falls, 1969-71; teaching asst. Iowa State U., Ames, 1971-72, U. Nebr., Lincoln, 1972-74; rsch. asst. Utah Water Rsch. Lab., Logan, 1977-79, rsch. chemist, 1980-84, lab. supr., 1984-86; lab. mgr. Portland (Oreg.) Water Bur., 1987—; quality assurance lab. cons. Ecosystems Rsch. Inst., Logan, 1982. Co-author/editor lab. procedures manual: Analytical Procedures for Selected Water Quality Parameters, 1981. Mem. APHA, Am. Water Wks. Assn. (standard methods com. 1980—). Home: 39920 Hall Ct Sandy OR 97055-9387 Office: Portland Water Bur 2010 N Interstate Ave Portland OR 97227-1756

SEIFEL, ELIZABETH MARGARET, business owner; b. Boston, Apr. 23, 1956; d. Norman and Mary Elizabeth (Gill) S.; m. Scott D. Morse, Aug. 19, 1990. BS in Urban Studies, Mass. Inst. Tech., 1978, M in City Planning, 1979. Exec. dir. Tent City Corp., Boston, 1979-81; planner, economist Blayney-Dyett, San Francisco, 1981-82; assoc.-in-charge Williams-Kuebelbeck, Belmont, Calif., 1982-89; prin. Seifel Assocs., San Francisco, 1990—; mem. Contra Costa County Home Tech. Adv. Commn., 1994—. Dir. Women's Philharm., San Francisco, 1990-94; mem. Leadership Calif., 1994—. Recipient Harold E. Kobdell Disting. Svc. award, MIT, 1995. Mem. Am. Inst. Cert. Planners, Calif. Redevel. Assn., Urban Land Inst., Non-Profit Housing Assn., MIT Alumni Assn. No. Calif. (officer 1982-94, dir. 1993—, nat. selection com. 1994-96, pres. 1995-96). Office: Seifel Assocs 220 Montgomery St Ste 448 San Francisco CA 94104

SEIFERT, STEPHEN WAYNE, lawyer; b. Washington, May 25, 1957; s. Arthur John and Frances E. (Smith) S. BA summa cum laude, Yale U., 1979; JD, Stanford U., 1982. Bar: Colo. 1982, U.S. Dist. Ct. Colo. 1982, U.S. Ct. Appeals (10th cir.) 1982, U.S. Ct. Appeals (5th cir.) 1987, U.S. Supreme Ct. 1988. Ptnr.. Fairfield and Woods P.C., Denver, 1982—; mng. dir. Fairfield & Woods P.C., Denver, 1990-92, 95-96. Author: Colorado Creditors' Remedies--Debtors' Relief, 1990; contbg. author: Colorado Methods of Practice; contbr. articles to profl. jours. Chmn. bd. Opera Colo., 1989-92; bd. trustees Denver Pub. Libr. Friends Found., Yale-Harvard Regatta Com., Allied Arts Inc., Denver World Affairs Coun. Mem. ABA, Am. Bankruptcy Inst., Colo. Bar Assn., Denver Bar Assn. Law Club Denver) v.p. 1992-93, pres. 1993-94), Phi Beta Kappa, Univ. Club. Office: Fairfield & Woods PC 1700 Lincoln St Ste 2400 Denver CO 80203-4524

SEIFF, STEPHEN S., ophthalmologist; b. L.A., Sept. 30, 1925; s. Max and Minnie F. (Feldman) S.; m. Gloria Louise Holtzman, Apr. 16, 1950; children: Stuart R., Sherri Seiff Sloane, Karen Seiff Sacks. AA, UCLA, 1945; AB, U. Calif., Berkeley, 1946; MD, U. Calif., San Francisco, 1949. Diplomate Am. Bd. Ophthalmology. Intern County Gen. Hosp., L.A., 1949-50; fellow in anesthesiology Lahey Clinic, Boston, 1950-51; resident in ophthalmology U. Calif., San Francisco, 1952-55; clin. prof. dept. ophthalmology UCLA, 1956—; pvt. practice Beverly Hills, Calif., 1955—; clin. chief divsn. ophthalmology Cedars/Sinai Med. Ctr., L.A., 1957—; attending ophthalmologist Children's Hosp., L.A., 1956-94; lectr. in field; assoc. examiner Am. Bd. Ophthalmology. Collaborating author: Clinical Anticoagulant Therapy, 1965; contbr. articles to profl. jours. Bd. dirs. That Man May See Inc., San Francisco; former exec. com. mem. UCLA Hosp. Lt. M.C. USNR, 1950-52. Recipient Sr. Honor award UCLA Dept. Ophthalmology, 1994. Fellow ACS, Am. Acad. Ophthalmologists; mem. L.A. Soc. Ophthalmology (past pres.), Fredericke Cordes Eye Soc. (past nat. pres.), L.A. County Med. Assn., Calif. Med. Assn., Am. Soc. Cataract and Refractive Surgery (founding mem.). Office: 435 N Roxbury Dr Ste 107 Beverly Hills CA 90210-5003

SEILER, STEVEN LAWRENCE, health facility administrator; b. Chgo., Dec. 30, 1941; married. B, U. Ariz., 1963; M, U. Iowa, 1965. Adminstrv. resident Rush-Presbyn.-St. Luke's Med. Ctr., Chgo., 1965, adminstrv. asst., 1965-68; asst. adminstr. Lake Forest (Ill.) Hosp., 1968-71, adminstr., 1971-73, pres., 1973-86; exec. v.p Voluntary Hosps. Am., Park Ridge, Ill., 1987-89, sr. v.p., 1986-92; CEO Good Samaritan Regional Med. Ctr., Phoenix, 1992—; adj. prof. Contbr. articles to profl. jours. Mem. AHA (svc. com.), Ill. Hosp. Assn. (chair 1980-81). Home: 3930 E Rancho Dr Paradise Valley AZ 85253-5025 Office: Good Samaritan Regional Med Ctr 1111 E Mcdowell Rd Phoenix AZ 85006-2612*

SEITZ, WALTER STANLEY, cardiovascular research consultant; b. L.A., May 10, 1937; s. Walter and Frances Janette (Schleef) S. BS in Physics and Math., U. Calif., Berkeley, 1959; PhD in Biophysics, U. Vienna, 1981, MD, 1982. Health physicist U. Calif. Radiation Lab., 1959-61; rsch. assoc. NIH at Pacific Union Coll., 1961-63; physicist Lockheed Rsch. Labs., Palo Alto, Calif., 1961-63; staff scientist Xerox Corp., Pasadena, Calif., 1963-66; sr. scientist Applied Physics Cons., Palo Alto, 1966-75; instr. clin. sci. U. Ill Coll. Medicine, Urbana, 1983-84; cons. cardiology Cardiovascular Rsch. Inst. U. Calif. Sch. Medicine, San Francisco, 1987—; sr. scientist Inst. Med. Analysis and Rsch., Berkeley, 1987—. Contbr. articles to profl. jours. Postdoctoral Rsch. fellow, U. Calif. San Francisco, 1984. Fellow Am. Coll. Angiography; mem. AAAS, Royal Soc. Medicine London, N.Y. Acad. Scis., Physicians for Social Responsibility. Office: IMAR Cons Inc 38 Panoramic Way Berkeley CA 94704-1828

SEJNOWSKI, TERRENCE JOSEPH, science educator; b. Cleve., Aug. 13, 1947; s. Joseph Francis and Theresa (Cudnik) S.; m. Beatrice Alexandra Golomb, Mar. 24, 1990. BS, Case Western Res. U., 1968; PhD, Princeton U., 1978. Rsch. fellow Harvard Med. Sch., Boston, 1979-82; prof. biophysics Johns Hopkins U., Balt., 1982-90; prof. U. Calif. San Diego, Salk Inst., La Jolla, 1988—; investigator Howard Hughes Med. Inst., 1991—; bd. dirs. San Diego McDonnell-Pew Ctr. for Cognitive Neurosci., 1990—, Inst. for Neural Computation, U. Calif. San Diego. Editor-in-chief Neural Computation; co-inventor: (with others) the Boltzmann machine and NET talk. Recipient Presdl. Young Investigator award NSF, 1984, Wright prize Harvey Mudd Coll., 1996; Sherman Fairchild Disting. scholar Calif. Inst. Tech., 1993. Mem. Soc. for Neurosci., Am. Phys. Soc., Internat. Neural Network Soc. (governing bd. 1988-92), IEEE, Am. Math. Soc., Assn. Rsch. in Vision and Ophthalmology, Am. Assn. Artificial Intelligence. Office: Salk Inst PO Box 85800 San Diego CA 92186-5800

SEKINE, DEBORAH KEIKO, systems analyst, programmer; b. Honolulu, Dec. 1, 1952; d. Yoshiteru and Yaeko (Matsuda) Isa; m. Andrew K. Sekine, May 8, 1993. BA in Math. with distinction, U. Hawaii, 1974, BEd with distinction, 1974, MS in Computer Sci., 1976, MBA, 1987. Data analyst, engr. in-charge Kentron, Honolulu, 1977-81; sys. analyst Am. Savs., Honolulu, 1981-82; analyst, programmer City and County of Honolulu, 1982—; cons. Am. Savs., Honolulu, 1982. Contbr. articles to profl. jours. Vol. Hawaii Dem. Conv., Honolulu, 1984, Mayoral campaign, 1988, 92; com. co-chair Hui Makaala, Honolulu, 1989—; caregiver Makiki Christian Ch., Honolulu, 1991—. Mem. IEEE, Assn. for Computing Machinery, Am. Fedn. State County Mcpl. Employees, U. Hawaii MBA Alumni Assn., Phi Kappa Phi. Mem. United Ch. of Christ. Home: 3322 George St Honolulu HI 96815-4319

SELANDIA, ELIZABETH, acupuncturist, Oriental medicine physician; b. Santa Barbara, Calif., Apr. 3, 1945; d. Fredrick Bunnell and Anna LaVerne (Welch) Pulling Jr.; m. William Kent Selandia, July 1966 (div. July 1977); 1 child, Karina Vanessa; m. Carsten Hennier, Feb. 4, 1981 (div. June 1986). Student, Sch. Holography, Emeryville, Calif., 1978; AA in French/Behavioral Sci./Humanities, Coll. of Marin, Kentfield, Calif., 1992; BA in Native Am. Studies and Linguistics, U. Calif., Berkeley, 1994. Diplomate NCCR; lic. acupuncturist, Calif. Astrology tchr. De Kosmos, Amsterdam, 1971-72; interpreter Langebortistan, Copenhagen, 1972-77; self-employed editor/writer, 1981—; acupuncturist Larkspur, Calif., 1987—; editl./adminstrv. asst. Unix/World Mag., Mountain View, Calif., 1985-91; test writer

Acupuncture Exam Com., Sacramento, Calif., 1996. Editor/author: Gently Whispered: Oral Teachings of V.V. Kalu Rinpoche, 1994; author/artist: Tiger Inside, Dragon Outside, 1996; artist cloth art in crocheted wool; exhbn. of textile collection Sophienholm Musée, Lyngby, Denmark, 1976, Smithsonian Mus., Washington, 1983. Art show coord. United Astrologers Congress, Monterey, Calif., 1995. Recipient highest honors in Native Am. Studies, U. Calif., Berkeley, 1994 (only person to have done so). Mem. Nat. Coun. Cascromie Rsch., Young Scandinavians Club, Alpha Gamma Sigma. Democrat. Buddhist. Home and Office: PO Box 827 Larkspur CA 94977

SELBY, JEROME M., mayor; b. Wheatland, Wyo., Sept. 4, 1948; s. John Franklin and Claudia Meredith (Hudson) S.; m. Gloria Jean Nelson, June 14, 1969; children: Tyan, Cameronn, Kalen. BS in Math., Coll. Idaho, 1969, MA in Ednl. Adminstrn., 1974; MPA, Boise State U., 1978. Assoc. engr. Boeing Co., Seattle, 1969-71; dir. evaluation WICHE Mountain States Regional Med. Program, Boise, 1971-74; dir. rsch., evaluation Mountain States Health Corp., Boise, 1974-76, with health policy analysis and accountability, 1976-78; dir. health Kodiak (Alaska) Area Native Assn., 1978-83; mgr. Kodiak Island Borough, 1984-85, mayor, 1985—; proprietor Kodiak Tax Svc., 1978—, Registered Guide, Kodiak, 1987—; cons. Nat. Cancer Inst., Washington, 1973-78, others. Contbr. articles to profl. jours. Treas. ARC, Kodiak, 1978-93, bd. dirs., 1978-95, chmn., 1989-90, mem. western ops. hdqrs. adv. bd., 1986-92, mem. group IV and V nat. adv. coj., 1986-89, nat. bd. govs., 1989-95, chmn. chpt. rels. com., 1994-95; pres. S.W. Alaska Mcpl. Conf., Anchorage, 1988-89, v.p., 1986-87, treas., 1996—, bd. dirs., 1986—; pres. Alaska Mcpl. League Investment Pool, Inc., 1992—; v.p. Alaska Mcpl. League, 1988-90, pres., 1990-91, bd. dirs., 1988—; bd. dirs. Alaska Mcpl. League Jt. Ins. Assn. Bd., 1995—, v.p., 1996—; mem. Alaska Resource Devel. Coun., 1987—, exec. com., 1989—; mem. policy com. of outer continental shelf adv. bd. U.S. Dept. Interior, 1990—, v.p., 1996—; co-chair Alaska Task Force, 1995—; mem. Com. on Oil Pollution Act, 1995; mem. Nat. Assn. Counties, Cmty. and Econ. Devel. Steering Com., 1990—, Alaska govtl. roles task force, 1991-92; mem. Alaska state/local govt. task force, 1996; chmn. Kodiak Island Exxon Valdez Restoration Com., 1991-95; dir. Kodiak Health Care Found., 1992—; co-chmn. Arctic Power, 1993—; mem. bd. dirs. Western Interstate Region Nat. Assn. of Counties, 1993—. Paul Harris fellow, 1987, 88, 91, 92, 96; recipient Outstanding Contbn. award Alaska Mcpl. League, 1994. Mem. Alaska Conf. Mayors, Nat. Soc. Tax Profls., Acad. Polit. Sci., Alaska Mcpl. Mgrs. Assn., Kodiak C. of C. (dir. 1983—), Rotary (bd. dirs. 1989—, treas. 1989-93, v.p. 1993-94, pres.-elect 1994-95, pres. 1995-96). Office: Kodiak Island Borough 710 Mill Bay Rd Kodiak AK 99615-6340

SELDNER, BETTY JANE, environmental engineer, consultant, aerospace company executive; b. Balt., Dec. 11, 1923; d. David D. and Miriam M. (Mendes) Miller; m. Warren E. Gray, June 20, 1945 (div. 1965); children: Patricia, Deborah; m. Alvin Seldner, Nov. 15, 1965; children: Jack, Barbara. BA in Journalism, Calif. State U., Northridge, 1975, MA in Communications, 1977. Dir. pub. info. United Way, Van Nuys, Calif., 1958-63; dir. edn. United Way, Los Angeles, 1963-68; dir. pub. relations, fin. San Fernando Valley Girl Scout Council, Reseda, Calif., 1968-73; asst. dir. pub. info. Calif. State U., Northridge, 1973-75; dir. environ. mgmt. HR Textron Corp., Valencia, Calif., 1975-87; environ. engr. Northrop Aircraft, Hawthorne, Calif., 1987-88, EMCON Assocs., Burbank, Calif., 1988-92, Atkins Environ., 1992-93, Seldner Environ., Valencia, Calif., 1993—; prin. Seldner Environ. Svcs., 1993—. Author non-fiction. Mem. Santa Clarita Valley Environ. Mgrs. Soc. (chmn. bd. dirs. 1984), San Fernando Valley Round Table (pres. 1971-72), Hazardous Materials Mgrs.' Assn., Zonta Internat. Republican. Jewish.

SELF, SUSAN CAROLYN, technical writer; b. Oakland, Calif., May 11, 1949; d. Charles William and Caroline Lillian (Omo) S. BA in English, Am. Lit., U. Calif., San Diego, 1972, PhD in Comparative Lit., 1982. Tech. editor Indsl. Software Components, San Diego, 1983-86, TechFoss, San Diego, 1986-94; tech. writer TeleSoft, San Diego, 1984-93, Alsys, San Diego, 1993-94, Thomson Software Products, San Diego, 1995-96, QUALCOMM, San Diego, 1996—. Author and editor: (anthology) Creative VOM, 1994. Vol. writer, editor, proofreader San Diego Earth Times, 1991-95; editor Zero Population Growth San Diego Newsletter, 1992-95, Save Our Forests and Ranchlands, San Diego, 1992; vol. Peter Navarro Campaign, San Diego, 1992, 93. Mem. IEEE (assoc.) Soc. for Tech. Comm. (sr.). Democrat. Office: QUALCOMM 6455 Lusk Blvd San Diego CA 92121

SELIGMAN, JAY ARNOLD, military officer, social worker; b. Bklyn., Apr. 29, 1968; s. Edward and Rita (Lisnoff) S. BS, Fla. State U., 1990, MSW, 1993. Lic. social worker, Mass. Child protective investigator Dept. Health and Rehab. Svcs., Pompano Beach, Fla., 1993-94; commd. 2d lt. USAF, 1994, advanced through grades to capt., 1995; family advocacy officer USAF, Lexington, Mass., 1994-95; social worker USAF, Tripler Army Med. Ctr., Hawaii, 1995-96; dir. substance abuse element USAF, Eglin AFB, 1996—. Contbr. articles to profl. jours. Chair Leisure and Social Svc. Adv. Bd., Sunrise, Fla., 1993-94. Mem. NASW. Democrat. Home: 228 Amberjack Dr #13 Fort Walton Beach FL 32548 Office: 96MDOS/SGOLIA 307 Boatner Rd Ste 114 Eglin AFB FL 32542

SELIGMANN, WILLIAM ROBERT, lawyer, author; b. Davenport, Iowa, Oct. 10, 1956; s. William Albert and Barbara Joyce (Carmichael) S.; m. Carole Lee Francis; children: D Anna, Matthew. BA, U. Calif., Santa Barbara, 1979; JD, Santa Clara U., 1982. Bar: Calif. 1983, U.S. Dist. Ct. (no. dist.) Calif. 1983. Assoc. Office of J.R. Dempster, Cupertino, Calif., 1983-85; city atty. City of Campbell, Calif., 1985—; ptnr. Dempster, Seligmann & Raineri, Los Gatos, Calif., 1985—; pro tem Mcpl. Ct. Calif., Los Gatos, 1992—. Bd. dirs. Los Galos C. of C. Mem. ABA, Santa Clara County Bar Assn., Am. Trial Lawyers Assn., Better Bus. Bur. Office: Dempster Seligmann & Raineri 3 1/2 N Santa Cruz Ave # A Los Gatos CA 95030-5916

SELINER, BARBARA ANN, elementary education educator; b. Salem, Oreg., July 4, 1950; d. Elmer Sylvester and Charlotte Marie (McKee) Meade; m. Donald Joseph Seliner, Aug. 11, 1985; children: Kayla Marie, Brandon Joseph. Bachelor's degree, Oreg. Coll. Edn., 1973, Master's degree, 1977. Cert. learning specialist, tchr. Elem. tchr. Tillamook (Oreg.) Sch. Dist., 1973-76; diagnostician Diagnostic Ctr., Oreg. Coll. Edn., Monmouth, 1977; specialist, tchr., devel. severely learning disabled program David Douglas Sch. Dist., Portland, Oreg., 1977-86; tchr. 5th and 3d grade David Douglas Sch. Dist., Portland, 1986-90, tchr. severe emotionally disturbed, 1991-92, tchr. 3d grade, 1992-93, tchr. 5th grade, 1993—; mem. Insvc. State Cadre Team Pub. Law 94-142, Oreg., 1978-81; chmn. supts. com. staff devel. David Douglas Sch. Dist., Portland, 1981-83; sch. store coord. Gilbert Park Elem., David Douglas Sch. Dist., Portland, 1994-95, 96-97, safety patrol coord., 1995-96. Co-developer web page for Gilbert Park Elem. Sch., 1996-97. Office: Gilbert Park Elem Sch 13132 SE Ramona St Portland OR 97236-4113

SELKIN, JAMES, psychologist; b. N.Y.C., Aug. 9, 1931; s. William J. and Estelle Selkin; m. Arlette Daniel, May 30, 1961; children: Phillip, Joelle. BS in Social Sci., CCNY, 1952, MS in Edn., 1953; PhD of Clin. Psychology, U. Colo., 1962. Cert. Am. Bd. Examiners in Profl. Psychology. Pvt. practice Denver, 1966—; psychologist, cons. Denver Gen. Hosp., 1966-84; staff Bethesda Hosp., Denver, 1974—, Presby.-St. Luke's Hosp., Denver, 1984—, founder, dir. Darrow Clinic, Inc., Denver, 1979—; cons. VA Hosp., Denver, 1980—; cons. U. Oreg. Med. Sch., Portland, Purdue U., Hammond, Ind., U. N.D., Bismarck, Northeastern U., Boston, N.Y.C. Police Dept., Kansas City Police Dept., U. No. Colo., Greeley, Boulder County Mental Health Ctr., Arapahoe County Mental Health Ctr., Adams County Mental Health Ctr., Weld County Mental Health Ctr., Denver County Jail, U. Colo. Med. Sch., VA Hosp., Luth. Hosp., Denver, Colo. State Hosp., Pueblo, Lakewood Police Dept., Fort Logan Mental Health Ctr.; expert witness in cts. Author: The Child Sexual Abuse Case in the Courtroom, 1987, 2d edit., 1991; co-author: (with Lisa Gaudia) Psychological Autopsy in the Courtroom: Contributions of the Social Sciences to Resolving Issues Surrounding Equivocal Deaths, 1987; peer reviewer Am. Psychiatric Assn., 1981—; contbr. articles to profl. jours. Mem. APA (peer reviewer 1981—), Am. Assn. Suicidology (pres. 1980-81, cert. com. 1983-89), Colo. Psychol. Assn. (bd. dirs. 1960, treas. 1961-63). Office: 190 E Ninth Ave Ste 480 Denver CO 80203

SELL, JOHN VICTOR, computer architect; b. Seattle, Aug. 19, 1950; s. John A. and Solvieg P. (Fiske) S. BS in Engring., Harvey Mudd Coll., 1972; MS in Elec. Engring. and Computer Sci., U. Calif., Berkeley, 1973. Project mgr. Hewlett-Packard Co., Palo Alto, Calif., 1973-80; founder, v.p. Ridge Computers, Inc., Santa Clara, Calif., 1980-88; disting. engr. Apple Computer, Inc., Cupertino, Calif., 1988-92; v.p., fellow The 3DO Co., Redwood City, Calif., 1992-96, v.p., chief tech. officer, 1996—. Office: The 3DO Co 600 Galveston Dr Redwood City CA 94063-4721

SELLER, GREGORY EROL, marketing executive, writer; b. Denver, Oct. 4, 1953; s. Otto Gustave and Dolores Louise (Crawford) S. BBA, U. Colo., 1975. Account exec. Gt.-West Life, L.A., 1975-79; asst. v.p. group devel. Gt.-West Life, Denver, 1980-84; v.p. sales and nat. accts. Great-West Life, L.A., 1988—; pres., chief exec. officer Benefits Communication Corp., Denver, 1985-87; bd. dirs. Benefits Communication Co. Editor newsletter Focus on 457, 1988—; mem. editorial bd., 457 Ind. Info. Svcs., 1990—. Mem. vestry, treas. St. Thomas Episc. Ch., Hollywood, Calif., 1989-93. Mem. Delta Upsilon. Democrat. Home: 37 New York Ct Monarch Beach CA 92629-4524 Office: Great-West Life 18101 Von Karman Ave Ste 1460 Irvine CA 92612-1043

SELLIN, PAUL ROLAND, retired English literature educator; b. Everett, Wash., Nov. 14, 1930; s. Petrus and F. Amelia (Josephson) S.; m. Agatha Weststrate, Sept. 21, 1957; children: Merk Eric, Christine Petra, Britt Amelia. BA, Wash. State U., Pullman, 1952; MA, U. Chgo., 1955, PhD, 1963. From lectr. to prof. Roosevelt U., Chgo., 1959-66; from asst. prof. to prof. UCLA, 1966-93, prof. emeritus, 1993—; vis. prof., vis. scholar Vrije U., Amsterdam, 1980-81, prof. English lit. after 1500, 81-88, Stockholm U., 1993. Author: Daniel Heinsus and Stuart England, 1968, John Donne and Calvinist Views of Grace, 1983, So Doth, So Is Religion, 1988; translator: Daniel Heinsus On Plot in Tragedy, 1971. Mem. sch. bd. Bethel Luth. Ch., Encino, Calif., 1989-91, 95—. 1st lt., inf. U.S. Army, 1952-54, Korea. Hendrick Willem Van Loon fellow, 1959-60; Roosevelt U. fellow, Amsterdam, 1963-64; grantee Am. Philos. Soc., 1970s, 1980s, ACLS, 1970s. 1980s; Fulbright travel grantee, 1980. Mem. MLA, Am. Assn. for Netherlands Studies (exec. bd.), Internat. Assn. for Neo-Latin Studies, Am. Assn. for Neo-Latin Studies, John Donne Soc., Milton Soc. Am. Democrat. Home: 4848 Alatar Dr Woodland Hills CA 91364 Office: UCLA Dept English Los Angeles CA 90024

SELVIN, PETER SAM, lawyer; b. L.A., Dec. 1, 1953. BA with highest honors, U. Calif., San Diego, 1975; MA, U. Chgo., 1976; JD, UCLA, 1980. Bar: Calif. 1980, U.S. Dist. Ct. (cen. dist.) Calif. 1981, U.S. Dist. Ct. (no. dist.) Calif. 1990, U.S. Ct. Appeals (9th cir.) 1987. Clk. to presiding justice Calif. Ct. Appeals (2d Appellate Dist., Divsn. 5), 1979; assoc. Loeb & Loeb, LLP, L.A., 1980-87; ptnr. Loeb and Loeb, LLP, L.A., 1987—, chair litigation dept., 1994-97. Contbr. articles to profl. jours. Mem. Calif. State Bar Assn. (com. on adminstrn. justice 1992-93, co-chair tech. subcom. state bar litigation sect. 1992-93), L.A. County Bar Assn. (litigation sect.), Fin. Lawyers Conf., Fed. Bar Assn., Assn. Bus. Trial Lawyers. Office: Loeb & Loeb LLP 1000 Wilshire Blvd Ste 1800 Los Angeles CA 90017-2475

SELZER, KENNETH A., neurologist, editor; b. N.Y.C., Mar. 2, 1954; s. Milton C. and Sylvia (Bennett) S.; m. Lynn Dunbar, Mar. 2, 1955; 1 child, Jenna Nicole. BA in Chemistry, SUNY, 1977; MD, UCLA, 1982; postgrad., Harvard Bus. Sch., 1987-90. Diplomate Am. Bd. Neurology and Psychiatry. Internship St. Mary's Hosp., Long Beach, Calif., 1982-83; med. dir. Mercy Carepoint Family Med. Group, San Diego, 1983-88; pres., CEO Integrated Healthcare Svcs., Inc., San Diego, 1983-88; gen. ptnr. La Jolla Cons. Group, San Diego, 1989-90; editor-in-chief Neuropractice, San Diego, 1993—; bd. dirs. Healthwatch, Inc., San Diego, Biomed. Rsch. Inst., San Diego; prin. investigator TPA trial for acute treatment Ischemic Strokes Vanderbilt U., 1992; biomed. rsch. asst. SUNY, Binghamton, 1974-76. N.Y. State Regents scholar, 1972-76. Home: 4062 Moratalla Ter San Diego CA 92130-2282 Office: Neuropractice 3525 Del Mar Heights Rd Ste 196 San Diego CA 92130-2123

SELZER, STEPHEN RASHAW, healthcare administrator; b. Alvin, Tex., Feb. 7, 1952; s. Ardine and Kathryn Eileen (Rashaw) S.; m. Robbynn Ellen Krenz, Aug. 10, 1974; children: Daniel Rashaw, Lucy Maegan, Margaret Lee. BS in Sociology and Biology, Stephen F. Austin State U., Nacogdoches, Tex., 1974; MS in Healthcare Adminstrn., U. Houston at Clear Lake City, 1977. Lic. nursing home adminstr., Colo. Asst. adminstr. Sharpstown Gen. Hosp., Houston, 1977, Shoal Creek Hosp., Austin, Tex., 1979-80; adminstr. Lockhart (Tex.) Hosp., 1977-79, Grant Buie Hosp., Hillsboro, Tex., 1981-84, HCA Cross Timbers Cmty. Hosp., Ft. Worth, 1984-85; assoc. adminstr. Eastwood Hosp., El Paso, Tex., 1980-81; v.p. Wesley regional network HCA Wesley Med. Ctr., Wichita, Kans., 1985-89; adminstr. Montezuma County Hosp. Dist., Cortez, Colo., 1989-96; pres., CEO Southwest Health Sys., Inc., Cortez, 1996—; mem. regional adv. coun. Colo. Found. for Med. Care, Denver, 1992-97. Mem. adv. bd. S.W. Campus, Pueblo (Colo.) C.C., 1992-96; bd. dirs. Hospice of Montezuma County; chmn. fin. com. 1st United Meth. Ch., Cortez, 1993-95, mem. adminstrv. bd. Staff sgt. USAFR, 1971-77. Named Outstanding Fund Raiser, Kiwanis, Hillsboro, Tex., Outstanding Employer of Yr. Colo. group Am. Legion, 1993. Mem. Colo. Hosp. Assn. (bd. dirs. 1993—), Am. Coll. Healthcare Execs. (assoc.), Cortez Area C. of C. (bd. dirs., co-pres. 1994). Office: Southwest Health System Inc 1311 N Mildred Rd Cortez CO 81321-2231

SEMEL, GEORGE HERBERT, plastic surgeon; b. N.Y.C., Apr. 20, 1938; s. Louis Bennett and Sara Sonja (Eutis) S. AB, Columbia U., 1959; MD, Boston U., 1963. Diplomate Am. Bd. Plastic Surgery. Intern L.A. County Gen. Hosp., 1963-64; resident gen. surgery Long Beach (Calif.) VA Hosp., 1964-67; residency in plastic surgery Mayo Clinic, Rochester, Minn., 1967-69; chief resident plastic surgery Med. U. S.C., Charleston, 1969-70; pvt. practice L.A., 1970—. Founder L.A. Music Ctr., 1978, Mus. Contemporary Art, 1980. With Calif. NG, 1964-69, USNG, 1969-73. Mem. AMA, Am. Soc. Plastic Surgery, Am. Lipoplasty Soc., L.A. Soc. Plastic Surgeons, L.A. County Med. Soc., Phi Gamma Delta. Office: 450 S Beverly Dr Beverly Hills CA 90212-4415*

SEMOS, WILLIAM, management consultant, educator; b. Manchester, N.H., May 16, 1940; s. Harry J. and Helen Semos; m. Constance Ione Kalogeras, Oct. 13, 1974; children: Mark H., Stephen P. AB, Dartmouth Coll., 1962; MBA, U. Chgo., 1967. Mktg. analyst, sr. mktg. analyst United Air Lines, Chgo. and San Francisco, 1967-73; assoc. Golightly & Co., Mgmt. Cons., N.Y.C., 1973-75; staff v.p. mktg. Marriott Corp., Washington, 1976-79; counsel senate aviation subcom. U.S. Govt., Washington, 1979-82; v.p. corp. comms. Western Airlines, L.A., 1983-87; v.p. corp. affairs worldwide Mattel Inc., L.A., 1988-91; mgmt. cons., educator Loyola Marymount U., L.A., 1991—; adv. dir. Wicat Corp., Orem, Utah, 1988-90; exec.-in-residence U. Wash., Seattle, 1987; mem. mktg. adv. coun. Calif. Tourism Corp., Sacramento, 1985-87. Corp. outreach Rep. Presdl. Campaign, L.A., 1988. 1st lt. U.S. Army, 1962-65. Greek Orthodox. Home: 6512 Monero Dr Rancho Palos Verdes CA 90275

SENDROWSKI, DAVID PETER, optometrist; b. Worcester, Mass., Jan. 8, 1959; s. Frank Stephen and Geneive Sophia (Watjkon) S.; m. Lori L. Floyd, June 6, 1993. BS, U. Mass., Amherst, 1981; D in Optometry, New Eng. Coll. of Optometry, 1985. Resident VA Hosp., L.A., 1986; asst. prof. So. Calif. Coll. Optometry, Fullerton, 1986—; dir. optometric svcs. North Orange County C.C., Anaheim, Calif., 1989—; chief ocular disease svc. So. Calif. Coll. Optometry, Fullerton, 1991—; ptnr. in pvt. practice Floyd/Sendrowski, Mission Viejo, Calif., 1993—; cons. Calif. State Bd. Optometry, Sacramento, 1990—. Author (book chpts. in) Emergency Medicine, 1994, Hyperthyroid Dysfunction, 1994, Thyroid Eye Disease, 1995. Am. Acad. Optometrist fellow, 1987. Mem. Am. Optometric Assn. (Continuing Edn. award 1987-88), Calf. Optometric Assn. (cons., bd. dirs. pathology edn. com. 1991—), Assn. Optometric Educators, Am. Diabetes Assn., Orange County Optometric Soc. (membership chair 1988-91, trustee 1988—), Beta Sigma Kappa. Republican. Roman Catholic. Office: Floyd/Sendrowski 24000 Alicia Pkwy Ste 11 Mission Viejo CA 92691-3929

SENDZIKAS, ALDONA MARIJA, museum curator; b. Toronto, Dec. 23, 1963. BA, U. Toronto, 1986, MA, 1990; cert. mus. studies, Humber Coll.; doct. student, U. Hawaii. Mil. interpreter Hist. Fort York, Toronto, 1986-87, curatorial asst., 1988-89, asst. curator, 1989-91; exhibit specialist USS Bowfin Submarine Mus. and Park, Honolulu, 1991-92, mus. curator, 1992—; organizing com. mem. War Along the Niagara Symposium, Buffalo, N.Y., St. Catharines, Ont., 1988, Western Mus. Assn. annual conf., 1994; lectr. in field. Contbr. articles to profl. jours. Judge state and local competitions Hawaii History Day, 1993, 94, 95. Mem. Hawaii Mus. Assn., Ontario Mus. Assn., Coun. on Am.'s Mil. Past, Historic Naval Ships Assn. Office: USS Bowfin Sub Mus & Park 11 Arizona Memorial Dr Honolulu HI 96818-3145

SENEVIRATNE, SONAL JERARD, systems analyst, program director, researcher. BS in Biol. Scis., U. So. Calif., 1986; MS in Sys. Mgmt., 1989; DPA, U. So. Calif., 1997. Teaching asst. programming and data processing U. So. Calif., 1984-86, info. mgr., 1986-88; cons. Citadel Rsch. Group, L.A., 1987-90; programmer, systems analyst U. So. Calif., 1988-96, dir. organizational devel. and learning, 1996—, Boaz rsch. prof. for organizational devel. and learning, 1996—. Mem. ASPA, Inst. Ops. Rsch. & Mgmt. Scis., Ops. Rsch. Soc. Am., Acad. Mgmt. Office: U So Calif 3550 Trousdale Pkwy Los Angeles CA 90089-0007

SENGUPTA, MRITUNJOY, mining engineer, educator; b. Cuttack, Orissa, India, Oct. 24, 1941; came to U.S., 1968; s. Chandi P. and Bani S.; m. Nupur Bagchi, Jan. 15, 1981; children: Shyam S. ME, Columbia U., 1971, MS, 1972; PhD, Colo. Sch. of Mines, 1983. Mining engr. Continental Oil Co., Denver, 1977-78, United Nuclear Corp., Albuquerque, 1978-80, Morrison-Knudson Co., Boise, Idaho, 1975-77, 80-82; assoc. prof. U. Alaska, Fairbanks, 1983-88, prof., 1989-95; cons. UN Devel. Program, 1987. Author: Mine Environmental Engineering, vols. I and II, 1989, Environmental Impacts of Mining, 1992; contbr. articles to profl. publs. Recipient Gold medal Mining Metall. Inst. of India, 1976, Nat. Merit scholarship Govt. of India, 1959-63. Mem. NSPE, So. Mining Engrs. Home: 20520 Bothel-Everett Hwy Bothell WA 98012

SENGUPTA, SAILES KUMAR, engineering researcher, statistical consultant; b. Bankura, India, Jan. 1, 1935; came to U.S., 1963; s. Bhabani Charan and Pratima Gupta Sen; m. Sumedha Choudhury Sengupta, Aug. 8, 1969; children: Dyuti, Chaitee. BSc, Calcutta U., India, 1953, MSc, 1956; PhD, U. Calif., 1969. Asst. prof. math. U. Mo., Kansas City, 1969-76; assoc. prof. math. S.D. Sch. of Mines, Rapid City, 1976-81, prof. math. and computer sci., 1981-90; sr. fellow Naval Rsch. Lab., Monterey, Calif., 1990-91; electronics engr. Lawrence Livermore Lab., Livermore, Calif., 1991—; statis. cons. Inst. Atmospheric Rsch., S.D. Sch. of Mines, Rapid City, 1985-91; sr. vis. fellow Univ. Corp. Atmospheric Rsch. at Naval Oceanographic Atmospheric Rsch. Lab., Monterey, 1990-91. Co-editor: Automated Pattern Analysis in Petroleum Exploration, 1992; contbr. numerous articles to profl. jours. Recipient Univ. Gold medal, Calcutta U., 1956. Mem. IEEE Sig. Processing Soc., Am. Stats. Assn., Sigma Xi. Hindu. Office: Lawrence Livermore Nat Lab Engring Rsch Divsn EE Dept L 156 Livermore CA 94550

SENN, DEBORAH, insurance commisioner; m. Rudi Senn. Rep. cmty. groups, consumers, labor and small bus.; Wash. state ins. commr. Olympia, 1992—. Named Best Ins. Commr. U.S., Ralph Nader, 1996. Office: Insurance Bldg PO Box 40255 Olympia WA 98504-0255

SENSABAUGH, GEORGE FRANK, JR., forensic sciences educator; b. Palo Alto, Calif., June 8, 1941; s. George Frank and Elizabeth Katherine (Ake) S.; m. Linda Sallander, Aug. 30, 1963; children: Jeffrey, Laura. BA, Princeton U., 1963; D of Criminology, U. Calif., Berkeley, 1969. Researcher U. Calif., San Diego, 1969-71, Nat. Inst. Med. Rsch., London, 1971-72; from. asst. prof. to prof. U. Calif., Berkeley, 1972—. Contbr. articles to profl. jours. Fulbright scholar, 1993. Fellow Am. Acad. Forensic Scis. (Paul L. Kirk award 1987); mem. Am. Chem. Soc., Am. Soc. Human Genetics, Calif. Assn. Criminalists, N.Y. Acad. Scis. Office: U Calif Sch Pub Health Berkeley CA 94720

SENUNGETUK, VIVIAN RUTH, lawyer; b. Syracuse, N.Y., Sept. 27, 1948; d. George Albert and Ethel Margaret (Hearl) Bender; children: Adam George Moore, William Guugzhuk Senungetuk. BA, SUNY, Binghamton, 1968; MAT, U. Alaska, 1972; JD, Boston U., 1984. Bar: Alaska 1985, Mass. 1985, U.S. Dist. Ct. Alaska 1985, N.Y. 1995, U.S. Dist. Ct. (so. dist.) N.Y. 1996. Adminstr. Indian Edn., Sitka, Alaska, 1974-76, Cook Inlet Native Assn., Anchorage, 1977-80; assoc. Erwin, Smith & Garnett, Anchorage, 1984-86; sole practice Anchorage, 1986—; adj. prof. constitutional law U. Alaska, Anchorage, 1986-88. Author: A Place for Winter, 1987. Mem. ABA, Alaska Acad. Trial Lawyers. Democrat. Pentecostal. Office: 880 N St Ste 203 Anchorage AK 99501

SEPPI, EDWARD JOSEPH, physicist; b. Price, Utah, Dec. 16, 1930; s. Joseph and Fortunata S.; m. Betty Stowell, Aug. 25, 1953; children: Duane Joseph, Kevin Darrell, Cynthia Rae. BS, Brigham Young U., 1952; MS, U. Idaho, 1956; PhD, Calif. Inst. Tech., 1962. Staff physicist Gen. Electric Co., Richland, Wash., 1952-58; rsch. fellow Calif. Inst. Tech., Pasadena, 1962; staff physicist Inst. for Def. Analysis, Washington, 1962-64; rsch. area dept. head SLAC, Stanford, Calif., 1966-68, head exptl. facility dept., 1968-74; mgr. med. diagnostic instrumentation Varian Assocs., Palo Alto, Calif., 1974-76, engring. mgr. radiation divsn., 1976-77, mgr. computer tomography divsn., 1977-78, tech. dir., 1978-80, sr. scientist, 1980-93; prin. scientist Ginston Rsch. Ctr., Palo Alto, 1993—; cons. Inst. Def. Analysis, Washington, 1964-72; scientist Superconducting Super Collider, Dallas, 1990-91. Author: (with others) The Stanford Two-Mile Accelerator, 1968; contbr. articles to more than 82 sci. publs.; holder more than 22 patents in med. instrumentation. Asst. scoutmaster Boy Scouts Am., Menlo Park, Calif., 1969-75; bd. dirs. Ladera Community Assn., 1988-90. Mem. Am. Phys. Soc. Home: 320 Dedalera Dr Portola Valley CA 94028-7509

SERAFINE, MARY LOUISE, psychologist, educator, lawyer; b. Rochester, N.Y., July 2, 1948. B.A. with honors in music, Rutgers U., 1970; Ph.D., U. Fla., 1975; JD, Yale U., 1991. Bar: Calif., D.C.; U.S. Tax Ct. Teaching and research fellow U. Fla., Gainesville, 1970-76; vis. asst. prof. U. Tex.-San Antonio, 1976-77; asst. prof. U. Tex.-Austin, 1977-79; postdoctoral fellow dept psychology Yale U., New Haven, 1979-83, lectr., 1981-83; asst. prof. dept. psychology Vassar Coll. Poughkeepsie, N.Y., 1983-88; with O'Melveny & Myers, L.A., 1988-96, Chadbourne & Parke, L.A. Author: Music as Cognition: The Development of Thought in Sound, 1988. Contbr. articles to profl. jours. Editorial reviewer Child Devel., Devel. Psychology, Am. Scientist, Jour. Experimental Child Psychology, Jour. Applied Developmental Psychology, Yale Law Jour. Grantee State of Fla., 1974-75, U. Tex.-Austin, 1977, Spencer Found., 1979-85. Office: Chadbourne & Parke 601 S Figueroa St Ste 1600 Los Angeles CA 90017-5721

SERAFINI, VICTOR RENATO, aerospace engineer; b. Chgo., June 9, 1934; s. Renato Victor and Stella (Koch) S.; m. Donetta Werre. BS in Aero. Engring., U. Ill., 1957, postgrad., 1957-65; postgrad., UCLA, 1957-65. Rsch. and project engr. Rocketdyne Div. N.Am. Aviation, Canoga Park, Calif., 1957-67; program/project mgr. TRW Inc., Redondo Beach, Calif., 1967-78; dir. spacecraft engring. Comms. Satellite Corp. (now Comsat Corp.), El Segundo, Calif., 1978-94; aerospace cons., pres. S.T.D. Assocs., Rancho Palos Verdes, Calif., 1995—; bd. dirs., cont. Autobahn West, Westlake Village, Calif.; mgmt. cons. Westoaks Realty, Westlake Village, 1975—; pres. STD Assocs., Rancho Palos Verdes, Calif., 1965—. Recipient award of recognition TRW Inc., 1965, Recognition of Outstanding Effort award NASA and TRW, 1963-64, Outstanding Contbn. award to recovery stranded Intelsat VI 603 satellite Intelsat Orgn., 1992. Mem. AIAA (liquid rocket tech. com. 1985-86). Mem. Christian Ch. Home and Office: STD Associates PO Box 2665 Rancho Palos Verdes CA 90275-8665

SERBEIN, OSCAR NICHOLAS, business educator, consultant; b. Collins, Iowa, Mar. 31, 1919; s. Oscar Nicholas and Clara Matilda (Shearer) S.; m. Alice Marie Bigger, Sept. 16, 1952; children: Mary Llewellyn Serbein Parker, John Gregory. BA with highest distinction, U. Iowa, 1940, MS, 1941; PhD, Columbia U., 1951. Grad. asst. math. U. Iowa, Iowa City, 1940-41; clk. Met. Life Ins. Co., N.Y.C., 1941-42; lectr. U. Calif., Berkeley, summer 1948, 50; lectr., asst. prof., assoc. prof. Columbia U., N.Y.C., 1947-59; prof. ins. Stanford (Calif.) U., 1959-89, dir. doctoral program Grad. Sch. Bus., 1960-64, prof. emeritus ins., 1989—; cons. Ins. Info. Inst., N.Y.C., 1971-78,

N.Am. Re-Assurance Life Service Co., Palo Alto, 1973, SRI Internat., Menlo Park, Calif., 1980-81, other bus.; cons., expert witness various law firms. Author: Paying for Medical Care in the U.S., 1953, Educational Activities of Business, 1961; co-author: Property and Liability Insurance, 4 ed., 1967, Risk Management: Text and Cases, 2 ed., 1983; also articles. Bd. dirs. Sr. Citizens Coord. Coun., Palo Alto, 1986-89, dir. emeritus, 1990—. Maj. USAF, WWII. Decorated Bronze Star, 1944. Mem. Am. Risk and Ins. Assn., Western Risk and Ins. Assn., Phi Beta Kappa, Sigma Xi, Beta Gamma Sigma. Democrat. Methodist. Club: Stanford Faculty. Home: 731 San Rafael Ct Stanford CA 94305-1007 Office: Stanford U Grad Sch Business Stanford CA 94305

SERES, JOEL LEONARD, neurosurgeon; b. Bronx, N.Y., Mar. 10, 1933; s. Joseph Charles and Gussie (Brodat) S.; m. Sandra Lamer, Sept. 18, 1988; children: David Stuart, Barbara Ellen Harrington, Steven Paul, Andrew Carl. BS in Chemistry, U. Del., 1954; MD, Jefferson Med. Coll., 1958. Diplomate Am. Bd. Neurological Surgery; lic. physician Alaska, Del., Oregon. Intern Del. Hosp., Wilmington, 1958-59; resident Del. Med. Ctr., Wilmington, U. Oreg. Med. Sch., Portland; gen. surgery physician Del. Hosp., Wilmington, 1961-63; pvt. practice Newark, 1959-61; neurosurgeon U. Oreg. Med. Sch., 1963-67; pvt. practice Portland, Oreg., 1967—; founder, dir. N.W. Occupational Medicine Ctr., Portland, Oreg., 1972—; clin. prof. neurosurgery U. Oreg. Health Scis. Ctr., Portland, 1990—; bd. dirs. Commn. on Accreditation Rehab. Facilities, Tucson; govs. psychosurgery bd. State of Oreg., 1973-82; subcom. on acupuncture Oreg. State Bd. Med. Examiners 1973—, chmn. 1979—; staff Good Samaritan Hosp. & Med. Ctr., Portland, Emanuel Hosp., Portland, Woodland Park Hosp., Portland., St. Vincent Hosp. & Med. Ctr., Portland, Providence Med. Ctr., Portland, Holladay Park Hosp., Portland, Oreg. Health Scis. U., Portland. Contbr. articles to profl. jours. Dir. Congregation Beth Israel, Portland, 1989—. Recipient Oliver J. Nesbit award for outstanding vol. faculty Oreg. Health Scis. U., 1971-75. Fellow ACS, Am. Coll. Pain Medicine; mem. AMA, Am. Pain Soc. (founding mem.), Am. Acad. Pain Medicine (founding mem., pres. 1985-86), Am. Assn. Neurolog. Surgeons (vice-chmn. sect. on pain 1988-89, chmn., 1990-91), Internat. Assn. for the Study of Pain (founding mem.), Western USA Pain Soc. (founding mem., pres. 1982-83), Oreg. Neurosurg. Soc. (v.p. 1975-76), Oreg. Med. Assn., Multnomah County Med. Soc., Congress Neurolog. Surgeons. Office: NW Occupl Med Ctr 15862 SW 72nd Ave Portland OR 97224-7974

SERNA, JOE, JR., mayor; b. Stockton, Calif.; m. Isabel Serna; children: Phillip, Lisa. BA in Social Sci., Govt., Sacramento State Coll., 1966; postgrad., U. Calif., Davis. Vol. Peace Corps., Guatemala, 1966; edn. advisor Lt.-Gov. Mervyn Dymally, 1975-77; prof. govt. Calif State U., Sacramento, 1969—; mayor City of Sacramento, 1992—. Mem. Sacramento City Coun. 5th Dist., 1981-92, law and legis. com., 1989-92, Housing & Devel. Commn., Sacramento, chmn. budget and fin. com., 1981-89, transp. and cmty. devel. com., 1989-92; dir. United Farmworkers Am.'s Support Com. in Sacramento County, 1970-75; co-trustee Crocker Art Mus. Assn.; founder Thursday Night Market, Mayor's Summer Reading Camp; mem. Sacramento Housing & Devel. Commn.; bd. dirs. Regional Transit. Office: Office of the Mayor 915 I St Sacramento CA 95814-2608*

SERNA, PATRICIO, state judge; b. Reserve, N.Mex., Aug. 26, 1939; m. Eloise Serna; 1 stepchild, John Herrera; children: Elena Patricia, Anna Alicia. BSBA with honors, U. Albuquerque, 1962; JD, U. Denver, 1970; LLM, Harvard U., 1971; postgrad., NYU, 1976, Nat. Jud. Coll., 1985, 90, 92, 94. Bar: N.Mex., Colo., U.S. Dist. Ct. N.Mex. Probation and parole officer State of N.Mex., Santa Fe, Las Cruces, 1966-67; spl. asst. to commn. mem. Equal Opportunity Commn., Washington, 1971-75; asst. atty. gen. State of N.Mex., Santa Fe, 1975-79; pvt. practice Santa Fe, 1979-85; dist. judge First Jud. Dist., Santa Fe, 1985-96; supreme ct. justice N.Mex. Supreme Ct., Santa Fe, 1996—; adj. prof. law Georgetown U., Washington, 1973, Cath. U., Washington, 1974-75; faculty advisor Nat. Jud. Coll., Reno, 1987. Exhibited at N.Mex. Mus. Fine Arts, Gov.'s Gallery, Santa Fe. Active Citizens Organized for Real Edn., Santa Fe, No. N.Mex. Martin Luther King Jr. State Holiday Commn., Santa Fe; past bd. dirs. Santa Fe Group Homes Inc.; past mem. Santa Fe Fiesta Coun., N.Mex. Bd. Edn. Fin., Santa Fe, Child Support Guidelines Rev. Commn., Santa Fe. With U.S. Army, 1963-65, col. USNG. Mem. N.Mex. Bar Assn., N.Mex. Hispanic Bar Assn., Nat. Hispanic Bar Assn., Nat. Coun. Juvenile and Family Ct. Judges, No. N.Mex. Am. Inns of Ct., Santa Fe Bar Assn., Elks, Fraternal Order of Eagles, Fraternal Order of Police, Phi Alpha Delta. Office: NMex Supreme Ct PO Box 848 Santa Fe NM 87504-0848

SEROT, DAVID ELLIOT, economist, consultant; b. Fresno, Calif., Nov. 24, 1944; s. Nathan and Queenie Rosalie (Feldman) S. BA, UCLA, 1966; MA, 1968; PhD, U. Calif., 1976. Economist U.S. Dept. Energy, Washington, 1976-86; rsch. economist Pacific Northwest Labs., Richland, Wash., 1986-90; prin. DES Research, Richland, Wash., 1990—. Contbr. articles to profl. jours. Mem. Tri-City Indsl. Devel. Coun., Kennewick, Wash., 1993—. With U.S. Army, 1968-70, Vietnam. Mem. Am. Economic Assn., Nat. Assn. Bus. Economists. Jewish. Home: 616 Fuller St Richland WA 99352-1819 Office: DES Research 2000 Logston Blvd Richland WA 99352-5300

SERRA, ROBERT EMMETT, newspaper editor; b. Chgo., Feb. 7, 1946; s. Jose Miguel and Kathryn Eleanor (Day) S.; m. Suzanne Louise Reyes, May 24, 1975; children: Kathryn Louise, Gabrielle Rose, John Robert. BA in English, Regis Coll., Denver, 1968. Asst. editor The Am. Field, Chgo., 1971-73; editor The Siuslaw News, Florence, Oreg., 1976—. Sgt. U.S. Army, 1969-74, Viet Nam. Recipient various awards for photography, editing and writing Soc. of Profl. Journalists, Oreg. Newspaper Pub. Assn., Nat. Newspaper Assn. Mem. Nat. Newspaper Assn., Oreg. Newspaper Publs. Assn. Office: The Siuslaw News PO Box 10 Florence OR 97439

SERVOSS, MARCUS EDWARD, public relations executive; b. Council Bluffs, Iowa, Feb. 21, 1940; s. Clair E. and Catherine (Nason) S.; children: Robert, Tracy. BA, U. S. D., 1965; MA, American U., 1967. Press aide Congressman John Hansen, Washington, 1965-66, U.S. Dept. HUD, Washington, 1967-73; pres. Darcy Comms., Denver, 1973-81; pres., CEO Servoss Pub. Rels., Denver, 1981—; pres. Pinnacle Worldwide, Mpls., 1993, chmn., 1994. Mem. Colo. Bus. Com. for the Arts, 1991—, chmn., 1991-92; vice chair Keep Denver Beautiful. Mem. Pub. Rels. Soc. Am. (counselors acad. credentials chmn. 1992-93), Denver C. of C. (comms. coun. 1991-94). Office: Servoss Pub Rels 455 Sherman St Denver CO 80203-4400

SESTINI, VIRGIL ANDREW, biology educator; b. Las Vegas, Nov. 24, 1936; s. Santi and Merceda Francesca (Borla) S. BS in Edn., U. Nev., 1959; postgrad., Oreg. State U., 1963-64; MNS, U. Idaho, 1965; postgrad., Ariz. State U., 1967, No. Ariz. U., 1969; cert. tchr., Nev. Tchr. biology Rancho High Sch., 1960-76; sci. chmn., tchr. biology Bonanza High Sch., Las Vegas, 1976-90; ret., 1990; co-founder, curator exhibits Meadows Mus. Nat. History, 1993-94; part-time tchr. Meadows Sch., 1987-94; ret., 1994; edn. specialist, cell biologist SAGE Rsch., Las Vegas, 1993; founder Da Vinci Enterprises, Las Vegas, 1995. Served with USAR, 1959-65. Recipient Rotary Internat. Honor Tchr. award, 1965, Region VIII Outstanding Biology Tchr. award, 1970, Nev. Outstanding Biology Tchr. award Nat. Assn. Biology Tchrs., 1970, Nat. Assn. Sci. Tchrs., Am. Gas Assn. Sci. Teaching Achievement Recognition award, 1976, 1980, Gustov Ohaus award, 1980, Presdl. Honor Sci. Tchr. award, 1983; Excellence in Edn. award Nev. Dept. Edn., 1983; Presdl. award excellence in math. and sci. teaching, 1984, Celebration of Excellence award Nev. Com. on Excellence in Edn., 1986, Hall of Fame award Clark County Sch. Dist., 1988, Excellence in Edn. award, Clark County Sch. Dist., 1987, 88, Spl. Edn. award Clark County Sch. Dist., 1988, NSEA Mini-grants, 1988, 89, 92, World Decoration of Excellence medallion World Inst. Achievement, 1989, Cert. Spl. Congl. Recognition, 1989, Senatorial Recognition , 1989, mini-grant Jr. League Las Vegas., 1989, Excellence in Edn. award, Clark County Sch. Dist., 1989; named Nev. Educator of Yr., Milken Family Found./Nev. State Dept. Edn., 1989; grantee Nev. State Bd. Edn., 1988, 89, Nev. State Edn. Assn., 1988-89. Author: Lab Investigations For High School Honors Biology, 1989, Microbiology: A Manual for High School Biology, 1992, Laboratory Investigations in Microbiology, 1992, Genetics Problems for High School Biology, 1995, Science Laboratory Report Data Book, 1995, Field and Museum Techniques for the Classroom Teacher, 1995, Selected Lab Investigations and Projects for Honors and AP Biology, Vol. I Microbiology, 1995, Telecommunications: A Simulation for Biology Using the Internet, 1995; co-author: A Biology Lab Manual For Cooperative Learning, 1989, Metrics and Science Methods: A Manual of Lab Experiments for Home Schoolers, 1990, Experimental Designs in Biology I: Botany and Zoology, 1993, Designs in Biology: A Lab Manual, 1993, Integrated Science Lab Manual, 1994; contbr. articles to profl. jours. Mem. AAAS, NEA, Nat. Assn. Taxidermists, Nat. Sci. Tchrs. Assn. (life, Nev. State chpt. 1968-70), Nat. Assn. Biology Tchrs. (life, OBTA dir. Nev. State 1991-93), Am. Soc. Microbiology, Coun. for Exceptional Children, Am. Biographic Inst. (rsch. bd. advisors 1988), Nat. Audubon Assn., Nat. Sci. Suprs. Assn., Am. Inst. Biol. Scis., Internat. Plastic Modelers Soc., So. Nev. Scale Modelers (Las Vegas coord. Modeloberfest, 1995). Avocations: scale models, military figures, scale model circus, photography, chess.

SETCHKO, EDWARD STEPHEN, minister, theology educator; b. Yonkers, N.Y., Apr. 27, 1926; s. Stephen John and Mary Elizabeth (Dulak) S.; m. Penelope Sayre, Nov. 18, 1950; children—Marc Edward, Kip Sherman, Robin Elizabeth, Jan Sayre, Dirk Stephen. B.S., Union Coll., 1948; M.Div. cum laude, Andover Newton Theol. Sch., 1953, S.T.M., 1954; Th.D., Pacific Sch. Religion, 1962. Ordained to ministry United Ch. of Christ, 1954; cert. profl. hosp. chaplain. Psychometrician, Union Coll. Character Research Project, Schenectady, N.Y., 1947-50; asst. pastor Eliot Ch., Newton, Mass., 1950-54; clin. tng. supr. Boston City Hosp., 1951-54; intern, chaplain Boston State Mental Hosp., 1953-54; univ. campus minister U. Wash., Seattle, 1954-58; Danforth grantee, 1958-59; grad. fellow in psychotherapy Pacific Sch. Religion, Berkeley, Calif., 1959-60, instr. dept. pastoral psychology, 1960-61, grad. fellow, lectr. theology and psychology, 1961-62, asst. prof. psychology and counseling, 1962-63, dir. continuing theol. edn., 1962-63; clin. psychologist Calif. Correctional Facility, Vacaville, Calif., 1961-62; field research sec. laity div. United Ch. Christ, Berkeley, Calif. and N.Y.C., 1963-68; vis. prof. psychology and sociology Starr King Ctr. for Religious Leadership, Berkeley, 1967-69; assoc. prof. religion and soc. Starr King Ctr., Grad. Theol. Union, Berkeley, Calif., 1969-71, prof., 1971-83; career counselor The Ctr. for Ministry, Oakland, Calif., 1986-89; mem. faculty, chmn. curriculum and faculty com. Layman's Sch. Religion, Berkeley, 1960-67; cons. and lectr. in field. Del. voter registration delegation, Miss., 1965; mem. peace del., Mid-East, 1983; lectr. Internat. Conf. on the Holocaust and Genocide, Tel Aviv, 1982, Nuclear Disarmament Conf., W.Ger., 1980, 81, 82, Internat. Ctr. for Peace in the Middle East, Resource Ctr. for Non-Violence, Clergy & Laity Concerned, Ecumenical Peace Inst., Internat. Peace Acad.; World Policy Inst., Inst. Peace and World Order, Am. Friends Service Com. (bd. dirs.), Berkeley Ctr. for Human Interaction, Ristad Found., Am. Friends Golan Heights, Pacific Inst. of Criminal Justice; dir. The Project for Peace and Reconciliation in the Middle East (non-profit Calif. Found. 1983-89); vol. South Berkeley Cmty. Ch. hunger project Alta Bates Hospice. Lt. (j.g.) USNR, 1944-46, WW II. Mem. Am. Psychol. Assn. (cert.), Calif. State Psychol. Assn., Assn. Clin. Pastoral Edn., World Future Soc., Soc. Sci. Study of Religion, Inst. Noetic Scis., Com. for Protection Human Subjects (U. Calif.-Berkeley). Democrat. Contbr. articles to profl. jours.; condr. seminars: Futurology; Intricacies of Being Human, Images of Women and Men; Changing Values in Roles Between the Sexes in a Technological Society, Cybernetics and Humanization of Man; developer curriculum: Peace and Conflict Studies (U. Calif., Berkeley).

SETEROFF, SVIATOSLAV STEVE, management and logistics company executive; b. Shanghai, People's Republic of China, Oct. 6, 1937; came to U.S., 1949; s. Leo G. and Olga D. (Pankova) S.; m. Deanna Catherine Rogers (div. 1964); children: Steven James, Richard Aubrey; m. Joyce Eileen Schieldge, Feb. 22, 1965; children: Barbara Lynn Seteroff Anderson, Leanne Marie Seteroff DeBroeck. AA, Chapman Coll., 1974, BA cum laude, 1975; MBA, U. Puget Sound, 1983; postgrad., Nova Southeastern U., 1995—. Enlisted USN, 1955-75, commd. warrant officer, 1976-85; sr. analyst McDonnell Douglas Astronautics Co., Rockville, Md., 1985-87; program mgr. Anadac, Inc., Arlington, Va., 1987; v.p. Systems Mgmt. Am. Corp., San Diego, 1987-89; project mgr. info. systems, logistics, sr. ops. analyst MERIT Systems, Inc., Bremerton, Wash., 1989-91; pres., CEO Mgmt. and Logistics Assocs., Inc., Poulsbo, Wash., 1990—; instr. Residence Edn. Ctr., Chapman U., Bangor, Wash., 1985—. Developer Scrivener Masonic Lodge Mgmt. Program, 1992. Mem. Am. Soc. Naval Engrs. (nat. chmn. logistics symposium 1991-93, Pres. award 1993), Am. Soc. Logistics Engrs. (symposium presenter, chmn. advanced tech. steering group 1994—, gen. chmn. internat. symposium 1998), Ret. Officers Assn., Masons. Office: 12890 Old Military Rd NE Poulsbo WA 98370-7972

SETON, JULIE ANNE, technical writer; b. Santa Fe, N.Mex., May 17, 1961; d. Robert Dale and Dee (Seton) Barber; m. Christopher Von Ham, May 16, 1981 (div. Dec. 1992); children: Roy Dale Ham, Katherine Marie Ham. AA, N.Mex. State U., 1981, BA, 1984, MA, 1986, PhD, 1996. Instr. comm. studies N.Mex. State U., Las Cruces, 1985-86, 90-91, instr. English, 1991-95, rsch. asst. civil engring., 1991-94; adult basic educator So. N.Mex. Correctional Facility, Las Cruces, 1989-90; tech. writer Mgmt. Assistance Corp. Am., El Paso, Tex., 1995-96; comm. cons. Istari Cons., Las Cruces, 1988-92; sec. Ernest Thompson Seton Inst., Santa Fe, 1990. Prin. Temple Beth El, Las Cruces, 1996—, tchr., 1979-85; fire svc. chief Dona Ana County Vol., Las Cruces, 1989-92. Mem. Am. Tchrs. Tech. Writing, Soc. Tech. Comm., Assn. for Study of Lit. and the Environment (publs. coord.). Republican. Jewish. Home: PO Box 3292 Las Cruces NM 88003

SETZEKORN, WILLIAM DAVID, retired architect, consultant, author; b. Mt. Vernon, Ill., Mar. 12, 1935; s. Merrett Everet and Audrey (Ferguson) S.; m. Georgia Sue Brown, Feb. 4, 1958 (div. 1968); children: Jeffrey Merle, Timothy Michael. BArch, Kans. State U., 1957; cert. in computer graphics, Harvard U., 1968; BA with MA equivalency in Humanities, Western Ill. U., 1982. Registered arch., Calif. Coord. design and constrn. Cal-Expo, Sacramento, 1968; pvt. practice, Los Altos and Redding, Calif., Seattle, 1968-85; cons. Contra Costa County, Martinez, Calif., 1985-89, El Dorado County, Placerville, Calif., 1985-89, Somerset, Calif., 1989—; cons. Fed. Emergency Mgmt. Agy., The Presidio, San Francisco, 1989-95, Gov. Keating's task force for disaster recovery, Oklahoma City, 1995; apptd. Calif. State Grand Jury, 1996—. Author: Formerly British Honduras: A Profile of the New Nation of Belize, 1975, 4 other titles; contbr. articles to mags. Recipient Ofcl. Commendation, State of Calif., 1968, U.S. Presdl. Medal of Merit, Ronald Reagan, 1988. Fellow Augustan Soc. (bd. dirs. 1994-96); mem. Noble Co. of the Rose (knight 1979, lt. magister rosae 1995—), Mil. and Hospitaller Order of St. Lazarus (comdr.), numerous other internat. orders of chivalry, Family Setzekorn Assn. (prin. officer 1979—), San Leandro (Calif.) Yacht Club (founding), Kiwanis. Republican. Unitarian. Home and Office: PO Box 706 Somerset CA 95684-0706

SEVERE, SALVATORE FRANCIS, school psychologist; b. Batavia, N.Y., Dec. 10, 1947; s. Anthony Wayne and Mary (Calarco) S.; m. Dianne M. Heckman; children: Anthony, Leah, Alyssa. BA, Canisius Coll., Buffalo, 1969; MS, Buffalo State U., 1973; PhD, Ariz. State U., 1981. Cert. sch. psychologist. Tchr. Connors Children's Ctr., Buffalo, 1970-76; sch. psychologist Cartwright Sch. Dist., Phoenix, 1976—. Author: How to Behave So Your Children Will Too!, 1996. With N.Y. State Air N.G., 1964-75. Recipient Golden Achievement award Nat. Sch. Pub. Rels. Assn., 1989. Mem. Ariz. Assn. Sch. Psychologists (pres. 1997—). Home: 1951 E Velvet Dr Tempe AZ 85284

SEVERINSEN, DOC (CARL H. SEVERINSEN), conductor, musician; b. Arlington, Oreg., July 7, 1927; m. Emily Marshall, 1980; children—Nancy, Judy, Cindy, Robin, Allen. Ptnr. Severinsen-Akwright Co.; pops condr. The Phoenix (Ariz.) Symphony Orchestra. Mem., Ted Fio Rito Band, 1945, Charlie Barnet Band, 1947-49, then with, Tommy Dorsey, Benny Goodman, Norro Morales, Vaughn Monroe; soloist network band: Steven Allen Show, NBC-TV, 1954-55; mem., NBC Orch. Tonight Show, 1962-67 , music dir., 1967-92 ; past host of: NBC-TV show The Midnight Special; recs., RCA Records, including; albums: Brass Roots, 1971, Facets, 1988, The Tonight Show Band, Night Journey. Address: care Thomas Cassidy Inc 11761 E Speedway Blvd Tucson AZ 85748 also: care William Morris Agency 151 S El Camino Dr Beverly Hills CA 90212-2704 also: care The Phoenix Symphony Orch 455 N 3rd St Ste 390 Phoenix AZ 85004*

SEVIER, ERNEST YOULE, lawyer; b. Sacramento, June 20, 1932; s. Ernest and Helen Faye (McDonald) S.; m. Constance McKenna, Apr. 12, 1969; children: Carolyn Stewart, Katherine Danielle. A.B., Stanford U., 1954, J.D., 1956. Bar: Calif. 1956, U.S. Supreme Ct. 1965. Asso. mem. firm Sedgwick, Detert, Moran & Arnold, San Francisco, 1958-62; mem. firm Severson & Werson, San Francisco, 1962—. Served with USAF, 1956-57. Fellow Am. Bar Found.; mem. ABA (chmn. tort and ins. practice sect. 1982-83, exec. coun. 1976-84, chmn. standing com. on assoc. comms. 1988-90, chmn. coord. com. on Outreach to Pub. 1989-90, chmn. standing com. on lawyers responsibility for client protection 1991-94, commn. on non-lawyer practice 1992-95), Calif. Bar Assn., Internat. Assn. Def. Counsel, Fedn. Ins. and Corp. Counsel. Office: Severson & Werson 1 Embarcadero Ctr Ste 2500 San Francisco CA 94111-3714

SEVILLA, CARLOS A., bishop; b. San Francisco, Aug. 9, 1935. Ed., Gonzaga U., Santa Clara U., Jesuiten Kolleg, Innsbruck, Austria, Cath. Inst. Paris. Ordained priest Roman Cath. Ch., 1966, bishop, 1989. Titular bishop Mina, 1989—; aux. bishop San Francisco, 1989—. Office: Archdiocese San Francisco 445 Church St San Francisco CA 94114-1720

SEWELL, CHARLES ROBERTSON, geologist, exploration company executive, investor; b. Malvern, Ark., Feb. 7, 1927; s. Charles Louis and Elizabeth (Robertson) S.; m. Margaret Helen Wilson, Dec. 26, 1953 (dec. July 1985); children: Michael Stuart, Charles Wilson, Marion Elizabeth; m. Louise T. Worthington, Nov. 29, 1985; 1 child, Ginger B. BS, U. Ark.-Fayetteville, 1950; MA, U. Tex.-Austin, 1955, postgrad., 1961-64. Registered geologist, Calif., Ariz. Well logging engr. Baroid, Houston, 1950; asst. metallurgist Magcobar, Malvern, Ark., 1951; geologist Socony-Mobil Petroleum Co., Roswell, N.Mex., 1955; sr. geologist Dow Chem. Co., Freeport, Tex., 1956-61; spl. instr. U. Tex., Austin, 1962-65; pvt. practice cons. geologist, Austin, 1962-65; dist. geologist, mgr. Callahan Mining Corp., Tucson, 1965-68; owner, cons. geologist Sewell Mineral Exploration, worldwide, 1968—, extensive work USSR-CIS, 1988—. Contbr. articles to profl. jours. Elder, Presbyn. Ch., Tucson, 1973—. With USN, 1944-46, 51-53. NSF grantee, 1962-64, 63. Mem. AIME, Ariz. Geol. Soc., Mining Found. Southwest (bd. govs. 1982-86, 90—, pres. 1984). Republican. Lodge: Masons. Discoverer/co-discoverer numerous metallic and non-metallic ore deposits. Home and Office: 260 S Sewell Pl Tucson AZ 85748-6700 *Personal philosophy: To win you must at sometime in life move out into harm's way.*

SEXSON, STEPHEN BRUCE, educational writer, educator; b. Silver City, N.Mex., May 29, 1948; s. Ralph Dale and Wanda Claudean (McMahan) S.; m. Barbara Jane Davis, May 24, 1968; children: David Paul, Linda Carol. BA in Rhetoric and Pub. Address, Pepperdine U., 1969, MA in Pub. Comm., 1975; EdD in Higher Edn., Okla. State U., 1990. Asst. to supt. Morongo Unified Sch. Dist., 29 Palms, Calif., 1973-77; corp. trainer Merrill Lynch Realty, Dallas, 1979-81; sch. psychologist Texhoma (Tex.) Sch. Dist., 1982-83; assoc. prof., dir. Christian Student Ctr. Okla. Panhandle State U., Goodwell, 1982-84; rsch. resident Okla. State U., Stillwater, 1984-87; mem. spl. programs staff L.A. Unified Sch. Dist., 1987-93; dir. Edwest Edn. Rsch., Burbank, Calif., 1991—; guest lectr. edn. Okla. State U., Stillwater, 1993-94, U. Tulsa, 1993-94; conv. spkr. Merrill Lynch Realty-Relo, Atlanta, 1979. Author: The Magic Classroom, 1995, The Values Rich Teacher, 1996; contbr. articles to profl. jours. Mem. ASCD, Am. Assn. Sch. Adminstrs., Nat. Assn. of Sch. Psychologists, Lions Club, Phi Delta Kappa. Home: 266 Backs Ln Apt B Placentia CA 92870-6036

SEXTON ATKINS, JAN, artist; b. Frankfurt, Germany, Sept. 10, 1951; d. Thomas Logan Sexton and Wanda Jean (Spurlock) Ingram; m. Charles E. Atkins, Apr. 13, 1985. AA, Kauai C.C., Hawaii, 1975; studied sculptural clay with Toshiko Takaezu, 1975; cert., Windtree Sch. Drawing and Illustration, 1990; studied monoprints with Rodney Konopaki, 1990, studied with David Passalacqua; BFA cum laude, U. Alaska, Anchorage, 1990, BA cum laude, 1992. Art educator various Alaskan arts orgns., Alaska, 1990—; art dir. ARCA Murals, 1993-94; dir. and owner Earthwind Studio, Anchorage, 1994—; curator of exhibits Alaska Pacific U., Anchorage, 1995—; leader various art workshops, 1991-94; bd. dirs. Visual Arts Ctr. Alaska, 1992-94, exhbn. coord., 1992; vol. juror asst. Anchorage Mus. History and Art, 1993; exhbn. coord. Grandview Gardens Cultural Ctr., Alaska, 1994; art juror reflections program Nat. PTA, 1995; display asst. Nordstroms, 1995-96; scenic artist Anchorage Opera, 1995-96; mural asst. Blaines Art Supply, 1996; adj. prof. art history Alaska Pacific U., Anchorage, 1996—. Exhibitions include Bunnell St. Gallery, Homer, Alaska, 1994, 96, Callanetics Studio, Anchorage, 1995, Stonington Gallery, Anchorage, 1995, Pratt Mus., Homer, 1996, Alaska Pacific U., Anchorage, 1996, Fireweed Gallery, Homer, 1996, Blaines Art and Frame, Homer, 1996; represented in permanent collections Pratt Mus.; represented in pvt. collections. Pol. advocacy advisor People First, Anchorage, 1993-95; rep. arts adv. commn. Municipality of Anchorage, 1994—. Recipient Ceramic award Kauai C.C. Arts Festival, 1975, Hon. Mention U. Alaska, Anchorage, 1988, 1989, Best Graphic Design/Illustration, 1990, hon. mention Am. Coll. Theatre Festival and Northwest Drama Competition, 1989, XXIV all Alaska juried, 1992; Alaska Found. scholar, 1984, 85, 86, 87; Chancellor's scholar, 1986, 87; Saradell Ard scholar, 1989, 90. Home and Office: 1747 Talkeetna St Anchorage AK 99508

SEYBERT, JANET ROSE, lawyer, military officer; b. Cin., Feb. 7, 1944; d. Peter Robert and Helen Rose (Young) S. BA in Classics, BS in Edn., U. Cin., 1966; MA in Classics, U. Iowa, 1968; JD, Chase Coll. Law, 1975; ML, Army JAG Sch., 1984. Bar: Ohio 1975, U.S. Ct. Mil. Appeals 1975, Colo. 1981, U.S. Ct. Claims 1985; cert. mortgage investor; cert. profl. clown. Instr. Latin, ancient history Salem Coll., Winston-Salem, N.C., 1968-70; instr. N.C. Gov.'s Sch., Winston-Salem, N.C., 1969; instr. phys. edn., Latin Kemper Hall, Kenosha, Wis., 1970-71; instr. in Latin Carthage Coll., Kenosha, Wis., 1970-71; commd. 2d lt. USMC, 1972; completed interservice transfer to USAF, 1978, advanced through grades to maj., 1982; lawyer USAF Acad. USAF, Colorado Springs, Colo., 1978-81; chief civil law Sheppard AFB, Tex., 1981-84; dep. staff judge adv., chief mil. justice Homestead AFB, Fla., 1984-88; chief civil law Lowry AFB, Colo., 1988-91; ret., 1991—, pvt. practice environ. law, 1991—; owner, pres. The Seybert Funding Cos., 1991—; atty., notary The Seybert Funding Cos., S & K Ent., 1994—; legal advisor Armed Forces Disciplinary Control Bd., Child and Family Advocacy Coun. USAF, Homestead AFB, 1984-88. Vol. Muscular Dystrophy Assn., Colorado Springs, 1978-81; contbr. Ellis Island Resoration Program, Homestead AFB, 1985-88; active Nat. Mus. Women in Arts, Nat. Air and Space Mus.; officer in charge Lowry Silver and Blue Choir; charter mem. Women in Military Svc. to Am. Meml. Mem. ABA, Judge Adv. Assn., Edn. Profl. Assn., Ohio Bar Assn., Fed. Bar Assn., Colo. Bar Assn., Colo. Women's Bar Assn., Am. Bus. Women's Assn. (chmn. audit com. Homestead charter chpt., hist. com. 1987, pres. Visions charter chpt. 1990-91, 91-92, Top 10 Bus. Women 1987, Woman of Yr. 1987), Am. Legion, Ret. Officers Assn., Phi Beta Kappa, Kappa Delta Pi. Home: 378 Florence St Aurora CO 80010-4223

SEYFER, ALAN ERIC, surgeon; b. Ft. Smith, Ark., Aug. 15, 1945; s. Robert Paranteau and Maria Teresa (Ortiz) S.; m. Glenna Lee Stuart, Oct. 26, 1968; children: Tara Lee, Jessie Lynn. BS in Engring., U.S. Mil. Acad., 1967; MD, La. State U., 1973. Diplomate Am. Bd Surgery, Am. Bd. Plastic Surgery, Am. Bd. Hand Surgery and Plastic Surgery. U.S. army officer Artillery/Missiles, U.S.A., Asia, 1967-69; surg. internship Fitzsimons Army Med. Ctr., Denver, 1973-74, gen. surg. residency, 1974-78; plastic surg. residency Walter Reed Army Med. Ctr., Washington, 1978-81, hand microsurg. fellowship, 1979-80; hand microsurg. fellowship Duke U., Durham, N.C., 1979-80; chief plastic surgery svc. and dir. residency Walter Reed Army Med. Ctr., Washington, 1983-89, chief orthpaedic hand surgery, 1985-89; prof. surgery, head divsn. plastic surgery Oreg. Health Scis. U., Portland, 1989—; dir. plastic surgery tng. Oreg. Health Scis. U., Portland, 1989—; cons. NIH, Bethesda, Md., 1988—. Author: Atlas of Chest Wall Construction, 1986; editor: Chest Wall Reconstruction, 1989, Depuytren's Contracture, 1991, Bone Repair and Regeneration, 1994; assoc. editor Annals of Plastic Surgery, 1993—; contbr. articles to profl. jours. and chpts. to books. Recipient Rsch. grants, Vis. professorships, Arthur Garnes lectureship Columbia U., 1991, Best Tchr. award Oreg. Health Scis. U., 1993. Fellow Am. Coll. Surgeons; mem. Soc. Univ. Surgeons, Am. Assn. Plastic Surgeons. Office: Oreg Health Scis U L352A Divsn Plastic Surgery 3181 SW Sam Jackson Park Rd Portland OR 97201-3011

SEYFERT, HOWARD BENTLEY, JR., podiatrist; b. Clifton Heights, Pa., July 10, 1918; s. Howard Bentley and Mabel (Ashenbach) S.; m. Anna Mary van Roden, June 26, 1942; 1 child, Joanna Mary Irwin. D of Podiatric Medicine, Temple U., 1940. Cert. Nat. Bd. Podiatry Examiners (past pres.), Ariz. State Bd. Podiatry Examiners (past pres.). Pvt. practice podiatry Phoenix, 1950-82, Sedona, Ariz., 1982—; mem. med. staff Marcus J. Lawrence Meml. Hosp., Cottonwood, Ariz. Served to capt. USAAF, 1942-46, ETO, lt. col. Res. ret. Decorated Bronze Star. Fellow Acad. Ambulatory Foot Surgery, Am. Coll. Foot Surgeons; mem. Ariz. Podiatric Med. Assn. (past pres.), Am. Podiatric Med. Assn. Republican. Presbyterian. Clubs: OakCreek Country (Sedona); Fairfield Flagstaff Country (Flagstaff, Ariz.). Home: Air Force Village W 21364 Westover Cir Riverside CA 92518-2923

SEYLE, ROBERT HARLEY, artist, educator; b. National City, Calif., Oct. 9, 1937; s. Robert Van and Kristine (Aam) S.; children: Preston Van Seyle, Bryn Leigh Seyle. Student, Loma Linda U., 1956-58, 59-60; BFA, Otis Art Inst., L.A., 1961, MFA, 1966; postgrad., Clairmont (Calif.) Coll., 1978. Tchr. painting and sculpture Camarillo (Calif.) Cmty. Ctr., 1970, Shasta Coll. Ext. Program, Hynpalm, Calif., 1974; faculty painting, design, sculpture, drawing Loma Linda U., Riverside, Calif., 1976-79; tchr. drawing and painting West Union (W.Va.) Cmty. Ctr., 1982; faculty ceramics, sculpture, drawing, design/composition Pacific Union Coll., Angwin, Calif., 1991—; one-man shows include Ankrum Gallery, L.A., 1968, Palm Springs Desert (Calif.) Mus., 1974; works in permanent collections at Palm Springs Desert Mus., MGM Studios, Hollywood, Calif., Otis Art Inst. Storm King Art Mus., N.Y., La Jolla Art Mus., San Pedro and Peninsula YMCA, Calif. and many pvt. collections. Exhibited in group shows at Calif. Mus. Sci. and Industry, 1966, Otis Art Inst., 1966, Krannert Mus., U. Ill., 1967, Calif. Design X, 1968, Calif. Expo, Sacramento, 1968, Newport Harbor Mus., Calif., 1969, La Jolla (Calif.) Art Mus., 1969, Sacramento Capitol Bldg., 1974, San Bernardino County Mus., Calif., 1978, 79, Riverside (Calif.) Art Ctr., 1978, Ankrum Gallery, 1978, Luther Burbank Ctr. for Arts, 1993, The Artful Eye, Calistoga, Calif., 1994. With U.S. Army, 1961-63. Home and Office: 545 Howell Mountain Rd Angwin CA 94508-9757

SEYMOUR, JEFFREY ALAN, governmental relations consultant; b. L.A., Aug. 31, 1950; s. Daniel and Evelyn (Schwartz) S.; m. Valerie Joan Parker, Dec. 2, 1973; 1 child, Jessica Lynne. AA in Social Sci., Santa Monica Coll., 1971; BA in Polit. Sci., UCLA, 1973, MPA, , 1977. Councilmanic aide L.A. City Coun., 1972-74; county supr.'s sr. dep. L.A. Bd. Suprs., 1974-82; v.p. Bank of L.A., 1982-83; prin. Jeffrey Seymour & Assocs., L.A., 1983-84; ptnr. Morey/Seymour & Assocs., 1984—; mem. comml. panel Am. Arbitration Assn., 1984—. Chmn. West Hollywood Parking Adv. Com., L.A., 1983-84; chmn. social action com. Temple Emanuel of Beverly Hills, 1986-89, bd. dirs. 1988-93, v.p., 1990-93; v.p. Congregation N'vay Shalom, 1994-95; mem. Pan Pacific Park Citizens Adv. Com., L.A., 1982-85; bd. dirs. William O'Douglas Outdoor Classroom, L.A., 1981-88; exec. sec. Calif. Fedn. Young Dems., 1971; mem. Calif. Dem. Cen. Com., 1979-82; pres. Beverlywood-Cheviot Hills Dem. Club, L.A., 1978-81; co-chmn. Westside Chancellor's Assocs. UCLA, 1986-88; mem. L.A. Olympic Citizens Adv. Com.; mem. liaison adv. commn. with city and county govt. for 1984 Olympics, 1984; v.p. cmty. rels. metro region, Jewish Fedn. Coun. of L.A., 1985-87, co-chmn. urban affairs commn., 1987-89, vice chmn., 1989-90, subcom. chmn. local govt. law and legislation commn., 1990—, chmn. campus outreach task force, 1994—; mem. adv. bd. Nat. Jewish Ctr. for Immunology & Respiratory Medicine, 1991—; bd. dirs. Hillel Coun. of L.A., 1991—; mem. platform on world peace and internat. rels. Calif. Dems., 1983; pres. 43d Assembly Dist. Dem. Coun., 1975-79; arbitrator BBB, 1984—; trustee UCLA Found., 1989—; pres. UCLA Jewish Alumni, 1992-95; mem. Santa Monica Mountains Conservancy, 1995-96, adv. com., 1996—; mem. cabinet Jewish Cmty. Rels. Com. Greater L.A., 1994—, chair campus outreach task force, 1994-95, govtl. rels. commn., 1995-96; mem. adv. bd. L.A. Peace Now. Recipient Plaques for services rendered Beverlywood Cheviot Hills Dem. Club, L.A., 1981, Jewish Fedn. Coun. Greater L.A., 1983; Certs. of Appreciation, L.A. Olympic Organizing Com., 1984, County of L.A., 1984, City of L.A., 1987; commendatory resolutions, rules com. Calif. State Senate, 1987, Calif. State Assembly, 1987, 96, County of L.A., 1987, City of L.A., 1987. Mem. Am. Soc. Pub. Adminstrn., Am. Acad. Polit. and Social Scis., Town Hall of Calif., So. Calif. Planning Congress, Urban Land Inst., UCLA Alumni Assn. (mem. govtl. steering com. 1983—, chair, 1995—, bd. dirs. 1995—, pres.-elect 1997—). Office: Morey/Seymour and Assocs 233 Wilshire Blvd Ste 290 Santa Monica CA 90401-1206

SEYMOUR, LISA, museum director; b. Oct. 30, 1962; m. E. David Seymour. BA in Mass Comms., U. Denver, 1984; MA in Mass Comms., 1985. Grad. teaching asst. U. Denver, 1985; records clk. typist Kingman (Ariz.) Police Dept., 1985-86; sec. First Presbyn. Ch., Elko, Nev., 1986-87; exec. dir. Elko (Nev.) County Against Domestic Violence, 1987; exec. dir. of found. Elko (Nev.) Gen. Hosp. Found., 1989-90; mgr. cmty. rels. Elko (Nev.) Gen. Hosp., 1987-90; adtg. mgr. Elko (Nev.) Ind., 1990-91, newspaper editor, reporter, photographer, 1991-94; archivist and oral historian Northeastern Nev. Mus., Elko, 1994-95; interim mus. adminstr., 1995, mus. dir., 1996—. Grantee Newmont Gold Co., E.L. Cord Found., E.L. Wiegard Found., 1996. Office: Northeastern Nevada Museum 1515 Idaho St Elko NV 89801

SEYMOUR, RICHARD BURT, health educator; b. San Francisco, Aug. 1, 1937; s. Arnold Burt-Oakley and Florence Marguerite (Burt) S.; m. Michelle Driscoll, Sept. 15, 1963 (div. 1972); children: Brian Geoffrey, Kyra Daleth; m. Sharon Harkless, Jan. 5, 1973. BA, Sonoma State U., 1969, MA, 1970. Freelance writer Sausalito, Calif., 1960—; coord., adminstr. Coll. of Mendocino, Boonville, Calif., 1971-73; bus. mgr. Haight Ashbury Free Clinics, San Francisco, 1973-77; exec. adminstr., dir. tng. and edn. projects Height Ashbury Free Clinics, San Francisco, 1977-87; instr. John F. Kennedy U., Orinda, Calif., 1986—; asst. prof. Sonoma State U., Rohnert Park, Calif., 1985—; pres., chief exec. officer Westwind Assocs., Sausalito, Calif., 1988—; cons. Haight Ashbury Free Clinics, San Francisco, 1987—, treas., bd. dirs.; chmn. World Drug Abuse Treatment Network, San Francisco, 1988—; bd. dirs. Slide Ranch. Author: Physician's Guide to Psychoactive Drugs, 1987, Drug Free, 1987, The New Drugs, 1989, The Psychedelic Resurgence, 1993; editor-in-chief Internat. Addictions Infoline, 1995; mng. editor Jour. of Psychoactive Drugs, 1996; contbr. articles to profl. jours. Mem. Calif. Health Profls. for New Health Policy, Washington, 1976-80; chmn. Marin Drug Abuse Adv. Bd., San Rafael, Calif., 1979-81, CalDrug Abuse Svcs. Assn., Sacramento, 1975-79; mem. Alcohol and Drug Counselors Edn. Project, 1985—, San Francisco Delinquency Prevention Commn., 1981—, Calif. Primary Prevention Network, 1980—. Grantee NIMH, 1974—, Nat. Inst. on Drug Abuse, 1974—. Mem. Internat. Platform Assn., Commonwealth Club of Calif. Democrat. Episcopalian. Office: Westwind Assocs 90 Harrison Ave Apt C Sausalito CA 94965-2240

SHACKELFORD, ANASTASIA MARIE, secondary school educator; b. L.A., Oct. 2, 1970; d. Gerald Alexander and Mary Ann Katherine (Ristic) Braun; m. Matthew David Shackelford, June 17, 1995. BA in Math., Calif. State U., San Bernardino, 1993. Cert. tchr., Calif. Tchr. math. Yucaipa (Calif.)-Calimesa Joint Unified Sch. Dist., 1994-96, Whittier (Calif.) Union H.S. Dist., 1996—. Soccer coach. Mem. Nat. Coun. Tchrs. Math. Democrat. Office: LaSerna HS 15301 Youngwood Dr Whittier CA 90605

SHACKELFORD, GORDON LEE, JR., physics educator; b. South Bend, Ind., Apr. 7, 1948; s. Gordon Lee and Leatha Mae (Andrews) S.; m. Janis Elizabeth Mead, Apr. 6, 1974. BS in Physics, San Diego State U., 1970, MS in Radiol. Physics, 1974. Electronic designer for physics dept. San Diego State U., 1969-70; electronic engr. Naval Electronics Lab., Point Loma, Calif., 1970; electronic engr. product design Info. Machine Corps., Santee, Calif., 1970-71; lectr. physics San Diego State U., 1971—, asst. dir. alumni and devel. Coll. of Scis., 1980-81, assoc. dean scis., external rels., 1981—, project mgr. Biomass Power Plant, 1984-87, 89—; project mgr. SDSU 100 Telescope, 1989—, Tijuana River Tidal Wetlands Restoration Project, chmn. faculty senate athletic sub-com.. Mem. quality life bd. City of San Diego, 1989-90; mem. Lakeside Community Planning Group; chmn. senate com. on acad. resources and planning. Home: 9716 Red Pony Ln El Cajon CA 92021-2343 Office: San Diego State U Physics Dept San Diego CA 92182 *Personal philosophy: Get involved in your community. Work to make things better.*

SHACKLETON, ROBERT JAMES, accounting executive; b. Louisville, Aug. 21, 1936; s. Robert James and Annelle (Barrett) S.; m. Mary Randall, Dec. 21, 1963; children: Scott Randall, David Eric, Nancy Lynne. BSc, U. Louisville, 1958; MBA, U. So. Calif., 1969. Acct. audit dept. KPMG Peat Marwick, L.A., 1961-69, audit ptnr., 1969, ptnr. in charge San Fernando Valley, 1970-71, mem. profl. practice review com., 1974-76, SEC reviewing ptnr., 1976—; ptnr. in charge audit dept. KPMG Peat Marwick, Orange County, Calif., 1976-88, ptnr. in charge profl. practice, 1988—. Co-Author: Audits of Airlines, 1981. Chmn. L.A. Jr. C. of C., 1967-68, dir., 1968-70, pres. Arts Found., 1970-71, trustee Arts Found., 1970-75; dir. L.A. Master Chorale So. Calif. Choral Music Assn., 1968-69; treas. Jr. Achievement So. Calif., 1972-74, bd. dirs., 1972-80, bd. dirs. Orange County chpt., 1986—, treas. Orange County chpt., 1989-93; bd. dirs. Newport Harbor Area C. of C., Calif., 1979-91, CFO, 1983-84, pres. orgnl. affairs divsn., 1988, vice chmn. bd. dirs., 1989, chmn. bd. dirs., 1990; exec. bd. dirs. Orange County coun. Boy Scouts Am., 1981—, chmn. Scout-O-Rama, 1982, chmn. camp promotion, 1986, dist. chmn. Rancho Del Mar, 1984-85, advisor Order of Arrow, 1984-86; bd. dirs. Orange County Lincoln Club, 1992; mem. Calif. State Bd. Accountancy, 1992, chmn. profl. conduct com. and bd. liaison to qualifications com., 1992-94, mem. enforcement program mgmt. com., 1993-95, mem. article 9 task force, 1993-94, v.p., 1995, pres., 1996—; assoc. mem. Calif. Rep. State Ctrl. Com. Lt. USN, 1958-61. Mem. AICPA (mem. fed. govt. panel advisors 1973-80, mem. subcom. civil aeronautics 1973-80), Nat. Assn. Accts. (bd. dirs. San Fernando Valley chpt. 1971-72), Nat. Assn. State Bds. Accountancy (mem. rels. with govt. agys. com. 1992-95, mem. legal liability task force 1992-95, chmn. privity subcom. 1992-95, mem. CPA adv. panel 1995-96, mem. audit com. 1995—, mem. future licensing, litig. and legis. com. 1995—), Fin. Mgrs. Soc. Savs. Insts. (assoc. mem.), Calif. Soc. CPA (chmn. aerospace and electronics industry com. L.A. chpt. 1972-74, mem. state savs. and loan com. 1980-92, chmn. savs. and loan conf. 1985), Balboa Bay Club, Ctr. Club, Newport Harbor Yacht Club (bd. dirs. 1989-90, treas. 1997), Am. Legion Yacht Club, St. Francis Yacht Club. Presbyterian. Home: 102 Linda Isle Newport Beach CA 92660 Office: KPMG Peat Marwick LLP 650 Town Center Dr Costa Mesa CA 92626

SHACTER, DAVID MERVYN, lawyer; b. Toronto, Ont., Can., Jan. 17, 1941; s. Nathan and Tillie Anne (Schwartz) S. BA, U. Toronto, 1963; JD, Southwestern U., 1967. Bar: Calif. 1968, U.S. Ct. Appeals (9th cir.) 1969, U.S. Supreme Ct. 1982. Law clk., staff atty. Legal Aid Found., Long Beach, Calif., 1967-70; asst. city atty. City of Beverly Hills, Calif., 1970; ptnr. Shacter & Berg, Beverly Hills, 1971-83, Selwyn, Capalbo, Lowenthal & Shacter Profl. Law Corp., 1984—; del. State Bar Conf. Dels., 1976—; lectr. Calif. Continuing Edn. of Bar, 1977, 82, 83, 86; judge pro tem L.A. and Beverly Hills mcpl. cts.; arbitrator L.A. Superior Ct., 1983—, also judge pro tem; disciplinary examiner Calif. State Bar, 1986. Bd. dirs. and pres. Los Angeles Soc. Prevention Cruelty to Animals, 1979-89. Mem. Beverly Hills Bar Assn. (bd. govs. 1985—, editor-in-chief jour., sec. 1987-88, treas. 1988-89, v.p. 1989-90, pres.-elect 1990-91, pres. 1991-92), Am. Arbitration Assn. (nat. panel arbitrators, NASD arbitration panel), City of Hope Med. Ctr. Aux., Wilshire C. of C. (bd. dirs., gen. counsel 1985-87). Office: Selwyn Capalbo Lowenthal & Shacter Profl Law Corp 8383 Wilshire Blvd Ste 510 Beverly Hills CA 90211-2404

SHADD, VICKI MARIE NAGOS, secondary education educator; b. Corning, Calif., Mar. 19, 1957; d. Thomas and Patricia (Smith) N.; m. Jim L. Shadd. BA, Calif. State U., Chico, 1979; MA, Calif. State U., Sacramento, 1986. Cert. tchr., Calif.; cert. clear adminstrv. credential. Spl. Day Class tchr., resource specialist, mentor tchr. Biggs (Calif.) Unified Sch. Dist., 1982-90; job developer Workability I Butte County Schs., Oroville, Calif., 1984-90; instr. credential program Chapman U., Yuba City, Calif., 1988—; vocat. educator coord. and program specialist Glenn County Office Edn., Willows, Calif., 1992. Home: 3914 Front St Chico CA 95928-8923

SHADDOCK, PAUL FRANKLIN, SR., human resources director; b. Buffalo, Apr. 7, 1950; s. William Edmund and Rhea (Riester) S.; m. Linda Jeannine Bauer, July 19, 1980; children: Paul Jr., Jessica. BS, State U. Coll. N.Y., Buffalo, 1973; MBA, SUNY, Binghamton, 1975. Warehouse mgr. Ralston Purina Co., Denver, 1976-77; prodn. supr. Samsonite Corp., Denver, 1978-79, labor rels. rep., 1979-83; dir. human resources NBI, Inc., Denver, 1984-89, United Techs. Corp., Colorado Springs, Colo., 1990-95, Rockwell Semiconductor Sys., Newport Beach, Calif., 1995-96; v.p. human resources CSG, Systems, Inc., Denver, Colo., 1996—. Mem. Colo. Alliance of Bus., Denver, 1983-85, 90—, exec. com. U. Colo., Colorado Springs, 1990—. Mem. Assn. of Quality Participation, Am. Personnel Assn., Colo. Human Resource Assn., Human Resource Electroncis Group, Mountain States Employers Coun., Rocky Mountain Human Resources Group, Colorado Springs C. of C. Republican. Roman Catholic. Home: 5400 S Park Terr # 11-103 Greenwood Village CO 80111

SHADE, LINDA BUNNELL, university chancellor; m. William Shade. BA in English and Comm., Baylor U., 1964; MA in English Lang. and Lit., U. Colo., 1967, PhD in English Lit., 1970. Asst. prof. English, acting assoc. dean Coll. Humanities U. Calif., Riverside, 1970-77; dean acad. affairs for acad. programs and policy studies Calif. State U., Riverside, 1977-87; vice chancellor acad. affairs Minn. State Univs., Mpls., 1987-93; chancellor U. Colo., Colorado Springs, 1993—; active Minn. Women's Econ. Round Table, 1989; mem. exec. com. Nat. Coun. for Accreditation Tchr. Edn., 1996-99. Bd. dirs. St. Paul chpt. ARC; active St. Paul Chamber Orch., Baylor U. Coun. Sesquicentennial Coun. of 150, 1990, Grace Episcopal Ch., Colorado Springs. Recipient Disting. Alumni award Baylor U., 1995; Woodrow Wilson dissertation fellow U. Colo. Office: U Colo 1420 Austin Bluffs Pkwy Colorado Springs CO 80918-3733

SHADEGG, JOHN B., congressman; b. Phoenix, Oct. 22, 1950; s. Stephen and Eugenia Shadegg; m. Shirley Shadegg; children: Courtney, Stephen. BA, U. Ariz., 1972, JD, 1975. Advisor U.S. Sentencing Commn.; spl. asst. atty. gen. State of Ariz., 1983-90; spl. counsel Ariz. Ho. Rep. Caucus, 1991-92; pvt. practice; mem. 104th Congress from 4th Ariz. dist., 1995—, mem. various coms., asst. whip; mem. Victims Bill of Rights Task Force, 1989-90; mem. Fiscal Accountability and Reform Efforts Com., 1991-92; counsel Arizonian's for Wildlife Conservation, 1992; chmn. Proposition 108-Two-Thirds Tax Limitation Initiative, 1992. Rep. Party Ballot Security chmn., 1982; active Corbin for Atty. Gen., 1982-86; Rep. Precinct committeeman; chmn. Ariz. Rep. Caucus, 1985-87; chmn. Ariz. Lawyers for Bush-Quayle, 1988; mem. steering com., surrogate spkr. Jon Kyl for Congress, 1988-92; former pres. Crime Victim Found.; founding dir. Goldwater Inst. Pub. Policy; chmn. Ariz. Juvenile Justice Adv. Coun.; mem. adv. bd. Salvation Army; mem. vestry Christ Ch. of Ascension, 1989-91; mem. class II Valley Leadership; bd. dirs. Ariz. State U. Law Soc. Office: US House Reps 503 Cannon House Office Bldg Washington DC 20515-0304*

SHADISH, WILLIAM R., plastic surgeon, retired; b. Bridgeville, Pa., May 16, 1924; s. Jacob and Elizabeth (Straus) S.; m. Karen Leigh Phillips, Oct. 25, 1972. MD, L.I. Coll. Medicine, 1949. Asst. chief plastic surgery svcs. Walter Reed Gen. Hosp., Washington, 1959-62; chief plastic surgery svcs. Letterman Gen. Hosp., San Francisco, 1962-66; pvt. practice Redding (Calif.) Hosps., 1966-92; ret., 1992; mem. adv. bd. Dept. Vets. Affairs, Washington, 1987-96. Lt. col. U.S. Army, 1949-66. Mem. VFW, DAV, No. Calif. Emergency Care Coun., Korean War Vets., Am. Ex-POW. Republican. Presbyterian. Home: 845 Redbud Dr Redding CA 96001

SHADRACH, (MARTHA) JEAN HAWKINS, artist; b. La Junta, Colo., Nov. 7, 1926; d. Lloyd Marion Hawkins and Martha May (Hawkins) Sudan; widowed, 1987; children: John M., Karolyn Sue Shadrach Green. BA, U. Colo., 1948. Owner Artique, Ltd. Gallery, Anchorage, Alaska, 1971-87; instr. Foothills Art Ctr., Golden, 1988-89, Prince William Sound C.C., Homer, Alaska, 1993, Kachemak Bay C.C., Homer, 1994, 97, VAA, 1996; facilitator mktg. art seminars; guest lectr. Cunard Cruise Lines, 1988-90, 95. Bd. dirs. Bird Treatment and Learning Ctr., Anchorage, 1994, Anchorage Art Selection Com., 1984. Recipient gov.'s award for excellence in art, Anchorage, 1970, drawing award All Alaska Juried Show, 1970, 1st prize Fairbanks Watercolor Soc., 1987, Paul Schwartz Meml. award Sumi-e Soc. Am., 1993. Mem. Alaska Watercolor Soc. (v.p. 1994—, award 1988). Home and Studio: 3530 Fordham Dr Anchorage AK 99508-4558

SHADWICK, VIRGINIAANN GREER, librarian; b. Danville, Ky., Oct. 10, 1942; d. William Frederick and Helen Louise (Smith) Greer; m. Gordon Leon Shadwick, Dec. 31, 1979 (dec. Jan. 1986); 1 child, Laila Jenan Uthman (dec.). BA, Mich. State U., 1964; MSLS, U. Ky., 1967; postgrad., U. Calif., Berkeley, 1983-86. Libr. San Francisco State U., 1968—. Mem. pers. commn. Laguna Salada Union Sch. Dist., Pacifica, Calif., 1979-91. Mem. Am. Birding Assn., Calif. Tchrs. Assn. (bd. dirs. 1995—, state higher edn. WHO 1995), Calif. Faculty Assn. (pres. 1985-89), Nat. Edn. Assn. Nat. Coun. Higher Edn. (pres. 1989-95). Democrat. Buddhist. Home: 483 Andover Dr Pacifica CA 94044 Office: San Francisco State U Libr 1630 Holloway Ave San Francisco CA 94044

SHAEFFER, CLAIRE BRIGHTWELL, writer, educator; b. Weston, Ga., Dec. 2, 1939; d. Louie and Juanita (Sumner) Brightwell; m. Charlie W. Shaeffer, Jr., Feb. 24, 1959; children: Charlie W. III, James Robert. AA with honors, Laney Coll., 1968; BA summa cum laude, Old Dominion U., 1974. Floor supt. Famous Barr, St. Louis, 1960-64; tchr. Montgomery County (Md.) Adult Edn., 1969-70; cons. Portsmouth (Va.) City Schs., 1972-74; tchr. Coll. of the Desert, Palm Desert, Calif., 1975—; lectr. various cities in U.S. and Europe various cities in U.S. and London, 1984—. Author: 101 Sewing Shortcuts, 1978, The Complete Book of Sewing Short Cuts, 1981, Sew Successful, 1984, Sew A Beautiful Gift, 1986, Price It Right: An Alterations Pricing Guide, 1986, Claire Shaeffer's Sewing S.O.S., 1989, Claire Shaeffer's Fabric Sewing Guide, 1989, Sew Any Patch Pocket, 1992, Sew Any Set-in Pocket, 1994, Couture Sewing Techniques, 1993, (with others) Great Sewn Clothes, 1991, Jackets, Coats, and Suits, 1992, Distinctive Details, Beyond the Pattern, 1995, High Fashion Sewing, 1997; contbr. articles to profl. jours. Pres. Navy Officer's Wives, Portsmouth Naval Hosp., 1971-72; v.p. Assistance League Palm Springs Desert Area, 1976-77, pres., 1977-78; bd. dirs. Riverside County (Calif.) Heart Assn., 1978-82, sec., 1979-81; chmn. ann. mtg. Calif. Heart Assn., Burlingame, 1982. Recipient Second Place award Nat. Fedn. Press Women, 1989, Third Place award, 1993, First Place award 1994; First Place award Calif. Press Women, 1989, 93, 94, Third Place award, 1993, Second Place award, 1995, Woman of Achievement award Soroptimist Internat. of Palm Desert, 1996. Mem. Fashion Group Internat. (sec. 1992-94), Profl. Assn. Custom Clothiers, Calif. Press Women. Office: PO Box 157 Palm Springs CA 92263-0157

SHAEUMIN, MINAYA, claims representative; b. San Francisco, July 11, 1928; d. John Jesse and Helen Elizabeth (Forsyth) McNeil; m. Maurice Loren Turner, July 28, 1949 (div. Nov. 1955); 1 child, Colleen Ann; m. Rayee Shaeumin, Feb. 13, 1973. Student, Santa Rosa (Calif.) Jr. Coll., 1958-60; AA, Tanana Valley C.C., Fairbanks, Ark., 1987; BS in Anthropology, Oreg. State U., 1992. Lic. life ins. agt., health and accident agt. Intern tchr. 2d grade Primrose Elem. Sch., Santa Rosa, 1961-62; floor clk. surg. wing Santa Rosa Meml. Hosp., 1962; lab. technician Optical Coating Labs., Santa Rosa, 1962-63; live-in practical nurse, housekeeper, sch. tchr. Healsburg, Calif., 1963-65; saleslady, mgr. cosmetic dept. Empire Drug Store, Santa Rosa, 1965-67; cmty. ctr. aide, coord. Cmty. Ctr., Ukiah, Calif., 1968-69; picture framer New Horizons Art Gallery, Fairbanks, Alaska, 1985; seed analyst Oreg. State U. Seed Lab., Corvallis, 1988; owner, operator Best Publs., 1991-92; customer svc. rep. Prequest Co., 1993-95; security officer Am. Protective Svcs., Inc., 1995-96. Inventor matchbook holder-dispensor; inventor-designer free standing mag. rack; writer songs. Active mem. Pro-Choice Orgn., 1991—; mem. The Planetary Soc., 1989-91, Nat. Space Soc., 1990-91; mem. gold club North Shore Animal League, N.Y., 1985—. Recipient Benefactor award North Shore Animal League, 1991, Cert. of Appreciation, Nat. Cm. to Preserve Social Security and Medicare, 1991. Mem. Amnesty Internat. USA, Ams. to Limit Congl. Terms, Am. Policy Inst. "We the People", LWV, Srs. Coalition, So. Poverty law Ctr., Nat. Com. to Preserve Social Security and Medicare. Home: 205 NW 11th St Apt 2 Corvallis OR 97330-6048

SHAFER, JAMES ALBERT, health care administrator; b. Chgo., Aug. 26, 1924; s. James Earl and Kathleen (Sutterland) S.; m. Irene Jeanne Yurcega, June 20, 1948; children: Kathleen Mary, Patricia Ann. Technician Zenith Radio Corp., Chgo., 1946-47; owner, operator Eastgate Electronics, Chgo., 1947-61; applications engr. Perfection Mica Co., Bensenville, Ill., 1961-71; pres. Electronics Unltd., Northbrook, Ill., 1972-73, Ariz. Geriatric Enterprises Inc., Safford, 1974-86; sec.-treas. Saguaro Care Inc., 1988—; bd. dirs. Mt. Graham Community Hosp., Safford. Republican. Roman Catholic. Home: Skyline Ranch 10729 W Cottonwood Rd Pima AZ 85543-0630 Office: Saguaro Care Inc PO Drawer H Pima AZ 85543

SHAFF, BEVERLY GERARD, educational administrator; b. Oak Park, Ill., Aug. 16, 1925; d. Carl Tanner and Mary Frances (Gerard) Wilson; m. Maurice A. Shaff, Jr., Dec. 20, 1951 (dec. June 1967); children: Carol Maureen, David Gerrard, Mark Albert. MA, U. Ill., 1951; postgrad., Colo. Coll., 1966, 73, Lewis and Clark Coll., 1982, Portland State U., 1975-82. Tchr. Haley Sch., Berwyn, Ill., 1948-51; assoc. prof. English, Huntingdon Coll., Montgomery, Ala., 1961-62; tchr. English, William Palmer High Sch., Colorado Springs, Colo., 1964-67, 72-76, dir., 1967-72; tchr. English, Burns (Oreg.) High Sch., 1976-78; tchr. English as 2d lang. Multnomah County Ednl. Svc. Dist., Portland, Oreg., 1979-85; coord. gen. studies Portland Jewish Acad., 1984-90; with Indian Edn. Prog./Student Tng. Edn. Prog. (STEP) Portland Pub. Schs., 1990-92, 95—; tchr. St. Thomas More Sch., Portland, 1992-95; tchr. Indian Edn. Act Program Portland Pub. Schs., 1995—. Del. Colorado Springs Dem. Com., 1968, 72; active Rainbow Coalition, Portland; ct. apptd. spl. adv. CASA; mem. Lake Oswego Libr. Bd., Citizens Rev. Bd. Mem. Nat. Assn. Admnstrs., Nat. Assn. Schs. and Colls., Nat. Coun. Tchrs. Math., Nat. Coun. Tchrs. English. Home: 1 Jefferson Pky Apt 125 Lake Oswego OR 97035-8810

SHAFFER, AUDREY JEANNE, medical records administrator, educator; b. Hutchinson, Minn., Nov. 24, 1929; d. Floyd R. and Edna C. (Seppman) Kleiman; m. Frank L. Shaffer, July 15, 1948; 1 child, Cynthia Louise Shaffer Wilkinson. BS, Loma Linda U., 1973; MA, Central Mich. U., 1982. Registered records adminstr. Med. records clk. San Bernardino County Hosp., Calif., 1948-50; radiology receptionist White Meml. Med. Ctr., Los Angeles, 1950-52; med. records clk. Portland Adventist Hosp., Oreg., 1952-53; med. record mgr. Tempe Community Hosp., Ariz., 1953-54; faculty Loma Linda U., Calif., 1975-96; dir. med. info. services Corona Community Hosp., Calif., 1973-89 ; med. records cons. Calif., Utah, Fla. and Philippines, 1981-93, China, 1993—, pilot and med. asst. Liga Internat., Mex., 1964-68; chmn. Corona Blood Bank, 1957-68; chmn. vols. Corona Community Hosp. Aux., 1965-68; archaeology supr. Caesarea Expdn., Am. Schs. Oriental Research, Israel, summers 1974—. Recipient Vol. Service award Corona Community Hosp., 1968, Congeniality award Caesarea Archeol. Expdn., 1975, Alumna of Yr. award Sch. Allied Health Professions Loma Linda U., 1992. Mem. Loma Linda U. Med. Record Alumni (pres. 1979-81), Am. Health Info. Mgmt. Assn., Calif. Health Info. Assn. (mem. quality assurance com. 1980-81, pub. rels. com. 1988-91), Inland Area Health Info. Assn. (pres. elect 1991-92, pres. 1992-93), Nat. Assn. Healthcare Quality, Archeol. Inst. Am., Inland Quality Assurance Network (pres. 1988). Clubs: Women's Improvement (program chmn. 1960-61), Corona Flying (sec. 1960-68) (Corona). Home: 880 Encanto St Corona CA 91719-3501

SHAFRAN, MICHAEL WAYNE, editor; b. Bklyn., Nov. 29, 1966; s. Sam and Harriet (Scherer) S. BA in Polit. Sci., U. Mass., 1989. Acct. asst. Lobsenz Stevens, N.Y.C., 1989-90; sports editor Dateline Jour., Clifton, N.J., 1990-91; asst. editor MetroSports Mag., N.Y.C., 1991-93; editor InLine Retailer and Industry News, Boulder, Colo., 1993—. Vol. Habitat for Humanity, Boulder County, 1996. Mem. Colo. InLine. Democrat. Jewish. Office: Sports & Fitness Publ 2025 Pearl St Boulder CO 80302-4429

SHAFRANSKE, EDWARD PAUL, psychologist, educator; b. Chgo., Dec. 29, 1951; s. Joseph Edward and Katherine (O'Brien) S.; m. Kathryn A. Westerbeck, May 29, 1976; children: Kristin, Karen. BA magna cum laude, Immaculate Heart Coll., L.A., 1973; MA and PhD in Clin. Psychology, U.S. Internat. U., San Diego, 1981; PhD in Psychoanalysis, So. Calif. Psychoanalytic Ins., Beverly Hills, Calif., 1995. Lic. psychologist. Sr. psychologist U. San Diego, 1983-86; prof. Pepperdine U., Irvine, Calif., 1986—; pvt. practice, 1982—. Editor: Religion and the Clinical Practice of Psychology, 1996; author: (book chpt.) Handbook of Religious Experience, 1995. Fellow APA (pres. divsn. 36 psychology of religion 1994, William Bier award 1997); mem. Am. Psychoanalytic Assn. Office: Pepperdine U # 165 2151 Michelson Dr Irvine CA 92612

SHAGAM, MARVIN HÜCKEL-BERRI, private school educator; b. Monongalia, W.Va.; s. Lewis and Clara (Shagam) S. AB magna cum laude, Washington and Jefferson Coll., 1947; postgrad., Harvard Law Sch., 1947-48, Oxford (Eng.) U., 1948-51. Tchr. Mount House Sch., Tavistock, Eng., 1951-53, Williston Jr. Sch., Easthampton, Mass., 1953-55, Westtown (Pa.) Sch., 1955-58, The Thacher Sch., Ojai, Calif., 1958—; English dept. head Kurasini Internat. Edn. Centre, Dar-es-Salaam, Tanzania, 1966-67; dept. head Nkumbi Internat. Coll., Kabwe, Zambia, 1967-68; vol. visitor Prisons in Calif., 1980-95, Calif. Youth Authority, 1983-93; sr. youth crisis counsellor InterFace, 1984-94. 1st lt. M.I. res. U.S. Army, 1943-56. Danforth Found. fellow, 1942; Coun. for the Humanities fellow, Tufts U., 1983. Mem. Western Assn. Schs. and Colls. (accreditation com.), Great Teaching (Cooke chair 1977—), Phi Beta Kappa, Delta Sigma Rho, Cum Laude Soc. Republican.

SHAH, BHAILAL MORARJI, pharmacist; b. Koday-Kutch, Gujarat, India, Jan. 18, 1945; came to U.S., 1969; s. Morarji T. and Laxmiben M. (Lalan) S.; m. Neela B. Gala, Dec. 21, 1975; children: Monali, Jatin. Diploma in Pharmacy, Bombay (India) Coll. Pharmacy, 1966; B. in Pharmacy, U. Shivaji, Karad, India, 1969; BS in Pharmacy, U. Kans., 1971. Registered pharmacist Ariz., Kans., Calif. Staff pharmacist St. Joseph Hosp., Kansas City, Mo., 1971-73, Rsch. Med. Ctr., Kansas City, 1974-75; in-charge of out patient clinic pharmacy Good Samaritan Regional Med. Ctr., Phoenix, 1976—. Mem. India Assn., Phoenix, 1981—. Mem. Ariz. Pharmacy Assn., Am. Hosp. Pharmacy Soc. Home: 8734 E San Esteban Dr Scottsdale AZ 85258-2603 Office: Good Samaritan Reg Med Ctr 1111 E Mcdowell Rd Phoenix AZ 85006-2612

SHAH, DEVANG KUNDANLAL, software engineer; b. Mombasa, Kenya, Oct. 2, 1963; s. Kundan B. and Saryu K. (Mehta) S. B Tech Electronics Engring. with honors, Inst. Tech. Banaras Hindu U., Varanasi, India, 1985; MA in Computer Sci., U. Tex., 1989; MBA, U. Calif., 1995. Software engr. Tata Consultancy Svcs., Bombay, India, 1985-86; staff engr. SunSoft, Inc. subs. Sun Microsystems, Inc., Mountain View, Calif., 1990—; Sun Microsystems rep. to Unix Internat. multiprocessor working group, Parsippany, N.J., 1990. Co-author: Programming with Threads, 1996; author tech. papers in field. Mem. IEEE (tech. com. on oper. systems & stds. 1990-91, stds. com. on threads ext. for portable oper. systems), Assn. for Computing Machinery. Home: 1031 Foster City Blvd Apt B Foster City CA 94404-2328 Office: SunSoft Inc M/S MPK17-301 2550 Garcia Ave Mountain View CA 94043-1109

SHAH, GIRISH POPATLAL, data processing services company executive; b. Junagadh, India, Apr. 11, 1942; came to U.S., 1963; s. Popatlal Gulabchand and Lalitaben Popatlas (Kamdar) S.; m. Devmani Manilal Jhaveri, June 18, 1968; children: Nivisha, Munjal, Bhavin. B in Tech., Indian Inst. Tech., Bombay, 1963; MS, U. Calif., Berkeley, 1965. Project analyst IBM Corp., Palo Alto, Calif., 1965-67; v.p. Optimum Systems, Inc., Palo Alto, 1967-72; pres. Banking Systems Internat. Corp., Jakarta, Indonesia and Campbell, Calif., 1972-76; dir. software services Tymshare Transactions Services, San Francisco, 1980-83; sr. scientist McDonnell Douglas Corp., Fremont, Calif., 1984-86; dir. corp. devel. Sysorex Internat., Inc., Cupertino, Calif., 1986-87; v.p. Sysorex Internat., Inc., Mountain View, Calif., 1987-96; sr. v.p. Sysorex Info. Systems Inc., Mountain View, 1987-91; project exec. IBM Global Svcs., 1996—. Mem. adv. bd. Goodwill Industries, San Francisco, 1980-82; bd. dirs. Gujarate Cultural Assn., 1982; chmn. temple bd. Jain Ctr., 1990-94; co-chmn. Jaina Conv., 1991-94; city gov. Fedn. Indo-Am. Assns., Fremont, Calif., 1991—; pres.'s coun. Fedn. Jain Assoc. N.Am., 1995—; mem. Jaina charitable trust, 1995—; bd. dirs. Jain Ctr. No. Calif., 1996—. J.N. Tata Trust nat. scholar, 1963. Mem. Assn. Indians in Am. (v.p. 1980). Democrat. Home: 4048 Twyla Ln Campbell CA 95008-3721 Office: IBM Global Svcs 1055 Joaquin Rd Mountain View CA 94043 *Personal philosophy: Be truthful in all dealing and maintain an absolute level of personal ethics. Reverance for all life forms, non-violence and vegetarianism.*

SHAHIN, THOMAS JOHN, dry cleaning wholesale supply company executive; b. Buffalo, July 30, 1943; s. Thomas Mark and Marie (Colletto) S.; m. Laraine Edna Clements, Feb. 25, 1967; 1 child, Lori Lynn. BSBA, Calif. State U., L.A., 1966. Asst. v.p. stock brokerage div. United Calif. Bank, L.A., 1969-76; v.p., gen. mgr., treas. Newhouse Splty. Co. Inc., Santa Ana, Calif., 1976—, also bd. dirs. Patentee belt buckle. Officer USN, 1966-69, Vietnam. Mem. Textile Care Allied Trade Assn., Laundry and Drycleaners Suppliers, Internat. Fabricare Inst., Internat. Drycleaners Congress, Calif. Fabricare Inst., Beta Gamma Sigma. Republican. Roman Catholic. Office: Newhouse Splty Co Inc 2619 Oak St Santa Ana CA 92707-3720

SHAKMAN, ROBERT ALLAN, public health physician. BA in History with honors, U. Pa., 1965; MD, Northwestern U., 1969; MPH, U. Calif., Berkeley, 1972. Diplomate Am. Bd. Preventive Medicine, Nat. Bd. Med. Examiners; lic. physician, surgeon Calif., Oreg. Intern Evanston Hosp., Northwestern U. Med. Ctr., Evanston, 1969-70; pub. health physician Alameda (Calif.) and Contra Costa County Health Depts., 1972, Ventura County, 1970-72, 76-77; physician Permanente Med. Group, Walnut Creek, Lancaster, Calif., 1972-75; pvt. practice Ojai, Calif., 1973; environ. health cons. Ojai, Ventura, Calif., 1973-77; dir. occupational and environ. health program Navy Missile Test Ctr. and Air Base, Point Mugu, Calif., 1977-80; med. affairs dir. Vetco Offshore, Inc., Ventura, Calif., 1980-85; med. cons. Calif. Dept. Health Svcs., L.A., 1985-86; med. dir. so. region Calif. Med. Rev., Inc., Bakersfield, 1986-87; asst. med. dir. Blue Cross of Calif., L.A., 1987-90, med. dir., 1990-93; v.p., med. dir. Blue Cross of Calif., 1993-96; v.p. clin. and sci. affairs Calif. Health Care Found. and Calif. Endowment, 1996, health care cons., 1996; bd. dirs. Am. Lung Assn., Ventura County, Calif., 1981-88, pres. 1986-87; clin. assoc. prof. preventive medicine U. So. Calif., L.A. Author: Poison Proof Your Body: Food, Pollution and Your Health, 1980; Where You Live May Be Hazardous to Your Health: A Health Index to American Communities, 1979.; contbr. articles and abstracts to profl. jours. Med. mem. and chmn. Ventura County Air Pollution Hearing Bd. Fellow Am. Coll. Preventive Medicine; mem. AMA, Ventura County Med. Assn., Calif. Med. Assn., Western Occupational Med. Assn., Am. Pub. Health Assn. Office: 3248 Island View Dr Ventura CA 93003

SHALLENBERGER, GARVIN F., lawyer; b. Beloit, Wis., Jan. 7, 1921; s. Garvin D. and Grace (Hubbell) S.; m. Mary L., May 5, 1945; children: Diane, Dennis Clark. BA in Pre-law, U. Mont., 1942; JD, U. Calif., Berkeley, 1949; LLD (hon.), Western State U., Fullerton, Calif., 1988. Bar: Calif. 1949, U.S. Dist. Ct. (cent. dist.) Calif. 1949, U.S. Ct. Appeals (9th cir.) 1949, U.S. Supreme Ct. 1961, U.S. Dist. Ct. (no. and so. dists.) Calif. 1963. Rutan & Tucker, Costa Mesa, Calif.; chmn. spl. adv. com. state bar legal svcs. program, 1979-89, pub. law ctr Orange County, 1979-90. Recipient distinguished svc. award Boalt Hall (U. Calif. Berkeley); Judge Learned Hand Human Rel. award Nat. Jewish Com., 1990. Fellow Am. Coll. Trial Lawyers; mem. Am. Bd. Trial Advs. (founder and 1st sec.),Calif. Bar Assn. (bd. govs. 1975-76, pres. 1977-78; mem. com. on jud. nominees 1978-79, pres. 1980), mem. Orange County Bar Assn. (bd. dirs. 1970-71, pres. 1972, Franklin West award 1979). Democrat. Office: Rutan & Tucker 611 Anton Blvd PO Box 1950 Costa Mesa CA 92626

SHAMBAUGH, STEPHEN WARD, lawyer; b. South Bend, Ind., Aug. 4, 1920; s. Marion Clyde and Anna Violet (Stephens) S.; m. Marilyn Louise Pyle; children: Susan Wynne Shambaugh Hinkle, Kathleen Louise Shambaugh Thompson. Student San Jose State Tchrs. Coll., 1938-40, U. Ark., 1951; LLB, U. Tulsa, 1954. Bar: Okla. 1954, Colo. 1964. Mem. staff Reading & Bates, Inc., Tulsa, 1951-54; v.p., gen. mgr., legal counsel Reading & Bates Drilling Co. Ltd., Calgary, Alta., Can., 1954-61; sr. ptnr. Bowman, Shambaugh, Geissinger & Wright, Denver, 1964-81; sole practice, Denver, 1981—; dir., fin. counsel various corps. Col. USAF ret. Mem. ABA, Fed. Bar Assn., Colo. Bar Assn., Okla. Bar Assn., Denver Bar Assn., P-51 Mustang Pilots Assn., Masons, Shriners, Elks, Spokane Club, Petroleum Club of Bakersfield, Phi Alpha Delta.

SHAMGOCHIAN, THERON, food products executive; b. 1947. BSBA, Stanislaus State Coll., 1970. Prin. Monte Cristo Packing Co., Livingston, Calif., 1970-88; pres. Shamgochian Theron Inc., Livingston, 1973—. Office: Shamgochian Theron Inc 11173 W Mercedes Ave Livingston CA 95334-9707*

SHAMLIAN, BARBARA SUE, religion educator, biblical researcher; b. Wewoka, Okla., Dec. 16, 1936; d. John Timothy and Myrtle Esther (Bruce) Davisson; m. Paul Little Shamlian, Mar. 1, 1958; children: Paul Little Jr., Anthony Ray, Frank Bruce, Richard Nahabed. ThD, Sch. Bible Theology, San Jacinto, Calif., 1992. Pres. Christian Warriors Ministries and Corr. Bible Sch., Reno, 1993—. Author: Record of the Boal Family, 1987, Tithing: A Religious Fraud, 1989, New Testament Parables, 1993, Old Testament Tabernacle, 1993. Republican. Home: 3865 Sandpiper Dr Reno NV 89506

SHANAHAN, MICHAEL GEORGE, police officer; b. Seattle, Oct. 14, 1940; s. Raymond Roderick and Carletta (Anderson) S.; m. Jo-Anne Genevieve David, Sept. 16, 1961; children: Patrick, Matthew, Raymond. BA in Psychology, Stanford U., 1962. Asst. police chief U. Wash., Seattle, 1971-75, vol. police cons. and mgmt. pvt. sector issues, 1995—; mem. law enforcement task force interim mcpl. com. Wash. State Legis., 1970-71, campus law enforcement task force-higher edn. com., 1970-71; co-chmn. Wash. Law Enforcement Standards Task Force; founding chmn. Washington Law Enforcement Exec. Forum, 1981, Operation Bootstrap, 1985, others. Author: Private Enterprise and the Public Police: The Professionalizing Effects of a New Partnership, 1985; contbr. articles to profl. jours. Mem. nat. exploring com. Boy Scouts Am., 1977, exec. bd., chief Seattle council, 1984-88; mem. Blanchet High Sch. Bd., Seattle, 1978-79, Gov.'s Coun. on Criminal Justice, 1980-81, Gov.'s Coun. Food Assistance, 1983-86. Major U.S. Army, 1963-70, Vietnam. Decorated Bronze Star; recipient award for pub. svc. U.S. Dept. Transp., 1984, Humanitarian award Seattle chpt. NCCJ, 1985, Silver Beaver award Boy Scouts Am., 1986, St. Matthew award Northwest Harvest, 1987, Paul J. Breslin award Internat. Security Mgrs. Assn., 1990, Criminal Justice award of excellence Wash. State U., 1989. Mem. FBI Nat. Acad. Assocs., Nat. Inst. Justice (peer rev. program), Internat. Assn. Chiefs of Police (life, bd. officers 1983-84, gen. chmn. divsn. state assns. 1983-84, co-chmn. pvt. sector liaison com.), Police Exec. Rsch. Forum, Wash. Assn. Sheriffs and Police Chiefs, Rotary Internat. (pres. Univ. Rotary Club Seattle 1985-86, founding chmn. Rotary Op. First Harvest, Svc. Above Self award 1988). Roman Catholic.

SHANAHAN, MIKE, professional football coach; b. Oak Park, Ill., Aug. 24, 1952; m. Peggy, children: Kyle, Krystal. BS Phys. Edn., Eastern Illinois U., Charleston, Ill., 1974; MS Phys. Edn., 1975. Student coach Eastern Illinois U.; asst. coach U. Oklahoma, 1975-76; offensive coord., No. Ariz. U., 1976-77, Ea. Ill. U., 1977-78, U. Minn., 1979-80, offensive coord., U. Fla., 1980-84, asst. head coach, 1983-84; receivers coach Denver Broncos, 1984-87; head coach Los Angeles Raiders, 1988-89; asst. coach Denver Broncos, NFL, 1989-91; offensive coordinator San Francisco 49ers, 1992-94; head coach Denver Broncos, 1995—. Office: care Denver Broncos 13655 Broncos Pkwy Englewood CO 80112-4150*

SHANAHAN, R. MICHAEL, securities dealer; b. 1939. Stanford U., 1960. With Capital Rsch. & Mgmt. Co., Inc., L.A., 1964—; with AMCAP Fund, Inc., 1970—, now pres. Office: AMCAP Fund Inc 333 S Hope St Los Angeles CA 90071-1406*

SHANAHAN, TERESA ANN, therapist; b. Scotia, Calif., Nov. 23, 1955; d. Laurence and Katherine (Nansel) S. BA, San Diego State U., 1981, MS in Counseling, 1983; PhD in Psychology, U. Humanistic Studies, 1994. Cert. fitness instr., health mgmt. Therapeutic recreation specialist Grossmont Hosp., La Mesa, Calif., 1980-85, Sharp Cabrillo Hosp., San Diego, 1984-89; owner, founder, operator Lifeline Healthcare, San Diego, 1986—; cons. to skilled nursing facilities and care mgmt. to geriatric and brain injury population, San Diego, 1982—; fitness instr. San Diego C.C., 1984—; lectr., educator in field. Author: The Psychosocial Almanac, 1997; columnist Calendar Mag., 1986-89. Chmn. San Diego Stroke Club Facilitators, Am. Heart Assn., 1987-89; mem. spl. events com., parade announcer La Jolla (Calif.) Town Coun., 1987—. Mem. APA, Am. Therapeutic Recreation Assn., Internat. Platform Assn., Geriatric Care Mgrs., Women in Arts, Toastmasters (pres. La Jolla chpt. 1985—, mentor chair 1994, Best Serious Spkr. award 1987). Home: 4914 Lamont St San Diego CA 92109-1403

SHANE, WILLIAM WHITNEY, astronomer; b. Berkeley, Calif., June 3, 1928; s. Charles Donald and Mary Lea (Heger) S.; BA, U. Calif., Berkeley, 1951, postgrad., 1953-58; ScD, Leiden (The Netherlands) U., 1971; m. Clasina van der Molen, Apr. 22, 1964; children: Johan Jacob, Charles Donald. rsch. assoc. Leiden U., 1961-71, sr. scientist, 1971-79; prof. astronomy, dir. Astron. Inst., Cath. U. Nijmegen, The Netherlands, 1979-88; guest prof. astronomy Leiden U., 1988-93; C.H. Adams fellow Monterey (Calif.) Inst. Rsch. Astronomy, 1994—. With USN, 1951-53. Fellow AAAS; mem. Internat. Astron. Union (commns. 33, 34), Am. Astron. Soc., Astron. Soc. Netherlands, Astron. Soc. of the Pacific, Phi Beta Kappa. Achievements include research on structure and dynamics of galaxies, observational astronomy. Home: 9095 Coker Rd Prunedale CA 93907-1401 Office: Monterey Inst Rsch Astronomy 200 8th St Marina CA 93933

SHANG, ER-CHANG, acoustician; b. Sheng Yain, Liaonin, China, Feb. 5, 1932; came to U.S., 1986.; BS in Theoretical Physics, Peking U., Beijing, China, 1958; PhD equivalent, Inst. Acoustics, Acad. Sinica, Beijing, 1982. Asst. prof. Inst. of Acoustics, Beijing, 1958-62, assoc. prof., 1962-75, prof., 1975-82, dep. dir., 1982-86; sr. rsch. assoc. AOML/NOAA, Miami, Fla., 1983-84, Wave Propagation Lab./NOAA, Boulder, Colo., 1987-88; NRC postdoctoral advisor Wave Propagation Lab./NOAA, 1991—; rsch. assoc. CIRES/U. Colo./NOAA, Boulder, 1988-91, rsch. prof., supervisor, 1991—; vis. scientist Scripps Inst. Oceanography, U. Calif. San Diego, La Jolla, 1982-83; vis. prof. U. Wis., Madison, 1983, Yale U., New Haven, 1986-87. Author: Underwater Acoustics, 1981. Recipient Nat. award for sci. Nat. Com. of Sci, Beijing, 1982, 89. Fellow Acoustical Soc. Am. Office: ETL/NOAA 325 Broadway St Boulder CO 80303-3337

SHANHOUSE, BILL, sculptor, educator; b. Rockford, Ill., July 10, 1926; s. Louis Jacob and Lois Francis (Miller) S.; m. Linda Joyce Fillingham; children: Susan, Laurie, Robin, Barbara, Nancy, Jennifer. Grad., U.S. Naval Acad., 1949; BSEE, Northwestern U.; postgrad., Hofstra U., Corcoran Sch. of Art, Washington. Chief engr. S.S. Hunter; pres. Internat. Sys. Rsch. Corp.; v.p. ops. Renwell Industries; v.p. corp. devel. P&F Industries; v.p. student affairs Hofstra U.; v.p. adminstrv. svcs. U. Iowa; GS-12 engring. supr. Office Naval Rsch.; dir. employment programs City of N.Y.; cons. Dept. State, Nat. Bur. Stds., Nat. Endowment of the Arts, Md. State Legis., Tex. Commn. on the Arts; lectr. U. Iowa, George Washington U., Hofstra U., Am. Mgmt. Assn., Am. Assn. Indsl. Mgmt.; writer Washington Post, King Features Syndicate, Jossey-Bass. Inventor metering and measuring equipment, navigational instrumentation, and relative motion devices; sculpture installations Mitchell Mus., Lowe Mus., U. Tex., Fordham U., Morehead State U., Phila. Internat. Gardens; one-man shows include Arts Coun., Grapeville, Tex., Dallas Design Ctr., Carroll Sch., Southlake, Tex., U. Tex., Dallas, Dallas Symphony Showhouse, Paige Gallery, Dallas, Md. Coll. Art, Silver Spring, Bloomingdale's, McLean, Va., Lakeforest, Gaithersburg, Md., Montgomery County Delegation, Annapolis, Md., Slavin Gallery, Washington, Montgomery Mall, Bethesda, Md., Community Fed. Assn., Washington, Fordham U., N.Y.C., Lincoln Ctr., N.Y.C., Diane Brown Gallery, Washington; exhibited in group shows at Hofstra Mus., Hempstead, N.Y., Wright Gallery, Dallas, Dimensions, Lenexa, Kans., Edith Baker Gallery, Dallas, Dallas Mus. Art, Britt-Neman, Stenhamra, Sweden, Republic Pl., Austin, Tex., D'Art, Dallas, Kelton Mathis, Arlington, Tex., LTV Ctr., Dallas, Frito-Lay, Plano, Tex., Montage, Dallas, Mitchell Mus., Mt. Vernon, Ill., Tex. Sculpture Assn., Dallas, Signature Pl., Dallas, Sculpture Resources Inc., Dallas, Samuell Grand Park, Dallas, Athena Gallery, N.Y.C., Dallas Design Ctr., Paige Gallery, Dallas, Morehead State U., Ky., Carrier Found., Belle Mead, N.J., Swimmer Gallery, Mt. Kisco, N.Y., numerous others. Bd. dirs. U. Iowa Mus. Art, Columbia Visual Arts Coll., Sculpture Resources, Inc., Tex. Sculpture Assn., Tex. Arts Alliance, Studio Theatre. With USN, 1943-52. Home and Office: PO Box 578 Angel Fire NM 87710

SHANK, BRYAN LEIGH, marketing executive; b. St. Louis, July 13, 1954. B Journalism, U. Mo., 1976; MS in Advt., Northwestern U., 1984. Various advt. and pub. positions, 1976-96; v.p. Grey Advt., Huntington Beach, Calif., 1995—.

SHANK, THOM LEWIS, real estate executive, entertainment consultant, author; b. Butler, Pa., Apr. 23, 1953; s. Berdyne Delmont and Florence Elizabeth (Glasser) S. BA in Sociology, U. Pa., 1974; MBA, Pepperdine U., 1981. Negotiator Worldmark Travel, N.Y.C. and Phila., 1971-76; retail ops. mgr. Just Plants, Inc., Roxborough, Pa., 1973-79; founder, mgr. The Best-direct mail sales, Edgemoor, Del., 1974-79; property mgr. Moss and Co., Westwood, Calif., 1977-82; talent mgr. Thom Shank Assocs., Brentwood, Calif., 1979-84; pres., founder The Great Am. Amusement Co., Palm Desert, Calif., 1979-84; sales exec. Fred Sands Realtors, Brentwood, 1981-85; sales and mktg. dir. Coldwell Banker, Newport Beach, Calif., 1985-86, Great Western Ranches, Burbank, Calif., 1988-95; dist. and regional mgr. E.R.A. Real Estate, Pasadena, Calif., 1986; owner Century 21 Realtors, Tarzana, Calif., 1987-89; resorts dir. Prudential Jon Douglas Co., Beverly Hills, Calif., 1996—. Lutheran. Office: 301 N Canon Dr Beverly Hills CA 90210-4722

SHANKS, BERNARD D., state official; b. El Paso, Ill., Apr. 4, 1940; s. Arthur and Grace (Arnold) S.; m. Anne Marie Ellis, Dec. 21, 1982; 1 child, Michael Cole. BS in Gen. Sci., Mont. State U., 1968, MS in Earth Sci., 1970; PhD in Natural Resource Devel., Mich. State U., 1974. Ranger six nat. parks; assoc. prof. resource planning Coll. Natural Resources, Utah State U., Logan, 1977-80; asst. dir. resources Calif. Gov.'s Office, Washington, 1980-83; mgr. land Marin Mcpl. Water Dist., Corte Madera, Calif., 1983-84; asst. dir. environ. policy Ariz. Gov.'s Office, Phoenix, 1984-86; chief planning coordination Ariz. State Parks, Phoenix, 1984-86; dir. Ctr. for Calif. Studies, Calif. State U., Sacramento, 1986-90; dir. Office of Environment, Health and Safety U. Calif., Davis, 1990-95; dir. regional environ. mgmt. Metro Regional Govt., Portland, Oreg., 1995—; lectr. in field. Author: This Land is Your Land, California Wildlife, Wilderness Survival; contbr. articles to profl. jours. with USMCR. Mem. The Wilderness Soc. (bd. dirs. 1978-82), Defenders of Wildlife (bd. dirs. 1983-92), Calif. Parks and Conservation Assn. (bd. dirs. 1987-89). Home: PO Box 21 Deer Harbor WA 98243 Office: Fish and Wildlife Dept 500 N Capitol Way Olympia WA 98501-1076

SHANNON, BERNARD JOSEPH, optometrist, vision care company executive; b. Mpls., Aug. 15, 1930; s. Bernard Joseph and Theresa E. (Murphy) S.; m. Edith Joanne Davis, Sept. 4, 1964; children: Sean, Maurya, Erin. BS, Ill. Coll., Chgo., 1954; OD, Ill. Coll. Optometry, Chgo., 1956; cert., Wharton Grad. Sch., Phila., 1976, U. Mo., 1991. Pvt. practice in clin. optometry Mauston, Wis., 1956-76; dir. profl. svcs. Bausch & Lomb, Inc., Rochester, N.Y., 1976-79, dir. internat. distbn., 1979-82; exec. dir. Ciba Vision Corp., Atlanta, 1983-92; v.p. PBH, Phoenix, 1992—; pres. North Cen. States Coun., Mpls., 1967-68; cons. U.S. Army Surgeon Gen., Washington, 1973-76. Co-author: (manpower study) Optometric Man Power, 1974; The Leader and, 1975; contbr. articles to profl. jours. Chmn. City Planning Commn., Wis., 1967, City Housing Authority, Wis., 1969; pres. Kiwanis Club, Wis., 1960; bd. dirs. State of Wis.-Regional Mgr., 1974. With USN, 1952-54. Mem. Am. Optometric Found. (past bd. dirs.), Am. Acad. Optometry, Am. Optometric Assn. (pres. 1974-75, Disting. mem.), Wis. Optometric Assn. (pres. 1966-67, Disting. mem., OD of Yr.), Tomb and Key, Beta Sigma Kappa. Roman Catholic. Home: 30068 N 77th Pl Scottsdale AZ 85262-2143

SHANNON, JONATHAN J., artist; b. Ariz., 1938. BFA, UCLA, 1960. Owner John Shannon Fashions, L.A. and Mendocino, Calif., 1968-75; co-owner Spreckels Mansion Inn, San Francisco, 1978-88, Archbishops Mansion Inn, San Francisco, 1982—. Exhibited in exhbns. at Nat. Quilting Assn., 1991 (Best of Show award), Mid-Atlantic Quilt Fest, 1993 (Best of Show), Am. Internat. Quilt Assn., Houston, 1993, 94 (Best of Show 1993), Brit. Nat. Patchwork Championships, 1994 (Best of Show), Forge Mill Needle Mus., Eng., 1995, Mus. San Diego History, 1996, travelling exhbn., 1990—. Co-founder Shannon-Ross scholarship endowment fund Mus. Am. Quilters, Paducah, Ky., 1993—; bd. dirs. Am. Mus. Quilts and Textiles, San Jose, Calif., 1995—; pres. Bed & Breakfast Innkeepers No. Calif., 1980-81. Mem. Nat. Quilting Assn. (mem. nat. scholarship com. 1991-93), Studio Quilt Art Assn. (bd. dirs. 1995—), Am. Quilters Soc., East Bay Heritage Quilters, Can. Quilt Study Group, Quilters Guild Britain, Quilters Guild Australia. Studio: 113o Brockman Dr Sonoma CA 95476

SHANNON, PATRICK KAVANAUGH, finance manager; b. Aurora, Colo., Dec. 22, 1955; s. Lawrence Kavanaugh and Dorothy Berneice (Holtry) S. BSBA cum laude, U. Colo., 1978; MBA, U. Denver, 1990. Assoc. analyst estimating Lockheed/Martin Marietta Corp., Denver, 1978-79; fin. specialist estimating Martin Marietta Corp., Denver, 1979-81, sr. fin. specialist estimating, 1981-83, fin. adminstr. estimating, 1983-86, chief maj. proposals, 1986-88, mgr. maj. proposals, 1988-89, mgr. overhead control, 1989-92, mgr. fin. planning and analysis, 1992-94; mgr. ind. estimating ATLAS Fin. Analysis, 1994-95; mgr. program fin. Atlas IIAR Program, 1995—; treas., bd. dirs. Red Rocks Fed. Credit Union, Littleton, Colo., 1993, vice-chmn. bd. dirs., 1994—. Treas. bd. dirs. Rue Royale Homeowners Assn., Denver, 1982-91; del. Colo. State Conf. Dem. Party, Denver, 1984; del. Denver County Assembly, 1984, 90, precinct committeeman, 1984-90. Mem. Beta Gamma Sigma. Presbyterian. Home: 809 Fillmore St Denver CO 80206-3849 Office: Martin Marietta Astronautics MS DC 2811 PO Box 179 Denver CO 80201

SHANNON, RICHARD STOLL, III, financial executive; b. N.Y.C., Mar. 22, 1943; s. Richard Stoll Jr. and Margaret (Cather) S.; m. Ann Wright Schmidt, June 14, 1965; children: Clea Cather, Kathryne Baltzelle, Arianna Wright. BA, Stanford U., 1966, MA, 1969; PhD, Harvard U., 1973. Asst. prof. U. Mich., Ann Arbor, 1973-78; mgr., trustee, gen. ptnr. various family trusts, partnerships and corps. Englewood, Colo., 1978-84; pres. Shannon Mgmt. Corp., Englewood, 1985—. Author: The Arms of Achilles, 1975; editor (with others) Oral Literature and The Formula, 1976. Bd. dirs. Cherryvale Sanitation Dist., Englewood, 1984—, pres., 1986-93; regional chmn. Stanford Ann. Fund/Keystone Project, 1985—; mem. Rackham Advancement Coun., U. Mich., 1992—. Teaching fellow Harvard U., 1970-73. Mem. Am. Philol. Assn., Denver C. of C., Cherry Creek Commerce Assn., Cherry Hills Country Club, Denver Petroleum Club, Phi Beta Kappa. Office: Shannon Mgmt Corp 3098 S Pennsylvania St Englewood CO 80110-1649

SHANNON, ROBERT RENNIE, optical sciences center administrator, educator; b. Mt. Vernon, N.Y., Oct. 3, 1932; s. Howard A. and Harriebell S.; m. Helen Lang, Feb. 13, 1954; children: Elizabeth, Barbara, Jennifer, Amy, John, Robert. B.S., U. Rochester, 1954, M.A., 1957. Dir. Optics Lab., ITEK Corp., Lexington, Mass., 1959-69; prof. Optical Scis. Ctr., U. Ariz., 1969—, dir., 1983-92, prof. emeritus, 1992—; cons. Lawrence Livermore Lab., 1980-90; trustee Aerospace Corp., 1985-94, 96—; mem. Air Force Sci. Adv. Bd., 1986-90; mem. NRC Commn. on Next Generation Currency, 1992-94, NRC Commn. on Optical Sci. and Engring., 1996-97; mem. com. on def. space tech. Air Force Studies Bd., 1989-93, com. on optical sci. and engring, 1996-97, Hubble Telescope recovery panel, 1990; bd. dirs. Precision Optics Corp. Editor: Applied Optics and Optical Engineering, Vol. 7, 1980, Vol. 8, 1981, Vol. 9, 1983, Vol. 10, 1987, Vol. 11, 1992, Art and Science of Optical Design, 1997; editor Engring. and Lab. Notes, 1995—. Fellow Optical Soc. Am. (pres. 1985, mem. engring. coun. 1989-91), Soc. Photo-Optical Instrumentation Engrs. (pres. 1979-80, recipient Goddard award 1982, Gold medal, 1996); mem. NAE, Tucson Soaring Club (past pres.), Sigma Xi. Home: 7040 E Taos Pl Tucson AZ 85715-3344 Office: U Ariz Optical Scis Ctr Tucson AZ 85721

SHANNON, THOMAS FREDERIC, German language educator; b. Cambridge, Mass., Mar. 16, 1948; m. Christine D. Höner. BA in German summa cum laude, Boston Coll., 1969; MA in German Lit., SUNY, Albany, 1973; MA in Theoretical Linguistics, Ind. U., 1975, PhD in Germanic Linguistics, 1982. Instr. in German Boston Coll., 1969-70; teaching fellow in German SUNY, Albany, 1971-73; univ. fellow Ind. U., Bloomington, 1973-74, assoc. instr., 1974-76, 79-80; acting asst. prof. in Germanic linguistics U. Calif., Berkeley, 1980-82, asst. prof., 1982-87, assoc. prof., 1987-94, prof., 1994—, dir. lang. lab., 1989-92, assoc. dir. Berkeley Lang. Ctr., 1994-95; co-organizer Berkeley Confs. on Dutch Lang. and Lit., 1987, 89, 91, 93, 95, 97; econs. presenter and spkr. in field. Contbr. articles to profl. jours. With USAR, 1970-76. Grantee Fulbright Found., 1976-78, U. Calif. Berkeley, 1983-84, 94-95, ACLS, 1987, Internat. Assn. Netherlandic Studies, 1988, 91, 94, 97, German Acad. Exch. Svc., summer 1996; NDEA fellow, 1969; Fulbright rsch./lectr. grantee Rijksuniversiteit Groningen, Netherlands, 1992-93;

Inst. fuer deutsche Sprache summer rsch. grantee, Mannheim, Germany, 1997. Mem. MLA (exec. com. discussion group in Germanic philology 1989-94, discussion group for Netherlandic Studies 1995—, divsn. on lang. change 1995—), Am. Assn. Netherlandic Studies (exec. com. 1988—, editor newsletter 1989-95, series editor publs. 1994—), Am. Assn. Tchrs. German, Internat. Assn. Netherlandic Studies, Internat. Assn. Germanstik, Internat. Soc. Hist. Linguistics, Linguistic Soc. Am., Netherlands Am. U. League, Pacific Ancient & Modern Lang. Assn., European Linguistic Soc., Soc. Germanic Philology (v.p. 1991-92, 95—), Interna. Cognitive Linguistics Soc., Alpha Sigma Nu. Home: 770 Rose Dr Benicia CA 94510-3709 Office: U Calif Dept German 5317 Dwinelle Hall Berkeley CA 94720-3243

SHANNONHOUSE, SANDRA LYNNE RIDDELL, sculptor; b. Petaluma, Calif., May 19, 1942; d. Robert Andreas and Ruth Hester (Soroker) Riddell; m. Robert Carston Arneson, May 19, 1973 (dec. Nov. 1992); 1 child, Tenaya Alexa Riddell Arneson. BS, U. Calif., Davis, 1969, MFA, 1973. One-woman shows include Quay Gallery, San Francisco, 1975, 78, 80, Stephen Wirtz Gallery, San Francisco, 1982, 84, 86, 89, 91, City Gallery, Sacramento, 1986, John Natsoulas Gallery, Davis, 1992; exhibited in group shows at San Francisco Mus. Art, 1973-74, Seattle Art Mus., 1973-74, Phoenix Art Mus., 1980-82, Renwick Gallery, Smithsonian Inst., 1980-82, Crocker Art Mus., Sacramento, 1989, Sonja Henie-Niels Onstad Mus., Oslo, Norway, 1990, Muckenthaler Cultural Ctr., Fullerton, Calif., 1991, Frumkin/Adams Gallery, N.Y.C., 1991, Palo Alto (Calif.) Cultural Ctr., 1993, 95-96, Oakland Mus., Calif., 1994, Galleria de Arte and the Ctr. for the Book Arts, Sao Paulo, Brazil, 1994; represented in pvt. collections. Office: Studio Shannonhouse 430 1st St Benicia CA 94510

SHANOR, CLARENCE RICHARD, clergyman; b. Butler, Pa., Dec. 26, 1924; s. Paul L. and Marion (McCandless) S.; B.A., Allegheny Coll., 1948; S.T.B., Boston U., 1951, Ph.D., 1958; m. Anna Lou Watts, June 23, 1948; 1 son, Richard Watts. Ordained to ministry Methodist Ch., 1950; pastor Meth. Ch., South Hamilton, Mass., 1951-54; research asso. Union Coll., Schenectady, 1954-55; prof. Christian edn. Nat. Coll., Kansas City, Mo., 1956-58; asso. minister First United Meth. Ch., St. Petersburg, Fla., 1958-61, First United Meth. Ch., Fullerton, Calif., 1961-66; coord. Metro dept. San Diego dist. United Meth. Union, San Diego, 1966-87, ret., 1987; pres. Human Svcs. Corp., 1972-77. Treas. San Diego County Ecumenical Conf., 1970-71, pres., 1975-77; chmn. Coalition Urban Ministries, 1970-71, Cultural and Religious Task Force Rancho San Diego, 1970-74; chmn. western jurisdiction Urban Network United Meth. Ch., 1978. Chmn. San Diego Citizens Com. Against Hunger, 1969-72; bd. dirs. Interfaith Housing Found., chmn., 1979, pres. 1988—; v.p. North County Interfaith Coun., 1987—; mem. Gaslamp Quarter Project Area Com., San Diego, 1978, mem. coun., 1980-84; chmn. bd. Horton House Corp., 1978; mem. Mayor's Task Force on the Homeless, 1983-84; chmn. Downtown Coordinating Coun., 1983-84; mem. regional Task Force on Homeless, 1986-87; vice-chmn. Community Congress, 1987, ret., 1987; bd. dirs. North County Interfaith Coun., 1987-92, Redwood Town Ct., 1995, v.p. 1996; pres., bd. dirs. North County Housing Found., 1987-96. Recipient San Diego Inst. for Creativity award, 1969, Boss of Yr. award Am. Bus. Women's Assn., 1972, Christian Unity award Diocesan Ecumenical Commn., 1984, Congl. Disting. Svc. award, 1984, Helen Beardsley Human Rights award, 1986, Mayor O'Connor's Seahorse award 1989, Ecumenical Conf. award San Diego County, 1991, Vol. Extraordinaire award No. County Interfaith Coun., 1993. Home: 1636 Desert Gln Escondido CA 92026-1849

SHANSTROM, JACK D., federal judge; b. Hewitt, Minn., Nov. 30, 1932; s. Harold A. and Willian (Wendorf) S.; m. June 22, 1957; children: Scott S., Susan K. BA in Law, U. Mont., 1956, BS in Bus., 1957, LLB, 1957. Atty. Park County, Livingston, Mont., 1960-65; judge 6th Jud. Dist. Livingston, 1965-82; U.S. magistrate Billings, Mont., 1983-90, U.S. Dist. judge, 1990—. Capt. USAF, 1957-60. Office: US Dist Ct Federal Bldg 316 N 26th St Rm 5405 Billings MT 59101-0985*

SHAPERO, HARRIS JOEL, pediatrician; b. Winona, Minn., Nov. 22, 1930; s. Charles and Minnie Sara (Ehrlichman) S.; m. Byong Soon Yu, Nov. 6, 1983; children by previous marriage: Laura, Bradley, James, Charles. AA, UCLA, 1953; BS, Northwestern U., 1954, MD, 1957. Diplomate and cert. specialist occupational medicine Am. Bd. Preventive Medicine; qualified med. evaluator, Indsl. Med. Coun.; ind. med. examiner, Calif.; cert. aviation medicine FAA. Intern, L.A. County Harbor Gen. Hosp., 1957-58, resident in pediatrics, 1958-60, staff physician, 1960-64; attending physician Perceptually Handicapped Children's Clinic, 1960-63; disease control officer for tuberculosis, L.A. County Health Dept., 1962-64; pvt. practice medicine specializing in pediatrics and occupational medicine, Cypress, Calif., 1965-85; pediatric cons. L.A. Health Dept., 1983-85, disease control officer sexually transmitted diseases, 1968-78; emergency room dir. AMI, Anaheim, Calif., 1968-85; mem. med. staff Anaheim Gen. Hosp., Beach Cmty. Hosp., Norwalk Cmty. Hosp.; courtesy staff Palm Harbor Gen. Hosp., Bellflower City Hosp.; pediatric staff Hosp. de General, Ensenada, Mex., 1978—; primary care clinician Sacramento County Health, 1987-88; pvt. practice medico-legal evaluation, 1986-92; founder Calif. Legal Evaluation Med. Group; apptd. med. examiner in preventive and occupational medicine State of Calif. Dept. of Indsl. Rels., 1989; health care provider, advisor City of Anaheim, City of Buena Park, City of Cypress, City of Garden Grove, Cypress Sch. Dist., Magnolia Sch. Dist., Savanna Sch. Dist., Anaheim Unified Sch. Dist., Orange County Dept. Edn.; pediatric and tuberculosis cons. numerous other orgns.; FAA med. examiner, founder Pan Am. Childrens Mission. Author: The Silent Epidemic, 1979. Named Headliner in Medicine Orange County Press Club, 1978. Fellow Am. Coll. Preventive Medicine; mem. L.A. County Med. Assn., L.A. County Indsl. Med. Assn., Am. Pub. Health Assn., Mex.-Am. Border Health Assn. Republican. Jewish. Avocations: antique books and manuscripts, photography, graphics, beekeeper. Home: PO Box 228 Wilton CA 95693-0228 Office: MedClinics 3160 Folsom Blvd Sacramento CA 95816-5219

SHAPIRO, ALISON ESTHER, software engineer; b. Newton, Mass., Dec. 6, 1963; d. Murray L. and Dorothy E. (Nebergall) S. BS in Math., U. Chgo., 1984, MS in Computer Sci., 1985; postgrad., U. Denver, 1994. Engr. Carnegie Group, Inc., Pitts., 1985-89, sr. engr., 1989-92; sr. engr. Carnegie Group, Inc., Denver, 1992-94, prin. knowledge engr., 1994—; presenter 4th Re-engring. Forum, 1994. Patentee in field. Bd. dirs Tues. Night Folk Dancers, Pitts., 1991-92. Mem. IEEE Computer Soc., Assn. for Computing Machinery (treas. Pitts. chpt. 1991-92), Am. Assn. Artificial Intelligence, Sierra Club (outing leader 1991-92, mem. steering com. So. Rockies ecosystem project 1996). Office: Carnegie Group Inc 707 17th St Ste 2100 Denver CO 80202-3404

SHAPIRO, DAVID, newspaper editor; b. Culver City, Calif., Sept. 1, 1948; m. Maggie Shapiro; children: Treena, Jared. BA in Am. History, U. Hawaii. Editorial asst. Star-Bulletin, Hilo, Hawaii, 1968-87; mng. editor Star-Bulletin, Honolulu, 1987—. Office: Star Bulletin 605 Kapiolani Blvd Honolulu HI 96802

SHAPIRO, LARRY JAY, pediatrician, scientist, educator; b. Chgo., July 6, 1946; s. Philip and Phyllis (Krause) S.; m. Carol-Ann Uetake; children: Jennifer, Jessica, Brian. A.B., Washington U., St. Louis, 1968, M.D., 1971. Diplomate Am. Bd. Pediatrics, Am. Bd. Med. Examiners, Am. Bd. Med. Genetics. Intern St. Louis Children's Hosp., 1971-72, resident, 1971-73; research assoc. NIH, Bethesda, Md., 1973-75; asst. prof. Sch. Medicine, UCLA, 1975-79, assoc. prof., 1979-83, prof. pediatrics and biol. chemistry, 1983-91; investigator Howard Hughes Med. Inst., 1987-91; prof., chmn. dept. pediat. U. Calif.-San Francisco Sch. Medicine, 1991—, chief pediat. svcs. U. Calif. San Francisco Med. Ctr., 1991—. Contbr. numerous articles to profl. publs. Served to lt. comdr. USPHS, 1973-75. Fellow AAAS, Am. Acad. Pediatrics (E. Mead Johnson award in rsch. 1982); mem. Inst. Medicine-NAS, Soc. Pediatric Rsch. (coun. 1984-87, pres. 1991-92), Western Soc. for Pediatric Rsch. (coun. 1983-87, Ross award in rsch. 1981, pres. 1989-90), Soc. for Inherited Metabolic Disease (coun. 1983-88, pres. 1986-87), Assn. Am. Physicians, Am. Soc. Human Genetics (council 1985-88, pres. elect 1995, pres. 1997), Am. Soc. Clin. Investigation, Am. Pediatric Soc., Am. Acad. Arts & Scis. Office: U Calif Third Ave & Parnassus San Francisco CA 94143

SHAPIRO, LEONARD, immunologist, allergist; b. Phila., Apr. 11, 1941; s. Nathan and Lottie (Ginsberg) S.; m. Linda Carol Adelman, June, 1964 (div. 1986); children: Lauren, Jonathan, Brett; m. Janet Susan Rubenstein, Nov. 7, 1987; 1 child, Eliana. AB, Temple U., 1963, MD, 1967. Diplomate Am. Bd. Allergy and Immunology, Am. Bd. Pediat. Intern Pa. Hosp., Phila., 1967-68; resident Children's Hosp., Phila., 1968-70; pvt. practice Reno, 1974—; fellow Nat. Jewish Hosp./Univ. Colo. Med. Sch., 1972-74; assoc. clin. prof. pediat. U. Nev. Med. Sch., 1974—; cons. VA Hosp., Reno, 1974—. Pres. Temple Emanu El, Reno, 1980, 81, 93, Jewish Cmty. Coun. No. Nev., 1982, 83. Major USAF, 1970-72. Recipient Maimonides award State of Israel, 1982. Fellow Am. Acad. Pediat., Am. Coll. Allergy Asthma Immunology, Am. Acad. Allergy Astmha Immunology; mem. Alpha Omega Alpha. Republican. Jewish. Office: Allergy Asthma Assocs 2005 Silverada Blvd Ste 250 Reno NV 89512-2057

SHAPIRO, MARGARET GOODWIN, astronomy educator; b. Maxton, N.C., Sept. 3, 1944; d. Harold and Marion Edna (Goodwin) S. BA, San Francisco State U., 1967, MA, 1971; Cert. Achievement, Simpson Coll., Modesto, Calif., 1976. C.C. lifetime credential, Calif. Instr. astronomy, phys. sci. San Francisco State U., 1968-71, 84; instr. astronomy, phy. sci. Modesto Jr. Coll., 1971-73; instr. geology Merritt Coll., Oakland, Calif., 1977; instr. astronomy Chabot Coll., Hayward, Calif., 1981-83, Los Medanos Coll., Pittsburg, Calif., 1982-84; instr. astronomy, phys. sci., physics Ohlone Coll., Fremont, Calif., 1982-91; instr. physics Calif. State U., Hayward, 1986; instr. astronomy, phys. sci. West Valley Coll., Saratoga, Calif., 1989-90; instr. astronomy City Coll. San Francisco, 1991—; advisor to astronomy club S.T.A.R.S., City Coll. San Francisco, 1994, advisor to bible study, 1995; paraprofl. San Francisco City Schs., 1970-71; instr. Coll. for Kids, Ohlone, Chabot colls., Fremont and Hayward, 1982-83, 85. Author 14 planetarium shows, 1982-86. Adv. Campus Girl Scouts, 1997. Mem. Astron. Soc. Pacific, San Francisco Amateur Astronomers (sec. 1960, editor monthly bull. 1962), Pacific Planetarium Assn., 1981-85. Democrat. Jewish. Office: City Coll San Francisco 50 Phelan Ave San Francisco CA 94112

SHAPIRO, RICHARD STANLEY, physician; b. Moline, Ill., June 11, 1925; s. Herbert and Esther Dian (Grant) S.; BS, St. Ambrose Coll., 1947; BS in Pharmacy, U. Iowa, 1951, MS in Preventive Medicine and Environ. Health, 1951, M.D., 1957; m. Arlene Blum, June 12, 1949; children: Michele Pamela, Bruce Grant, Gary Lawrence; m. Merry Lou Cook, Oct. 11, 1971. Pharmacist, Rock Island, Ill., 1951-53; research asst. U. Iowa Coll. Medicine, Iowa City, 1950-51, 53-57; practice medicine specializing in allergy, Beverly Hills, Calif., 1958-62, Lynwood, Calif., 1962—; attending physician Good Hope Found. Allergy Clinic, Los Angeles, 1958-62, Cedars of Lebanon Hosp., Hollywood, Calif., 1959-68, U. So. Calif.-Los Angeles County Med. Center, 1962—; physician St. Francis Hosp., Lynwood, 1962—; assoc. clin. prof. medicine U. So. Calif., 1978-84, emeritus, 1984—. Bd. dirs. Westside Jewish Community Center, 1961-65, Camp JCA, 1964-65. Served with USNR, 1943-45; PTO. Diplomate Am. Bd. Allergy and Immunology. Fellow Am. Geriatric Soc., Am. Coll. Allergy, Am. Assn. Clin. Immunology and Allergy; mem. Am. Soc. Tropical Medicine and Hygiene, Am. Acad. Allergy, Los Angeles Allergy Soc., AMA, Calif., Los Angeles County med. assns., West Coast Allergy Soc., AAAS, Am., Calif. socs. internal medicine, Calif. Soc. Allergy, Am. Heart Assn., Sierra Club, Sigma Xi. Jewish. Mason; mem. B'nai B'rith. Contbr. articles to profl. jours. Office: 8301 Florence Ave Ste 104 Downey CA 90240-3946

SHAPIRO, STEPHEN GEORGE, screenwriter, photographer; b. Bridgeton, N.J., Dec. 26, 1944; s. David Franklin Shapiro and Betty (Snyder) Rees; m. Patricia Jane Tiernan-Cox, Oct. 12, 1990. Student, Monterey (Calif.) Inst., 1967-68; BA in French, Utah State U., 1968; postgrad., UCLA, 1967-69. Cert. d'assuidité U. Grenoble, France, 1965; cert. of achievement Monterey (Calif.) Peninsula Coll., 1996. Photojournalist USNR, 1984-93; freelance screenwriter Pebble Beach, Calif., 1967—; freelance photographer Carmel, Calif., 1989—. Bd. mem. Monterey County Film Festival, 1987-88, Monterey Inst. Internat. Studies Alumni Assn., 1984-85; organizer, charter pres. Jr. United Nations, Palo Alto/Hillsborough, Calif., 1958. Recipient Squaw Valley (Calif.) Writing scholarship, 1979, continuing edn. grant Calif. State Dept. Rehab., Monterey, 1995-96. Democrat. Episcopal. Office: MM Designs PO Box 4391 Carmel CA 93921

SHAPIRO, SUMNER LEROY, psychoanalyst; b. Boston, May 15, 1926; s. Harry Alexander and Eva (Goldberg) S.; m. widowered; children: Paul Steven, Carolyne Amy, Leslie Susan. AB, Harvard U., 1946, MA, 1947; MD, Boston U., 1953. Intern New Eng. Ctr. Hosp., 1955-56; resident Worcester State Hosp., 1958-60, 63-65; with L.A. Psychoanalytic Inst., 1965—; psychoanalyst pvt. practice, L.A., 1967—; various teaching positions, UCLA. Author: Moment of Insight, 1969, Beyond Insight, 1973, Beyond Case Histories, 1984, Well-Kept Secrets, 1993, A Psychoanalytic Cookbook: Recipes to Season and Preserve Relationships, 1996. Home and Office: 16780 Oak View Dr Encino CA 91436-3238

SHAPIRO, YANINA, psychology educator; b. Moscow, Russia, Aug. 2, 1948; came to the U.S., 1975; p. Boris Yakoulevich and Irina Dmitrievna (Churikova) S. BS, Moscow Bauman U., MS in Mech. Engring.; EdM in Human Devel., Harvard U., 1986, EdD in Human Devel. and Psychology, 1991; BA in English, Coll. Fgn. Langs., Moscow; Cert. of German Studies, Vienna U., postgrad., 1981-82. Editor Inst. Info., Moscow, 1975, Gulf Pub. Co., Houston, 1975-76; engr. Ford Motor Co., Dearborn, Mich., 1976-79, Dowland Bach Co., Anchorage, Alaska, 1979; tech. cons. Exxon Rsch. and Engring., N.Y.C., 1980-81; engring. instr. dept. engring. Tufts U., Mass., 1982-83; engr. Dept. Transp., Cambridge, Mass., 1983-87; asst. prof. psychology St. Francis Coll., Loretto, Pa., 1992-93; asst. prof. psychology Ea. Oreg. State Coll., La Grande, 1993-94, rschr., writer, 1994-96; psychologist Fairview Tng. Ctr., Salem, Oreg., 1996—. Contbr. articles to profl. jours. Mem. AAAS, APA, Am. Psychol. Soc., Soc. for Neurosci. Democrat.

SHARBAUGH, W(ILLIAM) JAMES, plastics engineer, consultant; b. Pitts., Apr. 13, 1914; s. Oliver Michael and Sarah Marie (Wingenroth) S.; m. Eileen Carey, May 14, 1938; children: William James Jr., Eileen Sharbaugh Pinkerton, Susan Sharbaugh Coté. BS in Engring., Carnegie Inst. Tech., 1935. Project engr. MSA Corp., Pitts., 1935-46; founder, gen. mgr. ENPRO, Inc., St. Louis, 1947-62; mgr. plastics div. Vulcan Rubber and Plastic, Morrisville, Pa., 1962-67; v.p. engring. and mfg. FESCO div. Celanese, Pitts., 1967-72; exec. v.p. plastics div. Lenox, Inc., St. Louis, 1970-72; div. mgr. Crown Zellerbach, Inc., San Francisco, 1972-77; pres. Plastics Assocs., Cons., Newport Beach, Calif., 1977—; founder ISOBET USA, Inc., Newport Beach; dir. devel. and tech. Crown Zellerbach, Inc.; pres. Western Plastics Pioneers; cons. nat. and internat. plastics cos.; pres. Plastics Assics., Inc., 1996—. Author tech. papers, reports. Mem. Soc. of Plastics Engrs. (first pres. Pitts. sect.), Soc. Plastics Industry (profl. witness, forensics of plastic product failures). Republican. Roman Catholic. Home: 1516 Seacrest Dr Corona Del Mar CA 92625-1230 Office: Plastics Assocs Inc 4400 Macarthur Blvd Ste 500 Newport Beach CA 92660-2036

SHARIFF, ASGHAR J., geologist; b. Haft Kel, Iran, July 28, 1941; came to U.S., 1964, naturalized, 1978; s. Abdulwahab and Sakineh (Kamiab) S.; m. Kay L. Schoenwald, Aug. 9, 1969; 1 child, Shaun. B.Sc., Calif. State U., Northridge, 1971, M.Sc., 1983. Cert. profl. geologist, Va., Wyo. Petroleum geologist Iranian Oil Exploration and Producing Co., Ahwaz, 1971-74; geol. cons. D.R.L., Inc., Bakersfield, Calif., 1974-76, Strata-log, Inc., 1976-79, Energy Log, Inc., Sacramento, 1979-80; geologist U.S. Dept. Energy, Washington, 1980-81, Bur. Land Mgmt. Dept. Interior, Washington, 1981-89, asst. dist. mgr., Rawlins, Wyo., 1989-93, chief reservoir mgmt. team, Casper, Wyo., 1993—. Contbr. articles to profl. jours. Mem. Am. Assn. Petroleum Geologists, Soc. Profl. Well Log Analysts, Soc. Petroleum Engrs.

SHARKEY, RICHARD DAVID, product designer, architect, musician; b. Columbus, Ohio, May 8, 1957; s. John David and Beatrice Diane (Ziesler) S.; m. Melissa Duke Smith, Dec. 21, 1980 (div. 1995); children: Flax Allistair Linden, Ambrosia Rose Ashley. Student, U. No. Colo., 1975-77, Emporia State U., 1977-78, U. Denver, 1978-81. Music tchr., pvt. studio, piano, cello, composition theory Evergreen, Colo., 1978-82; pvt. bus., period residential restoration Sharkey and Assocs., Evergreen and Denver, 1978-86; stair apprentice Denver Stair Co., 1985-86; stair master Heidelberg Stair Co., Evergreen, 1986; pvt. bus., designer period staircases, millwork O'Searcaigh, Ltd., Evergreen and Denver, 1986-90; with Archtl. Artworks, Englewood, Colo., 1993-95, Form & Structure Ltd., Denver, 1995-96; prin. Adobe Homes, Denver, 1996—; cons. archtl. product design and devel. Heidelberg Stair, Evergreen, Frank's Woodworking, Lyons, Colo., Pierce Segerberg & Spaeh Architects, Vail, Colo., Charles Cunnifree & Assoc., Apsen, Colo., numerous manufacturers, contractor, architecture, design firms, 1987—; cons. archtl. design period features. Composer numerous piano compositions, 1972—; designer, inventor numerous archtl. products, machines, tools and accessories. Recipient scholarship Outward Bound Colo., Optimist Club of Evergreen, 1973, music grant, U. No. Colo., Greeley, 1975-76, Emporia (Kans.) U., 1977; scholar U. No. Colo., 1976. Mem. Internat. Soc. Archtl. Artisans (pres., founder 1988—), Denver Cherry Creek Club (charter mem.), Rotary. Mem. Christian Science Ch. Home and Office: 3975 Zenobia St Denver CO 80212

SHARMA, ARJUN DUTTA, cardiologist; b. Bombay, June 2, 1953; came to U.S., 1981; s. Hari D. and Gudrun (Axelsson) S.; m. Carolyn D. Burleigh, May 9, 1981; children: Allira, Eric, Harisson. BSc, U. Waterloo, Ont., Can., 1972; MD, U. Toronto, Ont., 1976. Intern Toronto Gen. Hosp., 1976-77, resident in medicine, 1978-80; resident in medicine St. Michael's Hosp., Toronto, 1980-81; residency medicine Toronto Gen. Hosp., 1977-78; Rsch. assoc. Washington U., St. Louis, 1981-83; asst. prof. pharmacy and toxicology U. Western Ont., London, 1985-89, asst. prof. medicine, 1983-89, assoc. prof. medicine, 1989-90; dir. interventional electrophysiology Sutter Meml. Hosp., Sacramento, 1990-95; abstract reviewer, faculty of ann. sci. sessions N.Am. Soc. for Pacing and Electrophysiology, 1993-94; assoc. clin. prof. U. Calif., Davis, 1990—; cons. Medtronic Inc., Mpls., 1985—, Telectronics Pacing Sys., Inc., 1990-94; mem. rsch. com. Sutter Inst. Med. Rsch., 1991—; mem. exec. com. Sutter Heart Inst., 1992; program dir. Update in Tachyarhythmia Mgmt., Palm Springs, 1996, Pacing Defibrillation and Electrophysiology, Squaw Valley, 1997. Reviewer profl. jours., including Circulation, Am. Jour. Cardiology; contbr. articles to profl. publs. Mem. coun. for basic sci. Am. Heart Assn., chmn. ann. sci. session, 1989. Recipient John Melady award, 1972, Dr. C.S. Wainwright award, 1973-75, Rsch. prize Toronto Gen. Hosp., 1979, 80, Ont. Career Scientist award Ont. Ministry of Health, 1983-89; Med. Rsch. Coun. Can. fellow, 1981-83. Fellow ACP, Am. Coll. Cardiology; mem. Am. Fedn. Clin. Rsch., Canadian Cardiovasc. Soc., N.Y. Acad. Scis., Sacramento Eldorado Med. Soc. Office: 3941 J St Ste 260 Sacramento CA 95819-3633

SHARMA, BRAHAMA D., chemistry educator; b. Sampla, Punjab, India, June 5, 1931; naturalized Am. citizen; s. Des Raj and Kesara Devi (Pathak) S.; m. Millicent M. Hewitt, Dec. 22, 1956 (div. 1996); children: Nalanda V. Sharma Bowman, Renuka D. BS with honors, U. Delhi, India, 1949, MS, 1951; PhD, U. So. Calif., 1961. Chemist Govt. Opium Factory, Ghazipur, India, 1951-52; lab. assoc., sci. asst. Nat. Chem. Lab., Poona, India, 1952-55; lab. assoc. U. So. Calif., L.A., 1955-61; research fellow Calif. Inst. Tech., Pasadena, 1961-65; asst. prof. chemistry U. Nev., Reno, 1963-64, Oreg. State U., Corvallis, 1965-70; asst. prof. chemistry Calif. State U., Northridge, 1973-75, assoc. prof., 1975-76; prof. L.A. Pierce Coll., Woodland Hills, Calif., 1976-96; part-time assoc. prof. chemistry Calif. State U., L.A., 1973-85, prof., 1985—; vis. assoc. Calif. Inst. Tech., 1979, 82; pres. L.A. Pierce Coll. Senate, 1981-82, chmn. profl. and acad. stds., 1989-92. Contbr. articles to profl. jours. Grantee E.I. duPont de Nemours, L.A., 1961, NSF, 1967-69. Mem. Royal Soc. Chemistry (chartered chemist), Am. Inst. Parliamentarians (sec., adminstr., lt. gov. region VII, exec. lt. gov.), Nat. Assn. Parliamentarians, Calif. Assn. Parliamentarians (pub. rels. chmn., statewide edn. chmn. So. area, pres. Calif. Sigma unit). Office: LA Pierce Coll Chem Dept Woodland Hills CA 91371

SHARMAN, WILLIAM, professional basketball team executive; b. Abilene, Tex., May 25, 1926; m. Joyce Sharman; children by previous marriage: Jerry, Nancy, Janice, Tom. Student, U. So. Calif. Basketball player Washington Capitols, 1950-51, Boston Celtics, 1951-61; coach Los Angeles/Utah Stars, 1968-71; coach Los Angeles Lakers, 1971-76, gen. mgr., 1976-82, pres., 1982-88, spl. cons., 1991—. Author: Sharman on Basketball Shooting, 1965. Named to Nat. Basketball Assn. All Star First Team, 1956-59, 2d Team, 1953, 55, 60, All League Team, 7 times; named Coach of Year Nat. Basketball Assn., 1972, Naismith Basketball Hall of Fame, 1976. Home: 27996 Palos Verdes Dr E Rancho Palos Verdes CA 90275 Office: LA Lakers PO Box 10 3900 W Manchester Blvd Inglewood CA 90306

SHARON, TIMOTHY MICHAEL, physicist; b. Portsmouth, Va., Aug. 21, 1948; s. Lester Clark and Ruth May (Banister) S.; student Santa Ana Coll., 1966-68; B.A., U. Calif.-Irvine 1970, M.A., 1972, Ph.D., 1976; m. Carla Deon Colley, Dec. 17, 1977. Jr. specialist solid state theory U. Calif.-Irvine, 1976, research asst. radiation physics Med. Center and Sch. Medicine, 1976-77, cons. to attending staff Research and Edn. Found., 1976-77; mktg. physicist Varian Assos., Irvine, 1977-78; prin. engr., program mgr. Spectra Research Systems, Newport Beach, Calif., 1977-82; v.p. Brewer-Sharon Corp., Newport Beach, 1981-86, Micor Instruments, Inc., Irvine, Calif., 1983-86; pres., chief exec. officer Medelec Instruments Co., Inc., Newport Beach, 1986-88; pres. Pacific Crest Enterprises, El Toro, Calif., 1988-91; pres., chief exec officer Novus Group NA, El Toro, Calif., 1991-96; pres. Instafil, Irvine, 1995—; adj. faculty physics and engring. Columbia Pacific U., San Rafael, Calif., 1981-87; dean Sch. Engring., Newport U., Newport Beach, Calif., 1983-87; mem. adv. panel on pub. Am. Inst. Physics, 1974-75. Brython P. Davis univ. fellow, 1973-74. Mem. AAAS, Am. Phys. Soc., Brit. Interplanetary Soc. (asso. fellow), Am. Assn. Physicists in Medicine, IEEE, Assn. Advancement Med. Instrumentation, Smithsonian Instn., Am. Film Inst., Nat. Hist. Soc., Nat. Geog. Soc., Festival of Arts Laguna Beach, Mensa, Intertel, Sigma Pi Sigma, Phi Theta Kappa, Alpha Gamma Sigma. Clubs: Acad. Magical Arts, Club 33. Contbr. articles to profl. jours.

SHARP, GEORGE LAWRENCE, counselor; b. Phila., Jan. 7, 1939; s. George Holly and Dorothy Marie (Brennan) S.; m. Jan Carol Lancaster, Oct. 3, 1973; 1 child, Jonathan Lawrence. AA, Atlantic C.C., Mays Landing, N.J., 1970; BA, Univ. Miami, 1972; MA, N.M. State Univ., 1975, PhD, 1978. Lic. profl. counselor, N.M. Counseling Therapy Bd. Instr. grad. sch. counseling, ednl. psychology N.M. State Univ., Las Cruces, 1979-80; asst. coord. devel. edn. Doña Ana Br. C.C. N.M. State Univ., Las Cruces, 1980-89, coord. ednl. success and disabled student svcs., 1989-94, coord. counseling and disabled student svcs., 1994—; mem. tech. coll. preparatory counselors com. County Consortium, N.M., 1993—. Mem. Casa Arriba Respite Care, Las Cruces, 1986—; chairperson gen. adv. bd. N.M. Divsn. Vocat. Rehab., 1984-87. Recipient Handicapped Employee of Yr. award Gov.'s Com., Las Cruces, 1976, Disting. Svc. award N.M. Coun. Exceptional Children, 1985, U.S. Sec. Edn. award, 1985, 92, Disting. Svc. award N.M. Protection and Advocacy Project, 1994. Mem. N.M. Vocat. Assn. (dir. 1985, Educator of Yr. 1988, 92, Am. Counseling Assn., Am. Coll. Counseling Assn., Am. Coll. Personnel Assn., Am. Vocat. Assn.,Phi Delta Kappa, Psi Chi, Epsilon Tau Lambda, Delta Theta Mu. Office: Dona Ana Br Cmty Coll NM State Univ 3400 S Espina St Las Cruces NM 88001

SHARP, JEAN HARRIET, retired physician and surgeon, antique dealer; b. Alameda, Calif., Sept. 30, 1923; d. Kenneth and Ann C. (Kelsey) Smith; m. Jack Kenton Sharp, May 28, 1949; children: David, Kathleen Lee. AA, U. Calif., Berkeley, 1942, BS, 1944, grad. in Nursing, 1944; grad. in Pub. Health Nursing, U. Calif., San Francisco, 1946; 1st degree in medicine, U. Heidelberg, Germany, 1957; MD, Johannes Gutenberg U., Mainz, Germany, 1961. RN, Calif. Physician Herrick Hosp., Berkeley, 1961-63; pvt. practice, Alameda, 1963-95; ret., 1995. With U.S. Army, WWII; ETO. Fellow Am. Acad. Family Practice; mem. Alameda Cancer League, Am. Legion (post comdr.), Lioness (pres.). Republican. Roman Catholic. Home: 2034 Santa Clara Ave Alameda CA 94501-2721

SHARP, LAURENCE NEWTON, diagnostic company executive; b. Providence, Dec. 4, 1932; s. Henry Freeman and Harriet Beth (Smira) S.; m. Nancy Ann Adle Sharp, June 8, 1963; 1 child, Theodore Douglas Sharp. BA, Boston U., 1954; MA, U. Kans., 1956. Salesman VW&R, Braun Div., Phoenix, 1956-59; regional mgr. VW&R, Braun Div., Tucson, 1959-63; clin. sales mgr. VW&R, Braun Div., L.A., 1963-66; mktg. mgr. B-D Labs., Cockeysville, Md., 1966-69; v.p. sales and mktg. Internat. Equipment Co., Needham Heights, Mass., 1969-70; gen. sales mgr. Micromedic Sys., Phila., 1970-74; gen. mgr. Micromedic Sys., Toronto, Can., 1974-84; dir. internat. sales ICN Biomedical, Costa Mesa, Calif., 1985-89, v.p. sales Asia/

Pacific, 1989-94; mng. dir. Australia ICN Biomedical, Costa Mesa, 1994—; pres. Novercal Consulting, Toronto, Can., 1981-83. Mem. Young Reps., Phoenix, 1956-59. Mem. Am. Air Mail Soc. Republican. Methodist. Office: ICN Biomedicals 3300 Hyland Ave Costa Mesa CA 92626-1503

SHARP, PAMELA ANN, quality assurance engineer; b. Pullman, Wash., Dec. 20, 1950; d. Robert Melvin and Vivian Lois (Steele) Olson; m. David William Sharp, June 16, 1973; children: Jaime David, Erik Scott. Student, Big Bend C.C., Moses Lake, Wash., 1969-70; BS in Zoology, Wash. State U., 1973; postgrad., Portland State U., 1976. Lab. technician The Carter Mining Co., Gillette, Wyo., 1977-79, lab. supr., 1979-80, quality control supr., 1980-81, engring. analyst, 1982-88; engr. quality control The Carter Mining Co., Gillette, 1988-89; owner Sharp Consulting, Gillette, 1989—, Landscape Design, 1993—; leader auditor tng. ISO 9000; owner Prairie Skullpture; obedience dog tng. instr., 1990—. Supt. Campbell County Fair, Gillette, 1985-87. Mem. AIME, ASTM (proximate analysis chmn. 1985-95, chmn. on-line analysis com., apptd. U.S.A. expert on on-line analysis to ISO), Am. Water Ski Assn. (regular judge 1974-91, ea. regional water ski trick record 1975, 3d nat. trick title 1962, state champion in tricks Wash., Idaho, Mont. 1961-73, 2d 1987 Western region women's III tricks). Republican. Presbyterian. Office: Sharp Consulting 2406 Hillcrest Dr Gillette WY 82718-5641

SHARP, ROBERT LEE, aerospace engineering consultant, test pilot; b. Indpls., Ind., Jan. 18, 1925; s. Floyd Neal and Nancy L. (Collett) S.; m. Margaret Maxine Deputy, June 28, 1947; children: Richard, Roger, William. BS in Aeronautics Engring., Purdue U., 1950, student, 1950. Fighter pilot USAF & Ind. ANG., 1944-63; test pilot McDonnell Aircraft Corp., St. Louis, 1956-62; chief spacecraft engr. pilot McDonnell Douglas Corp., St. Louis, 1962-74; sr. group engr. BDM Corp., Albuquerque, 1975-81; cons. Albuquerque, 1981-84; aerospace systems mgr. Gen. Dynamics Corp., San Diego, 1984-87; pres. Sharp Aerospace Assocs., Albuquerque, 1987—. Designer Gemini & Skylab Spacecraft Crew Stations, 1962-74. Maj. USAF & ANG. Recipient various awards NASA, 1965-74. Mem. AIAA. Home and Office: Sharp Aerospace Assocs 12324 Eastridge Dr NE Albuquerque NM 87112-4605

SHARP, ROBERT PHILLIP, geology educator, researcher; b. Oxnard, Calif., June 24, 1911; s. Julian Hebner Sharp and Alice Sharp Darling; m. Jean Prescott Todd, Sept. 7, 1938; adopted children—Kristin Todd, Bruce Todd. B.S., Calif. Inst. Tech., Pasadena, 1934, M.S., 1935; M.A., Harvard U., Cambridge, Mass., 1936, Ph.D., 1938. Asst. prof. U. Ill., Urbana, 1938-43; prof. U. Minn., Mpls., 1946-47; prof. Calif. Inst. Tech., Pasadena, 1947-79, chmn., 1952-67, prof. emeritus, 1979—. Author: Glaciers, 1960, Field Guide-Southern California, 1972, Field Guide-Coastal Southern California, 1978, Living Ice-Understanding Glaciers and Glaciation, 1988, (with A.F. Glazner) Geology Under Foot in Southern California, 1993. Served to capt. USAF, 1943-46. Recipient Exceptional Sci. Achievement medal NASA, 1971, Nat. Medal Sci., 1989, Charles P. Daly medal Am. Geog. Soc., 1991; Robert P. Sharp professorship Calif. Inst. Tech., 1978. Fellow Geol. Soc. Am. (councillor, Kirk Bryan award 1964, Penrose medal 1977, G.K. Gilbert and Disting. Career award 1996), Am. Geophys. Union; hon. fellow Internat. Glaciological Soc.; mem. NAS. Republican. Home: 1901 Gibraltar Rd Santa Barbara CA 93105-2326 Office: Calif Inst Tech 1200 E California Blvd Pasadena CA 91125

SHARP, SHARON LEE, gerontology nurse; b. Beatrice, Nebr., Jan. 14, 1939; d. Clarence Alfred and Edna Clara (Grosshuesch) Wolters; m. Philip Butler, June 27, 1959 (div. 1964); m. Ted C. Sharp, Sept. 21, 1966 (div. 1988); children: Sheryl Butler, Philip Butler. Diploma, Lincoln Gen. Hosp., 1959. RN Nebr. Charge nurse Mary Lanning Meml. Hosp., Hastings, Nebr., 1960-61; asst. head nurse Ingleside State Hosp., Hastings, Nebr., 1961-62; charge nurse Rio Hondo Meml. Hosp., Downey, Calif., 1969-71, Santa Barbara (Calif.) Cottage Hosp., 1974-78; supr. Marlora Manor Convalescent Hosp., Long Beach, Calif., 1979-80; supr. Marlinda Nursing Home, Lynwood, Calif., 1982-84, dir. nursing, 1984-89; dir. nursing Ramona Care Ctr., El Monte, Calif., 1989-90, Oakview Convalescent Hosp., Tujunga, Calif., 1990-91, North Valley Nursing Ctr., Tujunga, Calif., 1992—; asst. dir. nursing Skyline Health Care Ctr. (Gran Care), L.A., 1993-94; resident assessment coord. Country Villa Rehab. Ctr., L.A., 1994-95; case mgr. Vitas Innovative Hospice Care, West Covina, Calif., 1996—; mem. adv. bd. Regional Occupational Program, Downey, 1985-86. Home: 2875 E Del Mar Blvd Pasadena CA 91107-4314

SHARPE, ROLAND LEONARD, engineering company executive, earthquake and structural engineering consultant; b. Shakopee, Minn., Dec. 18, 1923; s. Alfred Leonard and Ruth Helen (Carter) S.; m. Jane Esther Steele, Dec. 28, 1946; children: Douglas Rolfe, Deborah Lynn, Sheryl Anne. BS in Civil Engring., U. Mich., 1947, MSE, 1949. Registered civil engr. and structural engr., Calif. Designer, Cummins & Barnard, Inc., Ann Arbor, Mich., 1947-48; instr. engring. U. Mich., 1948-50; exec. v.p. John A. Blume & Assocs., engrs., San Francisco, 1950-73; chmn., founder Engring. Decision Analysis Co., Inc., Cupertino, 1974-87; cons. earthquake engr., 1987—; mng. dir. EDAC, GmBH, Frankfurt, Germany, 1974-82; dir. EDAC; pres. Calif. Devel. & Engring. Co., Inc., Las Vegas, Nev., 1973-81; mem. nat. earthquake hazard reduction program adv. com. overviewing Fed. Emergency Mgmt. Agy., U.S. Geol. Survey, NSF and Nat. Inst. Stds. and Tech., 1990-93. Author: (with J. Blume, E.G. Kost) Earthquake Engineering for Nuclear Facilities, 1971. Mem. Planning Commn., Palo Alto, 1955-60; mng. dir. Applied Tech. Coun., Palo Alto, 1973-83; dir. Earthquake Engring. Rsch. Inst., 1972-75, now mem.; project dir., editor Tentative Provisions for Devel. of Seismic Regulations for Buildings, 1978; tech. mgr., contbr., editor Data Processing Facilities: Guidelines for Earthquake Hazard Mitigation, 1987. Served with USMC, 1942-46. Author, co-author over 200 engring. papers and reports; author of chpts.: (with others) DOE Seismic Safety Manual, 1995, 96. Fellow ASCE (hon. mem. 1994, chmn. dynamic effects com., 1978-80, exec. com. structural div. 1980-84, 89-93, chmn. 1983, mgmt. group B 1989-93, Earnest E. Howard award 1994); mem. Japan Structural Cons. Assn. (hon. mem. 1992), Structural Engrs. Assn. Calif. (dir. 1971-73, chmn. seismology com. 1972-74), Structural Engrs. No. Calif. (dir. 1969-71, life mem.), Am. Concrete Inst. (life), Structural Engrs. World Congress (pres. 1995—). Recipient citation for contbn. to constrn. industry Engring. News Record, 1978-79, 86-87; chmn. U.S. Joint Com. on Earthquake Engring., 1982-88. Home: 10320 Rolly Rd Los Altos CA 94024-6520 Office: Sharpe Struct Engrs 10320 Rolly Rd Ste 1 Los Altos CA 94024-6520 *Personal philosophy: One's conduct should be beyond reproach both morally and ethically and I should serve each of my clients to the best of my ability.*

SHARPE, SHANNON, professional football player; b. Chgo., June 26, 1968. Student, Savannah State U. Tight end Denver Broncos, 1990—; player AFC Championship Game, 1991. Named to Pro Bowl Team, 1992, 93, Sporting News NFL All-Pro Team, 1993. Office: Denver Broncos 13655 Broncos Pkwy Englewood CO 80112-4150*

SHARPE, WENONAH FINCH, writer, educator, editor; b. Penticton, B.C., Can., July 22, 1926; d. Sidney Gordon and Mabel Marguerite (Callaghan) Finch; m. Grant William Sharpe, Apr. 3, 1948; children: Christopher, Kathryn, Charles, Loretta, Paul, Patrick, Fred, Rosemary, Lena. BA, U. Wash., 1982. Corr. studies instr. U. Wash., Seattle, 1978-93. Co-author: (with others) Introduction to Park Management, 1983, Introduction to Advanced Park Management, 1994, Introduction to Advanced Forestry, 5th edit., 1986, Introduction to Forest and Renewable Resources, 6th edit., 1995. Mem. Wash. Women in Timber, Phi Beta Kappa.

SHARPE, WILLIAM FORSYTH, economics educator; b. Cambridge, Mass., June 16, 1934; s. Russell Thornley Sharpe and Evelyn Forsyth (Jillson) Maloy; m. Roberta Ruth Branton, July 2, 1954 (div. Feb. 1986); children: Deborah Ann, Jonathan Forsyth; m. Kathryn Dorothy Peck, Apr. 5, 1986. AB, UCLA, 1955, MA, 1956, PhD, 1961. Economist Rand Corp., 1957-61; asst. prof. econs. U. Wash., 1961-63, assoc. prof., 1963-67, prof., 1967-68; prof. U. Calif., Irvine, 1968-70; Timken prof. fin. Stanford U., 1970-89, Timken prof. emeritus, 1989-92; prin. William F. Sharpe Assocs., 1986-92; prof.fin. Stanford U., 1993-95, STANCO 25 prof. of fin., 1995—. Author: The Economics of Computers, 1969, Portfolio Theory and Capital Markets, 1970; co-author: Fundamentals of Investments, 1989, 2d edit., 1993, Investments, 5th edit., 1995. With U.S. Army, 1956-57. Recipient Graham and Dodd award Fin Analysts' Fedn., 1972, '73, '86-88. Nicholas Molodovsky award, 1989. Nobel prize in econ. scis., 1990. Mem. Am. Fin. Assn. (v.p. 1979, pres. 1980), Western Fin. Assn. (Enduring Contbn. award 1989), Ea. Fin. Assn. (Disting. Scholar award 1991), Am. Econ. Assn., Phi Beta Kappa.

SHARPTON, THOMAS, physician; b. Augusta, Ga., July 15, 1949; s. Thomas and Elizabeth (Dozier) S. BA, Northwestern U., 1971; MS, Stanford U., 1973, MD, 1977. Intern Martinez (Calif.) VAMC, 1977-78, resident, 1978-80; mem. staff Kaiser Permanente Med. Group, Oakland, Calif., 1980—; asst. clin. prof. medicine U. Calif., San Francisco, 1994—; cons. Berkeley (Calif.) Free Clinic, 1977—; chmn. peer review Kaiser Permanente Med. Group, Oakland, 1985-86; clin. mem. faculty U. Calif., San Francisco, 1992, asst. clin. prof., 1994; chair AIDS therapeutics com. No. Calif. Kaiser Hosps., 1996—. Mem. Alameda County Profl. Adv. Com., Oakland, 1984-88, Alameda County AIDS Task Force, Oakland, 1985-88. Fellow ACP; mem. Calif. Med. Assn., Alameda-Contra Costa Med. Assn., Mensa, Sigma Pi Sigma, Phi Beta Kappa. Democrat. Club: Phi Beta Kappa of No. Calif. Office: Kaiser PMG 280 W Macarthur Blvd Piedmont CA 94611-5642

SHARTIN, STACY D., lawyer; b. Mpls., Mar. 10, 1949. AB cum laude, U. Calif., L.A., 1970, JD, 1973. Bar: Calif. 1973. Mem. Seyfarth, Shaw, Fairweather & Geraldson, L.A. Mem. ABA, Calif. State Bar (exec. com. labor and employment sect.), Los Angeles County Bar Assn. Office: Seyfarth Shaw Fairweather & Geraldson 2029 Century Park E Los Angeles CA 90067-2901

SHATNEY, CLAYTON HENRY, surgeon; b. Bangor, Maine, Nov. 4, 1943; s. Clayton Lewis and Regina (Cossette) S.; div.; children: Tony, Andy. BA, Bowdoin Coll., 1965; MD, Tufts U., 1969. Asst. prof. surgery U. Md. Hosp., Balt., 1979-82; assoc. prof. U. Fla. Sch. Medicine, 1982-87; clin. assoc. prof. Stanford (Calif.) U. Sch. Medicine, 1987—; dir. traumatology Md. Inst. Emergency Med. Svcs., Balt., 1979-82; dir. trauma U. Hosp., Jacksonville, 1982-85; assoc. dir. trauma Santa Clara Valley Med. Ctr., 1992—; cons. VA Coop. Studies Program, Washington, 1980—. Mem. editl. bd. Circulatory Shock, 1989-94, Panam Jour. Trauma, 1995—. Maj. U.S. Army, 1977-79. State of Maine scholar Bowdoin Coll., 1961-65. Fellow ACS, Southeastern Surg. Congress, Southwestern Surg. Congress, Soc. Surg. Alimentary Tract, Am. Assn. Surg. Trauma, Soc. Critical Care Medicine, Soc. Internat. de Chirurgie, Western Surg. Assn., Pacific Coast Surg. Assn., Phi Kappa Phi. Home: 900 Larsen Rd Aptos CA 95003-2640 Office: Valley Med Ctr Dept Surgery 751 S Bascom Ave San Jose CA 95128-2604

SHAVER, CARL HUTCHENS, retail company executive; b. Richland, Oreg., June 10, 1913; s. Charles Jacob and Minne (Mary) S.; m. Georgia Bruce, Oct. 17, 1934 (dec. Apr. 1980); children—Carl B., Dennis G.; m. Laura Frazier, Aug. 12, 1983. Student N.W. Nazarene Coll., Nampa, Idaho, 1931-32. Clk., Stockwells, Nampa, 1935-36, mgr., Donnelly, Idaho, 1936-41; mgr. Shavers, Donnelly and New Meadows, Idaho, 1941-53; pres. Shaver's Inc., Boise, Idaho, 1953-80, chmn. bd., 1980—; pres. Boise Wholesale Drygoods Co., Inc., 1953-77; chmn. bd. Citizens Nat. Bank, Boise, 1981—; vice-chmn. Associated Food Stores, also bd. dirs.; bd. dirs., v.p. Shore Club Lodge Inc., McCall, Idaho. Bd. dirs. United First Meth. Ch., Boise, 1968-74. Named Small Businessman of Yr., State of Idaho, 1973; recipient Disting. Citizen award Idaho Daily Statesman, 1984. Mem. Nat. Assn. Textile and Apparel Wholesalers (bd. dirs. 1962-74, pres. 1974-76), Idaho Retailers (pres. 1951), Greater Boise C. of C. (bd. dirs. 1965-71). Republican. Clubs: Hillcrest Country, Arld (bd. dirs.) (Boise). Lodges: Masons, Shriners. Home: 3100 Crescent Rim Dr Apt 401 Boise ID 83706-2868 Office: Shavers Inc 705 S 8th PO Box 7278 Boise ID 83707-1278 other: Associated Food Stores Inc 3100 Crescent Rim Dr Boise ID 83706-2873*

SHAVER, PHILLIP ROBERT, psychologist, educator; b. Iowa City, Iowa, Sept. 7, 1944; s. Robert Richard and Frances Magdalene (Quinn) S.; m. Gail S. Goodman; children: Lauren and Danielle (twins). BA in Psychology, Wesleyan U., Middletown, Conn., 1966; PhD in Social Psychology, U. Mich., 1970. Asst. prof. psychology Columbia U., N.Y.C., 1971-75; assoc. prof. NYU, 1975-80; assoc. prof. U. Denver, 1980-84, prof. psychology, 1984-87; prof. psychology SUNY, Buffalo, 1988-92; prof. psychology U. Calif., Davis, 1992—, chmn. dept. psychology, 1993-96; coord. doctoral program in personality and social psychology NYU, 1978-80; pres. Societal Data Corp., N.Y.C., 1977-82; head experimental and social areas dept. psychology U. Denver, 1981-84, 87-88; vis. prof. U. Hawaii, Manoa, 1986; mem. grad. fellowship evaluation panel NSF, 1990-92; cons. to numerous orgns. Editorial bd.: Jour. Social and Personal Relationships, 1988—, Personality and Social Psychology Bull., 1985—, Rev. Personality and Social Psychology, 1979-82, 86—, Jour. Personality and Social Psychology, 1978-80, 85—, Behavioral Sci., 1972-80, Jour. Experimental Social Psychology, 1972-75; contbr. reviews and articles to profl. jours. Fundraiser Arthritis Found., Buffalo, 1991. Grantee NIMH, Russell Sage Found., Spencer Found., NSF, Nat. Inst. Alcoholism, Nat. Ctr. for Child Abuse and Neglect; Woodrow Wilson fellow, NSF fellow. Fellow Am. Psychol. Assn., Am. Psychol. Soc.; mem. Western Psychol. Assn., Soc. for Exptl. Social Psychology, Soc. for Psychol. Study Social Issues, Internat. Soc. for Rsch. on Emotion, Internat. Soc. for Study Personal Relationships, Internat. Network Personal Relationships, Phi Beta Kappa, Phi Kappa Phi, Sigma Xi. Democrat. Home: 3226 Grosbeak Ct Davis CA 95616-7510 Office: U Calif Dept Psychology Park Hall Davis CA 95616-8686

SHAW, A. PARK, III, commercial real estate broker; b. Hartford, Conn., May 1, 1947; m. Cassandra Claire Hudson, May 1, 1982. BA in Geol. Scis., Amherst Coll., 1974. Field/exploration geologist Union Carbide Corp., 1974-76; project geologist Chapman Wood & Griswold, Albuquerque, 1976-80; owner, mgr. Element of Time, Albuquerque, 1980-84; broker assoc. The Vaughan Co., Albuquerque, 1986-88; v.p. Hooten/Stahl Comml. Investment, Inc., Albuquerque, 1988—. Judge N.Mex. Sci. and Engring. Fair, 1975—, mem. bd. advisors, 1992—; master gardener N.Mex. dept. Agr., 1984, 85; bd. dirs. Albuquerque Boys Club, 1979-84; pres. Albuquerque Jaycees, 1981; J.C.I. senator # 34705, pres. senate N.Mex. Jr. Chamber Internat., 1983, nat. v.p., 1985, ambassador to Europe, 1985; dir. mktg. Albuquerque/S.W. Airlines Air Show, 1991; grad. Leadership Albuquerque, 1992, bd. dirs., 1993-96; chmn. N.Mex. Bus. Assistance Coun., 1992-95. With U.S. Army, 1967-70; mem. Gov.'s Bus. Adv. Coun., 1996—. Named Outstanding Vol. of N.Mex., Gov. of N.Mex., 1982, Mover and Shaker, N.Mex. Bus. Jour., 1990, 93. Mem. Nat. Assn. Realtors (cert. comml. investment mem.), Nat. Eagle Scout Assn. (life), N.Mex. Assn. Commerce and Industry (bd. dirs. 1992—), South Valley C. of C. (founder, pres. 1988-91), N.Mex. Vine and Wine Soc. (pres. Mid Rio Grande chpt. 1989), Nat. Assn. Watch and Clock Collectors (founding, pres. 1985), Albuquerque Geol. Soc. (pres. 1980), Albuquerque C. of C. (amb. 1987—), SAR, Disabled Am. Vat. (life), Nat. Rifle Assn. (life), Children Am. Revolution (sr. pres. N.Mex. Soc. 1977), Small Bus. Adv. Coun. to Senator Pete Demenici, 1995-96, Masons. Home: 2809 Chanate Ave SW Albuquerque NM 87105-6827

SHAW, ARTHUR E., conductor. Studied with, Sidney Harth; degree, Wichita State U.; postgrad. in Conducting, U. Mich., 1982-85. Asst. condr. Ark. Symphony Orch., 1977-79; music dir., condr. Adrian (Mich.) Symphony Orch., 1979-87, Rogue Valley Symphony, Ashland, Oreg., 1987—; condr. Rogue Opera, 1987-89; founding dir., guest condr. Youth Symphony So. Oreg.; guest condr. Little Rock Cmty. Theatre, 1979, Summer Music Camp No. Ariz. U., 1988, Ota (Japan) Jr. Symphony, 1990, Jalisco Philharm., Mex., 1992, Ctrl. Oreg. Symphony, 1994, Britt Festivals, 1996. James Robertson Meml. Conducting scholar, 1976-77. Office: Rogue Valley Symphony SOSC Music Hall 1250 Siskiyou Blvd Ashland OR 97520*

SHAW, CHARLES ALDEN, engineering executive; b. Detroit, June 8, 1925; s. Fred Alden and Amy (Ellis) S.; m. Barbara Loveland, Mar. 9, 1963 (div. 1979); children: Amy Elizabeth, Polly Nicole; m. Jeanne Steves Partridge, Apr. 22, 1989. BS, Harvard U., 1945; MSEE, Syracuse U., 1958. Test and design engr. G.E., Syracuse-Schenectady, N.Y., 1947-51; chief engr. Onondaga Pottery Co., Syracuse, 1951-60; mgr. semiconductor div. G.E., Syracuse-Schenectady, 1960-66; cons. to gen. dir. Bull-G.E., Paris, 1966-69; mgr. CAD sect. integrated cir. product dept. G.E., Syracuse, 1969-71, mgr. CAD ctr. solid state applied ops., 1971-78, mgr. computer support solid state applied ops., 1978-81; dir. CAD G.E. Intersil, Cupertino, Calif., 1981-88; cons. in field Cupertino, 1988-89; mgr. tech. program Cadence Design Systems, Santa Clara, Calif., 1989—. Trustee Hidden Villa, Los Altos Hills, Calif., 1986-92; vol. tech. KTEH Channel 54 pub. TV, 1984—. With USN, 1942-45, PTO. Mem. IEEE, Assn. Computing Machinery (chmn. spl. interest group SIGDA 1986-91), Design Automation Conf. (exec. bd. 1985-95), Harvard Club of Peninsula. Democrat. Unitarian. Home: 4925 Monaco Dr Pleasanton CA 94566-7671 Office: 555 River Oaks Pky San Jose CA 95134-1917

SHAW, CHRISTOPHER ALLEN, paleontologist, consultant; b. L.A., Apr. 1, 1952; s. Justin Charles and Joyce Betty (Long) S.; m. Martha Elaine Abell, Mar. 21, 1987; children: Gregory Martin, Charles Reese. BS in Zoology, Calif. State U., 1975, MS in Biology, 1981. Fossil excavator Natural History Mus. L.A., 1969-70, excavator, exhibit tech., 1975-77; mus. preparator Idaho Mus. Natural History, Pocatello, Idaho, 1970-72; curatorial asst. George C. Page Mus., L.A., 1977-87, project coord., excavation, 1984—, collection mgr., 1987—; cons. zooarcheologist, 1981—. Editor books; conbr. articles to profl. jours., chpts. to books. Office: George C Page Mus 5801 Wilshire Blvd Los Angeles CA 90036-4596

SHAW, DAVID LYLE, journalist, author; b. Dayton, Ohio, Jan. 4, 1943; s. Harry and Lillian (Walton) S.; m. Alice Louise Eck, Apr. 11, 1965 (div. Sept. 1974); m. Ellen Torgerson, July 17, 1979 (dec.); stepchildren: Christopher, Jordan; m. Lucy Stille, Apr. 14, 1988; 1 child, Lucas. BA in English, UCLA, 1965. Reporter Huntington Park Signal (Calif.), 1963-66, Long Beach Independent (Calif.), 1966-68; reporter L.A. Times, 1968-74, media critic, 1974—. Author: WILT: Just Like Any Other 7-Foot, Black Millionare Who Lives Next Door, 1973, The Levy Caper, 1974, Journalism Today, 1977, Press Watch, 1984, The Pleasure Police, 1996; contbr. numerous articles to mags. including Gentlemen's Quar., Cigar Aficionado, Esquire, TV Guide, New York. Recipient Mellet Fund Nat. award, 1983, PEN West award, 1990, Calif. Bar Assn. Gold Medallion, 1990, Pulitzer Prize for disting. criticism, 1991. Office: LA Times Times Mirror Sq Los Angeles CA 90012

SHAW, LILLIE MARIE KING, vocalist; b. Indpls., Nov. 27, 1915; d. Earl William and Bertha Louise (Groth) King; m. Philip Harlow Shaw, June 26, 1940. Student, Jordan Conservatory Music, Indpls., 1940-43; BA, Ariz. State U., 1959; MA, Denver U., 1962; pvt. vocal study, 1944-70. Educator, libr. Glendale (Ariz.) Schs., 1959-67; lectr. libr. sci. Ariz. State U., Tempe, 1962-68. Concertizing, oratorio, symphonic soloist, light opera, 1965-82; soloist First Ch. of Christ Scientist, Sun City West, Ariz., 1980—. Monthly lectr. Christian Women's Fellowship, Phoenix, 1989—; World Conf. del. Soc. of Friends, 1967. Mem. Nat. Soc. Arts and Letters (sec. 1990-94, nat. del. 1992), Am. Philatelic Assn. (life), Am. Topical Assn., Phoenix Philatelic Soc., Auditions Guild Ariz. (sec. 1989-92), Phoenix Opera League, Phoenix Symphony Guild, Sigma Alpha Iota Alumnae (Phoenix chpt., life, treas. 1988-96, Sword of Honor 1972, Rose of Honor 1982, Rose of Dedication 1995). Republican. Home: 6802 N 37th Ave Phoenix AZ 85019-1103

SHAW, MARK HOWARD, lawyer, business owner, entrepreneur; b. Albuquerque, Aug. 26, 1944; s. Brad Oliver and Barbara Rae (Mencke) S.; m. Ann Marie Brookreson, June 29, 1968 (div. 1976); adopted children: Daniel Paul, Kathleen Ann, Brian Andrew; m. Roslyn Jane Ashton, Oct. 9, 1976; children: Rebecca Rae, Amanda Leith. BA, U. N.Mex., 1967, JD, 1969. Bar, N.Mex. 1969. Law clk. to presiding justice N.Mex. Supreme Ct., Santa Fe, 1969-70; ptnr. Gallagher & Ruud, Albuquerque, 1970-74, Schmidt & Shaw, Albuquerque, 1974-75; sr. mem. Shaw, Thompson & Sullivan P.A., Albuquerque, 1975-82; chief exec. officer United Ch. Religious Sci. and Sci. Mind Publs., L.A., 1982-91; bus. owner, entrepreneur Santa Fe, N.Mex., 1991-94; mem. Coppler & Mannick, P.C., Santa Fe, N.Mex., 1994—. Trustee 1st Ch. Religious Sci., Albuquerque, 1974-77, pres. 1977; trustee Sandia Ch. Religious Sci., Albuquerque, 1980-82, pres. 1981-82; trustee United Ch. Religious Sci., Los Angeles, 1981-82, chmn. 1982; trustee Long Beach (Calif.) Ch. Religious Sci., 1983-86, chmn. 1983-86; chmn. Bernalillo County Bd. Ethics, Albuquerque, 1979-82. Served as sgt. USMCR, 1961-69. Mem. N.Mex. Bar Assn. Home: 2724 Puerto Bonito Santa Fe NM 87505-6534 Office: 645 Don Gaspar Ave Santa Fe NM 87501-4496

SHAW, RICHARD BLAKE, artist, art educator; b. Hollywood, Calif., 1941. Student, SUNY, Alfred, 1965; BFA, San Francisco Art Inst., 1965; MFA, U. Calif., Davis, 1968; DFA (hon.), San Francisco Art Inst., 1988. Instr. San Francisco Art Inst., 1966-87; lectr. U. Calif., Berkeley, 1970, U. Wis., Madison, 1971; Coll. of Marin, Kentfield, Calif., 1977, U. Calif., Davis, 1978; prof. art U. Calif., Berkeley, 1987—; panel chair Clay in the East Conf., Phila., 1988; lectr. Calif. Coll. Arts & Crafts, Oakland, 1986; juror Falkirk Ctr. Art Show, San Rafael, Calif., 1985; lectr. DeYoung Mus. Sch., San Francisco, 1983. One man shows include Boise (Idaho) Gallery of Art, 1982, Greenberg Gallery, St. Louis, 1982, Madison (Wis.) Art Ctr., 1983, Morgan Gallery, Kansas City, Mo., 1984, Braunstein/Quay Gallery, San Francisco, 1984, 88, 90, 93, 96, Asher/Faure Gallery, L.A., 1985, Huntsville (Ala.) Mus. Art, 1986, Everson Mus. Art, Syracuse, N.Y., 1986, Allan Frumkin Gallery, N.Y.C., 1986, 88, Tucson (Ariz.) Mus. Art, 1987, Foster/White Gallery, Seattle, 1987, Sierra Nev. Art Mus., Reno, 1988, U. Pacific, Stockton, Calif., 1988, Thomas Segal Gallery, Boston, 1989, Howard Yezerski Gallery, Boston, 1990, Garth Clark Gallery, L.A., 1990, Frumkin/Adams Gallery, N.Y.C., 1990, 92, Fullerton (Calif.) Mus. Ctr., 1991, Helander Gallery, Palm Beach, Fla., 1992, Perimeter Gallery, Chgo., 1995; exhibited in group shows at Calif. State U. Art Gallery, Hayward, 1993, 96, Transamerica, San Francisco, 1993, Toledo Mus. Art, 1993-94, Bank of Am. World Hdqs. Concourse Gallery, San Francisco, 1993-94, Nat. Mus. History, Republic of China, 1994, Oakland (Calif.) Mus., 1994, Perimeter Gallery, Chgo., 1994, Clay Studio, Phila., 1994, Fresno (Calif.) City Coll., 1994, Dublin (Calif.) Civic Ctr., 1994, Galerie Sho, Tokyo, 1994, San Francisco Internat. Airport, 1994, 95, John Natsoulas Gallery, Davis, Calif., 1994, 95, Bolinas (Calif.) Mus., 1995, 96, Palo Alto (Calif.) Cultural Ctr., 1995, Whitney Mus. Am. Art, 1995-96, City Coll. San Francisco, 1995-96, John Beggruen Gallery, San Francisco, 1996, Triton Mus. Art, Santa Clara, Calif., 1996; represented in permanent collections Oakland Mus., U. Miami, Fla., Palm Beach (Fla.) Mus., Smithsonian Instn., Washington, St. Louis Art Mus., L.A. County Mus. Art, U. N.Mex., Los Cruces, San Francisco Mus. Modern Art, Nat. Mus. Modern Art, Tokyo, Whitney Mus. Am. Art, N.Y.C., U. N.Mex., Albuquerque, Ariz. State U., Tempe, U. Wash., Seattle, Mpls. Inst. Arts. Recipient vis. artist grants Atelier Exptl. de Recherche et de Creation, Paris, 1987, 88, Clayworks, N.Y.C., 1977; recipient rsch. grant Union of Ind. Colls. of Art; Visual Arts fellow, NEA, 1971, 74. Office: Braunstein/Quay Gallery 250 Sutter St San Francisco CA 94108

SHAW, RICHARD EUGENE, cardiovascular researcher; b. Springfield, Ohio, Jan. 20, 1950; s. Eugene Russell and Marjorie Catherine S.; m. Nov. 26, 1976; 2 children. BA, Duquesne U., 1972; MA, U.S. Internat. U., San Diego, 1977; PhD, U. Calif., San Francisco, 1984. Cert. nuc. med. technologist. Nuclear Medicine Tech. Cert. Bd. Staff nuc. med. technologist Scripps Meml. Hosp., La Jolla, Calif., 1975-79; rsch. asst. U. Calif. San Francisco Sch. Medicine, 1980-85; mgr. rsch. programs San Francisco Heart Inst., Daly City, Calif., 1985-87, dir. rsch., 1988-90, dir. rsch. and ops., 1991—; sr. advisor steering com. for databases Daus. of Charity Nat. Health Sys., St. Louis, 1993—; cons. comm. informatics project HealthLink SmartPhone, San Francisco, 1992—. Editor-in-chief Jour. Invasive Cardiology, King of Prussia, Pa., 1989—; contbr. more than 200 articles and book chpts. to med. lit. Coach Am. Youth Soccer Orgn. and Youth Baseball Assn. (bd. dirs.), Burlingame, Calif., 1990—. Fellow Am. Coll. Cardiology; mem. Am. Heart Assn., Soc. for Clin. Trials, N.Y. Acad. Scis., Am. Statis. Assn., Am. Med. Informatics Assn., Soc. Behavioral Medicine. Office: San Francisco Heart Inst Seton Med Ctr 1900 Sullivan Ave Daly City CA 94015-2200

SHAW, RICHARD SCOTT, mental health therapist, educator; b. Alma, Nebr., Oct. 16, 1964; s. Larry Richard and Janice Carol (Wahl) S.; m. Karen Kay Shaw, Aug. 13, 1988. BS in Sociology and Psychology, U. Nebr., 1988; MA in Counseling, Asbury Theology Seminary, 1991; MA in Theology, Fuller Seminary, 1995, postgrad., 1995—. Staff therapist Calif. Christian Counseling Ctr., Monrovia, Calif., 1991-95; asst. dir. student svcs. Fuller Theol. Seminary, Pasadena, 1992-94; instr. Western Evang. Seminary, Portland, Oreg., 1995—; instr. marriage and family therapy George Fox U., Portland, 1996—; house mgr. Pasa Alta Manor Care, Altadena, Calif., 1991-

94; chaplain intern Charter Oak Hosp., Covina, Calif., 1995. Mem. Am. Counseling Assn., Am. Assn. Christian Counselors (charter mem.). Office: George Fox Univ 68th Ave PO Box 23939 Portland OR 97291

SHAW, STANFORD J., history educator; b. St. Paul, May 5, 1930; s. Albert G. Shaw and Belle (Paymar) Jaffey; m. Ezel Kural, June 15, 1938; 1 child, Wendy Miriam Kural. BA, MA, Stanford U., 1952; MA, PhD, Princeton U., 1958; MA (hon.), Harvard U., 1966; PhD (hon.), Bosporus U., Istanbul, Turkey, 1986. Asst. prof. Turkish history Harvard U., Cambridge, Mass., 1960-65, assoc. prof. Turkish history, 1965-68; prof. Turkish and Judeo-Turkish history UCLA, 1968—; vis. prof. U. Bosporus, 1990-91. Author: Between Old and New, 1971, History of the Ottoman Empire and Modern Turkey, 2 vols., 1976-77, Turkey and The Holocaust, 1992, The Jews of the Ottoman Empire and the Turkish Republic, 1992; editor-in-chief Jour. Mid. East Studies, 1967-80; contbr. articles to profl. jours. Recipient Medal of Honor, Am. Friends of Turkey, 1992, Medal of Honor, Rsch. Ctr. on Islamic History, Art and Culture, Istanbul, 1990, Guggenheim fellowship, 1966-67, NEH fellow, 1972-73, 78-80. Fellow Inst. Turkish Studies (sr.); mem. AAUP, Am. Hist. Soc., Turkish Hist. Soc. Jewish. Office: UCLA Dept History 405 Hilgard Ave Los Angeles CA 90024-1301

SHAWN, ERIC, software and consumer products company executive; b. L.A., May 6, 1966; s. Jerome Edward Resnick and Bonnye Mae (Kennard) Ford. Graphic designer Kahtom Corp., L.A., 1986-87; pres., CEO, Shawn, Co., Simi Valley, Calif., 1987—; computer programmer Doors, 1994, Scratch Pad, 1996. Inventor flat pack shaver; artist Computer Graphics World, 1993. Instr. art Simi Cultural Arts Assn., 1995—. Libertarian. Home and Office: 2860 Elizondo Ave Simi Valley CA 93065

SHAY, ROSHANI CARI, political science educator; b. Milw., Oct. 5, 1942; d. Walter John and Dorothee May (Dahnke) O'Donnell; 1 child, Mark Sather. Student, Willamette U., 1960-63; BA, U. Oreg., 1968, MA, 1971, PhD, 1974. Adminstrv. asst. Dept. of Youth Svcs., Lubbock, Tex., 1963; teaching asst., instr. U. Oreg., Eugene, 1969-72; vis. asst. prof. Oreg. State U., Corvallis, 1973-74, Willamette U., Salem, Oreg., 1973-79, Lewis and Clark Coll., Portland, Oreg., 1976, 78; from asst. prof. to prof. Western Oreg. State Coll., Monmouth, 1979—, chair history, polit. sci., pub. adminstrn. dept., 1991-94; chair social sci. divsn., 1994—. Author: (with others) The People of Rajneeshpuram, 1990, Annual Yearbook on the Sociology of Religion, 1995, (simulation) European Unity Project, 1982. Co-founder, v.p., sec.-treas Ind. Opportunities Unltd., Salem, 1986—; co-founder, sec. Inst. for Justice and Human Rights, San Francisco, 1988-94; bd. dirs. Oreg. UN Assn., Portland, 1982—, Salem UN Assn., 1982-91; v.p., pres., bd. dirs. Garten Found. for Disabled, Salem, 1989—; pres. Assn. Oreg. Faculties, 1989-91; mem. adv. bd. Connections Program for Disabled Deaf, Salem, 1989—; pres., bd. dirs. Model UN of the Far West, San Diego, 1981-84, 86-88, 95—; mem. Oreg. Women's Polit. Caucus. Danforth Found. fellow, 1968-74; named Woman of Achievement YMCA Tribute, Salem, 1990, Mem. of Yr., Oreg. Rehab. Assn., 1995. Mem. Am. Fedn. Tchrs. (v.p., legis. officer local 2278 1982-88), Western Polit. Sci. Assn., Communal Studies Assn., Mental Health Assn. Oreg., Oreg. Acad. Sci., Oreg. Internat. Coun., Phi Kappa Phi (hon.). Democrat. Home: 348 S Main St Falls City OR 97344-9763 Office: Western Oreg State Coll 345 Monmouth Ave N Monmouth OR 97361-1314

SHCOLNIK, ROBERT MILTON, insurance company executive; b. South Bend, Ind., Aug. 21, 1938; s. Harry and Esther (Baim) S.; m. Linda K. Egleberry, Aug. 10, 1972; children: Scott, Keith, Carin, Patricia. BS in Bus., Ariz. State U., 1960; grad., Am. Savings & Loan Inst., 1961; diploma in ins., Hartford Ins. Group Ins. Group, 1965. Loan officer, branch mgr., asst. to the pres. Home Savings & Loan Assn., 1959-61; pres. Harris/Shcolnik & Assocs., Inc., Phoenix, 1961—; ptnr. Harris/Shcolnik Properties; guest lectr. in ins. Phoenix Coll.; speaker Ind. Ins. Agts. Am. Contbr. articles to profl. jours.; designer interface mini-computer concept. Mem. nat. presidents circle Ctrl. Mutual Ins. Co., inter-circle, 1975, 76, 94, Ariz. Jonathan Trumbull Coun., Hartford Ins., 1979-80, Nat. Product Devel. Com. Hartford Inst., 1993-94, Nat. Great Am. Ins. Agts. Adv. Coun., 1979-81, chmn., 1979, Pacer (agts. coun., chmn. regional comml. lines, nat. coun. lines com. 1990-93), CNA group, agts. coun. Cigna Inst.; mem. Key Club, Continentatl Assurance Co., 1970-75; past pres. Am. Savs. and Loan Inst., Ariz.; bd. dirs. Jewish Cmty. Ctr., 1980-86, v.p., exec. com., 1983-85; mem. combined ops. coun. Jewish Ctrs. Greater Phoenix, 1987-88; mem. Mauor's Task Force on Graffiti, 1993-95; chmn. Anti-GRFFTI Hotline Maricopa County. Named Outstanding Agt. of Yr. Maricopa County Assn. Independent Ins. Agts., 1973, 76-78; recipient Jewish Community Ctr. Disting. Svc. award, 1981, 83, 85. Mem. Ind. Ins. Agts. Ariz. (pres. 1985), Phoenix Cmty. Alliance (bd. dirs., exec. com. 1992-97). Republican. Jewish. Office: Harris Shcolnik & Assocs 4808 N Central Ave Phoenix AZ 85012-1714

SHEA, B(ARBARA) CHRISTINE, communications educator, consultant; b. Washington, Nov. 28, 1961; d. Edward Vincent and Micheline Marie (Simplicio) S. BA summa cum laude, Towson State U., 1983; MA, Ohio U., 1985; PhD, U. Calif., Santa Barbara, 1995. Teaching assoc. Ohio U., Athens, 1983-84; instr. Clarion U. Pa., 1985; lectr. Calif. Poly. State U., San Luis Obispo, 1985—; cons. for corp. non-profit and ednl. orgns., 1984—, presenter in field. Assoc. editor Cross-Exam. Debate Yearbook, 1986-92; contbr. articles to scholarly jours., chpts. to books and procs.; reviewer scholarly jours. and books; reviewer Mgmt. Comm. Quarterly, 1995—, Jour. Applied Comm. Rsch., 1996—. Regents fellow U. Calif., 1994-95. Mem. AAUP, Am. Psychol. Assn., Am. Psychol. Soc., Internat. Comm. Assn., Internat. Soc. for Study Argummentation, Orgn. for Study Comm., Lang. and Gender, Speech Comm. Assn., Western States Comm. Assn., Acad. Mgmt., Nat. Coun. for Rsch. on Women, Phi Kappa Phi. Office: Calif Poly Speech Comm Dept San Luis Obispo CA 93407

SHEAFFER, RICHARD ALLEN, electrical engineer; b. Bronxville, N.Y., May 30, 1950; s. Harold Aumond and Carol Lois (Henry) Sweet; children: Alan Michael Sheaffer, Russell Logan Sheaffer, Neil Andrew Sheaffer. BSEE, Pa. State U., 1972; MSEE, U. So. Calif., 1975; MBA, Pepperdine U., 1996. Registered profl. engr., Calif., Fla. Elec. engr. So. Calif. Edison Co., Rosemead, 1973-79, 80-90, Harris Controls div., Melbourne, Fla., 1979-80; cons. to elec. utility industry, 1990-91; sr. transmission planner San Diego Gas & Electric, 1991—; project leader nomogram study for Pacific and S.W. transfer subcom. Western Systems Coordinating Coun., 1988, 91; project leader Ariz.-Calif. 7550 NW Path Rating, 1994-97. Author: 1984 West-of-the-River Operating Study, 1985, December 22, 1982 Disturbance Study, 1983. Mem. IEEE (Power Engring. Soc., Engring. Mgmt. Soc.), Phi Eta Sigma. Episcopalian.

SHEARER, RICK LELAND, academic administrator; b. Wichita, Kans., Jan. 8, 1955; s. Jack Leland and Marjorie Louise (Pearson) S. BSc, U. Calgary, Alberta, Can., 1979; MBA in Fin., Nat. U., 1984; MA in Edn., San Diego State U., 1992. V.p., gen. mgr. Direction Holdings Ltd., Calgary, 1979-81; cons. Ethic Mgmt. Ltd., Calgary, 1981-82; from dir. computer based edn. to dir. rsch. and evaluation Nat. U., San Diego, 1985-92, dir. instl. rsch., founding assoc. distance edn. system, 1992-96, dir. rsch. and instrnl. systems, 1996—; presenter conf. procs. Distance Teaching and Learning, 1993-94, 95-96, 96-97, Ed Media 93, 1993. Author: Am. Jour. Distance Edn., 1994. Mem. Assn. Edn. Comm. & Tech., Am. Coun. Distance Edn. Office: Nat Univ 4141 Camino Del Rio S San Diego CA 92108-4107

SHEARING, MIRIAM, justice; b. Waverly, N.Y., Feb. 24, 1935. BA, Cornell U., 1956; JD, Boston Coll., 1964. Bar: Calif. 1965, Nev. 1969. Justice of peace Las Vegas Justice Ct., 1977-81; judge Nev. Dist. Ct., 1983-92, chief judge, 1986; justice Nevada Supreme Ct., Carson City, 1993—. Mem. ABA, Am. Judicature Soc., Nev. Judges Assn. (sec. 1978), Nev. Dist. Ct. Judges Assn. (sec. 1984-85, pres. 1986-87), State Bar Nev., State Bar Calif., Clark County Bar Assn. Democrat. *

SHECHTER, PAGIEL, physician, internist, nephrologist; b. Tel Aviv, July 29, 1952; came to U.S., 1995; s. David and Nehama (Azulai) S.; m. Ofra Jacobson, June 10, 1984; children: Daphna, Nilly, Oren. MD cum laude, Tel Aviv U., 1977. Lic. physician, Maine, Calif. Intern, resident Sheba Med Ctr., Tel Hashomer, Israel; sr. nephrologist Sheba Med. Ctr., Tel Aviv, 1986-89; fellow in nephrology Stanford (Calif.) U., 1989-93; sr. nephrologist Sheba Med. Ctr., 1993-95; internal med., nephrology Medipace, L.A., 1995—. Surgeon Israeli Navy, 1985. Mem. Am. Soc. Nephrology, Internat. Soc. Nephrology. Jewish. Home: 6608 Colgate Ave Los Angeles CA 90048-4205 Office: Medipace 5901 W Olympic Blvd Los Angeles CA 90036-4667

SHEEHAN, MICHAEL JARBOE, archbishop; b. Wichita, Kans., July 9, 1939; s. John Edward and Mildred (Jarboe) S. MST, Gregorian U., Rome, 1965; D of Canon Law, Lateran U., Rome, 1971. Ordained priest Roman Cath. Ch., 1964. Asst. gen. sec. Nat. Coun. Cath. Bishops, Washington, 1971-76; rector Holy Trinity Sem., Dallas, 1976-82; pastor Immaculate Conception Ch., Grand Prairie, Tex., 1982-83; bishop Diocese of Lubbock, Tex., 1983-93; archbishop Archdiocese of Santa Fe, Albuquerqe, N.Mex., 1993—; past chmn. Am. Bd. Cath. Missions, 1989-91; trustee Cath. Relief Svcs., 1992—. Contbr. articles to New Cath. Ency. Trustee St. Mary Hosp., Lubbock, 1983-89; bd. dirs. Tex. Conf. of Chs. Mem. Serra Club (chaplain 1983-93). Office: Archdiocese of Santa Fe 4000 Saint Josephs Pl NW Albuquerque NM 87120-1714

SHEEHY, JEROME JOSEPH, electrical engineer; b. Hartford, Conn., Dec. 3, 1935; s. Jeremiah and Anna (Foley) S.; m. Jean Ann Baldassari, Oct. 13, 1962; children: Caroline, Jerome, Daniel, Carlene. BSEE, U. Conn., 1962, MSEE, 1967. Electronic engr. USN Underwater Sound Lab., New London, Conn., 1962-69; mem. tech. staff Rockwell Internat., Anaheim, Calif., 1969-74; staff engr. Hughes Aircraft Co., Fullerton, Calif., 1974-83; systems engr. Norden Systems, Santa Ana, Calif., 1983-89; advanced engring. specialist Lockheed Aircraft Svc., Ontario, Calif., 1990—. Contbr. articles to Jour. Acoustical Soc. Am. With USAF, 1954-57. Mem. Acoustical Soc. Am., Tau Beta Pi, Eta Kappa Nu. Home: 22951 Belquest Dr Lake Forest CA 92630-4007

SHEEN, PORTIA YUNN-LING, retired physician; b. Republic of China, Jan. 13, 1919; came to U.S., 1988; d. Y. C. and A. Y. (Chow) Sheen; m. Kuo, 1944 (dec. 1970); children: William, Ida, Alexander, David, Mimi. MD, Nat. Med. Coll. Shanghai, 1943. Intern, then resident Cen. Hosp., Chungking, Szechuan, China, 1943; with Hong Kong Govt. Med. and Health Dept., 1948-76; med. supt. Kowloon (Hong Kong) Hosp., 1948-63, Queen Elizabeth Hosp., Kowloon, 1963-73, Med. and Health Hdqrs. and Health Ctr., Kowloon, 1973-76, Yan Chai Hosp., New Territories, Hong Kong, 1976-87. Fellow Hong Kong Coll. Gen. Practitioners; mem. AAAS, British Med. Assn., Hong Kong Med. Assn., Hong Kong Pediatric Soc., N.Y. Acad. Sci. Methodist. Home: 1315 Walnut St Berkeley CA 94709-1408

SHEERAN, ANGELA MAUREEN, information specialist; b. Laredo, Tex., Apr. 3, 1961; d. Patrick Ritter and Elizabeth (Hornburg) S. BJ, U. Tex., 1983. Reporter, assignments editor The Daily Tex. U. Tex., Austin, 1983; reporter El Campo (Tex.) Leader-News, 1984, The South Jetty Newspaper, Port Aransas, Tex., 1984-85; asst. to city mgr. City of Port Aransas, 1985-86; devel. dir., dep. dir. Com. to Aid Abused Women, Sparks, Nev., 1988-94; information specialist Nat. Coun. Juvenile and Family Ct. Judges, Reno, 1994—. Vol. Com. to Aid Abused Women. Recipient 1st place award Gulf Coast Press Assn., 1984, 3d place award, 1984; recipient scholarship Leadership Reno, Class of 1992. Mem. Nat. Soc. Fund Raising Execs. (chair Philanthropy Day 1993, v.p. Sierra chpt. 1994), Nev. Network Against Domestic Violence. Home: 300 California Ave #16 Reno NV 89509 Office: Nat Coun Juvenile & Family Ct Judges Reno NV 89509

SHEERAN, LORI KAY, anthropology educator; b. Springfield, Ohio, Oct. 25, 1965; d. William B. and Marilyn P. (Murphy) Chiles; m. Joeseph R. Sheeran, Sept. 1, 1987. BSc, Wright State U., Dayton, Ohio, 1984; MA, Ohio State U., 1987, PhD, 1993. Lectr. anthropology Ohio State U., Columbus, 1993; prof. Calif. State U., Fullerton, 1993—; conservation edn. officer Internat. Ctr. for Gibbon Studies, Santa Clarita, Calif., 1994—; co-dir. with Royal Forest Dept. Thailand, Gibbon Rehab. Ctr., 1996—. Co-editor: The Neglected Ape, 1995; contbr. articles to profl. publs. Rsch. grantee Wenner Gren Found., 1990, Nat. Geol. Soc., 1990, 93, Primate Conservation Inc., 1994. Mem. AAUW, Am. Soc. Primatology (rsch. grantee 1994), Am. Assn. Phys. Anthropology, Internat. Primatology Soc., S.W. Anthropology Assn. Office: Calif State U PO Box 6846 Fullerton CA 92834

SHEFRIN, HAROLD MARVIN (HERSH SHEFRIN), economist, educator, consultant; b. Winnipeg, Man., Can., July 27, 1948; came to U.S., 1974, s. Samuel and Clara Ida (Danzker) S.; m. Arna Patricia Saper, June 28, 1970. B.Sc. with honors, U. Man., Winnipeg, 1970; M. of Math., U. Waterloo, Can., 1971; Ph.D., London Sch. Econs., 1974. Asst. prof. econs. U. Rochester, N.Y., 1974-79; asst. prof. U. Santa Clara, Calif., 1979-80, assoc. prof., 1981, chmn. econs., 1983-88, full prof., 1986—; cons. Nuclear Regulatory Commn., U.S. Dept. Energy, Livermore, Calif., 1979-82, Syntex Corp., Palo Alto, Calif., 1983-90. Contbr. articles to profl. jours. Mem. Am. Econ. Assn., Econometric Soc., Western Econ. Assn., Western Fin. Assn., Fin. Mgmt. Assn., European Fin. Assn. Jewish. Achievements include co-developed economic theory of self control, behavioral finance, behavioral life cycle hypothesis, behavioral approach to financial market regulation; capital asset pricing and portfolios; contributor economic theory of uncertainty, consumer aggregation, and Bayesian learning. Office: Santa Clara U Dept Econs Santa Clara CA 95053

SHEH, ROBERT BARDHYL, environmental management company executive; b. N.Y.C., July 29, 1939; s. Talat and Nedime (Karali) S.; m. Mary Cheney Fleming, Dec. 29, 1961; children—Andrea K., Jonathan C., Robert R., Elisabeth F., Theresa N. BS in Civil Engring, Rennselaer Poly. Inst., 1960; grad. program for Mgmt. Devel., Harvard U., 1974. With The Ralph M. Parsons Co., 1971—; sr. v.p., mgr. petroleum, chem., mining and metall. div. The Ralph M. Parsons Co., Pasadena, Calif., 1981-88, pres., 1989-92, also bd. dirs.; pres., CEO Internat. Tech. Corp., Torrance, Calif., 1992-96; mem. adv. bd. Sch. Chem. Engring., U. Calif., Berkeley, 1986—; bd. dirs. Davidson Assocs., 1993—; mem. adv. bd. Rensselaer Poly. Inst., 1995. Bd. regents Marymount Internat. Sch., London, 1979; bd. trustees Harvey Mudd Coll., 1992—. With USNR, 1960-64. Mem. Calif. Club (L.A.), Annandale Golf Club (Pasadena), L.A. Country Club. *

SHEIDLEY, WILLIAM EDWARDS, English language educator; b. Kansas City, Mo., May 29, 1940; s. Hubert O. and Betsey Josephine (Edwards) S.; m. Harlow W. Sheidley, June 19, 1962; children: Jennifer L., Nathaniel J. AB, Stanford U., 1962, AM, 1966, PhD, 1968. Asst. prof. English U. Conn., Storrs, 1966-72, assoc. prof. English, 1972-81, prof. English, 1981-93; asst. prof. English U.S. Air Force Acad., Colo., 1993-94; assoc. prof. and chair English and fgn. langs. U. So. Colo., Pueblo, 1994-95, prof., chair English and fgn. langs., 1995—; dir. Conn. Writing Project, Storrs, 1982-87; cons. Bedford Books, Boston, 1982—, Prentice-Hall, Englewood Cliffs, 1983—, St. Martin's Press, N.Y., 1985—; vis. lectr. English U. So. Colo., Pueblo, 1992-93. Author: Barnabe Googe, 1981; co-editor: Children's Literature jour., 1974-77; contbr. articles to profl. jours. Mem. MLA, Nat. Coun. Tchrs. English, Marlowe Soc. Am., Spenser Soc. Democrat. Home: 4307 Meadowview Ct Colorado Springs CO 80918-4313 Office: Univ So Colo English and Fgn Langs 2200 Bonforte Blvd Pueblo CO 81001-4901

SHEKHAR, STEPHEN S., obstetrician, gynecologist; b. New Delhi, India, Jan. 13, 1944; s. S.P. Jain and Shakuntala Mithal; came to U.S., 1972; m. Claudette Dorita, Jan. 6, 1978; children—Sasha, Stephen. MB BS, Govt. Med. Coll., Punjabi U., Patiala, India, 1966. Intern Columbia U. Coll. Phys. and Surgeons-Roosevelt Hosp. N.Y.C., 1972-73; surgeon, Nat. Health Service U.K., 1966-72; resident in ob-gyn. St. Clare's Hosp.-Margaret Hauge Maternity Hosp., N.Y.C. and N.J., 1973-76, Columbia U., Harlem Hosp., N.Y.C., 1976-77; practice medicine specializing in ob-gyn., North Hollywood, Calif., 1977—; mem. staff Los Angeles County-U. So. Calif. Med. Sch.; assoc. clin prof. ob-gyn. and family medicine U. So. Calif. Sch. Medicine. Fellow ACS, Am. Coll. Ob-Gyn., L.A. Soc. Ob-Gyn.; mem. AMA, Calif. Med. Assn., Los Angeles County Med. Assn. Jain. Office: PO Box 40013 Studio City CA 91614-4013

SHELBY, TIM OTTO, secondary education educator; b. Longview, Wash., Mar. 23, 1965; s. William Richard and Ruth (Masser) S. BA in Edn., Eastern Wash. U., 1989. Cert. grades 4-12 English tchr., Wash. English tchr. Kahlotus (Wash.) H.S., 1989-90; tchr. various dists., 1990-92; Eng. tchr. Kalama (Wash.) H.S., 1992-95; tchr. English, head basketball coach Frazier Mountain H.S., Lebec, Calif., 1995—; founder, co-exec. dir. Evergreen Environ. Working Ctr., Frazier Park, Calif., 1997—; asst. basketball coach Kalama H.S., 1992-95; head basketball and football coach Kahlotus High Sch., 1989-90. Mem. ASCD, Nat. Coun. Tchrs. Eng., Internat. Reading Assn., Nat. Assn. Basketballs Coachs, So. Calif. Interscholastic Coaches Assn., Calif. Edn. Assn. (bldg. rep.). Roman Catholic. Home: PO Box 113 Frazier Park CA 93225-0113 Office: El Tajon Unified Sch Dist Box 876 Lebec CA 93243

SHELDON, CHRISTOPHER CHARLES, food products executive; b. London, Mar. 15, 1943; came to U.S., 1948; s. Frank Michael and Marie Claire (Moiscescu) S.; m. Gloria Joan Weisberg, May 16, 1970; 1 child, Jeremy David. BA in Polit. Sci., Sir George William U., 1968. Sr. product mgr. new products Wise Foods divsn. Borden Inc., Berwick, Pa., 1978-81; pres. Westmount, Inc., Middlebury, Vt., 1981-88; v.p., gen. mgr. Borden, Inc., Columbus, Ohio, 1988-95; v.p., dir. mktg. Boyd Coffee Co., Portland, Oreg., 1995—. Office: Boyd Coffee Co 19730 NE Sandy Blvd Portland OR 97230-7310

SHELDON, GARY, conductor, music director; b. Bay Shore, N.Y., Jan. 21, 1953. Student, Wash. U., St. Louis, 1972; BMus, Juilliard Sch. Music, 1974; diploma, Inst. Hautes Etudes Musicales, Montreux, Switzerland, 1975. Prin. condr. Opera Theater, Syracuse, 1976-77; asst. condr. Syracuse Symphony Orch., 1976-77, New Orleans Symphony Orch., 1977-80; assoc. condr. Columbus (Ohio) Symphony Orch., 1982-89; music dir. Lancaster (Ohio) Festival, 1988—, Marin Symphony Orch., San Rafael, Calif., 1990—. Composer: Variations on a Theme of Handel, 1984, Mississippi River (for documentary film Miss. River Mus.), Memphis; rec. performances include Beauty and the Beast (with Frank DiGiacomo), 1977, Ballet Class with Karen Hebert, 1982. Recipient New Orleans Music and Drama Found. award, 1982, 3d prize Rupert BBC Symphony Found., London, 1982, 4th prize Leopold Stokowski Conducting Competition, 1986. Mem. Am. Symphony Orch. League (youth orch. div. bd. dirs. 1980—). Office: Marin Symphony Orchestra 4340 Redwood Hwy San Rafael CA 94903-2104*

SHELDON, MARK SCOTT, research engineer; b. Orange, Calif., May 19, 1959; s. Howard Lezurn and Vida Louise (Winegar) S.; m. Marti Reisman, Aug. 8, 1986. BS in Engring. and Applied Sci., Calif. Inst. Tech., 1981; MSME, Cornell U., 1985. Rsch. engr. Energy and Environ. Rsch. Corp., Irvine, Calif., 1985-91, sr. rsch. engr., 1991—. Mem. ASME (assoc.). Mem. Reorganized LDS Ch. Office: Energy and Environ Rsch Corp 18 Mason Irvine CA 92618-2798

SHELDON EPSTEIN, VIVIAN, author, publisher; b. N.Y.C., June 21, 1941; d. Herman and Hilde (Breslau) Sheldon; m. Ted Epstein, Jr., June 13, 1962; Ted III (dec.), Elizabeth Darien Epstein. BA in History, Edn., U. Denver, 1962. Cert. tchr., Colo. Tchr. Denver Pub. Schs., 1962-67; author, publisher VSE Publ. Co., Denver, 1975—; speaker, presenter to schs., univs., educator workshops, 1984—. Author: (books) History of Colorado for Children, 1975, The ABCs of What a Girl Can Be, 1980, History of Women for Children, 1984, History of Women Artists for Children, 1987 (CHOICES Best Books List 1987), History of Women in Science for Young People, 1994 (AAAS Best Sci. Books for children 1992-95). Mem. Nat. Mus. of Women in the Arts (sec. Denver chpt. 1987-93). Home and Office: VSE Publisher 212 S Dexter St Denver CO 80222

SHELLAN, RONALD A., lawyer; b. Everett, Wash., Oct. 17, 1949; s. Henry and Sondra Ilsa (Hess) S.; m. Rebecca Rae, March 24, 1972; children: Elisabeth S., David W. BA magna cum laude, U. Wash., 1972; LLM, Willamette U., 1975. Bar: Oreg. 1975, U.S. Dist. Ct. Oreg. 1979, U.S. Tax Ct. 1982; CPA, Oreg. 1978. Law clk. Oreg. Tax Ct., Salem, 1976; tax sr. Coopers & Lybrand, Portland, 1977-79; atty. Sussman, Shank, Wapnick, Caplan & Stiles, Portland, 1979-91, Weiss, Jensen, Ellis & Botteri, Portland, 1991; atty Miller, Nash, Wiener, Hager & Carlsen, Portland, 1991—. Author: G Reorganization Tax Free Acquisition of Financially Distressed Corporations; assoc. editor Willamette Law Jour., 1974-75. V.p. Nat. Multiple Sclerosis Soc. Oreg. Chapter, 1989-96, Robison Jewish Home, Portland, 1990-96. Mem. Oreg. State Bar (chair tax section), Oreg. Soc. CPA's (dir. 1978), Portland Tax Forum (pres.). Office: Miller Nash Wiener Hager Carlsen 111 SW 5th Ave Ste 3500 Portland OR 97204-3638

SHELLHORN, RUTH PATRICIA, landscape architect; b. L.A., Sept. 21, 1909; d. Arthur Lemon and Lodema (Gould) S.; m. Harry Alexander Kueser, Nov. 21, 1940. Student dept. landscape architecture, Oreg. State Coll., 1927-30; grad. landscape architecture program, Cornell U. Coll. Architecture, 1933. Pvt. practice landscape architecture, various cities Calif., 1933—; exec. cons. landscape architect Bullocks Stores, Calif., 1945-78, Fashion Sqs. Shopping Ctrs., Calif., 1958-78, Marlborough Sch., L.A., 1968—, El Camino Coll., Torrance, Calif., 1970-78, Harvard Sch., North Hollywood, Calif., 1974-90; cons. landscape architect, site planner Disneyland, Anaheim, Calif., 1955, U. Calif., Riverside Campus, 1956-64, numerous others, also numerous gardens and estates; landscape architect Torrance (Calif.) City Goals Com., 1969-70; cons. landscape architect City of Rolling Hills (Calif.) Community Assn., 1973-93. Contbr. articles to garden and profl. publs.; subject of Oct. 1967 issue Landscape Design & Constrn. mag. Named Woman of Year, Los Angeles Times, 1955, Woman of Year, South Pasadena-San Marino (Calif.) Bus. Profl. Women, 1955; recipient Charles Goodwin Sands medal, 1930-33, Landscape Architecture award of merit Calif. State Garden Clubs, 1984, 86, Horticulturist of the Yr. award So. Calif. Hort. Inst., numerous nat., state, local awards for excellence. Fellow Am. Soc. Landscape Architects (past pres. So. Calif. chpt.), Phi Kappa Phi, Kappa Kappa Gamma (Alumni Achievement award 1960). Home and Office: 362 Camino De Las Colinas Redondo Beach CA 90277-6435 *Integrity, honesty, dependability, sincerity, dedication, and a willingness to give more than is expected in service, are the basic principles which have guided my career. Never losing sight of the importance of the individual, I have tried to create total environments of harmony and beauty to which each individual can relate in a very personal and pleasureable way, and for a little while, can find a calm oasis in a busy and demanding world.*

SHELTON, JOEL EDWARD, clinical psychologist; b. Havre, Mont., Feb. 7, 1928; s. John Granvil and Roselma Fahy (Ervin) S.; m. Maybelle Platzek, Dec. 17, 1949; 1 child, Sophia. AB, Chico (Calif.) State Coll., 1951; MA, Ohio State U., 1958, PhD, 1960. Psychologist Sutter County Schs., Yuba City, Calif., 1952-53; tchr., vice prin. Lassen View Sch., Los Molinos, Calif., 1953-55; tchr. S.W. Licking Schs., Pataskala, Ohio, 1955-56; child psychologist Franklin Village, Grove City, Ohio, 1957; clin. psychologist Marion (Ohio) Health Clinic, 1958; intern Children's Mental Health Ctr., Columbus, Ohio, 1958-59; acting chief research psychologist Children's Psychiat. Hosp., Columbus, 1959-60; cons. to supt. schs. Sacramento County, Calif., 1960-63; mem. faculty Sacramento State Coll., 1961-69; clin. psychologist DeWitt State Hosp., Auburn, Calif., 1965; exec. dir. Children's Ctr. Sacramento, Citrus Heights, Calif., 1963-64, Gold Bar Ranch, Garden Valley, Calif., 1964-72; clin. psychologist El Dorado County Mental Health Ctr., Placerville, Calif., 1968-70, Butte County Mental Health Dept., Oroville, Calif., 1970-94; dir. dept. consultation, edn. and community services Butte County Mental Health Ctr., Chico, 1974-85, outpatient supr., 1986-94; mgmt. cons., 1972-94; advisor to pres. Protaca Industries, Chico, 1974-80; exec. sec. Protaca Agrl. Rsch., 1974-80; small bus. cons., 1983—; cons. on coll. scholarships and funding, 1991-92, computer cons., 1994—; freelance photographer, 1995—. With U.S. Army, 1946-47. Mem. APA, Western Psychol. Assn. Home: 1845 Veatch St Oroville CA 95965-4787

SHELTON, ROBERT CHARLES, electronics engineer; b. L.A., July 31, 1934; s. Weir Mitchell and Martalena (Scavarda); BSEE, Calif. State Poly. U., 1961; divorced; 1 son, Kevin Lyle. Ops. mgr. Halcyon, Palo Alto, Calif., 1971-74; mfg. mgr. Programmed Power, Menlo Park, Calif., 1974-78; pres. Shelton Electronics, Menlo Park, 1976—. Bd. dirs. Herbert Hoover Boys Club, Menlo Park; vol. Peninsula Meml. Blood Bank, St. Anthony Padua Dining Rm. Served with USN, 1952-56. Mem. IEEE, Profl. and Tech. Cons. Assn. Clubs: Elks (chmn. Palo Alto public relations); Rotary (bd. dirs., pres. 1981-82) (Menlo Park). Roman Catholic. Rsch. and publs. in telecommunication microwave and high energy physics, small computer systems and data communications; patentee various cryogenic and computer devices. Address: PO Box 2573 Menlo Park CA 94026-2573 Office: 1259-351 El Camino Real Menlo Park CA 94025-4227

SHELTON, ROBERT NEAL, physics educator, researcher; b. Phoenix, Oct. 5, 1948; s. Clark B. and Grace M. (McLaughlin) S.; m. Adrian Ann Millar, Aug. 30, 1969; children: Christian, Cameron, Stephanie. BS, Stanford U., 1970; MS, U. Calif., San Diego, 1973, PhD, 1975. Postdoctoral researcher U. Calif.-San Diego, La Jolla, 1975-76, asst. rsch. physicist, 1976-78; asst. prof. Iowa State U., Ames, 1978-81, assoc. prof., 1981-84, prof. physics, 1984-87; prof. physics, chmn. dept. U. Calif.-Davis, 1987-90, vice chancellor for rsch., 1990-96, vice provost for rsch., 1996—. Contbr. over 200 articles to profl. jours. Fellow Am. Phys. Soc.; mem. Sigma Xi. Office: U Calif Dept Physics Davis CA 95616

SHEP, ROBERT LEE, editor, publisher, textile book researcher; b. Los Angeles, Feb. 27, 1933; s. Milton and Ruth (Miller) Polen S. BA, U. Calif.-Berkeley, 1955; student Royal Acad. Dramatic Art, London, 1956; BFgn Trade, Am. Inst. Fgn. Trade, 1960. Asst. area mgr. fgn. dept. Max Factor, Hollywood, Calif., 1960-65; editor, pub. The Textile Booklist, Lopez Island, Wash., 1980-84; free-lance writer, book reviewer, library appraiser, book repairer. Author: Cleaning and Repairing Books, 1980, Cleaning and Care for Books, 1983, Bhutan - Fibre Forum, 1984, Civil War Gentleman, 1994, Late Victorian Women's Tailoring, 1997, Regency Etiquette, 1997; co-author: (annotated edit.) The Costume or Annals of Fashion, 1986, Dress and Cloak Cutter: Womens Costume 1877-1882, 1987; editor: The Handbook of Practical Cutting, 2d rev. edit., 1986, RAGS: Quarterly Revs. Cosume, Clothing & Ethnic Textile Books; pub. Ladies' Guide to Needle Work, 1986, Edwardian Ladies' Tailoring, 1990. Art of Cutting and History of English Costume, 1987; editor, pub. Tailoring of the Belle Epoque, 1991, Late Georgian Costume, 1991, Civil War Cooking, 1992, Art in Dress, 1993, Minister's Complete Guide to Practical Cutting, 1993, Freaks of Fashion, 1993; pub. Civil War Era Etiquette, 1988, Ladies Self Instr., 1988; mem. editl. rev. bd. The Cutter's Rsch. Jour. Bd. dirs AIDS Care and Edn. Svcs., Pacific Textiles. Mem. Costume Soc. (London), Costume Soc. Am. (bd. dirs. 1985-87), Costume Soc. Ont., Mendocino County HIV Consortium (mem. steering com.), Australian Costume and Textile Soc., U.S. Inst. Theatre Tech. Home: PO Box 668 Mendocino CA 95460-0668

SHEPARD, BRANDON WESLEY, secondary education educator; b. Miami, Fla., Oct. 22, 1963; s. William August and Edith Margaret (Rettberg) S.; m. Janice Marie Meltebeke, May 14, 1988; children: Julianne, Daniel, Heidi. BS, BBA, U. Oreg., 1985, MS in Geography and Edn., 1990. Std. tchr. cert. biology, math., social studies, Oreg. Tchr. sci., history Glendale (Oreg.) H.S., 1989—; jr. class advisor Glendale H.S., 1989—, mem. site coun., 1996—. Author: Cow Creek Historical, 1990; newspaper columnist Cow Creek Voice, 1996. Planning commr. Glendale City Govt., 1993-94, city councillor, 1994—; mem. hist. resource rev. bd. Douglas County Planning Dept., Roseburg, Oreg., 1995. Republican. Baptist. Home: PO Box 515 Glendale OR 97442-0515 Office: Glendale H S 10598 Azalea Glen Rd Glendale OR 97442-9764

SHEPARD, EARL ALDEN, retired government official; b. Aurora, Ill., Sept. 30, 1932; s. Ralph George and Marcia Louise (Phelps) S.; m. Carolyn Mae Borman, Sept. 1, 1959; 1 son, Ralph Lyle. AS in Bus. Adminstrn. magna cum laude, Southea. U., 1967, BSBA magna cum laude, 1969; MBA, U. Chgo., 1974. Chief program budget divsn. U.S. Army Munitions Command., Joliet, Ill., 1971-73; comptr., dir. adminstrn. U.S. Navy Pub. Works Ctr., Gt. Lakes, Ill., 1973-77; dep. comptr. U.S. Army Electronics Command/U.S. Army Communications Electronics Materiel Readiness Command, Ft. Monmouth, N.J., 1977-79; dir. resource mgmt., comptr., dir. programs U.S. Army, White Sands Missile Range, N.Mex., 1979-92; bd. dirs. 1st Nat. Bank of Dona Ana County, 1987—; mem. adv. com. Rio Grande Bancshares/First Nat. Bank of Dona Ana County, 1983-84; founding mem. White Sands Missile Range Hist. Found., 1992—. Mem. bd. govs. Southea. U. Ednl. Found., 1969-71; chmn. fin. com. No. Va. Assn. for Children with Learning Disabilities, 1966-67, treas., 1968-70; pres. West Long Branch (N.J.) Sports Assn., 1979. Fed. and local govt. employee scholar, 1967, Ammunition Procurement Supply Agy. fellow, 1974. Republican. Home: 2712 Topley Ave Las Cruces NM 88005-1334

SHEPARD, ROBERT CARLTON, English language educator; b. Akron, Ohio, Dec. 20, 1933; s. Robert and Mildred Lucille (Stewart) S.; m. Marjorie Alma Mackey, June 9, 1956; children: Robert Lincoln, Donald Ward. BA, U. Oreg., 1970, MA, 1971; postgrad., England, 1979, 1991. Prof. English Southwestern Oreg. C.C., Coos Bay, 1971-94, chair divsn. English, 1976-78, prof. emeritus, 1994—; liaison Oreg. Com. for Humanities, 1985-86; judge statewide writing contests Nat. Coun. Tchrs. English, Urbana, Ill., 1987-88; founder Willamette Valley Vineyards, Turner, Oreg., 1991; co-founder Nor 'Wester Brewing Co., Portland, 1993, Breweries Across Am., Portland, 1994. Author, photographer, producer: (multi-image show) Christmas Fiestas of Oaxaca (Mexico), 1985; developer ednl. software, 1993—. With USMCR, 1954-58. Grad. Teaching fellow U. Oreg., 1970-71. Democrat. Home: 3280 Sheridan Ave North Bend OR 97459-3043

SHEPARD, ROBERT ETHAN, literary agent; b. Ridgewood, N.J., 1961; s. Lawrence I. and Marjorie S. Shepard. BA, MA, U. Pa., 1983. Rsch. asst. U. Pa. Found., Phila., 1983-84; mgr. spl. markets and nat. accounts Addison-Wesley Pub. Co., Reading, Mass., 1985-93; prin. The Shepard Group, Washington, 1993-94, The Robert E. Shepard Agy., San Francisco, 1995—; trustee, bd. sec. Philomathean Endowment Trust, Phila., 1994. Mem. The Authors Guild, Philomathean Soc. (sr., archivist 1982). Office: The Robert E Shepard Agy Ste 3 4111 18th St San Francisco CA 94114

SHEPARD, ROBERT HENRY, retired oil company executive; b. N.Y.C., Dec. 6, 1926; s. Henry Joseph and Elfrieda (Allerhand) S.; m. Gloria June Caraway, July 16, 1950; children: Steven Douglas, Roger Neal, John Kirby. Cert. of Engring., Cornell U., 1944; BSc, Bklyn. Coll., 1949; Diploma Basico, U. Salamanca, Spain, 1995. Geologist U.S. Geol. Survey, Roswell, N.Mex., 1949, So. Petroleum Exploration/Malco, Roswell, 1950; field geologist Superior Oil Co., Midland, Tex., 1950-51; divsn. geologist Standard Oil Co. Tx., Houston, 1951-69; exploration mgr. Chevron Overseas Petroleum, Madrid, 1969-73; sr. staff geologist Chevron Overseas Petroleum, San Francisco, 1973-82; petroleum ops. mgr. Chevron Overseas Petroleum, Zagreb, Yugoslavia, 1982-89. Pres. sch. bd. Am. Sch. of Madrid, Spain, 1972-73. With USAF, 1943-44. Fellow Geol. Soc. Am.; mem. Am. Assn. Petroleum Geologists, Am. Geophys. Union, No. Calif. Geol. Soc., Soc. Exploration Geophysicists, Quintocentenario Toastmasters (v.p. edn. 1994—). Methodist. Home: 2 Blanket Flower Cir Santa Fe NM 87501

SHEPARD, THOMAS AKERS, physician assistant; b. Buffalo, N.Y., Oct. 4, 1948; s. Richard Marvin and Mabel Elizabeth (McVicker) S.; m. Ruth Virginia Heffleger Zebarth, June 5, 1971 (div. Nov. 1980); 1 child, Jared Nathaniel; m. Denise Hazel Donaldson, Sept. 25, 1993. BA, Franklin & Marshall Coll., 1971; AS in sci., Arapahoe Cmty. Coll., Littleton, Colo., 1977. RN, Colo.; lic. physician asst., Colo. Physician asst. Buffalo Park Medical Assn., Evergreen, Colo., 1975-82, ClearCreek Medical Ctr., Idaho Springs, Colo., 1982-85; occupational health dir. AMAX Inc. Henderson Mine, Empire, Colo., 1985-93; physician asst. urgent care Kaiser Permanente, Denver, 1988-96; mgr. med. svcs. Colo. Compensation Ins. Authority, Denver, 1993—. Co-author (book chpt.): Pain Treatment Centers At a Crossroads, 1996. Rule making testimony Colo. Dept. Labor, Denver, 1993, 94, 95; managed care task force Colo. Div. Workers Comp. Colo. Dept. Labor, 1993-94; apportionment working group, 1994. With Army, 1966-68, Vietnam. Fellow Am. Acad. Physicans Assts., Colo. Acad. Physicians Assts. Office: Colo Compensation Authority Ins 720 S Colorado Blvd Denver CO 80222-1904

SHEPARD, WILLIAM WAYNE, editor; b. Danville, Ill., Oct. 7, 1926; s. Carl Wayne and Mildred Leota (Ellingwood) S.; m. H. Joanne North, Nov. 1946; children: Gregory W., Mark W., Sue K. Portugal, Melinda A. Waltermire. BS, U. Ill., 1950. Advt. staff The Coloradoan, Fort Collins, 1950-52; co-pub. Espanola (N.Mex.) Valley News, 1952-53; advt. staff Sacramento Union, 1953-54; advt. staff, reporter Daily Dem., Woodland, Calif., 1954-63; info. specialist U. Calif., Davis, 1963-69; editor Rajo Publs., Mill Valley, Calif., 1969-80; editor Calif. Horse Rev. Paint Horse Jour., Sacramento and Ft. Worth, 1980-91; exec. dir., newsletter editor Livestock Publs. Coun., Eureka, Calif., 1991—. Author: (booklet) Root and Crown Diseases of Deciduous Fruit and Nut Trees, 1968; co-author: (booklet) News Photography for Extension Workers, 1966. Cpl. U.S. Army, 1945-46, PTO. Mem. Outdoor Writers Assn. Am., Outdoor Writers Assn. Calif. Democrat. Home and Office: 2631 Garland St Eureka CA 95501-3574

SHEPERSKY, MIMI, probate examiner; b. Portland, Oreg., Oct. 12, 1964; d. Sigman Roe and June Kim; m. Douglas M. Shepersky; children: Matthew Aaron, Katherine Ann, Grace Lee. Grad. high sch., Rancho Palos Verdes, Calif.; cert. legal asst. with honors, U. San Diego, 1989. Paralegal, office mgr. Law Offices Thomas Kagy, L.A., 1983, Law Office Tong S. Suhr, L.A., 1983-84; head litigation sect., paralegal def. litigation Wells Fargo Bank, N.A., L.A., 1984-85; paralegal bankruptcy and fed. litigation Pachulski, Stang & Ziehl, P.C., L.A., 1985-88; paralegal, office mgr. Law Offices Donald H. Glaser, San Diego, 1989—; paralegal probate, computer cons. Village Law Ctr., San Marcos, 1990-91; paralegal, probate, trust adminstrn. Law Offices Arthur S. Brown, Carlsbad, Calif., 1992-93, Higgs, Fletcher & Mack, San Diego, 1993-94. Editor newsletter Noteworthy, 1984-85. Sec.-elect Korean Am. Coalition, L.A., 1983-84; counselor Korean Am. Youth Found., 1974-82. Mem. San Diego Assn. Legal Assts., Nat. Notary Assn. (founding co-chair North County com.). Republican. Presbyterian. Home: 1503 Sundale Rd El Cajon CA 92019-3725 Office: Superior Ct County San Diego 201 W Broadway San Diego CA 92101

SHEPHERD, KAREN, former congresswoman; b. Silver City, N.Mex., July 5, 1940; m. Vincent P. Shepherd. BA, U. Utah, 1962; MA, Brigham Young U., 1963. Former instr. Brigham Young U., Am. U., Cairo; former pres. Webster Pub. Co.; former adminstr. David Eccles Sch. Bus., U. Utah; former dir. Salt Lake County Social Svcs., Utah; former dir. continuing edn. Westminster Coll.; former mem. Utah Senate; mem. 103d Congress from 2d Utah dist., Washington, 1993-95, Nat. Common Cause Governing Bd., Washington, 1995—; founding mem. Utah Women's Polit. Caucus, Project 2000; mem. Internat. Delegation to Monitor Elections in West Bank and Gaza, Israel. Former mem. United Way, Pvt. Industry Coun.; former mem. adv. bd. U.S. West Grad. Sch. Social Work; trustee Westminster Coll. Recipient Women in Bus. award U.S. Small Bus. Assn., Woman of Achievement award, Pathfinder award, YWCA Leadership award, 1st place award Nat. Assn. Journalists, Disting. Alumni award U. Utah Coll. Humanities. Fellow Inst. Politics Kennedy Sch Govt., Internat. Women's Forum; Salt Lake Area C. of C. (pub. rels. com.). Home: PO Box 1049 Salt Lake City UT 84110 Office: 21 G St Salt Lake City UT 84103-2949

SHEPHERD, WILLIAM C., pharmaceutical company executive; b. 1939. With Allergan Inc., Irvine, Calif., 1964—, pres., COO, 1984—, pres., CEO, 1992—, bd. dirs. Office: Allergan Inc PO Box 19534 2525 Dupont Dr Irvine CA 92713-9534*

SHEPPARD, BRETT C., surgeon; b. Harvey, Ill., Feb. 21, 1956; s. Neil N. and Rosyln C. (Constantine) S.; m. Julie Ann Schultz, May 26, 1987; children: Paige Constance, Scott Charles. BS, U. Wis., 1978; MS, Loyola U., Chgo., 1980; MD, Chgo. Med. Sch., 1984. Diplomate Am. Bd. Surgery. Fellow surgery br. NIH/Nat. Cancer Inst., Bethesda, Md., 1987-89; sr. resident Oreg. Health Scis. U., Portland, Oreg., 1989-90, chief resident, 1990-91; instr. surgery Oreg. Health Scis. U., Portland, 1991-92, asst. prof. surgery, 1992—. Contbr. articles to profl. jours., chpts. to books. Fellow ACS; mem. North Pacific Surg. Assn., Am. Assn. Cancer Rsch., Am. Gastroenterological Assn., Soc. Surgery of Alimentary Tract, Soc. Am. Gastrointestinal Endoscopic Surgeons, Soc. Surg. Oncology. Office: Oreg Health Scis Univ 3181 SW Sam Jackson Portland OR 97201

SHEPPARD, JACK W., retired air force officer; b. Parkersburg, W.Va., Aug. 8, 1931; s. James Lee and Audrey Irene (Heiney) S.; m. Norma Ann Stutler, Sept. 4, 1953; children—Bradley, Gregory. B.A.C., U. Akron, Ohio, 1955; M.A. in Pub. Adminstrn., George Washington U., 1965. Commd. lt. U.S. Air Force, 1955, advanced through grades to maj. gen.; vice comdr. 60 Mil. Airlift Wing, USAF, Travis AFB, Calif., 1977-79; comdr. 1606 Air Base Wing, USAF, Kirtland AFB, N.Mex., 1979-81; dir. internat. staff Inter Am. Def. Bd., USAF, Washington, 1981-82; dep. chief staff for personnel USAF Mil. Airlift Command, Scott AFB, Ill., 1982-83, chief of staff, 1983-85; comdr. Twenty First Air Force, McGuire AFB, N.J., 1985-87; asst. dep. chief staff programs and resources Hdqrs. USAF, Washington, 1987-88, ret., 1988. Mem. Order of Daedalians, Air Force Assn., Airlift Assn., Armed forces Adv. Assn. (pres. elect), Theta Chi. Presbyterian. Home: PO Box 908 21 Beaver Ln Cedar Crest NM 87008-0908

SHERIDAN, GEORGE EDWARD, manufacturing company executive; b. Emporia, Kans., July 4, 1915; s. George and Josephine Frances (Benson) S.; m. Edith Joye Card, July 4, 1940; 1 dau., Phyllis Lynne. Liberal arts student Coll. of Emporia, 1934-36; engring. student Nat. Schs., 1936-37, Los Angeles City Jr. Coll., 1937-38. Cert. mfg. engr.; registered profl. engr., Calif. With Douglas Aircraft, Santa Monica, Calif., 1939-40, Northrop Aircraft, Hawthorn, Calif., 1940-45; pres. Sheridan Products, Inc., Inglewood, Calif., 1940-87; ret., 1987. Active, YMCA, Inglewood, 1960—. Mem. Soc. Mfg. Engrs. (life, award 1979-80, Industrialist of Yr. 1982 past chmn.), U.S. Power Squadron, Am. Ordnance Def. Preparedness Assn., Nat. Rifle Assn., Smithsonian Assos., Cutting Tool Mfg. Assn., Nat. Fedn. Ind. Bus., Mech. Bank Collectors Am., Antique Toy Collectors Am. Republican. Quaker. Patentee double edge scraper. Home: 27692 Via Rodrigo Mission Viejo CA 92692-2019

SHERIDAN, GEORGE GROH, English and history educator; b. Balt., Mar. 18, 1947; s. Edward Walter and Mary Jane (Groh) S.; m. Catherine Elizabeth Heinz, May 25, 1968; children: Michael Edward, Elizabeth Makepeace, Peter Carlos, Tiffany Anne, Danielle Rebecca, Nicholas George. BA in Polit. Sci., Loyola U., L.A., 1969; MS in Edn., U. So. Calif., 1970. Std. elem. and secondary tchg. credentials, bilingual cert. competence. Tchr. intern Tchr. Corps Rural-Migrant, Tulare County, Calif., 1968-70; boycott organizer United Farm Workers AFL-CIO, Ohio, Mass., Conn., Cal., 1970-78; bilingual tchr. Lenox Sch. Dist., L.A., 1978-81; 5th-6th grade tchr. Black Oak Mine Unified Sch. Dist., Georgetown, Calif., 1981-87; 7th-8th grade tchr., mentor Black Oak Mine Unified Sch. Dist., Cool, Calif., 1987—; fellow Area 3 Writing Project, Davis, 1986—; tchr. leader, inst. dir. Calif. Reading & Lit. Project, Sacramento, 1987—; mem. State Instrnl. Resources Evaluation Panel, Sacramento, 1988, 94, 96; mem. State Lang. Arts Framework Com., Sacramento, 1996—. Author: First Papers in Migrancy and Rural Poverty, 1970; prin. author: Seeking Excellence in Education K-12, 1987; contbg. author: Picture Yourself in Local Government, 1995. Mem. ASCD, NEA, NAACP, NOW, ACLU, Nat. Coun. Tchrs. English, Calif. Tchrs. Assn., Black Oak Mine Tchrs. Assn. (pres. 1996—), Sierra Club. Home: 4467 Meadowbrook Rd Garden Valley CA 95633-9403 Office: Northside Sch PO Box 217 Cool CA 95614

SHERIDAN, JOHN BRIAN, librarian; b. N.Y.C., Aug. 20, 1947; s. John Bernard and Margaret Ann (Hefferon) S.; m. Dindy Reich, Aug. 20, 1972; children: Molly, Jonah, Liz Mary. BA in Classics, CCNY, 1970; AM in Classical Studies, Ind. U., 1972; MLS, U. Wis., Milw., 1973. Cataloguer, acquisitions librarian Kearney (Nebr.) State Coll., 1973-75; head tech. services Knox Coll., Galesburg, Ill., 1975-77; head librarian Transylvania U., Lexington, Ky., 1977-84, The Colo. Coll., Colorado Springs, 1984—; chmn. Colo. Council of Acad. Librarians, 1987-88. Contbr. articles to profl. jours. Commr. Environ. Improvement Commn., Lexington, 1978-81; coach Colorado Springs Youth Soccer and Basketball Assn., 1984-92; bd. dirs. North End Homeowners Assn., Colorado Springs, 1985-90, pres., 1988-90; adv. com. Lulac Nat. Ednl. Svcs. Ctr., 1991—; mem. Balbas Bandeleros Riding Club. Fellow U. Wis., Milw., 1972; recipient Ward medal in Latin, CCNY, 1970; Regents scholar, CCNY, 1965-69. Mem. ALA (councilor 1987-91, sec. social responsibilities roundtable 1984-85, chmn. 1985-86), Colo. Libr. Assn. (pres. Coll. and Univ. divsn. 1992-94), Rothman Rooters Club. Democrat. Home: 1731 N Nevada Ave Colorado Springs CO 80907-7456 Office: Colo Coll Charles Leaming Tutt Libr 1021 N Cascade Ave Colorado Springs CO 80903-3252

SHERIDAN, MARY STOEBE, social worker; b. Pasadena, Calif., Aug. 5, 1948; d. Jacob G. and Virginia Elizabeth (Gould) S.; m. Harold C. Sheridan, Aug. 23, 1969. BA, Northwestern U., 1969; MSW, U. Ill., Chgo., 1972; PhD, U. Hawaii, 1985. Caseworker Cook County Pub. Aid, Chgo., 1969-70; instr., asst. prof. social work U. Ill. Hosp., Chgo., 1972-77; social worker Hawaii Dept. Edn., Waipahu, 1978-80; social work edn. coordinator Kapiolani Med. Ctr. for Women and Children, Honolulu, 1980-82; home monitor coordinator Kapiolani Hosp. Med. Ctr. for Women & Children, Honolulu, 1982-88; instr. human services Hawaii Pacific Coll., Honolulu, 1987-91; instr., assoc. prof. psychology Hawaii Pacific U., Honolulu, 1995—; dir. social svcs. Pali Momi Med. Ctr., Aiea, Hawaii, 1989-93; rsch. coord. Straub Found., 1993-95; adj. instr. Hawaii Pacific Coll., Honolulu, 1978-79; instr./lectr. U. Hawaii, Honolulu, 1982-85, adj. instr., 1989-93. Author: (novel) To Michael with Love, 1977, Pain in America, 1992; editor: The NAAP Handbook of Infant Apnea and Home Monitoring, Vol. 1, 1992, Vol. 2, 1996; co-editor: (with Alex Levin) Munchausen Syndrome by Proxy, 1995; contbr. articles to profl. jours. Recipient Cert. Merit Council of Nephrology Social Workers, 1977, Continuing Edn. award March of Dimes, Honolulu, 1985. Mem. Nat. Assn. Social Workers (sec. Honolulu chpt. 1984-85, cert.), Nat. Assn. Apnea Profls. (pres., co-founder 1987-88, Hawaii bus. dir. 1989—), Hawaii Soc. Social Work Adminstrs. in Health Care (sec. 1991-93, 95—). Democrat. Roman Catholic. Office: Hawaii Pacific U 1188 Fort St Mall Honolulu HI 96813

SHERK, KENNETH JOHN, lawyer; b. Ida Grove, Iowa, Feb. 27, 1933; s. John and Dorothy (Myers) Sherk; m. Virginia Kay Taylor, June 28, 1958; children: Karin Fulton, Katrina, Keith, Kyle. BSC, U. Iowa, 1955; JD, George Washington U., 1961. Bar: Ariz. 1962, U.S. Dist. Ct. Ariz. 1962, U.S. Ct. Appeals (9th cir.) 1966, U.S. Supreme Ct. 1974. Assoc. Moore & Romley, Phoenix, 1962-67, ptnr., 1967-79; ptnr. Romley & Sherk, Phoenix, 1979-85; dir. Fennemore Craig, Phoenix, 1985—. Served as 1st lt. U.S. Army, 1955-58, Korea. Recipient Profl. Achievement Svcs. award George Washington Law Assn., 1986, Ariz. Judges Assn., 1989, Disting. Svc. award Phoenix Assn. Def. Counsel, 1990; named Mem. of Yr. State Bar of Ariz., 1994. Fellow Am. Coll. Trial Lawyers, Am. Acad. Appellate Lawyers, Am. Bar Found., Ariz. Bar Found.; mem. ABA (ho. of dels. 1990-93), Ariz. Bar Assn. (pres. 1985-86), Maricopa Bar Assn. (pres. 1978-79). Republican. Congregational. Home: 1554 W Las Palmaritas Dr Phoenix AZ 85012-2913 Office: Fennemore Craig 3003 N Central Ste 2600 Phoenix AZ 85012

SHERMAN, ALAN ROBERT, psychologist, educator; b. N.Y.C., Nov. 18, 1942; s. David R. and Goldie (Wax) S.; m. Llana Helene Tobias, Aug. 14, 1966 (div. 1989); children: Jonathan Colbert, Relissa Anne. BA, Columbia U., 1964; MS, Yale U., 1966, PhD, 1969. Lic. psychologist, Calif. Faculty psychology U. Calif., Santa Barbara, 1969—; clin. psychologist in pvt. practice Santa Barbara, 1981—; cons. in field. Author: Behavior Modification, 1973; contbr. articles to profl. jours. and chpts. in books. Pres. Santa Barbara Mental Health Assn., 1978, 84-85, 91, Mountain View Sch. Site Coun., Santa Barbara, 1978-84. Recipient Vol. of Yr. award Santa Barbara Mental Health Assn., 1979, Tchg. Excellence awards Delta Delta Delta, Alpha Chi Omega, Gamma Phi Beta, Santa Barbara; NIMH predoctoral rsch. fellow, 1964-69; grantee in field. Fellow Behavior Therapy and Rsch. Soc.; mem. APA, AAUP (chpt. pres. 1978-79), Calif. Psychol. Assn., Assn. for Advancement of Behavior Therapy, Santa Barbara County Psychol. Assn. (pres. 1985), Phi Beta Kappa (chpt. pres. 1977-78), Sigma Xi, Psi Chi (chpt. faculty advisor, 1979—). Office: Univ of Calif Dept Psychology Santa Barbara CA 93106-9660 *Pursuing a creative profession which allows one to help improve the condition of others, provides intrinsic rewards that make the work process satisfying in itself. I am fortunate to be involved in two such professions, college teaching and psychotherapy. When you genuinely enjoy what your are doing, you are likely to be successful at it.*

SHERMAN, ERIC, director, writer, educator; b. Santa Monica, Calif., June 29, 1947; s. Vincent and Hedda (Comorau) S.; m. Eugenia Blackiston Dillard, Apr. 1, 1978; children: Cosimo, Rocky. BA cum laude, Yale U., 1968. Film producer, dir., writer, photographer and editor; films include: Charles Lloyd-Journey Within, 1968; Paul Weiss-a Philosopher in Process, 1972; Waltz, 1980; Inside Out, 1982; Measure of America, 1983; Michael Reagan's Assault on Great Lakes, 1983, Futures, 1990 (Peabody Broadcast award 1990); represented in film festivals N.Y.C. Cine Golden Eagle, Melbourne, Australia, Bilbao, Spain, others; books include: (with others) The Director's Event, 1970; Directing the Film, 1976; Frame by Frame, 1987, Selling Your Film, 1990; pres. Film Transform; film tchr. Art Ctr. Coll. Design, Cal Arts, Pepperdine U., UCLA; guest lectr. Yale, Calif. Inst. Tech., U. So. Calif.; Andrew Mellon lectr. on arts Calif. Inst. Tech., 1977; chief cons. (motion picture industry) Gallup Orgn.; contbr. numerous articles to film publs. and distbn. catalogues, book dedication; works include three oral histories for Am. Film Inst. under Louis B. Mayer Found. grant. Trustee Am. Cinematheque; bd. dir. Film Forum. Mem. Soc. Motion Picture and TV Engrs. (asso.), Assn. Ind. Video and Filmmakers, Univ. Film Assn., Assn. Visual Communicators, Nat. Alliance Media Arts Ctrs. Home and Office: 4421 Dundee Dr Los Angeles CA 90027

SHERMAN, FREDERICK CHARLES, orthopedic surgeon; b. Marlboro, Mass., July 11, 1941; s. Frederick Louis and Dorothy (Field) S.; m. Susan Sherman; children: Kristin K., Frederick J. BA in Biology, Brown U., 1963; MD, Yale U., 1968. Resident orthopedist Fellowship Tng., 1972-76; med. dir. Carrie Tingley Hosp., Truth or Consequences, N.Mex., 1977-80; physician, founder N.Mex. Orthopedic Assocs., Albuquerque, 1980—; chmn. adv. com. Children's Med. Svcs., N.Mex., 1988—. Mem. editl. bd. Jour. Pediat. Orthopedics. Capt. U.S. Army, 1970-72. Fellow ACS, Am. Acad. Orthopedic Surgeons. Office: NMex Orthopedic Assocs 415 Cedar SE Albuquerque NM 87106

SHERMAN, FREDERICK HOOD, lawyer; b. Deming, N.Mex., Aug. 9, 1947; s. Benjamin and Helen (Hood) S.; m. Janie Carol Jontz, Oct. 23, 1973; children: Jerah Elizabeth, Frederick Jakub. BBA, Southern Meth. U., 1970, JD, 1972. Bar: Tex. 1972, N.Mex. 1973, U.S. Dist. Ct. N.Mex. 1973, U.S. Dist. Ct. (we. dist.) Tex. 1974, U.S. Supreme Ct. 1979; cert. mediator; bd. cert. civil trial advocate Nat. Bd. Trial Advocacy. Assoc. Sherman & Sherman, Deming, 1973-74, ptnr., 1974-78; prin. Sherman & Sherman P.C., Deming, 1978—; assoc. prof. Western N.Mex. U., Silver City, 1975-77; mem. specialization com. N.Mex. Supreme Ct., 1986-94; liaison N.Mex. Supreme Ct and Workers Compensation Bd., 1991-94; mem. jud. selection com. State Bar N.Mex., 1985-88, legal retreat com., 1986-88, co-chair, 1986-87, alternative dispute resolution com., 1980-91; owner Rio Mimbres Wine; apptd. guardian of assets State Fiscal Acctg. State N.Mex., 1992—; state coord. Nat. Bd. Trial Advocates for Bd. Cert. of Trial Specialist, 1994—. Contbr. articles to profl. jours. Chmn. Luna County Planning Commn., Deming, 1976-78; apptd. visitor to U. N.Mex. Law Sch., 1983—; treas. Luna County Econ. Devel. PSS, 1987-88, also bd. dirs.; bd. dirs. Luna County Hosp., 1991-94; bd. mem. Deming Pub. Sch., 1991-94, pres., 1991-92, elected bd. mem. 1991-95; chmn. bd. dirs. Luna County Charitable Found., 1991—; hon. dir. Deming Art Coun., 1989—; pres. Luna County Sch. Bd., 1991-92; pres., chmn. of the bd. Sherman Family Charitable Found., 1991—; mem. N. Mex. High Sch. Task Force, 1993-94; lector, communion minister Holy Family Catholic Ch. Named cert. civil trial adv. Nat. Bd. Trial Advocacy; recipient Svc. award N.Mex. Bd. Legal Specialization, 1994. Mem. ATLA (Notably Large award 1983, 84, 85), N.Mex. Trial Lawyers Assn. (bd. dirs. 1986—, sec. 1989, Amicus Curiae award, 1991), N.Mex. Bar Assn., State Bar N.Mex. (commr. 1978-86, com. on alt. dispute resolutions practice 1980-90, jud. selection com. 1985, com. for legal retreat 1989, Outstanding Svc. award, 1986, 94 and Dedication award 1986), Tex. Bar Assn., 6th Jud. Bar Assn., Am. Inns. of Ct. (master atty. 1995), Coll. State Bar Tex. (pro bono, 1995—), KC. Democrat. Roman Catholic. Office: Sherman & Sherman PC PO Box 850 Deming NM 88031-0850

SHERMAN, LINDA ARLENE, immunologist; b. N.Y.C., Feb. 27, 1950; d. Theodore and Helen (Tannenbaum) S.; m. Norman R. Klinman, June 18, 1978; children: Theodore, Matthew. BA, Barnard Coll., 1971; PhD, MIT, 1976. Postdoctoral fellow Albert Einstein Coll. Medicine, Bronx, 1976-77, Harvard Med. Sch., Boston, 1977-78; asst. mem. Scripps Clinic and Rsch. Found., La Jolla, Calif., 1978-85, assoc. mem., 1985—; adv. rev. panel NSF, Washington, 1985-89, Am. Cancer Soc., 1991-92; sci. adv. bd. Synbiotics, San Diego, 1988-90; mem. immunobiology study sect. NIH, 1992—. Section editor Jour. of Immunology, Bethesda, Md., 1990-94; contbr. articles to profl. jours. Rsch. grantee, Nat. Inst. on Aging, 1990—, NCI, 1989—, 1990—. Mem. Am. Assn. Immunologists. Home: 7766 Hillside Dr La Jolla CA 92037-3944 Office: Scripps Rsch Inst 10550 N Torrey Pines Rd La Jolla CA 92037-1027

SHERMAN, RANDOLPH, plastic and reconstructive surgeon, educator; b. St. Louis, May 27, 1951; s. Leon and Pearl (Lichtenfeld) S.; m. Sandra Lee Wackerman, May 3, 1992; 1 child, Max Lassen. BA, U. Rochester, 1973; MD, U. Mo., 1977. Intern in gen. medicine U. Wis., Madison, 1978; intern in surgery U. Calif., San Francisco, 1978-79, resident in surgery, 1979-81; resident in surgery SUNY, Syracuse, 1981-83; fellow in plastic and reconstructive surgery U. So. Calif., 1983-85; asst. prof. plastic and orthopedic surgery U. So. Calif. Sch. Medicine, L.A., 1985-90, assoc. prof. plastic, orthopedic and neurol. surgery, 1990-95, chmn. divsn. plastic and reconstructive surgery, 1994—; prof. plastic, orthop. and neurol. surgery U. So. Calif. Sch. Medicine, 1995—. Editor: Orthopedic Clinics, 1993; assoc. editor Jour. Hand Surgery, 1993-96, Am. Jour. Reconstructive Microsurgery, 1995—; contbr. articles to profl. jours. Founder L.A. chpt. Operation Smile Internat., 1993—. Recipient L.A. Humanitarian award Calif. Hosp., 1994. Fellow ACS, Am. Assn. Plastic Surgeons, Am. Assn. Hand Surgeons (bd. dirs. 1991-95), Am. Soc. Hand Surgery, Am. Soc. Reconstructive Microsurgery, Calif. Soc. Plastic Surgery. Office: U So Calif Divsn Plastic Surgery 1450 San Pablo St Los Angeles CA 90033-4615

SHERMAN, ROBERT B(ERNARD), composer, lyricist, screenwriter; b. N.Y.C., Dec. 19, 1925; s. Al and Rosa (Dancis) S.; student UCLA, 1943; BA, Bard Coll., 1949; MusD (hon.) Lincoln U., 1990; m. Joyce Ruth Sasner, Sept. 27, 1953; children: Laurie Shane, Jeffrey Craig, Andrea Tracy, Robert Jason. Popular songwriter, 1950-60, including Tall Paul, Pineapple Princess, You're Sixteen (Gold Record); songwriter Walt Disney Prodns., Beverly Hills, Calif., 1960-68, for 29 films including The Parent Trap, 1961, Summer Magic, 1963, Mary Poppins, 1964, That Darn Cat, 1965, Winnie The Pooh, 1965, Jungle Book, 1967, Bedknobs and Broomsticks, 1971; co-composer song It's A Small World, theme of Disneyland and Walt Disney World, Fla.; composer, lyricist United Artists, Beverly Hills, 1969—, songs for film Chitty, Chitty, Bang, Bang, 1969, Snoopy, Come Home!, 1972; song scores Charlotte's Web, 1972, Cabbage Patch Kids, 1974, Little Nemo, 1992, The Mighty Kong, 1996; composer for Walt Disney's Wonderful World of Color, TV, 1961—; co-producer NBC-TV spl. Goldilocks, 1970; v.p. Musi-Classics, Inc.; co-producer, composer, lyricist stage musical Victory Canteen, 1971; composer-lyricist Broadway show Over Here, 1975, Busker Alley, 1995; screenplay and song score Tom Sawyer, United Artists, 1972, Huckleberry Finn, 1974, The Slipper and the Rose, 1977, The Magic of Lassie, 1978. Served with inf. AUS, 1943-45; ETO. Decorated Purple Heart; recipient 2 Acad. awards best score for Mary Poppins, 1964, best song for Chim Chim Cheree, 1964; Grammy award, 1965; Christopher medal, 1965, 74; nine Acad. award nominations; Acad. award nomination for song score Bedknobs and Broomsticks, 1971, for best song The Age of Not Believing, 1971, others; 16 golden, 4 platinum and one diamond record album, 1965-83; first prize best composer song score Tom Sawyer, Moscow Film Festival, 1973, B.M.I. Pioneer award, 1977; Golden Cassette awards for Mary Poppins, Jungle Book, Bed Knobs and Broomsticks, 1983, Mouscar award Disney Studios, Disney Legend award, 1990, BMI Richard Kirk Achievment award, 1991. Mem. Acad. Motion Picture Arts and Scis. (exec. bd. music br. 12 yrs.), AFTRA, Nat. Acad. Rec. Arts and Scis., Composers and Lyricists Guild (exec. bd.), Dramatists Guild, Authors League. Office: 9030 Harratt St West Hollywood CA 90069-3858

SHERMAN, SIGNE LIDFELDT, portfolio manager, former research chemist; b. Rochester, N.Y., Nov. 11, 1913; d. Carl Leonard Broström and Herta Elvira Maria (Thern) Lidfeldt; m. Joseph V. Sherman, Nov. 18, 1944 (dec. Oct. 1984). BA, U. Rochester, 1935, MS, 1937. Chief chemist Lab. Indsl. Medicine and Toxicology Eastman Kodak Co., Rochester, 1937-43; chief rsch. chemist Chesebrough-Pond's Inc., Clinton, Conn., 1943-44; ptnr. Joseph V. Sherman Cons., N.Y.C., 1944-84; portfolio strategist Sherman Holdings, Troy, Mont., 1984—. Author: The New Fibers, 1946. Fellow Am. Inst. Chemists; mem. AAAS, AAUW (life), Am. Chem. Soc., Am. Econ. Assn., Am. Assn. Ind. Investors (life), Fedn. Am. Scientists (life), Union Concerned Scientists (life), Western Econ. Assn. Internat., Earthquake Engring. Rsch. Inst., Nat. Ctr. for Earthquake Engring. Rsch., N.Y. Acad. Scis. (life), Internat. Platform Assn., Cabinet View Country Club. Office: Sherman Holdings Angel Island 648 Halo Dr Troy MT 59935-9415

SHERRARD, RAYMOND HENRY, retired government official; b. Chgo., Mar. 8, 1944; s. Henry Loren and Minnie Valeria (Elrod) S.; m. Marsha L. McDermid, 1967 (div. 1971). AA, Long Beach City Coll., 1965; BA, Calif. State U., 1967; grad., Treasury Dept. Law Enforcement, Washington, 1970. Spl. dep. U.S. Marshal, L.A., 1970; pres. RHS Enterprises, Cypress, Calif., 1981-97; criminal investigator criminal investigation div. IRS, Santa Ana, Calif., 1969-94; story cons. Charles Fries Prodns., Hollywood, Calif., 1976—; instr. Fed. Law Enforcement Tng. Ctr., Glynco, Ga., 1977—; screenwriter Orion TV, Century City, Calif., 1984—; tech. advisor Paramount Pictures, Hollywood, 1987—; dir. speaker panel IRS, Laguna Niguel, Calif., 1984-92. Author: Federal Law Enforcement Patches, 1983, vol. 2, 1987, About Badges, 1987, Badges of the United Marshals, 1990, The Centurions Shield-A History of the Los Angeles Police Department, Its Badges and Insignia, 1996; columnist Police Colector News; contbr. articles to profl. jours. Recipient Presidential Commendation, Pres. U.S.A., Washington, 1980, Spl. Act award U.S. Treasury Dept., L.A., 1978, 87. Mem. Nat. Assn. Treasury Agts. (v.p. 1995-97), Fed. Criminal Investigators Assn. (life, regional v.p. 1978-80), Assn. Fed. Investigators, Fed. Law Enforcement Officers Assn., Calif. Narcotic Officers Assn. (life, sec. 1974). Republican. Home: PO Box 5779 Garden Grove CA 92846-0779

SHERRATT, GERALD ROBERT, university president; b. Los Angeles, Nov. 6, 1931; s. Lowell Heyborne and Elva Genevieve (Lamb) S. B.S. in Edn., Utah State U., 1953, M.S. in Edn. Adminstrn., 1954; Ph.D. in Adminstrn. Higher Edn., Mich. State U., 1975. Staff assoc. U. Utah, Salt Lake City, 1961-62; dir. high sch. relations Utah State U., Logan, 1962-64, asst. to pres., 1964-77, v.p. for univ. relations, 1977-81; pres. So. Utah U., Cedar City, 1982—; dir. Honeyville Grain Inc., Utah; mem. council pres. Utah System Higher Edn., 1982—; chmn. bd. Utah Summer Games, Cedar City, 1984—; chmn. pres.'s council Rocky Mountain Athletic Conf., Denver, 1984-85. Author hist. pageant: The West: America's Odyssey, 1973 (George Washington Honor medal 1973). Chmn. Festival of Am. West, Logan, Utah, 1972-82; chmn. bd. Utah Shakespearean Festival, Cedar City, 1982-86; chmn. bd. dirs. Salt Lake City Br. of the Fed. Res. Bank of San Francisco; bd. trustees Salt Lake Organizing Com. Winter Olympics 2002; chair bd. trustees Am. Folk Ballet; pres. Utah Higher Edn. Found. 1st lt. USAF, 1954-57. Recipient Editing award Indsl. Editors Assn., 1962, Robins award Utah State U., 1967, Disting. Alumnus award Utah State U., 1974, So. Utah U., 1991, Total Citizen award Cedar City C. of C., 1993; named to Utah Tourism Hall of Fame, 1989. Mem. Am. Assn. State Colls. and Univs., Cache C. of C. (bd. dirs. 1980-82), Phi Kappa Phi, Phi Delta Kappa, Sigma Nu (regent 1976-78). Mem. LDS Ch. Lodge: Rotary. Home: 331 W 200 S Cedar City UT 84720-3101 Office: So Utah U 351 W Center St Cedar City UT 84720-2470

SHERRIFFS, RONALD EVERETT, communication and film educator; b. Salem, Oreg., Apr. 10, 1934; s. Robert William and Margaret Kathleen (Tutt) S.; m. Mary Lona West, July 9, 1960; children: Ellen, Matthew. BA, San Jose State U., 1955, MA, 1957; PhD, U. So. Calif., 1964. Instr. theater Mich. State U., East Lansing, 1960-61; asst. prof. broadcasting Tex. Tech U., Lubbock, 1964-65; asst. prof. speech U. Oreg., Eugene, 1965-70, assoc. prof., 1970-79, prof. telecomm. and film, 1979-92, chmn. dept. speech, 1978-84, 88-90, prof. journalism and comm., 1993—. Author: (with others) Speech Communication via Radio and TV, 1971, TV Lighting Handbook, 1977, Small Format TV Production, 1985, 3d edit., Video Field Production and Editing, 1994, 4th edit., 1996; prodr., dir. TV programs, 1965—. Mem. Oreg. Pub. Broadcasting Policy Adv. Bd., 1980-88. Served to lt. comdr. USNR, 1957-68, PTO. Faculty enrichment program grantee Can., 1984, 91. Mem. Speech Communication Assn. Am., AAUP, Western States Communication Assn. Clubs: Oreg. Track; McKenzie Flyfishers (Eugene). Office: Univ Oreg Journalism Dept Eugene OR 97403

SHERRILL, BARBARA ANN BUKER, elementary school educator; b. Hamilton, Mont., July 11, 1952; d. Emery Orville and Helen (Hackett) Buker; m. Mark Warren Sherrill, Oct. 7, 1978; children: Kristopher Kain, Ashley Ann. BS in Elem. Edn., Western Mont. Coll., 1973, postgrad., 1984; M. Human Svcs., U. of Gt. Falls, 1991. Cert. tchr., Mont. Tchr. elem. grades Ramsay (Mont.) Sch., 1974-90; tchr. Sch. Dist. 1, Butte, Mont., 1990—; media coord. Creativity Factory Preschool, Butte, 1974-87; facilitator labor history workshop Internat. Brotherhood Teamsters, U. Wis., 1987, U. Calif. at Berkeley, 1988; writer, researcher, 1987-88. Co-author: Teaching Labor Studies in the Schools, vol. 1, 1988, Gezel Tester, 1991—. Parent vol. Silver Bow Amateur Wrestling Assn. Butte, pairings master. Mem. AAUW, Am. Fedn. Tchrs., Mont. Fedn. Tchrs., AFL-CIO, Ramsey Fedn. Tchrs. (pres. 1975-79), Butte Tchrs. Union, Mont. Energy Edn. Coun. (bd. dirs. 1991, v.p. 1995—, presenter workshop), Alpha Delta Kappa (pres. Mu chpt. 1994-96, corr. sec. Mont. chpt. 1996—). Democrat. Office: West Elem Sch Emmett And Steel St Butte MT 59701

SHERSHER, ZINOVY ISRAIL, artist; b. Birobidjan, USSR, Apr. 12, 1947; came to U.S., 1980; s. Israil and Adel (Schkliar) S.; m. Irina Levinson, Feb. 5, 1977; children: Roman, Lawrence. Student, Sch. of Fine Arts and Design, Kursk, Russia, 1962-65; MA, U. Fine/Applied Arts, Kursk, Russia, 1970; MusB, Mus. Coll., Kursk, Russia, 1975; student, Sch. of Visual Arts, N.Y.C., 1981-82. Fine artist various art galleries, 1980-91, Inspiration Art Studio, Hollywood, Calif., 1991—. One-man shows include Am.-Israeli Friendship Club, Bklyn., 1980, Metropol, Bklyn., 1985, Sherberg Gallery, L.A., 1989-90, Art Expo Calif. '90, L.A., 1990, Window Gallery, Beverly Hills, Calif., 1992, Security Pacific Bank, North Hollywood, Calif., 1992, Birch Gallery, L.A., 1993, pvt. show, Santa Barbara, Calif., 1993; exhibited in group shows All City Art Show, Oreol, USSR, 1973, Young Artist Group Show, Moscow, 1978, Regal Art Gallery, Bklyn., 1982-85, Installation One Gallery, Encino, Calif., 1989, Finegood Gallery, West Hills, Calif., 1989, Sherberg Gallery, L.A., 1989-90, Mussavi Gallery, South Hampton, N.Y., 1990, George Mayers Gallery, L.A., 1991, Ulf Breed Gallery, Munich, 1992, Barakat Gallery, Beverly Hills, Calif., 1992, Salmagundi Club, N.Y.C., 1992, Sloane Gallery, Denver, Opera Gallery, Singapore, others; represented in pvt. and pub. collections. Contbr. art Assn. for Breast Cancer Studies, Woodland Hills, Calif., 1994, Big Sisters Guild, L.A., 1994. Recipient Award of Appreciation, City of L.A., 1992, Internat. Inst. award, 1992. Mem. Oil Pastel Assn. Home: 6260 Morse Ave North Hollywood CA 91606-2920 Office: Zinovy Studio 4517 Mammoth Ave Sherman Oaks CA 91423

SHERWIN, NOEL V., psychologist, educator; b. Taft, Calif., Aug. 30, 1926. BA cum laude, Wheelock Coll., 1972; EdM, Harvard U., 1974; EdD, Boston U., 1979. Teaching fellow Boston U.; asst. prof. U. Maine, Augusta; pvt. practice in psychotherapy. Dir. Operation Reparation, Boston, 1968-78; chair bd. dirs. Ajo (Ariz.) Lukeville Health Dist., 1995—. Mem. Harvard Club Ariz. Democrat.

SHERWOOD, ALLEN JOSEPH, lawyer; b. Salt Lake City, Sept. 26, 1909; s. Charles Samuel and Sarah (Abramson) Shapiro; m. Edith Ziff, Jan. 19, 1941; children—Mary (Mrs. John Marshall), Arthur Lawrence. Student, UCLA, 1927-30; AB, U. So. Calif., 1933, LLB, 1933. Bar: Calif. 1933, U.S. Supreme Ct. 1944. Pvt. practice law L.A., 1933-54, Beverly Hills, 1954-95; legal counsel Internat. Family Planning Rsch. Assn., Inc., 1970-76; bd. dirs. Family Planning Ctrs. Greater L.A., Inc., 1968-84, pres., 1973-76. Mem. editorial bd. So. Calif. Law Rev., 1932-33. Contbr. articles to profl. jours. Mem. Calif. Atty. Gen.'s Vol. Adv. Coun. and its legis. subcom., 1972-78. Mem. Med.-Legal Soc. So. Calif. (bd. dirs. 1966-74), ABA, L.A. County Bar Assn., Beverly Hills Bar Assn., State Bar of Calif., Am. Arbitration Assn. (nat. panel arbitrators 1965—), Order of Coif, Tau Delta Phi, Brentwood Country Club (L.A.), Masons. Home: 575 Moreno Ave Los Angeles CA 90049-4840

SHERWOOD, ANNE LESLEY, molecular biologist; b. Chgo., May 10, 1954; d. William Milton and Maryon Renee (Bilodeau) Zilbersher; m. Yoshihide Sakuragi, July 25, 1981 (div. June 1989). BA, Kenyon Coll., 1976; MS, U. Ark., 1978; PhD, Purdue U., 1987. Rsch. microbiologist Cities Svc. Oil Co., Tulsa, Okla., 1976-77; rsch. asst. in immunology U. Ark., Fayetteville, 1979-81; postdoctoral sr. fellow dept. biochemistry U. Wash., Seattle, 1987-89; rsch. assoc. Pacific N.W. Rsch. Found., Seattle, 1989-95; asst. mem. dept. cell surface biochemistry N.W. Hosp., Seattle, 1996—. Contbr. articles to profl. jours. Del. Wash. Dem. Com., Seattle, 1992; musician Seattle Philharm. Orch., 1987—; mem. choir St. Stephen's Ch.; mem. folk groups Old Growth, Woodside. Mem. AAAS, Assn. Women in Sci., Puget Sound Biotech. Soc. (Puget Sound chpt.). Episcopalian. Home: 5304 228th St SW Mountlake Terrace WA 98043-3933 Office: Northwest Hosp Dept Cell Surface Biochem Seattle WA 98125

SHERWOOD, PATRICIA WARING, artist, educator; b. Columbia, S.C., Dec. 19, 1933; d. Clark du Val and Florence (Yarbrough) Waring; divorced; children: Cheryl Sherwood Kraft, Jana Sherwood Kern, Marikay Sherwood Taitt. BFA magna cum laude, Calif. State U., Hayward, 1970; MFA, Mills Coll., Oakland, Calif., 1974; postgrad., San Jose State U., 1980-86. Cert. tchr., Calif. Tchr. De Anza Jr. Coll., Cupertino, Calif., 1970-78, Foothill Jr. Coll., Los Altos, Calif., 1972-78, West Valley Jr. Coll., Saratoga, Calif., 1978—; artist-in-residence Centrum Frans Masereel, Kasterlee, Belgium, 1989. One-woman shows include Triton Mus., Santa Clara, Calif., 1968, RayChem Corp., Sunnyville, Calif., 1969, Palo Alto (Calif.) Cultural Ctr., 1977, Los Gatos (Calif.) Mus., 1992, Stanford U. faculty club, Palo Alto, 1993, d.p. Fong Gallery, San Jose, Calif., 1995, 97, Heritage Bank, San Jose, 1997, City Coll., San Jose, 1997; exhibited in group shows at Tressider Union Stanford U., 1969, Oakland (Calif.) Mus. Kaiser Ctr., 1969, Sonoma (Calif.) State Coll., 1969, Bank Am., San Francisco, 1969, San Francisco Art Festival, 1969, 70, U. Santa Clara, 1967, Charles and Emma Frye Mus., Seattle, 1968, Eufrat Gallery DeAnza Coll., Cupertino, 1975, San Jose Mus. Art, 1976, Lytton Ctr., Palo Alto, 1968 (1st award), Zellerbach Ctr., San Francisco, 1970, Works Gallery, San Jose, 1994; represented in permanent collections Mills Coll., Bank Am., San Francisco, Heritage Bank, San Jose. Art judge studnet show Stanford U., Palo Alto, 1977; mem. d.p. Fong Gallery, San Jose, Calif., 1994. Nat. Endowment for Arts/We. States Art Fedn. fellow, 1994. Mem. Calif. Print Soc., Womens Caucus for Arts, Internat. Platform Assn. Home: 1500 Arriba Ct Los Altos CA 94024-5941 Office: West Valley Jr Coll Art Dept 14000 Fruitvale Ave Saratoga CA 95070-5640

SHI, WENYUAN, microbiologist; b. Hangzhou, Zhejiang, China, June 26, 1962; came to U.S., 1985; s. Zhuxian Shi; m. Hanjing Yang, Sept. 3, 1987; 1 child, Jamie Young. BS in Genetics, Fudan U., Shanghai, China, 1984; PhD in Genetics, U. Wis., 1992. Rsch. asst. U. Wis., Madison, 1985-92; rsch. scientist U. Calif., Berkeley, 1992-95; prof. UCLA, 1995—. Author: Methods in Molecular Microbiology, 1994; contbr. articles to profl. jours. Pres. SOS China Edn. Fund, Calif., 1992-93, gen. sec., 1994; pres. Smargen Hitechland, Calif., 1994—. Mem. Am. Soc. Microbiology. Home: 7011 Kentwood Ave Los Angeles CA 90045-1253 Office: Sch Medicine and Dentistry Ctr for Health Scis 10833 Le Conte Ave Los Angeles CA 90024-1602

SHIDELER, ROSS PATRICK, foreign language and comparative literature educator, author, translator, poet; b. Denver, Apr. 12, 1936. B.A., San Francisco State U., 1958; M.A., U. Stockholm, 1963; Ph.D., U. Calif., Berkeley, 1968. Instr. in comparative lit. U. Calif., Berkeley, 1967-68; asst. prof. English Hunter Coll., N.Y.C., 1968-69; asst. prof. Scandinavian lang. and comparative lit. UCLA, 1969-73, assoc. prof., 1973-79, prof., 1979—; chmn. program in comparative lit., 1979-86, 92-96. Author: (monograph) Voices Under The Ground: Themes and Images in the Poetry of Gunnar Ekelof, 1973, Per Olov Enquist-A Critical Study, 1984; translator: (play) The Night of the Tribades (Per Olov Enquist), 1977, The Hour of the Lynx, 1990 (Per Olov Enquist), 1990; U.S. assoc. editor Swedish Book Rev., 1984—. Fellow NDFL, 1964; fellow NDEA, 1965; Fulbright-Hays fellow, 1966-67. Mem. MLA (exec. com. divsn. Scandinavian Langs. and Lits. 1993-97), Soc. Advancement Scandinavian Studies (exec. coun. 1985-89, v.p. 1997—), Am. Comparative Lit. Assn., Assn. Depts. and Programs Comparative Lit. (exec. com. 1993-94, 94—). Office: UCLA Dept Comparative Lit Los Angeles CA 90024

SHIELDS, DEBORAH JOANNE, accounting technician; b. New Haven, Aug. 22, 1962; d. Howard and Joan Carol (Goehring) Bensen; m. James Alexander Shields, Apr. 1, 1995; 1 child, Hannah Carol. BS in English, Calif. State U., Fullerton, 1987. Acctg. tech. U. N.Mex., Albuquerque, 1993—. Firefighter Edgewood (N.Mex.) Fire Dept., 1991-93. Capt. USAF, 1988-92. Office: Deejay Publs PO Box 361 Edgewood NM 87015

SHIELDS, JOSEPH DAVID, secondary school educator, guidance counselor; b. Walsenburg, Colo., July 10, 1945; s. Alexander and Lea Marie (Guerri) S.; m. Sylvia Ann Vanderwork, Aug. 28, 1965; children: Sean Alexander, Stacey Ann Riemenschneider, Stephanie Ann Sewell. BA, U. No. Colo., 1970, postgrad., 1990—. Indsl. arts instr. Boulder (Colo.) Valley Pub. Sch.; bldr., contr., rancher Ea. Colo.; tchr. BOCES, Yuma, Colo.; wrestling coach pub. schs., Boulder/Arickaree/Woodin, Colo.; vocat. tchr. Rebound Corp., Brush, Colo.; tchr., guidance counselor Plainview H.S., Sheridan Lake, Colo. Composer: (song) Lonely christmas/Echoes of the Past, 1982. Treas. Towner (Colo.) Bd., 1994-96. with USN, 1964-67. Mem. Elks (lecturing knight 1994). Republican. Roman Catholic. Home: 13855 3d St Towner CO 81071 Office: Plainview High School 1268 School House Rd Sheridan Lake CO 81071

SHIERS, FRANK ABRAM, lawyer; b. Marlboro, Mass., Oct. 23, 1920; s. Frank and Sarah (Chalk) S.; m. Sylvia A. Broz, Mar. 27, 1954; children: Frank A., Jane Marie Shiers Bryce. BA, Western Wash. U., 1942; JD, U. Wash., 1949. Bar: Wash. 1949, U.S. Dist. Ct. (we. dist.) Wash. 1950, U.S. Supreme Ct. 1969. Pvt. practice law Port Orchard, Wash., since 1949; ptnr. Greenwood & Shiers, Port Orchard, since 1950; now sr. ptnr. Shiers, Chrey, Cox & Caulkins, Port Orchard. Mem. Kitsap County Estate Planning Coun. Mem. Wash. State Bar Assn. (com. on profl. legal svcs. to armed forces and fee arbitration bd.), Kitsap County Bar Assn., VFWW, Am. Legion, Kitsap County-Wash. State Trial Lawyers Assn., Navy League (past pres. Bremerton coun.), Young Men's Bus. Club (past pres. Wash. chpt.), Elks (by-laws chmn. Wash. chpt.). Office: Shiers Chrey Cox & Caulkin 600 Kitsap St Ste 202 Port Orchard WA 98366-5394

SHIERSHKE, NANCY FAY, artist, property manager; b. St. Helens, Oreg., May 10, 1935; d. David Cline and Matilda Ruth (Pearce) Morrison; m. H. McNeal Kavanagh, Sept. 4. 1955 (dec. Dec. 1978); children: Marjorie L. Wood, David M. Kavanagh, Katherine F. Fiske; m. Richard M. Shiershke, Nov. 29, 1980. AA, Pasadena (Calif.) City Coll., 1956; BA, UCLA, 1965. Substitute elem. sch. tchr. Buena Park, Calif., 1967-69; property mgr. Pky. Cts., Arcadia, Calif., 1977—; libr. Reading Rm., Arcadia, 1979-87; freelance artist Kavanagh-Shiershke Art St., San Gabriel, Arcadia, Calif., 1985—; art gallery hostess Descanso Gardens, La Canada, Flintridge, Calif., 1990—; display and sales person Village Fine Arts Gallery, Arcadia, 1991-92; art instr. Tri Cmty. Adult Edn., Covina, Calif., 1994—. Group shows include Pasadena Presbyn. Ch., 1985—, Hillcrest Ch., 1992—, Descanso Gardens, 1994—, San Gabriel Fine Arts, 1994—. Named Artist of the Yr. Mid Valley art League, 1990; Recipient Best of Show San Gabriel Fine Arts, 1991, Hulsebus award Pasadena Prebyn. Ch., 1996. Mem. Nat. Watercolor Soc., San Gabriel Fine Arts, Mid Valley Fine Arts, East Valley Fine Arts, Valley Watercolor Soc., Foothill Creative Arts Group. Home: 505 Vaquero Rd Arcadia CA 91007 Office: 614 E Vine St West Covina CA 91722

SHIFFER, JAMES DAVID, retired utility executive; b. San Diego, Mar. 24, 1938; s. Kenneth Frederick and Thelma Lucille (Good) S.; m. Margaret Edith Rightmyer, Sept. 5, 1959 (div. July 1986); children: James II, Elizabeth Gonzales, Russell; m. Esther Zamora, Sept. 13, 1986; stepchildren: Bryan Boots, Jeremy Hellier, Marisol Boots. BS ChemE, Stanford U., 1960, MS ChemE, 1961. Registered profl. engr., Calif. Nuclear engr. Pacific Gas & Electric Co., Humboldt Bay Power Plant, Eureka, Calif., 1961-71; tech. mgr. Pacific Gas & Electric. Co., Diablo Canyon Power Plant, Avila Beach, Calif., 1971-80; mgr. nuclear ops. Pacific Gas & Electric Co., San Francisco, 1980-84, v.p. nuclear power generation, 1984-90, sr. v.p., gen. mgr. nuclear power generation bus. unit, 1990-91; exec. v.p. Pacific Gas & Electric, San Francisco, 1991-97; ret., 1997; pres., CEO PG&E Enterprises, San Francisco, 1994-95, also bd. dirs.; bd. dirs. Nuclear Energy Inst., U.S. Oper. Svcs. Co., Math., Engring., Sci. Achievement. Mem. AIChE, Commonwealth Club of Calif. (bd. govs. 1992-97). Republican. Episcopalian. Home: 2550 Royal Oaks Dr Alamo CA 94507-2227

SHIFFMAN, LESLIE BROWN, management executive; b. Fresno, Calif., Dec. 9, 1936; d. Albert Brown and Marion Jean (Riese) Brown-Propp; married, Jan. 20, 1957 (div. 1972); m. Sydney Shiffman, July 4, 1993; children: Susan, Steven, David, Thomas. BS, U. So. Calif., 1958. Office mgr. pvt. practice physician, Long Beach, Calif., 1971-73; cost acct. Panavision, Inc., Tarzana, Calif., 1974-76; exec. sec. Hartman Galleries, Beverly Hills, Calif., 1976-78; adminstrv. asst. Galanos Originals, L.A., 1978—. Named L.A. Alumnae Panhellenic Assn. Women of Yr., 1977. Mem. Alpha Epsilon Phi (nat. pres. 1985-89, trustee, sec. Alpha Epsilon Phi Found. Inc. 1990-91, pres. 1991-95, treas. 1996— Woman of Distinction award 1993), Order of Omega Honorary. Republican. Jewish. Home: 1745 S Bentley Ave # 1 Los Angeles CA 90025-4323 Office: Galanos Originals 2254 S Sepulveda Blvd Los Angeles CA 90064-1812

SHIFFMAN, MICHAEL A., lawyer; b. Newark, July 23, 1941. LLB magna cum laude, Lincoln U., 1973. Bar: Calif. 1973, U.S. Dist. Ct. (no. dist.) Calif. 1973; lic. real estate broker. Atty. Lanahan & Reilley, San Francisco. Editor: Lincoln U. Law Rev., 1972-73. Mem. ABA, Internat. Bar Assn., State Bar Calif., Bar Assn. San Francisco. Office: Lanahan & Reilly 500 Sansome St # 301 San Francisco CA 94111-1000

SHIH, HSIENCHENG, medicinal chemist; b. Pingtung, Taiwan, Feb. 13, 1947; came to U.S., 1975; s. Ching-nan and Ching-Jui (Wang) S.; m. Weiyung Yoko Chan, Nov. 26, 1983; children: Renshy Alexis, Renshuay Justin. BS in Pharmacy, Kaohsiung Med. Coll., 1969; MS in Medicinal Chemistry, U. R.I., 1977; PhD in Medicinal Chemistry, SUNY, Buffalo, 1982. Postdoctoral fellow M.D. Anderson Hosp. & Tumor Inst., Houston, 1982; group leader Food & Drug Bur., Taipei, Taiwan, 1983; postdoctoral fellow Med. U. S.C., Charleston, Taiwan, 1984; rsch. fellow Naylor Dana Inst. Am. Health Found., Valhalla, N.Y., 1984-86; rsch. assoc. Marshall U., Huntington, W.Va., 1986-89; asst. mem. The Whittier Inst., La Jolla, Calif., 1989-90; rsch. staff U. Calif., San Diego, 1991—. Patentee in field. Mem. Am. Chem. Soc., Am. Assn. Pharm. Scientists. Home: 10735 Passerine Way San Diego CA 92121-4216 Office: U Calif 9500 Gilman Dr La Jolla CA 92093-0663

SHIH, MARIE, metaphysical healer; b. Florence, Ariz., Jan. 24, 1959; d. John Cecil and Josephine Marie (Carter) Lewis; m. Ravi Sundervardan Candadai, Aug. 13, 1982 (div. Aug. 1984); m. Tony Hu-Tung Shih, July 11, 1987 (div. Sept. 1991); m. Jack Hunter Caldwell, Jan. 2, 1995; children: John Lewis Caldwell, James Carter Caldwell; step-children: Trevor Hunter, Levi Robert. BA, U. Ariz., 1982, postgrad., 1982-84. Musician, writer, illustrator, Tucson and Seattle, 1978-94; front desk clk. Ghost Ranch Lodge, Tucson, 1982-83; adminstrv. sec. Starnet Corp., Seattle, 1985-86; vol. U.S. Peace Corps, Mbalmayo, Cameroun, Africa, 1986; practitioner Christian Science Ch., 1994—, ch. vocalist, 1994; ind. team mgr. Noevir Natural Herbal Cosmetics, Seattle, 1987-92, author, editor mo. newsletter, 1989-92, attended nat. convs., 1989-92; lectr. So. Seattle Cmty. Coll., 1990-92. Author press releases, bus. forms local orgns., Tucson, Seattle, 1978-94; editor letters, speeches local orgns., Seattle; author, editor, designer mo. newsletter Fairmount News and Views, 1993-94; contbr. articles to jours. Bd. dirs., com. chmn. S.W. Seattle Literacy Coalition, 1989-90; active Arts-West, United Way, West Seattle Totem Theatre, 1990-94; bus. sponsor West Seattle Hi-Yu, 1991; active 6th Ch. of Christ, Scientist, Seattle, 1987-96, 1st reader, 1991-94; active 1st Ch. of Christ, Scientist, Boston, 1990—, Christian Sci. Soc. of Casa Grande, 1996—; mem. steering com. Constellation Park and Marine Res. at Ritchey Viewpoint, 1993-94; founding mem. Fairmount Ravine Preservation Group, 1993-94; substitute ch. soloist, Chehalis, 1994. Mem. NAFE, West Seattle C. of C. (area dir. 1990-91, com. mem. 1990-93, com. chair 1992-93), Neighborhood Promotion Com., Coolidge C. of C. Republican. Address: PO Box 1964 Coolidge AZ 85228

SHILLINGTON, KEITH ALLAN, principal, consultant; b. Palo Alto, Calif., Apr. 13, 1955; s. Dennis Frederick and Mary S. BA in Computer Sci., U. Calif., San Diego, 1978. Mgr. software distbn. U. Calif.-San Diego Inst. Info. Systems, 1977-78; operational and orgnl. designer, customer cons. SofTech Microsystems, San Diego, 1979-80; instr. Ada courses, designer software tools, mgr. validation testing & mktg. data TeleSoft, San Diego, 1980-90; instr. Ada courses, contractor Fastrak Tng. Inc., San Diego, 1992-95; cons. Aonix, 1997—; cons. Sci. Applied Internat. Corp. Editor: UCSD Pascal Users Manual, 1978-80; author Ada Compiler Validation Capability tests. Ind. contractor, Ada instr. and system troubleshooter, office mgr. San

Diego Earth Day, 1990-91, bd. dirs., 1993—. Mem. IEEE, Assn. for Computing Machinery.

SHIMA, LARRY MITSURU, health facility administrator; b. Tokyo, Nov. 17, 1958; came to U.S., 1970; s. Masa and Amy A. (Narisawa) S.; m. Fran T. Shinsato, July 14, 1991; 1 child, Austin Y. BS in Med. Tech., U. Hawaii, 1981; MS in Health Svcs. Adminstrn., Cen. Mich. U., 1994. Med. technologist Kuakini Med. Ctr., Honolulu, 1980-86; chemistry specialist Straub Clinic and Hosp., Honolulu, 1986-89; chemistry supr. Health Care Internat., Aiea, Hawaii, 1989; from ops. supr. to ops. mgr. Pali Momi Med. Ctr., Aiea, Hawaii, 1990-94; ops. mgr. Clin. Labs. Hawaii, Honolulu, 1994-96; ops mgr. Singapore divsn. Clin. Labs. Hawaii, 1996—; quality assurance coun. mem. Kapiolani Health Systems, Honolulu, 1993-94, tissueand transfusion mem., 1992-94, cons. cholesterol testing, 1991-94; cons. lab. computer sys., 1990-91. Mem. Clin. Lab. Mgmt. Assn., Am. Assn. for Clin. Chemistry, Am. Soc. Clin. Pathologists, Acad. Med. Arts & Scis., John A. Burns Sch. Medicine Alumni Assn. Republican. Home: 10 G Braddell Hill #02-25, Braddell View 579726, Singapore Office: Clins Labs Hawaii, 219 Henderson Rd #07-03, Henderson Industrial Park 159556, Singapore

SHIMEK, JOHN ANTON, legal investigation business owner, educator; b. Chgo., Sept. 1, 1925; s. John Anton Sr. and Florence Marie (Redman) S.; m. Corinne Gladys Hornburg, Mar. 1, 1947 (div. June 1988); m. Janet Lea Inghram Shyder, Sept. 10, 1988; children: Ronald Wayne, Scott Anthony, Brian Dean Snyder. AA, Phoenix Coll., 1963; BS, Grand Canyon Coll., 1967; M of Phys. Edn., Sussex (Eng.) Coll., 1974. Cert. sch. adminstr. Am. Police Acad.; cert. aquatic dir.; lic. pvt. investigator; lic. ins. agt. Patrolman Chgo. Police Dept., 1946-51; agt. Met. Life Ins., Colorado Springs/Phoenix, 1951-61; owner, head coach Ariz. Swim Devils, Phoenix, 1967-80; phys. dir., assoc. dir. Phoenix YMCA, 1957-67; sch. adminstr. Cartwright Sch. Dist., Phoenix, 1967-88; pres., owner Shimek & Assocs., Inc., Glendale, Ariz., 1988—; adj. prof. Grand Canyon Coll., Phoenix, 1963-83; spl. agt Internat. Intelligence and Organized Crime Investigations Assn., Washington, 1981-83; mem. AAU Regional Swimming Com., 1967-68; mem. coach AAU State Swim Com., chmn., 1966-67. Author: Physical Education Handbook, 1979, 80; co-author: An Annotated Bibliography of Experimental Research Concerning Competitive Swimming, 1970, (video) Desert Survival, 1983; contbr. articles to mags. Commdr., instr. search and rescue team Maricopa County Sheriff's Office, Ariz., 1980-89; counselor police acad. Ariz. Dept. Pub. Safety, Tucson, 1982. With USN, 1942-47, WWII. Named to Swimming Hall of Fame, Internat. Swimming Hall of Fame, 1971-72. Mem. Am. Legion (comdr. 1980—, Americanism citation 1980-81), Fraternal Order of Police (trustee 1980—), Arrowhead Country Club. Republican. Methodist. Home: 7827 W Julie Dr Glendale AZ 85308

SHIMM, DAVID STUART, medical educator; b. Chgo., Dec. 6, 1952; s. Melvin G. and Cynia A. (Brown) S. BA, Harvard U., 1973; MD, Duke U., 1977. Diplomate Am. Bd. Internal Medicine, Am. Bd. Radiology. House staff Duke Hosp., Durham, N.C., 1978-80, Mass. Gen. Hosp., Boston, 1981-83; instr. Harvard Med. Sch., Boston, 1985-89; asst. prof. U. Ariz., Tucson, 1985-89, assoc. prof., 1989—. Office: Dept Radiation Oncology U Ariz 1501 N Campbell Ave Tucson AZ 85724

SHIMODA, JERRY YASUTAKA, retired national historic park superintendent; b. Haleiwa, Hawaii, Mar. 21, 1930; s. Tamotsu and Sasai Shimoda; m. Clara H. Segawa, Aug. 7, 1954; children: Karen Marie K., Randall T., Shaun T., Teri Ellen H., Jacqueline Y., David Y. BA in Govt., U. Hawaii, 1952, MA in Far Ea. Area Studies, 1957; postgrad., St. Louis U., 1957-59. Historian Jefferson Nat. Expansion Meml. Nat. Hist. Site, St. Louis, 1957-60; chief historian, in charge hist. rsch. and visitor svcs. Saratoga Nat. Hist. Park, Stillwater, N.Y., 1960-66; chief historian Home of Franklin D. Roosevelt Nat. Hist. Site and Frederick Vanderbilt Nat. Hist. Site, Hyde Park, N.Y., 1966-69; instr. Nat. Park Svc. Stephen T. Mather Tng. Ctr., Harpers Ferry, W.Va., 1969-72; supt. Pu'uhonua o Honaunau (Hawaii) Nat. Hist. Park, 1972-96, Puukohola Heiau Nat. Hist. Site, Honaunau, 1972-96; ret., 1996; lectr. environ. edn. Pa. State U., U. W.Va., Shepherd Coll., 1969-72; acting supr. Kaloko-Honokohau Nat. Hist. Park, 1988-90; instr. environ. edn., interpretive and basic instructing techniques U. Hawaii, Hilo, Kapiolani C.C.; U.S. del. U.S.-Japan Panel on Nat. Parks and Equivalent Res., 1968—, World Conf. on Marine Parks, Tokyo, 1975; Japanese translator U.S. Nat. Park Svc.; mem. internat. bd. dirs. Heritage Interpretation Internat.; numerous presentations at confs. and tng. courses. Author booklets on nat. parks, mgmt. and history; contbr. numerous articles to profl. publs., mags. and newspapers. Bd. dirs. Volcano Art Ctr.; mem. adv. com. Wailoa State Ctr.; mem. Hawaii Gov.'s Task Force on Ocean and Recreation; chmn. restoration com. St. Benedict's Ch., Honounau, 1982-95; chmn. bd. dirs. Kahua Na'au 'Ao, 1996-97. Recipient spl. achievement award Nat. Park Svc., 1964, 68, 70, resolution W.Va. Senate, 1971, Hawaii Ho. of Reps., 1982, sec.'s cert. Dept. Interior, 1971, Exec. of Yr. award West Hawaii chpt. Profl. Secs. Internat., 1981, cert. Govt. of Japan, 1981, staff plaque Pu'uhonua o Honaunau Nat. Hist. Park, Puukohola Heiau Nat. Hist. Site and Kaloko-Honokohau Nat. Hist. Park, 1988, cert. Japan Nat. Parks Assn., 1989, cert. of appreciation South Kona Aloha Lions Club, 1990, Meritorious Svc. award Sec. Interior, 1996, also others. Mem. Hawaii Mus. Assn. (bd. dirs. 1988-92), Kona Hist. Soc. (bd. dirs. 1988-92), Big Island Ocean Recreation and Tourism Assn. (exec. com.), Kona Judo Club (pres. 1977—), Rotary (pres. Kona Nauka 1978-79, Paul Harris fellow 1991, Disting. Svc. award 1992).

SHIMPFKY, RICHARD LESTER, bishop; b. Albuquerque, Oct. 18, 1940; m. Jamel Shimpfky, 1966; children: Trevor, Allison, Joshua. Grad., U. Colo., 1963, Va. Theol. Seminary, 1970. Ordained to diaconate Episc. Ch., 1970. With William L. Philips Found., Richmond, Va., 1963-67; curate St. Peter's Ch., Arlington, 1970-72; vicar All Saints' Sharon Chapel, Alexandria, Va., 1972-73, rector, 1973-77; rector Christ Ch., Ridgewood, N.J., 1977-90; bishop Diocese El Camino Real, Monterey, Calif., 1990—. Office: Diocese of El Camino Real PO Box 1903 Monterey CA 93942-1093*

SHIN, SUK-HAN, geography educator, director Korean-American affairs; b. Seoul, Korea, Aug. 28, 1930; came to U.S., 1964; s. Kee Duk and Jung Sook (Shin) S.; m. Myung Jah Kim, Dec. 30, 1958; children: Yong Wook, Soo Hyun. BA, Seoul Nat. U., 1954; MA, Clark U., 1967; PhD, U. Pitts., 1975. Tchr. Jin Myung Girls Sr. High Sch., Seoul, 1954-61; urban planner Chonghab Architect Rsch. Ctr., Seoul, 1961-62; asst. planner S.W. Pa. Regional Planning Commn., Pitts., 1968; rsch. fellow Korea Rsch. Inst. of Human Settlements, Seoul, 1980; environ. scientist Engring.-Sci., Inc., Pasadena, Calif., 1982; prof. geography Ea. Wash. U., Spokane, Wash., 1969-92, prof. emeritus, 1992—; dir. Inst. Korean-Am. Affairs, Ea. Wash. U., Spokane, Wash., 1980-92; vis. prof. Seoul Nat. U., 1980, 82, 87; exch. prof. Dogguk U., 1986-87. Author: Journal of Environmental Conservation, 1977, Impact of Industrial Development, 1980, Environment: Conservation Management and B/C, 1983; (chpt. in book) Themes and Research Methods, 1983. Mem. Adv. Coun. on Peaceful Unification of Republic of Korea, Seoul, 1982-87, 91-93, Spokane Internat. Coordinating Coun., Spokane, 1986-88; pres. Spokane Korean Assn., 1978-84, Spokane Korean-Am. Citizens Assn., 1989-92; chmn. Seoul Olympic Supporting Com. of Spokane, 1986-88; advisor Korean Cmty. Counseling Ctr., Seattle, 1996—. Donnelly fellow Clark U., 1965-66; grantee Korea Rsch. Found.; recipient City Medal of Seoul, 1980, Disting. Korean Scientist Abroad, Min. Sci. and Tech., ROK, 1980, Cert. of Appreciation Korea Rsch. Inst. Human Settlements, 1981, Minister of Environ., Republic of Korea, 1983, Cert. of Achievement, Korean Consul Gen., 1986. Mem. Assn. Am. Geographers (session chmn., 1983, '84, '91), Assn. Pacific Coast Geographers (session chmn. 1984), N.W. Sci. Assn. (chmn. soc. sci. 1975-76), Western Regional Sci. Assn. (session chmn. 1983, '84), Korean Geog. Soc., Korean Sci. and Engring. Assn., Am. Regional Sci. Assn. Address: 16733 Cobblestone Dr Lynnwood WA 98037

SHIN, SUNG SIK, pathologist, educator, researcher; b. Pusan, Korea, Jan. 29, 1956; came to U.S., 1984; MD, Seoul Nat. U., 1980. Diplomate in anat. and clin. pathology and hematology Am. Bd. Pathology. Resident in pathology Rush Med. Ctr., Chgo., 1984-88; fellow in hematopathology City of Hope Med. Ctr., Duarte, Calif., 1988-90, staff pathologist, 1990-91; staff pathologist Kaiser Found. Hosp., Fontana, Calif., 1991-92, U. Calif. San Diego Med. Ctr., 1992—; assoc. prof. pathology U. Calif. San Diego Sch. Medicine, 1992—. Contbr. articles to med. jours. Am. Cancer Soc. clin. oncology fellow, 1990. Mem. U.S. and Can. Acad. Pathology, Soc. Hematopathology. Office: U Calif San Diego Med Ctr 200 W Arbor Dr San Diego CA 92103-1911

SHINDAY, MANNY SHRAWAN, architect; b. Dhaman, India, Apr. 28, 1941; came to U.S., 1971; s. Shrawan T. and Babitai (Shelkey) S.; m. Prabha Hande Shinday, Nov. 24, 1968 (dec. Jan. 1989); children: Netie, Nina; m. Nila Patel, Nov. 24, 1991; children: Nikhil, Nimisha. BArch, diplomate in Town Planning & Valuation, Bombay U., 1965; BArch, U. Ill., Chgo., 1974. Registered arch., Calif., Wis. Arch. Shinde and Assoc., Bombay, 1965-71; project arch. Belli and Belli, Chgo., 1971-74; arch. Manny Shinday, AIA Assoc., Chgo., 1974-78; project arch. Jecobs Engring., Pasadena, Calif., 1978-81; v.p. Constrn. Control Svc. Corp., L.A., 1981-84; pres., CEO Control Design Sys., L.A., 1984—; dir. Constrn. Control Svc. Corp., 1980-82. Trustee Control Design Syss. Profit Sharing Plan, L.A., 1989; dir. Quadrex Found., Hawthorne, Calif., 1993. Fellow Indian Inst. Arch.; mem. AIA (Best Paper award 1994), Constrn. Specifications Inst., Asian Am. Arch. and Engrs., Am. Gen. Contractors Assn., Constrn. Inspection Assn. Republican. Office: Control Design Sys 5777 W Century Blvd Los Angeles CA 90045-5600

SHINDLER, JACK THOMAS, finance company exececutive, lawyer; b. St. Louis, Jan. 18, 1924; s. Harold Allen and Marie (McCawley) S.; AB, Georgetown U., 1948; postgrad. Harvard Bus. Sch., 1945, U. Louvain (Belgium), 1949-51; LLB, Ind. U., 1963, JD, 1964. With Banque de Bruxelles, N.Y.C., 1951-53, Fidelity Bank and Trust Co., Indpls., 1954-58; admitted to Ind. bar, 1963, U.S. Dist. Ct. bar, 1963; asst. atty. gen. State of Ind., 1963-65; U.S. atty. Dept. Justice, Newburgh and Indpls. 1966-68; practice law, Evansville, Ind., 1968-75; v.p., gen. counsel The Thomas Co., Las Vegas, Nev., 1976—; dir. Nye Enterprises, Las Vegas, Francis Co., Pompano; vice-chmn. Fla. and Ind. League Voters, 1954-64. Lt. (j.g.), USNR, 1942-52. Recipient Freedom Found. award, 1948. Mem. Theater Arts Soc. of Las Vegas, Georgetown Alumni Assn., YMCA. Roman Catholic. Club: Theater Arts, Inc. (Las Vegas). Lectr. Office: The Thomas Co 3875 Cambridge St # 806 Las Vegas NV 89119-7474

SHINN, DUANE K., music publisher; b. Auburn, Calif., Nov. 13, 1938; s. Archie W. and Iola E. (Eisley) S.; m. Beverly J. Luman; children: Kurt, Kendra, Garin, Garth. BS, So. Oreg. State Coll., 1970, MS, 1977. Prin. Keyboard Workshop/Duane Shinn Pubs., Medford, Oreg., 1965—. Author, pub. instructional audio and video cassettes on piano playing, including: Piano Improvising, 1985, How to Dress Up Naked Music, 1988, Keyboard by Chords, 1982, Piano Tricks: author: Will Herk Go to Hell for Biting the Avon Lady, 1980. Office: Duane Shinn Publs PO Box 700 Medford OR 97501-0047

SHIPBAUGH, CALVIN LEROY, physicist; b. Huntington, Ind., Aug. 28, 1958; s. Paul and Marguerite (Pinkerton) S. BA, Rice U., 1980; PhD, U. Ill., 1988. Rsch. asst. U. Ill., Champaign-Urbana, 1981-88; analyst RAND Corp., Santa Monica, Calif., 1988—; mem. space and surface power panel RAND support to NASA Project Outreach, Santa Monica, 1990; vis. scientist Fermilab, Batavia, Ill.,1982-85; workshop leader biotech. group RAND; team mem. POET, Arlington, Va., 1989-92; mem. bioscis. panel AAN Workshop, 1997. Contbr. articles to Phys. Rev. Letters, Physics Letters, RAND Pub. Series, others. Mem. Am. Phys. Soc., Internat. Meteoritical Soc. Office: The RAND Corp 1700 Main St Santa Monica CA 90401-3208

SHIPMAN, KEITH BRYAN, sportscaster; b. Puyallup, Wash., Apr. 26, 1961; s. Richard James and Carol Esther (Christianson) S.; m. Julie Anne Poppe, June 30, 1984; children, Alicia Bryanne, Gregory Dane. BA in Comms., Wash. State U., 1983. Sportscaster/producer KOMO Radio/TV, Seattle, 1983-85; sports/pub. affairs dir. KCPQ TV, Tacoma-Seattle, 1986—; AM drive sports host KJR Radio, Seattle, 1991-93; play by play announcer RayCom Sports, Charlotte, N.C., 1992-95; disc jockey KPUG AM/KNWR FM Radio, Bellingham, Wash., 1978-81; play-by-play annoucer Turner Broadcasting System, Atlanta, 1990; host/prodr. "The Chuck Knox Show", Anderson/Baer Prodns., Bainbridge Island, Wash., 1987-88; host "The Chuck Knox Show", Andersen Ent., Bellevue, Wash., 1985-88, various other free-lance work; Edward R. Murrow Sch. of Comms. profl. adv. bd. Wash. State U., 1996—. Pres. bd. dirs. Plaza Hall, Tacoma, Wash., 1989-94; exec. com. Muscular Dystrophy Assn., Seattle, 1989-91; vol. Boys and Girls Club of King County, Seattle and Whatcom County, Bellingham, 1988—, Children's Hosp., Seattle, 1992—. Named Sportscaster of the Yr. for Wash., Nat. Sportscasters and Sportswriters Assn., 1986, 87, 88; recipient Emmy award NATAS, 1990, 92, 94. Mem. Nat. Sportscasters and Sportswriters Assn. (bd. dirs. 1989-96), NATAS, Radio TV News Dirs. Assn. Office: KCPQ TV 4400 Steilacoom Blvd SW Tacoma WA 98499-4002

SHIPPER, TODD JEFFREY, communications executive; b. Detroit, Nov. 18, 1946; s. Norman N. Shipper and Evaline (Spring) Krasner; m. Sherry E. Brown, May 30, 1968 (div. 1969). AA, L.A. Valley Coll., 1970; student, Calif. State U., Northridge, 1970-72. Announcer various radio stas., 1967-73; salesman, mgr. Standard Shoes, Encino, Calif., 1973-76; asst. mgr. K-Mart, Westminster, Calif., 1976-77; salesman Contractors Lic. Sch., Van Nuys, Calif., 1977-80; dir. mktg. Columbia Sch. Broadcasting, Hollywood, Calif., 1980-84; owner, operator Nat. Broadcasting Sch., Sacramento, Portland, Seattle, 1984-92, Las Vegas, 1984-94; owner, operator NBS Travel Tng. Sch., 1989-92, Nat. Career Tng. Ctr., Las Vegas, 1992-94; prin. Sound Ideas, Inc., Las Vegas, 1994—; prin. Nat. Advt. Agy., Las Vegas, 1986—, Nat. Ednl. Cons., Las Vegas, 1986—. With USAF, 1965-67. Mem. Nat. Assn. Trade and Tech. Schs., Assn. Broadcasters. Democrat. Jewish. Office: Sound Ideas PO Box 29063 Las Vegas NV 89126

SHIPPEY, SANDRA LEE, lawyer; b. Casper, Wyo., June 24, 1957; d. Virgil Carr and Doris Louise (Conklin) McC.; m. Ojars Herberts Ozols, Sept. 2, 1978 (div.); children: Michael Ojars, Sara Ann, Brian Christopher; m. James Robert Shippey, Jan. 13, 1991. BA with distinction, U. Colo., 1978; JD magna cum laude, Boston U., 1982. Bar: Colo. 1982, U.S. Dist. Ct. Colo. 1985. Assoc. Cohen, Brame & Smith, Denver, 1983-84, Parcel, Meyer, Schwartz, Ruttum & Mauro, Denver, 1984-85, Mayer, Brown & Platt, Denver, 1985-87; counsel western ops. GE Capital Corp., San Diego, 1987-94; assoc. Page, Polin, Busch & Boatwright, San Diego, 1994-95; v.p., gen. counsel First Comml. Corp., San Diego, 1995-96; legal counsel Next Wave Telecom Inc., San Diego, 1996—. Active Pop Warner football and cheerleading. Mem. Phi Beta Kappa, Phi Delta Phi. Republican. Mem. Ch. of Christ. Home: 11878 Glenhope Rd San Diego CA 92128-5002 Office: NextWave Telecom Inc 6256 Greenwich Dr Ste 500 San Diego CA 92122

SHIRAI, SCOTT, communications executive; b. Honolulu, June 5, 1942; s. George Yoshio and Thelma Takeko (Tominaga) S.; children: Todd, Kimberly, Lance, Lyle. MusB, U. Hawaii, 1983; exec. dir. news, reporter Sta. KHON-TV, Honolulu, 1974-81; asst. gen. mgr. Vanguard Investments, Berkeley, Calif., 1976-79; newscaster Sta. KPOI, Honolulu, 1979-80; news dir. Sta. KGU, Honolulu, 1981-82; owner Visual Perspectives, 1981—; dir. pub. rels. Hawaiian Electric Co., Honolulu, 1982-90; dir. cmty. rels., Hawaiian Electric Industries, 1990—; instr. U. Hawaii, 1984—; pres. Hawaii Cmty. TV, 1993—; dir. BBB of Hawaii, 1995, Hawaii Pub. Broadcasting, 1996—. Author: Karaoke: Sing Along Guide to Fun & Confidence, 1997. Bd. dirs., sec. Hawaii Com. For Freedom of Press, 1982—; bd. dirs. Mental Health Assn. in Hawaii, 1981—, Moanalua Gardens Found., 1981-84, Health and Cmty. Svcs. Coun., 1982-86, Friends of Father Damien, 1986; v.p. Mele Nani Singers, 1986—; mem. Mayors Adv. Com. on Mcpl. TV, 1987, Office of Hawaiian Affairs Pub. Rels. Adv. Com., 1987, (all Honolulu); sec., dir. Pro Geothermal Alliance, 1990-91. Recipient Jefferson award Honolulu Advertiser, 1985, Gold award Audio-Visual Producers Assn. Am., 1985, Audio-Visual Dept. of Yr. award Videography mag., 1986, Award of Excellence Nat. Hospice Orgn., 1987, Intre award Inst. Teleradial Atica Puerto Rico, Inc., 1988. Mem. ASTD, Internat. TV Assn. (pres. 1983—), Am. Film Inst., AFTRA (bd. dirs. 1980-83), Pub. Rels. Soc. Am. (immediate past pres. and del. 1995—), Hawaii Speakers Assn., Hawaii Film Bd., Honolulu Cmty. Media Council, Hawaii Cmty. TV Assn. (pres. 1990—). Clubs: Honolulu Press (bd. dirs. 1984—), Hui Luna (bd. dirs. 1986-90) (Honolulu). Avocations: martial arts, singing. Office: Hawaiian Electric Industries PO Box 730 1001 Bishop St Ste 811 Honolulu HI 96808

SHIRE, HAROLD RAYMOND, law educator, author, social scientist; b. Denver, Nov. 23, 1910; s. Samuel Newport and Rose Betty (Herman) S.; m. Cecilia Goldhaar, May 9, 1973; children: David, Darcy, Esti. MBA, Pepperdine U., 1972; LLD (hon.), 1975; JD, Southwestern U., L.A., 1974; M in Liberal Arts, U. So. Calif., 1977; PhD in Human Behavior, U.S. Internat. U., San Diego, 1980. Bar: Calif. 1937, U.S. Dist. Ct. (so. dist.) Calif. 1939, U.S. Supreme Ct. 1978. Dep. dist. atty. L.A. County, Calif., 1937-38; asst. U.S. atty. So. Dist. Calif., L.A. and San Diego, 1939-42; pvt. practice, L.A., 1946-56; pres., chmn. bd. Gen. Connectors Corp., U.S. and Eng., 1956-73; prof. mgmt. and law Pepperdine U., Malibu, Calif., 1974-75, U.S. Internat. U., San Diego, 1980-83; dir. Bestobell Aviation, Eng., 1970-74. Advisor U. S.C. Gerentology, Andrus Ctr., pre-retirement tng., 1976-80; bd. dirs. Pepperdine U., 1974-80; nat. bd. govs. Union Orthodox Jewish Congregations Am., 1973—. With U.S. Army, 1942-46. Author: Cha No Yu and Symbolic Interactionism: Method of Predicting Japanese Behavior, 1980; The Tea Ceremony, 1984. Patentee aerospace pneumatics; invented flexible connectors; designed, manufactured flexible integrity systems. Pres. Jewish Nat. Fund Legion of Honor, 1991—; mem. Presdl. Roundtable, Washington, 1989-93. Decorated chevalier du vieux moulin (France); companion Royal Aero. Soc. (U.K.); recipient Tea Name Grand Master Soshitsu Sen XV Urasenke Sch., Kyoto, Japan, 1976, Medal of Honor Jewish Nat. Fund, 1991, Legion of Honor, 1991. Mem. Am. Legion (svc. officer China #1), Masons (32 degree, Hiram award 1994), Royal Arch, Shrine. Republican. Achievements include designing and mfg. fluidic sys. flexible integrity for Saturn IV and welding in Apollo XI Landing on moon, 1969. Office: PO Box 1352 Beverly Hills CA 90213-1352

SHIREMAN, JOAN FOSTER, social work educator; b. Cleve., Oct. 28, 1933; d. Louis Omar and Genevieve (Duguid) Foster; m. Charles Howard Shireman, Mar. 18, 1967; 1 child, David Louis. BA, Radcliffe Coll., 1956; MA, U. Chgo., 1959, PhD, 1968. Caseworker N.H. Children's Aid Soc., Manchester, 1959-61; dir. research Chgo. Child Care Soc., 1968-72; assoc. prof. U. Ill., Chgo., 1972-85; prof. Portland (Oreg.) State U., 1985—, dir. PhD program, 1992—; interim exec. dir. Partnership for Rsch., Tng. and Grad. Edn. in Child Welfare, 1994; research cons. child welfare orgns., Ill., 1968-85, Oreg. 1985—; lectr. U. Chgo., 1968-72. Co-author: Care and Commitment: Foster Parent Adoption Decisions, 1985, Adoption: Theory, Policy and Practice, 1996; mem. editl. bd. Jour. Sch. Social Work, 1978-81, Social Work Rsch. and Abstracts, 1990-93, Children and Youth Svcs. Rev., 1990-95, Jour. Social Work Edn., 1990-95; contbr. articles to profl. jours., chpts. to books. Bd. dirs. Oreg. chpt. Nat. Assn. for Prevention Child Abuse, 1985-87; bd. dirs. Friendly House, Portland, 1991—, pres., 1995-96; mem. adv. com. children's svcs. divsn. State of Oreg., 1985-95. Grantee HEW, 1980-82, Chgo. Community Trust, 1982-86, Oreg. Children's Trust Fund, 1991-96. Mem. NASW, AAUP, Am. Profl. Soc. Abuse of Children, Children First Oreg., Acad. Cert. Social Workers, Coun. on Social Work Edn., Phi Beta Kappa. Home: 2535 SW Sherwood Dr Portland OR 97201-1679 Office: Portland State U Grad Sch Social Work PO Box 751 Portland OR 97207-0751

SHIRER, BRUCE EDWARD, pathologist; b. Chgo., Sept. 22, 1941; s. Benjamin Franklin and Thelma Katherine (Borgstrom) S.; m. Janett Margaret Jurasek, Sept. 16, 1967 (div. Nov. 1982); m. Linda Locke Sevcik, July 7, 1984; children: Brandt Stephen, Benjamin Stuart. Student, North Ctrl. Coll., Naperville, Ill., 1958-61; MD, U. Wis., 1965. Diplomate Am. Bd. Pathology. Resident internal medicine Northwestern U., Chgo., 1968-69, resident in pathology, 1969-73; pathologist, co-dir. San Diego Inst. Pathology, 1973-82; locum tenens pathologist various labs., San Diego, 1982-84; med. dir. Lab. Corp. Am., San Diego, 1984—; assoc. pathologist Yuma (Ariz.) Regional Med. Ctr., 1986—. Lt. comdr. USNR, 1966-68, Vietnam. Fellow Coll. AM. Pathologists, Am. Soc. Clin. Pathologists; mem. AMA, Calif. Med. Assn., San Diego County Med. Soc. Republican. Home: 5566 Rutgers Rd La Jolla CA 92037-7821 Office: Lab Corp Am 5601 Oberlin Dr San Diego CA 92121-3747

SHIRKEY, RONALD EARL, lawyer; b. Regina, Sask., Can., Jan. 21, 1945; s. Earl James and Agnes Berniece (Sweet) S.; m. Elizabeth Obrocki, Dec. 8, 1973; children: Timothy, Jennifer, Nichola. BA, U. Sask., 1967, LLB, 1968. Cert. auctioneer, 1964. Assoc. Griffin, Blakeney, Regina, 1969-71; ptnr. Odishaw, Shirkey & MacKay, Regina, 1971-73, Shirkey & MacKay, Regina, 1973-79, Shirkey, Ulmer, Ottenbreit, Regina, 1979-91, Shirkey, Willner, Megaw, Regina, 1991—; chmn. SSHC, Regina, 1988-92. Legal advisor Progressive Conservative Party of Sask., Regina, 1982-95; campaign mgr. Prime Minister of Can., Regina, 1993; active supporter, com. mem. United Way, Can. Cancer Soc.; dir., chmn. Sask. Roughrider Football club, Regina, 1979-83. Queen's Counsel, Govt. of Can., 1992, Sask, 1983; Hon. Consul for Sweden in Sask., 1991—. Mem. Can. Bar. Assn., Sask. Law Soc., Can. Tax Found., Ducks Unltd. (chmn.), Assiniboia Club. United Ch. Home: 170 Westfield Dr, Regina, SK Canada S4S 2S9 Office: Shirkey Ulmer Willner Megaw, 2550 15th Ave Ste 325, Regina, SK Canada S4P 1A5

SHIRLEY, JOHN JEFFERY, management information systems executive; b. Dallas, Jan. 28, 1955; s. John Albert Jr. and Margaret Louise (Webb) S.; m. Suzanne Scura, Feb. 10, 1996. BS in Computer Sci., Nat. U., 1987, MS in Software Engring., 1989. Engr. 3M Co., San Diego, 1973-82; sr. engr. Northrop Grumman Corp., Virginia Beach, Va., 1982-85; computer specialist Northrop Grumman Corp., San Diego, 1985-89, dir. computer ops. Western area, 1989—; owner Digital Concepts, San Diego, 1978—; instr. P.D. Pruden Votech, Chesapeake, Va., 1982-83; assoc. prof. Nat. U., San Diego, 1989—; instr. U. Calif., San Diego, 1989—. Republican. Office: Grumman Aircraft Svcs PO Box 45302 San Diego CA 92145

SHIRLEY, MICHAEL JAMES, ski area executive; b. Flagstaff, Ariz., Oct. 25, 1941, s. James Watson and Lorraine Elizabeth (Thomson) S.; m. Gloria Marie Bruni, Aug. 20, 1966; children: Brian Michael, Cynthia Marie. BS, No. Ariz. U., Flagstaff, 1969; MBA, U. Ariz., 1970. Sr. acct. Morrison-Knudsen Co., Inc., Boise, Idaho, 1970-72; asst. treas. Morrison-Knudsen Co., Inc., 1972-74, corp. treas., 1974-75, v.p. adminstrn., 1975-85; v.p. adminstrn. Morrison Knudsen Corp., 1985-89, v.p. fin., treas., 1989-91; gen. mgr. Bogus Basin Ski Area, Idaho, 1991—. Bd. dirs. United Way Ada County, 1975-81, Jr. Achievement of S.W. Idaho, 1978-86, pres., 1983-86; bd. dirs. Boise Philharm. Assn., 1982-85, Bogus Basin Recreation Assn., 1984—; bd. trustees Boise Art Mus., 1996—. Staff sgt. USAF, 1963-67. Recipient Wall St. Jour. award No. Ariz. U., 1969, Alumni Achievement award, 1978. Mem. Boise Area C. of C. (bd. dirs. 1985-89). Republican.

SHIRLEY, ROBERT CLARK, retired university president, strategic planning consultant, educator; b. Jacksonville, Tex., July 1, 1943; s. James Cullen and Mary Jim (Clark) S.; m. Terrie Thomas, June 17, 1967; children: Robin, Deron. B.B.A., U. Houston, 1965, M.B.A., 1967; Ph.D., Northwestern U., 1972. Asst. dean faculties U. Houston, 1974-76; asst. to pres. SUNY-Albany, 1976-77, assoc. v.p. acad. affairs, 1977-79; assoc. prof. Central U. Iowa, Pella, 1979-81; prof. Trinity U., San Antonio, 1981-84; pres. U. So. Colo., Pueblo, 1984-96, pres. emeritus, 1997—; cons. on strategic planning and mgmt. to numerous colls. and univs. Author: Strategy and Policy Formation, 1981; contbr. articles to profl. publs. Mem. Pueblo Econ. Devel. Bd. Bill Laufman Meml. scholar U. Houston, 1965-66; Northwestern U. fellow, 1969-71; HEW research asst. grantee, 1971, 72; La. State U. Found. grantee, 1972, 73. Mem. Acad. Mgmt., Soc. Coll. and Univ. Planning, Pueblo C. of C. Presbyterian. Lodge: Rotary. Office: U So Colo 2200 Bonforte Blvd Pueblo CO 81001-4901*

SHIROMA, GLADYS AKIKO, children's book author, retired educator; b. Honolulu, Nov. 25, 1935; d. Thomas Seigi and Grace Tsuruko (Shimabukuro) Yonashiro; m. Wilfred Tateshi Shiroma; children: Glenda Aiko Molina, Leigh Ann Sadako Gorai, Alison Harumi Adams, Wendy Kimie Smits, Ross Kazuo Shiroma. BEd, U. Hawaii, 1974; Diploma, Inst. Children's Lit., Redding Ridge, Conn., 1986. Elem. tchr. Windward Dept. Edn., Honolulu, 1975-90; tchr. ESL Windward Adult Sch., Kaneohe, Hawaii. Author: Taro and the Sea Princess, 1990, The Sea Dragon and the Lion Doy, 1991. Block rep. Keapuka Assn., 1963-95, v.p. Keapuka Cmty. Assn.; mem. Neighborhood Bd., Kaneohe, 1980. Mem. NEA, Hawaii Okinawa Ken Heritage Club, Hui Ohaulima, Hawaii Edn. Assn., Hawaii State Tchrs. Assn., Oahu Ret. Tchrs. Assn., Am. Assn. Ret. Persons, Farmington H.S. Alumni Assn. Mormon. Home: 45-726 Hinamoe Loop Kaneohe HI 96744-1817

SHIRTCLIFF, JOHN DELZELL, business owner, oil jobber; b. Roseburg, Oreg., Mar. 2, 1948; s. Henry Marion and Sheila Nell (Delzell) S.; m. Connie Lee Cantrell, June 13, 1975; children: Darcie, Danielle, Andrew. BS, Oregon State U., 1970. Pres. Shirtcliff Oil Co., Myrtle Creek, Oreg., 1971—. Engr. Myrtle Creek (Oreg.) Vol. Fire Dept., 1971—, emergency technician, 1981—; mem. Rep. Cen. Com., Roseburg, Oreg., 1982-88; chmn. Umpqua Community Coll. Budget Com., Roseburg, 1983-96; bd. dirs. Mercy Hospice, Roseburg, 1988-96. 2nd lt. U.S. Army, 1970-71. Named Citizen of Year, Myrtle Creek City, 1986, Vol. of Year, Douglas County C. of C., 1987. Mem. Petroleum Marketers Assn. Am. (dir. Oreg. 1988), Oreg. Petroleum Marketers Assn. (v.p. legis. chmn. 1986, pres. 1987, PMAA dir. 1988), Pacific Oil Conf. (bd. dirs., v.p. 1995, gen. chmn. 1997), Lions, Elks, Masons, Shriners. Republican. Office: Shirtcliff Oil Co 283 SW Western Ave PO Box 6003 Myrtle Creek OR 97457-0051

SHISHIM, FRANCIS G., artist, performer; b. Santa Monica, Calif., May 8, 1953; s. Francis A. and Margaret W. (Addes) Shishim. BFA in Painting, Art Ctr. Coll., 1975. lectr. Art Ctr. Coll. Design, Pasadena, Calif., Otis/Parson Sch. Design, Los Angeles, Calif. Inst. Arts, Valencia, U. Calif.-Berkeley Art Mus., San Francisco Art Inst., Trinity Coll., Hartford, Conn., 1986, Mus. Art, San Jose, 1985. Exhibitions with Paul Velick (The Light Bob) include Ruth S. Schaffner Gallery, Los Angeles, 1978, Swope Gallery/Art Garden, Venice, Calif., 1979, Los Angeles Inst. Contemporary Art, Los Angeles, 1979, Vanguard Gallery, Los Angeles, 1980, Espace Gallery, Los Angeles, 1981, Upstairs Gallery, Tryon, N.C., 1981, WPA Gallery, Washington, 1981, Marianne Deson Gallery, Chgo., 1982; exhibited in group shows at Los Angeles Inst. Contemporary Art, 1976, 81, Craft and Folk Art Mus., Los Angeles, 1980, Long Beach (Calif.) Mus. Art, San Francisco Internat. Video Festival, 1980, Mus. Contemporary Art, Chgo., 1981, Downtown Gallery, Los Angeles, 1981, Tortue Gallery, Santa Monica, 1981, Am. Gallery, Los Angeles, 1982, UCLA, 1982, WPA Gallery, 1982; solo exhibits as The Dark Bob Calif. State U., Long Beach, 1983, traveling exhibitions, Los Angeles, Buffalo, 1983, Cochise Fine Arts Gallery, Bisbee, Ariz., Kansas City (Mo.) Art Inst., Spaces Art Ctr. Cleve. State U., Film in the Cities Jerome Hill Theatre, St. Paul, Randolf St. Gallery, Chgo., Chgo. Art Inst., Inst. Contemporary Art, Boston, Painted Bride Art Ctr., Phila., Swain Sch. Design, New Bedford, Mass., Portland (Oreg.) Ctr. Visual Arts, L.A.C.E. Gallery, Los Angeles, New Langton Gallery, San Francisco, Inst. Contemporary Art, San Jose, Calif., Contemporary Arts Forum, Santa Barbara, Calif., Calif. State U., Long Beach., Sushi Art Gallery, San Diego, The Roxy, Hollywood, Calif., 1987, Diverse Works, Houston, 1987, D-Arts Gallery, Dallas, 1987, Utah Media Ctr, Salt Lake City, 1988, D.C. Spaces, Washington, 1988, Main Arts Festival, Portland, Minn., 1988, Barnsdall Gallery Theatre, L.A., 1988; exhibited with Rachel Rosenthal Mus. Contemporary Art, L.A., 1984; albums: One Bob Job, 1982, On Pico, 1983, Kabballamobile (with Rachel Rosenthal) 1984, Uncontrollable Love, 1987, An Ever Ominous Dream, 1995; films: The Fossil Dig, 1983, A Day and A Night in The Life and The Death, 1984, Good Morning Balcony, 1986, The Untold Origin of The Super The Dark Bob, 1987, Mister Whsker, 1988; appeared in numerous performances, radio interviews, recordings and videos, 1975—. Office: PO Box 6461 Beverly Hills CA 90212-1461

SHIVELY, HAROLD HASTINGS, JR., cardiologist; b. Newton, Mass., Mar. 13, 1937; s. Harold H. and Louise (Van Camp) S.;m. Carol Ann Steele, June 17, 1961; children: David, Debra, Karen. BA, Wesleyan U., 1959, U. Hartford, 1960; MD, George Washington U., 1965. Intern, resident Walter Reed Gen. Hosp., Washington, 1965-69; fellow in cardiology Letterman Army Hosp., San Francisco, 1969-71; interventional cardiologist Specialty Med. Clinic, La Jolla, Calif., 1974-94; pvt. practice interventional cardiology La Jolla, 1994—; from asst. prof. to assoc. prof. medicine U. Calif., San Diego, 1974—; cardiologist Scripps Meml. Hosp., La Jolla, 1974—, chief medicine, 1993-95, chief of staff, 1995—; aviation med. examiner FAA, Washington, 1979—. With U.S. Army, 1959-95, brig. gen. ret. Decorated Legion of Merit award U.S. Army, 1995. Fellow Am. Coll. Cardiology, Am. Coll. Physicians, Am. Heart Assn. Coun. Clin. Cardiology; mem. AMA, Calif. Med. Assn., San Diego Med. Assn., Res. Officers Assn., Sr. Army Res. Cmdr. Assn., Assn. Mil. Surgeons U.S., Soc. Cons. Mil. Surgeon. Republican. Home: 8596 Nottingham Pl La Jolla CA 92037-2124 Office: 9850 Genesee Ave # S780 La Jolla CA 92037-1224

SHIVELY, JUDITH CAROLYN (JUDY SHIVELY), office assistant, contract administrator; b. Wilkinsburg, Pa., Jan. 30, 1962; d. John Allen and Edith (Crowell) S. BA in English, U. Nev., Las Vegas, 1984. Circulation aide Charleston Heights Libr., Las Vegas, 1979-86; asst. food editor Las Vegas Sun Newspaper, 1985-88, asst. horse racing editor, 1985-90, features writer, page editor, 1988-89, editor youth activities sect., 1989-90; racebook ticket writer, cashier Palace Sta. Hotel Racebook, Las Vegas, 1989-92; contract adminstr., gen. office asst. Loomis Armored, Inc., Las Vegas, 1992—; propr. Creative Computing, Las Vegas, 1996—; horse racing historian, rschr., Las Vegas, 1985—; vol. rsch. asst. Dictionary of Gambling and Gaming, 1982-84; part-time clk. Hometown News, Las Vegas, 1994-96. Staff writer horse race handicaps, columns, articles, feature stories Las Vegas Sun Newspaper, 1985-90; freelance writer for monthly horse racing publ. Inside Track, 1992-94. Mem. Phi Beta Kappa. Republican. Home: PO Box 26426 Las Vegas NV 89126-0426

SHIVELY, MERRICK LEE, pharmaceutical scientist, consultant; b. Alamagordo, N.Mex., Dec. 12, 1958; s. Milton Lee and Dorothy Jean (Garlock) S.; m. Maureen Lynch, Dec. 28, 1985; 1 child, Sierra Lange. BS in Pharmacy, U. Conn., 1982, PhD in Pharmaceutics, 1986. Registered pharmacist, Colo., Mass. Sr. rsch. assoc. Baxter Healthcare, Morton Grove, Ill., 1985-87; asst. prof. U. Colo., Boulder, 1987-93; sr. rsch. scientist Atrix Labs., Inc., Ft. Collins, Colo., 1993-94; sr. scientist Nexagen, Inc., Boulder, 1994-96; founder, mng. ptnr. Drug Delivery Solutions LLC, Louisville, Colo., 1996—; pharm. cons. Glaxo, Synergen, Chemex, Cell Tech., Lilly; del. U.S. Pharmacopeia, 1988-94. Contbr. articles to Pharm. Rsch., Jour. Colloid Interface Sci., Drug Devel. and Indsl. Pharmacy, Internat. Jour. Pharmaceutics, others. Mem. Denver Econ. Com., 1989. Richardson-Vicks fellow, 1982-85. Mem. Am. Assn. Pharm. Scientists, Soc. of Controlled Release, Am. Chem. Soc., Rocky Mountain Devel. Forum (treas. 1989—), Phi Kappa Phi, Rho Chi. Home and Office: 10ll Turnberry Cir Louisville CO 80027-9594

SHKURKIN, EKATERINA VLADIMIROVNA (KATIA SHKURKIN), social worker; b. Berkeley, Calif., Nov. 20, 1955; d. Vladimir Vladimirovich and Olga Ivanovna (Lisenko) S. Student, U. San Francisco, 1972-73; BA, U. Calif., Berkeley, 1974-77; MSW, Columbia U., 1977-79; postgrad., Union Grad. Sch., 1986. Cert. police instr. domestic violence, Alaska. Social worker Tolstoy Found., N.Y.C., 1978-79, adminstr., 1979-80; program supr. Rehab. Mental Health Ctr., San Jose, Calif., 1980-81; dir. svc. counselor Kodiak (Alaska) Crisis Ctr., 1981-82; domestic violence counselor Abused Women's Aid in Crisis, Anchorage, 1982-85; pvt. practice social work specializing in feminist therapy Susitna Therapy Ctr., Anchorage, 1985—; pvt. practice, 1985-89; field instr. Abused Women's Aid in Crisis, Anchorage, 1983-88, Divsn. Family and Youth Svcs., State of Alaska, 1989-91, South Ctrl. Found.-Dena A. Coy Prematernal Alcohol Treatment Ctr., 1991-92; expert witness Anchorage Mcpl. Cts., 1982-96; interim faculty mem. U. Alaska, Anchorage, summer 1985, fall 1988-95, LaVerne U., Anchorage, 1986-96; family therapist Anchorage Ctr. for Families, 1994-96; clin. supr. New Parent Support Program, Ft. Lewis, Wash., 1997—. Coordinator Orthodox Christian Fellowship, San Francisco, 1972-76; pub. speaker Abused Women's Aid in Crisis, Anchorage, 1982—; active nat. and local election campaigns, 1968—. Mem. NASW (cert.). Democrat. Russian Orthodox. Home and Office: 1136 Summerfield Dr SE Olympia WA 98513-6684

SHMAVONIAN, GERALD S., entertainment executive; b. L.A., June 26, 1945; s. Sarkis Neshan and Berje-Lucia (der Hareutunyan) S. Student, U. Calif., Berkeley, 1964-70. Leader archaeol. excavation team Guatemala, Turkey, 1970-75; pub. City Mags., 1975-80; special advisor Bicentennial Commission, Washington, D.C., 1987; chmn. Am. Nationalities Coun., Stanford U., 1983-86; pres. L.A. Talent, 1986—. Mem. Calif. Scholarship Fedn. (life, pres. 1963), Nat. Forensic League (pres. 1963, degree of honor). Home: 6219 N Prospect Ave Fresno CA 93711-1658

SHNEIDER, JEFFREY A., architect; b. Lincoln, Nebr., Apr. 29, 1948; s. Sam and Rose (Block) S.; m. Anne Louise Shockley, Feb. 21, 1971; children: Sarah, Max. BS, U. Wis., 1971; MArch, U. Nebr., 1974. Pres. CSHQA Archs./Planners, Boise, Idaho, 1974-97. Active Leadership Boise, 1980-81; dir., exec. com. Boise Area Econ. Devel. Coun.; past. pres. Boise Art Mus. Recipient outstanding young man award, 1981, Mgmt. Magic for Design Profls. Profl. Svcs. Mgmt. Jour. Seminar, 1987. Mem. Am. Inst. Archs. (pres. 1977—), Ada Planning Assn. Office: CSHQA Archs/Planners Ctrl Sta 200 N 6th Boise ID 83702

SHNEOUR, ELIE ALEXIS, biochemist; b. Neuilly-sur-Seine, France, Dec. 11, 1925; came to U.S., 1941, naturalized, 1944; s. Zalman and Salomea (Landau) S.; m. Polly H. Henderson, Sept. 7, 1990; children from previous marriage: Mark Zalman, Alan Brewster. B.A., Columbia U., 1947; DSc (hon.), Bard Coll., 1969; M.A., U. Calif., Berkeley, 1955; Ph.D., UCLA, 1958. Teaching., research fellowship U. Calif., Berkeley, 1953-55, Am. Heart Assn. research fellow, 1958-62; teaching., research fellowship U. Calif., L.A., 1958; research fellow Nat. Cancer Inst., 1956-57; Am. Heart Assn. research fellow N.Y.U., 1958-59; research assoc. genetics Stanford U., 1962-65; assoc. prof. biology and neurosciences U. Utah, 1965-69; research neurochemist City of Hope Nat. Med. Ctr., Duarte, Calif., 1969-71; dir. rsch. Calbiochem., 1971-75; pres. Biosystems Insts., Inc., 1975—; dir. Biosystems Rsch. Inst., 1979—; mem. exec. com. Nat. Acad. Sci. Study Group on Biology and the Exploration of Mars, 1964; chmn. Western Regional coun. Rsch. in Basic Bioscis. for Manned Orbiting Missions, Am. Inst. Biol. Scis., NASA, 1966-69; fellow Com. Sci. Investigation Claims of Paranormal, 1996—. Author: Extraterrestrial Life, 1965, (with Eric A. Ottesen) National Academy of Sciences, National Rsch. Coun., 1966, (with S. Moffat) Life Beyond the Earth, 1966, The Malnourished Mind, 1974; contbr. numerous articles to sci. and lay jours. Chmn. citizens adv. coun. San Diego Pub. Schs., 1971-72; mem. adv. coun. Cousteau Soc., 1977—; bd. dirs. Am.-Ukraine Trade Coun., 1991—, Lunar Power System Coalition, 1993—, Transinnova S.A. France, 1990—; chmn. sci. adv. bd. County of San Diego, 1995—. With U.S. Army, 1944-45. Recipient William Lockwood prize, 1947. Mem. IEEE, AAAS (chmn. So. Calif. Skeptics soc. Pacific divsn. 1988-90), Am. Chem. Soc., N.Y. Acad. Scis., Am. Inst. Biol. Scis., Am. Soc. for Biochemistry and Molecular Biology (chmn. sci. advisors program 1973-75, mem. com. on pub. policy 1974-76, congl. liaison 1992—), Am. Soc. Neurochemistry (mem. coun. 1971-73), Soc. Neurosci., Internat. Soc. Neurochemistry, U.S. C. of C. (bd. dirs. 1993—), La Jolla Chamber Music Soc. (bd. dirs. 1994—), Internat. Coun. for Global Health Progress (N.Am. adv. bd. 1996—), Sigma Xi, Phi Sigma. Office: Biosystems Insts Inc CDM-608 700 Front St # Cdm-608 San Diego CA 92101-6000

SHOCKNEY, EDWIN ALLEN, psychotherapist, healthcare consultant; b. Winchester, Ind., Oct. 9, 1950; s. Robert Allen and Naomi Ruth (Geeding) S.; m. Shirley Rose Baldwin, Mar. 24, 1973 (div. Dec. 1988); children: Patrick, Elizabeth, Kellie. AS, SUNY, Albany, 1979; BA, Crossroads Coll., Muncie, Ind., 1985; PhD, Berean Coll., Long Beach, Calif., 1992, DHum (hon.), 1990. Registered med. technologist; cert. cognitive behavioral therapist; lic. pilot. Med. technologist Reid Hosp., Richmond, Ind., 1972-80, Meml. Hosp., Colorado Springs, Colo., 1980-83, Univ. Hosp., Tampa, Fla., 1983-84; healthcare cons. Rupp & Bowman Co., Tampa, 1984-87; instr. health scis. Denver Tech. Coll., 1988-91; psychotherapist in pvt. practice, Colorado Springs, Colo., 1992—. Author: Simlpified Aviation, 1979, A Tender Glimpse of My Soul, 1992. Bd. dirs. Make-A-Wish Found., Denver, 1989-94, Police Athletic League, Colorado Springs, 1991-93. With USNR, 1983-93. Mem. ACA, Internat. Assn. Marriage and Family Counselors, Phi Theta Pi. Republican. Office: 701 S Cascade Ave Colorado Springs CO 80903-4003

SHOE, STEPHEN CHARLES, marketing professional; b. Kansas City, Mo., Oct. 12, 1935; s. Charles Arthur and Mary Margaret (Skaggs) S.; m. Patricia Carmen Williams, Mar. 9, 1958; children: David Mark, Peggy Jo, Rebecca Lynn. BA, U. North Colo., 1958, MA, 1961. Tchr. art & advt. Borah (Idaho) High Sch., 1960-66; account exec. KEST Radio, Boise, Idaho, 1966-68, KBIO & KGDN Radio, Seattle, 1968-70; dir. sch. svcs. Nat. Assn. Christian Sch., Wheaton, Ill., 1970-73, dir., 1973-74; pub. rels. dir. Wheaton (Ill.) Christian High Sch., 1974-75; pub. relations dir. Rockmont Coll. (now Colo. Christian U.), Lakewood, 1975-78; cons. Lakewood, 1978—; pres. Railroad Promotions, 1990—; with pub. rels. dept. Georgetown Loop Railroad, 1984-94. Contbr. articles to profl. jours. Named Model Railroad Industry Person of Yr., 1993. Mem. Model R.R. Industry Assn. (exec. dir. 1987-96), South Lakewood Optimist Club (past pres.), Seattle Optimist Club (past pres.), Tourist Railway Assn. Inc. (exec. dir. 1995—). Republican. Home: 12235 W Texas Dr Lakewood CO 80228-3619

SHOEMAKER, BILL (WILLIAM LEE SHOEMAKER), retired jockey, horse trainer; b. Fabens, Tex., Aug. 19, 1931; s. B. B. and Ruby (Call) S.; 1 child, Amanda Elisabeth. Jockey, 1949-90, ret., 1990, trainer, 1990—. Author: Stalking Horse, 1994, Fire Horse, 1995, Dark Horse, 1996. Office: care Vincent Andrews Mgmt Ste 208 315 S Beverly Dr Beverly Hills CA 90212-4310*

SHOEMAKER, CAMERON DAVID JAMES, dean, educator; b. Honolulu, Dec. 15, 1940; s. John James and Belle Bird (Kellogg) S.; m. Catherine LaMoyne Prevost, May 23, 1966 (div. 1969); 1 child, David James; m. Leona Martha Wohlwend, May 18, 1972; 1 child, Jennifer Lee. BA in Polit. Sci., The Citadel, 1963; MA in History, San Jose State U., 1973; EdD, U. San Francisco, 1990. Commd. 2d lt. U.S. Army, 1963, advanced through grades to maj., 1971; fgn. area officer U.S. Army, U.S., Korea, Germany and Vietnam, 1972-84; ret. U.S. Army, 1984; mgmt. analyst Def. Lang. Inst., Monterey, Calif., 1985; ednl. tech. project mgr. Def. Lang. Inst., Monterey, 1985-86, dir. info. resources mgmt., 1986-90; evening coll. adminstr., instnl. researcher Monterey Peninsula Coll., 1990-92; dean of bus. Sacramento (Calif.) City Coll., 1992—; instr., Chapman Coll., Monterey, 1982-84, Monterey Inst., 1987; chmn. Asian Employment Program Com., Monterey, 1983-84; guest lectr., Naval Postgrad. Sch., Monterey, 1986-87; mem. Handicapped Individual Program Com., Monterey, 1986-90, treas., 1989-90. Contbr. articles to various publs. Pres., Creekside Community Assn., Salinas, Calif., 1985-86; mem. County Svc. Area Adv. Bd., Salinas, 1985-87, Flood Control Dist. Planning Com., Salinas, 1986-87; active Leadership Monterey Peninsula, grad., 1992. Decorated Silver Star medal; recipient Comdrs. award for Civilian Svc. Dept. of Army, 1990; Carl D. Perkins fellow, 1993. Mem. Royal Asiatic Soc., Monterey Peninsula Scottish Soc. (treas. 1986-92), Los Rios Mgmt. Assn. (pres. 1995-96), Caledonian Club of Sacramento (treas. 1994-, chief 1997—). Republican. Roman Catholic. Home: 11577 Melones Cir Gold River CA 95670-7738 Office: Sacramento City Coll 3835 Freeport Blvd Sacramento CA 95822-1318 *Personal philosophy: The solution to any organizational problem is known to those at the working level who struggle with the issue daily. Leadership is the ability to persuade these workers to share their best thoughts on the solution.*

SHOEMAKER, DOROTHY HAYS, technical writer; b. L.A., Nov. 4, 1959; d. David Glenn and Marguerite (Thompson) Hays; m. Lon Lawrence Shoemaker, Mar. 30, 1996. Student, Reed Coll., 1976-79; BA, Mills Coll., 1987; tech. writing cert., IBM, 1993. Tech. writer Mills C.C.M., Oakland, Calif., 1987; tchg. asst. Mills. Coll., Oakland, 1986-87; tech. sec. Hewlett-Packard, Palo Alto, Calif., 1988; tech. writer Cadre Techs., Saratoga, Calif., 1989-90, IBM R&D, San Jose, Calif., 1990-93. Writer, editor: (tech. manuals) Programmer's Guides, 1987-93. Mem. Bay Area Action, Palo Alto, 1991—, bd. trustees, 1995—; mem., journalist Jr. League, Palo Alto, 1994—. Mem. Computer Profls. for Social Responsibility. Home: # 18 559 Matadero Ave Apt 18 Palo Alto CA 94306-2759

SHOEMAKER, EUGENE MERLE, geologist; b. L.A., Apr. 28, 1928; s. George Estel and Muriel May (Scott) S.; m. Carolyn Jean Spellmann, Aug. 18, 1951; children: Christine Carol, Patrick Gene, Linda Susan. B.S., Calif. Inst. Tech., 1947, M.S., 1948; M.A., Princeton U., 1954, Ph.D., 1960; Sc.D., Ariz. State Coll., 1965, Temple U., 1967, U. Ariz., 1984. Geologist U.S. Geol. Survey, 1948-93, scientist emeritus, 1993—, exploration uranium deposits and investigation salt structures Colo. and Utah, 1948-50, regional investigations geochemistry, volcanology and structure Colorado Plateau, 1951-56, research on structure and mechanics of meteorite impact and nuclear explosion craters, 1957-60, with E.C.T. Chao, discovered coesite, Meteor Crater, Ariz., 1960, investigation structure and history of moon, 1960-73, established lunar geol. time scale, methods of geol. mapping of moon, 1960, application TV systems to investigation extraterrestrial geology, 1961—, geology and paleomagnetism, Colo. Plateau, 1969—, systematic search for planet-crossing asteroids and comets, 1973-94; with C.S. Shoemaker and D.H. Levy discovered Periodic Comet Shoemaker-Levy 9, 1993; with C.S. Shoemaker discovered 46 Trojan asteroids, 1985-94; geology of satellites of Jupiter, Saturn, Uranus and Neptune, 1978—, investigating role of large body impacts in evolution of life, 1981—, impact craters of Australia,, 1983—; organized br. of astrogeology U.S. Geol. Survey, 1961; co-investigator TV expt. Project Ranger, 1961-65; chief scientist, center of astrogeology U.S. Geol. Survey, 1966-68; prin. investigator geol. field investigations in Apollo lunar landing, 1965-70, also television expt. Project Surveyor, 1963-68; prof. geology Calif. Inst. Tech., 1969-85, chmn. div. geol. and planetary scis., 1969-72; sci. team leader Clementine Mission to the Moon, 1993-94; staff mem. Lowell Observatory, Flagstaff, Ariz., 1993—. Recipient (with E.C.T. Chao) Wetherill medal Franklin Inst., 1965, Arthur S. Flemming award, 1966, NASA medal for exceptional sci. achievement, 1967, 96, Honor award for meritorious svc. U.S. Dept. Interior, 1973, Disting. Svc. award, 1980, Disting. Alumni award Calif. Inst. Tech., 1986; co-recipient Rittenhouse medal, 1988, Nat. medal of Sci. Pres. Bush, 1992, McGovern award Cosmos Club Found., 1995. Mem. NAS, Internat. Astron. Union, Am. Acad. Arts and Scis., Geol. Soc. Am. (Day medal 1982, Gilbert award 1983), Mineral Soc. Am., Soc. Econ. Geologists, Geochem. Soc., Am. Assn. Petroleum Geologists (Spl. award 1997), Am. Geophys. Union (Whipple award 1993, Bowie medal 1996), Am. Astron. Soc. (Kuiper prize 1984), Meteoritical Soc. (Barringer award 1984, Leonard medal 1985). Home: RR 4 Box 998 Flagstaff AZ 86001-8346 Office: US Geol Survey 2255 N Gemini Dr Flagstaff AZ 86001-1637

SHOEMAKER, HAROLD LLOYD, infosystem specialist; b. Danville, Ky., Jan. 3, 1923; s. Eugene Clay and Amy (Wilson) S.; A.B., Berea Coll., 1944; postgrad. State U. Ia., 1943-44, George Washington U., 1949-50, N.Y. U., 1950-52; m. Dorothy M. Maddox, May 11, 1947 (dec. Feb. 1991). Research physicist State U., Ia., 1944-45, Frankford Arsenal, Pa., 1945-47; research engr. N.Am. Aviation, Los Angeles, 1947-49, Jacobs Instrument Co., Bethesda, 1949-50; asso. head systems devel. group The Teleregister Corp., N.Y.C., 1950-53; mgr. electronic equipment devel. sect., head planning for indsl. systems div. Hughes Aircraft Co., Los Angeles, 1953-58; dir. command and control systems lab. Bunker-Ramo Corp., Los Angeles, 1958-68, v.p. Data Systems, 1968-69, corp. dir. data processing, 1969-75; tech. staff R & D Assocs., Marina Del Rey, Calif., 1975-85; info. systems cons., 1985—. Served with AUS, 1945-46. Mem. IEEE. Patentee elec. digital computer. Home: PO Box 3385 Granada Hills CA 91394-0385

SHOJI, HIROMU, orthopedic surgeon, educator; b. Chiba-Ken, Japan; grad. Coll. Gen. Edn., 1959, U. Tokyo, grad. Faculty of Medicine, 1964. Intern, U. Tokyo Hosp., 1964-65, resident in orthopedic surgery, 1965-67; resident in surgery Bklyn. Cumberland Med. Ctr., 1967-68, N.Y. U. Med. Center, 1968-69; bone tumor clinic fellow Meml. Sloan-Kettering Med. Ctr., N.Y.C., 1969-70; orthopedic fellow Hosp. for Spl. Surgery, N.Y.C., 1971-72; resident orthopedic surgery Bowman Gray Med. Sch., Winston-Salem, N.C., 1973-74; practice medicine specializing in orthopedic surgery, Sacramento, 1974-76, New Orleans, 1976-90, Riverside, Calif., 1990—; mem. staff Parkview Hosp., Riverside Comty. Hosp., Corona Regional Hosp.; asst. prof. dept. orthopedic surgery U. Calif., Davis, 1974-76; assoc. prof. dept. orthopedic surgery La. State U. Med. Ctr., 1976-80, prof., 1980-90; clin. prof. Loma Linda U., 1990—. Diplomate Am. Bd. Orthopedic Surgery (examiner). Mem. AMA, NAS, Am. Acad. Orthopedic Surgeons, Am. Assn. Hip and Knee Surgeons, Japanese Orthopedic Assn., Orthopedic Rsch. Soc., Japanese Soc. for Connective Tissue Rsch., Japanese Rehab. Assn., Am. Orthopedic Assn., So. Med. Assn., Am. Rheumatism Assn., Calif. Orthopaedic Assn., Internat. Soc. for Orthopedics and Traumatology, Knee Soc., Internat. Soc. Knee Surgery. Contbr. numerous articles on orthopedic surgery to med. jours.; patentee orthopedic devices. Office: 3838 Sherman Dr Riverside CA 92503-4001

SHOLTIS, JOSEPH ARNOLD, JR., business owner, nuclear and aerospace engineer, consultant; b. Monongahela, Pa., Nov. 28, 1948; s. Joseph and Gladys (Frye) S.; m. Cheryl Anita Senchur, Dec. 19, 1970; children: Christian Joseph, Carole Lynne. BS in Nuc. Engring. (Disting. Mil. Grad.), Pa. State U., 1970; diplomas Air Univ., 1975, 78; MS in Nuclear Engring., U. N.Mex., 1977, postgrad., 1978-80. Lic. sr. reactor operator NRC, 1980-84. Mathematician, statistician, mine safety analyst U.S. Bur. Mines, Pitts., 1968-70; commd. 2d lt. USAF, 1970, advanced through grades to lt. col. 1988, ret., 1993; nuclear rsch. officer Fgn. Tech. Div., USAF, Wright-Patterson AFB, Ohio, 1971-74; chief space nucl. sys. safety branch Air Force Weapons Lab., Kirtland AFB, N.Mex., 1974-78; mil. mem. tech. staff, project officer Sandia Nat. Labs., Albuquerque, 1978-80; chief radiation sources div., reactor facility dir. Armed Forces Radiobiology Rsch. Inst., Bethesda, Md., 1980-84; program mgr. SP-100 space reactor power sys. tech. devel. program Air Force Element U.S. Dept. Energy, Germantown, Md., 1984-87; chief analysis and evaluation br. Air Force Safety Agy., Kirtland AFB, N.Mex., 1988-91, chief nuc. power and sources div., 1991-92, chief nuc. energy systems, 1992-93; dir. rsch. and engring., gen. mgr. N.Mex. ops. Oakton International. Corp., Va., 1993-96; cons. in field, 1993—; owner, chief exec. Sholtis Engring and Safety. Enterprises, 1997—; space shuttle nuclear payload safety assessment officer Air Force Weapons Lab., Kirtland AFB, 1976-78; instr. med. effects nuc. weapons Armed Forces Radiobiology Rsch. Inst., Bethesda, 1980-85, mem. reactor and radiation facility safety com., 1980-85; faculty, lectr. Uniformed Svcs. Univ. Health Scis., Bethesda, 1982-87; chmn. Power System Subpanel Interagency Nuclear Safety Rev. Panel risk assessments of Galileo and Ulysses nuclear-powered space missions, 1987-92; Dept. of Def. chmn. Interagency Nuclear Safety Rev. Panel Evaluation of Ulysses and Cassini nuclear-powered space missions for the office of the pres., 1989-93; mem. power system subpanel Interagency Nuc. Safety Rev. Panel for evaluation of Cassini, Mars Pathfinder, Mars Survey, and Pluto Express nuc.-powered space missions, 1993—; instr. Inst. for Space Nuc. Power Studies U. N.Mex., 1987-91; U.S. del., tech. advisor UN Sci. and Tech. Subcom. and Legal Subcom. Working Group on Nuclear Power Sources in Outer Space, 1984-88; mem. U.S. contingent U.S. and U.S.S.R. discussions on nuclear space power system safety, 1989-90; mem. adv. com., tech. program com. Symposia on Space Nuclear Power and Propulsion, U. N.Mex., 1989—; mem. Multimegawatt Space Reactor Power Project safety working group, 1988-91; mem. SP-100 Space Reactor Project safety adv. com., 1990-93; mem. space exploration initiative Nuclear Safety Policy Working Group, 1990-91; mem. Air Force Thermionic Space Power Program Safety com., 1990-93; mem. Strategic Def. Initiative Orgn. Ind. Evaluation Group, 1991-93; mem., ind. advisor U.S. Dept. Energy Ind. Safety Assessment of TOPAZ-II space reactor power system, 1993; mem. Ind. Rev. Team recert. evaluation Cassini space mission, 1994; mem. program com. Reactor Safety Divsn. Am. Nuclear Soc., 1992-94; lectr. N.Mex. Acad. of Sci. Vis. Scientist Program, 1991—. Author: (with others) LMFBR Accident Delineation, 1980, Military Radiobiology, 1987, Power System Subpanel Report for Galileo Space Mission, 1989, Power System Subpanel Report for Ulysses Space Mission, 1990, Safety Evaluation Report for Ulysses Space Mission, 1990, A Critical Review of Space Nuclear Power and Propulsion 1984-1993, 1994; contbr. articles, chpts. in books. Charter mem. N.Mex. Edn. Outreach Com., 1989-93; mem. sectional affairs com. USGA, N.Mex., 1996—; USGA rules official; bd. dirs., Com., 1989-93, USGA sectional affairs com. mem. for N.Mex., 1996—, USGA rules ofcl., mem. bd. dir., Sun Country Amateur Golf Assn., N.Mex., 1996—. Decorated Def. Meritorious Svc. medal (2), Air Force Meritorious Svc. medal (2) Air Force Commendation medal (3), Nat. Def. Svc. medal (2), U.S. Army Reactor Comdr. Badge, U.S. Air Force Missileman Badge, Air Force Master Space Systems Badge, Nat. Aeronautics and Space Administration Achievement awards (3); recipient White House citation. Mem. Am. Nuclear Soc. (Best Paper 1977), ASME, AIAA, AAAS, Planetary Soc., Nat. Space Soc., Nat. Orgn. Test, Rsch., and Tng. Reactors, Profl. Aerospace Contractors Assn. N.Mex., Sigma Xi. Republican. Avocations: hunting, fishing, camping, golfing, motorcycle touring. Office: PO Box 910 Tijeras NM 87059-0910

SHONK, ALBERT DAVENPORT, JR., advertising executive; b. L.A., May 23, 1932; s. Albert Davenport and Jean Spence (Stannard) S.; BS in Bus. Adminstrn., U. So. Calif., 1954. Field rep. mktg. div. Los Angeles Examiner, 1954-55, asst. mgr. mktg. and field supr. mktg. div. 1955-56, mgr. mktg. div., 1956-57; account exec. Hearst Advt. Svc., Los Angeles, 1957-59; account exec., mgr. Keith H. Evans & Assos., San Francisco, 1959-65;

owner, pres. Albert D. Shonk Co., L.A., 1965—; gen. ptnr. Shonk Land Co. LTD, Charleston, W.Va., 1989—; pres. Signet Circle Corp., Inc., 1977-81, dir., 1962-81, hon. life dir., 1981—, treas., 1989—. Bd. dirs. Florence Crittenton Ctr., sec., 1978, 1st v.p., 1978-79, exec. v.p., 1979-81, pres., 1981-83, chmn. bd., 1983-85, hon. life dir., 1986—, treas., 1997—; co-chair centennial com., founding chmn. Crittenton Assocs. Recipient Medallion of Merit Phi Sigma Kappa, 1976, Founders award, 1961, NIC Interfraternal award, 1989. Mem. Advt. Club Los Angeles, Pubs. Rep. Assn. of So. Calif., Nat. Assn. Pubs. Reps. (past v.p. West Coast 1981-83), Jr. Advt. Club L.A. (hon. life, dir., treas., 1st v.p.), Trojan Club, Skull and Dagger, U. So. Calif., U. S.C. Marshall Sch. Bus. Alumni Assn. (nat. bd. 1991-, treas. 1995—), U. S.C. Assocs., Inter-Greek Soc. (co-founder, hon. life mem. and dir., v.p. 1976-79, pres. 1984-86), Rotary, Phi Sigma Kappa (dir. grand council 1962-70, 77-79, grand pres. 1979-83, chancellor 1983-87, 90-91, recorder 1995—, v.p. meml. found. 1979-84, pres. 1984, trustee pres. Phi Sigma Kappa found. 1984-95, honorary and trustee emeritus 1995—), World Affairs Coun., Alpha Kappa Psi, Town Hall. Home: 3460 W 7th St Apt 806 Los Angeles CA 90005-2312 Office: Albert Shonk Co 3156 Wilshire Blvd Ste 7 Los Angeles CA 90010-1209

SHORE, DAVID LINCOLN, author; b. Cin., Feb. 12, 1942; s. George Joseph and Emma Lou (Swartz) Pildas; m. Patricia J. Campbell, Feb. 7, 1984. BA in Journalism, Ohio State U., 1970; MA in Pub. Rels., UCLA, 1976. Cert. organic grower. Asst. editor AFL-CIO Mag., Columbus, Ohio, 1969-70; pub. info. officer Gov. J.J. Gilligan, Columbus, 1971-74; freelance writer various mags., newspapers L.A., 1975—; advt. copy dir. Woolf Advt. Inc., L.A., 1977-79; author, pub. Shore-Campbell Publs., L.A. and Fallbrook, Calif., 1980—; grower Les Avocadeaux Ranch, Fallbrook, 1990—; fgn. travel cons. Shore-Campbell Publs., Fallbrook, 1980—. Author, pub.: Europe Free! The Car, Van and RV Travel Guide, 1985, Europe by Van and Motorhome, 1st edit., 1991; author: New Zealand by Motorhome, 1989. Campaign pub. info. officer H. Metzenbaum Senate Campaign, Ohio, 1970; speechwriter govs., congressmen, Ohio, Washington, 1970—. With USN, 1960-64. Mem. San Diego Zool. Soc., Nat. Orgn. to Stop Glutamates, Calif. Coop. Organic Growers, Cadillac-La Salle Club Internat., Pontiac-Oakland Club Internat. (editor 1984-87, Nat. award 1986). Democrat. Jewish.

SHORE, DIANA KAY, nutritionist; b. Parkersburg, W.Va., May 28, 1949; d. James Dana and Viola Mary (Bowen) McClanahan; m. Philip Shore, 1982; children: Adam, Allison. BGS, Ohio U., 1971, BS in Edn., 1972, PhD, 1989; MS, Murray State U., 1979. Registered dietitian, Ohio, Calif.; cert. elem., secondary, vocat. tchr. Grad. asst. Murray (Ky.) State U., 1978-80, Ohio State U., Columbus, 1980-81, 82-83; instr. Morehead (Ky.) State U., 1987-88; dietitian Women, Infants and children, Huntington, W.Va., 1985-87; dietitian wellness Carmel Hosp., Columbus, 1990-94; dietitian Shore Med. Ctr., Chatsworth, Calif., 1991-94; instr. L.A. Valley Coll., 1994-96; nutrition instr. Calif. State U., Northridge, 1996—. Mem. nominating com. L.A. Med. Aux., 1994—; steering com. Granada Hills (Calif.) Hosp. Found., 1993—; art docent Parent Faculty Assn. Round Meadow Sch., 1992—. Mem. Am. Dietetic Assn., L.A. Dietetic Assn. (chair pub. rels. 1993-94, Com. Chair of Yr. 1994), Toastmasters (CTM award). Office: Shore Med Ctr 10324 Mason Ave Chatsworth CA 91311-3305

SHORE, JOHN JAMES, III, materials and environmental engineering consultant; b. Rivesville, W.Va., July 27, 1930; s. John James II and Mary Elisbeth (Radcliffe) S.; m. Verne Jean Ashcraft, July 2, 1955 (div. 1978); children: Kimberlee, Leslie, Holly, John IV; m. Melba Odesa Beall, July 21, 1979. BSChemE, W.Va. U., 1955; student in engring. and mgmt. sch., U. Calif., L.A., 1989. Cert. hazardous materials responder, Calif; cert. in hazardous waste mgmt. U.S. EPA. Rural carrier U.S. Postal Dept., Rivesville, 1951-53; quality control engr. E.I. DuPont de Nemours, Parkersburg, W.Va., 1955-57; materials engr. Aerojet Gen., Sacramento, Calif., 1957-79; materials engr. Gen. Dynamics, Pomona, Calif., 1979-85, sect. head materials tech., 1985-92; sr. environ. engring. specialist Hughes Missile Systems, Pomona, Calif., 1992-94, ret., 1994; pvt. cons. Claremont, Calif., 1994—. Contbr. articles to profl. jours. and reports; co-patentee in field. Trailblazer, chief YMCA Indian Guides, Orangevale, Calif., 1971-74; adult leader YMCA Grey Y, Orangevale, 1974-76. With U.S. Army, 1950-51. Mem. Aerospace Industries Assn. (materials and structures com.), Soc. of Automotive Engring. (polymers, composites and elastomers coms. 1985—), Elks (past Exalted Ruler), Sigma Phi Omega, Phi Lambda Upsilon. Republican. Home and Office: 641 Rockford Dr Claremont CA 91711-2909

SHORENSTEIN, WALTER HERBERT, commercial real estate development company executive; b. Glen Cove, N.Y., Feb. 23, 1915; m. Phyllis J. Finley, Aug. 8, 1945 (dec.); children: Joan (Dec.), Carole, Douglas. Student, Pa. State U., 1933-34, U. Pa., 1934-36; D in Econs. (hon.), HanYang U., Seoul, Republic of Korea, 1988. With property sales mgmt. depts. Milton Meyer & Co., San Francisco, 1946-51, ptnr., 1951-60, owner, chmn. bd. dirs., 1960—; owner, chmn. bd. dirs. Shorenstein Group, San Francisco, Shorenstein Co., San Francisco, 1960—. Past chmn. bd. trustees Hastings Law Ctr., U. Calif., San Francisco; founding mem. exec. adv. com. Hubert H. Humphrey Inst. Pub. Affairs, U. Minn.; founder Joan Shorenstein Barone Ctr. on Press, Politics and Pub. Policy, Harvard U. Kennedy Sch. Govt.; past pres., hon. life bd. dirs. San Francisco Park and Recreation Commn.; chmn. Vietnam Orphans Airlift; bd. dirs. San Francisco Performing Arts Ctr.; trustee Asia Found.; fin. chmn. Dem. Nat. Conv., 1984; apptd. by Pres. Clinton to Nat. Svc. Commn., 1994; chmn. San Francisco UN50 nat. com., 1995, also numerous polit. activities. Maj. USAF, 1940-45. Named Leader of Tomorrow, Time mag., 1953, Calif. Dem. of Yr., 1985; recipient Nat. Brotherhood award NCCJ, 1982, Disting. Svc. award Dem. Nat. Com., 1983, Golden Plate award Am. Acad. Achievement, Lifetime Achievement award Dem. Party, 1997. Mem. Calif. C. of C. (bd. dirs.), San Francisco C. of C. (past chmn. bd. dirs., life bd. dirs. Office: Shorenstein Co 555 California St Ste 4900 San Francisco CA 94104-1714

SHORT, HAROLD ASHBY, imaging engineer; b. Cleve., Sept. 13, 1939; s. George Ashby and Irene June (Cibbs) S. BS in Photographic Sci., Rochester (N.Y.) Inst. Tech., 1961. Supr. quality control Cleve. Color Svc., 1959-61; assoc. engr. Lockheed Missiles & Space Co., Sunnyvale, Calif., 1961-63, micro photographer, 1970-74; photographic engr. Itek Corp., Palo Alto, Calif., 1963-68; project engr. Philco-Ford Corp., Palo Alto, 1968-70; sr. staff engr. Fairchild Semiconductor Corp., Mountain View, Calif., 1974-87; mgr., maskmaking engr. Nat. Semiconductor Corp., Santa Clara, Calif., 1987-89. Editor The Engraving Art of Czeslaw Slania, 1987, 90, 96, Bay Phil, 1994—. Mem. North Coast Beaches Adv. Com., County Bd. Suprs., County of Santa Cruz, Calif., 1991—, chair, 1993—. Mem. Sierra Club (forestry task force), Friends of The Sea Otter (editor Coast Project Recovery Effort), Aububon Soc., Cousteau Soc., Naturist Soc., Santa Cruz County Stamp Club (editor, treas. 1991—). Home: 1575 Tindall Ranch Rd Corralitos CA 95076-0127

SHORT, JAMES FRANKLIN, JR., sociology educator, researcher; b. Sangamon County, Ill., June 22, 1924; s. James Franklin and Ruth L. (Walbaum) S.; m. Kelma E. Hegberg, Dec. 27, 1947; children: Susan Elizabeth, James Michael. Student, Shurtleff Coll., Alton, Ill., 1942-43; B.A., Denison U., 1947, hon. degree, 1975; M.A., U. Chgo., 1949, Ph.D., 1951. Instr. Ill. Inst. Tech., 1950, Ind. U., South Bend extension, 1950-51; mem. faculty Wash. State U., Pullman, 1951—; prof. sociology Wash. State U., 1963-94, prof. emeritus, 1994—; dir. Sociol. Research Lab., 1962-65; dean Grad. Sch., 1964-68; dir. Social Research Center, 1970-85; vis. assoc. rsch. prof. U. Chgo., 1959-62; vis. prof. law and sociology Stanford, 1975; vis. scholar Inst. of Criminology, Cambridge U., 1976; disting. vis. prof. U. Colo., summer 1986; disting. vis. prof. (Hooker prof.) McMaster U., fall 1987, Beto chair prof. Criminal Justice Ctr. Sam Houston State U., spring, 1990; co.-dir. rsch. Nat. Commn. on Causes and Prevention of Violence, 1968-69; fellow Ctr. for Advanced Study in the Behavioral Scis., Stanford, 1969-70; cons. NIMH, 1961-76, mem. behavioral scis. fellowship rev. panel, 1963-66, mem. behavior sci. review panel, tng. grant br., 1967-71, chmn., 1970-71; mem. assembly behavioral and social scis. NRC, 1973-75, mem. com. on rsch. on law enforcement and adminstrn. of justice Commn. on Behavioral Scis. and Edn., 1984-89, mem. panel on understanding violence, 1989-92; Am. Sociol. Assn. rep. to NAS, 1970-72; cons. NSF, 1970—, mem. social adv. com., 1971-72, rsch. adv. com., 1973; cons. Ford Found., 1962-64. Author: (with A.F. Henry) Suicide and Homicide, 1954, (with F.L. Strodtbeck) Group Process and Gang Delinquency, 1965, 2d edit., 1974; Delinquency and Society, 1990, Poverty, Ethnicity, and Violent Crime, 1997; also articles chpts. in books; editor: Gang Delinquency and Delinquent Subcultures, 1968, Modern Criminals, 1970, 2d edit., 1973, The Social Fabric of Metropolis, 1971, (with Marvin Wolfgang) Collective Violence, 1972; editor, contbr. Delinquency, Crime and Society, 1976, The State of Sociology, 1981, The Social Fabric, 1986, (with Lee Clarke) Organizations, Uncertanties, and Risk, 1992; asso. editor Am. Sociol. Rev, 1960-63, 70-71; editor, 1972-74; asso. editor Social Problems, 1958-61, 67-69, Am. Jour. Sociology, 1964-72; adv. editor Jour. Life Threatening Behavior, 1971-75; mem. adv. bd. Jour. Rsch. in Crime and Delinquency, 1980—, Am. Sociologist, 1967-68, Jour. Criminal Law and Criminology, 1976—; assoc. editor Ann. Rev. Sociology, 1980-87; adv. editor Deviant Behavior, Sociol. Inquiry, contbr. to encys., yearbooks. Chmn. nat. peer rev. com. Clark County (Nev.) Nuclear Waste Divsn., 1991-95; mem. tech. rev. com. State of Nev. Nuclear Waste Project Office, 1995—. 2d lt. USMCR, 1943-46, PTO. Faculty Rsch. fellow Social Sci. Rsch. Coun., 1953-56; Guggenheim fellow, 1976, fellow Inst. Criminology and Kings Coll., Cambridge U., 1976, Centre for Socio-Legal Studies and Wolfson Coll., Oxford, 1986; NIMH, NSF grantee; recipient Regents Faculty Excellence award for rsch. Wash. State U., 1987, Outstanding Faculty Achievement award Coll. Sci. and Art, 1988; Bruce Smith award Acad. Criminal Justice Scis., 1987. Fellow Japan Soc. for Promotion Sci., Am. Soc. Criminology (pres.-elect 1995-96, pres. 1996-97), Edwin Sutherland award 1979), AAAS; mem. Western Soc. Criminology (Paul Tappan award 1977), mem. Am. Sociol. Assn. (chmn. research com. 1963, mem. council 1967-70, 76-80, com. on exec. office and budget 1971, 76-80, chmn. 1977-80, mem. publs. com. 1972-74, 76-80, sec. 1977-80, pres.-elect 1982-83, pres. 1983-84, Found. bd. trustees 1985-89, pres. 1989, chair adv. com. 1990-96, sect. on environ. and tech. Outstanding Achievement award 1990), Pacific Sociol. Assn. (pres. 1966-67), Soc. Study Problems (exec. com. 1965-66), Western Assn. Grad. Schools (exec. com. 1965-67), Sociologists for Women in Soc., Law and Soc. Assn. (trustee 1978-80), Sociol. Research Assn. (sec.-treas. 1982, pres. 1983), Phi Beta Kappa (hon.), Phi Kappa Phi (hon.). Home: 445 SE Crestview St Pullman WA 99163-2312

SHORT, JAY MILTON, biotechnology company executive; b. Lebanon, Ind., Mar. 5, 1958; s. Roy Milton and Patricia Ann (Brewer) S.; m. Heidi Patrice Messinger, July 26, 1980; children: Ryan Milton, Cole Evan. BA in Chemistry with honors, Taylor U., Upland, Ind., 1080; PhD in Biochemistry, Case Western Res. U., 1985. Tchg. asst. Taylor U., 1978-80, Kent (Ohio) State U., 1981, Case Western Res. U., Cleve., 1981-85; staff scientist R & D, Stratagene Cloning Systems, La Jolla, Calif., 1985-88, sr. staff scientist, 1988-89, v.p. long term rsch. and biol. ops., 1989-92, v.p. long term rsch. and ops., 1992-94; pres. Stratcyte, Inc., La Jolla, 1992-94; chief tech. officer Recombinant BioCatalysis, Inc., La Jolla, 1994—, also bd. dirs.; bd. dirs. Stressgen, Inc., Invitrogen, Indsl. Biocatalysis, Inc.; reviewer human genome project and patenting DNA sequences U.S. Congl. Office Tech. Assessment; chmn., ofcl. Instnl. Animal Care and Use Com.; mem. peer rev. com. Nat. Inst. Environ. Health Scis.; ewciwque Peoxa, NAS, Genetic Analysis Techniques, Analytical Biochemistry, Nucleic Acids Rsch.; cons. on transgenic toxicology testing EEC, 1991-94; lectr. in field; mem. adj. faculty U. Calif., San Diego, 1991; lectr. Ctr. for Drug Evaluation and Rsch., FDA, 1992, others. Editor Mutation Rsch.; contbr. numerous articles and abstracts to sci. jours.; numerous patents in field, including sys. for regulation of eukaryotic genes, methods for phenotype creation from multiple gene populations, transgenic non-human animals carrying test DNA sequences, mutagenesis testing using transgenic non-human animals carrying test DNA sequences, polycos mutagenesis sys., use of trans-acting proteins for devel. in situ expression screening system. Recipient 1st place award for innovation and entrepreneurship in biotech. U. Calif., 1990, 91; numerous grants including Nat. Inst. Environ. Health Scis., 1989-94, NIH, 1990-94, Nat. Cancer Inst., 1992-95. Mem. AAAS, Am. Soc. Biochemistry and Molecular Biology, Am. Soc. Microbiology, Environ. Mutagenesis Soc., Soc. Toxicology (chmn. conf. discussion group 1993), Japanese Environ. Mutagen Soc., N.Y. Acad. Scis. Office: Recombinant BioCatalysis Inc 10665 Sorrento Valley Rd San Diego CA 92121-4616

SHOSTAK, G. SETH, astronomer; b. Norfolk, Va., July 20, 1943; s. Arnold Aaron and Bertha (Gortenburg) S.; m. Karen Ann Claffey, Apr. 28, 1984. BA in Physics, Princeton U., 1965; PhD in Astronomy, Calif. Inst. Tech., 1972. Research assoc. Nat. Radio Astronomy Obs., Charlottesville, Va., 1972-74; sr. systems analyst Penn Cent. R.R., Phila., 1974-75; research assoc. State U., Groningen, Netherlands, 1975-85; bd. dirs. Found. DIGIMA Computer Animation, Groningen, The Netherlands, 1985-88; pub. programs scientist Search for Extraterrestrial Intelligence Inst., Mountain View, Calif., 1989—. Contbr. articles to profl. jours. Recipient Cindy award, 1975. Mem. Netherlands Assn. Sci. Film and TV (J.S. Niewenhuis 1984, Wubbo Ockels prize 1988), Soc. Motion Picture and TV Engrs. Jewish. Home: 1372 Cuernavaca Circle Mountain View CA 94040 Office: SETI Inst 2035 Landings Dr Mountain View CA 94043-0818

SHOTWELL, CHERRIE LEIGH, speech and language pathologist; b. Munich, Nov. 15, 1950; parents Am. citizens; d. William Bedford and Pauline Leona (Bainbridge) S. BA with distinction, U. Redlands, 1973, MS, 1975. Cert. lang., speech and hearing tchr., Calif. Speech and lang. therapist Hawaii Dept. Edn., Wahiawa, 1976-86; lang. and speech specialist L.A. County Dept. Edn., Downey, Calif., 1986-87; day treatment instr. Assn. Retarded Citizens, Honolulu, 1987-88; speech and lang. pathologist Honolulu Cmty. Action Program, 1988-89, Hawaii Speech Pathology, Honolulu, 1989-90, Med. Pers. Pool, Honolulu, 1990-94, Hawaii Dept. Edn., Waipahu, 1994—. Mem. Hawaii Speech Lang. Hearing Assn. (com. chairperson Licensure and Ethics 1978-79). Democrat. Home: 1015 Laakea Pl Honolulu HI 96818-1987

SHOVALD, ARLENE ELIZABETH, newspaper reporter; b. Stambaugh, Mich., Apr. 14, 1940; d. William Lawrence and Dorothy Mary (Scott) Mellstrom; m. Robert Paul Shovald, June 20, 1959; children: Robert, Terri, Richard, Anne. AA, Colo. Mountain Coll., 1992, AAS in Criminal Justice, 1996; B in Psychology, Regis U., 1996. Freelance writer, 1959—; editor The Reporter, Iron River, Mich., 1974-79; nurse aide and sec. to nursing svcs. Salida Hosp., 1979-81; reporter, photographer The Mountain Mail, Salida, 1981-87; reporter The Mountain Mail, Salida, Colo., 1989—; corr. The Pueblo (Colo.) Chieftain, 1987-89; creative writing tchr. Colo. Mountain Coll., Salida, 1992. Author: Kill the Competition, 1987; author numerous newspaper and mag. articles. Mem. Chaffee County Emergency, Med. Svcs. Coun., Salida, 1990-93. Mem. Colo. Author's League, Colo. Press Assn. Home: 1124 D St Salida CO 81201 Office: The Mountain Mail PO Box 189 Salida CO 81201

SHRADER, THOMAS HENRY, biologist; b. Marlinton, W.Va., July 12, 1943; s. George Henry and Lula Katherine (Wymer) S.; m. Michele H. Nguyen, Jan. 15, 1966; 1 child: Theodore Jack London. BS, U. Ariz., 1967, MS, 1972; postgrad., N.Mex. State U., 1972-77. Agronomist U.S. Bur. Reclamation, El Paso, Tex., 1972-73, conservation agronomist, 1974-77, ecologist, 1977-84, supervisory natural resource specialist, 1985-91; supervisory biologist U.S. Bur. Reclamation, Boulder City, Nev., 1991—; mem. Lower Colo. River Multi-Species Conservation Program, 1995—; lectr. in field. Contbr.: Herbicide Manual, 1983; contbr. articles to profl. jours. Dir. Celebrity Home Assn., Henderson, Nev., 1995; mem. Colo. River Work Group, 1993-95. Mem. Am. Soc. Agronomy, Weed Sci. Soc. Am., Ariz. Riparian Coun., Gamma Sigma Delta, Phi Kappa Phi. Home: 233 Jonquil Cir Henderson NV 89014-5244 Office: US Bureau of Reclamation PO Box 61470 Boulder City NV 89006-1470

SHRAIRMAN, RUTH, computer scientist, company executive; b. St. Petersburg, Russia, Mar. 29, 1947; came to the U.S., 1986; d. Miron and Riva (Belotserkovskaya) S.; m. Leonid Glotstein (div. Mar. 1966); m. Alexander Livshitz Landau, June 5, 1971; children: Igor, Daniel. MSc summa cum laude in Control and Optimization, Inst. Chem. Machine Engring., Moscow, 1964; diploma in Numerical Methods and Computer Programming, Inst. Advanced Tng. of Rschrs. and Mgrs., Moscow, 1973; MSc in Computer Sci., U. Colo., 1990, PhD in Computer Sci., 1995. Sr. rsch. engr. All-Union Sci. Rsch. Vitamin Inst., Moscow, 1965-77; sr. scientist Ministry of Comm., Telecom. Rsch. Ctr., Israel, 1978-86; rsch. assoc. Coll. Bus. and Adminstrn. U. Colo., Boulder, 1986-87, tchg. asst. dept. computer sci., 1987-89; sys. analyst AMICS Enterprises, Inc., 1989-90; chmn., founder VeriFax Corp., 1990—; tchg. asst. Tel-Aviv U., Sch. Math., 1984-85; lectr. and presenter in field. Contbr. articles to profl. jours.; patentee in field. Recipient NSF award, 1993. Mem. Assn. for Computing Machinery. Office: Univ Colo Computer Sci Dept PO Box 430 Boulder CO 80309-0430

SHREEVE, JEAN'NE MARIE, chemist, educator; b. Deer Lodge, Mont., July 2, 1933; d. Charles William and Maryfrances (Briggeman) S. BA, U. Mont., 1953, DSc (hon.), 1982; MS, U. Minn., 1956; PhD, U. Wash., 1961; NSF postdoctoral fellow, U. Cambridge, Eng., 1967-68. Asst. prof. chemistry U. Idaho, Moscow, 1961-65; assoc. prof. U. Idaho, 1965-67, prof., 1967-73, acting chmn. dept. chemistry, 1969-70, 1973, head dept., and prof., 1973-87, v.p. rsch. and grad. studies, prof. chemistry, 1987—; Lucy W. Pickett lectr. Mt. Holyoke Coll., 1976, George H. Cady lectr. U. Wash., 1993; mem. Nat. Com. Standards in Higher Edn., 1965-67, 69-73. Mem. editl. bd. Jour. Fluorine Chemistry, 1970—, Jour. Heteroatom Chemistry, 1988-95, Accounts Chem. Rsch., 1973-75, Inorganic Synthesis, 1976—; contbr. articles to sci. jours. Mem. bd. govs. Argonne (Ill.) Nat. Lab., 1992—. Recipient Disting. Alumni award U. Mont., 1970; named Hon. Alumnus, U. Idaho, 1972; recipient Outstanding Achievement award U. Minn., 1975, Sr. U.S. Scientist award Alexander Von Humboldt Found., 1978, Excellence in Teaching award Chem. Mfrs. Assn., 1980; U.S. hon. Ramsay fellow, 1967-68, Alfred P. Sloan fellow, 1970-72. Mem. AAAS (bd. dirs. 1991-95), AAUW (officer Moscow chpt. 1962-69), Am. Chem. Soc. (bd. dirs. 1985-93, chmn. fluorine divsn. 1979-81, Petroleum Rsch. Fund adv. bd. 1975-77, women chemists com. 1972-77, Fluorine award 1978, Garvan medal 1972, Harry and Carol Mosher award Santa Clara Valley sect. 1992), Göttingen (Germany) Acad. Scis. (corr. mem.), Phi Beta Kappa. Office: U Idaho Rsch Office 111 Morrill Hall Moscow ID 83843

SHREEVE, SUSANNA SEELYE, educational planning facilitator. BA in Dance, Arts and Humanities, Mills Coll.; MA in Confluent Edn., U. Calif., Santa Barbara, 1989; postgrad., U. Calif., 1990, San Diego State U., 1992. Cert. elem. tchr., C.C. adminstr., tchr., Calif. Comm. instr. Brooks Inst., 1982; initiator Santa Barbara County Arts and Aging Forum, 1982; co-plannter PARTners "How Kids Learn" Conf., 1985; dir. Los Ninos Bilingual Head Start Program, 1986-87; writing counselor Am. and internat. students S.B. City Coll., 1988, U. Calif., Santa Barbara, 1989-90; writing counselor Upward Bound, 1989-90; edn. coord. Santa Barbara County Urban Indian Project, Santa Barbara, 1990; instr. Santa Barbara Youth Cultural Arts, Santa Barbara, 1993; planner/staff Tri-County Regional Team Youth Summit, 1993-94, staff/planner Playshops, 1993—; planner SIG confluent edn. AERA, 1994—; DQ-U. math/sci. resources for tchrs. Indian Edn., 1992—; multi-cultural cmty. Regional Alliance Info. Network Internet Youth Programs, Santa Barbara, 1991—; Pro-Youth Coalition planner City Santa Barbara, NetDay 1996—, Native Ams., 1996—; planner, adv., website liaison Nuc. Age Peace Found, World Indigenous Peoples Edn. Confs. Mem. Kappa Delta Pi. Office: 527 Laguna St Santa Barbara CA 93101-1607

SHREVE, THEODORE NORRIS, construction company executive; b. St. Louis, Feb. 14, 1919; s. Truxtun Benbridge and Beulah (Dyer) S.; m. Caroline Prouty, Jan. 7, 1943; children: Sara Ann Caile, Suzanne Foster Shreve, Theo Carol. BS, U. Colo., 1942. Sec., treas. Trautman & Shreve, Inc., Denver, 1946-68, pres., 1965-86, chmn. bd., 1984—; pres. 4030 Corp., 1984—. Mem. Colo. U. Found. Bd., 1988—; Rep. County Assembly, 1962. Served with USNR, 1942-45. Registered profl. engr., Colo. Mem. Mech. Contractors Assn., Colo. Soc. Profl. Engrs., Rotary, Gyro Club, Denver Country Club, Sigma Phi Epsilon. Republican. Episcopalian. Home: 420 S Marion Pkwy # 1403 Denver CO 80209 Office: Trautman & Shreve 4406 Race St Denver CO 80216-3818

SHRONTZ, FRANK ANDERSON, airplane manufacturing executive; b. Boise, Idaho, Dec. 14, 1931; s. Thurlyn Howard and Florence Elizabeth (Anderson) S.; m. Harriet Ann Houghton, June 12, 1954; children: Craig Howard, Richard Whitaker, David Anderson. Student, George Washington U., 1953; LLB, U. Idaho, 1954; MBA, Harvard U., 1958; postgrad., Stanford U., 1969-70. Asst. contracts coordinator Boeing Co., Seattle, 1958-65, asst. dir. contract adminstrn., 1965-67, asst. to v.p. comml. airplane group, 1967-69, asst. dir. new airplane program, 1969-70, dir. comml. sales operations, 1970-73, v.p. planning and contracts, 1977-78; asst. sec. Dept. Air Force, Washington, 1973-76, Dept. Def., Washington, 1976-77; v.p., gen. mgr. 707/727/737 div. Boeing Comml. Airplane Co., Seattle, 1978-82, v.p. sales and mktg., 1982-84, pres., 1986—; pres., chief exec. officer The Boeing Co., Seattle, 1986—, chmn., chief exec. officer, 1988-96, chmn., 1996-97, chmn. emeritus, 1997—; bd. dirs. Citicorp, Boise Cascade Corp., 3M Co., Boeing, Chevron; mem. The Bus. Coun., 1987; vice chmn. New Am. Schs. Devel. Corp. Trustee Smithsonian Instn. 1st lt. AUS, 1954-56. Mem. Phi Alpha Delta, Beta Theta Pi. Clubs: Overlake Golf and Country, Columbia Tower. Office: Boeing Co 7755 E Marginal Way S Seattle WA 98108-4002*

SHROPSHIRE, DONALD GRAY, hospital executive; b. Winston-Salem, N.C., Aug. 6, 1927; s. John Lee and Bess L. (Shouse) S.; m. Mary Ruth Bodenheimer, Aug. 19, 1950; children: Melanie Shropshire David, John Devin. B.S., U. N.C., 1950; Erickson fellow hosp. adminstrn., U. Chgo., 1958-59; LLD (hon.), U. Ariz., 1992; EdD (hon.), Tucson U., 1994. Personnel asst. Nat. Biscuit Co., Atlanta, 1950-52; asst. personnel mgr. Nat. Biscuit Co., Chgo., 1952-54; adminstr. Eastern State Hosp., Lexington, Ky., 1954-62; assoc. dir. U. Md. Hosp., Balt., 1962-67; adminstr. Tucson Med. Ctr., 1967-82, pres., 1982-92, pres. emeritus, 1992—, bd. dirs., 1995; pres. Tucson Hosps. Med. Edn. Program, 1970-71, sec., 1971-86; pres. So. Ariz. Hosp. Council, 1968-69; bd. dirs. Ariz. Blue Cross, 1967-76, chmn. provider standards com., 1972-76; chmn. Healthways Inc., 1985-92; bd. dirs. Tucson Med. Found., Tucson Electric Power Co.; adv. bd. Steele Meml. Pediatric Rsch. Ctr., U. Ariz. Coll. Medicine, 1996—; chmn. bd. La Posada at Park Centre, Inc., Green Valley, Ariz., 1996—. Bd. dirs. Health Planning Coun. Tucson, 1992, mem. exec. com., 1969-74; chmn. profl. divsn. United Way, Tucson, 1969-70, vice chmn. campaign, 1988, Ariz. Health Faciltities Authority, bd. dirs., 1992—; chmn. dietary svcs. com., vice chmn., 1988, Md. Hosp. Coun., 1966-67; bd. dirs. Ky. Hosp. Assn., 1961-62, chmn. coun. profl. practice, 1960-61; past pres. Blue Grass Hosp. Coun.; trustee Assn. Western Hosps., 1974-81, pres., 1979-80; mem. accreditation Coun. for Continuing Med. Edn., 1982-87, chair, 1986; bd. govs. Piima C.C., 1970-76, sec., 1973-74, chmn., 1975-76, bd. dirs. Found., 1978-82, Ariz. Bd. Regents, 1982-90, sec., 1983-86, pres., 1987-88; mem. Tucson Airport Authority, 1987—, bd. dirs., 1990-95, pres., 1995; v.p. Tucson Econ. Devel. Corp., 1977-82; bd. dirs. Vol. Hosps. Am., 1977-88, treas., 1979-82; mem. Ariz. Adv. Health Coun. Dirs., 1976-78; bd. dirs. Tucson Tomorrow, 1983-87, Tucson Downtown Devel. Corp., 1988-95, Rincon Inst., 1992—, Sonoran Inst., 1992—; dir. Mus. No. Ariz., 1988—; nat. bd. advisors Coll. Bus. U. Ariz., 1992—, chmn. Dean's Bd. Fine Arts, 1992-96, pres. Ariz. Coun. Econ. Edn., 1993-95; vis. panel Sch. Health Adminstrn. and Policy Ariz. State U., 1990-92; bd. dirs. Tucson Cmty. Found., 1996—; mem. adv. bd. Steele Meml. Rsch. Ctr., U. Ariz. Coll. Medicine, 1996—. Named to Hon. Order Ky. Cols.; named Tucson Man of Yr. 1987; recipient Disting. Svc. award Anti-Defamation League B'nai B'rith, 1989. Mem. Am. Hosp. Assn. (nominating com. 1983-86, trustee 1975-78, ho. dels. 1972-78, chmn. coun. profl. svc. 1973-74, regional adv. bd. 1969-78, chmn. joint com. with NASW 1963-64, Disting. Svc. award 1989), Ariz. Hosp. Assn. (Salisbury award 1982, bd. dirs. 1967-72, pres. 1970-71), Ariz. C. of C. (bd. dirs. 1988-93), Assn. Am. Med. Colls. (mem. assembly 1974-77), Tucson C. of C. (bd. dirs. 1968-69), United Comml. Travelers, Nat. League for Nursing, Ariz. Town Hall (bd. dirs. 1982-92, chmn. 1990-92, treas. 1985), Pima County Acad. Decathlon Assn. (dir. 1983-85), The Rotary Ctr. of Tucson (pres. 1993-94). Baptist (ch. moderator, chmn. finance com., deacon, ch. sch. supt., trustee, bd. dirs. ch. found.). Home: 6734 N Chapultepec Circle Tucson AZ 85750 Office: Tucson Med Ctr 2195 E River Rd Ste 202 Tucson AZ 85718-6586 *It seems important to put something back into life - for all we take from it.*

SHROPSHIRE, HELEN MAE, historian; b. Prosser, Nebr., May 7, 1909; d. William Pearl and Dicy Belle (Myer) Stafford. Grad., Rogers Bus. Coll., Everett, Wash., 1928. Co-owner Camera Exchange, Pacific Grove, Calif., 1947-62; co-owner, photographer, writer Shropshire Film Prodns., Pacific Grove, 1950-76; pilot, co-owner Monarch Aviation, Monterey, Calif., 1962-63; co-founder, mgr. Calif. Heritage Guides, Monterey, Calif., 1971—. Mem. Ninety Nines Inc. (life), Nat. Aviation Hall of Fame (bd. nominations 1996—). Republican. Home: 1623 Josselyn Canyon Rd Monterey CA 93940-5273 Office: Calif Heritage Guides 535 Polk St Monterey CA 93940-2430

SHROYER, ROBERTA WAYMAN, music educator; b. Boise, Idaho, June 3, 1954; d. Robert Eugene and Fern Ann (Trotter) Wayman; m. Timothy McClain Shroyer, Oct. 2, 1976 (div. Dec. 1987); m. Kendall Loren Jensen, Dec. 31, 1992; 1 child, Jeffrey Michael. MusB, U. So. Calif., L.A., 1976; MBA, U. Hawaii Manoa, Honolulu, 1982. Cert. ORFF Schullwerk; elem. edn. and music edn. tchg. credential, Wash. Owner Mililani (Hawaii) Music Sch., 1980-82, Evergreen Music Sch., San Jose, Calif., 1983-86; mktg. program coord. Sun Microsystems, Mountain View, Calif., 1987-90; new product mktg. mgr. Technopoly, 1991-92; owner Queen Anne Music Studio, Seattle, 1994—; founder Queen Anne Arts Acad. Cmty. activist in land use and environ. issues Citizens for Permanent Greenbelt, Santa Cruz, Calif., 1990-91, Commons Park Campaign, Seattle, 1995-96. Mem. Music Tchrs. Nat. Assn., Phi Kappa Phi. Home: 1803 Bigelow Ave N Seattle WA 98109

SHUBART, DOROTHY LOUISE TEPFER, artist, educator; b. Ft. Collins, Colo., Mar. 1, 1923; d. Adam Christian and Rose Virginia (Ayers) Tepfer; m. Robert Franz Shubart, Apr. 22, 1950; children: Richard, Lorenne. *Dorothy Shubart's ancestors can be traced back to the days of Jefferson and Adams, with Christian Haufman (born January 1814). Her lineage also goes back to when humans came to America. Dorothy's great-grandfather, Ayers, gave up his knighthood in England and came to America to marry a Cherokee Indian princess. Her great-grandfather, Toepfer, a book binder, came to America in the 1870s from Altenstein, Germany. Many professions dot Dorothy's history, from a book binder to teacher, contractor, mid-wife to Dorothy's parents, who were homestead ranchers. Dorothy and her two sisters graduated from college as artists and art teachers. Several nieces and cousins are also musicians and artists.* Grad., Cleve. Inst. Art, 1944-46; AA, Colo. Women's Coll., 1944; grad., Cleve. Inst. Art, 1946; student, Western Res. U., 1947-48; BA, St. Thomas Aquinas Coll., 1974; MA, Coll. New Rochelle, 1978. Art tchr. Denver Mus., 1942-44, Cleve. Recreation Dept., 1944-50; ind. artist, portrait painter, ceramist-potter Colo., Cleve., N.Y., and N.Mex., 1944—; adult edn. art tchr. Nanuet (N.Y.) Pub. Schs., 1950-65, Pearl River (N.Y.) Adult Edn., 1950-51; rec. sec. Van Houten Fields Assn., West Nyack, N.Y., 1969-74. Exhbns. include Hopper House, Rockland Ctr. for Arts, CWC, Cleve. Inst. Art, Coll. New Rochelle, Rockland County Ann. Art Fair, Gonzalez Sr. Ctr., 1970-91. Leader 4-H Club, Nanuet, 1960-80, Girls Scouts U.S., Nanuet, 1961-68; mem. scholarship com., gen. com. PTA, Nanuet, 1964-68; rec. sec. Van Houten Fields assn., West Nyack, N.Y., 1969-74; com. mem. Eldorado (Santa Fe) Cmty. Improvement Assn.-Arterial Rd. Planning Com., 1992-94, Environ. Def. Fund, Union of Concerned Scientists, Nat. Com. to Preserve Social Security and Medicare; capt. Neighborhood Watch; local organizer Eldorado chpt.; mem. Eldorado Conservation Greenbelt Com., 1996-97; vol. Jim Baca Gov.'s campaign, 1994, Eric Serva's Campaign for Congress, 1996; mem. Eldorado Hist. Com., 1995-97; mem. El Dorado Arterial Road Planning Com., Habitat for Humanity. Gund scholar Cleve. Inst. Art, 1946. Mem. AAUW, NOW, Audubon Soc., Ams. for Dem. Action, Environ. Def. Fund, Union Concerned Scientists, Action on Smoking and Health, Wilderness Club, Delta Tau Kappa, Phi Delta Kappa. Democrat. Home: 8 Hidalgo Ct Santa Fe NM 87505-8898
Spring is eternal, life is very fragile.

SHUBB, WILLIAM BARNET, lawyer; b. Oakland, Calif., May 28, 1938; s. Ben and Nellie Bernice (Fruechtenicht) S.; m. Sandra Ann Talarico, July 29, 1962; children: Alisa Marie, Carissa Ann, Victoria Ann. AB, U. Calif., Berkeley, 1960, JD, 1963. Bar: Calif., 1964, U.S. Ct. Internat. Trade 1981, U.S. Customs Ct. 1980, U.S. Ct. Appeals (9th cir.) 1964, U.S. Supreme Ct. 1972. Law clk. U.S. Dist. Ct., Sacramento, 1963-65; asst. U.S. atty., Sacramento, 1965-71; chief asst. U.S. atty. (ea. dist.) Calif., 1971-74; assoc. Diepenbrock, Wulff, Plant & Hannegan, Sacramento, 1974-77, ptnr., 1977-80, 81-90; U.S. atty. Eastern Dist. Calif., 1980-81; judge U.S. Dist. Ct. (ea. dist.) Calif., 1990—; chmn. com. drafting of local criminal rules U.S. Dist. Ct. (ea. dist.) Calif., 1974, mem. speedy trial planning com., 1974-80; lawyer rep. 9th Cir. U.S. Jud. Conf., 1975-78; mem. faculty Fed. Practice Inst., 1978-80; instr. McGeorge Sch. Law, U. Pacific, 1964-66. Mem. ABA, Fed. Bar Assn. (pres. Sacramento chpt. 1977), Calif. Bar Assn., Assn. Def. Counsel, Am. Bd. Trial Advs., Sacramento County Bar Council. Office: US Courthouse 650 Capitol Mall Rm 2042 Sacramento CA 95814-4708*

SHUCK, LOLA MAE, retired elementary school educator; b. Eustis, Nebr., Mar. 22, 1929; d. Gust Adolf and Dora (Timm) Hueftle; m. Kenneth L. Shuck, Dec. 22, 1951 (div. Oct. 1969); children: David Lynn, Terri Kay, Lorie Jane Shuck Larson. BA, Nebr. Wesleyan U., 1951; MA, Ariz. State U., 1969. Elem. tchr. Springfield (Colo.) Pub. Sch., 1948-49; tchr. art David City (Nebr.) Pub. Schs., 1951-52, Alhambra Dist. 68 Pub. Schs., Phoenix, 1964-68, 69-92; ret., 1992. Vice pres. Women's Soc. Christian Svc., 1959-63; mem. ch. choir Meth. Ch., 1992—; committeewoman Phoenix Rep. Com., 1976-77. Named Ms. Personality, Ms. Nebr. Contest, 1949. Mem. Alpha Delta Kappa (pres. Xi chpt. 1981-82, chmn. bylaws 1991-93). Democrat. Home: 4766 W Palmaire Ave Glendale AZ 85301-2742

SHUGART, ALAN F., electronic computing equipment company executive; b. L.A., Sept. 27, 1930. BS in Engring. and Physics, U. Redlands, 1951. Dir. engring. IBM, San Jose, Calif., 1952-69; v.p. Memorex Corp., Sunnyvale, Calif., 1969-73; pres. Shugart Assocs., 1973-78; chmn., pres., chief exec. officer, coo Seagate Tech., Scotts Valley, Calif., 1978—, also bd. dirs. Office: Seagate Tech 920 Disc Dr Scotts Valley CA 95066-4544*

SHUKLA, PRADIP KANTILAL, academic administrator, educator, consultant; b. Ahmedabad, Gujarat, India, Sept. 7, 1956; came to U.S., 1961; s. Kantilal T. and Manju K. (Vyas) S.; m. Yatri P. Thaker, Jan. 6, 1983; children: Monica, Amy. BSc in Bus. Adminstrn., Calif. State U., Long Beach, 1978, BA in Econs., 1978, MBA, 1979; MSc in Bus. Adminstrn., U. So. Calif., 1983; MEd, UCLA, 1983, PhD in Ednl. Adminstrn., 1990. Cert. prodn. and inventory mgr. Coord. tutoring ctr. Compton (Calif.) Coll., 1976, instr. bus. and law, 1980-86, adminstrv. analyst, 1982-83, dir. instnl. rsch., 1986-88, asst. to pres., 1990—; night libr. Lynwood (Calif.) Adult Sch., 1974-78; lectr. in mgmt. Calif. State U., Long Beach, L.A., Northridge, 1978-91; mgmt. cons. P.K. Shukla & Assocs., Orange, Calif., 1979—; assoc. prof. mktg. and mgmt. Chapman U., Orange, 1985—; cons. various corps. and colls., Calif., 1979—; internat. cons. and speaker import/export ventures. Adv. bd. St. Francis Med. Ctr., Lynwood, Calif., 1979-81, Santa Ana (Calif) Zoo, 1988—; community breakfast chairperson City Lynwood, 1980; polit. cons. various candidates local and statewide, Calif., 1979—. Scholar Bank of Am., Soc. Calif. Edison Co., UCLA Grad. Sch. Mgmt.; grantee U.S. Dept. Edn., Compton Coll., Chapman U. Mem. Internat. Acad. Mgmt. Mktg., Internat. Acad. Bus. & Soc. (charter), Computer Using Instrs., Western Acad. Mgmt. (program reviewer, arrangements com., program com.), Western Mktg. Educators Assn. (program reviewer, session chmn.), Am. Mktg. Assn., Acad. Mgmt. (program reviewer). Republican. Home: 10492 Park Villa Cir Villa Park CA 92861-5318 Office: Chapman U 333 N Glassell St Orange CA 92866-1011

SHULER, SALLY ANN SMITH, telecommunications, computer services and software company executive; b. Mt. Olive, N.C., June 11, 1934; d. Leon Joseph and Ludia Irene (Montague) Simmons; m. Henry Ralph Smith Jr., Mar. 1, 1957 (div. Jan. 1976); children: Molly Montague, Barbara Ellen, Sara Ann, Mary Kathryn; m. Harold Robert Shuler, Aug. 2, 1987 (div. Mar. 1997). BA in Math., Duke U., 1956; spl. studies, U. Liège, Belgium, 1956-57; postgrad. in bus. econs., Claremont Grad Sch., 1970-72. Mgr. fed. systems GE Info. Svcs. Co., Washington, 1976-78; mgr. mktg. support GE Info. Svcs. Co., Rockville, Md., 1978-81; dir. bus. devel. info. tech. group Electronic Data Systems, Bethesda, Md., 1981-82; v.p. mktg. optimum systems div. Electronic Data Systems, Rockville, 1982-83; v.p. planning and communications Electronic Data Systems, Dallas, 1983-84; exec. dir. comml. devel. U.S. West Inc., Englewood, Colo., 1984-90; v.p. mktg. devel. Cin. Bell Info. Systems Inc., 1990-92; mgmt. cons. in mergers and acquisitions Denver, 1992-93; v.p. major accounts U.S. Computer Svcs., Denver, 1993-95; mgmt. cons. in mergers and acquisitions Mktg., Telecom., Denver, 1995—. Recipient GE Centennial award, Rockville, 1978. Mem. Women in Telecommunications, Rotary (fellow Internat. Found.), Phi Beta Kappa, Tau Psi Omega, Pi Mu Epsilon. Democrat. Presbyterian. Office: 1626 S Syracuse St Denver CO 80231-2691

SHULTS, MARY J., retail store owner; b. El Reno, Okla., July 25, 1944; m. Ray D. Shults, Jan. 17, 1964; children: E. Deanna, Jeffrey D. Student, Boise Jr. Coll., 1963. Owner retail clothing and horse equipment store, mgr. Highland Stables, Boise, Idaho, 1976-78; owner Horseman's Tac & Togs, Boise, 1978-79, Three Creek Ranch & Cattle Co., Ellensburg, Wash., 1982-84, Sagebrush Saddlery & Western Wear, Ellensburg, 1985—. Res. dep. sheriff Kittitas County Sheriff's Office, Ellensburg, 1993—. Mem. N.W. Cutting Horse Assn., Cascade Cow Cutters. Home and Office: 1310 S Ruby Ellensburg WA 98926

SHULTZ, C. E. (CHUCK SCHULTZ), exploration and production company executive. Degree in Geological Engring., Colo. Sch. of Mines, 1961; postgrad. U. Va., 1980, Harvard Bus. Sch., 1984. With Tenneco Oil Co., divsn. Tenneco Inc., 1961; v.p., gen. mgr. Western Gulf of Mex. divsn. Tenneco Oil Co., Lafayette, La., 1980-85; v.p., corp. planning and devel., officer Tenneco Inc., Houston, 1985-88; sr. v.p. Tenneco Oil Co., Houston, 1988-1989; pres., chief oper. officer Gulf Canada Resources Ltd., Calgary, 1989, pres., chief exec. officer, 1990—, also bd. dirs.; bd. dirs. Home Oil Co. Ltd., Interprovincial Pipe Line Co. Chmn. U.S. Nat. Energy Policy Coun., Nat. Petroleum Coun., selected study com., Teche API Chpt. (So. La.), Colo. Sch. Mines, pres.'s coun.; gov. Can. Petroleum Assn., exec. com., Oilmen's; chmn. Can-USSR Bus. Coun. Energy Group. Office: Gulf Can Resources Ltd, 401 9th Ave SW PO Box 130, Calgary, AB Canada T2P 2H7

SHULTZ, DELRAY FRANKLIN, oil company executive; b. South Bend, Ind., Apr. 4, 1948; s. Jack Raymond and Georgina Martha (Johnston) S.; m. Catherine Elizabeth Yontz, June 6, 1970; children: Jeremy Frank, Eric Bruce, Jon Karl. BS, USAF Acad., 1970; MS, Air U., 1978. Commd. 2d lt. USAF, 1970, advanced through grades to capt.; navigator USAF, Anchorage, 1972-77; adminstrv. contracting officer USAF, L.A., 1978-81; mgr. purchasing, contracts supr. BP Exploration, Anchorage, 1981-92; internal cons. BP Exploration, Bogotá, Colombia, 1992-93; mgr. contracts, internal cons. Alaska Petroleum Contractors, Anchorage, 1994-97; mgr. assurance and devel. Natchiq Inc., Anchorage, 1997—; adj. prof. U. Alaska, Anchorage, 1988-96. Bd. mem., vice chair bd. dirs. Family Connection, Inc., Anchorage, 1981-84; worsship dir., bd. elders Bethany Christian Cmty., Anchorage, 1982-93; del. Rep. Party of Alaska, Anchorage, 1988, 96. Named Outstanding Young Men of Am., U.S. Jr. C. of C., 1978. Mem. Nat. Contract Mgmt. Assn., Nat. Assn. Purchasing Mgrs. Home: 13495 Baywind Dr Anchorage AK 99516-3451

SHULTZ, FRED TOWNSEND, geneticist, biologist; b. Grinnell, Iowa, Mar. 3, 1923; s. J. Gordon and Katharine Lucia (Townsend) S.; m. Carolyn Covell June 24, 1961; children: Trina, Rebecca, Daniel, Brian. AB in Biol. Sci., Stanford U., 1947; PhD in Genetics, U. Calif.-Berkeley, 1952. Geneticist, biologist Animal Breeding Cons., Sonoma, Calif., 1952—; pres. Avian Allure; chmn. bd. dirs. Biol. Frontiers Inst. Inventor new life forms and prodn. systems. Served to 2nd lt. USAF, 1942-45. Recipient Poultry Sci. Research award Poultry Sci. Assn., 1954. Mem. Poultry Sci. Assn., World Poultry Sci., World Aquaculture Soc. Republican. Home: 19443 Marna Ln Sonoma CA 95476-6309 Office: Animal Breeding Cons PO Box 313 Sonoma CA 95476

SHULTZ, GEORGE PRATT, former government executive, economics educator; b. N.Y.C., Dec. 13, 1920; s. Birl E. and Margaret Lennox (Pratt) S.; m. Helena M. O'Brien, Feb. 16, 1946; children: Margaret Ann Shultz Tilsworth, Kathleen Pratt Shultz Jorgensen, Peter Milton, Barbara Lennox Shultz White, Alexander George. BA in Econs., Princeton U., 1942; PhD in Indsl. Econs., MIT, 1949; Hon. degree, Yeshiva U., U. Tel Aviv, Technion-Israel Inst. Tech., Keio U., Tokyo. Mem. faculty M.I.T., 1949-57; assoc. prof. indsl. relations MIT, 1955-57; prof. indsl. relations Grad. Sch. Bus., U. Chgo., 1957-68, dean sch., 1962-68; fellow Ctr. for Advanced Study in Behavioral Scis., 1968-69; U.S. sec. labor, 1969-70; dir. Office Mgmt. and Budget, 1970-72; U.S. sec. treasury, also asst. to Pres., 1972-74; chmn. Council on Econ. Policy, East-West Trade Policy com.; exec. v.p. Bechtel Corp., San Francisco, 1974-75, pres., 1975-77; vice chmn. Bechtel Corp., 1977-81; also dir.; pres. Bechtel Group, Inc., 1981-82; prof. mgmt. and pub. policy Stanford U., 1974-82, prof. internat. econs., 1989-91, prof. emeritus, 1991—; chmn. Pres. Reagan's Econ. Policy Adv. Bd., 1981-82; U.S. sec. of state, 1982-89; disting. fellow Hoover Instn., Stanford, 1989—; bd. dirs. Bechtel Group, Inc., Gulfstream Aerospace Corp., AirTouch Comm.; mem. Gilead Scis. Bd.; mem. adv. coun. GM; chmn. J.P. Morgan Internat. Coun.; chmn. adv. coun. Inst. Internat. Studies, Calif. Go.v's Econ. Policy Adv. Bd. Author: Pressures on Wage Decisions, 1951, (with Charles A. Myers) The Dynamics of a Labor Market, 1951, (with John R. Coleman) Labor Problems: Cases and Readings, 1953, (with T.L. Whisler) Management Organization and the Computer, 1960, (with Arnold R. Weber) Strategies for the Displaced Worker, 1966, (with Robert Z. Aliber) Guidelines, Informal Controls and the Market Place, 1966, (with Albert Rees) Workers and Wages in the Urban Labor Market, 1970, Leaders and Followers in an Age of Ambiguity, 1975, (with Kenneth W. Dam) Economic Policy Beyond the Headlines, 1977, Turmoil and Triumph: My Years as Secetary of State, 1993; also articles, chpts. in books, reports, and essays. Served to capt. USMCR, 1942-45. Mem. Am. Econ. Assn., Indsl. Relations Research Assn. (pres. 1968), Nat. Acad. Arbitrators. Office: Stanford U Hoover Instn Stanford CA 94305

SHUMAKER, JEANETTE ROBERTS, English language educator; b. Salinas, Calif., Dec. 24, 1958; d. Claude Herschel III and Dorothea Eileen (Hayes) Roberts; m. Andrew David Shumaker, July 26, 1985; 1 child, Nicholas. BA, U. Redlands, 1981; higher diploma, Trinity Coll., Dublin, Ireland, 1983; M English, Claremont Grad. Sch., 1985, PhD in English, 1990. Lectr. in writing programs UCLA, 1989-90; asst. prof. English Elizabethtown (Pa.) Coll., 1990-91, U. Tex.-Permian Basin, Odessa, 1991-92; assoc. prof. English San Diego State U.-Imperial Valley, Calexico, Calif., 1992—, dir. activity 1 title III, 1993—, faculty chair, 1994-95, asst. dean, 1995—. Contbr. articles to profl. jours. Recipient Outstanding Faculty Contbn. award San Diego State U. Alumni Assn., 1994; Rotary Internat. fellow, 1982-83, George Eliot fellow. Mem. MLA, Soc. for Study of Narrative Lit., Am. Coun. Irish Studies, Interdisciplinary 19C Studies Assn., Philol. Assn. of Pacific Coast. Democrat. Office: San Diego State U Imperial Valley 720 Heber Ave Calexico CA 92231

SHUMAN, THOMAS ALAN, correctional operations executive, consultant; b. Fairmont, W.Va., Dec. 31, 1946. BA, N.Mex. State U., 1969, 73; postgrad., U. N.Mex., 1988. Mgr. Drum Appliance, Inc., Las Cruces, N.Mex., 1971-75; classification supr. N.Mex. Corrections Dept., Santa Fe, 1976-80, mgmt. analyst supr., 1981-83, dir. classification, 1983-84, dep. sec., 1984-87; pres. Correctional Data Systems, Santa Fe, 1987—; owner Desktop Publ. Co., Santa Fe, 1988—; dir. N.Mex. Corrections Tng. Acad., 1991-95, probation, parole dir., 1995—; pres. Silicon Wizard Corp., 1989—; cons. Nat. Inst. Corrections, Washington, 1988, Am. Correctional Assn., Md., 1987—. Mem. Smithsonian Inst., U.S. Naval Inst. Served to lt. U.S. Army, 1969-71, Vietnam. Decorated Bronze Star, Presdl. Commendation. Mem. NRA, N.Mex. State U. Alumni Assn. Republican. Presbyterian.

SHUMATE, CHARLES ALBERT, retired dermatologist; b. San Francisco, Aug. 11, 1904; s. Thomas E. and Freda (Ortmann) S.; B.S., U. San Francisco, 1927, H.H.D., 1976; M.D., Creighton U., 1931. Pvt. practice dermatology, San Francisco, 1933-73, ret., 1973; asst. clin. prof. dermatology Stanford U., 1956-62; pres. E Clampus Vitus, Inc., 1963-64; hon. mem. staff St. Mary's Hosp. Mem. San Francisco Art Commn., 1964-67, Calif. Heritage Preservation Commn., 1963-67; regent Notre Dame Coll. at Belmont, 1965-78, trustee, 1977-93; pres. Conf. Calif. Hist. Socs., 1967; mem. San Francisco Landmarks Preservation Bd., 1967-78, pres., 1967-69; trustee St. Patrick's Coll. and Sem., 1970-86; dir. U.S. Catholic Hist. Soc., 1988—. Served as maj. USPHS, 1942-46. Decorated knight comdr. Order of Isabella (Spain); knight Order of the Holy Sepulchre, knight of St. Gregory, knight of Malta. Fellow Am. Acad. Dermatology; mem. U. San Francisco Alumni Assn. (pres. 1955), Calif. Book Club (pres. 1969-71), Calif. Hist. Soc. (trustee 1958-67, 68-78, pres. 1962-64), Soc. Calif. Pioneers (dir. 1979—), Drum Found. (v.p. 1986—). Clubs: Bohemian, Olympic, Roxburghe (pres. 1958-59) (San Francisco); Zamorano (Los Angeles). Author: Life of George Henry Goddard; The California of George Gordon, 1976, Jas. F. Curtis, Vigilante, 1988, Francisco Pacheco of Pacheco Pass, 1977; Life of Mariano Malarin, 1980; Boyhood Days: Y. Villegas Reminiscences of California 1850s, 1983, The Notorious I.C. Woods of the Adams Express, 1986, Rincon Hill and South Park, 1988, Captain A.A. Ritchie, Pioneer, 1991, Stormy Life of Major William Gouverneur Morris, 1993, Lord Sholter Douglas, Clamgen, 1996. Mem. St. Andrew Soc. (hon. mem.). Home: 1901 Scott St San Francisco CA 94115-2613 Office: 490 Post St San Francisco CA 94102-1401

SHURTLEFF, AKIKO AOYAGI, artist, consultant; b. Tokyo, Jan. 24, 1950; d. Kinjiro and Fumiyo (Sugata) Aoyagi; m. William Roy Shurtleff, Mar. 10, 1977 (div. 1995); 1 child, Joseph Aoyagi. Grad., Women's Coll. Art, Tokyo, 1971; student, Acad. Art, San Francisco, 1991-92. Fashion designer, illustrator Marimura Co. and Hayakawa Shoji, Inc., Tokyo, 1970-72; co-founder, art dir. Soyfoods Ctr. consulting svcs., Lafayette, Calif., 1976-94; freelance illustrator, graphic designer; lectr. U.S. Internat. Christian U., Tokyo, 1977, Japanese Tofu Mfrs. Conv., Osaka, 1978; presenter cooking demonstrations, tchr. cooking classes. Co-author, illustrator: The Book of Tofu, 1975, The Book of Miso, 1975, The Book of Kudzu, 1977, Tofu and Soymilk Prodduction, 1979, The Book of Tempeh, 1979, Miso Production, 1979, Tempeh Production, 1980; illustrator: Spirulina (by L. Switzer), 1982, The Bok of Shiatsu-The Healing Art of Finger Pressure (by S. Goodman), 1990, Staying Healthy with Nutrition (by E. Haas), 1992, Culinary Treasures of Japan (by John and Jan Belleme), 1992, Yookoso, An Invitation to Contemporary Japanese, Vols. 1 and 2 (by Hasu-Hiko Tohsaku), 1994-95, Blue Collar and Beyond (by Yana Parker), 1995, Damn Good Ready to Go Resumes, 1995, Homework (by Peter Jeswald), 1995, Vegetarian's A to Z Guide to Fruits and Vegetables (by Kathleen Robinson with Pete Luckett), 1996, Hubert Keller's Cuisine, 1996, Doctor Generic Will See You Now (by Oscar London), 1996, Everyday Pediatrics for Parents (by Elmer R. Grossman, M.D.), 1996. Office: Akiko Aoyagi Shurtleff PO Box 443 Lafayette CA 94549-0443

SHURTLEFF, C. MICHAEL, writer; b. Oslo, July 3, 1937; came to the U.S., 1940; s. Charles Joseph and Ruth (Mathison) S. BA, Lawrence U.; MFA, Yale U. Casting dir. David Merrick, Bob Fosse, Stuart Ostrow, Peter Glenville, Gower Champion, N.Y.C., 1959-79; pvt. Broadway casting cons. N.Y.C.; ret.; lectr., tchr. various locations. Author: Audition, 1979 (Best Seller), Taking Care of Yourself, 1997; author (plays) Call Me By My Rightful Name, 1961, Sailing, 1996, Entertaining Angels, 1996, Driving Yourself Crazy, The Mischief Makers, others. Home: 6619 Cahuenga Ter Hollywood CA 90068-2746

SHURTLEFF, WILLIAM ROY, food products executive; b. Oakland, Calif., Apr. 28, 1941; s. Lawton Lothrop and Barbara Anne (Reinhardt) S.; m. Akiko Aoyagi, Mar. 10, 1977 (div. May 1995); 1 child: Joseph Aoyagi. BS in Indsl. Engring. and Physics, Stanford U., 1962, MEd, 1966. Indsl. engr. U.S. Steel Corp., Pittsburg, Calif., 1963; with Peace Corps, Nigeria, 1964-66; founder, dir. Esalen program in human awareness Stanford (Calif.) U., 1967-68; founder, dir. Soyfoods Ctr., Lafayette, Calif., 1976—; speaker in field. Author: The Book of Tofu, 1975, The Book of Miso, 1976, Miso Production, 1981, The Book of Tempeh, 1985, Tofu and Soymilk Production, 1984, Tempeh Production, 1986, Soyfoods Industry and Market: Directory and Databook, 1984, Soymilk Industry and Market: Worldwide and Country-by-Country Analysis, 1984, History of Tempeh, 1985, Tofutti and Other Soy Ice Creams: Non-dairy Frozen Dessert Industry and Market, 1985, Thesaurus for SoyaScan, 1986, and others; compiler over 45 bibliographies on soybeans and soyfoods; prodr. computerized bibliographic database SoyaScan. Mem. Soyfoods Assn. Am. (bd. dirs.), Tofu Standards Com. (co-chair 1984-86), Earthsave Found. (bd. dirs.), Tau Beta Pi. Home and Office: 1021 Dolores Dr Lafayette CA 94549-2907 also: PO Box 234 Lafayette CA 94549-0234

SHUSHKEWICH, KENNETH WAYNE, structural engineer; b. Winnipeg, Man., Sept. 22, 1952; m. Valdine Cuffe, Sept. 28, 1980. BSCE, U. Man., Winnipeg, 1974; MS in Structural Engring., U. Calif., Berkeley, 1975; PhD in Structural Engring., U. Alta., Edmonton, Can., 1985. Engr. Wardrop and Assocs., Winnipeg, 1974-78, Preconsult Can., Montreal, Que., 1978-80; prof. U. Alta., 1981-85, U. Man., 1985-87; engr. T.Y. Lin Internat., San Francisco, 1988-90, H.J. Degenkolb Assocs., San Francisco, 1990-92, Ben C. Gerwick, Inc., San Francisco, 1993-94, J. Muller Internat., Chgo., 1994-95, T.Y. Lin Internat., San Francisco, 1995—; mem. bridge design com., prestressed concrete com. ASCE-Am. Concrete Inst. Prin. works include design of prestressed concrete segmental bridges, seismic strengthening of San Francisco Ferry Building damaged in Loma Prieta earthquake, seismic retrofit of Presidio Viaduct in San Francisco; design mgr. for long-span west approach bridge of Northumberland Strait Crossing in Can.; contbr. articles to profl. jours. Recipient award for design of Vierendeel truss bridge, Man. Design Inst., 1977. Mem. ASCE, Am. Concrete Inst., Prestressed Concrete Inst., Internat. Assn. Bridge and Structural Engrs. Office: PO Box 2590 San Francisco CA 94126-2590

SHUSTER, FRED TODD, journalist, commentator; b. Washington, Jan. 10, 1956; s. Alvin and Miriam (Schwartz) S. BA in English Literature, San Francisco State U., 1979. News asst. AP, L.A., 1985-87; reporter Simi Valley (Calif.) Enterprise, 1987-89; music critic L.A. Daily News, 1989—; radio corres. Greater London Radio, 1995—; west coast bur. chief Down Beat Mag., Chgo., 1993—. Recipient 2d pl. writing award Stuttering Found. Am., Memphis, 1996. Democrat. Jewish. Office: LA Daily News 21221 Oxnard St Woodland Hills CA 91367-5015

SHYMKUS, HAROLD, author; b. Chgo., May 6, 1926; s. Joseph N. and Hazel A. Shymkus; m. Mary Beth Shymkus, Sept. 16, 1951; children: David, Lisa. BA in Journalism, Franklin (Ind.) Coll., 1950. Mgr. field parts mktg. Cummins engine Co., Columbus, Ind., 1951-52, dir. sales promotion, 1952-69, dir. corp. advt., 1969-76, dir. adminstrv. svcs., 1976-83; pres. Halcom, Columbus, 1983-93. Author: Dance for the Fishermen, 1995, Nightcrawlers, Bait, Beer to Go, 1991; contbr. numerous articles to profl. jours. With U.S. Army Air Corps, 1944-46. Recipient First Place for short story Moreno Valley Writers Guild, 1995. Mem. Hoosier Outdoor Writers, N.Mex. Outdoor Writers/Photographers, Rocky Mountain Outdoor Writers/Photographers, Outdoor Writers Assn. Am. Presbyterian. Home: PO Box 1208 Espanola NM 87532

SIBERTS, DAWN ANNE, dietitian; b. Santa Clara, Calif., Aug. 31, 1969; d. Richard Jay and Sherry Kaye (Thompson) Gomes; m. Michael Scott Siberts, July 31, 1993. BS in Dietetics, San Jose (Calif.) State U., 1992. Registered dietitian. Dietary svcs. mgr. Hylond Healthcare Ctr., Sunnyvale, Calif., 1995—. Mem. Am. Dietetic Assn. Republican. Nazarene. Home: 760 Northrup St Apt 17 San Jose CA 95126

SIBLEY, PETER EDWARD, lawyer; b. Ft. Walton Beach, Fla., June 12, 1944. Student, St. Mary's Coll.; BA, U. Calif., Santa Barbara, 1966; JD, U. Calif., 1970. Bar: Calif. 1970. Ptnr. Cooper, White & Cooper, San Francisco. Office: Cooper White & Cooper 201 California St Fl 17 San Francisco CA 94111-5002

SICILIAN, JAMES MICHAEL, research engineer; b. Bronx, N.Y., May 25, 1947; s. Leonard James and Veronica Patricia (Reinwald) S. BS, MIT, 1969; MS, Stanford U., 1970, PhD, 1973. Tech. editor C.S. Draper Lab., Cambridge, Mass., 1968-69; research analyst Savannah River Lab., Aiken, S.C., 1973-76; staff Los Alamos (N.Mex) Scientific Lab, 1976-79, asst. group leader, 1979-80; sr. scientist Flow Science, Inc., Los Alamos, 1980—, sec. of corp., 1980—; v.p., 1990—. Mem. Cultural Ctr. adv. com., Los Alamos, 1987-89; vice chmn. Park and Recreation Bd., Los Alamos, 1989-90; treas. N.Mex. Theater Assn., 1983-85; pres. Los Alamos Little Theater, 1978-79; sec. Los Alamos Light Opera, 1990-91. Recipient AEC spl. fellowship, U.S. AEC, 1969-72. Mem. AIAA, ASME, Sigma Xi. Office: Remolinos 1345 Los Pueblos St Los Alamos NM 87544-2663

SICKEL, JOAN SOTTILARE, foundation administrator; b. Jersey City, Dec. 29, 1941; d. Peter S. and Rose M. (Maresca) Sottilare; m. Walter F. Sickel Jr., Jan. 4, 1964 (div. July 1979); children: Walter F. III (dec.), Linda Hilaire. AB, Georgian Ct. Coll., 1963. Dir. ann. giving Tucson Med. Ctr. Found., 1980-87; dir. devel. and pub. rels. Ariz. Children's Home, Tucson, 1987-93; exec. dir. Ariz. Children's Home Found., Tucson, 1993-94; curator edn. program devel. Ariz. Aerospace Found., Tucson, 1995-96; cons. Postal History Found., Tucson, 1996; ann. giving officer Nature Conservancy, Tucson, 1996—. Mem. women's studies adv. coun. U. Ariz. Mem. Nat. Soc. Fund Raising Execs., Nat. Assn. for Hosp. Devel., Pub. Rels. Soc. Am., Planned Giving Round Table of So. Ariz., AAUW, Ariz. Assn. for Hosp.

Devel. (treas. 1986-88), U. Ariz. Presidents Club, U. Ariz. Wildcat Club, Soroptimists Internat. (chair fin. com. 1985). Home: 4151 N Camino Ferreo Tucson AZ 85750-6358 Office: Nature Conservancy 300 E University Blvd Tucson AZ 85705

SIDEBOTTOM, DAVID KIRK, writer, former engineer; b. Kinseley, Kans., Aug. 20, 1955; s. Conard Jay and Harriet Louise (Bock) S. Student, U. Colo., 1973-75, U. So. Colo., 1981-83. Mech. draftsman Do-Ray Lamp Co. Inc., Colorado City, Colo., 1980-83; surveying technician Licensed Surveyors in Colo., Pueblo and La Junta, 1984-87; constrn. engr. H. W. Houston Co. Pueblo J. A. Walker Co., Denver, 1987-88; asst. supt. engr. C. P. Constrn. Co., Denver, 1988-90; asst. engr. Hensel-Phelps, Inc., Greeley, Colo., 1991; fed. safety engr. U.S. Bur. Land Mgmt., Pueblo, 1989. Author: Adventures in the Strike Zone, 1996; editor: (newsletter) Shift of the Earth News, 1997. With U.S. Army, 1976-79. Mem. U.F.O. Inst. Colo. Republican. Office: Shift of the Earth News PO Box 4712 Pueblo CO 81003-0712

SIDHU, GURMEL SINGH, geneticist, research scientist; b. Jullundur, Punjab, India, May 23, 1944; came to U.S., 1980; s. Naranjan Singh and Kartar Kaur (Hoti) S.; m. Baljit Aulakh, Mar.21, 1979; children: Vikramjit, Rupinderpal. BS, Punjab U., 1960, MS, 1966; PhD, U. B.C., Vancouver, Can., 1974. Postdoctoral fellow Simon Fraser U., Burnaby, B.C., 1973-75, rsch. scientist, 1975-80; asst. prof. genetics U. Nebr., Lincoln, 1980-86; prof. Calif. State U., Fresno, 1987—; rsch. dir. Germain's Inc., Fresno, 1992—. Editor: Genetics of Pathogenic Fungi, 1989; assoc. editor: (jours.) Phytopathology, 1980-86, Crop Improvement Sci., 1980—. Pres. Punjab Literacy Assn. Calif., 1994—. Rsch. fellow U. Wis., 1986-87. Mem. AAAS, Phytopathology Soc. Am., Genetics and Cytology Soc. Can. Home: 1637 Gettysburg Ave Clovis CA 93611-4509 Office: Calif State U Shaw and Cedar Fresno CA 93740

SIDHU, VICTOR S., investment executive; b. Pitts., Nov. 23, 1938; s. S. S. and Mary Elizabeth S.; m. Nancy Dayton; 1 child, Mary Sidhu Pittman. Student, Princeton U., 1956-59; BA, U. Chgo., 1961; MA, U. Ill., 1967. Chartered fin. analyst. Asst. to chmn. of dept. U. Ill., Champaign, 1963-65; account exec. Dean Witter Co., Chgo., 1967-70; pres., founder RMI Corp., Winnetka, Ill., 1970-72; investment mgr. Lincoln Nat. Investment Advisors, Chgo., 1972-73; lectr. Northeastern Ill. U., Chgo., 1971-73; v.p., div. mgr. Harris Bank, Chgo., 1973-87; v.p., chief investment officer First Interstate Bank of Calif., L.A., 1987-90; sr. v.p. Capital Rsch. and Mgmt. Co., L.A., 1990-97; pres. Sidhu Group, Santa Monica, 1997—. Bd. advisors Salvation Army, Santa Monica, Calif., 1988—; bd. dirs. U. Chgo. Alumni Assn., L.A., 1989-90; vice chmn. L.A. Met. bd. advisors Salvation Army, 1996—. Mem. L.A. Soc. Fin. Analysts (pres. 1992-93, gov. 1989-94), Am. Fin. Assn. (life), Inst. Chartered Fin. Analysts, Jonathan Club. Republican. Congregationalist. Home: 39 Sea Colony Dr Santa Monica CA 90405-5322 Office: Sidhu Group 39 Sea Colony Dr Santa Monica CA 90405-5322

SIEDENBURG, CARRIE, program manager; b. Chgo.; d. Reinhard and Carol Marie (Cheevers) S.; m. Michael R. Henn, Oct., 1991; 1 child, Charlotte Marie Henn. BS in Biochemistry with honors, Calif. Poly. Inst. Registered lead auditor. Space/brain rsch. asst. NASA/Ames, Mountain View, Calif., 1981-82; libr. rschr. Boston Consulting Group., Menlo Park, Calif., 1982-83; biotech. intern Atlantic Richfield Co. Plant Cell Rsch. Inst., Dublin, Calif., 1985; software quality assurance engr. Intelligenetics, Mountain View, 1986-87, mgr. quality assurance dept., 1987-88, project mgr., 1988-89; software designer Tandem Computers, Cupertino, Calif., 1989-92; lead auditor Nat. Stds. Authority of Ireland, 1993-96; program mgr. Borealis, Incline Village, Nev., 1996—; cons. Summit Quality Assocs., Tahoe City, Calif., 1992-93. Dir. Profl. Lifestyles Day, Cupertino, 1990-92. Sr. mem. Am. Quality Control (conf. chair 3d internat. conf. on software quality, software divsn. 1993); mem. AAUW, Santa Clara Valley Software Quality Assn. (bd. dirs., local task force 1991, newsletter editor 1992-94, chair internat. conf. SW divsn. 1992-93), Women in Technology Internat., Phi Kappa Phi. Address: PO Box 7548 Tahoe City CA 96145-7548

SIEGEL, DAVID AARON, accountant; b. Brizdowicz, Poland, June 10, 1913; came to U.S., 1920; s. Isaac and Malka (Pickholtz) S.; m. Rose Minsky, June 20, 1937; children: Stanley, Ira Theodore. BBA, St. Johns U., 1934; MBA, NYU, 1939. CPA, N.Y., Calif. Pvt. practice N.Y.C., 1929-49, L.A., 1974-96; chmn. bus. City of N.Y., 1950-73. Bd. govs., fin. sec. Ketubah Unit B'nai B'rith, L.A., 1980-96, pres., 1986-87; chmn. audit com. Congregation Mogen David, L.A., 1990-96. Recipient award for svc. B'nai Brith, L.A., 1990, 150th Anniv. Cert. of Appreciation, 1993, Plaque for Svc. N.Y. State Soc. CPA's, 1993-94; named Man of Yr. Congregation Mogen David, L.A., 1995. Mem. Knights of Pythias (chancellor comdr. 1981, chmn. fin. com. 1985). Home: 2175 S Beverly Glen Blvd Los Angeles CA 90025

SIEGEL, MO J., beverage company executive; b. Salida, Colo., Nov. 21, 1949; s. Joe E. and Betty Siegel; children—Gabriel, Sarah, Megan, Kate, Luke. Founder Celestial Seasonings Herb Tea Co., Boulder, Colo.; pres., chief exec. officer Celestial Seasonings Herb Tea Co., until 1984, Celestial Seasonings div. Dart and Kraft, 1984-86; founder, pres. Earthwise Corp., 1990; pvt. investor, lectr., TV talk show guest; CEO Celestial Seasonings Herb Tea Co., 1991—, chmn. bd.; bd. dirs. numerous orgns. Author numerous articles. Founder, pres. Inst. Advancement Internat. Fedn. Democracies, Jesusonian Non Profit Found.; founder Coors Classic Bicycle Race (formerly Red Zinger Bicycle Classic). named One of Best of New Generation, Esquire Mag.; Celestial Seasonings named One of 100 Best Cos. to Work For. Mem. Young Pres.' Orgn. Address: Celestial Sea Herb Tea Co 4600 Sleepytime Dr Boulder CO 80301*

SIEGEL, RICHARD LEWIS, political science educator; b. N.Y.C., Oct. 21, 1940; s. Samuel and Clara Siegel; children: Naomi Siegel Morse, Daniel, Jordan. BA, Brandeis U., 1961; PHD, Columbia U., 1967. From instr. to prof. U. Nev., Reno, 1965—, chairperson dept. polit. sci., 1988-92. Author: Employment and Human Rights, 1994, Evaluating the Results of Foreign Policy, 1969, (with others) Comparing Public Policies, 1977; contbr. articles to profl. jours. Nat. bd. dirs. ACLU, 1975-88; v.p. ACLU of Nev., 1996—; co-pres. Internat. Visitors Coun. of North Nev., 1995—. Recipient Hazel Erskine Lifetime Achievement award ACLU, 1989. Democrat. Jewish. Office: U Nev Dept Polit Sci Reno NV 89557

SIEGEL, SHELDON C., physician; b. Mpls., Jan. 30, 1922; s. Carl S.; m. Priscilla Rikess, Mar. 3, 1946; children—Linda, Nancy. A.A., Va. Jr. Coll., 1940; B.A., B.S., U. Minn., 1942, M.D., 1945. Intern U. Minn. Hosp., 1946, resident in pediatrics, 1947-48; fellow in pediatric allergy Rochester, N.Y., 1949-50; practice medicine specializing in pediatric allergy and pediatrics St. Paul, 1950-52, San Antonio, 1952-54, Los Angeles, 1954—; clin. instr. pediatrics U. Rochester, 1949-50, U. Minn., 1950-51; asst. prof. pediatrics U. Tex., 1952-54; asst. clin. prof. U. Calif. at Los Angeles Med. Sch., 1955, clin. asso. prof., 1957-62, clin. prof., 1963—, co-chief pediatric allergy clinic, 1957—; mem. staff Harbor Gen. Hosp., Torrance, Calif., Daniel Freeman Hosp., Inglewood, Calif., Centinela Valley Community Hosp., Inglewood, Hawthorne (Calif.) Community Hosp. Editorial bd.: Jour. Allergy, 1973-75; contbr. articles to med. jours. Fellow Am. Acad. Allergy (pres. 1974), Am. Coll. Allergists, Am. Acad. Pediatrics; mem. AMA, Allergy Found. Am. (pres. 1976), Calif., Los Angeles County med. assns., Los Angeles Pediatric Soc., Calif., Los Angeles socs. allergy, Western Pediatric Research Soc., Am. Bd. Med. Specialists, Sigma Xi. Office: 11620 Wilshire Blvd Los Angeles CA 90025-1706

SIEGEL, SHEPHERD, education administrator; b. Chgo., Apr. 5, 1953; s. Albert Bernard and Syvia (Pyes) S. BA, U. Calif., Santa Cruz, 1977; MA, San Francisco State U., 1985; PhD, U. Calif., Berkeley, 1988. Cert. tchr. Tchr., rschr., lectr. San Francisco State U., 1983-91; project mgr. Bridges From Sch. to Work, San Francisco, 1990-92; dir. Ladders to Success, Burien, Wash., 1995—; founder, dir. Career Ladders, San Francisco and Seattle, 1987—; dir. King County Vocat./Spl. Edn. Coop., Burien, 1991-96; exec. dir. Ctr. for Youth and Cmty. Svc., Puget Sound Ednl. Svcs. Dist., Burien, 1995-96; dir. sch.-to-work sys. Seattle Pub. Schs., 1996—; bus. liaison San Francisco U. Sch. Dist., 1989-92; cons., trainer local cmtys. across the nation, Calif., Kans., N.C., Iowa, 1991—. Author: Career Ladders, 1993; writer, prodr.; (video) Career Ladders, 1992 (Bronze Apple 1992); contbr. articles to profl. jours. Recipient Labor Investing for Tomorrow award U.S. Dept. Labor, San Francisco and Washington, 1990, Disting. Svc. award Wash. Assn. Vocat. Edn. Spl. Needs Pers., 1995. Mem. Am. Vocat. Assn., Coun. Exceptional Children (N.W. nat. rep. Divsn. Career Devel. and Transition, 1985), Coun. Children with Behavioral Disorders, Wash. Vocat. Assn. (outstanding svc. to vocat. edn. award 1995), Greater Seattle C. of C. Office: Seattle Pub Schs 815 4th Ave N Seattle WA 98109

SIEGEL, STUART ELLIOTT, physician, pediatrics educator, cancer researcher; b. Plainfield, N.J., July 16, 1943; s. Hyman and Charlotte Pearl (Freinberg) S.; m. Linda Wertkin, Jan. 20, 1968; 1 child, Joshua. BA, MD, Boston U., 1967. Diplomate Am. Bd. Pediatrics, Am. Bd. Pediatric Oncology. Intern U. Minn. Hosp., Mpls., 1967-68, resident, 1968-69; clin. assoc. NIH, Bethesda, Md., 1969-72; asst. prof. pediatrics U. So. Calif. Sch. Medicine, Los Angeles, 1972-76, assoc. prof., 1976-81, prof., 1981—; head div. hematology-oncology Childrens Hosp. L.A., 1976—, dep. physician-in-chief, 1987-90, vice chmn. dept. pediatrics, 1994—; dir. Childrens Ctr. for Cancer and Blood Diseases, L.A., 1996—; mem. clin. cancer program project com. NIH, Nat. Cancer Inst., HEW, Bethesda, Md., 1978-82; pres. So. Calif. Children's Cancer Services, L.A., 1977-95. Bd. dirs. Nat. Leukemia Broadcast Coun., 1987—, Ronald McDonald Children's Charities, 1988-95, Make-A-Wish Found., 1987-95, Children's Hosp. L.A. Found., 1994—, Ronald McDonald House Charities, 1995—, L.A. Regional Coun. Am. Cancer Soc., 1996—, Nat. Childhood Cancer Found., 1995—; pres. Ronald McDonald House Charities So. Calif., 1996—. Surgeon USPHS, 1969-72. Fellow Am. Acad. Pediatrics. Office: Childrens Hosp Los Angeles Div Hematology Oncology PO Box 54700 Los Angeles CA 90054-0700

SIEGLACK, JACK ALAN, mayor; b. Bismarck, N.D., Aug. 17, 1957; m. Brenda Lee Barsamian, 1983; children: Chris, Mark. AA, San Joaquin Delta Coll.; BA in Polit. Sci., U. Calif., Santa Barbara, 1980. Dist. rep. Congressman Norman D. Shumway, 1980; coun. mem. City of Lodi, Calif., 1990-93, mayor, 1993—; profl. svcs. dir. Option Care, 1992—; mem. group study exch. program Rotary Internat., Philippines, 1984. Active Temple Bapt. Ch., San Joaquin Partnership; bd. dirs. Lodi Boys and Girls Club, pres. 1990-93; trustee United Way. Named one of Outstanding Young Man Am., 1985. Mem. Lodi C. of C. (econ. devel. com.). Office: PO Box 3006 Lodi CA 95241

SIEGLER, RICHARD LOUIS, pediatric nephrologist, educator; b. Vallejo, Calif., May 5, 1939; s. Alfred Charles and Loyola Ann (Wolf) S.; m. Karen Koenig, June 25, 1963; children: Mark, Matthew, Amy. BA in Life Sci., Calif. State U., Sacramento, 1961; MD, Creighton U., 1965. Diplomate Am. Bd. Pediats., Am. Bd. Pediat. Nephrology. Intern in mixed medicine-pediatrics Creighton Meml. - St. Joseph's Hosp., Omaha, Nebr., 1965-66, resident in pediatrics, 1966-67; resident in pediatrics U. Utah Med. Ctr., 1969-71; fellowship in nephrology Dept. Medicine, U. Utah Med. Ctr., 1971-72; chief pediat. nephrology dept. pediats. Sch. Medicine, U. Utah, Salt Lake City, 1972—, acting chmn. dept. pediats., 1982-83, vice chair clin. affairs, 1983-87; mem. exec. com. Primary Children's Med. Ctr., Salt Lake City, 1982-83; dir. pediat. renal disease program U. Utah Health Scis. Ctr., Salt Lake City, 1982—. Contbr. articles to profl. jours., book chpts. Bd. trustees Utah Children, Salt Lake City, 1989-90. Capt. U.S. Army, 1967-68, Viet Nam. Decorated Bronze Star; recipient Rsch. awards So. Ariz. Found., 1990-91; Thrasher Rsch. Fund grantee, 1978-79, 82-85, RO1 grantee NIH, 1996-2001. Fellow Am. Acad. Pediats. (mem. exec. com. Utah chpt. 1986-90, pres. Utah chpt. 1988-90, chair legis. com. 1990-92); mem. Am. Soc. Nephrology, Am. Soc. Pediat. Nephrology, Internat. Soc. Nephrology, Internat. Soc. Pediat. Nephrology, Soc. Pediat. Rsch. Office: U Utah Health Scis Ctr Divsn Nephrology Dept Pediats 50 N Medical Dr Salt Lake City UT 84132-0001

SIEGMUND, MARK ALAN, editor, publisher, business consultant; b. Mpls., Oct. 19, 1942; s. Lucian Albert and Jeanette Katherine (Hayhoe) S.; m. Barbara Ann Cedergren, June 27, 1965 (div. Aug. 1971). BS, Sierra U., Santa Monica, Calif., 1985; PhD, World Peace Univ., Escazu, Costa Rica, 1989. Internat. bus. cons. Wanigatunga, Siegmund & Assocs., L.A., 1975-77; lang. tchr. Bilingual Inst., Mexico City, 1978-81; program coord. Univ. Without Walls, Santa Monica, 1981-84, faculty mem., 1984-86; asst. to pres. Sierra U., 1986-87; prof., vice chancellor for external affairs World Peace Univ., 1988-89; co-founder, dir. U. of Air, 1989; assoc. editor, mem. bd. Internat. Jour. Humanities and Peace, Flagstaff, Ariz., 1990—; cons. Min. Edn., Belize, Ctrl. Am., 1987-88; cons. Belize Nat. Libr., 1987-88; mem. adv. coun. for global edn., Calif. State U., L.A., 1982-85. Contbr. various articles to profl. jours. Co-chair fund distbn. com. Morongo Basin United Way, Yucca Valley, Calif., 1996, bd. dirs. 1996—, pres. 1997—. Recipient Cert. of Appreciation City of L.A. Dept. Aging, 1990. Mem. Humane Soc. Am., Calif. State Grange (environ. com. 1992-96), Wonder Valley Grange (exec. com. 1993-96), Wonder Valley TV Assn. (co-founder, chmn.), Wonder Valley Hiking Club. Home: HC 2 Box 434-h2 Twentynine Palms CA 92277-9802 Office: Internat Jour Humanities & Peace 1436 Evergreen Dr Flagstaff AZ 86001-1416

SIEMON-BURGESON, MARILYN M., education administrator; b. Whittier, Calif., Nov. 15, 1934; d. John Roscoe and Louise Christina (Secoy) Mason; m. Carl J. Siemon, Aug. 18, 1956 (div. Oct. 1984); children: Timothy G., Melanie A. Siemon Imes; Troy M.; m. James K. Burgeson, Jan. 24, 1987. BA, U. Redlands, 1956; MA, Pacific Oaks Coll., 1975; postgrad., Point Loma Coll., 1979-80. Cert. elem. and early childhood tchr. Tchr. Sierra Madre (Calif.) Community Nursery Sch., 1970-77; tchr. parent edn. and music Pasadena (Calif.) Unified Schs., 1977-79, project coordinator, 1980-82, tchr. curriculum resource dept., 1982-83, adminstr. Washington Children's Ctr., 1983—; endorsed trainer High Scope Found. Register, 1990—; trainer Program for Infant/Toddler Caregivers; instr. Citrus Coll., 1996—; conf. chair Calif. High Scope Educators, 1995—. Active Arcadia (Calif.) Bicentennial Commn., 1974-76; mem. policy coun. for cmty. housing svcs. Pasadena Head Start, 1992-95; life mem. Sierra Madre Sch. PTA; mem. Child Care Coalition, Pasadena; lay Eucharistic minister. Ednl. Professions Devel. fellow Pacific Oaks Coll., Pasadena, 1969. Mem. AAUW (past pres., co-chmn. Math.-Sci. Conf. 1983, chair Coll./Univ. Rels. 1988—, v.p. ednl. found. 1996—, grantee 1982, 83), Nat. Assn. Edn. Young Children (grantee 1970), Child Care Info. Svc. (bd. dirs., chmn. parent edn. and family affairs 1986—), Women Ednl. Leadership (asst. program v.p.), Calif. Child Devel. Adminstrs. Assn. (bd. dirs. 1994—), Coun. Women's Clubs (pres. 1995-97), Delta Kappa Gamma (pres. 1986-88, 92-94). Republican. Episcopalian. Home: 2266 Kinclair Dr Pasadena CA 91107-1022 Office: Washington Children's Ctr 130 E Penn St Pasadena CA 91103-1828

SIEPERMAN, KATHLEEN LOUISE, nurse; b. Morristown, N.J., June 21, 1962; d. Raymond Joseph and Doris Marie Louise (Scheppard) S.; m. William Grimm, May 11, 1991 (div. Oct. 1995). ADN, Scottsdale Cmty., Scottsdale, Ariz., 1984. RN; cert. registered nurse intravenous. Staff RN burn unit ICU Maricopa County Hosp., Phoenix, 1984-86, staff RN dialysis unit, 1986; staff charge RN intensive care Humana Hosp., Phoenix, 1987-88; clinical specialist IV therapy Infusion Care, Phoenix, 1988; discharge planner Humana Hosp., Phoenix, 1989-90; area mgr. infusion Kimberly Quality Care, Phoenix, 1990-91, regional mgr. infusion, 1991-92, divsn. mgr. infusion, 1993-95, western U.S. mgr. infusion, 1995—. Mem. Young Dem. Soc., Phoenix, 1995—. Recipient Nursing Excellence award Humana Hosp., 1988. Mem. Intravenous Nurses Soc., Soc. Pain Mgmt. Nursing, Nat. Assn. Vascular Acess Networks (1st Place Abstract award 1996), Am.-Soc. Parenteral & Enteral Nutrition. Methodist. Office: Olsten Kimberly Quality Care 711 E Missouri Ave Ste 300 Phoenix AZ 85014-2824

SIEVERS, ANN ELISABETH FURIEL, clinical nurse specialist in otolaryngology; b. Utica, N.Y., Mar. 26, 1950; d. Ralph Edward and Mary Paula (Delahunt) Furiel; m. Mark Scott Sievers, Apr. 29, 1979; children: Elisabeth Ann, Katherine Tanner. BSN, Russell Sage Coll., 1972; MA in Human Resource Devel., George Washington U., 1979. Cert. in otorhinolaryngology nursing; RN, Calif., D.C., N.Y. Staff/charge nurse Rome (N.Y.) Murphy Meml. Hosp., 1972-73; staff/charge nurse ICU George Washington U. Hosp., 1973-74, respiratory clin. specialist, 1974-79; otolaryngology clin. nurse specialist U. Calif. Davis Med. Ctr., Sacramento, 1979—, staff Skull Base Surgery Ctr.; adj. clin. prof. U. Calif., San Francisco; lectr., presenter in field; mem. nursing rsch. com. U. Calif., Davis, 1982-89, mem. nursing ethics and practice com., 1983-92, mem. instnl. rev. bd., 1984-90, chmn. hospice adv. bd., 1984-87, mem. skull base surgery programmatic subcom., 1990-93. Contbr. articles to profl. jours. Bd. dirs., vol. D.C. Lung Assn., 1974-79; vol. Am. Cancer Soc. of Immigrant Trails, Sacramento, 1980—; fundraiser Calif. hospice North Bay Med. Ctr., 1987—. Recipient S.O.H.N. Nat. Clin. Excellence award, 1995. Mem. AACN, Soc. Otorhinolaryngology Head and Neck Nurses (coord. nat. rsch. project 1990—, nat. bd. dirs. 1989-92, nat. v.p. 1992-94, chmn. rsch. com. 1980-90, edn. com. 1990, 92-94, Nat. Honor award 1991, 94), Sigma Theta Tau (Clin. Excellence award Zeta Eta chpt. 1982).

SIFFERMAN, THOMAS RAYMOND, speciality chemical researcher; b. Chgo., July 28, 1941; s. Joseph A. and Mary B. S.; m. Rose Mary Murphy, June 8, 1968; children: Nancy A., Joseph J., Laura M. BME, Marquette U., 1964; MSME, Purdue U., 1966, PhD, 1970. Registered profl. engr., Okla. Teaching/rsch. asst. Purdue U., W. Lafayette, Ind., 1968-70; rsch., sr. rsch. scientist Conoco, Ponca City, Okla., 1970-81; vis. assoc. prof. U. Tulsa, 1981-82; rsch. assoc. Mobil Rsch. - DRL, Dallas, 1982-87; activity leader Mobil Rsch.-CRL, Princeton, N.J., 1987-88; rsch. assoc. Mobil Rsch.-DRL, Dallas, 1988-91; planning assoc. Mobil Rsch. - DRL, Dallas, 1991-92; rsch. assoc. Mobil Rsch.-DRL, Dallas, 1992; rsch. fellow Kelco Rsch., San Diego, 1992-96; mgr. oil field applications Kelco Oil Field Group, San Diego, 1996—; cons. in field. Contbr. articles to profl. jours.; patentee in field. Mem. ASME, Soc. Petroleum Engrs. (sect. chmn. 1974), Soc. Rheology, Sigma Xi, Tau Beta Pi, Pi Mu Epsilon, Pi Tau Sigma. Roman Catholic. Office: Kelco Oil Field Group 8225 Aero Dr San Diego CA 92123-1716

SIFFORD, BENTON ALEXANDER, III, energy consultant; b. Evanston, Ill., Sept. 20, 1955; s. Benton Alexander Jr. and Gail Byrd (Sollender) S.; m. Saralynn Baker, Nov. 6, 1982. BA in Geography, U. Calif., Santa Barbara, 1978; MS in Geography, U. Idaho, 1984. Mgr. Oak Tree Antiques, London, 1978-80; geothermal specialist Idaho Office Energy, Boise, 1980; sr. assoc. Eliot Allen & Assocs., Salem, Oreg., 1981-84; program mgr. Oreg. Dept. Energy, Salem, 1984-94; pvt. practice Sifford Energy Svcs., Neskowin, Oreg., 1995—; pres. Wood Energy Coordination Group, Portland, 1988-90. Author: Geothermal Resources Council Transactions, Vol. 7, 1984, Vol. 14, 1990, Bioenergy Conversion Opportunities, 1988; also articles. Pres. Neskowin (Oreg.) Cmty. Assn., 1989-94; commr. Neskowin Regional Water Dist., 1993—. Recipient cert. of appreciation USDA Forest Svc., 1988, 89, Lions Internat., Salem, 1990. Mem. Geothermal Resources Coun. (pres. Pacific N.W. sect. 1985-88, bd. dirs. 1988-90), Assn. Pacific Coast Geographers, Internat. Dist. Heating Assn. Home: PO Box 760 Neskowin OR 97149-0760 Office: Sifford Energy Svcs Box 760 Neskowin OR 97149-0760

SIGLER, MARJORIE DIANE, computer programming executive, analyst; b. Fullerton, Calif., Sept. 19, 1943; d. Earl Lawrence Whipple and Ruth Juanita (Long) Purcell; children: Stephen, Deborah; m. William A. Sigler, June 10, 1995; Grad computer programming LaSalle U., Chgo., 1973; BSBA U. Phoenix, 1994. Computer programmer Los Alamos (N.Mex.) Nat. Lab., 1972-81, cons. control data, 1984-89, computer technician, 1989—; contract programmer Computer Assistance, Inc., Tulsa, 1981-82; profl. svcs. analyst Control Data Corp., Denver, 1982-84, Los Alamos, 1984-89. Mem. Order Eastern Star (past matron). Home: 90 Aspen Grove Jemez Springs NM 87025

SIGMAN, MELVIN MONROE, psychiatrist; b. N.Y.C., Dec. 15, 1935; s. Irving and Lillian (Pearlman) S. BA, Columbia U., 1956; MD, SUNY, N.Y.C., 1960; postgrad., William Alanson White Analytic Inst., N.Y.C., 1969. Staff psychiatrist Hawthorne (N.Y.) Cedar Knolls Sch., 1966-68; pvt. practice psychiatry N.Y.C., 1966-72, Fresno, Calif., 1974-87; staff psychiatrist Fresno County Dept. of Health, 1974-87, Psychol. Svcs. for Adults, L.A., 1987-93; psychiatrist pvt. practice, L.A., 1993—; attending staff psychiatry Bellevue Hosp., N.Y.C., 1966-68; cons. N.Y. Foundling Hosp., N.Y.C., 1966-72; assoc. attending staff Roosevelt Hosp., N.Y.C., 1967-72; asst. clin. prof U. Calif. San Francisco, Fresno, 1977; chmn. cen. Calif. com. Columbia Coll. Nat. Alumni Secondary Schs. Served to capt. USAF, 1961-63. Fellow Royal Soc. Health, Am. Orthopsychiat. Assn.; mem. Holiday Spa Clif., Fresno Racquet Club. Fresno Racquet. Office: 10780 Santa Monica Blvd Ste 250 Los Angeles CA 90025-4749

SIGOLOFF, SANFORD CHARLES, retail executive; b. St. Louis, Sept. 8, 1930; s. Emmanuel and Gertrude (Breliant) S.; m. Betty Ellen Greene, Sept. 14, 1952; children: Stephen, John David, Laurie. B.A., UCLA, 1950. Cons. AEC, 1950-54, 57-58; gen. mgr. Edgerton, Germeshausen & Grier, Santa Barbara, Calif., 1958-63; v.p. Xerox Corp., 1963-69; pres. CSI Corp., Los Angeles, 1969-70; sr. v.p. Republic Corp., Los Angeles, 1970-71; chief exec. officer Kaufman & Broad, Inc., Los Angeles, 1979-82; chmn., pres., chief exec. officer Wickes Cos. Inc., Santa Monica, 1982—. Contbr. articles on radiation dosimetry to profl. jours. Bd. govs. Cedars-Sinai Hosp. Served in USAF, 1954-57. Recipient Tom May award Nat. Jewish Hosp. and Research Ctr., 1972. Mem. AAAS, Am. Chem. Soc., AIAA, Am. Nuclear Soc., IEEE, Radiation Research Soc. Office: Sigoloff & Assocs Inc 3340 Ocean Park Blvd Santa Monica CA 90405-3204*

SIKAND, GEETA, dietitian; b. Udaipur, Rajasthan, India, Sept. 2, 1951; came to U.S., 1971; d. Anand Prakash and Shanti Devi Ahluwalia; m. Sharanpal Singh Sikand, June 6, 1971; children: Vikram, Kabir, Sunjeev. BS in Dietetics, Calif. State U., Long Beach, 1975, MS in Nutrition, 1976. Registered dietitian, Calif. Teaching dietitian St. Mary Med. Ctr., Long Beach, 1976-79; cons. dietitian Orange County Weight REduction Group, Anaheim, Calif., 1981, Los Alamitos (Calif.) Med. Ctr., 1981; teaching dietitian Baylor Coll. Medicine, Houston, 1981-86; clin. instr. medicine U. Calif., Irvine, 1989—; lipid rsch. dietitian U. Calif.-Irvine/VA Med. Ctr., Long Beach, 1989—; cons. dietitian San Clemente (Calif.) Hosp., 1986-93, Mission Viejo, Calif., 1989—. Chair Heart Fest com. Am. Heart Assn., Irvine, 1992-94; sec. United India Assn., Orange, Calif., 1991-92, v.p., 1992-94. Mem. Am. Dietetic Assn., Calif. Dietetic Assn. (treas. 1993—, chair fundraising com. 1992-93). Hindu. Home: 25201 Exmoor Mission Viejo CA 92692-2890

SIKORA, JAMES ROBERT, educational business consultant; b. Sacramento, July 8, 1945; s. George Robert and Marian Frances (Fears) S.; m. Marie Lynore Nyarady, June 22, 1968. BEE, U. Santa Clara, 1967; postgrad., U. Calif., Santa Cruz, 1979—. Electronic engr. GTE-Sylvania, Santa Cruz, 1967-69; sys. analyst GTE-Sylvania, 1969-71; sr. support analyst GTE-Sylvania, Mt. View, Calif., 1971-73; coord. bus. sys. Santa Clara County Office Edn., San Jose, Calif., 1973-76, dir. dist. payroll, pers. svcs., 1976-85, dir. dist. bus. svcs., 1985-95; self-employed sch. bus. cons. Omniserve, Ben Lomond, Calif., 1995—; cons. records mgmt. County Santa Clara, San Jose, 1982; vice-chmn. Edn. Mandated Cost Network Exec. Bd., 1991-95; mem. Schs. Fin. Svcs. subcom. 1987-94. Author, co-editor Howdy Rowdy Memorial, 1979. Affiliate San Jose/Cleveland Ballet; sponsor Dixieland Monterey; patrons cir. Monterey Bay Aquarium; dir. cir. San Jose Repertory Theater; fellow Cabrillo Music Festival; ptnr. Second Harvest Food Bank; vol. Mountain Pks. Found.; active Ctr. Photog. Arts, Napa Valley Wine Libr. Assn., Long Marine Lab., Silver Chancellor's Cir., U. Calif. Santa Cruz; sustaining mem. Omni Found., Team Shakespeare, Shakespeare Santa Cruz; bd. treas. Mountain Parks Found., 1997—. Mem. Pub. Agy. Risk Mgmt. Assn., Am. Diabetes Assn., Calif. Assn. Sch. Bus. Ofcls. (subsect. pres. 1984-85, sect. bd. dirs. 1987-93, sect. pres. 1991-92, state bd. dirs. 1991-92, state legis. com. 1989—, state risk mgmt. com. 1985-87, 96—, state strategic planning com. 1994), Norwegian Elkhound Assn. (pres. 1977-79), Wine Investigation for Novices and Oenephiles, Amnesty Internat., Calif. Trout, Trout Unltd., Calif. State Parks Found., Am. Dog Owners Assn., Sierra Club (life). Libertarian. Roman Catholic. Home and Office: 400 Coon Heights Rd Ben Lomond CA 95005-9711

SILAK, CATHY R., judge; b. Astoria, N.Y., May 25, 1950; d. Michael John and Rose Marie (Janor) S.; m. Nicholas G. Miller, Aug. 9, 1980; 3 children. BA, NYU, 1971; M in City Planning, Harvard U., 1973; JD, U. Calif., 1976. Bar: Calif. 1977, U.S. Ct. (no. dist.) Calif. 1977, D.C. 1979, U.S. Ct. Appeals (D.C. cir.) 1979, U.S. Dist. Ct. (so. dist.) N.Y. 1980, Idaho 1983, U.S. Dist. Ct. Idaho 1983, U.S. Ct. Appeals (2nd cir.) 1983, U.S. Ct. Appeals (9th cir.) 1985. Law clk. to Hon. William W. Schwarzer U.S. Dist. Ct. (no dist.), Calif., 1976-77; pvt. practice San Francisco, 1977-79, Washington, 1979-80; asst. U.S. atty. So. Dist. of N.Y., 1980-83; spl. asst. U.S. atty. Dist. of Idaho, 1983-84; pvt. practice Boise, Idaho, 1984-90; judge Idaho Ct. Appeals, 1990-93; justice Idaho Supreme Ct., Boise, 1993—;

assoc. gen. counsel Morrison Knudsen Corp., 1989-90; mem. fairness com. Idaho Supreme Ct. and Gov.'s Task Force on Alternative Dispute Resolution; instr. and lectr. in field. Assoc. note and comment editor Calif. Law Rev., 1975-76. Land use planner Mass. Dept. Natural Resources, 1973; founder Idaho Coalition for Adult Literacy; bd. dirs. Literacy Lab., Inc. Recipient Jouce Stein award Boise YWCA, 1992, Women Helping Women award Soroptimist, Boise, 1993. Fellow Idaho Law Found (ann., lectr.); mem. ABA (nat. conf. state trial judges jud. adminstrn. divsn.), Nat. Assn. Women Judges, Idaho State Bar (corp./securities sect., instr.). Office: PO Box 83720 Boise ID 83720-0101

SILBERGELD, ARTHUR F., lawyer; b. St. Louis, June 1, 1942; s. David and Sabina (Silbergeld) S.; m. Carol Ann Schwartz, May 1, 1970; children: Diana Lauren, Julia Kay. BA, U. Mich., 1968; M City Planning, U. Pa., 1971; JD, Temple U., 1975. Bar: N.Y. 1976, Calif. 1978, D.C. 1983, U.S. Ct. Appeals (2d, 9th and D.C. cirs.). Assoc. Vladeck, Elias, Vladeck & Lewis, N.Y.C., 1975-77; field atty. NLRB, Los Angeles, 1977-78; ptnr., head employment law practice group McKenna, Conner & Cuneo, L.A., 1978-89; ptnr., head labor and employment law practice group Graham & James, L.A., 1990-96; labor ptnr. Sonnenschein Nath & Rosenthal, L.A., 1996—; instr. extension divsn. UCLA, 1981-89. Author: Doing Business in California: An Employment Law Handbook, 2d edit. 1996, Advising California Employers, 1990, 91, 93, 94, 95 supplements; contbr. numerous articles to profl. jours. Founding mem. L.A. Mus. Contemporary Art; mem. Mus. Modern Art, N.Y., Art Inst. Chgo.; bd. dirs. Bay Cities unit Am. Cancer Soc., Calif., 1981-85, Jewish Family Svc. L.A., 1981-85, So. Calif. Employment Round Table, 1990-96, Leadership Coun., So. Poverty Law Ctr. Mem. ABA (com. on devel. law under NLRA 1975—), L.A. County Bar Assn. (exec. bd. labor law sect. 1984—, sect. sec. 1996-97). Office: Sonnenschein Nath & Rosenthal 601 S Figueroa St Fl 15 Los Angeles CA 90017-5704

SILBERMAN, IRWIN ALAN, public health physician; b. Newport News, Va., Sept. 1, 1932; s. Henry and Toby (Weiss) S.; m. Lynne Sussman, Feb. 1954 (div. 1961); children: Denise, Donn; m. Mitsue Fukuyama, May 1964 (div. 1984); children: Daniel, Dean, Dana; m. Andrea Z. George, Nov. 1993. BA, U. Calif., Berkeley, 1953; MD, U. Calif., San Francisco, 1956; MS, U. No. Colo., 1980. Intern L.A. County Harbor Gen. Hosp., Torrance, Calif., 1956-57; resident ob-gyn. Harbor/UCLA Med. Ctr., Torrance, 1957-61; commd. USAF, 1961, advanced through grades to col., 1973; staff obstetrician-gynecologist Tachikawa (Japan) Air Base, 1963-65; chief ob-gyn. Mather Air Force Base, Sacramento, 1965-66; chief aeromed. services Yokota Air Base, Tokyo, 1966-68; dir. base med. services Itazuke Air Base, Fukuoka, Japan, 1968-70, Kirtland Air Force Base, Albuquerque, 1970-72; chief hosp. services USAF Hosp. Davis-Monthan, Tucson, 1972-81; ret. USAF, 1981; med. dir. CIGNA Healthplan of Fla., Tampa, 1981-83; chief women's clinic H.C. Hudson Comprehensive Health Ctr., L.A., 1983-85; dir. maternal health and family planning programs Los Angeles County Dept. Health Svcs., L.A., 1985-91, dir. family health programs, maternal and child health, 1991—; mil. cons. to surgeon-gen. USAF, 1980-81; bd. dirs. L.A. Regional Family Planning Coun.; pres. Perinatal Adv. Coun. of L.A. Comtys., 1993-94. Chmn. health profls. adv. com. March of Dimes, Los Angeles, 1988; camp physician Boy Scouts Nat. Jamboree, Fort Hill, Va., 1985. Recipient Meritorious Service medal, USAF, 1972, 81, Air Force Commendation medal, 1980, Air medal, 1969. Fellow Am. Coll. Obstetricians and Gynecologists, Am. Coll. Physician Execs., Am. Coll. Preventive Medicine; mem. APHA, Am. Acad. Med. Dirs., So. Calif. Pub. Health Assn. Home: 3716 Beverly Ridge Dr Sherman Oaks CA 91423-4509 Office: LA County Dept Health Svcs 241 N Figueroa St Los Angeles CA 90012-2693

SILBERT, AMY FOXMAN, clinical art therapist; b. Augusta, Ga., July 11, 1953; d. Elliott and Anita Foxman; m. Philip Silbert, Sept. 6, 1987; children: Sean Kenneth, Karen Debra, Samantha Danielle. BA in Design, UCLA, 1976; MA, Loyola Marymount U., 1990. Art dir., advt. mgr. Unico Am. Corp., L.A., 1976-78; freelance graphic artist, art specialist, tchr., 1979-82; vol. coord., tchr. Craft and Folk Art Mus., L.A., 1983-86; art specialist Art Reach, UCLA Calif. Arts Coun., 1983-84; editor in chief Grad. Achievement Preparation Svc., Santa Monica, Calif., 1985-87; tchr. coordinator art exhibit Hebrew Union Coll., Los Angeles, 1984; guest children's TV programs, 1970-84. Gov. intern U.S. Congress, Washington, 1973. Recipient 1st Place award traffic light design City Monterrey, Calif., 1973. Democrat. Jewish. Home: 760 Briercliff Ln Lake Oswego OR 97034-1642

SILER, MICHAEL JOE, social sciences educator; b. Tacoma, Aug. 7, 1951; s. Maurice and Clara Inghram Parrish-Siler. BS, UCLA, 1975, MA, 1977; MPA, U. Wash., 1979; PhD, U. So. Calif., 1992. Adj. prof. U. Calif., Riverside, 1995-96; prof., polit. scis. Calif. State U., L.A., 1993—; cons. So. Calif. Assn. Govts., L.A., 1990-91, Golden State Mutual Life Ins., L.a., 1989-90; asst. coord. Roosevelt Ctr. for Am. Policy Studies and Allison Thomas Assocs., Sherman Oaks, Calif., 1989. Contbr. articles to profl. jours. Mem. Conf. Minority Pub. Adminstrs. (pres. So. Calif. chpt. 1995—). Home: 418 Wisteria Pl Altadena CA 91001-1935 Office: Calif State Univ 5151 State Univ Pl Los Angeles CA 90032

SILK, THOMAS, lawyer; b. Beaver, Pa., Dec. 12, 1937; s. Thomas and Alice Genevieve (Beck) S.; 1 child, Nicole Amory. AB, U. Calif.-Berkeley, 1959, LLB, 1963. Bar: Calif. 1964, U.S. Dist. Ct. (no. dist.) Calif. 1964, U.S. Ct. Appeals (D.C., 2-10th cirs.) 1966-68, U.S. Supreme Ct. 1967. Appellate atty. tax div. U.S. Dept. Justice, Washington, 1964-66; spl. asst. to asst. atty. gen. tax div., 1966-68; assoc. Brobeck, Phleger & Harrison, San Francisco, 1968-71; founder, sr. ptnr. Silk, Adler & Colvin, San Francisco, 1972—; adj. prof. Sch. Law, U. Calif., Berkeley; dir. comparative nonprofit law project of The Asia Found., 1995; trustee Jenifer Altman Found., Ctr. Citizen Initiatives, St. Francis Found.; author; lectr. tax-exempt orgns., nonprofit corps., charitable estate planning. Office: Silk Adler & Colvin 235 Montgomery St San Francisco CA 94104-2902

SILLIMAN, BRIAN ALLEN, commodities trader; b. Santa Monica, Calif., May 25, 1969; s. Richard Donald and Edith Lillian (Allen) S. Student, Occidental Coll., L.A. Regional mgr. San Carlos Cinemas, L.A., 1990-93; pres. BAS Rare Coin Gallery, Granada Hills, Calif., 1995—; cons. investment in rare coins, currency, historical documents, 1995—. Recipient osgood Hardy Meml. award for history Occidental Coll., 1996. Mem. Am. Numismatic Assn., Am. Numismatic Soc., West Valley Coin Club (2nd v.p.), So. Calif. Numismatic Assn., Occidental History Club, Occidental Russian Culture Club, Occident History Soc. (pres.), Wildlife Waystation (sponsor). Republican. Episcopalian. Office: BAS Coins PO Box 33411 Granada Hills CA 91394-3411

SILLIMAN, KATHRYN, nutrition educator; b. L.A., July 30, 1960; d. Edmund Neal and Beverly Jean (Martin) S.; m. Stephen Farrar Riley, Sept. 1, 1990; children: Audrey Hypatia, Willis Lorence. BS in Nutrition and Food Sci., Simmons Coll., Boston, 1984; MS in Nutrition, U. Calif. Berkeley, 1986, PhD in Nutrition, 1990. Registered dietician. Teaching asst. U. Calif. Berkeley, 1985-90; assoc. prof. Calif. State U., Chico, 1990—. Author: Nutrition and Fitness, 1996; author: (book chpt.) Sugars and Sweeteners, 1991; contbr. articles to profl. jours. Recipient Ellsworth C. Dougherty prize U. Calif. Berkeley, 1990. Mem. Am. Dietetic Assn. (New Researchers award 1992), Calif. Dietetic Assn. (Zellmer Scholarship award 1994, Legis. Contact award 1997, legis. liaison 1993—), North Valley Dietetic Assn. (cmty. nutrition officer 1991-92, pres. 1992-93, legis. liaison 1993—), Calif. Nutrition Coun. Democrat. Office: Calif State U Chico Dept Biol Scis Chico CA 95929-0515

SILLMAN, GEORGE DOUGLAS, computer programmer analyst; b. Dayton, Ohio, Mar. 13, 1957; s. Herbert Carl Sillman and Martha Carolyn Stump Greene. AA, Santa Monica City Coll., 1978; BA, Calif. State U., Northridge, 1981; AA, Pierce Coll., Woodland Hills, Calif., 1988. Programmer analyst Transamerica Ins. Group, Woodland Hills, 1989-92, Wellmark Inc., Westlake Village, Calif., 1993, Korn/Ferry Internat., L.A., 1993-96, Pentel of Am., Ltd., Torrance, Calif., 1996—; freelance computer cons., L.A., 1992—. Author software products. Home: 486 Palos Verdes Blvd Redondo Beach CA 90277-6514 Office: Pentel of Am Ltd 2805 Columbia St Torrance CA 90503-3804

SILVA, ED, food products executive; b. 1943. Prin. Dairy Bus., Gonzalis, Calif., 1964-75; pres. Silva Harvesting, Inc., Gonzalis, Calif., 1975—. Office: Silva Harvesting Inc PO Box Z Gonzales CA 93926*

SILVA, ERNEST R., visual arts educator, artist. BFA, U. R.I., 1971; MFA, Tyler Sch. Art, 1974. Instr. U. R.I., Kingston, 1977-79; lectr. dept. visual arts U. Calif. San Diego, La Jolla, 1979-87, prof. dept. visual arts, 1987—; represented by Jan Baum Gallery, L.A., Lenore Gray Gallery, Providence, R.I.; bd. dirs. Installation Gallery, San Diego, mem. arts adv. bd., 1992—, exec. com., 1993—; lectr. Phila. Coll. Art, 1973, U. R.I., 1974, 84, 91, RISD, 1977, Tyler Sch. Art, Elkins Park, Pa., 1979, U. Calif. Irvine, 1981, Southwestern Coll., Chula Vista, 1982, San Diego State U., 1985, Nat. Soc. Arts and Letters, Washington, 1986, Friends of Jung, San Diego, 1991. One-person exhbns. include Inst. Contemporary Art, Boston, 1972, Artists Space, N.Y.C., 1975, Anyart Contemporary Art Ctr., Providence, R.I., 1976, Lenore Gray Gallery, Providence, 1978, 79, 92, Roy Boyd Gallery, L.A., 1982, 84, 87, Quint Gallery, San Diego, 1982, 83, 86, Jan Baum Gallery, L.A., 1989, 91, Tuttle Gallery, McDonogh, Md., 1990, Porter Randall Gallery, La Jolla, 1994, Mus. Contemporary Art, Roskilde, Denmark, 1995, many others; group exhbns. include Mus. Phila. Civic Ctr., 1973, Cheltenham (Pa.) Art Ctr., 1973, Pratt Graphic Ctr., N.Y.C., 1975, Corcoran Art Gallery, Washington, 1975, Ft. Worth Art Mus., 1976, Baker Gallery, La Jolla, 1980, Ind. Contemporary Exhbns., L.A., 1982, Navy Pier, Chgo., 1983, 84, 85, Roy Boyd Gallery, Chgo., 1983, 85, 86, Heckscher Mus. Art, Huntington, N.Y., 1984, Indpls. Mus. Art, 1984, Forum Internat. Kunstmesse, Zurich, Switzerland, 1984, Nat. History Mus., San Diego, 1985, Visual Arts Ctr. Alaska, Anchorage, 1985, San Francisco Airport Mus., 1985, Sonrisa Gallery, L.A., 1985, Alaska State Mus., Juneau, 1986, Foire Internat. De L'Art Contemporain, Nice, France, 1986, Lyceum Theatre, San Diego, 1987, Installation Gallery, San Diego, 1986, 87, 88, Chgo. Internat. Art Exposition, 1987,L.A. Convention Ctr., 1987, Cmty. Arts, San Francisco, 1989, 90, Annex Gallery, La Jolla, 1990, Bill Bace Gallery, N.Y.C., 1991, David Lewinson Gallery, Del Mar, Calif., 1991, Southwestern Coll. Art, Chula Vista, Calif., 1992, Boehm Gallery Palomar Coll, San Marcos, Calif., 1993, Porter Randall Gallery, La Jolla, 1992, numerous others; represented in permanent collections Fogg Art Mus. Harvard U., Cambridge, Mass., Grand Rapids (Mich.) Art Mus., La Jolla Mus. Contemporary Art, Laguna Mus. Art, De Saisset Mus. U. Santa Clara, Newport Harbor Art Mus., Newport Beach, Calif., Mus. Contemporary Art, San Diego, La Jolla, San Jose Mus. Art, San Diego Mus. Art; subject reviews, articles, 1974—. Office: U Calif San Diego Visual Arts 0327 La Jolla CA 92093

SILVA, EVELYN, food products executive; b. 1947. V.p. Silva Harvesting Inc., Gonzales, Calif., 1975—. Office: Silva Harvesting Inc PO Box Z Gonzales CA 93926*

SILVA, LADON GAY, dietitian; b. Ft. Campbell, Ky., Oct. 22, 1954; d. Smiles Manning and Martha Jane (Porter) S.; m. Richard Peter Saval, Feb. 14, 1991. BS, Calif. Poly. State U., 1977; MBA, U. Redlands, 1994. Dir. food services Cottonwood (Calif.) Union Sch. Dist., 1977-78; dietetic intern U. Calif. Hosps. and Clinics, San Francisco, 1978-79; clin. dietician Bakersfield (Calif.) Meml. Hosp., 1979-89; pediat. territory specialist Wyeth-Ayers Labs., Newport Beach, Calif., 1989-96; quality assurance and compliance dietitian Horizon Health Care, Albuquerque, 1996—; cons. Centre for Neuroskills, Bakersfield, 1980-85, Dr. Shivinder Deol, Bakersfield, 1985-86, Bakersfield Cmty. Hosp., 1984-86, Kern Valley Hosp., Colonial Hosp., Hilltop Convalescent Hosp., 1985-86, Charter Hosp., Bakersfield, 1988-94. Mem. Bakersfield Rep. Assembly, 1987-96. Mem. Am. Dietetic Assn., Calif. Sch. Food Service Assn. (v.p. Shasta Cascade chpt. 1978), Nev. Dietetic Assn., Diabetic Educators Assn., Cons. Nutritionists Assn., Kern County Nutrition Council. Methodist. Home: 8432 Paseo Vista Dr Las Vegas NV 89128

SILVA, ROBERT OWEN, retired protective service official; b. La Junta, Colo., Sept. 5, 1935; s. Owen Delbert and Gertrude H. (Kerr) S.; m. Meredith Ann Ginn, Dec. 18, 1953; children—Edward, Andrew, Colleen. Student Pueblo Jr. Coll., 1953, FBI Nat. Acad., 1975, Police Found. Exec. Program, 1979-80. Cert. peace officer, Colo. Police officer Pueblo Police Dept., Colo., 1958-66, sgt., 1966-72, capt., 1972-77, chief of police, 1977-92, ret. dir. Colo. Police Officers Standards and Tng. Bd. dirs. Salvation Army, Pueblo, Easter Seals Soc., Pueblo, Community Corrections Bd., Pueblo, Served with U.S. Army, 1955-57; apptd. by gov. Colo. Crim. Justice Comsn., 1990. Mem. Pueblo Community Coll. Criminal Justice Adv. Bd., Leadership Pueblo Steering Com., Pikes Peak Community Coll. Criminal Justice Program (chmn. adv. bd. 1981), Organized Crime Strike Force (bd. dirs. 1977-84, chmn. 1982, 83, 84); Colo. Assn. Chiefs of Police (pres. 1984-85), Rocky Mountain Info. Network (chmn. bd. dirs. 1986—), Presbyterian (elder). Lodges: Kiwanis (bd. dirs. 1982-84), Elks.*

SILVER, BARNARD JOSEPH STEWART, mechanical and chemical engineer, consultant, inventor; b. Salt Lake City, Mar. 9, 1933; s. Harold Farnes and Madelyn Cannon (Stewart) S.; m. Cherry Bushman, Aug. 12, 1963; children: Madelyn Stewart Palmer, Cannon Farnes, Brenda Picketts Call. BS in Mech. Engring., MIT, 1957; MS in Engring. Mechanics, Stanford U., 1958; grad. Advanced Mgmt. Program, Harvard U., 1977. Registered profl. engr., Colo. Engr. aircraft nuclear propulsion div. Gen. Electric Co., Evandale, Ohio, 1957; engr. Silver Engring. Works, Denver, 1959-66, mgr. sales and tech. svcs., 1966-71; chief engr. Union Sugar div. Consol. Foods Co., Santa Maria, Calif., 1971-74; directeur du complexe SODESUCRE, Abidjan, Côte d'Ivoire, 1974-76; supt. engring. and maintenance U and I, Inc., Moses Lake, Wash., 1976-79; pres. Silver Enterprises Denver, Moses Lake, 1971—, Silver Energy Systems Corp., Moses Lake, 1980—; pres., gen. mgr. Silver Chief Corp., 1983—; pres. Silver Corp., 1984—; chmn. bd. Silver Pubs., Inc., 1986-87, 89—; chmn. bd. Agronomics Internat., McLean, Va., 1994—; mgr. Cascadian Inulin L.L.C., Sedro-Wooley, Wash., 1996—; mgr. Silver Inulin L.L.C., Moses Lake, 1996—; v.p. Barnard J. Stewart Cousins Land Co., 1987-88, 92—; dir. Isle Piquant Sugar Found., 1993-94; mem. steering com. World Botanical Inst., 1993—; instr. engring. Big Bend C.C., 1980-81. Explorer adviser Boy Scouts Am., 1965-66, 89-90, chmn. cub pack com., 1968-74, 94-96, chmn. scout troop com., 1968-74, vice chmn. Columbia Basin Dist., 1986-87; pres. Silver Found., 1971-87, v.p., 1987—; ednl. counselor MIT, 1971-89; pres. Chief Moses Jr. H.S. Parent Tchr. Student Assn., 1978-79; missionary Ch. of Jesus Christ of Latter-day Saints, Can., 1953-55, Hawaii, Puerto Rico Central & South America, Asia, 1959-68, West Africa, 1988, Côte d'Ivoire, 1988-89, Zaire, 1989, Holladay North Stake, 1991, 95—, dist. pres. No. B.C., No. Alberta, Yukon and N.W. Ters., 1955; stake high counselor, Santa Maria, Calif., 1971-72, Moses Lake, Wash., 1977-79; presiding elder Côte d'Ivoire, 1974-76, 88; 2d counselor Moses Lake Stake Presidency, 1980-88; bd. dirs. Columbia Basin Allied Arts, 1986-88; mem. Health Sci. Coun. U. Utah, 1991—; mem. Sunday sch. gen. bd. Ch. of Jesus Christ of Latter-Day Saints, 1991-93, com. for mems. with disabilities, 1992-93, CHOICE adv. bd., 1993-95; emergency preparedness dir. Holladay North Stake, 1993—. Served with Ordnance Corps, U.S. Army, 1958-59. Decorated chevalier Ordre National (Republic of Côte d'Ivoire). Patentee in field, including patent for extracting liquids soluable substances from subdivided solids, 1995. Mem. ASME, Assn. Energy Engrs., AAAS, Am. Soc. Sugar Beet Technologists, Internat. Soc. Sugar Cane Technologists, Am. Soc. Sugar Cane Technologists, Environ. Engrs. & Mgrs. Inst., Sugar Industry Technicians, Nat. Fedn. Ind. Bus.; Utah State Hist. Soc. (life), Mormon Hist. Assn., G.P. Chowder and Marching Soc., Western Hist. Assn., Sons of Utah Pioneers, Univ. Archeol. Soc. (life), Kiwanis, Cannon-Hinckley Study Group, Sigma Xi (life, sec., treas. Utah chpt. 1994—), Pi Tau Sigma, Sigma Chi, Alpha Phi Omega. Republican. Mormon. Home: 4391 South Carol Jane Drive Salt Lake City UT 84124-3601 Office: Silver Energy Systems Corp 13184 Road 3 SE Ste B Moses Lake WA 98837-9483 also: Silver Enterprises 4391 South 2275 E Carol Jane Dr Salt Lake City UT 84124-3601 also: Silver Corporation PO Box 17755 Salt Lake City UT 84117-0755 also: Silver Chief Corp 1433 S Skyline Dr Moses Lake WA 98837-2417 also: Agronomics Internat 6928 Butternut Ct Mc Lean VA 22101-1506 also: Silver Pubs Inc 4390 S 2300 E Salt Lake City UT 84124-3651

SILVER, ROBERTA FRANCES (BOBBI SILVER), special education educator, writer; b. Sedalia, Mo., Oct. 11, 1941; d. Elvin Joshua and Hilda M. (Abrams) Gordon; m. Wayne E. Mason, July 19, 1959 (div. 1974); m. Burton B. Silver, June 3, 1989 (div. 1992); children: Lori A., Philip A., Marc A. BA in Spl. Edn., Avila Coll., 1972; MA in Counselor Edn., U. Mo., 1974; MA in Spl. Edn., Santa Clara U., 1992. Cert. counselor, tchr., Calif.; specialist learning handicapped credential and multiple subject credential, 1992, C.L.A.D. Tchr. Learning Disabled Shawnee-Mission (Kans.) Sch. Dist., 1972-75; sch. counselor Hickman Mills Consolidated Sch. Dist. #1, Kansas City, Mo., 1975-77; tchr. Behavior Disorders Jefferson County Pub. Schs., Louisville, 1978-80; tchr. West Valley Ctr. for Edn. Therapy, Canoga Park, Calif., 1981-82, Ozanam Home for Boys, Kansas City, 1983-89; instr. in human svcs. and continuing edn. dept. Longview Community Coll., Lee's Summit, Mo., 1985-89; instr. learning handicapped Franklin-McKinley Sch. Dist., San Jose, Calif., 1990-95; chr. 2d grade Franklin-McKinley Sch. Dist., San Jose, 1995—; tng. bi-lingual Vietnamesetchr.; bi-lingual Vietnamese tchr.-in-tng. Author 2 novels; watercolorist. Docent Año Nuevo State Res. Home: 200 W Cliff Dr Unit 9 Santa Cruz CA 95060-6165

SILVERBERG, STUART OWEN, obstetrician, gynecologist; b. Denver, Oct. 14, 1931; s. Edward M. and Sara (Morris) S.; BA, U. Colo., 1952, MD, 1955; m. Joan E. Snyderman, June 19, 1954 (div. Apr. 1970); children: Debra Sue Owen, Eric Owen, Alan Kent; m. 2d, Kay Ellen Conklin, Oct. 18, 1970 (div. Apr. 1982); 1 son, Cris S.; m. 3d, Sandra Kay Miller, Jan., 1983. Intern Women's Hosp. Phila., 1955-56; resident Kings County Hosp., Bklyn., 1958-62; practice medicine specializing in obstetrics and gynecology, Denver, 1962—; mem. staff Rose Med. Ctr., N. Suburban Med. Ctr., U. Hosp., St. Anthony Hosp.; med. exec. bd., chmn. dept. obstetrics and gynecology, 1976-77, 86-87, dir. Laser Ctr., 1994-95; clin. instr. U. Colo. Sch. Medicine, Denver, 1962-72, asst. clin. prof., 1972-88, assoc. clin. prof., 1989—, dir. gynecol. endoscopy and laser surgery, 1988-90; v.p. Productos Alimenticos, La Ponderosa, S.A.; dir., chmn. bd. Wicker Works Video Prodns., Inc., 1983-91; cons. Ft. Logan Mental Health Ctr., Denver, 1964-70; mem. Gov.'s Panel Mental Retardation, 1966; med. adv. bd. Colo. Planned Parenthood, 1966-68, Am. Med. Ctr., Spivak, Colo., 1967-70. Mem. Colo. Emergency Resources Bd., Denver, 1965—. Served to maj. AUS, 1956-58; Germany. Diplomate Am. Bd. Obstetrics and Gynecology, Am. Bd. Laser Surgery. Fellow Am. Coll. Obstetricians and Gynecologists, Am. Soc. Laser Medicine and Surgery, ACS; mem. Am. Internat. fertility socs., Colo. Gynecologists and Obstetricians Soc., Hellman Obstet. and Gynecol. Soc., Colo. Med. Soc. (bd. dirs. 1987-95, speaker of the house 1989-95), Clear Creek Valley Med. Soc. (trustee 1978, 80, 87, 93—, pres. 1995), Phi Sigma Delta, Flying Physicians Assn., Aircraft Owners and Pilots Assn., Nu Sigma Nu, Alpha Epsilon Delta. Jewish. Mem. editorial rev. bd. Colo. Women's Mag.; editor in chief First Image, Physicians Video Jour., 1984-86.

SILVERMAN, ALAN H., lawyer; b. N.Y.C., Feb. 18, 1954; s. Melvin H. and Florence (Green) S.; m. Gretchen E. Freeman, May 25, 1986; children: Willa C.F., Gordon H.F. BA summa cum laude, Hamilton Coll., 1976; MBA, U. Pa., 1980, JD, 1980. Bar: N.Y. 1981, U.S. Dist. Ct. (so. and ea. dist.) N.Y. 1981, U.S. Ct. Internat. Trade 1981, D.C. 1986, U.S. Supreme Ct. 1990. Assoc. Hughes, Hubbard & Reed, N.Y.C., 1980-84; assoc. counsel Newsweek, Inc., N.Y.C., 1984-86; v.p., gen. counsel, sec., dir. adminstrn. Post-Newsweek Cable, Phoenix, 1986—. Contbr. articles to profl. jours. Mem. prevention adv. com. Gov. Pa. Justice Commn., 1975-79; bd. dirs. Lawyers' Alliance for N.Y., 1982-85, N.Y. Lawyers Pub. Interest, 1983-85, Nat. Assn. JD-MBA Profls., 1983-85, Bus. Vols. for Arts, Inc., Phoenix, 1989-93, Ariz. Vol. Lawyers for the Arts, Inc., 1994-97; mem. Maricopa County Citizens Jud. Adv. Coun., 1990-93. Mem. ABA, Assn. of Bar of City of N.Y., D.C. Bar Assn., Phi Beta Kappa. Home: 5833 N 30th St Phoenix AZ 85016 Office: Post-Newsweek Cable 4742 N 24th St Ste 270 Phoenix AZ 85016-4860

SILVERMAN, DALE KAREN, association administrator, educator; b. Phila., Dec. 27, 1943; d. Henry H. and Eleanor Luster; m. David L. Silverman, Nov. 2, 1962; children: Evelyn Sue, Sandra Gail. BA, UCLA, 1975, MBA, 1977. Cert. assn. exec.; sr. profl. in human resources certification Insts. Dep. dir. of adminstrn. Didi Hirsch Cmty. Mental Health Ctr., L.A., 1977-78; CFO Jewish Family Svc. of L.A., 1979-88, Gateways Hosps., L.A., 1988-90; exec. dir. Profls. in Human Resources Assn., L.A., 1990-94, Assn. of Woodworking and Furnishings Suppliers, Santa Fe Springs, Calif., 1994—; instr. UCLA, 1994—; vis. prof. U. Judaism, L.A., 1984; mem. adv. bd. U. Phoenix, 1993—, UCLA, 1995—; pres. Gateways Mental Health Ctr., L.A., 1973-74. Officer Equestrian Trails, Inc., L.A., 1990-91. Mem. Soc. of Human Resource Profls., Ctr. for Non Profit Mgmt., Profl. in Human Resources Assn. (chmn. comm.), So. Calif. Assn. of Assn. Execs. (coord. certifications). Office: Assn Wood Furnish Suplpiers Santa Fe Springs CA 90670

SILVERMAN, JEFFREY MICHAEL, radiologist; b. Columbus, Ohio, Mar. 28, 1960. BA, U. Calif. San Diego, 1981, MD, 1985. Diplomate Am. Bd. Radiology, Am. Bd. Med. Examiners. Intern Cedars-Sinai Med. Ctr., L.A., 1985-86, resident, 1986-90; vis. fellow UCLA, Stanford (Calif.) U., U. Calif./Irvine, San Francisco, 1991; radiologist Tower Imaging, L.A., 1991-92, Cedars-Sinai Med. Ctr., L.A., 1992—; active numerous coms. in field; assoc. editor Cedars-Sinai Med. Ctr. Rsch. Editl. Adv. Com., 1989; prsenter in field. Reviewer Jour. of Magnetic Resonance Imaging, 1994, Am. Jour. Roentgenology, 1995, Chest, 1993, others; contbr. articles to profl. jours. and pubs. Grantee in field. Mem. AMA, Am. Coll. Radiology, Radiol. Soc. N.Am., Am. Roentgen Ray Soc., Soc. Magnetic Resonance in Medicine, Soc. for Magnetic Resonance Imaging, Calif. Radiol. Soc., L.A. County Med. Assn., L.A. Radiol. Soc., Am. Coll. Chest Physicians, N.Am. Soc. Cardiac Imaging, Am. Heart Assn. Cardiovascular Radiology Coun. Office: Cedars Sinai Med Ctr 8700 Beverly Blvd Los Angeles CA 90048-1804

SILVERMAN, NORMAN HENRY, cardiologist, educator; b. Johannesburg, South Africa, Sept. 29, 1942; came to U.S., 1972; s. Simon Cecil and Jean (Krawitz) S.; m. Heather Silverman. DSc in Med., U. Witwatersrand, Johannesburg, 1985; postgrad., U. Witwatersrand. Diplomate Am. Bd. Pediatrics. Asst. prof. pediatrics Stanford U., Palo Alto, Calif., 1974-75; asst. prof. pediatrics U. Calif., San Francisco, 1975, assoc. prof. radiology, 1979, prof., 1985—. Co-author: Two Dimensional Echocardiography, 1982, Congenital Heart Disease, 1990; author: Pediatric Echocardiography, 1993. Lt. South African Def. Force, 1968-69. Grantee March of Dimes, 1977-79, Am. Heart Assn., 1978-80, 90-92. Fellow Am. Coll. Cardiology, Am. Acad. Pediatrics, Coll. of Physicians of South Africa, Soc. of Pediatric Rsch., Am. Pediatric Soc.; mem. Univ. Club (Palo Alto). Office: U Calif PO Box 0214 San Francisco CA 94143-0214

SILVERMAN, STEVEN LEE, aeronautical engineer; b. Boston, Dec. 23, 1953; s. Benjamin K. and Beverly (Miller) S. BS in Aerospace Engring., U. Va., 1977, MS, 1981. Cert. NetWare adminstr. Project scientist Princeton (N.J.) U., 1972-77; aerospace engr. Naval Surface Weapons Ctr., Dahlgren, Va., 1979-80; project engr. Rockwell Internat. Corp., Downey, Calif., 1981-85; rschr. Rockwell Internat. Corp., Seal Beach, Calif., 1985-87; project engr. Rockwell Internat. Corp., Downey, Calif., 1987-96, Boeing N.Am., Inc., Downey, 1996—; pres. Capricorn Computing, Downey, 1981-84; CEO Sports Line Systems, Seal Beach, 1983—. Recipient Customer Achievement award NASA, 1982. Mem. AIAA (2d Place award-Middle Atlantic Region 1977, 1st Place award 1981). Office: Boeing N Am Inc 12214 Lakewood Blvd Downey CA 90240-3458

SILVERMAN, TREVA, writer, producer, consultant; b. N.Y.C.; d. Nathan and Janno (Harra) S. Student, U. Chgo., 1956; BA, Bennington Coll., 1958. Staff writer: (TV) The Entertainers, 1964, The Monkees, 1966, 67, 68, Captain Nice, 1968, Room 222, 1969, The Mary Tyler Moore Show, 1970-75 (Emmy award Best Comedy Writer 1974, Writer of Yr. 1974); staff writer, prodr.: Fanelli Boys, 1991; episode writer He and She, 1968, Get Smart, 1968; writer: (TV pilots) Dates from Hell, 1991, Boy, Girl, Boy, 1991, Home Again, 1992, Ladies Night, 1992, The Rev, 1995, San Diego Presents, 1996; (features) A Nice Girl, 1980, Going All the Way, 1986, Act One, 1987; writer, prodr. children's musicals Theatre East, N.Y.C., 1960-63, Scandal, 1985, Hearts' Desire: Out of Town, 1992; contbg. writer: Julius Monk's Upstairs at the Downstairs, 1962-64; cons. Columbia pictures TV comedy programming, 1985-86, MTM Prodns., 1986, Just in Time, ABC-TV, 1987. Named one of TV Women of Yr., Ladies Home Jour., 1975. Mem. Dramatists Guild, Writers Guild Am. (Best Spl./Variety Writer 1969), Acad. TV Arts and Scis. Democrat. Office: Tudor Entertainment Inc 9437 Santa Monica Blvd Beverly Hills CA 90210

SILVERN, LEONARD CHARLES, retired engineering executive; b. N.Y.C., May 20, 1919; s. Ralph and Augusta (Thaler) S.; m. Gloria Marantz, June 1948 (div. Jan. 1968); 1 child, Ronald; m. Elisabeth Beeny, Aug. 1969 (div. Oct. 1972); m. Gwen Taylor, Nov. 1985. BS in Physics, L.I. U., 1946; MA, Columbia U., 1948, EdD, 1952. Registered profl. consulting engr., Calif. Tng. supr. U.S. Dept. Navy, N.Y.C., 1939-49; tng. dir. exec. dept. N.Y. Div. Safety, Albany, 1949-55; resident engring. psychologist Lincoln Lab. MIT for Rand Corp., Lexington, 1955-56; engr., dir. edn., tng., rsch. labs. Hughes Aircraft Co., Culver City, Calif., 1956-62; dir. human performance engring. lab., cons. engring. psychologist to v.p. tech. Northrop Norair, Hawthorne, Calif., 1962-64; prin. sci., v.p., pres. Edn. and Tng. Cons. Co., L.A., 1964-96, Sedona, Ariz., 1980, pres. Systems Engring. Labs. div., 1980-96; cons. hdqrs. Air Tng. Command USAF, Randolph AFB, Tex., 1964-68, Electronic Industries Assn., Washington, 1963-69, Edn. R and D Ctr., U. Hawaii, 1970-74, Ctr. Vocat. and Tech. Edn., Ohio State U., 1972-73, Coun. for Exceptional Children, 1973-74, Canadore Coll. Applied Arts and Tech., Ont., Can., 1974-76, Centro Nacional de Productividad, Mexico City, 1973-75, N.S. Dept. Edn., Halifax, 1975-79, Aeronutronic Ford-Ford Motor Co., 1975-76, Nat. Tng. Systems Inc., 1976-81, Nfld. Pub. Svc. Commn., 1978, Legis. Affairs Office USDA, 1980, Rocky Point Techs., 1986; adj. prof. edn., pub. adminstrn. U. So. Calif. Grad. Sch., 1957-65; vis. prof. computer scis. U. Calif. Extension Div., L.A., 1963-72. Dist. ops. officer, disaster communications svc. L.A. County Sheriff's Dept., 1973-75, dist. communications officer, 1975-76; bd. dirs. SEARCH, 1976—; mem. adv. com. West Sedona Community Plan of Yavapai County, 1986-88; councilman City of Sedona, 1988-92; rep. COCOPAI, 1988-89; vol. earth team Soil Conservation Svc., U.S. Dept Agr., 1989-92; Verde Resource Assn., 1988-90, Group on Water Logistics, 1989-90; chair publs. com. Ariz. Rural Recycling Conf., 1990. With USN, 1944-46. Mem. IEEE (sr.), APA, Am. Radio Relay League (life), Nat. Solid Waste Mgmt. Symposium (chmn. publs. com. 1988-89), Ariz. Rural Recycling Conf. (chair publs. com. 1990), Friendship Vets. Fire Engine Co. (hon.), Soc. Wireless Pioneers (life), Quarter Century Wireless Assn. (life), Sierra Club (treas. Sedona-Verde Valley Group 1991-93), Assn. Bldg. Coms., Vox Pop (chmn. bd. dirs. Sedona, 1983-93, dir. 1993-95), Nat. Parks and Conservation Assn., Wilderness Soc., Ariz. Ctr. Law in Pub. Interest, Old Old Timers Club. Contbg. editor Ednl. Tech., 1968-73, 81-85; reviewer ACM Computing Revs., 1962-92, 96—. Contbr. numerous articles to profl. jours. Office: PO Box 2085 Sedona AZ 86339-2085

SILVERS, E. RANDALL, information liaison; b. Somerville, N.J., July 8, 1951; s. William Joseph Silvers Sr. and Edna Rebecca (Pysher) Silvers-Brennan; m. Cynthia Lee Mulch, Aug. 6, 1974; children: Benjamin Judah, Deborah Lynn. AA summa cum laude, Palomar Coll., 1979; ASBA, Thomas Nelson Coll., 1984, AAS in Data Processing, 1984; postgrad., Christopher Newport, Newport News, Va., 1984-85. Cert. nat. registry EMT. Maintenance chief Escondido (Calif.) Convalescent Ctr., 1977-79; registrar, instr. Profl. Med. Inst., Hampton, Va., 1980-81; corps asst. Salvation Army, Logansport, Ind., 1985-88; computer system mgr. info. liason Salvation Army Harbor Light, L.A., 1988—; rep. divisional computer bd. (MIS) Salvation Army So. Calif., L.A., 1991—. Arranger orchestration for cantata; composer march; author poem. Scoutmaster Boy Scouts Am., San Diego, 1972-75, Camp Pendleton, Calif., 1975-76, Hampton, Va., 1980-84, Huntington Park, Calif., 1990-92, Whittier, Calif., 1992-94; commr., San Diego County, Calif., 1976-79; bandmaster Salvation Army, San Diego, 1970-71, 72-73, Escondido, 1974-77, Hampton, 1979-85, Logansport, 1985-88, Huntington Park, Calif., 1988-92, Long Beach Temple, 1994—; asst. dir., prin. euphonium Peninsula Community Band, Newport News, 1980-85; prin. euphonium LBCC Concert Band, 1994—; charter mem. Band of Calif. Bn. Civil War Reenactment Band, 1994—; instr./trainer ARC, Langley AFB, Va., 1979-85, 1st aid/CPR chmn., 1981-84. Sgt. USMC, 1969-77, Vietnam. Named Vol. of Month and Yr., ARC, 1980; decorated Air Force Achievement medal. Mem. Students Vets. Assn. (pres. 1982-84), Am. Legion (sgt. at arms 1974, 2d vice comdr. 1972—), Sons of Union Vets. of Civil War, VFW, Phi Beta Lambda (parliamentarian 1983-84). Republican. Office: Salvation Army Harbor Light 809 E 5th St Los Angeles CA 90013-2112

SILVERSTEIN, JOSEPH HARRY, musician; b. Detroit, Mar. 21, 1932; s. Bernard and Ida (Katz) S.; m. Adrienne Shufro, Apr. 27; children—Bernice, Deborah, Marc. Student Curtis Inst. Music, 1945-50; hon. doctoral degrees Tufts U., 1971, Rhode Island U., 1980, Boston Coll., 1981, New Eng. Conservatory, 1986, Susquehanna. Violinist, Houston Symphony Orch., Phila. Orch.; concertmaster Denver Symphony Orch., Boston Symphony Orch.; formerly chmn. string dept. New Eng. Conservatory Music; also chmn. faculty Berkshire Music Sch.; mem. faculty Boston U. Sch. Music, Yale U. Sch. Music; music dir. Boston Symphony Chamber Players, Boston U. Symphony Orch., Chautauqua (N.Y.) Instn., 1987—; interim music dir. Toledo Symphony Orch.; prin. guest condr. Balt. Symphony Orch., 1981; condr. Utah Symphony; mus. dir. Worcester Orch., Mass., until 1987. Recipient Silver medal Queen Elizabeth of Belgium Internat. contest, 1959, Naumberg found. award, 1960; named one of ten outstanding young men, Boston C. of C., 1962. Fellow Am. Acad. Arts and Scis. Office: care Utah Symphony Orch 123 W South Temple Salt Lake City UT 84101-1403

SILVERSTEIN, RICHARD, advertising agency executive. Grad., Parsons Sch. of Design. Prin., co-creative dir. Goodby, Silverstein & Ptnrs., San Francisco, 1983—. Office: Goodby Silverstein & Ptnrs 921 Front St San Francisco CA 94111-1426*

SILVERSTEIN, STEVEN B., railroad executive; b. Cleve., Sept. 21, 1951; s. Fred R. and Norma (Gillett) S.; m. Mary C. Straley, Aug. 6, 1988; children: Zachariah, Alisha. Student, Syracuse U., 1969-70, U. Rochester, 1972-73. Purchasing and warehouse mgr. Arctic Catering, Anchorage, 1979-80, field supr., 1980-82; freight auditor, then dir. in-bound logistics JB Gottstein Co., Anchorage, 1982-86; sr. logistics specialist, sr. supply mgmt. specialist ARCO Alaska, Inc., Anchorage, 1986-96; sr. dir. freight svcs. Alaska R.R. Corp., Anchorage, 1996—; speaker Atlanta Internat. Intermodal Expo, 1989, 91. Bd. dirs. Anchorage Ctr. for Performing Arts, 1993—. Mem. Am. Soc. Transp. and Logistics (cert., pres. 1982-88, Best Small Chpt. award 1986), Anchorage Concert Assn. (v.p., treas., bd. dirs. 1980—, now pres.), Coun. Logistics Mgmt. Jewish. Home: 1210 N St Anchorage AK 99501-4272

SILVERTHORN, LEE JAMES, clinical psychology; b. Atlanta, Nov. 27, 1929; m. Alma Inez, Aug. 28, 1971; children: Lee J. III, Judith A. BA, U. Mich., 1950; MA, U. Kans., 1953, PhD, 1957. Instr. U. Kans. Extension divsn., Leavenworth City and Fed. Prison, 1957-60; asst. chief psychology svc. VA Med. Ctr., Leavenworth, 1957-66; asst. prof. U. Kans., 1963-66; chief psychology svc. VA Med. Ctr., Memphis, 1967-75; Fulbright prof. U. Chiengmia, Thailand, 1966-67; asst. to assoc. clin. prof. divsn. psychology Dept. Psychiat Dept. Psychiatry, U. Tenn. Ctr. for Health Scis., Memphis, 1968-75; staff psychologist VA Med. Ctr., Palo Alto, Calif., 1975-85, cons., 1985—; forensic examiner Superior Ct. of Santa Clara county, San Mateo County, 1982—; pvt. practice, 1961—; cons. psychologist N.E. Kans. Guidance Ctr., Atchison, Kans., 1957-64; chief psychology svc. VA Hosp., Jefferson Barracks, St. Louis, 1966; adj. prof. dept. of psychology Memphis State U., 1967-75; mem. vice-chmn. Tenn. Bd. of Exminers in Psychology, 1972-75; presenter in field. Mem. Fellow AAAS, Am. Psychol. Soc.; mem. emeritus Sigma Xi. Home and Office: 3339 Kenneth Dr Palo Alto CA 94303-4216

SILVESTRI, PHILIP SALVATORE, lawyer; b. San Francisco, Nov. 10, 1944; s. Philip and Olga (Difilipo) S.; m. Dianne Loveland, June 22, 1968; children: Lauren, Steven, Karin. BA, U. San Francisco, 1966, JD, 1969. Bar: Calif. 1969; cert. family law specialist State Bar Calif. Assoc. Goth, Dennis & Aaron, Redwood City, Calif., 1969-84; ptnr. Goth, Aaron & Silvestri, Redwood City, 1984-87, Goth & Silvestri, A.P.C., Redwood City, 1987—. With N.G., 1969-75. Republican. Office: Goth & Silvestri APC 1000 Marshall St Ste B Redwood City CA 94063-2027

SILVIA, RAYMOND ALAN, librarian; b. Gustine, Calif., Apr. 10, 1950; s. Antonio and Mary (Viveiros) S.; m. Doris Elizabeth Newcomb, Jan. 9, 1972; children: Mary, Paul, Hilary, Dominic, Elizabeth. AA in English, Modesto (Calif.) Jr. Coll., 1970; BA in English summa cum laude, Calif. State U., Fresno, 1972, MA in English with distinction, 1982; MLS, San Jose State U., 1985. Cert. cmty. coll. tchr., Calif. Lectr. Calif. State U., Fresno, 1980-82; investor Clovis, Calif., 1982—; ref. libr./supr. King's County Libr., Hanford, Calif., 1986-90; libr./sr. libr. Calif. State Dept. Corrections, Sacramento, 1990-94; supervising libr. Calif. State Dept. Justice, Sacramento, 1994—; spkr./trainer, mem. statewide correctional law libr. task Calif. State Dept. Corrections, Sacramento, 1994; spkr. in field. Contbr. articles to profl. jours. Chmn. ref. com. San Joaquin Valley Libr. Sys., Fresno, 1989-90; mem. Secular Franciscan Order, Fresno, 1975—, novice master, 1984. Mem. MLA, Spl. Librs. Assn., Calif. State U. Fresno Alumni Assn., Phi Kappa Phi. Republican. Roman Catholic.

SILVIUS, DONALD JOE, educational consultant; b. Kingman, Kans., July 30, 1932; s. Henry Edgar and Gladys Mae (Beaty) S.; m. Jean Anne Able, Aug. 30, 1951; children: Laurie Dawn Silvius Gustin, Steven Craig, Jonathan Mark, Brian James. Student So. Calif. Coll., 1949-52; AA, Bakersfield Coll., 1962; BA, Fresno State Coll., 1963, MA, 1968. Radio/TV announcer, musician, music arranger and copyist, life ins. underwriter, other positions, 1953-62; jr. high sch. English tchr., elem. and jr. high counselor, child welfare, attendance and guidance supr., supr. pupil personnel svcs. Standard Sch. Dist., Oildale, Calif., 1963-92; ret. 1992; edn., guidance and computer cons., 1992—; tchr. counseling/guidance and spl. edn. various colls. Pres. North of the River Sanitation Dist. # 1. Recipient Standard PTA-Hon. Service award, Bakersfield "Up With People" Appreciation award, Golden Apple Service award Standard Sch. Dist. Tchrs. Assn., Innovations award Calif. Tchrs. Assn., Hon. Service award Kern chpt. Calif. Assn. Sch. Psychologists, Outstanding Ednl. Leader award West Kern chpt. Assn. Calif. Sch. Adminstrs., 1977-78, 7th Dist. PTA-Silver Service award, Continuing Service award Highland-Wingland PTA, Outstanding Community Service for Developmentally Disabled award. Mem. NEA, Calif. Tchrs. Assn., North of the River C. of C., Calif. Assn. Supervision of Child Welfare and Attendance, Assn. Calif. Sch. Adminstrs., Am. Assn. Curriculum Devel., Am. Assn. Counseling and Devel., ACES, ASCD, AMECD, ARVIC, Mental Health Assn. (Calif. exec. bd.), Assn. Kern County, Mensa, PTA, Calif. Assn. Counseling and Devel., Calif. Assn. for Counseling Edn. & Supervision, Calif. Assn. for Adult Devel. & Aging, Calif. Assn. for Measurement & Evaluation in Counseling, Calif. Assn. for Relig. Values & Issues in Counseling, v.p. Calif. Ret. Tchr. Assn., Oildale Lions Club, Phi Delta Kappa.

SIMAS, EDWARD ALFRED, chairman county board supervisors; b. Ripon, May 26, 1944; m. Sharon Simas, 1966; children: John, Gina. BBA, U. Pacific, 1966. Chmn. county seat Office of Bd. County Suprs., Stockton, Calif., 1988—; vice-chmn. bd. suprs. Office of Bd. County Suprs., Stockton, 1991, 96, chmn. bd. suprs., 1992, 97. Office: Bd of County Suprs Courthouse 222 E Weber Ave Rm 701 Stockton CA 95202

SIMEROTH, DEAN CONRAD, chemical engineer; b. Marysville, Calif., Mar. 21, 1946; s. Raphael Conrad and Mary Beatrice (Watson) S.; m. Phyllis Deborah Minakowski, Feb. 7, 1971 (div. Nov. 1994); 1 child, Brian Conrad. BS in Chem. Engring., U. Calif., Davis, 1968. From air pollution specialist to chief engr. evaluation br. Calif. Air Resources Bd., Sacramento, 1969-87; chief criteria pollutant br. Calif. Air Resources Bd., 1987—. Served in U.S. Army, 1969-71, Korea. Mem. AIChE, Air Waste Mgmt. Assn., Kiwanis (treas. Woodland, Calif. chpt. 1988-96). Democrat. Roman Catholic. Office: Calif Air Resources Bd PO Box 2815 2020 L St Sacramento CA 95812

SIMKHOVICH, BORIS ZALMAN, biochemist, researcher; b. Riga, Latvia, July 26, 1947; came to U.S., 1989; s. Zalman Israel and Sofia (Lipkina) S.; m. Mara Turets, May 30, 1991; 1 stepchild, Larry Adamsky. MD, Riga Med. Inst., 1971, PhD, 1974; DMS, Inst. for Gen. Pathology, Moscow, 1988. Rsch. assoc. Inst. of Organic Synthesis, Riga, 1975-85, head rsch. lab., 1985-89; rsch. assoc. U. So. Calif., L.A., 1989-90; dir. biochemistry Heart Inst. Good Samaritan Hosp., L.A., 1990—; asst. prof. rsch. medicine U. So. Calif. Sch. Medicine, L.A., 1995—. Contbr. scientific papers to profl. jours.; reviewer for rsch. jours. in the field of cardiology. Recipient 1st prize Annual Scientific award Latvian Acad. of Scis., 1985. Mem. Internat. Soc. for Heart Rsch. (Am. sect.), Am. Heart Assn. Office: Good Samaritan Hosp 1225 Wilshire Blvd Los Angeles CA 90017-1901

SIMMONS, ANN LORRAINE, actor; b. Kansas City, Mo., Feb. 8, 1952; d. Ronald Lee and Frances Jean (Smith) S.; m. Mithcell Duane Duckworth, Mar. 20, 1971 (div. Feb. 21, 1978); 1 child, Jason Bartholomew Duckworth; m. Russel Yates Mulock, July 25, 1986. BA, U. Calif., 1987; MFA, Calif. Inst. of the Arts, 1995. Appeared in plays Macbeth, The Comedy of Errors, Dancing at Lughnasa, Agamemnon, Twelth Night, The Glass Menagerie, The Rose Tattoo, Merchant of Venice, The Bacchae. Mem. Women in Theatre, Theatre Comms. Group. Home: 23835 Del Monte Dr # 102 Valencia CA 91355

SIMMONS, CHRISTOPHER LAIRD, graphic designer, art director; b. Iowa City, Iowa, Jan. 12, 1962; s. Jerry Laird and Nola Ann (Cox) S.; m. Paula Joan Polchert, July 25, 1992 (div. May 1996); 1 child, Abby Marie. Owner, graphic designer S.U. Graphics, Redondo Beach, Calif., 1978-82; prodn. mgr., art dir. Photoventures Graphics, Long Beach, Calif., 1982-87; owner, creative dir. Mindset Graphics, Manhattan Beach, Calif., 1987-92; advt. and mktg. mgr. Creative Computers, Torrance, Calif., 1992-94; dir. mktg. comms. NovaQuest Infosystems/DirectWare, Torrance, Calif., 1995-97; mktg. dir. CyberRam Memory Products, Irvine, Calif., 1997—. Editor: Galaxy Class, 1987-93; composer (theme music TV programs) Viewpoints on Video, 1988, KidVid Co., 1989, colorist: (comic book) Triad Universe, 1994; art dir. Computer Player Mag., 1994-95; art dir. Digital Imaging Mag., 1996—. Recipient Apple Computers Inc. ARPL Design/1st pl. award 1994, 2 Harvey Rsch. Orgn. Communications awards, 1994, Star of the Web award, 1996. Mem. L.A. Macintosh User Group, Direct Mktg. Assn. Independent.

SIMMONS, CLEDA-MARIE, artist; b. Douglas, Wyo., June 24, 1927; d. Neil and Hulda Louise (Anderson) Diehl; m. Alfred Allen Simmons, May 9, 1951 (dec. Dec. 1987); children: Alfred Allen Jr., Barry Neal, Nina Marie. Student, Casper (Wyo.) Jr. Coll., 1946-47, U. N.Mex., Albuquerque, 1947-51. Painter, illustrator, muralist, graphic artist Vista, Calif., 1978—; graphic artist Epsilon Sigma Alpha Women Internat., Ft. Collins, Colo., 1969-70; art editor ESA Women Int., Ft. Collins, Colo., 1970-73, art dir., 1973-77; artistic dir. Vista Iniatitive for Visual Arts, 1990-94, bd. dirs.; artistic dir. Murals of Vista, 1994-96. Illustrator Our Government, 1969, Beneath the Peaks, 1973; co-author: Art of Editorship, 1972; author: Design and Your World, 1995; one-woman shows include Ateneo de Belles Artes, Madrid, 1955-90 (Purchase award 1955), Art Ways-Design Ctr., San Diego, 1991, Creative Art Ctr., Burbank, Calif., 1986, Mark Reuben Gallery, San Francisco, 1985, Gallery of World Art, Newton Upper Falls, Mass., 1982, Ahmed's Gallery Lounge, Cambridge, Mass., 1981, The Catseye, Wellesley, Mass., 1979, Loveland (Colo.) Mus., 1978, and numerous others 1954—. Exhbn. dir. Women's Caucus for the Arts, L.A., 1985, Women Exhbns. in Boston, 1980-83. Home and Office: 724 Osborne St Vista CA 92084-1804

SIMMONS, GEOFFREY STUART, physician; b. Camp Gordon, Ga., July 28, 1943; s. Ted R. and Jane A. (Lavander) S.; m. Sherry Simmons, Sept. 7, 1985; children: Bradley, Anais. BS, U. Ill., 1965, MD, 1969. Intern U. So. Calif., L.A., 1969-70, resident, 1971-74; pvt. practice Astoria, Oreg., 1974-77, Eugene, Oreg.; chmn. internal medicine dept. PeaceHealth Med. Group, 1976—; bd. dirs. Lane County Med. Soc.; med. correspondent KUGN Radio, 1993-95. Author: The Z Papers, 1977, The Adam Experiment, 1978, Pandemic, 1980, Murdock, 1982, The Glue Factory, 1995; med. commentator KABC Radio, 1970. Office: 1200 Hilyard St Ste 200 S Eugene OR 97401-8133

SIMMONS, HOWARD LEE, education educator; b. Mobile, Ala.. BS in Secondary Edn., Spring Hill Coll., 1960; MAT in Slavic langs. and Lit., Ind. U., 1965; PhD in Design and Mgmt. of Postsecondary Edn., Fla. State U., 1975; LHD (honoris causa), Sojourner-Douglass Coll., 1995. Assoc. dir., asst. exec. sec. Commn. on Higher Edn. Middle States Assn. of Colls. & Schs., Phila., 1974-95, exec. dir., 1988-95; assoc. dean, prof., coord. edn. leadership in higher edn. Ariz. State U., Tempe, 1996—; vis. lectr. in Russian Lafayette Coll., Easton, Pa., 1970-71; part-time Russian/Spanish instr. Clayton (Mo.) High Sch., 1965-67; dean instructional svcs. Northampton Community Coll., Bethlehem, Pa., 1969-74; chmn. dept. fgn. lang. Forest Park Community Coll., Mo., 1964-69; sr. researcher Ariz. State U., nat. Ctr. for Postsecondary Governance and Fin., 1986-87; cons. in field; keynote speaker in field; researcher on accreditation and blacks in higher edn. Contbr. articles to profl. jours. NDEA grantee Spring Hill Coll., 1958-60, grantee Japan-U.S. Friendship Comm., 1993-94; NDEA fellow Ind. U., 1963-64, Edn. Professions Devel. Act fellow Fla. State U., 1973-75, fellow Am. Coun. Edn., 1972-73; USIA Acad. Specialist grantee, Quito, Ecuador, 1996. Mem. Am. Ednl. Rsch. assn., Am. Assn. for Community and Jr. Colls. (assoc.), Assn. for the Study of Higher Edn., Assn. of Tchrs. of Slavic and East European Langs., Assn. Caribbean Tertiary Instn., Internat. Accredition Specialist, 1996—, Am. Assn. for Higher Edn. (exec. bd. black caucus, nat. cultural diversity award by caucuses 1992), Phi Delta Kappa, Kappa Delta Pi. Home: 2008 N Squire Ave Tempe AZ 85281-1330 Office: Ariz State U Coll Edn PO Box 872411 Tempe AZ 85287-2411

SIMMONS, JANET BRYANT, writer, publisher; b. Oakland, Calif., Apr. 22, 1925; d. Howard Pelton and Janet Horn (McNab) Bryant; m. William Ellis Simmons, May 17, 1944 (div. 1979); children: William Howard, Janet Margaret Simmons McAlpine. BA, San Jose State U., 1965; MA, U. San Francisco, 1979. Social worker Santa Clara County Social Svcs., San Jose, Calif., 1965-91; editor, pub. Enlightenment Press, Santa Clara, 1994—. Author: The Mystical Child, 1996. Mem. Am. Booksellers Assn., Pubs. Mktg. Assn., Marin Small Pubs. Assn., Audubon Soc., Jacques Cousteau Soc. Office: Enlightenment Press PO Box 3314 Santa Clara CA 95055

SIMMONS, JULIE LUTZ, artist; b. San Diego, Dec. 25; d. Charles Ignatius and Latane (Mooring) Lutz; m. George Elliott Simmons, June 13, 1964 (div. Jan. 1989); children: Julie Elizabeth, George Elliott Jr. BS, Murray State U., 1964. Exhibits include Abstein Gallery, Atlanta, 1986, 87, 88, 89, 90, Shawnee Coll., Ullin, Ill., 1987, Ctrl. Coll., Union, Mo., 1988, D-zine, St. Louis, 1988, 91, 92, 93, Barucci's Gallery, St. Louis, 1990, Durfee Gallery, Scottsdale, 1992, Sun Cities Mus., 1992, 93, others; gallery representation Barucci's Gallery, St. Louis, Village Gallery, Scottsdale, S. Gregg Gallery, Cape Girardeau, Mo., Beyond the Horizon Gallery, Nashville; represented in pvt. collections Embassy Suites, La Jolla, Calif., Marriott Hotels, Atlanta, Orthodox Acad. Crete, Koympari, Greece, St. Louis Fed. Savs. and Loan, Electrolux Corp., Atlanta, PGA West Resort Golf Club, La Quinta, Calif., others. Ariz. Artists Guild, Ariz. Watercolor Assn. (sec. 1993-94), Soc. Layerists in Multi Media. Home: 11783 E Becker Ln Scottsdale AZ 85259

SIMMONS, KELLEY LYNN, mental health counselor, administrator; b. Shaker Heights, Ohio, May 2, 1965; d. Horace Bly Simmons and Sandra Gail (Pagana) Wright. BA in Psychology/Bus. magna cum laude, Ursuline Coll., Pepper Pike, Ohio, 1989; M in Counseling Psychology, St. Martin's Coll., Lacey, Wash., 1997. Adminstrv. asst. Stanspec Corp., Cleve., 1986-89; primary counselor, family therapist New Directions, Pepper Pike, Ohio, 1986-90; children's care specialist Adventure Nature Program, Yelm, Wash., 1991-93; exec. dir., founder Monarch Therapeutic Learning Ctr., Lacey, 1993—; vice-chair adv. bd. Partnership for Children, Youth, Families, Olympia, Wash., 1996—; mem. at large adv. bd. Ptnrs. for Prevention, Olympia, 1995-96; bd. mem. Child Protective Team, Thurston County, Wash., 1994—; mem. homeless child care policy task force Thurston County, Lacey, 1996—; mem. Elem. Sch. Health Planning Team, North Thurston, 1997—. Office: Monarch Therapeutic Learning Ctr PO Box 3541 Lacey WA 98509-3541

SIMMONS, NED LEE, landscape artist, art dealer, consultant; b. Carmel, Calif., Mar. 15, 1939; s. Ned Lee, Sr. and Grace Lucille (Sinclair) S.; m. Barbara June Yocom Simmons, Dec. 31, 1968 (div. June 1989); children: Valerie, Gaylene. BS in Forest Mgmt., Humboldt State U., Arcata, Calif., 1964; MS in Forest Mgmt., 1973. Cert. profl. forester, Calif. Cons. forester Western Timber Svcs., Inc., Arcata, Calif., 1965-89; pvt. practice Trinidad (Calif.) Art, 1989—. Editor: the Volunteer Trinidadian, 1988; author: A Trinidad Story, 1989, 93, Rainbow Ridge, 1991, Crystalization, 1995. Fireman Trnindad (Calif.) Vol. Fire Dept., 1989—. Mem. Trinidad Mus. Soc., Humboldt North Coast Landtrust, Redwood Art Assn., Trinidad C. of C. Home and Office: Trinidad Art PO Box 1233 Trinidad CA 95570-1233

SIMMONS, RICHARD J., lawyer; b. Brockton, Mass., Nov. 26, 1951. BA summa cum laude, U. Mass., 1973; JD, U. Calif., Berkeley, 1976. Bar: Calif. 1976. Mem. Sheppard, Mullin, Richter & Hampton, L.A.; lectr. State of Calif., 1977-88; instr. UCLA, 1980-87; appointed to bd. Calif. Minimum Wage Bds. 1982, 84, 87; adv. bd. U. Calif. Boalt Hall Law Sch. Indsl. Relations Law Journal, 1985—. Reviews editor, editor in chief: Indsl. Relations Law Jour. 1975-76; Author: Wrongful Discharge and Employment Practices Manual, 1989, Employee Handbook and Personnel Policies Manual, 1983, 87, 92, Wage and Hour Manual for California Employers, 1982, 86, 88, 89, 91, Employment Discrimination and EEO Practice Manual for California Employers, 1982, 85,91, Employer's Guide to the American with Disabilities Act, 1990, 91, 92, The Employer's Guide to the California Family Rights Act of 1991, 1992, Employer Obligations Under the Federal Plant Closing Law, 1989, 90, The New Federal Polygraph Law, 1989, The New Federal Immigration Law: The Immigration Reform and Control Act of 1986, 1987, COBRA: The Federal Health Insurance Rules for the 1990's, 1987,90. contbr. to profl mags. and jours. Commonwealth scholar. Mem. ABA (labor, employment law, tax sect.), L.A. County Bar Assn. (tax, labor sect.), The State Bar Calif., Calif. Soc. Health Care Attys., Am. Soc. Health Care Attys., Phi Kappa Phi. Office: Sheppard Mullin Richter & Hampton One Wilshire Blvd Ste 2000 Los Angeles CA 90017-3321

SIMMONS, ROY WILLIAM, banker; b. Portland, Oreg., Jan. 24, 1916; s. Henry Clay and Ida (Mudd) S.; m. Elizabeth Ellison, Oct. 28, 1938; children—Julia Simmons Watkins, Matthew R., Laurence E., Elizabeth Jane Simmons Hoke, Harris H., David E. Asst. cashier First Nat. Bank Layton, Utah, 1944-49; Utah bank commr., 1949-51; exec. v.p. Bank of Utah, Ogden, 1951-53; pres. Lockhart Co., Salt Lake City, 1953-64, Zion's First Nat. Bank, Salt Lake City, 1964-81; chmn. bd. Zion's First Nat. Bank, 1965—; chmn., CEO Zion's Bancorp, 1965-91, chmn. bd., 1991—; chmn. bd. Zion's Savs. & Loan Assn., 1961-69; pres. Lockhart Co., 1964-87; bd. dirs. Beneficial Life Ins. Co., Ellison Ranching Co. Chmn. Utah Bus. Devel. Corp., 1969-80. Mem. Utah State Bd. Regents, 1969-81. Mem. Salt Lake City C. of C. (treas. 1964-65), Sigma Pi. Republican. Mem. Ch. of Jesus Christ of Latter Day Saints. Home: 817 E Crestwood Rd Kaysville UT 84037-1712 Office: Zions Bancorp 1000 Kennecott Bldg Salt Lake City UT 84133

SIMMONS, SARAH R., lawyer; b. Ducktown, Tenn., Jan. 23, 1948. BA magna cum laude, U. Ariz., 1970, postgrad.; JD magna cum laude, U. Denver, 1973. Bar: Colo. 1974, Ariz. 1975. Mem. Molloy, Jones & Donahue, Tucson, Brown & Bain, P.A., Tucson. Trustee Tohono Club Park, 1995—, sec., 1997—; trustee Tucson Airport Authority, 1996—; mem. Law Coll. Assn. Bd., 1996—; fourth bd. Tucson Unified Sch., 1996—; bd. dirs. United Way of Tucson, 1995—, Family Advocacy Resource and Wellness Ctrs., Resources for Women, 1995—; mem. adv. bd. Ariz. for a Drug Free Workplace, 1991—, So. Ariz. Sports Devel. Corp., U. Ariz. Social and Behavioral Scis., 1994-96; sec. So. Ariz. Minutemen, 1996—. Recipient Tucson Woman of Yr. C. of C., 1994, Women on the Move award YWCA, 1995, Outstanding Alumni award U. Ariz., 1993. Fellow ABA, Ariz. Bar Assn.; mem. Nat. Assn. Bond Lawyers, State Bar Ariz. (bd. govs. 1987-95, sec.-treas. 1989-90, 2d v.p. 1990-91, 1st v.p. 1991-92, pres.-elect 1992-93, pres. 1993-94, employment law sect., profl. conduct com., fee arbitration com.), Ariz. Women Lawyers Assn. (charter), Colo. Bar Assn., Pima County Bar Assn. (bd. dirs. 1985-94), Am. Judicature Soc., So. Ariz. Legal Aid (bd. dirs. 1990—), Lawyers Against Hunger (bd. dirs., v.p. D-M 50 1996—), Order St. Ives, Phi Beta Kappa, Phi Kappa Phi, Phi Alpha Theta, Kappa Beta Pi. Office: Brown & Bain PA 19th Fl 1 South Church PO Box 2265 Tucson AZ 85702-2265

SIMMONS, TED CONRAD, writer; b. Seattle, Sept. 1, 1916; s. Conrad and Clara Evelyn (Beaudry) S.; m. Dorothy Pauline Maltese, June 1, 1942; children: lynn, Juliet. Student U. Wash., 1938-41, UCLA and Los Angeles State U., 1952-54, Oxford (Eng.) U., 1980. Drama critic Seattle Daily Times, 1942; indsl. writer, reporter-editor L.A. Daily News, 1948-51; contbr. Steel, Western Metals, Western Industry, 1951—; past poetry dir. Watts Writers Workshop; instr. Westside Poetry Center; asst. dir. Pacific Coast Writers Conf., Calif. State Coll. Los Angeles. Served with USAAF, 1942-46. Author: (poetry) Deadended, 1966; (novel) Middlearth, 1975; (drama) Greenhouse,

1977, Durable Chaucer, 1978, Rabelais and other plays, 1980, Dickeybird, 1981 (nominated TCG Plays-in-Progress award 1985), Alice and Eve, 1983, Deja Vu, Deja Vu, 1986, The Box, 1987, Ingrid Superstar, 1988, Three Quarks for Mr. Marks, 1989, Ingrid: Skier on the Slopes of Stromboli, 1990, A Midsummer's Hamlet, 1991, Hamlet Nintendo, After Hours, Dueling Banjoes, Viva el Presidente, Climate of the Sun, 1992, Nude Descending Jacob's Ladder, 1993, Almost an Opera, 1994, Landscape with Inverted Tree and Fred Astaire Dancing, 1995, O.J. Othello, Fast Track, Searching for Alice Liddell, Mr. Blue of Freaky Animals, Inc., 1997, Rosenstern & Guildencrantz II, 1997, Rosa/Rosa of the Centuries/Rosa of the Thorns, 1997, Joyce, 1997; writer short story, radio verse; book reviewer Los Angeles Times; contbr. poetry to The Am. Poet, Prairie Wings, Antioch Rev., Year Two Anthology; editor: Venice Poetry Company Presents, 1972. Grantee Art Commn. King County, 1993.

SIMMONS, VICTOR J., real estate broker, insurance agent; b. Vallejo, Calif., June 17, 1945; s. Victor J. Simmons; m. Martha Negash, June 6, 1996; children: Miriam Victoria, Jonathan Victor. BA, U. Nev., 1968. Bid coord. Dietary Products div. Am. Hosp. Supply Corp., Irvine, Calif., 1972-73; loan officer, appraiser Brentwood Savs., L.A., 1973-77; loan cons. Union Fed. Savs., L.A., 1978-79; real estate broker Far West Mortgage, L.A., 1980-81; ins. agt. Met. Life Ins., L.A., 1981-84; real estate broker Far West Mortgage, L.A., 1984-85; loan cons. Coast Savs., Beverly Hills, Calif., 1985-90; dist. agt., rep. Prudential Life Ins. Co., El Segundo, Calif., 1990-92; mortgage loan cons. Great Western Bank, Torrance, Calif., 1992-94; loan cons. Western Fin. Savings Bank, Beverly Hills, Calif., 1994-95; assessment appeals hearing officer L.A. County, L.A., 1995—. Contbr. articles to profl. jours., 1967-71. 1st lt. USMCR, 1968-71. Democrat. Baptist. Home: 3503 W 85th St Inglewood CA 90305-1616 Office: PO Box 78281 Los Angeles CA 90016-0281

SIMMS, MARIA ESTER, health services administrator; b. Bahia Blanca, Argentina; came to U.S., 1963; d. Jose and Esther (Guays) Barberio Esandi; m. Michael Simms, July 15, 1973 (Aug. 1993); children: Michelle Bonnie Lee Carla, Michael London Valentine, Matthew Brandon. Degree medicine, Facultad del Centenario, Rosario, Argentina, 1962; Physician Asst. Cert. (hon.), U. So. Calif., 1977. Medical diplomate. Pres. Midtown Svcs. Inc., L.A., 1973—; dir. internat. affairs, speaker Gov. of Papua, New Guinea, 1996—; dir., CFO World Film Inst., 1996—; dir. internat. affairs, speaker on humanitarian, cultural and econ. matters Govt. of Papua New Guinea; advocate, internat. spkr. for women, children and animal rights. Chmn. bd. Am.'s Film Inst., Washington; chmn. bd. trustees World Film Inst, Dir. Intl. Affairs, speaker-Humanitarian, Economic and Cultural Consulate of Papua New Guinea, Los Angeles, Calif. Nominated chairwoman of bd. trustees World Film Inst. Fellow Am. Acad. Physicians' Assts.; mem. Bus. for Law Enforcement (northeast divsn.), Physicians for Social Responsibility, Mercy Crusade Inc., Internat. Found. for Survival Rsch., Noetic Scis. Soc., Inst. Noetic Scis., So. Calif. Alliance for Survival, Supreme Emblem Club of U.S., Order Eastern Star, Flying Samaritans, Shriners.

SIMMS, MARIA KAY, publishing and computer services executive; b. Princeton, Ill., Nov. 18, 1940; d. Frank B. and Anna (Haurberg) S.; m. Neil F. Michelsen, Oct. 2, 1987 (dec. 1990); children: Shannon Sullivan Stillings, Molly A. Sullivan, Elizabeth Maria Jossick. BFA, Ill. Wesleyan U., 1962. Cert. cons. profl. astrologer; ordained min. L.A. Cmty. Ch. of Religious Sci. Elder priestess Covenant of the Goddess; art tchr. elem. and jr. high pub. schs., Dundee, Northbrook, Ill., 1962-65; high sch. art tchr. Danbury, Conn., 1975-76; self employed gallery painter various cities, 1962-77, free-lance comml. illustrator, 1972-74, 86-87; shop, gallery, café owner Conn., 1976-79; art dir. ACS Pubs., Inc., San Diego, Calif., 1987-90; pres. Astro Comm. Svcs., Inc. (formerly ACS Pubs.), San Diego, 1990—; conf. lectr. United Astrology Congress, 1986, 89, 92, 95, Am. Fedn. Astrologers Internat. Conv., 1982, 84, 86, 88, 90, 92, 94, 96. Author: Twelve Wings of the Eagle, 1988, Dial Detective, 1989; co-author: Search for the Christmas Star, 1989, Circle of the Cosmic Muse, 1994, Your Magical Child, 1994, Future Signs, 1996, The Witch's Circle, 1996; contbr. numerous articles to mags. High priestee Cir. of the Cosmic Muse; elder priestess Covenant of the Goddess, 2d officer Calafia Local Coun., 1995-96, pub. info. officer, 1996-97. Recipient numerous art awards. Mem. Nat. Assn. Women Bus. Owners, Nat. Coun. Geocosmic Rsch. Inc. (dir., pubs. dir. 1981-92, editor jour. 1984-92), Am. Fedn. Astrologers, Internat. Soc. Astrol. Rsch., New Age Pubs. Assn. Office: Astro Comm Svcs Inc 5521 Ruffin Rd San Diego CA 92123-1314

SIMMS, THOMAS HASKELL, police chief; b. Yuma, Ariz., Sept. 3, 1945; s. Jessie Lee and Mary Elizabeth (Servos) S.; divorced; m. Ginny Lee David, Mar. 26, 1988; children: Thomas Haskell Jr., Julie Marie. BA, St. Mary's Coll., Moraga, Calif., 1981; MS, Calif. Poly., Pomona, 1991. Officer Mountain View (Calif.) Police Dept., 1972-76; police sgt. East Bay Parks, Oakland, Calif., 1976-79; police lt. Town of Moraga, Calif., 1979-84, chief police, 1984-87; chief police City of Piedmont, Calif., 1987-91; chief of police City of Roseville, Calif., 1991—; mem. U. Calif.-Davis Med. Ctr. Leadership Coun.; bd. dirs. Child Abuse Prevention Coun. of Placer County, Sierra Family Svcs. Bd. dirs. Piedmont coun. Boy Scouts Am., 1988-89. Maj. U.S. Army, 1967-71, Vietnam. Mem. Calif. Chiefs Police Assn. (bd. dirs.), Calif. Peace Officers Assn., Calif. Peace Officers Meml. Found. (bd. dirs.), Rotary, Kiwanis (pres. Moraga 1982-83, Kiwanian of Yr. award 1983). Presbyterian. Office: Roseville Police Dept 311 Vernon St Roseville CA 95678-2634

SIMON, MAURYA, poet, educator; b. N.Y.C., Dec. 7, 1950; d. Robert Leopold Simon and Baila Goldenthal; m. Robert Edward Falk; children: Naomi Falk, Leah Falk. BA with honors, Pitzer Coll., 1980; MFA in English, U. Calif., Irvine, 1984. Creative writing lectr. U. Calif., Riverside, 1984-90, asst. prof. creative writing, 1991-94, assoc. prof. creative writing, 1995—; vis. poet Calif. Inst. Tech., Pasadena, 1991-97. Author: The Enchanted Room, 1986, Days of Awe, 1989, Speaking in Tongues, 1990, The Golden Labyrinth, 1995; contbr. poetry to various periodicals including The Georgia Review, Poetry, TriQuarterly, The Southern Review, Ironwood, Grand Street, The Kenyon Review, Salmagundi, The Hudson Review, The Missouri Review, Verse, The Gettysburg Review. Councilwoman San Antonio Canyon Town Hall, Mt. Baldy, Calif., 1988-92, mayor-moderator, 1992-93. Indo-Am. fellow Fulbright Found., Bangalore, India, 1989-90; recipient Gibbs Smith Poetry award Gibbs Smith Books, 1990. Mem. Poetry Soc. Am., Acad. Am. Poets, Poets & Writers. Home: PO Box 203 Mount Baldy CA 91759-0203 Office: U Calif Riverside Dept Creative Writing Calif 2116 Watkins Hal # U Riverside CA 92521

SIMON, RENEE BLATT, communications executive; b. N.Y.C., Mar. 25, 1928; d. Irving and Fanny (Miller) Blatt; m. Harry J. Simon, Mar. 22, 1949 (dec. Oct. 1977); children: Joel, Amy Simon Weiner, Matthew. BA, Adelphi U., 1947; MS, Stanford U., 1949; MLS, UCLA, 1966. Cert. tchr. jr. coll. Dir. med. libr. Comty. Hosp., Long Beach, Calif., 1966-72; elected mem. City Coun., Long Beach, 1972-78; prof. pub. adminstrn. Calif. State U., Long Beach, 1978-80; dep. dir. transp. So. Calif. Assn. Govts., L.A., 1980-87; pres. Inst. Mgmt. Comms., Long Beach, 1987—; bd. dirs. FHP Found., Long Beach, CRI Found. Articles editor: (jour.) Western Govtl. Researcher, 1988-92; contbr. feature columns to various bus. jours. and newspapers, articles to mags. Mem., past vice-chair Redevel. Agy., Long Beach, 1988—; bd. dirs. Housing Devel. Corp., Long Beach, 1991—, Internat. City Theater, Long Beach, 1992—, Long Beach Symphony Guild, 1994-95, fin. sec.; bd. dirs. Long Beach Heritage Coalition, 1989-90, pres. Recipient Ann. Susan B. Anthony award NOW, 1975, Disting. Achievement award Pi Alpha Alpha, 1981, Humanitarian award NCCJ, 1989. Mem. Am. Soc. Pub. Adminstrn. (bd. dirs., sec. 1991-92), Calif. Elected Women's Assn. for Edn. and Rsch. (founding mem.), Soroptimist Internat. (dir. comty. svc. 1993). Office: Inst Mgmt Comms 6475 E Pacific Coast Hwy # 242 Long Beach CA 90803-4296

SIMON, RICHARD DELOE, JR., internist; b. Toledo, Ohio, May 25, 1950; s. Richard DeLoe Sr. and Perla Lifsey (Hill) S.; m. Deborah Marie Simon, June 23, 1973; children: Michael Taylor, Anna DeLoe. AB in Chemistry, Whitman Coll., 1972; MD, U. Chgo., 1976; cert. in med. ethics, U. Wash., 1991. Diplomate Am. Bd. Internal Medicine, Am. Bd. Sleep Disorders Medicine. Intern internal medicine U. Chgo. Hosps. & Clinics, 1976-77, resident internal medicine, 1977-79, chief resident internal medicine, 1980; instr. in medicine U. Chgo., 1980; internist Walla Walla (Wash.) Clinic, 1981—; med. dir. Kathryn Severyns Dement Sleep Disorders Ctr. St. Mary Med. Ctr., Walla Walla, 1994—. Contbr. articles to profl. publs., chpt. to book. Saxophone soloist Walla Walla Symphony, 1994; mem. adv. bd. Walla Walla YMCA, 1982-94; mem. cmty. vision task force Walla Walla C. of C., 1995. Recipient Recognition cert. Wash. State Assn. Supervision & Curriculum Devel., 1996. Mem. ACP, Am. Soc. Law, Medicine and Ethics, Am. Sleep Disorders Assn., Walla Walla Valley Med. Soc. (pres. 1985, Physician Recognition award 1994), Wash. State Med. Soc., Walla Walla Jazz Soc. (founder, bd. dirs. 1992—). Democrat. Home: 733 Bryant St Walla Walla WA 99362-9322 Office: Walla Walla Clinic 301 W Poplar St Walla Walla WA 99362-2800

SIMON, SHEILA SANDRA, special education educator, administrator; b. N.Y.C., July 24, 1940; d. Leo and Frances (Wexler) Brown; children: Steven Marc, Scott Irwin, Sean Eric, Rebecca Shane. BA in Psychology, Lehman Coll., Bronx, 1974; MS in Spl. Edn., Coll. New Rochelle, N.Y., 1978; MS in Counseling, Loyola Marymount Coll., L.A., 1992; postgrad., UCLA, 1993—. Elem. tchr. spl. edn. N.Y.C. Pub. Schs., Bronx, 1974-79; tchr. spl. edn. Lincoln Spl. Sch., Palm Desert, Calif., 1979-83; tchr., chair dept. spel. edn. Mt. Vernon Jr. H.S. L.A. Unified Sch. Dist., 1983-86, resource specialist Revere Jr. H.S., 1986-91, outreach cons. Manual Arts H.S., 1991-94; exec. dir. spl. edn. commn. L.A. Unified Schs., 1994—. Mem. Los Angeles County Multicultural Collaborative, 1994, Los Angeles County Hate Crime Network, L.A. Roundtable for Children. Recipient Outstanding Sch. Svc. award Revere PTA, L.A., 1988. Mem. Coun. for Exceptional Children, Calif. Assn. of Resource Specialists, Calif. Assn. Counseling and Devel., Calif. Sch. Counselors, Kappa Delta Pi, Delta Kappa Gamma. Office: LA Unified Sch Dist Spl Edn Commn 450 N Grand Ave # H256 Los Angeles CA 90012-2100

SIMON, SHELDON WEISS, political science educator; b. St. Paul, Jan. 31, 1937; s. Blair S. and Jennie M. (Dim) S.; m. Charlann Lilwin Scheid, Apr. 27, 1962; 1 child, Alex Russell. BA summa cum laude, U. Minn., 1958, PhD, 1964; MPA, Princeton U., 1960; postgrad., U. Geneva, 1962-63. Asst. prof., then prof. U. Ky., 1966-75; prof. polit. sci. Ariz. State U., 1975—, chmn. dept., 1975-79, dir. Ctr. Asian Studies, 1980-88; vis. prof. George Washington U., 1965, U. B.C., Can., 1972-73, 79-80, Carleton U., 1976, Monterey Inst. Internat. Studies, 1991, 96, Am. Grad. Sch. Internat. Mgmt., 1991-92; cons. USIA Rsch. Analysis Corp., Am. Enterprise Inst. Pub. Policy Rsch., Hoover Instn., Orkand Corp., Nat. Bur. Asian Rsch. Author: Asian Neutralism and U.S. Policy, 1975, The ASEAN States and Regional Security, 1982, The Future of Asian-Pacific Security Collaboration, 1988; editor: The Military and Security in the Third World, 1978, East Asian Security in the Post-Cold War Era, 1993, Southeast Asian Security in the New Millenium, 1996; also others; contbr. articles to profl. jours., chpts. to books. Mem. Com. Fgn. Relations, Phoenix, 1976—; bd. dirs. Phoenix Little Theater, 1976-79. Grantee Am. Enterprise Inst., 1974, Earhart Found., 1979, 81, 92, 84, 88, U.S. Inst. Peace, 1994-96; Hoover Instn. fellow, 1980, 85. Mem. Am. Polit. Sci. Assn., Assn. Asian Studies, Internat. Studies Assn. (profl. ethics com. 1987-91, v.p. 1991-93), Asia Soc. (contemporary affairs com. 1987—), U.S. Coun. for Asia-Pacific Security, Phi Beta Kappa. Democrat. Jewish. Home: 5630 S Rocky Point Rd Tempe AZ 85283-2134 Office: Ariz State U Polit Sci Dept Tempe AZ 85287

SIMON, STEVEN ADAM, sculptor, educator; b. Encino, Calif., Apr. 16, 1959; s. Alvin Leonard and Simone Arlene (Hyman) S. BA in Polit. Sci., Calif. State U., Northridge, 1981, BA in 3-D Art, 1983. Pres. Monkey Man Press Pub. Co., L.A., 1980—; mem. staff tech. sculpture lab. UCLA, 1985—. One man show at Alexander Gallery, Studio City, Calif., 1987; exhibited in group shows at Orlando Gallery, Sherman Oaks, Calif., 1985, Karl Bornstein Gallery, Santa Monica, Calif., 1987, Found. for Art Resources, L.A., 1993, Venice, Calif., 1994, Drudis-Biada Art Gallery, Mount St. Mary's Coll., L.A., 1996; prin. works at Villa Buenaventura Sculpture Garden, San Juan Cosala, Mex., David Bermant Collection, Santa Ynez, Calif., Moorpark (Calif.) Coll., Cermak Plaza, Berwyn, Ill., Koke's Forest, Naperville, Ill., Fitzgerald's Park, Cork, Ireland; author: (poems) I'm Not Sure What You're Saying, But I Can Relate, 1980, Brace For The Impact, 1986. Recipient Ann. Conv. award Am. Lung Assn., 1986. Studio: 17945 Topham St Encino CA 91316-7125 Office: UCLA Dept Art 405 Hilgard Ave Los Angeles CA 90024-1301

SIMON, WILLIAM LEONARD, film and television writer and producer, author; b. Washington, Dec. 3, 1930; s. Isaac B. and Marjorie (Felsteiner) S.; m. Arynne Lucy Abeles, Sept. 18, 1966; 1 child, Victoria Marie; 1 stepson, Sheldon M. Bermont. BEE, Cornell U., 1954; MA in Ednl. Psychology, Golden State U., 1982, PhD in Comm., 1983. Writer features and TV movies, documentary and indsl. films, TV programs, 1958—; lectr. George Washington U., Washington, 1968-70; juror Coun. on Nontheatrical Events Film Festival, 1975-90, Cindy Festival Blue Ribbon Panel, 1985—; jury chmn., bd. dirs. CINE film festival, 1990—. Writer more than 600 produced works for motion pictures and TV, including (screenplays) Fair Woman Without Discretion, Majorca, Swindle, A Touch of Love, (teleplays and documentaries) From Information to Wisdom, Flight of Freedom II, Missing You, (home video) Star of India, Combat Vietnam series; writer, prodr.: The Star of India: Setting Sail; co-author: Profit from Experience—The Story of Transformation Management (best seller), 1995, Lasting Changes, 1997; author: Beyond the Numbers, 1996. Pres. Foggy Bottom Citizens Assn., 1963-65, mem. exec. bd., 1965-69; v.p. Shakespeare Summer Festival, 1966-67, trustee, 1965-70; mem. interview com. Cornell U., 1987-88. Lt. USN, 1954-58. Recipient 12 Golden Eagle awards Cine Film Festival, gold medal N.Y. Internat. Festival, gold medal Freedoms Found., IFPA Gold Cindy; awards Berlin, Belgrade and Venice film Festivals, numerous others. Mem. Nat. Acad. TV Arts and Scis. (gov. D.C. chpt. 1970-73), Writers Guild Am., Am. Film Inst., Internat. Documentary Assn., Rotary (bd. dirs., program chmn.), Eta Kappa Nu (chpt. pres. 1953-54), Tau Beta Pi. Republican. Home: 6151 Paseo Delicias PO Box 2048 Rancho Santa Fe CA 92067-2048

SIMONDS, JOHN EDWARD, newspaper editor; b. Boston, July 4, 1935; s. Alvin E. and Ruth Angeline (Rankin) S.; m. Rose B. Muller, Nov. 16, 1968; children—Maximillian P., Malia G.; children by previous marriage—Rachel F., John B. B.A., Bowdoin Coll., 1957. Reporter Daily Tribune, Seymour, Ind., 1957-58, UPI, Columbus, Ohio, 1958-60; reporter, asst. city editor Providence Jour. Bull., 1960-65, Washington Evening Star, 1965-66; corr. Gannett News Svc., Washington, 1966-75; mng. editor Honolulu Star Bull., 1975-80, exec. editor, 1980-87, sr. editor, editorial page editor, 1987-93; exec. Hawaii Newspaper Agy., Honolulu, 1993—. Served with U.S. Army, 1958. Mem. Am. Soc. Newspaper Editors, AP Mng. Editors, Soc. Profl. Journalists, Nat. Conf. Editorial Writers. Home: 5316 Nehu Pl Honolulu HI 96821-1941 Office: Hawaii Newspaper Agy 605 Kapiolani Blvd Honolulu HI 96813-5129

SIMONDS, PAUL EMERY, anthropologist; b. Ojai, Calif., Dec. 19, 1932; s. William Edward Simonds and Helen Adelia (Brandt) McGrew; m. Ann Gibson, Dec. 21, 1963; 1 child, William Edward. BA in Anthropology, U. Calif., Berkeley, 1954, MA in Anthropology, 1959, PhD in Anthropology, 1963. From instr. to assoc. prof. U. Oreg., Eugene, 1962-75, prof., 1975—, head dept. anthropology, 1989-93; pres. univ. senate U. Oreg., 1994-96. Sec. Lane Humane Soc., Eugene, 1968. Grantee NIH, India, 1961, 63, Nat. Geographic, India, 1975. Fellow Internat. Soc. Primatologists, Am. Soc. Primatologists, Am. Assn. Phys. Anthropologists, Royal Anthropol. Inst., Bombay Natural Hist. Soc. Republican. Office: U Oreg Anthropology Dept Eugene OR 97403

SIMONEIT, BERND ROLF TATSUO, geochemistry educator; b. Heilbronn, Republic of Germany, Sept. 7, 1937; came to U.S., 1952; s. Kurt Erich and Anna (Dietrich) S.; m. Lynda J. Wells, June 17, 1961 (div. Mar. 1966); m. Doreen Joy Gee, Sept. 7, 1968; 1 adopted child, Amanda Jane Houlding. BS, U. R.I., 1960; postgrad., MIT, 1961, 64; PhD, U. Bristol, Eng., 1975. Chemist A.C. Lawrence Leather Co., Peabody, Mass., 1962-63; spectroscopist space sci. lab. U. Calif., Berkeley, 1965-70, assoc. specialist space sci. lab., 1970-72, specialist space sci. lab., 1972-73; assoc. rsch. geochemist UCLA, 1976-81; assoc. prof. sch. oceanography Oreg. State U., Corvallis, 1981-83, prof. coll. oceanography, 1983—; cons. EG&G Idaho, Inc., Idaho Falls, 1983-92, Refineria de Petroleo, SA, Concon, Chile, 1990—, Chevron Petroleum Tech. Co., La Habra, 1992—; mem. NASA Exobiology Adv. Panel, Washington, 1980-85; mem., chmn. deep sea drilling project Joint Oceanographic Instns. for Deep Earth Sampling Orgn. Geochemisty Adv. Panel, Washington, 1978-83; vis. faculty assoc. Calif. Inst. of Tech., Pasadena, 1995—; vis. prof. Ctr. d'Investigacio Desenvolupement, Consell Superior d'Investigacions Sci., Barcelona, Spain, 199. Editor: Organic Geochemistry, 1982-87, 90—, Applied Geochemistry, 1992—; co-editor: Gulf and Peninsular Province of the Californias, 1990; contbr. articles to profl. jours. Recipient Best Paper of Yr. award Geochemical Soc., 1977, 81. Mem. AAAS, Internat. Assn. Geochemistry and Cosmochemistry, Am. Assn. for Aerosol Rsch., Internat. Soc. for the Study of the Orgin of Life, Am. Assn. Petroleum Geologists, Am. Chem. Soc., Am. Geophys. Union, Am. Soc. for Mass Spectrometry, European Assn. for Organic Geochemistry. Office: Oreg State U Coll Oceanic & Atmospheric Scis Oceanography Adminstrn Bldg 104 Corvallis OR 97331-5501

SIMON-GILLO, JEHANNE E., physicist; b. Liege, Belgium, Mar. 27, 1963; came to U.S., 1967; d. Nicolas Victor and Noelle Marie (Van Den Peereboom) Simon; m. Andrew James Gillo, June 9, 1990. BS, Juniata Coll., 1985; PhD, Tex. A&M U., 1991. Postdoctoral work Los Alamos (N.Mex.) Nat. Lab., 1991-94, staff mem., physicist, 1994—; project mgr. PHENIX Multiplicity Vertex Detector. Mem. Am. Chem. Soc., Am. Phys. Soc. Republican. Roman Catholic. Office: Los Alamos Nat Lab H846 LANL Los Alamos NM 87545

SIMONIAN, DEBRA LYN, dietitian, educator; b. Fresno, Calif., Sept. 27, 1951; d. Johnny Oscar and Louise Peggy (Nahabedian) S. BA in Home Econs., Calif. State U., Fresno, 1975, MBA, 1987. Registered dietitian. Staff dietitian, dietetic/nutrition svcs. Valley Children's Hosp., Fresno, 1978-80, asst. dir. dietetic/nutrition svcs., 1980-83, dir. dietetic/nutrition svcs., 1983—; lectr. Calif. State U., Fresno, 1988-93; instr. Kings River C.C., Reedley, Calif., 1992-93; self-employed lectr. and cons., Fresno, 1987—; sec.-treas. Calif. Dietetic Assn. Found., Playa del Rey, 1994-95. Author: Hunger in Fresno County, 1986, How to Start a Business in Fresno County, 1987; editor: Dietitian's Pediatric Handbook, 1990. Mem. Fresno Women's Network, 1987, Jr. League of Fresno, 1989. Mem. Calif. Dietetic Assn. (sec.-treas. 1994—, awards com. 1993-94), Calif. Dietetic Assn./Ctrl. Valley Dist. (pres. 1989-91). Democrat. Office: Valley Children's Hosp 3151 N Millbrook Ave Fresno CA 93703-1425

SIMONIAN, LANE PETER, history educator; b. Walnut Creek, Calif., Nov. 14, 1960; s. Simon and Cecelia (Arkelian) S. BA, U. Nev., Reno, 1982; MA, U. Calif., Davis, 1984; PhD, U. Calif., Santa Barbara, 1992. Tchg. asst. U. Calif., Davis, 1982-85, Santa Barbara, 1986-90; instr. Truckee Meadows C.C., Reno, 1993—. Author: Defending the Land of the Jaguar: A History of Conservation in Mexico, 1995; contbr. articles to profl. jours. U.S.-Mexus grantee, 1990. Mem. Am. Soc. for Environ. History, L.Am. Studies Assn., Am. Hist. Assn., Forest History Soc. Democrat. Home: 2800 W Moana Ln Reno NV 89509 Office: Truckee Meadows CC 4001 S Virginia St Reno NV 89502

SIMONOWITZ, DAVID ALAN, surgeon; b. New London, Conn., Dec. 4, 1946; s. George and Mary (Gilman) S.; m. Jean Weaver, Sept. 1967 (div. 1977); m. Barbara A. Joiner Lewandowski, Apr. 22, 1978; 1 child, Ethan Walter. Student, U. Conn., 1966; MD, U. Chgo., 1970. Lic. physician, Wash., Ill.; diplomate Am. Bd. Surgery. Intern dept. surgery straight surg. U. Chgo. Hosps., 1970-71, jr. asst. resident gen. surgery, 1971-72, asst. resident, 1974-75, sr. resident, 1975-76, chief resident, 1976-77; asst. prof. surgery U. Wash., 1977-82, clin. asst. prof., 1982-94; clin. assoc. prof. U. Chgo. Hosps., 1994—; clin. asst. prof. surgery Coll. Osteo. Medicine of Pacific, 1985-86; pvt. practice, 1982—; dir. Nutrition Support Svc., 1978-82, Out-Patient Surgery Clinics, 1978-82; sec.-treas. Overlake Hosp., 1984, chief surgery, 1986-88, chief quality assurance/utilization rev., 1988—; presenter various orgns. Contbr. articles to profl. jours. Maj. U.S. Army, 1972-74, Korea. Univ. scholar U. Conn., 1964-66; recipient Hilgar Perry Jenkins award for excellence in performance of acad. and patient oriented svc., 1972-77. Fellow ACS (program com. state chpt. 1981-82); mem. Am. Soc. Gen. Surgeons, Assn. Acad. Surgery, King County Med. Soc., Henry Harkins Surg. Soc., Am. Soc. Parenteral and Enteral Nutrition, Soc. for Surgery of Alimentary Tract, Seattle Surg. Soc., Collegium Internat. Chirurgiae Digestivae, North Pacific Surg. Assn., Pacific Coast Surg. Office: 1700 116th Ave NE Bellevue WA 98004-3022

SIMONS, ANNETTE, performing company executive; b. N.Y.C., June 7, 1953; d. Eloy and Mary (Quiñones) S. BA, Loyola-Marymount U., 1975; MFA, Bklyn. Coll., CUNY, 1990. Legal specialist Pettit & Martin, L.A., 1977-88; devel. adminstr. N.Y.C. Ballet, 1988-90; dir. grant writing The Music Ctr., L.A., 1990-93; mng. dir. L.A. Baroque Orch., Santa Monica, 1993—; permissions specialist Calliope Media, Santa Monica, 1995-96; dir. devel. comms. The Music Ctr., L.A., 1996—. Commr. Santa Monica Arts Commn., 1992—. Office: LA Baroque Orch 1223 Wilshire Blvd # 686 Santa Monica CA 90403-5400

SIMONS, RICHARD KEITH, medical educator; b. Leicester, U.K., Apr. 29, 1952; s. Robert William and Audry Joyce (Robinson) S.; m. Christine Mary Willick, May 12, 1984; children: Jonathan Robert, Mark Alexander, Philip Arthur. BA, Cambridge U., London, 1973, MA, 1976, MB, BCh, 1976. Diplomate Am. Bd. Surgery, U.K. Gen. Med. Coun.; MD Calif. Med. Bd. Clin. instr. U. Wash., Seattle, 1990-91; asst. prof. U. Calif., San Diego, 1991-96, U. B.C., Vancouver, 1996—; attending physician U. Calif. San Diego Med. Ctr., 1991-96, ethics com., 1993-96, infection control com., 1993-96; chair ATLS subcom. San Diego County ACS/COT, 1991-96. Contbr. articles to profl. jours. Grantee U. Calif. San Diego Acad. Senate, 1992-94. Fellow ACS, Royal Coll. Surgeons Eng., Royal Coll. Surgeons Can.; mem. Am. Assn. Surgery Trauma, Surg. Infection Soc. (fellow 1985-86), Shock Soc. Office: Univ BC Dept Surgery, 855 W 10th St, Vancouver, BC Canada V5Z 4E3

SIMONS, ROGER MAYFIELD, tax specialist; b. Portland, Oreg., Oct. 11, 1926; s. George M. and Ruth (Brunn) S. m. Abigail Wise, Aug. 23, 1954; children: Deborah, Sandra. BS, Stanford U., 1949; MS, MIT, 1950, PhD, 1955. Enrolled agt. Applied sci. rep. IBM, various locations, 1955-59; staff mathematician IBM, San Jose, 1959-63, sr. programmer, 1963-90; owner Simons Tax Svc., San Jose, 1980—. Contbr. articles to profl. jours. Instr. SeniorNet, San Jose, 1995—; dir. ACLU, San Jose, 1960. With USN, 1944-46. Mem. Mission Soc. Enrolled Agts. (dir. 1985), Assn. for Computing Machinery (Bay Area chpt. chmn. 1959). Home and Office: 20744 Scenic Vista Dr San Jose CA 95120-1212

SIMONS, STEPHEN, mathematics educator, researcher; b. London, Aug. 11, 1938; came to U.S., 1965; s. Jack Isidore Simons and Ethel Esther (Littman) Harris; m. Jacqueline Mania Berchadsky, Aug. 13, 1963; 1 son, Mark. BA, Cambridge U., Eng., 1959, PhD, 1962. Instr. U. B.C., Vancouver, Can., 1962-63; asst. prof. U. BC., Vancouver, Can., 1964-65; asst. prof. U. Calif., Santa Barbara, 1965-67, assoc. prof., 1967-73, prof., 1973—, chmn. dept., 1975-77, 88-89; trustee Math. Scis. Rsch. Inst., Berkeley, Calif., 1988-94. Peterhouse rsch. fellow, Cambridge U., 1963-64. Mem. Am. Math. Soc., Inst. for Ops. Rsch. and Mgmt. Scis. Office: Univ Calif Dept Math Santa Barbara CA 93106

SIMONSEN, RICHARD SEVERIN, retired aerospace engineer; b. Hollywood, Calif., Nov. 25, 1932; s. Irving P. and Margaret M. (Knox) S.; m. Marilynn Joy Johnson, June 1, 1955; children: Lynda G. Sheasley, Richard R. BS in Engring., UCLA, 1955; postgrad., Harvard U., 1984, U. Calif., Davis, 1980. Engr. Marquardt Aircraft Co., Van Nuys, Calif., 1955-56; engr., program mgr. Aerojet Gen. Corp., Sacramento, 1959-62, mgr. test ops., 1962-78, dir. product and environ. assurance, 1978-80, v.p., gen. mgr. propulsion divsn., 1980-86, pres. solid propulsion co., 1986-90, pres. propulsion co., 1990-93, corp. exec. v.p., 1993-95, ret., 1995. Pres. Sta. KVIE-TV, PBS, Sacremento, 1992-93, bd. dirs. 1987-93; v.p. fin. Boy Scouts Am. for Northern Calif., 1996. Named Engring. Alumnus of Yr. UCLA, 1993. Mem. Soc. Logistics Engrs. AIAA, Assn. U.S. Army, USAF Assn., mem. Boy's Scout of Am., 1996. Republican. Home: 101 Swift River Dr Folsom CA 95630-1521

SIMONSON, SUSAN KAY, hospital administrator; b. La Porte, Ind., Dec. 5, 1946; d. George Randolph and Myrtle Lucille (Opfel) Menkes; m. Richard

Bruce Simonson, Aug. 25, 1973. BA with honors, Ind. U., 1969; MA, Washington U., St. Louis, 1972. Perinatal social worker Yakima Valley Meml. Hosp., Yakima, Wash., 1979-81, dir. patient support and hospice program, 1981—, dir. social svc., 1982—; instr. Spanish, ethnic studies, sociology Yakima Valley Coll., Yakima, Wash., 1981—; pres. Yakima Child Abuse Council, 1983-85; developer nat. patient support program, 1981. Contbr. articles to profl. jours. Mem. Jr. League, Yakima; mem. adv. council Robert Wood Johnson Found. Rural Infant Health Care Project, Yakima, 1980, Pregnancy Loss and Compassionate Friends Support Groups, Yakima, 1982—, Teen Outreach Program, Yakima, 1984—. Recipient NSF award, 1967, discharge planning program of yr. regional award Nat. Glasrock Home Health Care Discharge Planning Program, 1987; research grantee Ind. U., 1968, Fulbright grantee U.S. Dept. State, 1969-70; Nat. Def. Edn. Act fellowship, 1970-73. Mem. AAUW, Soc. Med. Anthropology, Soc. Hosp. Social Work Dirs. of Am. Hosp. Assn. (regional award 1989), Nat. Assn. Social Workers, Phi Beta Kappa. Office: Yakima Valley Meml Hosp 2811 Tieton Dr Yakima WA 98902-3761

SIMONTACCHI, CAROL NADINE, nutritionist, retail store executive; b. Bellingham, Wash., July 6, 1947; d. Ralph Eugene and Sylvia Arleta (Tyler) Walmer; m. Bob Simontacchi, Oct. 3, 1981; children: Caryl Anne, Bobbie Anne, Melissa Anne, Laurie Anne. BS in Health and Human Svcs., Columbia Pacific U., 1996, postgrad., 1996—. Cert. nutritionist, Wash. CEO The Health Haus, Inc., Vancouver, Wash., 1985—; host radio program Back to the Beginning, Vancouver, 1990—; CEO The Natural Physician Ctr., Beaverton, Oreg., 1995—, Enique Internat., 1995—; chair bd. dirs. Enique Internat., 1996—. Author: Your Fat is Not Your Fault, 1994, 97, The Sun Rise Book: Living Beyond Depression, 1996. Mem. Soc. Cert. Nutritionists (pres. bd. 1992-93), Nat. Nutritional Foods Assn. (chair edn. com. 1996—), Internat. and Am. Assns. Clin. Nutritionists. Republican. Christian Ch. Office: The Health Haus Inc 101 E 8th St Ste 250 Vancouver WA 98660-3294

SIMPSON, ALAN KOOI, former senator; b. Cody, Wyo., Sept. 2, 1931; s. Milward Lee and Lorna (Kooi) S.; m. Ann Schroll, June 21, 1954; children—William Lloyd, Colin Mackenzie, Susan Lorna. BS, U. Wyo., 1954, JD, 1958; LLD (hon.), Calif. Western Sch. of Law, 1983, Colo. Coll., 1986, Notre Dame U., 1987; JD (hon.), Am. U., 1989. Bar: Wyo. 1958, U.S. Supreme Ct. 1964. Asst. atty. gen. State of Wyo., 1959; city atty. City of Cody, 1959-69; partner firm Simpson, Kepler, and Simpson, Cody, Wyo., 1959-78; mem. Wyo. Ho. of Reps., 1964-77, majority whip, 1973-75, majority floor leader, 1975-77, speaker pro tem, 1977; legis. participant Eagleton Inst. Politics, Rutgers U., 1971; mem. U.S. Senate from Wyo., 1978-96, asst. majority leader, 1985-87, asst. minority leader, 1987-95, chmn. vets. affairs com., chmn. fin. subcom. on Social Security and Family Policy, chmn. subcom. on immigration and refugee policy; mem. Sen. Rep. Policy Com. Spec. Com. on Aging; guest lectr. London exchange program Regent's Coll., London, 1987. Formerly v.p., trustee N.W. C.C., Powell, Wyo., 1968-76; trustee Buffalo Bill Hist. Ctr., Cody, Grand Teton Music Festival; del. Nat. Triennial Episcopal Ch. Conv., 1973, 76. With U.S. Army, 1954-56. Recipient Nat. Assn. Land Grant Colls. Centennial Alum award U. Wyo., 1987, Lifetime Svc. award Vietnam Vets. Am., 1993. Mem. Wyo. Bar Assn., Park County Bar Assn., Fifth Jud. Dist. Bar Assn., Am. Bar Assn., Assn. Trial Lawyers Am., U. Wyo. Alumni Assn. (pres. 1962, 63, Disting. Alumnus award 1985), VFW (life), Am. Legion, Amvets. (Silver Helmet award). Lodges: Eagles, Elks, Masons (33 deg.), Shriners, Rotary (pres. local club 1972-73). *

SIMPSON, ANDREA LYNN, energy communications executive; b. Altadena, Calif., Feb. 10, 1948; d. Kenneth James and Barbara Faries Simpson; m. John R. Myrdal, Dec. 13, 1986; 1 child, Christopher Ryan Myrdal. BA, U. So. Calif., 1969, MS, 1983; postgrad. U. Colo., Boulder Sch. Bank Mktg., 1977. Asst. cashier United Calif. Bank, L.A., 1969-73; asst. v.p. mktg. 1st Hawaiian Bank, Honolulu, 1973-78; v.p. corp. comm. BHP Hawaii, Inc. (formerly Pacific Resources, Inc.), Honolulu, 1978—. Bd. dirs. Arts Coun. Hawaii, 1977-81, Hawaii Heart Assn., 1978-83, Coun. Pacific Girl Scouts U.S., 1982-85, Child and Family Svcs., 1984-86, Honolulu Symphony Soc., 1985-91, Sta. KHPR Hawaii Pub. Radio, 1988-92, Kapiolani Found., 1990-95, Hanahauoli Sch., 1991—; bd. dirs., 2nd. v.p. Girl Scout Coun. Hawaii, 1994-96, adv. bd., 1996—; trustee Hawaii Loa Coll., 1984-86, Kapiolani Women's and Children's Hosp., 1988—, Hawaii Sch. For Girls at LaPietra, 1989-91, Kapiolani Med. Ctr. at Pali Momi, 1994—; commr. Hawaii State Commn. on Status of Women, 1985-87, State Sesquecentennial of Pub. Schs. Commn., 1990-91; bd. dirs. Hawaii Strategic Devel. Corp., 1991—, Children's Discovery Ctr., 1994—, Pacific Asian Affairs Coun., 1994-96, adv. dir. Hawaii Kids at Work, 1991—, Hawaii Mothers Against Drunk Driving, 1992-96. Named Panhellenic Woman of Yr. Hawaii, 1979, Outstanding Woman in Bus. Hawaii YWCA, 1980, Hawaii Legis., 1980, Outstanding Young Woman of Hawaii Girl Scouts Coun. of the Pacific, 1985, 86. Mem. Internat. Pub. Rels. Assn. (Golden World award 1997), Am. Mktg. Assn., Pub. Rels. Soc. Am. (bd. dirs. Honolulu chpt. 1984-86, Silver Anvil award 1984, Pub. Rels. Profl. Yr. 1991, Silver Anvil award of excellence 1996), Utilities Communicators Internat. (Communicator of Yr. 1984), Honolulu Advt. Fedn. (Advt. Woman of Yr. 1984), U. So. Calif. Alumni Assn. (bd. dirs. Hawaii 1981-83), Outrigger Canoe Club, Pacific Club, Rotary (pub. rels. chmn. 1988-97, Honolulu chpt.), Alpha Phi (past pres., dir. Hawaii), Hawaii Jaycees (Outstanding Young Person of Hawaii 1978). Office: BHP Hawaii Inc 733 Bishop St Ste 2700 Honolulu HI 96813-4022

SIMPSON, BOB G., retired quality assurance professional; b. DeWitt, Ark., Feb. 20, 1932; s. Fearmon Lambert Simpson and Myrtle Elsie (Lowrance) Simpson Palmer. BS in Physics., U. Ctrl. Ark., 1962. Quality/reliabilty engr. Motorola Inc., Phoenix, 1963-70; reliability engr. Motorola Inc., Mesa, Ariz., 1973-74; component engr. Control Data Corp., Tucson, 1971-73; mgr., supr. quality assurance Engineered Sys. Inc., Tempe, 1976-97, plant facilities mgr., 1996-97. Mem. Greater Phoenix Ch. of God; former chmn. coun. Phoenix Ch. of God Internat.With USN, 1951-55; with AEC Contractor, 1957-59.

SIMPSON, C. DENE, clinical neuropsychologist, psychophysiologist; b. Ashland, Ky., Sept. 16, 1936; s. Curtis Zotto and Clarice Loraine Simpson; m. Margaret Louise Cline, Aug. 17, 1956; children: René, Michelle, Yvonne. BA, Bethany Nazarene Coll., 1958; MA, U. Kans., 1962; PhD, U. Okla., Oklahoma City, 1974. Lic. psychologist, Idaho, Okla.; diplomate Nat. Registry Neurofeedback Providers; cert. polygraph examiner. Statis. analyst Ford Motor Co., Claycomo, Mo., 1959-63; prof. N.W. Nazarene Coll., Nampa, Idaho, 1963-66, head Dept. of Psychology, 1970-88; prof. Bethany (Okla.) Nazarene Coll., 1966-67; rsch. psychologist Okla. Med. Rsch. Found., Oklahoma City, 1967-68, Okla. Ctr. for Alcohol Related Studies, Oklahoma City, 1968-70; clin. neuropsychologist Boise, Idaho, 1976—; pres. Human Tech., Inc., Boise, 1985-94; cons. VA Med. Ctr., Boise; vis. prof. U. St. Andrews, Scotland, 1988; cons. neuropsychologist Intermountain Hosp. of Boise, 1983—. Contbr. sci. articles to profl. jours. Mem. The Nature Conservancy, 1988—, The Perringrine Fund, Boise, 1988—, World Ctr. for Birds of Prey. Fellow NSF-U. Mo., 1967, Nat. Def. Edn. Act-U. Okla., 1968-70; equipment grantee Nat. Sci. Found.-N.W. Nazarene Coll., 1978-79. Fellow Idaho Psychol. Assn. (pres. 1974-77, exec. bd. 1988); mem. Am. Psychol. Assn., Western Psychol. Assn., Internat. Neuropsychology Soc., Nat. Acad. Neuropsychology, Am. Polygraph Assn., Nat. Polygraph Assn., Am. Assn. Christian Counselors. Republican. Mem. Ch. of the Nazarene. Home: 979 Strawberry Ln Boise ID 83712-7724 Office: 317 Allumbaugh St Boise ID 83704-9208

SIMPSON, CAROLYN MARIE, critical care nurse; b. Boise, Idaho, Mar. 1, 1950; d. Thomas Michael and Eva Lucille (Hieter) Sliman; m. Jon E. Simpson, Feb. 17, 1973; children: Christy Lynn, David Jon. Diploma, St. Elizabeth Sch. Nursing, 1971. Cert. utilization rev. and managed care ACLS, CCRN, TNCC. Staff nurse St. Elizabeth's Hosp., Yakima, Wash., 1971-72, Vancouver Meml. Hosp., 1972-73; relief house supervisor Tri-State Meml. Hosp., Clarkston, Wash., 1973-75; charge nurse VA Hosp., Vancouver, 1975-83, Bess Kaiser, Portland, Oreg., 1984-96; staff nurse SW Wash. Med. Ctr., Portland, Oreg., 1995—; med.-legal cons., lectr. Bess Kaiser, AACN; owner And All That Stuff. Leader Girl Scouts U.S., Portland. Mem. AACN, Am. Homebusiness Assn., Oreg. Nurses Assn. (exec. com. 1988, gen. welfare 1989), Eagles Aux., Women of the Moose. Roman Catholic. Home: 5017 NE 139th Ave Vancouver WA 98682-6388

SIMPSON, CHARLES ROBERT, marketing professional. BS in Bus. Adminstrn., U. Tenn., 1971; MBA in Mktg., Bloomfield Coll., 1973. Gen. ptnr. Simpson Constrn. and Restoration, Paterson, N.J., 1972-79; v.p. sales and mktg. The Jim Walter Corp., Tampa, Fla., 1979-83; v.p. franchise mktg. Comml. Credit/Control Data, Mpls., 1983-84; v.p. acquisitions Equity Program Investment Corp., Falls Church, Va., 1984-85; pres., gen. mgr. Simpson Mktg. Group, Chandler, Ariz., 1985-87; v.p. mktg. and sales Hooker U.S.A., L.J. Hooker Homes, L.J. Hooker Internat., Phoenix, Atlanta, Dallas, 1987-91; cons. Resolution Trust Corp.-Oversight Bd., Phoenix, Denver, 1991—; lectr. Ariz. State U., Tempe, Harvard U. Grad. Sch. Bus. Contbg. editor of rsch. recommendations in weekly publs. Mem. Habitat for Humanities; adv. bd. Resolution Trust Corp.; mem. Greenspeace; past mem. bd. dirs. Verde Valley Sch., Sedona, Ariz. Recipient Pacesetter award Nat. Assn. Homebuilders, 1989, MIRM designation, 1988, MAME award in a career total of 21 categories, 1987-90, Nat. MIRM award, 1988. Mem. Nat. Trust for Hist. Preservation, Nat. Park and Wildlife Fedn., Benevolent Protective Order of Elks, Univ. Club, Essex County Hist. Soc. (past pres.). Office: PO Box 31203 Phoenix AZ 85046-1203

SIMPSON, DAVE, radio producer; b. Rantoul, Ill., Oct. 5, 1960; s. Ronald James and Janet Kay (Smith) S.; m. Karen Wilson, Nov. 3, 1984; children: Katherine, Allison. BS in Quantitative Psychology, UCLA, 1984. Program dir. Sierra Ski and Pack Club, L.A., 1983-88; co-dir. KVMR Broadcast Tng. Course, Nevada City, Calif., 1992—; ind. producer Nat. Pub. Radio Pub. Radio Satellite, Washington, 1993—. Producer, host The Morning Show, Mediawatch, Required Reading, Late Night Eclectica KVMR-FM, Nevada City, 1988—; author: The Art and Technique of Radio Broadcasting, 1993. Mem. Media Alliance, Soc. Profl. Journalists.

SIMPSON, GARY LAVERN, public health medical executive; b. St. Louis, Jan. 3, 1947; m. Sandra Cheryl Lapham; children: Cassandra Alyn, Courtney Meredith. BS, U. Ill., 1969, MS, 1970, PhD, 1973; MD, Rush Med. Coll., Chgo., 1974; MSc in Clin. Medicine, U. Oxford, Eng., 1977; MPH in Tropical Pub. Health, Harvard U., 1978. Diplomate Mass. Bd. Med. Examiners, Am. Bd. Internal Medicine, Calif. Bd. Med. Examiners, N.Mex. Bd. Med. Examiners. Intern Peter Bent Brigham Hosp., Boston, 1974-75, resident, 1975-76; sr. registrar in internal medicine/infectious diseases U. Oxford, Clin. Med. Sch., Radcliffe Infirmary, Eng., 1976-77; fellow infectious diseases divsn. infectious diseases Stanford (Calif.) U., 1978-79; asst. prof. medicine divsn. infectious diseases U. N.Mex., Albuquerque, 1979-83, clin. assoc. prof. medicine, 1983-88; attending physician Presbyn. Healthcare Svcs., Albuquerque, 1987-89; med. dir. infectious diseases Pub. Health divsn. Dept. Health, State of N.Mex., Santa Fe, 1992—; teaching asst. U. Ill., Champaign-Urbana, 1969-70, rsch. assoc., 1970-72; rsch. cons. U. N.Mex., Albuquerque, 1973-74, adj. assoc. prof. dept. biology, 1986-87; rsch. prof. dept. biology U. N.Mex., 1996—; rsch. scientist Rush Med. Sch., 1973-74; clin. fellow Harvard Med. Sch., Boston, 1974-76; dir., chief medicine Raymond Hosp., Wrentham, Mass., 1976; staff physician Children's Hosp. Med. Ctr., Boston, 1976; vis. prof. Instituto Nacional de Salud, Bogota, Colombia, 1979-80; attending physician U. N.Mex. Hosp., 1979-87, VA Med. Ctr., Albuquerque, 1980-87; assoc. scientist Lovelace Med. Found., Albuquerque, 1983-86; med. dir. Cottonwood de Albuquerque, Residential Treatment Ctr., Los Lunas, N.Mex., 1983-84, Jim Kelly Counseling Assocs., Albuquerque, 1984-86, Presbyn. Alcohol and Drug Treatment Ctr., Northside Presbyn. Hosp., Albuquerque, 1987-89; sr. cons. bur. communicable diseases AID, Dept. State, Washington, 1984—; cons. Am. Inst. Biol. Scis., Washington, 1984—; Eagleson lectr. Am. Biol. Safety Assn. 36th Annual Conf., Albuquerque, lectr. in field; vis. prof. dept. med. microbiology and sec. of infectious diseases Faculty of Medicine U. Man., Winnipeg, Can.; adj. prof. dept. biology U. M.Mex., Albuquerque, 1996—. Contbr. articles to profl. jours. Recipient Cert. award U.S. Indian Health Svc., 1995; Robert Wood Johnson fellow, 1977, Agy. for Internat. Devel. Edn. fellow, 1978, Palo Alto Med. Rsch. Found. fellow, 1979; hon. I award U. Ill. Fellow ACP; mem. AAAS, Oxford Med. Soc., Royal Soc. Tropical Medicine and Hygiene, Am. Soc. Microbiology, Am. Soc. Tropical Medicine and Hygiene, Am. Fedn. Clin. Rsch., Infectious Diseases Soc. Am., Am. Soc. Addiction Medicine (cert.). Home: 18 Senda Aliento Placitas NM 87043

SIMPSON, JOHN BERCHMAN, JR., clergy member, chaplain, retired law enforcement officer; b. Hartford, Conn., July 18, 1938; s. John Berchman Simpson and Gertrude Elizabeth; m. Yvonne Elaine McGruder, July 2, 1958 (div. May 1978); children: John B. III, Joan B. Gupton, Jeffery Brian, James Bryant, Jason Brent; m. Donna Jean Hadra, Dec. 27, 1978; children: Cheri Lynn DeBolt, Byrl Arthur Gibson, Michele Renee Thacker. BA in Journalism, Bklyn. Coll., 1963; BS in Divinity, Houston Divinity Coll., 1984, DD, 1989. Cert. protection profl., Ariz. Editor USAF, 1956-65; mng. editor Enfield (Conn.) Press, 1967; dir. pub. affairs U.S. Coast Guard Res., New London, Conn., 1970-89; pres. Loss Prevention Inst., Houston, 1980-84; asst. pastor Chapel of Prayer, Houston, 1982-84; officer, chaplain Maricopa County Sheriff's Office, Phoenix, 1985-96; pastor Chapel of Divine Faith, Scottsdale, Ariz., 1996—. Author: Retail Loss Prevention, 1983; editor Aetna-izer, 1969, The Deputy, 1986. Bd. dirs. Maricopa County Dep. Sheriff's Assn., Phoenix, 1986-93, Coun. of Chs., Houston, 1984, Phoenix, 1996; chaplain VA Hosp., Houston, 1980-84. Comdr. U.S. Coast Guard, 1989. Named Editor of Yr., Sigma Delta Chi, Hartford, 1966; recipient Medal of Valor, New Haven (Conn.) Police Dept., 1972, Disting. Svc. award VA Hosp., Houston, 1984. Mem. DAV (life), Res. Officers Assn. (life, chaplain 1993-94), U.S. Naval Inst. (life), Soc. Profl. Journalists (Pres.'s Club), Elks (1537), Fraternal Order of Police Lodge 5, Am. Legion (chaplain 1993-96, life), Ret. Officers Assn. Republican. Home: 6226 E Anaheim St Mesa AZ 85205

SIMPSON, LEWIS COLE (BUSTER SIMPSON), artist; b. Saginaw, Mich., May 29, 1942. Instr., guide Philmont Scout Ranch, Camarron, N.Mex., 1961-66; instr. Flint (Mich.) Jr. Coll., 1969; artist, cons. Redondo Seawall, Federal Way, Wash., 1988-92, New Denver Airport, 1990-91, Ctrl. Artery Tunnel, Boston, 1991-92, King Cross Railroad Lands, London, 1994-95; co-dir. Earthworks Woodstock Festival, Bethal, N.Y., 1969, Pilchuck Workshop, 1972-73; artist, cons., designer Post Alley Comp. Pike Pl. Mchts. Assn., Pike Devel. Auth., 1978-81; artist-in-residence ARTPARK, Lewiston, N.Y., 1978; artistic dir. City Fair Arts, Seattle, 1980; 1st Ave. Bus Stop Design Com., Seattle, 1983; commr. Pike Pl. Market Historic Dist. Commn., Seattle, 1983; artist Arts and Industry Program Kohler (Wis.) Co., 1984; collaborator 900 acre park Master Use Plan, Pontiac, Mich., 1987-88; vis. instr., lectr. U. N.C., Chapel Hill, 1992. Exhbns. include City Vancouver, B.C., Can., 1995, Kansas City, Mo., 1994, Miami Dade Metro, Fla., 1994, U. Wash., 1992—, Pratt Manhattan Gallery, N.Y.C., 1994, FIT Mus., N.Y.C., 1994, Honolulu Art Acad., 1994, CIA, Boston, 1994, Capp St. Project, San Francisco, 1993, Queens Mus., N.Y.C., 1992, Seattle Art Mus., 1991, Oreg. Conv. Ctr., Portland, 1991, Wash. State Conv. Ctr., Seattle, 1989, Hirshorn Mus. and Sculpture Garden, Washington, 1989, MBTA, Boston, 1986-87, Houston Festival, 1985, Portland Ctr. Visual Arts, 1985, The New Mus., N.Y.C., 1983, Pine Tree Tavern, Seattle, 1983, Spaxiozero, Rome, 1983, Inst. Art and Urban Resources, N.Y.C., 1983, Craft and Folk Art Mus., L.A., 1982, Smithsonian Mus., Washington, 1980-81, Western Front, Vancouver, 1980, Md. Inst. Coll. Art., Balt., 1980, Seattle Art Mus., 1989. Nat. Endowment Arts fellow, 1982. Home: 901 Yakima Ave S Seattle WA 98144-3146

SIMPSON, LINDA ANNE, retired police detective, municipal official; b. Greensburg, Pa., Oct. 23, 1953; d. Henry Theodore and Marceline (Krempasky) S.; m. Gail Montgomery, Jan. 10, 1977 (div. May 1981); m. Jeri Anne Sheely, July 10, 1981; children: Jessica Ann, Alexander Richard, Allison Dawn. BA, Calif. U. Pa., 1976, 78; cert., Pa. Police Acad., 1978. Asst. security supt. Rouse Svc. Co., Greensburg, 1971-77; asst. police chief Ellsworth (Pa.) Borough Police Dept., 1977-78; police officer Fallowfield Twp. Police Dept., Charleroi, Pa., 1978-80; police detective, trainer, instr., coord. field tng., supr. sex crimes unit Rock Springs (Wyo.) Police Dept., 1980-96; ret., 1996; rsch. asst. centennial com. Rock Springs Police Dept.; police instr. State of Wyo., 1982—; instr. Women's Inst., Western Wyo. Coll., Rock Springs, 1996—, actor, cons. tng. film series theater dept., 1987-88. Editor quar. newsletter Blue Knights News Wyo., 1986-92. Asst. basketball coach Spl. Olympics, Rock Springs, 1987; mem. Sweetwater County Child Protection Team, 1995-96; mem. Domestic Violence Coun., 1995-96. Recipient numerous commedations Rock Springs Police Dept., 1980-96, Outstanding Law Enforcement Officer award, 1985, Disting. Svc. medal, 1987, Svc. medal 1988. Mem. Nat. Assn. Field Tng. Officers, Police Protective Assn. (v.p. 1984-85, treas. 1990-94), Western Alliance Police Officers (v.p. 1985-87), Calif. U. Pa. Alumni Assn., Intermountain World War II Reenactment Assn., Shooting Stars Motorcycle Club (pres. 1980-84), Blue Knights Internat. Law Enforcement Motorcycle Club (pres. Wyo. chpts. 1985-92, bd. dirs. Wyo. chpt. 1 1992-96), High Desert Riders, Motorcycle Club (legis. officer 1991-94), Salt Lake Gender Consortium (mem. bd. protectors 1995-96). Home: 103 Agate St Rock Springs WY 82901-6601 Office: Rock Springs Police 221 C St Rock Springs WY 82901-6220

SIMPSON, PETER KOOI, university official; b. Sheridan, Wyo., July 31, 1930; s. Milward Lee and Lorna Helen (Kooi) S.; m. Lynne Alice Livingston, June 18, 1960; children: Milward Allen, Margaret Ann, Peter Kooi Jr. BA, U. Wyo., 1953, MA, 1962; PhD, U. Oreg., 1973. Pres. Western Hills, Inc., Billings, Cody, Wyo., 1959-61; asst. prof. history Ea. Oreg. Coll., La Grande, Oreg., 1962-65, Lane Community Coll., Eugene, Oreg., 1968-69, 70-72; instr. U. Oreg., Eugene, 1969-70; asst. to pres. Casper (Wyo.) Coll., 1974-77, coord. U.Wyo.-Casper Coll. upper div., 1976-77; dean instrn. Sheridan Coll., 1977-83, asst. to pres. for devel., dean instrn., 1983-84; v.p. for devel., alumni and univ. rels., exec. dir. Found., U. Wyo., Laramie, 1984-89, v.p. for institutional advancement, 1989-97, v.p. emeritus, 1997—; bd. dirs. Bank of Laramie. Author: The Community of Cattlemen, 1987; also articles. Mem. Wyo. Ho. of Reps., 1980-84; Rep. nominee for gov. of Wyo., 1986; bd. dirs. Wyo. Vol. Assistance Corp., Laramie, 1985-89, Casper Troopers Found., 1988—, Ivinson Meml. Hosp. Found., 1993—. Lt. USNR, 1954-60. Recipient award for signal contbn. to hist. preservation Wyo. Conservation Com., 1989; grantee Oreg. Edn. Coordinating Coun., 1971; named outstanding educator Am. Fuller and Dees, 1975, exemplary alumni U. Wyo. Coll. Arts & Scis., 1993. Mem. SAG, Wyo. Hist. Soc., Cowboy Joe Club (exec. com. 1984—), Rotary (chmn. Found. 1990-92), Masons (32 degree, K.C.C.H.), Shriners, Jesters. Episcopalian. Home: 812 Grand Ave Laramie WY 82070-3942 Office: U Wyo Found PO Box 3924 Laramie WY 82071-3924

SIMPSON, ROBERT HOUSER, orthodontist; b. Pratt, Kans., Aug. 14, 1938; s. George and Ruby Ethel (Houser) S.; m. Sally Marie Carney, Aug. 13, 1960; children: Erin Lynne, Jennifer Ashling. BA in Psychology, U. Kans., 1960; DDS, U. Mo., Kansas City, 1965, MS, 1968. Pvt. practice, orthodontist Englewood, Colo., 1968—. Past. trustee U. Mo. at Kansas City Sch. Dentistry. Mem. Am. Assn. Orthodontists, Pierre Fauchard Acad., Am. Dental Assn., Met. Denver Dental Soc. (past bd. dirs.), Arapahoe County Dental Soc. (past pres.), Rocky Mountain Dental Study Club (past pres.), Colo. Orthodontic Assn. (past pres.), U. Mo. at Kansas City Dental Sch. Alumni Assn. (past pres. Colo. chpt.), Phi Gamma Delta, Omicron Delta Kappa, Omicron Kappa Upsilon, Psi Omega Dental. Office: 7200 E Dry Creek Rd Ste A105 Englewood CO 80112-2556

SIMPSON, ROD R., city planning director; b. Ft. Knox, Ky., Jan. 14, 1962; s. Kenny Rex and Phyllis Ann (Kirk) S.; m. Janice Segars, May 19, 1990. BA in Sociology, Calif. State U.-Stanislaus, Turlock, 1985. Social worker Hemodialysis Inc., Glendale/Pasadena, Calif., 1986-88; program mgr. San Joaquin Valley Health Devel. Coun., Modesto, Calif., 1988-89; planning technician City of Patterson, Calif., 1989-90, city planner, 1990-92, planning dir., 1992—; mem., vice chair Downtown Task Force, Turlock, 1992-93; mem. consol. planning com. Stanislaus Area Assn. Govts., 1991—, mem. expressway project com., 1994-96. Mem. Am. Planning Assn., Stanislaus Planning Dirs. Assn., Kiwanis Club of Patterson. Home: 882 Whispering Pines Dr Turlock CA 95382-0458 Office: City of Patterson 33 S Del Puerto Ave Patterson CA 95363-2517

SIMS, BERNARD, food products executive; b. 1949. Grad., Gonzage U., 1971. With Virgil Hastings CPA, Moses Lake, Wash., 1971-72, Seattle First Nat. Bank, Seattle, Wash., 1972-73; v.p. fin., adminstrn. Snokist Growers, Yakima, Wash., 1973—. Office: Snokist Growers 18 W Mead Ave Yakima WA 98902-6026*

SIMS, DANIEL ALLEN, veterinarian; b. Evanston, Wyo., Feb. 25, 1943; s. Ronald Lee and Gilda Sims; m. Janice (Briggs) Sims, June 28, 1968; children: Lara Sue, Jennifer Lynn, Daniel Allen Jr., Heather Elizabeth, Jonathan David, Ronald Michael. Student, U. Wyo., 1963; DVM, Colo. State U., 1967. Owner, operator Bountiful (Utah) Dog and Cat Hosp., 1967-72; owner, operator Animal Med. Clinic, Bountiful, 1972-80, pres., CEO, 1980-90; pres., CEO Animal Clinic at 5th South Inc., Bountiful, 1990—. Coach South Davis Soccer, Bountiful, 1980-91. Mem. AVMA, Utah Vet. Med. Assn., South Davis C. of C. (bd. dirs. 1974-75), South Davis Sertoma (pres. 1976). Home: 669 N 900 E Bountiful UT 84010 Office: Animal Clinic at 5th South 463 W 500 South Bountiful UT 84010

SIMS, DARCIE DITTBERNER, grief management specialist, psychotherapist, clinical hypnotherapist; b. Milw., May 20, 1947; d. Van F. and Alicia (Haake) Dittberner; m. Robert A. Sims, Aug. 19, 1970; children: Alicia, Austin (dec.). BA in Journalism, U. N.Mex., 1969, MEd, 1971; MA in Mental Health Counseling, St. Mary's U., San Antonio, 1980; PhD, LaSalle U., 1991. Cert. counselor, N.Mex., Mich., Kans., Mo., La.; nationally cert. grief counselor, clin. hypnotherapist. Adj. prof. death and dying No. Mich. U., Marquette, 1978-79; cons. crisis mgmt. Northside Ind. Sch. Dist., San Antonio, 1981-82; adj. prof. sociology McMurry Coll., Abilene, Tex., 1983; psychotherapist Pastoral Care & Counseling Ctr., Abilene, 1983-84; dir. social svc. Hospice Abilene, 1983-84; counselor, therapist Albuquerque Pub. Sch. System, 1984-85, mental health specialist, 1985-88; dir. prevention program Crittenton Children's Psychotherapy Ctr., Kansas City, Mo., 1988-89; pvt. practice Slidell, La., 1989-91; pvt. practice, trainer N.D., 1991-92; pvt. practice, psychotherapist Albuquerque, 1992-94; hypnotherapist, psychotherapist Wenatchee, Wash., 1994 ; dir. tng. and program devel. Accord Aftercare Svcs., Louisville, 1995—; v.p. nat. bd. dirs. Compassionate Friends, Inc., Chgo.; dir. Big A and Co. Cons., Albuquerque; bd. v.p. Widowed Person's Svc. D. Dirs., Kansas City; co-chmn., keynote speaker World Gathering on Bereavement, Seattle, 1991; nat. trustee Nat. Cath. Ministries to the Bereaved, 1992—; v.p. EduVisions, Inc.; cons. in field. Author: Why Are the Casseroles Always Tuna?, 1990, Footsteps Through the Valley, 1993, Touchstones, 1993, The Other Side of Grief, 1993, Finding Your Way Through Grief, 1993, If I Could Just See Hope, 1994; author: (with others) Dear Parents; We Need Not Walk Alone, 1990, Young People and Death, 1991; author monthly column Bereavement Mag.: Grief and Humor Dept., 1987—. Troop cons. Girl Scouts Am.; state sec. Associated Care Children's Health, Albuquerque, 1985-87. Named Vol. of Yr. USAF Family Svcs., 1975. Mem. ACA, Am. Mental Health Counselor Assn., Assn. for Death Edn. and Counseling (cert. grief counselor 1983—, nat. bd. dirs. 1995—), Make Today Count Inc. (cons. 1975—, Nat. Appreciation award 1988). Office: Accord Aftercare Svcs 1941 Bishop Ln # 202 Louisville KY 40218-1927

SIMS, PAUL KIBLER, geologist; b. Newton, Ill., Sept. 8, 1918; s. Dorris Lee and Vere (Kibler) S.; m. Dolores Carsell Thomas, Sept. 15, 1940; children: Thomas Courtney, Charlotte Ann. AB, U. Ill., 1940, MS, 1942; PhD, Princeton, 1950. Spl. asst. geologist Ill. Geol. Survey, 1942-43; geologist U.S. Geol. Survey, 1943-61; prof. geology, dir. Minn. Geol. survey U. Minn., 1961-73; research geologist U.S. Geol. Survey, 1973-95, rsch. geologist emeritus, 1995—; pres. Econ. Geology Pub. Co., 1979-96; Bd. dirs. North Star Research and Devel. Inst., Mpls., 1966-73. Co-editor: Geology of Minnesota, 1972, 75th anniversary vo.. Economic Geology, 1981. Adviser Minn. Outdoor Recreation Resources Commn., 1963-67. Served with USNR, 1943-46. Recipient Meritorious Service award U.S. Dept. Interior, 1984; Goldich medal Inst. on Lake Superior Geology, 1985, Disting. Svc. award U.S. Dept. Interior, 1991. Fellow Geol. Soc. Am., Soc. Econ. Geologists (hon.; councilor 1965-68, pres. 1975, Ralph W. Marsden award medal 1989); mem. Internat. Assn. on Genesis of Ore Deposits, Internat. Union Geol. Sci. (subcom. Precambrian stratigraphy, sec. 1976-84), Assn. Am. State Geologists (hon.), Colo. Sci. Soc. (hon.). Home: 1315 Overhill Rd Golden CO 80401-4238 *Hard work and diligence can cover for a lot of deficiencies.*

SIMS, ROBERT REYNOLD, civil engineer; b. Milw., Aug. 22, 1939; s. Robert Forest and Ada (Pankow) S.; m. Nevette Mary Seaman, June 3, 1967. BSCE, U. Wis., 1963. Registered profl. engr., Calif., Nev., Ariz., Hawaii, Guam. Civil engr. assoc. County of L.A. Pub. Works, 1963-68; project mgr. VTN, Van Nuys, Calif., 1968-72; gen. mgr., exec. v.p. ESCO Internat., Guam, 1973-76; exec. v.p. Engring. Svc. Corp., Culver City, Calif.,

1976-92; pres. Robert R. Sims P.E., Inc., Rolling Hills Estates, Calif., 1991—, Land Design Cons., Inc., Pasadena, Calif., 1992—. Councilman L.A. Citizens Planning Coun., 1985—. Recipient Merit award San fernando Valley Bay Coun., 1980. Fellow Inst. for Advancement of Engring.; mem. NSPE, ASCE, Am. Cons. Engrs. Coun., Nat. Acad. Forensic Engrs., Calif. Soc. Profl. Engrs. (chpt. pres., state dir., state treas., Pres.'s award 1991, Outstanding Svc. award 1992), Calif. Soc. Profl. Engrs. Edn. Found. (founding bd. dirs. 1986-92, Outstanding Contbn. to Engring. in Sci. Cmty. award 1995). Republican. Home: 127 Cottonwood Cir Rolling Hills CA 90274-3430 Office: Land Design Cons Inc Ste 600, 225 201 S Lake Ave Pasadena CA 91101

SIMUNICH, MARY ELIZABETH HEDRICK (MRS. WILLIAM A. SIMUNICH), public relations executive; b. Chgo.; d. Tubman Keene and Mary (McCamish) Hedrick; m. William A. Simunich, Dec. 6, 1941. Student Phoenix Coll., 1967-69, Met. Bus. Coll., 1938-40. Exec. sec. sales mgr. Sta. KPHO radio, 1950-53; exec. sec. mgr. Sta. KPHO-TV, 1953-54; account exec. Tom Rippey & Assos., 1955-56; pub. rels. dir. Phoenix Symphony, 1956-62; co-founder, v.p. Paul J. Hughes Pub. Rels., Inc., 1960-65; owner Mary Simunich Pub. Rels., Phoenix, 1966-77; pub. rels. dir. Walter O. Boswell Meml. Hosp., Sun City, Ariz., 1969-85; pub. rels. cons., 1985—; pres. DARCI PR, Phoenix, 1994—, Cityscape, Inc. (formerly Citynet, Inc.), 1994—; instr. pub. rels. Phoenix Coll. Evening Sch., 1973-78. Bd. dirs. Anytown, Ariz., 1969-72; founder, sec. Friends Am. Geriatrics, 1977-86. Named Phoenix Advt. Woman of Year, Phoenix Jr. Advt. Club, 1962; recipient award Blue Cross, 1963; 1st Pl. award Ariz. Press Women, 1966. Mem. NAFE, Women in Comm., Internat. Assn. Bus. Communicators (pres. Ariz. chpt. 1970-71, dir.), Pub. Rels. Soc. Am. (sec., dir. 1976-78), Am. Soc. Hosp. Pub. Rels. (dir. Ariz. chpt. 1976-78), Nat., Ariz. Press Women. Home: 4133 N 34th Pl Phoenix AZ 85018-4771 Office: DARCI Group 2425 E Camelback Rd Ste 450 Phoenix AZ 85016-4236

SINCLAIR, SARA VORIS, health facility administrator, nurse; b. Kansas City, Mo., Apr. 13, 1942; d. Franklin Defenbaugh and Inez Estelle (Figenbaum) Voris; m. James W. Sinclair, June 13, 1964; children: Thomas James, Elizabeth Kathleen, Joan Sara. BSN, UCLA, 1965. RN, Utah; lic. health care facility adminstr.; cert. health care adminstr. Staff nurse UCLA Med. Ctr. Hosp., 1964-65; charge nurse Boulder (Colo.) Meml. Hosp., 1966, Boulder (Colo.) Manor Nursing Home, 1974-75, Four Seasons Nursing Home, Joliet, Ill., 1975-76; dir. nursing Home Health Agy of Olympia Fields, Joliet, Ill., 1977-79; dir. nursing Sunshine Terr. Found., Inc., Logan, Utah, 1980, asst. adminstr., 1980-81, adminstr., 1981-93; dir. divsn. health systems improvement Utah Dept. Health, Salt Lake City, 1993—; mem. long term care profl. and tech. adv. com. Joint Commn. on Accreditation Healthcare Orgns., Chgo., 1987-91, chmn., 1990-91; adj. lectr. Utah State u., 1991-93; mem. adj. clin. faculty Weber State U., Ogden, Utah; moderator radio program Healthwise Sta. KUSU-FM, 1985-93; spkr. Nat. Coun. Aging, 1993, Alzheimers Disease Assn. Ann. Conf., 1993; del. White House Conf. on Aging, 1995; chmn. Utah Dept. of Health's Ethics, Instnl. Rev. Bd. Com., 1995—, Utah Dept. Health Risk Mgmt. Com., 1995—; mem. Utah Long Term Care Coalition (exec. com. 1995, chmn. 1997), oversight com. and long term care tech. adv. group Utah Health Policy Commn., 1996—; Health Insight Utah State Coun, 1996—; presenter in field. Contbg. author: Associate Degree Nursing and The Nursing Home, 1988. Mem. dean's adv. coun. Coll. Bus. Utah State U., Logan, 1989-91, mem. presdl. search com., 1991-92; chmn., co-founder Cache Comty. Health Coun., Logan, 1985; chmn. bd. Hospice of Cache Valley, Logan, 1986; mem. Utah State Adv. Coun. on Aging, 1986-93; apptd. chmn. Utah Health Facilities Com., 1989-91; chmn. Bear River Dist. Adv. Coun. on Aging, 1989-91; chmn. health and human svcs. subcom. Cache 2010, 1992-93; mem. long term care tech. adv. group, oversight com. Utah Health Policy Commn., 1997; dir. Health Insight, 1996. Recipient Disting. Svc. award Utah State U., 1989. Fellow Am. Coll. Health Care Adminstrs. (presenter 1992-93, 95, 1996 ann. convocations, v.p. Utah chpt. 1992-94, convocation and edn. coms. 1992-93, region IX vice gov. 1994-96, bylaws com. 1996—); mem. Am. Health Care Assn. (non-proprietary v.p. 1986-87, region v.p. 1987-89, presenter workshop conv. 1990-93, exec. com. 1993, presenter ann. convocation 1995), Utah Health Care Assn. (pres. 1983-85, treas. 1991-93, Disting. Svc. award 1991, Svc. award for long term care 1996), Utah Gerontol. Soc. (bd. dirs. 1992-93, 95—, chmn. nominating com. 1993-94, chmn. ann. conf. 1996, pres. 1997), Cache C. of C. (pres. 1991), Logan bus. and Profl. Women's Club (pres. 1989, Woman of Achievement award 1982, Woman of Yr. 1982), Rotary (Logan chpt., chair cmty. svc. com. 1989-90); hon. mem. Golden Key Nat. Honor Soc. Office: Utah Dept Health Div Health Sys Improvement 288 N 1460 W Box 142851 Salt Lake City UT 84114-2851

SINCLAIR, WILLIAM DONALD, church official, fundraising consultant, political activist; b. L.A., Dec. 27, 1924; s. Arthur Livingston and Lillian May (Holt) S.; m. Barbara Jean Hughes, Aug. 9, 1952; children: Paul Scott, Victoria Sharon. BA cum laude, St. Martin's Coll., Olympia, Wash., 1975; postgrad. Emory U., 1978-79. Commd. 2d lt. USAAF, 1944, advanced through grades to col., USAF, 1970; served as pilot and navigator in Italy, Korea, Vietnam and Japan; ret., 1975; bus. adminstr. First United Methodist Ch., Colorado Springs, Colo., 1976-85; bus. adminstr. Village Seven Presbyn. Ch., 1985-87; bus. adminstr. Sunrise United Meth. Ch., 1987-89; vice-chmn. council fin. and adminstrn. Rocky Mountain conf. United Meth. Ch., U.S.A., 1979-83. Bd. dirs. Chins-Up Colorado Springs, 1983-86; chmn. bd. dirs. Pikes Peak Performing Arts Ctr., 1985-92; pres. Pioneers Mus. Found., 1985—; Rep. candidate for Colo. State Chmn., 1992-93, elected to Ho. of Reps., Colo. Legis., 1997—. Decorated Legion of Merit with oak leaf cluster, D.F.C., Air medal with 6 oak leaf cluster, Dept. Def. Meritorious Service medal, Vietnam Cross of Gallantry with Palms. Fellow Nat. Assn. Ch. Bus. Adminstrs. (nat. dir., regional v.p., v.p. 1983-85, pres. 1985-87; Ch. Bus. Adminstr. of Yr. award 1983, inducted hall of fame 1995), Colo. Assn. Ch. Bus. Adminstrs. (past pres.), United Meth., Assn. Ch. Bus. Admins. Adminstrs. (nat. sec. 1978-81), Christian Ministries Mgmt. Assn. (dir. 1983-85), USAF Acad. Athletic Assn. Clubs: Colorado Springs Country, Garden of the Gods, Met. (Denver), Winter Night Club. Lodge: Rotary (pres. Downtown Colorado Springs club 1985-86), Order of Daedalians. Home: 3007 Chelton Dr Colorado Springs CO 80909-1008 *Ten words of two letters each, spoken by a black clergyman during the civil rights crusade of the 60s, are my guide to the future: "If it is to be, it is up to me." Only with this in mind can change occur.*

SINCLITICO, DENNIS J., lawyer; b. St. Louis, Mo., Jan. 9, 1947. BA, U. San Diego, 1968; JD cum laude, U. Wis., 1971. Bar: Wis. 1971, Calif. 1972, U.S. Dist. Ct. (cen. and so. dists.) Calif. 1972. Prof. Calif. Coll. Law, 1972; ptnr. La Follette, Johnson, De Haas, Fesler & Ames, P.C., L.A.; arbitrator spl. arbitration plan Los Angeles County Superior Ct., 1975—. Mem. Am. Bd. Trial Advocates (nat. exec. com. 1978—, pres. L.A. chpt., editor newsletter), State Bar Wis., State Bar Calif., Assn. So. Calif. Def. Counsel (program chmn. 1980-81, bd. dirs. 1980—), Cal-Abota (chair 1994), Phi Alpha Delta. Office: La Follette Johnson De Haas Fesler & Ames PC 865 S Figueroa St Ste 3100 Los Angeles CA 90017-5472

SINCOFF, STEVEN LAWRENCE, science administrator, scientist; b. N.Y.C., Apr. 17, 1948; s. Murray B. and Lillian (Goldberg) S.; m. Marcella Seay, June 12, 1993; children by previous marriage: Kristina Lynne, Carolyn Suzanne. BSChemE, N.J. Inst. Tech., 1969, MSChemE, 1972; PhD in Analytical Chemistry, Ohio State U., 1980. Commd. 2d lt. USAF, 1969, advanced through grades to lt. col., 1987, retired, 1991; fuels mgmt. officer USAF, Albuquerque and Galena, Alaska, 1970-74; chem. engr. Aero. Systems Div., Wright-Patterson AFB, Ohio, 1974-77; assoc. prof. chemistry USAF Acad., Colorado Springs, Colo., 1980-84, dir. continuing edn. dept. chemistry, 1982-84; chief gas analysis lab. McClellan (AFB) Cen. Lab., Calif., 1984-88; exec. officer to comdr. Tech. Ops. Div. McClellan AFB, Calif., 1988-89, chief info. officer, 1989-91; gen. mgr. ChemWest Analytical Lab., Sacramento, 1991-92; dir. ops. Barringer Labs., Inc., Golden, Colo., 1992-94; instr. chemistry C.C. Aurora, Colo., 1995—; reviewer chemistry textbooks Saunders Pub., Phila., 1983-84. Mem. Am. Chem. Soc., Air Force Assn. Jewish. Home and Office: 9757 W Nova Ave Littleton CO 80127-3932

SINEGAL, JAMES D., variety store wholesale business executive; b. 1936. With Fed-Mart Corp., 1954-77, exec. v.p.; v.p. Builders Emporium, 1977-78; exec. v.p. Price Co., 1978-79; with Sinegal/Chamberlin & Assocs., 1979-83; pres., chief oper. officer Costco Wholesale Corp., 1983—, chief exec. officer, 1988—, bd. dirs. Office: Costco Wholesale Corp 999 Lake Dr Issaquah WA 98027*

SINES, RANDY DWAIN, business executive; b. Spokane, Jan. 16, 1948; s. Myron Jones and Paula Inez (Walls) S.; student Wash. State U., 1966-67, U. Wash., 1968-69; m. Irene Cheng, Mar. 18, 1981. With Boeing Co., 1967; with Winchell's Donut House, Inc., Seattle, 1968-71; owner, mgr. bakeries, Wash. and Mont., 1972-78; owner, mgr. Sonsine Inc., Great Falls, Mont., 1976-79; pres. Gardian Port Corp., Oxnard, Calif., 1980-82; pres., chmn. SNS Motor Imports, Inc., Oxnard, 1982-86; chmn. Karakal Corp. of Ams., Ventura, Calif., 1986-89; chief exec. officer, chmn. Steel Stix, U.S.A., 1990—; chmn. Mitt USA Corp., 1991—; mng. ptnr. Sharps Internat., 1993—; CEO Casinovations Inc., 1995—. Recipient alumni grant Wash. State U., 1967; lic. water well contractor, Wash., Mont. Patentee sports apparatus, over 20 patents worldwide. Home and Office: 4056 S Madelia St Spokane WA 99203-4227

SINGER, HERSH, marketing executive. Chmn. SMS Rsch. & Mktg. Svcs. Office: SMS Rsch & Mktg Svcs 1042 Fort St Mall Honolulu HI 96813*

SINGER, JANICE GAIL, psychotherapist, consultant; b. Chgo., Aug. 14, 1947; d. Harold and Dorothy (Kagen) S.; 1 child, Rachael Jacqueline. BA, U. Toledo, 1969; MSW, U. Wis., Milw., 1977; postgrad., Gestalt Inst., Cleve., 1982, Dreikers Relationship Ctr., Boulder, Colo., 1985; Reiki II, Nancy Retzlaff R.M., Milw., 1986. Program evaluator, project cons. Mental health Planning Council of Milw., 1976-78; counselor abortion WomanCare-West, Milw., 1978; treatment foster care worker Children's Service Soc. of Wis., Milw., 1978-81; mental health coordinator, primary psychotherapist Bread and Roses Women's Health Ctr., Inc., Milw., 1981-84; originator Friends' Psychotherapy Collective, Milw., 1984—; Santa Barbara Counseling Ctr., Calif., 1992-93, Family Therapy Inst., Santa Barbara, 1992—; radio talk show host Santa Barbara, 1994-95; group facilitator for vols. Santa Barbara AIDS/CAP Retreat, 1991-95; trainer Family Harmony Inst., Ojai, Calif., 1991; workshop presenter U. Calif. Santa Barbara Women's Ctr. Women's Spirituality Seminars, 1992; facilitator People to People, Waukesha, Wis., 1976-80; mem. coalition sexual misconduct by psychotherapists, Wis., 1984-86, 88-91; cons. Women to Women, Inc., Milw., 1981-92; adj. faculty Pacifica Grad. Inst., 1992, Antioch U. of Santa Barbara, 1996. Author: Women's Spirituality: Goddess & Native American Rituals & Traditions, 1992, Victim to Victim: Women Recovering from Childhood Sexual Abuse, 1992; co-author: (consumer guide) Making Therapy Work for You, 1986, revised, 1991; creator therapy mode Action Oriented Therapy, 1983; co-creator: (workshops) Living Your Godness Enhancing Self-Esteem Thru Action, 1988, Living in Balance-Integrating Male & Female Energy, 1987, Grieving: The Benefits of Being a Cry Baby, 1988, Seeking the Spirit-A Shamanic Tradition, 1989, Working With Abusive, Noncompliant, Obnoxious Patients, What Your Body's Saying Whether Your Lips are Moving or Not, 1989, Co-dependency: When Your Drug of Choice is Anyone But You, 1989, Discovering Your E/Sensual Body-Being Sensual is Essential to Life, 1989, Celebration in Living!, 1984, Living Beyond AIDS, 1987, Transforming Body Image, 1987, Finding Peace in Your Body, others. Co-creator, co-facilitator Santa Barbara Hearts, Hands, and Voices Metaphysical Healing Group for HIV Affected Persons, 1991-92; bd. dirs. Santa Barbara Rape Crisis Ctr., 1991-95, pres., 1993, 96, v.p., 1994; chair health com. Santa Barbara Women's Polit. Com., 1991-93; workshop leader Milw. AIDS Project, 1987; co-creator workshops Celebration in Living, 1984, Living Beyond AIDS, 1987, Transforming Body Image, 1987; active Maple Dale Sch. Human Sexuality, Milw., 1983-86; curriculum com. Nicolet High Sch. Human Sexuality, 1987. Mem. Feminist Therapy Network (pres. 1984-87), Nat. Assn. Social Workers, Assn. for Human Animal Bonding, Wis. Assn. Outpatient Mental Health Facilities (mem. ethics com. 1981-86). Democrat. Home and Office: 638 Calle De Los Amigos Santa Barbara CA 93105-4455

SINGER, JEFFREY ALAN, surgeon; b. Bklyn., Feb. 2, 1952; s. Harold and Hilda (Ginsburg) S.; m. Margaret Sue Gordon, May 23, 1976; children: Deborah Suzanne, Pamela Michelle. BA cum laude, Bklyn. Coll., 1973; MD, N.Y. Med. Coll., 1976. Diplomate Am. Bd. Surgery. Intern Maricopa County Gen. Hosp., Phoenix, 1976-77, resident, 1977-81, mem. teaching faculty, 1981—; trauma cons. John C. Lincoln Hosp., Phoenix, 1981-83; pvt. practice Phoenix, 1981-87; group pvt. practice Valley Surg. Clinics, Ltd., Phoenix, 1987-96, S.W. Surg. Clinics, P.C., Phoenix, 1996—; sec.-treas. med. staff Humana Desert Valley Hosp., Phoenix, 1987-89, chief surgery, 1985-87, 91-93, exec. com., 1993-95. Assoc. editor Ariz. Medicine. Rep. precinct committeeman, Phoenix, 1986—; bd. dirs. Goldwater Inst. for Pub. Policy Rsch. Fellow ACS, Internat. Coll. Surgeons, Southwestern Surg. Congress, Am. Soc. Abdominal Surgeons; mem. Ariz. Med. Assn. (bd. dirs. polit. com. 1985, chmn. bd. dirs. polit. com. 1991-93, legis. com. 1986—), Alpha Omega Alpha. Office: SW Surg Clinics PC 1728 W Glendale Ave Ste 401 Phoenix AZ 85021

SINGER, KURT DEUTSCH, news commentator, author, publisher; b. Vienna, Austria, Aug. 10, 1911; came to U.S., 1940, naturalized, 1951; s. Ignaz Deutsch and Irene (Singer) S.; m. Hilda Tradelius, Dec. 23, 1932 (div. 1954); children: Marian Alice Birgit, Kenneth Walt; m. Jane Sherrod, Apr. 9, 1955 (dec. Jan. 1985); m. Katherine Han, Apr. 8, 1989. Student, U. Zürich, Switzerland, 1930, Labor Coll., Stockholm, Sweden, 1936; Ph.D., Div. Coll. Metaphysics, Indpls., 1951. Escaped to Sweden, 1934; founder Ossietzky Com. (successful in release Ossietzky from concentration camp); corr. Swedish mag. Folket i Bild, 1935-40; founder Niemöller Com.; pub. biography Göring in Eng. (confiscated in Sweden), 1940; co-founder pro-Allied newspaper Trots Allt, 1939; corr. Swedish newspapers in, U.S., 1940; editor News Background, 1942; lectr. U. Minn., U. Kans., U. Wis., 1945-49; radio commentator WKAT, 1950; corr. N.Am. Newspaper Alliance, N.Y.C., 1953—; pres. Singer Media Corp., 1987—; dir. Oceanic Press Service, San Clemente, Calif. Author, editor: underground weekly Mitteilungsblätter, Berlin, Germany, 1933; author: The Coming War, 1934, (biog.) Carl von Ossietzky, 1936 (Nobel Peace prize), Germany's Secret Service in Central America, 1943, Spies and Saboteurs in Argentina, 1943, Duel for the Northland, 1943, White Book of the Church of Norway, 1944, Spies and Traitors of World War II, 1945, Who are the Communists in America, 1948, 3000 Years of Espionage, 1951, World's Greatest Women Spies, 1952, Kippie the Cow; juvenile, 1952, Gentlemen Spies, 1953, The Man in the Trojan Horse, 1954, World's Best Spy Stories, 1954, Charles Laughton Story; adapted TV, motion pictures, 1954, Spy Stories and Asia, 1955, More Spy Stories, 1955, My Greatest Crime Story, 1956, My Most Famous Case, 1957, The Danny Kaye Saga; My Strangest Case, 1958, Spy Omnibus, 1959, Spies for Democracy, 1960, Crime Omnibus Spies Who Changed History, 1961, Hemmingway-Life and Death of a Giant, 1961, True Adventures in Crime, Dr. Albert Schweitzer, Medical Missionary, 1962, Lyndon Baines Johnson-Man of Reason, 1964, Ho-i-man; juveniles, 1965; Kurt Singer's Ghost Omnibus, 1965; juvenile Kurt Singer's Horror Omnibus; The World's Greatest Stories of the Occult, The Unearthly, 1965, Mata Hari-Goddess of Sin, 1965, Lyndon Johnson-From Kennedy to Vietnam, 1966, Weird Tales Anthology, 1966, I Can't Sleep at Night, 1966, Weird Tales of Supernatural, 1967, Tales of Terror, 1967, Famous Short Stories, 1967, Folktales of the South Pacific, 1967, Tales of The Uncanny, 1968, Gothic Reader, 1968, Bloch and Bradbury, 1969, Folktales of Mexico, 1969, Tales of the Unknown, 1970, The House in the Valley, 1970, Hablan Los Artistas, 1970, Tales of the Macabre, 1971, Three Thousand Years of Espionage, 1971, El Mundo de Hoy, 1971, Cuentos Fantasticos del Mas, 1971, Aldous Huxley, El Camino al Infierno, 1971, Ghouls and Ghosts, 1972, The Unearthly, 1972, The Gothic Reader, 1972, Satanic Omnibus, 1973, The Plague of the Living Dead, 1973, Gothic Horror Omnibus, 1974, Dictionary of Household Hints and Help, 1974, Supernatural, 1974, They are Possessed, 1976, True Adventures into the Unknown, 1980, I Spied-And Survived, 1980, Great Adventures in Crime, 1982, The Oblong Box, 1982, Shriek, 1984, First Target Book of Horror, 1984, 2d, 1984, 3d, 1985, 4th, 1985, Solve A Crime, 1994, The Ultimate Quiz Book, 1994, The Complete Guide to Career Advancement, 1994, The Sex Quiz Book, 1994, The Marriage Quiz Book, The Psychology Quiz Book, The Teenage Quiz Book, Success Secrets, 1995, Conozcase Mejor y Triunfe, 1995, The Joy of Practical Parenting, 1995; editor: UN Calendar, 1959-58; contbr. articles to newspapers, popular mags., U.S., fgn. countries, all his books and papers in Boston U. Library-Spl. Collections. Mem. UN Speakers Research Com., UN Children's Emergency Fund, Menninger Found. Mem. Nat. Geog. Soc., Smithsonian Assos., Internat. Platform Assn. (v.p.), United Sch. Assemblies (pres.). Address: Singer Media Corp Seaview Business Pk 1030 Calle Cordillera # 106 San Clemente CA 92673-6234 *In the sunset years of my life, I feel stronger than ever that the most important contribution one makes in a lifetime is to plant as many seeds as possible with many people, and perhaps many countries. Who knows where the seeds of ideas survive and expand?.*

SINGER, MICHAEL HOWARD, lawyer; b. N.Y.C., Nov. 22, 1941; s. Jack and Etta (Appelbaum) S.; m. Saundra Jean Kupperman, June 1, 1962; children: Allison Jill, Pamela Faith. BS in Econs., U. Pa., 1962; JD, NYU, 1965, LLM in Taxation, 1968. Bar: N.Y. 1965, U.S. Ct. Claims 1968, U.S. Supreme Ct. 1969, U.S. Ct. Appeals (6th cir.) 1970, D.C. 1972, U.S. Tax Ct. 1972, Nev. 1973, U.S. Ct. Appeals (9th cir.) 1973. Law asst. Appellate Term Supreme Ct., N.Y.C., 1965-68; trial lawyer Ct. Claims Tax Div., Washington, 1968-72; tax lawyer Beckley, DeLanoy & Jemison, Las Vegas, 1972-74; ptnr. Oshins, Singer, Segal & Morris, Las Vegas, 1974-87; pvt. practice law Las Vegas, 1987; ptnr. Michael H. Singer Ltd., Las Vegas, 1987-96, Singer, Brown, and Barringer, LLC, Las Vegas, 1996—. Pres. Las Vegas chpt. NCCJ, 1980-82. Mem. ABA, ABI, Nev. Bar Assn., Las Vegas Country Club. Democrat. Jewish. Home: 4458 Los Reyes Ct Las Vegas NV 89121-5341 Office: Singer Brown and Barringer LLC 520 S 4th St Fl 2 Las Vegas NV 89101-6524 *Personal philosophy: A reasonable settlement is more economically beneficial for the client than protracted litigation of a great lawsuit.*

SINGER, ROBERT, plastic surgeon; b. Buffalo, Oct. 22, 1942; s. Murray and Fay Singer; m. Judith Harris. Student, SUNY, Buffalo, 1960-63; MD, SUNY, 1967. Lic. physician, Calif.; diplomate Am. Bd. Plastic and Reconstructive Surgery. Resident in gen. surgery Stanford Med. Ctr., Palo Alto, Calif., 1967-69, Santa Barbara Cottage and Gen. Hosp., 1972-74; resident in plastic surgery Vanderbilt U., 1974-76; pvt. practice specializing in emergency and trauma San Diego, 1971-72; pvt. practice plastic, reconstructive and aesthetic surgery La Jolla, Calif., 1976—; prior asst. clin. prof. plastic surgery U. Calif., San Diego; sr. staff, chief plastic surgery Scripps Meml. Hosp., La Jolla, 1980-86, vice chmn. dept. surgery, 1989-91. Contbr. articles to profl. jours. Active San Diego Opera, San Diego Mus. of Man, La Jolla Playhouse, Voices for Children, San Diego Zoo, Mus. Photog. Arts, KPBS, others; mem. exec. com. Anti-Defamation League. Fellow ACS; mem. AMA, Calif. Med. Assn., San Diego County Med. Soc., San Diego Internat. Soc. Plastic Surgeons (pres. 1988-89), Calif. Soc. Plastic Surgeons (pres. 1995), Am. Soc. Aesthetic Plastic Surgeons (pres. 1994-95), Internat. Soc. Clin. Plastic Surgeons, Am. Soc. Plastic and Reconstructive Surgeons, J.B. Lynch Soc., Royal Soc. Medicine, Am. Assn. for Accreditation of Ambulatory Surgery Facilities (v.p. 1994), San Diego Plastic Surgery Soc. (pres. 1989-90). Jewish. Office: 9834 Genesee Ave Ste 100 La Jolla CA 92037-1214

SINGER, ROSALIND RUTH, retired public health educator; b. N.Y.C., July 15, 1924; d. Jacob Loeb and Esther (Nadler) Schoenfeld; divorced; 1 child, Daniel Roberts. BA, Dominican Coll., 1956, MA in History, 1958; MPH, U. Calif., Berkeley, 1964. Instr. Dominican Coll., San Rafael, Calif., 1956-62; tchr. Berkeley (Calif.) Sch. Dist., 1965-70; lectr. dept. physiology and anatomy U. Calif., Berkeley, 1970-80, with Sch. Pub. Health, 1983-85; cons. health edn. various sch. dists., Napa, Albany, Oakland, Calif., 1971-80; lectr. health edn San Francisco State U., 1980-83; mem. bd. dirs. Calif. Med. Rev. Inc., San Francisco, 1992—. Author: (curriculum guide) K-8 Guide for Health, 1975; (with others) The Sexual and Gender Development of Young Children, 1976; (rev.) Jour. of Nutrition Edn., 1978. Pres. Commn. on Aging, Berkeley, 1985-88; bd. pres. Elders Network, Albany and Berkeley, Calif., 1989—; sr. adv. bd. mem. Kaiser Permanente, Oakland, Calif., 1993—; vol. tutor Berkeley Schs., 1995—. Mem. Am. Pub. Health Assn., Soc. Pub. Health Edn. Home: 731 Santa Barbara Rd Berkeley CA 94707

SINGH, LOREN CHAN, technical writing specialist; b. Palo Alto, Calif., Sept. 10, 1943; s. Shau Wing and Anna Mae (Chin) Chan; m. Frances Anastasia Chow, Apr. 19, 1975 (div. Jan. 1988); children: Karen Monique Chan, Pierre Benedict Chan, Marc Henri Chan. AB, Stanford U., 1965, AM, 1966; MS, Golden Gate U., 1988; PhD, UCLA, 1971. Teaching asst. UCLA, 1968-69, teaching assoc., 1969-70; lectr. in history Calif. State U., Northridge, 1970-71; lectr. in history San Jose (Calif.) State U., 1971-72, asst. prof. history, 1972-76, assoc. prof. history, 1976-80; lectr. history Calif. State U., Hayward, 1980-81; prodn. test technician Nicolet Paratronics Corp., Fremont, Calif., 1982; computer svc. technician Bell-Northern Rsch., Mountain View, Calif., 1982-83; rsch. analyst Bell-No. Rsch., Mountain View, 1984-85, tech. writer, 1985-87; sr. tech. writer StrataCom, Inc., Campbell, Calif., 1987-88; tech. writer Sun Microsystems, Mountain View, 1988-90, sr. tech. writer, 1990—. Author: Sagebrush Statesman, 1973, SPARCstation 1 Installation Guide, 1989, Collected Technical Support Notes, 1988, SPARCstation 2 Installation Guide, 1990, Desktop Storage Pack Installation Guide, 1989-90, SPARCstation 10 Installation Guide, 1992, SPARCstation 10 Networking and Communication Guide, 1993, SPARCstation 10SX VSIMMs Installation, 1993, SPARCstation 20 HyperSPARC Module Upgrade, 1995, SPARCstation 20 SuperSPARC-II Module Upgrade, 1995, Sun Ultra 1 Reference Manual, 1995-96, Sun Ultra 2 Reference Manual, 1996; editor: Chinese-American History Reader, 1976; contbr. articles to profl. jours. Radio sta. trustee ARC, Menlo Park, Calif., 1975-80. Recipient Presdl. Sports award Pres.'s Coun. on Phys. Fitness and Sports, 1973. Mem. Nat. Geog. Soc., Underwater Soc. Am., Am. Radio Relay League, Confederate Stamp Alliance, San Jose Aquatics Masters Swim Club. Democrat. Sikh. Home: 5719 Makati Cir Apt D San Jose CA 95123-6211

SINGH, RAJESH KUMAR, psychiatrist; b. 1948. MD, U. Santo Tomas, Manila, The Philippines. Diplomate Am. Bd. Psychiatry. Now with Las Encinas Hosp., Pasadena, Calif. Mem. APA, Soc. Calif. Psychiat. Assn. Office: Las Encinas Hosp 820 W Service Ave West Covina CA 91790*

SINGH, RASHMI SHARMA, writer; b. New Delhi, Sept. 1952; d. S.D. and S. Sharma; m. R.P. Singh; children: Anjali, Shalini, Arjun. BA with honors, Delhi U., 1972, MA, 1974. Author, pub. Berkeley, Calif., 1991—. Author, illustrator: The Blue Jackal, 1992, A Brahmin's Castles in the Air, 1994; author numerous tchr.'s guides, ednl. booklets, lesson plans; contbg. poet: Living in America, 1995. Founder, pres. Edn. about South Asia-Vidya, Inc., 1995—; former pres. PTA; former mng. editor non-profit newspaper. Office: PO Box 7788 Berkeley CA 94707-0788

SINGHAL, AVINASH CHANDRA, engineering administrator, educator; b. Aligarh, India, Nov. 4, 1941; s. Shiam Sunder and Pushpa Lata (Jindal) S.; m. Uma Rani Sharma, Sept. 5, 1967; children: Ritu Chanchal, Anita, Neil Raj. BSc, Agra U., India, 1957; BSc in Engring., St. Andrews U., Dundee, Scotland, 1959, BSC in Engring. with honors, 1960; MS, MIT, 1961, CE, 1962, ScD, 1964. Registered profl. engr., N.Y., Que., Ariz. Rsch. engr. Kaman Aircraft, Burlington, Mass., 1964-65; prof. Laval U., Quebec, Can., 1965-69; asst. program mgr. TRW, Redondo Beach, Calif., 1969-71; mgr. GE, Phila., 1971-72; mgr. tech. svcs. Engrs. India Ltd., New Delhi, 1972-74; project engr. Weidlinger Assocs., N.Y.C., 1974-77; prof. Ariz. State U., Tempe, 1977—; dir. Cen. Bldg. Rsch. Inst., 1992-93; dir. Earthquake Rsch. Lab., Tempe, 1978-89; grad. coord. structural engring. Ariz. State U., Tempe, 1991-92, senator acad. senate, 1995—, chmn. governance grievance, 1995-96, faculty ombudsman, 1996-97, ASU com. on coms., 1997—; cons. McDonnel Aircraft Corp., St. Louis, 1977-78, Sperry Corp., 1979-80, McDonnell Douglas Helicopter Co., 1990-91, Ariz. Nuclear Power Plant, 1991-92; reviewer of proposals NSF, Washington, 1980-91, 96-97, CSIR, India, 1990-93; U.S. del. U.S./China Workshop on Arch Dams, Beijing, 1987, Can. del. Shell Structures, USSR, 1964; session chmn. 5th Internat. Conf. on Soil Dynamics and Earthquake Engring., Karlsruhe, Fed. Republic of Germany, 1991; rsch. prof. Nat. Cen. U. Taiwan, Republic of China, 1990; vis. prof. U. Melbourne, Australia, 1983-84, U. Auckland, New Zealand, 1983-84; nodal dir. wood substitute rsch. program, India, 1992-93. Mem. editl. bd. Soil Dynamics and Earthquake Engring., 1991—, Advances in Earthquake Engring., 1995—; reviewer Jour. Psychol. Reports, Perceptual and Motor Skills; contbr. Nuclear Waste Storage, 1986, (proc. publ.) Earthquake Behavior of Buried Pipelines, 1989, Wood Substitute: A National Priority, 1992, System Flexibility and Reflected Pressures, 1993, Simulation of Blast Pressures on Flexible Panels, 1994; editor: Seismic Performance of Pipelines & Storage Tanks, 1985, Recent Advances in Lifeline Earthquake Engineering, 1987, Seismic Ground Motions Response, Repair and Instrumentation of Pipes and Bridges, 1992; contbr. articles to Jour. Performance of Constructed Facilities, ASCE, Jour. Computers and Structures, Jour. ASME, Jour. Aerospace Engring. ASCE; reviewer, bd. editors Jour. Earthquake Engring. and Structural Dynamics, Structural Engring. Papers Jour. ASCE. Mem. dos Estados Home Owner Assn. (bd. dirs., pres. 1996—), Tempe; chmn. bd. dirs. India Assn. Greater Phoenix, 1985-86; pres. India Assn. Greater Boston, 1964-65, das Estadas, Tempe, Ariz., 1996—; v.p., treas. Dobson Ranch Homeowners Assn., Mesa, Ariz., 1988-91; founding mem. Asian Am. Assn. Ariz., Phoenix, 1987-89; founding mem., pres. Asian Am. Faculty Assn., Ariz. State U., Tempe, 1986-88; cons. UN Devel. Program New Delhi, 1991-92. McLintock fellow MIT, 1960, Carnegie fellow MIT, 1960-63, fellow Royal Astron. Soc., London, 1961-64, rsch. fellow Kobe U., Japan, 1990; Denninson scholar Instn. Civil Engrs., London, 1959; Henry Adams Rsch. medal Structural Engrs., London, 1972; grantee Can. Def. Rsch. Bd., 1966-69, NSF, 1978-82, Engring. Found., 1978-79, U.S. Army Corps Engrs., 1984-86, U.S. Dept. Interior, 1986-88, Office Naval Rsch., 1994; recipient 1st prize bridge bldg. Instn. Strucural Engrs., Merit award Inst. Engrs., India. Fellow ASCE, Ctrl. Bldg. Rsch. Inst. (chmn. mgmt. coun., chmn. APEX com.), Sigma Xi, Tau Beta Pi, Chi Epsilon. Home: 2258 W Monterey Ave Mesa AZ 85202-7330 Office: Ariz State U Dept Civil Engring 5306 Tempe AZ 85287-5306 *Service to mankind and love for the family and friends is the key to success and happiness.*

SINGLETERRY, ROBERT CLAY, JR., nuclear engineer; b. Fayetteville, N.C., Jan. 4, 1961; s. Robert Clay and Phyllis Lea (Donovan) S.; m. Maria Star Groshner, May 18, 1984. BS in Nuclear Engring., U. Ariz., 1984, MS, 1990, PhD, 1993; postgrad., U. Idaho, 1986-91. Software-reactor engr. Ga. Power Co., Baxley, 1984-85; software engr. Energy Inc., Idaho Falls, 1985-89; grad. rsch. asst. U. Ariz., Tucson, 1989-93; nuclear engr. Argonne Nat. Lab., Idaho Falls, 1993—; principle mem. Quantum Solutions, LLC; rsch. asst. Argonne Nat. Lab., Idaho Falls, summers 1989-93; vis. scientist program coord. Idaho Acad. Sci., 1997—; adj. prof. nuclear sci. and engring. Idaho State U., 1994—. Vice-chair Young Women's Conf., Idaho Falls, 1993-94, chair, 1994-95. Mem. AAAS, Am. Nuclear Soc., The Planetary Soc., Idaho Acad. Sci., Idaho Falls Country Club. Office: Argonne Nat Lab PO Box 2528 Idaho Falls ID 83403

SINGLETON, HENRY EARL, industrialist; b. Haslet, Tex., Nov. 27, 1916; s. John Bartholomew and Victoria (Flores) S.; m. Caroline A. Wood, Nov. 30, 1942; children: Christina, John, William, James, Diana. S.B., S.M., Mass. Inst. Tech., 1940, Sc.D., 1950. V.p. Litton Industries, Inc., Beverly Hills, Calif., 1954-60; CEO Teledyne Inc., Los Angeles, 1960-86; chmn. Teledyne Inc., 1960-91, Singleton Group, Beverly Hills, Calif., 1991-96; chmn. exec. com. Teledyne, Inc., L.A., 1991—. Office: 335 N Maple Dr Ste 177 Beverly Hills CA 90210-3858

SINGLETON, JAMES KEITH, federal judge; b. Oakland, Calif., Jan. 27, 1939; s. James K. and Irene Elisabeth (Lilly) S.; m. Sandra Claire Hoskins, Oct. 15, 1966; children: Matthew David, Michael Keith. Student, U. Santa Clara, 1957-58; AB in Polit. Sci., U. Calif., Berkeley, 1961, LLB, 1964. Bar: Calif. 1965, Alaska, 1965. Assoc. Delaney Wiles Moore and Hayes, Anchorage, 1963, 65-68, Law Offices Roger Cremo, Anchorage, 1968-70; judge Alaska Superior Ct., Anchorage, 1970-80, Alaska Ct. Appeals, Anchorage, 1980-90; judge U.S. Dist. Ct. for Alaska, Anchorage, 1990-95, chief judge, 1995—; chmn. Alaska Local Boundary Commn., Anchorage, 1966-69. Chmn. 3d Dist. Rep. Com., Anchorage, 1969-70. Mem. ABA, Alaska Bar Assn., Phi Delta Phi, Tau Kappa Epsilon. Office: US Dist Ct 222 W 7th Ave Unit 41 Anchorage AK 99513-7504

SINGLETON, JOHN WEIR, gastroenterology educator, consultant; b. Denver, May 29, 1931; s. John Henry and Isabelle Douglas (Weir) S.; m. Louise Randolph Robinson, Oct. 3, 1959; children: John Robinson, Martha Weir Pennell, David Randolph, William Reynolds. BA, Yale U., 1953; MD, Harvard U., 1957. Diplomate in internal medicine and gastroenterology Am. Bd. Internal Medicine. Intern medicine Mass. Gen. Hosp., Boston, 1957-58, resident medicine, 1958-59, 61-62; clin. assoc. NIH, NIAMDD, Bethesda, Md., 1959-61; fellow gastroenterology Health Sci. Ctr. U. Colo., Denver, 1962-65, asst. clin. prof., 1965-68, asst. prof. medicine, 1968-74, assoc. prof. medicine, 1974-83, prof., 1983—; mem. rsch. tng. awards com. CCFA, N.Y.C., 1984-90; mem. subspecialty bd. Gastroenterology Am. Bd. Internal Medicine; bd. dirs. Rocky Mountain chpt. Crohn's & Colitis Found. Am. Mem. editl. bd. Inflamatory Bowel Diseases, 1995—; contbr. articles to profl. jours. Bd. dirs. Vis. Nurse Assn., Denver, 1980-82, Kent-Denver Country Day Sch., Denver, 1980-86. With USPHS, 1969-71. Fellow ACP; mem. Am. Gastroent. Assn., Inflammatory Bowel Disease Forum (pres. 1981-84, 88-93). Democrat. Presbyterian. Office: B-158 4200 E 9th Ave Ste B-158 Denver CO 80262

SINISCALCO, GARY RICHARD, lawyer; b. N.Y.C., Aug. 14, 1943. BA in Econs., Le Moyne Coll., 1965; JD, Georgetown U., 1969. Bar: Calif. Regional counsel, sr. trial atty. EEOC, San Francisco, 1969-78; ptnr. in charge of client rels. Orrick, Herrington & Sutcliffe, San Francisco, 1978—, co-chairperson employment law dept.; mem. adv. bd. Nat. Employment Law Inst.; lectr. in field. Co-author: Manager's Guide to Lawful Terminations, 1991; author: (with others) Employment Discrimination Law, 1979, 3rd edit., 1996; contbr. articles to profl. jours. Mem. ABA (mem. com. on internat. labor rels. and equal employment opportunity, mgmt. co-chairperson equal employment opportunity com. 1996—), State Bar Calif., Bar Commonwealth Va., Am. Employment Law Coun. (founder). Office: Orrick Herrington 400 Sansome St San Francisco CA 94111-3308

SINNEX, CEIL, nonprofit foundation founder, newsletter publisher; b. Washington, Dec. 31, 1944; d. John Robertson and Mary Elizabeth (Titsworth) Deatherage; m. W. John McCormick, Feb. 16, 1985. BA, U. Tenn., 1966. Reporter local weekly papers, Washington, 1967, Houston Post, 1968-70; Washington correspondent small news burs., Washington, 1970-75; staff writer AP, Honolulu, 1975-76; pub. info. specialist East-West Ctr., Honolulu, 1978-82; prin. Ceil Sinnex Comm., Paauilo, Hawaii, 1983—; founder, exec. dir. Ovarian Cancer Prevention and Early Detection Found., Paauilo, Hawaii, 1991-94; speaker to various orgns. on ovarian cancer, 1991—. Editor: (newsletter) Ovarian Plus Internat.: Gynecologic Cancer Prevention Quarterly, 1995—; commr. (TV pub. svc. announcement) Silent Killer, 1992 (Telly award 1993); presenter U.S. Army Ovarian Cancer Rsch. Program Stakeholder's Meeting, 1997; contbr. articles to pubis. Bd. dirs. Friends of the Waikiki Aquarium, Honolulu, 1980-90, Honolulu unit, Am. Cancer Soc., 1984-89. Recipient Outstanding Svc. cert. Montgomery County (Md.) Commn. on Status of Women, 1975, Jonquils award for efforts in the Fight Against Cancer, Duke U. Comprehensive Cancer Ctr., Durham, N.C., 1994. Office: PO Box 383 Paauilo HI 96776-0383

SINTON, WILLIAM MERZ, astronomer, educator; b. Balt., Apr. 11, 1925; s. Robert Nelson and Alma Merz (Summers) S.; m. Marjorie Anne Korner, June 4, 1960; children: Robert William, David Theodore, Alan Nelson. AB, Johns Hopkins U., 1949, PhD, 1953. Rsch. assoc. Johns Hopkins U., Balt., 1953-54; rsch. assoc., lectr. Harvard U., Cambridge, Mass., 1954-57; astronomer Lowell Obs., Flagstaff, Ariz., 1957-66; prof. physics and astronomy U. Hawaii, Honolulu, 1966-90; ret., 1990; adj. astronomer Lowell Obs., Flagstaff, Ariz., 1989—. Co-author: Tools of the Astronomer, 1961; contbr. articles to sci. jours. Sgt. U.S. Army, 1943-46, ETO. Fellow Optical Soc. Am. (Adolph Lomb medal 1954); mem. Am. Astron. Soc. (committeeman div. planetary sci. 1971-73), Am. Geophys. Union. Home: 850 E David Dr Flagstaff AZ 86001-4731

SIRI, JEAN BRANDENBURG, citizen advocate; b. Lakota, N.D., Mar. 11, 1920; d. Tunis Orville and Edith Marion (Molloy) Brandenburg; m. William E. Siri, Dec. 3, 1947; children—Lynn, Ann. B.S., Jamestown Coll., 1942; postgrad., U. Calif.-Berkeley, 1945-46, U. Calif., San Francisco, 1944. Biologist, Donner Lab., U. Calif., Berkeley, 1945-52. mem. State Solid Waste & Resource Recovery Adv. Coun., Sacramento, 1973-75; dir., chmn. Stege Sanitary Dist., El Cerrito, Calif., 1975-79; elected bd. dirs. ward 1 East Bay Regional Park, 1993—; coun. mem. El Cerrito City Coun., 1980-85, 87-91, mayor, 1982-83, 88-89. Mem. Save San Francisco Bay Assocs., Contra Costa Hazardous Waste Task Force, 1985-86, County Environ. Health Coordinating Council, 1985-88, County Hazardous Materials Commn., 1986-92, County Pub. and Environ. Health Adv. Bd., 1987—; founder, chmn. West County Toxics Coalition, 1986—; alternate solid waste West Contra Costa Joint Powers Authority, 1988-89. Served to lt. USNR, 1942-44. Recipient Sol Feinstone Environ. award U. Syracuse, 1977, Clean Air award Lung Assn. Santa Clara, 1976, Get Tough on Toxics Environ. award, 1986, Spl. award Homeless and Hungry, Vols. of Am., 1987, El Cerrito Wall of Fame, 1995. Mem. LWV, NAACP, Gray Panthers, Native Plant Soc., Sierra Club (city rep. to county homeless adv. com. 1988-93, Scope Environ. award 1986), Calif. State Local Emergency Planning Com. (rep. 1990-92), Audubon Soc., West Contra Costa Conservation League (pres.), League of Conservation Voters (dir 1978-79), West Contra Costa Transp. Joint Powers Authority. Democrat.

SISEMORE, CLAUDIA, educational films and videos producer, director; b. Salt Lake City, Sept. 16, 1937; d. Darrell Daniel and Alice Larril (Barton) S. BS in English, Brigham Young U., 1959; MFA in Filmmaking, U. Utah, 1976. Cert. secondary tchr., Utah. Tchr. English, drama and writing Salt Lake Sch. Dist., Salt Lake City, 1959-66; tchr. English Davis Sch. Dist., Bountiful, Utah, 1966-68; ind. filmmaker Salt Lake City, 1972—; filmmaker-in-residence Wyo. Coun. for Arts and Nat. Endowment for Arts, Dubois, Wyo., 1977-78; prodr., dir. ednl. films Utah Office Edn., Salt Lake City, 1979-93, Canyon Video, 1993—. Prodr., dir. Beginning of Winning, 1984 (film festival award 1984), Dancing through the Magic Eye, 1986, Se Hable Espanol, 1986-87; writer, dir., editor (film) Building on a Legacy, 1988, (videos) Energy Conservation, 1990, Alternative Energy Sources, 1990, Restructuring Learning, 1991, Kidsercise, 1991, Traditional Energy Sources, 1992, A State Government Team, 1992, Problem Solving Using Math Manipulative, 1993, Canyon Video, 1993—; videos Western Mountains and Basins, 1994, Bikes, Boards and Blades, 1994, Fitness After 50, 1995, Timescape, 1996, Splash of Color, 1996, A Winter's Hush: Understanding Depression, 1996; exhibited (abstract paintings) in group show Phillips Gallery; represented in numerous pvt. and pub. collections. Juror Park City (Utah) Arts Festival, 1982, Utah Arts Festival, Salt Lake City, 1982, Am. Film Festival, 1985-86, Best of West Film Festival, 1985-86; bd. dirs. Utah Media Ctr., Salt Lake City, 1981-87; mem. multi-disciplinary program Utah Arts Coun., Salt Lake City, 1983-87. Recipient award Utah Media Ctr., 1984, 85; Nat. Endowment for Arts grantee, 1978, Utah Arts Coun. grantee, 1980. Mormon.

SITILIDES, JOHN, government relations executive; b. Jersey City, Feb. 8, 1962; s. Louis and Frances (Sagiroglou) S. B, Queens Coll., N.Y.C., 1983; M Internat. and Pub. Affairs, Columbia U., 1986. Dep. press sec. D'Amato for Senate, N.Y.C., 1986; exec. dir. Maltese for State Senate, Middle Village, N.Y., 1988; comm. mgr. D'Amato for Senate, N.Y.C., 1992; exec. asst. comm. Sen Alfonse D'Amato, N.Y.C., 1986-93; founder The Sitilides Group, Sacramento, Calif., 1993—; chmn. The Western Policy Ctr., Sacramento, 1994—. V.p. devel. World Affairs Coun., Sacramento, 1994; mem. Rep. Nat. Com., Washington, 1984, Calif. Rep. Party, 1993. Mem. Am. Hellenic Edn. Progressive Assn. (chmn. Cyprus and Hellenic Affairs com. 1995-97), DYNAMIS, Nat. Wilderness Inst., Young Execs. Am., U.S. C. of C. Republican. Greek Orthodox. Office: The Sitilides Group 7801 Folsom Blvd Ste 106 Sacramento CA 95826-2303

SITNYAKOVSKY, ROMAN EMMANUIL, scientist, writer, inventor, translator; b. Kiev, Ukraine, Jan. 5, 1934; came to U.S., 1988; s. Emmanuil I. and Yevgeniya N. (Glazova) S. MS in Mech. and Heat Engring., Polytech. Inst., Kiev, Ukraine, 1956; PhD in Heat Theory/Engring., USSR Acad. Scis., Minsk, Belarus, 1967. Project engr. Ural Turbomotor, Sverdlovsk, USSR, 1956-58; mech. engr. Engring Factory, Kiev, Ukraine, 1958-61; project engr. Design Inst., Kiev, Ukraine, 1961-63; sr. engr. Heat & Mass Transfer Inst., Minsk, Belarus, 1963-68; prin. engr. Thermophysics Inst., Kiev, Ukraine, 1968-87; project engr. Hirt Combustion Engring., Montebello, Calif., 1989-90; cons. Socio-Econ. Sys., L.A., 1988-93; translator, Kiev, 1979-87, L. A., 1988—. Author: I Disagree with Guberman, 1995, Chernobyl is our Fate, 1996; contbr. numerous articles to jours., newspapers and mags.; 11 patents in field; over 70 inventions. Jewish.

SIVERTS, SHARON ANN, academic administrator; b. Pasco, Wash., June 2, 1946; d. Burton Frederick and Viola Mary (Zorr) Siverts. BS, Ohio U., 1967, MS, 1970; PhD, Pa. State U., 1974. Asst. prof. U. Tex., Austin, 1974-75; asst. prof. Oregon State U., Corvallis, 1975-78, ACE fellow in Acad. Adminstrn., 1981-82; coord. Oreg. State U., Corvallis, 1979-81, asst. dean Coll. of Home Econs., 1982-84; dean, professor of Home Econs. U. Nev., Reno, 1984-87; prof., dean of Acad. Resources Humboldt State U., Arcata, Calif., 1988-91; prof., v.p. for acad. affairs N.D. State U., Fargo, 1991-95; provost, v.p. Met. State Coll. of Denver, 1995—. Author various curriculum guides; contbr. articles to profl. jours. Mem. Assn. Internat. Edn. Adminstrs., AAUW, Am. Assn. Higher Edn.

SIYAN, KARANJIT SAINT GERMAIN SINGH, software engineer; b. Mauranipur, India, Oct. 16, 1954; came to U.S., 1978; s. Ahal Singh and Tejinder Kaur (Virdi) S.; m. Dei Gayle Cooper, Apr. 8, 1987. B in Tech. Electronics, Indian Inst. Tech., 1976, M in Tech. Computer Sci., 1978; MS in Engring., U. Calif., Berkeley, 1980; PhD of Computer Sci., Kennedy-Western U., Berkeley, 1994. Cert. enterprise netware engr.; cert. microsoft profl.; cert. master novell engr. Sr. mem. tech. staff Rolm Corp., San Jose, Calif., 1980-84; cons. Siyan Cons. Svcs., L.A., 1985-86, Emigrant, Mont., 1987—. Author, sr. instr. Learning Tree Internat., 1985—; author: Internet Firewalls and Network Security, Inside Java, Inside TCP/IP, Inside Visual J Netware-The Professional REference, Windows NT Server: The Professional Reference, Netware Training Guide-Network 4 Update, Building Intranets onto Netware Web Server, Netware Training Guide-Network 4 Update, Netware 4 Training Guide-Netware 4 Adminstration, CNE Training Guide-TCP/IP and NFS, Internetworking with Netware TCP/IP; co-author: Downsizing Netware, Implementing Internet Security, LAN Connectivity, Netware 4 for Professionals, Banyan Vines-The Professional Reference; author seminars on Novell Networking, TCP/IP Networks, Windows NT, Solaris-PC Network Integration. Mem. IEEE, ACM, Enterprise, Network Profl. Assn., Kappa Omicron Phi.

SIZEMORE, KENNETH LEE, county official; b. Salt Lake City, June 22, 1954; s. Allen DeVar and Myrna Lee (Syme) S.; m. Barbara Lynn Zolman, Dec. 18, 1975; children: Audrey, Jacob, Sarah, Kaye, Lance, Richard, Lee. BA, Utah State U., 1977, postgrad., 1979-83. Cert. econ. devel. fin. profl. Nat. Devel. Coun.; cert. cmty. devel. block grant mgr. Utah State Divsn. Cmty. Devel. Asst. county planner Cache County, Logan, Utah, 1977-80, county planner, 1980-86; dep. dir. Five County Assn. Govts., St. George, Utah, 1986—; Utah state rep. The Western Planner, Casper, Wyo., 1977-87, mem. editorial bd., 1994—. Co-author: Levels of Analysis in River Basin Planning, 1979, Integrating Water Resources and Land Use Planning, 1979. Voting dist. chmn. Rep. Com., Logan, Utah, 1975-77; chmn. Providence Utah Bd. Adjustment, 1985-86. Sgt. 1st class Utah Army N.G., 1984-93, with USAR, 1993—. Named Outstanding Young Men of Am., U.S. Jaycees, 1980; recipient Allen Stokes Conservation award Bridgerland Audubon Soc., 1986. Mem. Am. Planning Assn. (pres. 1984-86), Nat. Assn. County Planning Dirs. (Utah state rep. 1983-85). Republican. Mormon. Home: 2500 Arch Cir Santa Clara UT 84765-5538 Office: Five County Assn Govts 906 N 1400 W Saint George UT 84770-4989

SIZEMORE, NICKY LEE, computer scientist; b. N.Y.C., Feb. 13, 1946; s. Ralph Lee and Edith Ann (Wangler) S.; m. Frauke Julika Hoffmann, Oct. 31, 1974; 1 child, Jennifer Lee Sizemore; 1 stepchild, Mark Anthony Miracle. BS in Computer Sci., SUNY, 1989. Sgt. first class U.S. Army, 1964-68, 70-86; computer operator UNIVAC, Washington, 1968-69, programmer, 1969-70; programmer/analyst Ultra Systems, Inc., Sierra Vista, Ariz., 1986-87; computer scientist Comarco, Inc., Sierra Vista, 1987-92, ARC, Profl. Svcs. Group, Sierra Vista, 1992-93, Computer Scis. Corp., Ft. Huachuca, Ariz., 1994; sr. cons. Inference Corp., 1995; subject matter expert Northrop Corp., Sierra Vista, Ariz., 1995—; sr. info. sys. engr. Harris Corp., Sierra Vista, Ariz., 1996—; speaker numerous confs., seminars, symposia. Mem. AIAA (mem. artificial intelligence standard com.), Computer Soc. IEEE, Am. Assn. for Artificial Intelligence (co-dir. workshop on verification, validation, and test of knowledge-based sys. 1988), Assn. for Computing Machinery, Armed Forces Comms.-Electronics Assn., Am. Def. Preparedness Assn. Home: 880 E Charles Dr Sierra Vista AZ 85635-1611 Office: Harris Tech Svcs Corp 101 E Wilcox Dr Sierra Vista AZ 85635-2540

SJOLANDER, GARY WALFRED, physicist; b. Bagley, Minn., Dec. 5, 1942; s. Tage Walfred and Evelyn Mildred (Kaehn) S.; m. Joann Lorraine Tressler, June 18, 1966; 1 child, Toby Ryan. BS in Physics, U. Minn., 1970, MS in Physics, 1974, PhD in Physics, 1975. Rsch. assoc. U. Minn., Mpls., 1975-76; rsch. scientist Johns Hopkins U., Balt., 1977-78, sr. physicist, 1978-82; sr. engr. Westinghouse Electric Corp., Annapolis, Md., 1982-85; sr. staff engr. Lockheed Martin Astronautics, Denver, 1985-95; engring. scientist data techs. divsn. TRW, Aurora, Colo., 1996—; pres. Cypress Improvement Assn., Inc., Severna Park, Md., 1984-85; advisor Inroads/Denver, Inc., 1986-88. Author numerous articles in field. With USAF, 1960-64. Mem. AIAA, Internat. Soc. for Optical Engring., Am. Geophys. Union, The Planetary Soc. Lutheran. Home: 811 W Kettle Ave Littleton CO 80120-4443

SJOSTROM, JOAN SEVIER, travel consultant; b. Denver, Nov. 10, 1931; d. George Field and Martha Watson (Turnbull) Sevier; m. Rex William Sjostrom, Mar. 16, 1952; children: Sandra, Anne, John, Sharon. Student, Colo. State U., 1949-51. Bookkeeper U.S. Nat. Bank, Denver, 1951-52, First Nat. Bank, Ft. Collins, Colo., 1952, Larimer County Credit Assn., Ft. Collins, 1953-55, Fox Drug, Castle Rock, Colo., 1974-86; owner, mgr. Travel Haus Inc., Castle Rock, 1984—. Vol. Swedish Emergency Ctr., 1976-82, Douglas County Schs. Spl. Edn. Program, 1980-84; mem. Interfaith Task Force Bd., 1987-88; mem. Douglas County Bd. Edn., 1978-88; mem. Douglas County Placement Alternative Commn., Castle Rock., 1984—; mem. D.C. Schs. Sr. Program, Castle Rock, 1992—. Mem. Castle Rock Rotary (v.p. 1992—, pres. 1993-94, dist. scholarship 1991, 92, 93). Republican. Lutheran. Home: 2072 W Wolfensberger Rd Castle Rock CO 80104-9635 Office: Travel Haus Inc 317 3rd St Castle Rock CO 80104-1740

SKAAR, DANIEL (LEIF), engineering executive; b. Ridgecrest, Calif., July 21, 1949; s. Karsten Segred and Ellen Clara (Benson) S. BS, Calif. Polytech. State U., San Luis Obispo, 1972. Design engr. Applied Magnetics Corp., Goleta, Calif., 1973-75; staff engr. ISS Sperry/Univac, Cupertino, Calif., 1975-81; mgr. read write technicos Sugart Assoc., Sunnyvale, Calif., 1981-85; engring. mgr. Memorex, Santa Clara, Calif., 1985-86; dir. engring. Cipher Data Corp., San Diego, Calif., 1986-90, Verbatim Corp., San Diego, 1990-94; v.p. engring. Rexon Corp., Irvine, Calif., 1994-95, Telectronics, Englewood, Colo., 1995—; rep. ANSI X3B1 com., 1975-85, QIC com., 1986-94, Data Dat Com., 1994-95. Patentee: 3 U.S. patents magnetic tape cartridge, method for making tape cartridges, low stiffness spring for drag induction, 1994. With USNR, 1972-73. Mem. IEEE, S. Met. Denver C. of C., Audio Engring. Soc. Home: 5330 E 17th Ave Pkwy Denver CO 80220 Office: Telectronics 7400 S Tucson Way Englewood CO 80012

SKAGGS, BEBE REBECCA PATTEN, college dean, clergywoman; b. Berkeley, Calif., Jan. 30, 1950; d. Carl Thomas and Bebe (Harrison) P. BS in Bible, Patten Coll., 1969; BA in Philosophy, Holy Names Coll., 1970; MA in Bibl. Studies New Testament, Wheaton Coll., 1972; PhD in Bibl. Studies New Testament, Drew U., 1976; MA in Philosophy, Dominican Sch. Philosophy & Theology, 1990; postgrad., U. Calif., Berkeley, 1991-92. Ordained to ministry Christian Evang. Ch., 1963. Co-pastor Christian Cathedral, Christian Evang. Chs. Am., Inc., 1964—; assoc. prof. Patten Coll., Oakland, Calif., 1975-82, dean, 1977—, prof. N.T., 1982—; presenter in field. Author: Before the Times, 1980, The World of the Early Church, 1990; contbg. author: Internat. Standard Bibl. Ency., rev. edit., 1983. Active Wheaton Coll. Symphony, 1971-72, Drew U. Ensemble, 1971-75, Young Artists Symphony, N.J., 1972-75, Somerset Hill Symphony, N.J., 1973-74, Peninsula Symphony, 1977, 80-81, Madison Chamber Trio, N.J., 1973-75. Named one of Outstanding Young Women of Am., 1976, 77, 80-81, 82; St. Olaf's Coll. fellow, 1990. Mem. AAUP, Am. Acad. Religion, Soc. Bibl. Lit., Internat. Biographical Assn., Christian Evang. Chs. of Am., Inc. (bd. dirs. 1964—), Christian Assn. for Student Affairs, Assn. for Christians in Student Devel., Inst. for Bibl. Rsch., Phi Delta Kappa.

SKAGGS, DAVID E., congressman; b. Cin., Feb. 22, 1943; s. Charles and Juanita Skaggs; m. Laura Locher, Jan. 3, 1987; 1 child, Matthew; stepchildren: Clare, Will. BA in Philosophy, Wesleyan U., 1964; student law, U. Va., 1964-65; LLB, Yale U., 1967. Bar: N.Y. 1968, Colo. 1971. Assoc. Newcomer & Douglass, Boulder, Colo., 1971-74, 77-78; chief of staff Congressman Tim Wirth, Washington, 1975-77; ptnr. Skaggs, Stone & Sheehy, Boulder, 1978-86; mem. 100th-105th Congresses from 2d Colo. dist., Washington, 1987—; mem. Appropriations com., subcoms. Commerce and Justice, Interior; mem. Ho. Permanent Select Com. on Intelligence; mem. Colo. Ho. of Reps., Denver, 1980-86; minority leader, 1982-85. Former bd. dirs. Rocky Mountain Planned Parenthood, Mental Health Assn. Colo., Boulder County United Way, Boulder Civic Opera. Served to capt. USMC, 1968-71, Vietnam; maj. USMCR, 1971-77. Mem. Colo. Bar Assn., Boulder County Bar Assn., Boulder C. of C. Democrat. Congregationalist. Office: US House of Reps 1124 Longworth Bldg Washington DC 20515-0602 also: 9101 Harlan St Unit 130 Westminster CO 80030-2925

SKALAGARD, HANS MARTIN, artist; b. Skuo, Faroe Islands, Feb. 7, 1924; s. Ole Johannes and Hanna Elisa (Fredriksen) S.; came to U.S., 1942, naturalized, 1955. Pupil Anton Otto Fisher, 1947; m. Mignon Diana Haack Haegland, Mar. 31, 1955; 1 child, Karen Solveig Sikes. Joined U.S. Mcht. Marine, 1942, advanced through grades to chief mate, 1945, ret., 1965; owner, operator Skalagard Sq., Rigger Art Gallery, Carmel, 1966—; libr. Mayo Hays O'Donnel Libr., Monterey, Calif., 1971-73; painter U.S. Naval Heritage series, 1973—; exhibited in numerous one-man shows including Palace Legion of Honor, San Francisco, 1960, J.F. Howland, 1963-65, Fairmont Hotel, San Francisco, 1963, Galerie de Tours, 1969, 72-73, Pebble Beach Gallery, 1968, Laguna Beach (Calif.) Gallery, 1969, Arden Gallery, Atlanta, 1970, Gilbert Gallery, San Francisco, Maritine Mus. of Monterey, Calif., 1993, Rigger Art Gallery, Carmel, Calif., Stanton Ctr., Monterey, 1993, St. Francis Yacht Club, San Francisco, 1995, Monterey Nat. Mus., 1993; group shows: Am. Artists, Eugene, Oreg., Robert Louis Stevenson Exhibit, Carmel Valley Gallery, Biarritz and Paris, France, David Findley Galleries, N.Y.C. and Faroe Island, Europe, Martime Mus., Calif, 1993, 94, 95, Pacific Coast Lumber Schooners, 1994, numerous others; represented in permanent collections; Naval Post Grad. Sch. and Libr., Allen Knight Maritime Mus., Salvation Army Bldg., Monterey, Calif., Robert Louis Stevenson Sch., Pebble Beach, Anenberg Art Galleries, Chestlibrook Ltd., Skalagard Art Gallery, Carmel, 1984; work represented in numerous book including Modern Masters of Marine Art, 1993; profiled in profl. jours.; lectr. Bd. dirs. Allen Knight Maritime Mus., 1973—, mem. adv. and acquisition coms., 1973-77; founder Skalagard Square Rigger Gallery; chairperson Mayor's Choice Exhibit Carmel, Calif., 1995; co founder Carmel Gallery Alliance. Recipient Silver medal Tommaso Campanella Internat. Acad. Arts, Letters and Scis., Rome, 1970, Gold medal, 1972, Gold medal and hon. life membership Academia Italia dell Arti e del Honoro, 1980, Gold medal for artistic merit Academia d'Italia. Mem. Navy League (bd. dir. Monterey), Internat. Platform Assn., Sons of Norway (cultural dir. 1974-75, 76-77). Subject of cover and article Palette Talk, 1980, Compass mag., 1980. Home: 25197 Canyon Dr Carmel CA 93923-8329 Office: PO Box 6611 Carmel CA 93921-6611 also: Dolores At 5th St Carmel CA 93921

SKALAK, RICHARD, engineering mechanics educator, researcher; b. N.Y.C., Feb. 5, 1923; s. Rudolph and Anna (Tuma) S.; m. Anna Lesta Allison, Jan. 24, 1953; children: Steven Leslie, Thomas Cooper, Martha Jean, Barbara Anne. BS, Columbia U., 1943, CE, 1946, PhD, 1954; MD (hon.), Gothenburg U., Sweden, 1990. Instr. civil engring. Columbia U., N.Y.C., 1948-54, asst. prof., 1954-60, assoc. prof., 1960-64, prof., 1964-77, James Kip Finch prof. engring. mechanics, 1977-88, emeritus, 1988—, dir. Bioengring. Inst., 1978-88; prof. bioengring. U. Calif., San Diego, 1988—, dir. Inst. for Mechs. and Materials, 1992-96; Hunter lectr. Clemson U., 1994; mem. panel Gov.'s Conf. on Sci. and Engring., R&D, 1989-90. Contbr. articles to sci. jours. Bd. dirs. Biotech. Inst., Gothenburg, Sweden, 1978—; mem. adv. bd. Ctr. for Biomed. Engring., N.Y.C., 1994—. Recipient Great Tchr. award Columbia Coll. Soc. of Older Grads., 1972, Merit medal Czechoslovakian Acad. Scis., 1990. Fellow AAAS, ASME (Centennial medal 1980, Melville medal 1990, editor jour. 1984), Am. Acad. Mechanics, Soc. Engring. Sci., Am. Inst. Med. and Biol. Engring. (founding); mem. NAE, Soc. Rheology, Am. Heart Assn., Microcirculatory Soc., Internat. Soc. Biorheology (Poiseuille medal 1989), Biomed. Engring. Soc. (Alza medal 1983), Cardiovascular System Dynamics Soc., Am. Soc. for Engring. Edn., Tau Beta Pi, Sigma Xi. Democrat. Presbyterian. Home: 8916 Montrose Way San Diego CA 92122 Office: U Calif San Diego Dept Bioengring La Jolla CA 92093-0412

SKARDA, RICHARD JOSEPH, clinical social worker; b. Santa Monica, Calif., Jan. 2, 1952; s. Robert Ralph and Cathryn Marie (Tourek) S. AA, Los Angeles Valley Coll., Van Nuys, Calif., 1976; BA, U. Calif., Berkeley, 1978; MSW, UCLA, 1980. Lic. clin. social worker, Calif.; Diplomate Am. Bd. Clin. Social Workers. Children's svcs. worker L.A. County Dept. Children's Svcs., Panorama City, Calif., 1980-82; children's services worker Ventura (Calif.) County Pub. Social Svcs. Agy., 1983-85; head social work dept. Naval Med. Clinic, Port Hueneme, Calif., 1985-94; pvt. practice, 1996—. With USN, 1970-74. Fellow Calif. Soc. Clin. Social Work; mem. Nat. Assn. Social Workers (diplomate), Acad. Cert. Social Workers.

SKARIAH, MATTHEW, religious organization administrator; b. Punnackad, Kerala, India, Feb. 21, 1945; arrive in Canada; s. Mathai Skariah and Aleyamma (Chacko) Mathai; m. Susamma Mathew, Oct. 18, 1976; 1 child, Annie Susan. LLB, Blackstone Sch. Law, 1970, JD, 1972; DD, Am. Sch. of Bible, 1971. Ordained. Founder, dir. Outreach for Youth Internat., Inc., Tulsa, 1973-78; founder, dir. World Prayer Band, Tulsa, 1978-89, Roswell, N.Mex., 1978—. Author: Crispy Christians, 1984, Free But Not Cheap, 1985, Talk Less and Pray More, 1988, Inspirational Nuggets, 1994. Ordained minister Bapt. Ch., 1971. Republican. Baptist. Office: World Prayer Band 200 W 1st St Ste 531 Roswell NM 88201-4676

SKEEN, JOSEPH RICHARD, congressman; b. Roswell, N.Mex., June 30, 1927; s. Thomas Dudley and Ilah (Adamson) S.; m. Mary Helen Jones, Nov. 17, 1945; children: Mary Elisa, Mikell Lee. B.S., Tex. A&M U., 1950. Soil and water engr. Ramah Navajo and Zuni Indians, 1951; rancher Lincoln County, N.Mex., 1952—; mem. N.Mex. Senate, 1960-70, 97th-103rd Congresses from 2nd N.Mex. dist., Washington, D.C., 1981—; mem. appropriations com., subcom. agr., chmn. appropriations com., subcom. def., mem. subcom. interior. Chmn. N.Mex. Republican Party, 1963-66. Served with USN, 1945-46; Served with USAFR, 1949-52. Mem. Nat. Woolgrowers Assn., Nat. Cattle Growers Assn., N.Mex. Woolgrowers Assn., N.Mex. Cattle Growers Assn., N.Mex. Farm and Livestock Bur. Republican. Club: Elks. Office: House of Representatives Washington DC 20515

SKEFF, KELLEY MICHAEL, health facility administrator; b. Center, Colo., 1944. MD, U. Chgo., 1970. Diplomate Am. Bd. Internal Medicine. Intern Harbor Gen. Hosp., Torrance, Calif., 1970-71; resident in internal medicine U. Colo. Med. Ctr., Denver, 1974-75; resident in internal medicine Stanford (Calif.) U. Hosps., 1975-76, fellow in internal medicine, 1976; program dir. Stanford U. Recipient Alpha Omega Alpha award Assocs. Am. Med. Coll., 1994. Office: Stanford U Dept Med 300 Pasteur Dr Palo Alto CA 94304-2203

SKELLY, JOHN JOSHUA, clergyman, fundraiser; b. Central Falls, R.I., Oct. 25, 1932; s. Joshua Essa and Catherine (Hermiz) S.; m. Una C. Meadowcroft, June 21, 1959 (div.); children: Timothy John, Joan Louise, Steven Allan. BSBA, Pepperdine U., 1956; BD, San Francisco Theol. Sem., 1959, DS in Theology, 1981; DD, Tarkio Coll., 1971. Asst. pastor First Presbyn. Ch., Granada Hill, Calif., 1959-61; pastor Port Hueneme (Calif.) Presbyn. Ch., 1961-65; v.p. devel. Pikeville (Ky.) Coll., 1967-69; sr. pastor Westminster Presbyn. Ch., Topeka, 1969-72; v.p. seminary rels. San Francisco Theol. Sem., 1972-83; v.p. Pacific Homes Found., Woodland Hills, Calif., 1988—; area counselor The Fifty Million Fund, United Presbyn. Ch., Kans.-Mo., 1965-67; mission devel. cons., 1967—; cons. Model Cities Program, Pikeville, 1968; campaign cons. United Way, L.A., 1986-87. V.p. student body Pepperdine U., L.A., 1955-56; pres. Hueneme-Oxnard Ministerial Assn., Port Hueneme, 1962; chmn. law enforcement com. Ventura County Grand Jury, 1964-65; chaplain of the day Ho. of Reps., State of Kans., 1970. Staff sgt. U.S. Army, 1950-52. Named Most Inspirational Player, Pepperdine Rugby Club, L.A., 1955, Outstanding Young Men of Am., U.S. Jr. C. of C., Port Hueneme, 1964. Democrat. Home: 5974 Ruthwood Dr Calabasas CA 91302-1076 Office: Pacific Homes 21021 Ventura Blvd Ste 400 Woodland Hills CA 91364-2206

SKELTON, DOUGLAS H., architect; b. Cottage Grove, Oreg., Apr. 17, 1939; s. Harry Edward and Mary Jane (Caldwell) S.; m. Bonita L. Baker, June 17, 1961; children: Paul D., Cynthia J., Justin D. Student, Oreg. State U., 1957-59; degree in architecture, U. Oreg., 1963. Registered architect, Oreg. Draftsman Payne & Struble Architecture, Medford, Oreg., 1965-66; intern architect Wayne Struble Architect, Medford, Oreg., 1966-70, assoc., 1973-78; project architect William Seibert Architect, Medford, Oreg., 1970-73; ptnr. Struble & Skelton Architects, Medford, Oreg., 1978-83; owner Douglas Skelton Architect, Medford, Oreg., 1983-89; ptnr. Skelton, Straus & Seibert Architects, Medford, Oreg., 1989—; mem. law rev. com. State Bd. Architects, Oreg., 1991. Design bldg. renovation (911 Mag. award 1991, Excellence in Sch. Architecture AS&U mag. 1987). Bd. dirs. Rogue Valley Christian Ch., 1994. Recipient Outstanding Sch. Bldg. award Am. Sch. and Univ. mag., 1987. Mem. AIA (v.p. So. Oreg. chpt. 1972, pres. 1973), Architects Coun. Oreg. (del., treas. 1989), Rotary (v.p., bd. dirs. Jacksonville/Applegate chpt. 1994). Office: Skelton Straus & Seibert 26 Hawthorne St Medford OR 97504-7114

SKHISOV, EDUARD, systems analyst; b. Odessa, Ukraine, Aug. 29, 1971; came to the U.S., 1992; s. Yakov and Yevgeniya (Katsel) S. Student, Odessa Poly. U., 1988-91, Santa Monica Coll., 1992-93; BS in Computer Sci., Calif. State U., L.A., 1994. Software engr. Odessa (Ukraine) Inst. Power Engring. and Design, 1990-91; office project asst. Calif. State U., L.A., 1993-94; systems analyst Am. Mgmt. Systems, Inc., Denver, 1994—. Mem. Assn. for Computing Machinery, Golden Key Honor Soc., Phi Kappa Phi. Jewish. Home: 1050 S Monaco Pkwy Apt 89 Denver CO 80224

SKIDMORE, DONALD EARL, JR., government official; b. Tacoma, Apr. 27, 1944; s. Donald E. and Ingeborg (Johnsrud) S.; BSc, Evangel Coll., 1968. With Dept. Social and Health Svcs., State of Wash., Yakima, 1967-74; quality rev. specialist Social Security Adminstrn., Seattle, 1974-76, program analyst, Balt., 1976-79, Seattle, 1979-81, quality assurance officer, mgr. Satellite office, Spokane, Wash., 1981-84, program analyst, Seattle, 1984-90, mgmt. analyst, 1990—. Pres., bd. dirs. Compton Court Condo Assn., 1980-81; v.p., trustee Norwood Village, 1987-90; vice chair ops. subcom., mem. citizen's adv. com. METRO, 1987-89; mem. citizen's adv. com. land use planning, Bellevue, Wash., 1988-90. Grad. Bellevue Police Citizen's Acad., 1992. Office: Ste 510B 2201 6th Ave Seattle WA 98121-1832

SKIDMORE, REX AUSTIN, social work educator; b. Salt Lake City, Dec. 31, 1914; s. Charles H. and Louise (Wangsgaard) S.; m. Knell Spencer, Aug. 31, 1939; children: Lee Spencer, Larry Rex. BA, U. Utah, 1938, MA, 1939; PhD, U. Pa., 1941; PhD (hon.), U. Utah, 1996, HHD (hon.), 1996. Instr. sociology U. Pa., 1940-41, Utah State Agrl. Coll., Logan, 1941-42; spl. agt. FBI, Miami, Fla., San Francisco, San Antonio, 1943-45; dir. bur. student counsel U. Utah, 1947-57, asso. prof., 1947-50, prof., 1950-85, dean Grad. Sch. Social Work, 1956-75. Author: Mormon Recreation: Theory and Practice, 1941, Building Your Marriage, 1951, 3d edit., 1964, Marriage Consulting, 1956, Introduction to Social Work, 1964, 7th edit., 1997, Introduction to Mental Health, 1979, Social Work Administration, 1983, 3d edit., 1995; contbr. articles to sociol. jours. Chmn. Western Mental Health Council, Western Interstate Commn. Higher Edn., 1964-65; mem. Nat. Adv. Council Nat. Manpower and Tng. Recipient Disting. Svc. award Cmty. Svc. Coun., NASW, 1975, Utah Conf. on Human Svcs., 1976, U. Utah Prof. Emeritus Svc. award, 1994. Mem. Coun. on Social Work Edn., Phi Kappa Phi, Pi Kappa Alpha, Pi Gamma Mu. Mem. Ch. of Jesus Christ Latter-Day Saints. Home: 1444 S 20th E Salt Lake City UT 84108 *A significant idea for successful living is knowing that: Loving is the central ingredient in human relationships; and the essence of loving is giving, not getting.*

SKIELLER, CHRISTIAN, manufacturing executive; b. Copenhagen, Mar. 23, 1948; came to U.S., 1979; s. Erik C. and Vibeke (Tvilstegaard) S.; m. Kathleen E. Christman, Jan. 11, 1986; children: Claudia Christman, Christina Christman. MSc, Tech. U. Denmark, Copenhagen, 1971; MBA, Stanford U., Calif., 1981. Mgr. mfg. ops. Schou Mfg., Copenhagen, 1972-76; systems engr. IBM, Copenhagen, 1976-79; partner, gen. mgr. CSMC, Menlo Park, Calif., 1982-84; mfg. mgr. Oximetrix/Abbott Labs., Mountain View, Calif., 1984-87; prin. cons. Christian Skieller Cons., Menlo Park, 1987-90; v.p. ops. ABAXIS, Mountain View, 1990-91; v.p. mfg. Medtronic Cardio-Rhythm, San Jose, Calif., 1992-96; v.p. ops. Cardio Thoracic Systems, Cupertino, CA, 1996—. Mem. Am. Prodn. and Inventory Control Soc. Home: 55 Black Fox Way Woodside CA 94062-4103

SKILLIN, THERESE JENO, elementary school educator; b. San Jose, Calif., Feb. 16, 1956; d. Joseph John and Eloise Martha (Holden) Jeno; m. Robert Hance Skillin, Sept. 28, 1985; children: Paul Holden, Julia Rose, Anna Katherine. BA, San Francisco State U., 1978, MA, 1983. Cert. Calif. multiple subject life tchr. Tchr. Lost Hills (Calif.) Union Sch., 1979-81, Panama Unified Sch. Dist., Bakersfield, Calif., 1981-85, Santa Paula (Calif.) Sch. Dist., 1985-90; adult literacy tutor Family Literacy Aid to Reading Program, Bakersfield, 1986, 87; cons. Ventura (Calif.) County Farm Bus., 1987-88, Ventura County Supt. County Schs.; sci. specialist, chair Ventura County Environ. and Energy Edn. Coun., 1990; originator, presenter Farm Day, Kern and Ventura Counties; presenter Ventura County Creative Arts Seminar, 1990, Calif. Kindergarten Conf., San Francisco, 1995; tchr. agrl. seminar, Ker County, 1992-96. Author children's books. Recipient award of appreciation Kern Co. Farm Bur., 1996. Mem. AAUW (mem. Camarillo Creative Arts Workshop 1988), Ventura County Reading Assn., Northern Calif. Kindergarten Assn., So. Calif. Assn. Sci. Specialists, Wasco Jr. Woman's Club (sec. 1982-83, v.p. 1983-84, dir. Annual Fun Run, named Woman of Yr. 1982), Santa Barbara Cactus and Succulent Soc. (cons.), Petroleum Wives Assn. (com. chairperson 1993-94). Democrat. Roman Catholic. Home and Office: 2901 22nd St Bakersfield CA 93301-3237

SKINNER, E. MORGAN, JR., broadcast executive; b. Logan, Utah, Apr. 28, 1940; s. Earnest M. and Mabel Clarinda (Peterson) S.; m. Darlene Anice Coppinger, Aug. 31, 1986; children: Brad, Randy, Matthew, Suzanne, Earnest, Elizabeth, Jenifer, Ryan, Aaron. BA in Journalism, Ariz. State U., 1964; postgrad., U. Utah, 1964-67; JD, LaSalle U., 1970. Prodn. sales rep. Sta. KBRV Radio, Soda Springs, Idaho, 1956-58; program dir. Sta. KMOR Radio, Salt Lake City, 1964-65; news/agriculture divsn. Sta. KSL Radio-TV, Salt Lake City, 1965-66; news, pub. affairs rep. Sta. WNYW-WRFM, N.Y.C., 1966-69, Sta. KBIG AM/FM, L.A., 1969-72; sales mgr., sta. mgr. Sta. KOOL Radio-TV, Phoenix, 1972-79; pres. Sta. ABM Internat., Phoenix, 1979-81; v.p., gen. mgr. Sta. KORK AM/FM, Las Vegas, 1981-83; pres., gen. mgr. Frontier Media, Las Vegas, 1983-86; v.p. ops. Am. Mus. Hist. Documents, Las Vegas, 1986-89; pres., CEO Saturn Media Group, Inc., St. George, Utah, 1995—. Named Outstanding News Dir. AP, 1990-92, Best News and Sports Utah Broadcasters, 1992-93; recipient Disting. Svc. award Utah Sch. Bd. Assn., 1994. Mem. Rotary Internat., Boy Scouts Am., Utah Broadcasters Assn., Nat. Assn. Broadcasters. Mem. Ch. LDS. Office: Saturn Media Group Inc PO Box 1450 210 N 1000 East Saint George UT 84771-1450

SKINNER, KNUTE RUMSEY, poet, English educator; b. St. Louis, Apr. 25, 1929; s. George Rumsey and Lidi (Skjoldvig) S.; m. Jeanne Pratt; 1953; divorced 1954; 1 child, Frank; m. Linda Kuhn, Mar. 30, 1961 (div. Sept. 1977); children: Dunstan, Morgan; m. Edna Kiel, Mar. 25, 1978. Student, Culver-Stockton Coll., 1947-49; B.A., U. No. Colo., 1951; M.A., Middlebury Coll., 1954; Ph.D., U. Iowa, 1958. Instr. English U. Iowa, Iowa City, 1955-56, 57-58, 60-61; asst. prof. English Okla. Coll. for Women, 1961-62; lectr. creative writing Western Wash. U., Bellingham, 1962-71; asso. prof. English Western Wash. U., 1971-73, prof. English, 1973-97; pres. Signpost Press Inc., nonprofit corp., 1983-95. Author: Stranger with a Watch, 1965, A Close Sky Over Killaspuglonane, 1968, 75, In Dinosaur Country, 1969, The Sorcerers: A Laotian Tale, 1972, Hearing of the Hard Times, 1981, The Flame Room, 1983, Selected Poems, 1985, Learning to Spell "Zucchini," 1988, The Bears and Other Poems, 1991, What Trudy Knows and Other Poems, 1994, The Cold Irish Earth: New and Selected Poems of Ireland, 1965-1995, 1996; editor: Bellingham Rev., 1977-83, 93-95; contbr. poetry, short stories to anthologies, textbooks, periodicals. Nat. Endowment for the Arts fellow, 1975. Mem. Am. Conf. Irish Studies, Wash. Poets Assn. Office: Western Wash U HU 323 Bellingham WA 98225-9055

SKINNER, NATHAN LESTON, development chemist; b. Longview, Wash., Jan. 11, 1937; s. Nathan Leston and Lena (Gideon) S.; m. Sandra Celestine Hubka, July 1, 1959 (div. Jan. 1976); 1 child, Shannon Elizabeth; m. Susan Kay Brunkhorst, May 23, 1981; children: Niles Bentley, Kelci Nicole. Student, Lower Columbia Coll., 1955-56, Santiago Coll., 1956-57, Orange Coast Coll., 1957-64. Lab. technician Narmco, Costa Mesa, Calif., 1956-59, Crys-Tech., Santa Ana, Calif., 1960-61; engr. Western Semicondr., Santa Ana, 1962-66, Semco, Westminster, Calif., 1965-67; sr. rsch. asst. Hughes Rsch. Lab., Malibu, Calif., 1967-70; engr. Santa Barbara Rsch. Ctr., Goleta, Calif., 1970-76; rsch. dir., co-owner Sexwax, Inc., Carpinteria, Calif., 1970—; scientist III EG&G/EM, SBO, Goleta, 1976-91; tech. dir. Advanced Detectors, Inc., Santa Barbara, Calif., 1991—; co-owner, rsch. dir. Sumus Co., Santa Barbara, 1990—, Practichem Co., Carpinteria, 1991—, Bent Nickel Co., Carpinteria, 1993—; VCG sci. lead S.L.3 NASA, Marshall, Ala., 1978-85; invited speaker Nat. Tng. Inst. Pilot Program on Sci. and Tech., Albuquerque, 1991. Inventor surfboard wax, 1970, process for removing impurities from zone refined materials, 1975, direct vapor/solid synthesis of mercuric iodide using compounds of mercury and iodine, 1990; contbr. tech. papers to profl. jours. including Jour. Crystal Growth, 1988, Nuclear Instruments and Methods in Physics Rsch., 1989,NASA Conf. Publ., Jour. Spacecraft and Rockets 16, 1979. Founder REACTS (Rediscovery Educational Activities Create Tomorrow's Scientists)Goleta, 1990, exec. dir., 1990-93, resource leader; vol. sci. educator, demonstrator Santa Barbara County Schs., 1971—; trainer of sci. educators, 1992—. Recipient Letter of Commendation, NASA, 1985; Spl. Recognition award Adopt-a-Sch. com. Santa Barbara Industry Edn. Coun., 1990. Mem. Am. Chem. Soc., Mensa. Office: Xsirius Inc 815 E Mason St Santa Barbara CA 93103-3314

SKINNER, STANLEY THAYER, utility company executive, lawyer; b. Fort Smith, Ark., Aug. 18, 1937; s. John Willard and Irma Lee (Peters) S.; m. Margaret Olsen, Aug. 16, 1957; children—Steven Kent, Ronald Kevin. B.A. with honors, San Diego State U., 1960; M.A., U. Calif., Berkeley, 1961, J.D., 1964. Bar: Supreme Ct. Calif. bar 1965, U.S. Circuit Ct. Appeals for 9th Circuit bar 1966, 10th Circuit bar 1966. Atty. Pacific Gas and Electric Co., San Francisco, 1964-73; sr. counsel Pacific Gas and Electric Co., 1973, treas., 1974-76, v.p. fin., 1976, sr. v.p., 1977, exec. v.p., 1978-86, exec. v.p., chief fin. officer, 1982-85, vice chmn. bd., 1986-91, pres., chief oper. officer, 1991-94; pres., CEO Pacific Gas and Electric Co., San Francisco, 1994-95; chmn. bd. dirs., CEO Pacific Gas and Electric Co., 1995—; bd. dirs. Fed. Res. Bank of San Francisco, Pacific Gas Transmission Co. Bd. dirs. United Way of Bay Area, campaign chmn., 1992; trustee, former chmn. bd. dirs. Golden Gate U.; bd. dirs. Bay Area chpt. ARC, Bay Area Coun., Bay Area Econ. Forum. Mem. Calif. State Bar Assn., Calif. State C. of C. (bd. dirs.), San Francisco C. of C. (bd. dirs.), Bus. Coun., Bay Area Coun., Bus. Roundtable, Moraga Country Club. Republican. Presbyterian. Office: Pacific Gas & Electric Co 77 Beale St San Francisco CA 94105-1814

SKIRVIN, WILLIAM DAVID, artist, art director; b. Barstow, Calif., Mar. 8, 1952; s. Orval and Sylvia (Reynolds) S.; div.; children: Donovan Steven, Sarah Michelle, Dylan Thomas. Grad. high sch., Barstow. Tech. illustrator McDonnell Douglas Corp., Lemoore, Calif., 1973-80; freelance artist San Francisco, Calif., 1980—; fine artist, 1992-96; art dir. Virgin Interactive Entertainment, Irvine, Calif., 1992—, Inter-Game, Irvine, 1997—; art dir. Sierra On-Line, Inc., Oakhurst, Calif., 1987-91; freelance artist, 1997—. Pvt. collections include USN, Hewlett Packard, Apple Computers, and others. Republican.

SKLADAL, ELIZABETH LEE, elementary school educator; b. N.Y.C., May 23, 1937; d. Angier Joseph and Julia May (Roberts) Gallo; m. George Wayne Skladal, Dec. 26, 1956; children: George Wayne Jr., Joseph Lee. BA, Sweet Briar Coll., 1958; EdM, U. Alaska, 1976. Choir dir. Main Chapel, Camp Zama, Japan, 1958-59, Ft. Lee, Va., 1963-65; choir dir. Main Chapel and Snowhawk, Ft. Richardson, Alaska, 1968-70; tchr. Anchorage (Alaska) Sch. Dist., 1970—. Active Citizen's Adv. Com. for Gifted and Talented, Anchorage, 1981-83; mem. music com. Anchorage Sch. Dist., 1983-86; soloist Anchorage Opera Chorus, 1969-80, Cmty. Chorus, Anchorage, 1968-80; mem. choir First Presbyn. Ch., Anchorage, 1971—, deacon, 1988—, elder, 1996—, mission com. chair, 1996—; participant 1st cultural exch. from Anchorage to Magadan, Russia with Alaska Chamber Singers, 1992; participant mission trip to Swaziland, Africa with First Presbyn. Ch., Anchorage, summer 1995. Named Am. Coll. Theater Festival winner Amoco Oil Co., 1974; recipient Cmty. Svc. award Anchorage U. Alaska Alumni Assn., 1994-95. Mem. AAUW, Anchorage Concert Assn. Patron Soc. (assocs. coun. of dirs.), Alaska Chamber Singers, Am. Guild Organists (former dean, former treas., mem.-at-large). Republican. Presbyterian. Home: 1841 S Salem Dr Anchorage AK 99508-5156

SKLANSKY, JACK, electrical and computer engineering educator, researcher; b. N.Y.C., Nov. 15, 1928; s. Abraham and Clara S.; m. Gloria Joy Weiss, Dec. 24, 1957; children: David Alan, Mark Steven, Jeffrey Paul. BEE, CCNY, 1950; MSEE, Purdue U., 1952; D in Engring. Sci., Columbia U., 1955. Research engr. RCA Labs., Princeton, N.J., 1955-65; mgr. Nat. Cash Register Co., Dayton, Ohio, 1965-66; prof. elec. and computer engring. U. Calif., Irvine, 1966—; pres. Scanicon Corp., Irvine, 1980-89. Author: (with others) Pattern Classifiers and Trainable Machines, 1981; editor: Pattern Recognition, 1973, (with others) Biomedical Images and Computers, 1982; editor-in-chief: Machine Vision and Applications, 1987. Recipient best paper award Jour. Pattern Recognition, 1977; rsch. grantee NIH, 1971-84, Army Rsch. Office, 1984-91, NSF, 1992—, Office of Naval Rsch., 1995—. Fellow IEEE, Internat. Assn. for Pattern Recognition; mem. ACM. Office: U Calif Dept Elec-Computer Engring Irvine CA 92717

SKLAR, LOUISE MARGARET, service executive; b. L.A., Aug. 12, 1934; d. Samuel Baldwin Smith and Judith LeRoy (Boughton) Nelson; m. Edwynn Edgar Schroeder, Mar. 20, 1955 (div. July 1975); children: Neil Nelson, Leslie Louise Schroeder Grandclaudon, Samuel George; m. Martin Sklar, Oct. 17, 1983. Student, U. So. Calif., 1952-54, UCLA, 1977-79. Acct. Valentine Assocs., Northridge, Calif., 1976-78, programmer, 1978-79; contr. Western Monetary, Encino, Calif., 1979-81; pres. Automated Computer Composition, Chatsworth, Calif., 1984—. Mem. Am. Contract Bridge League (bd. govs. 1993—, mem. nat. charity com. 1982, mem. nat. goodwill com. 1994—), Assn. Los Angeles County Bridge Units (bd. dirs. 1990—, sec. 1984-86), DAR, Conn. Soc. Genealogists, Ky. Hist. Soc., So. Calif. Assistance League, Heart of Am. Geneal. Soc., Chatsworth C. of C., Greater L.A. Zoo Assn., Zeta Tau Alpha. Republican. Office: Automated Computer Composition Inc 21356 Nordhoff St Chatsworth CA 91311-6917

SKLAR, RICHARD LAWRENCE, political science educator; b. N.Y.C., Mar. 22, 1930; s. Kalman and Sophie (Laub) S.; m. Eva Molineux, July 14, 1962; children: Judith Anne, Katherine Elizabeth. A.B., U. Utah, 1952; M.A., Princeton U., 1957, Ph.D., 1961; UCLA. Mem. faculty Brandeis U., U. Ibadan, Nigeria, U. Zambia, SUNY-Stony Brook, UCLA; now prof. emeritus polit. sci. UCLA; mem. fgn. area fellowship program Africa Nat. Com., 1970-73; Simon vis. prof. U. Manchester, Eng., 1975, Fulbright vis. prof. U. Zimbabwe, 1984; Lester Martin fellow Harry S. Truman Rsch. Inst., Hebrew U. Jerusalem, 1979; fellow Africa Inst. of South Africa, 1994—. Author: Nigerian Political Parties: Power in an Emergent African Nation, 1963, Corporate Power in an African State, 1975; co-author: Postimperialism: International Capitalism and Development, 1987, African Politics and Problems in Development, 1991; contbr. articles to profl. jours. Served with U.S. Army, 1952-54. Rockefeller Found. grantee, 1967. Mem. Am. Polit. Sci. Assn., African Studies Assn. (dir. 1976-78, 80-83, v.p. 1980-81, pres. 1981-82), AAUP (pres. Calif. Conf. 1980-81). Home: 1951 Holmby Ave Los Angeles CA 90025-5905

SKLOVSKY, ROBERT JOEL, naturopath, pharmacist, educator; b. Bronx, N.Y., Nov. 19, 1952; s. Nathan and Esther (Steinberg) S. BS, Bklyn. Coll., 1975; MA in Sci. Edn., Columbia U., 1976; PharmD, U. of Pacific, 1977; D in Naturopathic Medicine, Nat. Coll. Naturopathic Medicine, 1983. Intern Tripler Army Med. Ctr., Honolulu, 1977; prof. pharmacology Nat. Coll. Naturopathic Medicine, Portland, Oreg., 1982-85; pvt. practice Milwaukie, Oreg., 1983—; cons. State Bd. Naturopathic Examiners, Oreg., Hawaii, Clackamas County Sherriff's Dept., Internat. Drug Info. Ctr., N.Y.C., 1983—, Albert Roy Davis Scientific Rsch. Lab, Orange Park, Fla. 1986. Recipient Bristol Labs. award, 1983. Fellow Am. Coll. Apothecaries; mem. Am. Assn. Naturopathic Physicians, Oreg. Assn. Naturopathic Physicians, N.Y. Acad. Sci. Office: 6910 SE Lake Rd Portland OR 97267-2196

SKOGEN, HAVEN SHERMAN, investment company executive; b. Rochester, Minn., May 8, 1927; s. Joseph Harold and Elpha (Hemphill) S.; m. Beverly R. Baker, Feb. 19, 1949; 1 child, Scott H. BS, Iowa State U., 1950; MS, Rutgers U., 1954, PhD, 1955; MBA, U. Chgo., 1970. Registered profl. engr., Wis. Devel. engr. E.I. duPont, Wilmington, Del., 1955-57; prof. Elmhurst (Ill.) Coll., 1957-58; chief engr. Stackpole, St. Marys, Pa., 1958-62; plant mgr. Magnatronics, Elizabethtown, Ky., 1962-65; mgr. Allen-Bradley, Milw., 1965-70; v.p. Dill-Clithrow, Chgo., 1970-74; oil co. exec. Occidental Oil Co., Grand Junction, Colo., 1974-92; ptnr. H&B Investment CO., 1992—. Author: Synthetic Fuel Combustion, 1984; inventor radioactive retort doping, locus retorting zone. Naval Rsch. fellow, 1951-55. Fellow Am. Inst. Chemists; mem. Internat. Platform Assn., Masons, Elks, Sigma Xi, Phi Beta Kappa, Phi Lambda Upsilon. Republican. Home: 3152 Primrose Ct Grand Junction CO 81506-4147

SKOLNIKOFF, ALAN ZACHARY, psychiatrist; b. N.Y.C., Aug. 25, 1932. MD, SUNY, 1959. Intern Madigan Gen. Hosp., Tacoma, Wash., 1959-60; resident Langley Porter, San Francisco, 1963-66; candidate San Francisco Psychoanalyst Inst., 1965-73; fellow Community Psychiat. Tng. Ctr., Berkeley, Calif., 1966-68; pvt. practice San Francisco; assoc. clin. prof. U. Calif.; tng. supr. analyst San Francisco Psychoanalytic Inst. Contbr. articles to profl. jours. Fellow Am. Psychiatric Assn. Office: 205 Edgewood Ave San Francisco CA 94117-3714

SKOOG, WILLIAM ARTHUR, former oncologist; b. Culver City, Calif., Apr. 10, 1925; s. John Lundeen and Allis Rose (Gatz) S.; m. Ann Douglas, Sept. 17, 1949; children: Karen, William Arthur, James Douglas, Allison. AA, UCLA, 1944; BA with gt. distinction, Stanford U., 1946, MD, 1949. Intern in medicine Stanford Hosp., San Francisco, 1948-49, asst. resident medicine, 1949-50; asst. resident medicine N.Y. Hosp., N.Y.C., 1950-51; sr. resident medicine Wadsworth VA Hosp., Los Angeles, 1951, attending specialist internal medicine, 1962-68; practice medicine specializing in internal medicine, Los Altos, Calif., 1959-61; pvt. practice hematology and oncology Calif. Oncologic and Surg. Med. Group, Inc., Santa Monica, Calif., 1971-72; pvt. practice med. oncology, San Bernardino, Calif., 1972-94; assoc. staff Palo Alto-Stanford (Calif.) Hosp. Center, 1959-61, U. Calif. Med. Center, San Francisco, 1959-61; asso. attending physician U. Calif. at Los Angeles Hosp. and Clinics, 1961-78; vis. physician internal medicine Harbor Gen. Hosp., Torrance, Calif., 1962-65, attending physician, 1965-71; cons. chemistry Clin. Lab., UCLA Hosp., 1963-68; affiliate cons. staff St. John's Hosp., Santa Monica, Calif., 1967-71, courtesy staff, 1971-72; courtesy attending med. staff Santa Monica Hosp., 1967-72; staff physician St. Bernardine (Calif.) Hosp., 1972-94, hon. staff, 1994—; staff physician San Bernardino Cmty. Hosp., 1972-90, courtesy staff, 1990-94; chief sect. oncology San Bernardino County Hosp., 1972-76; cons. staff Redlands (Calif.) Cmty. Hosp., 1972-83, courtesy staff, 1983-94, hon. staff, 1994—; asst. in medicine Cornell Med. Coll., N.Y.C., 1950-51; jr. rsch. physician UCLA Atomic Energy Project, 1954-55; instr. medicine, asst. rsch. physician dept. medicine UCLA Med. Center, 1955-56, asst. prof. medicine, asst. rsch. physician, 1956-59; clin. asso. hematology VA Center, Los Angeles, 1956-59; co-dir. metabolic rsch. unit UCLA Center for Health Scis., 1955-59, 61-65; co-dir. Health Scis. Clin. Rsch. Ctr., 1965-68, dir., 1968-72; clin. instr. medicine Stanford, 1959-61; asst. clin. prof. medicine, assoc. rsch. physician U. Calif. Med. Center, San Francisco, 1959-61; lectr. medicine UCLA Sch. Medicine, 1961-62, assoc. prof. medicine, 1962-73, assoc. clin. prof. medicine, 1973—. Served with USNR, 1943-46, lt. M.C., 1951-53. Fellow ACP; mem. Am., Calif. med. assns., So. Calif. Acad. Clin. Oncology, Western Soc. Clin. Research, Am. Fedn. Clin. Research, Los Angeles Acad. Medicine, San Bernardino County Med. Soc., Am. Soc. Clin. Oncology, Am. Soc. Internal Medicine, Calif. Soc. Internal Medicine, Inland Soc. Internal Medicine, Phi Beta Kappa, Alpha Omega Alpha, Sigma Xi, Alpha Kappa Kappa. Episcopalian (vestryman 1965-70). Club: Redlands Country. Contbr. articles to profl. jours. Home: 1119 Kimberly Pl Redlands CA 92373-6786

SKOUSEN, ROYAL JON, linguist; b. Cleve., Aug. 5, 1945; s. Leroy Bentley and Helen Louise (McCarty) S.; m. Sirkku Unelma Härkönen, June 24, 1968; children: Mikko, Lawrence, Angela, Christina, Nathaniel, Benjamin, Stephen. BA in English, Brigham Young U., 1969; MA in Linguistics, U. Ill., 1971, PhD in Linguistics, 1972. Instr. in linguistics U. Ill., Urbana,

1970-72; asst. prof. linguistics U. Tex., Austin, 1972-79; asst. prof. English Brigham Young U., Provo, Utah, 1979-81, assoc. prof. English, 1981-86, prof. English, 1986—; vis. prof. linguistics U. Calif., San Diego, 1981; Fulbright lectr. in linguistics U. Tampere, Finland, 1982; cons. Houghton Mifflin Pubs., Boston, 1978-82, WordPerfect Corp., Orem, Utah, 1984. author: Substantive Evidence in Phonology, 1975, Analogical Modeling of Language, 1989, Analogy and Structure, 1992; mem. editl. bd. Computers and the Humanities, 1987-97, Jour. of Quantitative Linguistics, 1993—. Spencer Found. rsch. grantee, 1974; James L. Barker lectr. Brigham Young U., 1985-86. Mem. Internat. Soc. Quantitative Linguistics (founding mem.), Found. for Ancient Rsch. and Mormon Studies (editor Book of Mormon Critical Text 1988—), Deseret Lang. and Linguistics Soc. (editor, pres. 1980-82). Mem. LDS Ch. Office: Brigham Young U Dept English Provo UT 84602

SKRATEK, SYLVIA PAULETTE, mediator, arbitrator, dispute systems designer; b. Detroit, Dec. 23, 1950; d. William Joseph and Helen (Meskauskas) S.; m. John Wayne Gullion, Dec. 21,1984. BS, Wayne State U., 1971; MLS, Western Mich. U., 1976; PhD, U. Mich., 1985. Media specialist Jackson (Mich.) Pub. Schs., 1971-79; contract specialist Jackson County Edn. Assn., 1976-79; field rep. Mich. Edn. Assn., E.Lansing, 1979-81; contract adminstr. Wash. Edn. Assn., Federal Way, 1981-85, regional coord., 1985-88, program adminstr., from 1988; dir. mediation svcs. Conflict Mgmt. Inst., Lake Oswego, Ore., 1986-87; exec. dir. N.W. Ctr. for Conciliation, 1987-88; served in Wash. State Senate, 1990-94; tng. cons. City of Seattle, 1986—; trustee Group Health Coop. of Puget Sound, Wash., 1984-87; sole proprietor Skratek & Assocs., 1980—; pres. Resolutions Internat., 1990-96; v.p. Mediation Rsch. and Edn. Project, Inc., 1990—. Contbr. articles to legal jours. Mem. Soc. for Profls. in Dispute Resolution, Indsl. Rels. Rsch. Assn.

SKROCKI, EDMUND STANLEY, II, health fair promoter, executive; b. Schenectady, N.Y., Sept. 6, 1953; s. Edmund Stanley I and Lorraine (Nocian) S.; m. Diane Carolyn Sittig, Sept. 6, 1976 (div. 1992); children: Carolyn, Michelle, Edmund III; 1 child, Johnathan Edmund. AA, LaValley Coll., 1981; BA, Sonoma State U., 1982, MA, 1987; postgrad., Am. Inst. Hypnotherapy. Pres. Skrocki's Philos. Svc., Lakeview Terrace, Calif., 1971-81, Redding, Calif., 1982—; pres., CEO Skrocki's Superior Svc., Lakeview Terrace, 1971-76, Redding, Calif., 1976—; pres., CEO, promoter, prodr. Realife Expositions, 1991—; producer Realife Expo Stars Over Hollywood, 1997. Bd. govs., deacon Ch. of Universal Knowledge, 1991—. Named one of Outstanding Young Men Am., 1980. Mem. Shasta Submarine Soc. (pres. 1984—). Home and Office: 755 Quartz Hill Rd Redding CA 96003-2118

SKROMEDA, STEVE, investment company executive; b. 1957. BS, Calif. State U., 1982. CFO Kennedy Cabot & Co., Beverly Hills, Calif., 1983—. Office: Kennedy Cabot & Co Inc 9470 Wilshire Blvd Beverly Hills CA 90212-2707*

SKROPOS, GUS JAMES, mayor. Grad. with honors in bus., Calif. Poly. Inst., Pomona, 1978; JD, U. La Verne, 1984. Bar: Calif. 1985. Mem. Ontario (Calif.) City Coun., Calif., 1984-85; elected mem. Ontario (Calif.) City Coun., 1990—, mayor pro tem, 1992-94; apptd. mayor City of Ontario, 1994, elected mayor, 1994—; dep. dist. atty. San Bernardino County, Calif., 1987—; mem. San Bernardino County bd. suprs., 4th dist., 1985-86. Major, USAFR, 1976—. Office: 303 E B St Ontario CA 91764

SKUD, BERNARD EINAR, marine biologist; b. Ironwood, Mich., Jan. 31, 1927; s. Ferdinand and Elma (Hendrickson) S.; m. Patricia Ruth Duffin, Aug. 20, 1950; children: Timothy, Ferd, Eric. BS, U. Mich., 1949, MS, 1950; postgrad., U. Wash., 1951-53; Fellow of Pub. & Internat. Affairs, Princeton U., 1968. Grad. asst. U. Mich., Ann Arbor, 1949-50; rsch. biologist U.S. Fish and Wildlife Svc., Seattle, 1950-56; supervisory fishery biologist U.S. Bur. Comml. Fisheries, Boothbay Harbor, Maine, 1956-58; asst. dir. U.S. Bur. Comml. Fisheries, Galveston, Tex., 1958-61; dir. U.S. Bur. Comml. Fisheries, Boothbay Harbor, 1961-70; dir. investigations Internat. Pacific Halibut Commn., Seattle, 1970-78; divsn. chief U.S. Nat. Marine Fisheries Svc., Washington, 1978-79; sr. scientist U.S. Nat. Marine Fisheries Svc., Narragansett, R.I., 1980-85; dir. Internat. North Pacific Fisheries Commn., Vancouver, B.C., Can., 1986-91; CEO Sisu Consulting, Oak Harbor, Wash., 1991—; affiliate prof. U. Wash., Seattle, 1971-78, U. R.I., Kingston, 1980-86. Editor (bull.) Internat. Pacific Halibut Commn. Scientific Reports, 1970-78, Jour. N.W. Atlantic Fishery Science, 1985-86. Bd. dirs. St. Andrews Hosp., Boothbay Harbor, 1965-70. With USN, 1945-46. Fellow Am. Inst. Fishery Rsch. Biologists (pres. 1981-83); mem. Am. Fisheries Soc. (book rev. editor 1965-70). Home and Office: 125 SW Jib St Oak Harbor WA 98277

SKWARA, ERICH WOLFGANG, novelist, poet, educator, literary critic; b. Salzburg, Austria, Nov. 4, 1948; came to U.S., 1975; s. Alois Gaigg and Hermine Maria Skwara; m. Victoria Anne Dufresne, July 10, 1974 (div. Mar. 1978); m. Gloria Elaine Winniski, June 8, 1978; children: Gabriella Maria, Alexandra Felicitas. BA, U. Paris VII, 1970; MA, Salzburg U., 1972; PhD, N.Y. State U., Albany, 1985. Instr. U. Md., Balt., 1975-77; freelance author Balt. and Paris, 1977-82; vis. lectr. Georgetown U., Washington, 1982-84; freelance author Salzburg, 1984-86; prof. humanities, comparative lit. and German San Diego State U., 1986—; dep. editor-in-chief for cultural affairs Die Weit, Berlin, 1993; cultural and lit. corr. for a number of German and Austrian newspapers and media, 1979—. Author: (novels) Black Sails, 1979, 97, The Cool Million, 1990, Tristan Island, 1992, Die Heimlichen Konige, 1995, Plague in Siena, 1994, 95, Ice on the Bridge, 1997, others; translator (from English to German) works by T. Williams, Thomas Wolfe, others. Mem. Internat. PEN Club, PEN Ctr. of German Speaking Authors Abroad (bd. dirs. 1985—), PEN Ctr. of Austria, PEN Ctr. of France. Roman Catholic. Office: San Diego State U Dept Classics/Humanities San Diego CA 92182

SKYLSTAD, WILLIAM S., bishop; b. Omak, Wash., Mar. 2, 1934; s. Stephen Martin and Reneldes Elizzbeth (Danzl) S. Student, Pontifical Coll., Josephinum, Worthington, Ohio; M.Ed., Gonzaga U. Ordained priest Roman Catholic Ch., 1960; asst. pastor Pullman, Wash., 1960-62; tchr. Mater Cleri Sem., 1961-68, rector, 1968-74; pastor Assumption Parish, Spokane, 1974-76; chancellor Diocese of Spokane, 1976-77; ordained bishop, 1977; bishop of Yakima, Wash., 1977-90, Spokane, Wash., 1990—. Office: Diocese of Spokane PO Box 1453 1023 W Riverside Ave Spokane WA 99210-1103 Home: 1025 W Cleveland Ave Spokane WA 99205-3320*

SLACK, DONALD CARL, agricultural engineer, educator; b. Cody, Wyo., June 25, 1942; s. Clarence Ralbon and Clara May (Beightol) S.; m. Marion Arline Kimball, Dec. 19, 1964; children: Jonel Marie, Jennifer Michelle. BS in Agrl. Engring., U. Wyo., 1965; MS in Agrl. Engring., U. Ky., 1968, PhD in Agrl. Engring., 1975. Registered profl. engr., Ky., Ariz. Asst. civil engr. City of Los Angeles, 1965; research specialist U. Ky., Lexington, 1966-70; agrl. engring. advisor U. Ky., Tha Phra, Thailand, 1970-73; research asst. U. Ky., Lexington, 1973-75; from asst. prof. to assoc. prof. agrl. engring. U. Minn., St. Paul, 1975-84; prof. U. Ariz., Tucson, 1984—, head dept. agrl. and biosystems engring., 1991—; tech. advisor Ariz. Dept. Water Resources, Phoenix, 1985—, Tucson active mgmt. area, 1996—; cons. Winrock Internat., Morrilton, Ark., 1984, Water Mgmt. Synthesis II, Logan, Utah, 1985, Desert Agrl. Tech. Systems, Tucson, 1985—, Portek Hermosillo, Mex., 1989—, World Bank, Washington, 1992—, Malawi Environ. Monitoring Project, 1996, Mex. Inst. for Water Tech., 1997; dep. program support mgr. Rsch. Irrigation Support Project for Asia and the Near East, Arlington, Va., 1987-94; mem. adv. team Cearan Found. for Meteorology and Hydrology, Fortaleza, Brazil, 1995—; mem. internat. adv. panel Matrou Resources Mgmt. Project, World Bank, Egypt, 1996—. Contbr. articles to profl. jours. Fellow ASCE (Outstanding Jour. Paper award 1988), Am. Soc. Agrl. Engrs. (Ariz. sect. Engr. of Yr. 1993); mem. Am. Geophys. Union, Am. Soc. Agronomy, Soil Sci. Soc. Am., Am. Soc. Engring. Edn., SAR, Brotherhood of Knights of the Vine (master knight), Sigma Xi, Tau Beta Pi, Alpha Epsilon, Gamma Sigma Delta. Democrat. Lutheran. Home: 9230 E Visco Pl Tucson AZ 85710-3167 Office: U Ariz Agrl Biosystems Engring Tucson AZ 85721 *Personal philosophy: Don't take yourself too seriously and don't take anyone else too seriously either.*

SLADE-LUNDY, BETTIE B., retired electronics professional; b. Marinette, Wis., Feb. 16, 1924; d. Adolph Gustav and Bertha Julian (Keller) Limberg; m. George Wesley Lundy II, Nov. 11, 1951 (div. 1956); children: George Wesley III, Genise Wynell, Charles Edward; m. Jim Donovan Slade, July 20, 1973. Lic. vocat. nurse, psychiat. technician, Calif. With Allis Chalmers, Milw., 1942-44, Gen. Dynamics, San Diego, 1959-65, Tetedyne Ryan, San Diego, 1966-76, Cubic, San Diego, 1976-86; ret., 1986. Author: (poetry) Do You Have a Minute, 1991, (biography) Growing Up on a Farm During the Depression, 1995; artist over 100 paintings, 1986—. Den mother Boy Scouts Am., San Diego; Sunday sch. tchr. Luth. Ch., San Diego. With USN Waves, 1944-50. Recipient Sen. Cashman award Marinette, Wis., 1937, Letter of Appreciation Mother Teresa, 1992, Gen. Norman Schwarzkoph, 1993, Queen Elizabeth, 1993. Mem. Internat. Soc. Poets (life), Nat. Parks & Conservation, Smithsonian Assocs., Peal Ctr. Christian Living, Nat. Audubon Soc., Nat. Mus. Women in Arts. Republican. Home: 6315 Thorn St San Diego CA 92115-6908

SLADICH, HARRY HAMILL, university administrator; b. Anaconda, Mont., Jan. 9, 1938; s. Joseph Francis and Caroline (Hamill) S.; m. Marguerite Dill, June 18, 1960; children: Harry G., Jennifer M., Suzanne. BBA, Gonzaga U., 1959, MBA, 1967. Asst. prof. Gonzaga U., Spokane, Wash., 1963—, dir. adminstrv. services, 1962-71, asst. to pres., 1972-83, v.p. adminstrn. and planning, 1983—. Bd. dirs. ARC, Spokane, 1978-95, chmn., 1981-83, adv. council western ops., Burlingame, Calif., 1983-86; mem. com. on nominations ARC, Washington, 1991-92; mem. exec. com. adv. bd. Wash. State Higher Edn. Bd., 1986-87; bd. dirs. Wash. State Catholic Conf., Seattle, 1980-84, Mus. Native Am. Culture, Spokane, 1989-92; chmn. edn. div. United Way, Spokane, 1983, bd. dirs. 1991—, vice chair adminstrn., 1995—. Roman Catholic. Home: 1103 W 17th Ave Spokane WA 99203-1108 Office: Gonzaga U 502 E Boone Ave Spokane WA 99258-1774

SLAGLE, MARJORIE WITMAN, occupational health program manager, educator; b. Bellefonte, Pa., July 13, 1950; d. Harold Francis and Carole Elizabeth Witman; children, Karl David Slagle, Michael Allen Slagle. BS, Gustavus Adolphus Coll., 1972; M in Nursing, U. Washington, 1993; FNP, Seattle Pacific U., 1996. RN, Wash. Commd. ensign USN, 1971, advanced through grades to capt., 1993, resigned, 1993; charge nurse, evening supr. U.S. Naval Hosp., Portsmouth, Va., 1972-77; staff nurse, ICU Gen. Hosp., Portsmouth, Va., 1978, staff nurse, maternal-child care dept, 1979-84; relief charge nurse Primacare Urgent Care Ctr., Carrolton, Tex., 1984; asst. charge nurse, pub. rels., maternal child-care dept. Adventist Hosp., Simi Valley, Calif., 1985-87; staff nurse emergency room, med. surg., maternal-child depts Nursefinders, Seattle, 1987-90; asst. dir. nursing svcs. U.S. Naval Hosp., Bremerton, Wash., 1989; tng. coord., headquarters, combat zone field hosp. USN, Seattle, 1987-90; relief dept. head maternal-child, and other duties U.S. Naval Hosp., Oakland, Calif., 1990-91; head, inpatient nursing svcs., combat zone field hosp. USN, Seattle, 1991-93; regional mgr., employee assistance program coord. USPHS Fed. Occupl. Health, Seattle, 1993-94, regional mgr. clin. ops., health educator, 1994—. Health and fitness speaker, Mt. Bachelor Acad., Prineville, Oreg., 1993-94. Mem. Assn. Mil. Surgeons U.S. (com. chmn. Navy Nurse Corps program of ann. conf. 1989-91, spkr. 1988-89), Res. Officers Assn., USN Meml. Found., Women in Mil. Svc. for Am. Meml. Found., Uniformed Svcs. Nurse Practitioner Assn., Am. Assn. Occupl. Health Nurses, USPHS Commd. Officers Assn., Wash. State Assn. Occupl. Health Nurses, Sigma Theta Tau. Home: 5736 S 238th Ct Apt E5 Kent WA 98032-3708

SLATER, DON AUSTIN, shipyard executive, consultant; b. Bay City, Mich., May 27, 1938; s. William Stuart and Inez Fern (Hagen) S.; m. Sara Belva Sanford, Feb. 3, 1962; children: Shandra Sanford, Nathan Dorman. BS in Naval Architecture and Marine Engring., U. Mich. Naval architect Western Boat Bldg. Corp., Tacoma, 1964; exec. v.p. and gen. mgr. Star Marine Industries, Tacoma; gen. mgr. Shipyard div. Marine Iron Works, Tacoma; pres., CEO Marine Industry N.W., Inc., Tacoma, 1976—; cons. to various law firms, Wash. and N.J., 1975—; arbitrator Am. Arbitration Assn., 1985—. 1st v.p. Va. V Found., Seattlem 1986; bd. dirs. Puget Sound Marine Hist. Soc., 1978-80. Mem. Soc. Naval Architects and Marine Engrs. Home: 30720 43rd Ave SW Federal Way WA 98023-2164 Office: Marine Industries NW Inc 313 E F St # 1275 Tacoma WA 98421-1821

SLATER, SHELLEY, communications executive; b. Ogden, Utah, June 26, 1959; d. Lynn Russell and Darlene (Allen) Slater; m. Dale Thomas Hansen, Jan. 26, 1977 (div. Feb. 1979); 1 child, Thomas Arthur; m. Eugene Allan DuVall, Mar. 8, 1981 (div. Dec. 1985); 1 child, Gregory Allan; m. Steven Blake Allender, June 9, 1990 (div. May 1993). BBA cum laude, Regis U., 1992, postgrad., 1992—. Installation, repair technician MT Bell, Clearfield, Utah, 1977-81; ctrl. office technician MT Bell, Salt Lake City, 1981-83, engring. specialist, 1983-86; engring. specialist U.S. West Comm., Englewood, Colo., 1986-93; network analyst, documentation and tng. mgr. Time Warner Comm., Englewood, Colo., 1993—; ops. process mgr. Time Warner Connect, Englewood, Colo.; bus. cons. Jr. Achievement, Denver, 1988-89. Day capt. AZTEC Denver Mus. of Natural History, 1992; loaned exec. Mile High United Way, 1993. Mem. Soc. Cable Telecomms. Engrs. (bd. dirs., pres. Rocky Mountain chpt.), Women in Cable and Telecomms. Democrat. Office: Time Warner Comm 160 Inverness Dr W Englewood CO 80112-5001

SLATT, ROGER MALCOLM, petroleum geologist; b. San Francisco, July 5, 1941; s. Earl and Helen (Nacht) S.; divorced; children: Andrew Martin, Thomas Wayne; m. Linda Hammond, Aug. 22, 1987; AA, San Francisco City Coll., 1961; BA, Calif. State U.-San Jose, 1965; MS, U. Alaska, 1967, Ph.D., 1970. Assoc. prof. geology Meml. U., Nfld., Can., 1970-76; vis. asst. prof. geology Ariz. State U., Tempe, 1976-78; sr. rsch. geologist Atlantic Richfield Co., Dallas, 1978-80; stratigraphy research mgr. Cities Svc. Exploration Prodn. Rsch., Tulsa, 1980-83; dir. reservoir geology Arco Oil & Gas Co., Plano, Tex., 1983-87, mgr. stratigraphic exploration rsch., 1987-90; mgr. formation evaluation Arco Internat. Oil & Gas Co., 1990-92; chmn. dept. geology and geol. engring. Colo. Sch. Mines, Golden, 1992—. Contbr. articles to profl. jours. NSF trainee, 1970; Ethan Allen scholar, 1965; fellow NDEA, 1968, Pan Am. Petroleum Found., 1970. Mem. Soc. Econ. Paleontologists and Mineralogists (rsch. com. 1983-88), Am. Assn. Petroleum Geologists (chmn. rsch. act. com. 1981-90, edn. com. 1986-91, devel. geol. com. 1987-91, chmn. rsch. com. 1991-94), Rocky Mountain Assn. Geol., Rocky Mountain Petroleum Tech. Trans. Coun. (dir. 1995—). Office: Colo Sch Mines Dept Geology & Geol Engring Golden CO 80401

SLAUGHTER, JOHN BROOKS, university administrator; b. Topeka, Mar. 16, 1934; s. Reuben Brooks and Dora (Reeves) S.; m. Ida Bernice Johnson, Aug. 31, 1956; children: John Brooks, Jacqueline Michelle. Student, Washburn U., 1951-53; BSEE, Kans. State U., 1956, DSc (hon.), 1988; MS in Engring., UCLA, 1961; PhD in Engring. Scis, U. Calif., San Diego, 1971; D Engring. (hon.), Rensselaer Poly. Inst., 1981; DSc (hon.), U. So. Calif., 1981, Tuskegee Inst., 1981, U. Md., 1982, U. Notre Dame, 1982, U. Miami, 1983, U. Mass., 1983, Tex. So. U., 1984, U. Toledo, 1985, U. Ill., 1986, SUNY, 1986; LHD (hon.), Bowie State Coll., 1987; DSc (hon.), Morehouse Coll., 1988, Kans. State U., 1988; LLD (hon.), U. Pacific, 1989; DSc (hon.), Pomona Coll., 1989; LHD (hon.), Alfred U., 1991, Calif. Luth. U., 1991, Washburn U., 1992. Registered profl. engr., Wash. Electronics engr. Gen. Dynamics Convair, San Diego, 1956-60; with Naval Electronics Lab. Center, San Diego, 1960-75, div. head, 1965-71, dept. head, 1971-75; dir. applied physics lab. U. Wash., 1975-77; asst. dir. NSF, Washington, 1977-79; dir. NSF, 1980-82; acad. v.p., provost Wash. State U., 1979-80; chancellor U. Md., College Park, 1982-88; pres. Occidental Coll., Los Angeles, 1988—; bd. dirs., vice chmn. San Diego Transit Corp., 1968-75; mem. com. on minorities in engring. Nat. Rsch. Coun., 1976-79; mem. Commn. on Pre-Coll. Edn. in Math., Sci. and Tech. Nat. Sci. Bd., 1982-83; bd. dirs. Monsanto Co., ARCO, Avery Dennison Corp., IBM, Northrop Grumman Corp.; chmn. advancement com. Music Ctr. of L.A. County, 1989-93. Editor: Jour. Computers and Elec. Engring, 1972—. Bd. dirs. San Diego Urban League, 1962-66, pres., 1964-66; mem. Pres.'s Com. on Nat. Medal Sci., 1979-80; trustee Rensselaer Poly. Inst., 1982; chmn. Pres.'s Com. Nat. Collegiate Athletic Assn., 1986-88; bd. govs. Town Hall of Calif., 1990; bd. dirs. L.A. World Affairs Coun., 1990. Recipient Engring. Disting. Alumnus of Yr. award UCLA, 1978, UCLA medal, 1989, Roger Revelle award U. Calif.-San Diego, 1991, Disting. Svc. award NSF, 1979, Svc. in Engring. award Kans. State U., 1981, Disting. Alumnus of Yr. award U. Calif.-San Diego, 1982; Naval Electronics Lab. Ctr. fellow, 1969-70; elected to Topeka High Sch. Hall of Fame, 1983, Hall of Fame of Am. Soc. Engring. Edn., 1993; named Kansan of Yr. by Kans. Native Sons and Daus., 1994. Fellow IEEE (chmn. com. on minority affairs 1976-80), Am. Acad. Arts and Scis.; mem. NAE, Nat. Collegiate Athletic Assn. (chmn. pres. commn.), Am. Soc. for Engring. Edn. (inducted into Hall of Fame 1993), Phi Beta Kappa (hon.), Tau Beta Phi, Eta Kappa Nu. Office: Occidental Coll 1600 Campus Rd Los Angeles CA 90041-3384

SLAWIATYNSKY, MARION MICHAEL, biomedical electronics engineer, software consultant; b. Phila., Nov. 21, 1958; s. Walter Wasyl and Maria Margaret (Sauer) S. BA in Biology, LaSalle U., 1980; MS in Biomed. Engring., Drexel U., 1984, BS in Electronics Engring. (hon.), 1982. Sr. systems engr. Innovative Med. Systems, Ivyland, Pa., 1983-95; sr. software engr. Advanced Tech. Labs., Bothell, Wash., 1995—. Soloist Male Chorus Prometheus, 1976-95; mem. Steuben Soc. Am., Phila., 1990-95. Mem. IEEE, Assn. for Advancement of Med. Instrumentation. Republican. Roman Catholic. Home: 20129 Hollyhills Dr NE Bothell WA 98011-7603 Office: ATL 22100 Bothell Everett Hwy PO Box 3003 MS265 Bothell WA 98041-3003

SLEDGE, REGINALD LEON, regulatory compliance analyst; b. Balt., July 8, 1954; s. Herbert Clifton and Juanita (Brantley) S. Grad., Lawrence Acad., 1972; student, Dartmouth Coll., 1968; BS, Boston U., 1976; MBA, Columbia U., 1984. Fin. analyst West Point-Pepperell, Inc., N.Y.C., 1976-77; fin. futures trader European Am. Bank, N.Y.C., 1978-82; portfolio mgr. Fuji Bank, N.Y.C., 1984-85; fin. cons. Control Assocs., N.Y.C., 1986-87; acct., fin. analyst Spicer & Oppenheim, N.Y.C., 1987-88; sr. regulatory compliance analyst BankAm. Bus. Credit Inc., San Diego, 1988—; mem. Columbia Bus. Sch. Alumni Counseling Bd., Lawrence Acad. Alumni Bd. Visitors. Mem. Rep. Nat. Com., 1986—, San Diego Rep. Party Century Club. Mem. Assn. for Investment Mgmt. and Rsch., Fin. Analysts Fedn., Columbia Bus. Sch. Club N.Y. (past v.p.), Columbia Univ. Club of San Diego. Republican. Roman Catholic. Home: 5225 Fiore Ter Apt D117 San Diego CA 92122-5647 Office: BankAm Bus Credit Inc 10124 Old Grove Rd San Diego CA 92131-1649

SLEEPER, ANDREW DUKE, electrical engineer, statistician; b. Oklahoma City, Okla., Mar. 21, 1959; s. Harold G. and Ann Sleeper; m. Julie Nguyen Phuoc Xuan Phuong, Nov. 2, 1981; children: Kim, Minh, Pascal. BSEE summa cum laude, Rice U., 1981; MS in Statistics, Colo. State U., 1994. Registered profl. engr., Colo. Engr. Hewlett-Packard Co., Corvallis, Oreg., 1981-87, Woodward Gov. Co., Loveland, Colo., 1987—; consulting statistician, 1991—; presenter Euro-EM '94, 1994. Contbr. articles to profl. jours. Precinct committeeman Rep. Orgn., Ft. Collins, Colo., 1988—. Mem. IEEE, Am. Soc. for Quality Control (cert. quality engr., cert. reliability engr.; trainer in statistics and quality engring. 1987—). Home: 1502 Mathews Fort Collins CO 80524 Office: Woodward Gov Co 3800 Wilson Ave Loveland CO 80538-2075

SLETTEN, KENNETH G., construction executive; b. 1929. BS in Engring., U. Colo.; MBA, Stanford U. Pres. Rudolph & Sletter, Inc., Foster City, Calif., 1961—, CEO. Office: Rudolph & Sletten Inc PO Box 4637 989 E Hillside Blvd Foster City CA 94404*

SLIKER, TODD RICHARD, accountant, lawyer; b. Rochester, N.Y., Feb. 9, 1936; s. Harold Garland and Marion Ethel (Caps) S.; BS with honors (Ford Found. scholar), U. Wis., 1955; PhD, Cornell U., 1962; MBA, Harvard, 1970; JD, U. Denver, 1982; m. Gretchen Paula Zeiter, Dec. 27, 1963; children: Cynthia Garland, Kathryn Clifton. Bar: Colo. 1983. With Clevite Corp., Cleve., 1962-68, head applied physics sect., 1965-68; asst. to pres. Granville-Phillips Co., Boulder, Colo., 1970; v.p., gen. mgr. McDowell Electronics, Inc., Metuchen, N.J., 1970-71; pres. C.A. Compton, Inc., mfrs. audio-visual equipment, Boulder, 1971-77; chief acct. C&S Inc., Englewood, Colo., 1977-80, v.p., 1980-82; sole practice law, Boulder, 1983-88; owner, mgr. real estate, 1972—. Del., Colo. Rep. Assembly, 1974, 76; Rep. dist. fin. coordinator, 1974-75; precinct committeeman, 1974-86, 92-94; chmn. Boulder County Rep. 1200 Club, 1975-79; mem. Colo. Rep. State Cen. Com., 1977-81, asst. treas., 1979-87; sect. corr. Harvard U., 1981—. Served to 1st lt. USAF, 1955-57. Recipient paper award vehicular communication group IEEE, 1966. Lic. real estate salesman, securities salesman; CPA, Colo. Mem. Colo. Soc. CPAs (govt. relations task force 1983-86), Colo. Bar Assn. (publs. com. 1982-84), Am. Phys. Soc., Optical Soc. Am. (referee Jour.), Colo. Harvard Bus. Sch. Club, Hist. Boulder Club, Rotary, Sigma Xi, Phi Kappa Phi, Theta Chi, Beta Alpha Psi. Contbr. articles to profl. jours. Patentee in field. Home: PO Box 715 12500 Oxford Rd Niwot CO 80544-0715 *Personal philosophy: The good will last.*

SLOAN, JERRY (GERALD EUGENE SLOAN), professional basketball coach; b. Mar. 28, 1942; m. Bobbye; 3 children: Kathy, Brian, Holly. Student, Evansville Coll., Evansville, Ind. Professional basketball player, Baltimore, 1965-66, Chicago Bulls, NBA, 1966-76; head coach Chicago Bulls, 1979-82; scout Utah Jazz, NBA, Salt Lake City, 1983-84, asst. coach, 1984-88, head coach, 1988—; player 2 NBA All-Star games; named to NBA All-Defensive First Team, 1969, 72, 74, 75. Office: care Utah Jazz Delta Ctr 301 W South Temple Salt Lake City UT 84101-1216*

SLOAN, LANNY GENE, municipal official; b. Denver, Aug. 30, 1945; s. Vincent Eugene and Leta Valma (Atwood) S.; m. Janet Cellen, July 5, 1968 (div. 1973); m. Patti Stucker, 1990. Student, U. Utah, 1963-68; BA in Bus. Mgmt., Lewis-Clark State Coll., 1990. Registered land surveyor, Idaho. Engr.'s technician Idaho Dept. Transp., Jerome, 1970-77; land surveyor Edwards-Howard-Martens, Engrs., Twin Falls, Idaho, 1977-80; project supt. J. Holley Constrn., Wells, Nev., 1981—; dir. pub. works City of Jerome, 1982-90, City of Coos Bay (Oreg.), 1990-93; city adminstr. City of Salmon, Idaho, 1993—; mem. adv. bd. N.W. Tech. Transfer Ctr., Olympia, Wash. Chmn. bd. dirs. Jerome City Libr., 1986-90; bd. trustees Coos Bay Libr., 1991—; bd. dirs. Jerome City Airport, 1986-90, Bay Area Rehab., 1990—. Mem. Am. Pub. Works Assn., Am. Water Works Assn. (trustee intermountain sect. 1987—), Pacific N.W. Pollution Control Assn., Green Drake Soc. Office: City of Salmon 200 Main St Salmon ID 83467-4111

SLOAN, MICHAEL DANA, information systems specialist; b. Santa Monica, Calif., Sept. 30, 1960; s. Avery and Beverly Rae (Krantz) S.; m. Barbara Rogers; 1 child, Ashley Harrison. BS in Bus. Adminstrn., Calif. State U., Northridge, 1983; MBA, Pepperdine U., 1987. Programmer/analyst TICOR, Inc., L.A., 1979-80; data processing analyst Deluxe Check Printers, Inc., Chatsworth, Calif., 1980-83; fin. systems analyst Wismer & Assocs., Inc., Canoga Park, Calif., 1983-84; sr. systems analyst Coast Savs. & Loan, Granada Hills, Calif., 1984-86; microcomputer systems specialist Litton Industries, Woodland Hills, Calif., 1986-87; systems mgr., info. resources mgr. TRW, Inc.- Space and Def., Redondo Beach, Calif., 1987-93; project mgr. Health Net, Woodland Hills, 1993-95; mgr. fin. and sales systems Merisel Ams. Inc., El Segundo, Calif., 1995—; cons. Data Most, Inc., Chatsworth, 1982-83, Home Savs. & Loan, North Hollywood, Calif., 1987, Micro Tech., L.A., 1987, TRW, Inc.-Space and Def., Redondo Beach, Calif., 1993—. Mem. IEEE Computer Soc., Salle Gascon Fencing Club, U.S. Fencing Assn., Delta Sigma Pi. Republican. Office: 200 Continental Blvd El Segundo CA 90245-4526

SLOAN, PATRICE S., artist; b. Banner Elk, N.C., Jan. 14, 1955; d. George Wallace and Edna Earle (Heaton) Shook; m. Michael L. Sloan, July 1, 1988; 1 child, George Walter Shook. BA in History, U. S.C., 1977, BA in English, 1977. Artist Myrtle Beach, S.C., 1980-88, Juneau, Alaska, 1988-94; artist, gallery owner Dutch Harbor, Alaska, 1994—; graphic cons. Aleutian-Pribilof Islands Assn., Unalaska, Alaska, 1996. Contbg. artist Dutch Harbor Fisherman, 1996; prin. works include pastels Still Water, 1996, The Law, 1996, acrylic Arctic Squirrel, 1996, oil Life in the Arctic, 1996. Mem. Nat. Assn. Fine Arts, Arts for Healthy Alaska, Bering Sea Exch. Home: PO Box 920212 Dutch Harbor AK 99692

SLOANE, BEVERLY LEBOV, writer, consultant; b. N.Y.C., May 26, 1936; d. Benjamin S. and Anne (Weinberg) LeBov; m. Robert Malcolm Sloane, Sept. 27, 1959; 1 child, Alison Lori Sloane Gaylin. AB, Vassar Coll., 1958; MA, Claremont Grad. Sch., 1975, doctoral study, 1975-76; cert. in exec. mgmt., UCLA Grad. Sch. Mgmt., 1982, grad. exec. mgmt. program., UCLA 1982; grad. intensive bioethics course Kennedy Inst. Ethics, Georgetown U., 1987, advanced bioethics course, 1988; grad. sem. in Health

Care Ethics, U. Wash. Sch. Medicine, Seattle, summer 1988-90, 94; grad. Summer Bioethics Inst. Loyola Marymount U., summer, 1990; grad. Annual Summer Inst. on Teaching or Writing, Columbia Tchrs. Coll., summer 1990; grad. Annual Summer Inst. on Advanced Teaching of Writing, summer, 1993, Annual Inst. Pub. Health and Human Rights, Harvard U. Sch. Pub. Health, 1994, grad. profl. pub. course Stanford U., 1982, grad. exec. refresher course profl. pub. Stanford U., 1994; cert. Exec. Mgmt. Inst. in Health Care, U. So. Calif., 1995, cert. advanced exec. program Grad. Sch. Mgmt. UCLA, 1995; cert. in ethics corps tng. program, Josephson Inst. of Ethics, 1991, cert.; ethics fellow Loma Linda U. Med. Ctr., 1989; cert. clin. intensive biomedical ethics, Loma Linda U. Med. Ctr., 1989. Circulation libr. Harvard Med. Libr., Boston, 1958-59; social worker Conn. State Welfare, New Haven, 1960-61; tchr. English, Hebrew Day Sch., New Haven, 1961-64; instr. creative writing and English lit. Monmouth Coll., West Long Branch, N.J., 1967-69; freelance writer, Arcadia, Calif., 1970—; v.p. council grad. students, Claremont Grad. sch., 1971-72, adj. dir. Writing Ctr. Speaker Series Claremont Grad. Sch., 1993—, spkr., 1996, 97; mem. adv. coun. tech. and profl. writing Dept. English, Calif. State U., Long Beach, 1980-82; mem. adv. bd. Calif. Health Rev., 1982-83; mem. Foothill Health Dist. Adv. Coun. L.A. County Dept. Health Svcs., 1987-93, pres., 1989-91, immediate past pres., 1991-92; vis. scholar Hastings Ctr., 1996; spkr. N.Y. Task Force, 1996. Ann. Key Mem. award, 1990. Author: From Vassar to Kitchen, 1967, A Guide to Health Facilities: Personnel and Management, 1971, 2nd edit. 1977, 3d edit., 1992. Mem. pub. relations bd. Monmouth County Mental Health Assn., 1968-69; chmn. creative writing group Calif. Inst. Tech. Woman's Club, 1975-79; mem. ethics com., human subjects protection com. Jewish Home for the Aging, Reseda, Calif., 1994-97; mem. task force edn. and cultural activities, City of Duarte, 1987-88; mem. strategic planning task force com., campaign com. for pre-eminence Claremont Grad. Sch., 1986-87, mem. alumni coun., 1993-96, bd. dirs., governing bd. alumni assn., 1993-96, mem. alumni coun., mem. steering com. annual alumni day 1994-96, mem. alumni awards com., 1994-96, mem. alumni events com., 1994-96, mem. vol. devel. com., 1994-96; Vassar Coll. Class rep. to Alumnae Assn. Fall Coun. Meeting, 1989,, class corr. Vassar Coll. Quarterly Alumnae Mag., 1993—; co-chmn. Vassar Christmas Showcase New Haven Vassar Club, 1965-66, rep. to Vassar Coll. Alumnae Assn. Fall Coun. Meeting, 1965-66; co-chmn. Vassar Club So. Calif. Annual Book Fair, 1970-71; chmn. creative writing group Yale U. Newcomers, 1965-66, dir. creative writing group Yale U. Women's Orgn., 1966-67; grad. AMA Ann. Health Reporting Conf., 1992, 93; mem. exec. program network UCLA Grad. Sch. Mgmt., 1987—; trustee Ctr. for Improvement of Child Caring, 1981-83; mem. League Crippled Children, 1982—, bd. dirs., 1988-91, treas. for gen. meetings, 1990-91, chair hostesses com., 1988-89, pub. rels. com., 1990-91; bd. dirs. L.A. Commn. on Assaults Against Women, 1983-84; chmn. 1st. ann. Rabbi Camillus Angel Interfaith Svc. Temple Beth David, 1978, v.p., 1983-86, spkr., 1997; mem. cmty. rels. com. Jewish Fedn. Council Greater L.A., 1985-87; del. Task Force on Minorities in Newspaper Bus., 1987-89; cmty. rep. County Health Ctrs. Network Tobacco Control Program, 1991; with N.Y. Citizens Com. Health Care Decisions. Recipient cert. of appreciation City of Duarte, 1988, County of L.A., 1988, Alumni Coun. Claremont Grad. Sch. 1996; Coro Found. fellow, 1979; named Calif. Communicator of Achievement, Woman of Yr. Calif. Press Women, 1992. Fellow Am. Med. Writers Assn. (pres. Pacific Southwest chpt. 1987-89, dir. 1980-93, Pacific S.W. del. to nat. bd. 1980-87, 89-91, chmn. various conv. coms., chmn. nat. book awards trade category 1982-83, chmn. Nat. Conv. Networking Luncheon 1983, 84, chmn. freelance and pub. relations coms. Nat. Midyr. Conf. 1983-84, workshop leader ann. conf. 1984-87, 90-92, 95—, nat. chmn. freelance sect. 1984-85, gen. chmn. 1985, Asilomar Western Regional Conf., gen. chmn. 1985, workshop leader 1985, program co-chmn. 1987, speaker 1985, 88-89, program co-chmn. 1989, nat. exec. bd. dirs. 1985-86, nat. adminstr. sects. 1985-86, pres.-elect Pacific S.W. chpt. 1985-87, pres. 1987-89, immediate past pres. 1989-91, bd. dirs., 1991-93, moderator gen. session nat. conf. 1987, chair gen. session nat. conf., 1986-87, chair Walter C. Alvarez Meml. Found. award 1986-87, Appreciation award for outstanding leadership 1989, named to Workshop Leaders Honor Roll 1991); mem. Women in Comm. (dir. 1980-82, 89-90, v.p. cmty. affairs 1981-82, N.E. area rep. 1980-81, chmn. awards banquet 1982, sem. leader, speaker ann. nat. profl. conf., 1985, program adv. com. L.A. chpt. 1987, v.p. activities 1989-90, chmn. L.A. chpt. 1st ann. Agnes Underwood Freedom of Info. Awards Banquet 1982, recognition award 1983, nominating com. 1982, 83, com. Women of the Press Awards luncheon 1988, Women in Comm. awards luncheon 1988), Am. Assn. for Higher Edn., AAUW (legis. chmn. Arcadia br. 1976-77, books and plays chmn. Arcadia br. 1973-74, creative writing chmn. 1969-70, 1st v.p. program dir. 1975-76, networking chmn. 1981-82, chmn. task force promoting individual liberties 1987-88, named Woman of Yr., Woman of Achievement award 1986, cert. of appreciation 1987), Coll. English Assn., APHA, Am. Soc. Law, Medicine and Ethics, Calif. Press Women (v.p. programs L.A. chpt. 1982-85, pres. 1985-87, state pres. 1987-89, past immediate past state pres. 1989-91, chmn. state speakers bur. 1989—, del nat. bd. 1989—, moderator ann. spring conv., 1990, 92, chmn. nominating com. 1990-91, Calif. lit. dir. 1990-92, dir. state lit. com. 1990-92, dir. family literacy day Calif., 1990, Cert. of Appreciation, 1991, named Calif. Communicator of Achievement 1992), AAUP, Internat. Comm. Assn., N.Y. Acad. Scis., Ind. Writers So. Calif. (bd. dirs. 1989-90, dir. Specialized Groups 1989-90, dir. at large 1989-90, bd. dirs. corp. 1988-89, dir. Speech Writing Group, 1991-92), Hastings Ctr. (vis. scholar 1996), AAAS, Nat. Fedn. Press Women, (bd. dirs. 1987-93, nat. co-chmn. task force recruitment of minorities 1987-89, del. 1987-89, nat. dir. of speakers bur. 1989-93, editor of speakers bur. directory 1991, cert. of appreciation, 1991, 93, Plenary of Past Pres. state 1989—, workshop leader-speaker ann. nat. conf. 1990, chair state women of achievement com. 1986-87, editor Speakers Bur. Addendum Directory, 1992, editor Speakers Bur. Directory 1991, 92, named 1st runner up Nat. Communicator of Achievement 1992), AAUW (chpt. Woman of Achievement award 1986, chmn. task force promoting individual liberties 1987-88, speaker 1987, Cert. of Appreciation 1987, Woman of Achievement-Woman of Yr. 1986), Internat. Assn. Bus. Communicators, Soc. for Tech. Comm. (workshop leader, 1985, 86), Kennedy Inst. Ethics, Soc. Health and Human Values, Assoc. Writing Programs, Authors Guild. Clubs: Women's City (Pasadena), Claremont Colls. Faculty House, Pasadena Athletic, Town Hall of Calif. (vice chair cmty. affairs sect. 1982-87, speaker 1986, faculty-instr. Exec. Breakfast Inst. 1985-86, mem. study sect. coun. 1986-88), Authors Guild. Lodge: Rotary (chair Duarte Rotary mag. 1988-89, mem. dist. friendship exch. com. 1988-89, mem. internat. svc. com. 1989-90, info. svc. com. 1989-90) Home and Office: 1301 N Santa Anita Ave Arcadia CA 91006-2419

SLOANE, ROBERT MALCOLM, healthcare consultant; b. Boston, Feb. 11, 1933; s. Alvin and Florence (Goldberg) S.; m. Beverly LeBov, Sept. 27, 1959; 1 dau., Alison. A.B., Brown U., 1954; M.S., Columbia U., 1958. Adminstrv. resident Mt. Auburn Hosp., Cambridge, Mass., 1957-58; med. adminstr. AT&T, N.Y.C., 1959-60; asst. dir. Yale New Haven Hosp., 1961-67; assoc. adminstr. Monmouth Med. Center, Long Branch, N.J., 1967-69; adminstr. City of Hope Nat. Med. Center, Duarte, Calif., 1969-80; pres. Los Angeles Orthopedic Hosp., Los Angeles Orthopedic Found., 1980-86; pres., CEO Anaheim (Calif.) Meml. Hosp., 1986-94; pres. Vol. Hosp. Am. West, Inc., L.A., 1995; healthcare cons. Arcadia, Calif., 1996—; mem. faculty Columbia U. Sch. Medicine, 1958-59, Yale U. Sch. Medicine, 1963-67, Quinnipac Coll., 1963-67, Pasadena City Coll., 1972-73, Calif. Inst. Tech., 1973-85, U. So. Calif., 1976-79, clin. prof. 1987—, UCLA, 1985-87; chmn. bd. Health Data Net, 1971-73; bd. dirs. Intervalley Health Plan; pres. Anaheim Meml. Devel. Found., 1986-94, InTech Health Sys., Inc., 1996—; sr. cons. APM, Inc., 1996—. Author: (with B. L. Sloane) A Guide to Health Facilities: Personnel and Management, 1971, 2d edit., 1977, 3d edit., 1992; mem. editl. and adv. bd. Health Devices, 1972-90; contbr. articles to hosp. jours. Bd. dirs. Health Systems Agy. Los Angeles County, 1977-78, Vol. Hosps. of Am., 1986-95, chmn., 1993-94, pres., 1995; bd. dirs. Calif. Hosp. Polit. Action Com., 1979-87, vice chmn., 1980-83, chmn., 1983-85. Served to lt. (j.g.) USNR, 1954-56. Fellow Am. Coll. Hosp. Adminstrs. (regent 1989-93, nominations com. 1994—); mem. Am. Hosp. Assn., Hosp Coun. So. Calif. (bd. dirs. , sec. 1982, treas. 1983, chmn. elect 1984, chmn. 1985, past chmn. 1986, 89), Calif. Hosp. Assn. (bd. dirs. exec. com. 1984-86, 89), Anaheim C. of C. (bd. dirs. 1994). Home: 1301 N Santa Anita Ave Arcadia CA 91006-2419 Office: 150 N Santa Anita Ave Ste 300 Arcadia CA 91006-3113

SLOANE, SARAH JANE, English educator; b. Tappan, N.Y., Oct. 5, 1957; d. Thomas Charles and Virginia Louise (French) S. BA in English cum laude, Middlebury Coll., 1979; MFA in English, U. Mass., 1987; MA in English, Carnegie-Mellon U., 1988; PhD in English, Ohio State U., 1991. Asst. prof. English, dir. women studies U. Puget Sound, Tacoma, Wash., 1991-97, assoc. prof. English, 1997—; vis. scholar U. Wash. HIT-Lab, Seattle, 1996—; lectr. in field. Author: Computing Fictions: Reading and Writing in a Material World; contbr. numerous articles to profl. jours., chpts. to books, poetry to lit. pubs.; editl. bd. Computers and Composition Jour., 1991—; reviewer Written Comm., 1991—, Postmodern Culture, 1994—. Recipient Mary Dunning Thwing Poetry award Middlebury Coll., 1979, Henry V. Larom 1st Prize Writing award Rockland C.C., 1982, Disting. Tchg. award U. Mass., 1986, Grad. Student Rsch. award Ohio State U., 1990, Hugh Burns Dissertation award Computers and Composition Jour., 1992, Enrichment Com. Rsch. award U. Puget Sound, summer 1993, 95, 96, Martin Nelson Summer Rsch. award, 1994, 97; Thomas J. Watson fellow , 1979-80, Carnegie-Mellon U. fellow, 1987-88; N.Y. State Regents scholar, 1975. Mem. MLA, Acad. Am. Poets (assoc.), Am. Assn. for Artificial Intelligence, Coll. Composition and Comm., Internat. Soc. for History of Rhetoric, Nat. Coun. Tchrs. English, Rhetoric Soc. Am., Wilkie Collins Soc. Office: Univ of Puget Sound Dept English Tacoma WA 98416

SLOMANSON, WILLIAM REED, law educator, legal writer; b. Johnstown, Pa., May 1, 1945; s. Aaron Jacob and Mary Jane (Reed) S.; m. Anna Maria Valladolid, June 24, 1972; children: Lorena, Michael, Paul, Christina. BA, U. Pitts., 1967; JD, Calif. Western U., 1974; LLM, Columbia U., N.Y.C., 1975. Bar: Calif. 1975. Assoc. Booth, Mitchel, Strange & Smith, L.A., 1975-77; prof. law Western State U., San Diego and Fullerton, Calif., 1977-95; prof. Thomas Jefferson Sch. of Law, 1996—; judge Provisional Dist. World Ct., L.A., 1990—. Author: (reference book) International Business Bibliography, 1989, (textbooks) Fundamental Perspectives on International Law, 1990, 2nd edit., 1995, California Civil Procedure, 1991, California Civil Procedure in a Nutshell, 1992, (practitioner's treatise) The Choice Between State and Federal Courts in California, 1994, supplement, 1996. Lt. USN, 1967-71, Vietnam. Mem. Am. Soc. Internat. Law (chair, editor newsletter on UN decade of internat. law), San Diego County Bar Assn. (co-chair internat. law sect. 1988-92). Office: Thomas Jefferson Sch Law 2121 San Diego Ave San Diego CA 92110-2905

SLONE, ERNIE L., journalist; b. Woodland, Calif., Apr. 30, 1950; s. Ernie L. Sr. and Ann W. (Wittry) S.; m. Victoria M. Higdon, Sept. 27, 1969; children: Michael, Rob. B of Mgmt., U. Louisville, 1982. Asst., bus. editor The Courier-Jour., Louisville, 1989-92, computer sys. editor, 1992-94; bus. editor The Indpls. News, 1994-95; investigative reporter The Orange County Register, Santa Ana, Calif., 1995—. Editor: A Voice Is Born, 1991. Recipient Pulitzer prize Columbia U., 1996, Polk award for med. reporting Polk Found., 1996, Roy Howard Pub. Svc. award Scripps-Howard, 1996. Mem. Soc. Profl. Journalists, Investigative Reporters and Editors Assn. (Top Investigative Report 1996), Orange County Press Club. Office: The Orange County Register 625 N Grand Santa Ana CA 92701

SLOUBER, JAMES KIRK, accountant; b. Chgo., Feb. 12, 1952; s. Robert James and Doris Marie (Olson) S.; m. Kerry Perry, Oct. 24, 1981; children: Erika, Kirsten, Bradon. BA in Acctg., Econs., and Bus., Augustana Coll., Rock Island, Ill., 1974; MS in Taxation, DePaul U., 1978. CPA, Calif., Ill. Acct. Procon, Inc., Des Plaines, Ill., 1974-75; tax supervising sr. Peat, Marwick, Mitchell & Co., Chgo., Newport Beach, Calif., 1977-80; tax mgr. Price Waterhouse, West Los Angeles, Calif., 1980-83; sr. tax mgr. Price Waterhouse, Washington, 1983-84; sr. mgr. in charge tax dept. Price Waterhouse, Riverside, Calif., 1984-89; tax ptnr. in charge Pannell Kerr Forster, L.A., 1989-91, Goldfarb, Whitman & Cohen, L.A., 1991-94; prin. Parks Palmer Turner & Yemenidjian, L.A., 1994—; mem. citizens univ. com. U. Calif., Riverside, 1985-89. Author: (booklet) Interest Expense Rules After Tax Reform, 1989; contbr. 7 articles to profl. jours. Bd. dirs. United Way Inland Valleys, Riverside, 1986-90; bd. dirs., treas. Luth. Sch. Foothills, 1993—. Mem. AICPA (tax divsn.), Calif. Soc. CPAs, Ill. Soc. CPAs, L.A. City Hdqrs. Assn., Kiwanis. Republican. Lutheran. Home: 9426 Carlynn Pl Tujunga CA 91042-3319 Office: Parks Palmer Turner & Yemenidjian 1990 S Bundy Dr Fl 6 Los Angeles CA 90025-5240

SLOVER, ARCHY F., chemist; b. Oshkosh, Wis., July 8, 1920; s. Archie F. and Josephine Petronella (Zindler); BA, UCLA, 1947; m. Mary Beatrice Corkill, May 25, 1946 (dec. June 17, 1987); 1 child, Mary Kay Slover Eckhardt. Devel. chemist Kelite Products Co., L.A., 1946-49; v.p., gen. mgr. Delco Chems. Inc., L.A., 1949-57; mgr. indsl. spltys. Pennwalt Corp., L.A., 1957-74; chemist Custom Chem. Formulators Inc., Cudahy, Calif., 1974—; mgr. Cherokee Chem. Co., Inc., Compton, Calif., 1976-89; cons. in field. Capt. U.S. Army, 1942-46. Fellow AAAS, Am. Inst. Chemists; mem. Nat. Assn. Corrosion Engrs., Am. Chem. Soc., Am. Electroplaters Soc., USAF Assn., Soc. Advancement Material Process Engrs., Res. Officers Assn., Sigma Alpha Epsilon, Ky. Cols. Patentee in field. Address: 21 Hacienda Dr Arcadia CA 91006-2347

SLOVIACZEK-SMYSER, MELINDA, counselor; b. Caldwell, Idaho, Oct. 29, 1958; d. Bill and Sandra (Corn) Sloviaczek; m. Skip Smyser, Aug. 22, 1981; childrn: Lincoln, Logan, Landon, Lauren. BS, Univ. Idaho, 1981; M in Guidance Counseling, Coll. Idaho, 1985. Tchr. Wilder (Idaho) Sch. Dist., 1982-84; counselor Parma (Idaho) Sch. Dist., 1984-89, Canyon Alternative Edn. Ctr., Nampa, Caldwell, Emmett, Idaho, 1989—; cons. State Dept. Edn., 1990-92, chair mentorship program, 1990-91, dir. mentorship program, 1991-92. Rep. precinct committeeperson, Canyon County; v.p. State Fedn. Rep. Women; elder, ch. leader Sterry Meml. Presbyn. Ch., 1990-94, dir. vacation bible sch., 1992-94; edn. coord. PEO, 1994-96. Recipient Gov. award State of Idaho, 1992-93. Mem. Am. Sch. Counselors Assn., Am. Assn. Counseling Devel. (del. 1990-91), Idaho Sch. Counselors Assn. (sec. profl. conf. 1987, chairperson pub. rels. 1988-89, pres.-elect 1989-90, pres. 1990-91, Sch. Counselor of Yr. 1992-93, Counselor Disting Svc. award, 1996—). Home: 26298 Lee Ln Parma ID 83640 Office: Caldwell Sch Dist 1117 Arthur St Caldwell ID 83605-3825

SLOVIC, STEWART PAUL, psychologist; b. Chgo., Jan. 26, 1938; s. Jacob S. and Blanche (Cohen) S.; m. Roslyn Judith Resnick, Aug. 30, 1959; children: Scott, Steven, Lauren, Daniel. BA, Stanford U., 1959; MA, U. Mich., 1962, PhD, 1964; D (hon.), Stockholm Sch. Econs., 1996. Rsch. assoc. Oreg. Rsch. Inst., Eugene, 1964-76; rsch. assoc. Decision Rsch., Eugene, 1976-86, pres., 1986—; prof. dept. psychology U. Oreg., Eugene, 1986—; bd. sci. dirs. Risk Sci. Inst., Washington, 1987-91; cons. EPA, Washington, 1987-90; adviser WHO, Geneva, 1991; bd. dirs. Nat. Coun. Radiation Protection and Measurement. Author: Acceptable Risk, 1981; editor: Judgment Under Uncertainty, 1982; contbr. articles to profl. publs. J.S. Guggenheim fellow, 1986-87; recipient Oreg. Acad. of Sci. Outstanding Contbn. to Sci. award, 1995. Fellow AAAS, APA (Disting. Sci. Contbn. award 1993), Am. Psychol. Soc. (charter), Soc. Risk Analysis (pres. 1983-84, Disting. Contbn. award 1991). Office: Decision Rsch 1201 Oak St Eugene OR 97401-3519

SLUSSER, ROBERT WYMAN, aerospace company executive; b. Mineola, N.Y., May 10, 1938; s. John Leonard and Margaret McKenzie (Wyman) S.; BS, MIT, 1960; MBA, Wharton, 1962; ERC, Ft. Belvior Def. Systems Mgmt. Sch., 1977; AMP, Claremont, 1982; m. Linda Killeas, Aug. 3, 1968; children: Jonathan, Adam, Robert, Mariah. Assoc. adminstr.'s staff NASA Hdqrs., Washington, 1962-65; with Northrop Corp., Hawthorne, Calif., 1965-96, adminstr. Space Labs., 1965-68, mgr. bus. and fin. Warnecke Electron Tubes Co. div., Chgo., 1968-71, mgr. bus. adminstrn. YF-17 Program Aircraft Div., 1971-75, mgr. adminstrn. F-18/Cobra programs, also mgr. F-18 design to cost program, 1975-79, mgr. engrng. adminstrn., 1980-82, acting v.p. engrng., 1982, v.p. info. resources, 1983-91, mgr. long range planning, 1991-93; program mgr.-bus. F/A-18E/F program, 1994-96, cons. 1996—. CFO, bd. dirs. So. Calif. Hist. Aviation Found., 1987-90, chmn. of bd., pres., 1990—; bd. dirs., contracting officer, PDES, 1988-91; mem. dirs. adv. bd. S.C. Rsch. Authority, 1991-95. Grumman Aircraft Engrng. scholar, 1956-60. Fellow AIAA (assoc.); mem. So. Calif. Soc. Info. Mgnt., (mem. exec. com. 1987-91), Northrop Mgmt. Club (bd. dirs. 1992-93, Man of Yr. 1991-92). Home: 7270 Berry Hill Dr Palos Verdes Peninsula CA 90275-4402

SMALLWOOD, BETTY, lawyer; b. Eagle Pass, Tex., Nov. 27, 1946; d. Charles Augustus and Helen Elizabeth (Stanford) S. BA, U. Tex., 1968, BS, 1970; grad., Med. Tech. Sch., 1970; JD, U. San Diego, 1986. Bar: Tex. 1992, Nev. 1987; lic. real estate agt. Nev.; cert. med. technologist. Med. technologist VA Med Ctr., Denver and Houston, 1977-83; atty. Clark & Sacco, Las Vegas, Nev., 1987-88, Jeffrey Burr & Assocs., Las Vegas, 1988-91; pvt. practice Henderson, Nev., 1991—; instr., coord. U. Nev. Las Vegas Ctr. for Internat. Bus., 1992. Exec. editor U. San Diego Law Rev., 1985-86. Campaign worker Nev. U.S. Senator, 1988, Clark County Attys. for Nev. Atty. Gen., Las Vegas, 1990; girls day vol. Las Vegas Boys and Girls' Club, 1991; bd. dirs. United Cerebral Palsey of South Nev., 1992-93. Named Disting. Women So. Nev. Careline Inc., 1990, 91. Mem. ABA, So. Nev. Internat. Bus. Coun. (bd. dirs 1994), Am. Bus. Women's Assn., So. Nev. Assn. of Women Attys. (sec. 1989-90), State Bar Nev., State Bar Tex., Henderson C. of C. (amb. corps 1992-93). Office: 6550 S Pecos Las Vegas NV 89120

SMARANDACHE, FLORENTIN, mathematics researcher, writer; b. Balcesti-Vilcea, Romania, Dec. 10, 1954; came to U.S., 1990; s. Gheorghe and Maria (Mitroiescu) S.; m. Eleonora Niculescu; children: Mihai-Liviu, Silviu-Gabriel. MS, U. Craiova, 1979; postgrad., Ariz. State U., 1991. Mathematician I.U.G., Craiova, Romania, 1979-81; math. prof. Romanian Coll., 1981-82, 1984-86, 1988; math. tchr. Coop. Ministry, Morocco, 1982-84; French tutor pvt. practice, Turkey, 1988-90; software engr. Honeywell, Phoenix, 1990-95; prof. math. Pima C.C., Tucson, 1995—. Author: Nonpoems, 1990, Only Problems, Not Solutions, 1991, numerous other books; contbr. articles to profl. jours. Mem. U.S. Math. Assn., Romania Math. Assn., Zentralblatt fur Math. (reviewer). Home: 2456 S Rose Peak Dr Tucson AZ 85710-7413

SMARTT, RICHARD A., museum director. Dir., sci. chmn. N.Mex. Mus. Natural History, Albuquerque. Office: 1801 Mountain Rd NW Albuquerque NM 87104-1375

SMEAD, BURTON ARMSTRONG, JR., lawyer, retired; b. Denver, July 29, 1913; s. Burton Armstrong and Lola (Lewis) S.; m. Josephine McKittrick, Mar. 27, 1943; children: Amanda Armstrong, Sydney Hall. BA, U. Denver, 1934, J.D., 1950; grad. Pacific Coast Banking Trust Sch., 1955. Bar: Colo., 1950. With Norwest Bank Denver (formerly Denver Nat. Bank), 1934-78, trust officer, 1955-70, v.p. and trust officer, 1970-78, sec. bd. dirs., 1976-78; pvt. practice law, Englewood, Colo., 1978—; of counsel Buchanan & Thomas, Lakewood, Colo., 1985—; bd. dirs., trust counsel, Resources Trust Co., Englewood, Colo. Author: History of the Twelfth Field Artillery Battalion in the European Theater of Operations, 1944-45, Captain Smead's Letters to Home, 1944-45; editor: Colorado Wills and Estates, 1965. Pres., trustee Stebbins Orphans Home Assn. Chmn. bd. dirs. Am. Cancer oc., N.Y.C., Colo. div., 1961-68. Maj. U.S. Army, 1941-45; ETO. Decorated Bronze Star, Croix de Guerre (France). Mem. ABA, Arapahoe Bar Assn., Colo. Bar Assn. (treas. 1970-88, chmn. probate and trust law sect. 1967-68, exec. coun., bd. govs. 1970-88, coun. bd. gov. 1970-88, hon. 1989—, award of merit 1979), Denver Estate Planning Coun. (co-founder, pres. 1971-72), Univ. Club (Denver). Republican. Episcopalian. Home and Office: 3130 Cherryridge Rd Englewood CO 80110-6057

SMEGAL, THOMAS FRANK, JR., lawyer; b. Eveleth, Minn., June 15, 1935; s. Thomas Frank and Genevieve (Andreachi) S.; m. Susan Jane Stanton, May 28, 1966; children: Thomas Frank, Elizabeth Jane. BS in Chem. Engrng., Mich. Technol. U., 1957; JD, George Washington U., 1961. Bar: Va. 1961, D.C. 1961, Calif. 1964, U.S. Supreme Ct. 1976. Patent examiner U.S. Patent Office, Washington, 1957-61; staff patent atty. Shell Devel. Co., San Francisco, 1962-65; patent atty. Townsend and Townsend, San Francisco, 1965-91, mng. ptnr., 1974-89; sr. ptnr. Graham and James, San Francisco, 1992—; mem. U.S. del. to Paris Conv. for Protection of Indsl. Property. Pres. bd. dirs. Legal Aid Soc. San Francisco, 1982-84, Youth Law Ctr., 1973-84; bd. dirs. Nat. Ctr. for Youth Law, 1978-84, San Francisco Lawyers Com. for Urban Affairs, 1972—, Legal Svcs. for Children, 1980-88; presdl. nom., Legal Svcs. Corp., 1984-90, 93—. Capt. Chem. Corps, U.S. Army, 1961-62. Recipient St. Thomas More award, 1982. Mem. Ct. of Appeals for Federal Ct. (adv. com. 1992-96), ABA (chmn. PTC sect. 1990-91, ho. of dels. 1988—, mem. standing com. Legal Aid and Indigent Defendants, 1991-94, chair sect. officer conf., 1992-94, mem. bd. govs., 1994-97), Nat. Coun. Intellectual Property Law Assn. (chmn. 1989), Nat. Inventors Hall Fame (pres. 1988), Calif. Bar Assn. (v.p. bd. govs. 1986-87), Am. Patent Law Assn. (pres. 1986), Internat. Assn. Intellectual Property Lawyers (pres. 1995—), Bar Assn. San Francisco (pres. 1978), Patent Law Assn. San Francisco (pres. 1974). Republican. Roman Catholic. Clubs: World Trade, Olympic, Golden Gate Breakfast (San Francisco); Claremont (Berkeley). Contbr. articles to publs. in field. Office: Graham & James 1 Maritime Plz Ste 300 Alco San Francisco CA 94111-3404

SMELCER, JOHN E., publishing company executive; b. July 2, 1963; s. charles and Marie (Green) S.; m. Pamela A. Maslyk, June 23, 1966; 1 child, Zara Rhyana. BA in English, Anthropology, U. Alaska, 1987; MLA in Lit. and Humanities, Alaska Pacific U., 1991; PhD in Comparative Lit., Greenwich U., Hilo, Hawaii, 1993. Asst. prof. U. Alaska, Anchorage, 1991-94, Embry-Riddle Aero. U., Anchorage, 1994—; pres., chief editor Salmon Run Pub., Anchorage, 1991—; disting. prof. Gorky Inst., Moscow, 1994; vis. Am. poet U. Sydney, Australia, 1996; poetry editor Rosebud mag., Cambridge, Wis., 1996—. Author: The Raven and the Totem, 1992, Changing Seasons, 1996; editor: Durable Breath: Contemporary Nature American Poetry, 1994, Tracks, 1997, In the Shadows of Mountains, 1997. Exec. dir. Ahtna Indian Heritage Found., Glennallen, Alaska, 1996—; asst. cubmaster Boy Scouts Am., Anchorage, 1994-96. With USAR, 1981-83. Home: 4101 University Dr # 328 Anchorage AK 99508 Office: PO Box 213 Glennallen AK 99588-0213

SMELICK, ROBERT MALCOLM, investment bank executive; b. Phoenix, Mar. 27, 1942; s. Valentine and Mary Helen (McDonald) S.; m. Gail Paine Sterling, Dec. 10, 1979; children: Christopher Paine, Alexandra McBryde, Gillian Sterling. BA, Stanford U., 1964; MBA, Harvard U., 1968; postgrad. U. Melbourne (Australia), 1965-66. v.p. Kidder Peabody & Co., Inc., N.Y.C. and San Francisco, 1968-79; mng. dir. First Boston Corp., San Francisco, 1979-89; mng. prin., founder Sterling Payot Company, San Francisco, 1989—; bd. dirs. Willamette Industries, Portland, Oreg., Accrue Software, Inc., Sunnyvale, Calif., Metricom, Inc., Los Gatos, Calif. Republican. Episcopalian. Office: 222 Sutter St Fl 8 San Francisco CA 94108-4445

SMELSER, NEIL JOSEPH, sociologist; b. Kahoka, Mo., July 22, 1930; s. Joseph Nelson and Susie Marie (Hess) S.; m. Helen Thelma Margolis, June 10, 1954 (div. 1965); children: Eric Jonathan, Tina Rachel; m. Sharin Fateley, Dec. 20, 1967; children: Joseph Neil, Sarah Joanne. B.A., Harvard U., 1952, Ph.D., 1958; B.A., Magdalen Coll., Oxford U., Eng., 1954; M.A., Magdalen Coll., Oxford U., 1959; grad., San Francisco Psychoanalytic Inst., 1971. Mem. faculty U. Calif., Berkeley, 1958-94, prof. sociology, 1962—, asst. chancellor edni. devel., 1966-68; assoc. dir. Inst. of Internat. Studies, Berkeley, 1969-73, 80-89; Univ. prof. sociology U. Calif., Berkeley, 1972-94; prof. emeritus, 1994—; dir. edn. abroad program for U. Calif., Berkeley, 1977-79, spl. advisor Office of Pres., 1993-94, dir. Ctr. for Advanced Study in Behavioral Scis., 1994—; bd. dirs. Found. Fund for Rsch. in Psychiatry, 1967-70; bd. dirs. Social Sci. Rsch. Coun., 1968-71, chmn., 1971-73, mem. com. econ. growth, 1961-65; trustee Ctr. for Advanced Study in Behavioral Scis., 1980-86, 87-93, chmn., 1984-86; trustee Russell Sage Found., 1990—; mem. subcom. humanism Am. Bd. Internal Medicine, 1981-85, 89-90, mem. adv. com., 1992—, chmn. adv. com., 1995—; chmn. sociology panel Behavioral and Social Scis. survey NAS and Social Sci. Rsch. Coun., 1967-69; mem. com. on basic rsch. in behavioral and social scis. NRC, 1980-89, chmn., 1984-86, co-chmn., 1986-89. Author: (with T. Parsons) Economy and Society, 1956, Social Change in the Industrial Revolution, 1959, Theory of Collective Behavior, 1962, The Sociology of Economic Life, 1963, 2d edit., 1975, Essays in Sociological Explanation, 1968, Sociological Theory: A Contemporary View, 1971, Comparative Methods in the Social Sciences, 1976, (with Robin Content) The Changing Academic Market, 1980, Sociology, 1981, 2d edit., 1984, 3d edit., 1987, 4th edit., 1991, 5th edit., 1995, Social Paralysis and Social Change, 1991, Effective Committee Service, 1993, Sociology, 1994, Problematics of Sociology, 1997; editor: (with W.T. Smelser) Personality and Social Systems, 1963, 2d edit., 1971, (with S.M. Lipset) Social Structure and Mobility in Economic Development, 1966, Sociology, 1967, 2d edit., 1973, (with James Davis) Sociology: A Survey Report, 1969, Karl Marx on Society and Social Change, 1973, (with Gabriel Almond) Public Higher Education in California, 1974, (with Erik Erikson) Themes of

Work and Love in Adulthood, 1980, (with Jeffrey Alexander et al) The Micro-Macro Lilnk, 1987, Handbook of Sociology, 1988, (with Hans Haferkamp) Social Change and Modernity, 1992, (with Richard Munch) Theory of Culture, 1992, (with Richard Swedberg) The Handbook of Economic Sociology, 1994; editor Am. Sociol. Rev., 1962-65, 89-90; adv. editor Am. Jour. Sociology, 1960-62. Rhodes scholar, 1952-54; jr. fellow Soc. Fellows, Harvard U., 1955-58; fellow Russell Sage Found., 1989-90. Mem. Am. Sociol. Assn. (coun. 1962-65, 67-70, exec. com. 1963-65, pres. elect 1995-96, pres. 1996-97), Pacific Sociol. Assn., Internat. Sociol. Assn. (exec. com. 1986-94, v.p. 1990-94), Am. Acad. Arts and Scis. (hon.), Am. Philos. Soc. (hon.), Nat. Acad. of Scis. (hon.). Home: 400 El Escarpado Stanford CA 94305

SMIGHT, ALEC DOW, film editor, consultant; b. N.Y.C., Aug. 30, 1959; s. Jack Ronald and Joyce (Cunning) S.; m. Tamara Marie Dal Degan, May 28, 1983; children: Daniel David, Colin Walter, Claire Marie. Student, U. Minn., 1977. Film editor MTM, 1987-88, Universal Studios, 1989-90, 20th Century Fox, L.A., 1988—; cons. Avid Techs., L.A., 1996. Film editor for Hill St. Blues, Quantum Leap, No. Exposure, Hooperman, Chgo. Hope, L.A. Law. Mem. Am. Cinema Editors, Acad. TV Arts and Scis., Motion Picture Editors Guild. Democrat. Episcopalian. Home: 27272 Rosemont Ln Valencia CA 91354 Office: 20th Century Fox Chgo Hope 10201 W Pico Blvd Los Angeles CA 90035

SMILEY, ROBERT WILLIAM, industrial engineer; b. Phila., Oct. 18, 1919; s. Albert James and Laura Emma (Hoiler) S.; children from previous marriage: Robert, James, Lauralee, Mary; m. Gloria Morais, June 30, 1990; stepchildren: Deborah, Sheila, Vicki, James, Sonja, Michelle. Certificate in Indsl. Engring, Gen. Motors Inst., 1942; student, U. Rochester, 1948; student mgmt. program for execs., U. Pitts. Grad. Sch. Bus., 1968; student, San Jose State Coll., 1969; BSBA, Coll. Notre Dame, Belmont, Calif., 1972, MBA, 1974. Registered profl. engr., Calif. With A.S. Hamilton (cons. engrs.), Rochester, N.Y., 1946-48; commd. lt. comdr. USN, 1952, advanced through grades to comdr., 1960; engaged in tech. contract mgmt. (Poseidon/Polaris and Terrier Missile Programs), 1952-64; officer in charge (Polaris Missile Facility Pacific), Bremerton, Wash., 1964-66; resigned, 1966; mgr. product assurance Missile Systems div. Lockheed Missiles and Space Co., Sunnyvale, Calif., 1966-72; mgr. materiel Missile Systems div. Lockheed Missiles and Space Co., 1972-77; mgr. product assurance McDonnell Douglas Astronautics, 1977-78; dir. product assurance Aerojet Tactical Systems, Sacramento, 1978-83; dir. quality assurance Aerojet Solid Propulsion Co., Sacramento, 1984-92, Tahoe Surg. Instruments, Inc., 1992—; frequent guest lectr. at colls. on quality control and reliability; chmn. Polaris/Minuteman/Pershing Missile Nondestruct Test Com., 1958-64; quality control cons. Dragon Missile Program, U.S. Army, 1971. Contbr. articles to sci. jours., chpt. to Reliability Handbook, 1966, Reliability Engineering and Management, 1988. Docent Calif. State Railroad and Mus., 1994—; chmn. sec. chpt. svc. Corps Retired Exec., 1992, dist. mgr., 1995. With USNR, 1942-46, 51-52; now capt. ret. Recipient letters of Commendation for work on Polaris/Poseidon Sec. of Navy, 1960, certificate of Honor Soc. for Nondestructive Testing, 1966. Fellow Am. Soc. Quality Control (chmn. San Francisco sect. 1969-70, exec. bd. 1966—, chmn. reliability divsn. 1971, 81, nat. v.p. 1984-85; mem. SCORE (chmn. Sacramento chpt. 1993-94, dist. mgr. 1996—), Aircraft Industries Assn. (chmn. quality assurance com.), Navy League, AAAS, Am. Mgmt. Assn. Home and Office: 9144 Green Ravine Ln Fair Oaks CA 95628-4110 *A man can consider himself successful only if he leaves the world better than he found it partly through his efforts.*

SMITH, ALBERT CROMWELL, JR., investments consultant; b. Norfolk, Va., Dec. 6, 1925; s. Albert Cromwell and Georgie (Foreman) S.; m. Laura Thaxton, Oct. 25, 1952; children: Albert, Elizabeth, Laura. BS in Civil Engring., Va. Mil. Inst., 1949; MS in Govtl. Adminstrn., George Washington U., 1965; MBA, Pepperdine U., 1975; PhD in Bus. Adminstrn. LaSalle U., 1994. Enlisted USMC, 1944, commd. 2d lt., 1949, advanced through grades to col., 1970; comdr. inf. platoons, companies, landing force; variously assigned staffs U.K. Joint Forces, U.S. Sec. Navy, Brit. Staff Coll., Marine Staff Coll., U.K. Staff Coll., U.K. Latimer Staff Coll.; adviser, analyst amphibious systems; ret., 1974; pres. A. Cromwell-Smith, Ltd., Charlottesville, Va., 1973, head broker, cons. A. Cromwell Smith, Investments, La Jolla and Coronado, Calif., 1975—. Bd. dirs. Reps. La Jolla, 1975-76; vestryman St. Martin's Episcopal Ch., 1971-73. Decorated Legion of Merit with oak leaf cluster with V device, Bronze Star with V device with oak leaf cluster, Air medal with 2 oak leaf clusters, Purple Heart, Vietnamese Galantry cross with gold star. Mem. ASCE, SAR, Nat. Assn. Realtors, Calif. Assn. Realtors, San Diego Bd. Realtors, Coronado Bd. Realtors, Stockbrokers Soc., So. Calif. Options Soc., Mil. Order Purple Heart. Club: Kona Kai. Author: The Individual Investor in Tomorrow's Stock Market, 1977, The Little Guy's Stock Market Survival Guide, 1979, Wake Up Detroit! The EVs Are Coming, 1982, The Little Guy's Tax Survival Guide, 1984, The Little Guy's Sailboat Success, 1996, The Little Guy's Business Success, 1997, Little Guy's Real Estate Success Guide, 1990, Little Guy's Stock Market Success Guide, 1992, Little Guy's Stock Market Future Effectiveness, 1994, Semper Fidelis in Peace and War, 1995, Sailboat Success, 1996, Business Success, 1997; contbr. articles to civilian and mil. publs. Office: PO Box 180192 1001 B Ave Ste 319/320 Coronado CA 92178

SMITH, ALEXIS, artist, educator; b. L.A., Aug. 24, 1949; d. Dayrel Driver and Lucille Lloyd (Doak) Smith; m. Scott Grieger, June 11, 1990. BA in Art, U. Calif., Irvine, 1970. Teaching position Calif. Inst. Arts, 1975, 96; teaching position U. Calif., Irvine, 1976, San Diego, 1977-78; teaching position UCLA, 1979-82, 85-88, Skowhegan (Maine) Sch. Painting and Sculpture, 1990, So. Meth. U., 1993; vis. artist and lectr. in field. One person exhbns. include Whitney Mus. Am. Art, N.Y.C., 1975, Nicholas Wilder Gallery, L.A., 1977, Holly Solomon Gallery, N.Y.C., 1977, 78, 79, 81, Walker Art Ctr., Mpls., 1986, Bklyn. Mus., 1987-88, Margo Leavin Gallery, L.A., 1982, 85, 88, 90, 93, 94, 95, Retrospective Whitney Mus. Am. Art, N.Y.C., 1991, MOCA, L.A., 1991-92, Gerald Peters Gallery, Dallas, 1995, Wexner Ctr. for the Arts, Columbus, Ohio, 1997; exhibited in group shows at Pasadena (Calif.) Art Mus., Mus. Modern Art, Whitney Mus. Am. Art, Musee d'art Moderne, Paris, Inst. Contemporary Art, Boston, Contemporary Arts Mus., Houston, Hirshhorn Mus. and Sculpture Garden, Washington, Mus. Contemporary Art, Chgo., Los Angeles County Mus. Art, UCLA, Getty Ctr for History of Art and Humanities, Santa Monica, Calif., others; numerous commns. including The Stuart Collection U. Calif., San Diego, slate and concrete pathway, La Jolla, Calif., terrazzo floor designs for L.A. Conv. Ctr. Expansion Project; subject of numerous articles. Mem. artist adv. coun. L.A. Mus. Contemporary Art, 1979-90; trustee Beyond Baroque Lit. Arts Ctr., 1990-95; bd. govs. Skowhegan Sch., 1990-93. Recipient New Talent award Los Angeles County Mus. Art, 1974; Nat. Endowment for the Arts grantee, 1976, 87. Office: Margo Leavin Gallery 812 N Robertson Blvd Los Angeles CA 90069-4929

SMITH, ANDREA JEAN, professional association executive; b. Port Arthur, Tex., Nov. 14, 1944; m. Richard H. Weelans, May 10, 1986. Student, Lamar U., Beaumont, Tex., 1963-64, Lamar U., Port Arthur, Tex., 1964-65, 70-71; Cert., Inst. Orgnl. Mgmt., Boulder, Colo., 1981. Cert. assn. exec. Asst. mgr. Lakewood (Colo.) C. of C., 1973-85; mgr. chamber rels. Colo. Assn. Commerce and Industry, Denver, 1985-87; mgr. membership svcs. Colo. Soc. CPAs, Denver, 1987—. Editor Lakewood Leader newsletter, 1976-85 (Award of Excellence 1977); author: Chamber Executives Handbook, 1980. Adv. com. Red Rocks C.C., Met. State Coll., Denver; coord. Sister Cities Internat. Exch., Lakewood, 1980, Trees for Tomorrow, 1982. Recipient Appreciation award trees for Tomorrow, 1983. Mem. Colo. Soc. Assn. Execs. (bd. dirs. 1994—), Colo. C. of C. Execs. (bd. dirs. 1980-87), Mountain States Assn. (bd. dirs. 1986-87), Met. C. of C. Execs. (pres. 1983-84). Office: Colo Soc CPAs 7979 E Tufts Ave Ste 500 Denver CO 80237

SMITH, ANDREW VAUGHN, telephone company executive; b. Roseburg, Oreg., July 17, 1924; s. Andrew Britt and Ella Mae (Vaughn) S.; m. Dorothy LaVonne Crabtree, Apr. 25, 1943; children: Janet L., James A. B.S. in Elec. Engring, Oreg. State U., 1950. Registered profl. engr., Oreg. With Pacific N.W. Bell Tel. Co., 1951-89; asst. v.p. ops. Pacific N.W. Bell Tel. Co., Seattle, 1965, v.p. ops., 1970-78; v.p., gen. mgr. Pacific N.W. Bell Tel. Co., Portland, Oreg., 1965-70; v.p. ops. Pacific N.W. Bell Tel. Co., 1970-78; pres. Pacific N.W. Bell Tel. Co., Seattle, 1978-88; pres. ops. U.S. West Communications, 1988-89; exec. v.p. U.S. West Inc., 1989; pres. Telephone Pioneers of Am., 1989-90; ret. U.S. West Inc., 1989; bd. dirs. Airborne Freight Corp., Seattle Prime Source, Pennsouken, N.J. Hon. trustee Oreg. State U. Found.; trustee U. Wash. Grad. Sch. Bus., 1985, chmn. bd. trustees, 1984-85; gen. chmn. United Way of King County, 1980-81; mem. Wash. State Investment Com., Olympia, 1989-92; mem. bd. regents U. Wash., 1989-95; trustee Horizon House, Seattle. With USNR, 1943-46. Mem. Seattle C. of C. (chmn. 1985-86). Mem. Wash. Athletic Club (pres. 1982-83), Seattle Yacht Club, Rainier Club, Overlake Golf and Country Club, Multnomah Club (Portland), Columbia Tower Club (Seattle), Desert Island Country Club (Palm Desert, Calif.), The Palm Springs (Calif.) Club. Episcopalian. Office: 1600 Bell Plz Rm 1802 Seattle WA 98191

SMITH, ANITA BINGHAM, accountant, tax preparer; b. Charlotte, N.C., July 11, 1919; d. Irving Westerman and Lula Vernon (McGregor) Bingham; m. Charles Marsden Smith Sr., Sept. 9, 1944; children: Anita Dempsey, Thomas, Charles M. Jr., Martha. Cert., Queens Coll., 1936. Lic. tax preparer, Calif. Acct. B. R. Sharp & Co., Riverside, Calif., 1953-59; asst. office mgr. Crail Fuller Co., Vandenberg AFB, Calif., 1959-61; tchr. Govt. Guam (Mich.), 1961-62; pvt. practice acct. and tax preparer Riverside, 1965—. Treas. Riverside County Rep. Ctrl. Com., 1975-83; v.p. and pres. Rubidoux Cmty. Svcs. Dist., Riverside, 1978—; treas. Riverside Art Mus., 1980-84; pres. Riverside Art Alliance, 1986-87; treas. Legislator and Senator, Calif. State Legislature, Riverside, 1987—; chairperson and vice chairperson bd. dirs. Calif. State Water, Riverside, 1983-95;. Anita B. Smith Treatment Facility named in her honor Rubidoux Cmty. Svcs. Dist., 1995; floral design chosen for floral arrangement calender Nat. Coun. State Garden Clubs Inc., 1997. Presbyterian. Home: 5881 Sandoval Ave Riverside CA 92509-6343

SMITH, ARTHUR, JR., pharmacist, pharmacy company executive; b. San Francisco, Aug. 28, 1924; s. Arthur O. Smith Sr. and Emily Marie (Biondi) Foss; m. Audrey Jane Thomas, June 14, 1947; children: Megan Jane, David Rhys, CeriLyn. BSc, U. So. Calif., 1949. Lic. pharmacist, Calif. Pharmacist Miller Pharmacy, Lompoc, Calif., 1949-51, pharmacist, mgr., 1951-60; v.p. Miller Pharmacy, Inc., Lompoc, 1960-82, pres., CEO, 1983—; bd. dirs. Santa Barbara Regional Health Authority, 1985-95; pharmacy cons. Lompoc Dist. Hosp. Convalescent Care Ctr.; mem. tripartite com. on continuing edn. Calif. Bd. Pharmacy, 1975-77. Editor (jour.) Capsule, 1965-85. Mem. Santa Barbara County Gen. Plans Bd. With U.S. Army, 1943-45 ETO. Decorated Purple Heart. Fellow Am. Coll. Apothecaries (bd. dirs. 1976-86); mem. Calif. Pharmacists Assn. (bd. dirs. 1974-76), Ctrl. Coast Pharmacists Soc., Lompoc C. of C., Lompoc Valley Club, Rotary (pres. Lompoc, Paul Harris fellow), Elks, KP (chancellor cmmdr. 1990-92). Republican. Episcopalian.

SMITH, BARBARA BARNARD, music educator; b. Ventura, Calif., June 10, 1920; d. Fred W. and Grace (Hobson) S. B.A., Pomona Coll., 1942; Mus.M., U. Rochester, 1943, performer's cert., 1944. Mem. faculty piano and theory Eastman Sch. Music, U. Rochester, 1943-49; mem. faculty U. Hawaii, Honolulu, 1949—; assoc. prof. music U. Hawaii, 1953-62, prof., 1962-82, prof. emeritus, 1982—; sr. fellow East-West Center, 1973; lectr., recitals in Hawaiian and Asian music, U.S., Europe and Asia, 1956—; field researcher Asia, 1956, 60, 66, 71, 80, Micronesia, 1963, 70, 87, 88, 90, 91, Solomon Islands, 1976. Author publs. on ethnomusicology. Mem. Internat. Soc. Music Edn., Internat. Musicol. Soc., Am. Musicol. Soc., Soc. Ethnomusicology, Internat. Coun. for Traditional Music, Asia Soc., Am. Mus. Instrument Soc., Coll. Music Soc., Soc. for Asian Music, Music Educators Nat. Conf., Pacific Sci. Assn., Assn. for Chinese Music Rsch., Phi Beta Kappa, Mu Phi Epsilon. Home: 581 Kamoku St Apt 2004 Honolulu HI 96826-5210

SMITH, BERNALD STEPHEN, retired airline pilot, aviation consultant; b. Long Beach, Calif., Dec. 24, 1926; s. Donald Albert and Bernice Merrill (Stephens) S.; m. Marilyn Mae Spence, July 22, 1949; children: Lorraine Ann Smith Foute, Evelyn Donice Smith DeRoos, Mark Stephen, Diane April (dec.). Student, U. Calif., Berkeley, 1944-45, 50-51. Cert. airline transport pilot, flight engr., FAA. Capt. Transocean Air Lines, Oakland (Calif.) and Tokyo, 1951-53, Hartford, Conn., 1954-55; 1st officer United Air Lines, Seattle, 1955, San Francisco, 1956-68; tng. capt. United Air Lines, Denver and San Francisco, 1961-68; capt. United Air Lines, San Francisco, 1968-86, 2d officer, 1986-93, ret., 1993; founder, v.p. AviaAm., Palo Alto, Calif., 1970-72, AviaInternat., Palo Alto, 1972-74; cons. Caproni Vizzola, Milan, 1972-84; prin., cons. Internat. Aviation Cons. and Investments, Fremont, Calif., 1985—; instr. aviation Ohlone Coll., Fremont, 1976; founder Pacific Soaring Coun.; founder, trustee AirSailing, Inc., 1970—, Soaring Safety Found., 1985—. Author/editor: American Soaring Handbook, 1975, 80; contbr. articles to profl. jours. Trustee Nat. Soaring Mus., 1975—, pres. 1975-78; active RTCA, SSA del., 1992—, FAI del., 1996. Comdr. USNR. Fellow Internat. GPS Svc. for Geodynamics; mem. AIAA (pub. bd. 1977-94), Soaring Soc. Am. (pres. 1969-70, chmn. pub. bd. 1971-84, ins. com. 1975-93, bd. dirs. 1963—, Warren Eaton Meml. trophy, 1977, Exceptional Svc. award 1970, 75, 82, 88, 91, Exceptional Achievement award 1996, named to Hall of Fame 1984), Soc. Automotive Engrs., Nat. Aero. Assn., Exptl. Aircraft Assn., Aircraft Owners and Pilots Assn., Airline Pilots Assn., Seaplane Pilots Assn., Orgn. Scientifique et Technique Internat. du Vol a Voile (bd. dirs., U.S. del. 1981—), Fedn. Aeronatique Internat. (Paul Tissandier diploma 1992, Lilienthal medal 1993), Commn. de Vol A Voile (U.S. del. 1970-71, 78, 85-97, v.p. 1988-96), U. Calif. Alumni Assn. (life), Inst. Navigation, Civil GPS Svc. Interace Com. Democrat. Methodist. Office: Internat Aviation Cons Investments PO Box 3075 Fremont CA 94539-0307

SMITH, BERNARD JOSEPH CONNOLLY, civil engineer; b. Elizabeth, N.J., Mar. 11, 1930; s. Bernard Joseph and Julia Susan (Connolly) S.; BS, U. Notre Dame, 1951; BS in Civil Engring., Tex. A&M U., 1957; MBA in Fin., U. Calif.-Berkeley, 1976; m. Josephine Kerley, Dec. 20, 1971; children: Julia Susan Alice Birmingham, Teresa Mary Josephine, Anne Marie Kathleen. Asst. Bernard J. Smith, cons. engr. office, Dallas, 1947-57; hydraulic engr. C.E., U.S. Army, San Francisco, 1957-59, St. Paul dist., 1959-60, Kansas City (Mo.) dist., 1960-63, Sacramento dist., 1963-65; engr. Fed. Energy Regulatory Commn., San Francisco Regional Office, 1965—. Served with U.S. Army, 1952-54. Registered profl. engr., Calif., Mo.; lic. real estate broker, Calif. Mem. ASCE (sec. power div. San Francisco sect. 1969), Soc. Am. Mil. Engrs. (treas. Kansas City post 1962), Res. Officers Assn. (chpt. pres. 1973). Club: Commonwealth of Calif. Home: 247 28th Ave San Francisco CA 94121-1001 Office: Fed Energy Regulatory Commn 901 Market St San Francisco CA 94103-1729

SMITH, BETTY DENNY, county official, administrator, fashion executive; b. Centralia, Ill., Nov. 12, 1932; d. Otto and Ferne Elizabeth (Beier) Hasenfuss; m. Peter S. Smith, Dec. 5, 1964; children: Carla Kip, Bruce Kimball. Student, U. Ill., 1950-52; student, L.A. City Coll., 1953-57, UCLA, 1965, U. San Francisco, 1982-84. Freelance fashion coordinator L.A., N.Y.C., 1953-58; tchr. fashion Rita LeRoy Internat. Studios, 1959-60; mgr. Mo Nadler Fashion, L.A., 1961-64; showroom dir. Jean of Calif. Fashions, L.A., 1965—; freelance polit. book reviewer for community newspapers, 1961-62; staff writer Valley Citizen News, 1963. Bd. dirs. Pet Assistance Found., 1969-76; founder, pres., dir. Vol. Services to Animals L.A., 1972-76; mem. County Com. To Discuss Animals in Rsch., 1973-74; mem. blue ribbon com. on animal control L.A. County, 1973-74; dir. L.A. County Animal Care and Control, 1976-82; mem. Calif. Animal Health Technician Exam. Com., 1975-82, chmn., 1979; bd. dirs. L.A. Soc. for Prevention Cruelty to Animals, 1984-94, Calif. Coun. Companion Animal Advocates, 1993-97; dir. West Coast Regional Office, Am. Humane Assn., 1988-97; CFO Coalition for Pet Population Control, 1987-92; trustee Gladys W. Sargent Found., 1997; cons. Jungle Book II, Disney Studios, 1997; mem. Coalition to Protect Calif. Wildlife, 1996—; mem. Calif. Rep. Cen. Com., 1964-72, mem. exec. com., 1971-73; mem. L.A. County Rep. Cen. Com., 1964-70, mem. exec. com., 1966-70; chmn. 29th Congl. Cen. Com., 1969-70; sec. 28th Senatorial Cen. Com., 1967-68, 45th Assembly Dist. Cen. Com., 1965-68; mem. speakers bur. George Murphy for U.S. Senate, 1970; campaign mgr. Los Angeles County for Spencer Williams for Atty. Gen., 1966; mem. adv. com. Moorpark Coll., 1988—; mem. adv. bd. Wishbone Prodn., 1995—. Mem. Internat. Platform Assn., Mannequins Assn. (bd. dirs. 1967-68), Motion Picture and TV Industry Assn. (govt. rels. and pub. affairs com. 1992-97), Lawyer's Wives San Gabriel Valley (bd. dirs. 1971-74, pres. 1972-73), L.A. Athletic Club, Town Hall. Home: 1766 Bluffhill Dr Monterey Park CA 91754-4533

SMITH, BILL, city manager; b. N.Y.C., June 24, 1940; s. Harry John and Catharine Marie (Wheeler) S.; m. Judith Ann Carroll, Mar. 18, 1961; children: Shawn, Kevin, Susan, Kurt, Eric. BA, Iona Coll., 1962; MS, USN Postgrad. Sch., 1971; MPA, Golden Gate U., 1982. Adminstrv. analyst City of Monterey (Calif.), 1982-84; city adminstr. City of Sonora (Calif.), 1984-86; asst. city mgr. City of Monterey, 1986-90; city mgr. City of Manhattan Beach (Calif.), 1990-94, City of Westminster, Calif., 1994-97; gen. mgr. Ventura (Calif.) Regional Sanitation Dist., 1997—; instr. USN Postgrad. Sch., Monterey, 1979-82; adj. prof. Golden Gate U., San Francisco, 1984-90. Contbr. articles to profl. jours. Bd. dirs. Monterey County AIDS Project, 1987-90. Lt. col. USMC, 1962-82. Decorated Silver Star, Bronze Star, PurpleHeart, Joint Svc. Commendation medal. Mem. Am. Soc. Pub. Adminstrn. (chpt. pres. 1983-84),Internat. City Mgrs. Assn., Retired Officers Assn., Disabled Am. Vets., VFW, Am. Legion. Home: 2551 Plaza Del Amo # 1 Torrance CA 90503-7312 Office: Ventura Regional Sanitation Dist Ste 150 1001 Partridge Dr Ventura CA 93003-5562

SMITH, BRADLEY ROWAN, computer scientist; b. Ann Arbor, Mich., Jan. 15, 1959; s. Willie and Marjorie (Joslyn) S. BA in Computer and Info. Scis., U. Calif., Santa Cruz, 1981, M in Computer Sci., 1996. Software engr. Avera Corp., Scotts Valley, Calif., 1982-83, CTX Internat., Sunnyvale, Calif., 1983-84, Hewlett Packard, Cupertino, Calif., 1985; Unix sys. mgr. computer scis. U. Calif., Santa Cruz, 1985-90, computer facilities dir. computer scis., 1991—; Unix sys. mgr. Ecole Polytechnic Fed. de Lausanne, Switzerland, 1990; pvt. Internet security cons., Santa Cruz, 1994—. Mem. IEEE (assoc.), Assn. for Computing Machinery, Usenix Assn. Office: U Calif Santa Cruz Dept Computer Scis 1156 High St Santa Cruz CA 95064

SMITH, CARIN A., veterinarian, writer; b. Moses Lake, Wash., Sept. 3, 1958; d. William and Katherine Smith; m. Jay Bender, May 19, 1990. BS in Microbiology, Oreg. State U., 1980; DVM, Oreg. State U., Wash. State U., 1984. Pres. Smith Vet. Svcs., Albuquerque, 1986-90, Leavenworth, Wash., 1990—; co-founder Childless by Choice, Leavenworth, 1992—. Author: Easy Health Care for Your Horse, 1990, Relief Veterinarian's Manual, 1990, rev. edit., 1996, Employer's Guide to Hiring, 1992, rev. edit., 1996, Get Rid of Fleas and Ticks, 1993, rev. edit., 1995, 101 Training Tips for Your Cat, 1994, The Housecall Veterinarian's Manual, 1996, Career Choices for Veterinarians, 1997; editor (newsletter) Childless by Choice, 1992—. Pres. bd. dirs. Leavenworth Libr., 1994-95, 97—. Recipient 1st Place nonfiction book award Southwest Writers Workshop, 1989, Top 25 of Yr. award Groom & Board mag., 1995, book award Cat Writers' Assn., 1995, media award Wash. State Vet. Med. Assn., 1996. Mem. Am. Vet. Med. Assn., Pubs. Mktg. Assn., Women Vets. Assn., Am. Endurance Ride Conf. Office: Childless by Choice PO Box 695 Leavenworth WA 98826-0695 also: SmithVet Svcs PO Box 254 Leavenworth WA 98826-0254

SMITH, CAROL LOUISE, elementary school director; b. Dayton, Ohio, Feb. 28, 1943; d. Richard Louis and Virginia Louise Smith. BS in Edn., Wittenberg U., Springfield, Ohio, 1965; MA, San Francisco State U., 1976; postgrad., U. Calif., Berkeley, Calif. State U. Tchr. Dayton pub. schs.; tchr. K-5 Oakland (Calif.) pub. schs.; tchr./asst. curriculum Prospect Sch., El Cerrito, Calif.; founder, dir., tchr. Aurora Sch., Oakland, Calif., 1988-94, Elem. Sch. Arts and Scis., Oakland, 1994—; math cons./workshop leader Bay Area Math. Project; curriculum developer archaeology and marine biology and botany Univ. Rsch. Expedition Programs and Earthwatch; mem. adv. panel Interactive R & D Project Far West Labs. San Francisco. Author: Addison Wesley Math Texts, Grades K-3, 1978. Tchr. ESL Peace Corps, The Philippines, 1965-67. Grantee, Walter S. Johnson Found., U. Calif., Berkeley. Mem. ASCD, Nat. Assn. Edn. Young Children, Nat. Coun. Tchrs. Math., Nat. Sci. Tchrs. Assn., Elementary Network Progressive Educators. Home: 1101 Fountain St Alameda CA 94501-5547

SMITH, CARTER BLAKEMORE, broadcaster; b. San Francisco, Jan. 1, 1937; s. Donald V. and Charlotte M. (Nichols) S.; children: Carter Blakemore, Clayton M. AA, City Coll. San Francisco, 1958; BA, San Francisco State U., 1960; postgrad. N.Y. Inst. Finance, 1969-70; Assoc. in Fin. PLanning, Coll. for Fin. Planning, 1984. Announcer, Sta. KBLF, Red Bluff, Calif., 1954-56; personality Sta. KRE-KRE FM, Berkeley, Calif., 1958-63, Sta. KSFO, San Francisco, 1963-72, Sta. KNBR, San Francisco, 1972-83, Sta. KSFO, San Francisco, 1983-86, Sta. KFRC, San Francisco, 1986-91, 93-94, Sta. KABL, San Francisco, 1996—; mem. faculty radio-TV dept. San Francisco State U., 1960-61. Mem. adv. bd. Little Jim Club Children's Hosp., 1968-71; bd. dirs. Marin County Humane Soc., 1968-73, San Francisco Zool. Soc., 1980-90; trustee Family Svc. Agy. Marin, 1976-85; mem. alumni bd. Lowell High Sch. Recipient award San Francisco Press Club, 1965; named one of Outstanding Young Men in Am. U.S. Jaycees, 1972. Mem. Amateur Radio Relay League (life), Quarter Century Wireless Assn., Alpha Epsilon Rho.

SMITH, CHARLES ANTHONY, businessman; b. Santa Fe, Sept. 16, 1939; s. Frances (Mier) Vigil; student various adminstrv. and law courses; m. Paula Ann Thomas, June 26, 1965; 1 dau., Charlene Danielle. Circulation mgr. Daily Alaska Empire, 1960-63; agt. Mut. of N.Y. Life Ins. Co., Juneau, Alaska, 1964-65; mng. partner Future Investors in Alaska and Cinema Alaska, Juneau, 1961-62; SE Alaska rep. K & L Distbrs., 1966-68; mgr. Alaska Airlines Newspapers, SE Alaska, 1969; dep. Alaska Retirement System, Juneau, 1970-71; apptd. dir. hwy. safety, gov.'s hwy. safety rep., Juneau, 1971-83; pres. Valley Service Ctr., Inc., 1984—. Alaska pres. Muscular Dystrophy Assn. Am.; pres. SE Alaska Emergency Med. Services Council, 1965-72. Served to major Army N.G., 1964-88. Named Alaska Safety Man of Yr., 1977. Mem. Am. Assn. Motor Vehicle Adminstrs., Alaska Peace Officers Assn., Nat. Assn. Gov.s' Hwy. Safety Reps., N.G. Assn., Internat. Platform Assn. Roman Catholic. Club: Elks (Juneau). Author various hwy. safety manuals and plans, 1971—. Home: PO Box 32856 Juneau AK 99803-2856 Office: Pouch N Juneau AK 99811

SMITH, CHARLES LEWIS, retired naval officer and association executive; b. Clarkston, Ga., Oct. 27, 1920; s. Robert Clyde and Emelyn (Bloodworth) S.; m. Mildred Lee Stilley, Sept. 5, 1947; children: Jan, Robert Eugene. Student, Ga. Sch. Tech., 1938-39. Enlisted USN, 1937, advanced through grades to comdr., 1968; various assignments including comdg. officer USS Chickasaw (ATF 83), 1962-64; leadership devel. officer Amphibious Force U.S. Pacific Fleet, 1964-66; comdg. officer USS Tioga County (LST 1158), 1966-68; dept. head Amphibious Sch. U.S. Naval Amhibious Base, Coronado, Calif., 1968-70, ret., 1970; dir. pub. rels. and fin. San Diego County coun. Boy Scouts Am., 1971-80, dir. pub. rels., 1980-82, dir. planned giving, 1982-85, ret., 1985; mem. nat. adv. bd. Am. Security Coun., 1994—. Trustee God Bless Am. Week, Inc., 1972-80, pres., 1977-78, co-chmn. San Diego Bicentennial Pageant, 1976; mem. adv. bd. Commd. Officers Mess (Open) U.S. Naval Sta., 1973-89; bd. dirs. Boys Club Chula Vista, Calif., 1985-87; devel. com. Alvarado Health Found., Alvarado Hosp. Med. Ctr., 1986-87; charter rev. com. City of Chula Vista, 1986-88; mem. accolades com. City of San Diego, 1988-90; rsch. bd. advisors Am. Biog. Inst., 1988—; vol. Boy Scouts Am. 1935-71, 85—; scout commr. San Diego County coun. 1969-71, mem. internat. rels. com. 1985-92, bd. dirs., 1995-97, scoutmaster 7th Nat. Jamboree, Farragut State park, Idaho, 1969, 13th World Jamboree, Japan, 1971, mem. nat. staff Nat. Jamboree, Ft. A.P. Hill, Va., 1986. Recipient svc. award Civitan Internat., 1968, Cmty. Svc. resolution Calif. Senate, 1970, Southwestern Coll., 1973, Silver Beaver award Boy Scouts Am., 1965, Svc. to Youth resolution Calif. Senate, 1985, award Armed Forces YMCA Century Club, 1988, Appreciation award United Way San Diego, 1974-82, citation for heroism Sheriff of San Diego, 1991, Recognition award San Diego Rotary Club, 1991, citation for svc. City of San Diego Accolades Com., 1992, Disting. Svc. award U.S.S. Chickasaw (ATF) 83 Assn., 1993, Svc. award U.S.S. Wickes (DD578), 1995; Scouter Chuck Smith Day proclaimed by City of San Diego, 1985; flagpole dedicated to Scouter Chuck Smith San Diego County Coun. Boy Scouts Am., 1992; named to Hon. Order Ky. Cols., 1985, bd. dirs., 1987—, pres., 1996. Mem. VFW (Cert. of Appreciation 1995, 96, 97), Nat. Soc. Fund Raising Execs. (bd. dirs. San Diego chpt. 1975-80, 84-85, hosp. com. 1984-85), UN Assn. (bd. dirs. San Diego chpt. 1972-85), Ret. Officers Assn. (life, bd. dirs. Sweetwater chpt. 1972-92, pres. 1975, 81), Navy League U.S. (bd. dirs. 1984—, greeters 1983—, Appreciation award 1985, Cert. of Merit 1991), Mil. Order World Wars (comdr. 1989-90, nat. citations 1987, 91, 92, Outstanding Chpt. Comdr. award Dept. So. Calif. 1990, Patrick Henry medallion and medal 1996), Am. Legion, Crazy Horse Meml. Found., Clarkston

Civitan Club (founding bd. dirs.), Eagle Scout Alumni Assn. (founder 1973, bd. dirs. 1986-88, life mem. 1985—), Hammer Club San Diego, Kiwanis (bd. dirs. 1984-88, chmn. fellowship com. 1983-84, boys and girls com. 1984-85, planned giving com. 1988-89), Order of the Arrow (vigil, Cross Feathers award 1968), Masons, Shriners, Order of Ea. Star (life), Nat. Sojourners. Methodist.

SMITH, CHARLES RICHARD, high technology marketing executive; b. Covington, Ohio, Nov. 5, 1932; s. Richard Weller and Harriet Rosalind (Minton) S.; m. Margaret Jean Porter, Aug. 7, 1954; children: David Paul, Kevin Richard, Jennifer Perlee, Melinda Jean. BA, Ohio Wesleyan U., Delaware, 1954; B Chem. Engring., Ohio State U., 1960. Product engr. Dow Corning Corp., Midland, Mich., 1960-63; tech. pub. rels. mgr. Clyde Williams & Co., Columbus, Ohio, 1963-66; dir. pub. rels. Chem. Abstracts Svc., Columbus, 1966-68; v.p. sales/mktg. Ventron Corp., materials div., Bradford, Pa., 1968-73; v.p. sales/svc. Applied Materials, Inc., Santa Clara, Calif., 1973-77; gen. mgr. Gyrex Corp., Santa Barbara, Calif., 1977-81; pres., CEO Auto/Recognition Systems, Santa Barbara, 1982-84; v.p. mktg./sales Tylan Corp., Torrance, Calif., 1984-85, Benzing Tech., Santa Clara, Calif., 1985-88; v.p. sales High Yield Tech., Sunnyvale, Calif., 1988-91; cons. Internat. Remote Imaging Systems, Chatsworth, Calif., 1981-82, Hakuto Co. Ltd., Tokyo, 1989—; dir. Micropulse Systems, Santa Barbara, Benzing Tech., Santa Clara; founder Action Pro Tem internat. bus. cons. co. Author: Plasma Jet Technology, 1962; contbr. articles to profl. jours. Mem. U.S. English, Washington, Citizens Against Waste, Washington. With USAF, 1955-57. Mem. Semiconductor Equipment and Materials Internat. (chmn. sales exec. coun. 1988-90, W.C. Benzing award 1990), Marines' Meml. Assn., Churchill Club. Republican. Home: 7933 Caledonia Dr San Jose CA 95135-2112 Office: Action Pro Tem 3315 San Felipe Rd # 7 San Jose CA 95135-2000

SMITH, CHARLES Z., state supreme court justice; b. Lakeland, Fla., Feb. 23, 1927; s. John R. and Eva (Love) S.; m. Eleanor Jane Martinez, Aug. 20, 1955; children: Carlos M., Michael O., Stephen P., Felica L. BS, Temple U., 1952; JD, U. Wash., 1955. Bar: Wash. 1955. Law clk. Wash. Supreme Ct., Olympia, 1955-56; dep. pros. atty., asst. chief criminal div. King County, Seattle, 1956-60; ptnr. Bianchi, Smith & Tobin, Seattle, 1960-61; spl. asst. to atty. gen. criminal div. U.S. Dept. Justice, Washington, 1961-64; judge criminal dept. Seattle Mcpl. Ct., 1965-66; judge Superior Ct. King County, 1966-73; former assoc. dean, prof. law U. Wash., 1973; now justice Wash. Supreme Ct., Olympia. Mem. adv. bd. NAACP, Seattle Urban League, Wash. State Literacy Coun., Boys Club, Wash. Citizens for Migrant Affairs, Medina Children's Svc., Children's Home Soc. Wash., Seattle Better Bus. Bur., Seattle Foundation, Seattle Symphony Orch., Seattle Opera Assn., Community Svc. Ctr. for Deaf and Hard of Hearing, Seattle U., Seattle Sexual Assault Ctr., Seattle Psychoanalytic Inst., The Little Sch., Linfield Coll., Japanese Am. Citizens League, Kawabe Meml. Hous, Puget Counseling Ctr, Am. Cancer Soc., Hutchinson Cancer Rsch. Ctr., Robert Chinn Found.; pres. Am. Bapt. Chs. U.S.A., 1976-77, lt. col. ret. USMCR. Mem. ABA, Am. Judicature Soc., Washington Bar Assn., Seattle-King County Bar Assn., Order of Coif., Phi Alpha Delta, Alpha Phi Alpha. Office: Wash Supreme Ct Temple of Justice PO Box 40929 Olympia WA 98504

SMITH, CHESTER, broadcasting executive; b. Wade, Okla., Mar. 29, 1930; s. Louis L. and Effie (Brown) S.; m. Naomi L. Crenshaw, July 19, 1959; children: Lauri, Lorna, Roxanne. Country western performer on Capitol records, TV and radio, 1947-61; owner, mgr. Sta. KLOC, Ceres-Modesto, Calif., 1963-81, Sta. KCBA-TV, Salinas-Monterey, Calif.7; owner, gen. ptnr. Sta. KCSO-TV, Modesto-Stockton-Sacramento, 1966-97, Sta. VU-TV, Paradise-Chico-Redding, Calif., 1986—, Sta.; owner Sta. KBVU-TV, Eureka, Calif., 1990—; owner Sta. KNSO-TV, owner KCSO-TV, 1966-97 Merced-Fresno, KDS TV, Chico, Calif., KES-TV, Sacramento, Calif., owner, KFWU-TV, 1996-97, Fort Bragg, Calif., KRVU-TV, Redding, Calif., 1997—. Mem. Calif. Broadcasters Assn. Republican. Mem. Christian Ch. original rec. Wait A Little Longer Please Jesus; rec. in Country Music Hall of Fame, Nashville, 1955, inductee Western Swing Hall of Fame, Sacramento, 1988.

SMITH, CLIFFORD NEAL, business educator, writer; b. Wakita, Okla., May 30, 1923; s. Jesse Newton and Inez Lane (Jones) S.; m. Anna Piszczan-Czaja, Sept. 3, 1951; children: Helen Inez Smith Barrette. BS, Okla. State U., 1943; AM, U. Chgo., 1948; postgrad. Columbia U., 1960. Selector, U.S. Displaced Persons Commn., Washington and Munich, Germany, 1948-51; auditor Phillips Petroleum Co., Caracas, Venezuela, 1951-58; planning analyst Mobil Internat. Oil Co., N.Y.C., 1960, 65-66, Mobil Oil A.G., Deutschland, Hamburg, Germany, 1961-63; asst. to v.p. for Germany, Mobil Inner Europe, Inc., Geneva, 1963-65; asst. prof. No. Ill. U. Sch. Bus., DeKalb, 1966-69, part-time prof. internat. bus., 1970—; owner Westland Publs.; lectr. in field. Author: Federal Land Series, vol. 1, 1972, vol. 2, 1973, vol. 3, 1980, vol. 4, part 1, 1982, vol. 4, part 2, 1986, Encyclopedia of German-American Genealogical Research, American Genealogical Resources in German Archives, 1977, numerous monographs in German-Am., Brit.-Am., French-Am. geneal. research series, German and Central European Emigration Series, Selections from the American State Papers; contbg. editor Nat. Geog. Soc. Quar., Geneal. jour. (Utah); contbr. articles to profl. jours. Mem. at large exec. com. Friends Com. on Nat. Legis., 1968-75; mem. regional exec. com. Am. Friends Service Com., 1969-76; v.p. Riverside Dem., N.Y.C., 1959-61; precinct committeeman, 1984—; mem. Ariz. State Central Com. of Dem. Party, 1984—; sec. Dem. Cen. Com. of Cochise County; mem. com. to Re-Elect Clinton for Pres. Recipient Distinguished Service medal Ill. Geneal. Soc., 1973, award for outstanding service to sci. genealogy Am. Soc. Genealogists, 1973; court appointed arbitrator for civil cases, 1992. Fellow Geneal. Soc. of Utah; mem. S.R., SAR, Soc. Descs. Colonial Clergy, Soc. Advancement Mgmt., Ill. Genealogic Soc. (dir. 1968-69), Phi Eta Sigma, Beta Alpha Psi, Sigma Iota Epsilon. Mem. Soc. of Friends. Club: American of Hamburg (v.p. 1962-63); contbr. articles to profl. jours. Address: PO Box 117 Mc Neal AZ 85617-0117

SMITH, COLLEEN See SMITH, LEE R.

SMITH, DAVID ADAM, congressman; b. Washington, June 15, 1965; m. Sara Bickle-Eldridge, 1993. BA, Fordham U., 1987; JD, U. Wash., 1990. Driver United Parcel Svc., 1985-87; mem. Wash. State Senate, 1990-96; atty. Cromwell Mendoza Belur, 1992-93; asst. prosecuting atty. City of Seattle, 1993-96; mem. 105th Congress from 9th dist. Wash., 1997—. Democrat. Office: 1505 Longworth Washington DC 20515

SMITH, DAVID ALAN, systems programmer; b. Williamsburg, Va., Dec. 1, 1949; s. Robert Edward and Anne Katherine (Klein) S.; m. Linda Lark Wasmer, May 28, 1977; children: Amanda Lark, Michael David. BS in Math., U. N.Mex., 1979. Programmer analyst EG&G Energy Measurements, Albuquerque, 1980-83; systems programmer EG&G ENergy Measurements, Albuquerque, 1983-89, sr. systems programmer, 1989-94; sr. systems programmer Allied Signal Aerospace, Albuquerque, 1994-95, sci. specialist, 1995-96, tech. programmer analyst, 1996—. Contbr. articles to profl. jours. Sgt. USAF, 1971-75, N.Mex. Air N.G., 1977-81, 83-96, N.Mex. Army N.G., 1996—. Mem. ACM, Am. Def. Preparedness Assn., Nat. Computer Graphics Assn. Home: 12017 Kashmir St NE Albuquerque NM 87111 Office: Allied Signal Aerospace Kirland Ops Sta A PO Box 4339 Albuquerque NM 87196

SMITH, DAVID ELVIN, physician; b. Bakersfield, Calif., Feb. 7, 1939; s. Elvin W. and Dorothy (McGinnis) S.; m. Millicent Buxton; children: Julia, Suzanne, Christopher Buxton-Smith, Sabree Hill. Intern San Francisco Gen. Hosp., 1965; fellow pharmacology and toxicology U. Calif., San Francisco, 1965-67, assoc. clin. prof. occupational medicine, clin. toxicology, 1967—, dir. psychopharmacology study group, 1966-70; practice specializing in toxicology/addiction medicine San Francisco, 1965—; physician Presbyn. Alcoholic Clinic, 1965-67, Contra Cost Alcoholic Clinic, 1965-67; dir. alcohol and drug abuse screening unit San Francisco Gen. Hosp., 1967-68; co-dir. Calif. drug abuse info. project U. Calif. Med. Ctr., 1967-72; founder, med. dir. Haight-Ashbury Free Med. Clinic, San Francisco, 1967—; rsch. dir. Merritt Peralta Chem. Dependency Hosp., Oakland, Calif., 1984—; chmn. Nat. Drug Abuse Conf., 1977; mem. Calif. Gov.'s Commn. on Narcotics and Drug Abuse, 1977—; nat. health adviser to former U.S. Pres. Jimmy Carter; mem. Pres. Clinton's Health Care Task Force on Addiction and Nat. Health Reform, 1993; with Office Drug Abuse Policy, White House Task Force Physicians for Drug Abuse Prevention; dir. Benzodiazepine Rsch. and Tng. Project, Substance Abuse and Sexual Concerns Project, PCP Rsch. and Tng. Project; cons. numerous fed. drug abuse agys. Author: Love Needs Care, 1970, The New Social Drug: Cultural, Medical and Legal Perspectives on Marijuana, 1971, The Free Clnic: Community Approaches to Health Care and Drug Abuse, 1971, Treating the Cocaine Abuser, 1985, The Benzodiazepines: Current Standard Medical Practice, 1986, Physicians' Guide to Drug Abuse, 1987; co-author: It's So Good, Don't Even Try it Once: Heroin in Perspective, 1972, Uppers and Downers, 1973, Drugs in the Classroom, 1973, Barbiturate Use and Abuse, 1977, A Multicultural View of Drug Abuse, 1978, Amphetamine Use, Misuse and Abuse, 1979, PCP: Problems and Prevention, 1981, Sexological Aspects of Substance Use and Abuse, Treatment of the Cocaine Abuser, 1985, The Haight Ashbury Free Medical Clinic: Still Free After All These Years, Drug Free: Alternatives to Drug Abuse, 1987, Treatment of Opiate Dependence, Designer Drugs, 1988, Treatment of Cocaine Dependence, 1988, Treatment of Opiate Dependence, 1988, The New Drugs, 1989, Crack and Ice in the Era of Smokeable Drugs, 1992, others; also drug edn. films; founder, editor Jour. Psychedelic Drugs (now Jour. Psychoactive Drugs), 1967—; contbr. over 300 articles to profl. jours. Mem. Physicians for Prevention White House Office Drug Abuse Policy, 1995; pres. Youth Projects, Inc.; founder, chmn. bd., pres. Nat. Free Clin. Coun., 1968-72. Recipient Rsch. award Borden Found., 1964, AMA Rsch. award, 1977, Cmty. Svc. award U. Calif.-San Francisco, 1974, Calif. State Drug Abuse Treatment award, 1984, Vernelle Fox Drug Abuse Treatment award, 1985, UCLA Sidney Cohen Addiction Medicine award, 1989, U. Calif. San Francisco medal of honor, 1995; named one of Best Doctors in U.S., 1995. Mem. AMA (alt. del.), CMA (alt. del.), Am. Soc. on Addiction Medicine (bd. dirs., pres. 1995), San Francisco Med. Soc., Am. Pub. Health Assn., Calif. Soc. on Addiction Medicine (pres., bd. dirs.), Am. Soc. Addiction Medicine, Sigma Xi, Phi Beta Kappa. Methodist. Home: 289 Frederick St San Francisco CA 94117-4051 Office: Haight Ashbury Free Clinics 612 Clayton St San Francisco CA 94117-1911

SMITH, DAVID EUGENE, business administration educator; b. Boise, Idaho, Dec. 14, 1941; s. Roy Arthur and Anna Margaret (Fries) S.; m. Patricia Stroy, Aug. 4, 1973; 1 child, Zachary Adam. BS in Applied Stats., San Francisco State Coll., 1964, MS in Mgmt. Sci., 1966; MBA, PhD in Bus. Adminstrn., U. Santa Clara, 1969. Asst. to dir. mgmt ctr. Grad. Sch. Bus., U. Santa Clara, Calif., 1966-69, lectr. mktg., 1968; asst. prof. bus. adminstrn. Mktg./Quantitative Studies Dept., San Jose State U., Calif., 1969-71, assoc. prof. bus. adminstrn., 1971-76, prof. bus. adminstrn., 1976—, chmn. dept., 1986-89. Author: Quantitative Business Analysis, 1977, Internat. Edit., 1979, 1982; contbr. articles to profl. jours. Mem. INFORMS, Phi Kappa Phi, Beta Gamma Sigma. Republican. Home: 22448 Tim Tam Ct Los Gatos CA 95030-8521 Office: San Jose State U Mktg/MIS/Decision Scis One Washington Sq San Jose CA 95192

SMITH, DAVID MICHAEL, financial planner; b. Fresno, Calif., Dec. 29, 1944; s. Ralph S. and Verla Fern (Tharpe) S.; m. Barbara J. Bryson, June 27, 1964; children: Brandon, Eric. AA, Fresno City Coll., 1964; AB, Calif. State U., Fresno, 1966. Tchr. English Fresno Unified Sch. Dist., 1967-79; registered rep. TMI Equities, Inc., Fresno, 1979-82; regional mgr. TMI Equities, Inc., Camarillo, Calif., 1982-85; fin. planner Associated Planners Securities Corp., Camarillo, 1985-89, David M. Smith & Assocs., Camarillo, 1989—; mayor City of Camarillo, 1991-95. Council mem. City of Camarillo, 1988-95; pres. Fresno Dem. Coaltion, 1979. Mem. Inst. Cert. Fin. Planners, Ventura County Internat. Assn. Fin. Planning, Camarillo Noontime Optimists Club. Office: David M Smith & Assocs 1200 Paseo Camarillo Ste 190 Camarillo CA 93010-6085

SMITH, DAVID WAYNE, psychologist, educator; b. Ind., Apr. 16, 1927; s. Lowell Wayne and Ruth Elizabeth (Westphal) S.; m. Marcene B. Leever, Oct. 20, 1948; children: David Wayne, Laurreen Lea. B.S., Purdue U., 1949; M.S., Ind. U., 1953, Ph.D., 1955. Prof. rehab., dir. Rehab. Center; asso. dean, later asst. v.p. acad. affairs Ariz. Health Scis. Center, U. Ariz., Tucson, 1955-80; research prof. rehab., adj. prof. medicine, cons. in research S.W. Arthritis Center, Coll. Medicine, 1980-87; prof. rehab. and rheumatology, dept. medicine U. Ariz., 1987—, also dir. disability assessment program; pres. allied health professions sect. Nat. Arthritis Found.; bd. dirs. Nat. Arthritis Found. (S.W. chpt.); nat. vice chmn. bd. dirs.; mem. NIH Nat. Arthritis Adv. Bd., 1977-84; also chmn. subcom. community programs and rehab.; mem. staff Ariz. Legislature Health Welfare, 1972-73; Mem. Gov.'s Council Dept. Econ. Security, 1978-85; pres., bd. dirs. Tucson Assn. for Blind, 1974-86; chmn. Gov.'s Council on Blind and Visually Impaired, 1987—; active Gov.'s Coun. on Arthritis and Musculoskeletal Disease, 1987—. Author: Worksamples; contbr. chpts. to books and articles to profl. jours. Recipient Gov.'s awards for leadership in rehab., 1966, 69, 72, 73; awards for sci. and vol. services Nat. Arthritis Found., 1973, 75; 1st nat. Addie Thomas award Nat. Arthritis Found., 1983, Benson award, 1989, Govt. Affairs award, 1989; Arthritis Found. fellow, 1983. Mem. Am. Psychol. Assn. (div. 17 counseling psychology), Assn. Schs. Allied Health Professions, Nat. Rehab. Assn., Ariz. Psychol. Assn. Home: 5765 N Camino Real Tucson AZ 85718-4213 Office: U Ariz Arizona Health Scis Ctr Tucson AZ 85724

SMITH, DEAN ORREN, physiology educator; b. Colorado Springs, Colo., May 28, 1944; s. Everett Ellsworth and Margaret Elizabeth Smith; m. Julie L. Rosenheimer, Dec. 30, 1985; children: Curtis Dean, Corey Bryant. BA, Harvard U., 1967; PhD, Stanford U., 1971. Prof. of physiology U. Wis., Madison, 1976-95, assoc. dean grad. sch., 1984-91; sr. v.p. rsch., dean grad. divsn. U. Hawaii, Honolulu, 1995—. Office: U Hawaii 2444 Dole St Honolulu HI 96822

SMITH, DICK MARTIN, oil field service company executive, owner; b. Alamosa, Colo., Nov. 20, 1946; s. Jack and Mary (Turnbull) S.; m. Janyce Wood Smith, Jan. 5, 1971 (div. May 1975); 1 child, DAnna Marie; m. Patricia Ann Connors, June 5, 1987; stepchildren: Shawna Parker, Scott Parker. Student, U. Md., 1969-72, U. York, Harrogate, Eng., 1969-72, U. N.Mex., 1975-79. With spl. ops. Nat. Security Agy., U.S. Govt., Ft. Meade, Md., 1969-74; with engring. rsch. U. N.Mex., Albuquerque, 1974-78; engr. fluids Internat. Mineral and Chem. Co., Houston, 1978-82; owner, pres., CEO Corrosions Monitoring Svcs. Inc., Capser, Wyo., 1981—; bd. dirs. Trenching Svcs., Casper, CMS Farms, Alamosa, Colo. With USN, 1964-68. Decorated Navy Unit Citation. Mem. Soc. Petroleum Engrs., Casper Wildcatters, Aircraft Owners Pilots Assn., DAV. Republican. Home: 4471 E 12th St Casper WY 82609-3247 Office: CMS Inc PO Box 9826 Casper WY 82609-0826

SMITH, DONALD E., broadcast engineer, manager; b. Salt Lake City, Sept. 10, 1930; s. Thurman A. and Louise (Cardall) S.; B.A. Columbia Coll., Chgo., 1955; B.S.; U. Utah, 1970; postgrad. U. So. Calif., U. Utah, PhD (hon.) Columbia Coll., 1985; m. Helen B. Lacy, 1978. Engr., Iowa State U., (WOI-TV), 1955-56; asst. chief engr. KLRJ-TV, Las Vegas, 1956-60; studio field engr. ABC, Hollywood, Cal., 1960; chief engr. Teletape, Inc., Salt Lake City, 1961; engring. supr. KUER, U. Utah, Salt Lake City, 1962-74, gen. mgr., 1975-85. Freelance cinematographer, 1950—; cons. radio TV (mgmt. engr. and prodn.), 1965—. Mem. Soc. Motion Pictures and TV Engrs., Lambda Chi Alpha. Home: 963 Hollywood Ave Salt Lake City UT 84105-3347

SMITH, DONALD EVANS, library consultant; b. Shanendoah, Iowa, Dec. 2, 1915; s. William Wesley and Bess Alice (Evans) S.; student Ricks Coll., 1939-40; BA, Hastings Coll., 1946; MLS, U. Wash., 1964. Tchr. English, librarian Tenino (Wash.) High Sch., 1950-51, Rochester (Wash.) High Sch., 1954-59; librarian North Thurston High Sch., Lacey, Wash., 1959-67; head librarian, coord. instructional materials Lakes High Sch., Lakewood Ctr., Wash., 1967-80; library cons., 1980—. Mem. awards com. Wash. Library Commn., 1964-66. With Signal Corps, AUS, 1942-45; to 1st lt., M.I., U.S. Army, 1951-54; to col. Wash. State Guard, 1971-80, now ret. Mem. Wash. Assn. Sch. Librarians (com. chmn.), Clover Park Edn. Assn. (com. chmn. 1970-71), Am. Legion, Phi Delta Kappa (del. nat. confs.). Home and Office: 4530 26th Loop SE Lacey WA 98503-3264

SMITH, DONALD RICHARD, editor, publisher; b. Stockton, Calif., Aug. 20, 1932; s. Robert Gordon and Gertrude (Schweitzer) S.; m. Darlene Ruth Thomas, May 7, 1961; children: Douglas Robert, Deborah Renae. Student, Coll. Pacific, 1951, Delta Coll., 1951-52. Editor, pub. Calif. Odd Fellow & Rebekah, Linden, 1950—; editor Elk Grove (Calif.) Citizen, 1953-55; asst. dir. U.N. Pilgrimage for Youth, N.Y.C., 1956-59; editor, pub. Linden (Calif.) Herald, 1959-86, Lockeford (Calif.)-Clements Post, 1960-62, Internat. Rebekah News, Linden, 1963-86, Internat. Odd Fellow & Rebekah, Linden, 1986—; dir. communications Sovereign Grand Lodge, Linden, 1990-92. Author: From Stagestop to Friendly Community, 1976, Leadership Manual, 1980, The Three Link Fraternity, 1993, Six Links of Fellowship, 1995. Bd. dirs. Odd Fellow-Rebekah Youth Camp, Inc., Long Barn, Calif., 1959-61; bd. dirs. The Meadows of Napa Valley, 1995—; bd. dirs., chmn., S.J. County 4-H Found., 1986—; chmn. Linden Rep. Com., 1962-66, Linden Centennial Observance, 1963, Linden Mcpl. Coun., 1981-90. Recipient Legion of Honor Order of Demolay, 1961, John Williams award S.J. Tchrs. Assn., 1963, 87, Golden Key award Stockton Tchrs. Assn., 1971, Achievement award County Bd. Suprs., 1970, Grand Decoration of Chivalry, 1969, Citizen of Yr. award Lions Internat., 1982. Mem. IOOF Internat. Press Assn. (pres. 1962-63), Desktop Pub. Assn., Berkeley Macintosh Users Assn., Linden Peters C. of C. (pres. 1968-69), S.J. Hist. Soc. (trustee 1986-90). Methodist. Lodges: Lions, Odd Fellows (Calif.) (grand master 1958-59), Odd Fellows Internat. (sovereign grand master 1969-70), Internat. Coun. 100F (sec. 1990—). Home: 5350 Harrison St Linden CA 95236-9630 Office: Linden Publ 19033 E Main PO Box 129 Linden CA 95236-0129

SMITH, DOUGLAS G., optometrist; b. North Conway, N.H., Nov. 26, 1948; s. Vernon E. and Rose L. (Zacker) S.; m. Hazel Anne Parker, July 10, 1971; children: Erin Kathleen, Ryan Douglas. BA in Psychology, Colby Coll., 1970; postgrad., Mont. State U., 1974-75; OD, Pacific U. Coll. Optometry, 1979. Lic. optometrist, Oreg., Mont., Calif. Clinic staff Pacific U. Coll. Optometry, 1979; optometrist pvt. practice, Medford, Oreg., 1979—; mem. Oreg. Commn. for Blind; mem. childrens's svcs. div. citizens adv. com. Oreg. Bd. Optometry, 1991—; chmn., ceo Oreg. Laser Eye Ctr. Chmn. So. Oreg. State Coll. Learning Disabilities Clinic, Jackson County Juvenile Svcs. Commn.; bd. dirs. Rogue Valley Alcohol Rehab. Ctr., Willaway Ranch for Handicapped; mem. Jackson County Task Force for Pres-sch. Handicapped, Jackson County Head Start Med. Adv. Bd., Oreg. Tchr. Standards and Practices Com. Task Force. Capt. USAF, 1970-74. Recipient William M. Feinbloom Low Vision award, 1979; named Oreg. Optometrist of Yr., 1982, Outstanding Young Men Am., 1978, 84. Mem. Am. Optometric Assn. (contact lens sect., low vision sect., Optometric Recognition award 1984, 91, 92, 93, 94, 95, 96), Oreg. Optometric Assn., Rotary Internat. (spl. rep. Kamchatka, Russia), Beta Sigma Kappa. Home: 383 Alta PO 253 Ashland OR 97520 Office: Bison Vision Ctr 585 Murphy Rd Medford OR 97504-8128

SMITH, DUNBAR WALLACE, retired physician, clergyman; b. Dunbar, Nebr., Oct. 17, 1910; s. Clarence Dunbar and Marie Christine (Eden) S.; m. Kathryn Avis Johnson, May 2, 1935; children: Dunbar Wesley, John Wallace. BSc, La Sierra Coll., Riverside, Calif., 1949; MD, Loma Linda U., 1950; DTM and Hygiene, Sch. of Tropical Med. London U., 1951; MPH, Columbia U., 1967. Diplomate Nat. Bd. Med. Examiners. Pastor 7th-day Adventist Chs., San Diego, Omaha, N.Y., India, Ceylon, 1935-44; med. dir. 7th-Day Adventist Mission Hosps., India, 1951-056; adminstr. Battle Creek (Mich.) Sanitarium, 1957-62; med. dir. Bates Meml. Hosp., Yonkers, N.Y., 1962-67; dep. commr. health Nassau County, N.Y., 1967-69; dir. dept. health for Africa, 7th-day Adventist Ch., 1969-76; dir. dept. health for Far East, 7th-day Adventist Ch., Singapore, 1976-80; adj. asst. prof. internat. health Loma Linda (Calif.) U., 1980-90; v.p. Emerald Health and Edn. Found., Loma Linda, 1986-91. Author: Report of CME (now Loma Linda U. Sch. Medicine) Rsch. to Date, 1946, (textbook) Home Health Aide, 1960, Autobiography of Dunbar W. Smith, 1994, (booklet) The Cold Turkey Way to Stop Smoking; contbr. numerous articles to various publs. V.p. Emerald Health and Edn. Found., 1991—. Recipient Honored Alumnus award Loma Linda U. Sch. Medicine, 1975, Golden award La Sierra U. Alumni Soc., 1992. Fellow AMA, SAR, Am. Coll. Nutrition, Royal Soc. Tropical Medicine, Royal Soc. Health, Internat. Med. Assn. (bd. dirs. 1987—); mem. N.Y. Acad. Scis. Republican. Home: 1414 Bella Vista Crest Redlands CA 92373-4907 Office: Emerald Health and Edn Found PO Box 8877 Redlands CA 92375-2077

SMITH, EILEEN PAZDERKA, dermatologist; b. Fort Belvior, Va., Sept. 17, 1956; d. Robert James and Diane Louis (Lotz) Pazderka; m. Martin James Smith, May 18, 1985; children: Tyler James, Dylan Russell. BS in Med. Tech., U. Nebr., 1978, MS, 1985, MD, 1990. Med. tech. U. Nebr. Med. Ctr., Omaha, 1984-89; intern, resident U. Utah Health Sci. Ctr., Salt Lake City, 1991, fellow divsn. dermatology, 1991-93, resident in dermatology, 1993—; staff urgent care dept. Family Health Plan, Salt Lake City, 1991-94. Contbr. chpts. to books and articles to profl. jours. Named one of Outstanding Young Women Am., 1989. Mem. Utah State Med. Soc., AMA (credentials com. 1987, state leadership steering com. 1988, rules com. 1988), Soc. Investigative Dermatology. Democrat. Roman Catholic. Home: 2729 E Wilshire Dr Salt Lake City UT 84109-1632 Office: U Utah Sch of Medicine Dept of Dermatology 50 N Med Dr Salt Lake City UT 84132

SMITH, ELDEN LEROY, recreational vehicle company executive; b. Berwyn, Ill., June 1, 1940; s. Frederick M. and Margaret I. (Larson) S.; B.A. in Bus. Adminstrn., Whittier Coll., 1962; m. Barbara G. Whaley, Apr. 4, 1963; children—Jill Marie, David Elden. Market analyst Autonetics div. N.Am. Aviation, Anaheim, Calif., 1963-66; sales mgr. Pendleton Tool Industries, Los Angeles, 1966-68; plant gen. mgr. Fleetwood Enterprises, Inc., Hancock, Md., 1969-71, v.p. recreational vehicle group, Riverside, Calif., 1972-88, sr. v.p., 1988—. Trustee Whittier (Calif.) Coll., 1991—. Served with USNR, 1962-63. Mem. Recreation Vehicle Industry Assn. (chmn. 1980-82, dir. 1975—). Office: Fleetwood Enterprises Inc 3125 Myers St PO Box 7638 Riverside CA 92503-5544*

SMITH, ELDRED GEE, church leader; b. Lehi, Utah, Jan. 9, 1907; s. Hyrum Gibbs and Martha E. (Gee) S.; m. Jeanne A. Ness, Aug. 17, 1932 (dec. June 1977); children: Miriam Smith Skeen, Eldred Gary, Audrey Gay Smith Vance, Gordon Raynor, Sylvia Dawn Smith Isom; m. Hortense H. Child, May 18, 1978; stepchildren: Carol Jane Child Burdette (dec.), Thomas Robert Child. Employed with sales div. Bennett Glass & Paint Co., Salt Lake City, 6 years; mech. design engr. Remington Arms Co., 2 years; design engr., prodn. equipment design Tenn. Eastman Corp., Oak Ridge, Tenn., 3 years; now presiding patriarch Ch. Jesus Christ of Latter-day Saints. Home: 2942 Devonshire Cir Salt Lake City UT 84108-2526 Office: 47 E South Temple Salt Lake City UT 84150-1005

SMITH, FERN M., judge; b. San Francisco, Nov. 7, 1933. AA, Foothill Coll., 1970; BA, Stanford U., 1972, JD, 1975. Bar: Calif. 1975. children: Susan Morgan, Julie. Assoc. firm Bronson, Bronson & McKinnon, San Francisco, 1975-81, ptnr., 1982-86; judge San Francisco County Superior Ct., 1986-88, U.S. Dist. Ct. for Northern Dist. Calif., 1988—; mem. U.S. Jud. Conf., Adv. Com. Rules of Evidence, 1993-96, chair, 1996—; mem. hiring, mgmt. and pers. coms., active recruiting various law schs. Contbr. articles to legal publ. Apptd. by Chief Justice Malcolm Lucas to the Calif. Jud. Coun.'s Adv. Task Force on Gender Bias in the Cts., 1987-89; bd. visitors Law Sch. Stanford U. Mem. ABA, Queen's Bench, Nat. Assn. Women Judges, Calif. Women Lawyers, Bar Assn. of San Francisco, Fed. Judges Assn., 9th Cir. Dist. Judges Assn., Am. Judicature Soc., Calif. State Fed. Judicial Coun., Phi Beta Kappa.

SMITH, GARRY LEE, marketing manager; b. Waterville, Kans., Apr. 20, 1944; s. Adolph Clifton Smith and Mabelle Josephine Kalous; m. Nancy Carol Grey, July 20, 1968 (div. Aug. 1986); children: Andrea, Eric. BS, Kans. State U., 1967; MBA, William and Mary U., 1970. Fin. mgr. Ford Assn., Kansas City, Mo., 1967; sales rep., field mgr. Am. Hosp. Supply, Chgo., 1970-86, Baxter Internat., Chgo., 1986—; v.p. mktg. S&T Health Modulars, Phoenix. Writer, pub.: (nonfiction) Yuppies Lifestyle, 1987. Pres. Gov. Recall, Ariz., 1987, organizer 50 1 Constnl. Reform, Ariz., 1988; bd. dirs. King of Glory Luth., Tempe, Ariz., 1985-86. 1st lt. U.S. Army, 1967-69; bd. dirs. Windsor Sq. Homeowners Assn., 1994—; mem. Team Ariz., pres., 1990-91. Recipient Bell of Freedom award Martin Luther King Holiday Com., 1990. Mem. Leading Edge Club (chair 1997—), Sierra Club, Mountain Preserve Club.

SMITH, GARY CHESTER, meat scientist, researcher; b. Ft. Cobb, Okla., Oct. 25, 1938; s. William Chester and Aneta Laura (Lisk) S.; m. Carol Ann Jackson (div. 1965); children: Todd, Toni; m. Kay Joy Camp, Feb. 12, 1965; children: Leaneta, Stephanie, Kristl, Leland. BS, Calif. State U., Fresno, 1960; PhD, Tex. A&M U., 1968. Asst. prof. dept. animal sci. Wash. State U., Pullman, 1968-69; from assoc. prof. to prof. dept. animal sci. Tex. A&M U., College Station, 1969-82, head dept. animal sci., 1982-90; prof. Nat. Meat Inspection Tng. Ctr., College Station, 1987-90; Monfort Endowed prof. dept. animal sci. Colo. State U., Ft. Collins, 1990—, univ. disting. prof., 1993—; chmn. irradiation com. NAS, 1977-79, mem. packaging com. Office Tech. Assessment, 1973-74. Author: Laboratory Exercises in Meat Science; contbr. numerous articles to over 340 Jour. Animal Sci., Jour. Food Sci., Meat Sci. Bd. dirs. Internat. Stockmen's Edn. Found., Houston, 1983-91. Recipient Disting. Svc. award Nat. Livestock Grading and Mktg. Assn. Mem. Am. Meat Sci. Assn. (pres. 1976-77, Disting. Rsch. award 1982, Disting. Teaching award 1984), Am. Soc. Animal Sci. (Meat Rsch. award 1974, Disting. Teaching award 1980), Inst. Food Technologists, Coun. Agrl. Sci. and Tech. Republican. Baptist. Home: 1102 Seton St Fort Collins CO 80525-9498 Office: Colo State U Dept Animal Scis Fort Collins CO 80523

SMITH, GARY THOMAS, fine arts educator, curator; b. Portland, Oreg., Nov. 25, 1949; s. Bobby H. and Winifred (Kortge) S. BA, Lewis and Clark Coll., 1971; MFA, U. Calif., Santa Barbara, 1975. Instr. Santa Barbara City Coll. Adult Edn., 1974-76; instr. Hartnell Coll., Salinas, Calif., 1976—, gallery dir., 1976—; coord., instr. London semester program Ctrl. Calif. Consortium of C.C., 1989-93, Paris semester program, 1993, London semester program, 1994, Florence semester program, 1995. One-man shows include pvt. galleries in Santa Barbara, San Francisco, Vienna, Austria, N.Y.C., Nanao (Japan), and others. Trustee, chmn. acquisitions com. Monterey (Calif.) Peninsula Mus. Art, 1982—; bd. dirs. Monterey County Culture Coun., 1986-89. Recipient Excellence in Teaching award Harden Found., 1990. Home: 27465 Vista Del Toro Pl Salinas CA 93908-8914 Office: Hartnell Coll Art Dept 156 Homestead Ave Salinas CA 93901-1628

SMITH, GEORGE LARRY, analytical and environmental chemist; b. Beloit, Kans., Oct. 11, 1951; s. Richard Bailey and Vonda Ellene (Cox) S.; m. Charlene Janell Musgrove, Sept. 4, 1973; 1 child, Brian Lawrence. BA, Augustana Coll., 1973. Cert. grade 3 water treatment operator, Calif. Lab. technician Sanitary Dist. of Hammond, Ind., 1973; chemist Federated Metals Corp., Whiting, Ind., 1973-77; rsch. technician Air Pollution Technology, Inc., San Diego, 1978-80, environ. chemist, 1980-81, sr. tech. asst., 1981; staff chemist I Occidental Research Corp., Irvine, Calif., 1981-82, receiving chemist, 1982-84; processing chemist Chem. Waste Mgmt., Inc., Kettleman City, Calif., 1984-87, analytical chemist, 1987-89, wet analytical chemistry group leader, 1989-90, inorganic lab. supr., 1990-94, quality assurance/quality control specialist, 1994-96; lab. mgr. Bolsa Rsch. Assocs., Inc., Hollister, Calif., 1996—; lab. analyst for published article in environ. sci. and tech., 1981. bd. dirs. Apostolic Christian Missions, Inc., San Diego, 1978-82. Mem. Am. Chem. Soc., Nat. Geog. Soc., Bibl. Archeology Soc., Internat. Union Pure and Applied Chemistry, Assn. Ofcl. Analytical Chemists Internat. Home: 991 Meridian St Hollister CA 95023-4170 Office: Bolsa Rsch Assocs Inc 8770 Hwy 25 Hollister CA 95024

SMITH, GEORGE VINAL, librarian; b. Chgo., May 14, 1943; s. Earl Wesley and Frances (Kenney) S.; m. Chrystal Jean Stillings, Jan. 29, 1966; children: Rebecca Tyson, Morgen Elizabeth. BA, Whitman Coll., 1965; MA, Wash. State U., 1967; PhD, No. Ill. U., 1974; MS, U. Ill., 1975. Reference libr. Illinet/U. Ill., Urbana, 1975-76; info. svcs. cons. Lincoln Trail Libr. System, Champaign, Ill., 1977-79; circular and network svcs. supr. Oreg. State Libr., Salem, 1979-81; adminstr. of libr. devel. Oreg. State Libr., 1983-85; dir. Canby (Oreg.) Pub. Libr., 1981-82, Woodburn (Oreg.) Pub. Libr., 1982-83; dep. dir. Alaska State Div. of Librs., Archives and Mus., Juneau, 1985—; vol. Peace Corps, Thailand, 1967-69; vis. asst. prof. Grad. Sch. Libr. Sci., U. Ill., 1977-78; instr. Chemekata C.C., Salem, 1980-83, Marylhurst Coll., Lake Oswego, Oreg., 1982; course mentor Grad. Sch. Libr. Sci., U. Ariz., Juneau, Alaska, 1992-94; mem. State of Alaska Personnel Reinvention Com., 1996. Author: The Dutch in 17th-Century Thailand, 1977; co-editor and author: Contributions to Asian Studies, 15, 1980. Pres., bd. dirs., coach Juneau Soccer Club, 1992-94; dir., adminstrv. staff Arctic Winter Games/Team Alaska, Fairbanks, 1992—; coach, referee, referee trainer, Juneau Parks and Recreation Dept., 1986—; vol., patron Alaska Folk Festival, 1986—. NDEA fellow No. Ill. U., 1972-73; recipient Gov.'s Mgmt. Recognition award, Gov. Oreg., 1985. Mem. ALA (Libr. fellow to Nat. Libr. Cambodia 1994-95), Pacific N.W. Libr. Assn. (pres., v.p. 1987-89), Alaska Libr. Assn., Oreg. Libr. Assn. (pres., v.p. 1984-85). Home: 124 Behrends Ave Juneau AK 99801-1457 Office: Alaska State Libr/Archives PO Box 110571 Juneau AK 99811

SMITH, GERALD KENNETH, rehabilitation nurse; b. Riverside, Calif., Sept. 30, 1947; s. Clyde W. and Beulah M. (Moberly) S.; m. Brenda S. Grannis Lilburn (div. 1981); 1 child, Aaron J.; m. Sharon A. Scott, Jan. 19, 1984; children: Jenifer B., Dustin Beeson, Sara M., Clyde S. AA, Crafton Hills Coll., Yucaipa, Calif., 1979; ASN, San Bernardino City Coll., Calif., 1988; BS in Health Care Mgmt., U. La Verne, Calif., 1996. Cert. rehab. registered nurse, cert. disability mgmt. specialist. Self-employed musician, 1968-86; nurse's aide various locations, 1978-86; fire fighter USDA Forestry Svc., El Cariso, Calif., 1966-67; staff rehab. nurse Loma Linda (Calif.) Rehab. Inst., 1988—, case mgr., 1993-94, charge nurse, 1994—. Mem. Assn. Rehab. Nurses, Am. Assn. SpinalCord Nurses, Nat. League Nursing. Libertarian. Baptist. Home: PO Box 649 Crestline CA 92325-0649 Office: Loma Linda Univ Med Ctr Rehab Inst 11234 Anderson St Loma Linda CA 92354-2804

SMITH, GLENN A., lawyer; b. Oakland, Calif., July 11, 1946. BA, Pomona Coll., 1968; JD, U. Calif., Berkeley, 1971; LLM in Taxation, NYU, 1973. Bar: Calif. 1972, D.C. 1975. Law clerk to Hon. William M. Drennen U.S. Tax Ct., 1973-75; mem. Heller, Ehrman, White & McAuliffe, Palo Alto, San Francisco, Calif. Office: Heller Ehrman White & McAuliffe 525 University Ave Ste 1100 Palo Alto CA 94301-1908

SMITH, GORDON EUGENE, pilot; b. Corpus Christi, Tex., Nov. 22, 1953; s. Orvis Alvin and Helen Lucille (Lockhart) A.; m. Crisanta Lacson Oqueriza, Jan. 5, 1979; children: Pia Marie, Helena Irita. AAS in Electronics, Riverside City Coll., 1985; BSEE, Calif. Polytech., 1987. Electronics technician Lear Siegler, Inc., Ontario, Calif., 1981-86, Rockwell Internat., Palmdale, Calif., 1986-87; pilot Orion Air Inc., Raleigh, N.C., 1987-90; pilot, dir. maintenance, asst. dir. ops. Nat. Air, Riverside, Calif., 1990-93; pilot MGM Grand Air, 1993-96, Sun Pacific Internat., Tucson, 1996—. With USAF, 1972-79, with Res. 1979—. Mem. Aircraft Owners and Pilots Assn., Team One (v.p. 1980—). Republican. Dunkard Brethren. Office: Sun Pacific Intl 2502 E Benson Hwy Tucson AZ 85706

SMITH, GRANT WILLIAM, English language educator, civic fundraiser; b. Bellingham, Wash., July 26, 1937; s. George Whitfield and Hazel (Speirs) S.; m. Lelia Dickinson, June 9, 1961; children: Kathryn, Gavin. BA, Reed Coll., 1964; MA, U. Nev., 1966; PhD, U. Del., 1975. Asst. prof. Eastern Wash. U., Cheney, 1968-76, assoc. prof., 1976-79, prof., 1979—; faculty pres. Eastern Wash. U., Cheney, 1976-77, chair English dept., 1978-84, acting vice provost, 1987-88, coord. humanities, 1979—, dir. cultural outreach, 1995—; host Pub. TV, Here's Shakespeare, 1980, 81. Contbr. articles to profl. jours. and conf. procs. Moderator Cheney United Ch. Christ, 1982-84. With U.S. Army, 1957-60. Grantee U.S. Geol. Survey, State Humanities Commn., NEH, others. Mem. MLA, AAUP, Placename Survey U.S. (chair 1990-96), Connoisseur Concerts Assn. (pres. 1992-95), Am. Dialect Soc. (regional sec. 1982—), Rocky Mountain MLA (program chair 1987), Internat. Coun. Onomastic Scientists, Internat. Soc. Dialectology and Geolinguistics, Am. Name Soc., others. Home: 905 Gary St Cheney WA 99004-1341 Office: Eastern Wash Univ Dept of English MS-25 Cheney WA 99004

SMITH, GREG BRUCE, journalist; b. Phila., Dec. 10, 1945; s. Robert S. and Ruth (Yost) S. Columnist Small Voices, 1992—; contbr. articles to profl. jours. Recipient First Pl. award Dog Writers Assn. Am.-Sandoz Pharmaceuticals-Jeffs Companion Animal Shelter, 1995, Nat. award Dog Writers Assn. Am., 1995, Quincy (Ill.) Writers Guild, 1995, Disting. Svc. award Ariz. Pet Guide Mag., 1995, Phoenix Mayors Media award, 1995. Home: 2507 W Augusta Ave Phoenix AZ 85051

SMITH, GREGORY LAURENCE, computer scientist, consultant; b. Youngstown, Ohio, Apr. 15, 1954; s. William Thomas and Joan Duane (Muir) S.; m. Donna Lois Dickover, Sept. 8, 1983; children: Michael, Michelle. BSEE, Mich. Tech. U., 1978; BS in Computer Sci. magna cum laude, Seattle Pacific U., 1988. Assoc. engr. Boeing Def. and Space Group, Seattle, 1978-79, engr., 1979-81, sr. engr., 1981-83, specialist engr., 1983-85, sr. specialist engr., 1985-89, lead prin. engr., 1989-95, sr. prin. engr., 1995—; prin. engr., cons. Tech. Rsch. Assoc., Renton, Wash., 1986—; invited mem. tech. adv. com. Seattle (Wash.) C.C., 1991—; presenter in field. Author various computer programs; contbr. articles to profl. jours. Mem. IEEE (sr. mem.), Assn. for Computing Machinery, Am. Assn. for Artificial Intelligence, N.W. Artificial Intelligence Forum. Republican. Home: 17952 W Spring Lake Dr SE Renton WA 98058-0610 Office: Boeing Def & Space Group MS-3E-73 PO Box 3999 Seattle WA 98124-2499

SMITH, GREGORY R., lawyer; b. Chgo., Jan. 9, 1944. BA summa cum laude, Claremont Men's Coll., 1965; JD magna cum laude, Harvard U., 1968; MS, London Sch. Econs., 1969. Bar: Calif. 1969. Mem. Irell & Manella, L.A.; vis. prof. U. Kansas Sch. Law, 1975. Mem. bd. editors Harvard Law Review, 1966-68. Mem. State Bar Calif., Phi Alpha Delta. Office: Irell & Manella 1800 Avenue Of The Stars Los Angeles CA 90067-4212

SMITH, HARRY MENDELL, JR., science educator; b. Wichita, Kans., Aug. 19, 1943; s. H. Mendell and Sevilla Mae (Cooper) S.; m. Cecile Marie Adams, Sept. 19, 1964; children: Jeff, Shauna, Noelle. AA, Pasadena Coll., 1966; BA, Calif. State U., L.A., 1970; Vocat. Credential, UCLA, 1979. Tchr. Glendora (Calif.) Unified Schs., 1970-80; instr. Citrus Coll., Azusa, Calif., 1978-82; mgr. Christian Chapel, Walnut, Calif., 1980-82; pres. Whitmore Printing, Inc., La Puente, Calif., 1982-85; mgr. Evang. Free Ch., Fullerton, Calif., 1985-87; prof. Mt. San Antonio Coll., Walnut, 1985—, chair divsn. applied sci. and tech., 1993—; dir. Faculty Senate, Mt. San Antonio Coll., 1989-91. Author: Electronic Devices and Circuits Lab Book, 1994. Treas. Sojourner Evangelical Free Ch., Fullerton, 1996—. Chancellor's Office Electronic Tech. grantee, 1990. Mem. Nat. Assn. Radio and Telecommunications Engrs., Home Bldrs. Fellowship (pres. 1990-92), Calif. Indsl. Arts and Edn. Assn. Republican. Home: 951 S Idaho St Apt 70 La Habra CA 90631-6649 Office: Mt San Antonio Coll 1100 N Grand Ave Walnut CA 91789-1341

SMITH, HEATHER KAY, freelance writer; b. LaCrosse, Wis., Oct. 31, 1964; d. Richard James and Kay Louise (Atchison) S. BA, U. Wis., 1988. Info. specialist Exec. Office State of Wis., Madison, 1989; legis. asst. State of Wis. Assembly, Madison, 1990, rsch. asst., 1991; communication specialist State of Wis. Assembly Rep. Caucus, Madison, 1991-92; campaign cons. Wis. 68th Assembly Campaign, 1990, 92; comms. dir. Wis. 3rd Dist. Congrl. Campaign, 1992; mem. acad. staff Coll. of Engring. and Applied Sci. U. Wis., Milw., 1993; student support svcs. mgr. Met. Milw. Assn. Commerce Scholarship Fund, 1993-1994. Member Rep. Party of Wis., 1990-91. Mem. Clan Douglas Soc. N.Am., No. Calif. Deerhound Club (sec., editor). Home & Office: 1150 Kapareil Dr Tracy CA 95376

SMITH, H(OWARD) DUANE, zoology educator; b. Fillmore, Utah, June 25, 1941; s. Howard Martell and Mary Ellen (Mitchell) S.; m.. Dahnelle Bower, Dec. 18, 1961; children: Cory, Neichol. BS, Brigham Young U., 1963, MS, 1966; PhD, U. Ill., 1969. From asst. prof. to prof. Brigham Young U., Provo, Utah, 1969—; pvt. practice Orem, Utah, 1973—; dir. Life Sci. Mus. Co-author: Special Publications-Mammalogy, 1994; contbr. articles to profl. jours. Mem. Am. Soc. Mammalogists (sec.-treas. 1987—), Wildlife Soc., Ecol. Soc. Am., Rocky Mountain Elk Found., Sigma Xi (pres. 1996). Republican. Mormon. Office: Brigham Young Univ 290 MLBM Provo UT 84602-1049

SMITH, IRBY JAY, film producer; b. San Antonio, Apr. 17, 1938; s. Irby Jay and Virginia Lee (Algee) S.; m. Elaine Nicholson, June 8, 1956; children: Kimberly, Carrie, Jay. Student, Occidental Coll., 1955-56; BA summa cum laude, U. Calif., Berkeley, 1960. Pub. info. spcialist, tv interview host, writer U.S. Dept. Health, Edn. and Welfare, L.A., 1960-66; writer, dir. CRM/McGraw-Hill Films, L.A., 1969-70; pvt. practice asst. dir., prodn. mgr., prodr., dir., 1966—. Prodr. City Slickers, Prefontaine, Wild America, Rookie of the Year, Angels in the Outfield, Enemies a Love Story, Major League, Young Guns I and II. Recipient ALA award for writing and directing ednl. films, 1970, 2 Cine Golden Eagle awards for writing and directing ednl. films, 1970. Mem. Dirs. Guild Am., Phi Beta Kappa. Democrat.

SMITH, JACK DARYL, accountant, travel company executive; b. Red Oak, Iowa, May 11, 1939; s. Willard Sylvanus and Elveda Caroline (Dean) S.; m. Gwendolyn Bowman, Sept. 28, 1964 (div. May 1976); children: JD Carleton, Lled Aaron; m. Gloria Kay Chiri, May 22, 1976. Grad. H.S., Long Beach, Calif. Pvt. practice Lake Elsinore, Calif., 1965—; enrolled agt. Triple Check Tax Svc., Sun City, Calif., 1990—; rep. Royal Alliance Assoc., Sun City, Calif., 1993—. Sch. bd. trustee Elsinore H.S. Dist., Lake Elsinore, 1974-75; cmty. adv. bd. City of Lake Elsinore, 1972-74; treas. Wildomar (Calif.) C. of C., 1992-94, Lake Elsinore C. of C., 1965-74, pres., 1972-73. Served with U.S. Army, 1962-64. Recipient Packman award Lake Elsinore C. of C., 1974. Mem. Elks, Am. Legion. Republican. Presbyterian. Home: 872 S Heatherstone St Orange CA 92869 Office: Royal Alliance Assoc 28238 Bradley Rd Sun City CA 92586-3022

SMITH, JACK LEE, bank executive; b. Yale, Okla., Feb. 2, 1948; s. George W. and Alta E. (Tilley) S.; m. Rose Mary Cantrell, Feb. 3, 1968 (div. Feb. 1980); children: Anissa Kay, Melany Elaine; m. Janice A. Houston, Aug. 2, 1981). BS, Okla. State U., 1972. Asst. v.p. Production Credit Assn., 1972-76; v.p., office mgr. Mountain Plains Prodn. Credit Assn., Ft. Collins, 1976-81; dist. mgr. Ralston Purina, St. Louis, 1981-83; 2d v.p. Omaha Nat. Bank, 1983-85; v.p., office mgr. FirsTier Bank, N.A., Omaha, Ft. Collins, 1985-93; mgr. western area agrl. lending FirsTier Bank, N.A., Omaha, Omaha, 1993-96; sr. v.p. agribus. fin. group Farm Credit Svcs., Greeley, Colo., 1996—; bd. dirs. Colo. Cattle Feeders Assn.; chmn. Allied Industry Coun. for Agr. Mem. Am. Bankers Assn., Colo. Bankers Assn., Nat. Cattlemen's Assn., Kans. Livestock Assn., Colo. Cattlemen's Assn., Elks. Republican. Home: 2613 Jewelstone Ct Fort Collins CO 80525 Office: AgriBusiness Finance Group Farm Credit Svcs 2308 29th St Greeley CO 80631-8514

SMITH, JAMES ALEXANDER, metal processing executive; b. Harvey, N.D., Jan. 16, 1926; s. James Kay MacKenzie and Palma Theresa (Johnson) S.; m. Cleo Lorraine, Sept. 1, 1948 (div. 1962); children: Deborah Kay Smith Hooper, Daryl Lynn Smith O'Neill, Darcey Amelia Smith Ryan; m. Louise Mae Hammer, July 21, 1979. BS, U. Minn., 1951. Ptnr., v.p. VIP, Phoenix, 1960-78; founder Therm-O-Low Inc., Phoenix, 1978-84; v.p., gen. mgr., pres. 3XKryogenics, Phoenix, 1984-86; founder, pres. Cryogenics Internat., Inc., Tempe, Ariz., 1987-90; lectr. and speaker on cryogenics. Patentee (U.S. and fgn.) in field. Staff sgt. U.S. Army, 1943-46. Decorated Bronze star, Combat Infantryman Badge with 2 battle stars. Mem. Soc. Mfg. Engrs. (Ariz. chpt. chmn. 1983, chmn. western states zone 1985, Pres.'s award 1984), Cryogenic Soc. Am., Am. Soc. Metals, VFW (life mem.). Republican. Lutheran.

SMITH, JAMES MICHEAL, marketing executive; b. Ft. Carson, Colo., July 14, 1951; s. Richard Allen Smith and Cathrine Clare (Kehl) Ryan; m. Amelia Joann Carr, June 7, 1973; children: Peter Micheal, Lisa Danielle. BS in Basic Scis., USAF Acad., 1973; MA in Bus. Mgmt., Ctrl. Mich. U., 1977. Sr. cons. Strategic Mktg. Group, Inc., Denver, 1986-87; dir. ops. U.S.A. Direct, Inc., Englewood, Colo., 1987; mktg. rep. Martin Marietta Corp., Denver, 1988-90, sr. mktg. rep., 1990-92, mgr. bus. devel., 1992-95; dir. mktg. Hughes Info. Tech. Corp., Aurora, Colo., 1995-97; dir. bus. devel. EDS, Plano, Tex., 1997—. Patroller Nat. Ski Patrol, 1985—; cub scout leader Boy Scouts Am., 1993—. Maj. USAF, 1973-86, col. USAFR. Recipient Purple Merit Star for life saving Nat. Ski Patrol, 1990. Mem. AIAA, Am. Mktg. Assn., Air Force Assn. (life), Res. Officer Assn. (life), Nat. Security Indsl. Assn. (corp. mem.). Republican. Mem. LDS Ch. Home: 1362 Meadow Trail Franktown CO 80116 Office: EDS PO Box 1034 Franktown CO 80116

SMITH, J(AMES) SCOTT, elementary education educator; b. Pittsfield, Ill., Oct. 8, 1951; s. James H. and Joan (Johnson) S.; 1 child, Sydney Jacquelyn. BA in Sociology, Elem. Edn., Sangamon State U., 1973, MA in Ednl. Adminstrn., 1976. Tchr. grades 3-6 Pleasant Hill (Ill.) Community Sch. Dist., 1973-79; tchr. grade 5 Colegio Internacional de Carabobo, Valencia, Venezuela, 1979-80; tchr. grades 3-7 Pleasant Hill Community Sch. Dist., 1980-88; tchr. grades 5, 6 Salt Lake City Sch. Dist., 1988—; adj. prof. U. Utah, Salt Lake City, 1989—. Mem. Nat. Edn. Asns., Utah Coun. for Self-Esteem, Salt Lake Tchrs. Assn. (associational rep. 1989-92). Republican. Baptist. Home: 3546 Apollo Dr Salt Lake City UT 84124-2260 Office: Washington Sch 420 N 200 W Salt Lake City UT 84103-1207

SMITH, JAMES THOMAS, mathematician; b. Springfield, Ohio, Nov. 8, 1939; s. Earl Gearhart and Betty Mae (McCartney) S.; m. Helen Marie Patteson, Jan. 26, 1963; 1 son, Jedediah. AB, Harvard U., 1961; MA, San Francisco State U., 1964; MS, Stanford U., 1967; PhD, U. Sask., Regina, Can., 1970. Mathematician U.S. Navy, San Francisco, 1962-67; asst. prof. math. San Francisco State U., 1969-72, assoc. prof., 1972-75, prof., 1975—; dir. software devel. Blaise Computing, Berkeley, 1984-85; vis. prof. Mills Coll., Oakland, Calif., 1982-83, U. Alaska-Fairbanks, 1983, Calif. State U.-Hayward, 1984, SUNY, 1988-89. Author tech. reports on mil. ops. analysis, 1963-67. Author: IBM PC/AT Programmer's Guide, 1986, Getting the Most from Turbo Pascal, 1987, Advanced Turbo C, 1989, C++ for Scientists and Engineers, 1991, C++ Applications Guide, 1992, C++ Toolkit for Scientists and Engineers, 1997; contbr. papers on math. rsch. to profl. publs. Mem. schs. com. Harvard Club, San Francisco, 1978—, v.p. schs., 1989-93. Mem. Am. Math Soc., Math. Assn. Am. (chmn. north Calif. sect. 1992-93, bd. govs. 1996—), Deutsche Mathematiker-Vereinigung. Home: 1363 27th Ave San Francisco CA 94122-1508 Office: San Francisco State U Math Dept San Francisco CA 98132

SMITH, JAMES WELDON, museum director; b. Richmond, Va., Sept. 7, 1933; s. James Weldon Jr. and Viola Jett (Elliott) S.; m. Nancy Linnaea Lee, July 9, 1955; children: Christian Linnaea, Marshall Taylor. BA, Yale U., 1955; PhD, Northwestern U., 1962. Prof. MacMurray Coll., Jacksonville, Ill., 1962-80, J.F. Kennedy U., Orinda, Calif., 1980-81; dir. Fiberworks, Ctr./Textile Arts, Berkeley, Calif., 1981-87, San Francisco (Calif.) Craft & Folk Art Mus., 1987—; instr. San Francisco (Calif.) Art Inst., 1986; bd. dirs. Calif. Assn. Mus., 1993—; cons. Calif. Arts Coun., Nat. Endowment for the Arts, NEH. Curator exhbns. of African art, various locations, 1980—. Office: San Francisco Craft & Folk Art Mus Fort Mason San Francisco CA 94123

SMITH, JANET HUGIE, lawyer; b. Logan, Utah, Aug. 1, 1945. BA cum laude, Utah State U., 1967; MA cum laude, Stanford U., 1969; JD, U. Utah, 1976. Bar: Utah 1976, U.S. Ct. Appeals (10th cir.) 1977. Shareholder, exec. com. Ray, Quinney & Nebeker, Salt Lake City. Mem. ABA, Utah State Bar (labor and employment law sect.), CUE/NAM (labor lawyers adv. coun.). Office: Ray Quinney & Nebeker Deseret Bldg 79 S Main St Salt Lake City UT 84111-1901

SMITH, JEAN, interior design firm executive; b. Oklahoma City; d. A. H. and Goldy K. (Engle) Hearn; m. W. D. Smith; children: Kaye Smith Hunt, Sidney P. Student Chgo. Sch. Interior Design, 1970. v.p. Billco-Aladdin Wholesale, Albuquerque, 1950-92, v.p. Billco Carpet One of Am, 1970. Pres. Opera Southwest, 1979-83, advisor to bd. dirs.; active Civic Chorus, 1st Meth. Ch.; pres. Inez PTA, 1954-55, life mem.; hon. life mem. Albuquerque Little Theater, bd. dirs. Republican. Clubs: Albuquerque County, Four Hills Country, Daus. of the Nile (soloist Yucca Temple). Home: 1009 Santa Ana Ave SE Albuquerque NM 87123-4232 Office: Billco-Aladdin Wholesale 7617 Menaul Blvd NE Albuquerque NM 87110-4647

SMITH, JEFFREY ALAN, international educator; b. Phila., June 30, 1942; s. Richard Somerville and Marguerite Irene (Gebler) S. BS, Yale U., 1965; AM, Harvard U., 1982, EdD, 1983. Field asst. Peabody Mus. and Dept. Anthropology Yale U., U.S., Kenya, Tanzania, Egypt, France, Eng., 1963-65; tchr., coach Webb Sch., Claremont, Calif., 1965-66; tchr. Mass. Correctional Instn., Walpole, 1968-69; founder, dir. Redington Pond Sch., Rangeley, Maine, 1970-76, V-V Ranch Sch., Wardlow, Alta., Can., 1973-75; instr. U. Sci. and Tech., Chengdu, Sichuan, China, 1984; exec. dir. Crisis Ctr., Monterey, Calif., 1985-86, Books to China Found., San Francisco, 1986-87; pres. Bridge to Asia Found., Oakland, Calif., 1987—; math. instr. Wang Labs., Tweksbury, Mass., 1969; tchr. Adult Edn. Ctr., Cambridge, Mass., 1969-70, sr. addiction specialsit Human Svcs. Adminstrn., N.Y.C., 1969-70; instr. Hurricane Island Outward Bound Sch., Rockland, Maine, 1973, Dept. Hosps. and Instns., Santa Fe, 1977; vis. prof. U. Sci. and Tech., Chengdu; vis. libr. Ocean U. Qingdao, Shandong; mem. Nat. Com. on U.S.-China Rels., N.Y. Active San Francisco Shanghai Sister City Com. Mem. Internet Soc. Office: Bridge to Asia 1214 Webster St # F Oakland CA 94612-3919

SMITH, JEFFRY ALAN, health administrator, physician, consultant; b. L.A., Dec. 8, 1943; s. Stanley W. and Marjorie E. S.; m. Jo Anne Hague. BA in Philosophy, UCLA, 1967, MPH, 1972; BA in Biology, Calif. State U., Northridge, 1971; MD, UACJ, 1977. Diplomate Am. Bd. Family Practice. Resident in family practice WAH, Takoma Park, Md., NIH, Bethesda, Md., Walter Reed Army Hosp., Washington, Children's Hosp. Nat. Med. Ctr., Washington, 1977-80; occupational physician Nev. Test Site, U.S. Dept. Energy, Las Vegas, 1981-82; dir. occupational medicine and environ. health Pacific Missile Test Ctr., Point Mugu, Calif., 1982-84; dist. health officer State Hawaii Dept. Health, Kauai, 1984-86; asst. dir. health County of Riverside (Calif.) Dept. Health, 1986-87, regional med. dir. Calif. Forensic Med. Group, Monterey, Calif., 1987-94; med. dir. Cmty. Human Svcs., Monterey, Calif., 1987-94, Colstrip (Mont.) Med. Ctr., 1994—. Fellow Am. Acad. Family Physicians; mem. AMA, Am. Occupational Medicine Assn., Flying Physicians, Am. Pub. Health Assn.

SMITH, JOEY SPAULS, mental health nurse, biofeedback therapist, bodyworker, hypnotist; b. Washington, Oct. 9, 1944; d. Walter Jr. and Marian (Och) Spauls; children: Kelly, Sean. BSN, Med. Coll. Va., 1966; MA in Edn., U. Nebr., Lincoln, 1975. RNC, ANA; cert. psychiat. and mental health nurse; cert. zero balancer, cert. hypnotist, cert. biofeedback therapist, cons. Staff nurse Booth Meml. Hosp., Omaha, 1969-71; asst. house supr. Nebr. Meth. Hosp., Omaha, 1971-72; head nurse, clin. instr. U. Calif., Davis, 1976-78; staff nurse Atascadero State Hosp., Calif. Dept. Mental Health, 1978-79; nurse instr. psychiat. technician Atascadero State Hosp., 1979-84, insvc. tng. coord., 1984-86; nursing coord. chem. dependency recovery program French Hosp. Med. Ctr., San Luis Obispo, Calif., 1986-87; relief house supr. San Luis Obispo County Gen. Hosp., 1982-88; regional program assoc. statewide nursing program Consortium Calif. Sate U., 1986-88; nurse instr., health svcs. staff devel. coord. Calif. Men's Colony, Dept. Corrections, San Luis Obispo, 1987-92; pvt. practice San Luis Obispo, Calif., 1990—; clin. instr. nursing divsn. Cuesta Coll., 1988—; relief house supr. San Luis Obispo County Gen. Hosp., 1982-88, regional program assoc. statewide nursing program Consortium Calif. State U., 1986-88. 1st lt. U.S. Army Nurse Corps., 1965-67. Mem. Assn. Applied Psychophysiology and Biofeedback, Central Coast Nurses Coop. Coun., Consol. Assn. Nurses in Substance Abuse (cert. chem. dependency nurse), Biofeedback Cert. Inst. Am. (cert. biofeedback therapist, stress mgmt. edn., cert. zero balancer), Alpha Sigma Chi, Phi Delta Kappa. Home: 1321 Cavalier Ln San Luis Obispo CA 93405-4905 Office: PO Box 4823 San Luis Obispo CA 93406-4823

SMITH, JOHN KERWIN, lawyer; b. Oakland, Calif., Oct. 18, 1926; 1 dau., Cynthia. BA, Stanford U.; LLB, Hastings Coll. Law, San Francisco. Ptnr., Haley, Purchio, Sakai & Smith, Hayward, Calif; bd. dirs. Berkeley Asphalt, Mission Valley Ready-Mix; gen. ptnr. Oak Hill Apts., City Ctr. Commercial, Creekwood I and Creekwood II Apts. Road Parks Commn., 1957, mem. city coun., 1959-66, mayor, 1966-70; chmn. Alameda County Mayors Conf., 1968; chmn. revenue taxation com. League Calif. Cities, 1968; vice-chmn. Oakland-Alameda County Coliseum Bd. Dirs.; bd. dirs. Coliseum Found., Mission Valley Rock, Rowell Ranch Rodeo; former pres. Hastings 1066 Found. (Vol. Svc. award 1990), Martin Kauffman 100 Club. Recipient Alumnus of Yr. award Hastings Coll. Law, 1989. Mem. ABA, Calif. Bar Assn., Alameda County Bar Assn., Am. Judicature Soc., Rotary. Office: 22320 Foothill Blvd # 620 Hayward CA 94541-2700

SMITH, KATHERINE THERESA, human resources specialist, small business owner; b. Berlin, Germany, Sept. 18, 1950; came to U.S., 1953; d. Clyde Lonnel and Marion Freda (Ilas) Short; m. Richard B. Smith, Sept. 21, 1980. BA in Sociology, U. Md., 1972; MS in Counseling, Barry U., 1982. Pers. specialist Dept. Defense, various locations, 1974-84; pers. officer Naval Aviation Engring. Svcs. Unit, Phila., 1984-86; recruitment mgr. Kirkland AFB, Albuquerque, N. Mex., 1986-89; tng. dir. Kirkland AFB, Albuquerque, 1989-91; spl. asst. to gov. Gov.'s Office, Santa Fe, N. Mex., 1994; pers. security mgr. U.S. Dept. Energy, Albuquerque, 1991-93, 95-96; pres. Employment & Tng. Network, Inc., Albuquerque, 1996—; pres. Kirkland Mgmt. Assn., 1991; mem. com. for systemic change in edn., State of N.Mex., 1994, Blue Ribbon Panel for N.Mex. Educators' Profl. Devel., chair Gov.'s Sch.-to-Work Com., 1994; bd. dirs. Career Svcs. for Persons with Disabilities, Albuquerque, 1996—. Mem. NAFE, N.Mex. Human Resource Mgmt. Assn. (v.p. 1997), Nat. Assn. Women Bus. Owners (bd. dirs. No. N.Mex. chpt.), Hispano C. of C., Greater Albuquerque C. of C., Rio Grande Minority Purchasing Coun. Democrat. Office: Employment & Tng Network Inc 8501 Candalaria NE Ste E-1 Albuquerque NM 87112

SMITH, KEITH LARUE, research company executive; b. Salida, Colo., Dec. 15, 1917; s. Leroy Holt and Verna Lea (Tunnell) S.; student Marion Coll., 1935-38; A.B. in Math., Ind. U., 1946; postgrad. DePauw U., 1946-47; M.A. in Internat. Affairs, Harvard U., 1955; M.P.A., Calif. State U.-Fullerton, 1979; m. Evelyn May De Bruler, Aug. 29, 1943; 1 son, Eric Douglas. Mil. intelligence research specialist Dept. of Army, Washington, 1951-60; staff engr. Librascope div. Gen. Precision, Inc., Glendale, Cal., 1960-61; sr. operations research analyst Space div. N.Am. Rockwell Corp., Downey, Cal., 1961-71; dir. research Am. Research Corp., Paramount, Calif., 1972-80; instr. math. and polit. sci. DePauw U., 1946-47; cons. model bldg. and gaming techniques, 1960—; mgmt. cons., 1970—; instr. math. and sci. Verbum Dei High Sch., 1974-85; CEO K.L. Smith and Assocs., 1988—. Adult leader Boy Scouts Am., Long Beach, Calif., 1961-75. Treas., UN Council Harvard, 1947-49, Young Democratic Club, Arlington, Mass., 1949-50. Served to capt. USAAF, 1941-46; ETO. Recipient scholarship award Inst. World Affairs, 1947, Outstanding Efficiency award Dept. Army, 1960, Apollo 11 medallion NASA, 1970. Mem. Am. Mus. Natural History, Nat. Geog. Soc., Harvard Alumni Assn., Pi Sigma Alpha. Mason. Research on mil. operations research and war game model bldg., rsch. mgmt. techniques. Home: 3451 E Curry St Long Beach CA 90805-3815

SMITH, KENT ESSAM, real estate developer, flower grower; b. Detroit, Nov. 12, 1953; s. Frank and Aurelia Smith. BS, San Diego State U., 1977. Wine wholesaler Wine Warehouse, L.A., 1979—; pres. Rolling Hills Ranch, San Diego, 1992—. Pres., founder Townspeople, Inc., San Diego, 1984. Democrat. Home: 977 Manor Way San Diego CA 92106-2035 Office: Rolling Hills Ranch 175 La Costa Ave Encinitas CA 92024-1108

SMITH, LANE JEFFREY, automotive journalist, technical consultant; b. Honolulu, May 17, 1954; s. Gerald Hague and JoEllen (Lane) S.; m. Susan Elizabeth Gumm, May 24, 1980 (div. 1997); children: Amber Elizabeth, Graham Hague. BS in Journalism, Iowa State U., 1978. Feature editor Car Craft mag. Peterson Pub., L.A., 1979—, tech. editor, sr. editor, editor Hot Rod Mag., 1987-93, exec. editor, 1993—; speaker in field. Home: 18320 Citronia St Northridge CA 91325-1717 Office: Hot Rod Mag 6420 Wilshire Blvd Los Angeles CA 90048-5515

SMITH, LE ROI MATTHEW-PIERRE, III, municipal administrator; b. Chgo., Jan. 11, 1946; s. Le Roy Matthew and Norma Buckner (McCamey) S.; 1 son, Le Roi Matthew Pierre. B.A. in Psychology, Idaho State U., 1969; Ph.D. in Psychology, Wash. State U., 1977. Instr. psychology Idaho State U., Pocatello, 1969-70, Wash. State U., Pullman, 1970-71; mem. faculty dept. psychology Evergreen State Coll., Olympia, 1971-81; dir. diversity program Port of Seattle, 1981—; cons. in field. Bd. dirs. Thurston-Mason County Community Mental Health Ctr., Olympia; v.p., Idaho State Human Rights Commn., Bannock County, Idaho, 1968-70. Office Edn. fellow, 1969-70; U.S. Dept. Labor grantee, 1968; NSF grantee, 1972; Lilly Found. fellow, 1980. Mem. Am. Psychol. Assn., Am. Personnel and Guidance Assn., Wash. State Black Econs. and Edn. Conf., Assn. Black Psychologists, Am. Assn. of Affirmative Action Officers, Phi Delta Kappa. Democrat. Roman Catholic. Home: 761 S 45th St Tacoma WA 98408-4962 Office: PO Box 1209 Seattle WA 98111-1209

SMITH, LEE L., hotel executive; b. Long Beach, Calif., Oct. 15, 1936; s. Lowell Llake and Violet Margaret (Chrissman) S.; m. Sharon M.C. Lanahan, (div. 1977). AA, Long Beach City Coll., 1958; BA in Music, Chapman Coll., 1965; postgrad., Calif. State U., Long Beach, 1966-67, U. Calif., Santa Barbara, 1974. Cert. tchr. Calif.; lic. ins. agt., Calif. Owner, mgr. Lee's Land Cattle Ranch, Cuyama Valley, Calif., 1960—; tchr. Cuyama Valley Schs., New Cuyama, Calif., 1967-79; owner, mgr. Cuyama Buckhorn Restaurant & Motel, New Cuyama, 1979-83; owner Allstate Ins. Agy., Desert Hot Springs, Calif., 1987-91; owner, mgr. Caravan Resort Spa, Desert Hot Springs, 1983-91; owner S & S Printing, 1990—, Lee's Land Bed & Breakfast, 1992—. Violinist Bakersfield (Calif.) Symphony, 1967—, Brook String Quartet, Palm Springs, Calif., 1984-91; dir. Planning Commn., Desert Hot Springs, 1985-87; chmn. Environ. Rev., Desert Hot Springs, 1986-88; mem. Redevel. Com., Desert Hot Springs, 1983-88; mem. exec. bd. growth and devel. Boys and Girls Club; bd. dirs. Food Now Program, 1988-91. Mem. Am. Fedn. Musicians, Desert Hot Springs C. of C. (Bus. Person Yr. 1987), Taft C. of C. (pres. 1997), Breakfast Rotary (pres. 1987-88), Taft Rotary, Elks. Republican. Home: HC 1 Box 185B Maricopa CA 93252-9629 Office: S & S Printing 606 Center St Taft CA 93268

SMITH, LEE R. (COLLEEN SMITH), family therapist, political breast cancer activist; b. Portland, Oreg., Sept. 6, 1932; d. George A. McClymont and Edna F. (McBride) Lamont; m. William R. Smith, Apr. 16, 1955 (dec. Nov. 1977); children: Mark W. (dec.), Steven R., Stuart J., Leslie Ann, David G. BA in English Lit., U. Calif., Berkeley, 1954; MA in Counseling Psychology, Chapman Coll., 1987. Lic. marriage and family therapist, Oreg. Pvt. practice Laguna Hills, Calif.; family therapist Eugene, Oreg. Mem. ACA, Oreg. Counseling Assn., Nat. Breast Cancer Coalition, Oreg. Breast Cancer Coalition (founder, state coord. 1992—), Internat. Assn. Marriage and Family Counselors. Office: Oreg Breast Cancer Coaltn 1430 Willamette St # 193 Eugene OR 97401-4049

SMITH, LEO GILBERT, hospital administrator; b. Oroville, Calif., July 29, 1929; s. Leo Paul and Laura Mae (Hoffschulte) S.; m. Marcia Elise Ernest, Jan. 26, 1952; children: Matthew Paul, Mara Lee, Bridget Mari, Leo Ernest. B.S.C., U. Santa Clara, 1951; M.P.H., U. Calif., 1958. Adminstrv. resident San Diego County Gen. Hosp., 1958-59; asst. hosp. adminstr. Santa Clara Valley Med. Center, 1959-67, adminstr., 1967-76, dir. planning, 1976-77; health care cons., 1977-80; adminstr. Puget Sound Hosp., 1980-82; mgr. Tacoma Family Medicine dept Multicare Med. Ctr., Tacoma, Wash., 1982-86, dir. clinic services, 1986-91; clinic mgr. Providence Factoria Family Healthcare div. Providence Med. Ctr., Seattle, 1992; ret. Bd. dirs. Children's Home Soc. of Calif., chmn. dist. bd., 1969-70; chmn. br. bd. Children's Home Soc. of Wash., 1986—. Served in mil. 1952-54. Mem. Cen. Coast Hosp. Conf. (pres. 1970), Hosp. Coun. No. Calif. (dir. 1970-73), Am. Coll. Hosp. Adminstrs., Med. Group Mgrs. Assn., Tacoma Sunrise Rotary (pres. 1982-83, Dist. 5020 Youth Exch. officer 1991-96). Home: 7122 Turquoise Dr SW Tacoma WA 98498-6431

SMITH, LESTER LEROY, poet; b. Mishawaka, Ind., Apr. 26, 1921; s. Henry Tilton and Arvilla Lydia (Lent) S.; m. Pauline Ina Elijah, Apr. 20, 1946; children: David, Daniel, Michael. Student, Spokane Falls Coll., 1970. Bus. cons. pvt. practice, Spokane, Wash., 1948-96; freelance poet. Author over 20,000 poems. Mem. Spokane Valley C.of C. (legis. com. 1989-96), Idaho C. of C. (legis.com. 1992-96). Home: 12324 E Maxwell Spokane WA 99216

SMITH, LINDA A., congresswoman, former state legislator; m. Vern Smith; children: Sheri, Robi. Office mgr.; former mem. Wash. State Ho. of Reps.; mem. Wash. State Senate; congresswoman, Wash. 3rd Dist. U.S. House Reps., Washington, D.C., 1995—; mem. nat. parks & pub. lands, water & power, small bus. coms. Republican. Home: 10009 NW Ridgecrest Ave Vancouver WA 98685-5159 Office: 1317 Longworth Washington DC 20515*

SMITH, MARGARET LINN, retired educator, writer; b. New Kensington, Pa., June 14, 1933; d. Herbert Horton and Ruth Effie (Arner) Linn; m. DeWitt Rogers Smith, Dec. 30, 1967. BS, Slippery Rock (Pa.) U., 1955; MEd, Indiana (Pa.) State U., 1965; reading cert., Ga. Inst. Tech., 1980. Permanent tchg. cert., Pa. Tchr. Mt. Lebanon Pub. Schs., Pitts., 1955-67, Charnley-Johelen Sch., Santa Monica, Calif., 1968, Granada Hills (Calif.) Bapt. Sch., 1973-74, Council Schs., Jackson, Miss., 1974-75, Country Day Montessori Sch., Largo, Fla., 1980-82; substitute tchr. L.A. Pub. Schs., 1969-72; tutor for students in Fla. and vis. students from Pa., Seminole, Fla., 1982-90. Danforth scholar, 1963. Mem. Profl. Writers Prescott, Tri Critique Group. Republican. Methodist. Home: 2944 Lindsey Dr Prescott AZ 86301

SMITH, MARIE EDMONDS, real estate agent, property manager; b. Quapaw, Okla., Oct. 5, 1927; d. Thomas Joseph and Maud Ethel (Douglas) Edmonds; m. Robert Lee Smith, Aug. 14, 1966 (dec. 1983). Grad. vocat. nurse, Hoag Hosp., Costa Mesa, Calif., 1953; BA, So. Calif. Coll., 1955; MS, U. Alaska, 1963. Lic. vocat. nurse, Calif.; cert. sci. tchr., Alaska. Nurse Calif. Dept. Nurses, Costa Mesa, 1952-60; tchr. Alaska Dept. Edn., Aniak and Anchorage, 1955-60; tchr. sci. Garden Grove (Calif.) Sch. Dist., 1960-87; property mgr. Huntington Beach, Calif., 1970—; agent Sterling Realtors, Huntington Beach, 1988—. Author: Ocean Biology, 1969. Bd. dirs., tchr. Harbor Christian Fellowship, Costa Mesa, 1966-83; com. chmn. Garden Grove Unified Sch. Dist. PTA, 1977. NSF grantee, 1960-62. Mem. AAUW, So. Calif. Coll. Alumnae Assn. Republican. Home: 8311 Reilly Dr Huntington Beach CA 92646 Office: L8153 Brookhurst St Fountain Valley CA 92708

SMITH, MARK EDWARD, music educator; b. Farmington, N.Mex, May 26, 1955; s. Merle Emerson and Marjorie (Powell) S. B in Music Edn., Eastern N.Mex. U., 1978; MMus, U. N.Mex., 1994. Cert. music educator, N.Mex., Ariz. Music tchr. Ctrl. Consolidated Schs., Shiprock, N.Mex., 1979-80; dist. wide music tchr. Mesa Vista Consolidated Schs., El Rito, N.Mex., 1984-85; music tchr. Window Rock (Ariz.) Elem. Sch., 1985-86, Many Farms (Ariz.) High Sch., 1986-89, Navajo Preparatory Sch., Farmington, N.Mex., 1991-93, Santa Fe Pub. Schs., 1993-94, Red Mesa Unified Schs., Teec Nos Pos, Ariz., 1994—; founding mem. Reservation Music Educators, Keyenta, Ariz., 1986-89; lectr. Title I Parent Workshops, Chinle, Ganado, Red Mesa, Ariz., 1994-96. Performer (opening act) B.W. Stevenson, 1982, Paul Carrack and Nick Lowe, 1982, Willie Dixon, 1983, Marshal Tucker Band, 1984. Performer Dan Quayle Visit to Farmington, 1992, Vietnam Vets. Benefit, Farmington, 1993, Wild Rose, 1993, Clay Walker, 1995, John Anderson, 1995, Aaron Tippin, 1997. Mem. Music Educators Nat. Conf., Kappa Kappa Psi. Democrat. Episcopalian. Home: 903 Hallett Cir Farmington NM 87401 Office: Box 40-4002 Teec Nos Pos AZ 86514

SMITH, MARK LEE, architect; b. L.A., Nov. 16, 1957; s. Selma (Moidel) Smith. BA in History of Architecture, UCLA, 1978, MA in Architecture, 1980. Registered architect Calif., Nev., Oreg., Wash., Tenn., Colo., N.Y., Ohio. Designer, drafter John B. Ferguson and Assocs., L.A., 1976-83, architect, 1983; pvt. practice architecture L.A., 1984—; mem. Los Angeles County Archtl. Evaluation Bd., 1990—. Contbr. articles to profl. jours. Bd. govs. UCLA John Wooden Ctr., 1978-80. Regents scholar, U. Calif., Berkeley, UCLA, 1975-78; UCLA Grad. Sch. Architecture Rsch. fellow, 1979-80. Mem. AIA (treas. San Fernando Valley chpt. 1986, bd. dirs. 1986—, v.p. 1987, pres. 1988, Design award 1988, 89, 90, 91, chmn. Design awards 1994, bd. dirs. Calif. coun. 1989-94, v.p. 1991-94, chmn. continuing edn. 1991-93, chmn. 1992 conf.), Phi Beta Kappa. Office: 18340 Ventura Blvd Ste 225 Tarzana CA 91356-4234

SMITH, MARTIN BERNHARD, journalist; b. San Francisco, Apr. 20, 1930; s. John Edgar and Anna Sophie (Thorsen) S.; m. Joan Lovat Muller, Apr. 25, 1953; children: Catherine Joan, Karen Anne. AB, U. Calif., Berkeley, 1952, M Journalism, 1968. Reporter, city editor Modesto (Calif.) Bee, 1957-64; reporter, mng. editor Sacramento Bee, 1964-75; polit. editor, columnist McClatchy Newspapers, Sacramento, 1975-92; ret., 1992. Episcopalian.

SMITH, MARTIN RONALD, psychotherapist, consultant; b. St. Augstine, Fla., Oct. 4, 1946; s. Charles Warren and Linda B. (Bishop) S. AA, Union Jr. Coll., 1967; BA in Psychology, Rutgers U., 1969; MEd in Counseling Edn., U. Va., 1976. Asst. dir. fin. aid U. Va., Charlottesville, 1977-80; therapist, rschr. Biofeedback Inst. L.A., 1983—; presenter in field, 1987-94. Contbr. articles to profl. jours. Trustee World Svc. Orgn. Adult Children Alcoholics, Torrance, Calif., 1984-89; mem., spkr. Los Angeles County Commn. Women's Task Force on Ritual Abuse, 1988-95. With U.S. Army, 1969-71. Office: Biofeedback Inst LA 3710 Robertson Blvd Ste 216 Culver City CA 90232-2351

SMITH, MARVIN ARTELL, biochemistry educator; b. Ogden, Utah, Apr. 8, 1926; s. Ariel Tucker and Mary Josephine (Evans) S; m. Grace Marie Warnick Smith, Aug. 4, 1960; children: Marie, Lynne, Charles, Conrad, Mark, Kyle, Leslie, Matthew. BS, Utah State U., 1969; MS, U. Wis., 1962, PhD, 1964. Post-doctoral fellow biochemistry dept. NYU Med. Ctr., 1964-66; asst. prof. chem. dept. Brigham Young U., 1966, assoc. prof., 1969; vis. scientist, special fellow, dept. chem. and biophysics U. Calif., Davis, 1972-73, Donald F. Jones rsch. fellow, 1972-73; vis. prof. dept. biochemistry Kuwait U., Kuwait, 1978-80; vis. scientist Inst. Plant Physiology Biol. Rsch. Ctr. Hungarian Acad. Sci., Szeged, Hungary, 1986-87; vis. prof.dept. physiology Carlsberg Lab., Copenhagen, Denmark, 1990-91; vis. sci. Institut für Pflanzen Genetik und Kulturpflanzenforschung, Gatersleben, Germany, 1994-95; prof. biochemistry Brigham Young U., Provo, 1974-96, prof. emeritus, 1996—; sci. Union Carbide, Buffalo, N.Y., Summer, 1964; vis. sci. dept. plant genetics Weizman Inst. Sci., Israel, Summer, 1981. Contbr. numerous sci. articles to profl. jours. Scoutmaster, explorer, adv., cubmaster Boy Scouts Am., Provo, Utah, 1973-92; chmn. Edgemont Neighborhood, Provo, Utah, 1993, 94. Mem. Am Soc. Biochemistry and Molecular Biology, AAAS, Internat. Soc. Plant Molecular Biology, Sigma Xi. LDS ch. Office: Brigham Young U Dept Chem & Biochem Provo UT 84602

SMITH, MARY B., medical and surgical nurse; b. Spartanburg, S.C., Oct. 22, 1951; d. Henry Williams and Laura Bell (Wright) Fernanders; m. Thomas D. Smith, Jan. 7, 1972; children: Cory, Kizzy. ADN, U. S.C., Spartanburg, 1971; BS in Bus. Mgmt., U. Md., 1987; MSN, George Mason U., Fairfax, Va., 1991. RN, Eng., Wales. Staff nurse Midlands Community Hosp., Papillion, Nebr.; clin. nurse U.S. Navy, Seattle; relief charge nurse Desert Springs Hosp., Las Vegas; clinician Potomac Hosp., Woodbridge, Va.; supr. Crestview (Fla.) Nursing Ctr.; staff nurse USAF Hosp., Eglin AFB, Fla.; nurse clinician Desert Springs Hosp., Las Vegas; nursing faculty U. Nev., Las Vegas, C.C. of So. Nev. Home: 6428 Eagle Creek Ln Las Vegas NV 89115-5915

SMITH, MARY OLIVIA, veterinary medicine educator; b. London, July 10, 1957; came to U.S., 1985; d. Francis William Gruyffyd and Margaret Mary (Sullivan) S. B. Vet. Medicine and Surgery, U. Edinburgh, Scotland, 1980; PhD, U. Calif., Davis, 1992. Diplomate Am. Coll. Veterinary Internal Medicine. Vet. practitioner Eng., 1980-85; resident in vet. neurology U. Calif., Davis, 1985-87, adj. instr. vet. anatomy, 1987-89, postgrad. rschr., 1989-92; asst. prof. Colo. State U., Fort Collins, 1992—. Contbr. articles to Am. Jour. Pathology, Am. Jour. Vet. Rsch. and other sci. jours. Mem. Am. Vet. Med. Assn., Royal Coll. Vet. Surgeons, Brit. Small Animal Vet. Assn., Brit. Goat Vet. Assn. Office: Colo State U Coll Vet Medicine Dept Clin Scis Fort Collins CO 80523

SMITH, MAUREEN MCBRIDE, chemist; b. Santa Monica, Calif., Mar. 4, 1952; d. Clayton Laird McBride and Luella (Sullivan) Boudreau; step-father Henry A Boudreau; m. Gary Howard Cothran, July 27, 1974 (div. Apr. 1982); m. Guy Gordon Smith, Feb. 12, 1983; stepchildren: Keri Lynn, Scott Allen. BS magna cum laude, Calif. State Coll., San Bernardino, 1978, MS, 1993. Analytical chemist Chalco Engring., Edwards AFB, Calif., 1978-79, 82; microbiol. lab. tech. AVEK Water Agy., Quartz Hill, Calif., 1979-81, chemist, lab. mgr., 1982—; instr. Antelope Valley Coll., Lancaster Calif., 1980-82. Mem. AAAS, Am. Chem. Soc. Address: 6500 W Ave N Palmdale CA 93551

SMITH, MICHAEL, biochemistry educator; b. Blackpool, Eng., Apr. 26, 1932. BSc, U. Manchester, Eng., 1953, PhD, 1956. Fellow B.C. Rsch. Coun., 1956-60; rsch. assoc. Inst. Enzyme Rsch., U. Wis., 1960-61; head chem. sect. Vancouver Lab. Fisheries Rsch. Bd. Can., 1961-66; med. rsch. assoc. Med. Rsch. Coun. Can., 1966-71, career investigator, 1971—; assoc. prof. biochem. U. B.C., Vancouver, 1966-70, prof., 1970—, Peter Wall distng. prof. biotech., 1994—. Recipient Gairdner Found. Internat. award, 1986, Nobel Prize in Chemistry, 1993. Fellow Chem Inst. Can., Royal Soc. (London), Royal Soc. Can., Royal Soc. Chemistry; mem. Sigma Xi, Order of British Columbia, Companion of the Order of Can. Office: U BC Biotech Lab, 6174 University Blvd, Vancouver, BC Canada V6T 1Z3

SMITH, MICHAEL CORDON, lawyer; b. Boise, July 30, 1954; s. Jay Myrven Jr. and Jena Vee (Cordon) S.; m. Candace Louise Langley, Dec. 10, 1977; children: Angela K., Nicole E., Jeremy L., Melanie D. BS with high honors, Brigham Young U., 1977; JD, UCLA, 1980. Assoc. Johnson & Poulson, L.A., 1980-87, ptnr., 1987-91; pvt. practice Torrance, Calif., 1992—; judge pro tem L.A. Mcpl. Ct., 1986-94, L.A. Superior Ct., 1991-95, ct. apptd. arbitrator, 1986-91. Mem. ATLA, Nat. Employment Lawyers Assn., Calif. Employment Lawyers Assn., L.A. County Bar Assn. (vice chair law office mgmt. sect. 1992-94, exec. com. 1985-95, state bar conv. del. 1995), Consumer Attys. Assn. L.A. Republican. Mem. LDS Ch. Office: 23133 Hawthorne Blvd Ste 300 Torrance CA 90505-3724

SMITH, MICHAEL ROBERT, electro-optical engineer, physicist; b. Tela, Honduras, Aug. 24, 1937; s. Ike Morgan and Edith Helen (Hudson) S.; m. Suzanne Ruth Hudgins, Aug. 20, 1960; children: Stephen, Monica, Meryl. BME, Ga. Inst. Tech., 1959, MS in Nuclear Engring., 1961; PhD, Case Inst. Tech., 1965. Mem. tech. staff Hughes Rsch. Labs., Malibu, Calif., 1965-68; v.p., dir. rsch. Britt Corp., L.A., 1968-73; sr. staff engr. Singer/Librascope divsn., Glendale, Calif., 1973-78; pres. Exocor Tech., Newbury Park, Calif., 1978-95; asst. prof., head physics program Calif. Luth. U., Thousand Oaks, 1990-96; optical engring. cons. Calif. Inst. Tech., Pasadena, 1996—. Contbr. articles to profl. jours.; Inventor: Burst Ion Laser, Wetfield CO2 Laser Surgical Technique; Emergency Traffic Light Warning System. Greek folk dance tchr. Arts Coun., Thousand Oaks, Calif., 1991—. Mem. IEEE, Laser Electro-Optic Soc. (chair 1995—), Sigma Xi, Pi Tau Sigma. Republican. Home: 693 Benson Way Thousand Oaks CA 91360

SMITH, NATHAN MCKAY, library and information sciences educator; b. Wendell, Idaho, Apr. 22, 1935; s. M. Blair and Vaunda H. (Hawkes) S.; m. Joyce A. Carman, July 5, 1953; children: Nathan M., Jeffrey M., Pamela J., Russell A., Kristen E. BS in Secondary Edn., Eastern Oreg. Coll., 1961; MS in Gen. Sci., Oreg. State U., 1965; MLS, Brigham Young U., 1969, PhD in Zoology, 1972. Tchr. sci. Dalles Jr. High Sch., The Dalles, Oreg., 1961-64; asst. sci. libr. Brigham Young U., Provo, Utah, 1968, life sci. libr., 1970-73, prof. Sch. Libr. and Info. Sci., 1973-82, dir. Sch. Libr. and Info. Sci., 1982-93, life sci. libr. Sch. Libr. and Info. Sci., 1993-97; cons. Weber County Library, Ogden, Utah, 1980—; back issues sec. Herpetologists League, 1976-81. Served to sgt. USAF, 1953-57. Yr. scholar NSF Acad., 1964; fellow NDEA Title IV, 1969; recipient research award Assn. Library and Info. Sci. Edn., 1983. Mem. ALA (councilor legis. council), Assn. Library Info. Sci. Edn., Mountain Plains Library Assn., Utah Library Assn. (exec. bd., pres.), N. Am. Soc. Adlerian Psychology, Phi Kappa Phi, Sigma Xi, Beta Phi Mu. Mem. LDS Ch. Office: Brigham Young U Bean Mus Provo UT 84602

SMITH, NINA MARIA, mental health nurse, administrator, consultant; b. Bethesda, Md., July 15, 1950; d. Albert Henry and Magdalena (Portusach) Geiken; m. Robert John Smith, Nov. 18, 1972; children: Cara Anne, Rachel Marie. ADN, Tarrant County Jr. Coll., 1984; BA in Psychology, U. Md., 1972; MEd, Tex. Christian U., 1990. Charge nurse Psychiat. Inst. Ft. Worth; adolescent program coord. Community Psychiat. Ctr. Oak Bend, Ft. Worth; adminstr. Life Ctrs., Ft. Worth; dir. nursing Community Psychiat. Ctr. Oak Bend, Ft. Worth; adminstr. Total Home Health Care, Ft. Worth; dir. clin. svcs. Mountain Crest Hosp., Ft. Collins, Colo., 1992-94; nat. dir. psychiat. home svcs. Western Med. Svcs., Ft. Collins, 1994-96; owner, cons. Integrated Behavioral Health Cons., Ft. Collins, 1996—; mem. psychiat. symposium planning com. U. Tex., Arlington, 1988-91; presenter in field. Guest editor, reviewer Continum: Devel. in Ambulatory Mental Health Care, 1996; co-author: Behavior Management Guide for Home Care, 1997. Mem. Am. Psychiat. Nurses Assn., Am. Assn. Partial Hosps., Partial Hosp. Assn. Colo. (pres. 1994-95), Assn. Ambulatory Behavioral Healthcare (nat. bd. dirs. 1995—), Home Healthcare Nurses Assn. Home: 1430 Hilburn Dr Fort Collins CO 80526-3425

SMITH, OTTO J. M., electrical engineering educator; b. Urbana, Ill., Aug. 6, 1917; s. Otto Mitchell and Mary Catherine (Carr) S.; m. Phyllis P. Sterling, Sept. 3, 1941; children: Candace B., Otto J.A., Sterling M., Stanford D. BS in Chemistry, Okla. State U., 1938; BSEE, U. Okla., 1938; PhDEE, Stanford U., 1941. Registered profl. engr., Calif. Instr. elec. engring. Tufts U., Medford, Mass., 1941-43; asst. prof. elec. engring. Denver U., 1943-44; rsch. engr. Westinghouse Rsch. Labs., Forest Hills, Pa., 1944-46; sr. rsch. fellow econs. and engring. Monash U., Melbourne, Australia, 1966-67; prof. elec. engr. U. Calif., Berkeley, 1947—; chief engr. Smith and Sun, Berkeley, 1976—. Author: Feedback Control Systems, 1958; contbr. articles to profl. jours.; patentee in field. Dist. commr. Boy Scouts Am., Berkeley, 1949-53; trustee South Campus Community Ministry, Berkeley, 1968-70, Wesley Found., Berkeley, 1969-72. Guggenheim fellow, 1960. Fellow AAAS, IEEE; mem. Soc. Social Responsibility Engring., Am. Solar Energy Soc., Internat. Solar Energy Soc., Am. Wind Energy Assn., Calif. Writer's Club (bd. dirs.). Democrat. Methodist. Club: Berkeley City Commons (pres. 1963). Home: 612 Euclid Ave Berkeley CA 94708-1332 Office: U Calif Dept Elec Engr & Computer Scis Berkeley CA 94720-1770

SMITH, PAMELA IRIS, consulting company executive; b. Pitts., Aug. 23, 1958; d. Robert Edward and Rae R. Kline. Cert., U. Paris, Sorbonne, 1979; AB magna cum laude, Harvard U., 1980, MBA, 1984. Asst. staff mgr. Bell of Pa., Phila., 1980-82; product mgr. Visa Internat., San Francisco, 1983; v.p. Prognostics, Palo Alto, Calif., 1984-91; dir. Diefenbach/Elkins, San Francisco, 1991-92; ptnr. The McKenna Group, 1992—. Vol. San Jose Civic Lights, 1987; dir. Harvard/Radcliffe Fundraising, Boston, 1980—; chmn. Harvard/Radcliffe Schs. com., San Mateo County, 1985—. Recipient twin award YWCA. Mem. Young Profl. Woman Assn., Radcliffe Club (dir. 1987—), Harvard Club. Republican. Home: 570 Beale St Apt 416 San Francisco CA 94105-2025 Office: Gemini McKenna Inc 1755 Embarcadero Rd Palo Alto CA 94303-3304

SMITH, PATRICIA JACQULINE, marketing executive; b. Orange, N.J., June 13, 1944; d. Michael Joseph and Helen Francis (Costello) S. BS, U. Md., 1967. Field dir. Colgate Palmolive Co., N.Y.C., 1967-71; account exec. Foote Cone & Belding, N.Y.C., 1971-72; dir. regional sales, dir. ARA Services, Inc., Phila., 1973-76; dir. federally funded programs Ogden Food Service, Boston, 1976-79; v.p. Smith Tool Co., Manesquan, N.J., 1979-84; chmn., CEO Hygolet Metro, Inc., New Canaan, Conn., 1984-87; mktg. cons. Smith Mktg. Svcs., La Jolla, Calif., 1988-94; pres. Tea for Two Inc., Laguna Beach, Calif., 1995—; ptnr. La Jolla Playhouse. Bd. dirs., treas. Big Sister League, San Diego; mem. exec. com. Multiple Sclerosis Brunch Soc.; ptnr. La Jolla Playhouse. Mem. Women in Sales, Nat. Assn. Profl. Saleswomen, Bus. and Profl. Women's Club (N.Y.), Victorian Tea Soc., The Discovery Mus., Women's Club Laguna Beach, AAUW, Laguna Beach C. of C. Republican. Home: PO Box 4994 Laguna Beach CA 92652-4994

SMITH, PEGGY ANNE, fundraising executive; b. San Francisco, May 1, 1954; d. Howard Carlton and Margaret Alice (Strauss) S. BA with honors, U. Calif., Santa Cruz, 1976; Cert. in Fund Raising, UCLA, 1995. Cert. fund raising exec., Nat. Soc. Fund Raising Execs. Bilingual interviewer U. Mich Inst. for Survey Rsch., Ann Arbor, 1976-77; exec. asst. to pres. Nat. Assn. for Hispanic Elderly, L.A., 1978-92; dir. devel. and cmty. rels. Goodwill Industries of So. Calif., L.A., 1992—. Editor: A National Study to Assess the Service Needs of Hispanic Elderly, 1980; co-editor: A National Study of Hispanic Support Systems and the Chronically Ill Older Hispanic, 1982. Mem. Nat. Assn. Fund Raising Execs. (mem. nat. philanthrophy day com., bd. dirs., Great L.A. chpt. Pres.'s award 1994, Mem. of Month Aug. 1996), Nat. Notary Assn.. Roman Catholic. Office: Goodwill Industries So Calif 342 N San Fernando Rd Los Angeles CA 90031-1730

SMITH, RALPH EARL, virologist; b. Yuma, Colo., May 10, 1940; s. Robert C. and Esther C. (Schwarz) S.; m. Sheila L. Kondy, Aug. 29, 1961 (div. 1986); 1 child, Andrea Denise; m. Janet M. Keller, 1988. BS, Colo. State U., 1961; PhD, U. Colo., 1968. Registered microbiologist Am. Soc. Clin. Pathologists. Postdoctoral fellow Duke U. Med. Ctr., Durham, N.C., 1968-70, asst. prof., 1970-74, assoc. prof., 1974-80, prof. virology, 1980-82; prof., head dept. microbiology Colo. State U., Ft. Collins, 1983-88, prof. microbiology, assoc. v.p. rsch., 1989—, interim v.p. rsch., 1990-91, prof. microbiology, assoc. v.p. rsch., 1991—; cons. Bellco Glass Co., Vineland, N.J., 1976-80, Proctor & Gamble Co., Cin., 1985-86, Schering Plough Corp., Bloomfield, N.J., 1987-89. Contbr. articles to profl. jours.; patentee in field. Bd. dirs. Colo. Ctr. for Environ. Mgmt., v.p. for rsch.; mem. pollution prevention adv. bd. Colo. Dept. Pub. Health and Environment; mem. Rocky Mountain U. Consortium on Environ. Restoration, Environ. Inst. Rocky Flats; asst. scoutmaster Boy Scouts Am., Durham, 1972-82, com. mem., Ft. Collins, 1986-91; mem. adminstrv. bd. 1st United Meth. Ch., Ft. Collins. Eleanor Roosevelt fellow Internat. Union Against Cancer 1978-79. Mem. AAAS, Am. Soc. Microbiology, N.Y. Acad. Scis., Am. Soc. Virology, Am. Assn. Immunologists, Am. Assn. Avian Pathologists, Am. Assn. Cancer Rsch., Gamma Sigma Delta. Democrat. Methodist. Home: 2406 Creekwood Dr Fort Collins CO 80525-2034 Office: Colo State U VP Rsch Fort Collins CO 80523

SMITH, RAYMOND EDWARD, retired health care administrator; b. Freeport, N.Y., June 17, 1932; s. Jerry Edward and Madelyn Holman (Jones) S.; BS in Edn., Temple U., 1953; MHA, Baylor U., 1966; m. Lena Kathryn Jernigan Hughes, Oct. 28, 1983; children: Douglas, Ronald, Kevin, Doris Jean, Raymond. Commd. 2d lt. U.S. Army, 1953, advanced through grades to lt. col., 1973; helicopter ambulance pilot, 1953-63; comdr. helicopter ambulance units, Korea, 1955, Fed. Republic of Germany, 1961; various hosp. adminstrv. assignments, 1963-73; pers. dir. Valley Forge (Pa.) Gen. Hosp., 1966; adminstr. evacuation hosp., Vietnam, 1967; dep. insp. Walter Reed Gen. Hosp., Washington, 1970; dir. personnel divsn. Office of Army Surgeon Gen., Washington, 1971-73, ret., 1973; adminstr. Health Care Ctrs., Phila. Coll. Osteo. Medicine, 1974-76; dir. bur. hosps. Pa. Dept. Health, Harrisburg, 1976-79; contract mgr. Blue Cross of Calif., San Diego, 1979-88, Cmty. Care Network, San Diego, 1989-95, ret. 1995. Decorated Bronze Star, Legion of Merit. Mem. Am. Hosp. Assn., Am. Legion, Ret. Officers Assn., Kappa Alpha Psi. Episcopalian. Club: Masons. Home: 7630 Lake Adlon Dr San Diego CA 92119-2518

SMITH, RAYMOND WILLIAM, management consultant; b. North Platte, Nebr., Oct. 12, 1948; s. Raymond Wilbur and Ida Alberta (Ohlsen) S.; m. Diane Simmons, Mar. 16, 1971; children: Amanda, Rebecca, Jonathan Benjamin, Kathryn. BS in Econs., Utah State U., 1970; MS in Mgmt., Naval Postgrad. Sch., 1982. Commd. ens. USN, 1970, advanced through grades to lt. comdr.; divsn. dir. NAVPRO USN, Npls., 1982-85; asst. prof. Naval Postgrad. Sch., Monterey, Calif., 1985-90; ret. USN, 1990; contracts and material mgr. Western Electrochem. Co., Cedar City, Utah, 1990-95; pvt. practice cons. gen. mgmt. Cedar City, 1995—. Mem. centennial schs. adv. bd. Iron County Sch. Dist., Cedar City, 1994-95. Fellow Nat. Contract Mgmt. Assn. (cert. profl. contract mgr.), Cedar City C. of C. (bd. dirs., exec. com. 1993-94). Republican. Mem. LDS Ch. Home: 785 S St James Pl Cedar City UT 84720 Office: WECCO PO Box 629 Cedar City UT 84721

SMITH, RICHARD ALAN, neurologist, medical association administrator. Grad., Brandeis U., 1961, U. Miami, 1965. Intern in medicine Jackson Meml. Hosp., Miami, Fla., 1965-66; resident in neurology Stanford U. Hosp., Palo Alto, Calif., 1966-69; head neurology br. Navy Neuropsychiatric Rsch. Unit, San Diego, 1969-71; mem. assoc. staff microbiology Scripps Clinic and Rsch. Found., La Jolla, Calif., 1972-79, mem. assoc. staff neurology, 1972-82; dir. Ctr. Neurologic Study, San Diego, 1979—; mem. sr. staff Scripps Meml. Hosp., La Jolla, 1982—; mem. CTNF protocol com. Regeneron Pharm. Corp.; med. adv. bd. Multiple Sclerosis Soc., San Diego; animal welfare com. Whittier Inst., fitness clinic mentally disabled San Diego State U. Editor: Interferon Treatment for Neurologic Disorders, 1988, Handbook of Amyotrophic Lateral Sclerosis, 1992; contbr. articles to profl. jours. Recipient Henry Newman award San Francisco Neurologic Soc., 1968. Mem. AAAS, Am. Acad. Neurology (assoc.). Office: Ctr for Neurologic Study 11211 Sorrento Valley Rd Ste H San Diego CA 92121-1324

SMITH, ROBERT BRUCE, former security consultant, retired army officer; b. De Quincy, La., Apr. 22, 1920; s. Malcolm Monard and Jewell (Perkins) S.; m. Gladys Opal Borel, Feb. 22, 1941; children: Susan, Richard, Bruce. B.J., La. State U., 1941; grad., Command and Gen. Staff Coll., 1951-52, Army War Coll., 1958-59. Commd. 2d lt. U.S. Army, 1941, advanced through grades to maj. gen., 1969; plans and ops. officer 83d Div. Arty., Europe, 1943-45; personnel officer Philippine-Ryukyus Command, Manila, 1947-49; prof. mil. sci. and tactics ROTC, Lanier High Sch., Macon, Ga., 1949-51; chief res. officers sect., procurement br. Dept. Army, 1952-55; chief troop info. Office Chief Info., Dept. Army, 1962-63, dep. chief info., 1968-69; comdg. officer 8th F.A. Bn., 25th Inf. Div., Hawaii, 1955-56; G-1 25th Inf. Div. and U.S. Army Hawaii, Hawaii, 1956-58; mem. staff, faculty Command and Gen. Staff Coll., Fort Leavenworth, Kans., 1959-62; chief Alt. Nat. Mil. Command Center, Fort Ritchie, Md., 1963-64; dep. dir. ops. Office Joint Chiefs of Staff, 1964-65; asst. div. comdr. 7th Inf. Div., Korea, 1965-66; dep. comdt. Army War Coll., Carlisle, Pa., 1966-68; dep. comdg. gen. Ryukyus Islands, 1969-72, 6th U.S. Army, Presidio of San Francisco, 1972-73; ret. active duty, 1973; reporter, news editor Lake Charles (La.), 1946-47; region adminstrv. mgr. Burns Security Service, Oakland, Calif., 1974-76; ptnr. constrn. co. Napa, Calif., 1976-77, Burns Security Service, 1978-81; now ret.; dir. 1st Am. Title Co., Napa, Calif., 1988-92. Trustee Queen of Valley Hosp. Found., 1987-89; mem. Nat. coun. Boy Scouts Am., 1969-70; pres. Silverado Property Owners Assn., Inc., 1990-92. Decorated D.S.M. with oak leaf cluster, Legion of Merit with 2 oak leaf clusters, Bronze Star with oak leaf cluster; inducted into La. State U.'s Manship Sch. of Mass Communication Hall of Fame, 1996. Club: Silverado Country (Napa, Calif.). Home: 350 St Andrews Dr Napa CA 94558-1544

SMITH, ROBERT CHARLES, political science educator, researcher; b. Benton, La., Feb. 12, 1947; s. Martin and Blanch (Tharpe) S.; m. Scottie Bess Gibson, May 6, 1952; children: Blanch, Jessica, Scottus-Charles. BA, U. Calif., Berkeley, 1970; MA, UCLA, 1972; PhD, Howard U., 1976. Asst. prof. Coll. at Purchase SUNY, 1976-80; assoc. prof. Howard U., Washington, 1980-88; prof. Prairie View (Tex.) Agrl. Mech., 1988-89, San Francisco State U., 1989—; rsch. assoc. Columbia U., N.Y.C., 1972-73, 78-80; guest scholar Joint Ctr. Polit. Studies, Washington, 1985-86. Author: Racism in the Post Civil Rights Era, 1995, We Have No Leader: African Americans, 1996; co-author: Race, Class and Culture, 1992; co-editor: Urban Black Politics, 1978. Co-founder Congress of Black Faculty, Washington, 1987; founding fellow Open Mind: Cultural Diversity, 1988; co-chair Bay Area Malcum 25th Anniversary Com., 1990. Mem. Am. Polit. Sci. Assn., Nat. Conf. Black Polit. Scientists, Ctr. for Study Presidency, Acad. Polit. Sci. Baptist. Home: 3809 Painted Pony Rd El Sobrante CA 94803 Office: San Francisco State U 1600 Holloway Ave San Francisco CA 94132-1722

SMITH, ROBERT F., congressman; b. Portland, Oreg., June 16, 1931; m. Kaye Smith; 3 childre. BA, Willamette U., 1953. Mem. Oreg. Ho. of Reps., 1960-73, spkr., 1969-73; mem. Oreg. State Senate, 1973-82, leader republican caucus, 1977-83; mem. 98th-105th Congresses from 2d dist. Oreg., 1983-94; pres. Smith West Co., Portland, 1995-96. Republican. Office: 843 E Main Ste 400 Medford OR 97504

SMITH, ROBERT HAMIL, author, fund raiser; b. Oak Park, Ill., Nov. 8, 1927; s. Henry Garfield and Mary Ellen (Hamil) S.; student U. Denver, 1946-48, LLB, 1953, JD, 1960; m. Mary Helen Kingsley, Dec. 29, 1948; children: David H., Mark K., Steven H., Rebecca Anne. Dep. clk. County Ct., City and County of Denver, 1948-53; with Colo. Ins. Group, 1953-59; mgr. claims dept. R.H. Smith & Assos., 1959-64; cons. Am. Bapt. Home Mission Soc., 1964-68; assoc. dir. devel. Ill. Wesleyan U., 1968-69; asst. to chancellor U. Calif., San Diego, 1969-77; exec. dir. devel. Scripps Clinic and Research Found., La Jolla, Calif., 1977-82, v.p. devel., 1982-88; pres. Cartographic Enterprises, 1981—; owner C Books, 1981; bd. dirs. Nat. Com. on Planned Giving, 1990-94; fund raising cons. deferred giving. Served with USNR, 1945. Mem. Nat. Soc. Fund Raising Execs., Internat. Yachting Fellowship of Rotarians (San Diego fleet comdr. 1979-81). Baptist. Club: Oceanside Yacht. Author: Guide to Harbors, Anchorages and Marinas So. and No. California edits., 1983, The Physician as a Fundraiser, 1984, Naval Inst. Guide to Maritime Museums in U.S./Canada, 1991, Smith's Guide to Maritime Museums U.S./Canada, 1993; pub. boating cruising guides for no. and so. Calif. and guides to maritime mus. Home: PO Box 176 Del Mar CA 92014-5785

SMITH, ROBERT LONDON, commissioner, retired air force officer, political scientist, educator; b. Alexandria, La., Oct. 13, 1919; s. Daniel Charleston and Lillie (Roberts) S.; m. Jewel Busch, Feb. 5, 1949; children: Jewel Diane, Robert London, Karl Busch. B.A., Coll. St. Joseph, 1954; M.A., U. Okla., 1955; Ph.D., Am. U., 1964. Commd. 2d lt. USAAF, 1941; advanced through grades to lt. col. USAF, 1961; various assignments in aircraft engring., command and logistics, 1941-60; rsch. logistics Hdqs. Office Aerospace Rsch., 1960-63; project sci., adminstr. postdoctoral rsch. program, asst. dir. NAS, Hdqs. Office Sci. Rsch., 1963-65; ret., 1965; asso. prof. polit. sci., head dept. eve. classes and corr. study U. Alaska, College, 1966-68, dean Coll. Bus., Econs. and Govt., 1968-70, prof., head dept. polit. sci., 1966-84, prof. emeritus, 1984—; commr. Alaska Dept. Health and Social Services, 1983—; mem. govt. panels and planning groups; dir. Arctic 1st Fed. Savs. & Loan Assn.; corporator Mt. McKinley Mut. Savs. Bank. Author: (with others) Squadron Adminstration, 1951; also publs. on nat. security and nat. def.; Contbr. to: (with others) The United Nations Peace University, 1965. Committeeman Western region Boy Scouts Am., 1968-73; mem. exec. bd. Midnight Sun council, 1973-74, committeeman-at-large nat. council, 1968—; mem. Alaska Gov.'s Employment Commn.; pres. United Service Orgn. Council, Fairbanks, Alaska; mem. active corps execs. SBA. Recipient Silver Beaver award Boy Scouts Am.; named Outstanding Prof. U. Alaska, 1975. Mem. Nat. Acad. Econs. and Polit. Sci., AAAS, Air Force Hist. Found., Nat. Inst. Social and Behavioral Scis., Nat. Inst. U.S. in World Affairs, Am. Polit. Sci. Assn., Assn. U.S. Army (bd. dirs. Polar Bear chpt.), Alaska C. of C. (edn. com.), Pi Gamma Mu, Pi Sigma Alpha. Roman Catholic. Club: Rotary. Home: Smithhaven 100 Goldizen Ave Fairbanks AK 99709-3634 also: Smithawaii Nani Kai Hale 73 N Kihei Rd Apt 607 Kihei HI 96753-8827 also: Costa Vida Unit #920-921, KM 4 456 Carr Apdo Postal 186, Puerto Vallarta Jalisco, Mexico

SMITH, ROBERT VICTOR, university administrator; b. Glendale, N.Y., Feb. 16, 1942; s. Robert Arthur and Marie Marlene (Florence) S. BS in Pharm. Sci., St. John's U., Jamaica, N.Y., 1963; MS in Pharm. Chemistry, U. Mich., 1964, PhD in Pharm. Chemistry, 1968. Asst. prof., then assoc. prof. U. Iowa, Iowa City, 1968-74; assoc. prof., asst. dir. U. Tex., Austin, 1974-77, area coordinator basic pharmaceutics, 1975-76, assoc. dir. Drug Dynamics Inst., 1977-78, dir. Drug Dynamics Inst., Coll. Pharmacy, 1979-85, James E. Bauerle Centennial prof. Coll. Pharmacy, 1983-85; prof., dean Coll. Pharmacy Wash. State U., Pullman, 1985-86, vice provost for research, dean Grad. Sch., 1987—; cons. E. R. Squibb, New Brunswick, N.J., 1979-82, Upjohn Co., Kalamazoo, Mich., 1982-85; external examiner U. Malaysia, Penang, 1981-82; mem. sci. adv. bd. Biodecision Labs., Pitts., 1985-86; Wash. Biotech. Found., 1989-90; mem. noms. com. Coun. Grad. Schs., Washington, 1990-91; accreditation evaluator Northwest Assn. Schs. and Colls., Seattle, 1991—; mem. exec. com. grad. deans African-Am. Inst., N.Y., 1992—. Author: Textbook of Biopharmaceutic Analysis, 1981, Graduate Research: A Guide for Students in the Sciences, 1990, Development and Management of University Research Groups, 1986. Bd. dirs. Wash. Tech. Ctr., 1990-92. Grantee NIH, 1974-83; fellow Acad. Pharm. Scis., 1981, Am. Assn. Pharm. Scientists, 1987; recipient Disting. Alumnus award Coll. Pharmacy U. Mich., 1990, Outstanding Svc. award Wash. State U., Grad. and Profl. Student Assn., 1993. Mem. Am. Assn. Colls. Pharmacy (chmn. research and grad. affairs com. 1983-84), U.S. Pharmacopeia (revision com. 1985-90), Acad. Pharm. Scis. (chmn., vice chmn. 1983-85, 90, Presdl. citation 1985), Wash. Rsch. Found. (bd. dirs. 1989—). Unitarian. Home: 862 Indian Hills Dr Moscow ID 83843 Office: Wash State Univ Grad Sch Pullman WA 99164

SMITH, ROGER ALEXANDER, surgeon; b. Smithfield, N.C., Dec. 16, 1922; s. Roger Alexander and Alice (McGee) S,; m. Lillian Willms, Dec. 15, 1952 (div. Sept. 1967); children: Candyce, Frank, Terry, Jerry, Roger; m. Elena Vega Humildad, Oct. 17, 1971. Student, U. N.C., 1945; MD, Washington U., 1945-47. Diplomate Am. Bd. Neurological Surgery. Internship Mpls. General Hosp., 1947-48; general surgery residency VA Sawtelle Hosp., L.A., 1949-50; fellow in neurophysiology U. Wis., Madison, 1950; neurosurgery residency U. Ill., 1951-52; pvt. practice neurology & neurosurgery San Bernardino, Calif., 1953-77; asst. clinical prof. neurosurgery Loma Linda U. Medical Ctr., 1966; dir. neurosurgery San Bernardino County Medial Ctr., 1970-89; chief of neurosurgery Jerry L. Pettis Meml. Vets. Hosp., 1989-91, cons. in neurosurgery & neurology, 1991—; courtesy staff St. Bernardine's Hosp., 1953, San Bernardino Cmty. Hosp., 1953; instr. of neurosurgery Henry Ford Hosp., Detroit, 1953, instr. anatomy U. Minn., Mpls., 1948-49. Contbr. articles to profl. jours. With U.S. Army, 1956-58. Mem. Congress Neurological Surgeons, Calif. Assn. Neurological Surgeons, Western Fedn. of Neurological Surgeons, San Bernardino County Med. Soc., Calif. Med. Soc. Home: 1865 Dale Ln San Bernardino CA 92404-1001 Office: 1384 N Waterman Ave San Bernardino CA 92404-5313

SMITH, RON, mayor; b. 1965. BA, U. So. Calif., 1988. Co-owner Kirkland (Wash.) Bldg. Co., 1989—; mem. Bellevue (Wash.) City Coun., 1993-96; mayor City of Bellevue, 1996—. Office: 1511 Main St PO Box 90012 Bellevue WA 98009

SMITH, RUBEN, mayor. BA, N.Mex. State U. Mayor City of Las Cruces (N.Mex.), 1991—. Office: 200 N Church PO Box 20000 Las Cruces NM 88001

SMITH, SAM CORRY, retired foundation executive, consultant; b. Enid, Okla., July 3, 1922; s. Chester Hubbert and Nelle Kate (Corry) S.; m. Dorothy Jean Bank, Sept. 21, 1945; children: Linda Jean, Nancy Kay, Susan Diane. Student, Phillips U., 1940-43; BS in Chemistry, U. Okla., 1947, MS in Chemistry, 1948; PhD in Biochemistry, U. Wis., 1951. Asst. and assoc. prof. U. Okla., Oklahoma City, 1951-55; assoc. dir. grants Research Corp., N.Y.C., 1957-65, dir., 1965-68, v.p. grants, 1968-75; exec. dir. M.J. Murdock Charitable Trust, Vancouver, Wash., 1975-88; foundation cons., 1988—; pres. Pacific Northwest Grantmakers Forum, 1983-84. Contbr. sci. articles to profl. jours. Trustee Nutrition Found., Washington, 1976-84, Internat. Life Scis. Inst., Washington, 1984-86; bd. councilors U. So. Calif. Med. Sch., L.A., 1977-82; mem. adv. com. Coll. Natural Scis. Colo. State U., 1977-80; pres. Cardiopulmonary Rehab. Programs Oreg., 1990-91; bd. dirs. Clark Coll. Found., 1993—. Named Boss of Yr., Am. Bus. Women's Assn., 1982, Bus. Assoc. of Yr., 1983. Fellow AAAS; mem. Am. Chem. Soc. Home: 5204 Dubois Dr Vancouver WA 98661-6617 *Personal philosophy: "There is no limit to what a man can do or where he can go if he doesn't mind who gets the credit." Author unknown.*

SMITH, SAMUEL DAVID, artist, educator; b. Thorndale, Tex., Feb. 11, 1918; s. Otto Frank and Jeanette (Joyce) S.; m. Elizabeth Marie Smith; children: Cezanne, Rembrandt, Michelangelo. Ed. pub. schs. Prof. art U. N.Mex., 1956-84, prof. art emeritus, 1984—. Illustrator: Roots in Adobe, 1967, Cowboy's Christmas Tree, 1956; also: Coronet mag; one man exhbns. include, Corcoran Gallery Art, Washington, 1949, Santa Fe Mus. Art, 1947, Roswell (N.Mex.) Mus. Fine Art, 1953, 64, Goodwell (Okla.) Hist. Mus., 1964, Panhandle Plains Mus., Canyon City, Tex., 1964, Biltomore Galleries, Los Angeles, 1946, First Nat. Bank, Los Alamos, 1968, group exhbns. include, Baker Galleries, Lubbock, Tex., 1964-73, Met. Mus., N.Y.C., 1944, Blue Door Gallery, Taos, N.Mex., 1946-53, Galeria del Sol, Albuquerque, 1968-73, Brandywine Galleries, 1972-73, Watercolor Workshop, Telluride, Colo., 1964; one-man show includes Retrospective Exhbn. U. of N.Mex., Albuquerque, 1986, World War II War Art Exhibit, Nat. Bldg. Mus., 1995. Served as combat artist AUS, 1942-45. Hon. life mem. N.Mex. Art League. Mem. Artist Equity Assn. (pres. N.Mex. chpt. 1957-58, 66-67, 70-71), Elks. Gallery: PO Box 2006 Telluride CO 81435-2006

SMITH, SAMUEL HOWARD, academic administrator, plant pathologist; b. Salinas, Calif., Feb. 4, 1940; s. Adrian Reed and Elsa (Jacop) S.; m. Patricia Ann Walter, July 8, 1960; children: Samuel Howard, Linda Marie. BS in Plant Pathology, U. Calif., Berkeley, 1961, PhD, 1964; D (hon.), Nihon U., Tokyo, 1989. NATO fellow Glasshouse Crops Research Inst., Sussex, Eng., 1964-65; asst. prof. plant pathology U. Calif., Berkeley, 1965-69; assoc. prof. Pa. State U., Arendtsville, 1969-71; assoc. prof. Pa. State U., University Park, 1971-74, prof., 1974-85, head dept. plant pathology, 1976-81, dean Coll. Agr., dir. Pa. Agrl. Expt. Sta. and Coop. Extension Service, 1981-85; pres. Wash. State U., 1985—; bd. dirs. Assoc. Western Univs.; adv. com. Wash. Sch. Employees Credit Union, 1993-95; mem. adv. com. Battelle Pacific N.W. Lab., 1993—; chair Pacific-10 Conf. CEOs, 1993-94; bd. dirs. All-Nations Alliance for Minority Participation; mem. pres.' commn. NCAA, 1994—, divsn. I chair, 1995-96; chair Pres.'s Commn., 1996—. Bd. dirs. Forward Wash., 1986-95, The Technology Alliance, 1996—, China Rels. Coun.; mem. Wash. Coun. Internat. Trade, Western Interstate Commn. Higher Edn.; bd. dirs. Assn. Western Univs., 1993—. Mem. AAAS, Am. Phytopath. Soc., Nat. Assn. State Univs. and Land-Grand Colls. (bd. dirs. 1994—, chair commn. info. tech. 1994-96), Gamma Sigma Delta, Alpha Zeta, Epsilon Sigma Phi, Sigma Xi, Omicron Delta Kappa, Golden Key, Pi Kappa Alpha (hon.). Home: 755 NE Campus St Pullman WA 99163-4223 Office: Wash State U French Adminstrn Bldg Pullman WA 99164-1048

SMITH, SELMA MOIDEL, lawyer, composer; b. Warren, Ohio, Apr. 3, 1919; d. Louis and Mary (Oyer) Moidel; 1 child, Mark Lee. Student U. Calif., 1936-39, U. So. Calif., 1939-41; JD, Pacific Coast U., 1942. Bar: Calif. 1943, U.S. Dist. Ct. 1943, U.S. Supreme Ct. 1958. Gen. practice law; mem. firm Moidel, Moidel, Moidel & Smith. Field dir. civilian adv. com. WAC, 1943; mem. nat. bd. Med. Coll. Pa. (formerly Woman's Med. Coll. Pa.), 1953—, exec. bd., 1976-80, pres., 1980-82, chmn. past pres. com., 1990-92. Decorated La Orden del Merito Juan Pablo Duarte (Dominican Republic). Mem. ABA, State Bar Calif. (servicemen's legal aid com., conf. com. on unauthorized practice of medicine, 1964, Disting. Svc. award 1993), L.A. Bar Assn. (psychopathic ct. com., Outstanding Svc. award 1993), L.A. Lawyers Club (pub. defenders com.), Nat. Assn. Women Lawyers (chmn. com. unauthorized practice of law, social commn. UN, regional dir. western states, Hawaii 1949-51, mem. jud. adminstrn. com. 1960, nat. chmn. world peace through law com. 1966-67, liaison to ABA sr. lawyers divsn. 1996—), League of Ams. (dir.), Inter-Am. Bar Assn., So. Calif. Women Lawyers Assn. (pres. 1947, 48), Women Lawyers Assn. L.A. (chmn. Law Day com. 1966, subject of oral hist. project, 1986), Coun. Bar Assns. L.A. County (charter sec. 1950), Calif. Bus. Women's Coun. (dir. 1951), L.A. Bus. Women's Coun. (pres. 1952), Calif. Pres.'s Coun. (1st v.p.), Nat. Assn. Composers U.S.A. (dir. 1974-79, ann. luncheon chmn. 1975), Nat. Fedn. Music Clubs (nat. vice chmn. for Western region, 1973-78), Calif. Fedn. Music Clubs (state chmn. Am. Music 1971-75, state conv. chmn. 1972), Docents of L.A. Philharm. (v.p. 1973-83, chmn. Latin Am. community rels. 1972-75, press and pub. rels. 1972-75, cons. coord. 1973-75), Assn. Learning in Retirement Orgns. in West (pres. 1993-94, exec. com. 1994-95, Disting. Svc. award 1995), Euterpe Opera Club (v.p. 1974-75, chmn. auditions 1972, chmn. awards 1973-75), ASCAP, Iota Tau Tau (dean L.A., supreme treas.), Plato Soc. of UCLA (Toga editor, 1990-93, sec. 1991-92, chmn. colloquium com. 1992-93, discussion leader UCLA Constitution Bicentennial Project, 1985-87, moderator UCLA extension lecture series 1990, Exceptional Leadership award 1994). Composer of numerous works including Espressivo-Four Piano Pieces (orchestral premiere 1987, performance Nat. Mus. Women in the Arts 1989). Home: 5272 Lindley Ave Encino CA 91316-3518

SMITH, SHERWOOD PAUL, plastic surgeon; b. Sault St. Marie, Ont., Can., May 25, 1941; came to U.S., 1972; s. Irwin and Sophie Edith (Freeman) S.; m. Judith Ann Gebhard, Jan. 24, 1966; 1 child, Stephen Barclay. MD, U. Toronto, 1965; MSc, McGill U., 1969. Diplomate Am. Bd. Plastic Surgery. Plastic surgeon Olympia (Wash.) Plastic Surgeons Inc. PS, 1972—. Vol. plastic surgeon Gen. Hosp. Columbo, Sri Lanka, 1985—. Fellow ACS, Royal Coll. Physicians and Surgeons of Can.; mem. Olympia Yacht Club, South Sound Sailing Soc. Office: Olympia Plastic Surg Inc PS 300 Lilly Rd NE # B Olympia WA 98506-5032

SMITH, STACY ARLENE, educational management administrator; b. Long Beach, Calif., Nov. 29, 1962; d. Richard Alan Sr. and Arlene Lorraine (Towne) S. BA in Broadcast Journalism, U. Utah, 1996. Asst. v.p. post prodn. Lorimar Film and TV, Culver City, Calif., 1988-91; adminstr. Winnart Gallery, L.A., 1991-92; programming asst. KSL Radio, Salt Lake City, 1993-96; entertainment reporter KSL TV, Salt Lake City, 1993-96, assoc. producer, 1993-96; prodn. coord. Ednl. Mgmt. Group, Scottsdale, Ariz., 1996—; ind. producer, L.A., 1991-92; actress in various prodns., L.A., 1970-92. Assoc. producer The Movie Show, 1995. Mem. Soc. Profl. Journalists (v.p. 1995-96). Home: 8603 N 22d Ave # 265 Phoenix AZ 85021 Office: Ednl Mgmt Group 6710 E Camelback Scottsdale AZ 85251

SMITH, STANFORD SIDNEY, state treasurer; b. Denver, Oct. 20, 1923; s. Frank Jay and Lelah (Beamer) S.; m. Harriet Holdrege, Feb. 7, 1947; children: Monta Smith Ramirez, Franklin Stanley. Student, Calif. Inst. Tech., 1941-42, Stanford U., 1942-43; BS, U.S. Naval Acad., 1946. Pres. Vebar Livestock Co., Thermopolis, Wyo., 1961—; mem. Wyo. Senate, 1974-76; pres. Wyo. Wool GrowersAssn., 1976-78; mem. Wyo. Ho. of Reps., Cheyenne, 1978-82; treas. State Wyo., Cheyenne, 1983—; dir. Coun. of State Govts., 1990-92; v.p. Wyo. Wool Growers, dir., 1976-82. County commr. Hot Springs County, Wyo, 1966-74. Lt. USN, 1943-54. Decorated Bronze Star. Mem. Nat. Assn. State Treas. (pres. 1990-91). Republican. Methodist. Office: State of Wyoming State Capital Cheyenne WY 82002

SMITH, STEPHEN RANDOLPH, aerospace executive; b. Des Moines, Apr. 17, 1928; s. Norvin Ellis and Helen (Heberling) S.; m. Margaret Anne Graves, Dec. 20, 1950; children: Stephen Randolph Jr., Susan Canning, Sara Kutler, Anne Barrette, Julia Carroll. BSME, Stanford U., 1951, MSME, 1952; MBA Advanced Mgmt. Program, Harvard U., 1974. Registered profl. engr., Calif. Sr. analyst, preliminary design engr. Northrop & Garrett Corps., L.A. and Hawthorne, Calif., 1952-55; propulsion lead design engr. Northrop Corp., Hawthorne, 1955-59; engring. rep. ea. dist. Northrop Corp., Washington, 1959-60; T-38/F-5/F-20 program mgr. Northrop Corp., Hawthorne, 1960-75; v.p. Iran ops. Northrop Corp., Tehran, 1975-78; v.p. advanced projects Northrop Corp., Hawthorne, 1978-83, v.p. engring. and advanced devel., 1983-86, v.p., program mgr. F-20/YF-23A, 1986-88, corp. v.p., gen. mgr. aircraft divsn., 1988-92; cons. tech. mgmt. Palos Verdes, Calif., 1992—; bd. mem. Quarterdeck Ptnrs., Inc., L.A. and Washington, 1992—, NASA Advanced Aeronautics Com., 1984-86; invited lectr. aircraft design USAF Acad., 1983. Author, designer, patentee in field. Bd. dirs. Boy Scouts Am., L.A. coun., 1986—, charter comm. chmn., 1996; pres. Penn Srs., Palos Verdes, Calif., 1996. Sgt. U.S. Army, 1946-48. Recipient Disting. Civilian Svc. medal U.S. Dept. Def., Washington, 1983. Fellow AIAA (chmn. L.A. sect. 1985-86, adv. bd. 1988—, Spl. Citation 1994), Inst. Advancement Engring.; mem. Soc. Automotive Engrs. (chmn. aerotech. 1986-87, honors 1987), Sierra Club, Trailfinders Conservation Coun. (life, coun. chief 1940). Republican. Episcopalian. Home and Office: 2249 Via Guadalana Palos Verdes Estates CA 90274

SMITH, STEVEN SIDNEY, molecular biologist; b. Idaho Falls, Idaho, Feb. 11, 1946; s. Sidney Ervin and Hermie Phyllis (Robertson) S.; m. Nancy Louise Turner, Dec. 20, 1974. BS, U. Idaho, 1968; PhD, UCLA, 1974. Asst. research scientist Beckman Research Inst. City of Hope Nat. Med. Ctr., Duarte, Calif., 1982-84, staff Cancer Ctr., 1983—, asst. research scientist depts. Thoracic Surgery and Molecular Biology, 1985-87, assoc. research scientist, 1987-95; rsch. scientist City of Hope Nat. Med. Ctr., Duarte, 1995—; dir. dept. cell and tumor biology Beckman Research Inst. City of Hope Nat. Med. Ctr., Duarte, Calif., 1990—; Wellcome vis. prof. in basic med. scis. Okla. State U., 1995-96; cons. Molecular Biosystems Inc., San Diego, 1981-84, Am. Inst. Biol. Scis., Washington, 1994. Contbr. articles to profl. jours. Grantee NIH, 1983-93, Coun. for Tobacco Rsch., 1983-92, March of Dimes, 1988-91, Smokeless Tobacco Rsch. Coun., 1992—, Office of Naval Rsch., 1994—; Swiss Nat. Sci. Found. fellow U. Bern, 1974-77, Scripps Clinic and Rsch. Found., La Jolla, Calif., 1978-82, NIH fellow Scripps Clinic, 1979-81. Mem. Am. Soc. Cell Biology, Am. Assn. Cancer Rsch., Am. Crystallographic Assn., Am. Chem. Soc., Am. Weightlifting Assn., Phi Beta Kappa. Office: City of Hope Nat Med Ctr 1500 Duarte Rd Duarte CA 91010-3000

SMITH, STUART ROBERT, foundation executive; b. South Amboy, N.J., Aug. 14, 1942; s. Stuart Conroy and Elizabeth Beatrice (Keenan) S.; m. Nancy Jo Roberts, Apr. 24, 1965; children: Mark Christopher, Melissa Jo. BA in Psychology, St. Vincent Coll., Latrobe, Pa., 1964; postgrad., Stanford U., 1986. Dist. exec. Raritan coun. Boy Scouts Am., Perth Amboy, N.J., 1965-68, Greater Niagara Frontier Coun., Buffalo, 1968-69; assoc. dir. devel. Canisius Coll., Buffalo, 1969-70; dir. devel. Kenmore (N.Y.) Mercy Hosp., 1971-74; dir. community rels. and devel. United Hosp., Port Chester, N.Y., 1974-77; exec. dir. Shadyside Hosp. Found., Pitts., 1977-79; exec. v.p. Samaritan Med. Found., Phoenix, 1979-87, pres., chief exec. officer, 1988—; cons. fundraising and found. mgmt.; founding bd. mem. Cert. Fund Raising Exec. (CFRE) Profl. Cert. Bd., 1996—. Contbr. articles to profl. jours., newsletters. Founding mem. bd. govs. LPGA Std. Register Ping Golf Tournament, 1983—; pres., bd. dirs. Crisis Nursery, Phoenix, 1990-91, v.p., 1987, 88, found. sec., 1993—; chmn. Fiesta Bowl Golf Classic, Phoenix, 1988, 89; mem. com. Fiesta Bowl, Phoenix, 1986—; bd. dirs. Palms Clinic & Hosp. Found., Phoenix, 1993, exec. com., v.p.; vol. com. chmn. Super Bowl XXX. Fellow Assn. for Healthcare Philanthropy (nat. v.p. 1977-80, bd. accreditation 1986—); mem. Ariz. Assn. Hosp. Devel. (pres. 1990, exec. com. 1989—), Nat. Soc. Fund Raising Execs. (cert. various offices local chpts., Outstanding Fundraising Exec. award Ariz. chpt. 1989), LPGA (sponsors bd., treas. 1988-92), Moon Valley Country Club. Republican. Roman Catholic. Office: The Samaritan Found 1441 N 12th St Phoenix AZ 85006-2837

SMITH, SUSAN KIMSEY, lawyer; b. Phoenix, Jan. 15, 1947; d. William Lewis and Margaret (Bowes) Kimsey; m. Alfred Jon Olsen, Apr. 15, 1979. Student U. Ariz., 1965-66; BA, Principia Coll., 1969; MA, U. Va., 1970; JD, Ariz. State U., 1975. Bar: Ariz. Atty. trust dept. Valley Nat. Bank Ariz., Phoenix, 1976-77; assoc. Lane & Smith, Ltd., Phoenix, 1977-78; mem. Olsen-Smith, Ltd., Phoenix, 1979—, pres., 1979—; mem. Phoenix Tax Workshop, 1976—, Tax Study Group, 1979—, 401 Com., 1982—; chmn. taxation sect. State Bar Ariz., 1985-86, mem. tax. adv. commn.; lectr. profl. confs. and univs., 1977, 80—. Author: Estate Planning Practice Manual, 1984; editorial adv. bd. Practical Tax Lawyer, 1985—; contbr. writings to profl. publs. Bd. dirs. Ariz. Community Found., Samaritan Found.; chair legal adv. com. Ariz. Community Found.; chair Samaritan Gift Planning adv. com. Samaritan Found. Recipient J.P. Walker Am. History award, Principia Coll., 1969, Ethics award, State Bar Ariz., 1974. Fellow Am. Coll. Trust and Estate Counsel (Ariz. chmn.), Am. Coll. Tax Counsel; mem. ABA (chmn. com. econs. of tax practice 1983-84, chmn. com. liaison with other ABA sects. and coms., sect. econs. of law practice 1983—, selection com. appts. to U.S. Tax Ct., com. mem. sect. taxation 1976—, com. mem. sect. real property probate and trust law 1982—, chmn. taxation task force on family partnerships, editorial bd. Practical Tax Lawyer), Internat. Acad. of Estate and Trust Law, State Bar Ariz. (chmn. taxation sect. 1985—, mem. tax adv. commn.), Maricopa County Bar Assn., Fed. Bar Assn. (vice chmn. estate and gift taxation com., taxation council 1979-80), Valley Estate Planners (pres., elected first life time mem.), Central Ariz. Estate Planning Council (bd. dirs. 1986-88), The Group, Alpha Lambda Delta, Phi Alpha Eta. Republican. Office: Olsen-Smith Ltd 301 E Virginia Ave Ste 3300 Phoenix AZ 85004-1218

SMITH, SUSAN LEE, history educator; b. Burbank, Calif., June 13, 1950; d. Robert Emmet and Dorothy (Nicholson) Smith; m. Michael Ward Melton, May 8, 1976 (div. Aug. 1981); m. Albert David Doum Jr., Dec. 12, 1993. BS in History, No. Ariz. U., 1972, MA in History, 1975. Instr. UCLA, 1976-79, Georgetown U., Washington, 1979, Boston & Cambridge Ctr. Adult Edn., 1980-85; prof. history Orange Coast Coll., Costa Mesa, Calif., 1985—. Prodr., author 12 part cable series: Reel Times, 1991. Vice pres. Citizen's Budget Adv. Com. Newport Mesa Unified Sch. Dist., Costa Mesa, 1995-96; vol. Mariner's Libr., Newport beach, 1993-96. Recipient Tchg. Excellence award Nat. Inst. Staff Orgnl. Devel., Austin, Tex., 1992, 93, 94, 97. Episcopalian.

SMITH, SYLVIA SUE, artist, sculptor; b. L.A., Aug. 26, 1939; s. Joseph and Nettie (Torres) S.; m. Roy Elm, 1966 (div. 1974); 1 child, Carrie. BA, U. Calif., Davis, 1989. Cert. C.C. instr., Calif. Art instr., mural painter Ctrl. Valley Oppty. Ctr., Merced, Calif., 1978-80; sculptor Sitre & Sierra Ceramics, Fresno, Calif., 1980-81; model, mold maker Santa Barbara (Calif.) Indsl. Form & Design, 1982-83; porcelain restorer Bradwicks Art Restoration, 1983-84; sculptor, model maker STX Pac Industries, Winters, Calif., 1985-88; sculptor Clay Art Ceramics, San Francisco, 1990-91; freelance sculptor Carmichael, Calif., 1991—; art instr. Los Banos (Calif.) Schs., 1977-78; art and craft instr. Los Banos Recreation Dept., 1977; ceramics instr. Fresno Rehab. Dept., 1976; sculptor Duncan Ceramics, Fresno, 1973-76. Exhibited in group shows at Faulkner Gallery, Santa Barbara, 1984, Pence Gallery, Davis, 1991, Persuasion Gallery, Sacramento, 1989, Peach Pvt. Bronze Invitation, Sacramento, 1994. Recipient Best of Show award Valley Ceramic Show, Dist. Fair, Hon. Mention award No. Calif. Arts, 1995. Mem. Carmichael Fine Arts Ctr., No. Calif. Artists. Office: 5740 Windmill Way # 11 Carmichael CA 95608

SMITH, T. WAYNE, education director, rodeo announcer, rancher; b. Carlsbad, N.Mex., Dec. 13, 1970; m. Shelly D. Jones, May 24, 1991; children: Sidne Brook, Jinsen Paige. AA, Ea. N.Mex. U., 1993, BA, 1994. Coord. distance learning N.Mex. Jr. Coll., Hobbs, 1994-95, dir. continuing edn. and cmty. svcs., 1995—; mem. DWI planning coun. Lea County, Lovinton, N.Mex., 1996—. Mem. edn. comm. Hobbs C. of C., 1995-96; pres.-elect Prof. Assn. Continuing Edn., N.Mex., Miss Rodeo Am. Pageant (state dir. 1993—). Republican. Methodist. Office: N Mex Jr Coll 5317 Lovington Hwy Hobbs NM 88240-9121

SMITH, THOMAS HARRY, counselor; b. Tonawanda, N.Y., Nov. 17, 1947; s. Richard Sleep and Elsie (Supparritts) S.; m. Linda Sharon Kerr, Nov. 11, 1985 (div. Aug. 1991); children: Nicole Katya, Zachary Thomas. BS, SUNY, Oneonta, 1969. Counselor Upstate Home for Children, Milford, N.Y., 1973; psychometrician Attica (N.Y.) Correctional Facility, 1974-75; tchr. Albion (N.Y.) Head Start, 1975-76, Marion House, Waterport, N.Y., 1976; counselor Otsego County Manpower, Cooperstown, N.Y., 1977-79, Deverenx Found., Santa Barbara, Calif., 1979-81, 89-95, Work Tng. Program, Santa Barbara, 1981-86; nurse asst. channel Cities Nurse Registry, Santa Barbara, 1987-89; bd. dirs. Lake Serene, Santa Barbara. Author: Qim Tunes, 1994. Mem. Am. Union Men (pres. 1983—), Goleta Valley Athletic Club. Home: PO Box 80131 Goleta CA 93117

SMITH, THOMAS JAMES, reference librarian; b. Oceanside, N.Y., Mar. 29, 1963; s. Kenneth Perry and Dorothy Louise (Breidenbach) S. BA in History, U. Nev., Las Vegas, 1985; MLS, Ind. U., 1988. Reference libr. Las Vegas-Clark County Libr., 1988—. Co-editor, compiler: Nevada Funding Directory, 1994. Mem. Phi Kappa Phi, Phi Alpha Theta, Phi Lambda Alpha. Office: Clark County Libr 1401 E Flamingo Rd Las Vegas NV 89119-5256

SMITH, THOMAS SHORE, lawyer; b. Rock Springs, Wyo., Dec. 7, 1924; s. Thomas and Anne E. (McTee) S.; m. Jacqueline Emily Krueger, May 25, 1952; children: Carolyn Jane, Karl Thomas, David Shore. BSBA, U. Wyo., 1950, JD, 1959. Bar: U.S. Dist. Ct. Wyo. 1960, U.S. Ct. Appeals (10th cir.) 1960, U.S. Tax Ct. 1969, U.S. Supreme Ct. 1971. Of counsel Smith, Stanfield & Scott, LLC, Laramie, Wyo., 1963—; atty. City of Laramie, 1963-86; instr. mcpl. law U. Wyo., 1987, mem. dean's adv. com. Law Sch.; dir. budget and fin. Govt. of Am. Samoa, 1954-56. Bd. dirs. Bur. Land Mgmt., Rawlins, Wyo., 1984-89, chmn. bd. dirs., 1989; pres. Ivinson Hosp. Found., 1994-95; bd. dirs. U. Wyo. Found., 1991—, pres., 1996-97. Francis Warren scholar, 1958. Mem Wyo. Bar Assn. (pres. 1984-85), Albany County Bar Assn., Western States Bar Conf. (pres. 1985-86), Elks. Republican. Episcopalian. Office: Smith Stanfield & Scott LLC PO Box 971 515 E Ivinson Ave Laramie WY 82070-3157

SMITH, THOMAS WINSTON, cotton marketing executive; b. Crosbyton, Tex., Mar. 16, 1935; s. Lance L. and Willie Mae (Little) S.; m. Patricia Mae Zachary, Dec. 13, 1958; children—Janna Olean, Thomas Mark. B.S., Tex. A&M U., 1957; P.M.D., Harvard U., 1964. Various positions Calcot Ltd., Bakersfield, Calif., 1957-77, exec. v.p., pres., 1977—; v.p. Amcot, Inc., Amcot Internat., Inc., Bakersfield, 1977—, also bd. dirs.; bd. mgrs. N.Y. Cotton Exchange, N.Y.C., v.p., Memphis. Bd. dir. Greater Bakersfield Meml. Hosp.; mem. pres.'s adv. commn. Calif. State Coll., Bakersfield; v.p. Nat. Cotton Coun., Memphis. Mem. Rotary.

SMITH, THORN MCCLELLAN, lawyer; b. Peoria, Ill., Feb. 19, 1958; s. Lester Berry and June Edda (Kopal) S. BS in Fgn. Service, Georgetown U., 1979; JD, Northwestern U., 1982. Bar: Ill. 1982, U.S. Dist. Ct. (ctr. dist.) Ill. 1983, S.C. 1984, U.S. Dist. Ct. S.C. 1985, Calif. 1990, U.S. Dist. Ct. Calif. (no. dist.), 1990, U.S. Ct. Appeals (9th cir.) 1990. Assoc. Law Offices of Lester Berry Smith, Peoria, 1982-83, Law Offices of C.R. Dunbar, Spartanburg, S.C., 1983-85; sole practice Spartanburg, 1985-87; mem. office of gen. counsel USN, 1987-91; of counsel Tank Protect Engring. No. Calif., Inc., 1992-93. Western field dir. Confederate Lawyer, Western Command, 1993—. Mem. ABA, Bar Assn. of San Francisco, Spartanburg County Bar Assn., Sons Confederate Vets. Office: 465 California St Ste 521 San Francisco CA 94104-1814

SMITH, VERNON LOMAX, economist, researcher; b. Wichita, Kans., Jan. 1, 1927; s. Vernon Chessman and Lula Belle (Lomax) S.; m. Joyce Harkleroad, June 6, 1950 (div. Aug. 1975); m. Carol Breckner, Jan. 1, 1980. BSEE, Calif. Inst. Tech., 1949; MA in Econs., U. Kans., 1952; PhD in Econs., Harvard U., 1955; D of Mgmt. (hon.), Purdue U., 1990. Asst. prof. econs. Purdue U., West Lafayette, Ind., 1955-58, assoc. prof., 1958-61, prof., 1961-65, Krannert prof., 1965-67; prof. Brown U., Providence, 1967-68, U. Mass., Amherst, 1968-75; prof. U. Ariz., Tucson, 1975—, Regents' prof.; Contbr. articles to profl. jours. Fellow Ctr. for Advanced Study in Behavioral Scis., Stanford, Calif., 1972-73; Sherman Fairchild Disting. Scholar Calif. Inst. Tech., Pasadena, 1973-74; adj. scholar CATO Inst., Washington, 1983—. Fellow AAAS, Am. Acad. Arts and Scis., Econometric Soc., Am. Econ. Assn. (Disting. fellow); me. Pvt. Enterprise Edn. Assn. (Adam Smith award), Nat. Acad. Sci. Home: 6020 N Pontatoc Rd Tucson AZ 85718 Office: U Ariz Econ Sci Lab Tucson AZ 85718

SMITH, VIN, sports editor, business owner, novelist; b. Whittier, Calif., May 19, 1944; s. M. Clifford and Anna Eugenia (Hill) S.; m. Marthea Karen Callaham, May 15, 1969 (div. 1979); children: Jayare Smith, Eric Smith; m. Ginger Hammon, Oct. 20, 1984; children: Amy Michelle, Stacey Erin, Kellie Rae. Student, Columbia Sch. Broadcasting, San Francisco, 1967; AA, Cuesta Coll., 1974; grad., Am. Sch. of Piano Tuning, 1978. Sales mgr. Sta. KTAT, Frederick, Okla., 1967-69; announcer KOCY, Oklahoma City, 1969; owner Melmart Markets, San Luis Obispo, Calif., 1971-73, Am. Direct Sales, Grover City, Calif., 1973-79; instr. piano Valley View Acad., Arroyo Grande, Calif., 1977-78; instr. piano Long Piano Co., San Luis Obispo, 1977-79, piano technician, 1978-79; owner Chocolate Piano, Yreka, Calif., 1979—; instr. piano Makah Indian Tribe, Neah Bay, Wash., 1981-82; sports editor New Words Digest, Bakersfield, Calif., 1988—; cons., stress evaluator seminar Yreka Stress Therapy Clinic, 1986-87. Sports columnist New Words Digest, 1987-91; guest columnist Siskiyou Daily News, 1991-94; nat publicist chamber music concerts So. Oreg. State Coll., 1993—; contbr. articles to profl. jours. Chmn. heart fund Tillman County Okla., 1968; pub. co-chmn. Siskiyou County No-Prop 174, 1973-93; campaign worker Ken Jourdan for sheriff, Yreka, 1986; publicity dir. Gene Breceda for supr., 1993-94. Recipient Cert. of Appreciation, Siskiyou County, 1988, Achievement award, 1988; winner Golden Poet award World of Poetry, 1989. Mem. Nat. Writers Club (chmn. student com. Yreka chpt. 1988), Author's Guild, Inc., Author's League of Am., Mystery Writers Am., Soc. Children's Book Writers, Jr. C. of C. (sgt.-at-arms Frederick chpt. 1967-69), Kiwanis, Moose. Home: 710 Knapp St Yreka CA 96097-2343 Office: Chocolate Piano Svcs PO Box 447 Yreka CA 96097-0447

SMITH, WALDO GREGORIUS, former government official; b. Bklyn., July 29, 1911; s. John Henry and Margaret (Gregorius) S.; m. Mildred Pearl Prescott, July 30, 1935 (dec. Jan. 1992); 1 dau., Carole Elizabeth Smith Levin. Student CCNY, N.Y., 1928-29; BS in Forestry, Cornell U., 1933. Registered prof. engr., Colo. Forester Forest Svc., U.S. Dept. Agr., Atlanta, 1933-41, Ala. Div. Forestry, Brewton, 1941-42; engr., civil engring. technician Geol. Survey, U.S. Dept. Interior, 1942-71, cartographic technician, 1972-75; chmn. Public Transp. Council, 1975-89; legislator aide to individuals Colo. State Legis. Internship Program, 1987-95. Recipient 40 Yr. Civil Service award pin and scroll; 42 Yr. Govt. Service award plaque. Fellow Am. Congress Surveying and Mapping (life, sec.-treas. Colo. chpt. 1961, program chmn. 1962, reporter 1969, mem. nat. membership devel. com. 1973-74, rep. to Colo. Engring. Council 1976-77); mem. AAAS (emeritus), Denver Fed. Center Profl. Engrs. Group (U.S. Geol. Survey rep. 1973-76, Engr. of Yr. award 1975), Nat. Soc. Profl. Engrs. (pre-coll. guidance com. 1986-91, life 92—), Profl. Engrs. Colo. (chpt. scholarship chmn. 1979—, advt. corr., service award 1983), Cornell U. Alumni Assn. (alumni secondary schs. com. Quadrangle Club), Common Cause, Colo. Engring. Council (chmn. library com. 1970—, spl. rep. Regional Transp. Dist., 1974-75; mem. sci. fair com. 1970-71; rep. ex officio Denver Pub. Library Found. Bd. Trustees 1975-80, mem. historic agreement with Denver Pub. Libr. 1993, Pres.'s Outstanding Service award 1987), Environ. Concerns (chmn. com. 1988—, treas. 1989-91, mem. site specific adv. bd., restoration adv. bd. Rocky Mountain arsenal cleanup 1994—), Fedn. Am. Scientists, Am. Soc. Engring. Edn., People for Am. Way. Contbr. articles to profl. jours. Home: 3821 W 25th Ave Denver CO 80211-4417 *Personal philosophy: A new acronym: T'n'T=Truth and Trust; give posterity a decent break.*

SMITH, WALTER J., engineering consultant; b. Climax, Kans., Feb. 8, 1921; s. Jacob Walter and Thelma Christina (Stark) S.; m. Wanda Jean Sandys, Apr. 20, 1944 (div. 1965); children: Walter Brooke, Judith Jean; m. Evadean Louise Smith, Sept. 21, 1965; stepchildren: Stephen Henslee, Kimberly Ann; 1 adopted child, Nancy Louise. BEE, Cleve. State U., 1948; postgrad., UCLA, 1955-58, Western State U. Law, Anaheim, Calif., 1970-71. Lic. profl. engr., Ohio, Calif. Field tech. rep. to Air Force Jack & Heintz, Inc., Maple Hts., Ohio, 1942-44; rsch. engr. Jack & Heintz, Inc., 1948-50, N. Am. Aviation Inc., Downey, Calif., 1950-54; asst. chief engr. Ala. Engring. & Tool Co., Huntsville, Ala., 1954-55; rsch. specialist to dir. prodn. ops. N. Am. Aviation Inc./Rockwell Internat., Anaheim, 1955-86; engring. mgmt. cons. Anaheim, 1986-93; engring. mgmt. cons., Palm Desert, Calif., 1993—. Contbr. articles to profl. jours. Mem. Anaheim Indsl. Devel. Bd., 1982-86, Anaheim Pub. Utilities Bd., 1987-92; bd. dirs. Rep. Ctrl. Com. of Orange County, 1976-78; pres., bd. dirs. Galerie Homeowners Assn., 1987-93; bd. dirs. Coun. on Environ. Edn. and Econ. Through Devel., Inc., 1974-86, Action Com. to Inform Orange Now, Inc. Mem. Anaheim C. of C. (bd. dirs. 1983-90, pres. 1983-84), Gladhanders Acad. Hospitality Internat. (bd. dirs. 1989-95, Man of Yr. 1989). Republican. Religious Science. Home and Office: 78615 Purple Sagebrush Ave Palm Desert CA 92211-1444

SMITH, WILLARD GRANT, psychologist; b. Sidney, N.Y., June 29, 1934; s. Frank Charles and Myrtle Belle (Empet) S.; m. Ruth Ann Dissly, Sept. 14, 1957; children—Deborah Sue Henri, Cynthia Lynn Koster, Andrea Kay Richards, John Charles. BS, U. Md., 1976; MS, U. Utah, 1978, PhD, 1981. Lic. psychologist, Utah; cert. sch. psychologist, sch. adminstr., tchr., Utah, nat. cert. sch. psychologist; bd. cert. forensic examiner; diplomate Am. Bd. Forensic Examiners. Rsch. asst. Med. Ctr., U. Utah, 1977, teaching asst. dept. ednl. psychology, 1976-78, rsch. cons. dept. edn., 1977; program evaluator Salt Lake City Sch. Dist.; program evaluator and auditor Utah State Bd. Edn., 1978; sch. psychologist Jordan Sch. Dist., Sandy, Utah, 1978-82, tchr., 1979-80; exec. dir. Utah Ind. Living Ctr., Salt Lake City, 1982-83; spl. edn. cons. Southeastern Edn. Svc. Ctr., 1983-85; sch. psychologist Jordan Sch. Dist., Sandy, 1985-96; assoc. psychologist Don W. McBride & Assocs., Bountiful, Utah, 1989-91; pvt. practice Salt Lake City, 1991—. Master sgt. USAF, 1953-76. Decorated Air Force Commendation medal with 2 clusters; recipient U. Md. scholastic achievement award, 1975. Mem. APA, Am. Coll. Forensic Examiners, Nat. Assn. Sch. Psychologists, Air Force Sgts. Assn., Ret. Enlisted Assn., Phi Kappa Phi, Alpha Sigma Lambda. Home: 8955 Quail Hollow Dr Sandy UT 84093-1903

SMITH, WILLIAM HUGH, SR., retired audit manager, consultant; b. Peoria, Ill., Feb. 12, 1920; s. Hugh N. and Catherine Litta (Obrien) S.; m. Betty Lou Uth Smith, June 4, 1941; children: Beverly Ann Clark, William H. Smith Jr., Millie Judkins, Hugh N. Smith, Patrick James Smith. BSBA with honors, U. Dayton. Cert. Fraud Examiner; cert. Fin. Mgr. Mgr. Hugh H. Smith CPA, Chgo., 1946-66; resident mgr. CPA Firms, Chgo., 1966-76; v.p., auditor United of Am. Bank, Chgo., 1976-79; audit mgr. City of Anaheim, Calif., 1979-96. Charter Life mem. Rep. Presidential Task Force, Washington, 1982—. Capt. U.S. Army, 1941-46. Mem. Inst. Internal Auditors (bd. govs. Orange County chpt., internat. com. on govt. affairs), Cert. Fraud Examiners. Republican. Roman Catholic. Home: 14415 Baker St Westminster CA 92683-4813

SMITH, WILLIAM K., real estate developer; b. 1944. BA, U. Redlands, 1966; JD, UCLA, 1969. With Mission Viejo (Calif.) Co., 1969—, officer, 1974—, now sr. v.p., gen. counsel. Office: Mission Viejo Co 26137 La Paz Rd Mission Viejo CA 92691-5309

SMITH, WILLIAM RAY, retired biophysicist, engineer; b. Lyman, Okla., June 26, 1925; s. Harry Wait and Daisy Belle (Hull) S. BA, Bethany Nazarene Coll., 1948; MA, Wichita State U., 1950; PhD, UCLA, 1967. Engr., Beech Aircraft Corp., Wichita, Kans., 1951-53; sr. group engr. McDonnell Aircraft Corp., St. Louis, 1953-60; sr. engr. Lockheed Aircraft Corp., Burbank, Calif., 1961-63; sr. engr. scientist McDonnell Douglas Corp., Long Beach, Calif., 1966-71; mem. tech. staff Rockwell Internat., L.A., 1973-86, CDI Corp.-West, Costa Mesa, Calif., 1986-88, McDonnell Douglas Aircraft Corp., Long Beach, 1988-93; ret., 1993. tchr. math. Pasadena Nazarene Coll. (now Point Loma Nazarene Coll., San Diego), 1960-62, Glendale Coll., Calif., 1972; asst. prof. math. Mt. St. Mary's Coll., L.A., 1972-73; math. cons. L.A. Union Rescue Mission Bank of Am. Learning Ctr., 1995—; docent Will Rogers State Park Nature Mus., 1995—; deacon Presbyn. Ch. Recipient Recognition certificate NASA, 1982. Mem. Town Hall Calif., Yosemite Assocs., L.A. World Affairs Coun., Sigma Xi, Pi Mu Epsilon. Republican. Avocations: sailing, photography, teaching Sunday sch. first grade. Home: 2405 Roscomare Rd Los Angeles CA 90077-1839

SMITH, ZACHARY ALDEN, political science and public administration educator; b. Stanford, Calif., Aug. 8, 1953; s. Alden Wallace and Lelia (Anderson) S. BA, Calif. State U., Fullerton, 1975; MA, U. Calif., Santa Barbara, 1979, PhD, 1984. Adj. lectr. polit. sci. U. Calif., Santa Barbara, 1981-82; asst. prof., dir. Ctr. for Island and Ocean Resources Mgmt. U. Hawaii, Hilo, 1982-87, assoc. prof., 1987-89; assoc. prof. No. Ariz. U., Flagstaff, 1989-93, prof., 1993—. Author: Groundwater and the Future of the Southwest, 1984, Groundwater Policy in the Southwest, 1985, Groundwater in the West, 1989, The Environmental Policy Paradox, 1992, 2d edit., 1995, Hawaii State and Local Government, 1992, Politics and Public Policy in Arizona, 1993, 2d edit., 1995, Environmental Politics and Policy in the West, 1993. Active campaign for various state propositions, 1970, 74, 76; elected to Orange County (Calif.) Dem. Cen. Com., 1976-78; councilman City of Flagstaff, 1996—. Rsch. grantee U. Calif., Los Alamos (N.Mex.) Sci. Lab., Water Resources Ctr., Davis, Calif., U.S. Dept. HUD. Mem. ASPA, Am. Water Resources Assn., Am. Polit. Sci. Assn., Southwestern Social Sci. Assn., Western Polit. Sci. Assn., Western Social Sci. Assn. (exec. coun. 1995—). Office: No Ariz U Dept Polit Sci Box 15036 Flagstaff AZ 86011

SMITH-THOMPSON, PATRICIA ANN, public relations consultant, educator; b. Chgo., June 7, 1933; d. Clarence Richard and Ruth Margaret (Jacobson) Nowack; m. Tyler Thompson, Aug. 1, 1992. Student Cornell U., 1951-52; BA, Centenary Coll., Hackettstown, N.J., 1983. Prodn. asst. Your Hit Parade Batten, Barton, Durstine & Osborne, 1953-54; pvt. practice polit. cons., 1954-66; legal sec., asst. Atty. John C. Cushman, 1966-68; field dep. L.A. County Assessor, 1968-69, pub. info. officer L.A. County Probation Dept., 1969-73; dir. consumer rels. Fireman's Fund, San Francisco, 1973-76; pvt. practice pub. rels. cons., 1976-77; spl. projects officer L.A. County Transp. Commn., 1977-78; tchr. Calif. State U.-Dominguez Hills, 1979-86; editor, writer Jet Propulsion Lab., 1979-80; pub. info. dir. L.A. Bd. Pub. Works, 1980-82; pub. info. cons. City of Pasadena, (Calif.), 1982-84; pub. rels. cons., 1983-90, community rels./Worldport L.A., 1990-92. Contbr. articles to profl. jours. Mem. First United Methodist Ch. Commn. on Missions and Social Concerns, 1983-89; bd. dirs. Depot, 1983-87; mem. devel. com. Pasadena Guidance Clinics, 1984-85. Recipient Pro award L.A. Publicity Club, 1978, Outstanding Achievement award Soc. Consumer Affairs Profls. in Bus., 1976, Disting. Alumni award Centenary Coll., 1992. Mem. Pub. Relations Soc. Am. (accredited mem.; award for consumer program 1977, 2 awards 1984, Joseph Roos Community Service award 1985), Nat. Press Women (pub. relations award 1986), Calif. Press Women (awards 1974, 78, 83, 84, 85, community relations 1stplace winner 1986, 87, 88, 89), Nat. Assn. Mental Health Info. Offices (3 regional awards 1986). Republican. Home and Office: Box 4300-41 24145 Jacaranda Tehachapi CA 93561

SMOCK, TIMOTHY ROBERT, lawyer; b. Richmond, Ind., June 24, 1951; s. Robert Martin and Thelma Elizabeth (Cozad) S.; m. Martha Carolene Middleton, Apr. 4, 1992; children: Andrew Zoller, Alison Pierce. BA, Wittenberg U., 1973; JD cum laude, Ind. U., 1977. Bar: Ind. 1977, Ariz. 1979, U.S. Dist. Ct. (so. dist.) Ind. 1977, U.S. Dist. Ct. Ariz. 1979, U.S. Ct. Apeals (7th cir.) 1977, U.S. Ct. Appeals (9th cir.) 1979. Jud. clk. Ct. of Appeals of Ind., Indpls., 1977-79; assoc. Lewis and Roca, Phoenix, 1979-82; assoc./shareholder Gallagher & Kennedy, Phoenix, 1982-89; ptnr. Scult, French, Zwillinger & Smock, Phoenix, 1989-94, Smock and Weinberger, Phoenix, 1994—; judge, pro tempore Maricopa County Superior Ct., Phoenix, 1989—; faculty, State Bar Course on Professionalism, Ariz. Supreme Ct./State Bar, Phoenix, 1992—; speaker, Continuing Legal Edn., Maricopa County and Ariz. State Bar, 1988—. Mem. ABA, Ariz. Bar Assn., Maricopa Bar Assn., Def. Rsch. Inst. Office: Smock and Weinberger 2700 N Central Ave Ste 1125 Phoenix AZ 85004-1149

SMOLAREK, WALDEMAR, artist, printmaker; b. Warsaw, Poland, Sept. 5, 1937; Came to Canada, 1971; Student, Warsaw Sch. Art, 1952-55, Warsaw Acad. Fine Arts, 1955-57. Instr. form and color composition Warsaw Sch. Art, 1957-60; instr. continuing edn. U. B.C., 1972. One-man shows include Warsaw, Poland, 1958-65, Artist Coop. Gallery, San Francisco, 1959, Kunsterhaus Wien, Vienna, Austria, 1961, Selected Artist Gallery, N.Y.C., 1962, Miami (Fla.) Mus. Modern Art, 1962, Gallerie Classigua, Stockholm, 1967, Gallery Herder, Stockholm, 1969, Presentation House, North Vancouver, B.C., Can., 1976, Langton Gallery, London, 1977, Kilakyushu (Japan) City Mus. Art, 1982, Galeria Fernando Vijande, Madrid, 1982, Gallery Silvia Menzel, Berlin, 1984, Galeria Daniel Templon, Paris, 1985, Harrison Galleries, Vancouver, B.C., Can., 1986, Osaka Found. of Culture, Japan, 1991, Montserrat Gallery, N.Y.C., 1992; represented in permanent collections Miami Mus. Modern Art, mus. ModernArt, Stockholm, Nat. Mus., Warsaw. Home and Studio: 807-1424 Nelson St, Vancouver, BC Canada V6G 1L9

SMOLKA, JAMES WILLIAM, aerospace research pilot; b. Mt. Clemens, Mich., July 31, 1950; s. Joseph William and Patricia Joan (Righetti) S. BS in Astronautics, USAF Acad., 1972; MS in Aero., Astronautics, MIT, 1980; engineers degree in aero. & astronautics, Stanford U., 1994. Commd. 2d lt. USAF, 1972, advanced through grades to col., 1996; resigned, 1983; served as pilot 3d Tactical Fighter Squadron, Korat RT AFB, Thailand, 1974, 21 Tactical Air Support Squadron, Shaw AFBSC, 1975-77; test pilot 6510 Test Wing, Edwards AFB CA, 1981-83; exptl. test pilot Ft. Worth div. Gen. Dynamics, Edwards AFB, 1984-85; aerospace rsch. pilot N.A.S.A. Dryden FRC, Edwards AFB, 1985—; col. USAFR, 1992—; adj. prof. Calif. State U., Fresno, 1984—. Author: Analysis and Testing of Aircraft Flight Control Systems, 1982. Mem. Soc. Exptl. Test Pilots. Home: PO Box 2123 Lancaster CA 93539-2123 Office: NASA Dryden Flight Rsch Ctr PO Box 273 Edwards CA 93523-0273

SMOOT, SKIPI LUNDQUIST, psychologist; b. Aberdeen, Wash., Apr. 10, 1934; d. Warren Duncan and Miriam Stephen (Bishop) Dobbins; m. Harold Richard Lundquist, June 2, 1951 (div. Mar. 1973); children: Kurt Richard, Mark David, Ted Douglas, Blake Donald; m. Edward Lee Smoot, June 14, 1975. BA in Psychology, Coll. of William and Mary, 1978; MA, Pepperdine U., 1980; PhD, Calif. Sch. of Profl., Psychology, San Diego, 1985. Lic. clin. psychologist, Calif.; lic. marriage and family therapist, Calif. Owner, operator McDonald's Restaurants, San Pedro and Torrance, Calif., 1965-76, Williamsburg, Va., 1965-76; psychotherapist Coll. Hosp., Cerritos, Calif., 1979-81, Orange County Child Guidance, Laguna Hills, Calif., 1981-82; psychotherapist Calif. State Police, Costa Mesa, 1982-83, Anaheim, 1983-84; psychologist Orange County Mental Health, Santa Ana, Calif., 1984-85, Psychol. Ctr., Orange and El Toro, Calif., 1985-91; clin. dir. Career Ambitions, Irvine and Laguna Hills, 1991-94, Psychol. Decisions, Irvine-Laguna

Hills, Calif., 1991-94; psychol. cons. seminars and workshops for bus., Irvine and Laguna Hills, 1991-94. Mem. APA, Calif. Psychol. Assn., Calif. Assn. Marriage and Family Therapists. Democrat. Office: Psychol Decisions Career Ambitions Unltd 23161 Lake Center Dr Ste 124 Lake Forest CA 92630-6822

SMUCKLER, HARVEY GLASGOW, financial consultant; b. Sturgeon Bay, Wis., Aug. 4, 1924; s. Joseph Max and Ruth Mary (Glasgow) S.; m. Harriet Carol Victor, June 28, 1949; children: Alan Lee, David Todd, Joel Jay. BBA, U. Wis., 1949; cert., The Am. Coll., Bryn Mawr, Pa., 1969, The Am. Coll., Bryn Mawr, Pa., 1984. CLU, ChFC; registered investment advisor, SEC and Calif. Asst. mgr. Mut. of N.Y., Chgo., 1955-59; gen. agt. Continental Assurance Co., Milw., 1959-64; pres. Mayflower Life of Wis., Milw., 1964-67; agy. v.p. Bankers Security Life Ins. Soc., Washington, 1967-70, sr. v.p., 1970-74; exec. v.p. Occidental Life Ins. N.C., Raleigh, 1974, pres., 1975-79; CEO Lincoln Am. Life Ins. Co., Memphis, 1979-80; pres., CEO Smuckler Fin., Tarzana, Calif., 1981—; registered rep. Titan Value Equities Group, Tustin, Calif., 1983—; chmn. SS Telecom Inc., Encino, Calif., 1991—. Home: 4623 El Caballero Dr Tarzana CA 91356-4812 Office: Smuckler Fin 18801 Ventura Blvd Ste 304 Tarzana CA 91356-3362

SMUKLER, KIM BENNETT, lawyer; b. Aurora, Ill., Oct. 27, 1952; s. Keith Smukler and Loraine (Hallenstein) Reichel. BA in Philosophy, U. Minn., 1980, JD cum laude, 1983. Bar: Calif. 1983, Minn. 1985. Supr. atty. Tulare County Pub. Defenders Office, Visalia, Calif., 1984—. Mem. Calif. Attys. for Criminal Justice, Porsche Club Am. Office: Tulare County Pub Defenders Office Rm G35 County Civic Ctr Cthouse Visalia CA 93291

SMULDERS, ANTHONY PETER, biology educator; b. Oss, North Brabant, The Netherlands, July 6, 1942; came to U.S., 1963; s. Arnoldus A.P. and Maria A.A. (Horsten) S. T.C. in Edn. and Psychology, St. Stanislaus T.T.C., Tilburg, The Netherlands, 1962; BS in Biology summa cum laude, Loyola U., Los Angeles, 1966; PhD in Physiology with distinction, UCLA, 1970. Joined Bros. of Our Lady Mother of Mercy, Roman Cath. Ch., 1959. Tchr. Loon op Zand (The Netherlands) elem. schs., 1962-63, Santa Clara High Sch., Oxnard, Calif., 1965-67; research physiologist UCLA, 1970—; prof. biology Loyola Marymount U., Los Angeles, 1970—, assoc. dean sci., 1972-94, dir. health professions info. program, 1995—; mem. L.A. County Narcotics and Dangerous Drugs Commn., 1973—, Calif. State Adv. Bd. on Drug Programs, 1982-92. Contbr. articles to profl. jours. Mem. AAUP, AAAS, The Biophys. Soc., Nat. Assn. Advisors for Health Professions (pres. 1978-84), Western Assn. Advisors for Health Professions, Sigma Xi, Sigma Pi Sigma. Democrat. Lodge: KC. Office: Loyola Marymount U 7900 Loyola Blvd Los Angeles CA 90045-8220

SMYRL, ELIOT KEMP, computer animation scientist; b. Berkeley, Calif., Jan. 3, 1966; s. William Hiram and Donna Kay (Clayton) S.; m. Laura Michelle Money, Apr. 9, 1994. BS, U. Calif., Berkeley, 1987, MS, 1989. Mem. tech. staff Pixar, Richmond, Calif., 1989-90, animation scientist, 1991-95, lead animation scientist, 1996—. Mem. Assn. for Computing Machinery (spl. interest group on graphics). Democrat. Presbyterian. Office: Pixar 1001 W Cutting Blvd Richmond CA 94804

SMYTH, BERNARD JOHN, retired newspaper editor; b. Renovo, Pa., Nov. 16, 1915; s. John Bernard and Alice C. (Russell) S.; m. Eva Mae Stone, Dec. 31, 1936; children: Constance, Joe, Pamela, Lisa. Grad., Dickinson Jr. Coll., 1935. Machinist helper Pa. R.R. Renovo Shops, 1936-39; mgr. Smyth Bros., Renovo, 1939-45; editor, pub., owner Renovo Daily Record, 1946-53; owner, editor, pub. Del. State News, Dover, 1953-70; chmn. bd. Independent Newspapers Inc., 1970-85; pres. Valley Newspapers Inc., Tempe, Ariz., 1971-85. Served with AUS, 1944-45. Mem. Soc. Profl. Journalists, Ariz. Newspaper Assn., Sigma Delta Chi. Home: 4200 N Miller Rd Apt 422 Scottsdale AZ 85251-3631*

SMYTH, CORNELIUS EDMONSTON, retired hotel executive; b. N.Y.C., Aug. 20, 1926; s. Cornelius Joseph and Roberta Ernestine (Anderson) S.; m. Jeanne Laura Dillingham, Nov. 25, 1950 (dec. Oct. 1996); children: Cornelius E. Jr., Loretta M., William D., James B., Laura I., Robert B. BS in Econs., U. Pa., Phila., 1946. Cert. Hospitality Acct. Exec. Contr. Caesars Palace Hotel and Casino, Las Vegas, Nev., 1970-73, fin. v.p., 1974, adminstrv. v.p., 1975-77, exec. v.p., 1977-81; pres. Sands Hotel and Casino, Las Vegas, Nev., 1981-83; exec. v.p. Latin Am. ops. Caesars World Internat., L.A., 1983-89, pres. Mexican ops., 1989-90; bd. dirs. Inland Casino Corp., La Jolla, Calif.; cons., Coronado, Calif., 1994-97. Co-author: A Uniform System of Accounts for Hotels, 7th rev. edit., 1977. Lt. (j.g.) USNR, 1944-49. Named to U.S. Table Tennis Hall of Fame, 1996. Mem. Pi Gamma Mu, Sigma Chi. Democrat. Roman Catholic. Home: 263 Plz Marquessa Ct Henderson NV 89014-1433

SMYTH, DAVID SHANNON, real estate investor, commercial and retail builder and developer; b. Denver, May 13, 1943; s. William James and Constance Ruth (Sherman) S.; student Regis Coll., 1967-69, USAF Acad., 1961-65, U. No. Colo., 1965-67; m. Sharon Kaye Swiderski, Jan. 3, 1980; children: Julia Caitlin, Alexander Jeremiah, Matthew Davis; 1 son by previous marriage, Shannon David. Accountant, Colo. Nat. Bank, 1966-69; bus. analyst Dun & Bradstreet, 1969-70; pres., dir. Georgetown Valley Water & Sanitation Dist., 1973-74, Realists, Inc., 1973-74, Silver Queen Constrn. Co., 1973-74; v.p., sec., dir. Georgetown Assocs., Inc. (Colo.), 1970-74; pres., chief ops. officer Lincoln Cos., Denver, 1975-76; project mgr., sales mgr., prin. Brooks-Morris Homes, Fox Ridge, Colo., 1976-77; project mgr. U.S. West Homes, Denver, 1977-78; pres., dir. Denver Venture Capital, 1978-81; prin., dir., exec. v.p. Shelter Equities, Inc., 1982-87; prin., dir., exec. v.p. Comml. Constrn. Mgmt. Services, Inc., 1987-88, Shelter Equities, Inc., 1984-87; owner, dir., exec. v.p. Maple Leaf Realty Corp.; v.p., dir. Gibraltar Devel. Corp., Dominion Properties Ltd., 1978-82; investment dir. Van Schaack & Co., 1987-91; prin. investor, head devel. The Farkas Group, 1991-92; sr. residential loan officer, Freedom Mortgage Co., 1992-93; sr. loan officer, dir. builder mktg. NVR Mortgage Co., Englewood, Colo., 1994-96; sr. loan officer Market St. Mortgage, 1996-97; dist. builder account mgr. N.Am. Mortgage Co., Denver, 1997—. Served with USAF, 1961-65. Lic. real estate broker. Home: 8680 S Aberdeen Cir Highlands Ranch CO 80126 Office: NAm Mortgage Co 4949 S Syracuse St # 500 Denver CO 80237

SMYTH, THOMAS JENNER, economist, state official; b. Belvidere, Ill., Nov. 19, 1936; s. Thomas Joseph and Edna Ellen (O'Connor) S.; children: Judith A. Stoots, Steven S., Susan. BSEE, Va. Mil. Inst., 1958; BS in Comm. Engring., U.S. Navy Postgrad. Sch., Monterey, Calif., 1964; M.Engring. Adminstrn., George Washington U., 1970. Cert. econ. developer. Commd. USMC, 1958-79, advanced through grades to Lt. Col., ret., 1979; dir. purchasing Pacific Resources, Inc., Honolulu, 1979-83; prin. Bus. Devel. Assocs., Honolulu, 1984-85; divsn. adminstr. Hawaii Dept. Bus., Honolulu, 1985—. Chmn. Ala Moana Neighborhood Bd., Honolulu, 1988-92; treas. Downtown Neighborhood Bd., Honolulu, 1995—; bd. dirs. Hawaii Heart Assn., com. chair, 1981-87; bd. dirs., v.p. Pacific divsn. March of Dimes, 1986-88; bd. dirs. Diamond Head Theatre, 1990—. Recipient Cert. of Merit, Honolulu City Coun., 1993; named Dept. Mgr. of the Yr., State of Hawaii, 1994. Mem. Hawaii Soc. Corp. Planners (dir., v.p. 1991—). Home: 700 Richards St #2303 Honolulu HI 96813 Office: Hawaii Dept Bus Econ Devel and Tourism 250 S Hotel St #500 Honolulu HI 69813

SMYTHE, TED CURTIS, communications educator; b. Tacoma, Wash., May 6, 1932; s. Ted M. and Hilda May (Mastrude) S.; m. Barbara Ann Matthews, June 1, 1956; children: Timothy Neil, Randall Kent, Kristin Ann. BS, Sterling Coll., 1954; MS, U. Oreg., 1962; PhD, U. Minn., 1967. Dir. pub. relations Sterling Coll., Kans., 1956-60; prof. communications Calif. State U.-Fullerton, 1963-92, prof. emeritus; dist. scholar in residence Sterling Coll., Kans., 1993-97, writing cons. So. Calif. Edison, Santa Ana, 1965-67. Editor: Readings in Mass Communications, 1972 (Frank Luther Mott-Kappa Alpha award 1972), 12th edit., 1996; Issues in Broadcasting, 1975; mem. editorial bd. Journalism Quar., 1974, Journalism History, 1977. Contbr. articles to profl. jours. Served with U.S. Army, 1954-56. Named Disting. Prof. Calif. State U.-Fullerton, 1984, Disting. Alumnus, 1997. Mem. Assn. for Edn. in Journalism and Mass Communication, Journalism Historians Assn. (bd. dirs. 1992-95), Soc. Profl. Journalist. Democrat. Mem. Evang. Free Ch. Am. Home: 519 Swanson Ave Placentia CA 92870-2032 Office: Calif State U Dept Communications Fullerton CA 92634

SMYTHE, VALERIE ANN, special education educator; b. Sterling, Colo., July 2, 1962; d. Robert Jerome Kircher and Jean Elizabeth Seckler Austin; m. William Richardson Smythe, June 10, 1989; children: Robby, Nathan. BA in Elem. Edn., U. No. Colo., Greeley, 1984, Ma in Spl. Edn., 1989. Thr. 4th grade, coach Flagler (Colo.) Pub. Schs., 1985-89; tchr. spl. edn. Weld Schs. Dist. 6, Greeley, 1989-93, tchr. 3d and/or 4th grade, 1993—; dist. accelerated reading facilitator Centennial Elem. Weld Schs. Dist. 6, Greeley. Mem. ASCD, Coun. for Exceptional Children, Internat. Reading Assn., Phi Delta Kappa. Congregationalist. Home: 1129 72d Ave Greeley CA 80643

SNASDELL, SUSAN KATHLEEN, computer company executive; b. St. Louis, July 17, 1948; d. Russell John and Gertrude Burnett (Gassman) S. BA, So. Nazarene U., 1972. Office adminstr. Lake, Van Dyke & Browne Med. Group, Pasadena, Calif., 1972-83; founder, ptnr., adminstr. ComputerEase, Oxnard, Calif., 1984—. Contbr. articles to profl. jours. Mem. Better Bus. Bur., Oxnard C. of C. Office: ComputerEase 2361 Fairway Ct Oxnard CA 93030-7774

SNEE, LAWRENCE WARREN, geologist; b. Grove City, Pa., Dec. 6, 1947; s. William Warren and Ruth Elizabeth (Goehring) S.; m. Karen Ivy Lund, May 27, 1985 (div. Dec. 1994); children: Jens Erik, Torsten Anders. BS in Geology, Chemistry and Biology, Fla. State U., 1974; MS in Geology, Ohio State U., 1977, PhD in Geology, 1982. Geologist U.S. Geol. Survey, Reston, Va., 1981-83; prof. geology Oreg. State U., Corvallis, 1983-86; rsch. geologist U.S. Geol. Survey, Denver, 1986—; supr. Argon geochronology lab. U.S. Geol. Survey, Denver, 1986—, mem. adv. bd., 1990—, rsch. chief, 1994—; chief scientist Nat. Coop. Geol. Mapping Team, Ctrl. REgion, 1995—. Author/editor: Emeralds of Pakistan, 1989; contbr. articles to profl. jours. Sgt. USMC, 1966-69, Vietnam. Decorated Bronze Star; Rsch. grantee NSF, U.S. Geol. Survey. Mem. Geo. Soc. Am., Am. Geophys. Union, Soc. Econ. Geologists. Office: US Geol Survey Box 25046 MS913 DFC Denver CO 80225

SNELL, CHARLES MURRELL, physicist, astrophysicist; b. Johnson City, Tenn., Aug. 19, 1946; s. Murrell Watkins and Ruth (Freeman) S. BS, Vanderbilt Univ., 1967; MS, Univ. Ariz., 1969. Physicist U.S. Army Corps. Engrs., Livermore, Calif., 1971-73, Lawrence Livermore Lab., Livermore, 1973-78, Los Alamos (N.M.) Nat. Lab., 1978—. Contbr. over 100 articles to profl. publs.; patentee in field. With U.S. Army, 1969-71. Mem. Phi Beta Kappa. Office: Los Alamos Nat Lab Los Alamos NM 87545

SNELL, NED COLWELL, financial planner; b. Cowley, Wyo., May 16, 1944; s. Jay Hatton and Freda Hope (Colwell) S.; m. Barbara Anne Frandsen, Apr. 24, 1969; children: Taylor Anthony, Trevor Cameron. BA, U. Utah, 1969; CLU, Am. Coll., 1983, ChFC, 1985. English tchr. Granite Sch. Dist., Salt Lake City, 1969-71; ins. agt. Prudential Ins. Co., Salt Lake City, 1971-76; pres. Snell Fin. Corp., Salt Lake City, 1976—. Bd. dirs. Utah chpt. Arthritis Found., Salt Lake City, 1980-82, pres. 1982-83; missionary Mormon Ch. 1963-66; chmn. voting dist. 2604 Rep. Nominating Convs., 1986, 90. Recipient Golden Key Soc. Devel. award, 1990. Mem. NALU (Nat. Sales Achievement award 1971-89, Nat. Quality award), Am. Soc. CLU and ChFC (bd. dirs. Utah chpt. 1990-93, treas. 1993-94, v.p. 1994-96, pres. 1996-97), Million Dollar Round Table (knight 1988—), Salt Lake Assn. Life Underwriters (bd. dirs. 1974-76, 80-82). Republican. Home: 1101 S 2000 E Salt Lake City UT 84108-1971 Office: 1800 S West Temple Ste 416 Salt Lake City UT 84115-1878

SNELL, PATRICIA POLDERVAART, librarian, consultant; b. Santa Fe, Apr. 11, 1943; d. Arie and Edna Beryl (Kerchmar) Poldervaart; m. Charles Eliot Snell, June 7, 1966. BA in Edn., U. N.M., 1965; MSLS, U. So. Calif., 1966. Asst. edn. libr. U. So. Calif., L.A., 1966-68; med. libr. Bedford (Mass.) VA Hosp., 1968-69; asst. law libr. U. Miami, Coral Gables, Fla., 1970-71; acquistions libr. U. N.Mex. Law Sch. Libr., Albuquerque, 1971-72; order libr. Los Angeles County Law Libr., 1972-76, cataloger, 1976-90; libr. Parks Coll., Albuquerque, 1990-92; records technician Technadyne Engring. Cons. to Sandia Nat. Labs., 1992-93; libr. Tireman Learning Materials Ctr. U. N.Mex., Albuquerque, 1993-96, instr. libr. sci. program Coll. Edn., 1991—; rsch. technician City of Albuquerque, 1996—. Ch. libr.. Beverly Hills Presbyn. Ch., 1974-90, ch. choir libr., 1976-90. Southwestern Library Assn. scholar 1965. Mem. ALA, N.Mex. Libr. Assn., Pi Lambda Theta. Office: U N Mex Coll Edn EM/LS Program Ed Admin B 29 Albuquerque NM 87131

SNELL, RICHARD, holding company executive; b. Phoenix, Nov. 26, 1930; s. Frank L. and Elizabeth (Berlin) S.; m. Alice Cosette Wiley, Aug. 1, 1954. BA, Stanford U., 1952, JD, 1954. Bar: Ariz. Ptnr. firm Snell & Wilmer, Phoenix, 1956-81; pres., chmn., chief exec. officer Ramada Inc., Phoenix, 1981-89; chmn., chief exec. officer Aztar Corp., 1989-90, chmn., bd. dirs., 1990-92; chmn., chief exec. officer, pres. Pinnacle West Capital Corp., Phoenix, 1990—, bd. dirs.; bd. dirs. Bank One Ariz. Corp., Bank One Ariz. NA, Aztar Corp.; bd. dirs., chmn. Ariz. Pub. Svc. Co. Trustee Am. Grad. Sch. Internat. Mgmt., Phoenix; past pres. YMCA Met. Phoenix and Valley of Sun. With U.S. Army, 1954-56. Mem. ABA, Ariz. Bar Assn., Paradise Valley Country Club, Phoenix Country Club. Republican. Lutheran. Office: Pinnacle West Capital Corp 400 E Van Buren St Phoenix AZ 85004 also: Arizona Public Service Co PO Box 53999 # 9960 Phoenix AZ 85072-3999*

SNIDER, JANE ANN, elementary school educator; b. Inglewood, Calif., Nov. 18, 1939; d. Percy E. and Mamie D. (Gorman) S. MusB, U. So. Calif., 1962; MS, Azusa Pacific U., 1987. Cert. gen. elem. and spl. secondary music tchr. Tchr. 5th grade Centralia Sch. Dist., Buena Park, Calif., 1963—, mentor, tchr. computer tech., 1983—. Home: 1433 Royer Ave Fullerton CA 92833-4719

SNIEZEK, PATRICK WILLIAM, real estate loan officer; b. Zainesville, Ohio, Apr. 25, 1964; s. Richard Anton and Wanda Lee (Sir) S. BSBA in Mktg., U. Ariz., 1987. Customer svc. rep. Great Am. Bank, Tucson, 1983-85, customer svc. rep. II, 1985-87, real estate loan officer, 1987-91; real estate loan officer Waterfield Fin. Corp., Tucson, 1991-93; asst. v.p., br. mgr. Norwest Mortgage Inc., Tucson, 1993-96; br. mgr. The Bank of Ariz., Tucson, 1996—. Bd. mem. So. Ariz. Kidney Found., Tucson, 1987-88; bus. cons. Jr. Achievement, Tucson, 1987—; treas. Active 20/30 Club, Tucson, 1987-88, sec. 1988-89, bd. dirs., 1989-90. Named Outstanding Young Man of Yr., Outstanding Young Men of Am., Montgomery, Ala., 1988, Future Bus. Leader of Yr., Future Bus. Leaders of Am., Phoenix, 1988. Republican. Roman Catholic. Home: 3725 N Calle Perdiz Tucson AZ 85718-7215 Office: The Bank of Ariz 2100 N Kolb Rd Tucson AZ 85711

SNOOK, QUINTON, construction company executive; b. Atlanta, July 15, 1925; s. John Wilson and Charlotte Louise (Clayson) S.; student U. Idaho, 1949-51; m. Lois Mullen, Jan. 19, 1947; children: Lois Ann Snook Matteson, Quinton A., Edward M., Clayson S., Charlotte T. Rancher, Lemhi Valley, Idaho, 1942—; owner, mgr. Snook Constrn., Salmon, Idaho, 1952—; owner Snook Trucking, 1967—, Lemhi Posts and Poles, 1980—. Mem. Lemhi County Commn., Dist. 2, 1980-93. Named to Idaho Agrl. Hall of Fame, 1996. Mem. Am. Quarter Horse Assn., Farm Bur., Nat. Rifleman's Assn., Idaho Assn. Commrs. and Clerks (sec. 1986, v.p. 1987, pres. 1988), Am. Hereford Assn., Idaho Cattlemen's Assn., Elks. Republican. Episcopalian. Home: RR 1 Box 49 Salmon ID 83467-9701

SNOW, ALAN ALBERT, publisher; b. Van Nuys, Calif., July 20, 1946; s. Perry William and Virginia (Show) S. BA, Pepperdine U., L.A., 1969; MA, Sch. of Theology, Claremont, Calif., 1974; Magister Operae Onerosae (hon.), Inst. Antiquity-Christianity, Claremont, 1972; ThD, Andersonville Bapt. Sem., 1994. Dir., min. Ch. of the Ams., Balboa Island, Calif.; pres. Alan Alber Snow Ins. Agy. Farmers Ins. Group of Cos., Fountain Valley, Calif.; bd. dirs. Inst. for Study of Judeo-Christian Origins Calif. State U., Long Beach; mem. Jesus seminar Weststar Inst. Contbg. author to anthologies: The Book Your Church Does Not Want You to Read, 1993, 95, Sydney Omarr's Astrol. Guides for Your, 1994, 95, 96, 97. Mem. Am. Assn. Christian Counselors, Assn. Ind. Clergy, Nat. Notary Assn. (ethics com., Cert. Accomplishment), Am. Soc. Notaries, Dead Sea Scroll Rsch. Coun., Bibl. Archaeology Soc. Democrat. Home: 518 S Bay Front Newport Beach CA 92662

SNOW, JAMES HARRY, metallurgist, educator, aircraft planning executive; b. Inglewood, Calif., Jan. 7, 1949; s. Jack Norman and Georgiann H. S.; m. Darlene Angeline Pollo, Aug. 27, 1976 (div. June 1979); m. Wilma Susan Lewis, Aug. 17, 1986; children: Megan, Jaclyn, Brendan. AA, Orange Coast Coll., Costa Mesa, Calif., 1981; BA, Calif. State U., Long Beach, 1990, MA with honors, 1993. Cert. tchr., Calif. Metall. tech. ARCO Metals, Paramount, Calif., 1973-81; sr. quality control supr. Phelps Dodge Brass Co., City of Commerce, Calif., 1981-84; sr. prodn. controller Cerro Metals Co., Paramount, 1985-86; prin. specialist, group leader McDonnel Douglas Aircraft, Long Beach, 1986-94; adj. prof. Calif. State Univ., Long Beach, 1994—; tchr. Lakewood (Calif.) H.S., 1994—. Author: The Design and Construction of a Solar Powered Refrigeration System, 1993, American Kaizen, 1997. With USN, 1969-71, Vietnam. Mem. Am. Solar Energy Soc., Internat. Tech. Edn. Assn., Internat. Solar Energy Soc., Am. Philatelic Soc., Epsilon Pi Tau (pres. Alpha Phi 1994-95), Phi Kappa Phi (bd. dirs. 1994—), Phi Delta Gamma (bd.d irs. 1994—). Home: 20951 Glencairn Ln Huntington Beach CA 92646 Office: Calif State Univ Long Beach 1250 Bellflower Blvd Long Beach CA 90840

SNOW, MARINA SEXTON, author; b. Boston, Apr. 9, 1937; d. Charles Ernest Snow and Katherine Alice Townsend; m. Richard DeVere Horton, Aug. 30, 1958 (div. 1968); children: Heather Kertchem, James Horton; m. Charles A. Washburn, Jan. 7, 1978 (div. 1979). BA, U. Iowa, 1958; MA in Speech Pathology, N.Mex. State U., 1967; MA in Librarianship, San Jose State U., 1976; MA in Theatre Arts, Calif. State U., Sacramento, 1979. Cert. clin. competence Am. Speech and Hearing Assn. Tchr. ESL Inst. Colombo-Americano, Cali, Colombia, 1958-59; tchr. Las Cruces (N.Mex.) Pub. Schs., 1964-66; speech therapist Sutter County Schs., Yuba City, Calif., 1967-72; reference libr. Calif. State U. Libr., Sacramento, 1976-95. Contbr. articles to profl. jours.; author 2 plays: Apricot Coffee, Alkali Flat. Pres. Alkali Flat Neighborhood Assn., Sacramento, 1987-94. Mem. Sacramento Old City Assn.

SNOW, W. STERLING, secondary education educator, retired sports coach; b. Devils Lake, N.D., Feb. 14, 1947; s. Morgan Williams and Josephine Elizabeth Ann (Erickstad) S.; m. Barbara Kay Jolley, Aug. 29, 1976; 1 child, Michelle Rene. AB, U. Calif., Santa Cruz, 1970; postgrad., U. Calif., Santa Barbara, 1970-71; MA, Chapman Coll., 1976. Cert. secondary sch. tchr., Calif., Alaska, Ariz.; cert. in adminstrn., Calif., Ariz. Tchr., coach Monterey (Calif.) Peninsula Unified Sch. Dist., 1972-76; tchr., coach Anchorage (Alaska) Sch. Dist., 1976-96, athletic dir., 1987-92, tchr., 1992-96; sabbatical, 1996—; conf. asst. U. Calif., Santa Cruz, 1971-78. Bd. dirs. Dimond Alumni Found., Anchorage, 1987-92. Recipient Merit award for outstanding athletic program Alaska Dept. Edn., 1990, Appreciation award Dimond Alumni Found., 1990, Hall of Fame award, 1995. Mem. AAAS, ASCD, NSTA, Am. Chem. Soc., Nat. Assn. Biology Tchrs. (life), Nat. Interscholastic Athletic Adminstrs. Assn. (life), Alaska Sci. Tchrs. Assn., Alaska Athletic Adminstrs. Interscholastic Assn. (Athletic Dir. of Yr. 1990), N.Y. Acad. Scis., Kappa Delta Pi. Lutheran.

SNOWDEN, DAVID L., protective services official. Chief of police Costa Mesa, Calif. Office: 99 Fair Dr Costa Mesa CA 92626

SNOWHOOK, ANN LAFERTY, social services administrator; b. N.Y.C., May 25, 1929; d. Paul Gause and Anna Gladys (Braun) Laferty; m. John David Snowhook, Sept. 13, 1952; children: Eileen M., Elizabeth J., David P., J. Jordan, Nancy P. BA in Math., UCLA, 1953, postgrad., 1965, 70. Mathematician missiles divsn. The Rand Corp., L.A., 1951-52; substitute tchr. math. Spastic Children's Found., L.A., 1958-60; sec. women's aux. Exceptional Children's Found., L.A., 1960-63; chmn. and treas. parents group, chmn. fundraising, subsitute tchr. Exceptional Children's Class Pacific Palisades, L.A., 1963-73; chmn. area guild, mgr. sch. lunch program Corpus Christi Ch., L.A., 1972-74; statistician, rsch. asst. in mental retardation, family therapy and anorexia nervosa Neuropsychiatric Inst. UCLA, 1974-90; mem. program/policy bd. Kennedy Regional Ctr. for Developmentally Disabled, L.A., 1974-78; del. program devel. fund grants review Los Angeles County Area Bd. X, 1978-82; del. We. Regional Ctr. Assn. Regional Ctr. Contracting Agys., L.A., 1981-82; bd. dirs., pres., corp. sec. We. Regional Ctr. for Developmentally Disabled, L.A., 1978-82; bd. dirs., corp. sec., treas. Home Ownership Made Easy, L.A., 1988-91, Found. for Developmentally Disabled, L.A., 1982—; bd. dirs., corp. treas. Marian Homes for Physically Handicapped and Devel. Disabled, L.A., 1992—; rsch. assoc. Family Therapy: An Overview, 1980, Anorexia Nervosa: A Body Image Disturbance, 1978, Autism: A Study for Chromosomal Abnormalities, 1979, Family Therapy Today, Estrogen Therapy in Menopausal Women, 1991; rsch. cons. Estrogen Therapy in Menopausal Women, Family Therapy Today; bd. mem. Programs for the Developmentally Handicapped, 1995—, Easter Seals So. Calif., 1996—. Mem. Autism Soc. L.A. (v.p., program chair 1993-95, pres. 1995—). Roman Catholic. Home: 901 Iliff St Pacific Palisades CA 90272-3826 Office: 3424 Wilshire Blvd Los Angeles CA 90015

SNYDER, BEVERLY ANN, counselor, educator, therapist; b. Winthrop, Mass., Sept. 15, 1941; d. Blaine Jr. and Elsie Georgia (Johanson) Sweatt; m. Clarence Duke Snyder, Sept. 19, 1964 (div. Jan. 1984); children: Karen, Greg, Jon. BA, U. Fla., 1963; MEd, U. Cen. Fla., 1985, EdD, 1992. Lic. mental health counselor; cert. counselor, sch. counselor, Fla., adminstr., addictions prevention profl. Tchr. Northmont Jr. High, Dayton, Ohio, 1976-80; pers. mgr. Circus World, Orlando, Fla., 1980-81; pers. rep. CNA Ins. Co., 1981-82, therapist House of Hope, 1987-90, Greenhouse Counseling Ctr., 1990-92, Episcopal Counseling Ctr., 1990-92; resource counselor Orange County Pub. Schs., 1983-92; cons. Career Cons., Inc., Orlando, 1989-90, Ctr. for Counseling and Cons., Winter Park, Fla., 1990-92, Charter Counseling Ctr., 1991-92, U. Nebr., Kearney, 1992-95, Univ. Colo., Colorado Springs, 1995—. Editor: Developmental Guidance, 1990, Peer Counseling, 1990, Guidance Handbook, 1990. Vol. counselor House of Hope, Orlando, 1987; mem. adv. bd. Christian Svc. Ctr.-Fresh Start, Orlando, 1988; Crisis Ctr. vol. Orange County Mental Health, Orlando, 1989. Named Orange County Counselor of Yr., Orange County Schs., 1991; rsch. grantee Fla. Ednl. Rsch. Coun., 1991-92, Nebr. Dept. Edn., 1993-95. Mem. ACA, ASCD, Am. Sch. Counselors Assn., Mid. Sch. Assn., Am. Assn. Religious and Values Issues in Counseling (pres. 1990-92, Fla. and Nebr. exec. bd. 1990-95, nat. exec. bd. 1995—), Phi Delta Kappa. Episcopalian. Office: U Colo at Colorado Springs Sch Edn Colorado Springs CO 80933

SNYDER, CAROLE MARIE, parochial school educator; b. Burbank, Calif., Feb. 6, 1946; d. Raymond Eugene and Bernice Helen (Vandries) S. BA, St. Joseph's Coll., Bklyn., 1973. Cert. tchr. learning handicapped. Tchr. Sacred Hearts of Jesus and Mary Sch., Bklyn., 1964-65, 67-69, St. Cosmas and Damien Sch., Conshohocken, Pa., 1966-67; ednl. therapist Applied Learning Systems Inc., North Hollywood, Calif., 1969-82, St. Jude the Apostle Sch., Westlake Village, Calif., 1982—. Mem. Orton Dyslexia Soc., Coun. Exceptional Children, Nat. Cath. Edn. Assn., Nat. Inst. Dyslexia, Children and Adults with Attention Deficit Disorder. Democrat. Roman Catholic. Office: St Jude the Apostle Sch 32036 Lindero Canyon Rd Westlake Village CA 91361-4224

SNYDER, DAVID ALLEN, naval officer, surgeon; b. Portsmouth, Va., Nov. 8, 1948; s. William Allen and Betty Jane (Coffman) S.; m. Jan Karen Mitchell; children: Robert Patrick, Elizabeth Caroline. BA, U. Calif., Berkeley, 1970; MD, U. So. Calif., L.A., 1974; MPA, Troy State U., 1993. Diplomate Am. Bd. Surgery, Am. Bd. Med. Mgmt., Am. Coll. Healthcare Execs. Commd. ensign USN, 1970, advanced through grades to capt., 1988; intern and resident in surgery Naval Regional Med. Ctr., San Diego, 1974-79; staff surgeon Naval Regional Med. Ctr., Yokosuka, Japan, 1979-82; staff surgeon, quality assurance coord. Naval Hosp., Camp Pendleton, Calif., 1982-85; head dept. surgery Naval Hosp., Long Beach, Calif., 1985-87; staff, surgeon gen. of the Navy Bur. of Medicine & Surgery, Washington, 1987-88; chmn. surgery, dir. surg. svcs. Nat. Naval Med. Ctr., Bethesda, Md., 1988-93; exec. officer, chief med. staff Naval Med. Ctr., Oakland, Calif., 1993-94; commdr. Naval Med. Ctr., Oakland, 1994-96; force surgeon Surface Forces U.S. Pacific Fleet, 1996—; physician adv. bd. mem. Office of Champus, Aurora, Colo., 1989-92; assoc. prof. clin. surgery Uniformed Svcs. U. of the Health Scis., 1989-96. Contbr. articles to profl. jours. Sponsor Navy

League, San Francisco, 1993-96, Combined Fed. Campaign, San Francisco, 1993-96; facility sponsor ARC, San FRancisco, 1993-96; mem. ase Closure Coordinating Com., San Francisco, 1994-96. Decorated Legion of Merit. Fellow ACS, Am. Coll. Physician Execs.; mem. San Francisco Surg. Soc., Alpha Omega Alpha, Phi Beta Kappa. Office: US Pacific Fleet Naval Surface Force 2841 Rendova Rd San Diego CA 92155-5490

SNYDER, FRANCINE, psychotherapist, registered nurse, writer; b. Balt., Mar. 13, 1947; d. Jack and Naomi (Rapoport) S. AA, C.C. Balt., 1968; BA in Psychology, Antioch Coll. W, 1973; MA in MFCC, Azusa Pacific Coll., 1975; PhD in Clin. and Ednl. Psychology, Internat. Coll., 1981. RN, Hawaii; lic. marriage, family, and child counselor, Calif.; instr., Calif.; counselor, Calif; cert. instr. in Basic Cardiac Life Support, Am. Heart Assn. Staff & reliefnurse, crisis counselor Midway Hosp., L.A., 1972-77; counselor So. Calif. Counseling Ctr., L.A., 1972-77; counselor, exec. bd. mem., steering com. mem. Healing Ctr. for the Whole Person, Northridge, Calif., 1974-75; counselor The Family Home, North Hollywood, Calif., 1976; pvt. practice Beverly Hills, Calif., 1975-86; counselor St. Johns Mental Health Ctr., Santa Monica, Calif., 1977-79, Calif. Family Study Ctr., Burbank, 1979-80; pvt. practice Kauai, Hawaii, 1986—; clin. dir., therapist Kauai YWCA Sex Abuse Treatment Program, Hawaii, 1989-90; clin. cons. Iniki Ohana Project, Kapaa, Hawaii, 1993; student nurse Johns Hopkins Hosp., Balt., 1965-68; head and relief nurse, team leader, 1966-70; nurse Nix Meml. Hosp., San Antonio, Tex., 1970; staff nurse, team leader Cmty. Hosp. Chandler, Ariz.; cons. Slim Bionics Med. Group, L.A., 1974-75; instr. Pierce Coll., Woodland Hills, Calif., 1977, Saint Johns Med. Ctr., Santa Monica, Calif., 1977-79, Maple Ctr., Beverly Hills, Calif., 1979-80. Speaker in field. Mem. Am. Anorexia Nervosa/Bulimia Assn., Inc., Am. Mental Affiliates for Israel (exec. bd., head of allocations com.), Internat. Platform Assn., Assn. for Humanistic Psychology, Children's Coalition for TV, Ctr. for the Healing Arts, Alliance for Survival, UCLA Alumni Assn.; cons. Help Anorexia, Inc., Performance Design Syss. Home: PO Box 1303 Hanalei HI 96714-1303 Office: Kauai Counseling & Edn Ctr PO Box 1303 Hanalei HI 96714

SNYDER, HENRY LEONARD, history educator, bibliographer; b. Hayward, Calif., Nov. 3, 1929; s. Henry Runyon and Mary (Rosenberg) S.; m. Janette Marie Hannus, July 21, 1961; children: Michael Jesse, Christopher Henry, David Lyle. BA, U. Calif., Berkeley, 1951, MA, 1960, PhD, 1963. Sr. buyer Dohrmann Comml. Co., San Francisco, 1951-59; instr. to prof. U. Kans., Lawrence, 1963-78; assoc. dean to dean research adminstrn. U. Kans., 1967-78; prof. history, dean arts and scis. La. State U., Baton Rouge, 1979-86; prof. history U. Calif., Riverside, 1986—; dir. Ctr. for Bibliog. Studies, 1989—; dean humanities and social scis. U. Calif., Riverside, 1986; vis. lectr. Bedford Coll., U. London, 1965-66; Fulbright lectr., research scholar U. Hamburg, Fed. Republic Germany, 1974; dir. English Short Title Catalogue for N.Am., 1978—. Editor: The Marlborough Godolphin Correspondence, 1975; co-editor: The Scottish Heritage, 1981. Pres. Baton Rouge Opera, 1981-83, Riverside Opera, 1987-90; pres. United Way, Lawrence, 1977; bd. dirs. Arts and Humanities Com., Baton Rouge, 1981-85; Sigmund, Martin, Heller Traveling fellow U. Calif.-Berkeley, 1962-63. Am. Council Learned Soc. sr. fellow, 1969-70. Fellow Royal Hist. Soc. Gt. Brit. Bibliog. Soc. London; mem. Am. Soc. 18th Century Studies (pres. 1980-81), Conf. Brit. Studies (exec. com. 1978-83), Am. Hist. Assn., Internat. Fed. Librs. (chair rarebooks and ms. sect. 1995—). Republican. Congregationalist. Home: 220 Trinity Ave Kensington CA 94708-1139 Office: U Calif- Riverside Ctr for Bibliog Studies Riverside CA 92521-0154

SNYDER, JO ANNA W., cartographer, computer graphics designer; b. Atlanta, July 10, 1961; d. Joseph Hans Werner and Ruby Lee (Patty) Horton; m. Edward H. Snyder, Feb. 4, 1992. Grad. high sch., Ooltewah, Tenn., 1979; cert. computer drafting and design specialist, Charter Coll., Anchorage, 1994. Freelance graphics designer; typesetter, artist Printer's Workshop, Anchorage, 1984-85, Pip Printing, Anchorage, 1985-87; computer graphics designer BP Exploration (Alaska) Inc., Anchorage, 1987-92, cartographer, 1990-92; owner desktop pub. firm Graphics Alaska; freelance graphics designer, Wasilla, Alaska, 1989-94; CAD technician, then mktg. specialist New Horizons Telecom., Inc., Palmer, Alaska, 1994-96. Editor: Alaska Parenting Mag., 1996—. Checker Iditarod Trail Sled Dog Assn., Wasilla, 1990-91. Mem. NAFE, nat. Contract Mgmt. Assn., Nat. Computer Graphics Assn., Computer Graphics Network (founder, chmn. 1989-91). Home: HC 89 Box 330 Willow AK 99688-9704

SNYDER, JOHN DAVID, pediatric gastroenterologist, epidemiologist; b. Bakersfield, Calif., Dec. 2, 1947; s. David Henry and Margaret Louise (Salber) S.; m. Michele Lorraine Mietus, June 21, 1985; children: Michael David, Matthew Alan, Gregory John. AA, Bakersfield Coll., 1968; BS in Chemistry, U. Calif., Santa Barbara, 1970; MD, UCLA, 1975. Diplomate Am. Bd. Pediatrics with subspecialty in pediatric gastroenterology. Pediatric resident Duke U., Durham, N.C., 1975-78; epidemic intelligence svc. staff CDC, Atlanta, 1978-80, med. epidemiologist, 1980-81; fellow in gastroenterology Mass. Gen. Hosp., Boston, 1981-83; instr. pediatrics Harvard Med. Sch., Boston, 1983-85, asst. prof., 1985-91; assoc. prof. pediatrics U. Calif., San Francisco, 1991-95, prof. pediatrics, 1995—; med. epidemiologist WHO, Geneva, 1980—; cons. in field. Author/editor: Common Problems in Pediatric Gastroenterology and Nutrition, 1989; co-editor: Gastroenterology Section: First: Pediatric Medicine, 1993. Lt. comdr. USPHS, 1978-81. UCLA Regent scholar, 1966, U. Calif.-Santa Barbara Regent scholar, 1968. Fellow Am. Acad. Pediatrics; mem. Am. Gastroenterol. Assn., N.Am. Soc. Gastroenterology and Nutrition. Home: 144 Paloma Ave San Francisco CA 94127-2610 Office: Univ of Calif Med Ctr Box 0136 Dept Pediatrics 500 Parnassus Ave San Francisco CA 94122-2723

SNYDER, JOHN HENRY, computer science educator, consultant; b. Wichita, Kans., Mar. 16, 1947; s. Melvin Henry and Cathleen Ann (Collins) S.; m. Patricia Reilly, Mar. 11, 1984; children: Matthew Melvin George, Mark John Joseph. BA, U. Kans., 1970; MS, Nova U., Ft. Lauderdale, Fla., 1984. Cert. tchr. Nev., N.D. Computer sci. tchr. Hyde Park Jr. High Sch., Las Vegas, Nev., 1981-86, Chapparal High sch., Las Vegas, 1986-91, Cimarron Meml. High Sch., Las Vegas, 1991-94; chair dept. sci. & tech. Advanced Tech. Acad., Las Vegas, 1994—; copywriter pub. info. office CCSD, Las Vegas, 1982-84; chmn. gifted children spl. interest group, Am. Mensa, 1984; mem. tech. com. Nev. 2000 Task Force, 1994—, Nev. State Network Internet Com., 1994—; mem. sch. dist. tech. coord. task force, 1994—; cons. Office Supt. Clark County Sch. dist., Las Vegas, 1984, 85, IBM Corp., Atlanta, 1991—; systems analyst Homes & Narver, 1988 (summer); adminstrv. aide EG&G Energy Measurements, Las Vegas, 1989 (summer); adj. instr. computer sci. Nova U., 1984-93, U. Nev. Las Vegas, 1990—, The Meadows Sch., 1991-96; bd. dirs. Ctr. for Teaching Resources, The Mazer Corp., N.Y., Akron, Ohio, 1990—. Newsletter editor Nat. State Tchrs. of Yr., 1991—; contbr. articles to profl. jours. Co-chmn. Ednl. Exposition, Las Vegas, 1984; tech. cons. Harry Reid for U.S. Senate, 1986, 92; mem. Nevada 2000 Tech. Subcom., 1994—, Nev. State Network Internet Com., 1993—. Named Tchr. of Yr., State of Nev., 1989-90, U. Nev., Las Vegas, Southland Tchr. of Yr., 1990, Tandy Tech. Scholar, 1991, Nev. Educator of Yr., Milliken Family Found., 1992, Nev. Tchr. of the Yr. Microsoft Corp./Technology & Learning Mag., 1995; recipient Innovative Teaching award Bus. Week Mag., 1990, Mc Caulufffe fellowship, 1994l Impact Innovator grantee, 1996. Mem. NEA (Instrn. and Profl. Devel. chmn. 1979-80), ASCD, KC (sec., v.p., pres., past pres., local lodge newsletter editor), Am. Legion, Phi Delta Kappa (newsletter editor Overall Excellence award 1990). Democrat. Roman Catholic. Office: Advanced Tech Acad 2501 Vegas Dr Las Vegas NV 89106-1643

SNYDER, JOHN JOSEPH, optometrist; b. Wonewoc, Wis., June 30, 1908; s. Burt Frederick and Alta Lavinia (Hearn) S.; A.B., UCLA, 1931, postgrad., 1931-32; postgrad. U. Colo., 1936, 38, 40, 41, U. So. Calif., 1945-46; B.S. in Optometry, Los Angeles Coll. Optometry, 1948, O.D., 1949. Tchr., La Plata County (Colo.) Pub. Schs., 1927-28; supt. Marvel (Colo.) Pub. Schs., 1932-33; tchr. Durango (Colo.) High Sch., 1933-41; pvt. practice optometry, Los Angeles, 1952-72, Torrance, Calif., 1972-78; now retired. Former bd. dirs. Francia Boys' Club, Los Angeles; former pres. Exchange Club South Los Angeles, also sec. Mem. AAAS, Am. Inst. Biol. Scis., Am., Calif., Optometric Assn., Internat. Biog. Assn. Republican. Home: 25937 Reynolds St Loma Linda CA 92354-3962

SNYDER, JOHN MILLARD, recreation resources executive, educator; b. Chelsea, Mass., Apr. 3, 1946; s. John Henry and Grace (Eby) S.; m. Barbara Ripple, Nov. 8, 1969 (div. 1979); 1 child, Logan; m. Glenda Allene Snyder, Sept. 10, 1983; children: Erika, Kimberly. BA, Franklin & Marshall Coll., 1968; MS, Colo. State U., 1974, PhD, 1982; cert., Harvard Sch. Design, 1987. Econ. rsch. asso. Coll. Natural Resources, Ft. Collins, Colo., 1972-76; econ devel. City Devel. Dept., Kansas City, Mo., 1976-77; v.p. Oblinger Smith Corp., Denver, 1977-79; sr. resource analyst Abt Assocs., Denver, 1979-80; dr. devel. analysis URS Engrs., Denver, 1980-83; pres. Strategic Studies, Inc., Littleton, Colo., 1983—; pres. Glacier Bay Outfitters, 1990—; co-founder Ecotourism Internat., 1994—; dir. environ. policy and mgmt. U. Denver, 1990—; econ. faculty Regis U., 1984—. Author: (poems) A Far Off Place, 1995, Best Poems of 1995, 1995; contbr. articles to profl. jours. Econ. advisor Treas. and Gov. Colo., Denver, 1979-84; officer YMCA Guides Program, LIttleton, 1984-85; sr. advisor Spl. Family Recreation, Denver, 1985-90; benefactor Le Bal de Ballet, Denver, 1989—. 1st lt. U.S. Army military intelligence, 1968-72. Fellow nat. The Explorers Club, N.Y. Mem. Ctr. for Whale Studies, Stanford Libr. (assoc.), Denver Zoological Found., Nat. Parks and Conservation Assn., several environ. orgns., Phi Kappa Phi, Xi Sigma Pi. Office: Strategic Studies Inc 2275 E Arapahoe Rd Ste 303 Littleton CO 80122-1540

SNYDER, KELLY ANN, engineering company administrator; b. Seattle, June 26, 1968; d. Harold Carl and Amelia Jeanne (Smith) Ensor; m. Virgil Leighton Snyder, May 29, 1993. AA, Shoreline C.C., Seattle, 1989; BA, U. Wash., 1991. Office mgr. Aircraft Stds., Inc., Seattle, 1989-91; intern Bellevue (Wash.) C. of C., 1991, Puget Sound Power and Light Co., Bellevue, 1991, 1992-93; intern City of Bellevue Planning Dept., 1992, office asst., 1993; govt. affairs liaison Hedges and Roth Engring., 1993—. Mem. Advance Bellevue Leadership Program, 1996-97; bd. dirs. City of Bothell (Wash.) Pks. and Recreation Bd., 1996—. Mem. Am. Planning Assn., Master Builders Assn., Wash. Assn. Sewer and Water Dists. Episcopalian.

SNYDER, RICHARD GERALD, research scientist, administrator, educator, consultant; b. Northampton, Mass., Feb. 14, 1928; s. Grant B. and Ruth (Putnam) S.; m. Phoebe Jones, Mar. 2, 1949; children: Dorinda, Sherrill, Paul, Jeff, Jon, David. Student Amherst Coll., 1946-48; BA, U. Ariz., 1956, MA, 1957, PhD, 1959. Diplomate Am. Bd. Forensic Anthropology. Teaching asst. dept. anthropology U. Ariz., Tucson, 1957-58, assoc. rsch. engr. Applied Rsch. Lab., Coll. Engring., 1958-60, mem. staff Ariz. Transp. and Traffic Inst., 1959-60, assoc. prof. systems engring., 1960; chief phys. anthropology Civil Aeromed. Rsch. Inst., FAA, Oklahoma City, 1960-66, rsch. pilot, 1962-66, acting chief Protection and Survival Labs., 1963-66; mgr. biomechanics dept. Office of Automotive Safety Rsch., Ford Motor Co., Dearborn, Mich., 1966-68, prin. rsch. scientist, 1968; assoc. prof. anthropology U. Mich., Ann Arbor, 1968-73, prof., 1973-85, rsch. scientist Hwy. Safety Rsch. Inst., 1968-85, head biomed. dept., 1969-84, dir. NASA Ctr. of Excellence in Man-Vehicle Systems, 1984-85, prof. emeritus, 1985—, rsch. scientist emeritus, 1989—; pres. Biodynamics Internat., Tucson, Ariz., 1986—; pres., bd. dirs. George Snively Rsch. Found., 1992—; adj. assoc. prof. U. Okla., 1963; rsch. assoc. Zoller Lab. U. Chgo., 1964-65, rsch. assoc. dept. anthropology, 1965-67; assoc. prof. Mich. State U., East Lansing, 1967-68; cons. USAF Aerospace Med. Rsch. Labs., Nat. Acad. Scis., U.S. Dept. Transp., adv. com. Office Naval Rsch. Dept. Navy, numerous others. Assoc. editor: Jour. of Communication, 1961-63; cons. editor: Jour. of Biomechanics, 1967-81; editorial bd. Product Safety News, 1973—; adv. bd. Aviation Space and Environ. Medicine, 1980-91, 94—; contbr. chpts. to books and numerous articles to profl. jours. Judge, Internat. Sci. Fair, Detroit, 1968; mem. coun. Explorer Scouts, Ann Arbor, 1968-70; dir. Am. Bd. Forensic Anthropology, 1978-84, 85-91; dir. Snell Meml. Found., 1990—; bd. dirs. N.Mex. Rsch. Inst., 1996—. 1st lt. USAF, 1949-54, Korea. Recipient Met. Life award, Nat. Safety Coun., 1970; Arch T. Colwell Merit award Soc. Automotive Engrs., 1973; Award for Profl. Excellence Aerospace Med. Assn., 1978; Admiral Luis de Flores Flight Safety award Flight Safety Found., 1981; named to Safety and Health Hall of Fame Internat., 1993. Fellow Aerospace Med. Assn. (Harry G. Moseley award 1975, John Paul Stapp award in aerospace biomechanics 1994), Royal Anthrop. Inst., AAAS, Am. Anthropl. Assn., Am. Acad. Forensic Scis. (T. Dale Stewart award 1992), AIAA (assoc.); mem. Am. Assn. Phys. Anthropologists, Ariz.-Nev. Acad. Sci., Soc. Automotive Engrs. (Aerospace Congress award 1982, Tech. contributions to Air Transport Safety), Internat. Soc. Aircraft Safety Investigators, Aerospace Physiologists Soc., Sigma Xi, Beta Beta Beta. Republican. Congregationalist. Avocations: aviation, aerospace medicine, forensic anthropology. Home: 3720 N Silver Dr Tucson AZ 85749-9709 Office: Biodynamics Internat Tucson AZ 85749

SNYDER, SHERRY ANN, university administrator; b. Rochester, N.Y., July 5, 1950; d. Charles Donald and Patricia (Alderman) S. BA, Ashland (Ohio) U., 1972; MS, Nazareth Coll., Pittsford, N.Y., 1976; EdS, U. Colo., 1982; PhD, Colo. State U., 1997. Cert. secondary edn. adminstrn., reading specialist K-12. Reading tchr./cons. Boches #1 Monroe County, Fairport, N.Y., 1973-78; counselor/registrar Adams #12 Schs., Northglenn, Colo., 1979-84; instr. Front Range C.C., Westminster, Colo., 1984-86; instr. Loretta Heights Coll., Denver, 1986-87, dir., 1987-88; coord. acad. skills program U. Colo., Boulder, 1988—; participant U. Colo. Fellows Program, 1992-93, Leadership for a New Century, Tempe, Ariz., 1991-92. Author: (booklet) Study Smarter, 1994. Recipient Outstanding Young Woman award Outstanding Young Women Am., 1987. Mem. Internat. Reading Assn., Colo. Coun. Adult Educators and Cmty. Educators, Nat. Inst. for Leadership Devel. in Women. Democrat. Office: U Colo C B 107 Boulder CO 80309-0107

SO, GEORGE J. K., radiologist, researcher; b. Hong Kong, Apr. 22, 1962; s. Peter and Mary (Lee) S. Student, U. Mich., 1984; MS in Engring., U. Calif., Berkeley, 1987; MD, U. Chgo., 1991. Physician Cedars-Sinai Med. Ctr., L.A., UCLA Med. Ctr., L.A. Recipient Franklin Mclean Rsch. award U. Chgo., 1987; Golden Key scholar, 1983; U. Calif. San Francisco fellow, 1987. Mem. Radiol. Soc. N.Am., Am. Roentgen Ray Soc., Soc. Magnetic Resonance, Golden Key, Tau Beta Pi, Eta Kappa Nu. Office: UCLA Med Ctr 10833 LeConte MC 172115 Los Angeles CA 90024

SOBECK, GERALD ROBERT, quality assurance professional, professional baseball scout; b. San Francisco, Mar. 13, 1951; s. Joseph Ferdinand and Ann Marie (Kennedy) S.; m. Hson Lin Lee, Nov. 14, 1987; 1 child, Daniel Lee. BS in Analytical Mgmt., U.S. Naval Acad., 1974. Quality mgr. Advance Circuit, Santa Clara, Calif., 1985-88; quality engr. Singer Link Flight Simulation, Sunnyvale, Calif., 1988-91; mfg. engr. Amdahl Corp., Fremont, Calif., 1991-94; quality mgr. Phase II, San Bruno, Calif., 1994-95; dir. quality assurance Acute Tech., Milpitas, Calif., 1995—. Lt. comdr. USN, 1974-83. Mem. No. Calif. Baseball Scouts Assn., U.S. Naval Acad. Alumni Assn. Roman Catholic. Home: 1055 Ridgemont Dr Milpitas CA 95035-7838

SOBELLE, RICHARD E., lawyer; b. Cleve., Mar. 18, 1935. BA, Stanford U., 1956, JD, 1960; LLM, U. So. Calif., 1967. Bar: Calif. 1961, U.S. Supreme Ct. 1969. Exec. Tracinda Corp., Las Vegas. Mem. ABA (mem. corp., banking and bus. law sect. 1969—), State Bar Calif. (del. to conf. state bar dels. 1965-77, mem. exec. com. bus. law sect. 1977-78), L.A. County Bar Assn. (mem. exec. coun., jr. barristers 1965-68, mem. exec. com. bus. and corps. sect. 1973-75). Office: Tracinda Corp 4835 Koval Ln Las Vegas NV 89109-7308

SOBERON, PRESENTACION ZABLAN, state bar administrator; b. Cabambangan, Bacolor, Pampanga, Philippines, Feb. 23, 1935; came to U.S., 1977, naturalized, 1984; d. Pioquinto Yalung and Lourdes (David) Zablan; m. Damaso Reyes Soberon, Apr. 2, 1961; children: Shirley,Sherman, Sidney, Sedwin. Office mgmt., stenography, typing cert. East Cen. Colls., Philippines, 1953; profl. sec. diploma, Internat. Corr. Schs., 1971; student Skyline Coll., 1979, LaSalle Ext. U., 1980-82; AA, cert. in Mgt. and Supervision, Diablo Valley Coll. With U.S. Fed. Svc. Naval Base, Subic Bay, Philippines, clerical, stenography and secretarial positions, 1955-73, adminstrv. asst., 1973-77; secretarial positions Mt. Zion Hosp. and Med. Center, San Francisco, 1977, City Hall, Oakland, Calif., 1978; with State Bar Calif., San Francisco, 1978-79; secretarial positions gen. counsel div. and state bar court divsn., adminstrv. asst. fin. and ops. div., 1979-81, office mgr. sects. and coms. dept., profl. and pub. svcs. div., 1981-83, appointment adminstr. office of bar rels., 1983-86; adminstr. state bar sects. bus. law sect., estate planning, trust and probate law sect., labor and employment law section, office of bar rels., 1986-89, adminstr. antitrust and trade regulation law sect., labor and employment law sect., workers' compensation sect., edn. and meeting svcs., 1989-96, criminal law sect., 1996—, labor and employment sect., 1996—, internat. law sect., 1996—, workers' compensation sect., 1996—, edn. and meeting svcs., 1996—; disc jockey/announcer Philippine radio stas. DZYZ, DZOR and DWHL, 1966-77. Organizer Neighborhood Alert Program, South Catamaran Circle, Pittsburg, Calif., 1979-80. Recipient 13 commendation certs. and outstanding pers. monetary awards U.S. Fed. Svc., 1964-77, 20 Yr. U.S. Fed. Svc. pin and cert., 1975; Nat. 1st prize award for community svc. and achievements Nat. Inner Wheel Clubs Philippines, 1975; several plaques and award certs. for community and sch. activities and contbrns. Olongapo City, Philippines. Mem. NAFE, Am. Soc. Assn. Execs., N.Y.C. Olongapo-Subic Bay Assn. No. Calif. (Pittsburg rep. 1982-87, bus. mgr. 1988—, pub. rels. officer 1993-94), Castillejos Assn. of No. Calif. Roman Catholic. Home: 207 S Catamaran Cir Pittsburg CA 94565-3613 Office: State Bar of Calif 555 Franklin St San Francisco CA 94102-4456

SOBEY, EDWIN J. C., museum director, oceanographer, consultant; b. Phila., Apr. 7, 1948; s. Edwin J. and Helen (Chapin) S.; m. Barbara Lee, May 9, 1970; children: Ted Woodall, Andrew Chapin. BS, U. Richmond (Va.), 1969; MS, Oreg. State U., 1974, PhD, 1977. Rsch. scientist Sci. Applications, Inc., Boulder, Colo., 1977-79, div. mgr., 1979-81; exec. dir. Sci. Mus., West Palm Beach, Fla., 1981-88, Mus. Sci. and History, Jacksonville, Fla., 1988, Nat. Invention Ctr., Akron, Ohio, 1989-92, Fresno (Calif.) Met. Mus., 1993-95; ednl. cons., 1995—; exec. prodr. (t.v. show) Idea Factory, KFSN-30, Fresno, 1995—. Alumni v.p. Leadership Palm Beach County; expdn. leader Expdn. Tng. Inst., S.E. Alaska, 1980; mem. U.S. Antarctic Research Program, 1974. Author: Complete Circuit Training Guide, 1980; Strength Training Book, 1981; (with others) Aerobic Weight Training Book, 1982, Increasing Your Audience, 1989, Inventing Stuff, 1995, Wrapper Rockets and Trombone Straws-Science at Every Meal, 1996, Car Smarts, 1997; mem. editorial adv. bd. Invent Mag., 1989-92. Founder, bd. dirs. Visually Impaired Sports Program, Boulder, 1978-81; fitness instr. YMCA Boulder, 1977-81; convener 1st Nat. Conf. Sports for the Blind, 1979; bd. dirs. Leadership Palm Beach; vice chmn. County Com. on Artificial Reefs; treas. Leaderdeship Akron Alumni Assn., 1990-91, class pres. Leadership Akron; v.p. Ohio Mus. Assn., 1991-92, pres., 1992-93; co-host Blow the Roof Off Ednl TV show, 1992; bd. dirs. Fla. Mus. Assn., 1988-89; mem. adv. bd. Marine Sci. Inst., 1990—. Lt. USN, 1970-73. Fellow Explorers Club; mem. Marine Tech. Soc. (sect. chmn. 1982-84), Coral Reef Soc. (chpt. pres. 1982-87), Nat. Inventive Thinking Assn. (bd. dirs. 1989—). Home: 8806 N 5th St Fresno CA 93720-1724

SOBOLEWSKI, JOHN STEPHEN, computer information scientist, consultant; b. Krakow, Poland, July 14, 1939; came to U.S., 1966; s. Jan Zygmund and Stefania (Zwolinska) S.; m. Helen Skipper, Dec. 17, 1965 (div. July 1969); m. Carole Straith, Apr. 6, 1974; children: Anne-Marie, Elisa, Martin. BE, U. Adelaide, Adelaide, South Australia, 1962, ME, 1966; PhD in Computer Sci., Wash. State U., 1971. Sci. officer Weapons Research Establishment, Salisbury, South Australia, 1964-66; asst. prof. computer sci. Wash. State U., Pullman, 1966-73; dir. research, assoc. prof. U. Wash., Seattle, 1973-80, dir. computer svcs., 1980-88; assoc. v.p. computing U. N.Mex., Albuquerque, 1988—; cons. govt. and industry, Seattle, 1973—; mem. bd. trustees Fisher Found., Seattle, 1984—. Author: Computers for the Dental Office, 1986; contbr. articles to profl. jours. Served as engr. with Royal Australian Army, 1957-60. Australian govt. scholar, 1954-60, Elec. Res. Bd. scholar CSIRO, Melbourne, Australia, 1961-64. Mem. IEEE, Computer Soc. Roman Catholic. Home: 8501 Northridge Ave NE Albuquerque NM 87111-2107 Office: U NMex CIRT 2701 Campus Ave NE Albuquerque NM 87131

SOCHYNSKY, YAROSLAV, lawyer; b. Feb. 5, 1946. BA in English, Colgate U., 1967; JD, Georgetown U., 1970. Bar: Calif., N.Y. Assoc. White & Case, N.Y.C., 1970-71; law clerk to Hon. William T. Sweigert U.S. Dist. Ct. (no. dist.) Calif., 1971-73; assoc. Landels, Ripley & Diamond LLP, San Francisco, 1973-76; sr. ptnr. Landels, Ripley & Diamond, San Francisco, 1976—; lectr. Calif. Continuing Edn. Bar, 1985, Equity Asset Mgr.'s Assn., 1987, Calif. Dept. Real Estate, 1986-89). Originator, co-author California ADR Practice Guide, 1992; co-author Real Property Practice and Litigation, 1990; case and notes editor, mem. editorial bd. Georgetown Law Jour.; contbr. articles and monographs to profl. jours. Mem. ABA (chair litigation and dispute resolution com. sect. on real property, probate and trust, lectr. 1988, 89, 91), Am. Arbitration Assn. (cert. mediator, large and complex case panel, internat. panel, real property valuation panel, No. Calif. adv. coun., lectr. 1990, speaker various panels, No. Calif. Outstanding Mediator award 1991), San Francisco Bar Assn., San Francisco Lawyers Com. for Civil Rights under Law. Office: Landels Ripley & Diamond 350 The Embarcadero San Francisco CA 94105-1250

SOCWELL, MARGARET GERTRUDE OSBORN HARRIS, reading and language arts educator, consultant; b. Avoca, Iowa, Oct. 7, 1946; d. Fay and Mary Gertrude (Grote) Osborn; m. Richard John Socwell, Mar. 11, 1971 (div. May 1979); 1 child, Benjamin Adam. BS, Ohio State U., Columbus, 1968; MS, U. Wis., 1979. Cert. reading specialist, libr. media specialist, Spanish and French tchr., Ariz. Tchr. French Mason (Ohio) Pub. Schs., 1969-70; tchr. Spanish and French St. Matthias Cath. Girls H.S., L.A., 1970-71; tchr. French Whitewater (Wis.) Pub. Schs., 1971-72, tchr. Spanish, 1972-78; reading specialist Chilton (Wis.) Pub. Schs., 1978-79, Tolleson (Ariz.) Elem. Schs., 1979-80; tchr. reading and Spanish Deer Valley Unified Schs., Phoenix, 1980-88; tchr. reading Rio Salado C.C., Phoenix, 1987-91, tchr. lang. arts, 1989-93, tchr. social studies, 1993-96, libr. media specialist, 1996—; state forensics judge Whitewater Pub. Schs., 1974—; test designer Deer Valley Reading Curriculum Com., Phoenix, 1986-87, participant lang. arts pilot program Deer Valley Unified Sch. Dist., 1989; designer integrated social studies curriculum, 1994-96. Recipient grant Deer Valley Edn. Found., Inc., 1992. Mem. Internat. Assn. Near-Death Studies, Ariz. Reading Assn. Democrat. Office: Deer Valley Pub Schs #97 20402 N 15th Ave Phoenix AZ 85027-3636

SOEDER, DANIEL JOHN, geologist, hydrologist; b. East Cleveland, Ohio, Sept. 22, 1954; s. Bernard Ernest and Pauline Katherine (Klucher) S.; m. Janice Elizabeth McIntire, Aug. 27, 1976 (div. Mar. 17, 1995); children: Matthew Arnold, Elizabeth Anne, Kathleen Patricia. BS in Geology, Cleve. State U., 1976; MS in Geology, Bowling Green U., 1978. Field geologist Cleveland-Cliffs Iron Co., Morgantown, W.Va., 1978-81; assoc. geologist Inst. Gas Tech., Chgo., 1981-84, staff geologist, 1984-86, lab. supr., 1986-90; lab. scientist Foothill Engring. Cons., Golden, Colo., 1990-91; hydrologist U.S. Geol. Survey, Mercury, Nev., 1991-93, field ops. mgr., 1993-95; dep. mgr. geology program Yucca Mountain project U.S. Geol. Survey, Mercury, 1995—. Mem. Geol. Soc. Am., Am. Geophys. Union. Office: US Geol Survey PO Box 327 Mailstop 721 Mercury NV 89023

SOFAER, ABRAHAM DAVID, lawyer, legal advisor, federal judge, legal educator; b. Bombay, India, May 6, 1938; came to U.S., 1948, naturalized, 1959; m. Marian Bea Scheuer, Oct. 23, 1977; children: Daniel E., Michael J., Helen R., Joseph S., Aaron R., Raphael J. BA in History magna cum laude, Yeshiva Coll., 1962; LLB cum laude, NYU, 1965. Bar: N.Y. 1965. Law clk. to Hon. J. Skelly Wright, U.S. Ct. Appeals, Washington, 1965-66; to Hon. William J. Brennan, Jr., U.S. Supreme Ct., Washington, 1966-67; asst. U.S. atty. So. Dist. N.Y., N.Y.C., 1967-69; prof. law Columbia U., N.Y.C., 1969-79; judge U.S. Dist. Ct. for So. Dist. N.Y., 1979-85; legal advisor Dept. State, Washington, 1985-90; ptnr. Hughes Hubbard & Reed, Washington, 1991-94; George P. Shultz disting. scholar, sr. fellow Hoover Instn., Stanford U., 1994—; hearing officer N.Y. Dept. Environ. Conservation, 1975-76. Author: War, Foreign Affairs and Constitutional Power: The Origins, 1976; contbr. articles to legal, polit., fgn. jours.; editor-in-chief: NYU Law Rev, 1964-65. Served with USAF, 1956-59. Root-Tilden scholar NYU, 1965. Mem. Fed. Bar Assn., Am. Bar Assn., N.Y. Bar Assn., Am. Law Inst. Jewish. Office: Stanford Univ The Hoover Instn Stanford CA 94305-6010

SOFOS, JOHN NIKOLAOS, food science and microbiology educator; b. Arachneon, Greece, June 14, 1948; came to U.S., 1972; s. Nicholas John and Marina (Paspaliaris) S.; m. Helen Stamatatos, Oct. 21, 1978; children: Marina, Elvera. BS in Agriculture, Aristotle U., Thessaloniki, Greece, 1971; MS in Animal Sci., U. Minn., 1975, PhD in Food Sci., 1979. Research asst.

U. Minn., St. Paul, 1973-78, research assoc., 1978-80; asst. prof. animal sci., food sci. Colo. State U., Ft. Collins, 1980-84, assoc. prof., 1984-87, prof., 1987—. Contbr. articles to profl. jours. Fellow Inst. Food Technologists; mem. AAAS, Am. Soc. Microbiology, Am. Soc. Animal Sci. (meat rsch. award 1995), Am. Meat Sci. Assn. (disting. rsch. award 1994), Am. Acad. Microbiology Fellow, Internat. Assn. Milk, Food, Environ. Sanitarians (sci. co-editor Jour. Food Protection), AOAC Internat., Rocky Mountain Inst. Food Tech. (chmn. 1985-86), Sigma Xi, Gamma Sigma Delta, Phi Tau Sigma. Home: 1601 Sagewood Dr Fort Collins CO 80525-2057 Office: Colo State U Dept Animal Sci Fort Collins CO 80523

SOH, CHUNGHEE SARAH, anthropology educator; b. Taegu, Korea, May 1, 1947; came to U.S., 1970; d. Sang Yung and Ock Yun (Choi) S.; m. Jerry Dee Boucher. BA summa cum laude, Sogang U., 1971; postgrad., U. Calif., Berkeley, 1971; MA in Anthropology, U. Hawaii, 1983, PhD in Anthropology, 1987. Staff instr. English Korean Air Lines, Edn. & Tng. Ctr., Seoul, 1978-79; instr. anthropology Ewha Womans U., Seoul, 1985; asst. prof. U. Hawaii, 1990; asst. prof. anthropology Southwest Tex. State U., San Marcos, 1991-94; asst. prof. anthropology San Francisco State U., 1994-96, assoc. prof. anthropology, 1996—; guest lectr. Chaminade U. Honolulu, 1988; vis. asst. prof. anthropology U. Ariz., 1990-91; adj. prof. Intercultural Inst. Calif., 1997—; cons. in field. Author: Women in Korean Politics; contbr. articles to profl. jours. East-West Ctr. scholar, 1981-87; grantee NSF, 1985-86; fellow Korea Found., 1993, Japan Found., 1997. Fellow Am. Anthrop. Assn.; mem. Am. Ethnological Soc., Soc. Psychol. Anthropology, Assn. Asian Studies (exec. bd. Com. Women Asian Studies), Western Social Sci. Assn., Korean Assn. Womens Studies, Royal Asiatic Soc. Korean Br. Office: San Francisco State U Dept Anthropology 1600 Holloway Ave San Francisco CA 94132-1722

SOH, JOHN JUNGGWON, film editor, producer; b. Seoul, Korea, Sept. 11, 1929; came to U.S., 1953; s. Byungil Soh and Busun Park; m. Margaret D. Firmstone; children: Sharon Ruth, Bryan John, Susan Christine, Carol Anne. BA, UCLA, 1959. Film editor David L. Wolper Prodns., L.A., 1963-75; film editor, prodr. 20th Century Fox, L.A., 1975-77, Cousteau Soc., L.A., N.Y.C. and Paris, 1977-85; film editor Landsburg Co., L.A., 1986-87, QED Comms., L.A., 1987-92, Tufts U., Medford, Mass., 1994-95, Telescene Film Group, Montreal, Que., Can., 1995. Mem. NATAS (mem. motion picture editors exec. bd. 1995-96, Emmy award 1969), Am. Cinema Editors (Eddie award 1972, 87, 95). Buddhist.

SOHM, IRENE MAXINE, interior designer; b. Modesto, Calif., Aug. 22, 1949; d. Daniel Winfield and Fern Lea (Streeter) Ingwerson; m. David Sohm, June 17, 1972; children: Sarah, Jill. BA, Occidental Coll., 1971; MA, Calif. State U., Hayward, 1974; design cert., Cañada Coll., 1983. Cert. interior designer, Calif. Subs. tchr. Fremont (Calif.) Unified Sch. Dist., 1971-72, elem. music tchr., 1973-79; designer Kitchen & Bath Assoc., Palo Alto, Calif., 1983-85; pvt. practice Palo Alto, Calif., 1985-92; designer, ptnr. Interiors at the Village, Santa Rosa, Calif., 1992—; instr. Cañada Coll., Redwood City, Calif., 1991-92; interior design adv. com. Santa Rosa Jr. Coll., 1993—. Contbr. photographs to various newspapers and mags. 2d v.p. Santa Rosa Symphony League, 1994-96, 5th v.p., 1996—; bd. dirs. Occidental Coll. Bay Area Alumni, San Francisco, 1980-90; active Sonoma Valley Chorale, 1993-96, Santa Rosa Symphonic Chorus, 1996—. Recipient 1st Place lighting design award Nat. Home Furnishings League, 1983. Mem. Am. Soc. Interior Designers (profl. mem.; pres. Peninsula chpt. 1989-90, sec. Calif. North chpt. 1994-95, pres. Calif. North chpt. 1995-96, other com. chairs), Phi Beta Kappa. Office: Interiors at the Village 4000 Bastoni Ln Santa Rosa CA 95404-1249

SOHNEN-MOE, CHERIE MARILYN, business consultant; b. Tucson, Jan. 2, 1956; d. D. Ralph and Angelina Helen (Spiro) Sohnen; m. James Madison Moe, Jr., May 23, 1981. BA, UCLA, 1977. Rsch. asst. UCLA, 1975-77; ind. cons. L.A., 1978-83; cons. Sohnen-Moe Assocs., Tucson, 1984—. Author: Business Mastery, 1988, 2d edit., 1991; contbr. to Compendium mag., 1987-90, Massage Mag., 1992-94, 96—, Am. Massage Therapy Assn. Jour., 1989—. Vol. Am. Cancer Soc., Tucson, 1984—; mem. Ariz. Sonora Desert Mus., Tucson; pres. Women in Tucson, 1989. Recipient Outstanding Instr. award Desert Inst. of Healing Arts, 1992. Mem. NOW, ASTD (dir. mem. svcs. 1988, Achievement award 1987, Disting. Svc. award 1988, dir. mktg.), Nat. Fed. Independent Bus., Internat. Assn. Ind. Pubs., Pubs. Mktg. Assn., New Age Pub. and Retailing Alliance, Sierra Club. Office: Sohnen-Moe Assocs 3906 W Ina Rd # 200-348 Tucson AZ 85741-2261 *Personal philosophy: It is imperative to live your life and run your business according to your values. Be certain to maintain balance, perspective, and a good sense of humor.*

SOKOL, JAN D., lawyer; b. N.Y., May 27, 1952. BS magna cum laude, Rutgers U., 1974; JD Northwestern Sch. of Law, Lewis and Clark Coll., 1977. Bar: Oreg. 1978, U.S. Dist. Ct. (dist. Oreg.), U.S. Ct. Appeals (9th cir.) 1981, U.S. Claims Ct. 1982, U.S. Supreme Ct. 1982. Law clerk to Hon. George A. Juba U.S. Dist. Ct. (dist. Oreg.), 1978-79, law clerk to Hon. Gus J. Solomon, 1979-80, law clerk to Hon. James A. Redden, 1980; mem. Stewart, Sokol & Gray. Case note and comment editor Environmental Law, 1976-77. Mem. ABA (mem. forum com. on the construction industry, fidelity and surety, forest resources com.), Multnomah County. Address: Stewart Sokol & Gray 1500 Benjamin Franklin Plz One SW Columbia Portland OR 97258

SOKOLOFF, NAOMI BERYL, Hebrew language and literature educator; b. Washington, Nov. 15, 1953; d. Leon and Barbara (Snow) S.; m. Douglas H. Berry, May 24, 1981; children: Rachel Berry, Michelle Berry. BA, Swarthmore Coll., 1975; MA, Princeton U., 1979, PhD, 1980. Asst. prof. U. Ariz., Tucson, 1980-82; asst. prof. U. Wash., Seattle, 1985-92, assoc. prof., chair Near Ea. langs. and civilization, 1992—. Author: Imagining the Child in Modern Jewish Fiction, 1992; co-editor: Gender and Text in Modern Hebrew and Yiddish Literature, 1992, Infant Tongues: The Voice of the Child in Literature, 1994; mem. editorial rev. bd. Hebrew Ann. Rev., 1984-87, Hebrew Studies, 1984-85, 88-89. Grantee ACLS, 1987, NEH, 1988, Fulbright-Hayes Found., 1989. Mem. MLA (mem. Hebrew lit. discussion com., exec. com. 1993—), Assn. for Jewish Studies (bd. dirs. 1986-94). Jewish. Office: U Washington 229 B Denny Hall Box 353120 Seattle WA 98195-3120

SOKOLOV, JACQUE JENNING, health care executive, nuclear cardiologist; b. L.A., Sept. 13, 1954; s. Albert I. and Frances (Burgess) S. BA in Medicine magna cum laude, U. So. Calif., 1974, MD with hons., 1978; postgrad., Mayo Clinic, Rochester, Minn., 1978-81, U. Tex., Dallas, 1981-83. Med. diplomate. Cardiologist, nuclear cardiologist Health Sci. Ctr. U. Tex., 1981-84; chief med. officer Baylor Ctr. for Health Promotion Wellness & Lifestyle Corp., Dallas, 1985-87; v.p., dir. health care dept., corp. med. dir. So. Calif. Edison Co., Rosemead, Calif., 1987-92; CEO Advanced Health Plans, Inc./Sokolov Strategic Alliance, L.A., 1992—; chmn. bd. Coastal Physician Group, Inc., 1994—; cons. Health Care Strategic Planning Southwestern Bell, AT&T, Wang, Rosewood Corp., Dallas, 1985-87; bd. dirs. Calif. Health Decisions. Contbr. articles to profl. jours. Tech. advisor Coun. Social Security; bd. dirs. Washington Bus. Group Health. Grantee NIH, Bethesda, Md., 1983. Office: 9000 W Sunset Blvd Ste 800 Los Angeles CA 90069-5808

SOKOLOW, MAURICE, physician, educator; b. N.Y.C., May 19, 1911; s. Alexander and Anna (Spiegelman) S.; m. Ethel Schwabacher, June 30, 1941 (dec. 1970); children: Gail Anne, Jane Carol (dec.), Anne May. A.B. cum laude, U. Calif., Berkeley, 1932; M.D., U. Calif., San Francisco, 1936. Intern San Francisco Gen. Hosp., 1935-36; resident U. Calif., San Francisco, 1936-37, research fellow, 1939-40; resident New Eng. Med. Ctr., Boston, 1937-38; research fellow Michael Reese Hosp., Chgo., 1938-39; gen. practice medicine San Francisco, 1946-62; mem. faculty cardiovascular div. Sch. Medicine, U. Calif., San Francisco, 1946—, assoc. prof. medicine, 1952-58, prof., 1958-78, prof. emeritus, 1978—, chief electrocardiograph dept., chief hypertension clinic, 1946-78, chief cardiovascular div., 1954-73; program and founding dir. cardiology tng. grant USPHS, San Francisco, 1960-73; sr. mem. Cardiovascular Rsch. Inst., 1957—; cons. in field. Author: Clinical Cardiology; Contbr. articles to med. jours., texts.; mem. editorial bd.: Jour. Cardiovascular Medicine, 1975—, Western Jour. Medicine, 1946-68. Bd. dirs. Fromm Inst Life Long Learning, U. San Francisco. Served to lt. comdr. M.C. USN, 1942-46. Nat. Heart Inst. grantee, 1950-78; named U Calif. San Francisco Alumnus of Yr., 1986. Fellow Am. Coll. Cardiology (hon.); mem. Am. Fedn. Clin. Research (v.p. 1948-49), Assn. Univ. Cardiologists, Am. Soc. Clin. Investigation, Brit. Cardiac Soc. (corr.), Am. Heart Assn., San Francisco Heart Assn. (pres. 1950-51). Club: Menlo Circus. Home: 3452 Jackson St San Francisco CA 94118-2021 Office: U Calif Sch of Medicine San Francisco CA 94143

SOLAND, LISA ANN (ELIZABETH SOLAND), playwright, actress; b. Cheyenne, Wyo., Nov. 10, 1961; d. Norman Jerome and Ann Nesbit (Coolidge) S. Student, Rockford Coll.; BFA, Fla. State U., 1984. Owner Rose's Name Game Prodns., Sherman Oaks, Calif., 1993—; founding mem. Playwright's Wing, North Hollywood, Calif., 1990—. Author: (plays) The Name Game, 1993 (Harmony Gold award 1993), The Rebirth, 1996 (Hawthornden fellow 1996), Happy Birthday, Baby!, 1996. Mem., practitioner Ch. of Religious Sci.

SOLARI, R. C., heavy construction company executive; b. 1925; married. With Granite Construction Co., 1946—, formerly pres.; now pres., chief exec. officer, dir. Granite Construction Co., Watsonville, Calif., chmn. bd. dirs. Office: Granite Constrn Co PO Box 50085 Watsonville CA 95077-5085*

SOLBERG, MORTEN EDWARD, artist; b. Cleve., Nov. 8, 1935; s. Morten Odvard and Violet Elizebeth (Lamphier) S.; m. Marianne Louise Lyngso, July 5, 1958 (div. 1967); children, Morten Edward Jr., Eric Edward Collander; m. Marcia Louise Cox, 1967 (div 1971); 1 child, Scott Christopher; m. Lynda Suzanne Reinhart, 1971 (div.); 1 child, Brandalyn Michelle; m. Theresa Lee Lynch, June 25, 1977; children: Monet Lorraine, Tauna Elizabeth. Student, Cleve. Inst. Art, 196466. Artist Am. Greetings, 1959-61, art dir., 1961-68; artist Federman, Adams & Collipy Design Studio, 1961; with Buzza Cardozo Corp., Calif., 1968; founder Calif. Graphics Design Studio, 1971—; pub. Graybear Pub., Sebastopol, Calif., 1992—; selected as one of 5 artists to paint for book The Waterhole, South Africa, 1992. contbr. art, articles to jours. in field; mem. adv. bd. Informart Mag., 1993—; one-man shows include Challis Galleries, Laguna Beach, Calif., 1976, Nicolayson Art Mus., Casper, Wyo., 1990; exhibited in shows at Am. Watercolor Soc., Nat. Acad. Design, N.Y.C., 1962; represented in permanent collections Am. Bicentennial Mus., Calif., Nat. Acad. Design, N.Y.C., Nat. Gallery Art (Smithsonian Instn.), Washington, Nat. Mus. Am. Art, Washington, Cleve. Mus. Art, The White House, Leigh Yawkey Woodson Mus. Art, Hunt Wesson Foods, Am. Greetings Corp., Am. Artist Mag., Home Savs. and Loan, numerous pvt. collections. With USMC, 1958-1964. Named to U.S. Art Mag. Hall of Fame, 1993. Mem. Nat. Watercolor Soc. (bd. dirs., 1st v.p., top award 1970), Am. Watercolor Soc. (2 awards 1967, award 1974), , Soc. Animal Artists (award of excellence 1979, 86, 87, 88), Knickerbocker Artists (signature). Home: 68 Hickory Way Solvang CA 93436

SOLDAHL-HERTZOG, NAN, architectural illustrator, artist; b. Redwing, Minn., Aug. 29, 1949; d. Thomas Alan and Florence Lillian (Holm) Soldahl; m. Stephen Paul Hertzog, Nov. 26, 1969; children: Stephanie Marie, Ross Thomas. BA in Fine Arts, Calif. State U., Hayward, 1972. Art studio asst., art educator, artist H.A.R.D. Adobe Art Ctr., Castro Valley, Calif., 1971-73; graphic artist Dahlin (Calif.) Group Architects, 1988; prodn. asst. Forum Publs., Castro Valley, 1991-92; propr. Nan Soldahl Art Svcs., Castro Valley, 1985—. Exhibited in solo show at Rios-Lovell Winery, Livermore, Calif., also in numerous group shows in U.S., Australia, Russia. Vol. local sch. dist.; advocate Family Emergency Shelter Coalition. Mem. Lydia Women's Cir. Democrat. Lutheran. Office: 18392 Center St Castro Valley CA 94546-1608

SOLDATI, JOSEPH AURTHUR, language and literature educator; b. Rochester, N.H., Sept. 27, 1939; s. Secondo Joseph and Edna Dunklin (Garibaldi) S.; m. April Falkin, June 15, 1989. BA in Liberal Arts, Oglethorpe U., 1961; MA in English, U. Calif. Santa Barbara, 1968; PhD of English, Wash. State U., 1972. Reporter The Atlanta Constn., 1961; newsman UPI, Atlanta, 1961; tchr. sci. Am. Internat. Sch., Vienna, Austria, 1965-66; tchg. asst., asst. prof. Wash. State U., Pullman, 1968-72; asst. prof., assoc. prof. We. Oreg. State Coll., Monmouth, 1972-80, prof., 1980—; assoc. editor Calapooya Coll., Monmouth, 1987—; Fulbright lectr. U.S. Fulbright Assn., Ivory Coast, Africa, 1989-90, Mansura, Egypt, 1983-84. Author: Configurations of Faust, 1984, (poetry) Making My Name, 1992. Mem. Legacy Club Nature Conservancy, Portland, Oreg., 1989—. With U.S. Army, 1962-64, Vietnam. Fellow Salzburg Seminars, 1984; NEH summer seminar, 1982, 79. Mem. Assn. Literary Scholars and Critics, Mountain Writers Ctr., Oreg. Literary Arts Assn., Phi Kappa Phi (chpt. pres. 1986-87), Phi Sigma Iota. Democrat. Home: 1330 SW 3d Ave #PO5 Portland OR 97201 Office: Humanities Divsn We Oreg State Coll Monmouth OR 97361

SOLER, DONA KATHERINE, poet, artist, educator, metaphysical counselor, researcher, activist; b. Grand Rapids, Mich., Mar. 7, 1921; d. Melbourne and Katherine Anne (Herbst) Welch; 1 child, Suzette Maria. G-rad. Cath. Ctrl., Grand Rapids, Mich. Author: What God Hath Put Together, 1979, Our Heritage From the Angels, 1981, Expose the Dirty Devil, 1984, For Love of Henry, 1985, Greyball, 1986, House of Evil Secrets, 1986, Treasure Book of Poetry, 1990. Founder, 1st pres. South Coast Art Assn., San Clement, Calif., 1963-65, Orange Coast Cath. Christian Singles, 1970-73, Psychic Exchange, Orange County, 1979; founder, chief Lake Riverside Estates Communicators, Riverside, 1974-79. Recipient First Place Poetry awards, 1991-96, Rep. Am. Presdl. Legion Merit award; named Woman of Yr. for Poetry, 1992. Mem. Calif. Tax Reduction Movement Rep. Nat. Com. Mem. Animal Protection Inst., Greenpeace, People for the Ethical Treatment of Animals, Internat. Fund for Animal Welfare, Humane Soc. U.S., Am. Soc. Prevention Cruelty Toward Animals, In Def. of Animals., Physicians for Responsible Medicine, Humane Farming Assn.

SOLHEIM, WILHELM GERHARD, II, anthropologist, educator; b. Champaign, Ill., Nov. 19, 1924; s. Wilhelm Gerhard and Ragnhild Risty S.; m. Ludy Montenegro, Sept. 10, 1973; children: Gary, Kristina, Valerie, Lisa, Mei Li, Siri, Edwin. Student, U. Wis., 1943, U. Chgo., 1943-44; BS, U. Wyo., 1947; MA, U. Calif., 1949; PhD, U. Ariz., 1959. Mus. preparator Mus. Anthropology, U. Calif., Berkeley, 1947-49; research assoc. Mus. Archaeology and Ethnology, U. Philippines, 1950-54; lectr. U. East, Manila, 1950-52; provincial public affairs officer USIA, Manila, 1953-54; asst. prof. anthropology Fla. State U., Talahassee, 1960-61; mem. faculty dept. anthropology U. Hawaii, Honolulu, 1961—; prof. U. Hawaii, 1967-91, prof. emeritus, 1992—; asso. archaeologist Social Sci. Research Inst., 1963-67, archaeologist, 1967-70, editor, 1976-87; vis. prof. Inst. Advanced Studies, U. Malaya, Kuala Lumpur, Malaysia, 1979-80; v.p. R&D Transpacific Assocs., Guam, 1992; rsch. in Sarawak, The Philippines, 1983, Ea. Indonesia, 1990; dir. Ctr. for S.E. Asian Studies, U. Hawaii, 1986-89; bd. dirs. Austro-Tai Studies Inst., Guam, 1992—; cons. Irian Jaya, Indonesia archaeology program Irian Jaya Studies (a priority programme of Netherland Orgn. for Sci. Rsch.), 1994—. Author: The Archaeology of Central Philippines, 1964, (with Avelino M. Legaspi and Jaime S. Neri), Archaeological Survey in Southeastern Mindanao, 1979; founding editor Asian Perspectives, 1957-91, Asian and Pacific Archaeology Series, 1967-91, Southeast Asia and Korea from the Beginnings of Food Production to the First States, History of Humanity Vol. I, UNESCO, Paris, Prehistory and the Beginnings of Civilization, 1994, (with Charles Higham) Southeast Asia and the Pacific in History of Humanity, Vol. II From the Third Millenium to the Seventh Century B.C., UNESCO, Paris, 1996; contbr. articles to profl. jours. Trustee Hawaii Found. for History and Humanities, 1969-74, 1st v.p., 1972, 2d v.p., 1974; bd. dirs. Balik Bahay, Inc., Honolulu, 1976-93, pres., 1977-93; mem. Hawaii Com. Humanities, 1978-79. With USAF, 1943-46. Fulbright grantee, 1958-59, 83, 90; NSF grantee, 1963-66, 69-72; NEH fellow, 1967-68; Ford Found. grantee, 1972, 75-76; Vis. Scholar Exchange Program fellow Com. on Scholarly Communication with Peoples Republic of China, 1986. Fellow Philippine Assn. Advancement Sci. (founding); mem. Siam Soc., Société des Etudes Indochinoises, Royal Asiatic Soc. (Malaysian br.), Burma Research Soc., Assam Sci. Soc., Indian Archaeol. Soc., Soc. for East Asian Archaeology (hon.), Far-Eastern Prehistory Assn. (pres. 1971-76), Indo-Pacific Prehistory Assn. (pres. 1976-80, hon. mem.), Sigma Xi, Phi Kappa Phi, Phi Delta Theta. Office: U Hawaii Dept Anthropology 2424 Maile Way Honolulu HI 96822-2223

SOLIDAY, MICHAEL DAVID, secondary school and special educator; b. Durant, Okla., Feb. 25, 1955; s. David Norman and Patsy Marceille (Mansfield) S.; 7 foster children. BS in Edn., Utah State U., 1979; MEd in Deaf Edn., Western Md. Coll., Westminster, 1982; postgrad., Drake U., Des Moines, 1986. Itinerant tchr. for hearing impaired Heartland, AEA II, Des Moines, 1979-80, tchr. for hearing impaired, 1983-85, 86-87; tchr. Fla. Sch. for the Deaf, St. Augustine, 1982-83; liaison State of Iowa/Deaf Svcs., Des Moines, 1985-86; tchr. resource and 4th grade White Pine County Sch. Dist., Ely, Nev., 1987-94; tchr. h.s. deaf Brevard County Sch. Bd., Titusville, Fla., 1994—; resource tchr. White Pine County Sch. Dist., 1995—; chairperson sch. improvement Nev. Dept. Edn., Ely, 1990-91. Soccer commr. Steptoe Valley Soccer Club, Ely, 1989-94, 95-96; foster parent Children's Svcs., State of Nev., 1989-93; bd. dirs. White Pine County Family Recreation Ctr., 1996—. Named Nev. Tchr. of the Yr., Dept. of Edn., Nev., 1993; recipient Supt.'s award White Pine County Sch. Dist., 1992, 93. Home: PO Box 1167 Mc Gill NV 89318-1167 Office: McGill Elem Sch PO Box 1296 25 Avenue F St Mc Gill NV 89318

SOLIN, DAVID MICHAEL, state official; b. Summit, N.J., Mar. 17, 1967; s. Kenneth K. and Lillian R. Solin. BS in Fin. and Econs., San Francisco State U., 1990. Mktg. staff Wells Fargo Bank, San Francisco; lender First Interstate Bank, Denver; dep. state treas. State of Colo., Denver, 1995—. Mem. Bob Goen Celebrity Golf Tournament com. Make-A-Wish Found. of Colo., 1995—; mem. investment adv. com. U. Colo., 1995—; adv. bd. Correctional Industries, 1995—; vol. fireman, EMT Elk Creek Fire Dept., 1995—. With USMC, 1985-89. Republican. Office: Dept of Treasury 140 State Capitol Denver CO 80203

SOLINGEN, ETEL, social sciences educator. BA in Polit. Sci. and History, Hebrew U., Jerusalem, 1974, MA with distinction, 1977; MA, UCLA, 1981, PhD, 1987. Instr. dept. internat. rels. Hebrew U., 1974-78; teaching fellow dept. polit. sci. UCLA, 1981-84; rsch. fellow UCLA Ctr. for Internat. and Strategic Affairs, 1987-92; asst. prof. dept. politics and society U. Calif., Irvine, 1989-95, assoc. prof. dept. politics and society, 1995—. Author: Industrial Policy, Technology and International Bargaining, 1996; editor: Scientists and the State: Domestic Structures and the International Context, 1994; contbr. chpts. to books, numerous articles to profl. jours. NSF grantee, 1985, Sloan Found. awardee, 1987-88, UCLA postdoctoral fellow, 1989, ACLS grantee, 1994, NSF/Am. Polit. Sci. Assn. grantee, 1994; recipient rsch. grante Ctr. for Latin Am. Studies, 1982, UCLA, 1989, Columbia Found., 1989, U. Calif. Inst. on Global Conflict and Cooperation, 1989-90, 93, 94, John D. and Catherine T. Mac Arthur Found. Peace and Internat. Coop. award, 1995-96, U.S. Inst. of Peace, 1997—, others. Mem. Internat. Polit. Sci. Assn. (rsch. com. on sci. and politics, armed forces and soc. com.), Am. Polit. Sci. Assn., Internat. Studies Assn., Soc. for Women in Internat. Polit. Economy, Women's Caucus for Polit. Sci., Acad. Polit. Sci., Am. Acad. Polit. and Social Sci., Latin Am. Studies Assn., Pugwash Confs. on Sci. and World Affairs, Women in Internat. Security, Brazilian Soc. History of Sci. Office: Univ of Calif Dept Politics and Society Irvine CA 92717

SOLINGER, DOROTHY JANE, political scientist, educator; b. Cin., Sept. 20, 1945; d. Nathan and Janet Louise (Weiland) S.; m. Joel Falk, Sept. 2, 1973 (div. 1981); m. Thomas Paul Bernstein, Dec. 23, 1990. BA, U. Chgo., 1967; MA, Stanford U., 1970, PhD, 1975. From asst. prof. to assoc. dir. Asian studies program U. Pitts., 1975-84, adj. assoc. prof. polit. sci., 1975-84; vis. assoc. prof. U. Mich., Ann Arbor, 1985-86; from asst. prof. to prof. U. Calif., Irvine, 1986—; vis. assoc. prof. Stanford (Calif.) U., 1989-90; sr. rsch. assoc. East Asian Inst./Columbia U., 1994—; mem. editorial bd. U. Calif. Press, Berkeley, 1988-93; cons. World Bank, Washington, 1988, 93, 94. Author: Regional Government and Political Integration, 1977, Chinese Business Under Socialism, 1984, From Lathes to Looms: China's Industrial Policy, 1991, China's Transition from Socialism, 1993; editor: Three Visions of Chinese Socialism, 1984; editl. bd. The China Quar., Modern China. Fellow Hoover Instn., 1981, Woodrow Wilson Internat. Ctr. for Scholars, 1985, Com. on Scholarly Communication with the People's Republic of China, 1984, 85, 91-92, Am. Coun. Learned Socs., 1993. Mem. Am. Polit. Sci. Assn., Assn. for Asian Studies (chair China and Inner Asia coun. 1987-89). Democrat. Jewish. Office: U Calif Sch Social Sciences Irvine CA 92693

SOLL, LARRY, retired pharmaceutical executive; b. South Bend, Ind., Apr. 26, 1942; s. Manuel and Helenjean (Weiss) S.; m. Jean Newman (dec. 1971); m. Nancy Canavan Maron; children: William, Joel, Jonathan. AB, Princeton U., 1964; PhD, Stanford U., 1971. Vis. asst. prof. MIT, Cambridge, Mass., 1973-74; asst. prof. U. Colo., Boulder, 1974-82; pres. Synergen, Inc., Boulder, 1981-89, chief exec. officer, 1984-89, chmn., 1987-94. Chmn. Colo. Advanced Tech. Inst., Denver, 1986-87.

SOLMER, RICHARD, surgeon; b. South Bend, Ind., Feb. 11, 1947. MD, U. Mich., 1972. Diplomate Am. Bd. Plastic Surgery. Surgical intern Hosp. of the U. Pa., Phila., 1972-73; gen. surgical resident Calif. Hosp. Med. Ctr., L.A., 1976-80; plastic surgery resident Allentown (Pa.) Affiliated Hosp., 1980-82; pvt. practice Huntington Beach, Calif., 1982—. Fellow Am. Coll. Surgeons; mem. Am. Soc. Plastic and Reconstructive Surgery. Office: 17742 Beach Blvd Ste 300 Huntington Beach CA 92647-6835

SOLOMON, DOROTHY JEANNE ALLRED, writer, communications executive; b. Salt Lake City, June 24, 1949; d. Rulon Clark and Mabel (Finlayson) Allred; m. Bruce Craig Solomon, Jan. 8, 1968; children: Denise, Layla, Jeffrey, Laurie. BA in Lit., Theater and Speech, U. Utah, 1971, MA in Lit. and Creative Writing, 1981. Cert. secondary edn. educator, Utah. Storyteller, libr. Salt Lake City Libr., 1971; tchr. Salt Lake Sch. Dist., 1971-74; instr. U. Utah/Columbia Coll., Salt Lake City, 1974-80; writer-in-residence Utah Arts Coun., Salt Lake City, 1980-93; human devel. trainer Lifespring, San Rafael, Calif., 1983-87; media specialist Rivendell Psychiat. Hosps., West Jordan, Utah, 1987-90; curriculum writer Positive Action Pub., Twin Falls, Idaho, 1990-96; v.p. Rising Star Comm. and Team Resource Assocs., Salt Lake City, 1994—; bd. dirs. Rising Star Comm. Author: In My Father's House, 1984 (1st prize Biography, 1981, Pub. prize 1982), Inside Out: Creative Writing, 1989, Of Predators, Prey and Other Kin, 1996 (1st prize Non-fiction 1996); author (stories in anthologies) Sister Wife, 1995, Manna in the Desert, 1996, Remember Who You Are, 1994; screenwriter: In My Father's House, 1986-87. Bd. dirs. The Children's Ctr., Salt Lake City, 1982-85, Writers at Work, Park City, Utah, 1986-89, Lifespring Found., San Rafael, Calif., 1985-89; mem. curriculum com. Salt Lake Sch. Dist., 1971-74; coord. (with Bruce Solomon) lit. arts Utah Arts Festival "Performing Word", Salt Lake City, 1982; vol. Big Sisters, Salt Lake City, 1970-71; coord. cmty. edn. Rivendell Conf., West Jordan, Utah, 1987-89. Recipient Disting. Journalism 1st prize Am. Acad. Pediat., San Francisco, 1979, 1st prize feature writing Sigma Delta Chi, Salt Lake City, 1979, 1st prize essay Utah Original Writing Contest, Salt Lake City, 1995. Mem. LDS Ch.

SOLOMON, EZRA, economist, educator; b. Rangoon, Burma, Mar. 20, 1920; came to U.S., 1947, naturalized, 1951; s. Ezra and Emily (Rose) S.; m. Janet Lorraine Cameron, May 7, 1949; children—Catherine Shan, Janet Ming, Lorna Cameron. A.B. (hons.), U. Rangoon, 1940; Ph.D., U. Chgo., 1950. Instr. U. Chgo., 1948-51, asst. prof. fin., 1951-55, assoc. prof., 1955-57, prof., 1957-61; Dean Witter prof. fin. Stanford U., 1961-71, 73-90; dir. Internat. Ctr. Mgmt. Edn.; mem. Coun. Econ. Advisers, 1971-73. Author: The Theory of Financial Management, 1963, Money and Banking, 5th edit, 1968, The Management of Corporate Capital, 1959, Metropolitan Chicago: An Economic Analysis, 1958, The Anxious Economy, 1975, An Introduction to Financial Management, 2d edit, 1980, Beyond the Turning Point, 1981; editor: International Patterns of Inflation— A Study in Contrasts, 1984, Jour. Bus. 1953-57; bd. editors Jour. of Finance, 1965-66, Jour. Bus. Finance, 1969-73, Jour. Quantitative and Financial Analysis, 1969-71. Served as lt., Burma div. Royal Naval Vol. Res., 1942-47. Mem. Am. Econ. Assn. Home: 775 Santa Ynez St Stanford CA 94305-8478 Office: Stanford Univ Grad School of Busines Stanford CA 94305

SOLOMON, JULIUS OSCAR LEE, pharmacist, hypnotherapist; b. N.Y.C., Aug. 14, 1917; s. John and Jeannette (Krieger) S.; student Bklyn. Coll., 1935-36, CCNY, 1936-37; BS in Pharmacy, U. So. Calif., 1949; postgrad. Long Beach State U., 1971-72, Southwestern Colls., 1979, 81-82, San Diego State U., 1994—; PhD, Am. Inst. Hypnotherapy, 1988; postgrad. San Diego State U., 1994—. m. Sylvia Smith, June 26, 1941 (div. Jan. 1975);

children: Marc Irwin, Evan Scott, Jeri Lee. Cert. hypnotherapist; cert. hypnoanaesthesia therapist. Dye maker Fred Fear & Co., Bklyn., 1935; apprentice interior decorator Dorothy Draper, 1936; various jobs, N.Y. State Police, 1940-45; rsch. asst. Union Oil Co., 1945; lighting cons. Joe Rosenberg & Co., 1946-49; owner Banner Drug, Lomita, 1949-53, Redondo Beach, Calif., 1953-72, El Prado Pharmacy, Redondo Beach, 1961-65; pres. Banner Drug, Inc., Redondo Beach, 1953-72, Thrifty Drugs, 1972-74, also Guild Drug, Longs Drug, Drug King, 1976-83; pres. Socoma, Inc. doing bus. as Lee & Ana Pharmacy, 1983-86, now Two Hearts Help Clinic, 1986—. Charter commr., founder Redondo Beach Youth Baseball Council; sponsor Little League Baseball, basketball, football, bowling; pres. Redondo Beach Boys Club; v.p. South Bay Children's Health Ctr., 1974, Redondo Beach Coordinating Coun., 1975; bd. dirs. So. Bay Assn. Little Theatres, 1972-75; actor in 8 shows; founder Redondo Beach Community Theater, 1975; actor Man of La Mancha Vangard Theatre, San Diego, 1995; active maj. gift drive YMCA, 1975; mem. SCAG Com. on Criminal Justice, 1974, League Calif. Environ. Quality Com., 1975; mem. Dem. State Cen. Com., Los Angeles County Dem. Cen. Com.; del. Dem. Nat. Conv., 1972; chmn. Redondo Beach Recreation and Parks Commn.; mem. San Diego County Parks Adv. Commn., 1982; mem. San Diego Juvenile Justice Commn., 1986-92; mem. San Diego County Adv. Com. Adult Detention, 1987-92; mem. human resource devel. com., pub. improvement com. Nat. League of Cities; v.p. Redondo Beach Coordinating Coun.; councilman, Redondo Beach, 1961-69, 73-77; treas. 46th Assembly Dist. Coun.; candidate 46 Assembly dist. 1966; nat. chmn. Pharmacists for Humphrey, 1968, 72; pres. bd. dirs. South Bay Exceptional Childrens Soc., Chapel Theatre; bd. dirs. so. div. League Calif. Cities, U.S.-Mex. Sister Cities Assn., Boy's Club Found. San Diego County, Autumn Hills Condominium Assn. (pres.), Calif. Employee Pharmacists Assn. (pres. 1985), Our House, Chula Vista, Calif., 1984-86; mem. South Bay Inter-City Hwy. Com., Redondo Beach Round Table, 1973-77; mem. State Calif. Commn. of Californias (U.S.-Mexico), 1975-78; mem. Chula Vista Safety Commn., 1978, chmn., 1980-81; chmn. San Diego County Juvenile Camp Contract Com., 1982-83; mem. San Diego County Juvenile Delinquency Prevention Commn., 1983-85, 89-91, San Diego County Juvenile Justice Commn., 1986-91, San Diego County Adv. Com. for Adult Detention, 1987-91; spl. participant Calif. Crime and Violence Workshop; mem. Montgomery Planning Commn., 1983-86; mem. Constnl. Observance Com., 1990-93, Troubled Teenagers Hypnosis Treatment Program, 1989—. With USCGR, 1942-45. Recipient Pop Warner Youth award, 1960, 1962, award of merit Calif. Pharm. Assn., 1962, award Am. Assn. Blood Banks, 1982. Diplomate Am. Bd. Diplomates Pharmacy Internat., 1977-81; Fellow Am. Coll. Pharmacists (pres. 1949-57); mem. South Bay Pharm. Assn. (pres.), South Bay Councilman Assn. (founder, pres.), Palos Verdes Peninsula Navy League (charter), Am. Legion, U. So. Calif. Alumni Assn. (life), Assn. Former N.Y. State Troopers (life), AFTRA, Am. Pharm. Assn., Nat. Assn. Retail Druggists, Calif. Pharmacists Assn., Calif. Employee Pharmacist Assn. (bd. dirs. 1980-81), Hon. Dep. Sheriff's Assn., San Ysidro C. of C. (bd. dirs. 1985-87), Fraternal Order of Police, San Diego County Fish and Game Assn., Rho Pi Phi (pres. alumni). Club: Trojan (life). Lodges: Elks (life), Masons (32 deg.; life), Lions (charter mem. North Redondo). Established Lee and Ana Solomon award for varsity athlete with highest scholastic average at 10 L.A. South Bay High Schs. in Los Angeles County and 3 San Diego area South Bay High Schs.

SOLOMON, MARK A., lawyer; b. Cedar Rapids, Iowa, Aug. 30, 1950. BA summa cum laude, Calif. State U., San Jose, 1972; JD magna cum laude, U. Santa Clara, 1975. Bar: Calif. 1975, Nev. 1976. Mem. Lionel Sawyer & Collins, Las Vegas, Nev. Mem. ABA, State Bar Calif., State Bar Nev., Clark County Bar Assn. Office: Lionel Sawyer & Collins 1700 Bank Am Plz 300 S 4th St Las Vegas NV 89101-6014

SOLOMON, NORMAN, author, columnist; b. Washington, July 7, 1951; s. Morris Jacobson and Miriam (Abramowitz) S.; m. Cheryl D. Higgins, May 31, 1996. Freelance journalist, 1974—; syndicated columnist Creators Syndicate, L.A., 1992—; exec. prodr. Nat. Radio Project, San Francisco, 1995—; pub. spkr. and lectr., 1977—; assoc. Fairness and Accuracy In Reporting, N.Y.C., 1989—. Author: The Power of Babble, 1992, False Hope: The Politics of Illusion in the Clinton Era, 1994; co-author: Adventures in Medialand, 1993 (Hugh M. Hefner 1st Amendment award), Wizards of Media Oz, 1997. Office: PO Box 13193 Oakland CA 94661

SOLOMON, RHONDA HOPE, school and educational psychologist; b. L.A., Dec. 1, 1962; d. Jerry and Lynn (Cabin) S. BA in Psychology and Child Devel., Calif. State U., Northridge, 1985, MA in Psychology, 1987; PhD in Psychology, Calif. Grad. Inst., 1994. Lic. ednl. psychologist, Calif. Play therapist, children's counselor family stress program San Fernando Valley Child Guidance Clinic, Van Nuys, Calif., 1981-84; sch. psychologist, cons., presenter L.A. Unified Sch. Dist., 1987—; pvt. practice ednl. psychology, 1987—. Crisis counselor, helpline worker Haven Hills Shelter for Battered Women, 1983-84. Mem. APA (assoc.), Nat. Assn. Sch. Psychologists, Calif. Assn. Sch. Psychologists, Calif. Psychol. Assn., Western Assn. Psychologists, L.A. Assn. Sch. Psychologists (pres.), L.A. County Psychol. Assn., Psi Chi. Home: PO Box 260726 Encino CA 91426-0726 Office: LA Unified Sch Dist Dept Spl Edn/Infant-Presch HeadStart Unit 936 Yale St Los Angeles CA 90012

SOLOMON, SUSANNA, electrical engineer, novelist; b. Boston, June 1, 1949; d. Arthur Kaskel and Jean Blanchard (Roth) S.; children: Alissa, Chris. BA, Sonoma State U., 1972; BS, San Francisco State U., 1987. Journalist various newspapers and mags., 1972-81; engr. Winzler & Kelly, Santa Rosa, Calif., 1993—. Spkr. to high schs., colls. and elem. schs., 1990—. Mem. IEEE-Indsl Application Soc. (treas., program chmn., publicity chmn. San Francisco 1992—). Office: Winzler & Kelly 495 Tesconi Cir Santa Rosa CA 95401

SOLOW, HERBERT FRANKLIN, film producer, writer; b. N.Y.C., Dec. 14, 1930; s. Morris David and Frances Louise (Birnbaum) S.; children: Jody, Bonnie, Jamie; m. Yvonne Fern, 1996. AB, Dartmouth Coll., 1953. Agt. William Morris Agy., N.Y.C., 1954-58; dir., exec. NBC, N.Y.C., 1958-59, Los Angeles, 1958-60, CBS, Los Angeles, 1961-63; v.p. Desilu Studios, Los Angeles, 1964-69; v.p. prodn. Paramount TV, Los Angeles, 1969; v.p. worldwide prodn. Metro-Goldwyn-Mayer, Los Angeles, 1969-73; pres. Solow Prodn. Co., Los Angeles, 1976-79; v.p. Sherwood Prodns., Los Angeles, 1980-83; ind. producer, writer Los Angeles, 1984—. Mem. Writers Guild Am., Dirs. Guild Am., Acad. Motion Picture Arts and Scis., Acad. TV Arts and Scis.

SOLOWAY, JAY STEPHEN, consulting firm executive; b. Bklyn., Mar. 19, 1956; s. Martin and Joan (Jacobs) S. BA, Columbia U., 1978; MBA, U. Pa., 1980. Buyer Abraham & Straus, Bklyn., 1980-84; divsn. mgr. May Co. Dept. Stores, L.A., 1985; mgr. tng. and devel. Hartmarx Specialty Stores, Western U.S., 1986-90; mgr. mgmt. devel. Thrifty Drug Stores, L.A., 1990-92; v.p., cons. Drake Beam Morin, L.A., 1992-96; sr. v.p., mng. dir. So. Calif., Nev. Drake Beam Morin, Pasadena, Calif., 1996—. Democrat. Jewish. Office: Drake Beam Morin 35 N Lake Ave Pasadena CA 91101-4110

SOMANI, ARUN KUMAR, electrical engineer, educator; b. Beawar, India, July 16, 1951; came to the U.S., 1985; s. Kanwar Lal and Dulari Devi (Mundra) S.; m. Deepa-Toshniwal, Jan. 21, 1976 (dec. 1985); children: Ashutosh, Paritosh; m. Manju-Kankani, July 6, 1987; 1 child, Anju. BS with honors, B.I.T.S., Pilani, India, 1973; MTech, IIT, Delhi, 1979; MSEE, McGill U., 1983, PhD, 1985. Tech. officer Electronics Corp. India, Hyderabad, 1973-74; scientist Dept. Electronics, Delhi, 1974-82; asst. prof. dept. elec. engring. U. Wash., Seattle, 1985-90, assoc. prof. elec. engring. and computer sci. and engring., 1990-95, prof. elec. enring. and computer sci. engring., 1995—. Designer Proteus multi computer system for automated classification of objects; patentee in field; contbr. over 100 articles to profl. jours., chpts. to books. Mem. IEEE (sr.), Assn. for Computing Machinery, Eta Kappa Nu. Hindu. Home: 16609 126th Ave NE Woodinville WA 98072-7979 Office: U Wash Dept Elec Engring Ft # 10 Seattle WA 98195

SOMERSET, HAROLD RICHARD, retired business executive; b. Woodbury, Conn., Sept. 25, 1935; s. Harold Kitchener and Margaret Mary (Roche) S.; m. Marjory Deborah Ghiselin, June 22, 1957 (dec. Jan. 1984); children: Timothy Craig, Paul Alexander; m. Jean MacAlpine DesMarais, Jan. 2, 1985; stepchildren: Cheryl Lyn DesMarais, James Fenelon DesMarais. B.S., U.S. Naval Acad., 1957; B.C.E., Rensselaer Poly. Inst., Troy, N.Y., 1959; LL.B., Harvard U., 1967. Bar: Mass. 1967, Hawaii 1973. Commd. ensign U.S. Navy, 1957, advanced through grades to lt., 1961; service in U.S. and Hawaii; resigned, 1964; with firm Goodwin, Procter & Hoar, Boston, 1967-72; corp. counsel Alexander & Baldwin, Inc., Honolulu, 1972-74, v.p., gen. counsel, 1974-78, group v.p.-sugar, 1978-79, exec. v.p.-agr., 1979-84; with Calif. & Hawaiian Sugar Co., San Francisco, 1984-93, exec. v.p., chief operating officer, 1984-88, pres., chief exec. officer, 1988-93, bus. cons., 1994—; bd. dirs. Longs Drug Stores Corp., Brown and Caldwell, PLM Internat., Inc., Cornnuts, Inc. Trustee San Francisco Nat. Maritime Mus., Carquinez Strait Preservation Trust (mgmt. com., pres.). Mem. St. Mary's Coll. Sch. Edn. (adv. coun.). Home and Office: 19 Donald Dr Orinda CA 94563-3646

SOMMER-BODENBURG, ANGELA, author, artist; b. Reinbek, Kreis Storman, Germany, Dec. 18, 1948; came to U.S., 1992; d. Karl-Heinz and Anneliese Schockert; m. Burghardt Bodenburg, Dec. 27, 1978; 1 child, Katja Sommer. Student, Secondary Sch. Econs., 1968, U. Hamburg, 1968-72. Cert. asst. master for intermediate and secondary schs. Tchr. Secondary Sch., Hamburg, Germany, 1972-84. Author: (book series) The Little Vampire, 1979-88, Anton and The Little Vampire, 1989, 1993, Schokolowski, 1991-93, numerous others; (picture book) Gerneklein, 1990, Benjamin Biber, 1994, others; (poetry) Ich lieb dich trotzdem immer, 1982, various others; exhibited in shows at San Diego Mus. Art, 1995, Athenaeum Music and Arts Libr., La Jolla, Calif., 1996, Arveda Gallery, La Jolla, 1996. Home: PO Box 1577 Rancho Santa Fe CA 92067

SOMMERS, KAREN ROSE, editor, writer; b. Auburn, Wash., June 17, 1947; d. Arthur Emil and Mary Kathlyn (Thomas) Jorgensen; m. Ronald D. Baird; children: Lori Baird, Nathan Baird. AAS, Edmonds C.C., Lynnwood, Wash., 1988; BA in Polit. Sci., Botany, U. Wash., 1992. Free lance editor, writer Seattle, 1986-93, Fullerton, Calif., 1993-94, Colo. Springs, Colo., 1994-96; tech. editor Loral Command and Control Systems, Colo. Springs, 1995-96; editor Univ. N. Mex. Engring. and Rsch. Divsn., Colo., Springs, 1996; tech. writer MCI, Colo. Springs, 1997. Author: (books) The Web, 1994, Suffer My Children, 1995, Breaking the Web, 1996; editor: (books) The Magical Tooth Fairy, 1996, Legacy of Peace: Mountain with a Mission, 1996; contbr. articles and essays to social and polit. sci. jours. Ch. pianist and cellist, various chs., Kent. Wash., 1976-82; vol. Women's Transitional Living Ctr., Fullerton, Calif., 1982-84; Sunday Sch. tchr. First Luth. Ch., Fullerton, 1983-84; vol. Woman's Polit. Caucus, Seattle, 1984-85; campaign worker Ken Eikenberry for Atty. Gen., Seattle, 1984, John B. Still for Dist. 1 Rep., Seattle, 1984-82; tchg. asst. Seattle and Edmonds pub. schs., 1985-92; founder food program for the homeless, Edmonds, Wash., 1987, others. Recipient Comty. Svc. scholarship Western State U., Coll. of Law, Fullerton, Calif., 1993. Mem. Phi Theta Kappa (v.p. 1987=88), Tri Beta. Home and Office: PO Box 8091 Colorado Springs CO 80931

SOMMERS, SHARI CATHERINE, management executive; b. Danville, Ill., July 31, 1950; d. Warren Albert and Shari Bernard (Hill) S.; m. Robert Wightman, Apr. 21, 1990; 1 child, Shane Anthony. BA in Polit. Sci. with distinction, U. Ill at Chgo., 1980; cert. legal asst., Roosevelt U., Chgo., 1980. Mgr., legal support AMOCO Corp., Chgo., 1981-86; legal asst. supr. Skadden, Arps, Slate, Meagher & Flom, Chgo., 1986-88; v.p., gen. mgr. Templeton & Assocs., Chgo., 1989-93; vol. St. Bonaventure Indian Mission and Sch., Thoreau, N.Mex., 1993-95; chairperson Strengthening Ministries Diocese Gallup, N.Mex., 1994-96; co-dir. Ctr. Action & Contemplation, Albuquerque, 1996—; mem. adv. bd. dirs. Roosevelt U. Lawyer's Asst. Program, 1985-88. Participant Conclave of Legal Assns., Baton Rouge, 1988. Mem. ABA, Ill. Paralegal Assn. Legal Asst. Mgmt. Assn. (v.p. Cen. region 1986, sec. 1987, adminstrv. v.p. 1988, bd. dirs. 1986-88). Republican. Roman Catholic.

SOMMERS, WILLIAM PAUL, management consultant, think tank executive; b. Detroit, July 22, 1933; s. William August and Mary Elizabeth (Baietto) S.; m. Josephine A. Sommers; children: William F., Clare M., John C. Hughes, Joanna M. Weems, Russell L. Hughes. B.S.E. (scholar), U. Mich., 1955, M.S.E., 1956, Ph.D. (Riggs fellow, Texaco fellow, Univ. fellow), 1961. Research asso. U. Mich. Inst. Sci. and Tech., Ann Arbor, 1958-61; chief chem. propulsion space and missile systems Martin Marietta Corp., Balt., 1956-58, 61-63; v.p. Booz, Allen & Hamilton, Inc., Bethesda, Md., 1963-70; pres. Tech. Mgmt. Group Booz, Allen & Hamilton, Inc., 1973-79, sr. v.p., 1979-92; exec. v.p. Iameter, Inc., San Mateo, Calif., 1992-94; pres., CEO SRI Internat., Menlo Park, Calif., 1994—; bd. dirs. Kember Fin. Svcs., Rohr Inc., Therapeutic Discovery Corp., Litton Inc. Contbr. articles to profl. jours., also chpt. in book. Pres. Washington chpt. U. Mich. Alumni Club, 1970-71; v.p. Wildwood manor Citizens Assn., 1968-70; chief Adventure Guide program YMCA, 1971-72; bd. visitors Coll. Engring. U. Calif., Davis; mem. nat. adv. bd. Coll. Engring. U. Mich.; mem. conf. bd. Internat. Coun. on Innovation and Tech. Mem. Columbia Country Club, Willow Bend Country Club, Sigma Xi, Tau Beta Pi, Pi Tau Sigma. Republican. Roman Catholic. Home: 2181 Parkside Ave Hillsborough CA 94010-6452 Office: SRI Internat 333 Ravenswood Ave Menlo Park CA 94025-3453

SONENBERG, MAYA, writer, educator; b. N.Y.C., Feb. 24, 1960; d. Jack Sonenberg and Phoebe (Rubin) Helman-Sonenberg. BA in English, Wesleyan U., Middletown, Conn., 1982; MA in Creative Writing, Brown U., 1984. Lectr. Sonoma State U., Rohnert Park, Calif., 1986; instr. Chabot Coll., Hayward, Calif., 1989-90; asst. prof. Oreg. State U., Corvallis, 1990-93; asst. prof. dept. English U. Wash., Seattle, 1993—; panelist Artist Trust, Seattle, 1994; editor Calyx Books, Corvallis, 1993—; manuscript reviewer St. Martin's Press, N.Y.C., 1992—. Author: Cartographies, 1989; contbr. stories to Chelsea, Grand Street, Am. Short Fiction. Recipient Drue Heinz Lit. prize U. Pitts. Press, 1989; MacDowell Colony fellow, Peterborough, N.H., 1987; Humanities Ctr. faculty fellow Oreg. State U., 1992-93; U. Wash. grantee, 1994. Mem. MLA, Assoc. Writing Programs, Pacific N.W. Am. Studies Assn. Office: University of Washington Dept English Box 354330 Seattle WA 98195

SONES, LEON ISAAC, psychiatrist; b. Chelsea, Mass., Jan. 9, 1928; s. Barnet and Rose (Lang) S.; m. Gittelle M. Sones, July 15, 1951; children: Aaron, Daniel, David. AA, UCLA, 1951; BA, U. Calif., Berkeley, 1952; MD, U. Calif., San Francisco, 1955. Diplomate Am. Bd. Psychiatry. Intern Harbor Gen. Hosp., Torrance, Calif., 1955-56; resident in psychiatry UCLA, 1956-59; staff psychiatrist Mental Hygiene Clinic, L.A., 1959-60; pvt. practice Beverly Hills, Calif., 1959—; clin. instr. psychiatry UCLA, 1959-72, asst. clin. prof., 1972—; attending psychiatrist Cedars-Sinai Hosp., L.A., 1962—, founder, dir. Consultation and Liaison Svc., 1966-77, attending chief, 1983-87. Tech. sgt. U.S. Army, 1946-48, Japan. Mem. Am. Psychiat. Assn., So. Calif. Psychiat. Soc. Office: 435 N Bedford Dr Ste 400 Beverly Hills CA 90210-4315

SONNENBERG, FRANCES, sculptor, educator; b. Bklyn.; children: Brad, Ronni. Collections and gallery exhibitions world-wide. Mem. Am. Soc. Contemporary Artists, Nat. Assn. Women Artists, N.Y. Soc. Women Artists. Home: 1010 Paseo De La Cuma Santa Fe NM 87501

SONNENFELD, ALBERT, French language and comparative literature educator, food historian; b. Berlin, July 22, 1934; came to U.S. 1938; s. Arthur and Anni (Lichtenstein) S.; m. Portia B. Leys, June 15, 1955 (div. 1986); children: Mark David, Carole Marie Geithner; m. Noel Riley Fitch, Aug. 23, 1987. AB, Oberlin (Ohio) Coll., 1955; AM, Princeton U., 1957, PhD, 1958. Prof. French and comparative lit. Princeton U., 1958-86; M.F. Chevalier prof. French and dept. chmn. U. So. Calif., L.A., 1986—; vis. prof. Dartmouth Coll., UCLA, U. Wis., NYU, CUNY, also others; cons. Linguaphone Inst., London, 1974—; food critic; restaurant cons.; chmn. exec. bd. City Smarts, Inc., 1996—. Author: L'Oeuvre poetique de Tristan Corbiere, 1961, Crossroads, 1982, Thirty-Six French Poems, 1961; co-author: Temoins de l'Homme, 1965. Fulbright fellow, 1966-67; NEH fellow, 1978-79, 80, 83; recipient Raubenheimer Outstanding Faculty award, U. So. Calif., 1990. Mem. Am. Inst. Wine and Food (bd. dirs. 1989-95), The Athenaeum (London), Phi Beta Kappa. Home: 11829 Mayfield Ave Apt 303 Los Angeles CA 90049-5791 Office: U So Calif 126 University Pk Los Angeles CA 90089

SONNENFELD, SANDI, writer; b. Queens, N.Y., May 22, 1963; d. Fred I. and Myra G. (Gever) S.; m. Warren A. Berry, Sept. 6, 1992. BA in English/Dance, Mount Holyoke Coll., 1985; MFA in Creative Writing, U. Wash., Seattle, 1989. Adj. English instr. Seattle Cmty. Coll., 1989-91, Pierce Coll., Puyallup, Wash., 1991-95; devel. coord. Hope Heart Inst., Seattle, 1995-96; dir. devel. Tacoma Actors Guild, 1996-97; freelance writer, Federal Way, Wash., 1989—; planning com. co-chair Northwest Bookfest, Seattle, 1995—. Author: Case Study Harvard Bus. Rev., 1994, 95; contbg. author Litary Anthology, 1995, (short story) Sex and the City, 1992. Mem. Nat. Assn. Am. Pen Women, Artist Trust, Mount Holyoke Coll. Club Puget Sound (pres. alumnae club 1996-97). Democrat. Jewish. Home: 37136 4th Ave SW Federal Way WA 98023

SOO HOO, WAYNE EDWARD, orthopedic trauma clinical nurse specialist; b. Oxnard, Calif., Oct. 16, 1959; s. Edward W. and Patricia J. (Latham) S. H. BSN, Azusa Pacific U., 1984, MS in Nursing, 1991; postgrad., U. So. Calif., 1993—. RN, Calif.; cert. in med.-surg. nursing ANCC. Staff nurse neurosurgery ward Los Angeles County-U. So. Calif. Med. Ctr., L.A., 1984-86, staff nurse orthopaedic stepdown unit and admitting area, 1986-88, asst. nurse mgr. orthopaedic stepdown unit, 1988-89, nursing care specialist orthopaedic complex, 1990-91, clin. nurse specialist, 1991—; mem. adj. faculty Los Angeles County Med. Ctr. Sch. Nursing, fall 1990. Recipient productivity award Los Angeles County Dept. Health Svcs., 1989, 90. Mem. Nat. Mgmt. Assn. (charter), Sigma Theta Tau (Iota Sigma). Office: LA Co - U So Calif Med Ctr Gen Hosp 1200 N State St Rm 10-141 Los Angeles CA 90033-4525

SOONG, MELVIN KAIPOLEIMANU, circuit court judge; b. Kapaa, Kauai, Hawaii, Aug. 24, 1934; s. Kion and Mary Ann (Wong) S.; m. Barbara Anne Nelson, Oct. 19, 1958; children: Sharon Kaiulani Odom, Michael Kaipoleimanu, Randall Kawelolani, David Kanoa. BA, San Jose State, 1957; JD, Santa Clara U., 1963. Policeman San Jose Police Dept., 1956-57; dep. atty. gen. State of Hawaii, Honolulu, 1963-69, dep. dir. of taxation Gov.'s Cabinet, 1969-74; lawyer Honolulu, 1974-78; asst. U.S. atty. Fed. Dist. Hawaii, Honolulu, 1978-81; dist. ct. judge Hawaii State Judiciary, Honolulu, 1981-90, cir. ct. judge, 1990—; adminstrv. judge Dist. Ct. 1st Cir., Honolulu, 1987-90. 1st lt. U.S. Army, 1957-59; with U.S. Army Res., 1957-87, col. ret. Mem. Hawaii Judges Assn., ROA, U.S. Army War Coll. Office: Hawaii State Judiciary 777 Punchbowl St Honolulu HI 96813-5018 Home: 422 Iliaina St Kailua HI 96734-1809

SOOS, RICHARD ANTHONY, pastor; b. Passaic, Calif., Apr. 24, 1955; s. Richard A. and Shirley M. (Schneider) S.; m. Beverly J. Dauphinais, Aug. 27, 1987; children: Leann, Erin, Sarah, Richie. Student, San Jose State U., 1982-86; Bachelors Degree, Bethany Bible Coll., 86; Masters Degree, Bethany Bible Sem., 1993. Editor Realities Libr., San Jose, 1969—; pastor Redwood Family Chapel, San Jose, 1990—; web programmer Poets Park, San Jose, 1994—. Author: Why Poetry, 1972 (Poetry Shell award 1972), A Foreign Landscape, 1988, Garden Songs, 1994; editor Poet's Park, 1994 (Yahoo award 1996). With U.S. Army, 1973-74. Home: 2745 Monterey Hwy Spc 76 San Jose CA 95111-3130

SOOTER, WILL JAMES, executive search consultant; b. Waynesville, Mo., Nov. 16, 1950; s. Will Jennings and Hilda A. (Makurath) S. BS in Natural Resources Mgmt., Calif. Poly. State U., 1976. Mem. U.S. Peace Corps., The Philippines, 1976-78; scientific technician NOAA, San Diego, 1978-83; staff Scripps Inst. Ocean, U. Calif., San Diego, 1983-84; dir. sales Voice Link Sys., San Diego, 1984-86; sales engr. AMP Product Corp., San Diego, 1986-87; mgr. western region Rochester Corp., San Diego, 1987-90; pres., founder WJ Sooter Assoc., Inc., San Diego, 1990—. Mem. IEEE, Pacific Telecomm. Coun.

SORBY, J(OSEPH) RICHARD, artist, educator; b. Duluth, Minn., Dec. 21, 1911; s. Joseph Austin and Lydia A. (Esterly) S.; m. P. Elizabeth Ferguson, Dec. 9, 1950. B.A., U. Northern Colo., 1937, M.A., 1952; postgrad., UCLA, 1953, U. of Americas, 1952, U. Colo., 1954. Instr. art Greeley High Sch., Colo., 1937-41; asst. prof. art U. Nebr., Lincoln, 1941-43; assoc. prof. art U. Denver, 1946-59; prof. design and painting Calif. State U., San Jose, 1959-72, prof. emeritus, 1972—; guest prof. Southern Utah U., Cedar City, June, July 1964; rep. by Spectrum Gallery, Estes Park, Colo.; artist in residence Casa de las Campanas, Rancho Bernardo, Calif., 1988—. Exhibited in numerous nat. competitive exhbns. including Rocky Mountain Nat. Watermedia Exhbn. and various publ. collections. Served with USN, 1943-46, lt. comdr. USNR, ret. Recipient Purchase award Joslyn Art Mus., Omaha, Mid-Am. Annual, William Rockhill Nelson Gallery, Kansas City, Nat. Watercolor Competition, Washington, Denver Art Mus., Mus. N.Mex., Southwestern Artist's Annual; selected for U.S. nat. traveling exhbn. Mem. Fifteen Colo. Artists (pres. 1957-58), Retired officers Assn., Mil. Order World Wars, East Bay Art Assn. (v.p. 1966-68), Group 21 (pres. Los Gatos, Calif. 1970-71). Home and Office: 18655 W Bernardo Dr San Diego CA 92127-3002 Studio (summer): Morningsun Studio 15 N Fork Rd Glen Haven CO 80532-3020

SOREIDE, DAVID CHRISTIEN, physicist; b. Arlington, Va., July 20, 1945; s. Louis Severin and Mae Marie (Barber) S.; divorced. BS, U. Colo., 1967; MS, U. Wash., 1969, PhD, 1978. Prin. engr. Boeing Co., Seattle, 1977—. Patentee for Laser Doppler Velocimetry, Normal Shock Sensing in the Focus of a Laser Beam. Mem. AIAA, Soc. Photo-Optical Instrumentation Engrs., Optical Soc. Am. Home: 5113 48th Ave NE Seattle WA 98105-2930

SOREN, DAVID, archaeology educator, administrator; b. Phila., Oct. 7, 1946; s. Harry Friedman and Erma Elizabeth (Salamon) Soren; m. Noelle Louise Schattyn, Dec. 22, 1967. B.A., Dartmouth Coll., 1968; M.A., Harvard U., 1972, Ph.D., 1973. Cert. Rome Classics Ctr. Curator of coins Fogg Art Mus., Cambridge, Mass., 1972; asst. prof. U. Mo., Columbia, 1972-76, assoc. prof., dept. head, 1976-81; prof. archaeology U. Ariz., Tucson, 1982-97, regents prof., 1997—, dept. head, 1984-89; guest curator Am. Mus.. Natural History, N.Y.C., 1983-90, lectr., 1993—; creator/dir. Kourion Excavations, Cyprus, 1982-89, Portugal, 1983-84, Am. Excavations at Lugnano, Italy, 1988-93; pot cons., field dir. Tunisia Excavations, Chgo. Oriental Inst./Smithsonian Instn., 1973-78; bd. dirs. humanities program U. Ariz., 1992-94; dir. excavations Chianciano Terme, Italy, 1995—; subject of The Learning Channel TV program: series "Archaeology", 1995. Author: (books) Unreal Reality, 1978, Rise and Fall of Fantasy Film, 1980, Carthage, 1990, French edit., 1994; co-author: Kourion: Search for a Lost Roman City, 1988, Corpus des Mosaiques de Tunisie, 1972, 3rd rev. edit., 1986, Carthage: A Mosaic of Ancient Tunisia, 1987; editor: Excavations at Kourion I, 1987; producer: (film) Carthage: A Mirage of Antiquity, 1987; creator and guest curator: (internat. traveling exhbn.) Carthage: A Mosaic of Ancient Tunisia, 1987-92; editor, founder Roscius, 1993—; creative cons. TV miniseries Lost Civilizations, 1994; contbr. articles to profl. jours. Subject of National Geographic spl. Archeological Detectives, 1985; work subject of feature articles in Newsweek, Conoisseur, National Geographic and others; recipient Cine Golden Eagle, 1980, Angenieux Film award Industrial Photography mag., 1980, Outstanding American Under 40 award C. Johns Hopkins-Britain's Royal Inst. Internat. Affairs, 1985; named Outstanding American Under 40 Esquire mag., 1985, hon. Italian citizen Lugnano, Italy, 1989; grantee NEH, 1979, 87, Fulbright, Lisbon, 1983. Mem. Nat. Geog. Soc. (project dir. 1983-84), Am. Sch. Oriental Rsch. (dept. rep. 1981-85), Archaeol. Inst. Tucson (pres. 1983-86), Luso-Am. Commn. (citation 1983-84), Explorer's Club. Office: U Ariz Dept Classics 371 MLB Tucson AZ 85721

SORENSEN, ELIZABETH JULIA, cultural administrator; b. Kenora, Ont., Can., Nov. 24, 1934; d. John Frederick and Irene Margaret (Dowd) MacKellar; m. O. Leo P. Sorensen, July 7, 1956 (div. 1963); children: Lianne Kim Sorensen Kruger. BA, Lakehead U., 1970; MA, Brigham Young U., 1972; Assoc. Royal Conservatory, U. Toronto, 1978; Assoc., Mt. Royal Coll., Calgary, AB, 1978. Sec. Canadian Med. Assn. Manitoba div., Winnipeg, 1956-59; legal sec. Filmore, Riley & Co., Winnipeg, 1961-63; tchr. Fort Frances (Ont.) High Sch., 1963-70; instr. drama, speech, English Lethbridge (Alta.) Community Coll., 1972-77; tchr. bus. edn. Henderson Coll. Bus., Lethbridge, 1978-80; supt. cultural svcs. City Medicine Hat, Alta., 1980—. Mem. Alta. Mcpl. Assn. for Culture (sec. 1982-87, treas. 1982-90, vice-chair 1990-92, chair 1992-96), Can. Conf. Arts, World Leisure and

Recreation Assn. Mormon. Office: City of Medicine Hat, 580 1 St SE, Medicine Hat, AB Canada T1A 8E6

SORENSEN, JEAN, artist; b. San Diego, Nov. 18, 1920; d. William James and Hallie (Moran) Hart; m. Ralph James Sorensen, Sept. 1, 1939; children: Ellen Marie Pacchetti, Ann Christine Coons, James Christian. Student, San Jose State U., 1938-39, U. Calif., Santa Cruz, 1972—. Tchr. watercolor workshop DeAnza State Coll., Cupertino, Calif., 1984, Santa Clara Valley Watercolor Soc., Yosemite Nat. Park, 1984; tchr. botany Stanford U., 1985; ptnr. View Points Art Gallery, Los Altos, Calif., 1972-92; pres. View Prints Art Gallery, Los Altos, Calif., 1988-90. Exhibitor at Palazzo Veccico, Florence, Italy, 1972, Soc. Western Arts, DeYoung Mus., San Francisco, 1970-75; guest exhibiter biennial Kofu Watercolor Exhibit, Japan, 1983; commd. painting "Landmark Sceene", City of Syktyvhear, Russia, 1990. Vol. docent Mid-Peninsula Regional Park Open Space Dist., San Mateo and Santa Clara counties, Calif., 1977-91. Mem. Nat. Assn. Women Artists, Soc. Western Artists, Allied Artists West (pres. 1990-92), Santa clara Valley Watercolor Soc., Monterey County Watercolor Soc., Calif. Native Plant Soc.

SORENSEN, LINDA, lawyer; b. Eureka, Calif., Mar. 3, 1945. BS, U. Wis., Madison, 1967; JD, U. Calif., 1976. Bar: Calif. 1976, U.S. Dist. Ct. (no. dist.) Calif. 1977, U.S. Ct. Appeals (9th cir.), U.S. Dist. Ct. (ea. dist.) Calif. Lawyer Feldman, Waldman & Kline, P.C., San Francisco. Mem. ABA (mem. subcom. on avoiding powers, bus. bankruptcy com. 1983—), Bar Assn. of San Francisco (chmn. comml. law and bankruptcy sect. 1984, editor fed. cts. com., no. dist. Calif. digest 1979-82). Office: Feldman Waldman & Kline 3 Embarcadero Ctr 28th Fl San Francisco CA 94111-4066

SORENSEN, SHEILA, state senator; b. Chgo., Sept. 20, 1947; d. Martin Thomas Moloney and Elizabeth (Koehr) Paulus; m. Wayne B. Slaughter, May, 1969 (div. 1976); 1 child, Wayne Benjamin III; m. Dean E. Sorensen, Feb. 14, 1977; (stepchildren) Michael, Debbie, Kevin, Dean C. BS, Loretto Heights Coll., Denver, 1965; postgrad. pediatric nurse practicioner, U. Colo., Denver, 1969-70. Pediatric nurse practicioner Pub. Health Dept., Denver, 1970-71, Boise, Idaho, 1971-72; pediatric nurse practicioner Boise (Idaho) Pediatric Group, 1972-74, Pediatric Assocs., Boise, 1974-77; mem. Idaho State Ho. Reps., 1987-92; mem. Idaho Senate, 1992—, chair senate health and welfare com., 1992-94, chair senate majority caucus, vice chair state affairs com., 1994—; state chair Am. Legis. Exchange Coun. Precinct committeeman Ada County Rep. Ctrl. Com., Boise, 1982-86, dist. vice chair, 1985-88; polit. chair Idaho Med. Assn. Aux., 1984-87, Ada County Med. Assocs., 1986-87; bd. dirs. Family Practice Residency Program, 1992-94, Univ./Cmty. Health Sci. Assn., Bishop Kelly Found., 1993—; chair Senate Majority Caucus, 1995, vice chair state affairs com. Recipient AMA Nathan Davis award for Outstanding State Legislator, 1994. Mem. Nat. Conf. State Legislators, Nat. Orgn. Women Legislators (state chair), Am. Legis. Exch. Coun. Roman Catholic.

SORENSON, RICK J. (RICHARD JOHN SORENSON, JR.), import company executive, artist, educator; b. Ontario, Oreg., May 1, 1965; s. Richard John and Donna Jean (Kendall) S. BFA, Montserrat Coll. Art, Beverly, Mass., 1993. Owner, mgr. Far East Art Imports, Meridian, Idaho, 1994—; advisor CAN Group, Boise, Idaho and Thimphu, Bhutan, 1995—. Mem. Nat. Art Materials Trade Assn. Office: Far East Art Imports 700 E Fairview # 52 Meridian ID 83642

SORENSON, SANDRA LOUISE, merchandising manager; b. Santa Monica, Calif., Nov. 30, 1948; d. Edward John and Gordon Dudley (Pollock) S. BA in Telecommunications, BS in Mktg., U. So. Calif., 1970. Merchandiser Montgomery Ward Inc., Los Angeles, 1970-82; sr. fin. planner Plums Co., Los Angeles, 1982-84; mgr. merchandising systems devel. and tng. Millers Outpost, Ontario, Calif., 1984-89; merchandising systems specialist Oshmans Sporting Goods, Santa Ana, Calif., 1989-90; dir. allocations Clothestime, Anaheim, Calif., 1990—; dir. planning and allocation Pacific Sunwear, Anaheim. Active Shakespeare Festival Guild, Garden Grove, Calif., 1985—; chairperson membership com. Gem Theatre Guild, Garden Grove, 1986—. Recipient Achievement award Bicentennial Com. Norwalk, Calif., 1976. Mem. Am. Soc. Tng. and Devel. (v.p.), Commerce Assocs., Assn. Retail Technologies, Mensa, Internat. Platform Soc., Casitas de San Jose, Chi Omega, Phi Chi Theta, Alpha Epsilon Rho. Republican. Mem. Reformed Ch. Am. Club: Players of Orange. Home: 76 Carriage Way Pomona CA 91766-6721 Office: Pacific Sunwear 5037 E Hunter Ave Anaheim CA 92807

SORIANO, DEBBIE ANN, educator; b. Montebello, Calif., Dec. 10, 1963; d. Peter and Bernice (Ewing) Villescas; m. Douglas Earl Roberts, June 6, 1981 (div. Mar. 1989); 1 child, Douglas Earl II; m. Marcos Soriano III, June 27, 1992. BA, Biola U., 1982; MA, Calif. State U., L.A., 1983; MBA, Devry-Keller Bus. Sch., 1997; PhD, Azusa Pacific U., 1997. Adminstrv. credential, single subject tchg. credential, multiple subjects tchg. credential, ESL credential. Script asst. Val Prodns., Arcadia, Calif., 1979; tchr., coord. Lang. Inst., Toyko, 1980, El Monte (Calif.) Union Schs., 1983-84; tchr. English Montebello (Calif.) Schs., 1984-96; state del. Calif. Tchrs. Assn., Montebello, 1994-95. Vol. Police Dept., Arcadia, 1993-94; mem. World Affairs Coun., L.A., 1995-96, UNIFEM, N.Y.C., 1995-96, The Noel Found., L.A., 1995-97. With USNR, 1996—. Recipient Summer Inst. award NEH, Long Beach, Calif., 1994, Summer Seminar award NEH, Amherst, Mass., 1995. Mem. AAUW, DAR, Navy Wives, Clan Ewen Soc., Pi Lambda Theta. Home: PO Box 2095 Arcadia CA 91077-2095

SOROM, TERRY ALLEN, ophthalmic surgeon; b. Lanesboro, Minn., Jan. 9, 1940; s. Martin John and Elvira (Lodahl) S.; m. Suzanne A. Johnson, children: Martin, Jeb, Abraham, Theodore. BS, Luther Coll., 1962; MD, U. Minn.-Mpls., 1966. Diplomate Am. Bd. Ophthalmology. Intern. U. Oreg., Portland, 1967, resident in ophthalmology, 1969-73; ophthalmic surgeon Eye and Ear Clinic, Inc., Wenatchee, Wash., 1973—. Chmn. bd. dirs. Wash. Health Plan, 1993—. Charter trustee Wenatchee Visitor and Conv. Bur., 1980; bd. dirs. Blue Cross Wash., and Alaska, 1983-91; pres. Wenatchee Valley Coll. Found., 1986-88. Capt. M.C., USAF, 1967-69. Mem. AMA, Am. Acad. Ophthalmology, Contact Lens Assn. Ophthalmology, Am. Intraocular Implant Soc., Wash. State Acad. Ophthalmology (trustee 1978-80, pres. 1996-97), Oregon Ophthalmologic Alumni Assn. (pres. 1988—), Greater Wenatchee Found. (bd. dirs.), Chelan-Douglas County Med. Assn., Rotary (pres. 1993-94). Republican. Lutheran. Office: Eye & Ear Clinic Wenatchee 600 Orondo Ave PO Box 3027 Wenatchee WA 98801

SORRENTINO, JOSEPH NICHOLAS, prosecutor; b. N.Y.C.; s. Nicholas A. and Angelina C. (Trezza) S.; 1 child, Joseph Jr. BA, U. Calif., Santa Barbara, 1963; MA, U. Calif., L.A., 1971; JD, Harvard Law Sch., 1967; doctorate, So. Vt. Coll., 1976. Bar: Calif. 1968. Prosecutor intern U.S. Dept. Justice, L.A., 1968; writer Prentice Hall, Englewood Cliffs, N.J., 1968-71; adj. prof. U. So. Calif., UCLA, U. Calif. Irvine, Pepperdine U., 1971-81; juvenile ct. judge (pro tem) L.A., 1974-76; prosecutor Office of Riverside/L.A. Dist. Atty., 1981—; lectr., nationwide, 1970-84; host, guest numerous TV programs including 60 Minutes, Newsmakers, Good Morning Am., Tonight Show, 1970-84. Author: Up From Never, 1971, 2nd edit., 1976, The Moral Revolution, 1973, The Concrete Cradle, 1975, The Gold Shield, 1980, (poems) The People Who Stopped for You, 1995; contbr. numerous articles to profl. jours. and mags. Chmn. United Way mentally disabled com. L.A. Human Rights Commn., 1970-72. With USMC, 1963-64, USMCR, 1964-67. Recipient Notable Book award ALA, 1971; named Outstanding Spkr. of Yr. Nat. Authors and Celebrities Forum, 1977. Mem. Calif. Bar Assn., Calif. Assn. Dist. Attys., Calif. Consumers Activist Group (bd. dirs.), Constl. Rights Found., Sugar Ray Robinson Found. (bd. dirs.). Home: 2350 Nichols Canyon Rd Los Angeles CA 90046-1733 *Born in the immigrant section of Brooklyn, he dropped out and worked for ten years in factories, warehouses, construction, piers, railroad yards, and fought as a middleweight boxer before enrolling in night school. Ten years later, competing in oratory he became valedictorian at Harvard Law School. In 1975, he was ranked in Forbes among top lecturers in U.S., appearances in 49 states. In 1981, he was honored for Outstanding Volunteer Service with youth by Human Relations Commission. In 1991, performance evaluation: "one of the best prosecutors in the branch;" he has won 238 trials and appeals. His life story memorialized in U.S. Congressional Record: "essence of the American ideal."*

SORSTOKKE, SUSAN EILEEN, systems engineer; b. Seattle, May 2, 1955; d. Harold William and Carrol Jean (Russ) S. BS in Systems Engring., U. Ariz., 1976; MBA, U. Wash., Richland, 1983. Warehouse team mgr. Procter and Gamble Paper Products, Modesto, Calif., 1976-78; quality assurance engr. Westinghouse Hanford Co., Richland, Wash., 1978-80; supr. engring. document ctr. Westinghouse Hanford Co., Richland, 1980-81; mgr. data control and adminstrn. Westinghouse Electric Corp., Madison, Pa., 1981-82, mgr. data control and records mgmt., 1982-84; prin. engr. Westinghouse Elevator Co., Morristown, N.J., 1984-87; region adminstrn. mgr. Westinghouse Elevator Co., Arleta, Calif., 1987-90; ops. rsch. analyst Am. Honda Motor Co. Inc., Torrance, Calif., 1990-95; project leader parts sys. Am. Honda Motor Co., Inc., Torrance, Calif., 1995-96, mgr. parts systems and part number adminstrn., 1996—; adj. prof. U. LaVerne, Calif., 1991-92. Advisor Jr. Achievement, 1982-83; literacy tutor Westmoreland Literacy Coun., 1983-84, host parent EF Found., Saugus, Calif., 1987-88, Am. Edn. Connection, Saugus, 1988-89, 91; instr. Excell, L.A., 1991-92; mem. Calif. Acad. Math. and Sci., 1996-97. Mem. Soc. Women Engrs., Am. Inst. Indsl. Engrs., Nat. Coun. Systems Engring., Optimists Charities, Inc. (bd. dirs. Acton, Calif. 1991-94). Republican. Methodist. Home: 2567 Plaza Del Amo Unit 205 Torrance CA 90503-8962 Office: Am Honda Motor Co Inc Dept Parts Quality and Systems 1919 Torrance Blvd Torrance CA 90501-2722

SORTLAND, TRUDITH ANN, speech and language therapist, educator; b. Butte, Mont., Dec. 3, 1940; d. Kenneth Hjalmer Sortland and Sigrid V. (Kotka) Strand. BS, Minot (N.D.) State U., 1965. Tchr. Westby (Mont.) Sch., 1960-61, Glasgow (Mont.) Southside Sch., 1962-65, Glasgow AFB, Mont., 1965-80; tchr., speech and lang. pathologist Mineral County Sch. Dist., Hawthorne, Nev., 1965-68, 78—; kindergarten tchr. Mineral County Sch. Dist., Mina, Nev., 1968-72; elem. tchr. Mineral County Sch. Dist., Mina, 1978-80; speech, language pathologist Mineral County Sch. Dist., Mina, Republic of Korea, 1980—; tchr. Dept. Def., Pusan, Republic of Kores, 1972-73, Illesheim, Fed. Republic Germany, 1973-78; tchr. Mohall (N.D.) Pub. Sch., 1964-65; cons. Mary Kay Cosmetics, tchr. Glasgow AFB, 1965-68. Supt. Sunday sch. Bethany Luth. Ch., Hawthorne, 1987—, sec. Ladies Aid, 1987—. Mem. NEA, Nev. Edn. Assn., AAUW (past sec., pres.), Pair O Dice Square Dance Club (sec. 1989—), Delta Kappa Gamma. Home: PO Box 816 Hawthorne NV 89415-0816 Office: Mineral County Sch Dist A St Hawthorne NV 89415

SOSOKA, JOHN RICHARD, consulting firm executive, engineer; b. L.A., Nov. 30, 1929; s. John and Mary (Kovach) S.; m. Audrey T. Trezona, Apr. 26, 1952; children: John Richard Jr., Cathie Ann, Karen Elizabeth. BS in Gen. Engring., UCLA, 1952; MBA, Calif. State U., 1975. Registered mech., elec., fire protection, metallurgy, control systems and civil engr., Calif. Project engr. Stathem Instrument, L.A., 1954-55; staff engr. Aerojet Gen., Azusa, Calif., 1955-60; tech. dir. Unitek Corp., Monrovia, Calif., 1960-65; staff engr. TRW Systems, Redondo Beach, Calif., 1965-69; engr. mgr. Allen-Jones Electronics, Gardena, Calif., 1969-70; sect. head City of Long Beach, Calif., 1970-79; pres. Sosoka & Assoc.s, Los Alamitos, Calif., 1979-90; exec. v.p. Sparvan, Inc., Long Beach, Calif., 1990-91; pres. PSI Engrs., Inc., Long Beach, Calif., 1991—. Fellow ASHRAE (dir. and regional chair 1990-93, Disting. Svc. award 1988); mem. Assn. Energy Engrs. (v.p. 1980-81, Energy Engr. of Yr. award 1985). Republican. Episcopalian. Home: 848 Roxanne Ave Long Beach CA 90815-5013 Office: PSI Engrs Inc 5000 E Spring St #800 Long Beach CA 90815

SOTER, NICHOLAS GREGORY, advertising agency executive; b. Great Falls, Mont., Apr. 26, 1947; s. Sam Nick and Bernice (Bennett) S.; m. Kathleen Lyman, Feb. 20, 1970; children: Nichole, Erin, Samuel Scott, Kara, Stephen Andrew, Riley Kyle. BS, Brigham Young U., 1971. With McLean Assocs., Provo, Utah, 1970-75; chmn. bd., CEO Soter Assocs. Inc., Provo, 1975—; founder, pres. RS Corp., 1986-88, Plum C Corp., 1988, Due Respect Corp., 1991; owner, developer Parkside Apts., 1994—; instr. advt. Utah Valley C.C., Orem, 1971-75, Brigham Young U., Provo, 1980-84. Publisher: Journal of Joseph, 1979, Journal of Brigham, 1980, LaVell Edwards, 1980, Amos Wright, 1981, Moments in Motherhood, 1981, What It Means to Know Christ, 1981, Mormon Fortune Builders, 1982, Utah History, 1982; contbr. articles to profl. jours. Active Utah Valley Pub. Comm. Coun. for LDS Ch., 1982-87; mem. adv. coun. Monte L. Bean Life Sci. Mus., 1987-89; Rep. dist. chmn.; v.p. exec. com. Am.'s Freedom Festival at Provo, 1990-91; jury chmn. Coun. for Advancement and Support Edn., 1989; vocalist Ralph Woodward Chorale, 1991-95, pres., 1992-94; mem. govt. rev. com., Provo, Orem, 1992-95; trustee, v.p. Greek Assn. Family History and Tradition, 1990-95; unit commr., advisor Explorer post Boy Scouts Am., 1995—; bd. advisors Am. Cancer Soc., 1996—. Recipient N.Y. Art Dir.'s The One Show award, Salt Lake Art Dirs. Communications Assn. of Utah Valley awards. Mem. Utah Advt. Fedn., Pub. Rels. Soc. Am., Communications Assn. Utah Valley (past pres.), Provo C. of C. (bd. dirs.), Innisbrook Network of Advt. Agys. (pres. 1986-87). Home: 1728 S 290 E Orem UT 84058-7928 Office: Soter Assocs Inc 209 N 400 W Provo UT 84601-2746

SOTO, GARY, poet, educator; b. Fresno, Calif., Apr. 12, 1952; s. Manuel Soto and Angie (Trevino) Oftedal; m. Carolyn Sadako Oda, May 24, 1975; children: Mariko Heidi. BA in English, Calif. State U., Fresno, 1974; MFA in Creative Writing, U. Calif., Irvine, 1976. Lectr. Chicano Studies U. Calif., Berkeley, 1977-81, asst. prof. English and Chicano Studies, 1981-85, assoc. prof. English and Chicano Studies, 1985-95; Bd. dirs. Coordinating Council of Literary Mags., N.Y.C., 1985—. Books: The Elements of San Joaquin, 1977 (U.S. Internat. Poetry Forum award), The Tale of Sunlight, 1978, Where Sparrows Work Hard, 1981, Black Hair, 1985, Living Up the Street, 1985 (Am. Book award 1985), Small Faces, 1986. Fellow Nat. Endowment for Arts, 1981, Gueggenheim, 1980; recipient Acad. Am. Poets Prize, 1975, The Discovery-The Nation Prize, 1975, Levinson award from Poetry, 1984. Home: 43 The Cres Berkeley CA 94708-1701

SOTO, SHIRLENE ANN, history educator, consultant; b. San Luis Obispo, Calif., Jan. 22, 1950; d. Vernon Ernest and Althea Lorraine S.; m. Walt Elliott, Sept. 1, 1985. BA, San Francisco State U., 1969; MA, U. N.Mex., 1971, PhD, 1977. Instr. U. N.Mex., Albuquerque, 1976-77; asst. prof. Calif. Poly. State U., San Luis Obispo, 1977-80; asst. v.p. Calif. State U., Northridge, 1981-85, prof., 1985—; postdoctoral fellow UCLA, 1985-86; coord. program for gender equality grant Coll. of the Canyons, Valencia, Calif., 1991-94; panelist Fulbright-Hays grants U.S. Dept. Edn., 1993, 94, 96. Author: Emergence of the Modern Mexican Woman, 1990; editl. adv. bd. (book) Notable Hispanic Am. Women, 1993; contbr. numerous articles to profl. jours. Mem. Hispanic adv. coun. Calif. Dept. Pks. and Recreation, Sacramento, 1982-95; adv. bd. New Horizons project Coll. of the Canyons, Valencia, Calif., 1994—. Adminintstrv. fellow Calif. State U. Sys., 1980-81, Ford. Found. fellow Ford Found., 1972-76; Recipient Leadership in Edn. award Atty. Gen. of Calif., 1986. Mem. Mujeres Activas en Letras y Cambio Social (So. Calif. Rep. 1987-88), Western Assn. of Women Historians (chair, Judith Lee Ridge prize 1991-92). Democrat. Roman Catholic. Home: 25025 3/4 Everett Dr Santa Clarita CA 91321-3465 Office: Calif State U 18111 Nordhoff St Northridge CA 91330-0001

SOTO, THOMAS DE, photographer; b. Pomona, Calif., Oct. 30, 1960; s. Eddie and Henrietta (Nunez) S. AA, Palomar Coll., San Marcos, Calif., 1984; student, U. So. Calif., 1987-88. Photojournalist The Citizen Newspaper, Solano Beach, Calif., 1980-82, The Blade Tribune, Oceanside, Calif., 1982-84; dir. photography World Comms. Inc., La Costa, Calif., 1984-87; auteur of photography, fine arts posters Eyes Closed Internat., Solana Beach, 1987—; motion picture camera operator World Wave Pictures, Cardiff, Calif., 1990—; lectr. at schs. and colls. nationwide. Works include documentaries, TV commls., album covers, feature films. Photographer, San Diego Youth and Community Svcs., 1992—, Campaign, Calif., Santa Monica, 1989-90, Performing Arts Theater, Carlsbad, Calif., 1982-86, United Way, AIDS Found., Nat. Wildlife Found., others. Recipient Silver Lone Star award Houston Film Festival, 1990, Van Guard award Am. Women in Radio and TV, 1986, Student Emmy for Gilbert Lost A Tooth, Motion Picture Acad. of Arts, 1987; Polaroid grantee, 1984-86. Mem. Am. Soc. Mag. Photographers, Profl. Photographers Am. Inc., Nikon Profl. Svcs. Libertarian.

SOULÉ, MICHAEL ELLMAN, biologist; b. San Diego, May 28, 1936; s. Alan Kenyon Soulé and Berenice Charlotte (Ellman) Bluestone; m. Judith Ann Burgess Bays, Aug. 9, 1965 (div.); children: Aaron, Noah, Ani; m. Joy Ellis McKinney, June 28, 1993. BA, Calif. State U., San Diego, 1959; MA, Stanford U., 1963, PhD, 1965. Lectr. in zoology U. Malawi, Blantyre, Malawi, 1965-67; from asst. prof. to prof. U. Calif., San Diego, 1967-80; dir. Inst. Transcultural Studies, L.A., 1979-83; adj., vis. prof. U. Mich., Ann Arbor, 1984-89; prof., chair U. Calif., Santa Cruz, 1989-96, rsch. prof., 1996—; pres. The Wildlands Project, Tucson, 1995—; mem. sci. adv. com. The Nature Conservancy, 1992—. Author: Conservation and Evolution, 1981; editor: Conservation Biology, 1986, Viable Populations for Conservation, 1987, Reinventing Nature?, Responses to Postmodern Construction, 1995. Fellow Guggenheim Found. Fellow AAAS, N.Y. Zool. Soc.; mem. Nat. Rsch. Coun. (biology bd.), Soc. Conservation Biology (1st pres. 1986-89, Disting. Achievement award 1993).

SOUTH, MATTHEW TODD, aerospace engineer; b. Sacramento, Dec. 30, 1959; s. Jack Roy and Dorothy (Orr) S.; m. Nancy Ann Fischer, Mar. 26, 1983. BS in Aero. Engring., Calif. Poly. State U., 1983. Aerospace engr. Pacific Missile Test Ctr., Pt. Mugu, Calif., 1983-85; unmanned aerial vehicle br. head Pacific Missile Test Ctr., Pt. Mugu, 1985-87; unmanned aerial vehicle sys. engr. Naval Air Warfare Ctr., Pt. Mugu, 1987-92, dep. for targets test and evaluation, 1992-94, lead test engr. for targets, 1994-97, br. head-test ops. br., 1997—. Mem. AIAA, Assn. Unmanned Vehicle Sys. Home: 364 Walnut Dr Ventura CA 93003-2034 Office: Naval Air Warfare Ctr Code 4KL200E Bldg 6-2 Point Mugu CA 93042-5001

SOUTHARD, BURTON M., political and public affairs consultant; b. Flint, Mich., Mar. 31, 1944; s. Burton S. and Lorraine (McCloy) S.; m. Donna C. Southard, Mar. 20, 1966; children: Jill Ann, Philip John. BS, Ball State U., 1968; postgrad., U. Ill., 1973. Legis. advisor, assoc. adminstr. congl., legis. affairs SBA, Washington, 1987-88; chief staff, dir. cmty. rels. svc. U.S. Dept. Justice, Washington, 1988-93, Assemblyman Jim Brulte, Rancho Cucamonga, Calif., 1996-97; chief of staff State Sen. Jim Brulte, 1997—; prin. asst. Calif. Assembly Rep. Leader, Sacramento, Calif., 1993-95; dep. campaign mgr. Morry Taylor Pres., Des Moines, 1995; campaign mgr. U.S. Sen. Bob Kasten, Milw., 1986; chief staff Congressman John Grotberg, Washington, 1985, Congressman Tom Lewis, Washington, 1983-84; campaign cons. Nat. Rep. Congl. Com., Washington, 1984. Exec. com. Calif. Rep. Party, Burbank, 1994—. NSF fellow, U. Tex., Austin, 1976. Presbyterian. Home: 6853 Pandino Ct Rancho Cucamonga CA 91701-8540 Office: 10681 Foothill Blvd Ste 325 Rancho Cucamonga CA 91730

SOUTHARD, JAMES BRUCE, lecturer, painter; b. Bklyn., Mar. 31, 1921. Student, NAD, 1939-41, Beaux Arts Inst. Design, 1941, Arts Students League, 1946-49, Escuela Pintura Escultura, Mex.; also studied with, Robert Brackman, 1946, Reginald Marsh, 1947, Kenneth Hayes Miller, 1947, Jon Corbino, 1949. With Stockton Mus. Art, San Joaquin, Calif., San Francisco Gen. Hosp.; represented by Maxwell Galleries, San Francisco, Georg Krevsky Art Gallery, San Francisco; instr. painting. One-man shows include Galleria Arte Moderno, Mexico City, 1951, Galleria Caracalla, Guadalajara, Mex., 1951, Three Arts, Poughkeepsie, N.Y., 1953, Lucian Labault Gallery, San Francisco, 1954, St. Mary's Coll., Moraga, Calif., 1964, San Joaquin Pioneer Mus., Stockton, Calif., 1965, San Francisco Art Commn., 1977; exhibited in group shows at Oakland Mus., 1962-63, John Bolles Gallery, San Francisco, 1976, Calif. State Fair, 1977-78, Kensington Gallery, Calif., 1981, Eleonore Austerer Gallery, San Francisco, 1990, others; represented in permanent collections City and Co. San Francisco, Home Savings, L.A., Health Ctr., San Francisco, Bancroft Libr. Univ. Calif., Berkeley, Palace Legion Honor, San Francisco, San Joaquin Pioneer Mus., Stockton, Calif., San Francisco Dept. Health, Carnegie Art Mus., Oxnard, Calif., 1992; four paintings given to Hudson River Mus. from pvt. collection, Yonkers, N.Y., 1997. Recipient Purchase award Home Savings, San Francisco Arts Commn., Award of Merit, San Francisco Arts Festival. Mem. Artists Equity Assn., Internat. Soc. Artists, Soc. Western Artists, East Bay Watercolor Soc., Duchess County Art Assn. Address: 555 Buena Vista Ave W San Francisco CA 94117-4132

SOUTHERN, RONALD D., diversified corporation executive; b. Calgary, Alta., Can., July 25, 1930; s. Samuel Donald and Alexandra (Cuthill) S.; m. Margaret Visser, July 30, 1954; children: Nancy, Linda. BSc, U. Alta., Edmonton, 1953; LLD (hon.), U. Calgary, 1976, U. Alberta, 1991. Pres., CEO ATCO Ltd., Calgary, 1954-85, dep. chmn., CEO, 1985-91, chmn., pres., CEO, 1985-93; chmn., CEO ATCO Ltd. and Can. Utilities Ltd., Calgary, 1994—, ATCO Ltd., Calgary, 1994—, Can. Utilities Ltd., Calgary, 1994—; chmn. Akita Drilling Ltd.; bd. dirs. Fletcher Challenge Can. Ltd., Can. Airlines Corp., Can. Pacific Ltd., Chrysler Can. Ltd., IMASCO Ltd., LaFarge, Royal Ins. Ltd., Xerox of Can. Inc., Fletcher Challenge Ltd., New Zealand; co-chmn. Spruce Meadows Tournaments; chmn. Spruce Meadows Round Table. Recipient Holland Trade award Gov. of The Netherlands, 1985, (with wife) Sportsmen of Yr. award Calgary Booster Club, Internat., Disting. Entrepreneur award U. Man. Faculty Mgmt., 1990; inducted into Can. Bus. Hall, 1995; named Businessman of Yr. U. Alta., 1986, to Order of Can. Brit. Empire, 1986, Comdr. Brit. Empire, 1995, CEO of the Yr. Fin. Post, 1996. Mem. Ranchmen's Club, Calgary Golf and Country Club. Home: 67 Massey Pl SW, Calgary, AB Canada T2V 2G7 Office: ATCO Ltd & Can Utilities Ltd, 1600 909-11 Ave SW, Calgary, AB Canada T2R IN6

SOUTHWELL, PHYLLIS ARLENE, medical transcriptionist; b. Havre, Mont., Dec. 29, 1938; d. Edwin G. and Virginia L. (Cross) Brandt; children: Jay M., Lezlie M. AAS, North Seattle C.C., 1974; BA in English Lit., U. Wash., 1983. Med. transcriptionist U. Wash., Seattle, 1986, Providence Med. Ctr., Seattle, 1988—. Author: Love's Shadow, 1990. Mem. Am. Assn. Med. Assts (cert.), Am. Assn. Med. Transcriptionist. Lutheran. Home: 600 7th Ave Apt 304 Seattle WA 98104-1932

SOUTHWICK, JAMES ALBERT, realtor; b. Ogden, Utah, Feb. 5, 1964; s. Edward Hale and Althea Beryl (Sylvester) S. BS in Psychology, Weber State U., 1988. Water distbn. assoc. Pine View Water Sys., Ogden, Utah, 1980-87; comml real estates sales SAJ Ltd.,, Las Vegas, Nev., 1987-91; prodn. assoc. Morton Internat., Ogden, 1992-93; broker asst. Prudential Securities, Honolulu, Hawaii, 1991-92; sales exec. The Franklin Group, Ogden, 1993—. Inventor Techsafe, 1990, Butter Spreadables, 1987. Mem. Am. Radio Relay League, Ogden Bd. Realtors (assoc.). Home: 1495 N 1225 E Layton UT 84040 Office: The Franklin Group 1702 E 5600 S Ogden UT 84403

SOUTHWORTH, ROD BRAND, computer science educator; b. Binghampton, N.Y., Aug. 24, 1941; s. William Tanner Southworth and Ruth Evelyn (Brabham) Woods; m. Patrice Marie Gapen, Jan. 10, 1978; children: Suzi Lynn, Judi Leigh, Megan Marie, Robin Ashley. BS in Bus., U. Ariz., 1965; MS in Mgmt. Sci. and Info Systems, Colo. State U., 1978. Mktg. rep. IBM, Denver, 1966-69; system analyst Colo. State U., Fort Collins, 1969-73, grad. teaching asst., 1978-79; project mgr. Systems and Computer Tech., Portland, Oreg., 1973-75; asst. dir. Systems and Computer Tech., Fairbanks, Alaska, 1975-77; instr. in computer info. systems Laramie County C.C., Cheyenne, Wyo., 1979—. Author: (software) PC-DOS/MS-DOS Simplified, 1st edit. 1988, 3rd edit. 1992, DOS Complete and Simplified, 1990, DOS Essentials, 1991, DOS 5 Simplified, 1992, DOS 6.2 Simplified, 1994. Mem. Civil Air Patrol, Cheyenne, 1991. Mem. Data Processing Mgmt. Assn. (mem. assoc. level model curriculum 1984-85), Assn. Computing Machinery (mem. assoc. level computer info. processing model curriculum 1991-92). Home: PO Box 5457 Cheyenne WY 82003-5457 Office: Laramie County Comm Coll 1400 E College Dr Cheyenne WY 82007-3204

SOUZA, JOAN OF ARC, educational administrator; b. Honolulu, Nov. 16, 1943; d. Peter B. and Helen Souza. AA, Maria Regina Coll., Syracuse, N.Y., 1967; BA in Theology, St. Joseph Coll., Rensselaer, Ind., 1970; MA in Adminstrn. of Religious Edn., LaSalle Coll., Phila., 1976. Joined Sisters of 3d Franciscan Order, Roman Cath. Ch., 1961. Youth minister Cath. Diocese, Syracuse, 1963-71, St. Peter's Parish, Riverside, N.J., 1971-73, IHM Parish, Liverpool, N.Y., 1984-91; tchr. St. Francis Sch., Honolulu, 1973-84, jr./sr. high sch. prin., 1991—. Author AIDS Ednl. Workshops, 1988-91, Kindergarten Religious Edn. Program, 1985. Mem. Pro-Life Com., Honolulu, 1980-84; buddy AIDS Buddy Program of Ctrl. N.Y., Syracuse, 1987-91; mem. Malama O Manoa, Honolulu. Mem. ASCD, AAUW, Nat. Cath. Ednl. Assn., Nat. Assn. for Year-Round Edn., Nat. Assn. of Secondary Sch. Prins., Hawaii Assn. Ind. Schs. Roman Catholic. Office: St Francis School 2707 Pamoa Rd Honolulu HI 96822-1838

SOWDER, ROBERT ROBERTSON, architect; b. Kansas City, Kans., Dec. 29, 1928; s. James Robert and Agnes (Robertson) S.; m. Joan Goddard, July 26, 1954; 1 dau., Lisa Robertson Lee. B.A., U. Wash., 1953; B.Arch., U. Va., 1958; grad. diploma in Architecture, Ecole Des Beaux Arts, Fontainebleau, France, 1952. Designer Architects Collaborative, Boston, 1958-59, Peirce & Pierce (architects), Boston, 1959-63; asso. Fred. Bassetti & Co. (architects), Seattle, 1963-67; partner Naramore, Bain, Brady & Johanson (architects), Seattle, 1967-81; pres. NBBJ Internat., 1976-81; architect TRA, Seattle, 1981-83; v.p. Daniel, Mann, Johnson & Mendenhall, San Francisco, 1983-93; prin. RRS Consulting, 1993—; archtl. design critic Boston Archtl. Ctr., 1961-62. Important works include Ridgeway III Dormitories, Bellingham, Wash. (Dept. Housing and Urban Devel. Honor award), Seattle Rapid Transit (HUD Excellence award), Safeco Ins. Co. Home Office Complex, Seattle, King County Stadium, Balt. Conv. Ctr., Oreg. Conv. Ctr., San Francisco (Moscone) Conv. Ctr. Expansion, Honolulu Conv. Ctr., Wilmington (Del.) Conv. Ctr. Served with CIC U.S. Army, 1954-56. Recipient Premier Prix D'Architecture Ecole Des Beaux Arts, Fontainebleau, 1951, 52, Prix D'Remondet Fontainebleau, 1952. Mem. AIA, Internat. Assn. Assembly Mgrs., Seattle Tennis Club, Scarab, Sigma Chi. Episcopalian. Home and Office: 17032 NE 135th Ct Redmond WA 98052-1715

SOWERWINE, ELBERT ORLA, JR., chemist, chemical engineer; b. Tooele, Utah, Mar. 15, 1915; s. Elbert Orla and Margaret Alice (Evans) S.; BS in Chemistry, Cornell U., 1937, MSChemE, 1938; m. Norma Borge; children: Sue-Ann Sowerwine Jacobson, Sandra Sowerwine Montgomery, Elbert Orla 3d, John Frederick, Avril Ruth Taylor, Albaro Francisco, Octavio Evans, Zaida Sowerine Roberts. Analytical chemist Raritan Copper Works, Perth Amboy, N.J., summers 1936, 37; rsch. chem. engr. Socony-Vacuum Oil Co., Paulsboro, N.J., 1938-43; prodn. supr. Merck & Co., Elkton, Va., 1943-45; asst. plant mgr. U.S. Indsl. Chems. Co., Newark, 1945-48; project engr. and rsch. dir. Wigton-Abbott Corp., Newark, 1948-50, Cody, Wyo., 1950-55; cons. engring., planning, indsl. and community devel., resource evaluation and mgmt. Wapiti, Wyo., also C.Am., Honduras, 1955—. Commr. N.J., Boy Scouts Am., 1938-43; mem. Wapiti and Park County (Wyo.) Sch. Bds., 1954-58; dir. Mont. State Planning Bd., 1959-61; exec. bd. Mo. Basin Rsch. and Devel. Coun., 1959-61. Fellow Am. Inst. Chemists; mem. AIChE, Am. Planning Assn., Nicaraguan Assn. Engrs. and Architects. Libertarian. Mem. Christian Ch. Rschr. desulfurization of petroleum products, process control, alternate energy projects; patentee in petroleum and chem. processes and equipment. Home: Broken H Ranch Wapiti WY 82450 Office: Sowerwine Cons Wapiti WY 82450

SOWINSKI, STANISLAUS JOSEPH, artist, retired naval officer; b. Milw., May 7, 1927; s. Francis Anthony and Stefania (Zakszewski) S.; m. R. Jackie Giddens, Oct. 2, 1948; children: Stephanie Ann, Lisa Renée. BA, San Diego State U., 1952; postgrad., Def. Intelligence Sch., 1964-65; cert., San Diego Sch. Arts, 1948-49. Ensign USN, 1952, advanced through grades to comdr., jr. officer, 1952-60; comdg. officer USS Abnaki, Oahu, Hawaii, 1960-62, USS Surfbird, Sasebo, Japan, 1962-64, USN, London, 1965-67; comdr. landing ship squadron USN, San Diego, 1967-69; comdg. officer U.S.S. Fresno, San Diego, 1969-71; ret. USN, 1971, enlisted, 1945-48; painting instr. San Diego Art Inst., 1973-75; painting demonstrator Grumbacher Art Supplies, Inc., N.Y., 1980-85, Inveresk Paper Co., Bath, Eng., 1980-85; instr. painting workshops, San Diego, Rapid City, S.D., 1980-85. One-man shows include Laguna Beach (Calif.) Mus. of Art, 1955, USN,1963, Dept.Def., Washington, 1964, Am. Embassy, London, 1967, San Diego Art Inst. Gallery, 1980, 86, Dahl Fine Art Ctr., Rapid City, S.D., 1982, Wind Gap Gallery of Fine Art, Sacramento, 1983, Art Ctr. Gallery , Rancho Santa Fe, Calif., 1984, Thackeray Gallery of Fine Art, San Diego, 1985, 87, San Diego Mus. of Art, 1985, A. Huney Gallery of Fine Art, San Diego, 1990; artist 23 major icons including Sts. Constantine and Helen Greek Orthodox Ch., 1985-90, Corpus Christi Cath. Ch., 1985-97. Curator major art exhibit Felicita Found. of the Arts, Escondido, Calif., 1985. Mem. Internat. Westerners, The Retired Officers Assn. Republican. Roman Catholic. Home and Office: 13040 Cedilla Pl San Diego CA 92128-1811

SPADA, JAMES, author, publisher; b. S.I., N.Y., Jan. 23, 1950; s. Joseph Vincent and Mary (Ruberto) S. Student, Wagner Coll., 1968-71, Calif. State U., 1979-80. Pres., Spada Pubs, Los Angeles, pub. Barbra Quar., Los Angeles, 1980-83. Mem. Authors Guild, ACLU. Democrat. Author: Barbra: The First Decade-The Films and Career of Barbra Streisand, 1974, The Films of Robert Redford, 1977, The Spada Report, 1979, Streisand-the Woman and the Legend, 1981, Monroe-Her Life in Pictures, 1982, Judy and Liza, 1983, Hepburn: Her Life in Pictures, 1984, The Divine Bette Midler, 1984, Fonda: Her Life in Pictures, 1985, Shirley and Warren, 1985, Grace: The Secret Lives of a Princess, 1987, Peter Lawford: The Man Who Kept the Secrets, 1991, More Than a Woman: An Intimate Biography of Bette Davis, 1993, Streisand: Her Life, 1995; book packager The 1984 Marilyn Monroe Pin-Up Calendar, 1983, The Telephone Book, 1984, Elizabeth Taylor: A Biography in Photographs, 1984, Bette Davis: A Biography in Photographs, 1985, Natalie Wood: A Biography in Photographs, 1986.

SPADE, GEORGE LAWRENCE, scientist; b. Sioux City, Iowa, Dec. 14, 1945; s. Walter Charles and LaVancha May (Green) S.; m. Carol Margaret Deaton, Mar. 14, 1966 (div. June 1985); children: Aaron Michael, Margaret. Mem. earthquake study group for China, U.S. Citizen Amb. Programs, 1989. Contbr. articles to profl. jours. Mem. AAAS, Am. Math. Soc., Math. Assn. Am., N.Y. Acad. Scis., Mensa. Home and Office: PO Box 2260 Columbia Falls MT 59912-2260

SPAEGEL, CHARLES (LOUIS S.J. SPIEGEL), psychology educator; b. Toronto, Mar. 27, 1921; came to U.S., 1938; s. Israel and Eva (Gilbert) S.; m. Ruth Kagan, Sept. 19, 1954 (div. Oct. 1970); 1 child, Laurence. BA, U. Toronto, 1948; MSc in Edn., U. So. Calif., L.A., 1951; cert., Inst. Gen. Semantics, Conn., 1950; postgrad., Unarius Acad. Sci., El Cajon, Calif., 1975-79. Lifetime cert. counseling, instr. psychology, gen. secondary cert. Aerial photographer RCAF, Toronto, 1939-42; instr. English, 1951-53; dir. fundraising United Jewish Appeal, Toronto, 1954-56; life ins. agt. Sunlife Ins. Co., Toronto and Boston, 1957-72; h.s. instr. English/math. San Diego Secondary Schs., 1972-75; instr. ednl. psychology San Diego C.C. Dist., 1975-81; instr. psychology Unarius Acad. Sci., El Cajon, Calif., 1981-93, psychology, physics dir., 1993—, past life therapy educator, 1981-96. Author: (autobiography) Confessions of I Bonaparte, 1985; editor: Interdimensional Physics, 1984; co-author 35 books on interdimensional physics and sci. of life. Sgt. USMC, 1942-46. Mem. Am. Psychol. Soc., Am. Phys. Soc. Office: Unarius Acad Sci 145 S Magnolia Ave El Cajon CA 92020-4522

SPAFFORD, MICHAEL CHARLES, artist; b. Palm Springs, Calif., Nov. 6, 1935. BA, Pomona Coll., 1959; MA, Harvard U., 1960. One man shows include Seattle Art Mus., 1982, 86, Reed Coll., 1984, Whtcom county Mus., 1987, U. Puget Sound, Tacoma, Wash., 1973, Tacoma Art Mus., 1975, 86, Utah Mus. Fine Arts, Salt Lake City, 1975, Francine Seders Gallery, Seattle, 1965—, Bellevue Art Mus., 1991, Cheney-Cowles Mus., Spokane, Wash., 1994; exhibited in group shows at Wilcox Gallery, Swarthmore Coll., Pa., 1977, Seattle Art Mus., 1977, 80, 84, Am. Acad. and Inst. Arts and Letters, N.Y.C., 1980, 83, 89, 95, Kobe, Japan, 1981, Eastern Wash. U., 1982, Henry Art Gallery, 1982, 86, Bellevue Art Mus., 1987, 95, Cheney Cowles Mus., 1988, Holter Mus. of Art, Helena, Mont. Recipient Rome Prize Am. Acad. in Rome, 1967-69, award Am. Acad. and Inst. Arts and Letters, 1983; Louis Comfort Tiffany Found. grantee, 1965-66; Neddy fellow, 1996. Home: c/o Francine Seders Gallery 6701 Greenwood North Seattle WA 98103

SPAMAN, MORGAN PATRICK, fire and safety specialist; b. Springfield, Mass., Feb. 27, 1960; s. Gerald Allen and Marilyn Jean (Rouselle) S.; m. Sherry Anita Jennings, Apr. 10, 1979; children: Michael Wayne, Lisette Amanda. A in Fire Sci., Cmty. Coll. Air Force, Maxwell AFB, Ala., 1985. Cert. fire officer II, fire instr. II.; accredited Internat. Fire Svc. Accreditation Congress. Fire protection supr. USAF, Anchorage, 1978-94; sr. fire and safety specialist Alyeska Pipline Svc. Co., Anchorage, 1994—; part-time tchr. U. Alaska, Galena, 1985-86. Sgt. USAF, 1978-94. Home: 905 Agate Ln Wasilla AK 99654 Office: Alyeska Pipeline Svc Co 1835 S Bragaw Anchorage AK 99512

SPANDER, ART, sportswriter; b. L.A., Aug. 30, 1938; m. Elizabeth Newman, June 17, 1962; children: Debbie, Wendy. BA in Polit. Sci., UCLA, 1960. With UPI, 1960; joined Santa Monica (Calif.) Evening Outlook, 1963-65, San Francisco Chronicle, 1965-79; columnist San Francisco Examiner, 1979—. Author: Golf: The Passion and the Challenge, 1978, The Art Spander Collection, 1989. Recipient AP Sports Editors awards, Profl. Football Writers Am. awards, 1st place awards San Francisco Press Club, 1st Place Golf Writers Assn. Am. awards, Hayward-Newland Lifetime Achievement award Calif. Golf Writers. Office: San Francisco Examiner 110 5th Ave San Francisco CA 94103-1310*

SPANGLER, LORNA CARRIE, pharmacy technician; b. San Jose, Calif., Feb. 4, 1938; d. Earl Albert and Elsie Carol (Lincoln) LaPorte; children: Kirk Earl, Eric Clair, David Paul, Linda Jean Spangler-Whiting. AA, Monterey Peninsula Coll., 1958; AS in Pharmacy Tech., Santa Ana (Calif.) Coll., 1982; BSBA, Calif. State U., Long Beach, 1986, MS in Vocat. Edn., 1992. Registered pharmacy technician, Calif.; cert. Pharmacy Technician Certification Bd., 1995; cert. C.C. instr., Calif. Pharmacy technician Meml. Med. Ctr., Long Beach, Calif., 1974-77, technician coord., 1979-87; pharmacy technician Hoag Meml. Hosp., Newport Beach, Calif., 1987-92, Sharp Health Care, Murrieta, Calif., 1992—; preceptor Pharmacy Technician Interns, 1992—; accreditation team Am. Bur. Health Edn. Schs., 1987-91; adv. com. Cerritos (Calif.) Coll., 1982—; speaker in field. Mem. ctrl. com. Libertarian Party, riverside County, 1996—, also treas. Mem. Assn. of Pharmacy Technicians (founder, treas. 1989-91), Valley Computer Soc. (founder 1991), So. Calif. Assn. Pharmacy Technicians (treas. 1990-92, sec. 1992-96, pres. 1996—), Am. Vocat. Assn., Calif. Soc. of Hosp. Pharmacy (task force mem. 1982, nominating com. technician div., 1988), Omicron Tau Theta (Nu chpt. 1988). Office: Sharp Health Care Murrieta 25500 Medical Center Dr Murrieta CA 92562-5965

SPANGLER, LYNICE SUE, software engineer; b. Morris, Ill., Oct. 28, 1962; d. Ralph Duain and Vera Jean (Gemmill) S.; m. Alan R. Hooton, 1994. BS in Computer Sci., Kans. U., 1984; MS in Computer Sci., Portland State U., 1994. System analyst-info. systems Southwestern Bell Telephone Co., St. Louis, Mo., 1984-92; software test engr. Rational Software Corp., Aloha, Oreg., 1993-94; software engr. Intel Corp., Hillsboro, Oreg., 1994—. Mem. Assn. Computing Machinery. Office: Intel Corp MS JF2-64 2111 NE 25th Ave Hillsboro OR 97124-6067

SPANGLER, NITA REIFSCHNEIDER, volunteer; b. Ukiah, Calif., Apr. 17, 1923; d. John Charles and Olga Augusta (Wuertz) Reifschneider; m. Raymond Luper Spangler, Sept. 22, 1946; children: Jon Martin, Mary Raymond, Thor Raymond. BA, Univ. Nev., 1944. News reporter Redwood (Calif.) City Tribune, 1944-46, Country Almanac, Woodside, Calif., 1969-77. Mem. bd. dirs. San Mateo (Calif.) County Hist. Assn., 1961-68, pres., 1964-66; founder, 1st pres. Portolá Expedition Bicentennial Found., 1966-70; chmn. San Mateo County Scenic Rds. Com., 1967-76; mem. San Mateo County Hist. Resource Adv.; mem. commn. San Mateo County Parks and Recreation, 1983-97, past chmn.; cons. hwy. aesthetics Cal Trans., 1981-83; mem. sch. coms. Recipient Commendation, County Bd. Suprs., 1968, 1977, 92. Mem. Sierra Club, Western History Assn., Mormon History Assn., Nev. State Hist. Soc. (life), San Mateo County Hist. Assn. (life, Resolution of Thanks 1968, 76, 94), Friends Redwood City, Kappa Alpha Theta. Democrat. Episcopalian. Home: 970 Edgewood Rd Redwood City CA 94062

SPANGLER, TIMOTHY CHESTER, meteorologist, program director; b. Stoughton, Wis., Sept. 7, 1948; s. Chester Walter and Jane T. (Jungbluth) S.; m. Ellen K. Pfund, Feb. 7, 1970 (div. Nov. 1976); m. Jill Bannon, Nov. 18, 1978; children: Jonathan, Matthew. BS in Meteorology, U. Wis., 1970; MS in Atmospheric Sci., U. Wyo., 1972; PhD in Biometeorology, Utah State U., 1984. Meteorologist North Am. Weather Cons., Salt Lake City, 1972-77, v.p., 1977-83; coastal zone studies group mgr. Westec Svc., Inc., San Diego, 1983-85; asst. prof. No. Ill. U., Dekalb, 1985-90, assoc. prof., 1991; dep. dir. and residence program mgr. Coop. Program Operational Meteorology Endl. Tng. Univ. Corp. Atmospheric Rsch., Boulder, Colo., 1990-92, dir. Coop. Program Operational Meteorology Ednl. Tng., 1992—; mem. edn. ctr. adv. com. Geol. Soc. Am., 1995—; mem. policy com. Unidata, 1987—; mem. coordinating com. Standing Conf. Heads Tng. Insts. Nat. Meteorol. Svcs., 1993—; mem. mgmt. program com. WMO Conf. on Meteorol. and Hydrological Tech., 1995, UN panel of experts on Edn. and Tng. in Meteorology, 1996-2001. Contbr. articles to profl. jours. Grantee Utah Power and Light Co., 1978, EPA, 1980, Nev. Power Co., 1980, Getty Trading and Trasp. Co., 1984, Am. Petroleum Inst., 1985, 89, AMOCO Oil Co., 1986, NSF, 1986, 87, 88, 96, Nat. Ctr. Atmospheric Rsch., 1989, NOAA, 1992, 95. Mem. Am. Meteorol. Soc. (cert. consulting meteorologist, mem. com. meteorol. aspects air pollution 1977-80, chmn. bd. pvt. sector meteorology 1983-84, chmn. bd. cert. consulting meteorologists, 1991-92, chmn. bd. meteorol. and oceanog. edn. in univs. 1993-95, mem. com. continuing edn. 1993-96), Phi Kappa Phi. Office: UCAR COMET PO Box 3000 Boulder CO 80307

SPANIER, NANCY LOUISE, artistic director, educator, choreographer; b. N.Y.C., Dec. 29, 1942; d. Joseph and Muriel (Terr) S.; m. Paul Stanley Oertel, July 11, 1975. B.A. cum laude, Middlebury Coll., 1964; M.A., Mills Coll., 1969. Artistic dir. Nancy Spanier Dance Theatre, 1974—; prof. dance U. Colo. 1969—; tchr. Nat. Theatre Conservatory, Denver, 1984-94. Choreographer including The Balcony, NYU Sch. Arts, over 80 dance, theater creations, 1969—, Le Cabaret de la Passion, 1994, Un Regard en Arciere, 1995, Etapes de ma Vie, 1996; dir. Escales, 1997; dir. (theater) 1 Man Hamlet, 1986, Fixing a Hole, Copenhagen, 1994, (video) Flesh Chronicles, 1989; movement designer The Traveler, L.A., 1987, On The Sunnyside: Cabaret, Denmark, 1991, The Cutting Edge, Denmark, 1991. Colo. Coun. on Arts grantee, 1974—, Nat. Endowment for Arts grantee, 1975-81, Boulder Arts Commn. grantee, 1979-91. Mem. Colo. Dance Alliance. Office: Nancy Spanier Dance Theatre PO Box 4631 Boulder CO 80306-4631

SPANOS, ALEXANDER GUS, professional football team executive; b. Stockton, Calif., Sept. 28, 1923; m. Faye Spanos; children: Dean, Dea Spanos Berberian, Alexis Spanos Ruhl, Michael. LLD (hon.), U. Pacific, 1984. Chmn. bd. dirs. A.G. Spanos Constrn. Inc., Stockton, Calif., 1960—; chmn. bd. dirs. A.G. Spanos Properties Inc., Stockton, Calif., 1960—, A.G. Spanos Mgmt. Inc., Stockton, Calif., 1967—, A.G. Spanos Enterprises Inc., Stockton, Calif., 1971—, A.G. Spanos Devel. Inc., Stockton, Calif., 1973—, A.G. Spanos Realty Inc., Stockton, Calif., 1978—, A.G. Spanos Jet Ctr. Inc., Stockton, Calif., 1980—, A.G.S. Fin. Corp., Stockton, Calif., 1980—; pres., chmn. bd. dirs. San Diego Chargers, 1984—; Chmn. bd. dirs. A.G.S. Spanos Land Co., Stockton, Calif., 1982—. Former trustee Children's Hosp., San Francisco, San Francisco Fine Arts Mus.; trustee Eisenhower Med. Ctr., Rancho Mirage, Calif.; hon. regent U. Pacific, Stockton, 1972-82; gov. USO, , Washington, 1982—. Served with USAF, 1942-46. Recipient Albert Gallatin award Zurich-Am. Ins. Co., 1973, Horatio Alger award Horatio Alger Found., 1982, medal of Honor Statue of Liberty-Ellis Islan Found., 1982. Mem. Am. Hellenic Ednl. Progressive Assn., Calif. C. of C. (bd. dirs. 1980-85). Republican. Greek Orthodox. Office: San Diego Chargers Jack Murphy Stadium PO Box 609609 San Diego CA 92160-9609 also: A G Spanos Constrn Co 1341 W Robinhood Dr Stockton CA 95207-5515*

SPARKS, DALE BOYD, allergist, health facility administrator; b. Springfield, Mo., July 14, 1929; s. Roscoe R. and Ruby V. (Boyd) S.; m. Caroline P. Porter, Aug. 3, 1956; children: Susan L., Laura A., Lisa M., Jennifer G. AB, BS, Southwest Mo. State U., 1951; BS in Medicine, U. Mo., 1953; MD, St. Louis U., 1955. Diplomate Am. Bd. Allergy and Immunology. Intern Kansas City (Mo.) Gen. Hosp. U. Med. Ctr., 1955-56; resident U. Mo. Hosp., 1958-60; fellow in allergy and immunology Northwestern U., 1960-61; mem. cons. staff Parkview Cmty. Hosp., 1961—; mem. med. staff Riverside (Calif.) Cmty. Hosp., 1961—, dir. respiratory therapy, 1968-85; dir. respiratory therapy and diagnostic svcs. Riverside Gen. Hosp. U. Med. Ctr., 1965—, chmn. dept. medicine, 1978—, chief med. staff, 1990—; acting dir., health officer Riverside Pub. Health Dept., 1991-93; clin. prof. medicine Loma Linda U. Mem. editl. bd. Immunology and Allergy in Practice, 1980—. Lt. USNR. Fellow ACP (coun. subspecialty Socs. 1988—), Am. Coll. Allergy and Immunology (disting., bd. regents 1989-93, pres. 1990-91, chmn. fin. com./treas. 1990-93, recert. com.), Coll. Allergy, Asthma and Immunology; mem. AMA, Am. Soc. Internal Medicine, Am. Lung Assn. (bd. dirs. 1990—), Am. Heart Assn. (bd. dirs. 1964-70, pres. 1966), Joint Coun. Am. Allergy and Immunology (bd. dirs. 1985-90), Calif. Med. Assn., Calif. Soc. Allergy, Inland Soc. Internal Medicine, Riverside County Med. Assn. (bd. councilors 1980—, alt. del. CMA 1988—), Riverside County Found. Med. Care (sec., past pres.). Office: 4500 Brockton Ave Ste 319 Riverside CA 92501-4028

SPARKS, JACK NORMAN, college dean; b. Lebanon, Ind., Dec. 3, 1928; s. Oakley and Geraldine Ruth (Edrington) S.; m. Esther Lois Bowen, Apr. 11, 1953; children: Stephen Michael, Robert Norman, Ruth Ann, Jonathan Russell. BS, Purdue U., 1950; MA, U. Iowa, 1951, PhD, 1960. Tchr. math. Leyden Community High Sch., Franklin Park, Ill., 1954-58; rsch. asst. U. Iowa, Iowa City, 1958-60; assoc. prof. applied stats., dir. bur. of rsch. U. No. Colo., Greeley, 1960-65; assoc. prof. ednl. psychology Pa. State U., State Coll., 1965-68; dir. corr. Campus Crusade for Christ, San Bernardino, Calif., 1968-69; dir. Christian World Liberation Front, Berkeley, Calif., 1969-75; pastor, ch. overseer New Covenant Apostolic Order, Berkeley, 1975-77; dean St. Athanasius Acad. Orthodox Theology, Santa Barbara, Calif., 1977-87, St. Athanasius Coll., Santa Barbara, 1987-93, St. Athanasius Acad. of Orthodox Theology, Ben Lomnd, Calif., 1993—; cons. Measurement Rsch. Ctr., Iowa City, 1959-60, Western States Small Schs. Project, Greeley, 1962-65, Colo. Coun. on Edn. Rsch., Denver, 1963-65. Author: Letters to Street Christians, 1971, The Mind Benders, 1977, 79, The Resurrection Letters, 1978, The Preaching of the Apostles, 1987, Victory in the Unseen Warfare, 1993; editor: Apostolic Fathers, 1978, 88; gen. editor: The Orthodox Study Bible, 1993, Virtue in the Unseen Warfare, 1995, Prayer in the Unseen Warfare, 1996. Trustee Rock Mont Coll., Denver, 1962-77, Thomas Nelson Co., Nashville, 1977-78. 1st lt. U.S. Army, 1952-54. Mem. Am. Scientific Affiliation, Assn. Orthodox Theologians, Conf. on Faith and History, Phi Delta Kappa (Epsilon chpt. pres. 1959-60). Democrat. Orthodox Christian. Home: 8763 Cling Ct Elk Grove CA 95624 Office: St Athanasius Acad Orthodox Theology Ste 170 10519 E Stockton Blvd Elk Grove CA 95642

SPARKS, WALTER CHAPPEL, horticulturist, educator; b. New Castle, Colo., Aug. 22, 1918; s. Lester Elroy and Jean Ivene (Murray) S.; m. Barbara Ferne Gardner, May 31, 1942; children: Robert, Richard, Eugene. Student, Western State Coll., 1936-37; BS, Colo. State U., 1941, MS, 1943; postgrad., U. Minn., 1945, Wash. State U., 1949, 56-57; DSc (hon.), U. Idaho, 1984. Instr., head dept. agr. Pueblo Jr. Coll., 1941; grad. asst. Colo. State U., 1941-43, instr. horticulture, 1943-44, asst. prof., 1944-47, assoc. prof., 1947; assoc. horticulturist U. Idaho, Aberdeen, 1947-57; acting supt. Aberdeen br. Agrl. Expt. Sta., 1951, 57, 65, horticulturist, 1957—, research prof. horticulture, 1968—, prin. liaison coordinator for potato program, 1976—; exchange prof. Research Inst., Kolding, Denmark, 1972-73; adviser and lectr. on potato problems to various fgn. govts.; cons., adv., Israel, 1980, Philippines, 1981, Jamaica, 1988; dir. Postharvest Inst. Perishables, 1980—. Contbr. articles to profl. jours. Recipient 50th Anniversary medal Fed. Land Banks, 1967, Disting. Svc. in Potato Industry award Gov. of Idaho, 1967, Alumni Svc. award 1980, Disting. Faculty award Phi Kappa Phi, 1980, Disting. Svc. award for rsch. in potato postharvest storage tech., 1987, Cert. of Appreciation Nat. Potato Rsch. Edn. Found., 1986, Agriculture Svc. award N.W. Food Processor Field Reps., 1987; named to Hall of Fame Potato Mus. Brussels, 1977, Idaho Agrl. Hall of Fame, 1983, Idaho Potato Hall of Fame for outstanding contbn. to Idaho Potato Industry, 1996; Eldred Jenne Rsch. fellow, 1957; named 1 of 100 "People Make the Difference" in Idaho, 1990. Mem. AAAS, Am. Inst. Biol. Scis., Am. Soc. Hort. Sci. (life), European Assn. Potato Research, N.W. Assn. Horticulturists, Entomologists and Plant Pathologists, Idaho Acad. Sci., Nat. Potato Research and Edn. Found. (cert. appreciation seed potato storage tech. 1986), N.W. Food Processors Assn. (Disting. Service award, 1987), N.W. Fieldman's Assn. (Disting. Agrl. Service award, 1987), Potato Assn. Am. (life mem., past pres., dir.), Western Regional Potato Improvement Group (past pres.), C. of C., Scabbard and Blade, Sigma Xi (Outstanding Research Paper award 1974), Gamma Sigma Delta (Outstanding Research Worker award 1977, award of merit 1978), Alpha Zeta, Beta Beta Beta, Epsilon Rho Epsilon. Club: Rotary. Home: 1100 Burnett Dr Apt 513 Nampa ID 83651-7578 Office: U Idaho Rsch and Extension Ctr Aberdeen ID 83210 *If the food losses occurring from the farmer to the consumer (including storage) could be minimized or completely eliminated, the food supply could be significantly increased without bringing one more acre of land into production, or using one more pound of fertilizer, or using one additional gallon of fuel. Proper handling and storage can accomplish this goal.*

SPARLIN, JULIE ANGELA, magazine editor; b. Roseburg, Oreg., Jan. 22, 1967; d. Roy Keith and Charlene Susan (Farrow) S.; m. Stephen William Orosz, Nov. 20, 1989 (div. May 1994); m. Yumio Dornberg, Jan. 18, 1997. BA, U. Oreg., 1994. Reporter Oreg. Daily Emerald, Eugene, 1992-93; sr. editor Bobit Pub. Co., Redondo Beach, Calif., 1994—. Editor Triton Yacht Club newsletter, 1992-93. Mem. Soc. Profl. Journalists. Office: Bobit Pub Co 2512 Artesia Blvd Redondo Beach CA 90278

SPARLING, REBECCA HALL, retired materials engineer, energy consultant; b. Memphis, June 7, 1910; d. Robert Meredith and Kate Wallace (Sampson) Hall; m. Edwin Kinmonth Smith, Oct. 30, 1935 (div. 1947); 1 child, Douglas Kinmonth; m. Joseph Sparling, July 10, 1948; B.A., Vanderbilt U., 1930, M.S., 1931. Registered profl. engr., Calif. Design specialist Gen. Dynamics, Pomona, Calif., 1951-68, Northrop Aircraft, Hawthorne, Calif., 1944-51; cons. engr., Detroit, 1936-44; tech. writer William H. Baldwin, N.Y.C., 1934-35; metallurgist Lakeside Malleable, Racine, Wis., 1933-34, Am. Cast Iron Pipe, Birmingham, Ala., 1931-32; energy cons., Laguna Hills, Calif., 1973-85. Author; contbr. articles to profl. jours. Officer, leader Fgn. Policy Assn. of Leisure World, Laguna Hills, 1980-84; bd. dirs. AAUW, 1974-84; mem. Air Pollution Control Bd., San Bernardino County, 1973; cons., intervenor Calif. Energy Commn., 1975-82. Recipient Engring. Merit award Orange County Council Engrs. Soc., 1978; named Outstanding Engr. Inst. Advancement of Engring., 1978, Los Angeles Engrs. Week, 1965. Fellow Soc. Woman Engrs. (Achievement award 1957), Inst. Advancement Engring.; mem. Am. Soc. Metals, Am. Soc. Nondestructive Testing, Delta Delta Delta. Republican. Religious Sci. Ch. Address: 650 Harrison Ave Claremont CA 91711-4595

SPARR, DANIEL BEATTIE, federal judge; b. Denver, June 8, 1931; s. Daniel John and Mary Isabel (Beattie) S.; m. Virginia Sue Long Sparr, June 28, 1952; children: Stephen Glenwood, Douglas Lloyd, Michael Christopher. BSBA, U. Denver, 1952, JD, 1966. Bar: Colo. U.S. Dist. Ct. Assoc. White & Steele, Denver, 1966-70; atty. Mountain States Telephone & Telegraph Co., Denver, 1970-71; ptnr. White & Steele, Denver, 1971-74; atty. Wesley H. Doan, Lakewood, Colo., 1974-75; prin. Law Offices of Daniel B. Sparr, Denver, 1975-77; judge 2d dist. Colo. Dist. Ct., Denver, 1977-90; judge U.S. Dist. Ct. Colo., Denver, 1990—. Mem. Denver Bar Assn. (trustee 1975-78), Denver Paralegal Inst. (bd. advs. 1976-88), William E. Doyle's/Am. Inns of Ct., Am. Bd. Trial Advs., ABA, Colo. Bar Assn. Office: US Dist Ct US Courthouse Rm 540C 1929 Stout St Denver CO 80294-0001*

SPATH, CHARLES EMMETT, state official; b. Washington, Jan. 12, 1936; s. Harry Wright Spath and Lillian Ada Baker Blackburn; m. donna Louise Beougher, Dec. 20, 1958; children: Curt Eugene, Sherri Jo. BA in Bus. Edn., U. No. Colo., Greeley, 1958; MA in Pub. Adminstrn., U. N.Mex., 1970. Dir. orgn. and pers. AEC, Albuquerque, 1973-75; dir. exec. devel. ctr. U.S. Dept. Energy, Oak Ridge, 1975-78, asst. mgr. info. mgmt., 1978-89; dir. intergovtl. and external affairs U.S. Dept. Energy, Albuquerque, 1989-91; spl. asst. to gov. State of N.Mex., Santa Fe, 1991-94; mem. N.Mex. Adult Parole Bd., Santa Fe, 1994-95; dep. state land commr. N.Mex. State Land Office, Santa Fe, 1995—; adj. prof. pub. adminstrn. U. N.Mex., U. Albuquerque, Coll. Santa Fe, 1967-75, U. Tenn., Knoxville, 1975-80. Mem. sch. bd. Clark County Schs., Las Vegas, 1966-67; dep. dir. pres. Carter Re-Orgn. Task Force, Washington, 1978. Cpl. U.S. Army, 1955-57. Mem. Am. Soc. for Pub. Adminstrn. (pres. 1967, 83), Am. Soc. Info. Sci. (pres. 1978), State Pers. Dirs. Soc. (sec. 1970-72), Soc. for Pers. Adminstrn. (pres. 1967-70), Rotary (v.p.), Toastmasters Internat. Democrat. Home: 1404 Pinnacle View Dr NE Albuquerque NM 87112 Office: NMex State Land Office PO Box 1148 Santa Fe NM 87504

SPAULDING, JOHN PIERSON, public relations executive, marine consultant; b. N.Y.C., June 25, 1917; s. Forrest Brisbine and Genevieve Anderson (Pierson) S.; m. Eleanor Rita Bonner, Aug. 18, 1947; children:

Anne Spaulding Balzhiser, John F., Mary T. Spaulding Calvert; m. 2d, Donna Alene Abrescia, May 15, 1966. Student Iowa State Coll., 1935-36, Grinnell Coll., 1936-38, U. Chgo., 1938-39. Reporter, Chgo. City News Bur., UPI, 1939-40; editor Cedar Falls (Iowa) Daily Record, 1940-41; picture editor Des Moines Register & Tribune, 1941-42, 47-50; pub. relations dir. Motor Club Iowa, Davenport, 1950-51; commd. 2d. lt. USAF, 1942, advanced through grades to maj., 1947, recalled, 1951, advanced through grades to lt. col.; ret., 1968; v.p. Vacations Hawaii, Honolulu, 1969-70; dir. pub. relations, mgr. pub. relations services Alexander & Baldwin, Inc., Honolulu, 1970-76; mgr. community relations Matson Navigation Co., Honolulu, 1976-81. Pres., Econ. Devel. Assn., Skagit County, Wash., 1983-85; pres., chmn. Fidalgo Island Ednl. Youth Found.; mem. Anacortes (Wash.) Sch. Bd., 1982-88; mem. Gov.'s Tourism Devel. Council, 1983-85; mem. adv. com. State Ferry System, 1982—, productivity coun., 1990—; chmn. Everett chpt. S.C.O.R.E., 1984-86, Bellingham chpt., 1991—; mem. citizens adv. com. Skagit County Transit, 1995—. Decorated Air medal. Mem. Pub. Relations Soc. Am. (pres. Hawaii chpt. 1974), Hawaii Communicators (pres. 1973), Nat. Def. Transp. Assn. (pres. Aloha chpt. 1980-81, Disting. Service award 1978-79), Air Force Assn., Can. Inst. Internat. Affairs, Anacortes C. of C., Sigma Delta Chi (life). Clubs: Propeller (pres. Port of Honolulu 1979-80), Honolulu Press, Fidelgo Yacht, Hawaii Yacht, Royal Hawaiian 400 Yacht (comdr. 1977-81), Rotary (sec. 1996—), Elks. Home: 6002 Sands Way Anacortes WA 98221-4015

SPEACE, OSCAR KIMBROUGH, television producer and director, writer; b. Phila., Mar. 11, 1948; s. Robert St. Clair and Janka (Festinger) S.; m. Janice Joy Noga, Aug. 8, 1981; 1 stepchild, John Nicklas. BA, Fresno State Coll., 1971. Asst. golf pro L.A. Country Club, 1972-73, Phila. Country Club, 1973-76; salesman Sears, Fresno, Calif., 1976-78; newspaper reporter Dinuba (Calif.) Sentinel, 1978-79; videotape libr. Unitel Prodn. Svcs., N.Y.C., 1979-80; freelance dir. Phila. and N.Y.C., 1980-81; producer, dir. Valley Pub. TV, Fresno, 1981—; producer, dir. Valley Press, 1990. Dir. TV documentary film Conquest of My Brother, 1992, Ray Appleton Talk Show, Calif. and London, 1995; prodr., writer ABC 30, 1997; screenwriter film scripts The Station, 1985, The Great Marble Shoot, 1987, The Last Hanging, 1996. Phila. Golf Assn. scholar, 1966-71. Mem. Nat. Acad. TV Arts and Scis., Ind. Feature Project/West, Sherwood Golf Club. Republican. Jewish. Home: 2715 N Van Ness Blvd Fresno CA 93704

SPEARS, JAMES WILLIAM, systems programmer, consultant; b. Mt. Clemens, Mich., Oct. 2, 1958; s. Arthur Jackson and Margaret Elizabeth (McLeod) S. Student, Oakland C.C., 1983-85, Northwestern U., 1976-78. Computer operator, tutor Oakland C. C., Farmington Hills, Mich., 1983-84; systems programmer, application programmer Nat. Wholesale Drug Co., Detroit, 1984-85; systems programmer Domino's Pizza, Inc., Ann Arbor, Mich., 1985-86; systems engr. Computer Assocs. Internat., Inc., Dearborn, Mich., 1987; cons. JWS and Assocs., Walled Lake, Mich., 1987-90; systems programmer Alexander Hamilton Life Ins., Inc., Farmington Hills, 1990-91; cons. level 2 support staff IBM, Poughkeepsie, N.Y., 1991-94; sr. tech. support rep. Legent Corp., Columbus, Ohio, 1994-95, Cross Access Corp., Sunnyvale, Calif., 1995—; mem. adj. faculty Oakland C.C., Farmington Hills, 1987-88. Mem. Nat. Systems Programmer Assn. Lutheran. Home: Apt J-114 655 S Fair Oaks Ave Sunnyvale CA 94086

SPECHT, CARL FREDERICK, chaplain; b. St. Louis, Nov. 25, 1947; s. Charles W. and Jeanette Ann (Beehan) S.; m. Deborah Jane Simonton. BA in Psychology, Fla. Internat. U., Miami, 1973; MDiv in Theology magna cum laude, Denver Bapt. Theol. Sem., 1979; Clin. Pastoral Edn. degree, Washington U. Med. Ctr., 1986; CPE, Prairie View Mental Health Ctr, 1987. Tchr. Adams City Christian Sch., Denver, 1979-81, Mill Rd. Christian Sch., Evansville, Ind., 1981-85; hosp. chaplain intern Washington U. Med. Ctr., St. Louis, 1986, Prairie View Mental Health Ctr., Newton, Kans., 1986-87; hosp. chaplain Charter Hosp., Wichita, Kans., 1987-88, Camarillo (Calif.) State Hosp., 1989—, Charter Hosp., Thousand Oaks, Calif., 1990-91; pastoral counselor Grace Bapt. Ch., Santa Barbara, Calif., 1993—; guest lectr. psychology internships program, Camarillo State Hosp., 1991-92, hosp. chaplain grief counseling Trauma Response Team, 1992-93. Mem. Am. Assn. Christian Counselors. Avocations: hiking, running, calisthenics, weight lifting. Office: Camarillo State Hosp PO Box 6022 Camarillo CA 93011

SPECK, EUGENE LEWIS, internist; b. Boston, Dec. 17, 1936; s. Robert A. and Anne (Rosenberg) S.; m. Rachel Shoshana; children: Michael Robert, Keren Sara. AB, Brandeis U., Waltham, Mass., 1958; MS, U. Mass., 1961; PhD, George Washington U., 1966, MD, 1969. Diplomate Am. Bd. Internal Medicine with subspecialty in infectious diseases. Intern N.Y. Hosp.-Cornell, 1969-70; rsch. assoc. NIH, Bethesda, Md., 1970-72; resident Barnes Hosp.-Washington U., 1972-73; instr. medicine Washington U., St. Louis, 1972-73; fellow Strong Meml. Hosp.-U. Rochester, 1973-75; instr. medicine U. Rochester, N.Y., 1973-75, asst. prof. medicine, 1975-80; asst. prof. medicine U. Nev., Las Vegas, 1980-85, assoc. prof., 1985-95, prof. medicine, 1995—; dir./co-dir. infectious disease unit U. Med. Ctr. of So. Nev., Las Vegas, 1980—; ptnr. Infectious Diseases Consultants, 1983—; cons. Clark County Health Dept., Las Vegas, 1980—, U. Med. Ctr. So. Nev., Las Vegas, 1980—, Sunrise Hosp., Las Vegas, 1980—, Valley Hosp., Las Vegas, 1980—. Contbr. articles to profl. jours., chpts. to books. Fellow ACP; mem. Am. Soc. Microbiology, Infectious Disease Soc. Am., Alpha Omega Alpha. Home: 2228 Chatsworth Ct Henderson NV 89014-5309 Office: Infectious Diseases Cons 3006 S Maryland Pkwy Ste 780 Las Vegas NV 89109-2246

SPECTER, RICHARD BRUCE, lawyer; b. Phila., Sept. 6, 1952; s. Jacob E. and Marilyn B. (Kron) S.; m. Jill Ossenfort, May 30, 1981; children: Lauren Elizabeth, Lindsey Anne, Allison Lee. BA cum laude, Washington U., St. Louis, 1974; JD, George Washington U., 1977. Bar: Mo. 1977, U.S. Dist. Ct. (ea. and we. dists.) Mo. 1977, U.S. Ct. Appeals (8th cir.) 1977, Ill. 1978, Pa. 1978, U.S. Dist. Ct. (ea. dist.) Ill. 1979, U.S. Ct. Appeals (7th cir.) 1979, Calif. 1984, U.S. Dist. Ct. (cen. dist.) Calif. 1985, U.S. Ct. Appeals (9th cir.) 1986, U.S. Dist. Ct. (so. dist.) Calif. 1987, U.S. Dist. Ct. (no. dist.) Calif. 1988. Assoc. Coburn, Croft, Shepherd, Herzog & Putzell, St. Louis, 1977-79; ptnr. Herzog, Kral, Burroughs & Specter, St. Louis, 1979-82; exec. v.p. Uniqey Internat., Santa Ana, Calif., 1982-84; pvt. practice law L.A. and Irvine, Calif., 1984-87; ptnr. Corbett & Steelman, Irvine, 1987—; instr. Nat. Law Ctr. George Washington U. 1975. Mem. ABA, Ill. Bar Assn., Mo. Bar Assn., Pa. Bar Assn., Calif. Bar Assn. Jewish. Home: 37 Bull Run Irvine CA 92620-2510 Office: 18200 Von Karman Ave Ste 200 Irvine CA 92612-1029

SPECTOR, PHIL, record company executive; b. Bronx, N.Y., Dec. 25, 1940; m. Veronica Bennett, 1968 (div. 1974); children: Gary Phillip and Louis Phillip (twins), Donte Phillip, Nicole and Phillip (twins). Student, UCLA. Producer with Atlantic Records, 1960-61; founder Philles Records, 1962; now pres. Warner-Spector Records, Inc.; also Mother Bertha Music. Mem. mus. group: Teddy Bears, 1958-59; producer records for Gene Pitney, Ike and Tina Turner, Ben E. King, the Beatles, Righteous Bros., Checkmates, Crystals, Ronettes, John Lennon, George Harrison, The Ramones, Yoko Ono, others; producer album A Concert for Bangladesh (Grammy award); composer songs including You've Lost That Lovin' Feelin' (7 million performances; named most performed song in radio and TV performance history 1997), others; appeared in films Tami, Easy Rider; prod., TV documentary film A Giant Stands 5 Ft. 7 In.; prod. film That Was Rock. Named to Rock and Roll Hall of Fame, 1989; named Country Music Song of Yr. Songwriter and Pub. for To Know Him Is To Love Him, 1989; recipient lifetime achievement award U. Calif., Berkeley, 1994, Phila. award Phila. Music Alliance, 1994 (includes star on Phila.'s Walk of Fame); inducted into Songwriters Hall of Fame, 1996. Office: Care Warner-Spector Records Inc 686 S Arroyo Pky Pasadena CA 91105-3233

SPEER, ANDREW KEVIN, art educator; b. Louisville, Dec. 8, 1951; s. Joseph Thomas and Virginia Marie (Anderson) S.; m. Susan Birmingham Garr, May 10, 1970 (div. June 1972); 1 child, Heather; m. Linda Lee Bukszar, Oct. 12, 1974. B Gen. Studies, U. Ky., 1975, MFA in Painting, 1978; postgrad., SUNY, Buffalo, 1976-77. Instr. dept. art U. Ky., Lexington, 1978-79, San Diego State U., 1979-82; instr. studio art Mira Costa (Calif.) Coll., 1981-85; vis. artist Allen R. Hite Art Inst., U. Louisville, 1989, instr., 1990; asst. prof. art Met. State Coll. Denver, 1990—; vis. artist Cornell U., Ithaca, N.Y., 1981. One-man shows include Swanson-Cralle Gallery, Louisville, 1988, Morris B. Belknap Jr. Galleries, U. Louisville, 1990, Auraria Higher Edn. Ctr. Libr., Denver, 1993; exhibited in group shows, 1984—, including Louisville Visual Art Assn., 1987, 88, 89, Mus. Modern Art of Casa de la Cultra, Cuenca, Ecuador, 1990, Headley-Whitney Mus., Lexington, Ky., 1991, Swanson-Cralle Gallery, 1993, Coleman Gallery, Albuquerque, 1994; represented in permanent collection J.B. Speed Art Mus., Louisville. Recipient purchase award J.B. Speed Art Mus., 1977, hon. mention Reader's Digest Artists at Giverny Program, France, 1988, COVision recognition award Colo. Coun. on Arts, 1994; So. Arts Fedn. Regional fellow Nat. Endowment for Arts, 1986, Al Smith fellow Ky. Arts Coun., 1987; grantee Pollock-Krasner Found., 1989, profl. travel grantee Met. State Coll. Denver, 1992. Democrat. Baptist. Office: Met State Coll Denver Art Dept Denver CO 80217

SPEER, JOHN ELMER, freelance paralegal, reporter; b. Conrad, Mont., Mar. 19, 1956; s. Elmer Constant and Mildred Saphronia (LaBelle) S.; m. Sharron D. Knotts, May 23, 1982 (div. Mar. 1986); 1 child, Jeremy Keith; 1 foster child, Casey. Paralegal assoc., Coll. of Great Falls, Mont., 1994. Bar: Mont. 1996; Constrn. Law CLE, 1997. Farmer Valier, Mont., 1956-73; janitor Shelby (Mont.) pub. schs., 1974-75; freelance news reporter Sta. KSEN, Shelby, 1980—, various TV stas., newspapers, Great Falls, 1980-90; office cleaner Parkdale Housing Authority, Great Falls, 1990-95; freelance paralegal, Great Falls, 1993—; law clk., paralegal Mont. State Dist. Judge Thomas McKittrick, Great Falls, 1993; rschr. line-up identification appeal binder to U.S. Supreme Ct., 1993; trial assistance atty. Chas. Joslyn, spring 1996. Contbr. victim-witness assistance program operating manual, 1992. Counselor and adv. Victim-Witness Assistance Svcs., Great Falls, 1991-93. Mem. Mont. Big Sky Paralegal Assn., Am. Counseling Assn. Jehovah's Witness. Home: 3308 Lower River Rd Trlr 19 Great Falls MT 59405-7273

SPELLMAN, DOUGLAS TOBY, advertising executive; b. Bronx, N.Y., May 12, 1942; s. Sydney M. and Leah B. (Rosenberg) S.; BS, Fairleigh Dickinson U., 1964; m. Ronni I. Epstein, Jan. 16, 1966 (div. Mar. 1985); children: Laurel Nicole, Daren Scott; m. Michelle Ward, Dec. 31, 1986, 1 child, Dallas Ward Spellman. Media buyer Doyle, Dane, Bernbach, Inc., N.Y.C., 1964-66, Needham, Harper & Steers, Inc., N.Y.C., 1966; media supr. Ogilvy & Mather, Inc., N.Y.C., 1967-69; media dir. Sinay Advt., L.A., 1969-70; chief ops. officer S.H.H. Creative Mktg., Inc., L.A., 1969—; assoc. media dir. Warren, Mullen, Dolobowsky, Inc., N.Y.C., 1970—; dir. West Coast ops. Ed Libov Assocs., Inc., Los Angeles, 1970-71; media supr. Carson/Roberts Advt. div. Ogilvy & Mather, Inc., L.A., 1971-72; assoc. media dir. Ogilvy & Mather, Inc., L.A., 1972-73; media dir. Vitt Media Internat., Inc., L.A., 1973-74; v.p., dir. West Coast ops. Ind. Media Svcs., Inc., L.A., 1974-75; owner Douglas T. Spellman, Inc., L.A., 1975-77, pres., chmn. bd., 1977-82; pres., chief operating officer Douglas T. Spellman Co. div. Ad Mktg., Inc., L.A., 1982-85; pres., chief exec. officer, chmn. bd. Spellbound Prodns. and Spellman Media divs. Spellbound Communications, Inc., L.A., 1984-86; gen. ptnr. Faso & Spellman, L.A., 1984-86; chief oper. officer, pres. Yacht Mgmt. Internat., Ltd., L.A., 1984-86; v.p. media Snyder, Longino Advt. div. Snyder Advt., L.A., 1985-86; advt./media cons., L.A., 1986-91; gen. ptnr., Nucleus Nuance, L.A., 1987-88; gen. ptnr. Convention Photos Unltd, Hawaii, 1988-89; v.p. mktg. Pacific Med. Products, Inc., L.A., 1990-91; media dir., Kennedy-Wilson Inc., L.A., 1991-94; dir. media and advt. svcs. Goddard & Claussen/First Tuesday, L.A., 1994—; guest lectr. sch. bus UCLA, 1975, U. So. Calif., 1976. Served with U.S. Army Res. N.G., 1964-69. Mem. Aircraft Owners and Pilots Assn., Nat. Rifle Assn., Calif. Pistol and Rifle Assn., Phi Zeta Kappa, Phi Omega Epsilon. Jewish. Clubs: Rolls Royce Owners, Mercedes Benz Am., Aston Martin Owners.

SPENCE, ANDREW MICHAEL, dean, finance educator; b. Montclair, N.J., 1943. BA in Philosophy summa cum laude, Princeton U., 1966; BA, MA in Maths., Oxford U., 1968; PhD in Econs. with honors, Harvard U., 1972. Asst. prof. polit. econ. Kennedy Sch. Govt. Harvard U., Cambridge, Mass., 1971-75, prof. econs., 1977-83, prof. bus. adminstrn., 1979-83, George Gund prof. econs. and bus. adminstrn., 1983-86, vis. prof. econs. dept., 1976-77, chmn. bus. econs. PhD program, 1981-83; chmn. econs. dept. Harvard U., 1983-84, dean Faculty Arts and Scis., 1984-90; assoc. prof. dept. econs. Stanford (Calif.) U., 1973-75, Philip H. Knight prof., dean Grad. Sch. Bus., 1990—; bd. dirs. BankAm. Corp., Gen. Mills, Inc., Nike, Inc., Siebel Syss., Sun Microsyss., VeriFone, Inc.; chmn. Nat. Rsch. Coun. Bd. on Sci., Tech. and Econ. Policy. Author: 3 books; mem. editl. bd. Am. Econs. Rev., Bell. Jour. Econs., Jour. Econ. Theory and Pub. Policy; contbr. over 50 articles to profl. jours. Mem. econs. adv. panel NSF, 1977-79; mem. econs. adv. com. Sloan Found., 1979—. Danforth fellow, 1966; Rhodes scholar, 1966; recipient J.K. Galbraith prize for excellence in tchg., 1978. Fellow AAAS, Econometric Soc.; mem. Am. Econ. Assn. (John Bates Clark medal 1981). Office: Stanford U Grad Sch Bus Bldg 350 Memorial Way Stanford CA 94305-5015

SPENCER, CAROLINE, library director. Past pres. Hawaii Libr. Assn. Office: HI State Public Lib 478 S King St Honolulu HI 96813-2901

SPENCER, DOROTHY ANN, library director, consultant; b. Yonkers, N.Y., Aug. 31, 1947; d. Joseph Edwin and Lillian (Botz) S. BA, Hope Coll., 1969; MLS, Western Mich. U., 1970; PhD, U. Nebr., 1981. Libr. Rombout Mid. Sch., Beacon, N.Y., 1970-71; chief audio visual svcs. libr., assoc. prof. Med. Coll. Ga., Augusta, 1971-79; logistics mgr. internat. tng. Darwin (Australia) C.C., 1982; libr. dir. Kern Med. Ctr., Bakersfield, Calif., 1985-88; dir. Kauffman libr. Calif. Sch. Profl. Psychology, Fresno, 1988-95; dir. Graziano Libr. Samuel Merritt Coll., Oakland, Calif., 1996—. Co-author: Biosocial Psychopathology, 1994. Mem. ALA, No. Calif./Nev. Med. Libr. Group, Med. Libr. Assn., Acad. Health Info. Profls. of Med. Libr. Assn. (disting.). Office: Samuel Merritt Coll 400 Hawthorne Ave Oakland CA 94609

SPENCER, DOUGLAS LLOYD, chemist, manufacturing executive; b. Berkeley, Calif., July 19, 1952; s. Alma Glenn and Anna Lea (Lloyd) S.; m. Connie Jeanette Whitesel, Aug. 23, 1974; children: Jeanette Dawn, Jared Douglas, Jilissa Annette, Janine Marie, Janelle Renee, Jeffrey Brian. AA, Diablo Valley Coll., 1971; BS, Brigham Young U., 1974. Lab. instr. chemistry dept. Brigham Young U., 1973-74; rsch. chemist Dow Chem. Western div., Pittsburg, Calif., 1975-80; pres. Sunset Distbg., Inc., Brentwood, Calif., 1980-82; pres. Maier & Assocs., Inc., Brentwood, 1982-83; pres. Doug Spencer & Assocs., Placerville, 1983-94; buyer major wholesale merchandise distbr., Bacar, Inc., San Jose, 1995—. Mem. Brentwood Planning Commn., 1980-81; missionary, dist. zone leader Eastern States Mission, 1971-73; active Boy Scouts of Am.. Rossmoor residents scholar, 1969-71, Brigham Young U. scholar, 1973-74. Republican. Mormon. Avocations: camping, fishing, gardening. Home: 2010 Clearview Dr Hollister CA 95023-6239 Office: PO Box 610130 San Jose CA 95161-0130

SPENCER, HERBERT WARD, III, air pollution control manufacturing company executive; b. Louisville, June 12, 1945; s. Herbert W. Jr. and Mary (Armstrong) S.; m. Elizabeth Ryan, Sept. 2, 1967 (div. Feb. 1984); children—Andrew Heath, Jennifer Coates; m. Amy R. Soejoto, Aug. 12, 1984. B.A., Vanderbilt U., 1967; M.S., Auburn U., 1969, Ph.D., 1974. Research physicist So. Research Inst., Birmingham, Ala., 1974-76; research engr. Joy Mfg., L.A., 1976-79, mgr. advanced tech., 1979-85, chief devel. engr., 1985-86, mgr. new tech., 1986-87, founder, exec. v.p. EC&C Techs., La Canada, Calif., 1988—; owner HWS Engring. and Rsch. Co., 1989—, pres., 1996—. Mem. bd. mgrs. Santa Clara Valley YMCA, 1986—. Contbr. articles to profl. publs. NDEA fellow Auburn U., Ala., 1971-73; NSF summer trainee Auburn U., 1969. Mem. Am. Phys. Soc., Air and Waste Mgmt. Assn., Sigma Xi. Republican. Presbyterian. Office: EC&C Techs 4234 Chevy Chase Dr La Canada Flintridge CA 91011-3844

SPENCER, HOWARD DALEE, art museum curator; b. Dayton, Ohio, Mar. 23, 1950; s. Herbert Leo and Nellie Kate (DaLee) S. BS, Ind. State U., 1972, MFA, 1976. Student asst., grad. asst., exhibits preparator Swope Art Mus., Terre Haute, Ind., 1969-78, interim dir., 1978; curator of collections and exhbns. Wichita (Kans.) Art Mus., 1979-89; curator collections and exhbns. Nev. Mus. Art, Reno, 1992—. Office: Nev Mus Art 160 W Liberty St Reno NV 89501-1916

SPENCER, MARY JOSEPHINE, pediatrician; b. Joliet, Ill., Oct. 19, 1936; d. Ray Miller and Marjorie Elizabeth (Tedens) Mason; m. Donald James Spencer, June 3, 1960; children: Kenneth Donald, Marjorie Elizabeth, Katherine Anne, Christine Mary. BA, U. Colo., 1958; MD, UCLA, 1964. Diplomate Am. Bd. Pediatrics; lic. physician, Calif. Intern L.A. County Gen. Hosp., 1964-65; health officer L.A. Count Health Dept., 1965-66; gen. practice Kaiser Permanente Med. Group, West Los Angeles, 1966-69; resident in pediatrics Harbor Gen. Hosp./UCLA, 1969-71; clin. faculty, instr. dept. pediatrics UCLA, 1971-73, fellow in infectious diseases, 1973-75, asst. prof. pediatrics, 1975-82; assoc. clin. prof. pediatrics U. Calif., San Diego, 1983—; pvt. practice pediatrics and infectious diseases San Diego, 1982—; staff ambulatory pediatrics L.A. County Health Dept., 1973; acting dir. Marion Davies Children's Clinic, 1973, chief divsn. ambulatory pediatrics and dir., 1975-81; physician Sex Abuse Team, Children's Hosp., San Diego, 1982-85; med. dir. child abuse program Palomar Med. Ctr., Escondido, Calif., 1985—; cons. and lectr in field; del. Statehouse Conf. on Children and Youth, 1981; cons. pub. adv. com. NIH, 1981; expert witness in ct. child abuse and neglect cases, L.A. Contbr. numerous articles and abstracts to profl. jours., chpts. to books; co-editor: Your Child's Health Care at the UCLA Marion Davies Children's Center, 1982; reviewer Am. Jour. Diseases of Childhood, 1981, Pediatric Infectious Diseases, 1982, 83, 86, Pediatrics, 1986; adv. com. med. World News. Bd. dirs. UCLA Day Care Ctr., Ocean Park Cmty. Ctr., Westside Child Trauma Coun.; mem. L.A. County Task Force on Child Abuse; choir mem. St. Bartholomew's Episcopal Ch., 1990—; mgr., sponsor Rancho Bernardo women's softball teams, 1990-93; coach, mgr. Rancho Bernardo girls' softball, 1987, 88, 90. Grantee HIN, 1974-75, Hoffman LaRoche Labs., 1977, Eli Lilly Co., 1978-80, 80, 81, USPHS, 1977, 78, 80-83, 80-81, 81-84; named Woman of Yr. Santa Monica YWCA, 1982; recipient Woman of Distinction Rancho Bernardo Soroptimist award, 1994, First Ann. Unity award Palomar-Pomerado Health Network, 1994. Mem. Am. Acad. Pediatrics, Western Soc. Pediatric Rsch., Ambulatory Pediatric Soc. (region IX co-chmn. 1978-79, vice-chmn. 1979-80, rsch. com. 1979-82), Infectious Disease Soc. Am., Pediatric Infectious Disease Soc. Republican. Home: 18675 Avenida Cordillera San Diego CA 92128-1529 Office: Childrens Med Group 910 E Ohio Ave Ste 103 Escondido CA 92025-3439

SPENCER, NEAL RAYMOND, entomologist; b. Honolulu, Hawaii, July 9, 1936; s. Henry Jackson and Florence Lillian (Evans) S.; m. Patricia Louise Wilbur, Feb. 15, 1965; children: Quentin Reynolds, Nathan Patrick, Lisa Louise, Creighton Reynolds. BS, U. Fla., 1961, postgrad., 1970-77; postgrad., U. Mo., 1965-67. Staff entomologist Govt. of Am.Samoa, Pago Pago, 1963-65, Govt of Guam, Agana, 1968-70; entomologist USDA/ARS, Gainesville, Fla., 1970-77, Rome, Italy, 1977-81, Stoneville, MS, 1981-88, Sidney, Mont., 1988—. Contbr. numerous articles to profl. jours. Scoutmaster, cubmaster, chief exec. officer Boy Scouts of Am. Mem. Entomol. Soc. Am., Weed Sci. Soc. Am. Republican. Office: USDA/ARS 1500 N Central Ave Sidney MT 59270-5519

SPENCER, ROBERT C., political science educator; b. Chgo., Mar. 28, 1920; m. Edith Maxham McCarthy, Sept. 13, 1941; children: Margaret, Catherine, Anne, Thomas More, David. AB, U. Chgo., 1943, MA, 1952, PhD in Polit. Sci. (Univ. fellow 1952-53), 1955. Instr. polit. sci. and sociology St. Michaels Coll., 1949-51, asst., then assoc. prof. polit. sci., 1953-60, prof. govt., 1960-63, dir. summer sessions, 1960-61, asst. to pres., 1963-65; prof. polit. sci., chmn. dept., dean summer sessions U. R.I., 1965-67; grad. dean U. R.I. (Grad. Sch.), 1967-69; founding pres. Sangamon State U., Springfield, Ill., 1969-78; prof. govt. and public affairs Sangamon State U., 1978-88, prof. emeritus, 1988—; research assoc. Indsl. Relations Center, U. Chgo., 1952-53; extension lectr. N.Y. State Sch. Indsl. and Labor Relations, Cornell U., 1956-57; vice chmn. West Central Ill. Ednl. Telecommunications Consortium, 1975-77, chmn., 1977-78; chmn. task force personnel Vt. Little Hoover Commn., 1957-58; mem. Ill. adv. com. U.S. Commn. on Civil Rights, 1979-87; bd. mgrs. Franklin Life Variable Annuity Funds, 1974—; vis. prof. polit. sci., sr. rsch. assoc. local govt. ctr. Mont. State U., Bozeman, 1985, 89, 90—. Author: (with Robert J. Huckshorn) The Politics of Defeat, 1971. Bd. dirs. City Day Sch., Springfield, 1979-83, Gt. Am. People Show Repertory Co., 1980-90; vice chmn. Petersburg Libr. Bd., 1982-88; chmn. Petersburg Zoning Bd. Appeals, 1984-90; mem. Vt. Senate, 1959-63; faculty fellow Ford Found.'s Nat. Ctr. for Edn. in Politics, rsch. dir. Dem. Nat. Com., 1962-63; mem. adv. bd. Landmark Preservation Coun. Ill., 1986-89; mem., treas. Gallatin County Coun. on Aging, 1993—. Roman Catholic. Home: 2303 S 3rd Ave Bozeman MT 59715-6009

SPENCER, TAMAR LISH, aerospace engineer; b. L.A., July 2, 1963; d. Merrill Arthur and Marganit (Vardi) Lish; m. Todd Steven Spencer, Sept. 2, 1984; children: Shira, Arielle. BA in Econs., UCLA, 1985; BSME, Calif. State U., Long Beach, 1989, MS in Engring., 1991. Mem. tech. staff Space Sys. Divsn. Rockwell Internat., Downey, Calif., 1987-92; math tutor, Huntington Beach and Lake Forest, Calif., 1992—. Mem. Huntington Beach Concert Band. Mem. AIAA, Tau Beta Pi.

SPENCER, TED, museum director. Exec. dir. Alaska Aviation Heritage Mus., Anchorage. Office: Alaska Aviation Heritage Mus 4721 Aircraft Dr Anchorage AK 99502

SPERBER, BURTON S., construction executive; b. 1929. Chmn., pres. Valley Crest Landscape, Inc., Calabasas, Calif., 1949—. Office: Valley Crest Landscape Inc 24121 Ventura Blvd Calabasas CA 91302-1449*

SPERRY, EDMUND LYNN, real estate broker; b. Salt Lake City, Dec. 11, 1948; s. Edmund T. and Marjory (Matheson) S.; m. Anna Grace Bellis, Sept. 1, 1978; 1 child, Heather Anne Harris. Student, U. Utah, 1967, 70-71, U. N.C., 1971-73. Cert. real estate broker Utah. Sales assoc. Hooper Ballstaedt Realtors, Salt Lake City, 1971-79; bus. devel. cons. Realty World Intermountain Region, Salt Lake City, 1979-81; mgr. Commerce Residential Properties, Salt Lake City, 1981-82; owner broker E.L. Sperry Group Realtors, Salt Lake City, 1982-88; cons. Nat. Note, Salt Lake City, 1988-89; mng. ptnr. Bellis Sperry Group, Salt Lake City, 1989—; dir. Hooper Ballstaedt, Salt Lake City, 1977-79, Commerce Properties, 1981-82, Utah Residential Real Estate, Salt Lake City, 1982-92. Author: Franchise Operations Manual, 1989; contbr. articles to profl. jours. Bd. dirs. Habitat for Humanity, Salt Lake City, 1981-84, Cmty. Housing Resource Bd., Salt Lake City, 1989-92, Utah Vet. Licensing Com., Salt Lake City, 1992-96, Physicians Licensing Bd., 1996—; mayors com. for critical needs housing Mayors Conf., Washington, 1993. Sgt. U.S. Army, 1967—. Mem. Salt Lake Bd. Realtors, Utah Assn. Realtors, Nat. Assn. Realtors. Office: Bellis Sperry Realtors PO Box 58951 Salt Lake City UT 84158-0951

SPEZZANO, CHARLES LEE, seminar leader, lecturer, trainer, writer; b. Schenectady, N.Y., Jan. 2, 1948; s. Peter Spezzano and Katherine (Shelton) Kane; m. Lency K. Abel, Oct. 13, 1984; children: Christopher, J'aime. BA in Psychology and Philosophy, Duquesne U., 1970, MA in Sociology, 1971; PhD in Counseling and Psychology, U.S. Internat. U., 1977. Cert. marriage, family and child counselor. Dir. cmty. rels., counselor Bradshear Assoc., Pitts., 1971-72; psychologist, therapy supr., workshop coord. Naval Drug Rehab. Ctr., NAS Miramar, San Diego, 1973-79; sr. trainer ARAS Tng. Corp., San Diego, 1979-80; interim minister Windward Unity Ch., Kailua, Hawaii, 1983-84; pvt. practice marriage, family and child counselor Calif. and Hawaii, 1980-92; founder, seminar leader Break-Through Seminars, Tokyo, 1985; pres., lectr., seminar leader, author Spezzano & Assocs., Ltd., Kaneohe, Hawaii, 1990—; tng. lectr. Spezzano & Assocs. Ltd., Vancouver, B.C., Can., 1980—, Switzerland, 1986, Eng., 1987, France, 1988; therapist, trainer, lectr., Tokyo, Nagoya, Osaka, Mt. Fuji, Fukuoka, and Nagasaki, Japan, 1983—; trainer and lectr., Taiwan, 1991—, Malaysia, 1992-96. Author: Awaken the Gods, 1991, 30 Days to Find Your Perfect Mate, 1994, 96, If it Hurts, It Isn't Love - Secrets of Successful Relationships, 1995, 30 Days To Getting Along With Absolutely Anyone, 1996, The Enlightenment Pack, 1996. Mem. Assn. for Humanistic Psychology. Office: Spezzano & Assocs Ltd 47-416 Waihee Pl Kaneohe HI 96744-4958

SPIEGEL, DAVID, psychiatrist; b. N.Y.C., Dec. 11, 1945; s. Herbert Spiegel and Natalie Shainess; m. Helen Margaret Blau, July 25, 1976; children: Daniel, Julia. PhB, Yale Coll., 1967; MD, Harvard Med. Sch., 1971. Lic. psychiatrist Calif., Mass., N.Y.; diplomate Am. Bd. Med. Examiners, Am. Bd. Psychiatry and Neurology. Resident Mass. Mental Health Ctr. and Cambridge Hosp., 1971-74; resident tutor, premedical advisor Winthrop House Harvard Coll., Cambridge, Mass., 1972-74; clin. instr. Stanford (Calif.) U. Sch. Med., 1974-75; staff psychiatrist San Mateo (Calif.) County

Mental Health Program, 1974-75; from acting asst. prof. to prof. psychiatry/behavioral scis. Stanford U. Sch. Med., 1975-94; chief brief treatment inpatient unit Palo Alto Vets. Adminstrn. Med. Ctr., Calif., 1975-76; dir. social psychiatry cmty. svcs. Palo Alto Vets. Adminstrn., 1976-80; dir. psychiatry clinic Stanford U. Med. Ctr., 1980-89; assoc. dir. psychiat inpatient therapeutic cmty. Stanford U. Med. Ctr., 1981-83; med. dir. Stanford U. Clinic, 1986-87; assoc. rsch. psychiatrist U. Calif., San Francisco, 1986-91; dir. faculty med. psychotherapy clinic Stanford U. Med. Ctr., 1989—; physician, cons. psychology svc. Dept. Vets. Affairs Med. Ctr., 1994—. Editor: Progress in Psychiatry Series, 1984—, mem. editl. bd., 1986-89; med. co-editor: Internat. Jour. Clin. Exptl. Hypnosis, 1988-95; assoc. editor: Am. Jour. Clin. Hypnosis, 1985—, Am. Jour. Psychiatry, 1991-95, The Breast, 1994—; consulting editor: Health Psychology, 1990-91; mem. editl. bd.: Jour. of Psychosocial Oncology, 1983—, Jour. Traumatic Stress, 1986-90, Dissociation, 1988—, Psycho Oncology, 1991, Consciousness and Cognition, 1991—, Health Psychology, 1992, Columbia U. Sch. Pub. Health Newsletter, 1994—. Mem. data processing policy com. Dept. Mental Health, Mass., 1972-73, bd. dirs. No. Calif. Burn Coun., 1976-84; pub. mem. Chief Justice's Spl. Com. to Study Appellate Practices in First Appellate Dist., 1977-81. Recipient Treya Killam Wilber award Cancer Support Cmty, 1993, Pierre Janet Wrting award Internat. Soc. for Study Dissociation, 1994, Edward A. Strecker, M.D. award The Inst. of Pa. Hosp. and Jefferson Med. Coll., 1995; 8th Annual Chrysalis Gala honoree CHEMOcare, 1993. Fellow Am. Coll. Psychiat. Assn., Am. Soc. Clin. Hypnosis, Am. Psychiat. Assn., Assn. for Clin. Psychosocial Rsch., Soc. Behavioral Medicine, Soc. for Clin. and Exptl. Hypnosis (pres. 1995-97, Schneck award 1986, Best Theoretical Paper award 1991); mem. Urgent Action Network, Amnesty Internat. Office: Stanford U Sch Med 401 Quarry Rd Rm 2325 Stanford CA 94305-5544

SPIEGEL, MARCIA COHN, writer; b. Chgo., Oct. 16, 1927; d. Alfred and Helen (Yankelowitz) Cohn; m. Sidney L. Spiegel; children: Linda Allen, Randi, Judy, Edward, Steven. BA in Psychology, Rockford (Ill.) Coll., 1949; MA in Communal Svc., Hebrew Union Coll., L.A., 1979; Cert. Beyond Classroom, U. So.Calif, L.A., 1980. Instr. U. Judaism, L.A., 1979-91, UCLA Ext., 1980-81; cons. in vol. devel., 1979-92; lectr., workshop facilitator in women's studies and spirituality, 1980—. Co-author: Women Speak to God, 1987, Jewish Women's Awareness Guide, 1992, Chemical Dependency: Catholic-Jewish Relfections, 1987; author: The Jewish Woman: A Portrait in Her Own Words, 1978, The Heritage of Noah: Alcoholism in the Jewish Community Today, 1980, Women in the Bible: A Study Course, 1983; contbr. articles to books, mags. and periodicals. Co-founder Jr. Great Books, Palos Verdes, Calif., 1960-75; co-founder, later pres. Alcoholism Coun. South Bay, Torrance, Calif., 1968-80; co-founder, pres. Women Writers West, L.A., 1980; commr. L.A. County Commn. on Alcohol, 1980-83; founder Jewish Arts Assocs., 1981—, Creative Jewish Women's Alliance, 1979, Alcohol/Drug Action Program, 1983—; mem. Bnot Eish Spiritual Cmty., 1981—; mem. Jewish task force Ctr. for Prevention of Sexual and Domestic Violence, 1993—, sec. Project Kesher, 1996—. Recipient Award of Distinction, Rockford Coll., 1984, Frances Henry award Hebrew Union Coll., L.A., 1978, Cmty. award Jewish Fedn. South Bay, 1992, Achievement award Nat. Fedn. Temple Sisterhoods, 1978, Alumni of Yr. award Hebrew Union Coll./Jewish Inst. Religion, 1994; named L.A. County Woman of Yr., 1997. Democrat.

SPIEGEL, RONALD STUART, insurance company executive; b. Chgo., Sept. 12, 1942; s. Arthur I. and Elaine M. (Young); m. Carol J. Lieberthal, July 25, 1964; children: Eric, Elissa. BA, Calif. State U., Los Angeles, 1966. Pres. Newhouse Automotive, Los Angeles, 1966-78; agt. N.Y. Life Ins. Co., Santa Fe Springs, Calif., 1978-82, sales mgr., 1982-86, assoc. gen. mgr., 1986-88, gen. mgr., 1989-91; assoc. gen. mgr. N.Y. Life Ins. Co., Fullerton, Calif., 1991—; v.p. Cerritos Valley Br. Life Underwriters Assn. of Los Angeles, 1984-86, pres., 1987-88. Pres. Temple Shalom, West Covina, Calif., 1975-77, 88-89, 93-94, treas., 1978-83; pres. Temple Ami-Shalom, West Covina, 1994-95, Jewish Fedn. Coun. Ea. Region, L.A., 1986-89, v.p., 1984-85. Mem. Am. Soc. CLUs, Gen. Agts. and Mgrs. Assn., Airline Owners and Pilots Assn., Nat. Assn. Life Underwriters. Democrat. Lodge: Kiwanis. Home: 5050 Coldwater Cyn # 401 Sherman Oaks CA 91423 Office: NY Life Ins Co 3230 E Imperial Hwy Ste 100 Brea CA 92821

SPIER, LUISE EMMA, film editor, director; b. Laramie, Wyo., Aug. 22, 1928; d. Louis Constantine Cames and Vina Jane Cochran; m. John Spier, Sept., 1957 (div. 1962). Student, U. Wyo., 1947, U. Calif., Berkeley, 1948-53. Head news film editor Sta. KRON-TV, San Francisco, 1960-70, film editor, 1980—; freelance film editor, director San Francisco, 1970-80, 83—. Edited and directed numerous news specials and documentaries, including The Lonely Basque, Whaler, The American Way of Eating. Recipient numerous awards for film editing and directing, including Cine Golden Eagle, Best Med. Res. Film award John Muir Med. Found., Chris Statuette, Bronze and Silver Cindy awards Info. Film Producers Am.

SPIES, KAREN BORNEMANN, writer, education consultant; b. Renton, Wash., Sept. 5, 1949; d. William Edward and Aina Jeanette (Johnson) Bornemann; m. Allan Roy Spies, July 18, 1970; children: Karsten, Astrid. BA, Calif. Luth. U., Thousand Oaks, 1970; MEd, U. Wash., 1974. Vice prin., tchr. Lake Washington Sch. Dist., Kirkland, Wash., 1971-79; tchr. various pub. schs. N.J., 1979-82; kindergarten tchr. Mt. Park Sch., Lake Oswego, Oreg., 1982-84; writer, seminar leader, cons. Wash., 1984-87, Oreg., 1984-87, Littleton, Colo., 1987—; lectr. Arapahoe Community Coll., Littleton, 1988—; ski instr. various locations, 1974—; curriculum writer Augsburg-Fortress Pubs.; lectr. in field. Author: Family Activities for the Christmas Season, 1988, Denver, 1988, Raffi: The Children's Voice, 1989, Visiting in the Global Village, Vol. I, 1990, Vol. II, 1991, Vol. III, 1992, Vol. IV, 1993, Vol. V, 1994, Everything You Need to Know About Grieving, 1990, Competitiveness, 1991, Barbara Bush, 1991, George Bush, 1991, Everything You Need to Know About Incest, 1992, Our National Holidays, 1992, Our Money, 1992, The American Family: Can It Survive, 1993, Everything You Need to Know About Diet Fads, 1993, Our Folk Heroes, 1994, Earthquakes, 1994, Our Presidency, 1994, Isolation vs. Intervention, 1995, others. Organist Wooden Cross Luth. Ch., 1977-79. Title III grantee, 1974. Mem. AAUW, Soc. Children's Book Writers and Illustrators, Mensa, Profl. Ski Instrs. Am., Pi Lambda Theta. Republican. Lutheran.

SPIKES, ROZELIA KATHERINE, speaker, consultant, author, poet; b. Eunice, La.; d. Dominic and Ozelia (Anderson) Simon; m. Isiah Spikes Jr., June 11, 1966 (div. 1985); children: Stacy G., Marcus A. BS in Instn. Mgmt., Grambling State U., 1966; MS, Tex. Women's U., 1977. Pres. R.K. Spikes Cons., Inc., Houston, 1978-92, R.K. Spikes Performance Mgmt. Cons., San Diego, 1992—; prof. bus. mgmt. U. Phoenix, San Diego, 1993—, Nat. U., San Diego, 1993—; prof. Internat. Bus. Exec. program San Diego State U., 1993; human resource devel. specialist Meth. Hosp., Hosuton, 1985-90; mgr. Baylor Coll. Medicine, Houston, 1981-85; exec. dir. African Am. Heritage Mus., Houston, 1989-90; cons. Ctr. for Creative leadership, San Diego, 1996; exec. dir., founder African Am. Bus. Network, San Diego, 1994. Author: Ultimate Partner, 1995, Winning at Relationships, 1995, Winning at Performance Reviews Through Partnering, 1995, Understanding the Power of Women: Words to Live By, 1996, Reflections, 1996, 52 Inspirational Thoughts for the Year, 1996, For the Children and Their Parents, 1996. Bd. dirs. Vista Hill Found., San Diego, 1995—, Land Eagle Project, San Diego, 1992-94; mem. cmty. outreach bd. La Jolla Playhouse, 1994. Mem. Nat. Coalition of 100 Black Women (bd. dirs. 1990, treas. 1988), Toastmasters (v.p. pub. rels. 1993, v.p. edn. Centre City chpt. 1993, Area 14 gov. 1994, pres. Communicators chpt. 1994, Outstanding Mentor Dist. 5 1994).

SPINDLER, GEORGE DEARBORN, anthropologist, educator, author, editor; b. Stevens Point, Wis., Feb. 28, 1920; s. Frank Nicholas and Winifred (Hatch) S.; m. Louise Schaubel, May 29, 1942; 1 dau., Sue Carol Spindler Coleman. B.S., Central State Tchrs. Coll., Wis., 1940; M.A., U. Wis., 1947; Ph.D., U. Calif. at Los Angeles, 1952. Tchr. sch. in Wis., 1940-42; research asso. Stanford, 1950-51, mem. faculty, 1951—, prof. anthropology and edn., 1960-78, exec. head dept., 1963-67, 84; vis. prof. U. Wis., Madison, 1979, 80, 81, 82, 83, 84, 85; editor Am. Anthropologist, 1962-66; cons. editor Holt, Rinehart & Winston, 1965-91, Harcourt, Brce, 1991—; vis. prof. U. Calif., Santa Barbara, 1986-91. Author: Menomini Acculturation, 1955, (with A. Beals and L. Spindler) Culture in Process, 1967, rev. edit., 1973, Transmission of American Culture, 1959, (with L. Spindler) Dreamers Without Power, 1971, rev. edit., 1984, Burgbach: Urbanization and Identity in a German Village, 1973, (with Louise Spindler) The American Cultural Dialogue and its Transmission, 1990; editor: Education and Anthropology, 1955, (with Louise Spindler) Case Studies in Cultural Anthropology, 1960—, Methods in Cultural Anthropology, 1965—, Case Studies in Education and Culture, 1966—, Basic Units in Anthropology, 1970; editor, contbr.: Education and Culture, 1963, Being An Anthropologist, 1970, Education and Cultural Process, 1974, rev. edit., 1987, The Making of Psychological Anthropology, 1978, 2nd edit., 1994, Doing the Ethnography of Schooling, 1982, Interpretive Ethnography of Schooling at Home and Abroad, 1987, Pathways to Cultural Awareness: Cultural Therapy with Students and Teachers, 1994. Pres. Peninsula Sch. Bd., Menlo Park, Calif., 1954-56. Served with AUS, 1942-45. Recipient Lloyd W. Dinkelspell award Stanford U., 1978, Disting. Svc. award Soc. Internat. Diplomacy and Third World Anthropologists, 1984, Disting. Career Contbn. award Com. on Role and Status of Minorities, Am. Edn. Rsch. Assn., Nat. Acad. Edn., 1994; fellow Ctr. Advanced Study of Behavioral Scis., 1956-57; subject of Vol. 17 Psychoanalytic Study of Soc. essays, 1992. Fellow Am. Anthrop. Assn.; mem. Southwestern Anthrop. Assn. (pres. 1962-63), Coun. for Anthropology and Edn. (pres. 1982, George and Louise Spindler award for outstanding contbns. to ednl. anthropology 1987), Nat. Acad. Edn. Home: 489 Kortum Canyon Rd Calistoga CA 94515-9703 Office: Ethnographics PO Box 38 Calistoga CA 94515-0038 *My major aims as a professional observer and interpreter of human behavior are to acquire knowledge by research and disseminate understanding to others by teaching, writing, and editing. As a person I try to keep love, work, play in balanced relationship to each other, and strive for tolerance at least, and hopefully appreciation for others who are different than myself.*

SPINWEBER, CHERYL LYNN, research psychologist; b. Jersey City, July 26, 1950; d. Stanley A. And Evelyn M. (Pfleger) S.; m. Michael E. Bruich, June 18, 1977; children: Sean Michael Bruich, Gregory Alan Bruich. AB with distinction, Cornell U., 1972; PhD in Exptl. Psychology, Harvard U., 1977. Lic. psychologist, Calif. Asst. prof. psychiatry Tufts U. Sch. Medicine, Medford, Mass., 1977-79; asst. dir. sleep lab. Boston State Hosp., 1973-79; dep. head dept. behavioral psychopharmacology Naval Health Research Ctr., San Diego, 1978-86, head dept. behavioral psychopharmacology, 1986-89; research asst. prof. dept. psychiatry Uniformed Svcs. U. of the Health Scis., Bethesda, Md., 1985—; lectr. workshop instr. U. Calif. San Diego, La Jolla, 1979-81, vis. lectr. 1979-86; assoc. adj. prof. Dept. Psychology, 1989-94, adj. prof., 1994—; courtesy clin. staff appointee dept. psychiatry Naval Hosp., San Diego, 1984-89, clin. dir. Sleep Disorders Ctr. Mercy Hosp., San Diego, 1991—; pediatric sleep specialist Children's Hosp., San Diego, 1992-95. Contbr. articles to profl. jours. Scholar Cornell U., Ithaca, N.Y., 1968-72, West Essex Tuition, 1968-72, Cornell U. Fedn. Women, 1917-72, Harvard U., 1972-73, 74-76, NDEA Title IV, 1973-74; postdoctoral associateship Nat. Research Council, 1978-80, Outstanding Tchg. award U. Calif. San Diego, 1994. Fellow Am. Sleep Disorders Assn., Clin. Sleep Soc., We. Psychol. Assn. (sec.-treas. 1986—); mem. Am. Men and Women of Sci., Sleep Rsch. Soc. (exec. com. 1986-89), Calif. Sleep Soc., Sigma Xi. Office: U Calif San Diego Dept Psychology 0109 La Jolla CA 92093

SPIRT, MITCHELL JEFFREY, internist, gastroenterologist, medical consultant; b. N.Y.C., June 14, 1963; s. Theodore and Leila (Glassman) S. BS, SUNY, Binghamton, 1985; MD, Mt. Sinai Sch. Medicine, 1989. Mktg. rsch. strategy specialist Hosp. Rsch. Assocs., Fairfield, N.J., 1986-87; med. cons. Tribune News Svc., N.Y.C., 1991-92, Med. World News, N.Y.C., 1991-93, Bradley Pharms., Fairfield, 1987—; intern in internal medicine Mt. Sinai Med. Ctr., N.Y.C., 1989-90, resident in internal medicine, 1990-92; fellow in gastroenterology UCLA, 1992-94; rschr. in field. Contbr. articles to profl. publs. Office: Ste 1605 2080 Century Park E Century City CA 90067

SPIRTOS, NICHOLAS GEORGE, lawyer, financial company executive; b. Youngstown, Ohio, Mar. 19, 1950; s. George Nicholas Spirtos and Tulla (Palaologos) Waldron; m. Andrea Carel DeFrane, Aug. 19, 1979. BA in Physics, Philosophy, UCLA, 1969, MA in Biochemistry, 1974, JD, 1978. Bar: Calif., 1978; cert. rape crisis counselor, Calif. Intelligence analyst, 1969-72; dir. product devel. Adolph's Food Products, Burbank, Calif., 1972-73; asst. to pres. Eckel Research and Devel., San Fernando, Calif., 1973-74; dep. State Public Defender Los Angeles, 1977-82; sole practice Pacific Palisades and Palm Desert, Calif., 1982—; co-founder Tekni-Query Cons., 1990; appellate lawyer Calif. and U.S. Supreme Ct., 1982; exec. v.p. Gen. Counsel Compensation Strategies Group, Santa Ana, Calif., 1988-89; pro bono legal counsel Junipero Serra H.S., Gardena, Calif., 1987-88; cons. to U.S. Govt., 1982—; bd. dirs. Myelin Project, Washington, 1993-95. Patentee solubilization of Sodium CMC at room temperature, 1972. Founder, fund raiser Pacific Multiple Sclerosis Research Found., Beverly Hills, Calif., 1982—, coordinator with Reed Neurology Ctr. at UCLA; bd. dirs. John F. Kennedy Ctr. Performing Arts, Very Spl. Arts for Cachella Valley, 1996—. Westinghouse Sci. scholar, 1965; recipient Gregor Mendell award in genetics, 1962; named Jr. Engr. of Yr. Am. Assn. Aero. Engrs., 1963, Outstanding Speaker U. So. Calif., 1965. Mem. State Bar Calif., Internat. Platform Assn. Republican. Greek Orthodox. Office: 44489 Town Center Way # D-404 Palm Desert CA 92260-2723

SPISTO, LOUIS G., performing company executive. BBA with honors, U. Notre Dame, 1978; MA Arts Adminstrn., U. Wis., 1979. Dir. mktg. Pitts. Symphony Orch., 1984-87; exec. dir. Pacific Symphony Orch., Santa Ana, Calif., 1987—; chmn. Group II Maj. Orchs. Am. Symphony Orch. League; spkr. in field; cons. numerous orgns. including New World Symphony, N.Mex. Symphony, Inland Empire Symphony, Santa Barbara Chamber Orch., Chorale Arts Soc., Washington. Mem. Calif. Symphony Orchs. (bd. dirs. 1988—). Office: Pacific Symphony Orch Orange County Perform Arts 1231 E Dyer Rd Ste 200 Santa Ana CA 92705

SPITALERI, VERNON ROSARIO, newspaper publisher, manufacturing company executive; b. Pelham, N.Y., Aug. 2, 1922; s. Rosario S. and Martha (Landerer) S.; m. Marjorie A. Ferrar, Oct. 14, 1952; children: Marc, Eric, Kris, Lynn. B.S., Carnegie Mellon U., 1942. Mgr. mech. dept. Am. Newspaper Pubs. Assn., N.Y.C., 1946-53; research dir., gen. adminstr. Miami Herald and Knight Newspapers (Fla.), 1953-57; chmn. bd., pres. Sta-Hi Corp., Newport Beach, Calif., 1957-74; v.p. Republic Corp., 1974-76, Sun Chem. Corp., 1976-79; chmn. bd. Sta-Hi Color Service, Sta-Hi Europe, Brussels, Concrete Floats-Huntington Engring. Corp., Huntington Beach, Calif.; editor, pub. Laguna Beach (Calif.) News-Post, 1967-81; pres. Laguna Pub. Co., Nat. Newspaper Found.; dir. Suburban Newspapers Am.; chmn. bd. Victory Profl. Products, Mango Surfware. Pres., Boys Club, Laguna Beach; mem. citizens adv. com. Laguna Beach; pres. Laguna Beach Library Bd., Laguna Playhouse, Laguna Coordinating Council; bd. dirs. Sta-Hi Found.; dir. Opera Pacific. Served to lt. comdr. USNR, 1942-46. Decorated Purple Heart. Mem. Am. Mgmt. Assn., Nat. Newspaper Assn. (dir.), Calif. Newspaper Pubs. Assn. (dir.), Laguna Beach C. of C. (bd. dir.), Alpha Tau Omega. Republican. Roman Catholic. Club: Dana Point Yacht.

SPITLER, LEE WILLIAM, banker; b. Racine, Wis., Feb. 14, 1919; s. Marion Albert and Agnes Elizabeth (Lowe) S.; m. Helen Deloris Krejci, Mar. 19, 1949; children—Susan D., Lee William, Anne M., James E. B.S., U. Md., 1956; M.B.A., George Washington U., 1962; postgrad. advanced mgmt. program, Harvard U., 1963; grad., U.S. Air Force War Coll., 1959, U.S. Air Force Command and Staff Coll., 1955. Commd. 2d lt. U.S. Air Force, 1943, advanced through grades to col., 1954; chief personnel stats. div. Hdqrs. U.S. Air Force, Washington, 1950-54; asst. dir. statis. services U.S. Air Force, 1958-63; asst. comptroller Hdqrs. U.S. European Command U.S. Air Force, Paris, 1955-58; asst. comptroller Hdqrs. Air Tng. Command U.S. Air Force, Randolph AFB, Tex., 1963-64; ret. U.S. Air Force, 1964; v.p. Computax Corp., El Segundo, Calif., 1965-69; exec. v.p. Irving Bank Corp., N.Y.C., 1969-84; sr. exec. v.p. Irving Trust Co., N.Y.C., 1969-84; ret., 1984; pres. Spitler Fin. Svcs., Monterey, Calif., 1985—; dir. Turkiye Tutunculer Bankasi AS, Izmir, Turkey, 1984-87. mem. nat. adv. bd. Am. Security Council. Decorated Legion of Merit. Mem. Internat. Assn. Fin. Planning, Am. Bankers Assn., Am. Mgmt. Assn., Soc. for Mgmt. Info. Systems, Ret. Officers Assn., Nat. Assn. Uniformed Services, Mil. Order World Wars, Am. Assn. Mil. Comptrollers, Am. Legion, Veterans of Fgn. Wars, Am. Assn. Ret. Personnel, Inst. Cert. Planners, Air War Coll. Alumni Assn., First Fighter Group Assn. Clubs: Harvard, West Point Officers. Home: 200 Glenwood Cir Apt 525 Monterey CA 93940-6747 Office: 200 Glenwood Cir Monterey CA 93940

SPITZE, STEVEN CLYDE, army officer; b. Las Vegas, July 16, 1965; s. Clyde Oliver and Marilyn Louise (Edwards) S.; m. Rebecca Ann Rivenbark. BA, U. Nev., Reno, 1987, MA, 1994, postgrad., 1995—. Cert. comml. pilot FAA. Commd. 2d lt. U.S. Army, 1987, advanced through grades to maj., 1996; ops. officer 99th Troop Command, Reno, 1995-96; exec. officer 1st bn., 221st Armor, Las Vegas, 1996—. Program asst., mem. First Congl. Ch., Reno, 1993-96; mentor Challenge/Youth At Risk, Reno, 1994-96. Decorated Meritorious Svc. medal with oak leaf cluster; recipient Gov.'s Leadership award Gov. of Nev., 1987, others; Brit. Army Staff Coll. exch. student, 1996. Mem. Assn. U.S. Army, Aircraft Owners and Pilots Assn., U.S. Army Ranger Assn., N.G. Assn. U.S. (bd. dirs., treas.), Pi Sigma Alpha.

SPITZER, MATTHEW L., retail store executive; b. Pitts., June 20, 1929; s. Martin and Ruth G. S.; student U. Buffalo, 1948-50; children: Mark, Edward, Eric, Joseph. Lic. airline transport pilot. Product line mgr. Gen. Dynamics, Rochester, N.Y., 1962-67; dir. contracts Friden div. Singer, San Leandro, Calif., 1968-69; asst. v.p. Talcott Computer Leasing, San Francisco, 1970-71; pres. Spitzer Music Mgmt. Co., Hayward, Calif., 1972-95; pres. Spitzer Helicopter Leasing Co., Hayward, Calif.; chmn. bd. Leo's Audio and Music Techs., Oakland, Calif.; Masons, Mensa. Office: 5447 Telegraph Ave Oakland CA 94609-1921

SPIVAK, JOEL A., lawyer; b. L.A., Feb. 19, 1958; s. Herbert Alan and Jacque R. (Briet) S. BA in Polit. Sci., UCLA, 1979; JD, Western State U., San Diego, 1981. Bar: Calif. 1982, U.S. Dist. Ct. (cen. dist.) Calif. 1983, U.S. Ct. Appeals (9th cir.) 1983, U.S. Tax Ct. 1984. Lawyer Halperin & Halperin p.c., L.A., 1982-85; pvt. practice L.A., 1985—; corp. counsel Producers Escrow Corp., Beverly Hills, Calif., 1988—; pres., corp. counsel Producers Exchange Corp., Beverly Hills, Calif., 1988—; counsel Victims for Victims, L.A., 1984-86, L.A. Chpt. Hadassah, L.A., 1989-94. Democrat. Jewish. Office: Ste 213 3760 Motor Ave Los Angeles CA 90034-6404

SPIVEY, ROBERTA LEE, paralegal, community counselor; b. Boulder, Colo., July 2, 1940; d. William Elwood Hopkins and Donna Rebecca (Owen) Hopkins Ellis; m. James O. Spivey, Dec. 23, 1961; children: Dawna Jenelle, Michael James. Student, U. Ams., Mex., 1959-61; BA in Philosophy, Ga. State U., 1964; MS in Counseling, Calif. State U., Sacramento, 1996. Spanish and English tchr. Henrico County Schs., Richmond, Va., 1966-67; legal sec., real estate specialist Gettle & Fraser, Attys., Atlanta, 1964-75; real estate specialist, closer Merrill Lynch Relocation, Atlanta, 1975-79; escrow sec. Western Title, Fidelity Title, Sacramento, Calif., 1979-83; exec. sec., legal asst. Evans Fin., Sacramento, Calif., 1983-86; legal sec., asst. Granite Fin., Sacramento, Calif., 1986-88; exec. sec. Infotec/Passar, Sacramento, Calif., 1988-90; real estate paralegal Taylor & Hooper, Attys., Sacramento, Calif., 1990—. Author short stories. Arbitrator auto-line BBB, Sacramento, 1986—.

SPIZIZEN, JOHN, microbiologist, b. Winnipeg, Man., Can., Feb. 7, 1917; came to U.S., 1939, naturalized, 1944; s. Nathan and Sarah Spizizen; m. Louise Myers, Apr., 1969; 1 child, Gary. B.A., U. Toronto, 1939; Ph.D., Calif. Inst. Tech., 1942. Assoc. in virus rsch. Merck, Sharp and Dohme, West Point, Pa., 1946-54; assoc. prof. dept. Microbiology Western Res. U., Cleve., 1954-61; prof., head dept. microbiology U. Minn., Mpls., 1961-65; chmn. dept. microbiology Scripps Clinic and Rsch. Found., La Jolla, Calif., 1965-79; prof., head dept. microbiology and immunology U. Ariz., Tucson, 1979-87, prof. emeritus, 1987—; bd. govs. Weizmann Inst. Sci., Israel, 1970-82. bd. sci. advisors La Jolla Cancer Rsch. Found., 1978—; mem. com. for rsch. and tng. NIH, 1962-79, Am. Cancer Soc., 1967—; mem. coms. NASA, 1970-78. Served to capt. U.S. Army, 1943-46. Recipient Career Devel. award NIH, Western Res. U., 1955; rsch. grantee NIH, NSF; fellow NRC; Fulbright scholar U. Lund, Sweden, 1992. Mem. Am. Soc. Microbiology, Am. Soc. Biochem. and Molecular Biology. Home: 2540 E Camino La Zorrela Tucson AZ 85718-3122 Office: U Ariz Sch Medicine Dept Microbiology 1501 N Campbell Ave Tucson AZ 85724-0001

SPLANE, RICHARD BEVERLEY, social work educator; b. Calgary, Alta., Can., Sept. 25, 1916; s. Alfred William and Clara Jane (Allyn) S.; m. Verna Marie Huffman, Feb. 22, 1971. BA, McMaster U., 1940, LLD (hon.), 1990; cert. social sci. and adminstrn., London Sch. Econs., 1947; MA, U. Toronto, 1948, MSW, 1951, PhD, 1961; LLD (hon.), Wilfrid Laurier U., 1988, U. B.C., Can., 1996. Exec. dir. Children's Aid Soc., Cornwall, Ont., Can., 1948-50; with Health and Welfare Can., Ottawa, 1952-72; exec. asst. to dep. minister nat. welfare Health and Welfare Can., 1959-60, dir. unemployment assistance, 1960-62, dir. gen. welfare assistance and services, 1960-70, asst. dep. minister social allowances and services, 1970-72; vis. prof. U. Alta., Edmonton, 1972-73; prof. social policy Sch. Social Work, U. B.C., Vancouver, 1973—; cons. Govt. Can., Govt. Alta., UNICEF. Author: The Development of Social Welfare in Ontario, 1965; (with Verna Huffman Splane) Chief Nursing Officers in National Ministries of Health, 1994, 75 Years of Community Service to Canada: Canadian Council on Social Development, 1920-1995. Served with RCAF, 1942-45. Recipient Centennial medal Govt. Can., 1967, Charles E. Hendry award U. Toronto, 1981, Commemorative medal for 125th anniversary of Confedn. of Can., 1992, Disting. Svc. award Internat. Coun. on Social Welfare, 1996. Mem. Can. Assn. Social Workers (Outstanding Nat. Svc. award 1985), Can. Inst. Pub. Adminstrn., Can. Hist. Assn., Can. Coun. on Social Devel. (Lifetime Achievement award 1995), Internat. Assn. Schs. Social Work, Internat. Confs. Social Devel. (pres.), World Federalists of Can. (pres. Vancouver br.), Vancouver Club, Order of Can. Mem. United Ch. Can. Office: U BC Sch Social Work, 208 West Mall, Vancouver, BC Canada V6T 1Z2

SPOERL, OTTO HEINRICH, psychiatrist, educator; b. Kronach, Germany, Feb. 25, 1933. Student, U. Goettingen Med. Sch., 1951-54, U. Freiburg Med. Sch., 1954-55, U. Heidelberg Med. Sch., 1955, U. Erlangen Med. Sch., 1955-58. Diplomate Am. Bd. Psychiatry and Neurology; lic. Wash. Intern dept. surgery U. Erlangen (Germany) Med. Sch., 1957-58; rotating intern Md. Gen. Hosp., Balt., 1959-60; asst. resident dept. psychiatry Duke U. Med. Ctr., Durham, N.C., 1960-62, resident dept. pschiatry, 1962-63; chief resident dept. psychiatry, asst. in psychiatry U. Wash. Sch. Medicine, Seattle, 1963-64, instr. psychiatry, 1964-68, asst. prof., 1968-70, clin. asst. prof. dept. psychiatry and behavioral scis., 1970—; attending physician psychiatric inpatient svcs. U. Hosp., Seattle, 1964-68; dir. psychiatric inpatient svc. King Country Harborview Hosp., 1968-70; chief mental health svcs. Group Health Eastside Med. Ctr., 1975-78, Group Health Coop., 1980-82; mgr. psychiatric svcs. Cen. Mental Health Svc. Group Health Coop., Seattle, 1989—; cons. Washington State Heart Assn., 1964-74, German Consulate Gen., Seattle, 1964—; coord. student vol. program Psychiatric Inpatient Svc. U. Hosp., 1966-68. Contbr. articles to profl. jours. Med. adv. bd. Seattle Planned Parenthood Ctr., 1967-80; exec. bd. mem. Mental Health Profls. for Human Rights and Responsibilities, 1968-70; med. adv. Stevens Pass Ski area, mem. Nat. Ski Patrol. Fellow Am. Psychiatric Assn. (life); mem. Am. Pub. Health Assn., Seattle Psychiatric Soc., U. Dist. Rotary Club. Home: 3368 E Laurelhurst Dr NE Seattle WA 98105-5336 Office: 1730 Minor Ave # 1400 Seattle WA 98101-1448

SPOFFORD, ROBERT HOUSTON, advertising agency executive; b. N.Y.C., Apr. 3, 1941; s. Robert Knowlton and Linda Prieber (Houston) S.; m. Susan Proctor Allerton; children—Margaret, Robert Christopher. B.E.E., Cornell U., 1964. Account exec. Batten, Barton, Durstine & Osborn, Inc., N.Y.C., 1964-71, v.p., 1971-84, sr. v.p., 1984-88, exec. v.p., dir. strategic planning, 1988—. Contbr. articles to advt. and data processing jours. Mem. Westchester County Democratic Com. N.Y. 1974-78; ch. organist. First recipient Founder's medal Batten, Barton, Durstine & Osborn, Inc., 1985. Unitarian. Home: 39 Glenside Way San Rafael CA 94903 Office: BBDO LA 10960 Wilshire Blvd Los Angeles CA 90024-3702

SPOHRER, JAMES HENRY, librarian, consultant; b. Jennings, La., Dec. 18, 1950; s. Henry Stanislaus and Rosalie (Ballard) S.; m. Elisabeth Marie Aurelle, Mar. 20, 1974; 1 child, Bela. BA, La. State U., 1975, MS, 1978; MA, U. Calif., Berkeley, 1983. Pvt. practice translator Freiburg, Germany, 1973-75; test constrn. specialist Louisian Civil Svc. Dept., Baton Rouge, 1975-76; serials libr. U. Nebr., Lincoln, 1978-81; instr. U. Calif., Berkeley,

1981-83, Germanic libr., 1983—, dept. chair, 1992-96, assoc. U. Libr. Humanities and Area Studies, 1996—; cons. linguistics dept. U. Calif., Berkeley, 1989. Author: Guide to Collection Development and Management, 1986; translator: Cajuns de la Louisiane, 1978. Mem. Nebr. Wesleyan Chamber Orch., Lincoln, 1979; bd. dirs. East Bay Suzuki Music Assn., Berkeley, 1981-83. Recipient Nijhoff prize Martinus Nijhoff Internat., The Hague, 1989; Title II-C grantee U.S. Dept. Edn., Washington, 1988-90, Finlandia Found., 1997. Mem. MLA, ALA, Western European Specialist Sect. (chair 1993-94), Medieval Assn. of the Pacific, Beta Phi Mu. Home: 4824 Full Moon Dr El Sobrante CA 94803-2138 Office: Univ Calif 390 Doe Library Berkeley CA 94720-6000

SPONSEL, LESLIE ELMER, anthropologist, ecologist; b. Indpls., Nov. 6, 1943; s. Elmer John and Else Marie (Ehrhardt) S.; m. Poranee Natadecha, May 1, 1984. BA in Geology, Ind. U., 1965; MA in Anthropology, Cornell U., 1973, PhD, 1981. Vis. lectr. U. Sask., Saskatoon, Can., 1968-70; vis. Fulbright prof. Venezuelan Inst. for Sci. Investigations, Caracas, 1977-78, 81; vis. instr. U. Mass., Amherst, 1978-79; asst. prof. U. Hawaii, Honolulu, 1981-86, assoc. prof., 1986-96, prof., 1996—; Fulbright vis. prof. Prince Songkla U., Pattani, Thailand, 1994-95. Co-editor: The Anthropology of Peace and Nonviolence, 1994, Tropical Deforestation: The Human Dimension, 1995; editor: Indigenous Peoples and the Future of Amazonia: An Ecological Anthropology of An Endangered World, 1995. Mem. Am. Anthrop. Assn. (chair commn. for human rights 1992-95), Siam Soc., Sigma Xi. Office: U Hawaii Dept Anthropology 2424 Maile Way Honolulu HI 96822-2223

SPOOR, JAMES EDWARD, human resouces executive, entrepreneur; b. Rockford, Ill., Feb. 19, 1936; s. Frank Kendall and Genevieve Eileen (Johnson) S.; BS in Psychology, U. Ill., 1958; m. Nancy E. Carlson, Sept. 8, 1962; children: Sybll K., Kendall P., Andrea K., Marcie K. Pers. mgr. Nat. Sugar Refining Co., N.Y.C., 1960-64, Pepsico, Inc., N.Y.C., Auburn, N.Y., 1964-67; mgr. internat. pers. Control Data Corp., Mpls., 1967-75; v.p. pers. and employee rels. Vetco, Inc., Ventura, Calif., 1975-79; v.p. employee rels. Hamilton Bros. Oil Co., Denver, 1979-84; pres., CEO Spectrum Human Resource Systems Corp., 1984—; cons., author, spkr. on human resources and entrepreneurism. Mem. adv. bd. Salvation Army, 1978-79; chmn. Spl. Commn. for Ventura County Bd. Suprs., 1978; mem. task force on human resources Colo. Sch. Mines, 1983; state chairperson Coun. Growing Cos., 1991-92, nat. pres., 1992-94; bd. dirs. Breckenridge Outdoor Edn. Ctr., 1994—, chmn., 1996—.

SPRAGUE, AMARIS JEANNE, real estate broker; b. Jackson, Mich., Feb. 18, 1935; d. Leslie Markham and Blanche Lorraine (Basnaw) Reed; student Mich. State U., 1952-53; B.S., Colo. State U., 1965; m. John M. Vetterling, Oct. 1985; children by previous marriage—Anthony John, James Stuart. Real estate sales Seibel and Benedict Realty, Ft. Collins, Colo., 1968-69; salesman Realty Brokers Exchange, Ft. Collins, 1969-72; broker, pres. Sprague and Assos., Inc., Realtors, Ft. Collins, 1972-80; broker assoc. Van Schaack & Co., Ft. Collins, 1980-86; broker ptnr. The Group, Inc., 1986—; dir. Univ. Nat. Bank. Mem. bus. adv. council Colo. State U., 1976-84, chmn. 1979-80, mem. adv. council Coll. of Engring., 1981. Cert. real estate broker. Mem. Nat. Assn. Realtors, Colo. Assn. Realtors, Ft. Collins Bd. Realtors, Ft. Collins C. of C. (bd. dirs. 1978-84, pres. 1982-83). Republican. Episcopalian. Home: PO Box 475 Fort Collins CO 80522-0475 Office: 401 W Mulberry St Fort Collins CO 80521-2839

SPRAGUE, DALE JOSEPH, writer; b. Portland, Oreg., July 8, 1946; s. Gerald William Sprague and Ruth Marie (Majerus) Williams; m. Linda Joselyn, Nov. 22, 1975 (div. Aug. 1993); children: Amber, Noah, Jonah, Rachel. BS in Biocybernetics, Western Wash. U., 1974. Tech. writer Boeing, Seattle, 1976—; Cyberspace mag. essayist. With USN, 1965-69. Home: 824 NW 52nd St # 6 Seattle WA 98107

SPRAGUE, PETER JULIAN, software company executive, lecturer; b. Detroit, Apr. 29, 1939; s. Julian K. and Helene (Coughlin) S.; m. Tjasa Krofta, Dec. 19, 1959; children: Carl, Steven, Kevin, Michael. Student, Yale U., 1961, MIT, 1961, Columbia U., 1962-66. Chmn. Wave Sys., Inc.; bd. dirs. Enlightened Software Inc. Trustee Strang Clinic. Mem. Yale Club. Home: 399 Under Mountain Rd Lenox MA 01240-2036 Office: Wave Sys Corp 540 Madison Ave New York NY 10022-3213

SPRAITZ, STEPHEN MICHAEL, ceramic tile contractor; b. Washington, Jan. 20, 1953; s. Edward Frederick and Josephine Marie (Kennedy) S. Printer Orange Coast Daily Pilot, Costa Mesa, Calif., 1972-75; owner Tile Contractors, Forest Knolls, Calif., 1976-87, Steve Spraitz the Tilesetter, Santa Fe, N.Mex., 1987—. Mem. N. Am. Hunting Club, N.Mex. Home Builders Assn., Santa Fe Home Builders Assn., Friends of the Palace Santa Fe, Planetary Soc., Santa Fe Habitat for Humanity, Nat. Assn. Home Builders. Democrat. Roman Catholic. Office: PO Box 2427 Santa Fe NM 87504-2427

SPREWELL, LATRELL FONTAINE, professional basketball player; b. Milw., Sept. 8, 1970; s. Latoska Fields and Pamela Sprewell; children: Aquilla, Page, Latrell II. Student, Three Rivers C.C., Poplar Bluff, Mo., 1988-90, Ala. U., 1990-92. Profl. basketball player Golden State Warriors, Oakland, Calif., 1992—. Office: Golden State Warriors 1221 Broadway 20th Flr Oakland CA 94612-1918*

SPRINCZ, KEITH STEVEN, financial services company professional; b. Whitewater, Wis., Mar. 8, 1956; s. Steven B. Sprincz and Mary Lou (Crotte) Zolli; m. Renee Michele Werner, Sept. 11, 1982; children: Nicholas, Cameron. BS in Mktg., Colo. State U., 1978; student, Am. Coll., 1985-86. CLU, ChFC. Agt. Prudential, Denver, 1978-83; ins. broker Nolen/Western, Denver, 1983-88, ptnr., 1988—; tchr. Life Underwriters Tng. Coun., Bethesda, Md., 1991-92. Chmn. bd. elders Bethlehem Luth. Ch., Lakewood, Colo., 1989; campmaster council. Boy Scouts Am., Denver, 1989—, scoutmaster, 1983—; capt. March of Dimes, Denver, 1981, Big Bros., Denver, 1984; pres. Centennial Assn. Life Underwriters, 1986-87; sch. bd. mem., 1993—, pres., 1995—. Recipient Outstanding Family award Boy Scouts Am., 1986. Office: Nolen Western 5690 Dtc Blvd Ste 140 Englewood CO 80111-3233

SPRING, GLENN ERNEST, composer; b. Hot Springs, Ark., Apr. 19, 1939; s. Glenn Ernest Sr. and Ellen (Maddox) S.; m. Ingrid Kathryn Olesen, Aug. 5, 1962 (dec. Jan. 1973); 1 child, Brian Glenn; m. Kathleen Marie Klein, Dec. 16, 1973; children: Christopher, Heidi. BA, La Sierra U., 1962; M.Mus., Tex. Christian U., 1964; D. Mus. Arts, U. Wash., 1972. Instr. music Otterbein Coll., Westerville, Ohio, 1964-65; prof. music Walla Walla Coll., College Place, Wash., 1965—; concertmaster Walla Walla (Wash.) Symphony, 1965-75, 87-90; sect. violionist (1st) Columbus (Ohio) Symphony, 1964-65; sect. violinist (1st and 2d) Ft. Worth Symphony, 1962-64. Composer: Shapes: A Short Symphony, 1973 (Indpls. Symphony award 1974), (orchestral composition) Perceptions, 1977, Dona nobis pacem for baritone and orch., 1984, Contrasts for organ, 1986, Hold in Your Memory the Land, 1990, (for chorus a cappella) Messe pour l'humanité, 1993, many other works; Co-author: Musical Form and Analysis, 1995. Recipient commn. Wash. State Arts Commn., 1973, Musiklager Margess, Switzerland, 1988, 89, Alienor Harpsichord Composition award SE Hist. Keyboard Soc., 1990. Mem. ASCAP (ann. awards 1988-96), ASTA (Burlington-No. award 1991). Office: Walla Walla Coll 204 S College Ave College Place WA 99324-1139

SPRINGER, CHARLES EDWARD, state supreme court justice; b. Reno, Feb. 20, 1928; s. Edwin and Rose Mary Cecelia (Kelly) S.; m. Jacqueline Sirkegian, Mar. 17, 1951; 1 dau., Kelli Ann. BA, U. Nev., Reno, 1950; LLB, Georgetown U., 1953; LLM, U. Va., 1984; student Grad. Program for Am. Judges, Oriel Coll., Oxford (Eng.), 1984. Bar: Nev. 1953, U.S. Dist. Ct. Nev. 1953, D.C. 1954, U.S. Supreme Ct. 1962. Pvt. practice law Reno, 1953-80; atty. gen. State of Nev., 1962, legis. legal adv. to gov., 1958-62; legis. bill drafter Nev. Legislature, 1955-57; mem. faculty Nat. Coll. Juvenile Justice, Reno, 1978—; juvenile master 2d Jud. Dist. Nev., 1973-80; justice Nev. Suprem Ct., Carson City, 1981—; mem. Jud. Selection Commn., 1981, Nev. Supreme Ct. Gender Bias Task Force, 1981—; trustee Nat. Coun. Juvenile and Family Ct. Judges, 1983—; mem. faculty McGeorge Sch. Law, U. Nev., Reno, 1982—; mem. Nev. Commn. for Women, 1991-95. With AUS, 1945-47. Recipient Outstanding Contbn. to Juvenile Justice award Nat. Coun. Juvenile and Family Ct. Judges, 1989, Midby-Byron Disting. Leadership award U. Nev., 1988. Mem. ABA, Am. Judicature Soc., Am. Trial Lawyers Assn., Phi Kappa Phi. Office: Nev Supreme Ct Capitol Complex 201 S Carson St Carson City NV 89701

SPRINGER, GERALD WILLIAM, sales executive; b. Amherst, Ohio, Nov. 13, 1943; s. Raymond W. and Ione J. (Myers) S.; m. Marilyn F. Gregg, Aug. 28, 1971. BBA, Kent State U., 1966. Dist. sales mgr. Flintkote Co., Kent, Ohio, 1970-72, US Gypson Co., Denver, 1972-75, Ameron Corp., Denver, 1975-79; nat. sales mgr. Blue Bird Internat. Co., Englewood, Colo., 1979-81; sales mgr. Smith & Wesson, Golden, Colo., 1981-85; pres. The West & Assocs., Inc., Hudson, Colo., 1985—. Served with Ohio N.G., 1963-67. Jeffco Posse Club. Republican. Congregationalist.

SPRINGER, SALLY PEARL, university administrator; b. Bklyn., Mar. 19, 1947; d. Nathaniel Margulies and Fanny (Schoen) S.; m. Hakon Hope; children: Erik Jacob Hope, Mollie Liv Hope. BS, Bklyn. Coll., 1967; PhD, Stanford U., 1971. Postdoctoral fellow Stanford U. Med. Sch., Calif., 1971-73; asst. prof. SUNY-Stony Brook, 1973-78, assoc. provost, 1981-85, assoc. prof., 1978-87; exec. asst. to chancellor U. Calif., Davis, 1987-92, asst. chancellor, 1992—. Author (with others): Left Brain, Right Brain, 1981 (Am. Psychol. Found. Disting. Contbr. award 1981), 4th rev. edit., 1993, How to Succeed in College, 1982; contbr. articles to profl. jours. Mem. Internat. Neuropsychol. Soc., Psychonomic Soc. Office: U Calif Office Chancellor Davis CA 95616

SPRING-MOORE, MICHELE LEA, poet; b. Johnson City, N.Y., June 5, 1963; d. Robert Alfred Moore and Saralynne (Spring) Mullen. BA, St. John Fisher Coll., 1985; MA, U. Colo., 1993. Freelance writer Rochester, N.Y., 1983-90; editl. asst. City Newspaper, Rochester, 1984-85; comm. dir. Rochester Peace and Justice Edn. Ctr., 1986-87; editor The Empty Closet Press, Rochester, 1987-89; office mgr. Metro-Act of Rochester, 1989-91; freelance writer Boulder, 1995—; writer in residence Cottages at Hedgebrook, Langley, Wash., 1994; instr. Feminist Women's Writing Workshops, Geneva, N.Y., 1994; artist in residence Ucross Found., Clearmont, Wyo., 1994, Helene Wurlitzer Found., Taos, N.Mex., 1997; editl. bd., poetry reader Many Mountains Moving Lit. Jour., 1996—. Contbr. numerous poems to lit. jours. and anthology. Mem. Rochester Women's Action for Peace, 1984-87; local organizer Nicaragua Network, Rochester, 1986-87; co-founder Rochester Bisexual Women's Network, 1988-91,Bisexual Women's Voice support group, 1995—; vol. Equal Protection Campaign of Colo., Boulder, 1992. Tuition scholar Aspen Writer's Conf., 1993; Associateship artist's grantee Rocky Mountain Women's Inst., 1993-94. Home and Office: 5323 NDCBU Taos NM 87571

SPRITZER, RALPH SIMON, lawyer, educator; b. N.Y.C., Apr. 27, 1917; s. Harry and Stella (Theuman) S.; m. Lorraine Nelson, Dec. 23, 1950; children: Ronald, Pamela. B.S., Columbia U., 1937, LL.B., 1940. Bar: N.Y. bar 1941, U.S. Supreme Ct. bar 1950. Atty. Office Alien Property, Dept. Justice, 1946-51; anti-trust div. Dept. Justice, 1951-54, Office Solicitor Gen., 1954-61; gen. counsel FPC, 1961-62; 1st asst. to solicitor gen. U.S., 1962-68; prof. law U. Pa., Phila., 1968-86, Ariz. State U., Tempe, 1986—; gen. counsel AAUP, 1983-84; Adj. prof. law George Wasington U., 1967; cons. Adminstrv. Conf. U.S., Ford Found., Pa. Gov.'s Justice Commn. Served with AUS, 1941-46. Recipient Superior Service award Dept. Justice, 1960; Tom C. Clark award Fed. Bar. Assn., 1968. Mem. Am. Law Inst. Home: 1024 E Gemini Dr Tempe AZ 85283-3004 Office: Ariz State Univ Coll Law Tempe AZ 85287

SPROSTY, JOSEPH PATRICK, weapons specialist, producer, writer, consultant; b. Cleve., Aug. 25, 1947; s. Joseph Patrick and Anna Margret (Loucka) S.; m. Sharon Marie Blair, Sept. 29, 1993. Grad., Midpark H.S., Middleburgh, Ohio, 1965; student, San Diego City Coll., 1972-73. Class 2 firearms lic. Prop builder The Goulardi Show WJW-TV8, Cleve., 1962-65; sub-agent Internat. Artists Agy., San Diego and L.A., 1982-83; casting dir. Cinemode Films, 1982; operator, owner Actors Artists Agy., L.A., 1983-87; founder, prodr., dir. Magnum Prodns., 1985; founder Sprosty Prodns., 1990; demonstrator weapons and handling of weapons Beth Holmes, Propmaster TV Co., Van Nuys, Calif., 1992; expert witness Laser Weapon Scam, 1984; vis. lectr. firearms safety, handling, rules and regulations governing use of firearms in motion picture, TV prodn. U. So. Calif., 1996—; animal wrangler specializing opossums. Scripwriter: (films) Vanishing Point II, The Apartment Manager, The Big House, Rambo III (optioned), Rambo IV (revised), Boneyard, Mister Ed - Talking Again, Mister Ed - Radio Talk, Brick, Life Plus One, Gun Slave, Fixation, Last Chance (renamed Terminal Virus), numerous others; prodr., dir. (video) Break Disc, 1985; location mgr., armorer, weapons splst.: (film) Heat from Another Sun (retitled Maladiction), 1988; armorer, 2nd asst. dir., assoc. prodr., weapons splst.: (film) Provoked, 1989; weapons splst., armorer: (film) Big City, 1990; co-prodr., animal wrangler, weapons splst.: (film) Opossum de Oro, 1996; weapons splst.: (tv shows) Jake and the Fat Man, Black's Magic, Hill Street Blues, Murder, She Wrote, On the Edge of Death, Emerald Point N.A.S., (7 episodes) America's Most Wanted, (3 episodes) FBI: The Untold Stories, numerous others, (films) Revolt, Rocky IV, Streets of Fire, Walk in the Sun, Cloak & Dagger, One Man's Poison, Killing Zoe, Desert Storm, The Movie, Live Shot, Outer Heat, Zipperhead, Four Minute Warning, The Robbery, Spirit, Texas Payback, High Adventure, The Waterfront, The Philadelphia Experiment II, Opossum de Oro, Harlem Nights, Tango & Cash, Die Hard, Provoked, Beverly Hills Cop II, Big City, numerous others. Spkr. Veterans Day Calif. State U., Dominguez Hills, 1993. Served with USN, 1965-67. Mem. AFTRA, SAG (charter mem. San Diego br.). Home: 305 S Lincoln St Burbank CA 91506-2612

SPROUL, JOHN ALLAN, retired public utility executive; b. Oakland, Calif., Mar. 28, 1924; s. Robert Gordon and Ida Amelia (Wittschen) S.; m. Marjorie Ann Hauck, June 20, 1945; children: John Allan, Malcolm J., Richard O., Catherine E. A.B., U. Calif., Berkeley, 1947, LL.B., 1949. Bar: Calif. 1950. Atty. Pacific Gas & Electric Co., San Francisco, 1949-52, 56-62, sr. atty., 1962-70, asst. gen. counsel, 1970-71, v.p. gas supply, 1971-76, sr. v.p., 1976-77, exec. v.p., 1977-89; gen. counsel Pacific Gas Transmission Co., 1970-73, v.p., 1973-79, chmn. bd., 1979-89, also bd. dirs.; atty. Johnson & Stanton, San Francisco, 1952-56; bd. dirs. Oreg. Steel Mills, Inc. Bd. dirs. Hastings Coll. of Law. Served to 1st lt. USAAF, 1943-46. Mem. Calif. Bar Assn. (inactive), Pacific Coast Gas Assn., World Trade Club, Pacific-Union Club, Orinda Country Club. Home: 8413 Buckingham Dr El Cerrito CA 94530-2531 Office: Pacific Gas and Electric Co Mail Code H17F PO Box 770000 San Francisco CA 94177

SPROWL, DALE RAE, English educator; b. N.Y.C., May 21, 1954; d. Raymond Makofske and Joan Elizabeth Beer; m. David Arthur Sprowl, Aug. 14, 1977; children: Brooke Lindsay, Barrett David, Bayley Laurie. Student, UCLA, 1971-72; BA in Humanities, History, Pepperdine U., 1975, MAT in History, 1980. Cert. secondary tchr., Calif. 5th, 6th grade tchr. Radcliffe Hall, Anaheim, Calif., 1977-78; History and English tchr. Newport Christian H.S., Newport Beach, Calif., 1978-80, Garden Grove (Calif.) Sch. Dist., 1980-82; English tchr. Irvine (Calif.) H.S., 1981-84; tchr., cons. U. Calif. Irvine Writing Project, 1981—. Contbr. articles to profl. jours and books. Vol. Mariners South Coast Ch., 1977—, Newport Mesa Sch. Dist., 1987—; short-term missionary New Life Ch., Ukraine, 1995. Mem. Newport Beach Tennis Club (team mem. 1994—). Christian.

SQUIRES, RICHARD LANE, paleontologist, educator; b. Mexico, Mo., Nov. 19, 1944; s. Carl Standefer and Dorothy (Lane) S.; m. Janet Lee Diskin, Dec. 18, 1976; children: Katherine Marie, Caroline Elizabeth. BS, U. N.Mex., 1966, MS, 1968; PhD, Calif. Inst. Tech., 1973. Postdoctoral assoc. Jet Propulsion Lab., Pasadena, Calif., 1973-74; asst. prof. dept. geol. scis. Calif. State U., Northridge, 1974-78, assoc. prof., 1978-82, prof., 1982—; rsch. assoc. Natural History Mus. Los Angeles County, 1977—. Editor several guidebooks; author monographs and jour. articles. Libr. vol. Emblem Elem. Sch., Santa Clarita, Calif., 1985—. Mem. Paleontological Rsch. Soc., Paleontological Rsch. Instn., Soc. Econ. Paleontologists and Mineralogists, We. Soc. Malacologists, Conchologists of Am., Conchological Club So. Calif. (pres. 1990), Sigma Xi. Democrat. Home: 26800 Espuma Dr Saugus CA 91350-2324 Office: Calif State U Dept Geol Scis 18111 Nordhoff St Northridge CA 91330-0001

STACK, GEOFFREY LAWRENCE, real estate developer; b. Trinidad, British West Indies, Sept. 16, 1943; s. Gerald Francis and V. Louise (Bell) S.; m. Victoria Hammack, 1970 (div. 1986); 1 child, Kathryn; m. Nancy J. Haarer, Apr. 19, 1987; children: Alexandra, Natalie. BA, Georgetown U., 1965; MBA, U. Pa., 1972. Dir. acquisitions J.H. Snyder Co., L.A., 1972-75; from project mgr. to exec. v.p. Richards West, Newport Beach, Calif., 1975-77; pres. Regis Homes Corp., Newport Beach, 1977-93; mng. dir. Sares-Regis Group, Irvine, Calif., 1993—; bd. dirs. Arral & Ptnrs., Hong Kong, Calif. Housing Coun., Sacramento. Mem. adv. bd. Coro So. Calif., Santa Ana, 1991—; bd. regents Franciscan Sch. of Theology, Berkeley, Calif., 1991—; bd. advisors Grad. Sch. Bus., U. Calif., Irvine, 1992; bd. dirs. Nat. Multihousing Coun., 1987—. Capt. USMC, 1967-70. Decorated 2 Bronze Stars, 20 Air medals, Navy Commendation medal, Purple Heart. Mem. Young Pres. Orgn., Big Canyon Country Club, Pacific Club, Ctr. Club. Democrat. Roman Catholic. Office: Sares Regis Group 18802 Bardeen Ave Irvine CA 92612-1521

STACK, KEVIN J., lawyer; b. N.Y.C., Aug. 12, 1951. BA cum laude, UCLA, 1973; JD cum laude, Loyola U., L.A., 1976. Bar: Calif. 1976, U.S. Dist. Ct. (ctrl. dist.) Calif. 1977. Atty. Knapp, Petersen & Clarke, Glendale, Calif. Office: Knapp Petersen & Clarke 500 N Brand Blvd Fl 20 Glendale CA 91203-1923

STACKELBERG, JOHN RODERICK, history educator; b. Munich, May 8, 1935; came to U.S., 1946; s. Curt Freiherr and Ellen (Biddle) von Stackelberg; m. Steffi Heuss, Oct. 10, 1965 (div. Apr. 1983); m. Sally Winkle, Mar. 30, 1991; children: Katherine Ellen, Nicholas Olaf, Emmet Winkle. AB, Harvard U., 1956; MA, U. Vt., 1972; PhD, U. Mass., 1974. Reading instr. Baldridge Reading Svcs., Greenwich, Conn., 1957-62; lang. tchr. Hartnackschule, Berlin, 1963-67; English and social studies tchr. Lake Region Union High Sch., Orleans, Vt., 1967-70; lectr. history San Diego State U., 1974-76; asst. prof. history U. Oreg., Eugene, 1976-77, U. S.D., Vermillion, 1977-78; asst. prof. history Gonzaga U., Spokane, Wash., 1978-81, assoc. prof. history, 1981-88, prof. history, 1988—. Author: Idealism Debased, 1981; contbr. articles to profl. jours. Pres. Spokane chpt. UN Assn., 1986-90. With U.S. Army, 1958-60. Leadership Devel. fellow Ford Found., 1969-70. Home: 9708 E Maringo Dr Spokane WA 99206-4429 Office: Gonzaga U Dept History Spokane WA 99258

STACY, BILL WAYNE, academic administrator; b. Bristol, Va., July 26, 1938; s. Charles Frank and Louise Nelson (Altwater) S.; m. Sue Varnon; children: Mark, Sara, James. B.S.Ed., S.E. Mo. State U., 1960; M.S., So. Ill. U., 1965, Ph.D., 1968. Tchr. Malden High Sch., Mo., 1960-64; faculty Southeast Mo. State U., Cape Girardeau, 1967-89, dean Grad. Sch., 1976-79, interim pres., 1979, pres., 1980-89; pres. Calif. State U., San Marcos, 1989—; dir. Boatmen's Nat. Bank. Bd. dirs. San Diego United Way. Mem. Am. Assn. state Colls. and Univs. (dir.), Am. Assn. Higher edn., PIC Policy Bd., San Diego Rotary, Pvt. Industry Coun. Presbyterian. *

STAEHELIN, LUCAS ANDREW, cell biology educator; b. Sydney, Australia, Feb. 10, 1939; came to U.S., 1969; s. Lucas Eduard and Isobel (Malloch) S.; m. Margrit Weibel, Sept. 17, 1965; children: Daniel Thomas, Philip Roland, Marcel Felix. Dipl. Natw., Swiss Fed. Inst. Tech., Zurich, 1963, Ph.D. in Biology, 1966. Research scientist N.Z. Dept. Sci. and Indsl. Research, 1966-69; research fellow in cell biology Harvard U., Cambridge, Mass., 1969-70; asst. prof. cell biology U. Colo., Boulder, 1970-73, assoc. prof., 1973-79, prof., 1979—; vis. prof. U. Freiburg, 1978, Swiss Fed. Inst. Tech., 1984, 92; mem. cellular biology and physiology study sect. NIH, Bethesda, Md., 1980-84; mem. DOE panel on rsch. directions for the energy bioscis., 1988, 92; mem. NSF adv. panel for cellular orgn., 1994-96. Editor Jour. Cell Biology, 1977-81, European Jour. Cell Biology, 1981-90, Plant Physiology, 1986-92, Plant Jour., 1991—, Biology of the Cell; editor: (with C.J. Antzen) Encyclopedia of Plant Physiology, Vol. 19, Photosynthesis III, 1986; contbr. numerous articles to sci. jours. Recipient Humboldt award Humboldt Found., 1978, Sci. Tchr. award U. Colo., 1984; grantee NIH, 1971—, USDA, 1994—, NASA, 1997—. Mem. AAAS, Am. Soc. Cell Biology, Am. Soc. Plant Physiology, German Acad. Natural Scis. Leopoldina. Home: 2855 Dover Dr Boulder CO 80303-5305 Office: U Colo Dept Molecular Cell/Devel Biology Campus Box 347 Boulder CO 80309-0347

STAEHLE, ROBERT L., foundation executive; b. Rochester, N.Y., Apr. 22, 1955; s. Henry Carl and Isabel Montgomery S. BS in Aero. and Astronautic Engring., Purdue U., 1977. Prin. investigator Skylab Expt. ED-31 (bacteria aboard Skylab), NASA/Marshall Space Flight Center, Huntsville, Ala., 1972-74; student trainee engring. Skylab Expt. ED-31 (bacteria aboard Skylab), NASA/Marshall Space Flight Center, 1974-77; sci. observation analyst Caltech/Jet Propulsion Lab., Pasadena, Calif., 1977-78; engr. advanced projects group, 1978-83, mem. tech. staff system integration sect. of Space Sta., 1983-87, mem. tech. staff and space sta., user ops. team leader, 1987-88; tech. mgr. Jet Propulsion Lab., Pasadena, Calif., 1988—, mgr. space sta. Freedom support office Pasadena ops., 1990-92, Pluto team leader, 1992-93, mgr. Pluto Express preproject, 1993-96; mgr. Ice and Fire preprojects Jet Propulsion Lab., Pasadena, 1996—; prin. founder, pres. World Space Found., South Pasadena, Calif., 1979—; founding dir. So. Calif. Space Bus. Roundtable, 1987-95. Co-author: Project Solar Sail, New Am. Libr., 1990; contbr. articles to profl. jours. Mem. Cmty. Leaders Adv. Bd. for Irvine Scholars, Occidental Coll., L.A., 1996—; bd. dirs. Caltech Y, 1987-93. Nat. Space Club Goddard scholar, 1977; Charles A. Lindbergh Fund grantee, 1986. Fellow Brit. Interplanetary Soc.; mem. AIAA, Tau Beta Pi, Sigma Gamma Tau. Office: Jet Propulsion Lab Pasadena CA 91109

STAFFORD, PATRICK PURCELL, poet, writer, management consultant; b. L.A., Mar. 13, 1954; s. Elsan H. Stafford and Ann (Ruelle) Lane; m. Liane Beale Stafford, Jan. 2, 1987; 1 child, David. Student, U.S. Armed Forces Inst., 1971, UCLA, 1980, 81. Head script writer Hollywood (Calif.) Radio Network, 1981-82; mgr. new bus. Harry Koff Agy., Encino, Calif., 1984-85; pres., mgr. Legal Experts, L.A., 1988-94, Creative Adminstrs., L.A., 1994—; office adminstr. Moneymaker & Kelley, L.A., 1989-90; sales rep. Now Messenger Svc., L.A., 1993—; staff mgr. Stafford Resume Svc., L.A., 1990—. Contbr. poems, articles, short stories to profl. publs. Mem. Big Bros. of Greater L.A., 1991. With USMC, 1971-78, Vietnam. Recipient Concept/Essay award L.A. Rtd., 1990, Poetry Contest award Tradition Mag., 1991, Hon. Mention award Iliad Press, 1992, Wash. State Coll., 1990, Winner in Play-Reading Series, Altered Stage Theatre Co., 1991. Mem. The Writer's Exch. (life), Marino's of Beverly Hills (charter), Highlander Club. Libertarian. Home and Office: 1624 Williams Hwy Ste 51 Grants Pass OR 97527-5660

STAFFORD-MANN, PATRICIA ANN, library and textbook consultant, writer; b. San Francisco, Aug. 14, 1919; d. Alfonce Henry and Regina Dorothy (Flynn) Heller; m. Paris Howard Stafford, Sept. 25, 1944 (dec. 1979); children: Philip, Michael, Teresa, Marie, Stephen; m. Roy Everett Mann, Dec. 16, 1986. AA, Moorpark Coll., 1972; tchrs. credential, UCLA, 1975. Mem. sales staff May Co., Ventura, Calif., 1972; library media specialist Ventura County Supt. Schs., Camarillo, Calif., 1972-85; textbook cons. Ventura County Supt. Schs., Camarillo, 1985—; library cons. Calif. Lutheran U., Thousand Oaks, 1986; freelance writer; cons. to textbook pubs., 1976-84. Author: People of Ventura County (with others), 1982, Your Two Brains, 1986, Dreaming and Dreams, 1991; contbr. articles to various mags.; spkr. on children's books. Cpl. USMC, 1943-44. Mem. Soc. Children's Book Writers, LWV (past pres. Monrovia chpt.), Am. Goldstar Mothers (past pres. Oxnard chpt.), Friends of Libr., San Clemente Women's Club, Kiawanis, Los Escribientes. Republican. Roman Catholic. Home: 23 Segovia San Clemente CA 92672-6057

STAGER, DONALD K., construction company executive. Chmn. Dillingham Constrn. Holdings Inc., Pleasanton, Calif. Recipient, Roebling award Am. Soc. of Civil Engineers, 1995. Office: Dillingham Constrn Corp 5960 Inglewood Dr Pleasanton CA 94588-8535

STAHELI, LYNN TAYLOR, pediatric orthopedist, educator; b. Provo, Utah, Nov. 13, 1933; s. Harvey Roulin and Letha (Taylor) S.; m. Ann Lee Smith, June 4, 1957 (div. 1976); children: Linda Ann, Diane Kay, Todd Kent; m. Lana Ribble, June 11, 1977. BS, Brigham Young U., 1956; MD, U. Utah, 1959. Intern U. Utah, Salt Lake City, 1960; resident in orthopedic surgery U. Wash., 1964-68; dir. rsch. and edn. Children's Hosp., Seattle, 1968-77, dir. dept. orthopedics, 1977-92; prof. dept. orthopedics U. Wash., Seattle, 1968—; mem. med. exec. com. Children's Hosp. and Med. Ctr., Seattle, 1977-92; cons. Fircrest Sch., Seattle, 1968-80, Boyer Children's clinic, Seattle, 1968-80, Seattle Pub. Schs. Spl. Edn. Program, 1968-80; invited speaker for more than 1000 individual presentations in 30 countries, 1960—; founder Duncan Seminar for Cerebral Palsy, 1980. Editor: Jour. Pediatric Orthopedics, 1981—; author: Med. Writing and Speaking, 1986, Fundamentals of Pediatric Orthopedics, 1992; contbr. articles to numerous profl. jours. Founding mem. bd. N.W. Inst. Ethics and Life Scis., Seattle, 1974—; bd. dirs. Rainier Found., Seattle, 1988—; founder Internat. Scholarship for Pediatric Orthopedics, Seattle, 1988-93. Capt. USAF, 1960-63. Mem. Pediatric Orthopedic Soc. N.Am., Am. Acad. Orthopedic Surgeons (pediatric orthopedics com. 1980-86), Am. Acad. Pediatrics (chmn. com. on shoewear 1985—, Disting. Svc. award 1995), Am. Acad. Cerebral Palsy and Devel. Medicine (chmn. instrnl. course com. 1982—), Alpha Omega Alpha. Home: 4116 48th Ave NE Seattle WA 98105-5116 Office: Childrens Hosp Dept Orthopedics 4800 Sand Point Way NE Seattle WA 98105-3901

STAHL, GREGORY LEE, physiologist, researcher; b. Waynesboro, Pa., Oct. 17, 1959; s. Emory Charles and Nellie Jean (Stouffer) S.; m. Rebecca Lynn Freeman, Aug. 27, 1983. BS, Juniata Coll., 1984; PhD, Thomas Jefferson U., 1988. Assoc. psychologist dept. anesthesia Brigham & Women's Hosp.; assoc. prof. dept. anesthesia Med. Sch. Harvard U., Boston. Contbr. articles to Jour. Pharm. Exptl. Therapeutics, Am. Jour. Physiology, Circulation Rsch., others. With USN, 1977-81. Recipient Award of Excellence U.S. Achievement Acad. Am., 1988, Dr. Harold Lamport award, 1994, Rsch. Career Enhancement award, 1996. Mem. Am. Physiol. Soc., Am. Heart Assn., Basic Sci. Coun. Republican. Office: Ctr Exptl Therapeutics Repertusion Injury Anesthesia BWH 75 Francis St Boston MA 02115

STAHL, GREGORY PHILIP, geologist; b. San Diego, Dec. 17, 1956; s. Philip Wilfred and Dorothy Lucille (Sturdevant) S.; m. Tracy Lynn Suiter, May 5, 1984; children: Eric Gregory, Chelsea Renee, Austin Philip. Student, U. Calif., San Diego, 1975-77; BS in Geology, San Diego State U., 1981; postgrad., Okla. State U., 1990. Registered geologist, Calif.; cert. hydrogeologist, Calif. Geophys. technician Rogers Explorations, Inc., Midland, Tex., 1980; wellsite geologist Petrolog, Ventura, Calif., 1981-82; exploration geologist Natura Energy Corp., Midland, 1982-84, Petrom Corp., Midland, 1984-85; sr. geologist Willow Creek Resources, Inc., Midland, 1985-88; prin., geologist Vanguard Primary Resources, Midland, 1988-90; sr. geologist, project mgr. Resna Industries, Inc., Escalon, Calif., 1990-94, tech. dir. scis., 1994-95; ops. mgr. Ground Zero Analysis, Inc., Stockton, Calif., 1995—. Mem. Am. Assn. Petroleum Geologists, Assn. Groundwater Scientists and Engrs., Stanislaus Geol. Soc. (charter mem.). Republican. Lutheran. Home: 1517 Montclair Dr Modesto CA 95350-0560 Office: Ground Zero Analysis Inc 2291 W March Ln Ste 127D Stockton CA 95207

STAHL, JACK LELAND, real estate company executive; b. Lincoln, Ill., June 28, 1934; s. Edwin R. and Edna M. (Burns) S.; m. Carol Anne Townsend, June 23, 1956; children: Cheryl, Nancy, Kellea. BS in Edn., U. N.Mex., 1957. Tchr. Albuquerque Public Schs., 1956-59; pres. House Finders, Inc., Albuquerque, 1959-65; v.p. N.Mex. Savs. & Loan Assn., Albuquerque, 1965-67; chmn. bd. Hooten-Stahl, Inc., Albuquerque, 1967-77; mem. N.Mex. Ho. of Reps., 1969-70; pres. The Jack Stahl Co., Albuquerque, 1977—; mem. N.Mex. Senate, 1981-86; lt. gov. State of N.Mex., 1987-90. Mem. N. Mex. Ho. of Reps., 1969-70, exec. bd. Gr. S.W. Coun. Boy Scouts Am, 1982-89; bd. dirs. BBB N. Mex., 1968-82, pres. 1975-76; trustee Univ Heights. Hosp.,1980-85; vice chmn. N. Mex. Bd. Fin., 1987-90, N. Mex. Cmty. Devel. Coun., 1987-90; bd. dirs. Ctr. for Entrepreneurship and Econ. Devel., 1994—; mem. Gov.'s Bus. Adv. Coun., 1995—. Named Realtor of Yr., Albuquerque Bd. Realtors, 1972. Mem. Nat. Assn. Realtors, Nat. Homebuilders Assn., N.Mex. Amigos, 20-30 Club (pres. 1963-64), Rotary. Republican. Methodist. Office: 1911 Wyoming Blvd NE Albuquerque NM 87112-2865

STAHL, LOUIS A., lawyer; b. Oct. 31, 1940; s. Louis A. and Dorothy (Cox) S.; m. Mary Kathleen Quinn, Apr. 4, 1960; children: Lisa, Suzanne, Gretchen, Nicole. BA magna cum laude, Wheeling Jesuit Coll., 1962; postgrad., Duquesne U., 1965-66; JD summa cum laude, Notre Dame U., 1971. Bar: Ariz. 1971, U.S. Dist. Ct. Ariz. 1971, U.S. Ct. Appeals (9th cir.) 1974, U.S. Supreme Ct. 1975. Ptnr. Streich Lang P.A., Phoenix, 1971—; mem. Maricopa County Superior Ct. Rule 26.1 Study Com., 1992—; Frances Lewis lawyer in residence Washington & Lee Univ. Law Sch., 1986; seminar panelist Ariz. Bankers Assn., 1987, Profl. Ednl. Systems, Inc., 1989; mediator, arbirtator U.S. Arbitration and Mediation of Ariz., Nev. and N. Mex., 1993—. Contbg. author: Arizona Attorneys' Fees Manual, 1987, Arizona Professionalism Manual, 1992; contbr. papers to law revs. and jours. Active Phoenix and Maricopa County Young Reps., Ariz. Rep. Party's Lawyers' Ballot Security Com., 1980, Vols. for Reagan-Bush, 1980, Re-elect Rep. Ernest Baird Fin. Com., 1992, Ariz. Rep. Caucus.; founding mem., v.p., dir., legal counsel Performing Arts Combined Talent. Mem. ABA (vice-chmn. health ins. com., sect. ins., negligence and compensation law 1973-79, contbg. editor The Forum 1976-79), State Bar Ariz. (mem. profl. liability com. 1979-86, chmn. 1983-86, mem. com. on rules of profl. conduct ethics com. 1981-93, com. on professionalism 1989-91, discipline task force 1991-92, co-chmn. peer rev. com. 1991—), Def. Rsch. Inst., Ariz. Assn. of Def. Counsel, Ariz. Bar Found., Phoenix C. of C. (military affairs com.), Am. Numismatic Assn., Phoenix Coin Club. Office: Streich Lang PA 2 N Central Ave Ste 200 Phoenix AZ 85004-2322

STAHL, LOUISE W., defense company executive; b. Atlanta, Tex., Mar. 22, 1942; d. John Bonaparte and Winnie (Hawkins) Whittington; m. Timothy T. Stahl, July 18, 1961 (div. Dec. 1982); children: Jeannine Louise, Sandra Ann. BA, So. Meth. U., 1964; postgrad., Rice U., 1972-76. Sr. contract adminstr. TRW Mission, Houston, 1979-86; contract adminstr. Day & Zimmermann Hawthorne (Nev.) Corp., 1987-95, mgr. prodn. planning and bus. devel., 1995—, asst. sec. corp., 1994—. Contbr. articles to profl. publs. Bd. dirs. Consol. Agys. of Human Svcs., Hawthorne, 1995—. Grad. fellow Rice U., 1972-76. Mem. Am. Prodn. and Inventory Control Soc. (cert. in prodn. and inventory mgmt.), Nat. Contract Mgmt. Assn. Democrat. Episcopalian. Office: Day & Zimmerman Hawthorne Corp Hwy 95S PO Box 15 Hawthorne NV 89415

STAHL, RICHARD G. C., journalist, editor; b. Chgo., Feb. 22, 1934; m. Gladys C. Weisbecker; 1 child, Laura Ann. Student, Northwestern U., U. Ill., Chgo. Editor Railway Purchases and Stores Mag., Chgo., 1960-63; editor pub. rels. dept. Sears Roebuck & Co., Chgo., 1963-68; dir pub. rels. dept. St. Joseph's Hosp. Med. Ctr., Phoenix, 1968-72; v.p. pub. rels. Consultation Svcs., Inc., Phoenix, 1972-73; creative dir. Don Jackson and Assoc., Phoenix, 1973; editor, pub. rels. mgr. Maricopa County Med. Soc., Phoenix, 1974-76; sr. editor Ariz. Hwys. mag., Phoenix, 1977—. Regional editor: (travel guides) Budget Travel, 1985, USA, 1986, Arizona, 1986; free-lance writer and editor. Mem. Soc. Profl. Journalists. Office: Ariz Hwys Mag 2039 W Lewis Ave Phoenix AZ 85009-2819 *Personal philosophy: Follow your dream and fulfill your potentialities.*

STAKELUM, RICHARD ALLEN, naval officer; b. New Orleans, La., Feb. 14, 1954; s. Patrick Paul and Dorothy Marie (Farnet) S.; m. Joann Christine Andrews, June 12, 1982; 1 child, Derek Patrick. Student, U. Southwestern La., 1976-78; BS in Computer Sci., Nat. U., San Diego, 1986, MBA, 1988. Enlisted USAF, 1972; med. svc. technician USAF, Craig AFB, Ala., 1972-76; resigned USAF, 1976; enlisted USN, 1979, commd., 1989, advanced through grades to lt., 1993; sonar technician instr. Fleet ASW, San Diego, 1984-87; chief sonar technician USS Truxton CGN 36, San Diego, 1987-89; electronics material officer USS Fletcher DD992, Pearl Harbor, Hawaii, 1989-92, Comdesron 33, San Diego, 1992-95; force electronics material officer Commdr Naval Surface Forces Pacific, San Diego, 1995—; mem. CNSP Force 21 Think Tank, San Diego, 1993—; leader Combat Systems Maintenance Working Group, San Diego, 1996—. Den leader Cub Scouts, Boy Scouts Am., San Diego, 1993—; bd. dirs. Pacifica H/O Assn., San Diego, 1993—. Home: 4584A W Pt Loma Blvd San Diego CA 92107

STALEY, JOHN FREDRIC, lawyer; b. Sidney, Ohio, Sept. 26, 1943; s. Harry Virgil and Fredericka May (McMillin) S.; m. Sue Ann Bolin, June 11, 1966; children—Ian McMillin, Erik Bolin. A.B. in History, Fresno State Coll., 1965; postgrad. in pub. adminstrn. Calif. State U.-Hayward, 1967-68; J.D., U. Calif. 1972. Bar: Calif. 1972. Ptnr. Staley, Jobson & Wetherell, Pleasanton, Calif., 1972—; lectr. Hastings Coll. Law, 1973-74; founding mem., Bank of Livermore; bd. dirs. Xscribe Corp. (NASOAQ XSCR)' del. U.S.-China Joint Conf. on Law, Beijing, 1987. Mem. Livermore City Coun., 1975-82, vice mayor, 1978-82; bd. dirs. Alameda County Tng. and Employment Bd., Alameda-Contra Costa Emergency Med. Svcs. Agy., Valley Vol. Ctr. With M.I., U.S. Army, 1966-67. Fellow Am. Acad. Matrimonial Lawyers; mem. ABA, Calif. State Bar, Alameda Bar Assn., Contra Costa Bar Assn., Amador Valley Bar Assn., Calif. Assn. Cert. Family Law Specialists (pres. 1988-89, Hall of Fame award, 1994), Lawyer Friends of Wine. Office: Staley Jobson & Wetherell 5776 Stoneridge Mall Rd Ste 310 Pleasanton CA 94588-2838

STALLEY, ROBERT DELMER, retired mathematics educator; b. Mpls., Oct. 25, 1924; s. Francis Charles and Florence Camille (Goode) S.; m. Dorothy Ann Jeffery, Aug. 27, 1950; children: Mark, Jeffery, John, Lorena. BS, Oreg. State U., 1946, MA, 1948; PhD, U. Oreg., 1953. Instr. U. Ariz., Tucson, 1949-51, Fresno (Calif.) State U., 1955-56; instr. Iowa State U., Ames, 1953-54, asst. prof., 1954-55; mathematician Sperry Rand, St. Paul, 1955; mathematician U.S. Naval Ordnance Test Sta., China Lake, Calif., 1956, cons., 1956-60; asst. prof., assoc. prof. math. Oreg. State U., Corvallis, 1956-66, prof., 1966-89, prof. emeritus, 1989—; jour. referee, reviewer; speaker, cons. in field, mem. various sci. panels; dir. Summer Insts. in Math., NSF, 1965-67. Contbr. articles to math. jours. Rsch. grantee NSF, 1967-71. Mem. Am. Math. Soc., Sierra Club, Sigma Xi, Pi Kappa Phi. Home: 1405 NW Forest Dr Corvallis OR 97330-1705 Office: Oreg State U Dept Math Corvallis OR 97331

STALLKNECHT-ROBERTS, CLOIS FREDA, publisher, publicist; b. Birmingham, Ala., Dec. 31, 1934; d. August and Sadie Bell (Wisener) Anton; m. Randall Scott Roberts; children: Yvonne Denise, April O'dell, Kurt William. Publicist Ms. Clois Presents, L.A., 1968—; advt. Engineered Magic, Advt., Santa Ana, Calif., 1976, 77, 81; pub. Internat. Printing, L.A., 1981—. Editor: Nostradamus, William Bartram, Apuleious, 1990-92, Metamorphoses L.A., 1996-97. Home: PO Box 165 Inyokern CA 93527-0165 Office: Engineered Magic 510 De La Estrella San Clemente CA 92672 also: PO Box 165 Inyokern CA 93527-0165

STALNAKER, JOHN HULBERT, physician; b. Portland, Oreg., Aug. 29, 1918; s. William Park II and Helen Caryl (Hulbert) S.; m. Louise Isabel Lucas, Sept. 8, 1946; children: Carol Ann, Janet Lee, Mary Louise, John Park, Laurie Jean, James Mark. Student, Reed Coll., Portland, 1936-38; AB, Willamette U., Salem, Oreg., 1941; MD, Oreg. Health Scis. U., 1945. Diplomate Am. Bd. Internal Medicine. Intern Emanuel Hosp., Portland, 1945-46; resident in internal medicine St. Vincent Hosp., Portland, 1948-51; clin. instr. U. Oreg. Med. Sch., 1951-54, 60-62; staff physician VA Hosp., Vancouver, Wash., 1970-79; cons. in internal medicine, 1951-79. Contbr. articles to profl. jours. Pianist various civic and club meetings, Portland; leader Johnny Stalnaker's Dance Orch., 1936-39. Lt. (j.g.) USNR, 1946-48. Fellow ACP; mem. AMA, Multnomah County Med. Soc., Oreg. State Med. Assn., N.Am. Lily Soc., Am. Rose Soc. Home: 2204 SW Sunset Dr Portland OR 97201-2068

STALZER, MARK ANTHONY, computer scientist; b. Canoga Park, Calif., June 11, 1962; s. Dennis L. and Barbara J. (Pierce) S.; m. Julie F. Hopkins, July 2, 1983; children: Ashley M. Brittany A. BS in Physics and Computer Sci., Calif. State U., Northridge, 1984; MS in Computer Sci., U. So. Calif., 1988, PhD in Computer Sci., 1993. Prin. engr., mgr. software engring. Trace Instruments, Canoga Park, 1981-91; assoc. Merrill Lynch, N.Y.C., 1995-96; staff computer scientist Hughes Rsch. Labs., Malibu, Calif., 1991-95, sr. staff computer scientist, 1996—; mng. ptnr. Oak Park Speculation, 1996—. Contbr. articles to sci. jours.; inventor in field. Mem. Assn. for Computing Machinery, Sigma Xi. Office: Hughes Rsch Labs 3011 Malibu Canyon Rd Malibu CA 90265

STAMBAUGH, LARRY G., finance executive; b. Topeka, Feb. 1, 1947; s. Merle J. and Eileen M. (Denslow) S.; m. Sallie M. Underwood, Jan. 18, 1969 (div. Oct. 1981); children: Matt, Julie; m. Suzanne Van Slyke, May 14, 1982; children: Todd, Scott, Andy. BBA, Washburn U., 1969. CPA, Kans. Mgr. Peat, Marwick, Mitchell Co., Kansas City, Mo., 1969-76; co-owner Automotive Investment & Devel. Co., Olathe, Kans., 1976-82; chief fin. officer CNB Fin. Corp., Kansas City, Kans., 1983-90; chief fin. officer ABC Labs., Columbia, Mo., 1990, pres., chief exec. officer, 1990-92; chmn., pres., CEO Maxim Pharms., San Diego, Calif., 1993—; dir. City Nat. Bank, Atchison, Kans., 1986-90; chmn. bd. dirs. Advent Enterprises. Pres., dir. Big Bros. and Sisters, Kansas City, 1986-88; bd. dirs. Internat. Forum Corp. Dirs., 1996—. Mem. AICPA, Am. Mgmt. Assn., Soc. Environ. Toxicology Edn. Found. (bd. dirs.), Nat. Assn. Corp. Dirs., Columbia C. of C., Rotary Internat. Republican. Presbyterian. Home: 17947 Corazon Pl San Diego CA 92127-1009 Office: Maxim Pharms Ste 150 3099 Science Park Rd San Diego CA 92121

STAMBLER, IRWIN, publishing executive; b. Bklyn., Nov. 20, 1924; s. Sidney and Bessie (Levine) S.; m. Constance Gay Lebowitz, Nov. 5, 1950; children: Amy Ruth Champeau, Alice Joan Seidman, Lyndon Sidney, Barrett Charles. Cert. in Mech. Engring., Tex. A&M, 1944; B in Aero. Engring., NYU, 1947, M in Aero. Engring., 1949. Design engr., project mgr. Chase Aircraft, N.Y.C., 1950-53; structures engr. Republic Aviation, Farmingdale, N.Y., 1953-54; engring. editor Space Aero., N.Y.C., L.A., 1954-66; western editor, corr. Rsch. & Devel., L.A., 1967—. Author: Encyclopedia of Pop, Rock and Soul Music, 1974, 89, Encyclopedia of Folk, Country and Western, 1969, 82, 97 (Reference Book of Yr., Libr. Jour. 1982); 45 other books; field editor Gas Turbine World, 1970—; pub., editl. dir. Tech. Forecasts, 1969—. Chmn. com. Boy Scouts Troop 17, Beverly Hills, 1968-70; coach Little League, Beverly Hills, 1976-80. With U.S. Army, 1944-46. Office: PWG Publ 205 S Beverly Dr Ste 208 Beverly Hills CA 90212-3827

STAMES, WILLIAM ALEXANDER, realtor, cost management executive; b. Douglas, Ariz., Mar. 26, 1917; s. Alex Basil and Teresa (Ruis) S.; AA, Long Beach Coll., 1941; postgrad. U. Calif., Berkeley, 1962-64; cert. mgmt. practices Naval Officers CIC Sch., Glenview, Ill., 1955; grad. Real Estate Inst., Calif.; m. Marguerite Winifred Nelson, June 11, 1943; 1 child, Wynn Lorain. Owner, Stames Beverage Co., Brawley, Calif., 1945-50; liaison engr. Lockheed Missiles & Space Co., Sunnyvale, Calif., 1958-60, liaison engr. sr., 1960, adminstr., 1960-62, staff adminstr., 1962-63, liaison engr., sr., design engr. sr., 1965-76; owner, mgr. Cost Reduction Equipment Sales & Tech., Sunnyvale, 1967-76; realtor Cornish & Carey, 1988—. Dir. ret. activities office Naval Amphibious Base, Coronado, Calif. Comdr. USNR, 1941-69, ret., World War II, Korea, Vietnam. Decorated D.F.C., Air medal with four gold stars, Presdl. citation; inductee D.F.C. Soc. Honor Roll. Mem. Am. Mgmt. Assn., Mountain View Real Estate Bd. (pres.), Calif. Assn. Realtors (bd. dirs.), Tailhook Assn. Clubs: Commonwealth San Francisco, Ret. Officers (past pres. Peninsula chpt.), Lions. Author: Polaris Electrical Subsystems Design History, 1964; Poseidon Subsystem Invention, 1971. Home: 1060 Coronado Ave Coronado CA 92118-2439

STAMPER, MALCOLM THEODORE, aerospace company executive; b. Detroit, Apr. 4, 1925; s. Fred Theodore and Lucille (Cayce) S.; m. Marion Philbin Guinan, Feb. 25, 1946; children: Geoffrey, Kevin, Jamie, David, Mary, Anne. Student, U. Richmond, Va., 1943-44; BEE, Ga. Inst. Tech., 1946; postgrad., U. Mich., 1946-49; DHumanities, Seattle U., 1994. With Gen. Motors Corp., 1949-62; with Boeing Co., Seattle, 1962-90; mgr. electronics ops., v.p., gen. mgr. turbine div. Boeing Co., 1964-66; v.p., gen. mgr. Boeing Co. (747 Airplane program), 1966-69, v.p., gen. mgr. comml. airplane group, 1969-71, corp. sr. v.p. ops., 1971-72; pres. Boeing Co., 1972-85, vice chmn., 1985-90; chief exec. officer Storytellers Ink Pub., Seattle, 1990—, also chmn. bd. dirs.; bd. dirs. Esterline Co., Chrysler Co., Pro-Air Corp., Whittaker Corp., Pro-Air Airline; trustee The Conf. Bd., 1988—. Candidate for U.S. Ho. of Reps., Detroit, 1952; trustee, chmn. Seattle Art Mus.; nat. bd. dirs. Smithsonian Assocs. With USNR, 1943-46. Named Industrialist of Year, 1967; recipient Educator's Golden Key award, 1970, Elmer A. Sperry award, 1982, AIEE award, Ga. Inst. Tech. award, Sec. Dept. Health and Human Services award, Silver Beaver award Boy Scouts Am., 1989, Literary Lions award, 1995; named to Engring. Hall of Fame. Mem. Nat. Alliance Businessmen, Phi Gamma Delta.

STAMPER, NORMAN H., police chief. BS, MS in Criminal Justice Adminstrn., San Diego State U.; PhD in Leadership and Human Behavior, U.S. Internat. U. Chief of police Seattle Police Dept., 1994—; exec. dir. Mayor Pete Wilson's Crime Control Commn.; apptd. (by U.S. Atty. Gen. and Sec. Health and Human Svcs.) Adv. Coun. Violence Against Women; mem. adv. panel on Excessive Force by Police, Police Exec. Rsch. Forum, Major Cities Chiefs; mem. steering com. Seattle Equal Justice Coalition; co-chair Ptnr's. in Pub. Edn's. Urban Scholar's Program; mem. bd. dirs. Leadership Tomorrow; trustee Ctr. for Ethical Leadership. Author: Removing Managerial Barriers to Effective Police Leadership, 1992; tchnical adv. Municipal Police Administration, 1992. Named to Alumni Hall of Fame Boys and Girls Club of Am.; recipient Katharine M. Bullitt award for Leadership Ptnrs. in Pub. Edn. Mem. Internat. Assn. Chiefs of Police. Office: Police Dept 610 3rd Ave Seattle WA 98104-1824*

STAMPER, ROBERT LEWIS, ophthalmologist, educator; b. N.Y.C., July 27, 1939; m. Naomi T. Belson, June 23, 1963; children: Juliet, Marjorie, Alison. BA, Cornell U., 1957-61; MD, SUNY-Downstate, 1965. Diplomate Am. Bd. Ophthalmology (assoc. examiner 1976-92, bd. dirs. 1992—, mem. glaucoma panel 1993—); lic. physician, Calif. Intern Mt. Sinai Hosp., N.Y.C., 1965-66; resident in ophthalmology Washington U.-Barnes Hosp., St. Louis, 1968-71; Nat. Eye Inst.-NIH fellow dept. ophthalmology Washington U., St. Louis, 1971-72, from instr. ophthalmology to asst. prof. dept. ophthalmology, 1971-72; asst. prof. dept. ophthalmology Pacific Presbyn. Med. Ctr., San Francisco, 1972-76, assoc. prof. ophthalmology, 1976-87; chmn. dept. ophthalmology Calif. Pacific Med. Ctr. (formerly Pacific Presbyn. Med. Ctr.), San Francisco, 1987-96; asst. opthalmologist Barnes Hosp., St. Louis, 1971-72, Harkness Hosp., San Francisco, 1973-74; dir. ophthalmic photography and fluorescin angiography, dept. ophthalmology Washington U., St. Louis, 1969-72; dir. resident tng. Pacific Presbyn. Med. Ctr., 1972-89, dir. glaucoma svc., vice-chmn. dept. ophthalmology, 1974-87; chief ophthalmology svc. Highland Hosp., Oakland, Calif., 1974-76; clin. instr. dept. ophthalmology U. Calif., San Francisco, 1974-77; clin. asst. prof. ophthalmology U. Calif., Berkeley, 1974-78, asst. clin. prof. ophthalmology, 1978-85; sr. rsch. assoc. Smith-Kettlewell Inst. Visual Scis., San Francisco, 1972-89; project co-dir. ophthalmic curriculum for med. students Nat. Libr. Medicine, 1973-75; commr. Joint Commn. on Allied Health Pers. in Ophthalmology, 1975-87, bd. dirs., 1978-88, sec., 1980, v.p., 1982-83, pres., 1984-85; provisional asst. chief dept. ophthalmology Mt. Zion Hosp., San Francisco, 1976-87, assoc. chief dept. ophthalmology, 1982-86; ophthalmic cons. Ft. Ord, Calif., 1976—, Oakland (Calif.) Naval Hosp., 1978-83; instr. Stanford (Calif.) U., 1977—; glaucoma cons. U. Calif., Davis, 1978-84; vis. lectr. dept. ophthalmology Hadassah Hebrew U. Med. Ctr., Jerusalem, 1978, Oxford (Eng.) U. Eye Hosp., 1986; ind. med. examiner State of Calif., 1979—; mem. appeals hearing panel Accreditation Coun. for Grad. Med. Edn., 1986-93, mem. residency rev. com. for ophthalmology, 1993—; mem. provisional courtesy staff Peralta Hosp., Oakland, 1988-92; mem. ophthalmic devices adv. panel USFDA, 1989-92; presenter, lectr. in field. Editor Ophthalmology Clinics of North Am., 1988—; mem. editl. adv. com. Ophthalmology, 1982-89, mem. editl. bd., 1983-94; contbr. articles to profl. jours. Chmn. bd. Agy. for Jewish Edn., Oakland, 1986-89; bd. dirs. Jewish Fedn. Greater East Bay, Oakland, 1992-94; bd. dirs. Found. for Glaucoma Rsch.; mem. glaucoma adv. com. Nat. Soc. to Prevent Blindness, 1981—; mem. Am. Diabetes Assn. Surgeon USPHS, 1966-68. Recipient Nat. Soc. for Performance and Instrn. award for self-instrnl. material in ophthalmology, 1975, Honor award Am. Acad. Ophthalmology, 1982, Sr. Honor award, 1992, Statesmanship award Joint Commn. on Allied Health Pers. in Ophthalmology, 1989; N.Y. State Regents scholar, 1961, N.Y. State scholar in medicine, 1965; Blalock student fellow UCLA Sch. Medicine, 1961, Fight for Sight student fellow dept. ophthalmology N.Y. Hosp. and Cornell Med. Ctr., 1962, 63, 64. Fellow Am. Acad. Ophthalmology and Otolaryngology (rep. to joint commn. on allied health pers., faculty home study course sect. X, chmn. sect. VIII 1983-85, bd. councilors, editl. adv. com. Opthalmology jour. 1982-89, editl. bd. Ophthalmology jour. 1983-94, and many others), ACS; mem. AMA (Physician's Recognition award 1989), Am. Ophthalmologic Soc., Assn. for Rsch. in Vision and Ophthalmology, Calif. Med. Assn. (asst. sec. sect. ophthalmology, chmn., sci. bd. rep. adv. panel on ophthalmology 1985-91), Nat. Soc. Prevent Blindness (mem. glaucoma adv. com. 1981—, bd. dirs. 1986—), No. Calif. Soc. Prevent Blindness, Calif. Assn. Ophthalmology, Pan Am. Ophthalmological Soc., N.Y. Acad. Scis., Las Vegas Ophthalmological Soc. (hon.), Am. Glaucoma Soc. (v.p. 1997—). Office: Calif Pacific Med Ctr 2100 Webster St # 214 San Francisco CA 94115

STAMPFLI, JOHN FRANCIS, logistics consultant; b. Dhahran, Saudi Arabia, Oct. 27, 1957; s. Edmund Francis and Luisa Marie (Saucedo) S.; m. Susan Frances Thiel, Mar. 1992. BA in History, Calif. State U., Fullerton, 1980. Substitute tchr. East Whittier (Calif.) City Sch. Dist., 1980-81; customshouse broker LAX/Port of Long Beach, Calif., 1981-87; mgr. logistics Unisys Corp., Blue Bell, Pa., 1987-93; cons. Irvine, Calif., 1993—; field dir. U.S. Naval Inst., 1992—; participant NASA Landsat Adv. Process, 1995. Contbr. articles to profl. jours. Olympic Torch Relay Marshal, 1984; staff mem. to Congressman William E. Dannemeyer, 39th Dist., Calif., 1977-78. Mem. Am. Def. Preparedness Assn., Armed Forces Comm. and Electronics Assn., Assn. Old Crows, Navy League of U.S., U.S. Naval Inst., Phi Alpha Theta. Republican. Home: 26191 La Real Mission Viejo CA 92691-2834

STANDING BEAR, ZUGGUELGERES GALAFACH, criminologist, forensic scientist, educator; b. Boston, Jan. 10, 1941; m. Nancy Lee Karlovic, July 13, 1978 (div. Aug. 1985); m. Virginia Anne Red Hawk, Mar. 22, 1988. BS, U. Nebr., 1971; MS in Forensic Sci., George Washington U., 1974; postgrad. cert. in forensic medicine, Armed Forces Inst. Pathology, 1974; MSEd, U. So. Calif., 1976; MPA, Jacksonville State U., 1981; PhD in Criminology, Fla. State U., 1986. Diplomate Am. Bd. Forensic Examiners, Am. Bd. Forensic Medicine; cert. coroner, Ga., 1988-92; cert. criminal justice instr., Calif., Ga. Criminal investigator U.S. Army, 1965; dist. comdr. 7th region U.S. Army Criminal Investigation Command, Seoul, 1974-77; course mgr. U.S. Army Mil. Police Sch., Ft. McClellan, Ala., 1978-81; ret. U.S. Army, 1981; instr. Fla. State U., Tallahassee, 1981-85; asst. prof. No. Ariz. U., Flagstaff, 1985-86; program coord., prof. Valdosta (Ga.) State U., 1986-95; assoc. prof. Colo. State U., Ft. Collins, 1995—; v.p. Bearhawk Cons. Group, Ft. Collins, 1986—. Editor Jour. Contemporary Criminal Justice, 1992. Mem., task group coord. Com. for Sexual Assault Evidence Stds., ASTM, 1993— Com. Colo State U.; mem. leadership coun. Cmty. Policing Project, Valdosta, Ga., 1993-95; treas. and v.p. edn. and rsch. No. Colo. WOLF rescue, edn., and rsch. project, LaPorte, Colo., 1995—; mem. Nat. Am. lang. preservation com. Colo. State Univ. Decorated Bronze Star medal, Meritorious Svc. medal (with oak leaf cluster). Fellow Am. Acad. Forensic Scis. (gen. sec. 1987-88, gen. chmn. 1988-90, gen. program co-chair 1995-96, Gen. Sec. Meritorious Svc. award, 1996), Am. Coll. Forensic Examiners, Internat. Assn. Forensic Nurses (disting. fellow, mem. exec. bd. dirs., cons. and permissions exec., chmn. ethics com.),; mem. ASTM (co-coord. sexual assault evidence stds. task group), Am. Sociol. Assn., Acad. Polit. Sci., Am. Soc. Criminology, Acad. Criminal Justice Scis. (program com. 1996—), Southern Criminal Justice Assn., Am. Assn. of U. Profs. Democrat. Haudenosaunee (Native Am.). Office: Colo State U Dept Sociology Fort Collins CO 80523

STANDRING, JAMES DOUGLAS, real estate developer; b. Fresno, Calif., Dec. 2, 1951; s. James Robert Pusey and Jacquelin (Moore); m. Paula Jean Monson, Oct. 27, 1972; children: Craig Douglas, Ryan Scott, Melinda Jean, Kevin Paul. BS, Calif. State U., Fresno, 1975. Pres. Westland Industries, Inc., Portland, Oreg., 1976—; ptnr. Aloha Land and Cattle, Inc., Portland, 1982—; bd. dirs. Homebuilders Assn. Metro Portland, v.p. 1988-90, pres. 1990-91; bd. dirs. Oreg. Bldg. Industry Assn., v.p. 1993-96, pres. 1996-97; bd. dirs. Nat. Assn. Homebuilders, Washington, Oreg. trustee BUILD-PAC, 1992—, exec. com., 1994—. Bd. dirs. Tualitin Valley Econ. Devel. Corp., Portland, 1988-95; co-founder, bd. dirs. People for Washington County Charities, Beaverton, Oreg., 1985-88; mem. Tualitin Valley Econ. Devel. Commn., 1000 Friends of Oreg.; steering com. Oreg. Med. Laser Ctr., 1995—. Named Portland Metro. Builder of Yr., 1992, Oregon Builder of Yr., 1992. Mem. Multnomah Athletic Club, Portland City Club, Portland Golf Club, Sierra Club, Univ. Club, Elks. Republican. Episcopalian. Home: 5 Nansen Smt Lake Oswego OR 97035-1029 Office: Westland 6655 SW Hampton St Ste 100 Portland OR 97223-8358

STANFILL, DENNIS CAROTHERS, business executive; b. Centerville, Tenn., Apr. 1, 1927; s. Sam Broome and Hattie (Carothers) S.; m. Therese Olivieri, June 29, 1951; children: Francesca (Mrs. Peter Tufo), Sara, Dennis Carothers. BS, U.S. Naval Acad., 1949; M.A. (Rhodes scholar), Oxford U., 1953; LHD (hon.), U. S.C. Corporate finance specialist Lehman Bros., N.Y.C., 1959-65; v.p. finance Times Mirror Co., Los Angeles, 1965-69; exec. v.p. 20th Century-Fox Film Corp., 1969-71, pres., 1971, chmn. bd., chief exec. officer, 1971-81; pres. Stanfill, Bowen & Co., 1981-90; chmn. bd. dirs., chief exec. officer AME, Inc., 1990-91; co-chmn., co-CEO Metro-Goldwyn-Mayer, Inc., 1992-93; sr. advisor Credit Lyonnais, 1993-95; pres. Dennis Stanfill Co., 1995—; bd. dirs. Dial Corp., Weingart Found. Trustee Calif. Inst. Tech. Served to lt. USN, 1949-59; politico-mil. policy div. Office Chief Naval Ops., 1956-59.

STANFILL, LATAYNE COLVETT, non-fiction writer; b. Atwood, Tenn., Apr. 23, 1914; d. Benjamin Franklin and Geneva Wilson (Carter) Colvett; m. Homer Lawrence Stanfill, June 4, 1932 (dec. Mar. 1990); children: Lawrence Colvett, Suzanne Latayne. Grad., Alamo (Tenn.) H.S., 1929. Pres., hist. rschr., cons. Heirloom Press, Glendale, Calif., 1990—. Author: Colvett Family Chronicles: The History of the Colvett Family of Tennessee 1630-1990, 1991; contbr. articles to hist. and geneal. mags. Dist. collection chmn. L.A. area ARC, 1950-52; active various ch. and mission activities, Los Angeles County, 1972-83. Mem. DAR (chaplain 1989-94, Calif. State Librs. award 1992), Daus. of War of 1812, Huguenot Soc. of Founders of Manakin in the Colony of Virginia 1699. Office: Heirloom Press PO Box 250916 Glendale CA 91225-0916

STANFILL, SHELTON G., performing arts administrator; m. Brigitte. BA in History and Social Scis., Colo. State U., postgrad. Exec. dir. Hopkins Ctr. Dartmouth Coll.; dir. cultural programs Colo. State U.; dir. Nat. Arts Festival 12th Winter Olympic Games; ptnr. Brown, Stanfill & Brown; pres., CEO Wolf Trap Found. for Performing Arts, Vienna, Va.; pres. Music Ctr. L.A. County, 1994—; chair panels, cons. Nat. Endowment for Arts, Lincoln. Ctr., Bklyn. Acad. Music, UCLA; advisor Telluride Film Festival. Office: Nicholas T Goldsborough West Temple St # 400 Los Angeles CA 90012

STANFORD, GINNY CROUCH, painter; b. Lamar, Mo., Sept. 3, 1950; d. Howard D. and Mary Elizabeth (Price) Crouch; m. Frank G. Stanford, Oct. 17, 1974 (dec. June 1978). Ind. study, Amsterdam and Brussels, 1972. One-person shows include Landau Gallery, L.A., 1983, San Marco Gallery, Dominican Coll., San Rafael, Calif., 1987, U. Pacific, Stockton, Calif., 1990, Reed Whipple Cultural Ctr., Las Vegas, Nev., 1992, Saginaw (Mich.) Art Mus., 1995, Somerhill Gallery, Chapel Hill, N.C., 1996; exhibited in group shows at Jan Holloway Gallery, San Francisco, 1988, 90, U. Ariz., Tucson, 1988, Downey (Calif.) Mus. Art, 1988, Angels Gate Cultural Ctr., San Pedro, Calif., 1989, Fla. State U., Tallahassee, 1993, Riverside (Calif.) Art Mus., 1995; represented in permanent collection Nat. Portrait Gallery, Smithsonian Instn., Fuqua Sch. Bus., Duke U., Durham, N.C. Recipient 1st Pl. awards Ft. Smith (Ark.) Art Ctr., 1974, 75, 76, 2nd Pl. award Auburn (Calif.) Art Ctr., 1988, Merit awards Ft. Hays State U., Hays, Kans., 1988; Sonoma Found. grantee, 1990, 91. Office: PO Box 2014 Sebastopol CA 95473-2014

STANFORD, JOSEPH BARNEY, medical educator, physician; b. July 9, 1961; s. Kathleen Barnett; children: Matthew Joseph, Jesse Barnett, Hyrum Porter, Caleb Dean, Thomas Barnett. BA magna cum laude, Mankato State U., 1984; MD, U. Minn., 1988. Diplomate Am. Bd. Family Practice. Resident family and cmty. medicine U. Mo.-Columbia, 1988-91, chief resident family and cmty. medicine, 1990-91, academic fellow, clinical instr. dept. family and cmty. medicine, 1991-93; asst. prof. dept. family and preventive medicine U. Utah, Salt Lake City, 1993—; part time staff physician Cherchez La Femme Birth Svcs. Ltd., Columbia, Mo., 1991-93; med. cons. U. Utah BirthCare HealthCare, 1994—; physician N.E. Family Health Ctr., Salt Lake Regional Med. Ctr., U. Utah Hosp., Primary Children's Med. Ctr., 1993; invited observer Pontifical Acad. Scis. Working Group on Natural Fertility Regulation, Vatican, Italy, 1994. Contbr to prof. jours. Mem. Soc. Tchrs. of Family Medicine (mem. group family centered perinatal care 1990—), Am. Acad. Family Physicians, Am. Acad. Natural Family Planning (chairperson sci. and rsch. com. 1993—), Am. Holistic Med. Assn., Am. Soc. Clinical Hypnosis, Collegium Aesculapium, North Am. Primary Care Rsch. Group, Alpha Omega Alpha, Phi Kappa Phi. Office: U Utah Dept Family Preventive Med 50 N Medical Dr Salt Lake City UT 84132-0001

STANGELAND, ROGER EARL, retail chain store executive; b. Chgo., Oct. 4, 1929; s. Earl and Mae E. (Shaw) S.; m. Lilah Fisher, Dec. 27, 1951; children: Brett, Cyndi Stangeland Meili, Brad. Student, St. Johns Mil. Acad., 1943-47, Carleton Coll., 1947-48; B.S., U. Ill., 1949-51. With Coast to Coast Stores, Mpls., 1960-78, pres., 1972-77; sr. v.p., exec. v.p. Household Merchandising, Chgo., 1978-84; chief exec. officer, chmn. bd. Vons Grocery Co., Los Angeles, 1984-85; past CEO The Vons Cos., Inc., Arcadia, Calif., chmn., 1986—, now chmn. emeritus. Chmn. Wauconda (Ill.) Bd. Edn., 1957-60, Hopkins (Minn.) Bd. Edn., 1968-74; bd. fellows Claremont (Calif.) U. Ctr. and Grad. Sch., 1986; bd. dirs. L.A. area Boy Scouts Am.; trustee Hugh O'Brian Youth Found.; mem. CEO bd. advisors U. So. Calif. Sch. Bus. Adminstrn.; trustee St. John's Mil. Acad; bd. visitors Peter F. Drucker Grad. Mgmt. Ctr. Mem. Am. Inst. Wine and Food (bd. dirs.), Food Mktg. Inst. (chmn. bd. dirs.), Food Employers Coun. (exec. com., bd. dirs.), Mchts. & Mfrs. Assn. (bd. dirs.), L.A. Area C. of C. (bd. dirs.), Jonathan Club (L.A.), Calif. Club. Home: 842 Oxford Rd San Marino CA 91108-1214 Office: Vons Grocery Co PO Box 3338 618 Michillinda Ave Arcadia CA 91007-6300*

STANLEY, FORREST EDWIN, fundraiser, university program director; b. Bakersfield, Calif., Sept. 6, 1942; s. James Edwin and Lucile Haworth (Sloan) S.; student UCLA, 1960-63, MS, 1970; BS, Calif. State U., Northridge, 1969; m. Suzanne Roberts, June 15, 1968 (div. 1984); children: John Forrest, Cheryl Suzanne; m. Virginia Louise Sorenson, Jan. 18, 1987. Sr. clk. So. Calif. Gas Co., 1963-65, programmer analyst, 1965-70; fin. analyst Continental Bldgs. Co., Burbank, Calif., 1970-72; fin. analyst McKinsey & Co., Inc., L.A., 1972-74; analyst Unionamerica Advisors, Beverly Hills, Calif., asst. v.p., asst. treas., 1974-75; dir. alumni and devel. Grad. Sch. Mgmt., UCLA, 1976-80; dir. spl. campaigns U. Calif., Berkeley, 1980-84; dir. devel. U. Colo., Colorado Springs, 1984-86; dir. devel. pub. affairs, Calif. State U., Bakersfield, 1987-92, asst. sec., 1989-92; v.p. U. Colo. Found., Inc., 1984-86; mgr. LH Stanley Trust, 1991—. Mem. Am. Inst. Cert. Computer Profls., Assn. for Computing Machinery, Coun. Advancement and Support of Edn., UCLA Mgmt. Alumni Assn. (v.p. 1974, pres. 1975-77), Sons Am. Colonists, Mensa, Lambda Chi Alpha (UCLA alumni chpt. pres. 1974-77, treas. 1977-80). Clubs: North Kern. Office: PO Box 10705 Bakersfield CA 93389-0705

STANLEY, GEORGE DABNEY, JR., geology educator; b. Chattanooga, Jan. 25, 1948; s. George Dabney and Lucille (Proctor) S. B.A., U. Tenn.-Chattanooga, 1970; Ph.D., U. Kans., 1977. Lectr. in geology U. Calif., Davis, 1977-78; geologist and/or rsch. assoc. Smithsonian Instn., Washington, 1978-81; sr. prof. Fulbright fellow, Germany, 1981-82; assoc. prof. U. Mont., Missoula, 1982-90, prof., 1990—; exch. fellow, Kumamoto (Japan) U., 1992-93; mem. organizing com. Internat. Com. on Fossil Corals; U.S. group leader Internat. Geol. Correlation Project 359; mem. Internat. Geol. Correlation Project 335. Author monograph; editor books; contbr. numerous articles in field to profl. jours. Named hon. research assoc. Smithsonian Instn.; recipient Burlington No. Found. award; Orgn. for Tropical Studies fellow, Fulbright-Hayes fellow, 1981-82; grantee NSF. Mem. Soc. Sedimentary Geology, Geol. Soc. Am., Paleontol. Soc. Washington D.C.(pres. 1980-81), Paleontol. Soc. (medal com. 1990-93, dist. lectr., 1993-94), Paleontol. Assn. Gr. Britain, Com. on Coral Reefs (founding mem.), Internat. Subcom. on Triassic Stratigraphy.

STANLEY, MARLYSE REED, horse breeder; b. Fairmont, Minn., Sept. 19, 1934; d. Glenn Orson and Lura Mabel (Ross) Reed; m. James Arthur Stapleton, 1956 (div. 1976); 1 child, Elisabeth Katharene; m. John David Stanley, Oct. 22, 1982. BA, U. Minn., 1957. Registered breeder Arabian horses in Spain, 1976-94. Chmn. bd. dirs. Sitting Rock Spanish Arabians, Inc., Greensboro, N.C., 1978-81; pres. Sitting Rock Spanish Arabians, Inc., Hollister, Calif., 1981-91, Stanley Ranch, Yerington, Nev., 1991—; bd. dirs. Glenn Reed Tire Co., Fairmont, Minn. Author Arabian hunter/jumper rules Am. Horse Shows Assn.; contbr. articles to horse jours. Named Palomino Queen of Minn., 1951, Miss Fairmont, 1954, Miss Minn., 1955. Mem. AAUW, Arabian Horse Registry Am., Internat. Arabian Assn. (bd. dirs. region 10, Minn. and Wis. 1973-76, nat. chmn. hunter-jumper com. 1976-81), Minn. Arabian Assn. (bd. dirs. 1972-75), Am. Paint Horse Assn. (nat. bd. dirs. 1967-70), Assn. Española de Criadores de Caballos Arabes (Spain), World Arabian Horse Assn., Alpha Xi Delta. Republican. Episcopalian.

STANLEY, RICHARD GRAHAM, geologist; b. Berkeley, Calif., Feb. 22, 1951; s. Roger Upson and Ruth Irene (Graham) S.; m. Helen Gibbons, June 22, 1985; children: Sarah Elizabeth, Jenna Louise. BA in Biology with honors, U. Calif., Santa Cruz, 1973, BS in Earth Scis. with honors, 1973, PhD in Earth Scis., 1984; MA in Geology, Rice U., 1976. Geologist Pennzoil Producing Co., Houston, 1975-77, U.S. Geol. Survey, Menlo Park, Calif., 1984—; lectr. U. Calif., Santa Cruz, 1979-81, Calif. State U., Fresno, 1983-84. Author, co-author over 80 reports, articles, maps and abstracts in field. H. L. Doherty fellow, 1973, U. Calif. fellow, 1977. Mem. Am. Assn. Petroleum Geologists (assoc. editor bull. 1993—), Geol. Soc. Am., Soc. for Sedimentary Geology. Office: US Geol Survey 345 Middlefield Rd MS969 Menlo Park CA 94025

STANO, MARY GERARDINE, writer, tax accountant; b. Milw., Sept. 28, 1953; d. Stephen A. and Vera D. (Gulas) S. Newsletter editor Lake Havasu City (Ariz.) Police Dept., 1984-85; entertainment columnist Today News, Lake Havasu City, 1985-87; hist. columnist Las Vegas Rev.-Jour., 1988-89; editor Guide to the Western Sunbelt, Lake Havasu City, 1989-92, Destination Havasu, Lake Havasu City, 1995—; article writer True West, Stillwater, Okla., 1988—, Wild West, Leesburg, Va., 1994—. Mem. Nat. Writers ASsn. Republican. Roman Catholic.

STANTON, LEWIS HARRIS, software company executive; b. London, Apr. 2, 1954; came to U.S., 1980; s. Gerald and Carole (Harris) S.;divorced; children: Graham, Joshua. BS, U. Birmingham, Eng., 1976. CPA, Calif.; chartered acct., Eng. Sr. mgr. Arthur Andersen & Co., L.A., London, 1976-88; chief fin. officer Data Analysis Inc., L.A., 1988-96; CEO WorldSite Networks Inc., Beverly Hills, Calif., 1996-97; exec. v.p., COO, CFO MAI Sys. Corp., Irvine, Calif., 1997—. Chmn. L.A. Youth non-profit orgn., 1997—. Fellow Inst. Chartered Accts.; mem. AICPA, Calif. Soc. CPAs (chmn. mems. in industry com. 1990-94), Assn. Western Securities Mgmt. (pres. 1989). Office: MAI Sys Corp 9601 Jeronimo Rd Irvine CA 92618

STANTON, WILLIAM JOHN, JR., marketing educator, author; b. Chgo., Dec. 15, 1919; s. William John and Winifred (McGann) S.; m. Imma Mair, Sept. 14, 1978; children by previous marriage: Kathleen Louise, William John III. BS, Ill. Inst. Tech., 1940; MBA, Northwestern U., 1941, PhD, 1948. Mgmt. trainee Sears Roebuck & Co., 1940-41; instr. U. Ala., 1941-44; auditor Olan Mills Portrait Studios, Chattanooga, 1944-46; asst. prof., asso. prof. U. Wash., 1948-55; prof. U. Colo., Boulder, 1955-90; prof. emeritus, 1990—; head mktg. dept. U. Colo., 1955-71, acting dean, 1963-64; assoc. dean U. Colo. (Sch. Bus.), 1964-67. Author: Economic Aspects of Recreation in Alaska, 1953; (with Richard H. Buskirk and Rosann Spiro) Management of a Sales Force, 9th edit., 1995 (also Spanish transl.), (with others) Challenge of Business, 1975, (with M. Etzel and B. Walker) Fundamentals of Marketing, 11th edit., 1997 (also Spanish, Portuguese and Indonesian transls.), (with M.S. Sommers and J.G. Barnes) Can. edit. Fundamentals of Marketing, 7th edit., 1995, (with K. Miller and R. Layton) Australian edit., 3d edit., 1994, (with R. Varaldo) Italian edit., 2d edit., 1990, (with others) South African edit., 1992; monographs on Alaska Tourist Industry, 1953-54; contbr. articles to profl. jours. Mem. Am. Mktg. Assn., Western Mktg. Assn., Beta Gamma Sigma. Roman Catholic. Home: 1445 Sierra Dr Boulder CO 80302-7846

STANWAY, PAUL WILLIAM, newspaper editor; b. Manchester, Eng., Apr. 22, 1950; arrived in Canada, 1976; s. William and Gladys (Wright) S.; m. Erina Danyluk, May 5, 1976; children: Scott, Nicole. Reporter Nottingham (Eng.) Post, 1969-72, Express and Star, Wolverhampton, Eng., 1972-76, Free Press, Winnipeg, Can., 1976-77; city editor Edmonton (Can.) Sun, 1978-80, news editor, 1980-81, mng. editor, 1981-84, assoc. editor, columnist, 1988-90; editor Calgary (Can.) Sun, 1988-90; European bur. chief Toronto Sun Pub., London, 1990-96; editor-in-chief Edmonton Sun, 1992—. Office: The Edmonton Sun, 4990 92d Ave Ste 250, Edmonton, AB Canada T6B 3A1

STAPLETON, BEVERLY COOPER, aerospace company executive; b. Birmingham, Ala., June 4, 1933; d. Herston MacAger and Virginia Cooper; m. John Parker Stapleton, Aug. 31, 1959 (div. July 1981); children: Lisa Karen, Lawrence Cooper. BBA magna cum laude, U. Miami, 1954; MA, U. Ala., 1960. Tchr. Miami Beach (Fla.) H.S., Dade County Pub. Schs., 1956-59; mem. behavior R&D program U. Ala., Tuscaloosa, 1959-61; contracts adminstr. Houghton Mifflin Co., Palo Alto, Calif., 1974-78; Calif. sales rep. Prentice-Hall Inc., Sunnyvale, 1978; contract adminstr., cost analyst United Technologies, Sunnyvale, 1978-82; mgr. contract adminstrn. Echo Sci. Corp., Mountain View, Calif., 1982; contracts mgr. Lockheed Martin Corp. Missiles & Space, Sunnyvale, 1982—; instr. master's program in contracts and material mgmt. St. Mary's Coll., Moraga, Calif., 1984-85; mem. adv. bd. grad. program in contracts and acquisition mgmt. Golden Gate U., San Francisco, 1984-85. Fellow in polit. sci. U. Ala., 1954-55; recipient Women of Achievement award Santa Clara County Commn. on Status of Women, 1985. Fellow Nat. Contract Mgmt. Assn. (cert., pres. San Francisco area chpt. 1984-85, nat. coun. fellows 1983—, nat. exec. com. 1986-88, nat. bd. dirs. 1985-86, nat. v.p. 1987-88), Beta Gamma Sigma. Democrat. Presbyterian. Home: 3728 Rhoda Dr San Jose CA 95117 Office: Lockheed Martin Corp Missiles & Space Orgn 25-22 Bldg 102 1111 Lockheed Way Box 3504 Sunnyvale CA 94089

STAPLETON, JAMES JAY, agricultural scientist, consultant; b. Santa Monica, Calif.. BS, U. Calif., Davis, 1978, MS, 1981, PhD, 1983. Rsch. plant pathologist USDA Agrl. Rsch. Svc., Beltsville, Md., 1983-85; vis. plant pathologist U. Calif., Davis, 1986-87; area IPM adv. U. Calif., Modesto, 1987-90; integrated pest plant pathologist U. Calif., Parlier, 1991—; Collaborator USDA Animal and Plant Health Inspection Svc., Hyattsville, Md., 1986—; agrl. cons., Oakdale, Calif., 1993—; lectr. Calif. State U., Fresno, 1995—; chair Internat. Workgroup Soil Solarization, 1997. Editor profl. jours. With USN, 1969-70, Vietnam. Host Scientist, Postdoctoral Fellow USA-Israel BARD Found., 1991-92; Fulbright scholar J. Wm. Fulbright Bd., 1995-96; Recipient disting. svc. award U. Calif., 1991; keynote address 2d Internat. Conf. Soil Solarization, 1997. Mem. Am. Phytopath Soc., Orgn. Nematologists of Tropical Am. Office: U Calif Kearney Agrl Ctr Parlier CA 93648

STAPLETON, KATHARINE HALL (KATIE STAPLETON), food broadcaster, author; b. Kansas City, Mo., Oct. 29, 1919; d. William Mabin and Katharine (Hall) Foster; m. Benjamin Franklin Stapleton, June 20, 1942; children: Benjamin Franklin, III, Craig Roberts, Katharine Hall. BA, Vassar Coll., 1941. Cookbook reviewer Denver Post, 1974-84; producer, writer, host On the Front Burner, daily radio program Sta. KOA-CBS, Denver, 1976-79, Cooking with Katie, live one-hour weekly, Sta. KOA, 1979-89; guest broadcaster Geneva Radio, 1974, London Broadcasting Corp., 1981, 82; tour leader culinaries to Britain, France and Switzerland, 1978-85. Eng., 1978. Chmm. women's div. United Fund, 1955-56; founder, chmn. Denver Debutante Ball, 1956, 57; hon. chmn. Nat. Travelers Aid Assn., 1952-56, 93-96; commr. Denver Centennial Authority, 1958-60; trustee Washington Cathedral, regional v.p., 1967-73; trustee, Colo. Women's Coll., 1975-80; sole trustee Harmes C. Fishback Found. Decorated chevalier de L'Etoile Noire (France); recipient People-to-People citation, 1960, 66, Beautiful Activist award Altrusa Club, 1972, Gran Skillet award Colo./Wyo. Restaurant Assn., 1981, Humanitarian of Yr. award Arthritis Found., 1995, Disting. Woman of Yr. award Rocky Mountain News, 1996; named Chevalier du Tastevin, 1989, Outstanding Vol. Fundraiser Nat. Philanthropy Day, 1995, Disting. Woman of Yr., Rocky Mountain News. Republican. Episcopalian. Clubs: Denver Country, Denver. Author: Denver Delicious, 1980, 3d edit., 1983; High Notes, 1984. Home: 8 Village Rd Cherry Hills Village CO 80110

STARCEVICH, JOHN (JOHN STARK), producer, writer; b. Rossland, B.C., Can., Feb. 14, 1936; came to U.S., 1978; s. Ivan and Vera S.; m. June Elizabeth Starcevich, Sept. 17, 1961 (dec. May 1, 1976); children: Lara, Tanya. BFA, U. Ariz., Tucson, 1958. Prodr., dir., writer, actor John Stark Prodns., Ojai, Calif., 1966—. Produced and directed more than 40 plays in N.Y.C., London, L.A. and Can. including In Agony, Family Glembay, The Iceman Cometh, Electra, Just Wild About Harry, Name Day; produced play, RCA album, PBS TV spl. An Evening with Stephen Leacock, 1982 (Juno award 1982, Critics' Choice Edinburgh Festival 1983). Mem. Screen Actors Guild, Actors Equity, Brit. Actors Equity. Home and Office: PO Box 1712 Ojai CA 93024-1712

STARING, GRAYDON SHAW, lawyer; b. Deansboro, N.Y., Apr. 9, 1923; s. William Luther and Eleanor Mary (Shaw) S.; m. Joyce Lydia Allum-Poon, Sept. 1, 1949; children: Diana Hilary Agnes, Christopher Paul Norman. A.B., Hamilton Coll., 1947; J.D., U. Calif.-Berkeley, 1951. Bar: Calif. 1952, U.S. Supreme Ct. 1958. Atty. Office Gen. Counsel, Navy Dept., San Francisco, 1952-53; atty. admiralty and shipping sect. U.S. Dept. Justice, San Francisco, 1953-60; assoc. Lillick & Charles, San Francisco, 1960-64, ptnr., 1965—; titulary mem. Internat. Maritime Com.; bd. dirs. Marine Exchange at San Francisco, 1984-88, pres. 1986-88; instr. pub. speaking Hamilton Coll., 1947-48; adj. prof. Hastings Coll. Law, 1996—. Author: Law of Reinsurance, 1993; assoc. editor Am. Maritime Cases, 1966-92, editor, 1992—; contbr. articles to legal jours. Mem. San Francisco Lawyers Com. for Urban Affairs, 1972-90; bd. dirs. Legal Aid Soc., San Francisco, 1974-90, v.p., 1975-80, pres., 1980-82. With USN, 1943-46, comdr. USNR. Fellow Am. Bar Found., Am. Coll. Trial Lawyers; mem. ABA (chmn. maritime ins. com. 1975-76, mem. standing com. admiralty law 1976-82, 86-90, chmn. 1990, ho. dels. 1986-90), Fed. Bar Assn. (pres. San Francisco chpt. 1968), Bar Assn. San Francisco (sec. 1972, treas. 1973), Calif. Acad. Appellate Lawyers, Maritime Law Assn. U.S. (exec. com. 1977-88, v.p. 1980-84, pres. 1984-86), Brit. Ins. Law Assn., Brit.-Am. C. of C. (bd. dirs. 1987—), World Trade Club San Francisco, Tulane Admiralty Inst. (permanent adv. bd.), Assocs. Maritime Mus. Libr. (dir. 1990-92, pres. 1992-94). Home: 195 San Anselmo Ave San Francisco CA 94127-1513 Office: 2 Embarcadero Ctr Ste 2600 San Francisco CA 94111-3823 *"How small, of all that human hearts endure,/That part which laws or kings can cause or cure!".*

STARK, ALLEN LYTTON, psychiatrist, educator; b. McAllen, Tex., Feb. 3, 1949; s. J. Howard and Harriette (Smith) S.; m. Carol Lynn Reynolds, May 14, 1971; children: Elizabeth Kathleen, David Thomas, Michael Christopher. BA, Rice U., 1971; MD, Baylor Coll. Medicine, 1974. Resident in psychiatry Baylor Affiliated Hosp., Houston, 1974-77; pvt. practice in gen. psychiatry, 1977—, pvt. practice psychoanalysis, 1984—; asst. prof. psychiatry Baylor Coll. Medicine, Houston, 1977-88; asst. prof. Oreg. Health Sci. U., 1991—; exec. com. West Br. Ctr., 1986-88; med. dir. adolescent unit Twelve Oaks Hosp., Houston, 1987-88; clin. dir. adolescent treatment program Portland Adventist Med. Ctr., 1988-89; chief profl. staff Pioneer Trail Residential Treatment Ctr., 1989-95, med. dir., 1993—; chief med. staff Pacific Gateway Hosp., 1992-94, 95—; chmn. med. records and utilization rev., 1992-95; med. dir. Evans & Sullivan Clin., 1994—. Mem. vestry St. John the Evangelist Episcopal Ch., Milw., 1991-93. Mem. Internat. Psychoanalytic Assn., AMA, Am. Psychiat. Assn., Am. Psychoanalytic Assn., Am. Soc. Addiction Medicine, Am. Acad. Psychoanalysis, Am. Soc. Adolescent Psychiatry, Tex. Med. Assn., Oreg. Med. Assn., Oreg. Psychiat. Assn., Oreg. Psychoanalytic Study Group, Houston Psychiat. Soc. (rep. to exec. coun. of Tex. Psychiat. Soc. 1983-85, active numerous coms.), Houston-Glaveston Psychoanalytic Soc., Portland Psychiatrists in Pvt. Practice. Office: 340 Oswego Pointe Dr Ste 205 Lake Oswego OR 97034-3230

STARK, FORTNEY HILLMAN (PETE STARK), congressman; b. Milw., Nov. 11, 1931; s. Fortney Hillman Sr. and Dorothy M. (Mueller) S.; children: Jeffrey Peter, Beatrice Ann, Thekla Brumder, Sarah Gallun, Fortney Hillman Stark III; m. Deborah Roderick. BS, MIT; MBA, U. Calif. Teaching asst. MIT, Cambridge, 1953-54; prin. Skaife & Co., Berkeley, Calif., 1957-61; founder Beacon Savs. & Loan Assn., Antioch, Calif., 1961; pres., founder Security Nat. Bank, Walnut Creek, Calif., 1963-72; mem. 93d-102nd Congresses from 9th Calif. dist., 1973—; chmn. ways and means subcom. on health 93d-103d Congresses from 13th dist. Calif., 1973—; mem., chmn. D.C. com., Ways and Means com., subcom. Health, Select Revenue Measures, joint econ. com. Bd. dirs. ACLU, 1971, Common Cause, 1971, Starr King Sch.; del. Dem. State Cen. Com.; trustee Calif. Dem. Coun. Capt. USAF, 1955-57. Mem. Delta Kappa Epsilon. Office: House of Representatives 239 Cannon Bldg Washington DC 20515-0003

STARK, JACK LEE, academic administrator; b. Urbana, Ind., Sept. 26, 1934; s. Lynn C. and Helen (Haley) S.; m. Jil Carolyn Harris, June 14, 1958; children: Janet, Jeffrey, Jennifer, Jonathan. BA, Claremont McKenna Coll., 1957; hon. degree, Redlands U., LDH, 1973. Asst. to pres. Claremont (Calif.) McKenna Coll., 1961-70, pres., 1970—. Active Pomona Valley Cmty. Hosp.; bd. dirs. Thacher Sch., Ojai, Calif. Capt. USMCR, 1957-60. Mem. Assn. Ind. Calif. Colls. and Univs. (chmn.), Ind. Colls. So. Calif. (bd. dirs.), Western Coll. Assn. (bd. dirs.). Club: California (Los Angeles). Home: 1679 Tulane Rd Claremont CA 91711-3426 Office: Claremont McKenna Coll Office of Pres 500 E 9th St Claremont CA 91711-5903

STARK, JOHN See STARCEVICH, JOHN

STARK, MILTON DALE, sports association executive; b. Fellows, Calif., Apr. 28, 1932; s. Ernest Esco and Ruth Hazel (Keeney) S.; m. Katherine Margaret Boyd, Dec. 17, 1955 (div. June 1978); children: Mark Boyd, Kimberly Kay, Matthew Scott, Martin Dean; m. Diana Lynn Mead, July 26, 1980; 1 child, Ryan. AA, Taft Coll., 1956; BA, Whittier Coll., 1958, MEd, 1963. Cert. ednl. adminstr., Calif. Sec. Western Softball Congress, Hollywood, Calif., 1962-70; commr. Internat. Softball Congress, Anaheim Hills, Calif., 1966-75, sec., 1975-83, exec. dir., 1983—; v.p. U.S. Fastpitch Assn., Colorado Springs, Colo., 1993—; mem. coun. Amateur Softball Assn., 1994—; sports cons. Whittier (Calif.) News, 1959-70. Editor-in-chief Softball Illus. mag., 1966-69; columnist The Fastpitch Chronicle, 1993—; contbg. author: FastPitch World, 1993; contbr. articles to softball mags. Served with USAF, 1951-55. Named to Internat. Softball Congress Hall of Fame, 1981, recipient Alumni Achievement award Whittier Coll. Lancer Soc., 1989. Mem. Whittier Coll. Alumni Assn. (bd. dirs. 1989-94). Republican. Home and Office: Internat Softball Congress 6007 E Hillcrest Cir Anaheim CA 92807-3921

STARK, RAY, motion picture producer. Student, Rutgers U. Publicity agt., lit. agt.; talent agt. Famous Artist Agy., to 1957; co-founder Seven Arts Prodn. Co., 1957; ind. film producer, 1966—. Producer : (films) The World of Suzie Wong, 1960, The Night of the Iguana, 1964, Reflections in a Golden Eye, 1967, Funny Girl, 1968, The Owl and the Pussycat, 1970, Fat City, 1972, The Way We Were, 1973, Funny Lady, 1975, The SUnshine Boys, 1975, Murder By Death, 1976, Smokey and the Bandit, 1977, The Goodbye Girl, 1977, The Cheap Detective, 1978, California Suite, 1978, Chapter Two, 1979, The Electric Horseman, 1979, Seems Like Old Times, 1980, Annie, 1982, Blue Thunder, 1983, Nothing in Common, 1986, Peggy Sue Got Married, 1986, The Secret of My Success, 1987, Biloxi Blues, 1988. Steel Magnolias, 1989, Revenge, 1990, Lost in Yonkers, 1993, Barbarians at the Gate, 1993 (Emmy award Outstanding Made to Television Movie 1993), Mr. Jones, 1993, Dr. Jekyll and Ms. Hyde, 1995, Mariette in Ecstacy, 1996, To Gillian on Her 37th Birthday, 1996, Harriet the Spy, 1996. Recipient Thalberg award Acad. Motion Picture Arts and Scis., 1980. Office: Hepburn Bldg W 10202 W Washington Blvd Culver City CA 90232-3119

STARK, S. DANIEL, JR., convention and visitors bureau executive; b. Port Hueneme, Calif., Mar. 26, 1953; s. S. Daniel and Eloise Marie (Fisher) S.; m. Pauline Stark, July 19, 1997; 1 child, Kaitlyn Elizabeth. BS, Calif. Poly. U., Pomona, 1981; cert. in exec. mgmt., Claremont Grad. Sch., 1989, MA in Mgmt., 1992. Driver-guide San Diego Wild Animal Pk./Zool. Soc. San Diego, Escondido, Calif., 1974-76; attractions host Disneyland divsn. The Walt Disney Co., Anaheim, Calif., 1976-80, mgmt. intern, 1981, supr. ops., 1981-82, area supr. ops., dept. mgr., 1982-87; mgmt. cons. S.D. Stark, Jr., Redlands, Calif., 1987—; dir. mktg. Ramada Express Hotel & Casino, Laughlin, Nev., 1988-89; exec. dir. San Bernardino (Calif.) Conv. and Visitors Bur., 1989—; part-time instr. mgmt. and mktg. So. Calif. campus U. Phoenix, 1997—; cons. Hemmeter Devel. Corp., Honolulu, 1985, Calif. Authority Racing Fairs, Sacramento, 1987-88, USIA for Latvian Ministry Transp., tourism divsn., 1992, U.S. Bur. Land Mgmt., tourism mgmt. project U. Alaska Sch. Mgmt.; adj. prof. Sch. Bus. and Pub. Adminstrn., Calif. State U., San Bernardino, 1992-93. Bd. dirs. Leadership So. Calif., 1993—, grad.

pub. affairs tng., 1993; congl. appointee del. White House Conf. on Travel & Tourism, 1995; mem. regional econ. strategies consortium So. Calif. Assn. Govts. Recipient resolution Calif. Assembly, 1989, San Bernardino County Bd. Suprs., 1989, City of San Bernardino Mayor and Coun., 1989, Calif. Senate, 1989; selected as one of 1991 Up and Coming Young Bus. Leaders in San Bernardino County; named one of Inland Empire Bus. All Stars, 1991; recipient World Champion Trail Horse award Am. Jr. Quarter Horse Assn., 1972, Calif. Tourism award for Best Spl. Event-Rt. 66 Rendevouz, 1997. Mem. Am. Horse Shows Assn. (life), Am. Quarter Horse Assn (life), Assn. Travel Mktg. Execs., Internat. Assn. Conv. and Visitors Burs. (cert. comm., conv. mktg., tourism mktg.), Pub. Rels. Soc. Am. (bd. dirs. Calif. Inland Empire chpt. 1990-95, Polaris award 1997), Travel Industry Assn. Am., Calif. Festivals and Events Assn. (pres. 1997—, bd. dirs. 1994—), Inland Empire Tourism Coun. (bd. dirs. 1996—, exec. com. 1996—, treas. 1997-98), Calif. Travel Industry Assn., Tourism Assn. So. Calif. (bd. dirs. 1990-95, vice chair 1992-95), Western Assn. Convs. and Vis. Bur. (chmn. Calif. coun. 1992-94), FarmHouse Fraternity (internat. bd. dirs. 1986-94, v.p. 1990-92, Snyder Alumni award 1984). Office: San Barnardino Conv and Visitors Bur 201 N E St Ste 103 San Bernardino CA 92401-1520

STARKEY, DON J., museum director. Exec. dir. The Space Ctr., Alamogordo, N.Mex., 1993—. Office: The Space Ctr PO Box 533 Alamogordo NM 88311

STARKEY, HARRY CHARLES, geologist; b. Wheeling, W.Va., Dec. 10, 1925; s. Burtice Johannes and Mary Irene (Hilton) S.; BS, W.Va. U., 1950; m. Ruth Woods, May 16, 1964. With U.S. Geol. Survey, 1955-84, geologist specializing in clay mineralogy, Denver, 1958-84. With inf. U.S. Army, 1944-46. Methodist. Research in clay mineralogy, ion-exchange in clay and zeolites, chem. reactions involving clays; contbr. articles to profl. jours. Home: 1636 S Yarrow Ct Denver CO 80232-6754

STARKS, ROSALYN JUNE, physical education and health educator; b. Phoenix, June 17, 1952; d. Ross Owen and Maribel Louise (Barnes) S. BS in Edn., U. Ariz., 1974; MA in Edn., No. Ariz. U., 1991. Tchr. Phys. Edn. K-12, Ariz. Phys. edn. tchr. Santa Cruz Valley Union High Sch., Eloy, Ariz., 1975-84; phys. edn., health tchr. Phoenix Union High Sch. Dist., 1985—; coach Santa Cruz Valley Union H.S. and So. Mountain H.S., Phoenix, 1975—, facilitator student assistance program, 1987—; Phoenix 5A Metro Region Rep. State Softball Adv. Bd., 1990-94; mem. HIV/AIDS articulation com. Phoenix Union H.S. Dist., 1994—; mem. crisis intervention team South Mountain H.S., 1995—, dir. studies com., 1993—, title I literacy strategies cadre, 1995—. Del. People to People Internat. Citizen Amb. Program, Berlin Reflections, 1994; del. Sports Devel. Delegation to South Africa, 1997. Named Softball Coach of Yr., A Ctrl. Divsn., 1980. Mem. AAHPERD, NEA, Ariz. Edn. Assn., Ariz. AHPERD, Phoenix Union H.S. Dist. Classroom Tchrs. Assn. Home: 4406 N 111th Dr Phoenix AZ 85037-5333 Office: S Mountain High School 5401 S 7th St Phoenix AZ 85040-3104

STARKWEATHER, FREDERICK THOMAS, data processing executive; b. Sioux City, Iowa, Feb. 24, 1933; s. Fred Ervin and Gertrude Faye (Madden) S.; m. Margot Glassen, Nov. 19, 1959; children: Thomas Frederick, Jerry Russell, Michael Glassen. BA in Math. and Physics, U. Nebr., Omaha, 1955. Mathematician Flight Determination Lab., White Sands Missile Range, N.Mex., 1955-56; supervisory mathematician Analysis & Computation, White Sands Missile Range, 1956-81; chief data scis. div. Nat. Range Ops., White Sands Missile Range, 1981—; Nat. council rep. Am. Def. Preparedness Assn., Washington, 1980—; pres. White Sands Pioneer Group, White Sands Missile Range, 1983-86; bd. dirs. Assn. U.S. Army, Washington. Author hist. and genealog. books; contbr. book reviews and articles to newspapers and mags. Chmn. El Paso (Tex.) City Planning Commn., 1980-84; bd. dirs. El Paso County Hist. Soc., 1983-87; mem. El Paso County Hist. Commn., 1983—. With USAR, 1955-63. Recipient Profl. Secs. Internat. Exec. of Yr. award, 1987, Conquistador award City of El Paso, 1980; named Disting. Alumnus U. Nebr., Omaha, 1985; named to Hon. Order of St. Barbara U.S. Field Arty. Assn., 1988; cited for svcs. to mankind El Paso chpt. Sertoma, 1985. Mem. Fed. Mgrs. Assn. (bd. dirs.), Freedom Found. at Valley Forge (pres. El Paso chpt., George Washington Hon. medal 1982), El Paso C. of C. (assoc. dir. 1984—, bd. dirs.), Toastmasters (dist. gov. 1970-71), Masons, Tau Kappa Epsilon (Hall of Fame 1986). Office: Nat Range Ops Chief Data Scis Div White Sands Missile Range NM 88002

STARR, GRIER FORSYTHE, retired pathologist; b. Jamestown, N.D., Oct. 6, 1926; s. Earl Grier and Grace (Forsythe) S.; m. Virginia Lucille Heidinger, June 25, 1948; children: William Grier, Joan Elizabeth Starr Barton. BS cum laude, Jamestown (N.D.) Coll., 1947; MD, Northwestern U., 1951; MS in Pathology, U. Minn., 1956. Diplomate Nat. Bd. Med. Examiners, 1952, Minn., Mich., Oreg. and Wash. state bds., Am. Bd. Pathology in Clin. Pathology, 1956, and in Pathol. Anatomy, 1957. Intern Evanston (Ill.) Hosp., 1951-52; sr. resident in pathology Henry Ford Hosp., Detroit, 1955-56; fellow in pathology Mayo Clinic, Rochester, Minn., 1952-55, cons. surgical pathology, 1956-59; cons., pathologist Lab. Pathology and Pathology Cons., Eugene, Oreg., 1959-91, pres., 1973-85; mem. staff McKenzie-Willamette Hosp., Springfield, Oreg., 1959-91—; mem. staff Sacred Heart Gen. Hosp., Eugene, Oreg., 1959-91, chief of staff, 1969-71, dir. labs., 1973-86, emeritus staff, 1992—; chmn. bd., chief ops. officer Oreg. Consol. Labs., Eugene, Oreg., 1986-89; bd. dirs. PeaceHealth (Sisters of St. Joseph of Peace), Bellevue, Wash., Peace Health Oreg.; affiliate in pathology Oreg. Health Scis. Ctr., Portland, 1972-88; assoc. prof. U. Oreg., Eugene, 1986. Contbr. articles to profl. jours. Served with USN, 1944-46. Fellow Am. Coll. Pathologists, Am. Soc. Clin. Pathologists; mem. AMA, Lane County Med. Soc. (pres. 1984-85), Am. Soc. Cytology, Internat. Acad. Pathologists, Pacific NW Soc. Pathologists (pres. 1979-80), Oreg. State Soc. Pathologists, Am. Soc. Dermatopathology (chmn. 1984, peer rev. com. 1976-91). Republican. Presbyterian. Home: 2455 S Louis Ln Eugene OR 97405-1026

STARR, JAMES EDWARD, logistics management executive; b. Iowa City, Iowa, June 12, 1944; s. Donald Edward and Lucille (Waggoner) S. BBA, U. Iowa, 1967; M in Sys. Mgmt., Colo. Tech. U., 1996. Supr. bus. ops. various orgns. Chgo., 1973-82; logistics prog. analyst 442 Fighter Wing, Richards-Gebaur AFB, Mo., 1983-87; dir. plans, logistics prog. analyst 302 Airlift Wing, Peterson AFB, Colo., 1987—. Capt. USAF, 1967-73, lt. col. res., 1975—. Recipient Finkbine Leadership award, Pres./U. Iowa, Iowa City, 1966, 67; named Resource Officer of Yr. USAF Res., Robins AFB, Ga., 1985, Unit of Yr., 1989. Mem. Air Force Assn., Res. Officers Assn. U.S. (pres. Colo. State 1990-91, nat. officer 1981-82, various state offices 1978—, chmn. nat. AF com. 1992-93, Air Force nat. exec. committeeman 1993-95), U.S. Space Found., Soc. Logistics Engrs., U. Iowa Alumni Assn., Colorado Springs Club (chmn. 1988-96), Am. Legion, Alpha Kappa Psi, others. Lutheran. Home: 9025 Aragon Dr Colorado Springs CO 80920-7543

STARR, MELVIN LEE, counseling organization executive; b. N.Y.C., Mar. 17, 1922; s. Herman and Martha (Aberman) S.; m. Eileen Ferne Kagan, Sept. 7, 1947; children: Marianne, Lisa Caren. BBA, U. Miami, 1947; post-grad. Columbia U., 1949-53, U. Denver, 1955-56, Ariz. State U., 1956-57; MA, U. Ariz., 1950; EdD, Western Colo. U., 1974. Faculty, adminstrn. Tucson Pub. Schs., 1950—; tchr. Doolen Jr. High Sch., 1951-53, counselor high sch., 1953-62, asst. prin. Alice Vail Jr. High Sch., 1962-64, Catalina High Sch., 1964-68; prin. Rincon High Sch., 1968-71, Tucson High Sch., 1971-74; asst. supt. Tucson Pub. Schs., 1974-78, assoc. supt., 1978-82; pvt. practice family counseling; pres., CEO Psychol. Engring. for Bus. and Industry, Tucson, 1984—. Mem. Tucson Mayor's Com. on Human Relations, 1969—; mem. Ariz. state com. Anti Defamation League, 1971; Ariz. state adv. bd. Good Shepherd Sch. for Girls, 1971; mem. Dem. Cen. Com., Pima City, Ariz., 1968—; bd. dirs., Mobile Meals of Tucson, Pima County Bd. Health, So. Arix. Girl Scouts U.S. Council; chmn. Tucson Community Ctr. Commn.; bd. dirs. Amigos de los Americanos, AnyTown, Ariz., Lighthouse YMCA, Beacon Found., Big Bros., NCCJ, Jr. Achievement, Tucson Community Center, Pacific Western region Anti-Defamation League, Handmaker Nursing Home Pima County, United Way, CODAC, Planned Parenthood, Girl Scouts Am., Ariz. Mobile Meals, Epilepsy Soc. So. Ariz., Drug Abuse and Alcohol Consortium; adv. bd. Tucson Free Med. Clinic; bd. dirs. Los Ninos Crisis Ctr., 1995—. Mem. Ariz. Assn. Student Teaching (state treas.), NEA, Ariz. Interscholastic Assn. (pres. conf. 1971, legis. council), Ariz. Personnel and Guidance Assn., Nat. Assn. Secondary Sch. Prins., Am. Assn. Sch. Adminstrs., Assn. Supervision and Curriculum Devel., Ariz. Sch. Adminstrs., Phi Epislon Pi, Phi Delta Kappa. Home: 7101 E River Canyon Rd Tucson AZ 85750-2111 Office: PO Box 30163 Tucson AZ 85751-0163 also: 482 Elm Dr Ste E Las Vegas NV 89109

STARR, NANCY BARBER, pediatric nurse practitioner; b. Carlsbad, N.Mex., Dec. 7, 1954; d. John Thomas and Janet Lee (Fleehart) B. BSN cum laude, Tex. Christian U., 1976; MS, U. Colo., 1980. Cert. pediatric nurse practitioner; RN, Colo., Tex. Staff nurse/team leader The Children's Hosp., Denver, 1976-79, clin. nurse specialist, 1980-83; pediatric nurse practitioner Nancy Byrd, M.D., P.C., Houston, 1984-89, Aurora (Colo.) Pediatric Assocs., 1989—; interim dir. edn. Nat. Assn. Pediat. Nurse Assocs. & Practitioners, Cherry Hill, N.J., 1995-96. Author: Pediatric Primary Care Textbook, 1996; mem. editl. bd., dept. editor Jour. Pediat. Health Care, 1994—; contbr. articles to profl. jours. Deacon, mem. outreach steering com. Greenwood Cmty. Ch., Denver, 1991-94; tchr. Bethel Ind. Ch., Houston, 1985-89; mem., leader Bible Study Fellowship, Houston and Denver, 1985-91, 94-95. Fellow Nat. Assn. Pediatric Nurse Assocs. and Practitioners (exec. bd., program chair 1989-93, Rocky Mt. chpt. AAP liaison 1989-95, Houston area chpt. pres. 1988-89); mem. Colo. Nurses Assn., Sigma Theta Tau. Office: Aurora Pediatric Assocs 830 Potomac Cir Unit 105 Aurora CO 80011-6751

STARR, PHILLIP HENRY, psychiatrist, educator; b. Poland, Nov. 16, 1920; arrived in Can., 1922; s. Harry and Jennie (Amsterdam) S.; children: Eric, Craig, Susan. MD, U. Toronto, Ont., Can., 1944. Diplomate Am. Bd. Psychiatry and Neurology, Am. Bd. Child Psychiatry. Intern Hamilton Gen Hosp., Can., 1944-45; residence St. Louis Children's Hosp., 1946-49; fellow St Louis Children's Hosp, 1949-51; dir. Cmty. Child Guidance Clinic, Washington U., St. Louis, 1952-54; chief children's outpatient clinic Nebr. Psychiat. Clinic, Omaha, 1955-60; private practice Omaha, Neb., 1955-84; pvt. practice, Scottsdale, Ariz., 1984—; staff psychiatrist Student Health Ctr., Ariz. State U., Tempe, 1992—. Capt. Can. Army, 1942-44. Fellow Am. Psychiat. Assn., AMA. Home and Office: 7246 E El Caminito Dr Scottsdale AZ 85258

STARR, RAYMOND G., history educator; b. San Antonio, Aug. 7, 1937; s. John B. and Edith Stella (Buckelew) S. BA, U. Tex., 1958, PhD, 1964. Prof. history San Diego State U., 1964—. Author: San Diego: A Pictoral History, 1986, San Diego State University: A History in Word and Image, 1995. Bd. dirs. Cabrillo Hist. Assn., San Diego, 1983-87, 90, Save Our Heritage Orgn., San Diego, 1987-88. Mem. Orgn. Am. Historians (life), Western Hist. Assn., Calif. Hist. Assn., Calif. Coun. Promotion of History (bd. dirs. 1986-89), San Diego Hist. Soc. Republican. Office: San Diego State Univ Dept History 5500 Campanile Dr San Diego CA 92182-0001

STARR, ROBERT IRVING, plant physiologist, chemist; b. Laramie, Wyo., Dec. 11, 1932; s. George Herman and Meriel Louise (Spooner) S.; m. Lavon Fabricius, June 10, 1956; children: Deborah Ann, Kenneth Irving. BS in Chemistry, U. Wyo., 1956, MS in Soil and Biochemistry, 1959, PhD in Plant Physiology and Chemistry, 1972. Ordained deacon and elder Presbyn. Ch. Chemist Shell Chem. Corp., Dominguez, Calif., 1956-57; biochemist Bur. Sport Fisheries and Wildlife, Denver, 1960-63; plant physiologist U.S. Bur. Sport Fisheries and Wildlife, Denver, 1968-74; plant physiologist Colo. State U., Ft. Collins, 1963-64, chemist toxic residue lab., 1965-68; analytical chemist FDA, Denver, 1964-65; environ. scientist coal mining U.S. Geol. Survey, Denver, 1974-77, chief environ. tech. unit, 1977-78; chief biol. and ecol. scis. br. Office of Surface Mining U.S. Dept. Interior, Denver, 1979-81, sr. tech. coord., cons. environ. chemistry, 1984-89; sr. scientist pesticide rsch. Wildlife Rsch. Ctr. USDA, Denver, 1989-93; cons. environ. chemistry Fort Collins, Colo., 1993—; pvt. practice cons. environ. chemistry, 1993—; cons. in environ. chemistry and fin. planning/real estate, 1982-84. Reviewer Jour. Agrl. Food Chemistry, 1970; editor, Reclamation Rev., 1981; contbr. articles to profl. jours. Served to 1st lt., AUS, 1957-64. Fellow Am. Inst. Chemists; mem. Am. Chem. Soc., Ft. Collins Swimming Club, Sigma Xi.

STARR, RUBY, counselor; b. Colonia Dublan, Chihuahua, Mexico, July 25, 1939; came to the U.S., 1957; d. Harvey Ashton and Ruth (McClellen) Longhurst; m. Max Vargas, Nov. 22, 1962 (div. Feb. 1975); children: Michael Kimball, Richard Ryan. BS, So. Ill. U., 1991; MA, Webster U., 1994. Registered counselor, adult tchr., NBCC. Saleswoman Jafra Cosmetics, San Ferdnando, Calif., 1967-72; fiscal sec. Dept. Game and Fish, Santa Fe, 1979-81; med. sec. VA, Albuquerque, 1981-86; sec., tchr. Kirtland AFB, Albuquerque, 1987-91; clk. Social Security Assn., Albuquerque, 1991-92; counselor Displaced Homemakers, Albuquerque, 1985—; support group founder Divorced Women, Albuquerque, 1986-92, A Cry for Help, Albuquerque, 1986-97; rd. com. organizer Edgewood (N.Mex.) Cmty., 1989—; Founder Woman Free, Albuquerque, 1986-90; adv. Crusaders for Legal Change, Albuqurque, Libertad, Albuquerque; mem. N.Mex. rep. 9-5 Women Work, Washington, 1993—, Making the Connections Intercultural Network, Abuse in the Work Place, 1994. Mem. ACA, Nat. Counseling Cert., Nat. Career Counseling, N.Mex. Career Counseling, Albuquerque Career Network. Home: 2585 Anchor Ave Port Hueneene CA 93041

STARSHAK, JAMES L., lawyer; b. Chgo., Feb. 3, 1945; s. Norbert Phillip and Enda (Reiter) S.; m. Susanne M. Smith, Oct. 25, 1969; children: Lesle M., Phillip E. BBA, U. Notre Dame, 1966, JD, 1969. Bar: Ill. 1969, Hawaii 1972, U.S. Dist. Ct. (no. dist.) Ill., U.S. Tax Ct., U.S. Supreme Ct. Atty. estate tax IRS, Chgo., 1969-71, Honolulu, 1971-77; ptnr. Steiner & Starshak, Honolulu, 1971-79; assoc. Conahan & Conahan, Honolulu, 1979-86; ptnr. Carlsmith, Ball et al, Honolulu, 1986—. Office: Carlsmith Ball et al Pacific Tower 22d Fl 1001 Bishop St Honolulu HI 96813-3429

STARTZ, RICHARD, economist; b. White Plains, N.Y., July 19, 1952; s. Arthur and Adele (Kersh) S.; m. Shelly Joyce Lundberg, Jan. 8, 1983; children: Meredith Lundberg, Glynis Lundberg. BA, Yale U., 1974; PhD, MIT, 1978. Asst. prof. fin. U. Pa., Phila., 1978-84; assoc. prof. U. Wash., Seattle, 1984-91, prof. econs., 1991—, chmn. dept. econs., 1995—. Author: 8087/80287/80387 For the IBM PC, 1983, 85, 87, Working with 1-2-3, 1985; co-author: Macroeconomics, 1997. Office: Univ of Washington Dept Econs Box 353330 Seattle WA 98195-3330

STASHOWER, ARTHUR L., lawyer; b. Cleve., Apr. 12, 1930; s. Joseph G. and Tillie (Merlin) S.; m. Joy Schary, Sept. 1, 1957 (div. 1982); children: Keren, Saul, David; m. Barbara Hayden, Jan. 17, 1985. AB, U. Mich., 1951, JD with distinction, 1953. Bar: Ohio 1953, Mich. 1953, Calif. 1957, U.S. Dist. Ct. (mid. dist.) Calif. 1957, U.S. Ct. Appeals (9th cir.) 1962. Assoc. Kaplan Livingston Goodwin & Berkowitz, Beverly Hills, Calif., 1957-64; exec. United Artists Corp., L.A., 1964-65, Artists Agy. Corp., L.A., 1965-67; assoc. Greenberg & Glusker, Beverly Hills, 1967-68; ptnr. Swerdlow Glikbarg & Shimer, Beverly Hills, 1968-71, Sklar Cohen & Stashower, L.A., 1971-84; of counsel Shea & Gould, L.A., 1985-88; ptnr. Chrystie & Berle, L.A., 1988-92, of counsel, 1993—; arbitrator Hughes Aircraft, E.A.S.T. Mem. Anti-Defamation League, 1961-79, exec. com. 1967-73; mem. Assn. Alternative Pub. Schs., L.A., 1973-79. Lt. USCGR, 1953-57. Mem. ABA, Am. Arbitration Assn., L.A. Bar Assn., State Bar Assn. Calif., Beverly Hills Bar Assn., L.A. Copyright Soc. (trustee 1986-90), Fed. Mediation and Conciliation Svc. Democrat. Jewish. Office: Chrystie & Berle 1925 Century Park E Ste 2200 Los Angeles CA 90067-2723*

STAUB, ANITA (ANITA KILPATRICK), management analyst, educator; b. Oakland, Calif., Dec. 24, 1947; d. Homer Lenel and Martha Bernice Kilpatrick; m. Jay Palmer Eickenhorst, Dec. 9, 1983. BA with honors, U. Calif., Berkeley, 1971, teaching cert., 1974; postgrad., Calif. State U., Hayward, 1972, U. Calif., Berkeley, 1973-74, Calif. Pacific U., 1986-90. Cert. secondary tchr., Calif. Substitute tchr. Marin County Schs., San Francisco, 1974—; civil engring. tech. U.S. Army C. E., Sausalito, Calif., 1974-76; substitute tchr. Hendersonville (N.C.) City Schs., 1976-78, Henderson County (N.C.) Schs., 1976-79; park technician Nat. Park Service, Flat Rock, N.C., 1978-81; park technician Nat. Park Service, San Francisco, 1981-83, voucher examiner, 1983-85; mgmt. analyst intern Headquarters 6th U.S. Army, San Francisco, 1985-86; mgmt. analyst Hdqrs. 6th U.S. Army, San Francisco, 1986-89, U.S. Dept. Treasury, San Francisco, 1989—; cons. for interpretive prospectus Golden Gate Nat. Recreation Area, Nat. Park Service, San Francisco, 1981, recording sec. EEO com., 1984-85. Co-designer: Alcatraz Island interpretive display, 1981. Mem. Am. Soc. Mil. Comptrollers. San Francisco Bay Area Fed. Adminstrv. Coun., San Francisco Bay Area Fed. Fin. Mgrs. Coun., Wilderness Soc., Nature Conservancy, Nat. Audubon Soc., Mus. Soc., San Francisco Opera Guild, Stinson Beach Allied Arts Guild, San Francisco Regional Fin. Ctr. Employees Assn. (bd. dirs. sec. 1990, pres. 1991), Marin Conservation League. Home: PO Box 913 Stinson Beach CA 94970-0913 Office: US Treasury Dept Fin Mgmt Svc San Francisco Regional Fin Ctr San Francisco CA 94119-3858

STAUBER, BRANDON FREDERICK, consultant information technology and communications; b. Los Angeles, June 15, 1970; s. Ronald Joseph Stauber and Doreen Lynn Wallach. Ba in Pub. Adminstrn., San Diego State U., 1992; M in Pub. Policy, U. So. Calif., 1995. Lic. real estate agt., Calif. Dir. mktg. Barrister Exec. Suites, L.A., 1992-95; pres. B. Stauber & Assocs., L.A., 1992—; assoc. dir. L.A. Regional Tech. Alliance, 1995-96; prin. Ascent Bus. Cons., L.A., 1996—; v.p. DirectNet-An Omnetrix Co. Mem. L.A. World Affairs Coun., Calif., 1993. Mem. U. So. Calif. Alumni Assn., Am. Soc. Pub. Adminstrn., San Diego State Univ. Alumni Assn. Republican. Jewish. Office: Ascent Bus Cons 8655 W Pico Blvd Ste 19 Los Angeles CA 90035-2706

STAUFFER, GREGORY L., program director; b. Milford, Nebr., Apr. 8, 1955; s. Edward Arthur and Dora Elaine (Miller) S. BBA, Washburn U., 1978; EdD, U. Kans., 1990; MBA, Southwest Mo. State U., 1980. Budget analyst Washburn U., Topeka, 1981-83; asst. budget dir. U. Idaho, Moscow, 1983-84; asst. Dean Coll. Arts & Scis. Washburn U., 1984-88, acting athletic dir., 1989-90, asst. v.p. acad. affairs, 1988-91; v.p.adminstrn. & fin. Peru (Nebr.) State U., 1991-95; v.p. fin. affairs So. Utah U., Cedar City, 1995—; bd.dirs. So. Utah U. Found.; treas. Peru State Coll. Bobcat Booster Club, 1991-93; exec. com. Washburn U. Ichabod Booster Club, 1989. Bd. dirs. Ednl. Credit Union, Topeka, 1991-95, Sigma Phi Epsilon Alumni Corp., Topeka, 1982-83; mem. budget & fin. com. Sunflower Music Festival, Topeka, 1988-91; mem. adv. com. Heartland Health Conf., Topeka, 1985-88; bd. commrs. Utah Summer Games, 1997—. Mem. Nat. Assn. Coll. & Univ. Bus. Officers, Nat. Assn. Coll. Aux. Svcs., Western Assn. Coll. & Univ. Bus. Officers, Coll. & Univ. Personnel Assn., Soc. Coll. & Univ. Planning, Phi Kappa Phi, Omicron Delta Epsilon. Office: So Utah U 351 W Center St Cedar City UT 84720-2470

STEAD, TIMOTHY, architect; b. Newark, N.J., July 6, 1958; s. Thomas Eugene and Hilda (Goncalves) S. BA, William Paterson Coll., 1984; BS in Architecture, Cath. U. Am., 1990. Registered architect, D.C., Colo. Project mgr. CDI Design, N.Y.C., 1983-86; project architect Giant Food, Inc., Washington, 1986-89, Martin Reddy Architects, Washington, 1990-93, SEM Architects, Englewood, Colo., 1993—. Architect: (bldgs.) Restoration of Main Lobby, Georgetown U. Hosp., Washington, 1992, Renovation of Gov. Ames Mansion, Boston, 1984, Bildner & Sons, Lenox Square, Ga., 1985, Giant Food Store, Potomac, Md., 1989. Mem. Inst. Store Planners (assoc.), Internat. Assn. Lighting Designers (sr. assoc. 1987-89), AIA, Tau Sigma Delta. Democrat. Roman Catholic. Office: SEM Architects 7935 E Prentice Ave Ste 102 Englewood CO 80111-2711

STEAD LEE, POLLY JAE See LEE, PALI JAE

STEARNS, SUSAN TRACEY, lighting design company executive, lawyer; b. Seattle, Oct. 28, 1957; d. Arthur Thomas and Roberta Jane (Arrowood) S.; m. Ross Alan De Alessi, Aug. 11, 1990; 1 child, Chase Arthur. AA, Stephens Coll., 1977, BA, 1979; JD, U. Wash., Seattle, 1990. Bar: Calif. 1990, U.S. Ct. Appeals (9th cir.) 1990, U.S. Dist. Ct. (no. dist.) Calif 1990, U.S. Dist. Ct. (we. dist.) Wash. 1991, Wash. 1991. TV news prodr. KOMO, Seattle, 1980-86; atty. Brobeck, Phleger & Harrison, San Francisco, 1990-92; pres. Ross De Alessi Lighting Design, Seattle, 1993—. Author periodicals in field. Alumnae Assn. Coun. Stephens Coll., Columbia, Mo., 1995—. Named Nat. Order of Barristers U. Washington, Seattle, 1990. Mem. ABA (mem. state labor and employment law subcom.), Wash. State Bar Assn. (mem. bench-bar-press com.), State Bar Calif., King County Bar Assn., Bar Assn.San Francisco, Wash. Athletic Club. Office: Ross De Alessi Lighting Design 2815 2nd Ave Ste 280 Seattle WA 98121-1261

STEBBINS, GREGORY KELLOGG, foundation executive, chairman; b. Lafayette, Ind., Jan. 10, 1951; s. Albert Kellogg and Nancy Ruth (Osborn) S. BS in Data Processing, Calif. Poly., Pomona, 1974; MBA, U. So. Calif., 1976; EdD, Pepperdine U., 1985. Account exec. ADP, Long Beach, Calif., 1977-78; salesman Grubb & Ellis, L.A., 1978-81; v.p. Grubb & Ellis, Beverly Hills, Calif., 1981-83; regional mgr. Hanes Co., Beverly Hills, 1983-85; treas. U. Santa Monica, L.A., 1983—; pres. Stebbins Consulting Group, Santa Monica, 1989—; chair Santa Monica Inst., 1994—. Chair exec. com. Educare Found., 1994—. Mem. ASTD, Sigma Xi. Home: 445 Washington Blvd Apt 15 Marina Del Rey CA 90292-5271 Office: Santa Monica Inst 4553 Glencoe Ave Ste 355 Marina Del Rey CA 90292-7901

STEBLAY, CRAIG DOUGLAS, real estate executive, entrepreneur; b. San Bernardino, Calif., Mar. 1, 1948; s. Ralph Edward and Grace J. (Rhody) S.; m. Amina Marie Nickell, Sept. 28, 1968; children: Lavee, Kari Ann, Jennifer. V.p. Phototron Corp., San Bernardino, Calif., 1982—, also dir.; pres. Sunmass Corp., Phoenix, 1987—; founder, CEO Archive Mgmt. Svc., 1995—. Served with USMC, 1969-71. Lodge: Knights of Malta (named Knight of Honor 1984), Cedam Internat.

STECKBAUER, JAMES J., technical assessment professional; b. Oshkosh, Wis., Jan. 23, 1947; s. William jacob and Mary Catherine (Binder) S. AA in Quality Assurance, Coastline Coll., Fountain Valley, Calif., 1980; BSBA in Mgmt., U. Nev., Las Vegas, 1986. Cert. quality auditor, Am. Soc. Quality Control. Mechanic Oshkosh, Wis., 1965-66; avionics tech. USMC, 1966-70; avionics instr. Naval Air Tech. Tng. Ctr., Millington, Tenn., 1970-72; USMC recruiter Milw., 1972-76; avionics supr. USMC Air Station, Santa Ana, 1976-77; elec. mechanic test tech. US Naval Shipyard, Long Beach, Calif., 1978-79; quality assurance specialist USAF Plant Rep. Office, Redondo Beach, Calif., 1979-80, Fullerton, Calif., 1980-82; with USAF Western Space and Missile Ctr., Vandenberg AFB, Calif., 1982-83; quality assurance specialist U.S. Dept. Energy, Mercury, Nev., 1983-86, U.S. Army Plant Rep. Office, Mesa, Ariz., 1988-90, U.S. Def. Plant Rep. Office, Mesa, Ariz., 1990-96, Def. Contract Mgmt. Command, Phoenix, 1996—; tng. specialist, instr. U. Nev. Sys., N. Las Vegas, 1987. Ssgt. USMC, 1966-77. Mem. Am. Soc. for Quality Control, Nat. Contract Mgmt. Assn., U. Nev.-Las Vegas Alumni Assn., Fraternal Order of Eagles # 3850, Am. Legion, Harley Owners Group, USMC/Vietnam Helicopter Aircrew Reunion. Roman Catholic. Home: 11431 E Broadway Ave Apache Junction AZ 85220-4729

STECKLER, CRAIG THEODORE, law enforcement official; b. Scottsfield, Ill., Feb. 3, 1944; s. Albert George and Mary Lorene (Johnston) S.; m. Karen Capellutto, Mar. 11, 1978; children: Theresa, Rachael, Suzanne, Mark. AA, Saddleback Coll., 1973; BA, Calif. State U., L.A., 1975; postgrad., U. Va., 1982, Peace Officer Standards & Tng., Pomona, Calif., 1986. Dist. mgr. Orange County Register, Santa Ana, Calif., 1962-68; police officer, sgt., then lt. City of San Clemente, Calif., 1968-80; police chief City of Piedmont, Calif., 1980-86; dep. police chief City of Fremont, Calif., 1986-92, chief of police, 1992—; instr., Cypress (Calif.) Coll., 1975-77, Los Mondos Coll., Pittsberg, calif., 1982-83. Mem. Am. Mgmt. Assn., Calif. Peace Officers Assn., Calif. Police Chiefs Assn. (bd. dirs.), Command Coll. Grads. (bd. dirs.), Rotary. Republican. Roman Catholic. Office: Fremont Police Dept 39710 Civic Center Dr Fremont CA 94538-2359 Office: Fremont Police Dept 2000 Steveson Blvd Fremont CA 94537-2359*

STECKLER, LARRY, publisher, editor, author; b. Bklyn., Nov. 3, 1933; s. Morris and Ida (Beekman) S.; m. Catherine Coccozza, June 6, 1959; children: Gail Denise, Glenn Eric, Kerri Lynn, Adria Lauren. Student, CCNY, 1951. Assoc. editor Radio-Electronics mag., N.Y.C., 1957-62, editor, 1967-85; pub., editor in chief Radio Electronics mag., 1985-92; electronics editor Popular Mechanics mag., N.Y.C., 1962-65; assoc. editor Electronic Products mag., Garden City, N.Y., 1965-67; editorial dir. Merchandising 2-Way Radio mag., N.Y.C., 1975-77; v.p., dir. Gernsback Publs., N.Y.C., 1975-84, pres., dir., 1984—; pub., editorial dir. Spl. Projects mag., 1980-84, Radio-Electronics Ann., 1982-84; pub., editor in chief Hands-On Electronics, 1984-88, Computer Digest, 1985-90, Experimenters Handbook, 1986-96, Modern

Short Stories, 1987-90, Video/Stereo Digest, 1989-91, Popular Electronics Mag., 1988—, GIZMO, 1988—, Hobbyists Handbook, 1989-96, Sci. Probe! mag., 1989-93, StoryMasters, 1989—, Electronics Shopper, 1990, Electronics Market Ctr., 1991—, Electronics Now Mag., 1992—, Radio Craft, 1993-96, Poptronix Handbook, 1996—; pres. Claggk, Inc., 1986—, Silicon Chip, 1993-94, Sci. Probe Inc., 1989-93, Poptronix Inc., 1997—; pub., editor-in-chief Poptronix online, 1997—; mem. electronics adv. bd. Bd. Coop. Ednl. Services, Nassau County, N.Y., 1975-77; pres. Electronics Industry Hall of Fame, 1985—; bd. dirs. Pub. Hall of Fame, 1987-89. Author books, handbooks; pub.; contbr. articles to profl. jours. Bd. dirs. Nassau County council Camp Fire Girls, 1971-72. Served with U.S. Army, 1953-56. Recipient Coop. award Nat. Alliance TV and Electronic Services Assns., 1974, 75; inducted into Electronics Industry Hall of Fame, 1985. Mem. IEEE, Internat. Soc. Cert. Electronic Technicians (chmn. 1974-76, 79-81, 93-95, Chmn.'s award 1985, dir.-at-large 1991-93, rep. to NESDA bd. 1991-93, Region 9 dir. 1995—), Nat. Electronics Sales and Svc. Dealers Assn. (rec. sec. N.Y. state 1976-78, Man of Yr. award 1975, 85, treas. 1991-94, M.L. Finneyberg Excellence award 1994), Am. Mgmt. Assn., Radio Club Am., Internat. Underwater Explorers Soc., Am. Soc. Bus. Press Editors (sr.), Internat. Performing Magicians (exec. dir.), Soc. Profl. Journalists, L.A. Press. Home: 9072 Lawton Pines Ave Las Vegas NV 89129 Office: Gernsback Pub Inc 500 BiCounty Blvd Farmingdale NY 11735-3918 *Do not be afraid to try the unaccepted. Do not be afraid to do the undesirable. Do what you enjoy. . .do it well. . .and after it is done. . .never regret having done it. . .only regret what you have not yet done.*

STECKLER, PHYLLIS BETTY, publishing company executive; b. N.Y.C.; d. Irwin H. and Bertha (Fellner) Schwartzbard; m. Stuart J. Steckler; children: Randall, Sharon Steckler-Slotky. BA, Hunter Coll.; MA, NYU. Editorial dir. R.R. Bowker Co., N.Y.C., Crowell Collier Macmillan Info. Pub. Co., N.Y.C., Holt Rinehart & Winston Info. Systems, N.Y.C.; pres., CEO Oryx Press, Scottsdale, Ariz., 1973-76, Phoenix, 1976—; adj. prof. mktg. scholarly publs. Ariz. State U., Tempe. Past chmn. Info. Industry Assn.; pres. Ariz. Ctr. for the Book; bd. dirs. Contemporary Forum of Phoenix Art Mus., Phoenix Pub. Libr. Friends; past pres. Friends of the Librs., U.S.A.; mem. edn. adv. coun. Senator John McCain; mem. Ariz. Women's Forum. Recipient Women Who Make a Difference award The Internat. Women's Forum, 1995; elected to Hunter Coll. Hall of Fame. Mem. ALA, Spl. Librs. Assn., Am. Soc. Info. Soc., Ariz. Libr. Assn., Univ. Club of Phoenix (bd. dirs.). Home: 5104 N 32d St Phoenix AZ 85018 Office: Oryx Press 4041 N Central at Indian School Rd Phoenix AZ 85012

STECKLEY, RICHARD ALLAN, SR., secondary school educator; b. Indpls., May 18, 1938; s. Robert A. and Edith B. (Brown) S.; m. Alice J. Yocum, Apr. 11, 1959; children: Richard A. Jr., James W. BSBA, U. Albuquerque, 1972; MBA, Auburn U., 1973; postgrad. cert., U. N.Mex., 1984. Cert. secondary edn. tchr., N.Mex. Commd. 2d lt. USAF, 1958, advance through grades to lt. col., 1976, retired, 1982; substitute tchr. Albuquerque Pub. Schs., 1982-84; tchr., chmn. dept. math Highland High Sch., Albuquerque, 1984—. Named Tchr. of Yr., Greater Albuquerque C. of C., 1993; nominee Crystal Apple award, 1995. Mem. Nat. Coun. Tchrs. Math., N.Mex. Coun. Tchrs. Math., Albuquerque Coun. Tchrs. Math. (v.p. 1988-89, pres. 1989-90, chmn. math. contest 1990-93). Methodist. Office: Highland High Sch 4700 Coal Ave SE Albuquerque NM 87108-2804

STEDMAN, WILLIAM PRESTON, music educator; b. Austin, Tex., Feb. 10, 1923; s. Nathan Alexander and Mary Lucille (Sneed) S.; m. Helen Margaret Slessor, Aug. 3, 1946 (div. May 1968); children: Preston Slessor, Alexander Winship; m. Leslie Clark McNeill, June 5, 1971. BA, Tex. Christian U., 1944, MMus, 1948; PhD, U. Rochester, N.Y., 1953. Asst. bus. mgr. Ft. Worth Civic Opera Assn., 1946-47; asst. prof. music Sul Ross State Coll., Alpine, Tex., 1947-51; asst. prin. viola El Paso (Tex.) Symphony Orch., 1948-51; teaching asst. Eastman Sch. Music, Rochester, 1952-53; instr. music Ind. U., Bloomington, 1953-55; music chair, prof. music Tex. A&I U., Kingsville, 1955-66; dean Conservatory of Music U. Pacific, Stockton, Calif., 1966-76; prof. music Calif. State U., Fullerton, 1976—; exec. dir. Pacific Symphony Orch., Fullerton, 1978-79; dir. Western Opera, San Francisco Opera, 1975-78; v.p. exec. bd. Pacific Symphony Orch., Costa Mesa, Calif., 1978-93; examiner Western Assn. Schs./Colls., Oakland, Calif., 1966-92; cons. Calif. Arts Coun., Sacramento, 1968-76; fiscal cons. Calif. Assn. Profl. Music Tchrs. Author: Intro to Stylistic Theory, 3 vols., 1988, The Symphony, Research and Information Guide, 1990, Mexico's Musical Evolution, 1992, The Symphony, 2nd edit., 1993. Lay reader Episcopal Ch., Alpine, Tex., Stockton, Calif., Kingsville, Tex., 1950-76; pres. Kingsville Cmty. Concerts Assn., 1964-66; bd. mem. Fine Arts Commn.,Fullerton, Calif., 1980-84. Lt. (j.g.) USN, 1943-46, PTO. Faculty rsch. grantee Ind. U., Bloomington, 1954, Tex. A&I U., Kingsville, 1963. Mem. Assn. Calif. Symphony Orchestra (bd. mem., v.p. 1988-90), Music Tchrs. Nat. Assn. (chmn. theory composition S.W. divsn. 1958-66). Home: 731 E Avocado Crest Rd La Habra Heights CA 90631-8132 Office: Calif State U Dept Music Fullerton CA 92634

STEEFEL, DAVID SIMON, lawyer; b. Mpls., June 27, 1951; s. Lawrence D. Jr. and Marion (Charlson) S.; m. Mary Ann Moody, May 24, 1981; children: Emily, Daniel, Katherine. BA, Carleton Coll., 1973; JD, U. Colo., 1978. Bar: Colo. 1978, U.S. Dist. Ct. Colo. 1978, U.S. Ct. Appeals (10th cir.) 1978. Assoc. Gorsuch, Kirgis, Denver, 1978-80; assoc. Holme Roberts & Owen, Denver, 1980-84, ptnr., 1984—; instr. U. Colo. Law Sch., Boulder, 1978, 91. Home: 1300 Green Oaks Dr Greenwood Village CO 80121-1331 Office: Holme Roberts & Owen 1700 Lincoln St Ste 4100 Denver CO 80203-4541

STEEL, DAWN, motion picture producer; b. N.Y.C., Aug. 19; m. Charles Roven; 1 child, Rebecca. Student in mktg., Boston U., 1964-65, NYU, 1966-67. Sportswriter Major League Baseball Digest and NFL, N.Y.C., 1968-69; editor Penthouse Mag., N.Y.C., 1969-75; pres. Oh Dawn!, Inc., N.Y.C., 1975-78; v.p. merchandising, cons. Playboy mag., N.Y.C., 1978-79; v.p. merchandising Paramount Pictures, N.Y.C., 1979-80; v.p. prodn. Paramount Pictures, L.A., 1980-83, sr. v.p. prodn., 1983-85, pres. prodn., 1985-87; pres. Columbia Pictures, 1987-90; formed Steel Pictures, 1990—; (with Charles Raven and Bob Cavallo) formed Atlas Entertainment (with exclusive movie prodn. agreement with Turner Pictures), 1994. Bd. dirs. Claremont Coll., Home Edn. Network; mem. dean's adv. bd. UCLA Sch. Theater, Film and TV, 1993—. Recipient Crystal award Women in Film, L.A., 1989. Mem. Acad. Motion Picture Arts and Scis., Am. Film Inst. (bd. dirs. 1988-90), NOW Legal Def. Fund. Democrat. Jewish. Office: Atlas Entertainment 9169 Sunset Blvd Los Angeles CA 90069-3129

STEEL, KUNIKO JUNE, retired artist; b. San Francisco, June 3, 1929; d. Jirohei and Moriyo (Shiraishi) Nakamura; m. John Schulein-Steel, Jan. 26, 1963 (dec. May 1978). Student, U. Calif., 1948-49; diploma, Am. Acad. Art, Chgo., 1951; student, Academic Julian, Paris, 1952-53, Art Inst. Chgo., 1954-55, Art Students League, N.Y.C., 1959-62, 79-85. Exhibited in group shows at Rafilson Gallery, Chgo., 1954, Arts of N.E., Silvermine, Conn., 1966, 79, 90, 92, Modern Maturity Traveling Exhibit, 1990-92, Schoharie Exhibit, Cobleskill, N.Y., 1993-94, Mus. of Modern Art, Miami, Coral Gables, Fla., 1993, 37th Chautaqua Nat. Exhibit of Am. Art, 1994, Montclair State U., 1994, 95. Vol., crafts tchr. Hosp. for Spl. Surgery, N.Y.C., 1967-84; vol. Japanese Gallery Met. Mus., 1994; past vol. costume conservation Met. Mus., N.Y.C., 1979-94. Recipient scholarship Palo Alto Quota Club, 1948, Art Students League, 1960. Mem. N.Y. Artists Equity.

STEELE, CHARLES GLEN, retired accountant; b. Faulkton, S.D., July 24, 1925; s. Clifford D. and Emily O. (Hanson) S.; m. Shirley June Ferguson, Nov. 9, 1947; children: Richard Alan (dec.), Deborah Ann Steele Most. B.B.A., Golden Gate U., San Francisco, 1951, M.B.A., 1962. With Deloitte Haskins & Sells, 1951-86, partner, 1963-86, partner charge Chgo. office, 1973-76; partner charge personnel and adminstrn. Deloitte Haskins & Sells, N.Y.C., 1976-78; chmn., chief exec. officer Deloitte Haskins & Sells, 1978-86; instr. evening program Golden Gate U., 1952-58. Served with USNR, 1943-48. Recipient Elijah Watts Sells Gold medal for highest grade in U.S. for C.P.A. exam., 1951. Mem. Am. Inst. C.P.A.s. Home and Office: 26349 Rio Ave Carmel CA 93923-9101

STEELE, CYNTHIA, literary critic, translator, educator; b. Colusa, Calif., Aug. 7, 1951; d. Ned and Lorraine (Heard) S. BA in English and Spanish, Calif. State U., Chico, 1973; MA in Spanish Lit., U. Calif., San Diego, 1979, PhD in Spanish Lit., 1980. Asst. prof. Spanish Ohio State U., Columbus, 1980-85, Columbia U., N.Y.C., 1985-86; from asst. prof. to assoc. prof. Spanish U. Wash., Seattle, 1986-96, prof. Spanish, Comparative Lit. and Internat. Studies, 1996—; mem. joint com. Latin Am. studies Social Sci. Rsch. Coun.-Am. Coun. Learned Socs., N.Y.C., 1994-96; del. West Coast MLA, N.Y.C., 1996—; bd. dirs. Inst. de Lit. Iberoamericana, Pitts., 1996—. Translator: Underground River and Other Stories by Inés Arnedondo, 1996; (with David Laur) City of Memory (José Emilio Pacheco), 1997. Advanced grantee Social Sci. Rsch. Coun., 1990-91; Royalty Rsch. grantee U. Wash. Grad. Sch., 1997—. Mem. Latin Am. Studies Assn. Democrat. Office: U Wash Dept Spanish and Portuguese Seattle WA 98195

STEELE, MICHAEL RHOADS, humanities and peace studies educator, writer; b. Norfolk, Va., June 8, 1945; s. Harry Eugene and Dorothy Norris (Rhoads) S.; m. Gerianne Gayle Steele, May 31, 1986; children: Erica, Jared, Matthew, Sean. BA in English, U. Notre Dame, 1967; MA in English, Mich. State U., 1971, PhD in English, 1975. Rschr. Brit. Mus., London, 1973; disting. prof. English and humanities Pacific U., Forest Grove, Oreg., 1975—, chmn. peace and conflict studies, 1987-96, dir. Humanitarian Ctr., 1993—; pres. Oreg. Holocaust Reource Ctr., 1992-96. Author: Knute Rockne: A Bio-Bibliography, 1983, The Fighting Irish Football Encyclopedia, 1992, Christianity, Tragedy, and Holocaust Literature, 1995. Alumni disting. fellow Mich. State U., 1967; grantee Oreg. Com. for Humanities, 1986, United Ch. of Christ, 1990. Mem. MLA, Nat. Coun. Tchrs. English, U.S. Handball Assn. (nat. commr. 1986-89). Home: 2936 Watercrest Rd Forest Grove OR 97116-1034 Office: Pacific U English Dept 2043 College Way Forest Grove OR 97116-1756

STEELE, TIMOTHY REID, English language educator, poet; b. Burlington, Vt., Jan. 22, 1948; s. Edward William Steele Jr. and Ruth Bell Reid Gjessing; m. Victoria Lee Erpelding, Jan. 14, 1979. BA, Stanford U., 1970; PhD, Brandeis U., 1977. Jones lectr. in poetry Stanford (Calif.) U., 1975-77; lectr. English UCLA, 1977-83, U. Calif., Santa Barbara, 1986; prof. English Calif. State U., L.A., 1987—. Author: Uncertainties and Rest, 1979, Sapphics Against Anger and Other Poems, 1986, Missing Measures, 1990, The Color Wheel, 1994, Sapphics and Uncertainties: Poems 1970-1986, 1995; editor: The Poems of J.V. Cunningham, 1997. Recipient Peter I.B. Lavan award The Acad. Am. Poets, 1986; Guggenheim fellow, 1984-85. Home: 1801 Preuss Rd Los Angeles CA 90035-4313 Office: Calif State Univ Dept of English 5151 State University Dr Los Angeles CA 90032

STEELE, WILLIAM ARTHUR, financial analyst, public utilities executive; b. Albuquerque, Dec. 21, 1953; s. William Robert and Lois Ellen (Garvett) S. BSBA, U. No. Colo., 1976; MBA, U. Phoenix, Denver, 1987. Buyer Joslins Dept. Stores, Denver, 1978-79; transp. specialist Colo. Pub. Utilities Commn., Denver, 1979-80, fin. analyst, 1980-83, sr. fin. analyst, 1983-87, prin. fin. analyst, 1987—. Mem. Colo. State Mgr. Assn., Nat. Assn. Regulatory Commn. (staff subcom. on mgmt. analysis). Office: Pub Utilities Commn 1580 Logan St Denver CO 80203-1939

STEELSMITH, MARY JOANNE, playwright, actress; b. Boise, Idaho, Mar. 16, 1956; d. Ernest Martin and Casilda Eva (Wright) S. Student, Boise State U., 1974-75. mem. Wordsmiths Playwriting Workshop, L.A. Theatre Ctr. Author: (plays) This Isn't Exactly How I Expected It (award Dramatics Mag. 1974), WACS in Khaki, 1980, Paperback Books, 1980, Bedside Companion, 1996, Behold a Pale Bronco, 1996; appeared in films Rabbit Test, 1978, H.O.T.S., 1979, Death Valley, 1980. Chatleader playwrights corner chat Am. On Line.

STEEN, PAUL JOSEPH, retired broadcasting executive; b. Williston, N.D., July 4, 1932; s. Ernest B. and Inez (Ingebrigtson) S.; m. Judith Smith; children—Michael M., Melanie. BA, Pacific Luth. U., 1954; MS, Syracuse U., 1957. Producer, dir. Sta. KNTV, San Jose, Calif., 1957-58, Sta. KVIE, Sacramento, 1958-60; asst. prof. telecommunications Pacific Luth. U., Tacoma, 1960-67; dir. ops. Sta. KPBS San Diego State U., 1967-74; gen. mgr., 1974-93, prof. telecommunications and film, 1974-93, dir. univ. telecommunications; co-chmn. Office of New Tech. Initiatives. Dir. (tel. program) Troubled Waters (winner Nat. Ednl. TV award of excellence 1970). With AUS. Named Danforth Assoc. Mem. Pacific Mountain Network (bd. dirs., chmn., bd. of govs. award 1993), NATAS, Assn. Calif. Pub. TV Stas. (pres.), Pi Kappa Delta. Home: 4930 Campanile Dr San Diego CA 92115-2331

STEENSGAARD, ANTHONY HARVEY, federal agent; b. Rapid City, S.D., Mar. 21, 1963; s. Harvey Hans and Dorothy Lorraine (Hansen) S. Student, U. Alaska, 1981-83, Anchorage C.C., 1983-84; AAS in Indsl. Security, C.C. Air Force, 1989; BS in Criminal Justice, Wayland U., 1989; MS in Computer Systems Engring., U. Calif., San Diego, 1996. Lic. pilot, radio operator. Bookseller B. Dalton Bookseller, Rapid City, S.D., 1978-81, Anchorage, Alaska, 1981-83; warehouseman Sears, Roebuck & Co., Anchorage, 1983-85; security specialist Alaska Air N.G., Anchorage, 1985-88; agt., draftsman, engring. cons. U.S. Border Patrol, El Centro, Calif., 1988—; pvt. computer cons., 1994—. Author: Unit Security Manager's Guide Book, 1988. Vol. U.S. Senator George McGovern's Campaign, Rapid City, 1980, Congressman Tom Daschle's Campaign, Rapid City, 1980, Spl. Olympics, Rapid City, 1981; observer CAP, Anchorage, 1981; public affairs officer Civil Air Patrol, Rapid City, S.D., 1996. With USMC, 1981-85, USAFR, 1985-95. Recipient Hon. Sci. award Bausch and Lomb, 1984. Mem. Am. Legion, Air Force Assn., VFW, Fraternal Order Eagles, Fraternal Order of Police. Democrat. Lutheran. Office: US Border Patrol 1111 N Imperial Ave El Centro CA 92243-1739

STEERS, GEORGE W., lawyer; b. N.Y.C., Jan. 29, 1941. BA, Yale U., 1963; LLB cum laude, Columbia U., 1966. Bar: Wash. 1970. Law clk. U.S. Ct. Appeals (2d cir.), 1966-67; mem. Stoel Rives Boley Jones & Grey, Bellevue, Wash. Mem. ABA, Wash. State Bar Assn., Seattle-King County Bar Assn. Office: Stoel Rives Boley Jones & Grey 600 University St Ste 3600 Seattle WA 98101-3197

STEFANKI, JOHN X., airline pilot; b. Chgo., July 14, 1920; s. Stephen and Anastasia (Stopak) S.; m. Dorothy Lancaster, Apr. 4, 1945; children: Cathy Ann, Steve, John, Mike, Judy, Larry, Mary, Megan, Dorothy. Student, Western Ill. U., 1940-41, Northwestern U., 1942, U. Iowa, Elmhurst Coll. Capt. United Air Lines, 1946-85, ret.; aviation safety cons. Lt. USN, 1942-46. Recipient Gen. Spruance award SAFE, 1973, Pfizer award of Merit U.S. Civil Def. Coun., 1974, Outstanding Alumni Achievement award Western Ill. U., 1975, Cert. Appreciation NFPA, 1976, Silver Plate award Internat. Assn. Airport and Seaport Police, London UK, 1977, cert. Commendation State of Calif., 1981, Annual Air Safety award, Air Line Pilot Assn., 1978, Laura Taber Barbour Air Safety award Flight Safety Found., 1990, others. Mem. NFPA (former chmn. 424 airport/community emergency planning, mem. planning com.), Ret. Airline Pilots Assn. (legis. chmn., v.p. legis. com., Am. Safety award 1978), others. Democrat. Roman Catholic. Home: 26901 Beatrice Ln Los Altos CA 94022-3406

STEFFIAN, EMILY ENDERS, artist; b. Boston, Mar. 20, 1966; d. John Ames and Sarah Bennet (Enders) S. BA in Anthropology, Macalester Coll., 1988; cert. in metalsmithing, Oreg. Coll. Arts and Crafts, 1993. Mem. house staff A Prairie Home Companion, Minn. Pub. Radio, St. Paul, 1984-86; rsch. asst. Peabody Mus. Archaeology and Ethnology, Harvard U., Cambridge, Mass., 1986; curator's asst. Rifle Sport Alternative Art Gallery, Mpls., 1988; prodn. jeweler Shelley Holl Jewelry, St. Paul, 1988-89; gallery asst. Hoffman Gallery, Oreg. Sch. Arts and Crafts, Portland, 1991-93, studio mgr., 1994; tchr.'s asst. Penland (N.C.) Sch. Crafts, 1993; owner, mgr. Emily Steffian Jewelry and Sculpture, Portland, 1994—; co-designer sculptural furniture project, Portland, 1995-96. Two-person show Carlos and Jones Gallery, Portland, 1993; exhibited in group shows Opus 5 Gallery, Eugene, Oreg., 1993, Katie Gingrass Gallery, Milw., 1993, Harmony Gallery, Taipei, Taiwan, 1993, Oreg. Sch. Arts and Crafts, 1994, Pacific N.W. Craft Fair, Bellue, Wash., 1994, Coll. of Redwoods, Eureka, Calif., 1994, BonaKeane Decorative Arts, Portland, 1995, Kittrell Rifkind Art Glass, Houston, 1995, 96; Savage Fine Art, Portland, 1995, also others; represented in permanent collection L.A. EyeWorks; commd. driveway gate, wall sconce lighting, copper tub, arbor; gallery representation Bonakeane Decorative Arts, Portland, OOP Gallery, Providence, Katie Gingrass GAllery, Kittrell Riffkind Art Glass, New Stone Age, L.A.; work represented in Metalsmith mag., Sprectacles, Op Art. Mem. Soc. N.Am. Metalsmiths, Am. Craft Coun.

STEGEMEIER, RICHARD JOSEPH, oil company executive; b. Alton, Ill., Apr. 1, 1928; s. George Henry and Rose Ann (Smola) S.; m. Marjorie Ann Spess, Feb. 9, 1952; children: Richard Michael, David Scott, Laura Ann, Martha Louise. BS in Petroleum Engring., U. Mo., Rolla, 1950, cert. petroleum engr. (hon.), 1981; MS in Petroleum Engring., Tex. A&M U., 1951; D of Engring. (hon.), U. Mo., Rolla, 1990. Registered profl. engr., Calif. Various nat. and internat. mgmt. positions with Unocal Corp. (formerly Union Oil Co.), L.A., 1951—, pres. sci. and tech. div., 1979-80, sr. v.p. corp. devel., 1980-85, pres., COO, 1985-88, CEO, also chmn. bd. dirs., 1988-94; bd. dirs. First Interstate Bancorp, Found. Health Corp., Halliburton Co., Northrop Corp., Outboard Marine Corp. Patentee in field. Bd. dirs. Calif. Econ. Devel. Corp.; bd. govs. Town Hall of Calif., The Music Ctr. of L.A. County; bd. overseers Exec. Coun. on Fgn. Diplomats, Huntington Libr.; chmn. L.A. World Affairs Coun., 1990-94; pres. World Affairs Coun. of Orange County, 1980-82; chmn. Brea (Calif.) Blue Ribbon Com., 1979-80 ; trustee Com. for Econ. Devel., U. So. Calif., Harvey Mudd Coll., Loyola Marymount U.; mem. adv. bds. Northwestern U. Kellogg Grad. Sch. of Mgmt.; bd. vis. UCLA Anderson Grad. Sch. of Mgmt., U. Mo., Rolla; mem. adv. bd. Calif. State U., Fullerton, adv. coun., Long Beach; bd. dirs. YMCA of L.A., L.A. Philharm. Assn., John Tracy Clinic; chmn. L.A. area coun. Boy Scouts of Am., Calif. C. of C. chmn., 1994; gen. campaign chmn. United Way of Greater L.A., 1990-91; trustee and immediate past pres. Hugh O'Brian Youth Found., 1993-94, L.A. Archidiocese Edn. Found. Recipient Merit award Orange County Engring. Coun., 1980, Outstanding Engr. Merit award Inst. Advancement Engring., 1981, Disting. Achievement medal Tex. A&M U., Hugh O'Brian Youth Found. Albert Schweitzer Leadership award, 1990, Human Rels. award Am. Jewish Com., 1990. Mem. AIChE (Disting. Career award So. Calif. sect. 1989), NAM (bd. dirs.), Nat. Acad. Engring., Am. Petroleum Inst. (bd. dirs.), Soc. Petroleum Engrs. (lectr. 1978), Nat. Petroleum Coun., 25 Yr. Club Petroleum Industry (past pres.), Calif. Bus. Roundtable, Calif. Coun. on Sci. and Tech., Calif. Club. Republican. Roman Catholic. Office: Unocal Corp 376 Valencia Ave Brea CA 92823-6345*

STEIDLE, EDWARD, humanities educator; b. Nice, France, Jan. 17, 1947; came to U.S., 1963; s. Edward Steidle and Alice Moffa; m. Linda Susan Graham, July 8, 1989; children: Michelle Graham, Catherine Alexandra. BA, Franklin and Marshall, 1970; student, Johns Hopkins U., 1970-71; MA, U. Calif., Berkeley, 1974, PhD, 1980. Lectr. Stanford (Calif.) U., 1984—; lectr. Sonoma State Univ., Rohnert Park, Calif., 1990—. Office: Stanford Univ English Dept Stanford CA 94305

STEILING, DANIEL PAUL, railroad conductor; b. San Jose, Calif., June 28, 1944; s. Paul Henry and Lois Kathryn (Barton) S.; m. Dorothy Elise Chaplin, Nov. 6, 1976 (div. July 1978). Right of way agt. Caltrans - Calif. State Dept. Transp., San Francisco, 1969-70; owner Dan's Bicycle Shop, Santa Cruz, Calif., 1970-83; soil insp. Soil Svcs., Inc. div. Applied Soil Mechanics, Inc., San Jose, 1983-84; sr. mfg. specialist disk products divsn. IBM, San Jose, 1984-92; R.R. condr. Amtrak, San Jose, 1993—. With USAF, 1966-68. Mem. Assn. Am. Geographers, Ford Falcon Club Am. Home: 755 C Chestnut St San Jose CA 95110

STEIN, BEVERLY, chairperson county board supervisors. BA, U. Calif., Berkeley; JD, U. Wis. Chair county seat Office Bd. Commrs., Portland, Oreg., 1993—. Office: Bd of Commrs Portland Bldg 1120 SW Fifth Ave Portland OR 97204

STEIN, ELLYN BETH, mental health services professional; b. Chgo.. BS, Ariz. State U., 1988, M of Counseling, 1991. Cert. profl. counselor, Ariz. Rsch. asst. Ariz. State U., Tempe, 1985, 87, practicum, 1990, grad. asst., 1990, 91; residential counselor/supr. Wayland Family Ctrs., Phoenix, Ariz., 1988-91; intern St. Luke's Behavioral Health, Phoenix, 1991, Phoenix Adolescent Recovery Ctr., 1991; intake specialist II ComCare, Phoenix, 1991-94; needs assessment and referral coord. Charter, Chandler, Ariz., 1993—; clin. case mgr. Contact, Tempe, 1994—; vol. crisis counselor Terros, Phoenix, 1989-95; vol. warm line ComCare, Phoenix, 1995—. Mem. Valley of the Sun Active 20/30 Club, Phoenix, 1993—; vol. Make-A-Wish Found., Phoenix, 1995—. Mem. Am. Counseling Assn., Am. Mental Health Counselors Assn., Phi Beta Kappa (2nd v.p. 1994—).

STEIN, GERALD S., psychiatrist; b. Pueblo, Colo., Oct. 31, 1943; s. Emanuel and Ruth (Dobin) S.; m. Carol A. Maliborski, Mar. 30, 1980; 1 child, Danielle Alexis. BMS, Northwestern U., 1965, MD, 1968. Diplomate Am. Bd. Psychiatry and Neurology; cert. psychoanalyst; cert. tng. and supervising psychoanalyst. Pvt. practice psychiatry, psychoanalysis and forensic psychoanalysis, Colorado Springs, Colo., 1980—; with dept. psychiatry Denver Inst. Psychoanalysis/U. Colo. Med. Ctr., 1986—; presenter in field. Author psychobiographic book on L.L. Dickerson, 1992; contbr. papers to The American Fly-Fisher, 1990, articles to profl. jours. Bd. dirs. Pikes Peak Regional Sci. Fair, Colorado Springs, 1982-85, So. Colo. Med. Practices Assn., Colorado Springs, 1986-88; del. ann. meeting Colo. Med. Assn., Denver, 1987; cons. to paramedics Colorado Springs Fire Dept., 1982-84. Recipient Hoedemaker award Psychoanalytic Soc. Seattle, 1985. Fellow APA, Colo. Soc. for Psychoanalysis and Psychotherapy; mem. Colo. Psychiat. Soc. (chmn. pvt. practice com.), Am. Mus. Fly Fishing, Denver Psychoanalytic Soc. (program chmn. 1988-90). Home and Office: 1415 S Cascade Ave Colorado Springs CO 80907

STEIN, HERBERT I., internist, educator; b. L.A., Dec. 23, 1933; s. Joseph and Cecilia K. Stein; m. Elaine E. Alpert, Dec. 28, 1969; children: Alison Jay, Lauren Denise. AB in Zoology, UCLA, 1955, MA in Zoology, 1957; MD, U. Pitts., 1961. Diplomate Am. Bd. Internal Medicine, Am. Bd. Cardiovascular Diseases. Resident in internal medicine Cedars of Lebanon Hosp., L.A., 1962-64, fellow in cardiovasc. diseases, 1965-66; pvt. practice, L.A., 1965—; co-dir. Regional Med. Program, L.A., 1966-68; asst. clin. prof. medicine UCLA Sch. Medicine, L.A., 1980—. Contbr. articles to med. jours. Fellow ACP, Am. Coll. Cardiology. Office: 2080 Century Park E Los Angeles CA 90067-2001

STEIN, KAREN, mayor. Mayor Corona, Calif. Address: PO Box 940 Corona CA 91718

STEIN, KARL N., plastic and reconstructive surgeon; b. Phila., July 1, 1940; m. Sandra Diane Segal; children: Laura, Leigh. BA in Chemistry, Temple U., 1962, MD, 1966. Diplomate Am. Bd. Plastic Surgery. Intern U. Pa. Grad. Hosp., 1966-67; resident in surgery Abington Meml. Hosp., 1967-68; resident in surgery SUNY Up-State Med. Ctr., 1970-71, instr. in surgery, 1970—; resident in plastic surgery Hosp. Albert Einstein Coll. Medicine, Bronx Mcpl. Hosp. Ctr., 1971-74, asst. instr. plastic surgery and hand surgery, 1974; pvt. practice in plastic surgery, 1974—; surgeon Sherman Oaks (Calif.) Burn Ctr., 1975—; cons. L.A. Dept. Water and Power. Author (patent) Treatment of Tar Burns, 1980. Capt. USAF, 1969-71. Fellow Am. Coll. Surgeons; mem. AMA, Am. Soc. Plastic and Reconstructive Surgeons, Am. Burn Assn., Am. Assn. Hand Surgery, Am. Soc. Aesthetic Plastic Surgery, Calif. Soc. Plastic Surgeons, Calif. Med. Assn., L.A. Soc. Plastic Surgeons, L.A. County Med. Assn. Office: 4910 Van Nuys Blvd Ste 302 Sherman Oaks CA 91403-1728

STEIN, MICHAEL P., protective services official. Chief police Escondido (Calif.) Police Dept. Office: Escondido Police Dept 700 W Grand Ave Escondido CA 92025

STEIN, PAUL E., superintendent; m. Carol Mannin; children: Christine, John, James. BS in polit. sci., U.S.A.F. Acad., Colo., 1966; MBA, Fla. State U., 1973; attended, Air War Coll., Maxwell Air Force Base, Ala., 1986. Commd. 2d lt. USAF, 1966, advanced through grades to lt. gen., 1994; asst. football coach USAF, Colo., 1966-67; chief personnel svcs. 7149th combat support group USAF, Spangdahlem Air Base, Germany, 1967-69; chief spl. svcs. divsn. 36th combat support group USAF, Bitburg Air Base, Germany, 1969-71; chief, spl. svcs. divsn. 2d combat support group USAF, Barksdale Air Force Base, La., 1971-72; ops. analyst AWACS Test Ops. The Boeing Co., Washington, 1974-80; requirements program officer USAF, Washinton,

1980, tactical fighter requirements officer, 1980-82, 86-91; comdr. Keesler Tech. Training Ctr., Miss., 1991-92; dir., legislative liaison Office of the Sec., Washington, 1992-94; supr. USAF Acad., Colo., 1994—. Decorated Disting. Svc. medal, Legion of Merit with one bronze oak leaf cluster. Office: USAF Legislative Liason SAF/LL Washington DC 20330

STEIN, ROBERT GEORGE, mathematics educator, author; b. N.Y.C., Apr. 16, 1939; s. Ernest and Doris (Blumenthal) S.; m. Veronika Kirschner, Nov. 13, 1970; children: Joseph, Lucy. B.A., Harvard U., 1961; M.A.T., Conn. Wesleyan U., 1962; M.A., Dartmouth Coll., 1967; Ph.D., U. Tex.-Austin, 1975. Math. tchr. Ethical Culture Schs., N.Y.C., 1962-64, Acad. la Castellana, Caracas, Venezuela, 1964-65; mem. faculty Calif. State U., San Bernardino, 1967—, prof., 1982—, chmn. math. dept., 1976-89; mem. coms. Entry Level Math. Test Devel. Com.; mem. Calif. State Maths. Framework Com., 1997—. Author: Mathematics, An Exploratory Approach, 1975; Fundamentals of College Algebra and Trigonometry, 1986, Fundamentals of College Algebra, 1986; also articles; reviewer; reader Advanced Placement Calculus Test. Bd. dirs. Crestline Community Ambulance Assn., Calif., 1979-91; mem. Rim of the World Bd. Edn., 1989—. Fellow Danforth Assn.; mem. San Bernardino County Math. Tchrs. Assn. (founding pres. 1984—), Math. Assn. Am., Nat. Coun. Tchrs. of Math. Republican. Home: PO Box 494 Crestline CA 92325-0494 Office: Calif State U 5500 State University Pky San Bernardino CA 92407

STEINBERG, JACK, lawyer; b. Seattle, Jan. 6, 1915; s. Solomon Reuben and Mary (Rashall) S.; widower; children: Roosevelt, Mary Ann Steinberg Shulman, Quentin. BA, U. Wash., 1936, JD, 1938. Bar: Wash. 1938, U.S. Dist. Ct. (we. dist.) Wash. 1938, U.S. Ct. Appeals (9th cir.) 1938. Ptnr. Steinberg & Steinberg, Seattle, 1938—. Former editor and pub. The Washington Examiner; contbr. numerous articles to legal jours. Judge pro tem Seattle Mcpl. Ct., Seattle, 1952; past pres. Emanuel Congregation, Seattle, Seattle chpt. Zionist Orgn. Am. Recipient Scrolls of Honor award (3) The State of Israel. Mem. Assn. Trial Lawyers Am., Am. Judicature Soc., Wash. Bar Assn., Wash. Assn. Trial Lawyers, Seattle-King County Bar Assn. Jewish Orthodox. Office: Steinberg & Steinberg 1210 Vance Bldg Seattle WA 98101

STEINBERG, JOAN EMILY, retired middle school educator; b. San Francisco, Dec. 9, 1932; d. John Emil and Kathleen Helen (Montgomery) S. BA, U. Calif.-Berkeley, 1954; EdD, U. San Francisco, 1981. Tchr., Vallejo (Calif.) Unified Sch. Dist., 1959-61, San Francisco Unified Sch. Dist., 1961-93, elem. tchr., 1961-78, tchr. life and phys. sci. jr. high sch., 1978-85, 87-93, sci. cons., 1985-87; lectr. elem. edn. San Francisco State U., 1993-94; ind. sci. edn. cons., 1993—. Contbr. articles to zool. and edn. books and profl. jours. Fulbright scholar U. Sydney (Australia), 1955-56; recipient Calif. Educator award, 1988, Outstanding Educator in Teaching award U. San Francisco Alumni Soc., 1989. Mem. ASCD, San Francisco Zool. Soc., Exploratorium, Astron. Soc. Pacific, Am. Fedn. Tchrs., Calif. Acad. Scis., Calif. Malacozool. Soc., Nat. Sci. Tchrs. Assn., Elem. Sch. Sci. Assn. (sec. 1984-85, pres. 1986-87, newsletter editor 1994—), Calif. Sci. Tchrs. Assn., Sigma Xi. Democrat.

STEINBERG, RUSSELL, composer. BA summa cum laude, UCLA, 1981; MusM with honors, New Eng. Conservatory, Boston, 1983; PhD in Music, Harvard U., 1987. Postdoctoral teaching asst. Harvard U., Cambridge, Mass., 1988-90; orch. dir. Temple Emanuel, Beverly Hills, Calif., 1990-93; composer-in-residence Music Festival Goucher Coll., Balt., 1993; dir. Music Media Lab. and prof. ext. sch. UCLA, 1993, vis. asst. prof. music theory and composition, 1991-93; pres. Five-One Prodns., Ltd., 1995; solo compositions include: Small Rain, Periods of Luminance, Tonal Whispers, Sequoia sonata, Dichroisms, Atonal Variations (all for piano); White Crane Study, Latigo Tides, Canticles, Double Stop Etude (violin); Five Preludes (guitar); duo compositions include Flute Sonata Six Duos for Violin, Fantasy for Flute and Piano, Classic Berlin; trios include Fanfares for Three Trumpets, Rings of Saturn, Piano Trio; quartets include String Quartet, Woodwind Quartet, Change of Heart, others. Film scores include: You Are What You Eat, 1993, Paper Flowers (documentary), 1993, Class (comedy-variety pilot), 1992, Fatal Charm (feature-length psycho-drama), 1991, Dressage Freestyle music, 1991, Amber Waves (documentary), 1990, others; author: (CD-Rom) Richard Strauss: Three Tone Poems, 1992, Microsoft's Multimedia Strauss, 1994; contbr. articles to profl. jours.; commns. include Sheridon Stokes, Flute Sonata, 1993, Endre Granat and Alex Horvath, Violin Duos, 1992, Aspen Ctr. for Advanced Composition, City Strains, 1993, others. Recipient Disting. teaching award Harvard U., 1987, 1st prize New World String Quartet Competition, 1987; Aspen fellow, 1992, 93, MacDowell fellow, 1991, Cummington Cmty. of the Arts fellow, 1985; ASCAP grantee for young composers, 1987. Mem. Musicians Union Local 47, Coll. Music Soc., Am. Music Ctr., Harvard Group for New Music (founding mem.), NuClassix Inc. (founding mem.), Nat. Assn. Composers (2nd prize 1984, 86), Phi Beta Kappa, Phi Kappa Lambda.

STEINBERG, WARREN LINNINGTON, school principal; b. N.Y.C., Jan. 20, 1924; s. John M. and Gertrude (Vogel) S.; student U. So. Calif., 1943-44, UCLA, 1942-43, 46-47, BA, 1949, MEd, 1951, EdD, 1962; m. Beatrice Ruth Blass, June 29, 1947; children: Leigh William, James Robert, Donald Kenneth. Tchr., counselor, coach Jordan High Sch., Watts, Los Angeles, 1951-57; tchr. athletic coordinator Hamilton High Sch., Los Angeles, 1957-62; boys' vice prin. Univ. High Sch., Los Angeles, 1962-67, Crenshaw Hig Sch., Los Angeles, 1967-68; cons. Ctr. for Planned Change, Los Angeles City Sch., 1968-69; instr. edn. UCLA, 1965-71; boys' vice prin. LeConte Jr. High Sch., Los Angeles, 1969-71, sch. prin., 1971-77; adminstrv. cons. integration, 1977-81, adminstr. student to student interaction program, 1981-82; prin. Gage Jr. High Sch., 1982-83, Fairfax High Sch., 1983-90. Pres. Athletic Coordinators Assn., Los Angeles City Schs., 1959-60; v.p. P-3 Enterprises, Inc., Port Washington, N.Y., 1967-77, Century City (Calif.) Enterprises, 1966-88. V.p. B'nai B'rith Anti-Defamation League, 1968-70; mem. adv. com. Los Angeles City Commn. on Human Relations, 1966-71, 72-76, commr., 1976—, also chmn. edn. com.; pres. Los Angeles City Human Relations Commn., 1978-87; mem. del. assembly Community Relations Conf. of So. Calif., 1975-91; mem. citizens adv. com. for student integration Los Angeles Unified Sch. Dist., 1976-79; chmn. So. Calif. Drug Abuse Edn. Month com., 1970. Bd. dirs. DAWN, The Seedling, 1993-95, Project ECHO - Entrepreneurial Concepts, Hands-On, 1996—. Served with USMCR, 1943-46. Recipient Beverly Hills B'nai B'rith Presdl. award, 1965, Pres.'s awardCommunity Rels. Conf. So. Calif., 1990; commended Los Angeles City Council, 1968, 88. Mem. West Los Angeles Coordinating Council (chmn. case conf., human relations), Beverly-Fairfax C. of C. (bd. dirs. 1986-88). Lodges: Lions (dir. 1960-62), Kiwanis. Contbr. articles on race relations, youth behavior to profl. jours. and newspapers. Home: 2737 Dunleer Pl Los Angeles CA 90064-4303

STEINBOCK, JOHN THOMAS, bishop; b. L.A., July 16, 1937. Student, L.A. Diocesan sems. Ordained priest Roman Cath. Ch., 1963. Aux. bishop Diocese of Orange, Calif., 1984-87; bishop Diocese of Santa Rosa, Calif., 1987-91; titular bishop of Midila, 1984; bishop Diocese of Fresno, Calif., 1991—. Office: Diocese of Fresno 1550 N Fresno St Fresno CA 93703-3711

STEINBRECHER, EDWIN CHARLES, writer, film executive producer; b. Chgo., Apr. 4, 1930; s. Edwin E. and Helen Clara (Siska) S.; m. Suzanne Gross, June 17, 1955. (div.). BFA, UCLA, 1965. Cert. Am. Fedn. Astrologers. Founder, dir. D.O.M.E. The Inner Guide Meditation Ctr., L.A., 1973—. Author: The Inner Guide Meditation, 6th edit., 1988; co-author: Gay Soul, 1994, Exploring Consciousness in the Horoscope, 1993; editor White Sun, 1973. With USN, 1955-59, Japan, exec. producer, Evicted, 1996. Office: DOME Ctr Po Box 46146 Los Angeles CA 90046

STEINBUCHEL, MAXIMILIAN FREDERICK, program manager; b. Wichita, Kans., July 1, 1942; s. Maximilian Hubert and Patricia Steinbuchel; m. Toni Kay Smith, Dec. 30, 1966; children: Julie Marie, Kerri Janae. BBA in Acctg., Wichita State U., 1971; MBA in Technology Mgmt., U. Phoenix, 1997. Cert. profl. cost estimator, cert. prof. cost analyst, cert. cost estimator/analyst. Sr. cost analyst Boeing Inc., Wichita, 1974-76; cost acctg. mgr. Gen. Portland Cement, Wichita, 1976-77; mgr. pricing compliance Boeing Inc., Wichita, 1977-89; contract mgr. Motorola, Inc., Chandler, Ariz., 1989-95; program mgr. Motorola, Inc., Chandler, 1995—; nat. v.p. Nat. Estimating Soc., Washington, 1983-85, nat. pres., 1985-87. Vol. fire fighter Derby (Kans.) Fire Dept., 1967-89, adminstr. firemen's relief assn., 1977-89; coun. mem. ward 2 Derby (Kans.) City Coun., 1972-74. With USN, 1960-64. Recipient Estimator of the Yr. Mgmt. awards Nat. Estimating Soc., Wichita, 1983, Washington, 1983, 1987. Mem. Soc. Cost Estimating and Analysis (ednl. conf. chmn. 1993), Internat. Soc. Parametric Analysts. Home: 1927 E Dawn Dr Tempe AZ 85284-3429 Office: Motorola Inc Satellite Comm Group 2501 S Price Rd Chandler AZ 85248-2802

STEINER, HERBERT MAX, physics educator; b. Goeppingen, Germany, Dec. 8, 1927; came to U.S., 1939, naturalized, 1944; s. Albert and Martha (Epstein) S. B.S., U. Calif., Berkeley, 1951, Ph.D., 1956. Physicist Lawrence Berkeley Lab., Berkeley, Calif., 1956—; mem. faculty U. Calif., Berkeley, 1958—, prof. physics, 1966—, William H. McAdams prof. physics, chmn. dept., 1992-95; vis. scientist European Center Nuclear Research, 1960-61, 64, 68-69, 82-83, Max Planck Inst. Physics and Astrophysics, Munich, 1976-77; vis. prof. Japanese Soc. Promotion Sci., 1978; vis. prof. physics U. Paris, 1989-90; vis. scientist Deutsches Electron Synchrotron Lab., 1995-96. Author articles in field. Served with AUS, 1946-47. Recipient Sr. Am. Scientist award Alexander von Humboldt Found., 1976-77; Guggenheim fellow, 1960-61. Fellow Am. Phys. Soc. Office: U Calif Berkeley Dept Physics Berkeley CA 94720

STEINER, KENNETH DONALD, bishop; b. David City, Nebr., Nov. 25, 1936; s. Lawrence Nicholas and Florine Marie (Pieters) S. B.A., Mt. Angel Sem., 1958; M.Div., St. Thomas Sem., 1962. Ordained priest Roman Catholic Ch., 1962, bishop, 1978; asso. pastor various parishes Portland and Coos Bay, Oreg., 1962-72; pastor Coquille Ch., Myrtle Point, Powers, Oreg., 1972-76, St. Francis Ch., Roy, Oreg., 1976-77; aux. bishop Diocese of Portland, Oreg., 1977—; pastor St. Mary's Ch., Corvallis, Oreg., 1986—; adminstr. Archdiocese Portland, 1995-96. Democrat. Office: Saint Marys Ch 501 NW 25th St Corvallis OR 97330

STEINER, MAUREEN, political organization worker; b. Oakland, Calif., May 10, 1951; d. Paul and Ruth Irene (Arnhold) S. BA in Anthropology, U. Calif., Davis, 1973; JD, Calif. Western Sch. Law, 1988. Bar: Calif. 1988, U.S. Dist. Ct. (so. dist.) Calif. 1988. Asst. dir. Calif. Archaeol. Inventory Sonoma State U., Rohnert Park, Calif., 1983-84; staff scientist Woodward-Clyde Consultants, Walnut Creek, Calif., 1984-86; pvt. practice atty. San Diego, 1987-93; coord. Women's Vote! Project, San Diego, 1992, Get Out The Vote for Alpert for Assembly, San Diego, 1992; chair San Diego County Dem. Party, 1995—. Sec., Citizen Adv. Panel, City of Coronado, Calif., 1988-90; advocate-rep. Nat. Orgn. Disability, City of Coronado, 1989-94, chair strategic planning bd., 1992-94; civil svc. commr., 1996-97, planning commr., 1997—; vice-chmn. Coronada-Imperial Beach chpt. ARC; co-chmn. GLAAD, San Diego, 1997—. Democrat. Office: San Diego County Dem Party 413 Laurel St Ste B San Diego CA 92101-1632

STEINER, RICHARD RUSSELL, linen supply company; b. Chgo., Feb. 26, 1923; s. Frank Gardner and Ruth (Cowie) S.; m. Colleen M. Kearns, Dec. 6, 1949; children—Robert C., Kevin K., Sheila M. B.A., Dartmouth Coll., 1948. With Steiner Corp., Salt Lake City, 1948—; divisonal dir., v.p. Steiner Corp., 1951-59, pres., 1959—; dir. Am. Uniform Co. Served with USAAF, 1942-46. Decorated D.F.C. Mem. Phi Beta Kappa. Clubs: Alta, Salt Lake Country. Office: 505 E South Temple Salt Lake City UT 84102-1004

STEINER, ROBERTA PEARL, not-for-profit foundation administrator; b. N.Y.C., July 11, 1948; d. Charles and Ethel (Fier) S. BA, U. Calif., Berkeley, 1969, MLS, 1973. Specialist community resources, Sch. Resource Vols. Berkeley Pub. Schs., 1975-77; chief librarian Am. Insts. for Research, Palo Alto, Calif., 1973-77; assoc. in bibliography and instr. library sch. U. Calif., Berkeley, 1975-77; dir. Cen. Pacific Region B'nai B'rith Women, Daly City, Calif., 1977-84; dir. Found. Ctr. San Francisco office. Bd. dirs. Jewish Vocat. Svcs., 1984-88, San Francisco Jewish Community Ctr., 1984-90, mem. exec. com.; trustee Brandeis Hillel Day Sch., San Francisco, Marin, Calif., 1996—. Jewish.

STEINERT, LEON ALBERT, mathematical physicist; b. Shattuck, Okla., May 2, 1930; m. Emanuela Giovanna Montauti, May 21, 1988. PhD, U. Colo., 1962. Theoretical physicist Nat. Bur. Standards, Boulder, Colo., 1953-65; sr. rsch. engr. Lockheed Missiles & Space Co., Sunnyvale, Calif., 1972-79, 83-86; staff physicist IRT Corp., San Diego, 1979-81; prin. engr.-scientist McDonnell Douglas Corp., Huntington Beach, Calif., 1967-70, 88-92; cons. scientist Phys. Synergetics Inst., Sunnyvale, Calif., 1981—. Contbr. theoretical physics articles to profl. jours.

STEINFELD, RAY, JR., food products executive; b. Portland, Oreg., Nov. 21, 1946; s. Ray and June Catherine (Cox) S.; m. Janis Bowen, Nov. 11, 1978; children: Erik, Blair. Student, Wheaton Coll., 1964-66, Drew U., 1967; BS in Polit. Sci., Lewis and Clark Coll., 1968. Sales rep. Continental Can Co., L.A., 1969-72; co-chmn. bd., CEO, Steinfeld's Products Co., Portland, Oreg., 1972—; chmn. Oreg. Mus. Sci. in Industry, 1992-94. Treas., bd. dirs. Portland Recycling Team, 1973—; pres. exec. bd. Stop Oreg. Litter and Vandalism, 1973-92, pres., 1976; chmn., exec. com. Oreg. Landmark of Quality, 1985-87, Oreg. Ballet Theatre, 1994—, bd. dirs., 1995—, v.p. devel., 1997—; pres. exec. com. William Temple House, 1985-91; vestry mem. Trinity Episcopal Ch., 1987-90; chmn. Oregn. Strategic Plan Agrl. Dept., 1988, World Trade Week, Portland, 1989; mem. Gov. Robert's Task Force, Salem, Oreg., 1991-92; bd. dirs. Oreg. Enterprise Forum, 1992—, chmn., 1995. Mem. Pickle Packers Internat. (chmn. mdse. com.), Portland C. of C. (bd. dirs. 1995—). Democrat. Espiscopalian. Office: 10001 N Rivergate Blvd Portland OR 97203-6526

STEINHARDT, HENRY, photographer; b. N.Y.C., Nov. 15, 1920; s. Maxwell and Ruth (Davis) S.; m. Elizabeth Smith, 1946 (dec. 1955); children: Elizabeth, Maxwell; m. Helene Fleck, Feb. 1, 1958; 1 child, Henry III. AB, Harvard U., 1942, MArch, 1949. Registered architect. Office mgr. R.H. Cutting, Architect, N.Y.C., 1951-53; ptnr., architect Steinhardt & Thompson, Architects, N.Y.C., 1953-61; architect The Cerny Assocs., St. Paul, 1961-63, John Graham & Co., Seattle, 1963-67, Morse/Kirk, Seattle, 1967-68, N.G. Jacobson & Assocs., Seattle, 1968-69; pvt. practice Mercer Island, Wash., 1969-75; architect USN, Bremerton, Wash., 1975-78; photographer Mercer Island, 1979—. Prin. works exhibited at Washington, Seattle and Andover, Mass.; contbr. articles to fgn. archtl. jours. 1st lt. U.S. Army, 1943-46; capt. USAF, 1950-52. Recipient Design award Progressive Architecture, 1959, Archtl. award Fifth Ave. Assn., 1960. Fellow AIA. Democrat. Home and Office: 7825 SE 63rd Pl Mercer Island WA 98040-4813

STEINHAUS, PATRICIA, university administrator; b. San Francisco, Oct. 7, 1949; d. James Laverne and Mildred Charlene (Howe) Steinhaus; m. Raymond R. Hammer, Dec. 29, 1973 (div. Nov. 1992); children: Heather, Michael, Brittany. BA in Social Sci. and Psychology, Calif. State U., Sacramento, 1971, MA in Psychology, 1973. Rsch. writer multi-ethnic com. Los Rios Coll. Dist., Sacramento, 1973; faculty Calif. State U., Sacramento, 1973; substitute tchr. Fairfield (Calif.) Unified Sch. Dist., 1975-77; part-time instr. Vacaville (Calif.) Adult Sch., 1976-77, Fairfield Adult Sch., 1976-77; from instr. to full prof. adj. psychology Chapman U., Sacramento; social sci. advisor Chapman U., Sacramento, Travis, 1974-80, program adminstr., 1990—. Recipient Calif. State U.-Sacramento Alumni Campus Advancement award, 1971. Mem. AAUP, AAUW, APA, NAFE, PTA (life), Silver Key. Home: 1868 Ridgeview Dr Roseville CA 95661-5837 Office: Chapman University 4020 El Camino Ave Sacramento CA 95821

STEINHAUSER, JOHN STUART (JACK STEINHAUSER), oil company executive; b. Grosse Pointe, Mich., Mar. 28, 1958; s. John William and Patricia Elizabeth (Mooney) S.; m. Barbara Jeanne Shirley, Aug. 23, 1985; children: Cassandra Lorraine, Robert William, Alexandra Elizabeth. BA in Econs., Claremont McKenna Coll., Claremont, Calif., 1979; M in Internat. Mgmt., U. Denver, 1982; postgrad., Inst. Superieur des Affairs, Jouy-en-Josas, France, 1981. Fin. analyst Martin Marietta, Denver, 1980; intern analyst UN, Vienna, Austria, summer 1981; land mgr. Sharon Resources Inc., Englewood, Colo., 1982-84; from exec. dir. to pres. Sharon Resources Inc., 1984-95, CEO, 1992—; exec. v.p. Sharon Energy Ltd., Vancouver, B.C., 1987-95; pres. Sharon Energy Ltd., Vancouver, B.C., 1995—; dir. Sharon Resources, Inc.; founder, prin., Claremont Energy Ptnrs. L.L.C., Parker, Colo., 1993-95; founder, mng. dir. Rocky Mountain Helium, L.L.C., Boulder, Colo., 1994-96; founder The Sophia Inst., 1995—. Advisor Jr. Achievement, Parker, Colo., 1985-86; dir. Student Entrepreneurs, Parker, 1987-88; pres. Claremont McKenna Coll. Colo. Alumni Assn., Denver, 1988-95. Mem. Racquet World. Republican. Unitarian. Office: Sharon Resources Inc 5995 Greenwood Plaza Blvd Cherry Hills Village CO 80111-4706

STEINHAUSER, JOHN WILLIAM, lawyer; b. Akron, Ohio, June 25, 1924; s. John Hugo and Francis Lillian (Pearson) S.; BSc in Bus. Adminstrn., Ohio State U., 1949; JD, U. Mich., 1950; m. Patricia E. Mooney, Dec. 1, 1956; children: John, Christian, Mark, Sharon. Bar: Colo. 1972, Mich. 1950. With Chrysler Corp., 1950-71, beginning as atty., successively dir. Latin Am., dir. export sales, gen. mgr. Africa-Far East, dir. Chrysler Internat., Geneva, dir. Africa-Far East, 1950-71; corp. atty., Denver, 1971—; founder, pres. Pearson Energy Corp., 1977; founder, chmn. Sharon Energy, Ltd., Denver, 1980, also dir., 1971—. Sponsor Denver Symphony; active Colo. Rep. Party; pres. John and Patricia Steinhauser Found. With USNR, 1943-46. Mem. Colo. Bar Assn., Mich. Bar Assn., ABA, Soc. Internat. Law, Rocky Mountain Mineral Law Found., Cherry Hills Country Club, Naples Sailing & Yacht Club, Royal Poinciana Golf Club, Rotary (Denver). Home: 46 Charlou Cir Englewood CO 80111-1103 Office: Sharon Resources Inc Ste 220 5995 Greenwood Plaza Blvd Englewood CO 80111-4714

STEINHAUSER, SHELDON ELI, sociology and gerontology educator, consultant; b. N.Y.C., Aug. 11, 1930; s. Charles W. and Helen (Rosenstein) S.; m. Frances Goldfarb, June 28, 1953 (div. 1963); children: Karen, Lisa Steinhauser Hackel; m. Janice M. Glass, May 2, 1965; children: Shayle, David, Susan Hirschman. BS, L.I. U., 1963; DPS (hon.), Regis U., 1994. Community cons. Anti-Defamation League, Columbus, Ohio, 1951-57; regional dir. Anti-Defamation League, Denver, 1957-85, dir. nat. field svcs., 1977-85, dir. nat. community svcs. divsn., 1979-81, western area dir., 1975-85; exec. v.p. Allied Jewish Fedn. of Denver, 1985-91; pres. Sheldon Steinhauser & Assocs., Denver, 1991—; instr. sociology Met. State Coll., Denver, 1969-71, assoc. prof., 1994—; arbitrator Am. Arbitration Assn., Denver, 1988—; pres. Anti-Defamation League profl. Staff Assn., Agy. Orgn., Denver, 1963; past cons. EEOC. Missions to Egypt and Israel, 1982, 83; staff dir. Mission to Israel, 1986, 87, 90; former mem. Denver Anti-Crime Coun.; chmn. Mountain States Inst. of Judaism, Denver, 1958-59; pres. Adult Edn. Coun. Met. Dever; past mem. cmty. adv. bd. Jr. League Denver; cons. U.S. Dept. Justice Cmty. Rels. Svc., 1994—; mem. Colo. Martin Luther King Holiday Planning Com., Latin Am. Rsch. and Svc. Agy.; cmty. working group Nat. Civilian Cmty. Corps.; congl. del. White House Conf. on Aging, 1995. Recipient M.L. King Jr. Humanitarian award Colo. M.L. King Commn., Denver, 1986, 1st Ann. Human Rels. award Colo. Civil Rights Commn., Denver, 1965, Humanitarian award NAACP, Denver, 1980, ADL Civil Rights Achievement award, 1989; named to Gallery of Fame, Denver Post, 1979, 80. Mem. Div. Assn. Internat., Western Social Sci. Assn., Am. Sociol. Assn., Colo. Jewish Reconstructionist Fedn., Am. Soc. on Aging, Sociol. Practice Assn., Assn. for Gerontology in Higher Edn. (nat. membership com.), Gerontol. Soc. Am., Colo. Gerontol. Soc., Am. Arbitration Assn. (Rocky Mountain adv. com.), B'nai B'rith (Columbus v.p., Denver).

STEINHOFF, PATRICIA GAYLE, sociology educator; b. Detroit, Dec. 9, 1941; d. David Leslie and Ruth (Isbell) Golden; m. William David Steinhoff, July 13, 1968; children: Laura Sacajawea, Thomas Tecumseh. BA in Japanese Lang. and Lit. with honors, U. Mich., 1963; PhD in Sociology, Harvard U., 1969. Asst. prof. U. Hawaii, Honolulu, 1968-72, assoc. prof., 1972-74, prof., 1974—, dir. ctr. Japanese Studies, 1986-94; vis. rsch. scholar Inst. Social Scis. Tokyo U., 1982-83, 90-91; mem. joint com. Japanese Studies Social Sci. Rsch. Coun., N.Y.C., 1982-87; chair N.E. Asia Coun. Assn. Asian Studies, Ann Arbor, Mich., 1984-87; mem. Am. adv. com. The Japan Found., N.Y., 1987-97; mem. Japan adv. bd. Social Sci. Rsch. Coun. N.Y.C., 1997—. Co-Author: Abortion Politics: The Hawaii Experience, 1977; author: Tenkō: Ideology and Societal Integration, 1991, Japanese Studies in the United States in the 1990's, 1996; co-editor: Conflict in Japan, 1984; mem. editl. bd. U. Hawaii Press, Honolulu, 1986-97. Fulbright Sr. Rsch. fellow Fullbright Commn., Japan, 1982-83, 90-91, Guggenheim Rsch. fellow Harry Frank Guggenheim Found., 1990-92. Mem. Am. Sociological Assn. (sociology of law sect.). Home: 3624 Woodlawn Dr Honolulu HI 96822 Office: U Hawaii Dept Sociology Porteus Hall 2424 Maile Way Honolulu HI 96822

STEINKE, BETTINA, artist; b. Biddeford, Maine, June 25, 1913; d. William and Alice Mary (Staples) S.; m. Don Blair, Mar. 21, 1946. Student, Sch. Fine Arts, Newark, 1930, Cooper Union, 1931-33, Phoenix Art Sch., 1934-35. Represented in permanent collections Indpls. Mus., Ft. Worth Mus., Nat. Cowboy Hall of Fame and Western Heritage; artist original drawings of Toscanini, 1938, Paderewski, 1939 (both now in Smithsonian Inst.); charcoal portraits NBC book on Toscanini and Orch., 1938; many portraits of well known personalities; retrospective shows Palm Springs Desert Mus., Gilcrease Mus., Tulsa, Okla., Nat. Cowboy Hall of Fame, 1995; subject of biography Bettina. Pres. bd. dirs. Harwood Found. U. N.Mex.; exec. bd. Nat. Cowboy Hall of Fame and Western Heritage. Recipient Gold and Silver medals Nat. Cowboy Hall of Fame, Oklahoma City, 1973-89, Gold medal award for Outstanding Contbn. to Painting, 1995, N.Mex. Gov.'s award, 1996, John Singer Sargant award Portrait Soc. (East Coast), 1996, others; scholar Phoenix Art Sch., N.Y.C., 1934-35. Mem. Nat. Acad. Western Artists (Prix de West award, Cowboy Hall of Fame). Home: PO Box 2342 Santa Fe NM 87504-2342

STEINLICHT, STEVEN, astrologer, minister, educator; b. Bloomington, Ill., Mar. 13, 1950; s. Henry Jr. and Mary Elizabeth (Ritter) S. Student, U. Ill., 1968; D in Metaphysics, Universal Life Ch., 1975. Lic. psychol. counselor, Universal Life Ch. Minister Temple of Truth, Universal Life Ch., Bloomington, Ill., 1977; co-founder Ascension, Bloomington, 1979; stockroom supr. Murray's Shoes, Bloomington, Ill., 1981-86; psychic Rainbow Place, Albuquerque, 1988-90; software mgr., corp. astrologer Computer Bazaar, Albuquerque, 1991-96; pres., founder Albuqueque Metaphys. Inst., 1993—; tchr., healer Gold Key Ctr., Albuquerque, 1987-88, pub. spkr. New Age Connection, Albuquerque, 1987—, psychic Metaphysical Crystal Palace, Albuquerque, 1987; detective N.M. Bur. Investigations, 1988. Author: Astarunum, The Portable Oracle, 1993; columnist Rainbow Place, 1988-90, Up Front! Mag., 1996-97; inventor. Min. Universal Life Ch., 1972—. Mem. Mensa Internat., Soc. for Creative Anachronism, S.W. Psychic Forum. *Steven Steinlicht is a metaphysician and seer; he works in spiritual, mental, emotional, and physical dimensions. In order to help people with human problems, he uses a wide variety of psychic tools. Steven is adept in astrology, runestones, tarot cards, Egyptian cartouche, I-ching, numerology, name meanings, palmistry, handwriting analysis, dream interpretation, crystal-gazing, biorhythms, astrological fertility and birth control, aura vision, healing with hands, white magical protection, house exorcism, Kabbalah, Meditation, and spiritual growth.*

STEINMAN, JOHN FRANCIS, psychiatrist; b. N.Y.C., May 5, 1916; s. David Barnard and Irene Stella (Hoffman) S.; m. Helen G. Meyer (div. 1963); children: James, Judith, Jill; m. Roxane Bear (div. 1972); m. Ellen M. Sears, Nov. 16, 1985. AB with hons., Columbia U., 1936, MD, 1940. Diplomate Am. Bd. Psychiatry and Neurology. Intern Strong Meml. Hosp., Rochester, N.Y. and Cin. Gen. Hosp., 1940-43; resident psychiatry Nebr. Psychiat. Inst., 1948, 58, R.I. Med. Ctr., 1961; psychiatrist, dir. Lincoln (Nebr.) and Lancaster County Child Guidance Ctr., 1948-61; instr. pediatrics, psychiatry and neurology U. Nebr., Lincoln, 1951-52; postdoctoral fellow in psychiatry Yale U., New Haven, Conn., 1962-64; psychiatrist U. Conn., Storrs, 1964-69, Community Mental Health Services, San Francisco, 1971-79; pvt. practice psychiatry San Francisco, 1979—. Delgate, chmn. Nebr. health com. White House Conf. Children and Youth, Washington, 1960. Served to capt. M.C., AUS, 1943-46, PTO. Mem. Am. Psychiat. Assn. (life), Am. Orthopsychiat. Assn., N.Y. Acad. Scis., Phi Beta Kappa. Home and Office: 164 Otsego Ave San Francisco CA 94112-2536

STEINMANN, JOHN COLBURN, architect; b. Monroe, Wis., Oct. 24, 1941; s. John Wilbur and Irene Marie (Steil) S.; m. Susan Koslosky, Aug. 12, 1978 (div. July 1989). BArch., U. Ill., 1964; postgrad. Ill. Inst. Tech., 1970-71; Project designer C.F. Murphy Assocs., Chgo., 1968-71, Steinmann

Architects, Monticello, Wis., 1971-73; design chief, chief project architect State of Alaska, Juneau, 1973-78; project designer Mithun Assos., architects, Bellevue, Wash., 1978-80; owner, prin. John C. Steinmann Assos., Architect, Kirkland, Wash., 1980-94; supr. head facilities sect. divsn. fin. Dept. Edn. State of Alaska, Juneau, 1994-96; docs. mgr. Loschky Marquardt and Nesholm, Architects, Seattle, 1996—; bd. dirs. Storytell Internat.; lectr. Ill. Inst. Tech., 1971-72; prin. works include: Grant Park Music Bowl, Chgo., 1971, Menomonee Falls (Wis.) Med. Clinic, 1972, Hidden Valley Office Bldg., Bellevue, 1978, Kezner Office Bldg., Bellevue, 1979, The Pines at Sunriver, Oreg., 1980, also Phase II, 1984, Phase III, 1986, The Pines at Sunriver Lodge Bldg., 1986, 2d and Lenora highrise, Seattle, 1981, Bob Hope Cardiovascular Research Inst. lab. animal facility, Seattle, 1982, Wash. Ct., Bellevue, 1982, Anchorage Bus. Park, 1982, Garden Townhouses, Anchorage, 1983, Vacation Internationale, Ltd. Corp. Hdqrs., Bellevue, 1983, Vallarta Torres III, Puerto Vallarta, Mex., 1987, Torres Mazatlan (Mex.) II, 1988, Canterwood Townhouses, Gig Harbor Wash., 1988, Inn at Ceres (Calif.), 1989, Woodard Creek Inn, Olympia, Wash., 1989, Northgate Corp. Ctr., Seattle, 1990, Icicle Creek Hotel and Restaurant, Leavenworth, Wash., 1990, Bellingham (Wash.) Market Pl., 1990, Boeing Hot Gas Test Facility, Renton, Wash., 1991, Boeing Longacres Customer Svc. Tng. Ctr. Support Facilities, Renton, 1992, Boeing Comml. Airplane Group Hdqs., Renton, 1996, also pvt. residences. Served to 1st lt. C.E., USAR, 1964-66; Vietnam. Decorated Bronze Star. Registered architect, Wash., Oreg., Calif., N.Mex., Ariz., Utah, Alaska, Wis., Ill. Mem. AIA, Am. Mgmt. Assn., Nat. Council Archtl. Registration Bds., Alpha Rho Chi. Republican. Roman Catholic. Clubs: U. Wash. Yacht, Columbia Athletic. Address: 4316 106th Pl NE Kirkland WA 98033

STEINMETZ, JOHN CHARLES, geologist, paleontologist; b. St. Paul, Sept. 26, 1947; s. Charles Leonard and Ruth Naomi (Osteraas) S.; m. Sarah Cook Tristán, May 29, 1982; children: Katherine Ruth, Elizabeth Margaret. BS, U. Ill., 1969, MS, 1975; PhD, U. Miami, 1978. Asst. prof. U. South Fla., St. Petersburg, 1977-82; advanced rsch. geologist Marathon Oil Co., Littleton, Colo., 1982-86, sr. geologist, 1986-90, advanced sr. geologist, 1990-94; dir. state geologist Mont. Bur. of Mines and Geology, 1994—. Mem. bd. advisors Micropaleontology Press, N.Y.C., 1986—. Trustee Paleontol. Rsch. Instn., Ithaca, N.Y., 1990—, v.p., 1992-94, pres. 1994-96. Mem. Assn. Am. State Geologists, Am. Assn. Petroleum Geologists, Geol. Soc. Am., Internat. Nannoplankton Assn. (U.S. treas. 1982-92), Mont. Geol. Soc., Paleontol. Soc., Soc. Econ. Paleontologists and Mineralogists.

STELLING, E. EDMUND, educator; b. Menfro, Mo., May 11, 1935; s. Edmund George and Leona Christiana (Newberry) S.; m. Diane Marie Ottesen, June 14, 1958; children: Jennifer, Scott, Adnrew. BS, Concordia U., 1958; MA, Azusa U., 1977. Tchr. Bethany Luth. Sch., Detroit, 1958-63; tchr., prin. Christ Luth. Sch., Costa Mesa, Calif., 1963-72; literacy missionary Luth. Bible Translators, Liberia, 1972-82; prin. Trinity Luth. Sch., San Jose, Calif., 1982-84, Emmanuel Luth. Sch., Kahalui Maui, Hawaii, 1984-87, Immanuel Luth. Sch., Orange, Calif., 1989-96; bd. dirs. Luth. Bible Translations. Author: (literacy manuals) Kuwaa Primers/Readers, 1973-79. Vol. SOS Free Med. Clinic, Costa Mesa, 1992—. Mem. ASCD, Luth. Edn. Assn. Office: Immanuel Luth Sch 147 S Pine St Orange CA 92866-1600

STELZRIED, CHARLES THOMAS, engineer; b. L.A., Sept. 14, 1928; s. Charles Edward Stelzried and Dorothy Claire (Morgan) Mercer; m. Virginia Stelzried, 1962 (div. Jan. 1974); children: Camile Traci, Charles Thomas; m. Keiko Kawakami, Apr. 4, 1977. BS, UCLA, 1957, MS, 1959; PhD, U. So. Calif., 1969. Program mgr. NASA/Jet Propulsion Lab., Pasadena, Calif., 1953—, team mem. deep space radio sci. Mariner 10, 1967-81, tracking and data sys. mgr. for various deep space missions, 1981-86, DSN advanced sys. dep. program mgr., 1986—. Contbr numerous articles to profl. publs. With USN, 1946-53. Fellow IEEE; mem. AAAS, Sigma Xi, Tau Beta Pi. Office: Jet Propulsion Lab MS303-402 4800 Oak Grove Dr Pasadena CA 91109-8001

STEM, DONALD EDWARD, JR., marketing educator, researcher; b. San Francisco, Dec. 13, 1943; s. Donald Edward and Alma Jewel (Hines) S.; m. Theresa (Deta) Anne Chicoine, Aug. 5, 1972; 1 child, Katherine Ellen. BA in Bus. Econs., U. Calif., Santa Barbara, 1967; MS in Mktg. & Info. Systems, San Diego State U., 1972; PhD in Mktg., U. Wash., 1975. Mgmt. trainee Rohr Corp., Chula Vista, Calif., 1971-72; teaching asst. San Diego State U., 1971-72; asst. prof. Tex. A & M U., College Station, 1975-78; asst. prof. Wash. State U., Pullman, 1978-81, assoc. prof., 1981-86, prof., 1986—, acting dept. chair mktg., 1989-90; vis. prof. Madrid (Spain) Bus. Sch., 1991-92; vis. prof. faculty of psychology dept. methodology U. Santiago de Compostela, Spain, 1992; vis. scholar Ctr. for Survey Methods and Analysis, Mannheim, Germany, 1992; book rev. editor Jour. of Mktg. rsch., Chgo., 1988—; mem. Univ. Minority Mentor program com. Wash. State U., 1991—, Coll. Bus. and Econs. tenure com., 1984—, chair, 1993, chair mktg. dept. behavioral lab. com., 1993—, univ. orgn. and structure com., 1994—, faculty affairs com., 1994—. Mem. editorial rev. bd. Jour. of Bus. Rsch., 1980-85, Jour. of Acad. of Mktg. Sci., Miami, Fla., 1980—, Jour. of Mktg. Rsch., Chgo., 1988—; contbr. articles to Jour. Mktg. Rsch., Jour. Am. Statis. Assn. and others. Capt. U.S. Army Chem. Corps & Infantry, 1967-69. Grantee Gen. Telephone Co., 1979, Washington Water Power, 1982, Bur. Indian Affairs, 1985, 87, The Puyallup Tribe of Indians, 1984-85. Mem. Am. Mktg. Assn., Assn. for Consumer Rsch., Acad. Mktg. Sci., Acad. Internat. Bus. Office: Washington State U Dept of Mktg Todd 367 Pullman WA 99164-4730

STEMMER, JAY JOHN, safety engineer, consultant; b. Wilkes-Barre, Pa., Apr. 29, 1939. BSCE, N.J. Inst. Tech., 1962; MBA, Calif. State U., Long Beach, 1969. Registered profl. engr., Calif.; cert. safety profl.; cert. hazard control mgmt. Engr. Factory Mut., N.J., 1973-77; cons. McKay & Assoc., Calif., 1977-81, Index Research, Calif., 1981-83, Fireman's Fund, Calif., 1983-85, AIG Cons., Calif., 1985-87; sr. cons. Argonaut, Calif., 1987—; assoc. prof. Sierra Coll., Los Angeles, 1979-80. Author: Medical Manual of Industrial Toxicology, 1965, Latin America, A Study of Air Transport Development and Potential in the Decade Ahead, 1970. Served to lt. USAF, 1962-65. Mem. NSPE, Calif. Soc. Profl. Engrs., Am. Soc. Safety Engrs., Am. Bd. Motion Pictures and TV Engrs., Screen Actors Guild, Actors Equity Assn., AFTRA. Home: 1935 Alpha Rd Apt 225 Glendale CA 91208-2135

STEMPLE, ALAN DOUGLAS, aerospace engineer; b. Elkins, W.Va., July 19, 1963; s. Stephen Warren and C. Phyllis (Cavalier) S. BS cum laude, Davis and Elkins Coll., 1984; BS in Aero. Engring. cum laude, W.Va. U., 1985; MS, U. Md., 1986, PhD, 1989. Rotorcraft fellow Ctr. for Rotorcraft Edn. and Rsch., U. Md., College Park, 1985-89; structures rsch. engr. McDonnell Douglas Helicopter Sys., Mesa, Ariz., 1989—; reviewer tech. papers, 1990—. Contbr. articles to profl. publs. Army Rotorcraft fellow U. Md., 1985-89. Mem. AIAA (tech. com. 1995—), Am. Helicopter Soc. (Vertical Flight Found. scholar 1988). Home: 1401 N Hobson St Mesa AZ 85203-3651 Office: McDonnell Douglas Mail Stop M530-B337 5000 E McDowell Rd Mesa AZ 85215-9707

STENBERG, STEPHEN JOSEPH, risk manager, retail store manager; b. Berkeley, Calif., Sept. 11, 1947; s. Willis Franklin and Constance Dolores (Richmond) S.; m. Linda Straube, Dec. 29, 1965 (div. Sept. 1967); 1 child, Kristine Renée; m. Marcia Kay Hinks, Mar. 10, 1979; stepchildren: Anthony Michael, Lisa Marie Castillo. BS, Armstrong Coll., 1971. Mgr. Safeway Stores, Oakland, Calif., Riyadh, Saudi Arabia, Dubai, United Arab Emirates; risk mgr. Safeway Stores, Walnut Creek, Calif. With USN, 1965-67. Republican.

STENDER, CHARLES FREDERICK, test pilot; b. East Orange, N.J., Nov. 17, 1940; s. Robert Conrad and Ruth Warne (Cobb) S. BSCE, Pa. State U., 1962; MS in Systems Mgmt., U. So. Calif., University Park, Calif., 1982. Commd. ensign USN, 1962; advanced through grades to capt. USNR, 1983, ret., 1991; naval aviator USN, various, 1962-72; test pilot Grumman Aerospace, Point Mugu, Calif., 1972-77; airline pilot TWA, L.A., 1977-80; mgr., test pilot Hughes Aircraft Co., L.A., 1980—. Decorated Disting. Flying Cross (3), Vietnam, Air medal (13), Vietnam, Navy Commendation medal. Mem. Soc. Exptl. Test Pilots (assoc. fellow), Tailhook Assn., Air Line Pilots Assn. Office: Hughes Aircraft Co 16101 Saticoy St Van Nuys CA 91406-2915

STENGELE, BRIAN JOEL, mental health nurse; b. Vallejo, Calif., Dec. 30, 1948; s. Harold David and Nancy (Skakun) Marcus; m. JoEllen Stengele, June 23, 1973; children: Kristi Ann, Alena, Joseph. AA, Contra Costa Coll., 1969, dipl. nursing, 1976; BS in Biol. Sci., Calif. State U., Hayward, 1972; MA in Psychology, Triunne Coll., 1986. RN; cert. clin. specialist in adult psychiatry and mental health. Psychiat. and drug abuse counselor Martinez (Calif.) County Hosp., 1974-76; critical care nurse Oakland (Calif.) Kaiser Med. Ctr., 1976-79; cons. Stengele & Assocs., Kingston, Seattle, Wash., 1979—; psychiat. specialist Evergreen Cmty. Courier Home Health Care, Seattle, 1993—; bd. dirs. Group Health Coop., Seattle; chmn. mental health courses ARC, Brementon, Wash., 1992—. Contbr. articles to profl. jours. Mem. U.S. Del. of Nurses Citizen Amb. Program to China, 1996. Mem. ARNP United, Advance Positive Practice Psychiat. Nurses (com. chmn., fellow), Wash. State Nurses Assn. (Cert. Excellence award 1992, 94, 95), Kitsap Nurses Assn. (treas. 1995). Home: PO Box 584 Kingston WA 98346-0584

STENNER, ROBERT DAVID, environmental and health research engineer, toxicologist; b. Fennimore, Wis., Mar. 12, 1946; s. Arno F. and Edna M. (Mill) S.; m. Vicki S. Muller, June 12, 1965; children: James Brian, Heidi Diane. BS in Power Mechanics with honors, U. Wis., Menomonie, 1970; MS in Nuclear Engring., Idaho State U., 1981; PhD in Toxicology, Wash. State U., 1996. Environ. engr. Gaston County Air Pollution Control, Gastonia, N.C., 1973-77; environ. engring. specialist environ. divsn. State of Idaho, Pocatello, 1977-81; chem. and radiation protection engr. Pacific Gas and Electric Co., San Francisco, Eureka, Calif., 1981-84; rsch. engr. sci. III and IV Battelle N.W. Labs., Richland, Wash., 1984—; mem. audit team Assurance Program for Remedial Action, Dept. of Energy, Washington, 1984-86; risk assessment rep. Environ. Mgmt. Ops. Cons. Selection Team, Richland, Wash., 1988-89; mem. chem. protection initiative team Battelle N.W. Labs., 1989-90, point of contact-Life Sci. Ctr., 1993-95. Contbr. articles to profl. jours. Sec. Lions Club, Bessemer City, N.C., 1974-77; youth program counselor United Meth. Chs., numerous cities, 1973-95; vol. ARC, Kennewick, Wash., 1989. Recipient Merit award Menomonie Area C. of C., 1970. Mem. Am. Soc. Testing Materials, Soc. Toxicology, Health Physics Soc., Pacific N.W. Assn. Toxicologists, Soc. Risk Analysis. Democrat. Home: 2517 Granada Ct Richland WA 99352-1619 Office: Battelle NW Labs PO Box 999 Richland WA 99352

STENNIS, WILLIAM, psychiatrist, educator; b. Meridian, Miss., Mar. 5, 1930; s. William Hardy and Amelia Lee (Bell) S.; m. Maria T. Schulcz, Nov. 23, 1968; children: Susan Maria, Jennifer Lee. BA, Vanderbilt U., 1950, MA, 1952; grad., U. Miss. Sch. of Medicine, 1954; MD, Jefferson Med. Coll., 1956. Diplomate Am. Bd. Psychiatry and Neurology (gen. psychiatry, child and adolescent psychiatry). Intern Colo. Gen. Hosp., Denver, 1956-57; resident in gen. psychiatry Norristown (Pa.) State Hosp., 1957-60; resident in child and adolescent psychiatry Ea. Pa. Psychiat. Inst., Phila., 1960-62; pvt. practice Phila., 1962-70, Santa Fe, 1970-96; clin. assoc. dept. psychiatry U. N.Mex., Albuquerque, 1972-76, clin. prof. psychiatry, 1981—; cons. Bucks County (Pa.) Schs., 1962-72, Ea. Pa. Psychiat. Inst., 1963-70, Buttonwood Farms Day Camp for Emotionally Disturbed Children, 1960-70, Los Alamos Schs., 1971-80, Brush Ranch Sch., 1970-73; clin. dir. children's svcs., Ea. Pa. Psychiat. Inst., 1963; asst. dir. sect. child psychiatry, Albert Einstein Med. Ctr., Phila., 1964-68; study com. prevention Gov. Coun. Criminal Justice Planning, 19732; chmn. Com. Liaison between Am. Acad. Child and Adolescent Psychiatry and Com. Cert. in Child and Adolescent Psychiatry, Am. Bd. Psychiatry and Neurology, 1974-77; nat. steering com. recertification in psychiatry, 1976-77. Contbr. chpts. to books, articles to profl. jours. Recipient Virgil Lusk Meml. scholarship, N.Mex. Mil. Inst., 1946, 47. Fellow APA, Am. Acad. Child and Adolescent Psychiatry (mem. continuing edn. com. 1974-77); mem. AMA, AAAS, N.Mex. Med. Soc., Psychiat. Med. Assn. N.Mex., Santa Fe County Med. Soc., Regional Coun. Child Psychiatry (pres.-elect 1969-70, pres. 1970), N.Mex. Psychiat. Assn. (pres.-elect 1971-72, pres. 1972-73), Phila. Assn. Psychoanalysis. Home: 116 Tano W Santa Fe NM 87501-7024 Office: 200 W De Vargas St Ste 4B Santa Fe NM 87501-2654

STEPANEK, JOSEPH EDWARD, industrial development consultant; b. Ellinwood, Kans., Oct. 29, 1917; s. Joseph August and Leona Mae (Wilson) S.; m. Antoinette Farnham, June 10, 1942; children: Joseph F., James B., Antoinette L., Debra L. BSChemE, U. Colo., 1939; DEng in Chem. Engring., Yale U., 1942. Registered profl. engr., Colo. Engr. Stearns-Roger Mfg., Denver, 1939-45; from asst. to assoc. prof. U. Colo., Boulder, 1945-47; from cons. to dir. UN, various countries, 1947-73; cons. internat. indsl devel., U.S.-China bus. relations Boulder, 1973—; bd. dirs. 12 corps., 1973—. Author 3 books on indsl. devel.; contbr. 50 articles to profl. jours. Exec. dir. Boulder Tomorrow, 1965-67. Recipient Yale Engring. award Yale Engring. Assn., 1957, Norlin award U. Colo. 1978, Annual award India League of Am., 1982. Mem. AAAS. Democrat. Unitarian. Home: 1622 High St Boulder CO 80304-4224

STEPHENS, ELISA, art college president, lawyer. Pres. Acad. Art Coll., San Francisco. Office: Acad Art Coll Office of President 79 New Montgomery St San Francisco CA 94105-3410

STEPHENS, LARRY DEAN, engineer; b. Sterling, Colo., Sept. 1, 1937; s. John Robert and Shirley Berniece (Rudel) S.; m. Carol Ann Wertz, Sept. 1, 1957 (div. May 1975); children: Deborah Lynn, Janell Diane, Dana Larry, Hilary Elizabeth Melton. BS in Engring., Colo. State U., 1960; MBA, U. Colo., 1967. Registered profl. engr., Colo. Engr. Bur. Reclamation, Denver, 1960-90, cons., 1991—; exec. v.p. U.S. Com. on Irrigation and Drainage, Denver, 1971—; exec. dir. U.S. Com. on Large Dams, Denver, 1986—. V.p. Internat. Commn. on Irrigation and Drainage, 1989-92. With USNG, 1961-62. Mem. Am. Soc. Agrl. Engrs., Assn. State Dam Safety Officials, Colo. River Water Users Assn., Coun. on Engring. and Sci. Soc. Execs. Republican. Methodist. Home: 1625 Larimer St Apt 1505 Denver CO 80202-1532 Office: USCID 1616 17th St Ste 483 Denver CO 80202-1277

STEPHENS, MICHAEL DEAN, hospital administrator; b. Salt Lake City, May 1, 1942; married. B, Columbia U., 1966, MHA, 1970. Adminstrv. resident Mt. Sinai Med. Ctr., N.Y.C., 1969-70; asst. administr. Greenville (S.C.) Gen. Hosp., 1970-71, assoc. adminstr., 1971-72, adminstr., 1972-75; pres. Hoag Meml. Hosp.-Presbyn., Newport Beach, Calif., 1975—. Mem. Am. Coll. Healthcare Execs. Home: 900 Alder Pl Newport Beach CA 92660-4121 Office: Hoag Meml Hosp Presbyn PO Box 6100 Newport Beach CA 92658-6100*

STEPHENSON, BARBERA WERTZ, lawyer; b. Bryan, Ohio, Dec. 10, 1938; d. Emerson D. and Beryl B. (Barber) Wertz; m. Gerard J. Stephenson Jr., June 22, 1960; 1 child, Thomas. Student, Smith Coll., 1956-57; BSEE, MIT, 1961; JD, U. N.Mex., 1981. Bar: N.Mex. 1981. Electronic engr. Digital Equipment Corp., Maynard, Mass., 1960-66; logic analyst Librascope, Glendale, Calif., 1966; electronic engr. Md. Dept. of Def., Ft. Meade, 1966-68; mem. tech. staff Xerox Data Systems, Rockville, Md., 1968; pvt. practice cons., Silver Spring, Md., 1969-78; pvt. practice law, Albuquerque, 1981—. Author: Financing Your Home Purchase in New Mexico, 1992; patentee analog to digital converter, kitchen calculator. Mem. N.Mex. Bar Assn. Office: 4221 Silver Ave SE Albuquerque NM 87108-2720

STEPHENSON, HERMAN HOWARD, retired banker; b. Wichita, Kans., July 15, 1929; s. Herman Horace and Edith May (Wayland) S.; m. Virginia Anne Ross, Dec. 24, 1950; children: Ross Wayland, Neal Bevan, Jann Edith. BA, U. Mich., 1950; JD with distinction, U. Mo., Kansas City, 1958, LLD (hon.), 1993. Bar: Kans. 1958. With City Nat. Bank, Kansas City, Mo., 1952-54, City Bond & Mortgage Co., Kansas City, 1954-59, Bank of Hawaii, Honolulu, 1959-94; ret., 1994; chmn., exec. com., CEO, bd. dirs. Pacific Century Fin. Corp. and Bank Hawaii; bd. dirs. Bank of Hawaii Internat. Inc., Hawaiian Trust Co. Ltd.; internat. treas., dir. Pacific Basin Econ. Coun. U.S. Mem. Com. Bd. dirs. Maunalani Found., Aloha United Way, Pacific Fleet Submarine Meml. Assn. With U.S. Army, 1950-52. Mem. Navy League of U.S., Pacific Forum/CSIS (bd. govs.), U.S.-Korea Bus. Coun., Kappa Sigma, Pi Eta Sigma, Oahu Country Club, Waialae Country Club, Rotary, Lambda Alpha Internat. Office: Bank of Hawaii PO Box 2900 Honolulu HI 96846

STEPHENSON, IRENE HAMLEN, biorhythm analyst, consultant, editor, educator; b. Chgo., Oct. 7, 1923; d. Charles Martin and Carolyn Hilda (Hilgers) Hamlin; m. Edgar B. Stephenson, Sr., Aug. 16, 1941 (div. 1946); 1 child, Edgar B. Author biorhythm compatibilities column Nat. Singles Register, Norwalk, Calif., 1979-81; instr. biorhythm Learning Tree Open U., Canoga Park, Calif., 1982-83; instr. biorhythm character analysis 1980—; instr. biorhythm compatibility, 1982—; owner, pres. matchmaking svc. Pen Pals Using Biorhythm, Chatsworth, Calif., 1979—; editor newsletter The Truth, 1979-85, Mini Examiner, Chatsworth, 1985—; researcher biorhythm character and compatibility, 1974—, biorhythm columnist Psychic Astrology Horoscope, 1989-94, True Astrology Forecast, 1989-94, Psychic Astrology Predictions, 1990-94, Trouble-Addict (Suicide) Type, 1997; author: Learn Biorhythm Character Analysis, 1980, Do-It-Yourself Biorhythm Compatibilities, 1982; contbr. numerous articles to mags.; frequent guests clubs, radio, TV. Office: PO Box 3893-ww Chatsworth CA 91313 *To be happy, you have to be what is natural for you, not what someone else wants you to be.*

STEPHENSON, LARRY KIRK, strategic planner, management and geography educator; b. Seattle, Sept. 22, 1944; s. Norman Eugene and Virginia Dare (Frost) S.; m. Margery Alsever, Aug. 15, 1992; children: Mathew Alan, Leah Anela. BS, Ariz. State U., 1966, MA, 1971; PhD, U. Cin., 1973; Manpower research analyst Employment Security Commn. of Ariz., 1969-70; asst. prof. dept. geography U. Hawaii, Hilo, 1973-76, assoc. prof., 1976-78, chmn. dept., 1975-77; vis. lectr. dept. geography Ariz. State U., 1978, adj. assoc. prof., 1979—; planner Ariz. Dept. Health Services, Phoenix, 1978-84; vis. assoc. prof. dept. geography, area devel. and urban planning U. Ariz., 1978; strategic plannner City of Glendale, Ariz., 1984-92; pub. health analyst Gila River Indian Community, 1992—; mem. faculty U. Phoenix, 1979—; adj. prof. Golden Gate U., 1981—; ptnr. Urban Research Assocs., Phoenix, 1981—; adj. prof. Coll. St. Francis, 1982—; mem. faculty Troy State U., 1990—. Mem. Hawaii Island Health Planning Council, 1974-78; mem. Glendale Community Colls. Pres.'s Council, 1986-92. Served with U.S. Army, 1966-68. NDEA fellow, 1971-72. Mem. Am. Inst. Cert. Planners, Am. Planning Assn., Assn. Am. Geographers, Ariz. Planning Assn. (pres. 1987—), Southwest Profl. Geog. Assn., Lambda Alpha. Unitarian. Author books in field; contbr. chpts. to textbooks, articles to profl. jours. Home: RR 1 Box 453-f Laveen AZ 85339-9654 Office: PO Box 7 Sacaton AZ 85247-0007

STEPHENSON, SCOT ALAN, English educator; b. Ames, Iowa, Sept. 4, 1968; s. Conrad Jr. Stephenson and Diana Virginia (Du Bois) Butzlaff; m. Patricia Monique Jane, July 9, 1994; 1 child, Shannon Renate. BA in German and Journalism, U. Iowa, 1991. English tchr. U.S. Peace Corps, Hungary, 1992-94, Lang. Pacifica, Palo Alto, Calif., 1994-96; internat. student adv. ELS Lang. Ctr., St. Paul, Minn., 1996—. Mem. Nat. Returned Peace Corps Assn. Democrat. Roman Catholic. Home: 78 10th St E Apt 1205 Saint Paul MN 55101-2249

STEPNER, MICHAEL JAY, architect; b. Chgo., Sept. 7, 1940; s. Lester Harry and Florence (Addison) S.; m. Rosemary Reiser, Apr. 2, 1965; children: Rachel, Jessica, Adam, Joshua, Rebekah. Student, U. Minn., 1961-62; BArch, U. Ill., 1964; postgrad., U. Calif., Berkeley, 1971; U.S. Navy Engring. Schs., 1965-66. Registered architect, Calif. Urban designer, planner Crosstown Assocs., Chgo., 1968-71; urban designer, planner planning dept. City of San Diego, 1971-81, asst. planning dir., 1981-88, acting planning dir., 1987-88, city architect, 1988-92, asst. to city mgr., spl. projects coord., 1992-94, city urban design coord., 1994—; vis. critic in urban design U. Ill, Chgo., 1970-71, San Diego State U. Grad. Sch. Planning and Pub. Adminstrn., Urban Design & Site Planning Inst., 1974-85; lectr. Urban Conservation Grad. Sch. History, U. San Diego, 1978, 81, 82, 87; asst. prof., lectr., design critic New Sch. Architecture, San Diego City U., 1980—; faculty assoc. for transp. and land use planning Lincoln Inst. Land Policy, Cambridge, Mass., 1993-95; mem. hist. bldg. code bd. State of Calif.; mem., dir. Community Planning and Design Ctr., San Diego, 1971-74. Bd. dirs. Citizens Coordinate for Century III, 1991—; mem. Regional Urban Design Assistance Team, Seattle, Washington, and Liverpool, Eng.; past bd. dirs. Californians for Preservation Action. Recipient Leadership in Planning award New Sch. Architecture, 1992, Gaslamp Pioneer award San Diego Gaslamp Quarter Found., 1993, Ellen and Roger Revelle award Citizens Coordinate for Century III, 1993. Fellow AIA (co-chair housing assistance team City of Washincton, 1990, bd. dirs. San Diego chpt. 1976-78, mem. nat. urban design com., past mem. Calif. coun., hist. preservation-urban conservation com., urban design commr. San Diego chpt. 1975-76, Spl. award for Excellence in Govt. 1983); mem. Am. Planning Assn. (Disting. Leadership award Calif. chpt. 1991), Am. Inst. Cert. Planners, Inst. for Urban Design, Urban Land Inst., Lambda Alpha. Home: 4260 Hortensia St San Diego CA 92103-1105

STEPP, WILLIAM EDWARD, retired military operations analyst; b. Turtle Creek, Pa., Feb. 23, 1930; s. William George and Emma Jean (McLean) S.; m. Barbara Johanna Barth, Oct. 23, 1965; children: Randal R., Roger W. BS in Physics, Carnegie-Mellon U., 1951; MS in Engring., U. So. Calif., 1977. Physicist Bell Aircraft Co., Buffalo, 1951-53, Convair Aircraft Co., San Diego, 1953-56, Bendix Co., North Hollywood, Calif., 1956-59; ops. analyst ORI, Santa Monica, Calif., 1959-61, Douglas Aircraft Co., Santa Monica, 1961-63; sr. mil. ops. analyst Lockheed Calif. Co., Burbank, 1963-91, ret., 1991.

STERBACH, CHARLES ROBERT, lawyer; b. Nagoya, Japan, June 21, 1955; came to the U.S., 1957; s. Edward Robert and Shizuko (Ishimutsu) S.; m. Kimberly Ann Burke, Sept. 26, 1992; 1 child, Justin Andrew Chard. BA, U. Pa., 1977, 79; JD, Rutgers U., 1983. Bar: Ariz. 1983. Assoc. Streich Lang, P.A., Phoenix, 1983-89; assoc. Gallagher & Kennedy, P.A., Phoenix, 1989-90, ptnr., 1991—; mem. evening faculty Phoenix Coll., 1988-92. Mem. Am. Bankruptcy Inst., Ariz. Bar Assn., Ariz. Bankruptcy Bar Assn., Phoenix Adult Hockey League. Office: Gallagher & Kennedy PA 2600 N Central Ave Phoenix AZ 85004-3050

STERBICK, PETER LAWRENCE, lawyer; b. Tacoma, Nov. 12, 1917; s. Anton John and Pearl (Medak) S.; m. Rita J. Morrell, Dec. 26, 1946; children: Marilyn, Lawrence, Thomas, David, Colleen. BBA, U. Wash., 1941, LLB, 1948. Bar: Wash. 1949. Adjuster Gen. Accidenty Ins. Co., Seattle, 1948-49, Farmers Ins. Group, Tacoma, 1949-50; dep. pros. atty. Pierce County, Tacoma, 1950-51; ptnr. Sterbick and Sterbick, Tacoma, 1951-57, Sterbick, Manza, Moceri and Sterbick, Tacoma, 1958-72, Sterbick, Abel and Sterbick, Tacoma, 1972—. 2d lt. USAAF, 1943-45. Mem. Wash. Bar Assn., Wash. State Trial Lawyers Assn., Tacoma-Pierce County Bar Assn., Kiwanis, KC, Elks. Roman Catholic. Home: 3143 Olympic Blvd W University Place WA 98466-1605 Office: 15 Oregon Ave Ste 303 Tacoma WA 98409-7464 *Personal philosophy: Work hard - keep the faith. There are no free lunches.*

STERLING, DONALD JUSTUS, JR., retired newspaper editor; b. Portland, Oreg., Sept. 27, 1927; s. Donald Justus and Adelaide (Armstrong) S.; m. Julie Ann Courteol, June 7, 1963; children: Sarah, William, John. A.B., Princeton U., 1948; postgrad. (Nieman fellow), Harvard U., 1955-56. Reporter Denver Post, 1948-52; news staff mem. Oreg. Jour., Portland, 1952-82; editor Oreg. Jour., 1972-82; asst. to pub. The Oregonian, 1982-92, ret., 1992. Pres. Tri-County Community Coun., 1972-73. Recipient Izaak Walton League Golden Beaver award, 1969, Edith Knight Hill award, 1978, Jessie Laird Brodie award Planned Parenthood Assn., 1983, McCall award Women in Communications, 1987, Roger W. Williams Freedom of Info. award Oreg. Newspaper Pubs. Assn., 1989; English-Speaking Union traveling fellow, 1959. Mem. Oreg. Hist. Soc. (pres. 1977-79), Mazamas, Lang Syne Soc., City Club (Portland, pres. 1973-74), Multnomah Athletic, Dial, Elm. Cannon (Princeton), Phi Beta Kappa. Home: 1718 SW Myrtle St Portland OR 97201-2300

STERLING, DONALD T., professional basketball team executive; b. Chgo.. Lawyer L.A. (formerly San Diego) Clippers, Nat. Basketball Assn., owner, also chmn. bd. Office: care LA Clippers LA Meml Sports Arena 3939 S Figueroa St Los Angeles CA 90037-1200*

STERMER, DUGALD ROBERT, designer, illustrator, writer, consultant; b. Los Angeles, Dec. 17, 1936; s. Robert Newton and Mary (Blue) S.; m. Jeanie Kortum; children: Dugald, Megan, Chris, Colin, Crystal. B.A.,

UCLA, 1960. Art dir., v.p. Ramparts mag., 1965-70; freelance designer, illustrator, writer, cons. San Francisco, 1970—; founder Pub. Interest Communications, San Francisco, 1974; pres. Frisco Pub Group Ltd.; chmn. illustration dept. Calif. Coll. Arts and Crafts, 1994—; bd. dirs. Am. Inst. Graphic Arts; mem. San Francisco Art Commn., 1997—. Cons. editor: Communication Arts mag., 1974-90; designer: Oceans mag., 1976-82; editor: The Environment, 1972, Vanishing Creatures, 1980; author: The Art of Revolution, 1970, Vanishing Creatures, 1980, Vanishing Flora, 1994, Birds and Bees, 1994; designer 1984 Olympic medals; illustration exhbn. Calif. Acad. Scis., 1986; one-man show Jernigan Wicker Gallery, San Francisco, 1996. Mem. Grand Jury City and County San Francisco, 1989; bd. dirs. Delancey St. Found., 1990—. Recipient various medals, awards for design and illustration nat. and internat. competitions. Office: 600 The Embarcadero # 204 San Francisco CA 94107

STERN, ANITA ENKEL, English language educator; b. Detroit, July 22, 1941; d. Harry and Ida (Goodman) Enkel; m. Josef Stern, June 25, 1968; children: Tsafrir, Michael. BA magna cum laude, Wayne State U., Detroit, 1963, MA, 1964; MA, Calif. State U., L.A., 1990. Lic. single subject-English and crosscultural lang. and acad. devel. specialist, Calif. Tchr. Highland Park (Mich.) Schs., 1964-65; instr. Bar Ilan U., Ramat Gan, Israel, 1966-68, Tel Aviv (Israel) U., 1965-67; tchr. Tel Aviv Mcpl. H.S., 1968-69, Shein Tchrs. Coll., Petach Tikva, Israel, 1984-85, Levinsky, Tel Aviv, 1981-82, Lynwood (Calif.) Unified Sch. Dist., 1986-90, Baldwin Park (Calif.) Unified Schs., 1990-92, L.A. Unified Schs., 1992—; instr. L.A. S.W. Coll., 1987-88. Author: World Folktales, 1994, Tales From Many Lands, 1996. Mem. TESOL, Calif. TESOL, Nat. Coun. Tchrs. English, Authors Guild, Soc. Children's Book Writers and Illustrators, Tex. and Acad. Authors Assn., Calif. Continuing Edn. Assn., Phi Beta Kappa. Home: 344 S Peck Dr Beverly Hills CA 90212-3715 Office: McAlister H S 2808 W Glassell Ave Los Angeles CA 90026

STERN, ARTHUR PAUL, electronics company executive, electrical engineer; b. Budapest, Hungary, July 20, 1925; came to U.S., 1951, naturalized, 1956; s. Leon and Bertha (Frankfurter) S.; m. Edith M. Samuel; children: Daniel, Claude, Jacqueline. Diploma in Elec. Engring., Swiss Fed. Inst. Tech., Zurich, 1948; MSEE, Syracuse U., 1955. Mgr. electronic devices and applications lab. Gen. Electric Co., Syracuse, N.Y., 1957-61; dir. engring. Martin Marietta Corp., Balt., 1961-64; dir. ops. Bunker Ramo Corp., Canoga Park, Calif., 1964-66; v.p., gen. mgr. advanced products div. Magnavox, Torrance, Calif., 1966-79, pres. Magnavox Advanced Products and Systems Co., Torrance, 1980-90; vice chmn., bd. dirs. Magnavox Govt. and Indsl. Electronics Co., Ft. Wayne, Ind., 1987-90; pres. Ea. Beverly Hills Corp., 1991—, Calif.-Israel C. of C., 1994—; non-resident staff mem. MIT, 1956-59; instr. Gen. Elec. Bus. Mgmt., 1955-57. Chmn. engring. div. United Jewish Appeal, Syracuse, 1955-57; mem. adv. bd. dept. elec. engring. U. Calif., Santa Barbara, 1980-92; mem. Sch. Engring. Adv. and Devel. Council Calif. State U., Long Beach, 1985-90. Co-author: Transistor Circuit Engineering, 1957, Handbook of Automation, Computation and Control, 1961; also articles; U.S., fgn. patentee in field. Fellow AAAS, IEEE (pres. 1975, bd. dirs., officer 1970-77, guest editor spl. issue IEEE Trans. on Circuit Theory 1956, invited guest editor spl. issue Procs. IEEE on Integrated Electronics 1964, Centennial medal 1984, chmn. com. on U.S. competitiveness policy). Jewish.

STERN, DAVID GERALD, philosophy educator; b. London, Sept. 19, 1958; came to U.S., 1979; BA, Oxford (Eng.) U., 1979; MA, U. Pitts., 1980; PhD, U. Calif., Berkeley, 1987. Postdoctoral rschr. U. Alta., Edmonton, Can., 1987-88; asst. prof. philosophy U. Iowa, Iowa City, 1988-93; asst. prof. rhetoric U. Calif., Berkeley, 1993—. Author: Wittgenstein on Mind and Language, 1995; editor: Cambridge Companion to Wittgenshein, 1996; contbr. articles to profl. jours. Killam postdoctoral scholar U. Alta., 1987; May Brodbeck Humanities fellow U. Iowa, 1993. Mem. MLA, Am. Philos. Assn., Philosophy of Sci. Assn. Office: U Calif Berkeley Dept Rhetoric 2125 Dwinelle Hall Spc 2670 Berkeley CA 94720-2670

STERN, JAMES COPER, sales executive; b. N.Y.C., Dec. 12, 1925; s. George Charles and Ruth (Coper) S.; m. Judith Vinson, Oct. 31, 1963 (div. Mar. 1974); children: Hillary Anne, Renee Jean; m. Ruth Nussbacker Szold, Aug. 22, 1982. BA, NYU, 1949. Trainee, exec. asst. Gardner Advt. Co., N.Y.C., 1949-50; advt. mgr. NOPCO Chem. Co., Harrison, N.J., 1950-53; account exec. Ziv TV Programs, N.Y.C., 1954-56; sales rep. United Artists Associated, N.Y.C., 1957-61; v.p., sales mgr. Allied Artists TV, N.Y.C., 1961-70; exec. v.p., gen. sales mgr. ITC Entertainment, Inc., Studio City, Calif., 1970-89; pres. JCS Syndication Svcs., L.A., 1990—. Cpl. U.S. Army, 1944-46, ETO. Mem. Internat. Radio and TV Soc., Nat. Assn. TV Program Execs., Ind. TV Program Execs. Republican. Jewish. Home: 8455 Fountain Ave Apt 515 Los Angeles CA 90069-2543 Office: JCS Syndication Svcs 8455 Fountain Ave Apt 515 Los Angeles CA 90069-2543

STERN, JOHN LOUIS, real estate development and management executive; b. L.A., Feb. 11, 1924; s. Harold Melrose and Marion (Levi) S.; m. Eleanor Brill, July 3, 1948; children: Deborah, John B. BS, Calif. Inst. Tech., 1945; MBA, Stanford U., 1948. Real estate appraiser Winter Mortgage Co., L.A., 1948-49; real estate broker, sales mgr. Walter H. Leiment Co., L.A., 1949-51; owner JOhn L. Stern S&M Devel. Co., L.A., 1951—. Mem. Stanford Alumni Exec. bd. 1970s. Served to lt. (j.g.) USN, 1943-45. Mem. Beach Club (Santa Monica, Calif.), Maroon Creek Club (Aspen, Colo.), Cal. Tech Assocs., Stanford Alumni Assn., Riviera Country Club. Democrat. Jewish.

STERN, KINGSLEY ROWLAND, botanist, educator; b. Port Elizabeth, South Africa, Oct. 30, 1927; s. Julius Charles and Vera Grace (Estment) S.; m. Janet Elaine McLeland, June 9, 1956; children: Kevin Douglas, Sharon Maureen. BS, Wheaton (Ill.) Coll., 1949; MA, U. Mich., 1950; PhD, U. Minn., 1959. Instr. botany Hamline U., St. Paul, 1956-57; rsch. fellow in botany U. Minn., Mpls., 1957-58, instr., 1958-59; asst. prof. Chico (Calif.) State Coll., 1959-63, assoc. prof., 1963-68; prof. Calif. State U., Chico, 1968-92, prof. emeritus, 1992—; vis. prof. botany U. Hawaii, Honolulu, 1987; cons. to fed., state and local agys., Calif., 1976—. Author: Introductory Plant Biology, 1978; co-author: Botany, 1995; contbr. articles. to profl. jours. Fellow Conway McMillan Found., 1957-58; NSF grantee, 1963-72. Mem. Botanical Soc. Am., Am. Soc. Plant Taxonomists, Calif. Botanical Soc. (v.p. 1990-92). Office: Calif State U Dept Biolog Scis Chico CA 95929

STERN, MATTHEW ARNOLD, technical writer; b. Encino, Calif., July 14, 1961; s. Sheldon Simon and Barbara Jean (Bloom) S.; m. Elizabeth Shawn Newman, Dec. 22, 1990; 1 child, Stephanie Harriet. BA in English, Calif. State U., Northridge, 1985. Pub. rels. rep. EnTech Software, Sun Valley, Calif., 1983-85; freelance writer Reseda, Irvine, Calif., 1984-87; tech. writer Haba/Arrays, Inc., Van Nuys, Calif., 1985-86; sr. tech. writer AST Rsch., Inc., Irvine, 1986-95, Platinum Software, Irvine, Calif., 1995—. Author: (screenplay) Gilmore Field, 1994; columnist: Family Computing, 1988, Run, 1987-88. Recipient award of Merit Soc. for Tech. Comm., 1989, 90, 93, award of Achievement, 1991, 94, award of Achievement Internat. Publs. Competition, 1996, award of Excellence, 1997, Disting. Tech. Comm. award, 1995. Mem. Irvine Toastmasters Club, Toastmasters Internat. (pres. 1997), Soc. Tech. Comm. (Orange County chpt.). Home: 25716 Nugget Lake Forest CA 92630-4324

STERN, STANLEY, psychiatrist; b. N.Y.C., Apr. 5, 1933; s. Frank and Gussie S.; children: Marcus F., David S. BA cum laude, N.Y. U., 1953; MD, SUNY, 1957. Intern Ohio State U. Hosp., Columbus, 1957-58; resident in psychiatry Inst. Living, Hartford, Conn., 1958-60, Austen Riggs Ctr., Stockbridge, Mass., 1960-61; psychoanalytic tng. We. New Eng. Inst. for Psychoanalysis, New Haven, Conn., 1965-73; asst. clin. prof. psychiatry Yale U., New Haven, Conn., 1975-81; assoc. clin. prof. psychiatry U. Calif., San Diego, 1982-84; pvt. practice New Haven, 1965-82, La Jolla, Calif., 1982-84, Phoenix, 1984—; mem. faculty San Diego Psychoanalytic Inst., 1980-84; pres. Ariz. Psychoanalytic Study Group, Phoenix, 1986-88, Phoenix Psychoanalytic Study Group, 1986-88; tng. and supervising analyst So. Calif. Psychoanalytic Inst., 1989; chmn. edn. com. Ariz. Psychoanalytic New Tng. Facility, 1990-91; lectr., presenter, participant seminars and confs. in field. Contbr. article to profl. jours. Trustee, Gesell Inst., New Haven, 1986-88, Ctr. for the Exceptional Patient, New Haven; bd. dirs. ACLU. Capt. USAF, 1961-63. Mem. Am. Coll. Psychoanalysts, Am. Psychoanalytic Assn. (cert.), Am. Psychiatric Assn., Am. Acad. Psychoanalysts, Irene Josselyn Group Advancement of Psychoanalysis, So. Calif. Psychoanalytic Inst. and Soc. (faculty), San Diego Psychoanalytic Inst., Council for the Advancement of Psychoanalysis (treas. 1972-73, pres.-elect 1973-74, pres. 1974-75, councillor 1975-80), Phi Beta Kappa, Beta Lambda Sigma, Psi Chi. Home and Office: Box 32685 Phoenix AZ 85064 Address: 4438 E Arlington Rd Phoenix AZ 85018 *Personal philosophy: "Be a little kinder to each other" Aldous Huxley.*

STERNITZKE-HOLUB, ANN, elementary school educator; b. Oklahoma City, Okla., May 5, 1952; d. James Francis and Doris Josephine (Lahr) Sternitzke; m. James Robert Holub, Apr. 4, 1987. AA, Golden West Coll., Huntington Beach, Calif., 1972; BS, Calif. State U., Fullerton, 1975, postgrad., 1976. Cert. secondary multiple subject, phys. edn. and English tchr. grades kindergarten-12, Calif.; life cert. educator Calif. Cmty. Colls. Phys. edn. and fencing instr. Fullerton Coll., 1976-82; fencing instr. Golden West Coll., Huntington Beach, 1977-83, Calif. State U., Fullerton, 1983-86; elem. phys. edn. specialist Placentia-Yorba Linda (Calif.) Unified Sch. Dist., 1989-93, elem. tchr. Bryant Ranch Sch., 1993—; puppeteer Adventure City Amusement Park, Anaheim, Calif. Mem. support staff 1984 Olympics, Long Beach, 1984; entertainer Stagelight Family Prodns., Brea, Calif., 1993—. Grantee Disneyland, 1993, 94, 95, 96, 97. Mem. AAHPERD, U.S. Fencing Assn., U.S. Olympic Soc., U.S. Fencing Coaches Assn., Calif. State U. Alumni Assn. Republican. Office: Bryant Ranch Sch 24695 Paseo De Toronto Yorba Linda CA 92887-5116

STERNS, PATRICIA MARGARET, lawyer, consultant; b. Phoenix, Jan. 30, 1952; d. Lawrence Page and Mildred Dorothy (Barbaras) S. BA, Ariz. State U., 1974; JD, U. Ariz., 1977. Bar: Ariz. bar, 1978, U.S. Dist. Ct. Ariz., 1978, U.S. Supreme Ct. 1986. With Sterns and Tennen, Phoenix, 1978—; judge pro tempore Superior Ct. Ariz., County of Maricopa, 1983—; mem. Domestic Rels. Study Com., 1984-86, judge Jessup Internat. Moot Ct. Competition and semi-finals rounds, 1984—, regional rounds, 1981—; cons. internat. law; lectr. Am. Grad. Sch. Internat. Mgmt., 1982, Princeton U. Space Mfg. Facilities Conf., 1979; participant Internat. Astronautical Fedn., 1978—. Fellow Ariz. Bar Found.; mem. AIAA, ABA (family law, internat. law sects., aerospace law com.), Am. Soc. Internat. Law (space law sect.), Maricopa County Bar Assn. (family law sect.), Internat. Inst. Space Law (bd. dirs., sec., bd. dirs. U.S. membership IISL), Internat. Bar Assn., Internat. Acad. Astronautics (corr.), Firm Mem. Soc., Internat. Astronautical Fedn., Aviation/Space Writers Assn., Ariz. Bar Assn., Profl. Rodeo Cowboys Assn. (assoc.), Am. Quarter Horse Assn. Contbr. articles to profl. publs.; mem. Ariz. Law Rev. Office: 849 N 3rd Ave Phoenix AZ 85003-1408

STERRETT, JAMES MELVILLE, accountant, business consultant; b. Chicago, Dec. 25, 1949; s. James McAnlis and Antoinette (Galligan) S.; m. Joyce Mieko Motoda, Sept. 1, 1989; 1 child, Victoria Hanako. BS in Acctg., Chaminade U., Honolulu, 1988; MBA, Chaminade U., 1991. CPA, Hawaii. Cons. Profitability Cons., Honolulu, 1985-87; pres. Sterrett Cons. Group, Honolulu, 1987-88; auditor Deloitte & Touche, Honolulu, 1988-90; acct., cons. pvt. practice, Honolulu, 1990—. Mem. Nat. Soc. Pub. Accts., Nat. Assn. Tax Practitioners, Hawaii Soc. CPA's, Delta Epsilon, Sigma. Office: 1314 S King St Ste 650 Honolulu HI 96814-1941

STETLER, CHARLES EDWARD, English language educator; b. Pitts., Sept. 12, 1927; s. Charles Edward and Catherine (Seidel) S.; m. Ellen Donovan, June 25, 1956; (div. Jan. 1981); children: Peter, Paul, Casey; m. Kristin Jill Brown, July 17, 1984 (div. 1993); m. Mary Grace Aquino, Aug. 25, 1994. BA, Duquesne U., 1950, MA, 1962; PhD, Tulane U., 1966. Reporter Pitts. Sun Telegraph, 1957-62; instr. in English Rollins Coll., Winter Park, Fla., 1962-63; asst. prof. English Loyola U., New Orleans, 1963-67; prof. English Calif. State U., Long Beach, 1967-95; exch. prof. English U. Hull, Eng., fall 1984. Author poetry; contbr. articles to profl. jours. With USN, 1945-46, 50-52. Mem. Honor Soc. for Internat. Scholars, Phi Beta Kappa. Democrat. Home: 302 Chancery Ln Columbia SC 29229

STEVENS, ANN L. HENSE, art educator, artist; b. Toledo, Nov. 16, 1950; d. Robert Elmer and Helen Louise (Davis) Hense; m. Hobart W. Stevens, June 18, 1988; children: Megan, Parker. BS in Edn., Ohio U., 1972; MS, U. Toledo, 1976; MA, Bowling Green State U., 1981, MFA, 1982. Cert. K-12 art tchr., Ohio, Calif., Colo. Publicity dir. Assoc. Women Students Miami U., 1969; elem. and secondary tchr. art Sylvania (Ohio) Schs., 1972-79; mus. educator Toledo Mus. Art, 1973-88, Kidspace Mus., Pasadena, Calif., 1990-91; instr. art Monroe (Mich.) C.C., 1984-86, Bowling Green (Ohio) State U., 1985-86; secondary tchr. art Springfield (Ohio) Local Schs., 1986-88; elem. tchr. Arcadia (Calif.) Unified Schs., 1989-90; mus. educator Denver Art Mus., 1992-94, 96; chmn. Fibers Alive Competitive Art Exhibit, Toledo, 1984. Docent Pacific Asia Mus., Pasadena, 1988-90. Recipient best of show award Toledo Area Handweavers Guild, 1978; named outstanding tchg. asst. Bowling Green State U., 1983; scholar Miami U., 1979; grantee Denver Art Mus., 1994; recipient 2d Place award State Weaving Competition, Ohio, 1984. Mem. Handweavers Guild Boulder.

STEVENS, CHARLES J., prosecutor. BA in English, Colgate U., 1979; JD, U. Calif., Berkeley, 1982. Assoc. Gibson, Dunn & Crutcher, L.A., 1982-84; ptnr. in charge Gibson, Dunn & Crutcher, Sacramento, 1987-93; asst. U.S. atty. Office U.S. Atty., L.A., 1984-87; U.S. atty. ea. dist. Calif. U.S. Dept. Justice, Sacramento, 1993-97; ptnr., lawyer Steven & O'Connell Law Office, Sacremento, 1997—; mem. Civil Justice Reform Act com. for ea. dist. Biden Com. of Ea. Dist., 1991—; panel spkr. and lectr. in field. Contbr. articles to profl. jours. Master Anthony M. Kennedy Am. Inn. of Ct.; mem. FBA (chair program com. Sacramento chpt. 1992-93), State Bar Calif. (bd. editors Criminal Law News 1991-93). Office: Steven & O'Connell Law Office 400 Capitol Mall Ste 1450 Sacramento CA 95814*

STEVENS, CLYDE BENJAMIN, JR., property manager, retired naval officer; b. Denver, Oct. 10, 1908; s. Clyde Benjamin and Maybelle Olive (Boot) S.; m. Lucile Lillian-Louise Kip, May 5, 1933; children: Jane Stevens White, Donald Kip, Patricia Louise Stevens Schley. BS, U.S. Naval Acad., 1930; postgrad., U.S. Naval Postgrad. Sch., Annapolis, Md., 1939, U.S. Naval War Coll., Newport, R.I., 1947. Registered profl. engr. Commd. ensign USN, advanced through grades to rear adm., 1959; comdg. officer USS R-20, S-33 Plaice and Platte, 1950-52; comdr. officer USS Platte 50-52 Destroyer Squad 6, 1954-55; with torpedo prodn. and undersea weapons div. Bur. Ordnance, Washington, 1947-59; with USS Platte, 1950-52, Destroyer squad., 1955-56; program dir. Bur. Ordnance, Washington, 1952-55, 56-59; ret., 1959; product mgr. TRW, Inc., Cleve., 1959-65; rsch. engr. Boeing Co., Seattle, 1965-74, torpedo cons., 1985; apt. owner and mgr. Seattle, 1965—; torpedo cons. Goodyear Aerospace Co., Akron, Ohio, 1965. Patentee automobile generator. Decorated Navy Cross, Silver Star with oak leaf cluster. Mem. Seattle Apt. Assn. (bd. dirs. 1967-91), Army and Navy Club, Rainier Club. Republican. Episcopalian. Home and Office: 2339 Franklin Ave E Seattle WA 98102-3356

STEVENS, DAVID ALEC, medical educator; b. N.Y.C., June 3, 1940; m. Julie Anne Teece, Aug. 15, 1964; children: Joseph John, Emily Beth Stevens Marsh. BA, Cornell U., 1960; MD, U. Rochester, 1965. Diplomate Nat. Bd. Med. Examiners, Am. Bd. Internal Medicine; med. lic. Wis., Calif. Intern, asst. resident dept. medicine U. Wis. Hosps., Madison, 1965-67; rsch. assoc. Nat. Cancer Inst., Bethesda, Md., 1967-69; resident dept. medicine UCLA Med Ctr., 1969-70; fellow divsn. infectious diseases, dept. medicine Stanford (Calif.) U., 1970-72, asst. prof. divsn. infectious diseases dept. medicine, 1972-78; chief divsn. infectious diseases Santa Clara County-Valley Med. Ctr., San Jose, Calif., 1972—, assoc. chief dept. medicine, 1972—, epidemiologist, 1972—; assoc. prof. divsn. infectious diseases, dept. medicine Stanford U., 1978-85, assoc. prof. divsn. geographic medicine, dept. medicine, 1984-85, prof., 1985—; co-dir. microbiology lab. Santa Clara Valley Med. Ctr., 1972—; prin. investigator Infectious Diseases Rsch. Lab., Calif. Inst. Med. Rsch., San Jose, 1973—, bd. regents, 1978-90, 92—, sec.-treas., 1979-81, sci. dir. coun., 1986-88, pres., 1992—; mycology ref. lab. Pub. Health Lab. Svcs. Dept. Microbiology, U. London, 1979; dir. clin. labs. Calif. Inst. Med. Rsch., 1980—; co-dir. AIDS program Santa Clara Valley Med. Ctr., 1986-88, assoc. dir., 1988—. Author: (with others) Coccidioidomycosis, 1980; Contbr. articles to profl. jours; patentee in field. With USPHS, 1967-69. Ian Murray Meml. lectr. British Soc. Mycopathology, Canterbury, Eng., 1985. Fellow ACP, Am. Soc. Microbiology (chair mycology 1992-93), Infectious Diseases Soc. Am., Am. Acad. Microbiology; mem. AMA, AAUP, AAAS, Am. Fedn. Clin. Rsch., Am. Soc. Clin. Investigation, Fedn. Am. Scientists, Med. Mycology Soc. Ams., Calif. Med. Assn., Western Assn. Physicians, Calif. Collaborative Treatment Group, Santa Clara County Med. Soc., Internat. Soc. Human and Animal Mycology (clin. mycology com. 1985-91). Home: 19070 Portos Dr Saratoga CA 95070-5169 Office: Santa Clara Valley Med Ctr 751 S Bascom Ave San Jose CA 95128-2604

STEVENS, DAVID KING, civil engineer, educator; b. Kans. City, Kans., Dec. 17, 1954; s. Arthur David and Patricia (Williams) S.; m. Margaret Marie Cashell, May 18, 1985; children: Michael James, Abby Elizabeth. BSCE, Tufts U., 1976; PhD, U. Wis., 1983. Registered profl. engr., Ohio. Engr. irrigation U.S. Peace Corps, Malacca, Malaysia, 1976-78; rsch. assoc. U. Cin., 1984-86; asst. prof. Utah State U., Logan, 1986-90, assoc. prof., 1990—; cons. Soap and Detergent Assn., N.Y.C., 1982, Peer Cons., Washington, 1987-88, Dynamac Corp., Rockville, Md., 1989—, Am. Petroleum Inst. Contbr. articles to profl. jours. Recipient Cen. States Water Pollution Control Assn. Acad. Excellence award, 1981, Lewis H. Kessler award U. Wis., 1982; grantee EPA, U.S. Geol. Survey, Battelle Meml. Inst., 1984—, Nat. Inst. Environ. Health Scis., Electric Power Rsch. Inst. Mem. ASCE (former assoc. editor Jour. Environ. Engring.), Am. Water Works Assn., Internat. Assn. Water Quality, Water Environ. Fedn., Sigma Xi, Phi Kappa Phi, Tau Beta Pi. Office: Utah State U Umc # 4110 Logan UT 84322

STEVENS, EDWARD FRANKLIN, college president; b. Newcastle, Wyo., Sept. 7, 1940; s. Edward Downey and Esther Elizabeth (Watt) S.; m. Linda Elaine Loewenstein, June 3, 1962; children: Carla Sue, Cathy Lynne. Student, U. Denver, 1959-60; BA in Edn., Physics, Chemistry cum laude, Nebr. Wesleyan U., 1963; MA in Ednl. Psychology, Stats. and Measurement, U. Nebr., 1967; PhD in Higher Edn., Mktg., Mgmt., U. Minn., 1983; postdoctoral, Harvard U., 1991. Tchr., head basketball coach Alvo-Eagle (Nebr.) High Sch., 1963-64, Madison (Nebr.) High Sch., 1964-65; asst. basketball coach U. Nebr., Lincoln, 1965-67; head basketball coach, asst. prof. edn. Augustana Coll., Sioux Falls, S.D., 1967-71; v.p., gen. mgr. tng. Iseman divsn. U.S. Inds., Sioux Falls, 1971-74; chief devel. and instl. advancement officer Sioux Falls Coll., 1974-79, asst. prof. to prof., 1980-83; from exec. v.p. to exec. asst. pres. Kearny (Nebr.) State Coll. Found., 1979-80; pres. George Fox U., Newberg, Oreg., 1983—. Chmn. campaign Yamhill County United Way, Newberg, 1988; bd. commrs. Newberg Community Hosp., 1988-91. NDEA fellow, 1965; recipient Young Alumni Achievement award, Nebr. Wesleyan U., 1973, Leadership Fellows award, Bush Found., St. Paul, 1976. Mem. Am. Assn. Pres. Indep. Colls. and Univs., Nat. Christian Coll. Consortium (chmn. 1987-88), Nat. Assn. Intercollegiate Athletics (council pres., exec. com. 1988-92, chmn. 1992), Nat. Assn. Evangelicals (Christian higher edn. com.), Nat. Assn. Indep. Colls. and Univs., Oreg. Ind. Colls. Assn. (bd. dirs. 1983-92, chmn. 1986-87), Oreg. Ind. Colls. Found. (bd. dirs. 1983-92, vice chmn. 1993), Coun. of Ind. Colls. (bd. dirs. 1990), N.W. Assn. Schs. and Colls. (commn. on colls.), Internat. Assn. Univs. Pres., New Life 2000 (internat. com. reference), Rotary. Republican. Mem. Soc. Friends. Office: George Fox U Office of Pres 414 N Meridian St Newberg OR 97132-2697

STEVENS, ELEANOR SANDRA, professional services executive; b. Oklahoma City, Nov. 1, 1932; d. Benjamin Franklin and Mary Lou (Smith) Williams; children: Fred W., Nathandra, Benjiman, Ola Enaid. AS in medicine, Fresno State U., 1954; student Fresno Adult Edn., Los Angeles Trade Tech., 1972-73. Radio disc jockey, Fresno, Calif., 1954-55; bookkeeper L.A. County Assessor, 1961-69; supervisor Holzman-Begue Real Estate Co., L.A., 1969-73; dist. mgr. United Systems, Inc., L.A., 1973-77; pub. relations cons. Harold G. Simon & Assoc., Vernon, Calif., 1977-81; pres. Stevens Personalized Svcs., L.A., 1982—. Recipient cert. profl. devel. State of Calif., 1983. Mem. NAFE, Van Nuys Women's Referral Svc., D.B. & O. Charity and Social Club, Los Angeles Good Neighbor Council, Order Ea. Star. Methodist. Office: 3202 W Jefferson Blvd Los Angeles CA 90018-3230

STEVENS, GERALD D., secondary education educator, consultant; b. Seattle, Apr. 9, 1941; s. James Edward and Olga Rubina (Olsen) S.; m. Michele Christine Hayek, June 16, 1973; children: Heather Corrine, Wendy Jeannette, Gerald Michael. Student, U. Wash., 1963-65; BA in Polit. Sci., Calif. State U., L.A., 1989; MA, U. So. Calif., 1995, postgrad., 1995—. Cert. tchr., Calif. Bank auditor Nat. Bank Commerce, Seattle, 1965-72; pvt. practice GEMIC L.A., 1972-86; tchr. L.A. Unified Sch. Dist., 1986-96; cons. model schs. program Fgn. Policy Assn., Washington, 1990; presenter coalition essential schs. L.A. Unified Sch. Dist., 1990-91. Author: Redistributive Econ. Justice, 1993. Vol. C.L.A.R.E. Found., Santa Monica, 1989-91. With USMC, 1960-63, PTO. Mem. So. Calif. Social Sci. Assn. (bd. dirs. 1990-94, v.p.), United Tchrs. L.A., Sierra Club. Home: Unit 2 2101 Ocean Ave Santa Monica CA 90405-2228 Office: LA Unified Sch Dist 450 N Grand Ave Los Angeles CA 90012-2100

STEVENS, HENRY AUGUST, insurance agent, educator; b. Frankfurt, Main, Germany, July 21, 1921; came to U.S., 1940; m. Rosemary O'Neil, Mar. 23, 1963; children: Michael, Patrick; 1 child from previous marriage, H. Jack Fay. Student, U. Wis., 1943-44; grad., Dale Carnegie Sch., Richland, Wash., 1974. Theatre mgr. Sterling Theatres, Seattle, 1946-54, Alliance Amusement Co., Chgo., 1955-68; ins. agt. N.Y. Life Ins. Co., Richland, 1968—; regional v.p. Washington Assn. Life Underwriters, Richland, 1980; mem. adv. com. Wash. State Ins., Olympia, 1983-89. Chmn. bd. Richland YMCA, 1968; commr. Benton County Dyking Dist., Richland, 1970; chmn. Benton-Franklin Counties Bi-Centennial Commn., Tri-Cities, Wash., 1976; dist. chmn. Rep. Party, Benton County, 1980-96. Staff sgt. U.S. Army 1943-46. Recipient Nat. Quality award, Nat. Sales Achievement award. Mem. Tri-Cities Life Underwriters Assn. (pres. 1975, bd. dirs.), Tri-Cities Estate Planning Coun. (pres. 1984), Wash. State Assn. Life Underwriters (chmn. 1997), Kiwanis (pres. Chgo. club 1963, Richland club 1986-87, lt. gov. Pacific N.W. dist. 1983, chmn. dist. conv. 1971, 81, 91, sec. Pacific N.W. Found. 1994—). Home: 712 Riverside Dr Richland WA 99353-5216 Office: NY Life Ins Co 8203 W Quinault St Kennewick WA 99336-7117

STEVENS, JANET, illustrator; b. Dallas, Jan. 17, 1953; d. Jack and Frances Stevens; m. Ted Habermann; children: Lindsey Habermann, Blake Habermann. BFA, U. Colo., 1975. Illustrator children's books, 1979—. Writer, illustrator: From Pictures to Words: A Book about Making a Book, 1995; reteller, illustrator: Animal Fair, 1981, The Princess and the Pea (Hans Christian Anderson), 1982. Recipient Parents Choice award 1987, Notable Children's Trade Book in the Field of Social Studies citation Nat. Coun. for Social Studies-Children's Book Coun., 1987, Caldecott Honor citation Am. Libr. Assn., 1996, Notable Children's Book citation, 1996; recipient several state children's book awards. Home and Office: 3835 Spring Valley Rd Boulder CO 80304

STEVENS, JEFFREY S., chief of nuclear medicine; b. Newark, Dec. 24, 1942. BA, UCLA, 1965; MD, Stanford U., 1968. Diplomate Am. Bd. Radiology, Am. Bd. Nuclear Medicine. Intern medicine L.A. VA Hosp., 1968-69, resident in radiology, 1971-72; resident in radiology L.A. County Martin Luther King, Jr. Gen. Hosp., 1972-74, fellow nuclear medicine, 1974-75; chief nuclear medicine Portland (Oreg.) Adventist Med. Ctr., 1975-89; chief nuclear medicine Oreg. Health Scis. U., Portland, 1989—, asst. prof. radiology, 1989—. Office: Oreg Health Scis U 3181 SW Sam Jackson Park Rd Portland OR 97201-3011

STEVENS, JOHN GERALD, nuclear engineer; b. Mt. Holly, N.J., Mar. 27, 1965; s. Richard Wilson and Jerry Lee (Aiken) S.; m. Amy Dirks, 1988. BS in Nuclear Engring., Purdue U., 1988, MS in Nuclear Engring., 1991, PhD, 1995. Undergrad. rsch. asst. Purdue U. Sch. Nuclear Engring., West Lafayette, Ind., 1986-88, U.S. Dept. Energy nuclear engring. fellow, 1989-93; sr. nuclear engr. Studvik of Am., Idaho Falls, Idaho, 1993—; Am. Nuclear Soc. Chgo. sect. bilateral student exch. program participant Commisarit de l'Energie Atomique, Centre d'Etudes Nucleaires Cadarache, St. Paul lez Durance, France, summer 1988. Contbr. articles to profl. jours. Purdue U. Mortar Bd. grad. fellow, 1988. Mem. Am. Nuclear Soc. (Idaho local sect., grad. v.p. 1990-91), Inst. for Ops. Rsch. and Mgmt. Scis., Nature Conservancy, Nat. Wildlife Fedn., Nat. Audubon Soc., Idaho Audubon Soc., Wilderness Soc., Idaho Conservation League, Alpha Nu Sigma. Home: 254

W 19th St Idaho Falls ID 83402-4439 Office: Studsvik of Am 477 Shoup Ave Ste 105 Idaho Falls ID 83402-3658

STEVENS, JOHN JOSEPH, physician; b. Hartford, Conn., Dec. 19, 1929; s. John Joseph and Florence Martha (Wenning) S.; m. Mary Catherine Zeuhlke, Sept. 20, 1956; children: Kathleen, John, Margaret, Erich. BS cum laude, Boston Coll., 1951; MD cum laude, Tufts U., 1955. Diplomate Am. Bd. Internal Medicine, Am. Bd. Allergy and Immunology. Intern U.S. Naval Hosp., Bethesda, Md., 1955-56; resident internal medicine U.S.N. Hosp., Oakland, Calif., 1959-61; fellow in allergy Scripps Clinic and Rsch. Found., La Jolla, Calif., 1962-63; asst. chest svc., head allergy clinic U.S. Naval Hosp., San Diego, 1962-64; head allergy clinic U.S. Naval Hosp., Oakland, 1964-66, asst. chief medicine, 1966; staff assoc. divsn. allergy imm. rheumatology Scripps Clinic and Rsch. Found., La Jolla, 1966-67; pvt. practice allergy and clin. immunology La Jolla, San Diego, 1967-95; from asst. clin. prof. to clin. prof. medicine and pediatrics U. Calif., San Diego, 1973-1991, clin. prof. medicine and pediatrics, 1991—. Capt. USNR ret. Fellow Am. Acad. Allergy, Am. Coll. Physicians, Am. Assn. Cert. Allergists; mem. AMA, Calif. Med. Assn. (mem. appeals com. 1973—, adv. panel on allergy 1976-78), San Diego Allergy Soc. (pres. elect 1969, pres. 1970, chmn. ethics and med. review com. 1973, 75, mem. liaison com. with Found. of Med. Care, 1974-84), San Diego County Med. Soc. (mem. med. review com. 1972-90, chair 1983-85, chair loss prevention 1983-90, seminar moderator, mem. profl. conduct com. 1985-90), San Diego Acad. Medicine (treas. 1969, 70, 71, v.p. 1973), The Lung Assn. San DIego and Imperial Counties (mem. bd. dirs. 1972-73, mem. physical conditioning for asthmatics com. 1968-73, chmn. 72-73), San Diego Soc. Internal Medicine (mem. liaison com. with Found. of Med. Care 1974), San Diego Found. for Med. Care (trustee 1993-95, mem. com. 1993-95), Internat. Assn. Allergology and Clin. Immunology, Alpha Omega Alpha Honor Soc. Roman Catholic. Office: 9610 Granite Ridge Dr Ste B San Diego CA 92123-2661

STEVENS, MICHAEL KEITH, artist; b. Gilroy, Calif., July 14, 1945; s. Robert Louis and Jane Elizabeth (McCreery) S.; m. Suzanne Adan, Sept. 5, 1970. AA, Am. River Coll., 1965; BA, Calif. State U., Sacramento, 1967; MA, Calif. State U., 1969. Cert. tchr. community coll., secondary edn., Calif. guest artist and lectr. various instns., including Michael Himovitz Gallery, Sacramento, 1993, Oakland Mus., 1992, Humboldt State U., Arcata, Calif., 1991, U. Calif., Davis, 1991, others; curator, panelist in field. One-person shows include Braunstein/Quay Gallery, San Francisco, 1977, 78, 79, 82, 84, 86, 89, 92, 94, 97, Ovsey Gallery, L.A., 1990, Am. River Coll., 1987, Calif. State U., Chico, 1986, Himovitz/Salomon Gallery, Sacramento, 1984, Betsy Rosenfield Gallery, Chgo., 1981, 83, 85, 88, Michael Himovitz Gallery, Sacramento, 1993; group shows include Crocker Art Mus., Sacramento, 1994, Am. Cultural Ctr., Brussels, 1992, Oakland (Calif.) Mus., 1992, 94, Meml. Union Gallery U. Calif., Davis, 1994, Ark. Art Ctr., Little Rock, 1995, numerous others; articles. Recipient James D. Phelan award in art for sculpture, Walnut Creek Civic Arts Gallery, 1982, Pub. Art Commn., Cherry Island Golf Course, Sacramento Met. Arts Commn., 1988.

STEVENS, MURIEL KAUIMAEOLE LEE, elementary educator; b. Hana, Hawaii, May 29, 1942; d. Charles Pohaku and Violet Leimamo (Wahihako) Lee; m. James Gary Stevens, 1964 (div. 1976); 1 child, James Todd (dec.). AS, Ch. Coll. Hawaii, 1962; BS in Edn., Brigham Young U., 1964; postgrad., U. Utah, 1969, U. Hawaii, 1974—, U. Ala., 1990. Cert. elem. tchr., Hawaii. 1st grade tchr. Woodstock Elem. Sch., Salt Lake City, 1965-69; kindergarten-1st grade team tchr. Ewa (Hawaii) Elem. Sch., 1971-78; kindergarten tchr. Honowai Elem. Sch., Waipahu, Hawaii, 1978—; aerospace tchr., coord. after sch. improvement program Honowai Elem. Sch., 1991, 95; mem. Citizen Amb. Program, Spokane, 1987-95; participant Tchr. in Space program NASA, 1985-86. Spiritual living tchr. LDS Ch., Kaneohe, 1994, choir mem., 1992-94, sem. tchr., single adult rep. Waipahu II ward, 1996; amb. People to People Internat., Spokane, Wash., 1987-95. With CAP, 1985-95. Recipient Aerospace Edn. Achievement award Aux. USAF CAP, 1985. Mem. ASCD, Hawaii Parent, Tchr., Student Assn., NEA, Hawaii State Tchrs. Assn., Wilson Ctr. Assocs., Acad. Polit. Sci., World Aerospace Edn. Orgn. Republican. Home: PO Box 658 Wahiawa HI 96786-0658 Office: Honowai Elem Sch 94-600 Honowai St Waipahu HI 96797-1307

STEVENS, SERITA DEBORAH MENDELSON, psychiatric and forensic nurse, writer; b. Chgo., Jan. 20, 1949; d. Albert Stanley and Frances Tzipporah (Rosenberg) Mendelson; m. Raymond Glassenberg, Aug. 29, 1971 (div. 1980); m. Barrie Barr, Oct. 20, 1992 (div. Oct. 15, 1993); 1 stepchild, Shaina Rose Barr; 1 adopted child, Tzipporah Alexandra Stevens. BSN, U. Ill., Chgo., 1971; MA in Lit. with honors, Antioch U., London, 1979. Cert. Sane-Sexual asst. nurse examiner, death scene investigation forensic nurse. Staff nurse Dept. of Psychiatry, 1990—; instr. U. So. Calif., L.A., 1983-84, Loyola U., 1981-82, Santa Monica Calif. City Coll., 1981-82; investigative reporter CBS; writer's digest instr., 1988—; Judge of Hemmett, Edgar and Malice awards. Author: This Bitter Ecstasy, 1981, Tame the Wild Heart, 1983, The Shriekings Shadows of Penporth Island, 1983, A Dream Forever, 19984, Cagney and Lacey, 1985, Bloodstone Inheritance, 1985, A Gathering Storm, 1986, Secrets at Seventeen, 1986, Days of Our Lives, 1986, Champagne for Two, 1986, Buttercup Dreams, 1987, Lighting and Fire, 1987, Daughters of Desire, 1987, Deceptive Desires, 1987, Lilac Dreams, 1986, Unholy Alliance, 1991, Deadly Doses: A Writer's Guide to Poisons, 1991, Red Sea, Dead Sea, 1991, Bagels for Tea, 1993; co-author: The Nurses, 1966, Fine Art of Murder, 1994 (Anthony award); numerous short stories; videos: Champagne for Two, Lilac Dreams; contbr. articles to writers' mags. and jours. Recipient Cape Cod Writer's scholarship, Best Synopsis award Dell Publishing. Mem. Soc. Children's Books Writers, Mystery Writers Am. (bd. dirs. S. Calif. chpt. 1987-88), Romance Writers Am. (regional bd. dirs.), Internat. Assn. Forensic Nurses, Sisters in Crime (speakers bur. coord., bd. dirs. 1993-95, Am. Crime Writers, Internat. Crime Writers, Pen Women. Democrat. Jewish. Office: PO Box 7908 Mission Hills CA 91346-7908

STEVENS, STEPHEN EDWARD, psychiatrist; b. Phila.; s. Edward and Antonia S.; BA cum laude, LaSalle Coll., 1950; MD, Temple U., Phila., 1954; LLB, Blackstone Sch. Law, 1973; m. Isabelle Helen Gallacher, Dec. 27, 1953. Intern, Frankford Hosp., Phila., 1954-55; resident in psychiatry Phila. State Hosp., 1955-58; practice medicine specializing in psychiatry Woodland Hills, Calif., 1958-63, Santa Barbara, Calif., 1970-77; asst. supt. Camarillo (Calif.) State Hosp., 1963-70; cons. ct. psychiatrist Santa Barbara County, 1974-77; clin. dir. Kailua Mental Health Ctr., Oahu, Hawaii, 1977—. Author: Treating Mental Illness, 1961, Survival and the Fifth Dimension, 1997. Served with M.C., USAAF. Diplomate Am. Bd. Psychiatry and Neurology. Decorated Purple Heart. Fellow Am. Geriatrics Soc. (founding); mem. Am. Acad. Psychiatry and Law, AMA, Am. Psychiat. Assn., Am. Legion, DAV (Oahu chpt. 1), Caledonia Soc., Am. Hypnosis Soc., Am. Soc. Adolescent Psychiatry, Hawaiian Canoe Club, Honolulu Club, Elks (BPOE 616), Aloha String Band (founder and pres.). Home: PO Box 26413 Honolulu HI 96825-6413

STEVENS, THEODORE FULTON, senator; b. Indpls., Nov. 18, 1923; s. George A. and Gertrude (Chancellor) S.; m. Ann Mary Cherrington, Mar. 29, 1952 (dec. 1978); children—Susan B., Elizabeth H., Walter C., Theodore Fulton, Ben A.; m. Catherine Chandler, 1980; 1 dau.; Lily Irene. B.A., U. Calif. at Los Angeles, 1947; LL.B., Harvard U., 1950. Bar: Calif., Alaska, D.C., U.S. Supreme Ct. bars. Pvt. practice Washington, 1950-52, Fairbanks, Alaska, 1953; U.S. atty. Dist. Alaska, 1953-56; legis. counsel, asst. to sec., solicitor Dept. Interior, 1956-60; pvt. practice law Anchorage, 1961-68; mem. Alaska Ho. of Reps., 1965-68, majority leader, speaker pro tem, 1967-68; U.S. senator for Alaska, 1968—, asst. Rep. leader, 1977-85; chmn. Sen. Appropriations Com. Served as 1st lt. USAAF, World War II. Mem. ABA, Alaska Bar Assn., Calif. Bar Assn., D.C. Bar Assn., Am. Legion, VFW. Lodges: Rotary, Pioneers of Alaska, Igloo #4. Home: PO Box 100879 Anchorage AK 99510-0879 Office: US Senate 522 Hart Senate Bldg Washington DC 20510

STEVENS, THOMAS EDWARD, aerospace engineer; b. Peoria, Ill., Mar. 16, 1965; s. Edward Lee and Dorothy Lorraine (Wozniak) S.; m. Kimberly Marie Scheirer, Sept. 23, 1989; children: Kyle Glen, Kevin Thomas, Megan Lorraine. AAS, Ill. Cen. Coll., 1985; BS in Astronaut. Engring., U. Ill., 1987; MS in Astronaut. Engring., West Coast U., 1991. With engr. profl. program, Western Space and Missile Ctr. USAF, Vandenberg AFB, Calif., 1987-88, telemetry monitoring officer 6595 Test/Evaluation Group, 1988-92, space launch test mgr. Space & Missile Systems Ctr., 1992-95, with Atlas 2 SLC-3E Activation divsn. Space & Missile Systems Ctr., 1995—. Assoc. fellow AIAA (treas. Vandenberg sect. 1988-93, chmn. elect 1993-94, chmn. 1994-95, chmn. honors and awards 1996-97, chmn. Lompoc Sci. Fair 1994-97). Office: Det 9 SMC/CLFA Ste 173 1515 Iceland Ave Vandenberg AFB CA 93437

STEVENS, WILBUR HUNT, accountant; b. Spencer, Ind., June 20, 1918; s. John Vosburgh and Isabelle Jane (Strawser) S.; m. Maxine Dodge Stevens, Sept. 28, 1941; children: Linda Maxine Piffero, Deborah Anne Augello. BS, U. Calif., Berkeley, 1949, MBA, 1949. CPA, Calif.; cert. fraud examiner. Staff acct. McLaren, Goode, West & Co., San Francisco, 1949-52; mng. ptnr. Wilbur H. Stevens & Co., Salinas, Calif., 1952-70; regional ptnr. Fox & Co., CPAs, Salinas, 1970-73; nat. dir. banking practice Fox & Co., CPAs, Denver, 1973-80; pres., chmn. Wilbur H. Stevens, CPA, PC, Salinas, 1980-94; chmn. Stevens, Sloan & Shah, CPAs, 1994—; adj. prof. acctg. U. Denver, 1975-78; faculty mem. Assemblies for Bank Dirs., So. Meth. U., Dallas, 1976-81, Nat. Banking Sch., U. Va., Charlottesville, 1979-87; chmn., dir. Valley Nat. Bank, 1963-71. Editor Issues in CPA Practice, 1975; contbr. articles to profl. jours. Capt. AUS, 1942-53. Decorated Bronze Star; Frank G. Drum fellow U. Calif., Berkeley, 1949. Mem. AICPA (v.p. 1971), Am. Acctg. Assn., Am. Assembly Collegiate Schs. Bus. (accreditation coun. 1975-78, 81-84), Nat. Assn. State Bds. Accountancy (pres. 1976-77), Calif. Soc. CPAs (pres. 1968-69, Disting. Svc. award 1988), Acctg. Rsch. Assn. (pres. 1973-75), Assn. Cert. Fraud Examiners, Burma Star Assn., CBI Vets. Assn., 14 AF Assn., Hump Pilots Assn., Acad. Acctg. Historians, Commonwealth Club Calif., Masons (master 1992, 97, grand lodge com. taxation), Knight Tamplar, 32 degree Scottish Rite, Nat. Sojourners (pres. Monterey Bay chpt. 1996), Heroes of '76 (comdr John C. Fremont chpt. 1996-97), Salinas High Twelve Club (pres. 1995), QCCC, London, Rotary (dist. gov. 1983, chmn. internat. fellowship accounts 1994-96, Paul Harris fellow 1978), Phi Beta Kappa, Beta Gamma Sigma (v.p. 1949), Beta Alpha Psi. Republican. Methodist. Home: 38 Santa Ana Dr Salinas CA 93901-4136 Office: 975 W Alisal St Ste D Salinas CA 93901-1148

STEVENSON, JAMES GEOFFREY, pediatrician and cardiologist; b. Long Beach, Calif., Feb. 22, 1945; s. James Terry and Marie Dorothy (Lovell) S.; children: Brittany Jennifer, Emily Andrea. AB, Occidental Coll., L.A., 1966; MD, Baylor Coll. Medicine, Houston, 1970. Diplomate Am. Bd. Pediatrics, Am. Coll. Cardiology. Intern Children's Hosp./U. Wash., Seattle, resident; pediatric cardiologist Naval Regional Med. Ctr., San Diego, 1974-76; asst. prof. pediatrics U. Wash., Seattle, 1976-80, assoc. prof., 1980-85; prof. pediatrics U. Wash., 1985—; hosp.-based practice pediatric cardiology Seattle; staff Children's Hosp. and Med. Ctr., Seattle, U. Wash. Med. Ctr., Seattle, Providence Med. Ctr., Seattle, Swedish Hosp. Med. Ctr. Contbr. numerous articles and abstracts to profl. jours.; lectr. in field. Lt. comdr. USN, 1974-76. Recipient Christian Doppler award in echocardiography Internat. Soc. Intraoperative Cardiovascular Ultrasound, 1992. Fellow Am. Coll. Cardiology; mem. Soc. Pediatric Echo (sec. 1983-85, treas. 1985-87), Am. Soc. Echocardiography (bd. dirs. 1985-88, 90-93), Am. Registry Diagnostic Med. Sonographers (bd. dirs. 1990-93), Internat. Cardiac Doppler Soc. (bd. dirs. 1984-92), Am. Heart Assn. (mem. coun. 1987—). Office: Children's Hosp Cardiology CH-11 4800 Sand Point Way NE Seattle WA 98105-3901

STEVENSON, JAMES RALPH, school psychologist, author; b. Kemmerer, Wyo., June 29, 1949; s. Harold Ralph and Dora (Borino) S.; m. Alice M. Paolucci, June 17, 1972; children: Tiffany Jo, Brian Jeffrey. BA, U. No. Colo., 1971, MA, 1974, EdS, 1975. Lic. elem. sch. counselor, sch. psychologist, Colo.; nationally cert. sch. psychologist. Sch. psychologist Jefferson County Pub. Schs., Golden, Colo., 1975-87, 89-91, Weld County Sch. Dist. 6, Greeley, Colo., 1987-89, Weld Bd. Coop. Edn. Svcs., LaSalle, Colo., 1991-95; spl. edn. coord. Weld Bd. Coop. Edn. Svcs., LaSalle, 1995; sch. psychologist Fort Lupton (Colo.) Schs., 1995—; ltd. pvt. practice sch. psychologist Pathways, Greeley, 1994—. Asst. coach Young Am. Baseball, Greeley, 1989, 90, head coach, 1992, 93; asst. basketball coach Recreation League for 6th-7th Grades, 1992, 93. U. No. Colo. scholar, 1974. Mem. NEA, NASP (alt. del. Colo. chpt. 1975-77, dir. Apple II users group Washington chpt. 1989-95), Colo. Soc. Sch. Psychologists (chmn. task force on presch. assessment 1991-96), Colo. Edn. Assn., Ft. Lupton Edn. Assn., Jefferson County Psychologists Assn. (sec. 1986-87), Colo. Assn. for Play Therapy, Am. Orthopsychiat. Assn. Democrat. Roman Catholic. Home: 1937 24th Ave Greeley CO 80631-5027 Office: Fort Lupton Schs 301 Reynolds St Fort Lupton CO 80621-1329

STEVENSON, JAMES RICHARD, radiologist, lawyer; b. Ft. Dodge, Iowa, May 30, 1937; s. Lester Lawrence and Esther Irene (Johnson) S.; m. Sara Jean Hayman, Sept. 4, 1958; children: Bradford Allen, Tiffany Ann, Jill Renee, Trevor Ashley. BS, U. N.Mex., 1959; MD, U. Colo., 1963; JD, U. N.Mex. 1987. Diplomate Am. Bd. Radiology, Am. Bd. Nuclear Medicine, Am. Bd. Legal Medicine, 1989; Bar: N.Mex. 1987, U.S. Dist. Ct. N.Mex. 1988. Intern U.S. Gen. Hosp., Tripler, Honolulu, 1963-64; resident in radiology U.S. Gen. Hosp., Brook and San Antonio, Tex., 1964-67; radiologist, ptnr. Van Atta Labs., Albuquerque, 1970-88, Radiology Assocs. of Albuquerque, 1988—, pres., 1994-96; radiologist, ptnr. Civerolo, Hansen & Wolf, Albuquerque, 1988-89; adj. asst. prof. radiology U. N.Mex., 1970-71; pres. med. staff AT & SF Meml. Hosp., 1979-80, chief of staff, 1980-81, trustee, 1981-83. Author: District Attorney manual, 1987. Participant breast screening, Am. Cancer Soc., Albuquerque, 1987-88; dir. profl. divsn. United Way, Albuquerque, 1975. Maj. U.S. Army 1963-70, Vietnam; col. M.C. USAR, 1988—. Decorated Bronze Star. Allergy fellow, 1960. Med.-Legal Tort Scholar award, 1987. Fellow Am. Coll. Radiology (councilor 1980-86, mem. med. legal com. 1990-96), Am. Coll. Legal Medicine, Am. Coll. Nuclear Medicine, Radiology Assn. of Albuquerque; mem. AMA (Physicians' Recognition award 1969—), Am. Soc. Law & Medicine, Am. Arbitration Assn., Albbuquerque Bar Assn., Am. Coll. Nuclear Physicians (charter), Soc. Nuclear Medicine (v.p. Rocky Mountain chpt. 1975-76), Am. Inst. Ultrasound in Medicine, N.Am. Radiol. Soc. (chmn. med. legal com. 1992-95), N.Mex. Radiol. Soc. (pres. 1978-79), N.Mex. Med. Soc. (chmn. grievance com.), Albuquerque-Bernalillo County Med. Soc. (scholar 1959), Nat. Assn. Health Lawyers, ABA (antitrust sect. 1986—), N. Mex. State Bar, Albuquerque Bar Assn., Sigma Chi. Republican. Methodist. Club: Albuquerque Country. Lodges: Elks, Masons, Shriners. Home: 3333 Santa Clara Ave SE Albuquerque NM 87106-1530 Office: Medical Arts Imaging Ctr A-6 Med Arts Sq 801 Encino Pl NE Albuquerque NM 87102-2612

STEVENSON, PATRICIA KENNARD, artist, journalist; b. Pitts., Mar. 15, 1932; d. Ernest Spencer and Alice Ethalinda (Thompson) Kennard; m. Larry Dale Arnhart, Mar. 16, 1949 (div. 1954); 1 child, Tom Ray; m. Donald Andrus Fife, July 9, 1961 (div. 1963), 1 child, Alisa Melita; m. William Arnold Stevenson, Nov. 10, 1964 (dec. Nov. 1991); stepchildren: Kathleen Bates, William Eugene, Carol A. Robbins. Student, Internat. Corr. Sch., Milw., 1954-57. Artist, instr. self-employed, Nampa, Idaho, 1961-65, Lovelock, Nev., 1965-68; reporter Rev.-Miner, Lovelock, 1967-68; reporter, columnist, photographer, advt. Fallon (Nev.) Eagle Standard, 1968-70; pub. rels. dir., editor newsletter Nev. State Edn. Assn., Carson City, 1970-71; founding pub., editor Lahontan Valley News, Fallon, 1971-75; editor Fallon Eagle-Standard, 1978-84; graphic artist, compositor Loganberry Press, Fallon, 1985-89; artist, instr. self-employed, Fallon, 1989—; rural corr. CBS Affiliate, Reno, 1971-75, Reno Newspapers, 1984-86; judge various speech competitions. Author articles; executed mural Scenes in Early Mining Camp, 1990. Charter pres. Rep. Fed. Women's Club, Fallon, 1968. Recipient awards Nev. State Press Assn., 1969, Churchill County Fair, 1989, Best of Show award Walker Lake Art Club, 1993, 1st place miniature, 1996, 1st place-acrylic ElDorado Gallery Miniature Show, 1993, Best of Show Purchase award Nev. C.C., 1996. Mem. Nev. Artists Assn. (past bd. dirs., editor newsletter 1991-93), Lahontan Valley Artists Assn. (pres. 1993), Sierra Watercolor Soc. Home: 4020 Reno Hwy Fallon NV 89406-9304

STEVENSON, ROBERT MURRELL, music educator; b. Melrose, N.Mex., July 3, 1916; s. Robert Emory and Ada (Ross) S. AB, U. Tex., El Paso, 1936; grad., Juilliard Grad. Sch. Music, 1938; MusM, Yale, 1939; PhD, U. Rochester, 1942; STB cum laude, Harvard U., 1943; BLitt, Oxford (Eng.) U.; Th.M., Princeton U.; DMus honoris causa, Cath. U. Am., 1991; LHD honoris causa, Ill. Wesleyan U., 1992; LittD honoris causa, Universidade Nova de Lisboa, 1993. Instr. music U. Tex., 1941-43, 46; faculty Westminster Choir Coll., Princeton, N.J., 1946-49; faculty research lectr. UCLA, 1981, mem. faculty to prof. music, 1949—; vis. asst. prof. Columbia, 1955-56; vis. prof. Ind. U., Bloomington, 1959-60, U. Chile, 1965-66, Northwestern U., Chgo., 1976, U. Granada, 1992; cons. UNESCO, 1977; Louis Charles Elson lectr. Libr. of Congress, Washington, 1969; inaugural prf. musicology Nat. U. Mex., 1996. Author: Music in Mexico, 1952, Patterns of Protestant Church Music, 1953, La musica en la catedral de Sevilla, 1954, 85, Music Before the Classic Era, 1955, Shakespeare's Religious Frontier, 1958, The Music of Peru, 1959, Juan Bermudo, 1960, Spanish Music in the Age of Columbus, 1960, Spanish Cathedral Music in the Golden Age, 1961, La musica colonial en Colombia, 1964, Protestant Church Music in America, 1966, Music in Aztec and Inca Territory, 1968, Renaissance and Baroque Musical Sources in the Americas, 1970, Music in El Paso, 1970, Philosophies of American Music History, 1970, Written Sources for Indian Music Until 1882, 1972, Christmas Music From Baroque Mexico, 1974, Foundations of New World Opera, 1973, Seventeenth Century Villancicos, 1974, Latin American Colonial Music Anthology, 1975, Vilancicos Portugueses, 1976, Josquin in the Music of Spain and Portugal, 1977, American Musical Scholarship, Parker to Thayer, 1978, Liszt at Madrid and Lisbon, 1980, Wagner's Latin American Outreach, 1983, Spanish Musical Impact Beyond the Pyrenees, 1250-1500, 1985, La Música en las catedrales españolas del Siglo de Oro, 1993; contbg. editor: Handbook Latin Am. Studies, 1976—; editor Inter-Am. Music Rev., 1978—; contbr. to New Grove Dictionary of Music and Musicians, 17 other internat. encys. Served to capt. U.S. Army, 1943-46, 49. Decorated Army Commendation ribbon; fellow Ford Found., 1953-54, Gulbenkian Found., 1966, 81, Guggenheim Found., 1962, NEH, 1974, Comité Conjunto Hispano-Norteamericano (Madrid), 1989; recipient Fulbright rsch. awards, 1958-59, 64, 70-71, 88-89, Carnegie Found. tchg. award, 1955-56, Gabriela Mistral award OAS, 1985, Heitor Villa Lobos Jury award OAS, 1988, OAS medal, 1986, Cert. Merit Mexican Consulate San Bernardino, Calif., 1987, Silver medal Spanish Ministry Culture, 1989, Gold medal Real Conservatorio Superior, 1994. Mem. Am. Musicol. Soc. (hon. life, Pacific SW chpt.), Real Academia de Bellas Artes, Hispanic Soc. Am., Am. Liszt Soc. (cons. editor), Heterofonia (cons. editor), Brazilian Musicol. Soc. (hon.), Portuguese Musicol. Soc. (hon.), Argentinian Musicol. Soc. (hon.), Orden Andrés Bello, Primera Clase, Venezuela, 1992. Office: UCLA Dept Music 405 Hilgard Ave Los Angeles CA 90024-1301 *American achievements are as nothing unless they are written about and remembered. My mission has been to rescue the musical past of the Americas. Present-day composers are too busy making their own music to worry about their predecessors. As a result, every new generation of composers thinks that they are the first ones to descry Mount Olympus. Not so. The past is a succession of musical and artistic glories.*

STEVENSON, SARAH SCHOALES, rancher, business owner; b. N.Y.C., Sept. 1, 1944; d. Dudley Nevison and Virginia Jocelyn (Vanderlip) Schoales; m. David Earl Hollatz, Jan. 27, 1968 (div. June 1985); children: Melissa Virginia, Peter David; m. Richard Stevenson, Sept. 1, 1995. BS, U. Wis., 1966; postgrad., U. So. Calif., L.A., 1966. Copywriter Max W. Becker Advt., Long Beach, Calif., 1966-67; advt. dir. officers news USN, Coronado, Calif., 1968-70; with syndicate dept. Morgan Stanley & Co., N.Y.C., 1970-72; lay-out asst. North Castle News, Armonk, N.Y., 1972-75; performer, writer Candy Band, Pound Ridge, N.Y., 1975-82; owner, mgr. Circle Bar Guest Ranch, Utica, Mont., 1983—; bd. dirs. Park Inn, Lewistown, Mont. Artist, composer: Play Me a Song, 1978, Going Home, 1980; composer: (mus. play) Elsie Piddock, 1979, Secret Garden, 1981, Windows, 1989. Soloist Hobson (Mont.) Meth. Ch., 1983—; founder What the Hay, Utica, 1990—. Mem. Mont. Emergency Med. Assn. (bd. dirs. 1990—), Dude Rancher's Assn. (bd. dirs. 1989—, pres. 1996, 97). Episcopalian. Home and Office: Circle Bar Guest Ranch Utica MT 59452

STEWARD, HAL DAVID, correspondent; b. East St. Louis, Ill., Dec. 2, 1918; s. Owen Bob and Margaret Alice (Martin) S.; m. Dawn Jochebed Bentata, Aug. 18, 1945 (dec. Apr. 1968). BS, Boston U., 1961; LLB, LaSalle Ext. U., 1949; PhD, Columbia Pacific U., 1979. Commd. sgt. U.S. Army, 1937, advanced through ranks to lt. col., ret., 1961; reporter Los Angeles Examiner, 1961-62, San Diego Union, 1962-64; writer San Diego, 1964-69, 72-74; asst. dir. dept. human resources devel. State of Calif., Sacramento, 1970-71; exec. editor The Daily Chronicle, Centralia, Wash., 1975-78; writer Denver, 1982—; roving corr. Newsletter on Newsletters, Rhinebeck, N.Y., 1985—; flight instr. Elma (Wash.) Airport, 1981-82; adjunct faculty Columbia Pacific U., 1981—. Author: The Successful Writer's Guide, 1970, Money-making Secrets of the Millionaires, 1972, Winning In Newsletters, 1989; contbr. articles to nat. mags. Asst. to Lt. Gov. Calif., 1971. Decorated Bronze Star medal with oak leaf cluster. Mem. Soc. Profl. Journalists, Authors Guild, Investigative Reporters and Editors, Nat. Press Club, Denver Press Club, San Diego Press Club. Home: 5240 Fiore Ter # J-306 San Diego CA 92122-5636

STEWARD, LESTER HOWARD, addictiologist, academic administrator; b. Burt, Iowa, Nov. 6, 1930; s. Walterand Helen Steward; m. Patricia Byrness Roach, June 17, 1953; children: Donald Howard, Thomas Eugene, Susan Elaine, Joan Marsha. BS, Ariz. State U., 1958, MA in Sci. Edn., 1969; PhD in Psychology, Calif. Coast U., 1974; postgrad., Escuela Nat. U., Mex., 1971-80; MD, Western U. Hahnemann Coll., 1980. Rscher. drug abuse and alcoholism Western Australia U., Perth, Australia, 1970-71; intern in psychiatry Helix Hosp., San Diego, Calif., 1971-72; rscher. drug addiction North Mountain Behavioral Inst., Phoenix, 1975-77; exec. v.p., chief exec. officer James Tyler Kent Coll., 1977-80; pres., chief exec. officer Western U. Sch. Medicine, 1980-86; instr. psychology USN Westpac, Subic Bay, Philippines, 1988-91; pvt. practice preventive medicine Tecate, Baja California, Mexico, 1971-88; instr. Modern Hypnosis Instrn. Ctr., 1974—, Maricopa Tech. Community Coll., Phoenix, 1975-77; mem. Nt. Ctr. Homeopathy, Washington, Menninger Found., Wichita, Kans. Contbr. numerous papers to profl. confs. Leader Creighton Sch. dist. Boy Scouts Am., Phoenix, 1954-58. Lt. Cmdr. USN, 1949-54, 60-63, Korea. Fellow Am. Acad. Med. Adminstrs., Am. Assn. Clinic Physicians and Surgeons, Internat. Coll. Physicians and Surgeons, Am. Coll. Homeopathic Physicians, Am. Counc. Sex Therapy; mem. numerous orgns. including Nat. Psychol. Assn., Am. Psychotherapy Assn., Royal Soc. Physicians, World Med. Assn., Am. Acad. Preventive Medicine, Am. Bd. Examiners in Psychotherapy, Am. Bd. Examiners in Homeopathy, Western Homeopathic Med. Soc. (exec. dir.), Ariz. Profl. Soc. Hypnosis (founder 1974). Home: 515 W Townley Ave Phoenix AZ 85021-4566

STEWARD, PATRICIA ANN RUPERT, real estate executive, management consultant; b. Panama City, Panama, Apr. 20, 1945 (parents Am. citizens); d. Paul S. and Ernestina M. (Ward) Rupert; grad. Sch. of Mortgage Banking, Grad. Sch. of Mgmt., Northwestern U., 1979; m. Robert M. Levine, Oct. 28, 1978; children by previous marriage: Donald F. Steward, Christine Marie Steward. V.p. Assoc. Mortgage & Investment Co., Phoenix, 1969-71; v.p., br. mgr. Sun Country Funding Corp., Phoenix, 1971-72, Freese Mortgage Co., Phoenix, 1972-74, Utah Mortgage Loan Corp., Phoenix, 1974-81; pres. Elles Corp., 1982-90, Elles Mgmt. Corp., 1987-90, Elles Approvals Corp., 1987-90; founder, The Elles Group, 1987, Property Profls., 1990—; condr. numerous seminars on mortgage fin. Author: A Realtors Guide to Mortgage Lending, 1972. State chmn. Ariz. Leukemia Dr., 1977-78, mem. exec. com., 1979-80; troop leader Cactus Pine coun. Girl Scouts U.S., 1979-80; bd. dirs. Nat. Mental Health Assn., 1986-87, Ariz. Mental Health Assn., pres., 1986-87, bd. dirs., treas. Maricopa Mental Health Assn., 1984-85, v.p., 1985-86, pres., 1986-87; apptd. by state supreme ct. to Ariz. Foster Care Rev. Bd., 1984—, chairperson Bd. 8, 1986-87. Recipient cert. of appreciation Multiple Listing Svc., Phoenix Bd. Realtors, 1975, Multiple Listing Svc., Glendale Bd. Realtors, 1977. Lic. mortgage broker, Ariz. Mem. Ariz. Mortgage Bankers Assn. (bd. dir. 1981-82, chmn. edn. com. 1981-82, founder continuing edn. seminar series 1981), Young Mortgage Bankers Assn. (chmn. exec. com. 1980-81), Cen. Ariz. Homebuilders Assn. Republican.

STEWART, BETTY JEAN, secondary school educator; b. Kansas City, Mo., Mar. 12, 1946; d. Alfrey Lee and Helen Elizabeth (Henderson) Hansen; m. John Wesley Stewart, Sept. 16, 1966; children: Rebecca Lynn Stewart Hirsch, Scott Allen, David Raymond. BS in Elem. Edn. with honors, U. Kans., 1967, MS in Mid. Sch./Jr. High, 1985. Cert. tchr. elem. edn., jr. high edn., Mo.; cert. tchr. elem., secondary and mid. sch. edn., Colo. Tchr. JFK Elem. Sch., Kansas City, Kans., 1968, Schwegler Elem. Sch., Lawrence, Kans., 1971-73, Brookridge Day Sch., Overland Park, Kans., 1979-80; writer pub. rels., grants St. Luke's Hosp., Kansas City, Mo., 1980-84; tchr. English

C.F. Yeokum Jr. H.S., Belton, Mo., 1984-87; secondary English tchr. U. No. Colo. Lab. Sch., Greeley, Colo., 1987—; drug/alcohol workshop facilitator Cmty. Dynamics, Loveland, Colo., 1988—; tchr. drug/alcohol prevention classes numerous orgns. Loveland, 1988—; English edn. adv. bd. State of Colo., 1991-95. Author, asst. editor Wornall St. Jour., 1981-84. Bd. dirs. Thompson Edn. Found., Loveland, 1991-96. Mem. AAUW, ASCD, Colo. Hist. Soc., Colo. Lang. Arts Soc. Home: 4306 Crane Ct Loveland CO 80537 Office: University Northern Colorado University High Sch Greeley CO 80639-0001

STEWART, DAVID WAYNE, marketing educator, psychologist, consultant; b. Baton Rouge, Oct. 23, 1951; s. Wesley A. Stewart, Jr. and Edith L. (Richhart) Moore; m. Lenora Francois, June 6, 1975; children: Sarah Elizabeth, Rachel Dawn. BA, N.E. La. U., 1972; MA, Baylor U., 1973, PhD, 1974. Rsch. psychologist HHS, La., 1974-76; rsch. mgr. Needham, Harper & Steers Advt., Chgo., 1976-78; assoc. prof. Jacksonville (Ala.) State U., 1978-80; assoc. prof. Vanderbilt U., Nashville, 1980-86, sr. assoc. dean, 1984-86; prof. U. So. Calif., L.A., 1986-90, Ernest W. Hahn prof. mktg., 1990-91, Robert Brooker rsch. prof. mktg., 1991—, chmn. dept. mktg., 1995—; mgmt. cons., 1978—. Author, co-author: Secondary Research: Sources and Methods, Effective Television Advertising: A Study of 1000 Commericals, Consumer Behavior and the Practice of Marketing, Focus Group: Theory and Practice, Attention, Attitude, and Affect in Repsonse to Advertising, Nonverbal Communication and Advertising; contbr. articles to profl. jours.; mem. edtl. bd. Jour. Mktg. Rsch., Jour. Consumer Mktg., Jour. Pub. Policy & Mktg., Jour. Mktg., Jour. Advt., Jour. Promotion Mgmt., Current Issues and Rsch. in Advt., Jour. Internat. Consumer Mktg., Jour. Managerial Issues, Jour. Promotion Mgmt.; past pres. policy bd. Jour. Consumer Rsch., Acad. Mgmt. Fellow APA (coun. rep.), Am. Psychol. Soc. (charter); mem. Soc. for Consumer Psychology (past pres.), Inst. Mgmt. Scis., Decision Sci. Inst., Am. Mktg. Assn. (pres.-elec. acad. coun.), Assn. for Consumer Rsch., Am. Statis. Assn. (chair sect. on stats. in mktg. 1997), Acad. of Mgmt. Republican. Baptist. Office: U So Calif Sch Bus Adminstrn Dept Mktg Los Angeles CA 90089

STEWART, GAIL BENITA, alumni development director, editor; b. Cin., June 19, 1950; d. Charles Arthur Stewart and Ida Bell (McKinney) Tucker. BA, Calif. State U., 1974. Publicity asst. Sta. KCOP Channel 13, L.A., 1975; editor S.W. Regional Lab, L.A., 1975-77; editor, columnist Herald Am. News, Bellflower, Calif., 1977—, columnist, ad rep., 1979-80; researcher, writer asst. Sidney Poitier, Beverly Hills, Calif., 1977-78; pub. info. officer Long Beach (Calif.) Cmty. Svcs., 1982-85; dir. pub. rels. St. Anthony H.S., Long Beach, 1986-91; dir. alumni rels. Long Beach City Coll., 1991—. Contbr. articles to profl. jours. Grantee L.B. Comms., 1983, 84, 85, 86. Home: 3817 Arbor Rd Lakewood CA 90712 Office: Long Beach City Coll 4901 E Carson St Long Beach CA 90808-1706

STEWART, GARY CRAWFORD, oil company executive; b. Pitts., Apr. 5, 1956; s. Donald Eugene and Alma (Crawford) S.; m. Teresa Ann McInturff, Nov. 14, 1958; children: Sara Ann, Jon William. BS, Ariz. State U., 1978; MS in Geology, U. Okla., 1981. Sr. geologist Exxon Co. U.S.A., Denver, 1981-86; v.p. Melange Assocs., Inc., Denver, 1986-94, pres., CEO, 1994—; mem. Pres. Clinton's Energy Team, Washington, 1992—. Author: The Belize Carbonate Complex, 1980, The Influence of tectonics on Modern Carbonate Deposition, 1981. Mem. Am. Assn. Petroleum Geologists, Denver Internat. Petroleum Soc., Future Am. Geologists Soc. (hon. mem.). Office: Melange 821 17th St Ste 600 Denver CO 80202-3021

STEWART, ISAAC DANIEL, JR., judge; b. Salt Lake City, Nov. 21, 1932; s. Isaac Daniel and Orabelle (Iverson) S.; m. Elizabeth Bryan, Sept. 10, 1959; children: Elizabeth Ann, Shannon. BA with high honors, U. Utah, 1959, JD with high honors, 1962. Bar: Utah 1962, U.S. Dist. Ct. Utah 1962, U.S. Ct. Appeals (10th cir.) 1962, U.S. Ct. Appeals (4th cir.) 1963, U.S. Ct. Appeals (9th cir.) 1964, U.S. Ct. Appeals (8th cir.) 1965, U.S. Supreme Ct. 1965. Atty. antitrust divsn. Dept. Justice, Washington, 1962-65; asst. prof., then assoc. prof. U. Utah Coll. Law, 1965-70; ptnr. Jones, Waldo, Holbrook & McDonough, Salt Lake City, 1970-79; assoc. chief justice Utah Supreme Ct., 1979—, 1986-88, 94—; lectr. in field; mem. Utah Bd. Oil, Gas and Mining, 1976-78, chmn., 1977-78; Utah rep. Interstate Oil Compact Commn., 1977-78, exec. com. 1978-79; mem. adv. com. rules of procedure Utah Supreme Ct., 1983-87; chmn. com. on bar-press guidelines Utah Bar; mem. U. Utah search com., 1968-70; legal advisor, 1966-68. Editor-in-chief Utah Law Rev.; contbr. articles to legal jours. Chmn. subcom. on legal rights and responsibilities of youth Utah Gov's Com. on Youth, 1972; pres. Salt Lake chpt. Coun. Fgn. Rels., 1982; mem. Salt Lake City C. of C., 1974-79, mem. govtl. modernization com., 1976-78; missionary for Mormon Ch. in Fed. Republic Germany, 1953-56; bd. dirs. U. Utah Alumni Assn., 1986-89. Recipient Alumnus of Yr. award U. Utah Coll. Law, 1989. Mem. ABA, Utah Bar Assn. (com. on law and poverty 1967-69, com. on specialization 1977-78, pub. rels. com. 1968-69, chmn. com. on antitrust law 1977-78, com. on civil procedure reform 1968, mem. exec. com. bd. of appellate judges 1990—, liaison to supreme and adv. coms. evidence & profl. conduct 1986—, Appellate Judge of Yr. 1986), Salt Lake County Bar Assn., Am. Judicature Soc., Order of Coif, Phi Beta Kappa, Phi Kappa Phi, Sigma Chi (Significant Sig award 1987). Office: 332 State Capitol Building Salt Lake City UT 84114-1202*

STEWART, JAMES IAN, agricultural water scientist, cropping system developer, consultant; b. San Diego, Jan. 9, 1928; s. Castle Elmore and Myrtle Catherine (Hasty) S.; m. Robbie Nell Oliver, Mar. 23, 1975; children: Virginia Lane Stewart Carton, Ian Castle Stewart, Kevin Scott Overby. BSc, U. Calif., Berkeley, 1950; PhD, U. Calif., Davis, 1972. Farm advisor Agrl. Extension Svc., U. Calif., Stockton and Merced, 1950-61; extension expert Irrigation, Food and Agrl. Orgn. UN, Nicosia, Cyprus, 1962-66; assoc. rsch. water scientist U. Calif., Davis, 1966-77; supervisory soil scientist USDA/Office for Internat. Cooperation and Devel., Nairobi, Kenya, 1977-83; team leader, agrometeorologist USAID/Kenya Mission, 1977-83; founder, pres. Found. for World Hunger Alleviation Through Response Farming (WHARF), Davis, 1984—; cons., agrometeorology AID, USDA, World Bank, FAO/UNDP, 35 countries of Ams., Europe, Asia, Africa, Australia, 1965—; sci. convocations, 15 internat. countries, 1969—. Author: Response Farming in Rainfed Agriculture, 1988; creator (computer programs) Wharf, Wharfdat, 1990; contbr. numerous articles to profl. jours. Mem. Internat. Soil Sci. Soc., World Assn. Soil and Water Conservation, Internat. Com. for Irrigation and Drainage (life, U.S. com.), Indian Soc. Dryland Agr. (life), Sigma Xi, Phi Delta Theta. Home: 640 Portsmouth Ave Davis CA 95616-2738 Office: World Hunger Allev Through Response Farming PO Box 1158 Davis CA 95617-1158

STEWART, JEFFREE ROBERT, environmental planner, artist; b. Concord, N.H., June 20, 1956; s. Robert Davison and Ruth Florence (Olney) S. BA, Evergreen State Coll., Olympia, Wash., 1983; postgrad., U. Wash., 1983-84, Inst. Creative Devel., 1989-91. River guide rafting Rio Bravo, Inc., Durango, Colo., 1981-82; forester, planner Wash. State Parks Commn., Olympia, 1983-84; fisheries biologist U. Wash., Seattle, Alaska and Aleutians, 1984-86; pub. affairs rschr. NOAA, Seattle, 1986; hazardous waste project mgr. Washington Ecology Dept., Olympia, 1987, marine waste disposal project mgr., 1988-92, interagy. liaison, facilitator policy and tech. adv. groups, 1989-90, shorelands planner, 1992—; mem. art exhbns. com. Ecology Dept., Olympia, 1994, 95; mem. adv. bd. Washington Heritage Conf., Olympia, 1992; exhbns. team coord. Arts Olympia, 1993-94, chmn. steering group, 1995-96. One man shows include Batdorf & Bronson, Olympia, 1989, 91, 93, 94, Colophon Cafe, Bellingham, Wash., 1987, 96, Dancing Goats, Olympia, 1992, Thompson Gallery, 1995; exhibited in group shows at Janet Huston Gallery, LaConner, 1991, 92, 93, Wash. State Capitol Mus., Olympia, 1991, 92, 93, Childhoods End Gallery, 1995, 96, 97, Artspace Gallery, Bay City, Oreg., 1996, 97, Lucia Douglas Gallery, Bellingham, Wash., 1996, Evergreen State Coll., 1993, Wash. Ctr. Performing Arts, 1992, 93, 94, 95, 96, 97, Valley Mus. N.W. Art, 1994, 95, 96, 97, Tacoma Art Mus., 1995, also pvt. collections. Bd. trustees Evergreen State Coll., Olympia, 1981. Recipient Competent/Able Toastmaster awards Toastmasters Internat., 1989, 91, Oil Painting award of Merit Wash. State Capitol Mus., Olympia, 1993, Wash. Pub. Employees Assn. (bd. dirs. 1992-93), Meridian Toastmasters (pres., v.p. 1989-91). Mem. Artist Trust, Arts Olympia (steering group 1994—), Profl. Geographers of Puget Sound, Mus. N.W. Art, Tacoma Art Mus., Belleuve Art Mus. Home: PO Box 7397 Olympia WA 98507-7397 Office: Wash Ecology Dept PO Box 47775 Olympia WA 98504

STEWART, JOANNE, secondary school educator; b. Vancouver, Wash., Mar. 10, 1944; d. Edward Charles and Claudine Marie (Meilleur) Spencer; m. William Lemley Stewart, Sept. 2, 1966 (dec. June 1983); children: Amy Diane, Nicholas William. BS, Wash. State U., 1966, MA, 1973. Cert. tchr., Mont., Idaho, Wash., Calif. Tchr. foods Seaside High Sch., Monterey, Calif., 1966-67; tchr. home econs. Marysville (Wash.) High Sch., 1967-68, Palouse (Wash.) High Sch., 1968-73, Ennis (Mont.) High Sch., 1973-76, Genesee (Idaho) High Sch., 1976-77; instr. young family Missoula (Mont.) County High Sch., 1983-84; tchr. home econs. Woodman Sch., Lolo, Mont., 1985-86; travel cons. Travel Masters, Missoula, 1984-87; ticketing mgr. Blue Caboose Travel, Missoula, 1987-91; tchr. family and consumer scis. Victor (Mont.) High Sch., 1991—; project dir. sch.-to-work implementation Victor Sch., 1996—. Co-pres. Lolo PTO, 1980-81; v.p. Lolo Community Ctr., 1981; sec. Lolo Mosquito Control Bd., 1988—; mem. telecommunications com. Conrad Burns & Gov. Racicot; sec. state supt. edn. task force on vocat. edn., 1995-96. Marysville Edn. Assn. scholar, 1962, Future Homemakers Am. scholar, 1962. Mem. AAUW (sec. 1986, program chmn. 1987), Forestry Triangle (pres. 1981, editor cookbook 1982), Washington State Future Homemakers Am. (hon. mem.), Am. Family and Consumer Scis. Assn., Mont. Family and Consumer Scis. Assn. (bylaws chair 1994, pres. elect 1995-96, pres. 1996-97, Profl. of Yr. 1997), Mont. Vocat. Tchrs. Assn. (returning Rookie of Yr. 1992, Am. Federated Tchrs., Mont. Vocat. Family and Consumer Scis. Tchrs. (v.p. 1993-94, pres. 1994-95). Republican. Methodist. Home: 1200 Lakeside Dr Lolo MT 59847-9705 Office: Victor High Sch Family and Consumer Scis 425 4th Ave Victor MT 59875-9468

STEWART, KENNETH MALCOLM, retired anthropologist, researcher; b. Tecumseh, Nebr., June 16, 1916; s. Kenneth Atwell and Alta Margaret S.; m. Mary Marguerite Reed, Jan. 7, 1942 (div. 1951); children: Kenneth Malcolm Jr., Geraldine Kay; m. Louise Garland Dyer, June 6, 1960. BA, U. Calif., 1938, MA, 1940, PhD, 1946. Asst. prof. Calif. State U., Fresno, 1946-47; prof. Ariz. State U., Tempe, Ariz., 1947-79, ret., 1979; cons. Mohave Indian Tribe, Needles, Calif., 1955-56, researcher Colo. River Reservation, 1970-71; tchr. Papago Indian Tribe, Sells, Ariz., 1946. Co-author: The Native Americans, 1965, 77, The Southwest, vol. 10, 1983. Fellow Am. Anthropol. Assn.; mem. AAUP, Soc. Am. Ethnology, Sigma Xi. Democrat. Home: 4353 Dowitcher Way Oceanside CA 92097

STEWART, LARRY RAY, engineer, financial director, quality consultant; b. Rock Springs, Wyo., Mar. 26, 1948; s. Raymond Melvin and Mary Jane (Fillin) S.; m. Della Jean Warren, Aug. 25, 1967; children: Stephanie M., Kara K., Gina R., Laura J. BS in Engring., U. Wyo., 1970, MS in Engring., 1972. Registered profl. engr., Ariz., Colo., Idaho, Mont., N.Mex., Oreg., Tex., Utah, Wyo. Mgr. apt. Willey Enterprises, Laramie, Wyo., 1966-70; grad. asst. U. Wyo., Laramie, 1970-72; systems analyst Dept. Def., Corona, Calif., 1972-73; engr. Mountain Bell, Cheyenne, Wyo., 1973-77; adminstr. Mountain Bell, Denver, 1977-79; mgr. Mountain Bell, Englewood, Colo., 1979-84; dist. mgr. Mountain Bell, Denver, 1985-87; dir. Bell TRICO Services, Englewood, 1984-85, U.S. West CGI, Denver, 1987-92; divsn. mgr. Hamlin Electric Services, Inc., Ft. Morgan, Colo., 1993-94; field engr. Colo. State U., Ft. Collins, 1994-95; state dir. MAMTC U. Wyo., Laramie, 1995—; mem. adv. bd. U. Wyoming Grad. Sch., Laramie, 1970-72; IOF co-chair AT&T/Bell System, Basking Ridge, N.J., 1980-83; curriculum advisor Network Tng., Englewood, 1980-83; fin. advisor Employee Suggestion Plan, Denver, 1984-86. Editor (coll. mag.) Enginews, 1970. Pres. Maplewood Homeowners, Arvada, Colo., 1986; key chair United Way, Denver, 1988. Served with USAF, 1970-76. Mem. IEEE, Nat. Soc. Profl. Engrs. Republican. Lodge: Optimist (lt. gov. of Colo./Wyo. Dist.). Office: MAMTC U Wyo Wyo Hall Room 420 PO Box 3362 Univ Station Laramie WY 82071-3362

STEWART, LESLIE MUELLER, editor, writer; b. Morristown, N.J., Oct. 25, 1942; d. Edward Arthur and Phyllis Virginia (Dohm) Mueller; m. James Alexander Stewart, Sept. 19, 1969; children: Alexander, Alison. BA in English Lit., Reed Coll., Portland, Oreg., 1964; postgrad., U. Calif., Berkeley, 1964-65. Libr. Golden Gate U., San Francisco, 1964-69, lectr., 1968-71; adminstrv. asst. Williams & Mocine, San Francisco, 1968-71; classroom aide Mt. Diablo Unified Sch. Dist., Concord, Calif., 1978-79, substitute libr., 1982-87; adminstrv. asst. Bay Area Monitor, Oakland and Lafayette, Calif., 1987-95; editor Bay Area Monitor, Lafayette, 1995—; mem. adv. coun. U. Calif. Toxic Substances Rsch. and Tchg. Program, 1995—; prep. Decision Makers Directory, LWV Bay Area, Lafayette, 1987-95. Chair County Hazardous Materials Com., Contra Costa County, 1995—. Mem. LWV Calif. (bd. dirs., sec. 1993-95), LWV Diablo Valley (bd. dirs., action chair 1996-98). Office: Bay Area Monitor 500 Saint Marys Rd Lafayette CA 94549-5431

STEWART, LUCILLE MARIE, special education coordinator; b. Pittsburgh, Feb. 24; d. William H. and Edna (Hoffman) S. BEd Duquesne U.; MEd, U. Pittsburgh; postgrad. courses Columbia U., U. Calif., Calif. State U. Cert. elem. and secondary tchr., spl. edn. tchr., supr., adminstr. Tchr. Lincoln (Ill). State Sch., 1953; group leader Retarded Education Alliance, N.Y.C., 1954-58; tchr. mentally retarded Ramapo Cen. Sch. Dist., Spring Valley, N.Y., 1958-60, seriously emotionally disturbed, 1960-64; program dir. Pomona (N.Y.) Camp for Retarded, summers 1960-63; tchr. Stockton Sch., San Diego, 1964-65, supr. presch. program for educationally disadvantaged Ramapo Ctrl. Sch. Dist., Spring Valley, N.Y., 1965-67; tchr. Cathdral City (Calif.) Sch., 1967-78; prin. elem. summer schs. Palm Springs (Calif.) Unified Sch. Dist., 1971-72; prin.-tchr. Summer Extended Sch. for Spl. Students, 1979—; mem. exec. com. U. Calif. Extension area adv. com. Mem. NEA, AAUW, Calif. Tchrs. Assn., Palm Springs Tchrs. Assn., Palm Springs Ednl. Leadership Assn., Calif. Assn. Program Specialists, Assn. for Supervision and Curriculum Devel., Am. Assn., Calif. Adminstrs. of Spl. Edn. (Desert community mental health childrens com.), Coun. Exceptional Children (admin., early childhood-learning handicap divsns.), Childhood Edn. Alpha Kappa Alpha, Phi Delta Kappa, Delta Kappa Gamma. Club: Toastmistress. Office: Palm Springs Unified Sch Dist 333 S Farrell Dr Palm Springs CA 92262-7905

STEWART, MARLENE METZGER, financial planner, insurance agent; b. Portland, Oreg., Nov. 1, 1937; d. Eddie Charles and Helen M. (Grant) Metzger; m. Robert W. Stewart, Aug. 1, 1964 (dec. Jan. 1967); m. Melvin N. McBurney, Feb. 14, 1985. BA, U. Oreg., 1959; MA, U. Tex., El Paso, 1971. Exec. dir. Summer 72 Youth Com. Office of Mayor, Portland, 1972; registered rep. Mut. Life Ins. Co. N.Y., Portland, 1973-76, Prudential Life Ins. Co., Portland, 1976-77; ptnr. N.W. Fin. Planning, Portland, 1977-79; pres. Horizons Unltd. Fin. Planning, Portland, 1979-86; prin. EMR Fin. Adv. Svcs., Inc., Portland, 1986-89; registered rep. KMS Fin. Svcs., Inc., Portland, 1979—; owner Stewart Fin. Group, 1991—. Mem.-at-large nat. bd. YMCA's, 1971-73; bd. dirs. Met. YMCA, Portland, 1971-75; bd. dirs. YWCA, Portland, 1989-92, treas., 1990-92, chmn. investment com.; chmn. planned giving com. Arthritis Found., 1984-86. Bill Bottler scholar Portland chpt. CLU and Chartered Fin. Cons., 1981. Mem. Inst. CFP's, Oreg. Soc. Inst. CFP's (treas. 1985-86), Internat. Assn. Fin. Planners (pres. Oreg. chpt. 1987-88), Nat. Assn. Life Underwriters, CLU's and ChFC's (treas. Portland chpt. 1985-86), Assocs. Good Samaritan (steering com., chmn. 1991-92), Rotary. Republican. Presbyterian. Office: 4380 SW Macadam Ave Ste 525 Portland OR 97201-6408

STEWART, PAUL ANTHONY, II, association executive, author; b. Oakland, Calif., Apr. 14, 1952; s. Paul Anthony Sr. and Hilda Hensley (Monger) S.; m. Stephanie Anne Pitts, July 8, 1972; children: Jana Lorraine, Robyn Lynne. BA, San Jose (Calif.) State U., 1974, MS, 1975. News editor various pubs., 1974-77; v.p. legis. svcs. Bldg. Industry Assn. of Superior Calif., Sacramento, 1977-82; exec. v.p. So. div. Bldg. Industry Assn. of No. Calif., San Jose, 1982-86; exec. v.p. Bldg. Industry Assn. of San Joaquin Valley, Fresno, Calif., 1986-90; CEO Bldg. Industry Assn. of Cen. Calif., Modesto, 1990-91, Rental Housing Assn. Contra Costa County, Walnut Creek, Calif., 1993—. Host (TV show) Stewarts Sports Challenge, 1974 (Emmy nomination 1975); contbr. articles to profl. jours. Chmn. Transp. 2000 Steering LCom., San Jose, 1985-87; transp. commr. County of Santa Clara, Calif., 1986-87; pres. San Joaquin Valley Community Housing Leadership Bd., Fresno, 1988-90. Recipient Assn. Achievement award Calif. Apt. Assn., 1996; named one of Outstanding Young Men of Am., U.S. Jaycees, 1984. Mem. Nat. Assn. Home Bldrs., Calif. Bldg. Industry Assn. (exec. officers coun., pres. 1990-91), Internat. Soc. Poets, Poetry Soc. Am., Calif. Writer's Club, Sigma Delta Chi. Baptist.

STEWART, SALLY, public relations practitioner; b. Phoenix, Mar. 1, 1955; d. Biven and Nancy Sue (Spurlock) S.; children: Padraic Haines, Colin Haines. BS in Broadcast Journalism, Ariz. State U., 1977, BA in Edn., 1980. Staff writer, media rep. Salt River Project, Phoenix, 1979-81; copy editor Mesa (Ariz.) Tribune, 1981-82; mktg. adminstrv. asst. Phoenix chpt. ARC, 1983; pub. info. asst. City of Scottsdale, Ariz., 1983-84; bus. editor, asst. city editor Scottsdale Progress Tribune, 1984-86; comms. mgr. Mesa Conv. and Visitors Bur., 1986-90; mgmt. asst. Neighborhood Improvement and Housing Dept., City of Phoenix, 1990-92, Pub. Info. Office, City of Phoenix, 1992-93; comm. cons. Ariz. Pub. Svc., Phoenix, 1993—. Mem. com. Fiesta Bowl, Phoenix, 1987-89; mem. pub. rels. com. Juvenile Diabetes Found., Phoenix, 1990; mem. pub. rels. com. Children's Garden Ground Breaking, Phoenix, 1993. mem. Pub. Rels. Soc. Am. (accredited, bd. dirs. 1991-93, assembly del. 1993-95, pres. Valley of the Sun chpt. 1997). Office: Ariz Pub Svc 2 Arizona Ctr 400 N 5th St Phoenix AZ 85004-3902

STEWART, SHARON DIANE, writer; b. Cleveland, Miss., June 16, 1951; d. Elton Stewart and Mary Ruth (Speights) Boyland. BS in Mktg., San Diego State U., 1974; MBA, U. San Diego, 1977; AA in Tech. Writing, Mesa Coll., 1985. Sr. acctg. specialist Motorola Corp., San Diego, 1977-79; supr. acctg. Security Pacific Fin., San Diego, 1979-84; sr. acctg. specialist Sun Savs. and Loan, San Diego, 1984-85; publs. specialist Sundstrand Power Systems, San Diego, 1985-91; sr. analyst/editor MANTECH Advanced Tech., Pasadena, Calif., 1991-92; owner SDS Prodns., San Diego, 1981—; tech. editor Parsons Co., Pasadena, 1992-93; engring. writer Teledyne Laars, Moorpark, Calif., 1994-95; writer Harris Corp., Camarillo, CA, 1996—; instr. Mesa Coll., 1989-91. Contbr. articles to profl. jours. Vol. San Diego Police Dept., 1990-91, Glendale Police Dept., 1991—; vol. COMBO, 1982-83, Sta. KPBS Pub. Radio, 1984-87; chmn. Community Coll. Tech. Writing Coun., 1985-91; pres. Soc. for Technical COmms., 1993-95; mem. bd. dirs., chmn. Simi Valley Cultural Arts Ctr. Commn. & Found., 1994-97; mem. Simi Valley Neighbor D Coun., 1993-95. Lt. comdr. USNR, 1985—. Copley Assoc. scholar, 1983, Grocery Industry scholar, 1974; decorated Nat. Def. Svc. medal USNR, 1992. Mem. Naval Res. Assn. (v.p. 1987-90, Diamond in the Rough award 1990), Res. Officers Assn., Soc. Tech. Communicators, San Diego Writers Guild, Nat. Acad. TV Arts (acting chair 1984, cert. 1985), Toastmasters (Toastmaster of Yr. 1983). Republican. Baptist. Home: 78 E Bonita Dr Simi Valley CA 93065-2914 Office: Harris Corp 809 Calle Plano Camarillo CA 93012

STEWART, WAYNE M., newspaper editor; b. Kansas City, Kans., Sept. 16, 1950; m.. Sherry Stewart; 1 child, Laura. BS in Journalism, Baker U. Staff Las Vegas Rev.-Jour., 1973-87; news editor Colorado Springs (Colo.) Gazette-Telegraph, 1987-88, dep. mng. editor, 1988-92, mng. editor, 1991-96, asst. editor, 1996—. Office: Colo Springs Gazette Telegraph 30 S Prospect St PO Box 1779 Colorado Springs CO 80901

STEZOSKI-RODRIGUEZ, LORISE ANN, critical care nurse, educator; b. Pitts., July 11, 1963; d. Walter and Pauline (Kurutz) S. ASN, Mt. San Antonio Coll., 1985; BSN, Calif. State U., L.A., 1987, postgrad., 1995. RN, Calif. Part-time mem. faculty Calif. State U., L.A.; staff nurse Huntington Meml. Hosp., Pasadena, Calif.; clin. edn. specialist Hosp. of the Good Samaritan, L.A.; mgr. staff devel., case mgr. Healthcare Ptnrs. Mem. AACN, AAACN, Sigma Theta Tau.

STICKEL, FREDERICK A., publisher; b. Weehawken, N.J., Nov. 18, 1921; s. Fred and Eva (Madigan) S.; m. Margaret A. Dunne, Dec. 4, 1943; children—Fred A., Patrick F., Daisy E., Geoffrey M., James E., Bridget A. Student, Georgetown U., 1939-42; BS, St. Peter's Coll., 1943. Advt. salesperson Jersey Observer daily, Hoboken, N.J., 1945-51; retail advt. salesperson Jersey Jour., Jersey City, 1951-55; advt. dir. Jersey Jour., 1955-66, publisher, 1966-67; gen. mgr. Oregonian Pub. Co., Portland, Oreg., 1967-72, pres., 1972—, publisher, 1975—. Bd. regents U. Portland; mem. adv. bd. Portland State U.; bd. dirs. Portland Rose Festival Assn., United Way Oreg.; chmn. Portland Citizens Crime Commn.; mem. adv. bd. St. Vincent's Hosp. Capt. USMC, 1942-45. Mem. Assn. for Portland Progress (dir.), Portland C. of C. (dir.), Oreg. Newspaper Pubs. Assn. (past pres.), Pacific N.W. Newspaper Assn. (pres.), Am. Newspaper Pubs. Assn., University Club, Multnomah Athletic Waverley Country Club, Arlington Club, Rotary. Office: Oregonian Pub Co 1320 SW Broadway Portland OR 97201-3411

STICKLER, JOHN COBB, publisher, journalist, author; b. Washington, July 18, 1937; s. Joseph Harding and Virginia Murray (Cobb) S.; m. Lucy Han, 1964; children: Stephen Han, Alexander Han. BA with honors, Yale U., 1959; cert. Peace Corps, Pa. State U., 1961. Stringer CBS Radio News, Seoul, Republic of Korea, 1967-76; owner, mgr. S/K Internat. Advt., Seoul, 1966-76; pub., owner Jour. Applied Mgmt., Walnut Creek, Calif., 1978-81; account exec. Cunningham & Walsh, San Francisco, 1981; dir. mktg. Neighborhood Housing Services, Tucson, 1982; dir. pub. relations Sheraton Tucson El Conquistador Resort, 1983-92. Editor, pub.: Advertising in Korea, 1973, 2d revised edit., 1975; (poetry) Growing Up Afraid, 1985; contbr.: Exporting to Mexico, 1992, Berlitz American Southwest, 1993, Fodor's B&B Guide, Southwest, 1994, 2d edit., 1996Fodor's Southwest's Best Bed & Breakfasts, 1996; author: Exporting to the USA, 1992; contbr. numerous articles to mags. Served with U.S. Army, 1962-64. Recipient advt. prize Hotel Sales and Mktg. Assn., 1974, CLIO award, 1975, poetry award Nat. Writers Club, 1977, poetry award World Order Narrative Poets, 1978. Mem. Pub. Rels. Soc. Am. (pres. So. Ariz. chpt. 1991), Am. Soc. Journalists & Authors, Internat. Assn. Bus. Communicators (pres. Tucson chpt. 1985-86), Soc. Southwestern Authors (pres. 1988-90), UNESCO Assn. U.S.A. (bd. dirs. 1981-90), Internat. Advt. Assn. (founder Korea chpt. 1967), Internat. Food, Wine and Travel Writers Assn., Soc. Am. Travel Writers, Royal Asiatic Soc. (Korea br.), Tucson Press Club, UN Assn. So. Ariz., Yale Club Tucson (v.p. 1988). Democrat. Office: 16550 Twin Lakes Dr Watsonville CA 95076-3639

STICKLES, BONNIE JEAN, nurse; b. Waukesha, Wis., Nov. 24, 1944; d. Donald William and Betty Jane S.; B.S. in Nursing, U. Wis., 1967; M.S. in Nursing, Midwifery, Columbia U., 1974. Mem. nursing staff Grace Hosp., Detroit, 1970-73; mem. faculty and staff U. Minn. Sch. Nursing and Nurse-Midwifery Svc., Mpls., 1974-76; chief nurse-midwife, clin. instr. St. Paul-Ramsey Med. Ctr., 1976-84; midwifery supr. IHS/PHS Chinle Hosp., 1984-85; program mgr. maternal health sect. N.Mex. Dept. Health and Environ., 1985-90; Lovelace Med. Ctr., 1990-91; St. Vincent's Hosp., 1991-94; NMC Dialysis Divsn., 1994-95; blackjack dealer, 1995—. Mem. FDA Anesthetics, Life Support Adv. Com.; adv. bd. Childbirth Edn. Assn., 1980-85. Served with USNR, 1965-70. Decorated Letter of Commendation. Mem. Am. Coll. Nurse-Midwives (chmn. profl. affairs com. 1975-80), Nurses Assn. Am. Coll. Obstetricians and Gynecologists (charter), Aircraft Owners and Pilots Assn., Gt. Plains Perinatal Orgn., Alpha Tau Delta. Author articles in field; patentee teaching model.

STICKNEY, PHILIP MICHAEL, accountant, educator; b. Columbus, Ohio, Sept. 9, 1949; s. Palmer Blaine and Esther Milton (Udell) S.; m. Michele Marie Lenihan, June 13, 1970. BS in Math. with high honors, Mich. State U., 1971; postgrad., U. Ariz., 1971-75; M in Acctg., Ohio State U., 1977. CPA, Ariz. Audit supr. Coopers & Lybrand, Tucson, 1977-82; mgr. strategic and fin. planning Burr-Brown Corp., Tucson, 1982-84; contr. P.F. West, Inc. & Lumber Country, Tucson, 1984-86; v.p. fin. Clifton Investment Co., Tucson, 1986-87; contr. Marston's Inc., Tempe, Ariz., 1987-88; acct. in pvt. practice, 1987, 88-89; dir. Community Campus, program coord. Small Bus. Devel. Ctr. Cochise Coll., Douglas and Sierra Vista, Ariz., 1989—. Formerly bd. dirs., treas., chmn. bd. Goodwill Industries of Tucson, Inc.; bd. dirs., v.p. Sierra Vista Econ. Devel. Found.; participant Gov.'s Conf. on Small Bus., 1993, Gov.'s Rural Devel. Conf., 1990-95. Mem. AICPA, Ariz. Soc. CPAs, Phi Kappa Phi, Pi Mu Epsilon, Phi Eta Sigma, Beta Alpha Psi. Home: 5539 S Shawnee Dr Sierra Vista AZ 85635-9639 Office: Cochise Coll 4190 W State Highway 80 Douglas AZ 85607-6100

STIEBER, TAMAR, journalist; b. Bklyn., Sept. 15, 1955; d. Alfred and Florence (Spector) S. Student, Rockland C.C., 1972-75, Rockland C.C.,

1972-75, West London (Eng.) Coll., 1973-74; BA in Film cum laude, U. Calif., Berkeley, 1985, postgrad. in comparative lit., 1985-86; grad. police reserve academycum laude, Napa Valley Coll., 1988. Office mgr., confidential sec. AP, San Francisco, 1981-83; stringer Daily Californian, Berkeley, Calif., 1983-84; film rsch. teaching asst. U. California, Berkeley, 1984-86; libr. and rsch. asst. Pacific Film Archive, Berkeley, 1984-86; intern San Francisco Examiner, 1984; reporter Sonoma (Calif.) Index-Tribune, 1987-88, Vallejo (Calif.) Times-Herald, 1988-89, Albuquerque Journal, 1989-94. Recipient Pulitzer prize for specialized reporting, 1990, first place pub. svc. divsn. N.Mex. Press Assn., 1990, pub. svc. award Albuquerque Press Club, 1990; first place newswriting N.Mex. Press Assn., 1991; honorable mention Assn. Press Managing Editors, 1994. Mem. AAUW, Soc. Profl. Journalists, Investigative Reporters and Editors, Internat. Platform Soc., Phi Beta Kappa. Home: PO Box 9835 Santa Fe NM 87504-9835

STIENMIER, RICHARD HAROLD, pathologist; b. Ft. Collins., Colo., June 24, 1936; s. Harold and Agnes M. (Hannah) S.; m. Saundra K. Young, Dec. 20, 1958; children: Richard B., Susan I., Julia T., Laura S. BA cum laude, U. Colo., Boulder, 1958; MD, U. Colo., Denver, 1961. Diplomate Am. Bd. Pathology. Commd. 2d lt. Med. Corp. U.S. Army, 1958, advanced through grades to col. Med. Corp., ret., 1980; intern U. Cin., 1961-62; resident in pathology Fitzsimmons Army Med. Ctr., Denver, 1964-68; chief pathology dept. Leonard Wood Hosp., Ft. Leonard Wood, Mo., 1968-69; pathologist Letterman Army Med. Ctr., San Francisco, 1970-72; chief pathology dept. William Beaumont Army Med. Ctr., El Paso, 1972-77; comdr. 10th Med. Lab. U.S. Army, Landstuhl, Germany, 1977-80; chief dept. pathology Ft. Carson Hosp., Colorado Springs, Colo., 1980-82; pathologist St. Francis Hosp., Colorado Springs, Colo., 1982-90, Porter Hosp., Denver, 1990—; cons. in pathology U.S. Army, Heidelburg, Germany, 1977-80. Contbr. articles to profl. jours. Decorated Soldier's medal, Legion of Merit, Meritorious Svc. medal. Fellow Coll. Am. Pathologists, Am. Soc. Clin. Pathologists; mem. AMA, AAAS, Am. Acad. Forensic Sci., Am. Assn. Blood Banks, Colo. State Med. Soc., Arapaho County Med. Soc., Nat. Assn. Med. Examiners, Assn. Mil. Surgeons of the U.S., Internat. Assn. Pathologists, Colo. Soc. Clin. Pathologists (pres. 1988-89), Flying Physicians Assn. Republican. Episcopalian. Home: 7955 Tangleoak Ln Castle Rock CO 80104-9299 Office: Porter Hosp Pathology Dept 2525 S Downing St Denver CO 80210-5817

STIFEL, FREDERICK BENTON, pastor, biochemist, nutritionist; b. St. Louis, Jan. 30, 1940; s. Carl Gottfried and Alma J. (Clark) S.; m. Gail Joane Stewart, Aug. 10, 1963; children: Tim, Faith, Seth, Elizabeth. BS, Iowa State U., 1962, PhD, 1967; MDiv., Melodyland Sch. Theol., Anaheim, Calif., 1979. Ordained to ministry Evang. Presbyn. Ch., 1981. Lab. supr., research chemist U.S. Army Med. Research and Nutrition Lab., Denver, 1968-74, Letterman Army Inst. Research, San Francisco, 1974-76; intern pastor Melodyland Christian Ctr., Anaheim, 1979-80; assoc. pastor Faith Presbyn. Ch., Aurora, Colo., 1980—; chmn. care of candidates com. Presbytery of West, Denver, 1985-88, 91-94; mem. Denver Seminary Commn., 1995—; bd. dirs., v.p. Love Inc. of Metro Denver, 1987-90; regional coord. Nat. Assn. Single Adult Leaders, 1987-90, coord. Denver area, 1990-95; Colo. Pregnancy Ctrs., Inc., 1992-94, Rocky Mountain Prayer Network, 1994-96, Christian Family Svcs., 1990—; bd. dirs. St. James Bible Coll., 1995—, Profile Publs.; mem. faculty St. James Bible Coll., Kiev, Ukraine. Contbr. clin. med. and nutritional articles to profl. jours. Del. Iowa State Rep. Conv., Denver, 1984; mem. parent adv. coun. IMPACT drug intervention team Rangeview High Sch., Aurora, 1985-89, accountability com., 1989-96; mem. Friends of the Arts, 1992-96; young life leader Hinkley High Sch., Aurora, 1968-74; vice chmn. Young Life Com., Marin County, Calif., 1974-76. Capt. U.S. Army Med. Svc. Corps, 1967-70. Ralston Purina Rsch. fellow, 1962-63; Borden Agrl. scholar, 1962; recipient Sci. Achievement award U.S. Army Sci. Conf., West Point, N.Y., 1968, 70, Parents of the Yr. award Rangeview High Sch., 1992-93. Mem. Am. Inst. Nutrition, Am. Soc. Clin. Nutrition, Am. Sci. Affiliation, Evang. Theol. Soc., Phi Eta Sigma, Phi Kappa Phi, Alpha Zeta, Gamma Sigma Delta, Kappa Sigma, Sigma Xi. Home: 3492 S Blackhawk Way Aurora CO 80014-3909 Office: Faith Presbyn Ch 11373 E Alameda Ave Aurora CO 80012-1023

STIFFLER, DANIEL FRANCIS, biology educator, researcher; b. Los Angeles, Nov. 27, 1942; s. Frank M. and Alice (Holsclaw) S.; m. Gail Helen Clark, June 30, 1967; children: Jason Daniel, Jared Warren, Peter Benjamin. BA, U. Calif.-Santa Barbara, 1968; MS, Oreg. State U., 1970, PhD, 1972. Instr. zoology Oreg. State U., Corvallis, 1970-72; postdoctoral trainee physiology U. Oreg. Med. Sch., Portland, 1972-74; lectr. physiology U. Calif.-Davis, 1974-75; prof. biology Calif. State Poly. U., Pomona, 1975—, assoc. dean sci., 1983-85. Contbr. articles in field to profl. jours. Served with U.S. Navy, 1960-63. Calif. State Poly. U. Kellogg Unit Found. grantee, 1980; Grantee NSF, 1981, 85, 87, Calif. State U.-Acad. Program Improvement, 1985. Mem. Am. Physiol. Soc., Soc. Integrative & Comparative Biology, Canadian Soc. Zoologists, Sigma Xi. Democrat. Office: Calif State Poly Univ Biol Scis Dept Pomona CA 91768

STIGLICH, JACOB JOHN, JR., engineering consultant; b. Milw., Dec. 21, 1938; s. Jacob John Sr. and Augusta (Prezel) S. BSME, Marquette U., 1961; PhD, Northwestern U., 1970. Chief engr. Boride Products, Traverse City, Mich., 1971-74; mgr. ceramic materials Valeron Corp., Madison Heights, Mich., 1974-76; group leader, asst. dir. tech. Eagle Picher, Miami, Okla., 1976-78; program mgr. San Fernando Lab., Pacoima, Calif., 1978-84; tech. specialist Aerojet Ordnance Co., Tustin, Calif., 1984-85; cons. Colo., 1985-95; sr. scientist Materials Modification, Inc., Fairfax, Va., 1995—. Contbr. articles to profl. jours.; patentee in field. Col. USAR, 1961-92. Mem. AIME, Am. Soc. Metals, Am. Ceramic Soc., Mensa, Sigma Xi.

STIGLITZ, JOSEPH EUGENE, economist; b. Gary, Ind., Feb. 9, 1943; s. Nathaniel David and Charlotte (Fishman) S.; m. Jane Hannaway, Dec. 23, 1978; children: Siobhan, Michael, Edward, Julia. B.A., Amherst Coll., Mass, 1964; DHL (hon.), Amherst Coll., 1974; Ph.D. in Econs., MIT, 1966; M.A. (hon.), Yale U., 1970; D in Econs. (hon.), U. Leuven, 1994. Prof. econs. Cowles Found., Yale U., New Haven, 1970-74; vis. fellow St. Catherine's Coll., Oxford, Eng., 1973-74; Joan Kenney professorship Stanford U., 1974-76, 88—; Oskar Morgenstern dist. fellow Inst. Advanced Studies Math., Princeton, N.J., 1978-79; Drummond prof. polit. economy Oxford U., Eng., 1976-79; prof. econs. Princeton U., 1979-88; mem. Pres.'s Coun. Econ. Advisers, 1993-95, chmn. coun. econ. advisers, 1995-97, sr. v.p. devel. econs. and chief econs., exec. dir.; cons. World Bank, State of Alaska, Seneca Indian Nation, Bell Communications Rsch. Editor Jour. Econ. Perspectives, 1986-93; Am. editor Rev. of Econ. Studies, 1968-76; assoc. editor Am. Econ. Rev., 1968-76, Energy Econs., Managerial and Decision Econs.; mem. editl. bd. World Bank Econ. Rev. Recipient John Bates Clark award Am. Econ. Assn., 1979, Internat. prize Accademia Lincei, 1988, Union des Assurances de Paris prize, 1989; Guggenheim fellow, 1969-70. Fellow Inst. for Policy Rsch. (sr. 1991-93), Brit. Acad. (corr.); mem. Am. Econ. Assn. (exec. com. 1982-84, v.p. 1985), Am. Acad. Arts and Scis., Nat. Acad. Sci., Econometric Soc.

STILES, KNUTE, artist; b. Hudson, Wis., Sept. 14, 1923; s. Charles and Lorena Emma (Weldon) S. Grad., Calif. Sch. Fine Arts; student, St. Paul Sch Art, Black Mountain Coll, New Sch. Social Rsch. Reviewer, feature writer Artforum, San Francisco, L.A., N.Y., 1963-71; tchr. painting and drawing San Francisco Art Inst., 1965-71, 1964-71; reviewer, feature writer KXKX-FM, San Francisco, 1968-69, Art in Am., N.Y.C., 1975-83; columnist art Calif. Voice, San Francisco, 1977-83. One-man shows include 6 Gallery, San Francisco, 1955-56, Brata Gallery, N.Y.C., 1957-61, San Francisco Mus. Modern Arts, 1964, Staniford Gallery, San Francisco, 1969. With U.S. Army, 1943-46. Home: Box 1337 Bisbee AZ 85603

STILLMAN, ALFRED WILLIAM, JR., design and support engineer; b. Biloxi, Miss., Sept. 11, 1942; s. Alfred William and Marie Ann (Hengen) S.; AA, Am. River Coll., 1966; BSEE, Calif. Poly. State U., 1970, BS in Applied Math., 1970, MS in Applied Math., 1973; ME in Indsl. Engring., Tex. A&M U., 1976; postgrad. elec. engring. N.J. Inst. Tech., 1977; PhD in Mgmt., Calif. Coast U., 1984; children: Shannon Lynn, Laura Marie. Cert. profl. logistician, instr. Calif. Community Colls. Engring. intern U.S. Army Material Command, Texarkana, Tex., 1973-75, electronic systems staff maintenance engr., Ft. Monmouth, N.J., 1975-77, mil. tactical data system integrated logistics support mgr. Office of Project Mgr., ARTADS, Ft. Monmouth, 1977-78, tactical ADP ILS Mgr., ILS dir. CORADOM, Ft. Monmouth, 1978-79, engring. mgr. regional dist. office Office of Project Mgr., Firefinder, Hughes Aircraft Co., Fullerton, Calif., 1979-80; prof. systems acquisition mgmt. Dept. Def. Systems Mgmt. Coll., Ft. Belvoir, Va., 1980-82; integrated logistics support engring. specialist, advanced systems div. Northrop Corp., Pico Rivera, Calif., 1982-83; program mgmt. rep. space systems group Rockwell Internat., Downey, Calif., 1983-84; product assurance project engr. Space Sta. Systems div. Rockwell Internat., Downey, Calif., 1984-85; mgr. product support, 1985-86; sr. mgr. ILS, Amex Systems, Inc., Compton, Calif., 1986-88; dir. ILS NavCom Def. Electronics Inc., Huntington Beach, Calif., 1988-91; pres. AWS Assocs. Calif., Inc., El Monte, 1983—; corp. v.p., div. pres. HOPE ssocs., Inc., Huntington Beach, 1983—. With USAF, 1962-66. Mem. IEEE, Am. Mgmt. Assn., Am. Inst. Indsl. Engrs. (sr.) Soc. Logistics Engrs. (sr.), Am. Def. Preparedness Assn., Am. Security Council, Acacia, Tau Beta Pi. Presbyterian. Home: 17301 Keelson Ln Apt 75 Huntington Beach CA 92647-5934 Office: 7011 Warner Ave Ste L199 Huntington Beach CA 92647-5469

STILLMAN, HOWARD NEIL, investment analyst, consultant, writer; b. Bklyn., Oct. 29, 1935; s. Max and Betty Stillman; m. Carol Lou Panzer, Feb. 17, 1962; children: Brad, Todd. BBA, CCNY, 1957; MBA, NYU, 1964. Jr. securities analyst Fitch Investment Svcs., N.Y.C., 1957-59, Parrish & Co., N.Y.C., 1959-61; security analyst Sirota Taylor & Co., N.Y.C., 1961-66; sr. security analyst Orvis Bros., N.Y.C., 1966-67; dir. rsch. Kern Securities, N.Y.C., 1967-70; v.p. rsch. Black Stein Kimball, Paramus, N.J., 1970-73; market analyst Lustra Lighting divsn. N.Am. Phillips, East Rutherford, N.J., 1973-75; fin. advisor Prentice Hall, N.Y.C., 1975-82; dir. rsch. Phillip Appel/Muller, N.Y.C., 1983-84; ind. investment analyst, fin. specialist New Milford, N.J., 1985—; asst. prof. fin. Montclair (N.J.) State Coll., 1981-82, Fairleigh Dickinson U., Teaneck, N.J., 1976; tchr. fin. Bergen C.C., Paramus, 1969-81; has appeared as an expert witness on investment and bus. fraud for the N.Y. Stock Exchange as well as other major companies. With USAR, 1958-64. Mem. N.Y. Soc. Security Analysts, B'nai B'rith. Home: 1884 Matin Cir Bldg 149 San Marcos CA 92069

STILLWELL, KATHLEEN ANN SWANGER, healthcare consultant; b. Glendale, Calif., Aug. 12, 1950; d. Robert Dowayne and Irene Margaret (Sawatzky) Swanger; m. Joseph Wayne Stillwell, Nov. 11, 1971; children: Shannon Kristine, Nathan Joseph. AA, Cypress Coll., 1971; AS & diploma, Golden West Coll., 1981; BA in English Lit., Long Beach State U., 1982; MPA, Health Svcs. Adminstrn., U. San Francisco, 1989. RN Calif. Staff nurse Long Beach (Calif.) Meml. Hosp., 1981-84; sr. claims analyst Caronia Corp., Tustin, Calif., 1984-87; dir. quality assurance & risk mgmt. St. Mary Med. Ctr., Long Beach, 1987-89; cons. quality assurance, risk mgmt. Am. Med. Internat., Costa Mesa, Calif., 1989-91; cons. healthcare, 1991—; adj. faculty U. San Francisco, Woodbury U., 1996; faculty Am. Soc. Healthcare Risk Mgrs. Cert. Program; v.p. Patient Care Assessment Coun., L.A., 1988-89, pres., 1989-90, bd. dirs.; pres. State Bd. Patient Care Coun., 1990-92, past pres., 1992-94; speaker in field. Vol. Calif. Health Decisions, Orange County, 1989—, PTA, Am. Cancer Soc., Patient Care Assessment Coun.; active Constnl. Rights Found.; mem. edn. com. Bus. in Soc., Bus. Leadership, 1995, World Future Soc., 1995. Mem. NLN, Am. Soc. Healthcare Risk Mgmt., Nat. Assn. Healthcare Quality (exec. fin. com. 1993-95), Am. Soc. Quality Control Profls. (sec. healhtcare divsn. 1995—, chair membership 1994-95, chair-elect healthcare divsn. 1996-97, chair 1997-98), Am. Soc. Healthcare Risk Mgrs., So. Calif. Assn. Healthcare Risk Mgrs. (sec. 1989-90, mem. chmn. 1989-90), Calif. League for Nurses (bd. dirs. 1993-95), Patient Care Assessment Coun. (v.p. So. Calif. 1988, pres. So. Calif. 1989-90, state bd. pres. 1990-92, state bd. dirs. 1992-94). Democrat. Lutheran. Home and Office: 825 Coastline Dr Seal Beach CA 90740-5810

STILMAN, BORIS, computer science educator, researcher; b. Moscow, Aug. 16, 1950; came to the U.S., 1991.; s. Mikhail and Raisa (Gurevich) S.; m. Zinaida Korenblat, July 11, 1979; 1 child, Michael. MS in Math., Moscow State U., 1972; PhDs in Elec. Engring. and Computer Sci., Nat. Rsch. Inst. Elec. Engring, Moscow, 1984. Sr. engr., mathematician dept. for complex search problems The Nat. Rsch. Inst. for Elec. Engring., Moscow, 1972-75, sr. scientist dept. for complex search problems, 1975-85, sr. scientist/group leader dept. for complex search problems, 1985-88; chief dept. for software design computer tech. divsn. Nat. Rsch. Geol. Inst. for Oil Devel., Moscow, 1988-90; prin. software designer Inst. Designers Coun. The Nat. Rsch. Geol. Inst. for Oil Devel., Moscow, 1988-90; vis. prof. McGill U., Sch. Computer Sci., Montreal, 1990-91; assoc. prof. computer sci. dept. computer sci. and engring. U. Colo., Denver, 1991-94, prof. computer sci. dept. computer sci. and engring., 1994—; sci. sec. The USSR Acad. Scis. Nat. Commn., 1981-88; local divsn. chief, of. computer sci. The USSR Acad. Scis. Temporary Rsch. Group, Moscow, 1985-89; presenter in field. Author: Programming Within Structured Frame of Algorithmic Language, 1988, Theory of Linguistic Geometry in the Field of Artificial Intelligence; reviewer Annals of Math. and Artificail Intelligence, IBM Sys. Jour., Jour. of Intelligent Mfg.; contbr. 150 articles to books and articles to profl. jours.; numerous papers and presentations. Recipient The USSR Acad. Scis. and Dept. Geology Joint Rsch. grant, 1988, The USSR Acad. Scis. Rsch. grant, 1988, Sandia Nat. Labs. rsch. grantee, 1995, AFOSR Summer Faculty fellow, 1995, Chancellor's New Urban U. Lecturship awar, 1996, others. Mem. IEEE Computer Soc., Assn. for Computing Machinery, Am. Assn. for Artificial Intelligence, N.Y. Acad. Scis.

STILSON, WALTER LESLIE, radiologist, educator; b. Sioux Falls, S.D., Dec. 13, 1908; s. George Warren and Elizabeth Margaret (Zager) S.; m. Grace Beall Bramble, Aug. 15, 1933 (dec. June 1984); children: Carolyn G. Palmieri, Walter E., Judith A. Stirling; m. Lula Ann Birchel, June 30, 1985. BA, Columbia Union Coll., 1929; MD, Loma Linda U., 1934. Diplomate Am. Bd. Radiology, Nat. Bd. Med. Examiners. Intern White Meml. Hosp., Los Angeles, 1933-34; resident radiology Los Angeles County Gen. Hosp., 1934-36; instr. radiology Loma Linda (Calif.) U. Sch. Medicine, 1935-41, asst. prof., 1941-49, exec. sec. radiology, 1945-50, assoc. prof., 1949-55, head dept. radiology, 1950-55, prof. radiology, 1955-83, chmn. dept. radiology, 1955-69, emeritus prof., 1983—; chief radiology service White Meml. Hosp., Los Angeles, 1941-65, Loma Linda U. Med. Ctr., 1966-69; chmn. dept. radiologic tech. Sch. Allied Health Professions, 1966-75, med. dir. dept. radiologic tech., 1975-83. Contbr. articles to health jours. Fellow Am. Coll. Radiology; mem. AAAS, Los Angeles Radiol. Soc. (sec. 1960-61, treas. 1961-62, pres. 1963-64), Radiol. Soc. N.Am., Am. Roentgen Ray Soc., N.Y. Acad. Sci., Inland Radiol. Soc. (pres. 1971), Alpha Omega Alpha. Republican. Adventist. Home: 25045 Crestview Dr Loma Linda CA 92354-3414 Office: Loma Linda Radiol Med Group 11234 Anderson St Loma Linda CA 92354-2804

STIRLING, CLARK TILLMAN, lawyer; b. Washington, July 4, 1956; s. Edwin Tillman and Genevieve (Ruffner) S.; m. Linda Poumirau, May 30, 1986; children: Stephen Tillman, Grace Elizabeth. BS, Vanderbilt U., 1979; JD, George Washington U., 1983. Bar: Washington D.C. 1984, Alaska 1984. Clk. to Judge Cutler, State of Alaska, Palmer, 1983-84; asst. dist. atty. State of Alaska, Anchorage, 1984-87; assoc. Archbald & Spray, Santa Barbara, Calif., 1987-91; ptnr. Law Offices Kristofer Kallman, Santa Barbara, 1991-95; pvt. practice, Santa Barbara, 1996—; Bar: Alaska 1983, Calif. 1987. Bd. dirs. Childrens Creative Project, Santa Barbara, 1992-95; pres. bd. dirs. Transition House, Santa Barbara, 1993—; mem. centennial com. All Sts.-By-Sea, Santa Barbara, 1996—. Mem. Calif. Bar Assn., Alaska Bar Assn., D.C. Bar Assn., Santa Barbara County Bar Assn. (co-chmn. litigation sect. 1996—), Santa Barbara Inns Ct., Soc. of Cincinnati. Republican. Office: 2019 State St Santa Barbara CA 93105

STITH, JOSEPH, computer infosystems specialist, author; b. Ann Arbor, Mich., Sept. 1, 1962; s. Raymond Joseph and Rosemary Theresa (Babione) S.; m. Paula Campbell-Stith; children: Erin Peterson, Charles. BS in Computer Sci., Aurora (Ill.) Coll., 1983. Computer programmer, operator Aurora Coll., 1980-83; system programmer Moline Corp., St. Charles, Ill., 1983-84; mgr. system tech. Longman Group USA, Inc., Chgo., 1984-87; system mgr. tech. tracking Fermi Nat. Accelerator Lab., Batavia, Ill., 1987-94; sys. mgr., sys. support specialist Intel, Chandler, Ariz., 1994—. Mem. Digital Equipment Computer User's Soc., Alpha Chi. Home: 842 W Horseshoe Ave Gilbert AZ 85233 *Personal philosophy: Family first!.*

STOBER, MASON FREDERICK, JR., retired air traffic control educator; b. Washington, Mar. 8, 1929; s. Mason Frederick and Georgiana Butler (Joyes) S.; m. Dolores Sylvia Determan, Apr. 18, 1950; children: Mason Frederick III, Mary Catherine. BBS, N.H. Coll., 1968. Lic. air traffic controller, FAA. Enlisted USAF, 1947, advanced through grades to major; grad. to 2d lt. Officer Candidate Sch., 1956; navigator, bombardier B-52D USAF, 1956-70, ret., 1970; air traffic controller Boston Air Route Traffic Control Ctr., Nashua, N.H., 1970-87; instr. Seattle Air Rt. Traffic Control Ctr., Auburn, Wash., 1987-94. Decorated DFC, Air medal with nine oak leaf clusters. Mem. Res. Officers Assn. (life, past pres. Nashua chpt.), Nat. Geog. Soc., Alaska Geog. Soc., Am. Legion, VFW, Mil. Order of World Wars, Air Force Assn., Air Force Hist. Soc., U.S. Curling Assn. (Granite Curling Club), AARP, KC (Grand Knight Nashua coun. 5472, 1972-73, 82-83, coun. activity dir. N.H. state coun. 1974-76, state program dir. 1976-78, cmty. activity dir. 1979-81, state program dir. N.H.), Kiwanis (past pres. Greater Fed. Way chpt. 1993-94), Smokey's. Home: 2622 SW 320th Pl Federal Way WA 98023-2268

STOCK, LINCOLN FREDERICK, stockbroker; b. Schenectady, N.Y., Nov. 21, 1917; s. Lincoln Frederick and Evelyn Vaughn (Smith) S.; m. Helen Margaret Harris, May 5, 1962; children: Lynne Frederica Phillips, Elena Harris Madsen. Student, Syracuse U., 1937. Airline ops. in civil aeronautics Washington, 1944-58; aviation cons. Blomquist & Assocs., N.Y.C., 1958-60; aviation rschr. Flight Safety Fedn., N.Y.C., 1960-62; aviation ops. Howard, Needles et al, N.Y.C., 1962-63; dir. planning Pacific Airlines, San Mateo, Calif., 1963-65; exec. v.p. Carco Air Svc., Las Vegas, Nev., 1965-68; stockbroker Wilson-Davis Co., Las Vegas, 1963-95; tax collector Dept. Taxation Nev., Las Vegas, 1968-78; bookkeeper, Las Vegas, 1978-96; stockbroker Presdl. Brokerage, Las Vegas, 1994—; bankruptcy cons. Robert Cochrane, Trustee, Las Vegas, 1982—. Coun. mem. Greek Orthodox Ch., Las Vegas, 1971; candidate Sec. of State, Nev., 1990. Republican. Home: 2213 Plaza del Prado Las Vegas NV 89102

STOCK, PEGGY A(NN), college president, educator; b. Jan. 30, 1936; married; 5 children. BS in Psychology, St. Lawrence U., 1957; MA in Counseling, U. Ky., 1963, EdD, 1969. Lic. psychologist, Ohio. Instr., research asst. dept. psychology and spl. edn. U. Ky., Lexington, 1958-59, 63-67, staff psychologist Med. Ctr., 1964-66; dir. edn. United Cerebral Palsy of the Bluegrass, Lexington, 1959-61; exec. dir. Community Council for Physically Handicapped and Mentally Retarded, Lexington, 1962-64; dir. clin. program No. Ky. Regional Community Mental Health Ctr., Covington, 1969-71; pres. Midwest Inst. Tng. and Edn., Cin., 1971-76; assoc. prof., counseling psychologist Mont. State U., Bozeman, 1975-77, asst. dean Office of Student Affairs and Service, 1977-79; spl. asst. to pres. U. Hartford, Conn., 1979-80, assoc. prof. Coll. of Edn., 1980-85, v.p. adminstrn., 1981-86; prof., pres. Colby-Sawyer Coll., New London, N.H., 1986-95; pres. Westminster Coll. of Salt Lake City, 1995—; vis. prof. dept. sociology and edn. Thomas Moore Coll., Fort Mitchell, Ky., 1970-71; panelist Nat. Inst. Edn., 1985; cons. and lectr. in field. Contbr. chpts. to books, articles to profl. jours. Mem. coun. N.H. Coll. and Univ.; nat. bd. dirs. Med. Coll. Pa.; mem. New London Bus. Adv. Bd.; active numerous other civic orgns. Recipient Disting. Alumna award St. Lawrence U., 1989; grantee in field, most recent George I. Alden Trust, Helen Fuld Health Trust, Surdna, Cogswell, U.S. Dept. Edn., 1981-89, numerous others; fellow U. Ky., 1966-68, Am. Council Edn., 1979-80, United Jewish Com., 1981. Mem. Am. Coun. on Edn., Am. Assn. for Higher Edn., Advancement Women in Higher Edn. Office: Westminster Coll 1840 S 1300 E Salt Lake City UT 84105-3617

STOCKING, SHERL DEE, retail executive; b. Boise, Idaho, Aug. 20, 1945; s. Parley Dean and Iola Merrill (Linford) S.; m. Debra Lynn Hunt, Sept. 5, 1982. BS, Brigham Young U., 1968. Automotive specialist Bradshaw Auto Parts, Provo, Utah, 1964-68, J.C. Penney Co., Salt Lake City, 1969-70; store mgr. Uniroyal Tire Co., Salt Lake City, 1970-71; corp. tng. coordinator Uniroyal Tire Co., Houston, 1971, corp. advt. coordinator, 1972; store supr. Uniroyal Tire Co., Norfolk, Va., 1973-76; mgr. automotive dept. K-Mart Corp., Rapid City, S.D., 1976-79; dist. mgr. automotive dept. K-Mart Corp., N.Mex., 1979-80; mgr. Service Mdse. subs. K-Mart Corp., Denver, 1980-88; pres., owner S. & H. Svcs. Inc., Lynnwood, Wash., 1990—; antiques, petroliana, automobilia, Coca Cola, nostalgia dealer, Seattle. Pres. Quail Crossing Homeowner Assn., Denver, 1990—. Mem. Samuel Hall Soc., Coca Cola Collectors Club. Mormon. Home and Office: 115 146th St SE Lynnwood WA 98037-6711

STOCKTON, JOHN HOUSTON, professional basketball player; b. Spokane, Wash., Mar. 26, 1962; m. Nada Stepovich, Aug. 16, 1986; 1 child, John Houston. Grad., Gonzaga U., 1984. With Utah Jazz, Salt Lake City, 1984—; mem. U.S. Olympic Basketball Team, 1992. Named to NBA All-Star team, 1989-94; holder NBA single season rec. most assists, 1991; NBA Assists leader, 1987-1992; NBA Steals leader, 1989, 92; named NBA All-Star Co-MVP, 1993, All-NBA First Team, 1994. Office: Utah Jazz 301 W South Temple Salt Lake City UT 84101-1216*

STOCKTON, RODERICK ALAN, chemist; b. Lafayette, La., Jan. 18, 1951; s. Herbert Raymond and Olivet (Smith) S.; m. Pamela Sue Jones, Aug. 1, 1981 (div. 1992). BS, Stephen F. Austin State U., Nacogdoches, Tex., 1974; PhD, Tex. A&M U., College Station, 1985. Rsch. assoc. Tex. A&M U., College Station, 1975-85; sr. chemist Midwest Rsch. Inst., Kansas City, Mo., 1985-87, EG&G Idaho, Idaho Falls, 1987-89; prin. chemist Westinghouse Hanford Co., Richland, Wash., 1989-92; owner SLR Systems, Richland, 1992—; owner Stockton Consulting Svc., Richland, 1990-92. Contbr. articles to profl. jours. Welch Found. fellow. Mem. Am. Chem. Soc. Home: 3100 George Washington Way Richland WA 99352 Office: SLR Systems 3100 George Washington Way Richland WA 99352-1663

STOCKWELL, SHELLEY LESSIN, writer, hypnotherapist, television personality; b. Torrance, Calif., Mar. 7, 1945; d. I. M. Lessin and E. Kapilese. Cert. hypnotist, Hypnosis Inst., Glendale, Calif., 1981, cert. hypnotherapist, 1982; cert. advanced hypnotherapist, Wenatchee Wellness Inst., 1990; DD (hon.), Am. Fellowship Ch., 1989; PhD in Psychology, Internat. U. Profl. Studies, 1997. Cert. transpersonal hypnotherapist. CEO, writer, hypnotherapist, motivational speaker Creativity Unlimited Press, Rancho Palos Verdes, Calif., 1979—, artist, 1989—. Author: Insides Out, 1982, Sex and Other Touchy Subjects, 1991 (Gift of Yr. award 1991), Time Travel: Do-It-Yourself Past Life, 1992, Denial Is Not a River in Egypt: Overcome Depression and Addiction, 1995, Automatic Writing and Hiero-Scripting: How to Tap My Creativity and Guidance, 1995, How to Put a Smile on Your Face and Money in Your Pocket: Everything You Ever Wanted To Know; star: (TV show) The Shelley Show, 1989. Recipient Angel award for Outstanding Cable TV Show, 1990; named Woman of Distinction Soroptimist Internat., 1990. Mem. Nat. Guild Hypnotists, Nat. Speakers Assn., Pubs. Mktg. Assn., Assn. Past Life Therapies, Toastmasters Internat. (pres. 1983—, Toastmaster of Yr. 1983, 84), Assn. Councilors and Therapists. Office: Creativity Unlimited Press 30819 Casilina Dr Palos Verdes Peninsula CA 90275

STOEBUCK, WILLIAM BREES, law educator; b. Wichita, Kans., Mar. 18, 1929; s. William Douglas and Donice Beth (Brees) S.; m. Mary Virginia Fields, Dec. 24, 1951; children: Elizabeth, Catherine, Caroline. B.A., Wichita State U., 1951; M.A., Ind. U., 1953; J.D., U. Wash., 1959; S.J.D., Harvard U., 1973. Bar: Wash. 1959, U.S. Supreme Ct. 1967. Pvt. practice, Seattle, 1959-64; asst. prof. law U. Denver, 1964-67; assoc. prof. U. Wash., Seattle, 1967-70, prof., 1970-95; Judson Falknor prof., 1995—; of counsel Karr, Tuttle, Campbell, Seattle, 1988—. Author: Washington Real Estate: Property Law, 1995, Washington Real Estate: Transactions, 1995, Basic Property Law, 1989, Law of Property, 1984, 2nd edit., 1993, Nontrespassory Takings, 1977, Contemporary Property, 1996; contbr. articles to legal jours. Bd. dirs. Cascade Symphony Orch., 1978-83, Forest Park Libr., 1975-80. Mem. Am. Coll. Real Estate Lawyers, Am. Coll. Mortgage Attys., Wash. State Bar Assn., Assn. Am. Law Schs., Order of Coif, Seattle Yacht Club. 1st lt. USAF, 1951-56. Home: 3515 NE 158th Pl Lk Forest Park WA 98155-6649 Office: U Wash Law Sch 1100 NE Campus Pkwy Seattle WA 98105-6617

STOECK, JENNIFER ELIZABETH, scientific institute administrator; b. Seattle, Sept. 2, 1970; d. Michael C. Fuller and Kathleen V. (Riegel) Thomas; m. John A. Stoeck, Sept. 2, 1989. BA, U. Wash., 1993. Sci. coord.

Biomembrane Inst., Seattle, 1990-95; coord. rsch. program Fred Hutchinson Ctr. Rsch. Ctr., Seattle, 1995—. Contbr. articles to profl. jours. Mem. Am. Chem. Soc., Women in Comm., Amnesty Internat. Democrat. Office: Fred Hutchinson Cancer Rsch Ctr 1100 Fairview Ave N Seattle WA 98109

STOECKER, LEONA, mayor. Chair Longmont (Colo.) Water Bd., 1982-92; mayor City of Longmont, 1993—; bd. dirs. First Nat. Bank Longmont, Denver Regional Coun. Govts., Metro Vision 2020 Task Force, Metro Mayors Caucus, Colo. Smart Growth & Devel. Initiative; mem. Boulder County Long Range Planning commn., 1975-85, Boulder County Planning Commn., 1977-85, chair, 1984-85, City of Longmont Charter Rev. Commn., 1973, Longmont Cable TV Study Commn., 1972. Office: Civic Ctr Complex 350 Kimbark St Longmont CO 80501

STOFFLET, MARY KIRK, museum curator, writer; b. Long Branch, N.J., Dec. 23, 1942; d. Norman Kirk and Virginia (Birdsall) S. BA in Art History, Skidmore Coll., 1964; MA in Art History, NYU, 1969. Coord. intern program Fine Arts Museums of San Francisco, 1977-80; asst. curator San Francisco Internat. Airport, 1982-85; edn. curator San Diego Mus. Art, 1985-88, modern art curator, 1988—. Editor newsletter Western Assn. Art Museums, Oakland, Calif., 1974-77; contbg. editor Artweek, Oakland, 1974-81, Images & Issues, L.A., 1980-85; author, coordinating editor (exhbn. catalog) California Cityscapes, 1991; essayist, coordinating editor (exhbn. catalog) Latin American Drawings Today, 1991; author (exhbn. catalog) Dr. Seuss From Then to Now, 1987; editor (book) Correspondence Art, 1984. Rockefeller/NEA fellow in mus. edn., 1975-76; recipient Critic's Grant, NEA, 1981. Mem. MLA, Internat. Assn. Art Critics, Am. Assn. Museums, Coll. Art Assn., ArtTable, San Diego Ind. Scholars. Office: San Diego Museum of Art PO 2107 Balboa Park San Diego CA 92112

STOJANIK, KATHRYN ANN, accounting manager; b. Portland, Oreg., Oct. 24, 1954; d. Alfred Frank and Naomi Rose (Wolf) S. BSBA, Portland State U., 1977. Gen. collections asst. Nat. Assn. Credit Mgmt., Portland, Oreg., 1972-77; jr. acct. Precision Castparts Corp., Milwaukie, Oreg., 1977-86; sr. acct. Greenbrier Leasing Corp., Lake Oswego, Oreg., 1986-89, supr. car hire acctg., 1989-92, sr. fleet coord., 1992—. Democrat. Roman Catholic. Office: Greenbrier Leasing Corp One Centerpointe Dr Ste 200 Lake Oswego OR 97035

STOKES, GORDON ARTHUR, educational company executive, author; b. Salt Lake City, Aug. 28, 1929; s. Lovell Arthur and Viola (Condie) S.; div.; 1 child, Michael Ross. Cert. in personology, Interstate Coll. Personology, Sacramento, 1965; cert., Inst. Counseling, San Dimas, Calif., 1977; cert. in psychodrama, Calif. Inst. Socioanalysis, Long Beach, 1978; cert. minister, The New Sem., N.Y.C., 1983. Mktg. mgr. parent effectiveness seminars Pace Seminars, Pasadena, Calif., 1970-72; internat. trainer Touch for Health, Pasadena, 1973-85; pres. Three in One Concepts, Burbank, Calif., 1976—. Co-author: Under the Code, 1980, Structural Neurology, 1984, Basic/Advanced One Brain, 1984, Body Circuits, Pain and Understanding, 1990, New Options for Decision Makers, 1992, Body Mind Integration, 1992, Without Stress Learning Can Be Easy, 1996 (Best Book North Am. Bookdealer Exchange, 1996). Pres. Internat. Assn. Specialized Kinesiology. Office: Three in One Concepts 2001 W Magnolia Blvd Bc Burbank CA 91506-1704

STOLL, LEONARD PETER, business consultant; b. Canton, Ohio, July 29, 1941; s. Peter J. and Florence A. Stoll; m. Sheila A. O'Halloran, Sept. 9, 1967; children: Christine M., Eric P., Kevin J., Brian R. BS in Indsl. Mgmt., San Diego State U., 1964; MS in Sys. Mgmt., U. So. Calif., 1971. Commd. USAF, 1964, advanced through grades to lt. col., ret., 1984; subcontract administr. Boeing Def. & Space, Seattle, 1984-93, Westinghouse Hanford, Richland, Wash., 1993-95; pvt. practice cons. Richland, 1995—; purchasing cons. Dowty Aerospace, Yakima, Wash., 1996—. Bd. dirs. ACAP Day-Care Ctr., Auburn, Wash., 1991-93. Fellow Nat. Contracts Mgmt. Assn. (cert. profl. contracts mgr., pres. Puget Sound chpt. 1983-85, editor newsletter Columbia Basin chpt. 1995-96). Home and Office: 1401 Brookwood Ave Richland WA 99352

STOLPE, DANIEL OWEN, artist, printmaking educator; b. L.A., Nov. 14, 1939; s. Andrew Gustave and Mary Magdeleine (Schwind) S.; m. Joyce Anita Berge, Dec. 22, 1960 (div. Sept. 1972); 1 child, Matthew Lloyd; m. Elizabeth Fisher, July 13, 1986 (div. Aug. 1988). AA, Pasadena City Coll., 1960; student, Los Angeles County Art Inst., 1960; studies with, Don La Viere Turner, Glendora, Calif., 1961-62, Joseph Funk, Venice, Calif., 1965-66. Studio worker with Herbert A. Fox Monticeto Press, Sierra Madre, Calif., 1963-69; lithographer with Herbert A. Fox Fox Graphics, Boston, 1972; field worker Swinomish Indian Reservation, La Conner, Wash., 1971-74; artist lithographer with Joe Funk Joseph Graphics, Boston, 1972; founder, dir. Native Images, Inc., Santa Cruz, Calif., 1979—; instr. art Oakes Coll., U. Calif., Santa Cruz, 1978; with CETA and SYEP tng. programs Native Images Print Workshops, Santa Cruz 1979—; instr. artistically gifted and talented program Cultural Coun. Santa Cruz County, Spring 1987; instr. printmaking Inst. Am. Indian Arts, Santa Fe, N.Mex., 1987, Coos Bay (Oreg.) Art Mus., 1987. Artist illustrator Smithsonian Mag., 1972, Atlantic Monthly, Boston, 1972, Houghton-Mifflin Pubs., Boston, 1973, Planet Drum Mag., San Francisco, 1974, Native Am. Series, Am. Indian Studies Ctr., UCLA, 1978, The Best of the Smithsonian...the first decade of Smithsonian Mag., Harmony Books, N.Y.C., 1981, Images & Myths, Coyote Suite I & II (Daniel O. Stolpe), 1982, Renegade Christmas, Poetry by William Everson, 1984, Saturday Rev. Mag., Washington, 1984, Monterey Life Mag., 1987; artist woodcuts plays, poetry; exhbns. include Salt Lake City Art Ctr., 1976, Fort Hall (Idaho) Reservation Ctr.-Shoshone-Bannock Tribe, 1976, McHenry Libr. U. Calif. Santa Cruz, 1978, American West Gallery, Tucson, 1978, U. Utah, 1980, Calif. State U. Hayward, 1981, Mus. Fine Arts, Sante Fe, 1985, Many Horses Gallery, L.A., 1985, Rose Rock Gallery, Carmel, Calif., 1987; juried exhbns. include Okla. Printmakers, Okla. City, 1967, U. N.D. Art Galleries, 1981, Chautauqua (N.Y.) Art Galleries, 1981, Hunterdon (N.J.) Art Ctr., 1982, U. Calif. Santa Cruz, 1987, Monterey (Calif.) Peninsula Mus. Art, 1987, others; represented in permanent collections Smithsonian Mus., Washington, Utah Mus. Fine Arts, Salt Lake City, Portland (Oreg.) Art Mus., Boston Pub. Libr., Huntington Mus. U. Tex., Austin, U. N.Mex., Albequerque, Fogg Art Mus. Harvard, Mass., Everson Mus. Art, Syracuse, many others. Instr. summer job program SYEP, Santa Cruz County, 1982—; supporter Am. Indian Movement, 1980—. Los Angeles County Art Inst. scholar, 1960; Calif. ARts Coun. grantee, 1978, Santa Cruz City Arts Commn. grantee, 1986. Office: Native Images Inc 2539 Mission St Santa Cruz CA 95060-5727

STOLPMAN, THOMAS GERARD, lawyer; b. Cleve., June 2, 1949; s. Joseph Eugene and Katherine Ann (Berry) S.; m. Marilyn Heise, Aug. 17, 1974; children: Jennifer, Peter. BA, UCLA, 1972; JD, Los Angeles, 1976. Bar: Calif. 1976, U.S. Dist. Ct. (ctrl. dist.) Calif. 1976, U.S. Dist. Ct (ea. dist.) Calif. 1985, U.S. Dist. Ct. (so. dist.) Calif. 1995, U.S. Ct. Appeals (9th cir.) 1993, U.S. Supreme Ct. 1994. Ptnr. Stolpman, Krissman, Elber, Mandel & Katzman, Long Beach, Calif., 1976—. Editor The Forum, 1978-84; editor-in-chief The Advocate, 1984-87; contbr. articles to profl. jours. Bd. dirs. Miraleste Recreation and Park Dist., Rancho Palos Verdes, Calif., 1982-96. Named Trial Lawyer of Yr. So. Calif., Verdictum Juris, 1984. Fellow Am. Coll. Trial Lawyers; mem. ATLA, State Bar of Calif. (bd. govs. 1993-97, chair com. client rels. and assistance 1994-95, v.p. 1995-96, pres. 1996-97, chmn. com. on courts and legis. 1995-96), L.A. Trial Lawyers Assn. (bd. govs. 1979-93, pres. 1989), Calif. Trial Lawyers Assn. (bd. govs. 1987-90, exec. com. 1989-90), L.A. County Bar Assn. (bd. trustees 1986-87, exec. com. litigation sect. 1990-94), Am. Bd. Trial Advocates, Nat. Bd. Trial Advocacy (cert.), South Bar Bar Assn., Long Beach Bar Assn. Democrat. Roman Catholic. Office: Stoplman Krissman Elber Mandel & Katzman PO Box 1118 111 W Ocean Blvd 19th Fl Long Beach CA 90802

STOLTE, CHARLES ALBERT, company executive; b. Blue Earth, Minn., Apr. 20, 1933; s. Everett L. and Alice Marie Stolte; m. Betty J. Clark, June 13, 1954; children: Daryl, Penny, Susan, David. BSEE, U. Minn., 1955, MSEE, 1958, PhDEE, 1966. Rsch. asst. U. Minn., Mpls., 1955-57, rsch. fellow, 1957-66; mem. tech. staff Hewlett-Packard Co., Palo Alto, Calif., 1966-76, project mgr., 1976-84; R&D sect. mgr. Hewlett-Packard Co., Santa Rosa, Calif., 1984-92, wafer fab mgr., 1992—. Inventor Electrostatic deflection sys. for extended emitter life, 1979. Leader Boy Scouts Am., Los Altos, Calif., 1969-82. Mem. IEEE. Home: 2619 Fir Park Way Santa Rosa CA 95404-1809 Office: Hewlett Packard 1412 Fountain Grove Pkwy Santa Rosa CA 95403-1738

STOLTZ, ERIC MICHAEL, public relations executive; b. Glendale, Calif., Apr. 13, 1960; s. George Philip and Rosemary (Dunham) S. Student, U. So. Calif., L.A., 1981-83. Account exec. Aaron Cushman & Assocs., L.A., 1985-86; account supr. Aaron Cushman & Assocs., 1986-87, Pollare/Fischer Communications, L.A., 1987-89; account grp. mgr. Pollare/Fischer Communications, 1989-90; communications mgr. Am. Found. for AIDS Rsch., 1991-93; v.p. The Rowland Co., L.A., 1993-94; instr. UCLA, 1994—; sr. v.p. Evans Group, L.A., 1995—; bd. dirs. Urban Fitness Mag.; lectr. and author in field. Mem. mktg. com. L.A. Conservancy, 1988—; steering com. Calif. Preservation Found., Oakland, 1988-89; bd. dirs. L.A. Shanti Found., vice chmn. 1995. Mem. Pub. Rels. Soc. Am. (pres. L.A. chpt., accredited, dir. 1991—, Silver Anvil award 1990, 94, chpt. awards 1986-94), Internat. Assn. Bus. Communicators (chpt. awards of excellence 1987-93), Publicity Club L.A. (Pro awardee 1990, Merit award 1990). Roman Catholic. Home: 613 S Ridgeley Dr # 201 Los Angeles CA 90036

STOLTZE, DAVID ALBERT, physician; b. San Francisco, Feb. 13, 1950; s. Albert C. and Marjorie L. (Born) S.; m. Rosemarie Drechsler, Oct. 25, 1980; 1 child, Karl. AB, U. Calif., Berkeley, 1972; MD, U. Calif., San Diego, 1976; MPH, U. Ill., 1983. Intern Cook County Hosp., Chgo., 1977-78; resident in family practice Merced Cmty. Med. Ctr.-U. Calif. Davis, 1979-81; family physician Health Ctrs. No. N.Mex., Las Vegas, 1982—, Northeastern Regional Hosp., Las Vegas, 1982—; asst. clin. prof. U. N.Mex. Med. Sch., Albuquerque, 1983—; Nicaragua tng. exch. vol. U. Nacional Autonoma de Nicaragua, Managua, 1989. Mem. steering com. Com. for Health Rights in the Ams., San Francisco, 1994—. Fellow Am. Acad. Family Physicians; mem. APHA, N.Mex. Med. Soc., Physicians for Social Responsibility. Office: Health Ctrs No NMex PO Box 1928 Las Vegas NM 87701

STONE, ALEXANDER PAUL, mathematics educator; b. West New York, N.J., June 28, 1928; s. Samuel Bradford and Violet Elizabeth (Schuessler) S.; m. Mary Ann Majeski, July 23, 1960; 1 child, Christopher Bradford. BSEE, Columbia U., 1952; MSEE, Newark Coll. Engring., 1956; PhD, U. Ill., 1965. Field engr. Western Elec./Bell Telephone Labs., Whippany, N.J., 1952-56; instr. in elec. engring. Manhattan Coll., Riverdale, N.Y., 1956-58; asst. prof. physics Dickinson Coll., Carlisle, Pa., 1958-60; asst. prof. math. U. Ill., Chgo., 1965-69; assoc. prof. math. U. Ill., 1969-70, U. N.Mex., Albuquerque, 1970-76; prof. math. U. N.Mex., 1976—, chmn. dept. math. and stats., 1991—; cons. Air Force Weapons Lab., 1984—. Editor: Improperly Posed Boundary Value Problems, 1976; author: Transient Lens Synthesis, 1990; contbr. articles to profl. jours. With USN, 1946-48, 2d lt. U.S. Army, 1951-52. NSF grantee, 1966-70, AFOSR grantee, 1984-85. Mem. Am. Math. Soc., Internat. Union of Radio Sci. (commn. E on electro-magnetic noise and interference). Office: Univ NMex Dept Math And Stats. Albuquerque NM 87131

STONE, ARLENE, writer; b. Phila.. Student, Boston U. Author: (poetry books) The Shule of Jehovah, 1972, The Image Maker, 1972, Through a Coal Cellar, Darkly, 1977, The Women's House, 1978, At The Gates of Hell, 1979, The Double Pipes of Pan, 1980, Son Sonnets, 1994.

STONE, DESIREÉ NAOMI, artistic director, film producer and director; b. Chgo., Mar. 2, 1965; d. Cecil Anthony and Bertha Naomi (Long) Johnson; married; children: Philip, Alan, James, Kye. Student, Evelyn Lee Dance Sch., Kansas City, Mo., 1979-83, U. Mo. Conservatory, Kansas City, 1983-84. Ballet dancer Mo. State Ballet, Kansas City, 1979-81; painter Kansas City (Mo.) Art Inst., 1980-83; artistic dir., founder Children's Drama Workshop, Portland, Oreg., 1992—; prodr., dir., founder Le Femme Noir Pictures, Portland, 1992—; drama instr. N.W. Children's Theatre, Portland, 1995—, asst. dir., 1996; actress Oreg. Shakespeare Festival, Ashland, 1994-95. Author, pub.: (book) Beware of Strangers, 1990; writer, dir., prodr.: (films) Bellow, 1996, A Christmas Menorah, 1996. Vol. tchr. theater Sabin Elem. Sch., Portland, 1992-96. Recipient Artistic Achievement award for watercolor, 1983. Mem. Am. Fedn. TV Radio Assn. Office: Le Femme Noir Pictures 63 NE Fremont Portland OR 97212

STONE, DONALD D., investment and sales executive; b. Chgo., June 25, 1924; s. Frank J. and Mary N. (Miller) Diamondstone; student U. Ill., 1942-43; B.S., DePaul U., 1949; m. Catherine Mauro, Dec. 20, 1970; 1 child, Jeffrey. Pres., Poster Bros., Inc., Chgo., 1950-71, Revere Leather Goods, Inc., Chgo., 1953-71; owner Don Stone Enterprises, Chgo., 1954—; v.p. Horton & Hubbard Mfg. Co., Inc. div. Brown Group, Nashua, N.H., 1969-71, Neevel Mfg. Co., Kansas City, Mo., 1969-71. Mem. adv. bd. San Diego Opera; founder Don Diego Meml. Scholarship Fund; mem. bd. overseers U. Calif., San Diego, chancellor's assoc.; mem. exec. bd. Chgo. Area council Boy Scouts of Am. Served with U.S. Army, 1943-46. Clubs: Bryn Mawr Country (Lincolnwood, Ill.) (dir.), Carlton, La Jolla Beach and Tennis, La Jolla Country, Del Mar Thoroughbred. Home: 8240 Caminito Maritimo La Jolla CA 92037-2204

STONE, GEORGE, artist, art educator. BA, Calif. State U., Long Beach, 1972; MFA, R.I. Sch. Design, 1974. Instr. R.I. Sch. Design, Providence, 1972-74; instr. sculpture Portsmouth (R.I.) Abbey Sch., 1973-74, Wayne State U., Detroit, 1974-75; vis. lectr., sculpture dept. Ohio U., Athens, 1976-77; instr., found. dept. Otis/Parsons Sch. Design, L.A., 1982-83; vis. lectr., sculpture dept. UCLA, 1986; assoc. prof. fine arts Art Inst. So. Calif., Laguna Beach, 1989-93; assoc. prof. visual art U. La Verne, Calif., 1994—; vis. artist Calif. State U. Long Beach, 1986, Crossroads H.S. for Arts and Sci., Santa Monica, 1987, Claremont (Calif.) Grad. Sch., 1987, 88, U. Calif. Santa Barbara, 1989, Art Ctr. Coll. Design, Pasadena, Calif., 1991, Yale U., New Haven, 1992, Chatham Coll., Pitts., 1992, Calif. State U. San Francisco, 1993; commd. artist City West Hollywood, 1986, City of L.A. Cmty. Redevel. Agy., 1987, Metro Art L.A. County Met. Transp. Auth., 1990-97, City of L.A. Cultural Affairs Dept., 1995-97. Solo exhbns. include Forsythe Bldg., Detroit, 1975, Cline Bldg., Athens, Ohio, 1976, Lake Hope, Athens, 1977, Otis/Parsons Gallery, 1981, East Gallery Claremont Grad. Sch., 1985, Calif. State U. Long Beach Art Mus., 1986, Meyers/Bloom Gallery, Santa Monica, Calif., 1988, 91, Laguna Art Mus., Costa Mesa, Calif., 1990, Capp St. Project, 1991, New Langton Arts, San Francisco, 1991, Ruth Bloom Gallery, Santa Monica, 1993, Pitts. Ctr. Arts, 1994; 2-person exhbns. L.A. Contemporary Exhbns., 1985, Claremont Grad. Sch. Gallery, 1988; group exhbns. include Lehigh U. Art Gallery, Bethlemen, Pa., 1975, Wayne State U., 1975, U. Calif. Santa Cruz, 1978, Vanguard Gallery, L.A., 1979, L.A. Inst. Contemporary Art, 1979, NYU Art Gallery, N.Y.C., 1980, Charles Kobler and Assoc. Architects, L.A., 1983, Design Ctr. L.A., 1984, Univ. Art Mus. Calif. State U. Long Beach, 1985, IDM Corp. and Pub. Corp. Arts, Long Beach, 1985, CRA, L.A., 1987, Newport Harbor Art Mus., Newport Beach, Calif., 1988, Meyers/Bloom Gallery, 1989, Galerie Antoine Candeau, Paris, 1990, Sezon Mus. Art, Tokyo and Osaka, Japan, 1991, Muckenthaler Cultural Ctr., Fullerton, Calif., 1991, Contemporary Arts Ctr., New Orleans, 1993, Next Thread Waxing Space, N.Y.C., 1993, Contemporary Arts Forum, Santa Barbara, 1996, Armand Hammer Mus. Art and Cultural Ctr., UCLA, 1997, others; subject numerous catalogs, publs., and revs., 1984—. Home: 1815 Laurel Canyon Blvd Los Angeles CA 90046

STONE, GREGORY ORVILLE, cognitive psychology educator; b. Chgo., Nov. 7, 1955; s. Orville Joseph and Margaret Elizabeth (Case) S. BA, Harvard U., 1979; PhD, U. Calif., San Diego, 1985. Rsch. psychologist Navy Pers. R&D Ctr., San Diego, 1982; postdoctoral fellow math. dept. Boston U., 1983-86; asst. prof. psychology dept. Ariz. State U., Tempe, 1986-93, assoc. prof. psychology dept., 1993—. Author: (with others) The Reality of Linguistic Rules, 1994; jr. co-author: Parallel Distributed Processing Vol. I, 1986; contbr. articles to profl. jours. Mem. Psychonomics Soc., Sigma Xi, Sigma Chi (Outstanding tchr. 1991). Office: Ariz State U Psychology Dept Tempe AZ 85287

STONE, JAMES ROBERT, surgeon; b. Greeley, Colo., Jan. 8, 1948; s. Anthony Joseph and Dolores Concetta (Pietrafeso) S.; m. Kaye Janet Friedman, May 16, 1970; children: Jeffrey, Marisa. BA, U. Colo., 1970; MD, U. Guadalajara, Mex., 1976. Diplomate Am. Bd. Surgery, Am. Bd. Surg. Critical Care. Intern Md. Gen. Hosp., Balt., 1978-79; resident in surgery St. Joseph Hosp., Denver, 1979-83; practice medicine specializing in surgery Grand Junction, Colo., 1983-87; staff surgeon, dir. critical care Va. Med. Ctr., Grand Junction, 1987-88; dir. trauma surgery and critical care, chief surgery St. Francis Hosp., Colorado Springs, Colo., 1988-91; pvt. practice Kodiak, Alaska, 1991-92; with South Denver Surg. Cons., Englewood, Colo., 1992-93, Summit Surg. Assocs., 1993-96; asst. dir. trauma Tristate Trauma System, Erie, Pa., 1996—; med. dir. LifeStar Aeromed, Erie, Pa., 1997—; asst. clin. prof. surgery U. Colo. Health Sci. Ctr., Denver, 1984—; pres. Stone Aire Cons., Grand Junction, 1988—; owner, operator Jjnka Ranch, Flourissant, Colo.; spl. advisor CAP, wing med. officer, 1992—; mem. advisor med. com. unit, 1990-92; advisor Colo. Ground Team Search and Rescue, 1994—. Contbr. articles to profl. jours.; inventor in field. Bd. dirs. Mesa County Cancer Soc., 1988-89, Colo. Trauma Inst., 1988-91. Colo. Speaks out on Health grantee, 1988; recipient Bronze medal of Valor Civil Air Patrol. Fellow Denver Acad. Surgery, Southwestern Surg. Congress, Am. Coll. Chest Physicians, Am. Coll. Surgeons (trauma com. Colo. chpt.), Am. Coll. Critical Care; mem. Am. Coll. Physician Execs., Soc. Critical Care (task force 1988—). Roman Catholic.

STONE, JOHN HELMS, JR., admiralty advisor; b. Andalusia, Ala., Dec. 3, 1927; s. John Helms and Ruth May (Barker) S.;m. Mary Ham, July 24, 1950; children: Malcolm, Mary Ruth, Ronald, John T. Student Ga. Mil. Coll., U.S. Merchant Marine Sch., 1945; student, Tulane U., 1975. Master mariner, USCG. Master capt. Sea-Land Steamship, Port Newark, N.J., 1947-60; Lt. (jg) USNR, 1948-62; sr. pilot Panama Canal Co., Balboa Canal Zone, 1960-73; chief of transit op. Panama Canal Commn., Balboa Canal Zone, 1973-76; chmn. bd. local inspection Panama Canal Commn., Balboa, Republic of Panama, 1976-85; admiralty cons. John H. Stone & Assocs., Boulder, Colo., 1985—, Am. Registry Arbitrators, 1994—; admiralty advisor Phelps-Dunbar, New Orleans, 1958-79, Fowler White, Tampa, Fla., 1984, Terriberry & Assocs., New Orleans, 1992. County treas. Dem. Party, Boulder, 1989. Mem. NRA (v.p. 1970, master pistol and rifle shot), Master, Mates and Pilots Union (v.p. 1970-72). Presbyterian. Home: 3795 Wild Plum Ct Boulder CO 80304-0460

STONE, MICHAEL DAVID, landscape architect; b. Moscow, Idaho, Apr. 11, 1953; s. Frank Seymour Stone and Barbara Lu (Wahl) Stone/Schonthaler; m. Luann Dobaran, Aug. 12, 1978; children: Stephanie Nicole, David Michael. B in Landscape Architecture, U. Idaho, 1976; postgrad., Oreg. State U., 1986, Harvard U., 1990; MA in Orgnl. Leadership, Gonzaga U., 1990. Registered landscape architect, Wash., cert. leisure profl.Nat. Recreation and Park Assn. Landscape designer Robert L. Woerner, ASLA, Spokane, Wash., 1976-77; pk. planner Spokane County Pks. and Recreation, 1977-82; landscape architect City of Spokane Pks. and Recreation, 1982-84, asst. pks. mgr., 1984-86, golf and cmty. devel. mgr., 1986-95, co-dir., 1995-96, spl. ops. mgr., 1996—; cons. Lake Chelan (Wash.) Golf Course, 1988. Pres. Sacred Heart Parish Coun., Spokane, 1987-89; v.p. Cataldo Sch. Bd. Dirs., Spokane, 1987-89; pres. South Spokane Jaycees, 1977-86; active Leadership Spokane, 1989, Nat. Exec. Devel Sch., 1993. Named Outstanding Young Man Am., 1980, 85, Outstanding Knight, Intercollegiate Knights, 1972-73, Jaycee of the Yr., South Spokane Jaycees, 1981, Vet. of the Yr., South Spokane Jaycees, 1984-85; recipient Holy Grail award Intercollegiate Knights, 1972-73. Mem. Nat. Recreation and Pk. Assn. (bd. dirs. golf mgmt. sect. 1995—), Am. Soc. Landscape Architects, Wash. Recreation and Pk. Assn., Nat. Inst. Golf Mgmt. (bd. dirs. 1995—), Beta Chi, Delta Tau Delta. Roman Catholic. Home: 2007 E 55th Ave Spokane WA 99223-8212 Office: City of Spokane 808 W Spokane Falls Blvd Spokane WA 99201-3333

STONE, NORMAN MICHAEL, psychologist; b. Balt., Mar. 23, 1949; s. Forrest Leon and Beverly Iola (Gendason) S.; m. Susan Foster Hoitt, May 18, 1981; children: Shannon, Caroline, Brittany Rain, Forrest. BA, UCLA, 1971; PhD, U. Iowa, 1976. Lic. psychologist, Tex., Calif. Chief youth and family svcs. Abilene (Tex.) Mental Health-Mental Retardation Regional Ctr., 1976-79; coord. family crisis team San Fernando Valley Guidance Clinic, Northridge, Calif., 1980-88, sr. clin. supr., 1989-95; sr. cmty. psychologist L.A. County Dept. Children's Mental Health, L.A., 1995—; mem. psychiat. panel of experts on dependency and family law Calif. Superior Ct., 1987-96; mem. adj. faculty Hardin-Simmons U., Abilene, 1977-79; vis. prof. UCLA, 1980-81; clin. prof. Fuller Theol. Sem., L.A., 1982-94. Contbr. numerous articles on psychology, psychiatry, law and social welfare to internat. profl. jours., books and film. USPHS fellow, 1972-76; Simon Found. rsch. grantee, 1982, 89. Mem. AAAPP, Am. Psychol. Soc., Sojourners. Office: LA County Dept Childrens Mental Health 505 S Virgil Ave Los Angeles CA 90020-1403

STONE, RUBY ROCKER, state legislator; b. Portal, Ga., Feb. 6, 1924; d. Eddie Lee and Della (Taylor) Rocker; widowed; children: Dianne Carolyn Stone Milhollin, Raymond Edward Stone. Office mgr., dental asst. to Dr. Richard W. Collins, 1962-68; asst. to mgr. Am. Machine & Foundry Spl. Missile project Vandenberg AFB, 1959-60; sec. Idaho House State Affairs, 1970; aide to Gov. Don Samuelson, 1970-71; senate jour. clk. Idaho Ho. Reps., 1971-84, mem., 1986—, chmn. local govt. com., 1991—. Active ARC, and numerous other cmty. projects and cmty. vol. orgns. Recipient Sportsmanship award Idaho State Women's Amateur Golf Tournament, 1980, Plantation Ladies Golf Assn., Outstanding Woman award, 1993; inducted into Idaho Sports Hall of Fame, 1993, Idaho New Agenda Hall of Fame, 1993; named Republicn Outstanding Legislator-House, 1994; 5 time golf champion Tri-Club Golf, 2 time champion Treasure Valley Ladies Golf. Mem. Nat. Orgn. Women Legislators, U.S. Golf Assn. (mem. jr. girls championship com. 1981—), Idaho Golf Assn. (bd. dirs. 1975-87, Ladies Sr. Golf champion 1982), Plantation Golf Club (13 time champion), Gowen Field Officers Club, Gowen Field Officers Wives Club, Daus. of Nile, El Korah Honored Ladies Club, Elks. Republican. Protestant. Home: 6604 Holiday Dr Boise ID 83709-2022

STONE, SAMUEL BECKNER, lawyer; b. Martinsville, Va., Feb. 4, 1934; s. Paul Raymond and Mildred (Beckner) S.; m. Shirley Ann Gregory, June 18, 1955; children: Paul Gregory, Daniel Taylor. BSEE, Va. Polytech. Inst. & State U., 1955; JD, George Wash. U., 1960. Bar: Md. 1960, Calif. 1963, Patent and Trademark Office. Patent examiner, 1955-58; patent adv. Naval Ordinance Lab., Silver Spring, Md., 1958-59; assoc. Thomas & Crickenberger, Washington, 1959-61, Beckman Instruments Inc., Fullerton, Calif., 1961-65; assoc. Lyon & Lyon, L.A., 1965-72, ptnr., 1972; mng. ptnr. Lyon & Lyon, Costa Mesa, Calif., 1982—; judge Disneyland Com. Svc. Awards, Anaheim, Calif., 1987. Mem. Orange County Bar Assn. (bd. dirs. 1988-91, travel seminar chair 1986-92), Orange County Patent Law Assn. (pres. 1987, bd. exec. com. 1987-90), Calif. Bar Assn. (intellectual property sect. bd. 1987-90), Am. Electronics Assn. (lawyers com. 1988—, co-chair 1996—), Orange County Venture Group (dir. 1985—, pres. 1997), Rams Booster Club (dir. 1984-90), Pacific Club (mem. legal adv. com., chair 1989-92). Republican. Home: 1612 Antiqua Way Newport Beach CA 92660 Office: Lyon & Lyon 3200 Park Center Dr Ste 1200 Costa Mesa CA 92626-7108

STONE, SANDRA, writer, artist; b. Portland, Oreg., Apr. 4, 1934. visual arts cons. to individual collectors; editor Breitenbush Books, Portland, 1977-81; artist cons. Green Tiger Press, 1985. Exhibited in group shows at Portland Art Mus., 1975-80, 95, White Bird Gallery, Cannon Beach, Oreg., 1980, White Bird Gallery, 1981, N.W. Artist's Workshop, 1981, Contemporary Crafts Gallery, Portland, 1983, Am. Inst. Architects Gallery, 1994, Ricciardi Gallery, Astoria, Oreg., 1994, Orlo Found., 1994, Marylhurst Coll., Portland, 1994, Am. Inst. Architects Gallery, Portland, 1994, Spokane Ctrl. Libr. Art Gallery, 1994, Broders Books, 1995, Old City Hall, Gresham, Oreg., 1996; commd. works by Oreg. State Archives Bldg., Salem, 1991-92, Tacoma Firehouse, 1993, Spokane Ctrl. Libr., 1993-95, Portland C.C. Libr., 1994-96, Midland Regional Libr., Portland, 1994-96, U.S. Fed. Courthouse, Portland, 1995-97, Riverfront Park, Salem, Oreg., 1996-97; author: (poems) Cocktails with Brueghel in the Museum Cafe, 1996, also essays for art catalogues. Active Young Audiences Bd., Portland Art Mus., N.W. Artist's Workshop, Portland Ctr. for Visual Arts, Contemporary Crafts Gallery, Oreg. Sch. Arts and Crafts, others. Artist's fellow Va. Ctr. for Creative Arts, 1986, Oreg. Lit. Arts, 1992; recipient Purchase award U. West Fla., 1995. Mem. N.W. Dramatist's Guild, Soc. Children's Book Writers and Illustrators, Acad. Am. Poets (assoc.).

STONE, WILFRED H., English educator, writer; b. Springfield, Mass., Aug. 18, 1917; s. Lester Lyman and Clara (Gilbreth) S.; m. Cary Lee Laird, Dec. 31, 1954 (div. 1972); children: Gregory I., Miriam Lee; m. Margaret

Davis Aiken, Oct. 20, 1985. BA, U. Minn., 1941, MA, 1946; PhD, Harvard U., 1950. Instr. Harvard U., Cambridge, Mass., 1950; asst. prof. U. Vt., Burlington, summer 1953; from asst. prof. to prof. emeritus English Stanford (Calif.) U., 1950—. Author: Religion and art of William Hale White (Mark Rutherford), 1956, The Cave and the Mountain: A Study of E.M. Forster, 1966, Prose Style, 4 edits., 1972-82, The Short Story: An Introduction, 1978, 2d edit., 1982. Lt. USN, 1942-45. Recipient Commonwealth Club medal, 1967, Dinkelspiel award Stanford U., 1962. Mem. MLA (Christian Gauss prize 1967), Lighter-Than-Air Assn. Democrat. Home: 36 Pearce Mitchell Pl Stanford CA 94305 Office: Stanford Univ Dept English Stanford CA 94305

STONE, WILLIAM COY, surgeon; b. Carlsbad, N.Mex., Sept. 22, 1934; s. Coy Smith and Mattye Marie (Swint) S.; m. Carolyn Vaughn, Nov. 3, 1963; children: Coy Steven, Allison Ann. BA, Baylor U., 1956; MD, Tulane Med. Sch., 1960. Diplomate Am. Bd. Surgery. Rotating intern Parkland Meml. Hosp., Dallas, 1960-61, resident gen. surgery, 1961-65; pvt. practice gen. surgery Hobbs, N.Mex., 1967—. Capt. U.S. Army, 1965-67, Korea. Fellow ACS, Southwestern Surg. Congress; mem. Am. Soc. Gen. Surgeons (founding), Lubbock Surg. Soc., Parkland Surg. Soc. (founding), Alpha Omega Alpha. Baptist. Office: St Mary Med Ctr 2410 N Fowler St Hobbs NM 88240-2332

STONE, WILLIAM GENE, psychiatrist; b. Chgo., May 8, 1931; s. James and Bertha (Freeman) S.; m. Florence Raby, Sept. 4, 1953 (dec. Nov. 1977); children: Janet, Barbara, Lawrence, Robert. BS in Chemistry, Physics, U. Ill., 1952, MS in Physiology, 1954, MD, 1962. Diplomate Am. Bd. Psychiatry and Neurology. Intern Decatur, Macon County Hosp., Ill., 1962-63; resident in psychiatry Mental Health Inst., Independence, Iowa, 1963-68; med. dir. Blackhawk County Mental Health, Waterloo, Iowa, 1968-73; staff psychiatrist St. Francis Hosp., Waterloo, Iowa, 1966-77; chmn. dept. psychiatry St. Francis Hosp., Waterloo, 1975-77; sr. psychiatrist Las. Vegas (Nev.) Mental Health Ctr., 1977. 78. 88; psychiatrist pvt. practice Las Vegas, 1978—; med. staff Valley Hosp., Las Vegsa, Cmty. Hosp., Las Vegas, Desert Springs Hosp., Las Vegas, 1978-94, So. Nev. Meml. Hosp., 1979-84, Monte Vista Hosp., Las Vegas, 1986-94; pres. Redrock Neuropsychiat. Inst., 1980-89; chief psychiat. cons. to substance abuse program, State of Nev., Dept. of Prisons, 1986; chief of staff, Monte Vista Hosp., Las Vegas, 1986; dir. dept. psychiatry Cmty. Hosp., 1988-89; prof. Univ for Humanistic Studies, 1980-85, adj. instr. med. students U. Nev., 1993-94. Author: (book) Does Everybody Need an Analyst?, 1968. Scoutmaster, commiteeman Boy Scouts Am., Chgo., 1955-56; bd. dirs. Planned Parenthood of Blackhawk County, Iowa, 1963-66, Unitarian Universalist Soc. of Blackhawk County, 1969-75, pres., 1975; bd. dirs. U. for Humanistic Studies, Las Vegas, 1981-85, Nat. Kids Kampus, Las Vegas, 1987. Fellow Am. Psychiat. Assn.; mem. Las Vegas Psychiatric Soc. (sec., treas. 1980-81, pres. 1982-83, v.p. 1994), Nev. Assn. Psychiat. Physicians, (v.p., pres. elect 1989, pres. 1990, dist. rep. to Am. Assn. Psychiat. Physicians). Home: PO Box 12477 Las Vegas NV 89112-0477

STONEBERG, CONNIE, educational administrator; b. Idaho Falls, Idaho, Jan. 3, 1934; d. S. Eddie and LaVera (Hill) Pedersen; m. Robert Stoneberg, Dec. 30, 1952; children: Holly Reed, Waid R., Jody Nielson. BS magna cum laude, Brigham Young U., 1970; MEd, Idaho State U., 1983. Cert. tchr., sch. adminstr., Idaho. Tchr. Osgood Elem. Sch., Idaho Falls, 1967-79, tchg. prin., 1979-89; prin. Linden Park Elem. Sch., Idaho Falls, 1989—. Bd. dirs. Mae Nueber Endowment Fund, Idaho Falls, 1988-96, Idaho Falls Hist. Soc., 1996—. Mem. ASCD (regional conf. planning com. 1979-96), Internat. Reading Assn. Mem. LDS Ch.

STONECYPHER, DAVID DANIEL, writer, retired psychiatrist and ophthalmologist; s. David Daniel and Imogene May (Poynter) S.; married, Oct. 6, 1978; children: Karen, Lance. Student, U. Nebr., 1948; MD, U. Chgo., 1953. Diplomate Am. Bd. Ophthalmology. Psychiatrist VA Hosp., Hines, Ill., 1956; asst. chief ophthalmology 97th Gen. Hsp., Frankfurt am Main, Germany, 1959-61; pvt. practice ophthalmology Nebraska City, Nebr., 1961-63, La Mesa, Calif., 1963-87. Author: Getting Older and Staying Young, 1974. Capt. U.S. Army, 1959-61. Fellow Am. Geriatrics Soc., Gerontol. Soc.

STONEY, RONALD J., vascular surgeon, educator; b. Carmel, Calif., Mar. 4, 1934; s. Ronald Burdette and Gertrude Mathilda (Schram) S.; m. Linda Jean Whaley, Sept. 30, 1972; children: Ronald Mark, David Collis, Steven Lyle, Kathleen Lynn, Jeanette Spencer. BS, U. Santa Clara, Calif., 1955; MD, U. Calif., San Francisco, 1959. Instr. surgery, adminstrv. resident U. Calif., San Francisco, 1965-66, asst. prof. surgery, 1966-73, assoc. prof., 1973-79, prof., 1979-94, dir. Blood Flow Lab., 1981-86, co-chief div. vascular surgery, 1982-87, prof. surgery emeritus, 1994—; dir. Lifeline Found., Manchester, Mass., 1991—; founder, pres. Pacific Vascular Rsch. Found., San Francisco, 1982—. Author: Manual of Vascular Surgery, Vol. I, 1980, Vol. II, 1986, Wylie's Atlas of Vascular Surgery, Vols. I-VI, 1992; mem. editl. bd. Jour. Vascular Surgery, 1993—; contbr. articles to profl. jours. 2d lt. M.C., USA, 1966-68. Fellow ACS; mem. AMA, Am. Surgical Assn., Calif. Med. Assn., Soc. for Vascular Surgery, Internat. Soc. Cardiovascular Surgery (pres. N.Am. chpt. 1993), Howard C. Naffziger Surg. Soc. (pres. 1980-81), Western Vascular Soc., Pacific Coast Surg. Assn. Democrat. Roman Catholic.

STONG, JOHN ELLIOTT, retail electronics company executive; b. Elkater, Iowa, Sept. 20, 1921; s. Elliott Sheldon and Nora Elizabeth (Daly) S.; m. Olive Miriam Foley, Dec. 11, 1943; children: Mary Myers, Jon, Miriam. Grad. U. Colo., 1943. Salesman, Purucker Music, Medford, Oreg., 1946-48, dept. mgr., 1949-56, store mgr., 1957, partner, 1958-61, owner, 1962-64; pres. Purucker Music Houses, Medford, 1965-67, Music West, Inc., Eugene, Oreg., 1968-70, Magnavox Centers, Medford, 1971—, exec. asst., Consultants Internat., 1972—. Served with USAF, 1943-45. Decorated Air medal. Mem. Nat. Assn. Music Mchts. (dir. 1969-72), Scull Mchts. Rsch. Group (dir., chmn.). Republican. Roman Catholic. Home: 2120 Woodlawn Dr Medford OR 97504-7678 Office: Cons Internat 111 N Central Ave Medford OR 97501-5925

STOOKER, HENDRIK CORNELIS, curator, gallery director; b. Rhenoy, Beesd, The Netherlands, Apr. 22, 1931; came to U.S., 1960; s. Hendrik Cornelis Sr. and Sanderina Maria (Dekker) S. Cert. Tchr. in Art Edn., Art Acad., Arnhem, The Netherlands, 1953; BA in Art History, Calif. State U., L.A., 1972; MA in Art History, U. Calif., L.A., 1976. Gallery dir. Miller Gallery Amerindian Art, Beverly Hills, 1977-79; ind. art dealer, 1980-83; gallery dir. Alpha Contemporary Exhibit, L.A., 1983-86; sr. curator, gallery dir. dept. art history and visual arts Occidental Coll., L.A., 1987—. Cofounder Arroyo Arts Collective, L.A., 1989; organizer 1st arts & crafts fair Muss. of Arroyo/Southwest Mus., L.A., 1990, artists' studios Highland Park and Mt. Washington L.A. Open Festival, 1990, discovery tour Hist. Soc. So. Calif., 1993, Sarah A. Gilman Meml. award Occidental Coll., 1995. Home: 5322 Granada St Los Angeles CA 90042-3312 Office: Occidental Coll Dept Art History 1600 Campus Rd Los Angeles CA 90041-3384

STOORZA GILL, GAIL, corporate professional; b. Yoakum, Tex., Aug. 28, 1943; d. Roy Otto and Ruby Pauline (Ray) Blankenship; m. Larry Sttorza, Apr. 27, 1963 (div. 1968); m. Ian M. Gill, Apr. 24, 1981; 1 child, Alexandra Leigh. Student, N. Tex. State U., 1961-63, U. Tex., Arlington, 1963. Stewardess Cen. Airlines, Ft. Worth, 1963; advt. and acctg. exec. Phillips-Ramsey Advt., San Diego, 1963-68; dir. advt. Rancho Bernardo, San Diego, 1968-72; dir. corp. communications Avco Community Developers, San Diego, 1972-74; pres. Gail Stoorza Co., San Diego, 1974—, Stoorza, Ziegaus & Metzger, San Diego, 1974—; CEO Stoorza, Ziegaust, Metzger, Inc., 1993—; chmn. Stoorza/Smith, San Diego, 1984-85, Stoorza Internat., San Diego, 1984-85; CEO ADC Stoorza, San Diego, 1987—, Franklin Stoorza, San Diego, 1993—. Trustee San Diego Art Found.; bd. dirs. San Diego Found. for Performing Arts, San Diego Opera, Sunbelt Nursery Groups, Dallas. Names Small Bus. Person of Yr. Selest Com. on Small Bus., 1984, one of San Diego's Ten Outstanding Young Citizens San Diego Jaycees, 1979; recipient Woman of Achievement award Women in Communications Inc., 1985. Mem. Pubs. Soc. Am., Nat. Assn. Home Builders (residential mktg. com.), COMBO. Methodist. Clubs: Chancellors Assn. U. Calif. (San Diego), Pub. Relations, San Diego Press. Home: PO Box 490 Rancho Santa Fe CA 92067-0490 Office: Franklin Stoorza 225 Broadway Ste 1800 San Diego CA 92101-5018*

STOREK, JAN, hematologist, oncologist, researcher; b. Prague, Czechoslovakia, Aug. 5, 1959; came to U.S., 1989; m. Stepanka Storkova, Mar. 8, 1994. MD, Charles U. Sch. Medicine, 1984. Resident in internal medicine Charles U. Hosp., Prague, 1984-87; scholar Inst. Hematology and Blood Transfusion, Prague, 1987-89; felow in hematology and oncology UCLA, 1989-92; rsch. assoc. Fred Hutchinson Cancer Ctr., Seattle, 1992—; resident in internal medicine U. Wash., Seattle, 1994-96. Mem. ACP, AAAS, Am. Soc. Hematology.

STORER, NORMAN WILLIAM, sociology educator; b. Middletown, Conn., May 8, 1930; s. Norman Wyman and Mary Emily (House) S.; m. Ada Joan Van Valkenburg, Aug. 19, 1951; children: Martin Wilson, Thomas Wyman; m. Mary Ashton Pott Hiatt, Mar. 7, 1975. A.B., U. Kans., 1952, M.A., 1956; Ph.D., Cornell U., 1961. Lectr., asst. prof. Harvard U., Cambridge, Mass., 1960-66; staff assoc. Social Sci. Research Council, N.Y.C., 1966-70; prof. sociology CUNY-Baruch Coll., N.Y.C., 1970-88; prof. emeritus CUNY-Baruch Coll., 1989—; dept. chmn. CUNY-Baruch Coll., N.Y.C., 1970-85, chmn. faculty senate, 1981-84. Author: The Social System of Science, 1966, Focus on Society, 1973, 2d edit., 1980, A Leer of Limericks, 1990, (with William Flores) Domestic Violence in Suburban San Diego, 1994; editor: The Sociology of Science, 1973; column editor San Diego Writers' Monthly, 1992-94. Vol. S.D. Sheriff's Dept., 1992—. Served to sgt. AUS, 1953-55. Mem. AAAS, Phi Beta Kappa, Sigma Xi. Democrat. Home: 1417 Van Buren Ave San Diego CA 92103-2339

STOREY, BRIT ALLAN, historian; b. Boulder, Colo., Dec. 10, 1941; s. Harold Albert and Gladys Roberta (Althouse) S.; m. Carol DeArman, Dec. 19, 1970; 1 child, Christine Roberta. AB, Adams State Coll., Alamosa, Colo., 1963; MA, U. Ky., 1965, PhD, 1968. Instr. history Auburn (Ala.) U., 1967-68, asst. prof., 1968-70; dep. state historian State Hist. Soc. Colo., Denver, 1970-71, acting state historian, 1971-72, rsch. historian, 1972-74; hist. preservation specialist Adv. Coun. on Hist. Preservation, Lakewood, Colo., 1974-88; sr. historian Bur. Reclamation, Lakewood, 1988—. Contbr. articles to profl. publs. Mem. Fed. Preservation Forum (pres. 1990-91), Nat. Coun. Pub. History (sec. 1987, pres.-elect 1990-91, pres. 1991-92), Orgn. Am. Historians (com. 1983-86, chmn. 1985-86), Victorian Soc. Am. (bd. dirs. 1977-79), Western History Assn. (chmn. com. 1982-86), Colo.-Wyo. Assn. Mus. (sec. 1974-76, pres. 1976-77), Cosmos Club (Washington). Home: 7264 W Otero Ave Littleton CO 80123-5639 Office: Bur Reclamation D 5300 Bldg 67 Denver Fed Ctr Denver CO 80225-0007

STOREY, FRANCIS HAROLD, business consultant, retired bank executive; b. Calgary, Alberta, Can., June 20, 1933; s. Bertwyn Morrell and Hilda Josephine (Masters) S.; m. Willomae Saiter, Apr. 25, 1954; children: Daryl, Elizabeth, Brian, Shelley. Student, Gonzaga U., 1953, Pacific Coast Bankers Sch., 1974-76. Designated Certified Profl. Cons. Bank trainee Wash. Trust Bank, Spokane, 1950-56; owner Storey & Storey, Spokane, 1956-64; agt. Bankers Life Nebr., Spokane, 1964-67; sr. v.p. Old Nat. Bank, Spokane, 1967-87, U.S. Bank of Wash., Spokane, 1987-90; pvt. practice cons. Spokane, 1990—; bd. dirs. Alloy Trailers Inc., Output Tech. Corp. Bd. dirs. Spokane Bus. Incubator, 1985-96, United Way of Spokane, 1987-95; bd.dirs., treas., fin. chair, gen. conv. dep. Episc. Diocese Spokane Dep., 1969—; trustee Spokane Symphony Soc., 1986-93, Spokane Area Econ. Devel. Coun., 1982-89; mem. adv. bd. Intercollegiate Ctr. Nursing Edn., 1990-96, chair, 1996. Mem. Acad. Profl. Cons. and Advisors, Inland N.W. Soc. Cons. Profls., Spokane Rotary, Spokane Country Club, Spokane Club. Episcopalian. Home: 214 E 13th Ave Spokane WA 99202-1115

STOREY, ISABEL NAGY, writer, television producer; b. Parry Sound, Ont., Can., July 2, 1955; came to U.S., 1961; d. Louis and Denise (Ktorza) N. Diploma in French lang. and lit., Inst. Etrangers, Aix-en-Provence, France, 1976; BA, Calif. State U., Northridge, 1979. Editor Burbank (Calif.) Scene, 1979; reporter Burbank Daily Rev., 1979; mng. editor San Fernando Valley Mag., Studio City, Calif., 1980; writer, producer Sta. KTLA News, L.A., 1980-82, Sta. KCBS News, L.A., 1982-87, Lifetime Med. TV, L.A., 1987-89; writer, producer Channel One Whittle Communications, 1989; segment producer Rescue 911 CBS, 1989-90; segment producer syndicated mag. program Preview TV Program Enterprises, 1990. Writer Stuck in Traffic, Sta. KCET, 1988, The National Driving Test, CBS, 1989, 2d Ann. National Driving Test, 1990, The National Emergency Test, ABC, 1990. Recipient Best Local TV Feature award Odyssey Inst., cert. appreciation Ctr. Improvement Child Caring, 1982. Mem. Writers Guild Am. (outstanding script award 1987), Acad. TV Arts Scis. (Emmy 1982), Internat. Documentary Assn.

STOREY, NORMAN C., lawyer; b. Miami, Fla., Oct. 11, 1943. BA cum laude, Loyola U., L.A., 1965; JD, U. Ariz., 1968. Bar: Ariz. 1968. Law clk. to Hon. James A. Walsh U.S. Dist. Ct. Ariz.; ptnr. Squire, Sanders & Dempsey, Phoenix. Mem. ABA, State Bar Ariz., Am. Arbitration Assn. (panelist). Office: Squire Sanders & Dempsey 40 N Central Ave Ste 2700 Phoenix AZ 85004-4424

STORMES, JOHN MAX, instructional systems developer; b. Manila, Oct. 7, 1927; s. Max Clifford and Janet (Heldring) S.; m. Takako Sanae, July 29, 1955; children: Janet Kazuko Stormes-Pepper, Alan Osamu. BS, San Diego State U., 1950; BA, U. So. Calif., 1957, MA, 1967. Cert. secondary and community coll. tchr. Editing supr. Lockheed Propulsion Co., Redlands, Calif., 1957-61; proposals supr. Rockwell Internat., Downey, Calif., 1961-62; publs. dir. Arthur D. Little, Inc., Santa Monica, Calif., 1962-63; publs. coord. Rockwell Internat., Downey, 1963-68; project dir. Gen. Behavioral Systems, Inc., Torrance, Calif., 1969-73; tng. and comm. cons. Media Rsch. Assocs., Santa Cruz, Calif., 1973—; tng. support svc. supr. So. Calif. Gas Co., L.A., 1985—; lectr. Calif. State U., Northridge, 1991—; tng. cons. Nat. Ednl. Media, Chatsworth, Calif., 1966-81, communications cons. Opinion Rsch. Calif., Long Beach, 1974—. Co-author: TV Communications Systems For Business and Industry, 1970; contbg. author: Designing Training Programs, 1996. Curriculum adv. bd. communications dept. Calif. State U., Fullerton, 1964-78. Sgt. U.S. Army, 1953-55, Japan. Mem. Soc. Tech. Communication (sr. mem., 2nd v.p. Orange County chpt. 1962-63), Internat. Soc. Performance and Instruction (v.p. L.A. chpt. 1989, pres. 1990). Democrat. Episcopal. Home: 9140 Brookshire Ave Apt 207 Downey CA 90240-2963 Office: So Calif Gas Co ML 15H1 Box 3249 Los Angeles CA 90051-1249

STORMONT, CLYDE JUNIOR, laboratory company executive; b. Viola, Wis., June 25, 1916; s. Clyde James and Lulu Elizabeth (Mathews) S.; m. Marguerite Butzen, Aug. 31, 1940; children: Bonnie Lu, Michael Clyde, Robert Thomas, Charles James, Janet Jean. BA in Zoology, U. Wis., 1938, PhD in Genetics, 1947; DVM (hon.) U. Veterinaria & Pharmaceutica, Brno, Czech Republic, 1994. Instr., lectr. then asst. prof. U. Wis.-Madison, 1946-50; asst. prof. dept. vet. microbiology U. Calif.-Davis, 1950-54, assoc. prof., 1954-59, prof., 1959-73, prof. dept. reprodn., 1973-82, prof. emeritus, 1982—; chmn. Stormont Labs., Inc., Woodland, Calif., 1981—. Contbr. articles to profl. jours. Lt. (j.g.) USNR, 1944-46, PTO. Fulbright fellow, 1949-50, Ellen B. Scripps fellow, 1957-58, 64-65. Mem. Am. Genetic Assn., Genetics Soc. Am., Nat. Bison Assn., N.Y. Acad. Sci., Am. Soc. Human Genetics, Soc. Exptl. Biology and Medicine, Internat. Soc. for Animal Genetics, Sigma Xi. Office: Stormont Labs Inc 1237 E Beamer St Ste D Woodland CA 95776-6000

STORMSHAK, FREDRICK, physiology educator; b. Enumclaw, Wash., July 4, 1936; s. John and Theresa (Vertocnik) S.; m. Alice Mary Burk, June 8, 1963; children: Elizabeth Ann, Laurie Jo. BS, Wash. State U., 1959, MS, 1960; PhD, U. Wis., 1965. Rsch. physiologist USDA, Beltsville, Md., 1965-68; asst. prof. physiology Oreg. State U., Corvallis, 1968-72, assoc. prof., 1972-79, prof., 1979—, Ferguson disting. prof., 1989, affiliate prof. biochemistry, acting assoc. dir. expt. sta., 1985, interim head dept. animal sci., 1994-95, disting. prof., 1997; NIH postdoctoral fellow in biochemistry U. Wis., 1976; mem. study sect. NIH, Bethesda, Md., 1982-86; mem. animal sci. panel USDA, Washington, 1988-90. Sect. editor Jour. Animal Sci., 1975-78, editor-in-chief, 1982-85; mem. editl. bd. Biol. Reproduction, 1978-82, Endocrinology, 1994—, Domestic Animal Endocrinology, 1994-96. Fellow Am. Soc. Animal Sci. (animal physiology and endocrinology award 1993); mem. Endocrine Soc., Soc. for Study Reproduction (bd. dirs. 1992-95, pres. elect 1996-97, pres. 1997-98), Soc. for Study Fertility, Phi Kappa Phi. Office: Oreg State U Dept Animal Sci Corvallis OR 97331-6702

STORZ, DONNA MARIE, clinical dietitian; b. San Mateo, Calif., Nov. 5, 1962; d. Leroy Ernest and Susan A. (Gallier) Friebel; m. Roger Kenneth Storz, Aug. 2, 1992. BS in Dietetics, U. Calif., Davis, 1985; MS in Nutrition Scis., San Jose State U., 1987. Registered dietitian. Clin. dietitian Alexian Bros. Hosp., San Jose, Calif., 1989—. Mem. Circle of Friends, dept. nutrition and food sci. San Jose State U., 1992—. Named one of Outstanding Young Women of Am., 1987. Mem. Am. Soc. Parenteral and Enteral Nutrition (cert. nutrition support dietitian), Am. Dietetic Assn., Dietitians in Nutrition Support, San Jose-Peninsula Dietetic Assn. (program chair 1997—, co-editor newsletter 1989-90, editor 1990-91), U. Calif.-Davis Alumni Assn. Office: Alexian Bros Hosp 225 N Jackson Ave San Jose CA 95116

STOSICH, DAVIDJOHN, company executive; b. Idaho Falls, Idaho, May 24, 1938; s. Vaughn T. and Esther (Smith) S.; m. Adeana Marshall, Aug. 28, 1962; children: Jennifer Lynne, Jacquelyn, Bryan, Jill, Jon, Anthony, Vaughndavid, Jelair, Hartman, Jeanne. BS, Brigham Young U., 1964; BPA in Profl. Illustrator, Art Ctr. Coll. Design, L.A., 1967. Graphic support Computer Scis. Corp., El Segundo, Calif., 1967-68; corp. communications staff Geotech, Salt Lake City, 1968-69; asst. to pres. Computer Update, Salt Lake City, 1969-70; corp. communications staff Omnico, Salt Lake City & Tacoma, 1970-71; support staff Big Sky of Mont., Big Sky, Mont., 1972-73; art dir. Artcraft, Bozeman, Mont., 1973-75; owner Stosich Advt., Idaho Falls, 1975-78; pres. Worldwide Achievements, Idaho Falls, 1980-81, Hive Systems, Idaho Falls, 1982-92; pres. Stosich Woodlock, Inc., Idaho Falls, 1986-94, CEO, 1994—. Graphic designer Tour Guide to Europe, 1988; sculptor woodlock wood sculptures. Graphic designer Crapo for U.S. Congress, Boise, 1992; active Idaho Falls Arts Coun., Exch. Club Am.; missionary to Switerland LDS Ch., 1958-61. Chosen one of Idaho's best QVC, 1995. Mem. Art Guild (Pocatello, Idaho). Republican. Home: 2300 S Charlotte Dr Idaho Falls ID 83402-5675

STOTLER, ALICEMARIE HUBER, judge; b. Alhambra, Calif., May 29, 1942; d. James R. and Loretta M. Huber; m. James Allen Stotler, Sept. 11, 1971. BA, U. So. Calif., 1964, JD, 1967. Bar: Calif. 1967, U.S. Dist. Ct. (no. dist.) Calif. 1967, U.S. Dist. Ct. (cen. dist.) Calif. 1973, U.S. Supreme Ct., 1976; cert. criminal law specialist. Dep. Orange County Dist. Atty.'s Office, 1967-73; mem. Stotler & Stotler, Santa Ana, Calif., 1973-76, 83-84; judge Orange County Mcpl. Ct., 1976-78, Orange County Superior Ct., 1978-83, U.S. Dist. Ct. (cen. dist.) Calif., L.A., 1984—; assoc. dean Calif. Trial Judges Coll., 1982; lectr., panelist, numerous orgns.; standing com. on rules of practice and procedure U.S. Jud. Conf., 1991—, chair, 1993-96; mem. exec. com. 9th Cir. Jud. Conf., 1989-93, Fed. State Jud. Coun., 1989-98, jury com., 1990-92, planning com. for Nat. Conf. on Fed.-State Judicial Relationships, Orlando, 1991-92, planning com for We. Regional Conf. on State-Fed. Judicial Relationships, Stevens, Wash., 1992-93; chair dist. ct. symposium and jury utilization Ctrl. Dist. Calif., 1985, chair atty. liason, 1989-90, chair U.S. Constitution Bicentennial com., 1986-91, chair magistrate judge com., 1992-93; mem. State Adv. Group. on Juvenile Justice and Delinquency Prevention, 1983-84, Bd. Legal Speciliazations Criminal Law Adv. Commn., 1983-84, victim/witness adv. com. Office Criminal Justice Planning, 1980-83, U. So. Calif. Bd. Councilors, 1993—; active team in tng. Leukemia Soc. Am., 1993, 95; legion lex bd. dir. U. So. Calif. Sch. Law Support Group, 1981-83. Winner Hale Moot Ct. Competition, State of Calif., 1967; named Judge of Yr., Orange County Trial Lawyers Assn., 1978, Most Outstanding Judge, Orange County Bus. Litigation Sect., 1990; recipient Franklin G. West award Orange County Bar Assn., 1985. Mem. ABA (jud. adminstrn. divsn.and litigation sect. 1984—, nat. conf. fed. trial judges com. on legis. affairs 1990-91), Am. Law Inst., Am. Judicature Soc., Fed. Judges Assn. (bd. dirs. 1989-92), Nat. Assn. Women Judges, U.S. Supreme Ct. Hist. Soc., Ninth Cir. Dist. Judges Assn., Calif. Supreme Ct. Hist. Soc., Orange County Bar Assn. (mem. numerous coms., Franklin G. West award 1984), Calif. Judges Assn. (mem. com. on judicial coll. 1978-80, com. on civil law and procedure 1980-82, Dean's coll. curriculum commn. 1981), Calif. Judges Found. Office: US Dist Ct PO Box 12339 751 W Santa Ana Blvd Santa Ana CA 92701-4509

STOTT, JAMES CHARLES, chemical company executive; b. Portland, Oreg., Sept. 5, 1945; s. Walter Joseph and Rellalee (Gray) S.; m. Caroline Loveriane Barnes, Dec. 7, 1973; children: William Joseph, Maryann Lee. BBA, Portland State U., 1969. Ops. mgr. Pacific States Express, Inc., Portland, 1970-73; bus. mgr. Mogul Corp., Portland, 1974-80; v.p. Market Transport, Ltd., Portland, 1980-85; pres., founder, chmn. bd. dirs. Chem. Corp. Am., Portland, 1985—, also bd. dirs.; chmn. bd. dirs. Carolina Industries, Portland. Mem. TAPPI. Republican. Roman Catholic. Club: University (Portland). Home: 3842 Wellington Ct West Linn OR 97068-3600 Office: Chem Corp Am 2525 SE 9th Ave Portland OR 97202-1048

STOTT, PETER WALTER, forest products company executive; b. Spokane, Wash., May 26, 1944; s. Walter Joseph and Rellalee (Gray) S.; m. Julie L. Neupert, Oct. 12, 1996; 1 child, Preston. Student Portland State U., 1962-63, 65-68, U. Americas, Mexico City, 1964-65. Founder, chmn. bd. dirs. Market Transport Ltd., Portland, Oreg., 1969—; bd. dirs., pres., CEO, prin. Crown Pacific, Oregon Independent Coll. Found., Inc., Bd. dirs. Sunshine divsn. Portland Police Bur. (hon.), Liberty Northwest; assoc. mem. adv. bd. Pacific Crest Outward Bound Sch.; mem. pres.'s adv. bd. for athletics Portland State U. With USAR, 1966-72. Mem. Nat. Football Found. and Hall of Fame, Oreg. Sports Hall Fame (lifetime), Oreg. Trucking Assn., Arlington Club, Astoria Golf and Country, Mazamas Club, Multnomah Athletic Club, Portland Golf Club, Univ. Club. Republican. Roman Catholic. Office: Crown Pacific 121 SW Morrison St Ste 1500 Portland OR 97204-3145

STOUGH, STEPHEN ALAN, aerospace and railroad company executive; b. Wichita, Kans., Sept. 13, 1950; s. David Allen and Ramona June (York) S.; m. Lydia Kow, Nov. 20, 1981. B. in Physics, U. Calif., Berkeley, 1972. Aerospace engr. Lockheed Missiles & Space, Sunnyvale, Calif., 1972-77; aerospace engr. internat. Lockheed Missiles & Space, 1977-82; group engr. Lockheed Missiles & Space, Sunnyvale, 1982—; dir. Scriptomation, 1981—, Expressway Corp., Cupertino, Calif., 1985-86; CFO Ascesis Corp., Sunnyvale, 1988—; new bus. mgr. Lockheed Missiles & Space, Sunnyvale, 1984-86, systems engring. mgr., 1986-89, dir. anti-submarine warfare systems, 1989-90, systems engring. mgr. Space Systems div., 1990—; exec. v.p., sec. Nev. Copper Belt RR, Stagecoach, Nev., 1992—; instr. in bus. mgmt. U. Calif. Ext., 1993—. Mem. Nat. Rep. Congl. Com., Washington, 1989—. Mem. Armed Forces Communications and Electronics Assn., Nat. Security Indsl. Assn., Security Affairs Support Assn., Commonwealth Club Calif., Alpha Gamma Sigma. Office: Lockheed Space Systems Div 30-02 1111 Lockheed Way Sunnyvale CA 94089-1212

STOUT, ELIZABETH WEST, foundation administrator; b. San Francisco, Mar. 4, 1917; d. Claudius Wilson and Sarah (Henderson) West; m. Bruce Churchill McDonald, Mar. 19 1944 (dec. 1952); children: Douglas, Anne; m. Charles Holt Stout, Oct. 27, 1958 (dec. 1992); stepchildren: Richard, George (dec.), Martha Stout Gilweit. Student, U. Nev., 1934-37; grad., Imperial Valley Coll., 1990. Cashier, acct. N.Y. Underwriters, San Francisco, 1937-42; sec. supply and accounts USN, San Francisco, 1942-44. Contbr. articles to profl. jours. Mem. adv. bd. Anza-Borrego Desert, Natural History Assn., 1974-84; founder Stout Paleontology Lab., Borrego Springs, Calif., 1982; found. trustee Desert Rsch. Inst., Reno, 1989—; active Black Rock Desert Project, 1989, Washoe Med. Ctr. League, 1953—, St. Mary's Hosp. Guild, 1953—. Named Disting. Nevadan U. Nev., 1993. Mem. Anza-Borrego Desert Natural History Assn. (dir. emeritus 1984), Soc. Vertebrate Paleontology, De Anza Desert Country Club, Kappa Alpha Theta. Republican. Episcopalian.

STOUT, GARY FRANCIS, inventor, entrepreneur; b. Bountiful, Utah, Sept. 12, 1962; s. Cleamont Francis and Connie (Lee) S.; children: Christina Mae, Jason Alexander; m. Stephanie Kehaulani Battad, July 10, 1993. Student, Sch. Engring. U. Utah, Maxwell AFB, Mo., 1987. Pres. Aladdin Enterprises, Salt Lake City; founder, owner Aladdin Lamp Co., Salt Lake City. Inventor magic lamp, discrete display devices. Staff sgt. USAF, 1981-85. Mem. Nat. Congress Inventors, Intermountain Soc. Inventors. Mem. LDS Ch. Office: Aladdin Enterprises PO Box 17453 Holladay UT 84117

STOUT, JAMES TILMAN, minister; b. Pitts., Feb. 20, 1942; s. Randall Stuart and Alice Margaret (Stevenson) S.; m. Leah Ann Hayden, June 24, 1967; children: James T. Jr., John Davis. Student, U. Pitts., 1960-63; BA, Miami U. of Ohio, 1965; MDiv, Gorden Conwell Sem., 1969; DMin, Fuller Sem., 1980. Ordained to ministry Presbyn. Ch., 1969. Assoc. pastor Key Biscayne (Fla.) Presbyn. Ch., 1969-74; pastor First Presbyn. Ch., North Palm Beach, Fla., 1974-81, St. Andrews Presbyn. Ch., Beaumont, Tex., 1981-83, Covenant Presbyn. Ch., Sharon, Pa., 1983-87; assoc. pastor St. Andrews Presbyn. Ch., Newport Beach, Calif., 1987-91; area dir. Gathering of Men, Costa Mesa, Calif., 1992—. Author: Winning Over Depression, 1992. Named Golden Glove Heavyweight Champion, Pitts., 1961. Mem. Exch. Club, Rotary. Office: Gathering of Men 2093 Santa Ana Ave Costa Mesa CA 92627-2140

STOUT, LOWELL, lawyer; b. Tamaha, Okla., July 23, 1928; s. Charles W. and Rosetta (Easley) S.; m. Liliane Josue, Nov. 29, 1952; children: Georgianna, Mark Lowell. Student, Northeastern State Coll., Tahlequah, Okla., 1946-49, U. Okla., 1949-51; LLB, U. N.Mex., 1952. Bar: N.Mex. 1952. Ptnr. Easley, Quinn & Stout, Hobbs, N.Mex., 1954-58, Girand & Stout, Hobbs, 1958-60; pvt. practice Hobbs, 1960-80; ptnr. Stout & Stout, Hobbs, 1980—. Cpl. U.S. Army, 1952-54. Perenially listed in Best Lawyers in America. Fellow Am. Coll. Trial Lawyers; mem. Assn. Trial Lawyers Am., State Bar N.Mex., N.Mex. Trial Lawyers Assn., Lea County Bar Assn. Home: 218 W Lea St Hobbs NM 88240-5110 Office: Stout & Stout PO Box 716 Hobbs NM 88241-0716

STOUT-PIERCE, SUSAN, clinical specialist; b. Denver, June 6, 1954; d. Joseph Edward and Esther Mae (Miller) Hull; m. Jerry Lee Stout, Nov. 3, 1979 (div. Aug. 1984); m. Gary Myron Pierce, Nov. 21, 1987. AS, Denver Community Coll., 1975; BS, Met. State Coll., 1986. Cert. Radiologic Technologist, Calif., Am. Registry Radiologic Technologists. Radiologic technologist The Swedish Med. Ctr., Englewood, Colo., 1975-79, The Minor Emergency Clinic, Lakewood, Colo., 1979-80, The Children's Hosp., Denver, 1980-86, Merit Peralta Med. Ctr., Oakland, Calif., 1986-87, Am. Shared Hosp. Svcs., Oakland, 1987, HCA South Austin (Tex.) Med. Ctr., 1987-88, U. Calif., San Francisco, 1988-89; clin. imaging specialist OEC-Diasonics, Salt Lake City, 1989-92; software applications specialist Cemax, Inc., Fremont, Calif., 1992-93; mktg. specialist ADAC Healthcare Info. Systems, Houston, Tex., 1993-96; clin. specialist Elekta Instruments Inc., Atlanta, 1996—. Mem. NAFE, Am. Bus. Women's Assn. Home: 264 Rachael Pl Pleasanton CA 94566-6228

STOVER, CAROLYN NADINE, middle school educator; b. Martinsburg, W.Va., May 30, 1950; d. Norman Robert and Garnet Agnes (Zombro) Whetzel; m. James Stenner Stover Sr., Nov. 20, 1971; children: Heather N., James S. Jr. BA in Home Econs., Shepherd Coll., 1972; cert. in advanced studies, W.Va. U., 1978; cert. in tchg. methods, Marshall U., 1973; cert. in spl. edn., Shippensburg Coll., 1972. Cert. tchr., W.Va., N.Mex.; reg. EMT. Substitute tchr. Berkeley County Schs., Martinsburg, W.Va., 1972, adult edn. instr., 1972-77, home econs. instr., 1973-83; substitute tchr. Ruidoso (N.Mex.) Mcpl. Schs., 1984-90, child find coord. Region 9 edn. coop., 1990, life skills and at-risk educator, 1991—, coord. coun., 1991-93, mem. budget com., 1993. Elder First Presbyn. Ch., Ruidoso, 1984-90, 94-96; sponsor Acad. Booster Club, Ruidoso, 1993—; instr. CPR, 1980. Named Outstanding Young Women of Am., 1981. Mem. NEA, Nat. Middle Sch. Assn., Ruidoso Edn. Assn., Rotary (youth leadership councilor 1991—). Democrat. Home: Box 7837 1007 Hull Rd Ruidoso NM 88355 Office: Ruidoso Mid Sch 100 Reese Dr Ruidoso NM 88345-6016

STOVER, MARK EDWIN, librarian; b. Newport News, Va., May 1, 1961; s. Arnold Clinton and Janet Louise (Sheldon) S.; m. Elaine Davis, June 10, 1984; children: Hannah Rose, Malka Gabrielle, Adam Jacob. BA, Biola U., 1983; MA in Religion, Westminster Sem., Phila., 1986; MLS, UCLA, 1988. Theol. libr. Calvin Coll. and Sem., Grand Rapids, Mich., 1988-90; libr. dir. Phillips Grad. Inst., Encino, Calif., 1990—; cons. St. George's Coll., Jerusalem, 1991-92. Author: (with others) The Reader's Advisor, 1993; editor Libr. Trends, 1992; contbr. articles to profl. jours. Mem. ALA, Calif. Acad. and Rsch. Librs. Office: Phillips Grad Inst 5445 Balboa Blvd Encino CA 91316

STOVER, MILES RONALD, manufacturing executive; b. Glendale, Calif., Dec. 23, 1948; s. Robert Miles and Alberta Mae (Walker) S.; m. Cynthia McNeil, Jan. 25, 1975; children: Christopher, Matthew. BS, U. So. Calif., 1974; MBA, Pepperdine U., 1979; D of Bus. Adminstrn., U.S. Internat. U., 1982. V.p., gen. mgr., CFO Johnson Controls Inc., L.A., 1974-82; gen. mgr. MG Products Inc., San Diego, 1982-84; exec. v.p., gen. mgr. ICU Med. Inc., Mission Viejo, 1984-86; v.p., COO B.P. John Inc., Santa Ana, Calif., 1986-88; gen. mgr. MG Products Inc., San Diego, 1988-90; pres. Lucks Co., Kent, Wash., 1991-96, also bd. dirs.; pres. Turnaround Mgmt. Group, 1996—; cons. Turnaround Mgmt. Assn., Tacoma, 1990. Bd. dirs. Big Bros. Am. With USN, 1967-71. Recipient Gallantry Cross medal USN, 1971, Award for Productivity U.S. Senate, 1978. Mem. Inst. Mgmt. Cons. (cert. mgmt. cons.), Inst. Mgmt. Accts., Mensa. Republican. Methodist. Home: 2727 41st St SE Puyallup WA 98374-1734

STOWELL, KENT, ballet director; b. Rexburg, Idaho, Aug. 8, 1939; s. Harold Bowman and Maxine (Hudson) S.; m. Francia Marie Russell, Nov. 19, 1965; children: Christopher, Darren, Ethan. Student, San Francisco Ballet Sch., Sch. Am. Ballet; Lead dancer San Francisco Ballet, 1957-62, N.Y.C. Ballet, 1962-68; ballet dir., ballet master Frankfurt (Fed. Republic Germany) Opera Ballet, 1973-77; artistic dir. Pacific N.W. Ballet, Seattle, 1977—; prof. dance Ind. U., Bloomington, 1969-70; bd. dirs. Dance/USA, Washington, 1986—. Choreographer: Cinderella, Carmina Burana, Coppelia, Time & Ebb, Fauré Requiem, Hail to the Conquering Hero, Firebird, Over the Waves, Nutcracker, The Tragedy of Romeo and Juliet, Delicate Balance, Swan Lake, Time and Ebb, Through Interior Worlds, Quaternary, Orpheus. Bd. dirs. Sch. of Am. Ballet, N.Y.C., 1981—; mem. Goodwill Games Arts Com., Seattle, 1987—; chmn. dance panel NEA, 1981-85. Grantee NEA, 1980, 85; fellow NEA, 1979. Recipient Arts Service award King County Arts Commn., 1985, Outstanding Contbn. to Pacific N.W. Ballet State of Was., 1987, Best Dance Co. award The Weekly Newspaper, Seattle, 1987, Gov. Arts award, 1988, Dance Mag. award, 1996. Office: Pacific NW Ballet 301 Mercer St Seattle WA 98109-4600

STOWELL, LARRY JOSEPH, agricultural consultant; b. San Pedro, Calif., June 12, 1952; s. James E. and Dorothy L. (Geiser) S.; m. Wendy D. Gelernter, Feb. 22, 1986. BS, U. Ariz., 1977, PhD, 1982. Rsch. assoc. U. Ariz., Tucson, 1976-82; postdoctoral rschr. U. Calif., Davis, 1982-84; group leader Mycogen Corp., San Diego, 1984-88; prin. Pace Cons., San Diego, 1988—; prin., rsch. dir. Pace Turfgrass Rsch. Inst., San Diego, 1993—. Author: (with others) Microbial Products For Medicine and Agriculture, 1989, Microbial Control of Weeds, 1991, Advanced Engineered Pesticides, 1993. U. Ariz. Alumni Assn. scholar, 1978; U. Ariz. grantee, 1981. Mem. Am. Phytopath. Soc., Agronomy Soc. Am., Weed Sci. Soc. Am., Nat. Alliance Ind. Crop Cons. (bd. dirs. 1992-95), Assn. Applied Insect Ecologists (bd. dirs. 1991-95), Am. Registry Cert. Profls. in Agronomy Crops and Soils (bd. dirds. 1993—), Nat. Plant Pathology Bd. Home and Office: Pace Cons 1267 Diamond St San Diego CA 92109-2645

STRACK, STEPHEN NAYLOR, psychologist; b. Rome, N.Y., Nov. 13, 1955; s. Ralph and Grace (Naylor) S.; m. Leni Ferrero. BA, U. Calif., Berkeley, 1978; PhD, U. Miami, Fla., 1983. Psychologist L.A. County Dept. Mental Health, 1984-85; staff psychologist VA Outpatient Clinic, L.A., 1985—, dir. tng., 1992-97; clin. assoc. U. So. Calif., L.A., 1986-95; adj. prof. Calif. Sch. Profl. Psychology, L.A., 1989—; clin. prof. Fuller Grad. Sch. Psychology, Pasadena, Calif., 1986—. Author (test): Personality Adjective Check List, 1987; co-author (book): Differentiating Normal and Abnormal Personality, 1994, Death and the Quest for Meaning, 1997; cons. editor Jour. Personality Disorders, N.Y.C., 1992—, Omega, 1997—. U.S. Dept. Vets Affairs grantee, 1986-93, 96—. Fellow APA, Soc. for Personality Assessment; mem. Internat. Soc. for the Study of Personality Disorders, Calif. Psychol. Assn., European Assn. Psychol. Assessment, Soc. for Rsch. in Psychopathology, Western Psychol. Assn., Sigma Xi. Office: VA Outpatient Clinic 351 E Temple St Los Angeles CA 90012-3328

STRADER, JAMES HARLOW, IV, entertainment executive, financial consultant; b. Mobile, Ala., Mar. 5, 1967; s. James Harlow III and Rosalie (Depaul) S. BS in Fin., Boston U., 1989. Dir. devel. Boston Comedy, 1989-90; ptnr. Tritech Prodns., Boston, 1990; prin. Strader Entertainment, L.A., 1991—; bd. dirs. Second Opinion Capital, Langhorne, Pa., DNA Prodns., Dallas; cons. Expanded Entertainment, L.A., 1994—. Co-creator (TV prodn.) Weird America, 1992; creator (TV prodn.) The Fringe, 1996. Mem. Boston U. Alumni Club. L.A. Republican. Office: Strader Entertainment PO Box 38457 Los Angeles CA 90038

STRAHAN, JULIA CELESTINE, electronics company executive; b. Indpls., Feb. 10, 1938; d. Edgar Paul Pauley and Pauline Barbara (Myers) Shawver; m. Norman Strahan, Oct. 2, 1962 (div. 1982); children: Daniel Keven, Natalie Kay. Grad. high sch., Indpls. With EG&G/Energy Measurements, Inc., Las Vegas, Nev., 1967—; sect. head EG&G Co., 1979-83, mgr. electronics dept., 1984—. Recipient award Am. Legion, 1952, Excellence award, 1986. Mem. NAFE, Am. Nuclear Soc. (models and mentors), Internat. Platform Assn. Home: 5222 Stacey Ave Las Vegas NV 89108-3078 Office: EG&G PO Box 1912 Las Vegas NV 89125-1912

STRAHILEVITZ, MEIR, inventor, researcher, psychiatry educator; b. Beirut, July 13, 1935; s. Jacob and Chana Strahilevitz; m. Aharona Nattiv, 1958; children: Michal, Lior. MD, Hadassah Hebrew U. Med. Sch., 1963. Diplomate Am. Bd. Psychiatry and Neurology, Royal Coll. Physicians and Surgeons Can. Asst. prof. Washington U. Med. Sch., St. Louis, 1971-74; assoc. prof. So. Ill. U., Springfield, 1974-77, U. Chgo., 1977, U. Tex. Med. Br., Galveston, 1978-81; chmn. dept. psychiatry Kaplan Hosp., Rehovot, Israel, 1987-88; clin. assoc. prof. U. Wash., Seattle, 1981-88; prof. U. Tex. Med. Sch., Houston, 1988-92. Contbr. articles to profl. jours. Fellow Am. Psychiat. Assn., Royal Coll. Physicians and Surgeons Can. Office: PO Box 190 Hansville WA 98340-0190

STRAHLER, ARTHUR NEWELL, former geology educator, author; b. Kolhapur, India, Feb. 20, 1918; s. Milton W. and Harriet (Brittan) S.; m. Margaret E. Wanless, Aug. 10, 1940; children: Alan H., Marjorie E. A.B., Coll. Wooster, 1938; A.M., Columbia U., 1940, Ph.D. (Univ. fellow), 1944. Faculty Columbia U., 1941-71, prof. geomorphology, 1958-68, adj. prof. geology, 1968-71, chmn. dept. geology, 1959-62. Author: Physical Geography, rev. edit., 1975, The Earth Sciences, rev. edit., 1971, Introduction to Physical Geography, rev. edit., 1973, Planet Earth, 1971, Environmental Geoscience, 1973, Introduction to Environmental Science, 1974, Elements of Physical Geography, 2d edit., 1979, 3d edit., 1984, 4th edit., 1989, Principles of Earth Science, 1976, Principles of Physical Geology, 1977, Geography and Man's Environment, 1977, Modern Physical Geography, 1978, 4th edit., 1992, Physical Geology, 1981, Science and Earth History—The Evolution/Creation Controversy, 1987, Investigating Physical Geography, 1989, Understanding Science: An Introduction to Concepts and Issues, 1992, Physical Geography-Science and Systems of the Human Environment, 1996. Fellow Geol. Soc. Am., Am. Geog. Soc.; mem. Am. Geophys. Union, Phi Beta Kappa, Sigma Xi. Home: 1039 Cima Linda Ln Santa Barbara CA 93108-1818

STRAIGHT, JAMES WESLEY, secondary education educator; b. Ely, Nev., Jan. 3, 1930; s. James Wesley Sr. and Mary Elizabeth (Hunter) S.; m. Gloria Frances Roysum, Aug. 22, 1954; children: James W. Jr., Elizabeth Straight Stevenson, Kathryn Straight Hernandez, Douglas Scott. BS in Geol. Engring., U. Nev., Reno, 1954. Cert. secondary tchr., Calif. Geol. engr. Kennecott Copper Corp., McGill, Nev., 1954-57; soil engr. John F. Byerly, Bloomington, Calif., 1967-82; foreman Eagle-Picher, Lovelock, Nev., 1957-61, Kaiser Steel, Fontana, Calif., 1962-67; tchr. indsl. arts Fontana Unified Schs., 1967-92; tchr. prospecting class Rialto (Calif) Unified Schs., 1969—; tchr. prospecting class U. Calif., Riverside, 1976. Author, pub.: Follow the Drywashers, 1988, vol. 2, 1990, vol. 3, 1993, Magnificent Quest, 1990; contbg. editor mags. Popular Mining, Treas. Found., Western and Ea. Treas., Treas. Gold and Silver, Treas. Seekers. Treas. San Bernardino (Calif.) Area Assn. for the Retarded, 1972. 1st lt. U.S. Army C.E., 1955-57. Mem. Masons. Republican. Episcopalian. Home and Office: 19225 Mesa St Rialto CA 92377-4558

STRAIN, JOHN THOMAS, electronics engineer; b. Raymondville, Mo., Oct. 25, 1939; s. Thomas and Lillie (Merckling) S.; m. Bonnie J. Cline, 1967 (div. 1980); children: Robert Vidmar, Anthony Vidmar. BSEE, U. Mo., Rolla, 1964. Electronics technician Exec. Aircraft Co., Kansas City, Mo., 1960-61; electronic engring. technician Wilcox Electric Co., Kansas City, 1963, sr. electronics technician, 1964-67; sr. electronics technician Exec. Aircraft Co., 1964; electronic engring. tech. Gianni Voltex Co., San Diego, 1967-68; electronic fabricator Bendix Atomic Energy Commn., Kansas City, 1968; electronics engr. Electronic Research Corp., Overland Park, Kans., 1968-69, Monitor Products Co., South Pasadena, Calif., 1969-73, NBC, Burbank, Calif., 1973--. Designed and developed original TV stereo encoder; responsible (with Ron Estes) for first recorded stereo TV program (nominated for Emmy 1983); developer first DIP style crystal controled oscillator for use in computer and areospace industries. With USAF, 1964-65. Home: 6450 Clybourn Ave North Hollywood CA 91606-2728 Office: NBC 3000 W Alameda Ave Burbank CA 91523-0001

STRALING, PHILLIP FRANCIS, bishop; b. San Bernardino, Calif., Apr. 25, 1933; s. Sylvester J. and Florence E. (Robinson) S. BA, U. San Diego, 1963; MS in Child and Family Counseling, San Diego State U., 1971. Ordained priest Roman Catholic Ch., 1959, consecrated bishop, 1978. Mem. faculty St. John Acad., El Cajon, Calif., 1959-60, St. Therese Acad., San Diego, 1960-63; chaplain Newman Club, San Diego State U., 1960-72; mem. faculty St. Francis Sem., San Diego, 1972-76; pastor Holy Rosary Parish, San Bernardino, 1976-78; bishop Diocese of San Bernardino, 1978-95; pub. Inland Cath. newspaper, 1979-95; chmn. com. on lay ministry U.S. Cath. Conf./Nat. Cath. Conf. Bishops, 1993—; bishop of Reno, Nev., 1995—; bd. dirs. Calif. Assn. Cath. Campus Mins., 1960s; exec. sec. Diocesan Synod II, 1972-76; Episcopal vicar San Bernardino Deanery, 1976-78. Mem. Nat. Cath. Campus Ministries Assn. (bishop rep. 1992—). Office: PO Box 1211 Reno NV 89504-1211

STRALSER, STEVEN MICHAEL, marketing educator, consultant; b. L.A., Nov. 7, 1945; s. Harold Louis and Janice Louise (Linch) S.; m. Carol Ann Kamenshine, Feb. 25, 1967 (div. Sept. 1981); children: Amy Jennifer, Marcy Linch. BS, U. Ariz., 1967; MBA, Ariz. State U., 1970; PhD, U. Mich., 1997. Rsch. economist Valley Nat. Bank, Phoenix, 1972-74; entrepreneur, Phoenix, 1974-81; mktg. assoc. Iliff, Thorn & Co., Phoenix, 1981-89; dir. mktg. DMB Assocs., Phoenix, 1989-94; instr., cons. U. Mich. Bus. Sch., Ann Arbor, 1994-96; adj. instr. mktg. dept. U. Ariz. Coll. Bus. and Pub. Adminstrn., Tucson, 1996—; cons. Mott Coll., Flint, Mich., 1995. Bd. dirs. men's arts coun. Phoenix Art Mus., 1981-93; bd. dirs. Jewish Cmty. Ctr., Phoenix, 1990-92. Mem. AAAS, Licensing Execs. Soc., Assn. Univ. Tech. Mgrs., Tech. Transfer Soc., Econ. Club Detroit.

STRAND, CHERYL MARIE, Spanish language, literature educator; b. Viborg, S.D., Aug. 27, 1944; d. Alfred Nicholi and Lillian Evelyn (Wilson) S.; m. Alan Louis Kalter, Feb. 14, 1981; 1 child, Christopher Michael Kalter-Strand. BS, S.D. State U., 1966; MA, Calif. State U., Fresno, 1969; PhD, U. Calif., L.A., 1989. Tchg. asst. Calif. State U., Fresno, 1968-69, U. Calif., L.A., 1969-72, 76; instr. Ohio State U., Columbus, 1976-77; assoc. U. Wash., Seattle, 1979-83, lectr., Spanish coord., 1983-84, 86-89; instr. Shoreline C.C., Seattle, 1985; assoc. prof. Western Oreg. U., Monmouth, 1989—; mem. Latin Am. Exec. Bd., Oreg. State Sys. of Higher Edn., 1989-96; chmn. dept. modern langs. Western Oreg. U., Monmouth, 1991-94; mem. Spanish Proficiency Stds. Commn., Chancellor's Office, Oreg. State Sys. Higher Edn., 1993-94; presenter rsch. papers Mid-Am. Conf., Kans., Nebr., 1989, 91, Confedn. Oreg. Fgn. Lang. Tchrs. Conf., 1996. Contbr. articles, reviews to profl. publs. Panelist Office of Fgn. Study Programs, Oreg. State System of Higher Edn., Corvallis, 1992, others. Recipient scholarship for study in Spain, Fulbright, 1972-73, fellowship for doctoral rsch. Del Amo Found., Spain, 1974-75. Mem. MLA, Twentieth Century Spanish Assn. of Am., Confedn. of Oreg. Fgn. Lang. Tchrs., AAUW, AAUP, Phi Sigma Iota, Sigma Delta Pi, Phi Kappa Phi. Office: Western Oreg U Dept Modern Langs Monmouth OR 97361

STRAND, ROGER GORDON, federal judge; b. Peekskill, N.Y., Apr. 28, 1934; s. Ernest Gordon Strand and Lisabeth Laurine (Phin) Steinmetz; m. Joan Williams, Nov. 25, 1961. AB, Hamilton Coll., 1955; LLB, Cornell U., 1961; grad., Nat. Coll. State Trial Judges, 1968. Bar: Ariz. 1961, U.S. Dist. Ct. Ariz. 1961, U.S. Supreme Ct. 1980. Assoc. Fennemore, Craig, Allen & McClennen, Phoenix, 1961-67; judge Ariz. Superior Ct., Phoenix, 1967-85, U.S. Dist. Ct. Ariz., Phoenix, 1985—; assoc. presiding judge Ariz. Superior Ct., 1971-85; lectr. Nat. Jud. Coll., Reno, 1978-87. Past pres. cen. Ariz. chpt. Arthritis Found. Lt. USN, 1955-61. Mem. ABA, Ariz. Bar Assn., Maricopa County Bar Assn., Nat. Conf. Fed. Trial Judges, Phi Delta Phi, Aircraft Owners and Pilots Assn. Lodge: Rotary. Home: 5825 N 3rd Ave Phoenix AZ 85013-1537 Office: US Dist Ct Courthouse and Fed Bldg 230 N 1st Ave Ste 3013 Phoenix AZ 85025-0002

STRAND, SALLY LEE (SALLY STRAND ELLIS), artist, educator; b. Denver, Oct. 11, 1954; d. Owen Sven and Harriet Alice (Minton) S.; m. Mark Howard Ellis, Mar. 16, 1985;children: Samuel, Nathaniel. BFA, Denver U., 1978. Mem. faculty Colo. Inst. of Art, Denver, 1978-79, Scottsdale (Ariz.) Artist's Sch., 1990—. Exhibited at The Pastel Invitational, Telluride, Colo., 1995, Diane Nelson Fine Art, Laguna Beach, Calif., 1996; contbg. artist: Pastels Masterclass, 1993, The Best of Pastel, 1996. Recipient Anna Hyatt Huntington Bronze medal Catharine Lorilland Wolfe 85th Ann. Open Exhbn., 1981, Margery and Thomas Leighton award Pastel Soc. of West Coast, 1992. Mem. Pastel Soc. of Am. (Bd. Dirs. award 1993, Canson-Talens award 1995). Home and Studio: 33402 Dosinia Dr Dana Point CA 92629

STRASEN, BARBARA ELAINE, artist, educator. BFA, Carnegie Mellon Univ.; MFA, Univ. Calif., Berkeley. Instr. visual arts Cabrillo Coll., Aptos, Calif., Southwestern Coll., Chula Vista, Calif.; asst. prof. visual arts U. Calif., San Diego, 1SD3-78; Bd. dirs. Angels Gate Cultural Ctr.; mem. arts adv. bd. Inner-City Arts, L.A., 1992—; mem. adv. com. arts in the workplace L.A. Jr. C. of C., 1995; lectr. in field. One-woman shows include San Jose (Calif.) State Univ., 1975, Parson-Dreyfus Gallery, N.Y.C., 1980, Wooster (Ohio) Coll., 1981, San Diego State Univ. Gallery, San Diego Natural History Mus., 1982, A.I.R. Gallery, N.Y.C., 1983, La Chambre Blanche, Quebec, Can., 1984, Fisher Gallery Univ. So. Calif., L.A., 1985, James Turcotte Gallery, L.A., 1986, Gallery Store, San Diego, 1988, Zem Zwaite Gsicht Gallery, Basel, Switzerland, 1989, Grey Art Gallery NYU, 1990, Het Apollohuis, Eindhoven, The Netherlands, 1990, D.P. Fong Gallery, San Jose, 1991, Wolfson Art Gallery Miami-Dade (Fla.) C.C., 1992, Lynn Crandall Art Svcs., L.A., 1993, R&B Mgmt. Corp., L.A., 1994, L.A. Artcore Ctr., L.A., 1995, Angel's Gate Cultural Ctr., L.A., 1996, others; exhibited in group shows at Whitney Mus. Am. Art, N.Y.C., 1975, Univ. Calif., La Jolla, 1976, Parsons-Dreyfuss Gallery, N.Y.C., 1977, 78, Newspace Gllery, L.A., 1978, Santa Barbara Mus. Art, 1979, Museu de Arte Contemporanea, Sao Paulo, Brazil, 1980, A.I.R. Gallery, N.Y.C., 1982, One Penn Plaza, N.Y.C., 1984, L.A. Design Ctr., 1985, Islip (N.Y.) Art Mus., 1987, 90, 93, James Turcotte Gallery, L.A., 1988, Fahey/Klein Gallery, L.A., 1989, Spce Gallery, L.A., 1994, 95, Univ. Tex. San Antonio Art Gallery, 1996, others; represented in permanent collections Nat. Gallery Art, Allen Meml. Art Mus., Best Products Collection, others; author: Desert Notes, 1980; contbr. chpts. to books, articles to profl. jours. Grantee NEA, 1975-76, Univ. Calif., San Diego, 1976, 77, Arts Recovery, L.A., 1992-93; Summer scholar Yale Univ. Sch. Art. Home: 1724 S Pacific Ave San Pedro CA 90731

STRATTON, BRUCE CORNWALL, writer, landscape photographer, publisher; b. San Francisco, Feb. 17, 1929; d, Ernest Kenneth and Dorothy Sinclair (Cornwall) S.; m. Isolde Helga Samovitch (div.). LLB, La Salle Coll., Chgo., 1960. With U.S. Dept. State, 1950-67; vice consul to Mex., 1964-67; educator "Center" (free sch.), Ibiza, Spain, 1975-87; landscape photographer San Miguel de Allende, Mex., 1987-91; author, publisher Fourth Dimension Press, Reno, Nev., 1991—. Author: (books) Yoni, 1992, The Last Boat to Barcelona, 1994; editor Works By Dr. Robert N. Spadaro, 1987—. Home: 1432 Silverada Blvd Reno NV 89512

STRATTON, GREGORY ALEXANDER, computer specialist, administrator, mayor; b. Glendale, Calif., July 31, 1946; s. William Jaspar and Rita Phyllis (Smith) S.; m. Yolanda Margot Soler, 1967 (div. 1974); 1 child, Tiffany; m. Edith Carter, Sept. 27, 1975; stepchildren: John Henkell, Paul Henkell, D'Lorah Henkell Wismar. Student, Harvey Mudd Coll., 1964-65; BS in Physics, UCLA, 1968; MBA, Calif. Luth. U., 1977. Elec. engr. Naval Ship Weapon System Engring. Sta., Port Hueneme, Calif., 1968-73; sr. staff mem. Univac, Valencia, Calif., 1973-74; v.p. Digital Applications, Camarillo, Calif., 1974-75; cons. Grumman Aerospace, Point Mugu, Calif., 1975-76; F-14 software mgr. Pacific Missle Test Ctr., Pt. Mugu, 1976-84; software mgr. Teledyne Systems, Northridge, Calif., 1984-92, dir. engring. software dept., 1992-93; dep. dir. software engring. Teledyne Electronic Systems, Northridge, Calif., 1993-94; software mgr. Litton Guidance and Controls, Northridge, Calif., 1995—. Mem. City Coun., City of Simi Valley, Calif., 1979-86, mayor, 1986—; alt. Rep. County Cen. Com., Ventura County, 1986-88; mem. Rep. State Cen. Com., Calif., 1990—; bd. dirs. Simi Valley Hosp., 1987—. Mem. Assn. Ventura County Cities (chair 1990-91), Rotary (Paul Harris award Simi Sunrise chpt. 1989), Jaycees (pres. Simi Valley chpt. 1974-75, nat. bd. dirs. 1975-76, v.p. Calif. state 1976-77). Republican. Lutheran. Home: 254 Goldenwood Cir Simi Valley CA 93065-6771 Office: Office of Mayor 2929 Tapo Canyon Rd Simi Valley CA 93063-2199

STRATTON, JOHN MACLEAN, air transport company executive; b. Rosedale, Kans., Nov. 1, 1916; s. George Weatherworth and Margaret Shearer (Maclean) S.; m. Kathryn McCrea Hines, Dec. 25, 1942 (dec.); children: Laura Kathryn, Mark Hines. BA, U. Kans., 1939; MA, Stanford U., 1940. Mgr. advt. & mktg. Spencer Chem. Co. (now Grace Chem.), 1945-48; v.p., mgr. Rogers & Smith Advt. Agy., Kansas City, Mo., 1948-49; with Ruthrauff & Ryan ADvt. Agy., N.Y.C., Chgo., Detroit, 1952-54, Ramsey, Stratton, Barley & Brown, 1954-58; owner, chmn. bd. dirs. JAMSCO Enterprises, Inc., L.A., 1958—; chmn. bd. dirs. The Circutone Co., Inc., L.A., 1966—; pres. JAMSCO-TV, Hollywood, Calif. Patentee in field. Maj. USAAC, 1941-45, WWII, lt. col. USAF, 1949-52, Korea. Mem. Nat. 210 Owners Assn. (pres., editor Airletter), Am. Vets. Med. Airlift Svc. (CEO). Home: 931 Flanders Rd La Canada Flintridge CA 91011-2518

STRATTON, JON, philosophy educator; b. Great Falls, Mont., Mar. 10, 1944; s. Scott Bartine and Virginia (Connolly) S.; m. Jane Sigwell, Nov. 20, 1967 (div. Aug. 1972); 1 child, Daphne Stratton Moran; m. Marleen Ramsey, July 6, 1996; children: Melissa Ramsey, Cami Ramsey. BA in Philosophy, Coll. of Great Falls, 1967; MA in Philosophy, So. Ill. U., 1970, PhD in Philosophy, 1972. Lectr. in philosophy So. Ill. U., Carbondale, 1971-72; asst. prof. philosophy Whitman Coll., Walla Walla, Wash., 1972-73, adj. faculty philosophy, 1977—; instr. in philosophy Walla Walla C.C., 1974—; rsch. assoc. philosophy SUNY, Stoney Brook, 1991-92; dir. Wash. State Critical Thinking Assessment Ctr., Walla Walla, 1995—. Co-author (with Marleen Ramsey): A Compendium of Cats, 1994, Critical Thinking: A Handbook for College Teachers, 1995. Del. Dem. State Conv., Spokane, 1980; pres. Walla Walla C.C. Faculty Assn., 1984-86. NEH fellow, 1980; NEH grantee, 1986. Mem. Wash. Edn. Assn. (local pres. 1984-86), N.W. Philosophy Conf., Am. Philos. Assn. Democrat. Office: Walla Walla CC 500 Tausick Way Walla Walla WA 99362

STRAUB, RICHARD NEAL, coach; b. Kewaskum, Wis., Dec. 5, 1968; s. Hugo John and Isabelle Laura (Miller) S. BS in Edn. cum laude, U. Wis., Whitewater, 1992; MA in Counselor Edn., MA in Phys. Edn., Adams State Coll., 1996. Counselor wrestling camp U. Wis., Whitewater, summers 1989-93, Marquette U., Milw., summers 1990-93; tchr. driver edn. Hartford (Wis.) High Sch., 1991, Waterford (Wis.) High Sch., 1992; tchr. English, head wrestling coach Kewaskum (Wis.) Mid. Sch., 1992-93; asst. wrestling coach Adams State Coll., Alamosa, Colo., 1993—; guidance counselor, head wrestling coach Strasburg (Colo.) H.S., 1995—. Irving Young scholar, Laura Ferris scholar. Mem. Am. Counseling Assn., Colo. Counseling Assn., Golden Key Honor Soc., Delta Kappa Pi. Home: 1678 Arapahoe St Strasburg CO 80136

STRAUBEL, JOHN FREDERICK, public relations executive; b. Green Bay, Wis., May 19, 1928; s. Clarence Weise and Ethel (Puchner) S. B.S. in English, Northwestern U., 1950. Dir. pub. relations Hiller Aircraft Corp., Palo Alto, Calif., 1956-64; dir. communications Fairchild Hiller Corp.,

Washington, 1964-66; owner, pres. Straubel Communications, Portola Valley, Calif., 1966—. Author, editor: Pacific Diary I, 1952; Pacific Diary II, 1953; One Way Up, 1963. Mgr. pub. relations Volunteers for Nixon-Lodge, Washington, 1960, br. v.p. Boys & Girls Clubs Am. Served to lt. USN, 1950-53; Korea. Mem. Pub. Relations Soc. Am. Presbyterian. Office: Straubel Communications 162 Sand Hill Cir Menlo Park CA 94025-7104

STRAUCH, HAROLD BENJAMIN, orthopaedic surgeon; b. Sacramento, June 15, 1934; s. Harold Rudolph and Dorothy Gertrude (Harrigan) S.; m. Lilla Lou Witharm, June 1, 1962; children: Michael, Kristin, Kimberly, Marc, Matthew. BA, Stanford U., 1956, MD, 1959. Diplomate Am. Bd. Orthopaedic Surgery. Intern Phila. Gen. Hosp., 1959-60; resident U. Calif., San Francisco, 1960-61, Pacific Presbyn. Med. Ctr., San Francisco, 1961-63, Shriners Hosp., L.A., 1963-64; pvt. practice Sacramento, 1964—. Chmn. bd. Sutter Cmty. Hosps., Sacramento, 1993-94. Mem. ACS, AMA, Am. Acad. Orthopedic Surgeons, Western Orthopedic Assn., Calif. Med. Assn., Sacramento Med. Soc. Office: 2801 K St Ste 400 Sacramento CA 95816-5119

STRAUS, LAWRENCE GUY, anthropology educator, editor-in-chief; b. Ga., Oct. 17, 1948; s. David Albert and Clotilde (Magnant) S.; María del Carmen Rapado, July 12, 1975; 1 child, Eva Angela Rapado. AB, U. Chgo., 1971, AM, 1972, PhD, 1975. Asst. prof. U. N.M., Albuquerque, 1975-81, assoc. prof., 1981-87, prof., 1987—, archeology subfield chair, 1983-95, asst. dept. chair, 1987-93, Snead-Wertheim lectr. anthropology, history, 1990-91; vis. prof. U. Buenos Aires, 1996; supr. student fellowships, rsch. grants NSF, Leakey Found., Belgian-Am. Ednl. Found., Irene Levi-Sala Found., Fulbright Found., Am. Ctr. Oriental Rsch. Author: El Solutrense Vasco-Cantábrico, 1983, Iberia Before the Iberians, 1992 (CHOICE/Am. Assn. U. and Rsch. Librs. award 1993); co-author, co-editor: La Riera Cave, 1986, The End of the Paleolithic in the Old World, 1986, Les Derniers Chasseurs de Rennes du Monde Pyreneen: L'Abri Dufaure, 1995, Humans at the End of the Ice Age, 1996, Le Trou Magrite, 1996, La grotte du Bois Loiterie, 1997; editor-in-chief: Jour. Anthropol. Rsch., 1995—; contbr. over 280 articles, revs. to profl. jours. Fellow NSF, 1968, 71-74, 76-92, Nat. Geographic Soc., 1979-80, 87-88, 90, 93-95, 97, L.S.B. Leakey Found., 1985, 87-88, 91-92, 94, 96, 97; travel grantee Am. Coun. Learned Socs., 1987, 96, Am. Geophys. Union, 1995, Smithsonian Instn., 1994, Internat. Rsch. and Exchs. Bd., 1994. Mem. Am. Anthropol. Assn., Soc. Am. Archeology, French Prehistoric Soc., Aranzadi Soc. Sci., S. African Archeol. Soc., Paleoanthropology Soc., Ariège-Pyrénées Prehistoric Soc., Internat. Union Quaternary Rsch. (sec. commn. paleontology early man 1992-95, chair working group archeology of the pleistocene-holocene transition 1992—, pres. com. human evolution and paleontology 1996—). Office: U NM Dept Anthropology Albuquerque NM 87131

STRAUS, LEONARD HIRSCH, retail company executive; b. 1914; married. LL.B., Harvard U., 1938. With Thrifty Corp., L.A., 1945—; officer legal dept. Thrifty Corp., Los Angeles, from 1948; chmn., CEO Thrifty Corp., L.A., 1979-90, chmn. emeritus, 1990—; also dir. Thrifty Corp., Los Angeles. Served with USCG, 1943-45. Address: Thrifty-Payless Inc 9275 SW Peyton Ln Wilsonville OR 97070-9200*

STRAUSS, PAUL EDWARD, English language educator; b. Houston, Sept. 7, 1941; s. James Henry and Lucy Mae (Seger) S.; m. Karen Johnson, 1964 (div. 1980); children: Rebecca, Michael; m. Sandra Howell Colomy, May 18, 1995. BA, St. Mary's U., San Antonio, 1963; MA, Ea. N.Mex. U., 1971; PhD, U. Nev., Las Vegas, 1991. Instr., battery comdr. U.S. Army Artillery, 1964-66, 68-72; adminstrv. asst./tech. publs. writer U.S. Bur. Reclamation, Redding, Calif., 1972-76, Amarillo, Tex., 1972-76; sr. writer U.S. Bur. Reclamation, Boulder City, Nev., 1977-89; lectr. in English U. Nev., Las Vegas, 1990—. Author: In Hope of Heaven, 1995; contbr. articles, planning reports, and statements to jours. and govt. publs. (Outstanding Performance awards U.S. Govt. 1981, 86). Capt. U.S. Army, 1964-66, 69-72, Vietnam. Decorated Bronze Star. Office: Univ Nev Las Vegas English Dept 4505 S Maryland Pkwy Las Vegas NV 89154-9900

STRAW, ELLEN KATRINA, English educator, writer; b. Covina, Calif., Sept. 9, 1965; d. Earl Wilson and Marie Ruth (Ulmer) S. AA in English, Mt. San Antonio Coll., 1985; BA in English, Calif. State Poly. U., Pomona, 1988, MA in English, 1991. Freelance writer, Covina, 1982—, freelance editor,, 1988—; English tutor Calif. Poly. State U., Pomona, 1986—, instr. English,, 1990-92; instr. English, Citrus C.C., Glendora, Calif., 1992—; staff writer Write Away/Valley Writers, Covina, 1995—. Author: Creative Writhing, 1993, (screenplays) Long Distance, 1996, The New Girl, 1996; co-author: The First Anthology, 1996; editor: Hard Copies, 1988. Mem. Valley Writers (refreshments officer 1990—). Home: 1341 N Armel Dr Covina CA 91722

STRAWA, ANTHONY WALTER, research scientist; b. Chgo., Apr. 22, 1950. BS, USAF Acad., Colorado Springs, Colo., 1973; PhD, MS, Stanford (Calif.) U., 1986. Rsch. asst. Stanford U., 1982-86; lead researcher ballistic range NASA-Ames Rsch. Ctr., Moffett Field, Calif., 1986-89, prin. investigator Aeroassist flight expt., 1990-91, rsch. scientist, 1991-93, acting br. chief atmospheric rsch. br., 1995—; mem. NASA Aerodynamic Sensors Working Group, 1989-93. Mem. AIAA (sec. aerodynamic measurement tech. com. 1989-93), AAAS, AMS, AGU. Office: NASA-Ames Rsch Ctr Mail Stop 245-4 Moffett Field CA 94035

STRAWN, EVELYN RAE, artist; b. Kerman, Calif., Nov. 24, 1921; d. Cloy Ray and Florence Grace (Angell) Hudson; m. Virgil Hollis Strawn, Sept. 19, 1940; children: C.J., Randall, Michael, Reagan. BA, U. Redlands, 1966. Artist freelance Grand Terrace, Calif., 1959—; probation officer San Bernardino (Calif.) County, 1966-89; developed and directed Sch. Based Teen Programs, San Bernardino, 1967-75, Pregnancy Program for Teens to Continue Schooling, 1967-68. Exhibited paintings and sculptures in pvt. collections and galleries. Bd. dirs., pres. Sexual Assault Svcs., San Bernardino, 1980-84; pres. Women in Mgmt., Inland Empire, 1983. Recipient Cert. of Commendation, San Bernardino County Probation Dept., 1989. Mem. Nat. Soc. DAR, Soroptimist Internat. of Riverside (bd. dirs. 1984).

STRENA, ROBERT VICTOR, retired university research laboratory manager; b. Seattle, June 28, 1929; s. Robert Lafayette Peel and Mary Oliva (Holmes) S.; m. Rita Mae Brodovsky, Aug. 1957; children: Robert Victor, Adrienne Amelia. AB, Stanford U., 1952. Survey mathematician Hazen Engrng., San Jose, Calif., 1952-53; field engr. Menlo Sanitary Dist., Menlo Park, Calif., 1954-55; ind. fin. reporter Los Altos, Calif., 1953-59; asst. dir. Hansen Labs. Stanford U., 1959-93, asst. dir. emeritus Ginzton Lab., 1993—; ind. fin. cons., Los Altos, 1965—; mem. Rehab. Adv. Bd., Moffett Fed. Airfield, 1994—. Active Edn. System Politics, Los Altos, 1965-80, local Boy Scouts Am., 1968-80, Maj. USAR, 1948-70. Mem. AAAS, Mus. Soc., Big X (Los Altos). Republican. Home: 735 Raymundo Ave Los Altos CA 94024-3139 Office: Ginzton Lab Stanford Univ Stanford CA 94305

STRENGER, GEORGE, surgeon; b. N.Y., Sept. 5, 1906; s. Philip and Tillie (Strassman) S.; m. Florence Serxner, June 9, 1931; children: Philip J., Laurence N. BA, Columbia U., 1928, MD, 1931. Diplomate Am. Bd. Surg., 1942. surgeon Bklyn. Jew. Hosp., N.Y., 1934-72, Goldwater Meml. Hosp., N.Y., 1939-53; chief surg. svc. N.Y. regional office VA, 1948-72; surgeon Coney Island Hosp., N.Y., 1953-72; instr. Long Island Med. Coll., N.Y., 1934-36. Mem. Ditmas Pk. Assn. (pres. 1953-54). Comdr. field hosp. U.S. Army, 1942-46, ETO. Recipient commendation Gen. Eisenhower, 1945. Fellow Am. Coll. Surgeons. Home: 31397 E Nine Dr Laguna Niguel CA 92677-2909

STRETCH, SHIRLEY MARIE, marketing educator; b. Wauneta, Nebr., May 6, 1949; d. Lloyd Ray and Roberta Marie (Schroeder) S. BS, U. Nebr., 1971; MS, Kans. State U., 1972; MBA, Ohio State U., 1977, PhD, 1982. Instr. clothing and textiles Bowling Green (Ohio) State U., 1972-75; grad. adminstrv. asso. Univ. Coll., Ohio State U., 1976-78, 80; asso. mgr. direct mktg. div. Ashland Petroleum Co. (Ky.), 1979-80; asst. prof. clothing and textiles Tex. Tech U., Lubbock, 1980-85; assoc. prof. mktg. Valdosta State Coll., Ga., 1985-87; prof. mktg. Calif. State U., L.A., 1987—, also chair dept. Profl. devel. fellow, 1971-73. Mem. NAFE, Am. Mktg. Assn., So. Calif. Assn. MBA Execs., Am. Home Econs. Assn., So. Mktg. Assn., Southwestern Mktg. Assn., Western Mktg. Assn. (bd. dirs., program coord., v.p., pres.), Am. Collegiate Retailing Assn., Atlantic Mktg. Assn. (program coord., pres.), Toastmasters, Omicron Nu, Phi Upsilon Omicron, Mu Kappa Tau. Republican. Methodist. Office: Calif State U Dept Mktg Los Angeles CA 90032

STRICHARTZ, JAMES LEONARD, lawyer; b. N.Y.C., Feb. 5, 1951; s. Morris Harvey and Estelle (Flatow) S. BA in Urban Studies, U. Mich., 1973, M in Pub. Policy, 1976, JD, 1977. Bar: Mich., 1977, D.C. 19878, Wash., 1980; diplomate Coll. of Comty. Assn. Lawyers. Law clk. Mich. Ct. Appeals, Detroit, 1977-78; assoc. atty. Weinrich, Gilmore & Adolph, Seattle, 1978-79; gen. counsel The 13th Regional Corp., Seattle, 1979-81; pvt. practice Seattle, 1981—; mem. Senate Jud. Com. Condo. Law Task Force, Seattle, 1986-87, Condo. Act Statutory Revision Com., 1987-91, Washington Common Interest Ownership Act Legis. Task Force, 1994-95; spkr. 22 and 23d nat. confs. Cmty. Assn. Inst., Alexandria, Va.; faculty Profl. Mgmt. Devel. Program, 1993. Pres., bd. dirs. Fremont Community Health Clinic, 1982-83, 45th St. Community Health Clinic, 1984-89; gen. counsel, trustee Wash. Trust for Hist. Preservation, 1982-87; mem. Corp. Coun. For The Arts, 1987-88, Coun. for Corp. Responsibility, 1984—; founding mem., founding dir. Shoreline Arts Coun., 1989-92. Mem. Comty. Assn. Inst., Nat. Conf. of Chpts. (vice chmn., N.W. region 1988-89, chmn. 1990-91), Comty. Assns. Inst. Wash. (bd. dirs. 1986-92, v.p. 1987, pres. 1988-90, faculty mem. ops. and mgmt. comty. assns. leadership tng. program 1987, 89, 90, 91, chmn. 1992, 93, faculty profl. mgmt. devel. program 1993—), Comty. Assn. Inst. Rsch. Found. (chmn. symposium on comty. 1990, bd. dirs. 1991-96, speaker symposiums 1991, 93, v.p. 1994, treas. 1995). Democrat. Unitarian. Office: 200 W Mercer St # 511 Seattle WA 98119-3958

STRICK, RUTH COCHRAN, career counselor; b. Cleve., May 3, 1932; d. Joseph Lynn and Eva Maxine (McKerrell) Cochran; m. Dale Everington Strick, June 18, 1960 (dec. 1981); 1 child, Lorna Susan. BFA, Cleve. Inst. Art, 1955; MA, Univ. of the Arts, Phila., 1972; postgrad. in edn., U. Pa., 1972-74. Instr. drawing, design, enameling Carnegie-Mellon U., Pitts., 1957-66; instr. enameling, art edn., art history Glassboro (N.J.) State Coll., 1969-72; instr. early childhood, child devel. and child psychology Camden (N.J.) County Coll., 1972-81; rsch. assoc. Rsch. for Better Schs., Phila., 1974-75; lectr. U. Pa., Phila., 1975-79; career counselor Univ. of the Arts, Phila., 1985-86; dir. career resources Art Ctr. Coll. Design, Pasadena, Calif., 1986-90; career mgmt. counselor Right Assocs., Pasadena, Calif., 1993—; career cons. Bob McCarthy, L.a., 1992-93; curriculum cons. Burlington (N.J.) County Cmty. Action Program, 1983-86; career cons. in the arts Walt Disney Imagineering, Glendale, Calif., 1990-94. Co-founder Orange-Villa Neighborhood Assn., Pasadena, 1993; commr. Pasadena Arts Commn., 1994-96; cmty. advocate, Pasadena, 1993—. Design Rsch. fellow, Towle Silversmiths, Newburyport, Mass., 1957. Mem. Assn. for Supervision and Curriculum Devel., Coll. Art Assn., Pi Lambda Theta. Home: 625 N Mar Vista Ave Apt 2 Pasadena CA 91106-1199 Office: Right Assocs 2 N Lake Ave Ste 1030 Pasadena CA 91101-1872

STRICKLIN, GUY MICHAEL, construction company executive; b. Amarillo, Tex., June 11, 1944; s. Guy Mike and Lola Elizabeth (Word) S.; m. Margaret Suzanne Wilhite, Dec. 20, 1967; children: Dalene M., Melia L., Margaret E., William M. BSCE, Tex. Tech. U., 1967. Civil engr. Morrison Knudsen Corp., various locations, 1967-75, constrn. project mgr., 1975-91; regional mgr. Morrison Knudsen Corp., San Francisco, 1985-88; mgr. constrn. Morrison Knudsen Corp., Denver Internat. Airport, 1991-94; pres. Silverado Constructors, Irvine, Calif., 1994—. Leadership positions with various evangel. chs., 1977—. Mem. Associated Gen. Contractors, Irvine C. of C., Design/Build Inst. Am. Republican. Office: Silverado Constructors 22 Executive Park Irvine CA 92614

STRINGER, WILLIAM JEREMY, university official; b. Oakland, Calif., Nov. 8, 1944; s. William Duane and Mildred May (Andrus) S.; BA in English, So. Meth. U., 1966; MA in English, U. Wis., 1968, PhD in Ednl. Adminstrn., 1973; m. Susan Lee Hildebrand; children: Shannon Lee, Kelly Erin, Courtney Elizabeth. Dir. men's housing Southwestern U., Georgetown, Tex., 1968-69; asst. dir. housing U. Wis., Madison, 1969-73; dir. residential life, asso. dean student life, adj. prof. Pacific Luth., Tacoma, 1973-78; dir. residential life U. So. Calif., 1978-79, asst. v.p., 1979-84, asst. prof. higher and post-secondary edn., 1980-84; v.p. student life Seattle U., 1984-89, v.p. student devel., 1989-92, assoc. provost, 1989-95, assoc. prof. edn., 1990—, chair educational leadership, 1994—. Author: How to Survive as a Single Student, 1972, The Role of the Assistant in Higher Education, 1973. Bd. dirs. N.W. area Luth. Social Services of Wash. and Idaho, pres.-elect, 1989, pres., 1990-91. Danforth Found. grantee, 1976-77. Mem. AAUP, Am. Assn. Higher Edn., Nat. Assn. Student Pers. Adminstrs. (bd. dirs. region V 1985—, mem. editl. bd. Jour. 1995—), Am. Coll. Pers. Assn., Phi Eta Sigma, Sigma Tau Delta, Phi Alpha Theta. Lutheran. Home: 4553 169th Ave SE Bellevue WA 98006-6505 Office: Seattle U Seattle WA 98122

STROBECK, KEN L., state legislator, healthcare organization executive; b. Eugene, Oreg., Dec. 25, 1951; s. Lewis August and Jessie Marian (Pruett) S.; m. Kay A. Larson, Aug. 28, 1971; 3 children. BA, U. Oreg., 1973. Prodr. news KATU-TV, KGW-TV, Portland, Oreg., 1979-84; mem. dept. pub. rels. Portland Rose Festival, 1984-88; mem. dept. cmty. rels. Emanuel Hosp., Portland, 1988-92; mem. dept. corp. comm. Bluecross Blueshield, 1992—; state rep. State of Oregon, 1995—, majority whip, 1997. Mem. Rep. precinct com., Beaverton, Oreg., 1994—; pub. safety advocate 9-1-1 operators, State of Oreg., 1996. Flemming fellow Ctr. for Policy Alternatives, Washington, 1996. Mem. Soc. Healthcare Strategy and Market Devel. (bd. dirs. 1994—). Mem. Ch. of Christ. Office: PO Box 6690 Beaverton OR 97007

STROBER, MYRA HOFFENBERG, education educator, consultant; b. N.Y.C., Mar. 28, 1941; d. Julius William Hoffenberg and Regina Scharer; m. Samuel Strober, June 23, 1963 (div. Dec. 1983); children: Jason M., Elizabeth A.; m. Jay M. Jackman, Oct. 21, 1990. BS in Indsl. Rels., Cornell U., 1962; MA in Econs., Tufts U., 1965; PhD in Econs., MIT, 1969. Lectr., asst. prof. dept. econs. U. Md., College Park, 1967-70; lectr. U. Calif., Berkeley, 1970-72; asst. prof. grad. sch. bus. Stanford (Calif.) U., 1972-86, assoc. prof. sch. edn., 1979-90, prof., 1990—, assoc. dean acad. affairs, 1993-95, interim dean, 1994; organizer Stanford Bus. Conf. Women Mgmt., 1974; founding dir. ctr. rsch. women Stanford U., 1974-76, 79-84, dir. edn. policy inst., 1984-86, dean alumni coll., 1992, mem. policy and planning bd., 1992-93, chair program edn. adminstrn. and policy analysis, 1991-93, chair provost's com. recruitment and retention women faculty, 1992-93, chair faculty senate com. on coms., 1992-93; mem. adv. bd. State of Calif. Office Econ. Policy Planning and Rsch., 1978-80; mem. Coll. Bd. Com. Develop Advanced Placement Exam. Econs., 1987-88; faculty advisor Rutgers Women's Leadership Program, 1991-93. Author: (with others) Industrial Relations, 1972, Sex, Discrimination and the Division of Labor, 1975, Changing Roles of Men and Women, 1976, Women in the Labor Market, 1979, Educational Policy and Management: Sex Differentials, 1981, Women in the Workplace, 1982, Sex Segregation in the Workplace: Trends, Explanations, Remedies, 1984, The New Palgrave: A Dictionary of Economic Theory and Doctrine, 1987, Computer Chips and Paper Clips: Technology and Women's Employment, Vol. II, 1987, Gender in the Workplace, 1987; editor: (with Francine E. Gordon) Bringing Women Into Management, 1975, (with others) Women and Poverty, 1986, (with Sanford M. Dornbusch) Feminism, Children and the New Families, 1988; mem. bd. editors Signs: Jour. Women Culture and Soc., 1975-89, assoc. editor, 1980-85; mem. bd. editors Sage Ann. Rev. Women and Work, 1984—; mem. editorial adv. bd. U.S.-Japan Women's Jour., 1991—; assoc. editor Jour. Econ. Edn., 1991—; contbr. chpt. to book. Mem. rsch. adv. task force YWCA, 1989—; chair exec. bd. Stanford Hillel, 1990-92; bd. dirs. Resource Ctr. Women, Palo Alto, Calif., 1983-84; pres. bd. dirs. Kaider Found., Mountain View, Calif., 1990-96. Fellow Stanford U., 1975-77, Schiff House Resident fellow, 85-87. Mem. NOW (bd. dirs. legal def. and edn. fund 1993—), Am. Econ. Assn. (mem. com. status of women in the profession 1972-75), Am. Ednl. Rsch. Assn., Indsl. Rels. Rsch. Assn., Internat. Assn. for Feminist Econs. (pres. 1997—). Office: Stanford U School of Education Stanford CA 94305

STROCK, DAVID RANDOLPH, brokerage house executive; b. Salt Lake City, Jan. 31, 1944; s. Clarence Randolph and Francis (Hornibrook) S.; m. Phyllis A. Tingley, Dec. 13, 1945 (div. June 15, 1982); children: Sarah, Heidi. AA, San Mateo Coll., 1967; BS, San Jose State U., 1970. Investment exec. Paine Webber, San Jose, Calif., 1970-78; corp. trainer Paine Webber, N.Y.C., 1978-79, rsch. coord., 1979-82; br. mgr. Paine Webber, Northbrook, Ill., 1982-84, Palos Verdes, Calif., 1984-89, Napa, Calif., 1989-90; investment exec. Paine Webber, Napa, 1990—. Contbr. articles to profl. jours. Mem. San Jose Jr. C. of C. (chmn. 1977, v.p. 1978), North Napa Rotary (past pres.), Moose. Republican. Home: 3324 Homestead Ct Napa CA 94558-4275 Office: Paine Webber 703 Trancas St Napa CA 94558-3014

STROCK, JAMES MARTIN, state agency administrator, lawyer, conservationist; b. Austin, Tex., Aug. 19, 1956; s. James Martin Strock Sr. and Augusta (Tenney) Mullins. AB, Harvard U., 1977, JD, 1981; postgrad, New Coll. Oxford U., 1981-82. Bar: Colo. 1983. Tchg. asst. Harvard U., 1980-81; spl. cons. to majority leader U.S. Senate, Washington, 1982-83; spl. asst. to adminstr. EPA, Washington, 1983-85, asst. adminstr. for enforcement, 1989-91; spl. counsel U.S. Senate Com. on Environment and Pub. Works, Washington, 1985-86; environ. atty. Davis, Graham & Stubbs, Denver, 1986-88; acting dir., gen. counsel U.S. Office Pers. Mgmt., Washington, 1988-89; sec. for environ. protection State of Calif., Sacramento, 1991—; adj. prof. U. So. Calif., 1996—, mem. bd. advisors Toxics Law Reporter, 1987-89, Greenwire, 1991—; mem. Intergovtl. Policy Adv. Com., rep. U.S. Trade, 1991—. Contbr. articles to profl. jours.; moderator, producer Lay It On The Line, Sta. WDSU-TV, New Orleans, 1973-74. Bd. dirs. Youth Svc. Am., Washington, 1988-89, Environ. Law Inst., 1992—; chair Calif. United State Employees Campaign, 1996—. Capt. JAGC USAR, 1987-96. Recipient Retsie Arco Future award, 1992, Ross Essay award ABA, 1985, Environ. Leadership award Calif. Environ. Bus. Coun., 1994, Fed. Republic Germany Fellowship award, 1996; Environ. Soc. India fellow, 1997; Charles Joseph Bonaparte scholar Harvard U., 1976, Rotary Internat. scholar, 1981-82. Mem. Commonwealth Club Calif., Phi Beta Kappa. Republican. Home: 400 Spear St Ste 107 San Francisco CA 94105 Office: 555 Capitol Mall Ste 525 Sacramento CA 95814-4503

STROH, GARY ROLAND, development company executive; b. Lima, Ohio, Sept. 28, 1951; s. Roland William and Margaret Jean (Newcomb) S.; m. Mary Jane Mamola, Sept. 22, 1990. Student, Miami U., 1974. V.p. Lucas Furniture, Mansfield, Ohio, 1974-84; owner GRS Constrn., Washington, 1987-94, Gary R. Stroh Constrn., Golden, Colo., 1994—; pres. Bend in the River Devel., Golden, 1996—; authorized dealer Internat. Homes Cedar, Woodinville, Wash., 1996—. Recipient Degree of Chevalier, Order DeMolay, 1969. Mem. Coal Creek Canyon Improvement Assn. Home: 11646 Crescent Park Dr Golden CO 80403 Office: Bend in the River Devel 11646 Crescent Park Dr Golden CO 80403

STROHMEYER, JOHN, writer, former editor; b. Cascade, Wis., June 26, 1924; s. Louis A. and Anna Rose (Saladunas) S.; m. Nancy Jordan, Aug. 20, 1949; children: Mark, John, Sarah. Student, Moravian Coll., 1941-43; A.B., Muhlenberg Coll., 1947; M.A. in Journalism, Columbia, 1948; L.H.D. (hon.), Lehigh U., 1983. With Nazareth Item, 1940-41; night reporter Bethlehem (Pa.) Globe-Times, 1941-43, 45-47; investigative reporter Providence Jour.-Bull., 1949-56; editor Bethlehem Globe-Times, 1956-84, v.p., 1961-84, dir., 1963-84; African-Am. journalism tchr. in Nairobi, Freetown, 1964; Atwood prof. journalism U. Alaska Anchorage, 1987-88, writer-in-residence, 1989—. Author: Crisis in Bethlehem: Big Steel's Struggle to Survive, 1986, Extreme Conditions: Big Oil and The Transformation of Alaska, 1993. Lt. (j.g.) USNR, 1943-45. Pulitzer Traveling fellow, 1948; Nieman fellow, 1952-53; recipient Comenius award Moravian Coll., 1971; Pulitzer prize for editorial writing, 1972; Alicia Patterson Found. fellow, 1984, 85. Mem. Am. Soc. Newspaper Editors, Pa. Soc. Newspaper Editors (pres. 1964-66), Anchorage Racquet Club. Home: 6633 Lunar Dr Anchorage AK 99504-4550

STROMBOM, CATHY JEAN, transportation planner, consultant; b. Bremerton, Wash., Nov. 4, 1949; d. Paul D. and Carolyn (Snitman) Powers; m. David Glen Strombom, June 17, 1972; 1 child, Paul Davis. BA summa cum laude, Whitman Coll., 1972; M in City and Regional Planning, Harvard U., 1977; postgrad., U. Wash., 1982-84. Urban planner Harvard Inst. for Internat. Devel., Tehran, Iran, 1977; sr. transp. planner Puget Sound Coun. Govts., Seattle, 1978-84; mgr. transp. planning/prin. profl. assoc. Parsons Brinckerhoff Quade and Douglas, Inc., Seattle, 1984—; v.p. Women's Transp. Seminar, Seattle, 1988-90 (Woman of Yr. 1989). Contbr. articles to profl. jours. Vol. U.S. Peace Corps, Marrakech, Morocco, 1973-75. Mem. Am. Inst. Cert. Planners (cert.), Am. Planning Assn., Inst. Transp. Engrs., Phi Beta Kappa. Home: 2580 W Viewmont Way W Seattle WA 98199-3660 Office: Parsons Brinckerhoff Quade and Douglas Inc 999 3rd Ave Ste 2200 Seattle WA 98104-4028

STROMER, PRISCILLA (PERKY STROMER), physical education educator; b. Denver, Mar. 11, 1950; d. Willard Carl and Myrtle Linnea (Carlson) Vetter; m. June 16, 1973; children: Linnea, Sara. BS, Calif. State U., Chico, 1972; MS, Calif. Poly. U., Pomona, 1979; PhD, U. Calif., Riverside, 1987. Coach Chico Recreation Dept., 1970-72, Laguna Beach (Calif.) H.S., 1976-79; instr., coach Trinity Western U., Langley, B.C., Can., 1972-73; tchr., coach Sutter (Calif.) H.S., 1974-76; tchr. Michael Kent Sch., Orange, Calif., 1976-78; mem. faculty dept KHP Calif. Poly. U., 1978—, dir. Motor Devel. Clinic, 1985—; mem. Calif. APE Coun., 1987—; v.p. PTS Cons., La Verne, Calif., 1990-94; chmn. stds. Calif. CTC, Sacramento, 1990-93; cons. in spl. edn. Calif. Dept. Edn., Sacramento, 1993—; ddddir. nat. conf. APE, Ontario, Calif., 1994. Author computer program APE Goals and Objectives, 1992. Dir. spl. Edn. Evang. Free Ch., Fullerton, Calif., 1976-85. Mem. Calif. Assn. Health, Phys. Edn., Recreation and Dance (scholarship chmn. Pomona Valley chpt. 1988—, budget chmn. 1990—). Office: Calif Poly U Dept KHP 3801 W Temple Ave Pomona CA 91768

STROMQUIST, DON LEONARD, rheumatologist; b. Salt Lake City, May 26, 1954; s. Donald M. and Jane (Layton) S.; m. Regina E. Rosenthal, May 21, 1989. BA, U. Utah, 1978; MD, Yale U., 1982. Diplomate Am. Bd. Internal Medicine. Resident Boston City Hosp., 1982-86; fellow Boston U. Arthritis Ctr., 1986-88; physician Hitchcock Clinic, Manchester, N.H., 1988-91; physician in pvt. practice pvt. practice, Salt Lake City, 1991—. Trustee Utah Heritage Found., 1993. Fellow Am. Coll. Rheumatology. Office: 324 10th Ave Ste 250 Salt Lake City UT 84103-2853

STRONG, DAVID WARREN, urologist; b. Lansing, Mich., May 30, 1943; s. Warren Murray and Kathleen Louise (Kieppe) S.; m. Jacquelene Sue Wallace, June 15, 1967; children: Kimberly Ann Strong Moss, Vicki Lynn. BA, Yale U., 1965; MD, Wayne State U., 1969. Diplomate Am. Bd. Urology. Intern Cleve. Metro. Gen. Hosp., 1969-70; resident gen. surgery, urology U. Oreg. Med. Sch., Portland, 1970-76; lt. cmdr. U.S. Navy, San Diego, 1976-78; pvt. practice urology Phoenix, 1978—. Fellow Am. Coll. Surgeons; mem. Internat. Soc. Urology, Am. Urol. Assn. Republican. Office: Canyon State Urology 4616 N 51st Ave Ste 206 Phoenix AZ 85031-1721

STRONG, JAMES THOMPSON, management, security, human resources consultant; b. Boca Raton, Fla., Oct. 26, 1945; s. Earl William and Mary Joe (Thompson) S.; m. Lenore Jean Stager, Feb. 2, 1974; 1 child, Daria Nicole. BA in Polit. Sci., U. Calif., Riverside, 1973; MS in Strategic Intelligence, Def. Intelligence Coll., Washington, 1982. Factoring specialist. Commd. USAF, 1968, advaned through grades to maj., ret., 1990; faculty Def. Intelligence Coll., Washington, 1982-86; dir. translations USAF, 1986-88, dir. info. svcs., 1988-90; proprietary security mgr. McDonnell-Douglas Technologies, San Diego, 1990-92; owner Employment Svcs. for Bus., San Diego, 1995—; adj. prof. internat. rels. U.S. Internat. U., 1996—; factor broker. Author: The Basic Industrial Counter-Espionage Cookbook, 1993, The Government Contractor's OPSEC Cookbook, 1993; co-author: The Military Intelligence Community, 1985; mem. bd. editors Internat. Jour. Intelligence and Counterintelligence, 1986—; contbr. articles to profl. jours. Recipient Disting. EEO award USAF, 1987, Def. Meritorious Svc. medal 1986, Meritorious Svc. medal, 1981, 90, Joint Svc. Commendation medal Def. Intelligence Agy./NATO, 1982, 85. Mem. Nat. Mil. Intelligence Assn. (bd. dirs. 1984—, chpt. pres. 1989, 94), Ops. Security Profls. Soc. (chpt. chair 1993, 94-96), Nat. Cargo Security Coun., San Diego Roundtable (exec. coord. 1994, 95), Assn. Former Intelligence Officers (nat. scholarship adminstr. 1994—), Am. Soc. for Indsl. Security, Air Force Assn., San Diego Soc. for Human Resource Mgmt. Republican. Home and Office: Employment Svcs for Bus 1142 Miramonte Glen Escondido CA 92026

STRONG, JOHN OLIVER, plastic surgeon, educator; b. Montclair, N.J., Feb. 1, 1930; s. George Joseph and Olivia (LeBrun) S.; m. Helen Louise Vrooman, July 19, 1958 (dec. Mar. 1973); m. Deborah Sperberg, May 20, 1978; children: John Jr., Jean LeB., Andrew D. BS, Yale U., 1952; MD, U. Pa., 1957. Practice medicine specializing in plastic and reconstructive surgery Santa Ana, Calif., 1964-97; asst. clin. prof. plastic and reconstructive surgery U. Calif., Irvine, 1970—; chief of staff Western Med. Ctr., Santa Ana, 1996—, interim chmn. bd., 1996-97, bd. dirs.; bd. dirs. United Western Med. Ctrs., Orange Health Found. Fellow ACS; mem. Calif. Med. Assn. (chmn. sci. adv. panel 1983-89), Calif. Soc. Plastic Surgeons (pres. 1991-92). Republican. Office: Box 94 Borrego Springs CA 92004-0094

STRONG, MAYDA NEL, psychologist, educator; b. Albuquerque, May 6, 1942; d. Floyd Samuel and Wanda Christmas (Martin) Strong; 1 child, Robert Allen Willingham. BA in Speech-Theatre cum laude, Tex. Western Coll., 1963; EdM, U. Tex., Austin, 1972, PhD in Counseling Psychology, 1978; lic. clin. psychologist, Colo., 1984; cert. alcohol counselor III, Colo., 1987, nat. master addiction counselor, 1996; diplomate, bd. cert. Forensic Examiner; diplomate Am. Bd. Disability Analysts. Asst. instr. in ednl. psychology U. Tex., Austin, 1974-78; instr. psychology Austin C.C., 1974-78, Otero Jr. Coll., La Junta, Colo., 1979-89; dir. outpatient and emergency svcs. S.E. Colo. Family Guidance and Mental Health Ctr., Inc., La Junta, 1978-81; pvt. practice psychol. therapy, La Junta, 1981—; exec. dir. Pathfinders Chem. Dependency program, 1985-94, clin. cons., 1994—, mem. adv. bd., 1995—; clin. psychologist Inst. Forensic Psychiatry, Colo. Mental Health Inst., Pueblo, 1989-94; adj. faculty Adams State Coll., 1992; dir. Allstrong Enterprises, Inc., 1992-94; Del. to County Dem. Conv., 1988. Appeared in The Good Doctor, 1980, On Golden Pond, 1981, Chase Me Comrade, 1989, Plaza Suite, 1987; co-dir. The Odd Couple, 1995. Bd. dirs. Picketwire Cmty. Theatre, 1995; dir. Brighton Beach Memoirs, Picketwire Cmty. Theatre, 1996. AAUW fellow, 1974-76. Mem. Am. Coll. Forensic Examiners, Bus. and Profl. People (legis. chairperson 1982-83, chmn. news election svc. 1982-88), Colo. Psychol. Assn. (legis. chmn. for dist.), Am. Contract Bridge League. Contbr. articles in field to profl. publs. Author poems in Chinook: Paths through the Puzzle, Decisions, Passion. Home: 24555 Co Rd 27 La Junta CO 81050 Office: 315 W 3rd St Ste 204 La Junta CO 81050-1465

STROPE, MICHAEL LEE, protective services official. BS cum laude, Drury Coll., 1975; MS, Cen. Mo. State U., 1978. From police officer to police lt. Mo. Police Dept., Springfield, 1970-84; chief of police City of Stillwater, Okla., 1984-87, City of College Station, Tex., 1987-92, Peoria (Ariz.) Police Dept., 1992—; instr. Ariz. State U., Phoenix, 1996—, Wayland U., Luke AFB, Ariz., 1993—; security-mgmt. cons. SSRS Properties, Inc., College Station, 1992; dept. chmn. criminal justice Blinn Coll., Brenham, Tex., 1992; project assessor Commn. on Accreditation for Law Enforcement Agencies, Inc., 1990; lectr. Okla. Mcpl. League, 1986; adj. faculty Columbia (Mo.) Coll., 1982-84, Drury Coll., Springfield, 1976-82; project dir. Mo. Police Dept., Springfield, 1979-81; adv. bd. chmn. Tex. A&M Engring. Ext. Svc. Police Acad., 1990-92. Contbr. articles to profl. jours. Criminal justice adv. com. Brazos Valley Cmty. Devel. Coun., 1987-92; exec. bd. dirs. Brazos Valley Coun. on Alcohol and Substance Abuse, 1987-91; dep. chmn. Brazos County Emergency Mgmt. Coun., 1987-92. Recipient Mayors award C. of C., 1996, Best of the West award Cmty. Svc., 1994, Cmty. Svc. award SAR, Tex., 1992, Spl. Recognition award Spl. Olympics, Okla., 1986, Outstanding Cmty. Svc. award Delta Tau Delta, 1985; named one of Outstanding Young Men of Am., 1983. Mem. Internat. Assn. Chiefs Police (tng. and edn. com. 1984-92, juvenile justice com. 1995—), FBI Nat. Acad. Assoc., Ariz. Police Chiefs Assn., Rotary. Office: Peoria Police Dept 8343 W Monroe St Peoria AZ 85380

STROUP, ELIZABETH FAYE, librarian; b. Tulsa, Mar. 25, 1939; d. Milton Earl and Lois (Buhl) S. BA in Philosophy, U. Wash., 1962, MLS, 1964. Intern Libr. of Congress, Washington, 1964-65; asst. dir. North Cen. Regional Libr., Wenatchee, Wash., 1966-69; reference specialist Congl. Reference div. Libr. of Congress, Washington, 1970-71, head nat. collections Div. for the Blind and Physically Handicapped, 1971-73, chief Congl. Reference div., 1973-78, dir. gen. reference, 1978-88; city libr., chief exec. officer Seattle Pub. Libr., 1988—; cons. U.S. Info. Svc., Indonesia, Feb. 1987. Mem. adv. bd. KCTS 9 Pub. TV, Seattle, 1988—; bd. visitors Sch. Librarianship, U. Wash., 1988—; bd. dirs. Wash. Literacy, 1988—. Mem. ALA (pres. reference and adult svcs. div. 1986-87, div. bd. 1985-88), Wash. Libr. Assn., D.C. Libr. Assn. (bd. dirs. 1975-76), City Club, Ranier Club. Office: Seattle Pub Libr 1000 4th Ave Seattle WA 98104-1109

STROUP, RICHARD LYNDELL, economics educator, writer; b. Sunnyside, Wash., Jan. 3, 1943; s. Edgar Ivan and Inez Louise (Kellet) S.; m. Sandra Lee Price, Sept. 13, 1962 (div. Sept. 1981); children—Michael, Craig; m. Jane Bartlett Steidemann Shaw, Jan. 1, 1985; 1 child, David. Student, MIT, 1961-62; B.A., M.A., U. Wash., 1966, Ph.D. in Econs., 1970. Asst. prof. econs. Mont. State U., Bozeman, 1969-74; assoc. prof. econs. Mont. State U., 1974-78, prof. econs., 1978—; dir. Office Policy Analysis, Dept. Interior, Washington, 1982-84; vis. assoc. prof. Fla. State U., Tallahassee, 1977-78; sr. assoc. Polit. Economy Research Ctr., Bozeman, 1980—/lectr. summer univ., U. Aix (France), 1985—. Co-author: Natural Resources, 1983, Economics: Private and Public Choice, 8th edit., 1997, Basic Economics, 1993, What Everyone Should Know About Economics and Prosperity, 1993; also articles, 1972—; mem. editorial adv. bd. Regulation, 1993—. Treas., dir. Gallatin Valley Cmty. Sch. Adj. scholar Cato Inst., 1993—. Mem. Am. Econ. Assn., Western Econ. Assn., So. Econ. Assn., Mont Pelerin Soc., Phila. Soc., Pub. Choice Soc., Assn. of Pvt. Enterprise Edn. Episcopalian. Home: 9 W Arnold St Bozeman MT 59715-6127 Office: PERC 502 S 19th Ave Ste 211 Bozeman MT 59718-6827

STRUEVER, STUART MCKEE, archaeologist; b. Peru, Ill., Aug. 4, 1931; s. Carl Chester and Martha McKee (Scobee) S.; m. Alice Ruzzell Melcher, Aug. 21, 1956 (div. June 1983); children: Nathan Chester, Hanna Russell; m. Martha Lee Hopkins, Nov. 12, 1988. AB, Dartmouth Coll., 1953; MA, Northwestern U., 1960; PhD, U. Chgo., 1968. Instr. U. Chgo., 1964-65; from asst. prof. to prof. Northwestern U., Evanston, Ill., 1965-84; pres. Ctr. Am. Archaeology, Evanston, Ill., 1964-84, Crow Canyon Archaeological Ctr., Denver, 1985-92; chair Crow Canyon Ctr., Denver, 1993-96; bd. archaeological cons. Tenn. Valley Authority, Knoxville, 1975-88. Author: Koster: Americans in Search of Their Past, 1979; editor: (book series) Studies in Archaeology Series, 1977-92. Recipient Alumni Achievement award U. Chgo., 1976; medal Hist. Preservation Garden Club Am., N.Y.C., 1994; Humanities fellow Ill. Humanities Coun., 1984. Mem. Soc. Am. Archaeology (pres. 1975-76, Disting. Svc. award, 1995), Soc. Profl. Archaeologists (bd. dirs. 1976), Phi Beta Kappa. Office: Crow Canyon Ctr 1777 S Harrison St PH # 1 Denver CO 80210-3925

STRUHL, STANLEY FREDERICK, real estate developer; b. Bklyn., Oct. 10, 1939; s. Isidore and Yvette (Miller) S.; BS with honors in Engring., UCLA, 1961, MBA in Data Processing, 1963; m. Patricia Joyce Wald, Feb. 26, 1966; children: Marc Howard, Lisa Lynn. Mem. tech. staff Hughes Aircraft Co., Fullerton, Calif., 1963-65; sr. asso. Planning Research Corp., Los Angeles, 1965-70; mgr. corporate info. systems Logicon, Inc., Torrance, Calif., 1970-73; mgr. operations analysis System Devel. Corp., Santa Monica, Calif., 1973-77; gen. partner TST Developers, Canyon Country, Calif., 1977-81; pres. Struhl Enterprises, Inc., Northridge, Calif., 1977-85; owner Struhl Properties, Northridge, 1979—. Mem. planning sub. com. 12th council dist., Los Angeles, 1986—. Lic. real estate broker, Calif. Mem. San Fernando Valley Bd. Realtors, Trail Dusters, Tau Beta Pi, Beta Gamma Sigma, Alpha Phi Omega. Home: 17074 Knapp St Northridge CA 91325-2637 *Personal philosophy: Word(s) to live by; "Think"!.*

STRUPP, JOSEPH P., reporter; b. LaCrosse, Wis., Oct. 29, 1965; s. James Joseph and Margo Louise (Snyder) S. BS in Journalism, Bklyn. Coll., 1988. Reporter The Daily Jour., Elizabeth, N.J., 1988-90, The Argus, Fremont, Calif., 1990-93, San Francisco Ind., 1993—; commentator TCI Cable, San Francisco, 1993—; anchor, reporter KPFA Radio, Berkeley, Calif., 1990—; writing coach San Francisco State U., 1996; freelance writer. Mem. Soc. Profl. Journalists. Home: 575 27th Ave San Francisco CA 94121 Office: San Francisco Independent 1201 Evans Ave San Francisco CA 94124

STRUTTON, LARRY D., newspaper executive; b. Colorado Springs, Colo., Sept. 12, 1940; s. Merril and Gladys (Sheldon) S.; m. Carolyn Ann Croak, Dec. 3, 1960; children—Gregory L., Kristen. A.A. in Electronics Engring., Emily Griffith Electronics Sch., 1968; B.S. in Bus. Mgmt. and Systems Mgmt., Met. State Coll., 1971; diploma in Advanced Mgmt. Program, Harvard U., 1988. Printer Gazette Telegraph, Colorado Springs, Colo., 1961-64; prodn. dir. Rocky Mountain News, Denver, 1964-80, pres., 1990, pres. and CEO, 1991—; exec. v.p. ops. and advt. Detroit Free Press, 1981-83; v.p. ops. Los Angeles Times, 1983-85, exec. v.p. ops., 1986-90. Mem. adv. com. Rochester Inst. Tech., 1984—. Mem. Am. Newspaper Pubs. Assn. (chmn. 1987, chmn. TEC com. 1985-86), R&E Council (research and engring. council of the Graphic Arts Industry Inc.). Club: Lakeside Golf (Los Angeles). Home: 50 Glenmoor Cir Englewood CO 80110-7121 also: Rocky Mountain News 400 W Colfax Ave Denver CO 80204

STRUTZEL, J(OD) C(HRISTOPHER), escrow company executive; b. L.A., Sept. 20, 1947; s. James Rudolph and Charlotte Elizabeth (Weiss) S.; m. Christine Melba Kemp, Dec. 28, 1969; children: Jason James, Jess Warren. BS in Bus. Mgmt., Calif. State U., Long Beach, 1970. Bellman Edgewater Hyatt House Hotel, Long Beach, 1970, night auditor, 1970-71; asst. mgr. Sands Resort Hotel, Palm Springs, Calif., 1971-72; gen. mgr. Sands Resort Hotel, Palm Springs, 1972-73; sales coordinator Bendix Home Systems, Santa Fe Springs, Calif., 1973-74; loan rep. J.E. Wells Fin. Co., L.A., 1974-75; v.p. Express Escrow Co., Huntington Beach, Calif., 1976-78; pres., chmn. bd., bd. dirs. Express Escrow Co., Westminster, Calif., 1978—; pres., chmn. bd., bd. dirs. Elsinore (Calif.) Escrow, Inc., 1977-79; bd. dirs. Sorrell Devel., Redondo Beach, Calif.; expert witness on escrow, litigation and cons., 1982—; chmn. liability reduction com. Escrow Agts. Fidelity Corp., 1983-84, legis. chmn., 1985-86, 87-90, 95-97, vice-chmn. bd., 1989-90, 94-95, treas., 1992-93; bd. dirs., sec. Discovery Escrow Co., 1989-94; drafted sections of Calif. Fin. Code, Health and Safety Code, Calif. Adminstrv. Code. Contbr. articles to trade publs. Campaign treas. Californians to Elect Ted Cook, 1982; bd. dirs. publicity chmn. Fountain Valley (Calif.) Youth Baseball, 1986-87; AD HOC com. on Escrow Regulations Dept. Housing and Cmty. Devel., 1980; escrow adv. com. Dept. Corps., 1990-93. Recipient J.E. Wells Meml. award, 1988, Chmn.'s award 1997. Mem. Escrow Agts. Fidelity Corp. (bd. dirs. 1983-90, 91—), Escrow Inst. of Calif. (bd. dirs. 1991), Calif. Manufactured Housing Assn. (treas., bd. dirs. 1984-86), Calif. Manufactured Housing Inst. (bd. dirs. 1986—, treas. 1986-87, legis. chmn. 1993—, Polit. Action Com. Man of Yr. award 1988, Orange County chpt. Man of Yr. award 1988). Republican. Office: Express Escrow Co 14441 Beach Blvd Ste 100 Westminster CA 92683-5342

STUART, BARBARA KATHRYN, real estate broker, consultant, genealogist; b. Havre, Mont., Oct. 21, 1945; d. David Maurice and Sarah Kathryn (Rickman) S.; m. Gerald Lee Trenholm, March 18, 1969 (div. 1971); 1 child, Dawn Bea Rogers. BS in Bus. Adminstrn., Regis Coll., 1990, MBA, 1992; student, U. Denver, 1995; grad. Real Estate, U. Colo., 1978. Leasing dir. Colo. Ctr. I & II, Denver, 1979-81, Environ. Developers, Inc., Aurora, 1981—; dir. Librian Legacies, Denver, 1986—; pres. Windflower & Co., Denver, 1983—; family history cons. LDS Ch., Denver, 1983—. Author: (book) Snowball's Gift, 1989, Stuarts From Scotland, 1995, (poetry) The White Rose, 1995; editor: (newsletter) Stu's News, 1994. Vol. chaplain Lutheran Hosp., Wheat Ridge, Colo., 1992—; vol archivist Nat. Archives at Denver Fed. Ctr., 1992—; docent Denver Pub. Library, 1995. Mem. BBB (arbitrator), Nat. Bd. Realtors, Colo. Bd. Realtors, Bd. Realtors Million Dollar Club, Daughters of the Am. Revolution. Office: Windflower & Co 9101 North Pearl St Wheat Ridge CO 80229

STUART, CYNTHIA MORGAN, university administrator; b. Harrisburg, Pa., June 29, 1949; d. Paul William and Bernice Leona (Boyer) M.; m. David Edward Stuart, June 14, 1971. Student, Elizabethtown (Pa.) Coll., 1967-69; BA, U. N.Mex., 1971, MPA, 1982. Admissions counselor U. N.Mex., Albuquerque, 1974-77, asst. dir. admissions, 1977-80, assoc. dir. admissions, 1980-83, dir. admissions, 1983—, univ. articulation officer, 1989—; dir. student outreach svcs. (secondary appointment) U. N.Mex., 1991-95; mem. N.Mex. Coordinating Coun. Secondary Schs. and Colls., 1983-92; chair Coun. for Common Concerns, Albuquerque, 1987-95; mem. N.Mex. Articulation Com., Santa Fe, 1983-95; mem. adv. bd. Albuquerque Tech. Vocat. Inst., 1991—. Compiler, editor Statewide Statistical Profile Report, N.Mex. H.Ss., 1983-90; cover photographer Prehistoric New Mexico, 2d edit., 1994, Glimpses of the Ancient Southwest, 1995. Coord. United Way, Albuquerque, 1980-81; elected del. N.Mex. Dem. Conv., 1982; mem. issues and advocacy com. Albuquerque Bus. Edn. Compact, 1991-93; mem. Am. Indian Edn. Initiative, Albuquerque, 1992—; Coll. Bd. del., 1991—. Recipient sys. devel. grant Commn. on Higher Edn., Santa Fe, 1995. Mem. Am. Assn. Collegiate Registrars and Admissions Officers (reporting officer of transfer credit N.Mex. 1979—), Rocky Mountain Assn. Collegiate Registrars and Admissions Officers (v.p. 1979-81, pres. 1983-84), N.Mex. Assn. Collegiate Registrars and Admissions Officers (sec.-treas. 1978-82, pres. 1991-92, Outstanding Svc. award 1990), N.Mex. Am. Coll. Testing Coun. (chair elect 1995-96). Democrat. Home: 423 Tulane Dr SE Albuquerque NM 87106 Office: Univ New Mex Office of Admissions Student Svcs Ctr Albuquerque NM 87131

STUART, DAVID EDWARD, anthropologist, author, educator; b. Calhoun County, Ala., Jan. 9, 1945; s. Edward George and Avis Elsie (Densmore) S.; B.A. (Wesleyan Merit scholar 1965-66), W.VA. Wesleyan Coll., 1967; M.A. in Anthropology, U. N.Mex., 1970, Ph.D., 1972, postdoctoral student, 1975-76; m. Cynthia K. Morgan, June 14, 1971. Research assoc. Andean Center, Quito, Ecuador, 1970; continuing edn. instr. anthropology U. N.Mex., 1971, research archeologist Office Contract Archeology, 1974, research coordinator, 1974-77, asst. prof. anthropology, 1975-77, assoc. prof. anthropology, 1984—, asst. v.p. acad. affairs, 1987-95, assoc. v.p. academic affairs, 1995—; asst. prof. Eckerd Coll., St. Petersburg, Fla., 1972-74; cons. archeologist right-of-way div. Pub. Service Co. N.Mex., Albuquerque, 1977-78; cons. anthropologist Bur. Indian Affairs, Albuquerque, 1978, Historic Preservation Bur. N.Mex., Santa Fe, 1978-81, Nat. Park Service, 1980, Albuquerque Mus., 1981; sr. research assoc. Human Systems Research, Inc., 1981-83, Quivira Research Center, Albuquerque, 1984-86; bd. dirs. Table Ind. Scholars, 1979-83, pres., bd. dirs. Rio Grande Heritage Found., Albuquerque and Las Cruces, 1985-87; advisor Human Systems Research, Inc., Tularosa, N.Mex., 1978-80, Albuquerque Commn. on Hist. Preservation, 1984-86. Grantee Eckerd Coll., 1973, Historic Preservation Bur., 1978-80. Essayist award N.Mex. Humanities Council, 1986. Mem. Am. Anthrop. Assn., Royal Anthrop. Inst. Gt. Britain, N.Mex. Archeol. Council, Albuquerque Archeol. Soc. (pres. 1986-88), Descs. Signers Declaration Independence, Sigma Xi, Phi Kappa Phi. Presbyterian. Co-author: Archeological Survey: 4 Corners to Ambrosia, N.Mex., 1976, A Proposed Project Design for the Timber Management Archeological Surveys, 1978, Ethnoarcheological Investigations of Shepherding in the Pueblo of Laguna, 1983; Author: Prehistoric New Mexico, 1981, 2d edit., 1984, 3d edit., 1988, Glimpses of the Ancient Southwest, 1985, The Magic of Bandelier National Monument, 1989, Power and Efficiency in Eastern Anasazi Architecture, 1994, others; columnist New Mexico's Heritage, 1983-87, others. Editor: Archeological Reports, No. 1, 1975, No. 2, 1981. Office: U NMex Rm 263 Student Svcs Ctr Albuquerque NM 87131 *Personal philosophy: In academics, as in life, reliability, integrity and compassion are far more precious than mere intellectual brilliance.*

STUART, DAVID R., academic administrator. Office: Faculty Assn Calif CC's 926 J St Ste 211 Sacramento CA 95814

STUART, DOROTHY MAE, artist; b. Fresno, Calif., Jan. 8, 1933; d. Robert Wesley Williams and Maria Theresa (Gad) Tressler; m. Reginald Ross Stuart, May 18, 1952; children: Doris Lynne Stuart Willis, Darlene Mae Stuart Cavalletto, Sue Anne Stuart Peters. Student, Calif. State U., Fresno, 1951-52, Fresno City Coll., 1962-64. Artist, art judge, presenter demonstrations at schs., fairs and art orgns. Calif., 1962—. Editor, art dir. Fresno High School Centennial 1889-1989, 1989; art advisor Portrait of Fresno, 1885-1985; contbg. artist Heritage Fresno, 1975; exhibited in group shows, including M.H. De Young Mus., San Francisco, 1971, Charles and Emma Frye Mus., Seattle, 1971, Calif. State U.-Fresno tour of China, 1974. Mem. adv. com. Calif. State Ken Maddy Ctrl. Calif. Conf. on Women, 1989—, Patrons for Cultural Arts, Fresno, 1987-92, bd. dirs., 1991-92. Recipient 53 art awards, 1966-84; nominated Woman of the Yr., Bus./Profl. of Fresno, 1990. Mem. Soc. Western Artists (bd. dirs. 1968-74, v.p. 1968-70), Fresno Womens Trade Club (bd. dirs. 1986-93, pres. 1988-90), Fresno Art Mus., Fresno Met. Mus., Native Daus. Golden West Fresno. Republican. Home and Office: 326 S Linda Ln Fresno CA 93727-5737 *Personal philosophy: Dedication to yourself, your work and to your community.*

STUART, GERARD WILLIAM, JR., investment company executive, city official; b. Yuba City, Calif., July 28, 1939; s. Gerard William and Geneva Bernice (Stuke) S.; student Yuba Jr. Coll., 1957-59, Chico State Coll., 1959-60; A.B., U. Calif., Davis, 1962; M.L.S., U. Calif., Berkeley, 1963; m. Lenore Frances Loroña, 1981. Rare book librarian Cornell U., 1964-68; bibliographer of scholarly collections Huntington Library, San Marino, Calif., 1968-73, head acquisitions librarian, 1973-75; sec.-treas., dir. Ravenstree Corp., 1969-80, pres., chmn. bd., 1980—; pres., chmn. bd. William Penn Ltd., 1981—. Councilman City of Yuma, 1992-96, also dep. mayor, 1995; bd. dirs. Ariz. Humanities Coun., 1993—. Lilly fellow Ind. U., 1963-64. Mem. Bibliog. Soc. Am., Phi Beta Kappa, Alpha Gamma Sigma, Phi Kappa Phi. Clubs: Rolls-Royce Owners; Grolier (N.Y.C.); Zamorano (Los Angeles). Office: 204 S Madison Ave Yuma AZ 85364-1421

STUART, JOSEPH MARTIN, art museum administrator; b. Seminole, Okla., Nov. 9, 1932; s. Arch William and Lillian (Lindsey) S.; BFA in Art, U. N.Mex., 1959, MA in Art, 1962; m. Signe Margaret Nelson, June 18, 1960; 1 dau., Lise Nelson Stuart. Dir., Roswell (N.Mex.) Museum and Art Center, 1960-62; curator U. Oreg. Mus. Art, 1962-63; dir. Boise (Idaho) Gallery Art, 1964-68, Salt Lake (City) Art Ctr., 1968-71, S.D. Art Mus., Brookings, 1971-93; prof. art S.D. State U., 1971-93; represented in permanent collections: Civic Fine Arts Ctr., Sioux Falls, S.D., Coll. Idaho, Eureka Coll., Salt Lake Art Ctr., Sioux City (Iowa) Art Ctr., U. N.Mex. Art Mus., West Tex. State U.. With USN, 1951-55. Mem. Phi Kappa Phi. Unitarian. Author: Index of South Dakota Artists, 1974; Art of South Dakota, 1974, Harvey Dunn: Son of the Middle border, 1984, Art for a New Century, 1989; The Legacy of South Dakota Art, 1990; author numerous exhbn. catalogs.

STUART, LAURIE K., English language educator, court transcriber; b. Denver, Apr. 10, 1971; d. Walter E. and Deborah K. Stuart. BA in History, U. Wyo., 1992; MA in English, U. Alaska, 1995. Tchg. asst. English/ESL U. Alaska, Anchorage, 1993-94, adj. prof. English/ESL, 1996—, adj. prof. dept. devel. edn., 1996—; English instr. Am. Eigo Gakuin, Wakayama City, Japan, 1995; court transcriber Anchorage, 1995, 96—; tutor ESL students, Anchorage, 1994—. Mem. MLA. Office: U Alaska English Dept 3211 Providence Dr Anchorage AK 99508

STUART, ROBERT LEE, English language educator; b. Berkeley, Calif., Apr. 22, 1937; s. R. Marvin and Mary Ella (Rose) S. BA, Stanford U., 1959, MA, 1967, PhD, 1970; ThM, Sch. Theology, Claremont, Calif., 1962. From asst. prof. to assoc. prof. English U. Redlands, Calif., 1969-82, prof. English, 1982—; dean grad. studies U. Redlands, 1979-82, asst. to pres., 1981-88, assoc. dir. Jameson Ctr. Study Religion and Ethics, 1990—; assoc. Fitzgerald, Graves & Co., San Francisco, 1980-89. Contbr. articles to profl. jours. Cons. bd. higher edn. Ministry United Meth. Ch., Nashville, 1975-78; bd. dirs. Redlands Symphony Assn., 1984-90; mem. strategic planning com., Redlands, 1988-91, mem. redevelopment adv. com., 1988-91, vice chair, 1991; sec. Com. Chaplaincy Lytton Gardens, Palo Alto, Calif., 1983-96. Recipient Foerster prize Modern Literature Assn., 1976. Mem. Phi Beta Kappa (sec., treas. 1977—, sec. western dist. 1994-95). Democrat. Home: 884 Ardmore Cir Redlands CA 92374-6245

STUBBLEFIELD, JAMES IRVIN, emergency medicine physician, health facility administrator; b. Phila., Aug. 17, 1953; s. James Irvin Sr. and Geri (Harvey) S.; m. Linda Marie Simms, Aug. 12, 1978; children: Lindsay, Shannon. BSEE, MS in Bioengring., U. Pa., 1977; MD, Hahnemann U., Phila., 1982. Diplomate Am. Bd. Emergency Medicine, 1991. Mgr. energy engring. Norcross, Inc., Bryn Mawr, Pa., 1977-78; commd. 2d lt. U.S. Army, 1977, advanced through grades to lt. col., 1993; intern in gen. surgery Letterman Army Med. Ctr., San Francisco, 1982-83; flight surgeon, brigade surgeon 101st Airborne Div., Ft. Campbell, Ky., 1983-87; resident in emergency medicine Madigan Army Med. Ctr., Ft. Lewis, Wash., 1987-90; chief dep. emergency medicine and primary care Silas B. Hays Army Hosp., Ft. Ord, Calif., 1990-94; flight surgeon attack helicopter battalion Operation Desert Storm, Persian Gulf, 1991. Decorated Bronze Star, Air medal. Fellow Am. Coll. Emergency Physicians; mem. AMA, U.S. Army Flight Surgeon Soc., Assn. Mil. Surgeons U.S., Tau Beta Pi, Eta Kappa Nu, Alpha Epsilon Delta. Roman Catholic. Home: 18506 Candace Ln Watsonville CA 95076-9179

STUBBLEFIELD, THOMAS MASON, agricultural economist, educator; b. Taxhoma, Okla., Apr. 16, 1922; s. Temple Roscoe and Martha Lacy (Acree) S.; BS, N.Mex. State Coll., 1948; MS, A. and M. Coll. Tex., 1951, PhD, 1956; postgrad. U. Ariz., 1954; m. Martha Lee Miller, Mar. 7, 1943; children: Ellen (Mrs. Richard Damron), Paula (Mrs. James T. Culbertson), Thommye (Mrs. Gary D. Zingsheim). Specialist cotton mktg. N.Mex. State Coll., 1948; extension economist, then asst. agrl. economist U. Ariz., Tucson, 1951-58, from assoc. prof. to prof., 1958-64, prof. and agrl. economist, 1964-83, emeritus prof., 1983—, acting asst. dir. agrl. expt. sta., 1966-68, asst. to dir. sta., 1973-74, chief party Brazil contract, 1968-70. Mem. Pima Council Aging, 1974-77, 80-90; chmn. adv. com. Ret. Sr. Vol. Program, Pima County, 1974-77, 80-90, mem. 1974-97. Chmn. bd. Saguaro Home Found., 1980-85. With AUS, 1942-45. Author bulls. in field. Adv. bd. Unified Cmty., 1994—. Home: 810 W Calle Milu Tucson AZ 85706-3925

STUDDERT, STEPHEN MARK, investment banker; b. Petaluma, Calif., Nov. 17, 1948; m. Bonnie Jane Beck, June 1, 1968; children: Mark, Christopher, Stephanie, David, Allyson, Michael. BS, Brigham Young U., 1970. Staff asst. to Pres. of U.S. White House, Washington, 1975-77, spl. asst. to Pres. U.S., 1981-85; asst. to Pres. U.S., 1989-90; founder, chmn., CEO Fonix Corp., 1993—; chmn. KLS Environ. Resources, 1996—; chmn. and dir. Fed. Home Loan Bank of Seattle, 1987—; founder, dir. Sailors & Mchts. Bank & Trust, Vienna, Va., 1984-87. Chmn. Nat. Mormon Pioneer Hist. Trail Commn., 1987-89; dir. advance Reagan-Bush Campaign, 1980, sr. campaign advisor, 1984; leader Boy Scouts Am., Utah, Va., 1970—; sr. advisor Presdl. Inaugural, Washington, 1981, 85, dir., 1989; stake pres. LDS Ch., Va., 1984-89, Utah, 1992—; chair Utah Statehood Centennial Com., 1992-97; co-chair New Am. Revolution, 1994-95. Named Outstanding Young Men of Am., 1972-82. Republican. Office: Studdert Cos 60 E South Temple Ste 1225 Salt Lake City UT 84111-1048

STUDEBAKER, IRVING GLEN, mining engineering consultant; b. Ellensburg, Wash., July 22, 1931; s. Clement Glen and Ruth (Krause) S.; (widowed); children: Ruth, Betty, Raymond, Karl, Donna. BS in Geol. Engring., U. Ariz., 1957, MS in Geology, 1959, PhD in Geol. Engring., 1977. Registered profl. engr., Wash., Nev., Ariz., Colo., Mont. Geophys. engr. Mobil, 1959-61; civil engr. City of Yakima, Wash., 1964-66; instr. Yakima Valley Coll., 1962-67; sr. rsch. geologist Roan Selection Trust, Kalulushi, Zambia, 1967-72; sr. mining engr. Occidental Oil Shale, Grand Junction, Colo., 1974-81; prof. Mont. Coll. Mining Sch., Butte, 1982-96; prof. emeritus, 1996—; cons. in field. Sgt. U.S. Army, 1951-54, Korea. Mem. N.W. Mining Assn., Geol. Soc. Am., Soc. for Mining and Metall. Engring., Soc. Econ. Geologists, Mont. Mining Assn., Sigma Xi (pres. Mont. tech. chpt. 1990-91). Home and Office: 165 S 340th St #A Federal Way WA 98003-6623

STUDENMUND, ARNOLD HARWOOD, economist, educator; b. Cooperstown, N.Y., Oct. 6, 1944; s. W. R. and Betsy (Harwood) S.; m. Jaynie M. Miller, July 12, 1980; children: Brent, Scott, Connell. AB, Hamilton Coll., 1966; MA, Cornell U., 1969, PhD, 1970. From instr. to Richard W. Millar prof. econs. Occidental Coll., L.A.; various positions Occidental Coll. including dir. core program liberal arts, assoc. dean of faculty, dir. instl. rsch., v.p. student svcs., dean admission and fin. aid. Author: Using Econometrics, 3d edit., 1997 (best selling econometrics textbook worldwide); contbr. articles to profl. jours. Office: Dept Econs Occidental Coll Los Angeles CA 90041

STUDLEY, HELEN ORMSON, artist, poet, writer, designer; b. Elroy, Wis., Sept. 8, 1937; d. Clarence Ormson and Hilda (Johnson) O.; m. William Frank Studley, Aug. 1965 (div.); 1 son, William Harrison. Owner RJK Original Art, Sherman Oaks, Calif., 1979—; designer Aspen Series custom greeting cards and stationery notes, lithographs Love is All Colors, 1982, Flowers for Ruth (Best of Art Show award), Tex. Series original paintings and custom greeting cards. One woman show includes Sherman Oaks, Calif., 1991, Toluca Lake Art Festival, 1991, Art Show for Srs., 1992, Art Show for Youth, 1991; represented in numerous pub. and pvt. collections throughout U.S., Can., Norway, Sweden, Austria, Germany, Eng., France; group exhibits include Art Show for Homeless, L.A., 1990; author poetry Love is Care, Changes, 1988; contbr. poems to publs. Active Luth. Brotherhood, Emmanuel Luth. Ch. Honors include display of lithograph Snow Dreams, Snow Queens, Olympic Games, Lake Placid, N.Y., 1980, lithograph Summer Dreams, Summer Queens, Olympic Games, Los Angeles, 1984, lithograph Go for the Gold, Olympic Games, Atlanta, 1996; named finalist in competition for John Simon Guggenheim fellowship; recipient Golden Poet award World Poetry, 1987-92, Art Show for Youth, 1991, Art Show for Srs., 1992, Art Show at the Park, 1992, Diamond Pin award Carter Hawley Hale, 1991, 92, Outstanding Achievements in Poetry award, 1993, named Woman of the Year, 1993 Am. Biog. Inst., 1993. Mem. Internat. Soc. Poets (publ. in Disting. Poets Am. 1993), Soc. Illustrators, Am. Watercolor Soc., Internat. Soc. Artists, Internat. Platform Assn., Calif. Woman's Art Guild, Sons of Norway Club. Office: RJK Original Art 5020 Hazeltine Ave Sherman Oaks CA 91423-1174 *Personal philosophy: "In order to be creative we must be curious. We must leave ourselves open to ideas, sometimes we learn joyfully, other times we must struggle. But, we must dare to move on and follow our creative force to understand love, nature, beauty, our friends and loved ones."*

STUEHRMANN, RAYMOND LOUIS, lawyer; b. Altadena, Calif., Dec. 5, 1947; s. Raymond Edward and Minnie Rosalia (Collomb) S.; m. Maria Leonor Santiago, Feb. 27, 1982; children: Anna-Liese, John Christopher, Paul Andrew. BA with highest honors, Calif. State Coll., L.A., 1969; JD cum laude, Marymount U., 1975. Bar: Calif. 1975, U.S. Dist. Ct. (ctrl. and so. dists.) Calif. 1976, U.S. Dist. Ct. (no. dist.) U.S. Dist. Ct. Calif. 1979, U.S. Dist. Ct. (ea. dist.) Calif., 1983. Assoc. Palmer & Bartenetti, L.A., 1975-78; assoc. counsel United Calif. Bank, L.A., 1978-81; ptnr. Biele & Stuehrmann, L.A., 1981-82; v.p., gen. counsel Am. Pacific State Bank, North Hollywood, Calif., 1983-89; mgr. legal dept. Mitsui Mfrs. Bank, L.A., 1989-93; assoc. Phelps, Schwarz & Phelps, Pasadena, Calif., 1993-96; pvt. practice Thousand Oaks, Calif., 1996—; instr. Am. Inst. Banking, San Francisco and Moorpark, 1981—; mem. legal affairs com. Calif. Bankers Assn., San Francisco, 1984-93. Dir. Concern/Am., Santa Ana, Calif., 1977—; mem. Calif. Ctr. Coast World Trade Assn., Oxnard, Calif., 1996—; sponsor World Affairs Coun., Ventura County, 1996—. Sgt. U.S. Army, 1970-72. Mem. ABA, L.A. County Bar Assn. (gov. barristers' sect. 1979-82), Ventura County Bar Assn. Roman Catholic. Home: 4206 Peach Slope Rd Moorpark CA 93021-2726 Office: 2660 Townsgate Rd Ste 600 Westlake Village CA 91361-2714

STUMBLES, JAMES RUBIDGE WASHINGTON, multinational service company executive; b. Harare, Zimbabwe, Aug. 13, 1939; came to U.S., 1980; s. Albert R.W. and Mary Dallas (Atherstone) S.; m. Vyvienne Clare Shaw, Dec. 19, 1964; children: Christopher, Timothy, Jonathan. BA, U. Cape Town, Republic of South Africa, 1960, LLB, 1962. Adv. Supreme Ct. of S. Africa. Mng. dir. Pritchard Services Group of South Africa, Johannesburg, 1972-80; dir. security, pres. subs. Pritchard Svcs. Group Am., Columbus, Ohio, 1980-83; exec. v.p., pres. subs. Mayne Nickless/ Loomis Corp., Seattle, 1984-87; v.p. N.W. Protective Svc. Inc., Seattle, 1987-91, pres., CEO, 1991—; pres., CEO Western Security Svc. Inc., Spokane, 1991—, Northwest Protective Svc. Inc.-Oreg., Portland, 1992—. Sec. Boy Scouts, Johannesburg, 1978-80. Mem. Rand Club, Rainier Club, Rotary, Kiwanis, Round Table (officer 1969-80). Office: NW Protective Svc Inc 2700 Elliott Ave Seattle WA 98121-1109 *Personal philosophy: Love thy God, love thy neighbor, and be true unto thyself.*

STUMP, BOB, congressman; b. Phoenix, Apr. 4, 1927; s. Jesse Patrick and Floy Bethany (Fields) S.; children: Karen, Bob, Bruce. B.S. in Agronomy, Ariz. State U., 1951. Mem. Ariz. Ho. of Reps., 1957-67; mem. Ariz. Senate, 1967-76, pres., 1975-76; mem. 95th-104th Congresses from 3rd Dist.Ariz., 1976—; mem. Nat. Security Com. With USN, 1943-46. Mem. Am. Legion, Ariz. Farm Bur. Republican. Seventh-day Adventist. Office: 211 Canon House of Representatives Washington DC 20515-0303 also: 230 N 1st Ave Rm 5001 Phoenix AZ 85025-0230*

STUMP, D. MICHAEL, librarian; b. Santa Monica, Calif., Dec. 22, 1947; s. H. Walter and Margaret June (Stetler) S. B.A. in History, Pasadena Coll., 1971; M.L.S., U. So. Calif., 1977. Library asst. Calif. Inst. Tech., Pasadena, Calif., 1970-74; librarian First Baptist Ch. of Van Nuys, Calif., 1974-81, 1982-87, Laurence/2000, Van Nuys, 1981-82; Van Nuys Christian Coll., 1975-76, Hillcrest Christian Sch., Granada Hills, Calif., 1987—. Asst. scoutmaster San Fernando council Boy Scouts Am., 1970-73. Named to Outstanding Young Men Am. U.S. Jaycees, 1976. Mem. ALA, Am. Assn. Sch. Librs., Evang. Ch. Libr. Assn. (So. Calif. chpt.). Republican. Baptist. Office: Hillcrest Christian Sch 17531 Rinaldi St Granada Hills CA 91344-3319

STUMPF, BERNHARD JOSEF, physicist; b. Neustadt der Weinstrasse, Rhineland, Germany, Sept. 21, 1948; came to U.S., 1981; s. Josef and Katharina (Cervinka) S. Diploma physics, Saarland U., Saarbrucken, West Germany, 1975, Dr.rer.nat., 1981. Rsch. asst. physics dept. Saarland U., Saarbrucken, 1976-81; rsch. assoc. Joint Inst. Lab. Astrophysics, U. Colo., Boulder, 1981-84; instr. physics, physics dept. NYU, N.Y.C., 1984-86, asst. rsch. scientist Atomic Beams Lab., 1984-85, assoc. rsch. scientist Atomic Beams Lab., 1985-86; vis. assoc. prof. physics dept. U. Windsor (Ont., Can.), 1986-88; assoc. prof. physics dept. U. Idaho, Moscow, 1988—; chmn. Conf. on Atomic and Molecular Collisions in Excited States, Moscow, 1990. Contbr. articles to profl. jours. German Sci. Found. postdoctoral fellow U. Colo., 1981-83. Mem. AAUP, German Phys. Soc., Am. Phys. Soc. Home: 825 W C St Moscow ID 83843-2108 Office: U Idaho Dept Physics Moscow ID 83844-0903

STUMPF, PAUL KARL, biochemistry educator emeritus; b. N.Y.C., N.Y., Feb. 23, 1919; s. Karl and Annette (Schreyer) S.; married, June 1947; children: Ann Carol, Kathryn Lee, Margaret Ruth, David Karl, Richard Frederic. AB, Harvard Coll., 1941; PhD, Columbia U., 1945. Instr. pub. health U. Mich., Ann Arbor, 1946-48; faculty U. Calif., Berkeley, 1948-58, prof., 1956-58; prof. U. Calif., Davis, 1958-84, prof. emeritus, 1984—; chief scientist Competitive Rsch. Grants Office USDA, Washington, 1988-91; cons. Palm Oil Rsch. Inst., Kuala Lumpur, Malaysia, 1982-92; mem. sci. adv. bd. Calgene, Inc., Davis, 1990-93; mem. sci. adv. panel Md. Biotech. Inst., 1990-92; Inaugural lectr. Tan Sri Dato'Seri B. Bek-Nielsen Found., Kuala Lumpur, 1996. Co-author: Outlines of Enzyme Chemistry, 1955, Outlines of Biochemistry, 5th edit., 1987; co-editor-in-chief Biochemistry of Plants, 1980; exec. editor Archives of Biochemistry/Biophysics, 1965-88; contbr. over 250 articles to profl. jours. Mem. planning commn. City of Davis, 1966-68. Guggenheim fellow, 1962, 69; recipient Lipid Chemistry award Am. Oil Chemists Soc., 1974, Sr. Scientist award Alexander von Humboldt Found., 1976, Superior Svc. Group award USDA, 1992, Award of Excellence, Calif. Aggie Alumni Found., 1996. Fellow AAAS; mem. NAS, Royal Danish Acad. Scis., Am. Soc. Plant Physiologists (pres. 1979-80, chmn. bd. trustees 1986-90, Stephen Hales award 1974, Charles Reid Barnes Life Membership award 1992), Yolo Fliers Country Club (Woodland, Calif.). Home: 764 Elmwood Dr Davis CA 95616-3517 Office: Univ of Calif Molecular/Cellular Biology Davis CA 95616

STUPPI, CRAIG, lawyer; b. San Francisco, Mar. 4, 1946. BA with honors, U. Calif., Santa Barbara, 1968; JD, Stanford U., 1971. Bar: Calif. 1972, U.S. Dist. Ct. (no., ctrl. and ea. dists.) Calif. 1972, U.S. Ct. Appeals (9th cir.) 1972, U.S. Supreme Ct. 1975. Mem. Bronson, Bronson & McKinnon, San Francisco. Mem. Am. Bankruptcy Inst., State Bar Calif., Bar Assn. San Francisco, Bar Area Bankruptcy Forum (bd. dirs.), San Mateo County Bar Assn. Office: Bronson Bronson & McKinnon 505 Montgomery St San Francisco CA 94111-2552

STUPSKI, LAWRENCE J., investment company executive; b. 1945. JD, Yale U., 1970. V.p. Bradford Nat. Corp., N.Y.C., 1971-78; with Western Bradford Tr. Inc., San Francisco, 1978-80; pres., COO, CEO Charles Schwab & Co. Inc. (formerly Charles Schwab Corp.), 1980—, vice chmn. bd. dirs. Office: Charles Schwab & Co Inc 101 Montgomery St San Francisco CA 94104-4122*

STURE, STEIN, civil engineering educator; b. Oslo, Norway, Nov. 12, 1947; came to U.S., 1970; s. Alf and Gunnvor (Een) S.; m. Karen J. Marley, June 3, 1989. Student, Schous Inst. Tech., Oslo, 1970; BSCE, U. Colo., 1971, MSCE, 1973, PhD, 1976. Asst. prof. Va. Polytechnic Inst., Blacksburg, 1976-80; rsch. scientist Marshall Space Flight Ctr. NASA, Huntsville, Ala., 1979; from asst. prof. to prof. civil engring. U. Colo., Boulder, 1980—, acting chmn. dept. civil engring., 1990-91; chmn. dept. civil engring., 1994—; sr. vis. dept. engring. sci. U. Oxford, Eng., 1985; vis. prof. Norway Inst. Tech., Trondheim, 1985-86. Editor Jour. Engring. Mechanics. Jenkin fellow, 1986. Mem. Am. Soc. Civil Engrs. (pres. Colo. sect. 1990-91, Walter Huber Civil Engring. Rsch. prize 1990), Am. Assn. Advancement Sci., Am. Geophys. Union, Am. Soc. Engring. Edn., NASA Ctr. Space Construction, Internat. Soc. Soil Mech. Found. Engrs., U.S. Nat. Comm./Theoretical and Applied Mechanics. Home: 1077 Diamond Ct Boulder CO 80303-3244 Office: Univ Colo Dept Civil Engring Boulder CO 80309

STURGEN, WINSTON, photographer, printmaker, artist; b. Harrisburg, Pa., Aug. 27, 1938; s. George Winston and Gladys Erma (Lenker) S.; m. Nancy Kathryn Otto, Jan. 23, 1959 (div. 1981); 1 child, Bruce Eugene Sturgen; m. Jessica Sheldon, Mar. 15, 1988. BS in Forestry, Pa. State U., 1960; postgrad., U. N.H., 1961-62; M of Forestry, Pa. State U., 1964; postgrad., U. Oreg., 1966-68. Cert. profl. photographer. Devel. engr. Weyerhaeuser Co., Longview, Wash., 1964-66; mgr. Wickes Lumber Co., Elkhorn, Wis., 1968-70; dir. ops. Wickes Wanderland, Inc., Delavan, Wis., 1970-72; owner, mgr. Sturgen's Cleaners, Delavan, 1972-80, Images by Sturgen, Delavan, 1980-84; instr. photography continuing edn. dept. Western N.Mex. U., 1988-90; juror numerous orgns., 1982—. One-man shows include Artesia (N.Mex.) Mus. and Art Ctr., 1992, Delavan Art Mus., 1984, Donnell Libr., N.Y.C., 1992; exhibited in group shows at Carlsbad (N.Mex.) Mus., 1992, Sister Kenny Inst., 1992, (3rd Pl.), 93 (1st Pl.), 94, Deming Ctr. for the Arts, N.Mex., 1991, Shellfish Collection, Silver City, N.Mex., 1989, 90, 91, 92, 93, Thompson Gallery, U. N.Mex., 1989, Profl. Photographers Assn. of N.Mex., 1985, 86, 87, 88 (awards), Union Gallery, U. N.Mex., 1987, Gallery Sigala, Taos, N.Mex., 1986, World Trade Ctr., N.Y.C., 1992, 93, 94, Internat. Exposition of Photography, 1983, 84, 85, 87, Beyond Photography Touring Exhibit, 1991-92, An Am. Collection Touring Exhibit, San Francisco, Washington, Brussels, Tokyo, 1993-95, Sapporo (Japan) Internat. Print Biennial, 1993, Very Spl. Arts/N.Mex. Touring Exhibit, 1993-94, Ctr. Contemporary Art, St. Louis, 1994 (Purchase award), many others; pub. poetry, numerous articles in field. Founder, chmn. Winter Arts Festival, Silver City, N.Mex., 1988-90; com. mem. Taos Fall Arts Festival, 1985; com. chair Oktoberfest, Delavan, 1976-80; donated personal work to Southwestern Regional Med. Ctr., N.Mex., 1996. Residency grant Wurlitzer Found., 1987, 89. Mem. Very Spl. Artists N.Mex., Very Spl. Artists Washington, Enabled Artists United, Fuller Lodge Art Ctr. Home: 3357 Cerrillos Rd # 111 Santa Fe NM 87505

STURGULEWSKI, ARLISS, state senator; b. Blaine, Wash., Sept. 27, 1927; B.A., U. Wash.; LLD (hon.) U. Alaska, Anchorage, 1993. Mem. Assembly Municipality of Anchorage, interim exec. dir. Alaska Sci. and Tech. Found., 1995; vice chmn. New Capital Site Planning Commn., mem. Capital Site Selection Com.; chmn. Greater Anchorage Area Planning and Zoning Commn.; mem. Alaska State Senate, 1978-93. Rep. nominee Office Gov. Alaska, 1986, 90. Home: 2957 Sheldon Jackson St Anchorage AK 99508-4469 Office: 3301 C St Ste 520 Anchorage AK 99503-3956

STURKEN, MARITA LOUISE, communications educator, writer, critic; b. Plainfield, N.J., Mar. 18, 1957; d. Robert Carl and Marie Jean (Ryan) S. Student, Cornell U., 1977-79; BA Visual Studies Workshop, Empire State Coll., 1979; PhD, U. Calif., Santa Cruz, 1992. Film/video cataloguer Mus. Modern Art, N.Y.C., 1981-83; prof. San Francisco Art Inst., 1990-91; lectr. dept. comm. U. Calif., San Diego, 1992-94; asst. prof. Annenberg Sch. Comm. U. So. Calif., L.A., 1994—. Author: Circulating Video Library, 1983, Tangled Memories: The Vietnam War, The AIDS Epidemic, and the Politics of Remembering, 1997; co-editor: Electronic Arts Intermix: Video, 1991; editor: Machine Media, 1996; contbr. articles to profl. jours. and periodicals. N.Y. State Coun. on the Arts writing grantee, 1982, 83, 85, Annanberg Ctr. grantee, 1995-97, Zumberge Fund grantee, 1996; recipient AAUW dissertation fellowship, 1991. Office: Univ of So Calif Annenberg Sch Comm Los Angeles CA 90089-0281

STURTEVANT, DAVID CHARLES, environmental management consultant; b. Erie, Pa., Nov. 1, 1958; s. Roger Granville and Martha Elizabeth (Bert) S.; m. Susan Rodgers, Dec. 3, 1988; children: Catherine Faye, Summer Anne. BA in Urban Studies, Coll. Wooster, Ohio, 1980. Planner Met. Svc. Dist., Portland, Oreg., 1980-82; cons. Gershman, Brickner, and Bratton, Washington, 1983; project mgr. Govt. Fin. Rsch. Ctr., Washington, 1983-86; dir. bus. devel. CH2M Hill, Bellevue, Wash., 1986—. Co-author: The McGraw Hill Recycling Handbook, 1993; contbr. articles to profl. jours. Mem. Wash. Citizens for Recycling (bd. dirs. 1991-93), Solid Waste Assn. of N.Am. (bd. dirs. 1991—), Overlake G. Country Club, Bellevue Athletic Club. Office: CH2M Hill 777 108th Ave NE Bellevue WA 98004-5118

STUTZMAN, THOMAS CHASE, SR., lawyer; b. Portland, Oreg., Aug. 1, 1950; s. Leon H. and Mary L. (Chase) S.; BA with high honors, U. Calif., Santa Barbara, 1972; JD cum laude, Santa Clara U., 1975; m. Wendy Jeanne Craig, June 6, 1976; children: Sarah Ann, Thomas ChaseJr. Bar: Calif. 1976; cert. family law specialist. Pvt. practice, San Jose, Calif., 1976-79; pres., sec., CFO Thomas Chase Stutzman, P.C., San Jose, 1979—; legal counsel, asst. sec. Ctrl. Valley Cirs., Inc., Cypress Human Resources, Inc., DMJ Pro Care, Inc., Sparacino's Foods, Tax Firm, Inc., United Charities, Marina Assocs. Inc., Midnight Fraction Mine Inc., Forbord Enterprises, D.A.M. Good Engring./Mfg., Inc., E.M.I. Oil Filtration Systems, Inc., China Villa, Inc., Creative Pacifica, Inc., Am. West Furniture Mfg., Inc., Cody Electronics, Inc., Advanfab Corp., Am. First Tech., Analop Engring., Inc., Excel-Law Video, Inc., First Am. Real Estate Financing Co., Hoffman Industries, Inc., Info. Scan Tech., Inc., PRD Construction Mgmt. Svcs., Unifed Homes, Inc., Marine Biogenic Pharm. USA, Inc., Miller Networks, Mi Pueblo Mt. View, Inc., others; instr. San Jose State U., 1977-78. Bd. dirs. Santa Cruz Campfire, 1978-80, Happy Hollow Park, 1978-80, 83-86, Pacific Neighbors, pres., 1991-92. Mem. Calif. Bar Assn., Santa Clara County Bar Assn. (chmn. environ. law com. 1976-78, exec. com. family law, exec. com. fee arbitration com.), Assn. Cert. Law Specialist, San Jose Jaycees (Dir. of the Year 1976-77), Almaden Valley Rotary Club, Lions (dir. 1979-81, 2d v.p. 1982-83, 1st v.p. 1983-84, pres. 1984-85), Masons, Phi Beta Kappa. Congregationalist Office: 1625 The Alameda Ste 309 San Jose CA 95126-2223

STYLES, ALAN, mayor. Mayor City of Salinas, Calif. Office: City of Salinas 200 Lincoln Ave Salinas CA 93901

STYLES, BEVERLY, entertainer; b. Richmond, Va., June 6, 1923; d. John Harry Kenealy and Juanita Russell (Robins) Carpenter; m. Wilbur Cox, Mar. 14, 1942 (div.); m. Robert Marascia, Oct. 5, 1951 (div. Apr. 1964). Studies with Ike Carpenter, Hollywood, Calif., 1965—; student, Am. Nat. Theatre Acad., 1968-69; studies with Paula Raymond, Hollywood, 1969-70; diploma, Masterplan Inst., Anaheim, Calif., 1970. Freelance performer, musician, 1947-81; owner Beverly Styles Music, Joshua Tree, Calif., 1971—; v.p. spl. programs Lawrence Program of Calif., Yucca Valley, Calif.; talent coord., co-founder Quiet Place Studio, Yucca Valley, 1994; mem. exec. bd., awards dir. Am. chpt. Diogenes Process Group, 1996—. Composer: Joshua Tree, 1975, I'm Thankful, 1978, Wow, Wow, Wow, 1986, Music for The Whispering, 1994, World of Dreams, 1996, Thank You God, 1996; piano arrangements include Colour Chords and Moods, 1995, Desert Nocturne, 1996; records include The Perpetual Styles of Beverly, 1978; albums include The Primitive Styles of Beverly, 1977; author: A Special Plan to Think Upon, The Truth as Seen by a Composer, 1978, A Special Prayer to Think Upon, 1983. Mem. ASCAP (Gold Pin award), Profl. Musicians Local 47 (life), Internat. Platform Assn. Republican. Office: PO Box 615 Joshua Tree CA 92252-0615

SUAREZ, ELISABETH CLEMENCE, secondary mathematics educator; b. N.Y.C., Apr. 1, 1960; d. Alfonso Joseph and Maria Cristina (Lacayo) S.; m. June 13, 1959; children: Elisabeth, Christine, Paul, John-Peter. BS in Materials Engring., Rensselaer Poly. Inst., 1982; Cert. of Biblical Studies, Columbia Biblical Sem., 1988; MST in Math., U. N.H., 1989; MA in Counselling, Denver Seminary, 1996. Cert. secondary math. educator, N.J. Tchr. math. Timothy Christian Sch., Piscataway, N.J., 1984-87; project coord. Dr. Joan Ferrini-Mundy, U. N.H., Durham, 1988-89; tchr. math. Phillips Exeter (N.H.) Acad., 1989-91; therapist Southwest Counselling Assocs., Littleton, Colo., 1995—. Mem. Am. Coun. Assn., Nat. Coun. Tchrs. Math. Home: 15 Brentwood Rd Matawan NJ 07747-3720 Office: Southwest Counselling Assocs 141 W Davies Ave N Ste 105 Littleton CO 80120-4287

SUBACH, JAMES ALAN, infosystems company executive, consultant; b. Lawrence, Mass., Mar. 24, 1948; s. Anthony John and Bernice Ruth (Pekarski) S. m. Marilyn Butler, Feb. 16, 1980. BS with distinction, U. Maine, 1970; MS, U. Ariz., 1975, PhD, 1979. Vis. scientist NASA Johnson Space Ctr., Houston, 1977-79; rsch. assoc. Baylor Coll. Medicine, Houston, 1977-79; pres. Subach Ventures, Inc., San Antonio, 1980-84, JAS & Assocs., Inc., Phoenix, 1984—, C.I.O. Inc., 1987-90; v.p. PTIMS, Inc., Phoenix, 1992-96; faculty assoc. Ariz. State U., Tempe, 1992-96; v.p. Multipoint Tax Systems, Scottsdale, Ariz., 1996—. Assoc. editor Jour. Applied Photog. Engring., 1973-78; author software Gen. Acctg. System, 1987; bus. computing columnist, 1987. Pres. Forest Trails Homeowners Assn., Phoenix, 1987-88. Mem. SPIE, Phoenix C. of C. (Pres.'s Roundtable), Toastmasters (treas. Phoenix chpt. 1984), Ariz. Progress Users Group, Tau Beta Pi, Sigma Pi Sigma. Republican. Office: JAS & Assoc Inc 3625 N 16th St Ste 100 Phoenix AZ 85016 *Personal philosophy: Go with your strengths and buttress your weaknesses.*

SUBER, ROBIN HALL, former medical and surgical nurse; b. Bethlehem, Pa., Mar. 14, 1952; d. Arthur Albert and Sarah Virginia (Smith) Hall; m. David A. Suber, July 28, 1979; 1 child, Benjamin A. BSN, Ohio State U., 1974. RN, Ariz., Ohio. Formerly staff nurse Desert Samaritan Hosp., Mesa, Ariz. Lt. USN, 1974-80. Mem. ANA, Sigma Theta Tau.

SUBRAMANI, SURESH, biology educator; b. Jabalpur, India, Feb. 21, 1952; came to U.S., 1974; s. Janakiraman and Gomathy S.; m. Feroza Ardeshir, Aug. 15, 1981; children: Anand Subramani, Praveen Subramani. BS in Chemistry, Ferguson Coll., Pune, Maharashtra, 1972; MS in Chemistry, Indian Inst. Tech., Kanpur, India, 1974; PhD in Biochemistry, U. Calif., Berkeley, 1978. Post-doctoral fellow Stanford U., Palo Alto, Calif., 1979-82; asst. prof. U. Calif., San Diego, 1982-87, assoc. prof., 1987-91, prof., 1991—; sci. adv. bd. Viagene, San Diego, 1986-91; cons. Astra, Bangalore, India, 1989—. Contbr. over 100 scientific articles in biochemistry, molecular biology and cell biology to profl. jours. Named Nat. Sci. Talent scholar, India, 1969-74; recipient Nat. scholarship, India, 1972, Rsch. Career Devel. award, Nat. Cancer Inst., 1985-90; Searle scholar, 1982-85; Jane Coffin Childs Fund fellow, 1979-81; John Simon Guggenheim fellow, 1993-94; Dr. Narayana Meml. lectr., 1990. Mem. AAAS, Am. Soc. Microbiology, N.Y. Acad. Sci. Office: Dept Biology UCSD 9500 Gilman Dr La Jolla CA 92093-5003

SUBRAMANIAN, SUNDARAM, electronics engineer; b. Emaneswaram, Madras, India, July 9, 1934; came to U.S., 1968; s. Sundaram and Velammal (Subbiah) S.; m. Hemavathy Vadivelu, Feb. 18, 1968; children: Anand Kumar, Malathy. BE, Madras (India) U., 1959; PhD, Glasgow (Scotland) U., 1967; MBA, Roosevelt U., Chgo., 1977. Research engr. Zenith, Inc., Chgo., 1968-75; project engr. Motorola, Inc., Chgo., 1975-77; prof. Chapman Coll., Orange, Calif., 1977-78; cons. MCS, Orange, 1978-80; project engr. Endevco, San Juan Capistrano, Calif., 1980-84; project mgr. Unisys Corp., Mission Viejo, Calif., 1984—; bd. dirs. P.S.B. Inc., Torrance, Calif., 1984-93. Patentee in field. Bd. dirs. Tamil Nadu Found. Inc., Balt. and Washington, 1976-79; pres. S. India Cultural Assn., Villa Park, Calif., 1977-78. Mem. IEEE, Inst. Environ. Sci. (sr.). Office: Unisys Corp 25725 Jeronimo Rd Mission Viejo CA 92691-2711

SUBRAMANYA, SHIVA, aerospace systems engineer; b. Hole-Narasipur, India, Apr. 8, 1933; s. S.T. Srikantaiah and S. Gundamma; m. Lee. S. Silva, Mar. 3, 1967; children: Paul Kailas, Kevin Shankar. BSc, Mysore U., Bangalore, India, 1956; MSc, Karnatak U., Dharwar, India, 1962; postgrad., Clark U., 1963; MBA, Calif. State U., Dominguez Hills, 1973; D in Bus. Adminstrn., PhD in Bus. Adminstrn., Nova Southeastern U., 1986. Sr. scientific officer AEC, Bombay, India, 1961-63; chief engr. TEI, Newport, R.I., 1964-67; prin. engr. Gen. Dynamics Corp., San Diego, 1967-73; asst. project mgr. def. and systems group TRW, Colorado Springs, Colo., 1973-87; asst. project mgr. space and def. group TRW, Redondo Beach, Calif., 1987—. Contbr. over 150 articles to profl. jours. V.p. VHP of Am., Berlin, Conn., 1984-88; pres. IPF of Am., Redondo Beach, 1981-88; appointed by Pres. of India to Atomic Energy Commn., India. Winner of dozens of awards and commendations from U.S. Dept. of Defense and the Aerospace Industry. Mem. Armed Forces Comm. and Electronics Assn. (v.p.-elect Rocky Mountain chpt. 1986—, Meritorious Svc. award 1985, Merit medal 1990), Am. Acad. Mgmt. Hindu. Home: 12546 Inglenook Ln Cerritos CA 90703 Office: TRW Def and Space Group 1 Space Park Blvd Redondo Beach CA 90278-1001

SUCHENEK, MAREK ANDRZEJ, computer science educator; b. Warsaw, Poland, May 2, 1949; came to U.S., 1986; s. Tadeusz Aleksander and Barbara Krystyna (Zych) S.; m. Ewa Aleksandra Czerny, July 30, 1974 (div. 1991). MSc in Math. Engring., Warsaw Tech. U., 1973, PhD in Tech. Scis. with distinction, 1979. Instr. Warsaw (Poland) Tech. U., 1973-79, asst. prof., 1979-88; vis. asst. prof. Wichita (Kans.) State U., 1986-88; assoc. Nat. Inst. for Aviation Rsch., Wichita, 1987-90; assoc. prof. Wichita (Kans.) State U., 1988-89, assoc. prof., chair, 1989-90; prof. Calif. State U.-Dominguez Hills, Carson, 1990-96, prof., co-chair, 1996, prof., chair, 1997—; mem. organizing com. Internat. Symposium on Methodologies for Intelligent Sys., 1989-90; program com. Ann. Ulam Math. Conf., 1990-91, Internat. Conf. on Computing and Info., 1992—; referee NSF, 1990-92, Annals of Math. and Artificial Intelligence, 1992-93, Jour. Logic Programming, 1992-94; presenter in field. Author: (with Jan Bielecki) ANS FORTRAN, 1980, (with Jan Bielecki) FORTRAN for Advanced Programmers, 1981, 2d edit., 83, 3d edit., 88 (Minister of Sci. Higher Edn. and Techs. prize 1982); reviewer Zentralblatt fur Mathematik, 1980-89, Math. Reviews, 1989-91; mem. editorial bd.: Ulam Quarterly, 1990—; contbr. articles to profl. jours. Recipient rsch. grants Polish Govt., 1974-76, 85-86, FAA, 1988-90. Mem. AAUP, The Assn. for Logic Programming, Computer Soc. IEEE, Assn. Symbolic Logic, Sigma Xi (chpt. pres.). Home: 830 N Juanita Ave Unit 4 Redondo Beach CA 90277-2270 Office: Calif State Univ Dominguez Hills 1000 E Victoria St Carson CA 90747-0001

SUCKIEL, ELLEN KAPPY, philosophy educator; b. Bklyn., June 15, 1943; d. Jack and Lilyan (Banchefsky) Kappy; m. Joseph Suckiel, June 22, 1973. A.B., Douglass Coll., 1965; M.A. in Philosophy, U. Wis., 1969, Ph.D. in Philosophy, 1972. Lectr. philosophy U. Wis., Madison, 1969-71; asst. prof. philosophy Fla. State U., Tallahassee, 1972-73; asst. prof. philosophy U. Calif., Santa Cruz, 1973-80, assoc. prof., 1980-95, prof., 1995—, provost Kresge Coll., 1983-89. Author: The Pragmatic Philosophy of William James, 1982, Heaven's Champion: William James's Philosophy of Religion, 1996, also articles, book introductions and chpts. Mem. Am. Philos. Assn., Soc. for Advancement Am. Philosophy. Office: U Calif Cowell Coll Santa Cruz CA 95064

SUDBECK, ROBERT FRANCIS, music educator, philosophy educator; b. Sioux City, Iowa, May 14, 1955; s. Gorman Francis and Lois Mae (Lawless) S.; m. Lorraine Suzanne Delgadillo, June 27, 1987; children: John Robert, Patrick Michael. MusB, Cath. U. Am., 1977, MusM, 1979; MusM, Cath. U. Am., 1979; MA in Philosophy, Calif. State U., Long Beach, 1989, MA in Edn., 1994. music, philosophy, ednl. admin., Calif. Sch. Leadership Acad. Music educator Santa Ana (Calif.) Sch. Dist., 1981—; adjunct prof. Calif. State U., 1991-92; elem. dir. Santa Ana Edn. Assn., 1993—; Calif. mentor tchr., Santa Ana Sch. Dist., 1989-90; adv. bd., edl. admin. dept., Calif. State U., 1994—. Mem. Santa Ana Edn. Assn. (bd. mem. 1993—, co-chair human rights 1995—, polit. action comm. mem. 1996—), Calif. Tchrs. Assn. (state del. to State Coun. of Edn., mem. state rights and responsibilities com., TA governing rep., Burlingame, Calif. 1996—). Home: 1145 Salvador St Costa

Mesa CA 92626 Office: Santa Ana Unified Sch. Dist 1601 E Chestnut Ave Santa Ana CA 92701-6322

SUDDOCK, FRANCES SUTER THORSON, grief educator, writer; b. Estelline, S.D., Oct. 23, 1914; d. William Henry and Anna Mary (Oakland) Suter; m. Carl Edwin Thorson, July 6, 1941 (dec. Apr. 1976); children: Sarah Thorson Little, Mary Frances Thorson; m. Edwin Matthew Suddock, Aug. 7, 1982 (dec. Sept. 1986). BA, Iowa State Tchrs. Coll., 1936; postgrad., Syracuse U., 1940-41, U. Iowa, 1946; MA, Antioch U., San Francisco, 1981. Cert. tchr. Tchr. various high schs., Correctionville and Eagle Grove, Iowa, 1936-38, 38-40, 41-43, 45-47; chief clk. War Price and Rationing Bd., Eagle Grove, 1943-45; instr. (part time) Eagle Grove Jr. Coll., 1953-61; adminstr. Eagle Grove Pub. Library, 1961-77; facilitator Will Schutz Assocs., Muir Beach, Calif., 1987-88. Author: Whither the Widow, 1981. Vol. Nat. Trainer Widowed Persons Svc. Am. Assn. Retired Persons, 1989—, ret. sr. vol. program, Anchorage, 1988—; pres., bd. dirs. Anchorage Widowed Persons Svc., 1992-94; bd. dirs. North Iowa Mental Health Ctr., Mason City, 1959-76, Eagle Grove Cmty. Chest, 1960, Help Line, Inc., Ft. Dodge, Iowa, 1976-77; chmn. Cmty. Mental Health Fund, Eagle Grove, 1966-73; charter pres. Eagle Grove Concerned, Inc., 1973-77; active various civic orgns. Mem. AAUW (charter pres. Eagle Grove br. 1973-75), Am. Soc. on Aging, Alaska Assn. Gerontology (treas. 1992-94), Anchorage Woman's Club, P.E.O., Kappa Delta Pi. Home: 333 M St Apt 404 Anchorage AK 99501-1902

SUE, ALAN KWAI KEONG, dentist; b. Honolulu, Apr. 26, 1946; s. Henry Tin Yee and Chiyoko (Ohata) S.; m. Ginger Kazue Fukushima, Mar. 19, 1972; 1 child, Dawn Marie. BS in Chemistry with honors, U. Hawaii, 1968; BS, U. Calif., San Francisco, 1972, DDS, 1972. Film editor, photographer Sta. KHVH-TV ABC, Honolulu, 1964-71; staff dentist Strong-Carter Dental Clinic, Honolulu, 1972-73; dentist Waianae Dental Clinic, Honolulu, 1972-73; pvt. practice Pearl City, Hawaii, 1973—; chief exec. officer Dental Image Specialists, Pearl City, 1975—; dental dir. Hawaii Dental Health Plan, Honolulu, 1987—; dental cons. Calif. Dental Health Plan, Tustin, 1987—, Pacific Group Med. Assn., The Queen's Health Care Plan, Honolulu, 1993—; dental cons. Pacific Group Med. Assn., 1994—; cons. Hawaii Mgmt. Alliance Assn., 1996—; bd. dirs. Kula Bay Tropical Clothing Co., Hawaiian Ind. Dental Alliance; mem. exec. bd. St. Francis Hosp., Honolulu, 1976-78, chief dept. dentistry, 1976-78; mem. expert med. panel Am. Internat. Claim Svc., 1995—. Mem. adv. bd. Health Svcs. for Sr. Citizens, 1976—; mem. West Honolulu Sub-Area Health Planning Coun., 1981-84; mem. dental task force Hawaii Statewide Health Coordinating Coun., 1980, mem. plan devel. com., 1981-84; vol. oral cancer screening program Am. Cancer Soc.; v.p. Pearl City Shopping Ctr. Merchants Assn., 1975-84, 92-93, pres., 1994—. Regents' scholar U. Calif., San Francisco, 1968-72. Fellow Pierre Fauchard Acad., Acad. Gen. Dentistry; mem. ADA, Acad. Implants and Transplants, Am. Acad. Implant Dentistry, Hawaii Dental Assn. (trustee 1978-80), Honolulu County Dental Soc. (pres. 1982), Am. Acad. and Bd. Head, Facial, Neck Pain and TMJ Orthopedics, Intertel, Internat. Platform Assn., Mensa, Porsche Club, Pantera Owners Club, Mercedes Benz Club. Democrat. Office: Dental Image Specialists 850 Kam Hwy Ste 116 Pearl City HI 96782-2603

SUE, MICHAEL ALVIN, physician; b. L.A., Apr. 15, 1956. MD, U. Chgo., 1980. Diplomate Am. Bd. Internal Medicine, Am. Bd. Allergy and Immunology. Intern, resident and fellow West Los Angeles VA Med. Ctr., L.A., 1980-86; allergist Kaiser Permanente, Panorama City, Calif., 1986—. Fellow Am. Coll. Allergy, Asthma, and Immunology; mem. Am. Acad. Allergy, Asthma, and Immunology. Office: Kaiser Permanente 13652 Cantara St Panorama City CA 91402-5423

SUERMONDT, HENRI JACQUES, research scientist; b. Leiden, The Netherlands, Sept. 2, 1965; s. Rudolf Gerard and Wilhelmina Gustavine (Fabius) S. BS, Stanford U., 1987, MS, 1989, PhD, 1992. Rsch. fellow Stanford (Calif.) U., 1987-92; rsch. scientist Hewlett-Packard Labs., Palo Alto, Calif., 1992—. Contbr. articles to profl. jours. Vol. Los Altos (Calif.) Pony Baseball, 1995—, So. Calif. Children's Cancer Soc., L.A., 1986—. Mem. Am. Med. Informatics Assn. (membership com., publs. com., Martin Epstein award 1992), Am. Assn. Artificial Intelligence, Phi Beta Kappa. Home: 2544 Mardell Way Mountain View CA 94043-2716 Office: Hewlett-Packard Labs 3500 Deer Creek Rd Palo Alto CA 94304-1317

SUFFET, IRWIN (MEL), environmental chemistry educator, consultant; b. N.Y.C., May 11, 1939; s. Charles and Lee (Kellerman) S.; m. Eileen H. Shusterman, July 1, 1962; children—Alison M., Jeffrey H. B.S., Bklyn. Coll., 1961; M.S., U. Md., 1964; Ph.D., Rutgers U., 1968. Asst. prof. Drexel U., Phila., 1968-73, assoc. prof., 1973-78, prof. environ. sci., 1978-88, P. Walton Purdom prof. environ. sci., 1988-90; prof. UCLA, 1991—; cons. and expert witness on hazardous waste, water treatment, environ. organic analysis and fate of chems. to govt. agys., corps; mem. safe drinking water com. Nat. Acad. Scis., 1978-81; mem. NATO environ. tech. workshop on hazardous wastes, 1985; mem. space sta. water quality and treatment panel NASA, 1986—; mem. panel on research needs Hazardous Waste and Disposal Workshop NSF, 1986—, EPA, 1987-95; mem. Denver Water Reuse Panel, 1980—; mem. Innovative Rsch. Grant Panel EPA, 1981—; mem. Document Peer Rev. EPA, 1985-86; leader of EPA workshop on Separation and Detoxification of Hazardous Material in Soils and Variable Strength Liquids, Cin., 1987; mem. CDC, EPA and State Health Dept. N.Y.-Love Canal Habitability Criteria Study, 1985-86, NATO-Organic Chemicals Contamination Groundwater Workshop, 1983; mem. adv. bd. Hazardous Waste Substance Rsch. Ctr., EPA region III/V, 1989—; mem. scientific planning rev. com. bay protection and toxic cleanup program Calif. State Wctea Resources Control Bd., 1995—. Editor: (with M.J. McGuire) 3 Vols. Activated Carbon Treatment: Water Process Applications, 1984-86, 2 Vols. Fate of Pollutants in the Air and Water Environment, 1977, (with M. Malayandi) Organic Pollutants in Water, 1987, (with J. Mallevialle) Identification and Treatment of Tastes and Odors in Drinking Water, 1987, (with P. MacCarthy) Influence of Aquatic Humic Substance on Fate and Treatment of Pollutants, 1989, (with J Mallevialle and S.N. Samm) Influents and Removal of Organics in Drinking Water Treatment, 1992, (with J. Mallevialle and E. Kawczynski) Advances in Taste and Odor Treatment and Control in Drinking Water, 1995; mem. editorial bd. Jour. Environ. Sci. and Health, Part B, 1976-77, guest editor Vol. A13, 2 and 4, 1978; mem. editorial bd. Chemosphere, 1979-82; mem. adv. bd. Chemtech Jour., 1981-84; contbr. over 125 articles to profl. jours. Recipient Drexel U. research award, 1981-82. Mem. Am. Chem. Soc. (environ. chemistry div. treas. 1983-86, F.J. Zimmerman award in environ. sci. 1983, P. Walter Purdom named professorship award 1988), Am. Water Works Assn. (organics contaminants com. research div., chmn. taste and odor com. water quality div., standard methods com., water quality monitoring com., water reuse com.), Assn. Environ. Engring. Profs. (research div., Univ. Council Water Resources, Internat. Humic Substance Soc., Internat. Assn. Water Pollution Rsch. and Control (mem. working group on fate and effect of pollutants 1982-89, working group off-flavours in aquatic environment 1987—), Sigma Xi. Home: 336 23rd St Santa Monica CA 90402-2514 Office: UCLA Env Sci and Engring Program Sch Pub Health Box 951772 Los Angeles CA 90095

SUGGS, PATRICIA ANN, artist; b. Reedley, Calif., Mar. 17, 1936; d. Charles and Dorothy Rema (Prouty) Kofoed; m. Robert Reed Suggs, July 28, 1961; 1 child, Richard William. Student, Leighton Fine Art Acad., San Francisco, 1974-81. judge fine arts Arts Clubs, The Peninsula, No. Calif. and San Joaquin Valley, Calif. county fairs, 1984-93, Santa Clara County, San Jose, 1991, Sonoma County Fair, Santa Rosa, 1990, Alameda County Fair, Pleasanton, 1990. One-woman shows include Group 21, Los Gatos, Calif., 1978, Gt. Western Savs. & Loan, Fremont, Calif., 1982, Rosicrucian Egyptian Museums, San Jose, Calif., 1982, Gadabout Gallery, Los Gatos, Calif., 1986; exhibited in group shows at Pastel Soc. Am., N.Y., 1980, Ashland (Ky.) Gallery, 1990, Pastel Soc. West Coast, Sacramento, 1989-94, Runnings Gallery, Seattle, 1990, Soc. Western Artists Anns., San Francisco, 1976-93, Fremont Art Assn., 1993; also pvt. collections. Recipient Best of show award Fremont (Calif.) Art Assn., 1993. Mem. Pastel Soc. Am. (Best Floral award 1980, Best Pastel Plaque 1993), Pastel Soc. West Coast (adv. bd. 1986-94, award of merit 1991), Soc. Western Artists (bd. trustees 1986-96, 1st Pl. pastels 1993), Allied Artists West (dir. exhbn. 1991-92), Internat. Assoc. of Pastel Soc., (treas. 1994-96), Nat. League Am. Pen Women (Grumbacher award medallion 1993). Home: 4127 Beebe Cir San Jose CA 95135-1010

SUGIKI, SHIGEMI, ophthalmologist, educator; b. Wailuku, Hawaii, May 12, 1936; s. Sentaro and Kameno (Matoba) S.; AB, Washington U., St. Louis, 1957, M.D., 1961; m. Bernice T. Murakami, Dec. 28, 1958; children: Kevin S., Boyd R. Intern St. Luke's Hosp., St. Louis, 1961-62, resident ophthalmology, Washington U., St. Louis, 1962-65; chmn. dept. ophthalmology Straub Clinic, Honolulu, 1965-70, Queen's Med. Ctr., Honolulu, 1970-73, 80-83, 88-90, 93—; assoc. clin. prof. ophthalmology Sch. Medicine, U. Hawaii, 1973—. Served to maj. M.C., AUS, 1968-70. Decorated Hawaiian NG Commendation medal, 1968. Fellow ACS; mem. Am., Hawaii med. assns., Honolulu County Med. Soc., Am. Acad. Ophthalmology, Contact Lens Assn. Opthalmologists, Pacific Coast Oto-Ophthal. Soc., Pan-Pacific Surg. Assn., Am. Soc. Cataract and Refractive Surgery, Am. Glaucoma Soc., Internat. Assn. Ocular Surgeons, Am. Soc. Contemporary Ophthalmology, Washington U. Eye Alumni Assn., Hawaii Ophthal. Soc., Rsch. To Prevent Blindness. Home: 2398 Aina Lani Pl Honolulu HI 96822-2024 Office: 1380 Lusitana St Ste 714 Honolulu HI 96813-2443

SUGRUE, DONAL, food products executive. Various positions Vacu-Dry Co., Sebastopol, Calif., 1963-69, v.p., 1969-82, exec. v.p., 1982-89, pres., CEO, 1989-96, also bd. dirs. Office: Vacu-Dry Co 7765 Healdsburg Ave Sebastopol CA 95472-3309*

SUITER, THOMAS, advertising executive. Exec. creative dir. CKS Partners, Cupertino, Calif. Office: 10443 Brandley Dr Cupertino CA 95014*

SUKO, LONNY RAY, judge; b. Spokane, Wash., Oct. 12, 1943; s. Ray R. and Leila B. (Snyder) S.; m. Marcia A. Michaelsen, Aug. 26, 1967; children: Jolynn R., David M. BA, Wash. State U., 1965; JD, U. Idaho, 1968. Bar: Wash. 1968, U.S. Dist. Ct. (ea. dist.) Wash. 1969, U.S. Dist. Ct. (we. dist.) Wash. 1978, U.S. Ct. Appeals (9th cir.) 1978. Law clk. U.S. Dist. Ct. Ea. Dist. Wash., 1968-69; assoc. Lyon, Beaulaurier & Aaron, Yakima, Wash., 1969-72; ptnr. Lyon, Beaulaurier, Weigand, Suko & Gustafson, Yakima, 1972-91, Lyon, Weigand, Suko & Gustafson, P.S., 1991-95; U.S. magistrate judge, Yakima, 1971-91, 95—. Mem. Phi Beta Kappa, Phi Kappa Phi. Office: PO Box 2726 Yakima WA 98907-2726

SUKOV, RICHARD JOEL, radiologist; b. Mpls., Nov. 13, 1944; s. Marvin and Annette Sukov; Susan Judith Grossman, Aug. 11, 1968; children: Stacy Faye, Jessica Erin. BA, BS, U. Minn., 1967, MD, 1970; student, U. Calif.-Berkeley, 1962-64. Diplomate Am. Bd. Radiology; lic. physician Minn., Calif. Intern pediatrics U. Minn., Mpls., 1970-71; resident radiology UCLA Ctr. for Health Sci., 1973-76; fellow in ultrasound and computed tomography UCLA, 1976-77; staff radiologist Centinela Hosp. Med. Ctr., Inglewood, Calif., 1977-85; staff radiologist Daniel Freeman Meml. Hosp., Inglewood, Calif., 1977—, dir. radiology, 1988-90; asst. clin. prof. radiology UCLA Ctr. for Health Scis., 1977-83; adv. bd. Aerobics and Fitness Assn. Am., 1983—. Contbr. articles to profl. jours. Vol. Venice Family Clinic, 1985—. Lt. comdr. USPHS, 1970-72. U. Minn. fellow, 1964-65, 66, 70. Mem. AMA, Soc. Radiologists in Ultrasound (charter), Minn. Med. Alumni Assn., L.A. County Med. Assn., Calif. Med. Assn. Radiol. Soc. N.Am., L.A. Radiol. Soc. (continuing edn. com. 1990—, mgmt. com. 1996—, chmn.), L.A. Ultrasound Soc., Am. Coll. Radiology. Office: Ingelwood Radiology Ste 160 323 N Prairie Ave Inglewood CA 90301-4502

SULICH, VASSILI, artistic director; b. Island of Brac, Yugoslavia, Dec. 29, 1929; came to U.S., 1964; s. Thomas and Vjekoslava (Orlandini) Sulic. From co. mem. to Dancer Etoile various dancing cos., Paris, 1952-64; prin. dancer Broadway prodn. Follies Bergere, N.Y.C., 1964; prin. dancer, ballet master Las Vegas prodn. Follies Bergere, 1964-72; ind. choreographer Europe and U.S., 1964—; artistic dir. Nev. Dance Theatre, Las Vegas, 1972—. Choreographer: Suite Lyrique, Oedipe roi, Idomeneo with Luciano Pavarotti; creator, choreographer numerous dance works including Mantodea, Walls in the Horizon, Cinderella; prin. dancer: La Dryade, L'Echelle, Combat, Cyrano de Bergerac, Lovers of Teruel; performer (TV show) Geraldine starring Geraldine Chaplin. Named Outstanding Individual Artist Gov. of Nev., 1981, Disting. Nevadan U. Nev. Bd. Regents, 1987. Office: Nev Dance Theater 4505 S Maryland Pky Las Vegas NV 89154-9900

SULLENS, MICHAEL, mayor. Mayor Whittier, Calif. Address: 13230 Penn St Whittier CA 90602

SULLIVAN, ANITA CHRISTINE, piano tuner; b. Boston, Sept. 29, 1942; d. James Norton and Agnes Elizabeth (Wallner) Thurston; m. Paul Blakeney Sullivan (div. July 1979); children: Patrick, Timothy. BA in English, Clemson U., 1963, MA in English, 1970. Instr. Oreg. State U., Corvallis, 1983-85; piano tuner Corvallis, 1981—; commentator Nat. Pub. Radio, Washington, 1989—; tchr. workshops Linn Benton C.C., Albany, Oreg., 1989—. Author: The Seventh Dragon, 1986, I Hear the Crickets Laughing, 1996. Recipient Book award We. States Arts Found., 1986. Mem. Piano Technicians Guild (assoc.), Fiction Writing Group, Poetry Writing Group, Willamette Literary Guild (bd. dirs.). Home and Office: 3180 NE Pilkington Ave Corvallis OR 97330

SULLIVAN, DEBRA KAE, elementary education educator; b. Iowa City, Iowa, Jan. 27, 1962; d. Raymond Francis and Jo Adele (Meyers) S. Cert. specialization in mgmt. devel., Am. Hotel & Motel Assn., 1985; BA, U. Iowa, 1989. Nev. tchg. lic. grades K-8. Reservations mgr. Holiday Inn, Iowa City, 1981-83; reservations clk. Holiday Inn Mart Plaza, Chgo., 1983-85; substitute tchr. grades K-12 Iowa City Sch. Dist., 1989-90; tchr. K-8 Clark County Sch. Dist., Las Vegas, Nev., 1990—; tchr. cons. Geog. Alliance in Nev., Las Vegas, 1994—; mem. geography curriculum task force Clark County Sch. Dist., Las Vegas, 1995; mem. geography task force State of Nev., Reno, 1996, mem. social studies task force, 1996; mem. Advanced Geography Inst., Geog. Alliance in Nev., Moscow, Russia, 1996. Host family Home Away From Home Program, U. Nev., Las Vegas, 1994—. Mem. NEA, Nat. Coun. Social Studies, Nat. Coun. for Geog. Edn., People to People Internat., Social Studies Coun. Nev. (Elem. Sch. Social Studies Tchr. of the Yr. 1995-96). Home: 5709 Berwick Falls Ln Las Vegas NV 89129 Office: CH Decker Elem Sch 3850 Redwood St Las Vegas NV 89103-2029

SULLIVAN, G. CRAIG, household products executive; b. 1940. BS, Boston Coll., 1964. With Procter & Gamble Co., 1964-69, Am. Express Co., 1969-70; regional sales mgr. Clorox Co., Oakland, Calif., 1971-76, v.p. mktg., 1976-78, mgr. food svc. sales devel., mgr. bus. devel., 1978-79, gen. mgr. food svc. products divsn., 1979-81, v.p. food svc. products divsn., 1981, v.p. household products, 1981-89, group v.p. household products, 1989-92, chmn. bd., pres., CEO, 1992—. Office: The Clorox Co PO Box 24305 Oakland CA 94623-1305*

SULLIVAN, JAMES KIRK, forest products company executive; b. Greenwood, S.C., Aug. 25, 1935; s. Daniel Jones and Addie (Brown) S.; m. Elizabeth Miller, June 18, 1960; children: Hal N., Kim J. BS in Chemistry, Clemson U., 1957, MS, 1964, PhD, 1966; postgrad. program for sr. execs., MIT, 1975; DSc (hon.), U. Idaho, 1990. Prodn. supr. FMC Corp., South Charleston, W.Va., 1957-62; tech. supt. FMC Corp., Pocatello, Idaho, 1966-69; mktg. mgr. FMC Corp., N.Y.C., 1969-70; v.p. govtl. and environ. affairs Boise (Idaho) Cascade Corp., 1971-97, mem. new dist. bd., 1997—; chmn. trust and investment com. Key Bank Idaho, 1983-90, exec. com., 1983-97; bd. dirs., chmn. audit com. Key Trust Co. of the West; chmn. adv. bd. U. Idaho Coll. Engring., 1966-70, 80-87, centennial campaign, 1987-89, rsch. found., 1980-82; mem. Accreditation Bd. Engring. and Tech., Inc., 1994—; bd. dirs. Pub. Employees Retirement Sys. of Idaho. Contbr. articles to profl. jours.; patentee in field. Mem. Coll. of Forest and Recreation Resources com. Clemson U., Idaho Found. for Pvt. Enterprise and Econ. Edn., Idaho Rsch. Found., Inc., Idaho Task Force on Higher Edn.; bd. dirs. Idaho Found. for Excellence in Higher Edn., Exptl. Program to Stimulate Competitive Rsch. NSF, N.W. Nazarene Coll., 1988-90, Boise Philharm., 1996—, Pub. Employees Retirement Sys. of Idaho, 1996—; mem. Len B. Jordan Pub Affairs Symposium; trustee Idaho Children's Emergency Fund, 1984—; trustee Bishop Kelly H.S., 1987-89; chmn. Bishop Kelly Found., 1972-79, 85-89; chmn. adv. bd. U. Idaho Coll. Engring., Am. Forest and Paper Assn., Govtl. Affairs Com., Environ. Com., Future Options Group; bd. dirs. Boise Master Chorale, 1995—. 1st lt. U.S. Army, 1958-59. Recipient Presdl. Citation U. Idaho, 1990. Mem. AIChE, Am. Chem. Soc., Bus. Week Found. (chmn. Bus. Week 1980), Am. Forest and Paper Assn. (environ. and health coun., product and tech. com., solid waste task force), Bus. Roundtable (environ. com.), Idaho Assn. Commerce and Industry (past chmn. bd. dirs.), C. of C. of U.S. (pub. affairs com.). Republican. Home: 5206 Sorrento Cir Boise ID 83704-2347 Office: Boise Cascade Corp 1111 W Jefferson St PO Box 50 Boise ID 83728

SULLIVAN, JAMES N., fuel company executive; b. San Francisco, 1937. Student, U. Notre Dame, 1959. Formerly v.p. Chevron Corp., until 1988, now vice chmn., dir., 1988—. Office: Chevron Corp 575 Market St San Francisco CA 94105-2823*

SULLIVAN, JAMES PATRICK, lawyer; b. Minot, N.D., Apr. 25, 1958; s. William Thomas and Marjorie (Ellison) S.; m. Sandra T. Collins, June 9, 1983 (div. 1992); 1 child, William Thomas II; m. Janice Mackelman, Aug. 31, 1994. BA in History cum laude, U. So. Calif., 1980; JD, UCLA, 1982. Bar: Calif. 1982. Assoc. Ferrington & Ferrington, San Diego, 1983-86, Calligari, Werik & Assocs., San Francisco, 1986-91; ptnr. Calligari, Werik & Sullivan (formerly Calligari, Werik & Assocs.), San Francisco, 1991—; lectr. U. So. Calif., 1990-92, UCLA, 1993. Contbr. articles to profl. jours. Vol. ARC, San Francisco, 1984-89, Youth on the Run program, San Francisco, 1994—. Recipient Disting. Alumni award U. So. Calif., 1994, Outstanding Svc. to Cmty. award Mayor San Francisco, 1996. Mem. ABA, State Bar Calif., Northshore Country Club. Democrat. Office: Calligari Werik and Sullivan 890 Wisconsin St San Francisco CA 94107-3347

SULLIVAN, JANICE E., accountant; b. Kelso, Wash., Mar. 9, 1940; d. John Ralph and Mable Stella Elizabeth (Shield) Bartell; m. John Thomas Sullivan, Dec. 5, 1956 (div. June 1994); children: John L., Dale E., Brian P. CPA, Calif. Acct. Cherokee Auto Body, Lodi, Calif., 1985-95; bookkeeper Accountable Enterprises, Lodi, 1995—. Named Woman of the Yr., City of Lodi, 1975. Mem. Lodi C. of C., Eagles (state pres. 1986), emblem Club (pres. 1992). Democrat. Office: Accountable Enterprises 314 N Cherokee Ln Lodi CA 95240

SULLIVAN, JOHN CHARLES, journalist, editor, publisher; b. Spokane, Wash., Feb. 25, 1946; s. Dalton B. and Helen L. (Schnitzler) S. AB in Journalism, Stanford U., 1968. Pub. rels. dir. Colo. Conv. Bur., Denver, 1968-70; reporter The Bend (Oreg.) Bull., 1970-71, Daily Times Call, Longmont, Colo., 1971; mng. editor Livingston (Mont.) Enterprise, 1972-73, editor, pub., 1973—; pres. The Star Printing Co., Livingston, 1975—; bd. dirs. First State Bank, Newcastle; pres., dir. Schnitzler Corp., Livingston, 1974—. Trustee Livingston (Mont.) Hosp., 1974-84, Buffalo Bill Mus., Cody, Wyo., 1980—; pres., trustee Livingston (Mont.) Depot Found., 1986—, Livingston (Mont.) Cmty. Trust, 1987—. Mem. Am. Soc. Newspaper Editors, Newspaper Assn. Am., Denver Univ. Club. Office: Livingston Enterprise PO Box 665 401 S Main Livingston MT 59047

SULLIVAN, JOHN HARVEY, ophthalmologist, plastic surgeon; b. Charleston, W.Va., Jan. 10, 1939; m. Susan O'Connor, 1975; children: Brian, Patrick, Katerine. BA, U. Notre Dame, 1960; MD, Georgetown U., 1964. Diplomate Nat. Bd. Med. Examiners, Am. Bd. Ophthalmology; lic. physician, Calif. Med. intern Ohio State U., Columbus, 1964-65; resident in ophthalmology U. Calif., San Francisco, 1968-71; fellow St. John's Ophthalmol. Hosp., Jerusalem, 1971-72, Melbourne (Australia) U., 1972-73; ophthalmologist in pvt. practice San Jose, Calif., 1973—; pvt. practice El Segundo, Calif., 1967-68; clin. instr. ophthalmology U. Calif., San Francisco, 1973-75, asst. clin. prof., 1975-83, assoc. clin. prof., 1983-89, clin. prof., 1989—; vol. clin. faculty Stanford (Calif.) U., 1992—. Contbr. articles to profl. jours. Pres. Prevent Blindness No. Calif., 1996; Capt. M.C. U.S. Army, 1965-67. Sr. Fulbright-Hays postdoctoral fellwo, 1972, Oculoplastic Surgery fellow U. Calif., San Francisco, 1994-95. Fellow Am. Acad. Ophthalmology, Am. Soc. Oculoplastic and Reconstructive Surgery; mem. AMA, Calif. Med. Assn., Peninsula Eye Soc. (sec. 1995-96), Fredrick C. Cordes Eye Soc. (exec. sec. 1982-87, pres. 1988-89), Santa Clara Med. Assn. (pub. svc. com.), Calif. Assn. Ophthalmology. Office: Eye Med Clinic 220 Meridian Ave San Jose CA 95126-2903

SULLIVAN, KAREN LAU, real estate company executive, campaign consultant, federal commissioner; b. Honolulu, Jan. 21, 1948; d. Ralph Karn Yee and Beatrice (Loo) Lau; m. Paul Dennis Sullivan, Apr. 24, 1976. BA, Whittier Coll., 1970; MA, U. Hawaii, 1987. Staff asst. to Congresswoman Patsy Mink U.S. Ho. Reps., Washington, 1974, staff asst. subcom. mines and mining, 1975-77, legis. asst. to Congressman Cec. Heftel, 1977-79; spl. asst. to asst. to Pres. for policy and women's affairs The White House, Washington, 1979; spl. asst. office of sec. of transp. U.S. Dept. Transp., Washington, 1979-81; regional dir. mid-Atlantic states Mondale-Ferraro Presdl. Campaign, Washington, 1984; dep. nat. field dir. Paul Simon Presdl. Campaign, Washington, 1987-88; Ill. dir. forum inst. Martin & Glantz Polit. Cons., San Francisco, 1988; regional dir. western states Clinton-Gore Presdl. Campaign, Little Rock, 1992; dep. dir. for pub. outreach Office of Pres.-Elect Bill Clinton, Little Rock/Washington, 1992-93; v.p. Hoaloha Ventures, Inc., Honolulu, 1981—. U.S. alt. rep. South Pacific Commn., 1995-97. Mem. Carter/Mondale Alumni Fund, The Carter Ctr. Home and Office: 810-K N Kalaheo Ave Kailua HI 96734

SULLIVAN, KEVIN PATRICK, lawyer; b. Waterbury, Conn., June 9, 1953; s. John Holian Sullivan and Frances (McGrath) Coon; m. Peggy Hardy, June 13, 1975 (div. Jan. 1985); m. Jarnine Welker, Feb. 15, 1985; children: S. Craig Lemmon, Michael Scott Lemmon, Lindsay Michelle Lemmon. BS in Polit. Sci., BS in Police Sci. cum laude, Weber State Coll., 1979; JD, Pepperdine U., 1982. Bar: Utah 1982, U.S. Dist. Ct. Utah 1982, U.S. Ct. Appeals (10th cir.) 1986, U.S. Supreme Ct. 1986. Assoc. Farr, Kaufman & Hamilton, Ogden, Utah, 1982-87; ptnr. Farr, Kaufman, Hamilton, Sulivan, Gorman & Perkins, Ogden, 1987-91, Farr, Kaufman, Sullivan, Gorman & Perkins, Ogden, 1991—; judge pro tem Utah 2d Cir. Ct.; city prosecutor of South Ogden, 1990-92. Mem. Eccles Community Art Ctr., Victim's Rights Com. of 2d Jud. Dist. Mem. ABA (criminal justice sect., litigation sect., justice and edn. fund lawyers' coun.), ACLU, ATLA, Utah Bar Assn. (criminal law, young lawyer, litigation sects., unauthorized practice law com.), Utah Trial Lawyers Assn., Utah Assn. Criminal Def. Lawyers, Weber County Bar Assn. (criminal law sect., pres.-elect 1993, pres. 1994), Weber County Pub. Defenders Assn. (assoc. dir. 1987), Weber State Coll. Alumni Assn., Amicus Pepperdine, Elks, Kiwanis, Phi Kappa Phi. Roman Catholic. Home: 2731 E 6425 S Ogden UT 84403-5461 Office: Farr Kaufman Sullivan Gorman & Perkins 205 26th St Ste 34 Ogden UT 84401-3109

SULLIVAN, LESLIE NOELLE, editor-in-chief; b. Laurium, Mich., Dec. 17, 1965; d. Daniel Joseph and Patricia Amanda (Kallio) S. BA, Trinity U., 1987; MA, U. N.Mex., 1990. Editor Trinity News Svc., San Antonio, 1985-87; prodr., pub. affairs dir. Sta. KRTU, San Antonio, 1985-88; intern reporter Sta. KMOL-TV, San Antonio, 1987; asst. news dir. Sta. KUUB, Bozeman, Mont., 1988; editor, colloquium coord. dept. history U. N.Mex., Albuquerque, 1989-91; editl. dir. Skyhouse Pubs./Falcon Press, Helena, Mont., 1992-94; editor-in-chief Agencia, Helena, 1994—; publs. cons. Rocky Mountain Trade Corridor, Helena, 1995-96, Falcon Press, Helena, 1994—; symposium panelist Kaleidoscope Arts Festival, Helena, 1996; Chautauqua performer N.Mex. Endowment for Humanities, Albuquerque, 1991-92. Author: (book) M-E Ecci Aashi Awadi, 1995, It Happened In Southern California, 1997; contbr.: (essay) Writing Montana, 1996; contbr. poetry to anthologies; editor: (mag.) The Corridor, 1995-96. Com. mem. Elect Dorothy Bradley, Park County, Mont., 1992. Recipient Benjamin Franklin award Pub.'s Mktg. Assn., 1993, Best Poetry award Trinity Rev., 1987. Mem. Acad. Am. Poets, Mont. Ctr. for the Book, Phi Beta Kappa. Democrat. Office: Agencia PO Box 54 Helena MT 59624

SULLIVAN, LINDA ANN, psychologist, researcher; b. Dublin, Ireland, Feb. 13, 1961; came to U.S., 1982; BA, Trinity Coll., Dublin, 1982; MA, Coll. of William and Mary, 1986; PhD, Mich. State U., 1989. Data mgr. Mich. State U., East Lansing, 1988-92; rsch. dir. The Schroer Mktg. Co., Battle Creek, Mich., 1992-93; rsch. cons. The Polk Co., Southfield, Mich.,

1993—. CContbr. to 1 book and articles to profl. jours. Mem. Am. Psychol. Soc., Am. Mktg. Assn. Home: 7405 Charmant Dr Apt 2232 San Diego CA 92122-5012 Office: The Polk Co 1921 Palomar Oaks Way Ste 305 Carlsbad CA 92008

SULLIVAN, MARTIN EDWARD, museum director; b. Troy, N.Y., Feb. 9, 1944; s. John Francis and Helen Edna (Lynch) S.; m. Katherine Mary Hostetter, May 9, 1981; children: Abigail, Bethany. BA in History, Siena Coll., 1965; MA in History, U. Notre Dame, 1970, PhD in History, 1974. Exec. dir. Ind. Commn. for Humanities, Indpls., 1972-75; dir. pub. programs NEH, Washington, 1976-81; pres. Inst. on Man and Sci., Rensselaerville, N.Y., 1981-83; dir. N.Y. State Mus., State Edn. Dept., Albany, N.Y., 1983-90, The Heard Mus., Phoenix, 1990—; trustee Am. Indian Ritual Object Repatriation Found., N.Y.C., 1992—; chair U.S. Govt. Cultural Property Adv. Com., 1995—. Author: Museums, Adults and the Humanities, 1981, Inventing the Southwest: The Fred Harvey Company and Native American Art, 1996; contbr. articles to profl. jours. Trustee Phoenix Cmty. Alliance, 1991—, Am. Fedn. Arts, 1994—; mem. Native Am. Repatriation Act Adv. Com., 1992—. Served in U.S. Army, 1966-68. Mem. Am. Assn. Mus. (v.p. 1990-93, mem. exec. com. internat. com. 1992—). Democrat. Home: 4601 E Solano Dr Phoenix AZ 85018-1280 Office: The Heard Mus 22 E Monte Vista Rd Phoenix AZ 85004-1433

SULLIVAN, MICHAEL EVAN, investment and management company executive; b. Phila., Dec. 30, 1940; s. Albert and Ruth (Liebert) S.; BS, N.Mex. State U., 1966, MA (Ednl. Research Tng. Program fellow), 1967; BS, U. Tex., 1969; MBA, U. Houston, 1974; MS, U. So. Calif., 1976, MPA, 1977, PhD in Adminstrn., 1983; BS in Acctg., U. La Verne, 1981. Sr. adminstrv. and tech. analyst Houston Lighting & Power Co., 1969-74; electronics engr. U.S. Govt., Point Mugu, Calif., 1974-77; mem. tech. staff Hughes Aircraft Co., El Segundo, Calif., 1977-78; staff program adminstr. Ventura div. Northrop Corp., Newbury Park, Calif., 1978-79; div. head engring. div. Navastrogru, Point Mugu, 1979-82; br. head, div. head spl. programs head operational systems integraton office Pacific Missile Test Ctr., Calif., 1983-90, head tech. devel. office, head capability devel., 1993—; CNO, Dir. Rsch., Devel., and Acquisition in the Pentagon, Washington, 1987-88, dir. rsch. devel. test and evaluation and tech. in the Pentagon, 1990-93; pres., chmn. bd. Diversified Mgmt. Systems, Inc., Camarillo, Calif., 1978—. Author: The Management of Research, Development, Test and Evaluation Organizations; Organizational Behavior Characteristics of Supervisors-Public versus Private Sectors, Organizational Behavior Characteristics of Supervisors, Public versus Private Sectors; Self-Actualization in RDT & E Organizations; Self-Actualization in a Health Care Agency; others. V.p., bd. dirs. Ventura County Master Chorale and Opera Assn; bd. dirs. So. Calif. Assn. of Pub. Adminstrn. (also mem. fin. com., programs com., student aid com., exec. bd. fed. lab. consortium). Served with U.S. Army, 1958-62. Ednl. Rsch. Info. Clearing House fellow, 1965-67. Mem. IEEE, Am. Math. Soc., Math. Assn. Am., Am. Statis. Assn., IEEE Engring. Mgmt. Soc., Am. Soc. Pub. Adminstrn., So. Calif. Assn. Pub. Adminstrn. (bd. dirs., various coms.), Am. Pers. and Guidance Assn., Assn. Fed. Tech. Transfer Execs., Fed. Mgrs. Assn., Am. Assn. Individual Investors, Mcpl. Mgmt. Assts. So. Calif., Fed. Lab. Consortium Exec. Coun., Acad. Polit. Sci., Internat. Soc. for the Systems Scis., Assn. MBA Execs., Tech. Transfer Soc., Internat. Fedn. for Systems Rsch., Phi Kappa Phi, Pi Gamma Mu. Home: PO Box 273 Port Hueneme CA 93044-0273 Office: PO Box 447 Camarillo CA 93011-0447

SULLIVAN, PATRICIA, journalist; b. Joliet, Ill., Feb. 2, 1955; d. William L. and Elizabeth J. (Reed) S. BA, Marquette U., 1977. Reporter Herald-News, Joliet, 1977-78, Ft. Lauderdale (Fla.) Sun-Sentinel, 1979-84; reporter, editor Missoulian, Missoula, Mont., 1985-95; freelancer Sullivan Freelance, Missoula, 1995-96; online editor Mercury Ctr., San Jose, Calif., 1996—. John S. Knight Fellow, Stanford U., 1992-93.

SULLIVAN, ROBERT SCOTT, architect; b. Alexandria, La., Sept. 8, 1955; s. Robert Wallace and Harriette Henri (Fedric) S. BA cum laude, Tulane U., 1979, BArch, 1979. Registered architect, N.Y., Calif., La.; cert. Nat. Coun. of Archtl. Registrations Bds. Staff architect Cavitt, McKnight, Weymouth, Inc., Houston, 1979-81, Hardy, Holzman, Pfeiffer Assocs., N.Y.C., 1981-83; ptnr. Sullivan, Briggs Assocs., N.Y.C., 1983-86; cons. Butler, Rogers, Baskett, N.Y.C., 1985-86; prin. R. Scott Sullivan AIA, Berkeley, Calif., 1986-89; ptnr. Talbott Sullivan Archs., Albany, Calif., 1989-94, Scott Sullivan, Arch., Berkeley, 1994—; cons. Neometry Graphics, N.Y.C., 1983-86, dir, 1986—; bd. dirs. Middleton/Sullivan Inc., Alexandria, 1981—. Works include specific design projects at N.Y. Hist. Soc. exhibit Grand Cen. Terminal, N.Y.C., 1982, The Houston Sch. of Performing Visual Arts, 1980, The Pingry Sch., Bernards Twp., N.J., 1982, Arts Ctr. at Oak Knoll Sch., Summit, N.J., 1986. Vestry St. Mark's Episc. Ch., Berkeley, 1988-89, 97—; bd. dirs. The Parsonage, Episcopal Diocese Calif., 1992-94; cons. Commn. Accessibility, Episcopal Diocese Calif., 1991-93, 95-96. Mem. AIA, Calif. Council Architects, Archtl. League N.Y.C., Nat. Trust for Hist. Preservation, Royal Archtl. Inst. of Can. (assoc.), Tau Sigma Delta. Democrat. Episcopalian.

SULLIVAN, SHAWN E., marketing and sales professional; b. Jan. 3, 1965. BSEE, DeVry Inst., L.A., 1986; postgrad., U. So. Calif. Product mktg. engring. Dense Pac Microsystems, Garden Grove, Calif., 1987-91; sales rep. Olson Tech. Sales, Bellevue, Wash., 1991-93; area sales mgr. Dense Pac Microsystems, Garden Grove, 1993-95, Electronic Designs Inc., L.A., 1995—. Office: Electronic Designs Inc 501 N El Camino Real Ste 200 San Clemente CA 92672-4761

SULLIVAN, STUART FRANCIS, anesthesiologist, educator; b. Buffalo, July 15, 1928; s. Charles S. and Kathryn (Duggan) S.; m. Dorothy Elizabeth Faytol, Apr. 18, 1959; children: John, Irene, Paul, Kathryn. BS, Canisius Coll., 1950; MD, SUNY, Syracuse, 1955. Diplomate Am. Bd. Anesthesiology. Intern Ohio State Univ. Hosp., Columbus, 1955-56; resident Columbia Presbyn. Med. Ctr., 1958-60; instr. anesthesiology Columbia U. Coll. Physicians and Surgeons, N.Y.C., 1961-62, assoc., 1962-64, asst. prof., 1964-69, assoc. prof., 1969-73; prof. dept. anesthesiology UCLA, 1973-91, vice chair anesthesiology, 1974-77, exec. vice chair, 1977-90, acting chmn., 1983-84, 87-88, 90-91, prof. emeritus, 1991—. Served to capt. M.C., USAR, 1956-58. Fellow NIH, 1960-61; recipient research career devel. award NIH, 1966-69. Mem. Assn. Univ. Anesthetists, Am. Physiol. Soc., Am. Soc. Anesthesiologists. Home: 101 Foxtail Dr Santa Monica CA 90402-2047 Office: UCLA Sch Medicine Dept Anesthesiology Los Angeles CA 90024

SULLIVAN, THOMAS JAMES, retired manufacturing company executive; b. Franklin, N.H., Mar. 26, 1923; s. James J. and Helen (Mullin) S.; m. Anne Clark, Aug. 31, 1963. A.B., Holy Cross Coll., 1947; J.D., Harvard U., 1949. With Gen. Dynamics Corp., 1949-61, asst. div. mgr., 1959-61; sr. assoc. Harbridge House, Cambridge, Mass., 1961-63; with Hydraulic Research & Mfg. Co., Valencia, Calif., 1963-71; v.p. Hydraulic Research & Mfg. Co., 1964-68, exec. v.p., 1968-69, pres., 1969-71; v.p. Textron, Inc., Providence, 1971-73; pres. Walker/Parkersburg (W. Va.) Co., 1973-81, Sprague Meter, Bridgeport, Conn., 1981-84, Dimetrics Inc., Diamond Springs, Calif., 1984-86. Served with USAAF, 1943-46. Fellow Nat. Contract Mgmt. Assn. Home: 2186 Augusta Ct San Luis Obispo CA 93401

SULLIVAN-BOYLE, KATHLEEN MARIE, association executive; b. Tulsa, Feb. 9, 1958; d. Thomas Anthony and Jeanne Lee (Agnew) Sullivan; m. Thomas C. Boyle. BS in Polit. Sci., Ariz. State U., 1980; MA in Govt., Coll. William and Mary, 1982. Sec. Ariz. Rep. Party, Phoenix, 1980-81; rsch. asst. Pete Dunn for U.S. Senate Campaign, Phoenix, 1982; adminstra. sec Ariz. Corp. Commn., Phoenix, 1983-84; pub. relations dir. Epoch Univs. Publ., Phoenix, 1984-86; membership dir. Tempe (Ariz.) C. of C., 1986-93; dir. legis. affairs, exec. dir. Ariz. Pharmacy Assn., 1994—. Sec., chmn. publicity Cactus Wren Rep. Women, Phoenix, 1983-89, Fiesta Bowl; bd. dirs. Tempe Leadership, Tempe YMCA; bd. govs. Tempe St. Luke's Hosp. Mem. Publ Rels. Soc. Am., Soroptimist (past pres.), Tempe C. of C. (bd. gos.), Alpha Phi (chmn. conv.). Republican. Office: Ariz Pharmacy Assn 1845 E Southern Tempe AZ 85282-5831

SULLWOLD, HAROLD H., geologist; b. St. Paul, Dec. 22, 1916; s. Harold Herman and Emma Cornelia (Sundkvist) S.; m. Mayla Carol Sandbeck, Aug. 31, 1940; children—Eric Verner, Wendy. B.A., UCLA, 1939, M.A., 1940, Ph.D., 1959. Registered profl. engr., Calif.; registered profl. geologist, Calif. Geologist, U.S. Geol. Survey, western states, 1942-44, W.R. Cabeen & Assoc., North Hollywood, Calif., 1944-52, G.H. Roth & Assoc., North Hollywood, 1960-80; tchr. UCLA, 1952-59; ind. geologist, L.A., 1958-60, Carpinteria, Calif., 1980-96; adj. prof. U. So. Calif., 1974. Author, publ.: cartoons Andy Cline, 1983. Editor: O & G Fields of L.A. and Ventura, 1958; regional editor: Stratigraphic Oil and Gas, 1972. Contbr. papers to profl. publs. Pres. Concha Loma Improvement Assn., Carpinteria, 1975; chmn. continuing edn. com. Coast Geol. Soc., Ventura, Calif., 1977; chmn. bldg. fund Carpinteria Hist. Soc., 1982-85; dir. Carpinteria County Water Dist., 1983-93; geologist pro bono, 1993—; dir. Thomas Dibblee Geol. Found., 1988—. Fellow Geol. Soc. Am.; mem. Am. Assn. Petroleum Geologists (emeritus; hon. life, v.p. Pacific sect., field trip chmn. 1958, ho. of dels. 1983—), Am. Inst. Profl. Geologists (emeritus; screening chmn. 1968—). Republican. Presbyterian. Avocations: golf, travel, sketching. Home: 900 Calle De Los Amigos Apt N11 Santa Barbara CA 93105-4436

SULTAN, LARRY, photographer. BA, U. Calif., San Francisco, 1968; MFA, San Francisco Art Inst., 1973. One-man shows include Ohio Silver Gallery, L.A., 1972, U. Calif. Gallery, San Francisco, 1974, Ctr. for Creative Photography, Tucson, 1977, Fogg Art Mus., Cambridge, Mass., 1978, Light Gallery, L.A., 1981, Blue Sky Gallery, Portland, Oreg., 1981, Portland (Maine) Sch. Art, 1982, U. Colo. Art Gallery, Boulder, 1982, R.I. Sch. Design, Providence, 1987, Janet Borden, Inc., N.Y.C., 1989, Headlands Ctr. for Arts, Sausalito, Calif., 1989, The Exploratorium, San Francisco, 1990, San Jose (Calif.) Mus. Art, 1992, Stephen Wirtz Gallery, San Francisco, 1992, Mus. Contemporary Art, San Diego, 1994, Chgo. Cultural Ctr., The Corcoran Gallery of Art, Washington, Scottsdale Ctr. Arts, Ariz., Bronx Mus. Art, 1996; exhibited in group shows at Fogg Art Mus., 1976, La Mamelle Gallery, San Francisco, 1976, San Francisco Mus. Modern Art, 1977, 82, 85, 89, 91, L.A. Inst. of Contemporary Art, 1978, Chgo. Mus. Contemporary Art, 1979, Santa Barbara Mus. Art, 1981, Seibu Mus. Art, Tokyo, 1982, Univ. Art Mus., Berkeley, Calif., 1983, Internat. Ctr. Photography, N.Y.C., 1984, Barbican Art Gallery, London, 1985, Mus. Modern Art, N.Y.C., 1985, 89, 91, U. Colo. Gallery, 1986, Los Angeles County Mus. Art, 1987, Burden Gallery, N.Y.C., 1988, Northlight Gallery, Tempe, Ariz., 1990, Birmingham (Ala.) Mus. Art, 1990, Met. Mus. Art, N.Y.C., 1991, Milw. Art Mus., 1991, Stephen Wirtz Gallery, San Francisco, 1991, 96, Dartmouth Coll. Art Gallery, Hanover, N.H., 1996, List Art Ctr., Providence, 1991, Transamerica Pyramid, San Francisco, Presentation House, Ctr. Visual and Performing Arts, Vancouver, BC, U. Art Mus. Berkeley, Calif., Weatherspoon Art Gallery, Greenville, N.C., 1995, others; represented in permanent collections at Art Inst. Chgo., Bibliotheque Nationale, Birmingham Mus. Art, Ctr. for Creative Photography, Chase Manhattan Bank, Frods Regional D'Art contemporain, J. Paul Getty Mus., The Mus. Modern Art, Milw. Art Mus., The Met. Mus. Art, The Nat. Mus. Art, San Francisco Mus. Modern Art, San Jose (Calif.) Mus. Art., U. Ala., U. Colo. Recipient Art in Pub. Places grant Nat. Endowment for the Arts, 1976, Photography fellowship Nat. Endowment for the Arts, 1977, 80, 92, Spl. Projects grant Calif. Arts Coun., 1978, Guggenheim fellowship, 1983, Artists fellowship Marin Arts Coun., 1986, Engelhard award Inst. Contemporary Art, 1988, Fleishhaker Found. Eureka fellowship Calif. Arts Coun., 1989, Pub. Arts award Oakland Cultural Arts, 1990, Louis Comfort Tiffany fellowship, 1991. Office: 49 Geary St San Francisco CA 94108-5705

SUMMER, LYLE C., state agency economist, economics educator; b. Rexburg, Idaho, Apr. 3, 1938; s. Benjamin Earl and Laurene (Christensen) S.; m. Carole Winters, May 25, 1957; children: Jeffery, Serri, Quin, Blake, Holly, Cody. AS, Ricks Coll., 1969; BS, Utah State U., 1972, MS, 1972. Mgr., co-owner Family Farm, Rexburg, 1962-68; economist Soil Conservation Svc., USDA, Salt Lake City, 1968-76; chief economist Utah Divsn. Water Resources, Salt Lake City, 1976—; adj. prof. econ. dept., Utah State U., Logan, 1990—; appraiser, cons. Water Appraisal Svcs. Co., West Jordan, Utah, 1986—. Contbr. articles to profl. jours. Chairperson West Jordan Planning and Zoning Commn., 1980-84; candidate for mayor City of West Jordan, 1988, mem. budget com., 1994. With USMC, 1957-60. Mem. Am. Water Resources Assn. (pres. Utah chpt. 1987). Republican. Mem. LDS Ch. Home: 3961 W 8010 S West Jordan UT 84088-4337 Office: Utah Divsn Water Resources 1636 W North Temple Salt Lake City UT 84116-3156

SUMMERS, CAROL, artist; b. Kingston, N.Y., Dec. 26, 1925; s. Ivan Franklin and Theresa (Jones) S.; m. Elaine Smithers, Oct. 2, 1954 (div. Aug. 1967); 1 son, Kyle; m. Joan Ward, May 6, 1974. B.A., Bard Coll., 1951, D.F.A. (hon.), 1974. Tchr. Hunter Coll., Sch. Visual Arts, Haystack Mountain Sch. Crafts, Bklyn. Mus. Art Sch., Pratt Graphic Art Ctr., Chelterham Twp. Art Ctr., Valley Stream Community Art Ctr., U. Pa., Columbia Coll., U. Calif., Santa Cruz, San Francisco Art Inst., U. Utah, Logan, Art Study Abroad, Paris, Casa de Espiritus Allegres Marfil, Mex., USIS workshop tour, India, 1974, 79. Represented in permanent collections at, Mus. Modern Art, Bklyn. Mus., N.Y. Pub. Libr., Libr. of Congress, Nat. Gallery, Victoria and Albert Mus., London, Bibliotheque Nationale, Paris, Kinstmuseum, Basil, Lugan (Switzerland) Art Mus. Grenchen (Switzerland) Art Mus., Malmo (Sweden) Mus., Los Angeles County Mus., Phila. Mus., Balt. Mus., Seattle Mus., Boston Mus., Art Inst. Chgo., Am. embassies in Russia, Can., India, Thailand, Fed. Republic Germany and Eng.; traveling exhibit, Mus. Modern Art, 1964-66; retrospective exhbn. Brooklyn Mus., 1977, Nassau County Mus. Art, 1990, Belles Artes, San Miquel de Allende, Mex., 1992, Miami U. Art Mus., Oxford, Ohio, 1995. Served with USMCR, 1944-48, PTO. Italian govt. study grantee, 1954-55; Louis Comfort Tiffany Found. fellow, 1955, 60; John Simon Guggenheim Found. fellow, 1959; Fulbright fellow, Italy, 1961; Coun. for Internat. Exch. Scholars rsch. grantee, India, 1993-94. Mem. NAD, Calif. Soc. Printmakers. Address: 2817 Smith Grade Santa Cruz CA 95060-9764

SUMMERS, CATHLEEN ANN, film producer; b. Chgo.; d. Cecil Paul and Elizabeth Ann S.; m. Patrick Timothy Crowley. BA, U. So. Calif., 1973. Film editor, comml. producer, dir.'s asst. Roman Polanski, Rome, 1972; story editor Albert S. Ruddy Prodns. Paramount Pictures, L.A., 1973-74; exec. asst. Columbia Pictures, Burbank, Calif., 1974; story editor Columbia Pictures, 1974-76; devel. exec., v.p., producer Martin Ransohoff Prodns. Columbia Pictures, 1976; sr. v.p. Tri-Star Pictures, Century City, Calif., 1984-87; motion picture producer Cathleen Summers Prodns., L.A., 1989—; motion picture producer, ptnr. Summers-Kouf Prodns., Burbank, 1986-87; motion picture producer Cathleen Summers Prodns., L.A., 1987, Summers-Quaid Prodns., Century City, Culver City, Calif., 1988—. Producer: (motion picture) Stakeout, 1987, DOA, 1991, Vital Signs, 1990, Mystery Date, 1991, Dogfight, 1991, The Sandlot, 1993, Stakeout II, 1993. Co-founder Diane Thomas Scholarship-UCLA, 1988—. Mem. Am. Film Inst. (pres. 3d Decade Coun. 1995, 96).

SUMMERS, STANLEY EUGENE, mechanical engineer; b. Sterling, Colo.; s. Matthew Marion and Hazel J. (Snider) S.; m. Dorothy E. Hanneman, June 15, 1944 (div. Oct. 1977); children: Daniel E., Shirley A.; m. Jaclyn A. Marquart, Oct. 15, 1977; children: Stephanie Ann, Jeffrey E. BSME, UCLA, 1964. Mech. engr. Interstate Engring., El Segundo, Calif., 1947-59, Ametek Calmec, L.A., 1959-90, Ketema A&E, El Cajon, Calif., 1990—. Recipient Douglas Aircraft VIP award, 1968, NASA Achievement award, 1971, MacDonnell Douglas Pres.'s award, 1991, Spirit of Excellence award, 1992. Mem. ASME. Republican. Home: 2576 Katherine Ct El Cajon CA 92020-2062 Office: Ketema A&E 790 Greenfield Dr El Cajon CA 92021-3101

SUMMERS, WILLIAM KOOPMANS, neuropsychiatrist, researcher; b. Jefferson City, Mo., Apr. 14, 1944; s. Joseph S. and Amy Lydia (Koopmans) S.; m. Angela Forbes McGonigle, Oct. 2, 1972(div. Apr. 1985); children: Elisabeth Stuart, Wilhelmina Derek. Student, Westminster Coll., Fulton, Mo., 1962-64; BS, U. Mo., 1966; MD, Washington U., St. Louis, 1971. Internal medicine intern Barnes Hosp-Washington U., St. Louis, 1971-72; resident in internal medicine Jewish Hosp., St. Louis, 1972-73; resident in psychiatry Rsch. Hosp., St. Louis, 1973-76; asst. prof. U. Pitts., 1976-78, U. So. Calif., L.A., 1978-82; asst. clin. prof. rsch. UCLA, 1982-88; rschr. Arcadia, Calif., 1988-92, Albuquerque, 1992—. Patentee in field. Mem. AMA, ACP, Am. Psychiat. Assn., Soc. Neurosci., N.Y. Acad. Scis., Am. Fedn. Clin. Rsch. Episcopalian. Office: 201 Cedar St SE Ste 404 Albuquerque NM 87106-4924

SUMRALL, HARRY, journalist; b. Palestine, Tex., Oct. 15, 1950; s. Harry Glenn and Sherea Sue (Selden) S.; m. Leslie Leizear, Dec. 19, 1954; 1 child, Samuel Harry. BA, George Mason U., 1974. Writer, critic The Washington Post, 1978-81; contbg. writer The New Republic, Washington, 1979; assoc. editor Rock Concert Mag., Washington, 1979; music writer San Jose (Calif.) Mercury News/Knight Ridder News Svc., 1982—; advisor New Music Am., Washington, 1983; lectr., guest San Francisco State U., 1991; guest critic Sta. KGO, San Francisco, 1991—. Author: Pioneers of Rock and Roll, 1994, Giants of Country Music, 1995; contbg. author: New Grove Dictionary of American Music, 1983; broadcaster: (radio program) Rockology, 1989. Paneslist Chatauquas for Congress, Washington, 1979. Fellow New Music Am., 1980. Office: San Jose Mercury News 750 Ridder Park Dr San Jose CA 95190*

SUN, BILL KAWO-HWA, energy consulting company executive; b. Shanghai, China, Oct. 11, 1944; came to U.S., 1967; s. Pao-Fa and Wen-Gin (Chen) S.; m. Meiling Tang, Aug. 10, 1969; children: Jennifer, Christine, Valerie. BS, Nat. Taiwan U., 1966; MS, U. Ky., 1969; PhD, U. Calif., Berkeley, 1973. Registered profl. engr. Tech. leader, sr. engr. GE Co., San Jose, Calif., 1972-77; program & project mgr. Elec. Power Rsch. Inst., Palo Alto, Calif., 1977-94; pres. Sunutech, Inc., Los Altos, Calif., 1994—; advisor to pres. Taiwan Power Co., Taipei, 1994—; advisor to chmn. Rep. of China Atomic Energy Coun., Taipei, 1995—; com. chmn. Internat. Atomic Energy Agy., Vienna, Austria, 1990—. Contbr. articles to profl. jours. Bd. dirs. Sister City Com., Los Altos, 1996. Mem. ASME, Am. Nuclear Soc. (life), N.Am. Tiawanese Engrs. Assn., Chinese Am. Econ. & Tech. Devel. Assn. (pres. 1993-94, bd. dirs.), Chinese Inst. Engrs. (pres., chmn. bd. dirs. 1989-90). Home: 12444 Robleda Rd Los Altos Hills CA 94022 Office: Sunutech Inc PO Box 978 Los Altos CA 94023

SUN, CHARLES CHANGKYUN, minister, college president; b. Seoul, Republic of Korea, Feb. 18, 1931; came to U.S., 1959-61, 65—; s. Chongwhan and Shyin A. (Kim) S.; m. Alice Aiwon Yoon, Apr. 5, 1954; children: Susanna Sun Choi, John H., Mary Sun Roh. BA, Tanbook U., 1955; M of Religious Edn., Conservative Bapt. Theol. Sem., 1966; DD (hon.), U. L.A., 1982. Ordained to ministry Korean Methodist Ch., 1954. Prof. Korean Meth. Theol. Sem., 1961-64; min. Korean Christian Ch., Denver, 1968—; comptr. World of Sleep Mgmt., Inc., Denver, 1970-81; chmn. bd. Korean Sch., Denver, 1972—; owner Korean Christian Book Ctr., 1981—; pres. Bible Correspondence Coll., 1981—, Christian World Mission Coll., 1982—. Contbr. articles to newspapers and mags. Served as chaplain Republic of Korea, 1951-55. Home: PO Box 6715 Denver CO 80206-0715 Office: Korean Christian Ch 1495 S University Blvd Denver CO 80210-2406

SUN, TERESA CHI-CHING, foreign languages educator; b. Chingdao, Shandon, China, Dec. 24, 1935; came to U.S., 1959, naturalized, 1969; d. Shin-Ching and Yu-Tze (Lee) Wang; m. Terry Tseng-Yao Sun, Dec. 12, 1959; children: Larry, Myra Sun Chung. BA in Chinese Lit., Taiwan Normal U., 1957; MA in Edn., UCLA, 1964, postgrad., 1972-76; postgrad., Claremont Grad. Sch. Edn., 1978; D in Edn., Seton Hall U., 1995. Cert. std. tchg. credential with specialization in jr. coll. tchg., Calif. Lectr. Mandarin Tng. Ctr. for Fgn. Scholars, Taiwan Normal U., 1956-57; tchr. Chinese lit. Taipei 1st Girl's H.S., 1957-58, Subordinate H.S. of Taiwan Normal U., 1958-69; tchg. asst. dept. East Asian studies U. So. Calif., L.A., 1962-64; instr. dept. fgn. langs. evening divsn. L.A. City Coll., 1965-67; instr., asst. prof. dept. fgn. langs. Calif. State U., L.A., 1967-78; intern Ctr. for Internat. Edn., Calif. State U., Long Beach, 1986-87; vis. lectr., adj. asst. prof. dept. fgn. langs. Whittier (Calif.) Coll., 1991—; mem. com. to administer exam. for high sch. tchrs. in Chinese, L.A. Unified Sch. Dist., 1971; mem. adv. coun. on bilingual edn. HEW, 1974-77. V.p. China Soc. So. Calif., 1973-74, pres., 1975-78, 89-91, program chmn., 1978-79, 82-83, 89-91; program chmn. Rolling Hills Estates Women's Club, 1981-82, 95-97, treas., 1989; trustee Palos Verdes Libr. Dist., Palos Verdes Peninsula, Calif., 1989-93. Named hon. citizen City of Albuquerque, 1976, City of Austin, Tex., 1977. Mem. Assn. Asian Studies (standing com. Asian studies on Pacific Coast 1977-80), Modern and Classical Langs. Assn. So. Calif. (chmn. for program 1970-75). Republican. Home: 28717 Trailriders Dr Rancho Palos Verdes CA 90275

SUNDBERG, NORMAN DALE, psychology educator; b. Aurora, Nebr., Sept. 15, 1922; s. Cedric William and Nellie Mae (Akerson) S.; m. Donna Varner, Sept. 25, 1948; children: Kent Alan, Gregory Paul, Scott Donald, Mark William. BA, U. Nebr., 1947; MA, U. Minn., 1949, PhD, 1952. Teaching asst. instr. U. Minn., Mpls., 1947-52; from asst. to prof. U. Oreg., Eugene, 1952-88, prof. emeritus, 1988—; vis. prof. U. Calif., Berkeley, 1959-61, LaTrobe U., Melbourne, Australia, 1976, 80, Macquarie U., Sydney, Australia, 1980, U. Hong Kong, 1984; dean Wallace Sch. Cmty. Svc. and Pub. Affairs, U. Oreg., Eugene, 1967-72; cons. VA, 1953-88; dir. clin. and cmty. psychology program U. Oreg., 1977-80, 84-88; lectr., cons. U.S. Ednl. Found., New Delhi, 1965-66, 73; external examiner U. Hong Kong, 1992-96. Author: Assessment of Persons, 1977; (with Leona Tyler) Clinical Psychology, 1962; (with Leona Tyler, Julian Taplin) Clinical Psychology, 1973, 83; contbr. articles to profl. jours.; editorial com. Annual Rev. Psychology, 1976-80. Field assessment officer Peace Corps, Oreg., 1963. 1st lt. arty. U.S. Army, 1943-46. Grantee Fulbright-Hays, 1965-66, 73. Fellow Am. Psychol. Assn. (ethics com. 1970-73), Soc. Personality Assessment (Walter Klopfer award 1987); mem. Oreg. Psychol. Assn. (pres. 1962-63), Internat. Coun. Psychologists, Internat. Assn. Cross-Cultural Psychology. Democrat. Office: Univ Oreg Dept Psychology Eugene OR 97403

SUNDEL, HARVEY H., marketing research analyst and consultant; b. Bronx, N.Y., July 24, 1944; s. Louis and Pauline (Brotman) S. BBA, St. Mary's U., San Antonio, 1969, MBA, 1970; PhD, St. Louis U., 1974. Asst. dir. research Lone Star Brewery, San Antonio, 1970-71; cons. Tri-Mark, Inc., San Antonio, 1972-73; asst. prof. mktg. Lewis and Clark Coll., Godfrey, Ill., 1973-74; asst. prof. mktg. Met. State Coll., Denver, 1974-77, chmn., prof. mktg., 1977-86; pres. Sundel Rsch., Inc., Denver, 1976—; cons. Frederick Ross Co., Denver, 1979-84, U.S. West Direct, Denver, 1986—, Monsanto Chems. Co., St. Louis, 1985—, Mountain Bell, Denver, 1979-88, U.S. West Comm., Denver, 1988—, AT&T, 1986-91, Melco Industries, 1987-90, Norwest Banks, 1990-94, PACE Membership Warehouse, 1992-93, U.S. Meat Export Fedn., 1992—, G.D. Searle, 1996—; expert witness in legal cases. Contbr. papers and proceedings to profl. jours. Com. mem. Mile High United Way, Denver, 1975-80, Allied Jewish Fedn. Cmty. Rels. Action Com., 1995—. Jewish. Home: 1616 Glen Bar Dr Lakewood CO 80215-3014 Office: Sundel Rsch Inc 1150 Delaware St Denver CO 80204-3608

SUNDT, HARRY WILSON, construction company executive; b. Woodbury, N.J., July 5, 1932; s. Thoralf Mauritz and Elinor (Stout) S.; m. Dorothy Van Gilder, June 26, 1954; children: Thomas D., Perri Lee Sundt Touche, Gerald W. BS in Bus. Adminstrn., U. Ariz., 1954, postgrad., 1957-59. Salesman ins. VanGilder Agys., Denver, 1956-57; apprentice carpenter M.M. Sundt Constrn. Co., Tucson, 1957-58, estimator, 1958-59; adminstrv. asst. M.M. Sundt Constrn. Co., Vandenberg AFB, 1959-62; sr. estimator M.M. Sundt Constrn. Co., Tucson, 1962-64, div. mgr., 1964-65, exec. v.p., gen. mgr., 1965-75, pres., chmn., 1975-79; pres., chmn. Sundt Corp., Tucson, 1980-83, chmn., chief exec. officer, 1983—; bd. dirs. Tucson Electric Power Co., Nations Energy Co. Pres. Tucson Airport Authority, 1982; bd. dirs. U. Ariz. Found. 1981. 1st lt. U.S. Army, 1954-56. Recipient Disting. Citizen award U. Ariz., 1982, Centennial Medallion award, 1989. Mem. Tucson Country Club. Republican. Episcopalian. Home: 6002 E San Leandro Tucson AZ 85715-3014 Office: Sundt Corp PO Box 26685 4101 E Irvington Rd Tucson AZ 85714-2118

SUPAN, RICHARD MATTHEW, health facility administrator; b. Palo Alto, Calif., June 22, 1953; s. James Arthur and Nancy Ann (Rhein) S.; m. Bernadette Joan Bayer, Sept. 8, 1979; children: Raymond, Valerie, Joanna. AA, Foothill Coll., 1973; BSC, Santa Clara U., 1975, MBA, 1979. Cost acctg. supr. Electron Devices div. Litton Industries, San Carlos, Calif., 1975-78; cost acctg. mgr. Microwave Tube div. Varian Assocs., Palo Alto, Calif., 1978-81, ops. controller, 1981-84; dir. acctg. Varian Assocs., Palo Alto, Calif., 1984-85; controller Electron Device & Systems Group, Varian Assocs., Palo Alto, Calif., 1985-89, Oncology Systems, Varian Assocs., Palo Alto, Calif., 1989-95; v.p. ops. & fin. Intraop Med., Inc., Santa Clara, Calif., 1995—. Mem. Beta Gamma Sigma (hon.). Home: 5915 Amapola Dr San Jose CA 95129-3058

SUPPES, PATRICK, statistics, education, philosophy and psychology educator; b. Tulsa, Mar. 17, 1922; s. George Biddle and Ann (Costello) S.; m. Joan Farmer, Apr. 16, 1946 (div. 1970); children: Patricia, Deborah, John Biddle; m. Joan Sieber, Mar. 29, 1970 (div. 1973); m. Christine Johnson, May 26, 1979; children: Alexandra Christine, Michael Patrick. BS, U. Chgo., 1943; PhD (Wendell T. Bush fellow), Columbia U., 1950; LLD, U. Nijmegen, Netherlands, 1979; Dr. honoris causa, Académie de Paris, U. Paris V, 1982. Instr., Stanford U., 1950-52, asst. prof., 1952-55, assoc. prof., 1955-59, prof. philosophy, statistics, edn. and psychology, 1959-92, prof. emeritus; founder, chief exec. officer Computer Curriculum Corp., 1967-90. Author: Introduction to Logic, 1957, Axiomatic Set Theory, 1960, Sets and Numbers, books 1-6, 1966, Studies in the Methodology and Foundations of Science, 1969, A Probabilistic Theory of Causality, 1970, Logique du Probable, 1981, Probabilistic Metaphysics, 1984, Estudios de Filosofía y Metodologí de la Ciencia, 1988, Language for Humans and Robots, 1991, Models and Methods in the Philosophy of Science, 1993; (with Davidson and Siegel) Decision Making, 1957, (with Richard C. Atkinson) Markov Learning Models for Multiperson Interactions, 1960, (with Shirley Hill) First Course in Mathematical Logic, 1964, (with Edward J. Crothers) Experiments on Second-Language Learning, 1967, (with Max Jerman and Dow Brian) Computer-assisted Instruction, 1965-66, Stanford Arithmetic Program, 1968, (with D. Krantz, R.D. Luce and A. Tversky) Foundations of Measurement, Vol. 1, 1971, (with M. Morningstar) Computer-Assisted Instruction at Stanford, 1966-68, 1972, (with B. Searle and J. Friend) The Radio Mathematics Project: Nicaragua, 1974-75, 1976 (with D. Krantz, R.D. Luce and A. Tversky) Foundations of Measurement, Vol. 2, 1989, Vol. 3, 1990, (with Colleen Crangle) Language and Learning for Robots, 1994, (with Mario Zanotti) Foundations of Probability with Applications, 1996. Served to capt. USAAF, 1942-46. Recipient Nicholas Murray Butler Silver medal Columbia, 1965, Disting. Sci. Contbr. award Am. Psychol. Assn., 1972, Tchrs. Coll. medal for disting. service, 1978, Nat. medal Sci. NSF, 1990; Center for Advanced Study Behavioral Scis. fellow, 1955-56; NSF fellow, 1957-58. Fellow AAAS, Am. Psychol. Assn., Am. Acad. Arts and Scis., Assn. Computing Machinery; mem. NAS, Math. Assn. Am., Psychometric Soc., Am. Philos. Assn., Am. Philos. Soc., Assn. Symbolic Logic, Am. Math Soc., Académie Internationale de Philosophie des Scis. (titular), Nat. Acad. Edn. (pres. 1973-77), Am. Psychol. Assn., Internat. Inst. Philosophy, Finnish Acad. Sci. and Letters, Internat. Union History and Philosophy of Sci. (div. logic, methodology and philosophy of sci., pres. 1975-79), Am. Ednl. Research Assn. (pres. 1973-74), Croatian Acad. Scis. (corr.), Russian Acad. Edn. (fgn.), Norwegian Acad. Sci. and Letters (fgn.), European Acad. Scis. and Arts, Chilean Acad. Scis., Sigma Xi.

SURABIAN, DENNIS G., food products executive; b. 1941. With Crocker Bank, San Francisco, 1962-63; various positions Surabian Packing Co., Reedley, Calif., 1963—, now pres. Office: Surabian Packing Co Inc 18700 E South Ave Reedley CA 93654-9711

SURBER, RUSSELL JAY, retired foreign service officer; b. Glendale, Calif., Aug. 4, 1942; s. Marion Shelby Surber and Vinola Christine (Larson) Neavill; m. Denise Elizabeth Girard, June 18, 1966. BS, Calif. State Poly. U., 1965; MA, U. Hawaii, 1982. Polit. officer bur. polit./mil. affairs U.S. Dept. State, Washington, 1977-78, spl. asst. to dept. counselor, 1978-80, dir. Pacific Island affairs, 1985-88, dir. jr. officer program, 1988-90, dir. Egyptian affairs, 1991-93, sr. advisor to sec., 1993-94; dep. amb. U.S. Embassy, Suva, Fiji, 1981-85; ret., 1994; writer and lectr., 1994—. Mem. Am. Fgn. Svc. Assn., Kiwanis. Home and Office: 507 18th St Paso Robles CA 93446

SURFACE, STEPHEN WALTER, water treatment chemist, environmental protection specialist; b. Dayton, Ohio, Feb. 25, 1943; s. Lorin Wilfred and Virginia (Marsh) S.; m. Suzanne MacDonald, Aug. 29, 1964 (div.); 1 child, Jennifer Nalani; m. Sinfrosa Garay, Sept. 16, 1978; children: Maria Lourdes, Stephanie Alcantara. BS, Otterbein Coll., 1965; MA, U. So. Calif., 1970; postgrad., U. Hawaii, 1971. Cert. profl. chemist. Tchr. Hawaii State Dept. Edn., Honolulu, 1970-71; staff chemist Del Monte Corp., Honolulu, 1971; head chemist USNPearl Harbor, Honolulu, 1971-76; staff chemist USN Pearl Harbor, Honolulu, 1976-90; chief office installation svcs., environ. protection Def. Logistics Agy., Camp Smith, Hawaii, 1990—. Contbr. articles to profl. jours. Recipient DuPont Teaching award, U. So. Calif., 1966. Fellow Am. Inst. Chemists; mem. Am. Chem. Soc., Am. Def. Preparedness Assn., N.Y. Acad. Scis., Sigma Xeta, Phi Lambda Upsilon. Democrat. Methodist. Home: 94-1139 Noheaiki St Waipahu HI 96797-4138 Office: Def Logistics Agy DPAC-W Camp Smith HI 96861-4110

SURRELL, KEVIN JOEL, insurance company official; b. L.A., Mar. 7, 1966; s. Joe Willis and Marie Louise (Johns) S.; m. Tracey Janelle Urling, Aug. 13, 1988; 1 child, Chantal Miria. BA in Psychology, UCLA, 1989. Field claim rep. Farmers Ins. Group, Glendale, Calif., 1989-91; realtor Internat. Real Estate Group, Walnut, Calif., 1990-92; realtor, CEO, Century 21 Young, West Covina, Calif., 1992-93; claims rep. ICW/Explorer Ins., Burbank, Calif., 1994-95; asst. mgr. Western Gen. Ins., Encino, 1995—. Mem. Am. Tchrs. Martial Arts Assn., Am. Kenpo Karate Assn (5th degree black belt), Mary B. Thorne Scholarship Club. Office: Western Gen Ins 16501 Ventura Blvd Ste 200 Encino CA 91436-2066

SUSSKIND, CHARLES, engineering educator, author, publishing executive; b. Prague, Czech Republic; came to U.S., 1945, naturalized, 1946; s. Bruno Bronislav and Gertruda (Seger) S.; m. Teresa Gabriel, May 1, 1945; children: Pamela Susskind Pettler, Peter Gabriel, Amanda Frances. Student, City U., London, 1939-40; B.S., Calif. Inst. Tech., 1948; M.Engring., Yale U., 1949, Ph.D., 1951. Research asst. Yale U., 1949-51; research assoc. Stanford U., 1951-55, lectr., asst. dir. Microwave Lab., 1953-55; mem. faculty U. Calif., Berkeley, 1955—; prof. U. Calif., 1964-91; prof. emeritus U. Calif., Berkeley, 1991—; asst. dean Coll. Engring. U. Calif., 1964-68, also statewide adminstr., 1969-74; vis. prof. U. London, 1961-62, U. Geneva, Switzerland, 1968-69; cons. EPA Sci. Adv. Bd., 1982-92; cons. electronics industry, govt., publishers; dir. San Francisco Press, Inc. Author: (with M. Chodorow) Fundamentals of Microwave Electronics, 1964, (with L. Schell) Exporting Technical Education, 1968, Understanding Technology, 1973, 74, 85 (transl. into Dutch, French, Italian, Korean, Spanish, Indian edit. in English), Twenty-Five Engineers and Inventors, 1976, (with F. Kurylo) Ferdinand Braun, 1981, (with M.E. Rowbottom) Electricity and Medicine: History of their Interaction, 1984, Janáček and Brod, 1985, Heinrich Hertz: A Short Life, 1995; editor: (with M. Hertz) Heinrich Hertz: Memoirs, Letters, Diaries, bilingual edit., 1977; editor-in-chief Ency. Electronics, 1962. Served with USAAF, 1942-45. Named to Hon. Order Ky. Cols. Fellow IEEE; mem. AAAS, Histor of Sci. Soc., Soc. for History of Tech., Instn. Elec. Engrs. (London), Faculty Club of Berkeley (bd. dirs. 1972-73), Sigma Xi (pres. Berkeley chpt. 1972-73), Tau Beta Pi. Office: U Calif Coll Engring Berkeley CA 94720-1770

SUSSMAN, BRIAN JAY, meteorologist, weather broadcaster; b. L.A., Apr. 3, 1956; s. Alan E. and Beverly A. (Carlson) S.; m. Sue Ann Rittenhouse, June 18, 1978; chilren: Elisa, Samuel, Benjamin. BS, U. Mo., 1978. Reporter, anchor Sta. KCBJ-TV, Columbia, Mo., 1977-80; weather anchor Sta. KOLO-TV, Reno, 1980-83; on-air meteorologist Sta. KNTV-TV, San Jose, Calif., 1983-87, Sta. KDKA-TV, Pitts., 1987-89; substitute weatherman CBS This Morning, N.Y.C., 1988-93; on-air meteorologist Sta. KPIX-TV, San Francisco, 1989—. Co-author: (textbook) For Spacious Skies, 1987, rev. edit., 1989. Recipient Best Weathercast award Radio-TV News Dirs. Assn., 1987, 90-95, AP, 1989, 90-96, Advancement of Learning Through Broadcasting award NEA, 1989. Mem. Am. Meteorol. Soc. (Seal of Approval cert.). Office: Sta KPIX-TV 855 Battery St San Francisco CA 94111-1503

SUSSMAN, NEIL A., lawyer; b. N.Y.C., Jan. 26, 1956; s. Herbert and Ruth S.; m. Suzanne R. Thompson, Aug. 31, 1990; children: Annabelle, Franklin. BS in Econs., U. Pa., 1978; JD, U. Wash., 1982. Bar: Wash. 1982. Atty. pvt. practice, Seattle, 1982—. Mem. Wash. State Bar Assn., King County Bar Assn. Office: 10727 Interlake Ave N Seattle WA 98133-8907

SUSSMAN, WENDY RODRIGUEZ, artist, educator; b. N.Y.C., June 3, 1949. BA, Empire State Coll., 1978; MFA, Bklyn. Coll., 1980. Lectr. Touro Coll., N.Y.C., 1985-86, Pratt Inst., Bklyn., 1987-89; asst. prof. U. Calif., Berkeley, 1989—. One-woman shows include Bowery Gallery, N.Y.C., 1982, 87, D.P. Fong Gallery, San Jose, Calif., 1994, The Jewish Mus., San Francisco, 1996; exhibited in group shows in Bowery Gallery, 1980-88, Platt Gallery U. of Judaism, L.A., 1995, Munson-Williams-Proctor Inst. Mus. Art, 1982, 86, Reading (Pa.) Pub. Mus. and Art Gallery, 1983, Queens Mus., N.Y.C., 1983, Colby Coll. Mus. Art, Waterville, Maine, 1983, Butler Inst. Am. Art, Youngstown, Ohio, 1983, Bklyn. Coll., 1983, Am. Acad. Inst. Arts and Letters, N.Y.C., 1984, Am. Acad. in Rome, 1987, John Berggruen Gallery, San Francisco, 1992, San Francisco Arts Commn. Gallery, 1992, 94, D.P. Fong Gallery, 1994, Boulder Mus. Art, 1995, Gallery Paule Anglin, San Francisco, 1996, Jan Baum Gallery, L.A., 1996. Rome Prize fellow in painting Am. Acad. in Rome, 1986-87, Visual Arts fellow Nat. Endowment for Arts, 1989; Pollock-Krasner grantee Pollock-Krasner Found., 1988. Office: U Calif Berkeley Dept Art Berkeley CA 94720

SUTHERLAND, BRUCE, composer, pianist; b. Daytona Beach, Fla.; s. Kenneth Francis and Norma (Williams) S.; Mus.B. cum laude, U. So. Calif., 1957, Mus.M., 1959; studies with Halsey Stevens, Ellis Kohs, Ethel Leginska, Amparo Iturbi. Harpsichord soloist with Telemann Trio in concert tour, 1969-70; tchr. master class for pianists U. Tex., Austin, 1971; dir. Bach festivals Music Tchrs. Assn. Calif., 1972-73, dir. Artists of Tomorrow Music Festivals Music Tchrs. Assn. Calif., 1984-88, compositions performed in numerous contemporary music festivals in U.S., 1957—; piano faculty Calif. State U. at Northridge, 1977—; tchr. master class for pianists UCLA, 1995—, adjudicator music competitions and auditions Nat. Guild Piano Tchrs. U. So. Calif., 1996, others; dir. Brentwood-Westwood Symphony ann. competition for young artists, 1981-88; composer: Allegro Fanfara for Orch., world premiere conducted by José Iturbi with Bridgeport Symphony Orch., 1970; Saxophone Quartet, 1971; Quintet for Flute, Strings, Piano, 1972; Notturno for Flute and Guitar, 1973; also string trio, piano and vocal works. Recipient grand prize Internat. Competition Louis Moreau Gottschalk, 1970; Stairway of Stars award Music Arts Soc., Santa Monica, 1973; named one of Los Angeles' Finest Piano Tchrs., New West Mag., 1977; honored as Dist. Tchr. of Anders Martinson, presdl. scholar in arts, 1991, Disting. Tchr. White House Commn. on Presidential Scholars, 1991; honored by Nat. Found. Advancement Arts 1989, 91, 93. Mem. Nat. Assn. Am. Composers and Condrs., Music Tchrs. Nat. Assn., Music Tchrs. Assn., Calif. Assn. Profl. Music Tchrs., Pi Kappa Lambda.

SUTHERLAND, DOUGLASS B., former mayor, tent and awning company executive; b. Helena, Mont., May 2, 1937; s. Chris and Marie Sutherland; m. Grace Sutherland, Sept. 5, 1986; children: Karen, Scott. B.A., Central Wash. U., 1959. Program specialist Boeing Co., Tacoma, Wash., 1960-71; owner, pres. Tacoma Tent & Awning, Inc., 1971-86; sec., pres., 1986—. Bd. dirs. Tacoma-Pierce County Bd. Health, Tacoma-Pierce County Employment and Tng. Consortium; mayor City of Tacoma, 1982-89; pres. Puget Sound Regional Coun.; chair Urban County Caucus, Wash. Assn. of Counties. Mem. Assn. Wash. Cities, Tacoma-Pierce County C. of C. Republican. Lodge: Rotary. Office: Tacoma Tent and Awning Inc 121 N G St Tacoma WA 98403-2226 Office: Pierce County Executive 930 Tacoma Ave S Rm 737 Tacoma WA 98402-2102*

SUTHERLAND, JOHN CAMPBELL, pathologist, educator; b. Tamingfu, Hopei, People's Republic of China, Oct. 28, 1921; came to U.S., 1926; s. Francis Campbell and Ann Findlay (Bowman) S.; m. Eunice Lucille Kindschi, June 16, 1950; 1 child, John Mark. AB, N.W. Nazarene Coll., 1941; MD, Med. Coll. Wis., 1946. Intern Milw. Hosp., 1946-47; resident in pathology St. Francis Hosp., Wichita, Kans., 1950-52, Barnes Hosp., St. Louis, 1952-54, Stanford (Calif.) Med. Ctr., 1967-68; gen. practitioner Mangum Clinic, Nampa, Idaho, 1949-50; gen. med. officer Raleigh Fitkin Meml. Hosp., Manzini, Swaziland, 1955-56, Ethel Lucas Meml. Hosp., Acornhoek, South Africa, 1956-61, 62-67; acting head biology dept. N.W. Nazarene Coll., Nampa, 1961-62; head rsch. pathology dept. Balt. Cancer Rsch. Ctr., 1968-74; asst. prof. dept. pathology U. Md., Balt., 1974-76, assoc. prof., 1976-84, mem. grad. faculty, 1982-84; vis. assoc. prof. dept. surgery U. Ariz., Tucson, 1984—; dep. med. examiner Mojave County, Ariz., 1996—. Co-author: Guinea Pig Doctors, 1984; contbr. articles to sci. jours. Capt. USAF, 1947-49. Mem. Alumni Assn. of N.W. Nazarene Coll. (Profl. Achievement award 1984), Toastmasters, Gideons. Republican. Mem. Nazarene Ch. Home: 3411 S Camino Seco Unit 337 Tucson AZ 85730-2829 Office: Univ Ariz Dept Surgery 1501 N Campbell Ave Tucson AZ 85724-0001

SUTHERLAND, MICHAEL CRUISE, librarian; b. Morgantown, W.Va., Aug. 29, 1938; s. Charles Fish and Mildred (Haymond) S. BA in English, San Fernando Valley State U., 1967, postgrad., 1968-69; postgrad., UCLA, 1967, MLS, 1970. Office asst., clk. Lindsay & Hall, L.A., 1959-60; libr. asst. I, bindery clk. Biomed. Libr. UCLA, 1961-65; jr. adminstrv. asst. Dept. Pub. Works City of L.A., 1967; intermediate clk. typist San Fernando Valley State U., Northridge, Calif., 1967-69; libr. I, tchg. asst. Grad. Sch. Libr. and Info. Sci. UCLA, 1970; spl. collections libr. Occidental Coll., L.A., 1970—; attendee numerous workshops and seminars; organizer Western Books Exhbn. at various librs. throughout the Western U.S., 1992, 96; judging organizer, 1993. Author numerous exhbn. catalog booklets; author: (with others) Encyclopedia of Library and Information Sciences, 1979, Western Books Exhibition Catalog, 1986, Striking Research Gold: Distinguished Collections in California Independent Academic Libraries, 1988; contbr. articles to profl. jours. Active Neighborhood Watch, AIDS Quilt Program. Mem. ALA (rare books and manuscripts divsn.), Assn. Coll. and Rsch. Librs., Rounce and Coffin Club (sec., treas.), Robinson Jeffers Assn., Tor House Found. Office: Occidental Coll Mary Clapp Libr 1600 Campus Rd Los Angeles CA 90041-3384

SUTTER, DIANE, television executive; b. Pitts., Dec. 9, 1950; d. George Edward and Dorothy Ann (Deckard) S.; m. James M. Stuart, Sept. 21, 1974 (div. Nov. 1984). BA in Polit. Sci., Allegheny Coll., 1972; MS in Pub. Rels., Am. U., 1974. Pub. rels. Congressman William S. Conover from 27th Dist. Pa., Washington, 1972; press sec. Congressman Robert P. Hanrahan from 3d Dist. Ill., Washington, 1973; dir. communications D.C. Bicentennial, Washington, 1975; acct. exec. Sta. WPEZ, Pitts., 1975-78, sales mgr., 1978-79; v.p., mgr. Sta. WTKN/WWSW, Pitts., 1979-83, v.p., gen. mgr., 1983-88; corp. v.p., gen. mgr. Sta. WWSW-AM-FM, 1988-89; corp. v.p., gen mgr. Sta. WTVQ-TV (ABC affiliate), Lexington, Ky., 1989-91; exec. v.p. ops. Shamrock Broadcasting, Inc., Burbank, Calif., 1991-93; pres. Shamrock Television, Burbank, Calif., 1994-95; pres., CEO Shooting Star Broadcasting, Sherman Oaks, Calif., 1996—; chmn. ABC Talk Radio Affiliate Bd., 1983-87. Contbr. articles to various newspapers. Mem. adv. bd. Women's Polit. Caucus, Allegheny County, Pitts., 1979-89; bd. dirs. United Way of Bluegrass, 1990-91, Jr. Achievement of Bluegrass, 1990-91, Support Ctr. for Cancer, 1988-90; devel. com. Holygrove Children's Home. Mem. Am. Women in Radio and TV (nat. sec., treas. 1982-84, nat. pres.-elect 1987-88, nat. pres. 1988-89, Nat. Achievement award 1994), Pitts. Radio Orgn. (pres. 1982-83), Pitts. Radio/TV Club (dir. 1979-84), Nat. Assn. Broadcasters (legis. com. 1983—), Pa. Assn. Broadcasters (dir. 1983-87), TV Assn. of Bluegrass (pres. 1989-90), Hollywood Radio and TV Soc., Hollywood Women's Polit. Com. Republican. Methodist. Office: ShootingStar Broadcasting 3606 Camino de la Cumbre Sherman Oaks CA 91423

SUTTERBY, LARRY QUENTIN, internist; b. North Kansas City, Mo., Sept. 11, 1950; s. John Albert and Wilma Elizabeth (Henry) S.; m. Luciana Risos Magpuri, July 5, 1980; children: Leah Lourdes, Liza Bernadette. BA in Chemistry, William Jewell Coll., 1972; MD, U. Mo., Kans. City, 1976. Diplomate Am. Bd. Internal Medicine with qualifications in geriatric medicine. Resident in internal medicine Mt. Sinai Hosp., Chgo., 1976-79; physician Mojave Desert Health Svc., Barstow, Calif., 1979-86; pvt. practice Barstow, 1986—; med. dir. Rimrock Villa Convalescent Hosp., Barstow, 1995—, Mojave Valley Hospice, 1983—, VNA Hospice, Barstow, 1994—, Optioncare Home Health Svcs., 1995—. Recipient Loving Care award Vis. Nurse Assn. Inland Counties, 1988. Mem. AMA, ACP, Am. Med. Dirs. Assn., Am. Diabetes Assn., Calif. Med. Assn., San Bernardino County Med. Soc., Am. Soc. Internal Medicine, Am. Geriatric Soc., Acad. Hospice Physicians, Nat. Hospice Orgn., Internat. Coll. Hospice and Palliative Care, Soc. Gen. Internal Medicine, Am. Numismatic Assn., Combined Orgns. Numismatic Error Collectors Am. Democrat. Roman Catholic. Office: 209 N 2nd Ave Barstow CA 92311-2222

SUTTERFIELD, KEVIN JAMES, lawyer, consultant; b. Long Beach, Calif., July 16, 1955; s. George Washington Sutterfield Jr. and Faun (Memmott) Hughes; m. Paula Sowards, May 20, 1987; children: Ashley, Hailey, Nathaniel, Taylor, Morgan. BA, Brigham Young U., 1979, JD, 1982. Bar: Utah 1982, U.S. Dist. Ct. Utah 1982, U.S. Ct. Appeals (10th cir.) 1984. Assoc. Dart & Stegall, Salt Lake City, 1982-83; assoc. Ray G. Martineau, Salt Lake City, 1983-86; mem. Howard, Lewis & Petersen, Provo, Utah, 1987-94; mem., founder Hickinger & Sutterfield, P.C., 1994—. Contbr. articles to profl. jours. Organizer, incorporator, gen. counsel, trustee Nat. Kidney Found. Utah, 1986-88. Mem. ATLA, Utah Trial Lawyers Assn. (bd. dirs. 1992—, editor in chief Utah Trial Jour. 1993—), Utah Bar Assn., Utah Cen. Bar Assn., Cougar Club, Riverside Country Club. Democrat. Mormon. Office: Flickinger & Sutterfield 2750 N University Ave Provo UT 84604-3805

SUTTLE, CLARK, performing company executive. Music dir. Monterey County Symphony. Office: Monterey County Symphony PO Box 3965 Carmel CA 93921*

SUTTLES, VIRGINIA GRANT, advertising executive; b. Urbana, Ill., June 13, 1931; d. William Henry and Lenora (Fitzsimmons) Grant; m. John Henry Suttles, Sept. 24, 1977; step-children: Linda Suttles Daniels, Peg Suttles La Croix, Pamela Suttles Diaz, Randall. Grad. pub. schs., Mahomet, Ill. Media estimator and Procter & Gamble budget control Tatham-Laird, Inc., Chgo., 1955-60; media planner, supr. Tracy-Locke Co., Inc., Dallas and Denver, 1961-68; media dir., account exec. Lorie-Lotito, Inc., 1968-72; v.p., media dir. Sam Lusky Assos., Inc., Denver, 1972-86; ind. media buyer, 1984-89; mktg. asst. mktg. dept. Del E. Webb Communities, Inc., Sun City West, Ariz., 1985-88, with telemarketing dept., 1989-90, homeowner coord., 1993-97; mktg. coord. asst./media buyer, Del Webb Corp., Phoenix, 1990-93; lectr. sr. journalism class U. Colo., Boulder, 1975-80; condr. class in media seminars Denver Advt. Fedn., 1974, 77; Colo. State U. panelist Broadcast Day, 1978, High Sch. Inst., 1979, 80, 81, 82, 83. Founder, Del E. Webb Meml. Hosp. Found.; patron founder Tree of Life Nat. Kidney Found. of Colo.- Rockies Snow Mountain YMCA Ranch, Winter Park, Colo., Sun Health Found. Sun Cities, Ariz. State U. Found. Sundome Perfroming Arts Ctr. Mem. Denver Advt. Fedn. (bd. dir. 1973-75, program chmn. 1974-76, 80-82, exec. bd., v.p. ops. 1980-81, chmn. Alfie awards com. 1980-81, advt. profl. of Yr. 1981-82), Denver Advt. Golf Assn. (v.p. 1976-77, pres. 1977-78), Colo. Broadcasters Assn., Sun City West Bowling Assn. (bd. dirs. 1987-88), Am. Legion Aux., VFW Aux., Air Force Sgt.'s Assn. Aux., Sun City Art Mus. Women's League. Republican. Congregationalist. Club: Denver Broncos Quarterback. Home: 20002 N Greenview Dr Sun City West AZ 85375-5579 *Personal philosophy: Over the years has been to work your full day, volunteer to help young people coming up in their profession, so they will be able to do their tasks properly and volunteer your services to help in any way you can to make this a good world to live in.*

SUTTON, MARCELLA FRENCH, interior designer; b. Prague, Czechoslovakia, Sept. 4, 1946; came to U.S., 1952, naturalized, 1956; d. Eugen E. and Frances V. (Pruchovia) French; BS in Profl. Arts, Woodbury U., 1971; m. Michael D. Sutton, Feb. 11, 1978; 1 child, Kevin Christopher. Mgr. design dept. W. & J. Sloane, Beverly Hills, Calif., 1972-76; project dir. Milton I. Swimmer, Beverly Hills, 1977-78; owner, interior designer Marcella French Designs, Woodland Hills and La Crescenta, Calif., 1969-94; owner designer project mgr., constrn. and design Marcella French Designs, 1994—, prin. designer; property mgmt. coord., interior designer Home Savs. and Loan., State of Calif., L.A., 1979-82; regional premises officer, asst. v.p. regional hdqrs. Bank Am., L.A., 1981-86; v.p. M.D. Sutton Ins. Agy.; cons. pvt. residences, comml. bldgs., office and banks. Project mgr., 1st v.p. fundraising Shephard of the Valley Sch., 1989-90, enrichment chmn., 1990-91, mem. enrichment program pub. sch. calendar, 1991; active Young Reps., Vinyard Ch.; treas. West Hills Baseball Aux., 1989-93; arcades coord. Theatre Arts Festival for Youth, Agoura, 1992-93, co-chmn. ways and means RTRWF, 1992-94, 1st v.p., 1995-97, program chmn., 1996-97; judge Sci. Fair, 1993-95; treas. Taxpayers United for Fairness, 1994—; co-organizer 9th and 10th Grade Parent Network Orgn. & Found., Chaminade, 1994-95, 1st v.p., program chmn., 1996-97. Recipient various scholarships.

SUTTON, PARKER FOREST, principal; b. Williams, Ariz., July 14, 1939; s. Parker George Jr. and Lorraine (Goodson) S.; m. Patricia Riggs, Aug. 25, 1963; children: Jeffrey, Kathleen. BS in Edn., North Ariz. U., 1963; MA, Calif. State U., L.A., 1970. Lifetime tchg. credential, lifetime elem. adminstrn. credential. Tchr. Torrance (Calif.) Unified Sch. Dist., 1963-64, Buena Park (Calif.) Sch. Dist., 1964-70; asst. prin. Santa Ana (Calif.) Unified Sch. Dist., 1970-74; prin. Bonita Unified Sch. Dist., San Dimas, Calif., 1974—; mem. dist. negotiating team Bonita Unified Sch. Dist., San Dimas, 1990-91, 94-95, 96-97. Chmn. YMCA Bd., San Dimas/Laverne, Calif., 1983-85. 1st lt. U.S. Army Res., 1963-70. Mem. Assn. Calif. Sch. Adminstrs. (pres.-elect region 15 1996-97, v.p. programs 1995-96, v.p legis. action 1993-95), Assn. Calif. Sch. Adminstrs., Individualized Instrn. Assn. (pres. 1982-83), Bonita Mgmt. Assn. (pres. 1978-79). Presbyterian. Office: Bonita Unified Sch Dist 115 W Allen Ave San Dimas CA 91773-1437

SUTTON, PHILIP D(IETRICH), psychologist; b. Ridgewood, N.J., June 20, 1952; s. Clifton C. and Ida-Lois (Dietrich) S.; m. Kathleen E. Duffy, June 17, 1973; children—Heather, Shivonne. B.A., So. Ill. U., 1974; M.A., U. Chgo., 1975; Ph.D., U. Utah, 1979. Lic. psychologist, Colo. Psychologist VA Hosp., Salt Lake City, 1975-76; psychology intern Salt Lake Community Mental Health Ctr., Salt Lake City, 1976-78; counselor, instr. Counseling Ctr., U. Utah, Salt Lake City, 1976-78; counselor, acting dir. spl. services program Met. State Coll., Denver, 1978-80; staff psychologist Kaiser-Permanente Health Plan, Denver, 1980-83; adj. prof. U. Colo., 1979-83; pvt. practice psychology, Boulder (Colo.) Med. Ctr., 1983—; cons. spl. programs for disadvantaged students in higher edn. Dept. HEW, 1980. Mem. Am. Psychol. Assn., Biofeedback Soc. Am., Soc. Behavioral Medicine. Home: 4185 Corriente Pl Boulder CO 80301-1626 Office: Boulder Med Ctr 2750 Broadway St Boulder CO 80304-3573

SUZUKI, BOB H., university president. Formerly v.p. acad. affairs Calif. State Univ., Northridge; pres. Calif. State Poly. Univ., Pomona, 1991—. Office: Calif State Polytech Univ Office of Pres 3801 W Temple Ave Pomona CA 91768-2557

SUZUKI, DAVID TAKAYOSHI, geneticist, science broadcaster; b. Vancouver, B.C., Can., Mar. 24, 1936; s. Kaoru Carr and Setsu (Nakamura) S.; m. Joane Setsuko Sunahara, Aug. 20, 1958 (div. 1965); children—Tamiko Lynda, Troy Takashi, Laura Miya; m. Tara Elizabeth Cullis, Dec. 10, 1972; children—Severn Setsu, Sarika Freda. BA cum laude, Amherst Coll., Mass., 1958; PhD, U. Chgo., 1961; LLD (hon.), U. P.E.I., 1974, Queen's U., Ont., 1987; DSc (hon.), Acadia U., N.S., 1979, McMaster U., Ont., 1987, U. Windsor, Ont., 1979, Trent U., Ont., 1981, Lakehead U., Ont., 1986; DHL (hon.), Gov.'s State U., Ill., 1986. Research assoc. Oak Ridge Nat. Lab., 1961-62; asst. prof. U. Alta., Edmonton, Can., 1961-63; asst. prof. dept. zoology U. B.C., Vancouver, 1963-65, assoc. prof., 1965-69, prof., 1969—; vis. prof. UCLA, 1966, U. Calif.-Berkeley, 1969, 1976-77, U. Utah, Salt Lake City, 1971-72, U. P.R., 1972, U. Toronto, 1978. Host TV programs Suzuki on Sci., CBC, Vancouver, 1971-72, Sci. Mag., Toronto, 1974-79, Quirks & Quarks, Vancouver, 1974-79, Nature of Things, Toronto, 1979—; host series on sci. TV programs Interface, 1974-75, Just Ask, Inc., 1980, Night Video, 1984, Futurescan, 1984; radio program Discovery, 1983—; author: (textbook) Introduction to Genetic Analysis, 1976, David Suzuki Looks at Plants, 1985, David Susuki Looks at Insects, 1986, David Suzuki Looks at Senses, 1986, Egg-Carton Zoo, 1986, Sciencescape: The Nature of Canada, 1986, British Columbia: Frontier for Ideas, 1986, From Pebbles to Computers, 1986; contbr. articles to profl. and popular publs. and mags. Bd. dirs. B.C. Civil Liberties Assn., 1973, Can. Civil Liberties Assn., 1982—. Decorated officer Order of Can.; recipient W.R. Steacie Meml. award Nat. Research Council Can., 1969-72; Sci. and Engring. medal Sci. Council B.C., 1981; UN Environ. Programme medal, 1985; grantee Can. Nat. Research Council, AEC, Nat. Cancer Inst. Can., NIH also others; recipient UNESCO Kalinga prize, 1986, Royal Bank award, 1986. Mem. Alliance of Can. TV and Radio Artists (award 1986), Genetic Soc. Am., Sci. Council Can. Mem. New Democratic Party. Address: # 219, 2211 W 4th Ave, Vancouver, BC Canada V6K 4S4*

SUZUKI, JOHN PATRICK, biochemist; b. Modesto, Calif., Mar. 21, 1952; s. Shigeru and Star (Kaji) S.; m. Belinda T.L. Fong, May 5, 1978; children:

Patricia T., Mark D. AS in Chemistry, Modesto Jr. Coll., 1972; BS, U. Calif., Berkeley, 1974. Assoc. rsch. chemist Western Regional Rsch. Lab., Albany, Calif., 1974; rsch. biochemist Chevron Chem. Co., Richmond, Calif., 1974-90, Chevron Rsch. & Tech. Co., Richmond, 1990—; environ. cons. Chevron, Richmond, 1991-94. Patentee in field. Republican. Methodist. Office: Chevron Rsch & Tech Co 100 Chevron Way Richmond CA 94801-2016

SVEE, GARY DUANE, newspaper editor, author, journalist; b. Billings, Mont., Nov. 11, 1943; s. Sigvart Oluf and Beatrice Evelyn (Lund) S.; m. C. Diane Schmidt, June 26, 1966; children—Darren Kirk, Nathan Jared. B.A., U. Mont., 1967. Unit mgr. Midland Bank, Billings, Mont., 1967-69; reporter Billings Gazette, 1969-76, opinion editor, 1982—; pub. Bridger (Mont.) Bonanza, 1976-77; feature editor Missoulian, Missoula, Mont., 1977-81. Author: Spirit Wolf, 1987, Incident at Pishkin Creek, 1989, Sanctuary, 1990 (Best Western novel Western Writers Am. 1990), Single Tree. vestryman St. Luke's Meml. Bd., Billings, 1989, Salvation Army, Missoula, 1980-82; vestryman Holy Spirit Parish, Missoula, 1980-82. Served to lt. USAR, 1966-72. Recipient Business Writing award U. Mo., 1974, Minority Affairs Reporting award N.W. region Sigma Delta Chi, 1980. Mem. Kiwanis (bd. dirs. Billings club 1988-89, 2d v.p. 1989, pres. 1990, 91-92), Theta Chi. Episcopalian. Home: 474 Indian Trl Billings MT 59105-2706 Office: Billings Gazette PO Box 36300 Billings MT 59107-6300

SVEEN, JAMES E., state official; b. Bremerton, Wash., June 11, 1953; s. Ernest J. and Laura Evelyn (Johnson) S.; m. Ann Lorraine Quinn, June 22, 1996; 1 child, Sarah Lorraine; children by previous marriage: James Christopher, Laurie Ann, Brita Denise. AAS, C.C. of Air Force, Tacoma, Wash., 1979; AS, St. Martin's Coll., Lacey, Wash., 1979, BA, 1982; MBA, U. S.D., 1985. Commd. lt. USAF, 1983-94, advanced through grades to capt.; chief policy devel. and compliance sect. 44th Strategic Missile Wing, Ellsworth AFB, S.D., 1983-87; dir. info. mgmt., human resource mgr., dir. edn., asst. prof U. Wash./Air Force Res. Officer Tng. Program, Seattle, 1987-91; contracts mgr. edn. with industry The Boeing Co. USAF, Seattle, 1991-92; contracts mgr. Milstar Satellite Comm. USAF, Hanscom AFB, Mass., 1992-94; contracts specialist Wash. State Mil. Dept., Fairchild AFB, 1995—; adj. faculty contract mgmt. cert. program Middlesex C.C., Bedford, Mass., 1994. Contbr. articles to profl. jours. Mem. ABA (govt. bus. assoc. pub. contract law sect.), Nat. Contract Mgmt. Assn. (cert., Boston chpt. awards chmn. 1993—, v.p. for edn. 1993-94, bd. dirs. 1993-94, pres.'s coun. 1993-94, contract mgmt. edn. and state and local govt. spl. topics com. 1993—, Puget Sound chpt. v.p. for ops. 1994-95), Nat. Assn. Purchasing Mgrs. (1st v.p. 1997—, Spokane affiliate, mem. MRO buyers group 1997—), Soc. of Fellows. Home: 3618 E 13th Ave Spokane WA 99202-5409 Office: 141 Civil Engring Squadron Bldg. 2001E 2 S Olympia Ave Fairchild AFB WA 99011-9431

SVETLIK, JOHN ANTHONY, entertainment company executive; b. Appleton, Wis., Apr. 27, 1963; s. Gerald Lawrence and Rita Wilhelmina (Vanden Berk) S. BA in Philosophy, Ariz. State U., 1985; MA in Philosophy, U. Calif., San Diego, 1990. Writer, prodr. Thistle Prodns., Phoenix, 1992-93; sci. writer ASU Rsch. Mag., Tempe, 1992-95, Intelecom, 1995; prodn. coord. CGI and EFX Walt Disney Future Animation, Glendale, Calif., 1993-94; ops. mgr. Encore Video, Hollywood, Calif., 1995-96; video technician Diva Post Prodn., Hollywood, 1997—; adj. prof. philosophy Maricopa County C.C., Phoenix, 1991-93. Contbr. articles to profl. jours. Grad. fellowship Mellon Fellowships in the Humanities, 1985. Mem. Am. Philos. Assn., Nat. Assn. Sci. Writers, Internat. Documentary Assn. Office: Diva Post Prodn 6671 Sunset Blvd Hollywood CA 90028

SVIKHART, EDWIN GLADDIN, investment banker; b. Chgo., July 12, 1930; s. Edwin Gabriel and Mildred Charlotte (Slapnicka) S.; m. Joann Barbara Frisk, Aug. 22, 1954; children: David E., Robert E. BA, Beloit (Wis.) Coll., 1952; postgrad., Bradley U., 1957-59. With Caterpillar Tractor Co., Peoria, Ill., 1956-66; chief fin. officer Berglund Inc., Napa, Calif., 1966-71; chief fin. officer, treas. Galion (Ohio) Mfg. Co., 1971-77; chief operating officer constrn. equip. internat. div. Dresser Industries, Inc., Columbus, Ohio, 1977-81; chief operating officer Rocky Mountain Machinery Co., Salt Lake City, 1981-87; chief oper. officer Custom Equipment Corp., Salt Lake City, 1989-92; ptnr. Travis Capital Mkts., Salt Lake City, 1992—. Served to lt. (j.g.) USN, 1952-56.

SWAFFORD, LESLIE EUGENE, physician assistant, consultant; b. Long Beach, Calif., Aug. 31, 1950; s. Leslie Eugene Swafford, Sr. and Kathryn Shirley (Gros) Jarvis; children: Jayson Patrick, Jonathan Allyn, Jude Christopher, Joshua Douglas; m. Cheryl Kaleen Killman, Apr. 10, 1993; 1 child, Lesli Tayte. BS in Allied Health, physician asst. degree of completion, George Washington U., 1978; postgrad. in Occupl. Medicine, U. Cin., 1994-95. Cert. physician's asst. NCCPA, ACLS, PALS, CDC AIDS Counselor, EBT (Alco-Sensor IV), EBT (EC/IR) QAP, TTT. Chief EEG technologist Group Health Assn., Washington, 1974-76; physician asst. Pediat. Assocs., Frederick, Md., 1978-81, Heart Inst. for Care, Amarillo, Tex., 1981-84, Maricopa County Medicine Assocs., Avondale-Goodyear, Ariz., 1984-89; mgr. Samarital Occupl. Health Svcs. Samaritan Health System, Phoenix, 1989-96; adminstr. drug test program Samaritan Health Svcs., Phoenix, 1991-95; mem. com. Ariz. Rural Health Conf., 1992-96; adj. asst. prof. physician asst. tng. program Kirksville Coll. of Osteo. Medicine, Phoenix, 1995—. Contbr. articles to profl. jours. Chmn. sex edn. com. North Ctrl. Accreditation-Aqua Fria H.S., Avondale, Ariz., 1991; physician asst. Camp Geronimo (Boy Scouts of Am.), Phoenix, 1989-94; team mem. Young People's Beginning Experience Grief Recovery Program for Children, Phoenix, 1989-93; mem. com. Ariz. Dept. Health Svcs.-Robert Wood Johnson Application, Phoenix, 1992-93. With USN, 1969-74. Recipient scholarship NIH, 1976, Squibb Pharm. Rural Physician Asst. of Yr. award honorable mention Am. Acad. Physician Assts., 1987, Dr. Paul L. Singer award for disting. cmty. svc. Samaritan Found., 1991. Fellow Ariz. State Assn. Physician Assts. (pres.-elect 1990-91, pres. 1991-92, chmn. Ariz. physician asst. tng. program task force 1990-94). Republican. Roman Catholic. Home: 17723 W Cactus Flower Dr Goodyear AZ 85338 Office: Samaritan Occupl Health Svcs Edwards Med Plz 1300 N 12th St Ste 407 Phoenix AZ 85006-2842

SWAIN, MELINDA SUSAN, elementary education educator; b. Sacramento, Oct. 30, 1944; d. William A. and Maxine (Wickberg) S. BA, Aurora U., 1967; MA, U. N.Mex., 1981. Cert. early adolescence/generalist Nat. Bd. Profl. Tchg. Standards, 1995. Tchr. 1st grade Crownpoint (N.Mex.) Elem. Sch., 1968-69, tchr. English as second lang., 1969-71; tchr. English as second lang. Church Rock (N.Mex.) Elem. Sch., 1971-72; tchr. kindergarten Sky City Elem. Sch., Gallup, N.Mex., 1972-73; program specialist Gallup-McKinley County Schs., 1973-82; tchr. 5th grade Lincoln Elem. Sch., Gallup, 1982-96; office for civil rights program compliance officer Gallup-McKinley County Schs., 1996—; mem. Dist. Task Force, Gallup, 1989—. Columnist N.Mex. Jour. Reading, 1991-97. Recipient N.Mex. World Class Tchrs. Project award, 1994-95. Mem. N.Mex. Coun. Internat. Reading Assn. (pres. 1984, state coord. 1991-97), Gallup Reading Coun. of Internat. Reading Assn. (pres., membership dir. 1977—). Home: 1000 Country Club Dr Gallup NM 87301 Office: Gallup-McKinley County Schs PO Box 1318 Gallup NM 87305-1318

SWAIN, NOLA V., foundation administrator, marketing professional; b. Tacoma, Wash., Mar. 10, 1942; d. Arthur and Viola Mafalda (Sirianni) De Caro; m. Lloyd E. Montgomery, Dec. 8, 1961 (div. 1971); children: Gina N. Montgomery, Melissa R. Montgomery; m. Walter B. Swain, Mar. 11, 1977. Student, U. Puget Sound, 1959-62. First woman cert. real estate appraiser, Wash. Appraiser/assesor Pierce County Assessors Office, Tacoma, 1971-77; chief appraiser Otero Savs. & Loan, Colorado Springs, 1977-78; pvt. fee appraiser, co-owner N.W.S. & Assocs., Colorado Springs, 1978—; pres., designer N.V.S. Enterprises, Colorado Springs, 1980-89; dir. mktg. U S WEST Edn. Found., Seattle, 1990-92, exec. dir. Northwest Baby Talk, 1993-95, fund devel., pub. rels. mgr. Child Abuse Prevention Resources, 1995—. Designer numerous gift items. Recipient Women at Work award Council on Working Women, 1985, Pub. Service award Colorado Springs Assn. Life Underwriters, 1985, Salesman With A Purpose Club Booster of Yr. award, 1986. Mem. NAFE, NOW, Urban League, Soc. Real Estate Appraisers (candidate, treas. 1978, bd. dirs. 1982-84), Chi Omega Alumnae. Democrat. Avocations: traveling, crafts, photography.

SWALLEY, ROBERT FARRELL, structural engineer, consultant; b. Ponca City, Okla., June 1, 1930; s. Robert Arthur and Jeannette Dean (Edwards) S.; children: Arthur Gentry, Susanne Evelyn. BS with distinction, U.S. Naval Acad., 1952; BSCE, U. Mo., 1958; MS, Stanford U., 1959. Registered profl. engr., structural engr. Sr. rsch. engr. USN Civil Engring. Lab., Port Hueneme, Calif., 1959-63; structural engr. Benham Blair & Affiliates, Oklahoma City, Okla., 1967-69; sr. project engr. AMF Inc., Advanced System Lab., Santa Barbara, Calif., 1969-73; structural engr. Penfield & Smith Engrs. Inc., Santa Barbara, 1973-77; structural engr., prin. engr., CEO Swalley Engring. Inc., Santa Barbara, 1978-93; cons., structural engr. Santa Barbara, 1993—. Contbr. tech. reports on Small Buried Arches, Design of a Cast in Place Personnel Shelter, Behavior of Buried Model Arch Structures, Loadings on Drydock Gates from Nuclear Explosions. Mem. ASCE (pres. 1976-77, v.p. 1983-84), NSPE (pres. 1978-84), Structural Engrs. Assn. Calif. Home: 4053A Foothill Rd Santa Barbara CA 93110-1209 Office: 500 E Montecito St Santa Barbara CA 93103-3245

SWAMINATHAN, VENKATES VADAKANCHERY, electrical engineer, software company executive; b. Bombay, Maharashtra, India, Dec. 31, 1963; came to U.S., 1985; s. Venkateswaran and Radha V. Iyer; m. Debra Kay Ragan, Dec. 20, 1991. B Tech. in Elec. Engring., Indian Inst. Tech., Delhi, India, 1985; MS in Elec. Engring., U. Ill., 1988. Software engr. Teknekron Comm. Systems, Inc., Berkeley, Calif., 1988-91; sr. software engr. Teknekron Comm. Systems, Inc., Berkeley, 1991-92, project mgr., 1992-94, program mgr., 1994-96; dir. mktg. Telesphere Solutions, Inc., Palo Alto, Calif., 1996—. Designer (computer software) schematic generator, 1985 (Best Project award 1985), chief architect NMS/Core, 1992; sr. architect Carrier Access Billing System, 1994. Bd. dirs. Beacon High Sch., Oakland, Calif., 1992. Recipient fellowship U. Ill., 1985. Mem. IEEE, Assn. Computing Machinery, U.S. Sailing Assn. Home: 3600 Balfour Ave Oakland CA 94610-1703 Office: Telesphere Solutions Inc 180 Grand Ave Ste 750 Oakland CA 94612

SWAN, ANNA, school nurse; b. Albuquerque, Mar. 14, 1953; d. Robert Stutz and Lupita (Lujan) Swan. BSN, U. N.Mex., 1985. Nurse Pres. Hosp., Albuquerque, Children's Psychiat. Hosp./Heights Psychiat. Hosp., Albuquerque; clin. instr. Albuquerque Tech.-Vocat. Inst.; sch. nurse Los Lunas (N.Mex.) Pub. Schs.; rsch. nurse dept. psychiatry U. N.Mex., Albuquerque; pub. health nurse, Albuquerque, dir. health unit/coord. program Albuquerque Tech.-Vocat. Inst.; mem. nursing practice adv. com. for N.Mex. Bd. of Nursing, 1993-95. Camp nurse Girl Scouts U.S., Albuquerque.

SWAN, JAMES ALBERT, environmental psychologist, writer, actor; b. Trenton, Mich., Feb. 25, 1943; s. Donald Miller and Evelyn Ann (Berdan) S.; m. Roberta June Arnett, Dec. 7, 1975; 1 child, Andrew Arnett. BS, U. Mich., 1965, MS, 1967, PhD, 1969. Environ. edn. coord. Ann Arbor (Mich.) Pub. Schs., 1965-69; lectr., rsch. assoc. U. Mich., Ann Arbor, 1969-72; asst. prof. Western Wash. State U., Bellingham, 1972-73; asst. prof., dept. chair U. Ore., Eugene, 1973-76; vis. lectr. U. Wash., Seattle, 1977-78; pres. Life Sys. Edn. Found., Seattle, 1978-82; project dir. Inst. for the Human Environment, San Francisco, 1983-84; assoc. prof. Calif. Inst. Integral Studies, San Francisco, 1988-92; pres. Inst. for Study of Natural Sys., Mill Valley, Calif., 1987-93; published writer in field, 1967—; bd. govs. U. Mich. Sch. Nat. Resources, Ann Arbor, 1993-96; adv. bd. Audubon Expedition Inst., N.Y.C., 1981-88; sec. Mich. Natural Areas Coun., Ann Arbor, 1967-72; bd. advisors Internat. Ctr. for Earth Renewal, Vancouver, B.C., Can., 1992—. Author: In Defense of Hunting, 1994; co-author: Bound to the Earth, 1994, Nature as Teacher and Healer, 1992 (award 1993), Sacred Places, 1990, Building Networks, 1985, Environmental Education, 1974; author, editor: The Power of Place, 1991, Dialogues with the Living Earth, 1996; edtl. adv. bd. Nat. Geog. Jour. of India, 1992—; assoc. editor Jour. of Environment & Behavior, N.Y.C., 1969-74. Mem. SAG, Assn. Songwriters, Composers & Performers, The Author's Guild. Office: PO Box 2460 Mill Valley CA 94942-2460

SWAN, JOE B., retired journalism educator, emeritus; b. Gorman, Tex., July 1, 1929; s. Jacob Calvin and Valeda Bee (Park) S.; m. Laura Mae Jones, June 14, 1952 (dec. Jan. 1996); children: Charles Richard (Dick), Deborah Lynn Swan Gorman. BA in English, Howard Payne U., 1954, MEd in English, 1957. Reporter Brownwood (Tex.) Bull., 1952-53; publicity dir. Howard Payne U., Brownwood, 1953-57, Superior (Wis.) State Coll., 1957-60; pub. rels. editor Texas A&M Coll., College Station, 1961-62; prof. journalism San Jose (Calif.) State U., 1962-94; ret., 1994. Co-author: Modern Journalism, 1961; co-editor: Emeritus Faculty Biographies, 1997; contbr. articles to Tex. Parade Mag. Photographer Calif. So. Baptist, 1972-82. Staff sgt. U.S. Army, 1948-52, Korea. Named Disting. Alumnus Howard Payne U., 1996. Mem. Nat. Press Photographers Assn. (founder student chpts. nat. program 1970, editor region 10 newsletter 1972-74, dir. student program 1973, dir. internship program 1974-75, Citation 1973, Award of Merit 1986), Soc. Profl. Journalism, Assn. Edn. Journalism and Mass Comm. Democrat. Home: 1680 Faraday Ct San Jose CA 95124-4701

SWAN, KENNETH CARL, surgeon; b. Kansas City, Mo., Jan. 1, 1912; s. Carl E. and Blanche (Peters) S.; m. Virginia Grone, Feb. 5, 1938; children: Steven Carl, Kenneth, Susan. A.B., U. Oreg., 1933, M.D., 1936. Diplomate: Am. Bd. Ophthalmology (chmn. 1960-61). Intern U. Wis., 1936-37; resident in ophthalmology State U. Iowa, 1937-40; practice medicine specializing in ophthalmology Portland, Oreg., 1945—; staff Good Samaritan Hosp.; asst. prof. ophthalmology State U. Iowa, Iowa City, 1941-44; asso. prof. U. Oreg. Med. Sch., Portland, 1944-45, prof. and head dept. ophthalmology, 1945-78; Chmn. sensory diseases study sect. NIH; mem. adv. council Nat. Eye Inst.; also adv. council Nat. Inst. Neurol. Diseases and Blindness. Contbr. articles on ophthalmic subjects to med. publs. Recipient Proctor Rsch. medal, 1953, Disting. Svc. award U. Oreg., 1963, Meritorious Achievement award U. Oreg. Med. Sch., 1968, Howe Ophthalmology medal, 1977, Aubrey Watzek Pioneer award Lewis and Clark Coll., 1979, Disting. Alumnus award Oreg. Health Scis. U. Alumni Assn., 1988, Disting. Svc. award, 1988, Mentor award Oreg. Health Scis. Found., 1996; named Oreg. Scientist of Yr. Oreg. Mus. Sci. and Industry, 1959. Mem. Assn. Research in Ophthalmology, Am. Acad. Ophthalmology (v.p. 1978, historian), Soc. Exptl. Biology and Medicine, AAAS, AMA, Am. Ophthal. Soc. (Howe medal for distinguished service 1977), Oreg. Med. Soc., Sigma Xi, Sigma Chi (Significant Sig award 1977). Home: 4645 SW Fairview Blvd Portland OR 97221-2624 Office: Ophthalmology Dept Oreg Health Scis U Portland OR 97201

SWAN, PETER ALFRED, systems engineer; b. San Antonio, Apr. 17, 1945; s. Frederic F. and Marion (Marriott) S.; m. Cathy Wood, July 5, 1968. BS in Engring., U.S. Mil. Acad., 1968; MS in Engring., Air Inst. Tech., Dayton, Ohio, 1970; MS in Mgmt., U. So. Calif., 1977; PhD in Engring., UCLA, 1984. Commd. 2d lt. USAF, 1968, advanced through grades to lt. col., 1984; test engr. USAF, Albuquerque, 1970-76; space systems engr. Office Sec. Air Force, L.A., 1976-79, satellite architect, 1984-88; asst. prof. astronautics USAF Acad., Colorado Springs, Colo., 1979-81; cons. Jet Propulsion Lab., Pasadena, Calif., 1982-84; ret., 1988; sr. systems engr. Motorola, Inc. (GEG), Phoenix, 1988-89; mgr. Washington Systems Office, Motorola, Inc. (GEG), McLean, Va., 1989-92; dir. Sunnyvale office Satellite Comms. Motorola Inc., Chandler, Ariz., 1993-94, systems devel. mgr., 1994—. Editor course books; contbr. articles to tech. jours. Bd. dirs. Ctr. for Critical Care, Washington, 1990-91. Fellow AIAA (assoc.), Brit. Interplanetary Soc.; mem. Internat. Acad. Astronautics. Home: 5865 E Sanna St Paradise Valley AZ 85253

SWAN, SUSAN LINDA, history educator; b. Everett, Wash., May 31, 1943; d. Joseph William Franckevitch and Doris Aline (Doolittle) Berry; m. Victor LaMarr Swan, June 19, 1965 (div. Apr. 1994); 1 child, Kerrigan Aline. BA in History, U. Wash., 1965, BA in English, 1965; MA in History, Western Wash. U., 1969; PhD in History, Wash. State U., 1976. Employment interviewer Wash. State Employment Security, Tacoma, 1971-72; asst. prof. history Wash. State U., Pullman, 1977-82, student affairs officer III, 1984-94, assoc. prof. gen. edn. program, 1994—; rsch. assoc. Nat. Coord. Spl. Hist. Projects, Mex., 1991-92. Co-author: Breve Historia de las Sequias en Mexico, 1995; co-editor: Reading About the World, I and II, 1995; contbr. articles to profl. publs. Chair acad. advising and reinstatement subcom. Wash. State U. chpt. Alpha Phi Omega, 1995—; vol. Pullman Meml. Hosp. Aux., 1983-92; group leader Sacajawea coun. Camp Fire, Pullman, 1984-90. Mem. AAUP, AAAS, Assn. Faculty Women, Phi Alpha Theta (pres. 1974-75), Phi Kappa Phi. Home: PO Box 3195 College Sta Pullman WA 99165 Office: Wash State U Dept History Pullman WA 99164-4030

SWANEY, THOMAS ROBBINS, venture capitalist; b. L.A., Apr. 28, 1952; s. George Robbins and Marian (Smoliga) S.; m. Ines Veronique Szilard, Aug. 31, 1974; children: Elizabeth Marian, Peter Thomas. BA in Econs. and Math., U. Calif., Berkeley, 1974; postgrad., U. Minn., 1974-75. Treasury analyst Fed. Home Loan Bank, San Francisco, 1976-78; fin. analyst Bank of Am., San Francisco, 1978-81; fin. cons. Chase Manhattan Bank, San Francisco, 1981-83, Am. Express, San Francisco, 1984-86; v.p. Bear Stearns, San Francisco, 1986-89; pres. Harwood Capital Inc., Oakland, Calif., 1989—; bd. dirs. West Oakland (Calif.) Devel. Assn., Am. Petroleum Inst., Sacramento. Bd. dirs. Kisha Soc., San Francisco, 1991-93. Mem. Sacramento Petroleum Assn., Calif. Ind. Petroleum Assn., World Affairs Coun. No. Calif., No. Calif. Geol. Soc., No. Calif. Cogeneration Assn., World Forum Silicon Valley, Indo Am. C. of C., U. Calif. Alumni Assn. (bd. dirs.), U. Calif. Berkeley Entrepreneurs Forum, Commonwealth Club, Ind. Petroleum Assn. Am. Office: Harwood Capital Inc 6161 Harwood Ave Oakland CA 94618-1339

SWANSON, ANNE BARRETT, dean; b. Joliet, Ill., Dec. 23, 1948; d. Wendell Burdett and Mary Marcella (Redmond) Barrett; m. David Keith Swanson, Aug. 30, 1969. BS in Chemistry, No. Ill. U., 1970; PhD in Biochemistry, U. Wis., Madison, 1975. Rsch. assoc. U. Wis., 1975-79; prof. chemistry, chair Edgewood Coll., Madison, 1979-88; assoc. program dir. NSF, Washington, 1985-86; assoc. acad. dean Coll. St. Catherine, St. Paul, 1988-92; dean Sch. Natural Scis. Sonoma State U., Rohnert Park, Calif., 1992—; grant proposal reviewer NSF, 1979—, adv. com. sci. edn., 1986-89, com. on equal opportunities, 1983-85, task force on disabled scientists, 1990; cons. Am. Chem. Soc., Washington, 1980—. Contbr. articles to profl. jours. Bd. dirs. Met. Ctr. for Ind. Living, St. Paul, 1988-92. W.K. Kellogg Found. fellow, 1990-93; grantee Bush Found., 1991, NSF, 1985, 87, Dr. Scholl Found., 1980; recipient Gallantry award Easter Seals Soc., 1984. Mem. Am. Chem. Soc., AAAS, Internat. Wheelchair Aviators, N.Y. Acad. Scis., Sci. for Handicapped Assn. (pres. 1981-82), Am. Assn. for Higher Edn., Grad. Women in Sci., Sigma Xi. Office: Sonoma State U Sch Natural Scis 1801 E Cotati Ave Rohnert Park CA 94928-3613

SWANSON, CAROLYN RAE, news reporter, counselor; b. Riverton, Wyo., Nov. 10, 1937; d. Leonard Rae Swanson and Ruby Francis Mulholland Laliberte; m. William Hamilton Glenn, Oct. 22, 1956 (dec. 1959); children: Donald, Rocky, Laurel; m. Larry T. Hess, Nov. 23, 1962; childre: Lance Hess, Aaron Hess. AA, West Valley Coll., Saratoga, Calif., 1970; BA, San Jose State U., 1975. Cert. substance abuse counselor. Counselor, program dir. Carson Regional Coun., Carson City, Nev., 1977-82; Women's Internat. News Gathering Svc. news reporter Radio for Peace Internat., Costa Rica, 1988-89; news reporter Cmty. Endeavor, Nevada City, Calif., 1990—; dir. Innovative Voices, Paradise, Calif., 1990—; mem. adv. bd. UN U. of Peace, Costa Rica, 1988-89; bd. dirs. No. Nev. Lang. Bank, 1978-80; cons. Intertribal Coun., Nev.-No. Calif., 1977-80; mem. exec. bd. Grandparent State Coun.,cCalif., 1992-96. Coord. shelter for battered women, Carson City, 1979; U.S. del. Soviet-Am. dialog, Washington, 1988; N.Am. del. Peace Conf., Costa Rica, 1989; leader Fellowship of Reconciliation, Chico-Paradise area, 1991-92; Butte County contact Green Party, 1991—. Recipient Promoting Arts award Villa Montalvo Theatre, Saratoga, Calif., 1975, award Nat. Inst. on Drug Abuse, Utah, 1978. Home: 5941 Camino Ln Apt 5 Paradise CA 95969-4721

SWANSON, DONALD ALAN, geologist; b. Tacoma, July 25, 1938; s. Leonard Walter and Edith Christine (Bowers) S.; m. Barbara Joan White, May 25, 1974. BS in Geology, Wash. State U., 1960; PhD in Geology, Johns Hopkins U., 1964. Geologist U.S. Geol. Survey, Menlo Park, Calif., 1965-68, 71-80, Hawaii National Park, 1968-71; sr. geologist Cascades Volcano Obs. U.S. Geol. Survey, Vancouver, Wash., 1980-90, rsch. scientist-in-charge, 1986-89; sr. geologist U.S. Geol. Survey, Seattle, 1990-96; assoc. dir. Volcano Systems Ctr. U. Wash., 1993-96; scientist-in-charge Hawaiian Volcano Obs., 1997—; affiliate prof. U. Wash., 1992—; cons. U.S. Dept. Energy, Richland, Wash., 1979-83; volcanologist New Zealand Geol. Survey, Taupo, 1984; advisor Colombian Volcano Obs., Manizales, 1986. Assoc. editor Jour. Volcanology and Geothermal Rsch., 1976—, Jour. Geophys. Rsch., 1992-94; editor Bull. of Volcanology, 1985-90, exec. editor, 1995—; contbr. numerous articles to profl. jours. Recipient Superior Service award U.S. Geol. Survey, 1980, Meritorious Service award U.S. Dept. Interior, 1985; postdoctoral fellow NATO, 1964-65. Fellow Geol. Soc. Am.; mem. AAAS, Am. Geophys. Union, Sigma Xi. Home: 417 Linaka St Hilo HI 96720 Office: US Geol Survey Hawaiian Volcano Obs PO Box 51 Hawaii National Park HI 96718

SWANSON, EMILY, state legislator; b. Oak Park, Ill., Jan. 12, 1947; m. Tim Swanson; 2 children. BA, Bennington Coll.; MA, U. Calif., Berkeley. Mem. Mont. Ho. of Reps. Home: 15042 Kelly Canyon Rd Bozeman MT 59715-9625 Office: Mont Ho of Reps State Capitol Helena MT 59620*

SWANSON, KENNETH J., museum administrator. Adminstr. Idaho State Hist. Mus., Boise. Office: Idaho State Hist Mus 610 N Julia Davis Dr Boise ID 83702

SWANSON, PAUL RUBERT, minister; b. Bakersfield, Calif., May 13, 1943; s. Roland Hilding and Myrtle Isabelle (Magnuson) S.; m. Mary Elizabeth Greene, June 18, 1967; children: Kristen Ann, Karlynn Marie, Jonathan Paul. BA, Pacific Luth. U., 1966; MDiv, Luth. Sch. Theology, 1970. Ordained minister, Luth. Ch. Pastor 1st Luth. Ch., Anaconda, Mont., 1970-76, King of Kings Luth. Ch., Milwaukie, Oreg., 1976-84; asst. to bishop Pacific N.W. Synod-Luth. Ch. in Am., Portland, Oreg., 1984-87; bishop Oreg. Synod-Evang. Luth. Ch. Am., Portland, 1987—; bd. dirs. Legacy Health System, Portland. Regent Pacific Luth. U., Tacoma, 1987—; bd. dirs. Emanuel Hosp., Portland, 1987; chmn. bd. dirs. Hearthstone, Inc., Anaconda, 1973-76; bd. dirs. Ecumenical Ministries Oreg., Portland, 1984—. Recipient Disting. Svc. award Pacific Luth. U., 1993.

SWANSON, RICHARD MARKER, electrical engineering company executive; b. Davenport, Iowa, May 13, 1945; s. Carroll A. and Betty M. (Marker) S.; children: Mark G., Craig A. BSEE, Ohio State U., 1969; PhD in Elec. Engring., Stanford U., 1974. Rsch. assoc. Stanford (Calif.) U., 1974-76, asst. prof., 1976-83, assoc. prof., 1983-91; v.p. SunPower Corp., Sunnyvale, Calif., 1989-92, pres., 1993—. Contbr. more than 100 papers to profl. jours. Named fellow NSF, 1970-74. Office: SunPower Corp 430 Indio Way Sunnyvale CA 94086-4202

SWANSON, RICHARD WILLIAM, statistician; b. Rockford, Ill., July 26, 1934; s. Richard and Erma Marie (Herman) S.; m. Laura Yoko Arai, Dec. 30, 1970. BS, Iowa State U., 1958, MS, 1964. Ops. analyst Stanford Rsch. Inst., Monterey, Calif., 1958-62; statistician ARINC Rsch. Corp., Washington, 1964-65; sr. scientist Booz-Allen Applied Rsch., Vietnam, 1965-67, L.A., 1967-68; sr. ops. analyst Control Data Corp., Honolulu, 1968-70; mgmt. cons., Honolulu, 1970-73; exec. v.p. SEQUEL Corp., Honolulu, 1973-75; bus. cons. Hawaii Dept. Planning and Econ. Devel., Honolulu, 1975-77, tax rsch. and planning officer Dept. Taxation, 1977-82; ops. rsch. analyst U.S. Govt., 1982-89; shipyard statisician U.S. Govt., 1989—. Served with AUS, 1954-56. Mem. Hawaiian Acad. Sci., Sigma Xi. Home: 583 Kamoku St Apt 3505 Honolulu HI 96826-5240 Office: Pearl Harbor Naval Shipyard PO Box 400 Honolulu HI 96809-0400

SWANSON, ROBERT KILLEN, management consultant; b. Deadwood, S.D., Aug. 11, 1932; s. Robert Claude and Marie Elizabeth (Kersten) S.; m. Nancy Anne Oyaas, July 19, 1958; children: Cathryn Lynn, Robert Stuart, Bart Killen. BA, U. S.D., 1954; postgrad., U. Melbourne, Australia, 1955. With Gen. Mills, Inc., Mpls., 1955-58, 71-79, v.p., 1971-73, group v.p., 1973-77, exec. v.p., 1977-79; with Marathon Oil Co., Findlay, Ohio, 1958-60; sr. v.p., dir. Needham, Harper & Steers, Inc., Chgo., 1961-69; joint mng. dir. S. H. Benson (Holdings) Ltd., Eng., 1969-71; pres., chief operating officer Greyhound Corp., Phoenix, 1980; chmn., chief exec. officer Del E. Webb Corp., Phoenix, 1981-87; chmn. RKS Inc., Phoenix, 1987—; bd. dirs. Am. S.W. Concepts Inc., Ariz. Desert Seguaro; chmn. Grossman's Inc., Boston, 1994—. 2d lt. U.S. Army, 1955. Fulbright scholar, 1954-55; Woodrow

Wilson scholar. Mem. U.S. Coun. Fgn. Rels., U.K. Dirs. Inst., U.S. Internat. Scholars Assn., English Speaking Union. Episcopalian. Office: RKS Inc 5600 N Palo Cristi Rd Paradise Valley AZ 85253

SWARD, ROBERT STUART, author; b. Chgo., June 23, 1933; s. Irving Michael and Gertrude (Huebsch) S.; life ptnr. Gloria K. Alford; children: Cheryl, Barbara, Michael, Hannah, Nicholas. BA with hons., U. Ill., 1956; MA, U. Iowa, 1958; postgrad., U. Bristol (Eng.), 1960-61, Middlebury (Vt.) Coll., 1956-60. Instr. English Conn. Coll., New London, 1958-59; writer-in-residence Cornell U., Ithaca, N.Y., 1962-64, U. Iowa, 1967-68; asst. prof. English/writer-in-residence U. Victoria (B.C.), 1969-73; editor/pubr. Soft Press, Victoria, 1970-79; radio broadcaster Can. Broadcasting Corp., Toronto, Ont., 1979-84; tech. writer Santa Cruz Op. (SCO), Santa Cruz, Calif., 1987-89; writer-in-residence extension program U. Calif., Santa Cruz, 1988—; writer-in-residence Cabrillo Coll., Aptos, Calif., 1988—; vis. poet creative writing program U. Calif., Santa Cruz, 1992—; writer in the schs. Ont. Arts Coun., Toronto, 1979-84, Cultural Coun., Santa Cruz, 1984—; cons. to pubs.; book reviewer Toronto Star, others. Author: Uncle Dog and Other Poems, 1962, Autobiography, CAAS, 1991, Poems: New and Selected, 1983, Four Incarnations: New and Selected Poems, 1957-91; (with Charles Atkinson, David Swanger and Tilly Shaw) Family, 1994, A Much-Married Man, A Novel, 1996; editor eSCENE, 1996, Blue Penny Quar., summer 1996. Tchr. Oak Bay Sr. Citizens, Victoria, 1973-74; editor, advisor Jazz Press, Poet Santa Cruz Pubs., 1985-87. With USN, 1951-54. Fulbright grantee, 1961, Guggenheim fellow, 1964-65, D.H. Lawrence fellow, U. N.Mex., 1966-67, Yaddo MacDowell Colony grantee, 1959-82; Djerassi Found. grantee, 1990—; recipient Villa Montalvo Lit. Arts award, 1989-90. Mem. League of Can. Poets, Writers Union of Can. (newsletter editor 1983-84), Nat. Writers Union. Democrat. Home: PO Box 7062 Santa Cruz CA 95061-7062 Office: 435 Meder St Santa Cruz CA 95060-2307

SWARTZ, MELVIN JAY, lawyer, author; b. Boston, July 21, 1930; s. Jack M. and Rose (Rosenberg) S.; children: Julianne, Jonathan Samuel. BA, Syracuse U., 1953; LLB, Boston U., 1957. Bar: N.Y. 1959, Ariz. 1961. Assoc., Alfred S. Julian, N.Y.C., 1957-59; ptnr. Finks & Swartz, Youngtown, Sun City, Phoenix, Ariz., 1961-70, Swartz & Jeckel, P.C., Sun City, Youngtown, Scottsdale, Ariz., 1971-82; exec. v.p. APPPRO, Inc., Scottsdale, Ariz. Bd. dirs. Valley of the Sun Sch. for Retarded Children, 1975-79. Mem. ABA, Ariz. Bar Assn., N.Y. Bar Assn., Maricopa County Bar Assn., Scottsdale Bar Assn., Central Ariz. Estate Planning Council. Jewish. Club: Masons (Phoenix). Author: Don't Die Broke, A Guide to Secure Retirement, 1974, Retire Without Fear, 1994, (book and cassettes) Keep What You Own, 1989, rev. edit., 1997, (computer program) Keeping What You Own, 1993, The Realtor's Title Analysis, 1994, Retire Without Fear, 1995; columnist News-Sun, Sun City, 1979-83; author column Swartz on Aging. Office: 6619 N Scottsdale Rd Scottsdale AZ 85250-4421

SWARTZ, RAY, data processing executive; b. Glendale, Calif., May 3, 1952; s. Albert and Ethel S. BA, U. Calif., Irvine, 1974; MBA, U. Calif., Berkeley, 1981. Mng. dir. Berkeley Decision Systems, Santa Cruz, Calif., 1981—; adj. lectr. U. Santa Clara, 1982-84; vis. lectr. U. Calif., Santa Cruz, 1984-87, India-sponsored by NIIT, 1988. Author: Doing Business with C, 1989, UNIX Application Development, 1990; editor conf. proc. Modeling and Simulation, 1984; columnist Answers on UNIX, 1989-95; creator tng. on video line of C Programming and UNIX system video tng. courses. Coach Cmty. Basketball League, Santa Cruz, 1987, co-facilitator men's group, 1993—; spkr. Santa Cruz AIDS Project, 1993—. Mem. USENIX, Uniforum. Office: Berkeley Decision/Systems 803 Pine St Santa Cruz CA 95062-2444

SWARTZ, ROSLYN HOLT, real estate investment executive; b. Los Angeles, Dec. 9, 1940; d. Abe Jack and Helen (Canter) Holt; m. Allan Joel Swartz, June 2, 1963. AA, Santa Monica (Calif.) Coll., 1970; BA summa cum laude, UCLA, 1975; MA, Pepperdine U., 1976. Cert. community coll. instr., student-personnel worker, Calif. Mgr. pub. relations Leader Holdings, Inc., L.A., 1968-75, pres., 1991—; sec., treas. Leader Holdings, Inc., North Hollywood, Calif., 1975-81, pres., 1981-91; chief exec. officer Beverly Stanley Investments, L.A., 1979—; pres. Leader Properties, Inc., The Leader Fairfax, Inc., Leader 358, Inc., Leader 359, Inc., Leader Ventura, Inc., 1996—. Condr. An Oral History of the Elderly Jewish Community of Venice, Calif. at Los Angeles County Planning Dept. Library, 1974. Founder L.A. County Mus. Art, Music Ctr. L.A. County, West Alumni Ctr., UCLA; mem. Hadassah (life), Friends of the Hollywood Bowl; bd. dirs. Am. Friends of Haifa Med. Ctr. L.A., West L.A. Symphony; capital patron Simon Wiesenthal Ctr. Fellow Phi Beta Kappa (bicentennial); mem. NAFE, AAUW, Am. Soc. Profl. and Exec. Women, Nat. Women's Hall of Fame, Am. Pub. Health Assn., Am. Pharm. Assn., Comml. Real Estate Women, L.A. World Affairs Coun., Town Hall (life), Century City C. of C., UCLA Alumni Assn. (life), UCLA Founders Circle, Women's Coun. Women's Guild Cedars-Sinai Med. Ctr., UCLA Prytanean Alumnae Assn., Santa Monica Coll. Alumni Assn. (life), Phrateres Internat., Order of Eastern Star, Phi Alpha Theta. Alpha Gamma Sigma, Alpha Kappa Delta, Phi Delta Kappa, Pi Gamma Mu. Office: PO Box 241784 Los Angeles CA 90024-9584

SWATT, STEPHEN BENTON, communications executive, consultant; b. L.A., June 26, 1944; s. Maurice I. and Lucille E. (Sternberger) S.; m. Susan Ruth Edelstein, Sept. 7, 1968; 1 child, Jeffrey Michael. BSBA, U. Calif., 1966, M in Journalism, 1967. Writer San Francisco Examiner, 1967; reporter United Press Internat., L.A., 1968-69; producer news Sta. KCRA-TV, Sacramento, Calif., 1969-70, reporter news, 1970-79, chief polit. and capitol corres., 1979-92; exec. v.p. Nelson-Lucas Communications, Sacramento, 1992—; guest lectr. Calif. State U., Sacramento. Contbr. articles to profl. jours. With USCG, 1966. Recipient No. Calif. Emmy NATAS, 1976-77, Pub. Svc. award Calif. State Bar, 1977, Exceptional Achievement Coun. advancement and Support of Edn., 1976, Nat. Health Journalism award Am. Chiropractic Assn., 1978. Mem. Soc. Profl. Journalists (8 awards), Capitol Corres. Assn., U. Calif. Alumni Assn., Sacramento Press Club. Office: Nelson Comms Group 1029 J St Ste 400 Sacramento CA 95814-2825

SWAYZE, MARGARET ANN, elementary education educator; b. Urbana, Ill., Oct. 5, 1940; d. William Martin and Mary Margaret (Miller) Cartmell; m. Robert Bonner Crawford, Sept. 1, 1962 (div.); children: Audrey Ann, Paul Howard; m. William Benjamin Swayze, Nov. 20, 1985; stepchildren: Rachel Noel, Jeffrey Edward, Ryan Dixon. MA in Elem. Edn., U. N.Mex., 1993. Cert. tchr., N.Mex. Clk. typist Sandia Corp., Albuquerque, summers 1958-61; counselor freshman dorm U. Okla., Norman, 1961-62; exec. sec. Inst. for Def. Analyses, Washington, 1962-64; sec. Am. Embassy, Tokyo, 1968-70; exec. sec. Am. Embassy and Am. Internat. Devel., Jakarta, Indonesia, 1977-79; exec. sec., adminstrv. asst. Martin Marietta Corp., Bethesda, Md., 1979-80; adminstrv. asst. WHO, Geneva, 1980-83, NIMH, Bethesda, 1984-85; intermediate tchr. Los Lunas (N.Mex.) Pub. Schs., 1991-92; elem. tchr. Albuquerque Pub. Schs., 1992—; math rep. Hubert Humphrey Elem., Albuquerque, 1993-94, sci. fair coord., 1995-96, tech. com., 1996-97. Established kindergarten Am. Embassy, Tokyo, 1967-68; vol. Red Cross Hosp. Camp Oji, Tokyo, 1968-69; vol. ballet tchr.Seisen Internat. Girls Sch., Tokyo, 1971-73; scout leader Cub Scouts, Bethesda, 1974-75; v.p., pres. Am. Recreation Club, Jakarta, 1976-78; vol. English tchr., med. asst. World Health Sch. for Nurses and Midwives, Jakarta, 1977-78; vol. asst. Albuquerque Pub. Schs., Albuquerque, 1989-90. Mem. Nat. Coun. Tchrs., N.Mex. Coun. Tchrs. English, Internat. Reading Assn., Environ. Edn. Assn. N.Mex., Nat. Humane Edn. Assn., Animal Humane Assn. N.Mex., Human Soc. U.S., Wilderness Soc. Home: 6601 Harper Dr NE Albuquerque NM 87109 Office: Hubert Humphrey Elem 9801 Academy Hills Dr NE Albuquerque NM 87111-1311

SWEARINGIN, KEVIN BRIAN, human resources administrator; b. San Bernardino, Calif., Feb. 7, 1968; s. James Edward and Pamela Sue (Swearingin) Waugh. AA, Ariz. Western Coll., 1996. Quality control inspector Bose Corp., Yuma, Ariz., 1992-95; human resources adminstr., coord. Bose Corp., Yuma, 1995—; safety com. chairperson Bose Corp., Yuma, 1994-96. Vol. sch. reading program HOSTS Help One Student to Succeed, Gwyneth Ham Elem. Sch., Yuma, 1994-96. With USN, 1986-92. Frier Found. scholar No. Ariz. U., Yuma, 1996. Mem. Golden Key. Republican. Home: 1600 W 12th St #626 Yuma AZ 85364

SWEENEY, CHRISTOPHER LEE, applied mathematics engineer; b. Denver, Oct. 14, 1959; s. Roger Lee Sweeney and Beverly Ann (Wagoner) Good; m. Susan Ann Merrell, May 24, 1986. Student, Community Coll. Denver; grad., U. Colo., 1988. Technican Ball Computer Products, Boulder, Colo., 1978-82, devel. engr., 1982-83; devel. engr. Ball Electronic Systems, Westminster, Colo., 1983-88; reliability engr. StorageTek, Louisville, Colo., 1989-94; mem. tech. staff Analysts Internat. Corp., Denver, 1994—. Inventor in field. Mem. Eta Kappa Nu, Tau Beta Pi. Home: 7974 W 108th Ave Broomfield CO 80021-2649 Office: Analysts Internat Corp 7800 E Union Ave Ste 600 Denver CO 80237-2755

SWEENEY, JAMES D., computer engineer; b. Lansing, Mich., June 20, 1949; s. Harold and Margaret Frances (Johnson) S.; m. Sharlene Margaret Kelly, Sept. 5, 1982. BSEE, U. Mich., 1971, MSE, 1972. Computer engr. Unisys, Salt Lake City, 1976—. Capt. USAF, 1972-76. Mem. ACM, IEEE, Wasatch Mountain Club.

SWEENEY, JOSEPH W., III, investment executive; b. New Rochelle, N.Y., Mar. 8, 1953; s. Joseph W. Jr. and Rita (McCarren) S.; m. Claudia Margaret Campbell, June 5, 1975; children: Joseph IV, Meredith, Peter. BSEE, U.S. Naval Acad., 1975; MS in Aero. Engring., Naval Postgrad. Sch., 1987. Commd. ensign USN, 1975, advanced through grades to lt. comdr., 1984; asst. schedule officer Patrol Squadron Five AV/ARM Divsn. Office, Jacksonville, Fla., 1977-80; enlisted programs officer USN, Albany, N.Y., Orlando, Fla., 1980-83; ops. officer COMDESRON USN, Pearl Harbor, Hawaii, 1983-85; OIC rsch. detachment staff ASWOC Sigonella, 1987-90; mil. instr. aero/astro. engring. dept. Naval Postgrad. Sch., Monterey, Calif., 1990-94; ret. USN, 1994; fin. cons. Merrill Lynch, Carmel, Calif., 1996—. Race dir. Big Sur Internat. Marathon, Carmel, 1990—. Mem. AIAA. Office: Merrill Lynch 3775 Via Nona Marie Carmel CA 93923

SWEENEY, MICHAEL, state representative; b. Oakland, Calif., 1950. BA, Calif. State U., MA in Polit. Sci. Elected to Hayward City Coun., 1982, re-elected, 1986; mayor pro tem City of Hayward, 1983-84, 88-89, mayor, 1990-94; mem. Calif. State Assembly, 1994—; vice chair local govt. com.; mem. edn. com., natural resources com., environ. safety and toxic materialscom.; guest speaker planning action conf. ABAG, 1988, Oceanic Soc., 1988. Chmn. Citizen/Industry Task Force, 1984; established Household Toxics Removal Day with League of Women Voters, 1984; chmn. Hayward Area Shoreline Planning Agy.; pres., city rep. Alameda County Waste Mgmt. Authority, 1992. Recipient Outstanding Svc. award to community Hayward Neighborhood Alert for Crime Prevention, 1985, 86. Office: Calif State Assembly 22320 Foothill Blvd Ste 130 Hayward CA 94541-2700*

SWEET, CHERYL ANN, small business owner; b. San Antonio, Dec. 23, 1950; d. Lidio E. and Rachel (Ruiz) Caballero; m. David Jensen Sweet, Oct. 23, 1970 (div. Nov. 1981); children: Monique, Jason. Student, Orange Coast Coll., 1969, 87, Golden West Coll., 1969-70, Girards Coll. of Beauty, Costa Mesa, Calif., 1970. Cert. nurse asst.; lic. cosmetologist, cosmetology instr. Salon owner Hair by M.S. Cheryl Sweet, Newport Beach, Calif., 1995—; cosmetology instr. James Albert Sch. Cosmetology, Costa Mesa, Calif., 1995. Author: War Letters - A Tour in The Nam, 1996. Democrat. Home and Office: 420 31st St B-9 Newport Beach CA 92659

SWEET, HARVEY, theatric, scenic and lighting designer; b. Detroit, Oct. 27, 1943; s. Sam and Rose Sweet; m. Susan Perrett, Mar. 16, 1964 (div. Mar. 1975); children: Deborah Anne, Rebecca Lynn, Jason Aaron; m. Patricia Ravn, Sept. 9, 1978 (div. July 1987). BS, Ea. Mich. U., 1965; MS, U. Wis., 1967, PhD, 1974. Instr. U. N.D., Grand Forks, 1967-69; asst. prof. Boise (Idaho) State Coll., 1972-73; instr. U. Wis., Madison, 1973-74; prof. of theater arts U. No. Iowa, Cedar Falls, 1974-89; dir. lighting Landmark Entertainment Group, L.A. and Tokyo, 1989-91; cons. Advanced Tech., Tokyo, 1991; tech. writer Walt Disney Imagineering, Glendale, Calif., 1992; owner, operator Sweet Studios Theatrical Equipment, Cedar Falls, 1981-89; dir. theater tech. and design U. No. Iowa, 1974-87; project mgr., sr. designer, tech. writer Tru Roll, Inc., Glendale, Calif., 1993—. Author: Graphics for the Performing Arts, 1982, Handbook of Scenery, Properties and Lighting I and II, 1988, 2nd edit., 1995, The Complete Book of Drawing for the Theatre, 1995; scenic designer Summer Repretory Theatre, 1988, Timberlake Playhouse, 1988-89; lighting designer, scenic designer, tech. dir. various coll. theatrical prodns., 1964-89; themed lighting designer Sanrio Puroland, Tokyo, 1989, exec. dir. lighting, 1990. Mem. U.S. Inst. for Theatre Tech. (vice commr. 1979-81, commr. 1981-87, mem. graphic stds. bd. 1979-86, evaluation commn. 1983-88, mem. publs. com. 1986-89, bd. dirs. 1989). Office: Tru-Roll Inc 622 Sonora Ave Glendale CA 91201-2339

SWEET, MARY FRENCH, artist; b. Cin., Oct. 10, 1937; d. Robert Houston and Dorothy May (Duff) French; m. James Newton Sweet, June 20, 1961; children: Dennis Robert, Nancy Foster, Elizabeth Valerie. AB in Art, Stanford U., 1959, MA in Art, 1960. One-woman shows include Univ. Club, Cin., 1961, Tuomala's Gallery, Ft. Bragg, Calif., 1965, Vallejo (Calif.) Art League Gallery, 1967, 69, Vacaville (Calif.) Art League Gallery, 1967, 1st Unitarian Ch., Albuquerque, 1978, 87, Meridian Gallery, Albuquerque, 1979, 80, 81, 83, 85, Gekas-Nicholas Gallery, Tucson, 1983-84, Hummingbird Originals Gallery, Ft. Worth, 1987, Damsite, Elephant Butte State Pk., N.Mex., 1991, Am. Home Furnishings Gallery, Albuquerque, 1995, Fisher Gallery, Albuquerque, 1997; exhibited in group shows at Weyrich Gallery, Albuquerque, 1985—, Tarbox Gallery, San Diego, 1984-95, Leon Loard Galleries, Montgomery, Ala., 1993, Laughing Bear Gallery, Placitas, N.Mex., 1993, Blankley Gallery, Albuquerque, 1993—, Snowgrass Inst., Cashmere, Wash., 1993, Coll. Santa Fe, 1993, Monothon, Coll. Santa Fe, 1995, No. Colo. Artist Assn. 5th Nat. Exhbn., Ft. Collins, 1996, Western Fedn. Watercolor Socs. 21st Ann. Best of Show and Traveling Exhibit, San Antonio, 1996, many others; represented in permanent collections at La Posada Hotel, Albuquerque, Carlsbad Art Mus., N.Mex., 1st Nat. Bank of Albuquerque, N.Mex. Educators Credit Union, numerous pvt. collections. Mem. Nat. Mus. of Women in Arts, Escribiente, N.Mex. Watercolor Soc., Albuquerque United Artists. Democrat. Home and Office: PO Box 280 Tijeras NM 87059-0280

SWEET, THOMAS IRA, physician; b. Mpls., Aug. 29, 1958; s. Douglas Morton and Elaine (Solon) S.; m. Lisa Susan Treger, June 5, 1988; children: Jeffrey Aaron, Lauren Melissa, Andrew Jordan. BS, Stanford U., 1980, MS, 1980; MD, U. Minn., 1984. Diplomate Am. Bd. Internal Medicine, Am. Bd. Med. Oncology, Am. Bd. Hematology. Intern U. Calif., San Diego, 1984-85; resident U. Calif. Med. Ctr., San Diego, 1984-87; fellow U. Md. Cancer Ctr., Balt., 1987-90; staff physician So. Calif. Permanente Med. Group, Anaheim, Calif., 1990—. Mem. ACP, Am. Soc. Clin. Oncology, Alpha Omega Alpha. Home: 25 Diamante Irvine CA 92620-1904 Office: 411 N Lakeview Ave Anaheim CA 92807-3028

SWEETWATER, SARAH ALICE, art educator; b. Roscoe, Tex., Feb. 18, 1940; d. William Bernard and Opal Pearl (Young) Whisenant; m. Leland Ray Campsey, Nov. 25, 1960 (div. Jan. 1975); children: Keri Opal, Alice Anne, Melissa Lee. BS in Art Edn., West Tex. State U., Canyon, 1965; MEd in Art and Human Rels., U. Utah, 1977. Chmn. dept. art No. Nev. C.C., Elko, 1971—; dir. Ednl. Travel, Elko, 1976—. Artist marble, stone and steel, metals, quilts, bronze. Dir. Pioneer Arts Crafts-Cowboy Poetry, Elko, 1975-85; bd. mem. Nev. State Art Educators, Elko, 1994—; bd. dirs. Crytasia, Elko, 1993—; dir., com. chair Mural Task Force, Elko, 1994-95. Named Woman of Yr. Elko County, Nev., 1979; NEH fellow U. Calif., Berkeley, 1980; recipient Gov. Arts award Nev. State Coun. on Arts, 1981, Excellence in Edn. award Nat. Inst. for Staff and Orgnl. Devel., U. Tex., No. Nev. C.C., 1994. Mem. Nev. State Art Educators (bd. mem., coll. rep. 1994—), Internat. Sculpture Soc. Home: 1375 Oak St Elko NV 89801-3433

SWEGER, GLENDA LEE, educator; b. Harrisburg, Pa., July 26, 1946; d. George Glenn and Bertha Alverta (Kitner) S. BS, Ind. U. of Pa., Indiana, Pa., 1968; MA, Calif. State U., Fullerton, 1981. Cert. tchr. Calif. Tchr. Greensburg-Salem (Pa.) Unifed Sch. Dist., 1968-69, Covina-Valley (Calif.) Unified Sch. Dist., 1969—; bd. dirs. SCSPA, San Diego, 1972-82, English Dept. chair, 1991—, sch. site coun. chair, 1992—; publs. advisor Northview High Sch., Covina, 1970, accreditation chmn., 1987; lectr. Great Am. Lecture Series, Covina, 1988; mentor tchr., 1989—; mem. Curriculum Devel. Adv. Bd.; Staff Devel. Com.; chair Sch. Environ. Com. Author: Male & Female Reporters: Differences in Readers' Perceptions, 1981. Active PTA, Covina, 1969—, SPRING, Seal Beach, Calif., 1987—, Orange County AIDS Found., Calif., 1987—, Ellis Island Found., N.Y.C., 1986—, Statue of Liberty Found., N.Y.C., 1984—. Recipient SCV Educators' grant, Covina-Valley Unifed Sch. Dist., 1986. Mem. AAUW, NEA, Calif. Tchrs. Assn., Covina Unifed Edn. Assn., Nat. Coun. Tchrs of English, Calif. Assn. for Tchrs of English, Calif. Scholastic Press Assn., Columbia Scholastic Press Advisors Assn., Journalism Edn. Assn., So. Calif. Journalism Edn. Assn., So. Calif. Scholastic Press Assn. (sec. 1976-82, bd. dirs.), So. Calif. Scholastic Publs. Assn., Southland Assn. for Tchrs. of English, IUP Alumni Assn., Fullerton Alumni Assn. Democrat. Evagelical Lutheran. Home: 3372 Rowena Dr Los Alamitos CA 90720-4844 Office: Northview High Sch 1016 W Cypress St Covina CA 91722-3145

SWENSON, DAVID AARON, computer scientist, educator; b. Fullerton, Calif., Mar. 22, 1965; s. Edwin Albert and Judith Lynn (Swanson) S. BS in Computer Sci., U. So. Calif., L.A., 1987; MS in Computer Sci., Rutgers U., 1990. Instr. N.Mex. State U., Carlsbad, 1990-92, asst. prof. computer sci., 1992—. Mem. Assn. Computing Machinery, Elks. Home: 1507 Monroe Carlsbad NM 88220 Office: New Mexico State Univ 1500 University Dr Carlsbad NM 88220

SWENSON, KATHLEEN SUSAN, music and art educator; b. Reno, Nev., Oct. 23, 1938; d. Harold Ruthaford McNeil and Hollyce Margaret (Scruggs) McNeil Biggs; m. James Michael Phalan, 1956 (div. 1974); children: David Michael, Jeanine Louise Phalan Lawrence, Gregory Shaun; m. Gerald Allen Swensen, Nov. 1976 (div. 1987); stepchildren: Craig Allen, Sarah Ann, Eric Sander. Student, U. Nev., Reno, 1956-58, Foothill Coll., 1966-68; AA, West Valley Coll.; BA, U. Calif., Santa Cruz, 1983. Concert pianist Nev.,Calif, 1950-64; pvt. piano instr. various locations, 1963—, pvt. art instr., 1970—, pvt. astrology instr., 1973—; founder, pres. AAM Triple Arts, Aptos, Calif., 1974—; founder, owner Aptos (Calif.) Acad. Music, 1993—. Producer, instr. art instrn. videos, music instrn. films, books. Mem. Soc Western Artists, Calif. Piano Tchrs. Assn., Los Gatos Art Assn. (pres. 1985-86), Saratoga Contemporary Artists (v.p. 1984-85), Nat. League Am. Pen Women (honorarian 1985), Soroptomists, Phi Beta Kappa. Republican. Episcopalian. Home and Office: AAM Triple Arts 3000 Wisteria Way Aptos CA 95003-3318 also: Aptos Acad Music 7000 Soquel Dr Ste 425 Aptos CA 95003-3647

SWENSON, MARY ANN, bishop. Bishop Rocky Mountain Conf., Denver. Office: Rocky Mountain Conference 2200 S University Blvd Denver CO 80210-4708

SWENSON, MICHAEL DAVID, internist; b. Willmar, Minn., July 19, 1960; s. Ronald L. and Mary Lou C. (Johnson) S.; m. Leslie J. Swenson, June 25, 1983; children: Rachel, Sara, David. BA, St. Olaf Coll., Northfield, Minn., 1982; PhD in Philosophy, U. Minn., Mpls., 1987, MD, 1987. Diplomate Am. Bd. Internal Medicine. Intern, resident U. Colo. Health Science Ctr., Denver, 1987-91; staff physician Norton Sound Health Corp., Nome, Alaska, 1991—, dir. hosp. lab., 1991—; clin. asst. prof. U. Alaska, Fairbanks, 1994—. Contbr. articles to profl. jours. Coun. mem., v.p. Our Saviors Ch. Coun., Nome, 1993—; vol. Iditarod Trail Commn., Nome, 1992—. Fellow ACP; mem. Soc. Gen. Internal Medicine. Lutheran. Home: PO Box 1352 Nome AK 99762-1352 Office: Norton Sound Health Corp PO Box 966 Nome AK 99762

SWENSON, RICHARD ALLEN, business owner, animal trainer; b. Willmar, Minn., Dec. 1, 1950; s. LeRoy Oswald Boe and Delores G. (Malghist) S.; children: Kristen, Richard Andrew, Kevin. Author: Secrets of Long Distance Sled Dog Racing. Treas. Pride, Alaska, 1993—. Recipient 1st pl. Iditarod, 1977, 79, 80, 81, 91 among others. Office: Denali Sled Dog Tours PO Box 86 Denali National Park AK 99755-0086*

SWENSON, SHIRLEY RUTH, elementary education educator; b. Provo, Utah, Dec. 22, 1935; d. Karl Warnick and Ruth Irene (Eldredge) S. BS, Brigham Young U., 1958, MEd, 1972. Cert. tchr. elem. edn., spl. edn., libr., Utah. Tchr. 2d grade Sevier Sch. Dist., Richfield, Utah, 1958-59, Jordan Sch. Dist., Sandy, Utah, 1959-61; tchr. 3d grade Alpine Sch. Dist., American Fork, Utah, 1963-71, resource tchr., 1971-97, team leader Barratt Elem., 1992—. Editor: Swen Swenson Descendants, 1955, Nebeker Family Book, 1979. Guide, Nauvoo (Ill.) Restoration, 1969-70; missionary LDS Ch., southern states, 1961-63. Mem. DAR, Mayflower Soc., Utah Ednl. Assn. Office: Barratt Elem Sch 168 N 900 E American Fork UT 84003-2059

SWENSON, SUSAN ANN, engineering recruiting company executive; b. Lansing, Mich., July 30, 1948; d. Milton Cecil and Dorothy Frances (Manuel) Taylor; m. John William Deutschmann, Apr. 17, 1982 (div. Oct. 1995); 1 child, Danielle Cecile. BA in Sociology, U. Wis., 1971; MSW, Mich. State U., 1974. Cert. social worker. Vocat. rehab. counselor Portland, Oreg., 1982-88; recruiter rschr. Corp. Builders, Portland, 1989; engring. recruiter Fran Low, Ltd., Portland, 1989-91; owner Swenson & Assocs., Scottsdale, Ariz., 1991—; social and rehab. svcs. trainee U.S. Govt. Mich. State U., East Lansing, 1972-73, 73-74. Asst. coach Arcadia Scottsdale United Soccer Club, 1995; soccer player N.W. United Women's Soccer, 1980-93, DiHearts Soccer Team, 1996—; soccer player, mgr. Misfits Soccer Team, 1993-95. Mem. AAUW, Nationwide Interchange Svc., Inc., Ariz. Assn. Pers. Svcs. Democrat. Home and Office: Swenson & Assocs 8502 E Cholla St Scottsdale AZ 85260

SWIFT, WILLIAM CHARLES, professional baseball player, Olympic athlete; b. Portland, Maine, Oct. 27, 1961. Student, Maine. Mem. U.S. Olympic Baseball Team, 1984; with Seattle Mariners, 1984-91; pitcher San Francisco Giants, 1991-94, Colo. Rockies, 1994—. Office: Colo Rockies 2001 Blake St Denver CO 80205*

SWIG, ROSELYNE CHROMAN, art advisor; b. Chgo., June 8, 1930; m. Richard Swig, Feb. 5, 1950; children—Richard, Jr., Susan, Marjorie, Carol. Student, U. Calif.-Berkeley, UCLA; DFA (hon.), San Francisco Art Inst., 1988. Pres. Roselyne C. Swig Artsource, San Francisco, 1977-94; apptd. by President Clinton as Dir. Art in Embassies program U.S. Dept. of State, 1994—. Trustee San Francisco Mus. Modern Art, U. Art Mus., Berkeley, Calif.; past bd. trustees Mills Coll., Oakland, Calif., United Jewish Appeal; ex officio bd. mem. Jewish Mus. San Francisco; bd. dirs. Am. Jewish Joint Distbn. Com.; vice chair fine art adv. panel Fed. Res. Sys.; past past pres., bd. dirs. Jewish Cmty. Fedn. San Francisco, the Peninsula, Marin and Sonoma Counties; past commr. San Francisco Pub. Libr.; past bd. dirs. San Francisco Opera, Am. Coun. for Arts, KQED Broadcasting Sys.; past. pres. Calif. State Summer Sch. Arts, past chair bd. trustees San Francisco Art Inst.; past pres. San Francisco Arts Commn.; past nat. v.p. Am./Israel Pub. Affairs Com.; past chair bd. trustees U. Art mus.

SWIHART, H. GREGG, real estate company executive; b. San Francisco, Sept. 25, 1938; s. Lawson Benjamin and Violet Mary (Watters) S.; B.A., U. Ariz., 1958; postgrad. U. Heidelberg (W.Ger.), 1958-59, Harvard U., 1959-60; M.A., Boston U., 1961; postgrad. U. Freiburg (West Germany), 1961-65; m. Ilse Paula Rambacher, Dec. 24, 1958; children—Tatjana Etta, Brett Marc, Natascha Theda. Stock broker Walston & Co., Tucson, 1966-71; with Solot Co., Tucson, 1971-74; pres. Cienega Properties, Inc., property mgmt. and investment, Tucson, 1975-77; pres. GT Realty Assocs., Ltd., Tucson, 1977—. Mem. Tucson Com. Fgn. Relations, 1973—; pres. Forum for Greater Outdoors, 1977-79; bd. dirs. Tucson Mus. Art, pres. 1969-70; pres. and trustee Canelo Hills Sch., 1977-79. Cert. property mgr. Mem. Tucson Bd. Realtors, Inst. Real Estate Mgmt. (pres. Tucson-So. Ariz. chpt. 1982, mem. nat. governing council 1985-87), Inst. Real Estate Mgmt. (governing council 1985-87, Property Mgr. of Yr. award So. Ariz. chpt. 1988), Realtors Nat. Mktg. Inst. Clubs: Harvard (pres. 1973-74), Active 20-30 (pres. 1969), Downtown Tucson. Home: Tunnel Springs Ranch PO Box 555 Sonoita AZ 85637 Office: 4003 E Speedway Blvd Ste 110 Tucson AZ 85712-4555

SWIHART, STEVEN TAYLOR, judge; b. Alexandria, Va., Sept. 7, 1942; s. Albert Taylor and Marian Dorothy (Lille) S.; 1 child, Sarah Ann Swihart. BA, Univ. Nebr., 1966, JD, 1972. Bar: Nebr. 1972. Staff atty. Panhandle Legal Svcs., Scottsbluff, Nebr., 1972-73, Lincoln (Nebr.) Legal

Aid Soc., 1974; atty., advisor Health/Human Svcs., Social Security Adminstrn. Office Hearing Appeals, Omaha, 1975-77; ptnr. Christian, Krieg & Swihart, Omaha, 1978-88; adminstrv. law judge SSA, Office Hearing Appeals, Denver, 1989—. 1st lt. U.S. Army, 1966-69, Vietnam. Mem. Nebr. State Bar Assn. Democrat. Office: Office Hearings Appeals 1244 Speer Blvd Denver CO 80204-3518

SWINDELLS, WILLIAM, JR., lumber and paper company executive; b. Oakland, CA, 1930; married. B.S., Stanford U., 1953. With Willamette Industries, Inc., Portland, Oreg., 1953—; sr. v.p. prodn., mktg. bldg. materials Willamette Industries, Inc., until 1978, exec. v.p., 1978-80, pres. forest products div., 1980-82, pres., chief exec. officer, 1982-96, also dir., chmn., 1984—; dir. Oreg. Bank, Portland. Office: Willamette Industries 1300 SW 5th Ave Portland OR 97201-5667*

SWINDLER, STEPHEN FRANCIS, distribution company executive; b. Indpls., Jan. 27, 1942; s. Frank J. and Greta Miskell (Gormley) S.; m. Sally Swindler, Sept. 1, 1970 (div. July, 1985); children: Lori, Scott; m. Carol Ann Obermeier; children: Jeremy, Brndon. Student, Purdue U., 1960-62; BS in Biology, Chemistry, History, Phys. Edn., Ball State U., 1970. Sales rep. Merck & Co., Inc., Janesville, Wis., 1970-72; sales ops. mgr. Merck & Co., Inc., Rahway, N.J., 1972-73; regional sales mgr. Merck & Co., Inc., Chgo., 1973-76; nat. sale mgr. Bayvet Divsn. Cutter Labs., Shawnee Mission, Kans., 1976-80; dir. mktg. svcs. Bayvet Divsn. Miles Labs., Shawnee Mission, 1980-85; gen. mgr. sales and mktg. Mobay (Bayvet) Animal Health Divsn., Shawnee Mission, 1986-92; cons. acquisitions SFS Consulting, Shawnee Mission, 1992; v.p., dir. mktg. and sales WALCO Internat., Inc., Porterville, Calif., 1992-94, COO, 1994-95, pres., bd. dirs., 1995—; leader quality process Miles Labs. Shawnee Mission, Kans., 1990-92. Author (manuals) Training a Proactive Rep., 1979, Evaluation for Achievement, 1982. Rep. councilman, Westfield, N.J., 1972-73; coach little league baseball, soccer, basketball, 1977-91. With USN, 1965-70. Mem. VFW, Am. Quarter Horse Assn. (sponsor), Animal Health Inst. (speaker), Nat. Cattlemens Assn., Tex. Cattle Feeders Assn. Roman Catholic. Office: Walco Internat Inc 15 W Putnam Ave Porterville CA 93257-3627

SWING, WILLIAM EDWIN, bishop; b. Huntington, W.Va., Aug. 26, 1936; s. William Lee and Elsie Bell (Holliday) S.; M. Mary Willis Taylor, Oct. 7, 1961; children—Alice Marshall, William Edwin. B.A., Kenyon Coll., Ohio, 1954-58; D.Div. (hon.), Kenyon Coll., 1980; M.A., Va. Theol. Sem., 1958-61, D.Div., 1980. Ordained priest Episcopal Ch. Asst. St. Matthews Ch., Wheeling, W.Va., 1961-63; vicar St. Matthews Ch., Chester, W.Va., 1963-69, St. Thomas Ch., Weirton, W.Va., 1963-69; rector St. Columba's Episcopal Ch., Washington, 1969-79; bishop Episcopal Ch. Calif., San Francisco, 1980—; chmn. bd. Ch. Div. Sch. of the Pacific, 1983-84; founder, chmn. Episcopal Found. for Drama, 1976—. Republican. Home: 2006 Lyon St San Francisco CA 94115-1610 Office: Episcopal Ch Diocesan Office 1055 Taylor St San Francisco CA 94115-2209

SWISLOCKI, ARTHUR L. M., physician, internist; b. L.A., May 4, 1951; s. Adam and Marie (Spanbock) S.; m. Ann Manheimer, June 16, 1974; children: Pauline, Allison. BA in Zoology, UCLA, 1972, MA in Biology, 1973, MD, 1979; student medicine, Free U. Brussels, Belgium, 1974-75. Diplomate Am. Bd. Internal Medicine, Am. Bd. Endocrinology and Metabolism. Intern in medicine LA County U. So. Calif. Med. Ctr., L.A., 1979-80; resident in medicine U. Calif. Davis Med. Ctr., Sacramento, 1980-82, chief resident in medicine, 1982-83; fellow in endocrinology Stanford (Calif.) U., 1984-86, fellow in clin pharmacology, 1986-88; staff endocrinologist VA Med. Ctr., Martinez, Calif., 1988—; acting chief med. svcs. VA Med. Ctr., Martinez, 1992-95; asst. prof. medicine U. Calif., Davis, 1989-95, assoc. prof. medicine, 1995—. Author: (with others) Endocrine Disorders of Pregnancy, 1989; contbr. articles to profl. jours. Recipient Nat. Rsch. fellowship NIH, 1987. Fellow Am. Coll. Physicians. Home: 822 Craft Ave El Cerrito CA 94530-2712 Office: VA No Calif Sys of Clinics Med Svcs III 150 Muir Rd Martinez CA 94553-4612

SWOFFORD, ROBERT LEE, newspaper editor, journalist; b. Berryville, Ark., Aug. 22, 1949; s. Andrew Madison and Verna Mae (England) S.; m. Karen King, Jan. 24, 1969 (div. 1977); children: Teri, Toby; m. Sandra Dunn, 1978 (div. 1979); m. B. Joanna Rongren, Feb. 14, 1981; 1 child, Tyler. AA, Coll. of the Sequoias, 1969; student, Calif. State U., 1969-71. Photographer, reporter, news editor The Advance-Register, Tulare, Calif., 1965-78; city editor The Record Searchlight, Redding, Calif., 1978-81; suburban editor, Neighbors editor The Sacramento Bee, 1981-86; assoc. metro. editor, cmty. editor The Orange County Register, Santa Ana, Calif., 1986-89; exec. news editor The Press Democrat, Santa Rosa, Calif., 1989-90, mng. editor, 1990—. Mem. Assoc. Press Mng. Editors, Calif. Soc. of Newspaper Editors (bd. dirs.). Office: The Press Democrat 427 Mendocino Ave Santa Rosa CA 95401-6313

SYDOR, RICHARD PAUL, social science educator; b. Welland, Ont., Can., Sept. 5, 1947; came to U.S., 1984.; s. Thomas and Olga (Dolishny) S.; m. Linda Joy Evans, Oct. 23, 1971 (div. Apr. 1983); m. Marcia LeDuc, Aug. 24, 1984. BA, Calif. State U., 1988. Distbn. mgr. Toyota Can., Inc., Calgary, Alberta, 1974-80; speech/mtgs. cons. Calgary, 1980-84; social sci. educator Sacramento (Calif.) City Schs., 1984—. Mem. Am. Inst. Parliamentarians, Toastmasters Internat. (dist. gov. 1981-82, internat. dir. 1996—), Calif. Coun. Social Studies, K. of C. Roman Catholic. Home: 1092 Salmon Dr Roseville CA 95661-4432

SYED, RASHID, protein crystallographer; b. Bombay, India, Jan. 28, 1960; came to U.S., 1983; m. Fehmida, June 1, 1989. BSc, U. Bombay, 1980, MSc, 1982; PhD, U. Toledo, 1987. Rsch. fellow The Scripps Rsch. Inst., San Diego, 1987-94; rsch. scientist Amgen, Inc., Thousand Oaks, Calif., 1994—. NIH fellow, 1991-93. Mem. Am. Crystallography Assn. Office: Amgen Inc M/S 14-2-B 1840 De Havilland Dr Thousand Oaks CA 91320-1789

SYKE, CAMERON JOHN, lawyer; b. Oak Park, Ill., Jan. 29, 1957; s. A. John and Rosemarie (Grasso) S.; m. Susan Royer, Jan. 2, 1982; children: Caroline, Jared. BSBA cum laude, U. Denver, 1977, LLM in Taxation, 1986; JD with honors, DePaul U., 1982. Bar: CPA, Colo. 1983, U.S. Tax Ct. 1985. Acct. Touche, Ross, Chgo., 1978-79, Denver, 1980-83; investment broker Boettcher & Co., Denver, 1983-84; CPA Laventhol & Horwath, Denver, 1984-85; assoc. Roath & Brega, Denver, 1985-87; dir. Terry, Skye & Graham P.C., Denver, 1987—; adj. prof. U. Denver, 1985; instr. Colo. Soc. CPAs, 1986-87; lectr. Nat. Bus. Inst., 1986-87. Candidate councilman City of Denver, 1987. Mem. Colo. Bar Assn., Colo. Soc. CPA's. Republican. Presbyterian. Home: 6942 E Costilla Pl Englewood CO 80112-1110 Office: Terry Syke & Graham PC 1610 Wynkoop St Ste 200 Denver CO 80202-1135

SYLVESTER, JUNE GLADDEN, English literature educator; b. Elizabeth City, N.C., Sept. 23, 1958; d. Dwight L. and Mary (Gray) S. BA, East Carolina U., Greenville, N.C., 1980; MFA, Bowling Green State U., 1982. Asst. prof. Sierra Nevada Coll., Incline Village, Nev., 1987—; adj. faculty U. Nev., Reno, 1994—. Editor lit. mag. Sierra Nevada Coll., 1990—; contbr. to lit. mags. including Tar River Poetry, CQ. Home: PO Box 10772 Truckee CA 96162

SYLVESTER, RICHARD RUSSELL, economist, management executive; b. Newton, Iowa, Jan. 10, 1938; s. Leslie Gardner and Effie (Williams) S.; BA, UCLA, 1959; MBA, U. So. Calif., 1962; PhD (fellow), UCLA, 1970, postdoctoral scholar in Engring., 1971-74; JD, Loyola U., 1981; m. Irene Elizabeth Lehman, Apr. 17, 1976; children: Bonnie Ann, Vicky Ellis, Juliesta Elaine. Designer corp. offices Gen. Motors Corp., Warren, Mich., 1958; sr. analyst Lockheed Aircraft Corp., Burbank, Calif., 1962-66; sr. planner corp. offices Hughes Aircraft Co., Culver City, Calif., 1966-68; sr. staff economist, staff mgr. TRW, Inc., Redondo Beach, Calif., 1969-70; pres. Def. Rsch. Co., 1970-81, Sylvester Consulting Group, PhD Pub. Co., Sylvester Appraisal Co., 1970—, U.S. Electropower Controls Corp., 1970-71; asst. prof. Calif. State U., 1970-73; mgr. corp. planning Brunswick Def./Celesco, Costa Mesa, Calif., 1973-75; staff specialist strategic planning Gen. Dynamics Corp., 1981-83; strategic analysis specialist Northrop Corp., 1983-89; cons. econs., engring. and fin., L.A., 1970—; lectr. Northrop U., U. Calif., U. So. Calif., Loyola U., La Verne U., 1961-81; asst. prof. Calif. State U., 1970-73, lectr., 1989—; assoc. prof. Pepperdine U., 1975-76, lectr., 1994—; co-founder Theta Cable TV, L.A., 1966-67. GM scholar, 1953-57, Ford Found. grantee, 1965, U.S. Fed. Govt. rsch. grantee, 1967-70. Mem. Westwood Hills Christian Ch. (bd. dirs. 1978-81, 1991-93), Beta Gamma Sigma, Alpha Kappa Psi. Author: Management Decisions and Actions, 3d edit., 1988; Investment Strategy, 1982; Tax Planning, 4th edit., 1980, Strategic Planning, 6th edit., 1990, Investment Planning and Tax Planning Software, 1983-93, Strategic Financial Planning, 1993, Future Challenge, Financial Strategy and Tax Planning, 1993, International Transfer Pricing, 1994; contbr. tech. reports to profl. lit. Home: 11606 Charnock Rd Los Angeles CA 90066-2806

SYMINGTON, J. FIFE, III, governor; b. N.Y.C., Aug. 12, 1945; s. John Fife Jr. and Martha (Frick) S.; m. Leslie Marion Barker, June 1, 1968 (div. Jan. 1973); children: Fife IV, Scott; m. Ann Pritzlaff, Feb. 7, 1976; children: Whitney, Richard, Tom. Student, Harvard U., 1968. Ptnr. Lincoln Property Co., Phoenix, 1972-76; chmn. of the bd. The Symington Co., Phoenix, 1976-89; gov. State of Ariz., 1991—. Precinct committeeman Ariz.'s Legis. Dist. 24, Paradise Valley; fin. chmn. State Republican Party, Phoenix, 1982-84; campaign advisor Rep. John Rhodes, Sen. John McCain, Ariz.; chmn. Phoenix Citizens Police Protection Bond Com., 1988; v.p. bd. trustees Heard Mus.; mem. Men's Art Coun., Environ. Quality Commn., 1971-73, Ariz. Children's Found.; dep. sheriff Maricopa County Air Posse; exec. bd. Phoenix Community Alliance. Capt. USAF, 1968-71. Mem. Western Govs.' Assn. (chmn. 1992—). Episcopalian. Office: Govs Office 1700 W Washington St Phoenix AZ 85007-2812*

SYMMES, DANIEL LESLIE, three-dimensional technology executive, producer, director; b. Los Angeles, June 26, 1949; s. Louis Leslie and Mary (Warkentine) S. Student, Columbia Coll., Hollywood, Calif., 1970-71. Co-founder Stereovision Internat., Inc., North Hollywood, Calif., 1971; cons. Dimension 3e, Beverly Hills, Calif., 1975-87; pres., chmn. Spatial Techs. Inc., 3D Video Corp., Hollywood, Calif., 1987-95; pres., CEO Dimension 3, Beverly Hills, 1995—; responsible for comml. 3D TV in U.S. and abroad; known worldwide as Mr. 3D. Author: Amazing 3-D; contbr. numerous articles to profl. jours.; dir. photography local 659 IATSE; patentee 3-D TV; inventor 1st reflex widescreen 3D filming system. Mem. SMPTE.

SYMMONS, CLARE PAYNE, foundation administrator; b. Portland, Oreg., Mar. 3, 1962; d. Roy Alpha and Anna Lee (Bozarth) Payne; m. Michael Laurence Symmons, Oct. 12, 1991. BA in English Lit., Bryn Mawr Coll., 1984. Asst. to dir. mktg. and devel. Portland Opera Assn., 1984-86; asst. found. dir. Holladay Park Med. Ctr. Found., Portland, 1987; dir. fin. devel. YWCA of Ctrl. Jersey, New Brunswick, 1988; cons. Portland, 1990-92; exec. dir. St. John's Luth. Hosp. Found., Libby, Mont., 1992-96, Cmty. Found. of Jackson Hole, Wyo., 1996—. Mem. Lincoln County Sustainability Task Force, Libby, Mont., 1993-96; chair bd. dirs. Literacy Vols. Am., Lincoln County, 1994; bd. dirs. Mont. Cmty. Found., 1993-96; mem. adv. bd. Habitat for Humanity, Lincoln, 1994. Mem. Soc. for Non-Profit Orgns., Western Mont. Fund Raisers Assn., Assn. for Healthcare Philanthropy, Mont. Soc. Mktg. and Cmty. Rels., Rotary. Home: PO Box 10396 Jackson WY 83002

SYMONDS, NORMAN LESLIE, computer programming specialist; b. Hawthorne, Calif., July 10, 1953; s. Malcolm F. and Nancy J. (Raab) S.; m. Catherine Anne Meades, Jan. 1, 1994. BA in Math., U. Calif., Berkeley, 1978; MBA in Mgmt. Sci., U. So. Calif., 1981. Programmer Burroughs Corp. (Unisys), Pasadena, Calif., 1978-81; sr. systems analyst Sungard Fin. Systems, Canoga Park, Calif., 1981-89; programming project leader Dames & Moore, L.A., 1989—. Home: 24120 Mariano St Woodland Hills CA 92367-5822 Office: Dames & Moore 911 Wilshire Blvd Ste 700 Los Angeles CA 90017-3436

SYMONS, JAMES MARTIN, theater and dance educator; b. Jacksonville, Ill., May 7, 1937; s. James and Pauline (Barton) S.; m. Judith White, Nov. 14, 1959; children: Tracy, Kelly, Carrie. BA, Ill. Coll., 1959; MA, So. Ill. U., 1964; PhD, Cornell U., 1970. Asst. prof. Yankton (S.D.) Coll., 1964-67; assoc. prof. Coll. St. Catherine, St. Paul, 1970-74, SUNY, Albany, 1974-77; prof., chair Trinity U., San Antonio, 1977-84; prof., chair theatre and dance dept. U. Colo., Boulder, 1984—; actor Off-Broadway, N.Y.C., 1959, Mo. Repertory Theatre, Kansas City, 1984; dir., actor Colo. Shakespeare Festival, Boulder, 1985—, producing artistic dir., 1994-95; leader People-to-People Del. of Theater Educators, USSR and Czechoslovakia, 1991. Author: Meyerhold's Theatre of the Grotesque, 1971 (Freedley Meml. award Theatre Libr. Assn. 1971); contbr. articles to scholarly jours. Lt. (j.g.) USN, 1960-63. Mem. Assn. for Theatre in Higher Edn. (pres. 1989-91), Assn. for Communication Adminstrn. (pres. 1990). Democrat. Methodist. Office: U of Colorado Dept Theatre And Dance Boulder CO 80309

SYMONS, ROBERT SPENCER, electronic engineer; b. San Francisco, July 3, 1925; s. Spencer W. and Avesia (Atkins) S.; m. Alice Faye Smith, Dec. 21, 1960; children: Julia Ann, Robert Spencer Jr. BS, Stanford U., 1946, MS, 1948. Engr. Eitel-McCullough, Inc., San Bruno, Calif., 1947, Heinz & Kaufman, South San Francisco, 1948, Pacific Electronics Co., Los Gatos, Calif., 1949; sr. engring. mgr. Varian Assocs., Palo Alto, Calif., 1950-83; tech. dir. Litton Industries, San Carlos, Calif., 1983—. Recipient Charles B. Thornton award for Advanced Technology Achievement, 1991. Patentee in field. Served to 1st lt. AUS, 1950-53. Fellow IEEE (assoc. editor Transactions on Electron Devices jour. 1980-83); mem. Phi Beta Kappa, Tau Beta Pi. Club: Commonwealth of Calif. Home: 290 Surrey Pl Los Altos CA 94022-2146 Office: Litton Industries 960 Industrial Rd San Carlos CA 94070-4116

SZABO, ZOLTAN, medical science educator, medical institute director; b. Szeged, Hungary, Oct. 5, 1943; came to U.S., 1967; s. Imre and Maria (Szikora) S.; m. Wanda Toy, Dec. 5, 1976; children: Eva, Maria. Student, U. Med. Sch., Szeged, 1962-65; PhD, Columbia Pacific U., 1983. Tech. dir. microsurgery lab. R.K. Davies Med. Ctr., San Francisco, 1972-80; dir. Microsurgery and Operative Endoscopy Tng. (MOET) Inst., San Francisco, 1980—; assoc. dir. advanced laparoscopic surgery tng. ctr. Sch. Medicine U. Calif., San Francisco, 1992-96; rsch. assoc. oral and maxillofacial surgery U. of Pacific, San Francisco, 1980-83, adj. asst. prof., 1983—. Author: Microsurgery Techniques, vol. 1, 1974, vol. 2, 1984 (1st Place award for excellence in med. writing 1982); co-author: Tissue Approximation in Endoscopic Surgery, 1995; editor-in-chief Surgical Technology Internationa, Vol. 3, 1994, Vol. 4, 1995, Vol. 5, 1996; contbr. chpt. books, articles to profl. jours. With U.S. Army, 1969-71. Recipient cert. of Merit, AMA, 1978, commendation Accreditation Coun. for Continuing Med. Edn., 1984, 90, 94, Spl. Recognition award Sch. Medicine Cen. U. Venezuela, 1988, Sci. Poste Sessions Hon. Mention award Am. Urol. Assn., 1992, 1st prize Roundtable for New Techs. and Innovations we. sect., 1992, James Barrett Brown award Am. Assn. Plastic Surgeons, 1993. Fellow Internat. Coll. Surgeons (Disting. Svc. award 1994); mem. Hungarian Gynecol. Soc. (hon.), Medico-Dental Study Guild Calif., Internat. Microsurg. Soc., Soc. Am. Gastrointestinal Endoscopic Surgeons (hon., 1st prize Residents and Fellows Rsch. and Sci. Presentation 1992), Am. Fertility Soc., Am. Soc. Reconstructive Microsurgery (assoc.), Am. Soc. for Peripheral Nerve. Office: Microsurgery Operative Endoscopy Tng Inst 153 States St San Francisco CA 94114-1403

SZCZERBA, VICTOR BOGDAN, electrical engineer, sales engineer; b. Chgo., Oct. 21, 1966; s. Bogdan and Zosia (Mika) S. BSEE, Marquette U., 1989; postgrad., U. Calif., Berkeley, 1996—. Sales engr. New Vision Computers, Milw., 1988-89; mktg. engr. Cypress Semicondr., San Jose, Calif., 1989-91; regional sales mgr. AMD/NEXGEN, Milpitas, Calif., 1991-96; sr. acct. mgr. Sun Micro Sys., Mountain View, Calif., 1996—; sales engr. Trinity Tech., Mountainview, Calif., 1991-92; cons. S3, Santa Clara, 1991-92; tutor Project Read. Mem. Knights of St. Patrick (pres. 1988-89), Sigma Phi Delta (v.p. 1987-88). Republican. Roman Catholic. Home: 827 University Ave Palo Alto CA 94301-2132

SZEGO, CLARA MARIAN, cell biologist, educator; b. Budapest, Hungary, Mar. 23, 1916; came to U.S., 1921, naturalized, 1927; d. Paul S. and Helen (Elek) S.; m. Sidney Roberts, Sept. 14, 1943. A.B., Hunter Coll., 1937; M.S. (Garvan fellow), U. Minn., 1939, Ph.D., 1942. Instr. physiology U. Minn., 1942-43; Minn. Cancer Research Inst. fellow, 1943-44; rsch. assoc. OSRD, Nat. Bur. Standards, 1944-45, Worcester Found. Exptl. Biology, 1945-47; rsch. instr. physiol. chemistry Yale U. Sch. Medicine, 1947-48; mem. faculty UCLA, 1948—, prof. biology, 1960—. Named Woman of Year in Sci. Los Angeles Times, 1957-58; Guggenheim fellow, 1956; named to Hunter Coll. Hall of Fame, 1987. Fellow AAAS; mem. Am. Physiol. Soc., Am. Soc. Cell Biology, Endocrine Soc. (CIBA award 1953), Soc. for Endocrinology (Gt. Britain), Biochem. Soc. (Gt. Britain), Internat. Soc. Rsch. Reprodn., Phi Beta Kappa (pres. UCLA chpt. 1973-74), Sigma Xi (pres. UCLA chpt. 1976-77). Home: 1371 Marinette Rd Pacific Palisades CA 90272-2627 Office: U Calif Dept Molecular Cell & Devel Biology Los Angeles CA 90095-1606

SZELENYI, IVAN, educator; b. Budapest, Apr. 17, 1938; came to the U.S., 1981; s. Gusztav and Julianna (Csapo) S.; m. Kataline Varady, Jan. 31, 1960; children: Szonja, Lilla, Balazs. PhD, Hungarian Acad. Scis., Budapest, 1973, DSc, 1990; hon. doctorate, Budapest U. Econs., 1992. Rsch. fellow Hungarian Acad. Scis., Budapest, 1963-75; found. prof. Flinders U., Adelaide, Australia, 1975-80; prof. U. Wis., Madison, 1981-86; disting. prof. CUNY Grad. Ctr., 1986-88; prof. UCLA, L.A., 1988—. Author: Urban Inequalities under State Socialism, 1983, Socialist Entrepreneurs, 1988 (C. Wright Mills award 1989); co-author: Intellectuals on the Road to Class Power, 1979. Mem. Hungarian Acad. Scis. *

SZENASI, GAIL, educational administrator; b. Portales, N.Mex., Dec. 26, 1946; d. Robert Claude Mersereau and Wanda (Sollock) Sims; m. James Joseph Szenasi, Sept. 2, 1968; children: Clay, Daniel, David. BS, Tex. Tech U., 1969, MEd, 1975; PhD, U. N.Mex., 1989. Cert. tchr., adminstr., N.Mex. Tchr. Denver Pub. Schs., 1969-70, Lubbock (Tex.) Pub. Schs., 1970-76, U. N.Mex. Lab. Sch., Albuquerque, 1981; cons. U. N.Mex., N.Mex., 1984-88; headmistress Sunset Mesa Schs., Albuquerque, 1988—; cons. Rsch., 1988-94, ETC, Cedar Crest, N.Mex., 1984—, sr. Training cons., Sandia Nat. Labs., Albuquerque, N.Mex.

SZETO, ERIK K., family practice physician; b. Sept. 17, 1949; s. Yat and Siu-Fong (Ng) S.; m. Anita Y. Chan; children: Matthew, Eileen, Amanda, Jacob. BA in Chemistry, U. Ore., 1972; MS in Biochem. & Molecular Biophysics, Yale U., 1974; DO, Kirksville Coll. Osteopathic, 1978. Intern Botsford Hosp., Farmington Hills, 1978-79; pvt. family practice Portland, Ore., 1979—; chmn. quality assurance com. Family Care PCO of Oreg., 1991-94, Evergreen PCO of Oreg., 1991-94; chmn. gen. practice dept. Eastmoreland Hosp., Portland, 1985-87; health com. Gov. Roberts transitional team, 1990; com. for appt. diversion program med. dir. State of Oreg., 1992. Chmn., founder, bd. dirs. Chinese Svc. Ctr., Portland, 1983—; Chinese Cmty. Devel. Corp., 1991—; mem. leaders round table, Portland, 1992; chmn., exec. com. Asian Am. Coalition, 1992—. Mem. Am. Osteopathic Assn., Osteopathic Physicians and Surgeons of Ore., Ore. Med. Assn. Presbyn. Office: 4130 SE Division St Portland OR 97202-1647

SZETO, HUNG, publisher; b. Hoyping, Canton, People's Republic of China, Sept. 8, 1936; s. Cheong Yee and Sau King(Kwan) S.; m. Sau Hing Chow, Jan. 27, 1962; children: Roland, Lisa, Nancy. B in adminstrn., Tsing Hua Coll., Hong Kong, 1969. Mgr. Far East Trade Ctr., Seattle, 1975-81; editor Seattle Chinese Post, 1982; pres. APC Group, Seattle, 1986—; pub. Chinese Bus. Jour., 1989—. Mem. Asian Am. Journalists Assn., Chinese-Lang. Press. Inst., Northwest Minority Pubs. Assn. Office: Chinese Bus Jour 659 S Weller St Seattle WA 98104-2944 *Personal philosophy: Serving the community by providing information.*

SZILAGYI, MIKLOS NICHOLAS, electrical and computer engineering educator; b. Budapest, Hungary, Feb. 4, 1936; came to U.S., 1981; s. Karoly and Ilona (Abraham) S.; m. Larissa Dorner, Feb. 23, 1957 (div. July 1970); 1 child, Gabor; m. Julia Levai, May 31, 1975; 1 child, Zoltan Charles. MS in Engring., Physics with honors, Tech. U. Leningrad, USSR, 1960; PhD, Electrotech. U. Leningrad, 1965; D Tech., Tech. U. Budapest, 1965; DSc with exceptional distinction, Hungarian Acad. Scis., 1979. Research asst. phys. electronics Tech. U. Leningrad, 1958-60; research assoc., Inst. Tech. Physics Hungarian Acad. Scis., 1960-66; head electron optics lab. Tech. U. Budapest, 1966-71; prof., head dept. phys. scis. K. Kando Coll. of Elec. Engring., Budapest, 1971-79, pres., 1971-74; cons. Deutsches Elektronen-Synchrotron DESY, Hamburg, Federal Republic of Germany, 1980-81; vis. sr. research assoc., applied and engring. physics Cornell U., 1981-82; prof. elec. and computer engring. U. Ariz., 1982—; sci. adv. Nat. Inst. Neurosurgery, Budapest, 1966-70; vis. prof. Enrico Fermi Inst., U. Chgo., Lawrence Berkeley Lab, U. Calif., Stanford Linear Accelerator Ctr., Stanford U., 1976-77, Inst. Physics, U. Aarhus, Denmark, 1979-81, 88, 89, 90, Delft U. Tech., The Netherlands, 1988-89, U. Heidelberg, Fed. Republic of Germany, Max Planck Inst. Nuclear Physics, Heidelberg, 1984, pres. The Tucson Inst., 1993—. Author eleven books, including Introduction to the Theory of Space-Charge Optics, 1974, Fachlexikon Physik, 1979, Electron and Ion Optics, 1988, How To Save Our Country, 1993; contbr. over 95 articles to profl. jours., also contbr. to internat. confs; editor The New Common Sense. UN Indsl. Devel. Orgn. fellow, 1976. Mem. IEEE (sr.), Am. Phys. Soc., Internat. Soc. Hybrid Microelectronics, European Soc. Stereotactic and Functional Neurosurgery, L. Eotvos Phys. Soc. (Brody prize 1964), J. Neumann Soc. for Computer Sci., Danish Phys. Soc., Danish Engring. Soc. Office: U Ariz Dept Elec And Computer Engring Tucson AZ 85721

SZOSTAK, EDWARD WALTER, JR., pharmaceutical company executive; b. New Brunswick, N.J., Jan. 6, 1957; s. Edward and Matilda Catherine (Seaman) S.; m. Teresa Marie Szostak, Sept. 24, 1988; children: Alexandra Noel, Edward Blake III. BS, Charleston So. U., 1979; MBA in Human Resources, Nat. U., 1987. Med. rep. Geigy Pharms., Sacramento, 1982-83; clin. conf. mgr. Ciba Geigy Pharm., Sacramento, 1983-85; mktg. cons. mgr. Ciba-Geigy Corp., Summit, N.J., 1985-87; nat. account mgr. Ciba Pharms., L.A., 1987-93; dir. strategic planning Ciba Pharms., Summit, 1994—; gen. mgr. Novartis Pharm. Corp., dir. strategic planning and analysis Ciba Geigy Corp., Basel, Switzerland, 1982, 94, dir. corp. nat. accounts Midwest-West, 1994. Recipient Nat. Best of the Best in Managed Care award Health Internat. Rsch. Corp., 1994. Republican. Roman Catholic. Home: 4504 S Hampton Cir Boulder CO 80301

TAAFE, PETER JAMES, financial consultant; b. Youngstown, Ohio, Sept. 26, 1956; s. Francis Edwin and Donna Marie (Haletek) G.; m. Lucretia Laurie Ferch, June 2, 1990. Student, Ohio U., 1975-78. Cert. investment and fin. cons.; cert. trainer NLP. Prof. Ben Franklin Internat. Sch., Barcelona, Spain, 1986-88; dist. mgr. First Investors Corp., Seattle, 1988-93; sr. fin. cons., founding mem. Sound Investment Svcs., Seattle, 1993—. Contbr. articles to profl. jours. Vol., supporter Seattle Commons, 1993, 94. Recipient Highest award for Achievement Dale Carnegie, Bellevue, Washington, 1992. Mem. Seattle C. of C. (Bus. Vols. for the Arts). Home: 1415 2nd Ave Unit 1408 Seattle WA 98101-2033 Office: Sound Investment Svcs 1501 Fourth Ave Ste 2270 Seattle WA 98101

TABRISKY, JOSEPH, radiologist, educator; b. Boston, June 23, 1931; s. Henry and Gertrude Tabrisky; BA cum laude, Harvard U., 1952; MD cum laude, Tufts U., 1956; m. Phyllis Eleanor Page, Apr. 23, 1955; children: Joseph Page, Elizabeth Ann, William Page. Flexible intern U. Ill. Hosp., 1956-57; resident in radiology Fitzsimons Army Hosp., 1958-60; instr. radiology Tufts U. Med. Sch., 1964-65; cons. radiologist Swedish Med. Center, Denver, 1966-68; chief radiologist Kaiser Found. Hosp., Harbor City, Calif., 1968-72; mem. faculty UCLA Med. Sch., 1972—, prof. radiol. scis., 1975-92, prof emeritus, 1993—, vice chmn. dept., 1976-92 , exec. policy com. radiol. scis.; chmn. radiology dept. Harbor-UCLA Med. Ctr., 1975-92 , pres. faculty soc., 1979-80, exec. dir. MR/CT Imaging Ctr., bd. dirs. Rsch. Ednl. Inst., Harbor Collegium/UCLA Found.; chief exec. officer Vascular Biometrics Inc.; steering com. Harvard U., 1952; cons. L.A. County Dept. Pub. Health; chmn. L.A. County Radiol. Standards Com., 1979. Mem. Harvard-Radcliffe Schs. Com.; chmn., bd. dirs., treas., Harbor-UCLA Med. Found.; chmn. UCLA Coun. for Ednl. Devel. Maj. M.C., U.S. Army, 1957-63. Recipient Silver Knight award Nat. Mgmt. Assn., 1992. Diplomate Am. Bd. Radiology. Fellow Am. Coll. Radiology, Univ. Radcom Assn. (chief exec. officer 1987-89); mem. Radiol. Soc. N. Am., Calif. Med. Assn., Calif. Radiol. Soc., L.A. Med. Assn., L.A. Radiol. Soc., Alpha Omega Alpha. Contbr. articles to med. jours. Office: 1000 W Carson St Torrance CA 90502-2004

TACAL, JOSE VEGA, JR., public health official, veterinarian; b. Ilocos Sur, Philippines, Sept. 5, 1933; came to U.S., 1969; s. Jose Sr. and Cristina (Vega) T.; m. Lilia Caccam, 1959; children: Joyce, Jasmin, Jose III. DVM, U. Philippines, Quezon City, 1956; diploma, U. Toronto, 1964. Diplomate

Am. Coll. Vet. Preventive Medicine; lic. vet., Calif. Provincial veterinarian Philippine Bur. Animal Industry, Manila, 1956-57; instr. vet. medicine U. Philippines, Quezon City, 1957-64, asst. prof., chmn. dept. vet. microbiology, pathology and pub. health, 1965-69; pub. health veterinarian San Bernardino (Calif.) County Dept. Pub. Health, 1970-83, sr. pub. health veterinarian, program mgr., sect. chief, 1984—; zoonotic diseases lectr. Calif. State U., San Bernardino, spring 1984; lectr. U. Calif. Extension, Riverside, spring, 1985; vis. prof. vet. pub. health U. Philippines at Los Banos, Laguna, 1988; participant 1st Internat. Conf. on Emerging Zoonoses, Jerusalem, 1996; presenter in field, including 4th Internat. Symposium on Ectoparasites of Pets, U. Calif., Riverside, 1997, program presenter, 1997. Columnist L.A. Free Press, 1991, Pilipinas Times, 1993, Mabuhay Times, 1994-95; contbr. more than 50 articles to profl. jours. Pres. Filipino Assn. of San Bernardino County, Highland, Calif., 1979; charter mem. Greater Inland Empire Filipino Assn., Highland, 1986—; del. First Filipino Media Conf. N.Am., L.A., 1993; participant 1st Internat. Conf. on Emerging Zoonoses, Jerusalem, 1996; mem. San Bernardino County Africanized Honey Bey Task Force, 1993—. Recipient Donald T. Fraser Meml. medal U. Toronto, 1964, Cert. of Merit, Philippine Vet. Med. Assn., 1965, Cert. of Appreciation Calif. State Bd. Examiners in Vet. Medicine, 1979, 84, Cert. of Recognition, Congressman George E. Brown Jr., 42d Congl. Dist. Calif., 1994, Assemblyman Joe Baca, 62d Assembly Dist., Calif. State Legis., 1994, Colombo Plan Study fellow Can./Philippine Govts., 1963-64. Mem. AAAS, AVMA, Orange Belt Vet. Med. Assn., Western Poultry Disease Conf., Soc. for Advancement of Rsch., Nat. Trust for Historic Preservation, N.Y. Acad. Scis., Phi Kappa Phi, Phi Sigma. Office: San Bernardino County Dept Pub Health 351 N Mountain View Ave San Bernardino CA 92415-0010

TACHA, DEANELL REECE, federal judge; b. Jan. 26, 1946. BA, U. Kans., 1968; JD, U. Mich., 1971. Spl. asst. to U.S. Sec. of Labor, Washington, 1971-72; assoc. Hogan & Hartson, Washington, 1973, Thomas J. Pitner, Concordia, Kans., 1973-74; dir. Douglas County Legal Aid Clinic, Lawrence, Kans., 1974-77; assoc. prof. law U. Kans., Lawrence, 1974-77, prof., 1977-85, assoc. dean, 1977-79, assoc. vice chancellor, 1979-81, vice chancellor, 1981-85; judge U.S. Ct. Appeals (10th cir.), Denver, 1985—; U.S. sentencing commr., 1994—. Office: US Ct Appeals 10th Cir Ste 100 4830 W 15th St Lawrence KS 66049-3846

TACKITT, JAMES WILLIAM, graphic arts and photography educator, genealogical researcher; b. Bell, Calif., Dec. 18, 1935; s. Howard Russell and Ilabess (Hebard) T.; m. Shirley Emma Van Gieson, Jan. 27, 1957; children: Heidi Lynn Tackitt Baker, Pamela Ann Tackitt Thornton, James William II, Eric Russell Iveson, Karen Ellen Tackitt Quinn. BA, Chico State U., 1965; student, U. Calif., Berkeley, 1980. Cert. tchr., cert. vocat. tchr., Calif. Vocat. tchr. offset printing/graphics Contra Costa County Regional Occupl. Program, Concord, Calif., 1980-90; tchr. Mt. Diablo Unified Sch. Dist., Concord, Calif., 1966-96. Co-compiler: Stafford County, Va., 1800-1850, 1982; compiler (family genealogy) Descendants of Allen J. Tackitt, 1958; editor, pub. Tackett Family Jour., 1963—. City councilman City of Live Oak, Calif., 1963-66; mem. commn. Local Agy. Formation Com., Sutter County, Calif., 1965. Named Ky. Col., Gov. Julian Carroll, 1978. Mem. Ky. Geneal. Soc., Va. Geneal. Soc., Contra Costa County Geneal. Soc. (pres. 1979-80, past editor). Democrat. So. Baptist. Home: 1830 Johnson Dr Concord CA 94520-3917

TACKOWIAK, BRUCE JOSEPH, lawyer; b. Milw., July 10, 1956; s. Eugene Charles and Bernadine (Van Engle) T.; m. Deborah A. Moore, Dec. 11, 1994. BA in History and Polit. Sci., U. Wis., 1979; cert. emergency med. technician, Madison Area Tech. Coll., 1981; Diploma in Internat. and Comparative Law, Magdalen Coll., U. Oxford, Eng., 1986; JD, U. San Diego, 1988. Bar: Calif. 1990, Ill. 1991, U.S. Dist. Ct. (ctrl. and so. dists.) Calif. 1990, U.S. Ct. Appeals (4th cir.) 1990. Atty. LaFollette, Johnson, De Haas, Fesler & Ames, L.A., 1990-92, Hillsinger & Costanzo, L.A., 1992-93, Roxborough, Pomerance & Gallegos, LLP, L.A., 1993—; assoc. Am. Inns of Ct., 1992—. Sr./mng. editor U. San Diego Jour. Contemporary Legal Issues, 1987-88. Mem. ABA, ATLA, Calif. Bar Assn., Los Angeles County Bar Assn., Ill. Bar Assn., Chgo. Bar Assn., World Futurist Soc. (profl.). Office: Roxborough, Pomerance & Gallegos LLP 10866 Wilshire Blvd Ste 1200 Los Angeles CA 90024-4336

TAFOYA, ARTHUR N., bishop; b. Alameda, N.Mex., Mar. 2, 1933; s. Nicholas and Rosita Tafoya. Ed., St. Thomas Sem., Denver, Conception (Mo.) Sem. Ordained priest Roman Cath. Ch., 1962. Asst. pastor Holy Rosary Parish, Albuquerque, 1962-65; pastor Northern N.Mex., from 1965, San Jose Parish, Albuquerque; rector Immaculate Heart of Mary Sem., Santa Fe; ordained bishop of Pueblo Colo., 1980—. Office: 1001 N Grand Ave Pueblo CO 81003-2915*

TAFUR, MARIO HUMBERTO, psychiatrist; b. Libano, Tolima, Colombia, June 22, 1940; came to U.S., 1972; s. Rafael and Clementina (Galvis) T.; m. Clemencia Tafur, Aug. 30, 1969; children: Mario, Joseph, Camilo. MD, U. Javeriana, Bogota, Colombia, 1968. Diplomate Am. Bd. Psychiatry. Psychiat. resident Menninger, Topeka, 1973-76; staff psychiatrist VA Med. Ctr., Topeka, 1976-77, chief acute svcs., 1977-79; mem. faculty Menninger Found., Topeka, 1977—; med. dir. adult svcs. St. Luke's Behavioral Ctr., Phoenix, 1981-87, pres. med. staff, 1984-85; med. dir. Menninger Phoenix, 1987-94; chmn. dept. psychiatry, med. dir. St. Joseph's Hosp. & Med. Ctr., Phoenix, 1988—; med. dir. St. Joseph's Behavioral Health Svcs., Phoenix, 1995—; med. dir. Generations Program St. Luke's Med. Ctr., Phoenix, 1996—. Mem. AMA, Am. Psychiat. Assn., Am. Acad. Med. Dirs., Menninger Alumni Assn. Office: 300 W Clarendon Ave Ste 215 Phoenix AZ 85013-3422

TAGGART, SONDRA, financial planner, investment advisor; b. N.Y.C., July 22, 1934; d. Louis and Rose (Birnbaum) Hamov; children: Eric, Karen. BA, Hunter Coll., 1955. Cert. fin. planner; registered investment advisor; registered prin. Nat. Assn. Securities Dealers. Founder, dir., officer Copyright Svc. Bur., Ltd., N.Y.C., 1957-69; dir., officer Maclen Music, Inc., N.Y.C., 1964-69, The Beatles Ltd., 1964-69; pres. Westshore, Inc., Mill Valley, Calif., 1969-82; investment advisor, securities broker, chief exec. officer The Taggart Co. Ltd., 1982—. Editor: The Red Tapes: Commentaries on Doing Business With The Russians and East Europeans, 1978. Mem. Internat. Assn. Fin. Planners, Registry Fin. Planning Practitioners. Republican. Club: Bankers. Office: 9720 Wilshire Blvd Ste 205 Beverly Hills CA 90212-2006

TAGGART, TOM, county administrator; b. L.A., July 24, 1953; s. Claude Edward and Patricia Louise (Stark) T.; m. Cynthia L., Oct. 3, 1976; children: Lindsay Allison, Megan Laural. BA in Radio & TV, Calif. State U., Long Beach, 1976. Tax auditor IRS, Carson, Calif., 1977-78, Lewiston, Idaho, 1978-79, Coeur D Alene, Idaho, 1979-84; tax cons. pvt. practice, Coeur D Alene, Idaho, 1984-91; restaurant owner Coeur D Alene, Idaho, 1986-87; clk. of dist. ct. Kootenai County, Coeur D Alene, Idaho, 1991-95; county adminstr. Kootenai County, Coeurd Alene, Idaho, 1995—. Trustee Lakeland Sch. Dist., Rathdrum, Idaho, 1982-88, chair 1984-88; mem. coun. City of Rathdrum, 1989-90. Mem. Am. Soc. Pub. Adminstrn., Govt. Fin. Officers Assn., Nat. Inst. Govt. Purchasing, The Election Ctr. Independent. Office: Kootenai County 501 Govt Way Coeur D Alene ID 83814

TAGOMORI, HOWARD H., protective services official. Chief of police Maui, Hawaii. Office: Maui Dept Police 55 Mahalani St Wailuku HI 96793

TAHMASSIAN, ARA ZARNEH, university director; b. Tehran, Iran, Apr. 15, 1953; came to U.S., 1981; s. Ohan Zarneh and Nashkoon (Asadourian) T.; m. Linda Khosrof Garabedian, Jan. 7, 1953; children: Levon Zarneh, Ani Verjeen. BSc in Nuclear Engring., London U., 1977; postgrad., Middlesex (Eng.) Poly. U., 1978; MSc in Radiol. Health, Salford (Eng.) U., 1980; PhD in Health Physics, Columbia Pacific U., 1984. Chief field ops. Nat. Safety Cons., Fremont, Calif., 1981-84, v.p. ops., 1987-88; dir. environ. health and safety Vets. Med. Ctr., San Francisco, 1984-87; mgr. radiation safety U. Calif., San Francisco, 1988-93, dir. environ. health and safety, 1993—; cons. various hosps., Calif., 1982—. Co-author papers in field, book chpt. Trustee St. Gregory's Ch., San Francisco, 1991-92; pres. Ararat Armenian Assoc., San Francisco, 1991, Armenian Cultural Found., San Francisco, 1989; bd. dirs. Calif. Radioactive Forum, San Francisco, 1993. Mem. Soc. Nuclear Medicine, North Calif. Health Physics Soc. Republican. Armenian Orthodox. Home: 39537 Benavente Ave Fremont CA 94539-3002 Office: U Calif 50 Medical Center Way San Francisco CA 94143-8050

TAI, FRANK, aerospace engineering consultant; b. Omaha, Apr. 10, 1955; s. Shou Nan and May (Chuang) T.; m. Lorraine Mae Fesq, May 14, 1988. BSME, U. Calif., Berkeley, 1977; MS in Automatic Controls Engring., MIT, 1979. Design engr. satellite attitude control systems Ball Aerospace, Boulder, Colo., 1979-84; mgr. satellite attitude control systems TRW, Redondo Beach, Calif., 1984-88; mgr. engring. Microcosm, Inc., Torrance, Calif., 1988-89; pres., engring. cons., founder Tech. Advancements, Inc., Playa del Rey, Calif., 1989—. Contbr. articles to profl. jours. Mem. AIAA, Am. Astronautical Soc., Sigma Xi, Tau Beta Pi, Pi Tau Sigma. Office: Tech Advancements Inc 6738 Esplanade St # 300 Playa Del Rey CA 90293-7525

TAIFEL, ROMAN S., mortgage company executive; b. Freiburg, Germany, Oct. 11, 1936; came to U.S., 1949; s. Valentine and Valerie (Fisher) T.; m. Millee L. Buttery, July (, 1966. BS, Capitol Radio Engring., Washington, 1970. Lic. in real estate; comml. pilot. Engring. technician Western Union, Oakland, Calif., 1962-66; equipment inspector Western Union, Seattle, 1966-76, resident engr., 1977-89; real estate agt. Century 21, Seattle, 1992-93; owner RST Mortgage Svc., Seattle, 1994—; sales mgr. U.S. Mortgage Reduction, Hilton Island, S.C., 1992-96; ind. distbr. Tex. Refinery Corp, Fort Worth, 1997—. Mem. Rep. Nat. Com., Washington, 1980. Lt. comdr. USCGR, 1984—. Mem. Confederate Air Force (fin. officer 1980-84), VFW, Am. Legion. Home: 4426 40th Ave SW Seattle WA 98116 Office: RST Mortgage Service 4426 40th Ave SW Seattle WA 98116

TAIMUTY, SAMUEL ISAAC, physicist; b. West Newton, Pa., Dec. 20, 1917; s. Elias and Samia (Hawatt) T.; BS, Carnegie Inst. Tech., 1940; PhD, U. So. Calif., 1951; m. Betty Jo Travis, Sept. 12, 1953 (dec.); children: Matthew, Martha; m. Rosalie Richards, Apr. 3, 1976. Physicist, U.S. Naval Shipyard, Phila. and Long Beach, Calif., 1942-46; rsch. asst. U. So. Calif., 1947-51; sr. physicist U.S. Naval Radiol. Def. Lab., 1950-52, SRI Internat., Menlo Park, Calif., 1952-72; sr. staff engr. Lockheed Missiles & Space Co., Sunnyvale, Calif., 1972-89; cons. physicist, 1971—. Mem. Am. Phys. Soc., Sigma Xi. Episcopalian. Contbr. articles to sci. publs. Patentee in field. Home: 3346 Kenneth Dr Palo Alto CA 94303-4217

TAIT, JOHN REID, lawyer; b. Toledo, Apr. 7, 1946; s. Paul Reid and Lucy Richardson (Ruddew) T.; m. Christina Ruth Bjornstad, Mar. 12, 1972; children: Gretchen, Mary. BA, Columbia Coll., 1968; JD, Vanderbilt U., 1974. Bar: Idaho 1974, U.S. Dist. Ct. Idaho 1974, U.S. Ct. Appeals (9th cir.), U.S. Supreme Ct., Nez Perce Tribal Ct. Assoc. Keeton & Tait, Lewiston, Idaho, 1974-76, ptnr., 1976-86, 89—, Keeton, Tait & Petrie, 1986-88, Keeton & Tait, 1989—. Chmn. bd. No. Rockies Action Group, Helena, Mont., 1985-86, bd. dirs. 1981-88, Lewiston Hist. Preservation Commn., Idaho, 1975-94, chmn., 1988-94; bd. dirs. Idaho Legal Aid Svcs., Boise, 1975—, Idaho Housing Agy., Boise, 1984-91, St. Joseph Regional Med. Ctr. Found., Inc., 1989-94, Lewiston Ind. Found. for Edn., Inc., 1996—; Dem. precinct committeeman, 1976-86, state committeeman, 1977-94; co-chmn. Idaho state re-election com. John V. Evans, 1978; Idaho del. Nat. Dem. Conv., N.Y., 1980, mem. standing com. on credentials, N.Y., 1980, San Francisco, 1984; regional dir. Idaho State Dem. Party, 1996—; treas. Larry LaRocco for Congress, 1990, 92; vestryman Episcopal Ch. of Nativity, 1996—. With U.S. Army, 1968-71. Recipient Pro Bono Svc. award Idaho State Bar 1988, Community Recognition award Lewiston Intergovtl. Coun., 1992, Spl. Recognition award Idaho Legal Aid Svcs., Inc., 1993. Mem. ABA, ATLA, NACDL, Idaho Trial Lawyers Assn. (regional dir. 1976-77, 86-88, 96—), Clearwater Bar Assn. (sec. 1974-76, pres. 1984-86), Consumer Attys. Calif. Democrat. Office: Keeton & Tait 312 Miller St Ste E Lewiston ID 83501-1944

TAIT, WILLIAM HENDERSON, artist; b. Edinburgh, Scotland, Apr. 1, 1942; came to U.S. 1948; s. John Shanks and Anne (Henderson) T. Student, Art Students League of N.Y., 1967-71, San Francisco Art Inst., 1974. Studio mgr. Kala Inst., Berkeley, Calif., 1982-85; Exhibited in group show at San Francisco Mus. Modern Art Rental Gallery, 1991, 94; one man show at Intuit, Inc., 1996; works in permanent collection at Calif. Palace of the Legion of Honor, San Francisco. Mem. art curriculum devel. com. Berkeley (Calif.) Unified Schs., 1984-85; developer curricular Lincoln County, Oreg., 1994-95. Mem. Art Students League N.Y. Home: 1357 93rd Ave Oakland CA 94603-1413

TAKAHASHI, GARY WAYNE, internist, hematologist, oncologist; b. Honolulu, Jan. 2, 1959; s. Kenneth Kiyoshi and Grace Setsuko (Ishigure) T. BS in Math. and Biology, Stanford U., 1980; MS in Anatomy/Reproductive Biology, U. Hawaii, 1983; MD, John A. Burns Sch. Medicine, Honolulu, 1984. Diplomate Nat. Bd. Med. Examiners, Am. Bd. Internal Medicine (Hematology, Med. Oncology). Intern, resident Oreg. Health Scis. U., Portland, 1984-87; chief resident St. Vincent Med. Ctr., Portland, 1987-88; fellow hematology/oncology U. Wash., Seattle, 1988-93; physician Hematology Clinic, Portland, Oreg., 1993-94, Oreg. Hematology Oncology Assocs., 1994—; clin. asst. prof. medicine Oreg. Health Scis. U., 1995—. Contbr. articles and abstracts to profl. publs. Recipient Achievement Rewards for Coll. Scientists scholarship, 1982, Merck, Sharp & Dohme Acad. award, 1982, Nat. Rsch. Svc. award fellowship NIH, 1990, March of Dimes Rsch. grant, 1993. Mem. Am. Coll. Physicians, Am. Soc. Hematology, Am. Soc. Clin. Oncology, Southwestern Oncology Group, Oreg. Med. Assn., Wash. Med. Assn., Oreg. Mycol. Soc. Office: Oreg Hematology Oncology Assocs 9155 SW Barnes Rd Ste 530 Portland OR 97225-6632

TAKASUGI, ROBERT MITSUHIRO, federal judge; b. Tacoma, Sept. 12, 1930; s. Hidesaburo and Kayo (Otsuki) T.; m. Dorothy O. Takasugi; children: Jon Robert, Lesli Mari. BS, UCLA, Los Angeles, 1953; LLB, JD, U. So. Calif., 1959. Bar: Calif. bar 1960. Practiced law Los Angeles, 1960-73; judge East Los Angeles Municipal Ct., 1973-75, adminstrv. judge, 1974, presiding judge, 1975; judge Superior Ct., County of Los Angeles, 1975-76; U.S. dist. judge U.S. Dist. Ct. (cen. dist.) Calif., 1976—; nat. legal counsel Japanese Am. Citizens League; guest lectr. law seminars Harvard U. Law Sch. Careers Symposium; commencement spkr.; mem. Legion Lex U. So. Calif. Law Ctr.; chmn. Pub. Defs. Indigent Def. & Psychiat. Panel Com.; mem. Affirmative Action Com., Habeas Corpus-Death Penalty Com., Exec. Com., Jury Com., Settlement Rule Com., Adv. Com. on Codes of Conduct of the Jud. Conf. of the U.S., 1988-92, Code of Conduct of Judges. Mem. editorial bd. U. So. Calif. Law Rev., 1959; contbr. articles to profl. jours. Mem. Calif. adv. com. Western Regional Office, U.S. Commn. on Civil Rights; chmn. blue ribbon com. for selection of chancellor L.A. C.C. With U.S. Army, 1953-55. Harry J. Bauer scholar, 1959; recipient U.S. Mil. Man of Yr. award for Far East Theater U.S. Army, 1954, Jud. Excellence award Criminal Cts. Bar Assn., cert. of merit Japanese-Am. Bar Assn., Disting. Svc. award Asian Pacific Ctr. and Pacific Clinics, 1994, Freedom award Sertoma, 1995, Pub. Svc. award Asian Pacific Am. Legal Ctr. So. Calif., 1995, Trailblazer award So. Calif. region NAPABA, 1995, Spl. award Mex. Am. Bar Assn., 1996; named Judge of Yr. Century City Bar Assn., 1995. Mem. U. So. Calif. Law Alumni Assn. (dir.). Office: US Dist Ct 312 N Spring St Los Angeles CA 90012-4701

TAKEI, TOSHIHISA, otolaryngologist; b. L.A., Apr. 19, 1931; s. Taketomi and Mitsue (Hagihara) T.; m. Emiko Kubota, Jan. 25, 1955; children: H. Thomas, T. Robert. BA, UCLA, 1954; MD, Boston U., 1962. Diplomate, Am. Bd. Otolaryngology. Intern L.A. County Harbor Gen. Hosp., 1962-63; resident in otolaryngology L.A. County/U. So. Calif. Med. Ctr., 1963-67; staff physician Covina (Calif.) Ear, Nose & Throat Med. Group, 1968—; asst. prof. Sch. Medicine, U. So. Calif., L.A., 1968—. 1st lt. U.S. Army, 1955-56, Korea. Fellow Am. Acad. Otolaryngology, Royal Soc. Medicine. Republican. Buddhist. Office: Covina ENT Med Group Inc 236 W College St Covina CA 91723-1902

TAKEMOTO, CORY NOBORU, mathematics educator; b. Honolulu, June 29, 1962; s. Nobuo and Ritsuko Takemoto; m. Karen Noriko Hara, Aug. 25, 1990. BS, U. Hawaii, 1985, profl. diploma, 1986, MA, 1990. Tchr. Kailua (Hawaii) High Sch., 1986-87; substitute tchr. Punahou Sch., Honolulu, 1990-91; lectr. math. Honolulu C.C., 1991-92, instr. math., 1993-94; instr. math. Leeward C.C., Pearl City, Hawaii, 1994—. Mem. Math. Assn. Am. Office: Leeward CC 46-045 Ala Ike Pearl City HI 96782

TALBERT, MELVIN GEORGE, bishop; b. Clinton, La., June 14, 1934; s. Nettles and Florence (George) T.; m. Ethlelou Douglas, June 3, 1961; 1 child, Evangeline. BA, So. U., 1959; MDiv, Interdenominational Theol. Ctr., Gammon Theol. Sem., Atlanta, 1962; DD hon., Huston Tillotson Coll., Austin, 1972; LLD (hon.), U. Puget Sound, Tacoma, 1987. Ordained deacon, Meth. Ch., 1960 , elder, 1962, elected to episcopacy, United Meth. Ch., 1980. Pastor Boyd Chapel, Jefferson City, Tenn., 1960-61, Rising Sun, Sunrise, Tenn., 1960-61, St. John's Ch., L.A., 1961-62, Wesley Ch., L.A., 1962-64, Hamilton Ch., L.A., 1964-67; mem. staff So. Calif.-Ariz. Conf. United Meth. Ch., L.A., 1967-68; dist. supr. Long Beach dist. So. Calif.-Ariz. Conf. United Meth. Ch., 1968-73; gen. sec. Gen. Bd. Discipleship, Nashville, 1973-80; resident bishop Seattle area Pacific N.W. conf. United Meth. Ch., 1980-88, resident bishop San Francisco area Calif.-Nev. Conf., 1988—, sec. coun. bishops, 1988—; mem. exec. com. World Meth. Coun., 1976-81, 84—; mem. governing bd. Nat. Coun. Chs., 1980—; v.p., chmn. funding com. Gen. Commn. on Religion and Race, 1980-84, pres., 1984-88; chmn. Missional Priority Coordinating com. Gen. Coun. Ministries, 1980-84; mem. Gen. Commn. on Christian Unity and Interreligious Concerns, 1984—, African Ch. Growth and Devel. Com., 1981-84; pres. elect Nat. Coun. Ch. Christ in the U.S.A., pres. Mem. steering com. Student Non-Violent Coordinating com. Atlanta U. Ctr., 1960-61; trustee Gammon Theol. Sem., Atlanta, 1976—, U. Puget Sound, Tacoma, 1980-88 , Sch. Theology at Claremont, Calif., 1981-88, Pacific Sch. Religion, 1988—; bd. dirs. Glide Found., 1988—. Recipient award of merit for outstanding svc. in Christian edn. Gen. Bd. Edn., 1971; recipient Spl. achievement award Nat. Assn. Black Bus. Women, 1971; Nat. Meth. scholar, 1960; Crusade scholar, 1961. Mem. Theta Phi. Democrat. Home: 8735 W Camden Dr Elk Grove CA 95624-3037*

TALBOT, STEPHEN H., television producer, writer; b. Hollywood, Calif., Feb. 28, 1949; s. Lyle and Margaret (Epple) T.; m. Pippa Gordon; children: Dashiell, Caitlin. BA, Wesleyan U., 1970. Asst. to pres., lectr. Am. studies SUNY, Old Westbury, 1970-73; reporter Internews, Berkeley, Calif., 1973-79; producer, reporter KQED-TV, San Francisco, 1980-89; producer, writer Frontline (PBS), San Francisco, 1992—. Appeared in Leave It To Beaver as Gilbert, 1958-63, also Twilight Zone, Perry Mason, Lassie, others; producer, co-writer (documentary) The Long March of Newt Gingrich, 1996; producer: (documentary) The Best Campaign Money Can Buy, 1992 (Dupont award), (PBS-TV) John Doz Passos, Maxine Hong, Kingston, Carlos Fuentes, Ken Kesey, Beryl Markham; producer, writer: (documentary) The Case of Dashiell Hammett, 1982 (Peabody award, Edgar Allen Poe award); co-producer, reporter: (documentary) Broken Arrow, 1980 (George Peabody & George Polk award), Columbia U., others. Recipient Thomas Storke International Journalism award World Affairs Coun. No. Calif., San Francisco, 1983, 86, Golden Gate award San Francisco Film Festival, 1986, 89, Emmy award, NATAS, 1980-81, 82-83, 87-88, 90-91. Mem. Writer's Guild Am. West, Am. Fedn. TV and Radio Artists. Office: Ctr Investigative Reporting 500 Howard St Ste 206 San Francisco CA 94105-3000

TALBOT, STEVEN RICHARDS, vascular technologist, consultant, writer; b. Salt Lake City, Jan. 30, 1954; s. Eldon V. and Cara Sidney (Stevenson) T.; m. Penny Marie Bennett, Apr. 6, 1977; children: Alesia, Scott, Brian, Robert. Student, U. Utah, 1973, 75. Registered vascular technologist. Respiratory therapy technician LDS Hosp., Salt Lake City, 1975-78, peripheral vascular technologist, 1978-79, tech. dir. peripheral vascular dept., 1979-96; clin. svcs. coord. Am. Wellness and Fitness Ctrs., Sandy, Utah, 1996-97; edn. dir. Diagnostic Health Svcs., Las Vegas, 1997—; internat. speaker and cons. for various cos. Author: (book and instrnl. video tape) Techniques of Venous Imaging, 1992; contbr. chpts. to books; mem. editorial rev. bd. Jour. Diagnostic Med. Sonography, 1986—, Jour. Vascular Tech., 1994—. Mem. Soc. Vascular Tech. (6 coms., Cert. of Appreciation 1990, Pioneer award 1992), Utah Soc. Diagnostic Med. Sonographers. Mormon. Home: 527 N 220 E Centerville UT 84014 Office: Diagnostic Health Svcs Ste D 2860 E Flamingo Las Vegas NV 89121

TALBOTT, GEORGE ROBERT, physicist, mathematician, educator; b. San Diego, Oct. 1, 1925; s. George Fletcher and Mary (Lanz) T.; BA with honors, UCLA, 1960; DSc, Ind. No. U., 1973. Physicist, mem. tech. staff Rockwell Internat. Co., Anaheim, Calif., 1960-85; mem. faculty thermodynamics Pacific States U., 1971-77, prof., 1972-80, chmn. dept. math. studies, 1973-80; lectr. computer sci. Calif. State U., Fullerton, 1979—; cons. physics, computer sci.; disting. guest lectr. Brunel U., London, 1974, 76; spl. guest Forschungsbibliothek, Hannover, W. Ger., 1979; assoc. editor KRONOS jour., Glassboro (N.J.) U., 1978—; chief computer scientist and ednl. videotape dir. Specialized Software, Wilmot, Wis., 1982—; phys. scientist and rsch. assoc. San Diego Mus. Man, 1993-96. With M.C., U.S. Army, 1956. Recipient Vis. Scholar's award Western Mich. U., 1979. Mem. Am. Soc. Med. Technologists, Am. Math. Soc., Math. Assn. Am., Am. Soc. Clin. Pathologists (lic. med. lab. technologist), Sigma Xi. Buddhist. Author: Electronic Thermodynamics, 1973; Philosophy and Unified Science, 1977, Computer Applications, 1989, Sir Arthur and Gravity, 1990, Fermat's Last Theorem, 1991; co-inventor burner. Home: 4031 E Charter Oak Dr Orange CA 92869-2611

TALBOTT, RICHARD DAVID, physician; b. Jackson, Mich., Dec. 31, 1930; s. James Ernest and Ellen (McGowan) T.; m. Katherine Marie Bonney, June 18, 1983; children: James M., William J., Judith M. AB, Yale U., 1952; MD, Northwestern U., 1956. Diplomate Am. Bd. Orthopaedic Surgery. Intern Denver Gen. Hosp., 1956-57; resident St. Luke's Hosp., Denver, 1957-58, Lahey Clinic, Boston, 1958-59, Shriners Hosp. for Crippled Children, Springfield, Mass., 1959-60, Boston City Hosp., 1960-61; pvt. practice Orthopaedic Assocs., P.C., Denver, 1961-86; dir. dept. orthopaedic surgery Denver Gen. Hosp., 1987-95; ptnr. InMed Evaluations, Denver, 1995-97, ret., 1997. Home: Four Polo Field Ln Denver CO 80209

TALIAFERRO, ROBERT See BROOKE, TAL

TALLMAN, JOHN GARY, biology educator; b. Sistersville, W.Va., Mar. 20, 1950. AB in Biology, West Liberty State Coll., W.Va., 1971; PhD in Biochem. Genetics, W.Va. U., 1976. Rsch. assoc. Divsn. Biochemistry Kans. State U., 1976-78; asst. prof. biology Pepperdine U., 1978-81, assoc. prof. biology, 1981-88, tenured, 1982—, prof. biology, 1988—, prof. biology, Taul Watanabe Endowed chair in sci., 1996—; vis. scholar dept. biol. scis., Stanford U., 1986—; vis. rsch. scientist U. Calif., L.A., 1994. Contbr. articles to profl. jours. Grantee NSF, 1988—, Univ. Rsch. Coun., 1985, 89, 90, 92, Ralph M. Parsons Found., 1988-89, John Stauffer Charitable Trust, 1983, 88-89, others; named to Outstanding Young Men of Am., 1982. Mem. AAAS, Am. Genetic Assn., Am. Soc. Plant Physiologists, Coun. Undergrad. Rsch., Chi Beta Phi, Alpha Phi Sigma. Office: Willamette Univ 900 State St Salem OR 97301

TALLMAN, RICHARD C., lawyer; b. Oakland, Calif., Mar. 3, 1953; s. Kenneth A. and Jean M. (Kemppe) T.; m. Cynthia Ostolaza, Nov. 14, 1981. BSC, U. Santa Clara, 1975; JD, Northwestern U., 1978. Bar: Calif. 1978, Wash. 1979, U.S. Dist. Ct. (no. dist.) Calif. 1979, U.S. Dist. Ct. (we. dist.) Wash. 1979, U.S. Ct. Appeals (9th cir.) 1979, U.S. Dist. Ct. Hawaii 1986. Law clk to Hon. Morrell E. Sharp U.S. Dist. Ct. (we. dist.) Wash., Seattle, 1978-79; trial atty. U.S. Dept. Justice, Washington, 1979-80; asst. U.S. atty. U.S. Dist. Ct. (we. dist.) Wash., Seattle, 1980-83; ptnr. Schweppe, Krug & Tausend, PS, Seattle, 1983-89; mem. Bogle & Gates, PLLC, Seattle, 1990—; chmn. western dist. Wash. Lawyer Reps. to Ninth Cir. Jud. Conf., 1996-97. Instr. Nat. Park Svc. Seasonal Ranger Acad., Everett and Mt. Vernon, Wash., 1983-93; chmn. Edmonds C.C. Found., Lynnwood, Wash., 1990-92; gen. counsel Seattle-King County Crime Stoppers, 1987—; mem. exec. bd., chief Seattle Coun. Boy Scouts Am., 1997—. Mem. ABA, FBA (trustee 1992-93, v.p. 1994, pres. 1995), Seattle-King County Bar Assn., Rainier Club, Wash. Athletic Club. Office: Bogle & Gates Two Union Sq 601 Union St Seattle WA 98101-2346

TALMADGE, PHILIP ALBERT, judge, former state senator; b. Seattle, Apr. 23, 1952; s. Judson H., Jr., and Jeanne C. T.; m. Darlene L. Nelson, Sept. 6, 1970; children: Adam, Matthew, Jessica, Jonathan, Annemarie. BA magna cum laude with high honors in Polit. Sci., Yale U., 1973; JD, U. Wash., 1976. Bar: Wash. 1976. Assoc. Karr Tuttle Campbell, 1976-89; pres. Talmadge & Cutler, P.S., 1989-95; senator State of Wash., 1979-95; judge Supreme Ct. Wash., 1995—; chair Senate Judiciary Com., 1981, 83-87,

Senate Health and Human Svcs. Com., 1992-95, Wash. Senate, 1978-94, ways and means com., children and family svc. com., edn. com.; bd. dirs. Seattle Consumer Credit Counseling Svc.; coach West Seattle Youth Baseball; mem. bd. South Seattle Cmty. Coll. Found., West Seattle Helpline. Fellow Am. Assn. Appellate Lawyers; mem. King County Bar Assn., Wash. State Bar Assn., Seattle-King County Bar Assn. Author: The Nixon Doctrine and the Reaction of Three Asian Nations, 1973; editor Law Rev., U. Wash., 1975-76; contbr. articles to profl. jours.*

TALMAGE, KENNETH KELLOGG, business executive; b. Morristown, N.J., Jan. 16, 1946; s. Edward Taylor Hunt and Dorothy Rogers Talmage. BA, Claremont Men's Coll., 1968; MBA, Boston U., Brussels, 1976. Asst. to chmn. Fin. Com. to Re-elect President Nixon, 1972-73; assoc., Hon. Leonard K. Firestone, L.A., 1973-74; attaché Am. Embassy, Brussels, 1974-77; mgmt. cons. strategic planning and fin. Arthur D. Little, Inc., Cambridge, Mass., 1977-80; sr. v.p. Boston Safe Deposit & Trust Co., 1980-87; pres. Lloyd's Furs, Inc., Denver, Colo., 1987-92; bd. dirs. Monterey Water Co., 1992—, pres., 1995—; bd. dirs. Pure West Industries, Inc., vice-chmn., 1993-95. Trustee Colo. Outward Bound Sch., 1990-96, vice chmn., 1995-96, bd. govs., 1996—. Vols. for Outdoor Colo., 1988-94, Breckenridge Outdoor Edn. Ctr., 1989-92; advisor Hurricane Island Outward Bound Sch., Maine, 1987—, trustee, 1979-87, chmn. bd. trustees, 1980-83; mem. exec. com. Outward Bound, U.S.A., 1980-85. With USNR, 1968-69. Mem. The Country Club (Mass.), Denver Country Club. Home: 458 High St Denver CO 80218-4024 Office: Monterey Water Co 1158 S Main St Manteca CA 95337

TALMI, YOAV, conductor, composer; b. Kibbutz Merhavia, Israel, Apr. 28, 1943; diploma Rubin Acad. Music, Tel Aviv; postgrad. diploma Juilliard Sch. Music; m. Erella Gottesmann; 2 children. Assoc. condr. Louisville Orch., 1968-70; co-condr. Israel Chamber Orch., 1970-72; artistic dir., condr. Gelders Symphony Orch., Arnhem, 1974-80; prin. guest condr. Munich Philharm. Orch., 1979-80; artistic dir., condr. Israel Chamber Orch., 1984-88; music dir. New Israeli Opera, 1985-89, San Diego Symphony Orch., 1990-96, Waterloo Festival, N.J., 1994-95 ret., 1996; guest condr. Berlin Philharm., Munich Philharm., London Philharm., Philharmonia, Royal Philharm., Concertgebouw, Rotterdam Philharm., Israel Philharm., Tokyo Symphony, New Japan Philharm., Vienna Symphony, St. Petersburg Philharm., Pitts. Symphony, Detroit Symphony, St. Louis Symphony, Houston Symphony, Dallas Symphony, N.Y. Chamber Symphony, L.A. Chamber Orch., Oslo Philharm., Tonhalle Orch. Zurich, others. Composer: Dreams for choir a capella, Music for Flute and Strings; Overture on Mexican Themes (recorded), 3 Monologues for Flute Solo (pub.), Inauguration Fanfare; recs. include: Bruckner 9th Symphony (Oslo Philharm.), Gliére 3rd Symphony, Brahms Sextet/4 Serious Songs, Rachmaninov's Isle of the Dead, Berlioz Overtures, Berlioz Romeo et Juliette, Berlioz Harold in Italy (San Diego Symphony), Tchaikowsky/Schoenberg, Bloch/Barber/Grieg/Puccini (Israel Chamber Orch.); (with Erella Talmi) works for flute and piano. Recipient Boskovitch prize for composition, Israel, 1965; Koussevitzky Meml. Conducting prize, Tanglewood, 1969; award Ruppert Found. Condr. competition, London, 1973. Home: PO Box 1384, Kfar Saba 44113, Israel Office: ICM Artists 40 W 57th St New York NY 10019

TALMO, REGINA MARIE, social studies educator; b. Inglewood, Calif., Dec. 25, 1965; d. Leonard Thomas Talmo and Maria Elena (Chavez) Broer. BA in History, Loyola Marymount, 1989; MA in Edn., Calif. State U., 1994. Asst. editor mktg. Hope Chapel, Hermosa Beach, Calif., 1986-88; tchr. social studies Colegio Americano, Puebla, Mexico, 1989-90, Paramount (Calif.) High Sch., 1990—; cons., presentor LA. Migrant Edn. Dept., L.A., 1993. Nat. Hispanic Scholarship Fund grantee 1996—. Mem. Calif. Tchrs. Assn., Tchrs. Assn. Paramount. Home: 3603 W 226th St Torrance CA 90505

TAMARKIN, KATE, conductor; b. Newport Beach, Calif.. Student, Academia Musicale Chigiana, Siena, Italy; MusB magna cum laude, Chapman U.; MusM, Northwestern U.; MusD, Peabody Conservatory. Conducting fellow Tanglewood Music Festival, L.A. Philharm. Inst.; music dir. Fox Valley Symphony, Appleton, Wis., 1982-90, Vt. Symphony Orch. Assn., Inc., Burlington; music dir. E. Tex. Symphony Orch.; guest condr. Okla. City Philharm., Riverside Symphony N.J., Okla. Sinfonia, Tulsa Philharm., Grant Pk. Festival Orch., Chgo., others; vis. assoc. prof. orchestral studies U. Minn.; assoc. condr. Dallas Symphony, 1989-94. Appeared in numerous TV prodns. including Christmas concerts, 1993, 94, CNN-TV, (CBS-TV) Today Show. Recipient Alunni Merit award Northwestern U., Alumni of Yr. award Chapman U., 1997. Office: Vt Symphony Orch Assn Inc 2 Church St Burlington VT 05401*

TAMEZ, LORRAINE DIANE, writer, nurse; b. Pueblo, Colo., Nov. 26, 1950; d. Daniel and Mary Ann (Abeyta) Tamez; children: David, Christopher, Lauren. Cert. in nursing, Trinidad State Jr. Coll., Colo., student. poetry editor Purgatoire Mag. Author: Prairie Woman, 1989; contbr. poetry (as L.D. Thames) various mags. With U.S. Army, 1969-71. Mem. PEN, Poets and Writers. Democrat. Roman Catholic. Home and Office: PO Box 181 Trinidad CO 81082

TAMKIN, CURTIS SLOANE, real estate development company executive; b. Boston, Sept. 21, 1936; s. Hayward and Etta (Goldfarb) T.; BA in Econs., Stanford U., 1958; m. Priscilla Martin, Oct. 18, 1975; 1 child, Curtis Sloane. V.p., treas., dir. Hayward Tamkin & Co., Inc., mortgage bankers, L.A., 1963-70; mng. ptnr. Property Devel. Co., L.A., 1970-82; pres. The Tamkin Co., 1982—. Bd. govs. Music Ctr. L.A., 1974—; pres. Los Angeles Master Chorale Assn., 1974-78; mem. vis. com. Stanford U. Libraries, 1982-86; bd. dirs. L.A. Philharm. Assn., 1985—. Served to lt. (j.g.) USNR, 1960-63. Mem. Founders League of L.A. Music Ctr. (pres. 1988—), L.A. Jr. C. of C. (dir. 1968-69). Republican. Clubs: Burlingame Country. Office: 9460 Wilshire Blvd Beverly Hills CA 90212

TAMURA, CARY KAORU, fundraiser; b. Honolulu, Jan. 9, 1944; s. Akira and Harue (Otake) T.; m. Denise Jeanne Mitts, Oct. 17, 1987; children from previous marriage: Jennifer Joy, Matthew D. Student, U. Hawaii, 1961-63; BA in Philosophy, Nyack Coll., 1966; MA in Theology, Fuller Sem., 1986. Cert. fund-raising exec. Dir. svc. tng. ops. Fin. Adv. Clinic of Hawaii, Honolulu, 1972-76; dir. planned giving The Salvation Army, Honolulu, 1976-78; planned giving cons. InterVarsity Christian Fellowship, Portland, Oreg., 1978-80; account exec. Am. Income Life, Portland, Oreg., 1980-81; dir. planned giving The Salvation Army, Portland, Oreg., 1981-84, L.A., 1984-85; dir. devel., planned giving U. So. Calif., 1985-90; dir. gift planning UniHealth America, Burbank, Calif., 1990-94; pvt. gift planning cons. Brea, Calif., 1995—; bd. dirs. Nat. Com. on Planned Giving, Indpls., 1991-93, sec. exec. com., 1993; mem. adv. com., adj. faculty UCLA Extension; lectr. in field. Bd. dirs. Japanese Evang. Missionary Soc., 1990-95, v.p., 1993; bd. deacons Evang. Free Ch., 1992-95. With U.S. Army, 1969-72. Mem. Planned Giving Round Table So. Calif. (pres. 1989-91, Pres.'s award 1992), Nat. Soc. Fund Raising Execs., (bd. dirs. Greater L.A. chpt. 1990—, v.p. 1993, 95, chmn. Fund Raising Day 1994, treas. 1996-97, Profl. Fund Raiser of Yr. award 1995), So. Calif. Assn. Hosp. Developers, Asian Pacific Legal Soc. (exec. adv. bd. 1995—). Republican. Home and Office: 1413 Robert Ct Brea CA 92821-2165

TAN, ALFONSO O., internist; b. Bay, Laguna, The Philippines, July 4, 1930; came to U.S., 1967; s. Miguel and Felicidad (Oliva) T.; m. Ameurfina Gatchialian; 1 child, Alfred. AA, U. Santo Tomas, Manila, 1949, MD, 1954. Diplomate Am. Bd. Internal Medicine. Intern St. Mary's Hosp., East St. Louis, Ill., 1955-56; resident in internal medicine Nashville Gen. Hosp., 1957-58, chief resident, 1958-59; fellow in cardiopulmonary disease Jewish Hosp., Cin., 1959-61; pvt. practice, Manila, 1961-67; staff physician Rutland Heights (Mass.) Hosp., 1967-69; asst. supt. Worcester County Hosp., Boyston, Mass., 1969-71; staff physician VA Med. Ctr., Columbia, S.C., 1971-78, Bonham, Tex., 1978-79, Roseburg, Oreg., 1979—. Mem. ACP, AMA, Mass. Med. Soc. Democrat. Home: 305 Thora Cir PO Box 534 Winchester OR 97495 Office: VA Med Ctr Roseburg OR 97470

TAN, ENG MENG, immunologist, biomedical scientist; b. Seremban, Malaysia, Aug. 26, 1926; came to U.S., 1950; s. Ming Kee and Chooi Eng (Ang) T.; m. Liselotte Filippi, June 30, 1962; children: Philip, Peter. B.A., Johns Hopkins U., 1952, M.D., 1956. Rsch. assoc. Rockefeller U., N.Y.C., 1962-65; asst. prof. Washington U. Sch. Medicine, St. Louis, 1965-67; assoc. mem. Scripps Rsch. Inst., LaJolla, Calif., 1967-70, mem., 1970-77, dir. Autoimmune Disease Ctr., 1982—; prof. U. Colo. Sch. Medicine, Denver, 1977-82; chmn. allergy and immunology rsch. com. NIH, Bethesda, Md., 1982-84; mem. nat. arthritis adv. bd. HHS, Washington, 1981-85. Contbr. chpts. to books, articles to profl. jours. Named to Nat. Lupus Hall Fame, 1984; recepient U.S. Sr. Scientist award Humboldt Found., Fed. Republic Germany, 1986, award Ciba-Geigy-Internat. League Against Rheumatism, 1989, Carol Nachman award Wiesbaden, Fed. Republic Germany, 1989, Paul Klemperer award and medal N.Y. Acad. Medicine, 1993, City of Medicine award, Durham, N.C., 1996. Fellow AAAS; mem. Arthri tis Found. (Lee Howley Sr. award 1989), Am. Coll. Rheumatology (pres. 1984-85, Disting. Investigator award 1991), Assn. Am. Physicians, Am. Soc. Clin. Investigation, Western Assn. Physicians (v.p. 1980-81), Am. Assn. Immunologists, Brazilian Soc. Rheumatology (hon.), Australian Rheumatism Assn. (hon.), Brit. Soc. Rheumatology (hon.). Rsch. on characterization of autoantibodies in autoimmune diseases, systemic lupus erythematosus, scleroderma, Sjogren's syndrome, myositis and mixed connective tissue disease; relationship of autoantibodies to pathogenesis. Home: 8303 Sugarman Dr La Jolla CA 92037-2224 Office: Scripps Rsch Inst 10666 N Torrey Pines Rd La Jolla CA 92037-1027

TAN, JOO SIM, medical officer; b. Kuala Lumpur, Malaysia, Aug. 8, 1937; came to U.S., 1954; d. Keng Teong T. and Pee Ging (Ding) Khew; children: Stepen S., PEter B., Karen, Clifford. MD, NYU, 1965. Lic. Utah,. Ariz., N.Y. Physician pvt. practice, Perry, N.Y., 1970-80; med. dir. FHP-Utah, Salt Lake City, 1980-85, Cigna, San Diego & Dallas, 1985-90, Travelers, San Diego, 1990-91; cons. pvt. practice, Santa Ysabel, Calif., 1990—; chief med. officer Nat. Med Inc., Modesto, Calif., 1996—. Mem. Am. Coll. Physician Execs. (bd. dirs. 1991-94), Rotary Internat. (bd. dirs. Ramona, Calif. chpt. 1992-94, bd. dirs. La Jolla, Calif. chpt. 1990-92). Home: 31277 Lone Tree Rd Oakdale CA 95361-9761 Office: 1005 W Orangeburg Ste B Modesto CA 95350

TAN, WILLIAM LEW, lawyer; b. West Hollywood, Calif., July 25, 1949; s. James Tan Lew and Choon Guey Louie; m. Shelly Mieko Ushio. BA, U. Pa., 1971; JD, U. Calif. Hastings Coll. Law, San Francisco, 1974. Bar: Calif. 1975, U.S. Dist. Ct. (cen. dist.) Calif. 1975, U.S. Ct. Appeals (9th cir.) 1975, U.S. Supreme Ct. 1979. Assoc. Hiram W. Kwan, Los Angeles, 1974-79; ptnr. Mock & Tan, Los Angeles, 1979-80; sole practice Los Angeles, 1980-81; ptnr. Tan & Sakiyama, L.A., 1981-86, 88—, Tan & Sakiyama, P.C., L.A., 1986-88; bd. dirs. Am. Bus. Network, L.A.; pres., bd. dirs. Asian Rsch. Cons., L.A., 1983-85; mem. adv. bd. Cathay Bank, 1990-91; bd. dirs. Asian Pacific Am. Legal Ctr. Co-founder Asian Pacific Am. Roundtable, L.A., 1981; chmn. bd. dirs. Leadership Edn. for Asian-Pacifics, L.A., 1984-87; alt. del. Dem. Nat. Conv., San Francisco, 1984; mem. Calif. State Bd. Pharmacy, Sacramento, 1984-92, v.p., 1988-91, pres., 1991-92; mem. L.A. City and County Crime Crisis Task Force, 1981, L.A. Asian Pacific Heritage Week Com., 1980-85, Asian Pacific Women's Network, L.A., 1981, L.A. City Atty.'s Blue Ribbon Com. of Advisors, 1981, cmty. adv. bd. to Mayor of L.A., 1984, allocations vol. liaison team health and therapy divsn. United Way, L.A., 1986, mem. nominating com. bd. dirs. 1994—; bd. dirs. Chinatown Svc. Ctr., L.A., 1983; conf. advisor U.S.-Asia, L.A., 1981-83; mem. L.A. city atty. Housing Adv. Com.; mem. Pacific Bell Consumer Product Adv. Panel, 1986-90; vice chair cmty. adv. bd. Sta. KCET-TV, PBA, 1993-94; mem. adv. commn. State of Calif. Com. on State Procurement Practices, 1989-90; mem. L.A. City Attys. Citizens' Task Force on Pvt. Club Discrimination, 1989-90; mem. Calif. Med. Summit, 1993; mem. Mayor's Commn. Children, Youth and Families, 1993-96; mem. pub. access subcom. Mayor's Spl. adv. Com. on Tech. Implementation, 1994-96. Named one of Outstanding Young Men of Am., 1979. Mem. ABA (mem. numerous coms.), ATLA, Calif. State Bar Assn. (vice chmn. com. ethnic minority rels. 1983-85, chmn. pub. affairs com. 1981-82, mem. others), L.A. County Bar Assn. (trustee 1984-86, vice chair human rights com. 1980-82, mem. numerous coms.), So. Calif. Chinese Lawyers Assn. (pres. 1980-81, chmn. 1987-88, mem. various coms.), Minority Bar Assn. (chmn. 1981-82, sec. 1980-81, chmn. adv. bd. 1982-83), Asian Pacific Bar of Calif., Nat. Asian Pacific Am. Bar, Japanese Am. Bar Assn., Bench and Bar Media Coun., Consumer Attys. of Calif., Soc. Intercultural Edn. (conf. coord., advisor panelist tng. and rsch. com. 1983). Office: 300 S Grand Ave Ste 2750 Los Angeles CA 90071-3137

TANAKA, JEANNIE E., lawyer; b. L.A., Jan. 21, 1942; d. Togo William and Jean M. Tanaka. BA, Internat. Christian U., Tokyo, 1966; MSW, UCLA, 1968; JD, Washington Coll. Law, 1984. Bar: Calif. 1984, U.S. Dist. Ct. (cen., no. dists.) Calif. 1985, U.S. Ct. Appeals (9th cir.) 1985, D.C. 1987. Instr. Aoyama Gakuin, Meiji Gakuin, Sophia U., Tokyo, 1968-75; with program devel. Encyclopedia Britannica Inst., Tokyo, 1976-78; instr. Honda, Mitsubishi, Ricoh Corps., Tokyo, 1975-80; with editorial dept. Simul Internat., Tokyo; assoc. Seki and Jarvis, L.A., 1984-86, Jones, Day, Reavis & Pogue, L.A., 1986-87, Fulbright, Jaworsky and Reavis, McGrath, L.A., 1987-89; asst. counsel Unocal, L.A., 1989-91; pvt. practice, L.A., 1991—; counsel Calif. Dept. Corps., L.A., 1993—. Active Japan-Am. Soc., L.A., 1984-95, Japanese-Am. Citizens League, L.A., 1981, 92—, Japanese Am. Cultural and Cmty. Ctr., 1986-89; vol. Asian Pacific Am. Legal Ctr. So. Calif., 1985-86. Mem. Japanese-Am. Bar Assn., Mensa. Democrat. Methodist.

TANAKA, JOE SUEO, state legislator; b. Maui, Hawaii, Sept. 15, 1941; m. Barbara Tanaka; children: Joanne, Aimee. AA, Golden West Coll.; BA in Econs. and Bus. Adminstrn., U. Hawaii, Hilo. Mem. Hawaii Senate, asst. majority leader, 1992-93, mem. various coms., 1992-96, chair tourism and recreation com., 1993-96, vice chair transp. com., 1994, vice chair transp. & govt. affairs com., 1995-96. Mem. County Bd. Water Supply, Hawaii Criminal Justice Commn., Mayor's Com. for Betterment of Youth; mem. PTSA and band boosters Lihikai Sch.; mem. adv. bd. Family Cmty. Leadership; bd. dirs. Maui Econ. Opportunity, Inc., Maui Visitors Bur., Maui Econ. Bus. Devel.; chmn. econ. devel. and water devel. County Coun., 1986-88, chmn. econ. devel. and agr., 1988-90, chmn. human svcs., pks. and housing com., 1990-92. With U.S. Army, Vietnam. Democrat. Office: State Office Tower 235 S Beretania St Honolulu HI 96813

TANAKA, RICHARD KOICHI, JR., architect, planner; b. San Jose, Calif., Oct. 16, 1931; s. Richard Inoru and Mae Yoshiko (Koga) T.; m. Barbara Hisako Kumagai, Oct. 7, 1961; children: Craig, Todd, Sandra, Trent. BArch, U. Mich., 1954; M in Urban Planning, Calif. State U., San Jose, 1978. Exec. v.p. Steinberg Group, San Jose, L.A., 1954—. Author: American on Trial, 1988. Dir. Human Rels. Com., San Jose, 1969-73; dir., pres. Bicentennial Com., San Jose, 1974-77; bd. dirs. Santa Clara County Sch. Bd. Assn., 1980—; pres. Internment of Local Japanese Ams., San Jose, 1984—; past pres., trustee East Side H.S. Dist., San Jose, 1971-92, Japanese Am. Citizens League, San Jose; mem. bd. govs. Boy Scouts Am., San Jose, 1978—, NCCJ, San Jose, 1976—; past pres. Tapestry and Talent, 1976-80; trustee San Jose/Evergreen C.C., 1992—, pres., 1993-94; bd. dirs., first v.p. Calif. C.C. Trustees, 1997—. Mem. AIA, Am. Planning Inst., Constrn. Specification Inst., Rotary. Home: 14811 Whipple Ct San Jose CA 95127-2570 Office: 60 Pierce Ave San Jose CA 95110-2819

TANAKA, T., health and medical products executive; b. 1947. BS, Shimane Nat. U., 1973. With Green Cross Corp., 1973-79, Alpha Therapeutic, 1979-84, Green Cross Corp., 1984-88; pres. Oncomenbrane, Inc., Seattle, 1988-91. Office: Oncomembrane Inc 1201 3rd Ave Ste 5300 Seattle WA 98101-3013*

TANAKA, TOGO W(ILLIAM), retired real estate and financial executive; b. Portland, Oreg., Jan. 7, 1916; s. Masaharu and Katsu (Iwatate) T.; m. Jean Miho Wada, Nov. 14, 1940; children: Jeannie, Christine, Wesley. AB cum laude, UCLA, 1936. Editor Calif. Daily News, 1935-36, L.A. Japanese Daily News, 1936-42; documentary historian War Relocation Authority, Manzanar, Calif., 1942; staff mem. Am. Friends Service Com., Chgo., 1943-45; editor to head publs. div. Am. Tech. Soc., 1945-52; pub. Chgo. Pub. Corp., 1952-56; pub. School-Indsl. Press, Inc., L.A., 1956-60; chmn. Gramercy Enterprises, L.A.; dir. T.W. Tanaka Co., Inc.; city commr. Community Redevel. Agy., L.A., 1973-74; dir. L.A. Wholesale Produce Market Devel. Corp., 1979-89, Fed. Res. Bank, San Francisco, 1979-89; mem. adv. bd. Calif. First Bank, L.A., 1976-78, bd. dirs. Meth. Hosp., So. Calif., 1978-93. Author: (with Frank K. Levin) English Composition and Rhetoric, 1948; (with Dr. Jean Bordeaux) How to Talk More Effectively, 1948; (with Alma Meland) Easy Pathways in English, 1949. Mem. citizens mgmt. rev. com. L.A. Unified Sch. Dist., 1976-77; adv. coun. to assessor L.A. County, 1981-84; bd. dirs. Goodwill Industries of So. Calif.; trustee Wilshire United Meth. Ch., 1976-78, Calif. Acad. Decathlon, 1978-81; adv. bd. Visitors and Conv. Bur., 1984-88, Am. Heart Assn., 1984-88, New Bus. Achievement, Inc., YMCA Met. L.A., 1977-91, Boy Scouts Am. Coun., 1980-86; mem. adv. council Calif. World Trade Commn., 1986-87; active Nat. Strategy Info. Ctr. N.Y., Nat. Wellness Community, Western Justice Ctr. Found.; trustee Whittier Coll.; chmn. L.A. chpt. Nat. Safety Coun.; Recipient merit award Soc. Advancement Mgmt., 1950, mag. award Inst. Graphic Arts, 1953, 1st award Internat. Council Indsl. Editors, 1955, UNESCO Literacy award, 1974, L.A. Archbishop's Ecumenical award, 1986, Frances Larkin award ARC, 1993, Spirit of Wellness award, 1995. Mem. L.A. Area C. of C. (dir. 1975-77), Japan-Am. Soc. So. Calif. (coun. 1960-78), L.A. Athletic Club, Lincoln Club, Masons, Shriners, Rotary (dir., pres. L.A. club 1983-84, Svc. award 1995), Phi Beta Kappa, Pi Sigma Alpha, Pi Gamma Mu. Home: 949 Malcolm Ave Los Angeles CA 90024-3113 Office: 626 Wilshire Blvd Los Angeles CA 90017-3209

TANCER, SHOSHANA B., lawyer, business educator; b. N.Y.C., May 30, 1935; d. Salo Wittmayer and Jeannette (Meisel) Baron; m. Robert Stephen Tancer, June 10, 1954; children: Sara Tancer Gordon, Manuel, Catherine Lewkowitz, Cynthia. BA, Barnard Coll., 1954; LLB, U. Mich., 1956; PhD, Columbia U., 1970. Researcher Inst. War and Peace Studies Columbia U., 1963-64; rsch. scientist Ctr. for Rsch. in Social Systems Am. U., Washington, 1965-68; with Tancer Law Offices, Ltd., Phoenix, 1976-90; of counsel O'Connor, Cavanagh, Anderson, Killingsworth, et al, Phoenix, 1992—; assoc. prof. Am. Grad. Sch. Internat. Mgmt., Glendale, Ariz., 1969-70, prof., 1970—; dir. NAFTA Ctr., 1995—; vis. prof. U. Pedro Henriquez Urena, Santo Domingo, Dominican Republic, 1968-69; bd. dirs. The Finova Group, Inc., Xantel Corp. Contbr. articles to profl. jours. Mem. adv. bd. U. Ariz. Coll. Bus. and Pub. Adminstrn., 1984—, bd. visitors Law Sch., 1982-85; founding mem. Phoenix Com. on Fgn. Rels., 1978—, mem. exec. com., 1990—; founder mem. Charter 100, treas., mem. exec. com., 1980—; trustee Phoenix Country Day Sch., 1976—; bd. dirs. Ariz. Theater Co., 1994—; active Ariz. Acad., 1978—; bd. visitors Stanford U. Librs., 1990-92; bd. dirs. United Way, v.p., 1976-82; also others. Mem. Assn. for Corp. Growth (bd. dirs. Ariz. chpt. 1994-96), Internat. Studies Assn., Ariz. Bar Assn. (various coms.), Bar Assn. D.C., Ariz. Bus. Leadership Assn. (bd. dirs. 1996—), Strategic Mgmt. Assn., Maricopa County Bar Assn., Internat. Indsl. Rels. Assn., Acad. Internat. Bus. Office: O Connor Cavanagh Anderson Killingsworth et al Westover Killingsworth et al 1 E Camelback Rd Ste 1100 Phoenix AZ 85012-1656

TANENBAUM, BASIL SAMUEL, engineering educator; b. Providence, R.I., Dec. 1, 1934; s. Harry Milton and Rena Ada (Herr) T.; m. Carol Binder, Aug. 26, 1956; children: Laurie, Stephen, David. B.S. summa cum laude, Brown U., 1956; M.S. (NSF fellow, 1956-60), Yale U., 1957, Ph.D. in Physics, 1960. Staff physicist Raytheon Co., Waltham, Mass., 1960-63; prof. engrng. Case Western Res. U., Cleve., 1963-75; dean of faculty Harvey Mudd Coll., Claremont, Calif., 1975-93, prof. engrng., 1975—; Norman F. Sprague, Jr. prof. of life scis. Harvey Mudd Coll., Claremont, 1996—; vis. scientist Cornell U., Arecibo (P.R.) Obs., 1968-69; vis. assoc. prof. Northwestern U., Evanston, Ill., 1970; vis. scholar U. Calif. Irvine Beckman Laser Inst., 1993-94; mem. sci. adv. com. Nat. Astronomy and Ionosphere Ctr., 1972-77, Calif. Poly. Inst., Pomona, 1976-87; mem. engrng. and sci. adv. com. Calif. State U., Fullerton, 1976-87; mem. nat. adv. com. Rowan Coll., Glassboro, N.J., 1993—, chmn. curriculum subcom.; mem. Eisenhower adv. com. Calif. Postsecondary Edn. Com., 1993—; dir. Minority Engrs. Indsl. Opportunity Program, 1973-75; dir. summer sci. program Thacher Sch., Ojai, Calif., 1977-82; cons. various corps., univ. labs., govt. agys. Author: Plasma Physics, 1967. Woods Hole Oceanog. Inst. fellow, 1959; sr. Sterling fellow Yale U., 1959; recipient Case Western Res. U. Wittke teaching award, 1974, Henry T. Mudd prize Harvey Mudd Coll., 1996. Mem. AAAS, Am. Phys. Soc., Am. Soc. for Engring. Edn., IEEE, AAUP, Sigma Xi (research award 1969). Home: 611 W Delaware Dr Claremont CA 91711-3458 Office: Harvey Mudd Coll 301 E 12th St Claremont CA 91711-5901

TANG, PAUL CHI LUNG, philosophy educator; b. Vancouver, B.C., Can., Jan. 23, 1944; came to U.S., 1971; s. Pei-Sung and Violet (Wong) T. BSc with high distinction, U. B.C., 1966; MA in Edn., Simon Fraser U., Vancouver, 1971; MA, Washington U., St. Louis, 1975, PhD, 1982; cert. in ethics, Kennedy Inst. Ethics, 1983; diploma in piano, U. Toronto, 1962. Teaching asst. philosophy of edn. Simon Fraser U., 1969-71; instr. philosophy St. Louis C.C. at Meramec, Kirkwood, Mo., 1975-82; instr., lectr. philosophy Washington U., 1972-76; adj. asst. prof. Harris-Stowe State Coll., St. Louis, 1980-82; asst. prof. philosophy Grinnell (Iowa) Coll., 1982-85; asst. prof. to assoc. prof. to prof. dept. philosophy Calif. State U., Long Beach, 1985—, chmn. dept. philosophy, 1988-94; vis. lectr. philosophy So. Ill. U., Edwardsville, 1978-79. Contbr. numerous articles and revs. to profl. publs.; editor Philosophy of Sci. Assn. Newsletter, 1985-90; asst. editor Philosophy of Sci. acad. jour., 1972-75. Senator Internat. Parliament for Safety and Peace, Palermo, Italy. Decorated knight Templar Order of Jerusalem, knight Order Holy Cross of Jerusalem, knight comdr. Lofsenic Ursinius Orer, chevalier Grand Croix de Milice du St. Sepulcre; recipient cert. of merit Student Philosophy Assn., 1988-90, 93-94, spl. award, 1992; named faculty advisor of yr. Assoc. Students, 1987, 90, 91, 95, Highland Lord of Camster, Scotland, 1995; Paul Tang prize in philosophy named in his honor, 1996—; fellow Washington U., 1971, summer rsch. fellow Calif. State U., 1988, NEH fellow Harvard U., 1988, NEH Summer Seminar fellow, 1968; internat. scholar Phi Beta Delta, interdisciplinary scholar Phi Kappa Phi, 1993; grantee vis. philosophers program Coun. for Philos. Studies, 1987, 91, 92; Disting. Vis. Scholars and Artists Fund, Calif. State U., 1988, 89, rsch. grantee, summer 1996. Fellow World Lit. Acad.; mem. Am. Philos. Assn. (Excellence in Tchg. award 1995, 97), Philosophy of Sci. Assn., History of Sci. Soc., Kennedy Inst. Ethics, Hastings Ctr., Iowa Philos. Soc. (pres. 1985-86), Internat. Platform Assn., Brit. Soc. Philosophy of Sci., Soc. Philosophy and Psychology, Maison Internat. des Intellectuels de l'Acad. Francaise, Internat. Order Merit (Eng.), Golden Key (hon., Internat. Man of Yr. 1995-96), Order Internat. Fellowship (Eng.), numerous others. Home: 5050 E Garford St Apt 228 Long Beach CA 90815-2859 Office: Calif State U Dept Philosophy 1250 N Bellflower Blvd Long Beach CA 90840-0006

TANIGUCHI, TOKUSO, surgeon; b. Eleele, Kauai, Hawaii, June 26, 1915; s. Tokuichi and Sana (Omaye) T.; BA, U. Hawaii, 1941; MD, Tulane U., 1946; 1 son, Jan Tokuichi. Intern Knoxville (Tenn.) Gen. Hosp., 1946-47; resident in surgery St. Joseph Hosp., also Marquette Med. Sch., Milw., 1947-52; practice medicine, specializing in surgery, Hilo, Hawaii, 1955—; chief surgery Hilo Hosp.; teaching fellow Marquette Med. Sch., 1947-49; v.p., dir. Hawaii Hardware Co., Ltd. Capt. M.C., AUS, 1952-55. Diplomate Am. Bd. Surgery. Fellow Internat., Am. colls. surgeons; mem. Am., Hawaii med. assns., Hawaii County Med. Soc., Pan-Pacific Surg. Assn., Phi Kappa Phi. Contbr. articles in field to profl. jours. Patentee automated catheter. Home: 277 Kaiulani St Hilo HI 96720-2530

TANIMOTO, GEORGE, agricultural executive, farmer; b. Gridley, Calif., Feb. 10, 1926; s. Hikoichi and Rewa Tanimoto; m. Hanami Yamasaki, Dec. 19, 1946; 1 child, Patricia. Grad., Coyne Electric Sch., Chgo., 1950. Elec. technician, 1951, owner peach and prune orchards, 1952; founder Kiwifruit Nursery, Calif., 1965; pres. Tanimoto Bros., Gridley, Calif., 1977—, Tanimoto Enterprises, Inc., Gridley, 1979—; bd. dirs. Blue Anchor, Inc., Sacramento; chmn. Calif. Fruit Exchange, Inc.; U.S. rep. Internat. Kiwifruit Orgn., Lake Tahoe, Calif., 1985, Rome, 1986, Biarritz, France, 1987, Hong Kong, 1988, chmn. Orgn.,Rome, 1986; dir. Butte County Agrl. Adv. Commn., Oroville, Calif.; founder, chmn. Calif. Kiwifruit Commn., 1980-84, 1988-89, vice chmn. 1985-87. Pres. South Shore Assn., Bucks Lake, Calif., 1989. Mem. Kiwifruit Growers Calif. (founder, bd. dirs., pres. 1973-80), Kiwifruit Mktg. Assn. Calif. (founder, chmn. 1989-97), Gridley Sportsman Club (founder, pres. 1975-78). Republican. Buddhist. Home: 948 River Ave Gridley CA 95948-9774

TANNEN, RICHARD LAURENCE, medical educator, nephrologist; b. N.Y.C., Aug. 31, 1937; s. Harold and Fannie (Rosenberg) T.; m. Elizabeth

Whitney Harriman, Aug. 8, 1964 (div. Apr. 1990); m. Vivien Baraban, Nov. 17, 1990; children: Bradford, Whitney, Jennifer, Alison, Julie. Student, Vanderbilt U., 1957; MD, U. Tenn., Memphis, 1960. Rsch. internist Walter Reed Inst. Rsch., Washington, 1966-69; assoc. prof., co-dir. nephrology unit U. Vermont, Burlington, 1969-78; prof., chief nephrology divsn. U. Mich., Ann Arbor, 1978-88; prof., chmn. dept. medicine U. So. Calif., L.A., 1988-95; vice dean for rsch., prof. medicine U. Pa., Phila., 1995—; established investigator Am. Heart Assn., 1971-76. Co-editor: Fluids and Electrolytes, 1986, 3d edit., 1996; mem. editorial bd. Am. Jour. Medicine; contbr. more than 130 sci. articles to profl. jours. Maj. U.S. Army, 1966-69. Recipient Merit award NIH, 1986-94, Disting. Alumnus award U. Tenn., 1991. Fellow ACP; mem. Am. Soc. Nephrology (pres. 1991-92), Am. Soc. Clin. Investigation, Assn. Am. Physicians, Nat. Kidney Found. (regional v.p. 1984-87, Pres.'s award 1986). Jewish. Office: U Pa Health System 3400 Spruce St Philadelphia PA 19104

TANNER, DAVID EARL, education educator; b. Lethbridge, Alberta, Canada, July 31, 1948; s. Earl Pingree and Betty (Bridge) T.; m. Susan Elizabeth Bodell, Aug. 21, 1972; children: Dylan, David, Gillian, John, Suzanna. BA, Brigham Young U., 1973, MA, 1977; PhD, Tex. A&M U., 1984. Tchr. Jordan Sch. Dist., Sandy, Utah, 1977-81; lectr. Tex. A&M U., College Station, 1981-84; asst. prof. U. Tex., Tyler, 1984-85; asst. prof. Calif. State U., Fresno, 1985-87, assoc. prof., 1987-90, prof., 1990—, chmn. dept. ednl. rsch., adminstrn. and founds., 1990-95; cons. Calif. Dept. Edn., 1985-86; coord. spl. projects div. grad. studies Calif. State U., Fresno, 1989-90. Editor: The Network Journal, 1986-89; contbr. articles to profl. jours. Mem. Am. Ednl. Rsch. Assn. Mem. Latter-day Saints. Office: Calif State U Fresno Ms # 2 Fresno CA 93740

TANNER, DEE BOSHARD, retired lawyer; b. Provo, Utah, Jan. 16, 1913; s. Myron Clark and Marie (Boshard) T.; m. Jane Barwick, Dec. 26, 1936 (div. Aug. 1962); children: Barry, Diane McDowell; m. Reeta Walker, Dec. 6, 1981. BA, U. Utah, 1935; LLB, Pacific Coast U., 1940; postgrad., Harvard U., 1936, Loyola U., L.A., 1937. Bar: Calif. 1943, U.S. Dist. Ct. (so. dist.) Calif. 1944, U.S. Ct. Appeals (9th cir.) 1947, ICC 1964, U.S. Dist. Ct. (ea. dist.) Calif. 1969, U.S. Supreme Ct. 1971. Assoc. Spray, Davis & Gould, L.A., 1943-44; pvt. practice L.A., 1944; assoc. Tanner and Sievers, L.A., 1944-47, Tanner and Thornton, L.A., 1947-54, Tanner, Hanson, Meyers, L.A., 1954-64; ptnr. Tanner and Van Dyke, L.A., 1964-65, Gallagher and Tanner, L.A., 1965-70; pvt. practice Pasadena, Calif., 1970-95; retired, 1995. Mem. L.A. Bar Assn., World Affairs Assn., Harvard Law Sch. Assn., Lawyers' Club L.A. Home and Office: 1720 Lombardy Rd Pasadena CA 91106-4127

TANNER, JOHN DOUGLAS, JR., history educator, writer; b. Quantico, Va., Oct. 2, 1943; s. John Douglas and Dorothy Lucille (Walker) T.; m. Jo Ann Boyd, Jan. 1964 (div. Aug. 1966); 1 child, Lorena Desiree; m. Laurel Jean Selfridge, Dec. 19, 1967 (div. Oct. 1987); children: John DouglasIII, Stephen Douglas, Elizabeth Jane; m. Karen M. Olson, Apr. 16, 1988. BA, Pomona Coll., 1966; MA, Claremont Calif. Grad. Sch., 1968; postgrad., U. Calif., Riverside, 1976, 84-86, U. Calif., San Diego, 1984-87, U. Pacific, 1993. Cert. tchr., Calif. Asst. swimming, water polo coach Pomona Coll., 1966-69; rsch. asst. history dept. Claremont Grad. Sch., 1967-69; assoc. prof. history Palomar Coll., San Marcos, Calif., 1969—, pres. faculty, 1970-71, v.p. faculty senate, 1971-72. Author: Olaf Swenson and his Siberian Imports jour., 1978 (Dog Writers Assn. Am. Best Series award 1979), Campaign for Los Angeles, 1846-47, 69; co-editor: Don Juan Forster, 1970, Alaskan Trails, Siberian Dogs, 1994; contbr. articles to profl. jours. Mem. citizens com. Fallbrook (Calif.) San. Dist., 1980; merit badge counselor Boy Scouts Am., 1975-85; Martin County Hist. Soc., Morgan County Hist. Soc., Fallbrook Hist. Soc., San Diego Opera Guild, San Diego Classical Music Soc., Opera Pacific Guild. Chautauqua fellow NSF, 1979. Mem. Nat. Assn. for Outlaw and Lawman History, Inc., Western Outlaw-Lawman History Assn., Custer Battlefield Hist. and Mus. Assn. (life), The Westerners, Siberian Husky Assn. Am. (bd. dirs. 1974-78, 1st v.p. 1978-79), So. Calif. Siberian Husky Assn. (pres. 1972-79), U.S. Shooting Team (Inner Circle), Sons of the Rep. of Tex. Republican. Episcopalian. Home: 2308 Willow Glen Rd Fallbrook CA 92028-9752 Office: Palomar Coll 1140 W Mission Rd San Marcos CA 92069-1415

TANNER, JORDAN, state legislator; b. Provo, Utah, July 26, 1931; s. Vasco Myron and Annie (Atkin) T.; m. Patricia Nowell, Sept. 16, 1960; children: Eric, Jeffrey, Timothy. BS, U. Utah, 1954; MBA, U. Calif., Berkeley, 1961. Fgn. svc. officer USIA, Washington, 1960-87; state rep. Utah Ho. of Reps., Salt Lake City, 1990—. Commr. Utah Centennial Commn., Salt Lake City, 1993—. Lt. USN, 1954-56. Republican. Mem. LDS Ch. Home and Office: 1871 N 1450 E Provo UT 84604

TANNER, PATRICIA RUTH, gerontology nurse; b. Trego, Mont., July 30, 1935; d. Elmer E. and Jennie M. (Dukeshire) Pomeroy; children: Michael F. Ehart, Crystal Y. Blair, Karen Alexander. AS, Walla Walla (Wash.) C.C., 1973. Dir. nursing edn. Desert Palms Convalescent Hosp., Indio, Calif.; dir. nursing svc. Leisure Lodge, Mountain Home, Ark.; day charge nurse Hill Brook Nursing Home, Clancy, Mont.; charge and staff relief nurse Nursing Profls. Inc. Nursing Agy., Yakima, Wash., 1989-92; charge nurse Selah (Wash.) Convalescent Facility, 1991-92; med. and treatment on-call nurse Yakima Convalescent, 1993-94, med. and treatment nurse, 1995—; part-time and on-call nurse, resident care coord. Chinook Convalescent Ctr., 1994—, p.m. charge nurse, 1995—; resident care coord., staff devel., infection control nurse Selah Convalescent, 1995; p.m. medication nurse Yakima (Wash.) Convalescent, 1995—. Mem. Wash. State Nurse's Assn., Nightingale Soc. (pres.). Home: 1411 Naches Heights Rd Yakima WA 98908-8849

TANNER, WILLIAM COATS, JR., business owner; b. Magna, Utah, Oct. 22, 1920; s. William Coats and Clara (Sutton) T.; m. Athelia Sears, Feb. 14, 1942; children: Roberta Graham, Athelia Woolley, Terri Mitchell, William Coats Tanner III, John Sears Tanner, Richard Sears Tanner, Mark Sears Tanner, Claralyn Palfreyman, Kaye Whitworth, Daken Sears Tanner, Scott Sears Tanner, Janet Perry, Bryan Sears Tanner. BS, U. Utah, 1943; MA, U. Minn., 1948; PhD, U. Utah, 1952. Lic. psychologist, Calif. Instr. Ea. Montana Coll. Edn., Billings, 1952; rsch./statis. assoc. Ednl. Testing Svc., L.A., 1952-54; prin. Tanner Thought Dynamics, L.A., 1954—, PAR ASK, Salt Lake City, 1992—; instr. U. So. Calif., L.A., 1972-76; therapist, therapists trainer; lecturer. Author in field. Pres. Mormons Ill. Chgo. Mission, Oakbrook, 1986-89. 1st lt. arty. U.S. Army, 1943-46. Mem. Rotary Club, Phi Kappa Phi. Republican. Home: 5055 Holladay Blvd Salt Lake City UT 84117-6307

TANNO, RONALD LOUIS, dentist; b. San Jose, Calif., Dec. 17, 1937; s. George Anthony and Rose Marie (Manghisi) T. BS magna cum laude, Santa Clara U., 1959; DDS, U. of Pacific, 1963. Dentist Santa Clara County Health Dept., San Martin, Calif., 1965-67, Alameda County Health Dept., Oakland, Calif., 1965-67; pvt. practice San Jose, 1966—; dental cons. Found. Med. Care, San Jose, 1977-81, Dental Ins. Cons., Saratoga, Calif., 1980-88, Santa Clara County Sch. Dists. Dental Plan, San Jose, 1983—; cons. quality rev. Delta Dental Plan Calif., San Francisco, 1983—; mem. dental staff Los Gatos (Calif.) Community Hosp., 1978-94, chief dental dept., 1983, 84. Capt. USAF, 1963-65. Mem. ADA, Calif. Dental Assn., Santa Clara County Dental Soc., Elks, Lions, Xi Psi Phi, Omicron Kappa Upsilon. Office: 1610 Westwood Dr Ste 3 San Jose CA 95125-5110

TANOUYE, MARIAN NATSUKO, accountant; b. Honolulu, July 30, 1965; d. Masao and Hanayo T. BS in Math., U. Hawaii, 1987; AS in acctg., Leeward C.C., Pearl City, Hawaii, 1988. Bookkeeper Enterprise Realty, Honolulu, 1985-87; acctg. clk. Wayne Choo, CPA, Honolulu, 1988-89; secondary mktg. clk. Am. Savs. Bank, Honolulu, 1989-90, acct., 1990-91, sr. acct., 1991-96; acctg. mgr. and cons. Chip and Water Office Automation, 1996; acct. State of Hawaii, 1996-97, Interpacific Hawaii Retail Group, 1997—.

TANZI, CAROL ANNE, interior designer; b. San Francisco, Apr. 9, 1942; d. Raymond Edward and Anne Marie Giorgi. BA, U. San Jose, Calif., 1966. Teaching credential, Calif.; cert. interior designer, Calif. Home furnishings coord. R.H. Macy's, San Francisco, 1966-72; owner, pres. Carol A. Tanzi & Assocs., Burlingame, Calif., 1972—; instr. interior design Recreational Ctrs., Burlingame/Foster City, Calif., 1972-85; design cons. Am. Cancer Soc., San Mateo, Calif., 1994-95; mem. adv. com. for interior design students Coll. San Mateo, 1984-87; head designer San Mateo Battered Women's Shelter Pro Bono, 1993. Interior designer mags. Sunset, 1982, House Beautiful, 1992, 1001 Home Ideas, 1983; monthly cable TV program Interior Design by Tanzi, 1994—. Pres. Aux. to Mission Hospice, Burlingame, 1988-89, Hist. Soc. Burlingame, 1992-93; pres. Cmty. for Edn., Burlingame, 1996; mem. adv. com. Breast Ctr./Mills Peninsula Hosp., 1994—; mem. Oaks Hist. Adv. Bd., 1993-94; commr., pres. San Mateo County Commn. on Status of Women, 1990-95. Recipient Recogniton of Outstanding Performance Rotary Club of Burlingame, 1988—, Congl. Recognition U.S.A., Burlingame, 1994, Commendation Bd. Suprs., County of San Mateo, 1994, Recognition Calif. Legis. Assembly, Burlingame, 1994; named Superior Interior Designer Bay Area San Francisco Examiner, 1991, Woman of Distinction Soroptimist Internat., Burlingame/San Mateo, 1994. Mem. Am. Soc. Interior Designers (v.p. 1988, Presdl. Citation for disting. svc. 1986, 87, 88, Calif. Peninsula Chpt. Design award 1995), Burlingame C. of C. Women's Forum (chair 1986-95), Rotary Club of Burlingame (sec. 1988—). Home: 1528 Columbus Ave Burlingame CA 94010-5512 Office: Carol A Tanzi & Assocs PO Box 117281 Burlingame CA 94011-7281

TANZI, RONALD THOMAS, artist, educator; b. Brookline, Mass., Mar. 3, 1949; s. Henry Francis and Jennie (Vicenza) T.; m. Patricia Marie Morrill, Mar. 16, 1974 (div. Apr. 1990); children: Jenni Grace, Jacob Thomas. Student, Chapman Coll., Orange, Calif., 1968-70, Ea. Wash. U., Cheney, 1970-72; BFA magna cum laude, U. Wash., 1984; MFA, U. Cin., 1986. Artist self-employed, Spokane, Boston, Seattle, 1970—; art editor Contbr.'s Copy Quar., Spokane, 1970-73; instr., lectr. U. Cin., 1984-86; instr. U. Wash., Seattle, 1986-87, Seattle Cmty. Colls. (North and Ctrl. campuses), 1987—, Edmonds (Wash.) C.C., 1992—, Bellevue (Wash.) C.C., 1993—; dir. R's Studio Gallery, Cheney, 1971-73; visual advisor Masque Theater Co., Everett, Wash., 1987-88; lectr. Seattle Art Mus., 1991, Seattle Art League, 1992, Bellevue Art Mus., 1995. Exhibited paintings in shows including Spokane City Arts, 1971, Pacific Northwest Annual, 1976, N.W. Traditions: A Retrospective, 1987, King County Arts Commn., 1988, Faculty Art Shows, North Seattle C.C. and Bellevue C.C., 1994, 95, 96; artist, pub. commn. Metro Bus Shelter Mural Program, 1991, Harborview Med. Ctr. Mural, 1995; represented in pvt. collections in U.S., Japan, Germany, Finland. Instr. City Arts Program, Lynnwood, Wash., 1987-93, Pike Place Sr. Ctr., Seattle, 1992-94, S.E. Seattle Sr. Ctr., 1993-94, Creative Retirement Ctr., Seattle, 1993-94. Sgt. USAF, 1966-70, Vietnam. U. Cin. Grad. scholar, 1984, 85, 86. Mem. Coll. Art Assn., Am. Fedn. Tchrs., Wash. State Fedn. Tchrs., Seattle Art Mus., Phi Beta Kappa. Office: 540 1st Ave S # 203A Seattle WA 98104-2804

TAO, CHIA-LIN PAO, humanities educator; b. Soochow, Kiangsu, China, July 7, 1939; came to U.S., 1961; d. Tsung-han and Hoi-chin Pao; m. Jing-shen Tao, Aug. 22, 1964; children: Rosalind, Jeanne, Sandy. BA, Nat. Taiwan U., Taipei, 1961; MA, Ind. U., 1963, PhD, 1971. Assoc. prof. Nat. Taiwan U., Taipei, 1969-76, 78-79; vis. assoc. prof. U. Ariz., Tucson, 1976-78, 79-85, assoc. prof., 1989—; v.p. Hist. Soc. for 20th Century China in N.Am., 1992-93, pres., 1993-94. Editor, author: Studies in Chinese Women's History 4 vols., 1979-95. Mem. Tucson-Taichung Sister-City Com., Tucson, 1984—; sec. Ariz. Asian Am. Assn., 1989, dir., 1989-93. Rsch. grantee Nat. Sci. Coun., Taipei, 1971-72, 73-74, Harvard-Yenching Inst., Cambridge, Mass., 1972-74, Pacific Cultural Found., Taipei, 1984-85. Mem. Assn. for Asian Studies (pres. Western conf. 1994), Tucson Chinese Am. Profl. Soc. (pres. 1996), Tucson Chinese Assn. (bd. dirs.). Democrat. Office: Dept East Asian Studies Univ Ariz Tucson AZ 85721

TAPIA, ARTHUR ALBERT, lawyer; b. San Jose, Calif., July 26, 1959; s. Amador E. and Martha (Gonzalez) T.; m. Rosalia Tapia. BS, U. Santa Clara, 1981; JD, U. Pa., 1984. Assoc. The Boccardo Law Firm, San Jose. Bd. dirs. Mexican-Am. Community Svcs. Agy., San Jose; commr. Consumer Affairs Adv. Commn. County of Santa Clara, San Jose. Mem. United Way (budget allocations rev. com.), Santa Clara County Bar Assn., Calif. Trial Lawyers Assn., Phi Alpha Theta. Democrat. Roman Catholic.

TAPPAN, JANICE RUTH VOGEL, animal behavior researcher; b. Pasadena, Mar. 13, 1948; d. Robert Samuel and Etta (Berry) Vogel; m. David Stanton Tappan IV, Dec. 20, 1970; children: Stacey, Christina, Danny. BA in Anthropology, U. Calif., Berkeley, 1970. Rsch. asst. L.A. Zoo, 1982—; owner Fiddlers Crossing, Pasadena, 1989—. Calif. Arts Coun. folklore grantee, 1989-90. Mem. Scottish Fiddling Revival (v.p. 1986—, judge fiddling 1989—), Scottish Fiddlers of Calif. (v.p. 1986—), Calif. Traditional Music Soc. (devel. dir. 1990-94, v.p. 1994—), Scottish Fiddlers of L.A. (music dir. 1990—), Phi Beta Kappa. Democrat. Soc. of Friends. Home: 1938 Rose Villa St Pasadena CA 91107-5046

TAPPER, DAVID, pediatric surgeon; b. Balt., Aug. 26, 1945; s. Herman A. and Sylvia Phyllis (Golomb) T.; m. Susan Irene Wagner, June 25, 1968; children: Joellen, Erica, Jacalyn, Aaron. BS, U. Md., College Park, 1966; MD, U. Md., Balt., 1970. Surg. intern and resident U. Calif. San Francisco Med. Ctr., 1970-73; pediatric surg. rsch. fellow Boston Children's Hosp., 1973-75; sr. and chief surg. resident U. Calif., San Francisco, 1975-77; sr. and chief pediatric surg. fellow Children's Hosp., Boston, 1977-79; asst. prof. surgery Harvard Med. Sch., Boston, 1979-83; surgeon-in-chief Children's Hosp. Med. Ctr., Seattle, 1983—; prof. surgery and pediatrics U. Wash., Seattle, 1983—, vice chmn. dept. surgery, 1986—; bd. dirs. Am. Bd. Surgery, Phila., 1991—. Served to maj. USAR, 1971-82. Fellow ACS; mem. Am. Surg Assn., Am. Pediatric Surgery Assn. (bd. govs. 1993-96), Soc. Univ. Surgeons, Pacific Coast Surg. Soc., Halsted Surg. Soc. Republican. Jewish. Office: Children's Hosp Med Ctr 4800 Sand Point Way NE Seattle WA 98105-3901

TAPPER, JOAN JUDITH, magazine editor; b. Chgo., June 12, 1947; d. Samuel Jack and Anna (Swoiskin) T.; m. Steven Richard Siegel, Oct. 15, 1971. BA, U. Chgo., 1968; MA, Harvard U., 1969. Editor manuscripts Chelsea House, N.Y.C., 1969-71, Scribners, N.Y.C., 1971; editor books Nat. Acad. Scis., Washington, 1972-73; assoc. editor Praeger Pubs., Washington, 1973-74; editor New Rep. Books, Washington, 1974-79; mng. editor spl. pubs. Nat. Geog. Soc., Washington, 1979-83; editor Nat. Geog. Traveler, Washington, 1984-88; editor-in-chief Islands, internat. mag., Santa Barbara, Calif., 1989—; editl. dir. Islands Pub. Co., Santa Barbara, 1996—. Recipient Pacific Asia Travel Assn. Journalist of the Yr. award, 1995. Mem. Am. Soc. Mag. Editors, Soc. Am. Travel Writers (editors' coun.), Channel City Club. Democrat. Jewish. Home: 603 Island View Dr Santa Barbara CA 93109-1508 Office: Islands Mag 3886 State St Santa Barbara CA 93105-3112

TARA, research chemist, publishing executive, writer; b. Kotdata, Punjab, India, June 11, 1921; came to U.S., 1966; naturalized, 1972; s. Nand and Isar (Kaur) Singh; m. Rani Surinder, Dec. 29, 1954; children: Nina, Roopinder, Sylvia, Sonya. BS with honors, Punjab U., 1944, MS with 1st class honors, 1946; AM, Harvard U., 1949, PhD, 1950. Post doctorate fellow with Prof. R.B. Woodward Harvard U., 1950-51; Post doctorate fellow NRC, Can., 1953-54; prof. chemistry govt. colls., Punjab, India, 1954-58; prin. govt. colls., India, 1958-64; rsch. and devel. chemist PEBOC Ltd., Northolt, Eng., 1964-65, Unilever Rsch. Lab., Isleworth, Eng., 1965-66; prin. investigator rsch. projects Aldrich Chem.Co., Milw., 1966-76; rsch. and devel. chemist Polyscis., Inc., Warrington, Pa., 1976-88, Calbiochem, La Jolla, Calif., 1989-94; pres. One World Publ. Co., San Diego, 1996—; prin. investigator rsch. projects. Author: The Educational Problem of India, 1955, An Outline of the Philosophy of Creative Education, 1959, Evolution of the Soul, 1970, Universal Creative Religion for Peace, Love and Light, 1978, 2d edit., 1994, Human Sacrifice and Cannibalism in the Holy Bible, 1996, Sex Stories of the Holy Bible, 1996; contbr. numerous articles to profl. jours. Mem. Am. Chem. Soc. Home: 4202 Appleton St San Diego CA 92117-1901 Office: One World Publ Co PO Box 178206 San Diego CA 92177

TARANIK, JAMES VLADIMIR, geologist, educator; b. Los Angeles, Apr. 23, 1940; s. Vladimir James and Jeanette Downing (Smith) T.; m. Colleen Sue Glessner, Dec. 4, 1971; children: Debra Lynn, Danny Lee. B.Sc. in Geology, Stanford U., 1964; Ph.D., Colo. Sch. Mines, 1974. Chief remote sensing Iowa Geol. Survey, Iowa City, 1971-74; prin. remote sensing scientist Earth Resources Observation Systems Data Ctr., U.S. Geol. Survey, Sioux Falls, S.D., 1975-79; chief non-renewable resources br., resource observation div. Office of Space and Terrestrial Applications, NASA Hdqrs., Washington, 1979-82; dean mines Mackay Sch. Mines U. Nev., Reno, 1982-87, prof. of geology and geophysics, 1982—, Arthur Brant chair of geology and geophysics, 1996—; pres. Desert Research Inst., Univ. and Community Coll. System Nev., 1987—; adj. prof. geology U. Iowa, 1971-79; vis. prof. civil engring. Iowa State U., 1972-74; adj. prof. earth sci. U. S.D., 1976-79; program scientist for space shuttle large format camera expt. for heat capacity mapping mission, liaison Geol. Scis. Bd., Nat. Acad. Scis., 1981-82; dir. NOAA Coop. Inst. Aerospace Sci. & Terrestrial Applications, 1986-94; program dir. NASA Space Grant consortium Univ. and Community Coll. System Nev., Reno, 1991—; team mem. Shuttle Imaging Radar-B Sci. Team NASA, 1983-88, mem. space applications adv. com., 1986-88; chmn. remote sensing subcom. SAAC, 1986-88; chmn. working group on civil space commercialization Dept. Commerce, 1982-84, mem. civil operational remote sensing satellite com., 1983-84; bd. dirs. Newmont Gold Co., 1986—; mem. adv. com. NASA Space Sci. and Applications Com., 1988-90, Nat. Def. Exec. Res., 1986—, AF studies bd., com. on strategic relocatable targets, 1989-91; mem. pre-launch rev. bd., NASA, Space Radar Lab., 1993-94; mem. fed. lab. rev. task force, NASA, 1994—; prin. investigator Japanese Earth Resources Satellite, 1991-94; mem. environ. task force MEDEA, Mitre Corp., McLean, Va., 1993—; cons. Jet Propulsion Lab. Calif., Hughes Aircraft Corp., Lockheed-Marietta Corp., Mitre Corp., TRW; developer remote sensing program and remote sensing lab. for State of Iowa, ednl. program in remote sensing for Iowa univs. and U. Nev., Reno; program scientist for 2d space shuttle flight Office Space and Terrestrial Applications Program; mem. terrestrial geol. applications program NASA, 1981—; co-investigator Can. Radarsat Program, 1995—. Contbr. to profl. jours. Served with C.E. U.S. Army, 1965-67; mil. intellegence officer Res. Decorated Bronze Star medal; recipient Spl. Achievement award U.S. Geol. Survey, 1978, Exceptional Sci. Achievement medal NASA, 1982, NASA Group Achievement award Shuttle imaging radar, 1990, NASA Johnson Space Ctr. Group Achievement award for large format camera, 1985; NASA prin. investigator, 1973, 83-88, prin. investigator French Spot-1 Program to Evaluate Spot 1986-88; NDEA fellow, 1968-71. Fellow AAAS, Geol. Soc. Am., Explorers Club, Am. Soc. Photogrammetry Remote Sensing; mem. IEEE, AIAA (sr.), Am. Astron. Soc. (sr.), Internat. Acad. Astronautics, Soc. Exploration Geophysicists, Am. Geophys. Union, Am. Assn. Petroleum Geologists, Soc. Mining Engrs. Am., Inst. Metallurgical Engrs., Soc. Econ. Geologists, Bohemian Club San Francisco. Home: PO Box 7175 Reno NV 89510-7175 also: 2108 Calle De Espana Las Vegas NV 89102-4013 Office: Univ & Community Coll Sys Desert Rsch Inst Pres Reno NV 89512 *I have always been in awe of the universe in which we live and the little time we have on earth to perceive and understand it.*

TARANTA, ANGELO (VISCA), physician, educator; b. Rome, 1927; came to U.S., 1952, naturalized, 1956; MD, U. Rome, 1949. Diplomate Am. Bd. Internal Medicine, also sub-bd. Rheumatology. Intern, dept. internal medicine and pediatrics Univ. Hosp., Rome, 1949-50, resident, 1950-52; resident in medicine St. Mary's Hosp., Rochester, N.Y., 1952-53; resident in cardiology Irvington (N.Y.) House, 1953-54, research assoc., 1955-59, research dir., 1959-62; assoc. dir. Irvington House Inst., N.Y.C., 1965-71; research fellow in microbiology NYU Sch. Medicine, 1955-56, instr. in microbiology, 1955-58, adj. asst. prof. microbiology, 1958-60, asst. prof. medicine, 1960-65, assoc. prof., 1965-75, on leave of absence, 1975-79; dir. medicine Cabrini Health Care Ctr., N.Y.C., 1973-93; prof. medicine, chief rheumatology and immunology div. N.Y. Med. Coll., 1979-85, chief div. humanities and ethics, 1985-88; co-chmn. study group on heart disease in the young Inter-Soc. Commn. on Heart Disease Resources, 1972-78; bd. dirs. Am. Heart Assn., 1975-77; chmn. Council on Cardiovascular Disease in the Young, 1975-77; cons. in field. Author: (with M. Markowitz) Rheumatic Fever; editor (with E. Kaplan) Infectious Endocarditis; contbr. numerous articles to profl. publs. and textbooks. Fulbright travel grantee, 1952; recipient Terence Cardinal Cooke medal N.Y. Med. Coll., 1985. Mem. Soc. Clin. Investigation, Am. Assn. Immunologists, N.Y. Acad. Medicine (chmn. sect. medicine 1980-87), Italian Rheumatology Soc. (hon.), Argentine Rheumatology Soc. (hon.).

TARBET, URANIA CHRISTY, artist, writer; b. Wheelright, Ky., Dec. 19, 1931; d. Howard Pearce and Ethel (Maloney) Christy; m. Robert L. Tarbet; children: Michael, Melody, John. Student, Pasadena (Calif.) Coll., 1978, Otis Art Inst., L.A., 1979-81, Sergei Bongart Sch. of Art, Santa Monica, Calif., 1981-83. judge various art exhbns.; instr. oil and pastel workshops; instr. art mktg. seminars. Author: Pastel Panache, 1996; contbg. writer ArtRevue Mag.; contbr. articles to profl. jours.; one-woman shows include World Trade Ctr. Club, San Francisco, 1993, Helen Jones Gallery, Sacramento, 1994, 95; exhibited in group shows at Panorama of Traditional Artists Invitational, Paramount, Calif., 1984-93, Nat. Arts Club-Pastel Soc. Am. Internat. Open Exhbn., 1984-94, Rosicrucian Mus., San Jose, Calif., 1987, Kans. Pastel Soc. Internat. Art Exhbn., Wichita, 1987-90, Am. Contemporary Outstanding Masters Dr. Sun Yat Sen Meml., Taiwan, 1987, 90, Société des Pastellistes de France, Copiegne, 1988, Lille, 1989, Umpqua Valley Mus., Roseburg, Oreg., 1989, Ashland (Ky.) Art Mus., 1990, Quincey (Ill.) Art Mus., 1990, Lauren Rodgers Mus. of Art, Laurel, Mich., 1990, Women Artists of the West Internat. Exhbn., Visalia, Calif., 1990-91, Chinese Culture Mus., Visalia, Calif., 1992, C.L. Clark Gallery, Bakersfield, Calif., 1994-95; represented in permanent collections in U.S. and internat. Pres. Jr. Woman's Club, Alhambra, Calif., 1959-60, PTA, San Gabriel, Calif., 1971-72. Recipient over 100 ribbons, trophies and cash awards including Daniel Greene award Kans. Pastel Soc., 1988, award of excellence Women Artists of the West, 1990. Mem. Internat. Assn. Pastel Socs. (co-founder, pres., advisor, bd. dirs. 1994-96), Pastel Soc. Am. (signature, life, Fred & Mary Trump award 1993), Pastel Soc. West Coast (co-founder), Knickerbocker Art Club (signature), Soc. Western Artists (signature, Neva Rall award 1st pl. pastel 1987, hon. mention 1988), Degas Pastel Soc. (signature, Award of Excellence 1992), Nat. League Am. Pen Women (arts and letters, pres. 1995-96), Calif. Art Club, Cassatt Pastel Soc. (founding pres., signature), Pastel Soc. Can. (signature), San Gabriel Fine Arts Assn., Otis Art Inst. Alumni Assn., Toastmasters, Calif. Writers Club. Republican. Home: Lazy UB Ranch PO Box 1032 Diamond Springs CA 95619

TARBI, WILLIAM RHEINLANDER, secondary education educator, curriculum consultant, educational technology researcher; b. San Bernardino, Calif., Feb. 23, 1949; s. William Metro and Sue (Rheinlander) T.; m. Jenny Workman, Apr. 10, 1980 (div. 1985); m. Michele Hastings, July 4, 1990; children: Amy, Melissa. AA, Santa Barbara City Coll., 1969; BA in History, U. Calif., Santa Barbara, 1976; MA, U. Redlands, 1992. Cert. secondary edn. social studies tchr., Calif. Reporter AP, Santa Barbara, Calif., 1976-80, UPI, Seattle, 1980-85, Golden West Radio Network, Seattle, 1980-85; tchr. Redlands (Calif.) Unified Sch. Dist., 1988—; cons. IMCOM, Redlands, 1985—. Mrm. E Clampus Vitus, Phi Delta Kappa.

TARBUCK, BARBARA JOAN, actor; b. Detroit, Jan. 15, 1942; d. George and Ruth Erma (Fillmore) T.; m. James Denis Connolly, May 17, 1980; 1 child, Jennifer Lane. B of Philosophy, Wayne State U., 1963; MA, U. Mich., 1965; postgrad., Ind. U., 1965-66. Author: (children's play) Who Am I?, 1972; author/actor: They Call Me Dr. Greer, 1994; guest star: (TV shows) Picket Fences, Civil Wars, Golden Girls, L.A. Law, Cagney & Lacey, Gen. Hosp., Pacific Blue, The Burning Zone, The Practice; (TV movies) Death of the Incredible Hulk, 1990, A Child Lost Forever, 1992, Jack Reed: Badge of Honor, 1993, Before He Wakes, 1997; feature films include Curly Sue, Short Circuit, Police Squad, others; Broadway shows include Brighton Beach Memoirs, Water Engine, Landscape and Silence; nat. tours: Broadway Bound, America Hurrah!. Fulbright grantee, 1966-67; recipient L.A. Drama Critics award, 1985. Mem. Zeta Phi Eta. Democrat.

TARIO, TERRY C(HARLES), broadcasting executive; b. Los Angeles, Aug. 28, 1950; s. Clifford Alexander and Marion Charlene (Olive) T.; m. Bonnie L. Eisen; children: Brian Paul, Caycee Nicole. Grad. high sch., Hermosa Beach, Calif., 1968. Gen. mgr. South Bay Power Tools, Hermosa Beach, 1973-76; v.p., gen. mgr. Sta. KEZJ FM, Twin Falls, Idaho, 1976—; dir. mktg. Pet Complex, Boise and Salt Lake City, 1985-90. Creator commls. John Lennon Meml. (Best of Yr. award 1982), Pets Unltd., 1983 (Best of Yr. award 1983), Depot Grill, 1984 (Best of Yr. award 1984), Eyecenter (Best of Yr. award 1986). Served with USN, 1968-72. Recipient Best of Yr. Pub. Svc. award, 1990. Mem. Idaho State Broadcasters Assn. (Best Pub. Svc. award 1990), Advt. and Mktg.Cons. (pres.), Broadcast Music Inc.; v.p. Admagination. Office: Stas KEZJ FM, KLIX AM/FM 415 Park Ave Twin Falls ID 83301-7752

TARKINGTON, DICKEY EDWARD, artist, educator; b. Russellville, Ark., Nov. 16, 1937; s. William Edward and Dessie Odell (Hallmark) T.; m. Patricia Ann Lincoln, May 2, 1960 (div.); children: D. Edward, Kimberly Dawn. Student, East L.A. Coll., 1962-64, Cerritos Coll., 1973-78, Rio Hondo Coll., 1978-83, Citrus Coll., 1984—. Printer Omaha Nat. Bank, 1958-59; press operator Western Electric, Omaha, 1959-60; systems analyst Bus. Systems Inc., L.A., 1960-64; comml. artist Compton (Calif.) Press, 1964-65; gen. clk. P and A Carloading Co., L.A., 1965-69; freight ops. supr. P.I.E. Trucking Co., L.A., 1969-74; owner, operator Tarkington/Harman, Bassett, Calif., 1974-79, Tarkington Ltd., Rosemead, Calif., 1978-84; freelance woodcarver, 1981—; tchr. Tri-Communities Adult Edn., West Covina, Calif., 1989—. Exhbns. include Fiesta de Artes, 1980 (Best of Show award), Calif. Ceramics and Craft Assn., 1983 (Best of Show award, 1st place award, Spl. Merit award, Best of Class award), Great Am. Irish Fair, 1990 (2nd place overall award). With USAF, 1955-58. Mem. East Valley Art Assn. (show chmn. 1992—), Mid Valley Art Assn., Calif. Carving Guild. Democrat. Home: 1054 W Hollyvale St Azusa CA 91702-3356

TARKOWSKI, LARRY MICHAEL, municipal official; b. Flint, Mich., May 15, 1952; s. Lavern Joseph and Barbara Ann (Wade) T.; m. Nancy Susan Ostapuk, May 7, 1983; children: Jonathon, Logan. B in Gen. Studies, U. Mich., Ann Arbor, 1974. Supt. Warren Smith Contracting, Flagstaff, Ariz., 1979-89; dir. pub. works Town of Prescott Valley, Ariz., 1989—. Chmn. No. Ariz. Coun. Govt. Transp. Bd., Flagstaff, 1990—. Named Profl. Man of Yr., Prescott Valley Rotary Club, 1993. Mem. Am. Pub. Works Assn. (pres. No. Ariz. br. 1995), Ctrl. Yavapai Transp. Planning Orgn., Prescott Valley C. of C., Lions (pres.1994), Yavapai Soccer Club (coord. 1992—).

TARLSON, NICK GLENN, financial advisor; b. Anchorage, May 31, 1955; s. Glenn Robert and Popi (Zafiri) T.; m. Mauna Anne Arnzen, Aug. 16, 1980; children: Claire, Diana, George. BBA, Seattle U., 1976. CPA, Calif., Wash., La. Mgr. Ernst & Whinney, San Francisco, 1976-83; v.p., sec., treas. Brayer Elec. Co., San Francisco, 1983-86; owner, mgr. Tarlson & Assoc., San Francisco, 1986—; bd. dirs. Brayer Electric Co., Brayer Lighting Co., San Francisco; pres.Jupiter Group, 1986-87, bd. dirs.; treas. Galacar & Co., 1987—, bd. dirs. Trustee Opera West Found., San Francisco, 1986—; trustee, treas. Patriarch Athenagoras Orthodox Inst.; pres. Bay Area Greek Am. Bus. Assn., 1996—; trustee Treasure Island Mus. Assn., 1996—; chmn. exptl. west dist. com. San Francisco Bay Area Coun. Boy Scouts Am., 1996—. Mem. Calif. Soc. CPAs (chmn. com. on taxation San Francisco chpt. 1995—, bd. dirs. 1996—, state tax com. 1995—), Rotary Club San Francisco (treas., dir. 1996—). Republican. Greek Orthodox. Home: 73 Orange Ave Larkspur CA 94939-1953 Office: Tarlson & Assoc 22 Battery St Ste 1100 San Francisco CA 94111-5525

TARN, NATHANIEL, poet, translator, educator; b. Paris, June 30, 1928; s. Marcel and Yvonne (Suchar) T.; children : Andrea, Marc. BA with honors, Cambridge (Eng.) U., 1948, MA, 1952; postgrad., U. Sorbonne, U. Paris, 1949-51; MA, U. Chgo., 1952, PhD, 1957; postgrad., London Sch. Econs., 1953-58. Anthropologist Guatemala, Burma, Alaska, and other locations, 1952—; prof. comparative lit. Rutgers U., 1970-85, prof. emeritus modern poetry, comparative lit, anthropology, 1985; vis. prof. SUNY, Buffalo and Princeton, 1969-70. Author: Old Savage/Young City, 1964, Where Babylon Ends, 1968, The Beautiful Contradictions, 1969, October, 1969, A Nowhere for Vallejo, 1971, Lyrics for the Bride of God: Section: The Artemision, 1972, The Persephones, 1974, Lyrics for the Bride of God, 1975, The House of Leaves, 1976, Birdscapes, with Seaside, 1978, The Desert Mothers, 1985, At the Western Gates, 1985, Palenque, 1986, Seeing America First, 1989, Flying the Body, 1993, Multitude of One, 1995, Scandals in the House of Birds, 1997, Views from the Weaving Mountain: Selected Essays in Poetics and Anthropology, 1991, Scandals in the House of Birds: Shamans & Priests on Lake Atitlan, 1997; co-author: (with Janet Rodney) The Forest, 1978, Atitlan/Alashka, 1979, The Ground of Our Great Admiration of Nature, 1978; contbg. author: Penguin Modern Poets No. Seven: Richard Murphy, Jon Silkin, Nathaniel Tarn, 1965, A.P.E.N. Anthology of Contemporary Poetry, 1966, The Penguin Book of Modern Verse Translation, 1966, Poems Addressed to Hugh MacDiarmid, 1967, Music and Sweet Poetry: A Verse Anthology, 1968, Frontier of Going: Anthology of Space Poetry, 1969, Shaking the Pumpkin, 1972, America: A Prophecy, 1973, Open Poetry, 1973, Active Anthology, 1974, Symposium of the Whole, 1983, Random House Book of Twentieth Century French Poetry, 1983, Beneath a Single Moon: Buddhism in American Poetry, 1991, American Poetry since 1950: Innovators and Outsiders, 1993; translator: The Heights of Macchu Picchu (Pablo Neruda), 1966, Stelae (Victor Segalen), 1969, Zapotec Struggles, 1993; editor, co-translator: Con Cuba: An Anthology of Cuban Poetry of the Last Sixty Years, 1969, Selected Poems (Pablo Neruda), 1970; editor Cape Edits. and founder-dir. Cape Goliard Press, J. Cape Ltd., 1967-69. Recipient Guinness prize for poetry, 1963. Office: PO Box 8187 Santa Fe NM 87504-8187

TARSON, HERBERT HARVEY, university administrator emeritus; b. N.Y.C., Aug. 28, 1910; s. Harry and Elizabeth (Miller) T.; m. Lynne Barnett, June 27, 1941; 1 son, Stephen. Grad., Army Command Gen. Staff Coll., 1942, Armed Forces Staff Coll., 1951, Adavnced Mgmt. Sch. Sr. Air Force Comdrs., George Washington U., 1954; B.A., U. Calif., Los Angeles, 1949; Ph.D., U.S. Internat. U., 1972. Entered U.S. Army as pvt., 1933, advanced through grades to maj., 1942; transfered to U.S. Air Force, 1947, advanced through grades to lt. col., 1949; adj. exec. officer Ft. Snelling, Minn., 1940-42; asst. adj. gen. 91st Inf. Div., 1942-43; chief of personnel, advance sec. Comd. Zone, ETO, 1944-45; dir. personnel services 8th Air Force, 1946-47; dep. dir. dept. info. and edn. Armed Forces Info. Sch., 1949-51; dir. personnel services Japan Air Def. Force, 1951-53, Continental Air Command, 1953-62; dir. adminstrv. services, spl. asst. to Comdr. 6th Air Force Res. Region, 1962-64; ret., 1964; asst. to chancellor L.I. U., Brookville, 1964-69; dean admissions Tex. State Tech. Inst., San Diego Indsl. Center, 1970-72; v.p. acad. affairs Nat. U., San Diego, 1972-75, sr. v.p., 1975-88, founding sr. v.p. emeritus, 1988—. Decorated Bronze Star medal with oak leaf cluster, Air Force Commendation medal with 2 oak leaf clusters. Fellow Bio-Med Research Inst.; mem. Doctoral Soc. U.S. Internat. U., Am. Soc. Tng., Devel., World Affairs Council, Air Force Assn., Navy League U.S., Pres.'s Assos. of Nat. U. (presidential life). Home: 4611 Denwood Rd La Mesa CA 91941-4803 *The greatest motivating force in my life is to explore the challenging frontiers of the future. Nothing can be compared to it.*

TARTER, BLODWEN, marketing and information technology executive; b. Sacramento, Dec. 2, 1954; d. Bill and Blodwen Edwards (Coburn) Tarter; m. Alan May, Aug. 6, 1983. BA, MA, Stanford U., 1976; MBA, U. Chgo., 1978; PhD, Golden Gate U., 1991. Mgr. mkt. rsch. Mead Products, Dayton, Ohio, 1978-79; assoc. mktg. mgr. Mead Products, 1979-80; mgr. mktg. svcs. Mead Paperboard Products, 1980-81; mgr. mktg. planning Mead Data Cen., N.Y.C., 1981-82; v.p. mktg. Info. Access Co., Belmont, Calif., 1982-86; dir. mktg. Channelmark Corp., San Mateo, Calif., 1986-87; v.p. mktg. Ins. Equities Corp., Palo Alto, Calif., 1987-89; dir. product mgmt. Charles Schwab & Co., Inc., San Francisco, 1989-91, v.p. applications devel. and info. systems divsn., 1991-93, v.p. telecom., 1993-94, v.p. electronic brokerage, 1994-96; v.p. Knight-Ridder Info., Inc., Mountain View, Calif., 1996-97; v.p. mktg. ops. Providian Bancorp, San Francisco, 1997—. Fundraiser Stanford Keystone campaign, 1988-91; vol. AIDS Meml. Grove. Mem. Stanford Profl. Women. Office: Providian Bancorp 201 Mission St San Francisco CA 94105

TARVER, BEN, mayor. Mayor City of Pleasanton, Calif. Office: PO Box 520 Pleasanton CA 94566

TARY, JOHN JOSEPH, engineer, consultant; b. Salem, Ohio, Oct. 28, 1922; s. John and Mary Elizabeth (Toth) T.; m. Elizabeth Jane Keyes, May 18, 1957; children: Mary Jude, Elizabeth Jane, Ann Kathleen. BS, Tri-State Coll., 1943. Cert. engr. Radio engr. Sta. WFAH, Alliance, Ohio, 1946-48; test engr. Babcock & Wilcox, Alliance, 1948-52; field engr. Bendix Radio, Balt., 1952-56; electronics engr. Nat. Bur. of Standards, Boulder, Colo., 1956-79; field svc. engr. St. Regis Paper, Denver, 1979-81; telecom engr. Tri-State Generation and Transmission Assn., Inc., Denver, 1981-93; cons. Tary Assocs., 1993—; exhibits chmn. Utilities Telecomm. Coun., Colorado Springs, 1990; registration chmn. Internat. Conf. on Comm., Denver, 1991; orlganizer 36 tech. confs. Co-author: A Guide for Telecommunication Specialists, 1962; contbr. articles to Electronic Mag. Bd. dirs. Colo. State Sci. Fair, Denver, 1976-79. With U.S. Army 1944-46. Recipient Avant Garde award Vehicular Tech. Soc., 1984, RAB Innovation award, 1992. Mem. IEEE (conf. chmn. region 5 1988—, chmn. Denver sect. 1975, editor RockIEEE Overlook 1993—, Centennial medal 1984), Armed Forces Comm. and Electronics Assn. (chpt. pres. 1974, awards chmn. 1974), Associated Pub.-Safety Communications Officers. Roman Catholic. Home and Office: 7739 Spring Dr Boulder CO 80303-5036

TASH, GRAHAM ANDREW, JR., automobile retail company executive; b. Seattle, Dec. 18, 1956; s. Graham Andrew and Charlotte Eleanor (Hawes) Tash; m. Julie Thompson Titus, Aug. 8, 1981; children: Jacqueline E., Katherine J., Graham A. III. BA, U. Puget Sound, 1979. Dist. mgr. Kenworth Truck Co., Atlanta, 1984-86; ops. mgr. Titus-Will Ford/Toyota, Tacoma, Wash., 1987-90, gen. mgr., 1991-94; pres. Titus-Will Ford/Toyota, Tacoma, 1994—, bd. dirs.; bd. dirs. Titus-Will Ent. Bd. dirs. Christian Brotherhood Acad., Tacoma, 1996—; mem. activities coun. Tacoma Art Mus., 1993, 94, 95. Recipient Chairman's award Ford Motor Co., 1986, 87, 92, Pres.'s award Toyota Motor Sales USA, 1991, 92, 94, 95, 96. Mem. Tacoma C. of C. (bd. dirs. 1996—), Tacoma Country and Golf Club, Wash. Athletic Club, Tacoma Lawn Tennis Club. Republican. Episcopalian. Office: Titus-Will Ford/Toyota Sales Inc 3606 S Sprague Ave Tacoma WA 98409

TASHIMA, ATSUSHI WALLACE, federal judge; b. Santa Maria, Calif., June 24, 1934; s. Yasutaro and Aya (Sasaki) T.; m. Nora Kiyo Inadomi, Jan. 27, 1957; children: Catherine Y., Christopher I., Jonathan I. AB in Polit. Sci., UCLA, 1958; LLB, Harvard U., 1961. Bar: Calif. 1962. Dep. atty. gen. State of Calif., 1962-67; atty. Spreckels Sugar divsn. Amstar Corp., 1968-72, v.p., gen. atty., 1972-77; ptnr. Morrison & Foerster, L.A., 1977-80; judge U.S. Dist. Ct. (ctrl. dist.) Calif., L.A., 1980-96, U.S. Ct. Appeals (9th cir.), Pasadena, Calif., 1996—; mem. Calif. Com. Bar Examiners, 1978-80. With USMC, 1953-55. Mem. ABA, State Bar Calif., Los Angeles County Bar Assn. Democrat. Office: US Ct Appeals 125 S Grand Ave Pasadena CA 91105-1621*

TASHJIAN, GREGORY KIMBALL THADDEUS, political consultant, writer; b. Petaluma, Calif., July 12, 1961; s. John Edward Tashjian and Barbara Deane Thornley McCutcheon. BA in Polit. Sci. and Psychology, Claremont McKenna Coll., 1985, postgrad., 1985—. Internship coord. Claremont (Calif.) McKenna Coll., 1983-85; youth min. L.A. Archdiocese, 1987-89; scholar in residence Claremont Inst./Rose Inst., 1985-89; vis. prof., cons. Cath. Relief Svcs./Edn. for Democracy, Vienna, 1989-91; exec. dir. Republican Party Hdqrs., 1992; exec. fellow Gov. Wilson's Adminstrn., Sacramento, 1995-96; cons. Dole/Kemp Campaign, Burbank, Calif., 1996—. Editor quar. jour. Sesqi Sentinel, 1996; writer for mag. Calif. Polit. Rev., 1994—, Nat. Rev., 1985—, First Things, 1991—. Chmn. Tulare County Young Reps., Visalia, 1982, 95, Claremont Colls. GOP, 1985, 94; mem. Tulare County Rep. Ctrl. Com., Visalia, 1980-83, 90—. Haynes Found. fellow, 1985; Calif. State U. Sys. fellow, 1995-96. Mem. Claremont Rugby Football Club (chair 1984-85), Concert and Chamber Choirs, Alpha Gamma Sigma. Roman Catholic. Home: 415 N Akers Rd Apt 123 Visalia CA 93291-5142 Office: Kimball Cons 1616 N St Ste 105 Sacramento CA 95814-5038

TASHJIAN, LEVON DONALD, psychiatrist; b. Phila., Aug. 18, 1934; s. Levon O. and Anna L. (Mahmarian) T.; m. Stefanie M. Halus, June 17, 1961; children: Audrey, Paul, Peter. BA magna cum laude, Harvard Coll., 1952-56; MD, U. Pa., 1956-60. Diplomate Am. Bd. Neurology and Psychiatry; med. lic., Pa. Rotating intern Pa. Hosp., Phila., 1960-61; neurology resident Jefferson Med. Coll. Hosp., 1961; psychiatry resident Hosp. U. Pa., 1963-66; Sol Ginsberg fellow Group for the Advancement of Psychiatry, 1965-67; clin. psychiatry instr. U. Pa., 1966-68, assoc., 1968-72, asst. prof., 1972-84; clin. assoc. prof. Temple U., 1989—, 1984—; attending psychiatrist The Inst. of Pa. Hosp., 1968-90, assoc. dir. adolescent treatment ctr., 1968-74, dir. young adult unit and program, 1973-80, sr. attending psychiatrist, 1990-93; cons. adolescent psychiatry, Phila. Child Guidance Ctr., 1971-78; dir. adult unit and program, attending psychiatrist The Horsham Clin, Ambler, Pa., 1980-84, med. dir., 1984-88; med. dir. The Consultation Ctr., Phila., 1982-83; chmn. dept. psychiatry Mt. Sinai Hosp., Phila, 1988-89; med. dir. continuum care svcs. Editor: (newsletter) Am. Soc. Adolescent Psychiatry, 1983-85; editorial bd. mem. Child and Adolescent Mental Health Care, 1991—; author: (with Harold Rashkis) Understanding Your Parents, 1978; presenter in field; contbr. articles to profl. jours. Named One of Best Physicians of Phila., Phila. Mag., 1979, 91. Fellow Coll. of Physicians of Phila.; mem. Phila. soc. Adolescent Psychiatry (pres.-elect 1972-73, pres. 1973-74), Pa. Psychiatric Soc., Phila. Psychiatric Soc. (program chmn. 1971, 83). Home: 82 Tano Rd Santa Fe NM 87501 Office: 200 W De Vargas St Ste 4 Santa Fe NM 87501-2654

TATA, GIOVANNI, publishing executive; b. Taranto, Italy, Apr. 26, 1954; came to U.S., 1974, naturalized, 1982; s. Vito and Angela (Colucci) T.; m. Brenda Susan Smith, Feb. 14, 1978; children: Elizabeth Ariana, Katherine Allison, Margaret Anne, Michael Anthony. BS cum laude (scholar), Brigham Young U., 1977, MA, 1980; grad. cert. area studies U. Utah, 1980; PhD, 1986; postgrad. U. Turin (Italy), 1980-81. Archaeologist, Utah State Hist. Soc., Salt Lake City, 1979; instr. dept. langs. U. Utah, Salt Lake City, 1983-85; Mediterranean specialist Soc. Early Hist. Archaeology, Provo, Utah, 1978-91; mus. curator Pioneer Trail State Park, Salt Lake City, 1982-83; instr. dept. art Brigham Young U., Provo, 1982-84; research fellow Direzione Generale per la Cooperazione Scientifica Culturale e Technica, Rome, 1980-81; research curator Utah Mus. Fine Arts, Salt Lake City, 1985-87; chmn. 35th Ann. Symposium on the Archaeology of the Scriptures, 1986; pres. Transoft Internat., Inc., 1988—, Mus. Info. Systems, 1987-93; chmn. Taras Devel. Corp., 1994—. Chmn. MuseuMedia, Inc., 1995—. Republican. Mem. Ch. Jesus Christ of Latter-day Saints. Mem. Am. Assn. Museums, Internat. Coun. Museums, Utah State Hist. Soc. Home: PO Box 2194 Provo UT 84603-2194 Office: Taras Devel Corp 117 #250 W Center St Provo UT 84603

TATARSKII, VALERIAN IL'ICH, physics researcher; b. Kharkov, USSR, Oct. 13, 1929; s. Il'ya A. and Elizabeth A. (Lapis) T.; m. Maia S. Granovskaia, Dec. 22, 1955; 1 child, Viatcheslav V. MS, Moscow State U., 1952; PhD, Acoustical Inst. Acad. Scis., 1957; DSc, Gorky State U., 1962. Scientific rschr. Geophys. Inst. Acad. Sci. USSR, Moscow, 1953-56; scientific rschr. Inst. Atmospheric Physics, Acad. Sci. USSR, Moscow, 1956-59, sr. scientific rschr., 1959-78, head lab., 1978-90; head dept. Lebedev. Phys. Inst. Acad. Sci., Moscow, 1990-91; sr. rsch. assoc. U. Colo. Coop. Inst. for Rsch. in Environ. Sci., Boulder, 1991—, NOAA/ERL. Environ. Tech. Lab., Boulder. Author: Wave Propagation in a Turbulent Medium, 1961, 67, The Effect of the Turbulent Atmosphere on Wave Propagation, 1971, Principles of Statistical Radiophysics, 1989; contbr. articles to profl. jours. Recipient of Max Born award, 1994, Optical Soc. of Am., USSR State prize, 1990. Fellow Optical Soc. Am. (Max Born award 1994); mem. Russian Acad. Sci., U.S.A. Nat. Acad. Engring. (fgn. assoc.), N.Y. Acad. Sci. Office: NOAA ERL ETL 325 Broadway St Boulder CO 80303-3337

TATE, RANDALL J. (RANDY TATE), former congressman; b. Puyallup, Wash., Nov. 23, 1965; m. Julie; 1 child. AA, Tacoma C. C., Wash.; BA in Econs. and Polit. Sci., We. Wash. U. Mem. Wash. Ho. of Reps., 1988-94, 104th Congress from 9th Wash. dist., 1994—; former mem. com. rules, com. fin. instns. and ins., judiciary com., Wash. Ho. Reps.; mem. Congrl. com. transp. and infrastructure, com. govt. reform. Home: 13011 Meridian E # 301 Puyallup WA 98373 address: 5616 99th St Ct E Puyallup WA 98374*

TATE, STAN DAVIS, priest, clinical bioethicist; b. Boise, Idaho, Dec. 5, 1932; s. John P. and Marjorie (Davis) T.; m. Lynn Campbell, June 10, 1955; children: Teri McCully, Scott, Phil. BA, U. Idaho, 1955; MDiv, Princeton (N.J.) Sem., 1958; DMin, San Francisco Theol. Sem., Berkeley, Calif., 1988. Ordained priest Episcopalian Ch., 1962. Chaplain Smokejumpers USFS, McCall, Idaho, 1953-63, N.J. Prison, Trenton, 1957-58; pastor Presbyn. Ch., Hysham, Mont., 1958-61; vicar Episc. Ch., McCall, 1961-70; probate judge Valley County, Cascade, Idaho, 1965-70; instr. Boise State Coll., 1970-74; dir. Youth Alternatives, Boise, 1974-78; chaplain Oreg. State U., Corvallis, 1978-81; rector St. Mark's Episc. Ch., Moscow, Idaho, 1981-88; clin. bioethicist Gritman Med. Ctr., Moscow, 1989—. Author: Pastoral Bioethics, 1989. Active Idaho Commn. on Juvenile Justice, Boise, 1989—. Home: 1423 Alpowa St Moscow ID 83843-2401 Office: Gritman Med Ctr 2000 S Main St Moscow ID 83843-8970

TATHAM, WILLIAM R., vintner; b. 1934. Pres., chmn. bd. Consol Industries, Inc., Clovis, Calif., 1962—. Office: Consolidated Industries Inc 2148 E Copper Ave Clovis CA 93611-9128*

TATUM, THOMAS DESKINS, film and television producer, director; b. Pineville, Ky., Feb. 16, 1946; s. Clinton Turner and Gaynelle (Deskins) T.; m. Laura Ann Smith, Aug. 15, 1968 (div. 1974); m. Suzanne Pettit, Sept. 29, 1983; children: Rhett Cowden, Walker Edwin. BA, Vanderbilt U., 1968; JD, Emory U., 1974. Bar: Ga. 1974, D.C. 1980. Spl. asst. City of Atlanta, 1974-76; dep. dir. fed. relations Fed. Relations Nat. League of Cities, Washington, 1977-78; dir. communications Office of Conservation and Solar Energy, Washington, 1979-80; chmn. exec. producer Tatum Communications, Inc., Telluride, and Burbank, Calif., 1981—; chmn., pres. Western Film & Video, Inc., Telluride, Colo., 1987—; pres., COO Planet Central TV, 1995-96. Prodr. feature film Winners Take All, 1987; prodr., dir. documentaries Double High, 1982 (award), Maui Windsurf, 1983, home videos Greenpeace in Action, Girls of Winter/Skiing mag., Am. Ultra Sports with Prime Network, 1989-94, various TV, cable and home video sports programs, 1982—, series Eco Sports, 1995—. Dep. campaign mgr. Maynard Jackson, 1973, Jimmy Carter campaign, 1976, staff conf. Dem. Mayors, 1974-75, media cons. Greepeace, 1988; bd. dirs. Atlanta Ballet, v.p., 1975; nat. urban affairs coord. Carter Mondale campaign 1976, mem. Carter Mondale transition team 1976-77; mem. adv. bd. Solar Electric Light Fund, Washington, 1990—. Mem. Ga. Bar Assn., Hollywood Film and TV Soc., L.A. Tennis Club. Presbyterian. Home: PO Box 944 Telluride CO 81435-0944 Office: Tatum Comm Inc 2219 W Olive Ave Ste 173 Burbank CA 91506-2648

TAUBE, HENRY, chemistry educator; b. Sask., Can., Nov. 30, 1915; came to U.S., 1937, naturalized, 1942; s. Samuel and Albertina (Tiledetski) T.; m. Mary Alice Wesche, Nov. 27, 1952; children: Linda, Marianna, Heinrich, Karl. BS, U. Sask., 1935, MS, 1937, LLD, 1973; PhD, U. Calif., 1940; PhD (hon.), Hebrew U. of Jerusalem, 1979; DSc (hon.), U. Chgo., 1983, Poly. Inst., N.Y., 1984, SUNY, 1985, U. Guelph, 1987; DSc honoris causa, Seton Hall U., 1988; Lajos Kossuth U. of Debrecen, Hungary, 1988; DSc, Northwestern U., 1990; hon. degree, U. Athens, 1993. Instr. U. Calif., 1940-41; instr., asst. prof. Cornell U., 1941-46; faculty U. Chgo., 1946-62, prof., 1952-62, chmn. dept. chemistry, 1955-59; prof. chemistry Stanford U., 1962-90; prof. emeritus chemistry Stanford U, 1990—; Marguerite Blake Wilbur prof. Stanford U., 1976, chmn. dept., 1971-74; Baker lectr. Cornell U., 1965. Hon. mem. Hungarian Acad., Scis., 1988. Guggenheim fellow, 1949, 55; recipient Harrison Howe award, 1961, Chandler medal Columbia U., 1964, F. P. Dwyer medal U. NSW, Australia, 1973, Nat. medal of Sci., 1976, 77, Allied Chem. award for Excellence in Grad. Tchg. and Innovative Sci., 1979, Nobel prize in Chemistry, 1983, Bailar medal U. Ill., 1983, Robert A. Welch Found. award in Chemistry, 1983, Disting. Achievement award Internat. Precious Metals Inst., 1986, Brazilian Order of Sci. Merit award, 1994. Fellow Royal Soc. Chemistry (hon.), Indian Chem. Soc. (hon.); mem. NAS (award in chem. scis. 1983), Am. Acad. Arts and Scis., Am. Chem. Soc. (Kirkwood award New Haven sect. 1965, award for nuclear applications in chemistry 1955, Nichols medal N.Y. sect. 1971, Willard Gibbs medal Chgo. sect. 1971, Disting. Svc. in Advancement Inorganic Chemistry award 1967, T.W. Richards medal NE sect. 1980, Monsanto Co. award in inorganic chemistry 1981, Linus Pauling award Puget Sound sect. 1981, Priestley medal 1985, Oesper award Cin. sect. 1986, G.M. Kosolapoff award Auburn sect. 1990), Royal Physiographical Soc. of Lund (fgn. mem.), Am. Philos. Soc., Finnish Acad. Sci. and Letters, Royal Danish Acad. Scis. and Letters, Coll. Chemists of Catalonia and Beleares (hon.), Can. Soc. Chemistry (hon.), Hungarian Acad. Scis. (hon. mem.), Royal Soc. (fgn. mem.), Brazilian Acad. Scis. (corr.), Engring. Acad. Japan (fgn. assoc.), Australian Acad. Scis. (corr.), Chem. Soc. Japan (hon. mem. 1993), Phi Beta Kappa, Sigma Xi, Phi Lambda Upsilon (hon.). Office: Stanford U Dept Chemistry Stanford CA 94305-5080

TAUER, PAUL E., mayor, educator; b. 1935; m. Katherine Eldredge, Sept. 1, 1956; children: Paul E. Jr., Edward, Roch, Eugene, Kathryn, Tammie, Andrew, Timothy. BA in Historyand Edn., Regis Coll., 1961; MA in Edn. Adminstrn., U. No. Colo., 1964. Tchr. Denver Pub. Schs., 1961-92; ret., 1992. Mayor City of Aurora, Colo., 1987—, mem. Aurora City Coun., 1979-1987; mem. Adams County Coordinating Com., Gov.'s Met. Transp. Roundtable; active Aurora airport coms. Mem. Noise. Office: Office of Mayor 1470 S Havana St Aurora CO 80012-4014

TAULBEE, AMY LOUISE, college administrator; b. Washington, Feb. 2, 1963; d. John Earl and Sylvia Ida (Beer) T.; m. Richard A. Fass. BA, Stanford U., 1985; MDiv, Fuller Theol. Sem., Pasadena, Calif., 1992. Coll. asst. Menlo Park (Calif.) Presbyn. Ch., 1985-88; pres. student govt. Sch. of Theol. Fuller Theol. Sem., Pasadena, Calif., 1989-90, dir. academic advising, 1990-93; dir. found. and corp. rels. Pomona Coll., Claremont, Calif., 1993—. Recipient Pres.'s award Fuller Theol. Sem., 1992. Mem. Coun. for Advancement and Support of Edn., L.A. Jr. C. of C. Presbyterian. Office: Pomona Coll 550 N College Ave Claremont CA 91711-4434

TAUSIG, MICHAEL ROBERT, college administrator, higher education planning consultant; b. L.A., May 3, 1948; s. Maurice James and Georgia Ann (Bullgreen) T.; m. Cheryl Irvin, Jan. 30, 1972; children: Michael Robert Jr., Matthew Paul. BA in Music, Whittier Coll., 1971; MA, Calif. State U., Sacramento, 1973; ABD, Nova U., 1987. Dir. summer music programs Anaheim (Calif.) Arts Dept., 1968-73; tchr. music Borrego Springs (Calif.) High Sch., 1973-75; div. chmn., asst. to v.p. instrn. Napa (Calif.) Valley Coll., 1975-88; v.p. planning and devel. Mt. San Jacinto (Calif.) Coll., 1988-92; v.p. student svcs., 1994—; Calif. chief Student Svcs. Officers; dir. C.C.'s Facilities Coalition; student svcs. liaison Calif. State Com. Coll. Task Force on Accountability. Author: Fundamentals of Music, 1985. Chmn., pres. Napa County Arts Coun., 1985; chmn. spl. issues San Jacinto Planning Commn., 1990-91; elder Presbyn. Ch., Napa, 1985-87; state bd. dirs. Calif. Chief Student Svcs. Officers Assn. Mem. Nat. Coun. Rsch. and Planning, Rsch. and Planning Group for Calif., C.C., Kiwanis (bd. dirs. Hemet, Calif. 1990-91, pres.-elect 1993-94, pres. 1994-95). Republican. Office: Mt San Jacinto Coll 42837 LaPiedra Rd Menifee CA 92584

TAUSSIG, ROBERT TRIMBLE, engineering executive; b. St. Louis, Apr. 26, 1938; s. Joseph Bondi and Frances Shackleford (McConnell) T.; m. Judith Ann Pryor, July 13, 1963; 1 child, Emily Barr. BA, Harvard Coll., 1960; MA, Columbia U., 1963, PhD, 1965. Rsch. assoc. Columbia U., N.Y.C., 1965-66, Inst. for Plasma Physics, Nagoya, Japan, 1966-67; lectr. Harvard U., Cambridge, Mass., 1968-69; assoc. prof. Sch. of Engring. Columbia U., 1969-75; v.p. Spectra Tech., Inc., Bellevue, Wash., 1975-90; bus. devel. mgr. Bechtel Rsch. and Devel., San Francisco, 1990-92, mgr. applied physics, 1992—; cons. Allerton Press, N.Y.C., 1974-76, Edison Electric Inst., N.Y.C., 1974-75; bd. dirs. Spectra Tech., Inc., Bellevue. Contbg. author: Efficient Electricity Use, 1976; referee and assoc. editor: Energy jour., 1978. Intern sponsor Seattle (Wash.) Sch. System, 1980-88. Recipient award for Acad. Excellence, Harvard Coll., 1957-58. Mem. IEEE, ASME, ANS. Democrat. Presbyterian. Office: The Bechtel Corp 50 Beale St San Francisco CA 94105-1813

TAVEGGIA, THOMAS CHARLES, management educator, management consultant; b. Oak Lawn, Ill., June 15, 1943; s. Thomas Angelo and Eunice Louise (Harriss) T.; m. Brigitte I. Adams, Jan. 23, 1965; children: Michaela, Francesca. BS, Ill. Inst. Tech., 1965; MA, U. Oreg., 1968, PhD, 1971. Prof., U. Oreg., Eugene, 1970, U. B.C. (Can.), Vancouver, 1970-73, U. Calif.-Irvine, 1973-74, Ill. Inst. Tech., Chgo., 1974-77; mgmt. cons. Towers, Perrin, Forster & Crosby, Chgo., 1977-80; ptnr. Manplan Cons., Chgo., 1980-81; ptnr. Coopers & Lybrand, San Francisco, 1981-86; ptnr. Touche Ross, San Francisco, 1986-88; prof. Calif. Sch. Profl. Psychology, Berkeley, 1988—. NDEA Title IV fellow, 1967-71; U. B.C. faculty rsch. grantee, 1970, 71, 73. Faculty Rsch. grantee Calif. Sch. Profl. Psychology, 1993—ss. Mem. Acad. Mgmt. Soc., Am. Sociol. Assn., Nat. Bur. Profl. Mgmt. Cons., Human Resource Mgmt. Soc., Inst. Mgmt. Cons. Presbyterian. Author: (with R. Dubin and R. Arends) From Family and School To Work, 1967; (with Dubin) The Teaching-Learning Paradox: A Comparative Analysis of College

Teaching Methods, 1968; (with Dubin and R.A. Hedley) The Medium May Be Related to the Message: College Instruction by TV, 1969; contbr. numerous articles to books and profl. jours. Home: 2188 Lariat Ln Walnut Creek CA 94596-6515 Office: Calif Sch Profl Psychology 1005 Atlantic Ave Alameda CA 94501-1148

TAVERNA, RODNEY ELWARD, financial services company executive; b. Springfield, Ill., Aug. 8, 1947; s. Jerome Thomas and Virginia (Holcomb) T.; m. Cheryl Ann Walters, Sept. 4, 1968 (div. 1983); children: Lara Lyn, Melinda Marie, Ryan Thomas; m. Caroline Whiffen, Apr. 1985. BA, U. Mo., 1969; MBA in Fin., Nat. U., 1988. Commd. 2d lt., supply officer USMC, 1969, advanced through grades to maj., 1979; supply officer Central Svcs. Agy., Danang, Vietnam, 1970-71, Marine Air Control Squadron, Futenma, Okinawa, 1977-78; logistics officer Hdqrs. Marine Corps Recruit Depot, Paris Island, S.C., 1972-75; support officer Marine Barracks, Treasure Island, San Francisco, 1975-77; regimental supply officer 1st Marine Div., Camp Pendleton, Calif., 1978-79; brigade supply officer 1st Marine Brigade, Kaneohe Bay, Hawaii, 1980-82; exec. officer 1st Maintenance Bn., Camp Pendleton, 1982-85; asst div. supply officer 1st Marine Div., 1985-88; pres. Freedom Fin. Group, 1991—; br. mgr. WMA Securities, Inc., 1991—; owner, mgr. Opportunities Unltd., Oceanside, Calif., 1985-91; cons. Incentive Leasing Corp., San Diego, 1985-86, The Profit Ctr., Santa Ana, Calif., 1991; founding mgr. Meditrend Internat., San Diego, 1987-88; founding dir. Am. 3-D Corp., Henderson, Nev., 1990-91. Republican. Home and Office: 1632 Avenida Andante Oceanside CA 92056-6905

TAVOULARIS, KATHERINE EFY, political organization coordinator; b. Montreal, Que., Can., Feb. 1, 1970; came to U.S., 1971; d. George and Maria (Tsaltas) T. BA, Calif. State U., Long Beach, 1992. Concierge Doubletree Hotel, Orange, Calif., 1990-91; client rep. Home Fed. F.S.B., Villa Park, Calif., 1991-93; contract coord. Bergen Brunswig, Orange, 1993; vol. coord. activities, campaign, cands. Rep. Party Orange County, 1993—. adminstr. 400 Club-Rep. Party Orange County, 1993—; coord. Richard Nixon Meml. Svc., Yorba Linda, Calif., 1994; mem. Orange County Young Reps., 1995-96, Calif. Rep. Assembly, Corona del Mar, 1996; 1st v.p. Rep. Women Fedn., Orange, 1996. Home: 1537 E Riverview Ave Orange CA 92665 Office: Rep Party Orange County Orange CA 92665

TAVOULARIS, MARJORIE OSTERWISE, psychiatrist; b. Mt. Pleasant, Pa., May 28, 1938; d. Robert Russell and Violet Jane (Watson) Osterwise; m. James Harry Tavoularis, May 23, 1962 (div. 1987); children: Laura, Suzanne, Diana, Patricia. BS, U. Pitts., 1961; MD, Pitts. Pschomalytic Inst., 1966; postgrad., Pitts. Psychoanalytic Inst., 1976-85; PhD, Calif. Psychoanalytic Inst., 1996. Rotating intern St. Francis Gen. Hosp., 1966-67; resident in psychiatry U. Pitts. Western Psychiat. Inst., 1967-70; staff psychiatrist St. Frances Med. Ctr., Pitts., 1972-85, Kern Med. Ctr., Bakersfield, Calif., 1986-89; sr. psychiatrist Calif. Correctional Inst., Teachapi, 1989-91, Calif. Parole Office, Bakersfield, 1991-96; psychiatrist pvt. practice, Pitts. & Bakersfield, 1972—; chief psychiatrist CPS-Corcoran, 1995-96, Pelican Bay State Prison, 1996—. Mem. Am. Psychiat. Assn., Ctrl. Calif. Psychiat. Soc., Kern County Med. Soc., Pa. Psychiat. Soc. (pres. 1984-85), Pitts. Psychiat. Soc. (pres. 1981-82).

TAYLOR, ANN, artist; b. Rochester, N.Y., Mar. 23, 1941. Student, Vassar Coll., 1958-61; BA, The New Sch. Social Research, 1962. Pvt. practice Scottsdale, Ariz. One-woman shows include Carl Solway Gallery, Cin., 1964, York Gallery, N.Y.C., 1967-69, Hunter Gallery, Aspen, Colo., 1970, Christopher Gallery, N.Y.C., 1975, 77, Miller Gallery, Cin., 1978, 83, Munson Gallery, Santa Fe., 1980, Oxford Gallery, Rochester, 1965-95, C.G. Rein Galleries, Mpls., 1981, Scottsdale, Ariz., 1982, 85, Houston, 1983, Yuma (Ariz.) Art Ctr., 1984, Gallery Henoch, N.Y.C., 1984, Scottsdale Ctr. for Arts, 1985, Kauffman Galleries, Houston, 1986, Marilyn Butler Fine Art, Scottsdale, 1987, others; solo exhibition or solo traveling exhibition: Rochester Mus. and Scis. Ctr., 1984-85, Palm Springs Desert Mus., 1984-85, Yuma Art Ctr., 1984-85, Reed Whipple Cultural Ctr., 1984-85, Scottsdale Ctr. for the Arts, 1984-85, Beaumont Art Mus., 1984-85; exhibited in group shows at Indpls. Ctr. for Contemporary Art, Gallery of Modern Art, N.Y.C., Fine Art Ctr., Tempe, Ariz., Everson Mus., Syracuse, N.Y., Walton-Gilbert Galleries, San Francisco, Adelle M. Fine Art, Dallas, Janet Fleischer Gallery, Phila., Peter M. David Gallery, Mpls., Mickelson Gallery, Washington, Julia Black Gallery, Taos, N.Mex., Palm Springs Desert Mus., Scottsdale Ctr. for the Arts, Ariz. State U.; represented in permanent collections Eastman Kodak Co., Bank of Am., Houston, Am. Express, Phoenix, Bausch & Lomb, Inc., Rochester, A.C. Nielsen Corp., Chgo., 1st Interstate Bank, Phoenix, Honeywell, Inc., Mpls., Xerox, Rochester, Lincoln Chase Trust Co., Rochester, Third Nat. Bank, Dayton, Ohio, Cen. Trust Co., Cin., Valley Nat. Bank, Phoenix, Butterfield Savs. & Loan, Santa Ana, Calif., Sohio Petroleum Co., Houston, A.C. Neilsen Corp., Chgo., others.

TAYLOR, BARRY E., lawyer; b. Mineola, N.Y., Mar. 14, 1948. BA magna cum laude, U. Va., 1970, JD, 1975. Bar: Calif. 1975. With Wilson, Sonsini, Goodrich & Rosati P.C., Palo Alto, Calif. Mem. ABA, State Bar Calif., Order Coif, Phi Beta Kappa. Office: Wilson Sonsini Goodrich & Rosati PC 650 Page Mill Rd Palo Alto CA 94304-1001

TAYLOR, BELINDA CAREY, magazine editor, writer; b. Dayton, Ohio, Dec. 18, 1940; d. Robert Edward and Dorothe (Carey) Doty; children: Jennifer, Alexi. BA, U. Calif., Berkeley, 1973. Reporter Novato (Calif.) Advance, 1973-77, mng. editor, 1977-79; mng. editor The Montclarion, Oakland, Calif., 1979-83; bus. editor The Oakland Tribune, 1983-86, metro editor, 1987-89, dep. mng. editor, 1989-93; mng. editor Callboard Mag., San Francisco, 1993—; bd. dirs. Bay Area Playwrights' Found., San Francisco, 1996. Recipient Elsa Knight Thompson award Media Alliance, San Francisco, 1984, award for column writing Peninsula Press Club, 1992. Office: Theater Bay Area 657 Mission St San Francisco CA 94105-4104

TAYLOR, BEVERLY LACY, stringed instrument restorer, classical guitarist; b. Denver, Mar. 1, 1928; d. Frederick Thurlow and Ruth (Rogers) Lacy; m. Arthur D. Taylor, Mar. 18, 1967. BA, Wheaton Coll., Norton, Mass., 1949; postgrad., U. Denver, 1951-53, U. Colo., 1953. Scene designer, tech. dir. Piper Players, Idaho Springs, Colo., 1949-51; art instr. Denver Art Mus., 1952; craft and speech instr. Wallace Sch., Denver, 1953; illustrator dept. native art Denver Art Mus., 1954-56; designer, owner The Art Studio, Santa Fe, 1956-58; instr., owner Classic Guitar Studio, Santa Fe, 1959—; instr. classical guitar Santa Fe Conservatory of Music, 1966-67, Coll. Sante Fe, 1971-72; stringed instrument restorer Lacy Taylor Studio, Santa Fe, 1967—. One-woman shows of mosaic panels include Mus. N.Mex., Santa Fe, 1959; exhibited in group shows at Mus. New Mex., 1962, 63; executed mosaic panels Denver Art Mus. Recipient Miriam Carpenter Art prize Wheaton Coll., 1949, prize N.Mex. State Fair, 1959, 61. Mem. Guild Am. Luthiers, Assn. String Instrument Artisans. Home: 1210 Canyon Rd Santa Fe NM 87501-6128

TAYLOR, CARROLL STRIBLING, lawyer; b. Port Chester, N.Y., Jan. 14, 1944; s. William H. Jr. and Anna P. (Stribling) T.; m. Nancy S. Tyson, Apr. 7, 1968; children: Heather, Kimberly, Tori, Tiffany, Tacy. AB, Yale U., 1965; JD, U. Calif., Berkeley, 1968. Bar: Hawaii 1969, Calif. 1969, U.S. Dist. Ct. Hawaii 1969, U.S. Dist. Ct. (cen. dist.) Calif. 1975, U.S. Ct. Appeals (9th cir.) 1975. Researcher Legis. Reference Bur., Honolulu, 1968-70; reporter Jud. Coun. Probate Code Revision Project, Honolulu, 1970-71; assoc. Chun, Kerr & Dodd, Honolulu, 1971-75; ptnr. Hamilton & Taylor, Honolulu, 1975-80; officer, dir. Char, Hamilton, Taylor & Thom, Honolulu, 1980-82, Carroll S. Taylor Atty. at Law, A Law Corp., Honolulu, 1982-86; ptnr. Taylor & Leong, Honolulu, 1986-91, Taylor, Leong & Chee, Honolulu, 1991—; adj. prof. Richardson Sch. Law U. Hawaii, Honolulu, 1981-86, 88-90, 97; mem. Disciplinary bd. of Supreme Ct. of Hawaii, 1994—; dir. Am. Nat. Lawyers Ins. Reciprocal, 1997—. Fellow Am. Coll. Trust and Estate Counsel; mem. ABA, Calif. Bar Assn., Hawaii Bar Assn., Hawaii Inst. Continuing Legal Edn. (pres. 1986-88), Pla. Club (Honolulu). Episcopalian. Home: 46-429 Hololio St Kaneohe HI 96744-4225 Office: 737 Bishop St Ste 2060 Honolulu HI 96813-3211

TAYLOR, CHARLES ELLETT, biologist; b. Chgo., Sept. 9, 1945; s. Stewart Ferguson and Barbara (Ellett) T.; m. Minna Glushiens, June 22, 1969. AB, U. Calif., 1968; PhD, SUNY, Stony Brook, 1973. Prof. U. Calif., Riverside, 1974-80, UCLA, 1980—; cons. artificial life and population genetics. Mem. Santa Fe Inst. Office: Dept Biology UCLA 405 Hilgard Ave Los Angeles CA 90024-1301

TAYLOR, CYNTHIA HINKEL, English literature educator; b. Lovell, Wyo., Dec. 23, 1954; s. Robert Harold Hinkel and Sandra Tippetts Dodds; m. Ted Michael Taylor, Dec. 31, 1977. B of English, U. Idaho, 1977, M of English, 1979; Phd in English, U. Minn., 1993. Instrnl. asst. U. Idaho, Moscow, 1977-79; teaching asst. U. Minn., Mpls., 1979-89, adminstrv. fellow, 1987-89; asst. prof. English U. So. Colo., Pueblo, 1989—. Mem. MLA, Rocky Mountain MLA (pres. we. lit. sect. 1991), We. Lit. Assn., Nat. Women's Studies Assn., Phi Beta Kappa, Sigma Tau Delta. Democrat. Home: 18 Arrowsmith Dr Pueblo CO 81008-1849 Office: U So Colo Pueblo CO 81001

TAYLOR, DEBORAH ANN, paralegal; b. Columbia, S.C.. Asst. long term care ombudsman State of Alaska Sr. Svcs., Anchorage, 1989-95, ins. counseling and asst. coord., 1993—, info. and referral officer, 1995—; Bd. dirs. N.W. Alliance Info. & Referral Sys., 1994-96. Bd. dirs. Coll. Rd. Svc. Dist., Fairbanks, Alaska, 1985-87, North Star Borough Planning and Zoning Com., Fairbanks, pres. Village Green Homeowners Assn. 1983-85, Fairbanks, Grand Larry Condominium Assn., Anchorage, 1987-96. Mem. Alaska State Employees Assn. (sec. treas. 1993-95, pres. Anchorage chpt., 1991-95, sec. 1988-91), Elder Law Section Alaska Bar. Office: Divsn Sr Svcs 3601 C St #310 Anchorage AK 99503

TAYLOR, DENNIS MERRILL, state official; b. Richmond, Calif., July 8, 1946; s. Merrill Edward and Bettey (Orthman) T.; m. Joan South, Oct. 25, 1974; children—Morgan Clare, Merrill South. B.A., U. Kans., 1968; postgrad. U. Mont., 1976-82. Vista vol. ACTION, Helena, Mont., 1972-74; health planner Dept. Health and Environ. Scis., Helena, 1974-76; rsch. Mont. Legis. Council, Helena, 1974-80; dir. Dept. Budget and Adminstrn., City of Helena, 1980-81; dir. Mont. State Personnel Div., Helena, 1981-85, dir. Mont. Devel. Disabilities Div., Helena, 1985-90, dep. dir. dept. family svcs., Helena, 1990—; chief adminstrv. officer City of Missoula, Mont., 1990-93; dep. dir., chief of staff Mont. dept. justice, Helena, 1993—; chmn. Mgmt. Devel. Council, Helena, 1983-85; chmn. State Employees Group Benefits Council, 1981-91; mem. Gov.'s adv. council on Health Care Cost Containment, Mont., 1985-88. Chmn. Lewis and Clark City-County Bd. Health, 1979-83, Helena Citizens Council, 1975-77, 84-89; chmn. bd. trustees Broad Valley Library Fedn., 1985-88; del. Democratic Nat. Conv., San Francisco, 1984, Atlanta, 1988; precinct committeeman Lewis and Clark County Dem. Central Com., Helena, 1975-85, chmn. 1985-87, state committeeman 1987-89, state rules com., 1984—; trustee Lewis & Clark Library Bd., 1985—, vice chmn., 1987-88; bd. dirs. Missoula Youth Homes, Inc., 1991-93; commr. Helena Reg. Airport Authority, 1994—; mem. bd. dirs. Mont. Spl. Olympics, 1987-93; pres. Mont. Coun. for Families, Inc., 1991-94, mem. bd. dirs. 1991-96; mem. bd. dirs. Mont. Youth Homes, Inc., 1994—; trustee Helena Sch. Dist. # 1, 1990-91; mem. bd. dirs. Lewis & Clark Libr. Pub. Found., Inc., 1988-90, 93—, Missoula Pub. Libr. Found., Inc., 1991-93; chmn. Mont. Pub. Safety Comm. Task Force, 1994—; charter mem. bd. dirs. D.A.R.E., Mont. Inc., 1995—, v.p., 1995—. Served to capt. USMC, 1968-71, Vietnam. Recipient Disting. Community Service award Helena Jaycees, 1981; named Employee of Yr. Helena area C. of C., 1983. Mem. Sigma Alpha Epsilon, Omicron Delta Kappa. Lodge: Rotary. Home: 2607 Gold Rush Ave Helena MT 59601-5622 Office: Dept Justice PO Box 201401 215 N Sanders St Helena MT 59601-4522

TAYLOR, EDNA JANE, employment program counselor; b. Flint, Mich., May 16, 1934; d. Leonard Lee and Wynona Ruth (Davis) Harvey; children: Wynona Jane MacDonald, Cynthia Lee Zellmer. BS, No. Ariz. U., 1963; MEd, U. Ariz., 1967. Tchr. high sch. Sunnyside Sch. Dist., Tucson, 1963-68; employment program rep. employment devel. State of Calif., Canoga Park, 1968—. Mem. adv. coun. Van Nuys Cmty. Adult Sch., Calif., 1983—, steering com., 1989-91, leadership coun., 1991-92; mem. adv. coun. Pierce C.C., Woodland Hills, Calif., 1979-81; first aid instr., recreational leader ARC. Mem. NAFE, Internat. Assn. of Pers. in Employment Security, Calif. Employment Counselors Assn. (state treas. 1978-79, state sec. 1980), Delta Psi Kappa (life). Office: State of Calif Employment Devel Dept 21010 Vanowen St Canoga Park CA 91303-2804

TAYLOR, ELDON, psychologist researcher; b. Anchorage, Utah, Jan. 27, 1945; s. Blaine Eldon and Helen Gertrude (George) T.; children: Roy, Angela, Eric, Cassandra, Hillarie, Preston. Student, Weber State Coll., Ogden, Utah, 1971-74; BS, MS, DD, U. Metaphysics, L.A., PhD in Pastoral Psychology, 1986; PhD in Clin. Psychology, St. John's U., Springfield, La., 1990; HHD (hon.), Sem. Coll., 1987; PhD in Pastoral Psychology (hon.), World U. Roundtable, Benson, Ariz., 1988. Dir. Bulwark, Salt Lake City, 1977-84; pres., dir. Progressive Awareness Rsch., Spokane, Wash., 1984—; bd. dirs. World U. Roundtable, Benson, Ariz.; co-founder Creative Living Inst., 1993; mem. adj. faculty St. John's U., 1989—. Author: Thinking Without Thinking, 1995, Subliminal Communication, 1986, Subliminal Learning, 1988, Simple Things and Simple Thoughts, 1989, Wellness: Just a State of Mind, 1993, others; contbr. numerous articles and poetry to various publs.; author numerous audiocassettes on self-improvement; patentee whole brain info. audio processor. Spiritual advisor Intermountain Hospice Ctr., Salt Lake City, 1987-88; counselor Utah State Prison, Draper, 1986-88; sports motivation trainer U.S. Judo Team, Colorado Springs, Colo., 1989—. Named Ky. Col., State of Ky., 1984; recipient Golden Poet award Am. Poetry Soc., 1985-87. Fellow Nat. Assn. Clergy Hypnotherapists; mem. Am. Psychol. Practitioners Assn., Am. Law Enforcement Officers Assn., Internat. Assn. for Forensic Hypnosis, Am. Counselors Soc., Internat. Soc. Stress Analysts, Am. Assn. Religious Counselors. Home: PO Box 13249 Spokane WA 99213-3249 Office: Progressive Awareness Rsch 21203 W Beechwood Rd Medical Lake WA 99022-8630

TAYLOR, ELOUISE CHRISTINE, artist; b. Berkeley, Calif., Sept. 17, 1923; d. Charles Vincent and Lola Lucile (Felder) T.; m. P.S. Carnohan, Sept. 8, 1947 (div. 1982); children: Marcus Jay, Max Todd, Cecilia Ann. Student, Chgo. Opera Ballet Sch., Hollywood, Calif., 1941, San Francisco Opera Ballet Sc., Oukrainsky Ballet Sch., 1938-41, San Francisco Opera Ballet Sc. Featured skater Sonja Henie Hollywood Ice Revue, 1941-51, Ctr. Theater, N.Y.; artist Reno, Nev.; instr. figure skating and painting. Oil paintings featured in numerous group and one-woman shows; portrait of Sonja Henie and several others in permanent collection at World Figure Skating Hall of Fame and Mus., Colorado Springs, Colo.; paintings exhibited local shows Los Altos, Calif., 1970-74, Santa Rosa, 1974-79, also Half Moon Bay-Shoreline Sta. Gallery & art shows, 1981, 82, Parklane Mall, Reno, Nev., 1993; numerous commd. paintings; skated as double for Ann Rutherford in film, 1945.

TAYLOR, GARY L., federal judge; b. 1938. AB, UCLA, 1960, JD, 1963. Assoc. Wenke, Taylor, Evans & Ikola, 1965-86; judge Orange County Superior Ct., 1986-90, U.S. Dist. Ct. (ctrl. dist.) Calif., Santa Ana, 1990—. With U.S. Army, 1964-66. Mem. Am. Coll. Trial Lawyers, State Bar Calif., Orange County Bar Assn. (bd. dirs. 1980-82, founder, chmn. bus. litigation com., Disting. Svc. award 1983). Office: US Dist Cts 751 W Santa Ana Blvd Rm 801 Santa Ana CA 92701-4599*

TAYLOR, GEORGE FREDERICK, newspaper publisher, editor; b. Portland, Oreg., Feb. 28, 1928; s. George Noble and Ida Louise (Dixon) T.; m. Georga Bray, Oct. 6, 1951; children—Amelia Ruth, Ross Noble. B.S., U. Oreg., 1950. Reporter Astoria (Oreg.) Budget, 1950-52, Portland Oregonian, 1952-54; copy reader Wall St. Jour., 1955-57, reporter, 1957-59, Detroit Bur. chief, 1959-64, Washington corr., 1964-68; asst. mng. editor Wall St. Jour., San Francisco, 1968-69; mng. editor Wall St. Jour., N.Y.C., 1970-77, exec. editor, 1977-86; pub. North Bend (Oreg.) News, 1986—, Prime Time, 1987—, Coquille Valley Sentinel, 1989—. Served to lt. USAF, 1955-57. Office: 1 Bartons Aly Coquille OR 97423-1270

TAYLOR, GREGORY HOBBS, publisher; b. Joplin, Mo., Jan. 27, 1946; s. George Vincent and Beverly (Sharp) T.; m. Sarah Hughes, Mar. 9, 1968; children: Gregory Hughes, Matthew Sharp. BS in Marketing, U. Mo., 1970. Mktg. rep. Internat. Paper Sales Co., Chgo., 1970-72; asst. to gen. mgr. The Joplin (Mo.) Globe, 1973-77, gen. mgr., 1979-86; asst. to pub. The News Times, Danbury, Conn., 1977-79; pub. Sharon (Pa.) Herald, 1986-93, Allied News, Grove City, Pa., 1986-93; pres., pub. Mail Tribune, Medford, Oreg., 1993—; ptnr. C&T Land Co., 1988—. Chmn. Sharon chpt. United Way, 1992, bd. dirs., 1995—; vice chmn. Indsl. Devel. Authority, Sharon, 1990; bd. dirs. So. Oreg. State Coll. Found., 1995—, Providence Hosp., 1995—. With U.S. Army, 1963-67. Mem. Mo. Pub. Assn. (bd. dirs. 1984—), Pa. Newspaper Pub. Assn. (bd. dirs.), Oreg. Newspaper Pub. Assn. (bd. dirs.), Am. Newspaper Pub. Assn., Sharon Social Fishing Club, Subscribers Encouraging Econ. Devel. (vice chmn. 1989—), Twin Hills Country Club (pres. 1985), Univ. Club of Medford, Rogue Valley Country Club; v.p. Medford United Way. Republican. Home: 1278 Gardner Way Medford OR 97504-9300 Office: Mail Tribune 111 N Fir St Medford OR 97501-2772

TAYLOR, GUY WATSON, symphonic conductor; b. Anniston, Ala., Dec. 25, 1919; s. Stokely Brackston and Ola Mae (Shaw) T.; m. Renee Lifton, Oct. 19, 1947; children: Eric Anthony, Ellen Jane. Diploma, Birmingham Conservatory of Music, 1941, Juilliard Sch. Music, 1948; pvt. studies and workshops with, Dimitri Mitropoulos, 1941-42, L'Ecole Monteux, 1949, Eugene Ormandy, 1953, George Szell, 1956. Conductor Springfield (Ohio) Symphony Orch., 1948-51, Nashville Symphony Orch., 1951-59, Phoenix Symphony Orch., 1959-69, Fresno Philharmonic Orch., 1969-84; guest conductor, U.S., Gt. Britain, Philippines, P.R., Can. and Mexico City; musical commentator Springfield News & Sun, 1948-51, Ariz. Republic, 1959-61, Fresno Bee, 1970-76. Has appeared on, BBC Radio, CBS-TV. Served with AUS, 1942-45. Recipient Conductor Recognition award Am. Symphony Orch. League, 1960, Alice M. Ditson Orch. award, 1961, citation for adventuresome programming of contemporary music ASCAP, 1977. Mem. Am. Symphony Orch. League, Phi Mu Alpha Sinfonia.

TAYLOR, HAL RICHARD, agricultural journalist; b. Columbia, Md., Feb. 22, 1925; s. John Foster and Helen (Farwell) T.; m. Margaret Ruth Kallsen, July 15, 1950; 1 child, Helen Lynn. BS in Agrl. Journalism, U. Mo., 1949; MA in Comm. Arts, Mich. State U., 1960. Asst. ext. editor N.Mex. State U., Las Cruces, 1949-51; ext. publs. editor Ohio State U., Columbus, 1951-53; agrl. editor, dir. info. U. Wyo., Laramie, 1953-58; tng. specialist Kellogg Found., Nat. Project in Agrl. Comm., East Lansing, Mich., 1958-60; pub. info. officer USDA, Washington, 1960-64; editor, head of dept. agrl. info. Tex. A&M U., College Station, 1964-69; dir. pub. affairs, dep. dir. comm., asst. dir. info. USDA, Washington, 1969-80; cons. BIFAD, U.S. Agy. for Internat. Devel., Washington, 1984, E.A. Jaenke & Assocs., Inc., Washington, 1983-84, USDA Agrl. Rsch. Svc., Washington, summer 1983, Internat. Svc. for Nat. Agrl. Rsch., The Hague, Netherlands, fall 1982, winter 1983, Internat. Agrl. Devel. Svc. (now named Winrock Internat.), Washington, 1981, 82. Contbr.: (series of chpts.) Communications Handbook, 1967, 70, 76, 83; contbr. articles to profl. jours. and encys. Cpl. U.S. Army, 1943-46, ETO, 2d lt., 1948. Decorated Purple Heart; recipient Alumni Merit award U. Mo., 1977. Mem. SAR (life Colo. chpt.), Agrl. Communicators in Edn. (life, coord. 1981-87, 1st Pioneer award 1956, Profl. award 1979, Spl. award 1986), Sigma Delta Chi. Methodist. Home: 2172 Rockridge Dr Grand Junction CO 81503

TAYLOR, HENRY STUART, financial consultant; b. Syracuse, N.Y., Oct. 21, 1931; s. Stuart Baldwin and Margurite (Brown) T.; m. Mira Takla, Aug. 14, 1970 (div. Sept 1989); children: Karima Ashley, Sharifa Naima. BA, Colgate U., 1957; MA, London Sch. Econs., 1960; MBA, Stanford U., 1959. Asst. to chmn. IBM Corp., 1950-52; assoc. Stewart, Dougall & Assocs., 1960-62; sr. mktg. cons. Economist Intelligence Unit Ltd., London, 1962-64; chmn., founder Taylor, Nelson Group, Ltd., Ewell, Eng., 1964-76; cons., advisor NISR Enterprises Ltd., London, 1976-82; spl. advisor to ptnrs. Karifa Capital Corp., Geneva, Switzerland, 1983—. Served in U.S. Army, 1952-54. Home: PO Box 1209 Menlo Park CA 94026-0256

TAYLOR, IRVING, mechanical engineer, consultant; b. Schenectady, N.Y., Oct. 25, 1912; s. John Bellamy and Marcia Estabrook (Jones) T.; m. Shirley Ann Milker, Dec. 22, 1943; children: Bronwen D., Marcia L., John I., Jerome E. BME, Cornell U., 1934. Registered profl. engr., N.Y., Mass., Calif. Test engr. Gen. Electric Co., Lynn, Mass., 1934-37; asst. mech. engr. M.W. Kellogg Co., N.Y.C., 1937-39; sect. head engrng. dept. The Lummus Co., N.Y.C., 1939-57; research engr. Gilbert and Barker, West Springfield, Mass., 1957-58, Marquardt Corp., Ogden, Utah, 1958-60, Bechtel, Inc., San Francisco, 1960-77; cons. engr. Berkeley, Calif., 1977-91; adj. prof. Columbia U., 1950-60, NYU, 1950-60. Contbr. articles to profl. jours. Fellow ASME (life, Henry R. worthington medal 1990); mem. Pacific Energy Assn., Soaring Soc. Am. (life), Sigma Xi (assoc.). Unitarian. Home: 300 Deer Valley Rd Apt 2P San Rafael CA 94903-5514

TAYLOR, JAMES WALTER, marketing consultant; b. St. Cloud, Minn., Feb. 15, 1933; s. James T. and Nina C. Taylor; m. Joanne Syktte, Feb. 3, 1956; children: Theodore James, Samuel Bennett, Christopher John. BBA, U. Minn., 1957; MBA, NYU, 1960; DBA, U. So. Calif., 1975. Mgr. research div. Atlantic Refining, Phila., 1960-65; dir. new product devel. Hunt-Wesson Foods, Fullerton, Calif., 1965-72; prof. mktg. Calif. State U., Fullerton, 1972-95; mng. dir. Innovative Mgmt. Devel. Co., Laguna Beach, Calif., 1995—; cons. Smithkline Beecham Corp., Tokyo, Govt. of Portugal, Lisbon, Austrade, Govt. of Australia, Hagenfeldt-Affarerna AB, Stockholm. Author: Profitable New Product Strategies, 1984, How to Create a Winning Business Plan, 1986, Competitive Marketing Strategies, 1986, The 101 Best Performing Companies in America, 1987, The Complete Manual for Developing Winning Strategic Plans, 1988, Every Manager's Survival Guide, 1989, Developing Winning Strategic Plans, 1990, How to Develop Successful Advertising Plans, 1993, Marketing Planning: A Step by Step Guide, 1996. Fulbright scholar Ministry of Industry, Lisbon, Portugal, 1986-87, U. We. Sydney, Australia, 1989-90; recipient Merit award Calif. State U., 1986-90. Mem. The Planning Forum, Am. Mktg. Assn., Strategic Mgmt. Assn., Assn. for Consumer Rsch., Acad. Mktg. Sci. Home: 3190 Mountain View Dr Laguna Beach CA 92651-2056

TAYLOR, JAMES WILLIAM, lawyer; b. Lincoln, Nebr., Apr. 16, 1947; s. James W. and Doris O. (Elliott) T.; m. Susan K. Baker, June 21, 1969; children: Jennifer, Jonathan, Geoffrey, Steven. BA, Miami U., Oxford, Ohio, 1969; MA, George Washington U., 1976, LLM in Labor Law, 1988; JD, U. of the Pacific, 1980. Bar: Calif. 1981, D.C. 1982, U.S. Supreme Ct. 1987, Va. 1988. Commd. 2d lt. USAF, 1969, advanced through grades to maj., 1980, resigned, 1983; lt. col. USAFR, 1990, ret., 1996; sr. atty. Martin Marietta Corp., Lompoc, Calif., 1983-84; sr. div. counsel Unisys Corp., McLean, Va., 1984-87; assoc. gen. counsel Planning Rsch. Corp., McLean, 1987-89; ptnr. Wilder & Taylor, Sacramento, Calif., 1989-92; sr. counsel Burger & Plavan, 1996—. Contbr. articles to profl. jours. With USAF, 1970-83, lt. col. USAFR. Fellow Nat. Contract Mgmt. Assn. (dir. 1983—, bd. advisors 1994—, editor Jour. 1994—); mem. ABA (chmn. com. 1981-89), Fed. Bar Assn.

TAYLOR, JEREMY MICHAEL GEORGE, statistician, educator; b. Newbury, Eng., Dec. 25, 1956; came to U.S., 1979; s. Arthur Eric and Ruth Mary (Elliott) T.; m. Elizabeth Pennywitt Korns, Dec. 27, 1986; children: Evan George, Graham Patrick. BA, Cambridge (Eng.) Coll., 1978, diploma in stats., 1979, MA, 1981; PhD in Stats., U. Calif., Berkeley, 1983. Asst. prof., dept. biostats, radiation oncology UCLA, 1983-89, assoc. prof., dept. biostats radiation oncology, 1989-93, prof., dept. biostats radiation oncology, 1993—. Contbr. articles to statistics and medical jours. Grantee NIH, Am. Found. for AIDS Rsch., U. Calif. AIDS Rsch. Program; recipient Michael Fry Radiation Rsch. award 1996, Mortimer Spiegelman award APHA, 1996. Fellow Am. Statis. Assn.; mem. Royal Stats. Soc., Radiation Rsch. Soc., Inst. of Math. Stats., Bernoulli Soc. Office: Dept Biostats UCLA Sch of Pub Health Los Angeles CA 90095 Home: 13025 Bloomfield St Studio City CA 91604-1404

TAYLOR, JOHN LOCKHART, city official; b. N.Y.C., Nov. 4, 1927; s. Floyd and Marian (Lockhart) T.; m. Barbara Becker, July 19, 1952; children: Catherine Fair, Robert, William, Susan. A.B., Middlebury Coll., 1952; M.Govtl. Adminstrn., U. Pa., 1956. Reporter Providence Jour.-Bull., 1952-54; adminstrv. intern City of Xenia, Ohio, 1955-56; mcpl. mgr. Borough of Narberth, Pa., 1956-60, Twp. of Lakewood, N.J., 1960-64; asst. city mgr. Fresno, Calif., 1964-65; city mgr., 1965-68, Kansas City, Mo., 1968-74, Berkeley, Calif., 1974-76; lectr. U. Pa., 1957-58, Golden Gate U., 1977; sr. urban mgmt. specialist Stanford Research Inst., 1977-80; dir. Internat. Devel. Center, 1980-82; clk. of bd. suprs. City of San Francisco, 1982—; pres. Calif. Clks. Bd. Suprs. Assn., 1988-89. Served with USN, 1945-48. Mem. Internat. City Mgrs. Assn., Am. Soc. Pub. Adminstrn., Mcpl. Execs. Assn. (pres. 1991-93). Office: City Hall Rm 308 401 Van Ness Ave San Francisco CA 94102-4522

TAYLOR, JOHN O'MARA, engineer; b. Birmingham, U.K., Aug. 11, 1953; came to U.S., 1990; s. Dennis O. and Renee (Franklin) T. BSc, U. Aston, Birmingham, 1975; PhD, U. Birmingham, Birmingham, 1983. Registered profl. engr., England. Core metallurgist Rolls Royce & Assocs., Derby, U.K., 1979-80; section mgr. GKN Tech. Ltd., Wolverhampton, U.K., 1980-90; sr. staff engr. Rohr Inc., Chula Vista, Calif., 1990—. Author (patent application) Crack Detecting Apparatus, 1989; contbr. articles to profl. publs. Mem. Am. Soc. for NDT, Acoustic Emission Working Group. Home: 5290 Vickie Dr San Diego CA 92109-1332

TAYLOR, JUDITH ANN, marketing and sales executive; b. Sheridan, Wyo., July 9, 1944; d. Milo G. and Eleanor M. (Wood) Rinker; m. George I. Taylor, Sept. 15, 1962; children: Monte G., Bret A. Fashion dept. mgr. Montgomery Ward, Sheridan, 1968-73; pers. mgr., asst. mgr. Dan's Ranchwear, Sheridan, 1973-80; sales/prodn. coord. KWYO Radio, Sheridan, 1981-83; sales mgr., promotions coord. KROE Radio, Sheridan, 1984-96; mng. editor BOUNTY Publ., 1993-96; dir. sales and marketing Best Western Sheridan Ctr., 1996—; notary pub. State of Wyo., 1985—; lectr., instr. BSA Merit U.; lectr. acad. achievement LVA Adv. Bd., 1993—, instr. Tongue River Middle Sch. Academic Enrichmen t Program, 1994-95; S.C. Ambs., 1980—, pres., 1995-96. Mng. editor BOUNTY Publ., 1993-96. Sec.-treas. Sheridan County Centennial Com., 1986-89; local sec.-treas. Wyo. Cenntennial Com., Sheridan, 1986-90; exec. dir. Sheridan-Wyo. Rodeo bd., 1983—; bd. dirs. Sheridan County Fair Bd., 1991-96, treas., 1995—; bd. dirs. "Christmas in April" Sheridan County, 1992—; mem. WJTP Coun., Cheyenne, 1990-92; mem. adv. coun. Tutor-Literacy Vols. of Am., 1993—; Sheridan High Sch. Key Club sponser, 1994—; Sheridan Jr. High Sch. Builders Club sponser, 1996—; City of Sheridan CVB bd.; Mrs. Santa Claus for local groups; vol. coord. AIDS Quilt; local chmn. March of Dimes Walkamerica, 1997—. Mem. Wyo. Assn. Broadcasters, S.C. C. of C. (dir. 1988—, pres. 1989-91), UMWA Aux. (pres. 1982-89), Kiwanis (v.p. 1992—, pres.-elect 1993, pres. 1994), S.C. Ambassadors (pres. 1995-96), Ft. Phil Kearney/Bozeman Trail (bd. dirs. 1995—). Democrat. Christian Ch. Office: Best We Sheridan Ctr PO Box 4008 Sheridan WY 82801

TAYLOR, KATHRYN LEE, bank officer; b. Beckley, W.Va., Nov. 16, 1946; d. Curtis Marshall and Bobbie Christine (Cox) Horton; divorced; children: D. Randy L. Jr., Laura Anne Taylor Darnell, Andrew Noel, Robert Marshall. BSBA, U. Phoenix, 1997. With GE Credit Corp., Albuquerque, Springfield, Mo., 1970-74; sec.-treas. Valley Mortgage Corp., Albuquerque, 1980-82; asst. v.p. Charter Bank for Savs. Fed. Savs. Bank, Albuquerque, 1986—. Contbg. poet Springfield Daily News, 1974-79. Singer Albuquerque Civic Chorus, 1993, 95, Albuquerque Women's Ensemble, 1994, Celebration Chorale, Albuquerque, 1996—. Mem. Ctrl. N.Mex. Homebuilder's Assn. Methodist.

TAYLOR, KENDRICK JAY, microbiologist; b. Manhattan, Mont., Mar. 17, 1914; s. William Henry and Rose (Carney) T.; BS, Mont. State U., 1938; postgrad. (fellow) U. Wash., 1938-41, U. Calif. at Berkeley, 1952, Drama Studio of London, 1985; m. Hazel Marguerite Griffith, July 28, 1945; children: Stanley, Paul, Richard. Rsch. microbiologist Cutter Labs., Berkeley, Calif., 1945-74; microbiologist Berkeley Biologicals, 1975-86. Committeeman Mount Diablo coun. Boy Scouts Am., 1955, dist. vice-chmn., 1960-61, dist. chmn., 1962-65, cubmaster, 1957, scoutmaster, 1966; active Contact Ministries, 1977-80; bd. dirs. Santa Clara Community Players, 1980-84; vol. instr. English as a Second Lang., 1979-80; vol. ARC Blood Ctr., VA Hosp., San Jose; life mem. PTA; census taker, 1980; mem. Berkely Jr. C. of C., 1946-49. Served with AUS, 1941-46, lt. col. Res., ret. Recipient Scout's Wood badge Boy Scouts Am., 1962; recipient Golden Diploma Mont. State U., 1988. Mem. Am. Soc. Microbiology (chmn. local com. 1953, v.p. No. Calif. br. 1963-65, pres. 1965-67), Sons and Daus. Mont. Pioneers, Mont. State Univ. Alumni Assn., Mont. Hist. Soc., Gallatin County Hist. Soc., Headwaters-Heritage Hist. Soc., Am. Legion Post 89, Parent-Tchrs. Assn. Calif. (life). Presbyterian (trustee 1951-53, elder 1954—). Home: 550 S 13th St San Jose CA 95112-2361

TAYLOR, LEE ROGER, JR., English language educator; b. Long Beach, Calif., Apr. 15, 1944; s. Lee Roger and Penny (Woody) T.; m. Gaye Diane Elliott, Aug. 20, 1968; children: Patrick Andrew, Jacqueline Yvonne. AB in English, East Carolina U., 1970, MA in English, 1972. English and reading specialist Beaufort C.C., Washington, N.C., 1973-76; asst. prof. Brevard (N.C.) Coll., 1976-78; assoc. prof. English, Western Wyo. Coll., Rock Springs, 1978—; columnist, film reviewer Casper (Wyo.) Star-Tribune, 1991—. Author: English Grammar Made Difficult, 1975; also articles. Mem. Wyo. Coun. for Humanities, Laramie, 1980-84, Rock Springs Downtown Adv. Com., 1991—. With USAF, 1962-65. Grantee NEH, 1986, NSF, 1991; Fulbright scholar, 1987. Office: Western Wyo Coll 2500 College Dr Rock Springs WY 82901-5802

TAYLOR, LEIGH HERBERT, college dean; b. Chgo., Oct. 23, 1941; s. Herbert and Leona Taylor; m. Nancy E. Young; children: Jennifer, Jeremiah. BA, U. Tulsa, 1964, JD, 1966; LLM, NYU, 1969. Bar: Okla. 1966, Ill. 1976. Trial atty. Civil Rights div. Dept. Justice, Washington, 1966-68; prof. DePaul U. Coll. Law, Chgo., 1969-77; asst. dean DePaul U. Coll. Law, 1972-73, assoc. dean, 1973-77; dean Coll. Law, Ohio No. U., Ada, 1977-78, Sch. Law Southwestern U., L.A., 1978—; mem. adv. bd. 1st Woman's Bank of L.A., 1981-85; dir. Law Sch. Admissions Svcs., Inc., 1982-86; chmn. audit com. Law Sch. Admissions Coun., 1989-91, trustee, 1991-98, chair-elect, 1994-95, chair, 1995-97; mem. bd. trustees Coun. on Legal Edn. Opportunity, 1993-96. Editor-in-chief Tulsa Law Jour., 1966; author: Strategies for Law-Focused Education, 1977; (with others) Law in a New Land, 1972; mem. editorial bd. Family Law Quarterly, 1977-78. Bd. dirs. Criminal Def. Consortium Cook County (Ill.), Inc., 1975-77, L.A. Press Club Found. With AUS, 1959. Fellow Am. Bar Found.; mem. ABA (accreditation com. 1991-95), Law in Am. Soc. Found., Ill. Bar Assn., Chgo. Bar Assn. (rec. sec.), L.A. County Bar Assn., Okla. Bar Assn. Office: Southwestern U Sch Law Office of Dean 675 S Westmoreland Ave Los Angeles CA 90005-3905

TAYLOR, LESLIE GEORGE, mining and financial company executive; b. London, Oct. 8, 1922; came to U.S., 1925; s. Charles Henry and Florence Louisa (Renouf) T.; m. Monique S. Schuster, May, 1964 (div. 1974); children: Leslie G. Anthony II, Sandra J. Mira, Linda S. Marshall; m. Wendy Ann Ward, July 4, 1979. BBA, U. Buffalo, 1952. Asst. to pres. Kelsey Co., 1952-60; pres. Aluminum Industries and Glen Alden Co., Cin. and N.Y.C., 1960-63; pres., chmn. bd. dirs. DC Internat. (and European subs.), Denver, 1963-68; prin. Taylor Energy Enterprises, Denver, 1968—, Taylor Mining Enterprises, Denver, 1968—, Leslie G. Taylor and Co., Denver, 1968—; sr. advisor Chartwell Internat., Denver; cons. Lucky Break Gold Inc., Vancouver, B.C.; bd. dirs. Amrion Inc., Boulder, Colo.; del. Internat. Astronautical Soc., Stockholm, 1968, London, 1969, Speditur Conv., 1976; advisor to Morgenthau Group - Ft. Lauderdale. Mem. USCG Aux. Mem. Soc. Automotive Engrs., Denver Country Club, Shriners, Masons, Scottish Rites. Republican. Episcopalian. Office: 5031 S Ulster St Ste 200 Denver CO 80237-2810

TAYLOR, LYNDON ELMER, planning and development consultant; b. L.A., Sept. 21, 1935; s. Lyndon Elmer and Mary Rita (Worth) T.; m. Hazel JoAnn Hamer, Dec. 26, 1983; children: Jodi Bowle, Jeff Whitener. BA in Biology and chemistry, Whittier (Calif.) Coll., 1957; MS in Biochemistry, Simmons Coll., Boston, 1964; PhD in Non-Verbal Comm., Claremont (Calif.) Grad. Sch., 1976; postgrad., Western State U., Fullerton, Calif., 1987-89, U. So. Calif., L.A., 1968-70. Vice prin., tchr. Santa Fe H.S., Santa Fe Springs, Calif., 1958-64; instr. Fullerton (Calif.) Coll., 1964-66; divsn. dean Cypress (Calif.) Coll., 1966-68, v.p., 1968-82; ptnr. GFB Assocs., Yorba Linda, Calif., 1983—; dir. human resources North Orange C.C., Fullerton, 1988-90, asst. chancellor, 1982-90; dir. Creative Computer Learning Ctrs., Villa Park, Calif., 1983-86; ptnr. child care ctr. devel. ChildCare Am., Perris, Calif., 1992—; ptnr. planning and devel. cons. Maas, Rao, Taylor & Assocs., Perris, 1990—; on-air host cable tV program: Pursuit of Excellence, Fullerton, 1987-90; cons. multi-media GT-70, Aspen, Colo., 1970; cons. media Western Audio Visual Svcs., Redlands, 1966-72. Author (video prodns.): Los Angeles Southwest College, 1994, A Walk into the future, 1989, Alternative Funding for Colleges, 1989, (monographs) The Education Mall, 1992, The Community College of the Future, 1992. Bd. dirs. L.A. Southwest Coll. Found., 1992—, Childcare Am., 1992—, Moment Assocs., Cypress, 1976-83, Pvt. Industry Coun., Anaheim, 1987-90, Woodhaven Homeowner's Assn., Palm Desert, Calif., 1993-95; adv. bd. pres. Orange Unified Sch. Dist., 1980-82; ofcl. Canyon Youth Soccer Assn., 1979-81. Recipient Svc. award Hispanic Assn., 1976, Cypress Coll., 1983, Fullerton Coll., 1988; named to Outstanding educators of Am.; NSF grantee, 1960-64. Mem. AAAS, Catalina Amateur Radio Assn. (bd. dirs.), Catalina Island Conservancy. Home: 4399 Camphor Ave Yorba Linda CA 92886-3146 Office: Maas Rao Taylor & Assocs 2161 Falcon Crest Dr Riverside CA 92506-3474

TAYLOR, MARIAN ALECIA, manufacturing development engineer; b. Kansas City, Mo., Apr. 26, 1961; d. M.A. and Ellen Ardena (Hume) Nossaman; m. Michael Keith Taylor, July 26, 1986; children: Alecia Ellen, Nathaniel Alexander. AA, Johnson County C.C., 1989; BSME, BS in Bus., U. Kans., 1993. Dental asst. SE Brotherson DDS, Kansas City, Kans., 1983-85; dental instr. Kansas City Coll. of Med. and Dental Careers, Overland Park, 1985-86; math tutor Overland Park, 1988-91; tech. writer ArComm, Lenexa, Kans., 1991-92; total quality mgmt. rschr. U. Kans., Lawrence, 1992-93; process engr. Symbios Logic Inc., Ft. Collins, Colo., 1993-95; mfg. devel. engr. Hewlett Packard, Loveland, Colo., 1995—; sec. Hilltop Child Devel. Ctr., Lawrence, 1991-93. Contbr. articles to profl. jours. Student senator U. Kans. Student Senate, Lawrence, 1992-93; com. mem. Kans. U. Child Care Com., Lawrence, 1991-93, work and family com., 1991-92. Recipient U. Kans. Hilltopper award, 1993. Mem. ASME (treas. 1992-93), Oaks Nontraditional Students Orgn. (pres. 1991-92, treas. 1990-91, editor 1990-92), Tau Beta Pi, Pi Tau Simga. Home: 1955 W Rangeley Ct Loveland CO 80538 Office: Hewlett Packard Loveland Mfg Ctr 815 14th St SW Loveland CO 80537-6330

TAYLOR, MARK JESSE, systems analyst; b. Phillipsburg, N.J., Feb. 5, 1957; s. Jesse Ireland Jr. and Eleanor Jane (Meeker) T.; m. Hilda Susan Valdivia, June 15, 1983; children: Alexandra, Monique, Elizabeth Jane, Jessica Courtney. BSCE, Norwich U., 1979; MS in Mgmt., Lesley Coll., 1985. Engr. in tng. Commd. officer USAF, 1979, advanced through grades to maj., 1991; dep. missile crew comdr. USAF, 400 Strategic Missile Squadron, F.E. Warren AFB, Wyo., 1980-82; standardization evaluation mgr. USAF, 90 Strategic Missile Wing, F.E. Warren AFB, 1982-83; missile combat crew commander USAF, 400 Strategic Missile Squadron, F.E. Warren AFB, 1983-84; chief code handler tng. USAF, 90 Strategic Missile Wing, F.E. Warren AFB, 1984-85; ICBM flight test mgr. Ballistic Missile Orgn., Norton AFB, Calif., 1985-88; advanced tech. project mgr. Ballistic Missile Orgn., Norton AFB, 1988-89; dir. maintenance, engring. 1st Space Launch Squadron, Cape Canaveral AFS, Fla., 1989-93; mgr. Ballistic Missile Tech. Program HQAFSPC, Peterson AFB, Colo., 1993-96; ret., 1996; syss. analyst ANSER, Inc., Colorado Springs, Colo., 1996—. Presenter in field. V.p. Parent-Tchrs. Assn., San Bernardino, Calif., 1987-89. Mem. ASCE, Soc. Am. Mil. Engrs., Air Force Assn. Republican. Home: 2127 Greenwich Cir E Colorado Springs CO 80909-1625 Office: 1250 Academy Park Loop Ste 223 Colorado Springs CO 80910

TAYLOR, MARY ELIZABETH, retired recreation administrator, retired dietitian; b. Medina, N.Y., Dec. 10, 1933; d. Glenn Aaron and Viola Hazel (Lansill) Grimes; m. Wilbur Alvin Fredlund, Apr. 12, 1952 (div. Jan. 1980); 1 child, Wilbur Jr.; m. Frederick Herbert Taylor, Mar. 15, 1981 (dec. Dec. 1996); children: Martha Dayton, Jean Grout, Beth Stern, Cindy Hey, Carol McLellan, Cheryl Dearborn, Robert. BS in Food and Nutrition, SUCB, Buffalo, 1973; MEd in Health Sci. Edn. and Evaluation, SUNY, 1978. Registered dietitian, 1977. Diet cook Niagara Sanitorium, Lockport, N.Y., 1953-56; cook Mount View Hosp., Lockport, N.Y., 1956-60, asst. dietitian, 1960-73, dietitian, food svc. dir., 1973-79, cons. dietitian, 1979-81; instr. Erie Community Coll., Williamsville, N.Y., 1979-81; sch. lunch coord. Nye County Sch. Dist., Tonopah, Nev., 1982-93; retired Nye County Sch. Dist., 1993; food svc. mgmt. cons., fin. mgmt. advisor pvt. practice, 1994—; activity dir. Preferred Equitity Corp. Recreation Vehicle Resort, Pahrump, Nev., 1993-95; ret., 1996; cons. dietitian Nye Gen. Hosp., Tonopah, 1983-88; adj. instr. Erie Community Coll., Williamsville, 1978-79; nutrition instr. for coop. extension Clark County Community Coll., 1990—; cons. Group Purchasing Western N.Y. Hosp. Adminstrs., Buffalo, 1975-79, vice-chmn. adv. com., 1976-78; cons. BOCES, Lockport, 1979-81. Nutrition counselor Migrant Workers Clinic, Lockports, 1974-80; mem. Western N.Y. Soc. for Hosp. Food Svc. Adminstrn., 1974-81; nutritionist Niagara County Nutrition Adv. Com., 1977-81. Recipient Outstanding Woman of the Yr., YWCA-UAW Lockport, 1981, Disting. Health Care Food Adminstrn. Recognition award Am. Soc. for Hosp. Food Svc. Adminstrs., 1979, USDA award Outstanding Lunch Program in Nev. and Western Region, 1986, 91. Mem. Am. Assn. Ret. Persons, Am. Sch. Food Svc. Assn. (bd. dirs. 1987, 92-93, cert. dir. II 1987, 5-yr. planning com. 1990, mem. ann. confs. 1988-93), Am. Dietetic Assn. (nat. referral system for registered dietitians 1992-93), So. Nev. Dietetic Assn. (pres. 1985-86), Nev. Food Svc. Assn. (participant ann. meetings 1990-93), Nutrition Today Soc., Nev. Sch. Food Svcs. Assn. (dietary guidelines com. 1991-93). Republican. Lutheran. Home: 481 N Murphy PO Box 656 Pahrump NV 89041-0656

TAYLOR, MINNA, lawyer; b. Washington, Jan. 25, 1947; d. Morris P. and Anne (Williams) Glushien; m. Charles Ellett Taylor, June 22, 1969; 1 child, Amy Caroline. BA, SUNY, Stony Brook, 1969; MA, SUNY, 1973; JD, U. So. Calif., 1977. Bar: Calif. 1977, U.S. Dist. Ct. (cen. dist.) Calif. 1978. Extern to presiding justice Calif. Supreme Ct., 1977; field atty. NLRB, L.A., 1977-82; dir. employee rels., legal svcs. Paramount Pictures Corp., L.A., 1982-85, v.p. employee rels., legal svcs., 1985-89; dir. bus. and legal affairs Wilshire Ct. Prodns., L.A., 1989-91; sr. counsel Fox Broadcasting Co., L.A., 1991-92, v.p. legal affairs, 1992-96, sr. v.p. legal affairs, 1996—. Editor notes and articles: U. So. Calif. Law Rev., 1976-77. Mentor MOSTE, L.A., 1986-87, 88-89; pres. Beverly Hills chpt. ACLU, L.A., 1985. Fellow ABA, Calif. State Bar (mem. copyright subcom. 1994-95), L.A. County Bar Assn.; mem. Beverly Hills Bar Assn., L.A. Bead Soc. (membership sec. 1992-94, mem. bd. dirs. 1994-95), Order of Coif. Office: Fox Broadcasting Co 10201 W Pico Blvd Los Angeles CA 90064-2606

TAYLOR, NIGEL BRIAN, financial planner; b. Winchester, June 17, 1953. Grad., Coll. Fin. Planning, Denver, 1993. Cert. Fin. Planner; lic. NASD Series 6, 7, 24; registered prin.; lic. to practice in European Cmty. Owner Family Trust Planners, domestic and internat. retirement, estate planning, asset protection, L.A. and Santa Monica, Calif., 1988—; mgr. Fin. Planning Expo '96, L.A. Author: Domestic and International Estate and Asset Protection for the Resident Alien, 1996; mem. editl. rev. bd. Jour. Fin. Planning. Mem. Santa Monica Bar (assoc.), Inst. CFPs (registered practitioner, bd. dirs. L.A. Soc.). Office: 1011 4th St Apt 209 Santa Monica CA 90403-3843

TAYLOR, PETER VAN VOORHEES, advertising and public relations consultant; b. Montclair, N.J., Aug. 25, 1934; s. John Coard and Mildred (McLaughlin) T.; m. Janet Kristine Kirkebo, Nov. 4, 1978; 1 son, John Coard III. BA in English, Duke U., 1956. Announcer Sta. WQAM, Miami, 1956; announcer, program dir. Sta. KHVH, Honolulu, 1959-61; promotion mgr. Sta. KPEN, San Francisco, 1962; with Kaiser Broadcasting, 1962-74, GE Broadcasting Co., 1974-78; program/ops. mgr. Sta. KFOG, San Francisco, 1962-66; mgr. Sta. WXHR AM/FM, Cambridge, Mass., 1966-67; gen. mgr. Sta. WJIB, Boston, 1967-70; v.p., mgr. FM div. Kaiser Broadcasting, 1969-72; v.p., gen. mgr. Sta. KFOG, San Francisco, 1970-78; pres. Taylor Communications, 1978-90, 97—, Baggott & Taylor, Inc., 1990-91, Taylor Advt. & Pub. Rels., 1991-96, Broadcast Skills Bank, 1975-76, Roast Host, 1993—. Trustee, WDBS, Inc., Duke U., 1974-80; bd. dirs. San Francisco BBB, 1976-78, 89-94, Calif. Broadcasters Assn., 1982-84, San Francisco Boys & Girls Club, 1991-93, Coast Guard Found., 1991—, Leukemia Soc., San Francisco, 1992-93, Duke Devel. Coun., 1992-96, Golden Gate Breakfast Club, 1995-96, v.p., 1995-96; bd. dirs. Commencement Bay Rowing Club, 1997—. Mem. Nat., Internat. and Long Wave Radio Clubs, Worldwide TV/FM Dx Assn., Rotary (San Francisco - bd. dirs. 1988-93, 1st v.p. 1990-91, pres. 1991-92, dist. 5150 - pub. rels. chmn. 1986-89, conf. chmn. 1990, area rep. 1992-93, bd. dirs. 1994-95, dist. governor nom., 1995-96). Lt. USCGR, 1957-63. Home and Office: 6002 Bayview Dr NE Tacoma WA 98422-1227

TAYLOR, R. ERVIN, JR., archaeologist; b. Los Angeles, Jan. 15, 1938; s. Royal Ervin and Francys Ellen (McMurtry) T.; m. Marilynn Julia Lampley, Aug. 22, 1959; children: Gregory Michael, Karen Louane. BA, Pacific Union Coll., 1960; MA, UCLA, 1965, PhD, 1969. Asst. prof. Calif. State U., Northridge, 1967-70; from assoc. prof. to prof. anthropology, chair dept. anthropology U. Calif., Riverside, 1970—. Author: Radiocarbon Dating, 1987; editor: Chronologies in New World Archaeology, 1978, Advances in Obsidian Glass Studies, 1980; co-editor: Radiocarbon After Four Decades, 1992. Grantee NSF, 1978—. Fellow AAAS, Am. Anthropol. Assn.; mem. Southwestern Anthropol. Assn. (pres. 1975-76), Soc. Archaeol. Scis. (pres. 1982, gen. sec. 1982—). Home: 25155 Crestview Dr Loma Linda CA 92354-3508 Office: U Calif Radiocarbon Lab Riverside CA 92521

TAYLOR, REESE HALE, JR., lawyer, former government administrator; b. Los Angeles, May 6, 1928; s. Reese Hale and Kathryn (Emery) T.; m. Lucille Langdon, Dec. 29, 1948 (div. 1959); children: Reese Hale (dec.), Stuart Langdon, Anne Kathryn, Lucille Emery; m. Jolene Yerby, June 30, 1972. B.A. with distinction, Stanford U., 1949; LL.B., Cornell U., 1952. Bar: Calif. 1954, Nev. 1966. Assoc. Gibson, Dunn & Crutcher, Los Angeles, 1952-58; pvt. practice Los Angeles, 1958-65; assoc. Wiener, Goldwater & Galatz, Las Vegas, Nev., 1966-67; chmn. Nev. Pub. Service Commn., Carson City, 1967-71; ptnr. Laxalt, Berry & Allison, Carson City, 1971-78, Allison, Brunetti, MacKenzie & Taylor, Carson City, 1978-81; chmn. ICC, Washington, 1981-85; ptnr. Heron, Burchette, Ruckert & Rothwell, Washington, 1986-90, Taylor & Morell, Washington and Long Beach, Calif., 1990-91, Taylor, Morell & Gitomer, Washington and Long Beach, 1992-94; of counsel Keesal, Young & Logan, Long Beach, 1994—; vice chmn. Nev. Tax Commn., Carson City, 1967-69; mem. Nev. Gov.'s Cabinet, Carson City, 1967-70, Carson City Bd. Equalization, 1979-81, chmn., 1979-80; bd. dirs. U.S. Rail Assn., Washington, 1981-85. Del. Republican Nat. Conv., Kansas City, Mo., 1976, mem. platform com., 1976, alt. del., Detroit, 1980; mem. Rep. Nat. Com., 1980-81. Mem. ABA, Am. Judicature Soc., Capitol Hill Club, Cornell Club (N.Y.), Order of Coif, Phi Gamma Delta, Phi Delta Phi. Episcopalian. Office: Keesal Young & Logan Union Bank Bldg 400 Oceangate PO Box 1730 Long Beach CA 90801-1730

TAYLOR, RICHARD EDWARD, physicist, educator; b. Medicine Hat, Alta., Can., Nov. 2, 1929; came to U.S., 1952; s. Clarence Richard and Delia Alena (Brunsdale) T.; m. Rita Jean Bonneau, Aug. 25, 1951; 1 child, Norman Edward. B.S., U. Alta., 1950, M.S., 1952; Ph.D., Stanford U., 1962; Docteur honoris causa, U. Paris-Sud, 1980; DSc, U. Alta., 1991; LLD (hon.), U. Calgary, Alta., 1993; DSc (hon.), U. Lethbridge, Alta., 1993, U. Victoria, B.C., Can., 1994. Boursier Lab. de l'Accelerateur Lineaire, Orsay, France, 1958-61; physicist Lawrence Berkeley Lab., Berkeley, Calif., 1961-62; staff mem. Stanford (Calif.) Linear Accelerator Ctr., 1962-68, assoc. dir., 1982-86, prof., 1968—. Fellow Guggenheim Found., 1971-72, von Humboldt Found., 1982; recipient Nobel prize in physics, 1990. Fellow AAAS, Am. Acad. Arts and Scis., Am. Phys. Soc. (W.K.H. Panofsky prize div. particles and fields 1989), Royal Soc. Can.; mem. Can. Assn. Physicists, Nat. Acad. Scis. (fgn. assoc.). Office: Stanford Linear Accelerator Ctr PO Box 4349, M/S 96 Stanford CA 94309

TAYLOR, RICHARD W., public relations executive. V.p. spl. projects ICPR, 1975-80; with Rogers & Cowan, 1980—, v.p. corp. div., 1980-81, sr. v.p. corp. div., 1981, pres. corp. div., 1982—, pres., chief exec. officer, 1986—; pres. bus. devel. and client svcs. Hill & Knowlton Inc., L.A., 1991—. Office: Hill & Knowlton 6500 Wilshire Blvd Fl 21 Los Angeles CA 90048-4920*

TAYLOR, ROY LEWIS, botanist, educator; b. Olds, Alta., Can., Apr. 12, 1932; s. Martin Gilbert and Crystal (Thomas) T. B.Sc., Sir George Williams U., Montreal, Que., Can., 1957; Ph.D., U. Calif. at Berkeley, 1962; DSc (hon.), U. B.C., Vancouver, Can. Pub. sch. tchr. Olds Sch. Div., 1949-52; jr. high sch. tchr. Calgary Sch. Bd., Alta., 1953-55; chief taxonomy sect., research br. Can. Agrl. Dept., Ottawa, Ont., 1962-68; dir. Bot. Garden, prof. botany, prof. plant scis. U. B.C., Vancouver, 1968-85; pres., CEO Chgo. Horticultural Soc., 1985-94; dir. Chgo. Bot. Garden, Glencoe, Ill., 1985-94; exec. dir. Rancho Santa Ana Bot. Garden, Claremont, Calif., 1994—; prof. botany, chmn. botany program Claremont Grad. Sch., 1994—; pres. Western Bot. Svcs. Ltd. Author: The Evolution of Canada's Flora, 1966, Flora of the Queen Charlotte Islands, Vols. I and II, 1968, Vascular Plants of British Columbia: A Descriptive Resource Inventory, 1977; The Rare Plants of British Columbia, 1985. Mem. State of Ill. Bd. Natural Resources and Conservation, 1987-94; trustee Nature Ill. Found., 1990-94. Fellow Linnean Soc. London; mem. Can. Bot. Assn. (pres. 1967-68), Biol. Coun. Can. (pres. 1973-74), Am. Assn. Mus. (accreditation com. 1980-85, chmn. 1985-91, chmn. ethics commn. 1991-93), Am. Assn. Bot. Gardens and Arboreta (pres. 1976, 77, award of merit 1987), Claremont C. of C. (bd. dirs. 1995-98), Ottawa Valley Curling Assn. (pres. 1968-69), B.C. Soc. Landscape Archs. (hon.), U. B.C. Bot. Garden (hon.), Chgo. Hort Soc. (life, medal 1994), Gov. Gen.'s Curling Club Can. (life), Univ. Club Claremont, Men's Garden Club L.A. Office: Rancho Santa Ana Bot Garden Claremont CA 91711-3157

TAYLOR, RUTH ANNE, lawyer; b. Honolulu, Feb. 18, 1961; d. Gerald Lou and Charlotte Anne (Nelson) Allison; m. Thomas Scott Taylor, Dec. 28, 1985; children: Kyle Thomas, Kelly Gerald. BA in Journalism, U. So. Calif., 1984; JD, N.Y. Law Sch., 1987. Bar: Calif. 1987, U.S. Dist. Ct. (so. dist.) Calif., U.S. Ct. Appeals (9th cir.). Assoc. Carlsmith, Wichman, Case Mukai & Ichiki, L.A., 1987-89, Christensen, White, Miller, Fink & Jacobs, L.A., 1989-93; sr. counsel Warner Bros. Records, Inc., 1993—. Mem. Los Angeles County Bar Assn., Beverly Hills Bar Assn. Republican. *

TAYLOR, SABRENA ANN, author, visual artist; b. Galesburg, Ill., Apr. 10, 1957; d. Lloyd Henry and Utako (Saito) T. BA, Knox Coll., Galesburg, 1979; MA, Sangamon State U., Springfield, Ill., 1982. Cert. cmty. coll. instr., Calif. Case mgmt. supr. Cath. Social Svc., Peoria, Ill., 1984-85; health educator, monitor Japanese Cmty. Youth Coun., San Francisco, 1986-88; tchg. asst. Upward Bound Program, San Francisco, 1988-89; counselor YMCA, San Francisco, 1989; adminstrv. asst. The Family Sch., San Francisco, 1990-93, U. Calif., San Francisco, 1994—; libr. page City and County of San Francisco Pub. Libr., 1995—; mem. adv. bd. Nobiru-Kai, Japanese Newcomers Svcs., San Francisco, 1988—. Author: (poetry) Fusion-Go, 1989, Watch Out! We're Talking, 1993, Skin Deep: Women Writing on Color, Culture and Identity, 1994; exhibited work in The Art of the Brotherhood of Man exhibit, Manor House Gallery, Belmont, Calif., 1992. Mem.-at-large African Asian Am. Roundtable, San Francisco, 1991. Recipient Cert. of Appreciation San Francisco Mayor's Youth Employment and Edn. Program, 1987, others. Home: PO Box 590114 San Francisco CA 94159

TAYLOR, SANDRA ORTIZ, artist, educator; b. L.A., Apr. 27, 1936; d. John Santry and Juanita Loretta (Shrode) T. BA in Art, UCLA, 1958; MA in Art, State U. Iowa, 1962. Instr. art State U. Iowa, Iowa City, 1961-62, Indian Valley Colls, Marin County, Calif., 1973-74, San Francisco C.C., 1966—; seminar guest speaker Nat. Book Conf., 1991; chair all-media nat exhibit Fine Arts Gallery Broward C.C., Davie, Fla., 1994, Humanities Art Gallery Palm Beach C.C. Exhibited in group shows Calif. Mus. Art, Santa Rosa, 1991-95, Falkirk Ctr., San Rafael, Calif., 1992, 93, Gallery Route One, Point Reyes Station, Calif., 1993, San Jose (Calif.) Inst. Contemporary Art, 1993-94, San Francisco Airport Com. & Corp. of Fine Arts Mus. of San Francisco, 1994, Women Artists Gallery, San Francisco, 1994, ACCI Gallery, Berkeley, Calif., 1995-96, Moreau Galleries, St. Mary's Coll., Notre Dame, Ind., 1995, Bedford Gallery, Walnut Creek, Calif., 1996, San Francisco Open Studios, 1996, Univ. Hawaii, Manoa, Austin Mus. Art, Tex., San Mateo County Arts Coun., Belmont, Calif., San Jose Contemporary Art & Performance Gallery; commd. for grad. program Chicano and Latino studies U. Calif., Irvine, 1992; work reviewed in various publs. Recipient jurors award Calif. Mus. Art, 1992; scholar Anderson Ranch Art Ctr., Snow Mass, Colo., 1991. Home and Office: Ephemera Studio 2854 Harrison St San Francisco CA 94110-4117

TAYLOR, STEVEN BRUCE, agriculture company executive; b. Salinas, Calif., Dec. 29, 1954; s. Edward Horton and Joanne (Church) T.; m. Kathryn Hagler, Dec. 17, 1978; children: Meghan Jean, Kyle Hagler, Christian Steven. BA, U. Calif., Berkeley, 1978; MBA, Harvard U., 1985. Pres.

Fresh Concepts, San Marino, Calif., 1985-87; mktg. staff Bruce Church, Inc., Salinas, Calif., 1987-91; pres. Fresh Express Retail Mktg., Salinas, 1991—; pres. Fresh Internat., Salinas, 1991—, CEO; v.p. Salinas Valley Lettuce Co-op, Salinas, 1990—; bd. dirs. Produce for Better Health, Del., 1991—. Bd. Elders First Presbyn. Ch., Salinas, 1989-92, personnel com. 1989-94, bldg. com. 1990—; founding mem. Lincoln Club of Monterey County, Salinas, 1990. Home: 515 Santa Paula Dr Salinas CA 93901-1517 Office: Fresh Internat 1020 Merrill St Salinas CA 93901-4409*

TAYLOR, T. RABER, lawyer; b. Colorado Springs, Colo., Dec. 31, 1910; s. Ralph Franklin and Mary Catherine (Burns) T.; m. Josephine Loretto Reddin, Sept. 20, 1938; children: Mary Therese, Carol Anne, Margaret Claire, Josephine R., Rae Marie, Kathleen Mae, Anne Marie. BA magna cum laude, Regis Coll., 1933; JD, Harvard U., 1937. Bar: Colo. 1937, U.S. Dist. Ct. Colo. 1937, U.S. Tax Ct. 1938, U.S. Ct. Appeals (10th cir.) 1940, U.S. Supreme Ct. 1950. Pvt. practice law Denver, 1937—. Bd. dirs. Denver Cath. Charities, 1946-71; v.p. Nat. Conf. Cath. Charities, 1956-57, 69-75; mem. gov.'s com., White House Conf. on Children and Youth, 1971. Lt. comdr. USNR, 1943-45, NATOUSA, ETO. Knight Order St. Gregory, 1971, Equestrian Order of Holy Sepulchre of Jerusalem, 1973; recipient St. Vincent de Paul medal St. John's U., Jamaica, N.Y., 1971, St. Thomas More award Cath. Lawyers Guild Denver, 1981. Fellow Am. Coll. Probate Counsel; mem. ABA, Colo. Bar Assn., Denver Bar Assn., Denver Estate Planning Coun. (pres. 1962-63), Greater Denver Tax Counsel Assn., Serra Club Denver, Denver Athletic Club. Home: 790 Fillmore St Denver CO 80206-3848

TAYLOR, VELMA JEAN, elementary education educator; b. Marshall, Tex., June 28, 1957; d. John LeRoy Taylor and Bobbie Jean (Fields) Taylor-White; 1 child, Rachel Victoria Ashley Luciano. BBA, Tex. So. U., 1979; MEd, Coll. St. Thomas, St. Paul, 1979. Cert. tchr., Calif. Tchr. Compton (Calif.) Unified Sch., 1987-89, L.A. Unified Sch., 1989—. Troop leader Girl Scouts U.S., L.A.; track coord. 20th St. Elem. Mem. Calif. Edn. Assn., Neighborhood Club, Phi Beta Lambda. Democrat. Methodist. Office: 20th St Elem 1353 E 20th St Los Angeles CA 90011

TAYLOR, WALTER WALLACE, lawyer; b. Newton, Iowa, Sept. 18, 1925; s. Carrol W. and Eva (Greenly) T.; A.A., Yuba Coll., 1948, A.B., 1950; M.A., U. Calif., 1955, J.D., McGeorge Coll. Law, 1962; m. Mavis A. Harvey, Oct. 9, 1948; children—Joshua Michael (dec. 1980), Kevin Eileen, Kristin Lisa, Jeremy Walter, Margaret Jane, Melissa E., Amy M. Adminstrv. analyst USAF, Sacramento, 1951-53; personnel, research analyst Calif. Personnel Bd., Sacramento, 1954-56; civil service, personnel analyst, chief counsel, gen. mgr. Calif. Employees Assn., Sacramento, 1956-75; staff counsel, chief profl. standards Calif. Commn. Tchr. Credentialing, 1975-88, ret. 1988; staff counsel State Office Real Estate appraiser Licensing and Certification, 1992-94, ret.; tchr. discipline civil service, personnel cons. Served USCGR, 1943-46. Mem. Calif. State Bar, Am., Sacramento County bar assns. Democrat. Author: Know Your Rights, 1963-64. Home: 4572 Fair Oaks Blvd Sacramento CA 95864-5336

TAYLOR, WILLIAM AL, judge; b. Lusk, Wyo., Nov. 2, 1928; m. Jane Y.; 3 children. BA, U. Wyo., 1951, LLB, 1959. Bar: Wyo. 1959. Teacher Lusk, 1950-51,54-55, pvt. practice, 1959-78; city atty. Town of Lusk, 1962-74; atty. Niobrara County, Wyo., 1964-77; judge Wyo. Dist. Ct. (8th dist.), Cheyenne, 1980—; justice Wyoming Supreme Ct., 1993—, chief justice, 1996—; Exec. dir. Wyo. State Bar, 1977-80. Staff sgt. U.S. Army, 1951-53. Mem. Wyo. State Bar (Civil Rules com.), Wyo. Judicial Conf. (chmn. 1984-85),Tenth Cir. Bar Assn., Nat. Trial Judges, Am. Legion, Sigma Alpha Epsilon. Office: Wyo Supreme Ct PO Box 66 Cheyenne WY 82003-0066

TAYLOR, WILLIAM MALCOLM, environmentalist, educator; b. South Hiram, Maine, June 18, 1933; s. William Myers and Gladys Marie (Weldy) T.; stepmother Edna (Tyson) Taylor; m. Carrie Mae Fiedler, Aug. 31, 1957 (div. Sept. 1980); children: William Stephan, Alyson Marie, Eric Fiedler; m. Elizabeth Van Horn, June 18, 1983. Student, George Sch., 1948-50; BA in Liberal Arts, Pa. State U., 1956; MEd, U. N.C., 1962. Instr. ESL Anatolia Coll., Am. Lang. Ctr., Salonica, Greece, 1956-58; tchr. biology-chemistry Coral Shores H.S., Tavernier, Fla., 1961-62; pk. naturalist Everglades Nat. Pk., Fla., 1962-65; tech. editor Nat. Pk. Svc., Washington, 1965-67; chief interpretation Canyonlands Nat. Pk., Utah, 1967-71; environ. edn. specialist western regional office Nat. Pk. Svc., Calif., 1971-77; dir. program devel. Living History Ctr., Novato, Calif., 1981-83; exec. recruiter, ptnr. Van Horn, Taylor & Assocs, Biotech-Biomed. Rsch., Santa Cruz, Calif., 1983-95; mem. 2d World Conf. on Nat. Parks and Equivalent Reserves, 10th Internat. Seminar on Nat. Parks, U.S., Can., Mex. Author: The Strands Walk, Exercises in Guided Inquiry for Children; founder, developer (with Sally Berlant) ednl. program Environ. Living Program, 1973 (Calif. Bicentennial Commn. award 1974, Don Perryman award Calif. Social Studies Coun., 1975, Nat. Bicentennial Adminstrn. sponsorship 1976). Bd. dirs. Internat. Sonoran Desert Alliance, 1996-97; with Novato Environ. Quality Com., 1973-76; mem. Calif. Conservation Com., 1973-76; mem. Utah Environ. Com., 1968-71; vol. AZ Sonora Desert Mus. Mem. Am. Bonanza Soc., Lighthawk, Flying Samaritans, Tucson Soaring Club, Mensa. Home: 2321 S Circle X Pl Tucson AZ 85713

TAYLOR-GRIGSBY, QUEENIE DELORES, minister, consultant; b. Oklahoma City, Aug. 21, 1948; d. Barnett C., Sr. and Bedell (Boles) Taylor; m. Walter Thomas White II, Nov. 26, 1966 (div. June 1976); children: Walter Thomas III, Robin Orlando; m. James O. Grigsby, Oct. 19, 1976 (dec. Dec. 1976); 1 child, James Juamaané. BS, Howard U., 1970. Ordained to ministry Ray Deliverance Found., 1989. Assoc. cons. Trust Inc., Richmond, Va., 1974-80, Orgnl. Devel. Cons., Richmond, 1980-82; cons., pres. Taylor & Co., Phoenix, 1974—; min. Man Child Ministries, Phoenix, 1988—; cons. MARTA Atlanta, 1980-82, Fredrick County, Md., 1974, Richmond Pub. Sch. System, 1977, Black Police Officers, Tulsa, 1986. Author poetess. Advocate child welfare Dept. of Corrections, Phoenix, 1990, advocate tchr. rights, 1991; active tchr. rights Phoenix Pub. Sch. System, 1992; supr. elections County Election Bd., Maricopa County, Ariz., 1987. Lucille McMahn scholar, 1965, Nellie Green scholar, 1965; recipient Danforth Leadership award, 1965, Golden Poet award, 1991. Mem. Soc. Tng. and Devel. (cert. housing specialist), Housing Specialist Inst. Office: Taylor & Co 1138 N Bath Oklahoma City OK 73117

TAYLOR-PICKELL, LAVONNE TROY, editor; b. Riverside, Calif., May 20, 1941; d. Troy Virgil Bradstreet and R. Victoria (Freeman) Chambers; m. Robert Martin Taylor, May 15, 1958 (div. 1975); children: Dana Freeman, Timothy Rene; m. Herman Pickell, Feb. 14, 1985; children: Marianne, Barry, David. Reporter Thousand Oaks (Calif.) Chronicle; with prodn. News Chronicle, Thousand Oaks, prodn. supr., 1979-81; with prodn. Ind. Jour., Thousand Oaks, Herald Examiner, L.A., L.A. Times; asst. mgr. Publ. Typography, Agoura, Calif., 1981-85; owner Excellence Enterprises, L.A., 1982—; sr. editor arts Glencoe/McGraw-Hill Sch. Pub., Mission Hills, Calif., 1987-96; actress, 1997—; speaker various writers clubs. Editor, pub. L.A. My Way, 1991, On the Wings of Song, 1994; mng. editor The Book-Woman, 1991-93. Mem. pub. rels. com. Conejo Players Theatre, Thousand Oaks, 1970-75, Betty Mann for 38th Assembly Dist., Agoura, 1975-76. Mem. NAFE, Nat. Writers Club (pres. 1990-91, Merit Svc. award 1991), Women's Nat. Book Assn. (L.A. chpt. pres. 1992-93, newsletter editor, bd. dirs.).

TEAGUE, LAVETTE COX, JR., systems educator, consultant; b. Birmingham, Ala., Oct. 8, 1934; s. Lavette Cox and Caroline Green (Stokes) T.; student Auburn U., 1951-54; B.Arch., MIT, 1957, M.S.C.E., 1965, Ph.D., 1968; MDiv with distinction Ch. Div. Sch. Pacific, 1979. Cert. computer profl. Inst. Cert. of Computer Profls. Archtl. designer Carroll C. Harmon, Birmingham, 1957, Fred Renneker, Jr., Birmingham, 1958-59; architect Rust Engrng. Co., Birmingham, 1959-62, Synergetics, Inc., Raleigh, N.C., 1962-64, Rust Engrng. Co., Birmingham, 1964-68; research asst., inst., research assoc. MIT, Cambridge, 1964-68; dir. computer services Skidmore, Owings & Merrill, San Francisco, Chgo., 1968-74; postdoctoral fellow UCLA, 1972; adj. assoc. prof. architecture and civil engrng. Carnegie-Mellon U., Pitts., 1973-74; archtl. systems cons., Chgo., 1974-75, Berkeley, Calif., 1975-80, Pasadena, Calif., 1980-82, Altadena, Calif., 1982—; lectr. info. systems Calif. State Poly. U., Pomona, 1980-81, prof., 1981—, asst. chair, 1990-91, chair, 1991-93, 96—. Fulbright lectr., Uruguay, 1985. Co-author: Structured Analysis Methods for Computer Information Systems, 1985. Recipient Tucker-Voss award M.I.T., 1967; Fulbright scholar, 1985. Mem. AIA (Arnold W. Brunner scholar 1966), Assn. Computing Machinery, Sigma Xi, Phi Eta Sigma, Scarab, Scabbard and Blade, Tau Beta Pi, Chi Epsilon, Beta Gamma Sigma. Episcopalian. Home: 1696 N Altadena Dr Altadena CA 91001-3623 Office: 3801 W Temple Ave Pomona CA 91768-2557

TEAL, DONALD F., physician, surgeon; b. N.Y.C., Oct. 9, 1939; s. Gordon Kidd and Lyda (Smith) T.; m. Judith Horton, July 19, 1969; children: Randall Frasier, Brent Christopher. BA in History, Rice U., 1961; MD, U. Texas, Dallas, 1965. Diplomate Am. Bd. Gen. Surgery, Am. Bd. Plastic and Reconstructive Surgery. Pvt. practice Eugene, Oreg., 1975-95; assoc. prof. surgery Health Sci. Ctr. U. Oreg., Portland, 1975-95. Visiting plastic surgeon, Oaxaca, Mex. Lt. USNR, 1966-68, Vietnam. Fellow: ACS; mem. Am. Soc. Surgery of Hand, Am. Soc. Reconstructive Microsurgery (founder), Internat. Soc. Reconstructive Microsurgery (founder), Am. Assn. Hand Surgery, Am. Soc. Plastic and Reconstructive Surgery. Office: 1200 Hilyard St Ste S 550 Eugene OR 97401-8122

TEARNAN, BLAKE HOESLEY, psychologist; b. Denver, Nev., Dec. 20, 1951; s. Clyde Hoesley and Evelyn McBride (Hammer) T.; m. Olivia Andrea Stafford, Nov. 24, 1979; children: Audray Danielle, Vanessa Keeley. BS in Psychology magna cum laude, U. Houston, 1975; MA in Psychology, U. Pacific, Stockton, Calif., 1978; PhD in Clin. Psychology, U. Ga., 1982. Diplomate Am. Acad. Pain Mgmt.; lic. psychologist, Nev., Calif. Acad. staff U. Wis. Med. Sch., Madison, 1982-84; clin. coord. U. Nev. Med. Sch./VA Med. Ctr., Reno, 1984-86, Sierra Pain Inst., Reno, 1986-92; dir. behavioral medicine Health-Plex Med. Clinic, Reno, 1992-93; program dir. Nev. Occupl. Health Clinic, Sparks, Nev., 1993-95; dir. behavior medicine functional restoration program Rehab. Hosp. of Nev., Reno, 1995—; cons. psychologist Am. Acad. Pain Mgmt., Modesto, Calif., 1994-96; pvt. practice Capital Sq. Assocs., Madison, 1984-85, Reno, 1985—; asst. prof. psychiatry U. Nev.-Reno Med. Sch., 1985-87, adj. asst. prof. dept. psychology, 1988—; program dir. Sonora Ctr. for Pain and Occupl. Rehab., Sparks, 1993—; pres. Pendrake Inc., Reno, 1992—; lectr. in field; condr. workshops in field. Contbr. articles to profl. jours.; guest reviewer Jour. Behavioral Assessment and Psychopathology, 1979, 80, 81, 86, 89, Am. Jour. Pain Mgmt., 1992; editl. bd. Phobia Practice and Rsch. Jour., 1987-91, Pain Mgmt., 1987-92. Lauri T. Callicutt scholar, 1974. Mem. APA, Nev. Psychol. Assn., Am. Acad. Pain Mgmt. (Continuing Edn. Excellence award 1996), Phi Kappa Phi. Democrat. Home: 2558 Arches Ct Reno NV 89509 Office: 255 Moana Ln # 206 Reno NV 89509

TEDFORD, CHARLES FRANKLIN, biophysicist; b. Lawton, Okla., June 26, 1928; s. Charles E. and Loula B. (Waters) T.; m. Julie Reme Sauret, Sept. 15, 1951; children: Gary Franklin, Mark Charles, Philip John. BS with distinction in Chemistry, S.W. Tex. State U., 1950, MS, 1954; postgrad. in radiobiology Reed Coll., 1957, in biophysics U. Calif., Berkeley, 1961-63. Enlisted USN, 1945-47, commd. ensign, 1950, advanced through grades to capt., 1968; biochemist U.S. Naval Hosp., San Diego, 1953-54, U.S. Naval Biol. Lab., Oakland, Calif., 1954-56; sr. instr., radiation safety officer Nuclear, Biol. and Chem. Warfare Def. Sch., Treasure Island, Calif., 1956-61; asst. chief nuclear medicine div. Navy Med. Sch., Bethesda, Md., 1963-66; adminstrv. program mgr. radiation safety br. Bur. Medicine and Surgery, Washington, 1966-72; dir. radiation safety and health physics program Navy Regional Med. Center, San Diego, 1972-74; mgr. Navy Regional Med. Clinic, Seattle, 1974-78, ret., 1978; dir. radiation health unit Ga. Dept. Human Resources, Atlanta, 1978-79; dir. Ariz. Radiation Regulatory Agy., Tempe, 1979-91; chief, Radiological Health Prog., Juneau, Alaska, 1991-93, ret. 1993; cons. 1993—. elected chmn. Conf. Radiation Program Dirs., 1987; named Ariz. Southwestern Low Level Radioactive Waste Compact Commr., 1990. Recipient Ariz. Adminstr. of Yr. award Ariz. Adminstrs. Assn., 1988; decorated Legion of Merit, Meritorious Service medal. Mem. Health Physics Soc., Am. Nuclear Soc. Contbr. articles on radiation safety to profl. publs.

TEDFORD, JACK NOWLAN, III, construction executive, small business owner; b. Reno, Jan. 1, 1943; s. Jack Nowlan Jr. and Elizabeth (Kolhoss) T.; m. Nancy Joanne Stiles, Feb. 27, 1971; children: Jack Nowlan IV, James Nathan. BS, U. Nev., 1966, MBA, 1969. Bus. mgr. Los Angeles Bapt. Coll., Newhall, Calif., 1969-71; v.p. Jack N. Tedford, Inc., Fallon, Nev., 1971—; owner/broker Tedford Realty, Fallon, 1974-94; owner/mgr. Tedford Bus. Systems, Fallon, 1978-94; pres. JNT, Inc., Fallon, 1994—. Author numerous computer programs. Mem. Selective Svc. Local Bd., Fallon, 1971-76; chmn. City of Fallon Bd. Adjustment, 1975-95, Churchill Co. Reps., Fallon, 1976-80; mem. ctrl. com. Nev. Reps., 1976—; del. Nat. Conv., Detroit, 1980, Dallas, 1984; former coun. ofcls. Western Nev. Devel. Dist.; former treas. Lahontan Valley Environ. Alliance. Mem. Assn. Gen. Contractors (v.p., former treas. Nev. chpt.), Nat. Bd. Realtors, State Bd. Realtors, Fallon Bd. Realtors, CEDA Bus. Coun. (bd. dirs.), Nev. Motor Transport Assn., Nat. Asphalt Pavement Assn. (quality improvement com.), Rotary (bd. dirs. 1969-71), Slavic Gospel Assn. (bd. dirs. 1995—), Nat. Assn. Gen. Contractors (open shop com., closely held bus. com.), Fellowship of Cos. for Christ Internat. Republican. Baptist. Home: 115 N Bailey St Fallon NV 89406-2720 Office: 235 E Williams Ave Fallon NV 89406-3027

TEEL, JOYCE, supermarket and drugstore retail executive; b. 1930. Dir. Raley's, West Sacramento, 1950—; co-chmn., 1991—. Office: Raley's 500 W Capitol Ave Broderick CA 95605-2624

TEERLINK, J(OSEPH) LELAND, real estate developer; b. Salt Lake City, July 16, 1935; s. Nicholas John and Mary Luella (Love) T.; student U. Utah, 1953-55; m. Leslie Dowdle, Nov. 5, 1975; children: Steven, David, Andrew, Suzanne, Benjamin. Sales rep. Eastman Kodak Co., Salt Lake City, 1960-69; founder Graphic Systems, Inc., Salt Lake City, 1969-82, pres., 1969-79, chmn. bd., 1979-82; founder Graphic Ink Co., Salt Lake City, 1973, pres., 1975-79, chmn. bd., 1979-82; founder G.S.I. Leasing Co., Salt Lake City, 1975, pres., 1975-82; chmn. bd. Graphic Systems Holding Co., Inc., Salt Lake City, 1978-82; dir. leasing and acquisitions Terra Industries, Inc., real estate developers, 1982-86, ptnr., 1986—; bd. dirs. ARC, Salt Lake City, 1979-82; co-founder, dir. Hope Living Ctr. Found. for Mothers and Children, 1993—; vice consulate of the Netherlands for Utah, 1977-92; mem. active corps of execs., SBA, 1979-83; mem. adv. bd. House of Hope Mothers and Children Utah Alcoholism Found., 1992-94. Recipient Masters award Salt Lake Bd. Realtors, 1993; named Small Businessman of the Yr. for Utah, SBA, 1978. Mem. Graphic Arts Equipment and Supply Dealers of Am. (dir. 1978-82), Printing Industry of Am., Nat. Assn. Indsl. and Office Parks (pres. Utah chpt., 1986-87), Nat. Fedn. Ind. Businessmen, Million Dollar Club (life). Republican. Mormon. Home: 2984 Thackeray Pl Salt Lake City UT 84108-2517 Office: 6925 Union Park Ctr Midvale UT 84047-4142

TEETS, JOHN WILLIAM, retired diversifed company executive; b. Elgin, Ill., Sept. 15, 1933; s. John William and Maudie Teets; m. Nancy Kerchenfaut, June 25, 1965; children: Jerri, Valerie Sue, Heidi Jayne, Suzanne. Student, U. Ill.; LLD (hon.), Trinity Coll., 1982; DBA in Foodsvc. Mgmt. (hon.), Johnson and Wales U., 1991; D in Comml. Sci. (hon.), Western Internat. U., 1992. Pres., ptnr. Winter Garden Restaurant, Inc., Carpenterville, Ill., 1957-63; v.p. Greyhound Food Mgmt. Co.; pres. Post Houses, Inc., and Horne's Enterprises, Chgo., 1964-68; pres., chief operating officer John R. Thompson Co., Chgo., 1968-71; pres., corp. v.p. pub. restaurant divsn. Canteen Corp., Chgo., 1971-75; divsn. pres. Jacques Restaurant Group, 1975; exec. v.p., CEO Bonanza Internat. Co., Dallas, 1975; group v.p. food svcs., pres. Greyhound Food Mgmt., Inc. (now named Restaura), Phoenix, 1975; vice chmn. The Greyhound Corp., Phoenix, 1980; chmn., CEO Greyhound Corp. (now The Dial Corp), Phoenix, 1981-96; chmn., pres., CEO The Dial Corp, Phoenix, 1996-97; vice chmn. Pres.' Conf. on Foodservice Industry. Recipient Silver Plate award, Golden Plate award Internat. Foodsvc. Mgrs. Assn., 1980, Bus. Leadership award Harvard Bus. Sch. Club Ariz., 1985, Order of the Crown, Kingdom of Belgium, 1990, Ellis Island medal of honor Nat. Ethnic Coalition of Orgns. Found., 1995; named Top Bus. Spkr. of Yr., Forbes Mag., 1990, Capt. of Achievement, Acad. of Achievement, 1992, CEO of Yr., Leaders Mag., 1986. Mem. Nat. Inst. Foodsvc. Industry (trustee), Am. Mgmt. Assn., Christian Businessmen's Assn. (chmn. steering com. 1977). Office: JW Teets Enterprises LLC 1850 N Central Ave Phoenix AZ 85077-6000

TEETS, WALTER RALPH, accounting educator; b. Boulder, Colo., Oct. 1, 1950; s. Otis E. and Elsie (Purchase) T.; m. Mary Anne Clougherty. B in Music Edn., U. Colo., 1973; MMus, U. Wis., Madison, 1976; MS in Edn., U. Wis., Whitewater, 1981, MS in Acctg., 1985; PhD, U. Chgo., 1989. CPA. Asst. prof. Wash. U., St. Louis, 1986-89, U. Ill., Urbana-Champaign, Ill., 1989-94, Gonzaga U., Spokane, Wash., 1994—; continuing profl. edn. spkr. Gonzaga U., 1996. Contbr. articles to profl. jours. Mem. Am. Acctg. Assn., K.C. (fin. sec. 1990-93). Office: Gonzaga Univ 502 E Boone Ave Spokane WA 99258-1774

TEHRANI, DIANE HAWKE, English as a second language educator; b. Indpls., Feb. 19, 1943; d. Donald George and Mary Elizabeth (Garst) Hawke; m. Kazem Tehrani, July 3, 1970. BA, Ind. U., 1966, MA, 1969; MA, Columbia U., 1974, MPhil, 1978. ESL cert. Portland State U., 1988. ESL instr. Iranian Inst. Advanced Acctg., Tehran, 1971; ESL dir., tutor ARC, Portland, 1976-80; instr. Portland State U., 1978, 80, 82; ESL instr. Lewis and Clark Coll., 1987, Portland C.C., 1987-91, Mt. Hood C.C., Gresham, Oreg., 1991-92, Mt. Angel Seminary, St. Benedict, Oreg., 1992—; tutor Help One Student to Succeed, Portland, 1986-87; asst. editor Across Towns-Portland C.C., 1990-91; sec., asst., newsletter staff Persia House, Portland, 1990—. Trainee Peace Corps, Austin, Tex., 1966; mem. citizens adv. com. Tri-Met, Portland, 1978; mem. art in the schs. com. AAUW, Portland, 1979. Summer intern Indpls. Star, 1959; A.V. Williams scholar Columbia U., N.Y.C., 1970. Mem. ASCD, TESOL, Nat. Coun. Tchrs. English, Soc. for Iranian Studies, Middle East Studies Assn., Oreg. Tchrs. to Spkrs. of Other Langs. Episcopalian. Home: 7120 SW Taylors Ferry Rd Portland OR 97223-1164 Office: Mt Angel Seminary Abbey Dr Saint Benedict OR 97373

TEHRANI, FLEUR TAHER, electrical engineer, educator, researcher; b. Tehran, Iran, Feb. 16, 1956; came to U.S., 1984; d. Hassan and Pourandokht (Monfared) T. BS in Elec. Engring., Sharif U. of Tech., Tehran, 1975; DIC in Comm. Engring., Imperial Coll. Sci. and Tech., London, 1977; MSc in Comm. Engring., U. London, 1977, PhD in Elec. Engring., 1981. Registered profl. engr., Calif. Comm. engr. Planning Orgn. of Iran, Tehran, 1977-78; lectr. A elec. engring. Robert Gordon's Inst. Tech., Aberdeen, U.K., 1982-83; lectr. II elec. engring. South Bank U., London, 1984; asst. prof. elec. engring. Calif. State U., Fullerton, 1985-91, assoc. prof. elec. engring., 1991-94, prof. elec. engring., 1994—; vis. assoc. prof. elec. engring. Drexel U., Phila., 1987-88; sys. cons. Telebit Corp., Cupertino, Calif., 1985; engring. cons. PRD, Inc., Dresher, Pa., 1989-92; mem. NASA/Am. Soc. Engring. Edn. summer faculty Jet Propulsion Lab., Calif. Inst. Tech., Pasadena, 1995, 96. Contbr. articles to profl. jours.; patentee in field. Recipient Best Ann. Rsch. Manuscript award Assn. for the Advancement of Med. Instrumentation, 1993, Outstanding Excellence in Rsch. Faculty award Calif. State U., 1993. Mem. IEEE, Women in Sci. and Engring. (chair Calif. State U. chpt. 1990-91), Assn. Profs. and Scholars of Iranian Heritage (pres. 1991-92), Sigma Delta Epsilon. Office: Calif State U Dept Elec Engring 800 N State College Blvd Fullerton CA 92831-3599

TEIRSTEIN, PAUL SHEPHERD, physician, health facility administrator; b. N.Y.C., July 5, 1955; s. Alvin Stanley and Alice Teirstein. BA in Biology, Vassar Coll., 1976; MD, CUNY, 1980. Diplomate Am. Bd. Internal Medicine and Cardiovascular Diseases. With Lab. of Vision Rsch. NIH, Bethesda, Md., 1977-79; intern and resident Brigham & Women's Hosp., Boston, 1980-83; fellow in cardiology Stanford (Calif.) U., 1983-86; fellow in advanced coronary angioplasty Mid-Am. Heart Inst., Kansas City, Mo., 1986-87; fellow in stents, artherectomy and lasers NIH, Bethesda, 1987; dir. interventional cardiology Scripps Clinic and Rsch. Found., La Jolla, Calif., 1987—; presenter at Am. Coll. Cardiology, 1987-94, Am. Heart Assn., 1990-93, The French Hosp., San Luis Obispo, Calif., 1989, St. Luke's Med. Ctr., Phoenix, 1989, Cardiology for the Cons., Rancho Santa Fe, 1989, U. Calif., Irvine, 1989, ACP, Scottsdale, Ariz., 1989, Presbyn. Hosp., Whittier, Calif, 1989, St. Jude Med. Ctr., Fullerton, Calif., 1990, Oscala Med. Ctr., Osaka, Japan, 1992, Cedars-Sinai Med. Ctr., L.A., 1993, European Congress of Cardiology, Nice, France, 1993, Tokyo U., 1993, Lenox Hill Hosp., N.Y., 1993, Japanese Soc. Internat. Cardiology, 1994, Nat. Hindu Hosp., Bombay, 1994, G.B. Pant Hosp., Delhi, India, 1994, Escort's Hosp., 1994, B.M. Birla Hosp., Calcutta, 1994, Shaare Zedek Med. Ctr., Jerusalem, 1994, XV Congresso da Sociedad de Cardiology de Sao Paulo, Ribeirao Preto, Brazil, 1994, and others. Grantee NSF, 1975. Fellow Am. Coll. Cardiology, Assn. for Rsch. in Vision and Ophthalmology, Beta Beta Beta, Alpha Omega Alpha. Office: Scripps Clinic & Rsch Found 10666 N Torrey Pines Rd La Jolla CA 92037-1027

TEITELBAUM, LEE E., law educator; b. New Orleans, Nov. 4, 1941. BA magna cum laude, Harvard Coll., 1963; LLB, Harvard U., 1966; LLM, Northwestern U., 1968. Bar: Ill. Staff atty. Chgo. Lawyer Project, 1966-68; asst. prof. law U. N.D., 1968-70; assoc. prof. law SUNY, Buffalo, 1970-73; vis. assoc. prof. law U. N.Mex. Law Sch., 1972, assoc. prof. law, 1973-74, prof. law, 1974-87; prof. law, dir. Ctr. for the Study of Legal Policy Relating to Children Ind. U. Law Sch., 1980-81, vis. prof., 1987; vis. prof. U. Utah Coll. Law, 1985, prof. law, 1986—, assoc. dean acad. affairs, 1987-90, acting dean, 1988, dean, 1990—, Alfred C. Emery prof. law, 1994—; fellow legal history program U. Wis., Madison, 1984; mem. test audit subcom. Law Sch. Admissions Coun. Author: (with A. Gough) Beyond Control: Status Offenders in the Juvenile Court, 1977 (with W.V. Stapleton) In Defense of Youth: The Role of Counsel in American Juvenile Courts, 1972; contbr. articles to profl. jours.; bd. editors Law & Soc. Rev., 1982-87, Law & Policy, Jour. Legal Edn., 1990-92. Fellow ABA (reporter ABA-IJA project on standards for juvenile justics, standards relating to the role of counsel for pvt. parties 1979); mem. Law & Soc. Assn. (bd. trustees 1977-80), Utah Minority Bar Assn. (award), Assn. Am. Law Schs. Office: Univ of Utah Office Dean Coll Law Salt Lake City UT 84112*

TEIWES, HELGA, photographer; b. Meerbusch, Germany, Jan. 19, 1930; came to U.S., 1960; d. Reinhold and Gertrud (Zaepke) Kulbe. MA, Handwerks Kammer, Dusseldorf, Germany, 1957; BA in Art History, U. Ariz., 1978. Photographic apprentice Hehmke-Winterer Studio, Dusseldorf, 1950-53, studio photographer, 1953-57; staff photographer Bagel Printing Co., Dusseldorf, 1957-60; freelance photographer N.Y.C., 1960-61; photographer Cartier Jeweler, N.Y.C., 1961-62; transparency retoucher Creative Color Svc., N.Y.C., 1962-64; staff photographer Ariz. State Mus., Tucson, 1965-93; photographer, rschr. O'odham, Hopi, Navajo, Apache, Ariz. Indian Tribes, 1965—; photographer Mission San Xavier del Bac Restoration Projects, Tucson, 1968-69, 79, 93, 94, 95, 96, 97; author, photographer: Hopi Basket Weaving, Artistry in Natural Fibers, 1996; photographer nat. and internat. exhbns. Author, photographer: Kachina Dolls, 1991; photographer: Navajo, 1991; designer, photographer posters S.W. Pottery and Cultural Material, 1980. Recipient Spur award Western Writers Am., 1982, Grand prize World Photography Soc., Calif., 1983, 2nd prize for photography Sangre de Cristo Art Ctr., Pueblo, Colo., 1986, 88, 90; Ariz. Humanities Coun. grantee, Phoenix, 1992. Home: 2611 N Teresa Ln Tucson AZ 85745

TELBAN, ETHEL, librarian; b. Renton, Wash., Mar. 31, 1914; d. Blase and Amelia (Podbregar) T. BA, Ctrl. Wash. U., Ellensburg, 1938; M Librarianship, Denver U., 1950. Cert. educator, libr. Elem. tchr. Thorp (Wash.) Sch. Dist., 1935-36; elem. tchr. Renton (Wash.) Sch. Dist., 1937-50, libr. supr., 1950-74; libr. Western Wash. U., Bellingham, 1965; instr. libr. U. Wash., Seattle, summers 1955, 58, 59, 60; libr. Ctrl. Wash. U., Ellensburg, summers 1941, 51, 53, 57; mem. Curriculum Commn., State Dept. Edn., Olympia, Wash., 1954-55. Editor: (history book) From Coal to Jets, 1976. Mem. Mcpl. Arts Commn., Renton, 1973-75; mem. bicentennial com. City of Renton, 1975-76. Named Renton Citizen of Yr., Elks, Renton, 1977, Vol of Yr., Assoc. King County Hist. Assn., Seattle, 1994; recipient Individual Excellence award Wash. Mus. Assn., Richland, 1994, Cert. of Commendation, Am. Assn. State and Local History, Nashville, 1995. Mem. ALA (mem. Newbery-Caldecott com. 1960-61), Sch. Librs. Assn. Wash. State (state pres. 1962-63), Renton Hist. Soc. (pres. 1966-96, editor newsletter 1970-94), Renton Retired Tchrs. (sec. 1950-96), PEO Sisterhood (sec. 1959-96), Soroptimist Internat. (pres. 1951-96), Delta Kappa Gamma. Home: 11448 Rainier Ave S # 205 Seattle WA 98178 Office: Renton Hist Mus 235 Mill Ave S Renton WA 98055-2133

TELLER, MARC JOEL, computer systems engineer, consulting researcher; b. Bklyn., Dec. 2, 1951; s. Philip and Lillian (Greenberg) T.; m. Mette Hansen, Aug. 24 1980. BS in Biology, Columbia U., 1972. Systems mgr., head systems devel. Brain Rsch. Labs., NYU Med. Ctr., N.Y.C., 1974-76; mem. programming staff Bell Labs., AT&T Long Lines, Holmdel, N.J., 1977-82; various positions, then sr. market specialist UNIX, Perkin-Elmer Data Systems, Tinton Falls, N.J., 1983-85, sr. tech. specialist, then strategic product plannerr, 1985, 87; sr. systems engr. UNIX, AT&T Bell Labs., Holmdel, N.J., 1985-86; mgr. operating systems engring. Unisoft Corp., Cambridge, Mass., 1987-89; cons. operating systems engr. Phoenix Techs., Norwood, Mass., 1989-90; prin. cons. engr., program mgr. operating systems rsch. Encore Computer Corp., Marlborough, Mass., 1990-91; leader operating systems rsch., prin. tech. rsch. cons. Worcester Poly. Inst. Ctr. High Performance Computing, Marlborough, Mass., 1991-93; ind. sys. cons. M.J. Teller Cons., Mansfield, Mass., 1993—; mgr. HSM devel. EMASS, Inc., Englewood, Colo., Eng., 1994—; project leader spl. projects EMASS, Inc., Englewood, Colo., 1997—. Contbr. articles to profl. jours. Mem. IEEE (Posix stds. group 1984-89, 88open binary compatibility stds. com. 1987-89, cert. of apprecition 1988), IEEE Computer Soc., NRA (instr. 1992—), Lionel Collectors Club Am., Colo. Symphony Assn., Mass. Hort. Soc., Boston Symphony Orch. Home and Office: 3694 Deer Creek Dr Parker CO 80134-4568

TELLINGTON, WENTWORTH JORDAN, engineer; b. Gorham, N.H., Oct. 11, 1916; s. Jesse James and Myrtle Meneleh (Jordan) T.; m. Elizabeth Haman-Ashley, Apr. 29, 1939 (div. 1956); children: Wentworth J. Jr., Joan Elizabeth Gabert. Grad., Phillips Andover Acad., 1935; student, Norwich U., 1939; AB, Columbia U., 1940, postgrad., 1946-47; postgrad., U. So. Calif., 1957-59, UCLA, 1959. Instr. U.S. Mil. Acad., West Point, N.Y., 1941-45; field supr. Century Geophys. Corp., Tulsa, 1946-48; chief geophysicist Pacific Petroleums Ltd., Calgary, Alberta, Can., 1949-51; exec. v.p. Overland Inds. Ltd., Edmonton, Alberta, Can., 1952-55; head math. dept. Chadwick Sch., Rolling Hills, Calif., 1956-60; proprietor Pacific Coast Equestrian Rsch. Farm, Badger, Calif., 1961-70, Whitehurst Products Co., San Francisco, 1970-75, Deep Moon Gold Mine, Downieville, 1982-92; CEO Seadeck Corp., Tucson, 1995—, 1995—; adj. prof. Prescott (Ariz.) Coll., 1972-75. Author: (books) Military Maps and Air Photos, 1979, Endurance and Competitive Trail Riding, 1979, Gold and a Hideaway of Your Own, 1993, Crazy in America, 1994; inventor: vehicle tracker, device for tracking and recording locations, 1944, floating airport, 1995, floating platform, 1996. Engr. ethics com. Soc. Profl. Engrs., Can., 1953-54; bd. govs. Western States Trail Assn., Auburn, Calif., 1962-80. Recipient Creative Citizenship in Calif. award Gov. Ronald Reagan, 1968. Mem. Am. Assn. Petroleum Geologists. Republican. Congregationalist. Office: Airdock Enterprise PO Box 68291 Tucson AZ 85737

TELLO, DONNA, tax strategist; b. Annapolis, Md., Mar. 23, 1955; m. Gregory Tello, July 5, 1975 (div. 1978); children: Jesse Elliott Timothy Tello, Kimberlle Shey Thommasson; m. Dennis R. Thompson, Apr. 1, 1987 (dec. Jan. 1994). Enrolled agt. Owner Tax Savers, San Diego, 1981—. Libertarian party candidate for state assembly, 1984; candidate Calif. State Senate, 1996. Mem. Inland Soc. Tax Cons. (sec. San Diego chpt. 1989, bd. dirs. 1990, 2d v.p. 1991, 1st v.p. 1992, pres. 1993, soc. chmn. govt. affairs 1991, 93, 94, soc. sec. 1992, soc. pres. 1995, 96), Nat. Taxpayers Union, Camelopard Club (co-founder, treas. 1988-90, pres. 1995-96), Toastmasters (v.p. edn. Liberty chpt. 1987). Office: 14168 Poway Rd Ste 109 Poway CA 92064-4938

TEMA, WILLIAM JOHN, librarian; b. June 23, 1937; married; 1 son. BS in Edn., U. Minn., 1959, MA, 1961. Lic. real estate broker. Reference libr. Cedar Rapids (Iowa) Pub. Libr., 1961-63; page supr., reference libr. Pasadena (Calif.) Pub. Libr., 1963-67; adult libr. La Pintoresca br. Pasadena Pub. Libr., 1967-69; br. libr. Allendale br. Pasadena Pub. Libr., 1969-70, Hastings br. Pasadena Pub. Libr., 1970-73; dist. libr. Altadena (Calif.) Libr. Dist., 1973—; pres. Pub. Libr. Film Circuit, 1976-77; v.p. Met. Coop. Libr. System, 1984, pres., 1985-86, exec. com. 1994-96; v.p./pres.-elect Pub. Libr. Video Circuit, 1988-89, pres., 1989-90. Pres. Pasadena Am. Sr. Little League, 1981; bd. dirs. Altadena Sr. Ctr., 1982-85. With U.S. Army Res., 1959-69. Mem. Am. Libr. Assn. (membership bd. mem. Pub. Libr. Assn. 1976-78), Calif. Libr. Assn. (nominating com. 1981, govt. rels. com. 1988-91, long range planning com. 1992-97), Pasadena Mcpl. Employee Assn. (dir. 1968), Pasadena Pub. Libr. Assn. (pres. 1970-71), Pub. Libr. Execs. Soc. Calif. (pres. 1977), Altadena Kiwanis Club (pres. 1976-77), Altadena Kiwanis Club (pres. 1976-77, disting. pres., sec. 1978—), Altadena C. of C. (2d v.p. 1978, v.p. 1979, pres. 1980, 96, co-chmn. Altadena's Old Fashioned Days 1981, 95, Altadena Citizen of Yr. 1995), Calif. Assn. Realtors, Nat. Bd. Realtors, Pasadena Bd. Realtors. Home: 1115 Sierra Madre Villa Ave Pasadena CA 91107-1528 Office: Altadena Libr Dist 600 E Mariposa St Altadena CA 91001-2211

TEMKO, ALLAN BERNARD, writer; b. N.Y.C., Feb. 4, 1924; s. Emanuel and Betty (Alderman) T.; m. Elizabeth Ostroff, July 1, 1950 (dec. Aug. 1996); children: Susannah, Alexander. AB, Columbia U., 1947; postgrad, U. Calif., Berkeley, 1949-51, Sorbonne, 1948-49, 51-52. Lectr. Sorbonne, 1953-54, Ecole des Arts et Metiers, Paris, 1954-55; asst. prof. journalism U. Calif., Berkeley, 1956-62, lectr. in city planning and social scis., 1966-70, lectr. Grad. Sch. Journalism, 1991; prof. art Calif. State U., Hayward, 1971-80; lectr. art Stanford U., 1981, 82; architecture critic San Francisco Chronicle, 1961-93, art editor, 1979-82; archtl. planning cons.; chmn. Yosemite Falls Design Workshop, 1992; Pulitzer Prize juror, 1991-92. Author: Notre Dame of Paris, 1955, Eero Saarinen, 1962, No Way To Build a Ballpark and Other Irreverent Essays on Architecture, 1993; contbr. articles to U.S. and fgn. mags. and newspapers; West Coast editor, Archtl. Forum, 1959-62. Served with USNR, 1943-46. Recipient Gold medal Commonwealth Club Calif., 1956, Silver medal, 1994, Journalism award AIA, 1961, Silver Spur award San Francisco Planning and Urban Renewal Assn., 1985, AIA Inst. Honor award, 1991, Nathaniel A. Owings award AIA Calif. Coun., 1995, 1st prize in archtl. criticism Mfrs. Hanover/Art World, 1986, Critic's award Mfrs. Hanover/Art World, 1987, Profl. Achievement award Soc. Profl. Journalists, 1988, Pulitzer Prize for criticism, 1990; grantee Rockefeller Found., 1962-63, 20th Century Fund, 1963-66, NEA, 1988, Graham Found., 1990; Guggenheim fellow, 1956-57. Home: 1015 Fresno Ave Berkeley CA 94707-2517 *My chief intellectual and professional goal has always been to create excellence in a democratic America and, where possible, in the world at large. This Jeffersonian aim, which came to me directly from Lewis Mumford, naturally includes architecture, environmental planning, the fine arts, and literature. Through education, in which history, criticism, and serious journalism play important roles, I think it is still possible to attain such excellence despite the complex problems of technological civilization.*

TEMPLE, JOHN, publishing executive. Mng. editor Rocky Mountain News, Denver. Office: Rocky Mountain News 400 W Colfax Ave Denver CO 80204

TEMPLIN, JOHN ALTON, historical theology educator, minister; b. Hoehne, Colo., Sept. 27, 1927; s. John Wesley and Stella Mable (Canterbury) T.; m. Dorothy Jean Lear, Dec. 31, 1952; children: Kayla Jean, Ann Revae, Bryce Alton. BA, U. Denver, 1950; ThM, The Iliff Sch. Theology, 1953, ThD, 1956; PhD, Harvard U., 1966. Ordained United Meth. Ch., 1951. Asst. prof. Southwestern Coll., Winfield, Kans., 1954-57; min. Meth. Ch., Mass., 1957-66; asst. prof. U. S.D., Vermillion, 1966-67; asst. to full prof. The Iliff Sch. Theology, Denver, 1967—. Author and editor: The United Methodist, Evangelical and United Brethren Churches in the Rockies, 1977; author: Ideology on a Frontier: The Theological Foundation of Afrikaner Nationalism, 1652-1910, 1984; author, editor: An Intellectual History of the Iliff School of Theology: A Centennial Tribute, 1892-1992, 1992. Cpl. USAF, 1945-47. Named Alumnus of Yr., The Iliff Sch. Theology, Denver, 1989. Mem. Am. Soc. Ch. History, Am. Soc. Reformation History, Am. Hist. Assn., Sixteenth Century Study Conf. Democrat. Office: The Iliff Sch Theology 2201 S University Blvd Denver CO 80210-4707

TENCER, ALLAN FRED, mechanical engineer, medical educator; b. Montreal, Que., Can., Aug. 23, 1949; came to U.S., 1981; m. Signe Steinbach; 1 child, Holly. BEng, McGill U., 1971, MEng, 1973, PhD in Mech. Engring., 1981. Registered profl. engr., Que., Tex. Asst. prof. bioengring. U. Tex., Arlington, 1981-84; asst. prof. orthops. U. Tex. Med. Br., Galveston, 1984-88; assoc. prof. orthops., adj. prof. bioengring. U. Wash., Seattle, 1988—. Author: Biomechanics in Orthopedic Trauma, 1994; contbr. numerous articles to profl. jours.; co-inventor fracture brace, spinal implant. Grantee NSF, 1982, NIH, 1987, VA, 1993, 96, Ctrs. Disease Control, 1993, 96. Mem. ASME, Orthop. Rsch. Soc., Soc. for Biomaterials. Office: Harborview Med Ctr Box 359798 325 9th Ave Seattle WA 98104-2420

TENG, SHENGYI, science researcher; b. Yuhuan, Zhejiang, China, Sept. 24, 1964; arrived in U.S., 1993; s. Fungkui and Aizhu (Zhuang) T.; m. Ying Jia Hu, Oct. 21, 1988; 1 child, Jesse. DDS, Zhejiang Med. U., 1985; MSc, West China U. Med. Scis., Chengdu, Sichuan, China, 1988. Intern Zhejiang Med. U., Hanzhou, 1983-85; resident West China U. of Med. Scis., Chengdu, 1985-91, lectr., 1991-93; rsch. assoc. U. Wash., Seattle, 1993—. Editor: (book) Practical Occlusion, 1990; author original rsch. Recipient 2nd prize for outstanding scientific rsch. Sichuan Province Govt., Chengdu, 1992. Mem. Internat. Assn. for Dental Rsch., Am. Assn. for Dental Rsch. Office: Univ of Wash Seattle WA 98195

TENISON, JOHN HUGHES, civil engineer, retired military officer; b. Dallas, Sept. 29, 1952; s. John H. Sr. and Anne L. (Welborn) T.; m. Antonette Rachel Tenison. BSCE, Tex. A&M U., 1978; MSCE, U. Calif., Berkeley, 1985. Registered profl. engr., N.Mex. Area engr. Asphalt Inst., Long Beach, Calif., 1980-81; pavement design engr. N.Mex. State Hwy. Dept., Santa Fe, 1981-84, rsch. engr., 1984-88, dist. traffic engr., 1989-93, tech. support engr., 1993-96, staff materials engr., 1996-97, Geotech/pavement design sect. chief, 1997—; asst. tng. and readiness officer 3d Naval Constrn. Brigade Detachment, Pt. Hueneme, Calif., 1994-96; various office assignments Naval Mobile Constrn. Bn. 22, Dallas, 1984-94. Lt. comdr. Civil Engr. Corps. USNR, 1984-96. W. Vernon Petroleum Asphalt scholar Tex. A&M U., 1977, Nat. Hwy. scholar Fed. Hwy. Adminstrn., 1986. Mem. Assn. Asphalt Paving Technologists (W.J. Emmons award 1985), Naval Res. Assn. Republican. Roman Catholic. Office: NMex State Hwy Dept PO Box 1149 Santa Fe NM 87504

TENNANT, HOWARD EDWARD, university president, management educator; b. Lethbridge, Alta., Can., May 13, 1941; s. Rex. Joseph and Jean Sylvia (Engle) T.; m. Sharon Lea Buckley, Sept. 7, 1963; children: Carmen, Patricia, Daniel. BBA cum laude, Gonzaga U., 1963; MBA, U. Oreg., 1964, PhD, 1970; LLD (hon.), Gonzaga U., 1997. Asst. prof. U. Sask., Saskatoon, Can., 1966-70, assoc. prof., 1970-74, prof. mgmt., head dept. mgmt. and mktg., 1972-77, assoc. dean grad. studies, prof. mgmt., 1977-84, dean grad. studies, assoc. v.p. rsch., 1984-87; pres., vice chancellor, prof. mgmt. U. Lethbridge, 1987—; chmn. bd. dirs. SED Sys. Inc., Saskatoon, 1980-90; bd. dirs. Assn. Univs. and Colls. Can., Ottawa, Ont., 1987—, chmn. bd., 1995-97; chmn. Univs. Coordinating Coun., Edmonton, Alta., 1989-91, 95; bd. dirs. Alta. Rsch. Coun., Edmonton, 1990—; instr. Banff Sch. Advanced Mgmt., 1970-87; labor mediator U. Sask., 1989; vis. scholar U. Wash. Grad. Sch. Bus., Seattle, 1974-75; bd. govs. U. Lethbridge, 1987—; dir. U. Lethbridge Found., 1990—. Dir. Saskatchewan Rsch. Coun., Saskatoon, 1984-87; bd. dirs. Can. Plains Rsch. Ctr., Regina, Saskatchewan, 1984—, Saskatchewan Expo 86 Corp., Regina., 1985-86. Named adopted son and chief Bull Horn Soc., 1987, 90, Kainai Chief by Blood Indians, 1991; decorated 125th Can. medal Gov. Gen., 1992. Mem. Rotary (Paul Harris fellow 1997), Beta Gamma Sigma. Roman Catholic. Home: 61 Ridgewood Cres W, Lethbridge, AB Canada T1K 6C3 Office: Univ Lethbridge, Pres Office, Lethbridge, AB Canada T1K 3M4

TENNANT, MARY JO, secondary education educator; b. Tacoma, Jan. 6, 1938; d. Glenn Everett and Adelia Maurine (Converse) Sigler; m. Charles Edward Tennant, June 27, 1959; children: Stephen Victor, Catherine J. Tennant Mc Guire, Susan M. Tennant Swenson, William G. AB, Cornell U., 1959; MT, U. Ariz., 1976. Tchr. Yuma (Ariz.) Dist. 1, 1975-77, Children's Way Sch., Fairfax, Va., 1977-78, St. Michael Sch., Annandale, Va., 1978-84; substitute tchr. Conejo Valley Unified Dist., Thousand Oaks, Calif., 1985; tchr. English Newbury Park High Sch., 1986-87, Redwood Intermediate Sch., Thousand Oaks, 1987—, chmn. dept. English, 1989—; mem. Dist. Secondary Curriculum adv. com.; mem. Dist. Writing Assessment com.; mem. Dist. Writing Portfolio assessment com.; mem. Tri-Dist. Celebration of Learning com.; mem. Cornell Club of Washington, 1979-84, Cornell Club So. Calif., 1984—; area chmn. Cornell Alumnae Amb., 1994—, area v.p. class of 1959, 1995—; v.p. sch. bd. Am. Sch. Vientiane, Laos, 1973-74, sec. sch. bd., 1972-73. Neighborhood chmn. Ariz. Cactus-Pine council Girl Scouts U.S., 1974-77, bd. dirs., 1976-77; mem. apostolic commn. St. Jude's Ch., Westlake Village. Recipient Service award Lao Mil. Wives, 1974. Mem. NEA, Calif. Tchrs. Assn., Alpha Phi (dist. alumnae chmn. 1985-89, ho. corp. bd. Calstate Northridge, 1995—). Republican. Roman Catholic. Avocations: reading, sewing, walking. Home: 1317 Breckford Ct Westlake Vlg CA 91361-1707 Office: Redwood Intermediate Sch 233 W Gainsborough Rd Thousand Oaks CA 91360-3442

TENNENT, VALENTINE LESLIE, accountant; b. Apia, Western Samoa, Apr. 5, 1919; came to U.S., 1922; s. Hugh Cowper and Madge Grace (Cook) T.; m. Jeanne Marie Elder, Dec. 10, 1941; children: Madeline Jeanne Walls, Hugh Cowper II, Michael Waller, Val Leslie, Paul Anthony. Student, U. Calif., Berkeley, 1938-40. CPA, Hawaii, La. Mgr. Tennent & Greaney, CPAs, Hilo, Hawaii, 1945-50; ptnr. Cameron, Tennent & Dunn, CPAs, Honolulu, 1950-56; ptnr. KPMG Peat Marwick LLP, Honolulu, 1956-79, cons., 1979-84; ind. rschr. pub. fin. and banking, politico-econ. sci., moral philosophy, San Diego, 1984—. Founding trustee, pres., treas. Tennent Art Found., Honolulu, 1955-77; trustee, treas. Watumull Found., Honolulu, 1963-90; bd. dirs. Iolani Sch., Inst. for Human Svcs., Honolulu, Lyman Mus., Hilo. Capt. USAF, 1941-45. Recipient Bishop's Cross for disting. svc. Protestant Episcopal Ch., Dist. Hawaii, 1965, G.J. Watumull award for disting. achievement Watumull Found., Honolulu, 1982. Mem. AICPA (governing coun. 1961-64), Hawaii Soc. CPAs (pres. 1960). Episcopalian. Home and Office: 700 Front St Apt 1607 San Diego CA 92101-6011 *Joy in life comes from knowing the things you want to accomplish within God's overall purpose, pursuing them to the end regardless of difficulties, and accepting full responsibility for inevitable failures.*

TENNEY, WILLIAM FRANK, pediatrician; b. Shreveport, La., June 5, 1946; s. William Bonds and Pat (Patton) T.; m. Elizabeth Carter Steadman, Oct. 4, 1973; children: Amy Karen, William Allen. BA, Vanderbilt U., 1968; MD, La. State U., New Orleans, 1972. Diplomate Am. Bd. Pediatrics, sub-Bd. Pediatric Nephrology. Intern Grady Meml. Hosp., Atlanta, 1972-73; resident in pediatrics Emory U. Affiliated Hosps., Atlanta, 1973-74, fellow in pediatric nephrology and inorganic metabolism, 1974-76; practice medicine specializing in pediatric nephrology St. Helens, Oreg., 1976-79, Shreveport, 1979-85, Seattle, 1985—; mem. staff Children's Orthopedic Hosp. and Med. Ctr., Seattle; chief dept. pediatrics Swedish Hosp. Med. Ctr., Seattle, 1987-90, 95—; clin. asst. prof. pediatrics La. State U. Sch. Medicine, 1979-85, U. Wash. Sch. Medicine, Seattle, 1985—; chmn. Renal com. Schumpert Med. Ctr., Shreveport, 1982, co-chmn. 1979-81, mem. 1983-84, co-dir. Renal Dialysis Unit, 1979-84, mem. renal transplantation com., 1984; cons. pediatric nephrology Shriner's Hosp. Crippled Children, Shreveport, 1979-84, Shreveport Regional Dialysis Ctr., 1979-84, Bossier Dialysis Ctr., Bossier City, La., 1983-84, Natchitoches (La.) Dialysis Facility, 1984. Author: (with others) Pediatric Case Studies, 1985; contbr. articles to profl. jours. Mem. Union Concerned Scientists, Cambridge, Mass., 1986—, Internat. Physicians for Prevention of Nuclear War, Boston, 1986—. Fellow Am. Acad. Pediatrics; mem. Am. Soc. Pediatric Nephrology, North Pacific Pediatric Soc., AMA, Wash. State Med. Assn., Internat. Soc. Peritoneal Dialysis, Empirical Soc. Emory U., King County Med. Soc., AAAS, Northwest Renal Soc., Southwest Pediatric Nephrology (mem. study group 1981-84). Home: 23915 SE 42nd Ct Issaquah WA 98029-7521 Office: 1221 Madison St Seattle WA 98104-1360

TENNISON, WILLIAM RAY, JR., financial planner, stockbroker, resort owner; b. Deming, N.Mex., July 22, 1941; s. William Ray and Mildred Rose (Frei) T.; m. Mary Kay Reid, Jan. 27, 1963; children: William Ervin, Bradley Joseph, Stephanie Kay (dec.). BS in Indsl. Mgmt., Ariz. State U., 1963; MBA in Econs., U. Ariz., 1966. Indsl. engr. USAF, 1963-71; from account exec. to br. office mgr., stockbroker E. F. Hutton & Co., Mesa, Ariz., 1971-88, first v.p., also mem. Dirs. Adv. Coun.; sr. v.p., stockbroker Kemper Security Group, Mesa, Ariz., 1988-92, sr. v.p. Boettcher divsn., also Kemper Exec. Coun.; bd. dirs. D.E. Frey, Denver, 1992—; pres. Tennison and Assocs., Inc., Mesa, Ariz., Sedona, Ariz., Paonia, Colo., Carbondale, Colo., 1992—; owner Crystal Meadows Ranch Resort, Inc., Somerset, Colo.; speaker in field at sales confs. and conventions. Author: (book/tng. program) Bill Tennison Master Class, 1990.; featured in Registered Representative Mag., 1989, 92, 95, Rsch. Mag., 1992, 93, 95, Broker Hall of Fame, 1995, Arizona Business Mag., 1993; contbr. articles to profl. jours; presenter weekly radio show Pub. Radio, Western Colo. Mem. East Valley Sr. Found., 1986-96; pres. Paonia (Colo.) C. of C., 1994-95, Stephanie Kay Tennison Meml. Scholarship Found. Mem. Paonia (Colo.) Rotary Club. Republican. Methodist. Home: Crystal Meadows Ranch Resort 30682 County Rd 12 Somerset CO 81434 Office: DE Frey & Co 40 N Center Ste 100 Mesa AZ 85201-7300

TENNYSON, PETER JOSEPH, lawyer; b. Winona, Minn., Mar. 18, 1946; s. Richard Harvey and Sylvia Josephine (Jadrich) T.; m. Mary Eileen Fay, Jan. 3, 1970; children: Mark Christian, Rachel Christine, Matthew Patrick, Erica Ruth/. BA, Purdue U., 1968; JD, U. Va., 1975. Bar: Calif. Assoc. atty. O'Melveny & Myers, L.A., 1975-82; v.p., gen. counsel Cannon Mills Co., Kannapolis, N.C., 1982-84; ptnr. Stradling, Yocca, Newport Beach, Calif., 1984-89, Jones, Day, Reavis & Pogue, Irvine, Calif., 1990-95, Paul, Hastings, Janofsky & Walker, Costa Mesa, Calif., 1995—; mem. Calif. Commn. on Future of Legal Profession and State Bar, 1994; lectr. in field. Mem. St. Joseph Hosp. Benefit, Orange, Calif., 1987-93; bd. dirs. Lincoln Club Orange County, 1991-93, South Coast Symphony, 1989-92. Capt. U.S. Army, 1968-72. Mem. Orange County Bar Assn., Performing Arts Bus. Alliance South Coast Repertory Silver Circle. Roman Catholic. Home: 2621 Circle Dr Newport Beach CA 92663-5616 Office: Paul, Hastings, Janofsky & Walker LLP 695 Town Center Dr 17th Fl Costa Mesa CA 92626

TERADA, ALICE MASAE, retired elementary school teacher, writer; b. Hilo, Hawaii, Nov. 13, 1928; d. David Matsuo and Mitsuko (Sekido) Marutani; m. Harry T. Terada, Aug. 25, 1951; children: Suzanne T. Henderson, Keith Y., Lance S. Diploma, Queen's Hosp. Sch. Nursing, 1950; BS, We. Res. U., 1953; MEd, U. Hawaii, 1971. Cert. tchr., Hawaii. Registered nurse County Meml. Hosp., Hilo, Hawaii, 1950-51, U. Hosps., Cleve., 1952-53; lang. arts tchr. Dept. Edn., Honolulu, 1967-68; reading tchr. Reading Ctr., Honolulu, Hawaii, 1968-82. Author: Under the Starfruit Tree, 1989, The Magic Crocodile, 1994. Mem. AAUW, Internat. Reading Assn., Zonta Club Internat., Zonta Club Honolulu (bd. dirs. 1996-97).

TERAMURA, ALAN HIROSHI, science educator; b. L.A., Dec. 26, 1948; s. Kuniyoshi and Mineko (Nakamura) T.; m. Karen Lee McKnight, Sept. 10, 1974; 2 children. BA, Calif. State U., 1971, MA, 1973; PhD, Duke U., 1978. Asst. prof. botany U. Md., College Park, 1979-82, assoc. prof. botany, 1982-88, prof. botany, 1988-93; dean coll. natural scis. U. Hawaii, Honolulu, 1994—; guest prof. Botanishes Inst., Karlsruhe, Germany, 1982-83; chmn. sci. adv. bd. Ctr. Global Change, College Park, 1989-93; cons. USDA, EPA, Nat. Acad. Sci., Washington, 1982—. Contbr. chpts. to 12 books and 80 articles to profl. jours. Grantee NSF, 1977, 1996, U.S. EPA, 1980-90, USDA, 1989-93. Mem. Am. Soc. Plant Physiologists, Botanical Soc. Am., Ecol. Soc. Am., Sigma Xi. Office: U Hawaii Office Dean Coll Natural Scis 102 Bilger Honolulu HI 96822

TERENCE, FRANK, financial executive; b. Panama, Mar. 9, 1959. BS in Fin., Internat. Bus., Spanish Lit., Fla. State U., 1981; M in Internat. Bus., U. S.C., 1983. Cert. mgmt. acct. Planning analyst, pricing analyst, mktg. planning analyst NCR Corp., Dayton, Ohio, 1983-86; capital investment analyst, info. system ctr. Rockwell Internat., Seal Beach, Calif., 1986-88; sr. ops. systems analyst to acctg. supr. franchise acctg. Taco Bell divsn. PepsiCo, Inc., Irvine, Calif., 1988-90; mgr. fin., contr. Ashton-Tate, Torrance, Calif., 1990-91; contr. Borland Internat., Scotts Valley, Calif., 1991-94; gen. mgr. Latin Am. Borland Internat., 1994; dir. internat. fin. Ingram Micro Inc., Santa Ana, Calif., 1994—. Mem. Inst. Mgmt. Accts. Office: Ingram Micro Inc 1600 E Saint Andrew Pl Santa Ana CA 92705-4931

TERESI, JOSEPH, publishing executive; b. Mpls., Mar. 13, 1941; s. Cliff I.A. and Helen Ione (Leslie) T.; divorced; 1 child, Nicholas. Chief exec. officer Jammer Cycle Products Inc., Burbank, Calif., 1968-80, Paisano Pubs. Inc., Agoura Hills, Calif., 1970—. Pub. (mags.) Easyriders, 1971—, In the Wind, 1974—, Biker Lifestyle, 1986—, Tatto, 1986—, Am. Rodder, 1987, Womens Enterprise, 1987-89, Eagles Eye, 1989—, Tattoo Flash, 1993—, Tattoo Savage, 1993—, VQ, 1994—, Early-Riders, 1994-96, Quick Throttle, 1995—, Roadware, 1995—. Office: Paisano Pubs Inc PO Box 3000 Agoura Hills CA 91376-3000

TERMINELLA, LUIGI, critical care physician, educator; b. Catania, Italy, Nov. 15, 1960; came to U.S., 1961; s. Roberto and Josephine (Bartolotta) T. MD summa cum laude, U. Catania, 1986. Pathology asst. Brotman Med. Ctr., Culver City, Calif., 1987-89; transitional resident Miriam Hosp./Brown U., Providence, 1989-90; resident in internal medicine U. Hawaii, Honolulu, 1990-92; tng. in critical care/internal medicine U. Hawaii/Queen's Med. Ctr., Honolulu, 1992-93; transfusion svc. physician Blood Bank of Hawaii, Honolulu, 1992-93; internal medicine physician Hawaii Physician Svcs., Honolulu, 1993—; critical care physician Queen's Med. Ctr., Honolulu, 1993—; mem. clin. faculty John H. Burns Sch. Medicine, U. Hawaii, Honolulu, 1994—; pres. Pualani Family Health, SRL, Corp., Honolulu. Recipient Clementi award U. Catania, 1986, others. Mem. ACP, AMA, Am. Soc. Internal Medicine, Hawaiian Soc. Critical Care, Soc. Critical Care Medicine. Office: Queen's Med Ctr 1301 Punchbowl QET 4B Honolulu HI 96813

TERMINI, OLGA ASCHER, music educator; b. Hamburg, Germany, May 19, 1930; came to U.S., 1952; d. Viktor and Martha M. (Schuett) Ascher; married, Nov. 20, 1955 (dec. July 1979). MusB, U. So. Calif., 1954, MusM, 1957, PhD, 1970. Instr. music Stevenson Jr. H.S., L.A., 1954-57, Fairfax H.S., L.A., 1957-72; asst. prof. music Calif. State U., L.A., 1972-76, assoc.prof. music, 1976-81, prof. music, 1981-96, part-time prof. music, 1996—; instr. voice classes L.A. City Coll., 1957-64; instr. music history and theory Pasadena (Calif.) City Coll., 1973-76; vis. prof. musicology Claremont (Calif.) Grad. Sch., 1986, 95, 97. Contbr. articles to music revs. and profl. publs.; translator various German-English articles for profl. jours. Mem. edit. bd. Jour. of the Arnold Schoenberg Inst., 1974-81; bd. dirs. Glendale (Calif.) Chamber Orch., 1985-89, CSULA Friends of Music; vp. bd. dirs. Pacific Contemporary Music Ctr., 1987-96, newsletter editor, 1988-96, pres., 1997; substitute soloist 1st Ch. Christian Scientist, Alhambra, Calif., 1990—. Music scholar Ebell Club, 1953-54, Fulbright grantee, Venice, Italy, 1966-67, Calif. State U. Instnl. grantee, 1974-75, 75-76. Mem. NEA, Am. Musicol. Soc. (Pacific S.W. chpt. sec. 1981-83, v.p. 1984-86, pres. 1986-88, elective counselor 1990-92), Coll. Music Soc. (life), Calif. Music Tchrs. Assn., Am. Handel Soc. (bd. dirs.), Music Tchrs. Assn. Calif. (Pasadena br.), Phi Beta Delta, Phi Kappa Phi (bd. dirs. CSULA chpt.), Phi Kappa Lambda. Democrat. Home: 4278 Sea View Ln Los Angeles CA 90065-3350 Office: Calif State U dept Music 5151 State University Dr Los Angeles CA 90032-4221

TERRELL, A. JOHN, university telecommunications director; b. Pasadena, Calif., Dec. 27, 1927; s. Harry Evans and Elizabeth (Eaton) T.; m. Elizabeth Schalk, June 6, 1949; children—Patricia Elyse, Marilee Diane, John Scott. Student, Chaffey Coll., 1947-48; B.B.A., U. N. Mex., 1952. Communications cons. Mountain States Tel. & Tel., Albuquerque, 1951-56; mgr. office and communications services A.C.F. Industries, Inc., Albuquerque, 1956-62; mgr. communications and services Norton Simon Industries, Inc., Fullerton, Ca., 1962-68; v.p. gen. mgr. Wells Fargo Security Guard Service Div. Baker Industries, Fullerton, Ca., 1968-71; adminstrv. mgr., budget adminstr. Hyland div. Baxter-Trevenol Labs. Inc., Costa Mesa, CA, 1971-77; exec. v.p. Am. Tel. Mgmt. Inst Inc., Newport Beach, Calif., 1977-78; telecommunications dir. UCLA, 1978-89, retired, 1989. Contbr. articles to profl. jours. Republican. candidate for state rep., Albuquerque, 1960; precinct chmn. and mem. Bernalillo County Rep. Central Com., 1961-62; Rep. candidate for N. Mex. State Bd. Edn., 2nd Jud. Dist., 1962; colonial aide-de-camp Gov. N. Mex., Santa Fe, 1968. Served with U.S. Mcht. Marine, 1944-45, U.S. Army, 1946-47, USAR, 1947-50. Mem. Nat. Assn. Accts. (dir. 1967-77) (Most Valuable mem. 1974-75), Telecommunications Assn., Am. Legion, VFW. Episcopalian. Lodges: Greater Irvine Lions (charter pres. 1975-76), Albuquerque Jaycees (v.p., treas. 1956-62). Home: 2727 Island View Dr Corona Del Mar CA 92625-1309

TERRELL, HOWARD BRUCE, psychiatrist; b. Cleveland, Calif., Feb. 19, 1952. BS magna cum laude, Calif. State U., Hayward, 1974; MD, U. Calif., San Diego, 1980. Diplomate Am. Bd. psychiatry and Neurology, Am. Bd. Forensic Examiners. Intern. Kaiser Found. Hosp., Oakland, Calif., 1980-81; resident in psychiatry U. Calif., San Francisco/Fresno, 1982-85; staff psychiatrist Kings View Corp., Reedley, Calif., 1985-87, sr. staff psychiatrist, 1987-88, dir. outpatient psychiatry, 1988-89; dir. dual diagnosis and affective disorders programs Sierra Gateway Hosp., Clovis, Calif., 1989-91. Contbr. articles to profl. jours. Fellow Am. Coll. Forensic Psychiatry; mem. Am. Acad. Psychiatry and the Law, Am. Psychiat. Assn., Ctrl. Calif. Psychiat. Soc. (pres. Sierra chpt. Office: 3100 Willow Ave Ste 102 Clovis CA 93612-4741

TERRILL, KAREN STAPLETON, retired medical planning consultant; b. Milw., Mar. 21, 1939; d. Thomas John and Olive Patrea (Thorbjornsen) Stapleton; m. Max Kurt Winkler, Dec. 18, 1965 (dec. June 1976); m. Richard Terrill, Jan. 23, 1991 (dec. May 1991). BS in Nursing, U. Mich., 1961; MBA, U. Nev., 1974. RN, Calif. Project nurse Langley Porter N.P.I., San Francisco, 1962-64; asst. dir. nursing Milw. County Mental Health Ctr., 1964-66; instr. Fond du Lac (Wis.) Sch. Dist., 1966-67; sch. nurse Inglewood (Calif.) Sch. Dist., 1968-69; instr. nursing U. Nev., Reno, 1969-74; health planner manpower State of Nev. Comp B. Agy., Carson City, 1974-75; planning analyst St. Mary's Hosp., Reno, 1974-76; sr. system analyst U. Calif., San Francisco, 1976-79; med. planning cons. Stone Marraccini & Patterson, San Francisco, 1979-93. Mem. citizen's adv. group City of Richmond, Calif., 1987-88; founding dir. of B.O.A.T. non-profit corp. to promote ferry transit on San Francisco Bay. Mountain State Regional Planning Commn. grantee, 1973-74. Home: 1308 Mallard Dr Richmond CA 94801-4113

TERRILL, W(ALLACE) ANDREW, international security analyst; b. Pasadena, Calif., Aug. 15, 1954; s. Wallace and Gloria (Acheson) T. BA in Polit. Sci., Calif. State Poly. U., 1975; MA in Polit. Sci., U. Calif., Riverside, 1976; PhD in Internat. Rels., The Claremont Grad. Sch., 1983. Rsch. asst. Analytical Assessments Corp., L.A., 1978-80, rsch. assoc., 1980-87; part-time instr. Calif. State Poly. U., Pomona, 1987-89; asst. prof. polit. sci. Old Dominion U., Norfolk, Va., 1989-93; sr. internat. security analyst Lawrence Livermore Nat. Lab., Livermore, Calif., 1993—; cons. Sys. Rsch. and Devel. Corp., L.A., 1987-89; adj. asst. prof. Occidental Coll., L.A., 1988-89; workshop leader; interviewed on TV, radio and in print media on Mid. Eastern and nonproliferation issues. Contbr. numerous book revs. and articles to acad. jours. Served with USAR, 1976—, lt. col., 1997. Decorated Meritorious Svc. medal; recipient Haynes Found. dissertation fellowship, 2 Claremont Grad. Sch. full-tuition fellowships.

TERRIS, DAVID JAMES, head and neck surgeon, research scientist; b. Rome, N.Y., May 12, 1962; s. Frederick Morton and Elaine Marie (Crimmins) T.; m. Martha Bernice Kennedy, Dec. 28, 1987; children: Trevor, Garrett. BA, Cornell U., 1984; MD, Duke U., 1988. Diplomate Am. Bd. Otolaryngology. Intern in surgery Stanford (Calif.) U. Med. Ctr., 1988-89, resident in surgery, 1989-93, fellow in head and neck oncologic surgery, 1993-94, asst. prof. surgery, 1994—. Author: (with others) Manual of Surgical Procedures, 1994; contbr. articles to profl. jours. Mem. AMA, Am. Acad. Otolaryngology, Am. Assn. Facial Plastic and Reconstructive Surgery, Phi Beta Kappa, Alpha Omega Alpha. Republican. Home: 1000 Border Rd Los Altos CA 94024-4724 Office: Stanford U Med Ctr R-135 Edwards Bldg Stanford CA 94305-5328

TERRY, FRANK JEFFREY, bishop. Bishop Diocese of Spokane, Wash., 1991—. Office: Episcopal Diocese of Spokane 245 E 13th Ave Spokane WA 99202-1114*

TERRY, MARTIN MICHAEL, visual artist, art therapist; b. Poughkeepsie, N.Y., Dec. 17, 1952; s. Gustave Paul Thury and Philomena (Casale) Terry; m. Loretta Mary Bunten, Oct. 6, 1990. AS, Dutchess C.C., 1972; attended, SUNY, New Paltz, 1973-90, U. N.Mex., 1991-96. Engraver's asst. Dell Pub. Co., Poughkeepsie, 1972-75; therapy aide Hudson River Psychiatric Ctr., Poughkeepsie, 1975-80; art therapist N.Y. State Dept. Corrections, Stormville, 1980-85; program dir. Dutchess Horizons, Poughkeepsie, 1980-91; artist-in-residence Albuquerque Pub. Schs., 1991-96. Mem. Cmty. Cultural Planning Com., Albuquerque, 1991-93. Mem. N.Mex. Art League (bd. pres. 1993-95, exhibit com. 1991-93, Best in Show award 1995), Albuquerque United Artists. Home and Studio: 2281 Wilbur Rd SW Albuquerque NM 87101

TERRY, PATRICIA A., literature educator; b. Hartford, Conn., Feb. 13, 1929; d. William Samuel and Sarah Harriet (Press) Blech; m. Robert Davis Terry, June 27, 1952; 1 child, Nicolas S. Terry. BA, Wellesley U., 1950; PhD, Columbia U., 1958. adj. prof. French Lit., Barnard Coll., N.Y.C., 1958-84, U. Calif. San Diego, La Jolla, Calif., 1984-91. Translator: (books) Poems of Jules LaForgue, 1958, reprinted 1986, Lays of Courtly Love, 1965, The Song of Roland, 1969, 2d edit. 1992, Modern European Poetry, 1966, Poems of the Vikings, 1969, 2d edit., 1992, Modern French Poetry, 1981, Roof Slates and Other Poems of Pierre reverdy (with Mary Ann Caws), 1981, The Romance of Renard, 1983, reprinted 1992, Pierre Reverdy, Selected Poems, 1991, The Romance of the Rose or Guillaume de Dole, 1993, others. Grantee Nat. Endowment for the Humanities, 1982. Home: 14868 High Valley Rd Poway CA 92064-2714

TERRY, RICHARD FRANK, data transcriber; b. Ogden, Utah, July 19, 1949; s. Frank Nebeker and Gertrude Angeline (Berghout) T. BA, Weber State Coll., 1979. Data transcriber IRS, Marriott, Utah, 1976—. Mem. Ch. of Jesus Christ of Latter Day Saints.

TERRY, STEVEN SPENCER, mathematics educator, consultant; b. Hoodriver, Oreg., July 9, 1942; s. Steven Bliss and Kathryn (Spencer) T.; m. Vivian Hickman, Aug. 20, 1964; children: Yvette, Kathryn, S. Matthew, Spencer, Stuart, Heather. BS, Utah State U., 1964, MS, 1967. Tchr. math Clayton Jr. High, Salt Lake City, 1964-67, 29 Palms (Calif.) High Sch., 1967-68; tchr. math, coach Yucca Valley (Calif.) High Sch., 1968-76; prof. math. Ricks Coll., Rexburg, Idaho, 1976—; chmn. dept. Author: (textbook) Elementary Teachers' Math, 1985. Pres. Yucca Valley City Coun., 1972-76, mem. water bd., fire and streets bd., lighting bd., recreation bd.; judge Young Woman of Yr. contests, Idaho; officer Madison County (Idaho) Baseball Assn.; mem. Rexburg Airport Bd. Recipient Outstanding Tchrs. award San Bernardino and Riverside Counties, Calif., 1976, Outstanding Secondary Educator, 1974, 75. Mem. Am. Math. Assn. Two-Yr. Colls. (v.p. 1980-86, dir. Summer Inst., Outstanding Contbn. award 1982, 94, 96, co-chair Summer Inst. at Ricks Coll., co-chair 1988 conv.), Nat. Coun. Tchrs. Math., NEA (life), Phi Delta Kappa (life, sec. 1974-76, Outstanding Contbn. award 1984). Republican. Mormon. Home: 221 S 2nd E # D Rexburg ID 83440-2202 Office: Ricks Coll Rexburg ID 83460-0515

TERZ, JOSE JUAN, physician, surgical educator; b. Buenos Aires, Apr. 18, 1929; came to U.S., 1954; s. Barbar and Eva (Alem) T.; m. Rosa Basilia Tomsich, Apr. 7, 1954; children: Roxanna, Joseph, David. BA, Sarmiento Coll., 1946; MD, U. Buenos Aires, 1952. Diplomate Am. Bd. Surgery. Intern Lincoln Hosp., 1954-55, resident in surgery, 1955-56; resident in surgery Mt. Sinai Hosp., 1956-59, Meml. Hosp. for Cancer and Allied Diseases and James Ewing Hosp., 1959-62; rsch. fellow Sloan-Kettering Inst. for Cancer Rsch., 1964-66; dir. dept. gen. and oncologic surgery City of Hope Med. Ctr., Duarte, Calif., 1980-91, chmn. div. surgery, 1988-91; prof. clin. surgery U. So. Calif., L.A., 1993—; mem. cancer clin. investigation review com. Nat. Cancer Inst., 1988-91; mem. Pacificare of Calif. Tech. Assessment Com., 1992-93; cons. Santa Teresita Hosp., Duarte, Calif., 1991-93, Meth. Hosp., Arcadia, Calif., 1991-93, Inter-Community Med. Ctr., Covina, Calif., 1991-93, Pomona (Calif.) Valley Hosp. Med. Ctr., 1991—, Queen of the Valley Hosp., West Covina, Calif., 1991—, Hosp. of Good Samaritan, L.A., 1991—, Kenneth Norris Jr. Cancer Hosp., L.A., 1993—, U. So. Calif. Univ. Hosp., L.A., 1993—, LAC/USC Med. Ctr., L.A., 1993—. Author, contbr. numerous chpts. and books; reviewer editl. bd. Jour. Surg. Oncology, 1989—, Cancer, 1992—; contbr. over 100 articles to profl. jours. Mem. AAAS, AMA, Am. Assn. for Cancer Rsch., Am. Coll. Surgeons, Am. Soc. Clin. Oncology, Internat. Soc. Surgery, Pacific Coast Surg. Assn., Soc. for Surgery of Alimentary Tract, Soc. Head and Neck Surgeons, Soc. Surg. Oncology, L.A. Surg. Soc., So. Calif. Acad. Clin. Oncology. Home: 700 S Lake Ave Apt 206 Pasadena CA 91106-3943 Office: Univ So Calif Med Ctr 1441 Eastlake Ste 7418 Los Angeles CA 90033

TERZIAN, SHOHIG GARINE SHERRY, mental health facility administrator; d. Ebraxe Momjian and Ardashes Garabed T. AB in Engl. Literature cum laude, Radcliffe Coll., 1937; MS in Libr. and Info. Sci., Columbia Univ., 1942, postgrad.; postgrad., UCLA, Univ. Wis., 1940-65. First libr. neurol. inst. Columbia Presbyn. Med. Ctr., N.Y.C., 1940-41; reference asst. Vassar Coll. Libr., Poughkeepsie, N.Y., 1942-43; picture editor, rsch. asst. U.S. Office War Info., N.Y.C., 1943-46; rsch. libr. Time, Inc., N.Y.C., 1947-48; libr. Prudential Ins. Co. Western Home Office, L.A., 1948-61; mem. faculty dept. psychiatry & biobehavioral scis. UCLA Med. Sch., 1961-86; dir. mental health info. svc. UCLA Neuropsychiatric Inst., 1986; rsch. cons., 1987—; picture editor, rsch. asst. U.S. War Dept. Civil Defense, U.S. Dept. of State, Office Internat. Info. and Cultural Affairs, N.Y.C., 1943-46. Bibliographer; contbr. Bertrand Russell Soc. Quarterly, Santayana Soc. Bulletin, Ararat Quarterly. Mem. Armenian Gen. Benevolent Union, UCLA Emeriti, UCLA Faculty Ctr., Spl. Libr. Assn. Washington, Saroyan Soc., Santayana Soc., Calif. Libr. Soc., Statue of Liberty Found. Armenian Orthodox. Home: 11740 Wilshire Blvd # A1602 Los Angeles CA 90025

TESH, JOHN, television talk show host; b. Garden City, N.Y., 1953; s. John and Mildred Tesh; m. Connie Sellecca, Apr. 4, 1992; children: Gib, Prima. Co-host Entertainment Tonight, 1986—; host One-On-One with John Tesh, 1991; co-host John and Leeza from Hollywood, 1993. Television appearances include: The U.S. Open Tennis Championship, 1985, Macy's Thanksgiving Day Parade, 1987, Wimbledon, 1991; film appearances include Shocker, 1989, Soapdish, 1991; albums include Tour de France, 1988, The Early Years, 1990, Ironman, 1992, The Games, 1992, Monterey Nights, 1993, A Romantic Christmas, 1993, Wintersong, Sax by the Fire, Sax on the Beach, John Tesh Live at Red Rocks, Discovery, Avalon; composers theme music Bobby's World, 1990, The Knife and Gun Club, 1990, One on One, 1991, NFL Live. Recipient 4 Emmy awards for composing, 2 Emmy awards for reporting. Office: care GTSP Records PO Box 6010-721 Sherman Oaks CA 91413*

TESS, ROY WILLIAM HENRY, chemist; b. Chgo., Apr. 25, 1915; s. Reinhold W. and Augusta (Detl) T.; m. Marjorie Kohler, Feb. 19, 1944; children: Roxanne, Steven. BS in Chemistry, U. Ill., 1939; PhD, U. Minn., 1944. Rsch. chemist, group leader Shell Devel. Co., Emeryville, Calif., 1944—, rsch. supr., 1959-61, 63-66; rsch. supr. Royal Dutch/Shell Plastics Lab., Delft, The Netherlands, 1962-63; tech. planning supr. Shell Chem. Co., N.Y.C., 1967-70; tech. mgr. solvents Shell Chem. Co., Houston, 1970-77, cons., 1977-79; ind. cons. Fallbrook, Calif., 1979—; pres. Paint Rsch. Inst., Phila., 1973-76. Editor, organizer: Solvents Theory and Practice, 1973; (with others) Applied Polymer Science, 1975, Applied Polymer Science, 2d edit., 1985. Pres. Assn. Indsl. Scientists, Berkeley, Calif., 1948-50, Minerinda Property Owners Assn., Orinda, Calif., 1965-67, Houston Camellia Soc., 1973-74. Fellow Am. Inst. Chemists; mem. Nat. Paint and Coatings Assn. (air quality com. 1967-79), Fedn. Socs. Coatings Tech. (bd. dirs. 1973-76, Roon award 1957, Heckel award 1978), Am. Chem. Soc. (divsn. polymeric materials chmn. 1978, established Roy W. Tess award in Coatings 1985, exec. com. 1977—, Disting. Svc. award 1993), Sigma Xi, Alpha Chi Sigma, Phi Kappa Phi, Phi Lambda Upsilon. Home and Office: 1615 Chandelle Ln Fallbrook CA 92028-1707

TESTA, STEPHEN MICHAEL, geologist, consultant; b. Fitchburg, Mass., July 17, 1951; s. Guiseppe Alfredo and Angelina Mary (Pettito) T.; m. Lydia Mae Payne, July 26, 1986; 1 child, Brant Ethan Gage. AA, Los Angeles Valley Jr. Coll., Van Nuys, 1971; BS in Geology, Calif. State U., Northridge, 1976, MS in Geology, 1978. Registered geologist, Calif., Oreg.; cert. profl. geol. scientist., Idaho, Alaska; cert. engring. geologist, Calif.; registered environ. assessor, Calif. Engring. geologist R.T. Frankian & Assocs., Burbank, Calif., 1976-78, Bechtel, Norwalk, Calif., 1978-80, Converse Cons., Seattle, 1980-82; sr. hydrogeologist Ecology Environment, Seattle, 1982-83; sr. geologist Dames & Moore, Seattle, 1983-86; v.p. Engring. Enterprises, Long Beach, Calif., 1986-89; CEO Applied Environ. Svcs., San Juan Capistrano, Calif., 1990-94; pres. Testa Environ. Corp., Foothill Ranch, Calif., 1994—. Author: Restoration of Petroleum Contaminated Aquifers, 1990, Principles of Technical Consulting and Project Management, 1991, Geological Aspects of Hazardous Waste Management, 1994, Reuse and Recycling of Contaminated Soil, 1997; editor Geologic Field Guide to the Salton Basin, 1988, Environmental Concerns in the Petroleum Industry, 1989; contbr. more than 60 articles to profl. jours., a preface and chpts. to books. Mem. AAAS, Am. Inst. Profl. Geologists (mem. profl. devel. com. 1986, mem. continuing edn. com. program chmn., 1988—, mem. nat. screening bd. 1992-94, chmn. 1995—, exec. bd. del. 1993, nat. v.p. 1994, trustee 1995—, pres.-elect 1997, presdl. Cert. of Merit 1987, 94), L.A. Basin Geol. Soc. (pres. 1991-92), Geol. Soc. Am., Am. Assn. Petroleum Geologists (Pacific sect. environ. com., co-chmn. 1993—, chmn. liaison com. divsn. environ. geoscis. 1997, cert. of merit 1997), Am. Mineral. Soc., South Coast Geol. Soc., Assn. Ground Water Scientists and Engrs., Assn. Engring. Geologists, Assn. Mil. Engrs., Environ. Assessment Assn., Mineral Soc. Can., Hazardous Materials Rsch. Inst., Calif. Water Pollution Control Assn., Sigma Xi. Roman Catholic. Home: 19814 Jesus Maria Rd Mokelumne Hill CA 95245 Office: Testa Environ Corp Ste 1E-446 27641 Portola Pky Foothill Ranch CA 92610-1743

TETELBAUM, SOLOMON DAVID, research engineer; b. Odessa, Ukraine, June 10, 1936; came to U.S., 1989; s. David Mossey and Dvoyra Peysach Tetelbaum; m. Shushana Barer, Dec. 29, 1962; children: Dina, Vladimir. MS in Mech. Engring., Polytechnic Inst., Odessa, 1958; PhD in Mech. Engring., Tech. Inst., Odessa, 1968. Cert. sr. scientist, USSR. Chief sci. rsch. dept., assoc. prof. Polytechnic Inst., Odessa, 1971-89; cons. Electric Power Rsch. Inst., Palo Alto, Calif., 1991-93; prin. engr. GE Co., San Jose, Calif., 1992-93; dir. engring. Ideation Internat., Santa Monica, Calif., 1995; rsch. engring. mgr. environ. svcs. dept. City of San Jose, 1995—; bd. dirs. Sci. Tech. Soc. USSR. Author: (with others) Gases as Working Fluids of the Power Nuclear Installations, 1978, Thermodynamic Cycles and Schematics of High Temperature Gas Cooled Reactors, 1983, Simulation and Substance—Field Analysis of the Inventive Problems, 1984; contbr. numerous articles to profl. jours.; inventor in field. Recipient award All-Union Sci. Tech. Soc., 1981, prize Shipboard Com., 1975. Mem. ASME.

TETERS, CHARLENE (JOUN), editor; b. Spokane, Wash., Apr. 25, 1952; d. George G. and Evelyn Agnes (Campbell) T.; children: George H. Raymond, Kristal Lea Raymond. A Fine Arts, Inst. Am. Indian Arts, 1986; BFA, Coll. of Santa Fe, 1988; MFA, U. Ill., 1991. Mem staff racial justice office Nat. Congress Am. Indians, Washington, 1991; dir. placement and alumni Inst. Am. Indian Arts, Santa Fe, N.Mex., 1992-95; sr. editor Indian Artist Mag., Santa Fe, 1995—. Art represented in permanent collections. Mem. founding bd. Nat. Coalition of Racism in Sports and Media, Indpla., 1992; mem. fine arts com., bd. dirs. N.Mex. Mus. Fine Arts, 1994. Recipient W. Ellison Chalmers award ACLU, Champaign, Ill., 1991, Racial Justice award YWCA, Champaign, 1991. Home: Rt 19 Box 112 DM Santa Fe NM 87505

TETHER, ANTHONY JOHN, aerospace executive; b. Middletown, N.Y., Nov. 28, 1941; s. John Arthur and Antoinette Rose (Gesualdo) T.; m. Nancy Engle Pierson, Dec. 27, 1963 (div. July 1971); 1 child, Jennifer; m. Carol Suzanne Dunbar, Mar. 3, 1973; 1 child, Michael. AAS, Orange County C.C., N.Y., 1961; BS, Rensselaer Poly Inst., 1963; MSEE, Stanford (Calif.) U., 1965, PhD, 1969. V.p., gen. mgr. Sys. Control Inc., Palo Alto, Calif., 1968-78; dir. nat. intelligence Office Sec. of Def., Washington, 1978-82; dir. strategic tech. DARPA, Washington, 1982-86; corp. v.p. Ford Aerospace, Newport Beach, Calif., 1986-90, LORAL, Newport Beach, 1990-92; corp. v.p., gen. mgr. Sci. Application Internat., Inc., San Diego, 1992-94; CEO Dynamics Tech. Inc., Torrance, Calif., 1994-96; CEO, pres. Sequoia Group, Newport Beach, Calif., 1996—; chmn., bd. dirs. Condyne Tech., Inc., Orlando, Fla., 1990-92; dir. Orincon, La Jolla, Calif. Contbr. articles to profl. jours. Recipient Nat. Intelligence medal DCI, 1986, Civilian Meritorious medal U.S. Sec. Def., 1986. Mem. IEEE, Cosmos Club, Sigma Xi, Eta Kappa Nu, Tau Beta Pi. Home: 4518 Roxbury Rd Corona Del Mar CA 92625-3125

TETLOW, WILLIAM LLOYD, computer consultant; b. Phila., July 2, 1938; s. William Lloyd and Mary Eleanor (Ferris) T.; m. Amber Jane Riederer, June 13, 1964; children: Jennifer Kay, Rebecca Dawn, Derek William. Student, Cornell U., 1956-60; B in Gen. Edn., U. Omaha, 1961; MA, Cornell U., 1965, PhD, 1973. Dir. instl. research Cornell U., Ithaca, N.Y., 1965-70; dir. planning U. B.C., Vancouver, Can., 1970-82; dir. NCHEMS Mgmt. Products, Boulder, Colo., 1982-85; pres., dir. Vantage Info. Products, Inc., Boulder, 1985-87; pres., propr. Vantage Computer Svcs., Boulder, 1986—; computer cons. U. Colo., 1986—; cons. various univs. U.S., Can. and Australia, 1970—. Editor/author: Using Microcomputers for Planning and Decision Support, 1984; contbr. numerous articles to profl. jours. Mem. Mt. Calvary Luth. Ch. Coun., 1985-86, 89—, pres., 1991-92. Served to 1st lt. AUS, 1961-63. Recipient U. Colo. medal, 1987; Kiwanis Hixon fellow, 1996, Kiwanis Lusche fellow, 1996. Mem. Assn. Inst. Rsch. (sec. 1973-75, v.p. 1980-81, pres. 1981-82), Concordia, Kiwanis (pres. 1996—). Home: 312 Diamond Circle Louisville CO 80027-3202

TETREAULT, MARK DAVID, nuclear engineer and financial planner; b. Torrington, Conn., June 12, 1959; s. David Ronald and Audrey Bernice (Mierzwa) T.; m. Linda Jean Tetreault, July 11, 1981. BS, New Sch. for Social Rsch., 1985. Lic. gen. securities rep., Hawaii; lic. ins. solicitor, Hawaii. Nuc. engr. Pearl Harbor (Hawaii) Naval Shipyard, 1988—; fin. planner E.A. Buck Co., Honolulu, 1993—; stock trader, 1983—. With USN, 1980-88. Mem. Am. Legion, Nat. Assn. Securities Dealers (registered rep.), Mus. of Natural History. Home: 1296 Kahili St Kailua HI 96734-4058

TETTEGAH, SHARON YVONNE, education educator; b. Wichita Falls, Tex., Jan. 14, 1956; d. Lawrence Guice and Doris Jean (Leak) Oliver; 1 child, Tandra Ainsworth; m. Joseph Miller Zangai, Dec. 22, 1978 (div. 1983); 1 child, Tonia Monjay Zangai; m. George Tettegah, Apr. 28, 1989; children: Nicole Jennifer, Michael Scott. AA, Coll. Alameda, 1985; BA, U. Calif., Davis, 1988, teaching cert., 1989, MA, 1991; PhD in Ednl. Psychology, U. Calif., Santa Barbara, 1997. Cert. elem. tchr., Calif. Clk. II Alameda County Mcpl. Ct., Oakland, Calif., 1976-77; acct. clk. Alameda County Social Svcs., Oakland, 1977-78, eligibility technician, 1978-82; supervising clk. Alameda County Health Care Svcs., Oakland, 1982-84; tchr. Davis (Calif.) Joint Unified Sch. Dist., 1988-89, L.A. Unified Schs., L.A., 1990-92; tchr. Oakland Unified Sch. Dist., Oakland, 1992—, tchr. sci. mentor, 1993—; teaching asst. U. Calif., Santa Barbara, 1993-94; adminstrv. intern Oxnard Unified Sch. Dist., 1994, U. Calif. Cultural Awareness Program, Santa Barbara, 1994—; rsch. cons. to vice chancellor students affairs, cons. tchr. edn. program, facilitor registrar's office U. Calif., Santa Barbara, 1995-96, rsch. asst. Grad. Sch. Edn., 1996—; cons. U. Calif. , Davis, 1988-89, Montessori Ctr. Sch., Santa Barbara, Calif., 1996; multicultural cons. Davis Unified Sch. Dist., 1988-89; edn. cons. Ednl. Testing Svc., Emeryville, Calif., 1994; chair diversity com. of Santa Barbara Village Charter Sch.; mem. academic senate com. undergrad enrollment and admissions U. Calif. Santa Barbara, 1995, tchr. cross-cultural interactions course, summer, 1995; mem. academic affairs affirmative action com. U. Calif. Santa Barbara, 1995-96, grad. sch. of edn., grad. affairs and affirmative action comms. U. Calif. Santa Barbara, 1995-96. Contbr. articles to profl. jours. Mem. U. Calif. Santa Barbara Acad. Senate Bd. Undergraduate Admissions and Records; co-chair Diversity Com. Montecito-Santa Barbara Charter Sch.; pres. African-Am. Grad. and Profl. Students Orgn., Davis, 1988-89. Recipient Charlene Richardson Acad. Honors award Coll. Alameda, 1985; Calif. State Acad. fellow, 1989-91, Grad. Opportunity Acad. Excellence fellow, 1994-95, Vice Chancellors Acad. Achievement fellowship U. Calif. Santa Barbara, 1995-96, Vice Chancellors Acad. Fellowship Grad. Divsn., 1995-96, 96-97. Mem. Am. Ednl. Researchers Assn., Calif. Sci. Tchrs. Assn., Calif. Advocacy for Math and Sci., Calif. Tchrs. Assn., Calif. Media Libr. Educators Assn., PTA, Multicultural Curriculum Assn., Supervision and Curriculum Leadership Assn., Bay Area Sci. and Tech. Educators Corsortium, Pan-African Students Assn., Kappa Delta Pi. Home: PO Box 1782 Santa Barbara CA 93116-1782 Office: U Calif Santa Barbara Sch Edn/Ednl Psychology Santa Barbara CA 93106

TEVIS, BARRY LEE, television producer, marketing executive; b. Pasadena, Calif., Feb. 5, 1956; s. John Larry Tevis and Renee Lydia Clement; m. Julie Marie Knauss, Mar. 31, 1990; children: Ben, Ann Marie, Hilary, Andrew. Student, Bates Vocat. Tech. Inst., Tacoma, 1973-75. Master control operator KTBN-TV, Santa Ana, Calif., 1975-76; producer, dir. KOTI-TV, Klamath Falls, Oreg., 1976-77, KPAZ-TV, Phoenix, Ariz., 1977-78; prodn. mgr., dir. advt. and promotion KTVL-TV, Medford, Oreg., 1978—. Sound dir. Rogue Valley Fellowship Ch., Medford. Recipient various broadcast awards. Mem. Promax Internat. (award of merit 1990). Republican. Office: KTVL-TV 1440 Rossanley Dr Medford OR 97501-1751

TEVRIZIAN, DICKRAN M., JR., federal judge; b. Los Angeles, Aug. 4, 1940; s. Dickran and Rose Tevrizian; m. Geraldine Tevrizian, Aug. 22, 1964; children: Allyson Tracy, Leslie Sara. BS, U. So. Calif., 1962, JD, 1965. Tax acct. Arthur Andersen and Co., Los Angeles, 1965-66; atty., ptnr. Kirtland and Packard, Los Angeles, 1966-72; judge Los Angeles Mcpl. Ct., Los Angeles, 1972-78, State of Calif. Superior Ct., Los Angeles, 1978-82; ptnr. Manatt, Phelps, Rothenberg & Tunney, Los Angeles, 1982-85, Lewis, D'Amato, Brisbois & Bisgaard, Los Angeles, 1985-86; judge U.S. Dist. Ct., Los Angeles, 1986—. Named Trial Judge of the Yr., Calif. Trial Lawyers Assn., 1987, L.A. County Bar Assn., 1994-95. Mem. Calif. Trial Lawyer's Assn. (trial judge of yr. 1987), L.A. County Bar Assn. (trial judge of yr. 1994-95). Office: US Dist Ct Royal Federal Bldg 255 E Temple St Los Angeles CA 90012-3334

TEXTOR, ROBERT BAYARD, cultural anthropology writer, consultant, educator; b. Cloquet, Minn., Mar. 13, 1923; s. Clinton Kenney and Lillian (Nickles) T.; divorced; children: Alexander Robertson, Marisa Elizabeth. Student, Lafayette Coll., 1940-41, Antioch Coll., 1941-43; B.A. in Asian Studies, U. Mich., 1945; Ph.D. in Cultural Anthropology, Cornell U., 1960. Civil info. and edn. officer Mil. Govt., Kyoto-Wakayama, Japan, 1946-48; rsch. fellow anthropology and S.E. Asia studies Yale U., 1959-60, assoc., 1960-61; rsch. fellow in stats. Harvard U., 1962-64; assoc. prof. edn. and anthropology Stanford U., 1964-68, prof. edn. and anthropology, 1968-86, prof. anthropology, 1986-90, prof. anthropology emeritus, 1990—; vis. prof. U. Saar, Saarbrücken, Germany, 1984-85; cons. Motorola U., 1991—; mem. S.E. Asia Coun., 1974-77; cons. cultural anthropology to govt. agys., 1957-58, 61-62. Author: (most recent) Roster of the Gods: An Ethnography of The Supernatural in a Thai Village, 6 vols., 1973, Austria 2005: Projected Sociocultural Effects of the Microelectronic Revolution, 1983, Anticipatory Anthropology, 1985, (with Sippanondha Ketudat) The Middle Path for the Future of Thailand, 1990; assoc. editor Jour. Conflict Resolution, 1965-70; mem. editorial bd. Human orgn., 1966-71, Jour. Cultural Futures, 1979-87; adv. editor Behavior Sci. Rsch., 1974-86. Bd. dirs. Vols. in Asia, Stanford, Calif., 1968-73; mem. Metro Portland Future Vision Commn., 1993-95; mem. ad hoc organizing com. 2005 Lewis and Clark Bicentennial Commemoration, 1996. Served with U.S. Army, 1943-46. Fellow Rockefeller Found., 1951-52, fgn. area tng. fellow Ford Found., Thailand 1955-58, Carnegie fellow, 1958-59, Fulbright West Europe rsch. fellow, 1984-85, East-West Ctr. fellow, 1988-90; NSF grantee, Thailand, U.S., 1969-73, Volkswagen Found. grantee, Thailand and Germany, 1984. Fellow Am. Anthrop. Assn. (life mem.); mem. Siam Soc. (life mem.), Assn. Asian Studies (life mem.), Council on Anthropology and Edn. (pres. 1974-75), AAUP (pres. Stanford chpt. 1975-76), Phi Kappa Phi.

THACKER, GARY WILLIAM, agricultural extension agent; b. Yuma, Ariz., Sept. 18, 1953; s. William Hubert and Betty (Nelson) T.; m. Linda Speer, Oct. 6, 1979; 1 child, Robert. BS in Agrl. Econ., U. Ariz., 1975, MS in Agronomy, 1979, MBA, 1993. Cotton farmer Thacker Farms, Yuma, 1979-82; mng. ptnr., grower Yuma Farming Co., 1982-85; agrl. ext. agt. U. Ariz., Tucson, 1985-96; pres., CEO Pegasus Machinery Co., Tucson, 1993—; chmn. peer review com. U. Ariz. Coop. Ext., Tucson, 1994. inventor stalk and root embedding apparatus, self-aligning herbicide sprayer. Advisor Pima Natural Resource Conservation Dist., Tucson, 1986-92. Recipient First place award 1992 Bus. Plans Competition, Karl Eller Grad. Sch. Mgmt. Coll. of Bus. and Pub. Adminstrn., U. Ariz. Mem. Soil and Water Conservation Soc. (sec. Ariz. chpt. 1991), Soc. for Range Mgmt., Farm Equipment Mfrs. Assn. Presbyterian. Home: 5255 N Avenida Largo Tucson AZ 85745-9498 Office: Pegasus Machinery Co 5255 N Avenida Largo Tucson AZ 85745-9498

THACKER, NETHA LYNN, editor; b. Sanger, Calif., Aug. 21, 1945; d. Derrel Wilbur and Ruth Marion (Henning) Houdashelt; m. Gerald William Thacker, Nov. 21, 1964; children: Cynthia Anne, Laura Ellen, Deborah Lynn. BA, San Jose State U., 1984. Editor Bus. Woman Mag., San Jose, Calif., 1984-86, CTB/McGraw Hill, Monterey, Calif., 1986-87, The Villager, San Jose, 1987-89, ETR Assocs., Santa Cruz, Calif., 1989-94; cons. editor ETR Assocs., 1994-96; sr. editor Toucan Edn., 1996—; cons. in field, bd. dirs. Future Families. Co-author: Abstinence: Health Facts. Home: 620 Breckinridge Ln Soquel CA 95073-9751

THALL, RICHARD VINCENT, school system administrator; b. San Francisco, Sept. 12, 1940; s. Albert Vincent and Alice Stella (O'Brien) T.; m. Ellyn Marie Wisherop, June 15, 1963; children: Kristen Ellyn, Richard Vincent Jr. AA, City Coll. San Francisco, 1961; BA, San Francisco State Coll., 1964; MA, San Francisco State U., 1971. Cert. elem. tchr., Calif.; cert. secondary tchr., Calif.; cert. community coll. tchr., Calif. Tchr. biology San Francisco Unified Sch. Dist., 1965-66; tchr. biology Mt. Diablo Unified Sch. Dist., Concord, Calif., 1966-79, program dir. water environ. studies program, 1979—; ranger/naturalist State of Calif., Branna Island, 1973-78; naturalist Adventure Internat., Oakland, Calif., 1979-81; lectr. Princess Cruise Lines, 1982-84, Sea Goddess, 1986—, Sun Lines, 1987, Sitmar Lines, 1989, RCCL, 1991-95; spkr. commencements U. Calif., Berkeley, 1989. Author: Ecological Sampling of the Sacramento-San Joaquin Delta, 1976; Water Environment Studies Program, 1986; co-author: Project MER Laboratory Manual, 1982. Mem. Contra Costa County (Calif.) Natural Resources Commn., 1975-78, vice-chmn., 1977-78; active Save Mt. Diablo, Concord, 1969-76, v.p., 1974-75; mem. citizens com. Assn. Bay Area Govt. Water Quality, 1979-82, vice-chmn., 1980-82; active John Marsh Home Restoration Com., Martinez, Calif., 1977-78; mem. edn. adv. com. Marine World/Africa USA, Vallejo, Calif., 1988—; troop com. chmn. Boy Scouts Am., Concord, 1984-86, asst. scoutmaster, 1985-87. Recipient Recognition and Excellence cert. Assn. Calif. Sch. Adminstrs., 1984, Wood Badge award Boy Scouts Am., 1986; grantee State Calif., 1982, 84, San Francisco Estuary Project, 1992, EPA, 1992, Shell Oil Co., 1993. Mem. AAAS, Nat. Assn. Biology Tchrs., Nat., Audubon Soc., Am. Mus. Natural Hist., Nat. Geog. Soc., Smithsonian Instn. (assoc.). Republican. Roman Catholic. Home: 1712 Lindenwood Dr Concord CA 94521-1109 Office: Mt Diablo Unified Sch Dist 1936 Carlotta Dr Concord CA 94519-1358

THAMES, CARROLL THOMAS, financial consultant; b. Webbers Falls, Okla., Sept. 26, 1938; s. Carroll Hilton and Opal (Gillespie) T.; m. Ramona Pepin, Dec. 16, 1961 (div. July 1980); children: Kimberly Ann, Gavin Thomas. BA, Coll. of Notre Dame, Belmont, Calif., 1972; MBA, U. Santa Clara, 1974. CLU, chartered fin. cons.; cert. fin. planner. Chief industr. engr. Kaiser Aluminum Chem. Corp., Oakland, Calif., 1966-83; registered prin. SunAmerica Securities, Inc., Phoenix, 1980—; pres. Capital Mgmt. Network, Inc., Woodbridge, Calif., 1985—; lectr. U. Calif., Santa Cruz, 1986, Golden Gate U., Monterey, Calif., 1984-85, Hartnell Coll., Salinas, Calif., 1986-87. Contbr. fin. planning articles to profl. jours. Bd. dirs. YMCA, Salinas, 1986-87. Mem. Internat. Assn. for Fin. Planning Inc. (pres.-chmn. Monterey Bay chpt. 1985-88), Am. Soc. CLU & Chartered Fin. Consultants (pres. Monterey Bay chpt. 1984-85), Calif. Assn. for Fin. Planning (sec. 1986-87), Inst. Cert. Fin. Planners, Internat. Bd. Cert. Fin. Planners, Alpha Gamma Sigma. Republican. Office: PO Box 1024 Woodbridge CA 95258-1024

THAPA, MUKUND NARAIN-DHAMI, software company executive; b. Bombay, India, Apr. 13, 1954; came to U.S., 1976; s. Narain Singh and Devi (Jhangiani) Thapa; m. Radhika Hegde; 1 child, Ishra Devi. BTech, Indian Inst. of Tech., Bombay, 1976; MS in Ops. Rsch., Stanford (Calif.) U., 1979, PhD in Ops. Rsch., 1981. Sr. analyst Applied Decisions Analysis, Inc., Menlo Park, Calif., 1980-83; pres. Stanford Bus. Software, Inc., Mountain View, Calif., 1984—. Author: (with George B. Dantzig) Linear Programming: Introduction, 1997. Office: Stanford Bus Software Inc 2680 Bayshore Pkwy Ste 304 Mountain View CA 94043

THATCHER, BLYTHE DARLYN, assistant principal; b. Kansas City, Mo., Aug. 15, 1947; d. Aubria DeVille and Irene Lois (Cowan) Thatcher. AA, Ricks Coll., Rexburg, Idaho, 1967; BS, Brigham Young U., 1971, MEd, 1983, EdS, 1985. Cert. elem., spl. edn., adminstr., Utah. Spl. edn. tchr. K-6 J. Allen Axson Sch. #8, Jacksonville, Fla., 1971-72; resource tchr., dept. chair Westland Elem. Sch., Sandy, Utah, 1972-78; resource English tchr. Mt. Jordan Mid. Sch., Sandy, Utah, 1978-80; resource tchr., dept. chair Butler Mid. Sch., Sandy, Utah, 1980-87, tchr. specialist/English tchr., 1987-89, adminstrv. asst./English tchr., 1989-90; asst. prin. Bonneville Jr. High Sch., Salt Lake City, 1990-93, Granger High Sch., Salt Lake City, 1993-96, Olympus High Sch., 1996—; presenter, instr. state-wide writing confs., workshops, 1987-89. Editor, contbg. author: Heroines of the Restoration, 1997; contbg. author: (poetry book) Where Feelings Flower, 1992, LDS Women's Treasury, 1997; editor The Am. Mother Mag., 1994-95; editor: A Fruitful Season, 1988; contbg. editor: Singular Life, 1987; editl. asst. The Legacy Remembered and Renewed 1914-70, 1982; chmn. nat. editl. bd. Am. Mothers, Inc., 1994-95; exec. editor: Mother Love, 1995. Mem. Utah Office of Edn. Quality Indicates in Utah Schs. Task Force, Salt Lake City, 1989-90; county del. Utah Rep. Party, Salt Lake City, 1978; vol. Am. Cancer Soc., Utah Heart Assn., Detention Ctr., 1977-79. Fellow Utah Prins. Acad.; mem. Granite Assn. of Sch. Adminstrs. (bd. dirs. 1992-94, editor Adminstrv. Advantage 1992-94), Granite Assn. Jr. High Asst. Prins. (pres. 1992-93), Jordan Edn. Assn. (editor, originator Good Apples newsletter 1984-85), Utah Assn. of Women (chpt. and region pres. 1978-79), Parent Tchr. Student Assn. (2nd v.p. 1987-88), Utah Assn. Secondary Sch. Prins., Utah Found., Utah Women's Ednl. Adminstrs. Assn. (secondary dist. rep. 1995—, newsletter editro 1997—), Utah Days of '47 (sub-com. chair Pioneer of Progress awards 1995—), Granite Assn. H.S. Asst. Prins. Mem. LDS Ch. Home: 1254 Cove Park Cir Murray UT 84123 Office: Granite Sch Dist 340 E 3545 S Salt Lake City UT 84115-4615

THATCHER, CAROL JEAN, sociology and psychology educator, writer; b. Bell, Calif., Sept. 11, 1937; d. Lloyd Thatcher and Nadine (Crismon) T.; m. Donald E. Ross, June 7, 1955 (div. 1969); children: Dawn Ross, Jeffrey Ross, Jannette Ross, Christopher Ross; m. Charles R. Waistell, Mar. 26, 1993. MA in Social Sci., Calif. State U., Chico, 1992. Owner, mgr. Pan Gallery, 1972-74, Body & Bath, 1976-80; mktg. dir. Olives Inc., 1980-82; contractors office mgr. Bob Burleson, 1983-87; maintenance and utilities supr. Chico Area Recreation/Parks Dist., 1988-90; adminstrv. asst., intern, counselor Family Svc. Assn., 1990-91; instr., writer, pub. speaker Calif. State U., Chico, 1993—. Author: Female Body Modification Practices, 1992; actress, singer. Treas. Chico Art Ctr., 1991; minister 1st Spiritual Sci. Ch., Chico, 1993—; active United We Stand, Chico, Pub. Citizens, 1989—, Chico Peace Ctr., 1980, Clergy and Laity Concerned, 1990. Mem. Chico Jazz Soc. (co-founder 1981), Chico Dem. Club. Office: Ctr Multicultural & Gender Studies Calif State U Chico CA 95928

THAYER, MICHAEL J., secondary education educator. Tchr. Las Cruces (N.Mex.) Mid. Sch., 1972-94, Las Cruces H.S., 1994—. Named N.Mex. Tchr. of Yr., 1992. Office: Las Cruces HS 1755 El Paseo St Las Cruces NM 88001-6011

THEIS, JAMES EDWARD, pastry chef, interior designer; b. Bellville, Ill., May 23, 1963; s. Clement John and Alice Florence (Schoeppner) T. AA, Crafton Hills Coll., 1983; BS in Wildlife Mgmt., Humboldt State U., 1987; A of Occupational Sci. in Culinary Arts, Calif. Culinary Acad., San Francisco, 1994. Wild animal trainer San Diego Zoo, 1983-84, Wild Animal Tng. Ctr., Riverside, Calif., 1980-85; jewelry salesperson J.C. Penney's, West Covina, Calif., 1987-88; display supr. Sherwood Mgmt., Inc., Bell Gardens, Calif., 1989-90; counselor State of Calif. Sch. for Deaf, Riverside, 1990—; mgr. fine jewelry Finlay Fine Jewelry Corp, Monclair, Calif., 1990; interior designer Theis Interiors, Calimesa, Calif., 1990-93; asst. banquet chef Ritz Carlton Hotel, Rancho Mirage, Calif., 1994-95; chef tournat Elcaris Restaurant, Palm Springs, Calif., 1995-97; exec. chef Cottage Garden Restaurant, Palm Springs, 1996—; pastry chef Wolfgang Puck's Cafe, San Diego, 1997—. Scoutmaster Boy Scouts Am., Athens, Greece, 1985-86; fundraiser Desert AIDS Project. Sgt. USAF, 1985-86. Named to Outstanding Young Men Am., 1986. Republican. Roman Catholic. Home and office: Theis Catering 4018 Alabama St Apt 2 San Diego CA 92104-2424

THEIS, JOAN C., accountant; b. Flushing, N.Y., Feb. 22, 1948; d. Phillip Martin and Juanita Elizabeth (Weigelt) Brown; m. John H. Theis, Jr., Mar. 24, 1979; children: Mathew, Jacqueline. BA, U. Denver, 1970; MA, U. Colo., 1978; BS summa cum laude, Met. State Coll., Denver, 1984. CPA, Colo.; cert. master tchr., Colo. Tchr. Englewood (Colo.) Pub. Schs., 1976-82; acct. Diane D. Blackman, CPA, Denver, 1984-88, Pester & Co., CPAs, P.C., Denver, 1989-91; v.p. Grubb, Theis & Assocs. PC CPAs, 1991—. Pres. Englewood Educators, 1981-82. Mem. AICPA, Colo. Soc. CPAs, Toastmasters (past pres.), Colo. Women C. of C. (paast chmn. bd.), Phi Beta Kappa. Office: Grubb Theis & Assocs PC CPAs 1660 S Albion St Ste 403 Denver CO 80222-4020

THENELL, JANICE CATHERINE, public relations director, educator; b. Stanley, Wis., Mar. 9, 1940; d. Donald Henry and Mabel Rose (Rademacher) Vandehey; div. 1981; children: Catherine, Karen, Scott. BA, U. Oreg., 1962, MA, 1982. H.s. tchr. Pub. Schs., Eugene, Oreg., 1962-81; adminstrv. faculty So. Oreg. State coll., Ashland, 1982-83; comms. asst. Office Gov., Salem, Oreg., 1983-86; pub. rels. dir. Multnomah County Libr. Sys., Portland, Oreg., 1986—; adj. prof. Dept. Comms. Maryhurst (Oreg.) Coll., 1989—. Contbr. article to profl. jour. Bd. dirs. Salem Libr. Bd., 1984-86; bd. dirs., chair Fern Ridge Cmty. Libr., Veneta Oreg., 1970-78; mem. Portland City Club. Tchg. fellow U. Oreg. Sch. Journalism, Eugene, 1981-82; recipient Citizenship award City Lake Oswego, Oreg., 1991. Mem. Am. Libr. Assn. (presenter crisis comms. workshop 1995, John Cotton Dana Libr. Pub. Rels. award 1990, 96), Pub. Rels. Soc. Am., Nat. Press Women, Oreg. Libr. Assn. Office: Multnomah County Libr 205 NE Russell St Portland OR 97212-3708

THEOBALD, GILLIAN LEE, artist; b. La Jolla, Calif., Nov. 17, 1944; d. John Richmond and Mary Lee (Nugent) T.; m. Yuris Zeltins, July 20, 1974 (div. 1985); m. L.A. Heberlein, Mar. 15, 1992; 1 stepdaughter, Elaine Elizabeth. BA, San Diego State U., 1968, MA, 1971. One-woman shows incude Cirrus Gallery, L.A., 1983, 86, 88, 89, 90, 93, 94, 96, Patty Aande Gallery, San Diego, 1987, Boehm Gallery, San Marcos, Calif., 1988, Occidental Coll., L.A., 1990, Mark Quint Gallery, La. Jolla, 1993, Fletcher Priest, Worcester, Mass., 1977, Rocket Gallery, London, 1997; exhibited in group shows in Linda Hodges Gallery, Seattle, 1997, Port Angeles Fine Art Ctr., Wash., 1997, L.A. County Mus. of Art, 1995, Fitchburg (Mass.) Mus., Contemporary Arts, 1993, David Lewinson Gallery, Del Mar, Calif., 1992, Biota Gallery, L.A., 1991, Rose Art Mus. Brandeis U., Waltham, Mass., 1991, many others. Home: 9610 7th Ave NE Seattle WA 98115-2115

THEODOSAKIS, JASON J., physician; b. Chgo., Feb. 17, 1963; s. John C. and Helen Theodosakis. BA in Chem./BS in Biology with honors, Fla. Internat. U., 1985; MD, Univ. Health Scis./Chgo. Med. Sch., 1989; M in Exercise Physiology summa cum laude, U. Ariz., 1991, MPH summa cum laude, 1994. Diplomate Am. Bd. Preventive Medicine and Pub. Health, Nat. Bd. Med. Examiners. Intern in internal medicine Tucson Hosp., 1989-90; resident in preventive medicine U. Ariz. Health Scis. Ctr., Tucson, 1990-92, chief resident, 1992, fellow in faculty devel. program, 1992-93, fellow in clin. sports medicine, 1992-93, asst. clin. prof., 1995—; dir. preventive medicine residency program U. Ariz. Health Scis. Ctr., 1996—; staff physician Canyon Ranch Med. Dept., Tucson, 1992—; team physician Tucson Area High Sch. Football, 1992—; designer, mfr., tester exercise/rehab. equipment; tchr., rschr. in field. Author: The Arthritis Cure, 1997. Acad. scholar Fla. Internat. U., 1981-85. Mem. AMA, Am. Coll. Sports Medicine (advanced cert. team physician), Am. Coll. Preventive Medicine, Am. Profl. Practice Assn., Assn. of Tchrs. of Preventive Medicine. Nat. Osteoporosis Found.

THEURER, BYRON W., aerospace engineer, business owner; b. Glendale, Calif., July 1, 1939; s. William Louis and Roberta Cecelia (Sturgiss) T.; m. Sue Ann McKay, Sept. 15, 1962 (div. 1980); children: Karen Marie, William Thomas, Alison Lee. BS in Engring. Sci., USAF Acad., 1961; MS in Aero. Sci., U. Calif., Berkeley, 1965; MBA, U. Redlands, 1991. Commd. USAF, 1961, advanced through grades to lt. col., ret. 1978; project officer Space Shuttle Devel. Prog., Houston, 1971-76; chief of test F-15 Systems Prog. Office Wright Patterson AFB, Ohio, 1976-78; sr. engr. Veda, Inc., Dayton, 1979-81, Logicon Inc., Dayton, 1981-83; project mgr. Support Systems Assocs., Inc., Dayton, 1983-84, CTA Inc., Ridgecrest, Calif., 1985-89; owner, operator The Princeton Rev. of Ctrl. Calif., Ridgecrest, 1989-92, San Luis Obispo, 1993—; cons. in field. Decorated Silver Star, D.F.C., Air Medals (16); named Officer of the Yr., Air Force Flight Test Ctr., Edwards AFB, 1970. Mem. Air Force Assn., Assn. Old Crows, USAF Acad. Assn. Grads. (nat. bd. dirs. 1972-75, chpt. pres. 1981-83). Republican. Episcopalian. Home: PO Box 697 Cayucos CA 93430-0697

THIELGES, BART ARTHUR, university adminstrator; b. Chgo., June 16, 1938; s. Bart Herbert and Norma Ethel (Ohlin) T.; m. Mary Judith McMullen, June 4, 1960; children: Bart C., Jon S., Patrick A. BS, So. Ill. U., 1963; M of Forestry, Yale Sch., 1964; MPhil, Yale U., 1967, PhD, 1968. Rsch. fellow Yale U., New Haven, 1964-67; asst. prof. Ohio State U., Wooster, 1967-71; assoc. prof. La. State U., Baton Rouge, 1971-76; prin. geneticist USDA-Forest Svc., New Orleans, 1976-77; prof., chmn. U. Ky., Lexington, 1977-90; assoc. dean Oreg. State U., Corvallis, 1990—; vis. prof. U. Oxford, Eng., 1983-84; program mgr. USDA Competitive Grants, Washington, 1985-86. Editor: Forest Tree Improvement, 1975, Cottonwood and Related Species, 1977. Mem. Soc. of Am. Foresters, Forest Products Soc., Sigma Xi. Office: Oreg State U Coll Forestry Peavy Hall Rm 150 Corvallis OR 97331-8566

THIES, LYNN WAPINSKI, elementary education educator; b. Pottsville, Pa., Aug. 11, 1946; d. Stanley Walter and Mary Etta (Stevens) Wapinski; m. Wynn Gerrard, June 14, 1969; children: Heather Anne, Kevin Leonard. BA in Edn., Assoc. Libr. Sci., U. S.C., 1968. Tchr. 5th grade Ft. Jackson (S.C.) Elem. Sch., 1968-70; tchr. 4th and 5th grades Groner Elem. Sch., Scholls, Oreg., 1970-72; tchr. 1st grade Welches (Oreg.) Elem., 1980; tchr. 6th grade Sandy (Oreg.) Elem. Sch. Dist. 46, 1983-87, tchr. 3rd grade, 1987-94, tchr. mixed-age class, ages 7 and 8, 1994-96, 2nd grade tchr., 1996—; mem. lang. arts curriculum com. Firwood Elem. Sch., Sandy Elem. Sch. Dist. 46, 1986-87, mem. 21st Century S.I.T.E. com., 1994—, sci. curriculum com., 1995—; active Oreg. Consortium Quality Sci., Portland, 1985-87, Oreg. Cadre Quality Sci. Edn., Sandy, 1987-89, Sci. Curriculum Consortium, Sandy, 1989-92. Leader, mem. Day Camp core staff Girl Scouts U.S., mem. hist. reenactment group, vol. Columbia River Girl Scout coun., Portland, 1972-92. Eisenhower grantee, 1994, 95, 96, 97, ODE Primary Math Project grantee, 1996-97. Mem. NEA, ASCD, Internat. Reading Assn., Oreg. State Tchrs. Assn., Oreg. Consortium for Quality in Sci. Edn., Oreg. Cadre for Assistance to Tchrs. Sci., Oreg. Sci. Tchrs. Assn., Clackamas County Sci. Tchrs. Assn., Barlow Trail Long Rifles. Democrat. Roman Catholic. Home: 51956 E Terra Fern Dr Sandy OR 97055-9415

THIESSEN, DWIGHT EVERETT, farmer; b. Sidney, Mont., June 22, 1953; s. Peter D. and Nancy Mae (Edes) T.; m. Diana L. Mansveld, Aug. 30, 1975; children: Peter Karel, Andrew Everett, Jessica Marie. Agr. bus., Dawson C.C., Glendive, Mont., 1975, livestock tech., 1975. Farmer, rancher Savage, Mont., 1971—; county commr. Richland County, Sidney, 1988—. Ch. bd. mem. Christian and Missionary Alliance Ch., Lambert, Mont., 1975—. Named Outstanding Young Farmer Jaycee, 1978. Republican. Home and Office: RR 2 Box 175 Savage MT 59262

THIROUX, EMILY LOFTON, English educator, theater director; b. Porterville, Calif., July 26, 1949; d. Thomas Orville and Hazel Marie (Ketcham) Lofton; m. Jacques Thiroux, Apr. 8, 1984; children: Jason Ragle, Abigale Ragle. AA, Mesa Coll., 1971, AS, 1975; BA, Calif. State U., Bakersfield, 1985, MA, 1988. Instr. Bakersfield (Calif.) Coll., 1986-92; staff developer Pacific Regency Care Ctr., Bakersfield, 1986-94; lectr. English composition Calif. State U., Bakersfield, 1987—; dir., designer Bakersfield (Calif.) Music Theatre, 1992—; cons. Pacific Regency Care Ctr., Bakersfield, 1994—; owner Imperial Ambulance Co., Porterville, Calif., 1995—. Author: Cultures: Diversity in Reading and Writing, 1993, 2d edit., 1997. Mem. Kern County (Calif.) Commn. on Self Esteem and Personal and Social Responsibility, 1991-95. Mem. AAUW (past. pres., bd. mem. 1986—, state com. mem. 1994-95, Barbara Leask award), Sigma Tau Delta. Democrat.

THISTLE, HAROLD WILLIAM, JR., engineer; b. New Haven, July 29, 1958; s. Harold William and Myrta Lenore (Irwin) T.; m. Gay Ellen Schlichting, Jan. 14, 1984; children: Andrew Gregory, Brian Harold. BA in Geography, U. Conn., 1980, PhD in Forest Meteorology, 1988; MS in Climatology, U. Del., 1983. Cert. cons. meteorologist, Am. Meteorol. Soc. Rsch. assoc. U. Conn., Storrs, 1988; sr. scientist TRC Environ. Co., Windsor, Conn., 1988-92; program leader tech. and devel. USDA Forest Svc, , Washington, Mont., 1992—; coop. observer NOAA, Coventry, Conn., 1983-88. Contbr. articles to profl. jours. Active Univ. Congl. Ch., Missoula, Mont. Fellow Ctr. for Environ. Health, 1987, U. Conn., 1985, 87; recipient Cert. Merit USDA, 1994. Mem. AAAS, ASCE, ASCE (affiliate), Am. Meteorol. Soc., Air and Waste Mgmt. Assn., Am. Geophys. Union. Office: Missoula Tech and Devel Fort Missoula Rd # 1 Missoula MT 59801-7203

THISTLETHWAITE, ALINE M., artist; b. Long Beach, Calif.; d. John and Hazel McQuiston; m. Tor Torland; children: Mark, Lote. BA, tchg. credential, UCLA, 1945; studied with, Barse Miller, Robert E. Wood, Mario Cooper, John Pike, Ed Whitney, Herb Olsen, Joan Irving, Rex Brandt. tchr. drawing, painting and photography Santa Ana H.S. One-person shows include Laguna Trust, Laguna Beach, Calif., Lido Island Yacht Club, Lido, Newport, Calif., Newport (Calif.) City Hall, Oxnard (Calif.) Plaza Gallery Fine Arts, Riverside (Calif.) Art Mus. Upstairs Gallery; exhibited in group shows All. Calif. State Show, 1992, 94, Calif. Small Works, 1992, 93, 94, Newport City Open, Conejo Valley Ann., Hunt Libr., Fullerton, Calif., Sherman Gardens, Newport Beach, Calif., The Islander Gallery, Newport Beach, Armida Winery, 1996, Hopkilm Winery, Heritage Gallery, Lafayette, La., Nat. Acad. Design, N.Y., Watercolor U.S.A., Springfield, Mo., El Paso (Tex.) Mus., Oakland (Calif.) Mus., Wichita Centennial, St. Raymond's Ann., Whittier, Calif., Santa Paula Exhbn., Edward Dean Mus., Beaumont, Calif., Palm Springs Desert Mus., Brea (Calif.) Civic Ctr., Cerritos (Calif.) Coll.; featured in books: Southern California 100, Arts of Southern California XVII Watercolor. Recipient 1st prize Laguna Beach Mus., Jurors award San Bernardino Fine Arts Inst., Grumbacher Gold medal, 1994, 2d prize for mixed media, 1992, 1st prize Long Beach Art Open, 1st prize Riverside Art Assn., Best in Show in watercolor, 1st in oil, 1st in watercolor Orange County Fair, 1st and 2d prize Torana Art Assn., 1st prize Santa Ana Ebell, others. Mem. Nat. Watercolor Soc., Southwestern Watercolor Soc., La. Watercolor Soc., Watercolor West. Home: 401 Oak Brook Pl Santa Rosa CA 95409

THOM, DAVID HINTON, family physician, medical educator; b. Pendleton, Oreg., Aug. 23, 1957; s. George Lloyd and Jane Kathrine (Hinton) T.; m. Lorene Marie Nelson, June 20, 1987. AB with distinction, Stanford U., 1979; MD, U. Calif., San Diego, 1983; MPH, PhD, U. Wash., 1991. Diplomate Am. Bd. Family Practice; lic. physician/surgeon, Calif. Family physician Kaiser Permanente of Calif., Santa Rosa, Calif., 1984-86; emergency rm. physician Kaiser of Colo., Denver, 1986-87; sr. fellow U. Wash., Seattle, 1987-91; asst. prof. medicine Stanford (Calif.) U., 1992—, asst. dir. Robert Wood Johnson Clin. Scholars Program, 1991-96. Contbr. articles to profl. jours.; editl. bd. Archives of Family Medicine, 1992—; sect. editor Western Jour. Medicine, 1993-94. Hartford Found. scholar, 1992-93, Picker/Commonwealth scholar, 1994-96. Mem. Soc. Tchrs. of Family Medicine, Phi Beta Kappa. Democrat. Office: Stanford Univ Sch of Medicine 703 Welch Rd Ste G1 Palo Alto CA 94304

THOMAN, JOHN EVERETT, architect, mediator; b. Dixon, Ill., Aug. 6, 1925; s. George Dewey and Agnes Katherine (Fane) T.; m. Paula Ann Finnegan, Oct. 31, 1953; children: Shawn Michael, Brian Gerard, Kevin Charles, Trace Marie, Patricia Ann, Ronan Patrick, Caron Lynn. AA, UCLA, 1948; BArch cum laude, U. So. Calif., 1955. Registered architect, Calif. Project dir. A. Quincy Jones & Frederick E. Emmons, L.A., 1956-57, assoc., 1958, dir. constrn., 1958-73; dir. specifications A. Quincy Jones, FAIA & Assocs., L.A., 1973-77; dir. specifications Albert C. Martin and Assocs., L.A., 1977-79, dir. constrn. and industry rels., 1979-95, assoc., 1979-90, sr. assoc., 1990—, dir. emeritus constrn. and industry rels., 1996—; guest lectr. U. So. Calif. Lusk Sch. Real Estate, UCLA Grad. Sch., also various student, trade and tech. groups. Mem., vice chmn. Culver City (Calif.) Planning Commn., 1959; mem. Calif. Gov.'s Housing Commn., L.A., 1960, Community Redevel. Agy., Culver City, 1992-94. With U.S. Army, 1943-45, USAF, 1950-51. Mem. AIA (chmn. design awards com. L.A. 1960), Constrn. Specifications Inst. (bd. dirs. 1977-80, guest lectr.), Phi Eta Sigma, Tau Sigma Delta. Office: Albert C Martin and Assocs 811 W 7th St Los Angeles CA 90017-3408

THOMAN, MARY E., business and marketing educator, rancher; b. Kemmerer, Wyo., Sept. 14, 1949; d. William J. and Mary A. (Ferentchak) T. AA, Western Wyo. C.C., Rock Springs, 1970; BS in Bus., U. Wyo., 1972; MEd in Mktg., Colo. State U., 1978, PhD in Vocat./Secondary Adminstrn., 1981. Profl. Teaching Cert., Wyo. Bus. edn. Green River (Wyo.) H.S., 1972-75; part time bus. and mktg. instr. Western Wyo. C.C., Green River, 1972-77, Rock Springs, Wyo., 1972-80, Kemmerer, Wyo., 1983—; mktg. and coop. educator Green River H.S., 1975-77; asst. dir. Nev. St. Coun. on Vocat. Edn., Carson City, Nev., 1977; exec. dir. Mont. St. Coun. on Vocat. Edn., Helena, Mont., 1981-82; cattle/sheep rancher Kemmerer, 1981—; sr. sales dir. Mary Kay Cosmetics, Kemmerer, Wyo., 1988—; ednl. cons. past chair Wyo. St. Coun. on Vocat. Edn., Cheyenne, 1984-93; bus. cons. Western Wyo. Coll., Rock Springs, 1983—; sch.-to-work, S.W. Wyo. Collaberative Team; edn. cons. Kemmerer Sch. Dist., 1993—, chair voc/tech prep bus. curriculum com.; mem. Wyo. Agr. in Classroom, 1992-96. Active western range issues; testifier on Range Reform Hearings; mem. Cumberland Allotment Coordinated Resource Mgmt. Team Bur. Land Mgmt.; mem. S.W. Wyo. Resource Rendezvous Steering Com. Ednl./Profl. Devel. Act fellow, 1977-78, Grad. Leadership Devel. awardee, 1978-81. Mem. Kemmerer C. of C. (edn. com., bd. dirs. 1992—). Roman Catholic. Home: PO Box 146 Green River WY 82935-0146

THOMAS, BRIAN CHESTER, state legislator, engineer; b. Tacoma, Wash., May 19, 1939; s. Ralph R. and Katheryne (Chester) T.; m. Judith Lynn Adams, Feb. 20, 1965; children: Jeffrey, Kyle, Cheryl. BS in Engring., Oreg. State U., 1961; postgrad., U. Wash., 1968-70; MBA, Pacific Luth. U., 1979. Civil engr. U.S. Coast Guard, Seattle, 1962-63; ops. officer U.S. Coast Guard, Astoria, Oreg., 1964-65; sr. sales engr. Puget Sound Power & Light Co., Bellevue, Wash., 1965-70, mgr. market rsch., 1971-80, rsch. adminstr., 1981-89, prin. engr., 1989-97; mem. Wash. Ho. of Reps., Olympia, 1993—, mem. forecast coun., 1996—, mem. joint select com. on edn. restructuring, 1995—, chmn. fin., energy, utilities coms., 1997—; chair EEI Rsch. Mgmt. Com., Washington, 1988-89, EPRI Renewable Com., Palo Alto, Calif., 1989-90; adv. bd. Nat. Renewable Energy Lab., Golden, Colo., 1990-92; mem. adv. bd. sch. elec. engring. Oreg. State U., Corvallis, 1991-97; dep. dir. region 10 U.S. Dept. Transp. Emergency Orgn., Seattle, 1989-93. Bd. dirs. Issaquah (Wash.), Sch. Dist., 1989-93. Capt. USCGR, 1961-84. Mem. Issaquah Rotary (pres. 1982-83). Republican. Home: 14715 182nd Pl SE Renton WA 98059-8028 Office: Wash Ho Reps PO Box 40610 Olympia WA 98504-0610

THOMAS, BRIAN GORDON, municipal finance executive; b. Pasadena, Calif., July 23, 1954. BS in Biology, BS in Econs., Calif. State Poly. U., 1977; MA in Econs., U. Calif., Riverside, 1981, PhD in Econs., 1986, cert. in exec. mgmt., 1992. Lectr. econs. Riverside City Coll., 1980-81, Calif. State U., Fullerton, 1985-89, Calif. State Poly. U., Pomona, 1988-91; assoc. in econs. Calif. State U., Riverside, 1982-83, rsch. asst. dept. econs., 1980-83; engr. power resource planning Dept. Pub. Utilities City of Anaheim, Calif., 1983-85, mgr. fin. requirements, 1985-88; with utilities acctg., mgr. fin. Dept. Utilities City of Riverside, 1988-89, asst. dir. utilities, fin./adminstrn. Dept. Utilities, 1989-93; asst. dir. fin. Met. Water Dist. So. Calif., L.A., 1993-94, asst. chief planning divsn., 1994—. Contbr. articles to profl. jours. Regents fellow U. Calif., 1981. Mem. Am. Econs. Assn., Western Econ. Assn., Am. Water Works Assn.

THOMAS, CLAUDEWELL SIDNEY, psychiatry educator; b. N.Y.C., Oct. 5, 1932; s. Humphrey Sidney and Frances Elizabeth (Collins) T.; m. Carolyn Pauline Rozansky, Sept. 6, 1958; children: Jeffrey Evan, Julie-Anne Elizabeth, Jessica Edith. BA, Columbia U., 1952; MD, SUNY, Downstate Med. Ctr., 1956; MPH, Yale U., 1964. Diplomate Nat. Bd. Med. Examiners, Am. Bd. Psychiatry. From instr. to assoc. prof. Yale U., New Haven, 1963-68, dir. Yale tng. program in social community psychiatry, 1967-70; dir. div. mental health service programs NIMH, Washington, 1970-73; chmn. dept. psychiatry U.M.D.N.J., Newark, 1973-83; prof. dept.

psychiatry Drew Med. Sch., 1983—, chmn. dept. psychiatry, 1983-93; prof. dept. psychiatry UCLA, 1983-94, vice chmn. dept. psychiatry, 1983-93, prof. emeritus dept. psychiatry, 1994—; med. dir. Tokanui Hosp., TeAwamutu, N.Z., 1996; cons. A.K. Rice Inst., Washington, 1978-80, SAMSA/PHS Cons., 1991—; mem. L.A. County Superior Ct. Psych. Panel, 1991—. Author: (with B. Bergen) Issues and Problems in Social Psychiatry, 1966; editor (with R. Bryce LaPorte) Alienation in Contemporary Society, 1976, (with J. Lindenthal) Psychiatry and Mental Health Science Handbook; mem. editorial bd. Internat. Jour. Mental Health, Adminstrn. In Mental Health. Bd. dirs. Bay Area Found., 1987—. Served to capt. USAF, 1959-61. Fellow APHA, Am. Psychoanalytic Assn. (hon.), Am. Psychiat. Assn. (life), Royal Soc. Health, N.Y. Acad. Sci., N.Y. Acad. Medicine; mem. Am. Sociol. Assn. Home and Office: 30676 Palos Verdes Dr W Palos Verdes Peninsula CA 90274 *Personal philosophy: Integrity sooner or later calls upon courage. If courage is not home integrity goes away.*

THOMAS, CRAIG, senator; b. Cody, Wyo., Feb. 17, 1933; s. Craig E. and Marge Oweta (Lynn) T.; m. Susan Roberts; children: Peter, Paul, Patrick, Alexis. BS, U. Wyo., 1955. V.p. Wyo. Farm Bur., Laramie, 1959-66; with Am. Farm Bur., 1966-75; gen. mgr. Wyo. Rural Elec. Assn., 1975-89; mem. Wyo. Ho. of Reps., 1984-89, 101st-103rd Congresses from Wyo., Washington, 1989-94; U.S. senator from Wyoming, 1995—. Former chmn. Natrona County (Wyo.) Rep. Com.; state rep. Natrona County Dist.; del. Rep. Nat. Conv., 1980. Capt. USMC. Mem. Am. Soc. Trade Execs., Masons. Methodist. Office: US Senate 302 Hart Senate Office Bldg Washington DC 20510*

THOMAS, DALTON, food products executive; b. 1942. Degree, U. Wash., 1965. Fruit inspector State of Wash., Wenatchee, 1965-66; with Oneonta Trading Co., Wenatchee, 1966—; pres. Custom Apple Packers, Inc., Brewster, Wash. Office: Custom Apple Packers Inc 9 Brewster Grange Rd Brewster WA 98812*

THOMAS, DAVID SNOW, plastic surgeon; b. Chgo., Feb. 7, 1951; s. Allan Perry and Verna Bea (Snow) T.; m. Becky Williams Thomas, Aug. 25, 1973; children: Nathan David, Abigail, Elizabeth. BA, U. Utah, 1974, MD, 1978. Diplomate Am. Bd. Plastic Surgery, Am. Bd. Surgery. Resident surgery UCLA, 1978-83, resident plastic surgery, 1983-85, fellow craniofacial surgery, 1985; pvt. practice Salt Lake City, 1986—; chief plastic surgery Primary Childrens Med. Ctr., Salt Lake City, 1988-90, Los Hosp., 1993—; clin. asst. prof. U. Utah Plastic Surgeons, Salt Lake City, 1986-89, assoc. prof. surgery, 1990-93, clin. assoc. prof., 1993—. Bd. Dirs. AMICUS, Salt Lake City, Utah, 1990-92. Fellow Am Coll. Surgeons; mem. Am. Soc. Plastic & Reconstructive Surgery, Am. Soc. Maxillofacial Surgery, Am. Cleft Palate Craniofacial Assn., Am. Soc. Aesthetic Plastic Surgery, Interplast (pres. Salt Lake City, 1992—, bd. dirs. Palo Alto, Calif., 1992—), The Country Club (Salt Lake City). Office: 370 9th Ave Ste 200 Salt Lake City UT 84103-2877

THOMAS, DAVID STANLEY, sales executive; b. Malad, Idaho, July 4, 1946; s. Stanley and Erma (Peterson) T.; m. Rochelle Skinner, Sept. 27, 1974; children: Aaron, Adam, Amanda. BS in Acctg., Brigham Young U., 1969. Ptnr. Emporium Gift Shop and Union Block Inc., Provo, Utah, 1971-73; prin. Keith Warshaw & Co., Salt Lake City, 1973-79; regional sales mgr. Eddie Parker Sales, Dallas, 1979-84; v.p. mktg. Country Cozy's Inc., Buena Park, Calif., 1984—. Bd. dirs. AYSO Soccer. Mem. Am. Legion, Kiwanis Club La Mirada. Republican. Mem. LDS Ch. Home: 13126 San Felipe St La Mirada CA 90638-3450 Office: Country Cozy's Inc 8011 Orangethorpe Ave Buena Park CA 90621-3801

THOMAS, DAVID TIMOTHY, marketing professional; b. Circleville, Ohio, Jan. 2, 1946; s. Verneal Marshall and Lucile Frances (May) T.; m. Nancy Sue Bradford Thomas, July 5, 1969 (div. 1984); m. Susan Rae Alreck Thomas, June 23, 1984; 1 child, Jennifer Sue. BA, Otterbein Coll., Westerville, Ohio, 1969. News dir. KSIR-AM, Estes Park, Colo., 1975-77; owner, mgr. The Oxen Yoke and Covered Wagon Crafts, Estes Park, Colo., 1976-80; news editor Estes Park Trail-Gazette, Estes Park, Colo., 1979-80; owner De Nada Prodns., Estes Park, Colo., 1978-82; station mgr. KSIR-AM, Estes Park, Colo., 1982-84; dir. comms. YMCA of the Rockies, Estes Park, Colo., 1984—. Author: PR: The Proof of the Pudding, 1982; contbr. articles to profl. jours. Dist. capt., mem. County Ctrl. Com. Larimer County Dem. Party, Colo., 1980-84; mem. Estes Park Planning Commn. Recipient 2nd Place Best Program Colo. Broadcasters Assn., 1975, 1st Place, 1976, Pub. Svc. Announcement, 1st Place, 1976, Best Promotion for a Client 2nd Place, 1976, Best Topical News Series, 1st Place, 1982, Best Spot News Coverage, 1st Place, 1982, Best Spot News Coverage United Press Internat. 1st Place, 1982, Best Program, 1st Place, 1983, Slide presentation 2nd Place Colo. Ednl. Media Assn., 1978, 1st Place, 1979. Mem. Internat. Assn. Conf. Ctr. Adminstrs., Soc. Govt. Meeting Planners, Assn. Profl. Dirs. YMCAs (past chpt. pres.), Christian Camping Internat. U.S.A. Democrat. United Methodist. Home: PO Box 4448 1560 Axminster Ln Estes Park CO 80517-4448 Office: YMCA of the Rockies 2515 Tunnel Rd Estes Park CO 80511

THOMAS, DOUGLAS GRAHAM, technology company executive, communications consultant; b. L.A., Aug. 18, 1938; s. Robert Oliver and Olive (Friend) T.; m. Laurel Catherine Kimen, Mar. 9, 1968; 1 child, Robert Stanley. AA in Bus. Adminstrn., Glendale (Calif.) Coll., 1965; student, Am. River Jr. Coll., Sacramento, 1957-58, No. Va. C.C., Woodbridge, 1972-73, U. N.Mex., 1982-85. Cert. leadership instr., facilitator, USMC. Radio team chief Calif. ANG, Sacramento, 1955-58; mgr. comm. USMC, 1958-81; coord. logistics Wang Labs., Inc., Albuquerque, 1981-85; contract logistics specialist Dunhill Temporaries, Albuquerque, 1985-86; mgr. sys. proposals Frequency Engring. Labs., Inc., Farmingdale, N.J., 1986-90; polit. fundraiser Gordon & Schwenkmeyer, Inc., Brea, Calif., 1990-92; prin., polit. cons., fundraiser Creative Concepts, Rio Rancho, N.Mex., 1993—; contracts adminstr. Gen. Tech. Corp., Albuquerque, 1994—; co-owner, cons. S-T Assocs., Anaheim, Calif., 1991; career planning cons., Anaheim and Rio Rancho, 1991-96; small bus. cons. Garrard Enterprises, Newport Beach, Calif., 1992; sec. Overseas Mktg. Group, Anaheim, 1993. Editor Menzia, 1985; asst. editor Deming Mgmt. Assn. Newsletter, 1993. Adult scouter Boy Scouts Am., 1975—; v.p. facilities condo. assn., Lakewood, N.J., 1988-89; chair publicity Sandoval County Reps., Rio Rancho, 1995—; del. Rep. state conv. N.Mex., 1994-96. Sgt. USMC, 1958-81. Recipient Campaign and Svc. medals USMC, 1958-91; scholar DAR, Glendale, 1963. Mem. Nat. Contract Mgmt. Assn. (v.p. Albuquerque chpt. 1996—), Am. Soc. Quality Control (publicity chair Albuquerque chpt. 1996—), Marine Corps Assn., Presbyn. Men of U.S. (synod rep. 1996—). Home: 109 Dakota Morning Rd NE Rio Rancho NM 87124 Office: Gen Tech Corp 6816 Washington St NE Albuquerque NM 87109

THOMAS, EDWARD DONNALL, physician, researcher; b. Mart, Tex., Mar. 15, 1920; married; 3 children. BA, U. Tex., 1941, MA, 1943; MD, Harvard U., 1946; MD (hon.), U. Cagliari, Sardinia, 1981, U. Verona, Italy, 1991, U. Parma, Italy, 1992, U. Barcelona, Spain, 1994, U. Warsaw, Poland, 1996, U. Jagiellonski, Cracow, Poland, 1996. Lic. physician Mass., N.Y., Wash.; diplomate Am. Bd. Internal Medicine. Intern in medicine Peter Bent Brigham Hosp., Boston, 1946-47, rsch. fellow hematology, 1947-48; NRC postdoctoral fellow in medicine dept. biology MIT, Cambridge, 1950-51; chief med. resident, sr. asst. resident Peter Bent Brigham Hosp., 1951-53, hematologist, 1953-55; instr. medicine Harvard Med. Sch., Boston, 1953-55; rsch. assoc. Cancer Rsch. Found. Children's Med. Ctr., Boston, 1953-55; physician-in-chief Mary Imogene Bassett Hosp., Cooperstown, N.Y., 1955-63; assoc. clin. prof. medicine Coll. Physicians and Surgeons Columbia U., N.Y.C., 1955-63; attending physician U. Wash. Hosp., Seattle, 1963-90; prof. medicine Sch. Medicine U. Wash., Seattle, 1963-90, head divsn. oncology Sch. Medicine, 1963-85, prof. emeritus medicine Sch. Medicine, 1990—; dir. med. oncology Fred Hutchinson Cancer Rsch. Ctr., Seattle, 1974-89, assoc. dir. clin. rsch. programs, 1982-89, mem., 1974—; mem. hematology study sect. NIH, 1965-69; mem. bd. trustees and med. sci. adv. com. Leukemia Soc. Am., Inc., 1969-73; mem. clin. cancer investigation review com. Nat. Cancer Inst., 1970-74; 1st ann. Eugene C. Eppinger lectr. Peter Bent Brigham Hosp. and Harvard Med. Sch., 1974; Lilly lectr. Royal Coll. Physicians, London, 1977; Stratton lectr. Internation Soc. Hematology, 1982; Paul Aggeler lectr. U. Calif., San Francisco, 1982; 65th Mellon lectr. U. Pitts. Sch. Medicine, 1984; Stanley Wright Meml. lectr. Western Soc. Pediatric Rsch., 1985; Adolfo Ferrata lectr. Italian Soc. Hematology, Verona, Italy, 1991. Mem. editl. bd. Blood, 1962-75, 77-82, Transplantation, 1970-76, Proc. of Soc. for Exptl. Biology and Medicine, 1974-81, Leukemia Rsch., 1977-87, Hematological Oncology, 1982-87, Jour. Clin. Immunology, 1982-87, Am. Jour. Hematology, 1985—, Bone Marrow Transplantation, 1986—. With U.S. Army, 1948-50. Recipient A. Ross McIntyre award U. Nebr. Med. Ctr., 1975, Philip Levine award Am. Soc. Clin. Pathologists, 1979, Disting. Svc. in Basic Rsch. award Am. Cancer Soc., 1980, Kettering prize Gen. Motors Cancer Rsch. Found., 1981, Spl. Keynote Address award Am. Soc. Therapeutic Radiologists, 1981, Robert Roesler de Villiers award Leukemia Soc. Am., 1983, Karl Landsteiner Meml. award Am. Assn. Blood Banks, 1987, Terry Fox award Can., 1990, Internat. award Gairdner Found., 1990, N.Am. Med. Assn. Hong Kong prize, 1990, Nobel prize in medicine, 1990, Presdl. medal of sci. NSF, 1990,. Mem. NAS, Am. Assn. Cancer Rsch., Am. Assn. Physicians (Kober medal 1992), Am. Fedn. Clin. Rsch., Am. Soc. Clin. Oncology (David A. Karnoksky Meml. lectr. 1983), Am. Soc. Clin. Investigation, Am. Soc. Hematology (pres. 1987-88, Henry M. Stratton lectr. 1975), Internat. Soc. Exptl. Hematology, Internat. Soc. Hematology, Academie Royale de Medicine de Belgique (corresponding mem.), Swedish Soc. Hematology (hon.), Swiss Soc. Hematology, Royal Coll. Physicians and Surgeons Can. (hon.), Western Assn. Physicians, Soc. Exptl. Biology and Medicine, Transplantation Soc., Nat. Acad. Medicine (hon.). Office: Fred Hutchinson Cancer Ctr 1124 Columbia St Seattle WA 98104-2015

THOMAS, ESTHER MERLENE, elementary education educator; b. San Diego, Oct. 16, 1945; d. Merton Alfred and Nellie Lida (Von Pilz) T. AA with honors, Grossmont Coll., 1966; BA with honors, San Diego State U., 1969; MA, U. Redlands, 1977. Cert. elem. and adult edn. tchr. Tchr. Cajon Valley Union Sch. Dist., El Cajon, 1969—; sci. fair coord. Flying Hills Sch.; tchr. Hopi and Navajo Native Americans, Ariz., Utah, 1964-74, Goose and Gander Nursery Sch., Lakeside, Calif., 1964-66; dir., supt. Bible and Sunday schs. various chs., Lakeside, 1961-87; mem. sci. com., math. coun. Cajon Valley Union Sch. Dist., 1990-91. Author: Individualized Curriculum in the Affective Domain; contbg. author: Campbell County, The Treasured Years, 1990, Legends of the Lakeside; contbg. songwriter Sing Hallelujah, 1997; songwriter for Amerecord Records, Hollywood, Calif., Hilltop Records, Hollywood, Hollywood Artists; songs released Never Trouble Trouble, Old Glory, Jesus is Our Lord, Daniel's Prayer, There Lay Jesus, Clear the Path Lord, Born to Win, Home Is Where The Heart is, Don't Let Them Step On Your Heart, No Place to Cry, Aqua Forte, In the Volume of the Book; contbr. articles to profl. jours. and newspapers. Tem. U.S. Senatorial Club, Washington, 1984—, Conservative Caucus, Inc., Washington, 1988—, Ronald Reagan Presdl. Found., Ronald Reagan Rep. Ctr., 1988, Rep. Presdl. Citizen's Adv. Commn., 1989—, Rep. Platform Planning Com., Calif., 1992, at-large del. representing dist. #45, Lakeside, Calif., 1992, 1995—, Am. Security Coun., Washington, 1994, Congressman Hunter's Off Road Adv. Coun., El Cajon, Calif., 1994, Century Club, San Diego Rep. Century Club, 1995; mem. health articulation com. project AIDS, Cajon Valley Union Sch. Dist., 1988—, Concerned Women Am., Washington, Recruit Depot Hist. Mus., San Diego, 1989, Citizen's Drug Free Am., Calif., 1989—, The Heritage Found., 1988—; charter mem. Marine Corps Mus.; mem. Lakeside Centennial Com., 1985-86; hon. mem. Rep. Presdl. Task Force, Washington, 1986; del. Calif. Rep. Senatorial Mid-Term Conv., Washington, 1994; mus. curator Lakeside Hist. Soc., 1992-93. Recipient Outstanding Svc. award PTA, 1972-74; recognized for various contbns. Commdg. Post Gen., San Diego Bd. Edn., 1989. Mem. Tchrs. Assn., Calif. Tchrs. Assn., Nat. Trust for Hist. Preservation, Cajon Valley Educators Assn. (faculty advisor, rep. 1980-82, 84-86, 87-88), Nashville Songwriters Assn., Christian Bus. and Profl. Women, Capitol Hill Women's Club, Am. Ctr. for Law and Justice, Internat. Christian Women's Club (Christian amb. to Taiwan, Korea 1974). Republican. Home: 13594 Highway 8 Business Apt 3 Lakeside CA 92040-5235 Office: Flying Hills Elem Sch 1251 Finch St El Cajon CA 92020-1433

THOMAS, FRANK JOSEPH, nuclear engineer; b. Pocatello, Idaho, Apr. 15, 1930; s. Emil C. and Jean (Jones) T.; m. Carol Jones, Feb. 4, 1949; children: Dale, Wayne, Keith. BSEE, U. Idaho, 1952; MS, U. Calif., Berkeley, 1957. Registered profl. mech. engr., Calif. Engr. Sandia Corp., Albuquerque, 1952-56; mgr. engring. div. Aerojet Gen., San Ramon, Calif., 1957-64; dir. nuclear program Office Sec. Defense, Washington, 1964-67; sr. scientist Rand Corp., Santa Monica, Calif., 1967-71; chmn. Pacific-Sierra Rsch. Corp., L.A., 1971—; lectr. U. Calif., Berkeley, 1956-58; chmn. treaty evaluation panel Def. Advanced Rsch. Projects Agy., Washington, 1969-71; clear sky panel USAF, Washington, 1967-73. Author: Evasive Foreign Nuclear Testing, 1971, Blackjack Strategy, 1961; contbr. articles to profl. jours. including Nature, Physics Letters. Recipient Master Design award Product Engring. Mag., 1963. Mem. AAAS, Am. Inst. Aeronautics and Astro. Office: Pacific Sierra Rsch Corp 2901 28th St Santa Monica CA 90405-2938

THOMAS, HAROLD WILLIAM, avionics systems engineer, flight instructor; b. Cle Elum, Wash., Sept. 29, 1941; s. Albert John and Margaret Jenny (Micheletto) T.; children: Gregg Wallace, Lisa Michele. BS, U. Wash., 1964; M of Engring., U. Fla., 1968; Cert. Aviation Safety, U. So. Calif., 1994. Sci. programmer Aerojet Gen. Corp., Sacramento, Calif., 1964-65; systems analyst GE Co., Daytona Beach, Fla., 1965-69; systems engr. GE Co., Phoenix, 1969-70; sr. software engr. Sperry Flight Systems, Phoenix, 1970-77; sr. systems engr. Honeywell, Inc., Phoenix, 1977-80; engr. section head Sperry Flight Systems, Phoenix, 1980-87; free lance flight instr., 1981—; tech. staff engr. Honeywell, Inc., Phoenix, 1987—; designated engring. rep. Fed. Aviation Adminstrn., Long Beach, 1987—. Mem. AIAA, SAE Internat. Internat. Soc. Air Safety Investigators, Am. Mensa Ltd. Home: 2514 W Pershing Ave Phoenix AZ 85029-1445 Office: Honeywell INc 21111 N 19th Ave Phoenix AZ 85027-2708

THOMAS, HAYWARD, manufacturing company executive; b. Los Angeles, Aug. 9, 1921; s. Charles Sparks and Julia (Hayward) T.; m. Phyllis Mary Wilson, July 1, 1943; children: H. David, Steven T. BS, U. Calif., Berkeley, 1943. Registered profl. engr. Staff engr. Joshua Hendy Corp., Los Angeles, 1946-50; prodn. mgr. Byron Jackson Co., Los Angeles, 1950-55; mgr. mfg. Frigidaire div. Gen. Motors Corp., Dayton, Ohio, 1955-70; group v.p. White Motor Corp., Cleve., 1971-73; sr. v.p. Broan Mfg. Co., Hartford, Wis., 1973-85; pres. Jensen Industries, Los Angeles, 1985-87; retired, 1987. Served to lt. USNR, 1943-46. Mem. Soc. Mfg. Engrs. (chmn. mfg. mgmt. council 1984-86). Republican. Episcopalian. Home: 1320 Granvia Altamira Palos Verdes Peninsula CA 90274-2006

THOMAS, HOWARD PAUL, civil engineer, consultant; b. Cambridge, Mass., Aug. 20, 1942; s. Charles Calvin and Helen Elizabeth (Hook) T.; m. Ingrid Nybo, Jan. 4, 1969; children: Kent Michael, Lisa Karen, Karina Michelle. BS in Engring., U. Mich., 1965, MS in Engring., 1966. Registered profl. engr., Alaska, Calif. Engr. Ove Arup & Ptnrs., London, 1966-67; project engr. Woodward-Clyde Cons., San Francisco, 1967-73; assoc. Woodward-Clyde Cons., Anchorage, 1975-89; spl. cons. Cowiconsult Cons., Copenhagen, 1973-75; prin. engr. Harding-Lawson Assocs., Anchorage, 1989-90; v.p., chief engr. EMCON Alaska, Inc., Anchorage, 1991-94; gen. mgr. Internat. Tech. Corp., Anchorage, 1994-96; assoc. GeoEngrs., Inc., Anchorage, 1996—; mem. Anchorage Mayor's Geotech. Adv. Commn., 1997—; chmn. Nat. Tech. Coun. Cold Regions Engring., 1988-89, chmn. com. program and publs., 1982-84; chmn. 4th Internat. Conf. Cold Regions Engring., Anchorage, 1986; liaison NAS/Nat. Rsch. Coun. Polar Rsch. Bd., 1989—; mem. Achorage Mayor's Geotech. Adv. Commn., 1997—. Contbr. articles to profl. jours. French horn musician Anchorage Civic Orch. Named Alaskan Engr. Yr., 1986. Fellow ASCE (pres. Anchorage chpt. 1985-86, chair mgmt. group A. 1996-97); mem. Soc. Am. Mil. Engrs., Cons. Engrs. Coun. Alaska (pres. 1989-90), Am. Cons. Engrs. Coun. (nat. dir. 1990-91), Project Mgmt. Inst. (v.p. Alaska chpt. 1991-95), Toastmasters (pres. Anchorage club 1984), Sons of Norway (v.p. Anchorage lodge 1997). Lutheran. Home: 2611 Brittany Dr Anchorage AK 99504-3332

THOMAS, JEANETTE MAE, accountant; b. Winona, Minn., Dec. 19, 1946; d. Herbert and Arline (Shank) Harmon; m. Gerald F. Thomas, Aug. 9, 1969; children: Bradley, Christopher. BS, Winona State U., 1968; postgrad., Colo. State U.; CFP, Coll. for Fin. Planning, Denver, 1985. Enrolled agt.; cert. fin. planner; registered rep. NASD; registered investment advisor; accredited tax advisor. Tchr. pub. schs. systems Colo., N.Mex., Mich., 1968-72; adminstrv. asst. Bus. Men's Svcs., Ft. Collins, Colo., 1974-75; tax cons. Tax Corp. Am., Ft. Collins, Colo., 1972-80; chief acct. Jayland Electric, La Porte, Colo., 1981-90; pres., CEO Thomas Fin. Svcs. Inc., Ft. Collins, 1980—. Contbr. articles to newspapers and profl. newsletters. Bd. dirs. local PTO, 1984-85; treas. Boy Scouts Am., 1985-88; master food safety advisor coop. ext. Colo. State U., 1988—; spkr., steering com. AARP Women's Fin. Info. Program, 1988—; chair adv. bd. Larimer County Coop. Ext., Colo. State U.; quality rev. com., career edn. adv. bd. Poudre R-1 Schs. Mem. Internat. Assn. Fin. Planning (past officer), Am. Soc. Women Accts. (bd. dirs. 1984-86, 96-97), Pvt. Industry Coun. (chair 1994-95), Nat. Soc. Pub. Accts., Colo. Soc. Pub. Accts., Inst. CFPs, Am. Notary Assn., Ft. Collins C. of C. (red carpet com. bus. assistance coun. 1989—). Home: PO Box 370 Laporte CO 80535-0370 Office: 400 S Howes St Ste 2 Fort Collins CO 80521-2802

THOMAS, JEFFERY MICHAEL, sales executive; b. Homestead, Fla., July 31, 1955; s. James Charles and Kay Diane (Reimer) T.; m. Maureen Ann Moriarty, Aug. 21, 1981 (div. Oct. 1985); m. Lisa Carroll Watson, Nov. 14, 1987; children: Wesley James, Elizabeth Kathryn. AA, Saddleback Community Coll., 1975; BA, Calif. State U., Fullerton, 1978; JD, Western State U., 1982. Law clerk freelance, Newport Beach, Calif., 1981-84; fin. cons. Ronson Fin. Svcs., Newport Beach, 1984-86; stockbroker, cons. Kidder Peabody & Co. Inc., Newport Beach, 1986-88; regional v.p. Lexington Capital Mgmt., L.A., 1988; v.p. devel. San Antonio Community Hosp., 1988-89; v.p., regional dir. Van Kampen Am. Capital, Oakbrook Terrace, Ill., 1989—; speaker in field, 1984—. Mem. Choc Padrinos, Childrens Hosp., Orange County, Calif., 1990, Laurelwood Homeowners Assn., Tustin, 1991-92, bd. dirs.; active Tustin Area Rep. Assembly, 1990, Orange County Parliamentarians, 1993—; coun. mem. City of Tustin, 1992—; regional coun. mem. So. Calif. Assn. Govts., 1992-94; bd. dirs. Calif. Housing Partnership Corp., 1993-95, Tustin Cmty. Found., 1993—; mem. tech. adv. com. Calif. Debt Adv. Commn., 1995-97; chmn. treasury oversight com. County of Orange., 1996—; mayor City of Tustin, 1997—. Office: Van Kampen Am Capital 24422 Avenida De La Carlota Laguna Hills CA 92653-3636

THOMAS, JIM, professional basketball team executive. Mng. gen. ptnr. Sacramento Kings. Office: Sacramento Kings 1 Sports Pky Sacramento CA 95834-2300*

THOMAS, JOSEPH FLESHMAN, architect; b. Oak Hill, W.Va., Mar. 23, 1915; s. Robert Russel and Effie (Fleshman) T.; m. Margaret Ruth Lively, Feb. 28, 1939 (dec.); children: Anita Carol, Joseph Stephen; m. Dorothy Francene Root, Apr. 29, 1967 (div.); m. Bonnie Abbott Buckley, June 15, 1991. Student, Duke, 1931-32; B.Arch., Carnegie-Mellon U., 1938. Practice architecture various firms W. Va., Va., Tenn., Calif., 1938-49; staff architect Calif. Div. Architecture, Los Angeles, 1949-52; prin. Joseph F. Thomas, architect, Pasadena, Calif., 1952-53; pres. Neptune & Thomas (architects-engrs.), Pasadena and San Diego, 1953-78; Mem. Pasadena Planning Commn., 1956-64, chmn., 1963-64; pres. Citizens Coun. for Planning, Pasadena, 1966-67; mem. steering com. Pasadena NOW, 1970-74; mem. Pasadena Design Com., 1979-86; mem. adv. bd. Calif. Office Architecture and Constrn., 1970-72; mem. archtl. adv. com. Calif. State U. System, 1981-84; mem. adv. coun. Sch. Environ. Design Calif. Poly. Inst., 1983—; mem. outreach for architecture com. Carnegie Mellon U., 1989—, pres.'s devel. com., 1991—. Prin. works include Meth. Hosp., Arcadia, Calif., Foothill Presbyn. Hosp., Glendora, Calif., master plans and bldgs., Citrus Coll., Azusa, Calif., Riverside (Calif.) Coll., Westmont Coll., Monticeto, Calif., Northrop Inst. Tech., Inglewood, Calif, Indian Valley Coll., Marin County, Calif., Pepperdine U., Malibu, Calif., UCLA, U. Calif., San Diego, Long Beach (Calif.) State U., Calif. Inst. Tech., Pasadena, Calif., other coll. bldgs. Pacific Telephone Co., Pasadena, L.A. County Superior Ct. Bldg., U.S. Naval Hosp., San Diego. Trustee Almansor Edn. Ctr., 1986-92; bd. dirs., co-founder Syncor Internat., 1973-83; founding dir. Bank of Pasadena, 1962-65. Lt. (j.g.) USNR, 1943-46. Recipient Service award City of Pasadena, 1964; Disting. Service award Calif. Dept. Gen. Services, 1972; Gold Crown award Pasadena Arts Council, 1981. Fellow AIA (4 awards honor, 13 awards merit 1957-78, dir. Calif. coun. 1966-68, exec. com. 1974-77, pres. Pasadena chpt. 1967, chmn. Calif. sch. facilities com. 1970-72, mem. nat. jud. bd. 1973-74, nat. dir. 1974-77, treas. 1977-79, exec. com., planning com., chmn. finance com.); mem. Breakfast Forum (chmn. 1983), Annandale Golf Club, Pi Kappa Alpha. Republican. Methodist. Home: 330 San Miguel Rd Pasadena CA 91105-1446

THOMAS, JOSEPH JAMES, JR., trade association administrator; b. Fairbanks, Alaska, Oct. 17, 1948; s. Joseph James Sr. and Myrtle Rose (Harris) T.; children: Damian, Natalie, Ryan. BS, W.Va. U., 1974. Constrn. worker Laborers Local 942, Fairbanks, bus. agt., bus. mgr.; trustee Alaska Laborers Trust, 1978—; v.p. Alaska State AFL-CIO, 1984-96; bd. regents U. Alaska, 1995—. Vol. various polit. campaigns. Democrat. Roman Catholic. Home: 879 Vide Way Fairbanks AK 99712 Office: Laborers Local 942 315 Barnette St Fairbanks AK 99712

THOMAS, KEITH VERN, bank executive; b. Provo, Utah, Oct. 21, 1946; s. Vern R. and Lois (Doran) T.; m. Sherrie Hunter, Oct. 7, 1969; children: Genevieve, Joshua, Rachel, William, Rebecca. AA, Dixie Coll., 1969; BS, Brigham Young U., 1971; MBA, St. Mary's Coll., 1980. From examiner to asst. dir. Fed. Home Loan Bank Bd., San Francisco, 1971-85; sr. v.p., dir. exams. and supervision Fed. Home Loan Bank, Seattle, 1985-88; exec. v.p., COO Frontier Savings Assn., Las Vegas, Nev., 1988-89, pres., CEO, dir., 1989-90; sr. v.p. Am. Fed. Savs. Bank, Las Vegas, 1991-96; pres., CEO Frontier Fin. Corp., Las Vegas, 1996—; bd. dirs., chmn. Nev. Cmty. Reinvestment Corp.; bd. dirs. So. Nev. Housing Corp., U.S. Savs. Bank. Editor: Real Estate Textbook, 1983-84. Trustee Nev. Sch. Arts; mem. fin. com. North Las Vegas Neighborhood Housing Svcs.; mem. cmty. reinvestment and housing com. Western League Savs. Instns.; bd. dirs., scoutmaster Boulder Dam Area coun. Boy Scouts Am.; active Leadership Las Vegas; bd. dirs. Nev. Cmty. Found., Local Initiatives Support Corp.; mem. Clark County Cmty. Housing Adv. Com.; mem. contract com. United Way; mem. Leadership Las Vegas Alumni Assn. Named Outstanding Instr., Inst. Fin. Edn. 1984. Mem. Nev. Clearing House Assn. (v.p., bd. dirs.), Nat. Assn. Rev. Appraisers and Mortgage Underwriters, Brigham Young Mgmt. Soc., So. Nev. Exec. Coun. (bd. dirs., past pres.), Las Vegas C. of C., Nev. Devel. Authority, So. Nev. Home Builders Assn., Las Vegas S.W. Rotary (bd. dirs.). Republican. Mem. Ch. Jesus Christ LDS. Office: Frontier Fin Corp PO Box 81796 Las Vegas NV 89180

THOMAS, LAURA FALER, nutrition educator; b. Wallace, Idaho, Mar. 6, 1961; d. Roy Lee and Kaarlene (Anderson) Faler; m. James Alan Thomas, Sept. 1, 1984; children: Matthew Faler, Michael Robert. BS in Home Econs., Food and Nutrition, U. Idaho, 1983, MEd in Vocat./Adult Edn., 1995. Therapeutic dietitian Idaho State Sch. and Hosp., Nampa, 1983-85; nutrition edn. cons. Idaho Dairy Coun., Boise, 1985-86, dir. nutrition edn., 1986—; instr. food svc. course Idaho State Dept. Edn./Boise (Idaho) State U., 1986; steering com. mem. Idaho's Ptnrs. in Health Through Nutrition, Boise, 1990-95. Co-author, co-editor: Body Walk Resource Manual, 1989; contbr. articles to profl. jours. Named Disting. Alumna U. Idaho Sch. Family and Consumer Scis., 1997. Mem. Am. Dietetic Assn. (registered dietitian, young dietitian of yr. 1987), Idaho Dietetic Assn. (pres. 1996-97), Am. Assn. Family and Consumer Sci. (new achiever award 1989), Idaho Assn. Family and Consumer Sci., Soc. for Nutrition Edn. (young nutrition educator of yr. 1992). Roman Catholic. Office: Idaho Dairy Coun 1365 N Orchard St Ste 203 Boise ID 83706-2249

THOMAS, LAURA HEBENSTREIT, English educator; b. Hornell, N.Y., Apr. 17, 1958; d. Henry Arthur Hebenstreit and Carole Anne (Clifford) Kimball; m. Timothy Allen Thom as, June 22, 1985. BA in English, St. Bonaventure U., 1980; Colo. Tchg. cert., Colo. State U., 1988, MA in English, 1994. Secondary lang. arts tchg. cert., Colo. Tchr. Estes Park (Colo.) H.S., 1988-92; grad. tchg. asst. Colo. State U., Ft. Collins, 1992-94, lectr., 1994-96; tchr. English Estes Park (Colo.) H.S., 1996; instr. Colo. State U., 1996—; bd. mem., scholarship coord., v.p. Colo. H.S. Press Assn., 1990-94; bd. student comm. Colo. State U., 1992-93. Mem. Nat. Coun. Tchrs. English, Colo. Lang. Arts Soc. (conf. registrar 1994—, Outstanding Tchr. of Yr. 1997), Conf. on Coll. Composition and Comm., Phi Kappa Phi. Home: 210 S Grant Ave Fort Collins CO 80521

THOMAS, LAURA MARLENE, artist, private antique dealer; b. Chico, Calif., Apr. 29, 1936; d. Boyd Stanley Beck and Lois Velma (Behrke) Lyons;

m. Charles Rex Thomas; children: Tracy Loraine, Jeffory Norris. AA in Fine Arts, Sacramento City Coll., 1978; BA in Fine Arts, Calif. State U., 1981. Tchrs. asst. Hanford Elem. Sch., Hanford, Calif., 1963-68; asst. dir. RSVP: Retired Sr. Vol. Program, Hanford, 1971-74; dir. of Art Bank Sacramento City Coll., Sacramento, 1976-78; pub. asst. Student Activities Calif. State Univ., Sacramento, 1978-81; antique dealer pvt. practice, Sacramento, 1981--, arts and crafts bus., 1976--; social worker Cath. Social Svcs., Sacramento, 1985--. Artist: weaving, Double Image, 1977, 2nd Place 1977; ceramic sculptor, Bird. Charter mem. YWCA, Sacramento, 1972, Folsum Hist. Soc., 1988. Cert. of appreciation, Carmellia City Ctr. Adv. Council, Sacramento, 1986. Mem. Statue of Liberty-Ellis Island Found., 1985, North Shore Animal League (Benefactors award 1985), Calif. State U. Alumni Assn., Hanford Sportsman Club (v.p. 1963-68). Republican. Protestant. Home: 2719 I St Apt 4 Sacramento CA 95816-4354

THOMAS, LINDA MARRI GANDY, programmer, analyst; b. Salt Lake City, Oct. 7, 1951; d. Rupert Kennedy and Marilyn Irma (Murdock) Gandy; m. Norman Clark Thomas, Feb. 23, 1968; children: Tina Sue, Tonya Marie, Norman Clark II. BS in Computer Sci., Westminster Coll., 1994. Supr. pers. lines underwriting Northwestern Nat. Ins. Co., Salt Lake City, 1976-85; sr. agy. mktg. rep. Aetna Life and Casualty, Salt Lake City, 1985-86; comml. lines customer rep. Affiliated Ins. Agy., Salt Lake City, 1987-89; adminstrv. asst. Westminster Coll., Salt Lake City, 1989-95; electronic data interchange coord., programmer analyst Huish Detergents, Salt Lake City, 1995—. Home: 4355 Alice Way West Valley City UT 84119-5867 Office: Huish Detergents 3540 West 1987 South Salt Lake City UT 84125

THOMAS, LOWELL, JR., author, lecturer, former lieutenant governor, former state senator; b. London, Oct. 6, 1923; s. Lowell Jackson and Frances (Ryan) T.; m. Mary Taylor Pryor, May 20, 1950; children: Anne Frazier, David Lowell. Student, Taft Sch., 1942; B.A., Dartmouth Coll., 1948; postgrad., Princeton Sch. Pub. and Internat. Affairs, 1952. Asst. cameraman Fox Movietone News, S.Am., 1939, Bradford Washburn Alaskan mountaineering expdn., 1940; illustrated lecturer, 1946—; asst. economist, photographer with Max Weston Thornburg, Turkey, 1947, Iran, 1948; film prodn. Iran, 1949; Tibet expdn. with Lowell Thomas, Sr., 1949; field work Cinerama, S.Am., Africa, Asia, 1951-52; travels by small airplane with wife, writing and filming Europe, Africa, Middle East, 1954-55; mem. Rockwell Polar Flight, first flight around the world over both poles, Nov., 1965; mem. Alaska State Senate, 1967-74; lt. gov. State of Alaska, 1974-79; owner Talkeetna Air Taxi, Inc., air contract carrier, Anchorage, Alaska, 1980-94. Producer series of films Flight to Adventure, NBC-TV, 1956; producer, writer TV series High Adventure, 1957-59; producer documentary film Adaq, King of Alaskan Seas, 1960; producer two films on Alaska, 1962, 63, film on U. Alaska, 1964, South Pacific travel documentary, 1965, film on Arctic oil exploration, Atlantic-Richfield Co., 1969. Author: Out of this World, A Journey to Tibet, 1950, (with Mrs. Lowell Thomas, Jr.) Our Flight to Adventure, 1956, The Silent War in Tibet, 1959, The Dalai Lama, 1961, The Trail of Ninety-Eight, 1962, (with Lowell Thomas Sr.) More Great True Adventures, 1963, Famous First Flights that Changed History, 1968. past pres. Western Alaska coun. Boys Scouts Am.; bd. dirs. Anchorage unit Salvation Army, Alaska Conservation Found. 1st lt. USAAF, 1943-45. Mem. Nat. Parks and Conservation Assn. (bd. dirs.), Alaska C. of C., Aircraft Owners and Pilots Assn. Clubs: Explorers, Marco Polo, Dutch Treat (N.Y.C.); Rotary, (Anchorage), Press (Anchorage); Dartmouth Outing; American Alpine. Address: 10800 Hideaway Lake Dr Anchorage AK 99516-1145

THOMAS, MARCELLA ELAINE, elementary education educator; b. Blythe, Calif., July 20, 1946; d. Will H. and Carrie E. (Mack) Ector Sr.; m. George Walter Thomas, July 10, 1982; 1 child, Danielle Elaine. AA, Palo Verde Community Coll., 1966; BA, Calif. State U., 1970; MA, Azusa Pacific U., 1972; postgrad., U. Calif. at Riverside. Cert. c.c. educator. Mentor tchr. 5th grade Palo Verde Unified Sch. Dist., Blythe, Calif. Named to Delta Kappa Gamma Soc. (past pres.); recipient Tchr. of Yr. award. Mem. ASCD, NEA, CTA, CEEA, Palo Verde Tchrs. Assn. Home: 331 Bristlecone Ave Blythe CA 92225-2415

THOMAS, MICHAEL STEVEN, software company executive; b. Denver, June 1, 1954; s. Robert A. and Marilyn Jo (Malloy) T.; m. Mary Shiela Conway, Dec. 29, 1958; children: Kelly Louise, Edward Joseph. BS in Bus. and Fin., U. Colo., 1976; MBA, Regis U., Denver, 1995. Cert. purchasing mgr. Subcontract adminstr. Martin Marietta Corp., Denver, 1985-93; sr. subcontract adminstr. Union Pacific Corp., Boulder, Colo., 1993-94; contract adminstrv. mgr. Environ. Sci. and Engring., Englewood, Colo., 1994-95; purchasing mgr. Space Imaging, Inc., Thornton, Colo., 1995-96; mgr. corp. purchasing and contracts J.D. Edwards & Co., Denver, 1996—. Contbr. articles to profl. jours. Leader Boy Scouts Am., Lakewood, Colo. Fellow Nat. Contract Mgmt. Assn.; mem. Am. Mgmt. Assn., Nat. Assn. Purchasing Mgmt. Republican. Roman Catholic. Home: 2407 S Holman Cir Lakewood CO 80228 Office: JD Edwards & Co 8055 E Tufts Ave Denver CO 80237

THOMAS, MICHAEL TILSON, performing company executive; b. 1945. Piano studies with John Crown, U. So. Calif., 1964. Asst. conductor to prin. guest conductor Boston Symphony Orch., 1969-74; music dir. Buffalo Philharmonic, 1971-79; prin. guest conductor L.A. Philharmonic, 1981-85; prin. conductor Gt. Woods Music Festival, 1985-88, London Symphony Orch., 1988-95; music dir. San Francisco Symphony, 1995—; artistic dir., founder The New World Symphony, 1988—. TV appearances with London Symphony Orch., numerous PBS programs. Recipient Koussevitsky prize Tanglewood, 1969; named Conductor of Yr. Mus. Am., 1995. Office: San Francisco Symphony 201 Van Ness Ave San Francisco CA 94102

THOMAS, MITCHELL, JR., aerospace company executive; b. Terre Haute, Ind., Nov. 25, 1936; s. Mitchell and Carolyn Amalia (Wolff) T.; m. Helen Steimle, June 28, 1970; children: Sheri Helen, Deborah Michal, Mitchell III. AB cum laude, Harvard U., 1958; MS, U. Ill., 1959; PhD, Calif. Inst. Tech., 1964. With McDonnell Douglas, Santa Monica, Calif., 1959-64, group leader launch vehicles, 1964-65, sect. chief ablation and applied rsch. sect., 1965-67; br. chief thermophysics lab. McDonnell Douglas, Huntington Beach, Calif., 1969-75; dir. rsch. and devel. L'Garde Inc., Newport Beach, Calif., 1975-76, pres., 1976-96; pres. Thomas Dynamics Modeling, Inc., Villa Park, Calif., 1996—; mem. adv. com. on Gossamer structures NASA, 1981. Contbr. articles to profl. jours. Mem. AAAS, AIAA (assoc. fellow thermophysics com., tech. program chmn. for 8th thermophysics conf.). Office: TDM Inc 9691 Villa Woods Dr Villa Park CA 96861

THOMAS, PEARL ELIZABETH, English educator; b. N.Y.C., Feb. 22, 1928; d. Humphrey S. and Frances (Collins) T. BS, CCNY, 1948, MA, 1952; PhD, Columbia U., 1977; postgrad., Union Grad. Sch. Chmn. English dept. N.Y.C. secondary schs.; asst. prof. CUNY, N.Y.C., 1977-83; prin. A.P. Randolph High Sch.; adj. prof. U. Calif., Irvine, 1983—, L.A. Coll., 1988-91. Author: (series) Adventures in Literature, 1980-90, College Video on Native Son, 1991. Recipient awards for Contbn. to Edn. 1976-83. Mem. MLA, Am. Tchrs. English, Global Network in Edn. Home: 5718 Ravenspur Dr Palos Verdes Peninsula CA 90275-3561

THOMAS, RICHARD MCKENNON, II, college administrator; b. Ft. Morgan, Colo., Nov. 5, 1961; s. Richard McKennon and Ann Rae (Douglass) T.; m. Shannon Lisa Wells, Jan. 10, 1987; children: Jamison Scott, Christopher Patrick, Madilynn Samantha. BS, Colo. State U., 1993, MS, 1995. Asst. mgr. Walsh Auto Parts, Englewood, Colo., 1979-83; mgr. D & S Auto Parts, Littleton, Colo., 1983-85; salesman Continental VW, Littleton, 1985-86; mgr. Auto Parts Profls., Denver, 1986-90; athletic parking coord. Colo. State U., Ft. Collins, 1990-95, asst. informal recreation coord., 1993-95; assoc. dir. housing and residence life Mesa State Coll., Grand Junction, 1996—; informal recreation rep. Colo. State U., Ft. Collins, 1993-94, chair recreation adv. bd., 1994-95; new residence hall com. mem. Mesa State Coll., Grand Junction, Colo., 1996—. Reader bd. mem. Jour. Student Affairs, 1994-95. Asst. coach Ft. Collins Soccer Club, 1993-95; league coord. Littleton Soccer Assn., 1995; coach T-ball Grand Mesa Little League, Grand Junction, 1996, Grand Mesa Youth Soccer Assn. U9-Boys, 1996—. Mem. Nat. Intramural Recreational Sports Assn., Nat. Assn. Student Pers. Adminstrs., Assn. Coll. and Univ. Housing Officers. Office: Mesa State Coll PO Box 2647 Grand Junction CO 81502

THOMAS, RICHARD VAN, state supreme court justice; b. Superior, Wyo., Oct. 11, 1932; s. John W. and Gertrude (McCloskey) T.; m. Lesley Arlene Ekman, June 23, 1956; children: Tara Lynn, Richard Ross, Laura Lee, Sidney Marie. B.S. in Bus. Adminstrn. with honors, U. Wyo., 1954, LL.B. with honors, 1956; LL.M., NYU, 1961. Bar: Wyo. 1956, U.S. Ct. Appeals (10th cir.) 1960, U.S. Ct. Mil. Appeals 1960, U.S. Supreme Ct. 1960. Law clk. to judge U.S. Ct. Appeals (10th Circuit), Cheyenne, 1960-63; asso. firm Hirst & Applegate, Cheyenne, 1963-64; partner firm Hirst, Applegate & Thomas, Cheyenne, 1964-69; U.S. atty. Dist. Wyo., Cheyenne, 1969-74; justice Wyo. Supreme Ct., Cheyenne, 1974—, chief justice, 1985-86. Pres. Laramie County United Way, 1972, trustee, 1973-74, chmn. admissions and allocations com., 1968-69, chmn. exec. com., 1973, chmn. combined fed. campaign, 1974; bd. dirs. Goodwill Industries Wyo., Inc., 1974-77; exec. com. Cheyenne Crusade for Christ, 1974; v.p., exec. com. Wyo. Billy Graham Crusade, 1987; bd. dirs. Cheyenne Youth for Christ, 1978-81; chancellor Episcopal Diocese of Wyo., 1972—, lay dep. gen. conv., 1973—, chmn. search evaluation nomination com., 1976-77, lay reader, 1969—; bd. dirs. Community Action of Laramie County, 1977-82; chmn. Cheyenne dist. Boy Scouts Am., 1977-78, mem. nat. council, 1982-84, mem. Longs Peak council, 1977—, v.p. dist. ops., v.p. membership relationships, 1979-81, pres., 1981-83; mem. North Cen. Region Exec. Bd., 1986—, pres. Old West Trails Area, 1988—; chmn. Laramie County Health Planning Com., 1980-84. Served with JAGC USAF, 1957-60. Named Boss of Year, Indian Paintbrush chpt. Nat. Secs. Assn., 1974; Civil Servant of Year, Cheyenne Assn. Govt. Employees, 1973; Vol. of Yr., Cheyenne Office, Youth Alternatives, 1979; recipient St. George Episcopal award, 1982, Silver Beaver award Boy Scouts Am., 1985. Mem. Am., Laramie County bar assns., Wyo. State Bar, Phi Kappa Phi, Phi Alpha Delta, Omicron Delta Kappa, Sigma Nu. Clubs: Kiwanis (Cheyenne) (program com. 1969-70, dir. 1970-72, chmn. key club com. 1973-76, disting. pres. 1980-81), Masons (Cheyenne) (33 deg., past master); Shriners; Nat. Sojourners (Cheyenne). Office: Wyo Supreme Ct Supreme Ct Bldg Cheyenne WY 82002

THOMAS, ROGER PARRY, interior designer, art consultant; b. Salt Lake City, Nov. 4, 1951; s. E. Parry and Peggy Chatterton T.; m. Marilyn Harris Hite, Nov. 21, 1976 (div. Apr. 1979); m. H. Andrea Wahn, Nov. 20, 1982 (div. Dec. 1996); 1 child, Andrew Chatterton. BFA, Tufts U., 1973. Pres. Miller-Thomas, Inc., Las Vegas, Nev., 1973-76; v.p. Yates-Silverman, Inc., Las Vegas, 1976-81; v.p. design Atlandia Design a Mirage Resorts Inc. Co., Las Vegas, 1981—. Mem. Nev. State Coun. on the Arts (chair), McCarren Arts Adv. Bd.; vice chmn. McCarren Arts. Office: Atlandia Design 3260 Industrial Rd Las Vegas NV 89109-1132

THOMAS, SHIRLEY, author, educator, business executive; b. Glendale, Calif.; d. Oscar Miller and Ruby (Thomas) Annis; m. W. White, Feb. 22, 1949 (div. June 1952); m. William C. Perkins, Oct. 24, 1969. BA in Modern Lit., U. Sussex, Eng., 1960, PhD in Comm., 1967; diploma, Russian Fedn. Cosmonautics, 1995. Actress, writer, producer, dir. numerous radio and TV stas., 1942-46; v.p. Commodore Prodns., Hollywood, Calif., 1946-52; pres. Annis & Thomas, Inc., Hollywood, 1952—; prof. technical writing U. So. Calif., L.A., 1975—; Hollywood corr. NBC, 1952-56; editor motion pictures CBS, Hollywood, 1956-58; corr. Voice of Am., 1958-59; now free lance writer; cons. biol. scis. communication project George Washington U., 1965-66; cons. Stanford Rsch. Inst., 1967-68, Jet Propulsion Lab., 1969-70. Author: Men of Space vols. 1-8, 1960-68, Spanish trans., 1961, Italian, 1962; Space Tracking Facilities, 1963, Computers: Their History, Present Applications and Future, 1965; The Book of Diets, 1974. Organizer, chmn. City of L.A. Space Adv. Com., 1964-73, Women's Space Symposia, 1962-73; foudner, chmn. aerospace hist. com. Calif. Mus. Sci. and Industry; chmn. Theodore von Karman Postage Stamp Com., 1965—, stamp issued 1992; bd. dirs. World Children's Transplant Fund. Recipient Aerospace Excellence award Calif. Mus. Found. 1991, Nat. Medal Honor DAR, 1992, Yuri Gagarin Medal Honor, 1995. Fellow Brit. Interplanetary Soc.; mem. AIAA, AAAS, Internat. Soc. Aviation Writers, Air Force Assn. (Airpower Arts and Letters award 1961), Internat. Acad. Astronautics, Nat. Aero. Assn., Nat. Asn. Sci. Writers, Soc. for Tech. Communications, Am. Astronautical Soc., Nat. Geog. Soc., Am. Soc. Pub. Adminstrn. (sci. and tech. in govt. com. 1972—), Achievement Awards for Coll. Scientists, Muses of Calif., Theta Sigma Phi, Phi Beta. Home: 8027 Hollywood Blvd Los Angeles CA 90046-2510 Office: U So Calif Profl Writing Program University Park Waite-Phillips Hall 404 Los Angeles CA 90089-4034

THOMAS, STEPHEN CECIL, Chinese politics educator, university official; b. Columbus, Ohio, Nov. 8, 1944; s. Cecil Albert and Frances Catherine (Smith) T.; m. Carol Isabel Dreselly, Aug. 25, 1982; children: Michael and Nicolas (twins), Matthew. BA in Polit. Sci., San Jose State U., 1967; MA in East Asian Studies, Stanford U., 1972, PhD in Polit. Sci., 1979. Mem. faculty U. Colo., Denver, 1976—, prof. Chinese politics, chmn. dept. polit. sci., 1984-90, co-dir. Internat. Affairs Office, 1987-92, dir. Office Internat. Edn., 1992-94, Fei Yi-Ming prof. politics Hopkins-Nanjing program, 1994-95; sec.-treas. Nat. Com. Internat. Studies and Programs Adminstrs., 1991-92. Bd. dirs. Nat. Com. on U.S.-China Rels., N.Y.C., 1972-74, Am. Friends Svc. Co., Phila., 1972-76. Grantee USIA, 1987-90, U.S. Dept. Edn., 1987-89, 90-92, NEH, 1992-95. Mem. Am. Polit. Sci. Assn., Internat. Studies Assn. Mem. Soc. of Friends. Home: 541 Arapahoe Ave Boulder CO 80302-5826 Office: U Colo Polit Sci Box 190 PO Box 173364 Denver CO 80217-3364

THOMAS, STEVE D., infosystem specialist; b. Butte, Mont., Aug. 8, 1951; s. William James and Catherine (Murphy) T.; m. Kathy Ann McCarthy, Aug. 22, 1971; children: Shawn, Heather. Programmer analyst Anaconda Co., Butte, 1973-81, systems analyst, 1981-82; systems programmer ARCO Metals, Columbia Falls, Mont., 1982-83, supr. ops. and tech. support, 1983-85; supt. of mgmt. info. systems Columbia Falls Aluminum Co., 1985-96, info. sys. mgr., 1996—. Office: CFAC 2000 Aluminum Dr Columbia Falls MT 59912-9424

THOMAS, SYLVIA ANN, community college dean; b. Hanford, Calif., Jan. 16, 1947; d. Antonio R. and Esperanza R. (Gonzales) Vallejo; m. Francis Thomas, June 28, 1970; 1 child, Aric Vincent. BA, UCLA, 1968; teaching degree, Fresno State U., 1970; MA, Pepperdine U., 1973, postgrad., 1992. Cert. tchr., elem. K-9, jr. coll. and adminstrn. Tchr. Colton (Ill.) Sch. Dist., 1970-83; dean instruction, 1994—; dean instrnl. support svcs. Moreno Valley Campus of Riverside C.C., 1993-94, dean instrn. Gazzette columnist Am. Kennel Club, 1996—. Mem. Jr. League of Riverside, 1985—. Mem. Akita Club Am. (sec., nat. liaison, mem. judges edn. com. 1996—), Kin Ken Akita Club (newsletter editor), Inland Empire Akita Club (newsletter editor), Lake Mathews Kennel Club (treas.), Channel Islands Akita Club, Orange Empire Dog Club, Lake Mathews Kennel Club, Samoyed Club Am. Democrat. Roman Catholic. Home: 2155 Hackamore Pl Riverside CA 92506-4616

THOMAS, TERESA ANN, microbiologist, educator; b. Wilkes-Barre, Pa., Oct. 17, 1939; d. Sam Charles and Edna Grace T. BS cum laude, Coll. Misericordia, 1961; MS in Biology, Am. U. Beirut, 1965; MS in Microbiology, U. So. Calif., 1973. Tchr., sci. supr., curriculum coord. Meyers High Sch., Wilkes-Barre, 1962-64, Wilkes-Barre Area Public Schs., 1961-66; rsch. assoc. Proctor Found. for Rsch. in Ophthalmology U. Calif. Med. Ctr., San Francisco, 1966-68; instr. Robert Coll. of Istanbul (Turkey), 1968-71, Am. Edn. in Luxembourg, 1971-72, Bosco Tech. Inst., Rosemead, Calif., 1973-74, San Diego Community Coll. Dist., 1974-80; prof. math., sci. and engring. div. Southwestern Coll., Chula Vista, Calif., 1980—, pres. acad. senate, 1984-85, del., 1986-89; chmn., coord., steering com. project Cultural Rsch. Educational and Trade Exchange, 1991—, Southwestern Coll.-Shanghai Inst. Fgn. Trade; coord. Southwestern Coll. Great Teaching Seminar, 1987, 88, 89, coord. scholars program, 1988-90; mem. exec. com. Acad. Senate for Calif. C.Cs., 1985-86, Chancellor of Calif. C.Cs. Adv. and Rev. Council Fund for Instrnl. Improvement, 1984-86; co-project dir. statewide, coord. So. Calif. Biotech Edn. Consortium, 1993-95, steering com., 1993—; adj. asst. prof. Chapman Coll., San Diego, 1974-83; asst. prof. San Diego State U., 1977-79; chmn. Am. Colls. Istanbul Sci. Week, 1969-71; mem. adv. bd. Chapman Coll. Community Center, 1979-80; cons. sci. curriculum Calif. Dept. Edn., 1986—; pres. Internat. Relations Club 1959-61; mem. San Francisco World Affairs Coun., 1966-68, San Diego World Affairs Coun., 1992—; v.p. Palomar Palace Estates Home Owners Assn., 1983-85, pres. 1994—. mem. editorial rev. bd. Jour. of Coll. Sci. Teaching, NSTA, 1988-92; bd. dirs. San Diego-Leon Sister Cities Soc., 1991-94. Mem. Chula Vista Nature Interpretive Ctr. (life), Internat. Friendship Commn., Chula Vista, 1985-95, vice chmn. 1989-90, chmn. 1990-92, Chula Vista, Calif., 1987-95; mem. U.S.-Mex. Sister Cities Assn., nat. bd. dirs., 1992-94, gen. chair 30th nat. conv., 1993; mem. City of Chula Vista Resource Conservation Commn., 1996—. NSF fellow, 1965; USPHS fellow, 1972-73; recipient Nat. Teaching Excellence award Nat. Inst. Staff and Orgnl. Devel., 1989; recognized at Internat. Conf. Teaching Excellence, Austin, 1989; Pa. Heart Assn. research grantee, 1962; named Southwestern Coll. Woman of Distinction, 1987. Mem. Am. Soc. Microbiology (So. Calif. Microbe Discovery Team 1995—), Nat. Sci. Tchrs. Assn. (life, internat. com., coord. internat. honors exchange lectr. competition sponsored with Assn. Sci Educators Great Britain, 1986), Nat. Assn. Biology Tchrs. (life), Soc. Coll. Sci. Tchrs. (life), S.D. Zool. Soc., Calif. Tchrs. Assn., NEA, Am. Assn. Community and Jr. Colls., Giraffes, Am.-Lebanese Assn. San Diego (chmn. scholarship com., pres. 1988-93), Am. U. of Beirut Alumni and Friends of San Diego (1st v.p. 1984-91), Lions Internat. (bull. editor 1991-93, best bull. award 1992, 93, 2nd v.p. 1992-93, 1st v.p. 1993-94, editor Roaring Times Newsletter 1993-94, chmn. dist. internat. rels. and cooperations com. 1993-95, pres. SW San Diego County chpt. 1994-95, Sweetwater Zone chmn. dist. 4-L6 1996-97), Chula Vista-Odawara (Japan) Sister Cities Assn. (founding pres. 1995—), Kappa Gamma Pi (pres. Wilkes-Barre chpt. 1963-64, San Francisco chpt. 1967-68), Sigma Phi Sigma, Phi Theta Kappa (hon. mem. 1994—), Alpha Pi Epsilon (founder, advisor Southwestern Coll. chpt. 1989-90, Am. Lebanese Syrian Ladies Club (pres. 1982-83). Office: Southwestern Coll 900 Otay Lakes Rd Chula Vista CA 91910-7223

THOMAS, VERNEDA ESTELLA, retired perfusionist; b. Chgo., June 21, 1936; d. Russel Huston and Verneda (Williams) T. BS, Graceland Coll., Lamoni, Iowa, 1973. Cardiovascualr technician Michael Reese Hosp., Chgo., 1962; cardiopulmonary technician Chgo. State Tuberculosis Sanitorium, Chgo., 1962-66, Loyola U. Sch. Medicine, Maywood, Ill., 1966-68; physiology technician Loyola U. Sch. Medicine, 1968-69; med. technologist Cook County Hosp., Chgo., 1969-71; rsch. assoc. Queen's Med. Ctr., Honolulu, 1973-78; intra aortic balloon pump technician Queen's Med. Ctr., 1973-95; perfusionist for pvt. med. practice Honolulu, 1978-82; perfusionist Mid Pacific Perfusion, Honolulu, 1982-88, Psicor, Inc., Honolulu, 1988-96; ret., 1996; referee, U.S. Volleyball Assn., 1978. Contbr. articles to med. publs. Mem. U.S. Pan-Am. high jump team, Mex., 1955; mem. U.S. Olympic volleyball team, Tokyo, 1964. Mem. Am. Soc. Cardiopulmonary Technology, Am. Bd. Cardiovascular Perfusion. Baptist. Home: 217 Prospect St Apt D7 Honolulu HI 96813-1755 Office: Psicor Inc 16818 Via Del Campo Ct San Diego CA 92127-1714

THOMAS, WILLIAM MARSHALL, congressman; b. Wallace, Idaho, Dec. 6, 1941; s. Virgil and Gertrude Thomas; m. Sharon Lynn Hamilton, Jan. 1968; children: Christopher, Amelia. B.A., San Francisco State U., 1963, M.A., 1965. Mem. faculty dept. Am. govt. Bakersfield (Calif.) Coll., 1965-74, prof., 1965-74; mem. Calif. State Assembly, 1974-78, 96th-105th Congress from 18th, now 21st Calif. Dist., 1979—; vice chmn. of House Task Force on Campaign Fin. Reform; mem. Ho. of Reps. Ways and Means Com.; chmn. Com. on House Oversight, Ways & Means Health Subcom.; mem. Ways & Means subcom on Trade; mem. del. to Soviet Union, by Am. Council Young Polit. Leaders, 1977; chmn. Kern County Republican Central Com., 1972-74; mem. Calif. Rep. Com., 1972-80; del. Republican Party Nat. Conv., 1980, 84, 88; mem. Rep. Leader's Task Force on Health Care Reform. Office: Ho of Reps 2208 Rayburn Ho Office Bldg Washington DC 20515

THOMAS-COTE, NANCY DENECE, office products manufacturing company executive; b. Long Beach, Calif., Feb. 20, 1959; d. Alan and Barbara Jean (Rush) Tuthill; m. Gary Cote. V.p. BTE, Inc., Long Beach, 1978-88; gen. mgr. BTE, Inc., Huntington Beach, Calif., 1982-88, pres., 1988-95, CEO, 1995—; pres. Omni Label, Inc., Huntington Beach, 1985-90; co-owner LeMac Leasing, La Canada, Calif., 1985-90; owner Dayspring Wedding Cons., Long Beach, 1991-93. V.p. Long Beach Spl. Charities, Inc., 1987; pres. Long Beach Spl. Charities, Inc., 1988. Mem. NAFE, Am. Health Info. Mgmt. Assn., Calif. Health Info. Assn., Bus. Products Industry Assn., Nat. Assn. Women Bus. Owners (bd. dirs. L.A. chpt. 1995-96). Office: BTE Inc 5672 Bolsa Ave Huntington Beach CA 92649-1113

THOMAS-JOHN, YVONNE MAREE, artist, interior designer; b. Leeton, New South Wales, Australia, Sept. 8, 1944; came to U.S., 1966; d. Percy Edward and Gladys May (Markham) Thomas; m. Michael Peter John, Aug. 20, 1966; children: Michael Christian, Stephen Edwin Dennis. Student, Buenaventura Coll., 1969, U. Calif., Santa Barbara, 1975; cert., United Design Guild, 1975; AA, Interior Design Guild, 1976; Diploma, Internat. Correspondence Sch., 1976. Designer Percy Thomas Real Estate, Leeton, 1960-66; cosmetologist, artist Bernard's Hair Stylists, Ventura, Calif., 1966-67, 74-73; cosmetologist Banks Beauty Salon, Chgo., 1968-69; owner, mgr. Yvonne Maree Designs, Ventura and Olympia, Wash., 1978—; owner, cosmetologist Mayfair Salon, Leeton, 1962-66; owner, mgr. Y.M. Boutique, Griffith, Australia, 1965-66. Contbr. numerous short stories and poems to newspapers; artist numerous pen and ink drawings; exhibited one-person show Royal Mus. Sydney, Australia, 1954; exhibited group shows Ventura County Courthouse, 1970, Wash. Women in Art, Olympia, 1990, Timberland Libr., Olympia, 1990, Maska Internat. Gallery, Seattle, 1991, Nat. Hqrs. of Am. Soc. Interior Designers, Washington, 1992, Michael Stone Collection, Washington, 1992, Funding Ctr., Alexandria, Va., 1992, Mus. Modern Art, Bordeaux, France, 1993, Abbey Galleries, N.Y.C., 1993, Mus. Modern Art Miami, 1993, Harbus Unique Gallery, Pomona, Calif., 1994, Gallery Brindabella, Oakville, Ont., Can., 1996, Art Comm. Internat., Phila., 1996, World Bank, Washington, 1996-97, UN Fourth World Conf. on Women, Beijing, China, 1995, others; 1st release of ltd. edit. prints, 1992; exhibited oil painting and drawing Hargis Unique Gallery, Pomona, Calif., 1994; works collected in Royal Mus. of Sydney, O'Toole Coll., Melbourne, Nat. Mus. of Women in Arts, Washington, Patterson Collection, Mich., Witherow Collection, Washington, Samaniego Collection, Calif., Ronald Reagan Collection, Calif. Artist Ventura County Gen. Hosp., 1970's. Recipient Cash and Cert. awards Sydney Newspapers, 1950's, Ribbon awards Sydney County Fairs, 1970's, 1st round winner painting Hathaway Competition, Ventura, Calif., 1970's. Mem. Am. Platform Assn. Office: Yvonne Maree Designs PO Box 2143 Olympia WA 98507-2143

THOMASMA, KENNETH RAY, author, storyteller; b. Grand Rapids, Mich., Sept. 2, 1930; s. Peter E. and Freda Louise (Jones) T.; m. Barbara Joan Veurink, June 16, 1955; 1 child, Daniel Ross. AB in Elem. Edn., Calvin Coll., 1953; MA, U. Mich., 1958. Tchr. Grand Rapids Pub. Schs., 1953-58, 64-70, prin., 1958-64, 72-74, media specialist, 1972-77; assoc. prof. Grand Valley State U., Allendale, Mich., 1970-72; tchr. Teton County Schs., Jackson, Wyo., 1977-87; producer Travelog Films, Grand Rapids, 1960-75; dir. Ken-O-Sha Nature Ctr., Grand Rapids, 1964-74. Author: Naya Nuki: Girl Wyo Ran, 1983 (Indian Paintbrush award 1986), Soun Tetoken: Nez Perce Boy, 1984, Om-Kas-Toe of the Blackfeet, 1986, Kunu, 1988, Mohowat, 1992, Zuni Boy, 1994, Patchki Nana, 1995, Amee Nan, 1996, Sakajewa, 1997. Mem. citizen's adv. com. Jackson Pub. Schs., 1978, 81, 87. Served with USN, 1950-51. Named Citizen of Yr., Jackson C. of C., 1988. Mem. Mich. PTA (life). Baptist. Home: PO Box 2863 Jackson WY 83001-2863*

THOMASSEN, PAULINE F., medical and surgical nurse; b. Cleve., Jan. 19, 1939; d. Henry Clifford and Mabel Pauline (Hill) Nichols; m. Ruben Thomassen, Nov. 10, 1979; children: Rhonda, Terry, Diana, Philipp, Jody, Barbara. AA in Nursing, So. Colo. State Coll., 1974, BA in Psychology with distinction, 1975; BSN magna cum laude, Seattle Pacific U., 1986. RN, Wash. Staff nurse III orthopedic unit, preceptor orientation RNs and student RNs Swedish Hosp. Med. Ctr., Seattle, 1975—; mem. planning task force and faculty National Nurses Conference, The Nurse and Spinal Surgery, Cleve. Author: Spinal Disease and Surgical Interventions. Mem. Nat. Assn. Orthop. Nurses.

THOMPSON, ANNA BLANCHE, retired educator; b. Ft. Worth, Oct. 8, 1914; d. George Lewis and Gula Gertrude (Cook) Turnbow; m. Jess Lee, May 27, 1939; children: Jess Lee II, Mary Ann Thompson Archbold. BA in Edn., Ariz. State U., Tempe, 1935; postgrad., U. Ariz., 1940, U. Hawaii,

1964, Pepperdine U., 1967. Tchr. Parke (Ariz.) Elem. Sch., 1935-40; tchr. music Parker High Sch., 1940-42; tchr. Scottsdale (Ariz.) Elem. Sch., 1948-71; tchr. U. Hawaii, Laie, 1971-72; tchr. U. Hawaii, 1972-79, ret., 1979. Mem. edn. bd. Phoenix Women's Club, 1983-84; pres. Ariz. Res. Officers Ladies, Phoenix, 1982-84, state pres., 1986-87; pres. Ladies of the Ribbon, Phoenix, 1987-90, Tempe Garden Club, 1987-88. Recipient Mus. plaque Phoenix Symphony Symphonette, 1982-83, Cert. of Appreciation, St. Luke's Hosp. Aux., 1985, Cert. of Appreciation, Mil. Order of World Wars, 1989. Mem. Ariz. Res. Officers Ladies (state sec. 1990—), Tri-City Angels of Ariz. (pres. 1984—), Collectors Club Am. (nat. pres. 1987—), Ikebana Internat., AAUW (historian Tempe chpt. 1987-90), Delta Kappa Gamma (pres. Phoenix chpt. 1974-76, 88-90, parliamentarian 1990—). Home: 533 E Fairmont Dr Tempe AZ 85282-3722

THOMPSON, ARLENE RITA, nursing educator; b. Yakima, Wash., May 17, 1933; d. Paul James and Esther Margaret (Danroth) T. BS in Nursing, U. Wash., 1966, Masters in Nursing, 1970, postgrad., 1982—. Staff nurse Univ. Teaching Hosp., Seattle, 1966-69; mem. nursing faculty U. Wash. Sch. Nurses, Seattle, 1971-73; critical care nurse Virginia Mason Hosp., Seattle, 1973—; educator Seattle Pacific U. Sch. Nursing, 1981—; nurse legal cons. nursing edn., critical care nurse. Contbr. articles to profl. jours. USPHS grantee, 1969; nursing scholar Virginia Mason Hosp., 1965. Mem. Am. Assn. Critical Care Nurses (cert.), Am. Nurses Assn., Am. Heart Assn., Nat. League Nursing, Sigma Theta Tau, Alpha Tau Omega. Republican. Presbyterian. Home: 2320 W Newton St Seattle WA 98199-4115 Office: Seattle Pacific U 3307 3rd Ave W Seattle WA 98119-1940

THOMPSON, BETTY JANE, small business owner; b. Ladysmith, Wis., Nov. 18, 1923; d. Edward Thomas and Mayme Selma (Kratwell) Potter; m. Frederick Sturdee Thompson, Apr. 19, 1945 (div. Apr. 1973); children: Denise Alana, Kent Marshall; m. J.R. Critchfield, Feb. 14, 1977 (div. 1989). Student, Jamestown (N.D.) Coll., 1946-47, U. Calif., Long Beach, 1964-69; AA, Orange Coast Coll., 1976; postgrad., Monterey Peninsula Coll., 1979-80; SBA Cert., Hartnell Coll., 1982. Cert. fashion cons. Owner, mgr., buyer Goodview (Minn.) Food Mart, 1947-50; dist. mgr. Beauty Counselor of Minn., Winona County, 1951-61; Boy Scout liaison J.C. Penney Co., Newport Beach, Calif., 1969-72; dept. mgr. and buyer boyswear At Ease, Newport Beach, 1972-77; mgr. Top Notch Boys Wear, Carmel, Calif., 1977-83, buyer, 1984-88; owner, mgr. Top Notch Watch, Sun City, Ariz., 1989-95; editor H&R Block, 1995—; v.p., chmn. Don Loper Fashion Show, 1967, pres., 1968, bd. dirs., 1969. Co-editor Aux. Antics mag., 1965. Vol. fundraising leadership Family Svc. Assn., Orange County, Calif., 1962-68, other orgns.; chmn. publicity, study group, Sunday sch. tchr., Congl. Ch., Winona, Minn., 1956-58, fellowship pres., Santa Ana, Calif., 1963-65; pres. Goodview Civic Club, 1948. Recipient Athena award Panhellenic Assn. Orange City, Calif., 1968, El Camino Real Dist. Svc. award Orange Empire coun. Boy Scouts Am., Baden-Powell award, Outstanding Leadership award, El Camino Real Dist., Calif., 1972J. Ringling North award, 1949; named Outstanding Svc. Vol. Family Svc. Assn., 1969. Mem. Carmel Bus. Assn. Home and Office: 10048 W Hawthorn Dr Sun City AZ 85351-2829

THOMPSON, BONNIE RANSA, secondary educator, chemistry educator; b. Charleroi, Pa., Oct. 12, 1940; d. William Edward and Edith Lorraine Ransa; m. Joel E. Thompson, June 15, 1963 (div. Dec. 1980). BA, Seton Hill Coll., Greensburg, Pa., 1963; MEd, Ariz. State U., 1979, postgrad. Cert. in secondary chemistry, anthropology, and gifted edn., Ariz. Tchr. chemistry Scotch Plains (N.J.)-Fanwood High Sch., 1963-74; tchr. chemistry and anthropology Tolleson (Ariz.) Union High Sch., 1974-93; tchr. chemistry Westview High Sch., Phoenix, 1992—; owner Drenen Solutions, Inc.-Material Handling Systems, 1996—; instr. anthropology and archaeology Rio Salado C.C., Sun City, Ariz., 1981-88; instr. chemistry Glendale (Ariz.) C.C., 1988—, Estrella Mt. Cmty. Coll., 1996—; pres. Brite Ednl. Programs, Ltd., Phoenix, 1988-91; mem. Ariz. Reagent and Task Force on Lab. Sci., Tempe, 1987; tchr., cons. Pitts. SuperComputer Project, Tolleson, 1992—; amb. People to People Sci. Exchange, Russia, Australia, New Zealand, summer 1989-92; rsch partnership High Sch./Coll. Flinn Found. Rsch. Corp., 1988-91. Editor: Starting at Ground Zero, 1988, others; editor: Energy Education Kits, 1985; contbr. articles to mags. V.p. Villa Casitas Townhouse Assn., Phoenix, 1991-92, pres., 1993—; vol. Perot Orgn. for Pres., Phoenix, 1992. Woodrow Wilson fellow, 1983; recipient Golden Bell award Ariz. Sch. Bd. Assn., 1985, 88; recipient Growth Incentives for Tchrs. award GTE Corp., 1987, Tech. Scholar award Tandy Corp., 1990; named Outstanding High Sch. Sci. Tchr. Ariz. Coun. for Engring. and Scientific Assocs., 1993. Mem. NEA, Ariz. Edn. Assn., Tolleson Edn. Assn. (pres. 1981-83), Nat. Sci. Tchrs. Assn., Ariz. Sci. Tchrs. Assn., Ariz. Alliance for Math., Sci. and Tech., S.W. Archeol. Team. Office: Westview High Sch 10850 W Gardenlakes Pkwy Avondale AZ 85041

THOMPSON, C. MICHAEL, state official; b. St. Helena, Calif., Jan. 24, 1951; s. Charles Thompson and Beverly (Forni) Powell; m. Janet Thompson, Mar. 8, 1982; children: Christopher, Jon. MA, Chico State U. Owner, maintenance supr. Beringer Winery; mem. Calif. State Senate, 1990—; chair select com. on Calif.'s Wine Industry; chair Senate budget com.; vice chair Senate natural resources com. Staff sgt. U.S. Army, Vietnam. Decorated Purple Heart. Named Freshman Legislator of the Yr. Calif. Sch. Bds. Assn., 1990, Legislatorof the Yr. Calif. Abortion Rights Action League, Legislator of the Yr. Calif. Assn. Persons with Handicaps, Legislator of the Yr. Police Officers Rsch. Assn. Calif., Legislator of the Yr. Disabled in State Svc., 1994, Senator of the Yr. Calif. Assn. Homes and Svcs. for Aging, 1995; Recipient Disting. Svc. award Calif. State Assn. Counties, Disting. Svc. award Calif. Assn. Hosps., Legis. Leadership award Calif. Assn. Health Svcs. Home, 1994, Disting. Svc. award Aids Project L.A., 1995, Outstanding Senator award Planned Parenthood Affiliates Calif., 1996, Outstanding Senator of the Yr. award Calif. Sch. Bds. Assn., 1996, Outstanding Senator of the Yr. award Calif. Profl. Firefighters, 1996. Democrat. Roman Catholic. Office: Calif State Legis State Capitol Rm 3056 Sacramento CA 95814

THOMPSON, CRAIG SNOVER, corporate communications executive; b. Bklyn., May 24, 1932; s. Craig F. and Edith (Williams) T.; m. Masae Sugizaki, Feb. 21, 1957; children: Lee Anne, Jane Laura. Grad., Valley Forge Mil. Acad., 1951; B.A., Johns Hopkins U., 1954. Newspaper and radio reporter Easton (Pa.) Express, 1954-55, 57-59, Wall St. Jour., 1959-60; account exec. Moore, Meldrum & Assocs., 1960; mgr. pub. relations Cen. Nat. Bank of Cleve., 1961-62; account exec. Edward Howard & Co., Cleve., 1962-67; v.p. Edward Howard & Co., 1967-69, sr. v.p., 1969-71; dir. pub. relations White Motor Corp., Cleve., 1971-76; v.p. pub. relations No. Telecom Inc., Nashville, 1976-77, White Motor Corp., Farmington Hills, Mich., 1977-80; v.p. corp. communications White Motor Corp., 1980-81; dir. exec. communications Rockwell Internat. Corp., Pitts., 1981-86, El Segundo, Calif., 1986-91; dir. exec. communications Rockwell Internat. Corp., Seal Beach, Calif., 1992-97, sr. communications exec., 1997—. Bd. dirs. Shaker Lakes Regional Nature Center, 1970-73. Served to 1st lt., inf. U.S. Army, 1955-57. Mem. Pub. Rels. Soc. Am. (accredited), Alumni Assn. Valley Forge Mil. Acad. (bd. dirs. 1988-94). Office: Rockwell Internat Corp 2201 Seal Beach Blvd Seal Beach CA 90740-5603

THOMPSON, DANIEL EMERSON, vending machine service company; b. Fairbanks, Alaska, Jan. 24, 1947; s. George Edmond and Emma Jean (Burns) T.; m. Yvette Clarice Brazeau, Aug. 16, 1980. Student, U. Notre Dame, 1965-67. Vice-pres. Music Inc., Fairbanks, 1965-67; pres. Music Inc. (doing bus. as Alaska Music Co.), Fairbanks, 1967-81; sec.-treas. Music Inc. (doing bus. as Alaska Music Co. and TLC Vend), Anchorage, 1981-84; sec. Music Inc. (doing bus. as Vend Alaska-Fairbanks), Fairbanks, 1984-87, pres., 1987—; pres. Vend Inc. (doing bus. as Vend Alaska-Anchorage), Anchorage, 1984—; bd. dirs. Music Inc., Fairbanks, Vend Inc., Anchorage, Denali State Bank, Fairbanks; ptnr. Thompson Investment Co., Fairbanks, 1976—. Trustee Hi Pow, Fairbanks, 1972—; pres. Fairbanks Downtown Assn., 1987-88, bd. dirs., 1984-94; bd. dirs. Alaska State Devel. Corp., Juneau, 1971-82, Monroe Found., Fairbanks, 1991—. Mem. Amusement Music Operators Am., Nat. Automatic Merchandising Assn., N.W. Automatic Vending Assn. (bd. govs. 1983-95), Rotary, Fairbanks C. of C. (co-chmn. local govt. com. 1988-90). Roman Catholic. Office: Vend Alaska 1890 Marika Rd Fairbanks AK 99709-5520

THOMPSON, DARLENE, vocational nurse; b. Detroit, May 5, 1950; d. Henry Clay and Sarah Ann (Latham) T.; 1 child, La Tonya Reneé Johnson; m. Carl Albert Finley, Nov. 24, 1979 (div. Dec. 1984). Cert. lic. vocat. nurse, South Mountain C.C., Phoenix, 1986; AA, Compton (Calif.) C.C., 1988. Lic. vocat. nurse, Calif. Lab. asst. St. Luke Hosp., Phoenix, 1981-85; staff lic. vocat. nurse Phoenix Meml., 1985-87; post-partum lic. vocat. nurse St. Francis Hosp., Lynwood, Calif., 1987-89; rehab. lic. vocat. nurse Kaiser Permanente, Inglewood, Calif., 1989-93; charge nurse, lic. vocat. nurse Glen Terrace Hosp., Norwalk, Calif., 1991-92; cardiac lic. vocat. nurse Daniel Freeman Hosp., Inglewood, 1993-95; home care lic. vocat. nurse Oxford Health Care, Long Beach, Calif., 1993—. Author of poetry. Vol. counselor YWCA Greater L.A., Compton, 1992—; mem. African Am. Genelogy, L.A., 1996. Mem. Internat. Poets Soc. (cert. 1995), Enlightened Circle (cert. 1995), Compton Coll. Journalism Club (sec. 1995). Muslim. Home: 454 W Palmer St Compton CA 90220-2014

THOMPSON, DAVID RENWICK, federal judge; b. 1930. BS in Bus., U. So. Calif., 1952, LLB, 1955. Pvt. practice law with Thompson & Thompson (and predecessor firms), 1957-85; judge U.S. Ct. Appeals (9th cir.), 1985—. Served with USN, 1955-57. Mem. ABA, San Diego County Bar Assn., Am. Bd. Trial Lawyers (sec. San Diego chpt. 1983, v.p. 1984, pres. 1985). Office: US Ct Appeals 940 Front St San Diego CA 92101-8994*

THOMPSON, DENNIS PETERS, plastic surgeon; b. Chgo., Mar. 18, 1937; s. David John and Ruth Dorothy (Peters) T.; m. Virginia Louise Williams, June 17, 1961; children: Laura Faye, Victoria Ruth, Elizabeth Jan. BS, U. Ill., 1957, BS in Medicine, 1959, MS in Physiology, MD, 1961. Diplomate Am. Bd. Surgery, Am. Bd. Plastic Surgery. Intern Presbyn.-St. Lukes Hosp., Chgo., 1961-62; resident in gen. surgery Mayo Clinic, Rochester, Minn., 1964-66, fellow in gen. surgery, 1964-66; resident in gen. surgery Harbor Gen. Hosp., Los Angeles, 1968-70; resident in plastic surgery UCLA, 1971-73, clin. instr. plastic surgery, 1975-82, asst. clin. prof. surgery, 1982—; practice medicine specializing in plastic and reconstructive surgery, Los Angeles, 1974-78, Santa Monica, Calif., 1978—; chmn. plastic surgery sect. St. John's Hosp., 1986-91; mem. staff Santa Monica Hosp., UCLA Ctr. Health Scis.; chmn. dept. surgery Beverly Glen Hosp., 1978-79; pres. Coop. of Am. Physicians Credit Union, 1978-80, bd. dirs., 1980—, chmn. membership devel. com., 1983—, treas., 1985—. Contbr. articles to med. jours. Moderator Congl. Ch. of Northridge (Calif.), 1975-76, chmn. bd. trustees, 1973-74, 80-82; bd. dirs. L.A. Bus. Coun., 1987-90. Am. Tobacco Inst. research grantee, 1959-60. Fellow ACS; mem. AMA (Physicians Recognition award 1971, 74, 77, 81, 84, 87, 90, 93, 96), Calif. Med. Assn., L.A. County Med. Assn. (chmn. bylaws com. 1979-80, chmn. ethics com. 1980-81, sec.-treas. dist. 5 1982-83, program chmn. 1983-84, pres. 1985-86, councilor 1988-96), Pan-Pacific Surgical Assn., Am. Soc. Plastic and Reconstructive Surgeons, Calif. Soc. Plastic Surgeons (chmn. bylaws com. 1982-83, chmn. liability com. 1983-85, councilor 1988-91, sec. 1993-95, v.p. 1995-96, pres.-elect 1996-97, pres. 1997—), L.A. Soc. Plastic Surgeons (sec. 1980-82, pres. 1982-97), Lipoplasty Soc. N.Am., UCLA Plastic Surgery Soc. (treas. 1983-84), Am. Soc. Aesthetic Plastic Surgery, Am. Assn. Accreditation of Ambulatory Surg. Facilities (bd. dirs. 1995—), Western Los Angeles Regional C. of C. (bd. dirs. 1981-84, 86-89, chmn. legis. action com. 1978-80), Phi Beta Kappa, Alpha Omega Alpha, Nu Sigma Nu, Phi Kappa Phi, Delta Sigma Delta, Omega Beta Pi, Phi Eta Sigma. Republican. Office: 2001 Santa Monica Blvd Santa Monica CA 90404-2102

THOMPSON, DWIGHT ALAN, vocational rehabilitation expert; b. Monterey Park, Calif., Mar. 2, 1955; s. Irvin Edward and Lydia (Busch) T.; m. Irene Anita Arden, June 18, 1977; children: Dwight Christopher, Meredith Irene, Hilda Arden. BA in Social Welfare, U. Wash., 1978, MSW, 1980. Registered vocat. rehab. counselor, Wash., Oreg.; cert. social worker, Wash.; cert. case mgr.; diplomate Am. Bd. Clin. Examiners in Social Work; cert. disability mgmt. Specialist Commn. Houseparent Parkview Home for Exceptional Children, Seattle, 1976-77; rsch. analyst Wash. State Ho. Reps., Olympia, 1979-81; v.p. The James L. Groves Co., Everett, Wash., 1982-86; exec. dir. Evaluation & Tng. Assocs., Seattle, 1984-86; CEO, owner Rehab. & Evaluation Svcs. Inc., Seattle, 1986—; pres., owner Next Generation Technologies, Inc., Seattle, 1994—; social work officer 50th Gen. Army Res. Hosp., Seattle, 1982-87, 91-93; med. adminstrv. officer Operation Desert Storm, Riyadh, Saudi Arabia, 1990-91; aide-de-camp 2d Hosp. Ctr., San Francisco, 1987-88, pub. affairs officer, 1988-90; acting commdr. 1972d MED DET-Combat Stress Control, 1993, exec. officer, 1994—. Co-author Correction Study Report, 1981. Registered lobbyist Wash. State, 1983-87; conf. pres. St. Vincent de Paul Soc., 1975-78; lt. Thurston County Fire Dist #6, East Olympia, Wash., 1980-83; alumni rep. COS Track Com. U. Wash., 1984-87; primary candidate Dem. Primary for State Rep., Renton, Wash., 1984; mem. Wash. Vocat. Rehab. adv. com. Dept. Labor Industries, 1992-96; pres. Sheridan Beach Cmty. Club, Inc., 1994-95; chair human svcs. commn. City Lake Forest Park, Wash, 1995; mem. city coun., 1996—; mem. Girl Scouts of Am.. Maj. USAR, 1982—, Persian Gulf. Fellow Am. Acad. Pain Mgmt. (cert.); Mem. NASW (cert.), Nat. Assn. Rehab. Profls. (pvt. sector, Wash. legis. chair), Acad. Cert. Social Workers, Wash. Self-Insurers Assn., Assn. Mil. Surgeons U.S., Res. Officers Assn., Nat. Eagle Scout Assn., Am. Bd. Forensic Examiners, Case Mgmt. Soc. Am., Boy Scouts Am., Nat. Assn. Rehab. Profls. (Kevin Karr award for Most Innovative Rehab. Program 1995), Theta Xi (pres. 1975-77). Roman Catholic. Home: 16270 Beach Dr NE Lake Forest Park WA 98155 Office: Rehab and Evaluation Svcs 226 Summit Ave E Seattle WA 98102-5619

THOMPSON, ELBERT ORSON, retired dentist, consultant; b. Salt Lake City, Aug. 31, 1910; s. Orson David and Lillian (Greenwood) T.; m. Gayle Larsen, Sept. 12, 1935; children: Ronald Elbert, Karen Thompson Toone, Edward David, Gay Lynne. Student, U. Utah, 1928-30, 33-35; DDS, Northwestern U., 1939; hon. degree, Am. Coll. Dentistry, Miami, Fla., 1958, Internat. Coll. Dentistry, San Francisco, 1962. Pvt. practice dentistry Salt Lake City, 1939-78; ret., 1978; inventor, developer and internat. lectr. post-grad./undergrad. courses various dental schs. and study groups, 1953-83; developer, tchr. Euthenics Dentistry Concept; also, sit-down dentistry, four handed dentistry, lounge-type dental chair, washed field dentistry, euthenics dental operating chair; cons. in field. Contbr. numerous dental articles to profl. jours. Life mem. Rep. Presdl. Task Force, Washington, 1985—. Recipient Merit Honor award U. Utah, 1985; named Dentist of the Yr. Utah Acad. Gen. Dentistry, 1991, Father of Modern Dentistry, 1991. Mem. ADA (life), Utah Dental Assn. (life, sec. 1948-49, Disting. Svc. award 1980, E.O. Thompson Recognition award 1995), Salt Lake City Dental Soc. (life, pres. 1945-46), Utah Dental Hygiene Soc. (hon.), Am. Acad. Dental Practice Adminstrn. (life, pres. 1965-66), Internat. Coll. Dentists, Am. Coll. Dentists, Sons of Utah Pioneers (life), Dinorators Club (charter), Northwestern U. Alumni Assn. (Merit award 1961), Omicron Kappa Upsilon. Mormons. Home: 5672 S 960 E Ogden UT 84405

THOMPSON, GARY W., public relations executive; b. Berkeley, Calif., July 15, 1947. BA, Northwestern U., England, 1969—. Acct. exec. Allen & Doward Advt., 1971-74; acct. exec. Hoefer-Amedei Assocs., 1978-81, acct. supr., 1978, v.p., 1978-81; v.p., exec. supr. dir. Ketchum, 1981-82, sr. v.p., dir., 1982-84, exec. v.p., 1984-87, exec. v.p., dir. we. region, 1987-89, exec. v.p., dir. U.S.A., 1989-90; pres., CEO Hi-Tech Comm., 1990-95, Golin/Harris Techs., 1995—. Mem. Pub. Rels. Soc. Am. (counselors acad., membership chmn. San Francisco chpt. 1983, placement, newsletter chmn. 1985), Internat. Assn. Bus. Communicators,. Office: Golin/Harris Techs 101 Howard St San Francisco CA 94105-1629

THOMPSON, GEORGE FREDERICK, JR., public management educator; b. Anderson, Ind., Oct. 29, 1942; s. George Frederick and Ellen Leah (Reuter) T.; m. Sharon O'Rand, Sept. 8, 1968 (div. Nov. 1978); children: MacKendree and Kyrie' O'Rand; m. Ruth Ann Crowley, June 20, 1980; 1 child, Jonathan Crowley. BA, Pomona Coll., 1964; PhD, Claremont Grad. Sch., 1972. Asst. to sr. analyst Dept. Fin. State of Calif., Sacramento, 1972-75; asoc. dep. dir. for fin. and capital outlay planning Calif. Postsecondary Edn. Commn., Sacramento, 1975-76; vis. asst./assoc. prof. U. British Columbia faculty commerce and bus. adminstrn., 1976-77; sr. rsch economist Econ. Coun. Can., Ottawa, Ont., 1978-79; vis. assoc. prof., acting chmn. Grad. Sch. Mgmt. Pub. and Not for Profit Mgmt. Group UCLA, 1981; assoc. prof. Columbia U. Sch. Internat. and Pub. Affairs MPA Program, N.Y.C., 1980-85; Grace and Elmer Goudy Prof. Pub. Mgmt. and Policy Analysis Atkinson Grad. Sch. Mgmt. Willamette U., Salem, Oreg., 1985—; bd. dirs. Fin. Pub., Inc.; mem. task force on state budgeting Nat. Ctr. for Higher edn. Mgmt. Systems, Boulder, Colo., 1975-76, adv. com. Calif. State Senate Judiciary Com. subcom. on Consumr Affairs, 1980-81, Gov.'s Task Force on Sch. Fin. Reform, Oreg., 1988-89, adv. com. on Tax Reform, Oreg., 1990, Govt. Standards and Practices Commn., Oreg., 1995—; cons. House of Commons Can., on Regulatory Reform, Pub. Svcs. Commn. N.Y. Atty. Gen.'s Office of Consumer Affairs, Defense Sec.'s Commn. on Base Realignment and Closure, Senate Armed Svcs. subcom. on mil. constrn., others. Co-author: (with W.T. Stanbury) Regulatory Reform in Canada, 1982, (with L.R. Jones) Regulatory Policy and Practices: Regulating Better and Regulating Less, 1982, Reinventing the Pentagon, 1994; translator (with Ruth Crowley) F. Scharpf's Crisis and Choice in European Social Democracy, 1991; editor: Regulatory Regimes in Conflict, 1984; co-editor: (with LeRoy Gramer) Reforming Social Regulation, 1982, (with W.T. Stanbury) Managing Public Enterprises, 1982; contbr. numerous articles, notes, essays, book revs. to profl. jours. Mem. acad. adv. bd. Cascade Policy Inst. Recipient Clara Ihrig Linhardt Traveling fellowship, Mexico, Cen. Am., 1970-71, Mayr Found. Essay award, Lincoln Inst. Pub. Fin., Claremont Grad. Sch., 1973; nominated for Koopman prize of ORSA spl. interest group of defense analysis, 1987. Mem. Assn. for Pub. Policy and Mgmt., Am. Soc. for Pub. Adminstrn. (exec. coun. sect. on pub. budgeting and fin. 1991—, sect. on rsch. and theory 1996—, Mosher award 1994), Pub. Choice Soc., western Polit. Sci. Assn., Am. Soc. Mil. Controllers (Gold medal 1994), Midwest Polit. Sci. Assn., Inst. Mgmt. Scis., Oreg. Acad. Scis. Home: 540 Tillman Ave SE Salem OR 97302-3786 Office: Willamette Univ Atkinson Grad Sch Mgmt Salem OR 97301

THOMPSON, GEORGIA BETH, university department administrator; b. Milford, Utah, Jan. 25, 1940; d. George E. and Berniece (Miller) Smith; m. Richard A. Thompson, July 22, 1972; children: Richelle Lynne Thompson. BS, Utah State U., 1962; MA, The Am. Univ., 1967. Copy editor, reader Utah State U., Logan, 1962-63, asst. info. specialist, 1963-65; staff writer Larry Hogan Assocs., Washington, 1966; dean of women, instr. Southern Utah State Coll., Cedar City, 1967-72, adj. instr., 1976-78; office mgr., case worker Congressman Wayne Owens, Cedar City, 1973-75; dir. ednl. opportunity programs So. Utah State U., Cedar City, 1986-89; asst. v.p. student svcs. Southern Utah U., Cedar City, 1989-92; assoc. v.p. student svcs. Southern Utah State Coll., Cedar City, 1992—. Co-editor (jour.) Western Anasazi Reports, 1976-85; bibliography editor Archeolog. jours., 1986; contbr. articles to Womens Exponent II., 1979. Chmn. Cedar City Planning Commn., 1979-86; mem., vice chair Cedar Dist. Adv. Bd., Bur. Land Mgmt., 1985-91; coord. Dem. County campaigns, Iron County, Utah, 1974—; mem. Women's Resource Com., Southern Utah U., Cedar City, 1993—; bd. dirs. Cedar City Housing Authority, 1991—, Women's Domestic Violence Shelter, Cedar City, 1994—. Mem. LWV (pres. local chpt.), Utah Consortium of Women in Higher Edn. Mem. LDS Ch. Office: Southern Utah U Student Svcs Dept Cedar City UT 84720

THOMPSON, GORDON, JR., federal judge; b. San Diego, Dec. 28, 1929; s. Gordon and Garnet (Meese) T.; m. Jean Peters, Mar. 17, 1951; children—John M., Peter Renwick, Gordon III. Grad., U. So. Calif., 1951, Southwestern U. Sch. Law, Los Angeles, 1956. Bar: Calif. 1956. With Dist. Atty.'s Office, County of San Diego, 1957-60; partner firm Thompson & Thompson, San Diego, 1960-70; U.S. dist. judge So. Dist. Calif., San Diego, 1970—, chief judge, 1984-91, sr. judge, 1994—. Bd. dirs. Sharp Meml. Hosp. Mem. Am. Bd. Trial Advocates, ABA, San Diego County Bar Assn. (v.p. 1970), Delta Chi. Club: San Diego Yacht. Office: US Dist Ct 940 Front St San Diego CA 92101-8994

THOMPSON, HERBERT ERNEST, tool and die company executive; b. Jamaica, N.Y., Sept. 8, 1923; s. Walter and Louise (Joly) T.; student Stevens Inst. Tech., 1949-51; m. Patricia Elaine Osborn, Aug. 2, 1968; children: Robert Steven, Debra Lynn. Foreman, Conner Tool Co., 1961-62, Eason & Waller Grinding Corp., 1962-63; owner Endco Machined Products, 1966-67, Thompson Enterprises, 1974—; pres. Method Machined Products, Phoenix, 1967; pres., owner Quality Tool, Inc., 1967-96. Served to capt. USAAF, 1942-46. Decorated D.F.C., Air medal with cluster. Home: 14009 N 42nd Ave Phoenix AZ 85023-5306 Office: 4223 W Clarendon Ave Phoenix AZ 85019-3618

THOMPSON, JAMES AVERY, JR., legal intern; b. Whiteville, N.C., Oct. 3, 1947; s. James Avery and Mary Elizabeth (Davis) T.; m. Julia Lee Stephens Thompson, June 7, 1969 (div. July 1979); 1 child, Marlee Amanda Elizabeth Thompson; m. Susannah Elizabeth Rupp Thompson, May 16, 1987; 1 child, Sarah Mary Elizabeth Thompson. AA (hon.), Marion (Ala.) Mil. Inst., 1967; BA, U. Ala., Tuscaloosa, 1969; MLS, 1973; MBA, So. Calif. Inst., Claremont, 1988; JD, Am. Coll. of Law, 1988. Mus. curator U. Ala., Birmingham, 1972-73, med. libr., 1973-82; asst. law libr. U. Laverne (Calif.) Law Sch., 1985-86; ref. libr. Western State U. Sch. Law, Fullerton, Calif., 1986-88; prof., instr. Am. Coll. Law, Brea, Calif., 1988-89; dir., instr. U. West L.A. Law Libr., 1988-90; legal intern Law Office Frank Phillips, Yorba Linda, Calif., 1990-91, Law Office Susannah Thompson, Temecula, Calif., 1991—. Author numerous periodicals in field. Campaign chmn. Med. Libr. United Way, Birmingham, Ala., 1979-80; mem. Lions Club, Tarrant, Ala., 1975-77; dir., spon. Tennis Assn. Pleasant Grove, Ala., 1980-82. Recipient Eagle Scout award, Order of Arrow Boy Scouts Am., 1963; named pres. Student Bar Assn., Am. Coll. Law, Brea, Calif., 1987-88, editor Law Review Am. Coll. Law, Brea, Calif., 1988. Mem. Royal Numismatic Soc. Can., Royal Philatelic Soc. Can., U.S. Tennis Assn., Am. Numismatic Assn., Delta Theta Phi, Alpha Sigma Phi. Democrat. Methodist. Office: Law Office Susan Thompson 41593 Winchester Rd Ste 212-B Temecula CA 92590-4857

THOMPSON, JAMES WILLIAM, lawyer; b. Dallas, Oct. 22, 1936; s. John Charles and Frances (Van Slyke) T.; BS, U. Mont., 1958, JD, 1962; m. Marie Hertz, June 26, 1965 (dec. 1995); children: Elizabeth, Margaret, John. Acct., Arthur Young & Co., N.Y.C., summer 1959; instr. bus. adminstrn. Eastern Mont. Coll., Billings, 1959-60, U. Mont., Missoula, 1960-61; admitted to Mont. bar, 1962; assoc. Cooke, Moulton, Bellingham & Longo, Billings, 1962-64, James R. Felt, Billings, 1964-65; asst. atty. City of Billings, 1963-64, atty., 1964-66; ptnr. Felt, Speare & Thompson, Billings, 1966-72, McNamer, Thompson & Cashmore, 1973-86, McNamer & Thompson Law Firm PC, 1986-89, McNamer, Thompson, Werner & Stanley, P.C., 1990-93, McNamer Thompson Law Firm PC, 1993—; bd. dirs. Associated Employers of Mont., Inc., 1989—. Mem. Billings Zoning Commn., 1966-69; v.p. Billings Community Action Program (now Dist. 7 Human Resources Devel. Council), 1968-70, pres., 1970-75, trustee, 1975—; mem. Yellowstone County Legal Services Bd., 1969-70; City-County Air Pollution Control Bd., 1969-70; pres. Billings Symphony Soc., 1970-71; bd. dirs. Billings Studio Theatre, 1967-73, Mont. Inst. of Arts Found., 1986-89, Downtown Billings Assn., 1986-90, Billings Area Bus. Incubator, Inc., 1991-94, Found. of Mont. State U., Billings, 1992—; mem. Diocesan exec. council, 1972-75; mem. Billings Transit Commn., 1971-73; mem. City Devel. Agy., 1972-73; bd. dirs. United Way, Billings, 1973-81. CPA, Mont. Mem. ABA, Am. Acad. Estate Planning Attys., Nat. Acad. Elder Law Attys., State Bar Mont., Yellowstone County Bar Assn. (bd. dirs. 1983-87, pres. 1985-86), C. of C., Elks, Kiwanis (pres. Yellowstone chpt. 1974-75), Sigma Chi (pres. Billings alumni assn. 1963-65). Episcopalian. Home: 123 Lewis Ave Billings MT 59101-6034 Office: 300 First Bank Bldg Billings MT 59101

THOMPSON, JEREMIAH BEISEKER, international medical business executive; b. Harvey, N.D., July 20, 1927; s. Linden Brown and Ferne Althea (Beiseker) T.; m. Paula Maria Ketchum, Feb. 5, 1960; children: Cole, Per, Gover, Susannah. BS, U. Minn., 1949, MD, 1966. Rsch. assoc. U. Colo. Med. Sch., Denver, 1955-56, U. Calif. Med. Sch., San Francisco, 1956-57, Stanford U., 1957-59; applications rsch. scientist Beckman/Spinco Co., Palo Alto, Calif., 1959-61; mgr. Asia and Africa Hewlett Packard Co., Palo Alto, 1966-72; med. cons. Alyeska Pipeline Co., Anchorage, 1973-76; mgr. Asia, Africa, Australasia Corometrics Med. Systems, Wallingford, Conn., 1976-82; dir. internat. ops. Oximetrix (Abbott), Mountain View, Calif., 1982-84, Novametrix Med. Systems, Wallingford, 1984-88; ptnr. TMC Internat., Tokyo and Concord, Calif., 1988—; advisor, cons. Yokogawa-Hewlett Packard, Tokyo, 1966-70; cons. Kupat Holim, Tel Aviv, Israel, 1967-92, Itochu, Tokyo, 1984-97, Nat. Heart-Lung Inst., Beijing, China, 1984-94. Project dir. Comparative Study of Western and Japanese Medicine in Taisho and Showa Eras, 1991—. With USN, 1945-46; PTO. Founding fellow Brit. Interplanetary Soc.; assoc. Japan Found., Assn. Asian Studies; mem. Kokusai Bunka Kaikan, Tokyo, World Affairs Coun., Mechanics Inst.

Home and Office: TMC Internat 3718 Barrington Dr Concord CA 94518-1614

THOMPSON, JOHN, museum director. Gen. mgr. Copper King Mus., Butte, Mont., 1990—. Office: Copper King Museum 219 W Granite Butte MT 59701

THOMPSON, JOHN WILLIAM, international management consultant; b. Hurricane, Utah, Oct. 14, 1945; s. Thomas Thurman and Lula (Brinkerhoff) T.; m. Pamela Ruth Williams, Sept. 14, 1991. BSEE, Utah State U., 1969, MBA, 1972; PhD, U. Oreg., 1978. Rsch. asst. Utah State U., Logan, Utah, 1967-69, tching. asst., 1971-72; elec. engr. Collins Radio, Newport Beach, Calif., 1969-72; tching. fellow U. Oreg., Eugene, 1972-78; tng. dir. Lifespring Inc., San Rafael, Calif., 1978-80; pres., CEO Human Factors Inc., San Rafael, Calif., 1980—; chmn. bd. Acumen Internat., San Rafael, Calif., 1985—. Author: The Human Factor: An Inquiry into Communication and Consciousness, 1983, Leadership in the 21st Century in New Traditions in Business, 1992, The Renaissance of Learning in Learning Organizations: Developing Cultures for Tomorrow's Workplace, 1994, The Human Factor, 1996; author of software based management assessment programs, system theory based management development courses, 1980-92. Rockefeller Found. grantee, 1971. Office: Human Factors Inc 4000 Civic Center Dr Ste 500 San Rafael CA 94903-4171

THOMPSON, JOSIE, nurse; b. Ark., Apr. 16, 1949; d. James Andrew and Oneda Fay (Watson) Rhoads; m. Mark O. Thompson, Feb. 14, 1980. Diploma, Lake View Sch. Nursing, 1970; student, Danville C.C., 1974-75, St. Petersburg Jr. Coll., 1979. RN, Ill., Wyo. Staff nurse St. Elizabeth Hosp., Danville, Ill., 1970-78, Osteopathetic Hosp., St. Petersburg, Fla., 1980-81, Wyo. State Hosp., Evanston, 1981-83; staff nurse Wyo. Home Health Care, Rock Springs, 1984—, adminstr., 1986-95; pres. Home Health Care Alliance Wyo., 1991-92; staff nurse home health Interim Health Care, Cheyenne, Wyo., 1996-97; staff nurse Rocky Mountain Home Health Care, Green River, Wyo., 1997—. Mem. nursing program adv. bd. Western Wyo. Community Coll.; mem. Coalition for the Elderly, Spl. Needs Com. Sweetwater County, 1992-93. Home: PO Box 1154 Rock Springs WY 82902 Office: Rocky Mountain Home Health Care 198 Anita Dr Green River WY 82935

THOMPSON, JOYCE MARIE, writer; b. Seattle, July 9, 1948; d. Howard Jesse and Anne Marie (Olson) T.; m. Paul Steele, July 4, 1976 (div. June 1986); children: Alexandra Thompson Steele, Ian Emmet Steele ; m. Schuyler Neal Ingle, May 4, 1996; 1 stepchild, Farrell L. Ingle. AB in English magna cum laude, Cornell U., 1970. Multimedia writer Microsoft Network, Redmond, Wash., 1994-96, dir. editl., head writer Rifff, 1996—; tchr. fiction various univs. and colls., 1982-94. Author: (novels) The Blue Chair, 1977, Merry-Go-Round, 1982, Conscience Place, 1984, Bones, 1991, (short fiction) East Is West of Here, 1988, others, (screenplays) Willie & Phil, 1980, Hothouse, 1981, Harry & The Hendersons, 1986. Trustee Tillamook Bay Cmty. Coll., Bay City, Oreg., 1981-83; bd. dirs. Wash. Lawyers for the Arts, Seattle, 1986-88; del. Wash. Dem. Conv., Olympia, 1988; mem. com. Ed. Materials Selection, Bainbridge Schs., 1990-92. Mem. PEN, Writers Guild Am. West. Office: Microsoft 1 Microsoft Way Redmond WA 98052

THOMPSON, JUDITH KASTRUP, nursing researcher; b. Marstal, Denmark, Oct. 1, 1933; came to the U.S., 1951; d. Edward Kastrup and Anna Hansa (Knudsen) Pedersen; m. Richard Frederick Thompson, May 22, 1960; children: Kathryn Marr, Elizabeth Kastrup, Virginia St. Claire. BS, RN, U. Oreg., 1958, MSN, 1963. RN, Calif., Oreg. Staff nurse U. Oreg. Med. Sch., Eugene, 1957-58; staff nurse U. Oreg. Med. Sch., Portland, 1958-61, head staff nurse, 1960-61; instr. psychiat. nursing U. Oreg. Sch. Nursing, Portland, 1963-64; rsch. asst. U. Oreg. Med. Sch., Portland, 1964-65, U. Calif., Irvine, 1971-72; rsch. assoc. Stanford (Calif.) U., 1982-87; rsch. asst. Harvard U., Cambridge, Mass., 1973-74; rsch. assoc. U. So. Calif., L.A., 1987—. Contbg. author: Behavioral Control and Role of Sensory Biofeedback, 1976; contbr. articles to profl. jours. Treas. LWV, Newport Beach, Calif., 1970-74; scout leader Girl Scouts Am., Newport Beach, 1970-78. Named Citizen of Yr. State of Oreg., 1966. Mem. Soc. for Neurosci., Am. Psychol. Soc. (charter), ANA, Oreg. Nurses Assn. Republican. Lutheran. Home: 28 Sky Sail Dr Corona Del Mar CA 92625-1436 Office: U So Calif University Park Los Angeles CA 90089-2520

THOMPSON, KENNETH RANDALL, evangelist; b. Aliceville, Ala., June 28, 1943; s. Ernest Jackson and Ruby Gay (Dillard) T.; m. Shirley Jeanne Baker, Aug. 21, 1965; children: Esther Martinez, John Kenneth, Sarah Jeanne. Student, N.Mex. Mil. Inst., Roswell, 1961-63; BA, Point Loma Nazarene Coll., 1966; MDiv, Southwestern Bapt. Theol. Sem., 1968. Ordained to ministry Bapt. Ch., 1968. Pastor Calvary Bapt. Ch., Jal, N.Mex., 1972-76, Bethel Bapt. Ch., Plainview, Tex., 1976-78, 1st Bapt. Ch., Higgins, Tex., 1978-84, Trinity Bapt. Ch., Albuquerque, 1984-86, Highland Bapt. Ch., Albuquerque, 1986-88; evangelist Ken Thompson Evangelism, Albuquerque, 1988—; chmn. missions com. Southeastern Bapt. Assn., Jal, 1974, Cen. Bapt. Assn., Albuquerque, 1987-88; chmn. evangelism com. Panhandle Bapt. Assn., Higgins, 1983-84. Contbr. poems to anthologies. Pastor to homeless Cen. Pl. Mission of 1st Bapt. Ch., Albuquerque, 1991-96; chmn. sch. improvement team Lavaland Elem., Albuquerque, 1985-86; mem. Higgins chpt. Higgins Against Drugs, 1983-84; coach baseball team Higgins H.S., 1980-82. Recipient Internat. Poet of Merit award Internat. Soc. Poets, 1995. Mem. Conf. So. Bapt. Evangelists. Home and Office: 6231 Gibson SE Apt 223 Albuquerque NM 87108

THOMPSON, LINDA LEE, educational consultant; b. Ottumwa, Iowa, Sept. 21, 1940; d. Clarence Adelbert and Ollie Mae (Easley) Andrews; m. Richard Bruce Thompson, Aug. 13, 1961 (div. Nov. 1986); children: Bruce Edward, Curtis Lowell. BA, U. No. Iowa, 1961; postgrad., U. Wis., 1962-66, U. Ariz., 1967-68. Cert. tchr. Math. tchr. Franklin Jr. High Sch., 1961-63; tchr., head math. dept. LaFollette High Sch., Madison, Wis., 1963-67; cons., editor, writer, 1968—; cons. Ariz. State Dept. Edn., Phoenix, 1981. Author: General Mathematics, 1977; co-author: Consumer Mathematics, 2d edit., 1986, McGraw-Hill Mathematics, 1987, You, The Consumer, 1987, Business Mathematics, 1988, Pre-Algebra, 1991, Prentice Hall Mathematics; Explorations and Applications, 1995; also articles. Chmn. bd. dirs. Tucson Jr. Strings, 1981-84; com. mem. Rincon-Univ. H.S. Drug Impact Group, Tucson, 1986-90, co-chmn., 1989-90; mem. Univ. H.S. Parents Bd., co-chmn., 1989-90; mem. Clatsop Cmty. Action Bd., 1993-96, chmn., 1994-96; mem. Surf Pines Homeowners' Bd., 1993-95, pres., 1994-95; mem. Pioneer House bd., 1994-96, chmn., 1995-96. Mem. Nat. Coun. Tchrs. Math. Home and Office: 2136 Manion Dr Warrenton OR 97146-9783

THOMPSON, LOIS JEAN HEIDKE ORE, psychologist; b. Chgo., Feb. 22, 1933; d. Harold William and Ethel Rose (Neumann) Heidke; m. Henry Thomas Ore, Aug. 28, 1954 (div. May 1972); children: Christopher, Douglas; m. Joseph Lippard Thompson, Aug. 3, 1972; children: Scott, Les, Melanie. BA, Cornell Coll., Mt. Vernon, Iowa, 1955; MA, Idaho State U., 1964, EdD, 1981. Lic. psychologist, N.Mex. Tchr. pub. schs. various locations, 1956-67; tchr., instr. Idaho State U., Pocatello, 1967-72; employee/orgn. devel. specialist Los Alamos (N.Mex.) Nat. Lab., 1981-84, tng. specialist, 1984-89, sect. leader, 1989-93; pvt. practice indsl. psychology and healthcare, Los Alamos, 1988—; sec. Cornell Coll. Alumni Office, 1954-55, also other orgns.; bd. dirs. Parent Edn. Ctr., Idaho State U., 1980; counselor, Los Alamos, 1981-88. Editor newsletter LWV, Laramie, Wyo., 1957; contbr. articles to profl. jours. Pres. Newcomers Club, Pocatello, 1967, Faculty Womens Club, Pocatello, 1968; chmn. edn. com. AAUW, Pocatello, 1969. Mem. APA, N.Mex. Psychol. Assn. (bd. dirs. divsn. II 1990, sec. 1988-90, chmn. 1990), N.Mex. Soc. Adlerian Psychology (pres. 1990, treas. 1991-95, bd. dirs. 1996—), Soc. Indsl. and Orgn. Psychology. Mem. LDS Ch. Home and Office: 340 Aragon Ave Los Alamos NM 87544-3505 *Honesty, dependability, spiritual inspiration, and always doing our best are ingredients that lead to a successful and happy life.*

THOMPSON, LYLE EUGENE, electrical engineer; b. Pocatello, Idaho, May 16, 1956; s. Clyde Eugene and Doris (Pratt) T.; m. Barbara Mae Dickerson, Dec. 31, 1986. Grad. high sch. Sr. diagnostic engr. Calma/GE, Santa Clara, Calif., 1978-83; mem. tech. staff Telecommunications Tech., Inc., Milpitas, Calif., 1983-84; proprietor/cons. Lyle Thompson Cons., Fremont, Calif., 1984-87; sys. analyst Raynet Corp., Menlo Park, Calif., 1987-88; proprietor/cons. Lyle Thompson Cons., Hayward, Calif., 1988-89; mgr. sys. design Raylan Corp., Menlo Park, Calif., 1989-90; dir. system design Raylan Corp., Menlo Park, 1990-91; pvt. practice cons. San Lorenzo, Calif., 1991-96; pres., CEO HelioSoft, Inc., San Lorenzo, Calif., 1996—; cons. in field. Patentee in field. Mem. ACM, IEEE. Home: 664 Paseo Grande San Lorenzo CA 94580-2364

THOMPSON, MARI HILDENBRAND, medical staff services executive; b. Washington, Apr. 26, 1951; d. Emil John Christopher Hildenbrand and Ada Lythe (Conklin) Hildenbrand-Kammer; m. R. Marshall Thompson, Sept. 27, 1970 (div. June 1981); 1 child, Jeremy Marshall. BA in Secondary Edn., Am. U., 1976, BA in Performing Arts, 1976. Cert. med. staff coord.; cert. profl. credentialing specialist. Employment interviewer Scripps Meml. Hosp., La Jolla, Calif., 1977-81; office mgr. Jacksina & Freedman Press Office, N.Y.C., 1982-83; staffing coord., med. staff asst. Am. Med. Internat. Clairemont Hosp., San Diego, 1983-85; adminstrv. asst. Am. Med. Internat. Valley Med. Ctr., El Cajon, Calif., 1985-88; med. staff coord. Sharp Meml. Hosp., San Diego, 1988-92; adminstrv. asst. Grossmont Hosp., La Mesa, Calif., 1992-93, coord. Sharp family practice residency program, 1993-94; mgr. Sharp Meml. Hosp. med. staff svcs., San Diego, 1994-96; cons. med. staff svcs. San Diego Rehab. Inst., 1997—; cons. and adminstrv. support for Legal Support, Inc., Del., 1989—; wardrobe mistress various cmty. theatres, San Diego, 1978-79, actress, San Diego, 1979-81. Appeared N.Y.C. (N.Y.) Playreaders Group, 1981-83, N.J. Shakespeare Theatre, Madison, 1982, Good Humor Improv Co., N.Y.C., 1982-83; contbg. writer to Poetry Revival: An Anthology, 1994. Mem. NOW, 1995, World Wildlife Fedn., Calif., 1991, Greenpeace, Calif., 1991, Sierra Club, Calif., 1991, 92, Audubon Soc., Calif., 1991, 92, Internat. Wildlife Fedn., 1992, Smithsonian, 1993, 94, Dem. Nat. Com., 1996. Included in Outstanding Young Women of Am., 1986. Mem. NAFE, AFTRA, Nat. Assn. Med. Staff Svcs., Calif. Assn. Med. Staff Svcs., Nat. Assn. Health Care Quality, Assn. Family Practice Adminstrs. Democrat. Home: 7951 Beaver Lake Dr San Diego CA 92119-2610

THOMPSON, PAUL HAROLD, university president; b. Ogden, Utah, Nov. 28, 1938; s. Harold Merwin and Elda (Skeen) T.; m. Carolyn Lee Nelson, Mar. 9, 1961; children: Loralyn, Kristyn, Shannyn, Robbyn, Daylyn, Nathan. BS, U. Utah, 1964; MBA, Harvard U., 1966, D Bus. Adminstrn., 1969. Rsch. assoc. Harvard U., Cambridge, Mass., 1966-69; asst. prof. Harvard U., Cambridge, 1969-73; assoc. prof. bus. Brigham Young U., Provo, Utah, 1973-78, prof., 1978-84, asst. dean, 1978-81, dean, 1984-89, v.p., 1989-90; pres. Weber State U., Ogden, Utah, 1990—; cons. Goodyear, Hughes Aircraft, Portland GE, Esso Resources Ltd., GE. Co-author: Organization and People: Readings, Cases, and Exercises in Organizational Behavior, 1976, Novations: Strategies for Career Management, 1986; also articles. Named Outstanding Prof. of Yr., Brigham Young U., 1981; Baker scholar Harvard U., 1966. Mem. Am. Assn. State Colls. and Univs. (com. 1991—), Ogden C. of C. (exec. com. 1990—), Rotary (prograam com. Ogden 1991—, Harris fellow 1992—), Phi Beta Kappa. Office: Weber State U 1001 University Cir Ogden UT 84408-0001

THOMPSON, PETER L. H., golf course architect; b. Modesto, Calif., Apr. 26, 1939. BS in East Asian Studies, U. Oreg., 1962, B in Landscape Architecture, 1971, M in Urban Planning, 1971; postgrad., U. Calif., Berkeley, 1975, Nat. U. Registered landscape arch., Calif., Oreg., Wash., Nev. With Oreg. Planning Commn., Lane County, 1965-70; commr. Oreg. Planning Commn., Eugene, 1981-83; sr. assoc. Ruff, Cameron, Lacoss, Eugene, 1971-75; prin. Peter L. H. Thompson & Assocs., Eugene, 1975-83, John H. Midby & Assocs., Las Vegas, Nev., 1983-86, Thompson-Wihlborg, Ltd., Corte Madera, Calif., 1982-89, Thompson Planning Group (now Thompson Golf Planning), Ltd., San Rafael, Calif., 1989—; with Oreg. Planning Commn., commr., 1981-83, Novato, Calif. Planning Commn., commr. 1989-93, pres. 1989-93; spkr. Oreg. Home Builders Conf., 1980, Pacific Coast Builders Conf., 1984, Tacoma Country Club Pro-Pres. Tournament, 1991, Madrona Links Men's Golf Club, 1991, Twin Lakes Country Club Pro-Pres. Tournament, 1992, Golf Expo, Palm Springs, Calif., 1993, 95, Golf Expo, Nashville, 1993, Golf Expo, Monterey, Calif., 1994, others. Contbr. articles to mags. Mem. citizen's adv. bd. City of Eugene, Oreg., City of Las Vegas. Mem. USGA, Am. Soc. Landscape Archs., Am. Assn. Planners, Nat. Golf Found., Urban Land Inst., Rotary Internat. Office: Thompson Golf Planning Ltd 2175 Francisco Blvd E Ste A San Rafael CA 94901-5524*

THOMPSON, RENA LOUISE, elementary education educator; b. Long Beach, Calif., Aug. 1, 1961; d. Cloyd Roy Bower and Melody Mae (Montgomery) Smith; m. Floyd Fewel Thompson, Nov. 15, 1986; children: Kyle Fewel, Collin Odell. AA, Cypress Jr. Coll., 1982; BA, Calif. State U., Long Beach, 1985; MA, Calif. State U., L.A., 1991. Preliminary adminstrv. credential, spl. edn.-learning handicapped credential, resource spl. program cert. of competence, multi-subject credential, Calif. 6-8 Special Day Class tchr. East Middle Sch. Downey (Calif.) Unified Sch. Dist., 1987-91, 4th grade tchr. Williams Sch., 1991-95, summer prin. Williams Sch., 1995, K-5 math mentor, 1995-97, K-5 RSP tchr. Imperial Sch., 1995-97; summer prin. Downey (Calif.) Unified Sch. Dist.-Lewis Sch., summer 1996; PQR cons. Freeway Consortium, Lakewood, Calif., 1995—. Mem. Delta Kappa Gamma (sec. 1995-97, pres. 1997—), Alpha Omicron Pi Alumnae (v.p. 1985—). Democrat. Home: 2121 W Crone Ave Anaheim CA 92804-3524 Office: Imperial Sch 8133 Imperial Hwy Downey CA 90242-3715

THOMPSON, RICHARD CRAIG, artist; b. McMinnville, Oreg., 1945. Student, Oreg. State U., 1963-64, U. N.Mex., 1967; BFA, MA in Painting, U. N.Mex., 1972. artist in residence U. Md., Balt., 1969, Living Arts Ctr., Corsicana, Tex., 1979, Roswell (N.Mex.) Mus. and Art Ctr., 1981, Gippsland Inst., Victoria and the Visual Arts Bd., Australia, 1982, Pacific N.W. Coll. Art, Portland, 1983. One-man shows include Monique Knowlton, N.Y., 1981, 82, 84, Spau Gallery, L.A., 1980-84, William Campbell Contemporary Art, Ft. Worth, 1986, 90, 93, Harris Gallery, Houston, 1985, 87, 90, 94, Art Base, Singapore, 1989, Robischon Gallery, Denver, 1991, others; exhibited in groups shows at Blue Star Art Space, San Antonio, 1988, Whitney Mus., N.Y., 1975, 81, Groninger (Netherlands) Mus., 1988, Robischon Gallery, 1990, Palm Desert Mus., Calif., 1990, Nat. Portrait Gallery, D.C., 1993, others; represented in permanent collections including Edunburg Mus. Modern Art, Scotland, Roswell (N.Mex.) Mus., Mus. Albuquerque, N.Mex., Modern Art Mus., Ft. Worth, Tex., Barrett Collection, Dallas, others. Recipient Alfred Morang award N.Mex. Bienniel, Mus. N.Mex., 1975, Mid-Am. Arts Alliance award-painting fellowship, 1986; individual fellow Nat. Endowment for the Arts, 1978; guest artist Printmaking, Anderson Ranch, Colo., 1994. Office: Robischon Gallery 1740 Wazee St Denver CO 80202-1232

THOMPSON, RICHARD DICKSON, lawyer; b. Lexington, Ky., Aug. 14, 1955; s. Lawrence Sidney and Algernon Smith (Dickson) T.; m. Bobbi Dale Magidoff, Aug. 3, 1980; children: Anne Katherine, Harrison Asher. AB, Harvard U., 1977; JD, Stanford U., 1980. Bar: Calif. 1980, U.S. Dist. Ct. (so. dist.) Calif. 1980. Assoc. Rosenfeld Meyer & Susman, Beverly Hills, Calif., 1980-83, Silverberg Rosen Leon & Behr, L.A., 1983-86; ptnr. Silverberg Rosen Leon & Behr, 1986-89; assoc., then ptnr. Silverberg Katz Thompson & Braun, L.A., 1989-95. Bd. trustees L.A. Copyright Soc. Mem. Order of the Coif, Phi beta Kappa. Office: Bloom, Hergott, Cook Diemer & Klein 150 S Rodeo Dr 3d Fl Beverly Hills CA 90212-2408*

THOMPSON, ROBERT CHARLES, lawyer; b. Council, Idaho, Apr. 20, 1942; s. Ernest Lavelle and Evangeline Montgomery (Carlson) T.; m. Marilyn Anne Wilcox, Jan. 17, 1960 (dec. Mar. 1962); m. Patricia Joan Price, June 1, 1963 (div. 1969); m. Jan Nesbitt, June 29, 1973; 1 child, Tanya. AB, Harvard U., 1963, LLB, 1967. Bar: Mass. 1967, Calif. 1983, U.S. Dist. Ct. (ea. dist.) Mass. 1975, U.S. Ct. Appeals (1st cir.) 1976, U.S. Ct. Appeals (9th cir.) 1984, U.S. Dist. Ct. (no. dist.) Calif. 1983, U.S. Dist. Ct. (ea. dist.) Calif., 1996. Assoc. Choate, Hall & Stewart, Boston, 1967-73; asst. regional counsel EPA, Boston, 1973-75, regional counsel, 1975-82, assoc. gen. counsel, 1979-82; regional counsel EPA, San Francisco, 1982-84; ptnr. Graham & James, San Francisco, 1984-91, LeBoeuf, Lamb, Greene & MacRae, San Francisco, 1992—. Contbr. articles to profl. jours. Bd. dirs. Peninsula Indsl. and Bus. Assn., Palo Alto, Calif., 1986—; chmn. Cambridge (Mass.) Conservation Commn., 1972-74; co-chmn. The Clift Confs. on Environ. Law, 1983-97. John Russell Shaw traveling fellow Harvard Coll., 1963-64; recipient Regional Adminstrs. Bronze medal EPA, 1976, 84. Mem. ABA (natural resources sect., com. on native Am. natural resources law, spl. com. on mktg.), Natural Resources Def. Coun., Sierra Club, Commonwealth Club, Phi Beta Kappa. Democrat. Episcopalian. Office: LeBoeuf Lamb Greene & MacRae One Embarcadero Ctr San Francisco CA 94111

THOMPSON, ROBERT FRANK, JR., career officer; b. Durnham, N.C., Sept. 25, 1959; s. Robert Frank Sr. and Betty Ross (Connelly) T.; m. Vickie Marie Fjone, Nov. 17, 1979; children: Robert Frank III, Kimberly Anne. BA in English and History, Met. State Coll. Denver, 1993. Commd. capt. U.S. Army Nat. Guard, 1993; stationed at Panama, Ft. Polk, La., 1983-87; rural rt. carrier U.S. Postal Svc., Brighton, Colo., 1988-93; adminstrv. officer Colo. Army Nat. Guard, Denver, 1993—; master fitness trainer Colo. Army Nat. Guard, Englewood, 1989—, advisor work climate improvement program, 1996—, facilitator increasing human effectiveness, 1996—. Editor The Adv., 1990-91. Deacon Crossroads Bapt. Ch., Northglenn, Colo., 1997—. Recipient Exceptional Acad. Achievement award ROTC, 1989. Mem. U.S. F.A. Assn. (Hon. Order St. Barbaras 1993), Nat. Guard Assn. U.S., Golden Key Nat. Honor Soc., Phi Alpha Theta, Pi Gammma Mu. Republican. Home: 2830 E 99th Way Thornton CO 80229-2618 Office: Colo Army Nat Guard Dept Mil Affairs 6848 S Revere Pky Englewood CO 80112-6703

THOMPSON, RONALD EDWARD, lawyer; b. Bremerton, Wash., May 24, 1931; s. Melville Herbert and Clara Mildred (Griggs) T.; m. Marilyn Christine Woods, Dec. 15, 1956; children—Donald Jeffery, Karen, Susan, Nancy, Sally, Claire. B.A., U. Wash., 1953, J.D., 1958. Bar: Wash. 1959. Asst. city atty. City of Tacoma, 1960-61; pres. firm Thompson, Krilich, LaPorte, Tucci & West, P.S., Tacoma, 1961—; judge pro tem Mcpl. Ct., City of Tacoma, Pierce County Dist., 1972—, Pierce County Superior Ct., 1972—. Chmn. housing and social welfare com. City of Tacoma, 1965-69; mem. Tacoma Bd. Adjustment, 1967-71, chmn., 1968; mem. Tacoma Com. Future Devel., 1961-64, Tacoma Planning Commn., 1971-72; bd. dirs., pres. Mcpl. League Tacoma; bd. dirs. Pres. Tacoma Rescue Mission, Tacoma Pierce County Cancer Soc., Tacoma-Pierce County Heart Assn., Tacoma-Pierce County Council for Arts, Econ. Devel. Council Puget Sound, Tacoma Youth Symphony, Kleiner Group Home, Tacoma Community Coll. Found., Pierce County Econ. Devel. Corp., Wash. Transp. Policy Inst.; Coalition to Keep Wash. Moving, precinct committeeman Republican party, 1969-73. Served with AUS, 1953-55; col. Res. Recipient Internat. Community Service award Optimist Club, 1970, Patriotism award Am. Fedn. Police, 1974, citation for community service HUD, 1974, Disting. Citizen award Mcpl. League Tacoma-Pierce County, 1985; named Lawyer of the Yr. Pierce County Legal Secs. Assn., 1992. Mem. Am. Arbitration Assn. (panel of arbitrators), ABA, Wash. State Bar Assn., Tacoma-Pierce County Bar Assn. (sec. 1964, pres. 1979, mem. cts. and judiciary com. 1981-82), Assn. Trial Lawyers Am., Wash. State Trial Lawyers Assn., Tacoma-Pierce County C. of C. (bd. dirs., exec. com., v.p., chmn.), Downtown Tacoma Assn. (com. chmn., bd. dirs. exec. com., chmn.), Phi Delta Phi, Sigma Nu. Roman Catholic. Clubs: Variety (Seattle); Lawn Tennis, Tacoma, Optimist (Tacoma, Internat. Pres. 1973-74). Home: 3101 E Bay Dr NW Gig Harbor WA 98335-7610 Office: 524 Tacoma Ave S Tacoma WA 98402-5416

THOMPSON, RONALD MACKINNON, family physician, artist, writer; b. N.Y.C., Oct. 19, 1916; s. George Harold and Pearl Anita (Hatfield) T.; m. Ethel Joyce Chastant, June 30, 1950; children: Phyllis Anita, Walter MacKinnon, Charles Chastant, Richard Douglas. BS, U. Chgo., 1947, MS, 1948, MD, 1949. Diplomate Am. Bd. Family Practice. Intern U. Mich., Ann Arbor, 1950-51; resident in psychiatry U. Tex., Galveston, 1951-52; pvt. practice, family and internal medicine South Dixie Med. Ctr., West Palm Beach, Fla., 1952-85; instr. Anatomy, U. Chgo., 1946-47, Pharmacology, 1948-49. Contbr. articles to profl. jours.; exhibited in 7 one-man shows (over 30 awards for painting in regional and nat. shows); represented in permanent collections at 5 mus. Mem. Civitan Club W. Palm Beach, Fla., 1951; former bd. dirs. Norton Gallery Mus. of Art, West Palm Beach. Mem. Fla. Nat. Guard, 1936-40; cadet Army Air Force, 1943-44. Over thirty awards for painting in juried regional and nat. shows. Fellow Am. Acad. Family Physicians; mem. AMA, Fla. Med. Assn., Fla. Acad. of Family Physicians, Palm Beach County Med. Soc., Nat. Watercolor Soc., Ariz. Watercolor Soc. Republican. Episcopalian. Home: 308 Leisure World Mesa AZ 85206-3142

THOMPSON, SANDRA JANE, secondary school educator; b. Clarion, Pa., Nov. 21, 1953; d. Robert Stewart and Dorothy Jean (Wishart) T. BS, Clarion U., 1975. Cert. secondary tchr., Idaho. Tchr. 8th grade sci. Edgewood (Md.) Mid. Sch., 1975-80; tchr. 9th grade math. Idaho Sch. Dist. #60, Shelley, Idaho, 1980-92, tchr. 10th-12th grades math. and AP calculus, 1992—; pvt. tutor, Shelley, 1983—; girls basketball coach, Shelley, 1984-88; mentor tchr. Idaho Sch. Dist. #60, Shelley, 1989-91. Mem. NEA, Idaho Edn. Assn., Shelley Edn. Assn., Harford County Edn. Assn. Home: 1173 E 1400 N Shelley ID 83274-5146 Office: Shelley High Sch 570 W Fir St Shelley ID 83274-1449

THOMPSON, SUSANNAH ELIZABETH, lawyer; b. Fullerton, Calif., May 20, 1953; d. Harry Lowell and Susannah Elizabeth (Glover) Rupp; m. James Avery Thompson, Jr., May 16, 1987; 1 child, Sarah Mary Elizabeth Thompson. BA, Calif. State U., Fullerton, 1980; JD with hons., Am. Coll. of Law, 1989. Bar: Calif. 1989, U.S. Dist. Ct. (cen. dist.) 1989, U.S. Dist. Ct. (so. dist.) 1991. Legal asst. Minyard & Minyard, Orange, Calif., 1987-89; assoc. Simon & Simon, San Bernardino, Calif., 1989-91; pvt. practice Temecula, Calif., 1991—. Asst. editor Law Rev./Am. Coll. Law, Brea, Calif., 1989. Sec. student bar assn. Am. Coll. Law, 1987-88. Mem. ABA, Riverside County Bar Assn., Calif. Women Lawyers Assn., Inland Empire Bankruptcy Forum, Women Lawyers Assn. (chmn. mem. 1994—), Temecula C. of C. Republican. Office: 41593 Winchester Rd Ste 201 Temecula CA 92590-4857

THOMPSON, TERENCE WILLIAM, lawyer; b. Moberly, Mo., July 3, 1952; s. Donald Gene and Carolyn (Stringer) T.; m. Caryn Elizabeth Hildebrand, Aug. 30, 1975; children: Cory Elizabeth, Christopher William, Tyler Madison. BA in Govt. with honors and high distinction, U. Ariz., 1974; JD, Harvard U., 1977. Bar: Ariz. 1977, U.S. Dist. Ct. Ariz. 1977, U.S. Tax Ct. 1979. Assoc. Brown & Bain P.A., Phoenix, 1977-83, ptnr., 1983-92; ptnr. Gallagher and Kennedy, P.A., Phoenix, 1992—; legis. aide Rep. Richard Burgess, Ariz. Ho. of Reps., 1974; mem. bus. adv. bd. Citibank Ariz. (formerly Great Western Bank & Trust, Phoenix), 1985-86. Mem. staff Harvard Law Record, 1974-75; rsch. editor Harvard Internat. Law Jour., 1976; lead author, editor-in-chief: Arizona Corporate Practice, 1996; contbr. articles to profl. jours. Mem. Phoenix Mayor's Youth Adv. Bd. 1968-70, Phoenix Internat.; active 20-30 Club, 1978-81, sec. 1978-80, Valley Leadership, Phoenix, 1983-84, citizens task force future financing needs City of Phoenix, 1985-86; exec. coun. Boys and Girls Clubs of Met. Phoenix, 1990—; bd. dirs. Phoenix Bach Choir, 1992-94; deacon Shepherd of Hills Congl. Ch., Phoenix, 1984-85; pres. Maricopa County Young Dems., 1982-83, Ariz. Young Dems., 1983-84, sec. 1981-82, v.p. 1982-83; exec. dir. Young Dems. Am., 1985, exec. com. 1983-85; others. Fellow Ariz. Bar Found.; mem. State Bar Ariz. (vice chmn. internt. law sect. 1978, sec. securities law sect. 1990-91, vice chmn. sect. 1991-92, chmn.-elect 1992-93, chmn. 1993-94, exec. coun. 1988—, sec. bus. law sect. 1992-93, vice chmn. 1993-94, chmn. 1994-95), Nat. Assn. Bond Lawyers, Am. Acad. Healthcare Attys., Nat. Health Lawyers, Blue Key, Phi Beta Kappa, Phi Kappa Phi, Phi Eta Sigma. Home: 202 W Lawrence Rd Phoenix AZ 85013-1226 Office: Gallagher & Kennedy PA 2600 N Central Ave Phoenix AZ 85004-3050

THOMPSON, WILLIAM BENBOW, JR., obstetrician, gynecologist, educator; b. Detroit, July 26, 1923; s. William Benbow and Ruth Wood (Locke) T.; m. Constance Carter, July 30, 1947 (div. Feb. 1958); 1 child, William Benbow IV; m. Jane Gilliland, Mar. 12, 1958; children: Reese Ellison, Belinda Day. AB, U. So. Calif., 1947, MD, 1951. Diplomate Am. Bd. Ob-Gyn. Resident Gallinger Mun. Hosp., Washington, 1952-53; resident George Washington U. Hosp., Washington, 1953-55; asst. ob-gyn. La. State U., 1955-56; asst. clinical prof. UCLA, 1957-64; assoc. prof. U. Calif.-Irvine Sch. Med., Orange, Calif., 1964-92; dir. gynecology U. Calif.-Irvine Sch. Med., 1977-92; prof. emeritus U. Calif.-Irvine Sch. Med., Orange, 1993—; vice chmn. ob-gyn. U. Calif.-Irvine Sch. Med., 1978-89; assoc. dean U. Calif.-Irvine Coll. Med., Irvine, 1969-73. Inventor: Thompson Retractor, 1976; Thompson Manipulator, 1977. Bd. dirs. Monarch Bay Assn. Laguna Niguel,

Calif. 1969-77, Monarch Summitt II A ssn. 1981-83. With U.S. Army, 1942-44, PTO. Fellow ACS, Am. Coll. Ob-Gyn. (life), L.A. Ob-Gyn. Soc. (life); mem. Orange County Gynecology and Obstetrics Soc. (hon.), Am. Soc. Law and Medicine, Capistrano Bay Yacht Club (commodore 1975), Internat. Order Blue Gavel. Office: UCI Med Ctr OB/GYN 101 The City Dr S Orange CA 92868-3201

THOMPSON STANLEY, TRINA, lawyer; b. Oakland, Calif., June 3, 1961; d. Woodrow Thompson and Dorothy Mae (Martin) McCullough; 1 child, Daniel Jackson Jr.; m. Calvester Ray Stanley. AB, U. Calif., Berkeley, 1983; JD, U. Calif., 1986. Bar: Calif. 1987, U.S. Dist. Ct. (no. dist.) Calif. 1990. Tchg. asst. coun. on legal edn. opportunities U. Calif., 1984; law clk. Nat. Ctr. for Youth Law, San Francisco, 1984; clin. law clk. Alameda County Dist. Atty.'s Office, Oakland, 1985; law clk. to Hon. Henry Ramsey Alameda County Superior Ct., Oakland, 1986; sr. legal asst. Alameda County Pub. Defender's Office, 1986-87; asst. pub. defender III, Alameda County Pub. Defender's Office, Oakland, 1987-91; pvt. practice, Oakland, 1991—. Editing mem. Black Law Jour., 1983-85. Bd. dirs. Oakland Ensemble Theatre, 1991-93, Family Law and Violence Ctr., Berkeley, 1990-92, First Appellate Project, 1996—, Women Defenders, 1996—; PAL softball team sponsor Thompson Stanley Steelers; vol. Boys and Girls Clubs of Oakland, 1993—. Fellow Coun. on Legal Edn. Opportunities, 1983-85, grad. minority fellow, 1983-85; Yee scholar, 1985-86. Mem. ABA, Nat. Bar Assn., Calif. Pub. Defenders Assn., Alameda County Bar Assn., Calif. Attys. for Criminal Justice (bd. dirs. 1994—, President's award 1994), Alpha Kappa Alpha. Democrat. Baptist. Office: Ste 820 1970 Broadway Oakland CA 94612

THOMSEN, DAVID ALLEN, lawyer; b. L.A., July 14, 1950; s. Henry Alfred and Ruth Virginia (McKinzie) T.; m. Janet Kay Thomas, June 25, 1972; children: Jennifer Marie, Carl Edward, Daniel Eric. BA, Loma Linda U., 1974; JD, U. Calif., Davis, 1978. Bar: Calif. 1978, N.Mex. 1979. Asst. city atty. City of Farmington, N.Mex., 1979-81, 88-90; city atty. City of Alamogordo, N.Mex., 1981-87; pvt. practice Alamogordo, 1987-88, Ruidoso, N.Mex., 1992—; village atty. Village of Ruidoso, 1990-92; CLE lectr. N.Mex. Mcpl. League, Santa Fe, 1989-90. Active Riverside (Calif.) County Dem. Ctrl. Com., 1973-75; mem. Farmington Early Bird, 1988-90, pres., 1990. Mem. Lions, Ruidoso Noon (pres. 1993-94). Home: 315 Spring Rd PO Box 1131 Ruidoso NM 88345 Office: 2810 Sudderth Dr Ste 206 Ruidoso NM 88345

THOMSON, GRACE MARIE, nurse, minister; b. Pecos, Tex., Mar. 30, 1932; d. William McKinley and Elzora (Wilson) Olliff; m. Radford Chaplin, Nov. 3, 1952; children: Deborah C., William Earnest. Assoc. Applied Sci., Odessa Coll., 1965; extension student U. Pa. Sch. Nursing, U. Calif., Irvine, Golden West Coll. RN, Calif., Okla., Ariz., Md., Tex. Dir. nursing Grays Nursing Home, Odessa, Tex., 1965; supr. nursing Med. Hill, Oakland, Calif.; charge nurse pediatrics Med. Ctr., Odessa; dir. nursing Elmwood Extended Care, Berkeley, Calif.; surg. nurse Childrens Hosp., Berkeley; med./surg. charge nurse Merritt Hosp., Oakland, Calif.; adminstr. Grace and Assocs.; advocate for emotionally abused children; active Watchtower and Bible Tract Soc.; evangelist for Jehovah's Witnesses, 1954—.

THOMSON, MARJORIE BELLE, sociology educator, consultant; b. Topeka, Dec. 4, 1921; d. Roy John and Bessie Margaret (Knarr) Anderson; m. John Whitner Thomson, Jan. 4, 1952 (div. June 9, 1963); 1 child, John Coe. Diploma hostess, Trans World Airlines, 1945; diploma, U.Saltillo, Mex., 1945; BS, Butler U., 1957; MS, Ft. Hays Kans. State U., 1966; postgrad., U. Calif., Santa Barbara, 1968, Kans. State U., 1972-73, Kans. U., 1973. Cert. elem. tchr., Calif., Colo., Ind., Kans., jr. coll. tchr. Tech. libr. N.Am. Aviation, Dallas, 1944-45; flight attendant TWA, Kansas City, Mo., 1945-50; recreation dir. U.S. Govt., Ft. Carson, Colo., 1951-52; elem. tchr. Indpls. Pub. Schs., 1954-57; jr. high tchr. Cheyenne County Schs., Cheyenne Wells, Colo., 1958-59; elem. tchr. Sherman County Schs., Goodland, Kans., 1961-62; lectr. Calif. Luth. U., Thousand Oaks, 1967-69; instr. Ft. Hays Kans. State U., 1969-71; dir. HeadStart Kans. Coun. of Agrl. Workers and Low Income Families, Inc., Goodland, 1971-72; supr. U.S. Govt. Manpower Devel. Programs, Plainville, Kans., 1972-74; bilingual counselor Kans. Dept. Human Resources, Goodland, 1975-82; leader trainee Expt. in Internat. Living, Brattleboro, Vt., 1967-71; cons. M. Anderson & Co., Lakewood, Colo., 1982—; participant Internat. Peace Walk, Moscow to Archangel, Russia, 1991, N.Am. Conf. on Ecology and the Soviet Save Peace and Nature Ecol. Collective, Russia, 1992, Liberators-The Holocaust Awareness Inst., Denver, 1993; amb. internat. Friendship Force, Tiblisi, Republic of Georgia, 1991, Republic South Africa, 1995, Republic of Turkey, 1996; presenter State Conv. AAUW, Aurora, Colo., 1992, presenter nat. conv. Am. Acad. Audiology, Denver, 1992; cons. Gov.'s Conf. in Libr. and Info. Svc., Vail, Colo., 1992; presenter annual conf. Nat. Emergency Number 911 Assn., Denver, 1996. Docent Colo. Gallery of the Arts, Littleton, 1989; spkr. Internat. Self Help for Hard of Hearing People, Inc., 1990—, mem. state recreation resource com. for Self Help for Hard of Hearing People Internat. Conv., Denver, 1991; mem. Denver Deaf and Hard of Hearing Access Com., 1991—; spkr. Ret. Sr. Vol. Program, Denver, 1992—; dir. Holiday Project, Denver, 1992; mem. Lakewood Access Com., 1994—, Arvada Ctr.'s Women's Voices com., 1995—; participant women readers com. Rocky Mountain News, Denver, 1995; trustee Internat. Self Help for Hard of Hearing People, Inc., Bethesda, Md., 1995—; Deaf Panel spkr. for Deaf Awareness Week, Denver, 1995; program co-chair Lakewood Woman's Club, 1996, 97; mem. accessibility com. Arvada Ctr. for Arts and Humanities, 1997; commr. Denver Commn. for People with Disabilities, 1997. Grantee NSF, 1970, 71; recipient Svc. award Mayor of Lakewood, 1995, Honorable Mention Four Who Dare, Colo. Bus. and Profl. Women and KCNC Channel 4, 1995, J.C. Penney Nat. Golden Rule award for cmty. vol. svc., 1996, Cmty. Svc. award Mayor Denver, 1996, City and County of Denver Proclamation for Marjorie Thomason Day, Mayor Wellington E. Webb, April 8, 1997. Mem. AAUW (life, v.p., program chairperson Lakewood br. 1996, Trailblazer award Denver br. 1997), AARP (pres. Denver-Grandview chpt. 1994), VFW Aux. (life), Sociologists for Women in Soc., Bus. and Profl. Woman's Club, Internat. Peace Walkers, Spellbinders, Denver Press Club, Lakewood Woman's Club, TWA Internat. Clipped Wings (cert.), Mile High Wings, Order Ea. Star (life), Sons of Norway, UNESCO, Toastmasters, PHAMALy, Pi Gamma Mu, Alpha Sigma Alpha (life). Democrat. Presbyterian. Home: 12313 W Louisiana Ave G Lakewood CO 80228-3829 Office: M Anderson & Co 6941 W 13th Ave Lakewood CO 80215-5285

THOMSON, VALERIE, artist; b. Bellshill, Lanarkshire, Scotland, Oct. 23, 1948; came to U.S., 1970; d. James and Ingeborg (Erichsen) T.; m. Lawrence B. Pedowitz, 1970 (div. 1984); m. William Anthony Haynes, 1990; stepchildren: Mary Ackermann, Eric A. Haynes. MA, St. Andrews (Scotland) U., 1970; AAS summa cum laude, Fashion Inst. Tech., N.Y.C., 1980; studied with Leo Manso, Richard Pousette-Dart, Arts Student League, N.Y.C., 1983-86. Legal asst. Cahill Gordon & Reindel, N.Y.C., 1970-79; prin. Wonder Ink, Seattle, 1986-90; leader creative writing workshops, PEN, Very Spl. Arts, Roosevelt Island, N.Y., 1985-86; lectr. U. Portland, Oreg., 1994. Design editor: LCQ Mag., 1987-90, (catalogue) Bumbershoot Visual Arts, 1988; featured cover artist numerous pubs. Bd. dirs. Lit. Ctr., Seattle, 1989-90. Recipient Critic's Choice art award The Oregonian, Portland, 1994. Mem. Nat. Womens Caucus For Art, Network Oreg. Artists (program com. 1996—), Oreg. Womens Caucus (designer newsletter 1994-96).

THOR, PAUL VIETS, computer science educator, software engineer, consultant; b. Schenectady, N.Y., Mar. 10, 1946; s. Donald D. and Eleanor B. (Viets) T.; m. Barbara K. Nelson, Mar. 27, 1982 (div. Dec. 1993). BSME, U. Denver, 1968; MS in Engring. Mgmt., UCLA, 1976; MS in Computer Sci., George Mason U., 1993; postgrad., 1996—. Engr. Martin Marietta Corp., Denver, 1968-69; commd. 2d lt. USAF, 1969, advanced through grades to maj., 1982; pilot trainee USAF-Williams AFB, Phoenix, Ariz., 1970-71; pilot C141A 15 MAS-Norton AFB, San Bernardino, Calif., 1971-75, pilot C141B, 1981-84; communications and computer officer 2044 CG-Pentagon, Washington, 1977-81; air field mgr. 18TFW-Kadena AB, Okinawa, Japan, 1984-86; pilot C12 1402 MAS-Andrews AFB, Washington, 1986-87; comm. and computer officer 7 Comm. Group-Pentagon, Washington, 1987-89; cons. George Mason U., Fairfax, Va., 1990-93; pvt. practice cons. Colorado Springs, Colo., 1993—; wing flight examiner 63 MAW-Norton AFB, San Bernardino, 1981-84; acquisitions officer 7th Comms. Group-Pentagon, 1987-89; assoc. prof. computer sci. Colo. Tech. U., Colorado Springs, 1993—. Mem. Computer Soc. of IEEE, Assn. Computer Machinery, Air Force Assn. (life), Ret. Officers Assn. Home: 5330 Slickrock Dr Colorado Springs CO 80918-7646 Office: Colo Tech U 4435 N Chestnut St Colorado Springs CO 80907-3812

THORN, JAMES DOUGLAS, safety engineer; b. Tyler, Tex., May 20, 1959; s. Douglas Howard and Patricia Ann (Kolb) T. Student, U. of Mary, Manama, Bahrain, 1982, S.W. Tex. State U., 1984-86, La. State U., 1989, W.Va. Tech., 1991-92, Berlitz Sch. Langs., 1993. Cert. EMT, BTLS, ACLS, CPR instr., hazardous materials ops., hazardous waste ops., hazardous and indsl. waste mgmt. 3d officer Jackson Marine S.A., Manama, 1981; constrn. foreman Brown & Root S.A., Manama, 1982-83; barge officer Rezayat/Brown & Root E.C., Manama, 1983-84; safety insp. Brown & Root U.S.A., Carson, Calif., 1987-88; sr. safety insp. Brown & Root U.S.A., Taft, La., 1988-89; project safety mgr. Brown & Root Braun, Institute, W.Va., 1989-93; mgr. safety and health Brown & Root Braun, Phila., 1993-94; safety supt. Brown & Root, Carson, Calif., 1994; safety/security mgr. L.A. Export Terminal, 1995—; safety cons. Assn. Builders and Contractors, Charleston, W.Va., 1990-93, chmn. safety seminar, 1991-93; drill monitor Kanawha Valley Emergency Preparedness Coun., South Charleston, W.Va., 1990-93; v.p. Arco Contractors Safety Coun., Carson, 1995-96. Youth counsellor Neon League, St. Albans, W.Va., 1991; den leader cub scouts Boy Scouts Am., 1991-93; v.p. Area Contractors Safety Coun., 1995—; bd. dirs. Johnnie Johnson Tennis Tournament for Boys and Girls Clubs, 1996—. Mem. Am. Soc. Safety Engrs., Nat. Assn. EMTs, Team 911, Great Wall of Tex. Soc., Angels Booster Club (bd. dirs. 1995—, 1st v.p. 1996—), Rams Booster Club (bd. dirs. 1995) now NFL Booster Club of Orange County (bd. dirs. 1996—). Office: Brown & Root PO Box 320 Long Beach CA 90801

THORNBURG, RON, newspaper editor. BA in Polit. Sci., Purdue U., 1971. Reporter Jour. and Courier, Lafayette, Ind., 1972-73; mng. editor The Evening Times, Melbourne, Fla., 1973-75; met. editor, asst. news editor, copy editor, bur. chief Today, Melbourne, 1975-78, mng. editor, 1978-80; exec. editor News Press, Fort Myers, Fla., 1980-86; news exec. Comty. Newspapers, Gannet Co., Inc., 1986-88; editor Burlington (Vt.) Free Press, 1988-94; mng. editor Standard Examiner, Ogden, Utah, 1994—. Office: Standard-Examiner 455 23d St Ogden UT 84401

THORNE, BARRIE, sociologist, educator; b. Logan, Utah, May 22, 1942; d. David Wynne and Alison (Comish) T.; m. Peter Lyman, Nov. 17, 1970; children: Andrew L. Thorne-Lyman, Abigail L. Thorne-Lyman. BA in Anthropology, Stanford U., 1964; MA in Sociology, Brandeis U., 1967, PhD in Sociology, 1971. From asst. prof. to prof. sociology Mich. State U., East Lansing, 1971-87; Streisand prof. gender studies and sociology U. So. Calif., L.A., 1987-95; prof. sociology and women's studies U. Calif., Berkeley, 1995—; cons. AAUW, Washington, 1993-96. Author: Gender Play: Girls and Boys in School, 1993; co-editor: Language, Gender and Society, 1983, Rethinking the Family, 1992, Feminist Sociology, 1997; mem. editl. bd. Signs: Jour. of Women in Culture and Soc., 1983—; assoc. editor Contemporary Sociology, 1994—; contbg. editor Theory and Society, 1990—; contbr. articles to profl. publs. Recipient Rsch. Network on Mid. Childhood award MacArthur Found., 1994—. Mem. NOW, Am. Sociol. Assn. (v.p. 1993-94), Soc. for Study of Social Problems (bd. dirs. 1987-90), Sociologists for Women in Soc. (chair social issues 1973-76, Outstanding Mentor 1993), Nat. Women's Studies Assn., Internat. Sociol. Assn., Sociol. Rsch. Assn., Women's Internat. League for Peace and Freedom. Democrat. Office: U Calif Dept Sociology Berkeley CA 94720

THORNE, DAVID W., lawyer; b. Walla Walla, Wash., Aug. 9, 1945. BA, Wash. State U., 1967; MBA, U. Wash., 1969, JD, 1974. Bar: Wash. 1974. Mem. Davis Wright Tremaine, Seattle. Mem. ABA, Am. Coll. Real Estate Lawyers, Am. Coll. Mortgage Attys., Am. Land Title Assn. Lender Counsel Group, Wash. State Bar Assn. (past mem. exec. com. real property, probate and trust sect., past chmn. 1991-92), Pacific Real Estate Inst. (past pres. 1994, founding trustee 1989—), Phi Delta Phi. Office: Davis Wright Tremaine 2600 Century Sq 1501 4th Ave Seattle WA 98101-1662

THORNE, GARY MARVIN, surgeon; b. Great Bend, Kans., Feb. 22, 1948; s. Marvin E. and Annebeth L. (Oeser) T.; m. Margarita Salazar, May 3, 1975; children: Mary, Marci. BA, Pasadena Coll., 1970; MD, U. Ariz., 1974. Diplomate Am. Bd. Surgery. Intern U. Tex., San Antonio, 1974-75; resident in surgery U. Calif., Davis, 1975-79; pvt. practice Lewiston, Idaho, 1980—; attending surgeon Tri-State Meml. Hosp., Clarkston, Wash., 1979—, chief of staff, 1983; attending surgeon St. Joseph's Regional Med. Ctr., Lewiston, 1979—, chief of surgery, 1987, chief of staff, 1995—. Fellow ACS; mem. Idaho Med. Assn., North Idaho Dist. Med. Soc. (pres. 1997), U. Calif.-Davis Surg. Assn. Republican. Nazarene. Home: 1624 Swallows Nest Loop Clarkston WA 99403-1726 Office: Gary M Thorne MD 307 Saint Johns Way Lewiston ID 83501-2435

THORNE, KATE RULAND, writer, publisher, editor; b. Del Norte, Colo., Dec. 15, 1937; d. Joseph Lydian Norman and Avis Frances Kiemstead; m. Edwin G. Ruland, Aug. 20, 1960 (div. 1984); children: Gregory, Jeanie, Rebecca. BA, So. Meth. U., 1976. Speech pathologist Shady Brook Sch., Dallas, 1960-61, Hillside Rehab., Grand Junction, Colo., 1962-72; pub. Thorne Enterprises Pub. Inc., Sedona, Ariz., 1989—; editor, pub. Thorne/Swiftwind Pub., Sedona, 1993—; lectr. in field. Author: Lion of Redstone, 1980, Experience Sedona: Legends and Legacies, 1990, (screenplay) Blood Oath; author, editor: Experience Jerome and the Verde Valley: Legends and Legacies, 1992, The Yavapai: People of the Red Rocks, 1993, The Legacy of Sedona Schnebly, 1994, Upon This Rock, 1995, The Butcherbirds, 1996; editor, columnist Sedona Mag., 1986-87; columnist Art Talk, Directions Mag.; contbr. numerous articles to mags. and newspapers; 1st woman editor Sedona Red Rock News, 1987-88. Founder, pres., Ariz. Indian Living Treasures, 1990-91; founding mem., sec. Western Am. Week, 1990-94. Mem. Ariz. Small Pub. Assn. (founding mem.), Sedona Hist. Soc. (pres.). Home and Office: 149 Gambel Ln Sedona AZ 86336-7119

THORNE, MIKE, state agency administrator. Exec. dir. Port of Portland, Oreg. Office: Port of Portland Office Exec Dir 700 NE Multnomah Portland OR 97232

THORNSLEY, RANDALL G., management consultant; b. Cleve., Apr. 20, 1954; s. Ronald N. and Evelyn Jean (Adams) T.; divorced; children: Calista Marie, Adam Garrett. Owner Capri-Consol. Industries, Anchorage, Alaska, 1974-87; CEO Silver Screen Mgmt. Corp., Anchorage, 1987—.

THORNTON, CAMERON MITCHELL, financial planner; b. L.A., Sept. 30, 1954; s. H. Walter and Naomi L. (Brown) T.; m. Jane Kubasak, June 18, 1978; children: Mitchell, Kathryn, Andrew. BA, U. So. Calif., L.A., 1976; MBA, U. La Verne, 1983. CFP. Planner Lockheed Calif. Co., Burbank, 1980-84; adv. assoc. Fin. Network Investment Corp., Burbank, 1983—, fin. cons., 1983—; prin. Cameron Thornton Assocs., Burbank, 1982—; lic. charitable gift planner Renaissance Inc., 1992—. Author: (manual) Computer Aided Planning System, 1982-83. Mem., vice chair St. Joseph Med. Ctr. Found., 1988-92, chmn. planned giving dept., 1991-92; mem., chair Burbank Police Commn., 1981-85, Burbank Planning Commn., 1989-93; with ARC, Burbank, 1984-88, chmn. 1985-87. Lt. comdr. USN/USNR, 1976-88. Named Friend of Campfire, Camp Fire Coun., Pasadena, Calif., 1989, 92. Mem. Nat. Assn. Renaissance Advisors, Inst. CFP's, Internat. Assn. for Fin. Planning, Cert. Fin. Planner Bd. Standards, Burbank C. of C. Republican. Roman Catholic. Office: Cameron Thornton Assocs 290 E Verdugo Ave Ste 205 Burbank CA 91502-1342

THORNTON, CHARLES VICTOR, lawyer; b. Takoma Park, Md., July 18, 1942; s. Charles Victor and Margaret Louise (Wiggins) T.; m. Suzanne Thorne, May 16, 1970; children: Christopher, Matthew, Joshua, Jeremy. AB, Cornell U., 1964; JD, U. Mich., 1967. Bar: Calif. 1969, U.S. Dist. Ct. (cen. dist.) Calif. 1969. Instr. U. Pa. Law Sch., Phila., 1967-68; assoc. Paul, Hastings, Janofsky & Walker, L.A., 1968-74; ptnr. Paul, Hastings, Janofsky & Walker, 1975—, mng. ptnr. L.A. office, 1992-96, mng. partner San Francisco office, 1997—. Contbr. articles to pubs. Pres. Info. and Referral Fedn. Los Angeles County, 1988-95; mem. exec. com. Los Angeles County United Way, 1988-92. Named Bd. Vol. of Yr. United Way, 1986. Mem. Calif. Club, Los Angeles Country Club. Office: Paul Hastings Janofsky & Walker 555 S Flower St Fl 23 Los Angeles CA 90071-2300

THORNTON, J. DUKE, lawyer; b. Murray, Ky., July 11, 1944; s. Arthur Lee and Ruth Maxine (Billings) T.; m. Carol Caceres, Dec. 26, 1966 (dec.); children: Jennifer, Carey. BBA, U. N.Mex., Albuquerque, 1966, JD, 1969. Bar: N.Mex. 1969, U.S. Ct. Appeals (10th cir.) 1969, N.Y. 1985, U.S. Supreme Ct. 1992. With Butt, Thornton & Baehr, P.C., Albuquerque, 1971—; legal counsel N.Mex. Jaycees, 1972; clk. N.Mex. Supreme Ct., Santa Fe, 1969; mem. com. N.Mex. Uniform Jury Instructions, 1987-88. Author: Trial Handbook for New Mexico Lawyers, 1992. Bd. dirs. N.Mex. Bd. of Dentistry, Santa Fe, 1987-88; commr. N.Mex. Racing Commn., Albuquerque, 1988-95. Mem. ABA, Assn. Coll. and Univ. Counsel, Internat. Assn. Ins. Counsel, Am. Bd. Trial Advs., Albuquerque Bar Assn. (bd. dirs. 1978-79), Nat. Collegiate Athletic Assn. (agt.). Office: Butt Thornton & Baehr PC PO Box 3170 Albuquerque NM 87110

THORNTON, JOHN S., IV, bishop. Bishop Diocese of Idaho, Boise, 1990—. Office: Episcopal Diocese of Idaho Box 936 510 W Washington St Boise ID 83701*

THORNTON, ROBERT LEE, aircraft manufacturing company executive; b. Santa Monica, Calif., Sept. 5, 1957; s. Bobby Lee and Lillian Kay (Sutherlin) T.; m. Deborah Louise Wehrli Hines, Sept. 25, 1977 (div. July 1988); children: Kristi, Robert, Steven; m. Norma Jean Hannahs Tasch, May 8, 1990; children: Josh, Jason. AA in Bus. Adminstrn., Long Beach (Calif.) City Coll., 1984; BS, Pepperdine U., Malibu, Calif., 1993; postgrad., U. Calif., Irvine, 1995—. Foreman Prodn. Control, Long Beach, 1978-84; br. mgr. Tool Control, Torrance, Calif., 1985-87; br. mgr. Fabrication, Long Beach, 1987-88, mgr., 1989-92; mgr. Fabrication/Inventory Ops., Long Beach, 1989; dep. gen. mgr. Assembly, Long Beach, 1992-94; dir. Procurement, Long Beach, 1995—. Mem. Mgmt. Club. Home: 1 Shearwater Irvine CA 92604-4618

THORP, EDWARD OAKLEY, investment management company executive; b. Chgo., Aug. 14, 1932; s. Oakley Glenn and Josephine (Gebert) T.; B.A. in Physics, UCLA, 1953, M.A., 1955, Ph.D. in Math., 1958; m. Vivian Sinetar, Jan. 28, 1956; children: Raun, Karen, Jeffrey. Instr., UCLA, 1956-59, C.L.E. Moore instr. MIT, Cambridge, Mass., 1959-61; asst. prof. N.Mex. State U., 1961-63, assoc. prof. math., 1963-65, U. Calif., Irvine, 1965-67, prof. math., 1967-82, adj. prof. fin., 1982-87; regents lectr. U. Calif., Irvine, 1992-93; vis. prof. UCLA, 1991; chmn. Oakley Sutton Mgmt. Corp., Newport Beach, Calif., 1972-91; mng. gen. ptnr. Princeton/Newport Ptnrs., Newport Beach, 1969-91, OSM Ptnrs., MIDAS Advisors, Newport Beach, 1986-89; gen. ptnr. Edward O. Thorp & Assocs., L.P., Newport Beach, 1989—; portfolio mgr., cons. Glenwood Investment Corp., Chgo., 1992-94; prin., cons. Grosvenor Capital Mgmt., Chgo., 1992-93; pres. Noesis Corp., 1994—. Grantee NSF, 1954-55, 62-64, Air Force Office Sci. Research, 1964-73. Fellow NSF, Inst. Math. Stats.; mem. Phi Beta Kappa, Sigma Xi. Author: Beat The Dealer: A Winning Strategy for the Game of Twenty-One, 1962, rev. edit., 1966, Elementary Probability, 1966, The Mathematics of Gambling 1984; co-author: Beat The Market, 1967; The Gambling Times Guide to Blackjack, 1984; columnist Gambling Times, 1979-84. Avocations: astronomy, distance running. Office: Edward O Thorp & Assocs LP 620 Newport Center Dr Ste 880 Newport Beach CA 92660-8008

THORPE, DOUGLAS L., lawyer; b. Wahoo, Nebr., Jan. 25, 1937. BSCE, U. Nebr., 1959; JD cum laude, So. Meth. U., 1968. Bar: Calif. 1969. Mem. Perkins Coie, L.A.; bd. dirs. Pub. Counsel, 1980-83. Mem. ABA (antitrust law sect., corp., banking and bus. law sect., litigation sect., econs. of law practice sect.), State Bar Calif., L.A. County Bar Assn. (del. to State Bar Conf. of Dels. 1981, 1983-84, exec. com. antitrust law sect. 1981-83), Century City Bar Assn. (bd. govs. 1982-85), Order of the Coif, Barristers, Phi Delta Phi, Sigma Tau, Tau Beta Pi, Chi Epsilon. Office: Perkins Coie 9th Fl 1999 Ave Of Stars Fl 9 Los Angeles CA 90067-6022

THORPE, GARY STEPHEN, chemistry educator; b. Los Angeles, Mar. 9, 1951; s. David Winston and Jeanette M. (Harris) T.; m. Patricia Marion Eison, Apr. 13, 1949; children: Kristin Anne, Erin Michelle. BS, U. Redlands, 1973; MS, Calif. State U., Northridge, 1975. Tchr. L.A. Schs., 1975-80, L.A. Community Colls., 1976-81, Beverly Hills (Calif.) High Sch., 1980—; instr. chemistry Coll of the Canyons, Santa Clarita, Calif., 1994—; gen. ptnr. High 5 AP Test Pres. Svc., Beverly Hills, Calif., 1994—. Author: AP Chemistry Study Guide, 1993. Res. police officer L.A. Police Dept., 1991. Recipient Commendation L.A. County Bd. Suprs., 1983, 84, Beverly Hills City Coun., 1983, 84, City of L.A., 1995, REsolution of Commendation State of Calif. Senate and Assembly, 1983, 84, Cert. of Appreciation L.A. County Bd. Edn., 1984-85, Gov. George Deukmejian, Sacrament, 1984-85. Mem. Am. Chem. Soc. (exec. dir. So. Calif. divsn. 1995—, slected as Outstanding Chemistry Tchr. of So. Calif. 1989, 92), NEA, Calif. Tchrs. Assn., Phi Delta Kappa. Republican. Lutheran. Lodge: Masons. Home: 6127 Balcom Ave Encino CA 91316-7207

THORPE, JAMES, humanities researcher; b. Aiken, S.C., Aug. 17, 1915; s. J. Ernest and Ruby (Holloway) T.; m. Elizabeth McLean Daniells, July 19, 1941; children: John D., Sally Jans-Thorpe. A.B., The Citadel, 1936, LL.D., 1971; M.A., U. N.C., 1937; Ph.D., Harvard U., 1941; Litt.D., Occidental Coll., 1968; L.H.D., Claremont Grad. Sch., 1968; H.H.D., U. Toledo, 1977. Instr. to prof. English Princeton, 1946-66; dir. Huntington Libr., Art Gallery and Bot. Gardens, San Marino, Calif., 1966-83; sr. research assoc. Huntington Libr., San Marino, Calif., 1966—. Author: Bibliography of the Writings of George Lyman Kittredge, 1948, Milton Criticism, 1950, Rochester's Poems on Several Occasions, 1950, Poems of Sir George Etherege, 1963, Aims and Methods of Scholarship, 1963, 70, Literary Scholarship, 1964, Relations of Literary Study, 1967, Bunyan's Grace Abounding and Pilgrim's Progress, 1969, Principles of Textual Criticism, 1972, 2d edit., 1979, Use of Manuscripts in Literary Research, 1974, 2d edit., 1979, Gifts of Genius, 1980, A Word to the Wise, 1982, John Milton: The Inner Life, 1983, The Sense of Style: Reading English Prose, 1987, Henry Edwards Huntington: A Biography, 1994, H.E. Huntington: A Short Biography, 1996, A Pleasure of Proverbs, 1996. Served to col. USAAF, 1941-46. Decorated Bronze Star medal.; Guggenheim fellow, 1949-50, 65-66. Fellow Am. Acad. Arts and Scis., Am. Philos. Soc.; mem. MLA, Am. Antiquarian Soc., Soc. for Textual Scholarship. Democrat. Episcopalian. Clubs: Zamorano, Twilight. Home: 1199 Arden Rd Pasadena CA 91106-4143 Office: Huntington Libr San Marino CA 91108

THORPE, OTIS HENRY, professional basketball player; b. Boynton Beach, Fla., Aug. 5, 1962. Student, U. Providence. Basketball player Kansas City Kings, 1984-85, Sacramento Kings (formerly Kansas City), 1985-88, Houston Rockets, 1988-94, Portland Trail Blazers, 1994—, now with Detroit Pistons. Mem. NBA championship team 1994. Address: Detroit Pistons Two Championship Dr Auburn Hills MI 48326*

THORPE, PATRICIA WATTS, secondary education educator; b. Ogden, Utah, Jan. 4, 1960; d. Wells LeRoy and Carmen (Belvedere) Watts; m. Bret Simpson Thorpe, July 19, 1983; children: Andrea Carmen, Jessica Sharon, Shealynn. BA, Weber State U., Ogden, Utah, 1994. Cert. secondary edn. tchr., Utah. English tchr. Washington H.S., Weber Sch. Dist., Ogden, Utah, 1994—; adult edn. instr. Weber Sch. Dist., Ogden, Utah, 1994—. Mem. Ogden Golf and Country Club. Democrat. Mormon. Office: Washington High School 3279 Washington Blvd Ogden UT 84401-3935

THORSEN, JAMES HUGH, aviation director, airport manager; b. Evanston, Ill., Feb. 5, 1943; s. Chester A. and Mary Jane (Currie) T.; m. Nancy Dain, May 30, 1980. BA, Ripon Coll., 1965. FAA cert. comml. pilot, flight instr. airplanes and instruments. Mem. Am. Assn. Airport Execs. (pres. N.W. chpt.), Rotary (Idaho Falls West club), Mensa, Quiet Birdmen, Sigma Alpha Epsilon. Home: 334 Westmoreland Dr Idaho Falls ID 83402 Office: Mcpl Airport Idaho Falls ID 83402

THORSON, MARGARET HELEN, farmer, librarian; b. Puyallup, Wash., Jan. 8, 1944; d. Roy Louis and Helen Margot (Doremus) Van Alstyne; m. John Hall Blethen, Oct. 31, 1963 (div. Oct. 1973); children: Jennifer Margaret Blethen Pittis, Marilla Pearl Blethen; m. Joel D. thorson, Dec. 27,

1986; 1 child, Siri Alice. BA, Western Wash. U., 1971. Cert. tchr., Wash. Owner Thousand Flower Farm, Waldron, Wash., 1986—; libr. Waldron Island Sch., 1989—. Mem. San Juan Island Farmers Market, Island Farmcrafters. Home: Thousand Flower Farm Waldron WA 98297

THORSTENSON, CLARK T., religious studies educator, administrator; b. Spanish Fork, Utah, Apr. 15, 1936; s. Goodman and Florence H. (Angus) T.; m. Colleen Powelson, Aug. 15, 1962; children: Kevin, Lisa, Elizabeth, Daniel, Jill. BS, Brigham Young U., 1962, MRE, 1965; PhD, U. Utah, 1969. Cert. gerontologist, Utah. Prin. Ch. Edn. Sys., Richfield-Orem, Utah, 1962-64; area coord. Ch. Edn. Sys., Albuquerque, 1964-65; dir. Inst. Religion Ch. Edn. Sys., Salt Lake City, 1965-69; prof. religious studies Brigham Young U., Provo, 1969-85, dir. coop. edn. and internships, 1985-97, assoc. dir. Jerusalem Ctr., 1997—; bd. dirs. UTRS-Utah Recreation Parks Assn., 1971-85. Co-author: (coll. text) Issues in Outdoor Recreation, 1977, Planning for Social Recreation, 1978. Consul of Iceland, Mountain States, 1995—; bd. dirs. Grand Theatre, Salt Lake City, 1994-97; mem. Utah Gov.'s Com. for the Handicapped, Salt Lake City, 1980-85; mem. Coun. on Aging, Provo City, 1992-96. Recipient Profl. Svc. award Utah Recreation Parks Assn., 1982, Disting. Svc. award, 1985. Nat. Recreation Parks and Assn. (bd. dirs. regional coun. 1972-79, Disting. fellow 1979), Scandanavian Scholarship Soc., Phi Kappa Phi (chpt. pres. 1985-86). Republican. LDS. Home: 2797 Apache Ln Provo UT 84604

THRASHER, JAMES BRANTLEY, surgeon; b. Anderson, S.C., Sept. 9, 1960; s. James Douglas and Margaret Ann (Erskine) T.; m. Laura Lesslie Church, Aug. 26, 1989; children: James Brantley Jr., Madeline Lee. BS, Clemson U., 1982; MD, Med. U. S.C., 1986. Diplomate Am. Bd. Urology, Nat. Bd. Med. Examiners. Attending urologist Fitzsimmons Army Med. Ctr., Aurora, Colo., 1991; cons. urol. surgery VA Hosp., Durham, N.C., 1991-92; attending urologist Madigan Army Med. Ctr., Tacoma, Wash., 1992-95, program dir. urology svc., 1995—; cons. Am. Lake VA Med. Ctr., Tacoma, 1992—; clin. asst. prof. surgery Uniformed Svcs. U. Health Scis., Bethesda, Md., 1993-96, U. Wash., Seattle, 1993—; cons. urol. surgery Naval Regional Med. Ctr., Bremerton, Wash., 1994—. Decorated army achievement medal, 1995. Mem. AMA, Am. Assn. Clin. Urologists, Am. Coll. Surgeons, Am. Urol. Assn., Soc. Govt. Svc. Urologists, Assn. Mil. Surgeons U.S., N.C. Med. Soc., Northwest Urol. Soc., Phi Kappa Phi. Office: Madigan Army Med Ctr MCHJ-SU Tacoma WA 98431

THRASHER, KARA SCOTT, art association director; b. Richmond, Va., Dec. 30, 1964; d. James Winfield and Janet Marie (Geldard) T.; m. Clifford Joseph Livingston, Aug. 8, 1988. BA, Rutgers, 1986. Mgr. The Futon Shop, Emeryville, Calif., 1990-93; arts cons. Blaine's Art and Graphic Supply, Anchorage, 1993-95; tech. asst. Sheila Wyne Sculptor, Anchorage, 1995-96; art program dir. The Arc of Anchorage, 1996, cmty. inclusion program dir., 1996-97; mem. Grandview Gardens Curatoral Com., Anchorage, 1995-96; art educator Very Spl. Arts Alaska, Anchorage, 1996, Artists in Schs., Anchorage, 1996—. One-man shows include Harmonics, 1995; writer, musician Parallax 1, 1997, (stage performance) Trial By Fire, 1997. Graphics cons. Dem. Party, Anchorage, 1994; vol. art educator The Arc of Anchorage, 1995, exhibit cons. The Arc of Anchorage, 1996. Democrat. Office: The Arc of Anchorage 2211 Arca Dr Anchorage AK 99508

THRELFALL, TIMOTHY ALLEN, theater arts educator, director; b. Chgo., Feb. 25, 1959; s. Ronald Edward Threlfall and Mary Anne (Shetzely) Nelson; m. Linda Susan Wright, May 22, 1981; children: Kami Lynne, Kody Michael, Kyla Janeal. BFA, U. Idaho, 1983; MFA, U. Wash., 1987. Artistic dir. N.W. Summer Playhouse, Coeur d'Alene, Idaho, 1990-93; edn. program coord. Seattle Children's Theatre, 1993; artistic dir. Seattle Civic Light Opera, 1993-96; asst. prof. theatre arts Brigham Young U., Provo, Utah, 1996—. Mem. AFTRA, SAG, Actors Equity Assn. Democrat. Mormon. Office: Brigham Young U Theatre/Film HFAC D-581 Provo UT 84602

THRELKELD, STEVEN WAYNE, civil engineer; b. La Jolla, Calif., Feb. 22, 1956; s. Willard Wayne and Sylvia Eileen (Daugherety) T.; m. Sheree Leslie Chabot, Nov. 17, 1984; children: Tristan David, Kayla Lee. BS in Geol. Scis., San Diego State U., 1985. Geophys. trainee Western Geophys., Bakersfield, Calif., 1985; civil engr. Dee Jaspar & Assocs., Bakersfield, 1986, Bement, Dainwood & Sturgeon, Lemon Grove, Calif., 1987, Calif. Dept. Transp., San Diego, 1988—; comml. scuba diver, San Diego, 1987-88. Photo editor Montezuma Life Mag., San Diego, 1981; portrait photographer Coast Prodns., San Diego, 1975. Mem. Profl. Engrs. in Calif. Govt. (San Diego chpt.), Planetary Soc., Union Concerned Scientists, Common Cause, Nat. Parks and Conservation Assn., World Wildlife Fund, Planning and Conservation League. Home: 4262 Bancroft Dr La Mesa CA 91941-6744

THRIFT, WILLIAM BOYD, retired lecturer; b. Mosier, Oreg., Nov. 7, 1912; s. Edward Jackson and Lena Mavourneen (McCormick) T.; m. Margaret Wilson, Aug. 2, 1941 (div. Feb. 1954); children: David Edward, Ann Louise, Mardi; m. Suzann Williams, Apr. 30, 1971. BA, Lewis and ClarkU., 1934; MDiv, San Francisco Theol. Sem., 1941; MA, St. Mary's U., 1966. Min. Presbyn. Ch., Morgan Hill, Calif., 1941-42; asst. prof. San Antonio Coll., 1966-69; lectr. English, Speech, Religious U. Md., 1969-95; lectr. English, Speech, Religion, U. Coll., U. Md. in Greece, Spain, Germany, Eng., Iceland, 1969-95. With USN, 1942-46. With USAF, 1947-66.

THRO, BROYDRICK (ELAINE THRO), science and psychology educator; b. Boston, Feb. 19, 1945; d. Fredrick and Mary Frances (Goggin) Broydrick; m. A. Brooker Thro, June 19, 1965. Student, Conn. Coll., 1963-65; BA, U. Calif., Berkeley, 1969; MA, UCLA, 1970, PhD, 1990. Tchg. asst. dept. philosophy UCLA, 1974-77, tchg. assoc. dept. philosophy, 1977-80; vis. scholar dept. psychology Ctr. Human Info. Processing U. Calif. San Diego, La Jolla, 1991-92, 92-93; rsch. scholar Ctr. for Medieval and Renaissance Studies, UCLA, 1994—; assoc. Behavioral and Brain Scis.: An Internat. Jour. Current Rsch. and Theory, Princeton, N.J., 1987—. Contbr. articles to profl. jours. Mem. Am. Philos. Assn. Home: 4771A La Villa Marina Marina Del Rey CA 90292

THROCKMORTON, REX DENTON, lawyer; b. Lima, Ohio, June 4, 1941; s. Francis and Jane (Corwin) T.; m. Barbara Catherine Poore, July 21, 1962; children: Scott, John. BS, Denison U., 1963; JD, Ohio State U., 1965. Bar: Ohio 1966, N. Mex. 1971, U.S. Dist. Ct. N. Mex. 1971, U.S. Ct. Appeals (10th cir.) 1973. Assoc. Squire, Sanders & Dempsey, Cleve., 1965-66; shareholder, bd. dirs. Rodey, Dickason, Sloan, Akin & Robb, P.A., Albuquerque, 1971—, chmn. litig. dept., 1985--. Editor Ohio State Law Jour., 1965. Pres. Albuquerque Civic Light Opera Assn., 1985. Capt. JAGC, USAF, 1966-71. Mem. ABA, N.Mex. Bar Assn. (bd. of bar commrs. 1990—, sec.-treas. 1994, v.p. 1995, pres.-elect 1996, pres. 1997), Albuquerque Bar Assn. (pres. 1982). Republican. Home: 9109 Luna De Oro Rd NE Albuquerque NM 87111-1640 Office: Rodey Dickason Sloan Akin & Robb PO Box 1888 Albuquerque NM 87103-1888

THROP, GEORGE LAWRENCE, secondary education educator, mathematics educator; b. Greenville, Ohio, Jan. 17, 1942; s. Walter Ray and Virginia Maude (Carpenter) T.; m. Janet Irene Parker, June 26, 1966; children: Randall Jay, Laura Kay. BS in Edn., Ball State U., 1965, MA in Edn., 1969; postgrad., U. Ariz., 1975-85. Cert. prin. K-12, std. secondary tchr. 7-12. Tchr. math./sci. Warren Twp. Schs., Indpls., 1966-69, Catalina Foothills Sch. Dist., Tucson, Ariz., 1969-85; adminstrv. asst., tchr. Santa Cruz Valley Union H.S., Eloy, Ariz., 1985-88; asst. prin., at-risk dir. Somerton (Ariz.) Elem. Sch. Dist., 1988-90; assoc. prin. Creighton Elem. Sch. Dist., Phoenix, 1990-91; tchr. math. Phoenix Union H.S. Dist., 1991—; asst. prof. math. U. Advancing Computer Tech., Phoenix, 1992-96; evaluation cons. Sunnyside Unified Sch. Dist., Tucson, 1980; mem. evaluation team North Ctrl. Accrediting Assn., Marana, Ariz., 1988; mem. discipline task force Ariz. Dept. Edn., Phoenix, 1989-90; curriculum developer Phoenix Union H.S. Dist., 1994-95. Author: Integrated and Individualized Math/Science Curriculum, 1969-72; (handbook) Public Relations for Teachers, 1985. Sch. coord. United Way of Tucson, 1983; mem. Somerton Substance Abuse Task Force, 1988-90, Ariz. Humane Soc., Phoenix, 1991-97; mem. exec. bd. Gov.'s Alliance Against Drugs, Phoenix, 1989-90. Recipient Mentor Program award Western Ariz. Area Health Edn. Ctr., Yuma, 1990; Dropout Prevention grantee Ariz. Dept. Edn., Somerton, 1988-90. Mem. ASCD, Catalina Foothills Edn. Assn. (pres. 1979-81), Phi Delta Kappa. Home: 4909 W Onyx Ave Glendale AZ 85302

THUERY, JACQUES H.A., space industry engineer; b. Rodez, France, Nov. 27, 1951; came to the U.S., 1989; s. Jean Pierre and Marguerite H.M.L. (Roubellat) T.; m. Beatriz Leonor Lopez, Aug. 25, 1983; children: Anne, Philippe, Guillaume. Ingénieur d'Etat, Enseeiht, Toulouse, France, 1974. R&D engr. Industries Microondes Internat., Epône, France, 1977-80; engr. Thomson-CSF, Meudon, France, 1981-82, Cannes, France, 1983-88; engr. Alcatel-Espace c/o Ford Aerospace, Palo Alto, Calif., 1989-92, Alcatel-Espace c/o Space Sys./Loral, Palo Alto, 1992—. Author: Les Microondes, 1983, Microwaves, 1992. Mem. IEEE. Home: 3866 Corina Ct Palo Alto CA 94303 Office: Space Systems/Loral M/S SP-1 3825 Fabian Way Palo Alto CA 94303

THUMMA, SAMUEL ANDERSON, lawyer; b. Emmetsburg, Iowa, May 2, 1962; s. H. Russell and Lanore Ava (Anderson) T.; m. Barbara J. Dawson. BS, Iowa State U., 1984; JD, U. Iowa, 1988. Bar: Iowa 1988, Ill. 1990, D.C. 1990, Ariz. 1992. Broadcaster Sta. WOI-AM, Ames, Iowa, 1982-84; print journalist Iowa Dept. Agr., Des Moines, 1985; law clk. to Hon. David R. Hansen, U.S. Dist. Ct. for No. Dist. Iowa, Cedar Rapids, 1988-90; assoc. Arnold & Porter, Washington, 1990-92; law clk. to Hon. Stanley G. Feldman, Ariz. Supreme Ct., 1992-93; mem. Brown & Bain, P.A., Phoenix, 1995—. Contbr. articles to profl. jours. Bd. dirs., purchasing coord. Gifts for Homeless, Inc., Washington, 1991-93; mem. study affairs devel. adv. coun. Iowa State U., 1993—; mem. Paradise Valley Village Planning Com., 1994—, sec., 1995—. Harry S. Truman Found. scholar, 1982-87. Mem. ABA, State Bar of Ariz. (fee arbitration com. 1994—), Maricopa County Bar Assn. (continuing legal edn. com. 1995—), Ill. Bar Assn., D.C. Bar Assn., Iowa Bar Assn., Ariz. Bar Assn., Order of Coif. Republican. Methodist. Office: Brown & Bain PA PO Box 400 2901 N Central Ave Phoenix AZ 85012-2700

THUMS, CHARLES WILLIAM, designer, consultant; b. Manitowoc, Wis., Sept. 5, 1945; s. Earl Oscar and Helen Margaret (Rusch) T. B. in Arch., Ariz. State U., 1972. Ptnr., Grafic, Tempe, Ariz., 1967-70; founder, prin. I-Squared Environ. Cons., Tempe, Ariz., 1970-78; designer and cons. design morphology, procedural programming and algorithms, 1978—. Author: (with Jonathan Craig Thums) Tempe's Grand Hotel, 1973, The Rossen House, 1975; (with Daniel Peter Aiello) Shelter and Culture, 1976; contbg. author: Tombstone Planning Guide, 5 vols., 1974. Office: PO Box 3126 Tempe AZ 85280-3126

THUNDER, SPENCER K., retired elementary school principal; b. Longview, Wash., Dec. 5, 1939; s. Maynard King and Aarah Avona (Hearn) T.; m. Joyce Marie Sjogren, June 22, 1959 (div. June 1972); children: Scott, Mark, Karen; m. Jeanine Louise Pratt. BA, Cen. Wash. U., 1962; MEd, U. Wash., 1975. Cert. elem. educator, prin., reality therapist. Tchr. jr. and sr. high Yakima (Wash.) Sch. Dist., 1962-66; tchr. elem. Olympia (Wash.) Sch. Dist., 1966-67; tchr. high sch. Edmonds (Wash.) Sch. Dist., 1967-71, program mgr., high sch. spl. edn., 1971-76; prin. Maplewood Handicapped Children's Ctr., Edmonds, 1976-87, Mountlake Terrace (Wash.) Elem. Sch., 1987-94; adj. prof. Seattle Pacific U., 1991—; supr. tchg. interns City U., Renton, Wash., 1994—, Western Wash. U., 1996; instr. Edmonds C.C., 1978-79, 96; vis. faculty Ctrl. Wash. U., Ellensberg, 1976; instr. Olympia Vocat. Tech., 1966-67, Yakima Valley Coll., 1964-66. Author: (pamphlet) Work Eval in Schools, 1975; contbr. articles to profl. jours. Bd. dirs. Smithwright Estates Group Home, Edmonds, 1980-96. Sgt. Wash. N.G., 1955-63. Home: 708 Hoyt Ave Everett WA 98201-1320

THURBER, EMILY FORREST, political consultant; b. Chgo,, Oct. 31, 1930; d. Maulsby and Harriette (Reichmann) Forrest; m. James Perry Thurber, Jr., Aug. 8, 1950. BA, Stanford U., 1964. Legis. aide Sen. Alan Cranston U.S. Senate, Washington, 1974-78, 82-83; fundraiser Cranston for Pres., Washington, 1983-84; program dir. Fgn. Student Svc. Coun., Washington, 1984-86; polit. cons. EJT Assocs., Los Altos, Calif., 1991-96; campaign mgr. Sher for Senate, Los Altos, 1996—. Elected mem., vice chair, dir. cmty. outreach Santa Clara County Dem. Ctrl. Com., Calif., 1992; mem. Calif. State Dem. Ctrl. Com., 1992-96, elected mem., 1995—; elected del. Dem. Nat. Com., 1996. Mem. Peninsula Dem. Coalition (treas. 1996—), Los Altos Sister Cities Inc. (sec. 1995-96), Mid-Peninsula YWCA (sec. 1995-96, chair pub. policy com. 1996—), Mid-Peninsula NAACP (polit. dir. 1993-95), Phi Beta Kappa. Home and Office: 694 Benvenue Ave Los Altos CA 94024-4013

THURMOND, AMY SUZANNE, physician, radiologist, educator; b. Santa Monica, Calif., May 14, 1956; d. Robert Lee Thurmond and Nancy Lou (Reganall) Ross; m. Richard Michael Scanlan, Apr. 3, 1982; children: Charles, Meredith, William. BA, Wellesley Coll., 1978; MD, UCLA, 1982. Diplomate Am. Bd. Radiology. Intern gen. surgery Oreg. Health Scis. U., 1982; resident in radiology Oreg. Health Scis. U., Portland, 1984-87; rsch. asst. Wellesley (Mass.) Coll., 1975, U. Calif., Berkeley, 1977, Harvard U., Cambridge, Mass.; asst. prof. Oreg. Health Scis. U., Portland, 1988-90, assoc. prof., 1991—; cons. Conceptus, Inc., San Carlos, Calif., 1991—; lectr. Riverdale Elem. Sch., Portland, 1992, 93. Editor: Women's Imaging, 1996; contbr. articles to profl. jours.; patentee in field. Parent participant 4-H Club, Wilsonville, Oreg., 1994—; basketball coach Lake Oswego, Oreg., 1994-96. Rsch. grantee Oreg. Health Scis. U., 1990; grantee Zimmerman Found., 1977. Mem. Soc. Uroradiology, Am. Coll. Radiology (expert panel on women's imaging 1993—), Radiol. Soc. N.Am. (reviewer 1990—, Editor's Distinction award 1991, 92, 93, Magna Cum Laude Sci. Exhibit com. award 1988), Am. Fertility Soc., Oreg. Med. Assn., Alpha Omega Alpha.

THURSTON, JACQUELINE BEVERLY, art educator; b. Cin., Jan. 27, 1939; d. John O. and Frances Beverly Thurston; children: Mark, Beverly Thurston-Baller. BFA in Painting, Carnegie-Mellon U., 1961; MA in Painting, Stanford U., 1962. Prof. art San Jose (Calif.) State U., 1965—. Co-author: Optical Illusions, 1965; one woman shows include San Jose Spiritus Gallery, 1995. Fellow Nat. Endowment for the Arts, 1976, 78. Office: San Jose State U Sch of Art and Design One Washington Sq San Jose CA 95112

THURSTON, WILLIAM RICHARDSON, oil and gas industry executive, geologist; b. New Haven, Sept. 20, 1920; s. Edward S. and Florence (Holbrooke) T.; m. Ruth A. Nelson, Apr. 30, 1944 (div. 1966); children: Karin R., Amy R., Ruth A.; m. Beatrice Furnas, Sept. 11, 1971; children: Mark P., Stephen P., Douglas P., Jennifer P. AB in Geol. Sci. with honors, Harvard U., 1942. Registered profl. engr., Colo. Field geologist Sun Oil Co., Corpus Christi, Tex., 1946-47; asst. to div. geologist Sun Oil Co., Dallas, 1947-50; chief geologist The Kimbark Co., Denver, 1952-59; head exploration dept. Kimbark Exploration Co., Denver, 1959-66; co-owner Kimbark Exploration Ltd., Denver, 1966-67, Kimbark Assocs., Denver, 1967-76, Hardscrabble Assocs., Denver, 1976-80; pres. Weaselskin Corp., Durango, Colo., 1980—. Bd. dirs. Denver Bot. Gardens, 1972—, Crow Canyon Ctr. for Archaeology, Cortez, Colo., 1980-92. Comdr. USNR, World War II, Korea. Decorated D.F.C. (with 3 stars). Mem. Am. Assn. Petroleum Geologists, Denver Assn. Petroleum Landmen, Rocky Mountain Assn. Petroleum Geologists, Four Corners Geol. Soc. Republican. Office: Weaselskin Corp 12995 Highway 550 Durango CO 81301-6674

THYDEN, JAMES ESKEL, diplomat, educator; b. L.A., Apr. 10, 1939; s. Eskel A. and Mildred Aileene (Rock) T.; m. Patricia Irene Kelsey, Dec. 15, 1959; children: Teresa Lynn, Janice Kay, James Blaine. BA in Biology, Pepperdine U., 1961; MA in Scandinavian Area Studies, U. Wash., 1992. Cert. secondary tchr., Calif., Wash. Tchr. Gompers Jr. High Sch., L.A., 1962-64; fgn. svc. officer U.S. Dept. State, Washington, 1964-90; rschr. U. Wash., Seattle, 1991-93; exec. dir. Seattle chpt. UN Assn., 1993-96; travel lectr. Cunard Lines', Royal Viking Sun, 1995, Royal Caribbean's Splendour of the Seas, 1997. Editor govt. report, ann. human rights reports, 1983-86; author, editor in-house govt. reports, documents. Dir. Office of Human Rights, 1983-86; counselor Embassy for Polit. Affairs, Am. Embassy, Oslo, Norway, 1986-90. Named Outstanding Young Man Am., 1969, Alumnus of Yr., Pepperdine U., 1984. Mem. Am. Fgn. Svc. Assn., World Affairs Coun. Seattle, UN Assn. Home: 5631 153rd Pl SW Edmonds WA 98026-4239

TIBSHRAENY, JAY, mayor; b. Chandler, Ariz.; m. Karen Tibshraeny; 1 child, Lauren. BS in Acctg., Ariz. State U. Owner property mgmt. firm, Chandler; citrus grower Chandler; mem. Chandler City Coun., 1986—; elected vice mayor City of Chandler, 1990—, elected mayor, 1994—; chmn. Regional Pub. Transp. Authority, City of Chandler; mem. Maricopa Assn. Govts. Regional Coun., Greater Phoenix Econ. Coun., Ariz. Mcpl. Water Users Assn., Ariz. League of Cities and Towns Resolutions Com., Williams Air Force Redevel. Partnership, Nat. League of Cities Transp. and Comm. Com. Mem. Chandler Friends of the Libr.; adv. bd. Chandler-Gilbert Assn. for Retarded Citizens, Child Crisis Ctr., Chandler; mem. City Coun. Pub. Safety com., Chandler Pub. Safety Retirement Sys. Bd., Chandler Vol. Firemen Pension bd. Mem. Chandler Hist. Soc., Chandler C. of C. (bd. dirs.). Office: Office of Mayor Mail Stop 603 PO Box 4008 Chandler AZ 85244-4008

TICE, BRADLEY SCOTT, humanities educator; b. Palo Alto, Calif., Oct. 6, 1959; s. Lilburn Trent and Paula Nanette (Osborne) T. AA, De Anza Coll., Cupertino, Calif., 1983; BA in History, San Jose State U., 1987; PhD in Chemistry, Fairfax U., Baton Rouge, 1996; Diploma in Ayurvedic Medicine, The Ayurvedic Inst.; Diploma in Stress therapy, Internat. Yoga Sch. Prof. Pacific Lang. Inst., Cupertino, Calif., 1992—; dir. rsch. Advanced Human Design, Cupertino, 1992—. Author: Poems, 1997; editor Jour. Pacific Lang. Inst., 1995-96. Admiral of the fleet Calif. Naval Militia, 1979-95; commandant (gen.) Calif. Marine Militia, 1979-95; gen. Calif. Militia, 1979-95; chief of staff Calif. Air Militia, 1979-95. Recipient Pres.'s award Nat. Author's Registry, 1996, editor's choice award (3), The Nat. Libr. of Poetry, 1995, (2), 1996. Mem. N.Y. Acad. Scis., Tchrs. English to Spkrs. of Other Langs., Calif. Assn. Bilingual Edn., Internat. Assn. tchrs. English as a Fgn. Lang., Internat. Soc. Poets. Office: Pacific Language Inst PO Box 2214 Cupertino CA 95015-2214

TICKELL, WILLIAM EARL, architect, educator; b. San Pedro, Calif., May 2, 1935; s. William Earl Sr. and Maybelle Annabelle (Lee) T.; m. Laurie Monroe, 1976 (div. 1988); m. Judith Allen, 1967 (div. 1969); children: Shawn Rice, William Earl III. BS i: Archtl. Engring., Calif. Poly. U., 1964, BArch, 1969. Registered arch., Calif. Draftsman designer Charles Warren Callister, Tiburon, Calif., 1955-60; designer, planner B.A. Berkus, L.A., 1961-62; prin. William Earl Tickell Arch. (W.E.T. Inc.), San Luis Obispo, Calif., 1967—; lectr. Calif. State Poly. U., San Luis Obispo, 1989-97. Prin. works include Stuart Condominium, Signal Hill, Calif. (Design Excellence award 1974). Bd. dirs. Mission Coll. Prep. Acad., San Luis Obispo, 1993-94. With USN, 1953-55. Home: 3233 Davis Canyon Rd San Luis Obispo CA 93405-8051

TIDBALL, LEE FALK, elementary education educator; b. Waukon, Iowa, Feb. 26, 1955; s. John Harlow and Katherine Jane (Falk) T.; m. Catherine Susan Cooper, June 14, 1975 (div. Aug. 1982); children: Aaron Matthew, Johathan Michael; m. Julia Jordan, June 21, 1997. BS, Le Tourneau U., Longview, Tex., 1979. Cert. elem. tchr., Calif., Miss. Youth dir. Centenary Meth. Ch., Modesto, Calif., 1979-80; recreation dir. Crestwood Manor Hosp., Modesto, Calif., 1980; substitute tchr. Modesto City Schs., 1981-83; 7th grade tchr. Orangeburg Christian Sch., Modesto, 1983-84; 5th & 6th tchr. Bret Harte Elem., Modesto, 1984-91, gifted edn. tchr., 1991-97; tchr. social studies Rowan Middle Sch., Jackson, Miss., 1997—. Head coach, pres. Silverwings Track Club, Modesto, 1982-97; actor Modesto Performing Arts, 1994-96. Named Outstanding Young Religious Leader, Mason City (Iowa) Jaycees, 1976. Mem. NEA, Calif. Assn. for the Gifted, Modesto Tchrs. Assn., Pacific Assn., U.S.A. Track and Field. Home: 711 Lake Harbor Dr Apt 1024 Ridgeland MS 39157 Office: Rowan Middle Sch 136 W Ash St Jackson MS 39203-1901

TIDWELL, GEOFFREY MORGAN, medical company executive; b. San Diego, Aug. 16, 1958; s. Morgan Alfred and Dorothy (Doolittle) T. BA in Psychology, U.S. Internat. U., 1991; MBA in Health Care Adminstrn., Nat. U., 1996. Rsch. asst. San Marcos (Calif.) Clinic, 1988-91; area svc. mgr. Nat. Med. Sys., Frederick, Md., 1993-94, Life Med. Svcs., San Diego, 1994-95; intern San Diego County Med. Soc., 1996; adminstrn. resident dept. interventional radiology U. Calif., San Diego, 1996—; vis. scholar U. Calif. Sch. Medicine, San Diego, 1996, 97; radio personality Sta. KOWF, Escondido, Calif., 1989-90, Sta. KKYY, San Diego, 1990-91, Sta. KRMX, San Diego, 1990-91, Sta. KGB, San Diego, 1991—; pres., CEO, v.p. sales and mktg. M&G Med. Svc., San Diego, 1995—. Vol. telethon Muscular Dystrophy Assn., San Diego, 1991, Easter Seals, San Diego, 1991. Mem. Am. Coll. Healthcare Execs. (assoc.), Med. Group Mgmt. Assn. (assoc.), Emergency Med. Assembly (assoc.), Healthcare Coalition San Diego County (assoc.), Psi Chi. Republican. Methodist. Office: M&G Med Svcs 4198 Convoy St San Diego CA 92111-3702

TIEDT, IRIS MCCLELLAN, emeritus university dean; b. Dayton, Ohio, Feb. 3, 1928; d. Raymond Hill and Ermalene (Swartzel) McClellan; children: Pamela, Ryan. BS in English Edn., Northwestern U., 1950; MA in Curriculum and Instrn., U. Oreg., 1961; PhD in Curriculum and Instrn., Stanford U., 1972. Cert. life K-12 adminstrn. and supervision, life secondary English and Spanish tchr., elem. English, Spanish and reading tchr., Calif. Tchr. pub. schs., Chgo., 1950-51, Anchorage, 1952-57, Eugene, Oreg., 1959-61; prof., dir. tchr. edn. Santa Clara (Calif.) U., 1968-75; prof., dir. South Bay Writing Project San Jose (Calif.) State U., 1975-87; supr. student teaching U. Oreg., Eugene, 1959-61; vis. prof. U. Wash., Seattle, 1964-65; dean edn. No. Ky. U., Highland Heights, 1987-89; dean edn. and regional svcs. Moorhead (Minn.) State U., 1989-94. Author: Exploring Books with Children, 1979, Multicultural teaching, 1979, 4th edit., 1995, The Writing Process: Composition and Applied Grammar, 1981, Teaching Writing in K-8 Classrooms, 1983, The Language Arts Handbook, 1983, Lessons from a Writing Project, 3 vols., 1987, Teaching Thinking in K-12 Classrooms, 1989, Writing: From Topic to Evaluation, 1989, Reading, Thinking, and Writing: A Holistic Language and Literacy Program, 1989; also articles. Mem. ASCD, AAUW (life), Nat. Coun. Tchrs. English (editor Lang. Arts 1972-76), Am. Assn. Colls. Tchr. Edn., Am. Ednl. Rsch. Assn., Coun. Rsch. in English, Sierra Club (life), Stanford Alumni Assn. (life), Phi Delta Kappa. Democrat. Home: 1654 Fairorchard Ave San Jose CA 95125-4934

TIEN, CHANG-LIN, chancellor; b. Wuhan, China, July 24, 1935; came to U.S., 1956, naturalized, 1969; s. Yun Chien and Yun Di (Lee) T.; m. Di-Hwa Liu, July 25, 1959; children: Norman Chihnan, Phyllis Chihping, Christine Chihyih. BS, Nat. Taiwan U., 1955; MME, U. Louisville, 1957; MA, PhD, Princeton U., 1959; PhD (hon.), U. Louisville, 1991, U. Notre Dame, 1992, Hong Kong U. Sci. and Tech., 1993, U. Conn., 1994, U. Waterloo, Can., 1995, U. Ill., 1995. Acting asst. prof. dept. mech. engring. U. Calif., Berkeley, 1959-60, asst. prof., 1960-64, assoc. prof., 1964-68, prof., 1968-88, 90—, A. Martin Berlin prof., 1987-88, 90—, dept. chair, 1974-81, also vice chancellor for research, 1983-85; exec. vice chancellor U. Calif., Irvine, 1988-90; chancellor U. Calif., Berkeley, 1990-97; chair exec. com. Internat. Ctr. for Heat and Mass Transfer, 1980-82; hon. prof., dir. Xi'an Jiatong U. Engring. Thermodynamics Rsch. Inst., 1987—; mem. adv. bd. Hong Kong U. Sci. and Tech., 1991—; chair internat. adv. panel U. Tokyo Inst. Indsl. Sci., 1995; bd. trustees Princeton (N.J.) U., 1991-95, Chiang Indsl. Charity Found., Ltd., Hong Kong, 1991—, The Asia Found., 1993—, U.S. Com. on Econ. Devel., 1994—, Carnegie Found. for Advancement of Tchg., 1994—; tech. cons. Lockheed Missiles and Space Co., GE; gov. bd. dirs. Com. of 100, 1991—; bd. dirs. Berkeley Cmty. Found., Wells Fargo Bank, Raychem Corp., 1996; mem. coun. Foreign Rels., 1996; active Aspen Inst. Domestic Strategy Group. Author one book; editor Internat. Commn. Heat and Mass Transfer, 1981—; editor-in-chief Exptl. Heat Transfer, 1987—; editor twelve vols.; contbr. articles to profl. jours. John Simon Guggenheim fellow, 1965, Sr. U.S. Sci. fellow Japan Soc. for Promotion of Sci., 1980; recipient Sr. U.S. Sci. award Alexander von Humboldt Found., 1979; named Most Disting. Chinese scholar, Soc. Hong Kong Scholars, 1989, Li Ka Shing Disting. Lectr., U. Hong Kong, 1994, Gordon Wu Disting. Lectr., Princeton U., 1995, Martin Martel Lectr., Brown U., 1996. Fellow AAAS (bd. dirs. 1992—), ASME (hon., chair exec. com. heat transfer divsn. 1980-81, v.p. basic engring. 1988-90, Heat Transfer Meml. award 1974, Gustus L. Larson Meml. award 1975, AIChE/ASME Max Jakob Meml. award 1981, Disting. Lectr. award 1987-89), AIAA (Thermophysics award 1977), Am. Acad. Arts and Scis. (hon.), Academia Sinica (hon., Taiwan); mem. NAE (mem. internat. affairs adv. com. 1987-90, chair mech. engring. peer com. 1989-90), Am. Soc. Engring. Edn. (mem. nat. adv. coun. 1993—), Heat Transfer Soc. Japan (hon.), Chinese Acad. Scis. (fgn. mem., Hon. Prof., Inst.

Thermophysics 1981—). Office: U Calif Berkeley Chancellor's Office 200 Calif Hall 1500 Berkeley CA 94720-1500

TIFFANY, SANDRA L., state legislator; b. Spokane, Wash., June 30, 1949; m. Ross M. Tonkens; 1 child, Courtney. Student, U. Calif. Mem. Nev. Assembly, 1993—. Mem. Nev. Rep. Women's Club, Green Valley Cmty. Assn. Home: 75 Quail Run Rd Henderson NV 89014-2151 Office: Nev Assembly State Capitol Carson City NV 89710 Address: 2289 Cassatt Dr Henderson NV 89014*

TILDEN, KEVIN ARCHER, political consultant; b. Huntsville, ala., Dec. 21, 1968; s. Douglas Iver and Mary Cecile (Monaghan) T. BA, U. Wash., 1991; MBA, Pepperdine U., 1997. Acct. exec. Nelson Comms. Group, San Diego, 1991-95; mem. Clinton/Gore Transition Team, Little Rock, 1992-93; mgr. pub. affairs Pacific Bell, San Ramon, Calif., 1995—. Bd. dirs. Divisionary Theater. Democrat. Home: 3795 Georgia St Apt 304 San Diego CA 92103-7612 Office: Pacific Bell 2410 Camino Ramon San Ramon CA 94583

TILDEN, WESLEY RODERICK, author, retired computer programmer; b. Saint Joseph, Mo., Jan. 19, 1922; s. Harry William and Grace Alida (Kinnaman) T.; m. Lorraine Henrietta Frederick, June 20, 1948. Grad., Harvard Univ., 1945; BS, UCLA, 1948; BA, Park Coll., Mo., 1990; postgrad., Navy Supply Corps Sch. Purchasing agent Vortox Co., Claremont, Calif., 1951-61; lang. lab. dir. Mount San Antonio Coll., Walnut, Calif., 1962-65; computer programmer, operator General Dynamics, Pomona, Calif., 1967-70; ret., 1970. Author: (book) Scota, The Egyptian Princess, 1994, Merit-Sekhet: Foster Mother of Moses?, 1996; photographer, textbooks, mags., newspaper, catalogs. Historian Claremont Sister City Assn., 1963-66. Lt. USNR, 1942-46 PTO. Recipient with Lorraine Tilden People to People award Reader's Digest Found., 1963-64, 1964-65; named Hon. Citizen Guanajuato, Mexico, 1963. Mem. Soc. Mayflower Descendants, Scottish Clans, UCLA Alumni Assn., Park Coll. Alumni Assn., Univ. Club of Claremont. Republician. Home: 351 Oakdale Dr Claremont CA 91711-5039

TILL, FRANKLIN L., school system administrator; b. San Diego, Jan. 20, 1947; s. Franklin L. Sr. and Luella Jane (Krough) T.; m. Barbara Jane Till, May 1, 1971; children: Marlo, Jeffrey. BA, San Diego State U., 1969, MA, 1973; EdD, U. So. Calif., 1981. Vice prin. secondary schs. San Diego United Sch. Dist., ops. mgr., prin. mid. level, dep. supt. Contbr. articles to profl. jours. Bd. dirs. YMCA, Cornerstone 2000, Weed and Seed, United Way; mem. exec. bd. ACSA Sch. to Career. Recipient three PTA Hon. Svc. awards. Mem. Assn. of Calif. Sch. Adminstrs. (Disting. Leaders award), Adminstrs. Assn. Home: 5851 Torca Ct San Diego CA 92124-1020

TILLE, JAMES EUGENE, army chaplain; b. Decatur, Ill., July 31, 1951; s. Charles Herman and Alice Elizabeth (Wochner) T.; m. Insuk Kay Ch'oe, Jan. 6, 1976; 1 child, Charles Andrew. BA in Liberal Studies, SUNY, Albany, 1977; Assoc. in Acctg., Ft. Steilacoom Community Coll., 1984; MDiv, Golden Gate Bapt. Theol. Sem., 1988; MA in Counseling, Liberty U., 1990. Nat. cert. counselor; nat. cert. family therapist; cert. mental health counselor, Wash. Enlisted U.S. Army, 1973-82; chaplain candidate U.S. Army, Individual Ready Res., St. Louis, 1985-89; mental health technician Western State Hosp., Ft. Steilacoom, Wash., 1982-89; assoc. pastor Harbor Baptist Ch., Gig Harbor, Wash., 1985-89; battalion chaplain 3-3 FA Bn 2AD, Ft. Hood, Tex., 1989-90, 1-3 FA Bn. 2AD&1CD, Ft. Hood, 1990-91, 3-5CAV Bn, Germany, 1991-94, 14th Engr. Bn, Ft. Lewis, Wash., 1995-96; with 555 CMBT EN GP, Ft. Lewis, 1996—. Decorated Army Meritorious Svc. medal, Army Commendation medal, Army Achievement medal. Mem. ACA, Am. Assn. Christian Counselors, Internat. Assn. Marriage and Family Counselors, 2d Armored Divsn. Hell on Wheels Assn. (life), 1st Cavalry Divsn. Assn. (life). Baptist. Home: 9109 Zircon Dr SW Lakewood WA 98498-4054 Office: HHC 555 CMBT EN GP Fort Lewis WA 98433

TILLMAN, JOSEPH NATHANIEL, engineering executive; b. Augusta, Ga., Aug. 1, 1926; s. Leroy and Canarie (Kelly) T.; m. Alice Lavonia Walton, Sept. 5, 1950 (dec. 1983); children: Alice Lavonia, Robert Bertram; m. Areerat Usahaviriyakit, Nov. 24, 1986. BA magna cum laude, Paine Coll., 1948; MS, Northrop U., 1975, MBA, 1976; DBA, Nova U., 1989. Dir. Rockwell Internat., Anaheim, Calif., 1958-84; pres. Tillman Enterprises, Corona, Calif., 1985—; guest lectr. UCLA, 1980-85. Contbr. articles to profl. jours. Capt. USAF, 1948-57, Korea. Recipient Presdl. Citation Nat. Assn. for Equal Opportunity in Higher Edn., 1986. Mem. Acad. Mgmt. (chmn. 1985-86), Soc. Logistics Engrs. (pres. 1985-86), Paine Coll. Alumni Assn. (v.p. 1976—), NAACP (pres. 1984-88). Office: Tillman Enterprises 1550 Rimpau Ave Trlr 45 Corona CA 91719-3206

TILLMAN, PEGGY LOUISE (PEGGY LOUISE LARSON), human factors and ergonomics company executive; b. Baldwin, Wis., Nov. 1, 1943; d. Richard Louis and Dorothy (Baland) Larson; m. Barry William Tillman, Mar. 3, 1967. BA in Psychology, Sonoma State Coll., Rohnert Park, Calif., 1967. Cert. tchr., Calif. Photographer Sonoma State Coll., 1964-67, mgr. lab., 1964-66; tchr. Union Sci. Dist., Los Gatos, Calif., 1967-79; pres. H.F. Engrng. Co., Fox Island, Calif., 1983—. Author: Human Factors Essentials, 1991; co-author: Human Factors Design Handbook, 2d edit., 1992; contbr. numerous articles to profl. jours. Founder, dir. Synchronized Swimming Team, Wheeler AFB, Hawaii, 1961-62; developer Water Babies Swim Course, San Jose, Calif., 1968; founder Concerned Citizens, Cachagua, Calif., 1987-89; mem. Pierce County Air Quality Bd. Tacoma, 1993; vol. tchr. Franke Tobey Jones Retirement Estates, Tacoma, 1994. Recipient Disting. Presentation award Soc. Auto. Engrs., 1988. Mem. AIAA, Inc., Calif. Tchrs. Assn. (membership chmn. 1977), Human Factors Soc., Fox Island Hist. Soc. (bd. dirs. 1992). Home and Office: PO Box 165 Fox Island WA 98333-0165

TILSON, DANIEL, elementary education educator. Tchr. Eastwood Elem. Sch., Roseburg, Oreg. Recipient Excellence in Sci. Tchg. award, 1990, Milken Nat. Edn. award, 1992, State Tchr. of Yr. elem. award Oreg., 1992; Christa McAuliffe fellow, 1988. Office: Eastwood Elem Sch 2550 SE Waldon Ave Roseburg OR 97470-3805

TILSON THOMAS, MICHAEL, symphony conductor; b. L.A., 1944; s. Ted and Roberta T. Studies with, Ingolf Dahl, U. So. Calif., others; student conducting, Berkshire Music Festival, Tanglewood, Mass.; student conducting (Koussevitsky prize 1968); LL.D., Hamilton Coll.; L.H.D. (hon.), D'Youville Coll., 1976. Asst. condr. Boston Symphony Orch., 1969, assoc. condr., 1970-72, prin. guest condr., 1972-74; also Berkshire Music Festival, summer 1970, 74; music dir., condr. Buffalo Philharmonic Orch., 1971-79; music dir., prin. condr. Great Woods Ctr. for Performing Arts, 1985-88; prin. condr. London Symphony Orch., 1988—; artistic dir. New World Symphony, Fla., 1988—. Condr., dir., N.Y. Philharmonic Young People's Concerts, CBS-TV, 1971-77; vis. condr. numerous orchs., U.S., Europe, Japan; chief condr. Ojai Festival, 1967, dir., 1972-77; opera debut, Cin., 1975; condr.: Am. premiere Lulu (Alban Berg), Santa Fe Opera, summer 1979; prin. guest condr., L.A. Philharm., 1981-85, Am. premiere Desert Music (Steve Reich), 1984; prin. condr. Gershwin festival London Symphony Orch., Barbcan Ctr., 1987; composer: Grace (A Song for Leonard Bernstein), 1988, Street Song (for Empire Brass Quintet), 1988, From the Diary of Anne Frank (for orchestra and narrator Audrey Hepburn and New World Symphony), 1990; commd. by UNICEF for Concerts for Life's European premiere, 1991; recording artist Sony Classical/CBS Masterworks, 1973—; co-artistic dir. Pacific Music Festival, 1990—, with Leonard Bernstein 1st ann. Pacific Music Festival, Sapporo, Japan, 1990; co-artistic dir. 2d ann. Pacific Music festival, 1991, Salzburg Festival, 1991; conducted Mozart Requiem. Named Musician of Year, Musical Am. 1970; recipient Koussevitsky prize, 1968, Grammy award for Carmina Burana with Cleve. Orch., 1976, for Gershwin Live with Los Angeles Philharm., 1983, Grammy nomination, Best Classical Album - Debussy: Le Martyre de Saint Sebastien (with the London Symphony Orchestra), 1994. Office: 888 7th Ave Fl 37 New York NY 10106-3799 Office: San Francisco Symphony Davies Symphony Hall San Francisco CA 94102*

TILTON, JOHN ELVIN, mineral economics educator; b. Brownsville, Pa., Sept. 16, 1939; s. John Elvin Sr. and Margaret Julia (Renn) T.; m. Elizabeth Martha Meier, June 18, 1966; children: Margaret Ann, John Christian. AB, Princeton U., 1961; PhD in Econs., Yale U., 1965. Staff analyst Office of Sec. of Def., Washington, 1965-67; rsch. assoc. Brookings Inst., Washington, 1967-70; asst. prof. econs. U. Md., College Park, 1970-72; assoc. prof. mineral econs. Pa. State U., University Park, 1972-75, prof., 1975-85; Coulter prof. Colo. Sch. Mines, Golden, 1985-94, dir. Divsn. Econs. and Bus., 1994—; officer econ. affairs commodities divsn. UN Conf. on Trade and Devel., Geneva, 1977; leader rsch. Internat. Inst. Applied Systems Analysis, Laxenburg, Austria, 1982-84; joint dir. mineral econs. and policy Program of Resources for Future, Colo. Sch. Mines, Washington, 1982—; vice chmn. bd. mineral and energy resources NRC, Washington, 1980-83, mem. nat. materials adv. bd., 1987-89. Author: International Diffusion of Technology, 1971, The Future of Nonfuel Minerals, 1977; editor: Material Substitution, 1983, World Metal Demand, 1990, Mineral Wealth and Economic Development, 1992, View from the Helm, 1995; co-editor: Economics of Mineral Exploration, 1987, Competitiveness in Metals, 1992. Capt. U.S. Army, 1965-67. Fulbright scholar Ecole Nat. Supérieure des Mines de Paris, 1992. Mem. Am. Econ. Assn., Am. Inst. Mining Metall. and Petroleum Engrs. (Mineral Econs. award 1985), Mineral Econs. and Mgmt. Soc. (pres. 1993-94), Mining and Metall. Soc. Am. Office: Colo Sch Mines Divsn Econs and Bus Golden CO 80401

TILTON, RONALD WILLIAM, naval officer; b. Brookline, Mass., Dec. 28, 1944; s. John Walter and Audrey Muriel (Rice) T.; m. Thuy-Nhi Tran, Jan. 2, 1993; 1 child, Kayla Alani. BA in Mgmt., Jacksonville U., 1967; cert., Naval War Coll., 1979, Air U., 1985; MS in Systems Mgmt., U. Southern Calif., 1985. Commd. ens. USN, 1967, advanced through grades to comdr., 1982; sr. pilot evaluator of Atlantic fleet patrol squadrons Patrol Squadron Thirty, Jacksonville, Fla., 1975-78; patrol plane comdr., maintenance officer Patrol Squadron 17, Barbers Point, Hawaii, 1980-82; ops. and plans officer Commander in Chief Pacific, Camp H.M. Smith, Hawaii, 1982-84; comptroller Naval Air Sta., Barbers Point, 1984-86; exec. officer, chief test pilot NAVPRO, Lockheed Aero. Systems Co., Burbank, Calif., 1986-90; pilot UPS, Louisville, 1990—. Loaned exec. United Way, Jacksonville, 1975. Mem. Naval Air Exec. Inst., Order of Daedalians, Phi Delta Theta. Home: 24660A Brighton Dr Santa Clarita CA 91355-4361

TIMM, OLIN HENRY, animal breeder, farmer; b. Dixon, Calif., Apr. 24, 1913; s. Henry R. and Emma Jane (Bowen) T.; m. Aaley Pistor (dec.); children: Aaley, Peter, Susan. BA, Stanford U., 1930; M.Econs., Cornell U. Asst. agrl. economist USDA, 1936-38; owner/rancher/farmer Dixon, 1939—; pres., bd. dirs. First No. Bank, Dixon, 1958-77; adv. com. on fgn. animal disease USDA, Washington. Past pres. Dixon Hist. Soc.; active Boy Scouts Am. Mem. U.S. Animal Health Assn. (com. on diseases of sheep and goats 1959—, com. on fgn. animal diseases 1972—, western region rep. on exec. com. 1961-65, com. on profl. oversight 1977-78, bluetongue and bovine leukosis com. 1980—, epizootic attach com. 1980—, biologics com. 1984—, pres. 1974), Rotary (past pres.), Masons, Calif. Wool Growers Assn. (Golden Fleece award 1975, Master Shepherd award 1993). Home and Office: PO Box 1000 Dixon CA 95620

TIMMER, ROBERT SCOTT, geologist; b. Danville, Ill., July 19, 1949; s. George William and Dorthey Ann (Henderson) T.; m. Margaret Holle Young, July 12, 1975 (div. Apr. 1983); children: Jessica Ann, Christopher Scott. BS in Geology, U. Alaska, 1971; MS in Geology, U. N.Mex., 1976. Registered geologist, Calif. Exploration geologist Earth Resources Co., Cuba, N.Mex., 1973-75; exploration geologist Mobil Oil/Uranium, Denver, 1975-78, geol. supr., 1978-83; geol. supr. Mobil Oil, Houston, 1983-85; geol. supr., advisor Mobil Oil, Midland, Tex., 1985-90; geol. advisor Mobil Oil, Bakersfield, Calif., 1990-96, geology technoscoot, 1996-97; knowledge mgmt. COE Mobil Oil, Dallas, 1997—. Contbr. articles, map to profl. publs.; co-inventor, patentee of formation fracturing, 1994, method of sand consolidation, 1994, method for producing low permeability reservoirs using steam, 1995. Recipient Coenosystis Timmeri award Stremple, Allison & Kline, 1971. Mem. Am. Assn. Petroleum Geologists (gen. chair Pacific sect. 1997 ann. conv.), San Joaquin Well Logging Soc. (v.p. 1994-95, pres. 95-96), Soc. Petroleum Engrs. Home: Apt 1307 1158 Hidden Ridge Dr Irving TX 75038 Office: Mobil Oil Co 3033 Irving Blvd Dallas TX 75247

TIMMINS, JAMES DONALD, venture capitalist; b. Hamilton, Ont., Can., Oct. 3, 1955; came to U.S., 1979; s. Donald G. and Myrna L. (Seymour) T. BA, U. Toronto, 1977; law degree, Queen's U., 1979; MBA, Stanford U., 1981. Investment banker Wood Gundy, Toronto, 1980, Salomon Bros., San Francisco, 1981-84; mng. dir. and chief exec. officer McKewon & Timmins, San Diego, 1984-87; ptnr. Hambrecht & Quist, San Francisco, 1987-90, Redwood Ptnrs., Menlo Park, 1991—; bd. dirs. Artios Corp., Irvine. Mem. Olympic Club of San Francisco. Home: 735 Laurelwood Dr San Mateo CA 94403-4058 Office: Redwood Ptnrs 3000 Sand Hill Rd Ste 230 Menlo Park CA 94025-7116

TIMMONS, CLARA ELIZABETH, chemist, educator; b. Columbia, Mo., Apr. 18, 1926; d. Elbert M. and Carla Gertrude (Walker) Gallemore; m. Richard Dean Abernathy Timmons, Aug. 14, 1954 (div. Dec. 1960); children: Beth, Pamela Kay. BS in chem. & music, Central Mo. State Coll., 1946; MS in chem., U. Okla., 1948. Analytical chemist Haver Glover Labs., Kansas City, Mo., 1948-49; sr. analyst Pacific Coast Borax Co., Boron, Calif., 1950-55; chemist, co-owner Agri-Lab, Inc., Kearney, Nebr., 1956-60; chief chemist dairy foods Iowa Dept. Agriculture, Des Moines, 1961-62; chemist Kaiser Chemical Co., Wendover, Utah, 1969-71, Nat. Lead, Salt Lake City, 1973-74, Rocky Mountain Arsenal, Commerce City, Colo., 1977, Hill Air Force Base, Ogden, Utah, 1977-93; bd. dirs. U-Vest, Salt Lake City, 1972-73. Mem. Am. Chem. Soc., Am. Assn. Univ. Profs., AAUW.

TIMMONS, TERRY LEE, photographer, educator; b. Santa Paula, Calif., Mar. 13, 1946; s. Alvin Odell and Patricia Cristel (Henry) T. AA, Venture Coll., 1966; BPA, Brooks Inst., 1973. Cert. C.C. tchr., Calif. Owner, operator Gallery Photographic Svc., Ventura, Calif., 1974-80; instr. photographic scis. Ventura Coll., 1975—; forensic specialist State of Calif. and local police agys., 1974—. Exhibited fine art photography in shows at Buena Ventura Art Assn., also throughout state, Camarillo Art Assn.; author: Introduction into the Photographic Process, 1993. Tribal healer Cherokee and Chumash Nation, Okla., Ariz., Calif.; candidate trustee Ventura C.C. Dist., 1991. Mem. SAG, Am. Fedn. Tchrs. (negotiator), Brooks Alumni Assn. Home: 406 Sespe Ave Fillmore CA 93015-2024

TIMMONS, WILLIAM MILTON, producer, freelance writer, retired cinema arts educator, publisher, film maker; b. Houston, Apr. 21, 1933; s. Carter Charles and Gertrude Monte (Lee) T.; m. Pamela Cadorette, Dec. 24, 1975 (div. 1977). BS, U. Houston, 1958; MA, UCLA, 1961; PhD, U. So. Calif., 1975. Child actor Houston Jr. Theater, 1945-46; staff announcer Sta. KMCO, Conroe, Tex., 1951-52; prodn. asst. Sta. KUHT-TV, Houston, 1953-54, 56-57; teaching fellow UCLA, 1960-61; ops. asst. CBS-TV, Hollywood, Calif., 1961-62; prof. speech and drama Sam Houston State U., Huntsville, Tex., 1963-67; chmn. dept. cinema Los Angeles Valley Coll., Van Nuys, Calif., 1970-91, ret., 1992; prodr. Sta. KPFK, L.A., 1959-60, 83-95; pub. Acad. Assocs., L.A., 1976; proofreader, cons. Focal Press Pub. Co., N.Y.C., 1983-92. Author: Orientation to Cinema, 1986; contbr. articles to mags.; prodr., dir.: (radio programs) Campus Comments, 1963-67, numerous ednl. films, 1963—; prodr. ednl. series for cable TV, 1993—. With USNR, 1954-56. Named Hon. Tex. Ranger, State of Tex., Austin, 1946; U. Houston scholar, 1957. Mem. Mensa, U. So. Calif. Cinema-TV Alumni Assn., Red Masque Players, Secular Humanists L.A., Alpha Epsilon Rho, Delta Kappa Alpha. Democrat.

TIMMRECK, THOMAS C., health sciences and health administration educator; b. Montpelier, Idaho, June 15, 1946; s. Archie Carl and Janone (Jensen) T.; m. Ellen Prusse, Jan. 27, 1971; children: Chad Thomas, Benjamin Brian, Julie Anne. AA, Ricks Coll., 1968; BS, Brigham Young U., 1971; MEd, Oreg. State U., 1972; MA, No. Ariz. U., 1981; PhD, U. Utah, 1976. Program dir. Cache County Aging Program, Logan, Utah, 1972-73; asst. prof. div. health edn. Tex. Tech U., Lubbock, 1976-77; asst. prof. dept. health care adminstrn. Idaho State U., Pocatello, 1977-78; program dir., asst. prof. health services program No. Ariz. U., Flagstaff, 1978-84; cons., dir. grants Beth Israel Hosp., Denver, 1985; prof. dept. health scis. and human ecology, coordinator grad. studies, coordinator health adminstrn. and planning Calif. State U., San Bernardino, 1985—; pres. Health Care Mgmt. Assocs., 1985—; presenter at nat. confs.; mem. faculty Loretto Heights Coll., Denver, Dept. Mgmt. U. Denver, Dept. Mgmt. and Health Adminstrn. U. Colo., Denver, dept. bus. adminstrn. U. Redlands (Calif.), U. So. Calif., L.A. Author: Dictionary of Health Services Management, rev. 2d edit., 1987, Health Services Cyclopedic Dictionary, 3d edit., An Introduction to Epidemiology, 1994, Planning and Program Development and Evaluation: A Handbook for Health Promotion, Aging, and Health Services, 1995; mem. editl. bd. Jour. Health Values, 1986—, Basic Epidemiological Methods and Biostats., Dictionary of Epidemiology and Public Health; contbr. numerous articles on health care adminstrn., behavioral health, gerontology and health edn. to profl. jours. Chmn., bd. dirs. Inland Counties Health System Agy.; mem. strategic planning com. chmn. Vis. Nurses Assn. of Inland Counties; bd. dirs. health svc. orgns. With U.S. Army, 1966-72, Vietnam. Mem. Assn. Advancement of Health Edn., Am. Acad. Mgmt., Assn. Univ. Programs in Health Care Adminstrn., Healthcare Forum. Republican. Mormon. Office: Calif State U Dept Health Scis and Human Ecology San Bernardino CA 92407

TING, CHIHYUAN CHARLES, chemist; b. Qingdao, China, Feb. 1, 1947; came to U.S., 1971, naturalized, 1979; s. Shu-Ren and Shu-Yin (Yin) T.; m. Margaret An, Aug. 6, 1971; children: Michelle, Michael. BS, Fu-Jen U., Taipei, Taiwan, 1970; MS, Wilkes U., 1973; PhD, Pa. State U., 1978. Sr. rsch. specialist Monsanto, St. Louis, 1977-88; sr. scientist, Scios, Mountain View, 1988-92; group leader ABAXIS, Sunnyvale, 1992-93. Patentee in field. Mem. Am. Chem. Soc., Sigma Xi. Avocations: Reading, music, sports. Office: Sequus Pharm Inc 1050 Hamilton Ct Menlo Park CA 94025-1423

TING, PANG-HSIN, linguistics educator; b. Ju-Kao, Chiang-Su, China, Oct. 15, 1937; came to U.S., 1989; s. Ting-I and Sou-Yu (Li) T.; m. Chi Chen, Nov. 11, 1963; children: Tsuo-Wen, Tsuo-Chi, Tsuo-Li. BA, Nat. Taiwan U., 1959, MA, 1963; PhD, U. Wash., 1972. Rsch. asst. Academia Sinica, Taipei, Taiwan, 1963-64, from asst. rsch. fellow to assoc. rsch. fellow, 1964-75, rsch. fellow, 1975-89; from assoc. prof. to prof. Nat. Taiwan U., Taipei, 1972-89; prof. Chinese linguistics U. Calif., Berkeley, 1989-94, Agassiz prof., 1994—; chmn. linguistics sect. Inst History & Philology, Academia Sinica, Taipei, 1973-81, dir., 1981-89; dir. Chao Yuen Ren Ctr. for Chinese Linguistics, U. Calif., Berkeley, 1993-95. Author: Chinese Phonology of the Wei-Chin Period--Reconstruction of the Finals as Reflected in Poetry, 1975 (award 1977), The Tan-chou Ts'un-hua Dialect, 1986; translator: A Grammar of Spoken Chinese, 1980. 2d lt. Taiwanese Army, 1959-61. Recipient Outstanding Scholar award NSF, 1985-89. Mem. Internat. Assn. Chinese Linguistics (v.p. 1992-93, pres. 1993-94), Chinese Lang. Tchrs. Assn. Office: U Calif Dept East Asian Langs Berkeley CA 94720

TINGLEY, WALTER WATSON, computer systems manager; b. Portland, Maine, July 24, 1946; s. Edward Allen Tingley and Ruth Annie (Howard) Tuttle; m. Elizabeth A. Fletcher, May 1970 (div. 1975). BS, U. Md., 1974. Programmer analyst U.S. Ry. Assn., Washington, 1974-80, Digital Equipment Corp., Maynard, Mass., 1980-81, Interactive Mgmt. Systems, Belmont, Mass., 1981; systems designer Martin Marietta Data Systems, Greenbelt, Md., 1982-84; mgr. computer ops. Genex, Rockville, Md., 1984; system mgr. Applied Rsch. Corp., Landover, Md., 1985; programmer analyst Input/Output Computer Svcs., Washington, 1986-87, Lockheed Engrng. and Scis., Las Vegas, Nev., 1987-91, Los Alamos (N.Mex.) Nat. Lab., 1992-96. Author tech. book revs., software revs. With USAF, 1964-68. Mem. IEEE Computer Soc., Assn. Computing Machinery. Home: PO Box 429 Los Alamos NM 87544-0429

TINGSTROM, JACK, mayor. Mayor City of San Buenaventura, Calif. Office: City of San Buenaventura PO Box 99 San Buenaventura CA 93002-0099

TINKER, IRENE, city and regional planning educator, women's studies educator; b. Milw., Mar. 8, 1927; d. John Marlin and Irene Laverty (Casto) T.; m. Millidge P. Walker, Febr. 2, 1952; children: Stuart Tjipto, Janet Shakuntala, Jennifer Njoro. AB magna cum laude, Radcliff/Harvard Colls., 1949; PhD, London Sch. Econs. and Polit. Sci., 1954. Rsch. polit. sci. U. Calif., Berkeley, 1954-57; asst. prof. govt. Howard U., 1961-67; asst. provost for curriculum devel., prof. Fed. City Coll., 1967-71; dir. Ednl. Policy Ctr., 1971-73; founding dir. office of internat. sci. AAAS, 1973-77; asst. dir., dir. office policy and planning ACTION, The U.S. Agy. for Vol. Svc., 1977-78; founder, dir. Equity Policy Ctr., Washington, 1978-89; prof. city and regional planning and women's studies U. Calif., Berkeley, 1989—; adj. prof. Sch. Internat. Studies Johns Hopkins U., 1966-67; vis. prof. Internat. Devel. Program The Am. U., Washington, 1985-89. Co-editor: Leadership and Political Institutions in India, 1959, rev. edit., 1968, Culture and Population Change, 1974, Population: Dynamics, Ethics and Policy, 1975, The Many Facets of Human Settlements: Science and Society, 1977; Engendering Wealth and Well-Being: Empowerment for Global Change, 1995; editor: Persistent Inequalities: Women and World Development, 1990; author: Street Foods: Urban Food and Employment in Developing Countries, 1997; contbr. chpts. to books, articles to profl. jours. Convenor numerous confs.; mem. adv. bd. Ency. of Third World Women, 1993-96, Ctr. for Women Policy Studies, 1985—, Inst. for Women's Policy Rsch., 1987-95; mem. internat. coun. adv. Healthy Cities Found., 1994—; various com. assignments UN; candidate for Md. Assembly, 1966; bd. dirs. Overseas Devel. Network. Recipient Fulbright Regional award Nepal and Sri Lanka, 1987-88; grantee Am. Inst. Indian Studies in India, 1964-65; Ford Found. Area and AAUW fellow, Indonesia, 1957-59. Fellow AAAS; mem. Nat. Coun. Rsch. on Women, Internat. Studies Assn., Rural Sociological Assn. (hon. life), Assn. for Women in Devel., Assn. Asian Studies, Assn. Collegiate Schs. of Planning. Home: 7515 Claremont Ave Berkeley CA 94705-1432 Office: Dept City & Regional Planning U Calif Berkeley CA 94720-1850

TINKER, JUDY MARIE NORTHROP, nutritionist, musician; b. Albuquerque, Oct. 13, 1955; d. Robert Ellsworth and Marian La Verne (Hughes) Northrop; m. Richard Roy Tinker, July 30, 1978 (div. 1989); children: Roy Timothy, Ray Nathanael. BMus, Pacific Union Coll., Angwin, Calif., 1978; BS in Nutrition and Dietetics, Loma Linda (Calif.) U., 1992. Computer typesetter Adventist Media Ctr., Newbury Park, Calif., 1981-82; with Concerned Comms., Arroyo Grande, Calif., 1982; piano tchr. Newbury Park/Yucaipa, Calif., 1980—; organist St. Alban's Episcopal Ch., Yucaipa, 1988—; nutritionist County of San Bernardino Pub. Health Dept., San Bernardino, 1992—. Recipient Fgn. Langs. Achievement award Bank of Am., 1974, Achievement award for outstanding accomplishment and performance in piano Dept. of Music, Pacific Union Coll., 1978; Ruth Little Nelson scholar, 1991, Am. Dietetic Assn. Corps Tested Advt. Techniques scholar, 1991; Soroptimist Internat. scholar, 1992. Mem. Am. Dietetic Assn. (registered), Calif. Dietetic Assn., Inland Dist. Dietetic Assn., Seventh-Day Adventist Dietetic Assn. SDA. Office: San Bernardino Pub Health WIC Program 351 N Mountain View Ave San Bernardino CA 92401-1609

TINKER, ROBERT EUGENE, minister, educational consultant; b. Lincoln, Kans., June 10, 1915; s. Eugene F. and Mildred Adelaide (Brown) T.; AB, Am. U., 1937; MDiv, Garrett Theol. Sem., 1942; postgrad. Northwestern U., 1942-46; m. Anne Elizabeth Hall, June 13, 1942; children: Anne Terrill, Robert Bruce, MaryBeth. Ordained to ministry Methodist Ch., 1942, Congregational Ch., 1947-77, United Ch. Christ; minister Oxen Hill, Md., Tuxedo, Md., 1934-37, Evergreen Park, Ill., 1940-41; assoc. minister 1st Presbyterian Ch., Evanston, Ill., 1942-44; minister Glenview Meth. Ch. (Ill.), 1944-46, Broadway Meth. Ch., Chgo., 1946-47; with Chgo. Theol. Sem., 1947-58, asst. sec., asst. treas., bd. dirs., 1947-58, asst. bus. mgr., 1947-50, bus. mgr., 1951-55, dir. devel., 1953-55, v.p. charge devel., 1955-58; assoc. Gonser and Gerber, 1958-64; ptnr. Gonser Gerber Tinker Stuhr, ednl. cons. in devel. and public relations, Chgo., 1964-82, cons., 1982—; pres. Tabco Corp., Chgo., 1983-85; lectr. Creighton U., Omaha, summers 1978-80. N.J. State scholar, 1933; Larry Foster scholar, 1933; Wanamaker scholar Lingnon U., Canton, Republic of China, 1935-36; Howes Meml. scholar, 1939-42. Bd. dirs. Hyde Park YMCA, Chgo., Hyde Park Union Ch., Porter Found., U. Chgo., 1947-58, Bryn Mawr Cmty. Ch., Habitat for Humanity, Tucson, 1992—, Phi Sigma Kappa, Phi Beta Zeta, Pi Gamma Mu. Republican. Contbr. articles to profl. books and jours. Mem. Oro Valley Townhouses Improvement Assn. (bd. dirs. 1993-94, pres. 1994). Home: 69 W Oro Pl Oro Valley AZ 85737-7625

TINKLENBERG, JARED RAY, psychiatrist, researcher; b. Madison, S.D., Nov. 25, 1939; s. Richard John and Frances (DeBruyn) T.; m. Mae Van Der Weerd, Aug. 8, 1964; children: Karla Jean, Julie Ann. BA with highest distinction, U. Iowa, 1962, MD, 1965. Intern Yale New Haven Med. Ctr., 1965-66; resident in psychiatry Stanford U. Sch. Medicine, 1966-69, from instr. to assoc. prof. psychiatry, 1969-84, prof. psychiatry and behavioral scis., 1984—; chief clin. svcs., psychiatry svc. VA Med. Ctr., Palo Alto, Calif., 1984-87, chief geriatric psychiatry, 1987-96; dir. Stanford/VA Alzheimer's Disease Ctr., Palo Alto, 1989—. Editor: Marijuana and Health Hazards, 1975; contbr. articles to profl. jours. Served to cpl. U.S. Army, 1958-59. Fellow Am. Psychiat. Assn., Am. Coll. Neuropsychopharmacology; mem. Phi Beta Kappa, Alpha Omega Alpha. Office: VA Palo Alto Health Care Sys 3801 Miranda Ave #116A3 Palo Alto CA 94304-1207

TINNEY, THOMAS MILTON, SR., genealogical research specialist; b. Waynesville, Ohio, Aug. 10, 1941; s. Prentice Thomas and Hazel Kathleen (Greene) T.; m. Sheila Mary Foxon, Feb. 10, 1961 (div. May 1971); children: Jennifer Sheila, Andrew Thomas, Phillip Alexander, Sylvia May, Cynthia Anne; m. Kim Barrett, July 29, 1971 (div. 1985); children: Teresa Ruth Anne, Michael Thomas, David Seth Ahlish, Nelson Mahonri Moriancumer; m. Vicki Rae Chris Baker, Apr. 8, 1986; children: Rebecca Sarah, Matthew Abraham, Thomas Milton Jr., Michelle Gabrielle, Jonathan Ray Elijah. Student, Utah Tech. Coll., 1968-71; BS in Econs., U. Utah, 1979, postgrad., 1979-85. Clk., carrier U.S. Postal Svc., 1961-69, 80-81; staff engr. Anthony B. Cassedy & Assocs., Ridgefield, Conn., 1980; lic. ins. agt. Colo., 1980-82; housing project mgr. Fort Douglas, Utah, 1981-84, Missoula, Mont., 1981-84; mgr., owner Tinney GenSearch Cons., 1971—. Contbr. articles to profl. jours. Active Utah Nat. Guard and Army Res. Mem. SAR, Jewish Geneal. Soc. Sacramento, Calif. Aggie Alumni Assn., Davis Genealogy Club and Libr. Mem. LDS Ch. Home: 2748 Ganges Pl Davis CA 95616-2922

TINNIN, THOMAS PECK, real estate professional; b. Albuquerque, May 15, 1948; s. Robert Priest and Frances (Ferree) T.; m. Jamie Tinnin Garrett, Dec. 12, 1986; children: Megan Ashley, Courtney Nicole, Robert Garrett. Student, U. Md., 1969-72; BA, U. N.Mex., 1973. Ins. agt. Occidental Life of Calif., Albuquerque, 1972—; gen. agt. Transamerica-Occidental Life, Albuquerque, 1978—; pres. Tinnin Investments, Albuquerque, 1978—, Tinnin Enterprises, Albuquerque, 1978—, Tinnin Real Estate & Devel., Albuquerque, 1989—; mem. N.Mex. State Bd. Fin., Santa Fe., 1985-87, 90—, sec. 1990-96; del. White House Conf. on Small Bus., Washington, 1986; bd. dirs. Albuquerque Econ. Devel., 1987-88. Bd. dirs. Albuquerque Conv. and Visitor's Bureau, 1982-84, St. Joseph's Hosp, Better Bus. Bur., 1983, Albuquerque, 1984-86, N.Mex. Jr. Livestock Found., pres. 1988, Presbyn. Heart Inst., 1989—, N.Mex. First Confs., 1992, chair-elect; chmn. Manzano Dist. Boy Scouts Am., 1981-82; chmn. Manzano Dist. Finance, 1983; del. White House Conf. Small Bus., 1986; pres. N.Mex. Jr. Livestock Investment Found., Albuquerque, 1988—; trustee N.Mex. Performing Arts Coun., 1989-90. Mem. NALU, N.Mex. Life Leaders Assn., Nat. Assn. Real Estate Appraisers, Albuquerqye Armed Forces Adv. Assn., Albuquerque C. of C. (bd. dirs. 1978-84, chmn. ambassador's com. 1983), N.Mex. Life Underwriters Assn., Albuquerque Country Club. Republican. Presbyterian. Home: 2312 Calle Del Estavan NW Albuquerque NM 87104-3072 Office: Tinnin Enterprises 20 First Plaza Ctr NW Ste 518 Albuquerque NM 87102-3352

TINSLEY, BARBARA SHER, historian, educator, writer; b. Gloversville, N.Y., Apr. 29, 1938; d. Max and Ruth Ida (Shpritzer) Sher; m. William Earl Tinsley, Dec. 30, 1959; children: Claire Jennifer, Yve Hillary. BA, U. Wis., Milw., 1959; MA, U. Calif., Berkeley, 1960; PhD, Stanford U., 1983. Instr. English and French Stephens Coll., Columbia, Mo., 1963-64; asst. prof. European history San Jose (Calif.) State U., 1969-71; prof. European history Foothill Coll., Los Altos Hills, Calif., 1974—; lectr. in history Santa Clara (Calif.) U., 1977-79; lectr. in western culture Stanford (Calif.) U., 1985, vis. scholar, 1989—. Author: History and Polemics in the French Reformation: Florimond de Raemond Defender of the Church, 1992; co-author (with Lewis S. Spitz) Johann Sturm and Education, 1995; contbr. articles to profl. jours. Woodrow Wilson fellow U. Calif.-Berkeley, 1959-60; NDEA fellow Mich. State U. and Emory U., 1961, 63; Jessie Speyer fellow Stanford U., 1965-67; Fulbright fellow U. Strasbourg, 1983-84; NEH fellow Duke U., 1988, Princeton, 1995. Mem. Am. Hist. Assn., Sixteenth Century Studies Conf., YMCA. Democrat. Home: 15550 Glen Una Dr Los Gatos CA 95030-2936

TINSLEY, WALTON EUGENE, lawyer; b. Vanceburg, Ky., Jan. 22, 1921; s. Wilbur Walton and Sarah Edith (Frizzell) T.; m. Joy Mae Matthews, Aug. 31, 1952; children—Merry Walton Tinsley Moore, Troy Eugene, Paul Richard. E.E., U. Cin., 1943; M.S. in Aero. Engring, NYU, 1947; J.D., U. So. Calif., 1953. Bar: Calif. 1954, U.S. Supreme Ct. 1971. Practiced in Los Angeles, 1954—; mem. firm Harris, Wallen, MacDermott & Tinsley, 1958-96; of counsel Pretty, Schroeder & Poplawski, L.A., 1996—. Author: (book) Tasmania: Stamps and Postal History, 1986. Pres. World Philatelic Exhbn., Pacific 97 Inc. Signatory Roll of Disting. Philatelists, 1983. Fellow Royal Philatelic Soc. London; mem. IEEE (assoc.), AIAA, ABA, L.A. County Bar Assn., Am. Philatelic Soc. (v.p. 1965-69, Luff award 1986), S.R., English Speaking Union (dir. L.A. br.), Mensa. Presbyterian (elder, trustee, chmn. trustees 1972). Home: 2210 Moreno Dr Los Angeles CA 90039-3044 Office: Pretty Schroeder et al Ste 2000 444 S Flower St Los Angeles CA 90071

TIPTON, GARY LEE, retired services company executive; b. Salem, Oreg., July 3, 1941; s. James Rains and Dorothy Velma (Dierks) T. BS, Oreg. Coll. Edn., 1964. Credit rep. Standard Oil Co. Calif., Portland, Oreg., 1964-67; credit mgr. Uniroyal Inc., Dallas, 1967-68; ptnr., mgr. bus. Tipton Barbers, Portland, 1968-94; ret., 1994. Mem. Rep. Nat. Com., 1980—, Sen. Howard Baker's Presdl. Steering Com., 1980; dep. dir. gen. Internat. Biog. Ctr., Cambridge, Eng., 1987—; mem. U.S. Congl. adv. bd. Am. Security Coun., 1984-93; mem. steering com. Coun. on Fgn. Rels. Portland Com., 1983-84, chmn. 1984-86, mem. exec. com., 1988-90, bd. dirs., 1990-91. Recipient World Culture prize Accademia Italia, 1984, Presdl. Achievement award, 1982, cert. Disting. Contbn. Sunset High Sch. Dad's Club, 1972, 73, Cert. of Perfection award Tualatin Valley Fire and Rescue Dist., 1994. Fellow Internat. Biog. Assn. (life, Key award 1983, U.K.); mem. Sunset Mchts. Assn. (co-founder, treas. 1974-79, pres. 1982-83), Internat. Platform Assn., Smithsonian Assocs., UN Assn. (steering com. UN day 1985), World Affairs Coun. of Oreg., City Club of Portland.

TIPTON, JAMES SHERWOOD, poet, beekeeper; b. Ashland, Ohio, Jan. 18, 1942; s. James Robert and Ruth Loucetta (Burcher) T. BA, Purdue U., 1964, MA, 1968. Assoc. prof. Alma (Mich.) Coll., 1970-83; investment cons. Thomson McKinnon, Denver, 1983-89, Kemper Securities, Denver and Grand Junction, Colo., 1989-94; owner High Desert Honey Co., Glade Park, Colo., 1994—; writer in residence Kalamazoo (Mich.) Coll., 1969-70; spkr. in field. Author: (poems) Matters of Love, 1970, Sentences, 1970, Bittersweet, 1975, the Giant Alphabet, 1987, The Wizard of Is, 1995; co-editor: the Third Coast: Contemporary Michigan Poetry, 1976, Contemporary Michigan Fiction, 1982; contbr. to anthologies New Generation: Poetry, 1971, The Haiku Anthology, 1974, 86, Heartland II: Poets of the Midwest, 1975, The Other Voice, 1976, The Third Coast: Contemporary Michigan Poetry, 1976, 82, The Penguin Book of Women Poets, 1978, The Haiku Handbook, 1985, 95; contbr. poems, stories, translations, articles and revs. to lit. jours., mags. Treas. Mesa County Friends of the Libr., Grand Junction, 1993—. Grantee NEH, 1969, Mich. Coun. for Arts, 1975, 82; recipient 1st prize Birmingham (Ala.) Festival of Arts, 1973. Home: 1742 DS Rd Glade Park CO 81523

TIRMAN, VALENTIN WOLDEMAR, JR., engineering executive and educator; b. Tallinn, Estonia, Sept. 15, 1940; came to U.S., 1949; s. Valentin Woldemar and Natalie (Barchow) T.; children: Valentin III, Grigori, Mark, Mike. BSEE, Ariz. State U., 1963; MS in Sys. Mgmt., U. So. Calif., L.A., 1969. Commd. lt. USAF, 1962, advanced through grades to lt. col., 1978; sys. software engr. Ford Aerospace, Colorado Springs, Colo., 1982-88; v.p. Productive DAta Sys., Englewood, Colo., 1988—; adj. prof. Webster U., Colorado Springs, 1984—; assoc. prof. USAF Acad., Colorado Springs, 1973-82. Mem. ACM, IEEE, Assn. Old Crows. Home: 3250 Parade Cir E Colorado Springs CO 80917-2927 Office: Productive Data Sys Inc 6143 S Willow Dr #200 Englewood CO 80111

TISBERT, STEPHEN JAMES, recording industry executive; b. San Francisco, Apr. 1, 1954; s. Raymond Richard and Bernice Laverne (Samson) T. Owner Imperial Sound Recorders, Whittier, Calif., 1975-77; rec. engr. Internat. Media, Irvine, Calif., 1977-78, Crystal Sound, Hollywood, Calif., 1978-82, Motown/Hitsville, Hollywood, 1982-88; prodn. coord. Prince St. Music, Hollywood, 1988-92; pres., founder Fearless Records, Westminster, Calif., 1993—; owner Hi-Tech WWW, Whittier, 1996—. Recipient numerous gold and multi-platinum awwards by recording Industry Assn. Am, Emmy award; Grammy nomination. Office: Steve James/Fearless Records PO Box 11111 Whittier CA 90603

TISDALE, DOUGLAS MICHAEL, lawyer; b. Detroit, May 3, 1949; s. Charles Walker and Violet Lucille (Battani) T.; m. Patricia Claire Brennan, Dec. 29, 1972; children: Douglas Michael, Jr., Sara Elizabeth, Margaret Patricia, Victoria Claire. BA in Psychology with honors, U. Mich., 1971, JD, 1975. Bar: Colo. 1975, U.S. Dist. Ct. Colo. 1975, U.S. Ct. Appeals (10th cir.) 1976, U.S. Supreme Ct. 1979. Law clk. to chief judge U.S. Dist. Ct. Colo., Denver, 1975-76; assoc. Brownstein Hyatt Farber & Madden, P.C. ; ptnr., dir. Brownstein Hyatt Farber & Strickland, P.C., 1976-92; shareholder Popham, Haik, Schnobrich & Kaufman, Ltd., 1992-97, dir. 1995-97; ptnr. Baker & Hostetler, LLP, Denver, 1997—; Home: 4662 S Elizabeth Ct Cherry Hills Village CO 80110-7106 Office: Baker & Hostetler LLP 303 E 17th Ave Denver CO 80203-1264

TITUS, ALICE CESTANDINA (DINA TITUS), state legislator; b. Thomasville, Ga., May 23, 1950. AB, Coll. William and Mary, 1970; MA, U. Ga., 1973; PhD, Fla. State U., 1976. Prof. polit. sci. U. Nev., Las Vegas; mem. Nev. Senate, 1989—; alt. mem. legis. commn., 1989-91, mem., 1991-93; minority floor leader, 1993—; chmn. Nev. Humanities Com., 1984-86; mem. Eldorado Basin adv. group to Colo. River Commn.; active Gov. Commn. Bicentennial of U.S. Constn.; former mem. Gov. Commn. on Aging. Author: Bombs in the Backyard: Atomic Testing and American Politics, 1986, Battle Born: Federal-State Relations in Nevada during the 20th Century, 1989. Mem. Western Polit. Sci. Assn., Clark County Women's Dem. Club. Greek Orthodox. Home: 1637 Travois Cir Las Vegas NV 89119-6283 Office: Nev State Senate State Capitol Carson City NV 89710*

TITUS, EDWARD DEPUE, psychiatrist, administrator; b. N.Y.C., May 24, 1931; s. Edward Kleinhans and Mary (Brown) Chadbourne; m. Virginia Van Den Steenhoven, Mar. 24, 1963 (div.); m. Catherine Brown, Apr. 22, 1990. BA, Occidental Coll., 1953; MS, U. Wis., 1955; MD, Stanford U., 1962; PhD, So. Calif. Psychoanalytic Inst., 1977. Mng. ptnr. Hacker Clinic Assn., Lynwood, Calif., 1968-90; chief psychiatrist parole outpatient clinic region III Calif. Dept. Corrections, L.A., 1991—; asst. clin. prof. psychiatry U. So. Calif., 1993—; chmn. dept. psychiatry St. Francis Hosp., Lynwood, 1979-80. Fellow Am. Psychiat. Assn.; mem. Calif. Med. Assn. (ho. of dels. 1981-95), So. Calif. Psychiat. Soc. (sec. 1984-85), Los Angeles County Med. Assn. (dist. pres. 1980-81, pres. sect. psychiatry 1990-92). Office: Parole Outpatient Clinic 307 W 4th St Los Angeles CA 90013-1104

TOBIAS, SHEILA, writer, educator; b. N.Y., Apr. 26, 1935; d. Paul Jay and Rose (Steinberger) Tobias; m. Carlos Stern, Oct. 11, 1970 (div. 1982); m. Carl T. Tomizuka, Dec. 16, 1987. BA, Harvard Radcliffe U., 1957; MA, Columbia U., 1961, MPhil, 1974; PhD (hon.), Drury Coll., 1994, Wheelock Coll., 1995. Journalist W. Germany, U.S. and Fed. Republic Germany, 1957-65; lect. in history C.C.N.Y., N.Y.C., 1965-67; univ. adminstr. Cornell U., Wesleyan U., 1967-78; lect. in women's studies U. Calif., San Diego, 1985-92; lect. in war, peace studies U. So. Calif., 1985-88. Author: Overcoming Math Anxiety, 1978, rev. edit., 1994, Succeed with Math, 1987, Revitalizing Undergraduate Science: Why Some Things Work and Most Don't, 1992, Science as a Career: Perceptions and Realities, 1995; co-author: The People's Guide to National Defense, 1982, Women, Militarism and War, 1987, They're Not Dumb, They're Different, 1990, (with Carl T. Tomizuka) Breaking the Science Barrier, 1992, Rethinking Science as a Career, 1995, (with Jacqueline Raphael) The Hidden Curriculum, 1997, Faces of Feminism, 1997. Chmn. bd. dirs. The Clarion newspaper. Mem. Am. Assn. Higher Edn. (bd. dirs. 1993—), Coll. Sci. Tchrs. Assn., Nat. Women's Studies Assn., Phi Beta Kappa.

TOBIASON, FREDERICK LEE, chemistry educator; b. Pe Ell, Wash., Sept. 15, 1936; s. Joseph Oliver and Beatrice Olivia (Olaveson) T.; m. Dorothy Anne Puotinen, Sept. 3, 1961; children: Laura Anne Riddle, Anne Marie Bessette, Joseph Daniel. BA, Pacific Luth. U., 1958; PhD, Mich. State U., 1963. Rsch. assoc. Emory U., Atlanta, 1963-64; rsch. chemist E.I. du Pont de Nemours, Waynesboro, Va., 1964-66; from asst. prof. chemistry to assoc. prof. chemistry Pacific Luth. U., Tacoma, 1966-72, prof., 1973-91; regency prof., 1975; prof. emeritus Pacific Luth. U., Tacoma, 1992—; cons. Reichhold Chems., Inc., Tacoma, 1967-87; vis. prof. Chengdu U. of Sci. & Tech., Sichuan, China, 1989-91; vis. rsch. prof. U. Sci. & Tech., Lille, France, 1992-93, 96; vis. scholar Dnepropetrovsk Chem. Inst., Ukraine, 1991, 92. Contbr. book chpt.: Handbook of Adhesives, 1989; contbr. articles to profl. jours., sci. papers, manuals and book chpts. Mem. stream restoration com. Clover Creek Coun., Tacoma, 1988—; bd. dirs. Tahoma Land Conservancy, 1993; assoc. Danforth Found., 1978-85; mem. Danforth N.W., Pacific N.W. region, 1986—. Recipient faculty teaching award Burlington No. Found., 1989. Mem. Am. Chem. Soc., Tahoma Audubon Soc. (pres., bd. dirs.). Lutheran. Office: Pacific Luth U Tacoma WA 98447

TOBIN, JAMES MICHAEL, lawyer; b. Santa Monica, Calif., Sept. 27, 1948; s. James Joseph and Glada Marie (Meisner) T.; m. Kathleen Marie Espy, Sept. 14, 1985. BA with honors, U. Calif., Riverside, 1970; JD, Georgetown U., 1974. Bar: Calif. 1974, Mich. 1987. From atty. to gen. atty. So. Pacific Co., San Francisco, 1975-82; v.p. regulatory affairs So. Pacific Communications Co., Washington, 1982-83; v.p., gen. counsel Lexitel Corp., Washington, 1983-85; v.p., gen. counsel, sec. ALC Communications Corp., Birmingham, Mich., 1985-87, sr. v.p., gen. counsel, sec., 1987-88; of counsel Morrison & Foerster, San Francisco, 1988-90, ptnr., 1990—. Mem. ABA, Calif. Bar Assn., Mich. Bar Assn., Fed. Communications Bar Assn. Republican. Unitarian. Home: 3134 Baker St San Francisco CA 94123-4303 Office: Morrison & Foerster 425 Market St San Francisco CA 94105

TOBIN, VINCE, football coach; b. Sept. 29, 1943; m. Kathy Kautzman; children: Ryan, Shannon. BE, U. Mo., 1965, M in Guidance and Counseling, 1966. Defensive coord. U. Mo., 1970-76; coach B.C. Lions, 1977-82, Phila./Balt. Stars, 1983-85, Chgo. Bears, 1986-92, Indpls. Colts, 1994-95; head coach Ariz. Cardinals, Phoenix, 1996—. Office: Ariz Cardinals PO Box 888 Phoenix AZ 85001-0888

TOBIN, WILLIAM JOSEPH, newspaper editor; b. Joplin, Mo., July 28, 1927; s. John J. and Lucy T. (Shoppach) T.; m. Marjorie Stuhldreher, Apr. 26, 1952; children—Michael Gerard, David Joseph, James Patrick. BJ, Butler U., 1948. Staff writer AP, Indpls., 1947-52, news feature writer, N.Y.C., 1952-54, regional membership exec., Louisville, 1954-56, corr., Juneau, Alaska, 1956-60, asst. chief of bur., Balt., 1960-61, chief of bur., Helena, Mont., 1961-63; mng. editor Anchorage Times, 1963-73, assoc. editor, 1973-85, gen. mgr., 1974-85, v.p., editor-in-chief, 1985-89, editor editorial page, 1990, asst. pub., 1991, senior editor Voice of the Times, 1991—; bd. dirs. Enstar Corp., 1982-84. Mem. devel. com. Anchorage Winter Olympics, 1984-91, bd. dirs. Anchorage organizing com., 1985-91; bd. dirs. Alaska Coun. on Econ. Edn., 1978-84, Boys Clubs Alaska, 1979-83, Anchorage Symphony Orch., 1986-87, Blue Cross Wash. and Alaska, 1987—, chmn. 1990-91; chmn. Premera Corp., 1994—; mem. adv. bd. Providence Hosp., Anchorage, 1974-91, chmn., 1980-85. Served to sgt. AUS, 1950-52. Mem. Alaska AP Mems. Assn. (pres. 1964), Anchorage C. of C. (bd. dirs. 1969-74, pres. 1972-73), Alaska World Affairs Council (pres. 1967-68), Phi Delta Theta. Clubs: Alaska Press (pres. 1968-69), Commonwealth North (Anchorage). Home: 2130 Lord Baranof Dr Anchorage AK 99517-1257 Office: Anchorage Times PO Box 100040 Anchorage AK 99510-0040

TODARO, MICHAEL JOSEPH, JR., military officer; b. Darby, Pa., Aug. 31, 1969; s. Michael Joseph and Judith Francis (Meehan) T. BS in Aerospace Engring., U. So. Calif., 1991. Engring. intern Teledyne Ryan Aero., San Diego, summer 1988, 89, Morton Internat., Ogden, Utah, 1991-92; commd. 2d lt. USAF, 1991; advanced through grades to 1st lt., 1993; asst. flight chief, peacekeeper missile mech. flight USAF, Cheyenne, Wyo., 1992-93, chief missile mech. flight, 1993, chief team tng. flight, 1993-94; promoted to capt., 1995; assigned 2d Space Ops. Squadron Delta Flight Comdr., Falcon AFB, Colo., 1995—. Mem. AIAA, Co. Grade Officers Assn., Air Force Assn. Roman Catholic.

TODD, FRANCES EILEEN, pediatrics nurse; b. Hawthorne, Calif., Aug. 20, 1950; d. James Clark and Jean Eleanor (McGinty) Nailen; m. Steven Charles Todd, Oct. 25, 1975; 1 child, Amanda Kathryn. ASN, El Camino Jr. Coll., 1974; BSN, Calif. State Coll., Long Beach, 1982, postgrad. RN, Calif.; cert. pub. health nurse, Calif.; cert. pediatric nurse practitioner; cert. pediatric advanced life support Am. Heart Assn. Nursing attendant St. Earne's Nursing Home, Inglewood, Calif., 1973; clinic nurse I Harbor-UCLA Med. Ctr., Torrance, Calif., 1974-77, evening shift relief charge nurse, clinic nurse II, 1977-85, pediatric liaison nurse, 1984-90, pediatric nurse practitioner, 1985—; steward Local Union 660, 1995—; tutor Compton (Calif.) C.C., 1988, clin. instr., 1987-88; lectr. faculty dept. pediatrics UCLA Sch. Medicine, 1980—; lectr. in field. Contbr. articles to profl. jours. Co-chair parent support group Sherrie's Schs., Lomita, Calif. Mem. Nat. Assn. Pediatric Nurse Assocs. and Practitioners, L.A. Pediatric Soc., Emergency Nurses Assn., Local 660 (shop steward), Svc. Employees Int. Union, local 660 (union steward), Peruvian Paso Horse Registry N.Am. (co-chair judge's accreditation com. 1989—, judge's Andalusian horses). Office: Harbor UCLA Med Ctr 1000 W Carson St PO Box 14-7W Torrance CA 90509

TODD, HAROLD WADE, association executive, retired air force officer; b. Chgo., Jan. 17, 1938; s. Harold Wade and Jeanne (Fayal) T.; m. Wendy Yvonne Kendrick, July 12, 1981; children by previous marriage: Hellen J. Wilson, Kenneth J., Stephen D., Joseph M., Michelle M. Adams, Mark A.; stepchildren: Jamie Y. White, James K. Mills, Timothy S. Emerson. B.S., U.S. Air Force Acad., 1959; grad., Nat. War Coll., 1975. Commd. 2d lt. U.S. Air Force, 1959, advanced through grades to maj. gen., 1982; aide to comdr. (2d Air Force (SAC)), Barksdale AFB, La., 1970-71; exec. aide to comdr.-in-chief U.S. Air Forces Europe, Germany, 1971-74; spl. asst. chief of staff USAF, 1975-76; chief Concept Devel. Div., 1976-77, chief Readiness and NATO Staff Group, Hdqrs. USAF, 1977-78; exec. asst. to chmn. Joint Chiefs Staff Washington, 1978-80; comdr. 25th region N. Am. Aerospace Def. Command McChord AFB, Wash., 1980-82; chief staff 4th Allied Tactical Air Force Heidelberg, 1982-85; commandant Air War Coll., 1985-89; vice comdr. Air U., 1985-89, ret., 1989; ind. cons. Colorado Springs, Colo., 1989-95; pres., CEO, Nat. Stroke Assn., Denver, 1995—. Founder, pres. Bossier City (La.) chpt. Nat. Assn. for Children with Learning Disabilities, 1970-71. Decorated Def. D.S.M., Air Force D.S.M. (2), Legion of Merit (2), D.F.C., Air medal (8), Air Force Commendation medal. Mem. Air Force Assn., USAF Acad. Assn. Grads., Nat. War Coll. Alumni Assn. Home: 1250 Big Valley Dr Colorado Springs CO 80919-1015

TODD, JAY MARLYN, editor; b. Granger, Utah, July 28, 1936; s. Kenneth Cristian and Gertrude A. (Viehweg) T.; m. Janet Cutrer Todd, Mar. 20, 1964; children: Deborah, Jay Randall, Deanna, Jason Cutrer, Sarah Janet. BS, U. Utah, 1961. Staff writer Desert News, Salt Lake City, 1960-61; tchr. various schs. Ch. Edn. Sys., various cities in Utah, Idaho, 1961-65; asst. editor, asst. mng. editor Improvement Era, Salt Lake City, 1966-70; mng. editor New Era, Salt Lake City, 1971-72, Ensign, Salt Lake City, 1972—. Author: Curtain Time USA: Ambassador of Inspiration, 1965, Saga of the Book of Abraham, 1968, (booklets) The Creed Haymond Story, 1979, A Historical Walking Tour of Holladay, 1996; editor: A Treasury of Edward J. Wood, 1983. Office: Ensign 50 E North Temple Salt Lake City UT 84150-0002

TODD, LINDA MARIE, nutrition researcher, financial consultant, pilot; b. L.A., Mar. 30, 1948; d. Ithel Everette and Janet Marie (Zito) Fredricks; m. William MacKenzie Cook, Jan. 11, 1982 (div. Oct. 1989); m. Robert Oswald Todd, Apr. 8, 1990; 1 child, Jesse MacKenzie Todd. BA in Psychology and Sociology, U. Colo., 1969; student Psychology Grad. work, U. No. Colo., 1970. Pilot lic., weather cert., FCC lic., Calif. life ins. lic., coll. teaching credential; registered with Nat. Assn. Securities Dealers. Counselor Jeffco Juvenile Detention Ctr., Golden, Colo., 1969-71; communications Elan Vital, Denver, 1971-81; legal sec. Fredman, Silverberg & Lewis, San Diego, 1980-82; escrow supr. Performance Mktg. Concepts, Olympic Valley, Calif., 1982-85; mgmt. commn. instr. Sierra Coll., Truckee, Calif., 1986-87; regional mgr. Primerica Fin. Svcs., Reno, 1987-91; air traffic, weather advisor Truckee (Calif.) Tahoe Airport Dist., 1986-96; student tour leader, air show organizer Truckee (Calif.) Tahoe Airport; fin. cons. Primerica Fin. Svcs., Truckee, 1987-91; gen. agt. TTS Fin., 1992—; co-founder Todd Nutrition, 1995—. Editor: (newsletter) Communications, 1975. Sec. gen. Arapahoe H.S. Model UN, Littleton, Colo., 1965; del. State Model UN, Colo., 1966; conv. del. Elan Vital, The Ninety-Nines, Inc. Recipient Univ. scholarship Littleton (Colo.) Edn. Assn., 1966, flight scholarship The Ninety-Nines Inc., Reno, 1990; named Recruiter of Month, Al Williams Primerica, Reno, 1987. Mem. Elan Vital, Plane Talkers, The Ninety Nines, Planetary Soc. Home and Office: PO Box 1303 Truckee CA 96160-1303

TODD, PAUL WILSON, biophysicist, educator; b. Bangor, Maine, June 15, 1936; s. Albert Clayton and Sylvia May (Preble) T.; m. Judith Stow Blackmer, June 16, 1957; children: Kevin, Dana, Trevor, Andrea. BA, Bowdoin Coll., Brunswick, Maine, 1959; BS, Mass. Inst. Tech., 1959; MS, U. Rochester, 1960; PhD, U. Calif., Berkeley, 1964. Lectr. U. Calif., Berkeley, 1964-66; asst. prof. Pa. State U., University Park, 1966-72; assoc. prof. Pa. State U., 1972-77, chmn. genetics program, 1974-79, prof., 1977-86; dir. Bioprocessing & Pharm. Rsch. Ctr., Phila., 1984-87; physicist Nat. Inst. Stds. and Tech., Boulder, Colo., 1988-91; adj. prof. U. Colo., Boulder, 1990-91, rsch. prof., 1991—, assoc. dir. BioServe Space Tech. Rsch. Ctr., 1994—. Co-editor: Space Radiation Biology, 1973, Frontiers in Bioprocessing, 1989, II, 1991, III, 1995, Gravity and the Cell, 1991, Cell Separation Science and Technology, 1991; contbr. articles to profl. jours.; inventor in field. Radiol. Physics fellow AEC, 1959, Eleanor Roosevelt fellow Am. Cancer Soc., 1967, Fogarty Internat. fellow NIH, Moscow, 1979, Yamagiwa-Yoshida fellow Internat. Union Against Cancer, Sweden, 1979, R & D 100 award, 1990, Tech. Briefs Recognition award NASA, 1996. Mem. AAAS, AIAA, AIChE, Am. Chem. Soc., Electrophoresis Soc. (assoc. editor 1986-92), Cell Kinetics Soc., Radiation Rsch. Soc. (assoc. editor 1975-79), Soc. for Analytical Cytology (assoc. editor 1979-88), Am. Soc. for Gravational and Space Biology (coun. 1988-91, editl. bd. 1992—), Tissue Culture Assn., Am. Soc. Engring. Edn., Com. on Space Rsch. Home: 2595 Vassar Dr Boulder CO 80303-5730 Office: U Colo Dept Chem Engring Campus Box 424 Boulder CO 80309-0424

TODD, SALLY MCCLAY, gifted and special education educator, psychologist; b. San Francisco, July 26, 1936; d. Guy Leon and Alta (Hopkins) McClay; m. Henry S. Todd, Dec. 20, 1957. BS, Brigham Young U., 1959; MA, U. Ariz., 1970, PhD, 1973. Assoc. prof. ednl. psychology Brigham Young U., Provo, Utah; U.S. del. World Coun. for Gifted Children, 1989-93, 95—. Co-author: You and the Gifted Child, 1983; contbr. numerous articles to profl. jours. Recipient Pres.'s citation Ramses II Exhibit Ednl. Outreach, Brigham Young U., 1986, Outstanding Tchg. award Coll. Edn., 1990, Karl G. Maeser Excellence in Tchg. award Brigham Young U., 1994. Mem. Nat. Assn. for Gifted Children (chmn. creativity divsn. 1991-92, bd. dirs. 1995—, governing bd.), Coun. for Exceptional Children (talented and gifted divsn.), Utah Assn. for Gifted and Talented, Phi Delta Kappa, Phi Kappa Phi (pres.-elect). Mem. LDS Ch. Office: Brigham Young U 320-F MCKB Box 25040 Provo UT 84602-1040

TODD, WILLIAM MICHAEL, counselor, educator; b. Dayton, Ohio, Jan. 4, 1957; s. J.T. and Bessie Kate (Lowe) T.; 1 child, Katie Janeese. BA in Psychology, Ottawa U., 1993, MA in Profl. Counseling, 1994. Cert. cmty. coll. tchr., 1995. Counselor Arrowstar Counseling, Phoenix, 1992—; prof. psychology Glendale (Ariz.) C.C., 1994; bus. owner Antique Market, MT Constrn., Arrowstar Cons., Phoenix, 1983—. Assoc. pastor Nazarene Ch., Phoenix, 1991-93, youth min., 1993; counselor Boys and Girls Club, Phoenix, 1993-94. Mem. Am. Counselors Assn., Am. Clin. Mental Health Assn., Marriage and Family Counseling Assn., Phi Theta Kappa. Home: 3507 E Windsor Ave Phoenix AZ 85008 Office: Arrowstar Counseling 3520 E Indian School Rd Phoenix AZ 85018-5115

TODSEN, THOMAS KAMP, botanist; b. Pittsfield, Mass., Oct. 21, 1918; s. Lorenz and Ellen Paula (Christensen) T.; m. Margaret Cumming Dorsey, Aug. 4, 1939 (dec. 1988); children: Thomas A., William L. BS, U. Fla., 1939, MS, 1942, PhD, 1950. Instr. N.Mex. Coll. of A & MA, State College,

1950-51; chief chemist White Sands Proving Ground, N.Mex., 1951-53; chief warheads and spl. projects White Sands Proving Ground, 1953-57; chief sci. adv. office White Sands Missile Range, 1957-59, chief surf-to-surf project, 1959-65, dir. test ops., 1965-68, chief land combat project, 1968-72, tech. dir. Army test and evaluation, 1972-78; asst. prof. botany N.Mex. State U., Las Cruces, 1978—; chmn. Joint AEC-DOD subcom., Washington, 1953-62; cons. in field. Contbr. articles to profl. jours., chpts. to books; co-editor: Rare and Endemic Plants of New Mexico; asst. editor the Heliograph Jour.; author: New Mexico Territorial Postmarks; editor La Posta jour., 1974-76. Elder First Presbyn. Ch., Las Cruces, 1960—; dir. Rio Grande Hist. Collections, Inc., Las Cruces, 1975-85; wildflower chmn. N.Mex. Garden Clubs, Inc., Albuquerque, 1987-91. Tenn. Corp. rsch. fellow, Atlanta, 1949. Fellow Ariz.-Nev. Acad. Scis.; mem. Am. Chem. Soc. (emeritus), Am. Soc. Media Photographers (emeritus), AAAS, Am. Soc. Plant Taxonomists, Assn. for Tropical Biology, Sigma Xi.

TOENJES, JONI ELIZABETH, gas and oil consultant, researcher; b. Dillon, Mont., Aug. 1, 1964; d. Charles W. and L. Francine (Cada) Hardy; m. Vincent G. Toenjes, May 10, 1992. BA in Bus., Colo. State U., 1986; MBA in Fin., Claremont Grad. Sch., 1991. Corp. auditor Shell Oil Co., L.A. and Houston, 1986-91; dir. BBC Rsch. & Cons., Denver, 1991—. Author newsletter series The High Road to Opportunity, 1995—; contbr. articles to profl. jours. Mentor Inroads, L.A., 1990; tchr. Jr. Achievement, L.A., 1989. Presdl. scholar Colo. State U. Mem. Colo. Women's C. of C. (chair econ. devel. com. 1996—). Office: BBC Rsch & Cons 3773 Cherry Creek N # 701 Denver CO 80209

TOEPPE, WILLIAM JOSEPH, JR., retired aerospace engineer; b. Buffton, Ohio, Feb. 27, 1931; s. William Joseph Sr. and Ruth May (Hipple) T. BSEE, Rose-Hulman Inst. Tech., Terre Haute, Ind., 1953. Engr. Electronics divsn. Ralph M. Parsons Co., Pasadena, Calif., 1953-55; pvt. practice cons. Orange, Calif., 1961-62; engring. supr. Lockheed Electronics Co., City of Commerce, Calif., 1962-64; staff engr. Interstate Electronics Corp., Anaheim, Calif., 1957-61; engring. supr. Interstate Electronics Corp., Anaheim, 1964-89, ret., 1989. Author: Finding Your German Village, 1990, Gazetteers and Maps of France for Genealogical Research, 1990, GGSA Library User's Guide, 1995. Pres. Golden Cir. Home Owners' Assn., Orange, 1989-95. With U. S. Army, 1955-57. Mem. Ohio Geneal. Soc. (life), So. Calif. Geneal. Soc., German Geneal. Soc. Am. (bd. dirs. 1993—). Home: 700 E Taft Ave Apt 19 Orange CA 92865-4400

TOFF, HOWARD DAVID, psychiatrist; b. Phila., July 26, 1947; s. Fred and Evelyn (Gross) T.; m. Carol Hope Saturansky, July 4, 1976; children: Stephen Andrew, Benjamin Jacob. BS, Pa. State U., 1968; MD, Jefferson Med. Coll., Phila., 1970; PhD, So. Calif. Psychoanalytic Inst, L.A., 1992. Asst. dir. outpatient clinic, tng. dir. child psychiatry Cedars Sinai Med. Ctr., L.A., 1978-84; pvt. practice L.A. and Tucson, Ariz., 1978—; tng. dir. child psychiatry U. Ariz., Tucson, 1990-92; cons. ACCM, Tucson, 1992—. Lt. USPHS, 1971-73. Mem. Am. Psychiat. Assn., Am. Psychoanalytic Assn., Am. Acad. Child & Adolescent Psychiatry, Ariz. Psychiat. Soc. Democrat. Jewish. Office: 1050 E River Rd Ste 202 Tucson AZ 85718-5736

TOFFLER, WILLIAM LOUIS, medical educator; b. Ft. Knox, Ky., Feb. 9, 1949; s. Alan R. and Rosemary Toffler; m. Marlene Toffler, Aug. 11, 1973; children: Emily, Elizabeth, Adrienne, Christopher, Alan, Susan, Mark. BS in Aerospace Engring. cum laude, U. Notre Dame, 1971; postgrad., Georgetown U., 1972; MD, U. Va., 1976. Diplomate Nat. Bd. Med. Examiners; lic. physician, Calif., Oreg., Va. Resident in family medicine dept. family practice Med. U. S.C., Charleston, 1976-79, clin. instr. dept. family practice, 1979; family physician Sweet Home (Oreg.) Family Practice, M.D., P.C., 1979-85; clin. asst. prof. dept. family medicine Oreg. Health Scis. U., Portland, 1981-85, asst. prof., dir. patient care dept. family medicine, 1985-88, asst. prof., dir. predoctoral edn. dept. family medicine, 1988-91, assoc. prof., dir. edn. sect. and predoctoral edn., 1991—; med. staff Lebanon Community Hosp., 1979-85, sec. med. staff, 1981-83, chmn. hosp. infection control com., 1983-84; mem. adv. com. pub. health grant Oreg. Health Scis. U., 1985-86, numerous offices and coms., 1990-91; physician, cons. Portland Sports Medicine Assocs., 1986-91; mem. Gov.'s Task Force on Field Burning, 1988-89; med. advisor Crisis Pregnancy Ctr., Beaverton, Oreg., 1987-89; physician, med. dir. Rosemont Adolescent Treatment Ctr., Portland, 1986—; vis. nurse Assn. Med. Adv. Bd., Portland, Oreg., 1986-93; faculty sponsor Am. Heart Assn. Fellowship, 1991-92, 92-93, Am. Cancer Soc. Rsch. Fellowship, 1987-88; aviation med. examiner FAA; presenter in field. Peer reviewer: Family Practice Rsch. Jour., 1990-95, Family Medicine, 1992—, Acad. Medicine, 1992—, Am. Family Physician, 1994—, others; mem. editl. bd. Jour. Family Practice, 1993-96. With U.S. Army, 1971; capt. USAR, 1971-79. Mem. AMA, Physicians for Compassionate Care (pres. 1995—), Am. Acad. Family Physicians, Am. Coll. Sports Medicine, Oreg. D.O.C., Oreg. Acad. Family Physicians (del. 1981—, chmn. rsch. com. 1985-88, chmn. student activities com. 1988-91, com. for advancement of family medicine), Oreg. Med. Assn. (com. on med. aspects of sch. sports 1979—, pub. edn. com. 1986—, ho. dels. reference com. 1992), Portland Regional Acad. Family Practice (treas. 1990—), Multnomah County Med. Soc. (sch. sports com. 1986-93, del. 1991—). Office: Oreg Health Scis U Dept Family Medicine 3181 SW Sam Jackson Park Rd Portland OR 97201-3011

TOFTNESS, CECIL GILLMAN, lawyer, consultant; b. Glasgow, Mont., Sept. 13, 1920; s. Anton Bernt and Nettie (Pedersen) T.; m. Chloe Catherine Vincent, Sept. 8, 1951. AA, San Diego Jr. Coll., 1943; student Purdue U., Northwestern U.; BS, UCLA, 1947; JD cum laude, Southwestern U., 1953. Bar: Calif. 1954, U.S. Dist. Ct. (so. dist.) Calif. 1954, U.S. Tax Ct. 1974, U.S. Supreme Ct. 1979. Pvt. practice, Palos Verdes Estates, Calif., 1954—; dir., pres., chmn. bd. Fisherman & Mchts. Bank, San Pedro, Calif., 1963-67; dir., v.p. Palos Verdes Estates Bd. Realtors, 1964-65. Chmn. Capital Campaign Fund, Richstone Charity, Hawthorne, Calif., 1983; commencement spkr. Glasgow H.S., 1981. Served to lt. (j.g.) USN, 1938-46, ETO, PTO. Decorated Silver Star; mem. Physicians for Prevention of Nuclear War which received Nobel Peace Prize, 1987; named Man of Yr., Glasgow, 1984. Mem. South Bay Bar Assn., Southwestern Law Sch. Alumni Assn. (class rep. 1980—), Themis Soc.-Southwestern Law Sch., Schumacher Founder's Circle-Southwestern Law Sch. (charter). Democrat. Lutheran. Lodges: Kiwanis (sec.-treas. 1955-83, v.p., pres., bd. dirs.), Masons, K.T. Participant Soc. Expedition thur the N.W. Passage. Home: 2229 Via Acalones Palos Verdes Estates CA 90274-1646 Office: 2516 Via Tejon Palos Verdes Estates CA 90274-6802

TOGERSON, JOHN DENNIS, computer software company executive, retired; b. Newcastle, England, July 2, 1939; arrived in Can., 1949; s. John Marius and Margaret (McLaughlin) T.; m. Donna Elizabeth Jones, Oct. 3, 1964 (div. 1972); children: Denise, Brenda, Judson; m. Patricia Willis, May 5, 1984. BME, GM Inst., Flint, Mich., 1961; MBA, York U., Toronto, Ont., 1971. Sr. prodn. engr. GM of Can., Oshawa, Ont., 1961-69; with sales, investment banking Cochran Murray, Toronto, 1969-72; pres. Unitec, Inc., Denver, 1972-79, All Seasons Properties, Denver, 1979-81, Resort Computer Corp., Denver, 1981—; mng. dir. VCC London (subs. of Resort Computer Corp.), 1992; retired, 1996; bd. dirs. VCC London (sub. of 1st Nat. Bank U.K.), London, 1989—, mng. dir., 1992; pres., bd. dirs. Resort Mgmt. Corp., Dillon, Colo., 1980-81; presenter Assn. of Resort Developers Nat. Conv., 1993, Internat. T.S. Found. Think Tank, 1993, and others. Contbr. articles to profl. jours.

TOGNETTI, GENE, protective services official, consultant; b. Watsonville, Calif., July 3, 1940; s. John Louis and Mary Louise (Vigliecca) T. AA, City Coll. San Francisco, 1962; student, U. Calif., San Francisco, 1977; BA cum laude, Golden Gate U., 1977, MPA, 1980. Cert. BLS, Calif. Mgr. Majectic Plastics, San Francisco, 1973; plastics mgr. Thomas Swan Sign Co., San Francisco, 1973-75; police officer Colma (Calif.) Police Dept., 1975-78; detective sgt. Hillsborough (Calif.) Police Dept., 1981-85, comdr. adminstrn. and svcs. divsn., 1986-92; interim fire chief Point Montara Fire Protection Dist., Moss Beach, Calif., 1992-93; res. police officer San Francisco Police Dept., 1969-70; police officer Broadmoor Police Dept., Colma, 1970-75; owner, cons. Epoch Enterprises, San Francisco; cons. IBM Corp., Armonk, N.H., Viking Freight Sys., Inc., San Jose, Calif., Pfizer, Inc., N.Y.C., Liberty House of Calif., San Francisco, J.C. Penney Inc., San Bruno, Calif.; chief moderator Western State Crime Seminar, 1990-96, asst. chief moderator, 1988, state coord., 1984-87. Mem. Calif. Burglary and Theft Investigators Assn. (pres. 1986, chmn. by-laws com. 1983-89), No. Calif. Safe and Burglary Investigators Assn. (pres. 1982), Calif. Peace Officers Assn., Peninsula Police Officers Assn., Calif. State Firefighters' Assn., Am. Soc. for Indsl. Security. Office: Epoch Enterprises 906 Edinburgh St San Francisco CA 94112-3818

TOKÉ, ARUN NARAYAN, editor, educator, electrical engineer; b. Indore, India, July 2, 1949; came to U.S., 1971; s. Narayan Ganesh and Laxmibai (Chinchalkar) T. BSEE, U. Indore, 1971; postgrad., U. Vt., 1974-75, U. Notre Dame, 1974; MSEE, U. Wis., Milw., 1974. Cert. energy auditor, Vt. Energy auditor State of Vt., Morrisville, 1979; design engr. N.C.R. Corp., Columbia, S.C., 1978-79; asst. prof. Vt. Tech. Coll., Randolph, 1980-84; rsch. asst. Ctr. for Sci. and Environment, New Delhi, 1985-86; editor, publs. mgr. Approvecho Inst., Cottage Grove, Oreg., 1987-89; exec. editor, founder Skipping Stones, multi-cultural mag. for young people, Eugene, Oreg., 1989—; also bd. dirs. Skippings Stones mag., Eugene, Oreg.; co-founder Eugene Internat. Hostel. Author: Song of Winter Wonderland, 1982; co-author: Energy, Economics and the Environment, 1984; contbr. articles to various mags. and newspapers. Organizer Ctrl. Am. Peacewalk, Ctrl. Am., 1984. Recipient Disting. Achievement award Ednl. Press Assn. Am., 1993, Golden Shoestring award, 1995, Golden Apple award, 1996. Office: Skipping Stones Mag PO Box 3939 Eugene OR 97403-0939

TOKHEIM, ROBERT EDWARD, physicist; b. Eastport, Maine, Apr. 25, 1936; s. Edward George and Ruth Lillian (Koenig) T.; m. Diane Alice Green, July 1, 1962; children: Shirley Diane, William Robert, David Eric, Heidi Jean. BS, Calif. Inst. Tech., 1958, MS, 1959; Degree of Engr., Stanford U., 1962, PhD, 1965. Rsch. asst. Hansen Labs Physics Stanford (Calif.) U., 1960-65; microwave engr. Watkins-Johnson Co., Palo Alto, Calif., 1965-73, staff scientist, head ferrimagnetic R&D dept., 1966-69; sr. physicist SRI Internat., Menlo Park, Calif., 1973—. Co-author: Tutorial Handbook on X-ray Effects on Materials and Structures, 1992; contbr. articles to Jour. Applied Physics, IEEE Transactions on Magnetics, conf. proceedings on shock compression, and others. Mem. IEEE (sr. mem.), Am. Phys. Soc., Toastmasters, Tau Beta Pi, Sigma Xi. Home: 1891 Mar West St Tiburon CA 94920-1901 Office: SRI International 333 Ravenswood Ave Menlo Park CA 94025-3453

TOKOFSKY, JERRY HERBERT, film producer; b. N.Y.C., Apr. 14, 1936; s. Julius H. and Rose (Trager) T.; m. Myrna Weinstein, Feb. 21, 1968 (div.); children: David, Peter; m. Fiammetta Bettuzzi, 1970 (div.); 1 child, Tatianna; m. Karen Oliver, Oct. 4, 1981. BS in Journalism, NYU, 1957, LLD, 1959. Talent agt. William Morris Agy., N.Y.C., 1953-59; v.p. William Morris Agy., L.A., 1959-64; exec. v.p. Columbia Pictures, L.A., 1964-69; v.p. Paramount Pictures, London, 1970; exec. v.p. MGM, London, 1971; pres. Jerry Tokofsky Prodns., L.A., 1972-82; exec. v.p. Zupnik Enterprises, L.A., 1982-92; pres. Jerry Tokofsky Entertainment, Encino, Calif., 1992—; prof. Sch. TV and Film U. So. Calif. Sch. Bus. Prodr. films: Where's Poppa, 1971, Born to Win, 1972, Dreamscape, 1985, Fear City, 1986, Wildfire, 1988, Glengarry Glen Ross, 1992, The Grass Harp, 1995, American Buffalo, 1995, Double Down, 1997, Life on Mars, 1997, God's Anul and Out on My Feet, 1997. With U.S. Army, 1959, res. 1959-63. Named Man of Yr. B'nai B'rith, 1981; recipient L.A. Resolution City of L.A., 1981. Mem. Variety Club Internat. *Passion for family, life, work, with patience and intelligence and you have a chance to grab that winning ring.*

TOKUNO, KENNETH ALAN, college dean; b. Tokyo, Nov. 2, 1947; came to U.S., 1948; s. Shiro and Asako (Maida) T.; m. Diane Emi Nushida, July 7, 1979; children Chelsea Kiyoko Alana and Jamie Asako Nalani (twins). AA, Am. River Coll., 1967; BS, U. Calif., Davis, 1969, MS, 1973; PhD, U. Hawaii, 1977. Lectr. U. Hawaii, Honolulu, 1978-80, asst. prof., 1980-85; acad. counselor U. Wash., Seattle, 1985-87, dir. student svcs. dept. sociology, 1987-89, dir. curriculum and programs, 1989-93; dean student svcs. Leeward C.C., Pearl City, Hawaii, 1993—, acting provost, 1995; invited colloquium on freshman interest group program U. Hawaii-Manoa, 1993; cons. devel. gen. edn. arch. U. Mo., Columbia, 1992; mem. selection com. Am. Acad. Achievement, 1990-93. Reviewer: Jour. of Freshman Yr. Experience, 1992—; textbook reviewer Worth Pub. Co., Houghton-Mifflin Co., Charles Merrill Pub. Co., 1983-91; proposal reviewer Biennial Meeting of the Society for Research in Child Development, 1983, Social and Devel. Psychology Program, NSF, 1982-85; cons. editor: Child Development, 1979-81; contbr. poetry to anthologies. Mem. Nat. Assn. Student Pers. Adminstrs. (chair com. on disability concerns region VI 1994-95, exec. bd. Hawaii state chpt. 1994—. Office: Leeward Cmty Coll 96-045 Ala Ike Pearl City HI 96782

TOLANEY, MURLI, environmental engineering executive; b. 1941. BS in Civil Engring., U. Kans., MS in Environ. Engring. Jr. engr. Coun. Sci. and Indsl. Resources, New Delhi, 1963-66; project engr. L.A. County Sanitary Dist., 1966-70; with Montgomery Watson Assn., Pasadena, Calif., 1970—, now pres., CEO. Office: Montgomery Watson Ams 300 N Lake Ave 12 Flr Pasadena CA 91101-4106*

TOLEDANO, JAMES, lawyer; b. N.Y.C., Apr. 26, 1944; s. Ralph Robert and Nora (Romaine) T.; m. Peggy Cashman, Dec. 18, 1971; children: Gwyn Alcock, Michael Howard. AB in Polit. Sci., U. Calif., Riverside, 1968; JD, U. Calif., Berkeley, 1971. Bar: Calif. 1972. Sole practice Irvine, Calif., 1976-88; lawyer mgr. ptnr. Toledano & Wald, Irvine, Calif., 1988—. Bd. dirs., pres. U. Calif. Riverside Alumni Assn., 1972-90; alumni regent U. Calif., 1985-87; candidate Calif. State Assembly, 1992, 94; chair Orange County Calif. Dem. Party, 1995-97. Mem. Religious Soc. of Friends. Democrat. Mem. Religious Soc. of Friends. Office: Toledano & Wald 18201 Von Karman Ave Ste 1000 Irvine CA 92612-1005

TOLENTINO, CASIMIRO URBANO, lawyer; b. Manila, May 18, 1949; came to U.S., 1959; s. Lucio Rubio and Florence (Jose) T.; m. Jennifer Masculino, June 5, 1982; 2 children: Casimiro Masculino, Cristina Cecelia Masculino. BA in Zoology, UCLA, 1972, JD, 1975. Bar: Calif. 1976. Gen. counsel civil rights div. HEW, Washington, 1975-76; regional atty. Agrl. Labor Relations Bd., Fresno, Calif., 1976-78; regional dir. Sacramento and San Diego, 1978-81; regional atty. Pub. Employment Relations Bd., Los Angeles, 1981; counsel, west div. Writers Guild Am., Los Angeles, 1982-84; dir. legal affairs Embassy TV, Los Angeles, 1984-86; sole practice Los Angeles, 1986-87; mediator Ctr. Dispute Resolution, Santa Monica, Calif., 1986-87; asst. chief counsel Dept. of Fair Employment and Housing, State of Calif., 1986-92, adminstrv. law judge dept. social svcs., 1992—. Editor: Letters in Exile, 1976; contbr. articles and revs. to Amerasia Jour. Chmn. adv. bd. UCLA Asian Am. Studies Ctr., 1983-90; chmn. bd. Asian Pacific Legal Ctr., L.A., 1983-93 (Decade award); pres. bd. civil svc. commrs. City of L.A., 1984-85, 90-93; bd. dirs. met. region United Way, 1987-95; bd. dirs. Rebuild L.A., 1992—; mem. Asian-Pacific Am. adv. coun. L.A. Police Commn. Mem. State Bar Calif. (exec. com. labor law sect. 1985-88), Los Angeles County Bar Assn., Minority Bar Assn. (sec. 1984-85), Philippine Lawyers of So. Calif. (pres. 1984-87, Award of Merit 1982). Democrat. Roman Catholic.

TOLIVER, HAROLD EARL, language professional, English; b. McMinnville, Oreg., Feb. 16, 1932; s. Marion E. and Mable A. (Mallery) T.; m. Mary Bennette, June 20, 1954; children: Tricia, Brooks. BA, U. Oreg., 1954; MA, Johns Hopkins U., 1958; PhD, U. Wash., 1961. Asst. prof. Ohio State U., Columbus, 1961-64, UCLA, 1965-66; asst. prof., prof. U. Calif., Irvine, 1966-94. Author: Marvell's Ironic Vision, 1965, Pastoral Forms and Attitudes, 1971, Animate Illusions, 1974, Lyric Provinces, 1985, The Past That Poets Make, 1981, Transported Styles, 1989, Herbert's Christian Narrative, 1993. Pvt. first class, U.S. Army, 1954-56. Recipient Guggenheim fellowship, 1964, 76. Home: 1405 Skyline Dr Laguna Beach CA 92651-1942 Office: U of Calif Dept Of English Irvine CA 92717

TOLIVER, LEE, mechanical engineer; b. Wildhorse, Okla., Oct. 3, 1921; s. Clinton Leslie and Mary (O'Neall) T.; m. Barbara Anne O'Reilly, Jan. 24, 1942; children: Margaret Anne, Michael Edward. BSME, U. Okla., 1942. Registered profl. engr., Ohio. Engr. Douglas Aircraft Co., Santa Monica, Calif., 1942, Oklahoma City, 1942-44; engr. Los Alamos (N.Mex.) Sci. Lab., 1946; instr. mech. engring. Ohio State U., Columbus, 1946-47; engr. Sandia Nat. Labs., Albuquerque, 1947-82; instr. computer sci. and math. U. N.Mex., Valencia County, 1982-84; number theory researcher Belen, N.Mex., 1982—. Author: (computer manuals with G. Carli, AF. Schkade) Experience with an Intelligent Remote Batch Terminal, 1972; (with C.R. Borgman, T.I. Ristine) Transmitting Data from PDP-10 to Precision Graphics, 1973, Data Transmission-PDP-10/Sykes/Precision Graphics, 1975. With Manhattan Project (Atomic Bomb) U.S. Army, 1944-46. Mem. Math. Assn. Am., Am. Math. Soc. Home: 206 Howell St Belen NM 87002-6225

TOLLIVER-PALMA, CALVIN EUGENE, violist, instructor, performer; b. Corpus Christi, Tex., Sept. 24, 1950; s. Jack Terrell Tolliver and Sara Lee (Palma) Denmon. MusB, Baylor U., 1973; MusD, U. Colo., 1981; studied with Mary Ellen Proudfit, Waco, Tex., 1969-71; studied with Wayne Crouse, Houston, 1971-72. Violist Corpus Christi (Tex.) Symphony, 1967-69, Waco (Tex.) Symphony, 1970-73, Tucson Symphony, 1971; union musician Denver and Boulder (Colo.) Locals, 1973-88; violist, violinist Boulder Philharmonic, 1974-88; pvt. music instr., performer Boulder, 1973—. Home: 664 Manhattan Dr Apt 3A Boulder CO 80303-4020

TOLMAN, RICHARD ROBINS, zoology educator; b. Ogden, Utah, Dec. 1, 1937; s. Dale Richards and Dorothy (Robins) T.; m. Bonnie Bjornn, Aug. 18, 1964; children: David, Alicia, Brett, Matthew. BS, U. Utah, 1963, MSEd, 1964; PhD, Oreg. State U., 1969. Tchr. sci. Davis County Sch. Dist., Bountiful, Utah, 1964-66; instr. Mt. Hood C.C., Gresham, Oreg., 1968-69; staff assoc., project dir. Biol. Scis. Curriculum Study, Boulder, Colo., 1969-82; prof. zoology Brigham Young U., Provo, Utah, 1982—, chair dept. of zoology, 1994—. Contbr. articles to profl. jours. Scoutmaster Boy Scouts Am., Orem, Utah, 1992. With USAR, 1956-63. Alcuin fellow Brigham Young U., 1991. Mem. Nat. Sci. Tchrs. Assn., Utah Sci. Tchrs. Assn. (exec. sec. 1991—), Nat. Assn. for Rsch. in Sci. Teaching, Nat. Assn. of Biology Tchrs. Mem. Ch. of LDS. Home: 174 E 1825 S Orem UT 84058-7836 Office: Brigham Young Univ Dept Zoology Provo UT 84602

TOLMAN, RUTH, personal care industry executive; b. Salt Lake City, July 20, 1919; d. James Albert and Evelyn (Roberts) Miller; m. Morton Stanley Male, Sept. 20, 1956 (dec. May 1979); children: Chad, Radon, Kim, James, Rari Lee. Owner John Robert Powers Modeling Sch., Salt Lake City, Denver, 1950-59, World Modeling Assn., N.Y.C., 1961—. Author: A Woman's Guide to Business and Social Success, Personally Yours, Success Insurance, Call Me Mister, Guide to Fashion Merchandise Knowledge, Fashion Marketing and Merchandising, Photo Modeling and Posing, European Looks for Portfolios. Mem. World Modeling Assn. (chmn. 1980-94). Democrat. Unitarian. Office: World Modeling Assn 4401 San Pedro Dr NE Apt 801 Albuquerque NM 87111

TOLSTOY, MAYA, marine seismologist; b. Nyack, N.Y., Apr. 20, 1967; d. Ivan and Margie Tolstoy. BSc with honors, U. Edinburgh, 1988; PhD, Scripp Instn. Oceanography, La Jolla, Calif., 1994. Postgrad. rschr. Scripps Instn. Oceanography, 1994—. Mem. Am. Geophys. Union. Democrat. Office: Scripps Inst Oceanography Inst Geophys/Planetary Phys La Jolla CA 92093-0225

TOM, CREIGHTON HARVEY, aerospace engineer, consultant; b. Oakland, Calif., Mar. 29, 1944; s. Harvey and Katherine (Lew) T. BS in Forestry, U. Calif., Berkeley, 1966; MS in Stats., Colo. State U., 1972, PhD in Computer Sci., 1978. Sr. environ. analyst HRB-Singer, Inc., Ft. Collins, Colo., 1977-78; staff scientist Sci. Applications, Golden, Colo., 1979-80; cons. Golden, 1981; scientist, specialist ConTel Info. Systems, Littleton, Colo., 1981-84; sr. staff engr. Hughes Aircraft Co., Aurora, Colo., 1984-91; shuttle astronaut cand. NASA, Houston, 1980; cons. to companies and schs. Contbr. articles to profl. jours. Adviser CAP, Golden, 1981—; mem. YMCA. Served to maj. U.S. Army, 1966-67, with Res. 1967—. Decorated Bronze Star and Air medals, U.S. Army, 1967. Mem. Am. Soc. Photogrammetry, AAAS, NRA, Mensa, Intertel, Sigma Xi, Xi Sigma Pi, Phi Kappa Phi. Republican. Methodist. Home: 4057 S Bannock St Littleton CO 80110-4603 Office: C&H Enterprises Littleton CO 80120-4432

TOM, LAWRENCE, engineering executive; b. L.A., Jan. 21, 1950; BS Harvey Mudd Coll., 1972; JD Western State U., San Diego, 1978; spl. diploma U. Calif., San Diego, 1991. Design engr. Rockwell Internat., L.A., 1972-73; design engr. Rohr Industries, Inc., Chula Vista, Calif., 1973-76, sr. design engr., 1980, computer graphics engring. specialist, 1980-83, chief engring. svs., 1989-91, chief engring. quality, 1991-93, project mgr. 1993—; sr. engr. Rohr Marine, Inc., Chula Vista, 1977-79; chief exec. officer Computer Aided Tech. Svcs., San Diego, 1983-87; software cons. Small Systems Software, San Diego, 1984-85; computer graphics engring. specialist TOM & ROMAN, San Diego, 1986-88; dir. Computervision Users Group, 1986-88, vice chmn. 1988-91, pres., 1991-93, exec. chmn., 1992-94, regional chmn., 1996—; bd. dirs. Exec. Program for Scientists and Engrs.-Alumni Assn. U. Calif., San Diego, 1991—; pres. Art to Art, San Diego, 1994—. cons. in field. George H. Mayr Found. scholar, 1971, Bates Found. Aero. Edn. scholar, 1970-72. Mem. Aircraft Owners and Pilots Assn., Infiniti Club. Office: 7770 Regents Rd Ste 113-190 San Diego CA 92122-1937 *Personal philosophy: To be the very best.*

TOMASI, DONALD CHARLES, architect; b. Sacramento, Calif., Oct. 24, 1956; s. Thomas M. and Anita (Migliavacca) T.; m. Loretta Elaine Goveia, Feb. 1, 1986; children: Jeffrey, Genna, Michael. AB in Architecture with honors, U. Calif., Berkeley, 1979; MArch, U. Wash., 1982. Registered architect, Calif. Project mgr. Robert Wells and Assocs., Seattle, 1982-84, Milbrandt Architects, Seattle, 1984, T.M. Tomasi Architects, Santa Rosa, Calif., 1984-86; prin. Tomasi Architects, Santa Rosa, 1986-93, Tomasi Lawry Coker De Silva Architecture, Santa Rosa, 1993—. Grad. Leadership Santa Rosa, 1992; mem. design rev. com. Sonoma County, 1988-90; chmn. Santa Rosa Design Rev. Bd., 1990—. Recipient Honor award Coalition for Adequate Sch. Housing, 1991, 93, 96, Merit award, 1991. Mem. AIA (chpt. bd. dirs. 1990-91, Merit award 1986).

TOMASSON, HELGI, dancer, choreographer, dance company executive; b. Reykjavik, Iceland, 1942; m. Marlene Rizzo, 1965; children: Kristinn, Erik. Student, Sigridur Arman, Erik Bidsted, Vera Volkova, Sch. Am. Ballet, Tivoli Pantomime Theatre, Copenhagen. With Joffrey Ballet, 1961-64; prin. dancer Harkness Ballet, 1964-70, N.Y.C. Ballet, 1970-85; artistic dir. San Francisco Ballet, 1985—, also dir. Debut with Tivoli Pantomime Theatre, 1958; created roles in A Season of Hell, 1967, Stages and Reflections, 1968, La Favorita, 1969, The Goldberg Variations, 1971, Symphony in Three Movements, 1972, Coppélia, 1974, Dybbuk Variations, 1974, Chansons Madecasses, 1975, Introduction and Allegro, 1975, Union Jack, 1976, Vienna Waltzes, 1977; choreographer Theme and Variations, Polonaise, Op. 65, 1982, Ballet d'Isoline, 1983, Menuetto (for N.Y.C. Ballet) 1984, Beads of Memory, 1985, Swan Lake, 1988, Handel-a Celebration, 1989, Sleeping Beauty, 1990, Romeo and Juliet, 1994, others. Decorated Knight Order of Falcon (Iceland), 1974, Comdr. Order of Falcon, 1990; recipient Silver medal Internat. Moscow Ballet Competition, 1969, Golden Plate award Am. Acad. Achievement, 1992, Dance Mag. award, 1992. Office: care San Francisco Ballet 455 Franklin St San Francisco CA 94102-4438

TOMBRELLO, THOMAS ANTHONY, JR., physics educator, consultant; b. Austin, Tex., Sept. 20, 1936; s. Thomas Anthony and Jeanette Lilian (Marcuse) T.; m. Esther Ann Hall, May 30, 1957 (div. Jan. 1976); children: Christopher Thomas, Susan Elaine, Karen Elizabeth; m. Stephanie Carhart Merton, Jan. 15, 1977; 1 stepchild, Kerstin Arusha. B.A. in Physics, Rice U., 1958, M.A., 1960, Ph.D., 1961; hon. D, Uppsala U., 1997. Research fellow in physics Calif. Inst. Tech., Pasadena, 1961-62, 64-65, asst. prof. physics, 1965-67, assoc. prof., 1967-71, prof., 1971—, tech. assessment officer, 1996—, William R. Kenan Jr. prof., 1997—; asst. prof. Yale U., New Haven, 1963; cons. in field; disting. vis. prof. U. Calif.-Davis, 1984; v.p., dir. rsch. Schlumberger-Doll Rsch., Ridgefield, Conn., 1987-89; mem. U.S. V.P.'s Space Policy Adv. Bd., 1992; mem. scientific adv. bd. Ctr. of Nanoscale Sci. and Technology, Rice U., 1995—. Assoc. editor Nuclear Physics, 1971-91, Applications of Nuclear Physics, 1980—, Radiation Effects, 1985-88, Nuclear Instruments and Methods B, 1993—. Recipient Alexander von Humboldt award von Humboldt Stiftung, U. Frankfurt, Federal Republic of Germany, 1984-85; NSF fellow Calif. Inst. Tech. 1961-62; A.P. Sloan fellow, 1971-73. Fellow Am. Phys. Soc.; mem. AAAS, Materials Rsch. Soc., Phi Beta Kappa, Sigma Xi, Delta Phi Alpha. Avocations: reading, jogging. Democrat. Office: Calif Inst Tech Dept Physics Mail Code 91125 Pasadena CA 91125

TOMCZYK, THEODORE CLAYTON, secondary education educator; b. Flint, Mich., Nov. 10, 1962; s. Stanley Anthony and Doris Lorraine (Erickson) T.; m. Laurie Ann Burke, Oct. 21, 1989; children: Kristen, Clayton. BS, Mich. State U., 1985; MS, Purdue U., 1987. Geophysicist Chevron Oil Co. USA, Houston, 1987-91; H.S. tchr. Denver (Colo.) County, 1992-94, Jefferson County, Golden, Colo., 1994—; rschr. Hughes Rsch. for Tchrs., Ft. Collins, 1993, Boulder, 1994. Grantee Pub. Edn. Coalition, Denver, 1993, Cub Foods, Denver, 1993, Rsch. for Tchrs. grantee Hughes Found., Ft. Collins, 1993. Home: 9436 W Geddes Pl Littleton CO 80123-4116 Office: D'Evelyn HS 13200 W 32nd Ave Golden CO 80401-1614

TOMISKA, CORA LORENA, civic worker; b. Fontana, Calif., July 30, 1928; d. Riley Royston and Winifred Lillian (Humphry) Green; m. Joseph Frank Tomiska, June 19, 1950; children: Jo Ann, William Joseph, Robert Royston, Charity Lillianne, Angelina Kathleen. AA, Chaffey Jr. Coll., 1948; BA, Calif. State Coll., San Bernardino, 1976, postgrad., 1976—. Owner Tomiska Aviaries, Fontana, 1963—. Pres. Redwood PTA, 1976, Sequoia Jr. High PTA, 1969-70, Fontana Council PTA, 1972-74; mem. exec. bd. 5th Dist. PTA, 1972-83, historian, 1976-79, v.p., dir. health, 1979-81, v.p., dir. parent edn., 1981-83; mem. Redwood PTA; sec. consol. projects adv. com. Fontana Unified Sch. Dist., 1972-81, sec. family life edn. project, 1982-86; mem. Mayoral Candidacy Com., 1978: counselor jr. gardening Fontana Redwood Blue Jays, 1964-83; pres. Fontana Garden Club, 1974-77; vol. Fontana Youth Svc. Ctr., Am. Heart Fund, Am. Cancer Soc., Christian Youth Edn., Valley Bible Ch., Fontana United Way; scholarship chmn. San Bernardino Valley dist. Calif. Garden Clubs, 1974-83; sec.-treas. Fontana Family Svc. Agy., 1976-79, pres., 1980-82; mem. Arthritis Found., Westside Bapt. Ch., tchr. trainer, 1991; mem., personal care provider, estate mgr. Fellowship of the Living Water, 1984-88; vol. Literacy Vol. Am., Inc., 1992—. Recipient 1st place award Calif. Jr. Flower Shows, 1969-73. Mem. AAUW (edn. chmn. 1981-82), ARC, San Bernardino County Mus. Assn., Fontana Hist. Soc. Address: 430 Woodmont Pl Oakley CA 94561-2501

TOMIZUKA, MASAYOSHI, mechanical engineering educator, researcher; b. Tokyo, Mar. 31, 1946; came to U.S., 1970; s. Makoto and Shizuko (Nagatome) T.; m. Miwako Tomizawa, Sept. 5, 1971; children: Lica, Yumi. MS, Keio U., Japan, 1970; PhD, MIT, 1974. Rsch. assoc. Keio U., 1974; asst. prof. U. Calif., Berkeley, 1974-80, assoc. prof., 1980-86, prof., 1986—, Roscoe and Elizabeth Hughes prof., 1996—. Assoc. editor: Internat. Fedn. Automation Control Automatica, 1993—; contbr. more than 100 articles to profl. jours. NSF grantee, 1976-78, 81-83, 86-89, 93—, State of Calif. grantee, 1984-86, 88-93. Fellow ASME (chmn. dynamic systems and control divsn. 1986-87, tech. editor Jour. Dynamic Systems Measurement and Control Systems mag. 1986-88), IEEE (editor-in-chief IEEE/ASME Transactions on Mechatronics 1995—), Soc. Mfg. Engrs. (sr. mem., mem. scientific com. 1993—). Office: U Calif Dept Mech Engring Berkeley CA 94720-1740

TOMLINSON, WILLIAM M., lawyer; b. Paris, France, Sept. 2, 1948. BA, Princeton U., 1970; JD, U. Oreg., 1974. Bar: Oreg. 1974, Wash. 1986. Atty. Lindsay, Hart, Neil & Weigler, Portland, Oreg. Mem. ABA (mem. torts and ins. practice sect.), Oreg. State Bar, Oreg. Assn. Def. Counsel, Wash. State Bar Assn., Multnomah County Bar Assn. Office: Lindsay Hart Neil & Weigler 1300 SW 5th Ave Ste 3400 Portland OR 97201-5640

TOMPANE, MARY BETH, management consultant; b. Hollywood, Calif., Sept. 27, 1928; d. Richard F. and Mary Elizabeth (McGregor) Goss; m. Eugene F. Tompane; children: Michael, Richard, Donald, John. MBA, U. Calif., Riverside, 1973; postgrad., Stanford U., 1981. Cert. mgmt. cons.; cert. vol. adminstr. Dept. head Boswell Hosp., Sun City, Ariz.; prin., owner Tompane Consulting, Phoenix & Tempe, Ariz., San Diego. Active Girl Scouts USA, 1972—. Named Phoenix Woman of Yr., Phoenix Ad Club, 1965. Mem. AAUW, Inst. Mgmt. Cons. (bd. mem.), Assn. Vol. Adminstrs. Office: Tompane Consulting Unit 912 8515 Costa Verde Blvd San Diego CA 92122-1156

TOMPKINS, CYNTHIA MARGARITA, women's studies educator; b. Alta Gracia, Cordoba, Argentina, Jan. 30, 1958; came to U.S., 1982; d. Harold Stanley Albert and Ines Leonor (Hawkins) T. Prof. English Lang. and Lit., Nat. U. Cordoba, 1979, Lic. in Modern Langs., 1981; MA in Comparative Lit., Pa. State U., 1985, PhD in Comparative Lit., 1989. Teaching asst. in Spanish and comparative lit. Pa. State U., University Park, 1983-88; instr. Spanish Dickinson Coll., Carlisle, Pa., 1988-89; asst. prof. Spanish U. Wis.-Parkside, Kenosha, 1989-92; asst. prof. women's studies Ariz. State U. West, Phoenix, 1992—; mem. pubs. com. Ariz. State U. Ctr. for L.Am. Studies. Editor, contbg. author: Utopias, ojos, azules, bocas suicidas la narrativa de Alina Diaconu, 1993; contbr. articles to profl. jours.; editor: Confluencia: Revista Hispanica de Cultura y Literature, 1994—, Newsletter of Feministas Unidas; reviewer: World Literature Today, 1989—. Mem. steering com. Sisters of Color Internat., 1991-96. Fulbright fellow, Pa. State U., 1982, E. Sparks fellow Coll. Liberal Arts, 1982-83. Mem. MLA, Am. Comparative Lit. Assn. Office: Ariz State U PO Box 37100 4701 W Thunderbird Rd Phoenix AZ 85069-7100

TOMPKINS, NICK, agricultural products executive; b. 1955. Farmer, 1976—; v.p., sec. APIO Inc., Guadalupe, Calif., 1979—. Office: APIO Inc PO Box 627 Guadalupe CA 93434-1659*

TONELLO-STUART, ENRICA MARIA, political economist; b. Monza, Italy; d. Alessandro P. and Maddalena M. (Marangoni) Tonello; m. Albert E. Smith; m. Charles L. Stuart. BA in Internat. Affairs, Econs., U. Colo., 1961; MA, Claremont Grad. Sch., 1966, PhD, 1971. Sales mgr. Met. Life Ins. Co., 1974-79; pres., CEO, ETS R&D, Inc., Palos Verdes Peninsula, Calif., 1977—; dean internat. studies program Union U., L.A. and Tokyo; lectr. internat. affairs and mktg. UCLA Ext., Union U. Pub., editor Tomorrow Outline Jour., 1963—, The Monitor, 1988; pub. World Regionalism-An Ecological Analysis, 1971, A Proposal for the Reorganization of the United Nations, 1966, The Persuasion Technocracy, Its Forms, Techniques and Potentials, 1966, The Role of the Multinationals in the Emerging Globalism, 1978; developed the theory of social ecology and econsociometry. Organizer 1st family assistance program Langley FB Tractical Air Command, 1956-58. Recipient vol. svc. award VA, 1956-58, ARC svc. award, 1950-58. Mem. Corp. Planners Assn. (treas. 1974-79), Investigative Reporters and Editors, World Future Soc. (pres. 1974-75), Asian Bus. League, Chinese Am. Assn. (life), Japan Am. Assn., L.A. World Trade Ctr., Palos Verdes C. of C. (legis. com.), L.A. Press Club (bd. dirs.), Zonta (chmn. internat. com. South Bay), Pi Sigma Alpha.

TONG, RICHARD DARE, anesthesiologist; b. Chgo., Oct. 20, 1930; s. George Dare and June (Jung) T.; student U. Calif., Berkeley, 1949-52; MD, U. Calif., Irvine, 1956. m. Diane Helene Davies, Apr. 12, 1970; children: Erin, Jason; m. Deanna Johnson, Jan. 5, 1993; stepchildren: Jeffery Johnson, Ryan Johnson. Intern, Phoenix Gen. Hosp., 1956-57; resident in anesthesiology UCLA, 1965-67; pvt. practice, Lakewood, Calif., 1967—; clin. instr. UCLA Sch. Medicine, 1968—. Dep. sheriff reserve med. emergency team, L.A. County. With USNR, 1947-53. Diplomate Am. Bd. Anesthesiology. Fellow Am. Coll. Anesthesiology; mem. Am. Soc. Anesthesiologists, AMA, Calif. Med. Assn., L.A. County Med. Assns. Office: PO Box 1131 Lakewood CA 90714-1131

TONG, SIU WING, computer programmer; b. Hong Kong, May 20, 1950; came to U.S., 1968; BA, U. Calif., Berkeley, 1972; PhD, Harvard U., 1979; MS, U. Lowell, 1984. Research assoc. Brookhaven Nat. Lab., Upton, N.Y., 1979-83; software engr. Honeywell Info. Systems, Billerica, Mass., 1984-85; sr. programmer, analyst Hui Computer Cons., Berkeley, Calif., 1985-88; sr. v.p. devel., chief fin. officer Surgicenter Info. Systems, Inc., Orinda, Calif., 1989-94; sr. sys. specialist Info. Sys. Divsn. Contra Costa County Health Svcs., MArtinez, Calif., 1995—. Vol. tchr. Boston Chinatown Saturday Adult Edn. Program of Tufts Med. Sch., 1977-79. Muscular Dystrophy Assn. fellow, 1980-82. Mem. AAAS, IEEE, Assn. Computing Machinery, N.Y. Acad. Scis. Home: 17 Beaconsfield Ct Orinda CA 94563-4203 Office: Contra Costa County Health Svcs 595 Center Ave Ste 210 Martinez CA 94553-4634

TONG, YIMING, import company executive, accountant; b. Shanghai, China, Nov. 26, 1957; came to U.S., 1987; s. Guanshou Tong and Zhuying Zhao; married, June 20, 1986. BS, Jiangsu Inst. Tech., China, 1982; MBA, Hawaii Pacific U., 1991. Acct. Centurion Security System, Inc., Honolulu, Hawaii, 1991—; gen. mgr. Silk Import, Inc., Honolulu, 1994—. Home: 411 Hobron Ln Honolulu HI 96815 Office: Silk Import Inc 2442 Kuhio Ave #502 Honolulu HI 96815

TONINI, LEON RICHARD, sales professional; b. Pittsfield, Mass., May 16, 1931; s. John Richard and Mabel Grayce (Rushbrook) T.; B.A. in Mgmt., U. Md., 1951; m. Helen Jo, Aug. 15, 1966; 1 son, John Richard, II. Enlisted in U.S. Army, 1947, advanced through grades to master sgt., 1968; service in W.Ger., Vietnam; ret., 1974; dir. vets. employment and assistance Non-Commd. Officers Assn., San Antonio, 1974-75; supr. security Pinkerton's Inc., Dallas, 1975-78; gen. mgr. civic center Travelodge Motor Hotel and Restaurant, San Francisco, 1978-85; sales representative Vernon Co., 1985—. Chmn. San Francisco Vets. Employment Com., 1981. Served as sgt. maj. Calif. N.G., res. Decorated Bronze Star; Republic Vietnam Honor medal 2d class. Mem. San Francisco Hotel Assn. (dir.), Non-Commd. Officers Assn. (dir. Calif. chpt.), Am. Legion, Regular Vets. Assn. (nat. sr. vice comdr.), Amvets, Patrons of Husbandry. Republican. Baptist. Club: Masons. Home and Office: 205 Collins St Apt 9 San Francisco CA 94118-3429 *Personal philosophy: You can be what you want to be, go beyond the rest.*

TONJES, MARIAN JEANNETTE BENTON, education educator; b. Rockville Center, N.Y., Feb. 16, 1929; d. Millard Warren and Felicia E. (Tyler) Benton; m. Charles F. Tonjes (div. 1965); children: Jeffrey Charles, Kenneth Warren. BA, U. N.Mex., 1951, cert., 1966, MA, 1969; EdD, U. Miami, 1975. Dir. recreation Stuyvesant Town Housing Project, N.Y.C., 1951-53; tchr. music., phys. edn. Sunset Mesa Day Sch., Albuquerque, 1953-54; tchr. remedial reading Zia Elem. Sch., Albuquerque, 1965-67; tchr. secondary devel. reading Rio Grande High Sch., Albuquerque, 1967-69; rsch. asst. reading Southwestern Coop. Ednl. Lab., Albuquerque, 1969-71; assoc. dir., vis. instr. Fla. Ctr. Tchr. Tng. Materials U. Miami, 1971-72; asst. prof. U.S. Internat. U., San Diego, 1972-75; prof. edn. Western Wash. U., Bellingham, 1975-94, dir. summer study, 1979-94, prof. emerita, 1994—; dir. summer study at Oriel Coll. Oxford (Eng.) U.; reading supr. Manzanita Ctr. U. N.Mex., Albuquerque, 1968; vis. prof. adult edn. Palomar (Calif.) Jr. Coll., 1974; vis. prof. U. Guam, Mangilao, 1989-90; speaker, cons. in field; invited guest Russian Reading Assn., Moscow, 1992; part-time prof. U. N.Mex., Albuquerque, 1995—. Author: (with Miles V. Zintz) Teaching Reading/Thinking Study Skills in Content Classrooms, 3d edit., 1992, Secondary Reading, Writing and Learning, 1991; contbr. articles to profl. jours. Tng. Tchr. Trainers grantee, 1975; NDEA fellow Okla. State U., 1969. Mem. Am. Reading Forum (chmn. bd. dirs. 1983-85), Adult and Adolescent Literacy Confs. (spkr. 1991-94), Internat. Reading Assn. (mem. travel, interchange and study tours com. 1984-86, mem. non-print media nd reading com. 1980-83, workshop dir. S.W. regional confs. 1982, mem. com. internat. devel. N.Am. 1991-96, Outstanding Tchrs. Educator 1988-90), U.K. Reading Assn. (spkr. 1977-93), European Conf. in Reading (spkr. Berlin 1989, Edinburgh 1991, Malmo 1993, Budapest 1995), European Coun. Internat. Schs. (The Hague, spkr. 1993), World Congress in Reading Buenos Aires (spkr. 1994), PEO (past chpt. pres.), Phi Delta Kappa, Delta Delta Delta.

TONN, ELVERNE MERYL, pediatric dentist, dental benefits consultant; b. Stockton, Calif., Dec. 10, 1929; s. Emanuel M. and Lorna Darlene (Bryant) T.; m. Ann G. Richardson, Oct. 28, 1951; children: James Edward, Susan Elaine Tonn Yee. AA, La Sierra U., Riverside, Calif., 1949; DDS, U. So. Calif., 1955; BS, Regents Coll., U. State N.Y., 1984. Lic. dentist; cert. tchr., Calif., dental ins. cons. Pediatric dentist, assoc. Walker Dental Group, Long Beach, Calif., 1957-59, Children's Dental Clinic, Sunnyvale, Calif., 1959-61; pediatric dentist in pvt. practice Mountain View, Calif., 1961-72; pediatric dentist, ptnr. Pediatric Dentistry Assocs., Los Altos, Calif., 1972-83; pediatric dentist, ptnr. Valley Oak Dental Group, Manteca, Calif., 1987—; from clin. instr. to assoc. prof. U. Pacific, San Francisco, 1964-84; assoc. prof. U. Calif., San Francisco, Calif., 1984-86; ; pediatric dental cons. Delta Dental Plan, San Francisco, 1985—; chief dental staff El Camino Hosp., Mountain View, 1964-65, 84-85; lectr. in field. Weekly columnist Manteca Bull., 1987-92; producer 2 teaching videos, 1986; contbr. articles to profl. jours. Lectr. to elem. students on dental health Manteca Unified Sch. Dist., 1982—; dental health screener Elem. Schs., San Joaquin County Pub. Health, 1989-92; dental cons. Interplast program Stanford U. Sch. Medicine. Capt. U.S. Army, 1955-57. Fellow Internat. Coll. Dentists, Am. Acad. Pediatric Dentistry, Am. Coll. Dentists, Royal Soc. Health (Eng.), Acad. of Dentistry for Handicapped, Pierre Fauchard Acad., Acad. Dental Materials; mem. ADA, Internat. Assn. Pediatric Dentistry, Internat. Assn. Dental Rsch., Fedn. Dentaire Internationale, Am. Soc. Dentistry for Children, Am. Assn. Dental Cons., Calif. Dental Assn., Calif. Soc. Dentistry for Children (pres. 1968), Calif. Soc. Pediatric Dentists, N.Y. Acad. Scis., Calif. Acad. Sci., Rotary Internat., Am. Bd. Quality Assurance and Utilization Rev. Physicians (diplomate, cert. dental benefits cons.), Nat. Assn. for Healthcare Quality. Republican. Home: 374 Laurelwood Cir Manteca CA 95336-7122 Office: Valley Oak Dental Group Inc 1507 W Yosemite Ave Manteca CA 95337-5159

TOOKEY, ROBERT CLARENCE, consulting actuary; b. Santa Monica, Calif., Mar. 21, 1925; s. Clarence Hall and Minerva Maconachie (Anderson) T.; BS, Calif. Inst. Tech., 1945; MS, U. Mich., 1947; m. Marcia Louise Hickman, Sept. 15, 1956; children: John Hall, Jennifer Louise, Thomas Anderson. With Prudential Ins. Co. Am., Newark, 1947-49; assoc. actuary in group Pacific Mut. Life Ins. Co., Los Angeles, 1949-55; asst. v.p. in charge reins. sales and service for 17 western states Lincoln Nat. Life Ins. Co., Ft. Wayne, Ind., 1955-61; dir. actuarial services Peat, Marwick, Mitchell & Co., Chgo., 1961-63; mng. partner So. Calif. office Milliman & Robertson, cons. actuaries, Pasadena, 1963-76; pres. Robert Tookey Assos., Inc., 1977—. Committeeman troop 501 Boy Scouts Am., 1969-72. Served to lt. (j.g.) USNR, 1943-45, 51-52. Fellow Soc. Actuaries, Conf. Consulting Actuaries; mem. Am. Acad. Actuaries, Pacific States Actuarial Club, Pacific Ins. Conf., Rotary Club (Pasadena), Union League Club (Chgo.). Home and Office: 3950 San Augustine Dr Glendale CA 91206-1232 also: PO Box 646 La Canada Flintridge CA 91012-0646

TOOLE, FLOYD EDWARD, manufacturing company executive; b. Moncton, N.B., Can., June 19, 1938; s. Harold Osman and Arilla Adeltha (Allen) T.; m. Noreen Beckie, June 31, 1961. BSc in EE, U. N.B., Fredericton, 1961; PhD in EE, U. London, 1965. Sr. rsch. officer NRC Can., Ottawa, Ont., 1965-91; v.p. engring. Harman Internat. Industries Inc., Northridge, Calif., 1991—. Contbr. articles to profl. jours. Fellow Audio Engring. Soc. (pres. 1992-93, Publs. award 1988, 90, Silver Medal award 1996); mem. Acoustical Soc. Am. Office: Harman Internat Industries 8500 Balboa Blvd Northridge CA 91329-0001

TOOLEY, CHARLES FREDERICK, communications executive, consultant; b. Seattle, Sept. 29, 1947; s. Creath Athol and Catherine Ella (Wainman) T.; m. Valerie Adele Gose, Mar. 7, 1981 (dec. Feb. 1991); children: Paige Arlene Chytka, Marni Higdon Tooley. BA, Lynchburg Coll., 1968. Producer, stage mgr., tech. dir. various theatre cos. and performing arts orgns., 1965-74; field underwriter N.Y. Life Ins. Co., Billings, Mont., 1974-77; market adminstr. Mountain Bell Telephone Co., Butte and Billings, Mont., 1978-83; pres. BCC Inc., Billings, Mont., 1983—. Active Mont. Arts Coun., 1982-92, Billings/Yellowstone County Centennial, 1981-82, Mont. Cultural Advocacy, 1982-92; bd. dirs. Yellowstone 89ers, 1987-89, Christian Chs. in Mont., 1983—, divsn. of overseas ministries Christian Ch. Disciples of Christ, 1997—; elder Ctrl. Christian Ch., Billings, 1983—, chmn. trustees, 1983-85; mem. Mont. Dem. Exec. Bd., 1982-87; mem. adv. bd. Salvation Army, Billings, 1984—; del. Dem. Nat. Conv., 1980; Dem. candidate Mont. Ho. of Reps., 1986; mem. Billings City Coun., 1988-94, mayor pro tem, 1992-94; mayor city of Billings, 1996—; mem. Common Global Missions Bd., 1997—. Sgt. U.S. Army, 1969-72, Vietnam. Mem. Billings Coun. Fgn. Rels., Toastmasters (Div. Gov.'s Cup 1978), Kiwanis (bd. dirs. 1981-88), Masons, Shriners, Elks. Mem. Disciples of Christ. Home: 502 Alderson Ave Billings MT 59101-5920 Office: BCC Inc PO Box 555 Billings MT 59103-0555

TOOLEY, WILLIAM LANDER, real estate company executive; b. El Paso, Tex., Apr. 23, 1934; s. William Lander and Virginia Mary (Ryan) T.; m. Reva Berger, Mar. 5, 1966; children: William Ryan, Patrick Boyer, James Eugene. BA, Stanford U., 1956; MBA, Harvard U., 1960. Treas., mgr. Pickwick Hotel Co., San Diego, 1960-63, David H. Murdock Devel. Co., Phoenix, 1963-66; ptnr. Ketchum, Peck & Tooley, L.A., 1967-74; chmn. Tooley & Co., L.A., 1974—; dir. Nat. Realty Com., Washington. Trustee Loyola Marymount U., L.A., 1975-82, bd. regents, 1982-94; bd. dirs. San Francisco Traditional Jazz Found., 1992—. Recipient Lifetime Achievement award L.A. Area C. of C., 1992, Civic Achievement award Am. Jewish Com., 1989. Mem. Urban Land Inst. (award 1988), Calif. Club, Calif. Yacht Club. Office: 11150 Santa Monica Blvd Los Angeles CA 90025

TOOMEY, HUGH EDWARD, orthopedist, surgeon; b. Visalia, Calif., Dec. 6, 1934; s. David J. and Catherine M. (Creegan) T.; m. Mary Patricia McGavick, June 28, 1958; children: Elizabeth, Patricia, Steven, Sean. BS, Wash. State U., 1956; MD, UCLA, 1963. Diplomate Am. Bd. Orthop. Surgery. Intern Harborview Hosp., Seattle, 1963-64; resident U. Wash., 1964-69; orthop. surgeon Orthop. Phys. Assocs., Seattle, 1969—. With U.S. Infantry, 1957-58. Office: Orthop Physicians Assocs 1229 Madison St Ste 1600 Seattle WA 98104-1357

TOON, OWEN BRIAN, earth scientist; b. Bethesda, Md., May 26, 1947; s. Owen Russell and Adrienne Joan (Van Burk) T.; 1 child, Christopher Russell. AB, U. Calif., Berkeley, 1969; PhD, Cornell U., 1975. Nat. Rsch. Coun. fellow, Ames Rsch. Ctr. Nat. Acad. Sci., Mountain View, Calif., 1975-78; sr. scientist, Ames Rsch. Ctr. NASA, Moffett Field, Calif., 1978—. Contbr. 150 articles to profl. jours. Recipient Leo Szilard award for physics in pub. interest Am. Phys. Soc., 1986. Fellow Calif. Acad. Sci., Am. Geophys. Union, Am. Meterol. Soc. Office: LASP Campus Box 392 Univ Colo Boulder CO 80309-0392

TOPE, DWIGHT HAROLD, retired management consultant; b. Grand Junction, Colo., Aug. 29, 1918; s. Richard E. and Elizabeth (Jones) T.; m. Carolyn Stagg, Apr. 29, 1949; children: Stephen R., Chris L. AS, Mesa Coll., 1940; student, George Washington U. With Fgn. Funds Control, a Div. of U.S. Treasury Dept.; staff adjuster Fire Cos. Adjustment Bur., Denver, Albuquerque, 1946-48; br. mgr. Gen. Adjustment Bur., Deming, N.Mex., 1948-50; spl. agt. Cliff Kealey State Agy., Albuquerque, 1950-56; pres. Dwight Tope State Agy., Inc., Albuquerque, 1956-84; with Fgn. Funds Control divsn. U.S. Dept. Treasury, Albuquerque; sr. cons. Dwight Tope State Agy., Inc., Albuquerque, 1985-87. Mem. adv. bd. Salvation Army, Albuquerque, 1974-97, Meals on Wheels, 1987-97; past chmn. bd., pres. Presbyn. Heart Inst., Albuquerque, 1977-94. Maj. Coast Arty. Anti-Aircraft, 1941-45. Mem. N.Mex. Ins. Assn. (past chmn.), Ins. Info. Inst. (past chmn.), N.Mex. Surplus Lines Assn. (past pres.), Air Force Assn., Assn. of U.S. Army, Am. Legion, Albuquerque C. of C. (mil. rels. com.), Rotary, Masons, Shriners, Albuquerque Country Club, Petroleum Club. Republican. Home: 1812 Stanford Dr NE Albuquerque NM 87106-2538 Office: 8100 Mountain Rd NE Ste 204E Albuquerque NM 87110-7833

TOPIK, STEVEN CURTIS, history educator; b. Montebello, Calif., Aug. 6, 1949; s. Kurt and Gertrude Irene (Kriszanich) T.; m. Martha Jane Marcy, Feb. 3, 1979; children: Julia, Natalia. BA, U. Calif., San Diego, 1971; MA, U. Tex., 1973, PhD, 1978. Asst. prof. Universidade Fed. Fluminense, Rio de Janeiro, 1978-81, vis. prof., 1984—; asst. prof. Colgate U., Hamilton, N.Y., 1981-84; vis. prof. Univ. Ibero Americana, Mexico City, 1982; prof. U. Calif., Irvine, 1984-96; vis. prof. Ecols des Hautes Etudes en Sci. Social, Paris, 1990; chair historydept., 1996—; cons. in field; mem. editorial com. U. Calif. Press, Berkeley, 1987-89. Author: The Political Economy of the Brazilian State, 1987, Trade and Gunboats, The United States and Brazil in the Age of Empire, 1996; contbr. articles, revs. to profl. publs. Mem. Mayor's Adv. Bd. on Sister Cities, Irvine, 1989-90; mem. adv. bd. Orange County (Calif.) Com. on Latin Am., 1989-90. Fellow NEH, 1987, 89-90, Rockefeller Found., 1977, Social Sci. Rsch. Coun. Mexico City, 1982-83, Fulbright-Hayes Found., 1978-79, 84, U. Calif., 1988-89. Mem. Latin Am. Studies Assn., Am. Hist. Assn., Conf. Latin Am. History (com. on hist. statistics, com. on projects and publs., chair Brazilian studies com. 1988-90), Pacific Coast Coun. on Latin Am. Studies (bd. govs. 1987-90).

TOPILOW, CARL S., symphony conductor; b. Jersey City, N.J., Mar. 14, 1947; s. Jacob Topilow and Pearl (Roth) Topilow Josephs; m. Shirley; 1 child, Jenny Michelle. B.Mus., Manhattan Sch. of Mus., 1968, M.Mus., 1969. Exxon/Arts Endowment Condr. Denver Symphony Orch., 1976-79, asst. condr., 1979-80; mus. dir. Denver Chamber Orch., 1976-81, Denver Youth Orch., 1977-80, Grand Junction Symphony, Colo., 1977-80, Nat. Repertory Orch., Breckenridge, Colo., 1978—; dir. orchs. Cleve. Inst. Mus., 1981—, condr. Summit Brass 1986—, Cleve. Pops Orch., 1995—. Recipient Conducting fellowship Nat. Orch. Assn., N.Y.C., 1972-75, Aspen Mus. Festival, Colo., 1976; winner 1st place Balt. Symphony Conducting Competition, Md., 1976.*

TOPJON, ANN JOHNSON, librarian; b. Los Angeles, Dec. 2, 1940; d. Carl Burdett and Margaret Elizabeth (Tildesley) Johnson; m. Gary M. Topjon, 1963; children: Gregory Eric and Cynthia Elizabeth (twins); m. Philip M. O'Brien, 1990. BA, Occidental Coll., 1962; MLS, UCLA, 1963. Reference asst. Whittier (Calif.) Pub. Library, 1973-78; pub. services and reference librarian Whittier Coll., 1981—. Author, bibliography: Carl Larsson. Faculty rsch. grantee Whittier Coll., 1987-88, 91-92, 95-96; grantee The Am.-Scandinavian Found., N.Y., 1991. Mem. Calif. Acad. and Rsch. Librs. (liaison at Whittier Coll. 1990—), AAUW (Whittier br. 1968-77, Brea-La Habra br., Calif. 1977—, chmn. lit. group, 1977—, chmn. scholarship fund raising 1988-89). Office: Whittier Coll Wardman Libr 7031 Founders Rd Whittier CA 90608

TOPP, ALPHONSO AXEL, JR., environmental scientist, consultant; b. Indpls., Oct. 15, 1920; s. Alphonso Axel and Emilia (Karlsson) T.; m. Mary Catherine Virtue, July 7, 1942; children: Karen, Susan, Linda, Sylvia, Peter, Astrid, Heidi, Eric, Megan, Katrina. BS in Chem. Engring., Purdue U., 1942; MS, UCLA, 1948. Commd. 2d lt. U.S. Army, 1942, advanced through grades to col., 1966, ret., 1970; environ. scientist Radiation Protection Sect., State of N.Mex., Santa Fe, 1970, program mgr., licensing and registration sect., 1978, chief radiation protection bur., 1981-83; cons., 1984—. Decorated Legion of Merit, Bronze Star with 2 oak leaf clusters. Mem. Health Physics Soc., Sigma Xi, Rotary. Republican. Presbyterian. Home and Office: 872 Highland Dr Los Osos CA 93402-3902

TORBET, LAURA, author, artist, graphic designer; b. Paterson, N.J., Aug. 23, 1942; d. Earl Buchanan and Ruth Claire (Ehlers) Robbins; B.A., B.F.A., Ohio Wesleyan U., 1964; m. Bruce J. Torbet, Sept. 9, 1967 (div. 1971); m. Peter H. Morrison, June 19, 1983 (dec. Nov. 1988); m. Salam Habibi, Aug. 23, 1995. Mng. editor Suburban Life mag., East Orange, N.J., 1964-65; asst. public relations dir. United Funds N.J., Newark, 1965-67; art dir. Alitalia Airlines, N.Y.C., 1967-69; propr. Laura Torbet Studio, N.Y.C., 1969-84; author: Macrame You Can Wear, 1972, Clothing Liberation, 1973, Leathercraft You Can Wear, 1975, The T-Shirt Book, 1976, The Complete Book of Skateboarding, 1976, How To Do Everything With Markers, 1977; (with Doug McLaggan) Squash: How to Play, How to Win, 1977; The Complete Book of Mopeds, 1978; (with Luree Nicholson) How to Fight Fair With Your Kids...and Win!, 1980; editor: Helena Rubenstein's Book of the Sun, 1979, The Encyclopedia of Crafts, 1980, (with George Bach) The Inner Enemy, 1982, A Time for Caring, 1982; (with Hap Hatton) Helpful Hints for Hard Times, 1982, The Virgin Homeowners Handbook, 1984, Helpful Hints for Better Living, 1984, (with James Braly) Dr. Braly's Optimum Health Program, 1985; (with Bernard Gittelson) Intangible Evidence, 1987; (with Harville Hendrix) Keeping the Love You Find, 1992, The Couples Companion, 1994, The Personal Companion, 1996, All Out Art; editor, ghost writer, co-author books. Bd. dirs. The Living/Dying Project. Mem. Boss Ladies. Home and Office: 1111 Butterfield Rd San Anselmo CA 94960-1181

TOREN, ROBERT, photojournalist; b. Grand Rapids, Mich., Oct. 9, 1915; s. Clarence J. and Helen (Holcomb) T.; student Winona Sch. Profl. Photography, 1957, West Coast Sch. Photography, 1959-62; m. Miriam Jeanette Smith, July 17, 1940. Photographer, Harris and Ewing, Washington, 1938-39, Versluis Studios, Grand Rapids, Mich., 1939-43, prodn. mgr., 1940-43; owner, photographer Toren Galleries, San Francisco, 1946-70;

photographer Combat Tribes of World, Rich Lee Orgn., 1978-84, Darien jungle expdn. Am. Motors, 1979; feature writer Auburn (Calif.) Jour., El Dorado Gazette, 1983-87, Georgetown Gazette, 1983-96. One man shows various univs.; prints in permanent collections: Photog. Hall of Fame, Coyote Point Mus., San Mateo County Hist. Mus.; photog. column San Mateo Times, Georgetown Gazette; lectr. Am. Pres. Lines, Coll. San Mateo, Peninsula Art Assn., Mendicino Art Ctr. Historian City of Foster City; vice chmn. Art Commn. Foster City. Trustee, West Coast Sch.; bd. dirs. Foster City Art League, Hillbarn Theatre, San Mateo County Arts Council; mem. art com. San Mateo County Fair, 1979-87; coord., dir. Georgetown (Calif.) Mountain Mus., 1982-88; founding pres. Music on The Divide, 1989; founder Georgetown CA. Ragtime Concerts, 1996; pres. El Dorado County Arts Coun. Served from pvt. to staff sgt. AUS, 1943-46. Mem. Calif. Writers (br. pres.), Profl. Photographers Am. Presbyn. Author: Peninsula Wilderness. Illustrator: The Tainted Tree, 1963. Editor: The Evolution of Portraiture, 1965; The Western Way of Portraiture, 1965, Conquest of the Darien, 1984, Two Cities, 1996. Home: 3140 Cascade Trl Cool CA 95614-2615

TORGENRUD, TERRY WAYNE, pediatrician; b. Wahpeton, N.D., Sept. 6, 1942; s. Lyle Jerome and Maxine Bird (Hoffman) T.; m. Janet Marie Kuchera, Aug. 1, 1965; children: Timothy, Matthew, Andrew. BS, U. N.D., 1964, BS in Medicine, 1966; MD, Bowman Gray Sch. Medicine, 1968. Diplomate Am. Bd. Pediatrics. Intern Madigan Army Med. Ctr., Tacoma, 1968-69, resident in pediatrics, 1969-72; fellow in adolescent medicine U. Wash., Seattle, 1971-72, chief adolescent svc., 1972-74; pediatrician University Pl. Pediatric Clinic, Seattle, 1974—; chief of staff Mary Bridge Children's Hosp., Tacoma, 1978. Chmn. Citizens for Better Dental Helath, Tacoma, 1991-92. Maj. M.C., U.S. Army, 1968-74. Fellow Am. Acad. Pediatrics; mem. North Pacific Pediatric Soc., Wash. State Med. Soc., Pierce County Med. Soc. (chair sch. health, pub. health com., Cmty. Svc. award 1994). Roman Catholic. Home: 4216 Bayview Pl W Tacoma WA 98466-1500 Office: Univ Pl Pediatric Clinic 1033 Regents Blvd Ste 102 Fircrest WA 98466-6030

TORKILDSON, RAYMOND MAYNARD, lawyer; b. Lake City, S.D., Nov. 19, 1917; s. Gustav Adolph and Agnes (Opitz) T.; m. Sharman Elizabeth Vaughn, Sept. 8, 1956; children—Stephen, Thomas. S.B., U. S.D., 1946; J.D., Harvard U., 1948. Bar: Calif. 1949, Hawaii 1950. Assoc. James P. Blaisdell, Honolulu, 1949-52; ptnr. Moore, Torkildson & Rice and successors, Honolulu, 1955-64; exec. v.p. Hawaii Employers Council, Honolulu, 1964-67; ptnr. Torkildson, Katz, Fonseca, Jaffe, Moore & Hetherington and predecessors, Honolulu, 1967-72, sr. ptnr., 1972-92, of counsel, 1993—. Mem. mgmt. com. Armed Forces YMCA, Honolulu, 1971; treas. Hawaii Republican Com. 1977-83. Served with U.S. Army, 1941-46; lt. col. Res. ret. Mem. ABA, Hawaii Bar Assn. Roman Catholic. Clubs: Oahu Country, Pacific (Honolulu).

TORLAKSON, JAMES DANIEL, artist; b. San Francisco, Feb. 19, 1951; s. Allen Daniel and Catherine Agnus (Leary) T.; 1 child, Elizabeth. BA with high distinction, Calif. Coll. Arts and Crafts, Oakland, 1973; MA, San Francisco State U., 1974. Fine artist/painter, printmaker, filmmaker Pacifica, Calif., 1971—; prof. of art Skyline Coll., San Bruno, Calif., 1982—, Coll. of San Mateo, Calif., 1986—, Calif. Coll. Arts and Crafts, 1978-85, City Coll. of San Francisco, 1996—. Solo exhibits include Horvath Gallery, Sacramento, Calif., 1993, Cudahy's Gallery, Inc., N.Y.C., 1992, John Berggruen Gallery, San Francisco, 1974, 78, 80, 83, 86, 88, 91, Concept Art Gallery, Pitts., 1987, Dubins Gallery, L.A., 1984, Mus. of Art, Carnegie Inst., Pitts., 1982, Getler/Pall, N.Y.C., 1981, others; mus. collections include San Francisco Mus. of Art, Oakland Mus., Achenbach Foun. for Graphic Arts/Calif. Palace of Legion of Honor, San Francisco, Bklyn. Mus., others.; contbr. to publs. Home: 433 Rockaway Beach Ave Pacifica CA 94044-3226

TORME, MARGARET ANNE, public relations executive, communications consultant; b. Indpls., Apr. 5, 1943; d. Ira G. and Margaret Joy (Wright) Barker; children—Karen Anne, Leah Vanessa. Student Coll. San Mateo, 1961-65. Pub. rels. mgr. Hoefer, Dieterich & Brown (now Chiat-Day), San Francisco, 1964-73; v.p., co-founder, creative dir. Lowry & Ptnrs., San Francisco, 1975-83; pres., founder Torme & Co. (now Torme & Kenney), San Francisco, 1983—; cons. in communications. Mem. Pub. Rels. Soc. Am., San Francisco C. of C. (outstanding achievement award for women entrepreneurs 1987), Jr. League (adv. bd.), Pub. Rsls Orgn. Internat. (v.p., dir.). Office: 545 Sansome St San Francisco CA 94111-2908

TORRACA, LOUIS A., JR., retired public relations executive; b. New Haven, May 13, 1935; s. Louis Anthony Sr. and Mary Elizabeth (Pyle) T.; m. Beryl Joyce Collins, Mar. 15, 1963. BS in Comm./Pub. Rels., Boston U.; MA in Journalism/Mass Comm., U. Okla. Commd. 2d lt. USAF, 1958, advanced through grades to Col., retired, 1983; pres. Internat. Pub. Rels. Ltd., Honolulu, 1983-89; assoc. fin. investment divsn. United Way, Honolulu, 1984-85; dir. Mayor's Office of Info. and Complaint, Honolulu, 1985-87; dir. comm. Dept. Edn., Honolulu, 1987-90; spl. asst. to the pres. Bishop Mus. Corp., Honolulu, 1991-96; ret., 1996; mem. comm. faculty Chaminade U. Honolulu, 1991—. Mem., sub-com. chair Gov.'s Traffic Safety Task Force; dir. Pkwy. Cmty. Assn.; mem. Armed Svcs. Bd. Mgmt.; bd. trustees Honolulu Theatre for Youth; bd. dirs. Play it Safe Internat.; mem. adv. com. Hawaii Criminal Justice Commn. Recipient Dept. Def. Superior Svc. medal, Legion of Merit, Bronze star, Meritorious Svc. medal with 1 oak leaf cluster, Air Force commendation with 3 oak leaf clusters. Mem. Pub. Rels. Soc. Am. (accredited, pres. Hawaii chpt. 1995—), Soc. Profl. Journalists, Internat. Assn. Bus. Communicators, Honolulu Press Club, Kappa Sigma, Tau Mu Epsilon, Kappa Tau Alpha. Episcopalian. Home: 184 Aikahi Loop Kailua HI 96734-1642

TORRANCE, ROBERT MITCHELL, comparative literature educator; b. Washington, May 9, 1939; s. Charles Mitchell and Ayma Jean (Sharpe) T.; m. Mildred D. Fischer, June 14, 1963 (div. July 1991); children: Benjamin Henry, Nicholas Aaron; m. Donna K. Reed, Aug. 24, 1991; stepchildren: Benjamin Reed-Lunn, Rebecca Reed-Lunn. BA Classics and English summa cum laude, Harvard U., 1961; MA in Comparative Lit., U. Calif., Berkeley, 1963; PhD in Comparative Lit., Harvard U., 1970. Asst. prof. comparative lit. Harvard U., Cambridge, 1971-75; assoc. prof. comparative lit. CUNY, Bklyn., 1975-76; prof. comparative lit. U. Calif., Davis, 1976—. Author: The Comic Hero, 1978, Ideal and Spleen, 1987, The Spiritual Quest, 1994; editor: Encompassing Nature, A Sourcebook, 1997; translator: Sophocles, The Women of Trachis and Philoctetes, 1966. Jr. fellow Soc. of Fellows, Harvard U., 1966-69, Humanities Inst. fellow U. Calif., Davis, 1990. Home: 2800 Corona Dr Davis CA 95616-0116 Office: U Calif Comparative Lit Program Davis CA 95616

TORRES, ESTEBAN EDWARD, congressman, business executive; b. Miami, Ariz., Jan. 27, 1930; s. Esteban Torres and Rena Baron (Gomez) T.; m. Arcy Sanchez, Jan. 22, 1955; children: Carmen D'Arcy, Rena Denise, Camille Bianca, Selina Andre, Esteban Adrian. Student, East Los Angeles Coll., 1960, Calif. State U., Los Angeles, 1963, U. Md., 1965, Am. U., 1966; PhD (hon.), Nat. U., 1987. Chief steward United Auto Workers, local 230, 1954-63, dir. polit. com., 1963; organizer, internat. rep. United Auto Workers (local 230), Washington, 1964; asst. dir. Internat. Affairs Dept., 1975-77; dir. Inter-Am. Bureau for Latin Am., Caribbean, 1965-67; exec. dir. E. Los Angeles Community Union (TELACU), 1967-74; U.S. ambassador to UNESCO, Paris, 1977-79; chmn. Geneva Grp., 1977-78; chmn. U.S. del. Gen. Conf., 1978; spl. asst. to pres. U.S., dir. White House Office Hispanic Affairs, 1979-81; mem. 98th-103rd Congresses from 34th Dist. Calif., 1983—, mem. appropriations com., subcom. fgn. ops., subcom. transp.; campaign coordinator Jerry Brown for Gov., 1974; Hispanic coordinator Los Angeles County campaign Jimmy Carter for Pres., 1976; mem. Sec. of State Adv. Group, 1979-81; v.p. Nat. Congress Community Econ. Devel., 1973-74; pres. Congress Mex.-Am. Unity, 1970-71, Los Angeles Plaza de la Raza Cultural Center, 1974; dir. Nat. Com. on Citizens Broadcasting, 1977; cons. U.S. Congress office of tech. assessment, 1976-77; del to U.S. Congress European Parliament meetings, 1984—; ofcl. congl. observer Geneva Arms Control Talks; chmn. Congl. Hispanic Caucus, 1987; speaker Wrights Del. to USSR, 1987; Dem. dep. Whip, 1990. Contbr. numerous articles to profl. jours. Co-chmn. Nat. Hispanic Dems., 1988—; chmn. Japan-Hispanic Inst. Inc.; bd. visitors Sch. Architecture U. Calif. at Los Angeles, 1971-73; bd. dirs. Los Angeles County Econ. Devel. Com., 1972-75, Internat. Devel. Conf., 1976-78; chmn. Congrl. Hispanic Caucus, 1985-86; pres. Plaza de la Raza Cultural Ctr., 1972-73; trustee Am. Coll. Paris, 1977-79. Served in AUS, 1949-53, ETO. Recipient Congrl. award Nat. Leadership award 1997. Mem. Americans for Dem. Action (exec. bd. 1975-77), VFW Post 6315, Pico Rivera, Calif., Am. Legion, Smithsonian Inst. (regent 1997—), S.W. Voter Inst. Office: House of Representatives Rayburn Bldg Rm 2269 Washington DC 20515-0005

TORREY, JAMES D., mayor, communications executive, consultant; b. Drayton, N.D., July 16, 1940; s. Howard J. Torrey and Gertrude (Carpenter) Steenson; m. Katherine Joann Kowal, Sept. 2, 1958; children: Tamara, Timonthy (dec.), Teresa, Todd. Student, U. Oreg., 1959-61. Mgr. Waldport (Oreg.) Food Market, 1959-67; dist. mgr. Obie Outdoor Advt., Aberdeen, Wash., 1967-68; dir. sales Obie Media Corp., Eugene, Oreg., 1968-71, exec. v.p., 1971-78, pres., CEO, 1980-88; pres., CEO Total Comm., Inc., Eugene, Oreg., 1989-91; N.W. area market mgr. 3M Nat. Advt., Eugene, Oreg., 1978-80; dir. mktg. State Accident Ins. Fund, Salem, Oreg., 1988-89; mem. exec. com. affiliate bd. Mut. Broadcasting, 1981-87. Pres. Waldport City Coun., 1962-67; coach Eugene Kidsports, 1968-92, Am. Softball Assn. Girls Softball Team, 1988; mem. adv. com. 4 J Sch. Dist., 1988-90; bd. dirs. Lane County United Way, 1983-86, dir., 1992, Lane County Goodwill Industries, 1989-90; mem. Eugene City Budget Com., 1992-94, Eugene City Coun., 1994-97; mayor City of Eugene, Oreg., 1997—. Named JCI senator, Oreg. State Jaycees, 1966, Citizen of Yr., City of Waldport, 1967, Outstanding Vol., City of Eugene, 1991. Mem. Oreg. Outdoor Advt. Assn. (pres. 1971-80), Oreg. Assn. Broadcasters (dir. 1984-87), Eugene C. of C. (bd. dirs., pres. 1991-92), Eugene Rotary (dir., pres. 1984, Paul Harris fellow 1985). Republican. Roman Catholic. Office: Mayor's Office 777 Pearl St Rm 105 Eugene OR 97401

TORREZ, NAOMI ELIZABETH, editor, librarian; b. Scranton, Pa., July 3, 1939; d. Sterling E. and Naomi (Reynolds) Hess; m. Lupe F. Torrez, Dec. 23, 1961; children: Sterling Edward, Stanley Marshall. BA, U. Ariz., 1961; MA, U. Calif., Berkeley, 1964, MLS, 1970; DRE, Golden State Sch. Theology, Oakland, Calif., 1988; cert. in travel industry, Vista C.C., 1993. Libr. asst. Oakland Pub. Libr., 1966-67, U. Calif. Libr., Berkeley, 1967-70; tutor-couns. Sonoma State Hosp., Eldridge, Calif., 1973-77, libr. tech. asst., 1977-79; health scis. libr. Kaiser Hosp., Vallejo, Calif., 1979-87; copyright rev. editor Kaiser Dept. Med. Editing, Oakland, 1987—; former instr. Bay Cities Bible Inst., Oakland; instr. Golden State Sch. Theology, Oakland, 1984—; participant Statewide Latino Congress, 1994. Author: Not in My Pew, 1990, GSST Research Manual, 1990; contbr. to Co-op Low Cost Cookbook, 1965. Active Albany 75th Anniversary Com., 1983, Women's Health Initiative, 1995—; officer Ariz. Fedn. of the Blind, Calif. Coun. of the Blind, 1959-66. Woodrow Wilson fellow, 1961; winner Nat. Spelling Bee, 1953; Nat. Merit scholar, 1957-61. Mem. Kaiser Permanente Latino Assn., Kaiser Affirmative Action Com., Kaiser Health Edn. Com., K.P. Regional Librs. Group (chair 1988), Phi Beta Kappa, Phi Kappa Phi. Baptist. Home: 1009 Murrieta Blvd # 15 Livermore CA 94550-4134 Office: Kaiser Dept Med Editing 1800 Harrison St Fl 16 Oakland CA 94612-3429

TORRISI, RALPH JOSEPH, labor union executive; b. Lawrence, Mass., Feb. 29, 1932; s. Sebastiano Edward and Nellie Marie (Laudani) T.; m. Mary Esperanza Guillen, June 26, 1954; children: Debra Ann Marie Torrisi Negrete, Denise Marie Bernadette Torrisi Nuno. Pres. Teamsters #296, San Jose, Calif., 1965-80, sec., treas., CEO, 1980—; sec., treas. Teamster Joint Coun. # 7, San Francisco, 1974—; mem. policy com. Western Conf. Teamsters, 1983-94. Mem. adv. bd. Santa Clara County Sheriff's Dept., San Jose, 1981—, reserve dep., 1994—; bd. dirs. State Compensation Ins. Fund, San Francisco, 1985—; trustee numerous pension and health trusts, 1972—. Sgt. USAF, 1951-55. Named Labor Man of Yr., Bay Area Union Labor Party, 1995. Mem. Calif. State Sheriffs' Assn. (charter), KC (various offices, award 1974), Capitol Club of Silicon Valley (charter). Democrat. Roman Catholic. Office: Teamsters Local Union # 296 Ste 322 3275 Steven Creek Blvd San Jose CA 95117

TOSTI, DONALD THOMAS, psychologist, consultant; b. Kansas City, Mo., Dec. 6, 1935; s. Joseph T. Tosti and Elizabeth M. (Parsons) Tosti Addison; m. Carol J. Curless, Jan. 31, 1957 (dec. 1980); children: Rene, Alicia, Roxanna, Brett, Tabitha, Todd Marcus; m. Annette Brewer, Dec. 29, 1989. BS in Elec. Engring., U. N. Mex., 1957, MS in Psychology, 1962, PhD in Psychology, 1967. Chief editor Teaching Machines Inc., Albuquerque, 1960-64; div. mgr. Westinghouse Learning Corp., Albuquerque, 1964-70; founder, sr. v.p. Ind. Learning Systems, San Raphael, Calif., 1970-74, pres., 1974-76; chmn. bd. Omega Performance, San Francisco, 1976-77; pres. Operants Inc., San Rafael, 1978-81; v.p. Forum corp., San Rafael, 1981-83; mng. ptnr. Vanguard Cons. Group, San Francisco, 1983—. Author: Basic Electricity, Advanced Algebra, Fundamentals of Calculus, TMI Programmed Series, 1960-63; Behavior Technology, 1970; A Guide to Child Development; Tactics of Communication; co-author: Learning Is Getting Easier, 1973; Introductory Psychology, 1981, Usibility Factors in Hardware and Software Design, 1982, Comparative Usibility, 1983, Performance Based Management, Positive Leadership, 1986, Strategic Alliances, 1990, The Professional Manager, 1995, Power and Governance, 1996. Mem. APA, Internat. Soc. for Performance Improvement (v.p. rsch. 1983-85, treas. 1997—, Outstanding Mem. award 1984, Life Membership award 1984, Outstanding Product award 1974). Home: 41 Marinita Ave San Rafael CA 94901-3443

TOTTINO, LESLIE, food products executive; b. 1956. Ptnr. Castroville (Calif.) Laundromat, 1969—, Ralph's Hardware, Castroville, 1969-93, Calif. Artichoke, Castroville, 1977—. Office: Ocean Mist Farms PO Box 1247 11500 Del Monte Ave Castroville CA 95012-3155*

TOUBER, JOSHUA SAMUEL, technology consultant; b. L.A., Feb. 28, 1963; s. Selwyn and Paula Harriett (Anderson) T. BS in Computer Sci., Dartmouth Coll., 1985. Sr. editor Encore Video, L.A., 1987-88, gen. mgr., 1989-91; v.p. ops. Xymox Sys., L.A., 1992-95; pres. Virtuosity, L.A., 1995—. Office: Virtuosity 520 Washington Blvd Ste 908 Marina Del Rey CA 90292

TOUCH, JOSEPH DEAN, computer scientist, educator; b. Bristol, Pa., Apr. 20, 1963; s. Ralph Benjamin and Filomena (Cianfrani) T. BS in Biophysics and Computer Sci., U. Scranton, 1985; MS in Computer Sci., Cornell U., 1987; PhD in Computer Sci., U. Pa., 1992. Cons., indsl. undergrad. rsch. participation program student GTE Labs., Inc., Waltham, Mass., 1983-85; cons. The Software Engring. Inst., Pitts., 1986; rsch. asst. Cornell U., Ithaca, N.Y., 1985-87; cons. Bell Comm. Rsch., Morristown, N.J., 1987-88; grad. rsch. fellow, AT&T Bell Labs. Rsch. assistantship U. Pa., Phila., 1988-92; cons. NASA Goddard Space Flight Ctr., Greenbelt, Md., 1992; computer scientist, project leader U. So. Calif. Info. Scis. Inst., Marina del Rey, Calif., 1992—; rsch. asst. prof. U. So. Calif., L.A., 1994—; mem. U. Scranton Acad. Computing Adv. Coun., 1983-85; univ. coun. com. on comm. U. Pa., 1989-90, com. on rsch. policy, 1990-91, acad. planning and budget com., 1990-91; reviewer various jours.; lectr. in field. Contbr. articles to profl. jours.; patentee in field. Mem. IEEE, Assn. for Computing Machinery (chpt. pres. 1984-85), IEEE Comm. Soc. (tech. program com. 1993), U. Scranton Phila. Alumni Soc. (v.p. 1990-91), Sigma Xi, Alpha Sigma Nu, Sigma Pi Sigma, Upsilon Pi Epsilon. Democrat. Roman Catholic. Home: 14005 Palawan Way Ph 23 Marina Del Rey CA 90292 Office: USC Info Scis Inst 4676 Admiralty Way Marina Del Rey CA 90292

TOUPIN, EDWARD BERNARD, engineer, mathematician and computer scientist; b. Houma, La., Mar. 2, 1964; s. Bernard Ovid and Edna Mae (Pennison) T. AAS, North Harris County Coll., Houston, 1986; BS in Math. and Computer Sci., Met. State Coll. of Denver, 1992. Bench tech. R&D Instrument Svcs., Inc., Houston, 1984-85; owner, technician Hi Res. Technologies, Houston, 1985-88; programmer/analyst Johnson & Higgins of Tex., Houston, 1988-89; programmer/analyst cons. Edward B. Toupin, Houston and Denver, 1988—; automation engr. Texaco Trading and Transp., Inc., Denver, 1990-96, tech. analyst, software engr., 1996—; tech. editor, author QED/John Wiley & Sons, Denver, 1993-94, Macmillan Pub., Indianapolis and Denver, 1993-95; cons. RTX, Inc., Denver and Loveland, Colo., 1994-95; contract developer Mabry Software, Inc., Seattle and Denver, 1995-96; condr. seminars in field; designer/developer comms. classes various software packages. Author: The Windows Expert System v1.01, 1992, Network Programming under VMS/DECNet Phases IV and V, 1993, Easy Programming with C, 1994, Easy Programming with Visual BASIC 4.0, 1995, Mabry Software's Internet Pack, 1996; lead author Special Edition, Using Turbo C 4.5 for Windows, 1995; contbg. author Visual BASIC 4.0 Expert Solutions, 1995, Building OCXs, 1995, Visual Basic 4 Unleashed, 1995, Visual Basic 4 Multimedia Adventure Set, 1995, Ultimate VB 4 Controls Sourcebook, 1995, Building Internet Applications with Visual C , 1995, Visual Basic Internet Programming, 1996, Windows Development Exchange, 1996, Developing Visual Basic 4 Communications Applications, 1996, Windows 95 Power Toolkit, 1996; tech. editor Visual C 1.5 by Example, 1994, Spl. Edition, Using C 2.0, 1994, Insider's Guide to Windows 95 Programming, 1995, VBA Database Solutions, 1996; inventor in field. Vol. toys for Denver Children's Hosp., 1993, 94. With USAF. Met. State Coll. Colo. Scholars awardee, 1991, 92. Mem. ACM, Microsoft Developers Network (Level 2), AI-CD Network, Am. Assn. Artificial Intelligence, Math. Assn. Am., The Internet Soc., Colo. Advanced Software Inst., Rocky Mountain Windows NT Users Group, U.S. Powerlifting Fedn., Gulf Coast Sailing Assn., Gulf Coast Cycling Assn., Golden Key. Roman Catholic.

TOUR, ROBERT LOUIS, ophthalmologist; b. Sheffield, Ala., Dec. 30, 1918; s. R.S. and Marguerite (Meyer) T.; m. Mona Marie Elien, Oct. 3, 1992. Chem.E., U. Cin., 1942, M.D., 1950. Intern, U. Chgo. Clinics, 1950-51; resident U. Calif. Med. Center-San Francisco, 1951-54; practice medicine, specializing in ophthalmology, occupational medicine and plasmapheresis, San Francisco, 1954-76, Fairbanks, Alaska, 1976-79, Phoenix, 1979—; clin. prof. ophthalmology U. Calif.-San Francisco, 1974-76. Maj. AUS, 1942-45. Diplomate Am. Bd. Ophthalmology. Fellow ACS, Am. Acad. Ophthalmology; mem. AMA, MENSA, Ariz. Ophthal. Soc., Phoenix Ophthal. Soc., Calif. Assn. Ophthalmology, Contact Lens Assn. Ophthalmologists, Pacific Coast Oto-Ophthal. Soc., Ariz. Med. Assn., Maricopa County Med. Soc. , F.C. Cordes Eye Soc., Masons, K.T., Lions, Shriners, Sigma Xi, Nu Sigma Nu, Alpha Tau Omega, Tau Beta Pi, Alpha Omega Alpha, Phi Lambda Upsilon, Omicron Delta Kappa, Kappa Kappa Psi. Home: 2201 E Palmaire Ave Phoenix AZ 85020-5633

TOURTELLOTTE, WALLACE WILLIAM, neurologist; b. Great Falls, Mont., Sept. 13, 1924; s. Nathaniel Mills and Frances Victoria (Charlton) T.; m. Jean Esther Toncray, Feb. 14, 1953; children: Wallace William, George Mills, James Millard, Warren Gerard. PhB, BS, U. Chgo., 1945, PhD, 1948, MD, 1951. Intern Strong Meml. Hosp. U. Rochester (N.Y.) Sch. Medicine and Dentistry, 1951-54; resident in neurology U. Mich. Med. Ctr., Ann Arbor, 1954-57, asst. prof. neurology, 1957-59, assoc. prof., 1959-66, prof., 1966-71; prof. UCLA, 1971—; prof. dept. neurology, 1996—; vis. assoc. prof. Washington U., St. Louis, 1963-64; mem. med. adv. bd. Nat. Multiple Sclerosis Soc., 1968—, So. Calif. Multiple Sclerosis Socs., 1972—; dir. Multiple Sclerosis Rsch. and Treatment Ctr., Nat. Neurol. Rsch. Specimen Bank, 1971—; vice chmn. dept. neurology UCLA, 1971-96, dir. brain rsch. inst.; chief neurology svc. West L.A. VA Med. Ctr., 1971—; Pritchard lectr., Belfast, Ireland, 1996. Editor: Multiple Sclerosis, Clinical and Pathogenetic Basis, 1997; mem. editorial bd. Jour. Neurol. Sci., Revue Neurologica, Italian Jour. Neurol. Sci., Multiple Sclerosis Jour. Lt. (j.g.) M.C., USN, 1952-54. Recipient Disting. Alumni Service award U. Chgo., 1982. Fellow Am. Acad. Neurology (S. Weir Mitchell Neurology Reseach award 1959); mem. Am. Assn. Univ. Neurol. Prof., Am. Neurol. Assn. (counselor 1982—, v.p. 1992), World Fedn. Neurology (founding mem.), Am. Assn. Neuropathologists, Internat. Soc. Neurochemistry (founding mem.), Am. Soc. Pharmacology and Exptl. Therapeutics, Am. Soc. Neurochemistry (founding mem.), Soc. Neurosci., Conferie de la Chaine des Rotisseur (chevalier Los Angeles chpt.), Argentier du Baillage de Los Angeles, Ordre Mondial des Gourmets Degustateurs Etats-Unis, Pasadena Wine and Food Soc., Physician Wine & Food Soc., Soc. Med. Friends of Wine, Sigma Xi. Republican. Presbyterian. Home: 1140 Tellem Dr Pacific Palisades CA 90272-2244 Office: West Los Angeles VA Med Ctr 11301 Wilshire Blvd Los Angeles CA 90073-1003

TOUSSAINT, CHRISTOPHER ANDRE, video producer, director, writer; b. Balt., Aug. 27, 1953; s. Andre Jean and Genevieve Stella (Drybola) T.; m. Nancy Jane Aasen, Aug. 6, 1988. BA in Speech and Dramatic Arts, U. Md., 1975. Film editor Joy Renchers Editl., Hollywood, Calif., 1988; sales mgr. 20/20 Video, Santa Monica, Calif., 1986-88; exec. dir., prodr. The Prodrs. Consortium, L.A., 1986-92; dir., prodr. Only New Age Music, L.A., 1988-91; editor, prodn. asst. Smith-Hemion Prodns., L.A., 1990-91; dir. acquisitions Lightworks Audio and Video, L.A., 1992-95; prodr., dir. Harry DeLigter Prodns., L.A., 1993—; advisor Creative Resources Guild, Santa Monica, 1990-92. Prodr., dir.: (video programs) Starflight, 1990 (Silver award Houston Film Festival 1990), Opening to Angels, 1994 (Telly award 1996, Angel award Excellence in Media 1995, award of Excellence, Film Adv. Bd. 1995), Free Energy: The Race to Zero Point, 1997, (video short) Columbus Go Home, 1992, (video documentary) Future Options, 1989. Mem. Internat. Documentary Assn., 1987-97, Union of Concerned Scientists, Cambridge, Mass., 1995-96. Mem. Nat. Assn. for the Self-Employed. Mem. Green Party. Home: 11720 La Maida St Valley Village CA 91607

TOVAR, NICHOLAS MARIO, mechanical engineer; b. Ogden, Utah, Jan. 18, 1960; s. Gerdo and Alice (Martinez) T.; m. Suzanne Oxborrow, Sept. 17, 1982; children: Ashley, Nicholas Brock, Clinton Gregory, Lance Edward, Marshall Prescott. BSME in Logistics Engring., Weber State U., 1986; BSME in Mech. Engring. and Mfg., Nat. U., 1990. Warehouseman R.C. Willey & Son Co., Syracuse, Utah, 1982-85; logistics contr. Utah-Idaho Supply Co., Salt Lake City, 1985-86; assoc. engr. Aerojet TechSystems Co., Sacramento, 1986-87, engr., 1988-89; mech. engr. Aerojet Solid Propulsion, Sacramento, 1990; sr. mech. engr. Aerojet Propulsion div. GenCorp, Sacramento, 1991-93, BP Chems. Adv. Materials Divsn., Stockton, 1993-94; dir. quality engring., indsl. testing Internat. (Akleinfelder Divsn.), 1994-95; project mgr. Siemens Transp. Systems, Sacramento, 1996—. Republican. Mormon. Home: 2360 Cobbleoak Ct Rancho Cordova CA 95670-4230 Office: Siemens Transp Systems divsn Kleinfelder Corp 7464 French Rd Sacramento CA 95828

TOWE, A. RUTH, museum director; b. Circle, Mont., Mar. 4, 1938; d. David and Anna Marie (Pedersen) James; m. Thomas E. Towe, Aug. 21, 1960; children: James Thomas, Kristofer Edward. BA, U. Mont., 1960; MA, Am. U., 1964. Bookkeeper, copywriter Sta. KGVO, Missoula, Mont., 1960-61; grad. asst. Sch. of Journalism U. Mont., Missoula, 1961-62; editorial asst. Phi Gamma Delta mag., Washington, 1964; reporter The Chelsea (Mich.) Standard, 1965-66; dir. Mont. Nat. Bank, Plentywood, 1966-73; bookkeeper, legal sec. Thomas E. Towe, Atty. of Law, Billings, Mont., 1967-68; dir. Mont. Nat. Bank, Browning, 1972-73; mus. exec. dir. The Moss Mansion Mus., Billings, 1988—. Mem. Mont. Coun. of Family Rels. & Devel., 1970; pres. Mont. Assn. of Symphony Orchs., 1987-88; sheriff Yellowstone Corral of Westerners, Billings, 1993; v.p. Yellowstone Hist. Soc.; vice-chmn. Yellowstone Dem. Ctrl. Com., Billings, 1983-84; judge flower show Nat. Coun. State Garden Clubs; mem. Billings Friends Mtg., 1986—. Mem. AAUW, PEO, Mus. Assn. Mont. (pres. 1990-92, bd. dirs. 1989—), Jr. League, Theta Sigma Phi (hon.). Office: The Moss Mus 914 Division St Billings MT 59101-1921

TOWER, KATHLEEN RUTH, librarian, consultant; b. St. Paul, May 26, 1945; d. Einar Egon and Justina (Janzen) Nelson; m. John William Tower, June 23, 1973 (dec. Mar. 1977); 1 child, Susan Christine. BME, U. Denver, 1967, MA, 1968; PhD, Tex. Woman's U., 1995. Libr. Western State Coll., Gunnison, Colo., 1968-70; substitute tchr. Sch. Dist. # 51, Grand Junction, Colo., 1970-71; news rm. libr. The Daily Sentinel, Grand Junction, 1971-72; spl. collections libr. Mesa State Coll., Grand Junction, 1972—. Rsch. fellow Mus. Western Colo., 1996. Mem. AAUW (v.p. membership 1982-84), ALA, Colo. Libr. Assn. (divsn. sec. 1978, 90), Delta Kappa Gamma (treas. Xi chpt. 1994—).

TOWNER, LARRY EDWIN, consulting company executive; b. Gallup, N.Mex., Sept. 27, 1937; s. Edwin Robert and Esther Kathryn (Kern) T.; m. D. Yvonne Turner, Mar. 12, 1966; children: Kristina Kay, Jennifer Kate. BS in Tech. Mgmt., Am. U., Washington, 1976. Project mgr. Wolf Research, Houston, 1965-66, Gulton SRG, Arlington, Va., 1966-67; dep. for database devel. USN, Washington, 1967-79; mgr., BTP teleprocessing RCA, Cherry Hill, N.J., 1979-80; mgr., data base adminstrn., solid state div. RCA, Somerville, N.J., 1980-82; mgr., systems devel. Hughes Aircraft, El Segundo, Calif., 1982-89; pres. TCSI, Richland, Wash., 1989—. Author: Ads/Online Cookbook, 1986, A Professionals Guide, 1989, Case: Concepts and Implementation, 1989, Oracle: The Professionals Reference, 1991; contbr. articles to profl. jours. Treas. Va. Hills Recreation Assn., Alexandria, 1970-72, pres. 1975-77; active Civil Air Patrol, Alexandria, 1968-79; bd. dirs. Northwest Citizens Radio Emergency Service, Spokane, Wash., 1960-63. Recipient Meritorious Service award Civil Air Patrol, 1976. Mem. IDMS User Assn. (bd. dirs., Outstanding Svc. award 1984, Hall of Fame award 1992), Amateur Radio Relay League, Assn. for Sys. Mgmt. (v.p. Columbia chpt. 1993, pres. 1994), Richland Rotary Club, Hughes Mgmt. Club. Methodist. Home and Office: TCSI 266 Adair Dr Richland WA 99352-9453

TOWNES, CHARLES HARD, physics educator; b. Greenville, S.C., July 28, 1915; s. Henry Keith and Ellen Sumter (Hard) T.; m. Frances H. Brown, May 4, 1941; children: Linda Lewis, Ellen Screven, Carla Keith, Holly Robinson. B.A., B.S., Furman U., 1935; M.A., Duke U., 1937; Ph.D., Calif. Inst. Tech., 1939. Mem. tech. staff Bell Telephone Lab., 1939-47; assoc. prof. physics Columbia U., 1948-50, prof. physics, 1950-61; exec. dir. Columbia Radiation Lab., 1950-52, chmn. physics dept., 1952-55; provost and prof. physics MIT, 1961-66, Inst. prof., 1966-67; v.p., dir. research Inst. Def. Analyses, Washington, 1959-61; prof. physics U. Calif., Berkeley, 1967-86, 94, prof. physics emeritus, 1986-94, prof. grad. sch., 1994—; Guggenheim fellow, 1955-56; Fulbright lectr. U. Paris, 1955-56, U. Tokyo, 1956; lectr., 1955, 60; dir. Enrico Fermi Internat. Sch. Physics, 1963; Richtmeyer lectr. Am. Phys. Soc., 1959; Scott lectr. U. Cambridge, 1963; Centennial lectr. U. Toronto, 1967; Lincoln lectr., 1972-73, Halley lectr., 1976, Krishnan lectr., 1992, Nishina lectr., 1992, Rajiv Gandhi lectr., 1997; dir. Gen. Motors Corp., 1973-86, Perkin-Elmer Corp., 1966-85; mem. Pres.'s Sci. Adv. Com., 1966-69, vice chmn., 1967-69; chmn. sci. and tech. adv. com. for manned space flight NASA, 1964-69; mem. Pres.'s Com. on Sci. and Tech., 1976; researcher on nuclear and molecular structure, quantum electronics, interstellar molecules, radio and infrared astrophysics. Author: Making Waves, 1996, (with A.L. Schawlow) Microwave Spectroscopy, 1955; author, co-editor: Quantum Electronics, 1960, Quantum Electronics and Coherent Light, 1964; editorial bd.; Rev. Sci. Instruments, 1950-52, Phys. Rev., 1951-53, Jour. Molecular Spectroscopy, 1957-60, Procs. Nat. Acad. Scis., 1978-84, Can. Jour. Physics, 1995—; contbr. articles to sci. publs.; patentee masers and lasers. Trustee Calif. Inst. Tech., Carnegie Instn. of Washington, Grad. Theol. Union, Calif. Acad. Scis.; mem. corp. Woods Hole Oceanographic Instn. Decorated officier Légion d'Honneur (France); recipient numerous hon. degrees and awards including Nobel prize for physics, 1964; Stuart Ballantine medal Franklin Inst., 1959, 62; Thomas Young medal and prize Inst. Physics and Phys. Soc., Eng., 1963; Disting. Public Service medal NASA, 1969; Wilhelm Exner award Austria, 1970; Niels Bohr Internat. Gold medal, 1979; Nat. Sci. medal, 1983, Berkeley citation U. Calif., 1986; named to Nat. Inventors Hall of Fame, 1976, Engring. and Sci. Hall of Fame, 1983; recipient Common Wealth award, 1993, ADION medal Observatory Nice, 1995. Fellow IEEE (life, Medal of Honor 1967), Am. Phys. Soc. (pres. 1967, Plyler prize 1977), Optical Soc. Am. (hon., Mees medal 1968, Frederick Ives medal 1996), Indian Nat. Sci. Acad., Calif. Acad. Scis.; mem. NAS (coun. 1968-72, 78-81, chmn. space sci. bd. 1970-73, Comstock award 1959, Carty medal 1962), Am. Philos. Soc., Am. Astron. Soc., Am. Acad. Arts and Scis., Royal Soc. (fgn. mem.), Russian Acad. Scis. (fgn. mem.), Pontifical Acad. Scis., Max-Planck Inst. for Physics and Astrophysics (fgn. mem.), N.Y. Acad. Scis. (hon. life). Office: U Calif Dept Physics Berkeley CA 94720

TOWNLEY, CHARLES THOMAS, librarian, educator; b. Oklahoma City, Okla., Feb. 7, 1946; s. Max Henry and Helen Betty (Hawk) T.; m. Joyce Wiedler Nissley, May 22, 1988. BA, U. Okla., 1968, MLS, 1969; MA, U. Calif., Santa Barbara, 1975; PhD, U. Mich., 1983. Asst. libr. U. Calif., Santa Barbara, 1969-72; asst. project dir., dir. Nat. Indian Edn. Assn. Libr. Project, Mpls., 1972-75; lectr. U. Mich., Ann Arbor, 1976-78; head libr. Pa. State U., Middletown, 1979-90; dean New Mex. State U., Las Cruces, 1990—; cons. Dept. Interior Libr., Washington, 1976-80; team mem. Mid. States Assn., Phila., 1989-95. Author: Human Relations in Library Network Development, 1988; contbr. articles to profl. jours. Rackham fellow U. Mich., 1975-79; grantee Dept. Edn., 1988; recipient Founders award Am. Indian Libr. Assn., 1997, Disting. Alumnus award U. Okla., 1997. Mem. ALA (chair, councilor 1972-76, Disting. Svc. award 1976), Internat. Fedn. Libr. Assns. (sect. chair 1991-93), N.Mex. Consortium of Acad. Librs. (pres. 1994-95), Rotary (com. chair 1993—), Beta Phi Mu. Democrat. Episcopalian. Home: 1766 Vista Montana Las Cruces NM 88005-6264 Office: NMex State U Box 300006 Dept 3475 Las Cruces NM 88003

TOWNSEND, ALVIN NEAL, artist; b. Rock Island, Tex., Oct. 26, 1934; s. Archie Lee and Synthia Ellen (Westbrook) T.; m. Phyllis Virginia Keyes, jan. 15, 1955 (div. Apr. 20, 1960); 1 child, Phyllis Lynn; m. Betsy Rose Brown, June 23, 1960; children: Brita, Lissi, Shana, Kristinn. BFA, U. N.Mex., 1961, MA in Fine Arts, 1962. Profl. artist pvt. studio, Albuquerque, 1958—; instr. art N.E. La. State Coll., Monroe, 1962; base crafts dir. Spl. Svcs. Arts and Crafts, Sandia Base, N.M., 1962-69; post crafts dir. Spl. Svcs. Arts and Crafts, Ft. Belvoir, Va., 1969-70; prof. art edn. U. N.M., Albuquerque, 1970-91; vis. instr. ceramics Vancouver (Can.) Sch. of Art, 1972; vis. prof. art U. No. Ariz., Flagstaff, 1984; cons., Albuquerque, Santa Fe, Flagstaff, 1970—. With USN, 1953-57. Democrat. Home: 2583 Ramirez Rd SW Albuquerque NM 87105 Studio: Harwood Art Ctr Albuquerque NM 87102

TOWNSEND, RUSSELL HENRY, lawyer; b. Ft. Lewis, Wash., Dec. 27, 1949; s. Peter Lee and Irma Matilda (Greisberger) T.; m. Patricia Susan Parks, Feb. 9, 1985; children: Alexander Peter, Jennifer Sabrina. BS, Calif. Maritime Acad., 1971; JD, Lincoln U., San Francisco, 1979. Bar: Calif., U.S. Dist. Ct. (no. and ea. dists.) Calif. Title examiner Western Title Ins. Co., Oakland, Calif., 1971-74; clk. Garrison, Townsend, Hall and predecessor, San Francisco, 1974-79; ptnr. Amberg & Townsend, San Francisco, 1980-83, Townsend and Bardellini, San Francisco, 1983-87, Townsend, Bardellini, Townsend and Wechsler, San Francisco, 1988-92. Lt.j.g. USNR, 1971-75. Mem. ABA, State Bar Calif., Marin County Bar Assn. Republican. Home: 5 Mae Ct Novato CA 94947-1961 Office: Townsend Law Offices 2169 Francisco Blvd E Ste D San Rafael CA 94901-5531

TOWNSEND, SANDRA LYNNETTE, nurse; b. Boise, Idaho, Nov. 16, 1957; d. Edward Elmo and Betty Jean (Maus) Letney; m. Richard Wayne Townsend, Apr. 2, 1982; 1 child, Mallory Jean. BSN, Boise State U., 1992. CNA. From claims approver to internal auditor, asst. supr. John Hancock Ins. Co., 1978-88; oncology/BMT unit nurse St Luke's Regional med. Ctr., Boise, 1993—, patient care coord. oncology unit, 1995—. Singer-dancer Mayors and Minors, Nampa, Idaho, 1988. Mem. Idaho Nurses Assn. (membership dir. 1993, treas. 1994—), Oncology Nurses So. Idaho (pres. 1995-96). Republican. Home: 11101 Hummingbird Dr Boise ID 83709-1371

TOWNSEND, STORM DIANA, sculptor; b. London, Aug. 31, 1937; came to U.S., 1963; d. Douglas Arthur and Winnifred Lilian (Collinson) T. BFA, London U., 1955, MFA, nat. diploma in design, 1962. Cert. art tchr. Instr. basic sculpture and ceramics Marlebone Inst., England, 1962; tech. asst. Nambe Mills Bronze Foundry, Santa Fe, 1968-70, Shidoni Bronze Foundry, Santa Fe, 1970-74; instr. sculpture Coll. Santa Fe, 1974-75; instr. sculpture U. Albuquerque, 1976-78, instr. basic design 2 and 3 dimensional, 1979-83; instr. adult beginning drawing Albuquerque Arts Ctr., 1977-78; instr. pvt. studio classes, 1977-78; instr. adult beginning and intermediate sculpture U. N.Mex. Community Coll., 1979-83; contractor to mold and cast dinosaur, fossil, and skeleton's for N.Mex. Mus. Natural History, 1986, 87, 88, 91. One-woman shows include Joya de Taos Gallery, Taos, N.Mex., 1965, Maitland-Stokes Gallery, Santa Fe, 1966, West Gallery, Santa Fe, 1970, Gallery Marquis, Denver, 1972, Discovery Gallery, Santa Fe, 1975, Gallery Eleven, Lubbock, Tex., 1976, Kimo Gallery, Albuquerque, 1984, Am. Inst. Architects, N. Mex., 1991; exhibited in group shows at Fine Arts Mus. N.Mex., Santa Fe, 1972, 1976, Atlanta Arts Mus., 1982, Salmagundi Club, N.Y.C., 1984, Gallery 16 East, N.Y.C., 1986, N.M.S.F. Fine Arts Gallery, Albuquerque, N.Mex., 1987, Coll. of Santa Fe, N.Mex., 1988, Gov. Gallery State Capital, Santa Fe, N.Mex., 1989, Rio Grande Outdoor Sculpture Show, N.Mex., 1991 and others; represented in permanent collections Genesse County Mus., Rochester, N.Y., 1983, City of Albuquerque, N.Mex., 1983, Sunwest Bank, N.Mex., 1988. Recipient First Prize Sculpture award N.Mex. Art League Exhibition, 1966; Resident fellow Jajasan Siswa Lokantara of Indonesia, 1960-61, Huntington Hartford Found., 1963, Helen Wurlitzer Found., 1964; grantee London County Coun., 1959. Home: PO Box 1165 Corrales NM 87048-1165

TOZER, WILLIAM EVANS, entomologist, educator; b. Binghamton, N.Y., July 7, 1947; s. William Evans and Gertrude Genevieve (Lewis) T. BS in Natural Sci., Niagara U., 1969; MS in Biology, Ball State U., 1979; PhD in Entomology, U. Calif., Berkeley, 1986. Cert. C.C. biology and zoology tchr. Calif. Jr. H.S. sci. and English tchr. St. Patricks Sch., Corning, N.Y., 1969-71; tchg. asst. biology Ball State U., Muncie, Ind., 1974-76; pvt. practice biol. eviron. cons. Berkeley, Calif., 1976-79, 86-88; rsch. asst. U. Calif., Berkeley, 1979-86; dept. head tng. USN Disease Vector Ecology and Control Ctr., Poulsbo, Wash., 1988—; mem., acting chmn. San Francisco Bay Area Mosquito Control Coun., Alameda, 1988-96; vice chmn. com., mem. Armed Forces Pest Mgmt. Bd., Washington, 1994—. Editor (field handbook) Navy Environmental Health Center, 1994; contbr. articles to profl. jours. With U.S. Army, 1971-73. Mem. Am. Entomol. Soc., Sigma Xi. Home: 1407 NW Santa Fe Ln Apt 304 Silverdale WA 98383 Office: USN Disease Vector Ecol Control Ctr 19950 7th Ave NE Ste 201 Poulsbo WA 98370-7405

TRABITZ, EUGENE LEONARD, aerospace company executive; b. Cleve., Aug. 13, 1937; s. Emanuel and Anna (Berman) T.; m. Caryl Lee Rine, Dec. 22, 1963 (div. Aug. 1981); children: Claire Marie, Honey Caryl; m. Kathryn Lynn Bates, Sept. 24, 1983; 1 stepchild, Paul Francis Rager. BA, Ohio State U., 1965. Enlisted USAF, 1954, advanced through grades to maj.; served as crew commdr. 91st Stragetic Missile Div., Minot, S.D., 1968-70; intelligence officer Fgn. Tech. Div., Dayton, Ohio, 1970-73; dir. external affairs Aero Systems Div., Dayton, 1973-75; program mgr. Air Force Armament Div., Valparaiso, Fla., 1975-80; dir. ship ops. Air Force Ea. Test Range, Satellite Beach, Fla., 1980-83; dep. program mgr. Air Force Satellite Text Ctr., Sunnyvale, Calif., 1983-84; ret., 1984; sr. staff engr. Ultrasystems Inc., 1984-86; pres. TAWD Systems Inc., Palo Alto, Calif., 1986-92, Am. Telenetics Co., San Mateo, Calif., 1992—; cons. Space Applications Corp., Sunnyvale, 1986-87, Litton Computer Svcs., Mountain View, Calif., 1987-91, Battelle Meml. Inst. Columbus, 1993—. V.p. Bd. County Mental Health Clinic, Ft. Walton Beach, Fla., 1973-75. Decorated Bronze Star. Mem. DAV (life), World Affairs Coun., U.S. Space Found. (charter), Air Force Assn. (life), Assn. Old Crows, Nat. Sojourners, Commonwealth Club Calif., Masons (32 degree). Home: 425 Anchor Rd Apt 317 San Mateo CA 94404-1058

TRACY, JAMES JARED, JR., accountant, law firm administrator; b. Cleve., Jan. 17, 1929; s. James Jared and Florence (Comey) T.; m. Elizabeth Jane Bourne, June 30, 1953 (div. 1988); children: Jane Mackintosh, Elizabeth Boyd, James Jared IV, Margaret Gardiner; m. Judith Anne Cooper, Feb. 18, 1989. AB, Harvard U., 1950, MBA, 1953. CPA, Ohio. Acct., mgr. Price Waterhouse & Co., Cleve., 1953-65; treas., CFO Clevite Corp., Cleve., 1965-69; asst. treas. Republic Steel Corp., Cleve., 1969-70, treas., 1970-75; v.p., treas. Johns-Manville Corp., Denver, 1976-81; v.p., treas., CFO I. T. Corp., L.A., 1981-82; exec. dir. Hufstedler, Miller, Carlson & Beardsley, L.A., 1983-84, Shank, Irwin & Conant, Dallas, 1984-85, Pachter, Gold & Schaffer, L.A., 1985-86; v.p., sr. cons. Right Assocs., L.A., 1987-91; dir. adminstrn. Larson & Burnham, Oakland, Calif., 1991-95; retired Larson & Burnham, 1995; adminstrv. dir. Law Offices of Thomas E. Miller, Newport Beach, Calif., 1996—; trustee and v.p. Miss Hall's Sch., Pittsfield, Mass., 1970-78; dir. Union Commerce Bank, Cleve., 1971-76; adv. bd. mem. Arkwright-Boston Ins. Co., Boston, 1976-81. Trustee and v.p. Cleve. Soc. for Blind, 1965-76; trustee Western Res. Hist. Soc., Cleve., 1972-76; treas. St. Peters by the Sea Presbyn. Ch., Palos Verdes, Calif., 1981-91. Recipient Alumni award Harvard U., Denver, 1981. Mem. AICPA, Ohio Soc. CPAs, Assn. Legal Adminstrs., Piedmont Montclair Rotary Club (pres. 1995-96), Harvard Club San Francisco, Harvard Bus. Sch. Club No. Calif. Home: 2204 Fortuna Newport Beach CA 92660-4011

TRAFTON, STEPHEN J., bank executive; b. Mt. Vernon, Wash., Sept. 17, 1946; m. Diane Trafton; children: John, Roland. BS in Zoology, Wash. State U., 1968. V.p., mgr. dept. money market Seattle-First Nat. Bank, 1968-79; v.p., mgr. bank consulting group Donaldson Lufkin Jennrette, N.Y.C., 1980; exec. v.p., treas. Gibraltar Savings Bank, L.A., 1980-84; banking cons., 1984-86; v.p., treas. Hibernia Bank, San Francisco, 1986-88; sr. v.p., treas. Goldome Bank, Buffalo, N.Y., 1988-90; sr. exec. v.p., CFO Glenfed Inc., 1990-91, vice chmn., CFO, 1991—, pres., 1992—; sr. exec. v.p., CFO Glendale Fed. Bank, 1990-91, vice chmn., CFO, 1991, pres., COO, 1991-92, chmn. bd., pres., CEO, 1992—, also bd. dirs. Mem. Phi Eta Sigma. Office: Glendale Fed Bank 414 N Central Ave Glendale CA 91203-2002

TRAGER, RUSSELL HARLAN, advertising consultant; b. Cambridge, Mass., Sept. 26, 1945; s. Nathan Allan and Shirley (Gibbs) T.; m. V. Jan Adams, Aug. 19, 1968 (div. July 1975); 1 child, Eric Todd; m. Edna Marie Sanchez, Feb. 16, 1980; children: Felice Rosanne, Justin Tomas. AA, Newton Jr. Coll., 1965; BS, U. Miami, 1968; postgrad., Harvard U., 1968-69. Account rep. Hervic Corp., Sherman Oaks, Calif., 1972-75, Canon USA, Lake Success, N.Y., 1975-78; key account sales rep. Yashica Inc., Glendale, Calif., 1978-79; sales rep. Region I United Pubs. Corp., Beverly Hills, Calif., 1979-81, sales mgr., 1981-83; regional pres. United Pubs. Corp., Carson, Calif., 1983-86, region v.p., 1986-88; v.p. sales United Pubs. Corp. divsn. of Nynex Co., El Segundo, Calif., 1988-91; dir. sales Yelex Corp., L.A., 1991-92; sales mgr. Trader Pub. Co., L.A., 1992-93; cons. Russ Trager & Assocs., Manhattan Beach, Calif., 1994—. Home and Office: Russ Trager & Assocs 1201 11th St Manhattan Beach CA 90266-6025

TRAM, KENNETH KHAI KT, internist; b. Saigon, Vietnam, Oct. 29, 1961; came to U.S., 1978; s. Felix Ngan and Lisa Hong (Pham) T.; m. Christine Tram-Hong Tran, June 19, 1993. BS summa cum laude, U. Calif., Irvine, 1984; MD, UCLA, 1988. Diplomate Am. Bd. Internal Medicine, Am. Bd. Geriatric Medicine. Resident in internal medicine UCLA-San Fernandy Valley, 1988-91; geriatric medicine fellow UCLA Sch. Medicine, 1992-94; clin. instr./assoc. investigator Sepulveda (Calif.) VA Med. Ctr., 1991-94, acting med. dir., 1994; internist Facey Med. Group, Sepulveda, 1994—. Contbr. articles to profl. jours. Mem. CPAG/CHOMS, Calif., 1991—. Recipient Solomon Scholars Resident award UCLA Sch. Medicine, 1991, Nat. Kidney Found. Fellowship award, 1991-92, VA Rsch. and Devel. Career Devel. award, 1992-94. Mem. ACP, AAAS, AMA, Am. Soc. for Bone and Mineral Rsch., U.S. Table Tennis Assn., Nat. Geog. Soc., Mus. Heritage Soc. Home: 6 Malaga Irvine CA 92614-7304 Office: Facey Medical Group Inc 11211 Sepulveda Blvd Mission Hills CA 91345-1115

TRANER, NORMAN, food products executive. Grower Organo Farms, Orange County, Calif., 1961-74; sec., treas. Eco Farms Avocados, Inc., Temecula, Calif., 1974—. Office: Eco Farm Corp 28790 Las Haciendas St Temecula CA 92590-2614*

TRANQUADA, ROBERT ERNEST, medical educator, physician; b. Los Angeles, Aug. 27, 1930; s. Ernest Alvro and Katharine (Jacobus) T.; m. Janet Martin, Aug. 31, 1951; children: John Martin, James Robert, Katherine Anne. B.A., Pomona Coll., 1951; M.D., Stanford U., 1955; D.Sc. (hon.), Worcester Poly. Inst., 1985. Diplomate Am. Bd. Internal Medicine. Intern in medicine UCLA Med. Center, 1955-56, resident in medicine, 1956-57; resident Los Angeles VA Hosp., 1957-58; fellow in diabetes and metabolic diseases UCLA, 1958-59; fellow in diabetes U. So. Calif., 1959-60, asst. prof. medicine, 1960-63, assoc. prof., 1964-68, chmn. dept. community medicine, 1967-70; med. dir. Los Angeles County/U. So. Calif. Med. Center, 1969-74; regional dir. Central Region, Los Angeles County Dept. Health Services, 1974-76; assoc. dean UCLA Sch. Medicine, 1976-79; chancellor and dean U. Mass. Med. Sch., 1979-86; dean U. So. Calif. Sch. Medicine, 1986-91; prof. medicine U. So. Calif., L.A., 1986-92, Norman Topping/Nat. Med. Enterprises prof. med./pub. policy, 1992-97; prof. emeritus, 1997—. mem., chair L.A. County Task Force on Health Care Access, 1992-94. Trustee Pomona Coll., 1969—, vice chmn., 1987-91, chmn., 1991—; mem. bd. fellow Claremont U. Ct., 1971-79, 91—; bd. trustees Grad. Inst. Applied Life Scis., Claremont U., 1997—, vice-chmn., 1997—; corporator Worcester Art Mus., 1980-86; bd. dirs. Nat. Med. Fellowships, Inc., 1973—, chmn., 1980-85; trustee Charles Drew U. Med. and Sci., 1968-79, 86-95, Orthopaedic Hosp., 1986-91, Barlow Hosp., 1987-89; bd. dirs. Worcester Acad., 1984-86, U. So. Calif. Univ. Hosp., 1988-91, Alliance for Childrens Rights, 1991-95; bd. dirs. Good Hope Med. Found., 1994—; mem. Ind. Commn. on L.A. Police Dept., 1991-92; mem. governing bd. L.A. County Local Initiative Health Authority, 1994—. Milbank faculty fellow, 1967-72. Fellow AAAS, Am. Antiquarian Soc.; mem. AMA, Am. Diabetes Assn., Western Soc. Clin. Investigation, Los Angeles County Med. Assn., Los Angeles Acad. Medicine, Calif. Med. Assn., Inst. Medicine of Nat. Acad. Scis., Phi Beta Kappa, Sigma Xi, Alpha Omega Alpha. Office: U So Calif VKC # 368A Los Angeles CA 90089-0041

TRAPP, GERALD BERNARD, journalist; b. St. Paul, May 7, 1932; s. Bernard Edward and Lauretta (Mueller) T.; m. Bente Joan Moe, Jan. 29, 1954; children—Eric Gerald, Lise Joan, Alex Harold. B.A., Macalester Coll., St. Paul, 1954. Editor Mankato (Minn.) Free Press, 1954-57; with AP, 1957-80; nat. broadcast exec. charge sales AP, East of Miss., 1966-68; gen. broadcast news editor AP, N.Y.C., 1968-79; dep. dir. broadcast services AP, 1979-80, liaison broadcast networks, 1968-80; v.p., gen. mgr. Intermountain Network, Salt Lake City, 1980-87; v.p., dir. mktg. Travel Motivation, Inc., Salt Lake City, 1987-88; ops./program mgr. Mountain Cable Network, Inc., Salt Lake City, 1988-89; sr. v.p. Travel Motivation, Inc., Salt Lake City, 1990-92; mktg. specialist Morris Travel, 1992-95, pricing analyst, 1995—. Bd. dirs. Westminster Coll. Found. Mem. Radio TV News Dirs. Assn., Oratorio Soc. Utah (bd. dirs.), Pro Musica, Sigma Delta Chi. Mem. United Ch. Christ. Home: 785 Three Fountains Cir # 17 Salt Lake City UT 84107-5085 Office: 240 Morris Ave Salt Lake City UT 84115-3223

TRASK, ROBERT CHAUNCEY RILEY, author, lecturer, foundation executive; b. Albuquerque, Jan. 2, 1939; s. Edward Almon Trask and Florence Jane (White) Jones; m. Katie Lucille Bitters (div. 1981); m. Mary Jo Chiarottino, Dec. 1, 1984; 1 child, Chauncey Anne. Student pub. schs., San Diego. Lic. master sea capt. Entertainer, singer, comedian, 1964--; founder, pres. Nat. Health & Safety Svcs., San Francisco, 1968-71, ARAS Found., Issaquah, Wash., 1978—; capt., dive master San Diego Dive Charters, 1972-75; sr. capt., dive master Pacific Sport Diving Corp., Long Beach, Calif., 1975-77; lectr., bus. cons., 1978—; cons., tng. developer Nissan, Gen. Dynamics, AT&T, religious orgns., also other corps., 1978--. Author: (manual) Tulip, 1971, Living Free, 1982, God's Phone Number, 1987, (video program for adolescents) Breaking Free, also seminar manuals. Mem. SAG. Office: ARAS Found # 93 3020 Issaquah Pine Lk Rd SE Issaquah WA 98029

TRAUGOTT, ELIZABETH CLOSS, linguistics educator and researcher; b. Bristol, Eng., Apr. 9, 1939; d. August and Hannah M.M. (Priebsch) Closs; m. John L. Traugott, Sept. 26, 1967; 1 dau., Isabel. BA in English, Oxford U., Eng., 1960; PhD in English lang., U. Calif., Berkeley, 1964. Asst. prof. English U. Calif., Berkeley, 1964-70; lectr. U. East Africa, Tanzania, 1965-66, U. York, Eng., 1966-67; lectr., then assoc. prof. linguistics and English Stanford U., Calif., 1970-77, prof., 1977—, chmn. linguistics dept., 1980-85; vice provost, dean grad. studies Stanford U., 1985-91, mem. grad. record examinations bd., 1989-93, mem. test of English as a fgn. lang. bd., 1989-91, chmn. test of English as a fgn. lang. bd., 1991-92; mem. higher edn. funding coun. Eng. Assessment Panel, 1996. Author: A History of English Syntax, 1972, (with Mary Pratt) Linguistics for Students of Literature, 1980, (with Paul Hopper) Grammaticalization, 1993; editor: (with ter Meulen, Reilly, Ferguson) On Conditionals, 1986, (with Heine) Approaches to Grammaticalization, 2 vols., 1991; contbr. numerous articles to profl. jours. Am. Coun. Learned Socs. fellow, 1975-76, Guggenheim fellow, 1983-84, Ctr. Advanced Study of Behavioral Scis. fellow, 1983-84. Mem. MLA, AAUP, AAUW, Linguistics Soc. Am. (pres. 1987, sec.-treas. 1994—), Internat. Soc. Hist. Linguistic (pres. 1979-81). Office: Stanford Univ Dept Linguistics Bldg 460 Stanford CA 94305-2150

TRAVERS, JUDITH LYNNETTE, human resources executive; b. Buffalo, Feb. 25, 1950; d. Harold Elwin and Dorothy (Helsel) Howes; m. David Jon Travers, Oct. 21, 1972; 1 child, Heather Lynne. BA in Psychology, Barrington Coll., 1972; cert. in paralegal course, St. Mary's Coll., Moraga, Calif., 1983; postgrad., Southland U., 1982-84. Exec. sec. Sherman C. Weeks, P.A., Derry, N.H., 1973-75; legal asst. Mason-McDuffie Co., Berkeley, Calif., 1975-82; paralegal asst. Blum, Kay, Merkle & Kauftheil, Oakland, Calif., 1982-83; CEO, bd. dirs. Dela Pers. Svcs. Inc., Concord, Calif., 1983—; pres. All Ages Sitters Agy., Concord, 1986-95; CEO, bd. dirs. Guardian Security Agy., Concord, Calif., 1992—; sec., bd. dirs. TK Allied Systems, Inc., Per Diem Staffing Systems, Inc. Vocalist record album The Loved Ones, 1978. vol. local Congl. campaign, 1980, Circle of Friends, Children's Hosp. No. Calif., Oakland, 1987—; mem. Alameda County Sheriff's Mounted Posse, 1989, Contra Costa Child Abuse Prevention Coun., 1989; employer adv. coun. Ctrl. Contra Costa County, 1993—. Mem. NAFE, Am. Assn. Respiratory Therapy, Soc. for Human Resource Mgmt., Am. Mgmt. Assn., Gospel Music Assn., Palomino Horse Breeders Am., DAR, Barrington Oratorio Soc., Commonwealth Club Calif., Nat. Trust Hist. Preservation, Alpha Theta Sigma. Republican. Baptist. Home: 3900 Brown Rd Oakley CA 94561-2664 Office: Delta Pers Svcs Inc 1820 Galindo St Ste 3 Concord CA 94520-2447

TRAVIS, LUCINDA LOUISE, display designer, writer, editor; b. Holdrege, Nebr., June 28, 1948; d. Dale Edward Travis and Betty Louise (Watts) Travis McCreadie. Cultural diploma, U. Stranieri di Perugia, Italy, 1969, ITESM, Monterey, Mex., 1969, U. Granada, Spain, 1971; BA in Italian, UCLA, 1970; cultural diploma, U. Salamanca, Spain, 1971; BA in Spanish with high honors, Calif. State Coll., San Bernardino, 1972; MEd., U. Hawaii, 1975. Cert. secondary tchr., Calif. Producer, dir. promotions, programming Hawaii Pub. TV KHET, Honolulu, 1972-78; producer, writer Direcion Gen. Radio, TV y Cinemagrafia del Gobierno de Mex., Mexico City, 1978-80; dir. World's Children's Art Exhbn., L.A., 1983-89; coord. grant applications ind. filmmaker program Am. Film Inst., L.A., 1982-87; creative/pub. rels. specialist Ohio Art, Bryan, 1987-90; product designer Hama, Inc., Nokøbing Mors, Denmark, 1991-96; editor Wee Deliver newsletter for Office of Literacy U.S. Postal Svc., Washington, 1991-93; instr. Payap Coll., Chiang Mai, Thailand, 1983, 84; designer, curator traveling mus. exhibit Gumby Exhibit, 1991-92; programming cons. Internat. Mass-Comm. Svc., Kvinesdal, Norway, 1984. Author: (poetry) Aire y Alma, 1971, Animation: A Resource Book, 1986; co-editor: Film/Television: Grants, Scholarships and Special Programs, 1985; patentee beading system for craft market. Speaker for various svc. and ednl. orgns.; Bible study tchr. Presbyn. and Bapt. Chs., Ontario, Calif., Bryan, Ohio, 1982-91; vol. missionary refugee work Am. Bapt. Chs., Thailand. Calif. Arts Coun. grantee, 1985. Mem. Alpha Gamma Delta.

TRAVOUS, KENNETH E., state agency administrator. Exec. dir. Ariz. State Parks Bd., Phoenix. Office: Ariz State Parks Bd 1300 W Washington Phoenix AZ 85007

TRAXLER, BUCK, newspaper editor; b. Missoula, Mont., Jan. 9, 1948; s. Jack Eugene and Dorothy (Shepherd) T.; m. Elizabeth Marie Traxler, Apr. 15, 1972 (div. 1984). Degree in photography, San Diego City Coll., 1974. Editor Phillips County News, Malta, Mont., 1985-86, Independent Observer, Conrad, Mont., 1986—. Ctrl. committeeman Rep. Party, Conrad, 1988—. With USN, 1968-72. Decorated Meritorious Unit commendation, Nat. Def. Svc. medal, Combat Action ribbon. Mem. Conrad C. of C. (pres. 1991, 93), Conrad Crimestoppers (sec. 1988-91), Pondera Golf Club (v.p., dir. 1990-93), Lions (sec. 1995-96), Moose, VFW. Home: 616 S Delaware Conrad MT 59425 Office: Independent Observer PO Box 966 Conrad MT 59425

TRAYLOR, WILLIAM ROBERT, publisher; b. Texarkana, Ark., May 21, 1921; s. Clarence Edington and Seba Ann (Talley) T.; m. Elvirez Sigler, Oct. 9, 1945; children: Kenneth Warren, Gary Robert, Mark Daniel, Timothy Ryan. Student, U. Houston, 1945-46, U. Omaha, 1947-48. Div. mgr. Lily-Tulip Cup Corp., N.Y.C., 1948-61; asst. to pres. Johnson & Johnson, New Brunswick, N.J., 1961-63; mgr. western region Rexall Drug & Chem. subs. Dart Industries, L.A., 1963-67; pres. Prudential Pub. Co., Diamonds Springs, Calif., 1967—; cons. to printing industry, 1976—; syndicated writer (under pseudonym)s. Bill Friday's Bus. Bull., 1989—. Author: Instant Printing, 1976 (transl. into Japanese), Successful Management, 1979, Quick Printing Encyclopedia, 1982, 7th edit., 1988, How to Sell Your Product Through (Not to) Wholesalers, 1980; pubr. Professional Estimator and Management Software for Printing Industry, 1992, Small Press Printing Encyclopedia, 1994. With USCG, 1942-45. Named Man of Yr. Quick Printing Mag., 1987. Mem. Nat. Assn. Quick Printers (hon. lifetime), C. of C., Kiwanis, Toastmasters. Democrat.

TRAYNOR, GARY EDWARD, association administrator; b. Ponca City, Okla., Aug. 7, 1944; s. Paul Edward and Berniece Dolores (Hanon) T. Diploma, Ponca City Bus. Coll., 1963. Acctg. supr. Army Air Force

Exch. Svc., Norton AFB, Calif., 1966-94; charities chmn. Fraternal Order Eagles, 1995-96, sec. San Bernardino (Calif.) Aerie 506, 1996—. Mem. Am. Philatelic Soc., Smithsonian Instn. (assoc.). Republican. Baptist. Home: 7706 Golondrina Dr San Bernardino CA 92410 Office: San Bernardino Aerie 506 Fraternal Order Eagles 895 E 9th St San Bernardino CA 92410

TRAYNOR, J. MICHAEL, lawyer; b. Oakland, Calif., Oct. 25, 1934; s. Roger J. and Madeleine (Lackmann) T.; m. Shirley Williams, Feb. 11, 1956; children: Kathleen Traynor Millard, Elizabeth Traynor Fowler, Thomas. B.A., U. Calif., Berkeley, 1955; J.D., Harvard U., 1960. Bar: Calif. 1961, U.S. Supreme Ct. 1966. Dep. atty. gen. State of Calif., San Francisco, 1961-63; spl. counsel Calif. Senate Com. on Local Govt., Sacramento, 1963; assoc. firm Cooley Godward, LLP, San Francisco, 1963-69, ptnr., 1969—; adviser 3d Restatement of Unfair Competition, 1988-95, 3d Restatement of Torts; Products Liability, 1992—, Apportionment, 1994—, 1988 Revs. 2d Restatement of Conflict of Laws, 2d Restatement of Restitution, 1981-85; lectr. U. Calif. Boalt Hall Sch. Law, Berkeley, 1982-89, 1996—; chmn. Sierra Club Legal Defense Fund, 1989-91, pres. 1991-92, adv. bd., 1996—, Trust for Pub. Land, 1997—. Mem. bd. overseers Inst. for Civil Justice The RAND Corp., 1991-97; bd. dirs. Environ. Law Inst., 1992—, Sierra Legal Defence Fund, 1990-96. Served to 1st lt. USMC, 1955-57. Fellow AAAS, Am. Bar Found. (life); mem. Am. Law Inst. (coun. 1985—, 2d v.p. 1993—), Bar Assn. San Francisco (pres. 1973). Home: 3131 Eton Ave Berkeley CA 94705-2713 Office: Cooley Godward LLP 1 Maritime Plz Ste 2000 San Francisco CA 94111-3580

TRAYNOR-KAPLAN, ALEXIS ELAINE, biomedical researcher; b. Chgo., Aug. 22, 1952; d. Gerald Edmund and Ruth Eleanor (Fritsche) Traynor; m. Richard Jay Kaplan. BS, U. Mich., 1974; PhD, U. Calif., San Diego, 1979. Postdoctoral fellow The Salk Inst., San Diego, 1979-83; rsch. assoc. The Scripps Rsch. Inst., La Jolla, Calif., 1984-88; asst. rsch. biochemist U. Calif., San Diego, 1989-90, asst. prof., 1990-95; assoc. prof., 1995—; founder Inologic, 1996. Contbr. articles to profl. jours., chpts. to books. Recipient Miles and Shirley Fiterman Basic Rsch. award AGA Found., 1994; grantee NIH, Washington, 1994. Mem. AGA, Internat. Soc. Immunomodulation (charter mem.), Internat. Soc. Neurochemistry, Am. Soc. Biochemistry and Molecular Biology, Gastroenterology Rsch. Group. Office: U Calif San Diego The Whittier Inst 9894 Genesee Ave La Jolla CA 92037-1221

TREADWAY-DILLMON, LINDA LEE, athletic trainer, actress; b. Woodbury, N.J., June 4, 1950; d. Leo Elmer and Ona Lee (Wyckoff) Treadway; m. Randall Kenneth Dillmon, June 19, 1982. BS in Health, Phys. Edn. & Recreation, West Chester State Coll., 1972, MS in Health and Phys. Edn., 1975; postgrad., Ctrl. Mich. U., 1978; Police Officer Stds. Tng. cert. complaint dispatcher, Goldenwest Coll., 1982. Cert. in safety edn. West Chester State Coll.; cert. EMT, Am. Acad. Orthopaedic Surgeons. Grad. asst., instr., asst. athletic trainer West Chester (Pa.) State Coll., 1972-76; asst. prof., program dir., asst. athletic trainer Ctrl. Mich. U., Mt. Pleasant, 1976-80; police dispatcher City of Westminster, Calif., 1980-89; oncology unit sec. Children's Hosp. Orange County, Orange, Calif., 1989-96; control clk. food & beverage Marriott Hotel, Anaheim, Calif., 1996—. Stuntwoman, actress United Stunt Artists, SAG, L.A., 1982—; dancer Disneyland, Anaheim, Calif., 1988—; contbr. articles to profl. jours. Athletic trainer U.S. Olympic Women's Track and Field Trials, Frederick, Md., 1972, AAU Jr. World Wrestling Championships, Mt. Pleasant, Mich., 1977, Mich. Spl. Olympics, Mt. Pleasant, 1977, 78, 79. Named Outstanding Phys. Educator, Delta Psi Kappa, Ctrl. Mich. U., 1980, Outstanding Young Woman of Am., 1984; named to Disneyland Entertainment Hall of Fame, 1995. Mem. SAG, Nat. Athletic Trainers Assn. (cert., women and athletic tng. ad hoc com. 1974-75, placement com. 1974-79, program dirs. coun. 1976-80, ethics com. 1977-80, visitation team 1978-80, 25 Yr. award 1997), U.S. Field Hockey Assn. (player), Pacific S.W. Field Hockey Assn. (player, Nat. Champion 1980, 81, 82), L.A. Field Hockey Assn. (player), Swing Shift Dance Team (dancer). Presbyterian. Home: 15400 Belgrade St Apt 152 Westminster CA 92683-6962

TREASTER, MELBA MAUCK, education consultant; b. Langdon, Kans., Dec. 10, 1929; d. Phillip Alvis and Bessie F. (Holmes) Mauck; m. W. Arlen Treaster, Dec.16, 1950 (dec. Nov. 1985); children: Paul Arlen, Andrew Philip. BA in Edn., Sterling (Kans.) Coll., 1951; MS in Psychology, Emporia State U., 1964. Cert. elem. tchr., reading endorsement, Colo. Elem. tchr. Union Five Sch., Reno County, Kans., 1951-52, Sterling (Kans.) Pub. Schs., 1952-53; kindergarten tchr. sub Lucas (Kans.) Pub. Schs., 1956-61; elem. tchr. Sunny Grove Sch., Atchison County, Kans., 1963-64; H.S. tchr. English/social studies Atchison County Cmty. H.S., Effingham, Kans., 1964-67; chpt. I tchr./supr. Poudre Sch. Dist., Ft. Collins, Colo., 1967-90; ednl. cons. Ft. Collins, 1990—; developer, demonstrator Prior Project Nat. Diffusion Network, 1979-81; presentor nat., regional profl. confs. Internat. Reading Assn., 1983-92. Co-author: (videos) Reading Aloud to Children, 1989, Listening to Children Read, 1990. Elder Westminster Presbyn. Ch., Ft. Collins, 1989-91; bd. dirs. Ft. Collins READ-Aloud, 1994—. Recipient Recognition award Chpt. I/Title I, U.S. Dept. Edn., Washington, 1990. Mem. ASCD, Internat. Reading Assn. (local pres., chair Colo. Commn., 1965—), Nat. Dissemination Assn. Home: 3414 Seneca B Fort Collins CO 80526

TREECE, JAMES LYLE, lawyer; b. Colorado Springs, Colo., Feb. 6, 1925; s. Lee Oren and Ruth Ida (Smith) T.; m. Ruth Julie Treece, Aug. 7, 1949 (div. 1984); children—James (dec.), Karen Treece, Teryl Wait, Jamilyn Smyser, Carol Crowder. Student Colo. State U., 1943, Colo. U., 1943, U.S. Naval Acad., 1944-46; B.S., Mesa Coll., 1946; J.D., U. Colo., 1950; postgrad. U. N.C., 1976-77. Bar: Colo. 1952, U.S. Dist. Ct. Colo. 1952, U.S. Ct. Appeals (10th cir.) 1952, U.S. Supreme Ct. 1967. Assoc., Yegge, Hall, Treece & Evans and predecessors, 1951-59, ptnr., 1959-69; U.S. atty., Colo., 1969-77; pres. Treece & Bahr and predecessor firms, Littleton, Colo., 1977-91; mcpl. judge, 1967-68; mem. faculty Nat. Trial Advocacy Inst., 1973-76, Law-Sci. Acad., 1964. Chmn. Colo. Dept. Pub. Welfare, 1963-68; chmn. Colo. Dept. Social Services, 1968-69; mem. Littleton Bd. Edn., 1977-81. Served with USNR, 1944-46. Recipient awards Colo. Assn. Sch. Bds., 1981, IRS, 1977, FBI, 1977, DEA, 1977, Fed. Exec. Bd., 1977. Mem. Fed. Bar Assn. (pres. Colo. 1975, award 1975), Colo. Bar Assn. (bd. govs.), Denver Bar Assn. (v.p., trustee). Republican. Episcopalian. Home: 12651 N Pebble Beach Dr Sun City AZ 85351-3327

TREGLE, LINDA MARIE, dance educator; b. Fort Sill, Okla., Sept. 8, 1947; d. Franklin and Helen Marie (Diggs) T. BA, Mills Coll., Stockton, Calif., 1970, MA, 1974; life credential, U. Calif., 1974. founder, dir., choreographer Internat. Studios, Inc., Stockton, 1970—; dance instr. San Joaquin Delta Coll., Stockton, 1970—; program cons., choreographer Alpha Kappa Alpha, Stockton, 1984—, choreographer SDW Motion Pictures, Stockton, 1983—; advisor Internat. Dance Club San Joaquin, 1970—; founder, dir. Tregles Internat. Dance Co., 1970—; mem. Ruth Beckford's Dance Studio. Directed and choreographed numerous dance prodn. videos. Mem. NAACP, Black Employment Trends (community rep. 1988—), Calif. Tchrs. Assn., Alpha Kappa Alpha. Home: 2411 Arden Ln Stockton CA 95210-3256 Office: San Joaquin Delta Coll 5151 Pacific Ave Stockton CA 95207-6304

TRELOAR, HARRIETTE ELLEN, lawyer; b. Mpls., Feb. 21, 1950; d. Alan Edward and Dorothy Elizabeth (Buchanan) T. BA, Oberlin Coll., 1972; JD, U. Calif., Davis, 1976. Bar: Calif. 1977. Legis. rsch. asst. U.S. Senate (John V. Tunney), Washington, 1971-73; law clk. Yolo County Superior Ct., Woodland, Calif., 1975-77; asst. regional counsel U.S. Dept. Health and Human Svcs., San Francisco, 1978—. Author, editor: (book) University of California, Law Review, 1974-75, 75-76. Chair adv. bd. Volunteers-in-Parole, San Francisco, 1989-95. Recipient Exemplary Svc. award U.S. Surgeon Gen., 1993. Mem. Calif. Women Lawyers (bd. gov. 1994—, sec. 1996-97), Queen's Bench (bd. dirs. 1994—, sec. 1996, 1st v.p. 1997). Democrat.

TREMBLAY, WILLIAM ANDREW, English language educator; b. Southbridge, Mass., June 9, 1940; s. Arthur Achille and Irene (Fontaine) T.; m. Cynthia Ann Crooks, Sept. 28, 1962; children: William Crooks, Benjamin Philip, John Fontaine. BA, Clark U., 1962, MA, 1969; MFA in Poetry, U. Mass., 1972. English tchr. Southbridge (Mass.) High Sch., 1962-63, Sutton (Mass.) High Sch., 1963-65, Tantasqua Regional High Sch., Sturbridge, Mass., 1965-67; asst. prof. Leicester (Mass.) Jr. Coll., 1967-70; teaching asst. U. Mass., Amherst, 1970-72; instr. Springfield (Mass.) Coll., 1972-73; prof. English Colo. State U., Fort Collins, 1973—, dir. MFA program in creative writing; Fulbright-Hays lectureship, Lisbon, Portugal, 1979, NEH summer program, 1981; mem. program dirs. coun. Associated Writing Programs, Norfolk, Va., 1984-86. Author: The June Rise: The Apocryphal Letters of Antoine Janis, 1994, (poetry) Duhamel: Ideas of Order in Little Canada, 1986, other books; editor-in-chief: Colo. Rev., 1983-91. Summer writing fellow Corp. of Yaddo, 1989, Creative Writing fellow Nat. Endowment for Arts, 1985; recipient Pushcart prize Pushcart Prize Anthology, 1987. Mem. Puerto del Sol (bd. advisors). Home: 3412 Lancaster Dr Fort Collins CO 80525-2817 Office: Colo State U Dept English Fort Collins CO 80523

TREMBLY, CRISTY, television executive; b. Oakland, Md., July 11, 1958; d. Charles Dee and Mary Louise (Cassidy) T. BA in Russian, German and Linguistics cum laude, W.Va. U., 1978, BS in Journalism, 1978, MS in Broadcast Journalism, 1979; advanced cert. travel, West L.A. Coll., 1982; advanced cert. recording engring., Soundmaster Schs., North Hollywood, Calif., 1985. Videotape engr. Sta. WWVU-TV, Morgantown, W.Va., 1976-80; announcer, engr. Sta. WVVW Radio, Grafton, W.Va., 1979; tech. dir., videotape supr. Sta. KMEX-TV, L.A., 1980-85; broadcast supr. Sta. KADY-TV, Oxnard, Calif., 1988-89; news tech. dir. Sta. KVEA-TV, Glendale, Calif., 1985-89; asst. editor, videotape technician CBS TV Network, Hollywood, Calif., 1989-90; videotape supr. Sta. KCBS-TV, Hollywood, 1990-91, mgr. electronic news gathering ops., 1991-92; studio mgr., engr.-in-charge CBS TV Network, Hollywood, 1992—; radio operator KJ6BX Malibu Disaster Comm., 1987—. Prodr. (TV show) The Mountain Scene, 1976-78. Sr. orgn. pres. Children of the Am. Revolution, Malibu, Calif., 1992—; chmn. adminstrv. coun. Malibu United Meth. Ch., 1994—; sec., mem. adv. com. Tamassee (S.C.) Sch., 1992—; vol. Ch. Coun., L.A. Riot Rebldg., Homeless shelter work, VA Hosps., Mus. docent; sponsor 3 overseas foster children. Named one of Outstanding Young Women of Am., 1988; recipient Asst. editor Emmy award Young and the Restless, 1989-90, Golden Mike award Radio/TV News Assn., 1991, 92. Mem. ATAS (mem. exec. com. on electronic prodn. 1992—, mem. nat. awards com. 1994—), DAR (state chair jr. membership 1987-88, state chair scholarships 1992-94, state chmn. jr. contest 1994-96, others, Malibu chpt. regent 1991, state chair motion pictures radio and TV Calif. 1988-90, Mex. 1990—, Nat. Outstanding Jr. 1993, nat. vice-chair broadcast media 1995—), Am. Women in Radio and TV (so. Calif. bd. 1984-85, 93-95, pres.-elect 1995-96, pres. 1996-97), Soc. Profl. Journalists, Women in Comms., Travelers Century Club (program chair 1987—), Soc. Broadcast Engrs. (1995—), Mensa (life), Soc. Motion Picture/TV Engrs. (pres. 1995—), Beta Sigma Phi. Democrat. Methodist. Home: 2901 Searidge St Malibu CA 90265-2969 Office: CBS TV City 7800 Beverly Blvd Los Angeles CA 90036-2165

TREMBOUR, FRED WILLIAM, foreign service officer, metallurgist; b. Watervliet, N.Y., Sept. 19, 1912; s. Max Rudolf and Margaret Rose (Ellinger) T.; m. Margaret Culbertson (div. June 1951); children: Richard, William; m. Mary Leone Egerman, Dec. 1, 1951; children: Alice, Karla Trembour Irvin. BS in Metall. Engring., Carnegie Inst. Tech., 1940; postgrad., U. Colo., 1971-73. Rsch. engr. Westinghouse Electric & Mfg. Co., East Pittsburgh, Pa., 1938-42; prodn. engr. Ferrotherm Co., Cleve., 1942-46; fgn. svc. officer Dept. Commerce, Dept. War, USIA, Dept. Def., Dept. State, various locations, 1946-69; rsch. assoc. U.S. Geol. Survey Dating Lab., Denver, 1974—; rsch. affiliate U. Colo. Inst. Arctic and Alpine Rsch., Boulder, 1988—. Contbr. articles to profl. jours. Carnegie Inst. Tech. scholar. Mem. AAAS, Archaeol. Inst. Am. Democrat. Home: 365 S 43d St Boulder CO 80303

TRENARY, RALPH HIRAM, III, federal agency administrator, human resources manager; b. Hardtner, Kans., June 20, 1961; s. Ralph Hiram Trenary Jr. and Ardath Ann (Bruner) Meyer; m. Holly Ann Hershman, June 15, 1985; children: Caroline, Erik. BA, U. No. Colo., 1985. Exec. adminstrv. asst. Mortgage Plus, Inc., Denver, 1989-90; adminstrv. officer Colo. Nat. Guard, Fed. Civil Svc., Aurora, Colo. Springs, 1990-93; human resources mgr. Fed. Civil Svc., Englewood, 1993-96; tng. adminstr. Ft. Carson, Colo., 1996—. 1st lt. U.S. Army, 1985-89; capt. Colo. NG, 1993-95. Democrat. Home: 1390 Masthead Way Monument CO 80132-9005 Office: Colo Regional Tng Inst Bldg 6286 Fort Carson CO 80913-6600

TRENBERTH, KEVIN EDWARD, atmospheric scientist; b. Christchurch, New Zealand, Nov. 8, 1944; came to U.S., 1977; s. Edward Maurice and Ngaira Ivy (Eyre) T.; m. Gail Neville Thompson, Mar. 21, 1970; children: Annika Gail, Angela Dawn. BSc with honors, U. Canterbury, Christchurch, 1966; ScD, MIT, 1972. Meteorologist New Zealand Meteorol. Service, Wellington, 1966-76, supt. dynamic meteorology, 1976-77; assoc. prof. meteorology U. Ill., Urbana, 1977-82, prof., 1982-84; scientist Nat. Ctr. Atmospheric Research, Boulder, Colo., 1984-86, sr. scientist, 1986—, leader empirical studies group, 1987, head sect. climate analysis, 1987—; dep. dir. climate and global dynamics divsn. Nat. Ctr. Atmospheric Rsch., Boulder, Colo., 1991-95; mem. joint sci. com. for world climate programme, com. climate changes and the ocean Tropical Oceans Global Atmosphere Program Sci. Steering Group, 1990-94; mem. Climate Variability and Predictability Sci. Steering Group, 1995—, co-chair, 1996—. Editor: Climate System Modeling, 1992, Earth Interactions, 1996—; contbr. articles to profl. jours. Grantee NSF, NOAA, NASA. Fellow Am. Meteorol. Soc. (editor sci. jour. 1981-86, com. chmn. 1985-87, Editor's award 1989), AAAS (coun. del. sect. atmosphere and hydrosphere sci. 1993-97), Royal Soc. New Zealand (hon.); mem. NAS (earth scis. com. 1982-85, tropical oceans global atmosphere adv. panel 1984-87, polar rsch. bd. 1986-90, climate rsch. com. 1987-90, global oceans atmosphere land sys. panel 1994—), Atmosphere Obs. Panel of Globe Climate Observing Sys., Meterol. Soc. New Zealand. Home: 1445 Landis Ct Boulder CO 80303-1122 Office: Nat Ctr Atmospheric Research PO Box 3000 Boulder CO 80307-3000

TRENT, DONALD STEPHEN, thermo fluids engineer; b. Cloverdale, Oreg., Mar. 29, 1935; s. James Charles and Emma (Bauer) T.; (div. Jan., 1986); children: Steve, Lynn Trent Wooldridge, Greg; m. Alta Mae Brown, Aug. 20, 1994. BSAE, Oregon State U., 1962, MSME, 1964, PhD in Mech. Engring., 1972. Chief scientist (emeritus) Battelle Meml. Inst., Richland, Wash., 1965-96; retired, 1996, cons., 1996—; cons. in field, 1996—; courtesy prof. Oreg. State U., Corvallis, 1987—; rsch. affiliate MIT, Cambridge, Mass., 1990—; mem. tchg. staff Wash. State U., Richland, 1991—; vis. U. Md., College Park, 1995—. Sgt. U.S. Army, 1958-61. Recipient Fed. Lab. Consortium award, 1992. Mem. ASME, Phi Kappa Phi, Sigma Xi. Home: 721 Lynnwood Loop Richland WA 99352

TRENTALANGE, JOHN JOSEPH, counselor, educator; b. Waterbury, Conn., Apr. 20, 1959; s. John Pasqual and Regina Ann (Obarowski) T. BS, U. Oreg., 1991; MA, U. Colo., 1996. Bookkeeper House of Ruth, East L.A., 1989-90; pre-sch. tchr. U. Oreg., Eugene, 1990-91; crisis counselor The Compass Ctr., Seattle, 1991-94; therapist A Children's Counsel Ctr., Colorado Springs, 1994—; counselor Univ. Oreg. Base Program, Eugene, 1990-91; rsch. asst. Oreg. Rsch. Inst., Eugene, 1990-91; case aide DSHS, Bellevue, Wash., 1992-94; CCP instr. Inst. Bus., Colorado Springs, 1994-96; child advocate Jacob Ctr., Colorado Springs, 1994—. Home: 144 Crystal Pk Rd # 3 Manitou Springs CO 80829

TRESELER, KATHLEEN MORRISON, retired nursing educator; b. Tacoma, Wash., Apr. 28, 1925; d. Charles T. and Elizabeth M. (McDermott) Morrison; m. Donald K. Treseler, July, 1949; children: Michael S., C. Maureen, Patrick A. BS, Seattle Coll., 1946; MSN, U. Wash., 1966. Prof. Seattle U. Sch. Nursing, 1968-91, prof. emeritus, 1991—. Author: Clinical Laboratory and Diagnostic Tests, 1982, 3d edit., 1995. Home: 17401 17th Pl NE Shoreline WA 98155-5201

TREVITHICK, RONALD JAMES, underwriter; b. Portland, Oreg., Sept. 13, 1944; s. Clifford Vincent and Amy Lois (Turner) T.; m. Delberta Russell, Sept. 11, 1965; children: Pamela, Carmen, Marla, Sheryl. BBA U. Wash., 1966. CLU, CPA, ChFC, accredited estate planner. Mem. audit staff Ernst & Ernst, Anchorage, 1966, 68-70; pvt. practice acctg., Fairbanks, Alaska, 1970-73; with Touche Ross & Co., Anchorage, 1973-78, audit ptnr., 1976-78; exec. v.p., treas., bd. dirs. Veco Internat., Inc., 1978-82; pres., bd. dirs. Petroleum Contractors Ltd., 1980-82; bd. dirs. P.S. Contractors A/S, Norcon, Inc., OFC of Alaska, Inc., V.E. Systems Svcs., Inc., Veco Turbo Services, Inc., Veco Drilling, Inc., Vemar, Inc., 1978-82; with Coopers & Lybrand, Anchorage, 1982-85; field underwriter, registered rep. New York Life Ins., 1985—; instr. acctg. U. Alaska, 1971-72; lectr. acctg. and taxation The Am. Coll., 1972, instr. adv. sales Life Underwriters Tng. Coun., 1988-89; bd. dirs. Ahtna Devel. Corp., 1985-86. Div. chmn. United Way, 1975-76, YMCA, 1979; bd. dirs., fin. chmn. Anchorage Arts Coun., 1975-78, Am. Diabetes Assn., Alaska affiliate, 1985-91, chmn. bd. 1988-89, chmn. hon. bd. 1992-96, Am. Heart Assn., Alaska affiliate, 1986-87, Anchorage dist. com., 1994-96, treas. 1996—. With dist. com., treas. Alaska State Youth Soccer Assn.; mem. Anchorage Estate Planning Coun., 1996—. With U.S. Army, 1967-68. Mem. Fin. Execs. Inst. (pres. Alaska chpt. 1981-83), Am. Soc. CLUs & ChFCs (v.p. Alaska chpt. 1993-94, pres. 1994-96), Alaska Assn. Life Underwriters (sec., treas. 1987-90), Alaska Planned Giving Counc., Beta Alpha Psi. Clubs: Alaska Goldstrikers Soccer (pres. 1992-93), Petroleum (treas. 1996—). Home: 4421 Huffman Rd Anchorage AK 99516-2211 Office: 1400 W Benson Blvd Anchorage AK 99503-3660

TRIBBLE, RICHARD WALTER, brokerage executive; b. San Diego, Oct. 19, 1948; s. Walter Perrin and Catherine Janet (Miller) T.; m. Joan Catherine Sliter, June 26, 1980. BS, U. Ala., Tuscaloosa, 1968; student, Gulf Coast Sch. Drilling Practices, U. Southwestern La., 1977. Stockbroker Shearson, Am. Express, Washington, 1971-76; ind. oil and gas investment sales, Falls Church, Va., 1976-77; pres. Monroe & Keusink, Inc., Falls Church and Columbus, Ohio, 1977-87; instnl. investment officer FCA Asset Mgmt., 1983-85; fin. cons. Merrill Lynch Pierce, Fenner & Smith, Inc., Phoenix, 1987—, cert. fin. mgr., 1989—, sr. fin. cons., 1992—, asst. v.p., 1993—. Served with USMC, 1969-70. Republican. Methodist. Office: 2525 E Camelback Rd Phoenix AZ 85016-4219

TRIEWEILER, TERRY NICHOLAS, justice; b. Dubuque, Iowa, Mar. 21, 1948; s. George Nicholas and Anne Marie (Oastern) T.; m. Carol M. Jacobson, Aug. 11, 1972; children: Kathryn Anne, Christina Marie, Anna Theresa. BA, Drake U., 1970, JD, 1972. Bar: Iowa 1973, Wash. 1973, U.S. Dist. Ct. (so. dist.) Iowa 1973, U.S. Dist. Ct. (we. dist.) Wash. 1973, Mont. 1975, U.S. Dist. Ct. Mont. 1977. Staff atty. Polk County Legal Services, Des Moines, 1973; assoc. Hullin, Roberts, Mines, Fite & Riveland, Seattle, 1973-75, Morrison & Hedman, Whitefish, Mont., 1975-77; sole practice, Whitefish; justice Mont. Supreme Ct., Helena, 1991—; lectr. U. Mont. Law Sch., 1981—; mem. com. to amend civil proc. rules Mont. Supreme Ct., Helena, 1984, commn. to draft pattern jury instrns., 1985; mem. Gov.'s Adv. Com. on Amendment to Work Compensation Act, adv. com. Mont. Work Compensation Ct. Mem. ABA, Mont. Bar Assn. (pres. 1986-87), Wash. Bar Assn., Iowa Bar Assn., Assn. Trial Lawyers Am., Mont. Trial Lawyers Assn. (dir., pres.). Democrat. Roman Catholic. Home: 1615 Virginia Dale St Helena MT 59601-5823 Office: Mont Supreme Ct 414 Justice Bldg 215 N Sanders St Rm 323 Helena MT 59620-3003 also: 215 N Sanders St Helena MT 59601-4522*

TRIFFET, TERRY, college dean; b. Enid, Okla., June 10, 1922; B.A., U. Okla., 1945; B.S., U. Colo., 1948, M.S., 1950; Ph.D. in Structural Mechanics, Stanford U., 1957; married; 3 children. Instr. engring. U. Colo., 1947-50; gen. engr. rocket and guided missile research U.S. Naval Ordnance Test Sta., 1950-55; gen. engr. radiol. research, head radiol. effects br. U.S. Naval Radiol. Def. Lab., 1955-59; assoc. prof., then prof. mech. and materials sci. Mich. State U., 1959-76; assoc. dean research Coll. Engring., U. Ariz., Tucson, 1976-84, acting dean, 1984, 87; prof. materials sci. engring., dir. NASA/UA Space Engring. Resch. Ctr., 1988-93; prof. emeritus U. Ariz., 1993—. mem. apex com. U.S. Naval Research Labs., 1959-65; cons. to govt. and industry. Grantee Australian Research Grants Com., 1966-67, 72-73. Mem. Am. Phys. Soc., Am. Math. Soc., Soc. Engring. Sci., Soc. Industry and Applied Math., IEEE, AIAA, Assn. Computing Machinery. Office: U Ariz Coll Engring Tucson AZ 85721 also: 5871 North Pontatoc Rd Tucson AZ 85718-4319

TRIGIANO, LUCIEN LEWIS, physician; b. Easton, Pa., Feb. 9, 1926; s. Nicholas and Angeline (Lewis) T.; children: Lynn Anita, Glenn Larry, Robert Nicholas. Student Tex. Christian U., 1944-45, Ohio U., 1943-44, 46-47, Milligan Coll., 1944, Northwestern U., 1945, Temple U., 1948-52. Intern, Meml. Hosp., Johnstown, Pa., 1952-53; resident Lee Hosp., Johnstown, 1953-54; gen. practice, Johnstown, 1953-59; med. dir. Pa. Rehab. Center, Johnstown, 1959-62, chief phys. medicine and rehab., 1964-70; fellow phys. medicine and rehab. N.Y. Inst. Phys. Medicine and Rehab., 1962-64; dir. rehab. medicine Lee Hosp., 1964-71, Ralph K. Davies Med. Center, San Francisco, 1973-75, St. Joseph's Hosp., San Francisco, 1975-78, St. Francis Meml. Hosp., San Francisco, 1978-83; asst. prof. phys. medicine and rehab. Temple U. Sch. Medicine; founder Disability Alert. Served with USNR, 1944-46. Diplomate Am. Bd. Phys. Medicine and Rehab. Mem. AMA, A.C.P., Pa., San Francisco County Med. socs., Am. Acad. Phys. Medicine and Rehab., Am. Congress Phys. Medicine, Calif. Acad. Phys. Medicine, Nat. Rehab. Assn., Babcock Surg. Soc. Author various med. articles. Home: 1421 Casa del Rey Ct Las Vegas NV 89117 Office: 1150 Bush St Ste 4B San Francisco CA 94109-5920

TRIMBLE, DONNA DENISE, counselor; b. Tokyo, Sept. 15, 1967; came to U.S., 1970; d. Dennis Leroy and Ok Son (Kim) T. BS in Sociology, So. Calif. Coll., Costa Mesa, 1989; MA in Counseling, Regent U., 1996. Primary counselor I Olivecrest Treatment Ctrs., Anaheim, Calif., 1989-90; cmty. svc. officer Costa Mesa Police Dept., 1990-92; residence dir. So. Calif. Coll., Costa Mesa, 1992-93; admissions counselor So. Calif. Coll., 1993-94; case mgr., intake specialist Cmty. Diversion Incentive, Chesapeake, Va., 1994-95; residential counselor Children's Ark, Green Mountain Falls, Colo., 1996; dir. residence and freshman programming, housing coord. Menlo Coll., Atherton, Calif., 1996—. Mem. ACA, Am. Assn. Christian Counselors. Office: Menlo Coll Student Life 1000 El Camino Real Atherton CA 94027

TRINKL, FRANK HERMAN, economist, educator; b. Cudahy, Wis., July 3, 1928; s. Frank and Celia (Damhazel) T.; m. Barbara Ruth Henry, June 9, 1951; children: Peter, Garth, Alison. MA in Econs., U. Mich., PhD in Econs.; MS in Statistics, Stanford U. Staff scientist Ramo-Wooldridge Corp., L.A., 1956-57; staff mem. RAND Corp., Santa Monica, Calif., 1957-61; spl. asst. to asst. sec. def. U.S. DOD, Washington, 1961-65; cons. various orgns., 1966-70, 74-79; sr. lectr. grad. sch. pub. policy U. Calif., Berkeley, 1970-74; pres., dir. for planning and econ. analysis Ctr. for Policy Studies, Inc., Berkeley, 1979-83; prin. cons. Calif. Legislature, Sacramento, 1983-85; dir. pub. law rsch. inst., adj. prof. U. Calif. Hastings Coll. Law, San Francisco, 1986-93, ret. Contbr. articles to profl. jours. Fellow AAAS; mem. Am. Econ. Assn.

TRIPOLI, MASUMI HIROYASU, financial consultant and diplomat; b. Fukuyama, Japan, Apr. 23, 1956; d. Yoshimi and Suzuko Hiroyasu; 1 child, Mona Lisa Tripoli. BA cum laude, U. Wash., 1978; MA, Sophia U., Tokyo, 1981; MBA, Ecole des Hautes Etudes Comml, Jouy-en-Josas, France, 1983. Cert. fin. planner, chartered fin. cons. Corp. planning mgr. Kowa Corp., Osaka, Japan, 1983-85; internat. bond trader Banque Baribas, Tokyo, 1985-86, Westpac Bank, Tokyo, 1987-88; fin. cons. CIGNA Fin. Advisors, Glendale, Calif., 1989—, Masumi Tripoli & Assocs., Glendale, Calif., 1989—; anchor newscaster United TV, L.A., 1989-92; condr. seminars in field. Contbr. articles to profl. jours. Grantee Sophia U., 1979, H.E.C., 1983. Mem. Internat. Bd. Cert. Fin. Planners, Ritz-Carlton Fitness Club. Office: Masumi Tripoli and Assocs 330 N Brand Blvd Ste 400 Glendale CA 91203-2308

TRISKA, JAN FRANCIS, retired political science educator; b. Prague, Czechoslovakia, Jan. 26, 1922; came to U.S., 1948, naturalized, 1955; s. Jan and Bozena (Kubiznak) T.; m. Carmel Lena Burastero, Aug. 26, 1951; children: Mark Lawrence, John William. J.U.D., Charles U., Prague, 1948; LL.M., Yale U., 1950, J.S.D., 1952; Ph.D., Harvard U., 1957. Co-dir. Soviet treaties Hoover Instn., Stanford, Calif., 1956-58; lectr. dept. polit. sci. U. Calif.-Berkeley, 1957-58; asst. prof. Cornell U., Ithaca, N.Y., 1958-60; assoc. prof. Stanford U., Calif., 1960-65, prof. polit. sci., 1965-89, assoc. chmn. dept., 1965-66, 68-69, 71-72, 74-75, emeritus prof. polit. sci., 1990—; cons. Inst. State and Law, Czech Acad. Scis., Prague, 1996—. Co-author: (with Slusser) The Theory, Law and Policy of Soviet Treaties, 1962, (with Finley) Soviet Foreign Policy, 1968, (with Cocks) Political Development and Political Change in Eastern Europe, 1977, (with Ike, North) The World of Superpowers, 1981, (with Gati) Blue Collar Workers in Eastern Europe, 1981, Dominant Powers and Subordinate States, 1986; bd. editors: East

European Quar. Comparative Politics, Internat. Jour. Sociology, Jour. Comparative Politics, Studies in Comparative Communism, Soviet Statutes and Decisions, Documents in Communist Affairs. Recipient Rsch. award Ford Found., 1963-68, Josef Hlavka Commemorative medal Czechoslovak Acad. Scis., 1992, M.A. Comenius 1592-1992 Meml. medal Czechoslovak Pedagogical Mus., Prague, 1991; fellow NSF, 1971-72, Sen. Fulbright fellow, 1973-74, Woodrow Wilson fellow Internat. Ctr. for Scholars, 1980-81. Mem. Am. Polit. Sci. Assn. (sec. pres. conf. on communist studies 1970-76), Assn. Advancement Slavic Studies (bd. dirs. 1975-83), Am. Soc. Internat. Law (exec. coun. 1964-67), Czechoslovak Soc. Arts and Scis. (pres. 1978-80, 90-92), Inst. for Human Scis. Vienna (acting for Commn. European Communities, Brussels, com. experts on transformation of nat. higher edn. and rsch. system in Ctrl. Europe, Brussels 1991—). Democrat. Club: Fly Fishers (Palo Alto, Calif.). Home: 720 Vine St Menlo Park CA 94025-6154 Office: Stanford U Dept Polit Sci Stanford CA 94305

TRITT, LINCOLN C., writer, educator, musician; b. Salmon River, Alaska, Oct. 18, 1946; s. Isaac Albert and Naomi (Peter) T. Grad., Mt. Edgecombe H.S., 1966; student, U. Alaska, 1972, 84-87; student electricity and electronics, Naval Tng. Ctr., 1967, student radioman class A sch., 1967; studied with traditional tchrs. Exploration worker, driver, driller asst. Kandik Oil Field Parker Exploration, Fairbanks, Alaska, 1977; negotiator Venetie (Alaska) Tribal Govt., 1980, heavy equipment operator, 1982; phone survey rep. Mental Health Program and U. Alaska, 1984; curriculum developer Yukon Flats (Alaska) Sch. Dist., 1985; laborer Peter Kewitt and sons, Deadhorse, Alaska, 1985; bookkeeper Tanana Chiefs Conf., Inc., on-site supr., 1985; translator fed. Indian law Fed. Indian Law workshop, Venetie, Alaska, 1986; grant contract negotiator with fed. agys., 1987; grant adminstr., overall project dir. Arctic Village Traditional Coun., 1988-89; liaison, coord. U.S. Geophys. Inst./U. Alaska, Fairbanks, 1989; instr. rural coll. U. Alaska, 1990; tribal adminstr. Native Vill. Venetie (Alaska), 1994-95; carpenter Bur. Indian Affairs Sch., Arctic Vill., Alaska, 1970; postal clk. U.S. Postal Svc., Fairbanks, Alaska, 1971, substitute postmaster, 1984—; tchr. Gwich'in lang., 1974; store mgr. Midnight Sun Native Store, Arctic Village, Alaska, 1975. Author screenplay on Native Am. alcohol experience; contbr. essays, stories to Raven Tells Stories: An Anthology of Alaska Native Writings, Coyote Bark, Alaska Mag., Alaskan Epiphany, All Alaska Weekly, Talking Leaves, Tundra Times, The Turtle Quarterly, The Council, Nimrod; columnist Fairbanks Daily News Miner, Northland News; composer (song) Belief; mem. of cast: Earth and the Great Weather, 1993, 95, 97; performed at Athabascan Old-Time Fiddling Festival, Summer Folk Festival, Fairbanks Folk Festival, Plate and Palate Restaurant, Native Village at Alaskaland; cons. (videos, films) Wisdom of the Elders, Caribou People. Firefighter Dept. Natural Resource, Fairbanks, Alaska, 1984; lobbyist Gwich'in People, 1986-87; mem. restructuring com. Howard Luke Alternative Sch., 1993, 94; Rural Campuses U. Alaska, 1990; coord. first Gwich'in Gathering in Arctic Village, Alaska, 1988; mem. coun. Native Village of Venetie (Alaska) Govt., 1974-86; mem. Arctic Village Traditional Coun., 1973-89, chief, 1987-89; mem. sch. bd. Arctic Village, 1974-76. Served with USN, 1966-70, Vietnam. Mem. Native Writers Circle of Ams., Internat. Conf. Higher Edn. Indigenous People, Internat. Conf. Hunting and Gathering Socs., Alaska Native Viet Nam Vets, Fairbanks Folk Fest. Home: PO Box 22016 Arctic Village AK 99722

TRIVEDI, NARENDRA SHANTILAL, physician, educator, researcher; b. Jalia, Gujarat, India, June 24, 1955; came to U.S., 1982; s. Shantilal P. and Sushilaben S. (Mehta) T.; m. Trupti N. Trivedi, Feb. 1, 1983; children: Akash, Nikunj. MB, BS, NHL Mcpl. Med. Coll., Ahmedabad, India, 1979. Diplomate Am. Bd. Anesthesiology, Am. Bd. Pain Mgmt. Resident in orthopedic surgery KM Sch. of PG Medicine, Ahmedabad, 1978-80; house officer orthopedic surgery Kitwe (Zambia) Ctrl. Hosp., 1980-82; med. asst. allergy Jefferson Med. Ctr., Pitts., 1982-84; house physician surgery Brookdale Med. Ctr., Bklyn., 1984-85; resident in surgery Mt. Sinai Med. Sch., N.Y.C., 1985-87; resident in anesthesiology Maimonides Med. Ctr., Bklyn., 1987-90; fellow cardiac anesthesiology Cleve. Clin. Found., 1990; asst. clin. prof. U. Calif., Irvine, 1991-94, assoc. clin. prof., 1994—; lectr. in field, 1991—. Author: (chpt.) Textbook of Critical Care, 1989, Textbook of Thoracoscopic Surgery; edtl. bd. Clin. Anesthesia Jour., 1992—; contbr. articles to profl. jours. Mem. Am. Soc. Indian Anesthesiologists (bd. dirs. 1993—), Am. Soc. Anesthesiologists, Internat. Anesthesia Rsch. Soc., Soc. Cardiovascular Anesthesia, Calif. Soc. Anesthesiologists, Orange County Soc. Anesthesiologists. Hindu. Home: 1011 S Mountcrest Ct Anaheim CA 92808-2127 Office: Univ Calif 101 The City Dr S Orange CA 92868-3201

TROGDON, DOROTHY WEBER, interior designer; b. Waterville, Maine, Feb. 25, 1926; d. Carl Jefferson and Clara Whitehouse (Carter) Weber; m. William Henry Trogdon, June 23, 1952; children: Benjamin William, Peter Whitehouse, William Henry. BA, Wheaton Coll., 1947; MARch, Harvard U., 1952. Interior designer Joel, Inc., Spokane, Wash., 1956-76; interior designer, co-dir. Inscape, Spokane, 1976-83; interior designer N.W. Arch. Co., Seattle, 1983-87, Dorothy Trogdon Interior Design, Olga, Wash., 1987—; mem. accreditation com. Found. for Interior Design Edn. Rsch., Grand Rapids, Mich., 1984-91, chmn. bd., 1997. Bd. dirs. Orcas Ctr., Orcas Island, Wash., 1992-96. Mem. Am. Soc. Interior Designers (profl. mem.). Home and Office: Star Route Box 107 Olga WA 98279

TRONE, DONALD BURNELL, investment company executive; b. Gettysburg, Pa., Jan. 22, 1954; s. Donald Burnell and Mary Ann (Moreau) T.; children:from previous marriage Tara C., Donald Timothy. BS in Govt., USCG Acad., 1977; MS in Fin. Svcs., Am. Coll., Bryn Mawr, Pa., 1989. Registered investment adviser. Commd. ensign USCG, 1977, advanced through ranks to lt. comdr., 1988, aviator, 1977-87; resigned, 1987; sr v.p. Investment Adv. Svcs. of Raymond James, St. Petersburg, Fla., 1987-89, USF&G, Cin., 1989; v.p. mktg. SEI Wealth Mgmt., 1989-91; dir. investment mgmt. coun. divsn. div. Callan Assocs. Inc., San Francisco, 1991—. Pilot (film) Cocoon, 1985; co-author: Procedural Prudence, 1991, The Management of Investment Decisions, 1995. Recipient Sikorsky Heroism award United Techs., 1981. Republican. Episcopalian. Home: 3 Rose Ct Sausalito CA 94965-2065 Office: Callan Assocs Inc 71 Stevenson St Ste 1300 San Francisco CA 94105-2938

TROST, BARRY MARTIN, chemist, educator; b. Phila., June 13, 1941; s. Joseph and Esther T.; m. Susan Paula Shapiro, Nov. 25, 1967; children: Aaron David, Carey Daniel. B.A. cum laude, U. Pa., 1962; Ph.D., MIT, 1965; D (hon.), U. Claude Bernard, Lyons, France, 1994, Technion, Israel, 1997. Mem. faculty U. Wis., Madison, 1965—, prof., chemistry, 1969—, Evan P. and Marion Helfaer prof. chemistry, from 1976; Vilas rsch. prof. chemistry U. Wis.; prof. chemistry Stanford U., 1987—, Tamaki prof. humanities and scis., 1990, chmn. dept., 1996—; cons. Merck, Sharp & Dohme, E.I. duPont de Nemours.; Chem. Soc. centenary lectr., 1982. Author: Problems in Spectroscopy, 1967, Sulfur Ylides, 1975; editor-in-chief Comprehensive Organic Synthesis, 1991—, ChemTracts/Organic Chemistry, 1993—; editor: Structure and Reactivity Concepts in Organic Chemistry series, 1972—; assoc. editor Jour. Am. Chem. Soc., 1974-80; mem. editl. bd. Organic Reactions Series, 1971—, Chemistry A European Jour., 1995—, Sci. of Synthesis, Houben-Weyl Methods of Molecular Transformations, 1995—; contbr. numerous articles to profl. jours. Recipient Dreyfus Found. Tech.-Scholar award, 1970, 77, Creative Work in Synthetic Organic Chemistry award, 1981, Baekland medal, 1981, Alexander von Humboldt award, 1984, Guenther award, 1990, Janssen prize, 1990, Roger Adams award Am. Chem. Soc. 1995; named Chem. Pioneer, Am. Inst. Chemists, 1983; NSF fellow, 1963-65, Sloan Found. fellow, 1967-69, Am. Swiss Found. fellow, 1975—, Zencca fellow, 1997; Cope scholar, 1989. Mem. AAAS, Am. Chem. Soc. (award in pure chemistry 1977, Roger Adams award 1995), Nat. Acad. Scis., Am. Acad. Arts and Scis., Chem. Soc. London. Office: Stanford U Dept Chemistry Stanford CA 94305

TROTT, STEPHEN SPANGLER, federal judge, musician; b. Glen Ridge, N.J., Dec. 12, 1939; s. David Herman and Virginia (Spangler) T.; divorced; children: Christina, Shelley. B.A., Wesleyan U., 1962; LL.B., Harvard U., 1965; LLD (hon.), Santa Clara U., 1992. Bar: Calif. 1966, U.S. Dist. Ct. (cen. dist.) Calif. 1966, U.S. Ct. Appeals (9th cir.) 1983, U.S. Supreme Ct. 1984. Guitarist, mem. The Highwaymen, 1958—; dep. dist. atty. Los Angeles County Dist. Atty.'s Office, Los Angeles, 1966-75; chief dep. dist. atty. Los Angeles County Dist. Atty.'s Office, 1975-79; U.S. dist. atty. Central Dist. Calif., Los Angeles, 1981-83; asst. atty. gen. criminal div. Dept. Justice, Washington, 1983-86; mem. faculty Nat. Coll. Dist. Attys., Houston, 1973—; chmn. central dist. Calif. Law Enforcement Coordinating Com., Houston, 1981-83; coordinator Los Angeles-Nev. Drug Enforcement Task Force, 1982-83; assoc. atty. gen. Justice Dept., Washington, 1986-88; chmn. U.S. Interpol, 1986-88; judge U.S. Ct. of Appeals 9th Cir., Boise, Idaho, 1988—; chmn. U.S. Interpol. Trustee Wesleyan U., 1984-87; bd. dirs. Children's Home Soc., Idaho, 1990—, Boise Philharm. Assn., 1995—. Recipient Gold record as singer-guitarist for Michael Row the Boat Ashore, 1961, Disting. Faculty award Nat. Coll. Dist. Attys., 1977. Mem. Am. Coll. Trial Lawyers, Wilderness Fly Fishers Club (pres. 1975-77), Brentwood Racing Pigeon Club (pres. 1977-82), Magic Castle, Internat. Brotherhood Magicians, Idaho Classic Guitar Soc. (founder, pres. 1989—). Republican. Office: US Ct Appeals 9th Cir 666 US Courthouse 550 W Fort St Boise ID 83724-0101

TROTTER, F(REDERICK) THOMAS, retired academic administrator; b. L.A., Apr. 17, 1926; s. Fred B. and Hazel (Thomas) T.; m. Gania Demaree, June 27, 1953; children—Ruth Elizabeth, Paula Anne (dec.), Tania, Mary. AB, Occidental Coll., 1950, DD, 1968; STB, Boston U., 1953, PhD, 1958; LHD, Ill. Wesleyan U., 1974, Cornell Coll., 1985, Westmar Coll., 1987; LLD, U. Pacific, 1978, Wesleyan Coll., 1981; EdD, Columbia Coll., 1984; LittD, Alaska Pacific U., 1987. Exec. sec. Boston U. Student Christian Assn., 1951-54; ordained elder Calif.-Pacific, Methodist Ch., 1953; pastor Montclair (Calif.) Meth. Ch., 1956-59; lectr. So. Calif. Sch. Theology at Claremont, 1957-59, instr., 1959-60, asst. prof., 1960-63, assoc. prof., 1963-66, prof., 1966, dean, 1961; prof. religion and arts, dean Sch. Theology Claremont, 1961-73; mem. Bd. Higher Edn. and Ministry, United Meth. Ch., 1972-73, gen. sec., 1973-87; pres. Alaska Pacific U., Anchorage, 1988-95; ret., 1995; dir. Inst. for Antiquity and Christianity at Claremont. Author: Jesus and the Historian, 1968, Loving God with One's Mind, 1987, weekly column local newspapers; editor-at-large: Christian Century, 1969-84. Trustee Dillard U. Served with USAAF, 1944-46. Kent fellow Soc. for Values in Higher Edn., 1954; Dempster fellow Meth. Ch., 1954. Mem. Rotary Internat. (Anchorage Downtown), Commonwealth North. Home: 75-136 Kiowa Dr Indian Wells CA 92210

TROUNSTINE, PHILIP J., editor, journalist; b. Cin., July 30, 1949; s. Henry P. and Amy May (Joseph) Trounstine; children: Jessica, David; m. Deborah Williams, May 1, 1993; children: Amy, Ryan, Patrick Wilkes. Student, U. Vt., 1967-68, Stanford U., 1968-70; BA in Journalism, San Jose State U., 1975. Graphic artist Eric Printing, San Jose, Calif., 1972-75; reporter Indpls. Star, Ind., 1975-78; reporter San Jose Mercury News, Calif., 1978-83, editl. writer, 1983-86, polit. editor, 1986—; ednl. cons. Teen Recovery Strategies, 1995—. Co-author: Movers & Shakers: The Study of Community Power, 1981. Creator, writer SPJ Gridiron Show, San Jose, 1981-91. Pulliam fellow, 1975, Duke U., 1991, J.S. Knight Stanford U., 1993-94. Mem. Soc. Profl. Journalist (mem. nat. ethics com. 1993—). Jewish. Home: 960 Asbury St San Jose CA 95126-1805 Office: San Jose Mercury News 750 Ridder Park Dr San Jose CA 95190

TROUSDALE, STEPHEN RICHARD, newspaper editor; b. L.A., May 29, 1963; s. Richard Gardner Trousdale and Geraldine Barbara Wisdom. AB, Stanford U., 1985. News editor L.A. Daily Commerce, 1986-87; edit. page editor L.A. Daily Jour., 1987-89, mng. editor, 1989-96; bus. editor Copley L.A. Newspapers, 1996—. Mem. Soc. Profl. Journalists (past pres. L.A. chpt.), AP Mng. Editors, Calif. Soc. Newspaper Editors, Soc. Newspaper Design, Soc. Am. Bus. Editors and Writers, Toastmasters Internat. Home: 10933 Huston St Apt 203 North Hollywood CA 91601-5135 Office: Copley LA Newspapers 5215 Torrance Blvd Torrance CA 90503

TROUT, LINDA COPPLE, judge; b. Tokyo, Sept. 1, 1951. BA, U. Idaho, 1973, JD, 1977. Bar: Idaho 1977. Judge magistrate divsn. Idaho Dist. Ct. (2d jud. divsn.), 1983-90; dist. judge Idaho Dist. Ct. (2d jud. divsn.), Lewiston, 1991-92; acting trial ct. adminstr. Idaho Dist. Ct. (2d jud. divsn.), 1987-91; justice Idaho Supreme Ct., 1992—, chief justice, 1997—; instr. coll. law U. Idaho, 1983, 88. Mem. Idaho State Bar Assn., Clearwater Bar Assn. (pres. 1980-81).

TROVER, ELLEN LLOYD, lawyer; b. Richmond, Va., Nov. 23, 1947; d. Robert Van Buren and Hazel (Urban) Lloyd; m. Denis William Trover, June 12, 1971; 1 dau., Florence Emma. AB, Vassar Coll., 1969; JD, Coll. William and Mary, 1972. Asst. editor Bancroft-Whitney, San Francisco, 1973-74; owner Ellen Lloyd Trover Atty.-at-Law, Thousand Oaks, Calif., 1974-82; ptnr. Trover & Fisher, Thousand Oaks, 1982-89; pvt. practice law, Thousand Oaks, 1989—. Editor: Handbooks of State Chronologies, 1972. Trustee, Conejo Future Found., Thousand Oaks, 1978-91, trustee emeritus, 1992—, vice chmn., 1982-84, chmn., 1984-88; pres. Zonta Club Conejo Valley Area, 1978-79; trustee Hydro Help for the Handicapped, 1980-85, Atlantis Found., 1994—. Mem. State Bar Calif., Va. State Bar, Phi Alpha Delta. Democrat. Presbyterian. Home: 11355 Presilla Rd Camarillo CA 93012-9230 Office: 1107E E Thousand Oaks Blvd Thousand Oaks CA 91362-2816

TROXELL-GURKA, MARY THERESA (TERRY TROXELL-GURKA), geriatrics services professional; b. Syracuse, N.Y., Aug. 29, 1950; d. Henry and Mary (McDermott) Flynn; m. Richard Gurka, Apr. 2, 1994; 1 child, Melissa Lee. BSN, U. Pa., 1971. Cert. quality improvement specialsit; cert. gerontol. nurse specialist; cert. case mgr. Supr. neonatal ICU St. Joe's, Syracuse, 1976-79; dir. nursing Hillhaven, Phoenix, 1979-81; quality assurance nurse long term care Maricopa County, Phoenix, 1981-83; dir. nursing Desert Haven Nursing Home, Phoenix, 1983-84; team leader, surveyor health care licensure State of Ariz., Phoenix, 1985-87, program mgr. long term care licensure and certification, 1987-89, program mgr. enforcement and compliance licensure and cert., 1989-91; dir. profl. svcs. SunQuest Healthcare, Phoenix, 1991-94, v.p. clin. ops., 1994-96; sr. v.p. clin. and ancillary ops. Unison Healthcare, 1996—. Author: (manuals) Licensure Procedures, 1990, Quality Improvement, Restorative Nursing: A Key to Quality, 1992, Director of Nursing Manual, 1996. Developer legislation for adult care homes, health care licensure laws State of Ariz., 1990. Mem. Ariz. Health Care Assn. (chair legis. com. 1992-94, chair devel./revision nursing facility laws 1992-94), Am. Health Care Assn. (nat. facility stds. com. 1992-96, nat. multifacility com. 1993-96, LTC nurses coun. 1995, nat. quality com. 1996—), Quality Improvement Nurses Assn., Gerontol. Nurses Assn. Home: 3608 E Woodland Dr Phoenix AZ 85044-7330 Office: Unison Health Care 7272 E Indian School Rd Ste 214 Scottsdale AZ 85251-3948

TRUAX, DONALD ROBERT, mathematics educator; b. Mpls., Aug. 29, 1927; s. William Raymond and Hermina Wilhelmina (Sobolick) T.; m. Barbara June Eckton, Sept. 16, 1950; children: Mary, Catherine, Patricia, Gail. BS in Math., U. Wash., 1951, MS in Math., 1953; PhD in Statistics, Stanford U., 1955. Rsch. fellow Calif. Inst. Tech., Pasadena, 1955-56; asst. prof. math. U. Kans., Lawrence, 1956-59, U. Oreg., Eugene, 1959-62; assoc. prof. math. U. Oreg., 1962-69, prof. math., 1969—. Mng. editor Inst. Math. Statistics, 1975-81; contbr. articles to profl. jours. With USN, 1945-47. Fellow Inst. Math. Statistics; mem. Am. Statis. Assn. Home: 2323 University St Eugene OR 97403-1547 Office: University of Oregon Dept Of Mathematics Eugene OR 97403

TRUBNER, HENRY, museum curator; b. Munich, Ger., June 10, 1920; s. Jorg and Gertrude T.; m. Ruth Trubner, July 10, 1948; children: Susan, Karen. BA, Harvard U., 1942, MA, 1944; postgrad., Fogg Art Mus., 1942-47. Curator Oriental art L.A. County Mus. Art, 1947-58; curator Far Eastern dept. Royal Ont. Mus., Toronto, 1958-68; curator Asian art Seattle Art Mus., 1968-87, assoc. dir. and curator Asian Art, 1976-87, sr. curator emeritus, 1987—; dir. Son of Heaven Exhbn. Imperial Arts of China, Seattle, 1988; mem. art adv. com. The Asia Soc., Japan Soc. Gallery, China Inst. in Am., Inc.; mem. Am. adv. com. The Japan Found., Tokyo, 1978-80. Contbr. articles to profl. jours. Recipient Fujio Koyama Meml. prize, Idemitsu Mus. Art, Tokyo, 1988. Mem. Am. Assn. Mus., Oriental Ceramic Soc. London, The Asia Soc. N.Y., The Japan Soc. N.Y., China Inst. in Am., Acad. Laquer Rsch. Tokyo, Soc. for Japanese Arts. Home: 9341 Vineyard Cres Bellevue WA 98004-4028

TRUCKER, ALBERT, plastic surgeon; b. St. Joseph, Mich., Aug. 5, 1924; s. Albert and Louise (Goebel) T. BA, Johns Hopkins U., 1951; MD, U. Md., 1956. Diplomate Am. Bd. Plastic Surgery. Intern in gen. surgery U. Calif., San Francisco, 1956-59; resident in plastic surgery Mayo Clinic, Rochester, Minn., 1959-62; pvt. practice Santa Rosa, Calif., 1962—. Mem. Am. Soc. Plastic Surgery, Calif. Soc. Plastic Surgery. Office: 200 Montgomery Dr Santa Rosa CA 95404-6633

TRUDEL, JOHN DAVIS, management consultant; b. Trenton, N.J., Aug. 1, 1942; s. Leroy and Elizabeth (Reading) T. BEE cum laude, Ga. Inst. Tech., 1964; MSEE, Kans. State U., 1966. Cert. profl. cons.; cert. mgmt. cons. Engr. Collins Radio, Richardson, Tex., 1966-67, sr. engr., 1969-70; sr. engr. Sanders Assoc., Nashua, N.H., 1967-68, LTV E-Systems, Inc., Greenville, Tex., 1968-69, F&M Systems, Inc., Dallas, 1970; pres. Sci. System Tech., Inc., Dallas, 1970-74; mgr. mktg. Tektronix, Inc., Beaverton, Oreg., 1974-83, mgr. bus. devel., 1983-89; v.p. mktg. Cable Bus. Systems Corp., Beaverton, 1981-83; owner, mng. dir. The Trudel Group, Scappoose, Oreg., 1988—; v.p. TCI, Portland, Oreg., 1992-94; adj. prof. Oreg. Grad. Inst. and U. Oreg. Author: (software) MAGIC CAE, (book) High Tech with Low Risk, 1990; writer regular columns for Upside and Electronic Design mags.; inventor Waveform Storage, 1984. Aviation com. mem., OMSI, Portland, 1986-87. Mem. Am. Mgmt. Assn., Inst. Mgmt. Cons., Acad. Profl. Cons. and Advisors, Am. Electronics Assn., Nat. Avionics Soc., IEEE, Product Devel. and Mgmt. Assn. (nat. examiner for outstanding corp. innovator award), Assn. Old Crows, Aircraft Owners and Pilots Assn. Office: The Trudel Group 33470 Chinook Plz Scappoose OR 97056-3726

TRUE, DAN JAMES, writer, photographer; b. Nashville, Tenn., Dec. 8, 1924; s. David Crowley and Mildred Doris (Tuggle) T.; m. Betty E. Krauel, Aug. 1950 (div. Mar. 1985); children: Greg (dec.), Jeff, Dawn, Terri, Teresa, Todd. Student, John Brown U., 1948-50, U. Ill., 1950-51, Amarillo Coll., 1957-58, U. Okla., 1963-65, U. N.Mex., 1984-86. Meteorologist/pilot KGNC-TV, Amarillo, Tex., 1953-60, KFDA-TV, Amarillo, Tex., 1960-75, KOB-TV, Albuquerque, 1979-82, KGGM-TV, Albuquerque, 1982-86; weather cons. Robert Redford Movie Group, Santa Fe, N.Mex., 1988. Author: A Family of Eagles, 1980; Flying Free, 1984; Hummingbirds of North America, 1993; What Do Women Want from Men? 1994. Sgt. U.S. Army, 1943-46, Europe, PTO. Home and Office: 1000 Hondo Clovis NM 88101

TRUE, VIRGIL, retired government official; b. Richview, Ill., July 21, 1925; s.Robert Thurman and Beulah Hazel (Wilson) T.; m. Ruth Louise Hotle, Oct. 7, 1949; children: Kenneth Allen, Virgil David. BSEE, Washington U., St. Louis, 1950. Electronic scientist Naval Rsch. Lab., Washington, 1950-54; supervisory electronic scientist Naval Rsch. Lab., Port Huenene, Calif., 1954-58; br. head Navy Missile Test Ctr., Point Mugu, Calif., 1958-61; sta. dir. Navy Missile Range, Kauai, Hawaii, 1961-65; sta. dir. NASA Network, Kauai, 1965-78, White Sands, N.Mex., 1978-89; cons. NASA, Las Cruces, N.Mex., 1990—. Chmn. Kauai Econ. Devel. Com., 1974-76. With USMCR, 1943-46, PTO. Recipient Exceptional Svc. medal NASA, 1984, 89. Home: 701 Frank Maes Ave Las Cruces NM 88005-1230

TRUEBLOOD, MARK, systems engineer; b. Cin., Feb. 23, 1948; s. William Oliver and Opal Lauretta (Hamilton) T.; m. Patricia Ann Bulman, May 16, 1981. AB-ScB in Physics, Brown U., 1971; MS in Astronomy, U. Md., 1983. Lab. technician Smithsonian Instn., Rockville, Md., 1972-74; mem. tech. staff Computer Scis. Corp., Silver Spring, Md., 1974-78; sr. computer programmer The Dilks Co., Herndon, Va., 1978-79; sr. computer analyst GE Space Div., Lanham, Md., 1979-81; program mgr. Ford Aerospace Corp., Seabrook, Md., 1981-90; sr. sci. programmer Nat. Optical Astronomy Obs., Tucson, 1990-94; project engr. U.S. Gemini Program, Nat. Optical Astronomy Observatory, 1994—; computer cons. pvt. practice, Potomac, Md., 1974-87; sci. dir. Winer Mobile Observatory, Sonoita, Ariz., 1983—. Co-author (with Russell M. Genet) Microcomputer Control of Telescopes, 1985; contbr. 21 articles on telesccope control to profl. jours. Grantee Am. Astronomical Soc., 1987. Mem. Internat. Amateur Profl. Photoelectric Phometry Group, Am. Astron. Soc., Tucson Amateur Astronomy Assn. Democrat. Home: PO Box 797 Sonoita AZ 85637-0797 Office: Nat Optical Astro Observtrs PO Box 26732 Tucson AZ 85726-6732

TRUEBLOOD, PAUL GRAHAM, retired English educator, author, editor; b. Macksburg, Iowa, Oct. 21, 1905; s. Charles E. and Adele (Graham) T.; m. Helen Churchill, Aug. 19, 1931; children—Anne Williams, Susan Stuart. BA, Willamette U., 1928; MA, Duke U., 1930, Ph.D., 1935; Litt.D. (hon.), Willamette U., 1984. Instr. Friends U., 1931-34; English master Mohonk Sch. Boys, Lake Mohonk, N.Y., 1935-37; instr. U. Idaho, 1937-40; asso. prof. Stockton Coll., 1940-46; asst. prof. U. Wash., 1947-52; vis. prof. U. Oreg., 1954-55; prof. English, head dept. Willamette U., 1955-70, prof. emeritus, 1971—; vis. lectr. U. B.C., summer 1963. Author: The Flowering of Byron's Genius, 2d edit, 1962, Lord Byron, 2d edit, 1977; Editor: Byron's Political and Cultural Influence in Nineteenth-Century Europe: A Symposium, 1981; Contbr. to charter issues Keats-Shelley Jour, 1952, Byron Jour, 1973. Pendle Hill fellow, 1934-35; fellow Am. Council Learned Socs., 1952-53; recipient Disting. Alumni citation Willamette U., 1975. Mem. MLA, Keats-Shelley Assn. Am., Philol. Assn. Pacific Coast (exec. com. 1964-65), Byron Soc. (founding mem. Am. com. 1973, bd. dirs. 1975, delivered lecture to Byron Soc. in Ho. of Lords 1975). Home: Capitol Manor 1955 Dallas Hwy NW Apt 903 Salem OR 97304-4496

TRUJILLO, ARTHUR BENJAMIN, journalism educator; b. Las Vegas, Apr. 21, 1939; s. Jose Demosthenes and Marie Remijia (Medina) T.; m. Bonnie Caroline Coppock, June 12, 1966; children: Stanley Adam, Diego Coppock, Benjamin Vernon. BA in English/Speech, N.Mex. Highlands U., 1966; MA in English, U. Va., 1971; MA in Journalism, U. Mo., 1979. Reporter, photographer Las Vegas Daily Optic, 1957-60, Naperville (Ill.) Sun, 1960-61, Aurora (Ill.) Beacon News, 1961-62; owner, publ. Warrenville (Ill.) News, 1962-64; tchr. reading Zuni (N.Mex.) H.S., 1966-67; tchr. English, speech, journalism Cuba (N.Mex.) H.S., 1967-70; prof. English N.Mex. Highlands U., Las Vegas, 1971-72, prof. journalism, 1972—; vis. prof. journalism No. Ariz. U., Flagstaff, summers, 1982-91. Author (Macintosh database) Shakespeare Hyperquotes, 1994. Mem., com. chair Gambling Study Commn., Las Vegas, 1995-96; vol. newsletter editor Animal Welfare Soc., Las Vegas, 1995-96; mem. corp. bd. Northeastern Regional Hosp., 1995—. Recipient Nat. Tchg. award Poynter Inst. Media Studies, St. Petersburg, Fla., and Am. Assn. Newspaper Editors, 1985. Mem. State Bar Com. Consumer Advocacy. Presbyterian. Home: 555 N Luna Dr Las Vegas NM 87701 Office: NMex Highlands U 1000 University Ave Las Vegas NM 87701

TRUJILLO, AUGUSTINE, university administrator; b. Swink, Colo., May 5, 1940; s. Roque and Manclovia (Chavez) T.; m. Martha cordelia Velasquez, June 19, 1969; children: Augustine Christopher, Melissa Ann, Brian Anthony, Clarissa Frances. AA, Otero Jr. Coll., La Junta, Colo., 1968; BA, Adams State Coll., 1971; PhD, U. Colo., 1983. Tchg. cert., Colo. Social studies tchr. Swink H.S., 1971-72; southwest regional fellow Leadership Devel. Program/Ford Found., Albuquerque, 1972-73; athletic dir. Naco (Ariz.) Elem./Jr. H.S., 1973-74; asst. dir. spl. svcs. program U. So. Colo., Pueblo, 1975-76; coord. STW program L.Am. Rsch. and Svc. Agy., Denver, 1980-81; asst. dir. high sch. equivalency U. So. Colo., Pueblo, 1981-84; dir. Ctr. for Ethnic Student Affairs U. Utah, Salt Lake City, 1984—. Mem. Bd. of State History, Utah, Salt Lake City, 1995; chmn. Hispanic adv. bd. Utah State Office Edn., Salt Lake City, 1987-92, chmn. coalition of minority coun., 1991; bd. dirs. math, engring, sci. achievement bd. U. Utah, 1988-94. With USAF, 1961-64. Ford Found. fellow, 1972-73, Title III Bilingual fellow Dept. HEW, 1976-80; Adams State U. grad. assistantship, 1975. Democrat. Roman Catholic. Home: 647 E 800 S Salt Lake City UT 84102 Office: University of Utah Ad16 14 318 Union Bldg Salt Lake City UT 84112-1192

TRUJILLO, LORENZO A., lawyer, educator; b. Denver, Aug. 10, 1951; s. Filbert G. and Marie O. Trujillo; children: Javier Antonio, Lorenzo Feliciano. BA, U. Colo., 1972, MA, 1974, postgrad.; EdD, U. San Francisco, 1979; JD, U. Colo., 1993. Bar: Colo. 1994, U.S. Dist. Ct. Colo. 1994, U.S. Ct. Appeals (10th cir.) 1994; cert. edn. tchr., prin., supt., Colo., Calif. Exec. assoc. Inter-Am. Rsch. Assocs., Rosslyn, Va., 1980-82; exec. dir. humanities Jefferson County Pub. Schs., Golden, Colo., 1982-89; pvt. practice edn. cons. Lakewood, Colo., 1989-93; gen. corp. counsel Am. Achievement Schs., Inc., Lakewood, Colo., 1994-96; atty. Frie, Arndt & Trujillo Law Firm, Arvada, Colo., 1994-96, ptnr., 1995-97; in-house counsel/hearing officer, dir. of instrn. Adams County Sch. Dist. 14, 1997—; co-chair Mellon fellowships The Coll. Bd., N.Y.C., 1987-93; cons. U.S.I.A. Fulbright Tchr. Exch. Program, Washington, 1987-93; editorial advisor Harcourt, Brace, Jovanovich Pub., Orlando, Fla., 1988-93. Contbr. numerous articles to profl. jours. Mem.

panel of arbitrators Am. Arbitration Assn., 1994. Recipient Legal Aid Clinic Acad. award Colo. Bar Assn., 1993, Pro Bono award, 1993, Loyola U. Acad. award, 1993, Gov.'s award for excellence in the arts State of Colo., 1996. Mem. Colo. chpt. Am. Assn. Tchrs. of Spanish and Portuguese (pres. 1985-88), Am. Immigration Lawyers Assn., Nat. Sch. Bds. Coun. Sch. Attys., Nat. Assn. Judiciary Interpreters and Translators, Colo. Bar Assn. (family law sect., probate and trust sect., grievance policy com. 1995—, ethics com. 1995-96), Soc. Security Benefits Panel, U. San Francisco Alumni Assn. (founder, pres. 1987-90), Phi Delta Kappa (chair internat. edn. com. 1988-89), Phi Alpha Delta. Home: 1556 S Van Dyke Way Lakewood CO 80228 Office: Adams County Sch Dist 14 Divsn Ednl Svcs 4720 E 69th Ave Commerce City CO 80022

TRUJILLO, LUCY ANN, elementary education counselor and educator; b. Trinidad, Colo., July 9, 1965; d. Robert Anthony James and Rose Helen DeCarolis; m. Michael Rafael Trujillo, June 20, 1992; 1 child, Annelore Lynn. BS in Elem. Edn., U. So. Colo., 1987; MA in Elem. Counseling, Adams State Coll., 1996. Cert. elem. tchr., Colo. Kindergarten tchr. Trinidad (Colo.) Sch. Dist. #1, 1987-94, elem. counselor, 1994-96, fifth grade tchr., 1996—. Mem. ACA, Am. Fedn. Tchrs.

TRUJILLO, MICHAEL JOSEPH, elementary school principal; b. L.A., May 14, 1939; s. Damacio and Helen (Rubalcava) T.; m. Yolanda Flores, June 23, 1973; children: Roberto Miguel, Antonio Miguel. BA in Spanish, Iona Coll., 1961; MA in Counseling Psychology, Santa Clara U., 1973. Cert. tchr., adminstr., supr., pupil pers., Calif. Tchr. St. Laurence H.S., Chgo., 1961-62, Christian Bros. H.S., Butte, Mont., 1962-64, Damien Meml. H.S., Honolulu, 1964-68, St. Patrick's H.S., Vallejo, Calif., 1968-71; jr. H.S. tchr., elem. sch. counselor, vice prin. jr. H.S. Pajaro Valley Unified Sch. Dist., Watsonville, Calif., 1971-77; elem. sch. prin. Natividad Sch. Salinas (Calif.) City Sch. Dist., Salinas, 1977-96; elem. sch. prin. Loma Vista Sch. Salinas (Calif.) City Sch. Dist., Salinas, 1996—; cons., presenter in planning for year round edn. Bd. dirs. North Monterey Unified Sch. Dist., Moss Landing, Calif., 1983-91. Recipient Cert. of Recognition, Calif. Senator Henry Mello, 1992. Mem. ASCD, NAESP, Calif. Assn. Yr. Round Edn. (pres. 1994-95), Assn. Calif. Sch. Adminstrs. Democrat. Roman Catholic. Home: 14597 Charter Oak Blvd Salinas CA 93907-1015 Office: Loma Vista Sch 757 Sausal Dr Salinas CA 93906

TRUJILLO, TEÓFILO-CARLOS, writer, publisher, history educator; b. Durango, Mex., Oct. 22, 1950; s. Teófilo and Consuelo (Martínez) T. BA in History, San Diego State U., 1986. Prof. history Colegio Luis Cervantes, Guadalajara, Mex., 1987-88, Inst. de Estudios Superiores de Occidente, Guadalajara, Mex., 1987-88; founder Editorial San Diego, 1992—; subs. tchr. San Diego and Miami pub. schs., 1990—; cons. to writers and journalists, Mexico City. Author, pub.: Teoria de la Historia, 1993; author: Elvis: Rey del Rock 'n Roll, 1996; editl. writer (daily) El Mexicano, 1976-86, (weekly) Zeta, 1987-89. Hon. Rep. Presdl. Task Force, 1992. Roman Catholic. Home and Office: Editl San Diego 232C Otay Valley Rd Chula Vista CA 91911

TRUMAN, EDWARD CRANE, real estate manager, consultant, composer; b. Des Moines, Dec. 28, 1915; s. Wright Edward and Annie Louise (Cate) T.; m. Maxine LeVon Hemping, June 28, 1947 (dec. Apr. 1983); 1 child, Robert E.C. Student, UCLA, 1966, 72; BA in English, Immaculate Heart Coll., 1978; MA in Psychology, U. Redlands, 1980. Asst. program dir. Cowles Broadcasting, Des Moines, 1938-44; pub. rels. writer Armed Forces Radio Svcs., Hollywood, Calif., 1944-46; staff musician Don Lee Mut. Radio, Hollywood, Calif., 1946-48, ABC-TV, Hollywood, Calif., 1948-53; music dir., composer TV series NBC-TV, Burbank, Calif., 1955-60; freelance organist, composer Hollywood, 1960—, real estate property mgr., owner, 1974—; bd. dirs. Gen. Affiliates U. Calif., Santa Barbara, chair scholarship com., 1988—; co-founder Artasia Seminars, L.A., 1972-75. Composer: Matinee, 1956, Broadcast Mood Music, Bowie Knife, 1958, Songs for Builders, 1960. Endowment grantor in religious studies U. Calif., Santa Barbara, 1984—, mem. pres.'s ctr., 1993—; endowment grantor in humanities Drake U., Des Moines, 1994, mem. pres.'s cir., 1995—; mem. judging panels acad. advancement program UCLA, 1994—. Recipient citation Dept. Edn., 1976, commendation City Atty. Office, L.A., 1993. Mem. Nat. Acad. TV Arts and Scis. (Emmy panels, music br.), Pacific Pioneer Broadcasters (bd. dirs. 1988-91, Golden Circle award 1991), Musician's Union (asst. to pres. Local 47 1969-77). Democrat. Episcopalian. Home: 1826 Jewett Dr Los Angeles CA 90046-7702 Office: Compass-Am Group 1826 Jewett Dr Los Angeles CA 90046-7702

TRUNDLE, W(INFIELD) SCOTT, publishing executive newspaper; b. Maryville, Tenn., Mar. 24, 1939; s. Winfield Scott and Alice (Smith) T.; m. Elizabeth Latshaw, Oct. 14, 1989; children: Stephen, Allison. B.A., Vanderbilt U., 1961, J.D., 1967. Bar: Tenn. 1967. Spl. agt. U.S. Secret Service, 1963-66; asso. to partner firm Hunter, Smith, Davis & Norris, Kingsport, Tenn., 1967-72; pub. Kingsport (Tenn.) Times-News, 1972-78; pres. Greensboro (N.C.) Daily News, 1978-80; exec. v.p. Jefferson Pilot Publs., Inc., Greensboro and Clearwater, Fla., 1980-82; v.p., bus. mgr. Tampa Tribune (Fla.), 1982-91; sr. v.p. Hillsborough Community Coll., 1991-93; publisher Ogden (Utah) Standard Examiner, 1993—; assoc. prof. E. Tenn. State U., 1973-77. Bd. dirs. Downtown Ogden, Inc. Mem. Tenn. Bar Assn., Utah Press Assn. (pres., bd. dirs.), Weber Ogden C. of C. (bd. dirs.). Methodist. Home: 1580 Maule Dr Ogden UT 84403-0413 Office: Ogden Publ Corp 455 23d St PO Box 951 Ogden UT 84402

TRUSLER, JAMES HALL, oil company research and development technician; b. Newton, Iowa, Dec. 2, 1940; s. Clifford Wayne and Wanda Elizabeth (Bowen) T.; widowed 1995; children: Heather Eileen, James Benjamin. BA in English, Iowa State U., Ames, 1965. Lab. technician Colgate-Palmolive Co., Jersey City, 1960-61; sr. rsch. technician Chevron, Richmond, Calif., 1967—. Co-Authored articles "Deleterious Effects of Caustic Cleaner Solution Contamination on Paper Machine Lubricant Properties", 1996, Lubrication Engring. Patentee processes for pelletizing. Head trustee United Meth. Ch., Martinez, Calif., 1985—.

TRUSSELL, R(OBERT) RHODES, environmental engineer; b. National City, Calif; s. Robert L. and Margaret (Kessing) T.; m. Elizabeth Shane, Nov. 26, 1969; children: Robert Shane, Charles Bryan. BSCE, U. Calif.-Berkeley, 1966, MS, 1967, PhD, 1972. With Montgomery Watson, Inc. (formerly J.M. Montgomery Cons. Engrs.), Pasadena, Calif., 1972—, v.p., 1977, sr. v.p., 1986, dir. applied tech., 1988-92, sr. v.p., dir. of corp. devel., 1992— Mem. com. on water treatment chems. Nat. Acad. Sci., 1980-82, mem. com. 3d part cert., 1982-83, com. on irrigation-induced water quality problems, 1985-88, indirect potable pense, 96—, Am. Water Work Commn. on mixing of water treatment chems., 1988-90; mem. U.S./German rsch. com. on corrosion of water systems, 1984-85; mem. U.S./Dutch rsch. com. on organics in water, 1982-83; mem. U.S./USSR rsch. com. on water treatment, 1985-88, U.S./E.C. Com. Corrosion in Water, 1992-94. Mem. joint editl. bd. Standards Methods for Examination of Water and Wastewater, 1980-89; mem. editl. adv. bd. Environ. and Sci. and Tech., 1977-83; contbr. articles to profl. publs. Mem. AIChE, NAE, Water Works Assn. (mem. editl. adv. bd. jour. 1987-94, EPA sci. adv. bd. com. on drinking water 1988-91, 94—, cons. radon disinfectant by products 1993, cons. on disinfection and disinfection byproducts 1994, ad hoc sci. adv. com. on arsenic 1995-96), Internat. Water Supply Assn. (U.S. rep. to standing com. on water quality and treatment 1990-94, chmn. com. on disinfection and mem. sci. and tech. coun. 1994—), Water Pollution Control Fedn., Internat. Water Pollution Rsch. Assn., Am. Chem. Soc., Nat. Assn. Corrosion Engrs., Sigma Xi. Office: Montgomery Watson 300 N Lake Ave Ste 1200 Pasadena CA 91101-4106

TRUTA, MARIANNE PATRICIA, oral and maxillofacial surgeon, educator, author; b. N.Y.C., Apr. 28, 1951; d. John J. and Helen Patricia (Donnelly) T.; m. William Christopher Donlon, May 28, 1983; 1 child Sean Liam Riobard Donlon. BS, St. John's U., 1974; DMD, SUNY, Stonybrook, 1977. Intern The Mt. Sinai Med. Ctr., N.Y.C., 1977-78, resident, 1978-80, chief resident, 1980-81; asst. prof. U. of the Pacific, San Francisco, 1983-85, clin. asst. prof., 1985-94; asst. dir. Facial Pain Rsch. Ctr., San Francisco, 1986-92; pvt. practice oral and maxillofacial surgery Peninsula Maxillofacial Surgery, South San Francisco, Calif., 1985—, Burlingame, Calif., 1988—, Redwood City, Calif., 1990-95, San Carlos, Calif., 1995—. Contbr. articles to profl. jours., chpts. to textbooks. Mem. Am. Assn. Oral Maxillofacial Surgeons, Am. Dental Soc. Anesthesiology, Am. Soc. Cosmetic Surgery, Am. Assn. Women Dentists, Western Soc. Oral Maxillofacial Surgeons, No. Calif. Soc. Oral Maxillofacial Surgeons, San Mateo County Dental Soc. (bd. dirs. 1995). Office: Peninsula Maxillofacial Surgery 1860 El Camino Real Ste 300 Burlingame CA 94010-3114

TSAI, CHIH-LING, management educator; b. Taipei, Republic of China, Jan. 7, 1952; came to U.S., 1976; s. Liang-Chih and Chen-Ling (Lu) T.; m. Yu-Yen Ho, Sept. 27, 1952; children: Wen-Lin, Wen-Ting. BS, Tankang Univ., Taipei, 1974; MS, Univ. Ill., 1978; PhD, Univ. Minn., 1983. Asst. prof. bus. NYU, N.Y.C., 1983-85; lectr. Univ. Tex., Austin, 1985-86; from assoc. prof. to prof. mgmt. Univ. Calif., Davis, 1988-93, prof. mgmt., 1993—. Contbr. articles to profl. jours. Office: Grad Sch Mgmt Univ Calif Davis Davis CA 95616-8609

TSCHACHER, DARELL RAY, mortgage banking executive; b. Wendell, Idaho, Oct. 17, 1945; s. Lewis Edward and Erma Irene (Parmely) T.; m. Judith Allyn Evers, Dec. 30, 1966; children: Kendall Ray, Kristin Allyn. Grad. high sch. Cert. bus. counselor; lic. real estate broker, Calif., Idaho. Ptnr. KD Air Svc., Apple Valley, Calif., 1967-68; real estate broker Calif., 1968-73; v.p., dir. mktg. Chism Homes, Inc., Las Vegas, Nev., 1973-78; self-employed real estate, fin., bus. cons., 1978-87; reg. v.p. br. ops. Nat. First Mortgage Co., 1987-88; sr. v.p., western reg. mgr. Nat. First Mortgage Co., Rancho Cordova, Calif., 1988-91; v.p., div. mgr. Ryland Mortgage Co., Rancho Cordova, 1991-94; v.p., regional mgr. Ryland Mortgage Co., Woodland Hills, Calif., 1995; v.p., project mgr., prodn. redesign Ryland Mortgage Co., Columbia, Md., 1996—; pres. Premier Escrow Co., Woodland Hills, Calif., 1996; self employed business cons., 1997—; pres. Home Acquisition Systems, Inc. Bd. dirs. Tomorrow's Hope, Boise, Idaho, 1985; exec. com. MDA of No. Calif., Sacramento, 1991. With USAF, 1963-67. Mem. Homebuilders of S.W. Idaho (bd. dirs. 1976-78), Idaho Home Owners Warranty Coun. (bd. dirs. 1977), Treasure Valley Exchangors (bd. dirs. 1980-84, Exchangor of the Yr. 1982), Soc. Exchange Counselors. Republican. Home: 792 N Nicklaus Ln Eagle ID 83616

TSCHANG, TAI-PO, pathologist; b. Taipei, Taiwan, Republic of China, Feb. 14, 1947; came to U.S., 1965; s. Hsi-Lin and Ping (Ching) T.; m. Pui-Suen Wong (dec. 1984); children: Chi-Chu, Chi-Young, Chi-Jia; m. Grace C. Huang. BA, So. Ill. U., 1969; MD, Duke U., 1972. Diplomate Am. Bd. Anatomic and Clin. Pathology. Pathologist St. Elizabeth Hosp., Beaumont, Tex., 1977-86; dir. pathology St. Agnes Med. Ctr., Fresno, Calif., 1986—. Contbr. articles to profl. jours. Fellow Coll. Am. Pathologists, Am. Soc. Clin. Pathology; mem. Am. Assn. Blood Banks. Office: St Agnes Med Ctr 1303 E Herndon Ave Fresno CA 93720-3309

TSCHERNISCH, SERGEI P., academic administrator. BA, San Francisco State U.; MFA in Theatre, Stanford U.; student, San Francisco Actors' Workshop, Stanford Repertory Theatre. Founding mem. Calif. Inst. of Arts, 1969, mem. faculty, assoc. dean Sch. Theatre, dir., 1969-80; prof. dept. theatre U. Md., College Park, 1980-82; dir. divsn. performing and visual arts Northeastern U., Boston, 1982-92; dean Coll. of Comm. and Fine Arts Loyola Marymount U., L.A., 1992-94; pres. Cornish Coll. of Arts, Seattle, 1994—; advisor NEA; mem. com. USIA; cons. to many festivals. Office: Cornish Coll of Arts 710 E Roy St Seattle WA 98102-4604*

TSE, KELVIN ANTHONY, dentist; b. Cleve., Dec. 29, 1962; s. Kenneth K. and Joyce (Auyeung) T.; m. Cynthia Lee Weideman, Aug. 20, 1994; 1 child, Carleen Ann. BS in Marine Biology, Loyola Marymount U., 1984; DDS, U. Pacific, 1989; cert. esthetic dentistry, UCLA, 1994. Lic. dentist, Calif. Pvt. practice Alhambra, Calif., 1990-94, Citrus Heights, Calif., 1995—; dir. Am. Soc. Dentistry for Children. Mem. ADA, Am. Acad. Cosmetic Dentistry, Internat. Congress Oral Implantologists, Sacramento Dist. Dental Soc., Rotary Club. Office: 7916 Pebble Beach Dr Ste 103 Citrus Heights CA 95610-7790

TSENG, FELIX HING-FAI, accountant; b. Kowloon, Hong Kong, May 11, 1964; s. Hin-Pei and Selena Suk-Ching Tseng; m. Rachel Wai-Chu, Feb. 16, 1992; children: Walter Fan-Kong, Riley Fan-Wei. BS, Pepperdine U., 1985, MBA, 1989. CPA. Acct. Ronald A. Stein CPA, Woodland Hills, Calif., 1989-93; contr. Benebase Investment Inc., Monterey Park, Calif., 1991—; also bd. dirs. Benebase Investment Inc., Monterey Park, Calif., Hong Kong; ptnr. Lilly Property Mgmt., L.A., 1995—; bd. dirs. YTT Corp., Monterey Park. Editor (newsletter) El Toro, 1993-96. Mem. AICPA, Inst. Mgmt. Accts. (v.p. comm. 1994-95, pres. 1995-96), Calif. Soc. CPA, So. Calif. Soc. CMAs, Assn. MBA Execs. Office: Benebase Investment Inc 108 N Ynez Ave Ste 209 Monterey Park CA 91754-1680

TSINIGINE, ALLEN, educator; b. Tuba City, Ariz., Feb. 25, 1952; s. Claw and Desbah (Martin) T.; 1 child, Ryan Allen. BS in Elem. Edn., No. Ariz. U., 1974. Cert. tchr., Ariz. Tchr. Page (Ariz.) Unified Sch. Dist. # 8, 1974-85; asst. dir., instr. LeChee Vocat. Tech. Ctr., Page, 1987-93; instr. prealgebra, algebra Coconino County C.C., Page, 1992—; instr. math. Coconino C.C., Page, 1992—; presdl. appointee, exec. staff asst. Navajo Dept. Edn., 1993-95; mem. Nat. Indian Policy Ctr., George Washington U., 1995-96; edn. com. co-chair Nat. Congress Am. Indians, 1995-96. Mem. gov. bd. dirs. Page Unified Sch. Dist. #8, 1987-93, pres., 1988-90, 91-92, clk., 1990-91, 92-93; sec.-treas. LeChee chpt. Navajo Nation, 1979-87; mem. Navajo Way, Inc., Window Rock, Ariz., 1987-92. Mem. Nat. Sch. Bds. Assn., Native Am. Caucus, Nat. Ind. Edn. Assn. (pres.). Home: PO Box 292 Page AZ 86040-0292 Office: LeChee Vocat Tech Ctr Coppermine Rd-LeChee Page AZ 86040

TSUJIO, HIROKAZU, computer consultant; b. Tokyo, Oct. 7, 1955; came to U.S., 1995; s. Hiroshi and Kazuko (Kimoto) T.; m. Marjolaine Gagnon, Oct. 4, 1980; children: Jonathan, Stephanie. Student, Prince Hotel Sch., Tokyo, 1976. Maitre'd Restaurant Katsura, Montreal, 1977-83; MIS dir. Scotbage, Montreal, 1983-92; cons. Techsyscom Inc., Montreal, 1992-95; ind. Oracle database cons. Beaverton, Oreg., 1995—. Home and Office: 16295 NW Schendel Ave # 14-b Beaverton OR 97006-8307

TSUNG, CHRISTINE CHAI-YI, financial executive, treasurer; b. Nanking, China, Mar. 23, 1948; came to U.S., 1970; d. Chi-Huang Tsung and Siao-Tuan Huang; m. Icheng Wu, Aug. 14, 1971 (div. Dec. 1989); m. Jerome Chen, Aug. 10, 1990; children: Jonathan, Julia. BBA, Nat. Taiwan U., Taipei, 1970; postgrad., Washington U., St. Louis, 1970-71; MBA, U. Mo., 1973. Acct. Capital Land Co., St. Louis, 1972-74; chief acct. Servis Equipment Co., Inc., Dallas, 1974-75; acctg. supr. Calif. Microwave, Sunnyale, 1975-76; budget and sales mgr. Columbia Pictures TV Internat., Burbank, Calif., 1976-77; acctg. mgr. Husquarna, San Diego, 1977-82; sr. acct. City of Poway, Calif., 1982-88, fin. mgr., 1988-95; pres., treas. Jade Poly Investment, Beverly Hills, Calif., 1989—; cons. assoc. Metro Properties, San Diego, 1989—. Tchr. San Diego North County Chinese Sch., 1985-86; v.p. San Diego Chinese Culture Assn., 1982-86, bd. dirs., 1988-90, 93-94. Mem. Govt. Fin. Officers Assn. (Cert. of Achievement 1988-94), Calif. Soc. Mcpl. Fin. Officers (standing com. membership devel., Cert. of Award 1988-94), Mcpl. Treas. Assn. U.S. and Can., Taiwanese C. of C. of N.Am. (bd. dirs. 1994-95). Home: 808 N Bedford Dr Beverly Hills CA 90210 Office: Jade Poly Investments PO Box 3719 Beverly Hills CA 90212

TSUO, ANNE LI, database specialist; b. Taipei, Taiwan, Republic of China, June 5, 1950; d. Bing-Ching Benn and Chong-Jye (Liang) Lee; m. Yuan-Huai Simon Tsuo, Apr. 7, 1974; children: Lee Kirjohn, Leo Kirtie. M in Computer Info. Sci., U. Denver, 1989; postgrad., NYU. Therapeutic dietitian Coney Island Hosp., Bklyn., 1974-75; dietitian Carlton Nursing Home, Bklyn., 1975-76; therapeutic dietitian Flatbush Gen. Hosp., Bklyn., 1976-78; clin. dietitian Johnston-Willis Hosp., Richmond, Va., 1978-79, Mercy Med. Ctr., Denver, 1982-87; cons. nutritionist Nutrition Cons. Svc., Golden, Colo., 1982—; data analyst Colo. Found. for Med. Care, Denver, 1989-90, tech. program coord., 1990-92; database specialist Nat. Renewable Energy Lab., Golden, 1992-96; mem. tech. staff application software engr., technical lead info. tech. U.S. West Com., Denver, 1996—; speaker for health and nutrition subjects The Rocky Mountain Engring. and Sci. Coun., Denver, 1989-92. Contbr. articles to profl. jours. Bd. dirs. The Colo. Chinese Club, Denver, 1991-93; record custodian The Boy Scout of Am., Troop 166, Lakewood, Colo., 1992—. Fellow The Am. Dietetic Assn.; mem. The Colo. Dietetic Assn., The Denver Dietetic Assn., The Data Processing Mgmt. Assn. Democrat. Roman Catholic. Home: 2850 Joyce St Golden CO 80401-1323

TSUTAKAWA, DEEMS AKIHIKO, musician, composer, record producer; b. Seattle, Jan. 21, 1952; s. George and Ayame Tsutakawa; m. Jean Tsutakawa, July 17, 1982. Owner J-Town Records, Seattle, 1980—; profl. jazz pianist, Seattle, 1970—. Recorder albums, cassette recordings, CDs, 1977—. Mem. Seattle Tennis Ctr. Home: PO Box 78035 Seattle WA 98178

TSUTAKAWA, EDWARD MASAO, management consultant; b. Seattle, May 15, 1921; s. Jin and Michiko (Oka) T.; student U. Wash., 1941, Wash. State U., 1949; m. Hide Kunugi, Aug. 11, 1949; children: Nancy Joyce Tsutakawa Seigel, Margaret Ann Langston, Mark Edward. Free-lance comml. artist, Spokane, 1943-47; artist Maag & Porter Comml. Printers, Spokane, 1947-54; organizer Litho Art Printers, Inc., Spokane, 1954—, gen. mgr., pres., 1965-80; charter organizer, dir. Am. Comml. Bank, 1965-80; prin. E. M. Tsutakawa Co., bus. cons. and dir., 1980—; v.p., operation officer, dir. Mukogawa Ft. Wright Inst. Pres. emeritus Spokane-Nishinomiya Sister City Soc., Sister Cities Assn. of Spokane; mem Eastern Wash. State Hist. Soc.; bd. dirs., chmn. Spokane Regional Internat. Trade Alliance, Intercollegiate Nursing Edn., Leadership Spokane. Recipient Disting. Svc. medal Boy Scouts of Japan, 1967, Cultural medal in Edn., Japan, 1985, Disting. Svc. award City of Nishinomiya, 1971, Disting. Svc. to Expo '74 State of Wash., 1974, Book of Golden Deeds award Exchange Club, 1978, Disting. Community Scv. award UN Assn., 1979, Whitworth Coll., 1987, Svc. to Youth award Spokane YMCA, 1988; decorated Order of Sacred Treasure medal Govt. of Japan, 1984. Mem. Japanese Am. Citizens League. Methodist. Clubs: Kiwanis (Spokane). Home: 4116 S Madelia St Spokane WA 99203-4229

TSVANKIN, ILYA DANIEL, geophysics educator; b. Moscow, Apr. 6, 1956; came to U.S., 1990; s. Daniel and Maya (Slonimskaya) T.; m. Olga Dashevskaya, July 27, 1985; children: Edward, Daniel. MS in Geophys. Exploration, Moscow State U., 1978, PhD in Geophysics, 1982. Rsch. scientist Inst. Phys. of the Earth, Moscow, 1978-86, dep. chief of lab., 1986-89; cons. Rsch. Ctr. Amoco Prodn. Co., Tulsa, 1990-92; assoc. prof. Colo. Sch. Mines, Golden, 1992—; co-leader Ctr. for Wave Phenomena rsch. project. Contbr. articles to profl. publs.; patentee in field. Recipient Gold medal in Geophysics for Young Scientists, Soviet Acad. Scis., 1988. Mem. Am. Geophys. Union, Denver Geophys. Soc., Soc. Exploration Geophysicists (translation com. 1990—, Virgil Kauffman Gold Medal award 1996), European Assn. Exploration Geophysists.

TU, JOHN, engineering executive; b. 1941. With Motorola Co., Wiesbaden, Germany, 1966-74; pres. Tu Devel., L.A., 1975-82, Camintonn Corp., Santa Ana, Calif., 1982-85; v.p., gen. mgr. AST Rsch., Irvine, Calif., 1985-87; pres. Newgen Systems Corp., Fountain Valley, Calif., 1987—; CEO Kingston Tech., Fountain Valley, 1988—. Office: 17600 Newhope St Fountain Valley CA 92708-4220

TU, SAMSON W., computer science researcher; b. Taipei, Taiwan, Jan. 31, 1954; came to U.S., 1972; s. Grant T. and Lillian L. T.; m. Polly Lien, Feb. 20, 1987 (div. July 1992). AB in Math., Harvard U., 1977; MS in Computer Engring., Stanford U., 1985. Mem. tech. staff Sytek, Inc., Mountain View, Calif., 1982-83; rsch. scientist Stanford (Calif.) U., 1985—. Group coord. Amnesty Internat. U.S.A., Palo Alto, Calif., 1994. Mem. Am. Assn. Artificial Intelligence, Assn. Computing Machinery.

TUAZON, JESUS OCAMPO, electrical engineer, educator, consultant; b. Manila, Jan. 2, 1940; came to U.S., 1963; s. Filomeno and Patrocino (Ocampo) T.; m. Norma Mamangun, Oct. 12, 1963; children: Maria, Noel, Norman, Mary, Michelle. BSEE, Mapua Inst., Manila, 1962; MSEE, Iowa State U., 1965, PhD, 1969. Elec. prof. Calif. State U., Fullerton, Calif., 1969—; scientist Jet Propulsion Lab., Pasadena, Calif., 1984—; computer cons. Hughes Aircraft, Fullerton, 1977, Gen. Dynamic, Pomona, Calif., 1983, U.S. Naval Weapon Sta., Seal Beach, Calif., 1978-83. Author of papers for profl. confs. Mem. IEEE, Am. Assn. Engring Educators. Democrat. Roman Catholic. Home: 816 S Verona St Anaheim CA 92804-4035 Office: Calif State Univ 800 N State College Blvd Fullerton CA 92831-3547 also: Jet Propulsion Lab 4800 Oak Grove Dr Pasadena CA 91109-8001

TUBBS, JANET CAROLYN, educational consultant; b. Mineola, N.Y.; d. Gale Huntington and Janet McKinnon (Sloan) Rice; children: Linda, John, Robert, Debra. Founder Arcadia Press; founder, pres. Children's Resource Ctr., Scottsdale, Ariz., 1988—; condr. workshops in field; lectr. in field. Author: Don't Worry, They'll grow Up - A Parent's Survival Guide, If You Can't Pronounce It, Don't Eat It, All Children Are Special; developer: The Phrenogarten Method of Education, 1991, Middle Aged Children, A Survival Guide for Kids Ages 9 to 12. Bd. dirs. Very Spl. Arts; exhibit chair World Congress, 1992. Mem. Nat. Assn. for Edn. Young Children, World Orgn. for Early Childhood Edn. (exhibit chmn.). Office: Children's Resource Ctr PO Box 8697 Scottsdale AZ 85252-8697

TUBBS, WILLIAM REID, JR., public service administrator; b. Johnson Air Base, Japan, June 1, 1950; s. William Reid and Roberta Daisy (Krenkel) T.; m. Ellen Lee Duccini, May 19, 1984; 1 child, Catlin Alyse. BA, Calif. State U., Sacramento, 1973, MPA, 1981. Assoc. analyst adminstrn. and fin. agy. County of Sacramento, 1975-84, program coordinator emergency ops., 1984-85; adminstrv. dir. Sacramento County Mental Health Treatment Ctr., 1985—. Chmn. Cable TV Adv. Commn., West Sacramento, Calif., 1987-90; pipe maj. City Sacramento Pipe Band. Lt. comdr. USCGR. Mem. Am. Soc. Pub. Adminstrn., Res. Officers Assn., U.S. Naval Inst., Am. Radio Relay League. Republican. Office: Sacramento Co Mental Health 2150 Stockton Blvd Sacramento CA 95817-1337

TUCH, RICHARD HOWARD, psychoanalyst, psychiatrist; b. L.A., Apr. 14, 1949; s. Irving and Shirley Josephine (Edelstein) T.; m. Sunnye Louise Jaffe, oct. 31, 1952. BA, U. Calif., Santa Barbara, 1971; MD, U. So. Calif. 1975. Diplomate Am. Bd Psychiatry and Neurology; cert. in psychoanalysis. Intern Children's Hosp., L.A., 1975-76; resident Neuropsychiat. Inst. UCLA, 1976-79; asst. clin. prof. psychiatry, mem. faculty Grad. Ctr. for Child Devel. and Psychotherapy; v.p. med. staff Van Nuys (Calif.) Psychiat. Hosp., 1981-82; med. dir. Treatment Ctrs. of Am., San Fernando Valley, 1984-87; clin. dir. adult program Westwood Hosp., 1988-93; pvt. practice L.A., 1979—; tng. and supervision psychoanalyst L.A. Psychoanalytic Soc. and Inst., 1992—; presenter in field. Contbr. articles to profl. jours. Past bd. dirs. Family Svcs. L.A. Mem. Am. Psychiat. Assn., So. Calif. Psychiat. Soc. (program com. 1981-84, co-chair program 1986-87, treas. elect 1990, treas., 1991), Am. Psychoanalytic Assn., L.A. Med. Assn., Calif. Med. Assn. Office: 1800 Fairburn Ave Ste 206 Los Angeles CA 90025-4968

TUCK, EDWARD FENTON, business consultant, venture capitalist; b. Memphis, July 5, 1931; s. Edward Fenton and Jane Florence (Lewis) T.; m. Janet Allene Barber, July 6, 1957; children: Jean, Ann. BSEE, Mo. Sch. Mines, 1953; elec. engr. (hon.), U. Mo., 1980. Registered profl. engr., Calif., Mo., Ala. Various engring. and mfg. mgmt. positions Lenkurt Elec. Co. div. GTE, San Carlos, Calif., 1957-62; v.p., co-founder Kebby Microwave Corp., San Carlos, 1962-64; v.p., tech. dir. ITT Telecommunications, N.Y.C., 1965-72; gen. mgr., pres. Tel-Tone Corp., Kirkland, Wash., 1972-74; v.p. mktg. and engring. Am. Telecommunications Corp., El Monte, Calif., 1975-79; pres. Edward Tuck & Co., Inc., West Covina, Calif., 1979-86; gen. ptnr. The Boundary Fund, West Covina, 1986-95; dir. Peninsula Wireless, Inc., San Carlos, Calif., Applied Digital Access, San Diego, TriQuint Semiconductors, Beaverton, Oreg.; chmn. Endgate Corp., Sunnyvale, Calif.; vice-chmn. Teledesic Corp., Kirkland, Wash. Contbr. articles to profl. jours. Trustee U. Mo., Rolla. Served with U.S. Army, 1954-56. Named mem. Acad. Elec. Engring. U. Mo. Fellow Instn. Radio, Elec. and Electronic Engrs. Australia; mem. IEEE (sr., 1st prize for article 1962), Assn. Profl. Cons. (pres., bd. dirs. 1979-86), AAAS. Democrat. Office: Kinship Partners II Ste 200 1900 W Garvey S West Covina CA 91790

TUCK, MICHAEL RAY, technical services executive; b. Pocatello, Idaho, Aug. 9, 1941; s. Amos R. and Phyllis (Day) T.; m. Heather K. Fowler, Oct. 22, 1962; children: Lisa M., Jennifer A., M. Mark. BS in Math., Idaho

State U., 1964; MS in Math., U. Idaho, 1971. Programmer analyst Argonne Nat. Labs., Idaho Falls, Idaho, 1964-69; computer scientist Argonne Nat. Labs., Idaho Falls, 1969-76; engr., mgr. computer div. Montana Energy Inst., Butte, Mont., 1976-81; v.p. MultiTech Inc. div. MSE Inc., Butte, 1981-82, pres., 1982-83, v.p., 1983-87; sr. v.p., COO MSE Tech. Applications, Inc., Butte, 1987-94; pres. MSE Tech. Applications Inc., Butte, 1994—, also bd. dirs.; cons. TMA Assocs., Butte, 1982-83. Mem. Exchange Club. Methodist. Office: MSE Tech Applications Inc PO Box 4078 Butte MT 59702-4078

TUCKER, ANNABELLE DORIS, medical device company executive; b. Whittier, Calif., Jan. 11, 1922; d. Raymond Kleeman and Violet N. (Arnold) Covington; m. John Warren Tucker, Aug. 29, 1948 (dec. Apr. 1995); children: Richard Warren, Brian Lee. Degree in Nursing, Bishop Johnson Coll. Nursing, L.A., 1946. RN, Calif. Maternal and child health nurse Foster Mem. Hosp., Ventura, Calif., 1946; med. and cardioly ward Birmingham Vets. Hosp., Van Nuys, Calif., 1946-47; maternal and child health nurse Hosp. Good Samaritan, L.A., 1947-50; nurse various drs. offices, 1950-73; maternal and child health nurse Tarzana (Calif.) Regional Med. Ctr., 1973-87; pres., owner, innovator RN/MDs, Inc., Sherman Oaks, Calif., 1992—; cons. in field. Editor (newsletter) Clin. Voice; contbr. articles to profl. jours.; patentee in field. Mem. Assn. Practitioners in Infection Control, Calif. Women Bus. Owners, Hosp. Good Samaritan Alumni Assn. Republican. Episcopalian. Home and Office: 4480 Sherman Oaks Cir Sherman Oaks CA 91403-3829

TUCKER, JAMES RAYMOND, primary education educator; b. Pueblo, Colo., Apr. 18, 1944; s. James George and Pauline F. (Sena) T.; m. Kathie Owens; 1 child, Brittany. BA, U. So. Colo., 1966; MA, U. No. Colo., 1990, postgrad., 1991. Tchr. Sinclair Mid. Sch., Englewood, Colo., 1971-93, Denver Pub. Schs., 1993—; co-dir. Nick Bolleteri Tennis Acad., Boulder, Colo., 1986; head tennis coach Englewood High Sch., 1971—. Sgt. U.S. Army, 1967-70. Mem. NEA, U.S. Profl. Tennis Assn., U.S. Profl. Tennis Registry, Internat. Platform Assn., Colo. Edn. Assn., Meadow Creek Tennis and Fitness, Colo. H.S. Coaches Assn. (Achievement award 1989, 92, Tchr. of Yr. 1973, 78, 86, Coach of Yr. 1986, 87, 90, 93, 96, Franklin award 1988, 89). Home: 2316 S Harlan Ct Denver CO 80227-3962

TUCKER, JOEL LAWRENCE, aviation company executive; b. Berkeley, Calif., Feb. 23, 1932; s. Lawrence Otis Tucker and Edythe Lauretta (Pye) Connolly; m. Constance Nadine Finnick, Oct. 19, 1951 (div. Sept. 1975); 1 child, John Lawrence; m. Cristita Gozarin, Feb. 15, 1992. BS, U. Wash., 1953. Statistician Bell Telephone System, Seattle, 1953-61, AID, Washington, 1961-64; dir. sales Boeing Comml. Airplanes, Seattle, 1965-87; pres. J.E.T. Cons. Ltd., Kirkland, Wash., 1987—; mng. dir. Lorad Boeing Ltd., Hamilton, Bermuda, 1988-89. Chmn. Citizens Sch. Adv. Coun., Bellevue, Wash., 1969-71. With U.S. Army, 1954-56. Republican. Presbyterian.

TUCKER, MARCUS OTHELLO, judge; b. Santa Monica, Calif., Nov. 12, 1934; s. Marcus Othello Sr. and Essie Louvonia (McLendon) T.; m. Indira Hale, May 29, 1965; 1 child, Angelique. BA, U. So. Calif., 1956; JD, Howard U., 1960. Bar: Calif. 1962, U.S. Dist. Ct. (cen. dist.) Calif. 1962, U.S. Ct. Appeals (9th cir.) 1965, U.S. Ct. Internat. Trade 1970, U.S. Supreme Ct. 1971. Pvt. practice, Santa Monica, 1962-63, 67-74; dep. atty. City of Santa Monica, 1963-65; asst. atty. U.S. Dist. Ct. (Cen. Dist.) Calif., 1965-67; commr. L.A. Superior Ct., 1974-76; judge mcpl. ct. Long Beach (Calif.) Jud. Dist., 1976-85; judge superior ct. L.A. Jud. Dist., 1985—; supervising judge L.A. County Dependency Ct. L.A. Superior Ct., 1991-92, presiding judge Juvenile divsn., 1993-94; asst. prof. law Pacific U., Long Beach, 1984, 86; justice pro tem U.S. Ct. Appeals (2nd cir.), 1981; mem. exec. com. Superior Ct. of L.A. County, 1995-96. Mem. editl. staff Howard U. Law Sch. Jour., 1959-60. Pres. Community Rehab. Industries Found., Long Beach, 1983-86, Legal Aid Found., L.A., 1976-77; bd. dirs. Long Beach coun. Boy Scouts Am., 1978-92. With U.S. Army, 1960-66. Named Judge of Yr. Juvenile Cts. Bar Assn., 1986, Disting. Jurist Long Beach Trial Trauma Coun., 1987, Honoree in Law Handy Community Ctr., L.A., 1987, Bernard S. Jefferson Jurist of Yr. John M. Langston Bar Assn. Black Lawyers, 1990, Judge of Yr. Long Beach Bar Assn., 1993; recipient award for Law-Related Edn. Constl. Rights Found./L.A. County Bar Assn., 1992, commendation L.A. County Bd. Suprs., 1994. Fellow Internat. Acad. Trial Judges; mem. ABA, Calif. Judges Assn. (chmn. juvenile law com. 1986-87), Langston Bar Assn. (pres. bd. dirs. 1972, 73), Calif. Assn. Black Lawyers, Santa Monica Bay Dist. Bar Assn. (treas. 1969-71), Am. Inns of Ct., Selden Soc. Office: 7281 E Quill St Dept 250 Downey CA 90242

TUCKER, MARY LINDA, management educator, consultant; b. Andalusia, Ala., Dec. 7, 1945; d. Bennett D. and Pearl A. T.; children: Mandi Shayne Tucker, Matthew Little. BS, Nicholls State U., Thibodaux, La., 1984; MEd summa cum laude, Nicholls State U., Thibodeau, La., 1985; PhD in Ednl. Leadership and Founds., U. New Orleans, 1990. Tchrs. aide St. Clements Episc. Sch., El Paso, 1975-76; co-owner sporting goods store, Marianna, Fla., 1976-82; prof. Nicholls State U., 1984-93; prof. dept. mgmt. Colo. State U., Ft. Collins, 1993—; cons. to banks, La., 1984-93. Contbr. chpts. to books, articles and book revs. to bus. jours. and newspapers; presenter at confs. Friend New Orleans Ctr. for Creative Arts, 1984-93; del. La. Gov.'s Conf. on Women, 1992-93. Mem. The Acad. of Mgmt. (Ocis divsn. exec. bd., membership chair 1993—, Best Paper award 1994), Assn. Bus. Comms. (reviewer), Ft. Collins C. of C., Phi Kappa Phi (sec. 1991, pres. 1992-93), Delta Sigma Pi, Delta Kappa Gamma, Alpha Kappa Si (faculty mem.). Episcopalian. Office: Colo State U Dept Mgmt 315 Rockwell Hall Fort Collins CO 80523

TUCKER, PIERCE EDWARD, air force officer; b. East St. Louis, Ill., Oct. 11, 1961; s. Kenneth Edward and Delores Ida Mae (Crawford) T.; m. Julie Ann Lutz, Dec. 26, 1981; children: Justin Pierce, Jordan Paige, Preston James. BS in Fin. Mgmt., So. Ill. U., 1988; MS in Human Resources Mgmt., Lesley Coll., 1992. ICBM crew comdr. USAF, Ft. Warren AFB, Wyo., 1989-94; edn. with industry USAF, Rancho Cordova, Calif., 1994-95; contract negotiator USAF, McClellan AFB, Calif., 1995—. Mem. BBB, Nat. Contract Mgmt. Assn., Air Force Assn. Office: SM ALC PKLT 5039 Dudley Blvd Mcclellan AFB CA 95652

TUCKER, ROY ANTHONY, electro-optical instrumentation engineer, consultant; b. Jackson, Miss., Dec. 11, 1951; s. Roy Anthony and Marjorie Faye (Human) T. BS in Physics, Memphis State U., 1978; MS in Sci. Instrumentation, U. Calif., Santa Barbara, 1981. Planetarium tech. Memphis (Tenn.) Mus. Planetarium, 1976-78; engring. tech. Kitt Peak Nat. Obs., Tucson, 1979; electro-optical engr. Multiple Mirror Telescope Obs., Tucson, 1981-83; rsch. engr., dept. physiology Univ. Ariz., Tucson, 1988-92; electro-optical engr. Applied Tech. Assocs., Inc., Albuquerque, N.Mex., 1992-94; founder Southwest Cryostatics, Albuquerque, 1993-94; Tucson, 1994—; electronics engr. Phase Shift Tech., Tucson, 1995—; cons. Roy Tucker and Assocs., Vancouver, Wash., 1983-84, Tucson, 1984—. Sgt. USAF, 1972-76. Mem. Am. Astron. Soc. Home and Office: 5500 W Nebraska St Tucson AZ 85746-9533

TUCKEY, JOHN DAVISON, artist, commercial photographer; b. Phila., June 12, 1950; s. John Calvin and Ruth Jacqueline (Davison) T.; m. Leslie Hunn, Aug. 18, 1973 (div. Apr. 1976); m. Barbara Anne Snyder, June 18, 1995. BA in History, Moravian Coll., 1971; postgrad., U. Alaska, Anchorage, 1992, San Francisco Art Inst., 1992-93. Carpenter Anchorage, Boulder, Colo., 1976-92; mountain guide Genet Expeditions, Anchorage, 1984-90; freelance photographer Anchorage, 1994—. One man shows include Grant Hall Gallery, Alaska Pacific U., Anchorage, 1996, Main Street Gallery, Ketchikan, Alaska, 1996; exhibited in group shows at Benham Street Gallery, Seattle, 1996, Anchorage Mus. History and Art, 1996, Alaska State Mus., Juneau, 1996. Recipient Scenic Nature Student Photographer of the Yr. award U. Mo., 1992, Recognition award Alaska State Mus., 1996; Career Opportunity grantee Alaska Coun. Arts, 1996; Merit scholar San Francisco Art Inst., 1993. Home: 3454 Sagan Cir Anchorage AK 99517

TUDDENHAM, W(ILLIAM) MARVIN, chemist, metallurgist, consultant; b. Salt Lake City, July 8, 1924; s. William Calder and Laura (Pack) T.; m. Dorothy Evelyn Snelgrove, May 1, 1945; children: William Marvin Jr. (dec.), Mary Alice, Evelyn, Laurie. BA in Chemistry, U. Utah, 1947, MS in Chemistry, 1948, PhD in Fuels, 1954, teaching cert., 1984. Rsch. chemist Eastman Kodak Co., Rochester, N.Y., 1948-50; dept. mgr. Kennecott Rsch., Salt Lake City, 1953-83; v.p., gen. mgr. Master Travel, Salt Lake City, 1984-91; pres. Mining & Metall. Assocs., Salt Lake City, 1991—. Editor: Sampling and Analysis Copper, 1983; contbr. articles to tech. jours. and encys., chpts. to books; patentee in electrowinning and refining field. Chmn. Salt Lake City Adv. Com. on Waste Disposal, 1981, Salt Lake City Pub. Utilities Adv. Bd., 1983-90; mem. Salt Lake City Mayor's Budget Adv. Com., 1985-90. Ensign USNR, 1944-46, PTO. Recipient Silver Beaver award Gt. Salt lake coun. Boy Scouts Am., 1978. Mem. AIME (sr.), Metall. Soc. of AIME (past chmn. nat. electrolytic process com.), Am. Chem. Soc. (emeritus, chmn. nat. membership affairs com. 1980-82, various offices 1953—, Utah award Salt Lake-Cen. Utah sects. 1973), Sigma Xi, Alpha Chi Sigma. Republican. Mem. LDS Ch. Office: 1828 Lincoln St Salt Lake City UT 84105-3308

TUELL, JACK MARVIN, retired bishop; b. Tacoma, Nov. 14, 1923; s. Frank Harry and Anne Helen (Bertelson) T.; m. Marjorie Ida Beadles, June 17, 1946; children—Jacqueline, Cynthia, James. B.S., U. Wash., 1947, LL.B., 1948; S.T.B., Boston U., 1955; M.A., U. Puget Sound, 1961, DHS, 1990; D.D., Pacific Sch. Religion, 1966; LLD, Alaska Pacific U., 1980. Bar: Wash. 1948; ordained to ministry Meth. Ch., 1955. Practice law with firm Holte & Tuell, Edmonds, Wash., 1948-50; pastor Grace Meth. Ch., Everett, Wash., 1950-52, South Tewksbury Meth. Ch., Tewksbury, Mass., 1952-55, Lakewood Meth. Ch., Tacoma, 1955-61; dist. supt. Puget Sound dist. Meth. Ch., Everett, 1961-67; pastor 1st United Meth. Ch., Vancouver, Wash., 1967-72; bishop United Meth. Ch., Portland, Oreg., 1972-80, Calif.-Pacific Conf., United Meth. Ch., L.A., 1980-92; interim sr. pastor First United Meth. Ch., Boise, Idaho, 1995; Mem. gen. conf. United Meth. Ch., 1964, 66, 68, 70, 72; pres. coun. of Bishops United Meth. Ch., 1989-90. Author: The Organization of the United Methodist Church, 1970, 7th edit. 1993. Pres. Tacoma U.S.O., 1959-61, Vancouver YMCA, 1968; v.p. Ft. Vancouver Seamens Cnt., 1969-72; vice chmn. Vancouver Human Rels. Commn., 1970-72; pres. Oreg. Coun. Alcohol Problems, 1972-76; trustee U. Puget Sound, 1961-73, Vancouver Meml. Hosp., 1967-72, Alaska Meth. U., Anchorage, 1972-80, Willamette U., Salem, Oreg., 1972-80, Willamette View Manor, Portland, 1972-80, Rogue Valley Manor, Medford, Oreg., 1972-76, Sch. Theology at Claremont, Calif., 1980-92, Methodist Hosp., Arcadia, Calif., 1983-92; pres. nat. div. bd. global ministries United Meth. Ch., 1972-76, pres. ecumenical and interreligious concerns div., 1976-80, Commn. on Christian Unity and intereligious concerns, 1980-84, Gen. Bd. of Pensions,1984-92, Calif. Coun. Alcohol Problems, 1985-88. Jacob Sleeper fellow, 1955. Mem. Lions. Home and Office: 2697 S North Bluff Rd Greenbank WA 98253-9713

TUKEY, HAROLD BRADFORD, JR., horticulture educator; b. Geneva, N.Y., May 29, 1934; s. Harold Bradford and Ruth (Schweigert) T.; m. Helen Dunbar Parker, June 25, 1955; children: Ruth Thurbon, Carol Tukey Schwartz, Harold Bradford. B.S., Mich. State U., 1955, M.S., 1956, Ph.D., 1958. Research asst. South Haven Expt. Sta., Mich., 1955; AEC grad. research asst. Mich. State U., 1955-58; NSF fellow Calif. Inst. Tech, 1958-59; asst. prof. dept. floriculture and ornamental horticulture Cornell U., Ithaca, N.Y., 1959-64, assoc. prof., 1964-70, prof., 1970-80; prof. urban horticulture U. Wash., Seattle, 1980—, dir. Arboreta, 1980-92, dir. Ctr. Urban Horticulture, 1980-92; cons. Internat. Bonsai mag., Electric Power Rsch. Inst., P.R. Nuclear Ctr., 1965-66; mem. adv. com. Seattle-U. Wash. Arboretum and Bot. Garden, 1980-92, vice chmn., 1982, chmn., 1986-87; vis. scholar U. Nebr., 1982; vis. prof. U. Calif., Davis, 1973; lectr. U. Western Sydney-Hawkesburg U. Melbourne, Victoria Coll. Agrl. and Horticulture, 1995, Massey U., 1996; Hill prof. U. Minn., 1996; mem. various coms. Nat. Acad. Scis.-NRC; bd. dirs. Arbor Fund Bloedel Res., 1980-92, pres., 1983-84. Mem. editorial bd. Jour. Environ. Horticulture, Arboretum Bull. Mem. nat. adv. com. USDA, 1990—; pres. Ithaca PTA; troop advisor Boy Scouts Am., Ithaca. Lt. U.S. Army, 1958. Recipient B.Y. Morrison award USDA, 1987; NSF fellow, 1958-59; named to Lansing (Mich.) Sports Hall of Fame, 1987; grantee NSF, 1962, 75, Bot. Soc. Am., 1964; hon. dr. Portuguese Soc. Hort., 1985. Fellow Am. Soc. Hort. Sci. (dir. 1970-71); mem. Internat. Soc. Hort. Sci. (U.S. del. to coun. 1971-90, chmn. commn. for amateur horiticulture 1974-83, exec. com. 1974-90, v.p. 1978-82, pres. 1982-86, past pres. 1986-90, chmn. comm. Urban Horticulture 1990-94, hon. mem. 1994), Wash. State Nursery and Landscape Assn. (hon. mem. 1995), Internat. Plant Propagators Soc. (hon., ea. region dir. 1969-71, v.p. 1972, pres. 1973, internat. pres. 1976), Am. Hort. Soc. (dir. 1972-81, exec. com. 1974-81, v.p. 1978-80, citation of merit 1981), Royal Hort. Soc. (London) (v.p. hon. 1993—), Bot. Soc. Am., N.W. Horticulture Soc. (dir. 1980-92), Arboretum Found. (dir. 1980-92), Rotary, Sigma Xi, Alpha Zeta, Phi Kappa Phi, Pi Alpha Xi, Xi Sigma Pi. Presbyterian. Home: 3300 E St Andrews Way Seattle WA 98112-3750 Office: U Wash Ctr Urban Horticulture Box 354115 Seattle WA 98195

TULIS, RONALD LEE, airport consultant; b. Bklyn., Jan. 19, 1946; s. Theodore Gabriel and Ella (Kornberg) T.; m. Susan D. Dulebohn, Oct. 29, 1966; children: Jason Michael, Corey Scott. BArch, U. Calif., Berkeley, 1968. Urban designer City of Mpls., 1968-72; urban planner Sedway Cooke, San Francisco, 1972-73, Livingston & Blaney, San Francisco, 1973-74, Livingston & Assocs., San Francisco, 1974-77; airport cons. KPMG Peat Marwick, San Francisco, 1977-93, Leigh Fisher Assocs., San Francisco, 1993—; mem. steering com., environ. com. Airports Coun. Internat.-N.Am., Washington, 1992—. Recipient HUD Urban Design award Mpls. Downtown Assn., 1974, Am. Assn. Planners, 1978. Office: Leigh Fisher Assocs PO Box 8007 San Francisco CA 94128

TULL, STEVEN GERALD, secondary education educator; b. Peoria, Ill., Dec. 18, 1954; s. Ralph Gerald Tull and Maella Christean (Daugherty) Bridgeman; m. Virginia Marie Kimmet, July 30, 1983. BA, So. Ill. U., 1982; postgrad., Coll. Great Falls, 1983-90; MA, San Diego State U., 1996. Cert. tchr., Mont. Commd. officer USAF, 1973, advanced through grades to 1st lt., translator, 1973-79; intelligence specialist Ill. Air N.G., Springfield, 1979-80; missile launch comdr. USAF, Great Falls, Mont., 1982-86; English educator Superior (Mont.) Sch. Dist. #3, 1990—. Cmty. rep. Acad. Yr. U.S.A. Internat., San Francisco, 1994—. Mem. ASCD, NEA, Nat. Coun. Tchrs. English, Internat. Reading Assn., Superior Edn. Assn. (local pres. 1996—). Home: 639 4th Ave East Superior MT 59872 Office: Superior High Sch 410 Arizona Ave Superior MT 59872

TULL, TANYA, social scientist; b. San Francisco, Mar. 22, 1943; d. Samuel Adams and Clare Sara (Weitzman) Cherry; widowed; children: Daniel, Deborah, Rebecca. BA, Scripps Coll. for Women, 1964; tchg. credential, UCLA, 1971; D Social Sci. (hon.), Whittier Coll., 1992. Founder, exec. dir. Para Los Niños, L.A., 1980-86, Beyond Shelter, L.A., 1988—; co-founder, co-dir. L.A. Family Housing Corp., L.A., 1983-88; founder, acting exec. dir. A Cmty. of Friends, L.A., 1988-90; cons. in field., 1986—. Recipient Jefferson award Nat. Inst. Pub. Svc., 1982, Pub. Affairs award Coro Found., 1983, Ethics in Action award Ethical Culture Soc., 1984, Disting. Alumna award Scripps Coll. for Women, 1986, Ralph Bunche Peace award UN Orgn., 1987, Founder's award NAFE, 1988, Woman of Yr. award Robinson's, 1993, Nonprofit Sector award Nat. Alliance to End Homelessness, 1996, Citizen Activist award Gleitsman Found., 1996; named one of A Hundred Heroes of Our Time, Newsweek mag., 1986, one of 26 leaders Visions for Future of Met. L.A., L.A. Mega-Cities Project, 1995. Democrat. Jewish. Home: 227 S Windsor Blvd Los Angeles CA 90004-3819 Office: Beyond Shelter 3255 Wilshire Blvd Ste 902 Los Angeles CA 90010-1413

TULLIS, PAUL ROWAN, journalist; b. Chgo., Aug. 21, 1968; s. Robert Wood Tullis and Robin (Rowan) Clarke. BA, U. Calif., Berkeley, 1992. Sr. editor Might mag., San Francisco, 1994—. Contbg. writer New York mag., New Yorker mag., Details mag., L.A. Times Mag., L.A. Weekly, Columbia Journalism, rev., Mademoiselle mag. Office: 77 Federal St 2nd Fl San Francisco CA 94107-1414

TULLY, JOHN PETER, land use planner; b. Mineola, N.Y., Sept. 27, 1952; s. John and Doris (Sealander) T; m. Linda Howard, Apr. 11, 1987: children: Nathan, Caroline. BS, Calif. Poly., San Luis Obispo, 1978; AA, San Marcos (Calif.) Jr. Coll., 1974. Lic. landscape arch., Calif. Sr. project mgr. Hogan & Roy Ptnrs., Irvine, Calif., 1978-81; prin. CYP, Inc., Irvine, 1981-91; founding ptnr., exec. v.p. KTGY Group, Inc., Irvine, 1991—. Awards judge sr. housing Nat. Assn. Home Builders, Washington, 1996; panelist Pacific Coast Builders Conf., San Francisco, 1994, 95; advisor zoning ordinance City of San Clemente, Calif., 1993-95. Recipient Parade of Homes Best Site Plan Over 25 Acres award Hawaii Bldg. Assn., Honolulu, 1990, Parade of Homes Best Residential Home award Utah Bldg. Assn., St. George, 1996, Homer award for residential home Las Vegas Builders Assn., 1996. Mem. Bldg. Industry Assn. (spkr. 1989-91), Am. Planning Assn., Urban Land Inst., Rotary (founding, San Clemente Sunrise chpt., bd. dirs. 1993—). Republican. Lutheran. Office: KTGY Group 2 Executive Cir Irvine CA 92714

TULLY, SUSAN BALSLEY, pediatrician, educator; b. San Francisco, July 12, 1941; d. Gerard E. Balsley Sr. and Norma Lilla (Hand) Carey; m. William P. Tully, June 19, 1965; children: Michael William, Stephen Gerard. BA in Premed. Studies, UCLA, 1963, MD, 1966. Diplomate Am. Bd. Pediatrics, Am. Bd. Pediatric Emergency Medicine. Intern L.A. County-U. So. Calif. Med. Ctr., 1966-67, jr. resident pediatrics, 1967-68; staff pediatrician, part-time Permanente Med. Group, Oakland, Calif., 1968; sr. resident pediatrics Kaiser Found. Hosp., Oakland, 1968-69; sr. resident pediatrics Bernalillo County Med. Ctr., Albuquerque, 1969-70, chief resident pediatric outpatient dept., 1970; instr. pediatrics, asst. dir. outpatient dept. U. N.Mex. Sch. Medicine, 1971-72; asst. prof. pediatrics, dir. (ambulatory pediatrics) U. Calif., Irvine, 1972-76, asst. prof. clin. pediatrics, vice chair med. edn., 1977-79; staff pediatrician Ross-Loos Med. Group, Buena Park, Calif., 1976-77; assoc. prof. clin. pediatrics and emergency medicine U. So. Calif. Sch. Medicine, 1979-86; dir. pediatric emergency dept. L.A. County/U. So. Calif. Med. Ctr., 1979-87; prof. clin. pediatrics and emergency medicine U. So. Calif. Sch. Medicine, 1986-89; dir. ambulatory pediatrics L.A. County/U. So. Calif. Med. Ctr., 1987-89, L.A. County-Olive View/UCLA Med. Ctr., 1989—; clin. prof. pediatrics UCLA, 1989-93, prof. clin. pediats., 1993-97; prof. emeritus, 1997—; dir. ambulatory pediatrics UCLA, 1989-96, chief pediatrics, 1996-97; pediatric toxicology cons. L.A. County Regional Poison Control Ctr. Med. Adv. Bd., 1981-97; clin. faculty rep. UCLA Sch. Medicine, 1992-93; pediatric liaison dept. emergency medicine Olive View/UCLA Med. Ctr., 1989-96, dir. lead poisoning clinic, 1993—; mem. quality assurance com. Los Angeles County Cmty. Health Plan, 1986-89; mem. survey team pediatric emergency svcs. L.A. Pediatric Soc., 1984-86; mem. adv. bd. preventive health project univ. affiliated program Children's Hosp. L.A., 1981-83; active numerous coms. Author: (with K.E. Zenk) Pediatric Nurse Practitioner Formulary, 1979; (book chpt. with W.A. Wingert) Pediatric Emergency Medicine: Concepts and Clinical Practice, 1992, 2d edit., 1996; (with others) Educational Guidelines for Ambulatory/General Pediatrics Fellowship Training, 1992, Physician's Resource Guide for Water Safety Education, 1994; reviewer Pediatrics, 1985-89; editl. cons. Advanced Pediatric Life Support Course and Manual, 1988-89, Archives Diseases of Childhood, 1996—; dept. editor Pediatric Pearls Jour. Am. Acad. Physician Assts., 1989-94; tech. cons., reviewer Healthlink TV Am. Acad. Pediatrics, 1991; reviewer Pediatric Emergency Care, 1992—, Archives of Pediatrics and Adolescent Medicine, 1995—; question writer sub-bd. pediatric emergency medicine Am. Bd. Pediatrics, 1993—; assoc. editor: Curriculum for the Training of General Pediatricians, 1996; cons. to lay media NBC Nightly News, Woman's Day, Sesame Street Parents, Parenting, Los Angeles Times; author numerous abstracts; contbr. articles to profl. jours. cons. spl. edn. programs Orange County Bd. Edn., 1972-79; mem. Orange County Health Planning Coun., 1973-79; co-chairperson Orange County Child Health and Disability Prevention Program Bd., 1975-76; mem. Orange County Child Abuse Consultation Team, 1977-79; mem. project adv. bd. Family Focussed "Buckle Up" Project, Safety Belt Safe, U.S.A., 1989—;. Fellow Am. Acad. Pediatrics (life, active numerous sects. and coms., active Calif. chpt.); mem. APHA, Ambulatory Pediatric Assn., L.A. Pediatric Soc. (life), L.A. Area Child Passenger Safety Assn. Democrat. Office: Olive View UCLA Med Ctr Pediatrics 3A108 14445 Olive View Dr Sylmar CA 91342-1495

TUMAN, WALTER VLADIMIR, Russian language educator, researcher; b. Heidelberg, Germany, Jan. 21, 1946; came to U.S., 1949; s. Val Alexander Tuman and Valida (Zedins) Grasis; m. Helena Eugenia Makarowsky, June 6, 1970; children: Gregory Vladimir, Larissa Alexandra. BA, Fordham U., 1967; MS in Russian, Linguistics, Georgetown U., 1970, PhD in Russian, 1975. Supr. Russian dept. Def. Lang. Inst., Washington, 1972-75; developer course-curriculum Def. Lang. Inst., Monterey, Calif., 1975-78; asst. prof. Russian Hollins (Va.) Coll., 1978-84; dir. fgn. lang. lab. La. State U., Baton Rouge, 1984-90; assoc. prof., coord. Russian program Thunderbird Campus Am. Grad. Sch. Internat. Mgmt., Glendale, Ariz., 1990-95, prof., 1995—; cons. various univs.; grant participant, cons. US AID Consortia Am. Buss., NIS, 1993—, U.S. Commerce Dept., Nizhny Novgorod, Volgograd, Am. Bus. Ctrs., 1994—. Author: Think Russian: Level I, 1993; editor: A Bibliography of Computer-Aided Language Learning, 1986; contbg. editor Jour. Ednl. Techniques and Techs., 1987—; mem. editl. bd.: Jour. Lang. in Internat. Bus.; author book revs., computer programs, conf. presentations; contbr. articles to profl. jours. Georgetown U. fellow, 1969; recipient Prof.'s Exch. award Internat. Rsch. and Exchs. Bd. (USSR), 1979; Mednick Meml. Fund grantee Va. Found. for Ind. Colls. (Australia), 1983, Apple Computer grantee, 1989, U.S. Dept. Edn. grantee Ctr. Internat. Bus. Edn. and Rsch., 1993—. Mem. Am. Assn. Tchrs. Slavic and East European Langs. (v.p. 1981-84, founder Monterey, Calif. chpt.), Am. Coun. on the Teaching Fgn. Langs., Am. Coun. Tchrs. Russian (bd. dirs. 1992—), Internat. Assn. Learning Lab. Dirs., Assn. Internat. Linguistique Appliquée. Russian Orthodox. Office: Am Grad Sch Internat Mgmt 59th and Greenway Glendale AZ 85306

TUMMONS, LOIS PATRICIA, writer, editor; b. Springfield, Mo., Jan. 3, 1950; d. Norris Benjamin and Mary Alice (Glenn) T.;. BA, SUNY, Buffalo, 1971, MA, 1976. Mng. editor Telos, St. Louis, Mo., 1976; copy editor, news St. Louis Post Dispatch, 1976-83, editl. writer, 1983-89; writer, publisher Environment Hawaii, Honolulu, Hilo, 1990—; bd. dirs. Environment Hawaii, Hilo, 1990—. Mem. U.S. Marine Fisheries adv. com., Washington, 1996-99, Hawaii Environ. Coun., Honolulu, 1996-98. Recipient Gannett fellowsip, Gannett Found., U. Hawaii, 1985, Hon. Mention, Newsletter Publishers Found., Va., 1992, Exemplary Pub. svc. Common Cause, Honolulu, 1992, Media award, Am. Planning Assn., 1993. Mem. LWV, Big Island Press Club, Soc. Environ. Journalists, Sierra Club, Phi Beta Kappa. Office: 200 Kanoelehua Ave # 103-325 Hilo HI 96720-4648

TUNE, SUELYN CHING, secondary education educator; b. Palo Alto, Calif., June 7, 1944; d. Hung Leong and Mabel Chun Kiam (Tom) Ching; m. Gerald Robert Tune, Aug. 9, 1968; 1 child, Padraic Man Ching Tune. BA in Comparative Lit., Occidental Coll., 1965; MA in Ednl. Psychology, NYU, 1966; Profl. Diploma, Calif. State Coll., 1967. Cert. secondary educator, Calif.; cert. elem. educator, Hawaii. Tchr. L.A. City Schs., 1967-70, Hawaii State Dept. of Edn., Honolulu, 1970-71, Kamehameha Schs. Bishop Estate, Honolulu, 1971—. Co-author: (book) Made in Hawaii, 1983; author: (book) How Maui Slowed the Sun, 1988, Maui and the Secret of Fire, 1991, (booklet) Hawai'i in 1819: The Breakdown of the Kapu System, 1985, (booklet) Furs, Sandalwood, and Whales, 1989, (booklet) Liholiho, Kamehameha II, 1991. Mem. ASCD, Internat. Reading Assn., Honolulu Acad. Arts, Bishop Mus. Office: Kamehameha Schs Unit 7-8 2125 Alii Rd Honolulu HI 96817-1501

TUNG, PRABHAS, plastic surgeon; b. Ubol, Thailand, Apr. 3, 1944; s. Sathee and Seng (Ngium) T.; m. Patarin C. Sinjin; children: Tony, Tommy. MD, Mahidol U., Bangkok, 1968. Diplomate Am. Bd. Plastic Surgery. Plastic surgeon pvt. practice, Flint, Mich., 1980-82, Sacramento, Calif., 1982—. Office: 2801 K St Ste 200 Sacramento CA 95816-5118

TUNISON, ELIZABETH LAMB, education educator; b. Portadown, Northern Ireland, Jan. 7, 1922; came to U.S., 1923; d. Richard Ernest and Ruby (Hill) Lamb; m. Ralph W. Tunison, Jan. 24, 1947 (dec. Apr. 1984); children: Eric Arthur, Christine Wait, Dana Paul. BA, Whittier Coll., 1943, MEd, 1963. Tchr. East Whittier (Calif.) Schs., 1943-59; tchr. T.V. TV Channels 13 and 28, So. Calif. Counties, 1960-75; dir. curriculum Bassett (Calif.) Schs., 1962-65; elem. sch. prin. Rowland Unified Schs., Rowland Heights, Calif., 1965-68; assoc. prof. edn. Calif. State Poly. U., Pomona, 1968-71; prof. Whittier Coll., 1968-88, prof. emerita, 1988—; bd. dirs. Restless Legs Syndrome Found., facilitator for So. Calif. Orgn. Bd. dirs. Presbyn. Intercmty. Hosp. Found.; founder Restless Legs Support Group (chmn. 1995—). Recipient Whittier Coll. Alumni Achievement award 1975; Helen Hefernan scholar 1963. Mem. AAUP, Assn. Calif. Sch. Adminstrs. (state bd., chmn. higher edn. com. 1983-86, region pres. 1981-83, Wilson Grace award 1983), PEO (pres. 1990-92), Assistance League of Whittier (v.p.

1994-96), Delta Kappa Gamma (v.p. 1996-97). Home: 5636 Ben Alder Ave Whittier CA 90601-2111

TUPIN, JOE PAUL, psychiatry educator; b. Comanche, Tex., Feb. 17, 1934; m. Betty Thompson, June 19, 1955; children: Paul, Rebecca, John. BS in Pharmacy, U. Tex., 1955, postgrad., 1955; MD, U. Tex., Galveston, 1959, Wash. Sch. Psychiatry, 1962, NIH Grad. Sch., 1962-64. Lic. physician, Tex., Calif. Intern U. Calif. Hosps., San Francisco, 1959-60; resident U. Tex. Med. br., Galveston, 1960-62, asst. prof. psychiatry, 1964-68, mem. staff John Sealy Hosp., 1964-69, dir. psychiatric consultation service, 1965-66, dir. psychiatric research, 1965-69, asst. dean medicine, 1967-68, assoc. prof., 1968-69, assoc. dean, 1968-69; resident NIMH div NIH, 1963-64; assoc. prof. psychiatry U. Calif., Davis, 1969-71, mem. staff Davis Med. Ctr., 1969—, vice-chmn. dept. psychiatry, 1970-76, prof., 1971-93, prof. emeritus, 1993, acting chmn. dept. psychiatry, 1977, acting dir. admissions sch. medicine, 1977-78, chmn. dept. psychiatry, 1977-84; med. dir. U. Calif. Davis Med. Ctr., 1984-93; cons. staff St. Mary's Infirmary, Galveston, 1967-69, Moody House Retirement Home for the Aged, Galveston, 1967-69, VA Hosp., Martinez, 1977-82, Yolo Gen. Hosp., 1980-81; dir. psychiatric consultation service U. Calif., Davis, 1969-74, co-director 1974-77; vis. prof. King's Coll. Med. Sch., London, 1974; acting dir. admissions sch. medicine, U. Calif., Davis, 1977-78; chief div. mental health U. Calif. Davis Med. Ctr., 1977-84, also mem. quality care com., 1979-85, chmn. com., 1981-85; med. dir. and assoc. dir. Hosp. and Clinics U. Calif., Davis, 1984-93; cons. U. Calif., Davis, 1993; cons. to pres. U. Calif., head clin. policy rev. team, 1996—. Referee and book reviewer numerous publs.; mem. sci. editorial bd. Am. Jour. Forensic Psychiatry, 1985-88, Jour. Clin. Psychopharmacology, 1981—, Psychiatry, 1985, Tex. Reports on Biology and Medicine, 1965-67, 68-69; Western Jour. Medicine, 1979-89; contbr. numerous articles to profl. jours. Mem. Academically Talented Child com. Galveston City Sch. Bd., 1966-67; chmn. bd. dirs. William Temple Found., Galveston, 1967-68; bd. dirs. Citizens for Advancement of Pub. Edn., Galveston, 1967-69, pres., 1968-69, Moody House Retirement Home for the Aged, 1968, Cal Aggie Athletic Assn., 1978-82; mem. Davis Master Plan com., 1971. Served to lt. commdr. USPHS, 1962-64, with Res. 1964-80. Recipient Career Teaching award NIMH, 1964-66; named to Friars Soc. U. Tex., 1954; Mosby scholar U. Tex., Ginsberg fellow Group for Advancement of Psychiatry, 1960-62, Nat. Found. Infantile Paralysis fellow, 1957; grantee U. Tex. Med. br., 1964-69, NIMH, 1965-68. Fellow Am. Psychiat. Assn., Am. Coll. Psychiatrists (mem. com., editl. com., fin. com.); mem. Am. Acad. Psychiatry and the Law, Alpha Omega Alpha. Home: 108 Kent Dr Davis CA 95616 Office: U Calif Davis Med Ctr Office of the Dir 2315 Stockton Blvd Sacramento CA 95817-2201

TURGEL, STUART CHARLES, hospital administrator; b. Boston, June 15, 1948; m. Lynn Greenberg, Mar. 28, 1976; children: Mindy Sue, Ariel David, Sarah Ruth. Student, Marietta Coll., N.E. Broadcasting Sch., U.S. Def. Dept. Schs. Journalism and Broadcasting, U. Denver. Music dir. Sta. WCMO-FM, Marietta, Ohio, 1966-67; news dir., chief announcer Armed Forces Radio and TV Network, Johnston Island, 1968-70; external media liaison, sr. info. officer Fitzsimons Gen. Hosp., Denver, 1970-71; pub. rels. asst. Nat. Jewish Hosp. and Rsch. Ctr., Denver, 1971-72, devel. assoc., 1972-73, area dir. fin. devel., 1973-74, asst. dir. fin. devel., 1974-78; exec. dir. Menorah Med. Ctr. Found., Kansas City, Mo., 1978-80; exec. v.p. The Children's Hosp. Found., Denver, 1980-87; pres. The Sheridan (Wyo.) Inn, 1985-87; sr. v.p. external affairs, exec. dir. Children's Hosp. Found. Children's Hosp. and Health Ctr., San Diego, 1987-93; sr. v.p. mktg. and external affairs Lucile Salter Packard Children's Hosp. Stanford, Palo Alto, Calif., 1993—. Active LEAD San Diego, 1991; past pres. Congregation Beth Am, Solana Beach, Calif.; former trustee Rocky Mountain Philanthropy Fund, Osmond Found.; bd. dirs. Congregation Kol Emeth, Palo Alto, Calif. Recipient Presdl. letter of commendation, 1969, McEachern award, 1970, Gold Pick award Pub. Rels. Soc. Am., 1983, regional Emmy award, 1984. Mem. Am. Soc. Health Care Mktg. and Pub. Rels. of Am. Hosp. Assn., Acad. Health Svcs. Mktg. of Am. Mktg. Assn., Nat. Assn. Children's Hosps. and Related Instns. (mem. child health policy coun.), Assn. Healthcare Philanthropy, Colo. Assn. Fund Raisers (past pres.), Knights of Pythias. Address: 2938 Waverley St Palo Alto CA 94306-2440 Office: Lucile Salter Packard Children's Hosp Stanford 725 Welch Rd Palo Alto CA 94304-1601

TURK, ROBERT LOUIS, radiologist; b. Lima, Ohio, Oct. 30, 1940; s. Herman Matthew and Daphne Carol (Stout) T.; m. Penelope Bryant, Mar. 25, 1964; children: Marjorie Carol Turk Desmond, Susan Elizabeth Turk Charles. BA, Stanford U., 1962; MD, UCLA, 1966. Diplomate Am. Bd. Radiology, Am. Bd. Nuclear Medicine. Rotating intern U. Iowa, Iowa City, 1966-67; resident in radiology Harbor Gen.-UCLA Hosp., Torrance, Calif., 1967-70; radiologist, chief staff, vice chief, head radiology El Cajon (Calif.) Valley Hosp., 1972-83; pvt. practice, El Cajon, 1983—. Elder Presbyn. Ch., 1966—. Maj. M.C., USAR, 1970-72, Vietnam. Mem. Am. Coll. Radiology, Radiol. Soc. N.Am., Calif. Radiol. Soc., San Diego Radiol. Soc. (pres. 1990-91, past treas., rep.), Calif. Med. Soc., San Diego Med. Soc. Democrat. Home: 1760 Key Ln El Cajon CA 92021-1507 Office: El Cajon X-Ray Imaging 1663 Greenfield Dr El Cajon CA 92021-3520

TURKS, VICTOR LEONARD, English language educator; b. LÜbeck, Germany, Feb. 18, 1946; came to U.S., 1950; s. John Leonard and Helena (Ruskulis) T.; m. Laurie Jane Larson, June 8, 1968 (div. 1988); m. Michiko Adachi, June 8, 1988; children: Aaron, Terence, John. AA, San Francisco City Coll., 1965; BA, San Francisco State U., 1968, MA, 1969. Cert. lifetime jr. coll. lang. arts and lit. tchr., Calif. Instr. English Sprach-Inst. Cologne, Hamburg, Germany, 1970-72; instr. English and composition San Francisco C.C.-City Coll. San Francisco, 1973—; instr. English lang. San Francisco State U.-Am. Lang. Inst., summer 1980; instr. English composition and lit. Eugene J. McAteer H.S., San Francisco, 1987-92; instr. English Nagoya (Japan) Sch. Bus., 1985; adminstr. in charge evening-Saturday-summer programs Mission Comty Coll. Ctr., San Fancisco, 1977, 78, 79. Editor: ESLetter, 1994—; contbr. poetry to anthologies, articles to profl. jours. Democrat. Home: 775 23rd Ave San Francisco CA 94121-3736 Office: City Coll San Francisco 50 Phelan Ave San Francisco CA 94112-1821

TURKUS-WORKMAN, CAROL ANN, educator; b. Balt., Nov. 12, 1946; d. Stanley Phillip and Catherine Anna (Koppleman) Turkus; m. William Thomas Workman, Apr. 23, 1973 (div. 1983); children: Devin Thomas, Timothy Michael. BA in History, Calif. State U., Long Beach, 1969; spl. cert. classroom mgmt., Centralia Sch. Dist., 1980, crosscultural devel. and acad. devel. cert., 1994; M in Adminstrn. Mgmt., U. La Verne, 1997; M in Adminstrv. Mgmt., U. LaVerne, 1997. Cert. crosscultural lang. and acad. devel.; cert. adminstrv. credential. Educator Centralia Sch. Dist., Buena Park, Calif., 1970—; ednl. tech. Centralia Sch. Dist., Buena Park, 1986—; cons. U. Sch.-Space Sci. Acad., Cleve., 1991. Unit commr. Boy Scouts Am., Orange County Coun., 1989-96; co. systems officer Starfleet Bulletin Bd. System, Long Beach, 1990-94; life mem. PTA, Buena Park. Recipient Gold Leaf, PTA Nat., 1991, Woodbadge Beads, Boy Scouts Am., 1991. Mem. Computer Using Educators, Order of Arrow, Kappa Delta Pi. Republican. Roman Catholic. Office: Centralia Sch Dist 6215 San Rolando Way Buena Park CA 90620-3635 Address: 11762 Argyle Dr Los Alamitos CA 90720-4226

TURLEY-MOORE, SUSAN GWEN, minister; b. Boston, June 19, 1952; d. Calvin Earl and Marilyn (Anderson) Turley; m. Clifford Jesse Moore, Jr., Jan. 7, 1978; 1 child, Keith Jesse. BA in Sociology, Urbana (Ohio) U.; MEd, Suffolk U. Lic. cert. social worker, Mass.; ordained to ministry Swedenborgian Ch. Pvt. practice as pastoral psychotherapist Turley and Assocs., Newton, Mass., 1979-81; pastor Swedenborgian Ch., Portland, Maine, 1981-84; pastor on ministerial team Wayfarer's Chapel, L.A., 1984-87; founder, dir. Swedenborigan Social Action Concerns Com., 1987-92; guidance counselor Fairbanks Elem. Sch., Sacramento, Calif., 1987-89; interim assoc. pastor Swedenborgian Ch., San Francisco, 1989-90; chaplain and pastoral staff New Ch. Youth League West Coast, 1990-92; founding exec. dir. of living waters HIV ministry Swedenborgian Ch., San Francisco, 1992—. Mem. ACA, Nat. Coun. of Chs. (counseling com. 1977—),. Office: Swedenborgian Ch Living Waters PO Box 460388 San Francisco CA 94146-0388

TURLIP, JAMES DOUGLAS, career officer; b. Decatur, Ill., Jan. 15, 1961; s. John David and Joyce Ann (Pierce) T.; m. Joan Elizabeth Hampton, Sept., 1993. BA, Rice U., 1983; MBA, Albany State U., 1990. Commd. 2d lt. USMC, 1983, advanced through grades to maj., 1994; computer sys. team leader USMC, Albany, Ga., 1988-91; sr. supply/logistics advisor U.S. Mil. Tng. Mission, Riyadh, Saudi Arabia, 1992-93; head supply analysis sect. USMC, Camp Pendleton, Calif., 1993-96; officer in charge of supply ops. and customer svc. sect. USMC, Camp Pendleton, 1996—. Scoutmaster Boy Scouts Am., Hawaii, Japan, Ga., Saudi Arabia, 1984-94. Mem. KC, Marine Corps Assn. Naval Inst., Nat. Eagle Scout Assn., Mission San Luis Rey Parish, Camp Pendleton Officer's Club. Republican. Roman Catholic. Home: 5276 Hubbert St Oceanside CA 92056-2355 Office: 1st Supply Bn 1st Force Svc Support Group Box 555627 Camp Pendleton CA 92055-5627

TURNAGE, JEAN A., state supreme court chief justice; b. St. Ignatius, Mont., Mar. 10, 1926. JD, Mont. State U., 1951; D Laws and Letters (non.), U. Mont., 1995. Bar: Mont. 1951, U.S. Supreme Ct. 1963. Formerly ptnr. Turnage, McNeil & Mercer, Polson, Mont.; formerly Mont. State senator from 13th Dist.; pres. Mont. State Senate, 1981-83; chief justice Supreme Ct. Mont., 1985—. Mem. Mont. State Bar Assn., Nat. Conf. Chief Justices (past pres.), Nat. Ctr. State Courts (past chair). Office: Mont Supreme Ct 215 N Sanders St Helena MT 59601-4522

TURNBULL, WILLIAM, JR., architect; b. N.Y.C., Apr. 1, 1935; s. William and Elizabeth (Howe) T. A.B., Princeton U., 1956, M.F.A. in Architecture, 1959; student, Ecole des Beaux Arts Fontainebleau, France, 1956. With Skidmore, Owings & Merrill, San Francisco, 1960-63; founding ptnr. Moore, Lyndon, Turnbull, Whitaker, 1962; partner-in-charge Moore, Turnbull (San Francisco office), 1965-69; mem. design group Pres.'s Adv. Coun. Pennsylvania Ave., 1963; lectr. U. Calif.-Berkeley, Berkeley, 1965-69; vis. prof. U. Oreg., 1966-68; dir. MLTW/Turnbull Assocs., 1970-83; dir. William Turnbull Assocs. William Turnbull Assocs., 1983—; lectr. Stanford U., 1974-77, vis. design critic MIT, 1975, U. Calif., Berkeley, 1977-81, 95; Mobil vis. design critic Yale U., 1982, Bishop vis. prof. archtl. design, 1986; Hyde prof. excellence U. Nebr., 1994; design cons. Formica Corp., 1977-84, World Savs. and Loan, 1976-95; mem. design rev. bd. U. Calif., San Diego, 1988-93, City of Sausalito, Calif., 1976-77; mem. fgn. bldgs. adv. bd. Dept. of State, 1991—; design critic Calif. Coll. Arts & Crafts, 1997. Author: Global Architecture Series: Moore, Lyndon, Turnbull & Whitaker: The Sea Ranch, The Sea Ranch Details, The Poetics of Gardens, 1988; illustrator: The Place of Houses; prin. works include Sea Ranch Condominium I, 1965, Sea Ranch Swim Tennis Club, 1966, Lovejoy Fountain Plaza, Portland (assoc. architect), Faculty Club at U. Calif.-Santa Barbara, Kresge Coll. at U. Calif.-Santa Cruz, Biloxi (Miss.) Library, Am. Club, Hong Kong, Ariz. State U. Sonora Ctr., Tempe, Foothill Student Housing, U. Calif., Berkeley, Mountain View City Hall and Community Theater, Calif., Grace Cathedral Close, San Francisco, St. Andrews Ch., Sonoma, Calif.; mem. editl. adv. bd. Architecture California, 1986-92. Mem. tech. adv. com. Calif. Legislature Joint Com. Open Space Lands, 1968-71; mem. regional honor awards (90) jury AIA, 1968—, nat. honor awards jury, 1969, chmn. jury, 1977, 1988; chmn. jury C.E. honor award, 1973, 79; mem. Progressive Architecture Honor Awards Jury, 1975, Pres.'s Jury for Nat. Design Excellence, 1984; bd. dirs. Pub. Sculpture Pub. Places, 1981-85. Served with AUS, 1959-60. Recipient Calif. Gov. award Planned Communities, 1966, citation Progressive Architecture Design awards, 1962-66, 68-70, 81, 1st honor award, 1971, 74, 1st honor award Homes for Better Living, 1963, Merit award, 1966; Honor award Western Home awards, 1961-62, 62, 63, 66-67, 88, 89, 93, 95; Merit award, 1966-67; House of Yr. award Archtl. Record, 1961, 67, 69, 70, 72, 83; award of Honor San Francisco Art Commn., 1982; Am. Wood Coun. Design award, 1984, Honor award, 1985, 89, 92, 93, 94; Firm of Yr. award Calif. Coun. AIA, 1986, Maybeck award, 1993, cited for continuous distinctive practice of architecture in Calif. by an individual; Am. Wood Coun. Merit award, 1991; Honor award San Francisco AIA, 1988, 91, 93. Fellow AIA (dir. chpt. 1981, Nat. Honor award 1967, 68, 73, 79, 90, 91, 95, award of merit Bay Region honor awards 1963, 67, 7, 78, 82, Nat. 25 Yr. Honor award 1991), Am. Acad. in Rome. Office: William Turnbull Assocs Pier 1 1/2 The Embarcadero San Francisco CA 94111

TURNER, BONESE COLLINS, artist, educator; b. Abilene, Kans.; d. Paul Edwin and Ruby (Seybold) Collins; m. Glenn E. Turner; 1 child, Craig Collins. BS in Edn., U. Idaho, MEd; MA, Calif. State U., Northridge, 1974. Instr. art L.A. Pierce Coll., Woodland Hills, Calif., 1964—; prof. art Calif. State U., Northridge, 1986-87; art instr. L.A. Valley Coll., Van Nuys, 1987-89, Moorpark (Calif.) Coll., 1988—, Arrowmont Coll. Arts & Crafts, Gatlinburg, Tenn., 1995-96; advisor Coll. Art and Arch. U. Idaho, 1988—; juror for numerous art exhbns. including Nat. Watercolor Soc., 1980, 91, San Diego Art Inst., Brand Nat. Watermedia Exhbn., 1980, 96-97, prin. gallery Orlando Gallery, Sherman Oaks, Calif. Prin. works exhibited in The White House, 1984, 85, Smithsonian Inst., 1984, 85, Olympic Arts Festival, L.A., 1984, Royal Birmingham Soc. of Artists Gallery, Birmingham, Eng., 1996; one-woman shows include Angel's Gate Gallery, San Pedro, Calif., 1989, Art Store Gallery, Studio City, Calif., 1988, L.A. Pierce Coll. Gallery, 1988, Brand Art Gallery, Glendale, Calif., 1988, 93, Coos (Oreg.) Art Mus., 1988, U. Nev., 1987, Orlando Gallery, Sherman Oaks, Calif., 1993, others; prin. works represented in pub. collections including Smithsonian Inst., Hartung Performing Arts Ctr., Moscow, Idaho, Home Savs. and Loan, San Bernardino Sun Telegram Newspapers, Oreg. Coun. for the Arts, Newport, Nebr. Pub. Librs., Lincoln (Nebr.) Indsl. Tile Corp. Recipient awards Springfield (Mo.) Art Mus., 1989, Butler Art Inst., 1989, Nat. award Acrylic Painters Assn. Eng. and U.S.A., 1996. Mem. Nat. Acrylic Painters Assn. of Eng. (award 1996), Nat. Mortar Bd. Soc., Nat. Watercolor Soc. (life, past pres., Purchase prize 1979), Watercolor U.S.A. Honor Soc. (award), Watercolor West.

TURNER, DAVID WINBURN, aerospace engineer; b. Havre, Mont., Sept. 12, 1946; s. David Henry and Mary Fay (Winburn) T.; m. Irene McLean Miller, Sept. 12, 1986. BS in Physics, Mont. State U., 1968; MS in Systems Engring., Calif. State U., Fullerton, 1971; PhD in Engring., U. Calif., Irvine, 1979; M Engring. in Aeronautics, Calif. Poly. Inst., Pomona, 1989. Mem. tech. staff Autonetics, Anaheim, Calif., 1968-79, Lear Siegler Astronics, Santa Monica, Calif., 1979-83; sr. tech. specialist Northrop Grumman Corp., Hawthorne, Calif., 1983—. Contbr. articles to profl. publs. Mem. AIAA, IEEE. Office: Northrop Grumman Corp 1 Northrop Ave # 710 90 Hawthorne CA 90250-3236

TURNER, FLORENCE FRANCES, ceramist; b. Detroit, Mar. 9, 1926; d. Paul Pokrywka and Catherine Gagal; m. Dwight Robert Turner, Oct. 23, 1948; children: Thomas Michael, Nancy Louise, Richard Scott, Garry Robert. Student, Oakland C.C., Royal Oak, Mich., 1975-85, U. Ariz., Yuma, 1985, U. Las Vegas, 1989—. Pres., founder Nev. Clay Guild, Henderson, 1990-94, mem. adv. bd., 1994—; workshop leader Greenfield Village, Dearborn, Mich., 1977-78, Plymouth (Mich.) Hist. Soc., 1979, Las Vegas Sch. System, 1989-90, Detroit Met. area, 1977-85. Bd. dirs. Las Vegas Art Mus., 1987-91; corr. sec. So. Nev. Creative Art Ctr., Las Vegas, 1990-94. Mem. So. Nev. Rock Art Enthusiasts, Las Vegas Gem Club, Nev. Camera Club, Golden Key, Phi Kappa Phi. Office: Nev Clay Guild PO Box 50004 Henderson NV 89016-0004

TURNER, GARRISON F., lawyer; b. Modesto, Calif., Nov. 8, 1947; s. Paul William and Raylene F. (Smith) T.; m. Pamela Ann Burkholder, Oct. 11, 1981; 1 child, Abigail. BA, U. Calif., Berkeley, 1969; JD, Hastings Coll of Law, 1972. Bar: Calif. 1972, Oreg. 1985. Dep. pub. defender San Joaquin County, Calif., 1973-80; assoc. Freeman, Rishwain & Hall, Stockton, 1981-82; ptnr. Freeman, Hall, Turner & Brown, Stockton, 1982-85; assoc. Frohnmayer, Deatherage, deSchweinitz, Pratt & Jamieson, Medford, Oreg., 1985-88; ptnr. Frohnmayer, Deatherge, Pratt, Jamieson & Turner, Medford, 1988-94; sole practice Ashland, Oreg., 1994—; instr. Humphreys Coll. Law, Stockton, 1974-75. Capt. U.S. Army, 1969-77. Mem. State Bar Calif., State Bar Oreg., Jackson County Bar Assn., Oreg. Assn. Def. Counsel. Democrat. Office: 108 N 2nd St Ashland OR 97520-1935

TURNER, HAL WESLEY, state agency administrator; b. Winchester, Mass., Nov. 18, 1932; s. Wesley Francis and Anna Louise (Hodgkins) T.; m. Jean Marie Turner; children: Julie, Karen. BA, U. Sioux Falls, S.D., 1955. Cert. Govtl. Fin. Mgr. Mem. tech. and mgmt. staff Boeing Computer Svcs., Seattle, 1958-69; mgr. prodn. systems Kennecott Copper Corp., Salt Lake City, 1970-71; dir. MIS State of Idaho, Boise, 1971-74, adminstr. of budget, 1974-77; sales assoc. White Riedel Realtors, Boise, 1978-81; chief dep. Idaho State Controller's Office, Boise, 1981—; pres., Student Loan Fund Idaho, Inc., Fruitland, 1978—. Mem. Boise Samaritan Village Health Facility Adv. Bd.; region 4 chmn. Idaho Com. for Employer Support of Guard and Res. With U.S. Army, 1955-57. Mem. Nat. Assn. State Auditor's Comptr. and Treas., Nat. Assn. Govtl. Accts., Elks, Broadmore Country Club. Democrat. Methodist. Home: 3512 S Brookshore Pl Boise ID 83706-5582 Office: State Contrs Office PO Box 83720 Boise ID 83720-0011

TURNER, LILLIAN ERNA, nurse; b. Coalmont, Colo., Apr. 22, 1918; d. Harvey Oliver and Erna Lena (Wackwitz) T. BS, Colo. State U., 1940, Columbia U., 1945; cert. physician asst., U. Utah, 1978. Commd. 2d lt. Nurse Corps, U.S. Army, 1945; advanced through grades to lt. comdr. USPHS, 1964; 1st lt. U.S. Army, 1945-46; U.S. Pub. Health Svc., 1964-69; dean of women U. Alaska, Fairbanks, 1948-50; head nurse Group Health Hosp., Seattle, 1950-53; adviser to chief nurse Hosp. Am. Samoa, Pago Pago, 1954-60; head nurse Meml. Hosp., Twin Falls, Idaho, 1960-61; shift supr. Hosp. Lago Oil and Transport, Siero Colorado, Aruba, 1961-63; nurse adv. Province Hosp., Danang, South Vietnam, 1964-69, Cho Quan Hosp., South Vietnam, 1970-72; chief nurse, advisor Truk Hosp., Moen, Ea. Caroline Islands, 1972-74; nurse advisor Children's Med. Relief Internat., South Vietnam, 1975; physician's asst. U. Utah, 1976-78, Wagon Circle Med. Clinic, Rawlins, Wyo., 1978-89, Energy Basin Clinic Carbon County Meml. Hosp., Hanna, Wyo., 1989-96; ret., 1996. Named Nat. Humanitarian Physician Asst. of Yr., 1993, Wyo. Physician Asst. of Yr., 1992, Disting. Alumnus of Yr., Columbia U.-Presbyn. Hosp., N.Y.C., 1977. Mem. Wyo. Acad. Physician Assts. (bd. dirs. 1982-83), Am. Acad. Physician Assts., Nat. Assn. Physician Assts. Home: PO Box 337 Hanna WY 82327-0337 *Personal philosophy: You only go this way once so get as much out of it and put as much in as possible in the time allotted.*

TURNER, NANCY ELIZABETH, artist, designer; b. Cumberland Mountains, Ky.; d. Earl K. and Mary Lee (Jones) T.; m. Peter Alvet, Mar. 31, 1989. BA in Liberal Arts, U. Southwestern La.; Master Painter and Restorer, Yelland Acad. Fine Art, Calif.; cert. completion, Interior Decorators Inst. of L.A., 1990. Owner, chmn. The Turner Studio, Los Angeles; head artist/designer The Art Connection, Beverly Hills, Calif. Work includes fine paintings, artwork and decorative svcs. for residential and comml. interiors, trompe l'oeil murals, huge comml. fine art murals and signs, The Creator of "Fine Art Naturalism"; A Method of Painting very Realistic Lifesize Flowers and Foliage in Large Scale Setting, hand painted furniture and standing screens; creator bestselling collector's plates Michael's Miracle, 1982, Susan's World, 1983, illustrations appearing in the L.A. Times, and Sunset Mag. Leader nat. multi-ch. religious freedom crusade, 1985-86. Winner Lithograph of Yr. award, 1982. Mem. Am. Inst. Fine Arts, Am. Soc. Interior Designers (accessorizing cons.), The Calif. Arboretum Found. and The Nat. Mus. of Women in Arts. Address: 3240 McCarthy Dr Los Angeles CA 90065

TURNER, RALPH JAMES, artist; b. Ashland, Oreg., Oct. 24, 1935; s. Ralph Edwin and Ruth Marie (DeLap) T.; m. Phyllis Irene Wilson, Feb. 25, 1956; children: Sage Russell, Theresa Dawn, Rosalind Ruth, Alys Renee. Diploma, Pacific N.W. Coll. of Art, 1958; BA, Reed Coll., 1958; MFA, U. Oreg., 1962. Tchr. Seward (Alaska) Pub. Schs., 1959-60; teaching asst. Univ. Oreg., Eugene, 1961-62; instr. Univ. Ariz., Tucson, 1962-65, rsch. assoc. Lunar & Planetary Lab., 1964-75; asst. prof. Syracuse (N.Y.) Univ., 1966-70; instr. Pima Community Coll., Tucson, 1970-72, Linfield Coll., McMinnville, Oreg., 1975-80, Chemeketa Community Coll., Salem, Oreg., 1976-80; dir. Rock Creek Experimental Sta., Sheridan, Oreg., 1973—; coord. Art Program, Pima Coll., Tucson, 1970-71. Group shows include 150 Years of Martian Cartography, Staatsbibliothek, Berlin, 1993; permanent exhbns. of planetary models include Smithsonian Instn., NASA hdqs., U. Ariz., Griffith Obs., 1972-83, Beverly Hills, Calif., 1979, Syracuse U., 1966; pvt. collections in Homer, Alaska, Salishan, Oreg.; murals include Greeley, Colo., Wilsonville, Oreg., Corvallis, Oreg., Portland, Oreg., 1982-92. Pres. Willamina (Oreg.) Sheridan Grand Ronde Kiwanis, 1984-85. Recipient fellowship Nat. Endowment for Humanities, Washington, 1972-73. Mem. Oreg. Art Inst., Internat. Soc. for the Arts, Sci. and Tech., Internat. Sculpture Ctr. Democrat. Unitarian. Home and Office: Rock Creek Experimental Sta 14320 Rock Creek Rd Sheridan OR 97378-9735

TURNER, ROBERT ELWOOD, physicist; b. Covington, Ky., Dec. 8, 1937; s. Elwood Fletcher and Margaret Belle (Gunn) T. BS in Physics, U. Cin., 1959, MS in Physics, 1960; MA in Physics, Columbia U., 1963; PhD in Physics, Washington U., St. Louis, 1970. Research physicist U. Mich., Ann Arbor, 1970-73, Environ. Research Inst. Mich., Ann Arbor, 1973-77; sr. scientist Sci. Applications Internat. Corp., Hampton, Va., 1977—; rsch. assoc. Inst. for Space Studies, NASA, N.Y.C., 1962, Washington U., 1964-69; astronomer McDonnell Planetarium, St. Louis, 1965-68; lectr. U. Mich., 1971-77; Gordon Conf. lectr., 1980. Contbr. articles to profl. jours. and books. Rep. precinct leader, Ann Arbor, 1972. Laws fellow, 1959; recipient Group Achievement award NASA, 1976. Mem. AAAS, Am. Assn. Physics Tchrs., Optical Soc. Am., N.Y. Acad. Scis., Toastmasters (ednl. v.p. Dayton 1986, pres. 1987, sec. 1989, treas. 1991), Sigma Xi (programs co-chair Air Force chpt. 1988-89). Methodist. Club: Toastmasters (ednl. v.p. Dayton 1986, pres. 1987, sec. 1989). Home: 930 Casanova Ave #40 Monterey CA 93940 Office: Sci Applications Internat One Enterprise Pkwy Ste 250 Hampton VA 23666

TURNER, STEPHEN WAYNE, library director; b. Sacramento, Calif., July 31, 1945; s. George Rodgers and Louise Betty (Baumgart) T.; m. Patricia Ann Robison, June 25, 1972; children: Dorothy L., Elizabeth N., Peter E., Emily Jane. BA, U. Rochester, 1967; MA, U. Calif., Irvine, 1969; MLS, U. Denver, 1972. Head reference Lake Oswego (Oreg.) Pub. Libr., 1972-82, libr. dir., 1982-90; libr. dir. Wilsonville (Oreg.) Pub. Libr., 1990—. Author: Tracing Your Ancestors: A Guide to Research, 1978. Mem. Oreg. Libr. Assn. Office: Wilsonville Pub Libr 8200 SW Wilsonville Rd Wilsonville OR 97070-7727

TURNER, WALLACE L., reporter; b. Titusville, Fla., Mar. 15, 1921; s. Clyde H. and Ina B. (Wallace) T.; m. Pearl Burk, June 12, 1943; chldren: Kathleen Turner, Elizabeth Turner Everett. B.J., U. Mo., 1943; postgrad. (Nieman fellow), Harvard U., 1958-59. Reporter Springfield (Mo.) Daily News, 1943, Portland Oregonian, 1943-59; news dir. Sta. KPTV, Portland, 1959-61; asst. sec. HEW, Washington, 1961-62; reporter N.Y. Times, San Francisco, 1962—; bur. chief N.Y. Times, 1970-85, Seattle bur. chief, 1985-88. Author: Gamblers Money, 1965, The Morman Establishment, 1967. Recipient Heywood Broun award for reporting, 1952, 56; Pulitzer Prize for reporting, 1957. Office: Box 99269 Magnolia Sta Seattle WA 98199-4260

TURNER, WARREN AUSTIN, state legislator; b. Berkeley, Calif., Dec. 21, 1926; s. Warren Mortimer and Rebecca Oline (Noer) T.; m. Beverly Daune Mackay, Mar. 29, 1952; children: Daune Scott, Warren Adair, Alan Corey. BA, U. Calif., Berkeley, 1950, BS, 1952, MPH, 1958. Pub. acct. Price Waterhouse, San Francisco, 1951-52, AW Blackman, Las Vegas, Nev., 1952-56; asst. adminstr. Marin Gen. Hosp., San Rafael, Calif., 1958-60; assoc. dir. UCLA Hosp., 1960-68; founding adminstr. Walter O. Boswell Meml. Hosp., Sun City, Ariz., 1968-81; pres. Sun Health Corp., 1981-89; mem. Ariz. Senate, Phoenix, 1993-97, chmn. rules com., vice chair health com., mem. appropriations, family svcs. and transp. com., 1995-97; chmn. appropriation subcom. K-12, C.C.'s and natural resources. With USN, 1944-46. Mem Ariz. Acad., Rotary Internat. Republican. Home: 18432 W Glendale Ave Waddell AZ 85355-9737

TURNER, WILLIAM COCHRANE, international management consultant; b. Red Oak, Iowa, May 27, 1929; s. James Lyman and Josephine (Cochrane) T.; m. Cynthia Dunbar, July 16, 1955; children: Scott Christopher, Craig Dunbar, Douglas Gordon. BS, Northwestern U., 1952, LLD (hon.), Am. Grad. Sch. Internat. Mgmt., 1993. Pres., chmn. bd. dirs. Western Mgmt. Cons., Inc., Phoenix, 1955-74, Western Mgmt. Cons. Europe, S.A., Brussels, 1968-74; U.S. amb., permanent rep. OECD, Paris, 1974-77, vice chmn. exec. com., 1976-77, U.S. rep. Energy Policy Com., 1976-77, mem. U.S. dels. internat. meetings, 1974-77; mem. western internat. trade group U.S. Dept. Commerce, 1972-74; chmn., CEO Argyle Atlantic Corp., Phoenix, 1977—; chmn. European adv. coun., 1981-88, Asia Pacific adv. coun. AT&T Internat., 1981-88; founding mem. Pacific Coun. Internat. Policy, L.A., 1995—; mem. U.S.-Japan Bus. Coun., Washington, 1987-93, European adv. coun.

IBM World Trade Europe/Mid. East/Africa Corp., 1977-80; mem. Asia Pacific adv. coun. Am. Can Co., Greenwich, Conn., 1981-85, GE of Brazil adv. coun. GE Co., Coral Gables, Fla., 1979-81, Caterpillar of Brazil adv. coun. Caterpillar Tractor Co., Peoria, Ill., 1979-84, Caterpillar Asia Pacific Adv. Coun., 1984-90, U.S. adv. com. Trade Negotiations, 1982-84; bd. dirs. Goodyear Tire & Rubber Co., Akron, Ohio, Rural/Metro Corp., Microtest, Inc., Phoenix; chmn. bd. dirs. GO Wireless Internat. Ltd., Melbourne, Fla., 1995—; chmn. internat. adv. coun. Avon Products, Inc., N.Y.C., 1985—; mem. Spencer Stuart adv. coun. Spencer Stuart and Assocs., N.Y.C., 1984-90; chmn., mem. internat. adv. coun. Advanced Semiconductor Materials Internat. NV., Bilthoven, The Netherlands, 1985-88; bd. dirs. The Atlantic Coun. of U.S., Washington, 1977-92; co-chmn. internat. adv. bd. Univ. of Nations, Kona, Hawaii, 1985—; bd. dirs. World Wildlife Fund/U.S., 1983-85, World Wildlife Fund/The Conservation Found., 1985-89, Nat. Coun., 1989-95, 1996—; bd. govs. Joseph H. Lauder Inst. Mgmt. and Internat. Studies, U. Pa., 1983—; trustee Heard Mus., Phoenix, 1983-86, mem. nat. adv. bd., 1986-93; trustee Am. Grad. Sch. Internat. Mgmt., 1972—, chmn. bd. trustees, 1987-89; bd. govs. Atlantic Inst. Internat. Affairs, Paris, 1977-88; adv. bd. Ctr. Strategic and Internat. Studies, Georgetown U., 1977-81; dir. Pullman, Inc., Chgo., 1977-80, Nabisco Brands, Inc., Parsippany, N.J., 1977-85, Salomon Inc., N.Y.C., 1980-93, AT&T Internat., Inc., Basking Ridge, N.J., 1980-84, Atlantic Inst. Found., Inc., N.Y.C., 1984-90; mem. European Cmty.-U.S. Businessmen's Coun., 1978-79; bd. govs. Am. Hosp. of Paris, 1974-77; trustee Nat. Symphony Orch. Assn., Washington, 1973-83, Am. Sch., Paris, 1976-77, Orme Sch., Mayer, Ariz., 1970-74, Phoenix Country Day Sch., 1971-74; mem. nat. coun. Salk Inst., 1978-82; mem. U.S. Adv. Com. Internat. Edn. and Cultural Affairs, 1969-74; nat. rev. bd. Ctr. Cultural and Tech. Interchange between East and West, 1970-74; mem. vestry Am. Cathedral, Paris, 1976-77; pres., bd. dirs. Phoenix Symphony Assn., 1969-70; chmn. Ariz. Joint Econ. Devel. Com., 1967-68; exec. com., bd. dirs. Ariz. Dept. Econ. Planning and Devel., 1968-70; chmn. bd. Ariz. Crippled Children's Services, 1964-65; treas. Ariz. Rep. Com., 1956-57; chmn. Ariz. Young Rep. League, 1955-56; chmn. bd. Mercy Ships Internat., Inc., A Ministry of Youth With A Mission, Lindale, Tex., 1985—; mem. trade and environment com. Nat. Adv. Coun. for Environ. Policy and Tech.-U.S. EPA, Washington, 1991-95; dir. exec. com., chmn. internat. com. Ariz. Econ. Coun., Phoenix, 1989-93; dir. exec. com. Orgn. for Free Trade and Devel., Phoenix, 1991-93; chmn. Internat. Adv. Coun. Plasma Tech., Inc., Sante Fe, 1992—. Recipient East-West Ctr. Disting. Svc. award, 1977. Mem. U.S. Coun. Internat. Bus. (trustee, exec. com.), Coun. Fgn. Rels., Coun. of Am. Ambs. (vice chmn. bd.), Nat. Adv. Coun. on Bus. Edn., Coun. Internat. Edn. Exchange, Greater Phoenix Leadership, Govs. Strategic Partnership Econ. Devel., Phoenix, 1992-95, Met. Club, Links Club (N.Y.C.), Plaza Club (Phoenix), Paradise Valley (Ariz.) Country Club, Bohemian Club. Episcopalian. Office: 4350 E Camelback Rd Ste 240B Phoenix AZ 85018-2722

TURNER, WILLIAM JOSEPH, retired psychiatrist; b. Wilkinsburg, Pa., Sept. 22, 1907; s. William Moore and Phoebe Emma (Smith) T.; m. Kathryn Morrow, Aug. 12, 1925 (div. May 1959); children: William Morrow, James Quigly. BS, Pa. State Coll., 1927; MA, Johns Hopkins U., 1933. Cert. in medicine. Rotating intern Harriburg Hosp., Harrisburg, Pa., 1933-34; asst. resident pathology Balt. City Hosp., 1934-35; asst. resident medicine Billings Hosp., U. Chgo., 1935-36; staff physician Cresson The Hosp., Cresson, Pa., 1936-37; staff psychiatrist VA Hosp., N. Little Rock, Ark., 1937-40; psychiatrist VA Hosp., L.A., 1940-41, Northport, N.Y., 1941-50; rsch. psychiatrist Cen. Islip State Hosp., Cen. Islip, N.Y., 1954-76, SUNY, Stony Brook, 1976-82; prof. emeritus psychiatry, 1982-90, ret.; med. dir. Dreyfus Med. Found., N.Y.C., 1964-68, cons., 1966—. Author papers on subjects in field. Pres., various positions Suffolk County Dist. br. Am. Psychiat. Assn., 1960-92; chmn. com. for liaison with lay groups S.C.D.P. Lt. col. U.S. Army, 1943-46. Fellow Am. Psychiat. Assn. (life); mem. AMA (life), Am. Coll. Neuropsychopharmacology (life), AAAS, N.Y. Acad. Sci., Am. Chem. Soc., Soc. Biol. Psychiatry.

TURNER, WILLIAM WEYAND, author; b. Buffalo, N.Y., Apr. 14, 1927; s. William Peter and Magdalen (Weyand) T.; m. Margaret Peiffer, Sept. 12, 1964; children: Mark Peter, Lori Ann. BS, Canisius Coll., 1949. Spl. agt. in various field offices FBI, 1951-61; free-lance writer Calif., 1963—; sr. editor Ramparts Mag., San Francisco, 1967—; investigator and cons. Nat. Wiretap Commn., 1975; U.S. del. J.F.K. Internat. Seminar, Rio de Janeiro, 1995. Author: The Police Establishment, 1968, Invisible Witness: The Use and Abuse of the New Technology of Crime Investigation, 1968, Hoover's F.B.I.: The Men and the Myth, 1970, Power on the Right, 1971, (with Warren Hinckle and Eliot Asinof) The Ten Second Jailbreak, 1973, (with John Christian) The Assassination of Robert F. Kennedy, 1978, (with Warren Hinckle) The Fish is Red: The Story of the Secret War Against Castro, 1981, updated, expanded, retitled as Deadly Secrets: The CIA-Mafia War Against Castro and the Assassination of JFK, 1992; contbg. author: Investigating the FBI, 1973; contbr. articles to popular mags. Dem. candidate for U.S. Congress, 1968. Served with USN, 1945-46. Mem. Authors Guild, Internat. Platform Assn., Press Club of San Francisco. Roman Catholic. Home and Office: 163 Mark Twain Ave San Rafael CA 94903-2820

TURNEY, STEVEN CRAIG, architect; b. Lima, Ohio, Sept. 18, 1958; s. Paul Raymond and Barbra Jean (Metzger) T.; m. Mary Hollis Von Dach, July 24, 1991. AS, Boise State U., 1982; BArch, U. Idaho, 1990. Iron worker, welder Hartman Mfg., Boise, Idaho, 1976-80; crew chief T.W. Blasingame & Assocs., Boise, 1982-86; intern architect Walter H. Miller AIA, Clarkston, Wash., 1989-90; project mgr. Hosford & Larson AIA, Boise, 1990-91; project architect AGA Archs. Planners, Boise, 1991—. Mem. Local Govt. Com., Boise, 1992. Mem. AIA, NCARB, Constrn. Specifications Inst. (v.p. Idaho chpt. 1995, pres.-elect 1996, pres. 1997), Boise C. of C., Golden Key, Tau Sigma Delta. Home: 4096 E Driftwood Dr Meridian ID 83642 Office: 815 Park Blvd Ste 350 Boise ID 83712-7740

TURNEY, THOMAS CHARLES, civil engineer; b. Santa Fe, N. Mex., May 21, 1949; s. William Forbes and Mary Aileen (McCauley) T.; m. Patricia Ann Melick, June, 1973; 1 child, Scott. BSCE, N.M. State U., 1972, MSCE, 1974. Tech. Mescalero (N.Mex.) Apache Tribe, 1973-74; jr. engr. Camp Dresser McKee, Denver, 1974-76; engr. William F. Turney & Assoc., Santa Fe, N. Mex., 1976-77; prin. Turney & Sayre, Santa Fe, N. Mex., 1977-86, Thomas C. Turney, PE, Santa Fe, N. Mex., 1986-89; N.Mex. state engr. Cielo Corp., Santa Fe, 1989-95; state engr. State of N.Mex., Sante Fe, 1995—. Mem. NSPE, Am. Water Works Assn., Host Linon's Club (pres. 1982). Democrat. Roman Catholic. Office: State Engr Interstate Stream PO Box 25102 Santa Fe NM 87504-5102

TURPEN, LOUIS A., airport terminal executive. Pres., CEO Greater Toronto Airports Authority (formerly Lester B. Pearson Internat. Airport), Ont., Can., 1996—; dir., San Franciso Airports Commn. *

TURPIN, CALVIN COOLIDGE, retired university administrator, educator; b. Granite City, Ill., Nov. 8, 1924; s. Golden and Gertrude (West) T.; m. Eudell Coody, June 29, 1944; children: Susan Turpin Jones, John Thomas. BA, Baylor U., 1949, MA, 1952; BD, So. Bapt. Theol. Sem., 1955, M of Religious Edn., 1958; MA, Vanderbilt U., 1962; MDiv, So. Bapt. Theol. Sem., 1973; DSc in Theology, Golden Gate Bapt. Theol. Sem., 1967. Prof. history and Greek Jacksonville Coll., Tex., 1950-52; prof. religion Belmont Coll., Nashville, 1955-56, Austin-Peay State U., Clarksville, Tenn., 1956-57; assoc. libr. Inst. of Old Testament Golden Gate Bapt. Theol. Sem., Mill Valley, Calif., 1961-66; dir. librs., prof. libr. sci. Minot (N.D.) State Coll., 1966-67; dir. librs., prof. religion Judson Coll., Marion, Ala., 1967-70; dir. librs. Hardin-Simmons U., Abilene, Tex., 1970-77; vis. prof. Tex. Woman's U., Denton, 1974-75. Author: Beyond My Dreams: Memories and Interpretations, 1992, Writings and a Selected Bibliography of Calvin C. Turpin, 1995; co-author: Rupert N. Richardson: The Man and His Works, 1971, History of the First Baptist Church, Gilroy, California, 1995; contbr. numerous articles to profl. publs. Nat. dep. chief chaplains CAP-USAF Aux., 1990-92; Calif. dept. chaplain Am. Legion, San Francisco, 1990-92, 94-95; vets. pk. commr. San Benito County, Hollister, Calif., 1990-92; rent control commr. City of Hollister, 1993-95. Brigadier gen. USSC, 1992—. Lilly Endowment scholar Lilly Found., 1962. Mem. Rotary Club, Lions Club, Beta Phi Mu, Phi Delta Kappa, Gamma Iota. Republican. Baptist. Home: 188 Elm Dr Hollister CA 95023-3430

TURPIN, JOSEPH OVILA, counselor, educator; b. Rockford, Ill., July 11, 1943; s. D. John and Mona Belle (Albright) T.; m. Hester R. Thompson, June 26, 1969; children: Matthew, Michael. AB in Sociology, Ind. U., 1965, MS in Mental Retardation, 1966, postgrad., 1966-67; PhD in Rehab. Psychology, U. Wis., 1986. Rsch. assoc. Ind. U., Bloomington, 1966-67; instr. U. Wis. Parkside Extension, Kenosha, 1967-71; tchr. Kenosha Unified Sch. Dist., 1967-71; coord. Racine area Gov.'s Com. on Spl. Learning State of Wis. Dept. Adminstrn., 1971-73; dir. Racine County Comprehensive Mental Health, Mental Retardation, Alcohol and Other Drug Abuse Svcs. Bd, 1973-78; vocat. cons., counselor supr. Industrial Injury Clinic, Neenah, Wis., 1978-83; owner, vocat. expert Vocat. Counseling Svc., Inc., Madison, Wis., 1983-88; teaching intern, counseling supr., student tchr. supr. U. Wis., Madison, 1983-86; asst. prof. rehab. counselor edn. Ohio U., Athens, 1986-89; assoc. prof. rehab. counseling program Calif. State U., San Bernardino, 1989-94, prof. rehab. counseling program, 1994—, coord. rehab. counseling program, 1990-94; mem. sch. psychologist exam. com. Dept. Edn. State of Ohio, 1989; rschr., presenter, cons. in field. Contbr. articles to profl. publs. Bd. dirs. United Cerebral Palsy of Racine County, 1969-73, Children's House, Inc., Racine, 1971-73, Ctrl. Ohio Regional Coun. on Alcoholism, 1987-89, Inland Caregivers Resource Ctr., 1993—, Health and Hosp. Planning Com. of Racine County, 1976; treas. Cub Scout Pack # 68, Boy Scouts Am., Neenah, 1981-83, Whitcomb Village Assn., Inc., 1984; bd. dirs. Aquinas H.S., 1992-94, pres. 1994; H.S. liaison West Point Parents Club of Inland Empire, 1992-94; budget rev. com. United Fund Racine County, 1975. Grantee Rehab. Svcs. Adminstrn., 1985-88, Ohio U., 1987-88, Ohio U. Coll. Osteo. Medicine and Coll. Edn., 1989, Office Spl. Edn. and Rehab., 1989-92. Mem. ACA (pub. policy and legis. com. 1992-94, various subcoms.), APA, Assn. Counselor Educators and Suprs. (we. region legis. chair 1996—), Am. Rehab. Counseling Assn. (exec. coun. 1992-94, ethics com. 1990-91, chair coun. on profl. preparation and stds. 1992-94), Nat. Rehab. Counseling Assn. (bd. dirs. 1993-94, chmn. grievance com., pres. 1997). Office: Calif State U 5500 University Pky San Bernardino CA 92407-2318

TURRILL, FRED LOVEJOY, surgeon; b. Redlands, Calif., Sept. 14, 1922; s. Gardner Stilson and Virginia Marie (Johnson) T.; m. Edith Mae Brown, Mar. 17, 1951; children: Brian Casey, Kevin Michael, Ann Louise, Mark. AS, Glendale Coll., 1942; BSE, U. Mich., 1944; MD, U. So. Calif., 1950. Diplomate Am. Bd. Surgery. Intern L.A. County/U. So. Calif. Med. Ctr., 1950-52, resident surgery, 1952-56; surgeon Turrill, Shader & Myles, Glendale, Calif., 1956—; prof. surgery U. So. Calif., L.A., 1974—. Contbr. articles to profl. jours. With U.S. Army, 1942-46. Grantee USPS, 1956-57. Mem. ACS (gov. 1977-84), Collegium Internat. Chirurgiae, Pacific Coast Surg. Assn. (councillor 1980-83), We. Surg. Assn., Soc. Grad. Surgeons (life hon., pres. 1970-71), L.A. Surg. Soc. (pres. 1975). Republican.

TURTURRO, JOHN, actor; b. Brooklyn, Feb. 28, 1957; s. Nicholas and Katherine Turturro; m. Katherine Borowitz; 1 child, Amadeo. Grad., SUNY (New Paltz), 1978; student, Yale Drama Sch. Worked in regional theater and off-Broadway in Danny and the Deep Blue Sea (Obie award 1985), Men Without Dates, Tooth of the Crime, La Puta Vida, Chaos and Hard Times, The Bald Soprano, Of Mice and Men, The Resistable Rise of Arturo Ui, 1991; appeared in Broadway prodn. Death of a Salesman, 1984; appeared in films Raging Bull, 1980, The Flamingo Kid, 1984, To Live and Die in L.A., 1985, Desperately Seeking Susan, 1985, Hannah and Her Sisters, 1986, Gung Ho, 1986, Offbeat, 1986, The Color of Money, 1986, The Sicilian, 1987, Five Corners, 1988, Do the Right Thing, 1989, Miller's Crossing, 1990, Men of Respect, Mo Better Blues, 1990, Jungle Fever, 1991, Barton Fink, 1991 (winner best actor award, Cannes Film Festival, 1991, David Donatello award Montreal Film Festival-Best Actor), Backtrack, 1991, Brain Donors, 1992, Fearless, 1993, Being Human, 1994, Quiz Show, 1994, Grace of My Heart, 1994, Search and Destroy, 1995, Unstrung Heroes, 1995, Clockers, 1995, Box of Moonlight, 1996, Girl 6, 1996, The Big Lebowski, 1997, Animals, 1997; film dir. (debut) Mac (Camera d'Or award Cannes Film Festival, 1992). Office: care ICM 8942 Wilshire Blvd Beverly Hills CA 90211-1934 also: 16 N Oak St # 2 A Ventura CA 93001-2631*

TUSHER, THOMAS WILLIAM, retired apparel company executive; b. Oakland, Calif., Apr. 5, 1941; s. William C. and Betty J. (Brown) T.; m. Pauline B. Kensett, Jan. 1, 1967; children: Gregory Malcolm, Michael Scott. B.A., U. Calif., Berkeley, 1963; M.B.A., Stanford U., 1965. Asst. to v.p. internat. Colgate Palmolive Co., N.Y.C., 1965-67; product mgr. Colgate-Palmolive P.R., 1967-68; supt. corp. planning Levi Strauss & Co., San Francisco, 1969; pres. Levi Strauss Internat., 1977-84; sr. v.p. Levi Straus & Co., before 1984, exec. v.p., chief operating officer, dir., from 1984, pres., chief oper. officer; now ret.; regional gen. mgr., Australia/N.Z., Levi Strauss Australia, 1970-74; area gen. mgr. Levi Strauss No. Europe, London, 1974-75; pres. European div. Levi Strauss Internat., San Francisco, 1976; dir. various subs's. Levi Strauss Internat.; dir. Gt. Western Garment Co., Can. Bd. dirs. Calif. Council Internat. Trade, 1977—, U. Calif. Grad. Bus. Sch. Served with Intelligence Corps. USAR, 1966-67. Mem. San Francisco C. of C. (dir.). Republican. Presbyterian. Clubs: World Trade, Bay. Office: Levi Strauss & Co 1155 Battery St San Francisco CA 94111-1230

TUSKA, JON, author, publisher; b. South Milwaukee, Wis., Apr. 30, 1942; s. Andrew and Florence Catherine (Tommet) T.; m. Vicki Piekarski, May 24, 1980; 1 child, Jennifer Lee. BA, Marquette U., 1965. Owner Pers. Cons., Milw., 1969-74; editor, pub. Views & Revs. mag., 1969-75; freelance writer, 1975--91; co-owner, agt. Golden West Literary Agy., Portland, Oreg., 1992—; mem. adj. faculty MA and tchg. program and undergrads. Lewis and Clark Coll., 1979-88' staff music critic Ovation mag., 1987-89, Fanfare mag., 1989-95; spl. film. cons. Images of Indians, PBS, 1980, Images of Appalachia, PBS, 1984, Mommy, Who's Winning Now? The Cold War in America, Turner, 1986, Say It with Music: Irving Berlin's America, PBS, 1986, Broadway's Eternal Romantics: Lerner and Loewe, PBS, 1988, John Wayne: Standing Tall, PBS, 1989, Big Guns Talk, Turner, 1997; prodr. classical music programs, art and news features and interviews with musicians and motion picture personalities, and film revs. for radio stas. Oreg. Pub. Broadcasting. Author: Philo Vance: The Life and Times of S.S. Van Dine, 1973, The Films of Mae West, 1973, The Filming of the West, 1976, The Detective in Hollywood, 1978, The Vanishing Legion: A History of Mascot Pictures 1927-35, 1982, 2d edit., 1986, Billy the Kid: A Bio/Bibliography, 1983, Dark Cinema: American Film Noir in Cultural Perspective, 1984, The American West in Film: Critical Approaches to the Western, 1985, In Manors and Alleys: A Case-Book on the American Detective Film, 1988, A Variable Harvest: Essays and Reviews in Literature and Film, 1989, Encounters with Filmmakers: Eight Career Studies, 1991, The Complete Films of Mae West, 1992, Billy the Kid: His Life and Legend, 1994, (with Vicki Piekarski) The Frontier Experience: A Reader's Guide to the Life and Literature of the American West, 1984; editor-in-chief (with Piekarski) Ency. of Frontier and Western Fiction, 1983; also editor numerous books. Home and Office: 2327 SE Salmon St Portland OR 97214-3943

TUTASHINDA, ABD KARIM KWELI (BRIAN P. ALTHEIMER), chiropractic physician, educator; b. Wynne, Ark., May 14, 1956; s. Joe Porché and Lura Ella (Darden) Altheimer; divorced; 1 child, Chinyere R.; m. Leonor Quiñonez, June 13, 1987; children Xihuanel, Rukiya, Jomoké. BA in Philosophy magna cum laude, U. Ark., 1978; D of Chiropractic cum laude, Life Chiropractic Coll. West, San Lorenzo, Calif., 1989. Tchr. English Oakland (Calif.) Pub. Schs., 1984-86; tchr. spl. programs U. Calif., Berkeley, 1984-92, 94-95; instr. phys. diagnosis and chiropractic tech. Life Chiropractic Coll. West, San Lorenzo, Calif., 1989—; pvt. practice chiropractic physician Oakland, Berkeley, 1990—; owner Imhotep Chiropractic & Wellness Clinic; dir. Imhotep Wellness Workshops & Seminars. Editor, pub. Foresight Mag., 1982-84; author, pub. Toward a Holistic Worldview, 1985; contbr. articles to Chiropractic History. Recipient 1st degree Black Belt Tae Kwon Do, 1976. Mem. Assn. Chiropractic History, Somatics Soc. Mem. Sufi Order of the West, Naqshbandi Sufi Order. Islam. Office: 3358 Adeline St Berkeley CA 94703-2737

TUTT, MARGARET HONNEN, retail store owner; b. Garden City, Kans., Oct. 11, 1951; d. Russell Thayer and Louise (Honnen) T.; m. Frank John Steinegger, Sept. 7, 1974 (div. Aug. 1981); children: John F. Steinegger, Elisabeth Sophia Tutt Steinegger. BA, U. Denver, 1974. Owner Foster & Son-The Gift Collection, Denver, 1992—. Docent Denver Zoo Assocs., 1976-81, chair, 1979-80; bd. dirs. Hist. Denver, Inc., 1986-92; chmn. fundraising Newborn Hope, Inc., Denver, 1990, treas., 1996—; fundraiser Kent Denver Sch., 1993—; spl. events chair Colo. Preservation, Inc., 1995—; pres. Historic Denver Guild, 1996—. Mem. Jr. League of Denver (lectr. on volunteering for cmty. orgns. 1991, 92), Glenmoor Country Club (golf com.), Centennial Club (chair 1989-90). Republican. Episcopalian. Home: 5925 E Princeton Cir Cherry Hl Vlg CO 80111-1038 Office: Foster & Son The Gift Collection 235 Steele St Denver CO 80206-5208

TUTTLE, FRANK DOUGLAS, marketing executive; b. Peterborough, N.H., Sept. 30, 1957; s. Robert Perry and Marion Laura (Edoy) T.; m. Valerie Marie Ogrodski, July 29, 1989; children: Lauren Elizabeth, Rebecca Marie, Ryan Douglas. BS in Electrical Engring., Vanderbilt U., 1979; MBA, Pepperdine U., 1983; postgrad., Calif. Coast U. Project engr. Hughes Aircraft Co., Fullerton, Calif., 1979-91; secondary mktg. Renet Fin. Co., Anaheim, Calif., 1991-94; with Pioneer Savs. & Loan, 1994-95, Tuttle Fin Sys., 1995—. Mentor Big Brothers of Am., Fullerton, 1981-85. Home: 20756 Ivy Cir Yorba Linda CA 92887-3323

TUUL, JOHANNES, physics educator, researcher; b. Tarvastu, Viljandi, Estonia, May 23, 1922; came to U.S., 1956, naturalized, 1962; s. Johan and Emilie (Tulf) T.; m. Marjatta Murtoniemi, July 14, 1957 (div. Aug. 1971); children: Melinda, Melissa; m. Sonia Esmeralda Manosalva, Sept. 15, 1976; 1 son, Johannes. B.S., U. Stockholm, 1955, M.A., 1956; Sc.M., Brown U., 1957, Ph.D., 1960. Research physicist Am. Cyanamid Co., Stamford, Conn., 1960-62; sr. research physicist Bell & Howell Research Center, Pasadena, Calif., 1962-65; asst. prof., assoc. prof. Calif. State Poly. U., Pomona, 1965-68; vis. prof. Pahlavi U., Shiraz, Iran, 1968-70; chmn. phys. earth sci. Calif. State Poly. U., Pomona, 1971-75, prof. physics, 1975-91, prof. emeritus, 1992—; cons. Bell & Howell Research Center, Pasadena, Calif., 1965, Teledyne Co., Pasadena, 1968; guest researcher Naval Weapons Center, China Lake, Calif., 1967, 72; resident dir., Calif. State U. Internat. Programs in Sweden and Denmark, 1977-78. Author: Physics Made Easy, 1974; contbr. articles in field to profl. jours. Pres. Group Against Smoking Pollution, Pomona Valley, Calif., 1976; foster parent Foster Parents Plan, Inc., Warwick, R.I., 1964—; block capt. Neighborhood Watch, West Covina, Calif., 1982-84. Brown U. fellow, 1957-58; U. Namur (Belgium) research grantee, 1978; Centre Nat. de la Recherche Scientifique research grantee, France, 1979; recipient Humanitarian Fellowship award Save the Children Fedn., 1968. Mem. AAAS (life), N.Y. Acad. Scis. Am. Phys. Soc., Republican. Roman Catholic. Research in energy conservation and new energy technologies.

TWARDZIK, DAVE, manager professional athletics; b. Middletown, N.Y.. Student, Old Dominion U., 1972. Player Va. Squires, 1972-76; free agent Portland Trail Blazers, 1976-81, dir., 1981; asst. coach Ind., 1986-89, L.A. Clippers, 1989-90; dir. scouting Charlotte Hornets, 1990-91, dir. player personnel, 1991; gen. mgr. Golden State Warriors, Oakland, Calif. Office: Golden State Warriors 1221 Broadway 20th Fl Oakland CA 94612-1918

TWENEY, GEORGE HARRISON, aeronautical engineer; b. Moosejaw, Sask., Can., Sept. 16, 1915; s. Charles Rank and Mary Elizabeth (Peirce) T.; m. Maxine Calvert, July 11, 1955; 1 child, Craig Peirce. B Aero. Engring., U. Detroit, 1938, profl. degree in Aero. Engring., 1942; MS, U. Mich., 1942. Test engr. Pan Am. World Airways, N.Y.C., 1938-41; Aero. Engr. U. Detroit and Wayne State U., Detroit, 1941-54; staff engr. in charge tech. Sci. Rsch. Labs., Boeing Co., Seattle, 1955-73; pvt. practice cons. in field.; vis. sr. prof. engring. Trinity Coll., Dublin, Ireland, 1985. Author: American Student Flyer, 1942, Jack London - A Bibliography, 1966, 2d edit., 1973, The Washington 89, 1989 (Rounce and Coffin award 1990), ; editor BSRL Sci. Rev., 1964-70, Univ. Rsch. Newsletter, 1964—; contbr. articles to profl. jours. Chmn. Wash. State Nat. Libr. Week, 1968; chmn. Wash. State Lewis and Clark Com., 1973—; trustee U. Mich. Clements Libr., 1965-72; life mem., past pres. bd. trustees Seattle Pub. Libr.; bd. dirs. Lewis and Clark Trail Heritage Found. Fellow AIAA (assoc.); mem. Am. Antiquarian Soc., Am. Soc. Engring. Edn. (chmn. aeros divsn. 1978), Grolier Club, Monday Club. Home: 16660 Marine View Dr SW Seattle WA 98166-3210

TWIGG-SMITH, THURSTON, newspaper publisher; b. Honolulu, Aug. 17, 1921; s. William and Margaret Carter (Thurston) Twigg-S.; m. Bessie Bell, June 9, 1942 (div. Feb. 1983); children: Elizabeth, Thurston, William, Margaret, Evelyn; m. Laila Roster, Feb. 22, 1983 (div. Dec. 1994); m. Sharon Smith, Feb. 28, 1996. B.Engring., Yale U., 1942. With Honolulu Advertiser, 1946—, mng. editor, 1954-60, asst. bus. mgr., 1960-61, pub., 1961-86; pres., dir., chief exec. officer Honolulu Advertiser, Inc., 1962-93, chmn., 1993—; chmn., dir., CEO Persis Corp.; bd. dirs. Atalanta/Sosnoff Capital Corp., N.Y. Trustee Punahou Sch., Old Sturbridge Inc., Honolulu Acad. Arts, The Contemporary Mus., Hawaii, Mus. Contemporary Art, L.A., The Skowhegan Sch., Maine, Yale Art Gallery, New Haven, Philatelic Found., N.Y., Whitney Mus. Am. Art, N.Y. Maj. AUS, 1942-46. Mem. Honolulu C. of C., Waialae Country Club, Pacific Club, Oahu Country Club, Outrigger Canoe Club. Office: Persis Corp PO Box 3110 96802 605 Kapiolani Blvd Honolulu HI 96813

TWIST, ROBERT LANPHIER, farmer, rancher, cattle feeder; b. Memphis, Dec. 27, 1926; s. Clarence C. and Edith G. Twist; student Springfield (Ill.) Jr. Coll., 1943; B.S. in Agr., U. Ill., 1950; postgrad. U. Edinburgh (Scotland); m. Joy Twist; 1 child Marilyn Edith Ten Hope. Owner, operator farm lands, Twist, Ark., 1949—, Bow Fiddle Ranch, Laramie, Wyo., 1961—, Lost Creek Ranch, Masters, Colo., 1963, Rolling T Ranch, Ft. Morgan, Colo., 1965—, R.L. Twist Ranches Cattle Feeding Enterprises, Greeley, Colo. and Ft. Morgan, 1974—; prin. R.L. Twist Land & Investments, Paradise Valley, Ariz., 1974—; Rocker M Ranch, Douglas, Ariz., 1981—, Circle J Ranch, Gunnison, Colo., 1993; cons. agrl. mgmt. Justice of Peace, Twist, Ark., 1954. Served with USAAF, 1944-46. Mem. Colo. Farm Bur., Wyo. Farm Bur., Nat. Cattlemen's Assn. (charter). Republican. Presbyterian. Home: 4612 E Sparkling Ln Paradise Valley AZ 85253

TWITCHELL, CLEVELAND EDWARDS, journalist, writer; b. N.Y.C., May 8, 1937; s. Hanford Mead and Virginia (Sterry) T.; m. Linda Elaine Johnson, Aug. 20, 1977; children: Peter, Wendy, Richard, Kathryn. Grad., Phillips Exeter Acad., 1955. Editor, pub. Bay Window, San Francisco, 1957-59; asst. city editor Post Advocate, Alhambra, Calif., 1959-61; regional editor Mail Tribune, Medford, Oreg., 1961-64, news editor, 1964-83, lifestyles editor, 1983-95; editor and columnist Mail Tribune, Medford, 1996—. Author: The UFO Saga, 1966, Living & Other Good Ideas, 1977, Daytrips, 1992, Dining Out in Southern Oregon, 1994. Mem. Soc. Profl. Journalists (treas. So. Oreg. chpt. 1976-78), Soc. of Mayflower Descendants (dep. gov. Cascade County chpt. 1992-95, lt. gov. 1995—). Office: Mail Tribune 111 N Fir St Medford OR 97501-2772

TWITCHELL, KENT, mural artist; b. Lansing, Mich., Aug. 17, 1942; s. Robert E. and Wilma Doris (Berry) T.; m. Susan Catherine Fessler, Dec. 27, 1975 (div. 1986); m. Pandora Seaton, Feb. 23, 1990; children: Rory, Artie. AA, East L.A. Coll., 1969; BA, Calif. State U., 1972; MFA, Otis Art Inst., 1977; DA (hon.), Biola U., 1989; DFA (hon.), Otis Coll. Art and Design, 1996. Illustrator USAF, 1960-65; display artist J.C. Penney Co., Atlanta, 1965-66; abstract artist, painter L.A., 1968-70, mural artist, 1971—; instr. L.A. County High Sch. for the Arts, L.A., 1987-90, Otis/Parsons Art Inst., L.A., 1980-83; cons. Olympic Murals Program, L.A., 1983-84. Executed exterior murals at Union at 12th St. (Steve McQueen monument), L.A., 1971, Hollywood Fwy. (The Freeway Lady), L.A., 1974, Hill St. at Olympic (Edward Ruscha monument), 1987, 405 Fwy. (La Marathon mural), Inglewood, Calif., 1987, 1420 Locust St. (Dr J monument), Phila., 1989, Harbor Fwy. (La Chamber Orch.), L.A., 1991-93, Calif. Theater, San Bernardino, Calif., 1997; one-man shows include: L.A. Mcpl. Art Gallery, 1980, Loyola Marymount U., L.A., 1985, Thinking Eye Gallery, L.A., 1986, Valparaiso (Ind.) U. Art Mus., 1987, Westmont Coll. Art Gallery, Santa Barbara, Calif., 1987, Biola U. Art Gallery, La Mirada, Calif., 1987, Vincent Price Gallery-East L.A. Coll., 1990, Lizardi-Harp Gallery, Pasadena, Calif., 1991, U. Redlands Art Gallery, 1997; exhibited in group shows at L.A. Mcpl. Art Gallery, 1977, 81, 94, 96, Calif. Polytech. U., Pomona, 1978, Santa Monica Coll., 1978, L.A.C.E. Gallery, L.A., 1981, Otis/Parsons Art Inst., L.A., 1987, Mayer Schwarz Gallery, Beverly Hills, 1988, 90, Principia Coll., Elsah, Ill., 1989, Koplin Gallery, Santa Monica, 1992, 95, L.A. County Mus. Art, 1992, Robert Berman Gallery, Santa Monica, 1995, Art Ctr./Coll. Design, Pasadena, 1996, Riverside (Calif.) Art Mus., 1996. Mem. adv. bd. Artists Equity Assn., 1980—, Mural Conservancy of L.A., 1988—. Grantee

Calif. Arts Coun., 1978, Nat. Endowment for Arts, 1986. Studio: 9429 Main St PO Box 145 Upper Lake CA 95485-0145

TWITCHELL, THEODORE GRANT, music educator and composer; b. Melrose, Kans., Jan. 26, 1928; s. Curtis and Sarah Frances (Lane) T.; m. Rebecca Janis Goldsmith, Nov. 18, 1989; stepchildren: Ralph Norman, Russell Norman, Dawn Jiricek. AA in Music, L.A. City Coll., 1949; BA in Social Studies, Calif. State U., L.A., 1951, MA in Secondary Edn., 1955; EdD in Secondary and Higher Edn., U. So. Calif., L.A., 1964. Tchr. Barstow (Calif.) Union High Sch., 1952, Burbank (Calif.) Unified Sch. Dist., 1954-66; dean instrn., dir. evening divsn., dir. summer sessions, 1966-69; pres. Palo Verde Coll., Blythe, Calif., 1969-70; adult tchr. L.A. Unified Sch. Dist., 1977-78; faculty Columbia West U., L.A., 1993—; pvt. English tutor, 1979—. Composer: The Gettysburg Address, Tidewater, The Pride of Monticello, Labor Day March, Valley Forge, Normandy Prayer, Christmas in L.A., L.A., Overture to Tidewater, The Joy of Snow, Walt Whitman and Friends, over 90 others; contbr. articles to profl. jours.; author: Dear Mr. President, 1982, Courage, Conflict and Love, 1988, The Magnificent Odyssey of Michael Young, 1992. With U.S. Army, 1952-53. Recipient Coll. Faculty Senate Award for Achievements for the coll., Palo Verde Coll., Student Body award. Mem. Internat. Poetry Hall Fame, Cmty. Coll. Pres.'s Assn., Am. Assn. Composers, Authors and Pubs., Calif. PTA (hon. life mem.), Rho Delta Chi. Republican. Methodist. Home: 2737 Montrose Ave Apt 10 Montrose CA 91020-1318

TWOGOOD, RICHARD EDWARD, electrical engineer; b. National City, Calif., May 29, 1951; s. Frederick John and Gladys Ruth (Belttary) T.; m. Beth Ellen Norman, June 11, 1972; children: Kate, Sara, Richard. BS, U. Calif., Davis, 1972, MS, 1973, PhD, 1977. Engr. Lawrence Livermore (Calif.) Nat. Lab., 1972-79, group leader, 1979-83, div. leader, 1983-88, prog. leader, 1988-96, dep. assoc. dir. for electronics engring., 1996—. Contbr. articles to profl. jours. Mem. IEEE. Office: Lawrence Livermore Labs PO Box 808 Livermore CA 94551-0808

TWOMLEY, BRUCE CLARKE, commissioner, lawyer; b. Selma, Ala., Jan. 23, 1945; s. Robert Clarke and Eleanor Jane (Wood) Anderson T.; m. Sara Jane Minton, June 13, 1979; children: Christopher Mario, Jonathan Marion. BA in Philosophy, Northwestern U., 1967; LLM, U. Calif., San Francisco, 1970; postgrad. Nat. Jud. Coll., Reno, Nev., 1983, 88. Bar: Calif. 1972, Alaska 1973, U.S. Dist. Ct. Alaska, 1973, U.S. Ct. Appeals (9th cir.) 1982. VISTA vol., Anchorage, 1972-73; lawyer Alaska Legal Services Corp., Anchorage, 1973-82; commr. Alaska Comml. Fisheries Entry Commn., Juneau, 1982-83, chmn., 1983—; mem. Gov.'s Fisheries Cabinet, 1983—, Child Support Enforcement Divsn. Rural Task Force, 1985—, Alaska Fedn. of Natives Task Force on IRS and Alaska Native Fishermen, 1994; cons. IRS, Sta. WNED-TV, Buffalo, 1988; mem. Bristol Bay Native Assn. Blue Ribbon Commn. on Ltd. Entry, 1994—; presenter in field. Contbr.: Limited Access Management: A Guidebook to Conservation, 1993. Recipient Alaska Legal Services Disting. Service award, 1983, 92. Mem. Juneau Racquet Club (adv. bd. 1989—), Kappa Sigma (pres. interfraternity council 1966-67). Home: PO Box 20972 Juneau AK 99802-0972 Office: Alaska Comml Fisheries Entry Commn 8800 Glacier Hwy Ste 109 Juneau AK 99801-8079

TWOREK, RICHARD KENNETH, dean; b. Buffalo, Jan. 14, 1943; s. Anthony and Sophie (Jozwiak) T.; m. Theodora Jean Swietlik, Nov. 27, 1965; children: Todd Mitchell, Tammy Lynn. BS in Mgmt., SUNY, Buffalo, 1970, MS in Health Scis., 1973; PhD in Edn., U. Ill., Urbana, 1979. Lab. tech. Millard Fillmore Hosp., Buffalo, 1964-66, Roswell Park Meml. Inst., Buffalo, 1965-66; product mktg. specialist Am. Optical Corp., Buffalo, 1965-71; enzyme analysis tech. Mercy Hosp., Buffalo, 1966-72; program. coord., instr. dept. medicine Albany (N.Y.) Med. Coll., 1972-75; staff assoc., basic med. scis. U. Ill. Coll. Medicine, Urbana, 1975-77; dean, health scis. Chgo. City-Wide Coll., 1977-91; dean health scis. and profl. studies Malcolm X Coll. City Coll. Chgo., Chgo., 1991-93; dean instrn. Riverside C.C., Moreno Valley, Calif., 1993—; chmn. Dept. of Health and Human Svcs., 1996—; bd. trustees, Michael Reese HMO, Chgo., 1984-87, vice chmn., review com., 1987-93. Contbr. articles to profl. jours. Bd. dirs. Moreno Valley Cmty. Hosp. Found., 1997—. Named Outstanding Teaching Intern, SUNY, 1972; nominated Outstanding Jour. Article, Jour. Allied Health, 1978, Charles A. Dana award, Assn. Am. Colls. Mem. Am. Soc. Allied Health Profls. (bd. dirs. 1981-83), Moreno Valley March Field Rotary Club (founder, bd. dirs. 1994—). Office: Riverside CC 16130 Lasselle St Moreno Valley CA 92551-2045

TYBURCZY, JOHN ADRIAN, surgeon; b. Alameda, Calif., Dec. 24, 1953; s. Joseph Andrew and Irene Janet (Christo) T. BS, Lewis and Clark Coll., 1975; MD, N.Y. Med. Coll., 1979. Diplomate Am. Bd. Surgery. Resident in gen. surgery Oreg. Health Scis. U., Portland, 1979-83; resident in gen. surgery San Joaquin Gen. Hosp., Stockton, Calif., 1985-87, chief resident, 1987-88; pvt. practice, Elko, Nev., 1989—; chief surgery Elko Gen. Hosp., 1992-94, chief staff, 1994-95. Vice pres. for med. affairs Elko chpt. Am. Cancer Soc., 1990-92. Fellow ACS (participant 2d group of 100 1995), Southwestern Surg. Congress; mem. Am. Soc. Gen. Surgeons (charter), Boondocks Med. Soc. Office: Elko Clinic 762 14th St Elko NV 89801-3413

TYCHOWSKI, CHRISTOPHER ROMAN, engineer; b. Chorzow, Poland, Sept. 20, 1937; came to U.S., 1973; s. Feliks and Maria Jadwiga (Napierala) T.; m. Slavomira Maria Zbierska, Sept. 16, 1975 (div. Mar. 1979). Bachelors Degree, Poznan (Poland) Tech. Coll., 1958; Masters Degree, Poznan Politechnik, 1965; PhD, Warsaw (Poland) Inst. Tech., 1972. Sr. project engr. Warsaw Inst. Tech., 1969-73; project engr. Arthur G. McKee, San Mateo, Calif., 1974-76; pvt. practice cons. Phoenix, 1976-78; civil engr. W.B.C. Cons., Phoenix, 1978-79; project engr. Peter A. Lendrum Architects, Phoenix, 1979-80; sr. structural engr. Sullivan-Mason, Inc. Architects-Engrs., Phoenix, 1981-83; plans rev. engr. City of Phoenix Bldg. Safety Dept., 1981-83; sr. project engr. Magadini Alagia Assoc., Phoenix, 1983-84; pres. C.R.T. Corp., Tempe, Ariz., 1984—; realtor Realty Experts, Inc., Phoenix, 1987—; pres. Alliance Bldg. Corp., Phoenix, 1988—, Acorn Bldg. Corp.; exec. v.p. Gemcraft Constrn. Co., Inc., Phoenix, 1988—. Patentee in field. Recipient Recognition awards, Polish Assn. of Architects, 1968, 70, Tech. Excellence award Polish Normalization Com., 1971, Best Sports Pub. of Yr. award Polish Nat. Olympic Com., 1972. Mem. Am. Inst. Steel Constrn., Structural Engrs. Assn., Phoenix Bd. Realtors. Republican. Roman Catholic. Office: CRT Corp 1370 E 8th St Ste 2 Tempe AZ 85281-4383

TYKESON, DONALD ERWIN, broadcasting executive; b. Portland, Oreg., Apr. 11, 1927; s. O. Ansel and Hillie Martha (Haveman) T.; m. Rilda Margaret Steigleder, July 1, 1950; children: Ellen, Amy, Eric. BS, U. Oreg., 1951. V.p., dir. Liberty Communications, Inc., Eugene, Oreg., 1963-67, pres., chief exec. officer, dir., 1967-83; chmn. bd. Bend Cable Communications, Inc., 1983—, Telecomm Systems, Inc., 1983—; pres. Telecomm Svcs. Inc., 1988—; chmn. bd. Ctrl. Oreg. Cable Advt., Inc., 1992—; chmn., CEO Bend Cable Comm. Inc., 1983—. Bd. dirs. Nat. Coalition Rsch. in Neurol. and Communicative Disorders, 1984-89, Sacred Heart Med. Ctr. Found., 1995—; chmn. Nat. Coalition in Rsch. pub. and govt. info. com., 1986-89, C-SPAN, 1980-89; mem. bus. adv. coun. U. Oreg. Coll. Bus. Adminstrn., 1973—; trustee U. Oreg. Found., 1996—; vice-chmn. we. area Nat. Multiple Sclerosis Soc., 1983—, dir., mem. rsch. and med. programs com., 1986—; trustee Eugene Art Found., 1980-85, Oreg. Health Scis. U. Found., 1988-91, mem. investment com., 1992—; mem. Oreg. Investment Coun. State of Oreg., vice chmn., 1988-92. Mem. Nat. Assn. Broadcasters, Nat. Cable TV Assn. (dir. 1976-83), Chief Execs. Orgn., Vintage Club (bd. dirs. 1996—, chmn. fin. com., treas. 1996—, pres. 1997—), Eugene Country Club (dir. 1975-77, sec. 1976, v.p. 1977), Multnomah Athletic Club, Arlington Club, Rotary, Elks. Home: 447 Spyglass Dr Eugene OR 97401-2091 Office: Bend Cable Comm Inc PO Box 70006 Eugene OR 97401-0101*

TYLER, CECILIA K., army officer; b. McCall, Idaho, May 18, 1956; d. Cecil Edward and Ruby Ilene (Wine) Oatney; m. Nelvin Eugene (Gene) Tyler Jr., Dec. 24, 1991. BBA in Acctg., Idaho State U., 1978; MS in Econs. and Ops. Research, Colo. Sch. Mines, 1987. Commd. 2d lt. U.S. Army, 1978, advanced through grades to lt. col., 1995; platoon leader A, B and C Cos. 8th Signal Battalion U.S. Army, Bad Kreuznach, Fed. Republic of Germany, 1978-81, logistics officer, 1981; promoted to capt., 1982; div. radio officer 142d Signal Battalion U.S. Army, Ft. Hood, Tex., 1982-83, comdr. C Co. 142d Signal Battalion, 1983-85, asst. ops. officer, 1985; chief market analysis 6th Recruiting Brigade U.S. Army, Ft. Baker, Calif., 1987-89; with command and gen. staff coll. U.S. Army, Leavenworth, Kans., 1989-90; promoted to maj., 1990; chief strategic systems plans br. 5th Signal Command U.S. Army, Fed. Republc of Germany, 1990-91, chief plans & programs div., 1991; exec. officer 509th Signal Battalion U.S. Army, Italy, 1991-92; exec. officer office dep. chief staff, info. mgmt. U.S. Army, Germany, 1992-94; promoted to lt. col. U.S. Army, 1995; dep. brigade comdr. 2d Sig BDE, Germany, 1995-96; commdr. 504th Signal Battalion, Fort Huachuca, Ariz., 1996—. Pres. 4-H Club, Valley County, Idaho, 1973-74. Mem. Armed Forces Communication-Electronics Assn., Assn. U.S. Army. Home: 2211 Lara Dr Sierra Vista AZ 85635 Office: 504th Signal Battalion Fort Huachuca AZ 85613

TYLER, DARLENE JASMER, dietitian; b. Watford City, N.D., Jan. 26, 1939; d. Edwin Arthur and Leola Irene (Walker) Jasmer; BS, Oreg. State U., 1961; m. Richard G. Tyler, Aug. 26, 1977 (dec.); children: Ronald, Eric, Scott. Clin. dietitian Salem (Oreg.) Hosp., 1965-73; sales supr. Sysco Northwest, Tigard, Oreg., 1975-77; clin. dietitian Physicians & Surgeons Hosp., Portland, Oreg., 1977-79; food svc. dir. Meridian Park Hosp., Tualatin, Oreg., 1979—. Registered dietitian. Mem. Am. Dietetic Assn., Oreg. Dietetic Assn., Portland Dietetic Assn., Am. Soc. Hosp. Food Svc. Adminstrs. Episcopalian. Home: 9472 SW Hume Ct Tualatin OR 97062-9039 Office: 19300 SW 65th Ave Tualatin OR 97062-7706

TYLER, DONALD EARL, urologist; b. Ontario, Oreg., Oct. 3, 1926; s. Charles Maurice and Iva (Hess) T.; 1 child, Paul Donald. MD, U. Oreg. Med. Sch., 1950; JD, U. Denver Coll. Law, 1967. Diplomate Am. Bd. Urology, Am. Coll. Legal Medicine. Fellow in gen. surgery, urology The Mayo Found., Rochester, Minn., 1952, 55-58; clin. instr. in urology U. Utah Med. Sch., Salt Lake City, 1959-64. Author: A New and Simple Theory of Gravity, 1970, Originations of Life from Volcanoes and Petroleum, 1983, Earliest Man of America in Oregon, USA: With Photographs of Paleolithic Artifacts, 1986, The Other Guy's Sperm: The Cause of Cancer and Other Diseases, 1994. Served to lt. USNR, 1944-45, 52-55, WWII, Korea. Mem. Alpha Omega Alpha, Phi Eta Sigma. Home: 1092 SW 2nd Ave Ontario OR 97914-2121

TYLER, GAIL MADELEINE, nurse; b. Dhahran, Saudi Arabia, Nov. 21, 1953 (parents Am. citizens); d. Louis Rogers and Nona Jean (Henderson) Tyler; m. Alan J. Moore, Sept. 29, 1990; 1 child, Sean James. AS, Front Range C.C., Westminster, Colo., 1979; BS in Nursing, U. Wyo., 1989. RN. Ward sec. Valley View Hosp., Thornton, Colo., 1975-79; nurse Scott and White Hosp., Temple, Tex., 1979-83, Meml. Hosp. Laramie County, Cheyenne, Wyo., 1983-89; dir. DePaul Home Health, 1989-91; field staff nurse Poudre Valley Hosp. Home Care, 1991—; parish nurse Cornerstone Evangelical Free Ch., 1996—. Avocations: collecting internat. dolls, sewing, reading, travel.

TYLER, RICHARD R., marketing executive; b. Denver, June 27, 1935; s. George Franklin and Josephine (Grassi) T.; m. Marcella Leonetti, Nov. 12, 1960; children: Marcella, Mark, Scott, Christine. BA, Calif. State U., San Jose, 1957. Reporter Daily News, L.A.; pub. rels. rep. Ford Motor Co., L.A.; account exec. Carl Byoir & Assocs., L.A.; west coast pub. rels. dir. Am. Airlines, L.A. and other cities; dir. corp. pub. rels. Six Flags Corp., L.A.; regional v.p. N.W. Ayer Pub. Rels., L.A., 1984-87; mktg. v.p. Triple Check Cos., L.A., 1987—. Pub. rels. adv. L.A. City Fire Chief, 1988—. Fellow Pub. Rels. Soc. Am. (Disting. Profl. 1987); mem. Pub. Rels. Soc. Am. L.A. (pres. 1986), L.A. Press Club (bd. mem. 1993-95), San Fernando Valley Press Club (pres. 1966), San Fernando Valley Press Club (pres. 1966), Soc. Profl. Journalists. Home: 15400 Valley Vista Blvd Sherman Oaks CA 91403-3812 Office: Triple Check Cos 727 S Main St Burbank CA 91506-2528

TYLER, STEVEN ANTHONY, mechanical engineer; b. Chgo., July 8, 1964; s. Edwin Chester and Lillian Josephine (Mierzwinski) Drzymkowski; m. Debra Jean Gaetke, June 15, 1991. BSME, U. Ill., 1986; MSME, Stanford U., 1992. Registered profl. engr., Calif. Design engr. Argonne (Ill.) Nat. Lab., 1986-87; flight test engr. Lockheed - Missiles div., Sunnyvale, Calif., 1987-88; infrared phenomenologist Lockheed - Rsch. & Devel., Palo Alto, Calif., 1988-96; sr. electro-optical engr. Lockheed Martin Advanced Tech. Ctr., Palo Alto, 1996-97; project engr. Styrker Endoscopy, Santa Clara, Calif., 1997—. Mem. NSPE, ASME, AIAA. Democrat.

TYLER-PARKER, SYDNEY BILLIG, publishing executive, author, educational consultant; b. L.A., May 11, 1938; d. Harvey Ellsworth Jr. and Sidney Roberta (Woolslair) Billig; m. Thomas True Tyler, July 11, 1969 (div. 1986); 1 child, Lee Harris Tyler Argabrite; m. Minot Harold Parker, Dec. 30, 1988. BA in English Lit., Coll. William and Mary, 1960; MSC in Sci. Edn., U. So. Calif., 1968; post masters, Tavistock Inst. Human Rels., London, 1975. cert. elem. and secondary tchr., U.S., U.K., West Germany, Canada. Tchr. math., social studies Torrance (Calif.) Unified Sch. Dist., 1966-68; math rsch. assoc. southwest Reg. Fed. Lab., Inglewood, Calif., 1967-68; tchr. Am. lit., Latin, great issues of man Palos Verdes USD, Rolling Hills, Calif., 1968-69; tchr. math. Mayfield Comprehensive Sch., London, 1970; tchr. AFCENT NATO Internat. Sch., Brunssum, The Netherlands, 1970-75; internat. primary coord., rsch. head, 1972-74; tchr., program dir. RAF Alconbury (U.K.) U.S. Air Force Schs., 1975-81; pres. Thomas Geale Pubs., Inc., Montara, Calif., 1982—; tchr. Laguna Salada Union Sch. Dist., 1997—; gifted and talented cons., tchr. Cabrillo Unified Sch. Dist., Half Moon Bay, Calif., 1991-96; cons., counselor U.S. Air Force Offices of Social Actions, Alconbury, 1976-79; project dir. The Think Bridge, Inc. Author: Young Think, 1980—, Just Think, 1980—, Stretch Think, 1982—, Think Quest, 1990—; editorial adv., article contbr. THINK Magazine, San Antonio, Tex., 1990—. Recipient 200 Women of Achievement in England award United Kingdom Soc., 1970, Outstanding World-wide Social Actions Cons. Counselor award U.S. Air Force, Alconbury, 1978. Mem. NEA, ASCD, Overseas Edn. Assn., Phi Delta Kappa (U.K. chpt. treas. 1978-81). Home and Office: PO Box 370540 Montara CA 94037-0540

TYLLIA, FRANK MICHAEL, principal; b. Rossiand, B.C., Can., Dec. 1, 1942; came to U.S., 1942; s. Alex J. and Lenora M. (Janni) T.; m. Kathryn A. McWalter, Mar. 21, 1970. BBA, Gonzaga U., 1965, BA in Edn., 1967; MA in Edn., Seattle U., 1972. Tchr. pub. schs., Seattle, 1967-72, prin., 1972-78; prin. Edmonds Sch. Dist., Lynnwood, Wash., 1978—; adj. prof. Seattle Pacific U., 1990—. Active Gonzaga Alumni Mentoring Program, Seattle, 1993—. Mem. ASCD, Assn. Wash. Sch. Prins. (various coms.), Lions, Washington Athletic Club, Phi Delta Kappa. Home: 4527 103d Ln NE Kirkland WA 98033 Office: Edmonds Sch Dist 9601 220th St SW Edmonds WA 98020-4557

TYNES, JOHN COWAN, publisher, writer; b. Memphis, Feb. 25, 1971; s. Guy Allan and Claudia Karen (Blackwell) T. BA in Journalism, U. Mo., 1993. Pres. Pagan Pub., Columbia, Mo., Seattle, 1990—; continuity editor Wizards of the Coast, Seattle, 1994-95; editor-in-chief Daedalus Entertainment, Seattle, 1995-96; prodn. designer Movie Maker Mag., Seattle, 1996—. Pub./editor: The Golden Dawn, 1996, Coming Full Circle, 1995; editor: Feng Shui, 1996; editor/pub. The Unspeakable Oath mag., 1990—; author: Puppetland, 1997. Mem. Universal Life Ch.

TYSON, ERIC, personal finance writer, finance counselor. BS, Yale U., 1984; MBA, Stanford U., 1989. Mgmt. cons. Bain & Co., Boston, 1984-87, San Francisco, 1987-90. Author: Personal Finance for Dummies, Investing for Dummies; syndicated columnist Investor's Guide, 1996—.

TYTLER, MORTON MAYNARD, lawyer, retired state assistant attorney general; b. Poulsbo, Wash., Dec. 30, 1932; s. George Fitzroy and Annie (Hokonson) T.; m. Sylvia Virginia Komedal, May 29, 1957; children: Ian Morton, Karen Marie. BA, U. Wash., 1954, JD, 1961. Bar: Wash. 1961. Pvt. practice Tonasket, Wash., 1961-62; asst. atty. gen. State of Wash., Olympia, 1962-93; pvt. practice Olympia, 1994—; Bd. trustees Thurston County Legal Svcs. Assn., Olympia, 1969-73; mem. planning com. Pacific Coast Labor Law Conf., Seattle, 1980-83; liaison to state bar assn. Govt. Lawyers Bar Assn., Olympia, 1990-93. Author: Enforcement of Law Governing Public Drinking Water in Washington, 1985; contbr. chpt. to book. Mem. Constl. Revision Commn., Olympia, 1968-69. With U.S. Army, 1955-58. Democrat. Home and Office: 3303 Fairfield Rd SE Olympia WA 98501-6103

UBERSTINE, MITCHELL NEIL, bank executive; b. N.Y.C., Apr. 27, 1956; s. Elliott and Barbara Marilyn (Wernick) U.; m. Janice Diane Wemple, Dec. 26, 1987; children: Jeffrey Aaron, Andrew Louis. AA, Pierce Coll., Woodland Hills, Calif., 1975. Purchasing agt. Workshop West, Inc., Beverly Hills, Calif., 1975-78, Allianz Ins., L.A., 1978-79, Allstate Savs., Glendale, Calif., 1979-80; gen. svc. supr. First Fed. Bank Calif., Santa Monica, 1980-83, asst. v.p., 1983-86, v.p., 1986-93, sr. v.p., 1994—. Contbr. articles to profl. jours. Bd. dirs., v.p. Jewish Family Svc., Santa Monica, 1991—; bd. dirs. Santa Monica region NCCJ. Mem. Purchasing Mgmt. Assn. L.A. Republican. Jewish. Office: First Fed Bank Calif 401 Wilshire Blvd Ste 220 Santa Monica CA 90401-1430

UCHITEL, NEIL, composer; b. N.Y.C., July 19, 1968; s. Robert Nathan and Sandra Kay (Holt) U. MusB, U. So. Calif., 1990, MusM, 1994. Owner Slappo Music & Sound Design, L.A., 1996—. Composer for TV and film, as well as various instrumental and choral works, TV commls., film. Mem. ASCAP, Nat. Assn. Scholars, Am. Musicol. Soc.

UDALL, CALVIN HUNT, lawyer; b. St. Johns, Ariz., Oct. 23, 1923; s. Grover C. and Dora (Sherwood) U.; m. Doris Fuss, Dec. 11, 1943; children: Fredric, Margaret Udall Moses, Julie (Mrs. Blair M. Nash), Lucinda (Mrs. Douglas Johnson), Tina Udall Rodriguez. LL.B., U. Ariz., 1948. Bar: Ariz. 1948. Ptnr. Fennemore Craig, 1953—; Ariz. spl. counsel Arizona v. California, 1954-62; mem. Coun. on Legal Edn. Opportunity, 1983-93. Mem. cast Phoenix Mus. Theatre, 1959-65. Fellow Am. Bar Found. (bd. dirs. 1986-89, fellows chmn. 1988-89), Ariz. Bar Found. (Disting. Svc. award 1993), Am. Coll. Trial Lawyers; mem. ABA (ho. dels. 1962-92, bd. govs. 1981-84, exec. com. 1983-84, chmn. task force on minorities 1984-86), Maricopa County Bar Assn. (pres. 1957, Disting. Pub. Svc. award 1986), State Bar Ariz. (bd. govs. 1960-65), Ariz. Law Coll. Assn. (founding bd. dirs. 1967-80, pres. 1978-79, U. Ariz. Disting. Citizen award 1984, bd. visitors 1991—). Office: Fennemore Craig One Renaissance Sq 2 N Central Ave Ste 2200 Phoenix AZ 85004-4406

UDALL, THOMAS, state attorney general; b. Tucson, May 18, 1948; s. Stewart and Lee Udall; m. Jill Z. Cooper; 1 child, Amanda Cooper. BA, Prescott Coll., 1970; LLB, Cambridge U., Eng., 1975; JD, U. N.Mex., 1977. Law clk. to Hon. Oliver Seth U.S. Ct. Appeals (10th cir.), Santa Fe, 1977-78; asst. U.S. atty. U.S. Atty.'s Office, 1978-81; pvt. practice Santa Fe, 1981-83; chief counsel N.Mex. Health & Environ. Dept., 1983-84; ptnr. Miller, Stratvert, Togerson & Schlenker, P.A., Albuquerque, 1985-90; atty. gen. State of N.Mex., 1990—. Dem. candidate U.S. Ho. Reps., 1988; past pres. Rio Chama Preservation Trust; mem. N.Mex. Environ. Improvement Bd., 1986-87; bd. dirs. La Compania de Teatro de Albuquerque, Santa Fe Chamber Music Festival, Law Fund. Mem. Nat. Assn. Attys. Gen. (pres. 1996), Kiwanis. Office: Atty Gen Office PO Box 1508 Galisteo St Santa Fe NM 87504-1508

UDLAND, DUANE S., protective services official; m. Judi Udland; 1 child, Eric. Grad., Spokane Police Acad., 1973; BA in Sociology, Ea. Washington State Coll., 1973; grad., FBI Nat. Acad., 1987. From law enforcement officer to detective Spokane (Wash.) County Sheriffs Office, 1972-78; from patrol officer to sgt. Soldotna Police Dept., 1978-82; from patrol officer to dep. chief Anchorage Police Dept., 1988-97, apptd. chief, 1997—; bd. dirs. Alaska Native Justice Ctr.; past chmn. Cen. Peninsula 911 Bd.; mem. Govs. Juvenile Justice Conf. on Youth and Justice; criminal justice adv. bd. State of Alaska; we. states working group FBIs Criminal Justice Info. Sys.; dept. rep. Police Minority Rels. Task Force. Mem. FBI Nat. Acad. Assn., Internat. Assn. Chiefs of Police, Alaska Assn. Chiefs of Police, Alaska Peace Officers Assn., Anchorage C. of C. (crime com.). Home: 1743 W 15th Ave Anchorage AK 99501 Office: Anchorage Police Dept 4501 S Bragraw St Anchorage AK 99507

UDVAR-HAZY, STEVEN F., leasing company financial executive; b. Budapest, Hungary, Feb. 23, 1946; came to U.S., 1958.; m. Christine L. Henneman, June 7, 1980; 3 children. BA, UCLA, 1968; HHD (hon.), U. Utah (Dixie Coll.), 1990. Cert. airline transp. jet pilot. Pres. Internat. Lease Fin. Corp., Beverly Hills, Calif., 1973—; bd. dirs. Sky West Inc., St. George, Utah. Mem. Wings Club (Achievement to Aviation award 1989).

UDWADIA, FIRDAUS ERACH, engineering educator, consultant; b. Bombay, Aug. 28, 1947; came to U.S., 1968.; s. Erach Rustam and Perin P. (Lentin) U.; m. Farida Gagrat, Jan. 6, 1977; children: Shanaira, Zubin. BS, Indian Inst. Tech., Bombay, 1968; MS, Calif. Inst. Tech., 1969, PhD, 1972; MBA, U. So. Calif., 1985. Mem. faculty Calif. Inst. Tech., Pasadena, 1972-74; asst. prof. engring. U. So. Calif., Los Angeles, 1974-77, assoc. prof., 1977-83, prof. mech. engring., civil engring. and bus. adminstrn., 1983-86; prof. engring. bus. adminstrn. U. So. Calif., 1986—; also bd. dirs. Structural Identification Computing Facility U. So. Calif.; cons. Jet Propulsion Lab., Pasadena, 1978—, Argonne Nat. Lab., 1982-83, Air Force Rocket Lab., Edwards AFB. Calif., 1984—; vis. prof. applied mechanics and mech. engring. Calif. Inst. Tech., Pasadena, 1993. Assoc. editor: Applied Mathematics and Computation, Jour. Optimization Theory and Applications, Jour. Franklin Inst., Jour. Differential Equations and Dynamical Sys., Nonlinear Digest, Jour. Mathematical Analysis and Applications, Jour. Mathematical Problems in Engring.; mem. adv. bd. Internat. Jour. Tech. Forecasting and Social Change; mem. publs. com. Jour. Aerospace Engring.; contbr. articles to profl. jours. Bd. dirs. Crisis Mgmt. Ctr., U. So. Calif. NSF grantee, 1976—; recipient Golden Poet award, 1990. Mem. AIAA, ASCE, Am. Acad. Mechanics, Soc. Indsl. and Applied Math., Seismological Soc. Am., Sigma Xi (Earthquake Engring. Research Inst., 1971, 74, 84). Home: 2100 S Santa Anita Ave Arcadia CA 91006-4611 Office: U So Calif 430K Olin Hall University Park Los Angeles CA 90007

UEHLING, BARBARA STANER, educational administrator; b. Wichita, Kans., June 12, 1932; d. Roy W. and Mary Elizabeth (Hilt) Staner; children: Jeffrey Steven, David Edward. B.A., U. Wichita, 1954; M.A., Northwestern U., 1956, Ph.D., 1958; hon. degree, Drury Coll., 1978; LLD (hon.), Ohio State U., 1980. Mem. psychology faculty Oglethorpe U., Atlanta, 1959-64, Emory U., Atlanta, 1966-69; adj. prof. U. R.I., Kingston, 1970-72; dean Roger Williams Coll., Bristol, R.I., 1972-74; dean arts scis. Ill. State U., Normal, 1974-76; provost U. Okla., Norman, 1976-78; chancellor U. Mo.-Columbia, 1978-86, U. Calif., Santa Barbara, 1987-94; sr. vis. fellow Am. Council Edn., 1987; mem. Pacific Rim Pub. U. Pres. Conf., 1990-92; exec. dir. Bus. and Higher Edn. Forum, Washington, 1995—; cons. North Ctr. Accreditation Assn., 1974-86; mem. nat. educator adv. com. to Compt. Gen. of U.S., 1978-79; mem. Commn. on Mil.-Higher Edn. Rels., 1978-79, Am.Coun. on Edn., bd. dirs. 1979-83, treas., 1982-83, mem. Bus.-Higher Edn. Forum, 1980-94, exec. com. 1991-94; Commn. on Internat. Edn., 1992-94, vice chair 1993; bd. dirs. Coun. of Postsecondary Edn., 1986-87, 90-93, Meredith Corp., 1980—; mem. Transatlantic Dialogue, PEW Found., 1991-93. Author: Women in Academe: Steps to Greater Equality, 1979; editorial bd. Jour. Higher Edn. Mgmt., 1986—; contbr. articles to profl. jours. Bd. dirs., chmn. Nat. Ctr. Higher Edn. Mgmt. Sys., 1977-80; trustee Carnegie Found. for Advancement of Teaching, 1980-86, Santa Barbara Med. Found. Clinic, 1989-94; bd. dirs. Resources for the Futrue, 1985-94; mem. select com. on athletics NCAA, 1983-84, also mem. presdl. commn.; mem. Nat. Coun. on Edn. Rsch., 1980-82. Social Sci. Research Council fellow, 1954-55; NSF fellow, 1956-57; NIMH postdoctoral research fellow, 1964-67; named one of 100 Young Leaders of Acad. Change Mag. and ACE, 1978; recipient Alumni Achievement award Wichita State U., 1978, Alumnae award Northwestern U., 1985, Excellence in Edn. award Pi Lambda Theta, 1989. Mem. Am. Assn. Higher Edn. (bd. dirs. 1974-77, pres. 1977-78), Western Coll. Assn. (pres.-elect 1988-89,k pres. 1990-92), Golden Key, Sigma Xi. Office: Bus-Higher Edn Forum One Dupont Cir Ste 800 Washington DC 20036*

UFFNER, BETH M., television and film agent; b. N.Y.C., Sept. 30, 1942; d. George and Lillian (Becker) U.; 1 child, Darlene. BA, NYU, 1964. Asst. producer Tony Awards, N.Y.C., 1967-69; assoc. producer Emmy Awards, Los Angeles, 1969-74; casting dir. Barney Miller, Hollywood, Calif., 1974-76; casting exec. NBC-TV, Burbank, Calif., 1977; dir. comedy devel. Warner Bros. TV, Burbank, 1977-79; agt., exec. Internat. Creative Mgmt., Los

Angeles, 1979-82; v.p. MTM Enterprises, Studio City, Calif., 1982-85; pres. Beth Uffner & Assocs., Studio City, 1985-88; ptnr. Broder, Kurland Webb Uffner, 1988—. Office: Broder Kurland Webb & Uffner 9242 Beverly Blvd # 200 Beverly Hills CA 90210-3710

UFIMTSEV, PYOTR YAKOVLEVICH, physicist, electrical engineer, educator; b. Ust'-Charyshskaya Pristan', Altai Region, Russia, July 8, 1931; s. Yakov Fedorovich and Vasilisa Vasil'evna (Toropchina) U.; m. Tatiana Vladimirovna Sinelschikova; children: Ivan, Vladimir. Grad., Odessa State U., USSR, 1954; PhD, Cen. Rsch. Inst. of Radio Industry, Moscow, 1959; DSc, St. Petersburg State U., Russia, 1970. Engr., sr. engr., sr. scientist Cen. Rsch. Inst. of Radio Industry, Moscow, 1954-73; sr. scientist Inst. Radio Engring. & Electronics Acad. Scis., Moscow, 1973-90; vis. prof., adj. prof. UCLA, 1990—; mem. Sci. Bd. of Radio Waves, Acad. Scis., Moscow, 1960-90. Author: Method of Edge Waves in the Physical Theory of Diffraction, 1962; contbr. articles to profl. jours. Recipient USSR State Prize, Moscow, 1990, Leroy Randle Grumman medal for outstanding sci. achievement, N.Y.C., 1991. Mem. AIAA, IEEE, Electromagnetics Acad. (U.S.), A.S. Popov Sci. Tech. Soc. Radio Engring., Electronics & Telecommunication (Russia). Office: UCLA Dept Elec Engring 405 Hilgard Ave Los Angeles CA 90024-1301

UHALLEY, STEPHEN, JR., history educator; b. Akron, Ohio, Sept. 22, 1930; s. Stephen and Julia Clara (Kovac) U.; m. Allene Mable Lyons (dec. May 1959); children: Kathryn Allene, Stephen III; m. Joan Carol Mooney, Nov. 7, 1964; children: Mark Christopher, Dawn Therese, David Alexander. AA, San Bernardino Valley Coll., 1954; BA, U. Calif., Riverside, 1956; MA, Claremont Grad. Sch., 1957; PhD, U. Calif., Berkeley, 1967. Program officer, asst. rep. The Asia Found., San Francisco, 1960-67; asst. prof. U. Ariz., Tucson, 1967-68; assoc. prof. Duke U., Durham, N.C., 1968-70; sr. fellow East-West Ctr., Honolulu, 1970-71; prof., chmn. U. Hawaii, Honolulu, 1972-77; faculty assoc. Am. Univs. Field Staff, 1977-78; scholar in residence The Asia Soc., N.Y.C., 1978; dir., prof. U. Hawaii, Honolulu, 1980-85, prof., 1985-95, chair, 1991—, prof. emeritus, 1995—; Kiriyama disting. prof. for Pacific Rim studies U. San Francisco, 1996-97; rsch. assoc. Ctr. for Chinese Studies U. Calif., Berkeley, 1996—; vis. prof. Peking U., Beijing, 1993, internat. hon. resch. fellow, 1993—; pres. Pacific Basin Assocs., 1995—. Author: Critical Biography of Mao Tse-tung, 1975, History of the Chinese Communist Party, 1988; editor: Sino-Soviet Documents 1989, 1993, (jour.) Hong Kong Br. Royal Asiatic Soc., 1965-66; contbr. articles to profl. jours. Bd. mem. Pacific and Asian Affairs Coun., Honolulu, 1975-85, pres., 1976-77. Sgt. USMC, 1949-52, Korea. Woodrow Wilson fellow Woodrow Wilson Found., Claremont Grad. Sch., 1957-58. Mem. Am. Assn. for Chinese Studies (bd. mem. 1990—), Assn. for Asian Studies, Phi Beta Kappa. Office: U Hawaii Dept History 2284 Vineyard Rd Novato CA 94947-3779

UHDE, LARRY JACKSON, joint apprentice administrator; b. Marshalltown, Iowa, June 2, 1939; s. Harold Clarence and Rexine Elizabeth (Clemens) U.; m. Linda-Lee Betty Best, Nov. 19, 1960; children: Mark Harold, Brian Raymon. Student, Sacramento City Coll., 1966, Am. River Coll., Sacramento, 1975. Equipment supr. Granite Constrn., Sacramento, 1962-69; truck driver Iowa Wholesale, Marshalltown, Iowa, 1969-70; mgr. Reedy & Essex, Inc., Sacramento, 1970-71; dispatcher Operating Engrs. Local Union 3, Sacramento, 1971-73; tng. coord. Operating Engrs. Joint Apprenticeship Com., Sacramento, 1973-83, apprenticeship div. mgr., 1983-87, adminstr., 1987-95; ret., 1995; chmn. First Women in Apprenticeship Seminar, 1972, Calif. Apprentice Coun., 1992, chair Blue Ribbon com.; com. mem. Sacramento Gen. Joint Apprenticeship Com., 1973-74; rep. Sacramento Sierra's Bldg. and Constrn. Trades Coun., 1973-75; com. mem. Valley Area Constrn. Opportunity Program, 1974-77; commr. State of Calif. Dept. Indsl. Rels., Calif. Apprenticeship Coun., chmn. 1992; mem. Apprenticeship Adv. Com. Internat. Union Oper. Engrs. Contbr. articles to trade papers. Mgr., v.p. Little League, 1971-75; co-chmn. Fall Festival St. Roberts Ch., 1973-75; v.p. Navy League Youth Program, 1978-81; instr. ARC, 1978-87; counselor United Way 1980—; bd. mem. County CETA Bd., 1981-82; coun. mem. Calif. Balance of State Pvt. Industry Coun., 1982-83, Sacramento Pvt. Industry Coun., 1982-83; coord. Acholic Recovery Program, 1984—. With USN, 1956-60. Inducted into Calif. Apprenticeship Hall of Fame, 1996. Mem. Western Apprenticeship Coords. Assn. (statewide dir. 1987—), U.S. Aprenticeship Assn., Sacramento Valley Apprenticeship Tng. Coords. Assn. (rep.), Rancho Murieta County, U.S. Golf Assn., Bing Maloney Golf Club. Democrat. Roman Catholic.

UHL, PHILIP EDWARD, marine artist; b. Toledo, Aug. 19, 1949; s. Philip Edward and Betty Jean (Mayes) U. Student, Dayton Art Inst., 1967-68, Art Students League, 1974. Creative dir. Ctr. for Civic Initiative, Milw., 1969-71; VISTA vol. Office Econ. Opportunity, 1969-71; artist, photographer Assn. Honolulu Artists, 1974-77; pres. Uhl Enterprises div. Makai Photography, Honolulu, 1977—, Videoscapes div. Channel Sea TV, Honolulu, 1977—; cons. Pan Am. Airways, N.Y.C., Honolulu, 1979-84, ITTC Travel Ctr., Honolulu, 1982-83, Royal Hawaiian Ocean Racing Club, Honolulu, 1984—, Sail Am.-Am's Cup Challenge, Honolulu, 1985-86, Am. 3 Found., Am. Cup Def., San Diego, 1991-92, Am. 3 Found. Womens Team, 1994-95. Co-prodr. video documentary White on Water, 1984 (Emmy 1984), Racing the Winds of Paradise (Golden Monitor award Internat. TV Assn. 1989); prodr.: Joy of Life (Golden Monitor award Internat. TV Assn. 1988), Sailors on the Sea, 1990, Teamwork, Talent, Technology (Tele award 1993); cameraman: Pan Am. Clipper Cup, 1980, 82, 84, Kenwood Cup, 1986, 88, 90, 92, 94, 96 (2 Tele awards 1994), ESPN Kenwood Cup, 1990, 92, 94, ESPN Am.'s Cup, 1991-92, 94-95, Transpac, 1991, 93, 95, (video documentary) Rocking the Boat, 1994-95, Datelinbe NBC Setting Sail, 1994-95, numerous spls., reports on ABC-TV, NBC-TV, CBS-TV, PBS, NHK, BBC, TFI, F1, TVNZ and numerous other major worldwide broadcast networks; photographer: (book) Nautical Quar. (Soc. Pub. Designer award 1984); contbr. numerous articles, photos to yachting publs. Mem. Am. Film Inst., Internat. Platform Assn., Soc. Internat. Nautical Scribes, Am. Soc. Media Photographers, Honolulu Printmakers, Hawaii Computer Art Soc., U.S. Sailing Assn., Royal Hawaiian Ocean Racing Club, Tutukaka S. Pacific Yacht Club, Waikiki Yacht Club. Office: UHL Enterprises 1750 Kalakaua Ave Honolulu HI 96826-3766

UHRICH, RICHARD BECKLEY, hospital executive, physician; b. Pitts., June 11, 1932; s. Leroy Earl and Mabel Hoffer (Beckley) U.; m. Susan Kay Manning, May 25, 1985; children by previous marriage—Mark, Karen, Kimberly. BS, Allegheny Coll., 1954; MD, U. Pa., 1958; MPH, U. Calif.-Berkeley, 1966. Diplomate: Am. Bd. Preventive Medicine. Intern Lancaster Gen. Hosp., (Pa.), 1958-59; commd. asst. surg. USPHS, 1959, advanced through grades to med. dir., 1967; resident U. Calif., 1965-66; various adminstrv. positions regional and service unit levels Indian Health Services, until 1971; dir. div. programs ops. Indian Health Service, Health Services Adminstrn. USPHS, Washington, 1971-73; assoc. dir. div. profl. resources Office Internat. Health, Office Asst. Sec. for Health, HEW, Washington, 1973-74; assoc. dir. for program devel. and coordination Office Internat. Health, 1974-78; dir. Phoenix Indian Med. Ctr. and Phoenix Services Unit, 1978-81, ret., 1982; sr. adminstr. Good Samaritan Med Ctr., Phoenix, 1981-82, chief exec. officer, 1982-89; v.p. for managed care programs Samaritan Health Svcs., Phoenix, 1989-90; cons. health care systems Phoenix, 1990-93; dir. S.E. Asia, internat. dir. Med. Ambs. Internat., Modesto, Calif., 1993-95, ret., 1995; mem. Phoenix Regional Hosp. Coun., 1981-88, pres., 1982-83; bd. dirs. Med. Ctr. Redevel. Corp., Phoenix, Med. Ambs. Internat.; v.p. Samaritan Redevel. Corp., 1983-88. Bd. dirs. Phoenix Symphony Orch., 1984-89, Ariz. Sr. Olympics Bd., 1985-89, Med. Ambs. Internat., 1995—. Recipient Meritorious Service medal USPHS, 1973; recipient citation USPHS, 1973, Commd. Officers award, 1981. Mem. Ariz. Hosp. Assn. (bd. dirs. 1980-86, chmn. council on planning 1980-81, council on human resources 1982-83, council on patient care 1983-84, fin. com. 1984-86), Am. Coll. Health Care Adminstrs., Am. Pub. Health Assn., Christian Med. Soc.

ULAM, FRANÇOISE, retired freelance writer, editor; b. Paris, Mar. 8, 1918; came to U.S., 1938, naturalized, 1945; d. Pierre and Madeleine (Carcassonne) Aron; m. Stanislaw M. Ulam, Aug. 19, 1941 (dec. May 1984); 1 child, Claire Anne. BA, Mills Coll., 1939; MA, Mt. Holyoke Coll., 1941. Data analyst Los Alamos (N.Mex.) Nat. Lab., 1946-67; freelance writer book revs., profiles, feature stories, 1965—. Editor: Adventures of a Mathematician (Stanislaw M. Ulam), Analogies Between Analogies (Stanislaw M. Ulam).

ULEP, LEI ANN ESTAMPADOR, political campaign manager; b. Honolulu, Oct. 7, 1967; d. Diosdado and Nerita (Estampador) U. BA, Trinity Coll., 1992. Intern for polit. ops. Bush/Quayle '92, Washington, 1992; asst. to campaign mgr. Huffington for U.S. Senate, Costa Mesa, Calif., 1994; mgr., event coord. Richard Nixon Libr., Yorba Linda, Calif., 1994-95; br. adminstr. Cable & Connector Warehouse, Irvine, Calif., 1995-96; campaign mgr. Susan Brooks for Congress, 1996. Republican. Roman Catholic. Home: 18 18th St Hermosa Beach CA 90254

ULIN, SAMUEL ALEXANDER, computer systems developer; b. Nov. 8, 1955; s. Webster Beattie Ulin and Ann (Fletcher) Rainier; m. Lida Ohan, May 30, 1992. Student, U. Del., 1973-78. Systems design cons. Alpha Ro Inc., Wilmington, Del., 1982-83, Command Computer Svcs., N.Y.C., 1983-84; systems designer DBS Films, Inc., Malvern, Pa., 1984-86; dir. engring. Flight Safety Inc., ISD, Malvern, 1986-87, Irving, Tex., 1987-89; sr. system designer Litigation Scis., Culver City, Calif., 1989-96; v.p. engring. IDEA, Inc., Seattle, 1996—. Designer software for interactive tng. on aircraft sys., 1983, one of first interactive ct. evidence presentation systems used in fed. ct., 1987. Home: 449 E Providencia Ave Apt K Burbank CA 91501-2916 Office: IDEA Inc 11351 Blue Heron Ln Bainbridge Island WA 98110

ULLIMAN, JOSEPH JAMES, forester, educator; b. Springfield, Ohio, July 19, 1935; s. Joseph James Sr. and Iola Mae (Roth) U.; m. Barbara Blessing Gish, Apr. 29, 1961; children: Kathryn Nicole, Barbara Anne, Mark Joseph. BA in English, U. Dayton, 1958; MF in Forest Mgmt., U. Minn., 1968, PhD in Forest Mgmt., 1971. Research asst. U. Minn., Mpls., 1966-68, from instr. to asst. prof., 1968-74; mem. staff land use planning Willamette Nat. Forest, Eugene, Oreg., 1973; from assoc. prof. to prof. U. Idaho, Moscow, 1974-79; dir. U. Idaho FWR Remote Sensing Ctr.; co-dir. U. Idaho Remote Sensing Rsch. Unit, assoc. dean 1988-89, dept. head of forest resources, 1989-96; cons. USAID, 1979—. Contbr. numerous articles on forestry and remote sensing to profl. jours. and books. Chmn. Natural Resources Com., Moscow, 1980-81, Environ. Commn., South St. Paul, Minn., 1972-74; pres. Moscow Swim Team Parents Assn., 1976. Recipient Phi Kappa Phi Disting. Faculty award, 1985, German Acad. Exchange Program award, 1985. Mem. Am. Soc. Photogrammetry and Remote Sensing (pres. Minn. chpt. 1974, dep. dir. 1983-85, Ford Bartlett award 1981), Soc. Am. Foresters (counselor 1981-84, chmn. remote sensing working group 1982-84), Internat. Soc. Photogrammetry (chmn. working group 1981-84). Democrat. Roman Catholic. Home: 2226 Weymouth St Moscow ID 83843-9618 Office: U Idaho Coll of Forestry Moscow ID 83844-1133

ULLMAN, MYRON EDWARD, III, retail executive; b. Youngstown, Ohio, Nov. 26, 1946; s. Myron Edward Jr. and June (Cunningham) U.; m. Cathy Emmons, June 20, 1969; children: Myron Cayce, Denver Tryan, Peter Brynt, Benjamin Kyrk, Kathryn Kwynn. BS in Indsl. Mgmt., U. Cin., 1969; postgrad. Inst. Ednl. Mgmt., Harvard U., 1977. Internat. account mgr. IBM Corp., Cin., 1969-76; v.p. bus. affairs U. Cin., 1976-81; White House fellow The White House, Washington, 1981-82; exec. v.p. Sanger Harris div. Federated Stores, Dallas, 1982-86; mgr. dir., chief oper. officer Wharf Holdings Ltd., Hong Kong, 1986-88; chmn., CEO, dir. R.H. Macy & Co. Inc., N.Y.C., 1986-95; dir. Federated Dept. Stores, Inc.; chmn., CEO, dir. DFS Group Ltd., San Francisco, 1995—; mng. dir. Lane Crawford Ltd., Hong Kong, 1986-88; bd. advisors Gt. Traditions Corp., Cin.; dep. chmn. Omni Hotels, Hampton, N.H., 1988; vice chmn. bd. dirs. Mercy Ships Internat. Internat. v.p. U. Cin. Alumni Assn., 1980—; bd. dirs. Nat. Multiple Sclerosis Soc., N.Y.C.; bd. dirs. Brunswick Sch., Greenwich, Conn., U. Cin. Found., Lincoln Ctr. Devel. Mem. White House Fellow Alumni Assn., Econ. Club N.Y.C. (bd. dirs., exec. com. 1993—), Nat. Retail Fedn. (vice chmn., bd. dirs., exec. com. 1993—), Delta Tau Delta (treas. 1967-68). Republican. Office: DFS Group Ltd 655 Montgomery St San Francisco CA 94111-2635

ULLMANN, LEONARD PAUL, psychologist, educator, author, artist; b. N.Y.C., May 28, 1930; s. Siegfried and Irma (Lichtenstadter) U.; m. Rina Kalb, June 5, 1951 (div. Apr. 19, 1972); children: Michael, Nancy; m. Wendy S. Ullmann, May 17, 1978. AB, Lafayette U., 1951; AM, Stanford U., 1953, PhD, 1955. Coord. psychiatric evaluation VA Hosp., Palo Alto, Calif., 1956-63; prof. psychology U. Ill., Urbana, 1963-72, U. Hawaii, Honolulu, 1972-81, U. Houston, 1981-88. Author: Case Studies in Behavior Modification, 1965, A Psychological Approach to Abnormal Behavior, 1969, 75, Institution and Outcome, 1968, Behavior Influence and Personality, 1973. Home: PO Box 9240 Incline Village NV 89452-9240

ULLOA, EUNICE, mayor. Mayor City of Chino, Calif. Office: 13220 Central Ave Chino CA 91710

ULMER, FRANCES ANN, state official; b. Madison, Wis., Feb. 1, 1947; m. Bill Council; children: Amy, Louis. BA in Econs. and Polit. Sci., U. Wis.; JD with honors, Wis. Sch. Law. Polit. advisor Gov. Jay Hammond, Alaska, 1973-83; former mayor City of Juneau, Alaska; mem. 4 terms, minority leader Alaska Ho. Reps.; lt. gov. State of Alaska, 1995—. Home: 1700 Angus Way Juneau AK 99801-1411 Office: State Capitol PO Box 110015 Juneau AK 99811

ULNICK, KEITH MITCHELL, physician, health care administrator; b. L.A., Sept. 11, 1962; s. Melvin Arthur and Helane (Pearlman) U.; m. Sheryl Lynn Ward, June 25, 1988; 1 child, Katrina Mykelle. AA in Liberal Arts, SUNY, Albany, 1985; BS in Health Care Mgmt. with honors, So. Ill. U., 1986; MS in Health Care Adminstrn., Calif. State U., Northridge, 1988; DO, Coll. of Osteo. Medicine of the Pacific, 1992. Diplomate Am. Bd. Osteopathy. Commd. USN, 1980, advanced through grades to lt. comdr., 1996; leading petty officer ENT Naval Hosp. Phila., 1981-83; leading petty officer Naval Weapons Sta. Br. Clinic, Colts Neck, N.J., 1983-84; leading petty office ENT Naval Hosp. Long Beach, Calif., 1984-86; adminstn./tng. officer Naval Hosp. Camp Pendleton Det 819, Santa Barbara, Calif., 1986-87; officer-in-charge Med. Det "D" wd Bn. 23d Marines, Los Alamitos, Calif., 1987-88; student med. sch. COMP, Pomona, Calif., 1988-92; intern in surgery Portsmouth (Va.) Naval Hosp., 1992-93; bn. surgeon 1st Tank Bn., Twenty-nine Palms, Calif., 1993-95; regimental surgeon 7th Marine Regiment, Twenty-nine Palms, Calif., 1995-96; mem. exec. ocm. med. staff Naval Hosp., Twenty-nine Palms, 1996—; resident Otorhinolaryngology Madigan Army Med. Ctr., Ft. Lewis, Wash. Mem. admissions/interview com. Coll. Osteopathic Medicine of the Pacific, Pamona, 1993—. Ensign USNR, 1986. Mem. Assn. Mil. Osteo. Physicians and Surgeons, Assn. of Mil. Surgeons of U.S., Am. Osteo. Assn., Golden Key Honor Soc. Republican. Roman Catholic. Home: 4002 214th Street Ct E Spanaway WA 98387-6852 Office: Madigan Army Med Ctr Madigan Hospital WA 98431-5000

ULRICH, JOHN AUGUST, microbiology educator; b. St. Paul, May 15, 1915; s. Robert Ernst and Mary Agnes (Farrell) U.; m. Mary Margaret Nash, June 6, 1940 (dec. May 1985); children: Jean Anne, John Joseph, Robert Charles, Karl James, Mary Ellen, Lenore Alice; m. Mary Matkovich, July 19, 1986. BS, St. Thomas Coll., 1938; PhD, U. Minn., 1947. Instr. De La Salle High Sch., Mpls., 1938-41; rsch. asst. U. Minn., Mpls., 1941-45, 49, Hormel Inst., U. Minn., Austin, 1945-49; instr. Mayo Clinic, U. Minn., Rochester, 1949-55; asst. prof. Mayo Found., U. Minn., Rochester, 1955-66; assoc. prof. U. Minn., Mpls., 1966-69; prof. U. N.Mex., Albuquerque, 1969-82, prof. emeritus, 1982—; chmn. Bacteriology & Mycology Study Sect., NIH, Washington, 1961-64, Communicable Diseases Study Sect., Atlanta, 1968-69; cons. VA Hosp., Albuquerque, 1970—, Sandia Labs., Albuquerque, 1971—, U.S. Hosp. Supply, 1978, Internat. Chem. Industries, U.S., 1979—, Minn. Mining and Mfg. Co., 1980—, Johnson and Johnson, 1981; mem. com. on surface sampling APHA, 1974; mem. FDA-Over the Counter Drugs Panel, 1975-77, FDA-Hosp. and Personal Use Device Panel, 1978-80; mem. internat. working group on air handling in hosps. and energy conservation U. Minn., 1978-79; rsch. chmn. in field; others. Chmn. Zumbo Valley exec. bd. Boy Scouts Am., Rochester, 1953-55; mem. Gamehaven exec. bd. Boy Scouts Am., Rochester, 1952-62, Dem. Com., Olmsted County, Minn., 1964-69. Recipient Silver Beaver award Boy Scouts Am., 1962, Bishop's award Winona Diocese, 1962, Katahli award U. N.Mex., 1980. Mem. Am. Soc. Microbiology (coun. mem. 1978-80), Am. Chem. Soc., Am. Bd. Med. Mycology, Am. Acad. Microbiology, Am. Acad. Dermatology (affiliate) Elks. Democrat. Roman Catholic. Home: 3807 Columbia Dr Longmont CO 80503-2122

ULRICH, PAUL GRAHAM, lawyer, author, publisher, editor; b. Spokane, Wash., Nov. 29, 1938; s. Donald Gunn and Kathryn (Vandercook) U.; m. Kathleen Nelson Smith, July 30, 1982; children—Kathleen Elizabeth, Marilee Rae, Michael Graham. BA with high honors, U. Mont., 1961; JD, Stanford U., 1964. Bar: Calif. 1965, Ariz. 1966, U.S. Supreme Ct. 1969, U.S. Ct. Appeals (9th cir.) 1965, U.S. Ct. Appeals (5th cir.) 1981. Law clk. judge U.S. Ct. Appeals, 9th Circuit, San Francisco, 1964-65; assoc. firm Lewis and Roca, Phoenix, 1965-70; ptnr. Lewis and Roca, 1970-85; pres. Paul G. Ulrich P.C., Phoenix, 1985-92, Ulrich, Thompson & Kessler, P.C., 1992-94, Ulrich & Kessler, P.C., Phoenix, 1994-95, Ulrich, Kessler & Anger, P.C., Phoenix, 1995—; owner Pathway Enterprises, 1985-91; judge pro tem Divsn. 1, Ariz. Ct. Appeals, Phoenix, 1986; instr. Thunderbird Grad. Sch. Internat. Mgmt., 1968-69, Ariz. State U. Coll. Law, 1970-73, 78, Scottsdale C.C., 1975-77, also continuing legal edn. seminars. Author and pub.: Applying Management and Motivation Concepts to Law Offices, 1985; editor, contbr.: Arizona Appellate Handbook, 1978—, Working With Legal Assistants, 1980, 81, Future Directions for Law Office Management, 1982, People in the Law Office, 1985-86; co-author, pub.: Arizona Healthcare Professional Liability Handbook, 1992, supplement, 1994, Arizona Healthcare Professional Liability Defense Manual, 1995, Arizona Healthcare Professional Liability Update Newsletter, 1992—; co-author: Federal Appellate Practice Guide: Ninth Circuit, 1994, supplement, 1997; contbg. editor Law Office Econs. and Mgmt., 1984—, Life, Law and the Pursuit of Balance, 1996. Mem. Ariz. Supreme Ct. Task Force on Ct. Orgn. and Adminstrn., 1988-89; mem. com. on appellate cts. Ariz. Supreme Ct., 1990-91; bd. visitors Stanford U. Law Sch., 1974-77; adv. com. legal assisting program Phoenix Coll., 1985-95. With U.S. Army, 1956. Recipient continuing legal edn. award State Bar Ariz., 1978, 86, 90, Harrison Tweed spl. merit award Am. Law Inst./ABA, 1987. Fellow Ariz. Bar Found. (founding 1985—); mem. ABA (chmn. selection and utilization of staff pers. com., econs. of law sect. 1979-81, mem. standing com. legal assts. 1982-86, co-chmn. joint project on appellate handbooks 1983-85, co-chmn. fed. appellate handbook project 1985-88, chmn. com. on liaison with non-lawyers orgns. Econs. of Law Practice sect. 1985-86), Am. Acad. Appellate Lawyers, Am. Law Inst., Am. Judicature Soc. (Spl. Merit citation 1987), Ariz. Bar Assn. (chmn. econs. of law practice com. 1980-81, co-chmn. lower ct. improvement com. 1982-85, co-chmn. Ariz. appellate handbook project 1976—), Coll. Law Practice Mgmt., Maricopa County Bar Assn. (bd. dirs. 1994-96), Calif. Bar Assn., Phi Kappa Phi, Phi Alpha Delta, Sigma Phi Epsilon. Democrat. Home: 2529 E Lupine Ave Phoenix AZ 85028 Office: 3030 N Central Ave Ste 1000 Phoenix AZ 85012-2717

ULRICH, THEODORE ALBERT, lawyer; b. Spokane, Wash., Jan. 1, 1943; s. Herbert Roy and Martha (Hoffman) Ulrich; m. Nancy Allison, May 30, 1966; children: Donald Wayne, Frederick Albert. BS cum laude, U.S. Mcht. Marine Acad., 1965; JD cum laude, Fordham U., 1970; LLM, NYU, 1974. Bar: N.Y. 1971, U.S. Ct. Appeals (2nd cir.) 1971, U.S. Supreme Ct. 1974, U.S. Ct. Claims 1977, U.S. Customs Ct. 1978, U.S. Ct. Internat. Trade 1981, U.S. Ct. Appeals (5th cir.) 1988, U.S. Ct. Appeals (D.C. cir.) 1992, Colo. 1993, U.S. Ct. Appeals (10 cir.) 1994. Mng. clk. U.S. Dept. Justice, N.Y.C., 1968-69, law clk. to federal dist. judge, 1969-70; assoc. Cadwalader, Wickersham & Taft, N.Y.C., 1970-80, ptnr., 1980-94; ptnr. Popham, Haik, Schnobrich & Kaufman, Ltd., Denver, 1994-96. Co-author: Encyclopedia of International Commercial Litigation, 1991, Arbitration of Construction Contracts, V, 1991; contbg. author: Mainre Engineering Economics and Cost Analysis, 1995; author, editor Fordham Law Rev., 1969. Leader Boy Scouts Am., Nassau County, N.Y., 1984-94, Denver, 1994—. Lt. comdr. USCGR, 1965-86. Mem. ABA, Colo. Bar, Denver Bar, Maritime Law Assn., Am. Soc. Internat. Law, Soc. Naval Architects and Marine Engrs., U.S. Naval Inst., Am. Arbitration Assn. Home and Office: 4300 E 6th Ave Denver CO 80220

UMAN, STEPHEN JONAS, physician; b. Jersey City, Jan. 26, 1947; m. Gwen C. Uman, 1971; 1 child, Russell Eli. Ed., Palm Beach Jr. Coll., 1963-64, U. Fla., 1964-65; MD, Tulane U., 1969. Diplomate Am. Bd. Internal Medicine, Am. Bd. Infectious Disease. Intern Charity Hosp. of La., New Orleans, 1969-70; resident in medicine, chief resident Cedars-Sinai Med. Ctr., L.A., 1970-73; fellow in infectious disease U. Wis., 1973-75; pvt. practice L.A., 1975—; past chmn. infectious disease com. Cedars-Sinai Med. Ctr., L.A., 1977-84, mem. med. adv. com., 1978—, chief of staff, 1994-95, mem. med. exec. com.; attending physician Midway Hosp. Med. Ctr., past chmn. infectious diseases com., 1981-85; past mem. internal medicine com.; cons. Century City Hosp., past mem. pharmacy and therapeutics com.; assoc. clin. prof. medicine UCLA Med. Ctr. Author: (with others) Medical Management of the Cardiac Surgical Patient, 1990; contbr. articles to profl. jours. Mem. AMA, Am. Soc. for Microbiology, Infectious Disease Soc. Am., Calif. Med. Assn., L.A. County Med. Assn. (past pres. Beverly Hills, Calif. dist.).

UMBERG, THOMAS JOHN, lawyer; b. Cin., Sept. 25, 1955; s. John H. and Joan (Jansen) U.; m. Robin Bailey; children: Erin, Brett, Tommy. BA, UCLA, 1977; JD, U. Calif., San Francisco, 1980. Bar: Calif. 1980, U.S. Dist. Ct. (ctr. dist.) Calif. 1981, U.S. Dist. Ct. (so. dist.) Calif. 1986, U.S. Ct. Appeals (9th cir.) 1988. Asst. U.S. atty. Dept. Justice, L.A., 1987-90; mem. Calif. Assembly, Sacramento, 1990-94; atty. Morrison & Foerster, Irvine, Calif., 1995—. With U.S. Army, Korea, Italy, lt. col. USAR. Roman Catholic. Office: Morrison & Foerster 19900 Macarthur Blvd Irvine CA 92612-2445

UMEBAYASHI, CLYDE SATORU, lawyer; b. Honolulu, Sept. 2, 1947; s. Robert S. and Dorothy C. Umebayashi; m. Cheryl J. Much, June 27, 1975. BBA in Travel Industry Mgmt., U. Hawaii, 1969, JD, 1980. Spl. dept. atty. gen. Labor and Indsl. Rels. Appeals Bd., Honolulu, 1980-81; atty., dir., shareholder Kessner Duca Umebayashi Bain & Matsunaga, Honolulu, 1981—; commr. Hawaii Criminal Justice Commn. Bd. dirs. Wesley Found., Honolulu, 1993-97. Mem. Hawaii State Bar Assn. Office: Kessner Duca Umebayashi 220 S King St Fl 19 Honolulu HI 96813-4526

UMEZAWA, ADO, physicist; b. Tokyo, Japan, Sept. 17, 1962; arrived in U.S., 1986; s. Hiroomi and Tamae (Yamagami) U.; m. Yukako Akiyama, Jan. 23, 1988; children: Andrea Mikiko, Justin Hiroshi. BSc, U. Alberta, 1984, MSc, 1986, PhD, 1991. Rsch. asst. Argonne (Ill.) Nat. Lab., 1986-91; postdoctoral fellow U. Wis., Madison, 1991-93; sr. applications physicist Quantum Design, San Diego, 1993—. Contbr. articles to profl. jours. Mem. Am. Phys. Soc., Sigma Xi.

UNDERWOOD, MARTHA JANE MENKE, artist, educator; b. Quincy, Ill., Nov. 28, 1934; d. Francis Norman Menke and Ruth Rosemary (Wells) Zoller; divorced; children: Leslie, Stephen. BA, Scripps Coll., 1956; MFA, Otis Art Inst., 1958. Cert. adult edn. and post secondary tchr. Designer staineglass windows Wallis-Wiley Studio, Pasadena, Calif., 1959-60; mural asst., designer Millard Sheets Murals, Inc., Claremont, Calif., 1960-68; art instr. adult edn. Monrovia, Pomona and Claremont Sch. Dists., Calif., 1967-69; prof. art Chaffey C.C., Alta Loma, Calif., 1970-96; ret., 1996; free lance illustrator Claremont, 1975—, watercolorist, 1970—; lectr. and demonstrator in field. Contbr. photographs to: How to Create Your Own Designs, 1968, Weaving Without Loom, 1969; illustrator: Opening a Can of Words, 1994, coloring books about baseball team mascots, 1995, 96; contbr. illustrations to Wayfarers Jour. Co-chmn. Recording for the Blind annual fundraiser, Upland, Calif., 1995, 96, 97; mem. Scripps Fine Arts Found. Recipient Strathmore award, 1985, Grumbacher award Assoc. Artists of Upland, Calif., 1990, 92, 95, 96 Associated Artists of Inland Empire; Faculty Initiated Projects Program grantee, 1991-92. Mem. Associated Artists, Soc. Children's Book Writers and Illustrators, Pomona Valley Art Assn.

UNDERWOOD, RALPH EDWARD, computer systems engineer; b. Houston, Sept. 26, 1947; s. Harry Anson and Ethel Jackson Underwood; m. Linda Sue Merkel, Apr. 10, 1976. BS in Biology, Baker U., 1969; JD, Washburn U., 1973; MS in Computer Sci., Kans. U., 1984. Bar: Kans, 1973. Free-lance stock and options trader Prairie Village, Kans., 1974-79; mem. staff BDM Corp., Leavenworth, Kans., 1982-84; sr. research and devel. engr. Ford Aerospace and Communications Corp., Colorado Springs, Colo., 1984-87, subcontract adminstr., 1987-89; sr. engr., program mgr. CTA Inc., Colorado Springs, 1989-93; sr. staff system engring. MCI Telecomms. Corp.,

Englewood, Colo., 1993-95; cons. in computer security and risk mgmt. Colorado Springs, 1995—. Patentee in field. Mem. Kans. Bar Assn., Upsilon Pi Epsilon, Sigma Phi Epsilon (social chmn. 1968, asst. house mgr. 1968, sec./treas. sr. coun. 1969), Phi Alpha Delta. *Personal philosophy: Treat every person with equal respect and dignity, without regard to their position or personal achievements.*

UNDERWOOD, THOMAS WOODBROOK, communications company executive; b. Royal Oak, Mich., Nov. 29, 1930; s. Elmer and Della Marie (Zimmer) U.; m. Louise Virginia, May 24, 1953 (dec. Feb. 1979); children: Ann Marie Underwood Shuman, Dan and Dave (twins). BAS in Elec. Engring., Milw. Sch. Engring., 1957. Service analyst, writer ITT Gillfillan, Los Angeles, 1958-60; sr. tech. editor, writer Smithkline Beckman, Fullerton, Calif., 1960-78; tech. com. mgr. Smithkline Beckman, Brea, Calif., 1978-85; pres. Tranwood Communications, Santa Ana, Calif., 1985—. Tech. editor, writer manuals for manned space flights to Mars and the moon. Served to staff sgt. USAF, 1950-54, Korea. Fellow Soc. Tech. Comms. (Orange County chpt., assoc., pres. 1992, 93, treas. 1966, 88), Am. Med. Writers Assn, U.S. C. of C., Santa Ana C. of C. Democrat. Office: Tranwood Communications PO Box 5578 Buena Park CA 90622-5578

UNDERWOOD, VERNON O., JR., grocery stores executive; b. 1940. With Youngs Market Co., L.A., pres., from 1976, chmn. bd., 1989—, also chief exec. officer. Office: Young's Market Co 2164 N Batavia St Orange CA 92865-3104*

UNGAR, LISA ELAINE, school counselor, education educator; b. Youngstown, Ohio, Apr. 13, 1951; d. Herbert Leonard and Selma (Deitchman) U.; m. Rober E. Fridrich, May 13, 1996. MEd in Ednl. Psychology, U. Ariz., 1975, MEd in Counseling and Guidance, 1976. Tchr. Cin. Pub. Schs., 1972-74; religious sch. tchr. Congregation Chaverim, Tucson, 1976-85, Congregation Anshei Israel, Tucson, 1985-89; sch. counselor Tucson Unified Sch. Dist., 1977—; mem. edn. faculty U. Phoenix, Tucson; ednl. counselor, Tucson, 1988-92; mem. Ariz. State Sch. Counselor Cadre, Dept. Edn., Phoenix, 1990-93. Editor/co-editor resource manuals, including Remediation Counseling Manual, 1982, Developmental Counseling Resource Manual, 1986-87, Sex Role Stereotyping Implementation Manual. Chair women's div. Jewish Fedn. So. Ariz., Tucson, 1987-89, now solicitation trainer, div. chair; bd. dirs. Tucson Jewish Cmty. Ctr., 1984-87; vol., com. mem. United Way, Tucson, 1993-94. Named Young Woman of Yr., Jewish Fedn. So. Ariz., 1984, Mid. Sch. Counselor of Yr., Ariz. Sch. Counselors Assn., 1997. Mem. ASCD, ACA, Ariz. Counselors Assn. (past v.p. mid. sch. counselors), Nat. Mid. Sch. Assn., Nat. Bd. Cert. Counselors. Democrat. Home: 2282 W Rapallo Way Tucson AZ 85741

UNGAR, ROSELVA MAY, primary and elementary educator; b. Detroit, Oct. 31, 1926; d. John and Elva (Mutchler) Rushton; m. Kenneth Sawyer Goodman, Dec. 26, 1946 (div. 1950); m. Fred Ungar, June 22, 1952 (div. 1977); children: Daniel Brian, Carol Leslie, Lisa Maya. Student, U. Mich., 1946-48; BA, UCLA; postgrad., Pacific Oaks Coll. Cert. elem. tchr., early childhood tchr., bilingual cert. of competency in Spanish. Recreation dir. Detroit City Parks and Recreation, 1946-50; recreation dir. L.A. Unified Sch. Dist., 1950-52, tchr., 1953-84; mentor tchr. elem. edn. L.A. Unified Sch. Dist., L.A., 1988-94; tchr. head start Found. Early Childhood Edn., L.A., 1965-73; staff organizer Early Childhood Fedn. Local 1475 AFT, L.A., 1973-79; staff rep. Calif. Fedn. Tchrs., L.A. contbr. articles to profl. jours. Com. mem. Gov.'s Adv. Com. Child Care, L.A., 1980-83; mem. Nat. Parks and Conservation Assn., Washington, 1988—, Sierra Club, 1978—; vol. So. Calif. Libr. Social Studies, L.A., 1989—; charter mem. Mus. Am. Indian Smithsonian Inst., 1994—; Nat. Ctr. Early Childhood Workforce, Children's Def. Fund, S.W. Mus., Ctr. Sci. in Pub. Interest, Internat. League for Peace and Freedom, ACLU, So. Poverty Law Ctr., Meiklejohn Civil Liberties Inst.; bd. dirs. Found. for Early Childhood Edn., 1997—. Mem. Calif. Assn. Bilingual Edn., So. Calif. Assn., Assn. Edn. Young Children, Early Childhood Fedn. (pres. emeritus 1979—), United Tchrs. L.A. (chpt. chair 1984-96, east area dir. and UTLA bd. dirs. 1996—), Coalition Labor Union Women (bd. mem. 1980-86). Home: 3131 Hamilton Way Los Angeles CA 90026-2107 Office: Glen Alta Sch LA Unified Sch Dist 3410 Sierra St Los Angeles CA 90031-2137

UNIS, RICHARD L., state supreme court justice; b. Portland, Oreg., June 11, 1928. Grad., U. Va., U. Oreg. Bar: Oreg. 1954, U.S. Dist. Ct. Oreg. 1957, U.S. Ct. Appeals (9th cir.) 1960, U.S. Supreme Ct. 1965. Judge Portland Mcpl. Ct., 1968-71; judge Multnomah County Dist. Ct., 1972-76, presiding judge, 1972-74; former judge Oreg. Cir. Ct. 4th Judicial Dist., 1977; former sr. dep. city atty. City of Portland; adj. prof. of local govt. law and evidence Lewis & Clark Coll. Northwestern Sch. Law, 1969-76, 77—; faculty mem. The Nat. Judicial Coll., 1971—; former faculty mem. Am. Acad. Judicial Edn. Author: Procedure and Instructions in Traffic Court Cases, 1970, 101 Questions and Answers on Preliminary Hearings, 1974. Bd. dirs. Oreg. Free from Drug Abuse; mem. Oreg. Adv. Com. on Evidence Law Revision, chmn. subcom., 1974-79. Maj. USAFR, JAGC, ret. Recipient Meritorius Svc. award U. Oregon sch. Law, 1988; named Legal Citizen of Yr. Oreg. Law Related Edn., 1987; inducted into The Nat. Judicial Coll. Hall of Honor, 1988. Mem. Am. Judicature Soc. (bd. dirs. 1975), Am. Judges Assn., Multnomah Bar Found., Oregon Judicial Conf. (chmn. Oreg. Judicial Coll. 1973-80, legis. com. 1976—, exec. com. of judicial edn. com., judicial conduct com.), N.Am. Judges Assn. (tenure, selection and compensation judges com.), Dist. Ct. Judges of Oreg. (v.p., chmn. edn. com.), Nat. Conf. Spl. Ct. Judges (exec. com.), Oreg. State Bar (judicial adminstrn. com., sec. local govt. com., com. on continuing certification, uniform jury instrn. com., exec. com. criminal law sect., trial practice sect. standards and certification com., past chmn., among others), Oreg. Trial Lawyers Assn. (named Judge of Yr. 1984). Office: US Dist Ct House 620 SW Main St Portland OR 97205

UNSER, AL, professional auto racer; b. Albuquerque, May 29, 1939; s. Jerry H. and Mary C. (Craven) U.; m. Wanda Jesperson, Apr. 22, 1958 (div.); children: Mary Linda, Debra Ann, Alfred; m. Karen Barnes, Nov. 22, 1977 (div.). Auto racer U.S. Auto Club, Speedway, Ind., 1964-94. Home: 7625 Central Ave NW Albuquerque NM 87121-2115

UNVERRICH, LENA SHIRLEY, contracting and purchasing executive; b. West Berlin, Federal Republic of Germany, Jan. 10, 1962; d. Stephen Sr. and Ursula (Eichstädt) Serbeniuk; m. Don August Unverrich, Aug. 4, 1984; children: Nicole, Marc. BBA, McKendree Coll., 1984; MA in Procurement and Materials Mgmt., Webster U., 1988. Cert. profl. contracts mgr. Commd. Capt. USAF, 1984; acquisition contracting officer USAF, Scott AFB, Ill., 1984-88; contract adminstr. quality assurance dept. USAF, Garden City, N.Y., 1988-91; dep. chief, Operational Contracting Div. USAF, Oklahoma City, 1991-95; adminstrv. contracting officer USAF, Tuscon, 1995-96. Mem. Air Force Assn., Nat. Contract Mgmt. Assn. (treas. 1994-95, tng. co-facilitator 1995). Home: 3705 N Ridgewood Dr Midwest City OK 73110-3707

UPP, ROBERT DEAN, lawyer; b. Allerton, Ill., Feb. 6, 1916; s. Dean Foreman Upp and Ruby (Armstrong) Upp Mason; m. Margaret Bernice Thiel, July 1, 1939 (div. June 1951); children: Dolores Dean Upp Boutin, Robert Rexford; m. Jane McIntosh Dinneen, Dec. 26, 1953. BS in Journalism, U. Ill., 1937; JD, U. So. Calif., 1948, MA in Social Sci., 1948, MS in Edn., 1949. Bar: Calif., U.S. Supreme Ct. Commd. 2d lt. U.S. Army, 1941, advanced through grades to Maj., 1951; asst. mgr. W.T. Grant Co., 1939-41; pvt. practice L.A., 1948—; prof. law L.A. City Coll., 1949-79. Contbr. articles to profl. jours. Pres. Hollywood (Calif.) Dem. Club, 1957-58. Brigadier gen. JAGC, USAR, 1970-76. Decorated Bronze Star with V oak leaf cluster, Legion of Merit. Mem. VFW (life), Res. Officers Assn. U.S. (pres. 1972-73, Calif. state pres. 1960), Interallied Confederation Res. Officers/NATO (past v.p.), Am. Legion (life), Retired Officers Assn., U.S. Army Assn., Mil. Order of World Wars, Judge Advocate's Assn., Inter-Am. Bar, San Diego Bar Assn., U. So. Calif., Alumni Assn., U. Ill. Alumni Assn. Democrat. Home and Office: 341 Pacific Ave Solana Beach CA 92075-1147

URBAN, JEFFREY C., financial analyst, portfolio manager; b. Lawton, Okla., Oct. 10, 1969; s. Robert Eugene and Marian Bertha (Vandeberg) U.; m. Lynn Michelle Clark, June 19, 1992; 1 child, Amanda. BA in Econs., Managerial Studies, Rice U., 1990. Assoc. The Capital Group, L.A., N.Y.C., Washington, 1990-92; investment analyst Capital Rsch. Co., L.A., 1992—. Office: The Capital Group 333 S Hope St 54th Flr Los Angeles CA 90071

URBIGKIT, WALTER C., JR., state supreme court chief justice; b. Burris, Wyo., Nov. 9, 1927. BA, U. Wyo., 1949, JD, 1951. Bar: Wyo. 1951. Ptnr. Urbigkit, Whitehead, Zunker & Davidson and predecessors; justice Wyo. Supreme Ct., Cheyenne, 1985-93, chief justice, 1990-92. Chmn. Wyo. State Selective Services Appeal Bd., 1960-70; rep. Wyo. State Legislature, 1973-84. Mem. ABA, Wyo. Trial Lawyers, Laramie County Bar Assn. Office: 1107 W 6th Ave Cheyenne WY 82001

URCIA, INGEBORG, English language educator; b. Nurnberg, Germany, Apr. 6, 1934; came to U.S., 1952; d. Werner Edward and Ilse (Lebermann) O.; m. Jose Urcia, July 25, 1958; children: Benjamin Urcia, Gwendolyn Urcia. BA in English, U. Wash., 1955, MA in English, 1956, PhD in English, 1960. Instr. Yakima Valley Coll., Yakima, Wash., 1962-63; asst. prof. U. Nev., Las Vegas, 1963-65, Calif. Poly. U., Pomona, 1965-68; assoc. prof. Eastern Wash. U., Cheney, 1969-83, prof., 1983—; book reviewer and critical adv. Eastern Wash. Book Review Coun., Spokane Sch. Dists., 1983—. Author: All About Rex Cats, 1983, This is the Russian Blue, 1984, For the Love of Cats, 1985, The American Shorthair Cat, 1992, The Russian Blue Cat, 1992, Big Sky Country, 1994. Bd. dirs. Spokanimal Humane Soc., 1985-88; editor Spokanimal newsletter, 1985-88; adv. and judge Spokane area 4-H clubs. Mem. Nat. Conf. Tchrs. and Educators, Modern Lang. Assn., Phi Beta Kappa, Cat Writers of Am. Lutheran. Home: PO Box 36 Cheney WA 99004-0036 Office: Ea Wash U Dept English Cheney WA 99004

URENA-ALEXIADES, JOSE LUIS, electrical engineer; b. Madrid, Spain, Sept. 5, 1949; s. Jose L. and Maria (Alexiades Christodulakis) Urena y Pon. MSEE, U. Madrid, Spain, 1976; MS in Computer Science, UCLA, 1978. Rsch. asst. UCLA, 1978; systems analyst Honeywell Info. Systems, L.A., 1978-80; mem. tech. staff Jet Propulsion Lab., Pasadena, Calif., 1980-91; exec. dir. Empresa Nacional de Innovacion S.A., L.A., 1991-96; sr. technologist Hughes Space & Comm., L.A., 1996—. Contbr. various articles to profl. jours. Two times recipient NASA Group Achievement award. Mem. IEEE, IEEE Computer Soc., IEEE Communications Soc., Assn. for Computer Machinery, World Federalist Assn., Spanish Profl. Am. Inc. Roman Catholic. Home: 904 Dickson St Marina Dl Rey CA 90292-5513 Office: Hughes Space & Comm Mail Stop: S50-x366 1700 E Imperial Hwy Los Angeles CA 90045

URETZ, MICHAEL ALBERT, health and fitness executive; b. Chgo., Oct. 19, 1942; s. George and Frances (King) U. JD, DePaul U., 1966. Asst. states atty. Ill. States Atty., Chgo., 1967-70; atty. pvt. practice, L.A., 1972-88; pres. World Gym Lic. Ltd., Santa Monica, Calif., 1983—. Mem. Eldorado Polo Club, Empire Polo Club, Sigma Chi (life). Independent. Office: World Gym Lic Ltd 2210 Main St Santa Monica CA 90405

URI, GEORGE WOLFSOHN, accountant; b. San Francisco, Dec. 8, 1920; s. George Washington and Ruby Uri; m. Pamela O'Keefe, May 15, 1961. AB, Stanford U., 1941, IA, 1943, MBA, 1946; postgrad., U. Leeds, Eng., 1945. CPA, Calif.; CFP. CMA, ChFC; Accredited Estate Planner. Mem. acctg., econs. and stats. depts. Shell Oil Co., Inc., San Francisco, 1946-48; ptnr. Irelan, Uri, Mayer & Sheppie, San Francisco; pres. F. Uri & Co., Inc.; instr. acctg. and econs. Golden Gate Univ., 1949-50. Contbr. articles to profl. jours. Chmn. San Rafael Redevel. Adv. Com., 1977-78, mem., 1978-91, mem. emeritus, 1991— ; bd. dirs. San Francisco Planning and Urban Renewal Assn., 1958-60. Served with AUS, 1942-46, to col. Res. (ret.). Recipient Key Man award San Francisco Jr. C. of C.; Meritorious Service medal Sec. of Army, 1978. Mem. AICPA (hon., cert. personal fin. specialist), INFORMS (treas. No. Calif. chpt. 1961-62), Calif. Soc. CPAs (hon.; sec.-treas. San Francisco chpt. 1956-57, dir. 1961-63, state dir. 1964-66, mem. Forbes medal com. 1968-69, chmn. 1969-71), Am. Econs. Assn., Inst. Mgmt. Accts., San Francisco Estate Planning Coun. (dir. 1965-68, Am. Soc. Mil. Comptrollers, Execs. Assn. San Francisco (pres. 1965-66), Inst. Cert. Mgmt. Accts. (Disting. Performance cert. 1978), Inst. Cert. Fin. Planners, Am. Soc. CLUs and ChFC, World Trade Club (San Francisco), Commonwealth Club (quar. chmn. 1971), Stanford (San Francisco; dir. 1990-97), Army and Navy (Washington). Home: 11 McNear Dr San Rafael CA 94901-1545 Office: 100 Pine St Ste 2300 San Francisco CA 94111-5530

URRUTY, KATHERINE JEAN, secondary school educator; b. Buffalo, Apr. 3, 1948; d. Sauveur and Stella (Washut) Inchauspe; m. John M. Urruty, Dec. 10, 1969; 1 child, Terry John. BA in English, Gonzaga U., Spokane, Wash., 1970; MA in Curriculum and Instrn., U. Wyo., 1978, postgrad.; postgrad., Ea. Mont. State U., Seattle Pacific U. Cert. tchr., Wyo. Tchr. lang. arts, head dept. chair NCA accreditation Clear Creek Mid. Sch., Buffalo; secondary tchr. Johnson County Sch. Dist., Buffalo, 1970; pvt. tchr. kindergarten, Buffalo, 1971-74; mid. sch. tchr. lang. arts Johnson County Sch. Dist., Buffalo, 1974—; mem. Instrnl. and Profl. Devel. Commn., Profl. Standards and Practices Commn., Spl. Svcs. and Membership Commn.; tchr. trainer Six-trait Analytical Scoring Model for Student Writing; mentor tchr. coach Essential Elements of Edn. Mem. ASCD, Nat. Coun. Tchrs. English, Wyo. Assn. Tchrs. English (pres. 1988-89), Wyo. Edn. Assn. (assembly del., edn. com., chpt. pres., sec., bldg. rep., treas.), Rocky Mountain Mid. Schs. Assn. (pres. 1987-88), Wyo. ASCD, Delta Kappa Gamma (treas. 1987-90), Phi Delta Kappa. Office: 58 N Adams Ave Buffalo WY 82834-1809

URSYN, ANNA Z., computer graphics artist, educator; b. Warsaw, Poland, Feb. 11, 1955; came to U.S., 1986; MFA, Fine Arts U., Warsaw, 1983, U. Wyo., 1988; PhD, U. Wyo., 1994. Instr. art Bielany Art Ctr., Warsaw, 1983-86; tchg. asst. U. Wyo., 1986-93; asst. prof. U. No. Colo., Greeley, 1993-95; assoc. prof. U. No. Colo., 1995—; presenter confs. in field. Exhbns. include SIGGRAPH (Assn. Computing Machinery Spl. Interest Group on Computer Graphics), Internat. Computer Art Shows, Boston, 1989, Dallas, 1990, Chgo., 1992, Orlando, Fla., 1994, L.A., 1995, 97, Der Prix Ars Electronica Internat. Computer Graphics Contests, Linz, Austria, 1988-97, Eurographics Internat. Computer Graphics Contest, Slide, Video and WWW Competitions, Vienna, Austria, 1991, Poitiers, France, 1996, Internat. Symposia on Electronic Art, Groningen, The Netherlands, 1990,, Sydney, Australia, 1992, Helsinki, 1994, Rotterdam, The Netherlands, 1996, Small Computers in the Arts Symposia, Phila., 1990, 92, 93, ArCADE Internat. Exhbn. Computer in Art and Design, Brighton, Eng., 1995, 97, Ann. N.Y. Digital Salon Visual Arts Mus., N.Y.C., 1995, 96, 20th Century Matrix, Tokyo; contbr. art to numerous publs. Recipient Best of Show award U. Wyo. Art Mus., Laramie, 1989, Fine Art Achievement award Binney & Smith Inc. Liquitex, 1991; grantee U. No. Colo. Found., Greeley, 1996. Mem. Assn. Computing Machinery (Spl. Interest Group on Computer Graphics grantee 1990), Artist Using Sci. and Tech./YLEM, Internat. Soc. for Arts, Scis. and Tech. (assoc.), Inter-Soc. for Electronic Arts, Am. Ednl. Rsch. Assn., Nat. Art Edn. Assn., Colo. Art Edn. Asn., Kappa Delta Pi (hon.), Phi Delta Phi (hon.). Office: U No Colo Dept Visual Arts Greeley CO 80639

URY, CLAUDE MAX, educational consultant, book reviewer; b. Paris, May 5, 1937; Came to U.S., 1941.; s. George Lewis and Genia Ury. AB in Econs., San Francisco State U., 1962, MA in Counseling, 1966; MA in Social Sci., U. Colo., 1981; PhD in History of Edn., U. Santa Barbara, 1993. Tchr. San Francisco Schs., 1973-79; ednl. cons. San Francisco, 1980—, rschr., 1980—. Book reviewer for 22 maj. pub. firms in U.S.; contbr. articles to profl. jours. Mem. Ednl. Rsch. Assn., Am. Econ. Assn., Am. Hist. Assn. Democrat. Jewish. Home: 906 Lake St San Francisco CA 94118-1121

USUI, LESLIE RAYMOND, clothing executive; b. Wahiawa, Hawaii, Feb. 2, 1946; s. Raymond Isao and Joyce Mitsuyo (Muramoto) U.; m. Annie On Nor Hom, Oct. 23, 1980; 1 child, Atisha. BA in Zool., U. Hawaii, 1969, MA in Edn., 1972. Cert. tchr., Hawaii. Flight steward United Airlines, Honolulu, 1970; spl. tutor Dept. Edn., 1971-73; v.p. Satyuga, Inc., Honolulu, 1974-80; pres. Satyuga, Inc., 1980—; also bd. dirs.; cons. Hawaii Fashion Guild, 1978-79. Composer: Song to Chenrayzee, Song to Karmapa. Co-founder, bd. dirs. Kagyu Thegchen Ling Meditation Ctr., 1974—, Maitreya Inst., 1983-86; bd. dirs. Palpung Found., 1984—; mem. U.S. Senatorial Bus. Adv. Bd., Washington, 1988; charter mem. Citizens Against Govt. Waste, 1988—, Citizens for Sound Economy, 1987-91, Nat. Tax Limitation Com., 1988-89. Mem. Nat. Fedn. Ind. Bus., Am. Biog. Inst. (life, bd. govs. 1990), Hawaii Bus. League, Internat. Biog. Centre (life), Internat. Platform Assn., World Inst. Achievement (life), Cousteau Soc., Nature Conservancy, Honolulu Zool. Soc., Waikiki Aquarium. Republican. Buddhist. Home: 1417 Laamia Pl Honolulu HI 96821-1403 Office: Satyuga Inc 248 Mokauea St Honolulu HI 96819-3110

UTHOFF, MICHAEL, dancer, choreographer, artistic director; b. Santiago, Chile, Nov. 5, 1943; came to U.S., 1962; s. Ernst and Lola (Botka) U.; m. dau., Michelle. Grad. biology, high sch., Chile; dance tng. with Juilliard Sch., 1962-65, Martha Graham, 1962-63, Joffrey Ballet, 1965-68, Sch. Am. Ballet, 1962-64; Laureate in Humanities, St. Joseph Coll., Hartford, Conn. Leading dancer Jose Limon Dance Co., 1964-65, City Center Joffrey Ballet, 1965-68, N.Y.C. Opera, 1968-69; leading dancer, asst. dir. First Chamber Dance Co. N.Y., from 1969; artistic dir. Hartford Ballet Co., 1972-92, Ballet Ariz., 1992—; mem. faculty Juilliard Sch. Music, N.Y.C., from 1969; guest artist, tchr. Princeton Ballet Soc.; prof. dance SUNY, Purchase, 1972-74; instr. dance and drama movement, Yale U.; works premiered by Compania Nacional de Danzas, Mexico City, 1989; guest choreographer Shanghai Ballet, Republic of China, 1986; led Hartford Ballet on 3-week 11-city tour of Peoples Republic of China by invitation of Shanghai Internat. Culture Assn., 1988, 5-week 9-country tour Latin Am., 1991. Choreographer, dancer-actor film Seafall, 1968; opera prodns. Aida and La Cenerentola, Honolulu, 1972, Conn. Opera Romeo et Juliette, 1989, Pitts. Opera Aida, 1988; choreographer Quartet, City Center Joffrey Ballet, 1968, The Pleasure of Merely Circulating, Juilliard Sch. Music, 1969, Windsong, Reflections, Dusk, Promenade, First Chamber Dance Co., 1969-70, Mozart's Idomeneo for Caramoor Music Festival, 1970, Concerto Grosso for Ballet Clasico 70 of Mexico, also restaged Dusk, 1972, Aves Mirabiles, 1973, Danza a Quattro, 1973, Marosszek Dances, 1973, Duo, 1974, Pastorale, 1974, Brahms Variations, 1974, Autumalal, 1975, Mir Ken Geharget Veren, 1976, Tom Dula, 1976, Unstill Life, 1977, Songs of a Wayfarer, 1977, Ask Not..., 1977, White Mountains Suite, 1978, Bach Cantata, 1978, The Nutcracker, 1979, Romeo and Juliet, 1981, Cachivaches, 1981, Reflections on the Water, 1981, Weeping Willow, 1982, Carmencita Variations, 1982, Hansel and Gretel, 1983, Coppelia, 1986, Speak Easy, 1986, New England Triptych, 1986, Los Copihues, 1988, Petrouchka, 1988, RFD #1, 1989, Classical Symphoniette, 1990, Alice in Wonderland, 1991, Nocturnes, 1991, Sinfonia Danzante, 1991; Nat. Endowment Arts commns. for choreography: Primavera, Minn. Dance Theatre, 1975, Panvezitos, Greater Houston Civic Ballet, 1976, Sonata, The Prodigal Son, Hartford Ballet, 1977, 79. Recipient award for best choreography for Murmurs of the Stream, Chilean Nat. Press, 1983, Critic's Circle Best of Yr. in Arts award, Chile, 1984, Milagno en la Alameda award for Chilean Nat. Women, 1995; grantee various founds. Office: Ballet Ariz 3645 E Indian School Rd Phoenix AZ 85018-5126

UTNE, JOHN RICHARD, retired radiation oncologist; b. Fergus Falls, Minn., Oct. 2, 1924; s. John Arndt and Dagney Louise (Thyse) U.; m. Bernice Gertrude Kiefer, June 19, 1948; children: John Stephen, Susan Elizabeth, Barbara Ellen, Linda Louise. Student, Marquette U., 1943; BS, U. Ill., Chgo., 1946, MD, 1948; MS, U. Minn., 1955. Diplomate Am. Bd. Radiology. Intern Mpls. Gen. Hosp., 1948-49; pvt. practice, Mpls., 1948-50, Northfield, Minn., 1951-52; resident in radiology Mayo Clinic, Rochester, Minn., 1953-55; radiologist, chief staff St. John's Mercy Hosp., Mason City, Iowa, 1956-74; radiologist Scripps Meml. Hosp., La Jolla, Calif., 1974-85; locum tenens radiologist, 1985—. Former mem. Mason City Sch. Bd.; former dist. pres. Boy Scouts Am., Mason City; radiologist Project Hope, Managua, Nicaragua, 1965, Tunis, Tunisia, 1969. Lt. M.C., USN, 1951-53, Korea. Named Man of Yr., Sertoma Club, Mason City, 1968. Fellow Am. Coll. Radiology; mem. Radiol. Soc. N.Am. (emeritus). Republican. Lutheran. Home: 220 Coast Blvd La Jolla CA 92037-4617

UTTAL, WILLIAM R(EICHENSTEIN), psychology and engineering educator, research scientist; b. Mineola, N.Y., Mar. 24, 1931; s. Joseph and Claire (Reichenstein) U.; m. Michiye Nishimura, Dec. 20, 1954; children: Taneil, Lynet, Lisa. Student, Miami U. Oxford, Ohio, 1947-48; B.S. in Physics, U. Cin., 1951; Ph.D. in Exptl. Psychology and Biophysics, Ohio State U., 1957. Staff Psychologist, mgr. behavioral sci. group IBM Research Center, Yorktown Heights, N.Y., 1957-63; assoc. prof. U. Mich., Ann Arbor, 1963-68, prof. psychology, 1968-86, research scientist, 1963-86, prof. emeritus, 1986—; grad. affiliate faculty dept. psychology U. Hawaii, 1986—; research scientist Naval Ocean Systems Ctr.-Hawaii Lab., Kailua, 1985-88; prof., chmn. dept. psychology Ariz. State U., Tempe, 1988-92, prof. dept. indsl. and mgmt. systems engring., 1992—, affiliated prof., Dept. of Computer Sci. and Engring., 1993—; vis. prof. Kyoto (Japan) Prefectural Med. U., 1965-66, Sensory Sci. Lab., U. Hawaii, 1968, 73, U. Western Australia, 1970-71, U. Hawaii, 1978-79, 80-81, U. Auckland, 1996; pres. Nat. Conf. on On-Line Uses Computers in Psychology, 1974. Author: Real Time Computers: Techniques and Applications in the Psychological Sciences, 1968, Generative Computer Assisted Instruction in Analytic Geometry, 1972, The Psychobiology of Sensory Coding, 1973, Cellular Neurophysiology and Integration: An Interpretive Introductin, 1975, An Autocorrelation Theory of Visual Form Detection, 1975, The Psychobiology of Mind, 1978, A Taxonomy of Visual Processes, 1981, Visual Form Detection in Three Dimensional Space, 1983, Principles of Psychobiology, 1983, The Detection of Nonplanar Surfaces in Visual Space, 1985, The Perception of Dotted Forms, 1987, On Seeing Forms, 1988, The Swimmer: A Computational Model of a Perceptual Motor System, 1992, Toward a New Behaviorism: The Case Against Perceptual Reductionism, 1997; also numerous articles; editor: Readings in Sensory Coding, 1972; assoc. editor Behavioral Research Method and Instrn., 1968-90, Computing: Archives for Electronic Computing, 1963-75, Jour. Exptl. Psychology; Perception and Performance, 1974-79; cons. editor Jour. Exptl. Psychology: Applied, 1994—. Served to 2d lt. USAF, 1951-53. USPHS spl. postdoctoral fellow, 1965-66; NIMH research scientist award, 1971-76. Fellow AAAS, Am. Psychol. Soc. (charter), Soc. Exptl. Psychologists (chmn. 1994-95); mem. Psychonomics Soc. Office: Ariz State U Dept Indsl and Mgmt Systems Engring Tempe AZ 85287-1104

UTTER, ROBERT FRENCH, retired state supreme court justice; b. Seattle, June 19, 1930; s. John and Besse (French) U.; m. Elizabeth J. Stevenson, Dec. 28, 1953; children: Kimberly, Kirk, John. BS, U. Wash., 1952; LLB, 1954. Bar: Wash. 1954. Pros. atty. King County, Wash., 1955-57; individual practice law Seattle, 1957-59; ct. commr. King County Superior Ct., 1959-64, judge, 1964-69; judge Wash. State Ct. Appeals, 1969-71; judge Wash. State Supreme Ct., 1971-95, chief justice, 1979-81; ret., 1995; lectr. in field, leader comparative law tour People's Republic of China, 1986, 87, 88, 91, USSR, 1989; adj. prof. constl. law U. Puget Sound, 1987, 88, 89, 90, 91, 92, 93, 94; cons. CEELI, 1991, 93—, USIA, 1992; visitor to Kazakhstand and Kyrgystan Judiciary, 1993, 94, 95, 96; lectr. to Albanian Judiciary, 1994, 95. Editor books on real property and appellate practice. Pres., founder Big Brother Assn., Seattle, 1955-67; pres., founder Job Therapy Inc., 1963-71; mem. exec. com. Conf. of Chief Justices, 1979-80, 81-86; pres. Thurston County Big Bros./Big Sisters, 1984; lectr. Soviet Acad. Moscow, 1991; USIA visitor to comment on jud. system, Latvia, 1992, Kazakstan, 1993-94; trustee Linfield Coll. Named Alumnus of Yr., Linfield Coll., 1973, Disting. Jud. Scholar, U. Ind., 1987, Judge of Yr., Wash. State Trial Lawyers, 1989, Outstanding Judge, Wash. State Bar Assn., 1990, Outstanding Judge, Seattle-King County Bar Assn., 1992, Conder-Faulkner lectr. U. Wash. Sch. Law, 1995, Disting. Alumnus Sch. Law U. Wash., 1995. Mem. ABA (commentator on proposed constns. of Albania, Bulgaria, Romania, Russia, Lithuania, Azerbaijan, Uzbekistan, Byelarus, Kazakhstan & Ukraine), Am. Judicature Soc. (Herbert Harley award 1983, sec. 1987—, chmn. bd. dirs., mem. exec. com.), Order of Coif. Baptist.

UTTERBACK, DAVID, financial aid counselor; b. Champaign, Ill., June 4, 1963; s. James William and Melba (Kountz) U. BA, Purdue U., 1986; MS, U. So. Calif., 1994. Wellness program coord. Spelman Hosp., Smithville, Mo., 1988-91; acad. asst. athletic acad. svcs. U. So. Calif., L.A., 1991, facilities mgr., 1992-97, fin. aid counselor, 1997—. Republican. Baptist. Office: U So Calif Dept Dept Fin Aid Los Angeles CA 90089

UYEHARA, CATHERINE FAY TAKAKO (YAMAUCHI), physiologist, educator, pharmacologist; b. Honolulu, Dec. 20, 1959; d. Thomas Takashi and Eiko (Haraguchi) Uyehara; m. Alan Hisao Yamauchi, Feb. 17, 1990. BS, Yale U., 1981; PhD in Physiology, U. Hawaii, Honolulu, 1987. Postdoctoral fellow SmithKline Beecham Pharms., King of Prussia, Pa., 1987-89; asst. prof. in pediatrics U. Hawaii John Burns Sch. Medicine,

Honolulu, 1991—; rsch. pharmacologist Kapiolani Med. Ctr. for Women and Children, Honolulu, 1990—; statis. cons. Tripler Army Med. Ctr., Honolulu, 1984-87, 89—, chief rsch. pharmacology, 1991—, dir. coop. rsch. and devel. projects, 1995—; asst. prof. pharmacology U. Hawaii John A. Burns Sch. Medicine, 1993—; grad. faculty Interdisciplinary Biomed. Sci. program, 1995—. Contbr. articles to profl. jours. Mem. Am. Fedn. Clin. Rsch., Am. Physiol. Soc., Soc. Uniformed Endocrinologists, Endocrine Soc., We. Soc. Pediatric Rsch., N.Y. Acad. Scis. Democrat. Mem. Christian Ch. Office: Tripler Army Med Ctr Dept Clin Investigation MCHK-CI 1 Jarrett White Rd Rm 131 Tripler Army HI 96859-5000

UZIELLI, ALESSANDRO FORD, movie producer; b. N.Y.C., Nov. 23, 1966; s. Giancarlo Uzielli and Anne Ford. BFA, Boston U., 1989; MFA, Am. Film Inst., 1993. Pres., prodr. Alph Prodns., L.A., 1993—. Prodr.: (films) In the Name of the Father, 1993 (awards 1993-94), Shakespeare's Sister, 1996. Office: Alph Prodns 369 S Doheny Dr Beverly Hills CA 90211

VACCARINO, ROBIN, artist; b. Seattle. BFA, MFA, Otis Art Inst. Faculty Calif. State U., Northridge, 1970-72, Otis Art Inst., L.A., 1972-93, Parsons Sch. Design, Paris, 1981-92; grad. faculty Art Ctr. Sch. Design. Maestra grantee Calif. Arts Coun., 1978, Individual Artist grantee NEA, Washington, 1980.

VADEN-NEUENSCHWANDER, SHERRY MAE, broadcaster, poet; b. Farmington, N.Mex., May 1, 1967; d. Jerry M. and Cherie G. (Donham) Vaden; m. William E. Neuenschwander, Feb. 15, 1991; children: Krystle, Amanda, Timothy, Brittany, Donovan. Work study KSJE-FM, Farmington, N.Mex., 1991-93, broadcast prodn. clerk, 1993-95, ops. dir., 1995—. Mem. Four Corners Lit. Alliance, Phi Theta Kappa.

VAGNINI, LIVIO LEE, chemist, forensic consultant; b. North Bergen, N.J., Apr. 26, 1917; s. Frank S. and Margaret (Avondo) V.; m. Daniele Hogge, Sept. 29, 1949; children: Frank, Stephen, Eric. BS in Chemistry, Fordham U., 1938; postgrad., U. Md. Med. Sch., 1938-39. Diplomate Am. Bd. Forensic Examiners. Chemist H.A. Wilson Co. div. Englehard Industries, Inc., 1940-42; chief chemist U.S. Army Graves Registration, Liege, Belgium, 1946-48; chief forensic chemist U.S. Army Criminal Investigation Lab., Frankfurt, Fed. Republic Germany, 1948-60; sr. chemist FDA, Washington, 1960-62, CIA, Washington, 1963-73; project engr. Mitre Corp., McLean, Va., 1973-75; staff scientist Planning Research Corp., McLean, 1975-77; program dir. L. Miranda Assocs., Washington, 1978-81; forensic cons. Carmel, Calif., 1981—. Contbr. articles to profl. publs. Mem. Ft. Ord (Calif.) Retireee Coun., 1988, 89—, Monterey County Vets. Svcs. Adv. Commn.; treas. Alliance Francaise Monterey Peninsula; adv. commn. Monterey County Commn. Veterans Svcs., 1990, 91, 92. Decorated Bronze Star. Fellow Am. Inst. Chemists, Am. Acad. Forensic Scis.; mem. Nat. Assn. for Uniformd Svcs. (Monterey chpt.)Internat. Soc. Blood Transfusion, Internat. Soc. Forensic Scientists, Ret. Officers Assn. (pres. Monterey County chpt. 1985), Sons in Retirement (pres. Pebble Beach br. 1986), Am.-Scandinavian Soc. (1st v.p., program dir. Monterey County 1989). Roman Catholic. Home: 26069 Mesa Dr Carmel CA 93923-8952

VAIL, MICHAEL GEORGE, academic director; b. Fullerton, Calif., Oct. 3, 1950; s. Harold Ford and Mabel (Williams) V.; m. Laura Marie Yeoman, Mar. 31, 1973. AA, Fullerton Coll., 1970; BA, Calif. State U., Fullerton, 1973. Planner City of Irvine, Calif., 1980-83; dir. facilities planning Capistrano Unified Sch. Dist., San Juan Capistrano, Calif., 1983-89; sr. dir. facilities Santa Ana (Calif.) Unified Sch. Dist., 1989—. State chair Calif. for Schs., Sacramento, 1988, Coalition for Adequate Sch. Housing, Sacramento, 1991-92; mem. State Supt's Sch. Facilities Adv. Com., Sacramento, 1989-92, State Treas.'s Sch. Facilities Task Force, Sacramento, 1990-92; pres. Coun. Ednl. Facility Planners, S.W. region Calif., 1990-91; treas. Nat. Com. for Adequate Sch. Housing, Washington, 1994-96. Democrat. Office: Santa Ana Unified Sch Dist 1601 E Chestnut Ave Santa Ana CA 92701-2414

VALDERRAMA, ALEXANDER STANLEY, graphic designer; b. Trujillio, Peru, S.Am., Feb. 25, 1964; came to U.S., 1974; s. Louis Alehandro and Judith Lee (Bucklu) V.; m. Laurie Beth Touch, May 8, 1986; children: Nathan Alexander, Sarah. AA, Des Moines Area C.C., 1988. Owner Valderrama Design, Des Moines, 1989-91; ptnr. Thingk Spot Creative, Des Moines, 1991-92; owner X Design Co., Greenwood Village, Colo., 1992—. Mem. Art Dirs. Assn. of Iowa. Republican. Roman Catholic. Home: 16854 Dandelion Way Parker CO Office: X Design Co Ste 204 2525 W Main St #201 Littleton CO 80120

VALDEZ, ARNOLD, dentist, lawyer; b. Mojave, Calif., June 27, 1954; s. Stephen Monarez Jr. and Mary Lou (Esparza) V.; m. Brandy Radovich, Dec. 31, 1994; children: Bayleigh, Briton. BS in Biol. Sci., Calif. State U., Hayward, 1976; BS in Dental Sci. and DDS, U. Calif., San Francisco, 1982; MBA, Calif. State Poly. U., 1985; BS and JD, Pacific West Coll. Law, 1995. Bar: Mex., 1996; Cert. ind. med. examiner, qualified med. examiner, Calif. Pvt. practice specializing in temporomandibular joint and Myofascial Pain Dysfunction Disorders Pomona, Calif., 1982, Claremont, Calif., 1982—; CEO Valcom, 1994—; assoc. Marin, O'Connell & Meché, 1996; CEO Valcom-A Telecom. Corp.; mem. adv. com. dental assisting program Chaffey Coll., Rancho Cucamonga, Calif., 1982—; mem. staff Pomona Valley Hosp. Med. Ctr.; ptnr. Marin, O'Connell & Meché. Vol. dentist San Antonio Hosp. Denal Clinic, Rancho Cucamonga, 1984—, Pomona Valley Assistance League Dental Clinic, 1986—; bd. dirs. Pacific West Coll. Law, 1993—, v.p. fgn. devel., 1996—. Fellow Acad. Gen. Dentistry (mastership 1994); mem. ADA, Am. Equilibration Soc., The Cranial Acad., Newport Harbor Acad. Dentistry, Calif. Dental Assn., Tri-County Dental Soc. (co-chmn. mktg. 1986, chmn. sch. screening 1987, Golden Grin award), Acad. Gen. Dentistry, U. Calif.-San Francisco Alumni Assn., U. So. Calif. Sch. Dentistry Golden Century Club, Psi Omega, Delta Theta Phi. Democrat. Roman Catholic. Home: 515 Seaward Rd Corona Del Mar CA 92625-2600 Office: 410 W Baseline Rd Claremont CA 91711-1607 *Personal philosophy: Life is a journey, not a destination!.*

VALDEZ, JAMES GERALD, automotive aftermarket executive; b. Vallejo, Calif., Jan. 26, 1945; s. Charles Arthur and Margaret Ellen (Chavez) V.; m. Cathy Evelyn Gudiewski, Oct. 9, 1970; children: Mitchell Charles, Jason Garrett. BS in Engring. Tech., Calif. Poly. U., 1967; MBA in Mktg., Pepperdine U., 1975. Sales engr. Shell Oil Co., L.A., 1969-70; regional mgr. Ethyl Corp., L.A., 1970-76; dir. product engring. Pennzoil Co., Houston, 1976-84; owner, operator Valco Enterprises, L.A., 1984-86; sr. v.p. mktg. Analysis, Inc., L.A., 1986-88; dir. sales and mktg. Castrol Inc., L.A., 1988-93; v.p., gen. mgr. CSF, Inc., L.A., 1993—, also dir.; cons. in field, 1984-86. Major USAR, 1967-80. Decorated Commendation medal. Mem. SAE (chmn. various coms., gen. materials coun. 1980), Am. Petroleum Inst. (chmn. lubricants com. 1980-84). Republican. Home: 5850 E Trapper Trl Anaheim CA 92807-4734

VALDEZ, JESSE NAJERA, psychologist; b. La Pryor, Tex., Nov. 17, 1944; s. Jose Cordova and Margarita (Najera) V.; m. Gloria Mary Ruiz, Sept. 27, 1969; children: Richard Kenneth, James Roderick, David Joseph. AA, Southwest Tex. Jr. Coll., 1966; BA, Southwest Tex. State U., 1969; MEd, Sul Ross State U., 1972; PhD, U. Wis., 1985. H.S. tchr. Uvalde (Tex.) Consolidated Ind. Sch. Dist., 1969-76; counselor Developmental Edn. Svcs., Uvalde, 1976-79; asst. prof. dept. psychology Colo. State U., Ft. Collins, 1984-88; psychologist U. Calif., Santa Barbara, 1988-95; asst. prof. counseling psychology dept. U. Denver, 1995—; lectr. U. Wis., Madison, 1983; cons. Psychotherapy Svcs., Ft. Collins; psychotherapist Cmty. Mental Health, Loveland, Colo. Cubmaster Boy Scouts Am., Madison, 1980-81. Mem. APA, Soc. for Psychol. Study of Ethnic Minority Issues, Pi Lambda Theta, Sigma Delta Pi. Home: 544 Sussex Ct Goleta CA 93117-1614 Office: U Denver Counseling Psychology 2450 S Vine St Denver CO 80208

VALDEZ, JOSEPH VINCENT, II, state government information management executive; b. Oakland, Calif., Aug. 13, 1955; s. Joseph Vincent and Joann Marinda (Dunn) V.; m. Teresa Ann Casaus, Apr. 9, 1984; children: Joseph Vincent III, Kristi Amber. AA with honors, Merritt Coll., Oakland, 1980; BA in History, U. Calif., Berkeley, 1982. Asst. mgr., caterer Soup Pot/Party Makers, Oakland, 1981-82; client svc. agt. Social Svc. div. N.Mex. Human Svcs., Santa Fe, 1983-85; ctrl. office unit records mgr. N.Mex. Corrections Dept., Santa Fe, 1985-86, parole records mgr., 1986-88, asst. substance abuse program dir., 1988-89; city records mgr. City of Santa Fe, 1989—; mem. records task force City of Santa Fe, 1994—. Author: La Iglesia de Santa Ana: Celebra Cinquenta Anos de Gloria, 1992, (booklet) City of Santa Fe: A Centennial Publication, 1991; featured in The 96/97 Santa Fe Directory of the Arts. Chmn. fiesta float com. N.Mex. Green Party, Santa Fe, 1994. Recipient Cert. of Honor/Councilor's award Merritt Coll., 1980, Silver Plaque, La Entrada Alternative Sch. Bd., 1985, Olsten award for excellence in records mgmt., 1990; named col., aide-de-camp Gov.'s Office, N.Mex., 1976, 80, 84, 91. Mem. Assn. Records Mgrs. and Adminstrs. (chmn. legis. com. No. N.Mex. chpt. 1990-91, historian 1990-92, bd. dirs. 1990-91, 93—, pres. 1993-94), Nat. Assn. Govt. Archives and Records Adminstrs., Eagles (v.p. 1993-94, chaplain 1995-96). Democrat. Roman Catholic. Home: 3944 Los Milagros Santa Fe NM 87505-1613 Office: City of Santa Fe 200 Lincoln Ave PO Box 909 Santa Fe NM 87504

VALEK, BERNARD MICHAEL, accounting executive; b. Joliet, Ill., Nov. 19, 1945; s. Peter Anthony and Ann Monica (Hertko) V.; m. Kathleen Mary Clarke, Aug. 16, 1969; 1 child, Emily Ann. BS, No. Ill. U., 1968, MBA, 1969. CPA, Calif., Ill. Asst. prof. Ferris State U., Big Rapids, Mich., 1969-72; staff mgr. Arthur Andersen & Co., Chgo., 1972-78; dir. Calif. CPA Fedn., Palo Alto, 1979-84; pres. Alliance of Practicing CPAs, Long Beach, Calif., 1985—; cons. ANA, L.A., 1984-86. Author: ANA Practice Management Manuals, 1985; pub. (newsletter) The CPAdvocate, 1990—. Bd. dirs. Am. Heart Assn., Long Beach, 1993-94; bd. dirs., treas. Cities in Schs. Long Beach, 1988—, Long Beach Phone Friend, 1988-93. Named One of 100 Most Influential People in Acctg., Acctg. Today newspaper, 1996. Mem. AICPA (bd. dirs. 1982-84), Calif. CPA Soc. (bd. dirs. 1979-84). Roman Catholic. Office: Alliance of Practicing CPAs 3909 California Ave Long Beach CA 90807-3511

VALENCIA-CASTILLO, MARIBEL, social worker; b. Zacapu, Michoacan, Mex., Sept. 17, 1971; came to U.S., 1987; d. Baltazar Valencia and Martha (Escobedo) Castillo. AA in Gen. Studies, Merced Coll., 1994. Immigration educator One Stop Immigration and Ednl. Ctr., Merced, Calif., 1990-92, tchr. E.S.L., 1990-94, legal asst. Servimex, 1994; educator HIV and AIDS Loving AIDS Mgmt. Program, Merced, 1994—, case mgr., 1996—; Activist migrant rights United Farm Workers, Merced, 1993-94; adv. San Francisco AIDS Found., Merced, 1994—. Office: Loving Aids Mgmt Program 1744 G St Ste C Merced CA 95340

VALENTINE, CHRISTINE SPICER JONES, human services counselor; b. Newbury, Berks, Eng., Jan. 20, 1942; came to U.S., 1964; d. Percy W. and Mary E. (Brooks) Spicer; m. Robert H. Jones, Dec. 17, 1965 (dec. Nov. 1972); m. Stephen Valentine III, May 11, 1974; stepchildren: Stephen, Cary, John, Samuel, Sarah. Student, Reading Tech. Coll., 1961-64; Assocs. in Human Svcs., Dull Knife Coll., 1986-89. Cert. chem. dependency counselor, Mont., Nat. Assn. Alcohol & Drug Abuse Counselors. Med. rsch. technician histology dept. radiobiol. unit Atomic Energy Rsch. Establishment, Harwell, Eng., 1958-62, med. rsch. technician genetics dept., 1962-64; head tchr. Headstart Program No. Cheyenne Headstart, Birney, Mont., 1969-72; counselor No. Cheyenne Recovery Ctr., Lame Deer, Mont., 1979-82, sr. counselor, 1982-89, tng. and devel. coord., 1990-92; tech. asst. Billings (Mont.) Area Office, Indian Health Svcs., 1992-93; tech. writing and chem. dependence cons. Cons. Svcs., Birney, Mont., 1993—. Mem. No. Cheyenne Interdisciplinary Core Team, IHS Clinic, Lame Deer, 1986-89; coord. St. Judes Bikeathon, Birney, 1987-94. Recipient Svc. award No. Cheyenne Bd. Health, Lame Deer, 1987, 91, Cmty. Svc. award, 1996, Community Svc. award No. Cheyenne Tribe Community Com., Lame Deer, 1988. Mem. Range Writers Assn. Sheridan Wyo. Home and Office: Cons Svcs PO Box 547 Birney MT 59012-0544

VALENTINE, GENE C., securities dealer; b. Washington, Pa., June 19, 1950; s. John N. and Jane S. Valentine. BS in Psychology, Bethany Coll., 1972; student, U. Vienna, Austria, 1971-72. Commd. ensign USN, 1972, advanced through grades to lt., 1987, hon. discharged, 1978; owner Horizon Realty, San Francisco, 1978-82; dir. land acquisitions Windfarms Ltd. subs. Chevron, U.S.A., San Francisco, 1980-82; v.p. mktg. Christopher Weil & Co., Sherman Oaks, Calif., 1982-85; co-chmn., CEO Pacific Asset Group Inc. (name now Fin. West Group, Inc.), Pasadena, Calif., 1985—; bd. dirs. Fin. West Group, Inc., Paradox Holdings, Kennsington Holdings; founder, chmn., dir. Second Byte Found. Chmn., founder Second Byte Found.; mem. Rep. Party, L.A. Mem. NASD, Internat. Assn. Fin. Planning (bd. dirs. L.A. chpt. 1982—). Episcopalian. Office: Fin West Group Inc 600 Hampshire Rd Ste 200 Westlake Village CA 91361-2500

VALENTINE, JANE LEE, environmental health sciences educator; b. Nashville, July 29, 1945; d. Ollie Carter and Lillian Bernice (Scruggs) V.; 1 child, Catherine Elizabeth Sweetser. BS in Chemistry, Tenn. State U., 1967; MS in Water Chemistry, U. Wis., 1970; PhD in Environ. Health, Pub. Health, U. Tex., 1973. Postdoctoral fellow in preventive medicine, program of environ. toxicology N.J. Coll. Medicine and Dentistry, Newark, 1973-74; from asst. prof. to assoc. prof. pub. health, divsn. environ. and nutritional scis. Sch. Pub. Health UCLA, 1974-83, assoc. prof. pub. health Dept. Environ. Health Scis., Sch. Pub. Health, 1983—; mem. Calif. State Sanitarian Registration Adv. Com., 1984—, pub. health subcom. San Joaquin Valley Drainage Program U.S. Bur. Reclamation, 1986-90, pub. health strategic planning environ. health panel County of L.A. Dept. Health Svcs., 1987-88, pub. health assessment work group San Joaquin Valley Post-Drainage Programs, 1992—; cons. in field; presenter papers in field. Reviewer profl. jours.; contbr. chpts. to books, articles to profl. jours. Mem. AAAS, Internat. Soc. Trace Element Rsch. in Humans (founding mem.), Am. Pub. Health Assn., Am. Water Resources Assn., Internat. Soc. Environ. Epidemiology, Delta Omega, Sigma Xi. Democrat. Roman Catholic. Home: 1721 Las Lunas St Pasadena CA 91106-1304 Office: UCLA Sch Pub Health 10833 Le Conte Ave Los Angeles CA 90024-1602

VALENTINE, JOHN LESTER, state legislator, lawyer; b. Fullerton, Calif., Apr. 26, 1949; s. Robert Lester and Pauline C. (Glood) V.; m. Karen Marie Thorpe, June 1, 1972; children: John Robert, Jeremy Reid, Staci Marie, Jeffrey Mark., David Emerson, Patricia Ann. BS in Acctg. and Econs., Brigham Young U., 1973, JD, 1976. Bar: Utah 1976, U.S. Dist. Ct. Utah, U.S. Ct. Appeals (10th cir.), U.S. Tax Ct.; CPA. Atty. Howard, Lewis & Petersen, Provo, Utah, 1976—; mem. Utah Ho. Reps., 1988—; instr. probate and estates Utah Valley State Coll.; instr. fin. planning., adj. prof. law Brigham Young U.; mem. exec offices, cts., corrections and legis. appropriations subcom., 1988-90, capital facilities subcom., 1988-90, retirement com., 1988-90, judiciary com., 1988-92, strategic planning steering com., 1988-90, interim appropriations com., 1988-94, tax. review commn., 1988-96, ethics com., 1990-92, human svcs. and health appropriations subcom., 1990-92, revenue and taxation com., 1988—, vice chmn. 1990-92; vice chmn. exec. appropriations., 1990-92; chmn. exec. appropriations com., 1992-94, chmn. rules com., 1994-96, higher edn. appropriations com. 1994-96, asst. majority whip, 1996—; bd. dirs. Utah Corrections Industries. Mem. adv. bd. Internat. Sr. Games, 1988—; active Blue Ribbon Task Force on Local Govt. Funding, Utah League Cities and Towns, 1990-94, Criminal Sentencing Guidelines Task Force, Utah Judicial Coun., 1990-92, Access to Health Care Task Force, 1990-92, Utah County Sheriff Search and Rescue, Orem Met. Water Bd., Alpine Sch. Dist. Boundary Line Com., Boy Scouts Am.; bd. regents Legis. Adv. Com. UVCC.; mem. exec. bd. Utah Nat. Parks Coun.; mem. adv. coun. Orchard Elem. Sch., Mountainlands Com. an Aging; bd. trustees Utah Opera Co.; judge nat. and local competitions Moot Ct.; voting dist. chmn.; state, county del.; lt. incident command sys. Utah County Sheriff. Recipient Silver Beaver award Boy Scouts Am., Taxpayer Advocate award Utah Taxpayer Assn. Mem. ABA (tax sect.), Utah State Bar, CPA Com., Tax Sect. Specialization Com., Bicentennial Com. Republican. Mormon. Office: Howard Lewis & Petersen 120 E 300 N Provo UT 84603

VALENTINO, STEPHEN ERIC (IL CONTÉ VALENTINO), production and entertainment company executive, actor, singer; b. N.Y.C., Apr. 2, 1954; s. Joseph and Ina Mae (Diamond) V. Student, Hofstra U., N.Y.C., 1972-74, San Francisco Conservatory Music, 1974-78, Am. Inst. Mus. Studies, Graz, Austria, 1982. Gen. dir., chmn. bd. Mastic Community Theatre, Mastic Beach, N.Y., 1971-74; dir. advt. Marin Opera Co., San Rafael, Calif., 1979-80, Marin Ctr., San Rafael, 1983-85; pres., chief exec. officer Valentino & Assocs., Novato, Calif., 1978—; pres., CEO, co-founder Celebrity Events Internat., 1992—. Food and wine critic, contbg. editor San Francisco Mag., 1995—; contbg. author: Come Barefoot Eating Sensuous Things, 1979; prodr. Miss Julie, San Francisco; appeared in Firestorm, 1992, La Boheme, Daughter of the Regiment, (world premier) Calisto and Melibea, U. Calif., Davis, La Cenerentola, La Nozze de Figaro, The Merry Widow, La Traviata, The Bartered Bride, The Twelfth Night, Barber of Seville, Carmen, Die Fledermaus, Gianni Schicchi, I Pagliacci, Hansel and Gretel, The Magic Flute, Old Maid and the Thief, The Mikado, The Merry Wives of Windsor, (comml.) Ind. Live Ins. Corp. Am., (play) Feuerbach, Mary Stewart as Earl of Leister, 1996. Celebrity coord. Kids Say No To Drugs, 1987, MADD, 1987, ARC, San Jose, Calif., 1989; entertainment coord. Earthquake Relief Fund, San Francisco, 1989, Christmas Tree Program for the Needy, San Francisco, 1986, San Francisco Grand Prix BMW Polo Classic, Marin Suicide Prevention Ctr., 1987, Calif. Health Rsch. Found., 1988, UNICEF San Francisco, 1985, Little Sisters of The Poor, 1985, San Francisco Child Abuse Coun., 1988, 92; fundraiser Easter Seals, Marin County, Calif., 1988, Toys for Tots, Bay Area, Calif., 1987—, Global Youth Resource Orgn., Sunnyvale, Calif., 1989-90; mem. Dem. Nat. Com., 1988-90; commr. Bus. Ins. Adv. Commn., 1989; dir. celebrity basketball game Special Olympics, 1992, celebrity basketball game Easter Seals Soc., 1993; entertainer Shelters for the Homeless of L.A. Earthquake, 1994. Recipient Cert. of Honor, Bd. Suprs., City and County San Francisco, 1986, Awards of Appreciation Easter Seals Soc., 1988, Spl. Olympics, 1992; named Right Honourable H.R.H. Prince Leonard of the Hutt River Principality, Queensland, Australia, 1995. Mem. AFTRA, SAG. Home and Office: Valentino and Assocs 20 Prestwick Ct Novato CA 94949-5841

VALENZUELA, MANUEL ANTHONY, JR., lawyer; b. L.A., Dec. 4, 1955; s. Manuel and Artimesa B. (Ruiz) V.; m. Guadalupe Roa, Nov. 8, 1980; children: Manuel Anthony III, Nancy Christine. BA in Polit. Sci., UCLA, 1978; MPA, U. So. Calif., 1982; JD, Southwestern U., L.A., 1987. Bar: Calif. 1987, U.S. Dist. Ct. (cen. dist.) Calif. 1987, U.S. Ct. Appeals (9th cir.) 1988, U.S. Supreme Ct. 1991. Legis. analyst L.A. City Coun., 1981-88; legal extern ACLU, L.A., 1985; assoc. county counsel County of Los Angeles, 1988-89, sr. assoc county counsel, 1989-90, dep. county counsel, 1990-94; sr. dep. county counsel, 1994—. Mem. L.A. County Bar Assn. (exec. com. govtl. law sect. 1990-91, 95-96, 96—, sec. govtl. law sect. 1991-92, 2d vice chair govtl. law sect. 1992-93, 1st vice chair govtl. law sect. 1993-94, chair govtl. law sect. 1994-95, bd. trustees 1995-96), Mexican Am. Bar Assn. (bd. dirs. 1990, 91), L.A. County Counsel Assn. (bd. dirs. 1989—), UCLA Latino Alumni Assn. (founder, bd. dirs. 1989-90, scholarship com. 1996). Democrat. Roman Catholic. Home: 9647 Val St Temple City CA 91780-1438 Office: Office of County Counsel 648 Hall of Adminstrn 500 W Temple St Los Angeles CA 90012-2713

VALLA, ROBERT, aeronautical engineer, aerodynamicist; b. Milan, Italy, Mar. 11, 1967; came to U.S., 1983; s. Gian Edoardo and Lucilla (Petrazzini) V.; m. Kristi Lynette Loenser, June 6, 1992. BS in Aerospace Engring., Northrop U., L.A., 1989; MS in Aeronautical Engring., Stanford U., 1990. Physics lab. instr. Northrop U., 1986-87; asst. design engr. Downs Crane & Hoist Co., L.A., 1987-88; aerodynamicist McDonnell Douglas Aerospace, Long Beach, Calif., 1991—. John K. Northrop scholar, 1985-89. Mem. AIAA, Soc. Automotive Engrs., Tau Beta Pi, Sigma Gamma Tau. Office: McDonnell Douglas Corp M/C CO71-0035 2401 E Wardlow Rd Long Beach CA 90807-5309

VALLBONA, MARISA, public relations counselor; b. Houston, Tex., Jan. 2, 1964; d. Carlos and Rima (Rothe) Vallbona; m. Don R. Rayner Jr., July 12, 1986 (div.); children: Donald R. Rayner III, Timothy Carlos Rayner. Student, U. Colo., U. de Dijon, France; BS in Journalism, U. Tex. Account exec. Jae Stefan & Assocs., Austin, Tex., 1987-88; media rels. asst. America's Cup XXVII, 1988; sr. account exec. pub. rels. Berkman & Daniels, 1988-90; prin. Rayner & Vallbona Inc. Advt. & Pub. Rels., San Diego, 1990-97; pres. CIM, Inc., San Diego, 1997—. Editor: Flowering Inferno, 1994, Soldiers Cry By Night, 1994, Assumed Name, 1994, People on the Prowl, 1995; contbr. articles to profl. jours. Pub. rels. chair, bd. dirs. Women of St. James Episc. Ch., 1994, 1st v.p., 1995; mem. pub. affairs disaster task force ARC, 1993—; pub. rels. chair Sunkist Am. Cancer Soc. Cup Regatta, 1989; mem. elections mktg. task force City of San Diego, 1989. Mem. Pub. Rels Soc. Am. (accredited, San Diego chpt. chair accreditation com. 1994, dir.-at-large 1995, bd. dirs. 1996—, sec. 1997), Am. Soc. Health Care Mktg. and Pub. Rels., Health Care Communicators San Diego (v.p., bd. dirs. 1994, sec. 1993, numerous awards), Pub. Rels. Club San Diego (exec. bd. dirs. 1991-92, various awards), Jr. League San Diego. Office: CIM Inc 6961 Petit St San Diego CA 92111-3303

VALLEE, JACQUES FABRICE, venture capitalist; b. Pontoise, France, Sept. 24, 1939; came to U.S., 1962; s. Gabriel and Madeleine (Passavant) V.; m. Janine M. Saley, Oct. 19, 1960; children: Olivier, Catherine. BS in Math., U. Paris Sorbonne, 1959; MS in Astrophysics, U. Lille, France, 1961; PhD in Computer Sci., Northwestern U., 1967. Sr. software specialist RCA Corp., Cherry Hill, N.J., 1969-70; mgr. infosystems Stanford U., Palo Alto, Calif., 1970-71; rsch. engr. SRI Internat., Menlo Park, Calif., 1971-72; sr. rsch. fellow Inst. for Future, Menlo Park, 1972-76; chmn. Infomedia Corp., Palo Alto, 1976-81; v.p. Sofinnova, Inc., San Francisco, 1982-86; pres. Eurolink Internat., San Francisco, 1987—; gen. ptnr. Euro-Am. Group, San Francisco, 1996—; bd. dirs. Accuray Inc., Sunnyvale, IXYS Inc., San Jose, Diametrix Detectors, San Diego, Class Data Sys., Ra'anana, Israel. Author: Computer Message Systems, 1984, Dimensions, 1988, Confrontations, 1990, Revelations, 1991, Forbidden Science, 1992, FastWalker, 1996. Recipient Jules Verne prize, Paris, 1961. Office: Eurolink Internat 690 Market St Ste 702 San Francisco CA 94104

VALLERAND, PHILIPPE GEORGES, sales executive; b. Montreal, Que., Can., June 12, 1954; came to U.S., 1982; s. Louis Philippe and Beatrice (Goupil) V.; m. Laura Jean Frombach, Sept. 25, 1979; children: Harmonie May, Jeremy Thomas, Emilie Rose. Student, U. Montreal, 1974, U. Sherbrooke, 1975, U. Que., 1976, White Mgmt. Sch., London, 1981. Dir. resort Club Mediterranee Inc., Bahamas, Switzerland,, Africa,, Guadelupe, West Indies, 1978-80; v.p. Franglo/Sunsaver Inc., London and Hyeres, France, 1980-82; v.p. sales Source Northwest, Inc., Woodinville, Wash., 1982-93; pres. Prime Resource Group. Sr. comdr. Royal Rangers Boys Club, Monroe, Wash., 1988—; bd. mem. Christian Faith Ctr., Monroe, 1988-94; mem. Rep. Nat. Com. Named to 500 Inc. Mag., 1983, 89; recipient Disting. Sales & Mktg. Exec. award Internat. Orgn. Sales & Mktg. Execs., 1993, 96. Mem. Am. Mktg. Assn. (new mem. adv. bd.).

VALNER, RUDY, lawyer; b. Mexico City, Dec. 23, 1960; came to U.S., 1979; s. Benito and Lia (Sod) V.; m. Marci Lynn Zweben, June 22, 1985; children: Danielle Kasey, Alexander Jason, Gabriela Bryn. BA in Polit. Sci. cum laude, UCLA, 1983; JD, Loyola U., L.A., 1987. Bar: Calif. 1989. Assoc. Smylie & Leven, L.A., 1989-90, Warren & Marks, Calabasas, Calif., 1990-92; pvt. practice L.A., 1992—; cons. Mex.-U.S. bus. and real estate devel., transactions, investments, gen. bus.; spkr. on NAFTA opportunities and cultural aspects of doing bus. in Latin Am. Contbr. articles to profl. jours. Mem. ABA (real property, bus. and internat. law sects.), L.A. County Bar Assn. (real property, bus. and internat. law sects.), State Bar Calif. Office: Law Offices of Rudy Valner 10100 Santa Monica Blvd Ste 945 Los Angeles CA 90067-4013

VAMPOLA, ALFRED LUDVIK, aerospace consultant; b. Dwight, Nebr., July 10, 1934; s. Ludwig Anton and Pauline Christine (Trousil) V.; m. Karen Agnes Kirkwood, Apr. 7, 1956; children: Joseph, John, Elaine, Mary, Mark, Robert, James, Donald. BS, Creighton U., 1956; MS, St. Louis U., 1958, PhD, 1961. Sr. physicist Convair, San Diego, 1961-62; sr. staff scientist Aerospace Corp., El Segundo, Calif., 1962-90; cons. Space Environ. Effects, Torrance, Calif., 1990—; vis. fellow Otago U., Dunedin, New Zealand, 1986-87; guest rsch. fellow Max Planck Inst. for Aeronomie, Lindau, Germany, 1991. Assoc. editor Jour. Spacecraft and Rockets, 1984-96; contbr. articles to profl. jours. Fellow AIAA (assoc.); mem. Am. Geophys. Union. Office: Space Environ Effects PO Box 10225 Torrance CA 90505-1025

VAN ALLEN, PHILIP ANDREW, multimedia production company executive, educator; b. Santa Monica, Calif., Jan. 15, 1958; s. William Allen and Dorothy (Wright) van A. BA in Exptl. Psychology highest honors, U. Calif., Santa Cruz, 1988. Freelance audio engr. L.A., 1975-81; programmer analyst Santa Monica Coll., 1981-83; sr. mktg. support analyst Prime Computer, Culver City, Calif., 1983-85; software developer PVA Rsch., Santa Cruz, 1985-88; sr. software engr., mgr. tech. design Philips Interactive Media, L.A., 1988-91, sr. producer, 1991-93; pres., founder Commotion New Media, Santa Monica, 1993—; tech. dir. Interval Rsch., Palo Alto; adj. prof. McGill U., Montreal, 1994-95. Prodr. CD-ROM and On-line titles, interactive music products. Mem. Phi BEta Kappa. Democrat. Unitarian. Office: Commotion New Media 1424 4th St Ste 604 Santa Monica CA 90401-3413

VAN ARSDALE, DICK, professional basketball team executive; b. Indpls., Feb. 22, 1943; m. Barbara V.; children: Jill, Jason. AB in economics, Indiana U., 1965. Player New York Knicks (Nat. Basketball Assn.), N.Y.C., 1965-68; with Phoenix Suns, Phoenix, Ariz., 1968-77; color commentator, TV broadcasts Phoenix Suns, from 1977, interim mgr., 1987, v.p., player personnel, dir. player personnel. Named "Mr. Basketball" of Indiana during high school, NCAA All-American, Indiana U. Office: care Phoenix Suns 201 E Jefferson St Phoenix AZ 85004-2412*

VANARSDEL, ROSEMARY THORSTENSON, English studies educator; b. Seattle, Sept. 1, 1926; d. Odin and Helen Catherine (McGregor) Thorstenson; m. Paul P. VanArsdel Jr., July 7, 1950 (dec. Jan. 1994); children: Mary M., Andrew P. BA, U. Wash., 1947, MA, 1948; PhD, Columbia U., 1961. Grad. tchg. asst. Columbia U., N.Y.C., 1948-50; acting instr. U. Wash., Seattle, 1961-63; asst. prof. U. Puget Sound, Tacoma, Wash., 1967-69; assoc. prof. U. Puget Sound, Tacoma, 1970-77, prof. English, 1977-87, disting. prof. emeritus, 1987—, dir. Writing Inst., 1976-86, dir. semester abroad, 1977, dir. Legal English program Sch. Law, 1973-77; vis. prof. Gonzaga U., Pacific Luth. U., Whitman Coll., Willamette U., 1977. Author: Victorian Periodicals: A Guide to Research, Vol. I, 1978, Vol. II, 1989, George Eliot: A Centenary Tribune, 1982, Victorian Periodicals and Victorian Society, 1994, Periodicals of Queen Victoria's Empire, An Exploration, 1996; mem. editl. bd. Wellesley Index for Victorian Periodicals, 1968-89; contbr. articles to profl. jours. Recipient Doris Bronson Morrill award Kappa Kappa Gamma, 1982, Disting. Alumnae award Broadway H.S., Seattle, 1991. Mem. MLA, Royal Soc. Lit., Oxford Bibliog. Soc., Nat. Coun. Tchrs. English (Achievement awards, dir. 1974-77), Rsch. Soc. for Victorian Periodicals (pres. 1981-83). Home: 4702 NE 39th St Seattle WA 98105-5205

VAN ASPEREN, MORRIS EARL, banker; b. Wessington, S.D., Oct. 5, 1943; s. Andrew and Alyce May (Flagg) Van A.; m. Anne Virginia Merritt, July 2, 1966; 1 child, David Eric. BS in Math., U. Okla., 1966; MBA, Pepperdine U., 1979. Mgr. western dist. Svc. Rev. Inc., Northbrook, Ill., 1970-77; v.p. Hooper Info. Systems Inc., Tustin, Calif., 1977-78; v.p., chief fin. officer ATE Assocs. Inc., Westlake Village, Calif., 1978-84; mgmt. cons. Thousand Oaks, Calif., 1984-94; sr. v.p. Nat. Bank Calif., L.A., 1986—; chmn. liaison com. region IX SBA, 1990-94; adj. faculty U. Phoenix, 1997—. Nat. advocate fin. svcs. SBA, 1989. Lt. USN, 1966-70. Mem. Nat. Assn. Govt. Guaranteed Lenders (bd. dirs. 1990-93), Robert Morris Assocs., Nat. Assn. Credit Mgmt., Am. Legion (bd. dirs. Post 339 1995). Office: Nat Bank Calif 145 S Fairfax Ave Los Angeles CA 90036-2166

VANATTA, MERRY JANICE, accountant; b. Mpls., July 18, 1938; d. Lief Erick and Lucille Evelyn (Tucker) Larson; m. Larry Lee VanAtta, Oct. 12, 1956 (div. Dec. 1981); children: Jan Luell, Lori Lee, Erick Donald. Student, Linn Benton Community Coll., 1973-78. Lic. tax cons., Oreg. With various acctg. firms, Lebanon, Oreg., 1956-64, Sharp, Young et al CPAs, Lebanon, Oreg., 1964-72; sole propr. M.J. VanAtta, Acct., Lebanon, Oreg., 1972—. Treas. Oreg. Fedn. Women's Clubs, 1972-74; sec. Lebanon Rural Fire Protection Dist., Lebanon, 1978-87. Mem. Nat. Soc. Pub. Accts. (state dir. 1988-92), Oreg. Assn. Ind. Accts. (pres. 1988-89, 1st v.p. 1987-88, 2d v.p. 1986-87, sec. 1985-86, Martin Fitzgerald award 1988-89, William Blair award 1986-87), Oreg. Assn. Pub. Accts. (sec. bd. dirs. scholarship found. 1994—).

VAN AUKEN, STUART, marketing educator; b. Sherman, Tex., July 19, 1941; s. Frank Monroe and Sally (McCormick) Van A.; m. Linda Lou Nance, June 1, 1963 (div. Jan. 1980); children: Paige, Steve, Stacie. BBA, U. North Tex., 1964, PhD, 1970; MBA, So. Meth. U., 1966. Asst. prof. mktg. Tex. Tech U., Lubbock, 1969-72; disting. prof. mktg., chair dept. mktg. and bus. stats. U. Louisville, 1972-86; prof. mktg. Calif. State U., Chico, 1986—, dean Coll. Bus., 1986-90. Contbr. articles to profl. jours. Mem. Am. Mktg. Assn., Assn. for Consumer Rsch., Am. Acad. Advt. Republican. Presbyterian. Home: 761 Bridlewood Ct Chico CA 95926 Office: Calif State U Chico Dept Fin and Mktg Chico CA 95929-0051

VAN BAAK, ANTHONY EDWARD, resort executive; b. Shanghai, Mar. 26, 1949; came to U.S., 1949; s. Edward Anthony and Frances Ruth (Ribbens) Van B.; BA in History, Calvin Coll., 1970; postgrad. Western Mich. U., 1970-71; m. Arlene Florence Dewey, Aug. 7, 1982; children: Edward Anthony, Florence Ribbens, Rachel Dewey. Owner Sounds Unlimited, Steamboat Springs, Colo., 1976-83; asst. contr. LTV Corp., 1971-76, Utah Internat., Craig, Colo., 1976-77, Mountain Resorts, Steamboat Springs, 1978-80, Steamboat Resorts, 1980-89; owner Resort Group Cos., 1983—, Hotel Bristol, 1994—. Chmn. fin. com. Meth. Ch., 1991-94, chmn. trustees, 1994—; bd. dirs. Steamboat Springs Pub. Sch. Dist. RE-2, 1995—. Republican. Home: PO Box 1809 65 Park Ave Steamboat Springs CO 80477-4671

VAN BARSELAAR, LESLIE FRANCES, private school director; b. Boston, Jan. 23, 1952; d. Arie and Edith Grace (Leslie) van den Barselaar; m. David Randolph Kallgren, Nov. 12, 1976. B in Individual Concentration, U. Mass., 1973. Field instr. Wyo. and Wash. Nat. Outdoor Leadership Sch., Lander, Wyo., 1973-79; Kenya br. co-dir. Nat. Outdoor Leadership Sch., Lander, 1979-82, field instr. Alaska and Baja, 1982-86, Mexico br. co-dir., 1986—. Mem. Am. Birding Assn., Wyo. Carriage Club. Office: Nat Outdoor Leadership Sch 288 W Main St Lander WY 82520-3128

VAN BRUNT, EDMUND EWING, physician; b. Oakland, Calif., Apr. 28, 1926; s. Adrian W. and Kathryn Anne (Shattuck) Van B.; m. Claire Monod, Feb. 28, 1949; children: Karin, Deryk, Jahn. BA in Biophysics, U. Calif., Berkeley, 1952; MD, U. Calif., San Francisco, 1959; ScD, U. Toulouse, France, 1978. Postdoctoral fellow NIH, 1961-63; rsch. assoc. U. Calif., San Francisco, 1963-67; staff physician Kaiser Permanente Med. Ctr., San Francisco, 1964-91; dir. div. rsch. Kaiser Permanente Med. Program, Oakland, Calif., 1979-91; assoc. dir. Kaiser Found. Rsch. Inst., Oakland, 1985-91, sr. cons., 1991—; adj. prof. U. Calif., San Francisco, 1975-92; chmn. instnl. rev. bd. Kaiser Found. Rsch. Inst., 1986—; pres. bd. trustees French Found. Med. Rsch. and Edn., San Francisco, 1992—. Contbr. articles to profl. books and jours. With U.S. Army, 1944-46. Fellow ACP, Am. Coll. Med. Informatics; mem. AAAS, Calif. Med. Assn., U. Calif. Emeritus Faculty Assn., Sigma Xi.

VAN BUSKIRK, EDMUND MICHAEL, ophthalmologist; b. Lafayette, Ind., July 13, 1941; s. Edmund Linford and Dorothy Elizabeth (Deming) Van B.; m. Bette Jo Lueck, June 19, 1965; children: Audrey Elizabeth, Sarah Lynn, Amy Louise. AB cum laude, Harvard U., 1963, AM in Anthropology, 1964; MD, Boston U., 1968. Diplomate Am. Bd. Ophthalmology. Intern Santa Barbara (Calif.) Cottage-Gen. Hosp., 1968-69; resident in ophthalmology Boston U. Med. Ctr., 1969-72; fellowship Mass. Eye and Ear Infirmary, Harvard Med. Sch., 1972-74; asst. prof. ophthalmology Milton S. Hershey Med. Ctr., Pa. State U., 1974-79; assoc. prof. ophthalmology Oreg. Health Scis. U., Portland, 1979-84, prof. ophthalmology, 1984-94, vice chmn. ophthalmology, 1984-94; chmn. dept. ophthalmology Devers Eye Inst., Good Samaritan Hosp. and Med. Ctr., Portland, 1990—, Richard G. Chenoweth chair, 1990—; assoc. examiner Am. Acad. Bd. of Ophthalmology, 1986, 88, 89, 91; mem. visual scis. study sect. NIH, 1986-89; glaucoma adv. bd. Nat. Soc. to Prevent Blindness, 1987—; glaucoma rsch. rev. bd. Am. Health Assistance Found.; chief dept. ophthalmology Legacy Portland Hosps., 1992—; lectr. in field. Author: Clinical Atlas of Glaucoma, 1986, A Color Atlas of Ophthalmic Surgery: Surgery, 1991; founding editor, editor-in-chief Jour. of Glaucoma, 1991—; editl. bd. Am. Jour. Ophthalmology, 1985-91, modules program, 1986-89, Glaucoma Forum, 1989—, Focus on Glaucoma, 1990—; contbr. chpts. to books and articles to profl. jours. Capt. U.S. Army Res. Spl. fellowship NIH, Nat. Eye Inst., 1972-74, Mass. Lions Club, EB Dunphy Eye rsch. fellowship Mass. Eye and Ear Infirmary, 1973-74; Rsch. Career Devel. award Nat. Eye Inst., 1976-81, Faculty Excellence award Oreg. Health Scis. U., 1986, Achievement award Alcon Rsch. Inst., 1988. Fellow ACS, Am. Acad. Ophthalmology (com. ethics 1987, dir. spl. focus course on glaucoma surgery, 1986, 88, chmn. regional update program 1988-92, Honor award 1986), Coll. Physicians Phila.; mem. AMA, Am. Glaucoma Soc. (sec. 1992-94, v.p. 1994-96, pres. 1996—), Assn. for Rsch. in Vision and Ophthalmology (mem. program planning com. 1986, 88, chmn. glaucoma sect. 1987-88), Chandler Grant Soc., Internat. Glaucoma Soc., Mass. Eye and Ear Infirmary Alumni Assn., Oreg. Acad. Ophthalmology, Am. Ophthalmol. Soc. Office: Devers Eye Assocs PC 1040 NW 22nd Ave Portland OR 97210-3057

VAN DAM, HEIMAN, psychoanalyst; b. Leiden, The Netherlands, Feb. 5, 1920; s. Machiel and Rika (Knorringa) van D.; m. Barbara C. Strona, Oct. 6, 1945; children: Machiel, Claire Ilena, Rika Rosemary. AB, U. So. Calif., 1942, MD, 1945. Fellowship child psychiatry Pasadena (Calif.) Child Guidance Clinic, 1950; gen. practice psychiatry and psychoanalysis L.A., 1951—; instr. L.A. Psychoanalytic Inst., 1959—, co-chmn. com. on child psychoanalysis, 1960-67, tng. and supervising psychoanalyst, 1972—; supr. child and adolescent psychoanalysis So. Calif. Psychoanalytic Inst., 1986—; cons. Reiss Davis Child Study Center, 1955-76, Neighborhood Youth Assn., Los Angeles, 1964-69; asso. clin. prof. psychiatry UCLA Sch. Medicine, 1960—, clin. prof. psychiatry and pediats., 1996—; vis. supr. child psychoanalysis San Francisco Psychoanalytic Inst., 1969-79, Denver Psychoanalytic Inst., 1972-74; mem. adv. bd. Western State U. Coll. Law, Fullerton, Calif., 1965-83. Corr. editor Arbeits Hefte Kinderanalyse, 1985—; contbr. articles to profl. jours. Trustee, mem. edn. com. Center for Early Edn., 1964-92, v.p., 1978-79; bd. dirs. Child Devel. and Psychotherapy Tng. Program, Los Angeles, 1975-80, pres., 1975-77; bd. dirs. Los Angeles Child Devel. Center, 1977-86, treas., 1978-80; mem. cult clinic Jewish Family Service, Los Angeles, 1978-86; bd. dirs. Lake Arrowhead Crest Estates, 1990—. Served to capt. M.C. AUS, 1946-48. Mem. Am. Psychoanalytic Assn. (com. on ethics 1977-80), Assn. Child Psychoanalysis (councillor 1966-69, sec. 1972-74, mem. nominating com. 1978-84, membership com. 1988—, Marianne Kris lectr. 1995), Internat. Assn. Infant Psychiatry (co-chmn. program com. 1980-83), Internat. Soc. Adolescent Psychiatry (sci. adv. com. 1988—), Phi Beta Kappa. Office: 1100 Glendon Ave Ste 941 Los Angeles CA 90024-3513

VANDE BERG, MARSHA JOAN, journalist, columnist, author; b. Sheldon, Iowa, Dec. 20, 1946; d. Theodore Martin and Esther Margaret (Terpstra) V. Student, Va. Poly. Inst., U. Iowa; MA in German Studies/Comparative Lit., Duke U., 1970; PhD in Internat. Studies/Fine Arts, Vanderbilt U., 1978. City editor, columnist, reporter The Tennessean, Nashville, 1972-86; planning dir. CBS affiliate, Nashville, 1986-87; assignment editor Orange County (Calif.) Register, 1988-89; opinion page editor San Francisco Chronicle, 1989-94; self-employed editor/analyst internat. confs., 1994—, freelance columnist on fgn. affairs nationwide, 1989—; editor-in-chief Ferndale (Calif.) Enterprise, 1996; pub. The Vande Berg World Report, 1996—; vis. lectr. internat. studies dept. U. Calif., 1993; seminar leader on media and ethics Acad. Specialist Program, USIA, Pakistan, 1995, Lusaka, Zambia, 1994; adj. faculty U. Calif., Berkeley, 1989; guest lectr. Bosch Found., Stuttgart, Germany, 1992, World Affairs Coun. and UN Assn., San Francisco, 1991; participant various symposia, seminars and confs. Author: America's Rising Star Chefs, 1994; writer articles for jours. and mags. including New York Times, Newsweek, The Cong. Quar., Nieman Reports, Calif. Jour., Golden State Report, Orange County Mag., Nashville!, others; editl. cons. various projects including: Agents of change, 1995. Mem. Coun. on Fgn. Rels., N.Y. chmn. San Francisco Com. on Fgn. Rels., 1995—; adv. bd., exec. com. Inst. Internat. Edn., 1993—, editor newsletter, 1993—; docent San Francisco Mus. Modern Art. Mem. Coun. on Fgn. Rels., Women in Internat. Security, Inst. of Current World Affairs, Nat. Assn. Opinion Page Editors (pres. 1993-94), Commonwealth Club, Pacific Coun. on Internat. Policy. Democrat. Episcopalian. Office: 2584 Filbert St San Francisco CA 94123

VAN DE KAMP, ANDREA LOUISE, academic administrator; b. Detroit, July 28, 1943; m. John K. Van De Kamp; 1 child, Diana. BA, Mich. State U., 1966; MA, Columbia U., 1972. Dir. recruitment Columbia U., N.Y.C., 1968-71; asst. dean admissions Dartmouth Coll., Hanover, N.H., 1971-74; assoc. dean admissions Occidental Coll., L.A., 1974-77; exec. dir. Internat. Acad. Estate Trust Law, L.A., 1976-79, Coro Found., L.A., 1977-80; dir. devel. Mus. Contemporary Art, L.A., 1980-81; dir. pub. affairs Carter Hawley Hale Stores, Inc., L.A., 1981-87; pres. Ind. Colls. So. Calif., L.A., 1987-89; v.p., mng. dir. west coast Sotheby's N.Am., Beverly Hills, Calif., 1989—. Bd. dirs., KCET, L.A., L.A. County Mus. Art; bd. dirs., officer, Music Ctr. Operating Co., L.A.; co-chmn. Arts Task Force, L.A.; mem. L.A. 2000. Mem. L.A. Pub. Affairs Officers' Assn. (chmn. 1987-88), Women in Pub. Affairs, Town Hall, Ind. Coll. Fund Am. Democrat. Office: 308 N Rodeo Dr Beverly Hills CA 90210-5106

VAN DE KAMP, JOHN KALAR, lawyer; b. Pasadena, Calif., Feb. 7, 1936; s. Harry and Georgie (Kalar) Van de K.; m. Andrea Fisher, Mar. 11, 1978; 1 child, Diana. BA, Dartmouth Coll., 1956; JD, Stanford U., 1959. Bar: Calif. 1960. Asst. U.S. atty. L.A., 1960-66, U.S. atty., 1966-67; dep. dir. Exec. Office for U.S. Attys., Washington, 1967-68, dir., 1968-69; spl. asst. Pres.'s Commn. on Campus Unrest, 1970; fed. pub. defender L.A., 1971-75; dist. atty. Los Angeles County, 1975-83; atty. gen. State of Calif., 1983-91; with Dewey Ballantine, L.A., 1991-96, of counsel, 1996—; pres. Thoroughbred Owners, Calif., 1996—; bd. dirs. United Airlines. Mem. Calif. Dist. Attys. Assn. (pres. 1975-83), Nat. Dist. Attys. Assn. (v.p. 1975-83), Peace Officers Assn. L.A. County (past pres.), Nat. Assn. Attys. Gen. (exec. com. 1983-91), Conf. Western Attys. Gen. (pres. 1986). Office: Dewey Ballantine 333 S Hope St Ste 3000 Los Angeles CA 90071-3039

VANDENBERG, PETER RAY, magazine publisher; b. Geneva, Ill., Sept. 8, 1939; s. Don George and Isabel (Frank) V.; m. Kathryn Stock, June 1973 (div. Apr. 1977). BBA, Miami U., 1962. Creative administr. E.F. McDonald Incentive Co., Dayton, Ohio, 1966-73; mfrs.' rep. Denver, 1974-75; mgr. Homestake Condominiums, Vail, Colo., 1975-76; desk clk. Vail Run Resort, 1976-77; sales rep. Colo. West Advt., Vail, 1977-79, pres., 1980-83; pres. Colo. West Publ., Vail, 1983—. With U.S. Army, 1963-66. Mem. Sigma Chi.

VAN DEN BERG, SARA JANE, English educator; b. St. Paul, May 19, 1942; d. Henry John and Edith Ann (Hutchins) Streich; m. Kent Talbot van den Berg, June 12, 1976; 1 child, David Talbot. BA summa cum laude, U. Minn., 1964; MA, Yale U., 1965, PhD, 1969. Instr. Fordham U., N.Y.C., 1968-70; asst. prof. Fairfield (Conn.) U., 1970-73, Occidental Coll., L.A., 1973-76, Ohio State U., Columbus, 1976-80; asst. prof. U. Wash., Seattle, 1980-87, assoc. prof. English, 1987—, chmn. curricular policy bd., 1996—. Mem. editl. bd. Modern Lang. Quar., 1995—, Psyart: The Jour., 1997—; author: The Action of Ben Jonson's Poetry, 1987. Huntington Libr. fellow, 1987, NEH fellow, summer 1987. Mem. MLA (chmn. divsn. lit. and psychology 1990-94), Renaissance Soc. Am., Milton Soc. Am., Pacific Ancient and Modern Lang. Assn. (exec. com. 1997—). Office: Univ of Washington Dept English Box 354330 Seattle WA 98195

VANDENBERGHE, RONALD GUSTAVE, accountant, real estate developer; b. Oakland, Calif., July 1, 1937; s. Anselm Henri and Margaret B. (Bygum) V.; B.A. with honors, San Jose State Coll., 1959; postgrad. U. Calif. at Berkeley Extension, 1959-60, Golden Gate Coll., 1961-63; CPA, Calif.; m. Patricia W. Dufour, Aug. 18, 1957; children: Camille, Mark, Matthew. Real estate investor, pres. VandenBerghe Fin. Corp., Pleasanton, Calif., 1964—. Instr. accounting U. Cal., Berkeley, 1963-70; CPA, Pleasanton, 1963—. Served with USAF. Mem. Calif. Soc. CPAs. Republican. Presbyterian. Mason (Shriner). Home: PO Box 803 Danville CA 94526-0803 Office: 20 Happy Valley Rd Pleasanton CA 94566-9714

VANDER DUSSEN, SHERI TULLEY, city official; b. Inglewood, Calif., Mar. 21, 1959; d. Harry Alexander Tulley and Dorothy Ann (Herder) Pagenstecher; m. Nicholas Paul Vander Dussen, June 20, 1981; children: David Nicholas, Matthew John. BA in Social Ecology, U. Calif., Irvine, 1980. Assoc. planner City of Newport Beach, Calif., 1980-85; sr. planner City of Norwalk, Calif., 1985-86; sr. planner City of Irvine, 1986-89, prin. planner, 1989-90, mgr. devel. svcs., 1990-93, mgr. planning and devel. svcs., 1993-96, acting dir. cmty. devel., 1996—; devel. cons. Faith Reformed Ch., Norwalk, 1991; spkr. Am. Planning Assn., Newport Beach, 1990, Palm Springs, Calif., 1996; guest lectr. U. Calif., Irvine, 1992, 96. Mem. task force Orange County Affordable Housing, Santa Ana, Calif., 1992; coord. ann. drive, United Way, Irvine, 1991; mem. Bellflower (Calif.) Christian Sch. Soc., 1989—; mem. Orange County Forum, 1994—. Mem. Am. Inst. Cert. Planners, Am. Planning Assn., Nat. Assn. Housing and Redevel. Ofcls. Office: City of Irvine PO Box 19575 Irvine CA 92713-9575

VANDERGRIFF, CHRISTINA RAI, controller; b. Prineville, Oreg., Nov. 13, 1964; d. Marvin Ronald and Virginia Lucille (Warren) Craig; m. Kenneth Wayne Vandergriff, Aug. 23, 1987. Cert. legal adminstrn. with honors, Trend Coll., Eugene, Oreg., 1989; BA in Acctg., Morrison Coll., Reno, Nev., 1996; Assoc. Bus. Adminstrn. in Bus. Mgmt., B of Bus. Adminstr. in Acctg. Shipper, asst. loan processor Centennial Mortgage Co., Inc., Eugene, 1989-90; asst. acct. Kimwood Corp., Cottage Grove, Oreg., 1990-91; sec., asst. Bill Vollendorff Appraisal, Walla Walla, Wash., 1991-92; inventory supr., purchaser Sierra Office Concepts/Nev. Copy Systems, Reno, 1992-95, mem. employee adv. com., 1993-94; with Tahoe Office Sys. Nev. Copy Sys., Tahoe City, Calif., 1995-96; asst. adminstrn., asst. contr. Interstate Safety and Supply, Inc., Sparks, Nev., 1996—. Active Adopt-A-Sch. Program, Reno, 1992;co-sponsor Nev. Women's Fund, Reno, 1993. Democrat. Baptist. Office: Water Safety Corp 320 Coney Island Dr Sparks NV 89431

VANDERGRIFF, JERRY DODSON, retired computer store executive; b. Ft. Leonard Wood, Mo., Nov. 6, 1943; s. Oliver Wyatt Vandergriff and Mary Ella (Perkins) Myers; m. Donna Jean Niehof, Aug. 14, 1976 (div. Nov. 1987); children: Robert Lee II, William Oliver; m. Lisa Ann Marrett, Aug. 10, 1996. BS in Bus., Emporia State U., 1974. Customer svc. mgr. Pictures, Inc., Anchorage, 1975-83, v.p., gen. mgr., 1983-87; gen. mgr. Pictures-The Computer Store, Anchorage, 1987-96; ret., 1996. Bd. dirs. Community Schs. Coun., Anchorage, 1986-87; mem. Gov.'s Coun. on Edn., 1989-90; bd. dirs. Romig Jr. High Sch., 1989-90, pres. PTSA, 1990-92; mem. exec. bd. Alaska's Youth Ready for Work, 1989-92. Mem. VFW. Republican. Home: 3831 Balchen Dr Anchorage AK 99517-2446

VANDERHEIDEN, RICHARD THOMAS, government official, lawyer; b. Omaha, Nov. 10, 1947; s. Frederick Joseph and Margaret (Burke) V.; m. Mary Margaret Schuster, June 1, 1969; children: Brian, Paul. BS, U. Nebr., 1970, JD, 1973. Bar: Nebr. 1974. Dep. county atty. Merrick County, Central City, Nebr., 1974-75; ptnr. Phares Torpin Vanderheiden & Mesner, Central City, 1976-87; v.p. Founders Bank of Ariz., Scottsdale, 1987-88, Chase Trust Co. of Ariz., Scottsdale, 1988-91; pub. fiduciary Maricopa County, Phoenix, 1991—; jud. nominating commn. 21st Jud. Dist., Nebr., 1984-86; bd. dirs. Merrick County Mental Health Ctr., 1975-82, Mericopa County Justice Com., 1991—, exec. team, 1991; chmn. Maricopa County Deferred Compensation Bd., 1994—, NaCo Deferred Compensation Adminstrv. Com., 1995—. Pres. Bd. Edn., Central City, 1975-82; chpt. chmn. ARC, Central City, 1976-80; co-chair United Way Campaign, Maricopa County; chmn. cert. com. Nat. Guardianship Assn. Mem. ABA, Nat. Guardianship Assn. (bd. dirs. 1992—, v.p. 1995), Scottsdale Bar Assn., Valley Estate Planners (pres. 1990-91), Ariz. Bankers Assn. (trust com. 1989-91), Sertoma Internat. (pres. 1979), Central City C. of C. (bd. dirs. 1980-84). Roman Catholic. Office: First Am Title Bldg 111 W Monroe St Fl 5 Phoenix AZ 85003-1728

VANDERHEYDEN, MIRNA-MAR, resort management and services executive; b. Freeport, Ill., Oct. 8, 1932; d. Orville Ray and Frances Elmira (Miller) Van Brocklin; m. Roger Eugene Vanderheyden, Dec. 23, 1950 (div. 1983); children: Romayne Lee, Adana Dawn, Grayling Dwayne, Willow B., Tiffany LaMarr. Cert., Brown's Bus. Coll., Freeport, Ill., 1949; BA, Milliken U., 1953. Paralegal various locations, 1953-93; pres. Carlin Bay Corp., Coeur d'Alene, Idaho, 1981—. Lobbyist PTA, Springfield, Ill., 1972. Home and Office: 609 W Apple Dr Delta CO 81416-3062

VANDERHOEF, LARRY NEIL, academic administrator; b. Perham, Minn., Mar. 20, 1941; s. Wilmar James and Ida Lucille (Wothe) V.; m. Rosalie Suzanne Slifka, Aug. 31, 1963; children: Susan Marie, Jonathan Lee. B.S., U. Wis., Milw., 1964, M.S., 1965; Ph.D., Purdue U., 1969. Postdoctorate U. Wis., Madison, 1969-70; research assoc. U. Wis., summers 1970-72; asst. prof. biology U. Ill., Urbana, 1970-74; assoc. prof. U. Ill., 1974-77, prof., 1977—, head dept. plant biology, 1977-80; provost Agrl. and Life Scis., U. Md., College Park, 1980-84; exec. vice chancellor U. Calif., Davis, 1984-91, exec. vice chancellor, provost, 1991-94; chancellor, 1994—; vis. investigator Carnegie Inst., 1976-77, Edinburgh (Scotland) U., 1978; cons. in field. NRC postdoctoral fellow, 1969-70, Eisenhower fellow, 1987; Dimond travel grantee, 1975, NSF grantee, 1972, 74, 76, 77, 78, 79, NATO grantee, 1980. Mem. AAAS, Am. Soc. Plant Physiology (bd. editors Plant Physiology 1977-82, trustee, mem. exec. com., treas. 1982-88, chmn. bd. trustees 1994—), Nat. Assn. State Univ. and Land Grant Colls. Home: 615 Francisco Pl Davis CA 95616-0210 Office: U Calif Davis Office Chancellor Davis CA 95616

VANDER HOUWEN, BOYD A., marketing and management executive; b. Yakima, Wash., Jan. 17, 1946; s. John W. and Elsie W. (Lanfear) V.; m. Loma Alene Madsen, June 27, 1970; children: Garth John, Dana Madsen. BA in Journalism, U. Mont., 1968; BA in Econs., U. Wash., 1971, MA in Communications/Bus., 1978; grad., Northwest Intermediate Banking Sch., Portland, Oreg., 1985. Edn., city hall reporter Idaho Falls (Idaho) Post-Register, 1971-72; farm bus. writer Tri-City Herald, Kennewick, Wash., 1973-74; bur. mgr., editor Yakima Valley Tri-City Herald, Sunnyside, Wash., 1974-76; editor Jour. Contemporary Bus., mgr. bus. publs. Grad. Sch. Bus. Adminstrn. U. Wash., Seattle, 1978-81; asst. v.p., mgr. communications Rainier Nat. Bank, Seattle, 1981-88; prin. Hawkins Vander Houwen, Inc., Seattle, 1988-89, Vander Houwen Pub. Rels., Bellevue, Wash., 1989—. Mem. publs. redesign com. Hist. Seattle, 1982, selection com. merit scholarship Rainier Nat. Bank, 1983; publicity chmn. United Way One to One Program, 1983, United Way Cabinet, 1982; chmn. comms. com. United Way of King County, mem. mktg. com., 1985-90; chmn. fiscal adv. com. Mercer Island Pub. Schs., 1985-89; mem. Mercer Island Sch. Bd., 1991-95, pres. 1992-93, strategic planning com. 1994-95; chmn. CMU Com. United Way of King County, 1985-88, mem. awards com. Washington Gives, 1988-90. With U.S. Army, 1969-71. Named IABC Communicator of Yr., 1982, NEH grantee, 1979; recipient Excellence in Publs. award Soc. Tech. Publs., 1979, 81, Merge-Communicator awards IABC, 1987, First Pl. Employee Comm. award Washington Press Assn., 1997. Mem. am. Mktg. Assn. (v.p. mktg. Puget Sound chpt. 1990-91, pres. elect 1991, pres. 1992-93), Pub. Rels. Soc. Am., Internat. Assn. Bus. Communicators (Pacesetter awards com. 1981-83, Internal Communications award of excellence Pacific N.W. chpt. 1982, Silver 6 and Totem awards employee pubs., Puget sound chpt. 1983, 84, 88, 90, award of excellence Northwest Classics 1995), Soc. Profl. Journalists (bus. writing, editing awards 1971, 73, 74). Home: 8575 SE 76th Pl Mercer Island WA 98040-5706 Office: Vander Houwen Pub Rels 11747 NE 1st St Ste 101 Bellevue WA 98005-3018

VANDERLINDEN, CAMILLA DENICE DUNN, telecommunications industry manager; b. Dayton, July 21, 1950; d. Joseph Stanley and Virginia Danley (Martin) Dunn; m. David Henry VanderLinden; Oct. 10, 1980; 1 child, Michael Christopher. Student, U. de Valencia, Spain, 1969; BA in Spanish and Secondary Edn. cum laude, U. Utah, 1972, MS in Human Resource Econs., 1985. Asst. dir. Davis County Community Action Program, Farmington, Utah, 1973-76; dir. South County Community Action, Midvale, Utah, 1976-79; supr. customer service Ideal Nat. Life Ins. Co., Salt Lake City, 1979-80; mgr. customer service Utah Farm Bur. Mutual Ins., Salt Lake City, 1980-82; quality assurance analyst Am. Express Co., Salt Lake City, 1983-86, quality assurance and human resource specialist, 1986-88; mgr. quality assurance and engring. Am. Express Co., Denver, 1988-91; mgr. customer svc. Tel. Express Co., Colorado Springs, Colo., 1991—; mem. adj. faculty Westminster Coll., Salt Lake City, 1987-88. mem. adj. faculty, mem. quality adv. bd. Red Rocks Community Coll., 1990-91. Vol. translator Latin Am. community; vol. naturalist Roxborough State Park; internat. exch. coord. EF Fgn. Exch. Program. Mem. Internat. Customer Svc. Orgn. (officer call ctr. chpt.), Colo. Springs Customer Svc. Assn. (officer). Christian. Home: 10857 W Snow Cloud Trl Littleton CO 80125-9210

VAN DER MEULEN, JOSEPH PIERRE, neurologist; b. Boston, Aug. 22, 1929; s. Edward Lawrence and Sarah Jane (Robertson) VanDer M.; m. Ann Irene Yadeno, June 18, 1960; children—Elisabeth, Suzanne, Janet. A.B.,

Boston Coll., 1950; M.D., Boston U., 1954. Diplomate: Am. Bd. Psychiatry and Neurology. Intern Cornell Med. div. Bellevue Hosp., N.Y.C., 1954-55; resident Cornell Med. div. Bellevue Hosp., 1955-56; resident Harvard U., Boston City Hosp., 1958-60, instr., fellow, 1962-66; assoc. Case Western Res. U., Cleve., 1966-67; asst. prof. Case Western Res. U., 1967-69, assoc. prof. neurology and biomed. engring., 1969-71; prof. neurology U. So. Calif., L.A., 1971—; also dir. dept. neurology Los Angeles County/U. So. Calif. Med. Center; chmn. dept. U. So. Calif., 1971-78, v.p. for health affairs, 1977—, dean Sch. Medicine, 1985-86, 95—, vice dean med. affairs, 1995—; vis. prof. Autonomous U. Guadalajara, Mex., 1974; pres. Norris Cancer Hosp. and Research Inst., 1983—. Contbr. articles to profl. jours. Mem. med. adv. bd. Calif. chpt. Myasthenia Gravis Found., 1971-75, chmn., 1974-75, 77-78; med. adv. bd. Amyotrophic Lateral Sclerosis Found., Calif., 1973-75, chmn., 1974-75; mem. Com. to Combat Huntington's Disease, 1973—; bd. dirs. Calif. Hosp. Med. Ctr., Good Hope Med. Found., Doheny Eye Hosp., House Ear Inst., L.A. Hosp. Good Samaritan, Children's Hosp. of L.A., Barlow Respiratory Hosp., USC U. Hosp., chmn., 1991—; bd. govs. Thomas Aquinas Coll.; bd. dirs. Assn. Acad. Health Ctrs., chmn., 1991-92; pres. Scott Newman Ctr., 1987-89; pres., bd. dirs. Kenneth Norris Cancer Hosp & Rsch. Inst. Served to lt. M.C. USNR, 1956-58. Nobel Inst. fellow Karolinska Inst., Stockholm, 1960-62; NIH grantee, 1968-71. Mem. AMA, Am. Neurol. Assn., Am. Acad. Neurology, L.A. Soc. Neurology and Psychiatry (pres. 1977-78), L.A. Med. Assn., Mass. Med. Soc., Ohio Med. Soc., Calif. Med. Soc., L.A. Acad. Medicine, Alpha Omega Alpha (councillor 1992—), Phi Kappa Phi. Home: 39 Club View Ln Palos Verdes Peninsula CA 90274-4208 Office: U So Calif 1540 Alcazar St Los Angeles CA 90033-4500

VANDER MOLEN, JACK JACOBUS, engineering executive, consultant; b. Assen, Drenthe, Netherlands, May 28, 1916; came to U.S., 1947, naturalized 1952; s. Evert Moll and Victorina Sweelssen; m. Ina Mary Auerbach, 1946. ME, M.T.S., Haarlem, 1940; postgrad. computer program specialist, Ariz. Tech., 1982. Draftsman, designer Fokker Aircraft, Amsterdam, Netherlands, 1939-40; asst. plant mgr. Bruynzeel's Deuren Fabriek, Zaandam, Netherlands, 1941-44; civilian mgr. Allied Hdqrs. Rest Ctrs., Maastricht, Amsterdam, Netherlands, 1944-45; cen. staff tech. efficiency and orgn. Philips Radio, Eindhoven, Holland, 1945-47; indsl. engr. N.Am. Philips, Dobbs Ferry, N.Y., 1947-48; supr. methods and standards Otis Elevator Co., Yonkers, N.Y., 1948-51; staff engr., material handling and distbn., cons. Drake, Startzman, Sheahan & Barclay, N.Y.C., 1951-55; mgr. material handling engring. Crane Co., Chgo., 1955-60; assoc., cons. A.T. Kearney & Co., Inc., Chgo., 1960-67; pres., cons. J.J. Vander Molen & Co., Internat., Oak Park, Ill. and Sun City, Ariz., 1967—. Conceptual developer of plants, warehouses and terminals, computerized conversion of inventory into space requirements for food chains. With Dutch resistance, U.S. and Can. Armed Forces, 1940-45. Mem. ASME (life), Internat. Materials Handling Soc. (nat. dir., past pres. Chgo. chpt.). Home: 10629 W Willowcreek Cir Sun City AZ 85373-1345 Office: PO Box 1656 Sun City AZ 85372-1656

VANDERPOEL, JAMES ROBERT, lawyer; b. Harvey, Ill., Sept. 27, 1955; s. Waid Richard and Ruth (Silberman) V.; m. Deanne Czabaranek, May 1987; children: Jacqueline, Robert, Jennifer. BS in Fin., Ind. U., 1978; JD, Santa Clara U., 1982. Bar: Calif. 1982, U.S. Dist. Ct. (no. dist.) Calif. 1982. Group contracts mgr. Motorola Computer Group, Tempe, Ariz., 1984—. Office: Motorola Computer Group 2900 S Diablo Way Tempe AZ 85282-3214

VANDERSPEK, PETER GEORGE, management consultant, writer; b. The Hague, Netherlands, Dec. 15, 1925; came to U.S., 1945; s. Pieter and Catherine Johanna (Rolf) V.; m. Charlotte Louise Branch, Aug. 18, 1957. Student, Tilburg (Netherlands) U., 1944; MA in Econs., Fordham U., 1950, PhD in Econs., 1954; postgrad., George Washington U., 1967-68. Internat. economist Mobil Oil Corp., N.Y.C., 1956-59; mgr. internat. market rsch. Celanese Corp., N.Y.C., 1959-63; internat. economist Bethlehem (Pa.) Steel Corp., 1964-65; sr. tech. adviser Battelle Meml. Inst., Washington, 1965-66; indsl. adviser Inter-Am. Devel. Bank, Washington, 1967-69; economist Fed. Res. Bank, N.Y.C., 1970-72; mgr. internat. market rsch. Brunswick Corp., Skokie, Ill., 1973-76; mgr. advanced planning Sverdrup Corp., St. Louis, 1979-87; cons. Sverdrup Corp., 1988-90; pres. OBEX, Inc., San Luis Obispo, Calif., 1988—. Author: Planning for Factory Automation, 1993; contbr. to profl. jours. Thomas J. Watson fellow, IBM-Fordham U., 1945-49. Mem. Nat. Assn. Bus. Economists, Mensa. Home and Office: 1314 Vega Way San Luis Obispo CA 93405-4815

VANDERTUIN, VICTORIA ELVA, book seller; b. New Bedford, Mass., Oct. 16, 1933; d. Harry Robinson and Elva Gladys (Ramsay) Belot; m. David Kent Roy, Dec. 13, 1983 (div.); children: Lowell Ramsay, Jewell Pauline. Book seller New Age World Svcs. & Books, Joshua Tree, Calif.; min. Internat. Evangelism Crusades, 1964, Inst. Mentalphysics, 1982. Editor/pub. New Age World Polaris newsletter, 1994.

VAN DERVEER, TARA, university athletic coach; b. Niagara Falls, N.Y., 1954. Grad., Indiana U., 1975. Coach women's basketball Stanford U. Cardinals, 1985—, U.S. Nat. Women's Team, 1995—. Office: Family Sports Ctr Stanford Univ Stanford CA 94305-6150*

VAN DER WERFF, TERRY JAY, management consultant, professional speaker, futurist; b. Hammond, Ind., May 16, 1944; s. Sidney and Johanna (Oostman) van der W.; m. Renee Marie Leet, Mar. 2, 1968; children: Anne Cathleen, Valerie Kay, David Edward, Michele Renée, Julia Leigh. SB and SM, MIT, 1968; DPhil, Oxford (Eng.) U., 1972. Registered profl. engr., Colo., South Africa; chartered profl. biomed. engr., South Africa. Staff engr. ARO, Inc., Tullahoma, Tenn., 1968; asst. prof. mech. engring., physiology and biophysics Colo. State U., Ft. Collins, 1970-73; vis. asst. prof. medicine U. Colo., Denver, 1973-74; head biomed. engring. U. Cape Town/Groote Schuur Hosp., Cape Town, South Africa, 1974-80; dean of sci. and engring. Seattle U., 1981-90; exec. v.p. for acad. affairs St. Joseph's U., Phila., 1990-91; pres. van der Werff Global Ltd., Seattle, 1991—. Co-author: Mathematical Models of the Dynamics of the Human Eye; author 150 book revs., monthly newspaper and mag. columns; contbr. over 40 articles to profl. jours. Recipient Ralph R. Teetor award Soc. Automotive Engrs., Detroit, 1972. Fellow Royal Soc. South Africa, Biomed. Engring. Soc. South Africa; mem. AAAS, Nat. Spkrs. Assn., Inst. Mgmt. Cons., Strategic Leadership Forum, Sigma Xi. Republican. Roman Catholic. Home: 2410 NE 123rd St Seattle WA 98125-5241

VANDERWOOD, PAUL JOSEPH, history educator; b. Bklyn., June 3, 1929; s. Joseph and Mildred (Horstmann) V. BA, Bethany Coll., 1950; MA, Memphis State U., 1956; PhD, U. Tex., 1970. Reporter Scripps-Howard Newspapers, Memphis, 1956-64; prof. San Diego State U., 1969—. Author: Night Riders of Reelfoot Lake, 1970, Disorder and Progress, 1981, Los Rurales Mexicanos, 1983, Border Fury, 1988, War Scare on the Rio Grande, 1992, Los Rostros de la Batalla, 1993. 1st lt. U.S. Army, 1951-53. Recipient Hubert Herring awards Pacific Coast Coun. Latin-Am. studies, 1981, 82, Southwest Book award Regional Libr. Assn., 1989. Mem. Conf. Latin Am. Studies, Historians Film Com., Pacific Coast and Rocky Mountain Coun. Latin Am. Studies (pres. 1970—). Democrat. Home: 8705 Jefferson Ave La Mesa CA 91941-5145 Office: San Diego State U History Dept San Diego CA 92182

VAN DEVENTER, JESS, municipal official. Chmn. bd. commrs. San Diego Unified Port Dist. Office: San Diego Unified Port Dist 3165 Pacific Hwy San Diego CA 92101

VANDEVER, JUDITH ANN, county official; b. Hemstead, N.Y., Aug. 6, 1941; d. John Anthony Klym and Kathryn M. (Lane) Trexler; children: Garret, Kimberlee Vandever Johnson. Student, U. Nev. Dep. recorder Clark County Recorder, Las Vegas, Nev., 1979-91, chief dep. recorder, 1991-93, asst. recorder, 1993-94, county recorder, 1995—. State chair. Nev. Young Woman of the Yr., 1991; mem. S.M.A.R.T. Team Clark County Sch. Dist., 1994-95, ctrl. com. State/County Dem. Ctrl. Com., 1988—; state dir. Women Officials NACo, 1997. Recipient Leadership Dedication award Amigos De HIP, 1996, Women Elected Ofcls. Spotlight award Women's Dem. Club, 1996. Mem. ASPA, Nat. Assn. County Recorders and Clks., Assn. of Profl. Mortage Women,Assn. of Recorders Mgrs. and Adminstrs., U. Nev.-Las Vegas Jean Nidetch Women's Ctr. (original founder), Leadership Las Vegas Alumni Assoc., Las Vegas C. of C. (bd. of trustees, cmty. coun. 1995—). Office: Clark County Recorder 500 S Grand Central Pkwy Las Vegas NV 89106-4506

VANDEVERE, CHRISTIAN, fashion model, writer; b. Newport, R.I., Jan. 22, 1971; s. John and Clara (Kunyck) Van D. Fashion model Vanity Ltd. Modeling Agy., L.A., Chgo., N.Y., 1987-90, Unlimited Glamour, SCA Modeling Agy., Milan, Italy, 1990—; Author: What Moves the Heavens? (nominated for 1997 Pulitzer prize), 1996. Office: Unlimited Glamour PO Box 691754 Los Angeles CA 90069

VANDIVER, LINTON MITCHELL, II, publisher; b. Rome, Ga., Sept. 7, 1937; s. Edmund Marshall and Mary Betty (Bradshaw) V.; m. Gail Hemmeter, Aug. 13, 1975 (div. Nov. 1985); children: Leslie, Linton Mitchell III. BSc, Georgetown U., 1960. Editorial dir. Butterworth, Inc., Washington, 1961-65; assoc. dir., sr. editor The Pa. State U. Press, University Park, 1966-72; pres., CEO University Park Press, Balt., 1967-85; exec. v.p., COO College Hill Press, San Diego, 1985-88; exec. v.p. First Liberty Bancorp, Inc., Washington, 1988-90; pub., COO Singular Pub. Group, Inc., San Diego, 1990-92; pres., pub., dir., CEO Index Pub. Group, Inc, San Diego, 1992—; bd. dirs. First Liberty Bancorp, Inc., Washington; bd. dirs., treas. Singular Pub. Group, Inc., San Diego. Home: 1706 MacKinnon Ave Cardiff By The Sea CA 92007 Office: Index Pub Group Inc 3368 Governor Dr Ste 273 San Diego CA 92122-2936

VAN DUSEN, PETER, artist; b. Syracuse, N.Y., Nov. 27, 1929; s. William Judson and Ruth Thayer (Burnham) Van D.; m. Mary Estelle Hougesen, June 14, 1962; 1 child, Kristin Lee. BA, U. Fla., 1958; MA, U. Oreg., 1962; PhD, U. Mich., 1971. Tchr. sci. Roosevelt Jr. High Sch., Eugene, Oreg., 1961-63; instr. Eastern Oreg. Coll., LaGrande, 1963-64; asst. prof. Colo. State Coll., Greeley, 1964-65; chmn. dept. geography Eastern Oreg. Coll., 1968-72; assoc. prof., chmn. dept. geography U. Mich., Flint, 1972-76, environ. cons., 1972-80; free-lance artist Scottsdale, Ariz., 1980—; instr. art, cons., Scottsdale, 1986—. With USN, 1951-55. Republican. Home and Office: 7643 E Chaparral Scottsdale AZ 85250

VANE, SYLVIA BRAKKE, anthropologist, cultural resource management company executive; b. Fillmore County, Minn., Feb. 28, 1918; d. John T. and Hulda Christina (Marburger) Brakke; m. Arthur Bayard Vane, May 17, 1942; children: Ronald Arthur, Linda, Laura Vane Ames. AA, Rochester Jr. Coll., 1937; BS with distinction, U. Minn., 1939; postgrad., Radcliffe U., 1944; MA, Calif. State U., Hayward, 1975. Med. technologist Dr. Frost and Hodapp, Willmar, Minn., 1939-41; head labs. Corvallis Gen. Hosp., Oreg., 1941-42; dir. lab. Cambridge Gen. Hosp., Mass., 1942-43, Peninsula Clinic, Redwood City, Calif., 1947-49; v.p. Cultural Systems Rsch., Inc., Menlo Park, Calif., 1978—; pres. Ballena Press, Menlo Park, 1981—; cons. cultural resource mgmt. So. Calif. Edison Co., Rosemead, 1978-81, San Diego Gas and Elec. Co., 1980-83, Pacific Gas and Elec. Co., San Francisco, 1982-83, Wender, Murase & White, Washington, 1983-87, Yosemite Indians, Mariposa, Calif., 1982-91, San Luis Rey Band of Mission Indians, Escondido, Calif., 1986-89, U.S. Ecology, Newport Beach, Calif., 1986-89, Riverside County Flood Control and Water Conservation Dist., 1985-95, Infotec, Inc., 1989-91, Alexander & Karshmer, Berkeley, Calif., 1989-92, Desert Water Agy., Palm Springs, Calif., 1989-90, Metropolitan Water Dist., Nat. Park Svc., 1992—. Author: (with L.J. Bean), California Indians, Primary Resources, 1977, rev. edit., 1990, The Cahuilla and the Santa Rosa Mountains, 1981, The Cahuilla Landscape, 1991; contbr. chpts. to several books. Bd. dirs. Sequoia Area coun. Girl Scouts U.S., 1954-61; bd. dirs., v.p., pres. LWV, S. San Mateo County, Calif., 1960-65. Fellow Soc. Applied Anthropology, Am. Anthropology Assn.; mem. Southwestern Anthrop. Assn. (program chmn. 1976-78, newsletter editor 1976-79), Soc. for Am. Archaeology. Mem. United Ch. of Christ. Office: Ballena Press 823 Valparaiso Ave Menlo Park CA 94025-4206

VAN EATON, ERROL HAY, career officer; b. Yakima, Wash., Sept. 9, 1947; s. Howard Hopkins and Jane Ann (Karr) van E.; m. P. Suzan Bandy, Oct. 25, 1969; children: Jason Lee, Joshua Hay. BS in Profl. Aeronautics, Embry-Riddle Aero. U., 1978; grad., U.S. Army War Coll., 1991. Cert. airline transport pilot. S-4 logistics officer 174th Gen. Support Group U.S. Army, Ft. Lawton, Wash., 1980-82, comdr. 324th Mil. Police Battalion, 1982-85, chief TMED, DCST 124th U.S. Army Res. Command, 1985-87, ADCS for Pers., 1987-88, comdr. 1397th Trans Terminal Unit, 1988-92; comdr. 540th Aviation Group Camp Murray, Tacoma, 1992-93, comdr. 66th Aviation Brigade (corps), 1993—; chief army aviation support facility 124th Army Res. Command, U.S. Army, Everett, Wash., 1972-84; supervisory aviation safety insp. FAA, Seattle, 1984-94, ret.; agt. for svc. Nat. Charter Network, Inc., Seattle, 1994—; v.p. aviation ops. Global Safety Svcs., Inc., Fayetteville, Ga., 1994—. Decorated 26 Air medals, 2 DFCs, Bronze star; Paul Harris fellow Rotary Internat. Mem. Internat. Soc. Air Safety Investigators, NG Assn., Res. Officers Assn. Home: 111-137th St SW Everett WA 98208

VAN EMBURGH, JOANNE, lawyer; b. Palmyra, N.J., Nov. 18, 1953; d. Earl Henry and Clare (Kemmerle) Van E.; m. Samuel Michael Surloff, July 6, 1993. BA summa cum laude, Catholic U., 1975; JD cum laude, Harvard Law Sch., 1978. Bar: Calif. 1978. Assoc. atty. Agnew Miller & Carlson, L.A., 1978-82; ptnr. Sachs & Phelps, L.A., 1982-91, Heller, Ehrman, White & McAuliffe, L.A., 1991-93; with Toyota Motor Sales, USA, Inc., Torrance, 1993—. Mem. ABA. Office: Toyota Motor Sales USA Inc 1900 S Western Ave Torrance CA 90509

VAN HALDEREN, LAUREL LYNN, dietitian; b. Milw., June 27, 1951; d. Vern LeRoy and Elizabeth (Siegel) Johnson; m. Robert John Van Halderen, Aug. 7, 1971; children: Nickolas James, Christine Kate. BS, U. Ariz., 1973. Registered dietitian, Ariz. Intern Houston VA Med. Ctr., 1973-74; clin. dietitian Miami (Fla.) VA Med. Ctr., 1974-76; ambulatory care dietitian Tucson VA Med. Ctr., 1976-78; chief clin. dietetic sect. Battle Creek (Mich.) VA Med. Ctr., 1978-79, chief adminstrv. dietetic sect., 1979-81; chief dietetic svc. Am. Lake VA Med. Ctr., Tacoma, Wash., 1981-84; chief dietetic svc. Phoenix VA Med. Ctr., 1984-96, adminstr. inpatient care, 1996—; chairperson VA Dietetic Decentralized Hosp. Computer Program Expert Panel, 1987-96; vice chair VA Nat. Adv. Group for Info. Security Officers, 1994. Mem. Am. Dietetic Assn., Ariz. Dietetic Assn. (bd. dirs. 1994—), Am. Soc. for Hosp. Food Svc. Adminstrs. Office: VA Medical Center 650 E Indian School Rd Phoenix AZ 85012-1839

VAN HISE, JAMES NICHOLAS, writer, editor; b. North Tonawanda, N.Y., Dec. 20, 1949; s. James Nicholas and Marianne (Hoelperl) Van H.; m. Della Cornelia Hawks, Feb. 5, 1977. Editor/publisher: (mag.) Midnight Graffiti, 1988-94; editor: (book) Midnight Graffiti, 1992; author: (book) The New SFTV, 1995; author/editor: (book) Edgar Rice Burroughs Fantastic Worlds, 1996. Home: 57754 Onaga Trail Yucca Valley CA 92284

VAN HOOMISSEN, GEORGE ALBERT, state supreme court justice; b. Portland, Oreg., Mar. 7, 1930; s. Fred J. and Helen F. (Flanagan) Van H.; m. Ruth Madeleine Niedermeyer, June 4, 1960; children: Geroge T., Ruth Anne, Madeleine, Matthew. BBA, U. Portland, 1951; JD, Georgetown U., 1955, LLM in Labor Law, 1957; LLM in Jud. Adminstrn., U. Va., 1986. Bar: D.C. 1955, Oreg. 1956, Tex. 1971, U.S. Dist. Ct. Oreg. 1956, U.S. Ct. Mil. Appeals 1955, U.S. Ct. Customs and Patent Appeals 1955, U.S. Ct. Claims 1955, U.S. Ct. Appeals (9th cir.) 1956, U.S. Ct. Appeals (D.C. cir.) 1955, U.S. Supreme Ct. 1960. Law clk. for Chief Justice Harold J. Warner Oreg. Supreme Ct., 1955-56; Keigwin teaching fellow Georgetown Law Sch., 1956-57; dep. dist. atty. Multnomah County, Portland, 1957-59; pvt. practice Portland, 1959-62; dist. atty. Multnomah County, 1962-71; dean nat. coll. dist. attys., prof. law U. Houston, 1971-73; judge Cir. Ct., Portland, 1973-81, Oreg. Ct. Appeals, Salem, 1981-88; assoc. justice Oreg. Supreme Ct., Salem, 1988—; adj. prof. Northwestern Sch. Law, Portland, Willamette U. Sch. Law, Portland State U.; mem. faculty Am. Acad. Judicial Edn., Nat. Judicial Coll.; Keigwin Teaching fellow Georgetown U. Law Sch. Mem. Oreg. Ho. of Reps., Salem, 1959-62, chmn. house jud. com. With USMC, 1951-53; col. USMCR (ret.). Recipient Disting. Alumnus award U. Portland, 1972. Master Owen M. Panner Am. Inn of Ct.; mem. ABA, Oreg. State Bar, Tex. Bar Assn., Oreg. Law Inst. (bd. dirs.), Arlington Club, Multnomah Athletic Club, Univ. Club. Roman Catholic. Office: Oreg Supreme Ct 1163 State St Salem OR 97310-1331

VAN HORN, O. FRANK, retired counselor, consultant; b. Grand Junction, Colo., Apr. 16, 1926; s. Oertel F. and Alta Maude (Lynch) Van H.; m. Dixie Jeanne MacGregor, Feb. 1, 1947 (dec. Nov. 1994); children: Evelyn, Dorothy. AA, Mesa Coll., 1961; BA, Western State Colo., 1963; MEd, Oreg. State U., 1969. Counselor, mgr. State of Oreg.-Employment, Portland and St. Helens, 1964-88; pvt. practice counselor and cons. St. Helens, 1988-96; chair Task Force on Aging, Columbia County, 1977-79; advisor Western Interstate Commn. on Higher Edn., Portland, 1971, Concentrated Employment and Tng., St. Helens, 1977, County Planning Bd., Columbia County, Oreg., 1977-80, City Planning Bd., St. Helens, 1978, Youth Employment Coun., St. Helens, 1978, Task Force on Disadvantaged Youth, St. Helens, 1980; counselor Career Mgmt. Specialists Internat.; instr. Portland C.C. Mem. ACA, Oreg. Counseling Assn., Internat. Assn. Pers. in Employment Svc. (Outstanding Achievement award 1975), Nat. Employment Counselors Assn. Democrat. Home: 1111 St Helens St Saint Helens OR 97051

VAN HORSSEN, CHARLES ARDEN, manufacturing executive; b. Mpls., June 28, 1944; s. Arden Darrel and Margaret E. (Ellingsen) V H.; m. Mary Katherine Van Kempen, Sept. 11, 1967 (div. 1975); children: Lisa, Jackie; m. Mary Ann Pashuta, Aug. 11, 1983; children: Vanessa, Garrett. BSEE, U. Minn., 1966. Design engr. Sperry Univac, Mpls., 1966-68; sr. project engr. Sperry Univac, Salt Lake City, 1975-80; systems engr. EMR Computer, Mpls., 1968-75; pres. A&B Industries Inc., Phoenix, 1980—. Patentee in field. Mem. Ariz. Tooling and Machining Assn. (bd. dirs., v.p. 1987-89, pres. 1989-91). Republican. Episcopalian. Office: A&B Industries Inc 9233 N 12th Ave Phoenix AZ 85021-3018 *Personal philosophy: The secret of success in business is attention to detail. The attainment of very high levels of quality, which is now a prerequisite for success, is the result of a correspondingly high level of attention to detail. Mistakes are like rabbits... they multiply.*

VAN KARNES, KATHLEEN WALKER, realtor; b. Providence, June 17, 1944; d. Robert Edward Walker and Mary Antoinette (Brouillard) Holl; m. Eugene Sergei Tolegian, Dec. 3, 1966 (div. 1987); children: Elisabeth Ani, Aram Eugene; m. Karl Robert Van Karnes, Mar. 31, 1990. Student, East L.A. Coll., 1970-71, Pan Am. Coll., 1962-63. Sec. 3M Co., Los Angeles, 1963-68; office adminstr. Imperial Clin. Lab., Inc., Lynwood, Calif., 1978-80, v.p., chief fin. officer, 1980-87; realtor Bliss Keeler, Inc., San Marino, Calif., 1986-90, Fred Sands Realtors, San Marino, 1990—; co-owner VK Enterprises, Pasadena, 1997—. Co-chmn. program Los Angeles chpt. founding mem. Foothill affiliate Am. Diabetes Assn., 1987. Mem. White Ho. Confederacy Mus. (founding), Nat. Assn. Realtors, Calif. Assn. Realtors, Braille Aux. Pasadena (pres. 1991-93). Republican. Presbyterian. Office: Fred Sands Realtors 751 E Cordova St Pasadena CA 91101

VAN KIRK, JOHN ELLSWORTH, cardiologist; b. Dayton, Ohio, Jan. 13, 1942; s. Herman Corwin and Dorothy Louise (Shafer) Van K.; m. Patricia L. Davis, June 19, 1966 (div. Dec. 1982); 1 child, Linnea Gray. BA cum laude, DePauw U., Greencastle, Ind., 1963; BS, Northwestern U., Chgo., 1964, MD with distinction, 1967. Diplomate Am. Bd. Internal Medicine, Am. Bd. Internal Medicine subspecialty in cardiovasc. disease; cert. Nat. Bd. Med. Examiners. Intern Evanston (Ill.) Hosp., 1967-68; staff assoc. Nat. Inst. of Allergy & Infectious Diseases., Bethesda, Md., 1968-70; resident internal medicine U. Mich. Med. Ctr., Ann Arbor, 1970-72, fellow in cardiology, 1972-74, instr. internal medicine, 1973-74; staff cardiologist Mills Meml. Hosp., San Mateo, Calif., 1974—, vice-chief medicine, 1977-78, dir. critical care, 1978-96, critical care utilizaton rev., 1988—, dir. pacemaker clinic, 1976—; dir. trantional care, mem. courtesy staff Sequoia Hosp., 1996—. Contbr. rsch. articles to profl. jours. Recipient 1st prize in landscaping Residential Estates, State of Calif., 1977. Fellow Am. Coll. Cardiology; mem. AMA (Physician's Recognition award 1968, 72, 75, 77, 80, 82, 85, 87, 89, 93), Calif. Med. Assn., San Mateo County Med. Soc., Am. Heart Assn., San Mateo County Heart Assn. (bd. dirs. 1975-78, mem. Bay area rsch. com. 1975-76, mem. edn. com. 1975-77, pres.-elect 1976-77, pres. 1977-79), Alpha Omegaa Alpha. Republican. Mem. United Brethren Ch. Office: Unified Med Clinics of Peninsula 50 S San Mateo Dr Ste 270 San Mateo CA 94401-3859

VAN LEEUWEN, KATO, psychiatrist; b. Rotterdam, The Netherlands, June 23, 1917; came to U.S., 1940; d. Henry Bernard and Evalina (van Zwanenberg) van L.; m. Sydney Lawrence Pomer, Mar. 6, 1948; children: Judith, Karen, Lisa. Student, U. Leiden Med. Sch., 1935-40; MD, Johns Hopkins U., 1943. Intern in pediat. Strong Meml. Hosp., Rochester, N.Y., 1943-44; intern in psychiatry Bellevue Hosp., N.Y.C., 1944; staff pediat. Permanente Hosp., Vancouver, Wash., 1944-45, Oakland, Calif., 1945; resident psychiatrist Mt. Zion Hosp., San Francisco, 1946-48; mental health program organizer Oakland City Health Dept., 1948-49; tng. and supervising analyst in adult and child analysis So. Calif. Psychoanalytic Inst., L.A., 1961—, former chair child and adolescent analysis sect.; staff UCLA Med. Sch., 1958—. Former bd. dirs. Little Village Nursery Sch., San Fernando Valley Child Guidance Clinic. Grantee NIMH, 1947-48, 1960s. Home: 430 S Bundy Dr Los Angeles CA 90049-4032 Office: 10444 Santa Monica Blvd Los Angeles CA 90025-5057

VAN LOUCKS, MARK LOUIS, venture capitalist, business advisor; b. Tampa, Fla., June 19, 1946; s. Charles Perry and Lenn (Bragg) Van L.; m. Eva Marianne Forsell, June 10, 1986; children: Brandon, Charlie. BA in Comm. and Pub. Policy, U. Calif., Berkeley, 1969. Sr. v.p. mktg., programming and corp. devel. United Cable TV Corp., Denver, Colo., 1970-81, advisor, 1983-89; sr. v.p., office of chmn. Rockefeller Ctr. TV Corp., N.Y.C., 1981-83; advisor United Artists Commun. Corp., Englewood, 1989-91; investor, business advisor in pvt. practice Englewood, 1983—; founder, prin. owner Glory Hole Saloon & Gaming Hall, Central City, Colo., 1990—, Harrah's Casino, Black Hawk, Colo., 1990—; chmn., CEO Bask Internat., Englewood, 1990—; bd. dirs. Wild West Devel. Corp., Denver; sr. v.p., bd. dirs. GSI Cable TV Assocs., Inc., San Francisco, 1984-90; guest lectr. on cable TV bus., 1985-91; cons. Telecommunications, Inc., Denver, 1989-93. Producer HBO spl. Green Chili Showdown, 1985; producer TV spl. 3 Days for Earth, 1987; producer, commd. artist nuclear war armament pieces; contbr. articles to profl. jours. Chmn. Cops in Crisis, Denver, 1990—; bd. dirs. The NOAH Found., Denver, 1976—; founding dir. Project for Responsible Advt., Denver, 1991-92; chmn. mayor's mktg. adv. bd., Central City, Colo. Named hon. capt. Denver Police Dept., 1991—, fin. advisor L. Rose Co., 1995—. Mem. Casino Owners Assn. (founding dir. 1989—), Colo. Gaming Assn. (dir. 1990—), recipient S'nnaeel Evol award, 1995), Glenmoor Country Club, The Village Club. Republican. Jewish. Office: MLVL Inc 333 W Hampden Ave Ste 1005 Englewood CO 80110-2340

VAN MAERSSEN, OTTO L., aerospace engineer, consulting firm executive; b. Amsterdam, The Netherlands, Mar. 2, 1919; came to U.S., 1946; s. Adolph L. and Maria Wilhelmina (Edelmann) Van M.; m. Hortensia Maria Velasquez, Jan. 7, 1956; children: Maria, Patricia, Veronica, Otto, Robert. BS in Chem. Engring., U. Mo., Rolla, 1949. Registered profl. engr., Tex., Mo. Petroleum engr. Mobil Oil, Caracas, Venezuela, 1949-51; sr. reservoir engr. Gulf Oil, Ft. Worth and San Tome, Venezuela, 1952-59; acting dept. mgr. Sedco of Argentina, Comodoro Rivadavia, 1960-61; export planning engr. LTV Aerospace and Def., Dallas, 1962-69, R & D adminstr. ground transp. div., 1970-74, engr. specialist new bus. programs, 1975-80; mgr. cost and estimating San Franciso and Alaska, 1981-84; owner OLVM Cons. Engrs., Walnut Creek, Calif., 1984—; cons. LTV Aerospace and Def., Dallas, 1984—. Served with Brit. Army. Intelligence, 1945, Germany. Mem. Soc. Petroleum Engrs. (sr.), Toastmasters (sec.-treas. Dallas chpt. 1963-64), Pennywise Club (treas. Dallas chpt. 1964-67). Democrat. Roman Catholic. Home and Office: OLVM Cons Engrs 1649 Arbutus Dr Walnut Creek CA 94595-1705

VAN MOLS, BRIAN, publishing executive; b. L.A., July 1, 1931; s. Pierre Matthias and Frieda Carthyll (MacArthur) M.; m. Barbara Jane Rose, Oct. 1, 1953 (dec. 1968); children—Cynthia Lee, Matthew Howard, Brian; m. Nancy Joan Martell, June 11, 1977; children—Thomas Bentley, Cynthia Bentley, Kristi. A.B. in English, Miami U., Oxford, Ohio, 1953. Media supr. McCann-Erickson Inc., 1955-58; salesman Kelly Smith Co., 1959; with sales Million Market Newspaper Inc., 1959-63; sales mgr. Autoproducts

Mag., 1964; sr. salesman True Mag., 1965-68, Look Mag., 1969-70; regional advt. dir. Petersen Pub. Co., Los Angeles, 1971-74; pub. Motor Trend, 1982-84; nat. automotive mktg. mgr. Playboy Enterprises, Inc., N.Y.C., 1984-85, nat. sales mgr., 1985—; western advt. dir. Playboy mag., 1985-86; assoc. pub., advt. dir. Cycle World CBS, Inc., Newport Beach, Calif., 1974-81, pub., 1981; v.p., advt. dir. Four Wheeler Mag., Canoga Pk., Calif., 1986-88; v.p., dir. advt. western div. Gen. Media, Inc., 1988-91; v.p., dir. new bus. devel. Paisano Pub., Inc., Agoura Hills, Calif., 1991-92; dir. mktg. Crown Publs., 1993-94; exec. v.p. Voice Mktg. Inc., Thousand Oaks, Calif., 1994, DMR The Reis Co., Tustin, Calif., 1995-96; COO Mesa Exhaust Prodn., Inc., Costa Mesa, Calif., 1996—. Served with U.S. Army, 1953-55. Mem. Los Angeles Advt. Club, Adcraft Club Detroit, Advt. Sportsmen of N.Y. Republican. Episcopalian. Home: 5 Odyssey Ct Newport Beach CA 92663-2349

VANNIX, C(ECIL) ROBERT, programmer, systems analyst; b. Glendale, Calif., June 14, 1953; s. Cecil H. Jr. and Gloria Jenny (Zappia) V.; married, 1980; 1 child, Robert Jeremy. AS in Plant Mgmt., BS in Indsl. Arts, Loma Linda U., 1977; AS in Info. Systems, Ventura City Coll., 1985. Instr. indsl. arts Duarte (Calif.) High Sch., 1977-79, Oxnard (Calif.) High Sch., 1979-81; computer cons. Litton Data Comand Systems, Agoura, Calif., 1976-81, sr. engr. instr., 1981-85; computer cons. McLaughlin Research Corp., Camarillo, Calif., 1976-77, sr. program analyst, 1985-88; sr. program analyst Computer Software Analysts, Camarillo, Calif., 1988-90; sr. systems analyst, mgr. S/W systems devel. V.C. Systems, 1990—. Recipient Spl. Achievement award One Way Singers, Glendale, 1975. Mem. Apple PI Computer Club, Litton Computer Club (pres. 1975-76), West Valley Xbase Users Group. Republican. Adventist. Home and Office: 407 Appletree Ave Camarillo CA 93012-5125

VAN NOY, TERRY WILLARD, health care executive; b. Alhambra, Calif., Aug. 31, 1947; s. Barney Willard and Cora Ellen (Simms) V.; m. Betsy Helen Pothen, Dec. 27, 1968; children: Bryan, Mark. BS in Bus. Mgmt., Calif. State Poly. U., 1970; MBA, Pepperdine U., 1991. CLU. Group sales rep. Mutual of Omaha, Atlanta, 1970-74, dist. mgr., 1974-77; regional mgr. Mutual of Omaha, Dallas, 1977-82; nat. sales mgr. Mutual of Omaha, Omaha, Neb., 1982-83; v.p. group mktg. Mutual of Omaha, Omaha, 1983-87; div. dir. Mutual of Omaha, Orange, Calif., 1987-95; pres., CEO, Amil Internat., Las Vegas, 1995—. Presenter in field. Vice chmn. Morning Star Luth. Ch., Omaha, 1987; mem. adv. bd. Chapman U. Sch. Bus.; mem. exec. com. ABL Orgn.; trustee Desert Rsch. Inst. Mem. Am. Soc. CLU, Orange County Employee Benefit Coun., We. Pension and Benefits Conf. Republican. Home: 2312 Prometheus Ct Henderson NV 89014 Office: Amil Internat 1050 E Flamingo Ste E120 Las Vegas NV 89119

VAN OTTEN, GEORGE ARNOLD, geography and public planning educator; b. Dallas, Oreg., Nov. 30, 1944; s. George Cecil and Kathryn May (Reed) Van O.; m. Cecilia Santiago, Aug. 20, 1966 (div. June 1981); 1 child, Robert Ryan; m. Ruth Narcho, Jan. 28, 1982; children: Nicole E., Penny A., Charles M., Mark George. BS, Oreg. Coll. Edn., 1967, MS, 1975; PhD, Oreg. State U., 1977. Tchr. Woodburn (Oreg.) H.S., 1972-73; prof. dept. geography and pub. planning No. Ariz. U., Flagstaff, 1977-93, chair dept. geography and pub. planning, 1993—. Contbr. articles to profl. jours. Mem. Ariz. Commn. on Environ., 1983-85, grad. stds. com. Ariz. State Bd. Edn., 1985, Flagstaff Multi-Cultural Coalition, 1994—. With USAF, 1967-72, USAFR, 1972-82; lt. col. USAR, 1982-96; ret. Mem. Nat. Coun. Geog. Edn., Assn. Am. Geographers (splty. group leader 1985-95), Pacific Coast Geographers, Ariz. Geog. Alliance, Phi Kappa Phi. Democrat. Baptist. Office: No Ariz U Dept Geography Pub Planning PO Box 15016 Flagstaff AZ 86011-5016

VAN PELT, TAMISE JO, English educator; b. Wichita, Kans., Apr. 22, 1947; d. Joseph and E. Gayle (Bozeman) Van P. BA, Kans. State U., 1969; MA, U. Nev., 1988; PhD, U. Ill., 1994. Instr. U. Nev., Reno, 1987-90; tchg. asst. U. Ill., Urbana-Champaign, 1990-94; asst. prof. theory Idaho State U., Pocatello, 1994—. Author: Birth Pattern Psychology, 1985; contbr. articles to profl. jours. Mem. MLA, Shakespeare Assn. Am., Marlowe Soc., Assn. Psychoanalysis of Culture & Soc., Internat. Assn. Philosophy and Literature, Internat. Soc. Study of European Ideas. Democrat. Office: Dept English Idaho State U PO Box 8056 Pocatello ID 83209-8056

VAN REMMEN, ROGER, management consultant; b. Los Angeles, Sept. 30, 1950; s. Thomas J. and Elizabeth (Vincent) V.; B.S. in Bus., U. So. Calif., 1972. Account mgr. BBDO, Los Angeles, 1972-78; account mgr. Dailey & Assocs. Advt., L.A., 1978—, v.p., mgmt. supr., 1980-84, sr. v.p., 1985-90; dir. Aux. Aids Inc., Richstone Family Ctr; dir. mktg. communications, Teradata, 1990-91, ptnr. Brown, Bernardy, Van Remmen Exec. Search, L.A., 1991—. Chmn. adv. bd. El Segundo (Calif.) First Nat. Bank; bd. dirs. Advt. Emergency Relief Fund., Richstone Family Ctr. Mem. Univ. So. Calif. Alumni Assn., Advt. Club of Los Angeles. Roman Catholic. Home: 220 9th St Manhattan Beach CA 90266-5506 Office: Brown Bernardy Van Remmen 12100 Wilshire Blvd Ste 40M Los Angeles CA 90025-7109

VAN RIPER, KENNETH ALAN, astrophysicist and researcher; b. New Brunswick, N.J., Feb. 7, 1949; s. Raymond Walsh Van Riper and Beulah Mae Higgins Scheer. AB, Cornell U., 1970; PhD, U. Pa., 1976. Rsch. assoc. U. Chgo., 1976, U. Ill., Urbana, 1978-81; mem. tech. staff Los Alamos (N.Mex.) Nat. Lab., 1981-95. Editor: Isolated Pulsars, 1993; contbr. articles to profl. jours. Mem. Am. Astron. Soc., Am. Phys. Soc., Internat. Astron. Union, New Eng. Sonett Club.

VANSELL, SHARON LEE, nursing administrator, nursing educator, researcher, obstetrical and psychiatric clinical nurse; b. Indpls., Feb. 7, 1944; d. Leo Roland and Mimadel (Klipsch) VanSell; m. Thomas Wayne Davidson, Apr. 10, 1967 (div. Nov. 1978); 1 child, Daniel Zane; m. Glenn William Meintz, Mar. 17, 1982 (div. Mar. 1995). BSN, Murray State U., 1968; MEd in Health Edn., Memphis State U., 1971; MS in Nursing Administrn., U. Colo., 1985; EdD in Guidance Counseling, U. Denver, 1986. Sr. rsch. assoc. Planning and Human Systems, Inc., Washington, 1975-77; ob-gyn coord. Meml. Hosp., Colorado Springs, Colo., 1978-79; indsl. nurse Ramport Industries, Colorado Springs, 1979-80; psychiat. nurse N.E.E.D. Jr./Sr. High Sch., Colorado Springs, 1980-84; dir. rsch. Ireland Corp., Englewood, Colo., 1984; staff nurse perinatal float pool Univ. Hosp., Denver, 1985; dir. reproductive and pediatric nursing, asst. dir. patient care svcs. U. Calif. Med. Ctr., San Diego, 1986-90; relief charge nurse Charter Hosp., Las Vegas, 1990-94; assoc. prof. U. Nev., Las Vegas, 1990-96; relief charge nurse Manti Vista Hosp., 1994-95; maternal child nurse Sunrise Med. Ctr., 1995-96; dir. nursing Pueblo (Colo.) Cmty. Coll., 1996—; nursing cons. Comprehensive Health Care Devel., Inc., Fairfax, 1974—, Bur. Quality Assurance and Profl. Svcs. Revises Orgn., DHEW, Rockville, Md., 1972-75; pres., ceo C.P.E., Colorado Springs, 1977-80; founder NURMETRICS and computational nursing, 1990—; pres. Omega Techs., Inc., Las Vegas, 1995—. Editor: PSRO: Utilization and Adult, 1976, Alcoholism and Health, 1980; sr. author: Nursing Care Evaluation: Concurrent and Retrospective, 1977, Obstetrical Nursing, 1980; co-author: PSRR: The Promise Perspective, 1981; mem. editl. bd. RN, Family and Cmty. Health Jour.; contbr. articles to profl. jours. 1dst lt. U.S. Army Nurse Corps, 1966-69. U. Colo. Gannett scholar for excellence in nursing, 1985-86; recipient March of Dimes So. Nev. Nurse of the Yr. award in Edn., 1992, Disting. Women of Nev. award, 1995, Future Vision Sci. award, 1995. Mem. Nev. Nurses Assn., Western Inst. Nursing (nominating com. 1988-90), Phi Kappa Delta, Sigma Theta Tau. Office: Pueblo CC 900 W Orman Pueblo CO 81004

VAN SICKLE, FREDERICK L., federal judge; b. 1943; m. Jane Bloomquist. BS, U. Wis., 1965; JD, U. Wash., 1968. Ptnr. Clark & Van Sickle, 1970-75; prosecuting atty. Douglas County, Waterville, Wash., 1971-75; judge State of Wash. Superior Ct., Grant and Douglas counties, 1975-79, Chelan and Douglas Counties, 1979-91; judge U.S. Dist. Ct. (ea. dist.) Wash., Spokane, 1991—; co-chair rural ct. com. Nat. Conf. State Trial Judges, 1987-91. 1st lt. U.S. Army, 1968-70. Mem. ABA (nat. conf. fed. judges jud. adminstrn.), Am. Adjudicature Soc., Wash. State Bar Assn., Masons (pres. Badger mountain lodge 1982-83), Scottish Rite, Spokane Rotary, Shriners. Office: US Dist Cts US Courthouse PO Box 2209 920 W Riverside Ave Rm 914 Spokane WA 99201-2209

VAN STEKELENBURG, MARK, food service executive. Pres., CEO G.V.A., The Netherlands; chmn., CEO Rykoff-Sexton Inc., Wilkes-Barre, Pa. Office: Rykoff-Sexton Inc 613 Baltimore Dr Wilkes Barre PA 18702-7944*

VAN VELZER, VERNA JEAN, retired research librarian; b. State College, Pa., Jan. 22, 1929; d. Harry Leland and Golda Lillian (Cline) Van V. BS in Library Sci., U. Ill., 1950; MLS, Syracuse U., 1957. Head librarian Orton Library, Ohio State U., Columbus, 1952-54; serials assoc. Syracuse (N.Y.) U. Library, 1954-57; head cataolger SRI Internat., Menlo Park, Calif., 1957-58; head librarian GE Microwave Lab., Palo Alto, Calif., 1958-64, Fairchild Rsch. and Devel. Lab., Palo Alto, 1964-65, Sylvania Intelligence Library, Mountain View, Calif., 1965-66; rsch. librarian ESL Inc. subs. TRW, Sunnyvale, Calif., 1966-92; cons. in field. Vol. Lantos Re-election Campaign, San Mateo, Calif., 1972—, Wildlife Rescue, Palo Alto, 1980—; mem. Barron Park Assn., Palo Alto, 1975—; mem. Calif. Polit. Action Com. for Animals, San Francisco, 1986—. Recipient Commemorative medal of Honor, Am. Biographical Inst., 1946, Paul Revere Cup, Santa Clara Camellia Soc., 1968, Internat. Cultural Diploma of Honor, Am. Biographical Inst., 1988. Mem. Spl. Librs. Assn., IEEE, AIAA, Calif. Holistic Vet. Assn., Internat. Primate Protection League, People for Ethical Treatment of Animals, Assn. Old Crows, In Def. of Animals, Primarily Primates, Sierra Club, World Wildlife Club, Greenpeace. Home: 4048 Laguna Way Palo Alto CA 94306-3122

VAN WHY, REBECCA RIVERA, retired guidance counselor; b. Casa Blanca, N.Mex., Sept. 14, 1932; d. Charles and Doris (Thompson) Rivera; m. Raymond Richard Van Why, Aug. 27, 1955; children: Raymond R., Ronald R., Randall R. BS, U. N.Mex., 1959. Tchr. Bur. of Indian Affairs, Albuquerque, 1960-62, guidance counselor, 1969-94, tchr., supr., 1973-74, acting dir. student life, 1987, ret., 1994; head tchr. Laguna (N.Mex.) Headstart OEO, 1967-69, acting dir., 1969. Appt. N.Mex. Youth Conservation Corps Commn., 1992-97. Recipient Cert. of Recognition, Sec. of Interior, 1975, Cert. of Appreciation, State of N.Mex., 1986, N.Mex. Commn. on the Status of Women, 1993; named honoree Internat. Women's Day, U. N.Mex., 1987. Republican. Home: 14417 Central Ave NW Albuquerque NM 87121-7756

VAN WINKLE, WESLEY ANDREW, lawyer, educator; b. Kansas City, Mo., Sept. 22, 1952; s. Willard and Cleone Verlee (O'Dell) Van W.; m. Ruth Kay Shelby, Apr. 10, 1984. B. U. Nebr., 1972; JD, San Francisco Law Sch., 1987. Bar: Calif. 1987, U.S. Dist. Ct. (no. dist.) Calif. 1987, U.S. Supreme Ct. 1994. Atty. Bagetelos & Fadem, San Francisco, 1987-91; pvt. practice Berkeley, Calif., 1991—; prof. law San Francisco Law Sch., 1990—; apptd. mem. Calif. Appellate Indigent Def. Oversight Adv. com., 1997—. Editor (legal newspaper/rev.) Res Ipsa Loquitur, 1986. Mem. Calif. Attys. for Criminal Justice, Calif. Appellate Def. Counsel (v.p., appellate indigent def. oversight adv. com.), San Francisco Law Sch. Alumni Assn., Delta Theta Phi. Democrat. Office: PO Box 5216 Berkeley CA 94705-0216

VARGA, STEVEN CARL, reinsurance company executive, consultant; b. Columbus, Ohio, Jan. 19, 1952; s. Stephen Thomas and Eva Jeney V.; BA in Psychology and Philosophy magna cum laude, Carthage Coll., 1977, MSA with honors Cen. Mich. U., 1986; m. Michelle L. Auld, Nov. 17, 1973; children: Zachary Steven, Joshua Lewis. Svc. mgr. Chem-Lawn Corp., Columbus, 1972-75; respiratory therapist St. Catherine's Hosp., Kenosha, Wis., 1975-77; policy analyst Nationwide Ins. Cos., Columbus, 1978-79, asst. mgr. Corp. Tng. Ctr., 1979-86; dir. ednl. tng. Sullivan Payne Co., Seattle, 1986-88, asst. v.p. human resource devel., 1989-93; v.p. Reinsurance Solutions, Inc., Seattle, 1994-95; sr. v.p. Unltd. Potential, Inc., 1995—. Mem. civic action program com., 1979-86, Nat. Mental Health Assn., 1972-79; mem. occupational adv. coun. Bellevue C.C., 1989—; v.p. Kenosha County chpt., 1975-77; mem. Franklin County (Ohio) Mental Health Assn., 1978-86. Rhodes scholar, 1976-77. Mem. Am. Soc. Tng. and Devel., Soc. Broadcast Engrs., Ins. Inst. Am. (contbg. author Principles of Reinsurance, vol. I and II, nat. advisory com. assoc. in reinsurance program), Brokers and Reinsurers Markets Assn. (edn. and tng. co-chair), Am. Psychol. Assn., Am. Mgmt. Assn., Soc. of Ins. Trainers and Educators (chmn. regional area planning com.), Carthage Coll. Alumni Assn., Phi Beta Kappa, Psi Chi. Home: 15586 Sandy Hook Rd NE Poulsbo WA 98370-7823 Office: Unltd Potential Inc 400 Warren Ave Ste 410 Bremerton WA 98337-1408

VARGAS, AL GARCIA, building contractor; b. Fresno, Calif., Apr. 21, 1943; s. Aurelio Villegas and Anita (Garcia) V.; m. Luci Guerrero Cruz, Sept. 22, 1968; children: Sylvia, Al Jr., George. AA, Fresno City Coll., 1974; BS in Bus. Adminstrn., Calif. State U., Fresno, 1977. Acctg. clerk Anderson/Clayton, Fresno, 1968-70; constrn. salesman Wilson Constrn., Fresno, 1974-76; bldg. contractor Vargas Homes, Fresno, 1981-82; mktg. exec. Econ. Opportunity Commns. Fresno County, 1983-90; bldg. contractor Sequoia Homes, Fresno, 1990—. Recipient Ambassador award Calif.-Nev. Weatherization Bd., Sacramento, 1985, Superior Performance award, Fresno County Econs. Opportunity Commns. Weatherization Project, 1985. Republican. Mem. Assembly of God Ch. Home and Office: 6643 Latonia PO Box 751 Laton CA 93242-0751

VARGAS, FIDEL A., mayor. AB in Soc. Studies cum laude, Harvard U.; tchg. cert., Harvard U. Grad. Sch. Edn. Cert. tchr., Calif. Bus. analyst McKinsey & Co., N.Y.C.; edn. specialist Nat. Coun. La Raza; exec. asst. to dir. European ops. Little League Baseball Inc.; sr. policy analyst L.A. Mayor Richard J. Riordan; prin. The Mountaintop Group (mgmt. consulting firm); elected mayor City of Baldwin Park, Calif.; apptd. by Pres. Clinton to adv. coun. on Social Security, 1994-95. Named one of top 50 U.S. leaders under 40 yrs of age, Time Mag.; named Person of Week, KCBS, KABC; profiled in Wall St. Jour., L.A. Times, Newsweek, Hispanic (mag.), Hispanic Bus. (mag.), and Swing (mag.). Office: Office of Mayor 14403 E Pacific Ave Baldwin Park CA 91706

VARGO, GEORGE JAMES, JR., health physicist; b. Pitts., July 3, 1956; s. George James and Lois Irene (Sammer) V.; m. Janet Ormiston Humphrey, Dec. 7, 1996. BS, Duquesne U., 1978; MS, Ga. Inst. Tech., 1988; PhD, Columbia Pacific U., 1989. Diplomate Soc. Radiol. Protection, Am. Bd. Health Physics (comprehensive and power reactor splty.), Nat. Registry Radiation Protection Technologists; cert. hazart control mgmt., hazardous materials mgr. Sr. health physicist Radiation Svc. Orgn., Laurel, Md., 1978-79; instr. tng. N.Y. Power Authority, Lycoming, 1979-80, shift tech. advisor, 1980-81, radiol. tng. supr., 1981-84; lead radiol. specialist N.Y. Power Authority, White Plains, 1984-85; radiol. engring. gen. supr. N.Y. Power Authority, Lycoming, 1985-89; radiol. and environ. svcs. mgr. N.Y Power Authority, Lycoming, 1989-91; staff scientist Battelle-Pacific N.W. labs., Richland, Wash., 1991—; adj. asst. prof. nuclear engring. and engring. physics Rensselaer Poly. Inst., 1990-94; adjuct assoc. prof. nuclear engring. and engring. Physics Rensselaer Poly Tech. Inst., 1994—. Editorial bd. Health Physics jour., 1993—, software editor, 1993—; author conf. papers; inventor directional radiation probe. Mem. ASTM (chair subcom. E10.04 radiation protection methodology 1993—), Health Physics Soc. (admissions com. 1989-92, manpower and profl. edn. com. 1992-93, continuing edn. com. 1993), Am. Nuclear Soc., Am. Indsl. Hygiene Assn., Soc. Radiol. Protection (U.K.), N.Y. Acad. Scis., Am. Bd. Health Physics (power reactor splty panel of examiners 1987-91, panel chair 1991, bd. dirs. 1993-95, sec. 1996, vice chair 1997), Can. Radiation Protection Assn., Soc. for Risk Analysis. Home: PO Box 338 Richland WA 99352-0338 Office: Battelle-Pacific Nat Lab Health Protection Dept K3-56 PO Box 999 # 56 Richland WA 99352-0999

VARMUS, HAROLD ELIOT, government health institutes administrator, educator; b. Oceanside, N.Y., Dec. 18, 1939; s. Frank and Beatrice (Barasch) V.; m. Constance Louise Casey, Oct. 25, 1969; children: Jacob Carey, Christopher Isaac. AB, Amherst Coll., 1961, DSc (hon.), 1984; MA, Literature, Harvard U., 1962; MD, Columbia U. Med. Sch., 1966. Lic. physician, Calif. Intern, resident Presbyn. Hosp., N.Y.C., 1966-68; clin. assoc. NIH, Bethesda, Md., 1968-70; lectr. dept. microbiology U. Calif., San Francisco, 1970-72, asst. prof., depts. microbiology and immunology, biochemistry and biophysics, 1972-74, assoc. prof., 1974-79, prof., 1979-83, Am. Cancer Soc. research prof., 1984-93; dir. NIH, Bethesda, Md., 1993—; chmn. bd. on biology NRC. Editor: Molecular Biology of Tumor Viruses, 1982, 85; Readings in Tumor Virology, 1983; assoc. editor Genes and Development Jour., Cell Jour.; mem. editorial bd. Cancer Surveys. Named Calif. Acad. Sci. Scientist of Yr., 1982; co-recipient Lasker Found. award, 1982, Passano Found. award, 1983, Armand Hammer Cancer prize, 1984, GM Alfred Sloan award 1984, Shubitz Cancer prize, 1985, Nobel Prize in Physiology or Medicine, 1989. Mem. AAAS, NAS, Inst. Medicine of NAS, Am. Soc. Virology, Am. Soc. Microbiology, Am. Acad. Arts and Scis. Democrat. Office: National Istitutes of Health Bldg 1 Rm 126 1 Center Dr MSC 0148 Bethesda MD 20892-0148*

VARO, MARTON-GEZA, sculptor; b. Szekelyudvarhely, Hungary, Mar. 15, 1943; came to U.S., 1989; s. Gyorgy and Viola (Tomori) V.; 1 child, Kata; m. Ilona Magdolna Kalmar, Sept. 25, 1979; children: Marton, Ilona. Diploma in Fine Arts, Ion Andreescu U., Cluj, Romania, 1966. Sculptor in limestone and marble. Works include sculptures at Conv. Ctr. Budapest, 1984, Breaking Free, Brea, Calif., 1990, Peace Meml., Palm Desert, Calif., 1992, Dallas Plaza of the Americas, 1992, marble sculpture at Volos, Greece, 1988, Tustin Ranch Market Place, Calif., Art Inst. of So. Calif., Laguna Beach, Calif. Recipient award Studio of Young Artists, Hungary, 1976, Munkacsy prize Ministry of Culture, Hungary, 1984; Derkovits grantee Ministry of Culture, 1972-75; Fulbright scholar, 1989-91. Home: 2 Charity Irvine CA 92612-3255

VAROGLU, MARY, wholesale distribution executive; b. Mt. Vernon, N.Y., Apr. 11, 1960; d. Jack Walter and Jean (Kish) Milder; m. Salih Varoglu, Oct. 9, 1982. Student, Pace U., 1979-81. Adminstrv. dir. Jingles Internat., N.Y.C., 1982-85; pres. Elite Salon Svcs., Colorado Springs, Colo., 1985—. Mem. Beauty and Barber Supply Inst. Roman Catholic. Home: 2955 Electra Dr Colorado Springs CO 80906

VASCHE, MARK, editor. Mng. editor Modesto (Calif.) Bee. Office: Modesto Bee 1325 H St Modesto CA 95352

VÁSQUEZ, BEN L., school guidance counselor; b. Vancouver, Wash., Jan. 31, 1945; s. Eusebio and Dora (Ortiz) V.; m. Rose M. Martinez; 1 child, Nadia R. BS, Weber State U., Ogden, Utah, 1967; MA, N.Mex. State U., 1974. Cert. sch. counselor, K-12 tchr. elem. and secondary social studies, Spanish. Tchr. Colegio Americano, Ibagué, Colombia, 1970; intern/tchr. Tchr. Corp./N.Mex. State U., Las cruces, 1972-74; tchr. Santa Fe (N.Mex.) Pub. Schs., 1974-77; tchr./master tchr. Albuquerque Pub. Schs., 1977-80; program specialist bilingual program N.Mex. Boys Sch., Springer, N.Mex., 1980-82; sch. counaselor Springer Mcpl. Schs., 1983-90, Las Vegas (N.Mex.) City Schs., 1990—; dir. Head Start, Mora, N.Mex., 1971, Helping Hands, Inc., Mora, 1972; cons. in field. Editor Sunspots newsletter, 1994-96, Agua Pura newsletter, 1996; author/co-author various curriculum guides, 1972-95. Adv. bd. San Miguel Mora Mental Health, Las Vegas; coord. Grads Dads, Las Vegas City Schs.. Recipient Gov.'s Accomendation for Svc. to Edn. and Youth, State of N.Mex., 1994. Mem. ASCD, N.Mex. Counseling Assn. (exec. bd., pub. chmn.), Kiwanis (newsletter editor 1995-96, program chair, bd. dirs.), Masons (scholarship chair). Republican. Presbyterian. Home: PO Box 126 Chacon NM 87713

VASSALLI, SHORTY See COLLINGS, CELESTE LOUISE

VASSBERG, JOHN CHARLES, aerospace engineer; b. Lyford, Tex., Jan. 28, 1959; s. Charles John and Carole Shere (Sundra) V.; m. Claire Ann Land, Dec. 31, 1982; 1 child, Dylan Land. BS in Aerospace Engring., Tex. A&M Univ., 1980, MS in Aerospace Engring., 1981; PhD in Aerospace Engring., Univ. So. Calif., 1992. Engr. asst. Gen. Dynamics, Ft. Worth, 1979; engr. scientist McDonnell-Douglas Corp., Long Beach, Calif., 1982-83; engr. scientist specialist McDonnell-Douglas Corp., Long Beach, 1983-87, sr. engr., scientist, 1987-94, prin. engr., scientist, 1994-96, sr. prin. engr., 1996—; student rsch. asst. Tex. A&M Univ., College Station, 1978-79, grad. rsch., tchg. asst., 1980-81; grad. rsch. asst. Univ. So. Calif., L.A., 1985-90; cons. in field, 1987—. Boeing scholar Tex. A&M Univ., 1978. Mem. AIAA, Douglas Aircraft Mgmt. Club, Phi Kappa Phi, Sigma Gamma Tau, Tau Beta Pi. Home: 5918 Bixby Village Dr # 106 Long Beach CA 90803 Office: McDonnel Douglas Corp MS 800 33 3855 Lakewood Blvd Long Beach CA 90846

VASUDEVAN, RAMASWAMI, engineering consultant; b. Trichi, Tamil Nad, India, Nov. 28, 1947; came to U.S. 1970; s. Rajagopal and Jembakalakshmi; m. Padmini Vasudevan, mar. 20, 1980 (div. 1992). BE, Madras U., India, 1970; MS, UCLA, 1972. Registered profl. engr., Calif.; cert. plant engr., Calif. Project engr. Anco Engrs., Culver City, Calif., 1971-77; mgr. Wyle Labs., Norco, Calif., 1977-78, EDAC, Palo Alto, Calif., 1978-82; project mgr. Los Alamos (N.Mex.) Tech. Assocs., 1982-85; assoc. EQE Inc., Irvine, Calif., 1985-87; pres. Sidhi Cons., Inc., Santa Ana, Calif., 1987—. Contbr. articles to profl. jours. Mem. ASME, IEEE (stds. com. 1982-84), EERI, NFPA, EPRI-EQAG, Am. Inst. Plant Engrs., Am. Facilities Engrs., Nat. Elec. Testing Assn. Republican. Office: Sidhi Cons Inc 4642 E Chapman Ave # 210 Orange CA 92869-4111

VATH, RAYMOND EUGENE, psychiatrist, educator; b. Butte, Mont., Aug. 2, 1931; s. Gustave Henry and Clara Wilhelmina (Meyers) V.; m. Joanne Vath, June 7, 1952; children: Connie, Christy, Brian. BS, Coll. Great Falls, 1952; MD, U. Wash., 1965. Diplomate Nat. Bd. Med. Examiners, Am. Coll. Forensic Examiners, Am. Coll. Forensic Medicine; lic. physician, lic. surgeon, Wash. Meteorologist USAF, 1952-61; intern Madigan Gen. Hosp., Tacoma, 1965-66; lectr. family counseling Seattle Pacific U., 1969-80; prof. counseling Seattle br. Fuller Theo. Sem., 1971-74; rsch. asst. dept. psychiatry U. Wash., Seattle, 1962-65, resident in psychiatry, 1966-69, clin. instr. psychiatry and preventive medicine, 1965-82, clin. asst. prof. psychiatry, 1982—; cons. King County Pub. Health Nurses, 1969-72, MEDEX/U. Wash. and Wash. State Med. Assn., 1969-72, Cath. Children's Svcs., 1969-79, Teen Challenge Drug Program, 1970-80, Youth With a Mission, 1974-85, Neighbors Who Care program area ch., 1974-87; condr. seminars Marrying for Life, 1980, 81; active Student Rsch. Soc., Sch. Medicine U. Wash. Author: Counseling Those with Eating Disorders, 1986, (with D. O'Neill) Marrying for Life, 1982; contbr. chpt. to: Eating Disorders: Nutritional Therapy in the Recovery Process, 1992; contbr. articles to profl. pubs.; guest appearances various radio and TV programs, including Seattle Today, 1981, Regis Philbin Show, NBC, 1982, others. Chmn. bd. dirs. Mercy Corps, Internat., 1981—, N.W. Found. for Eating Disorders, 1981-85. Capt. USAF, 1952-61, capt. M.C. U.S. Army, 1965-66. Mem. AMA, Wash. State Med. Soc., Am. Psychiat. Assn., Wash. State Psychiat. Assn., King County Med. Soc., Am. Soc. Clin. Psychopharmacology, Kappa Pi Lambda. Home: 5009 134th Pl NE Bellevue WA 98005-1019 Office: 1715 114th Ave SE # 208 Bellevue WA 98004

VATTER, HAROLD GOODHUE, economics educator; b. Glen Rock, N.J., Dec. 18, 1910; s. George C. and Della Goodhue V.; children: Marguerita, Theresa, Marc. B.A., U. Wis.-Madison, 1936; M.A., Columbia U., 1938; Ph.D., U. Calif.-Berkeley, 1950. Assoc. prof. econs. Oreg. State U., Corvallis, 1948-56, U. Mass., Amherst, 1956-58; assoc. prof. Carleton Coll., Northfield, Minn., 1958-64; prof. econs. Portland State U., Oreg., 1965-79, prof. econs. emeritus, 1980—. Author: U.S. Economy in the 1950s, 1960, Drive to Industrial Maturity, 1975, U.S. Economy in World War II, 1985, (with John Walker) The Inevitability of Government Growth, 1990. Lilly fellow, U. Chgo., 1964. Mem. Am. Econ. Assn., Econ. History Assn., Assn. Evolutionary Econs. Home: 3041 NE 25th Ave Portland OR 97212-3462 Office: Portland State U PO Box 751 Portland OR 97207-0751

VAUGHAN, MARK BASS, naval officer; b. Norfolk, Va., Oct. 9, 1958; s. Edgar III and Patricia (Bass) V.; m. Donna Ruth Hallberg; children: Anna, Nathan, Rachel. BS in Aerospace Engring., U.S. Naval Acad., 1980. Commd. ensign USN, 1980, advanced through grades to comdr., 1995; divsn. officer Naval Air Test Ctr., Patuxent River, Md., 1980; flight instr. naval aviator Tng. Squadron 3, Milton, Fla., 1981-83; leadership instr. Naval Tech. Tng. Ctr., San Francisco, 1983-86; ops. officer Naval Air Facility, Washington, 1986-87; aircraft maintenance officer, logistics support Squadron 48, Washington, 1987-89; ops. officer logistics support Squadron 59, Dallas, 1989-92; ops. desert shield desert storm, 1990-91; tng. officer Logistics Support Wing, Dallas, 1992-93; officer in charge logistics support Squadron 57, San Diego, 1993-95; program mgr. Naval Air Reserve Force, New Orleans, La., 1995-96; exec. officerlogistics support Squadron 57, San Diego, Calif., 1996—; master tng. specialist USN, San Francisco, 1986, transport aircraft comdr., 1987-94; airline transport pilot FAA, Dallas, 1992. Asst. coach Tierra Santa Little League, San Diego, 1994. Mem. SAR,

Jamestowne Soc., Soc. Mayflower Descendants, Huguenot Soc. Presbyterian. Address: 234 Bearing Ln El Cajon CA 92019 Office: VR 57 PO Box 357108 NAS NI San Diego CA 92135

VAUGHAN, ROBERT OREN, lawyer; b. Elko, Nev., Mar. 19, 1925; m. Barbara Schreiner, 1950 (dec. June 1996); children: Meg, Brad. BA, U. Nev., Reno, 1950; JD cum laude, U. Denver, 1952; Assoc. degree (hon.), Gt. Basin Coll., 1996. Bar: Nev. 1952, U.S. Dist. Nev. 1955, U.S. Supreme Ct. 1961, U.S. Ct. Appeals (9th cir.) 1973. Ptnr. Vaughan & Hull, Ltd. and predecessor firms, Elko, 1953—; mem. Nev. State Assembly, 1955-58, minority floor leader, 1958; city atty. City of Wells, Nev., 1957-75; dep. city atty. City of Elko, 1962-82; gen. counsel Wells Rural Electric Co., 1958—, Mt. Wheeler Power, Inc., 1963-92, Nev. Rural Electric Assn., 1974; mem. Nev. Jud. Selection Commn., 1981-89; ptnr. AAA Self Storage, Western Enterprises; owner Vaughan Ranch, Ruby Valley, Nev., 1958-95. Bd. editors U. Denver Law Rev., 1952. Trustee Elko County Libr. Bd., 1959-63; bd. dirs. Elko Knife and Fork Club, 1962; dir. Heart Fund, 1957-85; active youth sports; trustee No. Nev. C.C. Found., 1981—, mem. exec. com., planned giving com., 1991—, chmn. spkrs. bur., 1989-90, chmn. major gifts com., 1991—; mem. devel. com. Gt. Basin Coll. Found., 1992—; deacon, ruling elder 1st Presbyn. Ch. of Elko. 1st lt. USAF, 1943-47; with Nev. N.A.G., 1948-50. Mem. ABA, Nev. State Bar Assn. (adminstrv. com. 1956-66, adminstrv. com. 1961-66, probate and property practice com., unauthorized practice of law com., fee dispute com.), Elko County Bar Assn. (pres. 1963-64), Elko C. of C. (past bd. dirs., treas.), Rotary (pres. 1964-65), Masons, Royal and Select Masters, Royal Arch, K.T., Shriners, Ea. Star. Republican. Home: 1065 Dotta Dr Elko NV 89801-2707 Office: Vaughan & Hull Ltd 530 Idaho St PO Box 1420 Elko NV 89803

VAUGHN, BILLY ELDRIDGE, psychology educator, publisher; b. Houston, Mar. 2, 1951; s. David Isaac Vaughn and Willie Beatrice (Barzeron) Ward; m. Elizabeth Francis, Aug. 22, 1984 (div. Oct. 1995); 1 child, David Torrey; m. Karin Margareta Ingvarsdotter, Aug. 11, 1996. BS, U. Calif., San Diego, 1978, MS, 1984, PhD, 1986. Mem. faculty Calif. Sch. of Profl. Psychology, San Diego, 1987—, Calif. State U., Fullerton, 1989-96. Author: Walking on Multicultural Eggs, 1996, Ethnic Diversification of Psychology, 1990; inventor cultural game. Bd. dirs. Elem. Inst. of Sci., San Diego, 1993—. Mem. APA, Nat. Coun. Profl. Schs. of Psychology, Soc. for Psychol. Studies of Social Issues, Nat. Assn. for Multicultural Edn. (pres. 1996—). Home: PO Box 720207 San Diego CA 92172-0207 Office: Calif Sch Profl Psychology 6160 Cornerstone Ct E San Diego CA 92121

VAUGHN, KATHY, municipal official. Pres. bd. commrs. Pub. Utility Dist., Everett, Wash. Office: Office Bd Commrs Pub Utility Dist 2320 California St Everett WA 98201

VAUGHN, MICHAEL JAMES, arts critic, poet; b. Brunswick, Maine, Jan. 1, 1962; s. Harold James and Grace Winifred (Maze) V. BA in Journalism, San Jose (Calif.) State U., 1984. Dir. publicity Montalvo Ctr. for the Arts, Saratoga, Calif., 1989-92; opera and theater critic Palo Alto (Calif.) Weekly, 1993—; dir. Poetry Ctrl. Reading Series, Campbell, Calif., 1991—; outreach artist Tapestry in Talent, San Jose, 1995—. Author: (novel) Frozen Music, 1995; contbr. poetry to Eclectic Literary Forum, North Atlantic Rev., Orange Coast Rev.

VAUGHT, TONY STEVEN, aquaculturist; b. Susanville, Calif., July 15, 1954; s. Tommie Gene and Sulvia Louise Vaught; m. Rebecca Lou Allen, Sept. 9, 1978; children: Ryan Eugene, Megan Rebecca. AA, Lassen C.C., Susanville, 1975; student, Chico State U., 1976-78. Instr. Lassen C.C., 1985; mgr. Chico (Calif.) Game Fish Farm, 1978-85; gen. mgr. Arrowhead Fisheries, Gerber, Calif., 1985-87; owner Profl. Aquaculture Svcs., Chico, 1987—; chmn. adv. bd. Calif. Dept. Fish and Game, 1980-95; instr. Calif. State U., Chico, 1991-95; speaker at profl. confs. and workshops. Rschr. propagation of first domestic striped bass in U.S. Elder, Bidwell Meml. Presbyn. Ch., Chico, 1990—. Mem. Calif. Aquaculture Assn. (past pres.). Office: Profl Aquaculture Svcs 971 East Ave Chico CA 95926

VAUX, DORA LOUISE, sperm bank official, consultant; b. White Pine, Mont., Aug. 8, 1922; d. Martin Tinus and Edna Ruth (Pyatt) Palmlund; m. Robert Glenn Vaux, Oct. 25, 1941; children: Jacqueline, Cheryl, Richard, Jeanette. Grad. high sch., Bothell, Wash. Photographer Busco-Nestor Studios, San Diego, 1961-68; owner, mgr. Vaux Floors & Interiors, San Diego, 1968-82; cons., mgr. Repository for Germinal Choice, Escondido, Calif., 1983-91; adminstr. Found. for the Continuity of Mankind, Spokane, 1991—. Republican. Home: 2727 S Skipworth Rd Spokane WA 99206-5874 Office: Found Continuity of Mankind 1209 W 1st Ave Spokane WA 99204-0601 *Personal philosophy: It does not matter what our start in life has been, we can set goals and by our own hard work, achieve them. We must find our own answers to our problems and with this will come great pride and enjoyment.*

VAVROSKY, MARK JAMES, career officer, educator; b. Vancouver, Wash., July 4, 1962; s. Donald James and Edna Mae (Englehardt) V.; m. Connie Jean White Itatani, Nov. 27, 1981 (div. Jan. 1987); 1 child, Shannon Jean; m. Gail Cooper, July 7, 1990; 1 child, Paige Marie. BA in Bus. Mgmt., Seattle U., 1984; MA in Edn., Chapman U., Concord, Calif., 1994. Asst. mgr. Household Fin. Corp., Oakland, Calif., 1985-86; commd. 2d lt. U.S. Army, 1985, advanced through grades to capt., 1989; pers. officer 185th Mill. Police Bn., Pittsburg, Calif., 1989-91; comdr. 340th Forward Support Bn., San Lorenzo, Calif., 1991-95; asst. prof. mil. sci. Claremont (Calif.) McKenna Coll., 1995—. V.p. Shadowood Homeowners Assn., Pleasant Hill, Calif., 1991-92. Decorated Army Commendation medal (2). Mem. Assn. U.S. Army (treas. chpt. 1990-91). Roman Catholic. Office: Claremont McKenna Coll Dept Mil Sci 500 E 9th St Claremont CA 91711-5903

VAWTER, DONALD, retired personnel management consultant; b. Spokane, Wash., May 19, 1920; s. Edgar F. and Lina M. Vawter; m. Margaret Schroeder, May 5, 1950; children: Charlotte, Sara. Student in Polit. Sci., Wash. State U., 1946-49. Supr. employer svcs. Wash. State Employment Svc., Seattle, 1950-58; employment mgr. Sundstrand Data Control, Redmond, Wash., 1958-72; profl. recruiter DBA Bellevue Employment Agy., Bellevue, Wash., 1972-73; pers. mgr., workers compensation adminstr. Crown Zellerbach, Omak, Wash., 1973-82; bd. dirs. Pacific N.W. Pers. Mgmt. Assn. 1974-78; apptd. Gov's Svcs. Coun., 1977-83. Served with USCGR, 1942-46, 50-53, comdr. Res. ret., 1968. Mem. Am. Soc. Pers. Adminstrn. (accredited pers. mgr.). Home: PO Box 296 Tonasket WA 98855-0296 *Personal philosophy: If everyone would treat others as they wished to be treated, the whole world would be a better place to live.*

VEA, HENRY WALTER, radiologist, nuclear medicine specialist; b. Henderson, Nev., May 22, 1953; s. Matthew Johnson and Ethelyne Elvira (Hendrickson) V.; m. Julia Allen Grothaus, June 14, 1980; children: Kathleen Arvilla, Hollister Charles. BS in Nuclear Engring. cum laude, Rensselaer Poly. Inst., 1975, M in Engring., 1976, BS in Physics, 1976; MD, U. Wash., 1980. Diplomate Am. Bd. Internal Medicine, Am. Bd. Nuclear Medicine, Am. Bd. Radiology. Resident in internal medicine U. Wash., Seattle, 1980-83, resident in nuclear medicine, 1983-84, chief resident in nuclear medicine, 1984-85; resident in diagnostic radiology Oreg. Health Scis. U., Portland, 1985-88; staff radiologist Good Samaritan Hosp./Med. Ctr., Portland, 1988—. Contbr. articles to profl. jours. NSF grad. fellow, 1975-76. Mem. AMA, Soc. Nuclear Medicine, Radiol. Soc. N.Am., Am. Coll. Radiology, Am. Coll. Nuclear Physicians, Oreg. Med. Assn., Tau Beta Pi, Alpha Omega Alpha. Presbyterian. Office: Good Samaritan Hosp Med Ctr 1015 NW 22nd Ave Portland OR 97210-3025

VEATCH, JOHN WILLIAM, Reiki educator, educational administrator; b. Mitchell, S.D., Dec. 9, 1923; s. William Homer and Helen Gwendolyn (Lowther) V.; m. Doris Lavelle Guthrie (dec. 1978); children: Dean, Joan; m. Joy Sullivan, Aug. 21, 1993. BA in Speech, Wash. State U., 1946, BEd, 1951; MA in Speech, U. Wash., 1950; DEd, U. Idaho, 1970. Pvt. practice speech pathology Spokane, Wash., 1950-79; pvt. practice speech pathology and ednl. cons. Tacoma, 1980-93; dir. rsch., edn. and bus. Sullivan Ctr. & Phys. Therapy, Puyallup, Wash., 1993—; tchr., master Reiki and Mind/Body Healing; lectr. in speech pathology Gonzaga U., Spokane, Wash., 1963-70; adj. prof. Wash. State U., 1972-77, Applied Psychology, Eastern Wash. U., 1977; chief exec. officer and dir. rsch. Espial Inst., Tacoma, 1982-92; mem. home health adv. bd. Spokane County Health Dept., past. pres. Wash. State Health Dept. Crippled Children's Svc. Adv. Bd. Maxillofacial Defects; co-dir. Sullivan Ctr., 1992—; cons. in field; workshops and training in energy medicine techniques; co-developer V.E.A.T.C.H. Technique. Author: (with D. Hughes) Teacher Qualities, 1947; (test profiles) Personal Stress Balance Profile, 1982, Info. Processing Style, 1984, The Deep Screening Profile of Tongue Thrusting Activity, 1985, The Tongue Thrust Screening Test, 1986, Learning Style Profile, 1986; writer, contbr. guides, workbooks, studies and films in field. Fellow Northwest Acad. Speech Pathology (pres. 1978-82, 86-91); mem. Am. Speech-Lang.-Hearing Assn. (life, pres. bd. Oakbridge U. 1989-90). Office: 2717 E Main Ave Puyallup WA 98372-3165

VEBLEN, JOHN ELVIDGE, lawyer; b. Seattle, Feb. 14, 1944. AB magna cum laude, Harvard U., 1965; BA, MA with first class honors, Oxford U., Eng., 1967; JD, Yale U., 1971. Bar: Wash. 1971, N.Y. 1973. Law clerk U.S. Ct. Appeals (9th cir.), 1971-72; lawyer Stoel Rives LLP, Seattle. Mem. ABA, Wash. State Bar Assn., Seattle-King County Bar Assn., Phi Beta Kappa. Office: Stoel Rives LLP One Union Sq 600 University St Ste 3600 Seattle WA 98101-3197

VECCI, RAYMOND JOSEPH, airline industry consultant; b. N.Y.C., Jan. 22, 1943; s. Romeo John and Mary (Fabretti) V.; m. Helen Cecelia Clampett, Sept. 3, 1967; children: Brian John, Damon Jay. BBA, CCNY, 1965; MBA, NYU, 1967. Adminstrv. asst. Internat. Air Transport Assn., N.Y.C., 1961-66; econ. analyst United Airlines, Chgo., 1967-74; asst. v.p. planning and regulatory affairs Alaska Airlines Inc., Seattle, 1975-76, staff v.p. planning and regulatory affairs, 1976-79, staff v.p. planning, 1979, v.p. planning, 1979-85, exec. v.p., chief operating officer, 1986-90, pres., chief exec. officer, 1990—; chmn., dir. Alaska Airlines Inc., 1991—; also chmn., pres., chief exec. officer, dir. Alaska Air Group Inc.; pres. Carnival Airlines, Danica, Fla., 1997—. Served with U.S. Army, 1968-69, Vietnam. Decorated Bronze Star. Roman Catholic. Office: Carnival Airlines 1815 Griffin Rd Ste 205 Dania FL 33004*

VEGA, BENJAMIN URBIZO, retired judge, television producer; b. La Ceiba, Honduras, Jan. 18, 1916; m. Janie Lou Smith, Oct. 12, 1989; AB, U. So. Calif., 1938, postgrad., 1939-40; LLB, Pacific Coast U. Law, 1941. Bar: Calif. 1947, U.S. Dist. Ct. (so. dist.) Calif. 1947, U.S. Supreme Ct. 1958. Assoc. Anderson, McPharlin & Connors, L.A., 1947-48, Newman & Newman, L.A., 1948-51; dep. dist. atty. County of L.A., 1951-66; judge L.A., County Mcpl. Ct., East L.A. Jud. Dist., 1966-86, retired, 1986; leader faculty seminar Calif. Jud. Coll. at Earl Warren Legal Inst., U. Calif-Berkeley, 1978. Mem. Calif. Gov.'s Adv. Com. on Children and Youth, 1968; del. Commn. of the Califs., 1978; bd. dirs. Los Angeles-Mexico City Sister City Com.; pres. Argentine Cultural Found., 1983. Recipient award for outstanding services from Mayor of L.A., 1973, City of Commerce, City of Montebello, Calif. Assembly, Southwestern Sch. Law, Disting. Pub. Service award Dist. Atty. L.A. Mem. Conf. Calif. Judges, Mcpl. Ct. Judges' Assn. (award for Outstanding Services), Beverly Hills Bar Assn., Navy League, L.A. County, Am. Judicature Soc., World Affairs Council, Rotary (hon.), Pi Sigma Alpha. Home: 101 California Ave Apt 1207 Santa Monica CA 90403-3525

VEGA, JOSE GUADALUPE, psychologist, clinical director; b. San Benito, Tex., June 4, 1953; s. Jose Guadalupe and Bertha (Saenz) V.; children: Lilian Anna, Jose Guadalupe III; m. Alberta L. Valdez, Oct. 5, 1990. BA, Pan. Am. U., Edinburg, Tex., 1975; MA, U. Denver, 1976, PhD, 1979. Lic. psychologist, Colo., 1983, profl. counselor, Tex., 1982; diplomate Am. Bd. Med. Psychotherapists, Am. Bd. Vocat. Neuropsychology, Am. Bd. Profl. Disability Cons., Am Bd. Forensic Examiners, Am. Bd. Psychol. Specialties (forensic neuropsychology); cert. adminstrn. Halste ad-Reitan Neuropsychology test batteries. With Oasis of Chandala, Denver, 1978-79, Maytag-Emrick Clinic, Aurora, Colo., 1979; psychologist Spanish Peaks Mental Health Ctr., Pueblo, Colo., 1980-85; pvt. practice Assocs. for Psychotherapy and Edn., Inc., 1985-86; co-owner Affiliates in Counseling, Psychol. Assessment and Consultation, Inc., Pueblo, 1986-87; psychologist Parkview Psychol. Testing Clinic, Pueblo, 1987-93, Colo. Dept. Corrections, 1994—; pvt. practice, Pueblo, 1993—; mem. state grievance bd. Psychology Augment Panel, 1988-95. Active Colo. Inst. Chicano Mental Health Community Youth Orgn., Boys Club Pueblo; mem. health and human svcs. com. City of Pueblo. Mem. APA, ACA, Nat. Acad. Neuropsychology, Internat. Neuropsychol. Soc., Colo. Neuropsychol. Soc., Reitan Soc., Colo. Psychol. Assn. (bd. dirs. non-metro rep. 1995—), Nat. Hispanic Psychol. Assn., Hispanic Neuropsychol. Soc., Phi Delta Kappa, Kappa Delta Pi. Democrat. Roman Catholic. Office: 222 West B St Pueblo CO 81003

VEIGELE, WILLIAM JOHN, physicist; b. N.Y.C., June 18, 1925; s. William John and Lena (Dorn) V.; m. Sue Jane Schwagerman, Jan. 25, 1956; children: William, Kris, Dyana, Lucy. BA, Hofstra U., 1949, MA, 1951; PhD, U. Colo., 1960. Instr. physics Williams Coll., Williamstown, Mass., 1951-52; instr. engring. and physics Hofstra U., Garden City, N.Y., 1952-57; instr. physics U. Colo., Boulder, 1957-58; thermodynamicist Nat. Bur. Stds., Washington, 1958-59; prof., head dept. physics Parsons Coll., Iowa, 1960-61; sr. scientist Martin Marietta Aerospace Corp., 1961-64; sr. scientist, program mgr. Kaman Scis. Corp., 1964-74; founder, pres. Resource Sci. Inc., 1974-78; program mgr., sr. scientist, product line mgr. Santa Barbara (Calif.) Rsch. Ctr., 1978-84; dept. dir. GRC, 1984-89; owner Astral Pub. Co., Santa Barbara, 1993—; part-time lectr. physics U. Colo., Colorado Springs, 1966-77; part-time lectr., vis. assoc. prof. physics, nuc. and chem. engring., electrical computer engring., mech. and environ. engring. U. Santa Barbara, 1978-92; invitee Internat. Atomic Physics Conf., Gordon Rsch. Conf.; faculty affiliate atmospheric sci. Colo. State U.; sci. jour. referee Phys. Rev., Jour. Applied Physics, Jour. Chem. Physics, Am. Jour. Physics, Jour. Atmospheric Environment; cons. environ. divsn. County of Santa Barbara, Colo. Dept. Hwys., Denver, Med. Care and Rsch. Found., Denver, GRC, Santa Barbara, dept. elec. and computer engring. U. Calif. Santa Barbara, Raytheon Electromagnetics Sys. Divsn., Santa Barbara, SBRC, Goleta, Calif., Fairchild Camera and Instrument Corp., L.I., N.Y. Contbr. numerous articles to profl. jours. With USNR, 1943-46, with Res., 1947-68. NSF Sci. Faculty fellow; recipient hon. mention Writer's Digest Short Story Contest. Mem. AAAS, Am. Phys. Soc. (life), Am. Assn. Physics Tchrs., U.S. Naval Inst. (life), Navy League, Patrol Craft Sailors Assn. (life, bd. dirs.), PC 793 Assn. (pres., historian), Sigma Xi, Sigma Pi Sigma, Sigma Alpha. Home: 333 Old Mill Rd Spc 324 Santa Barbara CA 93110-3655

VEIS, FRED ALAN, special education educator; b. L.A.; s. Eric Norbert and Anne (Rauscher) V.; m. Nora Gallardo McDonnell, May 6, 1972 (div. Jan. 1981); children: Vanessa Maria, Andrea Elizabeth; m. Lydia del Carmen Chavez,Sept. 28, 1985; children: Fred Alan, Edward. BA, Calif. State U., Northridge, 1969; MA, San Jose State U., 1981, Calif. State U., Long Beach, 1988. Reading coord. Camp Fenner Probation Camp, Valyermo, Calif., 1974-76; multiple subjects tchr. Mojave (Calif.) Unified Sch. Dist., 1976; tchr. English and reading Pataro Valley United Sch. Dist., Watsonville, Calif., 1976-83; multiple subjects tchr. L.A. Unified Sch. Dist., 1983—; spl. edn. tchr. L.A. Unified Sch. Dist., Huntington Park, Calif., 1983—; salesperson IMED, L.A., 1972-74. Author: Ring Around the Rosie, 1975. WithUSNR, 1968-70, 83-84, Vietnam. Democrat. Roman Catholic. Home: 8455 Garden View Ave South Gate CA 90280 Office: LA City Schs 2880 E Gage Ave Huntington Park CA 90255

VEIT, CLAIRICE GENE TIPTON, measurement psychologist; b. Monterey Park, Calif., Feb. 20, 1939; d. Albert Vern and Gene (Bunning) Tipton; children: Steven, Barbara, Laurette, Catherine. BA, UCLA, 1969, MA, 1970, PhD, 1974. Asst. prof. psychology Calif. State U., L.A., 1975-77, assoc. prof. psychology, 1977-80; rsch. psychologist The Rand Corp., Santa Monica, Calif., 1977—; rsch. cons. NATO Tech. Ctr., The Hague, The Netherlands, 1980-81; faculty Rand Grad Sch., Santa Monica, 1993—. Developer subjective transfer function (STF) method to complex sys. analysis. Mem. LWV, NOW, Mil. Ops. Rsch. Soc. Am., Inst. Mgmt. Sci., Soc. Med. Decision-Making, Soc. for Judgement and Decision-Making, L.A. World Affairs Coun., L.A. Opera League. Office: The Rand Corp 1700 Main St Santa Monica CA 90401-3208

VEIT, WILLIAM ARTHUR, financial planner; b. Altadena, Calif., July 10, 1947; s. Richard Earl and Sally Nell (Brown) V.; m. Maureen Alice Connors, Sept. 13, 1969; children: Stephen, Shereen. BS, Ariz. State U., 1969. Cert. fin. planner. Assoc. v.p. Prudential-Bache, Phoenix, 1983-88; asst. v.p. Kidder, Peabody & Co., Phoenix, 1988-90; v.p. fin. planner Cushman Ramras Cornelius & Crowe, Scottsdale, Ariz., 1990-91; dir., sr. cons. Anasazi Investment Group Inc., Phoenix, 1991—. Coach Little League, Scottsdale, 1979-83, Pop Warner Football, Scottsdale, 1979-82. Mem. Internat. Bd. Cert. Fin. Planners (Phoenix chpt.), Inst. Cert. Fin. Planners, Internat. Assn. Fin. Planning. Republican. Roman Catholic. Office: Anasazi Investment Group Inc 11801 N Tatum Blvd Ste 240 Phoenix AZ 85028-1613

VEITH, RICHARD CHARLES, geriatric psychiatrist, educator; b. Seattle, May 23, 1947; s. Michael C. Veith and Barbara E. (Maguire) Seaman; m. Marcella Pascualy, Sept. 9, 1988; children: Ryan, Carly, David. BA, Western Wash. U., 1969; MD, U. Wash., 1973. Diplomate Nat. Bd. Med. Examiners, Am. Bd. Psychiatry and Neurology (mem. examination com. 1989-93), Am. Bd. Geriatric Psychiatry. Intern in internal medicine Sch. Medicine, U. Wash., Seattle, 1973-74, resident in psychiatry, 1974-77; chief psychiat. consultation and liaison sect. psychiat. svc. Seattle VA Med. Ctr., 1977-79, staff rsch. psychiatrist, geriatric rsch., edn. and clin. ctr., 1977-87, dir., 1987—, fellowship dir. geriatric psychiatry fellowship program, 1991—; instr. dept. psychiatry and behavioural scis. Sch. Medicine U. Wash., 1977-80, asst. prof., 1980-83, assoc. prof., 1983-89, prof., 1989—, head divsn. gerontology and geriatric psychiatry, 1991—; active Nat. Inst. on Aging Task Force on Reversible Causes of Dementia, 1978-80; rsch. program specialist in psychiatry dept. medicine and surgery med. rsch. svc. Dept. VA, Washington, 1989-92, mem. rev. com. geriatric psychiatry fellowship program tng. sites, 1990, mem. regional geriatric psychiatry working group region 4, 1990; study sect. reviewer biochem. endocrinology study sect. Nat. Inst. Aging-NIH, Bethesda, Md., 1990; mem. adv. bd. U. Wash. Alzheimer's Disease Rsch. Ctr., 1988—, chair, 1991—; grant investigator in field; presenter in field. Mem. editl. bd. Geriatric Cons., 1984—; ad hoc rev. numerous jours.; contbr. articles to profl. jours. Bd. dirs. Norwest Day Care Ctr., Seattle, 1978-82, pres., 1980;. Fellow Am. Psychiat. Assn. (mem. psychopharmacology subcom. Psychiat. Knowledge and Skills Self-Assessment Program 1983-84); mem. Am. Geriatrics Soc. (mem. editl. bd. Jour. Am. Geriatric Soc. 1989-91, Internat. Jour. Geriatric Psychiatry 1990—), Am. Assn. Geriatric Psychiatry, Gerontol. Soc., Psychiat. Rsch. Soc., Soc. Neurosci., Soc. Biol. Psychiatry. Office: Geriatric Rsch Edn and Clinic Ctr VA Med Ctr 1660 S Columbian Way Seattle WA 98108-1532

VEJSICKY, CATHLEEN LYNN, management executive, educator; b. Columbus, Ohio, June 25, 1958; d. Eugene Joseph and Jane Ann (Thomas) V. BS, U. So. Calif., L.A., 1981, MBA, 1987, postgrad. Cert. tchr., bus. mgmt. and mktg. tchr., C.C. tchr., Calif. Sr. product mgr. Dataproducts Corp., Woodland Hills, Calif., 1980-86; product mktg. mgr. Light Signatures, Century City, Calif., 1987-88; mgr., sr. mgmt. cons. KPMG Peat Marwick, L.A., 1988-92; v.p. Stranberg & Assocs., Newport Beach, Calif., 1993—; substitute tchr. Long Beach (Calif.) Unified Sch. Dist., 1993-95; tchr. Anaheim (Calif.) City Sch. Dist., 1994-97; guest mktg. lectr. U. So. Calif., 1986—; developer, leader U. So. Calif. Western Europe's Grad. Bus. Exch. Program, 1987; dir. Platinum Interchange Tricom Mgmt., 1997. Polit. campaign vol., Long Beach, Calif., 1989—; mem. Patrick Henry Leadership Team, Anaheim Unified Sch. Dist. Ins. Com., P.Q.R. sci. Team; leader Anaheim Math. Mem. Town and Gown of U. So. Calif. Republican. Presbyterian. Home: 6016 Bixby Village Dr Long Beach CA 90803-6304

VELASQUEZ, ANA MARIA, languages educator; b. Callao, Lima, Peru, Nov. 18, 1947; came to U.S. 1980; d. Victor and Yolanda (Reinoso) V.; m. Scott Mathew Nakada, Mar. 19, 1981; 1 child, Victor Min Nakada. Bachelor's Degree, San Marcos U., Lima, 1969; student French Paris VI U., 1971-72, student English Prince George Coll., 1983-84, student Quechua Yachay Wasi Coll., Lima, 1986. Cert. tchr., Peru. Educator San Jose de Cluny, Lima, 1968-71; translator Aubert & Duval, Paris, 1972-76; linguistic coordinator Ser. de Maquinaria, Lima, 1977-80; educator, cons. IN-LINGUA, Washington, 1981-83, CACI, Inc., Arlington, Va., 1982-89; educator Diplomatic Lang. Svcs., Inc., Arlington, Va., 1990-94; dir. AKTA Internat., San Diego, 1984—. Author: Pronunciacion Basica Universal, 1974; South American Dialects, 1977; Abbreviated Telephone Communications System, 1984; Teaching Languages to Adults, 1985; Languages 365 Days, 1986. Coord. literacy campaign, Puno, Peru, 1969. Mem. Intertel, Am. Assn. Applied Linguistics, Mensa. Republican. Roman Catholic. Avocations: chess, skiing. Home and Office: PO Box 502884 San Diego CA 92150-2884

VELORIA, VELMA ROSETE, state legislator; b. The Philippines, Oct. 22, 1950; came to U.S., 1961; d. Apelino and Patrocinio (Rosete) V. BS in Med. Tech., San Francisco State U., 1976. Office mgr. First Hill Phys. Therapy, Seattle, 1985-89; field coord. Dolores Sibonga for Mayor, Seattle, 1989; staff organizer N.W. Nat. Union of Hosp. and Health Care Employees, Seattle, 1989-90; organizer Svc. Employees Internat. Union, 1995—; rep. dist. 11 Wash. State Legis., Olympia, 1992—, ranking minority mem. trade and econ. devel., past vice chmn. state govt., healthcare, labor/commerce; mem. nat. environ. justice adv. coun. U.S. EPA, 1994—; co-chmn. jobs creation subcom. Duwamish Coalition, 1994-96; leader, organizer Wash. State Trade and Investment Mission to Vietnam, Cambodia and Thailand, 1995, to Philippines and Indonesia, 1994, The Philippines, 1993; participant summer seminar for tchrs. Wash. State in Global Economy, 1995. Oral historian Alaskeros, 1987; del. Dem. Nat. Conv., Atlanta, 1988, Chgo., 1996; mem. transition team Mayor of Seattle, 1989; mem. Filipino Am. Polit. Action Group of Washington, 1991-92; bd. dirs. Wing Luke Asian Mus., 1991-92; Wash. state adv. com. mem. U.S. Civil Rights Commn., 1991—; mem. steering com. Cultural Unity Coalition, 1991—; chmn. Asian Elected Ofcls. of Wash., 1994—; mem. Asian Pacific Islander Women's Polit. Caucus, 1994—, Wash. Law and Justice Adv. Coun., 1994—; mem. Wash. Econ. Devel. Fin. Authority, 1995-96; bd. dirs. Wash.-Pangasinan Sister State Assn., 1995—; mem. cmty. adv. bd. U. Wash. Women's Ctr., 1995—. Office: House of Representatives Legis Bldg Dist 11 Olympia WA 98504

VELTFORT, THEODORE ERNST, electrical engineer, physicist; b. Cambridge, Mass., Feb. 23, 1915; s. Theodore Ernst and Helen (Gaston) V.; m. Helene Rank, Oct. 27, 1941 (div. Jan. 1952); children: Ruhama Danielle, Susan Marlene; m. Leonore Valeton, Oct. 14, 1954; children: Anna Cornelia, Kevin Daniel. BA in Econ., Columbia U., 1940; MS in Physics, Stanford U., 1947. Registered profl. engr., Calif. Chief devel. engr. Shand and Jurs Co., Berkeley, Calif., 1955-58; sr. project engr. Lynch Comm. Systems, San Francisco, 1958-59; chief electronics engr. Shockley Unit Clevite Corp, Stanford, Calif., 1960-61; sr. cons. engr. Sierra Electronics Corp., Menlo Park, Calif., 1961; prof. physics, dir. dept. solid state physics U. Havana, Cuba, 1962-68; chief engr. Bioelectric Instruments, Inc., Yonkers, N.Y., 1968-70; electronics systems engr. Mt. Sinai Med. Ctr., N.Y.C., 1970-80; cons. engr. Veltek, Oakland, Calif., 1981—; adj. prof., course advisor CCNY, 1971-78. Ambulance driver Cuerpo Sanitario de la Republica Espanola, 1937-38. Sgt. Signal Corps U.S. Army, 1942-45. Mem. IEEE (life), AAAS, Vets. the Abraham Lincoln Brigade (exec. sec. San Francisco chpt. 1983-84, fgn. corres. sec. 1985—), Sigma Xi (assoc.). Home and Office: 6534 Whitney St Oakland CA 94609-1028

VENEMA, JON ROGER, educator, pastor; b. Modesto, Calif., Apr. 11, 1953; s. Roger Edwin and Marilyn Ailene (Johnson) V.; m. Shelley Elizabeth, Mar. 29, 1974; children: Jordan Christopher Wilder, Susanna Lee. AA, Modesto (Calif.) Jr. Coll., 1974; BA magna cum laude, Simpson Coll., 1976; MDiv, Mennonite Brethren Bibl. Sem., 1980; PhD, Golden Gate Bapt. Theol. Sem., 1995. Instr. bibl. and religious studies Fresno Pacific Coll., Modesto, 1980-84; sr. pastor 1st Bapt. Ch., So. San Francisco, 1984-94; adj. faculty Fresno Pacific Coll., 1984-87, Simpson Coll., San Francisco, 1987-88; instr. St. James Coll., Pacifica, Calif., 1987-90; adj. prof. Golden Gate Bapt. Theol. Sem., Marin, Calif., 1992, Highland Christian Coll., San Bruno, Calif., 1992-93, We. Conservative Bapt. Theol. Sem., 1994—; acad. dean, devel. coord. We. Seminary, Sacramento, 1996—, asst. prof. N.T. lang. and lit., 1996—. Mem. Soc. Bibl. Lit., Delta Epsilon Chi. Republican. Home: 2228 Canadian Cir Modesto CA 95356 Office: We Conservative Baptist Sem 2924 Becerra Way Sacramento CA 95821-3939

VENNUM, WALT, geology educator; b. Seattle, May 10, 1941; s. Francis Lorenzo and Myrle Marie (Paisley) V.; m. Barbara Louise Young, June 9, 1964 (div. Sept. 1990). BA in Geology with honors, U. Mont., 1964; PhD in

Geology, Stanford U., 1971. Smoke jumper Bur. Land Mgmt., Fairbanks, Alaska, 1962-66; rsch. asst. Found. for Glacier Rsch., Juneau, Alaska, 1967; geologist U.S. Geol. Survey, Denver and Menlo Park, Calif., 1971-89; teaching asst., acting instr. geology Stanford (Calif.) U., 1967-71; prof. geology Sonoma State U., Rohnert Park, Calif., 1971—; participant 5 geol. expeditions unexplored areas in Antarctica, geological mapping Alaskan wilderness areas, 1971, 72, 74; igneous petrologist on 2 cruises on deep sea drilling ship The Glomar Challenger, 1974, 76; vis. prof. geology U. Mont., Missoula, 1978; geology lectr., naturalist Seaquest, Quark & Clipper Cruise Lines, and Marine expdns., Antarctica, Alaska, New Zealand, and Russian Far East, 1990-96; mountain climbing guide Palisades Sch. Mountaineering, Lone Pine, Calif., 1968-69, 78-79; dir. gold exploration project, Saudi Arabia, 1988. Contbr. papers to sci. jours. With USAF, 1965. Recipient Antarctic Svc. medal, 1978; Penrose grantee Geol. Soc. Am., 1969, Small Coll. Sci. Equipment grantee NSF, 1988; geographic feature in Antarctica named Mt. Vennum. Mem. Nat. Speological Soc., Am. Alpine Club, Geol. Hon. Soc., Sigma Gamma Epsilon. Presbyterian. Home: 3925 Kim Ct Sebastopol CA 95472-5736 Office: Sonoma State U Dept Geology 1801 E Cotati Ave Rohnert Park CA 94928-3613

VENN-WATSON, PATRICIA, psychiatrist; b. L.A., Aug. 14, 1944; d. Joseph Harry and Yetta (Margarick) Bernhard; 1 child, Eric Joseph. BA, UCLA, 1966; MD, U. Calif., Irvine, 1970. Intern U. N.Mex., Albuquerque, 1970-71, resident in psychiatry, 1971-75; cons. Cath. Family Svcs., San Diego, 1975-78; pvt. practice psychiatry San Diego, 1975—. Fellow Am. Psychiat. Assn.; mem. Am. Women's Med. Soc., Calif. Psychiat. Assn., San Diego County Med. Soc., San Diego Soc. Psychiat. Physicians (rep. 1993—), San Diego Soc. Adolescent Psychiatry (pres., treas. 1985-93). Office: 15644 Pomerado Rd Ste Gse Poway CA 92064-2418 also: 3242 4th Ave San Diego CA 92103-5702

VENTURO, FRANK A., academic affairs administrator, communications educator; b. Gunnison, Colo., May 24, 1940; s. Peter J. and Theresa (Luchetta) V.; m. Margaret Patricia Palmer, July 1, 1967; children: Paul, Angela, Laura. BA, Western State Coll., Gunnison, 1964; MA, U. Colo., 1971, PhD, 1987. Tchr. English, speech South Routt County H.S., Oak Creek, Colo., spring 1965; tchr. speech and drama Grand Junction (Colo.) Ctrl. H.S., 1965-68; instr. comm. U. Colo., Boulder, 1969-71, St. Louis U., 1971-74; prof. comm. Western State Coll., Gunnison, 1974—, assoc. v.p. acad. affairs, 1991—; mediator, facilitator, arbitrator GV Assocs., Gunnison, 1988—; pres. Colo. Drama Speech Assn., 1978-79, Western State Coll. Edn. Assn., Gunnison, 1987-88. Chair Gunnison County Dems., 1981-84; mem. Gov.'s Econ. Adv. Coun., State of Colo., Denver, 1990-91; gov. appointee, mem. 7th Jud. Dist. Performance Review Com., Colo. State Cts., 1995. Mem. Am. Assn. Higher Edn., Colo. Edn. Assn. (bd. dirs. 1988-92), Colo. Coun. Mediators and Mediation Orgns., Western State Coll. Alumni Assn. (pres. 1986-88). Democrat. Home: 179 Tomichi Ln Gunnison CO 81230 Office: Western State Coll Colo College Heights Gunnison CO 81231

VENZKE, RAY FRANK, psychotherapist; b. Wood County, Wis., Sept. 7, 1933; s. Herman A. and Christina (Sojka) V.; m. Dawn Woltman, June 14, 1953 (div. Feb. 1972); 1 child, Diane W. Doersch; m. Joy Leadbetter, June 21, 1972 (div. Nov. 1985); m. DeMaris Hafner Unruh, May 31, 1986. BA in Ednl. Psychology, Wartburg Coll., 1955; MDiv, Trinity Sem., Columbus, Ohio, 1959; MA in Psychology, U. N.D., 1974. Lic. clin. profl. counselor, Mont. Pastor Bearlake Luth. Parish, Twin Lakes, Minn., 1959-63; missionary Thailand Luth. Mission, 1963-64; pastor First Luth. Parish, Washburn, N.D., 1965-67; addiction counselor Heartview Found., Mandan, N.D., 1971-74; therapist, program evaluator Badlands Human Svc. Ctr., Dickinson, N.D., 1975-85; psychotherapist Dickinson, N.D., 1985-87, Chrysalis Counseling Svcs., Helena, Mont., 1988—; cons. Lewis and Clark County Law Enforcement Chaplains, Helena, 1988-95. Narrator Mont. Libr. for the Blind, Helena, 1990—; chair task force CISM Mont. Dept. Disaster, 1994—; mem. Mont. Gov.'s Task Force on Mental Health Medicaid, Helena, 1993—. Mem. Am. Counselors Assn., Am. Mental Health Counselors, Mont. Clin. Mental Health Counselors (treas. 1992-94, counselor of yr. award 1996), Mont. Counselors Assn., Lions (Dist. Gov. 5NW award 1983), Am. Philatelic Soc. Home: 2019 Missoula Ave Helena MT 59601-3245 Office: Chrysalis Counseling Svc 3117 Cooney Dr Apt 201 Helena MT 59602-0200

VEOMETT, COLLEEN MICHELLE, librarian; b. Ft. Monmouth, N.J., June 17, 1957; d. Willis K. and Norma G. (Mulcahy) V. BA, Oreg. Coll. Edn., 1979; MLS, U. Hawaii, 1982. Head libr. Yakama Indian Nation Libr., Toppenish, Wash., 1987—. Active Amnesty Internat. Mem. ALA. Democrat. Roman Catholic. Office: Yakama Indian Nation Libr PO Box 151 Toppenish WA 98948-0151

VERANT, WILLIAM J., state agency administrator; b. Washington, Dec. 19, 1941; m. Donna M. Verant; children: Bill Jr., Sharon. BSBA, Am. U. Various sr. mgmt. positions various comml. banks, savs. and loan and mortgage banks, Washington, Calif., N.Mex.; dir. fin. instns. divsn., regulation and licensing dept. State of N.Mex., Santa Fe, 1995—, acting dir. securities divsn.; acting dir. securities divsn. State of N.Mex. Office: State of New Mexico PO Box 25101 725 St Michaels Dr Santa Fe NM 87504

VERBIEST, CLAIRE SCHROEVEN, artist; b. Brussels, Brabant, Belgium, July 4, 1948; came to U.S., 1982; d. Richard Andre Anna and Claire Marie Ghislaine (De Fooz) S.; m. Noel, Dec. 24, 1970; children Katrien, Peter. Pvt. practice, 1988—; art instr. Los Gatos Art Supplies, Calif., 1996, 97; judge Fine Arts League of CUpertino, Calif., 1997; art instr. Hakone Gardens, Saratoga, Calif., 1996, 97, Santa Clara County Fair, 1997. Recipient award Fremont Art Assn., 1996, Knickerbocker Artists, Joan Cawley Gallery, 1997; Arts Students League scholar, Denver, 1995. Mem.Calif. Watercolor Assn., Allied Artists West (dir. of exhbns., 1994-95, bd. mem. corr. sec., 1997); signature mem. Pastel Soc. Am., Pastel Soc. West Coast. Home: 3126 Brightwood Ct San Jose CA 95148

VERGER, MORRIS DAVID, architect, planner; b. Ft. Worth, Mar. 25, 1915; s. Joseph and Dora (Bunyan) V.; m. Florence Brown, June 21, 1939; children: Paul, Alice. B.Arch., U. Calif., Berkeley, 1943. Naval architect U.S. Navy Bur. Ships, San Pedro, Calif., 1943-45; draftsman various archtl. firms So. Calif., 1946-50; pvt. practice as architect and planner Los Angeles, 1951—; lectr. architecture UCLA Extension; vis. critic Calif. State U., San Luis Obispo; leader Seminar on Interactive Planning, San Francisco; cons. to legal profession, tech. witness. Works include program for City of Hope, Duarte, Calif., 1972, Terman Engring. Ctr., Stanford U., 1974, and design of Huntington Dr. Sch., L.A., 1975, Flax Artist Materials Bldg., L.A., 1976, Frank D. Lanterman H.S., L.A., 1978, exec. offices S.E. Rykoff & Co., L.A., 1982, condominiums, Stoneman Corp., L.A., 1988, 91; developed DiscoveryBased Planning, 1994. Recipient design awards Westwood C. of C., 1974, 75. Fellow AIA (pres. So. Calif. chpt. 1975, v.p. environ. affairs Calif. council 1976, v.p. Calif. council 1979-80, pres. Calif. council 1980). Home: 1362 Comstock Ave Los Angeles CA 90024-5315

VERHAEGEN, TERRI LYNN FOY, middle school educator; b. Monrovia, Calif., May 25, 1960; d. Gordon Lawrence and Vivian Lou (Smith) Foy; m. William Francis Verhaegen, Dec. 19, 1992. BA, U. So. Calif., 1981; postgrad., Calif. State U., L.A., 1983; MA, Chapman U., Orange, Calif., 1990. Office mgr. Bradley Ins. Svc., Pasadena, Calif., 1981-83; tchr. English and drama Valley H.S., Santa Ana, Calif., 1983-87; tchr. Lang. Arts, Journalism Spurgeon Intermediate Sch., Santa Ana, 1987—; Technology fellow Calif. Ctr. for Sch. Restructuring, 1995—. Bd. dirs. Huntington Beach (Calif.) Playhouse, 1991-96. Mem. ASCD, Nat. Coun. Tchrs. English, Computer Using Educators. Office: Spurgeon Intermediate 2701 W 5th St Santa Ana CA 92703-1821

VERHEY, JOSEPH WILLIAM, psychiatrist, educator; b. Oakland, Calif., Sept. 28, 1928; s. Joseph Bernard and Anne (Hanken) V.; BS summa cum laude, Seattle U., 1954; MD, U. Wash., 1958; m. Darlene Helen Seiler, July 21, 1956. Intern, King County Hosp., Seattle, 1958-59; resident Payne Whitney Psychiatric Clinic, N.Y. Hosp., Cornell Med. Center, N.Y.C., 1959-62, U. Wash. Hosp., Seattle, 1962-63; pvt. practice, Seattle, 1963-78; mem. staff U. Providence Hosp., 1963-78, Fairfax Hosp., 1963-78, VA Med. Center, Tacoma, 1978-83, chief inpatient psychiatry sect., 1983—; clin. instr. psychiatry U. Wash. Med. Sch., 1963-68, clin. asst. prof. psychiatry, 1968-82, clin. assoc. prof., 1982—; cons. psychiatry U.S. Dept. Def., Wash. State Bur. Juvenile Rehab.; examiner Am. Bd. Psychiatry and Neurology. Diplomate Am. Bd. Psychiatry and Neurology. Fellow N. Pacific Soc. Psychiatry and Neurology, Am. Psychiat. Assn.; mem. AMA, Am. Fedn. Clin. Rsch., World Fedn. Mental Health, Soc. Mil. Surgeons of U.S., Wash. Athletic Club, Swedish Club (life). Home: 1100 University St Seattle WA 98101 Office: VA Med Ctr Tacoma WA 98493

VERLOT, FRANK OSCAR, aerospace executive; b. Ghent, Belgium, Oct. 18, 1941; came to U.S., 1946; s. Max Gustave and Eva Emily (Danilevits) V.; m. Marian Elizabeth Berkner, June 24, 1967; children: Nancy Elizabeth, Susanne Marie. BSME, MIT, 1963; MSME, Stanford U., 1964. Thermodynamics engr. Grumman Aircraft, Bethpage, N.Y., 1964-65; sr. thermodynamics engr. Lockheed Missiles & Space Co., Sunnyvale, Calif., 1966-68; project engr. program mgmt. United Tech. Ctr. divsn. of United Aircraft, Sunnyvale, 1968-72, mgr. procurement liaison engring., 1972-76; mgr. procurement liaison engring. Chem. Systems divsn. United Techs., Sunnyvale, 1976-82; dir. strategic and bus. planning Chem. Systems divsn. United Techs., San Jose, Calif., 1982-94; dir. strategic bus. planning Pratt & Whitney Space Propulsion Ops., San Jose, 1994-96, dir. bus. devel. and planning, 1996—. Planning commr. City of Los Altos, 1978-82, mem. city coun., 1982-89, mayor, 1983-84; chmn. Santa Clara County (Calif.) Rep. Com., 1971, 72; state precinct chmn. Calif. Rep. Party, 1973-74. Mem. AIAA (space transp. tech. com. 1994—). Roman Catholic. Home: 634 S Springer Rd Los Altos CA 94024-4105 Office: United Tech Pratt & Whitney Space Propulsion Ops PO Box 49028 San Jose CA 95161-9028

VERNIERO, JOAN EVANS, special education educator; b. Wilkes-Barre, Pa., Nov. 30, 1937; d. Raymond Roth and Cary Hazel (Casano) Evans; m. Daniel Eugene Verniero Jr., Jan. 7, 1956; children: Daniel Eugene III, Raymond Evans. BA, Kean Coll., 1971; MS in Edn. Adminstrn., Monmouth U., West Long Branch, N.J., 1974; postgrad., Calif. Coast U., 1986-92. Cert. elem. sch. tchr., spl. edn. tchr., sch. adminstr., N.J., N.Mex., Colo.; nat. registered emergency med. technician. Tchr. Children's Psychiat. Ctr., Eatontown, N.J., 1965-69; tchr. Arthur Brisbane Child Treatment Ctr., Farmingdale, N.J., 1969-71, prin., 1971-75; prin. S.A. Wilson Ctr., Colorado Springs, Colo., 1976-82; tchr. pub. schs. Aurora, Colo., 1982-93; retired, 1993; edn. rep. Aurora Pub. Schs. Crew leader Black Forest (Colo.) Rescue Squad 1979-85, treas., bd. dirs. Fire Protection Dist., 1980-85; evaluator Arson divsn. Aurora (Colo.) Fire Dept., 1993—. Mem. Phi Delta Kappa. Republican. Presbyterian. Home: 671 S Paris St Aurora CO 80012-2315 *Personal philosophy: Enjoy life and continue to seek as much knowledge of life as you can. "Who dares to teach must never cease to learn."*

VERNON, GAYLE (LUMARI), psychic consultant, author, publisher; b. Boston, Mar. 13, 1951; d. Edward and Esta (Freedman) V. BFA, Mass. Coll. Art, Boston, 1974. Artist, sculptor Boston, 1974-88, writer, author, 1974—; psychic cons. for individual, bus. and corp. clients Mass., 1980-92, Santa Fe, 1992—; pub. Heart of the Goddess, Santa Fe, 1995—; channel, conscious medium and healer. Author: The Magic of Incense, 1994, Alawashka, The Mother Tongue, 1996. Founder pres. Artists Salon, Inc., Boston, 1982-83, Women Art Profls., Inc., Boston, 1980-82. Internat. Arts Fellowship grantee Meml. Found. for Jewish Culture, 1979-80; Artists Found. fellow, 1980-81; pub. art commn. First Night, Boston, 1985, 96. Office: PO Box 22565 Santa Fe NM 87502-2565

VERRONE, PATRIC MILLER, lawyer, writer; b. Glendale, N.Y.C., Sept. 29, 1959; s. Pat and Edna (Miller) V.; m. Margaret Maiya Williams, 1989; 1 child, Patric Carroll Williams. BA, Harvard U., 1981; JD, Boston Coll., 1984. Bar: Fla. 1984, Calif. 1988, U.S. Dist. Ct. (mid. dist.) Fla. 1984, U.S. Dist. Ct. (ctrl. dist.) Calif. 1995, U.S. Ct. Appeals (9th cir.) 1995. Assoc. Allen, Knudsen, Swartz, DeBoest, Rhoads & Edwards, Ft. Myers, Fla., 1984-86; writer The Tonight Show, Burbank, Calif., 1987-90; temp. judge L.A. Mcpl. Ct., 1995—. Dir., producer, writer The Civil War--The Lost Episode, 1991; writer The Larry Sanders Show, 1992-94, The Critic, 1993-95; producer, writer The Simpsons, 1994-95, Muppets Tonight!, 1995-97; editor Harvard Lampoon, 1978-84, Boston Coll. Law Rev., 1983-84, Fla. Bar Jour., 1987-88, L.A. Lawyer, 1994—; issue editor: Ann. Entertainment Law Issue, 1995-97; contbr. articles to profl. jours. including Elysian Fields Quar., Baseball and the American Legal Mind. Bd. dirs. Calif. Confedn. of Arts, Mus. Contemporary Art. Mem. ABA (vice chair arts, entertainment and sports law com.), Calif. Bar, Calif. Lawyers for Arts, L.A. County Bar Assn. (sec. barristers exec. com., chair artists and the law com., steering com. homeless shelter project, intellectual property and entertainment law sect., state appelate jud. evaluation com., legis. activity com.), Fla. Bar Assn., Writers Guild Am. West (exec. com. animation writers caucus), Harvard Club Lee County (v.p. 1985-86), Harvard Club So. Calif. Republican. Roman Catholic. Home and Office: PO Box 1428 Pacific Palisades CA 90272-1428

VERRY, WILLIAM ROBERT, mathematics researcher; b. Portland, Oreg., July 11, 1933; s. William Richard and Maurine Houser (Braden) V.; m. Bette Lee Ronspiess, Nov. 20, 1955 (div. 1981); children: William David, Sandra Kay Verry Londregan, Steven Bruce, Kenneth Scott; m. Jean Elizabeth Morrison, Oct. 16, 1982; step-children: Lucinda Jean Hale, Christine Carol Hale Fortner, Martha Jean Johnson, Brian Kenneth Lackey, Robert Morrison Lackey. BA, Reed Coll., 1955; BS, Portland State U., 1957; MA, Fresno State U., 1960; PhD, Ohio State U.-Columbus, 1972. Instr. chemistry Reedley (Calif.) Coll., 1957-60; ops. rsch. analyst Naval Weapons Center, China Lake, Calif., 1960-63; ordnance engr. Honeywell Ordnance, Hopkins, Minn., 1963-64; sr. scientist Litton Industries, St. Paul., 1964-67; project mgr. Tech. Ops., Inc., Alexandria, Va., 1967-70; rsch. assoc. Ohio State U., Columbus, 1970-72; prin. engr. Computer Sci. Corp., Falls Church, Va., 1972-77; mem. tech. staff MITRE Corp., Albuquerque, 1977-85; C3 program dir., assoc. prof. math. sci. Clemson U., S.C., 1985-87; dep. dir. Riverside Rsch. Inst., Rosslyn, Va., 1987-91; mgr. Hillcrest Gardens, Livermore, Calif., 1992—. Founder, minister Christian Love Ctr.; founder, v.p. Interfaith Sharing, Inc., 1994—. Mem. Inst. for Ops. Rsch. and the Mgmt. Scis. Home and Office: 550 Hillcrest Ave Livermore CA 94550-3769

VERSCHOOR, JOHN, IV, physician assistant; b. Phoenix, Mar. 19, 1949; s. John Verschoor III and Dorothy (Killman) Hibbard; m. Nancy Lorel Welsh, Jan. 24, 1970; children: Bianca Dawn, Jared Moroni, Renee Ann, Benjamin Thayer. AS, Ariz. Western Coll., Yuma, 1972; Assoc. Med. Sci., Emory U., 1975; MD, Spartan Health Sci. U., St. Lucia, West Cast, 1985. Lic. nurse, Ariz., Ga., Tex., physician asst., Ariz. Orderly Yuma Regional Med. Ctr., 1967-68, emergency rm. nurse, 1970-72; commd. U.S. Army, 1972, advanced through grades to maj., 1990; physician asst. S.W. Med., Yuma, 1975-80; comdr. 12th Spl. Force Group, Albuquerque, 1980-85; exec. officer 996th Med. Co., Glendale, Ariz., 1985-88; bn. comdr. indsl. facility Fitzsimmons Army Hosp., 1988-92; physician asst. Deseret Diagnostic Ctr., Mesa, Ariz., 1990—; med. svc. officer CIA, Langley, Va., 1988—; exec. officer Tripler Army Med. Ctr., HI, 1992—; Lectr. U. Utah, Salt Lake City, 1990-94; bd. dirs. Lazerus Group, Inc., Las Vegas, 1989—. V.p. Clnica de Mormona, Guadalajara, Mexico, 1981. Mem. Wilderness Med. Soc., Am. Acad. Physician Assts. Republican. LDS Ch. Office: Deseret Diagnostic Ctr 215 S Power Rd Ste 106 Mesa AZ 85206-5236

VER STEEG, DONNA LORRAINE FRANK, nurse, sociologist, educator; b. Minot, N.D., Sept. 23, 1929; d. John Jonas and Pearl H. (Denlinger) Frank; m. Richard W. Ver Steeg, Nov. 22, 1950; children: Juliana, Anne, Richard B. BSN, Stanford, 1951; MSN, U. Calif., San Francisco, 1967; MA in Sociology, UCLA, 1969, PhD in Sociology, 1973. Clin. instr. U. N.D. Sch. Nursing, 1962-63; USPHS nurse rsch. fellow UCLA, 1969-72; spl. cons., adv. com. on physicians' assts. and nurse practitioner programs Calif. State Bd. Med. Examiners, 1972-73; asst. prof. UCLA Sch. Nursing, 1973-79, assoc. prof., 1979-94, asst. dean, 1981-83, chmn. primary ambulatory care, 1976-87, assoc. dean, 1983-86, prof. emeritus (recalled 1994-96), chair primary care, 1994-96, emeritus, 1996—; co-prin. investigator PRIMEX Project, Family Nurse Practitioners, UCLA Extension, 1974-76; assoc. cons. Calif. Postsecondary Edn. Commn., 1975-76; spl. cons. Calif. Dept. Consumer Affairs, 1978; accredited visitor Western Assn. Schs. and Colls., 1985; mem. Calif. State Legis. Health Policy Forum, 1980-81; mem. nurse practitioner adv. com. Calif. Bd. RNs, 1995—. Contbr. chpts. to profl. books. Recipient Leadership award Calif. Area Health Edn. Ctr. System, 1989, Commendation award Calif. State Assembly, 1994; named Outstanding Faculty Mem. UCLA Sch. Nursing, 1982. Fellow Am. Acad. Nursing; mem. AAAS, ANA (pres. elect Calif. 1977-81, pres. Calif. 1979-81), ANA C interim chair Calif. 1995-96, Am. Soc. Law and Medicine, Nat. League Nursing, Calif. League Nursing, N.Am. Nursing Diagnosis Assn., Am. Assn. History Nursing, Assn. Health Svcs. Rsch., Stanford Nurses Club, Sigma Theta Tau (Gamma Tau chpt. Leadership award 1994), Sigma Xi. Home: 708 Swarthmore Ave Pacific Palisades CA 90272-4353 Office: UCLA Sch Nursing 700 Tiverton Ave Box 956919 Los Angeles CA 90095

VERTS, LITA JEANNE, university administrator; b. Jonesboro, Ark., Apr. 13, 1935; d. William Gus and Lolita Josephine (Peeler) Nash; m. B. J. Verts, Aug. 29, 1954 (div. 1975); 1 child, William Trigg. BA, Oreg. State U., 1973; MA in Lingustics, U. Oreg., 1974; postgrad., U. Hawaii, 1977. Librarian Forest Research Lab., Corvallis, Oreg., 1966-69; instr. English Lang. Inst., Corvallis, 1974-80; dir. spl. svcs. Oreg. State U., Corvallis, 1980—, faculty senator, 1988-96. Editor ann. book: Trio Achievers, 1986, 87, 88; contbr. articles to profl. jours. Precinct com. Rep. Party, Corvallis, 1977-80; adminstrv. bd. 1st United Meth. Ch., Corvallis, 1987-89, mem. fin. com., 1987-93, tchr. Bible, 1978—; bd. dirs. Westminster Ho., United Campus Ministries, 1994-95; adv. coun. Disabilities Svc., Linn, Benton, Lincoln Counties, 1990—, vice-chmn., 1992-93, chmn. 1993-94. Mem. N.W. Assn. Spl. Programs (pres. 1985-86), Nat. Coun. Ednl. Opportunities Assn. (bd. dirs. 1984-87), Nat. Gardening Assn., Alpha Phi (mem. corp. bd. Beta Upsilon chpt. 1990-96). Republican. Methodist. Home: 530 SE Mayberry Ave Corvallis OR 97333-1866 Office: Spl Svcs Project Waldo 337 OSU Corvallis OR 97331

VESS, RONALD WAYNE, librarian; b. Richmond, Va., Oct. 12, 1947; s. Clarence Hiram and Elaine (Ayres) V.; m. Claudia Vess, Apr. 21, 1990; children: Stacey Noel, Forrest Matthew, Lisa Marie Staples. BA, Calif. State U., Fullerton, 1973, MLS, 1974. Instr. credential Calif. Cmty. Colls. Libr. Mira Costa Coll., Oceanside, Calif., 1984-86, Palomar Coll., San Marcos, Calif., 1984-86; libr. Southwestern Coll., Chula Vista, Calif., 1985—, pres. acad. senate, 1994-96; mem. curriculum com. acad. senate Calif. Cmty. Colls., Sacramento, 1995—, libr. adv. com. chancellor's office, 1995—, libr. and learning resources com. acad. senate, 1993-95. Co-author: (CD-ROM Program) Interactive CD-Rom Orientation to Southwestern College Library, 1993-96 (Ebesco award 1996). Pres. Grace Covenant Ch., Vista, Calif., 1995—. Sgt. U.S. Army, 1966-68. Mem. U.S. Golf Assn. Republican. Office: Southwestern Coll 900 Otay Lakes Rd Chula Vista CA 91910-7223

VESSELS, KEVIN DARYL, mental health clinician, inventor; b. Denver, Jan. 5, 1958; s. Clinton Cleveland Jr. and Etta Berniece (Jacobs) V. Student, Wiley Coll., Marsh, Tex., 1976-78, U. D.C., Washington, 1978-85. Recreation counselor Laradon Tng. and Residential Ctr., Denver, 1986-87; counselor Devel. Pathways, Aurora, Colo., 1986-87; clinician Aurora Cmty. Mental Health Ctr., 1986—; bd. dirs. Rocky Mountain Inventors and Entrepreneurs Congress, Denver, 1995—. Author: The Academic Success of Varsity Athletes, 1985; TV producer Mile High Cablevision Pub. Access Sta., 1985—. Mem. Ch. of Christ. Avocations: tennis, skiing, fishing. Home: 11235 E Alameda Ave Apt 22 Aurora CO 80012-1011

VEST, ROSEMARIE LYNN TORRES, secondary school educator; b. Pueblo, Colo., Jan. 16, 1958; d. Onesimo Bernabe and Maria Bersabe (Lucero) Torres; m. Donald R. Vest, May 1, 1982. BA, U. So. Colo., 1979, BS, 1991; cert. travel agt., Travel Trade Sch., Pueblo, 1986. Cert. secondary tchr., Colo.; cert. travel agt., Colo. Tutor U. So. Colo., Pueblo, 1977-79; sales rep. Intermountain Prodns., Colorado Springs, Colo., 1979-80; tutor, Pueblo, 1980-82, 84-85; travel agt. So. Colo. Travel, Pueblo, 1986-88; children's program facilitator El Mesias Family Support Program, Pueblo, 1987-88; substitute tchr. social studies Sch. Dist. 60, Pueblo, 1990—, Freed Mid. Sch., Pueblo, 1991, 92; Chpt. 1 Summer Reading Program, 1992, 93, 94, 95; instr. Travel and Tourism Dept. Pueblo C.C., 1994-95, Dept Social Studies, 1996-97. Tchr. Sunday sch., chairperson adminstrv. bd. cert. lay spkr., lay rep. to ann. conf. Ch. Evangelism, co-chmn. Trinity United Meth. Ch., Pueblo, 1989-94, parish coun. rep. to Trinity/Bethel Coop. Parish; sponsor United Meth. Youth United Meth. Ch.; tchr. Sunday Sch., co-coord. vacation Bible sch., pastoral asst., edn. chairperson, 1994—, cert. lay spkr., ministerial program asst., lay leader Bethel United Meth. Ch., 1994—; craft facilitator Integrated Health Svcs., Pueblo, 1991—; spiritual devotions/worship leader Pueblo Manor Nursing Home, 1993—; vol. resident svcs. Pueblo County Bd. for Developmental Disabilities, 1989—; mem. conf. leadership team, parliamentarian Rocky Mountain Conf. United Meth. Ch., 1995, dist. rep., 1997—; ministerial candidate United Meth. Ch.; conf. rep. Rocky Mountain Conf. Coun. on Fin. and Adminstrn., 1996. Recipient Excellence in Tchg. award Freed Mid. Sch., 1992, Vol. of Yr. award IHS of Pueblo, 1995. Mem. Assn. Am. Geographers, Nat. Oceanog. Soc., Nat. Geog. Soc. Democrat. Home: 125 W Grant Apt C Pueblo CO 81004-2000

VESTAL, JOSEPHINE BURNET, lawyer; b. Iowa City, June 13, 1949; d. Allan Delker and Dorothy (Walker) V. Student Williams Coll., 1970; B.A., Mount Holyoke Coll., 1971; J.D., U. Wash., 1974. Bar: Wash. 1974, U.S. Dist. Ct. (we. dist.) Wash. 1974, U.S. Ct. Appeals (9th cir.) 1984, U.S. Ct. Appeals (D.C. cir.) 1984, U.S. Dist. Ct. (ea. dist.) Wash. 1993. Ptnr. Selinker, Vestal, Klockars & Andersen, Seattle, 1974-80; assoc. Williams, Lanza, Kastner & Gibbs, Seattle, 1981-87, ptnr., 1988—. Mem. Wash. State Bar Assn. (trustee young lawyers sect. 1974—), Seattle-King County Bar Assn. (trustee young lawyers sect. 1974—), Wash. Women Lawyers. Office: Williams Kastner & Gibbs 2000 Skyline Tower 10900 NE 4th St PO Box 1800 Bellevue WA 98009-1800

VETTO, JOHN TYSON, surgeon, educator; b. Cin., May 11, 1956; s. R. Mark and Marianne (Tyson) V.; m. Irene Perez, Jan. 11, 1992. BS in Biology with highest honors, Portland State U., 1978; MD summa cum laude, Oreg. Health Scis. U., 1982. Intern, jr. resident Brigham and Women's Hosp., Boston, 1982-84; fellow Nat. Cancer Inst., Bethesda, Md., 1984-86; resident UCLA, L.A., 1986-89; fellow Meml. Sloan-Kettering Cancer Ctr., N.Y.C., 1989-91; asst. prof. surgery Oreg. Health Scis. U., Portland, 1991—; chief sect. of surg. oncology Portland VA Med. Ctr., 1991—; co-chmn. Oreg. Breast & Cervical Cancer Coalition, Portland, 1993—. Recipient Lange award Lange Publs., 1981, Mosby award Mosby Publs., 1982. Fellow Am. Coll. Surgeons (liaison com. on cancer 1992—), Soc. Surg. Oncology, Am. Bd. Surgery; mem. Assn. Acad. Surgery, Soc. Head & Neck Surgeons, Pacific Coast Surg. Assn., North Pacific Surg. Assn.

VEVERKA, MICHAEL J., diagnostic radiologist; b. Mitchell, S.D., May 5, 1947; s. Joe and Dorothy (Schiltz) V.; m. Kathleen Sullivan, Sept. 26, 1970; children: David, Marie. BS cum laude, St. John's U., 1969; MD, U. Minn., 1975. Diplomate Am. Bd. Radiology. Intern in surgery Oreg. Health Scis. U., Portland, 1976-77, resident in diagnostic radiology, 1977-80, instr. in radiology, 1980; radiologist Legacy Portland Hosp., 1981—; chmn. dept. imaging Northwest Magnetic Imaging, 1992—; radiologist Meridian Park Hosp., Tualatin, Oreg., 1981—; consulting radiologist Northwest Magnetic Imaging, Portland, 1984—; med. advisor Portland C.C., 1992—; clin. asst. prof. dept. diagnostic radiology Oreg. Health Scis. U., 1986—. Mem. Am. Coll. Radiology, Soc. Breast Imaging, Radiol. Soc. N.Am., Oreg. Radiol. Soc. (pres. 1993-94), Oreg. Med. Assn. Office: Radiology Cons Inc PO Box 10768 Portland OR 97210

VIANCO, PAUL THOMAS, metallurgist; b. Rochester, N.Y., Dec. 28, 1957; s. George William and Josephine Rose (Sardisco) V.; m. Karen Elaine Claghorn. BS in Physics, SUNY, 1980; MS in Mechanical and Aeronautical Engring., U. Rochester, 1981, PhD in Materials Sci., 1986. Sr. mem. tech. staff Sandia Nat. Labs., Albuquerque, 1987—. Mem. ASME, Am. Welding Soc. (chmn. subcom. 1992—), ASM Internat., The Metalurgical Soc., Sandia Skeet Club (treas.). Home: 4012 Shenandoah Pl NE Albuquerque NM 87111-4158 Office: Sandia Nat Labs PO Box 5800 MS 1411 Albuquerque NM 87185

VICCARO, JAMES RICHARD, marketing executive; b. Sewickley, Pa., Dec. 12, 1945; s. James Edward and Frances (Mastro) V.; m. Linda Schutte, May 14, 1966; children: James Richard Jr., Christy, Gina. BS, Indiana U. Pa., 1967; MBA, U. Phoenix, 1986. Vice pres. mktg. and sales Lee Pharms., South El Monte, Calif., 1973-78; pres., cons. Corp. Mktg. Dynamics, Huntington Beach, Calif., 1977—; dir. sales and mktg. chem. packaging div. Ga.-Pacific Co., Newport Beach, Calif., 1980-83; pres., chief operating officer Arnco Mktg., Ltd., Irvine, Calif., 1987-91; pres., owner Poly-Tak, Huntington Beach, Calif., 1992—. Mem. Am. Mktg. Assn., U. Phoenix Network for Profl. Devel., Tau Kappa Epsilon. Home: 6891 Loyola Dr Huntington Beach CA 92647-4053

VICE, CHARLES LOREN, electromechanical engineer; b. LaVerne, Okla., Jan. 2, 1921; s. Cyrus Christopher and Ethel Sewatch (Hoy) V.; m. Katherine Margaret Maxwell, July 14, 1949; children: Katherine Lorene, Charles Clark, Ann Marie. Cert., Oreg. State U., 1944, BSME, 1947; postgrad., U. So. Calif., 1948-55. Registered profl. engr., Calif. Mgr. magnetic head div. Gen. Instrument Corp., Hawthorne, Calif., 1959-62; sr. staff engr. magnetic head div. Ampex Corp., Redwood City, Calif., 1962-66; chief mech. engr. Collins Radio Corp., Newport Beach, Calif., 1967-69; pres. FerraFlux Corp., Santa Ana, Calif., 1970-78; sr. staff engr. McDonnell Douglas Computer Systems Co., Irvine, Calif., 1979-89, Santa Ana, Calif., 1989; ret. McDonnell Douglas Computer Systems Co., 1989; cons. Teac Corp. Japan, 1974-78, Otari Corp. Japan, 1975-77, Univac Corp., Salt Lake City, 1975-76, Crown Radio Corp. Japan, 1979-80, Sabor Corp. Japan, 1982, Empire Corp., Tokyo, 1987-89, DIGI SYS Corp., Fullerton, Calif., 1988-89, Puritan Bennett Aerosystems, El Segundo, Calif., 1989-94, Avox Corp., Van Nuys, Calif., 1995—. Patentee in field. Served with U.S. Army Engrs., 1943-46. Decorated Bronze Star. Mem. NSPE, Toastmasters. Republican. Office: Precision Cons Inc 5902 E Bryce Ave Orange CA 92867-3305

VICKERMAN, PAULA MARIE, marketing professional, consultant; b. Colo. Springs, Colo., July 8, 1968; d. Robert Eugene V. and Sharon May Lowney. BSBA in Orgn. Mgmt., U. Colo., 1990; MBA in Market Strategy, Regis U., 1996. Econ. devel. splst. Office Econ. Devel. City of Colo. Springs (Colo.), 1990-96, dir. mktg. program dept. transp., 1996—. Dir. Colo. Springs (Colo.) Film Commn., 1990-96; adv. bd. Colo. Motion Picture and TV Adv. Commn., Denver, 1992-96, Colo. Springs Film Adv. Commn., 1991-96; founding mem. Colo. Springs Sister Cities Internat., 1992-96, treas., 1992-93, chair mktg. com., 1993-95. Mem. Am. Econ. Developers Coun., Assn. Film Commrs. Internat. (award of Achievement 1990), Colo. Film and Video Assn., Econ. Developers Coun. Colo. Democrat. Office: City of Colorado Springs Transportation PO Box 1575 MC 450 Colorado Springs CO 80901

VICKERY, BYRDEAN EYVONNE HUGHES (MRS. CHARLES EVERETT VICKERY, JR.), retired library services administrator; b. Belleview, Mo., Apr. 18, 1928; d. Roy Franklin and Margaret Cordelia (Wood) Hughes; m. Charles Everett Vickery, Jr., Nov. 5, 1948; 1 child, Camille. Student, Flat River (Mo.) Jr. Coll., 1946-48; BS in Edn., S.E. Mo. State Coll., 1954; MLS, U. Wash., 1964; postgrad. Wash. State U., 1969-70. Tchr. Ironton (Mo.) Pub. Schs., 1948-56; elem. tchr. Pasco (Wash.) Sch. Dist. 1, 1956-61, jr. high sch. libr., 1961-68, coord. librs., 1968-69; asst. libr. Columbia Basin Community Coll., Pasco, 1969-70, head libr., dir. Instructional Resources Ctr., 1970-78, dir. libr. svcs., 1979-87, assoc. dean libr. svcs., 1987-90, ret., 1990; owner Vickery Search & Research, 1990—; chmn. S.E. Wash. Libr. Svc. Area, 1977-78, 88-90. Bd. dirs. Pasco-Kennewick Community Concerts, 1977-88, pres., 1980-81, 87-88, Pasco-Kennewick Community Concerts, treas., 1991—; bd. dirs. Mid-Columbia Symphony Orch., 1983-89; trustee Wash. Commn. Humanities, 1982-85; bd. mem. Arts Coun. Mid-Columbia Region, 1991-93. Author, editor: Library and Research Skills Curriculum Guides for the Pasco School District, 1967; author (with Jean Thompson), also editor Learning Resources Handbook for Teachers, 1969. Recipient Woman of Achievement award Pasco Bus. and Profl. Women's Club, 1976. Mem. ALA, AAUW (2d v.p. 1966-68, corr. sec. 1969), Wash. Dept. Audio-Visual Instrn., Wash. Libr. Assn., Am. Assn. Higher Edn., Wash. Assn. Higher Edn., Wash. State Assn. Sch. Librs. (state conf. chmn. 1971-72), Tri-Cities Librs. Assn., Wash. Libr. Media Assn. (community coll. levels chmn. 1986-87), Am. Assn. Rsch. Libr., Soroptimist Internat. Assn. (rec. sec. Pasco-Kennewick chpt. 1971-72, treas. 1973-74, pres. 1978-80, v.p. 1989-90, treas. 1991, found. & awards chmn. 1995-96), Columbia Basin Coll. Adminstrs. Assn. (sec.-treas. 1973-74), Pacific N.W. Assn. Ch. Libr., Women in Communications, Pasco Bus. and Profl. Women's Club, PEO, Beta Sigma Phi, Delta Kappa Gamma, Phi Delta Kappa (sec. 1981-82, Outstanding Educator award 1983). Home: 3521 S Fisher Ct Kennewick WA 99337-2559

VICTOR, ANDREW CROST, physicist, consultant, small business owner; b. N.Y.C., Nov. 4, 1934; s. Joseph and Stella (Crost) V.; m. Dorothy Tresselt, Dec. 9, 1955; children: Lisa Ann, Jean Sylvia Victor Lindsteadt, Joseph Andrew. BA in Chemistry, Swarthmore (Pa.) Coll., 1956; MS in Physics, U. Md., 1961. Physicist Nat. Bur. Standards, Washington, 1956-62; physicist Naval Weapons Ctr., China Lake, Calif., 1962-67, br. head, 1967-80, program mgr., 1980-89; physicist, owner Victor Tech., San Rafael, Calif., 1990—; mem., chmn. exhaust plume subcom. Joint Army, Navy, NASA, Air Force Propulsion Group, Laurel, Md., 1964-89; mem., leader exhaust plume and propulsion hazards com. The Tech. Coop. Program, U.S., UK, Can., Australia, New Zealand, 1967-89; mem. plume working group Adv. Group Aerospace Rsch. and Devel./NATO, Brussels, 1987-90. Contbr. articles to profl. jours. Fellow AIAA (assoc.); mem. Am. Def. Preparedness Assn., System Safety Soc., Internat. Pyrotechnics Soc., Sigma Xi.

VIDAL, ALEJANDRO LEGASPI, architect; b. Kawit, Cavite, The Philippines, May 3, 1934; came to U.S. 1954; s. Antonio and Patrocinia Santonil (Legaspi) V.; m. Fe Del Rosario, Aug. 16, 1962; 1 child, Alex Anthony. BS in Architecture, Mapua Inst. Tech., 1962. Registered arch., The Philippines. Prin. A.L. Vidal Arch., Manila, The Philippines, 1962-63; staff arch. Vinnell Wall & Green, Agana, Guam, 1963-64; project engr. Dillingham Corp. of Nevada, Hawaii and Guam, 1964-74; sr. project mgr., preconstrn. svc. mgr. Fletcher-Pacific Constrn. Co. Ltd., Honolulu, 1974-96; prin. A.L. Vidal Constrn. Cons., Honolulu, 1996—, A.L. Vidal Arch., Cavite, The Philippines, 1996—. Designer, builder first application of integrated aluminum forming sys. for high rise concrete construction. Active Rep. Presdl. Task Force, Washington, 1980-88, Rep. Senatorial Com., Washington, 1980-88. With USN, 1954-58, Korea. Mem. Am. Concrete Inst., Am. Mgmt. Assn., Soc. Am. Mil. Engrs., Am. Legion, U. Hawaii Found., Chancellor's Club, Disabled Am. Vets., Comdrs. Club, Oxford Club. Roman Catholic. Home: 1051 Kaluanui Rd Honolulu HI 96825-1321

VIDAR, KENNETH MILES, real estate company executive; b. Hollywood, Calif., June 17, 1948; s. Nils-Uno and Margareta (Svensson) V.; m. Linda Susan Ragozzino Cooper, Aug. 26, 1966 (div. 1985); children: Stacey Diane, Jennifer Lynn; m. Mary Ellen Cross, Aug. 23, 1986. Student, Coll. of San Mateo, Calif., 1966-74. Cert. comml. investment mem., cert. residential specialist. Salesperson Century 21, San Rafael, Calif., 1974-76; owner/broker Kenneth M. Vidar Realtor, San Rafael, 1976-81, Vidar/Wrisley/Pace Realtors, San Rafael, 1981-86; ptnr. Triad Internat., Walnut Creek, Calif., 1981-86; pres. Vidar Cos., Inc., San Rafael, 1981-92, Incline Village, Nev., 1990—; pres. Meken Corp., Manhattan, Mont., 1992—. With USAF, 1968-72. Mem. Nat. Assn. Realtors (Campbell Trophy 1981), Soc. Exchange Counselors. Republican. Office: Vidar Companies Inc 3200 Nixon Gulch Rd Manhattan MT 59741

VIDGEN, RICK, food products executive; b. 1941. With C.S.R. Ltd., Sydney, Australia, 1962-83, Ram Group, Inc., Oakland, Calif., 1983-86; with Macadamia Farms of Hawaii, Inc., Captain Cook, 1986—, now pres.; bd. dirs. Internat. Nutrition Coun., chmn. nutrition com. Office: Mac Farms of Hawaii Inc Honomalino District Captain Cook HI 96704

VIEIRA, LINDA MARIE, endoscopy technician; b. San Jose, Calif., July 8, 1961; d. Albert Sequeira and Catherine Marie (Souza) Vieira; m. John Bettencourt Ramos, June 12, 1982 (div. July 1993). AA, De Anza Coll., 1986; BA, St. Mary's Coll. Calif., Moraga, 1988. Cert. gastrointestinal clinician, aerobic instr. Endoscopy technician O'Connor Hosp., San Jose, 1979-94, Good Samaritan Health Sys., Los Gatos, Calif., 1994—, Alexian Bros. Hosp., San Jose, Calif., 1995—; aerobic instr. Mountain View (Calif.) Athletic Club, 1984-95, Decathlon Club, Santa Clara, 1991—, Golds Gym, Mountain View, 1994—, Silicon Valley Athletic Club, Santa Clara, 1995—. Contbr. articles to profl. jours. Vol. O'Connor Hosp., 1975-79; active campaign Santa Clara City Council, 1980-81. Fellow Irmandade Da Festa Do Espirito Santo (sec. 1974-82, queen 1975-76), Soc. Gastrointestinal Assts., No. Soc. Gastrointestinal Assts., Soc. Espirito Santo of Santa Clara, Luso Am. Fraternal Fedn. (state youth pres. 1979-80, youth leader local coun. Santa Clara Mountain View 1979-87, scholar, 1979, founder, organizer Mountain View-Santa Clara chpt. 1980, pres. local region 1980-84, state 20-30 pres. 1984-85, state dir. youth programs 1988-94, state dir. 1994—); mem. Aerobics and Fitness Assn. Am. Republican. Roman Catholic. Home: 1618 Roll St Santa Clara CA 95050-4024 Office: Good Samaritan Health Sys 15066 Los Gatos Almaden Rd Los Gatos CA 95032-3909

VIEIRA, ROBERT, composer; b. Newark, Apr. 22, 1957; s. Joseph Robert and June Lucielle (Perry) V. AB, U. Calif., Berkeley, 1983, MA, 1986, CPhil, 1988. Computer analyst Flexi-Van, San Francisco, 1980-82; composer, audio engr. ATARI, Sunnyvale, Calif., 1981-84; composer, cons. various clients, 1984-92; composer/sound designer The 3DO Co., Redwood City, Calif., 1992-97; composer, designer Prolific Pub., 1997—. Composer on more than 50 titles of electronic entertainment games, 1981-96. Mem. Commonwealth Club. Democrat. Office: The 3DO Co 600 Galveston Dr Redwood City CA 94063-4721

VIERHELLER, TODD, software engineering consultant; b. Winter Park, Fla., June 22, 1958; s. Irvin Theodore and Jeanne Marie (Zeller) V.; m. Susan Lindhe Watts, Dec. 22, 1984; children: Renate Jeanne, Clark, Lindhe Marie, Kent. BS in Computer Sci., U. Mo., Rolla, 1980; MA in Bibl. Studies, Multnomah Sch. Bible, Portland, Oreg., 1986. Tech. writer, software engr. Tektronix, Beaverton, Oreg., 1981-86, software engring. mgr., 1988-89; software engr., supr. Intel Corp., Hillsboro, Oreg., 1986-88; software engring. mgr. Summation, 1989-90; software cons. Quality First, Lynnwood, Wash., 1990—; software engring. cons. Digital Equipment Corp., Bellevue, Wash., 1990-91, GTE, Bothell, Wash., 1990-91, Frank Russell Co., Tacoma, Wash., 1992-93, InterConnections, Inc., Bellevue, 1993, Novell, San Jose, Calif., 1993, Heartstream, Inc., 1996, N.Am. Morpho Sys., Inc., 1996, Air Touch Cellular, 1996-97; software engring. mgmt. cons. Weyerhauser, Federal Way, Wash., 1991-92, Frank Russell, Tacoma, Wash., 1994, ConnectSoft, Inc., Bellevue, 1994, Microsoft, Redmond, Wash., 1995-96; tech. writer, cons. Air Touch Cellular, Bellevue, Wash., 1996-97. Mem. IEEE, NRA, Upsilon Pi Epsilon, Kappa Mu Epsilon. Republican. Mem. Evang. Christian Ch. Home: 23617 36th Pl W Brier WA 98036-8411 Office: Quality First PO Box 6212 Lynnwood WA 98036-0212

VIERLING, JOHN MOORE, physician; b. Bellflower, Calif., Nov. 20, 1945; s. Lester Howard and Ruth Ann (Moore) V.; m. Gayle Aileen Vandermast, June 30, 1968 (div. 1984); children: Jeffrey M., Janet A; m. Donna Marie Sheps, May 4, 1985; children: Matthew R., Mark L. (dec.). AB in Biology with great distinction, Stanford U., 1967, MD, 1972. Intern then resident Strong Meml. Hosp. U. Rochester, N.Y., 1972-74; clin. assoc. liver unit NIH, Bethesda, Md., 1974-77; gastroenterology fellow U. Calif., San Francisco, 1977-78, instr. medicine, 1978-79; from asst. to assoc. U. Colo. Sch. Medicine, Denver, 1979-90; dir. hepatology, med dir. liver transplantation Cedars-Sinai Med. Ctr., L.A., 1990—; assoc. prof. medicine UCLA, 1990-96, prof. medicine, 1996—; lectr. Schering Corp., Kenilworth, N.J., 1990—; mem. sci. adv. bd. Am. Digestive Health Found., Digestive Health Initiative. Assoc. editor: Prinicples and Practice of Gastroenterology and Hepatology, 1992; editorial bd. Hepatology, 1985-90, Gastroenterology, 1993—; co-patentee in hybridization assay for hepatitis virus, 1992. With USPHS, 1974-77. Fellow ACP; mem. Am. Assn. Study Liver Diseases, Am. Gastroenterolog. Assn., Internat. Assn. for Study Liver, European Assn. for Study Liver, Am. Liver Found. (chmn. bd. dirs. 1994—). Office: Cedars-Sinai Ctr Liver Diseases and Transpl 8635 W Third St Ste 590W Los Angeles CA 90048

VIGDOR, JAMES SCOTT, distribution executive; b. Bklyn., Oct. 12, 1953; s. Irving and Betty Jean (Wolkenbrod) V.; m. Mindy Sue Neirs, May 30, 1982; 1 child, Rachel Dyan. BA, Ohio State U., 1975. Regional distbn. mgr. Gestetner Corp., L.A., 1979-83; asst. ops. mgr. Wall-Pride, Inc., Van Nuys, Calif., 1983-88; ops. mgr. Opportunities for Learning, Inc., Chatsworth, Calif., 1988-89; dir. ops. Image Entertainment, Chatsworth, 1989-91; ops mgr. Cal-Abco and Legend Computer Products, Woodland Hills, Calif., 1991-95; dir. ops. HW Electronics, Van Nuys, Calif., 1995-97; v.p. ops. Micro Age Computer Ctr./Advanced Optical Distbn., Encino, Calif., 1997—. Office: Micro Age Computer Ctr Advanced Optical Distbn 16530 Ventura Blvd Ste 105 Encino CA 91436

VIGIL, DANIEL AGUSTIN, academic administrator; b. Denver, Feb. 13, 1947; s. Agustin and Rachel (Naranjo) V.; m. Claudia Cartier. BA in History, U. Colo., Denver, 1978, JD, 1982. Bar: Colo. 1982, U.S. Dist. Ct. Colo. 1983. Project mgr. Mathematics Policy Rsch., Denver, 1978; law clk. Denver Dist. Ct., 1982-83; ptnr. Vigil and Bley, Denver, 1983-85; asst. dean sch. law U. Colo., Boulder, 1983-89; assoc. dean sch. law U. Colo., 1989—; apptd. by chief justice of Colo. Supreme Ct. to serve on Colo. Supreme Ct. Ad Hoc Com. on miniority participation in legal profession; adj. prof. U. Colo. Sch. Law; bd. dirs. Continuing Legal Edn. in Colo., Inc.; mem. Gov. Colo. Lottery Commn. Editor (newsletter) Class Action, 1987-88; co-editor (ethics com. column) Colo. Lawyer. Bd. dirs. Legal Aid Soc. Met. Denver, 1986—; past v.p. Colo. Minority Scholarhip Consortium, pres. 1990-91; mem. Task Force on Community Race Rels., Boulder, 1989-94; past mem. jud. nomination rev. com. U.S. Senator Tim Wirth. Mem. Colo. Bar Assn. (mem. legal edn. and admissions com. 1989-94, chmn. 1989-91, bd. govs. 1991), Hispanic Nat. Bar Assn. (chmn. scholarship com. 1990-95), Colo Hispanic Bar Assn. (bd. dirs. 1985-89, pres. 1990), Denver Bar Assn. (joint com. on minorities in the legal profession), Boulder County Bar Assn. (ex-officio mem., trustee), Phi Delta Phi (faculty sponsor). Roman Catholic. Home: 828 3d Ave PO Box 518 Lyons CO 80540 Office: U Colo Sch Law PO Box 401 Boulder CO 80303

VIGIL, DOUGLAS ELLIOTT, lawyer; b. Denver, Jan. 19, 1953; s. Joseph M. and Sally A. (Roberts) V.; m Gloria M. Kephart, May 30, 1981; 1 child, Aislinn Elizabeth. BFA, Utah State U., 1977; AD in Radiol. Sci., U. N.Mex., 1981, BSN, 1984, JD, 1989. Bar: N.Mex. 1989, U.S. Ct. Appeals N.Mex. 1991, U.S. Ct. Appeals (10th cir.) 1991, Colo. 1996. Self employed ceramic potter Logan, Utah, 1975-79, San Jose, Calif., 1975-79; radiol. tech. Albuquerque, 1981-84; staff nurse trauma ICU U. N.Mex. Hosp., Albuquerque, 1984-89; staff nurse St. Josephs Hosp. Intensive Care Unit, Albuquerque, 1984-85; atty. Simon, Cuddy & Friedman, Santa Fe, 1989-90, Branch Law Firm, Albuquerque, 1990-96; pvt. practice Albuquerque, 1996—. Mem. ABA, N.Mex. Trial Lawyers. Home: 9709 Fostoria Rd NE Albuquerque NM 87111-1251 Office: 620 Roma NW Albuquerque NM 87103

VIGIL, MICHAEL J., school system administrator; b. Espanola, N.Mex., Sept. 30, 1957; s. Edward E. and Luz E. (Gallegos) V.; m. Lucy J. Glover, Aug. 18, 1979; children: Victoria L., Michael J. II, Mark J. BBA, U. N.Mex., 1980. CPA, N.Mex., Ariz. Securities specialist N.Mex. Securities Bur., Santa Fe, 1980-81; staff acct., securities specialist Ariz. Securities Divsn., Phoenix, 1981-85; chief auditor Am. Fed. Savs. & Loan Assn., Albuquerque, 1985-89; tax auditor State N.Mex., Albuquerque, 1989; dir. internal audit Albuquerque Pub. Schs., 1990-93, CFO, 1993—; Mem. State Dept. Edn. Com., Albuquerque, 1994-95. Mem. Risen Savior Pastoral Coun., Albuquerque, 1992-93. Mem. AICPA, Assn. Sch. Bus. Officers, Inst. Internal Auditors (dir., treas. 1987-88), N.Mex. Assn. Sch. Bus. Officers, K.C. (grand knight 1991-92, fin. sec. 1995-97). Office: Albuquerque Pub Schs 725 University Blvd SE Albuquerque NM 87106-4329

VIGIL, VELOY JOSEPH, artist; b. Denver, Mar. 5, 1931; s. Cipriano Cornealous and Andrea Agatha (Rodriquez) V.; m. Elean Montoya, Apr. 12, 1952; children—Daniel John, Rita Marie, Sandra Louise, Michael Veloy. Student pub. schs., Greeley, Colo. Art dir. Creative West, Orange, Calif., 1972-75, Buzza-Gibson, Anaheim, Calif., 1965-72; artist Am. Greeting, Cleve., 1959-64, LooArt Design, Colorado Springs, 1964-65; one man shows include: Segal Gallery, N.Y.C., 1984, 86, Suzanne Brown Gallery, Scottsdale, Ariz., 1985, 97, Retropective Exbhn. Millicent Rogers Mus., Taos, New Mex., Ontario (Calif.) Mus. of History and Art; exhibited in group shows including: Smithsonian Instn., 1983, Masters of Southwest, 1984; represented in permanent collections including, Heard Mus., Phoenix, Portland Mus., IBM Corp., Phoenix, Simuflite Corp., Dallas. Served with USMC, 1950-53. Recipient Winslow Homer award, Springfield Art Mus., 1969; Purchase award Colorado Springs Fine Arts, 1964; Avery Meml. award, Heard Mus., Phoenix, 1976; Ann award Nat. Watercolor Soc., 1969. Mem. Nat. Watercolor Soc. (v.p. 1973-74). Home: 224 North Guadalupe Santa Fe NM 87501 Office: 111 Morada Ln Taos NM 87571

VIGLIONE, EUGENE LAWRENCE, automotive executive; b. Paterson, N.J., Nov. 23, 1931; s. Fred and Caroline (Cantilina) V.; m. Vera Yonkens, June 12, 1954 (div. June 1976), m. Evila (Billie) Larez Viglione, Sept. 19, 1976; children: Victoria, David, Valerie, Vanessa, Francine, Margaret, Robert. Student, Cooper Union, N.Y., 1950-51. Pres. Lahaina News, Ridgewood, N.J., 1995—; sales mgr. Carlton Motors, Frankfurt, Germany, 1966-67, Jones Minto Ford, Burlingame, Calif., 1967-72, Terry Ford, Pompano Beach, Fla., 1974-75; gen. mgr. Kohlenberg Ford, Burlingame, 1975-76; v.p. Morris Landy Ford, Alameda, Calif., 1976-80, Burlingame Ford, 1980-85; emeritus chmn. bd. Valley Isle Motors, Wailuku, Hawaii, 1985—; pres. Marriott Luau, Lahaina, Hawaii, 1989—; gen. mgr., v.p. Jim Falk Lexus of Beverly Hills, 1996—; pres. Maui Auto Dealers Assn., Wailuku, 1986-87, pres. VIG Music C., 1996. Del. Rep. State Conv., Honolulu, 1988, State House of Reps.; 1992; v.p. Rep. Party Precinct, Lahaina, 1988, trustee Rep. Presdl. Task Force, Washington, 1983-88; pres. Maui County Rep. Party, 1983; pres. Big Bros./Big Sisters, 1993; pres. Light Bringers; bd. dirs. Following Maui Symphony, Lahaina Action Com., Maui United Way, Homeless Resource Ctr. Named Top 250 Exec. Hawaii Bus. Mag., 1986-92. Mem. Nat. Auto Dealers Assn., Internat. Auto Dealers Assn., Nat. Fed. of Ind. Bus., Maui Rotary, Lahaina Yacht Club, Maui Country Club, Frairs Club of Calif., Gideons, Maui C. of C. Home: 2481 Kaanapali Pky Lahaina HI 96761-1910 Office: Valley Isle Motors 221 S Puunene Ave Kahului HI 96732-2426 also: 9230 Wilshire Blvd Beverly Hills CA 90212

VIGNE, JEAN-LOUIS, biochemist; b. Pertuis, Vaucluse, France, Nov. 8, 1945; came to U.S., 1976; s. Francis Fortuné and Denise (Sube) V.; m. Josefina Maria Naya, Sept. 8, 1976; 1 child, Carole. D in Specialité, U. d'Aix-Marseille I, France, 1972; D in Phys. Scis., U. d'Aix-Marseille II, France, 1981. Postdoctoral fellow U. Calif., San Francisco, 1976-78; attaché de recherches Institut National de la Santé et de la Recherche Medicale, Marseille, 1978-81; charge de recherches INSERM, Marseille, 1981-84; scientist project leader Calif. Biotech. Inc., Mountain View, Calif., 1984-88; vis. asst. endocrinologist U. Calif., San Francisco, 1988-90, co-dir. analytical lab., 1990—; vis. asst. prof. Fed. U., Rio de Janeiro, 1973-76; vis. scientist Cardiovascular Rsch. Inst., San Francisco, 1982-84. Contbr. articles to profl. jours.; inventor pharmaceutical microemulsions and mature apoA1 protein production. Fellow Brazilian Nat. Rsch. Coun., 1972-76, French Fgn. Affairs, 1976-78, NATO, 1982-83, Phillipe Found., 1982-83; grantee HHS, 1986. Mem. N.Y. Acad. Scis., Endocrine Soc. Home: 201 Dellbrook Ave San Francisco CA 94131-1210

VILARDI, AGNES FRANCINE, real estate broker; b. Monson, Mass., Sept. 29, 1918; d. Paul and Adelina (Mastrioanni) Vetti; m. Frank S. Vilardi, Dec. 2, 1939; children: Valerie, Paul. Cert. of dental assisting Pasadena Jr. Coll., 1954. Lic. real estate broker. Real estate broker, owner Vilardi Realty, Yorba Linda, Calif., Placentia, Calif., Fullerton, Calif., 1968—; cons. in property mgmt. Mem. Am. Dental Asst. Assn., North Orange County Bd. Realtors (sec./treas. 1972), Yorba Linda Country Club, Desert Princess Country Club. Home and Office: 18982 Villa Ter Yorba Linda CA 92886-2610

VILLA, CARLOS PEDRO, artist, activist, educator; b. San Francisco, Dec. 11, 1936. BFA in Edn., San Francisco Art Inst., 1961; MFA in Painting, Mills Coll., 1963. Assoc. prof. Calif. State U. art dept., 1969-79; lectr. Calif. Coll. of Arts and Crafts, Oakland, 1988-95, San Francisco State U., 1990, Mills Coll., Oakland, Calif., 1992; prof. San Francisco Art Inst., 1969—; guest curator Emmanuel Walter Gallery, San Francisco, 1976; bd. dirs. Coll. Art Assn., N.Y.C., 1992-94, pres., artist, dir. Filipino Am. Art Exposition, San Fancisco, 1992-94; chief adminstr. rsch. art exhbn. Four Bay Area Pioneer Filipino Artists, 1994-96. Publisher: (book) Worlds in Collision, 1994; artist: numerous solo and group exhbns., nat. and internat., 1958—. Advisor, founder Wolds inCollision Web Site, San Francisco, 1996. With U.S. Army, 1954-57, Korea. Recipient Hon. Mention Richmond (Calif.) Art Ctr., 1959, Adelaide Kent award, San Francisco Art Inst., 1974, Disting. Alumni award, 1989; grantee NEA, 1973. Office: San Francisco Art Inst 800 Chestnut St San Francisco CA 94133

VILLA, THEODORE B., artist, educator; b. Santa Barbara, Calif., Sept. 28, 1936; s. Theodore G. Villa and Josephine Melendez Willette; m. Judith Ann McConnell Villa, Aug. 21, 1963; children: Rebecca Lynn, Paul Andrew. BA, U. Calif., Santa Barbara, 1963, MFA, 1974. Cert. tchr. secondary and cmty. coll. Art instr. U. Calif., Santa Barbara, Santa Barbara City Coll., Sun Valley Ctr. for the Arts; One man shows at U. Calif. Art Mus., Santa Barbara, 1974, Esther Bear Gallery, Santa Barbara, 1975, 77, Jodi Scully Gallery, L.A., 1977, Mekler Gallery, L.A., 1980, Niles Gallery, Santa Barbara, 1981, 82, Sun Valley Ctr. for Arts and Humanities, 1982, 83, Kneeland Gallery, Sun Valley, Idaho, 1984, 85, 86, 87, 88, 89, Bridgitte Schluger Gallery, Denver, 1988, Anne Reed Gallery, Ketchum, Idaho, 1989, 90, 91, 92, Broschofsky Gallery, Ketchum, 1992, 93, many others. Exhibited in numerous group shows including L.A. County Mus. Art, 1975, 77, 78, 80, 81, 82, M. Shore and Sons Gallery, Santa Barbara, 1980, Sacred Circles Gallery, Seattle, 1982, 83, 85, Palais de Nations, Geneva, Switzerland, 1984, Nimbus Gallery, Dallas, 1985, Harcus Gallery, Boston, 1987, Munson Gallery, Santa Fe, N.Mex., 1987, 88, Lakota Gallery, Santa Monica, Calif., 1988, 89, Brigitte Schluger Gallery, Denver, 1990, Gallery 10, Santa Fe, 1991, Ctr. for Cont. Art, Seattle, 1992, Heard Mus., Phoenix, 1991, Mus. No. Ariz., Flagstaff, Ariz., 1995, Heard Mus., Phoenix, 1993, Kimball Art Ctr., Park City, Utah, many others; one man shows include Centro Washington Irving, Madrid, 1993, Millicent Rogers Mus., Taos, N.Mex., 1990, Broschofsky Gallery, Ketchum, Idaho, Ctr. Gallery, Jackson, Wyo., Telluride (Colo.) Gallery. Bd. dirs. Contemporary Art Forum, 1987-94; dir. Atkinson Gallery, Santa Barbara City Coll., 1986-87, coord., 1979-83, dir. smallimages exhbn., 1979-83; lectr. in field.

VILLABLANCA, JAIME ROLANDO, medical scientist, educator; b. Chillàn, Chile, Feb. 29, 1929; came to U.S., 1971; naturalized, 1985; s. Ernesto and Teresa (Hernàndez) V.; m. Guillermina Nieto, Dec. 3, 1955; children: Amparo C., Jaime G., Pablo J., Francis X., Claudio I. Bachelor in Biology, Nat. Inst. Chile, 1946; licentiate medicine, U. Chile, 1953, MD, 1954. Cert. neurophysiology. Rockefeller Found. postdoctoral fellow in physiology John Hopkins and Harvard Med. Schs., 1959-61; Fogarty internat. rsch. fellow in anatomy UCLA, 1966-68, assoc. research anatomist and psychiatrist, 1971-72; assoc. prof. psychiatry and biobehavioral scis. UCLA Sch. Medicine, 1972-76; prof. psychiatry and biobehavioral scis. UCLA, 1976—, prof. neurobiology, 1977—; mem. faculty U. Chile Sch. Medicine, 1954-71, prof. exptl. medicine, 1970-71; vis. prof. neurobiology Cath. U. Chile Sch. Medicine, 1974; cons. in field. Author numerous rsch. papers, book chpts., abstracts; chief regional editor Developmental Brain Dysfunction, 1988—. Decorated Order Francisco de Miranda (Venezuela); recipient Premio Reina Sofia, Madrid, 1990, Fgn. Scientist Traveling grant Tokyo (Japan) Met. Govt., 1995; fellow Rockefeller Found., 1959-61, Fogarty Internat. Rsch. fellow NIH, 1966-68; grantee USAF Office Sci. Rsch., 1962-65, Found. Fund Rsch. Psychiatry, 1969-72, USPHS-Nat. Inst. Child Human Devel., 1972-96, USPHS-Nat. Inst. Drug Abuse, 1981-85, USPHS-Nat. Inst. Neurol. Disorders and Stroke, 1988-92. Mem. AAAS, AAUP, Am. Assn. Anatomists, Mental Retardation Rsch. Ctr., Brain Rsch. Inst., Internat. Brain Rsch. Orgn., Am. Physiol. Soc., Soc. for Neurosci., Assn. Venezolana Padres de Niños Excepcionales, Sci. Coun. Internat. Inst. Rsch. and Advice in Mental Deficiency (Madrid), Soc. Child and Adolescent Psychiatry and Neurology (Chile) (hon.), Sigma Xi. Home: 200 Surfview Dr Pacific Palisades CA 90272-2911 Office: UCLA Dept Psychiatry & Biobehavioral Scis Los Angeles CA 90024

VILLEGAS, RICHARD JUNIPERO, artist; b. Santa Monica, Calif., Apr. 19, 1938; s. Robert Narciso and Jessie (Rodrigues) V. Student, Art Students League, N.Y.C., 1965-66. Artist Joseph Sarosi Inc., N.Y.C., 1961-62, Vozzo & Binetti, N.Y.C., 1962-64, Siegman-Ambro, N.Y.C., 1964-77; chief artist Greenbaum Bros., Paterson, N.J., 1978-89; owner The Villegas Art Studio, Thousand Oaks, Calif., 1989—. Mem. Westlake Village (Calif.) C. of C., C.G. Jung Found., Am. Mus. Natural History, Nat. Geog. Soc., Nat. Trust for Hist. Preservation, Gold Coast Bus. and Profl. Alliance, Conejo Valley Archers, Nat. Archery Assn. Home and Studio: 980 Camino Flores Thousand Oaks CA 91360-2367

VILNROTTER, VICTOR ALPÁR, research engineer; b. Kunhegyes, Hungary, Nov. 8, 1944; came to U.S., 1957; s. Nicholas and Aranka (Vidovits) V.; m. Felicia D'Auria, Jan. 20, 1974; children: Katherine, Brian. BSEE, NYU, 1971; MS, MIT, 1974; PhD in EE, U. So. Calif., L.A., 1978. Teaching asst. MIT, Cambridge, Mass., 1972-74; rsch. engr. Jet Propulsion Lab., Pasadena, Calif., 1979—. Contbr. articles to profl. jours.; patentee in field. Mem. IEEE (referee in communications soc. 1980—), N.Y. Acad. Scis., Sigma Xi, Eta Kappa Nu. Home: 1334 Greenbriar Rd Glendale CA 91207-1254

VINCENT, DAVID RIDGELY, management consulting executive; b. Detroit, Aug. 9, 1941; s. Charles Ridgely and Charlotte Jane (McCarroll) V.; m. Margaret Helen Anderson, Aug. 25, 1962 (div. 1973); children: Sandra Lee, Cheryl Ann; m. Judith Ann Gomez, July 2, 1978; 1 child, Amber; stepchildren: Michael Jr., Jesse Joseph Flores. BS, BA, Calif. State U.-Sacramento, 1964; MBA, Calif. State U.-Hayward, 1971; PhD Somerset U, 1991. Cert. profl. cons. to mgmt., 1994. Sr. ops. analyst Aerojet Gen. Corp., Sacramento, 1960-66; contr. Hexcel Corp., Dublin, Calif., 1966-70; mng. dir. Memorex, Austria, 1970-74; sales mgr. Ampex World Ops., Switzerland, 1974-76; dir. product mgmt. NCR, Sunnyvale, Calif., 1976-79; v.p. Boole & Babbage Inc., gen. mgr. Inst. Info. Mgmt., Sunnyvale, Calif., 1979-85; pres., CEO The Info. Group, Inc., Santa Clara, Calif., 1985—. Deacon Union Ch., Cupertino, Calif.; USSF soccer referee emeritus. Author: Perspectives in Information Management, Information Economics, 1983, Handbook of Information Resource Management, 1987, The Information-Based Corporation: stakeholder economics and the technology investment, 1990, Reengineering Fundamentals: Business Processes and the Global Economy, 1994-96; contbr. monographs and papers to profl. jours. Mem. Nat. Alliance Bus. Economists, Am. Electronics Assn., Soc. Competitive Intelligence Profls. Home: 2803 Kalliam Dr Santa Clara CA 95051-6838 Office: PO Box Q Santa Clara CA 95055-3756

VINCENT, EDWARD, mayor; b. Steubenvill, Ohio, 1934. Student, State U. Iowa; BA in Corrections and Social Welfare, Calif. State U. With L.A. County Probation Dept. Mcpl. and Superior Cts.; mayor City of Inglewood, Calif., 1982-96; Calif. State assemblyman 51st Dist. Bd. dirs. Inglewood Neighbors, Inglewood Neighborhood Housing Svcs., Inc.; mem. Urban League, New Frontier Dem. Club, Inglewood Dem. Club, Morningside High Sch. PTA, Monroe Jr. High Sch. PTA, Kew-Bennett PTA; pres. Morningside High Sch. Dad's Club. With U.A. Army, 1957-1959. Mem. NAACP, Calif. Probation Parole Corrections Assn., Black Probation Officers Assn., Calif. Narcotic Officers Assn., Mexican-Am. Corrections Assn., S.W. Horeseman, Assn., Imperial Village Blck Club, Inglewood Block Club (chmn. human affairs). Office: 1 W Manchester Blvd 6th Fl Inglewood CA 90301-1750*

VINCENT, MARK KENT, lawyer; b. Murray, Utah, May 10, 1959; s. Kent Bryan and Edith Theone (Paxton) V. BA, Brigham Young U., 1984; JD, Pepperdine U., 1987. Corp. sec. Vincent Drug Co. Inc., Midvale, Utah, 1980-87; dep. dist. atty. Office of Dist. Atty. County of Ventura, Calif., 1987-89; asst. U.S. atty. U.S. Dept. of Justice, Salt Lake City, 1989—; law clk. Utah State Supreme Ct., Salt Lake City, 1986; v.p. Barrister's Bar Orgn., Ventura, 1988-89. Margaret Martin Brock scholar Pepperdine U., 1986-87. Mem. Calif. Bar Assn., Utah Bar Assn. Mormon. Office: US Attys Office Ste 400 185 S State St Salt Lake City UT 84111

VINCENT, STEVE, environmental engineer; b. 1951. BS in Oceanography, U. Wash., 1974. With Weyerhaeuser, Tacoma, 1974-85; with Columbia Analytical Svcs., Kelso, Wash., 1986—, now pres. Office: Columbia Analytical Svc 1317 S 13th Ave Kelso WA 98626-2845*

VINCENT, VERNE SAINT, protective services official. Chief police Aurora (Colo.) Police Dept. Office: Aurora Police Dept 15001 E Alameda Dr Aurora CO 80012

VINCENTI-BROWN, CRISPIN RUFUS WILLIAM, engineering executive; b. Epsom, Surrey, England, Sept. 20, 1951; came to U.S., 1989; s. Douglas Hector and Joan Margaret Patricia (Lowe) Brown; m. Terry Doreen Bennett, May 20, 1978 (dec. Oct. 1992); children: Genevieve Louise, Juliette Alexandra; m. Margaret Anna Vincenti, Feb. 13, 1993. BSc in Engring. Prodn., U. Birmingham, 1974. Mgr. Soc. M.O.M, Grans, France, 1975; prin. cons. Ingersoll Engrs. Inc., Rugby, England, 1975-79; pres., dir. Ingersoll Engrs. SA, Annecy, France, 1979-89; sr. ptnr. Ingersoll Engrs. Inc., Los Altos, Calif., 1989—; v.p. Groupe de Talloires, Geneva, 1987-89; bd. dirs. Ops. Mgmt. Assn., Waco, Tex. Fellow Inst. Elec. Engrs. (chartered engr.). Home: 1098 Eastwood Ct Los Altos CA 94024-5015 Office: Ingersoll Engrs 5100 E State St Ste 4 Rockford IL 61108-2398

VINCENZI, FRANK FOSTER, pharmacology educator; b. Seattle, Mar. 14, 1938; s. Frank Vincenzi and Thelma C. (McAllister) Olson; m. Judith I. Heimbigner, Aug. 27, 1960; children: Ann Marie, Franklin R., Joseph P. BS in Pharmacy, U. Wash., 1960, MS in Pharmacology, 1962, PhD in Pharmacology, 1965. NSF postdoct. fellow U. Bern, Switzerland, 1965-67; asst. prof. U. Wash., Seattle, 1967-72, assoc. prof., 1972-80, acting chair, pharmacology, 1975-77, prof., 1980—. Contbr. articles to profl. jours. Mem. Am. Med. Informatics Assn., Am. Soc. of Hypertension, Am. Soc. for Pharmacology Exptl. Therapeutics, Biophys. Soc., Oxygen Soc., Western Pharmacology Soc. (pres. 1988-89). Office: Univ Wash Pharmacology Box 357280 Seattle WA 98195-7280

VINSON, CONNIE SUE, aerospace engineer; b. Gardner, Kans., May 3, 1956; d. Vernon L. and Beatrice Marie Messer; m. John Willliam Vinson, Jan. 24, 1987; children: Kyla Marie, Richard Glenn. BS in Physics, Baker U., Baldwin City, Kans., 1977; MS, Trinity U., San Antonio, 1979; MBA, Harvard U., 1983. Engr. Armstrong Machine Works, New Braunfels, Tex., 1979-81; asst. to v.p. Barnes and Jones, Newton, Mass., 1982; engr. Boise Cascade Corp., DeRidder, La., 1983-84; ops. mgr. Geneva Group Inc., Woburn, Mass., 1984-87; product mgr. TLB, Inc., Findlay, Ohio, 1987-88; tech. staff Rocketdyne div. Rockwell Internat. Corp., Canoga Park, Calif., 1990-96; tech. staff Rocketdyne divsn. Boeing N.Am. Inc., Canoga Park, 1996—; mem. adv. bd. Geneva Group, 1986-88. Recipient Leadership award Rocketdyne and YWCA of L.A., 1994. Mem. Harvard Bus. Sch. Assn. So. Calif. Republican. Presbyterian. Home: 2668 Velarde Dr Thousand Oaks CA 91360-1337 Office: Rocketdyne 6633 Canoga Ave Canoga Park CA 91303-2703

VINTAS, GUSTAV, actor, psychiatrist; b. Buenos Aires, Argentina, Nov. 27, 1948; came to U.S., 1976; s. Mauricio and Zelmira (Silbert) V. BS, U. Poitiers, France, 1967; MD, U. Buenos Aires, 1973. Resident in psychiatry McGill U., Montreal, 1976; fellow in child psychiatry Cornell U., N.Y.C., 1978; instr. psychiatry N.Y. Hosp.-Cornell U., N.Y.C., 1978-84; assoc. psychiatrist Cedars-Sinai Med. Ctr., L.A., 1986—; Diplomate in psychiatry and child psychiatry Am. Bd. Psychiatry and Neurology, Royal Coll. Physicians and Surgeons of Canada. Appeared in films including Lethal Weapon, Mickie and Maude, Vampire at Midnight, Midnight, Fair Game; TV appearances include Drug Wars, Tales From the Crypt, Beauty and the Beast, Mistress, Murder She Wrote, Madonna video Express Yourself; performer one-man show Merci Maurice, Evoking the Memory of Maurice Chevalier. Mem. Royal Coll. Physicians and Surgeons, Am. Psychiat. Assn. Office: 462 N Linden Dr # 230 Beverly Hills CA 90212

VINTON, ALICE HELEN, real estate company executive; b. McMinnville, Oreg., Jan. 10, 1942; d. Gale B. and Saima Helen (Pekkola) V. Student, Portland State Coll., Northwestern Sch. Commerce. Lic. real estate broker, Hawaii. Owner, prin. broker Vinton Realty, Honolulu, 1988—. Founder, bd. dirs. Kekuaanaui, Hawaii Big Sisters, 1972-76; former vol. Child and Family Svc., women's divsn. Halawa Prison; bd. dirs. Kindergarten and Children's Aid Assn., 1977-88, advisor, mem. long-range planning com. 1988-90; former mem. tuition aid com., chmn. nominating com. and capital improvements com. Laura Morgan Pre-Sch.; bd. dirs. Hawaii Theatre Ctr., 1985-86; mem. Lyon Arboretum Assn. Recipient proclamation Hawaii Ho. of Reps., cert. of merit for disting. svc. to community, Dictionary of Internat. Biography, Vol. XXI, 1990. Mem. Nat. Assn. Realtors, Hawaii Assn. Realtors, Honolulu Bd. Realtors, Honolulu C. of C., Acad. Arts, Bishop Mus. Assn., Wildlife Fedn., Honolulu, Friends of Iolani Palace, Smithsonian Inst., Honolulu Press Club (membership chmn. 1988-90), Rainbow Girls Club (life), Hawaii Humane Soc., Sierra Club, Hist. Hawaii, Cen. Bus. Club Honolulu, Nature Conservancy Hawaii, YWCA, Coustea Soc., Wolf Haven, Honolulu Polo Club, Orchid Soc. Manoa, North Shore Animal League, Nat. Pks. and Conservation Assn., Wilderness Soc. Republican. Episcopalian. Office: 650 Ala Moana Blvd Ste 211 Honolulu HI 96813-4907

VIOLET, WOODROW WILSON, JR., retired chiropractor; b. Columbus, Ohio, Sept. 19, 1937; s. Woodrow Wilson and Alice Katherine (Woods) V.; student Ventura Coll., 1961-62; grad. L.A. Coll. Chiropractic, 1966; m. Judith Jane Thatcher, June 15, 1963; children: Woodina Lonize, Leslie Alice. Pvt. practice chiropractic medicine, Santa Barbara, Calif., 1966-73, London, 1973-74, Carpinteria, Calif., 1974-84; past mem. coun. roentgenology Am. Chiropractic Assn. Former mem. Parker Chiropractic Rsch. Found., Ft. Worth. Served with USAF, 1955-63. Recipient award merit Calif. Chiropractic Colls., Inc., 1975, cert. of appreciation Nat. Chiropractic Antitrust Com., 1977. Mem. Nat. Geog. Soc., L.A. Coll. Chiropractic Alumni Assn., Scripps Rsch. Coun., Delta Sigma. Patentee surg. instrument.

VIOLETTE, GLENN PHILLIP, construction engineer; b. Hartford, Conn., Nov. 15, 1950; s. Reginald Joseph and Marielle Theresa (Bernier) B.; m. Susan Linda Begam, May 15, 1988. BSCE, Colo. State U., 1982. Registered profl. engr., Colo. Engring. aide Colo. State Hwy. Dept., Glenwood Springs, Colo., 1974-79, hwy. engr., 1980-82; hwy. engr. Colo. State Hwy. Dept., Loveland, Colo., 1979-80; project engr. Colo. State Hwy. Dept., Glenwood Canyon, Colo., 1983—; guest speaker in field. Contbg. editor, author, photographer publs. in field. Recipient scholarship Fed. Hwy Adminstrn., 1978. Mem. ASCE, Amnesty Internat., Nat. Rifle Assn., Internat. Platform Assn., Siera Club, Audubon Soc., Nature Conservancy, World Wildlife Fund, Cousteau Soc., Chi Epsilon. Office: Colo Dept Transp 202 Centennial Dr Glenwood Springs CO 81601-2845

VIRGILIO, JOANNE, oncologist, hematologist; b. Bklyn., Sept. 9, 1958; d. James and Rita (Rakowski) V.; m. George D. Gromke, May 13, 1989; children: Megan, Mikaela, George. BA in Biology, NYU, 1981; DO, Chgo. Coll. Osteo. Medicine, 1986. Diplomate Nat. Bd. Osteopathic Medicine in Internal Medicine, Oncology, Hematol ogy. Intern Grandview Hosp., Dayton, Ohio, 1986-87; resident in internal medicine Grandview Hosp., Dayton, 1987-89; fellow in oncology U. Cin., 1989-91; fellow in hematology-oncology U. S. Fla., Tampa, 1991-92; pvt. practice Grand Junction (Colo.) Oncology Group, 1992—. Mem. Am. Osteopathic Assn. Roman Catholic. Office: Saint Marys Hosp 2635 N 7th St Grand Junction CO 81501-8209

VISCO, KIM KELLY, biologist, educator; b. L.I., N.Y., Feb. 15, 1965; d. Francis John and Elizabeth Veronica (Gambino) Kelly; m. Frank Joseph Visco, Sept. 10, 1988; stepchildren: Lisa Marie, Michelle Marie. AA, Orange Coast Coll., 1983; BA, Calif. State U. Fullerton, 1988. Cert. Calif. C.C. lifetime credential, 1988. Sec.-treas. ALWS, Inc., Stanton, Calif., 1987-93; instr. biology Orange Coast Coll., Costa Mesa, Calif., 1988—; lab. dir. Benz/Gabbita Cons., Westminster, Calif., 1989-91; environ. cons. Benz Group, Pasadena, Calif., 1991—; fin. cons. FLD Corp., Pasadena, 1995—. Editor, contbr.: Biology 100 Lab Manual, 1995, Biology 181 Lab Manual, 1996; cons., contbr. (video) Soil Wash Technologies, 1996; patentee in field. Republican. Roman Catholic. Home: 21171 Amberwick Ln Huntington Beach CA 92646 Office: Orange Coast Coll 2701 Fairview Rd Costa Mesa CA 92628

VISTNES, LARS M., plastic surgeon; b. Stavanger, Norway, 1927. MD, U. Man., Can., 1957. Intern Winnipeg (Man., Can.) Gen. Hosp., 1956-57; resident in surgery St. Luke's Hosp., 1962-65; resident in plastic surgery St. Francis Meml. Hosp., San Francisco, 1965-68; plastic surgeon Stanford (Calif.) U. Hosps., 1971—. Fellow ACS, Royal Coll. Surgeons Can., Am. Assn. Plastic Surgery. Office: Stanford U Med Ctr Divsn Plastic Surgery NC 104 Stanford CA 94305*

VITALE, ROBERT LOUIS, electrical engineer; b. Inglewood, Calif., Apr. 13, 1961. BSEE, Calif. State U., Sacramento, 1985; MSEE, Naval Postgrad. Sch., 1997. Registered profl. engr., Calif. Elec. engr. Mare Island Shipyard, Vallejo, Calif., 1985-90, sys. engr., 1990-94; gen. mgr. Rockville Lights, Vallejo, 1993—; lab. dir. Naval Postgrad. Sch., Monterey, Calif., 1994—. Mem. IEEE, Rusty Bindings Ski Club (bd. dirs.). Office: Naval Postgrad Sch 833 Dyer Rd Code EC/EL Monterey CA 93943

VITRAC, JEAN-JACQUES CHARLES, international marketing consultant; b. Paris, May 31, 1942; came to U.S., 1972; s. Jean Bernard Vitrac and Paulette Aimée (Buisson) Mannerheim; m. Roswitha Kahling, Sept. 11, 1965; children: Emmanuel, François, Catherine. Diploma, Faculty of Law, Aix, France, 1963; post grad. in mktg., Institut National Du Marketing, Paris, 1972; post grad. in econ. scis., Institut Superieur Sciences Economiques, Paris, 1979. Mktg. cons. Bernard Krief Internat., Paris, 1973-79; strategy cons. Euro-PacRim Internat., Walnut Creek, Calif., 1980—; chair task force on multinat. strategies Ctrl. Bank of France, Paris, 1974-78; mktg. cons. Aérospatiale, Paris, 1978; bd. dirs. Capsule Française Inc., Napa, Calif. Author: Discover Export, 1974; co-author: Doing Business in California, 1989. Mem. E. Bay Internat. Trade Coun., 1996-97. Mem. KC, Art Ranaissance Found. (hon., chair Calif. chpt. 1994—), Classical Philharmonic (v.p. 1995-96), Cal-France Coun. (v.p. 1996-97), Kiwanis Internat (gov.'s cabinet, dir. com. svc. 1996-97), French War Vets. (No. Calif. chpt. pres. 1996-97), Napa Kiwanis Club (disting. pres. 1993). Republican. Roman Catholic. Home: Becket's Ranch PO Box 467 Valley Springs CA 95252 Office: Cal-France Coun PO 3028 9 Parnell Ct Walnut Creek CA 94598

VITT, LISA OSBURN, archivist; b. Bellflower, Calif., Feb. 1, 1965; d. James Charles Osburn and Diane Marie (Austrum) Shannon; m. Christopher Eric Vitt, Jan. 22, 1996. BA in Art History and Anthropology, U. Calif., Santa Barbara, 1989; MA in History, Calif. State U., Northridge, 1996. Archives tech. Pacific S.W. region Nat. Archives, Laguna Niguel, Calif., 1989-91, Ronald Reagan Presdl. Libr., Simi Valley, Calif., 1991—. Melba Barry Bennett scholar Palm Springs Hist. Soc., 1986-89, Pan Hellenic Soc. Coachella Valley scholar, 1985-88. Mem. Soc. Calif. Archivists. Office: Ronald Reagan Presdl Libr 40 Presidential Dr Simi Valley CA 93065-0600

VITTI, ANTHONY MARK, secondary education educator; b. Stamford, Conn., Sept. 6, 1961; s. Anthony Frank and Joanne Marie (Milano) V. BS, Conn. State U., 1984; student, Mt. St. Mary's Sem., Emmitsburg, Md., 1987-89; MS in Instrnl. Leadership, Nat. U., 1996. Cert. tchr. Dir. edn., dir. music Diocese St. Petersburg, Fla., 1984-86; behavior mgmt. specialist Savannah (Ga.) Chattam Schs., 1986-87; designated mentor tchr. Poway (Calif.) Unified Schs., 1990—. poet, songwriter. Coord. March of Dimes, San Diego, 1994—. Mem. ASCD, Nat. U. Alumni Assn. (Pres. award 1993), Danbury H.S. Alumni Assn. (George W. Perry award 1978), KC, Elks (scholar 1986). Home: PO Box 501954 San Diego CA 92150-1954 Office: Poway Unified Schs 13626 Twin Peaks Rd Poway CA 92064-3034

VIVIAN, LINDA BRADT, sales and public relations executive; b. Elmira, N.Y., Nov. 22, 1945; d. Lorenz Claude and Muriel (Dolan) Bradt; m. Robert W. Vivian, Apr. 5, 1968 (div. Sept. 1977). Student, Andrews U., 1963-66. Adminstrv. asst. Star-Gazette, Elmira, 1966-68; editor Guide, staff writer Palm Springs (Calif.) Life mag., 1970-75; dir. sales and mktg. Palm Springs Aerial Tramway, 1975—; sec. Hospitality and Bus. Industry Coun. Palm Springs Desert Resorts, 1989-91, 1997—, vice-chmn. 1991-94, chmn., 1994-95. Mem. Hotel Sales and Mktg. Assn. (allied nominating chmn. Palm Springs chpt. 1986-88), Am. Soc. Assn. Execs., Travel Industry Assn., Hospitality Industry and Bus. Coun. of Palm Springs Resorts (sec. 1989-91, vice-chmn. 1991-94, chmn. 1994-95), Nat. Tour Assn. (co-chair Team Calif. promotions com. 1993-97), Calif. Travel Industry Assn., Hospitality Bus. Industry Coun., Palm Springs C. of C. (bd. dirs. 1984-85). Republican. Office: Palm Springs Aerial Tramway One Tramway Rd Palm Springs CA 92262

VIVIER, MARY LOUISE, mayor. Mayor City of Visalia, Calif. Office: City of Visalia 707 W Acequia St Visalia CA 93291

VLASAK, WALTER RAYMOND, state official, management development consultant; b. Hartsgrove, Ohio, Aug. 31, 1938; s. Raymond Frank and Ethel (Chilan) V.; m. Julia Andrews, Feb. 25, 1966; children: Marc Andrew, Tanya Ethel. BSBA, Kent State U., 1963; MA, U. Akron, 1975. Commd. 2d lt. U.S. Army, 1963; platoon leader, anti-tank platoon leader and battalion adjutant 82d Airborne Div., 1963-65; combat duty Viet Nam, 1965-66, 68-69; exec. officer, co. comdr. and hdqrs. commandant of the cadre and troops U.S. Army Sch. Europe, Oberammergau, Fed. Republic Germany, 1966-68; asst. prof. Mil. Sci. Kent (Ohio) State U., 1970-74; infantry battalion exec. officer 9th Infantry Div., Ft. Lewis, Wash., 1976-77, orgnl. effectiveness cons. to commanding gen., 1977-79, brigade exec. officer, 1980-82; orgnl. effectiveness cons. to commanding gen. 8th U.S. Army, U.S. Forces, Korea, 1979-80; advanced through ranks to lt. col. U.S. Army, 1980, ret., 1984; pres. Comsult, Inc., Tacoma, 1984—; mgr. employee devel. tng. dept. social and health svcs. State of Wash., Tacoma, 1985—. Decorated Legion of Merit, Bronze Star with V device and two oak leaf clusters, Air medal, Purple Heart, Vietnamese Cross of Gallantry with Silver Star. Mem. Am. Soc. for Tng. and Devel., Assn. U.S. Army (bd. dirs. Tacoma 1984—). Home: 10602 Hill Terrace Rd SW Tacoma WA 98498-4337 Office: State of Wash Dept Social and Health Svcs 8425 27th St W Tacoma WA 98466-2722

VLOSKY, MARK ALAN, psychologist; b. N.Y.C., Dec. 23, 1944; s. Victor Victoroff and Margery (Weintraub) V.; m. Bertha Dinger, Aug. 25, 1968 (div. Jan. 1987); children: Robin, Karen; m. Louise Benson, July 25, 1987; 1 child, Eric. BA, NYU, 1967; MA, New Sch. for Social Rsch., 1977, PhD, 1979. Lic. psychologist, N.Y., Colo. Clin. dir. Wyo. Mental Health Ctr., Douglas, 1980-83; staff psychologist Kaiser-Permanente, Denver, 1983-86, Family Psychology Assocs., Longmont, Colo., 1989—; pvt. practice Broomfield, Colo., 1984—; clin. assoc. U. Denver, 1986—; cons. Parents of Murdered Children, Denver, 1986-90. Inventor (game for child therapists) Our Game, 1986. Cons. City of Broomfield, 1988. Recipient Values in Wyo. award Wyo. Coun. for Humanities, Cheyenne, 1981; Hiram Halle fellow New Sch. for Social Rsch., N.Y.C., 1979. Mem. APA, Colo. Psychol. Assn. (dist. coord.), Boulder Interdisciplinary Com. Home: 3308 W 11th Avenue Pl Broomfield CO 80020-6764 Office: 11975 Reed St # 1 Broomfield CO 80020-2818

VO, HUU DINH, pediatrician, educator; b. Hue, Vietnam, Apr. 29, 1950; came to U.S., 1975; s. Chanh Dinh and Dong Thi (Pham) V.; m. Que Phuong Tonnu, Mar. 22, 1984; children: Katherine Hoa-An, Karyn Bao-An. MD, U. Saigon, 1975. Diplomate Am. Bd. Pediat. Adminstr. bilingual vocat. tng. Cmty. Care and Devel. Svc., L.A., 1976-77; resident in pediat. Univ. Hosp., Jacksonville, Fla., 1977-80; physician, surgeon, chief med. officer Lanterman Devel. Ctr., Pomona, Calif., 1980-92, chief med. staff, 1984-88, coord. med. ancillary svc., 1984-88, 91—; physician Pomona Valley Cmty. Hosp., 1988-90; asst. clin. prof. Loma Linda (Calif.) Med. Sch., 1985-92; chief med. officer So. Reception Ctr. and Clinic., Norwalk, Calif., 1992—; bd. dirs. Pomona Med. Clinic Inc. Pres. Vietnamese Cmty. Ponoma Valley, 1983-85, 87-95, chmn., 1993-95; nat. co-chair mem. Vietnamese Am. Cmty. in U.S.A., 1993-95; bd. dirs. YMCA, Pomona, 1988-92, Sch.-Cmty. Partnership, Pomona, 1988-92. Mem. AMA (Physician recognition award 1989, 1992), L.A. Pediat. Soc., Vietnamese-Am. Physicians Assn. La. and Orange County (founding mem., sec. 1982-84, bd. dirs. 1987-90). Republican. Buddhist. Home: 19036 Stonehurst Ln Huntington Beach CA 92648-6122 Office: So Reception Ctr and Clinic 13200 Bloomfield Ave Norwalk CA 90650-3253

VOBEJDA, WILLIAM FRANK, aerospace engineer; b. Lodgepole, S.D., Dec. 5, 1918; s. Robert and Lydia (Stefek) V.; m. Virginia Parker, Oct. 24, 1942; children—William N., Margaret, Mary Joan, Barbara, Lori. B.C.E., S.D. Sch. Mines and Tech., 1942. Registered profl. engr., Colo. Stress analyst Curtiss Wright Corp., Columbus, Ohio, 1942-45; civil/hydraulic engr. Bur. Reclamation, Denver, 1945-54; mech. supr. Stearns Roger Corp., Denver, 1954-62; mgr. Martin Marietta Corp., Denver, 1962-86, mgr. engring. M-X Program, 1978-86; pres. BV Engring., Inc., Englewood, Colo., 1986-89. Active Boy Scouts Am. Recipient Silver Beaver award. Mem. Englewood City Council 1984-87, Englewood Water and Sewer Bd., 1990—. Mem. AIAA. Democrat. Roman Catholic. Clubs: St. Louis Men's, K.C., Martin Marietta Chess, Lions Internat. (sec.).

VOELKER, ELIZABETH ANNE, artist; b. Pitts., Oct. 17, 1931; d. Stanley Howard and Ruth Julia (Weber) V. BFA, Coll. Fine Arts, Carnegie Inst. Tech., 1953. lectr. U. Calif., San Francisco, 1972, Assoc. Artists Winston-Salem, 1987; art tchr. San Francisco Cmty. Sch., 1975-76, workshop Santa Barbara (Calif.) Mus. Art, 1982; vis. artist Am. Acad., Rome, 1992. One-person shows include Kalla Gallery, Pitts., 1954, Pitts. Playhouse Gallery, 1956, Art Mus., Carnegie Inst., Pitts., 1957, Calif. Palace of Legion of Honor, San Francisco, 1960, Gumps Gallery, San Francisco, 1965, U. Calif., San Francisco, 1967, Scaife Galleries, Pitts., 1968, Protetch/McIntosh Gallery, Washington, 1978, Parsons/Dreyfuss Gallery, N.Y., 1978, Concourse Gallery, San Francisco, 1979, Cantor/Lemberg Gallery, Birmingham, Mich., 1981, San Jose Mus. Art, 1982, Santa Barbara Mus. Art, 1982, Allport Assocs. Gallery, San Francisco, 1983, 84, Gallery 30, San Mateo, Calif., 1984, 89, Gensler & Assocs. Gallery, San Francisco, 1984, 86, Hewlett Packard Galleries, Palo Alto, Calif., 1986, Susan Conway Carroll Gallery, Washington, 1990; exhibited in group shows Kalla Gallery, 1954, Cin. Art Mus., 1955, 58, Hewlitt Gallery, Carnegie Inst. Tech., Pitts., 1956, Mus. Art, Carnegie Inst., 1956, 57, 58, 59, 77, Butler Art Inst., Youngstown, Ohio, 1956, 57, 58, Calif. Palace of Legion of Honor, 1960, 61, 62, 63, 78, 87, San Francisco Art Inst., 1961, 62, 63, 64, 65, 66, 67, L.A. County Mus. Art, 1961, San Francisco Mus. Modern Art, 1961, 62, 65, 79, 90, Kingpitcher Gallery, 1976, Parsons/Dreyfuss Gallery, N.Y., 1977, Nat. Collection Fine Arts, Washington, 1978, Baum/Silverman Gallery, L.A., 1979, Impressions Gallery, Boston, 1979, Miss. Mus. Art, 1981-83, Brook House Gallery, Orinda, Calif., 1983, Santa Barbara Mus. Art, 1983, 89, Palo Alto Cultural Ctr., 1984, Va. Ctr. Creative Arts, 1987, 88, Winston-Salem Arts Assn. Gallery, 1987, Art Corridor Gallery, Menlo Park, Calif., 1988, DeYoung Mus., San Francisco, 1989, Susan Conway Carroll Gallery, 1989, San Francisco Craft and Folk Art Mus., 1990, Calif. Crafts Mus., San Francisco, 1990; represented in permanent collections Phillips Collection, Washington, Nat. Mus. Am. Art, Washington, San Francisco Mus. Modern Art, Art Mus., Carnegie Inst., Achenbach Found., Calif. Palace of Legion of Honor, Hunt Inst. Botanical Documentation, Carnegie Mellon U., Pitts., Skidmore, Owings and Merrill, Chgo., Jones and Laughlin, Pitts, Itel Corp., Chgo., Bank of Am., San Francisco, Incom Internat., Pitts., Alexander and Alexander, Washington, World Savings and Loan Assn., Oakland, Calif., Genstar, San Francisco, Brown Wood Ivey Mitchell and Petty, San Francisco, VISA, N.Y., San Mateo, Merrill Lynch, San Francisco, Southeast Banking Corp., Miami, Fla., Hogue and Assocs., San Francisco, Hewlett Packard Corp., Palo Alto, Detroit Inst. Arts, Nat. Mus. Women in the Arts, Washington, Santa Barbara Mus. Art, Nat. Collection Fine Arts, Washington, San Jose Mus. Art. Carnegie Inst. Tech. scholar, 1949-51; recipient Carnegie Inst. Purchase prize, 1958; fellow MacDowell Colony, 1970, 72, 73, 75, 76, 77, 79, Ossabaw Island project, 1977, Va. Ctr. Creative Arts, 1982, 83, 84, 85, 87, 88, 89, 90, 91, 92, 95, Ragdale Found., 1983, Djerassi Found., 1988, 90, 91, Blue Mountain Ctr., 1991, ; Hereward Lester Cooke Found. grantee, 1977, Ludwig Vogelstein Found. grantee, 1987, Pollock-Krasner Found. grantee, 1989-90, 96-97, Gottlieb Found. grantee, 1996, Artists' Fellowship Found. grantee, 1996; Rockefeller Found. scholar, 1988. Home: 301 Bloomfield Rd Burlingame CA 94010

VOELKER, MARGARET IRENE (MEG VOELKER), gerontology, medical, surgical nurse; b. Bitburg, Germany, Dec. 31, 1955; d. Lewis R. and Patricia Irene (Schaffner) Miller; 1 child, Christopher Douglas. Diploma, Clover Park Vocat.-Tech., Tacoma, 1975, diploma in practical nursing, 1984; ASN, Tacoma (Wash.) C.C., 1988; postgrad., U. Washington Tacoma, Tacoma, 1992-95; student nurse practitioner program, U. of Wash., 1995—. Cert. ACLS. Nursing asst. Jackson County Hosp., Altus, Okla., 1976-77; receptionist Western Clinic, Tacoma, 1983; LPN, Tacoma Gen. Hosp., 1984-88, clin. geriatric nurse, 1988-90, clin. nurse post anesthesia care unit perioperative svcs., 1990—; pre-admit clinic nurse, 1995—; mem. staff nurse coun. Tacoma Gen. Hosp., 1990-91, procedural sedation nurse, 1996—. Recipient G. Corydon Wagner endowment fund scholarship. Mem. PostAnesthesia Nurses Assn., Phi Theta Kappa, Sigma Theta Tau.

VOGEL, NADINE ORSOFF, estate planner; b. Bronx, N.Y., Oct. 21, 1963; d. Eli H. and Phyllis S. (Landskroner) Orsoff; m. Douglas Albert Vogel,

June 15, 1985; 1 child, Gretchen Ashley. Student, U. South Fla., 1981-83; BS, Coll. of Charleston, 1985; MBA, Golden Gate U., 1987. Account rep., asst. mgr. Met Life, L.A., 1987-89, br. agy. mgr., 1989-93, account exec., 1993—; pres., founder Spl. Needs Advocate for Parents, L.A., 1993—; instr. Life Underwriter Tng. Coun., Monterey, Calif., 1988-89; spkr. on spl. needs to numerous orgns., 1993—. Author: Special Needs Planning, The Process, 1996. Fin. Liason Lea Baeck Temple FYC Com., Belair, Calif., 1994-96; creator, bd. dirs. Spl. Needs Awareness Day, Beverly Hills, Calif., 1994; v.p. Good Beginnings neonatal ICU Cedars Sinai Med. Ctr., 1993-96; mem. adv. bd. Computer Access Ctr., 1994-95; mem. region C planning bd. L.A. Unified Sch. Dist., 1994; bd. dirs. Westside Coastal Early Start Joung Coun., 1993-95, Profl. Women's Network, Monterey, 1987-90. Recipient Vol. award Cedars Sinai Med. Ctr., 1994. Mem. Nat. Assn. Life Underwriters (v.p. 1988-93, 93-96, Achievement award 1988, 89, 94, 95, Agt. of Yr. award 1988, 89), Nat. Orgn. Rare Disorders, Calif. Perinatal Assn. (mem. coun., bd. dirs. 1994-96), Nat. Assn. Security Dealers, Million Dollar Round Table (mem. conf. com. 1988, 95, 96), Parent Care, Bus. and Profl. Women's Assn. (bd. dirs. 1987-90, Outstanding Young Profl. Woman of Yr. award 1988, 89). Home: 2227 Midvale Ave Los Angeles CA 90064

VOGEL, RICHARD WIEDEMANN, business owner, ichthyodynamicist, educator; b. N.Y.C., Apr. 12, 1950; s. Jack and Edna Jeanne (Wiedemann) V.; m. Pamela Jane Gordon, Aug. 7, 1974; children: Amy Jane, Katy Lynn, Gina Marie, Krista Jeanne. Grad. high sch., Calif. Owner, operator ichthyol. rsch. and comml. fishing vessel Santa Barbara, Calif., 1973-88; designer advanced hydrodynamic curvature Clark Foam Factory, Laguna Beach, Calif., 1994—; lectr. Surfrider Found. Conf., U. Calif., San Diego, 1994. Inventor in field. Episcopalian. Office: Ichthyodynamics PO Box 1167 Hanalei HI 96714-1167

VOGEL, SUSAN CAROL, nursing administrator; b. Hartford, Conn., Oct. 9, 1948; d. Morton B. and Esther (Riback) Worshoufsky. Diploma in nursing, Grace Hosp., New Haven, 1969; B in Healthcare Mgmt., U. La Verne, 1991, M in Health Adminstrn., 1994. RN, Calif.; cert. nephrology nurse, Nephrology Nurse Cert. Bd. Oper. rm. nurse New Britain (Conn.) Gen. Hosp., 1970-72; staff nurse oper. rm. Parkview Cmty. Hosp., Riverside, Calif., 1972-74; staff nurse dialysis, IV team Cedars-Sinai Med. Ctr., L.A., 1974-82; clin. nurse III dialysis UCLA, 1982-88; nurse mgr. inpatient dialysis UCLA Med. Ctr., 1988-93; adminstr. South Valley Regional Dialysis Ctr., Encino, Calif., 1993—; pres. Renal Replacement Therapies, Inc. Author: (with others) Review of Hemodialysis for Nurses and Dialysis Personnel, 1993, Vascular Access, Principles & Practices, 3rd edit., 1996. Mem. NAFE, Am. Orgn. Nurse Execs., Am. Nephrology Nurses Assn. (pres. L.A. chpt. 1990-92, 96—, nat. chairperson hemodialysis spl. interest group 1993-95), Nat. Kidney Found. Office: South Valley Regional Dialysis Ctr 17815 Ventura Blvd Ste 100 Encino CA 91316-3612

VOGEL, WALTER PAUL, priest, college counselor; b. Encinitas, Calif., Mar. 7, 1935; s. Walter Albert and Ruth Emily (Maurer) V. BA, Villanova U., 1959; MA, Augustinian Coll., Washington, 1963. Ordained priest Roman Cath. Ch., Feb. 9, 1963. Tchr. math. Msgr. Bonner H.S., Phila., 1963-66; tchr. math, ASB moderator St. Augustine H.S., San Diego, 1966-68; tchr., chmn. dept. math. Ctrl. Cath. H.S., Modesto, Calif., 1975-76; asst. headmaster Villanova Prep. Sch., Ojai, Calif., 1968-75, tchr., chmn. dept. math., 1976-78, headmaster, 1979-82; chmn. dept. math., dorm master Woodside Priory, Portola Valley, Calif., 1982-85; tchr. math., counselor St. Augustine H.S., San Diego, 1985-92, coll. counselor, 1992—. Mem. Western Assn. Coll. Counselors, Nat. Assn. Student Coun. Advisors, Nat. Cath. Edn. Assn., Augustinian Ednl. Assn. Roman Catholic. Home: 1605 28th St San Diego CA 92102 Office: Saint Augustine H S 3266 Nutmeg St San Diego CA 92104

VOGELSANG, PHILIP JOHN, pathologist; b. Oakland, Calif., Sept. 3, 1954; s. Otto C. and Margaret Vogelsang; m. Kathleen Fischer, Oct. 14, 1979; children; Kirsten, Emily, Laura. AB in Zoology, Humboldt State U., 1978; MD, U. Calif., San Diego, 1984; PhD in Comparative Pathology, U. calif., Davis, 1993. Diplomate Am. Bd. Pathology with subspecialty in anatomic and clin. pathology, qualfications in cytopathology. Intern U. Calif. Affiliate Cmty. Hosp., Santa Rosa, 1984-85; resident clin. pathology U. Calif., Davis, 1985-90, Dean's scholar, 1986-88; hon. clin. fellow in cytopathology U. Alberta, Edmonton, Can., 1990-91; staff pathologist Mad River Cmty. Hosp., Arcata, Calif., 1991—.

VOGET, JANE J., city official, lawyer; b. Montréal, Que., Can., Jan. 2, 1949; d. Frederick Wilhelm and Mary Kay (Mee) V.; m. Frederick Walton Hyde, Oct. 9, 1988. BA in German and Anthropology, So. Ill. U., 1971, MS in Planning and Cmty. Devel., 1977; JD, Lewis and Clark Coll., 1990. Bar: Wash. 1991. Program mgr. Ill. Dept. Local Govt. Affairs, Springfield, 1975-78, U.S. Dept. Housing and Urban Devel., Washington, 1978; mem. staff The White House, Office Asst. to Pres. for Intergovtl. Affairs, Washington, 1979-80; exec. dir. Ctr. for Collaborative Problem Solving, San Francisco, 1981-83; hotel asst. mgr. Hyatt Regency Waikiki, Honolulu, 1983-85; housing project mgr. Multnomah County, Portland, Oreg., 1985-88; sr. project mgr. City of Seattle, 1989—; pvt. practice, Seattle, 1991—. Co-author govtl. publs. Vol. lawyer West Seattle Legal Clinic, 1994—; active 11th Dist. Dems., Seattle, 1993-95, Na Hanu 'O Kapuaku'ulei Aloha, 1996—. Mem. ABA (mem. affordable housing fin. com. 1991-96, forum housing & cmty. devel. law, probate and real property sect., state and local govt. sect.), Wash. State Bar Assn. (legal aid com.), King County Bar Assn. (mem. legis. com., govt. ops. subcom. 1995). Avocations: swimming, Hawaiian music and dance, animal rights advocate. Home: 5946 39th Ave SW Seattle WA 98136 Office: City of Seattle 618 2nd Ave Seattle WA 98104-2222

VOIGT, JOHN LOUIS, advertising and marketing executive; b. Appleton, Wis., June 1, 1935; s. John Louis and Anne (Strommen) V.; m. Beverley Jean Hilleque, June 16, 1957; children: Cynthia Anne Voigt Scanland, John Louis III. BBA in Mktg., U. Wis., 1957; postgrad., Lake Forest Coll., 1967-70. Mktg. rsch. analyst Smith Kline and French Labs., Phila., 1957; mktg. specialist Abbott Labs., North Chicago, Ill., 1969; dir. mktg. Hycel, Inc., Houston, 1973-77; account supr. Baxter, Gurian and Mazzei, Inc., L.A., 1977-81; exec. v.p. Reavis Comms., Inc., Cardiff by the Sea, Calif., 1981-87, Beach Internat., Inc., San Diego, 1987-90; v.p. mktg. Forsythe Marcelli Johnson Advt., Inc., Newport Beach, Calif., 1990-93; pres. Medmar Comms., Inc., Carlsbad, Calif., 1993—. Capt. U.S. Army, 1958-61. Mem. Med. Mktg. Assn., Biomed. Mktg. Assn., Mktg. Rsch. Assn. Office: Medmar Comms Inc 2638 Unicornio St Carlsbad CA 92009-5333

VOIGT, LYNDA FAY, cancer researcher, former nurse; b. Longview, Wash., Feb. 6, 1945; d. Leseray and Bessie Edna (Steadman) Norris; m. George Q. Voigt Jr., Dec. 25, 1966 (div. Dec. 1988); children: Cathleen Marie, Barbara Jean; m. Michael Rolland Turner, Sept. 8, 1991. BSN, U. Wash., 1967; BS, Seattle Pacific U., 1967; MSN, Emory U., 1969; PhD, U. Wash., 1990. Pub. health nurse Seattle-King County Dept. Health, Seattle, 1967-68, Atlanta Comprehensive Health Ctr., 1969-70; staff nurse neonatal unit Presbyn. Hosp., Dallas, 1970-71; pub. health nurse Vis. Nurse Svcs., Seattle, 1977-83; teaching asst. epidemiology and biostats. U. Wash., Seattle, 1982-83; rsch. asst. Fred Hutchinson Cancer Rsch. Ctr., Seattle, 1983, statis. rsch. assoc., 1984-92, sr. staff scientist, 1992—. Author: (book chpt.) Epidemiology of Endometrial Cancer, 1989; editl. cons. Am. Jour. Epidemiology, Cancer Causes and Control, Internat. Jour. Epidemiology, Am. Jour. Ob-Gyn.; contbr. articles to med. jours. Sunday sch. tchr. Bapt. and Episcopal Ch., 1964—; vol., bd. dirs. student activities PTA, Renton, Wash., 1975-92; foster parent Dept. Social Svcs., Bellevue, Wash., 1985-88; vol. leader, day camp worker Camp Fire Girls, Renton, 1977-83; vol. Humane Soc., Bellevue, 1994; mem. Nature Conservancy, Habitat for Humanity, ASPCA, Nat. Stuttering Project. Weyerhaeuser scholar, 1963. Mem. Soc. Epidemiologic Rsch., Eastside Astronomical Soc., Issaquah Alps Trail Club., Am. Statis. Assn., Am. Assn. Pub. Opinion Rsch. Office: Fred Hutchinson Cancer Ctr 1124 Columbia St # P381 Seattle WA 98104-2015

VOLBERG, HERMAN WILLIAM, electronics engineer, consultant; b. Hilo, Hawaii, Apr. 6, 1925; s. Fred Joseph and Kathryn Thelma (Ludloff) V.; m. Louise Ethel Potter, Apr. 26, 1968; children: Michael, Lori. BSEE, U. Calif., Berkeley, 1949. Project engr. Naval Electronics Lab., San Diego, 1950-56; head solid state rsch. S.C. div. Gen. Dynamics, San Diego, 1956-60; founder Solidyne Solid State Instruments, La Jolla, Calif., 1958-60; founder, v.p. electronics divsn. Ametek/Straza, El Cajon, Calif., 1960-66; founder, cons. H.V. Cons., San Diego, 1966-69; sr. scientist Naval Ocean Systems Ctr., Oahu, Hawaii, 1970-77; chief scientist Integrated Scis. Corp., Santa Monica, Calif., 1978-80; founder, pres. Acoustic Sys. Inc., Goleta, Calif., 1980-84; founder, pres. Invotron, Inc., Lafayette, Calif., Murray, Utah, 1984—; tech. dir. Reson, Inc., Santa Barbara, Calif., 1992—; cons. U. Utah Ctr. for Engring. Design, 1991; cons. on autonomous underwater vehicle sonar systems Mitsui/U. Tokyo, 1992; lectr. solid state course UCLA and IBM, 1956-62; instr. Applied Tech. Inst., Columbia, Md., 1988—; contbr. to undersea acoustical rsch. and devel. programs European Union, 1990—. Contbr. articles to IRE Bull., IEEE Ocean Electronics Symposium. Mem. adv. panels for advanced sonar systems and for high resolution sonars, USN, 1970-77. 1st lt. U.S. Army, 1944-47, ETO. Recipient award of merit Dept. Navy, 1973, 94. Mem. IEEE, AAAS, NRA, Acoustical Soc. Am., Mine Warfare Assn., N.Y. Acad. Scis., Marine Tech. Soc., U.S. Naval Inst., Planetary Assn., Old Crows, Masons, Elks. Home and Office: 41 W 6830 S Murray UT 84107-7124

VOLENSKI, ANTHONY ALEXANDER, poet; b. Kalamazoo, Oct. 14, 1941; s. Anthony Michael and Sophia Maria (Ugliantza) V.; m. Julie Ann Clampitt (div. Apr. 1966). Grad. H.S., Kalamazoo. Owner, mgr. Alexander Pub., Port Angeles, Wash., 1994—. Author: The Mountain, 1994, Journeys of the Mind, 1994, Journeys 2, 1995, Concepts, 1995, Love Verse, 1995, Love Verse 96, 1996; author poetry, fiction and non-fiction. Lutheran. Home and Office: 216 E 10th St Port Angeles WA 98362

VOLK, GREG T., secondary education educator; b. Salem, Oreg., June 7, 1951; s. Henry Jacob and Dorothy Jean (Ballard) V. BA, Calif. State U., Turlock, 1977; MFA, U. Utah, 1979. Cert. secondary edn. tchr. Tchr. Turlock H.S., 1984—. Producer: (plays) Where Have All the Lightening Bugs Gone, 1993 (1st place superior award 1993), Scarecrow, 1994 (1st place superior award 1994), Joined at the Head, 1995 (1st place superior award 1995), Jack, 1996 (1st place superior award 1996). Exec. dir. Miss Stanislaus County, Calif., 1992-94; bd. dirs. Turlock H.S. Auditorium Restoration Com., 1993—; producer Miss Merced County, Calif., 1995. Recipient Outstanding Contribution to the Arts award Nat. Arts Coun., 1994, Educator of Yr. award C. of C., Turlock, 1995. Mem. Internat. Thespian Soc. (advisor 1983—). Democrat. Roman Catholic. Home: 2220 Mira Flores Turlock CA 95380 Office: Turlock High Sch 1600 E Canal Dr Turlock CA 95380

VOLK, ROBERT HARKINS, aviations company executive; b. East Orange, N.J., Nov. 27, 1932; s. Harry Joseph and Marion (Waters) V.; m. Barbara June Klint, Sept. 10, 1954; children: Christopher G., William W., Laura L., Elisabeth M. BA, Stanford U., 1954, LLB, 1958. Bar: Calif. 1959. Assoc. Adams Duque & Hazeltine, L.A., 1959-62; ptnr. Adams Duque & Hazelyine, L.A., 1962-67; commr. of corps. State of Calif., Sacramento, 1967-69; pres. Union Bancorp, L.A., 1969-73; pres., chmn. Union Am., L.A., 1973-79; owner, chief exec. officer Martin Aviation Inc., Santa Ana, Calif., 1980-90, Media Aviation L.P. Burbank, 1984—. Sgt. USAF, 1955-57. Mem. Calif. Bar Assn. Republican. Episcopalian. Home: 332 Conway Ave Los Angeles CA 90024-2604 Office: Media Aviation LP 3000 N Clybourn Ave Burbank CA 91505-1012

VOLLACK, ANTHONY F., state supreme court justice; b. Cheyenne, Wyo., Aug. 7, 1929; s. Luke and Opal Vollack; m. D. Imojean; children: Leah, Kirk. Bar: Colo. 1956. Pvt. practice law Colo., from 1956; former state senator; judge Colo. Dist. Ct. (1st jud. dist.), 1977-85; justice Colo. Supreme Ct., 1986—, chief justice, 1995—. Office: Colo Supreme Ct 2 E 14th Ave Denver CO 80203-2115*

VOLPE, EILEEN RAE, special education educator; b. Fort Morgan, Colo., Aug. 23, 1942; d. Earl Lester and Ellen Ada (Hearting) Moore; m. David P. Volpe, July 28, 1965 (div. 1980); children: David P. Jr., Christina Marie. BA, U. No. Colo., 1964, MA, 1978. Cert. fine art tchr., learning handicapped specialist, resource specialist. 5th grade tchr. Meml. Elem. Sch., Milford, Mass., 1967-68; fine arts jr./sr. high tchr. Nipmuc Regional Jr. Sr. H.S., Mendon, Mass., 1968-69; spl. edn. tchr. Saugus (Calif.) High Sch., 1979—; publicity dir. Sacred Heart Ch. Sch., Milford, Mass., 1974-75, float coord. bicentennial parade, 1975. Author: (poetry) Seasons to Come, 1994, Best Poems of 1997, The Other Side of Midnight, 1997. Mem. Calif. Tchr. Assn., Coun. for Exceptional Children, DAR, Phi Delta Kappa, Kappa Delta Pi. Republican. Office: Saugus High Sch 219000 W Centurion Way Santa Clarita CA 91350

VOLPE, ELLEN MARIE, middle school educator; b. Bronx, N.Y., Aug. 2, 1949; d. George Thomas and Mary (Popadinecz) Soloweyko; m. Ronald Edward Volpe, May 22, 1971; children: Keith, Daniel, Christopher, Stephanie. BBA, Pace U., 1971; MA in Teaching, Sacred Heart U., 1986. Tchr. Conn. Bus. Inst., Stratford, 1979-80, Katherine Gibbs Sch., Norwalk, Conn., 1980-89; adj. instr. So. Cen. Community Coll., New Haven, 1986-87, Salt Lake C. C., Phillips Jr. Coll., Salt Lake City, 1992-93; instr. Bryman Sch., Salt Lake City, 1990-92; tchr. Indian Hills Mid. Sch., Sandy, Utah, 1993—; mem. reaccreditation and tech. coms. Indian Hills Mid. Sch.; mem. curriculum rev. com. Katharine Gibbs Sch., 1989-90. Mem., NEA, Am. Vocat. Assn., Nat. Bus. Edn. Assn., Western Bus. Edn. Assn. Home: 8390 Sublette Cir Sandy UT 84093-1164

VOLPE, RICHARD GERARD, insurance accounts executive, consultant; b. Swickley, Pa., Apr. 10, 1950; s. Ralph Carl and Louise P. (Cosentino) V.; m. Janet Lynn Henne, May 10, 1986; 1 child, John Ralph. BA, Vanderbilt U., 1972. CPCU. Trainee, asst. mgr. Hartford (Conn.) Ins. Group, 1973-74; v.p. sales Roy E. Barker Co., Franklin, Tenn., 1975-80; asst. v.p., product mgr. comml. ins. Nat. Farmers Union Ins., Denver, 1980-82; prin. R.G. Volpe & Assocs, Denver, 1982-85; account exec. Millers Mut. Ins., Aurora, Colo., 1985-89; pres, chief exec. officer AccuSure, Inc., Arvada, Colo., 1989—; account exec. J.R. Misken, Inc., Denver, 1990-92, The Prudential, Colorado Springs, 1992—; edn. chmn. Insurors Tenn., Nashville, 1978-79; new candidate chmn. Mid-Tenn. chpt. CPCU, Nashville, 1979-80; cons. Bennett Nat. Bank Colo., mktg. mgr., 1989-90; cons. Plains Ins., Inc., 1987-90. Contbr. articles to profl. jours. Dem. chmn. Williamson County, Tenn., 1979; campaign mgr. legis., Franklin, 1979. Named Hon. Col. Gov. Tenn., 1979. Mem. Soc. Property and Casualty Underwriters, South Metro Denver C. of C. Roman Catholic. Home: 10908 W Snow Cloud Trl Littleton CO 80125-9083 Office: The Prudential 5225 N Academy Blvd Ste 310 Colorado Springs CO 80918-4084

VON, DENNIS, actor, producer; b. Tulsa, Aug. 21, 1944; s. Paul Dennis and Catherine Susan (Krischan) B. BFA, Kans. U., 1967; postgrad., London Coll. Homeopathy, 1980; diploma, Royal Acad. Dramatic Arts, London, 1971; assoc. deg., Pasadena (Calif.) Playhouse, 1973; PhD in Nutrition, Donsbach Sch., 1981. Actor, contract player 20th Cent. Fox Studios, Century City, Calif., 1973-74; actor Universal Studios, Universal City, Calif., 1974-84, Embassy TV, Universal City, 1984-86; exec. producer D.W. Prodns., Hollywood, 1986—; dir. and instr. Pasadena Playhouse, 1983-85; instr., Hollywood, Calif., 1983—; bd. dirs. USO, Hollywood. Author: Basic Health and Nutrition, 1986; screenwriter Sunset Heaven, 1978, The Illuminati, 1984; appeared in films Silent Movie, 1975, Gypsy Warriors, 1978, Truce in the Forest, 1979; TV appearances include Nancy Walker Show, 1976, Mary Hartman, Mary Hartman, 1976, Maude, 1976, Operation Petticoat, 1977, Bionic Woman, 1978, E/R, 1984 (Emmy award 1985). Founding mem. Hollywood Preservation Orgn., 1985; mem. Hollywood Heritage, Inc., 1985, Orgn. Police & Sheriffs; mem. com. Save Medicare and Social Security, 1986—; hon. consulate Principality of Wahlstatt. Recipient Resolution award City of L.A., 1985, Disting. Svc. award Hollywood Heritage, Inc., 1985, Bronze Halo award So. Calif. Motion Picture Coun., Star Sapphire award So. Calif. Motion Picture Coun., 1986; named Celebrity of Yr. Calif. Spl. Olympics, 1984; nominated Emmy award, 1985. Mem. ADLER, Royal Acad. Dramatic Arts, Monarchist League London.

VON BARTHELD, CHRISTOPHER STEPHEN, neurobiologist; b. Denver, June 5, 1959; s. Robert August and Hanna (Baumann) Von B.; m. Sonia K. Budhecha, Sept. 18, 1993. MD, U. Goettingen, Germany, 1983. Vis. scholar Scripps Instn. Oceanography, La Jolla, Calif., 1983-84; instr. U. Goettingen, 1985-87; postdoctoral fellow U. Wash., Seattle, 1987-92; rsch. asst. prof. U. Wash., 1992-97; assoc. prof. U. Nev., Reno, 1997—. Ad hoc reviewer Jour. Comparative Neurology, 1991—, Jour. Neuroscience, 1996—; contbr. articles to profl. jours. Active German Scholarship Found., Bonn, Germany, 1980—, cons., 1986—. Recipient Nat. Rsch. Svc. award NIH, 1989-92, R29 First award, 1992-97; Max Kade fellow Max Kade Orgn., 1987-88. Mem. Soc. Neuroscience, J.B. Johnston Club. Office: U Nev Dept Physiology & Cell Bio Reno NV 89557-0046

VONDERHEID, ARDA ELIZABETH, nursing administrator; b. Pitts., June 19, 1925; d. Louis Adolf and Hilda Barbara (Gerstacker) V.; diploma Allegheny Gen. Hosp. Sch. Nursing, 1946; B.S. in Nursing Edn., Coll. Holy Names, Oakland, Calif., 1956; M.S. in Nursing Adminstrn., UCLA, 1960. Head nurse Allegheny Gen. Hosp., Pitts., 1946-48; staff nurse Highland-Alameda County Hosp., Oakland, Calif., 1948-51, staff nurse poliomyelitis units, 1953-55; pvt. duty nurse Directory Registered Nurses Alameda County, Oakland, 1951-53; adminstrv. supervising nurse Poliomyelitis Respiratory and Rehab. Center, Fairmont, Alameda County Hosp., Oakland, 1955-58; night supr., relief asst. dir. nursing Peninsula Hosp., Burlingame, Calif., 1960, adminstrv. supr., 1961-62, inservice educator, 1963-69; staff nurse San Francisco Gen. Hosp., 1969, asst. dir. nurses, 1969-72; mem. faculty continuing edn. U. Calif., San Francisco, 1969-71; dir. nursing services Kaiser Permanente Med. Center, South San Francisco, 1973-1982, asst. adminstr. Med. Center Nursing Services, 1982-85; asst. adminstr. Kaiser Hosp., San Francisco, 1985-87; ret. 1987. Chmn. edn. com. San Mateo County (Calif.) Cancer Soc., 1962-69; bd. dirs. San Mateo County Heart Assn., 1968-71; mem., foreman pro tem San Mateo County Civil Grand Jury, 1982-83; mem. San Mateo County Health Council, 1982-85, vice chmn., 1984; mem. all ch. coms. Cert. advanced nursing adminstrn. Mem. AAAW (bd. dirs.), San Mateo County (dir. 1964-69, pres. elect 1967-68, pres. 1968-70), Golden Gate (1st v.p. 1974-78, dir. 1974-78), Calif., Am. nurses assns., Nat. League Nursing, Soc. for Nursing Service Adminstrs., State Practice and Edn. Council, Maui Hospice Assn. (vol.), San Mateo County Grand Jury Assn., Calif. Grand Jury Assn., AARP (chpt. 3184 Lahaina, Hawaii 1995—), Maui Christian Women's Club (bd. dirs. 1995—, chmn. 1966-67), Sigma Theta Tau. Republican. Club: Kai-Perm. Contbr. articles in field to profl. jours. Home: 150 Puukolii Rd Apt 47 Lahaina HI 96761-1961 *Personal philosophy: Develop belief in self, people and a power beyond you (in God). Develop and fashion work and savings ethic and get involved.*

VON DOEPP, CHRISTIAN ERNEST, psychiatrist; came to U.S., 1949; s. Philip and Elizabeth von Doepp; m. Janet Carol Brown, Jan. 2, 1994; children: Heidi Louise von Doepp Lemon, Peter Anders, Niels Christian. Student, U. Heidelberg, Germany, 1955; BA, DePauw U., 1957; MD, Stanford U., 1961; intern, Boston City Hosp., Tufts U., 1962. Diplomate Am. Bd. Psychiatry and Neurology, Nat. Bd. Med. Examiners. Resident psychiatry Langley Porter Psychiat. Inst. U. Calif., San Francisco, 1968; house call physician Permanente Med. Group, San Francisco, 1966-68; consulting psychiatrist Somerville (Mass.) Child Guidance Ctr., 1969; brig psychiatrist and cons. to correctional program Boston Naval Sta., 1968-69; lectr. and preceptor Calif. Dept. Health, Health Tng. Resource Ctr., Berkeley, Calif., 1970-77; dir. day hosp. and aftercare programs San Mateo (Calif.) Ctrl. County Psychiat. Svcs., 1970-87; sr. psychiatrist San Mateo County Mental Health Divsn., 1987—; cons. psychiatrist Calif. Med. Facility,CDC, Vacaville, 1995—; fellow Inst. Pathology, U. Freiberg, Germany, 1960, Lab. Cmty. Psychiatry, Harvard Med. Sch., Boston, 1969; supr., coord. cmty. psychiatry rotation for residents U.S. Naval Hosp., Oakland, Calif., 1970-81; med. examiner State of Calif., 1971-78; cons. Counseling and Assistance Ctr., U.S. Naval Sta., Treasure Island, Calif., 1974-76; asst. clin. prof. dept. psychiatry U. Calif., San Francisco, 1971—; chmn. or mem. numerous coms. San Mateo County Mental Health Div., 1970—. Bd. dirs. Tahoma Meadows Homeowners Assn., 1986-92, pres., 1980-81; pres. Tahoma Mut. Water Co., 1978-80. With M.C., USN, 1962-65; capt. USNR, 1965—. Mem. Am. Psychiat. Assn., No. Calif. Psychiat. Soc., San Mateo County Psychiat. Soc. (sec.-treas. 1987-89, bd. dirs. 1987-93), Calif. Med. Assn., San Mateo County Med. Assn., Faculty-Alumni Assn. Dept. Psychiatry U. Calif. San Francisco (bd. dirs. 1985-90). Office: 19 W 39th Ave Ste 4 San Mateo CA 94403-4549

VON FRIEDERICHS-FITZWATER, MARLENE MARIE, health communication educator; b. Beatrice, Nebr., July 14, 1939; d. Paul M. and Velma B. (von Friederichs) Fitzwater; children: Richard Nielson, Kevin T. Young, James L. Nielson, Paul M. Nielson. BS, Westminster Coll., 1981; MA, U. Nebr., Omaha, 1981; PhD, U. Utah, 1987; cert. in death edn., Temple U., 1982. Various pub. rels., writing and editing positions, 1957-78; teaching fellow in comm. U. Nebr., Omaha, 1978-83, U. Utah, Salt Lake City, 1978-83; asst. prof. mass comm. U. So. Colo., Pueblo, 1983-85; prof. comm. studies Calif. State U., Sacramento, 1985—, chair comm. studies, 1996—; asst. clin. prof. family practice Sch. Medicine U. Calif., Davis, 1987—; condr. workshops on communication skills for health care profls. Bergan Mercy Hosp., Omaha, 1980-81, Mercy Care Ctr., Omaha, 1980-81, Am. Cancer Soc., 1981-82, Hospice of Salt Lake, Utah, 1981-82; condr. seminars, workshops and courses on health communication, death and dying, patient edn. and compliance, other related topics, 1983—; presenter in health communication various profl. orgn. meetings and confs., 1981—; dir., co-founder The Health Communication Rsch. Inst., Sacramento, 1988—. Contbr. articles to profl. jours. Trainer United Way, Sacramento, project mgr., 1986—; pres. bd. dirs. Hospice Care Sacramento, Inc., 1986-87; instr. vol. tng. program Hospice Consortium Sacramento; hospice vol. 1980—. Recipient numerous state, regional and nat. awards for writing, editing, publ. design and photography. Fellow Am. Acad. on Physician & Patient; mem. Internat. Communication Assn. (health communication div., newsletter editor 1987-89, sec. 1989-91), AAUP, Assn. Behavioral Scis. and Med. Edn., Assn. Women in Sci., Pub. Rels. Soc. Am. (bd. dirs. Calif. Capital chpt. 1987-91), Soc. Tchrs. Family Medicine, Soc. Health Care Pub. Rels. and Mktg. No. Calif. Home: 5020 Hackberry Ln Sacramento CA 95841-4765 Office: Calif State U Communication Studies Dept 6000 J St Sacramento CA 95819-2605

VON KALINOWSKI, JULIAN ONESIME, lawyer; b. St. Louis, May 19, 1916; s. Walter E. and Maybelle (Michaud) von K.; m. Penelope Jayne Dyer, June 29, 1980; children by previous marriage: Julian Onesime, Wendy Jean von Kalinowski. BA, Miss. Coll., 1937; JD with honors, U. Va., 1940. Bar: Va. 1940, Calif. 1946. Assoc. Gibson, Dunn and Crutcher, L.A., 1946-52, ptnr., 1953-62, mem. exec. com., 1962-82, adv. ptnr., 1985—; CEO, chmn. Litigation Scis., Inc., Culver City, Calif., 1991-94, chmn. emeritus, 1994-96; chmn. emeritus Dispute Dyamics, Inc., Culver City, 1996—; bd. dirs., mem. exec. com. W.M. Keck Found.; mem. faculty Practising Law Inst., 1971, 76, 78, 79, 80; instr. in spl. course on antitrust litigation Columbia U. Law Sch., N.Y.C., 1981; mem. lawyers dels. com. to 9th Cir. Jud. Conf., 1953-73; UN expert Mission to People's Republic China, 1982. Contbr. articles to legal jours.; author: Antitrust Laws and Trade Regulation, 1969, desk edit., 1981; gen. editor: World Law of Competition, 1978, Antitrust Counseling and Litigation Techniques, 1984. With USN, 1941-46, capt. Res. ret. Fellow Am. Bar Found., Am. Coll. Trial Lawyers (chmn. complex litigation com. 1984-87); mem. ABA (ho. of dels. 1970, chmn. antitrust law sect. 1972-73), State Bar Calif., L.A. Bar Assn., U. Va. Law Sch. Alumni Assn., Calif. Club, L.A. Country Club, La Jolla Beach and Tennis Club, N.Y. Athletic Club, The Sky Club (N.Y.C.), Phi Kappa Psi, Phi Alpha Delta. Republican. Episcopalian. Home: 12320 Ridge Cir Los Angeles CA 90049-1151 Office: Litigation Scis Inc 6167 Bristol Pkwy Culver City CA 90230-7633

VON KRENNER, HANA R., artist; b. Berlin, Germany, Sept. 20, 1940; d. Erhard and Hildegard (Haar) Geue; m. Walther G. von Krenner, Sept. 2, 1960; children: Michael P., Karen P. Hotel Mgmt., Hotel Sch., Coburg, Germany, 1959. Artist Kapalua Bay Hotel, Maui, Hawaii, 1977-80; Am. Indian Trad. Design and Techs.; rschr. pvt. practice, 1988—. Exhibited in group show at Mus. of Native Am. Cultures, Spokane, Wash., 1987-88. Office: PO Box 1338 Kalispell MT 59901

VON KRENNER, WALTHER G., artist, writer, art consultant and appraiser; b. W. Ger., June 26, 1940; s. Frederick and Anna-Marie (von Wolfrath) von K.; m. Hana Renate Geue, 1960; children—Michael P., Karen P. Privately educated by Swiss and English tutors; student Asian studies, Japan, 1965-68; student of Southeast Asia studies, Buddhist U., Bankok, Thailand, Cambodia. Curator, v.p. Gallery Lahaina, Maui, Hawaii; pres. Internat. Valuation Honolulu, 1980—; owner Al Hilal Arabians; instr. aikido, 1962—; founder, dir. Sandokan Aikido Schs. Mem. Am. Soc. Appraisers (sr. mem.;

pres., dir.). Author books on Oriental art. Home: PO Box 1338 Kalispell MT 59903-1338

VON LINSOWE, MARINA DOROTHY, information systems consultant; b. Indpls., July 21, 1952; d. Carl Victor and Dorothy Mae (Quinn) von Linsowe; m. Clayton Albert Wilson IV, Aug. 11, 1990; children: Kira Christina von Linsowe, Lara Carla von Linsowe-Wilson, Tami Cheri von Linsowe-Wilson. Student Am. River Coll., Portland State U. Verbal operator Credit Bur. Metro, San Jose, Calif. and Portland, Oreg., 1970-72; computer clk. Security Pacific Bank, San Jose, 1972-73; proof operator Crocker Bank, Seaside, Calif., 1973-74; proof supr. Great Western Bank, Portland, 1974-75; bookkeeper The Clothes Horse, Portland, 1976-78; computer operator Harsh Investment Co., Portland, 1978-79; data processing mgr. Portland Fish Co., 1979-81; data processing mgr. J & W Sci. Inc., Rancho Cordova, Calif., 1981-83; search and recruit specialist, data processing mgr. Re:Search Exec. Recruiters, Sacramento, Calif., 1983; sr. systems analyst Unisys Corp. (formerly Burroughs), 1983-91; sr. systems cons. FileNet Corp., Portland, Oreg., 1991-92; owner Optimal System Svcs., Portland, Oreg., 1992—; mfg. specialist, computer conversion cons., bus. sys. analyst Portland. First violinist Am. River Orch. Recipient Bank of Am. Music award, 1970. Mem. NAFE, Am. Prodn. and Inventory Control Soc. (CPIM 1989), Am. Mgrs. Assn., MENSA, Data Processing Mgmt. Assn. Republican. Lutheran.

VON PASSENHEIM, JOHN B., lawyer; b. Calif., Nov. 25, 1964; s. Burr Charles and Kathryn E. (Kirkland) Passenheim. BA in English with honors, U. Calif.-Santa Barbara, 1986; JD, U. Calif., Hastings, 1989. Bar: Calif. 1989, U.S. Dist. Ct. (so. dist.) Calif. 1991. Pvt. practice San Diego, 1990—; organizer Rock The Vote, San Diego, 1992; primary atty. Calif. Lawyers for the Arts, San Diego; panelist Ind. Music Seminar, 1992, 93, 94; mem. Surfrider Found. Nat. Adv. Bd., 1995—; gen. counsel Greyboy Records, Poptones Records, Alchemical, Inc. Contbg. staff DICTA mag., 1990-94; editor (legal column) It's the Law, 1990-93. Exec. counsel San Diego chpt. Surfrider Found., 1991-95; vol. atty. San Diego Vol. Lawyer Program, 1990-93. Office: 4425 Bayard St Ste 240 San Diego CA 92109-4089

VON PRINCE, KILULU MAGDALENA, occupational therapist, sculptor; b. Bumbuli, Lushoto, Tanzania, Jan. 9, 1929; came to U.S., 1949; d. Tom Adalbert and Juliane (Martini) Von Prince. BA in Occupational Therapy, San Jose State U., 1958, MS in Occupational Therapy, 1972; EdD, U. So. Calif., 1980. Registered occupational therapist; cert. work evaluator, work adjustment specialist. Commd. 2d lt. U.S. Army, 1959, advanced through grades to lt. col.; staff asst. U.S. Army, Denver, 1959-62; hand rehab. asst., hand therapy Walter Reed Army Med. Ctr., 1962-65; hand rehab. asst. occupational therapist 97th Gen. Hosp., U.S. Army, Frankfurt, Fed. Republic Germany, 1965-68; occupational therapist Inst. Surg. Rsch. U.S. Army, Ft. Sam Houston, Tex., 1967-70; occupational therapy dir., cons. U.S. Army, Honolulu, 1972-75; adminstr. occupational therapy clinic, cons. LAMC U.S. Army, Presido, Calif., 1975; asst. evening coll. program San Jose (Calif.) C.C., 1976-77; postdoctoral fellow allied health adminstrn. SUNY, Buffalo, 1978, Commonwealth U., Richmond, Va., 1978-79; project dir. Ctr. of Design, Palo Alto, 1980; part-time staff project developing pre-retirement program older adults De Anza Coll., Cupertino, Calif., 1980-81; part-time instr. Stroke Activity Ctr. Cabrillo Coll., Santa Cruz, Calif., 1981; dir. occupl. therapy Presbyn. Med. Ctr., 1981-86; ptnr., mgr. retail store, 1986-89; dir. rehab. therapy Merrithew Meml. Hosp. Contra Costa Med. Ctr., Martinez, Calif., 1990-93; sculptor, 1993—; part-time activity program coord. Calif. Women's Detention Facility, Chowchilla, Calif., 1994—; researcher, presenter workshops and seminars in field. Co-author: Splinting of Burned Patients, 1974; producer videos: Elbow Splinting of the Burned Patient, 1970, Self-Instruction Unit: Principles of Elbow Splinting, 1971; contbr. articles to profl. jours. Decorated Legion of Merit; recipient Disting. Alumni Honors award San Jose State U., 1982; grad. scholar U.S. Surgeon Gen.; Kellogg Found. postdoctoral fellow, 1979. Mem. Am. Occupational Therapy Assn., Occupational Therapy Assn. Calif. (award of excellence 1986, v.p. 1981-84, state chair pers. 1981-84, state chair continuing edn. 1984-86, Lifetime Achievement award 1994), Am. Soc. Hand Therapists (hon., life). Home: 36141 Manon Ave Madera CA 93638-8613 Office: Calif Women's Detention Facility Chowchilla CA 93610-1501

VON STAR, BRENDA LEE, primary care family nurse practitioner; b. Lakeview, Oreg., Feb. 5, 1948; d. Leslie Darrell and May Mabel (Hirsch) Denstedt; m. Jimmie E. Muro, Aug. 20, 1977 (div. Nov. 1990); children: Michael, Christine. AS, Lane C.C., Eugene, Oreg., 1972; BSN, Met. State U., Denver, 1978. Cert. FNP; ACLS. Staff nurse med. unit Presbyn. Intercmty. Hosp., Kalmath Falls, Oreg., 1972-73; surg. ICU nurse St. Luke's Hosp., Denver, 1973-76; burn unit nurse U. Colo. Health Sci. Ctr., Denver, 1976-80; family pediatric nurse practitioner Tri-County Health Dept., Denver, 1980-85; pvt. collaborative practice Luth. Family Practice, Arvada, Colo., 1985-90; clin. dir. rsch. Family Futures Project, Denver, 1990-91; pvt. practice FNP Arbor Family Medicine, Thornton, Colo., 1991-95. With USN, 1967-70. Mem. Am. Acad. Nurse Practitioners, Colo. Nurses Assn. Unity Ch. Office: Family Medicine 1022 Depot Hill Rd Broomfield CO 80020-1068

VON STUDNITZ, GILBERT ALFRED, state official; b. Hamburg, Germany, Nov. 24, 1950; came to U.S., 1954.; s. Helfrid and Rosemarie Sofie (Kreiten) von S.; m. Erica Lynn Hoot, May 26, 1990. BA, Calif. State U., L.A., 1972. Adminstrv. hearing officer State of Calif., Montebello, 1987-91; mgr. III driver control policy unit Dept. Motor Vehicles State of Calif., Sacramento, 1991-93; ops. mgr. Driver Safety Review, 1993-95; contract mgr. State Dept. Health Svcs., 1995-97; staff mgr. licensing ops. policy Dept. Motor Vehicles, Sacramento, 1997—. Author: Aristocracy in America, 1989; editor publs. on German nobility in U.S., 1986—. Active L.A. Conservancy, West Adams Heritage Assn., dir., 1989-91. Mem. Calif. State Mgrs. Assn., Assn. German Nobility in N.Am. (pres. 1985—), Driver Improvement Assn. Calif. (v.p. 1992-96, dir. media rels. 1996—), Benicia Hist. Soc., Sierra Club, Intertel, Mensa, Orders and Medals Soc. Am., Nat. Assn. Managed Care Regulators, Phi Sigma Kappa (v.p. chpt. 1978). Roman Catholic. Home: 1101 W 2nd St Benicia CA 94510-3125

VON TILSIT, HEIDEMARIE, information management specialist; b. Heinrichswalde, Germany, Sept. 26, 1944; came to U.S., 1967; d. Heinz and Kaethe Krink; m. Leonard Wierzba, May 14, 1969 (div. 1980). Buchhandel, Dt. Buchh. Schule, Kiel, Germany, 1965; profl. cert., Coll. of Further Edn., Oxford, Eng., 1966; BA, Calif. State U., Fullerton, 1979. Library asst. Allergan, Inc., Irvine, Calif., 1975-76; info. analyst Allergan Pharms., Irvine, Calif., 1976-79, library supr., 1979-81, mgr. corp. info. ctr., 1982—; cons. in field, Irvine, 1980—; owner, pres. Unitran, Corona, Calif., 1980—; mem. adv. bd. CB&S Career Cons., Orange, Calif., 1987—; mem. adv. bd. for univ.-industry rsch. and tech. U. Calif., Irvine, 1992—; mem. adv. bd. Sch. Libr./Info. Sci., Continuing Edn., Calif. State U., Fullerton. Editor/writer articles sci. and information mgmt. Vol. AIDS Svcs. Found., 1994—. Mem. Am. Soc. Info. Sci., Spl. Librs. Assn., Pharm. Edn. & Rsch. Inst. (com. info. mgmt. sect. 1985—). Democrat. Home: 1543 San Rafael Dr Corona CA 91720-3795 Office: Allergan Inc 2525 Dupont Dr Irvine CA 92612-1531

VOORHEES, JOHN LLOYD, columnist; b. DeWitt, Iowa, Aug. 30, 1925; s. Lloyd William and Elsie Irene (Bousselot) V. BA in History, U. Iowa, 1951; BA in Journalism, U. Wash., 1953. Tchr. Oelwein (Iowa) High Sch., 1951-52; columnist Seattle Post-Intelligencer, 1953-71; columnist, critic Seattle Times, 1971—. With U.S. Army, 1946-48. Democrat. Office: The Seattle Times Fairview Ave N & John St Seattle WA 98111

VORIS, WILLIAM, academic administrator emeritus; b. Neoga, Ill., Mar. 20, 1924; s. Louis K. and Faye (Hancock) V.; m. Mavis Marie Myre, Mar. 20, 1949; children: Charles William II, Michael K. BS, U. So. Calif., 1947, MBA, 1948; PhD, Ohio State U., 1951; LLD, Sung Kyun Kwan U. (Korea), 1972, Eastern Ill. U., 1976. Teaching asst. Ohio State U., Columbus, 1948-50; prof. mgmt. Wash. State U., Pullman, 1950-52; prof., head dept. mgmt. Los Angeles State Coll., 1952-58, 60-63; dean Coll. Bus. and Pub. Adminstrn., U. Ariz., Tucson, 1963-71; pres. Am. Grad. Sch. Internat. Mgmt., Glendale, Ariz., 1971-89, pres. emeritus, 1989—, adj. prof., 1994—. Ford Found. research grantee Los Angeles State Coll., 1956; prof. U. Tehran (Iran), 1958-59; Ford Found. fellow Carnegie Inst. Tech., Pitts., 1961; prof. Am. U., Beirut, Lebanon, 1961, 62; cons. Hughes Aircraft Co., Los Angeles, Rheem Mfg. Co., Los Angeles, Northrop Aircraft Co., Palmdale, Calif., Harwood Co., Alhambra, Calif., ICA, Govt. Iran. Served with USNR, 1942-45. Fellow Acad. Mgmt.; mem. Ariz. Acad., Beta Gamma Sigma, Alpha Kappa Psi, Phi Delta Theta. Author: Production Control, Text and Cases, 1956, 3d edit., 1966; Management of Production, 1960. Research in indsl. future of Iran, mgmt. devel. in Middle East. Home: Thunderbird Campus Glendale AZ 85306

VORPAGEL, WILBUR CHARLES, historical consultant; b. Milw., Feb. 26, 1926; s. Arthur Fred and Emma (Hintz) V.; Betty J. Hoch, June 19, 1952; stepchildren: Jerry L., Sharon Belveal Sullenberger. Student Army specialized tng. program, U. Ill., 1943-44; BBA, U. Wis., 1949; MBA, U. Denver, 1953. Cert. tchr., Colo. Instr. Montezuma County High Sch., Cortez, Colo., 1949-51; coord. bus. edn. Pueblo (Colo.) Pub. Schs., 1951-56; pvt. practice bus. cons. Pueblo and Denver, 1956—; tchr. bus. edn. Emily Griffith Opportunity Sch., Denver, 1959-69; various positions with Denver & Rio Grande Western R.R. Co., Denver, 1959-88; cons. in field. Bd. dirs. Colo. Ret. Sch. Employees Assn., Denver, 1988—; rep. Custer Battlefield Hist. & Mus. Assn. Sgt. U.S. Army, 1944-46, ETO. Mem. Augustan Soc., St. John Vol. Corp., S.E. Colo. Geneal. Soc., Rio Grande Vets. Club (bd. dirs. Pueblo chpt.), Biblical Archaeol. Soc. (contbg. writer), Nat. Huguenot Soc., Colo. Huguenot Soc. (organizing pres. 1979-95), 70th Inf. Divsn. Assn., Shriners, Masons. Republican. Mem. Christian Ch. Home and Office: 335 Davis Ave Pueblo CO 81004-1019 *Personal philosophy: We really live twice when we can enjoy the past and the present. Born into a world unbidden, assailed by forces beyond our ken, carried out protesting - life is still worth living. The best is yet to come.*

VOS, THOMAS JAMES, career officer, criminal investigator; b. Muskegon, Mich., Aug. 21, 1953; s. Millard William and Frances Marie (Nemgar) V.; m. Claudia Ann Simes, Oct. 25, 1979 (div. July 1991); children: Stephanie; m. Janet Kay Knuth, May 29, 1993; step-children: Shawnee Montgomery, Alicia Berg, Jason Montgomery. Assoc., Robedrt Morris Coll., 1974; Bachelor, Western Ill. U., 1976. Dormitory dir. Robert Morris Coll., Carthage, Ill., 1972-74; enlisted U.S. Army, 1977, advanced through grades to chief warrant officer 3; mil. policeman U.S. Army, Ansbach, Germany, 1977-81; spl. agt. U.S. Army Criminal Investigation Command, Ft. Carson, Colo., 1981-84, Ft. Lee, Va., 1984-85, Taegu, Korea and Ft. Dix, N.J., 1985-89; ops. officer U.S. Army Criminal Investigation Command, Ft. Dix, 1989-90, spl. agt. in charge, 1990-92; spl. agt. U.S. Army Criminal Investigation Command, Vancouver, Wash., 1992-93; spl. agt. in charge U.S. Army Criminal Investigation Command, San Francisco, 1993-94, Oakland, Calif., 1994-96; spl. agt. in charge 44th MP Det C10, Ft Lewis, Wa., 1996—; instr. Prosecutor's Office, Cape May, N.J., 1991. Author (manual) Crime Scene Investigation, 1991. Mem. Young Reps., Muskegon, Mich., 1967. Recipient Army Commendation medal, 1980, 85, 90, 91, 94, Meritorious Svc. medal, 1984, 87, awarded Rank CW3, 1992. Mem. Criminal Investigation Dept. Agts. Assn., 8-Ball Assn. Roman Catholic. Home: 30320 19th Place SW Federal Way WA 98023 Office: US Army Criminal Investigation 44 MP Det CID Fort Lewis WA 98433

VOSBECK, ROBERT RANDALL, architect; b. Mankato, Minn., May 18, 1930; s. William Frederick and Gladys (Anderson) V.; m. Phoebe Macklin, June 21, 1953; children: Gretchen, Randy, Heidi, Macklin. BArch, U. Minn., 1954. Various archtl. positions, 1956-62; ptnr. Vosbeck-Vosbeck & Assocs., Alexandria, Va., 1962-66, VVKR Partnership, Alexandria, 1966-79; exec. v.p. VVKR Inc., 1979-82, pres., 1982-88; prin. Vosbeck/DMJM, Washington and Alexandria, Va., 1989-94; archtl. cons., 1994—; mem. Nat. Capital Planning Commn., 1976-81, U.S./USSR Joint Group on Bldg. Design and Constrn., 1974-79; mem. Nat. Park System Adv. Bd., 1984-88. Archtl. works include Pub. Safety Ctr., Alexandria, Va., 1987, Yorktown (Va.) Visitors Ctr, 1976, Frank Reeves Mcpl. Office Bldg., Washington, 1986, Fed. Bldg., NOrfolk, Va., 1979, Jeff Davis Assocs. Office Complex, Arlington, Va., 1991, Westminster Continued Care Retirment Community, Lake Ridge, Va., 1993. Served as engr. officer USMC, 1954-56. Recipient Plaque of Honor Fedn. Colegios Architects (Republic of Mexico); named Acadamecian, Internt. Acad. Architecture, hon. fellow Royal Archtl. Inst. Can., Soc. Architects of Mexico; recipient hons. Colegios Architects Spain, Union Bulgarian Architects. Fellow AIA (bd. dirs. 1976-78, v.p. 1979-80, pres. 1981), Internat. Union Architects (coun. 1981-87), Nat. Trust Hist. Preservation, Alexandria C. of C. (pres. 1974-75). Presbyterian. Home and Office: Unit A 770 Potato Patch Dr Vail CO 81657-4441

VOSEVICH, KATHI ANN, technical writer and editor, scholar; b. St. Louis, Oct. 12, 1957; d. William and Catherine Mildred (Kalinowski) V.; m. James Hughes Meredith, Sept. 6, 1986. AB with honors, St. Louis U., 1980, MA, 1983; PhD, U. Denver, 1988. Tchg. fellow St. Louis U., 1980-83, acad. advising fellow, 1983-84; tchg. fellow U. Denver, 1985-87; prof. ESL, BNM Talensch., Uden, The Netherlands, 1988-91; instr. English, mentor U. Ga., Athens, 1992-94; vis. asst. prof. Colo. Coll., Colorado Springs, 1994; sr. tech. writer and editor Titan Client/Server Techs., Colorado Springs, 1994-96, head documentation, libr., 1996—; forensic judge USAF Acad., Colo., 1987-88; edn. officer Volkel (The Netherlands) Air Base, 1988-91; instr. English European divsn. U. Md., The Netherlands and Belgium, 1989-91. Author: Customer Care User's Guide, 1996; editor: Subscription Services System Documentation, 1996; contbr. over 100 electronic texts and articles to profl. jours. Colo. scholar U. Denver, 1985-86, grad. dean scholar, 1988; NEH fellow U. Md., 1994. Mem. MLA, Phi Beta Kappa, Alpha Sigma Nu. Roman Catholic. Office: Titan Client/Server Techs 1115 Elkton Dr Ste 200 Colorado Springs CO 80907

VOTH, ALDEN H., political science educator; b. Goessel, Kans., May 4, 1926; s. John F. and Helena (Hildebrandt) V.; m. Norma E. Jost, Aug. 18, 1956; children: Susan, Thomas. BA, Bethel Coll., 1950; MS in Econs., Iowa State U., Ames, 1953; PhD in Internat. Rels., U. Chgo., 1959. Assoc. prof. polit. sci. Upland (Calif.) Coll., 1960-63; prof. polit. sci. San Jose (Calif.) State U., 1963-65, 67-91, prof. emeritus, 1991—; vis. prof. polit. sci. Am. U. in Cairo, 1965-67. Author: Moscow Abandons Israel, 1980, (with others) The Kissinger Legacy, 1984. Trustee Pomona (Calif.) Valley Am. Assn. UN, 1963. Am. U. in Cairo Rsch. grantee, 1966; Nat. Coun. on U.S.-Arab Rels. fellow, 1990—. Home: 1385 Kimberly Dr San Jose CA 95118-1426 Office: San Jose State U One Washington Sq San Jose CA 95192

VREE, DALE, editor; b. L.A., Feb. 25, 1944; s. Henry and Marion (Wyma) V.; m. Elena Maria Reyes, June 18, 1965; children: Maria, Pieter, Magdalena, Pilar. BA, U. Calif., Berkeley, 1965, MA, 1967, PhD, 1972; student, Humboldt U., East Berlin, Germany, 1966. Editor New Oxford Rev., Berkeley, 1977—. Author: On Synthesizing Marxism and Christianity, 1976, From Berkeley to East Berlin and Back, 1985; contbg. editor Nat. Cath. Register, 1980—. Rockefeller Found. humanities fellow Inst. Internat. Studies, U. Calif., Berkeley, 1975-76, NEH fellow, Hoover Instn., Stanford (Calif.) U., 1976-77. Roman Catholic.

VREELAND, ROBERT WILDER, electronics engineer; b. Glen Ridge, N.J., Mar. 4, 1923; s. Frederick King and Elizabeth Lenora (Wilder) V.; m. Jean Gay Fullerton, Jan. 21, 1967; 1 son, Robert Wilder. BS, U. Calif., Berkeley, 1947. Electronics engr. Litton Industries, San Carlos, Calif., 1948-55; sr. devel. electronics engr. U. Calif. Med. Ctr., San Francisco, 1955-89; ret.; cons. electrical engring; speaker 8th Internat. Symposium Biotelemetry, Dubrovnik, Yugoslavia, 1984, RF Expo, Anaheim, Calif., 1985, 86, 87. Contbr. articles to profl. jours., also to internat. meetings and symposiums; patentee in field. Recipient Chancellor's award U. Calif., San Francisco, 1979; cert. appreciation for 25 years' service U. Calif., San Francisco, 1980. Mem. Nat. Bd. Examiners Clin. Engring. (cert. clin. engr.), IEEE, Assn. Advancement Med. Instrumentation (bd. examiner), Am. Radio Relay League (pub. service award 1962). Home: 45 Maywood Dr San Francisco CA 94127-2007 Office: U Calif Med Ctr 4th and Parnassus Sts San Francisco CA 94143

VU, DUNG QUOC, systems analyst; b. Vungtau, Vietnam, Sept. 12, 1963; came to U.S., 1980; s. Tu Duy and Ha Chieu (Phan) V.; m. Tisa Nguyen; 1 child, Alexander. BS in Math./Computer Sci., UCLA, 1986; MS in Computer Sci., Calif. State U., Fullerton, 1992. Sys. analyst L.A. County Sanitation Dists., 1985—; cons. VNI, Inc., Westminster, Calif., 1987—; pvt. tutor, Huntington Beach, Calif., 1982-83; writer, Anaheim, Calif., 1988—. Chmn. Vietnamese New Year Festival com., Santa Ana, Calif., 1989. Recipient Community Svc. award UCLA Community Svc. Commn., 1985. Mem. IEEE, Assn. for Computing Machinery, Ice Skating Inst. Am., Union Vietnamese Student Assns. So. Calif. (internal regulation com.). Republican.

VU, ERIC TIN, neurobiologist, researcher; b. Saigon, Vietnam, Apr. 8, 1963; came to U.S., 1975; s. Van and Bich-Chi (Ha) Vu-Thuong; m. Yu-Chien Kuo, July 16, 1994. BA, U. Tex., 1985; PhD, UCLA, 1990. Postdoctoral fellow Calif. Inst. Tech., Pasadena, 1991-93, sr. rsch. fellow, 1994-95; staff scientist Barrow Neurol. Inst., Phoenix, 1995—. Author: (with others) Frontiers in Crustacean Neurobiology, 1990; contbr. articles to profl. jours. Scholar U. Tex., 1983-85; Chancellor's fellow UCLA, 1985, NSF fellow, 1986, Alfred P. Sloan Rsch. fellow, 1996; recipient Nat. Rsch. Svc. award NIH, 1991, Capranica Found. Prize in Neuroethology, 1995. Mem. Soc. for Neuroscience, Internat. Soc. for Neuroethology, Internat. Brain Rsch. Orgn., Soc. Neural Control Movement. Office: Barrow Neurol Inst Divsn Neurobiology 350 W Thomas Rd Phoenix AZ 85013

VUCANOVICH, BARBARA FARRELL, former congresswoman; b. Fort Dix, N.J., June 22, 1921; d. Thomas F. and Ynez (White) Farrell; m. Ken Dillon, Mar. 8, 1950 (div. 1964); children: Patty Dillon Cafferata, Mike, Ken, Tom, Susan Dillon Stoddard; m. George Vucanovich, June 19, 1965. Student, Manhattanville Coll. of Sacred Heart, 1938-39. Owner, operator Welcome Aboard Travel, Reno, 1968-74; Nev. rep. for Senator Paul Laxalt, 1974-82; mem. 98th-104th Congresses from 2d Nev. dist., 1983-97; chmn. appropriations subcom. on military construction. Pres. Nev. Fedn. Republican Women, Reno, 1955-56; former pres. St. Mary's Hosp. Guild, Lawyer's Wives. Roman Catholic. Club: Hidden Valley Country (Reno). Office: US Ho of Reps 2202 Rayburn Washington DC 20515*

VUJOVIC, MARY JANE, education and employment training planner; b. Huntington, N.Y., Dec. 3, 1951; d. Carl David Sr. and Alice Lucille (Hanson) B. BS in Psychology cum laude, U. Wash., 1973, postgrad., 1980-84. Spl. edn. tchr. Town of Huntington, 1972; adminstrv. asst. Daishowa Am. Corp., Seattle, 1973-74; with King County Work Tng. Program, Seattle, 1973-85, records sect. mgr., 1977-84, contracts mgr., 1984-85; tech. cons., program mgr. Refugee Ctr. of Clark County, Vancouver, Wash., 1985-87; instr., counselor S.W. Wash. Pvt. Industry Coun., Vancouver, 1986-87; planner Wash. Human Devel., Seattle, 1987, dir. planning and MIS, 1987-94; tech. cons. SJL and Assocs., Seattle, 1990—; dir. prog. devel. and evaluation Yakima Valley Opportunities Industrialization Ctr., 1994—; mem. planning and adv. com. Seattle-King County Pvt. Industry Coun., 1987-94; mem. Partnership for Tng. and Employment Careers, Washington, 1991-94. Bd. dirs. Slavia, Seattle, 1990—, St. James Refugee Program, Seattle, 1993-95. Mem. Phi Beta Kappa. Office: Yakima Valley Opportunities Indsl Ctr 815 Fruitvale Blvd Yakima WA 98902-1467

VYAS, GIRISH NARMADASHANKAR, virologist, immunohematologist; b. Aglod, India, June 11, 1933; came to U.S., 1965, naturalized, 1973; s. Narmadashankar P. and Rukshmani A. (Joshi) V.; m. Devi Ratilal Trivedi, Apr. 3, 1962; children: Jay, Shrikrishna. B.Sc., U. Bombay, 1954, M.Sc., 1956, Ph.D., 1964. Postdoctoral fellow Western Res. U., 1965-66; mem. faculty U. Calif., San Francisco, 1967—, chief blood bank, 1969-88; prof. lab. medicine U. Calif., 1977—; dir. transfusion rsch. program, 1985—; WHO cons., S.E. Asia, 1980; cons. in field; mem. com. viral hepatitis NRC, 1974-76; mem. task force blood processing Nat. Heart and Lung Inst., 1972-73; sci. program com. Am. Assn. Blood Banks, 1971-76; com. immunoglobulin allotypes WHO, 1974—; mem. U.S. del. immunologists to Romania and Hungary, 1980; mem. FDA com. on blood and blood products, 1987-92; cons. to VA on med. rsch., 1985, UN Devel. Program in India, 1986; and others; chmn. Transmed Biotech Inc., South San Francisco, 1989-95. Author: Hepatitis and Blood Transfusion, 1972, Laboratory Diagnosis of Immunological Disorders, 1975, Membrane Structure and Function of Human Blood Cells, 1976, Viral Hepatitis, 1978, Viral Hepatitis and Liver Disease, 1984, Use and Standardization of Chemically Defined Antigens, 1986, Transfusion-associated Infections and Immune Response, 1988, Molecular Approaches to Laboratory Diagnosis, 1996; also research papers. Recipient Julliard prize Internat. Soc. Blood Transfusion, 1969; named Outstanding Immigrant in Bay Area Communities Mayor of Oakland, Calif., 1969; Fulbright scholar France, 1980. Mem. AAAS, Am. Soc. Hematology (chmn. com. on transfusion medicine 1989-90), Am. Assn. Immunologists, Am. Soc. Clin. Pathologists, Internat. Assn. for Biol. Standarization (coun. 1992-96). Democrat. Hindu. Office: U Calif Lab Med S-555 San Francisco CA 94143-0134 *Truth alone wins. Truth in our actions manifests beauty in character. Beauty in character brings harmony into the home. Harmony in the home produces order in our society. Order in our society leads to peace in the nation. And peace in the nation can win for us universal prosperity and happiness for mankind, only if individuals practice truth in their actions.*

WACHBRIT, JILL BARRETT, accountant, tax specialist; b. Ventura, Calif., May 27, 1955; d. Preston Everett Barrett and Lois JoAnne (Fondersmith) Batchelder; m. Michael Ian Wachbrit, June 21, 1981; children: Michelle, Tracy. AA, Santa Monica City Coll., 1975; BS, Calif. State U., Northridge, 1979; M in Bus. Taxation, U. So. Calif., 1985. CPA. Supervising sr. tax acct. Peat, Marwick, Mitchell & Co., Century City, Calif., 1979-82; sr. tax analyst Avery Internat., Pasadena, Calif., 1982-83; tax mgr., asst. v.p. First Interstate Leasing, Pasadena, 1983-88, Gibraltar Savs., 1988, Security Pacific Corp., L.A., 1988-92; tax mgr., acct. El Camino Resources Ltd., Woodland Hills, Calif., 1992-95; tax mgr. Herbalife Internat. of Am., Century City, Calif., 1995—. Republican. Jewish.

WACHNER, LINDA JOY, apparel marketing and manufacturing executive; b. N.Y.C., Feb. 3, 1946; d. Herman and Shirley W.; m. Seymour Applebaum, Dec. 21, 1973 (dec., 1983). BS in Econs. and Bus., U. Buffalo, 1966. Buyer Foley's Federated Dept. Store, Houston, 1968-69; sr. buyer R.H. Macy's, N.Y.C., 1969-74; v.p. Warner divsn. Warnaco, Bridgeport, Conn., 1974-77; v.p. corp. mktg. Caron Internat., N.Y.C., 1977-79; chief exec. officer U.S. divsn. Max Factor & Co., Hollywood, Calif., 1979-82, pres., chief exec. officer, 1982-83; pres., chief exec. officer Max Factor & Co. Worldwide, 1983-84; mng. dir. Adler & Shaykin, N.Y.C., 1985-86; pres., CEO, chmn. Warnaco Inc., N.Y.C., 1986—; chmn., CEO Authentic Fitness Corp., 1991—; bd. dirs. The Travellers, Inc. Presdl. appointee Adv. Com. for Trade, Policy, Negotiations; trustee U. Buffalo Found., Carnegie Hall, Aspen Inst., Thirteen/WNET; bd. overseers Meml. Sloan-Kettering Cancer Ctr. Recipient Silver Achievement award L.A. YWCA; named Outstanding Woman in Bus. Women's Equity Action League, 1980, Woman of Yr., MS. Mag., 1986, one of the Yr.'s Most Fascinating Bus. People, Fortune Mag., 1986, one of 10 Most Powerful Women in Corp. Am., Savvy Woman Mag., 1989, 90, Am.'s Most Successful Bus. Woman, Fortune Mag., 1992, Queen of Cash Flow, Chief Exec. Mag., 1994. Mem. Am. Mgmt. Assn., Am. Apparel Mktg. Assn. (bd. dirs.), Bus. Roundtable, Coun. on Fgn. Rels. Republican. Jewish. Office: Warnaco Inc/Authentic Fitness Corp 90 Park Ave New York NY 10016

WACHS, MARTIN, urban planning educator, author, consultant; b. N.Y.C., June 8, 1941; s. Robert and Doris (Margolis) W.; m. Helen Pollner, Aug. 18, 1963; children: Faye Linda, Steven Brett. B.C.E., CUNY, 1963; M.S., Northwestern U., 1965, Ph.D., 1967. Asst. prof. U. Ill.-Chgo., 1967-69, Northwestern U., Evanston, Ill., 1969-71; assoc. prof. urban planning UCLA, 1971-76, prof., 1976-96; dir. UCLA Inst. Transp. Studies, 1993-96; prof. civil and environ. engring and city and regional planning U. Calif., Berkeley, 1996—; dir. U. Calif. Transp. Ctr., 1996—; vis. disting. prof. Rutgers U., New Brunswick, N.J., 1983-84; mem. exec. com. Transp. Rsch. Bd., 1995—. Author: Transportation for the Elderly: Changing Lifestyles, Changing Needs, 1979, Transportation Planning on Trial, 1996; also numerous articles; editor: Ethics in Planning, 1984, The Car and the City, 1992. Mem. steering com. Los Angeles Parking Mgmt. Study, 1976-78; bd. dirs. Los Angeles Commuter Computer, 1978-94, mem. Calif. Commn. on Transp. Investment, 1995. Served to capt. Ordnance Corps, U.S. Army, 1967-69. Recipient Pike Johnson award Transp. Research Bd., 1976, Disting. Teaching award UCLA Alumni Assn., 1986, Disting. Planning Educator award Calif. Planners Found., 1986, vis. fellow Oxford U. (Eng.), 1976-77; Guggenheim fellow, 1977; Rockefeller Found. humanities fellow, 1980. Fellow Am. Coun. Edn.; mem. Am. Planning Assn., Am. Inst. Cert. Planners, Architects, Designers, Planners for Social Responsibility. Jewish. Home: 1106 Grizzly Peak Blvd Berkeley CA 94708-1704 Office: U Calif Transp Ctr 108 Naval Arch Bldg Berkeley CA 94720-1720

WACHTEL, ALAN LARRY, writer, transportation consultant; b. Cin., Aug. 14, 1947; s. Jacques Louis and Rose (Edlin) W.; m. Cathleen Clarice Moran, Sept. 12, 1984; children: Elizabeth Jean, Anna Rebecca. BA, Yale U., 1968; postgrad., Stanford U., 1970-77. Vol. Peace Corps, Kenya, 1969; tchr. Lawrence Acad., Groton, Mass., 1969-70; teaching asst. Dept. of Physics, Stanford U., 1970-77; instr. Dept. Physics, San Francisco State U., 1977-78; instr. vacuum tech. tng. program Stanford Mid-Peninsula Urban Coalition, 1978-81; engring. trainer Racal-Vadic, Milpitas, Calif., 1981-85; ind. tech. writer/cons. Palo Alto, Calif., 1985—; cons. 3Com Corp., Santa Clara, Calif., 1986-88, 91-92, 94-95, County of Santa Clara, 1986-87, SynOptics Comm., Santa Clara, 1988-91, Alantec Internetworking Sys., San Jose, Calif., 1992-93, City of Berkeley (Calif.), 1992-93, County of Marin, Calif., 1993-94, City of San Francisco, 1994-95, Cisco Sys., San Jose, 1995—, City of Palo Alto, 1995-96. Author computer user and adminstr. manuals; contbr. articles to profl. jours. Mem. Am. Nat. Stds. Inst. Z90 Com. on Vehicular Head Protection, 1982—; mem. Palo Alto Bicycle Adv. Com., 1978—, chmn., 1983-86; chmn. Mountain View (Calif.) Bikeway Com., 1985; mem. Proposition 116 Bicycle Program Tech. Adv. Com., 1992-93; vice chair State of Calif. Bicycle Adv. Com., 1992—; mem. Regional Bicycle Adv. Com. of San Francisco Bay Area. Mem. Nat. Writers Union, Soc. for Tech. Comm. (sr.), Inst. Transp. Engrs., Calif. Assn. Bicycling Orgns. (govt. rels. dir. 1986—, pres. 1982-84, 85-86), League Am. Bicyclists (state legis. rep. 1987—, Effective Cycling Instr. cert. 1983, regional dir.'s Disting. Svc. award 1991), Western Wheelers Bicycle Club (pres. 1980), Adventure Cycling Assn., Silicon Valley Bicycle Coalition. Home and Office: 3446 Janice Way Palo Alto CA 94303-4212

WACHTEL, ALBERT, writer, educator; b. N.Y.C., Dec. 20, 1939; s. Jacob and Sarah Rose (Kaplansky) W.; m. Sydelle Farber, Mar. 9, 1958; children: Sally Rose, Seth Laurence, Stephanie Allyson, Synthia Laura, Jonathan Benjamin, Jessica Eden, Jacob Ethan. BA, CUNY, 1960; PhD, SUNY, Buffalo, 1968. Instr. SUNY, Buffalo, 1963-66, asst. to dean, 1966-68; asst. prof. U. Calif., Santa Barbara, 1968-74; prof. English, creative writing Pitzer Coll., The Claremont (Calif.) Colls., 1974—. Playwright: Paying the Piper, 1968, Prince Hal, 1995; co-editor Modernism: Challenges and Perspectives, 1986; author: The Cracked Lookingglass: James Joyce and the Nightmare of History, 1992; contbr. stories, creative essays to lit. jours. NDEA fellow, 1960-63, fellow Creative Arts Inst., U. Calif., Berkeley, 1970, NEH Summer Inst., Dartmouth Coll., 1987; Danforth Found. assoc., 1978. Jewish. Office: Pitzer Coll Claremont Colls Claremont CA 91711-6101

WADDELL, JOHN HENRY, sculptor; b. Des Moines, Feb. 14, 1921; s. William Wilder and Isabel Catherine (McGee) W.; m. Leslie Owen, 1942 (div. 1948); children—Sean, Seamus, Seanchan; m. Ruth Holland, Mar. 24, 1949; children—Lindsey, William, Amy. BFA, Art Inst. Chgo., 1948; B in Art Edn., 1949, MFA, 1949, M in Art Edn., 1951; DFA (hon.), Nat. Coll. Edn., 1979. Instr. Nat. Coll. Edn., Evanston, Ill., 1949-55; asst. prof. Ill. Inst. Tech., Chgo., 1955-57; prof. Ariz. State U., Tempe, 1957-64; head Waddell Sculpture Fellowship, Cornville, Ariz., 1971—. Executed sculpture Dance, Phoenix Civic Ctr., 1974, The Family, Maricopa County, Phoenix, 1967, That Which Might Have Been, Birmingham, 1963, Unitarian Ch., Paradise Valley, Ariz., 1964, Dance Mother, Kenyon Coll., Gambier, Ohio, 1969, Seated Flutist and Relief Dancers, Nat. Coll. Edn., Evanston, Ill., 1979, Backwalkover, Phoenix Sports Medicine Ctr., 1985, Apogee and Momentum, USTA Nat. Tennis Ctr., Flushing Meadows, N.Y., 1988, Seated Harpist, Ravinia, Highland Park, Ill., 1990, Touchstone, Boswell Meml. Hosp., Sun City, Ariz., 1994, Life's Celebration, 1985-95; represented Scottsdale (Ariz.) Ctr. For the Arts, 1984, others. Served with AUS, 1943-45. Grantee Valley Beautiful Commn., Phoenix, 1965, Nat. Endowment Arts/Commn. Arts and Humanities, 1969-74, Nat. Endowment Arts, 1978; recipient Gov. Artist award, 1995. Unitarian. Home: 10050 E Waddell Rd Cornville AZ 86325-6010

WADDELL, THEODORE, painter; b. Billings, Mont., Jan. 6, 1941. Student, Bklyn. Mus. Art Sch., 1962; BS, Ea. Mont. Coll., 1966; MFA, Wayne State U., 1968. One-man shows include U. Calif., San Diego, 1984, Cheney Cowles Meml. Mus., Spokane, Wash., 1985, The New West, Colorado Springs, 1986, Bernice Stein Baum Gallery, N.Y., 1992; exhibited in group shows 38th Corcoran Biennial, Corcoran Gallery, Washington, 1983; represented in permanent collections Ea. Mont. Coll., Yellowstone Art Ctr., Billings, Sheldon Meml. Art Gallery, U. Nebr., Lincoln, City of Great Falls, Mont., Dallas Mus. Art, San Jose (Calif.) Mus. Office: care Stremmel Gallery 1400 S Virginia St Reno NV 89502-2806*

WADDINGHAM, JOHN ALFRED, artist, journalist; b. London, Eng., July 9, 1915; came to U.S., 1927, naturalized, 1943; s. Charles Alfred and Mary Elizabeth (Coles) W.; m. Joan Lee Larson, May 3, 1952; children: Mary Kathryn, Thomas Richard. Student, Coronado (Calif.) Sch. Fine Arts, 1953-54, Portland Art Mus., 1940-65, U. Portland, 1946-47; pupil, Rex Brandt, Eliot Ohara, George Post. Promotion art dir. Oreg. Jour., Portland, 1946-59; with The Oregonian, Portland, 1959-81; editorial art dir. The Oregonian, 1959-81; tchr. watercolor Ore. Soc. Artists, 1954-56; tchr. art Oreg. Sch. Arts and Crafts, 1981—, Portland Community Coll.; represented by several galleries, Oreg. and Wash. One man show includes Art in the Gov.'s Office Ore State Capitol, 1991; rep. mus. rental collections, Portland Art Mus., Bush House, Salem, Ore., U. Oreg. Mus., Vincent Price collection, Ford Times collection, also, Am. Watercolor Soc. Travelling Show; judge art events, 1946—, over 50 one-man shows; ofcl. artist, Kiwanis Internat. Conv., 1966; designed, dir. constrn. cast: concrete mural Genesis, St. Barnabas Episcopal Ch., Portland, 1960; spl. work drawings old Portland landmarks and houses; propr. John Waddingham Hand Prints, fine arts serigraphs and silk screen drawings, 1965—; featured artist: Am. Artist mag., May 1967, June 1990, published in numerous mags. Served with USAAF, 1942-46. Recipient gold medal Salone Internazionale dell' Umorismo, Italy, 1974, 76, 80; honored with a 45 yr. retrospective Assignment: The Artist as Journalist Oreg. Hist. Soc., 1991. Artist mem. Portland Art Mus.; mem. Portland Art Dirs. Club (past pres.), N.W. Watercolor Soc., Watercolor Soc. Oreg., Oreg. Soc. Artists (watercolor tchr.), Multnomah Athletic Club, Jewish Community Ctr., Univ. Oreg. Med. Sch., Art in the Mounts., Oreg. Old Time Fiddlers, Clan Macleay Bagpipe Band. Home and Studio: 955 SW Westwood Dr Portland OR 97201-2744*

WADE, KENNETH ALAN, physician assistant; b. Salt Lake City, Oct. 22, 1948; s. Lester Heber and Carol (Braby) W.; m. Denice Stratford, Dec. 17, 1970; children: Kenneth Andrew, Dennis Curtis, Christopher Aaron. BS, Okla. Univ., 1981, U. Utah, 1973; AS, Weber State Coll., 1971. Staff acct. Elwood & Barnes, CPAs, Salt Lake City, 1973-79; physician asst. U.S. Army, 1979-81, Utah Army Nat. Guard, Salt Lake City, 1981—; mgr. Logan (Utah) Med. Ctr., 1983—; adj. instr. U. Utah, Salt Lake City, 1982-87; physician's asst. Logan Woman's Clinic, 1981—. Co-author: Prenatal Development. Bd. dirs. Cache County Sch. Bd., North Logan, 1992—, Cache Edn. Found., North Logan, 1992—. Fellow Am. Acad. Physician Assts., Utah Acad. Physician Assts.; mem. Assn. Mil. Surgeons U.S. Mem. Ch. Jesus Christ Latter Day Saints. Home: 175 W 100 S Smithfield UT 84341 Office: Logan Women's Clinic 550 E 1400 N Ste K Logan UT 84341-2450

WADE, LEROY GROVER, JR., chemistry educator; b. Jacksonville, Fla. Oct. 8, 1947; s. Leroy Grover and Margaret Lena (Stevens) W.; m. Patricia Andrews; children: Christine Elizabeth, Jennifer Diane. BA summa cum laude, Rice U., 1969; AM, Harvard U., 1970, PhD, 1974. Resident research fellow Du Pont Corp., Wilmington, Del., 1969; teaching fellow in chemistry Harvard U., Cambridge, Mass., 1969-74, sr. adviser to freshmen, 1971-74; resident sci. tutor Radcliffe Coll., Cambridge, 1970-74; asst. prof. chemistry Colo. State U., Ft. Collins, 1974-80, assoc. prof., 1980-89; prof. chemistry Whitman Coll., Walla Walla, Wash., 1989—. Author: Annual Reports in Organic Synthesis, 1975-82, 8 vols., Compendium of Organic Synthetic Methods, Vols. III, IV, V, 1977, 80, 84, Organic Chemistry, 1987, 3d edit., 1995; contbr. articles to sci. jours.; reviewer profl. jours., papers. Mem. Am. Chem. Soc., AAAS, Catgut Acoustical Soc., Am. Acad. Forensic Scis., Phi Beta Kappa (pres. Colo. State U. chpt. 1983-84), Sigma Xi. Home: 1123 Sturm Ave Walla Walla WA 99362-3831 Office: Whitman Coll Chemistry Dept Walla Walla WA 99362

WADE, MICHAEL ROBERT ALEXANDER, marketing specialist; b. N.Y.C., June 29, 1945; s. Burton Jean and Celia (Handleman) W.; student U. Rennes, France, 1964; AB, U. Chgo., 1967; postgrad. in pub. adminstrn., Am. U., 1967-71; MBA in Fin., N.Y. U., 1975; m. Carole Kay West, Aug. 25, 1974. Program analyst, mgmt. intern HUD, 1967-71; dep. dir. Mgmt. Communications and Briefing Center, U.S. Price Commn., 1972; asst. exec. sec. policy coordination U.S. Cost of Living Council, 1973-74; asso. dir. U.S. Indochina Refugee Program, 1975-76; pres. China Trade Devel. Corp. of Chgo., 1977—: participant with W.R. Grace & Co. in Okla. oil and gas prodn. Recipient Meritorious Service award Exec. Office of the Pres., 1972, Disting. Service award U.S. Cost of Living Council, 1974. Mem. Soc. Contemporary Art, Internat. Bus. Council MidAm. (bd. dirs.). Office: China Trade Devel Corp 2049 Century Park E Ste 480 Los Angeles CA 90067-3106

WADE, MICHAEL STEPHEN, management consultant; b. Mesa, Ariz., Sept. 13, 1948; s. William Conrad and Geraldine (Pomeroy) W.; m. Mary Ann Kraynick, Aug. 30, 1971; children: Jonathan, Hilary. BA, U. Ariz., 1970, JD, 1973. Command equal opportunity officer U.S. Army Criminal Investigation Command, Washington, 1974-76; EEO investigative specialist City of Phoenix, 1977-79, EEO adminstr., 1979-84; cons. Phoenix, 1984—; instr. Ariz. Govtl. Tng. Service; ptnr. Sanders & Wade Consulting Inc. Author: The Bitter Issue: The Right to Work Law in Arizona, 1976. Active Ch. of the Beatitudes, Ariz. Rep. Caucus. With U.S. Army, 1974-76. Recipient Phoenix Mayor's Com. on Employment of Handicapped award, 1984, Cert. Appreciation award Phoenix Fire Dept. Mem. Nat. Assn. Pub. Sector EEO Officers (founding pres. 1984-85, Pres.'s award 1989), Am. Soc. Equal Opportunity Profls. (v.p.), Ariz. Dispute Resolution Assn., Soc. Southwestern Authors. Home: 7032 N 3rd Ave Phoenix AZ 85021-8704 Office: PO Box 34598 Phoenix AZ 85067-4598

WADE, RODGER GRANT, financial systems analyst; b. Littlefield, Tex., June 25, 1945; s. George and Jimmie Frank (Grant) W.; m. Karla Kay Morrison, Dec. 18, 1966 (div. 1974); children: Eric Shawn, Shannon Annelle, Shelby Elaine; m. Carol Ruth Manning, Mar. 28, 1981. BA in Sociology, Tex. Tech. U., 1971. Programmer First Nat. Bank, Lubbock, Tex., 1971-73, Nat. Sharedata Corp., Odessa, Tex., 1973; asst. dir. computing ctr. Odessa Community Coll., 1973-74; programmer/analyst Med. Sci. Ctr., Tex. Tech U., Lubbock, 1974-76; sys. mgr. Hosp. Info. Sys., Addison, Tex., 1976-78; programmer, analyst Harris Corp., Grapevine, Tex., 1978-80, Joy Petroleum, Waxahachie, Tex., 1980-82; owner R&C Bus. Sys./Requerdos de Santa Fe, N.Mex., 1982-84; fin. sys. analyst Los Alamos (N.Mex.) Tech. Assocs., 1984-95; cons. mngr. Unidata Corp., Denver, 1995—; owner El Rancho Herbs, Santa Fe, 1988-91, Wade Gallery, Santa Fe, 1990-91, Wade Systems, Santa Fe, 1992—. Vol. programmer Los Alamos Arts Coun., 1987-88; mem. regulations task force N.Mex. Gov.'s Health Policy Adv. Com.; vol. systems support Amigos Unidos of Taos, 1990—. Republican. Home: 7160 Berthoud St Westminster CO 80030 Office: Unidata Corp 1099 18th St Ste 2500 Denver CO 80202-1908

WADIA, MANECK SORABJI, management consultant, writer; b. Bombay, Oct. 22, 1931; came to U.S., 1953.; s. Sorabji Rattanji and Manijeh M. (Pocha) W.; m. Harriet F. Schilit, Nov. 21, 1962; children: Sara Wadia Fascetti, Mark Sorab. MBA, Ind. U., 1958, PhD in Anthropology, 1957. Mem. faculty Ind. U., Bloomington, 1958-60; Ford Found. fellow U. Pitts., 1960-61; prof. Stanford U., Palo Alto, Calif., 1961-65; mgmt. and personal cons., pres. Wadia Assoc., Del Mar, Calif., 1965—; cons., lectr. presenter in field. Author: The Nature and Scope of Management, 1966, Management and the Behavioral Sciences, 1968, Cases in International Business, 1970, Holistic Management: A Behavioral Philosophy of Successful Leadership, 1990; co-author: (with Harper W. Boyd, Jr.) Cases from Emerging Countries, 1977, Shurkriya America: Adventures of a Sophisticated Immigrant, 1997; contbr. articles to profl. publs. Fellow Soc. Applied Anthropology; mem. Soc. Advancement Mgmt., Acad. Mgmt., Ind. Acad. Sci. (pres. anthropology sect.), Sigma Xi (assoc.), Sigma Iota Epsilon. Home and Office: 1660 Luneta Dr Del Mar CA 92014-2435

WADLEY, M. RICHARD, consumer products executive; b. Lehi, Utah; s. Merlyn R. and Verla Ann (Ball) W.; m. Nancy Zwiers; children: Lisa Kathleen, Staci Lin, Eric Richard, Nicole Marie. BS, Brigham Young U., 1967; MBA, Northwestern U., 1968. Brand asst. packaged soap and detergent div. Procter & Gamble Co., Cin., 1968-69, asst. brand mgr. packaged soap and detergent div., 1970-71, brand mgr. Dawn detergent, 1972-73, copy supr. packaged soap and detergent div., 1974-75, brand mgr. Tide detergent, 1975-77, assoc. advt. mgr. packaged soap and detergent div., 1977-81; corp. product dir. Hallmark Cards, Inc., Kansas City, Mo., 1982-83, corp. product dir. Ambassador Cards div., 1983-85; v.p., gen. mgr. feminine protection div. Tambrands Inc., Lake Success, N.Y., 1986-88; sr. v.p. Bongrain, Inc., N.Y.C., 1988-89; pres., CEO Alta-Dena Inc., Divsn. of Bongrain, Inc., 1989-91; pres. The Summit Group, 1991—; chmn., CEO T-Chem Products Inc., 1993—; bd. dirs. T-Chem Products. Bd. dirs. Long Beach Opera, 1991-95, L.I. Friends of the Arts, 1986-88; mem. adv. bd. Bus. Sch. Calif. State U., Long Beach, 1991-93.

WADLINGTON, W. M., software company executive; b. Madisonville, Ky., Oct. 28, 1944; s. W. Milton and Ellen Christine (Bryan) W.; m. Anne R. Lewis, Apr. 29, 1979; children: Andrew Stephen, Michael Edward, Thomas Scott. BA, Vanderbilt U., 1967. Commd. 2d lt. U.S. Army, 1967, advanced through grades to capt., 1970, field artillery officer, 1967-78, resigned, 1978; CFO Tech. Tools Inc., Boca Raton, Fla., 1992—. Decorated Silver Star. Republican. Home and Office: 10981 Twinleaf Ct San Diego CA 92131-3643

WADLINGTON, WILLIAM JEWELL, principal, secondary education educator; b. Princeton, Ky., Aug. 29, 1954; s. James Alvin and Virginia Irene (Storm) W.; m. Janet Louise Minshall, June 16, 1979; 1 child, Rebecca Minshall. AAS in Environ. Protection, Colo. Mountain Coll., Leadville, 1978; BS in Environ. Edn., Colo. State U., Ft. Collins, 1981; MNS in Biol. Scis., U. Idaho, Moscow, 1985. Cert. sci. tchr., prin., Wash. Teaching asst. U. Idaho, Moscow, 1983-85; adj. sci. prof. Spokane C.C., Republic, Wash., 1987-92; teaching scientist Glenns Ferry (Idaho) H.S., 1985-87, Republic (Wash.) H.S., 1987-93; teaching scientist Cascade H.S., Leavenworth, Wash., 1993-96, prin., teaching scientist, 1996—; co-dir. Wenatchee Valley Environ. Edn. Coalition, Wenatchee, Wash., 1993-96. Contbr. articles to profl. jours.; presenter in field. Mem. recreation dist. com. Ferry County Govt., Republic, 1991-92; bd. dirs. Rural Girls in Sci., Seattle, 1994-96; advisor Cascade Ednl. Found., Leavenworth, 1996—, Cascade Key Club, Leavenworth, 1996—. With USN, 1972-76. Recipient Christie MacAuliffe award, Wash. State, 1992, Pacific Sci. Tchr. of Yr. award Pacific Sci. Ctr., Seattle, 1996, Golden Apple award KCTS/PEMCO Ins., Seattle, 1996. Mem. ASCD, Nat. Sci. Tchrs. Assn., Wash. Sci. Tchrs. Assn. (small rural schs. rep. 1994-95, pres. 1996—), Trout Unltd. (edn. advisor), Kiwanis Club (past sec. and pres.). Home: 221 West St Leavenworth WA 98826-1044 Office: Cascade HS 10190 Chumstick Hwy Leavenworth WA 98826-9267

WADLOW, JOAN KRUEGER, academic administrator; b. LeMars, Iowa, Aug. 21, 1932; d. R. John and Norma I. (IhLe) Krueger; m. Richard R. Wadlow, July 27, 1958; children: Dawn, Kit. B.A., U. Nebr., Lincoln, 1953; M.A. (Seacrest Journalism fellow 1953-54), Fletcher Sch. Law and Diplomacy, 1956; Ph.D. (Rotary fellow 1956-57), U. Nebr., Lincoln, 1963; cert., Grad. Inst. Internat. Studies, Geneva, 1957. Mem. faculty U. Nebr., Lincoln, 1966-79; prof. polit. scis. U. Nebr., 1964-79, assoc. dean Coll. Arts and Scis., 1972-79; prof. polit. scis., dean Coll. Arts and Scis., U. Wyo., Laramie, 1979-84, v.p. acad. affairs, 1984-86; prof. polit. sci., provost U. Okla., Norman, 1986-91; chancellor U. Alaska, Fairbanks, 1991—; cons. on fed. grants; bd. dirs. Key Bank Alaska; mem. Commn. Colls. N.W. Assn. Author articles in field. Bd. dirs. Nat. Merit Scholarship Corp., Lincoln United Way, 1976-77, Bryan Hosp., Lincoln, 1978-79, Washington Ctr., 1986—, Key Bank of Alaska; v.p., exec. commr. North Cen. Assn., pres., 1991; pres. adv. bd. Lincoln YWCA, 1970-71; mem. def. adv. com. Women in the Svcs., 1987-89; mem. community adv. bd. Alaska Airlines. Recipient Mortar Board Teaching award, 1976, Disting. Teaching award U. Nebr., Lincoln, 1979; fellow Conf. Coop. Man, Lund, Sweden, 1956. Mem. NCAA (divsn. II subcom. of pres. commn. 1997—), Internat. Studies Assn. (co-editor Internat. Studies Notes 1978-91), Nat. Assn. State Univs. and Land-Grant Colls. (exec. com. coun. acad. affairs 1989-91, chair internat. affairs counsel 1996-97), Western Assn. Africanists (pres. 1980-82), Assn. Western Univs. (pres. 1993), Coun. Colls. Arts and Scis. (pres. 1983-84), Greater Fairbanks C. of C., Gamma Phi Beta. Republican. Congregationalist. Office: U Alaska Fairbanks Singers Hall Ste 320 Fairbanks AK 99775

WADMAN, WILLIAM WOOD, III, educational director, technical research executive, consulting company executive; b. Oakland, Calif., Nov. 13, 1936; s. William Wood, Jr., and Lula Fay (Raisner) W.; children: Roxanne Alyce Wadman Hubbling, Raymond Alan (dec.), Theresa Hope Wadman Boudreaux; m. Barbara Jean Wadman; stepchildren: Denise Ellen Varine Skrypkar, Brian Ronald Varine. M.A., U. Calif., Irvine, 1978. Cert. program mgr. tng. Radiation safety specialist, accelerator health physicist U. Calif. Lawrence Berkeley Lab., 1957-68; campus radiation safety officer U. Calif., Irvine, 1968-79; dir. ops., radiation safety officer Radiation Sterilizers, Inc., Tustin, Calif., 1979-80; prin., pres. Wm. Wadman & Assocs. Inc., 1980—; mem. operational review team Princeton U. Rsch. Campus TOKOMAK Fusion Test Facility, 1993-94; technical project mgr. for upgrades projects Los Alamos Nat. Lab. 1994-96, tech. project mgr. for 3 projects, 1995—; mem. team No. 1, health physics appraisal program NRC, 1980—, operational readiness review team to Princeton U. Rsch. Campus TOKOMAK Fusion Test Facility, 1993-94; cons. health physicist to industry; lectr. sch. social ecology, 1974-79, dept. community and environ. medicine U. Calif., Irvine, 1979-80, instr. in environ. health and safety, 1968-79, Orange Coast Coll., in radiation exposure reduction design engring. Iowa Electric Light & Power; trainer Mason & Hanger-Silas Mason Co., Los Alamos Nat. Lab.; instr. in medium energy cyclotron radiation safety UCLBL, lectr. in accelerator health physics, 1966, 67; curriculum developer in field; subject matter expert Los Alamos Nat. Lab., Earth and Environ. Scis., Tech. Support Office. Active Cub Scouts; chief umpire Mission Viejo Little League, 1973. Served with USNR, 1955-63. Recipient award for profl. achievement U. Calif. Alumni Assn., 1972, Outstanding Performance award U. Calif., Irvine, 1973. Mem. Health Physics Soc. (treas. 1979-81, editor proc. 11th symposium, pres. So. Calif. chpt. 1977, Professionalism award 1975), Internat. Radiation Protection Assn. (U.S. del. 4th Congress 1977, 8th Congress 1992), Am. Nuclear Soc., Am. Public Health Assn. (chmn. program 1978, chmn. radiol. health sect. 1979-80), Campus Radiation Safety Officers (chmn. 1975, editor proc. 5th conf. 1975), ASTM, Project Mgmt. Inst. Club: UCI Univ. (dir. 1976, sec. 1977, treas. 1978). Contbr. articles to tech. jours. Achievements include research in radiation protection and environmental sciences; Avocations: sailing, Tae Kwon Do, wood working, numesmantics. Home: 3687 Red Cedar Way Lake Oswego OR 97035-3525 Office: 675 Fairview Dr Ste 246 Carson City NV 89701-5468 *Personal philosophy: The continuous practice of patience, openmindedness, and open communication provide the essential ingredients for a full, satisfying personal and professional life. The timing of major decisions is not a matter of heart, but the culmination of the effective use of the practices above.*

WADSTROM, ANN KENNEDY, retired anesthesiologist; b. Slippery Rock, Pa., Aug. 5, 1931; d. James Alton and Eva Mildred (Fleming) Kennedy; m. Howard T. Wadstrom, June 23, 1956; children: Barbara Ann, Jeffrey George, Mark Howard, Carol V. Wadstrom Levandoski. Student, Warren Wilson Jr. Coll., Swannanoa, N.C., 1949-51; BS, Wheaton Coll., 1953; MD, Women's Med. Coll. Pa., 1958. Diplomate Am. Bd. Anesthesiology. Staff anesthesiologist Holy Cross Hosp., Salt Lake City, 1962-65, Los Alamos (N.Mex.) Med. Ctr., 1965-93; pres. Am. Coll. Med. Quality, Bethesda, Md., 1992-94; mem. adv. coun. physicians against family violence, AMA, Chgo., 1993—, alt. del., 1994—. Campaign chair United Way, Los Alamos, 1986, 96; mem. N.Mex. adv. coun. and atty. gen.'s task force Violence Against Women, 1994—; bd. dirs. Los Alamos Retirement Cmty., 1994—. Recipient Disting. Alumni award Warren wilson Coll., 1994. Fellow Am. Soc. Anesthesiologists; mem. Am. Med. Soc., N.Mex. Med. Soc. Home: 42 Loma Del Escolar Los Alamos NM 87544

WADSWORTH, JACQUELINE DORÈT, private investor; b. San Diego, June 15, 1928; d. Benjamin H. Dilley and Georgia E. (Elliott) Dilley Waters; m. Charles Desmond Wadsworth Jr., June 16, 1954 (dec. 1963); 1 child, Georgia Duncan Wadsworth Barber. BS, U. Oreg., 1946-50; MA, San Diego State U., 1950-52. Cert. tchr. Calif., Oreg. Dir. Jr. Red Cross, San Diego County chpt. ARC, 1952-59; asst. dir. leadership ctrs. for 8 western states ARC, Calif., 1954-59; pvt. investor, comml. real estate and property devel., 1974—; interior designer J. Wadsworth Interiors, La Jolla, Calif., 1990—. Vol. chairperson nat. conv. ARC, San Diego, 1966; vol., fundraiser San Diego Symphony Orch. Orgn., 1974-83; mem. Gold Ribbon Patron com. San Diego Symphony, 1995—; friends mem., vol. San Diego Mus. Art, 1958—, Asian Arts Com., 1996—; mem. Scripps Found. for Medicine and Sci., 1990—; life mem., bd. dirs. programs chairmanships, Mercy Hosp. Aux., 1965—; life mem., chairperson, bd. dirs. Social Svc. Aux., 1968—. Recipient Svc. awards Mercy Hosp. Aux., 1967-70. Mem. Caridad Internat., Globe Gilders Theatre Aux. (activity chairperson 1966-85), San Diego Zool. Soc. (curator 1976—), Country Friends Charities La Jolla Group, Mus. Contemporary Art San Diego. Republican.

WAFER, THOMAS J., JR., newspaper publisher. Pub. The Daily Breeze, Torrance, Calif. Office: 5215 Torrance Blvd Torrance CA 90509

WAGEMANN, DOUGLAS GERALD, banker; b. Oshawa, Ont., Can., Oct. 5, 1954; s. Edward and Sylvia Ella Wagemann; m. Rita Viola Hillock, Dec. 27, 1973; children: Shawna Lynn, Christine Renee, Douglas Gerald II. BS in Bus. magna cum laude, Calif. State Poly. U., 1984; MBA, Calif. State U., San Bernardino, 1987. Adminstrv. trainee PFF Bank & Trust, Pomona, Calif., 1984-85, asst. br. mgr., 1985-87, corp. rsch. analyst, 1987-90, v.p. rsch. planning mgr., 1990-93, v.p. mktg./planning dir., 1993—; lectr. Calif. State Poly U., 1992, La Sierra U., Riverside, Calif., 1995. Dir., v.p. Inland Hospice Assn., Claremont, Calif., 1991; lectr. Jr. Achievement, Anaheim, Calif., 1990. Named Vol. of Yr. Jr. Achievement, 1990. Mem. Internat. Soc. Strategic Mgmt. and Planning, Nat. Investor Rels. Inst., Bank Mktg. Assn., Western League of Savs. Inst. (chmn. mktg. com.), Phi Kappa Phi, Delta Mu Delta. Office: PFF Bank & Trust 350 S Garey Ave Pomona CA 91766-1722

WAGENER, ROBERT JOHN, bioethicist, mediator; b. Buffalo, N.Y., Mar. 6, 1946; s. Philip John and June Augusta (Bartels) W. BA, Houghton Coll. and SUNY, Buffalo; MDiv, McCormick Theol. Sem., Chgo.; MA, Canisius Coll. Founder, pres. Ctr. for Med. Ethics and Mediation, San Diego, 1992—; mediation coord. Am. Arbitration Assn., 1993—; cons. U. Calif. San Diego Ethics Consultation Svc., 1985—; lectr., mediator, mentor, trainer in field. Contbr. articles to profl. jours. Bd. dirs. Hospice Buffalo, Victim Offender Reconciliation Program, San Diego, UCSD Med. Ctr. Ethics Com.; cons. San Diego Hospice Chaplaincy Project; vice chair Hotel Dieu Hosp. Hospice, New Orleans; v.p. Sudden Infant Death Found. Western N.Y. Mem. ABA (dispute resolution sect.), Am. Soc. Law, Medicine and Ethics, Soc. Profls. in Dispute Resolution, So. Calif. Mediation Assn., Internat. Bioethics Inst., Hastings Ctr. for Bioethics. Office: Ctr for Med Ethics & Mediation Ste 106 1081 Camino del Rio S San Diego CA 92108-3545

WAGGENER, MELISSA, public relations executive; b. 1954. With Tektronix Inc., Beaverton, Oreg., 1975-80, Regis McKenna, Portland, 1980-83; with Waggener Edstrom, Inc., 1983—, now pres. Office: Waggener Edstrom Inc 6915 SW Macadam Ave Ste 300 Portland OR 97219-2398*

WAGGENER, THERYN LEE, law enforcement professional; b. Cedar Rapids, Iowa, Sept. 7, 1941; s. Hollis Angisa (Fowler) Hogan; m. Zoetta Jean Hamilton, May 30, 1967; 1 child, Drugh Kincade. BBA, Nat. U., 1977, MBA, 1979; JD, Western State Coll. Law, 1980. Traffic officer Calif. Hwy. Patrol, San Diego, 1966-72; owner, operator Am. Nat. Chem., San Diego, 1972-82; chief investigator N.Mex. Real Estate Commn., Albuquerque, 1983-86, Nev. Real Estate Div., Carson City, 1986-89; lt., shift comdr. Nev. Dept. Prisons, Ely, 1989—; prof., Sierra Nev. Coll., Incline Village, 1988-89, Western Nev. Community Coll., Carson City, 1987-89; No. Nev. C.C., 1992—. Mem. Washoe County (Nev.) Rep. Cen. Com., 1989. With USN, 1960-65. Mem. Nat. Assn. Real Estate Lic. Law Ofcls. (enforcement and investigative com. 1987-89), Toastmasters, Rotary, Lions, Masons, Shriners, Nu Beta Epsilon.

WAGNER, DAVID JAMES, lawyer; b. Cleve., Feb. 7, 1946; m. Martha Wilson, June 22, 1979; 1 child, Diana Jane. BS, USAF Acad., 1969; JD, Georgetown U., 1973. Bar: Colo. 1973, U.S. Supreme Ct. 1975, U.S. Dist. Ct. of Colo. 1973, U.S. Tax Ct. 1974. Asst. assoc. gen. counsel Presdl.

Clemency Bd., Washington, 1974-75; sec., gen. counsel Cablecomm-Gen. Inc., Denver, 1975-77; adj. prof. law Metro. State Coll., Denver, 1975-80; atty., mng. prin. Wagner & Waller, P.C., Denver, 1977-84; chmn. bd. GILA Comm., Inc., Denver, 1987; pvt. practice David Wagner & Assocs., P.C., Englewood, Colo., 1984—. Editor Am. Criminal Law Rev., Georgetown U. Law Sch., 1972-73. Trustee Kent Denver Sch., Cherry Hills Village, Colo., 1990-96, treas., 1992, pres., 1992-96; treas., dir. Denver Chamber Orch., 1979-81; dir. Leadership Denver Assn., 1978-80. Capt. USAF, 1973-75. Republican. Episcopalian. Office: David Wagner & Assocs PC Penthouse 8400 E Prentice Ave Englewood CO 80111-2912

WAGNER, DIANE MASTERS, newspaper editor; b. Corvallis, Oreg., May 7, 1938; d. Donald William and Marjorie Irene (Masters) Wagner; widowed; children: Victoria D. Masters, Dana L. Herbert, Benjamin D. Herbert. BA in Comms., Wash. State U., Pullman, 1961. Newspaper reporter Bellingham (Wash.) Herald, 1961-63; pub. info., vol. program dir. Douglas County Health Dept., Roseburg, Oreg., 1978-80; exec. dir. Umpqua Cmty. Action Coun., Roseburg, 1980-85; prodn. mgr. Pry Pub., Portland, Oreg., 1985-90; comms. coord. City of Vancouver, Wash., 1990—. Mem. SW Washington Writers, Oreg. Writers Colony (bd. dirs. 1993-94, newsletter editor 1994—). Office: City of Vancouver PO Box 1995 210 E 13th St Vancouver WA 98668

WAGNER, JOHN LEE, food products executive; b. Mt. Vernon, Wash., Aug. 24, 1943; s. John Orville and Gladys Annina (Hansen) W.; m. Judith Ann Murray, June 17, 1965 (div. Oct. 1991); 1 child, Trevor John; m. Claudia Ruth Littleton, Feb. 27, 1996. BA, U. Wash., 1965. Bank official Seattle First Nat. Bank, 1970-78; pres. Bank of Wash., Bellingham, 1978-83, Talbot Investment Co., Seattle, 1982-83; pres., owner Resource Pacific, Inc., Seattle, 1982—. Pres. Bellingham C. of C., 1980, Whatcom County Devel. Coun., 1981; bd. dirs. Western Wash. U. Western Found., 1984-88. Capt. USMC, 1965-70. Recipient Paul Harris Fellowship award Rotary Internat., 1989. Mem. Columbia Tower Club, Seattle Club, Rotary (pres. local dist. 1984). Republican.

WAGNER, JUDITH BUCK, investment firm executive; b. Altoona, Pa. Sept. 25, 1943; d. Harry Bud and Mary Elizabeth (Rhodes) B.; m. Joseph E. Wagner, Mar. 15, 1980; 1 child, Elizabeth. BA in History, U. Wash., 1965; grad. N.Y. Inst. Fin., 1968. Registered Am. Stock Exch., N.Y. Stock Exch., investment advisor. Security analyst Morgan, Olmstead, Kennedy & Gardner, L.A., 1968-71; security analyst Boettcher & Co., Denver, 1972-75; pres. Wagner Investment Mgmt., Denver, 1975—; chmn., bd. dirs. The Women's Bank, N.A., Denver, 1977-94, organizational group pres., 1975-77; chmn. Equitable Bankshares Colo., Inc., Denver, 1980-94; bd. dirs. Equitable Bank of Littleton, 1983-88, pres., 1985; bd. dirs. Colo. Growth Capital, 1979-82; lectr. Denver U., Metro State, 1975-80. Author: Woman and Money series Colo. Woman Mag., 1976; moderator 'Catch 2' Sta. KWGN-TV, 1978-79. Pres. Big Sisters Colo., Denver, 1977-82, bd. dirs., 1973-83; bd. fellows U. Denver, 1985-90; bd. dirs. Red Cross, 1980, Assn. Children's Hosp., 1985, Colo. Health Facilities Authority, 1978-84, Jr. League Community Adv. Com., 1979-92, Brother's Redevel., Inc., 1979-80; mem. agy. rels. com. Mile High United Way, 1978-81, chmn. United Way Venture Grant com., 1980-81; bd. dirs. Downtown Denver Inc., 1988-95; bd. dirs., v.p., treas. The Women's Found. Colo., 1987-91; treas., trustee, v.p., Graland Country Day Sch., 1990—, pres. 1994—; trustee Denver Rotary Found., 1990-95; trustee Hunt Alternatives Fund, 1992—. Recipient Making It award Cosmopolitan Mag., 1977, Women on the Go award, Savvy mag., 1983, Minouri Yasoui award, 1986, Salute Spl. Honoree award, Big Sisters, 1987; named one of the Outstanding Young Women in Am., 1979; recipient Woman Who Makes A Difference award Internat. Women's Forum, 1987. Fellow Assn. Investment Mgmt. and Rsch.; mem. Women's Forum of Colo. (pres. 1979), Women's Found. Colo., Inc. (bd. dirs. 1986-91), Denver Soc. Security Analysts (bd. dirs. 1976-83, v.p. 1980-81, pres. 1981-82), Colo. Investment Advisors Assn., Rotary (treas. Denver chpt. found., pres. 1993-94), Leadership Denver (Outstanding Alumna award 1987), Pi Beta Phi (pres. U. Wash. chpt. 1964-65). Office: Wagner Investment Mgmt Inc Ste 240 3200 Cherry Creek South Dr Denver CO 80209-3245

WAGNER, PATRICIA HAMM, lawyer; b. Gastonia, N.C., Feb. 1, 1936; d. Luther Boyd and Mildred Ruth (Wheeler) Hamm; married; children: David Marion, Michael Marion, Laura Marion. AB summa cum laude, Wittenberg U., 1958; JD with distinction, Duke U., 1974. Bar: N.C. 1974, Wash. 1984. Asst. univ. counsel Duke U., Durham, N.C., 1974-75, assoc. univ. counsel health affairs, 1977-80; atty. N.C. Meml. Hosp., 1975-77; assoc. N.C. Atty. Gen. Office, 1975-77; assoc. Powe, Porter & Alphin, Durham, 1980-81, prin., 1981-83; assoc. Williams, Kastner & Gibbs, 1984-86, Wickwire, Goldmark & Schorr, 1986-88; spl. counsel Heller, Ehrman, White & McAuliffe, 1988-90, ptnr., 1990—; arbitrator Am. Arbitration Assn., 1978—; arbitrator, pro tem judge King County Superior Ct., 1986—; tchr. in field. Mem. bd. vis. Law Sch. Duke U., 1992—; bd. dirs. Seattle Edn. Ctr., 1990-91, Metroctr. YMCA, 1991-94, Cmty. Psychiat. Clinic, Seattle, 1984-86; bd. dirs., sec.-treas. N.C. Found. Alternative Health Programs, Inc., 1982-84; bd. dirs., sec.-treas. N.C. Ctr. Pub. Policy Rsch., 1976-83, vice-chmn., 1977-80; mem. task force on commitment law N.C. Dept. Human Resources, 1978; active Def. Rsch. Inst. 1982-84; bd. dirs. Law Fund, 1992—, v.p., 1993—. Fellow Am. Bar Found.; mem. ABA (mem. ho. dels. Seattle-King County Bar Assn. 1991-94, mem. litigation sect.), Am. Soc. Hosp. Attys., Wash. State Bar Assn. (mem. domestic rels. task force 1991-93), Seattle-King Bar Assn. (mem. bd. trustees 1990-93, sec. bd. 1989-90, chair judiciary and cts. com. 1987-89, mem. King County Superior Ct. delay reduction task force 1987-89, mem. gender bias com. 1990-94, chair 1990-91), Wash. Def. Trial Lawyers (chmn. ct. rules and procedures com. 1987, co-editor newsletter 1985-86), Wash. State Soc. Hosp. Attys., Wash. Women Lawyers (treas. 1986, 87). Office: Heller Ehrman White & McAuliffe 6100 Columbia Ctr 701 5th Ave Seattle WA 98104-7016

WAGNER, RICHARD, artist; b. Trotwood, Ohio. BFA, U. Colo., 1950, MFA, 1952. Instr. Mansfield Art Ctr., Steamboat Springs, Colo., Castle Hill Art Ctr., Ispwich, Mass., U. Colo., 1950-53, Dartmouth Coll., 1953-66; gallery reps. El Prado Galleries, Santa Fe and Sedona, Ariz., The Darvish Collection, Naples, Fla., Courtyard Gallery, New Buffalo, Mich., Elinoff-Cote Gallery, Telluride, Colo. One-man shows include Grand Central Galleries, N.Y.C., Shore Gallery, Boston, Dartmouth Coll., DeCordova Mus., Lincoln, Mass., Fairleigh Dickinson U., N.J., Middlebury Coll., Telluride Gallery Fine Art, Colo., El Prado Art Galleries, Santa Fe, Sedona, Ariz., Western Colo. Ctr. Arts, Invitational Colorado Springs Rotary Show, 1995, 96, numerous others; group shows at Mus. Modern Art, Pa. Acad. Fine Arts, Joslyn Art Mus., Libr. Congress, Madison Square Gardens, Butler Art Inst.; contbr. articles to profl. jours.; represented in private collections. Recipient Colo. Springs Fine Arts Guild Juror's award, 1989, Pinon Arts Show First Pl., 1992, Naples Fla. Art Assn. First Pl., and others. Home: 13980 County Road 29 Dolores CO 81323-9356

WAGNER, RICHARD, business executive, former baseball team executive; b. Central City, Nebr., Oct. 19, 1927; s. John Howard and Esther Marie (Wolken) W.; m. Gloria Jean Larsen, May 10, 1950; children—Randolph G., Cynthia Kaye. Student, pub. schs., Central City. Gen. mgr. Lincoln (Nebr.) Baseball Club, 1955-58; mgr. Pershing Mcpl. Auditorium, Lincoln, 1958-61; exec. staff Ice Capades, Inc., Hollywood, Calif., 1961-63; gen. mgr. Sta. KSAL, Salina, Kans., 1963-65; dir. promotion and sales St. Louis Nat. Baseball Club, 1965-66; gen. mgr. Forum, Inglewood, Calif., 1966-67; asst. to exec. v.p. Cin. Reds, 1967-70, asst. to pres., 1970-74, v.p. adminstrn., 1975, exec. v.p., 1975-78, gen. mgr., 1977-83, pres., 1978-83; pres. Houston Astros Baseball Club, 1985-87; spl. asst. Office of Baseball Commr., 1988-93; asst. to chmn. Major League Exec. Coun., 1993-94; pres. RGW Enterprises, Inc., Phoenix, 1978—. Served with USNR, 1945-47, 50-52. Named Exec. of Yr., Minor League Baseball, Sporting News, 1958. Mem. Internat. Assn. Auditorium Mgrs. Republican. Methodist.

WAGNER, SUE ELLEN, state official; b. Portland, Maine, Jan. 6, 1940; d. Raymond A. and Kathryn (Hooper) Pooler; m. Peter B. Wagner, 1964 (dec.); children: Kirk, Kristina. B.A. in Polit. Sci., U. Ariz., 1962; M.A. in History, Northwestern U., 1964. Asst. dean women Ohio State U., 1963-64; tchr. history and Am. govt. Catalina High Sch., Tucson, 1964-65; reporter Tucson Daily Citizen, 1965-68; mem. Nev. Assembly, 1975-83; mem. Nev. Senate from 3d dist.; elected lt. gov. of Nev., 1990-94. Author: Diary of a Candidate, On People and Things, 1974. Mem. Reno Mayor's Adv. Com., 1973-84; chmn. Blue Ribbon Task Force on Housing, 1974-75; mem. Washoe County Republican Central Com., 1974-84, Nev. State Rep. Central Com., 1975-84; mem. Nev. Legis. Commn., 1976-77; del. social service com. Council State Govts.; v.p. Am. Field Service, 1973, family liaison, 1974, mem.-at-large, 1975. Kappa Alpha Theta Nat. Grad. scholar, also Phelps-Dodge postgrad. fellow, 1962; named Outstanding Legislator, Nev. Young Republicans, 1976. Mem. AAUW (legis. chmn. 1974), Bus. and Profl. Women, Kappa Alpha Theta. Episcopalian. Home: 845 Tamarack Dr Reno NV 89509-3640*

WAGNER, TERESA ANN, handwriting analyst; b. Spokane, Wash., Jan. 5, 1954; d. Alexander Lazarus and Pauline Joyce (Hodgson) Birch; m. Robert Earl Hurt, Aug. 11, 1973 (div. Jan. 1986); 1 child, Melinda Eslie Ann; m. Gary William Wagner, Aug. 25, 1996. AAS in Paralegal Studies, Spokane C.C., 1995. Cert. in behavioral profiling and forensic document exams., Am. Bd. Forensic Examiners, 1993; cert. in document exam., Nat. Assn. Document Examiners, 1995. Owner Profl. Handwriting Analysis, Spokane, 1986—; instr. Spokane Falls C.C., 1989-92, 92-94. Mem. Am. Handwriting Analysis Found. (cert., com. mem.), Coun. Graphological Soc., Nat. Assn. Document Examiners (treas., cert. document examiner), Northwest Fraud Investigators Assn. Office: Profl Handwriting Analysis 10 N Post St Ste 550 Spokane WA 99201-0705

WAGNER, WILLIS HARCOURT, vascular surgeon; b. Long Beach, Calif., May 13, 1955; s. William Franklin and Caroline (Willis) W.; m. Diane Elaine Benkert, Sept. 14, 1982; children: Daniel, Samuel, Alison, Matthew. BS in Biol. Sci., Stanford U., 1977; MD, U. So. Calif., L.A., 1981. Intern U. So. Calif. Med. Ctr., L.A., 1981-82, resident, 1982-86; instr. in surgery U. So. Calif., 1986-87; fellow in vascular surgery U. N.C., Chapel Hill, 1987-88; vascular surgeon Cedars Sinai Med. Ctr., L.A., 1988—, chief div. vascular surgery, 1994—; clin. asst. prof. surgery U. So. Calif., 1988—. Author chpts. to books; contbr. articles to profl. jours. Mem. So. Calif. Vascular Surgery Soc., So. Assn. for Vascular Surgery (Pres. award 1988), Western Vascular Soc., Peripheral Vascular Surg. Soc., Internat. Soc. Vascular Surgery, Alpha Omega Alpha. Office: 8631 W 3rd St Ste 615-e Los Angeles CA 90048-5901

WAGONER, DAVID EVERETT, lawyer; b. Pottstown, Pa., May 16, 1928; s. Claude Brower and Mary Kathryn (Groff) W.; children: Paul R., Colin H., Elon D., Peter B., Dana F.; m. Jean Morton Saunders; children: Constance A., Jennifer L., Melissa J. B.A., Yale U., 1950; LL.B., U. Pa., 1953. Bar: D.C. 1953, Pa. 1953, Wash. 1953. Law clk. U.S. Ct. Appeals (3d cir.), Pa., 1955-56; law clk. U.S. Supreme Ct., Washington, 1956-57; ptnr. Perkins & Coie, Seattle, 1957-96; panel mem. of arbitration forum worldwide including Republic of China, B.C. Internat. Comml. Arbitration Ctr., Hong Kong Internat. Arbitration Centre, Asian/Pacific Ctr. for Resolution of Internat. Bus. Disputes and the Ctr. for Internat. Dispute Resolution for Asian/Pacific Region. Mem. sch. com. Mcpl. League Seattle and King County, 1958—, chmn., 1962-65; mem. Seattle schs. citizens coms. on equal ednl. opportunity and adult vocat. edn., 1963-64; mem. Nat. Com. Support Pub. Schs.; mem. adv. com. on community colls., to 1965, legislature interim com. on edn., 1964-65; mem. community coll. adv. com. to state supt. pub. instrn., 1965; chmn. edn. com. Forward Thrust, 1968; mem. Univ. Congl. Ch. Council Seattle, 1968-70; bd. dirs. Met. YMCA Seattle, 1968; bd. dirs. Seattle Pub. Schs., 1965-73, v.p., 1966-67, 72-73, pres., 1968, 73; trustee Evergreen State Coll. Found., chmn. 1986-87, capitol campaign planning chmn.; trustee Pacific NW Ballet, v.p. 1986. Served to 1st lt. M.C., AUS, 1953-55. Fellow Am. Coll. Trial Lawyers (mem. ethics com., legal ethics com.), Chartered Inst. Arbitrators, Singapore Inst. Arbitrators; mem. ABA (chmn. standing com. fed. jud. imprisonment, chmn. appellate advocacy com., mem. comm. on separation of powers and jud. independence), Wash. State Bar Assn., Seattle-King County Bar Assn., Acad. Experts, Swiss Arbitration Assn., Comml. Bar Assn. London, Nat. Sch. Bds. Assn. (bd. dirs., chmn. coun. Big City bds. edn. 1971-72), English-Speaking Union (v.p. Seattle chpt. 1961-62), Chi Phi. Home: 3403 E Shore Dr Seattle WA 98112 Office: Internat Arbitration Chambers US BankCtr 1420 5th Ave 22d Fl Seattle WA 98101

WAHLER, DENNIS DANIEL, business studies educator, administrator; b. Freeport, Ill., Oct. 20, 1938; s. Robert Richard and Elizabert A. (Schubert) W.; m. Beverly A. Davis, June 30, 1961 (div. 1972); children: Richard, Rene; m. Maryam Behbod, June 30, 1978; 1 child, Yusuf Ali. BS in Gen. Engring., Met. Colgate Inst., London, 1968; MBA, U. Phoenix, San Jose, Calif., 1984; D Bus. Adminstrn., So. Calif. U., 1995. Project engr. Hughes Aircraft, L.A., 1974-76, Iran Electronics, Shiraz, Iran, 1976-78; owner, pres. Delta Design, San Jose, 1976-80, D.D. Wahler Design Group Ltd., San Jose, 1980—; prof. bus. studies San Jose City Coll., 1982—, dir. internat. bus. studies, 1993—. Co-author: Drafting for Electronics, 1985, 93, The Small Business Challenge, 1992, Mechanical Design, 1994, International Business Terrorism and Personal Security, 1994. Mem. Am. Inst. Bldg. Designers, San Jose Met. C. of C. Office: San Jose City Coll 2100 Moorpark Ave San Jose CA 95128-2723

WAHLKE, JOHN CHARLES, political science educator; b. Cin., Oct. 29, 1917; s. Albert B.C. and Clara J. (Ernst) W.; m. Virginia Joan Higgins, Dec. 1, 1943; children: Janet Parmely, Dale. A.B., Harvard U., 1939, M.A., 1947, Ph.D., 1952. Instr., asst. prof. polit. sci. Amherst (Mass.) Coll., 1949-53; assoc. prof. polit. sci. Vanderbilt U., Nashville, Tenn., 1953-63; prof. polit. sci. SUNY, Buffalo, 1963-66, U. Iowa, 1966-71, SUNY, Stony Brook, 1971-72, U. Iowa, Iowa City, 1972-79; prof. polit. sci. U. Ariz., Tucson, 1979-87, prof. emeritus, 1987—. Author: (with others) The Legislative System, 1962, Government and Politics, 1966, The Politics of Representation, 1978; co-author: Introduction to Political Science—Reason, Reflection, and Analysis, 1997;. Served to capt., F.A. AUS, 1942-46. Decorated Air medal with 2 oak leaf clusters. Mem. AAAS, Am. Polit. Sci. Assn. (past pres.), Internat. Polit. Sci. Assn., So. Polit. Sci. Assn., Midwest Polit. Sci. Assn. (past pres.), Western Polit. Sci. Assn., Southwestern Polit. Sci. Assn., Assn. Politics and the Life Scis. Home: 5462 N Entrada Catorce Tucson AZ 85718-4851 Office: U Ariz Dept Polit Sci Tucson AZ 85721

WAIN, CHRISTOPHER HENRY FAIRFAX MORESBY, actuary, insurance and investment consultant; b. Toronto, Ont., Can., Nov. 21, 1918; came to U.S., 1923; s. Andrew Martin and Eve Margaret (Fairbain) W.; m. Jeane Crawford Thomas, June 26, 1948; children: Christopher H. Jr., Margot Crawford. BA, UCLA, 1940. CLU. Actuarial student Occidental Life of Calif., L.A., 1946-48; various positions including v.p., actuary Prudential Ins. Co. Am., Newark and L.A., 1948-83; ins. and investment cons. L.A., 1984—; mem. various coms. Am. Coun. Life Ins., Washington, 1965-83. Capt. U.S. Army, 1941-45. Regents scholar UCLA, 1938-39. Fellow Soc. Actuaries; mem. Am. Acad. Actuaries.

WAINESS, MARCIA WATSON, legal management consultant; b. Bklyn., Dec. 17, 1949; d. Stanley and Seena (Klein) Watson; m. Steven Richard Wainess, Aug. 7, 1975. Student, UCLA, 1967-71, 80-81, Grad. Sch. Mgmt. Exec. Program, 1987-88, grad. Grad. Sch. Mgmt. Exec. Program, 1988. Office mgr., paralegal Lewis, Marenstein & Kadar, L.A., 1977-81; office mgr. Rosenfeld, Meyer & Susman, Beverly Hills, Calif., 1981-83; adminstr. Rudin, Richman & Appel, Beverly Hills, 1983; dir. adminstrn. Kadison, Pfaelzer, L.A., 1983-87; exec. dir. Richards, Watson and Gershon, L.A., 1987-93; legal mgmt. cons. Wainess & Co., Beverly Hills, 1993—; faculty mem. UCLA Legal Mgmt. & Adminstrn. Program, 1983, U. So. Calif. Paralegal Program, L.A., 1985; mem. adv. bd. atty. asst. tng. program, UCLA, 1984-88; adj. faculty Univ. of West L.A. Sch. Paralegal Studies, 1997—. Mem. ABA (chair Displaywrite Users Group 1986, legal tech. adv. coun. litig. support working group 1986-87), Inst. Mgmt. Consultants, L.A. County Bar Assn. (exec. com. law office mgmt. sect.), San Fernando Valley Bar Assn., Assn. Legal Adminstrs. (bd. dirs. 1990-92, asst. regional v.p. Calif. 1987-88, regional v.p. 1988-89, pres. Beverly Hills chpt. 1985-86, membership chair 1984-85, chair new adminstrn. sect. 1982-84, mktg. mgmt. sect. com. 1989-90, internat. conf. com.), Beverly Hills Bar Assn. (exec. com. law practice mgmt. sect.), Internat. Platform Assn., Cons. Roundtable of So. Calif. Office: 415 N Camden Dr Beverly Hills CA 90210

WAINIO, MARK ERNEST, insurance company consultant; b. Virginia, Minn., Apr. 18, 1953. BA, Gustavus Adolphus Coll., 1975. Cert. safety profl., assoc. loss control mgmt., assoc. risk mgmt., assoc. claims, CPCU. Carpenter ABI Contracting Inc., Virginia, 1975-77; co-owner Mesabi Builders, Albuquerque and Eveleth, Minn., 1977-79; sr. engring. rep. Aetna Life & Casualty, Albuquerque, 1979-86; loss control specialist CNA Ins. Cos., Albuquerque, 1986-91, loss control cons., 1991-94, mgr. loss control svcs., 1994-95, dir. los control svcs., 1995—; owner MEW Safety and Risk Mgmt., 1989—; pres. MW Enterprises, 1990—. Mem. Am. Soc. Safety Engrs., CPCU. Office: CNA Ins Cos 8500 Menaul Blvd NE Albuquerque NM 87112-2298

WAINIONPAA, JOHN WILLIAM, computer equipment company executive; b. Quincy, Mass., July 13, 1946; s. Frank Jacob and Jennie Sofia (Kaukola) W.; m. S. Linda Rapo, Oct. 18, 1969; children: Heidi Liisa, Erik David, Sinikka Lin. BSEE, U. N.Mex., 1972; MS in Aero. Engring., Naval Postgrad. Sch., 1981. Engr.-in-tng., Colo. Enlisted USN, 1968, commd. ens., 1972, advanced through grades to lt. comdr., 1982; flight instr. Tng. Squadron 27, Corpus Christi, Tex., 1973-75; aircraft, mission comdr. Patrol Squadron 49, Jacksonville, Fla., 1976-79; ops. officer Anti-Submarine Warfare Ops. Ctr., Kadena, Okinawa, Japan, 1982-84; launch and control systems officer Naval Space Command, Dahlgren, Va., 1984-86; naval space systems ops. officer U.S. Space Command, Colorado Springs, 1986-88; ret. USN, 1988; sys. engr. CTA Inc., Colorado Springs, 1988-95, tng. coord., 1993-94, profl. devel. orgn. mgr., 1994-95; product mgr. Digital Equipment Corp., Colorado Springs, 1995—. Merit badge counselor Boy Scouts Am., Colorado Springs, 1986—; clasroom instr. Jr. Achievement, Colorado Springs, 1995—. Mem. AIAA (sr.), IEEE, U.S. Naval Inst., Sigma Tau, Eta Kappa Nu. Office: Digital Equipment Corp CX01-2/P22 301 S Rockrimmon Blvd Colorado Springs CO 80919-2398

WAITE, JOANNE LISCHER, systems analyst; b. N.Y.C., July 17, 1938; d. Carl Fredrick and Blanche Edna (Hestwood) Lischer; m. William McCastline Waite, June 18, 1960; 1 child, William Frederick. AB, Oberlin Coll., 1960; MSEE, U. Colo., 1970. Systems analyst Mut. of N.Y., N.Y.C., 1960-65, U. Sydney, Australia, 1965-66; sr. network analyst U. Colo., Boulder, 1974—. Mem. Eta Kappa Nu (bd. dirs. 1979-81, v.p. 1984-85, pres. 1985-86). Office: U Colo at Boulder Computing and Network Svcs Box 455 Boulder CO 80309-0455

WAKATSUKI, LYNN Y., commissioner. Commr. fin. instns. Honolulu. Office: 1010 Richards St Rm 602A Honolulu HI 96813

WAKE, DAVID BURTON, biology educator; b. Webster, S.D., June 8, 1936; s. Thomas B. and Ina H. (Solem) W.; m. Marvalee Hendricks, June 23, 1962; 1 child, Thomas Andrew. BA, Pacific Luth. U., 1958; MS, U. So. Calif., 1960, PhD, 1964. Instr. anatomy and biology U. Chgo., 1964-66, asst. prof. anatomy and biology, 1966-69; assoc. prof. zoology U. Calif., Berkeley, 1969-72, prof., 1972-89, prof. integrative biology, 1989-91, John and Margaret Gompertz prof., 1991—; dir. Mus. Vertebrate Zoology U. Calif., Berkeley, 1971—. Author: Biology, 1979; co-editor: Functional Vertebrate Morphology, 1985, Complex Organismal Functions: Integration and Evolution in the Vertebrates, 1989. Mem. nat. bd. Nat. Mus. Natural History. Recipient Quantrell Teaching award U. Chgo., 1967, Outstanding Alumnus award Pacific Luth. U., 1979; grantee NSF, 1965—; Guggenheim fellow, 1982. Fellow AAAS, NRC (bd. biology 1986-92); mem. Internat. Union for Conservation of Nature and Natural Resources (chair task force on declining amphibian populations 1990-92), Am. Soc. Zoologists (pres. 1992), Am. Soc. Naturalists (pres. 1989), Am. Soc. Ichthyologists and Herpetologists (bd. govs.), Soc. Study Evolution (pres. 1983, editor 1979-81), Soc. Systematic Biology (coun. 1980-84), Herpetologist's League (Disting. Herpetologist 1984), Am. Philos. Soc., Am. Acad. Arts & Scis., (1997). Home: 999 Middlefield Rd Berkeley CA 94708-1509

WAKS, DENNIS STANFORD, lawyer; b. Decatur, Ill., Apr. 2, 1949; s. Paul and Regina (Geisler) W.; m. Jaclyn Hoyle; 1 child, Kelly. BA, U. Wis., 1971; JD, U. Miss., 1973; LLM, U. Mo., Kansas City, 1975. Bar: Miss. 1973, Ill. 1975, U.S. Dist. Ct. (no. dist.) Miss. 1973, U.S. Dist. Ct. (so. dist.) Ill. 1975, U.S. Dist. Ct. (ea. dist.) Calif. 1988, U.S. Ct. Apeals (9th cir.) 1989, Calif. 1989. Dir. prison legal svcs. project So. Ill. U. Sch. Law, Carbondale, Ill., 1976-77; asst. pub. defender Jackson County Pub. Defenders Office, Murphysboro, Ill., 1977-80, chief pub. defender, 1980-85; spl. prosecutor Perry County States Atty. Office, Pinckneyville, Ill., 1985; prof. dept. law enforcement So. Ill. U., Carbondale, 1978-87; pvt. practice Murphysboro, 1985-87; asst. atty. Fed. Pub. Defenders Office Ea. Dist. Calif., Sacramento, 1988—, supervising sr. atty., 1990-96; chief asst. Fed. Pub. Defender, 1996—; faculty Ill. Defender Program, Chgo., 1982-86, bd. dirs.; faculty masters thesis and doctoral com. So. Ill. U., Carbondale, 1978-87. Editor Miss. Law Rev., 1973. Organizer Paul Simon for Senator, Carbondale, 1984; bd. dirs. Hill Ho. Resdl. Ctr. for Substance Abuse, Carbondale, 1981-87, v.p. 1984-87. Named Outstanding Young Man of Am., 1985. Mem. ABA, Nat. Assn. Criminal Def. Attys., Ill. Pub. Defender Project, Ill. Pub. Defenders Assn., Calif. Attys. for Criminal Justice, Calif. Pub. Defenders Assn. Democrat. Office: Fed Defenders Office 801 K St Ste 1024 Sacramento CA 95814-3518

WALASEK, OTTO FRANK, chemical engineer, biochemist, photographer; b. Park Falls, Wis., Mar. 11, 1919; s. Frank Otto and Mary (Swoboda) W.; m. Annie May Stockton (div. Nov. 1959); 1 child, Richard A.; m. Joan Constance Ashton, Sept. 18, 1965; children: Arthur, Carl. BS in Chem. Engring., U. Wis., 1946; MS in Biochemistry, U. Ill., 1968; postgrad., Loyola U., 1968-72. Penicillin processing product engr. I Abbott Labs., North Chgo., Ill., 1946-49; antibiotic process rsch. and devel. Abbott Labs., North Chgo., 1950-55, biochemical rsch., 1956-68, sr. biochemist, 1968-77, staff Leukemia project, 1978-80; pvt. photographer Sonora, Calif., 1981—. Patentee in field; contbr. articles to profl. jours. Recipient Excellence award Fedn. Internat. of Art Photographic, Switzerland, 1972; named Hon. Master of Profl. Photography, Profl. Photographic Assns., Taiwan, 1990. Mem. Photographic Soc. Am. (associateship), Royal Photographic Soc., Nat. Stereoscopic Soc., Internat. Stereoscopic Union. Democrat. Office: 10165 US Highway 49 Sonora CA 95370-9456

WALCOTT, WILLIAM OLIVER, family practice physician; b. Waterbury, Conn., Jan. 7, 1938; s. Ray William and Ruth Turza (Eggleton) W.; m. Anne Tremaine Bennett, Aug. 27, 1960 (div. Dec. 1981); children: William B., Christopher V.; m. Linda June Nilsen, Jan. 18, 1987. BArch, U. Mich., 1961; MD, U. Conn., 1974. Bd. cert. ob-gyn., family practice. Commd. 2d lt. U.S. Army, 1964, advanced through grades to col., 1988, ob-gyn. physician, 1978-88, family practice physician, 1988-92, ret., 1992; family practice physician Group Health Coop., Seattle, 1992—. Mem. Am. Acad. Family Physicians. Office: Group Health Coop 10452 Silverdale Way Silverdale WA 98383

WALD, ROBERT DAVID, psychiatrist; b. Cleve., Dec. 8, 1924; s. Herman and Dorothy (Sherower) W.; m. Martha Jan Fuller, Oct. 15, 1947 (div. Feb. 1963); children: Jean, Malie, M. Daniel, Shanti, Rebecca; m. Nicole diPadua, Feb. 8, 1981. Student, U. Calif., Berkeley, 1950-52; MD, Wash. U., 1956. Diplomate Am. Bd. Psychiatry & Neurology. Intern U. Calif., 1957; resident Langley Porter Neurologist, 1957-59, fellow, 1959-61; assoc. prof. U. Calif. Sch. Medicine, San Francisco, 1961-93; med. dir. outpatient divsn. Charter North Hosp., Anchorage, Alaska, 1993—. Office: Charter No Counseling Ctr 2530 DeBarr Rd Anchorage AK 99508

WALDEN, JOSEPH LAWRENCE, army officer; b. Paducah, Ky., Oct. 2, 1956; s. Thomas Lorenzo and Betty Jo (Miller) W.; m. Julia Kay Johnson, Oct. 9, 1982; children: Amber Marie, Bobbi Michelle. BS in Rural Sociology, N.C. State U., 1978; MBA, Fla. Inst. Tech., Melbourne, 1988; MS in Sys. Mgmt., Fla. Inst. Tech., 1989. Commd. U.S. Army, 1978, advanced through grades to lt. col., to date; supply platoon leader 25th Inf. div. U.S. Army, Schofield Barracks, Hawaii, 1979-81; supply control officer U.S. Army, 1981-82; installation supply officer Signal Sch. U.S. Army, Ft. Gordon, Ga., 1983; brigade logistics officer 2d Signal Brigade U.S. Army, Ft. Gordon, 1983-84; co. comdr. Co. B, 3rd Batallion, 2d Signal Brigade, Ft. Gordon, 1984-86; logistics plans officer Combat Devel., Quartermaster Sch., Ft. Lee, Va., 1988-89; chief gen. support U.S. Army Quartermaster Sch., Ft. Lee, 1989-91; assigned to U.S. Army Command and Gen. Staff Coll., Ft. Leavenworth, Kans., 1991-92; exec. officer 19th Corps Materiel Mgmt. Ctr., Wiesbaden, Germany, 1992-94; chief supply mgmt. 3D Corps Support Command, Wiesbaden, 1994-95; comdr. Materiel Mgmt. Ctr., Ft. Irwin, Calif., 1995—; mem. adj. faculty St. Leo Coll., Ft. Lee, 1988-91; mem. faculty City Coll. of Chgo., 1994-95; pres. Walden Fitness Systems, Ft. Leavenworth, 1984—. Contbr. articles to profl. jours. Mem. Bldg. Code Appeals Bd., City of Hopewell, 1988-91. Mem. Nat. Strength Conditioning

Assn., Va. Assn. of U.S. Powerlifting Fedn. (pres. 1989-91), Am. Sunbathing Assn., Fellowship Christian Athletes, Fla. Sheriffs Assn., San Diego Zool. Soc., Assn. Quartermasters, Las Vegas Sun Club, Save the Manatee Club, Delta Mu Delta. Republican. Methodist.

WALDEN, RICHARD KEITH, agri-business executive; b. Santa Paula, Calif., July 4, 1913; s. Arthur Frisbie and Eva Juanita (Southwick) W.; m. Barbara Eldredge Culbertson, Sept. 25, 1938 (div.); 1 son, Richard Sheffield; m. 2d, Dorothy Dayton Beck, July 5, 1967. B.A., Pomona Coll., 1936; postgrad. UCLA, 1934, 39. With Limoneira Ranch Co., Santa Paula, 1936-40; mgr. Ford-Craig Ranch Co., San Fernando, Calif., 1940-46; founder, chmn. bd. Farmers Investment Co., Calif., Ariz. and Fla., 1946—; dir. Ariz. Feeds Co., 1950-74, 1st Interstate Bank, 1962-84 , Cotton, Inc., 1961-73; cons. Ford Found., Pakistan, 1969; dir. agr. adv. com. Stanford Research Inst., 1960-66; chmn. Pima County Agr. and Stblzn. Com., 1956-61. Bd. trustees Pomona Coll., 1978-81, Continental Sch. Bd., 1950-67; bd. advisors U. Ariz. Coll. Bus., 1983-88; bd. dirs. Tucson C. of C.; chmn. Ariz. Oil and Gas Commn., 1960-66, Green Valley Community Health Ctr., 1981—; mem. Gov.'s Emergency Resources Planning Com., 1964. Recipient Disting. Citizen award U. Ariz. Alumni Assn., 1973, Outstanding Citizen award Ariz. State Farm Bur., 1988; named Citizen of Yr., Rotary Club, 1980, Agrl. of the Year, U. Ariz., 1994. Mem. Nat. Pecan Council, Ariz. Cotton Growers, Nat. Cotton Council (dir. 1960), Western Pecan Growers Assn. (dir. 1972-82), Ariz. Cattle Growers Assn. (dir. 1954-60), U. Ariz. Pres.'s Club, Cotton Council Internat. (chmn., pres. 1961-66), Town Hall Ariz., Balboa Club (Mazatlan, Sinaloa, Mex.), Green Valley (Ariz.) Country Club, Mountain Oyster Club. Republican. Home: 635 W Twin Buttes Rd PO Box 504 Green Valley AZ 85622-0504 Office: PO Box 7 Sahuarita AZ 85629-0007

WALDMANN, RAYMOND JOHN, aerospace executive; b. Walton, N.Y., Nov. 28, 1938; s. Raymond George and Flora Elizabeth (Gannon) W.; m. Jane Imper (div.); 1 child, Christine; m. Mary Nimmo, July, 1983; children: Elizabeth, John, Emily. SB in Chem. Engring., MIT, 1960, SB in Humanities, 1961; JD, Harvard U., 1964. Bar: Mass. 1964, D.C. 1970. Cons. Arthur D. Little, Cambridge, Mass., 1964-70; staff asst. to Pres. The White House, Washington, 1970-73; special asst. to Pres. The White House, 1975-76; dep. asst. sec. U.S. Dept. State, Washington, 1973-75; of counsel Schiff, Hardin & Waite, Washington, 1979-81; asst. sec. U.S. Dept. Commerce, Washington, 1981-83; pres. Transnat. Investments, Washington, 1983-85; dir. govt. affairs The Boeing Co., Seattle, 1985-95, v.p. internat. bus., 1995—; chmn. Aerospace Trade Adv. Bd., U.S. Dept. Commerce, Washington, 1990-94. Author: Regulating Business Through Codes of Conduct, 1980, Business Investment in U.S., 1984, Managed Trade, 1986; co-author: Investment Incentives of Pacific, 1980. Bd. dirs. Wash. Coun. on Internat. Trade, Seattle, 1992—, U. Wash. Bus. Sch., Seattle, 1991-96; advisor Rep. Platform Com., 1976, 80. Home: 2038 78th Ave NE Medina WA 98039-2321

WALDRON, RICHARD FREDERICK, musician, educator; b. Kelso, Wash., Mar. 1, 1952; s. Richard Alan and Marjorie (Tenoll) W.; m. Charlene Bevry, June 19, 1982; children: Jason, Jonathan, Ricky. MusB summa cum laude, Cornish Inst., 1980; MusM, North Tex. State U., 1984. Instr., chair music dept. Everett (Wash.) C.C., 1986—; musician, composer, rec. artist. Composer, performer rec. Twist of Fate, 1995. Mem. Nat. Assn. Music Educators, Snohomish Music Tchrs. Assn. (adjudicator), Music Educators Nat. Conf., Phi Kappa Lambda, Phi Beta. Office: Everett CC 801 Wetmore Ave Everett WA 98201

WALDRON, VANIS ROY, artist, educator; b. Parkersburg, W.Va., Sept. 19, 1936; s. James Michael and Edna Marie (Caplinger) W. Diploma, Oakland (Calif.) Art Inst., 1970, Bongart Sch. Art, L.A., 1979; teaching credential, U. Calif., Berkeley, 1981. Pvt. tchr. art, San Leandro, Calif., 1970-80; tchr. San Leandro Unified Sch. Dist., 1980—; art judge numerous orgns. countrywide, 1985—; tchr. St. Mary's Art Ctr., Virginia City, Nev., 1979—. One-man shows include Jack London Sq., Oakland, Calif., 1988, 89, 90, 91, 95, 96, 97; group shows include Casa Peralta, San Leandro, Calif., 1985-91, Who's Who in Art, Monterey, Calif., 1989—, Pennfield Fine Arts, San Ramone, Calif., 1991—, Collector's Gallery, Carmel, Calif., 1992—, The Gallery, Burlingame, Calif., 1994—, Diablo Fine Arts, Concord, Calif. and San Ramone, Calif., 1994—. With U.S. Army, 1960-66. Recipient over 300 art awards from numerous nat. orgns., 1975—. Home: 240 Bristol Blvd San Leandro CA 94577-1611 Office: San Leandro Unified Sch Dist 2000 Bancroft Ave San Leandro CA 94577-6112

WALEN, JOANNE MICHELE, secondary education educator, consultant; b. Reno, Nev., July 8, 1942; d. John Baptista and Helen Hattie (Laakkonen) Pollastro; m. Wallace Donald Walen, Feb. 20, 1961; children: Lisa M. Mays, Kevin M. Walen. BA, U. Nev., Reno, 1965, MA, 1974. Cert. secondary sch. tchr., curriculum supr., Nev. Tchr. Washoe County Sch. Dist., Reno, Nev., 1965-85; English program coord. Washoe County Sch. Dist., Reno, 1985-95; dir. WCSD Shakespeare in the Schs., Reno, 1985-95; cons. Holt, Rinehart & Winston, N.Y.C., 1994—, Shakespeare Express, Reno, 1995—; head reader, trainer Nev. State Dept. Edn., Carson City, 1980—; co-dir. Lit. Inst. U. Nev., Reno, 1986-90; essay reader ETS, Princeton, N.J., 1990-94; cons. IBEU, Rio de Janiero, Brazil, 1996. Sr. editor (book) Secondary Writing Guide, 1995; author: (booklet) Handbook for Writing Traits, 1993; also articles. Founder, dir. Shakespeare Performance Festival, Reno, 1986-95; co-dir. Washoe K-16 Coun. Lang. Consortium, Reno, 1995-96. Recipient Humanities award Nev. Humanities Com. State of Nev., 1991; grantee Summer Seminar NEH, Stratford Upon Avon, UK, 1994. Mem. NEA, Nat. Coun. Tchrs. of English (liason officer 1994—, chair CEE commn 1996—), Internat. Reading Assn., No. Nev. Writing Project, Alpha Delta Kappa (pres. 1982-84). Lutheran. Home: 11500 Pickens Dr Reno NV 89511-9445

WALENDOWSKI, GEORGE JERRY, accounting educator; b. Han-Minden, Germany, Mar. 25, 1947; came to U.S., 1949; s. Stefan (dec.) and Eugenia (Lewandowska) W. AA, L.A. City Coll., 1968; BS, Calif. State U., L.A., 1970, MBA, 1972. Cert. community coll. instr. acctg. and mgmt., Calif. Acct. Unocal (formerly Union Oil Co. Calif.), L.A., 1972-76, data control supr., 1976-78, acctg. analyst, 1978-79; sr. fin. analyst Hughes Aircraft Co., El Segundo, Calif., 1979-83, fin. planning specialist, 1983-84, program controls specialist, 1984-86; adj. instr. bus. math. L.A. City Coll., 1976-80, adj. instr. acctg., 1980—, mem. acctg. adv. com., 1984, 87, 89; bus. mgmt. specialist, 1986-92; bus. analyst, 1993-95; adj. instr. acctg. Pasadena City Coll., 1996—; reviewer conf. papers Western Acad. Mgmt., 1996. Contbr. articles to profl. jours. Mem. commn. Rep. Pres. Task Force, 1986; softball co-organizer Precious Blood Ch., L.A., 1979. Recipient Medal of Merit, Rep. Presdl. Task Force, 1984, cert. of merit, named registered life mem. commn., 1986, named Honor Roll life mem., 1989; recipient Vice-Presdl. Cert. of Commendation, Rep. Nat. Hall of Honor, 1992, Rep. Congl. cert. of Appreciation, 1993, Rep. Congl. Order of Freedom award Nat. Rep. Congl. Com., 1995. Mem. Acad. Mgmt. (reviewer social issues in mgmt. divsn. 1991, rev. panelist bus. policy and strategy divsn. 1994, 95, 96), Inst. Mgmt. Accts. (author's cir. L.A. chpt. 1980, Robert Half author's trophy 1980, cert. of appreciation 1980, 83), Am. Acctg. Assn., Nat. Bus. Edn. Assn., Nat. Mgmt. Assn., Strategic Leadership Forum (recognition award L.A. chpt. 1983), Am. Fin. Assn., Fin. Mgmt. Assn., Strategic Mgmt. Soc., U.S. Chess Fedn., Beta Gamma Sigma. Republican. Roman Catholic. Home: 426 N Citrus Ave Los Angeles CA 90036-2632 Office: LA City Coll 855 N Vermont Ave Los Angeles CA 90029

WALIZE, REUBEN THOMPSON, III, health research administrator; b. Williamsport, Pa., May 28, 1950; s. Reuben Thompson Jr. and Marion Marie (Smith) W.; m. Kathleen Anne Smith, Aug. 13, 1979; children: Heather, Amanda, Reuben IV. BS, Pa. State U., 1972; MPH magna cum laude, U. Tenn., 1975; cert. exec. mgmt., Boston U., 1978. Manpower planner North ctrl. Pa. Area Health Edn. Sys. The Inst. for Med. Edn. and Rsch. Geisinger Med. Ctr., Danville, Pa., 1975-76; asst. dir. Northcentral Pa. Area Health Edn. System, Danville, 1976, exec. dir., 1976-78; health mgr. Seda-Cog, Timberhaven, Pa., 1978-81; exec. asst. VA Med. Ctr., Erie, Pa., 1978-81; trainee VA Med. Ctr., Little Rock, 1981; adminstrv. officer rsch. svc. VA Med. Ctr., White River Junction, Vt., 1981-88; mgmt. analyst Dept. Vets. Affairs Med. Ctr., Roseburg, Oreg., 1988-90, health systems specialist, 1990-92; adminstrv. officer rsch. Vets. Affairs Med. Ctr. Am. Lake, 1992-95; EEO investigator Dept. Vet. Affairs, Washington, 1995—; adminstrv. officer rsch. dept. vets. affairs Am. Lake divsn. VA Puget Sound Health Care System, Tacoma, 1995—; exec. dir. American Lake Biomed Rsch. Inst., 1996—; exec. dir. Am. Lake Biomed. Rsch. Inst., 1996—; mem. Pa. Coun. Health Profls., 1975-77, Ctrl. Pa. Health Sys. Agy. Manpower Com., 1975-77; mem. Interagy. Coun. Geisinger Med. Ctr., Danville, 1976-78; liaison for rsch. Dartmouth Med. Sch., Hanover, N.H., 1981-88; mem. instnl. rev. bd. Madigan Army Med. Ctr., 1994—; EEO investigator; cons. in field. Recipient Man of Achievement award Queens Coll., Eng., 1978, Student Am. Med. Assn. Found. award, 1975; 1st pl. Douglas County Lamb Cooking Contest, 1992. Mem. APHA, AAAS, N.Y. Acad. Scis., Soc. Rsch. Adminstrs., Assn. Hosps., Pa. State Alumni Assn., Nat. Audubon Soc., Steamboaters, Nat. Wildlife Fedn., Record Catch Club, VIP Club. Home: 1103 25th Ave SE Puyallup WA 98374-1362

WALKER, BURTON LEITH, engineering writer, psychotherapist; b. Mt. Morris Twp., Mich., Oct. 23, 1927; s. Dalton Hugh and Muriel Joyce (Black) W.; m. Norva Jean Trochman, June 28, 1949; children: Paul, Cynthia Halverson, Mark; m. Carol Jean D'Andrea, July 31, 1981. Cert. psychology. tchr., lic. psychotherapist, hypnotherapist, Calif. A.A., Allan Hancock Coll., 1971; B.A., Chapman Coll., 1974, M.A., 1975. Contract estimator Ryan Aeronaut., San Diego, 1949-59; logistics rep. GD/A, San Diego, 1960-62; systems engr., cons. fgn. svc. Ralph M. Parsons, L.A., 1962-68; lead engring. writer, sr. analyst Fed. Electric, Vandenberg AFB, Calif., 1969-86; psychotherapist Access, Vandenberg Village, Family Guidance Svc., Santa Ynez, Calif.; part time prof. Allan Hancock Coll., Santa Maria, Calif., 1974-93, ret.; small bus. owner 1974-86. Active Santa Ynez Valley Presbyn. Ch.; mem. Republican Nat. Com. Served with USN, 1946-48. Mem. Am. Assn. Christian Counselors, Nat. Mgmt. Assn. (Outstanding Svc. award 1982), Calif. Assn. Marriage and Family Therapists, Assn. Advancement Ret. People. Republican. Home: 3149 E Hwy 246 Santa Ynez CA 93460-9634

WALKER, CAROLYN LOUISE, nursing researcher, educator; b. Ft. George, Wash., Apr. 4, 1947; d. Marvin John and Louise Olive (Billings) W.; m. Simon I. Zemel, Apr. 6, 1968 (div. 1981); children: Michelle, Brent Zemel. AA, Fullerton (Calif.) Coll., 1968; BSN, Calif. State U., Fullerton, 1976; MSN, Calif. State U., L.A., 1979; PhD in Nursing, U. Utah, 1986. RN, Calif. Staff nurse Children's Hosp. Orange (Calif.) County, 1969-71; instr. nursing Cypress (Calif.) Coll., 1978-81, 81-82, Saddleback Coll., Mission Viejo, Calif., 1979-80; nurse oncology Children's Hosp. Orange County, 1980-81; asst. prof. U. Utah, Salt Lake City, 1984-85; asst. prof. San Diego State U., 1986-90, assoc. prof., 1990-94, prof., 1994—. Mem. editorial rev. bd. Am. Jour. Continuing Edn. in Nursing, 1987-90, Oncology Nursing Forum, 1988-91, Jour. Pediatric Oncology Nursing, 1991-96. Mem. children's com. Am. Cancer Soc., San Diego, 1988—. Mem. ANA, Assn. Pediatric Oncology Nurses (chair rsch. 1988-91, exec. bd. dirs. 1992-94, pres. 1994—), Oncology Nursing Soc. Democrat. Episcopalian. Office: San Diego State U Sch Nursing San Diego CA 92182

WALKER, DAPHINE BROADHEAD, construction executive; b. Nephi, Utah, Oct. 29, 1903; d. Hyrum and Polly Victoria (Jennings) Broadhead; widowed Oct. 1930; children: Raymond Walker, Darrell Walker, Jacqueline Nadel. LittD (hon.), Willamette U., 1992. Aircraft mechanic Fla. Aircraft Corp., Orlando, 1941-46; sec. Air Force Operational Test Ctr., Elgin AFB, Fla., 1947; manuscript reproduction and layout specialist supr. Air Rsch. and Devel. Ctr., Elgin AFB, Fla., 1948; sec. Bonneville Power, Eugene, Oreg., 1948-50; dist. clk. Forest Svc., Eugene, 1950-55; mgr. various apt. houses, Eugene; owner and mgr. constrn. bus. Eugene. Author and editor: Through the Years, 1970, My Last Chapter, 1994. Named Woman of the Yr. and one of Top Ten Women Am. Bus. Women's Assn., 1968. Home: 16057 NW Claremont Portland OR 97229

WALKER, DEBRA, artist; b. Omaha, Nebr., Apr. 23, 1953; d. Lowell Lampert and Margaret Mary (Ball) W.; life ptnr. Saundra Marie Ardito. Student fine arts, Riverside City Coll., 1972-74, UCLA, 1974-75; student painting, Skyline Coll., 1981-83; student, Visual Arts Access, 1993-94; student intaglio etching, U. Calif., 1995. Represented by George Krevsky Fine Art, San Francisco, CSK, Inc., Denver, Evelyn Seigel Gallery, Ft. Worth; designer United Artists Records, 1975-76; art dir. L.A. Times, 1976-78; owner Comml. Design Advtsg. Agy., 1978-81; art cons. Bowles-Hopkins Gallery, 1981-82; print cons., 1985-91; bus., prodn. mgr. Redgate Comms., 1991-92. One-woman exhbns. include Riverside Art Mus., 1974, Cowell Theater, San Francisco, 1995, George Krevsky Fine Art, San Francisco, 1995, 96, CSK, Inc., Denver, 1996, Evelyn Seigel Gallery, Ft. Worth, 1997; group exhbns. Riverside Press Enterprise, 1974 (Purchase prize 1974), Shenendoah Gallery, Plymouth, 1987. Studio Show, San Francisco, 1990, Bay Arts Gallery, San Francisco, 1992, 93, Riverside Art Mus., 1993, George Krevsky Fine Art, 1993, 94, Nat. Assn. Women Artists, Athens, Greece, 1996, San Francisco Mus. Modern Art, 1996; permanent collections Twentieth Century Fox, numerous pvt. collections. Mem. Nat. Assn. Women Artists. Democrat.

WALKER, DEWARD EDGAR, JR., anthropologist, educator; b. Johnson City, Tenn., Aug. 3, 1935; s. Deward Edgar and Matilda Jane (Clark) W.; m. Candace J. Arroyo; children: Alice, Deward Edgar III, Mary Jane, Sarah, Daniel, Joseph Benjamin. Student, Ea. Oreg. Coll., 1953-54, 56-58, Mexico City Coll., 1958; BA in Anthropology with honors, U. Oreg., 1960-61, PhD in Anthropology, 1964; postgrad., Wash. State U., 1962. Asst. prof. anthropology George Washington U., Washington, 1964-65; asst. prof. anthropology Wash. State U., Pullman, 1965-67, research collaborator, 1967-69; assoc. prof., chmn. dept. Sociology/Anthropology, lab. dir. U. Idaho, Moscow, 1967-69; prof. U. Colo., Boulder, 1969—, research assoc. in population processes program of inst. behavioral sci., 1969-73, assoc. dean Grad. Sch., 1973-76; v.p. Walker Rsch. Group, Ltd., Boulder, Colo. Founder, coeditor Northwest Anthropol. Rsch. Notes, 1966—; editor, Plateau Vol.: Handbook of North American Indians, 1971; author, co-author 135 books, reports, articles and papers. Mem. tech. steering panel Hanford Environ. Dose Reconstrn. Project, 1988-95, Basalt Waste Isolation Project, Hanford, 1986-88; advisor on Native Am. affairs. With U.S. Army, 1954-62. Fellow NSF, 1961, NDEA, 1961-64. Fellow Am. Anthropol. Assn. (assoc. editor Am. Anthropologist 1973-74), Soc. Applied Anthropology (hon. life, exec. com. 1970-79, treas. 1976-79, chmn. 1980-95, cons., expert witness tribes of N.W., editor Human Orgn. 1970-76, rsch. over 65 projects with 135 monographs, articles, reports, and papers); mem. AAAS, Am. Acad. Polit. and Social Scis., N.W. Anthropol. Conf. Home: PO Box 4147 Boulder CO 80306-4147 Office: U Colo PO Box 233 Boulder CO 80309-0233 *I have been both lucky and happy to have had the opportunities to do so many wonderful things in my life as an anthropologist.*

WALKER, DUNCAN EDWARD, retired air force officer; b. Washington, Aug. 2, 1942; s. Edward John and Katherine Edith (Duncan) W. BA in Indsl. Psychology, N.Mex. State U., 1965; MS in Systems Mgmt., U. So. Calif., 1978; MPA, Golden Gate U., 1980. Commd. 2d lt. USAF, 1965, advanced through grades to lt. col., 1981; grad. Squadron Officers Sch., 1973, Air Command and Staff Coll., 1974, Indsl. Coll. Armed Forces, 1977; chief devel. and deployment br. ICBM requirements SAC, Offutt AFB, Nebr., 1981-84; dep. for ICBM ops. and evaluation Air Force Operational Test and Evaluation Ctr., Vandenberg AFB, Calif., 1984-88; program engr. Fed. Svcs. Corp., Western Space and Missile Ctr., Vandenberg AFB, Calif., 1988-92; ret., 1992, pvt. cons., 1992—. Mission coun. exec. Boy Scouts of Am., 1993-95. Decorated Bronze Star, Meritorious Service medal with two oak leaf cluster, Air Force Commendation medal with three oak leaf clusters. Mem. AIAA, VFW, Order Pour Le Merite, Internat. Test and Evaluation Assn., Air Force Assn., Mil. Order of World Wars, Am. Legion, Elks (past exalted ruler), Order Moose, Vietnam Vets. of Am. Republican. Methodist. Home: 113 N Y St Lompoc CA 93436-5514

WALKER, E. JERRY, retired clergyman; b. Seattle, May 31, 1918; s. Septimus and Mae Ruth (Roys) W.; m. Holly Rae Harding, Nov. 10, 1941; children: Jerrianne, Dale Harding, Barbara Rae. AB, Seattle Pacific U., 1940; MDiv, Garrett Theol. Sch., 1945; DD, Wiley Coll., 1958, Northland Coll., 1971. Ordained to ministry United Meth. Ch. Teaching fellow State Coll. Wash., 1940-41; dir. edn. Prairie Farmer Sta. WLS, Chgo., 1942-45; dir. radio Internat. Coun. Religious Edn., 1945-48; freelance writer, dir. radio and TV Sta. WBKB-TV, Chgo., 1948-53; pastor St. James Meth. Ch., Chgo., 1953-62, First United Meth. Ch., Duluth, 1962-74; freelance daily commentary Sta. KDAL-TV, Duluth, Minn., 1964-76; exec. dir. Ctr. for Family Studies, Duluth, 1972-82; ptnr. SoundVideo Prodns., Tahuya, Wash., 1987—; cons. environ. grants, 1987—; project dir. Hood Canal Wetlands Interp Ctr., 1988—; bd. dirs. Pacific N.W. WRiters Conf., Wash., 1983-88; mem. gen. bd. Nat. Coun. Chs., 1954-66. Author: Five Minute Stories from the Bible, 1948, Stories from the Bible, 1955, Seeking a Faith of Your Own, 1961, Sinner's Parish, 1963, (plays) Checkerboard, Kyrie, The Unpainted Wall; also numerous articles. Bd. dirs. Chgo. chpt. NCCJ, 1955-62, nat. bd. trustees, 1974-76; mem. Kenwood-Ellis Cmty. Renewal Commn., 1957-62, Gov. Ill.'s Adv. Commn. on Aged, 1958-62, S.E. Chgo. Commn., 1958-62, United Fund Survey Com., 1968-70; co-chmn. Duluth Citizens Com. Secondary Edn., 1963-64; bd. dirs. Mary E. Theler Cmty. Ctr., Belfair, Wash., 1988-91; cons. Mason County United Way, 1990-94, co-chmn. needs assessment com., 1992-94; cons. Bremerton Hist. Ships Assn., 1994—. Recipient Human Rels. award Chgo. Commn. Human Rels., 1954, Friend of Youth award Southside Community Com., 1955, Disting. Citizen award Com. of One Hundred, 1962, Achievement award Freedom Found., 1963-65, Broadcast Journalism award Minn. Coun. Chs., 1971, Appreciation award North Mason Sch. Dist., 1990, Environ. Pride award Pacific Northwest Mag., 1992; named Chicagoan of Yr. Chgo. Jaycees, 1962. Mem. Internat. Platform Assn., Seattle Free Lances, Kiwanis. Democrat. Home: 18341 E State Highway 106 Belfair WA 98528-9588 Office: North Mason Sch Dist PO Box 167 Belfair WA 98528-0167

WALKER, EDWARD DONALD (RUSTY WALKER), artist, educator; b. Danville, Ill., Oct. 31, 1946; s. Edward Glennen and Hazel Mary (Castledine) W.; m. Kelli Suzanne Walker; children: Melody Robin, Courtney Elizabeth, Hunter Nicholas. BA in Illustration, Queensland Inst. Tech., Brisbane, Australia, 1966; MFA in Studio Art, Greenwich U., Hilo, Hawaii, 1990, PhD in Art Edn., 1992. Art dir. SAC Hdqs., Offutt AFB, Nebr., 1967-71; artist, illustrator Walker Studio, San Francisco, 1971-89; assoc. prof. Al Collins Graphic Design Sch., Tempe, Ariz., 1989—; awards juror Calif. State Fair, Sacramento, 1979; condr. Hewitt Painting Workshops, San Miguel de Allende, Mex., 1982, Asilomar Watercolor Workshops, Monterey, Calif., 1977-79. One-man show Jalisco Mus., Guadalajara, Mex., 1974, Scott Gallery, Orinda, Calif., 1977-81, John Pence Gallery, San Francisco, 1981; exhibited in group shows C.G. Rein Galleries, Scottsdale, Ariz., Mpls., Denver, Houston, 1985-94; represented in permanent collection San Francisco Mus. Modern Art; author: Writer's Digest Transparent Watercolor, 1985, Classroom Companion, 1993; portrait commd. John Steinbeck Found., 1974, also others. Recipient Emily Lowe award Am. Watercolor Soc., 1977, Tchr. of Yr., Career Coll. Assn., 1990.

WALKER, ELJANA M. DU VALL, civic worker; b. France, Jan. 18, 1924; came to U.S., 1948; naturalized, 1954; student Med. Inst., U. Paris, 1942-47; m. John S. Walker, Jr., Dec. 31, 1947; children: John, Peter, Barbara. Pres., Loyola Sch. PTA, 1958-59; bd. dirs. Santa Claus shop, 1959-73; treas. Archdiocese Denver Catholic Women, 1962-64; rep. Cath. Parent-Tchr League, 1962-65; pres. Aux. Denver Gen. Hosp., 1966-69; precinct committeewoman Arapahoe County Republican Women's Com., 1973-74; mem. re-election com. Arapahoe County Rep. Party, 1973-78, Reagan election com., 1980; block worker Arapahoe County March of Dimes, Heart Assn., Hemophilia Drive, Muscular Dystrophy and Multiple Sclerosis Drive, 1978-81; cen. city asst. Guild Debutante Charities, Inc. Recipient Distinguished Service award Am.-by-choice, 1966; named to Honor Roll, ARC, 1971. Mem. Cherry Hills Symphony, Lyric Opera Guild, Alliance Franciase (life mem.), ARC, Civic Ballet Guild (life mem.), Needlework Guild Am. (v.p. 1980-82), Kidney Found. (life), Denver Art Mus., U. Denver Art and Conservation Assns. (chmn. 1980-82), U. Denver Women's Library Assn., Chancellors Soc, Passage Inc., Friends of the Fine Arts Found. (life), CHildren's Diabetes Found. (life). Roman Catholic. Clubs: Union (Chgo.); Denver Athletic, 26 (Denver); Welcome to Colo. Internat. Address: 2301 Green Oaks Dr Greenwood Village CO 80121

WALKER, FRANCIS JOSEPH, lawyer; b. Tacoma, Aug. 5, 1922; s. John McSweeney and Sarah Veronica (Meechan) W.; m. Julia Corinne O'Brien, Jan. 27, 1951; children: Vincent Paul, Monica Irene Hylton, Jill Marie Nudell, John Michael, Michael Joseph, Thomas More. B.A., St. Martin's Coll., 1947; J.D., U. Wash., 1950. Bar: Wash. Asst. atty. gen. State of Wash., 1950-51; pvt. practice law, Olympia, Wash., 1951—; gen. counsel Wash. Cath. Conf., 1967-76. Lt. (j.g.) USNR, 1943-46; PTO. Home and Office: 2723 Hillside Dr SE Olympia WA 98501-3460

WALKER, FRANKLIN CURTIS, national park administrator; b. Sept. 10, 1945; s. Howard and Edna Walker; m. Judy Provins, May 29, 1967; children: Mark, Kathy, Phillip. BS in Biology, N.Mex. State U., 1967. Park ranger White Sands Nat. Monument Nat. Park Svc., 1970-72, park ranger Jefferson Nat. Expansion Meml., 1972-73, park ranger Gulf Islands Nat. Seashore, 1973-77, naturalist south dist. Yellowstone Nat. Park, 1977-80, chief of interpretation Carlsbad Caverns Nat. Park, 1980-85, park supt. Ft. Clatsop Nat. Meml., 1985-90; supt. Nez Perce Nat. Hist. Park Nat. Park Svc., Idaho, Oreg., Wash., Mont., 1990—. 1st lt. U.S. Army, 1967-69. Home: 3510 7th St E Lewiston ID 83501 Office: Nez Perce Nat Hist Park Rte 1 Box 100 Spalding ID 83540

WALKER, GWENDOLYN KAYE, librarian assistant, small business owner; b. Houston, Aug. 11, 1956; d. Willie Lee Sr. and Juanita W.; 1 child, Nika Ayanna Sewell. Student, U. Nev., 1973-74, Massey Bus. Coll., Houston, 1978-79; grad., So. Nev. Sch. Cosmetology, Las Vegas, 1988. Lic. manicurist. Mgr. snack shop St. Lukes Hosp., Houston, 1976-80; svc. rep. Centel Tel., Las Vegas, 1980-85; owner Nika's Gifts, Las Vegas, 1985-87; co-owner Genesis Nails and Gifts, 1987-89; libr. asst. Clark County Libr. Dist., Las Vegas, 1988—; co-owner Nika's Aftrocentric Gifts, Las Vegas, 1992—. Author: (books of poetry) Feelings, 1996, Memories, Book II, 1997; columnist Las Vegas Sentinel Newspaper, 1988-95. Mem. bd. City North Las Vegas Crime Prevention Task Force, 1992-95; mem. adv. bd. Kyle Ranch, 1982-84; capt. neighborhood watch Valley View Estates, 1984—; founder, pres. The Walker African-Am. Mus. and Rsch. Ctr., Las Vegas, 1992—; sec., chmn. souvenir booklet and food basket com. Dr. Martin Luther King Jr. Com., 1985-88; mem. Mems. and Advs. for Minority Adoptions, 1982-84, Dem. Ctrl. Com., 1984-85, Nev. Black C. of C., various election coms.; leader 4-H, 1969-73; leader Swappett drill team, 1970-73. Recipient Cmty. Svc. award North Las Vegas City Coun., 1992, Clark County Commn., 1997, Outstanding Mem. and Sec. award Dr. Martin Luther King Jr. Com., 1987-88. Mem. NAACP, Nat. Assn. African-Am. History Preservation, Nev. Women in History, Tuskegee Airmen, Inc. (Nev. Chpt. sec. 1996—). Baptist. Office: Walker African-Am Mus 705 W Van Buren Ave Las Vegas NV 89106

WALKER, JEANNE CLAIRE, retired English educator, writer; b. Bklyn., Nov. 2, 1924; d. Itys Vaux and Dona (Marshall) Johnson; m. Thomas M. Walker, Oct. 29, 1943 (dec. Oct. 1990); 1 child, Karen L. (dec.). BA, U. So. Calif., 1945. Tchr. English, Alta Loma H.S., Rancho Cucamonga, Calif., 1963-69; prof. English, Chaffey Coll., Rancho Cucamonga, 1970-86, prof. emeritus, 1986—, supr. part-time English faculty, 1990-96; writer promotional material Unsolved Mysteries, 1994, Oprah, 1996, Larry King Live, 1996. Author: (nonfiction) Always, Karen (alt. selection Lit. Guild 1975), More Alive Than Ever, 1995; contbr. articles to profl. jours. Recipient 1st place award for outstanding program writing in computer tech. classroom Nat. Coun. Instrnl. Assn. for C.C.'s, 1996. Home: 1285 W Cheshire St Rialto CA 92377

WALKER, JOHN SUMPTER, JR., lawyer; b. Richmond, Ark., Oct. 13, 1921; s. John Sumpter, Martha (Wilson) W.; m. Eljana M. duVall, Dec. 31, 1947; children: John Stephen, Barbara Monika Ann, Peter Mark Gregory. BA, Tulane U., 1942; MS, U. Denver, 1952, JD, 1960; diploma Nat. Def. U., 1981. Bar: Colo. 1960, U.S. Dist. Ct. Colo. 1960, U.S. Supreme Ct., 1968, U.S. Ct. Appeals (10th cir.) 1960, U.S. Tax. Ct., 1981. With Denver & Rio Grande Western R.R. Co., 1951-61, gen. solicitor, 1961-89 ; pres. Denver Union Terminal Ry. Co. Apptd. gen. counsel Moffat Tunnel Commn., 1991; life mem. Children's Diabetes Fund. With U.S. Army, 1942-46. Decorated Bronze Star. Mem. Colo. Bar Assn., Arapahoe County Bar Assn., Alliance Francaise (life), Order of St. Ives, U. Denver Chancellors' Soc., Cath. Lawyers Guild. Republican. Roman Catholic. Club: Denver Athletic.

WALKER, JOYCE MARIE, secondary school educator; b. Kansas City, Kans., Jan. 24, 1948; d. Frank Cornelius and Inez (Pennington) W.;

divorced; 1 child, Kevin Cornelius. BS, U. Ark., Pine Bluff, 1972. Cert. ch. adminstr. Bus. tchr. U.S. Trade Sch., Kansas City, 1972-74; exec. sec. Kansas City Mo. Sch. Dist., 1974-77; tchr. vocat. bus. Aurora (Colo.) Pub. Sch., 1977—; vocat. bus. tchr. Pioneer Community Coll., 1975-77. Mem. Aurora Human Rels. Martin Luther King Jr. Com., 1986—; asst. sec. Sunday sch. Macedonia Bapt. Ch., 1985—, evangelism counselor, 1992—; 2d v.p. E.L. Witchfield Missionary Soc., 1989; chmn. We. States Fgn. Mission, 1990. Mem. Nat. Coun. Negro Women, Nat. Assn. Bus. Educators, NAACP (Aurora br. 1990—), Delta Sigma Theta. Home: 12948 E 48th Ave Denver CO 80239-4408 Office: Aurora Pub Schs 11700 E 11th Ave Aurora CO 80010-3758

WALKER, LINDA ANN, financial planner; b. Denver, May 10, 1956; d. John Bruce Elmer and Ruth Evelyn (Rogers) Metsker; m. Sidney Carr Walker III, Feb. 9, 1992; 1 child. BA, U. Colo., 1978. CFP. Account exec. E.F. Hutton, Boulder, 1980-84; with Fin. Planning and Mgmt., Boulder, 1984-91, pres., 1989-91; pres. Premier Planning Assocs., Boulder, 1991-95; pvt. practice, 1995—; cons. Lighting Co., Boulder, 1987-88. Actress (play) Shadow of a Gunman, 1991, La Ronde, 1992 (dancer) Who's There, 1991. Bd. dirs. Nancy Spanier Dance Theatre, Boulder, 1986-91; mem. Win/Win, Boulder, 1989-91. Mem. Internat. Assn. Fin. Planners, Inst. CFP. Democrat. Office: Linda A Walker CFP Linsco/Pvt Ledger 4730 Walnut St Ste 208 Boulder CO 80301-2558

WALKER, MARGARET SMITH, real estate company executive; b. Lancashire, Eng., Oct. 14, 1943; came to U.S., 1964; d. Arthur Edward and Doris Audrey (Dawson) Smith; m. James E. Walker, Feb. 6, 1992. Lic. real estate agt., Hawaii. Broker Lawson-Worrall Inc. (now Worrall-McCarter), Honolulu, 1974-81; pres. Maggie Parkes & Assocs., Inc., Honolulu, 1981—. Bd. dirs. Hawaii Combined Tng. Assn., Honolulu, 1985—; com. chmn. Hist. Hawaii Found., Honolulu, 1990, Hawaii Opera Theatre, 1997. Mem. Am. Horse Shows Assn., Hawaii Horse Shows Assn., Outrigger Canoe Club. Episcopalian. Office: PO Box 25083 Honolulu HI 96825-0083

WALKER, MICHAEL MAURICE, secondary education educator; b. Euclid, Ohio, Aug. 22, 1956; s. Joseph Dwight and Elnora (Raleigh) W.; m. Megumi Tanaka, May 12, 1984; children: Debra, Denise. BS, Marquette U., 1978; tchrs. credential, Nat. U., San Diego, 1986; EdM, Harvard U., 1994. Cert. tchr. math., Calif. Instr. math. Yucca Valley (Calif.) H.S., 1987-94, math. dept. chairperson, 1994—; v.p. Morongo Tchrs. Assn., 1994—, mem. negotiating com., 1990—; mem. acad. coun. Yucca Valley, 1990—. Site chmn. United Way, Yucca Valley High Sch., 1989—. Lt. col. USMCR, 1996—. Mem. ASCD, Math. Assn. Am., Am. Math. Soc., Nat. Coun. Tchrs. Math., Nat. Geog. Soc., Smithsonian Nat. Assocs. Office: Yucca Valley High Sch 7600 Sage Ave Yucca Valley CA 92284-3624

WALKER, MOIRA KAYE, sales executive; b. Riverside, Calif., Aug. 2, 1940; d. Frank Leroy and Arline Rufina (Roach) Porter; m. Timothy P. Walker, Aug. 30, 1958 (div. 1964); children: Brian A., Benjamin D., Blair K., Beth E. Student, Riverside City Coll., 1973. With Bank of Am., Riverside, 1965-68, Abitibi Corp., Cucamonga, Calif., 1968-70; with Lily div. Owens-Illinois, Riverside, 1970-73; salesperson Lily div. Owens-Illinois, Houston, 1973-77; salesperson Kent H. Landsberg div. Sunclipse, Montebello, Calif., 1977-83, sales mgr., 1983-85; v.p., sales mgr. Kent H. Landsberg div. Sunclipse, Riverside, 1985—. Mem. NAFE, Women in Paper (treas. 1978-84), Kent H. Landsberg President's Club (1st female to make club, 1994, 95, 96). Lutheran. Office: Kent H Landsberg Div Sunclipse 1180 W Spring St Riverside CA 92507-1327

WALKER, OLENE S., lieutenant governor; b. Ogden, Utah, Nov. 15, 1930; d. Thomas Ole and Nina Hadley (Smith) W.; m. J. Myron Walker, 1957; children: Stephen Brett, David Walden, Bryan Jesse, Lori, Mylene, Nina, Thomas Myron. BA, Brigham Young U., 1954; MA, Stanford U., 1954; PhD, U. Utah, 1986. V.p. Country Crisp Foods; mem. Utah Ho. of Reps. Dist. 24; lt. gov. State of Utah, 1993—. Mem. Salt Lake Edn. Found. bd. dirs. 1983-90; dir. community econ. devel.; mem. Ballet West, Sch. Vol., United Way, Commn. on Youth, Girls Village, Salt Lake Conv. and Tourism Bd. Mormon. Office: Lieutenant Governor 203 State Capitol Building Salt Lake City UT 84114-1202*

WALKER, RAYMOND FRANCIS, business and financial consulting company executive; b. Medicine Lake, Mont., Nov. 9, 1914; s. Dennis Owen and Rose (Long) W.; m. Patricia K. Blakey, May 15, 1951; children: Richard A., Mark D., Maxie R. Forest, Victoria L. Le Huray, Suzanne J. Buhl, Tracy Walker Stampanoni. Grad. pub. schs.; student, Edison Vocat. Sch., 1935-39. Truck mgr. Pacific Food Products, Seattle, 1939-42; machinist Todd Shipyard, Seattle, 1943-45; owner Delbridge Auto Sales, Seattle, 1945-48; pres. Pacific Coast Acceptance Corp., 1949-60; v.p. West Coast Mortgage, Seattle, 1960-67, United Equities Corp., Seattle, 1965-69; pres. Income Mgmt. Corp., Seattle, 1970-90; v.p. Internat. Mint and Foundry, Redmond, Wash., 1983-87; pvt. practice bus. and fin. cons. Sequim, Wash., 1987—; cons. Life Ins. Co. Am., Bellevue, Wash., 1982-87, Consumer Loan Svc., Lynwood Wash., 1980-92; dir., cons., v.p. fin. Am. Campgrounds, Bellevue, 1971-79; cons., bd. dirs. Straits Forest Products, Inc. , Port Angeles, Wash.; dir., cons. Synergy Techs., Inc., Sequim, 1990—, co-founder, dir. Sequim Tech., Inc., 1994—. Mem. Nat. Assn. Security Dealers. Methodist. Lodge: Elks. Home: 3347 W Sequim Bay Rd Sequim WA 98382-9031

WALKER, RICHARD ALLEN, multimedia computing executive, consultant; b. Flushing, N.Y., Sept. 24, 1935; s. John Randall and Estella Viola (Stephenson) W.; m. Jauhree Ann Sparks, July 14, 1973. BA in Econs. and History, U.S. Internat. U., 1963, MS in Mgmt. Sci., 1968; PhD in Instructional Sci., Brigham Young U., 1978. Commd. ensign USN, 1958, advanced through grades to comdr., ret., 1976; sr. instructional psychologist Courseware, Inc., 1978-82, mgr. electronics pub. group, 1982-83; founder, pres., acting v.p. instrnl. devel. Interactive Tech. Corp., 1983-86, chmn., 1986; pvt. practice, 1986-87; dir. tng. svcs. WICAT Systems, Inc., 1987-90; group dir. Jostens Learning Corp., 1990-92; pres. Multimedia Group, Coronado, Calif., 1992—. Mem. Soc. for Applied Learning Tech. (sr.), Am. Ednl. Rsch. Assn., Assn. Aviation Psychologists, Eagle Scout Assn., Arlberg Ski Club (silver medal), Crown Club (v.p. 1985). Republican. Presbyterian. Home: 740 Olive Ave Coronado CA 92118-2136 Office: Multimedia Group 740 Olive Ave Coronado CA 92118-2136

WALKER, RICHARD HUGH, orthopaedic surgeon; b. Elgin, Ill., Jan. 29, 1951; m. Wendy Allen; children: Ashley Elizabeth, Blake Allen, Emily Paige. AB cum laude, Occidental Coll., 1973; MD, U. Chgo., 1977. Diplomate Nat. Bd. Med. Examiners, Am. Bd. Orthopaedic Surgery. Jr. resident in surgery UCLA, 1977-79; jr. resident in orthopaedic surgery Stanford (Calif.) U., 1979-81, sr. resident, 1981-82, chief resident, 1982-83; clin. mem. divsn. orthopaedic surgery, sect. lower extremity reconstructive surgery Scripps Clinic and Rsch. Found., La Jolla, Calif., 1983—, co-dir. lower extremity reconstructive surgery fellowship, divsn. orthopaedic surgery, 1989—, assoc. head. divsn. orthopaedic surgery, 1990—; staff physician dept. surgery Green Hosp. of Scripps Clinic, La Jolla, 1983—, chief of staff, 1995-97; staff physician Pomerado Hosp., Poway, Calif., 1983-92; team physician San Diego Padres, 1983-86, 95—; clin. instr. dept. orthopaedics and rehab. U. Calif., San Diego, 1983-92, asst. clin. prof., 1992—; mem. bd. dirs. Scripps Clinic Med. Group, La Jolla; mem. bd. govs. Scripps Clin. and Rsch. Found., 1992—, mem. joint exec. bd., 1992-93; mem. joint coun. Scripps Health, 1995-97; mem. physicians coun. Scripps Insts. of Medicine and Sci., 1995-97; presenter, lectr. in field. Cons. reviewer Clin. Orthopaedics and Related Rsch., 1989—, Jour. Bone and Joint Surgery, 1994—; contbr. articles to profl. jours. Mem. AMA, Am. Acad. Orthopaedic Surgeons, We. Orthopaedic Assn. (program chmn. San Diego chpt. 1994-95, treas. 1995-96, v.p. 1996-97, pres. 1997—, Resident Paper award 1983), Calif. Orthopaedic Assn., Assn. Arthritic Hip and Knee Surgery (charter mem. 1991), Am. Assn. Hip and Knee Surgeons, Assn. Bone and Joint Surgeons (Nicholas Andry Rsch. award 1997). Office: Scripps Clinic and Rsch Found Divsn Orthopaedic Surgery 10666 N Torrey Pines Rd La Jolla CA 92037-1027 also: Scripps Clinic and Rsch Found 15025 Innovation Dr San Diego CA 92128-3409

WALKER, RICHARD K., lawyer; b. Knoxville, Tenn., Oct. 21, 1948. BA with honors, U. Kans., 1970, JD, 1975; student, U. Bonn, Germany. Bar: Ariz. 1975, D.C. 1977, U.S. Supreme Ct. 1977. Asst. prof. law U. S.C., 1977-81, assoc. prof. law, 1981-82; ptnr. Bishop, Cook, Purcell & Reynolds, Washington, 1981-90, Winston & Strawn, Washington, 1990-93; dir. Streich Lang, Phoenix, 1993—. Bd. trustees Ariz. Theatre Co., 1995—. Fulbright scholar. Mem. ABA, Labor and Employment Law Sec. (mem. equal employment opportunity law com. 1979—), Ariz. Assn. Def. Counsel (bd. dirs. 1997—). Office: Streich Lang Renaissance One 2 N Central Ave Phoenix AZ 85004-2391

WALKER, ROBERT EUGENE, aerospace engineer; b. San Francisco, May 19, 1926; s. Paul Kessler and Roberta Adelia (Cole) W.; m. Joyce Selma Ecklund, Sept. 7, 1950; children: Lynette D. Walker Chaney, Bryan R., Craig A. BS, U. Minn., 1946, BME, 1948. Registered profl. engr., Wash. Design engr. The Boeing Co., Seattle, 1949-71, engring. mgr., 1972, 84; pres. Walker Engring., Inc., Mercer Island, Wash., 1984—; aircraft sys. designer; cons. in field. Lt. comdr. USNR. Mem. Probus. Republican. Baptist. Home and Office: Walker Engring Inc 6 Wambley Ln Mercer Island WA 98040

WALKER, ROGER ALFRED, lawyer; b. Norman, Okla., Feb. 9, 1958; s. John Adams and Norma Jean (English) W.; m. Amy Bess Rupprecht, Aug. 9, 1980; children: Marie Elizabeth, Caitlin Ruth, John Alfred. BS in Secondary Edn. with honors, U. Ill., 1980, JD cum laude, 1989. Bar: N.Mex. 1989, U.S. Dist. Ct. N.Mex. 1991, U.S. Ct. Appeals (10th cir.) 1994. Assoc. Modrall, Sperling, Roehl, Harris & Sisk, P.A., Albuquerque, 1989-96, shareholder, 1997—; tchr. jr. high lang. arts and social studies Comty. Christian Sch., Savoy, Ill., 1981-83. Contbr. articles to profl. jours. and treatises; presenter seminars on legal issues. Primary Sunday sch. tchr. Trinity Ch., Albuquerque, 1993—; bd. dirs. Little Shepherd Child Care, Albuquerque, 1990-93; vol. Men's Winter Emergency Shelter, Champaign, Ill., 1978-84, Mercy Hosp. Hospice Care, Urbana, Ill., 1980-83. Office: Modrall Law Firm 500 4th St NW Ste 700 Albuquerque NM 87102-2183

WALKER, VAUGHN R., federal judge; b. Watseka, Ill., Feb. 27, 1944; s. Vaughn Rosenworth and Catharine (Miles) W. AB, U. Mich., 1966; JD, Stanford U., 1970. Intern economist SEC, Washington, 1966, 68; law clk. to the Hon. Robert J. Kelleher U.S. Dist. Ct. Calif., L.A., 1971-72; assoc. atty. Pillsbury Madison & Sutro, San Francisco, 1972-77, ptnr., 1978-90; judge U.S. Dist. Ct. (no. dist.) Calif., San Francisco, 1990—; mem. Calif. Law Revision Commn., Palo Alto, 1986-89. Dir. Jr. Achievement of Bay Area, San Francisco, 1979-83, St. Francis Found., San Francisco, 1991—. Woodrow Wilson Found. fellow U. Calif., Berkeley, 1966-67. Fellow Am. Bar Found.; mem. ABA (jud. rep., antitrust sect. 1991-95), Lawyers' Club of San Francisco (pres. 1985-86), Assn. Bus. Trial Lawyers (dir. 1996—), Am. Law Inst., Am. Saddlebred Horse Assn., San Francisco Mus. Modern Art, Bohemian Club, Olympic Club. Office: US Dist Ct 450 Golden Gate Ave San Francisco CA 94102

WALKER, VIRGINIA L., art educator; b. Elkridge, W.Va., June 29, 1926; d. William Frank and Margaret Elizabeth (Scott) Birchfield; m. Onyx Robbley Walker, Mar. 13, 1946; 1 child, Elaine Helene Walker Evans. BS, Morris Harvey Coll., 1954; MA, W.Va. U., 1967. Cert. art tchr., K-12, elem. tchr., W.Va. Tchr. Fayette County Bd. Edn., Elkridge, W.Va., Beards Fork, W.Va.; tchr. Oak Hill and Greenbrier Sch., Crighton, W.Va.; tchr. art 7-12 Kanawna County Schs., Cedar Grove, W.Va.; county art supr. Kanawna County Schs., Charleston, W.Va.; curriculum devel. specialist W.Va. Dept. Edn., Charleston; mem. adj. faculty W.Va. State Coll. Artist: (watercolor/acrylic) Through the Glass Darkly (award 1968), Spring (reviewed in Art Rev. jour. 1967), Mama! Mama! the Bridge (Appalachian Corridors 1968); contbr. articles to profl. jours.; exhibitor numerous shows. Past chmn. W.Va. Arts for Handicapped, W.Va. Alliance for Arts Edn. Mem. Nat. Art Edn. Assn., NEA, W.Va. Art Edn. Assn. (pres. 1976-78). Home: 2123 Ronda Granada Unit A Laguna Hills CA 92653-2447

WALKER, WALTER FREDERICK, professional basketball team executive; b. Bradford, Pa., July 18, 1954; m. Linda Walker. Diploma, U. Va.; MBA, Stanford U., 1987; BA, U. Va., 1976. Chartered Fin. Analyst. Player Portland (Oreg.) Trail Blazers, 1976-77; player Seattle SuperSonics, 1977-82, pres., gen. mgr., 1994—; player Houston Rockets, 1982-84; with Goldman Sachs and Co., San Francisco, 1987-94; prin. Walker Capital, Inc., San Francisco, 1994; mem. USA gold medal World Univ. Games basketball team, 1973; broadcaster basketball Raycom Network, 1989-94; cons. Seattle SuperSonics, 1994. Vice chmn. Capital Campaign; bd. dirs. Red Hook Ale Brewery; bd. dirs. Interpoint Corp., Gargoyles Performance Eyeware. Named 1st team Acad. All-Am. U. Va.; named to Pa. State Sports Hall of Fame. Office: Seattle SuperSonics 490 5th Ave N Seattle WA 98109-9711

WALKUP, KATHLEEN ANN, English language educator; b. Portland, Oreg., Apr. 10, 1946; d. Lowell Edward and Dorothy Olive (Tyrrell) W.; m. Walter L. Martin, Dec. 15, 1978; children: Owen Lowell, Nora Lennox, Claire Elizabeth. BA, Temple U, 1967. Founder, ptnr. Hovey Street Press, Cambridge, Mass., 1971-72; prodn. coord. Jupiter Thermographers, San Francisco, 1972-76; founder, ptnr. Five Trees Press, Printers and Pubs., San Francisco, 1973-79, Peartree Printers, Commissioned Printers, San Francisco, 1976-79; lectr. Mills Coll., Oakland, Calif., 1978-83, program coord. grad. book arts, 1983-89, asst. prof. in English, 1993—; instr. topography and book arts City Coll., San Francisco, 1996—; founder, owner Matrix Press, Printer and Pub., Palo Alto, Calif., 1979—; vis. asst. prof. in fine arts and letters, Mills Coll., 1983-93; vis. lectr. Calif. Coll. of Arts and Crafts, Oakland, 1978-79; program cons. MA Book Arts Camberwell Coll. Art, London. Book/presses exhibits include Sci. Imagined, Berkeley (Calif.) Arts Ctr., 1996, Bay Area Bookmaking: Art and Craft Tradition, Oakland, 1991, Eighty from the Eighties, N.Y. Pub. Libr., 1990-91, The Arts of the Book, The Univ. of the Arts, Phila., 1988, Forwarding the Book in Calif., Victoria and Albert Mus., London, 1988, Literate Letterpress, Ctr. for Book Arts, N.Y., 1987, Oxford Polytechnic, eng., 1986, numerous others; curator and cons. numerous book arts exhbns.; contbr. to profl. jours. and publs. Adv. coun. Menlo-Atherton Sch. dist., 1992—; pres. site coun., Menlo Park Pub. Sch. Dist., 1992-93; bd. dirs. Friends of the Palo Alto Children's Theatre, 1992-93; trustee Keys Sch., Palo Alto, 1987-89. Recipient fellowship Ctr. for Book at the Brit. Libr., 1993, faculty devel. grant Mills Coll., 1987, 90, 91, 93, 94, 95, 96, Book design award Bookbuilders West, San Francisco, 1984, award of merit for book design Western Books, L.A., 1984, others. Mem. Pacific Ctr. for the Book Arts (founding dir.), Am. Printing History Assn. Office: Mills Coll 5000 Macarthur Blvd Oakland CA 94613-1301

WALL, BRIAN RAYMOND, forest economist, business consultant, researcher, author, policy analyst, telemarketing sales; b. Tacoma, Wash., Jan. 26, 1940; s. Raymond Perry and Mildred Beryl (Pickert) W.; m. Joan Marie Nero, Sept. 1, 1962 (div. Aug. 1990) children: Torden Erik, Kirsten Noel. BS, U. Wash., 1962; MF, Yale U., 1964. Forestry asst. Weyerhaeuser Timber Co., Klamath Falls, Oreg., 1960; inventory forester West Tacoma Newsprint, 1961-62; timber sale compliance forester Dept. Nat. Resources, Kelso, Wash., 1963; rsch. forest economist Pacific N.W. Rsch. Sta., USDA Forest Svc., Portland, Oreg., 1964-88, cons. 1989—; co-founder, bd. dirs. Cordero Youth Care Ctr., 1970-81; owner Brian R. Wall Images and Communications; owner, Nikken ind. distbr. Sage Mentor Lifestyles; owner Sage Mentors Bus. Consultancy; ind. distbr. NIKKEN; cons. to govt. agys., Congress univs., industry, small bus.; freelance photographer. Co-author: An Analysis of the Timber Situation in the United States, 1982; contbr. articles, reports to profl. publs., newspapers. Interviewed and cited by nat. and regional news media. Recipient Cert. of Merit U.S. Dept. Agr. Forest Service, 1982. Mem. ACLU, Soc. Am. Foresters (chmn. Portland chpt. 1973, Forester of Yr. 1975), Conf. of Western Forest Economists Inc. (founder, bd. dirs. 1988-91, treas. 1982-87), Portland Photographic Forum, Common Cause, Oregon Economists Assn., Nat. Audubon Soc., Amnesty Internat., Zeta Psi. Home: 989 Netzel St Oregon City OR 97045-3405 Home and Office: Sage Mentors Consultancy F-1162 10117 SE Sunnyside Rd Clackamas OR 97015-7708

WALL, DAVID ELLIOTT, substance abuse specialist; b. Evanston, Wyo., Aug. 27, 1965; s. Max Melvin and Wilma Ann (Slover) W.; m. Barbara Joy Webster, Sept. 30, 1964; children: David Lewis, Alexandria Elizabeth. BS, U. Utah, 1987. Sales mgr. Tinder Box, Inc., Salt Lake City, 1985-88; sr. rsch. tech. Gull Lab., Inc., Salt Lake City, 1988-92; from chemist to confirmation analyst ARUP, Salt Lake City, 1992—; lab. tech. Bioremediation Tech., Inc., Salt Lake City, 1991; instr. biology Salt Lake C.C., 1991-92. Mem. AAAS, Associated Regional and Univ. Pathologists, Masons, Shriners, Scottish Rite. Republican. Presbyterian. Home: 4353 Larson Way Salt Lake City UT 84124-2717

WALL, JANET E., assessment, testing and evaluation professional; b. Chgo., Dec. 15, 1946; d. Al Evans and Josephine (Evinskas) Simpson; m. Robert G. Gard Jr., July 26, 1984. BS, No. Ill. U., 1968; MEd, Tex. A&M U., 1970; EdS, U. Ga., 1973; EdD, Nova U., 1979. State specialist testing and evaluation Del. Dept. Pub. Instrn., Dover, 1975-79; coord. rsch. and evaluation Dept of Defense Dependents Schs., Alexandria, Va., 1979-81; dir. rsch. adminstrn. Naval Postgrad. Sch., Monterey, Calif., 1981-84; vis. prof. Johns Hopkins U., Sch. Adv. Internat. Studies, Bologna, Italy, 1984-87; dep. div. dir. Sci. Applications Internat. Corp., Monterey, 1987-89; mgr. Dept. of Defense student testing program Def. Manpower Data Ctr., Monterey, 1989—. Developer: (assessment program) Delaware Objective Referenced Testing Program, 1979, (career guidance program) Armed Svcs. Vocat. Aptitude Battery Career Exploration Program, 1992, ASVAB Career Exploration System, 1995, The Interest Finder, 1995. Bd. dirs. Americorps, Nat. Civilian Cmty. Corps, 1995—. Mem. ACA, Assn. for Assessment in Counseling (com. chair, mem. exec. coun.), Am. Vocat. Assn. (sch. to work ptnrs. 1995—, DOD rep. to mil. liason, 1997—), Nat. Career Devel. Assn., Sch. Sci. and Math. (officer), Phi Delta Kappa (officer). Home: 3053 Forest Way Pebble Beach CA 93953-2904 Office: Def Manpower Data Ctr DOD Ctr Monterey Bay 400 Gigling Rd Seaside CA 93955-6771

WALL, JUDITH LINDLEY, data entry professional; b. Burley, Idaho, Oct. 18, 1943; d. Raymond Earl and Helen Margaret (Knettle) W. BA, U. Calif., Berkeley, 1964; MA, Calif. State U., Chico, 1976. Life tchg. credentials elem., secondary, jr. coll., Calif. Tchr. Enterprise Elem. Sch. Dist., Redding, Calif., 1968-79; computer terminal operator 1st Ch. of Christian Scientist, Boston, 1979-82; substitute tchr. Boise (Idaho) Ind. Sch. Dist., 1983-91; data entry professional State of Idaho, Boise, 1991—. Patentee structural object; contbr. articles to profl. publs. Mem. Ada County Rep. Women's Club, Boise, 1996; charter mem. Women in the Arts Mus., Washington, 1990s. Mem. AAUW (bd. dirs. 1990), U.S. Naval Inst., Edelweiss Club. Christian Scientist. Home: 2209 Brumback St Boise ID 83702

WALL, KAREN ELISABETH, editor; b. Radford, Va., Dec. 16, 1966; d. Martin Robert and Mary Jo (Zeh) W. BA in Journalism, Mich. State U., 1988. Copy editor intern Asbury Park Press, Neptune, N.J., 1987, news copy editor, 1988-94, sports copy editor, 1994-95, columnist sports tv, 1995; sports copy editor Sacramento (Calif.) Bee, 1995—. Mem. Soc. Profl. Jours., Assn. Women in Sports Media. Home: 7054 Fifth Ave Rio Linda CA 95673

WALL, LLOYD L., geological engineer; b. Jerome, Idaho, Feb. 2, 1936; s. Lloyd and Ola (Buck) W.; m. Myrna Bradshaw, Aug. 25, 1954; children: Jeffrey B., Julie, Neil S., Charlene, Gail, Matthew W., Suzzane, Michael L., Connie. AS in Chemistry, Coll. Eastern Utah, 1956; BS in Geology, Brigham Young U., 1958. Pres., owner Cons. Geologist, Salt Lake City and Brigham City, 1958—; plant mgr. Thiokol, Brigham City, Utah, 1958-66; mgr. ops. Sealcraft, Salt Lake City, 1966-68; mgr. programs Eaton-Kenway, Bountiful, Utah, 1968-76; pres., owner HydraPak, Inc., Salt Lake City, 1976-86; pres. Kolt Mining Co., Salt Lake City, 1979—; owner Lloyd L. Wall & Assocs., Salt Lake City, 1986—. Author: Seal Technology, 1993; developer largest rocket motor vacuum casting system in free world, only high pressure water reclaimation system for solid propellant rocket motors in free world, only acceptable seal mfg. process for NASA Space Shuttle rocket motor. Vol. tchr. Alta Acad., Salt Lake City, 1983—. Served as sgt. N.G., 1954-62. Mem. Geol. Soc. Am., Utah Geol. Assn. Republican. Mormon. Home: 2180 Claybourne Ave Salt Lake City UT 84109-1727

WALLACE, BRENDA ANN, human service community planner; b. Riverton, Wyo., May 30, 1961; d. Thomas Dell and Barbra Lou (Beackman) Wilson; m. Jeff William Wallace, May 4, 1994; children: Jennifer Carol, Melissa Mae. B in Behavioral Sci., U. Ariz., Tucson, 1992. Cert. tchr. K-12, Ariz. and Cmty. Coll.; nat. issues forums facilitator. Collections supr. Bekins Internat., 1980-82, ADVO, 1982-85; personal asst. NAF/U.S. Navy, Groton and New London, Conn., 1987-89; human svc. specialist Pinal County Nursing Home, Florence, Ariz., 1993-94; with child protective svcs. Decon. Econ. Security/Stae of Ariz., Pinal-Gila County, 1994-95; human svc. cmty. planner Ctrl. Ariz. Assn. Govts., Florence, 1995—; mem. adv. bd. Ariz. State Family Preservation/Support, 1995—; chair Florence Family Preservation, 1995—; cons. Ctrl. Ariz. Coun. on Devel. Disabilities, 1995—, My Brothers Resources (HIV), Casa Grande, Ariz., 1994—; grants writer for nonprofit agys., 1994—. Mem. allocation bd. United Way of Pinal County/Casa Grande, 1996; bd. dirs. Fed. Emergency Mgmt. Adminstrn., Pinal County, 1996; cmty. leader 4-H, Florence, 1995—; mem. adv. bd., sec. Florence Little League, 1996; mem. adv. bd. Coolidge Alliance Against Drugs, 1994-95; Sunday sch. dir. First Bapt. Ch., Florence, 1992-95; leader Girl Scouts Am., 1992—. Recipient Vol. awrd of excellence Florence C. of C., 1996, Cmty. Mem. award Florence Head Start, 1995, Grants Teaming Honors, Cochise Pvt. Industry Coun., 1995. Home: 800 Butte # 33 Florence AZ 85232 Office: Ctrl Ariz Assns Govt PO Box 560 Florence AZ 85232

WALLACE, DANIEL JEFFREY, rheumatologist; b. L.A., Oct. 27, 1949; s. Leon and Fern (Wixen) W.; m. Janice Brock. BS, U. So. Calif., 1970, MD, 1974. Diplomate Am. Bd. Med. Examiners, Am. Bd. Internal Medicine. Med. intern R.I. Hosp., Providence, 1974-75; med. resident Cedars-Sinai Med. Ctr., L.A., 1975-77; rheumatology fellow UCLA Sch. of Medicine, 1977-79; chief rheumatology cons. City of Hope Med. Ctr., Duarte, Calif., 1980-88; chief of rheumatology, cons. physician Century City Hosp., 1982-84; clin. chief of rheumatology Cedars Sinai Med. Ctr., L.A., 1992-96; divsn. of rheumatology reappointment/peer rev. Cedar Sinai Med. Ctr., L.A., 1988-96, hosp. peer rev. com., 1986-89, 92-94, med. adv. com., 1985-88, 92-96, intern selection com., 1979-93, chmn. med. peer rev., 1985-87, mem., 1982-89, attending physician; assoc. clin. prof. UCLA Sch. Medicine, 1988-94, clin. prof., 1994—; asst. clin. prof. U. So. Calif., 1979-81, prof. medicine, 1995—. Editl. bd. Jour. of Clin. Apheresis, 1982—; reviewer Jour. of Rheumatology, Lupus, Arthritis and Rheumatism, Jour. of Clin. Apheresis, Artificial Organs, Jour. of Musculoskeletal Medicine, Annals of Internal Medicine, New England Jour. of Medicine, Scandanaivan Jour. of Rheumatology; editor Current Opinion in Rheumatology, 1994—; co-author: Dubois Lupus Erythematosus, 3rd edit., 1987, 4th edit., 1993, 5th edit., 1997, The Lupus Book, 1995; contbr. numerous articles to profl. jours. Fellow ACP, Am. Coll. Rheumatology (com. on rheumatologic practice 1982-85, lupus coun. 1986—, chmn. 1990-91, nomination com. 1991—, rsch. and edn. found bd. dirs. 1993—, chmn. 1995—); mem. AMA, Royal Coll. of Physicians, L.A. County Med. Assn., Calif. Med. Assn., So. Calif. Rheumatism Soc., Gerontology Soc., Lupus Found of Am. (bd. dirs. 1991—, v.p. 1996—, L.A. chpt. med. adv. bd., co-chair 1989—), Am. Lupus Soc. (nat. med. adv. bd. 1988—), Am. Soc. for Apheresis (med. exec. com. 1987-89, editor ASFA newsletter 1987-89), Am. Fibromyalgia Syndrome Assn. (med. adv. bd. 1994—), United Scleroderma Found. (bd. dirs. 1990—), Arthritis Found. (L.A. metro com. chmn. 1989-94, cmty. svcs. com. 1989-94, med. and scientific com. 1989-94, institutional grants com. 1989-94, fibromyalgia subcom. 1988—, chmn. 1990-95, rep. nat. ho of dels. 1987, 90, bd. dirs. So. Calif. 1994—). Home: 8737 Beverly Blvd Ste 203 Los Angeles CA 90048-1828

WALLACE, HELEN MARGARET, physician, educator; b. Hoosick Falls, N.Y., Feb. 18, 1913; d. Jonas and Ray (Schweizer) W. AB, Wellesley Coll., 1933; MD, Columbia U., 1937; MPH cum laude, Harvard U., 1943. Diplomate Am. Bd. Pediatrics, Am. Bd. Preventive Medicine. Intern Bellevue Hosp., N.Y.C., 1938-40; child hygiene physician Conn. Health Dept., 1941-42; successively jr. health officer, health officer, chief maternity and new born div., dir. bur. for handicapped children N.Y.C. Health Dept., 1943-55; prof., dir. dept. pub. health N.Y. Med. Coll., 1955-56; prof. maternal and child health U. Minn. Sch. Pub. Health, 1956-59; chief prof. tng. U.S. Children's Bur., 1959-60, chief child health studies, 1961-62; prof. maternal and child health U. Calif. Sch. Pub. Health, Berkeley, 1962-80; prof., head divsn. maternal and child health Sch. Pub. Health San Diego State U., 1980—; Univ. Research lectr. San Diego State U., 1985—; cons. WHO numerous locations, including Uganda, The Philippines, Turkey, India, Geneva, Iran, Burma, Sri Lanka, East Africa, Australia, Indonesia, China, Taiwan, 1961—, traveling fellow, 1989—; cons. Hahnemann U., Phila., 1993,

Ford Found., Colombia, 1971; UN cons. to Health Bur., Beijing, China, 1987; fellow Aiiku Inst. on Maternal and Child Health, Tokyo, and NIH Inst. Child Health and Human Devel., 1994; dir. Family Planning Project, Zimbabwe, 1984-87. Author, editor 14 textbooks; contbr. 325 articles to profl. jours. Mem. coun. on Disabled Children to Media, 1991; dir. San Diego County Infant Mortality Study, 1989—, San Diego Study of Prenatal Care, 1991. Recipient Alumnae Achievement award Wellesley Coll., 1982, U. Minn. award, 1985; Ford Found. study grantee, 1986, 87, 88; fellow World Rehab. Fund, India, 1991-92, Fulbright Found., 1992—, NIH Inst. Child Health and Human Devel., 1994, Aiiku Inst. of Maternal-Child Health, Tokyo, 1994. Fellow APHA (officer sect., Martha May Eliot award 1978, chair com. on internat. MCH), Am. Acad. Pediatrics (Job Smith award 1980, award 1989); mem. AMA, Assn. Tchrs. Maternal and Child Health, Am. Acad. Cerebral Palsy, Ambulatory Pediatric Assn., Am. Sch. Preventive Medicine. Home: 850 State St San Diego CA 92101-6046

WALLACE, J. CLIFFORD, federal judge; b. San Diego, Dec. 11, 1928; s. John Franklin and Lillie Isabel (Overing) W.; m. Elaine J. Barnes, Apr. 8, 1996; 9 children. B.A., San Diego State U., 1952; LL.B., U. Calif., Berkeley, 1955. Bar: Calif. 1955. With firm Gray, Cary, Ames & Frye, San Diego, 1955-70; judge U.S. Dist. Ct. (so. dist.) Calif., 1970-72; judge U.S. Ct. Appeals (9th cir.), 1972-91, sr. circuit judge, 1996. Contrbr. articles to profl. jours. Served with USN, 1946-49. Mem. Am. Bd. Trial Advocates, Inst. Jud. Adminstrn. Mem. LDS Ch. (stake pres. San Diego East 1962-67, regional rep. 1967-74, 77-79). Office: US Ct Appeals 9th Cir 940 Front St Ste 4192 San Diego CA 92101-8918 *My principles, ideals and goals and my standard of conduct are embodied in the Gospel of Jesus Christ. They come to fruition in family life, service, industry and integrity and in an attempt, in some small way, to make my community a better place within which to live.*

WALLACE, JEANNETTE OWENS, state legislator; b. Scottsdale, Ariz., Jan. 16, 1934; d. Albert and Velma (Whinery) Owens; m. Terry Charles Wallace Sr., May 21, 1955; children: Terry C. Jr., Randall J., Timothy A., Sheryl L., Janice M. BS, Ariz. State U., 1955. Mem. Los Alamos (N.Mex.) County Coun., 1981-82; cons. County of Los Alamos, 1983-84; chmn., vice chmn. Los Alamos County Coun., 1985-88; cons. County of Los Alamos, Los Alamos Schs., 1989-90; rep. N.Mex. State Legislature, 1991—; mem. appropriations and fin. govt. and urban affairs, N.Mex., 1991—, legis. fin. com., Indian affairs, radioactive and hazardous materials, co-chmn. Los Alamos County's dept. energy negotiating com., 1987-88; mem. legis. policy com. Mcpl. League, N.Mex., 1986-88. Bd. dirs. Tri-Area Econ. Devel., 1988-94, 96—, Crime Stoppers, Los Alamos, 1988-92, Los Alamos Citizens Against Substance Abuse, 1989-94; mem. N.Mex. First, Albuquerque, 1989-96; legis. chmn. LWV, 1990; mem. Los Alamos Rep. Women, pres., 1989-90. Mem. Los Alamos Bus. & Profl. Women (legis. chmn. 1990), Los Alamos C. of C., Mana del Norte, Kiwamis. Methodist. Home: 146 Monte Rey Dr S Los Alamos NM 87544-3826

WALLACE, JOHN BARRY, lawyer; b. N.Y.C., June 14, 1954; s. Bert H. and Carol (Lomnitz) W.; m. Deborah Madden. BA, SUNY, Stony Brook, 1975; JD, U. So. Calif., 1980. Bar: Calif. 1980, U.S. Dist. Ct. (ctrl. dist.) Calif. 1980, U.S. Ct. Appeal (9th cir.) 1985. Assoc. Egerman, Brown & Rosen, Beverly Hills, Calif., 1980-81, Mazlrow, Forer, Lawrence, Cunningham & Giden, Inc., Century City, Calif., 1981-82, Bronson, Bronson & McKinnon, L.A., 1983-85, Kircher & Nakazato, L.A., 1985-86, Contos & Bunch, Woodland Hills, Calif., 1986-91, Matthew B.F. Biren & Assocs., L.A., 1991-92; pvt. practice Agoura Hills, Calif., 1992—. Author: Attorney's Calendar Reference, 1982-83, The Witness Preparation Book, 1995; contbr. articles to law rev. Mock trial coach Constnl. Rights Found., 1991—; vol., fundraiser L.A. Bar Assn. Lawyer Referral Svc. Mem. Sierra Club (life).

WALLACE, JULIA DIANE, newspaper editor; b. Davenport, Iowa, Dec. 3, 1956; d. Franklin Sherwood and Eleanor Ruth (Pope) W.; m. Doniver Dean Campbell, Aug. 23, 1986; children: Emmaline Livingston Campbell, Eden Jennifer Campbell. BS in Journalism, Northwestern U., 1978. Reporter Norfolk (Va.) Ledger-Star, 1978-80, Dallas Times Herald, 1980-82; reporter, editor News sect. USA Today, Arlington, Va., 1982-89, mng. editor spl. projects, 1989-92; mng. editor Chgo. Sun-Times, 1992-1996; exec. editor Statesman Jour., 1996—. Mem. Am. Soc. Newspaper Editors. Office: Statesman Journal 280 Church St Salem OR 97301

WALLACE, KENNETH ALAN, investor; b. Gallup, N.Mex., Feb. 23, 1938; s. Charles Garrett and Elizabeth Eleanor (Jones) W. A.B. in Philosophy, Cornell U., 1960; postgrad. U. N.Mex., 1960-61; m. Rebecca Marie Odell, July 11, 1980; children: Andrew McMillan, Aaron Blue, Susanna Garrett, Megan Elizabeth, Glen Eric. Comml. loan officer Bank of N.Mex., Albuquerque, 1961-64; asst. cashier Ariz. Bank, Phoenix, 1964-67; comml. loan officer Valley Nat. Bank, Phoenix, 1967-70; pres. WWW, Inc., Houston, 1970-72; v.p. fin. Hometels of Am., Phoenix, 1972-77, Precision Mech. Co., Inc., 1972-77; ptnr. Schroeder-Wallace, 1977-93; chmn. Shalako Corp., Phoenix; mng. ptnr., pres. Blackhawk, Inc., Phoenix, 1977—, also, bd. dirs.; pres., chmn. bd. AlphaSat Corp., Phoenix, 1990—; pres. chmn. bd. dirs. Black Diamond Cable Co., LLC, Park City, Utah; gen. ptnr. Wallco Enterprises, Ltd., Mobile, Ala., Am. Entertainment Network, LLC, Phoenix; mng. gen. ptnr. The Village at University Heights, Flagstaff; mem. AEN Cable Ventures, LLC. Loaned exec. Phoenix United Way, 1966, Tucson United Way, 1967; mem. Valley Big Bros., 1970—; bd. dirs. Phoenix Big Sisters, 1985-87; mem. Alhambra Village Planning Com.; fin. dir. Ret. Sr. Vol. Program, 1973-76; mem. Phoenix Men's Arts Coun., 1968—, dir., 1974-75; mem. Phoenix Symphony Coun., Packards Internat. Campaign committeeman Rep. gubernatorial race, N.Mex., 1964; mem. AEN CableVentures, LLC; treas. Phoenix Young Reps., 1966; mem. Cornell U. adv. coun., 1996—, Coll. Arts and Scis. Coun. Cornell U., 1996—; bd. dirs. Devel. Authority for Tucson, 1967. Mem. Soaring Soc. Am. (Silver badge), Am. Rifle Assn. (life), Nat. Mktg. Assn. (Mktg. Performance of Year award 1966), Nat. Assn. Skin Diving Schs., Pima County Jr. C. of C. (bd. dir. 1967), Phoenix Little Theatre, Phoenix Musical Theatre, S.W. Ensemble Theatre (bd. dir.), Wheelmen of Am., Cornell Univ. Coun., Cornell Univ. Arts & Scis., Packards Internat., Masons, Shriners, Kona Kai Club (San Diego), Paradise Valley Country Club, Alpha Tau Omega. Office: The Wallace Group of Cos PO Box 7703 Phoenix AZ 85011-7703

WALLACE, MARK RAYMOND, physician; b. Seattle, Feb. 22, 1955; s. George Warren and Grace Joann (Balch) W.; m. Kathleen Cornell, Jan. 19, 1985; 1 child, Luke Randall. BA in Chemistry, Whitman Coll., Walla Walla, Wash., 1977; MD, St. Louis U., 1981. Diplomate Am. Bd. Internal Medicine, sub-bd. Infectious Diseases; cert. added competence in clin. tropical medicine. Intern Med. Ctr. Hosp. of Vt., Burlington, 1981-82; resident U. Wash., Seattle, 1982-84; staff physician Naval Hosp., Long Beach, Calif., 1984-85, head internal medicine dept., 1986-87; fellow in infectious diseases Naval Hosp., San Diego, 1987-89, staff physician, 1989-90, head HIV unit, 1990-93, dir. infectious disease fellowship, 1993—. Author/co-author 85 jour. articles and 60 abstracts. Served to comdr. USN, 1984—. Decorated Navy Commendation medal, Meritorious Svc. medal; Nat. Merit scholar, 1973. Fellow ACP, Infectious Disease Soc. Am.; mem. AMA, Am. Soc. Microbiology (Weigelt-Wallace award in clin. medicine named in his honor 1992), Physicians Assn. for AIDS Care, Phi Beta Kappa, Alpha Omega Alpha. Office: Naval Med Ctr San Diego CA 92134

WALLACE, MATTHEW WALKER, entrepreneur; b. Salt Lake City, Jan. 7, 1924; s. John McChrystal and Glenn (Walker) W.; m. Constance Cone, June 22, 1954 (dec. May 1980); children—Matthew, Anne; m. Susan Struggles, July 11, 1981. B.A., Stanford U., 1947; M.C.P., MIT, 1950. Prin. planner Boston City Planning Bd., 1950-53; v.p. Nat. Planning and Research, Inc., Boston, 1953-55; pres. Wallace-McConaughy Corp., Salt Lake City, 1955-69; pres. Ariz. Ranch & Metals Co., Salt Lake City, 1969-84; chmn. Wallace Assocs., Inc., Salt Lake City, 1969—; dir. 1st Interstate Bank, Salt Lake City, 1956—, dir. Arnold Machinery Co., 1988—, dir. Roosevelt Hot Springs Corp., 1978—; mem. adv. bd. Mountain Bell Telephone Co., Salt Lake City, 1975-85. Pres., Downtown Planning Assn., Salt Lake City, 1970; chmn. Utah State Arts Coun., Salt Lake City, 1977; mem. Humanities and Scis. Coun., Stanford U., also mem. athletic bd., bd. vis. sch. law; mem. nat. adv. bd. Coll. Bus., U. Utah; lifetime dir. Utah Symphony Orch.; chmn. arts adv. coun. Westminster Coll. Lt. (j.g.) USN, 1944-46; PTO. Recipient Contbn. award Downtown Planning Assn., 1977, Govs. Award in the Arts, 1991, Utah Nat. Guard Minuteman award, 1994. Mem. Am. Inst. Cert. Planners (charter), Am. Arts Alliance (bd. dirs. 1991), Alta Club (dir.), Cottonwood Club (pres. 1959-63), Salt Lake Country Club (dir.), Flat Rock Club (Island Pk., Idaho pres. 1994-95), Phi Kappa Phi. Home: 2510 Walker Ln Salt Lake City UT 84117-7729 Office: Wallace Assocs Inc 165 S Main St Salt Lake City UT 84111-1918

WALLACE, WILLIAM, composer, educator; b. Salt Lake City, Nov. 25, 1933; s. Henry Ashley and Dorothy (Robinson) W.; m. Harriette Kippley, June 7, 1957; children: Peter Matthew, David William. BMus, U. Utah, 1957, PhD, 1962. Asst. prof. Rutgers U., New Brunswick, N.J., 1962-67; assoc. prof., prof. McMaster U., Hamilton, Ont., Can., 1967-89; honors faculty U. Utah, Salt Lake City, 1989—. Composer for recs. including Dances and Variations, recorded by London Symphony Orch., 1990, Warsaw Chamber Orch., 1993. Recipient commissions various performing groups, 1967—. Mem. Can. Music Centre, Can. League Composers (v.p. 1979), Soc. Composers, Authors and Music Pubs. Can., Phi Beta Kappa. Democrat. Home: Box 203 Wilson WY 83014 Office: U Utah Honors Divsn Sill Centre Salt Lake City UT 84112

WALLACE, WILLIAM ARTHUR, JR., environmental engineering executive; b. N.Y.C., Dec. 6, 1942; s. William Arthur and Helene Marie (Hoene) W.; m. Diane Marie Guillot, July 11, 1964; children: Kathleen Marie, Jane Coventry. BSChemE, Clarkson U., 1964; MS in Mgmt., Rensselaer Poly. Inst., 1971; advanced mgmt. program course, Harvard U., 1989. Chief plans and programs U.S. Naval Ammunition Depot, Hawthorne, Nev., 1973-75; chief hazardous waste enforcement EPA, Washington, 1975-78; chief enforcement br. U.S. Dept. Interior, Washington, 1978-79; v.p. Fred C. Hart Assocs., N.Y.C., 1979-81; engring. exec. mktg. and strategic planning CH2M Hill, Bellevue, Wash., 1981—; testified Overview of Superfund Cleanup Techs. U.S. Ho. Reps., Washington, 1985, Overview of Superfund, 1988, 91, Soil Contaminants: PCB, 1988, U.S. Senate inquirey into environ. tech., 1993. Bd. dirs. Hazardous Waste Action Coalition, 1986—, treas., 1990-91, pres., 1996—; invited panel mem. Office of Tech. Assesment Nuclear Waste Remediation Workshop, Washington, 1990; mem. sci. adv. com. Western Regional Hazardous Substance Rsch. Ctr. Stanford U., 1989-95; mem. panel ad hoc criteria group environ. tech., We. Govs.' Assn., 1993-95; mem. Enterprise for the Environment, 1996—. Recipient George A. Hogaboom award Am. Electroplaters Soc., 1968, Bronze Medal award EPA, 1978, Outstanding Citizenship award Met. Law Enforcement Assn., Denver, 1980. Mem. Met. Club, Greenwood Athletic Club. Office: CH2M Hill 6060 S Willow Dr Greenwood Village CO 80111-5142

WALLACH, HOWARD FREDERIC, psychiatrist; b. Chgo., Sept. 4, 1923; s. Leo and Mildred (Ebert) W.; m. Laurie Rochelle Gettleman, Sept. 15, 1945 (div. July 1968); children: Joan, John, Richard; m. Gloria Bunny Jackman, July 15, 1968; children: Rand, Steve, Beth. MD, U. Ill., Chgo., 1946; M.Social Psychiatry, UCLA, 1969. Diplomate Am. Bd. Psychiatry and Neurology. Intern Cook County Hosp., Chgo., 1946-47; asst. clin. prof. psychiatry UCLA, 1968-80, assoc. clin. prof., 1980—; chief allied mental health Brentwood VA Hosp., L.A., 1970-72; chief psychiatry Sepulveda VA Hosp., L.A., 1972-74; pvt. practice L.A.; resident internal medicine Cook County Hosp., Chgo., 1947-49; bd. govs. Cedars-Sinai Med. Ctr., L.A., 1985—; cons. VA Med. Ctr., L.A., 1982-90. Contbr. articles to profl. jours. Sec. Am. Psychiat. Found., Washington, 1990—; bd. dirs. Nat. Mus. Health and Medicine, Washington, 1989—. 1st lt. U.S. Army, 1943-46. Recipient Bronze award Boys Clubs of Am., 1962, Pres.'s Spl. Achievement award So. Calif. Psychiat. Assn., 1991. Fellow Am. Coll. Psychoanalysts, Am. Psychiat. Assn. (exec. com. 1982-88), Am. Acad. Psychoanalysis; mem. Calif. Psychiat. Assn. (pres. 1986-88), Alpha Omega Alpha. Office: 2080 Century Pk East Los Angeles CA 90067

WALLACH, LESLIE ROTHAUS, architect; b. Pitts., Feb. 4, 1944; s. Albert and Sara F. (Rothaus) W.; m. Susan Rose Berger, June 15, 1969; 1 child, Aaron. BS in Mining Engring., U. Ariz., 1967, BArch, 1974. Registered architect, Ariz.; registered contractor, Ariz. Prin. Line and Space, Tucson, 1978—. Representative projects include Ariz. Sonora Desert Mus. Restaurant Complex, Tucson, Elgin Elem. Sch., Ariz., Hillel Student Ctr. U. Ariz., Tucson, Boyce Thompson Southwestern Arboreteum Vis. Ctr., Superior, Ariz., San Pedro Riparian Ctr., Sierra Vista, Ariz., Nat. Hist. Trails Ctr., Casper, Wyo., 1996; contbr. Sunset Mag., Architecture Mag. and Fine Homebuilding; exhibited at U. Ariz., AIA Nat. Conv., Washington. Bd. dirs Tucson Regional Plan, Inc. Recipient Roy P. Drachman Design award, 1982, 85, 93, Electric League Ariz. Design award, 1987, 88, Gov. Solar Energy award, 1989, Desert Living awards citation, 1991, Ariz. Architect's medal, 1989, also 25 additional design awards, including 4 received in 1995. Fellow AIA (Ariz. Honor award 1989, 92, 96, AIA/ACSA Nat. Design award 1991, Western Mountain region Design award 1992, 96, CA AIA/Phoenix Homes and Gardens Home of the Yr. Honor award 1992, 96, Western Region Silver medal 1996); mem. SAC AIA (past pres., Design award 1985, 88, 90). Office: Line and Space 627 E Speedway Blvd Tucson AZ 85705-7433

WALLACH, PATRICIA, mayor; b. Chgo.; m. Ed Wallach; 3 children. Grad., Pasadena City Coll. Mem. city coun. City of El Monte, Calif., 1990-92, mayor, 1992—; tchr.'s aide Mountain View Sch. Dist. Past trustee El Monte Union High Sch. Dist., L.A. County High Sch. for the Arts; chief amb. of goodwill Zamora, Michoacan, Mex., Marcq-en-Baroeul, France, Yung Kang, Hsiang, Republic of China, Minhang, Peoples Republic of China; mem. L.A. County Libr. Commn.; mem. air quality com. West San Gabriel Valley; chairperson of bd. Cmty. Redevel. Agy.; mem. bd. El Monte Cmty. Access TV Corp.; mem. PTA, Little League Assns.; mem. exec. bd. Foothill Transit. Mem. League of Calif. Cities, San Gabriel Valley Assn. of Cities, Independent Cities Assn., Bus. and Profl. Women, U.S./Mex. Sister Cities Assn., Sister Cities Internat. Office: 11333 Valley Blvd El Monte CA 91731-3210

WALLACH-LEVY, WENDEE ESTHER, secondary school educator; b. N.Y.C., Dec. 29, 1948; d. Leonard Morris and Annette (Cohen) W.; m. David Levy, Mar. 23, 1997; 1 child, Nanette Renè. BS in Edn., SUNY, Cortland, 1970; MA in Teaching, N.Mex. State U., 1975. Cert. tchr., N.Mex. Tchr. phys. edn. Las Cruces (N.Mex.) Pub. Schs., 1970-96; mem. Shoemaker-Levy Observing Team, 1996—; coord. Jarnac Obs., Vail, Ariz., 1997—; intramural and athletic coord. White Sands Sch., 1970-93; instr. swimming N.Mex. State U. Weekend Coll., Las Cruces, 1986-96; dir., coord. learn to swim program ARC, Las Cruces, 1973-96; instr. phys. edn., coach volleyball and track, athletic coord. Sierra Mid. Sch., 1993-96. Instr. trainer water safety ARC, 1973—, CPR, 1974—; instr. life guard, trainer, health and safety specialist, 1988-96, instr., trainer standard first aid, 1991—; chair com. health and safety svcs. Don Ana County Red Cross. Named Water Safety Instr. of Yr. ARC, Las Cruces, 1986, 89, 25 Yr. Svc. award, 1992. Mem. AAHPERD, N.Mex. Alliance Health, Phys. Edn. Recreation and Dance (spkr. 1988, 92, 93, aquatic chmn. 1990-92), Nat. Intramural-Recreational Sports Assn., N.Mex. H.S. Athletic Dirs. Assn. Democrat. Jewish. Home and Office: 2500 E Wetstones Rd Vail AZ 85641

WALLEN, CARL, education educator; b. Glendale, Calif., Dec. 12, 1931; s. Carl Joseph and Winifred (Batten) W.; m. LaDonna Leigh Stanley, Nov. 29, 1959; children: Erik Stanley, Todd Alan, Michael Carl. BA, U. Calif., Santa Barbara, 1956; MA, San Francisco State U., 1960; EdD, Stanford U., 1962. Tchr. 5th grade Mt. Eden Sch. Dist., Hayward, Calif., 1956-58; tchr. 3d and 6th grades Pacifica (Calif.) Sch. Dist., 1958-60; grad. asst. Stanford U., Palo Alto, Calif., 1960-62; asst. prof. Oreg. State U., Corvallis, 1962-65; assoc. prof. Oreg. Sys. Higher Edn., Monmouth, 1965-67, U. Oreg., Eugene, 1967-73; prof., chmn. dept. elem. edn. Ariz. State U., Tempe, 1973-78, prof., 1978—; cons. to schs., dists. and state depts. edn. in Oreg. and Ariz., 1962—. Author: Competency in Teaching Reading, 1973, 82, Cognition and Effective Instruction, 1993, 94, 95, 96; co-author: Effective Classroom Management, 1978, Fraud Recognition: Claims Adjustors, 1993; also monographs and jour. articles. Mem. com. Am. Friends Svc. Com., Oreg. and Ariz., 1963—; co-founder, pres. Ariz. Ctr. to Reverse Arms Race, Phoenix, 1978-82; rep. Ariz. Ecumenical Coun., 1978—, pres., 1990-93. Cpl. U.S. Army, 1953-54. U.S. OfficeEdn. fellow, 1972-73. Mem. Am. Ednl. Rsch. Assn., Phi Delta Kappa. Democrat. Quaker. Home: 525 E Alameda Dr Tempe AZ 85282-0311

WALLEN, LINA HAMBALI, educator, consultant; b. Garut, West Java, Indonesia, Mar. 24, 1952; came to U.S., 1986; d. Mulyadi and Indra (Hudiyana) Hambali; m. Norman E. Wallen, Apr. 16, 1986. BA, IKIP, Bandung, Indonesia, 1975, DRA, 1984; PhD in Psychology, Columbia Pacific U., San Rafael, Calif., 1990; MA in Economics, San Francisco State U., 1993. Cert. tchr. Clk. PT Radio Frequency Communication, Bandung, 1972-74; adminstrv. mgr. CV Electronics Engring., Jakarta, Indonesia, 1974-76; exec. sec. PT Tanabe Abadi, Bandung, 1977-81; br. mgr. PT Ama Forta, Bandung, 1982-84; tchr. SMA Pembangunan, Bandung, 1976-83, Patuha Coll., Bandung, 1980-84.

WALLER, KIRSTEN ORLETTE, epidemiologist; b. Mpls., Dec. 1, 1958; m. Kai John Hagen. BA, St. Olaf Coll., 1980; MD, U. Minn., 1985, MPH, 1988. Diplomate Am. Bd. Preventive Medicine. Epidemic intelligence svc. officer Ctrs. Disease Control, Atlanta, 1988-90; pub. health med. officer Calif. Dept. Health Svcs., Berkeley, 1990—. Lt. commdr. USPHS, 1988-90. Home: 1464 Dockside Ct Frederick MD 21701-9117 Office: Environ Health Invest 5900 Hollis St Ste E Emeryville CA 94608

WALLER, LARRY GENE, mortgage banking executive; b. Corpus Christi, Tex., Nov. 18, 1948; s. Paul Hobson and Marie (Armellini) W.; m. Mary Sandra Cupp, Dec. 27, 1969 (div. 1987); children: Stacey Ann, Jaime Lynn; m. Sharon Elizabeth Falls, Jan. 28, 1988; 1 child, Lisa Suzanne Cantello. AA, Bakersfield Jr. Coll., 1970. Lic. real estate broker, Calif. Asst. v.p. Bank of Am., Stockton, Calif., 1970-78, Wells Fargo Mortgage Co., Sacramento, 1978-81; regional v.p. Weyerhaeuser Mortgage Co., Sacramento, 1981-89; sr. v.p. Koll Realty Advisors, Sacramento, 1989-91; pres. L. G. Waller Co., 1991-93; pres., CFO Waller, Kaufman & Sutter, Sacramento, 1991—, Waller, Kaufman & Sutter of Nev., Reno, 1995—. Mem. Nat. Assn. Indsl. and Office Parks (bd. dirs. Sacramento chpt.), Mortgage Bankers Assn. (income property com.), Calif. Mortgage Bankers Assn., North Tahoe Bus. Assn. Home: PO Box 2810 Kings Beach CA 96143-2810 Office: 2277 Fair Oaks Blvd Ste 400 Sacramento CA 95825-5533 also: PO Box 670 Incline Village NV 69450-6670

WALLER, PETER WILLIAM, public affairs executive; b. Kewanee, Ill., Oct. 1, 1926; s. Ellis Julian and Barodel (Gould) W.; m. Anne-Marie Appelius van Hoboken, Nov. 10, 1950; children: Catherine, Hans. BA with hons., Princeton U., 1949; MA with hons., San Jose State U., 1978. Bur. chief Fairchild Publs., San Francisco, 1953-55; freelance writer Mountain View, Calif., 1956-57; pub. relations coord. Lockheed Missiles and Space, Sunnyvale, Calif., 1957-64; info. mgr. for 1st missions to Jupiter, Saturn, Venus NASA Ames Rsch. Ctr., Mountain View, 1964-83, mgr. pub. info., 1983-95; cons. NASA-Ames Galileo, Lunar Prospector, 1996-97; speechwriter for pres. Lockheed Missiles and Space, 1960-64. Producer (documentary) Jupiter Odyssey, 1974 (Golden Eagle, 1974); producer, writer NASA Aero. program, 1984; contbr. articles to profl. jours, encyclopedias. Cons. on preservation of Lake Tahoe, Calif. Resources Agy., Sacramento, 1984. Mem. No. Calif. Sci. Writers Assn., Sierra Club. Democrat. Congregationalist. Home: 3655 La Calle Ct Palo Alto CA 94306-2619 Office: NASA Ames Rsch Ctr Moffett Field CA 94035

WALLER, STEPHEN, air transportation executive; b. 1949. Student, New Zealand U., 1970-74. Courier, country mgr., european mktg. mgr. DHL Airways, Inc., London, 1975-80, Tehran, Iran, 1975-80; sr. v.p. DHL Airways, Inc., Redwood City, Calif., 1981—. Office: DHL Airways Inc 333 Twin Dolphin Dr Redwood City CA 94065-1401

WALLERSTEIN, JUDITH SARETSKY, marriage and divorce researcher; b. N.Y.C., Dec. 27, 1921; d. Samuel Saretsky and Augusta (Tucker) Weinberger; m. Robert S. Wallerstein, Jan. 27, 1949; children—Michael, Nina, Amy. B.A., Hunter Coll., N.Y.C., 1943; M.S., Columbia U., 1946; Ph.D. in Psychology, Lund U. (Sweden) 1978. Sr. lectr. U. Calif.-Berkeley, 1966-91, sr. lectr. emeritus, 1991—; dir. Calif. Children of Divorce Project, Marin County, Calif., 1971—; mem. task force on family equity Calif. Senate, 1986; founder, former exec. dir. Judith Wallerstein Ctr. Family in Transition, Corte Madera, Calif., 1980-93. Prin. investigator follow-up study Effects of Divorce on Children and Their Parents. Mem. adv. com. on family law Calif. Senate Subcom. on Adminstrn. of Justice, 1977-79; mem. task force on Family equity Calif. State Senate, 1986. Author 3 books; contbr. 80 articles to profl. jours. Recipient Koshland award in Social Welfare San Francisco Found., 1975, René Spitz award Denver Psychoanalytic Soc., 1991, Geri Taylor Meml. award No. Calif. Psychiat. Soc., 1993, Presdl. Citation Am. Psychol. Assn. Divsn. of Family Psychol., 1995, Dale Richmond award Am. Acad. Pediat., 1996; others. Fellow Ctr. Advanced Study in the Behavioral Scis., Stanford, Calif., 1979-80, Rockefeller Found. Study Ctr., Bellagio, Italy, 1992. Mem. NASW, Am. Psychoanalytic Assn. (hon.), N.Y. Freudian Soc. (hon.), San Francisco Psychoanalytic Soc. (interdisciplinary mem.), Am. Orthopsychiatric Assn., Assn. Child Psychoanalysis (mem. exec. council 1977-80), Assn. Family Conciliation Courts, Phi Beta Kappa.

WALLERSTEIN, RALPH OLIVER, physician; b. Dusseldorf, Germany, Mar. 7, 1922; came to U.S., 1938, naturalized, 1944; s. Otto R. and Ilse (Hollander) W.; m. Betty Ane Christensen, June 21, 1952; children: Ralph Jr., Richard, Ann. A.B., U. Calif., Berkeley, 1943; M.D., U. Calif., San Francisco, 1945. Diplomate Am. Bd. Internal Medicine (bd. govs. 1975-83, chmn. 1982-83). Intern San Francisco Hosp., 1945-46, resident, 1948-49; resident U. Calif. Hosp., San Francisco, 1949-50; research fellow Thorndike Meml. Lab., Boston City Hosp., 1950-52; chief clin. hematology San Francisco Gen. Hosp., 1953-87; mem. faculty U. Calif., San Francisco, 1952—, clin. prof. medicine, 1969—. Served to capt. M.C. AUS, 1946-48. Mem. AMA, ACP (gov. 1977-87, chmn. bd. govs. 1980-81, regent 1981-87, pres. 1988-89), Am. Soc. Hematology (pres. 1978), San Francisco Med. Soc., Am. Clin. and Climatol. Assn., Am. Fedn. Clin. Rsch., Am. Soc. Internal Medicine, Am. Assn. Blood Banks, Inst. Medicine, Calif. Acad. Medicine, Internat. Soc. Hematology, Western Soc. Clin. Rsch., Western Assn. Physicians, Gold Headed Cane Soc. Republican. Home: 3447 Clay St San Francisco CA 94118-2008

WALL HOFER, MARJORIE SELMA, career specialist, consultant; b. Chilliwack, B.C., Can., Feb. 2, 1959; came to U.S., 1986; d. Peter and Selma (Klassen) Wall; m. Peston LeRoy Hoffer, Aug. 31, 1986; children: Audra, Peyton, Mason, Adele. BHe, U. B.C., Vancouver, Can., 1982, MEd, 1987. Job developer, employment counselor Can. Employment & Immigration Commn., Vancouver, Chilliwack, 1979-86; career counselor and tng. coord. women's ctr. Red Rocks C.C., Lakewood, Colo., 1986-91; pres. and owner OPTiM Devel. Sys., Denver, 1991—; vice chair Ten Thousand Village Store, Denver, 1994—. Chair adv. bd. Jefferson Social Svc., Lakewood, 1988-90; mem. Mennonite Econ. Devel. Internat., 1992—; sec. Ch. Coun., Aurora, Colo., 1995—. Mem. ACA, ASTD, Colo. Career Devel. Assn. Office: OPTiM Devel Sys Inc 465 A Krameria St Denver CO 80220

WALLIN, LAWRENCE BIER, artist; b. Norwalk, Conn., Apr. 23, 1944; s. Edward and Anita (Bier) W.; m. Bettine Celia Kinney, May 14, 1936; children: Alizon Ossman Harris, Devis Ossman. BFA, MFA, Otis Art Inst., 1966. v.p. L.A. Artists Equity, 1982. Exhibited works in solo shows at The Ash Grove, L.A., Green Apple Gallery, Las Vegas, Centennial Galleries, Westlake, Calif., Bolen Gallery, Santa Monica, Calif., Senior Eye Gallery, Long Beach, Calif., Peter Nahum, London, Carnegie Mus., Oxnard, Calif., Montecito (Calif.) Pub. Libr., Karpeles Manuscript Libr., Santa Barbara, Calif., Art Angles Gallery, Orange, Calif., Oliver & Espig, Santa Barbara, others; group shows include Litton Ctr. Visual Arts, L.A., Meridith Hunter Gallery, Santa Fe, Fine Arts Gallery, Durango, Colo., Robertson Galleries, Riverside, Calif., Louis Newman Galleries, Beverly Hills, Calif., The Outsiders Gallery, Santa Barbara, Santa Barbara Mus. Natural History, L.A. Mcpl. Gallery. Tchg. adult literacy program Santa Barbara Pub. Libr., 1996. Home and Office: 895 Toro Canyon Rd Santa Barbara CA 93108-1641

WALLING, DOUGLAS DEAN, retired airline pilot; b. Arcadia, Fla., Dec. 22, 1934; s. Curtis Eugene and Thelma Paulene (Johnson) W.; m. Shirley Anne Thomas, Sept. 7, 1956 (div. 1967); m. Anne Bernadete Lindberg, Feb. 5, 1980 (div. 1985). Student, U. Md., 1956-59, Coll. of Great Falls, Mont., 1960-62, Tex. Christian U., 1963-67. Commd. 2nd lt. USAF, 1954, advanced through grades to lt. col., 1966, ret., 1967; from pilot to capt. Western Airlines, L.A., 1967-86; from pilot to capt. Delta Airlines, Atlanta, 1986-92, ret. Republican. Lutheran.

WALLIS, ERIC G., lawyer; b. Astoria, N.Y., Jan. 8, 1950. AB magna cum laude, U. Pacific, 1972; JD, U. Calif., Hasting Coll. of Law, 1975. Bar: Calif. 1975. Mem. Crosby, Heafey, Roach & May P.C., Oakland, Calif. Editorial assoc. Hastings Law Jour., 1974-75. Mem. ABA (sect. litigation), State Bar Calif., Alameda County Bar Assn. Office: Crosby Heafey Roach & May PC PO Box 2084 Oakland CA 94604-2084

WALLISCH, CAROLYN E., principal; b. Denver, Aug. 23, 1939; d. Morgan Franklin and Margaret C. (Kopf) White; m. Darrell Dean Wallisch, June 9, 1963; children: Michael Dean, Kerri Elise. BA in Elem. Edn., U. No. Colo., 1961, MA in Elem. Edn., 1965; postgrad., Denver U., 1989. Cert. tchr. grades K-8, adminstrn. grades K-12. Tchr. grade 1 San Jose Unified Sch. Dist., 1961-62, Greeley (Colo.) Pub. Schs., 1962-69; tchr. grades 2-8, dean of students Jefferson County Schs., Lakewood, Colo., 1984-94; prin. grades K-5 Littleton (Colo.) Pub. Schs., 1994—. Contbr. articles to profl. jours. Leader 4-H Clubs of Am., Littleton, 1982-84, Girl Scouts U.S.A., Littleton, 1979-82; den leader Boy Scouts Am., Littleton, 1976-78; precinct committeewoman Littleton, 1984-90. Named one of Outstanding Young Women of Am., 1965, Model Tchr., ABC News Peter Jennings Who's Happening in Edn., 1993, Instr. Mag., 1993. Mem. ASCD, Internat. Reading Assn. (Colo. coun. 1989—), Colo. Coun. Tchrs. Math. (conf. presenter), Colo. Assn. Sch. Execs. (conf. presenter), PTO (v.p. 1994—), Kiwanis, Kappa Delta Pi (bd. dirs.), Sigma Sigma Sigma (bd. dirs.), Alpha Delta Kappa (bd. dirs.), Phi Delta Kappa (bd. dirs., rsch. chmn. 1987—). Republican. Home: 5549 W Hinsdale Ave Littleton CO 80123 Office: Highland Elementary School 711 E Euclid Ave Littleton CO 80121

WALLMANN, JEFFREY MINER, author; b. Seattle, Dec. 5, 1941; s. George Rudolph and Elizabeth (Biggs) W.; BS, Portland State U., 1962; PhD, U. Nev., 1997. Pvt. investigator Dale Systems, N.Y.C., 1962-63; asst. buyer, mgr. pub. money bidder Dohrmann Co., San Francisco, 1964-66; mfrs. rep. electronics industry, San Francisco, 1966-69; dir. pub. rels. London Films, Cinelux-Universal and Trans-European Publs., 1970-75; editor-in-chief Riviera Life mag., 1975-77; cons. Mktg. Svcs. Internat., 1978—; instr. U. Nev., Reno, 1990—; books include: The Spiral Web, 1969, Judas Cross, 1974, Clean Sweep, 1976, Jamaica, 1977, Deathtrek, 1980, Blood and Passion, 1980; Brand of the Damned, 1981; The Manipulator, 1982; Return to Conta Lupe, 1983; The Celluloid Kid, 1984; Business Basic for Bunglers, 1984, Guide to Applications Basic, 1984; (under pseudonym Leon DaSilva) Green Hell, 1976, Breakout in Angola, 1977; (pseudonym Nick Carter) Hour of the Wolf, 1973, Ice Trap Terror, 1974; (pseudonym Margaret Maitland) The Trial, 1974, Come Slowly, Eden, 1974, How Deep My Cup, 1975; (pseudonym Amanda Hart Douglass) First Rapture, 1972, Jamacia!, 1978; (pseudonym Grant Roberts) The Reluctant Couple, 1969, Wayward Wives, 1970; (pseudonym Gregory St. Germain) Resistance #1: Night and Fog, 1982, Resistance #2: Maygar Massacre, 1983; (pseudonym Wesley Ellis) Lonestar on the Treachery Trail, 1982, numerous others in the Lonestar series; (pseudonym Tabor Evans) Longarm and the Lonestar Showdown, 1986; (psyeudonym Jon Sharpe) Trailsman 58: Slaughter Express, 1986, numerous others in Trailsman series; also many other pseudonyms and titles; contbr. articles and short stories to Argosy, Ellery Queen's Mystery Mag., Alfred Hitchcock's Mystery Mag., Mike Shayne's Mystery Mag., Zane Grey Western, Venture, Oui, TV Guide; also (under pseudonym William Jeffrey in collaboration with Bill Pronzini) Dual at Gold Buttes, 1980, Border Fever, 1982, Day of the Moon, 1983. Mem. Mystery Writers of Am., Sci. Fiction Writers Am., Western Writers Am., Nat. Coun. Tchrs. English, Crime Writers Assn., Nev. State Coun. Tchrs. English, Esperanto League N.Am., Western Literature Assn., Internacia Societo De Amikeco Kaj Bonvolo, Science Fiction Rsch. Assn., Internat. Assn. of the Fantastic in the Arts, Nat. Assn. Sci. Tech. & Sci., Soc. Internat. d'Amitié et Bonne Volonté, Nat. Coun. Tchrs. English, Western Lit. Assn. Office: Jabberwocky Lit Agy 41-16 47th Ave Ste 2D Sunnyside NY 11104-3040

WALLO, STEVEN F., physical education and athletics director; b. Portland, Oreg., July 22, 1957; s. Ed and Rosemarie (Rennie) W.; m. Cynthia Ann Chevalier, May 8, 1982; children: Bryan, Megan. BS, Lewis and Clark Coll., 1979, MAT, 1996. Tchr., coach Beaverton (Oreg.) Sch. Dist., 1980-83, Portland Pub. Schs., 1983-85, Jesuit High Sch., Portland, 1985-89; coach, sports info. dir. Lewis and Clark Coll., Portland, 1989-91, asst. dir. athletics, 1991-93, dir. of phys. edn. and athletics, 1993—. Bd. dirs. Beaverton Ave. Little League. Mem. AAHPERD, Nat. Assn. Coll. Dirs. of Athletics, Am. Baseball Coaches Assn., U.S. Golf Assn., Oreg. Coaches Assn., Multnomah Athletic Club. Office: Lewis & Clark Coll Athletics 0615 SW Palatine Hill Rd Portland OR 97219

WALLS, JOSEPH PATRICK, orthopaedic surgeon; b. Phila., Nov. 3, 1955; s. Thomas Francis and Margaret Mary Walls; m. Ellen Vera Eliassen, July 29, 1989. BA in Biology summa cum laude, Temple U., 1978; MD, Thomas Jefferson Med. Coll., 1982. Diplomate Am. Acad. Orthopaedic Surgeons. Resident in orthpaedic surgery Med. Coll. of Va., Richmond, 1982-87; attending orthpaedic surgeon, maj. Luke AFB, Glendale, Ariz., 1987-91; orthopaedic surgeon with 363rd Tactical Fighter Wing USAF, Middle East, 1990-91; fellowship in sports medicine Penn State U., Hershey, Pa., 1991-92; pvt. practice orthopaedic surgeon Carson-Douglas Orthopaedic and Sports Medicine Ctr., Carson City, Nev., 1992-95; established Capitol Orthopedics and Sports Medicine, 1995. Contbr. articles to profl. jours. Mem. AMA, Am. Acad. Orthopaedic Surgeons, Carson City Rotary (bd. dirs. 1994, 96). Office: Capitol Orthopaedics & Sports Medicine 1000 N Division St Carson City NV 89703-3929

WALLSTRÖM, WESLEY DONALD, bank executive; b. Turlock, Calif., Oct. 4, 1929; s. Emil Reinhold and Edith Katherine (Lindberg) W.; student Modesto Jr. Coll., 1955-64; certificate Pacific Coast Banking Sch., U. Wash., 1974; m. Marilyn Irene Hallmark, May 12, 1951; children: Marc Gordon, Wendy Diane. Bookkeeper, teller First Nat. Bank, Turlock, 1947-50; v.p. Gordon Hallmark, Inc., Turlock, 1950-53; asst. cashier United Calif. Bank, Turlock, 1953-68, regional v.p., Fresno, 1968-72, v.p., mgr., Turlock, 1972-76; founding pres., dir. Golden Valley Bank, Turlock, 1976-84; pres. Wallström & Co., 1985—. Campaign chmn. United Crusade, Turlock, 1971; chmn., founding dir. Covenant Village, retirement home, Turlock, 1973-94, treas. Covenant Retirement Communities West; founding pres. Turlock Regional Arts Coun., 1974, dir., 1975-76. Served with U.S. N.G., 1948-56. Mem. Nat. Soc. Accts. for Coops., Ind. Bankers No. Calif., Am. Bankers Assn., U.S. Yacht Racing Union, No. Calif. Golf Assn., Turlock C. of C. (dir. 1973-75), Stanislaus Sailing Soc. (commodore 1980-81), Pacific Inter-Club Yacht Assn. (bd. dirs. 1994—, regatta chmn.), Turlock Golf and Country Club (pres. 1975-76, v.p., 1977, dir. 1977, 83), Stockton Sailing Club, Grindstone Joe Assn., Masons, Rotary. Republican. Mem. Covenant Ch. Home: 1720 Hammond Dr Turlock CA 95382-2850 Office: Wallstrom & Co 2925 Niagra St Turlock CA 95382-1056 *Personal philosophy: "Faith is the substance of things hoped for, the evidence of things not seen".*

WALNER, WILLIAM DENNIS, school system administrator; b. Monterey Park, Calif., July 16, 1954; s. James Frederic and Joyce Hope Walner; m. Carol Rathbun, Nov. 22, 1980. BA in Music Edn., Seattle Pacific U., 1976; MA in Adminstrn., Biola U., LaMirada, Calif., 1985; postgrad., Pepperdine U., 1996—. Tng. rep. Broadway Dept. Store, Downey, Calif., 1978-80; tchr. Santa Fe Springs (Calif.) Christian Sch., 1976-82, prin., 1982-90; supt. Santa Fe Springs/Woodruff Christian Schs., 1990; asst. regional dir. so. Calif. region Assn. Christian Schs. Internat., Whittier, Calif., 1991—. Mem. ASCD, Toastmasters. Office: Assn Christian Schs Internat PO Box 4097 Whittier CA 90607-4097

WALRAD, CHARLENE CHUCK, management consultant; b. Palm Beach, Fla., Feb. 21, 1946; d. Jack Maynard and Marian (Davenport) W. BA, Ariz. State U., 1967, MA, 1969; MS, U. Calif., San Diego, 1971. Linguist LATSEC, Inc., La Jolla, Calif., 1971-75, sr. linguist, 1975-84; v.p. World Translation Ctr., La Jolla, 1981-84; dir. mktg. Automated Lang. Processing Systems, Provo, Utah, 1984-85; dir. R & D, WICAT Systems, Orem, Utah, 1985-86; dir. quality mgmt. Ingres, Alameda, Calif., 1986-87; software engring. cons. San Francisco, 1987—; pres. Davenport Cons., Inc., 1994—; cons. Xerox Corp., Webster, N.Y., 1983-84, Sci. Applications, Inc., La Jolla, 1984, Dept. Commerce, 1988, CIA, 1989, NAS, 1989, Control Data Corp., 1989, Word Star, 1990, Ford Motor Co., 1990-91, Dialog/Knight-Ridder, 1991, IBM, 1991-94, Esprit de Corps, 1992-93, Calif. State Automobile Assn., 1994, So. Pacific R.R., 1994, Frame Tech., 1994-95, Adobe Sys., 1995, Microsoft, 1996, Ceridian, 1996; presenter in field. Co-author: Introduction to Luiseno, 1972. Bd. dirs. Shelter Ridge Assn., Mill Valley, Calif., 1988-90, v.p., 1989-90, pres., 1990; mem. Mill Valley Bus. Task Force, 1990-91; bd. dirs. Marin Mus. of Am. Indian; chmn. Bus. Advocacy Ctr., Mill Valley, 1992-93; bd. dirs. Mill Valley Fall Arts Festival, 1994—. Mem. Ariz. State U. Alumni Assn. (pres. San Diego chpt. 1982-83, pres. Utah chpt. 1985-86), Mensa. Home: 438 Hillcrest Rd San Carlos CA 94070

WALRATH, HARRY RIENZI, minister; b. Alameda, Calif., Mar. 7, 1926; s. Frank Rienzi and Cathren (Michlar) W.; AA, City Coll. San Francisco, 1950; BA, U. Calif. at Berkeley, 1952; MDiv, Ch. Div. Sch. of Pacific, 1959; m. Dorothy M. Baxter, June 24, 1961; 1 son, Gregory Rienzi. Dist. exec. San Mateo area council Boy Scouts Am., 1952-55; ordained deacon Episcopal Ch., 1959, priest, 1960; curate All Souls Parish, Berkeley, Calif., 1959-61; vicar St. Luke's, Atascadero, Calif., 1961-63, St. Andrew's, Garberville, Calif., 1963-64; asso. rector St. Luke's Ch., Los Gatos, 1964-65, Holy Spirit Parish, Missoula, Mont., 1965-67; vicar St. Peter's Ch., also headmaster St. Peter's Schs., Litchfield Park, Ariz., 1967-69; chaplain U. Mont., 1965-67; asst. rector Trinity Parish, Reno, 1969-72; coordinator counciling svcs. Washoe County Council Alcoholism, Reno, 1972-74; adminstr. Cons. Assistance Svcs., Inc., Reno, 1974-76; pastoral counselor, contract chaplain Nev. Mental Health Inst., 1976-78; contract mental health chaplain VA Hosp., Reno, 1976-78; mental health chaplain VA Med. Ctr., 1978-83, staff chaplain, 1983-85, chief, chaplain service, 1985-91, also triage coord. for mental health, ret., 1991; per diem chaplain Washoe Med. Ctr., Reno, 1993; assoc. priest Trinity Episcopal Ch., Reno, 1995; assoc. Mountain Ministries, Susanville, Calif., 1995—; dir. youth Paso Robles Presbytery; chmn. Diocesan Commn. on Alcoholism; cons. teen-age problems Berkeley Presbytery; mem. clergy team Episcopal Marriage Encounter, 1979-85, also Episc. Engaged Encounter. Author: God Rides the Rails-Chapel Cars on American Railroads at the Turn of the Century, 1994. Mem. at large Washoe dist. Nev. area council Boy Scouts Am., scoutmaster troop 73, 1976, troop 585, 1979-82, asst. scoutmaster troop 35, 1982-92, assoc. adviser area 3 Western region, 1987-89, regional com. Western Region, 1989-90; lodge adviser Tannu Lodge 346, Order of Arrow, 1982-87; docent coun. Nev. Hist. Soc., 1992; South Humboldt County chmn. Am. Cancer Soc. Trustee Community Youth Ctr., Reno. Served with USNR, 1944-46. Decorated Pacific Theater medal with star, Am. Theater medal, Victory medal, Fleet Unit Commendation medal; recipient dist. award of merit Boy Scouts Am., St. George award Episc. Ch.-Boy Scouts Am., Silver Beaver award Boy Scouts Am., 1986, Founders' award Order of the Arrow, Boy Scouts Am., 1985; performance awards VA-VA Med. Ctr., 1983, 84; named Arrowman of Yr., Order of Arrow, Boy Scouts Am. Cert. substance abuse counselor, Nev. Mem. Ch. Hist. Soc., U. Calif. Alumni Assn., Nat. Model R.R. Assn. (life), Sierra Club Calif., Missoula Council Chs. (pres.), Alpha Phi Omega. Democrat. Club: Rotary. Home: 4822 Ramcreek Trail Reno NV 89509-8029 *The study of history has taught me one thing: that human nature has not changed, only the means of its execution. This same study has also taught me that human nature reveals the glory of God in our quest for our future.*

WALSDORF, DONALD P., art show producer, gallery director; b. Ladysmith, Wis., Apr. 22, 1931; s. Leland Peter and Elizabeth Opal Walsdorf; m. Gertrude Mary Thompson, Jan. 28, 1955; children: Mark Thomas, Kurt Lee. Student, Coll. St. Thomas, St. Paul, 1950. Intelligence specialist USAF, Yokota AFB, Japan, 1950-54; dir. Rusk Mut. Ins. Co., Ladysmith, 1957-67; v.p. Ladysmith agy., 1954-67; mgr., agy. dir. Weyerhauser Co., Tacoma, Wash., 1968-72; account exec. Marsh-McLennan, Spokane, Wash., 1968-72; owner Lincoln Assocs., Spokane, 1985—, Art Shows-Walsdorf Gallery, Spokane, 1985—. Pres. Cath. Diocese of Spokane, 1969-73; commr. Spokane City Art Commn., 1991-94; assoc. MIA/POW Korean War Group, 1991-96. Mem. Spokane Chamber Art Dirs. Assn. (bd. dirs. 1992-94). Republican. Office: Art Shows PO Box 245 Spokane WA 99210-0245

WALSER, MILTON WESLEY (BUDDY WALSER), systems engineer; b. Orlando, Fla., Dec. 2, 1958; s. Milton Wesley and Carolyn Wenona (Blake) W.; m. Zoe Dimassis (div.); m. Tammy Jo Beil, Mar. 5, 1994. BS in Ecology and Evolutionary Biology, U. Ariz., 1980, MS in Sys. Engring., 1983. Teaching asst. U. Ariz., Tucson, 1981-83; project engr. Hughes Aircraft Co., Tucson, 1983-89; sys. engr. The Mitre Corp., Ft. Huachuca, Ariz., 1989-91; group leader The Mitre Corp., San Antonio, 1992-93; site leader Mitretek Sys., Sacramento, Calif., 1993—; oceanographer USNR, 1986—. Vol. instr. Rendokan Dojo, Tucson, 1986-91, Calif. Muscle Dojo, Sacramento, 1993—. Named Jr. Officer of Yr. San Diego area Reserve Officer's Assn. Mem. Am. Soc. Quality Control, Am. Geophys. Union, U.S. Judo Assn. (life), U.S. Judo Fedn. Home: 305 Withington Ave Rio Linda CA 95673-3345 Office: Mitretek Syss 5050 Dudley Blvd Ste 3 Mcclellan AFB CA 95652-1385

WALSH, BERNARD LAWRENCE, JR., retired physicist; b. Detroit, Jan. 11, 1932; s. Bernard Lawrence Sr. and Catherine Bridget (McCarthy) W.; m. Margaret Barbara Milko, Feb. 16, 1957; children: Bernard Lawrence III, Catherine Teresa. AB, U. Detroit, 1954. With Hughes Aircraft Co., L.A., 1954--, sr. scientist, 1968-75, chief scientist, 1975-97; ret., 1997. Contbr. articles to profl. jours.; patentee in field. Mem. IEEE, Am. Phys. Soc., ASM Internat., Profl. Group Electron Devices, Profl. Group Microwave Theory and Techniques. Home: 9609 Wystone Ave Northridge CA 91324-1858

WALSH, DANIEL FRANCIS, bishop; b. San Francisco, Oct. 2, 1937. Grad., St. Joseph Sem., St. Patrick Sem., Catholic U. Am. Ordained priest, Roman Catholic Ch., 1963. Ordained titular bishop of Tigia, 1981; aux. bishop of San Francisco, 1981-87, bishop of Reno-Las Vegas, 1987—. Home: 2809 Cameo Cir Las Vegas NV 89107-3213 Office: Diocese of Reno-Las Vegas Office of Bishop PO Box 18316 Las Vegas NV 89114-8316*

WALSH, JOHN, museum director; b. Mason City, Wash., Dec. 9, 1937; s. John J. and Eleanor (Wilson) W.; m. Virginia Alys Galston, Feb. 17, 1962; children: Peter Wilson, Anne Galston, Frederick Matthiessen. B.A., Yale U., 1961; postgrad., U. Leyden, Netherlands, 1965-66; MA, Columbia U., 1965, PhD, 1971. Lectr., rsch. asst. Frick Collection, N.Y.C., 1966-68; assoc. higher edn. Met. Mus. Art, N.Y.C., 1968-71; assoc. curator European paintings Met. Mus. Art, 1970-72, curator dept. European paintings, 1972-74, vice-chmn., 1974-75; adj. asso. prof. art history Columbia U., N.Y.C., 1969-72; adj. prof. Columbia U., 1972-75; prof. art history Barnard Coll., Columbia U., N.Y.C., 1975-77; Mrs. Russell W. Baker curator paintings Mus. Fine Arts, Boston, 1977-83; dir. J. Paul Getty Mus., Malibu, Calif., 1983—; vis. prof. fine arts Harvard U., 1979; mem. governing bd. Yale U. Art Gallery, 1975—, Smithsonian Coun., 1990—. Contbr. articles to profl. jours. Mem. Dem. County Com., N.Y.C., 1968-71; mem. vis. com. Fogg Mus., Harvard U., 1982-87; bd. fellows Claremont U. Ctr. and Grad. Sch., 1988—. With USNR, 1957-63. Fulbright grad. fellow The Netherlands, 1965-66. Mem. Coll. Art Assn., Am. Assn. Mus., Archaeol. Inst. Am., Am. Antiquarian Soc., Assn. Art Mus. Dirs. (trustee 1986—, pres. 1989-90), Century Assn. N.Y.C. Office: J Paul Getty Museum PO Box 2112 Santa Monica CA 90407

WALSH, KENNETH ANDREW, biochemist; b. Sherbrooke, Que., Can., Aug. 7, 1931; s. George Stanley and Dorothy Maud (Sangster) W.; m. Deirdre Anne Clarke, Aug. 22, 1953; children: Andrew, Michael, Erin. BSc in Agr., McGill U., 1951; MS, Purdue U., 1953; PhD, U. Toronto, 1959. Postdoctoral fellow U. Wash., Seattle, 1959-62, from asst. prof. to assoc. prof. Biochemistry, 1962-69, prof. Biochemistry, 1969—, chair, 1990—. Author (book) Methods in Protein Sequence Analysis, 1986. Mem. The Protein Soc. (sec.-treas. 1987-90), Am. Soc. Biochemistry/Molecular Biology. Office: U Wash Dept Biochem Box 357350 Seattle WA 98195

WALSH, MADGE RICHARDSON, editor, writer; b. Berkeley, Calif., Mar. 1, 1931; d. Russell David and Jessie Dewey (Cutting) Richardson; m. Bert Thompson Walsh, Dec. 20, 1958; children: David, Caitilin. BA in Dramatic Lit. cum laude, U. Calif., Berkeley, 1952, MA in Anthropology, 1959. Cons. Redding (Calif.) Mus. Art & History, 1986—, Dogtown Territorial Quarterly, Paradise, Calif., 1993—; Shasta Hist. Soc. rep., Assn. Redding Museums, 1987-88. Author: A Century of Saints, 1878-1978, 1978, Carpenter With a Camera, 1993; compiler: Shasta County Voters, 1866-1884, 1993; contbr. articles to hist. jours.; editor Shasta Hist. Soc., 1987—; script writer, dir. Shasta Hist. Soc. Presents video programs, 1996. Cataloger, v.p. Shasta Hist. Soc., Redding, Calif., 1974-75, bd. dirs., 1975-76, 88-90. Named Woman of Yr. St. Andrews Presbyn. Ch., Portland, 1983. Mem. Calif. Hist. Soc., Calif. Native Plant Soc., Assn. for Northern Calif. Records and Rsch., Redding Mus. Art & History, Shasta Natural Sci. Assn., Shasta Hist. Soc., Anderson Hist. Soc., Horsetown-Clear Creek Preserve. First Christian Disciple. Office: Shasta Historical Soc PO Box 990277 1449 Market St Redding CA 96099-0277

WALSH, MASON, retired newspaperman; b. Dallas, Nov. 27, 1912; s. Herbert C. and Margaret (Hayes) W.; m. Margaret Anne Calhoun, Mar. 7, 1947; children: Margaret Anne (Mrs. James G. Dunn), Timothy Mason, Kevin Calhoun. B.A. in Polit. Sci., So. Meth. U., 1934. Staff Dallas Evening Jour., 1929-37; staff Dallas Dispatch-Jour. (later Dallas Jour.), 1938-42; editor Austin (Tex.) Tribune, 1942; dir. employee relations N.Am. Aviation, Dallas, 1942-45; with Dallas Times-Herald, 1945-60, mng. editor, 1952-60; mng. editor Phoenix Gazette, 1960-66; gen. mgr. Phoenix Newspapers, Inc., 1966-75, asst. pub., 1975-78; pub. Ariz. Republic and Phoenix Gazette, 1978-80, pub. emeritus, 1980—. Profl. musician, 1929-35. Chmn. Ariz. Dept. Econ. Planning and Devel. Bd., 1968-71; bd. dirs., v.p. Goodwill Industries Central Ariz., 1978-84, v.p., 1982-83; bd. dirs. Western Newspaper Found., 1974-81; trustee Desert Found., Scottsdale, 1982-85; mem. Nat. Def. Exec. Res., 1964-80. Mem. A.P. Mng. Editors Assn. (dir. 1956-63, pres. 1963), A.P. Assn. Calif., Ariz., Hawaii and Nev. (pres. 1976-77), Ariz. Acad. (dir. 1973-81, v.p. 1980-81), Valley Forward Assn. (dir. 1970-87), Newcomen Soc., Phoenix 40, Sigma Delta Chi. Episcopalian. Club: Arizona. Home: 4102 N 64th Pl Scottsdale AZ 85251-3110

WALSH, MICHAEL JOSEPH, security director; b. Boston, Aug. 19, 1947; s. James Patrick and Margaret Mary (Watson) W.; m. Linda Susan Newton, Dec. 29, 1971 (div. Oct. 1987); m. Esperanza Gonzales, June 1, 1991 (div. June 1996). AA in Spanish, Southwestern S.C., Chula Vista, Calif., 1975, AS in Bus. Mgmt., 1975; BS in Edn., So. Ill. Univ., 1978. Lt. comdr. USN, 1966-93; mem. Seal Team One, Coronado, Calif., 1968-73; platoon comdr. Seal Team Two, Norfolk, Va., 1978-80; combat craft officer in charge Spl. Boat Unit Twenty, Norfolk, 1980-82; command tng. officer Seal Team Four, Norfolk, 1982-84; chief exercise divsn. USN So. Command, Panama, 1984-87; dir. logistics Naval Spl. Warfare Group Two, Norfolk, 1987-89; dep. dir. intelligence Spl. Ops. Command Atlantic, Norfolk, 1989-93; dir. security Symmetry By Design, Inc., Castle Rock, Colo., 1996-97; chief navy rep. Counter Terror Work Group, Panama, Latin Am., 1981-87; task unit commdr. Naval Spl. Warfare Task Unit 1-84, Beirut, Lebanon, 1983-84; radio guest. Author: SEAL!, 1995; contbg. editor Polinews, 1995—. Decorated Bronze Star with 3 combat V, Purple Heart, Def. Meritorious Svc. medal, Navy Commendation medal with 2 combat V, Navy Achievement with combat V, 24 others. Mem. Am. Soc. Indsl. Security, Spl. Ops. Assn., UDT/SEAL Assn. (life, pres. 1992-93).

WALSH, THOMAS FRANCIS, JR., producer, writer, director; b. N.Y.C., Aug. 15, 1956; s. Thomas Francis and Catherine Alice (May) W.; m. Adriana Mia Stastny, Oct. 19, 1996. BFA, NYU, 1977. Pres. Tom Walsh Prodns. Inc., N.Y.C. and Del., 1977-89; chmn., CEO I.D.L. Inc., N.Y.C. and Calif., 1989-91, Wonderland Dream Factory Inc., Calif. and Del., 1991-93, Enteraktion, Inc., Calif. and Del., 1993—. Prodr.: (feature film) Denial, 1991, (CD-ROM) The Arrival, 1996; exec. prodr.: (TV spl.) We Dare You!, 1982, House to House, 1982, Mismatch, 1979; prodr., dir.: The Whole Truth, 1977. Scholar Helena Rubenstein Co., N.Y.C., 1976-77; recipient 1st prize for best TV show Conn. Assn. Profl. Communicators, 1974, Bronze and Silver awards Nat. Forensic League, 1977. Mem. Psi Upsilon (Delta chpt.), Alpha Epsilon Rho. Office: Enteraktion Inc 15200 Sunset Blvd Pacific Palisades CA 90272

WALSH, TIMOTHY JOHN, geologist; b. L.A., Aug. 9, 1952; s. Edward Francis and Lenore (Beerli) W.; m. Pamela Jeanne Shaffer, Sept. 10, 1977; children: Maureen Elizabeth, Brigid Eileen. BS, UCLA, 1976, MS, 1979. Staff geologist Dept. Natural Resources, Divsn. Geology and Earth Resources, Olympia, Wash., 1980-88; chief geologist, environ. sect. Dept. Natural Resources, Divsn. Geology and Earth Resources, 1988—. Contbr. numerous articles to profl. jours. Recipient Honor by Resolution, Wash. State Ho. of Reps., 1988, Disting. Lectr., N.W. Petroleum Assn., 1990. Mem. Am. Geophys. Union (sec. Pacific N.W. Br. 1986-87, pres. 1987-88), Am. Assn. Petroleum Geologists, Soc. Econ. Paleontologists and Mineralogists (Pacific sect.), Assn. Engring. Geologists. Office: Wash Dept Natural Resources PO Box 47007 Olympia WA 98504-7007

WALSH, WILLIAM, former football coach; b. Los Angeles, Nov. 30, 1931. Student, San Mateo Jr. Coll.; BA, San Jose State U., 1954, MA in Edn., 1959. Asst. coach Monterey Peninsula Coll., 1955, San Jose State U., 1956; head coach Washington Union High Sch., Fremont, Calif., 1957-59; asst. coach U. Calif., Berkeley, 1960-62, Stanford U., 1963-65, Oakland Raiders, Am. Football League, 1966-67, Cin. Bengals, 1968-75, San Diego Chargers, Nat. Football League, 1976; head coach Stanford U., 1977-78; head coach, gen. mgr. San Francisco 49ers, NFL, 1979-89, exec. v.p., 1989; broadcaster NBC Sports, 1989-91; head coach Stanford U., 1992-95; cons. San Francisco Forty Niners, 1996—. Named NFL Coach of Yr., Sporting News, 1981; coached Stanford U. winning team Sun Bowl, 1977, Bluebonnet Bowl, 1978, Blockbuster Bowl, 1993, San Francisco 49ers to Super Bowl championships, 1981, 84, 88; elected to Pro Football Hall of Fame, 1993. Office: Bill Walsh Enterprises Bldg 2 Ste 200 3000 Sand Hill Rd Menlo Park CA 94025

WALSHAW, L. SCOTT, commissioner. BA in Art History, Calif. State U., BA in Econ.; MBA, U. Nev. Sr. examiner Nev. Fin. Instns., Carson City, Nev.; asst. nat. bank examiner Office the Comptr. the Currency, Carson City, Nev.; commr. Fin. Instns., Carson City, Nev., 1983—; past chmn. Am. Coun. State Savs. Supr.; past. chmn., trustee Inst. Supr. Edn.; past mem. state liaison com. Fed. Fin. Instns. Examination Coun. Office: State of Nev Fin Instns Divsn 406 E Second St Carson City NV 89710

WALSTON, RODERICK EUGENE, state government official; b. Gooding, Idaho, Dec. 15, 1935; s. Loren R. and Iva M. (Boyer) W.; m. Margaret D. Grandey; children: Gregory Scott W., Valerie Lynne W. A.A., Boise Jr. Coll., 1956; B.A. cum laude, Columbia Coll., 1958; LL.B. scholar, Stanford U., 1961. Bar: Calif. 1961, U.S. Supreme Ct. 1973. Law clk to judge U.S. Ct. Appeals 9th Cir., 1961-62; dep. atty. gen State of Calif., San Francisco, 1963-91, head natural resources sect, 1969-91, chief asst. atty. gen. pub. rights div., 1991—; spl. dep counsel Kings County, Calif., 1975-76; mem. environ. and natural resources adv. coun. Stanford (Calif.) Law Sch. Contbr. articles to profl. jours.; bd. editors: Stanford Law Rev., 1959-61, Western Natural Resources Litigation Digest, Calif. Water Law and Policy Reporter; spl. editor Jour. of the West. Co-chmn. Idaho campaign against Right-to-Work initiative, 1958; Calif. rep. Western States Water Coun., 1986—; environ. and natural resources adv. coun., Stanford Law Sch. Nat. Essay Contest winner Nat. Assn. Internat. Rels. Clubs, 1956, Stanford Law Rev. prize, 1961; Astor Found. scholar, 1956-58. Mem. ABA (chmn. water resources com. 1988-90, vice chmn. and conf. chmn. 1985-88, 90—), Contra Costa County Bar Assn., U.S. Supreme Ct., Hist. Soc., Federalist Soc., World Affairs Coun. No. Calif. Office: Calif Atty Gen's Office 1300 I St Ste 1720 Sacramento CA 95814-2913

WALTER, JACQUELINE JO, elementary educator; b. Oklahoma City, Mar. 22, 1962; d. Otto Wallace and Geraldine Jo (Tonkin) W.; m. Mark Sasser, Apr. 1, 1980 (dec. Mar. 1996); 1 child, Guthrie Kamil Sasser-Silkwood. BA, Evergreen State Coll, Oly, Wash., 1986; tchg. cert., U. Puget Sound, Tacoma, Wash., 1986. Cert. elem. edn. K-8, endorsement in earth sci. 4-12. Periodicals libr. The Evergreen State Coll., Oly, 1979-80; children's activity dir. Apple Program Cmty. Action Coun., Oly, 1984-86; substitute tchr. local sch. dists., Oly, Lacey, Tumwater, Wash., 1986-88; tchr. Upward Bound Program, Oly, summer 1988, Lincoln Elem. Sch., Oly, 1988-89, Olympic Elem. Sch., Chehalis, Wash., 1989-90, Meadows Elem. Sch., Oly, 1990—; tchr., counselor Thurston County Off-Campus Secondary Sch., Oly, 1981-84. Author philosophy statements sch. documents (Meadows), 1996. Mem. NEA, Wash. Edn. Assn., North Thurston Edn. Assn. (Polit. Action Com. rep. 1993—), Learning Disabilities Assn. Wash. Democrat. Methodist. Office: Meadows Elem Sch 836 Deerbrush Dr Se Olympia WA 98513

WALTER, MICHAEL CHARLES, lawyer; b. Oklahoma City, Nov. 25, 1956; s. Donald Wayne and Viola Helen (Heffelfinger) W. BA in Polit. Sci.,

BJ, U. Wash., 1980; JD, Univ. Puget Sound, 1983. Bar: Wash. 1985, U.S. Dist. Ct. (9th cir. 1985). Ptnr. Keating, Bucklin & McCormack, Seattle, 1985—; instr. Bellevue (Wash.) C.C., 1983—. Mem. ABA, Wash. State Bar Assn., Reporters Com. for Freedom of Press, Seattle-King County Bar Assn., Wash. Assn. Def. Counsel, Seattle Claims Adjustors Assn., Wash. Assn. Mcpl. Attys. Home: 11920 27th Pl SW Burien WA 98146-2438 Office: Keating Bucklin & McCormack 4141 SeaFirst 5th Ave Pla Seattle WA 98104

WALTER, PATRICIA ANN, graphic designer; b. Oshkosh, Wis., Nov. 17, 1948; d. Edgar Harvey and Jeanne Ann (Schermerhorn) W. BS in Secondray Edn., U. Wis., Oshkosh, 1970, postgrad., 1970-71. Graphic artist I and II, U. Wis., 1973-74, 78-80; with DDM & Assocs., advt. publs., Madison, Wis., 1974-76; designer Baxandall Co./Work Force Publs., Oshkosh, 1976-78; freelance graphic artist, Breckenridge, Colo., 1980-83; art dir. Cope Daley McCrea, advt. agy., Breckenridge, 1983-84, Hesdorfer Assocs., advt. agy., Denver, 1987-88, The Clifton Group, Denver, 1988-89; owner, designer The Art Dept., Breckenridge, 1984-87; exec. art dir. Wiesner Pub., Englewood, Colo., 1990-91; owner, mgr. Pat Walter Art & Design, Englewood, 1991—. Office: 4137 S Hazel Ct Englewood CO 80110-4327

WALTERS, DAVID WAYNE, history and government educator, tennis coach; b. Corona, Calif., Aug. 7, 1956; s. Kenneth Richard Walters and Ellen Louise (Masters) Deitrick; m. Shelia Faye Young, June 25, 1977; children: Jeremy Andrew, Joshua Allen. BA, Calif. Poly. U., 1990; MEd, Azusa Pacific U., 1997. Cert. social sci. tchr., Calif. Salesmen United Van Lines, Monrovia, Calif., 1980-84; mktg. dir. Chino (Calif.) Valley Chamber, 1986-89; tchr. Bloomington (Calif.) H.S., 1991-96; asst. prin. Ruth O. Harris Mid. Sch., Bloomington, 1996—. Mem. Calif. Coun. Social Scis. (Student Tchr. of Yr. 1990), Calif. Tchr.'s Assn.

WALTERS, KENNETH C., retired educator; b. Constantine, Mich., Apr. 2, 1913; s. Roy Irvin and Pearl Valentine (Ashbaugh) W. Student, Western Mich. U., 1931-35; MA in Math., MA in Edn., U. Mich., 1948; PhD in Math., U. Fla., 1952. Tchr. coll. level, 1980-96. One man shows, Thousand Oaks, Calif.; author: (novels) Gone with the Winter, 1980, I, the President, 1980, (comedy, play) Irene, The Nurse's Aide, 1980, (instrnl.) Beginners Play Piano in 60 Minutes, 1996; copywright 2,000 songs. Advisor to Bill Clinton. 4-yr. scholar Western Mich. U., 1931-35. Mem. Catalina Art Assn. (pres.), San Fernando Art Club. Home: 2233 N Catalina St Burbank CA 91504

WALTERS, PAUL, protective services official; b. Reading, Eng., 1945; (parents Am. citizens); m. Linda; children: Gary, Michael. Attended, Orange Coast Coll.; BA in Criminal Justice, Calif. State U., Fullerton; MPA, U. So. Calif.; JD, Am. Coll. of law; grad., Calif. Command Coll., 1986, Police Exec. Rsch. Forum, Sr. Mgmt. Inst., Harvard U. From patrol officer to capt. City of Santa Ana (Calif.) Police Dept., 1971-88, chief of police, 1988—. Sgt. USAF. Recipient Appreciation cert. Orange County Bar Assn., 1990, Commendation cert. Orange County Human Rels. Commn., 1990, Orange County Cmty. Policing award, 1994. Mem. Orange County Chiefs of Police and Sheriff's Assn. (mem. exec. com., past pres.). Office: Santa Ana Police Dept PO Box 1981 Santa Ana CA 92702*

WALTHER, LESLIE RAE, nurse administrator; b. Torrance, Calif., Apr. 12, 1962; d. Reinhold A. and Nora M. (Webb) Ullrich; m. Curt Robert Walther, Aug. 23, 1986. BSN, U. So. Calif., L.A., 1986. Clin. med. nurse Mercy Hosp., San Diego, adminstrv. nurse III, asst. mgr. oncology unit, clin. nurse surg.-med. ICU, discharge planner; utilization rev. nurse U.S. Naval Hosp., Yokosuka, Japan. Home: 4680 Zelda Ave La Mesa CA 91941

WALTON, BRIAN, labor union executive; b. London, Dec. 24, 1947; came to U.S., 1966; s. Frank William and Irene Mary (Thornton) W.; (div.); children: Robert, Sarah; m. Deborah R. Baron. BA with honors, Brigham Young U., 1969, MA in Polit. Sci., 1971; JD, U. Utah, 1974. Bar: Calif. 1974, U.S. Dist. Ct. (ctrl., so. and no. dists.) Calif. 1974. Law clk. to Hon. J. Allan Crockett Utah Supreme Ct., 1974; assoc. Reavis & McGrath and predecessor firms, L.A., 1974-82; ptnr. Selvin and Weiner, L.A., 1982-85; exec. dir. Writers Guild Am., West, Inc., L.A., 1985—; teaching asst. Coll. Law, Utah U., 1973, asst. to v.p. of spl. projects, 1971-73, rsch. asst. Coll. Law, 1972-74, tchr., dir. legal skills seminar Coll. Law, 1974. Contbr. articles to law jours. Edwin S. Hinckley scholar. Mem. ABA (antitrust sect.), L.A. County Bar Assn. (antitrust sect., intellectual property and unfair competition sect.), Assn. Bus. Trial Lawyers, Internation Assn. des Avocats du Droit d'Auteur. Office: Writers Guild of Am 7000 W 3d St Los Angeles CA 90048

WALTON, (DELVY) CRAIG, philosopher, educator; b. L.A., Dec. 6, 1934; s. Delvy Thomas and Florence (Higgins) W.; m. Nancy Young, June 6, 1965 (div. May 1977); children: Richard, Kerry; m. Vera Allerton, Aug. 30, 1980; children: Matthew, Ruth, Peter, Benjamin. BA, Pomona Coll., 1961; PhD, Claremont Grad. Sch., 1965. Asst. prof. U. So. Calif., L.A., 1964-68; asst. prof. No. Ill. U., DeKalb, 1968-71, assoc. prof., 1971-72; assoc. prof. U. Nev., Las Vegas, 1972-75, prof., 1975—, chmn. dept. philosophy, 1986-89, dir. Inst. for Ethics and Policy Studies, 1986—. Author: De la recherche du Bien, 1972, Philosophy & the Civilizing Arts, 1975, Hobbes's Science of Natural Justice, 1987; translator: (intro.) Treatise on Ethics (Malebranche), 1992; bd. dirs. Jour. History of Philosophy, 1978—; contbr. articles to profl. jours. V.p. Nev. Faculty Alliance, 1984-86, pres. 95-97; mem. Clark County Sch. Dist. Task Force on Ethics in schs., 1987, 96-97. 1st lt. USAF, 1956-59. Recipient NDEA Title IV fellowship Claremont Grad. Sch., 1961-64, rsch. sabbaticals U. Nev., 1978, 85, 92; named Barrick Disting. scholar U. Nev., 1988. Mem. AAUP (pres. Nev. chpt. 1983-84), Internat. Hume Soc. (exec. com. 1979-81), Am. Philos. Assn., Soc. for Study History of Philosophy (founder and mem. exec. com. 1974-91), Internat. Hobbes Soc., Phi Beta Kappa. Democrat. Home: 6140 Eisner Dr Las Vegas NV 89131-2303 Office: U Nev Inst Ethics Policy Studies 4505 S Maryland Pky Las Vegas NV 89154-9900

WALTON, JAMES STEPHEN, research scientist; b. Kingston-upon-Thames, Eng., Nov. 27, 1946; came to U.S., 1968, permanent resident, 1975, citizen, 1996; s. Ronald Walter and Jean Edna (Hudson) W.; m. Dorcas Ann Graham, July 20, 1974; children: Kirstyn Amy, Lars Timothy. Diploma in Phys. Edn., Leeds U., 1968; MA in Exercise Physiology, Mich. State U., 1970; MS in Applied Mechanics, Stanford U., 1976; PhD in Biomechanics, Pa. State U., 1981. Cert. tchr., Eng. Research asst. Stanford (Calif.) U., 1974-76; tchr. Gaynesford High Sch., Carshalton, Eng., 1969-70; dir. engring. Computerized Biomech. Analysis Inc., Amherst, Mass., 1979; sr. biomed. research scientist Gen. Motors Research Labs., Warren, Mich., 1979-85; applications engring. and product planning mgr. Motion Analysis Corp., Santa Rosa, Calif., 1985-87, v.p. applications engring., 1987-88; pres. 4D Video, Sebastopol, Calif., 1988—; cons. Sci. mag., 1982, 83, Mich. State U., 1984-85; trampoline coach several gymnastics clubs and univ. teams, 1968—. Contbr. articles to profl jours. Mem. Nat. Boy's Club Gt. Britain, London, 1964—. Recipient Research award Nat. Collegiate Gymnastics Assn., 1968-69. Fellow Brit. Assn. Phys. Tng. (hon.); mem. AAAS, Internat. Soc. Biomechanics, Internat. Soc. Biomechanics in Sports, Am. Acad. Forensic Scis., Am. Coll. Sports Medicine, Am. Soc. Biomechanics, Am. Soc. Photogrammetry and Remote Sensing (cert. photogrammetrist), Human Factors Soc., N.Y. Acad. Scis., Soc. Photo-Optical Instrumentation Engrs. (chmn. high speed photography working group, 1994—), Digital Equipment Computer Users' Soc., Sun Users' Group, Mensa, U.S. Gymnastics Fedn., Brit. Trampoline Fedn., Stanford Alumni Club, Sigma Xi. Home: 3136 Pauline Dr Sebastopol CA 95472-9741 Office: 4D Video Ste 4 825 Gravenstein Hwy N Sebastopol CA 95472

WALTON, LINDA GAIL, nursing administrator; b. Long Beach, Calif.; 1 child, Rachel Kathleen Audrey. BSN, Calif. State U., Long Beach, 1968; MS, Calif. State U., L.A., 1982. Asst. nursing dir. L.A. County -USC Med. Ctr., L.A.; dir. nursing SW cluster personal health svcs. County of L.A. Dept. Health Svcs., L.A. Mem. Am. Acad. of Ambulatory Care Nursing. Home: 11365 Walcroft St Lakewood CA 90715-1143

WALTON, ROGER ALAN, public relations executive, mediator, writer; b. Denver, June 25, 1941; s. Lyle R. and Velda V. (Nicholson) W.; m. Helen Anderson. Attended, U. Colo., 1960-63. Govt. rep. Continental Airlines, Denver, 1964-72; dir. pub. affairs Regional Transp. Dist., Denver, 1972-77; pub. affairs cons. Denver, 1977—; res. pub. info. officer Fed. Emergency Mgmt. Agy., 1995-96; pres. Colo. Times Pub. Co. Author: Colorado-A Practical Guide to its Government and Politics, 1973, 6th rev. edit., 1990, Colorado Gambling - A Guide, 1991; columnist The Denver Post newspaper, 1983—, The Rocky Mountain Jour., 1977-81. Mem. U.S. Presdl. Electoral Coll., Washington, 1968; commr. U.S. Bicentennial Revolution Commn., Colo., 1972-76, U.S. Commn. on the Bicentennial of U.S. Constn., Denver, 1985-90, pres.; trustee Arapahoe County (Colo.) Libr. Bd., 1982-86; chmn. lobbyist ethics com. Colo. Gen. Assembly, 1990-91. Republican. Home and Office: 12550 W 2nd Dr Lakewood CO 80228-5012

WALTZ, KENNETH NEAL, political science educator; b. Ann Arbor, Mich., June 8, 1924; s. Christian Benjamin and Luella (Braun) W.; m. Helen Elizabeth Lindsley, June 4, 1949; children: Kenneth L., Thomas E. (dec.), Daniel E. AB, Oberlin Coll., 1948; MA, Columbia U., 1950, PhD, 1954; D honoris causa, Copenhagen U., 1995. Instr., then asst. prof. Columbia U., 1953-57; from assoc. prof. to prof. politics Swarthmore Coll., 1957-66; research assoc. Center Internat. Affairs, Harvard, 1963-64, 68-69, 72; prof. politics Brandeis U., Waltham, Mass., 1966-71, Adlai E. Stevenson prof. internat. politics, 1967-71; Ford prof. polit. sci. U. Calif., Berkeley, 1971-94, Ford prof. emeritus, 1994—; vis. sr. research assoc. King's Coll., U. London, 1986-87; cons. govt. agys.; vis. scholar philosophy London Sch. Econs., 1976-77; vis. scholar Rsch. Sch. Pacific Studies, Australian Nat. U., 1978; vis. scholar dept. internat. politics Beijing U., 1982, 91, 96, Fudan U., Shanghai, 1991, USAF Acad., 1991-92. Author: Man, The State and War, 1959, Foreign Policy and Democratic Politics, 1967, Theory of International Politics, 1979, The Spread of Nuclear Weapons, 1981; co-author: The Spread of Nuclear Weapons: A Debate, 1995; co-author, co-editor: Conflict in World Politics, 1971, The Use of Force, 1971, 4th edit., 1993; mem. edtl. bd. Jour. Strategic Studies, ABC Polit. Sci. Served to 1st lt. AUS, 1944-46, 51-52. NSF grantee, 1968-71; Guggenheim fellow, 1976-77; fellow Woodrow Wilson Center, Internat. Center for Scholars, 1979-80; Heinz Eulau award for best article in the Am. Polit. Sci. Rev., 1990. Fellow Am. Acad. Arts and Scis.; mem. Am. Polit. Sci. Assn. (sec. 1966-67, pres. 1987-88), Internat. Studies Assn. (pres. New Eng. sect. 1966-67), Coun. Fgn. Rels., Am. Acad. Arts and Scis., Phi Beta Kappa. Office: U Calif at Berkeley Polit Sci Dept 210 Barrows Hall Berkeley CA 94720-1950

WALTZ, MARCUS ERNEST, retired prosthodontist; b. Brownsville, Oreg., July 29, 1921; s. Roswell Starr and Eva Ione (Cherrington) W.; m. Constance Jean Elwood, May 31, 1952 (div. Nov. 1973); children: Melody Ann, Martha Louise, Kathryn Jean, Holly Jay, Joy Evalyn, Ross Elwood; m. Shelby Annette Schwab, June 10, 1975. AB, Willamette U., 1942; DMD, U. Oreg., 1945. Cert. Nev. State Bd. Dental Examiners. Practice dentistry Forest Grove, Oreg., 1946-52; practice dentistry specializing in prosthodontics Reno, 1954-95, ret., 1995; councillor Pacific Coast Dental Conf.; pres. Pacific Coast Soc. of Prosthodontics, 1983. Mem. State of Nev. Selective Svc. Appeals Bd., 1970-76, pres., 1974-76. Lt. USN, 1945-46, 52-54, Korea. Decorated Combat Medics award, Battle Stars (oak leaf cluster). Fellow Internat. Coll. Dentistry, Acad. Dentistry Internat.; mem. ADA, Northern Nev. Dental Soc. (pres. 1959), Nev. Dental Assn., Nev. Acad. Gen. Dentistry (pres. 1974), Sigma Chi, Omicron Kappa Upsilon. Democrat. Methodist. Club: Reno Exec. (dir. 1960-66, pres. 1964-65). Lodges: Sigma Tau (pres. 1941-42), Masons (32 degree), Shriners. Home: 715 Manor Dr Reno NV 89509-1944

WALTZER, KENNETH BRIAN, physician, marketing consultant; b. N.Y.C., Feb. 10, 1959; s. Bernard and Blanche Bernice (Zwillenberg) W.; m. Jennifer Ann Mason, June 24, 1990. AB, Harvard U., 1980, MPH, 1985; MD, Baylor U., 1984. Diplomate Am. Bd. Internal Medicine, Am. Bd. Geriatrics. Clin. fellow in medicine Harvard U. Med. Sch., Boston, 1985-88, 89-90; asst. physician Harvard U. Health Svcs., Cambridge, Mass., 1989-90; employee physician So. Calif. Permanente Group, L.A., 1990-92; ptnr. physician So. Calif. Permanente Group, 1992—, regional coord. preventive care, 1995—; dir. med. edn. Kaiser-Permanente West L.A., 1993—; chmn. profl. edn. com. Kaiser-Permanente West L.A., 1993—; ptnr., med. dir. Global Alliance, L.A., 1994—; v.p. Bay Dist. L.A. County Med. Assn., 1995—. Mem. ACP, Calif. Med. Assn., Am. Pub. Health Assn. Democrat. Jewish. Office: Kaiser Permanente 6041 Cadillac Ave Los Angeles CA 90034

WALUCONIS, CARL JOSEPH, English language educator, humanities educator; b. Balt., Oct. 27, 1946; s. George Jospeh and Alberta Mary (Romanouski) W.; m. Susan M. Beardsley, Aug. 30, 1970 (div. June 1975); m. Joan Leslie McBride, June 2, 1979; children: Gabriel, Lilian, Jacob. BA, Towson State U., 1968; MA, Western Wash. State U., 1970. Adj. faculty humanities Bellevue (Wash.) C.C., 1970-75, 83-87; prof. humanities Seattle (Wash.) Ctrl. C.C., 1988—; workshop presenter; keynote spkr. Internat. Symposium on Modern Ednl. Thought, Hunan, Peoples Republic of China, 1996. Author: (novel) Whispers of Heavenly Death, 1980; contbr. chpts. to books on learning in higher edn.; author of short stories and poetry. Recipient award of excellence Wash. Fedn. Tchrs., 1992, Exemplary Status award Wash. C.C. Humanities Assn., 1992. Mem. Am. Assn. Higher Edn., Ctr. for Devel. Undergrad. Edn., Nat. Coun. Tchrs. English, Am. Gen. Liberal Studies. Democrat. Home: 6536 102nd Ave NE Kirkland WA 98033-6922 Office: Seattle Ctrl CC BE 4128 1701 Broadway Seattle WA 98122-2413

WAMBOLT, THOMAS EUGENE, financial consultant; b. Scottsbluff, Nebr., Aug. 9, 1938; s. Andrew, Jr. and Anne (Altergott) W.; B.S., Met. State Coll., Denver, 1976; cert. Total Quality Mgmt. m. Linda E. Shifflett, Oct. 31, 1967; 1 son, Richard Duane King. Pres. Universal Imports Co., Westminster, Colo., 1967-71; printer Rocky Mountain News, Denver, 1967-78; propr., accountant Thomas E. Wambolt Co., Arvada, Colo., 1974-77, fin. cons., 1977—. Baptist. Address: 6035 Garrison St Arvada CO 80004-5345

WAN, YU-JUI YVONNE, educator, scientist; b. Taipei, Taiwan, Sept. 8, 1956; came to U.S., 1979; d. Shin-Chang and Yat-Gen (Shiu) W. BS, Taipei Medical Coll., Taipei, Taiwan, 1979; MSc in pathology, Hahnemann U., 1981, PhD in pathology, 1983. Rsch. asst. electron microscopy and immunochemistry Hahnemann U., Phila., 1980-82; postdoctoral fellow, lab. devel. and molecular immunity NICHD, NIH, Bethesda, Md., 1984-86, staff and sr. staff fellow sect. on cellular differentiation, 1986-89; assoc. morphology core dir. Population Rsch. Ctr. Harbor-UCLA Med. Ctr., Torrance, Calif., 1989-91; co-dir. molecular biology diagnostic lab. Harbor UCLA Med. Ctr., Torrance, Calif., 1989-95; asst. prof. dept. pathology UCLA Sch. Medicine, 1989-95, assoc. prof dept. pathology, 1995—; instr. U. Calif. Riverside, 1993—, adj. assoc. prof. biomed. program, 1996—; sec., bd. dirs. Torrance Chinese Sch., 1996—; cons. NIH, 1992—. Contbr. numerous articles to profl. jours.; expert in retinoic acid, cancer and devel. Mem. exec. com. Population Rsch. Ctr., 1989-92. Recipient Upjohn scholarship award Hahnemann U., 1980-82, Purvis Martin M D award, 1992, Richard Weitzman Rsch. award Faculty Soc./Harbor-UCLA Rsch. and Edn. Inst., 1996, numerous rsch. grants. Mem. The Endocrine Soc., Am. Assn. Cancer Rsch., Am. Soc. Microbiology, Am. Assn. Advancement Sci., Soc. Chinese Bioscientists in Am. Office: Harbor UCLA Medical Ctr Dept Pathology 1000 W Carson St Torrance CA 90502-2004

WANDS, ROBERT JAMES, art educator; b. Denver, June 24, 1939; s. Alfred James and Dorothy L. (Payne) W.; m. Carol Louise Longgrear, Aug. 12, 1966; children; Kirby Lynn Marquez, Cassandra Leann Wands. BFA, Denver U., 1961, MA, 1962-63; postgrad., Western Res. U., 1961-62, Cleve. Art Inst., 1961-62. Instr. Denver U., 1962-63; art prof. U. So. Colo., Pueblo, 1963-96; prof. emeritus U. So. Colo., 1996—; artist in residence YMCA Ctr., Estes Park, Colo., 1972-77; dir. Wands Art Studio and Gallery, Estes Park, 1978—. One-man shows include Western Colo. Ctr. for Arts, Grand Junction, 1974, El Pueblo Mus., Pueblo, 1976, Off Broadway Art Galleries, Pueblo, 1986, The Colo. Gallery, Pueblo, 1994, Sangre de Cristo Art Ctr., Pueblo, 1996, others; group shows include Colo. State Fair Exhibition, Pueblo, 1986, 93, Perry Coldwell Gallery, Ft. Worth, Tex., 1986, Colo. Art Educators Exhibit, Pueblo, 1988, 1989, Colo. Tchrs. Exhibition, Manitou Springs, 1989, Estes Park Art Ctr., 1990, and others; represented in permanent collections U. Denver, Colo. Women's Coll., We. Colo. Ctr. for Arts, U. So. Colo., Dain Bosworth, United Bank, Intrawest Bank, Colo. Nat. Bank, Pueblo Bank & Trust, Pueblo Tchrs. Credit Union, Sangre de Cristo Art Ctr. Bd. dirs. Sangre de Cristo Art Ctr., Pueblo, 1981-87. Home: 1306 W Abriendo Ave Pueblo CO 81004-1006

WANG, CHARLES PING, scientist; b. Shanghai, Republic of China, Apr. 25, 1937; came to U.S., 1962; s. Kuan-Ying and Ping-Lu (Ming) W.; m. Lily L. Lee, June 29, 1963. BS, Taiwan U., Republic of China, 1959; MS, Tsinghua U., Singchu, Republic of China, 1961; PhD, Calif. Inst. Tech., 1967. Mem. tech. staff Bellcomm, Washington, 1967-69; research engr. U. San Diego, 1969-74; sr. scientist Aerspace Corp., Los Angeles, 1976-86; pres. Optodyne, Inc., Compton, Calif., 1986—; adj. prof. U. Calif., San Diego, 1979-90; pres. Chinese-Am. Engr. and Scientists Assn. So. Calif., Los Angeles, 1979-81; program chmn. Internation Conf. of Lasers, Shanghai, 1979-80; organizer and session chmn. Lasers Conf., Los Angeles, 1981-84, program chmn., Las Vegas, 1985. Editor in chief Series in Laser Tech., 1983-91; contbr. articles to profl. jours.; inventor discharge excimer laser. Calif. Inst. Tech. scholar, 1965. Fellow Am. Optical Soc., AIAA (assoc., jour. editor 1981-83). Office: Optodyne Inc 1180 W Mahalo Pl Compton CA 90220-5443

WANG, CHEN CHI, electronics company executive, real estate executive, finance company executive, investments services executive, international trade executive; b. Taipei, Taiwan, Aug. 10, 1932; came to U.S., 1959, naturalized, 1970; s. Chin-Ting and Chen-Kim Wang; m. Victoria Rebisoff, Mar. 5, 1965; children: Katherine Kim, Gregory Chen, John Christopher, Michael Edward. B.A. in Econs., Nat. Taiwan U., 1955; B.S.E.E., San Jose State U., 1965; M.B.A., U. Calif., Berkeley, 1961. With IBM Corp., San Jose, Calif., 1965-72; founder, chief exec. officer Electronics Internat. Co., Santa Clara, Calif., 1968-72, owner, gen. mgr., 1972-81, reorganized as EIC Group, 1982, now chmn. bd., chief exec. officer; dir. Systek Electronics Corp., Santa Clara, 1970-73; founder, sr. ptnr. Wang Enterprises (name changed to Chen Kim Entrprises 1982), Santa Clara, 1974—; founder, sr. ptnr. Hanson & Wang Devel. Co., Woodside, Calif., 1977-85; chmn. bd. Golden Alpha Enterprises, San Mateo, Calif., 1979—; mng. ptnr. Woodside Acres-Las Pulgas Estate, Woodside, 1980-85; founder, sr. ptnr. DeVine & Wang, Oakland, Calif., 1977-83; Van Heal & Wang, West Village, Calif., 1981-82; founder, chmn. bd. EIC Fin. Corp., Redwood City, Calif., 1985—; chmn. bd. Maritek Corp., Corpus Christi, Tex., 1988-89; chmn. EIC Internat. Trade Corp., Lancaster, Calif., 1989—, EIC Capital Corp., Redwood City, 1990—. Served to 2d lt., Nationalist Chinese Army, 1955-56. Mem. Internat. Platform Assn., Tau Beta Pi. Mem. Christian Ch. Author: Monetary and Banking System of Taiwan, 1955, The Small Car Market in the U.S., 1961. Home: 195 Brookwood Rd Woodside CA 94062-2302 Office: EIC Group Head Office Bldg 2055 Woodside Rd Redwood City CA 94061-3355

WANG, COLLEEN IONA, medical association administrator, writer; b. Mpls., Oct. 23, 1953; d. Dillard Wayne and Nova Bardeen (Vaught) Greenwood; m. Hansen Stephen Wang, Aug. 22, 1976; children: Hansen Jeremiah, Nathaniel Stephen. AS in Nursing, Loma Linda U., 1994. Registered nurse, Calif. Staff nurse cardio-thoracic ICU Loma Linda (Calif.) U. Med. Ctr., 1975-77, staff nurse pediats. ICU, 1978-80; staff nurse med.-surg. cardio-thoracic ICU St. Bernardine's Hosp., San Bernardino, Calif., 1977-78; nurse medically fragile, high risk infants, foster care San Bernardino County, Alta Loma, Calif., 1980-87; coord. support group San Bernardino-Riverside County Tourette Syndrome Assn. So. Calif. chpt., Loma Linda, 1987—; med. liaison Tourette Syndrome Assn. So. Calif. chpt., Redlands, 1991—, nursing edn., 1993—; bd. dirs. med. liaison Encino, 1993-96; chmn. we. regional med. conf. Pasadena, 1994; bd. dirs., pres. Encino, 1996—; host chair with Tourette Syndrome Assn. N.Y. Burbank, 1996. Co-author, editor: Tourette Syndrome: A Continuing Education Program for Nurses, 1993, updated, 1996 (Outstanding Chpt. Achievement award Nat. Tourette Syndrome Assn. Inc. 1994); contbr. articles to profl. jours. Vol. instr. gifted and talented math Mariposa Elem. Redlands (Calif.) Sch. Dist., 1990-91; mem. PTA Mariposa Elem., Redlands, Calif., 1992—, vol. instr. first aid Flash Class, 1990-92; presenter-in-svc. edn. Multiple Schs. San Bernardino County, Riverside County, 1992—; mem. PTA Moore Middle Sch., Redlands, 1992, Redlands H.S., 1994—. Mem. Ams. for Nonsmoker's Rights, Tourette Syndrome Assn. (nat. membership Bayside, N.Y. emm. com. underserved area conf. 1986—). Office: Tourette Syndrome Assn So Calif 30733 E Sunset Dr S Redlands CA 92373

WANG, HUAI-LIANG WILLIAM, mechanical engineer; b. Hsinchu, Taiwan, Republic of China, Apr. 4, 1959; came to U.S., 1984; s. Feng-Chi and Hu-Mei (Chou) W.; m. Wen-Pei Chen, June 28, 1986; children: James, Edward. BSME, Tatung Inst. of Tech., Taipei, Taiwan, 1981; MSME, Okla. State U., 1985. Asst. engr. Teco Electric and Machinery Corp., Taipei, Taiwan, 1984; electro-mech. engr. Microsci. Internat. Corp., Sunnyvale, Calif., 1987-89; engr. Lockheed Engring. and Scis. Co., Houston, 1989-91, sr. engr., 1991-92; mgr. mech. engring. Orbiter Tech. Co., Fremont, Calif., 1992; sr. engr. Avatar Sys. Corp., Milpitas, Calif., 1993, Quantum Corp., Milpitas, 1994—. Mem. IEEE, ASME. Office: Quantum Corp 500 Mccarthy Blvd Milpitas CA 95035-7908

WANG, I-TUNG, atmospheric scientist; b. Peking, People's Republic of China, Feb. 16, 1933; came to U.S., 1958; s. Shen and Wei-Yun (Wen) W.; m. Amy Hung Kong; children: Cynthia P., Clifford T. BS in Physics, Nat. Taiwan U., 1955; MA in Physics, U. Toronto, 1957; PhD in Physics, Columbia U., 1965. Rsch. physicist Carnegie-Mellon U., Pitts., 1965-67, asst. prof., 1967-70; environ. systems engr. Argonne (Ill.) Nat. Lab., 1970-76; mem. tech. staff Environ. Monitoring and Svcs. Ctr. Rockwell Internat., Creve Coeur, Mo., 1976-80, Newbury Park, Calif., 1980-84; sr. scientist, combustion engr. Environ. Monitoring and Svcs. Inc., Newbury Park, Camarillo, 1984-88; sr. scientist ENSR Corp (formerly ERT), 1988; pres. EMA Co., Thosand Oaks, Calif., 1989—; tech. advisor Bur. of Environ. Protection, Republic of China, 1985; environ. cons. ABB Environ, 1989-92, ARCO, 1990-91, Du Pont (SAFER Sys. Divsn.), 1992-93, So. Calif. Edison, 1993-95, So. Coast Air Quality Mgmt. Dist., 1995—. Contbr. papers to profl jours. Grantee Bureau of Environ. Protection, Taiwan, 1985. Mem. N.Y. Acad. of Scis., Air and Waste Mgmt. Assn., Sigma Xi. Office: EMA Co Ste 435 2219 E Thousand Oaks Blvd Thousand Oaks CA 91362-2930 *Personal philosophy: The pursuit of science is much like the pursuit of art. It requires one's complete involvement and devotion.*

WANG, WEIQUN, cancer researcher, biochemist; b. Tai-Zhou, Jiang-Su, China, June 20, 1961; s. Min-sun and Houlin (Zou) W.; m. Qianqian Su; children: Sushu, Sophie. BS, Nanjing U., 1983; MS, Nanjing Agrl. U., 1987, PhD, 1990. Rsch. assoc. Biol. Rsch. Inst. Shanghai, 1983-85; asst. prof. in biology Nanjing (China) U., 1990-91; postdoctoral fellow in animal sci. U. Hawaii, Honolulu, 1991-92; jr. rschr. Cancer Rsch. Ctr. Hawaii, Honolulu, 1992—; seminar presenter, spkr. U. Hawaii, Honolulu, 1992, 93, 95, 96, Ann. Biomed. Scis. Symposium, Honolulu, 1994, Third Internat. Conf. on Phytoestrogens, Little Rock, 1995, Second Internat. Conf. on Soy, Belgium, 1996. Contbr. articles to profl. jours. Grantee Am. Heart Assn., 1995—, Am. Assn. Cancer Rsch., 1994, Nat. Cancer Inst., 1992-94, Hawaii Cmty. Found., 1996-97; Mead Johnson award, 1994, Travel award, 1995. Mem. NEA, AAAS, Am. Assn. Cancer Rsch. Home: 707 16th Ave Honolulu HI 96816-4121 Office: Cancer Rsch Ctr Hawaii 1236 Lauhala St Honolulu HI 96813-2424

WANGBERG, ELAINE GREGORY, university administrator; b. Huntington, W.Va., Aug. 4, 1942; d. Bradford Wade and Freda (Smith) Gregory; children: Brigitte, Leslie. BS with highest distinction, U. Minn., 1964; MA, U. Mich., 1970, PhD, 1979. Lang. arts specialist Ann Arbor (Mich.) Pub. Schs., 1971-75, interim dir., 1975-76, staff devel. specialist, 1976-79; vis. prof. Ea. Mich. U., Ypsilanti, 1976-78; asst. prof. U. New Orleans, 1979-82, assoc. prof., dir. rsch. and devel., 1983-85; vice provist for rsch., dean the grad. sch. Calif. State U., Chico, 1986-96; exec. dir. grants and contracts Calif. State U., Monterey, 1996-97, asst. v.p. rsch. and acad. resources, 1997—; bd. dirs., cons. Coun. of Grad. Schs., Washington, 1992-93. Contbr. articles to profl. jours., literacy software. Mem. Western Assn. Grad. Schs. (pres. 1992-93), C. of C., Rotary. Home: 608 Acorn Ct Pacific Grove CA 93950

WANGER, OLIVER WINSTON, federal judge; b. L.A., Nov. 27, 1940; m. Lorrie A. Reinhart; children: Guy A., Christopher L., Andrew G., W. Derek, Oliver Winston II. Student, Colo. Sch. Mines, 1958-60; BS, U. So. Calif., 1963; LLB, U. Calif., Berkeley, 1966. Bar: Calif. 1967, U.S. Dist. Ct. (ea. dist.) Calif. 1969, U.S. Tax Ct. 1969, U.S. Dist. Ct. (cen. dist.) Calif. 1975,

U.S. Dist. Ct. (so. dist.) Calif. 1977, U.S. Dist. Ct. (no. dist.) Calif. 1989, U.S. Ct. Appeals (9th cir.) 1989. Dep. dist. atty. Fresno (Calif.) County Dist. Atty., 1967-69; ptnr. Gallagher, Baker & Manock, Fresno, 1969-74; sr. ptnr. McCormick, Barstow, Sheppard, Wayte & Carruth, Fresno, 1974-91; judge U.S. Dist. Ct. (ea. dist.) Calif., Fresno, 1991—; adj. prof. law Humphreys Coll. Law, Fresno, 1968-70. Fellow Am. Coll. Trial Lawyers, Internat. Acad. Trial Lawyers; mem. Am. Bd. Trial Advs. (pres. San Joaquin Valley chpt. 1987-89, nat. bd. dirs. 1989-91), Am. Bd. Profl. Liability Attys. (founder, diplomate), Calif. State Bar (mem. exec. com. litigation sect. 1989-92, mem. com. on fed. cts. 1989-90), San Joaquin Valley Am. Inn of Ct. (pres. 1992-93), Beta Gamma Sigma. Office: US Dist Ct 5104 US Courthouse 1130 O St Fresno CA 93721-2201

WANGSGARD, CHRIS PRINCE, lawyer; b. Ogden, Utah, July 16, 1941; s. Scott Maughn and Elizabeth (Prince) W.; m. Erica Gwilliam, June 25, 1979; children: Kirk, Sten, Dane. BS, U.S. Military Acad., 1963; JD, U. Utah, 1972. Bar: Utah 1972, U.S. Dist. Ct. (Utah) 1972, U.S. Ct. Appeals (10th cir.) 1972. Commd. 2d lt. U.S. Army, 1963, advanced through grades to capt., resigned, 1969; atty. Van Cott, Bagley, Cornwall & McCarthy, Salt Lake City, 1972-91, ptnr., 1977-91; ptnr. Parsons Behle & Latimer, Salt Lake City, 1991—; adj. prof. Coll. of Law U. of Utah, 1983-87. Mem. Am. Inns of Ct. (Master of the Bench). Office: Parsons Behle & Latimer 201 S Main St Ste 1800 Salt Lake City UT 84111-2218

WANIE, DON, state government official. Dir. finance State of Alaska, 1991—. Office: PO Box 110204 Juneau AK 99822-0204

WARBLE, BONNIE CHERYL, massage therapist, holistic educator; b. El Paso, Tex., Apr. 10, 1957; d. Richard Holmes and Ida Angela (Dominguez) Bowen; m. Mark Robin Payne, Aug. 28, 1977 (div. May 1984); 1 child, Caleb Z. Payne; m. Kent Vonn Warble, Oct. 10, 1989. Student, Southwestern Union Coll., 1974-75, Loma Linda U., 1976-77, Mesa C.C., 1986, Inst. Natural Therapies, 1989-90. Sec. El Paso Natural Gas Co., 1976-77; English tchr. Seoul English Lang. Sch., Korea, 1978-79; E.W. signals comdr. U.S. Army Intelligence, San Antonio, 1982-86; adminstrv. asst. Motorola Inc., Scottsdale, Ariz., 1986-88, Mitchell Internat., San Diego, 1988-90; massage therapist, owner Body Harmony, Mesa, Ariz., 1990—; workshop tchr. in field, 1991—. Author: (poetry) Beyond the Horizon, 1994. Sgt. U.S. Army, 1982-86. Home and Office: 6551 E Preston St Mesa AZ 85215

WARD, ALBERT EUGENE, research center executive, archaeologist, ethnohistorian; b. Carlinville, Ill., Aug. 20, 1940; s. Albert Alan and Eileen (Boston) W.; m. Gladys Anena Lea, Apr. 26, 1961 (div. Apr. 4, 1974); children—Scott Bradley, Brian Todd; m. Stefanie Helen Tschaikowsky, Apr. 24, 1982. AA, Bethany Luth. Jr. Coll., Mankato, Minn., 1961; BS, No. Ariz. U., 1968; MA, U. Ariz., 1972. Lab. asst., asst. archeologist Mus. No. Ariz., Flagstaff, 1965-67; research archeologist Desert Research Inst., U. Nev., Las Vegas, 1968; research archeologist Archeol. Survey, Prescott Coll., Ariz., 1969-71, research assoc., 1971-73; research archeologist Ariz. Archeol. Ctr., Nat. Park Service, Tucson, 1972-73, research collaborator Chaco Ctr., Albuquerque, 1975; founder, dir. archaeol. research program Mus. Albuquerque, 1975-76; founder, dir., 1976-79 pres. bd. dirs. Ctr. Anthrop. Studies, Albuquerque, 1976—; lectr. U. N.Mex. C.C., 1974-77, others; contract archaeol. salvage and research projects in N.Mex. and Ariz. Editorial adv. bd. Hist. Archeology, 1978-80; editor publs. Ctr. Anthrop. Studies, 1978—. Contbr. articles to scholarly jours. Grantee Mus. No. Ariz., 1972, S.W. Monuments Assn., 1973, CETA, 1975-79, Nat. Park Service, 1978-79. Mem. Soc. Am. Archeology, Soc. Hist. Archeology, No. Ariz. Soc. Sci. and Art, Ariz. Archeol. and Hist. Soc., Archeol. Soc. N.Mex., Albuquerque Archeol. Soc., Am. Anthrop. Assn., S.W. Mission Research Ctr., Am. Soc. Conservation Archeology, Soc. Archeol. Scis., Southwestern Anthrop. Assn., N.Mex. Archeol. Council, Living Hist. Farms and Agrl. Mus. Assn. Republican. Lutheran.

WARD, BARRY JOHN, historian; b. West Covina, Calif., Nov. 25, 1964; s. Bobby Joe Ward and Eileen June (McCormick) Allred. BA, U. Pacific, 1988. Loan officer Fin. Ctr. Bank, Stockton, Calif., 1986-88; asst. curator Haggin Mus., Stockton, 1988-91, devel. officer, 1991, spl. projects archivist, 1993-95; asst.-underwriter Trillium Mortgage Bank, Lake Oswego, Oreg., 1992-93; dir. freshman honors program U. Pacific, Stockton, 95—; hist. cons. Duraflame, Inc., Stockton, 1993—; featured speaker Mystic (Conn.) Seaport Mus., 1991, St. Francis Yacht Club, San Francisco, 1992, Nat. Maritime Mus., San Francisco, 1993, Seattle Yacht Club, 1995. Feature writer: The Cen. Valley Harvester, 1994. Bd. dirs. Historic Records Commn., San Joaquin County, Calif., 1992, Cultural Heritage Bd., Stockton, 1994; mem. bd. trustees Land Utilization Trust, 1995. Republican. Home: 3601 Pacific Cir # Price Stockton CA 95211-0110

WARD, CARL EDWARD, research chemist; b. Albuquerque, Oct. 16, 1948; s. Joe E. and Loris E. (Wenk) W.; m. Bertha R. Schloer, June 9, 1970. BS in Chemistry, N.Mex. Inst. Mining and Tech., 1970; MS in Chemistry, Oreg. Grad. Ctr., 1972; PhD in Chemistry, Stanford U., 1977. Research chemist Union Carbide Corp., Charleston, W.Va., 1977-79, Dynapol Corp., Palo Alto, Calif., 1979-80; research chemist Chevron Chem. Co., Richmond, Calif., 1980-85, sr. research chemist, 1986-88; apptd. supr. chemical synthesis Chevron Chem. Co., Richmond, 1988-90; sr. rsch. assoc. Chevron Rsch. & Tech. Co., Richmond, 1990-91, staff scientist, 1991—; staff scientist Chevron Products Co.-Global Lubricants, Richmond, 1997—. Referee Jour. Organic Chemistry, 1983—; patentee in field; contbr. articles to profl. jours. Recipient NSF traineeship, Stanford U., 1972-73; Upjohn fellow, Stanford U., 1976-77; recipient Clarence E. Earle Meml. award, 1995. Mem. Soc. Tribologists and Lubrication Engrs., Nat. Lubricating Grease Inst. (Clarence E. Earle Meml. award 1995), Am. Chem. Soc., Calif. Acad. Sci., N.Mex. Inst. Mining and Tech. Pres. Club, Stanford U. Alumni Assn. Democrat. Home: 1355 Nisich Dr San Jose CA 95122-3061 Office: Chevron Rsch & Tech Co PO Box 1627 Richmond CA 94802-1796

WARD, DAVID CHARLES, police chief; b. Glendive, Mont., Aug. 12, 1948; s. Charles Maxwell and Harriet Cora (Oellermann) W.; m. Valerie Jean Remfert Ward, Mar. 20, 1971; children: Kimberlee, Kyla, Kelley. BA in gen. bus., Mont. State U., 1970. Police officer Billings (Mont.) Police Dept., 1972-79, patrol sgt., 1979-84, detective sergant, 1984-89, patrol lt., 1989-92, asst. chief, 1992-94, police chief, 1994—; cmty. policing task force Mont. Bd. of Crime Control, 1994; criminal hist. improvement task force, 1995. Bd. mem. Rimrock Credit Union, Billings, Mont., 1987—; mem. Mont. PTSA, Billings. Chief Warrant Officer USAR. Mem. U.S. Army Warrant Officers Assn., Internat. Assn. Chiefs of Police, FBI Nat. Acad. Assn., Mont. Assn. Chiefs of Police (v.p. 1993-95, pres. 1995—), Billings Police Protective Assn. (pres., v.p., sec.), Lions Club Internat. (v.p., dir.), Bd. of Private Investigators, Helena, Mont., Atty. Gen. Law Enforcement Adv. Com., Helena, Mont., Police Cmty. Adv. Com., Billings, Mont.; bd. mem. Eastern Coal County DARE. Mem. Evangelical Ch. of N.Am. Office: Billings Police Dept 220 N 27th St Billings MT 59101-1938

WARD, DENNIS FRANCIS, librarian; b. Redwood City, Calif., Dec. 13, 1946; s. Thomas Francis and Dorothy Blanche (Coates) W.; m. Anne Marie Pierce, Feb. 12, 1977; children: Lisa Anne, Matthew Thomas, Patrick Timothy. BA in History cum laude, Santa Clara U., 1969; MLS, U. Calif., Berkeley, 1973. Libr. Kratter Law Libr. U. San Diego, 1973-74; libr. Calif. State Law Libr., Sacramento, 1974-78; sr. libr. Sierra Conservation Ctr., Jamestown, Calif., 1978—; legal ref. instr. Calif. Dept. Corrections, Sacramento, 1989—. Catechist, rite of Christian initiation of adults St. Patrick's Ch., Sonora, Calif., 1983—. With U.S. Army, 1970-72. Edwin Brown fellow U. Santa Clara, 1969-70. Mem. Ctrl. Assn. Librs. (vice chair, chair elect 1984-85, chmn. 1985, 91). Office: Sierra Conservation Ctr 5100 O'Byrnes Ferry Rd Jamestown CA 95327

WARD, JOHN J., bishop; b. Los Angeles, 1920. Student, St. John's Sem., Camarillo, Calif., Catholic U. Am. Ordained priest, Roman Catholic Ch., 1946. Apptd. titular bishop of Bria, aux. bishop Diocese of Los Angeles Roman Cath. Ch., 1963—; vicar gen. Roman Cath. Ch., Los Angeles., 1963—. Office: 3224 Wilshire Blvd Los Angeles CA 90010-2241*

WARD, KATHERINE MARIE, school system administrator; b. Raton, N.Mex., Oct. 31, 1936; d. Robert Lee and Lucille (Gasperetti) Davis; m. Leonard Carlin Ward, Aug. 30, 1953; children: Kathy Ann, Ronnie, Tonia, Jess. BS, Ea. N.Mex. U., 1972, MEd, 1977; edn. specialist, U. N.Mex., 1981. Data reduction tech. phys. sci. lab. N.Mex. State U., Las Cruces, 1955-61; 3d and 4th grade tchr. Clayton Pub. Schs., Amistad, N.Mex., 1972-74; 4th grade tchr. Grants/Cibola County (N.Mex.) Schs., 1974-76, Title I reading tchr., 1976-77, Title I coord., 1977-82, Chpt. I coord., 1982-89, coord. Chpt. I and drug free sch. and cmtys., 1989-90, coord. Chpt. I, drug free, DARE and Title II, 1990-92, coord. Chpt. I, Title I, drug free and Title II, 1992-96, fed. program coord., 1996—. Leader Girl Scouts U.S., Las Cruces, 1966-67, 4-H, Grants, 1977-80; mem., sec. Fighting Back Robert Wood Johnson Found. Prevent Drug and Alcohol Use Grants, 1991-96. Recipient Adminstrn. award N.Mex. Study and Rsch. Coun., 1986, Chpt. I Exemplary award U.S. Dept. Edn., 1988, Merit award DARE program Grants Police Dept., 1991. Mem. Internat. Reading Assn., Malpais Internat. Reading Assn. (pres. 1977-79, Literacy award 1979), N.Mex. Internat. Reading Assn. (Land of Enchantment Book award com. 1983-86). Home: PO Box 188 2100 Ann St Grants NM 87020 Office: Grants Cibola County Schs Grants NM 87020

WARD, MICHAEL, mayor; b. Calif., Apr. 8, 1946; m. Teri Ward; 1 child, Alison. Planning commr. City of Irvine, Calif., 1992, mayor, 1992—; pvt. practice mfg. rep. metal finishing; chmn. El Toro Reuse Planning Authority; bd. dirs. Orange County Fire Authority, Transp. Corridor Agy., Orange County Gixed Guideway Agy., Orange County Transp. Authority, fin. com., Orange County Coun. Govts. Treas. Woodbridge Village Assn., pres., bd. dirs.; vol. girls softball rep. Woodbridge H.S. Athletic Booster Club; com. mem. Woodbridge Softball Tournament, Irvine Softball Classic Tournament Organizing Com.; past pres., coach South Irvine Bobby Sox Orgn. Office: City of Irvine Office of Mayor PO Box 19575 Irvine CA 92713

WARD, MICHAEL ALAN, public information consultant; b. L.A., Oct. 10, 1936; s. Carl Franklin and Verna Grace (Somerton) W.; m. Barbara Lee Maziarz, July 22, 1972; 1 child, Jennifer Lorraine. BA, Calif. State U., L.A., 1959; MS in Journalism, UCLA, 1962. Asst. city editor San Gabriel Valley Tribune, West Covina, Calif., 1965-72; reporter L.A. Times, 1972-93; co-owner Ward Pub. Rels., Upland, Calif., 1993—; lectr. Calif. State U., Fullerton, 1993, Calif. State U., San Bernardino, 1993-94. Mem. Soc. Profl. Journalists. Home: 1582 Maywood Ave Upland CA 91786-2135

WARD, MICHAEL DEAN, marriage and family therapist, minister; b. Oklahoma City, June 28, 1961; s. Jarreld Dean Ward and Billie Jean (Percy) Brindley; m. Raye Ann Roberts, May 19, 1984; children: Jeffrey, David, Jennifer. BA in Psychology cum laude, Bethany Nazarene Coll., 1984; MDiv, Nazarene Theol. Sem., 1990; MA in Counseling Psychology, George Fox U., 1996. Ordained elder Ch. of Nazarene, 1993. Youth pastor Western Oaks Ch., Oklahoma City, 1984-85; assoc. pastor Blue Valley Ch., Overland Park, Kans., 1987-89; dist. assigned min. Oreg. Pacific Dist., Ch. of Nazarene, Portland, 1990—; sr. pastor Restoration Cmty. Ch., Portland, 1990—; exec. dir. Restoration Cmty., Inc., Portland, 1995—. Active cmty. svc., organizer Brentwood-Darlington Cmty., Portland, 1990—. Mem. ACA, Am. Assn. Marriage and Family Therapists. Office: Restoration Cmty Inc PO Box 82562 Portland OR 97282

WARD, MILTON HAWKINS, mining company executive; b. Bessemer, Ala., Aug. 1, 1932; s. William Howard and Mae Ivy (Smith) W.; m. Sylvia Adele Randle, June 30, 1951; children: Jeffrey Randle, Lisa Adele. BS in Mining Engring., U. Ala., 1955, MS in Engring., 1981; MBA, U. N.Mex., 1974; DEng (hon.), Colo. Sch. of Mines, 1994. Registered profl. engr., Tex., Ala. Supr., engr. San Manuel (Ariz.) Copper Corp., 1955-60; mine supt., divsn. supt., gen. supt. of mines, divsn. engr. Kerr-McGee Corp., Oklahoma City and Grants, N.Mex., 1960-66; gen. mgr. Homestake Mining Co., Grants, 1966-70; v.p. ops. Ranchers Exploration & Devel. Corp., Albuquerque, 1970-74; pres., bd. dirs. Freeport Minerals Co., N.Y.C., 1974-85; pres., COO Freeport-McMoRan, Inc., New Orleans, 1985-92, also bd. dirs.; chmn., pres. CEO Cyprus Amax Minerals Co., Englewood, Colo., 1992—; chmn., CEO Amax Gold Inc., 1993—; bd. dirs. Mineral Info. Inst., Inc., Internat. Copper Assn. Contbr. articles to profl. jours. Bd. trustees Western Regional Coun.; bd. dirs. Smithsonian Nat. Mus. Natural History, Nat. Mining Hall of Fame and Mus.; mem. adv. bd. bus. coun. Tulane U. Sch. Bus.; disting. engring. fellow U. Ala., also mem. mining engring. adv. coun., mem. Pres.'s cabinet. Recipient Daniel C. Jackling award and Saunders gold medal Soc. Mining, Metallurgy and Exploration, 1992; inductee Am. Mining Hall of Fame, State of Ala. Engring. Hall of Fame, 1996. Fellow Inst. Mining and Metallurgy (London); mem. NAE, AIME (former sect. chmn., Disting. Mem. award), Am. Mining Congress, Nat. Mining Assn. (dir.), Am. Australian Assn., Mining and Metall. Soc. Am. (pres. 1981-83, exec. com.), Can. Inst. Mining and Metall., NAM (natural resources com.), Internat. Copper Assn. (bd. dirs.), Copper Club, Cherry Hills Country Club (Englewood), Met. Club (Washington), Met. Club (Englewood). Republican. Presbyterian. Office: Cyprus Amax Minerals Co 9100 E Mineral Cir Englewood CO 80112-3401

WARD, PATRICK STANLEY, applications engineer; b. San Bernardino, Calif., Mar. 23, 1971; s. Thomas P. and Rosemary T. Ward. BS in Computer Sci., U. Calif., Irvine, 1992, BS in Math., 1993. Applications engr. Logicon, Inc., San Pedro, Calif., 1993-96, Jet Propulsion Labs., Pasadena, Calif., 1996—. Republican. Roman Catholic.

WARD, R(OBERT) SCOTT, physical therapist; b. Boston, Dec. 17, 1955; s. John Robert and Norma (Harris) W.; m. Diane McVey, Dec. 19, 1983; children: Kristin Anne, Sarah McVey. BA in Phys. Therapy magna cum laude, U. Utah, 1980, PhD in Physiology, 1994. Lic. phys. therapist, Utah. Phys. therapist dept. phys. medicine and rehab. U. Utah Med. Ctr., Salt Lake City, 1980-81, phys. therapist, assoc. dir. burn therapy dept., 1981-84; pres., co-owner Continuing Edn. Assocs., 1982-83; phys. therapist Lewis-Hamblin Health Care, Salt Lake City, 1982-85; clin. instr. Weber State Coll., Ogden, Utah, 1983-84; clin. instr. divsn. phys. therapy U. Utah, 1982-84; phys. therapist Mountain States Hemophilia Ctr. U. Utah Health Scis. Ctr., Salt Lake City, 1987—, staff phys. therapist Intermountain Burn Ctr., 1986—; co-dir. divsn. phys. therapy Coll. Health U. Utah, Salt Lake City, 1990—, clin. asst. prof., 1987-94, asst. prof., 1994—; vis. asst. prof. divsn. phys. therapy Coll. Health, U. Utah, 1984-87; Am. Phys. Therapy Assn. liaison to Am. Burn Assn., 1993—; mem. med. adv. bd. Utah chpt. Nat. Hemophilia Found., 1988—; cons. Hemophilia and AIDS/HIV Network for Dissemination of Info., Nat. Hemophilia Found., 1992—; cons., physiology lab. coord. U. Utah Sch. Medicine, Salt Lake City, 1988—. Abstracter, book reviewer Phys. Therapy; contbr. articles to profl. jours., chpts. to books. Grantee Cutter Biol., 1991, Dumke Found., 1992, J-Tech, 1993, Internat. Assn. Fire Fighters, 1993. Mem. Am. Phys. Therapy Assn. (del. ho. of reps. 1993, chief del. 1994, mem. Task Force on Americans With Disabilities Act 1992-94), Am. Burn Assn. (trustee 1994—, Burn Ctr. verification com. 1995—), Nat. Hemophilia Found. (edn. com. 1992—, regional rep. Mountain States region phys. therapy com., 1989—), Soc. Neurosci., Internat. Soc. Burn Injuries. Office: U Utah Phys Therapy Annex Building # 1130 Salt Lake City UT 84112-1116

WARDEN, PATRICIA STARRATT, writer, actress, composer; b. Boston, Nov. 7, 1943; d. Alfred Byron and Anna (Mazur) S.; m. David W. Warden, Dec. 20, 1995; AB, Smith Coll., 1965; grad. prep. dept. Peabody Conservatory Music, 1961. Teaching asst. Harvard U. Grad. Sch. Bus. Aminstrn., 1965-67; mng. dir. INS Assocs., Washington, 1967-68; adminstrv. asst. George Washington U. Hosp., 1970-71; legal asst. Morgan, Lewis & Bockius, Washington, 1971-72; profl. staff energy analyst Nat. Fuels and Energy Policy Study, U.S. Senate Interior Com., 1972-74; cons., exec. asst. energy resource devel. Fed. Energy Adminstrn., Washington, 1974-75; sr. cons. energy policy Atlantic Richfield Co., 1975-76; energy cons., Alaska, 1977-78; govt. affairs assoc. Sohio Alaska Petroleum Co., Anchorage, 1978-85; legal asst. Hughes, Thorsness, Gantz, Powell and Brudin, Anchorage, 1989-90; writer, media specialist corp. affairs Alyeska Pipeline Svc., Co., 1990-95; legal asst. Hughes Thorsness Powell Huddleston & Bauman LLC, 1996—, pres. Starratt Monarch Prodns., 1986—; Econ. Devel. Commn., Municipality of Anchorage, 1981; actress/asst. dir. Brattle St. Players, Boston, 1966-67, Washington Theater Club 1967-68, Gene Frankel, Broadway 1968-69; actress Aspen Resident Theater, Colo. 1985-86, Ranyevskya (The Cherry Orchard), Anchorage, 1994, Bonfila (SLAVS!), Frau Schmidt (The Sound of Music), Anchorage, 1995; writer and assoc. producer Then One Night I Hit Her, 1983; screenwriter, prodr., actress, composer/pianist A Call to Live, 1995, Marmee (Little Women), 1997; appeared Off-Broadway in To Be Young, Gifted and Black; performed as Mary in Tennessee, Blanche in A Streetcar Named Desire, Stephanie Dickinson in Cactus Flower, Angela in Papa's Wine, Elizabeth Procter in The Crucible, Candida in Candida, Zeuss in J.B., Martha in Who's Afraid of Virginia Woolf, Amy in Dinny and The Witches, as Columbina in Servant of Two Masters, as Singer in Death of Morris Biederman, as Joan in Joan of Lorraine, as Mado in Amadee, as Mrs. Rowlands in Before Breakfast, as the girl in Hello Out There, as Angela in Bedtime Story, as Hannah in Night of the Iguana, as Lavinia in Androcles and the Lion, as Catherine in Great Catherine, as Julie in Lilliom, as First Nurse in Death of Bessie Smith, as Laura in Tea and Sympathy, as Amelia Earheart in Chamber Music; appeared at Detroit Summer Theatre in Oklahoma, Guys and Dolls, Carousel, Brigadoon, Kiss Me Kate, Finnian's Rainbow; asst. to dir. Broadway plays A Cry Of Players, A Way Of Life, Off-Broadway play To Be Young, Gifted, and Black; screenwriter Challenge in Alaska, 1986, Martin Poll Films; asst. dir. Dustin Hoffman, 1974; contbr. articles on natural gas and Alaskan econ. and environ. to profl. jours. Bd. dirs. Anchorage Community Theatre, Alaska Assn. Legal Assts., 1996—; industry rep. Alaska Eskimo Whaling Commn.; mem. Alaska New Music Forum. Mem. Actors' Equity. Episcopalian. Avocations: skiing, horseback riding, biking, hiking. Home: 1054 W 20th Ave Apt 4 Anchorage AK 99503-1749

WARDER, MICHAEL YOUNG, think tank executive; b. Buffalo, June 29, 1946; s. Thomas Grayston and Norma A. (Young) W.; m. Cheryl Lynn Gilkerson, Feb. 8, 1975; children: Maureen, Amy, Michael Jr. BA, Stanford U., 1968. Tchr. Drew Sch., San Francisco, 1968-69; pres. Internat. Re-edn. Found., San Francisco, 1970-73; sec.-gen. Internat. Conf. on the Unity of Scis., N.Y.C., 1974-79; pres., pub. Newsworld Comm., N.Y.C., 1976-69; dir. adminstrn. Heritage Found., Washington, 1980-83; exec. v.p. Ethics and Pub. Policy Ctr., Washington, 1983-84, The Rockford (Ill.) Inst., 1985-95; v.p. devel. The Claremont (Calif.) Inst., 1995—; radio commentator (bi-weekly) Sta. WNIJ-FM NPR Affiliate, DeKalb, Ill., 1991-95, (weekly) KMNY-AM, Pomona, Calif., 1996—; del. leader People to People, USSR, 1991, Rockford Inst., Lithuania, Latvia, Estonia, 1994; del. to London Claremont Inst., 1996, del. Hong Kong, 1997, Claremont Inst., Hong Kong, 1997; spkr. in field. Op-ed columnist The Wall Street Jour., USA Today, The Chgo. Tribune, Chgo. Sun Times, San Francisco Chronicle, St. Louis Post Dispatch, Indpls. Star, 1985—; host/prodr. (TV weekly public affairs show) Stateline Newsmakers, 1990-92; columnist (weekly) Rockford Register Star, 1991-92, Herald Tribune, Pasadena, 1997—. Recipient Silver Dome award Ill. Broadcasters Assn., 1993, 95, 96; grantee Earhart Found., 1988. Mem. Nat. Strategy Forum (mem. rsch. comm.), Phila. Soc., L.A. World Affairs Coun., Sigma Delta Chi. Republican. Office: The Claremont Inst 250 W 1st St Ste 330 Claremont CA 91711

WARDER, WILLIAM, artist; b. Guadalupita, N.Mex., July 23, 1920; s. Julian and Benita (Cordova) W.; m. Sylvia Ann Shipley, May 1, 1942 (div. June 1947); children: Alice O., Benita A., Thomas S.; m. Betty Lorena Caldwell, Oct. 2, 1947; children: Susan J., Rebecca J., Margaret E., Emily A. BFA, U. N.Mex., 1946; postgrad., UCLA, Art Students League, N.Y.C., Taos (N.Mex.) Sch. Fine Arts. Tchr. APS, Albuquerque, 1948-50; artist-in-residence Las Vegas, Espanola & Albuquerque Pub. Schs., 1971-84. Author: Art as an Alternative Approach to Education, Answering an Inner Voice, 1993; writer, prodr., host tv art series How to be an Artist. Chmns. grantee Nat. Endowment for the Arts. Home: 400 Sandstone Dr Rio Rancho NM 87124

WARDLAW, KIM A.M., judge; b. San Francisco, July 2, 1954; m. William M. Wardlaw Sr., Sept. 8, 1984. Student, Santa Clara U., 1972-73, Foothill C.C., Los Altos Hills, Calif., 1973-74; AB in Comm. summa cum laude, UCLA, 1976, JD with honors, 1979. Bar: Calif., U.S. Dist. Ct. (cen. dist.) Calif. 1979, U.S. Dist. Ct. (so. dist.) Calif. 1982, U.S. Dist. Ct. Nev. 1985, U.S. Dist. Ct. (no. dist.) Calif. 1992, U.S. Dist. Ct Mont. 1993, U.S. Dist. Ct. Minn. 1994, U.S. Dist. Ct. (no. dist.) Ala. 1994, U.S. Dist. Ct. (so. dist.) Miss. 1995, U.S. Supreme Ct. Law clk. U.S. Dist. Ct. Cen. Dist. Calif., 1979-80; assoc. O'Melveny and Myers, 1980-87, ptnr., 1987—; presdl. transition team Dept. Justice, Washington, 1993; mayoral transition Team City of L.A., 1995—; bd. govs., vice-chair UCLA Ctr. for Comm. Policy, 1994—; cons. in field. Co-author: The Encyclopedia of the American Constitution, 1986; contbr. articles to profl. jours. Pres. Women Lawyers Pub. Action Grant Found., 1986-87; del. Dem. Nat. Conv., 1992; founding mem. L.A. Chamber Orchestra, 1992—; active Legal Def. and Edn. Fund, Calif. Leadership Coun., 1993—, Blue Ribbon of L.A. Music Ctr., 1993—. Named one of Most Prominent Bus. Attys. in L.A. County, L.A. Bus. Jour., 1995; recipient Buddy award NOW, 1995. Mem. ABA, NOW, Mex.-Am. Bar Assn. L.A. County, Calif. Women Lawyers, Women Lawyers Assn. L.A., L.A. County Bar Assn. (trustee 1993-94), Assn. Bus. Trial Lawyers (gov. 1988—), Orgn. Women Execs., Downtown Women Ptnrs, Chancery Club, Breakfast Club, Hollywood Womens Polit. Com., City Club Bunker Hill, Phi Beta Kappa. Office: US Dist Ct Calif 255 E Temple St Rm 730 Los Angeles CA 90012

WARD-SHAW, SHEILA THERESA, nurse; b. N.Y.C., June 20, 1951; d. Arthur and Cynthia Melba (Mapp) Jenkins; m. Howard J. Ward, Nov. 1977 (div. 1981); m. Thomas N. Shaw, Sept. 1988; children: Tanyatta, Barbara, Thomas. Student, Rockland Community Coll., 1973, U. Nev., Las Vegas, 1984, San Jose State U., 1994-95; BSN, San Jose State U., 1995. Charge nurse Hillcrest (N.Y.) Nursing Home, 1973-74; infirmary nurse St. Agatha's Home for Children, Nanuet, N.Y., 1974-75; temp. bldg. charge nurse Letchworth Village, Thiells, N.Y., 1976; charge nurse New Paltz (N.Y.) Nursing Home, 1977; non secure detention, foster bdg. parent St. Agatha's Home for Children, Nanuet, 1977-79; asst. nursing supr., inservice coord., infection control nurse So Nev. Mental Retardation, Las Vegas, 1979-84; psychiat. nurse II evening duty officer Harbor View Devel. Ctr., Valdez, Alaska, 1987-89; infection control, employee health nurse, unit coord. North Star Hosp., Anchorage, 1989-92; psychiat. nurse, infection control Oak Creek Hosp., San Jose, Calif., 1992-93, writer, producer OSHA precaution tng. staff video, 1993; psychiat. nurse Menlo Park divsn. VA Hosp., Palo Alto, 1992-95, psychiat. nurse Palo Alto divsn., 1995-96, nursing supr. Livermore divsn., 1996—. Campaign worker Nev. Gov. Bryan Dem. Candidate, Las Vegas, 1983-84, Pearson for County Commn. Race, Las Vegas, 1984; pres. Clark County Health Educators, 1983; mem. APIC., 1980-85. Mem. Nat. Assn. Black Nurses, South Bay Black Nurses Assn. (corr. sec. 1996-97), San Jose State U. Students of African Descent Assn. (chmn. pub. affairs, newsletter editor 1995), Sant Jose State U. Coll. Applied Sci. and Art Friends and Alumni Sch. Nursing (editor newsletter 1995-96), Sant Jose State U. Alumni Assn., Assn. for Practioners of Infection Control, Nat. Assn. Black Nurses., San Jose State U. Alumni Assn., San Jose State U. Sch. Nursing Alumni and Friends. Roman Catholic. Office: VA Hosp Palo Alto MPD 3801 Miranda Ave Palo Alto CA 94304-1207

WARE, DAVID JOSEPH, financial consultant; b. Oberlin, Ohio, Dec. 1, 1928; s. Elmer Edwin and Jessie VanStone (Potter) W.; m. Diane Sue Adams, Sept. 12, 1958 (dec. July 1980); m. Mary Ann Spadafora, Aug. 15, 1981; children: Stacey Whitman, Joel Potter. BA, DePauw U., 1950; postgrad., Miami U., 1950-51, 53-54. CFP. Grain trader Glidden Co., Chgo., 1955-57; dept. mgr. Merrill Lynch, San Francisco, 1958-59; br. and regional mgmt. Dean Witter Reynolds, San Francisco, 1969-92; prin. Experts Co., Mill Valley, Calif., 1992—; panelist, guest lectr. U. Calif., Berkeley, 1970-71; instr. Golden Gate U., San Francisco, 1987-89; adj. prof. Coll. Fin. Planning, Denver, 1986-87. Counselor Jr. Achievement, San Francisco, 1963; bd. dirs. Jr. C. of C., Mill Valley, 1964, Joint Powers Authority, Marin County, Calif., 1992-96, Marin County Local Agy. Formation Commn., 1995—; com. chmn. San Francisco C. of C., 1975-78; v.p. Marin County Spl. Districts Assn., Calif., 1995; bd. chmn. Strawberry Dist., Marin County, 1996. Recipient Achievement award Chgo. Bd. of Trade, 1956. Mem. Internat. Assn. Fin. Planners, Assn. Cert. Fin. Planners, Am. Arbitration Assn. (panelist), Nat. Futures Assn. (panelist), N.Y. Stock Exch. (disciplinary com. 1975-92), Olympic Club (chmn. house com. 1987), Phi Beta Kappa, Alpha Delta Sigma. Republican. Home and Office: 248 E Strawberry Dr Mill Valley CA 94941

WARE, JAMES W., federal judge; b. 1946. BA, Calif. Luth. U., 1969; JD, Stanford U., 1972. Assoc. Blase, Valentine & Klein, Palo Alto, Calif., 1972-

77, ptnr., 1977; judge Santa Clara County Superior Ct., U.S. Dist. Ct. (no. dist.) Calif., 1990—; pro bono East Palo Alto Law Project. Active Am. Leadership Forum; mem. bd. visitors Stanford Law Sch.; active Martin Luther King Papers Project. 2nd lt. USAR, 1969-86. Office: US Dist Cts US Courthouse Rm 4150 280 S 1st St San Jose CA 95113-3002

WARE, PEGGY JENKINS, photographer, writer, artist, dancer; b. Santa Monica, Calif., Sept. 6, 1947; d. Stanley Lauder Mahony and Patricia Lou Chapman Covo; m. James Michael Jenkins, Feb. 5, 1966 (div. May 1982) 1 child, Cheryl Denise Jenkins; m. Wiley Neal Ware, Jan. 1, 1988. Dance student of Eugene Loring, U. Calif., Irvine, 1979; dance student Valentina Oumansky, Dramatic Dance Ensemble, North Hollywood, Calif., 1969-72; dance student, Jerry Bywaters Cochran, Dallas, 1972-75; photography student of James Baker, U. Tex., Dallas, Richardson, 1984-86; BA in English, U. Tex. at Dallas, Richardson, 1986, postgrad., 1987. Propr. Mahony/Jenkins & Assocs., Richardson, 1980-82; mng. editor, writer Happenings Mag., Dallas, 1983; prodn. supr. Publishing Concepts, Dallas, 1983-85; mem. book prodn. team David Marquis/Robin Sachs-Corp. for Edn., Dallas, 1990; freelance photographer and artist Dallas, 1984-95, Sedona, Ariz., 1995—; rsch. editor Prin. Fin. Securities, Dallas, 1994; dance rsch. interviewer Simon Semenoff, Ballet Russe, Sol Hurok, Impressario. Exhbns. include Allen St. Gallery, Dallas, 1985, Oak Cliff Art Festival, Dallas, 1991, 500 Inc. Artfest, Dallas, 1992, Sedona Art and Wine Festival, 1993, Good Dog/Bad Dog, Dallas, 1994, Internat. FotoFest, 1994, Lakewood Svc. League, Dallas, 1995, Bath House Cultural Ctr., 1995, Irvine (Calif.) Fine Arts Ctr., 1995-96, Select Art Gallery, Sedona, 1996, Sedona Arts Festival, 1996; transcribing editor: I Am a Teacher, A Tribute to America's Teachers, 1990; photographer: Photo Essay of the Berlin Wall, 1988; contbr. articles and photos to mags. Exec. bd. Friends of Photography, Dallas Mus. Art, 1993-94; bd. dirs., trustee Dancers Unltd. Repertory Co., Dallas, 1990-91; contbr. photographer Lakewood Svc. League, Dallas, 1992; writer, video producer Women's Conf., Women's Caucus for Art, Dallas, 1986. Home: 62 Morning Sun Dr Sedona AZ 86336 Office: PO Box 1891 Sedona AZ 86339-1891

WAREHALL, WILLIAM DONALD, art educator; b. Detroit, July 12, 1942; s. John P. and Helen (Szymanski) W.; 1 child, Eric Ryder; m. Kathryn Coolbaugh, Dec. 21, 1985; 1 child, Elle Lauren, Chloé Ann. BFA, Wayne State U., 1968; MFA, U. Wis., 1971. Instr. of art U. Minn., Mpls., 1971-73; artist in residence L.I. U., 1972-73; asst. prof. of art Calif. State U., San Bernardino, 1973-77; artist in residence U. So. Calif., 1974-75; asst. prof. of art La. State U., Baton Rouge, 1977-78; assoc. prof. art Calif. State U., San Bernardino, 1978-82, prof., 1982—, chair, 1988-90, 95-97; exchange prof. Va. Commonwealth U., Richmond, Va., 1986; artist in residence Buckingham Coll. Art & Design, High Wycomb, England, 1993—. Executed reproduction of 1000 A.D. shipping bottles Inst. of Nautical Archaeology, 1990. Mem. Coll. Art Assn., Am. Crafts Coun., Nat. Coun. Art Adminstrs. Office: Calif State U 5500 University Pky San Bernardino CA 92407-2318

WAREING, THOMAS HIGHTOWER, cardiothoracic surgeon, educator; b. Homestead, Fla., Aug. 26, 1953; s. Thomas Wareing and Nellie Alice (Hightower) Pate; m. Sally Anne Thomas, Dec. 6, 1986; children: Anne Hightower, Thomas Robert, William Patrick. BS, Auburn U., 1975; MD, U. Ala., 1979. Diplomate Am. Bd. Surgery, Am. Bd. Thoracic Surgery. Intern surgery Vanderbilt U. Sch. Medicine, Nashville, 1979-80, jr. resident surgery, 1980-81, rsch. fellow vascular surgery, 1981-82, rsch. fellow cardiac surgery, 1982-83, sr. resident surgery, 1983-85, chief resident surgery, 1985-86, resident cardiac surgery, 1986-88; asst. prof. cardiovascular surgery Jewish Hosp. at Washington U. Med. Ctr., St. Louis, 1988-94; dir. cardiovascular/thoracic surgery Phoenix Meml. Hosp., 1994-95, chmn. dept. cardiovascular and thoracic svcs., 1995—; pvt. practice Scottsdale Cardiovascular Ctr., 1995—; prin. investigator Thoratec Corp., Berkeley, Calif., 1988-94; cons. SESATS V, St. Louis, 1992—. Author: (with others) Complications in Cardiothoracic Surgery, 1990; guest reviewer Annals of Thoracic Surgery, Chgo., 1988—; contbr. numerous articles to profl. jours. Fellow ACS, Am. Coll. Angiology, Am. Coll. Cardiology; mem. AMA, Am. Heart Assn., Assn. for Acad. Surgery, Internat. Coll. Surgeons, Soc. Thoracic Surgeons (moderator circulatory support symposium 1991), So. Thoracic Surg. Assn., Am. Soc. for Artificial Internal Organs. Office: Scottsdale Cardiovasc Ctr 3099 N Civic Center Plz Scottsdale AZ 85251-6903

WARK, ROBERT RODGER, art curator; b. Edmonton, Can., Oct. 7, 1924; žame to U.S., 1948, naturalized, 1970; s. Joseph Henry and Louise (Rodger) W. B.A., U. Alta., 1944, M.A., 1946, LLD (hon.), 1986; A.M., Harvard, 1949, Ph.D., 1952. Instr. art Harvard U., 1952-54; instr. history art Yale U., 1954-56; curator art Henry E. Huntington Library and Art Gallery, San Marino, Calif., 1956-90; lectr. art Calif. Inst. Tech., 1960-91, UCLA, 1966-80. Author: Sculpture in the Huntington Collection, 1959, French Decorative Art in the Huntington Collection, 1961, Rowlandson's Drawings for a Tour in a Post Chaise, 1963, Rowlandson's Drawings for the English Dance of Death, 1966, Isaac Cruikshank's Drawings for Drolls, 1968, Early British Drawings in the Huntington Collection 1600-1750, 1969, Drawings by John Flaxman, 1970, Ten British Pictures 1740-1840, 1971, Meet the Ladies: Personalities in Huntington Portraits, 1972, Drawings from the Turner Shakespeare, 1973, Drawings by Thomas Rowlandson in the Huntington Collection, 1975, British Silver in the Huntington Collection, 1978; editor: Sir Joshua Reynolds: Discourses on Art, 1959. Served with RCAF, 1944-45; Served with RCNVR, 1945. Mem. Coll. Art Assn. Home: 1330 Lombardy Rd Pasadena CA 91106-4120 Office: Huntington Library San Marino CA 91108

WARNAS, JOSEPH JOHN, municipal official; b. Boston, Aug. 31, 1933; s. Augustas and Nellie (Pipiras) W.; m. Bernice Gearlene Sarver (dec. July 1983); children: Robert John, Kimberly Joanne; m. Ruth Ellen Haaker, Jan. 12, 1985. BS in Mgmt., Boston Coll., 1955; MBA in Mgmt., Ariz. State U., 1971. Adminstr. subcontract Gen. Motors, Oak Creek, Wis., 1958-65; mgr. purchasing Sperry Rand Corp., Phoenix, 1965-70; dir. material mgmt. dept. Maricopa County, Phoenix, 1971-93; Mem. Joint Fed., State and local Govt. Adv. Bd GSA, Washington, 1974; mem. exptl. tech. adv. com. Nat. Inst. Govt. Purchasing & GSA, Washington, 1975; guest lectr. Ariz. State U., Tempe, Glendale Community Coll.; instr. seminars Nat. Inst. Govt. Purchasing, Washington. Assoc. editor Aljian's Purchasers Handbook, 4th rev. edit., 1982; contbr. articles to profl. jours. Mem. State Ariz. Purchasing Rev. Bd., Phoenix, 1980, Men's Zoo Aux., Phoenix, 1976—. Served as 1st lt. U.S. Army, 1956-58. Mem. Nat. Inst. Govtl. Purchasing (pres. 1971, bd. dirs. 1972—, sr. del. to Internat. Fedn. Purchasing and Mgmt. 1983), Ariz. State Capitol Chpt. Nat. Inst. Govtl. Purchasing Inc. (founder, pres. 1977), Purchasing Mgmt. Assn. Ariz. (pres. 1973), Sigma Iota Epsilon. Republican. Roman Catholic. Home: 12511 N 76th Pl Scottsdale AZ 85260-4839 *Personal philosophy: To strive, survive and flourish even in the face of adversity.*

WARNER, DAVID P., council member; b. Lodi, Calif., Oct. 24, 1949; m. Kathy Warner; children: Jason, Tara Staal. BA in Polit. Sci. and Adminstrn., Sacramento State Coll., 1971; JD, Humphreys Coll., 1975. Bar: Calif. Pvt. practice; councilman City of Lodi, 1994—; com. mem. San Joaquin County Transp.; mayor pro temp City of Lodi, 1994-95. Rep. No. Calif. Power Assn.; past. pres. Lakewood Sch. Parents Club; active First United Meth. Ch., Lodi, Kids Can't Wait Program; vol. United Way. Mem. San Joaquin County Bar Assn., Masons, Elks, Rotary (past. pres.). Office: PO Box 3006 Lodi CA 95241

WARNER, FRANK SHRAKE, lawyer; b. Ogden, Utah, Dec. 14, 1940; s. Frank D. and Emma (Sorensen) W.; m. Sherry Lynn Clary; 1 child, Sheri. JD U. Utah 1964. Bar: Utah 1964. Assoc. Young, Thatcher, Glasmann & Warner, and predecessor, Ogden, 1964-67, ptnr., 1967-72; chmn. Pub. Svc. Commn. Utah, Salt Lake City, 1972-76; ptnr. Warner & Wikstrom, Ogden, 1976-79, Warner, Marquardt & Hasenyager, Ogden, 1979-82; pvt. practice, Ogden, 1982—. Mem. Utah Gov.'s Com. on Exec. Reorgn., 1978-80. Mem. Utah Bar Assn. (ethics and discipline com. 1981-90), Ogden Gun Club (past pres.). Office: 868 25th St Ogden UT 84401-2611

WARNER, LINDA MARIE, elementary education educator; b. Corvallis, Oreg., June 2, 1950; d. Everett and Bea (Cosner) W.; divorced. BS, U. Oreg., 1972, postgrad. Tchr. fifth grade, phys. edn. Klamath Falls (Oreg.) City Schs., 1974-78; tchr. fourth and fifth grades Klamath County Schs., Klamath Falls, 1978-82, tchr. fifth grade, 1982—; cons. in field; rep. strategic action coms. Klamath County Sch. Dist.; trainer Hands-On elem. sci. through NDN program. Nominated for Christa McAuliffe award, 1989, Catalyst award, 1991. Mem. ASCD. Democrat. Home: 243 Rogers Klamath Falls OR 97601 Office: Shasta Elem Sch 1951 Madison St Klamath Falls OR 97603-5135

WARNER, PAUL WELLMAN, film and theater director, educator; b. Pt. Jefferson, N.Y., Apr. 1, 1962; s. Wellman Joel and Ida Mastri Warner. BA, Harvard U., 1984; MFA, Am. Film Inst., 1992. Artistic assoc. Second Stage Theatre, N.Y.C., 1986-88; instr. acting and directing, artistic cons. L.A. County H.S. for Arts, L.A., 1991—, co-chair film dept., 1995—; film dir. Am. Film Inst., L.A., 1991-92; stage dir. L.A. Theatre Festival, 1993; dir. film Live Entertainment, L.A., 1993-94; lectr. Gail Abbot Enterprises, 1991—; artistic cons. Opera-At-The Acad., N.Y.C., 1988-89; guest dir. Swarthmore Coll., 1996-97; dir. Paul Warner Workshops, Piedmont Coll., Durham, N.C., 1996, Swarthmore Coll., 1996. Dir. (films): In the Name of the Father, 1992, FallTime, 1995; dir stage play Chinese Cabaret 1993; asst. dir. film Glory 1989 (Acad. award 1990), (play) The Wedding Dress, Am. Premiere Theatre 40, 1997, (film) Beyond the Pale, 1997. Bd. dirs. L.A. H.S. for the Arts, 1991—; vol. AIDS Project L.A., 1991—, Comty. Works, L.A., 1993—. Recipient Gold Hugo awrd Chgo. Film Festival, 1993, Gold awrd Houston Film Festival, 1993, 95, Sundance Internat. Film Festival, 1993, Brit. Internat. Film and Video Festival. Mem. Dirs. Guild Am., Harvard-Radcliffe Club. Democrat. Home: 734 S Sycamore Ave Los Angeles CA 90036-4317 Office: Krost/Chaplain Mgmt 9911 W Pico Blvd # PH I Los Angeles CA 90035-2703

WARNER, RICHARD, psychiatrist; b. London, Sept. 6, 1943; s. Reginald William and Kathleen Violet (Garvey) W.; m. Barbara Lucy Salinger, Dec. 9, 1970; children: Adam Paul, David Stephen. MB BS, London U., 1967; MA in Anthropology, U. Colo., 1975. Sr. house officer Littlemore Hosp., Oxford, Eng., 1968-70; registrar Dingleton Hosp., Melrose, Eng., 1971; staff psychiatrist Ft. Logan Mental Health Ctr., Denver, 1971-74, Jefferson County Mental Health Ctr., Denver, 1974-76; med. dir. Mental Health Ctr. of Boulder County, Boulder, Colo., 1976—; clin. prof. psychiatry U. Colo., Denver, 1995—; adj. prof. anthropology U. Colo., Boulder, 1995—. Author: Recovery from Schizophrenia, 1994; co-author: Epidemiology of Mental Disorders: Schizophrenia, 1995; editor: Alternatives to the Hospital for Acute Psychiatric Treatment, 1995. Mem. Royal Coll. Physicians, Am. Psychiat. Assn., Am. Assn. Cmty. Psychiatrists (bd. dirs. 1990-94). Office: Mental Health Ctr Boulder County 1333 Iris Ave Boulder CO 80304

WARNER, ROLLIN MILES, JR., economics educator, real estate broker; b. Evanston, Ill., Dec. 25, 1930; s. Rollin Miles Warner Sr. and Julia Herndon (Polk) Clarkson. BA, Yale U., 1953; cert. in law, Harvard U., 1956; MBA, Stanford U., 1960; cert. in edn. adminstrn., U. San Francisco, 1974. Lic. real estate broker, Calif. Asst. to v.p. fin. Stanford U., 1960-63; instr. history Town Sch., San Francisco, 1963-70; instr. econs. and math., dean Town Sch., 1975—; prin. Mt. Tamalpais, Ross, Calif., 1972-74; dir. devel. Katharine Branson Sch., Ross, 1974-75, instr. econs./math., outdoor edn., computer-aided design; cons. Nat. Ctr. for Fin. Edn., San Francisco, 1986—. Author: America, 1986, Europe, 1986, Africa, Asia, Russia, 1986, Greece, Rome, 1981, Free Enterprise at Work, 1986. Scoutmaster to dist. commr. Boy Scouts Am., San Francisco, 1956—. Recipient Silver Beaver award Boy Scouts Am., 1986, Town Sch. medal Town Sch. for Boys Alumni Coun., 1995. Mem. Math. Assn. Am., Am. Econs. Assn., Assn. for Asian Studies, Grolier Club N.Y., Univ. Club San Francisco, San Francisco Yacht Club (Belvedere, Calif.), Old Oundelian Club (London). Office: Town Sch 2750 Jackson St San Francisco CA 94115-1144

WARNER, THOMAS MARTIN, advertising executive; b. Eugene, Oreg., July 20, 1963; s. George Custer and Ruth (Heuter) W. BS, U. Oreg., 1986. Art dir. Pacific Coast Mktg., Eugene, 1988-90; sales rep., mgr. Newspaper Sales Inc., Eugene, 1992-96; advt. exec. Willamette Valley Publs., Junction City, Oreg., 1996—. Office: Willamette Valley Publs 25027 Dunham Rd Veneta OR 97487-9791

WARNER, VINCENT W., bishop. Bishop Diocese of Olympia, Seattle, 1990—. Office: Diocese of Olympia PO Box 12126 1551 10th Ave E Seattle WA 98102-4298*

WARNER, WALTER DUKE, corporate executive; b. Davenport, Iowa, Feb. 26, 1952; s. Robert Martin and Opal Louise (Gibbons) W.; m. Susan Dee Hafferkamp, Nov. 15, 1975 (div. 1982); 1 child, Natalie. BS, Drake U., 1975. Ops. officer Iowa-Des Moines Nat. Bank, 1975-78; from v.p. ops. to v.p. mktg. and pub. rels. Cen. Savs. and Loan Assn., San Diego, Calif., 1978-84; pres. The Lomas Santa Fe Cos., Solana Beach, Calif., 1985-91; pres., co-founder Ebert Composites Corp., San Diego, 1991—, also bd. dirs.; bd. dirs. Torrey Pines Bank, Solana Beach, Lomas Group Inc., Del Mar, Calif., Madison Valley Properties, Inc., La Jolla, Calif., Nature Preserved of Am. Inc., San Clemente, Calif.; pres., bd. dirs. Regents Pk. Comml. Assns., La Jolla. Bd. dirs. Inst. of the Ams., La Jolla, 1986—, mem. internat. council, 1986—; chmn. bd. dirs., pres. San Diego chpt. Arthritis Found., 1985-87; dir., pres. Gildred Found., Solana Beach, 1986—; founding dir., treas. Golden Triangle Arts Found. Mem. The Exec. Com., Calif. League of Savs. and Loans (mem. mktg. and ops. com. 1982-84), Internat. Forum for Corp. Dirs., Iowa Club of San Diego (founding dir. 1984-85). Republican. Protestant.

WARREN, BACIL BENJAMIN, writer, publisher; b. Leupp, Ariz., Oct. 21, 1915; s. Bacil Augustine and Margaret Adell (Norman) W.; m. Annelle Griffin, May 26, 1938 (dec. Apr. 1990); children: Jannelle Jedd, Bacil Christopher. BA, U. Ariz., 1938. Pub. info. officer U. Ariz., Tucson, 1937-38, Ariz. Dept. Social Security, Phoenix, 1938-42; supr. of continuity Ariz. Broadcasting Sys., Tucson, 1942-45; investigations supr. U.S. Civil Svc. Commn., Tucson, 1945-64; dir. pubs. U.S. Civil Svc. Commn., Washington, 1964-76; pub. Aileen Griffin Press, Tucson, 1976—. Supervising writer: Biography of an Ideal, 1974; author: Young at Any Age, 1978, Ernie, the Fast Horse (children's book), 1979, A History of Errors, 1984, On the Anacoluthe, 1994, Think Left, Look Right, 1996; contbr. articles to profl. jours. Mem. Oral History Assn., Western History Assn., Ariz. Hist. Soc., Internat. Air Passenger's Assn., Royal Oak Soc., Nat. Press Club (founding mem. Found.), Phi Beta Kappa. Democrat. Presbyterian. Office: Aileen Griffin Press 2509 N Campbell Ste 201 Tucson AZ 85719

WARREN, BARBARA KATHLEEN (SUE WARREN), wildlife biologist; b. Appleton, Wis., Oct. 3, 1943; d. Richard Grant and Beatrice Marie (Kath) Henika. Diploma, St. Luke's Sch. Nursing, San Francisco, 1965; AS in Forest Tech., Green River Community Coll., Auburn, Wash., 1976; BS in Wildlife Biology, U. Calif., Davis, 1990. RN, Calif.; cert. merit wildlife program devel. Nurse ICU, Ross (Calif.) Gen. Hosp., 1965-66; nurse emergency room CCU, St. Luke's Hosp., 1966-68; head nurse ICU and CCU, Valley Gen. Hosp., Auburn, 1971-76; forest technician Wash. Dept. Natural Resources, Husum, 1976-77; nurse emergency room ICU, Marshall Hosp., Placerville, Calif., 1977-78; forestry and wildlife biology technician U.S. Forest Svc., Pioneer, Calif., 1978-89, trainer for critical incident stress, Region 5, 1987—, dist. wildlife biologist, 1989-90, career advisor, 1990—; asst. forest wildlife biologist U.S. Forest Svc., 1990-91, asst. dist. ranger, 1991-92. Chmn. outdoor program com. Girl Scouts U.S.A., Sacramento, 1981-85, master planning cons., 1984-86; vol. ARC, Sacramento, 1985—, vol. disaster nurse, 1986—. With Nurse Corps, U.S. Army, 1968-71. Recipient award for outstanding svc. Girl Scouts U.S.A., 1987, Role Model of Yr. award, 1989; Sustained Superior Performance and Host of Yr. award Eldorado Nat. Forest, 1988, Regional Affirmative Action award U.S. Forest Svc., 1990, Outstanding Woman award YWCA, 1991. Democrat. Office: PO Box 559 Prather CA 93651-0559

WARREN, CHRISTOPHER CHARLES, electronics executive; b. Helena, Mont., July 27, 1949; s. William Louis and Myrtle Estelle (Moren) W.; m. Danette Marie Geordge, Apr. 21, 1972; 1 child, Jeffrey Scott. Grad. high sch., Helena, 1967. Electrician Supreme Electronics, Helena, 1972-81; v.p., svc. technician Capital Music Inc., Helena, 1981—; state exec. Amusement & Music Operators Assn. Coun. of Affiliated States, Chgo., 1990-92. Sgt. USAF, 1968-72, Vietnam. Mem. Internat. Flipper Pinball Assn. (sec./treas. 1991-92, pres. 1993-94), Mont. Coin Machine Operators Assn. (pres. 1989-91), Mont. Coin Machine Operators State 8-Ball (chmn.), Valley Nat. 8 Ball Assn. (charter), Amusement and Music Operators Assn. (bd. dirs. 1992—), Ducks Unltd., Eagles, Moose, Rocky Mountain Elk Found. Home: 8473 Green Meadow Dr Helena MT 59602-8312 Office: Capital Music Inc 3108 Broadwater Ave Helena MT 59602-9222

WARREN, DALE ANDREW, publishing company executive; b. Auburn, Wash., July 29, 1949; s. Jack Vernon and Thelma Jean (McMasters) W.; m. Sue May Yee, June 14, 1975 (div. Dec. 1981); 1 child, David; m. Lani Meah Kennard, June 5, 1982; children: Michelle, Eric. AA, Northwest Coll., Kirkland, Wash., 1976, BA, 1977, ThB, 1978; postgrad., Calif. Grad. Sch. Theology, Glendale, 1979, Fuller Sem., Pasadena, Calif., 1979. Cert. tchr., Wash.; lic. minister Harvestime Ch., 1974. Property mgr. Coldwell Banker, Seattle, 1975-79; assoc. pastor Queen Anne Assembly of God, Seattle, 1977-79; youth pastor United Meth. Ch., Woodinville, Wash., 1979; co-owner Fast Foto Co., Tacoma, 1980-84; owner Capital Quest Inc., Tacoma, 1984—, Magic Touch Limosine, Federal Way, Wash., 1989—; mgr. sales Pacific Coast Pub., Tacoma, 1994—; dir. express lane com. Gull Oil Corp., Seattle, 1988-89; chmn. Gull brand Automotive United Trade Orgn, Olympia, Wash., 1987-89. Contbr. articles to local newspapers. Chmn. coll. support Billy Graham Crusade, Seattle, 1975; chmn., founder Fair Tobacco Ordinance Assn., Seattle, 1988; vol. pastor Wash. State Prison, Monroe, 1973-74. Recipient various awards. Mem. Limousine Assn. Wash. (pres. 1990-94), Nat. LImousine Assn., Federal Way C. of C., Tacoma Elks. Christian. Office: Pacific Coast Pub 1551 Broadway Ste 400 Tacoma WA 98402

WARREN, GERALD LEE, retired newspaper editor; b. Hastings, Nebr., Aug. 17, 1930; s. Hie Elias and Linnie (Williamson) W.; m. Euphemia Florence Brownell, Nov. 20, 1965 (div.); children: Gerald Benjamin, Euphemia Brownell; m. Viviane M. Pratt, Apr. 27, 1986. A.B., U. Nebr., 1952. Reporter Lincoln Star, Nebr., 1951-52; reporter, asst. city editor San Diego Union, 1956-61; bus. rep. Copley News Service, 1961-63; city editor San Diego Union, 1963-68, asst. mng. editor, 1968-69, editor, 1975-92; editor San Diego Union-Tribune, 1992-95; ret., editor at large, 1995 (ret.); dep. press sec. to Pres. Gerald Ford, 1974-75. Mem. bd. Pacific coun. internat. policy Eureka Found., Freedoms Found. Lt. (j.g.) USNR, 1952-56. Mem. Am. Soc. Newspaper Editors, Coun. Fgn. Rels., Sigma Delta Chi, Sigma Nu. Republican. Episcopalian. Office: care Copley Press Inc 350 Camino De La Reina San Diego CA 92108-3003*

WARREN, JAMES RONALD, retired museum director, author, columnist; b. Goldendale, Wash., May 25, 1925; stepson H.S. W.; m. Gwen Davis, June 25, 1949; children: Gail, Jeffrey. B.A., Wash. State U., 1949; M.A., U. Wash., 1953, Ph.D., 1963. Adminstrv. v.p. Seattle Community Coll., 1965-69; pres. Edmonds Community Coll., Lynnwood, Wash., 1969-79; dir. Mus. of History and Industry, Seattle, 1979-89; lectr. in field. Author history books; columnist Seattle Post Intelligencer, 1979-92, Seattle Times, 1992-96. Served with U.S. Army, 1943-45, ETO, prisoner-of-war, Germany. Mem. VFW, Am. Ex-POW Assn., 42d (Rainbow) Div. Vets., Rotary, also others. Home and Office: 3235 99th Ave NE Bellevue WA 98004-1803

WARREN, KATHERINE VIRGINIA, art gallery director; b. Balt., Aug. 10, 1948; d. Joseph Melvin and Hilda Virginia (Thiele) Heim; m. David Hardy Warren; 1 child, Gabriel Kristopher Coy; 1 stepchild, Michael Jonathan Warren. BA, U. Calif., Riverside, 1976, MA, 1980. Asst. curator Calif. Mus. Photography, Riverside, 1979-80, acting dir., 1980-81, asst. dir., curator of edn., 1981-84; dir. univ. art gallery U. Calif., Riverside, 1980—. Bd. dirs. Riverside Arts Found., 1980-89, chmn. bd., 1986-88. Marius De Brabant fellow U. Calif., 1977-79. Mem. Am. Assn. Mus., Western Mus. Conf. Office: Art Gallery Sweeney Univ California Riverside CA 92521

WARREN, LARRY MICHAEL, clergyman; b. Bonne Terre, Mo., Nov. 25, 1946; s. Orson Wesley and Ruth Margaret (Stine) W.; m. Bonnie Jean Monk Chandler, Apr. 9, 1983; children: Samantha Chandler, John, Abigail Chandler, Anne, Meredith. BA cum laude, Lincoln U., 1969; MDiv with honors, St. Paul Sch. Theology, Kansas City, Mo., 1976; D of Ministry, San Francisco Theol. Sem., 1987. Ordained elder United Meth. Ch., 1978. Pastor Cainsville (Mo.) United Meth. Ch., 1975-76, Lakelands Parish, Rathdrum, Idaho, 1976-78; assoc. pastor Audubon Park United Meth. Ch., Spokane, Wash., 1978-83; pastor Faith United Meth. Ch., Everett, Wash., 1983-90, Tacoma First United Meth. Ch., 1990-95; co-pastor Renton First United Meth. Ch., 1995—; adviser Kairos Prison Ministry Wash., Monroe, 1984-92; conf. rep. grad. bd. St. Paul Sch. Theology, Kansas City, 1984, 94-96. Contbr. to col. Dialogue Everett Herald, 1984-88. Adviser DeMolay, Spokane, 1979-81; team mem. Night-Walk, inner-city ministry, Spokane, 1979-82; coord. Ch. Relief Overseas Project Hunger Walk, Spokane and Everett, 1981, 85; vol. chaplain Gen. Hosp. Everett, 1983-90; trustee Deaconess Children's Svcs., Everett, 1983-88. Recipient Legion of Honor DeMolay Internat., 1982. Mem. Fellowship of Reconciliation, North Snohomish County Assn. Chs. (v.p. 1985-89), Pacific N.W. Ann. Conf. Bd. Global Ministries (sec. 1988-92, pres. 1993—), Renton Ecumenical Assn. Chs. (pres. 1992-96). Democrat. Home: 121 Monterey Pl NE Renton WA 98056-4032 Office: Renton First United Meth Ch 2201 NE 4th St Renton WA 98056 *Personal philosophy: To seek peace and reconciliation among all people and nations, and with the creation given to us as stewards.*

WARREN, LISA LYNNE, telecommunications executive; b. Düsseldorf, Germany, Nov. 24, 1964; came to U.S., 1966; d. Leonard Lewis and Helen Ruth (Dombrowski) W. BFA, Ohio State U., 1991. Acctg. clk. Paine Webber, N.Y.C., 1984-85; account exec. Advest Inc., N.Y.C., 1986-88; assoc. KCET TV, L.A., 1992-96; multimedia cons. L.A., 1996-97; internet sales engr. Worldsite Networks, Beverly Hills, Calif., 1997—; adv. bd. Multimedia Exec. Stakeholders, L.A., 1996—, KCET/ISI Multimedia Tng. Corp., L.A., 1995—. Mem. Young Calif. Reps., L.A., 1992-94; mem. L.A. Area Spl. Olympics, 1993—. Recipient Spl. Recognition award L.A. Spl. Olympics, 1993, 94; Ohio State U. scholar, 1988-91. Mem. Internet Interactive Comm. Soc., Internet Developers Assn., Women in Film, L.A. Jr. C. of C. (Ann. Project Leader award 1995, 96), Ohio State U. Alumni Club, Pi Sigma Alpha. Office: 8670 Wilshire Blvd Beverly Hills CA 90211

WARREN, RICHARD WAYNE, obstetrician and gynecologist; b. Puxico, Mo., Nov. 26, 1935; s. Martin R. and Sarah E. (Crump) W.; m. Rosalie J. Franzola, Aug. 16, 1959; children: Lani Marie, Richard W., Paul D. BA, U. Calif., Berkeley, 1957; MD, Stanford U., 1961. Intern, Oakland (Calif.) Naval Hosp., 1961-62; resident in ob-gyn Stanford (Calif.) Med. Ctr., 1964-67; practice medicine specializing in ob-gyn, Mountain View, Calif., 1967—; mem. staff Stanford and El Camino hosps.; pres. Warren Mexical Corp.; assoc. clin. prof. ob-gyn Stanford Sch. Medicine. Served with USN, 1961-64. Diplomate Am. Bd. Ob-Gyn. Fellow Am. Coll. Ob-Gyn; mem. AMA, Am. Fertility Soc., Am. Assn. Gynecologic Laparoscopists, Calif. Med. Assn., San Francisco Gynecol. Soc., Peninsula Gynecol. Soc., Assn. Profs. Gynecology and Obstetrics, Royal Soc. Medicine, Shufelt Gynecol. Soc. Santa Clara Valley. Contbr. articles to profl. jours. Home: 102 Atherton Ave Menlo Park CA 94027-4021 Office: 2500 Hospital Dr Mountain View CA 94040-4106

WARREN, SANDRA LYN, quality assurance professional; b. Castro Valley, Calif., Oct. 30, 1958; d. Harold J. and Anneliese (Ohlwerther) W. BS in Phys. Sci., Calif. State U., Hayward, 1993. Supr. escrow dept. Union Bank, Oakland, Calif., 1978-80; mgr. quality assurance Aerotest Ops., Inc., San Ramon, Calif., 1980—. Mem. Am. Nuclear Soc., Am. Soc. for Non-Destructive Testing (level III), Horsemen's Benevolent and Protective Assn., Calif. Thoroughbred Breeders Assn. Republican. Office: Aerotest Ops Inc 3455 Fostoria Way San Ramon CA 94583-1317

WARRICK, BROOKE, marketing executive. MS in Psychology, San Francisco State U. Past mktg. dir. VALS program Stanford Rsch. Inst.; pres. Am. Lives, San Francisco; internat. spkr. in field; condr. tng. sessions. various orgns. Author: The Builder's Guide to Moveup Buyers; prodr. (video) An American Portrait. Office: Am Lives 2512 Filbert St San Francisco CA 94123*

WARSINKE, NORMAN GEORGE, interior designer, sculptor; b. Wichita, Kans., Mar. 4, 1929; s. Norman and Gladys Elmira (Thompson) W.; m. Jackye Lagen, Dec. 20, 1970 (dec. Apr. 1980); children: Marc, Debbie, Brian;

m. Sheila Gay Brockway, Mar. 17, 1984; 1 child, Erica. BA in Journalism, U. Mont., 1949; BA in Art, U. Wash., 1959; postgrad., Kunstwerk Sch., Darmstadt, Germany, 1951. Photographer Western Livestock Reporter, Billings, Mont., 1950-55; interior designer, co-owner Miller-Pollard, Seattle, 1959-84; pvt. practice Bellevue, Wash., 1984—. Pres. N.W. Craft Ctr., Seattle, 1965-70, Seattle Art Commn., 1970. Staff sgt. USAF, 1951-54. Recipient 1st pl. sculpture award Bellevue Art Festival, 1960; named Best all Catagories, Henry Art Gallery, 1966. Home: 3823 94th Ave NE Bellevue WA 98004-1321

WASHBURN, DOROTHY A., entrepreneur; b. Detroit, Oct. 28, 1934; d. Dajad and Mary (Pevrenkjian) Katchadoorian; m. Floyd Donald Washburn, June 23, 1956; children: Mary Susan, Dorothy Ann, Sherry Lynn, Tina Marie. Addressograph and graphotype instr. Burrough's Corp., Detroit, 1952-54; sec. to wire divsn. mgr. Mich. Oven Co., Detroit, 1954-58; exec. sec. to pres. Walch Metal Products, Detroit, 1961-62; sec. and treas. Record Distbrs. Corp., Detroit, 1963-65; fundraiser and trip coord. Edison High Sch., Huntington Beach, Calif., 1972-90; pres. Sunset Sales, Huntington Beach, 1977—. Editor: Annual Assembly Booklet of Ladies Society of the Armenian Church of North America Western Diocese, 1993-96. Campaign com. Gov. George Deukmejian, Doris Allen Campaign com.; chair band boosters Edison High Sch., 1975-77, chair choir boosters, 1988-90; vice chair parish coun. St. Mary Armenian Apostolic Ch., 1994, treas., social and entertainment com., 1993, advisor Ladies Soc., 1994—, advisor cultural com., 1993-96, tchr. Sunday sch., 1992-96; corr. sec. Armenian ch. N.Am., Western Diocese, Ladies Ctrl. Coun., 1985—. Recipient Hon. Svc. award Calif. Congress of Parents, Tchrs. and Students, 1990. Armenian Orthodox.

WASHBURN, JON, artistic director. Founder, condr., artistic dir. Vancouver (B.C., Can.) Chamber Choir, 1971—; condr., artistic dir. Phoenix (Ariz.) Bach Choir, 1992—; condr. CBC Vancouver Orch., Masterpiece Ensemble, Phoenix Chamber Orch., Calgary, Edmonton, Nova Scotia, Phoenix and Vancouver Symphony Orchs.; guest condr. Sata Fe Desert Chorale, Estonian Philharmonic Chamber Choir, L.A. Master Chorale; assoc. composer Can. Music Ctr.; mem. artistic juries Can. Coun.; mem. adv. coun. Internat. Music Festivals in U.S.; tchr. in field. Composer, arranger Rossetti Songs, The Star, A Stephen Foster Medley, Chinese Melodies, Rise!Shine!, Noel Sing We; co-author God's Lamb; gen. choral editor Jaymar Music Ltd. Co-recipient Music award Vancouver Awards; recipient Govt. of Can. Celebration 88 cert. of merit, Queen Elizabeth's Silver Jubilee medal, Disting. Svc. award Assn. Can. Choral Condrs. Mem. Chorus Am. (bd. dirs.). Office: Vancouver Chamber Choir, 1254 W Seventh Ave, Vancouver, BC Canada V6H 1B6

WASHINGTON, JAMES WINSTON, JR., artist, sculptor; b. Gloster, Miss., Nov. 10, 1909; s. James and Lizie (Howard) W.; m. Janie R. Miller, Mar. 29, 1943. Student, Nat. Landscape Inst., 1944-47; D.F.A., Center Urban-Black Studies, 1975. tchr. summer class N.W. Theol. Union Seattle U., 1988. One man shows U.S.O. Gallery, Little Rock, 1943, Foster-White Gallery, Seattle, 1974, 78, 80, 83, 89 (also at Bellevue Art Mus., 89), Charles and Emma Frye Art Mus., Seattle, 1980, 95, Mus. History and Industry, Seattle, 1981; exhibited in group shows Willard Gallery, N.Y.C., 1960-64, Feingarten Galleries, San Francisco, 1958-59, Grosvenor Gallery, London, Eng., 1964, Lee Nordness Gallery, N.Y.C, 1962 Woodside Gallery, Seattle, 1962-65, Foster-White Gallery, Seattle, 1974, 76, 89, 92, Smithsonian Instn., 1974, San Diego, 1977, others; retrospective exhbn. Bellevue Art Mus., Washington, 1989; represented in permanent collections Seattle, San Francisco, Oakland art museums, Seattle First Nat. Bank, Seattle Pub. Libr. YWCA, Seattle, Meany Jr. H.S., Seattle World's Fair, Expo 70 Osaka, Japan, Whitney Mus. Am. Art, N.Y.C.; commd. sculpture: Bird With Covey, Wash. State Capitol Mus., Olympia, 1983, Obelisk with Phoenix and Esoteric Symbols of Nature in granite, Sheraton Hotel Seattle, 1982, Life Surrounding the Astral Alter, In Matrix, owner T.M. Rosenblume, Charles Z. Smith & Assocs., Seattle, 1986, The Oracle of Truth (6 1/2 ton sculpture) Mt. Zion Bapt. Ch., Seattle, 1987, commd. sculptures King County Arts Commn., 1989, Bailey Gatzert Elem. Sch., Seattle, 1991, Twin Eaglets of the Cosmic Cycle (Quincy Jones), 1993, Fountain of Triumph (Bangasser Assocs. Inc.), 1992-93, Seattle, 1993-94, 94-95, Child in Matrix, 1995, Blunt Tail Owl, 1996, Bunny Rabbit and Robbin, 1996. Passover leader Mt. Zion Baptist Ch., Seattle, 1974-87; founder James W. Washington, Jr. and Mrs. Janie Rogella Washington Found. Recipient Spl. Commendation award for many contbns. to artistic heritage of state Gov., 1973, plaque City of Seattle, 1973, plaque Benefit Guild, Inc., 1973, arts service award King County Arts Commn., 1984, cert. of recognition Gov. of Wash., 1984, Editor's Choice award Outstanding Achievement in Poetry Nat. Libr. Poetry, 1993; named to Wash. State Centennial Hall of Honor, Wash. State Hist. Soc., 1984; home and studio designated historic landmark (city and state), 1991. Mem. Internat. Platform Assn., Internat. Soc. Poets (life, awards 1993), Profl. Artists Phila., Masons (33d degree). Home: 1816 26th Ave Seattle WA 98122-3110

WASHINGTON, MAURIECE E., senator; b. Albuquerque, July 25, 1956; s. Willy Edward and Marion (Moore) W.; m. Donna Marie Bartee, Mar. 3, 1978; children: Michelle Denise, Jason Maurice, Angelise Marie, Dennis Bartee. Journeyman electrician IBEW Local 401, Nev., 1978-84; owner D&M Enterprises, Reno, Nev., 1984-86; sales rep. Gierra Office Concepts, Reno, 1986-90, Reno-Gazette Jour., 1990-94; pastor/founder Ctr. of Hope, Sparks, Nev., 1989—; senator Nev. State Senate, Washoe, 1994—, mem. standing com. judiciary, human resources, 1995—, vice chmn. transp. com., 1995—, asst. majority whip, 1997—; adjutant State Bishops Cabinet, Cogie, Nev., 1993; bd. dirs. Safe Harbor Ministries, Sparks, Nev., 1995; mem. steering com. Grace Project, Reno, 1994. Contbr. articles to profl. jours. Mem. Reno Citizens Policy Planning Adv. Commn., 1988; mem. platform com. Washoe County Rep. Ctrl. Com., Reno, 1994; chmn. Nat. Panel on Welfare Reform, 1996. Recipient Outstanding Svc. award Families of Murder Victims and Stop DUI, 1995. Mem. Am. Coun. Young Polit. Leaders (delegation to Israel 1996), Nat. Black Rep. Roundtable (Fredrick Douglass award 1996), Rotary. Office: Nevada State Senate PO Box 1166 Sparks NV 89430

WASHINGTON, REGINALD LOUIS, pediatric cardiologist; b. Colorado Springs, Colo., Dec. 31, 1949; s. Lucius Louis and Brenette Y. (Wheeler) W.; m. Billye Faye Ned, Aug. 18, 1973; children: Danielle Larae, Reginald Quinn. BS in Zoology, Colo. State U., 1971; MD, U. Colo., 1975. Diplomate Nat. Bd. Med. Examiners, Am. Bd. Pediatrics, Pediatric Cardiology. Intern in pediatrics U. Colo. Med. Ctr., Denver, 1975-76, resident in pediatrics, 1976-78, chief resident, instr., 1978-79, fellow in pediatric cardiology, 1979-81, asst. prof. pediatrics, 1982-1988, assoc. prof. pediatrics, 1988-90, assoc. clin. prof. pediatrics, 1990—; staff cardiologist Children's Hosp., Denver, 1981-90; v.p. Rocky Mountain Pediatric Cardiology, Denver, 1990—; chmn. dept. pediatrics Presbyn./St. Luke's Med. Ctr.; mem. admissions com. U. Colo. Sch. Medicine, Denver, 1985-89; chmn., bd. dirs. Coop. Health Care Agreements, 1994—; chmn. dept. pediatrics Presbyn./St. Lukes MC, Denver. Cons. editor Your Patient and Fitness, 1989-92. Chmn. Coop. Health Care Agreements Bd., State of Colo., 1994—; adv. bd. dirs. Equitable Bank of Littleton, Colo., 1984-86; bd. dirs. Ctrl. City Opera, 1989-95, Cleo Parker Robinson Dance Co., 1992-94, Rocky Mountain Heart Fund for Children, 1984-89, Raindo Ironkids, 1989—; nat. bd. dirs. Am. Heart Assn., 1992-96; bd. dirs. Nat. Coun. Patient Info. and Edn., 1992—, Children's Heart Alliance, 1993-94, Regis U., Denver, 1994—, Colo. State U. Devel. Coun., 1994—; trustee Denver Ctr. Performing Arts, 1994—; mem. Gov.'s Coun. Phys. Fitness, 1990-91; bd. trustees Regis U.; mem. Colo. State Bd. Agr., 1996—. Named Salute Vol. of Yr. Big Sisters of Colo., 1990; honoree NCCJ, 1994, Physician of Yr., Nat. Am. Heart Assn., 1995. Fellow Am. Acad. Pediatrics (cardiology subsect.), Am. Coll. Cardiology, Am. Heart Assn. (coun. on cardiovascular disease in the young, exec. com. 1988-91, nat. devel. program com. 1990-94, vol. of yr. 1989, pres. Colo. chpt. 1989-90, Torch of Hope 1987, Gold Heart award Colo. chpt. 1990, bd. dirs. Colo. chpt., exec. com. Colo. chpt. 1987—, grantee Colo. chpt. 1983-84, mem. editorial bd. Pediatric Exercise Scis. 1988—, Nat. Physician of the Yr., 1995), Soc. Critical Care Medicine; mem. Am. Acad. Pediatrics/Perinatology, , Am. Acad. Pediatrics/Pediatric Cardiology (exec. com. 1996—), N.Am. Soc. Pediatric Exercise Medicine (pres. 1986-87), Colo. Med. Soc. (chmn. sports medicine coun. 1993-94), Leadership Denver 1990, Denver Athletic Club, Met. Club, Glenmoor Golf Club. Democrat. Roman Catholic. Home: 7423 Berkeley Cir Castle Rock CO 80104-9278 Office: Rocky Mountain Pediatric Cardiology 1601 E 19th Ave Ste 5600 Denver CO 80218-1255

WASHINGTON-KNIGHT, BARBARA J., military officer, nurse; b. Chgo., July 13, 1948; d. Lewis and Carrie Mae (Randolph) Washington; m. William S. Knight, Aug. 23, 1986; children: Carlton, Carrie. Diploma, St. Elizabeth's Hosp., Chgo., 1971; B in Health Scis., Chapman Coll., 1979, postgrad. CCRN. Commd. lt. USAF, 1972, advanced through grades to lt. col.; asst. head nurse med. unit USAF, Fairfield, Calif., 1976-78, asst. head nurse orthopedic unit, 1978-79; asst. head nurse spl. care unit USAF, Montgomery, Ala., 1979-80, head nurse spl. care unit, 1980-82; head nurse spl. care unit USAF, Riverside, Calif., 1982-85; head nurse surg. ICU USAF, San Antonio, 1985-87, clin. supr. dept. of critical care, 1987-88; head nurse spl. care unit USAF, Riverside, Calif., 1988-91, coord. quality improvement, 1990-92; asst. chief nurse, clin. nurse specialist inpatient svcs. USAF, Tinker AFB, Oklahoma City, 1992-93; clin. nurse post critical care unit Moreno Valley (Calif.) Cmty. Hosp., 1993—. Mem. Soc. Ret. Air Force Nurses, Am. Assn. Critical Care Nurses, Air Force Assn., Air War Coll. Assn., Women's Meml. Found., Nat. Coun. Negro Women, Ret. Officers Assn., Citizen Amb.

WASON, BETTY (ELIZABETH WASON), author; b. Delphi, Ind., Mar. 6, 1912; d. James Paddock and Susan Una (Edson) W.; divorced; 1 child, Ela Bannick; 1 stepson, Lance Hall. BS, Purdue U., 1933. Cert. home economist. Radio cooking sch. hostess WLAP Radio, Lexington, 1934; asst. food editor McCall's mag., 1935; publicist R. C. Mayer, 1936-38; roving corr. Transradio Press, 1938-40; war corr. CBS, Stockholm, spring 1940, Athens, 1940-41; stringer Newsweek, 1940-41; spl. corr. PM Newspaper, N.Y., 1940-41; editor Voice of Am., 1942-43; talk show moderator WINX Radio, 1945-46; prodn. mgr. Am. Forum Mutual Broadcasting of Air, 1947; women's editor Voice of Am., 1948-52; editor food booklets Gen. Foods Corp., 1954; asst. food editor Women's Home Companion, 1955-56; publicist Spanish olive oil Selvage & Lee, N.Y., 1956-68; author, freelance writer, 1968—. Author: Miracle in Hellas, 1943, Cooking Without Cans, 1944, Dinners That Wait, 1954, Language of Cookery, 1956, Travel Fair, 1960, Cooks, Gluttons & Gourmets, 1962, It Takes Jack to Build a House, 1963, Bride in the Kitchen, 1964, Hair Today, Gone Tomorrow, 1964, Art of Vegetarian Cookery, 1965, A Salute to Cheese, 1966, Art of German Cooking, 1967, Mediterranean Cook Book, 1969, Betty Wason's Greek Cook Book, 1969, Cooking to Please Finicky Kids, 1969, Everything Cook Book, 1970, Low Calorie Hors d'Oeuvres, 1970, Giving Cheese & Wine Party, 1974, High Fiber Cookbook, 1975, Remodelling For Pleasure & Profit, 1976, Ellen, A Mother's Story, 1976, (with Ela Bannick) Heads You Lose, 1971; editor: F-Plan Diet, 1982. Mem. Nat. Press Club (mem. libr. com., travel com., new club com., arts com., hon. life mem.), Seattle Freelancers, English Speaking Union, C. S. Jung Soc. Democrat. Episcopalian. Home: 3011 NW 56th St Apt 3 Seattle WA 98107-4249

WASSERMAN, BARRY L(EE), architect; b. Cambridge, Mass., May 25, 1935; s. Theodore and Adelaide (Levin) W.; m. Wilma Louise Greenfield, June 21, 1957 (div. 1971); children: Tim Andrew, Andrew Glenn; m. Judith Ella Michalowski, Apr. 22, 1979. B.A., Harvard U., 1957, M. Arch., 1960. Registered architect, Calif. Assoc. John S. Bolles Assocs., San Francisco, 1960-69; prin. Wasserman-Herman Assocs., San Francisco, 1969-72; prin., dir. Office Lawrence Halprin U Assocs., San Francisco, 1972-76; dep. state architect State of Calif., Sacramento, 1976-78, state architect, 1978-83; prof. dept. architecture, dir. Inst. Environ. Design, Sch. Environ. Design Calif. State Poly. U., Pomona, 1983-87, chair dept. architecture, Coll. Environ. Design, 1988-96; cons. architecture, Sacramento, 1983—; program advisor Fla. A&M U., Tallahassee, 1981-83. Architect Wasserman House, San Rafael, Calif., 1963 ((AIA-Sunset Mag. award of Merit) 1965-66), Anna Waden Library, San Francisco, 1969 ((AIA award of Merit 1970)), Capitol Area Plan, Sacramento, 1977 (Central Valley chpt. AIA Honor award 1979). Recipient Awards citation Progressive Architecture 26th awards Program, 1979. Fellow AIA chmn. architecture in govt. com. (1979). Democrat. Jewish. Home: 6456 Fordham Way Sacramento CA 95831-2218

WASSERMAN, BRUCE ARLEN, dentist, mail order company executive; b. San Mateo, Calif., June 7, 1954; s. Albert and Dunia (Frydman) W.; children: Rachael, Rebecca, Meir, Keren; m. Debra Elizabeth Wright, Apr. 14, 1996. BA in Mass Communications, Winona State U., 1981; DDS, U. Pacific, 1985. Apprentice blacksmith Reuben Syhre Blacksmith Shop, Pine River, Minn., 1973-74; blacksmith Walden Forge, Pine River, 1974-79; founding dir. Team Redeemed, San Mateo, 1984-92; pvt. practice dentistry San Mateo, 1985—; pres. Manx USA, San Mateo, 1987-92. Editor: (quar. jour.) Cycle Lines, 1983-85, Good News, 1984-92, No. Calif. Reporter, 1987-90; assoc. editor: Internat. Communicator, 1988-89, editor, 1990; editor: (mo. jour.) The Mouthpiece, 1986-89; author: A Manual of Uniforming. Cubmaster Boy Scouts Am., San Mateo, 1986-87; fund raiser Am. Lung Assn., San Mateo County, 1986-90, bd. dirs., 1989-94, chmn. Bike Trek, 1989, fund devel. com., 1989-90, membership com., 1991; chmn. Sofitel Bastille Tour, 1992-93. Recipient Disting. Young Alumni award Winona State U., 1988; Mosby scholar Tau Kappa Omega, 1985. Fellow Am. Acad. Dentistry Internat. (editor 1990, mem. bylaws com. 1990), Am. Coll. Dentists, Royal Soc. Health, Pierre Fauchard Acad. (chmn. No. Calif. sect. 1992-95); mem. ADA (cert. recognition 1987, 89, 90), Calif. Dental Assn. (Disting. Svc. award 1987), San Mateo County Dental Soc. (exec. bd. 1986-89, editor 1986-89, Pres. award 1989, Bd. Dirs. award 1987, bd. dirs. 1991-92), Christian Classic Bikers Assn. (Calif. rep. 1983-94), Order Ky. Cols., 78th Fraser's Highlanders Regiment (lt./capt., recruiting officer 1993-94, maj. O.C. 77th Montgomery Highlanders Regiment Headquarters Garrison), Pacific Road Riders (pres., editor 1983-85). Office: 410 N San Mateo Dr San Mateo CA 94401-2418

WASSERMAN, LEW R., film, recording and publishing company executive; b. Cleve., Mar. 15, 1913; m. Edith T. Beckerman, July 5, 1936; 1 dau., Lynne Kay. D (hon.), Brandeis U., NYU. Nat. dir. advt. and publicity Music Corp. Am., 1936-38, v.p., 1938-39, became v.p. charge motion picture div., 1940; now chmn., chief exec. officer, dir., mem. exec. com. MCA, Inc., also chmn. bd., chief exec. officer, dir. subsidiary corps.; now chmn. emeritus; chmn. emeritus Assn. Motion Picture and TV Producers. Trustee John F. Kennedy Libr., John F. Kennedy Ctr. Performing Arts, Jules Stein Eye Inst., Carter Presdl. Ctr., Lyndon Baines Johnson Found.; pres. Hollywood Canteen Found.; chmn. Rsch. to Prevent Blindness Found.; hon. chmn. bd. Ctr. Theatre Group L.A. Music Ctr.; bd. dirs. Amateur Athletic Found. of L.A. (chmn. fin. com.), L.A. Music Ctr. Found.; bd. gov.'s Ronald Reagan Presdl. Found. Recipient Jean Hersholt Humanitarian award Acad. Motion Picture Arts and Scis., 1973. Democrat. Office: Universal City Studios Inc 100 Universal City Plz Universal City CA 91608-1002

WASSERMAN, MARTIN STEPHEN, psychiatrist, psychoanalyst, child psychiatrist; b. N.Y.C., Jan. 19, 1938; s. Sol and Frances (Levine) W.; m. Ann Beckett, June 8, 1963 (div. June 1976); children: Gregory, Eric; m. Francine B. Heller, June, 1976. AB, Columbia Coll., 1959; sr. elective student, Trinity Coll., Dublin, Ireland, 1963; MD, SUNY, Bklyn., 1963. Diplomate Am. Bd. Psychiatry and Neurology (psychiatry, child psychiatry), Nat. Bd. Examiners. Intern Albany (N.Y.) Med. Ctr., 1963-64; resident in psychiatry Kings County Med. Ctr. Hosp., Bklyn., 1964-67, fellow in child psychiatry, 1966-67; fellow in child psychiatry U. Mich. Med. Ctr., Children's Psychiat. Hosp., Ann Arbor, 1969-70; instr. psychiatry SUNY, Bklyn., 1966-67; asst. prof. psychology L.I. U., Southampton, N.Y., 1966-68; asst. prof. psychiatry, asst. dir. student psychiat. svcs. U. So. Calif. Sch. Medicine, L.A., 1970-75, assoc. clin. prof. psychiatry and child psychiatry, 1975—; faculty L.A. Psychoanalytic Soc. and Inst., 1977-88, sr. faculty, 1989—; staff psychiatrist Sisters of Mercy Orphanage, Bklyn., 1965-67, Little Flower House of Providence, Ctr. Forensic Psychiatry, Ypsilanti, Mich., 1969-70; cons. Operation Head Start, San Diego, 1967-69, Oceanside (Calif.) Union Sch. Dist., 1967-69; consulting psychiatrist Ingham County Mental Health Ctr., Lansing, Mich., 1969-70, U.S. Pub. Health Svc., Milan, Mich., 1969-70; field supr. St. John's Seminary, Plymouth, Mass., 1969-70; attending psychiatrist L.A. County Hosp., 1970—; dir. postgrad. edn. L.A. Psychoanalytic Soc. and Inst., 1975-78, sec. bd. dirs., 1977-78, candidates evaluation com., 1990—; dir. rotating six internship U. So. Calif., L.A., 1970-72; profl. staff C.P.C. Westwood Hosp., L.A., 1975-92; examiner Am. Bd. Psychiatry and Neurology, 1977-82, sr. examiner, 1982; cons. MGM Film Corp., Columbia Pictures, 20th Century Fox Films, Carolco Pictures, Jaffe-Lansing Prodns., Indie Prodns., The Landsburg Co., 1975—. Bd. dirs. Anna Freud Found., L.A., 1975-78. Lt. comdr. M.C., USNR, 1967-69. NIMH psychiat. rsch. fellow, 1962; recipient Career Tchr. award NIMH, 1972. Fellow APA; mem. Am. Psychoanalytic Assn., L.A. Psychoanalytic Soc. and Inst., So. Calif. Psychiat. Soc. (chmn. continuing edn. com., program com. 1970-73, counselor 1974-77), Am. Coll. Psychiatrists, Am. Acad. Child Psychiatry, Am. Assn. Psychiatry Clinic for Children, AAUP, Med. Com. for Human Rights. Office: 510 E Channel Rd Santa Monica CA 90402-1342

WASSERMAN, STEPHEN IRA, physician, educator; b. Los Angeles, Dec. 17, 1942; m. Linda Morgan; children: Matthew, Zachary. BA, Stanford U., 1964; MD, UCLA, 1968. Diplomate Am. Bd. Internal Medicine, Am. Bd. Allergy and Immunology. Intern, resident Peter B. Brigham Hosp., Boston, 1968-70; fellow in allergy, immunology Robert B. Brigham Hosp., Boston, 1972-75; asst. prof. medicine Harvard U., Boston, 1975-79, assoc. prof., 1979; assoc. prof. U. Calif.-San Diego, La Jolla, 1979-85, prof., 1985—, chief allergy tng. program Sch. Medicine, 1979-85, chief allergy div. Sch. Medicine, 1985-93, acting chmn. dept. medicine, 1986-88, chmn. dept. medicine, 1988—, Helen M. Ranney prof., 1992—; co-dir. allergy sect. Robert B. and Peter B. Brigham Hosps., 1977-79; dir. Am. Bd. Allergy and Immunology, Am. Bd. Internal Medicine. Contbr. articles to profl. jours. Served to lt. comdr. USPHS, 1970-72, San Francisco. Fellow Am. Acad. Allergy and Immunology; mem. Am. Soc. Clin. Investigation, Assn. Am. Physicians, Am. Assn. Immunologists, Collegium INternationale Allergologicum, Phi Beta Kappa, Alpha Omega Alpha. Office: U Calif Med Ctr 402 Dickinson St Ste 380 San Diego CA 92103-6902

WASSERMANN, FRANZ WALTHER, physician; b. Munich, Sept. 11, 1920; arrived in U.S., 1938; s. Friedrich and Margarete (Schmidgall) W.; m. Sarah Hortense Webster, Jan. 4, 1945; children: Paul F., Margaret Marie Wassermann Bone. BS, U. Chgo., 1941, MD, 1943. Diplomate Am. Bd. Psychiatry and Neurology. Staff psychiatrist VA Hosp., Palo Alto, Calif., 1948-49; psychiatrist Piedmont Psychiatric Clinic, Oakland, Calif., 1949-51, Walnut Creek, Calif., 1951—; staff psychiatrist Agnew (Calif.) State Hosp., 1951-52; staff psychiatrist Contra Costa County Mental Health Svcs., Martinez, Calif., 1952-93, program chief, 1959-65; chief, east county mental health Contra Costa County Mental Health Svcs., Pittsburg, Calif., 1965-89, med. dir., east county mental health, 1989-93. Co-founder Many Hands, Inc., Pittsburg, 1970. Capt. Army M.C., 1944-46, ETO. Fellow APA; mem. No. Calif. Psychiat. Soc. (v.p. 1982-83), East Bay Psychiat. Assn. (pres. 1977-78), Contra Costa Coun. Alcoholism (chmn. 1969-71), Contra Costa County Mental Health Assn. (v.p. 1958), Concord Mount Diablo Trail Ride Assn., AMA. Democrat. Home: 58 Terrace Rd Walnut Creek CA 94596-3462 Office: 177 La Casa Via Ste 2 Walnut Creek CA 94598-3009

WASTERLAIN, CLAUDE GUY, neurologist; b. Courcelles, Belgium, Apr. 15, 1935; s. Desire and Simone (De Taeve) W.; m. Anne Marguerite Thomsin, Feb. 28, 1967; 1 child, Jean Michel. Cand. Sci., U. Liege, 1957, MD, 1961; LS in Molecular Biology, U. Brussels, 1969. Resident Cornell U. Med. Coll., N.Y.C., 1964-67, instr. neurology, 1969-70, asst. prof., 1970-75, assoc. prof., 1975-76; assoc. prof. UCLA Sch. Medicine, 1976-79, prof., 1979—, vice chair dept. neurology, 1976—; chief neurology svc. VA Med. Ctr., Sepulveda, Calif., 1976—; cons. neurologist Olive View Med. Ctr., Sylmar, Calif., 1976—; attending neurologist UCLA Ctr. Health Scis., 1976—. Author, editor: Status Epilepticus, 1984, Neonatal Seizures, 1990, Molecular Neurobiology and Epilepsy, 1992; contbr. articles to med. jours. William Evans fellow, U. Auckland, New Zealand, 1984; recipient N.Y. Neurol. Soc. Young Investigator award, 1965, Rsch. Career Devel. award NIH, 1973-76, Worldwide AES award, 1992, Golden Hammer Teaching award, 1996. Fellow Am. Acad. Neurology; mem. Am. Neurol. Assn., Am. Soc. Neurochemsitry (coun. mem. 1991—), Internat. Neurochemistry, Am. Epilepsy Soc., Royal Soc. Medicine. Office: VA Med Ctr 1611 Plummer St Sepulveda CA 91343

WATANABE, CORINNE KAORU AMEMIYA, lawyer, judge, state official; b. Wahiawa, Hawaii, Aug. 1, 1950; d. Keiji and Setsuko (Matsumiya) Amemiya; m. Edwin Tsugio Watanabe, Mar. 8, 1975; children: Traciann Keiko, Brad Natsuo, Lance Yoneo. BA, U. Hawaii, 1971; JD, Baylor U., 1974. Bar: Hawaii 1974. Dep. atty. gen. State of Hawaii, Honolulu, 1974-84, 1st dep. atty. gen., 1984-85, 87-92, atty. gen., 1985-87; assoc. judge Hawaii Intermediate Ct. Appeals, Honolulu, 1992—. Mem. ABA, Hawaii Bar Assn. Democrat. Office: Hawaii Intermediate Ct Appeals PO Box 2560 Honolulu HI 96804-2560

WATERHOUSE, RUSSELL RUTLEDGE, artist, painter; b. El Paso, Aug. 11, 1928; s. Charles Ewing and Lucille (Rutledge) W.; children: Robert M., Quentin. BS, Tex. A&M U., 1950; postgrad. Art Ctr., Coll. Design, Pasadena, Calif., 1953-56. Art dir. El Paso Nat. Gas Co., 1956-71; adv. dir. Tony Lama Co., El Paso, 1971-72; free-lance painter, El Paso, 1972—. One man shows include El Paso Mus. of Art, Wichita Falls Mus. Art, Americana Mus., Tex. A&M U., Game Conservation Internat. Exhibit, San Antonio, 1982, 84, 86; represented in permanent collections El Paso Mus. Art, Tex. Tech U., Tex. A&M U. Mem. Tex. Commn. Arts and Humanities, 1970-75. Served to 1st lt. U.S. Army, 1951-53. Home and Studio: PO Box 6 Lincoln NM 88338

WATERMAN, MIGNON REDFIELD, public relations executive, state legislator; b. Billings, Mont., Oct. 13, 1944; d. Zell Ashley and Mable Erma (Young) Redfield; m. Ronald Fredrick Waterman, Sept. 11, 1965; children: Briar, Kyle. Student, U. Mont., 1963-66. Lobbyist Mont. Assn. Chs., Helena, 1986-90; senator State of Mont., Helena, 1990—; with pub. rels. dept. Mont. Coun. Tchrs. Math., Helena, 1991-96; mem. edn., pub. welfare and instns. sub-com. fin. and claims commn. Mont. Senate, rev. oversight com., 1995—, post-secondary policy & budget com., 1995—. Sch. trustee Helena (Mont.) Sch. Dist. 1, 1978-90; bd. dirs. Mont. Hunger Coalition, 1985—; pres. Mont. Sch. Bds. Assn., 1989-90; active Mont. Alliance for Mentally Ill (Mon Ami award 1991). Recipient Marvin Heintz award Mont. Sch. Bds. Assn., 1987, Friends of Edn. award Mont. Assn. Elem. and Middle Sch. Prins., 1989, Child Advocacy award Mont. PTA, 1991, award Mont. Alliance for Mentally Ill, 1991. Mem. Mont. Sch. Bds. Assn. (Marvin Heintz award 1988, pres.1989-90), Mont. Elem. Sch. Prins., Mont. Parent, Teacher, Student Assn. (child advocacy award 1991). Democrat. Methodist. Home and Office: 530 Hazelgreen Ct Helena MT 59601-5410 Office: Mt State Senate State Capitol Helena MT 59620

WATERS, J. KEVIN, university administrator, educator; b. Seattle, June 24, 1933; s. Thomas and Eleanor (Hynes) W. BA in Classics, Gonzaga U., Spokane, Wash., 1957; MA in Philosophy, Gonzaga U., 1958; MA Theology, Santa Clara (Calif.) U., 1963; BA in Music, U. Wash., 1964, D of Music Arts, 1970. Asst. prof. Seattle U., 1969-74; vis. prof. Gonzaga-in-Florence, Italy, 1971; assoc. prof. Seattle U., 1974-81, prof. fine arts, 1981-83; prof. music Gonzaga, 1983—, dean arts and scis., 1983-96; sec., trustee Seattle U., 1971-73, presiding officer, bd. dirs., 1975-77; pres. Seattle Archdiocesan Music Com., 1978-80; chmn. Jesuit Inst. For Arts, Washington, 1980—; panelist Nat. Endowment Arts, 1991—. Composer various musical compositions; commn. work Hearst Found. The Mask of Hiroshima, 1970, Job: A Play with Music, 1971, Solemn Liturgy, 1973, Dear Ignatius, Dear Isabel, 1978, Edith Stein, 1987, Psalm 150, 1991, A Child's Psalm of Creation, 1993, In Dulci Jubilo, 1994, Clare Symphony, 1996. Mem. Am. Guild Organists. Home: 502E E Boone Ave Spokane WA 99202-1713 Office: Music Dept Gonzaga U Spokane WA 99258

WATERS, JONATHON HALE, anesthesiologist; b. Cin., July 21, 1959; s. Robert Charles and Frances Elyse (Reynolds) W.; m. Janet Frances Robinson, Aug. 16, 1990; children: Samuel, Sarah. BS, U. Mo., 1981; MD, George Washington U., 1986. Diplomate Nat. Bd. Med. Examiners, Am. Bd. Anesthesiology. Intern Roanoke (Va.) Meml. Hosp., 1987; resident NYU, Bellevue Hosp. Ctr., N.Y.C., 1987-90; staff anesthesiologist Naval Hosp., San Diego, 1990-94, dir. obstetrical anesthesia, 1990-94, coord. dept. rsch., 1990-94; asst. clin. prof. U. Calif., Irvine, 1994—; presenter in field. Contbr. articles to profl. jours. Lt. comdr. USN, 1983—. Decorated Navy Commendation medal. Mem. Internat. Anesthesia Rsch. Soc., Am. Soc. Anesthesiology, Calif. Soc. Anesthesiology, Soc. Obstet. Anesthesia and Perinatology. Office: U Calif Irvine Dept Anesthesiology 101 The City Dr S Orange CA 92868-3201

WATERS, M. BRUCE, engineering technician; b. Houston, Apr. 17, 1950; s. Wayland O. and Snellah G. (Holt) W.; m. Jean H. Sudduth, June 26, 1971; 1 child, Tegan Joy. Student, La. State U., 1968-69, 70-74, U. Houston, 1969, San Jacinto Jr. Coll., Deer Park, Tex., 1969. Engring. aide I La. Dept.

Highways, Baton Rouge, 1971-73, engring. aide II, 1973-74; sta. mgr. Cliff Brice Gas Stas., Boulder, Colo., 1975; mill worker Red Dale Coach, Longmont, Colo., 1975; engring. aide B Colo. Dept. Highways, Boulder, 1975-76, engring. aide C, 1976-91, engring tech. I, 1991—. Blood donor Belle Bonfils, Boulder, Colo., 1975—; mem. Vols. for Outdoor Colo.; sec. Libertarian Party of Boulder County, 1991-93, 95-96. Eagle Scout, 1967. Mem. Nat. Inst. Cert. Engring. Techs., Chpt. C Freewheelers (sec. 1993-95), Am. Motorcyclist Assn., Soc. for Preservation and Encouragement of Barbershop Quartet Singing in Am. Office: Colo Dept Transp 1050 Lee Hill Dr Boulder CO 80302-9404

WATERS, MAXINE, congresswoman; b. St. Louis, Aug. 15, 1938; d. Remus and Velma (Moore) Carr; m. Sidney Williams, July 23, 1977; children: Edward, Karen. Grad. in sociology Calif. State U., L.A.; hon. doctorates, Spelman Coll., N.C. Agrl. & Tech. State U., Morgan State U. Former tchr. Head Start; mem. Calif. Assembly from dist. 48, 1976-91, Dem. caucus chair, 1984; mem. 102nd-104th Congresses from Dist. 35, Calif., 1991—; mem. Banking, Fin., Urban Affairs com., Ho. subcom. on banking, capitol subcom. on banking, employment and tng. subcom. on vets., veterans affairs com. Mem. Dem. Nat. Com., Dem. Congrl. Campaign com.; del. Dem. Nat. Conv., 1972, 76, 80, 84, 88, 92, mem. rules com. 1984; mem. Nat. Adv. Com. for Women, 1978—; bd. dirs. TransAfrica Found., Nat. Women's Polit. Caucus, Ctr. Nat. Policy, Clara Elizabeth Jackson Carter Found. Spellman Coll., Nat. Minority AIDS Project, Women for a Meaningful Summit, Nat. Coun. Negro Women, Black Women's Agenda; founder Black Women's Forum. Office: US Ho of Reps 330 Cannon HOB Washington DC 20515*

WATKINS, CHARLES REYNOLDS, medical equipment company executive; b. San Diego, Oct. 28, 1951; s. Charles R. and Edith A. (Muff) W.; children: Charles Devin, Gregory Michael. BS, Lewis and Clark Coll., 1974; postgrad., U. Portland, 1976. Internat. salesman Hyster Co., Portland, Oreg., 1975-80, Hinds Internat. Corp., Portland, 1980-83; mgr. internat. sales Wade Mfg. Co., Tualatin, Oreg., 1983-84; regional sales mgr. U.S. Surg., Inc., Norwalk, Conn., 1984-86; nat. sales mgr. NeuroCom Internat., Inc., Clackamas, Oreg., 1986-87; pres. Wave Form Systems, Inc., Portland, 1987—. Bd. dirs. Portland World Affairs Coun., 1980. Mem. Am. Soc. Laser Medicine and Surgery, Am. Fertility Soc., Am. Assn. Gynecol. Laparoscopists, Portland City Club. Republican. Office: Wave Form Systems Inc PO Box 3195 Portland OR 97208-3195

WATKINS, EUGENE LEONARD, surgeon, educator; b. Worcester, Mass., Jan. 4, 1918; s. George Joseph and Marcella Katherine (Akels) W.; A.B. with honors in biology, Clark U., 1940; M.D. (Hood scholar), Harvard U., 1943; m. Victoria Peake, Sept. 23, 1944; children—Roswell Peake, Priscilla Avery. Intern, Roosevelt Hosp., N.Y.C., 1944; resident in surgery, 1944-46, sr. asst. resident in surgery, 1948-49, resident surgery, 1949-50; fellow in surgery, clin. research fellow, Mass. Gen. Hosp., Boston, 1947-48; practice medicine specializing in surgery, N.Y.C., 1950-56, Morristown, N.J., 1950—, Denville, N.J., 1956-85, Boonton, N.J., 1961-85; mem. staff Morristown Meml. Hosp., 1950, vice chmn. dept. surgery, 1974-77, chmn., 1959-61, mem. corp.; cons. surgeon St. Clare's Hosp., Denville, N.J., Riverside Hosp., Boonton, N.J., Community Med. Center, Morristown; courtesy surg. staff St. Luke's-Roosevelt Hosp. Center, N.Y.C.; asst. clin. prof. surgery Rutgers U. Coll. Medicine and Dentistry, New Brunswick, N.J., 1972-85; asst. clin. prof. surgery Columbia Coll. Phys. and Surg., 1985—; v.p. chmn. fin. com. Morristown Bd. Health, 1954-56. Served to 1st lt., AUS, 1946. Diplomate Am. Bd. Surgery. Fellow ACS (chmn. N.J. Adv. Com. 1965-77, chmn. N.J. State com. Trauma, 1960); mem. N.J., Morris County med. socs., AMA, Soc. Surgeons N.J. (1st v.p. 1982, pres. 1983), Am. Thoracic Soc., AAAS, Harvard Med. Soc. N.Y. (pres. 1960-61), West Side Med. Soc., Roosevelt Hosp. Alumni Assn. Republican. Presbyterian. Clubs: Harvard (N.Y.C.), Morristown, Morristown Field. Development spring-loop surg. suture holder. Home: PO Box 1037 Buffalo WY 82834-1037

WATKINS, GLORIA THOMAS, health care worker; b. Memphis, May 25, 1937; d. James Victor and Louise (Bowers) Thomas; m. William Edward Carnes, Dec. 2, 1953 (div. May 1972); children: Denzil Carnes (dec.), Vincent Carnes, Francesca Brande, Trent Carnes; m. Calvin Floyd Watkins, June 17, 1972. BS, Calif. State U., 1978. Wirer, solderer Douglas Aircraft, Ocean Park, Calif., 1962; teller Bank Am., Westwood, Calif., 1962-63, City Nat. Bank, Beverly Hills, Calif., 1963-64; tchr. Project Headstart Delta Sigma Theta, L.A., 1964-73; instr. Southwest Industries, Gardena, Calif., 1974-76; care provider Los Angeles County Sys., L.A., 1979—. Author: Definitions of Common Words and Phrases in The King James Bible, 1994; inventor Back Zipper Opener, 1995. Home: 1918 W 81st St Los Angeles CA 90047-2639

WATKINS, JOHN GOODRICH, psychologist, educator; b. Salmon, Idaho, Mar. 17, 1913; s. John Thomas and Ethel (Goodrich) W.; m. Evelyn Elizabeth Browne, Aug. 21, 1932; m. Doris Wade Tomlinson, June 8, 1946; m. Helen Verner Huth, Dec. 28, 1971; children: John Dean, Jonette Alison, Richard Douglas, Gregory Keith, Rodney Philip, Karen Stroobants, Marvin R. Huth. Student, Coll. Idaho, 1929-30, 31-32; BS, U. Idaho, 1933, MS, 1936; PhD, Columbia U., 1941. Instr. high sch. Idaho, 1933-39; faculty Ithaca Coll., 1940-41, Auburn U., 1941-43; assoc. prof. Wash. State Coll., 1946-49; chief clin. psychologist U.S. Army Welch Hosp., 1945-46; clin. psychologist VA Hosp., American Lake, Wash., 1949-50; chief clin. psychologist VA Mental Hygiene Clinic, Chgo., 1950-53, VA Hosp., Portland, Oreg., 1953-64; prof. psychology U. Mont., Missoula, 1964-84; prof. emeritus U. Mont., 1984—, dir. clin. tng., 1964-80; lectr. numerous univs.; clin. asso. U. Oreg. Med. Sch., 1957; pres. Am. Bd. Examiners in Psychol. Hypnosis, 1960-62. Author: Objective Measurement of Instrumental Performance, 1942, Hypnotherapy of War Neuroses, 1949, General Psychotherapy, 1960, The Therapeutic Self, 1978, (with others) We, The Divided Self, 1982, Hypnotherapeutic Techniques, 1987, Hypnoanalytic Techniques, 1992; contbr. articles to profl. jours. Mem. Internat. Soc. Clin. and Exptl. Hypnosis (co-founder, pres. 1965-67, recipient awards 1960-65), Soc. Clin. and Exptl. Hypnosis (pres. 1969-71, Morton Prince award), Am. Psychol. Assn. (pres. divsn. 30 1975-76, recipient award 1993), Sigma Xi, Phi Delta Kappa. Home and Office: 413 Evans Ave Missoula MT 59801-5827 *For a complete life one needs a job, a home, a love, a friend, and an enemy. My "enemies" are injustice, war, poverty, illness, and suffering, not people. Make your existence as meaningful as possible. Enjoy life fully, and when it comes time to leave, have no fear or regrets. Seek to leave this world a little better off because you lived. These are my values. Would that I were mature enough always to live up to them.*

WATKINS, JUDITH ANN, nurse administrator; b. Chgo., Mar. 11, 1942; d. Russell and Louise Bernadine (Aloy) Keim; m. Thomas H. Watkins III, Dec. 24, 1961; children: Tamara Sue, Randall Scott. Grad. in nursing, Knapp Coll. Nursing, Santa Barbara, Calif., 1963; BSN, Pacific Union Coll., 1991, PHN cert., 1991; MHA, U. LaVerne, 1995. Cert. CPR instr., vocat. edn. instr. Obstetrics supr. Bowling Green (Ky.) Warren County Hosp., 1963-67; clin. staff nurse Chula Vista (Calif.) Med. Clinic, 1967-69; nurse aide instr. Sawyers Coll., Ventura, Calif., 1972; ob-gyn. supr. Westlake (Calif.) Community Hosp., 1972-77; RN acute patient care Medical Personnel Pool, Bakersfield, Calif., 1984; med. asst. instr., dir. of allied health San Joaquin Valley Coll., Bakersfield, 1984-88; dir. nurses Bakersfield Family Med. Ctr., 1988-91, dir. client svcs., 1991-94, asst. adminstr. clin. svcs., 1994—. Named Mother of the Yr., Frazier Pk. (Calif.) Community Ch., 1979, Instr. of the Yr., 1986. Mem. Kern County RN Soc., Kern County Trade Club, Pine Mt. Golf Club (founder Lilac Festival 1982, Lady of the Yr. 1983) Sundale Country Club, Seven Oaks Country Club, Toastmasters Internat. Home: 9513 Steinbeck Ln Bakersfield CA 93311-1445 Office: Bakersfield Family Med Ctr 4580 California Ave Bakersfield CA 93309-1104 *Personal philosophy: All things are possible through Christ who strengthens me.*

WATKINS, SYDNEY LYNN, sports administrator; b. Hartford, Conn., Sept. 12, 1964; s. Robert Lee and Joan (Hardy) W. BS, Howard U., 1986, MS, 1989. Cert. U.S. Olympic Acad., Sport Adminstrn. Facility Mgmt. Inst. Water safety instr. Howard U. Satellite Youth Program, Washington, 1986; water safety instr. D.C. Dept. Recreation, Washington, 1986-87, phys. therapeutic recreation specialist, 1987-88; account rep. AT&T, Silver Spring, Md., 1988-90; program assoc. Amateur Athletic Found., L.A., 1991-95; program mgr. L.A. Team Mentoring, 1995-96; ind. cons., 1996—; pharm. sales cons. Wyeth-Ayerst Labs., 1997—; spl. asst. to pres. Dr. LeRoy T. Walker Found., Durham, N.C., 1993. African Am. Summit fellow NAACP, L.A., 1994; Patricia Roberts Harris grantee Howard U., 1989. Mem. AAHPERD, Alpha Kappa Alpha. Home: 1233 1/2 S Citrus Ave Los Angeles CA 90019-1603

WATKINSON, W. GRANT, distribution company executive; b. Seattle, Oct. 17, 1941; s. Percy John and Betty Lou (Grant) W.; m. Diane Weiblen, June 25, 1966; children: Brett, Tara. BS, Oreg. State U., 1964; MBA, U. Oreg., 1966, PhD, 1971. Asst. prof. Pacific Luth. U., Tacoma, 1970-72; v.p. fin. Stiles Enterprises, Portland, Oreg., 1972-76, Discount Fabrics, Portland, 1976; pres. Paulsen & Roles Labs., Portland, 1977—; bd. dirs. Internat. Sanitary Supply Assn., Chgo.; past pres. Preferred Distbrs., Inc., San Antonio, 1988-89. Office: Paulsen & Roles Labs 1836 NE 7th Ave Portland OR 97212-3904

WATLAMET, AUROLYN RENEE, casino management professional; b. Prineville, Oreg., Sept. 18, 1957; d. Arnold Stwyer Sr. and Neda (Brown) Wesley; m. Farley S. Eagle Speaker, Nov. 10, 1980 (div. Nov. 1984); 1 child, Ty A. Eagle Speaker; m. Rick Watlamet; 1 child, Jonathan. AA, Ctrl. Oreg. C.C., 1986; BS, Marylhurst (Oreg.) Coll., 1990; MBA, U. Minn., 1992. Budget technician Bonneville Power Adminstrn., Portland, Oreg., 1977-78; sr. staff acct. Conf. Tribes of Warm Springs, Oreg., 1979-86, internal auditor, 1986-90; auditor Bur. Indian Affairs, Portland, 1984; summer intern 3M Chief Contr. Div., St. Paul, 1991; strategic planner Little Six, Inc., Prior Lake, Minn., 1992-94; gen. mgr. Confederated Tribes of Warm Springs, Warm Springs, Oreg., 1994—; cons. Guerin Logging, Inc., Warms Springs, Oreg., 1985-89, Thunder Spirit Lodge, St. Paul. Coach Youth Softball, Warm Springs, 1988; mentor Oreg. Indian Women's Mentorship, Portland, 1988-90; mem. Community Health Planning Com., Warm Springs, 1989-90; chmn. Johnson O'Mally Edn. Com., Warm Springs, 1987-90; co-chairperson Twin Cities Adv. Bd., U. Minn., Mpls., 1991—; bd. mem. Indian Neighborhood Club on Alcohol and Drugs, Mpls., 1991-92; mem. bishops com. All Saints Episc. Ch., 1993—. Named Miss Indian N.W., 1980, Adult Learner of Yr. Assn. for Continuing Higher Edn., Washington, 1989; TCEMP fellow First Nations/U. Minn., 1990-92. Mem. Nat. Congress Am. Indians, Nat. Indian Edn. Assn., Am. Indian Sci. and Engring. Soc., Nat. Assn. Native Am. Adult Children of Alcoholics, Oreg. Assn. Minority Enterprises, Minn. Am. Indian C. of C. Democrat. Roman Catholic. Office: Confederated Tribes of Warm Springs PO Box C Warm Springs OR 97761

WATRING, WATSON GLENN, gynecologic oncologist, educator; b. St. Albans, W.Va., June 2, 1936; m. Roberta Tawell. BS, Washington & Lee U., 1958; MD, W.Va. U., 1962. Diplomate Am. Bd. Ob-Gyn, Am. Bd. Gynecol. Oncology. Intern The Toledo Hosp., 1963; resident in ob-gyn Ind. U., Indpls., 1964-66, Tripler Gen. Hosp., Honolulu, 1968-70; resident in gen. and oncologic surgery City of Hope Nat. Med. Ctr., Duarte, Calif., 1970-71, assoc. dir. gynecol. oncology, sr. surgeon, 1973-77; fellow in gynecol. oncology City of Hope Nat. Med. Ctr. and UCLA Med. Ctr., 1972-74; asst. prof. ob-gyn UCLA Med. Ctr., 1972-77; assoc. prof., sr. gynecologist, sr. surgeon Tufts New Eng. Med. Ctr. Hosp., Boston, 1977-80, asst. prof. radiation therapy, 1978-80; practice medicine specializing in ob-gyn Boston, 1980-82; assoc. prof. ob-gyn U. Mass., Worcester, 1982; regional dir. gynecol. oncology So. Calif. Permanente Med. Group, Los Angeles, 1982—, asst. dir. residency tng., 1985—; dir. gynecol. oncology St. Margarets Hosp. for Women, Dorchester, Mass., 1977-80; clin. prof. ob-gyn U. Calif., Irvine, 1982—. Contbr. articles to profl. jours. Mem. ch. council Luth. Ch. of the Foothills, 1973-75. Served to lt. col. M.C., U.S. Army, 1965-71. Fellow Am. Coll. Ob-Gyn, Los Angeles Obstet. and Gynecol. Soc.; mem. AAAS, ACS (Calif. and Mass. chpts.), Boston Surg. Soc., AMA, Mass. Med. Soc., Mass. Suffolk Dist. Med. Soc., Internat. Soc. Gynecol. Pathologists, Western Soc. Gynecologists and Obstetricians, Am. Soc. Clin. Oncology, Soc. Gynecol. Oncologists, Western Assn. Gynecol. Oncologists (sec.-treas. 1976-81, program chmn. 1984, pres. 1985—), New Eng. Assn. Gynecol. Oncologists (chmn. charter com.), New Eng. Obstet. and Gynecol. Soc., Obstet. Soc. Boston, Am. Radium Soc., Soc. Study Breast Disease, New Eng. Cancer Soc., Internat. Gynecol. Cancer Soc., Daniel Morton Soc., Sigma Xi. Republican.

WATSON, ALVIN, JR., educational administrator; b. Monroe, La., June 25, 1948; s. Alvin and Marsella (Anderson) W.; m. Genevieve Thomas, June 16, 1972; children: Alvin Latrel, Gene LaMar, Thomas LaRon. Grad., Grambling (La.) State Coll.; MS, Drake U., 1974. Adminstrv. cert. Tchr. Des Moines Ind. Sch. Dist., 1972-86; asst. prin. Tucson Unified Sch. Dist., 1987—. With USN, 1968-70. Mem. ASCD, NEA, Ariz. Edn. Assn., Tucson Edn. Assn., Ednl. Leaders Inc., Kappa Alpha Psi. Home: 87 S Bonanza Ave Tucson AZ 85748

WATSON, DAVID COLQUITT, electrical engineer, educator b. Linden, Tex., Feb. 9, 1936; s. Colvin Colquitt and Nelena Gertrude (Keasler) W.; m. Flora Janet Thayn, Nov. 10, 1959; children: Flora Janeen, Melanie Beth, Lorrie Gaylene, Cheralyn Gail, Nathan David, Amy Melissa, Brian Colvin. BSEE, U. Utah, 1964, PhD in Elec. Engring. (NASA fellow), 1968. Electronic technician Hercules Powder Co., Magna, Utah, 1961-62; rsch. fellow U. Utah, 1964-65, rsch. asst. microwave devices and phys. electronics lab., 1964-68; sr. mem. tech. staff ESL, Inc., Sunnyvale, Calif., 1968-78, head dept. Communications, 1969-70; sr. engring. specialist Probe Systems, Inc., Sunnyvale, 1978-79; sr. mem. tech. staff ARGO Systems, Inc., Sunnyvale, 1979-90; sr. mem. tech. staff GTE Govt. Systems Corp., Mountain View, Calif., 1990-91; sr. cons. Watson Cons. Svcs., 1991-92; sr. staff engr. ESL, Inc., 1992— ; mem. faculty U. Santa Clara, 1978-81, 1992—, San Jose State U., 1981—, Coll. Notre Dame, 1992—, Chapman U., 1993—. Contbr. articles to IEEE Transactions, 1965-79; co-inventor cyclotron-wave rectifier; inventor gradient descrambler. Served with USAF, 1956-60. Mem. IEEE, Phi Kappa Phi, Tau Beta Pi, Eta Kappa Nu. Mem. LDS Ch. Office: ESL/TRW 495 E Java Dr Sunnyvale CA 94089-1125 *Personal philosophy: I believe in hard work and strict honesty, in giving full value for consideration received, to God and fellow man or woman.*

WATSON, HAROLD GEORGE, ordnance company executive, mechanical engineer; b. Phoenix, Oct. 19, 1931; s. Clarence Elmer and Eunice A. (Record) W.; m. Ruth May Thomas, Aug. 30, 1951 (dec.); children: Patricia Ruth, Linda Darlene, Harold George; m. Katherina Anna Kish, Sept. 22, 1990. B.S., U. Ariz., 1954. Engr. Shell Oil Co., L.A., 1954; project engr. Talco Engring. Co., Hamden Conn., 1956, area mgr., Mesa, Ariz., 1956-57, chief engr. Rocket Power, 1958-61, dir. engring., 1961-64; dir. engring. Space Ordnance Systems, El Segundo, Calif., 1964-68; dir. engring. Universal Propulsion Co., Riverside, Calif., 1968-70, gen. mgr., v.p. engring., Tempe, Ariz., 1970-76, v.p., mgr., 1976-77, pres., gen. mgr., Phoenix, 1977—. Patentee in field. 1st lt. USAR, 1954-56. Mem. Am. Mgmt. Assn., SAFE Assn. (past pres.), AIAA, Air Force Assn., Internat. Pyronetics Soc., Am. Def. Preparedness Assn. Office: Universal Propulsion Co Inc 25401 N Central Ave Phoenix AZ 85027-7899

WATSON, JULIA, women's studies and liberal studies educator; b. Detroit, Jan. 4, 1945; d. Walter J. and Florence M. (Ryan) W.; 1 child, Evan Orion. BA, Western Mich. U., 1967; MA, U. Calif., Irvine, 1971, PhD, 1979. Assoc. in English U. Calif., Irvine, 1972-73; instr. U. Mass., Amherst, 1974-75; asst. prof. English Hobart & William Smith Colls., Geneva, N.Y., 1979-86; sr. assoc. Lutz Assocs., Inc., Detroit, 1986-87; assoc. prof. English Elizabethtown (Pa.) Coll., 1987-88; assoc. prof. liberal studies, dir. women's studies U. Mont., Missoula, 1988-96; chair dept. women's studies Calif. State U., Northridge, 1996—; sr. lectr. Fulbright Assn., Dakar, Senegal, 1992-93. Co-editor: Women's Autobiography: A Reader in Sheorils, 1997, Getting a Life, 1996, (with Sidonie Smith) De-colonizing the Subject, 1997; mem. edit. bd. Auto/Biography Studies, 1990—. NEH grantee, 1979, 83, 87, 88, 92, 95; DAAD fellow German Acad. Exch. Assn., 1973-74. Mem. MLA (regional del. 1993—, exec. bd. autobiography divsn. 1988-92), Autobiographical Soc. (editorial bd. 1990—), Soc. for Study of Narrative Lit., Am. Comparative LIt. Assn., Nat. Women's Studies Assn. Office: Calif State U Women's Studies Program 18111 Nordhoff St Northridge CA 91330-0001

WATSON, KENNETH MARSHALL, physics educator; b. Des Moines, Sept. 7, 1921; s. Louis Erwin and Irene Nellie (Marshall) W.; m. Elaine Carol Miller, Mar. 30, 1946; children: Ronald M., Mark Louis. B.S., Iowa State U., 1943; Ph.D., U. Iowa, 1948; Sc.D. (hon.), U. Ind., 1976. Rsch. engr. Naval Rsch. Lab., Washington, 1943-46; mem. staff Inst. Advanced Study Princeton (N.J.) U., 1948-49; rsch. fellow Lawrence Berkeley (Calif.) Lab., 1949-52, mem. staff, 1957-81; asst. prof. physics U. Ind., Bloomington, 1952-54; asso. prof. physics U. Wis., Madison, 1954-57; prof. physics U. Calif., Berkeley, 1957-81; prof. oceanography, dir. marine physics lab. U. Calif., San Diego, 1981-93; cons. Mitre Corp., Sci. Application Corp.; mem. U.S. Pres.'s Sci. Adv. Com. Panels, 1962-71; adviser Nat. Security Coun., 1972-75; bd. dirs. Ctr. for Studies of Dynamics, 1979-88; mem. JASON Adv. Panel; mem. sci. adv. bd. George C. Marshall Inst., 1989—. Author: (with M.L. Goldberger) Collision Theory, 1964, (with J. Welch and J. Bond) Atomic Theory of Gas Dynamics, 1966, (with J. Nutall) Topics in Several Particle Dynamics, 1970, (with Flatté, Munk, Dashen) Sound Transmission Through a Fluctuating Ocean, 1979. Mem. Nat. Acad. Scis. Home: PO Box 9726 Rancho Santa Fe CA 92067-4726 Office: U Calif Marine Physics Lab La Jolla CA 92093

WATSON, LARRY SULLIVAN, editor, educator; b. Oklahoma City, May 3, 1941; s. Levi Sullivan and Betty Wilma (Galyean) W. BA, Okla. State Univ., 1963; MA, Ctrl. Mo., 1964; student, Northwestern Univ., 1964-65. Asst. prof. Carson-Newman Coll., Jefferson City, Tenn., 1965-66; prof., rschr., writer U. Mo., Columbia, 1969-79; editor, owner HISTREE, Yuma, Ariz., 1979—; instr. Cen. Mo., Warresnburg, 1964, Northwestern Univ., Evanston, Ill., 1965; assoc. faculty Western Ariz. Coll., Yuma, 1995—. Author over 200 books; contbg. editor Heritag Quest, Orting, Wash., 1995; contbr. articles to profl. publs. Dir. Key Club, 4-H, Okla., 1959-64; sec. Ariz. Geneal. Adv. Bd., 1995-96, comms. chmn., 1997. With U.S. Army, 1964-68. Fellow Ark.-La.-Tex. Genealogy Soc.; mem. Nat. Genealogy Soc., New Eng. Hist. Soc., Genealogy Soc. Yuma (v.p. 1996, pres. 1997), Ariz. Genealogy Soc. (adv. bd.). Republican. Office: HISTREE PO Box 5982 Yuma AZ 85366

WATSON, MARY ANN, psychologist, educator; b. St. Clairsville, Ohio, Jan. 27, 1944; d. William Glenn and Jeanette (Shannon) W.; m. Robert Montgomery (div. 1974); m. Dennis A. Whitlock, Oct. 6, 1978; children: Suzanne, Matthew Montgomery. BA, Grove City (Pa.) Coll., 1966; PhD, U. Pitts., 1969; postgrad., Johns Hopkins U., Balt., 1972-73. Lic. psychologist, Colo. Rsch. assoc. dept. biophysics and genetics/psychiatry U. Colo. Med. Ctr., Denver, 1973-77; prof. psychology Met. State Coll., Denver, 1974—, U. Colo., Denver, 1979-82; pvt. practice clin. psychology, 1975—; clin. psychologist Pub. Health Svc., Navajo and Hopi Reservations, Ariz., 1970-72; asst. prof. psychology Community Coll. of Phila., 1969-70; lectr. in field; cons. in field; mem. State Bd. Psychologist Examiners, 1979-85, chmn., 1981-83. Author: Breaking the Bonds, 1981, Your Sexuality Workbook, 1996; prodr., author: Video Cases in Human Sexuality, 1996; editor: Reading in Sexology, 1986, 2d edit. 1991; contbr. articles to profl. jours. Home: 6840 Richthofen Pky Denver CO 80220-4848 Office: Met State Coll Denver Dept Psychology Campus Box 54 PO Box 173362 Denver CO 80217-3362 also: 1732 E 17th Ave Denver CO 80218

WATSON, MARY ELLEN, ophthalmic technologist; b. San Jose, Calif., Oct. 29, 1931; d. Fred Sidney and Emma Grace (Capps) Doney; m. Joseph Garrett Watson, May 11, 1950; children: Ted Joseph, Tom Fred, Pamela Kay Watson. Cert. ophthalmic med. technologist and surg. asst. Ophthalmic technician Kent W. Christoferson, M.D., Eugene, 1965-80; ophthalmic technologist, surg. asst., adminstr. I. Howard Fine, M.D., Eugene, 1980—; course dir. Joint Commn. Allied Health Pers. in Ophthalmolgy, 1976—, lectr., mem. faculty, 1983—, skill evaluator and site coord., Eugene, 1988—; internat. instr. advanced surgical techniques. Contbr. articles to profl. jours. Recipient 5-Yr. Faculty award Joint Commn. for Allied Health Pers. in Ophthalmology, 1989. Mem. Allied Tech. Pers. in Ophthalmology, Internat. Women's Pilots Assn. Home: 2560 Chaucer Ct Eugene OR 97405-1217 Office: I Howard Fine MD 1550 Oak St Eugene OR 97401-7701

WATSON, MILTON RUSSELL, retired surgeon; b. Silverton, Oreg., July 14, 1934; s. Milton R. and Alice Violet (Sommers) W.; m. Shirley Ilene Kiel, June 20, 1958; children: Mark R., Tamara Faye. BA in Biology, Whitman Coll., Walla Walla, 1956; MD, U. Wash., 1960. Intern, then resident Santa Clara County Medical Ctr., San Jose, Calif., 1960-65; pvt. practice Walla Walla Clinic, 1969-96. Contbr. articles to profl. jours. Capt. U.S. Army, 1965-69. Paul Harris fellow Rotary, 1980. Fellow ACS; mem. AMA, North Pacific Surg. Soc., Soc. Clin. Vascular Surgery, Internat. Cardiovascular Soc., Christian Med. Soc. (del. 1989). Presbyterian. Home: 545 Edgewood Dr Silverton OR 97381-2277

WATSON, NOEL G., construction executive; b. 1936. BSChemE, U. N.D., 1958; postgrad., Colo. Sch. Mines, 1958-60. With Jacobs Engring., 1960-62, AMAX Inc., 1962-65; pres., COO Jacobs Engring. Group Inc., Pasadena, Calif., 1965-92, pres., CEO, 1992—. Office: Jacobs Engring Group Inc 251 S Lake Ave Pasadena CA 91101-3003*

WATSON, OLIVER LEE, III, aerospace engineering manager; b. Lubbock, Tex., Sept. 18, 1938; m. Judith Valeria Horvath, June 13, 1964; 1 child, Clarke Stanford. BSEE, U. Tex., 1961; MSEE, Stanford U., 1963; MBA, Calif. State U., Fullerton, 1972; cert., U. So. Calif., 1980. Mgr. ballistic analysis Rockwell Internat. Autonetics Div., Anaheim, Calif., 1973-78, mgr. minuteman systems, 1978-83, mgr. preliminary engring., 1983-84; mgr. analysis group autonetics divsn. Rockwell Internat., Anaheim, Calif., 1984-85, mgr. aircraft sys. autonetics dept., 1985-93, dep. dir. integrated product devel. N.Am. aircraft aircraft modification divsn., 1993-94, dep. dir. engring. N.Am. aircraft modification divsn., 1994-96; dep. dir. engring. comm. and combat sys. divsn. Boeing N.Am., Anaheim, 1996—; lectr. engring. Calif. State U., Fullerton, 1981-90, mem. indsl. adv. bd., 1994—, vice chmn., 1995—. Co-author Digital Computing Using Fortran IV, 1982; Fortran 77, A Complete Primer, 1986. Bd. dirs. Olive Little League, Orange, 1980; vol. Stanford U. Engring. Fund, Orange County, Calif., 1983, regional chmn. 1984-86, So. Calif. chmn. 1986-91; mem. Stanford Assocs., 1988—. Recipient Stanford Assocs. Centennial Medallion award, 1991; fellow N.Am. Aviation Sci.-Engring., L.A., 1962, 63, Inst. Advancement Engring., L.A., 1976. Mem. IEEE (sr., sec. v.p. 1974-75, sect. chmn. 1975-76), Jaycees (v.p. Orange chpt. 1973-74), Rockwell-Calif. State Univ. Alumni Club (v.p. 1993, pres. 1993-94), Lido Sailing Club. Republican. Office: Boeing NAm 031-DA62 3370 E Miraloma Ave Anaheim CA 92806-1911

WATSON, REBECCA M., elementary school educator; b. Miami, Okla., July 13, 1958; d. Charles C. and Lena Mae (Jackman) W. BS, Okla. State U., 1981; MA, Northeastern Okla. State U., 1981, Northeastern Okla. State U., 1987; adminstrv. cert., Nova U., 1990. Cert. elem. tchr., Okla., Nev.; K-12 reading tchr., Nev. Elem. tchr. Afton (Okla.) Pub. Sch., 1981-84, Chandler (Okla.) Pub. Sch., 1984-85, Cushing (Okla.) Pub. Sch., 1985-86; elem. tchr. Clark County Sch. Dist., Las Vegas, Nev., 1986—, asst. prin., 1993—; adminstrv. asst. prin., Clark County Sch. Dist., Nev.; mem. curriculum commn., multicultiral task force Clark County Sch. Dist., Nev.; asst. site adminstr. Nova Univ., Fla.; workshop presenter. Named Outstanding Classroom Tchr.; grantee NEH. Mem. NEA, Nev. Edn. Assn., Internat. reading Assn., Clark County Tchrs. Assn., native Am. Educators Clark County Sch. Dist. (sec.), Native Ams. for Edn. (tchr. rep.), Phi Delta Kappa, Nat. Geography Assn. Home: 5684 Titanium Ave Las Vegas NV 89120 Office: 2801 Ft Sumter Dr North Las Vegas NV 89109-3106

WATSON, SHARON GITIN, psychologist, executive; b. N.Y.C., Oct. 21, 1943; d. Louis Leonard and Miriam (Myers) Gitin; m. Eric Watson, Oct. 31, 1969; 1 child, Carrie Dunbar. B.A. cum laude, Cornell U., 1965; M.A., U. Ill., 1968, Ph.D., 1971. Psychologist City N.Y. Prison Mental Health, Riker's Island, 1973-74; psychologist Youth Services Ctr., Los Angeles County Dept. Pub. Social Services, Los Angeles, 1975-77, dir. clin. services, 1978, dir. Youth Services Ctr., 1978-80; exec. dir. Crittenton Ctr. for Young Women and Infants, Los Angeles, 1980-89, Assn. Children's Svcs. Agys. of So. Calif., L.A., 1989-92, L.A. County Children's Planning Coun., 1992—. Contbr. articles to profl. jours. Mem. Commn. for Children's Svcs. Family Preservation Policy Com., Mayor's Com. on Children, Youth and Families, L.A. Learning Ctrs. Design Team, Interagy. Coun. Child Abuse and Neglect Policy Com., L.A. Unified Sch. Dist. Bd. Edn.'s Com. on Student Health and Human Svcs.; bd. dirs. L.A. Roundtable for Children, 1988-94, Adolescent Pregnancy Childwatch, 1985-89; trustee L.A. Ednl. Alliance for

Restructuring Now; co-chmn. Los Angeles County Drug and Alcohol Abuse Task Force, 1990; mem. Cmty. Adv. Coun. Dept. Children's Svcs., 1989-90; mem. steering com. western region Child Welfare League Am., 1985-87. Mem. APA, Calif. Assn. Svcs. for Children (sec.-treas. 1983-84, pres. elect 1985-86, pres. 1986-87), Assn. Children's Svcs. Agys. So. Calif. (sec. 1981-83, pres. elect 1983-84, pres. 1984-85), Town Hall Calif., U.S. Figure Skating Assn. (bd. dirs., chair, membership com., sanctions and eligibility com. 1993-96), Pasadena Figure Skating Club (bd. dirs., pres. 1985-87, 89-90), So. Calif. Inter-Club Assn. Figure Skating Clubs (vice chair 1989-91, chair 1991-93). Home: 4056 Camino Real Los Angeles CA 90065-3928 Office: LA County Children's Planning Coun 500 W Temple St Rm B-26 Los Angeles CA 90012-2713

WATSON, WILLIAM D., lawyer; b. Buffalo, Sept. 1, 1943; s. William E. and Dorothy J. (Bowman) W.; m. Andrea L. Ehudin, Dec. 18, 1971; children: William A., Graham H. BA, Princeton U., 1965; LLB, Harvard U., 1968. Atty. Holme Roberts & Owen, LLP, Denver, 1970—; dir. Colo. Oil & Gas Assn. Author: The Gas Sellers Companion, 1992; editor Public Land and Resource Law Digest, 1990—. Capt. U.S. Army, 1968-70, Vietnam. Decorated 8 Bronze stars. Mem. Colo. Bar Assn., Fed. Energy Bar Assn., Rocky Mountain Princeton Club (pres. 1991-94). Office: Holme Roberts & Owen LLP 1700 Lincoln St Ste 4100 Denver CO 80203-4541

WATTS, CHRISTOPHER JOHN, artist, educator; b. London, Oct. 12, 1947; s. Victor George and Maureen (Olver) W.; m. Karen Denise Larson. Student, Plymouth Coll. Art, 1964-66; BFA in Art, U. London, 1969; MFA with honors, Ohio U. Grad. asst. Ohio U., Athens, 1969-71; instr. in sculpture and drawing U. R.I., Kingston, 1971-73; lectr. Trent Poly., Nottingham, Eng., 1973-74; chair art dept., gallery dir. Cornish Inst., Seattle, 1978-84; chair art dept. Mid. Tenn. State U., Murfreesboro, 1984-88; chair fine arts dept. Wash. State U., Pullman, 1988—; speaker, lectr. in field; vis. artist Trent Poly., 1974-78, Gloucester (Eng.) Coll. of Art, 1973-74, Dartington (Eng.) Coll. of Arts, 1974, U. Reading, Eng., 1975-76, Slade Sch. Fine Art, London, 1975-78; art dir., coord., mem. adv. bd. Gov.'s Sch. for Arts of Tenn., 1986-88; external assessor rev. dept. fine arts Weber State U., 1990; mem. various panels in field; bd. advisors And/Or Gallery, Seattle, 1980; mem. Contemporary Arts Coun., Seattle, 1981-82. Exhibited in numerous one person shows, including Cornish Inst., Seattle, 1979, Traver Gallery, Seattle, 1980, Mus. Art, Carnegie Inst., Pitts., 1981, Seattle Pacific U., 1982, 86, Traver/Sutton Gallery, 1981, 83, Seattle Ctr., 1983, Mid. Tenn. State U., 1984, Cumberland Gallery, 1985, 86, 90, in many group shows, including Wash. State U., 1989, Linda Farris Gallery, Seattle, 1989, Cumberland Gallery, 1987, 88, 89, 90, 92, U. Idaho, Moscow, 1991, Seattle Pacific U., 1993, , Vladivostok, Artetage, Russia, 1994, Seattle Pacific U., 1994, Art Fair, Seattle, 1995, Bellevue Art Mus., Wash., 1995, Prichad & Acceny, Moscow, 1995, Grand Forks Art Gallery, B.C., Can., 1996, Art Gallery of South Okanagan, B.C., 1996, Norwich Gallery, Eng., 1996, Reed's Wharf Gallery, London, 1996, others; represented in permanent collections U.S. and Europe including 1st Nat. Bank, Providence, R.I., Seattle 1st Nat. Bank, Honeywell, Inc., Seattle, Carnegie Mus., Pitts., Arts Coun. Great Britain, Seattle Arts Commn., Hartt Sch. Music Libr., Hartford, Conn., H.C.A., Nashville, 3d Nat. Bank, Nashville, Endata, Nashville, No. Telecom, Nashville, J.D. Nichols Assoc., Atlanta, Bass, Berry, Conners & Sims, Nashville, Wash. State Arts Commn., Ea. Wash. U./Spokane Ctr. Office: Wash State U Dept Fine Arts Pullman WA 99164

WATTS, DAVID H., construction company executive; b. Newark, 1938. Grad., Cornell U., 1960. Pres., CEO Granite Constrn. Inc., Watsonville, Calif. Office: Granite Constrn Co 585 W Beach St Watsonville CA 95076-5125*

WATTS, JILL MARIE, history educator; b. Pomona, Calif., May 28, 1958; d. Thomas H. and Doris Ruth (Hohlfeld) W. BA, U. Calif., San Diego, 1981; MA, UCLA, 1983, PhD, 1989. Asst. prof. Weber State U., Ogden, Utah, 1989-91; asst. prof. Calif. State U., San Marcos, 1991-94, assoc. prof., 1994—, dir. history program, 1994-96. Author: God, Harlem USA: The Father Divine Story, 1992; contbr. articles to profl. publs. (Theodore Salautos award). Carey McWilliams fellow, 1986-87, Rosecrans fellow, 1986-87, Inst. for Am. Cultures fellow, 1986-87, Cornell U. Soc. for Humanities fellow, 1994-95. Mem. Am. Hist. Assn., Orgn. Am. Historians, Am. Studies Assn., Western Assn. Women Historians, Oral History Assn. Office: Calif State U History Program San Marcos CA 92096

WATTS, OLIVER EDWARD, engineering consultancy company executive; b. Hayden, Colo., Sept. 22, 1939; s. Oliver Easton and Vera Irene (Hockett) W.; m. Charla Ann French, Aug. 12, 1962; children—Erik Sean, Oliver Eron, Sherilyn. BS, Colo. State U., 1962. Registered profl. engr., Colo., Calif.; profl. hand surveyor, Colo. Crew chief Colo. State U. Rsch. Found., Ft. Collins, 1962; with Calif. Dept. Water Resources, Gustine and Castaic, 1964-70; land and water engr. CF&I Steel Corp., Pueblo, Colo., 1970-71; engring. dir. United Western Engrs., Colorado Springs., Colo., 1971-76; ptnr. United Planning and Engring Co., Colorado Springs, 1976-79; owner Oliver E. Watts, Cons. Engr., Colorado Springs, 1979—. Dir. edn. local Ch. of Christ, 1969-71, deacon, 1977-87, elder, 1987-96. 1st lt. C.E., AUS, 1962-64. Recipient Individual Achievement award Colo. State U. Coll. Engring., 1981. Fellow ASCE (v.p. Colorado Springs br. 1975, pres. 1978); mem. NSPE (pres. Pike's Peak chpt. 1975, sec. Colo. sect. 1976, v.p. 1977, pres. 1978-79, Young Engr. award 1976, Pres.'s award 1979), Cons. Engrs. Coun. Colo. (bd. dirs. 1981-83), Am. Cons. Engrs. Coun., Profl. Land Surveyors Colo., Colo. Engrs. Coun. (del. 1980—), Colo. State U. Alumni Assn. (v.p., dir. Pike's Peak chpt. 1972-76), Lancers, Lambda Chi Alpha. Home: 7195 Dark Horse Pl Colorado Springs CO 80919-1442 Office: 614 Elkton Dr Colorado Springs CO 80907-3514

WATTS, VAN, retired career navy officer; b. Mooers, N.Y., Aug. 26, 1920; s. Bert and Margaret (Baker) W.; m. Lilie Remoreras, 1971; children: Michelle Remie, Philip, Charlotte, Britt, Lance, Douglas. With USN, 1937-62. prodr. TV and radio shows Sailor of the Week, Month, Quarter and Year Programs, Norfolk, Va., 1952-54. Mem. adv. bd. World War II Nat. Commemorative Assn., 1996—. Decorated battle stars Nat. Def. Svc., Am. Def. Svc., Am. Campaign, Asiatic-Pacific Campaign, WWII Victory, Navy Occupl., Navy Occupl. Svc. (Europe), Armed Forces Expeditionary (Lebanon), Guadal Canal and New Guinea; recipient letter of commendation Nat. Trust for Hist. Preservation, 1975, Naval Aviation Schools, 1994; honored by Navy League Hollywood Coun., 1988; recipient Gold Plaque Hollywood Coun., others. Mem. VFW, Am. Legion, U.S. Naval Inst., USS Albany CA123 Assn., USS Enterprise CV6 Assn., USS Fremont APA44 Assn., USS Sierra AD18 Assn., Nat. Chief Petty Officers Assn., Tin Can Sailors Assn., Surface Navy Assn. (San Diego chpt.), Guadalcanal Campaign Vets. Assn., Naval Hist. Found., Navy Supply Corps Assn., Fleet Res. Assn., Botsford Family Hist. Assn., N.H. Hist. Soc., Brattleboro (Vt.) Hist. Soc., Chesterfield (N.H.) Hist. Soc., Burbank (Calif.) Hist. Soc., Hollywood Coun. Navy League (life).

WAUGH, KATHLEEN MARY, archivist; b. Bellingham, Wash., Feb. 2, 1952; d. Robert Burton and Shirley Kathleen (Stewart) W.; m. David Warren Hastings, Aug. 23, 1975; children: Rebecca, Ian. BA in History, Western Wash. U., 1973, BA in Anthrop., 1976; BS in Geology, Evergreen State Coll., 1983. Surveyor hist. records Wash. State Hist. Records Survey, Olympia, 1977-79; archival clk. Wash. State Archives, Olympia, 1979—. Author, editor: (catalogs) Index to Mining Surveys, 1985, Roll On, Columbia, 1987, Galloping Gertie, 1993, Guide to Records of Dixie Lee Ray, 1994. Mem. Mason County Heritage Bd., Shelton, Wash, 1993.

WAXMAN, HENRY ARNOLD, congressman; b. Los Angeles, Sept. 12, 1939; s. Louis and Esther (Silverman) W.; m. Janet Kessler, Oct. 17, 1971; children: Carol Lynn, Michael David. B.A. in Polit. Sci, UCLA, 1961, J.D., 1964. Bar: Calif. 1965. Mem. Calif. State Assembly, 1969-74, chmn. com. on health, until 1994; mem. 94th-104th Congresses from 24th (now 29th) Calif. dist., 1975—, ranking minority mem. house subcom. on health and environment, 1979—; mem. govt. reform & oversight com. Pres. Calif. Fedn. Young Democrats, 1965-67. Mem. Calif. Bar Assn., Guardians Jewish Home for Aged, Am. Jewish Congress, Sierra Club, B'nai B'rith, Phi Sigma Alpha. Office: US Ho of Reps 2408 Rayburn HOB Washington DC 20515

WAYBURN, EDGAR, internist, environmentalist; b. Macon, Ga., Sept. 17, 1906; s. Emanuel and Marian (Voorsanger) W.; m. Cornelia Elliott, Sept. 12, 1947; children: Cynthia, William, Diana, Laurie. AB magna cum laude, U. Ga., 1926; MD cum laude, Harvard U., 1930. Hosp. tng. Columbia-Presbyn. Hosp., N.Y.C., 1931-33; assoc. clin. prof. Stanford (Calif.) U., 1933-65, U. Calif., San Francisco, 1960-76; practice medicine specializing in internal medicine San Francisco, 1933-1985; mem. staff Pacific Presbyn. Med. Ctr., San Francisco, 1959-86, chief endocrine clinic, 1959-72, vice chief staff, 1961-63, hon. staff, 1986—. Editor: Man Medicine and Ecology, 1970; contbr. articles to profl. and environ. jours. Mem. Sec. of Interior's Adv. Bd. on Nat. Park System, 1979-83, commn. on nat. parks and protected areas Internat. Union for Conservation Nature and Natural Resources; leader nat. campaigns Alaska Nat. Interest Lands Conservation Act; trustee Pacific Presbyn. Med. Ctr., 1978-86; chmn. People For a Golden Gate Nat. Recreation Area, 1971—; mem. citizens' adv. commn. Golden Gate Nat. Recreation Area, San Francisco, 1974—, leader nat. campaigns, 1978-86; prin. citizen advocate Redwood Nat. Park, 1968, 78; dir. The Antarctica Project; mem. adv. bd. Pacific Forest Trust; hon. chmn. Tuolomne River Preservation Trust; bd. dirs. Garden Sullivan Hosp., 1965-78; prin. adv. Enlargement of Mt. Tamal Pais State Pk.; leader campaign to establish Golden Gate Nat. Recreation Area, 1972. Maj. USAF, 1942-46. Recipient Douglas award Nat. Pks. and Conservation Assn., 1987, Leopold award Calif. Nature Conservancy, 1988, Fred Packard award Internat. Union Conservation Nature, 1994, Laureate of Global 500 Roll of Honour award U.N. Environment Programme, 1994, 1st Conservation award Ecotrust, 1994, Albert Schweitzer prize, 1995. Fellow ACP; mem. AMA, Am. Soc. Internal Medicine, Calif. Med. Assn. (del. 1958-83, Recognition award 1986, Leadership and Quality awards 1986), San Francisco Med. Soc. (pres. 1965, Resolution of Congratulations 1986), Sierra Club (pres. 1961-64, 67-69, John Muir award 1972, hon. pres. 1993), Fedn. Western Outdoor Clubs (pres. 1953-55). Home: 314 30th Ave San Francisco CA 94121-1705

WAYBURN, PEGGY (CORNELIA ELLIOTT WAYBURN), author, editor; b. N.Y.C., Sept. 2, 1917; d. Thomas Ketchin and Cornelia (Ligon) E.; m. Edgar Wayburn Sept. 12, 1947; children: Cynthia, William, Diana, Laurie. BA cum laude, Barnard, 1942. Copywriter Vogue Mag., N.Y.C., 1943-45, J. Walter Thompson, San Francisco, 1945-47; self employed freelance writer, San Francisco, 1948—; Author: Adventuring in the San Francisco Bay Area, Adventuring in Alaska; (prize-winning audio visual series) Circle of Life; contbr. articles to mags. and profl. jours. Mem. bd. advisors Am. Youth Hostels; trustee Sierra Club Found. Recipient annual award Calif. Conservation Assn., 1966. Mem. Sierra Club (spl. svc. award 1967, women's award 1989), Phi Beta Kappa. Home: 314 30th Ave San Francisco CA 94121-1705

WAYLAND, NEWTON HART, conductor; b. Santa Barbara, Calif., Nov. 5, 1940; s. L.C. Newton and Helen Bertha (Hart) W.; m. Judith Anne Curtis, July 3, 1969 (div. 1986). MusB, New Eng. Conservatory Music, 1964, MusM, 1966. Host, composer, performer Sta. WGBH-TV, Boston, 1963-82; pianist, harpsichordist Boston Symphony Orch., 1964-71; music dir. Charles Playhouse, 1965-67; pianist, guest condr., arranger Boston Pops Orch., 1971-74; resident Pops condr. Midwest Pops Orch., South Bend, Ind., 1979-91, Oakland Symphony Orch., Calif., 1980-85, Houston Symphony Orch., 1986-93; prin. Pops condr. Denver Symphony Orch., 1987-89, Vancouver (B.C.) Symphony Orch., 1993—; guest condr. numerous orchs. U.S. and Canada, 1977—. Recs. include: Music for Zoom (PBS Emmy-winning TV show), 1971-78, Music for Nova (award-winning PBS-TV show), 1972-78, America Swings, 1987, Gershwin Plays Gershwin, 1987, Pop Go the Beatles, 1987, Classical Jukebox, 1988, Stompin' at the Savoy, 1988, Sophisticated Ladies, 1988, A Touch of Fiedler, 1989, Prime Time, 1989; arranger, performer: Jazz Loves Bach, 1968, Fiedler in Rags, 1974; arranger, condr.: Berlin to Broadway with Kurt Weill, 1972; condr. Oedipus Tex (Grammy award 1991); arranger, composer, performer (songs A&M Records) Come On and Zoom, Zoom Tunes. Recipient highest honors New Eng. Conservatory Music, 1974, Chadwick Disting. Achievement medal New Eng. Conservatory Music, 1966. Home and Office: 2970 Hidden Valley Ln Santa Barbara CA 93108-1619

WAYMAN, COOPER HARRY, environmental legal counsel; b. Trenton, N.J., Jan. 29, 1927; s. Cooper Ott and Helen Viola (Unverzagt) W.; m. Ruth Treier, June 16, 1951; children: Carol Beth Withers, Andrea Lee Daschbach. BS, Rutgers U., 1951; MS, U. Pitts., 1954; PhD, Mich. State U., 1959; JD, U. Denver, 1967. Bar: Colo. 1969, Tex. 1972; registered profl. engr., Colo.; cert. real estate broker, Colo. Rsch. chemist U.S. Geol. Survey, Lakewood, Colo., 1960-65; assoc. prof. chemistry Colo. Sch. Mines, Golden, 1965-70; regional counsel EPA, Dallas, 1971-74; asst. to regional adminstr. EPA, Denver, 1974-83; exec. asst. to mayor City of Denver, 1981-85; dir. environment compliance Cord Labs., Inc., Broomfield, Colo., 1986-88; environ. and permits mgr. Chem. Waste Mgmt. Inc., Port Arthur, Tex., 1988-92; regional regulatory mgr. Chem. Waste Mgmt., Inc., Houston, 1992-94; compliance branch mgr. Adv. Scis., Inc., Carlsbad, N.Mex., 1994-95; area office legal counsel Waste Isolation Project, Dept. Energy, Carlsbad, N.Mex., 1995—; dir. energy office EPA, Denver, 1974-78; adj. prof. law U. Denver, 1981-84; mem. State of Colo. Air Pollution Commn., Denver, 1969-70. Author: Detergents and Environment, 1965, Permits Handbook, 1981; contbr. articles to profl. jours. V.p. WE Lockwood Civic Assn., Lakewood, 1985-86. With USNR, 1945-46. Grantee U.S. Fish and Wildlife Svc., 1967; fellow, rsch. assoc. MIT, 1956-58. Fellow Am. Inst. Chemists, 1993. Home: 901 Fountain Dr Carlsbad NM 88220 Office: US Dept Energy Carlsbad Area Office PO Box 3090 Carlsbad NM 88221

WAYNE, KYRA PETROVSKAYA, writer; b. Crimea, USSR, Dec. 31, 1918; came to U.S., 1948, naturalized, 1951; d. Prince Vasily Sergeyevich and Baroness Zinaida Fedorovna (Fon-Haffenberg) Obolensky; m. George J. Wayne, Apr. 21, 1961; 1 child, Ronald George. BA, Leningrad Inst. Theatre Arts, 1939, MA, 1940. Actress, concert singer, USSR, 1939-46; actress, U.S., 1948-59; enrichment lectr. Royal Viking Line cruises, Alaska-Can., Greek Islands-Black Sea, Russia/Europe, 1978-79, 81-82, 83-84, 86-87, 88. Author: Kyra, 1959, Kyra's Secrets of Russian Cooking, 1960, 93, The Quest for the Golden Fleece, 1962, Shurik, 1971, 92, The Awakening, 1972, The Witches of Barguzin, 1975, Max, The Dog That Refused to Die, 1979 (Best Fiction award Dog Writers Assn. Am. 1980); Rekindle the Dreams, 1979, Quest for Empire, 1986, Li'l Ol' Charlie, 1989, Quest for Bigfoot, 1996. Founder, pres. Clean Air Program, Los Angeles County, 1971-72; mem. women's coun. KCET-Ednl. TV; mem. Monterey County Symphony Guild, 1989-91, Monterey Bay Aquarium, Monterey Peninsula Mus. Art, Friends of La Mirada. Served to lt. Russian Army, 1941-43. Decorated Red Star, numerous other decorations USSR; recipient award Crusade for Freedom, 1955-56; award Los Angeles County, 1972, Merit award Am. Lung Assn. L.A. County, 1988. Mem. Soc. Children's Book Writers, Authors Guild, P.E.N., UCLA Med. Faculty Wives (pres. 1970-71, dir. 1971-75) UCLA Affiliates (life), L.A. Lung Assn. (life), Friends of the Lung Assn. (pres. 1988), Carmel Music Soc. (bd. dirs. 1992-94), Idyllwild Sch. Music, Art and Theatre Assn. (trustee 1987), Los Angelenos Club (life). Home: 561 E Mariners Cir Fresno CA 93720-0848 *Personal philosophy: I believe in total loyalty. Loyalty to one's family and friends, to one's colleagues and to one's country. In my case - to my chosen country, the U.S.A.*

WAYNE, ROBERT, surgeon; b. N.Y.C., Aug. 14, 1943; s. William and Dorothy (Gear) W.; m. Jean Wayne. Diplomate Am. Bd. Surgery. Resident in surgery Creighton U., Omaha, 1971-74; pvt. practice, Astoria, Oreg., 1978—. Office: 2055 Exchange St Astoria OR 97103-3419

WAYNE, VALERIE, English language educator; b. Chgo., Aug. 2, 1945; d. Robert August and Eleanor Margaret (Kalow) W.; m. David Lee Callies, June 18, 1966 (div. Mar. 1986); 1 child, Sarah Anne. BA in Philosophy cum laude, DePauw U., 1966; MA in English, U. Chgo., 1972, PhD in English, 1978. Tchg. asst. in humanities U. Chgo., 1973-74; lectr. in composition Chgo. State U., 1974; lectr. U. Ill., Chgo., 1976-78; from vis. asst. prof. to assoc. prof. English U. Hawaii at Manoa, Honolulu, 1978-93, prof. English, 1993—, dir. grad. program English, 1994-97; vis. lectr. U. Liverpool, Eng., 1988; vis. scholar Alice F. Holmes Inst., U. Kans., 1997. Editor: The Matter of Difference: Materialist Feminist Criticism of Shakespeare, 1991, The Flower of Friendship: A Renaissance Dialogue Contesting Marriage, 1992, A Trick to Catch the Old One in the Collected Works of Thomas Middleton; contbr. articles and poetry to profl. jours. and anthologies. Mem. Shakespeare Assn. Am., Modern Lang. Assn., Early Modern Women, Renaissance Eng. Text Soc. Home: 2406 Oahu Ave # A Honolulu HI 96822-1967 Office: Univ Hawaii English Dept 1733 Donaghho Rd Honolulu HI 96822-2315

WEAGRAFF, PATRICK JAMES, psychologist, educator; b. Buffalo, May 27, 1940; s. Harry Edward and Donnabelle (O'Brien) W.; m. Michael, Patrick Jr., Kim Marie, Susan Lynn. BS, SUNY, Buffalo, 1963; MEd, U. Md., 1965; EdD, UCLA, 1970, PhD, 1971. Cert. psychology, post secondary edn., secondary edn., ednl. adminstrn., drug and alcohol counseling. Assoc. dir. U.S. Peace Corps, Lagos, Nigeria, 1965-68; ednl. adminstr. Calif. Dept. Edn., Sacramento, 1971-75; assoc. commr. edn. Mass. Dept. Edn., Boston, 1975-76; psychologist Sierra View Mental Health, Auburn, Calif., 1978-81; chief clin. svcs. Calif. Dept. Mental Health, Sacramento, 1981-93; clin. dir. St. Joseph's Hosp., Stockton, Calif., 1993-95; core faculty psychology Profl. Sch. Psychology, Sacramento, 1993-96; assoc. prof. Nat. U., Stockton, Calif., 1983—. Author 9 books including Careers in Focus, 1993, Communications, 1993, Public Service Occupations, 1993, Construction Occupations, 1993, Decision Making, 1995, Making Decisions Work, 1997. Trustee Crossroads Inc., Sacramento, 1982-90; bd. dirs. Golden Empire Scouts, Sacramento, 1985-91. Edn. Profession Devel. Act fellow UCLA, 1970. Mem. Phi Delta Kappa, Epsilon Pi Tau. Jewish. Home: 9338 Framington Way Elk Grove CA 95758-4013

WEARING, J.P., English language educator; b. Birmingham, Eng., Mar. 1, 1945; s. Jhn and Joan (Hall) W. BA with honors, U. Wales, Swansea, 1967, PhD, 1971; MA, U. Sask., Can., 1968. Lectr. U. Alta., Edmonton, 1971-74; asst. prof. English U. Ariz., Tucson, 1974-77, assoc. prof., 1977-84, prof. English, 1984—; cons. NEH, Washington, 1978—. Author: The Collected Letters of Sir Arthur Pinero, 1974, The London Stage 1890-1959: A Calendar of Plays and Players, 16 vols., 1976-93, English Drama and Theatre, 1800-1900, 1978, American and British Theatrical Biography: A Directory, 1979, G.B. Shaw: An Annotated Bibliography of Writings About Him: Vol. I: 1871-1930, 1986, many others; editor: 19th Century Theatre Rsch., 1972-86; adv. editor English Literature in Transition, 1976—, 19th Century Theatre, 1986-96; gen. editor The London Stage 1960-1999 Project, 1996—; contbr. articles to profl. jours. Killam Found. fellow, 1971-73, Guggenheim Found. fellow, 1978-79; NEH grantee, 1987-91. Mem. Soc. for Theatre Rsch. (Eng.). Office: U Ariz Dept English Tucson AZ 85721

WEARY, THOMAS MARTIN, investment company executive; b. Kansas City, Mo., July 21, 1960; s. Daniel Croft and Barbara Anne (Tindall) W.; m. Helen Jenkins Van Metre, June 25, 1983; children: Evelina Underhill, Taylor Evans, Brandt Pearson. AB cum laude, Harvard U., 1982. CFA. Planning analyst John Hancock Internat., Boston, 1983-86; dir. strategic planning John Hancock Internat. Svcs., Hong Kong, 1987-89; 2d v.p. John Hancock Mut. Funds, Boston, 1990-92; v.p. Sovereign Asset Mgmt., Berwyn, Pa., 1993-96; chief equity officer Farmers Group, L.A., 1996—. Mem. Assn. for Investment Mgmt. and Rsch., World Affairs Coun. of Phila., L.A. Soc. Fin. Analysts, Harvard-Radcliffe Club of So. Calif., Phoenix-S. K. Club. Home: 314 22nd St Santa Monica CA 90402-2508 Office: Farmers Investment Rsch and Mgmt 4680 Wilshire Blvd Los Angeles CA 90010-3807

WEATHERHEAD, LESLIE R., lawyer; b. Tacoma, Sept. 28, 1956; s. A. Kingsley and Ingrid A. (Lien) W.; m. Anali C. Torrado, June 24, 1985; children: Spencer, Madeleine, Audrey. BA, U. Oreg., 1977; JD, U. Wash., 1980. Bar: Wash. 1980, Oreg. 1996, U.S. Ct. Appeals (9th cir.) 1981, U.S. Dist. Ct. (ea. dist.) Wash. 1984, U.S. Ct. Internat. Trade 1984, Hawaii 1987, U.S. Dist. Ct. (we. dist.) Wash. 1989, Idaho 1989, U.S. Dist. Ct. Idaho 1989, U.S. Supreme Ct. 1994, Colville Tribal Ct. 1993, U.S. Ct. Apeals (10th cir.) 1995, U.S. Ct. Fed. Claims 1995. Asst. terr. prosecutor Territory of Guam, Agana, 1980-83; spl. asst. U.S. Atty. Dist. of Guam and No. Marianas, Agana, 1982-83; atty. Witherspoon, Kelley, Davenport & Toole, Spokane, 1984—; lawyer-rep. 9th cir. jud. conf., 1989-95, lawyer-rep. chmn., 1995; adj. faculty Gonzaga U. Sch. of Law, 1994-95. Contbr. articles on Indian law and administrv. investigations to profl. jours. Bd. dirs. Spokane Uptown Opera, 1989-96, pres., 1992-94. Mem. ABA, Fed. Bar Assn. (pres. ea. dist. 1997—), Hawaii Bar Assn., Idaho Bar Assn., Wash. State Bar Assn., Oreg. State Bar Assn. Office: Witherspoon Kelley Davenport & Toole 428 W Riverside Ave Spokane WA 99201-0301

WEATHERLEY-WHITE, ROY CHRISTOPHER ANTHONY, surgeon, consultant; b. Peshawar, India, Dec. 1, 1931; S. Roy and Elfreda (Milward) Boehm, m. Dorian Jeanne Freeman Weatherley-White, Dec. 27, 1961; children: Carl Christopher, Matthew Richard, Larissa Chantal. MA, Cambridge U., 1953; MD, Harvard U., 1958. Surgeon Biomedical Cons., Denver, 1970—; pres., 1992—; chmn. Plastic Surgery Rsch. Coun., 1975-76; pres. Rocky Mountain Assn. Plastic Surgeons, 1973-74; v.p. Am. Cleft Palate Assn. Author: Plastic Surgeru of the Female Breast, 1982; contbr. over 45 articles to profl. jours. Cons. Colo. Biomedical Venture Ctr., Denver, 1993—. Recipient Rsch. award Am. Soc. Plastic Surgery, 1962, 64. Mem. Harvard Club of N.Y., Oxford-Cambridge Club, Denver Country Club, Denver Athletic Club. Episcopalian. Home: 100 S Humboldt St Denver CO 80209-2516 Office: 4500 E 9th Ave Ste 470 Denver CO 80220-3923

WEATHERUP, WENDY GAINES, graphic designer, writer; b. Glendale, Calif., Oct. 20, 1952; d. William Hughes and Janet Ruth (Neptune) Gaines; m. Roy Garfield Weatherup, Sept. 10, 1977; children—Jennifer, Christine. B.A., U. So. Calif., 1974; Lic. ins. agt. Freelance graphic designer, desktop pub., Northridge, Calif. Mem. Nat. Assn. Female Execs., U. So. Calif. Alumni Assn., Alpha Gamma Delta. Republican. Methodist. Avocations: photography; travel; writing novels; computers. Home: 17260 Rayen St Northridge CA 91325-2919

WEAVER, HOWARD C., newspaper executive; b. Anchorage, Oct. 15, 1950; s. Howard Gilbert and Lurlene Eloise (Gamble) W.; m. Alice Laprele Gauchay, July 16, 1970 (div. 1974); m. Barbara Lynn Hodgin, Sept. 16, 1978. BA, Johns Hopkins U., 1972; MPhil, Cambridge U., 1993. Reporter, staff writer Anchorage Daily News, 1972-76, columnist, 1979-80, mng. editor, 1980-83, editor, 1983-95; editor, owner Alaska Advocate, Anchorage, 1976-79; asst. to pres., McClatchy Newspapers, 1995-97, editor of editl. pages, 1997—; internat. co-chair Northern News Svc., 1989-94; disting. lectr. journalism U. Alaska, Fairbanks, 1991. Pulitzer Prize juror, 1988, 89, 94, 95. Recipient Pulitzer prize, 1976, 89, Pub. Svc. award AP Mng. Editor's Assn., 1976, 89, Headliner award Press Club of Atlantic City, 1976, 89, Gold medal Investigative Reporters and Editors, 1989. Mem. Am. Soc. Newspaper Editors, Investigative Reporters and Editors, Sigma Delta Chi (Nat. award 1989), Alaska Press Club (bd. dirs. 1972-84), Upper Yukon River Press Club (pres. 1972). Avocations: ice hockey, foreign travel, opera.

WEAVER, MAX KIMBALL, social worker, consultant; b. Price, Utah, Apr. 4, 1941; s. Max Dickson and Ruth (Kimball) W.; m. Janet Hofheins, Sept. 13, 1963; children: Kim, Cleve, Chris, Wendy, Michael, Amyanne, Heather. Student, So. Utah State Coll., 1959-60; BS, Brigham Young U., 1965; MSW, U. Utah, 1967. Lic. clin. social worker and marriage counselor, Utah. Cons. Utah State Tng. Sch. (now Devel. Ctr.), American Fork, 1966; dir. Dept. Pub. Welfare, Cedar City, Utah, 1967-70; social worker Latter Day St. Social Services, Cedar City, 1970-75; with Mental Retardation Devel. Disabled Adult Services Dept. Social Services, Cedar City, 1975—; cons. nursing homes, Utah, 1974-95; tchr. So. Utah State Coll., Cedar City, 1972, 77; home health social worker, 1993—. Contbr. articles to mags. Pres. Am. Little League Baseball, 1977-84, 86, Cedar High Booster Club, 1984-95; chmn. Rep. Precinct #1, 1984; v.p. Big League Baseball, 1986-95. Recipient Silver Beaver award, 1996. Mem. Nat. Assn. Social Work (nominating com., licensing com.), Am. Pub. Welfare Assn., Utah Pub. Employees Assn. Mormon. Lodge: Rotary. Home: 116 N 200 E Cedar City UT 84720-2617 Office: Dept Social Svcs 106 N 100 E Cedar City UT 84720-2608

WEAVER, MICHAEL JAMES, lawyer; b. Bakersfield, Calif., Feb. 11, 1946; s. Kenneth James and Elsa Hope (Rogers) W.; m. Valerie Scott, Sept. 2, 1966; children: Christopher James, Brett Michael, Karen Ashley. AB, Calif. State U., Long Beach, 1968; JD magna cum laude, U. San Diego, 1973. Bar: Calif., 1973, U.S. Dist. Ct. (so. dist.) Calif. 1973, U.S. Ct. Appeals (9th cir.) 1975, U.S. Supreme Ct. 1977. Law clk. to chief judge U.S. Dist. Ct. (so. dist.) Calif., San Diego, 1973-75; assoc. Luce, Forward,

Hamilton & Scripps, San Diego, 1975-80, ptnr., 1980-86; ptnr. Sheppard, Mullin, Richter & Hampton, San Diego, 1986—; judge pro tem San Diego Superior Ct.; master of the Bench of the Inn, Am. Inns of Ct., Louis M. Welch chpt.; lectr. Inn of Ct., San Diego, 1981—, Continuing Edn. of Bar, Calif., 1983—, Workshop for Judges U.S. Ct. Appeals (9th cir.), 1990; mem. task force on establishment of bus. cts. sys. Jud. Coun. Calif., 1996-97. Editor-in-chief: San Diego Law Rev., 1973; contbr. articles to profl. jours. Bd. dirs., pres. San Diego Kidney Found., 1985-90; bd. dirs. San Diego Aerospace Mus., 1985—; trustee La Jolla (Calif.) Playhouse, 1990-91. Served to lt. USNR, 1968-74. Fellow Am. Coll. Trial Lawyers; mem. San Diego Assn. Bus. Trial Lawyers (founding mem., bd. govs.), San Diego Def. Lawyers Assn. (dir.), Am. Arbitration Assn., 9th Cir. Jud. Conf. (del. 1987-90), Safari Club Internat. (San Diego chpt.), San Diego Sportsmen's Club. Republican. Presbyterian. Office: Sheppard Mullin Richter & Hampton 501 W Broadway Fl 19 San Diego CA 92101-3536

WEAVER, VELATHER EDWARDS, small business owner; d. Willie and Ethel Edwards; m. Ellerson Weaver; children: Frank Mattox Jr., Terence Mattox, Christopher Williams, Sharon, Shelley, Stephanie. Student, Sonoma State Coll., 1972, U. Calif., Berkeley, 1972; BA, Calif. State U., Hayward, 1973; MBA, St. Mary's Coll., Moraga, Calif., 1989. Coach, counselor Opportunities Industrialization Ctr., Oakland, Calif., 1967-69; tchr. Berkeley Headstart, 1969-70; instr., cons. external degree program Antioch Coll.-West, San Francisco, 1971-74; market analyst World Airways, Inc., Oakland, 1972-75, affirmative action adminstr., 1975-78; cons. A.C. Transit, Oakland, 1982; owner, mgr. Val's Designs and Profl. Svcs., Lafayette, Calif., 1980—; mgr. adminstrn., tng. supr. North Oakland Pharmacy, Inc., 1970—, also bd. dirs.; adv. bd. The Tribune, Oakland, 1982-88. Author RAPRO Self Mgmt. Program, 1985. Program coord., mem. publicity com. Lafayette Arts and Sci. Found., 1982-83; mem. admission bd. St. Mary's Coll. Grad. Sch. Bus., 1990; bd. dirs. Acalanes H.S., Lafayette, 1980-82, Lafayette Elem. Sch., 1975-80; mem. Lafayette Econ. Devel. Task Force, 1994-95; vice chmn. Lafayette Econ. Devel. Commn., 1995—. Mem. Calif. State Pharmacists Assn. Aux. (pres. Contra Costa Aux. 1980, pres. state aux. 1986-88, recognition award 1987), Calif. Pharmacists Polit. Action Com. (appreciation award 1988), Diablo Valley Bus. and Profl. Women (pub. rels. com. 1986-87, best local orgn. award 1987, author yearbook 1987), No. Calif. Med., Dental and Pharm. Assn. Aux. (bd. dirs., com. chair 1975—, pres. elect 1991, pres. 1991-93), Internat. Platform Assn., Links, Inc. Office: North Oakland Pharmacy Inc 5705 Market St Emeryville CA 94608-2811

WEAVER, WILLIAM SCHILDECKER, electric power industry executive; b. Pitts., Jan. 15, 1944; s. Charles Henry and Louise (Schildecker) W.; m. Janet Kae Jones, Mar. 7, 1981. BA, Hamilton Coll., 1965; JD, U. Mich., 1968. Bar: Wash. 1968. Assoc. Perkins Coie, Seattle, 1968-74; ptnr. Perkins COIE, Seattle, 1975-91; exec. v.p., CFO Puget Sound Power & Light Co., Bellevue, Wash., 1991—; bd. dirs. Puget Sound Power & Light Co., Hydro Electric Devel. Co., Bellevue, Connex T, Inc., Seattle. Bd. dirs. Wash. Rsch. Coun., Seattle, 1991—, chmn., 1995—; trustee Seattle Repertory Theatre, 1992-95, Corp. Coun. Arts, 1995-97. Mem. ABA, Wash. State Bar Assn., Seattle Yacht Club, Rainier Club. Office: Puget Sound Power & Light Co PO Box 97034-obc- Bellevue WA 98009

WEBB, ERIC SETH, physician; b. Lexington, Ky., Mar. 2, 1958; s. Ross Allen and Ruth Evangeline (Keil) W. BA, Coll. of Charleston, 1980; MD, Med. U. S.C., 1986. Diplomate Am. Bd. Family Practice. Emergency dept. physician Good Samaritan Hosp., Lexington, Ky., 1989-90, Ashland (Oreg.) Comty. Hosp., 1991—; physician and med. dir. Comty. Health Ctr., Medford, Oreg., 1991-94; physician Aptos, Calif., 1996—. Mem. Am. Acad. Family Physicians, World Orgn. of Family Drs., Sierra Club.

WEBB, LEWIS M., retail executive; b. 1934. Owner Webb's Texaco Svc., Los Alamitos, Calif., 1960-72; pres. Bargain Rent-A-Car Inc., Cerritos, Calif., 1960—, L.M. Webb & Sons, Inc., Mission Viejo, Calif., 1988—; pres., CFO Webb Automotive Group, Inc., Cerritos, Calif., 1989—; pres. Buick Mart Inc., Cerritos, Cerritos Body Works, Inc., Irvine, Calif., Kit Fit Inc., Buena Park, Calif., Lew Webb's Irvine Toyota, Mr. Wheels Inc., Cerritos. Office: Webb Automotive Group Inc 18700 Studebaker Rd Cerritos CA 90703-5335*

WEBB, MARLO L., automobile executive, banking executive; b. Miami, Ariz., Nov. 21, 1924; s. Max R. Webb and Glenna L. (Layton) Smoak; m. Louise McClure; children: Margo W. Allee, Perry M. Webb, Lisa W. Rogers. Student, U. N.Mex., 1941-44. Chmn. Webb Automotive Group, Farmington, N.Mex., 1958—; v.p. Farmington (N.Mex.) Oil Co., 1958—; dir. Burns Nat. Bank, Durango, Colo., 1991—; chmn. First Place Fin. Corp., Farmington, 1993—, First Nat. Bank, Farmington, 1993—. City councilman City of Farmington, 1968-72, mayor, 1974-78, chmn. utility commn., 1978-94; dir. San Juan Med. Found., Farmington, 1985—; chmn. San Juan Boy Scout Dist., Farmington; founder, dir. San Juan Coll. Found., Farmington; dir. N.Mex. Mcpl. League, Albuquerque. Lt. USNR, 1943-46. Recipient Silver Beaver award Boy Scouts Am., 1968; named Citizen of Yr., C. of C., Farmington, 1975, Dealer of the Yr., Time Mag. and Nat. Automobile Dealers Assn., Washington, 1993, Hall of Honor, Farmington H.S., 1995. Mem. Nat. Chevrolet Dealer Coun., Mason, Shrine. Republican. Mem. LDS Ch. Office: Webb Automotive Group Inc PO Box 5550 Farmington NM 87499

WEBB, RICHARD L., air industry service executive; b. 1932. With USAF, 1948-69; dir. Dynair Svc. Inc., McLean, Va., 1969—; pres., CEO Dynair Tech. Ariz., Inc., Phoenix, 1988—.

WEBB, ROY, television producer, writer; b. N.Y.C., Aug. 30, 1951; s. Earl and Eleanor Webb. BA, Rockhurst Coll., 1973; postgrad., UCLA, 1977-79. Prodr. Webb Prodns., Marina Del Rey, Calif. Author: (play) The Comic Touch, 1990, (screenplay) The Envoy, 1992, (TV series) Club MVS, 1996-97, (TV series) Rythmn of the Heart, 1995. Office: Webb Prodns 520 Washington Blvd Ste 265 Marina Del Rey CA 90292

WEBB, WELLINGTON E., mayor; BA in Edn. Colo. State Coll., 1964, MA in Edn. Univ. No. Colo., 1970; teacher, 1964-76; elected Colo. House of Reps., 1972, 74, 76; regional dir. HEW, 1977-81, governor's cabinet, 1981-87; elected auditor City of Denver, 1987-91, mayor, 1991—. Chmn. U.S. Conf. of Mayor's Task Forces on Violence, 1993—. Office: Office of Mayor City & County Bldg Rm 350 1437 Bannock St Denver CO 80202-5308*

WEBBER, MARILYN ASPEN KAY, writer; b. Abilene, Tex., Nov. 22, 1961; d. George Caswell Sleep and Barbara Maxine (Vick) W. BA in Journalism, U. Okla., 1984; MFA in Screen Writing, Am. Film Inst., 1991. Tchrs. asst. Tarleton State U., Stephenville, Tex., 1988-89; writer, assoc. producer AFI, L.A., 1989-91; TV animation writer Gunther-Wahl Prodns.-ABC, L.A., 1992, Ruby/Spears-ABC, L.A., 1993-94; TV writer children's programs ABC-Greengrass Prodns., L.A., 1993-94, CBS-Allegra Films, L.A., 1994; children's programs animation writer ABC, L.A., 1994; Saturday morning animation writer DIC Entertainment-ABC, L.A., 1994; cons., Tex., 1993. Writer: (screenplays) How to Kill Howie?, 1987 (best screenplay), Mouth of the Cat, 1993 (semi-finalist Am.'s best), Captain Zoom: Zoom On Trial; writer/dir. ind. film A Place Called Harmony. Mem. World Wildlife Fund, 1991; supporter Union Rescue Mission, L.A., 1991, Feed the Children, Oklahoma City, 1994, Habitat for Humanity Internat., Americus, Ga., 1994. Recipient Acad. award nomination Motion Picture Acad., 1992, Most Notable Children's Video award Am. Libr. Assn., 1993, nomination Humanitas, 1994, award for advancement of learning in broadcasting NEA, 1994. Episcopalian.

WEBBER, PATRICK NEIL, diversified financial services company executive; b. Hanna, Alta., Can., Apr. 17, 1936; s. Charles and Katherine (McAuliffe) W.; m. Dorothy Platzer, Aug. 3, 1957; children: Barbara, Carol, Len, Lorne, Dianne. BS, U. Alta., 1957, BEd, 1962, PhD, 1973; MA, U. Mont., 1963. Mem. Alta. Legis. Assembly, 1975-90; former min. of energy Govt. of Alta., former min. of edn., former min. social svcs. and cmty. health, former assoc. min. telephones for Alta.; pres. Webber Acad., 1989—; chmn. Telus Corp., AGT Ltd.; former chmn. Alta. Govt. Telephones Commn.; bd. dirs. SNC-Lavalin Group Inc., Calgary Rsch. and Devel. Authority. Former mem. Mt. Royal Coll.; bd. govs. Can. Math. Congress. Mem. Assn. Inst. Rsch. Progressive Conservative. Roman Catholic. Home: 210 Edgeview Dr NW, Calgary, AB Canada T3A 4X5 Office: Webber Acad, 4935 40th Ave NW, Calgary, AB Canada T3A 2N1*

WEBBER, PEGGY MCCLORY, actress, director, producer; b. Laredo, Tex., Sept. 15, 1925; d. Mathew Edward and Margaret Ann (Pierce) W.; m. Robert Marshall Sinskey, Aug. 8, 1951 (div. Aug. 1968); children: Teresa Dickinson, Patricia Wynn, Robert M. Jr.; m. Sean Joseph McClory, Mar. 17, 1983. Student, U. So. Calif., 1941-44, Cuesta Coll., 1971-73, Calif. Poly, 1974-75; tchg. credential, UCLA, 1980. Lic. FCC. Actress radio various, 1942—; dir., prodr., writer KFI TV, L.A., 1948, 49, Calif. Artists Radio Theatre; TV program director Sta. WTIK-TV; exec. dir. Rustin Canyon Theatre, L.A., 1957-71; founder Calif. Artists Repertory Theatre, New Hope Inn, Rustin Canyon Theatre; artistic dir., co-owner New Hope Inn Dinner, Theatre (with Ted Cassidy), 1967-70. Actress: appeared in 8000 radio shows, 300 TV shows, 21 feature films: appeared in network radio Sherlock Holmes, The Man Called X, The Saint, The Peter Lorre Mystery In the Air, One Man's Family, Sam Spade, Suspense, The Life Of Riley, Harold Lloyd Comedy Theater, Lux Radio Theater, Fibber McGee and Molly, Dragnet, Director's Playhouse, numerous others; dir. Colgate Comedy Hour Going Home, 1949 (first woman dir. for filmed TV). Recipient Outstanding Prodn. Most Popular Series award Acad. TV Arts and Scis., 1945-49, Best Supporting Actress award Radio TV Life, 1950, Best Radio Drama Actress award Conf. Christians and Jews, 1950, Best Prodn. award, L.A. Reader, 1985, Meml. Soc. Preservation Radio award, L.A., 1986, 14 awards (6 gold, 2 silver) Internat.. Radio Festival, N.Y., 1989-96, 2 Gold awards Corp. for Pub. Broadcasting, 1992; Ahmanson Found. grant, L.A., 1991-96, Gale Mahonney grant, 1994, Conrad Found. grant, L.A., 1996. Mem. AFTRA, SAG, Equity, Pacific Pioneer Broadcasters (bd. dirs. 1994-97). Home: 6612 Whitley Ter Los Angeles CA 90068 Office: Evolving Minds Calif Artists Radio Theatre 2950 31st St Santa Monica CA 90405

WEBBER, WILLIAM ALEXANDER, university administrator, physician; b. Nfld., Can., Apr. 8, 1934; s. William Grant and Hester Mary (Constable) W.; m. Marilyn Joan Robson, May 17, 1958; children—Susan Joyce, Eric Michael, George David. M.D., U. B.C., Can., Vancouver, 1958. Intern Vancouver Gen. Hosp., 1958-59; postdoctoral fellow Cornell U. Med. Coll., N.Y.C., 1959-61; asst. prof. medicine U. B.C., 1961-66, assoc. prof., 1966-69, prof., 1969—, dean faculty medicine, 1977-90, assoc. v.p. acad., 1990-96. Mem. B.C. Med. Assn., Can. Assn. Anatomists, Am. Assn. Anatomists. Home: 2478 Crown St, Vancouver, BC Canada V6R 3V8 Office: U BC, 2177 Westbrook Mall, Vancouver, BC Canada V6T 1Z3

WEBEL, CHARLES PETER, human science and psychology educator; b. L.A., Dec. 23, 1948; s. James Webel and Jeanne (Herbert) Mackavanagh. BA, U. Calif., Berkeley, 1969, PhD, 1976; postgrad. in pub. health/social medicine, Harvard U., 1989-91. Chair Ctr. Ednl. Change, Berkeley, 1968-70; filmmaker Nat. Ednl. TV, N.Y.C., 1969-70; lectr. social scis. U. Calif., Berkeley, 1976-78; dir. grad. programs Western Inst. Social Rsch., Berkeley, 1977-78; asst. prof. sociology New Coll., Sarasota, Fla., 1978-79; exec. editor social scis. Columbia U. Press, N.Y.C., 1980-83; asst. prof. philosophy Calif. State U., Chico, 1984-89; teaching fellow gen. edn. Harvard U., Cambridge, Mass., 1990-91; gen. editor scholarly book series Peter Lang Pub., N.Y.C., 1990—; rsch. assoc. dept. anthropology U. Calif., Berkeley, 1990—; prof. human sci. and psychology Saybrook Inst., San Francisco, 1990—. Author, editor: Marcus Critical Theory and The Promise of Utopia, 1988; filmmaker: Lifestyle, 1969. Organizer Congress Racial Equality, N.Y.C., 1965-66; West Coast sec. Internat. Philosophers for Prevention Nuclear Omnicide, 1985-89. Fulbright scholar Fulbright Commn., Germany, 1971-72; regents fellow U. Calif., Berkeley, 1972-73, dissertation fellow Social Sci. Rsch. Coun., N.Y.C., 1974-76, grad. fellow Harvard U., 1989-91, NEH summer fellow Harvard U., 1986. Mem. Am. Philos. Assn., Am. Sociol. Assn., Internat. Soc. Polit. Psychology, Commonwealth Club Calif., World Affairs Coun. Office: Saybrook Inst 450 Pacific Ave San Francisco CA 94133-4640

WEBER, ALOIS HUGHES, principal; b. Clay County, Mo., Dec. 19, 1910; d. William Swan and Nora Mildred (Elam) Hughes; m. Frank Thomas Ewing Weber, May 28, 1934 (dec. 1980); children: Patricia Katherine Weber Brusuelas, Susan Weber Mills. BA, William Jewell Coll., Liberty, Mo., 1932; MA, U. Mo., Kansas City, 1971. Elem. prin. Linden (Mo.) Sch. Dist. #72, 1931-34; elem. tchr. Eugene (Mo.) Sch. Dist., 1935-38, Sycamore Sch., Boone County, Mo., 1938-41; reserve tchr. Kansas City (Mo.) Schs., 1941-55, contract tchr., 1955-63; head tchr. Allen Sch., Kansas City, 1963-67; remedial reading tchr. Benjamin Franklin Sch., Kansas City, 1967-69; reading cons. Div. Urban Edn., Kansas City, 1969-73; coord. Title I Elem. Reading and Compensatory Edn., Kansas City, 1974-79; ret.; instr., trainer Staying Healthy After Fifty, State of N.Mex., 1987-89, Growing Old with Health and Wisdom, 1991-95; tutor Literacy Vols. of Am., Inc., Corrales, N.Mex., 1990-93; spkr. AARP Health Care Reform, Health Care Am., 1992—; Lovelace sr. adv. group, 1993—. Instr. ARC, Am. Assn. Ret. Persons; vol. Corrales Libr., 1980-88; bd. dirs. Read West, Literacy Vols. Am., Rio Rancho, 1989-92; bd. dirs. Adobe Comty. Theatre, Corrales, 1989-90; lectr. in field; mem. Bernalillo County steering com. Growing Old with Health and Wisdom, 1988—; asst. state coord. Am. Assn. Ret. Persons, Health Advocacy Svcs., N.Mex., 1995—. Recipient Area Comty. Svc. award AARP, State of N.Mex., 1988, Cert. of Appreciation, ARC, 1988, Cert. of Appreciation for outstanding comty. svc. N.Mex. State Senate Legislature, 1997, Cert. of Appreciation Rio Rancho, N.Mex. Dept. Pub. Safety Srs. and Law Enforcement Together, 1997; NSF grantee, 1973. Mem. AAUW, N.Mex. Assn. Edn. Retirees (exec. com. 1987-89), Albuquerque Assn. Edn. Retirees (exec. sec., bd. dirs. 1990-95), PEO (chpt. BD chaplain, 1990—), West Mesa Assn. Ednl. Retirees (membership chmn. 1991, v.p. 1993, pres. 1994), Grad. Club Albuquerque. Democrat. Baptist. Home: 3321 Esplanade Cir SE Rio Rancho NM 87124-2198

WEBER, ARNOLD I., lawyer; b. Little Cedar, Iowa, Oct. 4, 1926; divorced; children: Katherine Weber Hickle, Thomas, Margaret Weber Robertson. PhB magna cum laude, Marquette U., 1949; MA, Harvard U., 1950; JD, George Washington U., 1954, LLM, 1956. Bar: D.C. 1954, Md. 1961, Calif. 1962, U.S. Dist Ct. D.C. 1954, (no. dist.) Calif. 1962, (cen. dist.) Calif. 1992, U.S. Ct. Claims 1960, U.S. Tax Ct. 1965, U.S. Ct. Appeals (D.C. cir.) 1954, (9th cir.) 1962, (fed. cir.) 1991, U.S. Supreme Ct. 1959. Lawyer Housing and Home Fin., Washington, 1954; pvt. practice Washington, 1954-55; lawyer Tariff Commn., Washington, 1954-55, FCC, Washington, 1955-56, IRS, Washington, 1956-61; assoc. Brobeck, Phleger & Harrison, San Francisco, 1961-64; sr. gen. atty. So. Pacific Transp., San Francisco, 1964-84; western tax counsel Santa Fe Pacific Corp., San Francisco, 1985-88; pvt. practice San Francisco, 1988—. With USNR, 1944-46, PTO. Mem. Olympic Club, San Francisco C. of C., ABA, Bar Assn. San Francisco, State Bar of Calif. Office: 57 Post St Ste 612 San Francisco CA 94104-5023

WEBER, DAVID OLLIER, writer; b. Cin., Feb. 28, 1938; s. George W. Jr. and Eleanor Marchant (Kilby) W.; m. Christine Heath Leigh-Taylor, Nov. 28, 1964; children: Alexandra Leigh-Taylor, Peter Christian, Erec-Michael Ollier. Cert. Norwegian studies, U. Oslo, 1958; BA in Philosophy, U. Cinn., 1959; postgrad., Columbia U., 1959-60, U. Calif., Berkeley, 1964. Gen. assignment reporter The Daily Review, Hayward, Calif., 1964-66; freelance sci. writer and tech. editor, 1966-74; pub. rels. rep. Port of Oakland, Calif., 1975-79; sr. editor Pacific Gas and Electric Co., San Francisco, 1979-80; freelance writer and editor, 1980—. Author: Health for the Harvesters, 1970, Oakland: Hub of the West, 1981; contbg. editor: The Healthcare Forum Jour., 1994—, Strategies For Healthcare Excellence, 1994—. Lt. (j.g.) USNR, 1961-64. Recipient Gold Quill awards Internat. Assn. Bus. Communicators, 1975, 79, Best Bus. Mag. Feature award L.A. Press Club, 1980, Best Feature Story award Assn. Area Bus. Publs., 1984, Golden Hammer award Nat. Assn. Home Builders, 1985; fellow Woodrow Wilson Fellowship Found., Princeton, N.J., 1959. Mem. Phi Beta Kappa. Home: 1186 Euclid Ave Berkeley CA 94708-1640

WEBER, EICKE RICHARD, physicist; b. Muennerstadt, Germany, Oct. 28, 1949; s. Martin and Irene (Kistner) W.; m. Magdalene Graff (div. 1983); m. Zuzanna Liliental , June 10, 1985. BS, U. Koeln, Fed. Republic of Germany, 1970, MS, 1973, PhD, 1976, Dr.Habil., 1983. Sci. asst. U. Koeln, 1976-82; rsch. asst. U. Lund, Sweden, 1982-83; asst. prof. Dept. Material Sci. U. Calif., Berkeley, 1983-87, assoc. prof., 1987-91, prof. materials sci., 1991—; prin. investigator Lawrence Berkeley Lab., 1984—; vis. prof. Tohoku U., Sendai, Japan, 1990; cons. in field; internat. fellow Inst. for Study of Defects in Solids, SUNY, Albany, 1978-79; chmn. numerous confs.; mem. founding com. CAESAR Found., Bonn, 1995—; lectr. in field. Editor: Defect Recognition and Image Processing in III-V Compounds, 1987, Imperfections in III-V Compounds, 1993; co-editor: Chemistry and Defects in Semiconductor Structures, 1989, others; series co-editor: Semiconductors and Semimetals, 1991—; contbr. over 300 articles to profl. jours. Recipient IBM Faculty award, 1984, Humboldt U.S. Sr. Scientist award, 1994; rsch. grantee Dept. of Energy, 1984—, Office Naval Rsch., 1985—, Air Force Office Sci. Rsch., 1988—, NASA, 1988-90, Nat. Renewable Energy Lab., 1992—. Mem. IEEE (sr.), Am. Phys. Soc., Materials Rsch. Soc. Office: 587 Evans Hall Dept Materials Sci U Calif Berkeley CA 94720

WEBER, EUGEN, historian, educator, author; b. Bucharest, Romania, Apr. 24, 1925; came to U.S., 1955; s. Emanuel and Sonia (Garrett) W.; m. Jacqueline Brument-Roth, June 12, 1950. Student, Inst. d'études politiques, Paris, 1948-49, 51-52; M.A., Emmanuel Coll., Cambridge U., 1954, M.Litt., 1956. History supr. Emmanuel Coll., 1953-54; lectr. U. Alta., 1954-55; asst. prof. U. Iowa, 1955-56; asst. prof. history UCLA, 1956, assoc. prof., 1959-63, prof., 1963—, Joan Palevsky prof. modern European history, 1984—, chmn. dept., 1965-68; dir. study center U. Calif., France, 1968-70; dean social scis. UCLA, 1976-77, dean Coll. Letters and Scis., 1977-82; Ford faculty lectr. Stanford U., 1965; Patten lectr. Ind. U., 1981; vis. prof. Collège de France, Paris, 1983; dir. d'études Ecole des hautes études, Paris, 1984-85; Christian Gauss lectr., Princeton U., 1990. Author: Nationalist Revival in France, 1959, The Western Tradition, 1959, Paths to the Present, 1960, Action Française, 1962, Satan Franc-Maçon, 1964, Varieties of Fascism, 1964; (with H. Rogger) The European Right, 1965, A Modern History of Europe, 1970, Europe Since 1715, 1972, Peasants into Frenchmen, 1976 (Commonwealth prize Calif. 1977), La Fin des Terroirs, 1983 (Prix de la Société des gens de lettres 1984), France Fin-de-siècle, 1986 (Commonwealth prize Calif. 1987), The Western Tradition (WGBH/PBS TV series), 1989, My France, 1990, Movements, Currents, Trends, 1991, The Hollow Years, 1994, La France des années trente (Prix littéraire Etats-Unis/France, 1995, Prix Maurice Baumont 1995, Prix de Jeux Floraux 1997), 1995; adv. editor Jour. Contemporary History, 1966—, French History, 1985—, French Cultural Studies, 1990—, Am. Scholar, 1992—. Served as capt. inf. Brit. Army, 1943-47. Recipient Luckman Disting. Teaching award UCLA Alumnae Assn., 1992; decorated Ordre Nat. des Palmes Academiques, France; Fulbright fellow, 1952, 82-83; research fellow Am. Philos. Soc., 1959, Social Sci. Research Council, 1959-61, Am. Council Learned Socs., 1962; Guggenheim fellow, 1963-64; NEH sr. fellow, 1973-74, 82-83. Fellow Netherlands Inst. Advanced Studies, Assn. française de science politique, Am. Acad. Arts and Scis.; mem. Am. Hist. Assn., Soc. d'histoire moderne, Soc. French Hist. Studies, Phi Beta Kappa (hon., Ralph Waldo Emerson prize 1977, senator 1988—).

WEBER, FRANCIS JOSEPH, archivist, museum director; b. Jan. 22, 1933; s. Frank J. and Katherine E. (Thompson) W. Student, L.A. Coll., 1953, St. Johns Coll., 1955, St. Johns Seminary, 1959, Cath. U. Am., 1962, Am. U., Washington. Ordained priest Roman Cath. Ch., 1959. Archivist Archdiocese L.A., 1962—; prof. history Queen Angels Sem., 1962-72; chaplain St. Catherine Mil. Sch., 1972-75; pastor San Buenaventura Mission, 1975-81; dir. Borromeo Guild, 1984-87; dir. San Fernando Mission, 1981—. Editor The Tidings, 1990, Hoja Volante, 1984-95, Miniature Book Soc. Newsletter, 1995-97; contbr. articles to profl. jours. Pres. Zamorano Club, 1991-93; sheriff L.A. Corral Westerners, 1995; hist. rev. commn. Diocese of Monterey. Decorated Grand Cross Isabel la Catolica, 1993, Knighthood of The Holy Sepulchre; recipient Commendation award El Pueblo do L.A. State Historic Park, 1970, L.A. County Bd. Supr., 1972, L.A. City Coun., 1981, L.A. County Bd. Supr., 1992, Merit award Rounce and Coffin Club, 1969, 71, 75, 77, 79-80, 84-86, 88, 92-95, Archivist Excellence award Calif. Heritage Preservation Commn., 1995. Fellow Calif. Hist. Soc. (Merit award 1972, 83), Hist. Soc. So. Calif. (bd. dirs.); mem. Assn. Cath. Diocesan Archivists (pres. 1996-97), Santa Barbara Mission Archves (bd. dirs.), Assn. Cath. Diocesan Archives (bd. dirs.). Democrat. Roman Catholic. Office: Hist Mus Archival Ctr 15151 San Fernando Mission Mission Hills CA 91345

WEBER, FRED J., retired state supreme court justice; b. Deer Lodge, Mont., Oct. 6, 1919; s. Victor N. and Dorothy A. (Roberts) W.; m. Phyllis M. Schell, June 2, 1951; children: Anna Marie, Donald J., Mark W., Paul V. B.A., U. Mont., 1943, J.D., 1947. Bar: Mont. 1947. Atty. Kuhr & Weber, Havre, Mont., 1947-55, Weber, Bosch & Kuhr, and successors, 1956-80; justice Supreme Ct. Mont., Helena, 1981-95. Served to capt. inf. U.S. Army, 1943-46. Fellow Am. Bar Found., Am. Coll. Probate Counsel; mem. ABA, Am. Judicature Soc.

WEBER, GEORGE RICHARD, financial consultant, writer; b. The Dalles, Oreg., Feb. 7, 1929; s. Richard Merle and Maud (Winchell) W.; m. Nadine Hanson, Oct. 12, 1957; children: Elizabeth Ann Weber Katooli, Karen Louise Weber Zaro, Linda Marie. BS, Oreg. State U., 1950; MBA, U. Oreg., 1962. CPA, Oreg. Sr. trainee U.S. Nat. Bank of Portland (Oreg.), 1950-51; jr. acct. Ben Musa, CPA, The Dalles, 1954; tax and audit asst. Price Waterhouse, Portland, 1955-59; sr. acct. Burton M. Smith, CPA, Portland, 1959-62; pvt. practice, Portland, 1962—, assoc. World Mktg. Alliance, 1996—; lectr. acctg. Portland State Coll.; expert witness fin. and tax matters. Sec.-treas. Mt. Hood Kiwanis Camp, Inc., 1965. Exec. counselor SBA; mem. fin. com., powerlifting team U.S. Powerlifting Fedn., 1984, amb. People to People, China, 1987. Arty. officer AUS, 1951-53. Decorated Bronze Star. Mem. AICPA, Internat. Platform Assn., Oreg. Hist. Soc.,Oreg. City Traditional Jazz Soc., Order of the Holy Cross Jerusalem, Order St. Stephen the Martyr, Order St. Gregory the Illuminator, Knightly Assn. St. George the Martyr., World Literary Acad., Portland C.S. Lewis Soc., Beta Alpha Psi, Pi Kappa Alpha. Republican. Lutheran. Clubs: Kiwanis, Portland Track, City (Portland); Multnomah Athletic; Sunrise Toastmasters. Author: Small Business Long-term Finance, 1962, A History of the Coroner and Medical Examiner Offices, 1963, CPA Litigation Service References, 1991, Letters to a Friend, 1995; contbr. to profl. publs. and poetry jours. Home: 2603 NE 32d Ave Portland OR 97212-3611 Office: 4380 SW Macadam Ave Ste 210 Portland OR 97201-6404 *My basic beliefs are in faith, family and freedom through limited government and personal responsibility, with personl responsibility including development and use of capabilities.*

WEBER, JOAN L., library director; b. Renton, Wash., June 21, 1948; d. Karl J. and Mildred C. Weber. Br. clk., head bookmobile, pub. info. officer Spokane (Wash.) County Libr. Dist., 1971-74; part-time tech. lab. asst. U. Denver, 1976-77; dir. Learning Resource Ctr. Northeastern Jr. Coll., Sterling, Colo., 1977-80; dir. Pend Oreille County Libr. Dist., Newport, Wash., 1980-81; br. libr. Manito br. and East Side br. Spokane Pub. Libr., 1981-89, acting mgr. facilities, 1989, mgr. Manito br., 1990-91, mgr. Shadle br., 1991-92; dir. libr. and media svcs. Yakima (Wash.) Valley C.C., 1992—; tchr. mgmt. courses Nat. Mgmt. Assn., Inst. Cert Profl. Mgrs., Spokane; mem. Wash. State Coun. on Continuing Edn.; mem. Wash. State Adv. Coun. on Librs. Apptd. facilitator Wash. State Libr. Gov.'s Conf. on Libr. and Info. Svcs.; charter commr. Greater Spokane Women's Commn.; apptd. chair Older Women's Task Force; mem. Spokane City Women's Issues Adv. Com. Recipient Nat. Mgmt. Chpt. Exec. of Yr., City of Spokane, 1991-92. Mem. ALA, Am. Assn. Women in C.C.s, Assn. Coll. and Rsch. Librs., Nat. Coun. Instnl. Adminstrs., Wash. Libr. Assn. (1st v.p. com. 1994-96, publicity chair 1994 ann. conf., pres. 1996—), P.E.O. (state chair scholar award, chpt. pres., pre. internat. conv.), Rotary (exec. bd., chair scholarship com.), Beta Phi Mu. Office: Yakima Valley CC PO Box 1647 Yakima WA 98907-1647

WEBER, LAVERN JOHN, marine science administrator, educator; b. Isabel, S.D., June 7, 1933; s. Jacob and Irene Rose (Bock) W.; m. Shirley Jean Carlson, June 19, 1959 (div. 1992); children: Timothy L., Peter J., Pamela C., Elizabeth T.; m. Patricia Rae Lewis, Oct. 17, 1992. AAS, Everett Jr. Coll., 1956; BA, Pacific Luth. U., 1958; MS, U. Wash., 1962, PhD, 1964. Instr. U. Wash., Seattle, 1964-67, asst. prof., 1967-69, acting state toxicologist, 1968-69; assoc. prof. Oreg. State U., Corvallis, 1969-75, prof., 1976—, asst. dean grad. sch., 1974-77; dir. Hatfield Marine Sci. Ctr. Oregon State U., Newport, 1977—, supt. Coastal Oreg. Marine Exptl. Sta., 1989—. Pres., trustee Newport Pub. Libr., 1991-92, Yaquina Bay Econ. Found., Newport, 1991-92; chmn. Oreg. Coast Aquarium, 1983-95. Recipient Pres. award Newport Rotary, 1984-85. Mem. South Slough

Mgmt. Commn., Am. Soc. Pharm. and Exptl. Therapy, West Pharm. Soc., Soc. Toxicology, Soc. Exptl. Biol. Med. (n.w. divsn., pres. 1978, 82, 87), Pacific N.W. Assn. Toxicologists (chair 1985-86, coun. 1991-93), Western Assn. Marine Lab. (pres. 1993). Office: Oregon State Univ Hatfield Marine Sci Ctr Aquarium 2030 SE Marine Science Dr Newport OR 97365-5229

WEBER, MARIAN FRANCES, laboratory administrator, educator; b. L.A., Mar. 25, 1951; d. Charles Robert and Dorothy Elizabeth (Welch) Howseman; m. Daniel Mark Babcock, July 13, 1972 (div. 1977); 1 child, Angela Dawn Babcock; m. Michael Patrick Weber, July 24, 1984; 1 child, Benjamin Michael. ScB in Chemistry, Brown U., 1973. Lab. tech. Med. Coll. Ga., Augusta, 1973; analytical sci. United Mchts. & Mfg., Langley, S.C., 1973-75; analytical chemist Sav River Ecology Lab., Aiken, S.C., 1976-82; chief chemist Enwright Lab., Greenville, S.C., 1983-86; chief chemist Laidlaw Environ. Svcs., Roebuck, S.C., 1986-90, lab. mgr., 1990-92; lab. mgr. U.S. Pollution Control, Inc., Salt Lake City, 1993-95; lab. supervisor FMC Wyo. Corp., Green River, 1995—. Mem. Am. Chem. Soc., S.C. Lab. Mgmt. Soc. (v.p. 1986, pres. 1992), Am. Assn. Lab. Analysts. Baptist. Office: FMC Westvaco Rd Green River WY 82935

WEBER, MARK EDWARD, editor, historian; b. Portland, Oreg., Oct. 9, 1951; s. Stanley Edward and Yvonne (Bernard) W.; m. Priscilla Marie Gray, Oct. 29, 1994; 1 child, Laura Marie. BA with high honors, Portland State U., 1976; MA, Ind. U., 1978. Editor Jour. Hist. Rev., Newport Beach, Calif., 1992—; dir. Inst. for Hist. Rev., Newport Beach, 1995—. Roman Catholic.

WEBER, SAMUEL, editor, retired; b. N.Y.C., July 31, 1926; s. Bernard and Gertrude (Ellenberg) W.; m. Eileen Gloria Hornstein, Mar. 5, 1950; children—Bruce Jay, Robert Matthew. B.S. in Elec. Engring, Va. Poly. Inst., 1947. Engr. N.Y. Bd. Transp., 1948-50, U.S. Naval Shipyard, Bklyn., 1950-52, Barlow Engring. Co., N.Y.C., 1952-54; engring. supr. Curtiss Wright Corp., Woodridge, N.J., 1954-56; electronics engr. Loral Electronics Corp., N.Y.C., 1957-58; with Electronics mag., N.Y.C., 1958-67, assoc. mng. editor, 1968-70, exec. editor, 1970-79, editor in chief, 1979-84, exec. tech. editor, 1984-88, editor-at-large, 1988-92; editor in chief Electrotechnology mag., N.Y.C., 1968—; pres. Samuel Weber & Assocs., 1988-91, Samuel Weber & Assocs., Inc., 1991-96; contbg. editor Asic & Eda Magazine, 1991-94; spl. projects editor Electronic Engring. Times, 1992-96, ret., 1997. Author: Modern Digital Circuits, 1964, Optoelectronic Devices and Circuits, 1968, Large and Medium Scale Integration, 1974, Circuits for Electronics Engineers, 1977, Electronic Circuits Notebook, 1981. Served with AUS, 1944-46. Mem. IEEE (life). Home and Office: 4242 E Allison Rd Tucson AZ 85712-1039

WEBER, STEPHEN LEWIS, university president; b. Boston, Mar. 17, 1942; s. Lewis F. and Catherine (Warns) W.; m. Susan M. Keim, June 27, 1965; children: Richard, Matthew. BA, Bowling Green State U., 1964; postgrad., U. Colo., 1964-66; PhD, U. Notre Dame, 1969; EdD (hon.), Capital Normal U., China, 1993. Asst. prof. philosophy U. Maine, Orono, 1969-75, assoc. prof., 1975-79, asst. to pres., 1976-79; dean arts and scis. Fairfield (Conn.) U., 1979-84; v.p. acad. affairs St. Cloud (Minn.) State U., 1984-88; pres. SUNY Oswego, 1988-95; interim provost SUNY, Oswego, 1995-96; pres. San Diego State U., 1996—; participant Harvard Inst. Ednl. Mgmt., Cambridge, Mass., 1985; cons. Sloan Found., 1981. Contbr. numerous articles on philosophy and acad. adminstrn. to profl. jours. Mentor Am. Coun. Edn. Fellowship Program; co-chair Minn. State Bd. Edn. Curriculum Task Force on Educating the Black Learner, 1988; mem. Minn. Tech. Alliance, 1987; mem. program adv. com. Minn. Higher Edn. Coordinating Bd., 1986-88; mem. Gov.'s Commn. on Internat. Edn., 1988. Named Outstanding Humanities Tchr., U. Maine, 1975; Rsch. fellow U. Notre Dame, 1968-69. Mem. Am. Philos. Assn., Am. Assn. Higher Edn. Democrat. Office: Office of President San Diego State Univ San Diego CA 92182-8000

WEBER-SHADRICK, DOROTHY JO, management consultant; b. Denver, Nov. 3, 1951; d. Herbert Eugene and Marian Rose (Walsh) Forbis; 1 child, Dawn Michele. BBA, U. Denver, 1985. Cert. exhbn. mgr., Colo. Asst. dir. meetings Assn. Operating Rm. Nurses, Denver, 1978-87; v.p. Price & Assocs., Denver, 1987; pres. Assn. Conf. and Exhbn. Mgmt., Aurora, Colo., 1987—. Contbr. articles to profl. jours. Recipient Spl. Recognition award U. Denver, 1985. Mem. Colo. Soc. Assn. Execs. (bd. dirs., Pres.'s award 1995), Am. Soc. Assn. Execs., Nat. Assn. Exhbn. Mgrs. (v.p. 1981, pres. 1982, Pres.'s award 1982). Office: Assn Confs and Exhbns Mgmt 11275 E Mississippi Ave Ste 2e3 Aurora CO 80012-2818

WEBSTER, JEFFERY NORMAN, technology policy analyst; b. Erie, Pa., Oct. 23, 1954; s. Norman A. and Betty B. (Bessetti) W.; m. Harriet Marie McGinley, Nov. 27, 1982; 1 child, Jessica Marie. BA, Pa. State U., 1980; MPA, U. So. Calif., 1985. Sr. evaluator, technologist U.S. Gen. Acctg. Office, L.A., 1981—. Co-author numerous technology assessment reports to the Congress, 1983—. Mem. AIAA. Home: 1191 E Mendocino St Altadena CA 91001-2524 Office: US Gen Acctg Office 350 S Figueroa St Ste 1010 Los Angeles CA 90071-1306

WEBSTER, JOHN KINGSLEY OHL, II, health administrator, rehabilitation manager; b. L.A., July 27, 1950; s. John Kingsley Ohl and Inez (Gilbert) W.; m. Marcia Lanier McKnight, June 16, 1977; children: David Lilly, Jason Kingsley McKnight. AA, Pasadena (Calif.) City Coll., 1973; BS, San Jose (Calif.) State U., 1975; MS, Calif. State U., L.A., 1989. Registered occupational therapist, Calif. Supervising occupational therapy cons. San Gabriel Valley Regional Ctr., 1976-79; supr. II occupational therapy cons. San Diego Regional Ctr., 1979-83; sr. occupational therapist Mesa Vista Hosp., 1983-84; pvt. practice Vista, Calif., 1983-85; occupational therapy cons. Calif. Children Svcs., State Dept. Health Svcs., L.A., 1985-86, regional adminstrv. cons., 1986-90; dir. occupational therapy Eureka Gen. Hosp., 1990; dir. ops. and mktg. Life Dimensions Inc., Newport Beach, Calif., 1990; occupational therapy cons., licensing and cert. Calif. Dept. Health Svcs., 1990-93; program dir. rehab. svcs. Scripps Meml. Hosp., Encinitas, Calif., 1993-94; dir. rehab. Vista (Calif.) Knoll, 1994; clin. dir. occupational therapy Sundance Rehab., San Diego, 1994-95; regional dir. ops. Quest Rehab, L.A., 1995-96; area mgr. Am. Therapy Svc., 1996; western divsn. dir. of ops. Accelerated Care Plus, L.A., 1996—; cons. Hopi and Navajo Tribes, Winslow, Ariz., 1978; dir. Imperial County SPRANS grant, El Centro, Calif., 1986-88; pres., owner Kingsley Constrn., Vista, 1988—. Artist (sculpture) Free Form (3d pl. award 1973), (oil painting) Jamaican Woman (3d pl. award 1979). Recipient Esquire title Lady Elliott of STOBS, Edinburough, Scotland, 1973, spl. dept. recognition Calif. State U., 1989. Mem. Am. Occupational Therapy Assn., Inst. Profl. Health Svc. Adminstrs., Student Assn. of Am. Coll. Health Care Execs.

WEBSTER, MERLYN HUGH, JR., manufacturing engineer, information systems consultant; b. Beaver Falls, Pa., Nov. 7, 1946; s. Merlyn Hugh and Helen Ruth (Dillon) W.; m. Linda Jeanne Gundlach, June 14, 1969; children: Matthew Jason, Nathaniel Kevin. AA, Palomar Coll., San Marcos, Calif., 1975; BA, Chapman Coll., 1978. Registered profl. engr., Calif. Sr. cons., pres. WEB Internat. Corp., 1992—; mfg. analyst NCR Corp., Rancho Bernardo, Calif., 1968-72, indsl. engr., 1972-76, sr. indsl. engr., 1976-78; sr. project mgr. Tektronix, Beaverton, Oreg., 1978-83, corp. distbn. I.E. mgr., 1983-86; sr. info. systems cons. Intel Corp., Hillsboro, Oreg., 1986—; pres. WEB Internat. Corp., Tualatin, Oreg., 1992—; cons. material handling Intel Mfg., Puerto rico and Ireland, 1989-92; cons. info. systems M.I.S.I., N.Y.C., 1992-93. Chmn. United Way Hillsboro, Oreg., 1986. With USMC, 1964-68, Vietnam. Mem. NSPE, Inst. Indsl. Engrs. (cert.), Shelby Car Club Am. Republican. Office: WEB Internat Corp Ste 101 5200 SW Joshua St Tualatin OR 97062

WEBSTER, RONALD LEWIS, structural engineer; b. Salt Lake City, Aug. 23, 1936; s. Wesley Owen and Ruth (Holmes) W.; m. Linda Helen Hall, Apr. 16, 1960; children: Mark, Adeena, David, Ronna, Ann, John, Paul, Scott, Brent, Lori Jo, Brian, Adam, Chelsea. Student, U. Utah, 1955-57; BS in Math., Utah State U., 1965; MS in Mech. Engring., Brigham Young U., 1969; PhD in Civil Engring., Cornell U., 1976. Registered profl. engr., N.Y. Rsch. technician Raytheon Co., Lawrence, Mass., 1960; asst. engr. Thiokol Chem. Corp. (name now Thiokol Corp.), Brigham City, Utah, 1960-64, engr., 1966-67, sr. staff engr., 1977—; scientific programmer Boeing Airplane Co., Seattle, 1965-66; engr. Lockheed Propulsion Co., Redlands, Calif., 1967-68, GE Co., ESD, Syracuse, N.Y., 1969-77; cons. Brigham City, 1977—. Author: (computer program) SEADYN, 1976; contbr. articles to profl. jours. Mem. AIAA (assoc. fellow), ASME, Phi Kappa Phi. Home: 720 Eliason St Brigham City UT 84302-2268

WECHSLER, MARY HEYRMAN, lawyer; b. Green Bay, Wis., Jan. 8, 1948; d. Donald Hubert and Helen (Polcyn) Heyrman; m. Roger Wechsler, Aug. 1971 (div. 1977); 1 child, Risa Heyrman; m. David Jay Sellinger, Aug. 15, 1981; 1 stepchild, Kirk Benjamin; 1 child, Michael Paul. Student, U. Chgo., 1966-67, 68-69; BA, U. Wash., 1971; JD cum laude, U. Puget Sound, 1979. Bar: Wash. 1979. Assoc. Law Offices Ann Johnson, Seattle, 1979-81; ptnr. Johnson, Wechsler, Thompson, Seattle, 1981-83; pvt. practice Seattle, 1984-87; ptnr. Mussehl, Rosenberg et al, Seattle, 1987-88, Wechsler, Besk, Erickson, Ross & Roubik, Seattle, 1988—; bd. dirs. U. Wash. Law Sch. Child Advocacy Clinic; mem. Walsh Commn. on Jud. Selection, 1995-96; mem. commn. on domestic rels. U.S. Supreme Ct., 1996-97, mem. law-related edn. com., 1997; chair edn. com. Access to Justice Bd., 1996-97; presenter in field. Author: Family Law in Washington, 1987, rev. edit., 1988, Marriage and Separation, Divorce and Your Rights, 1994; contbr. articles to legal publs. Mem. Wash. State Ethics Adv. Com., 1992-95; bd. dirs. Seattle LWV, 1991-92. Fellow Am. Acad. Matrimonial Lawyers (trustee Wash. state chpt. 1994, sec.-treas. 1996-97 profl. com. 1996-97; mem. ABA (chmn. Wash. state 1987-88), Wash. State Bar Assn. (exec. com. family law sect. 1985-91, chair 1988-89, legis. com. 1991-96, Outstanding Atty. of Yr. family law sect. 1988), Wash. Women Lawyers, King County Bar Assn. (legis. com. 1985—, vice-chair 1990-91, chair family law sect. 1986-87, chair domestic violence com. 1986-87, trustee 1988-90, policy planning com. 1991-92, 2d v.p. 1992-93, 1st v.p. 1993-94, pres. 1994-95), Nat. Conf. of Bar Pres. (commn. com. 1994-95, long range planning com. 1996). Office: Wechsler Besk Erickson Ross & Roubik 701 5th Ave Seattle WA 98104-7016

WECHSLER, SUSAN LINDA, software design engineer; b. Burbank, Calif., Oct. 7, 1956; d. Robert Edward and Sharron Ilene Wechsler; m. Gary Daniel Grove, Aug. 24, 1975 (dec. Dec. 1980); m. Dane Bruce Rogers, Feb. 28, 1987; children: Shayna Marneen Rogers, Ayla Corinne Rogers. BA in Math., Calif. State U., Long Beach, 1979. R&D software engr. Hewlett-Packard Co., Corvallis, Oreg., 1980—; Presenter N.W. Software Quality Conf., 1984. Contbr. articles to profl. publs.; co-developer nine calculators and handheld computers; patentee in field; co-designer HP 200LX Palmtop PC/Organizer, 1994; writer user interface DMI and BIOS software for laptop computers. Pres. Gifts for a Better World, Corvallis, Oreg., 1994, bd. dirs. 1990-1995. Democrat. Office: Hewlett-Packard 1000 NE Circle Blvd Corvallis OR 97330-4239

WEDDLE, JUDITH ANN, social services administrator; b. Burlington, Iowa, Aug. 28, 1944; d. Kenneth Ivan and Betty Ruth (Neiswanger) Shipley; 1 child, Brian Douglas. BA, Midland Coll., 1966. Social worker Dodge County Welfare Dept., Fremont, Nebr., 1967-68; social worker L.A. County Dept. Pub. Social Svcs., 1969-71, appeals hearing specialist, 1971-78; supr., appeals hearing specialist L.A. Welfare Dept., 1978-86; human svcs. adminstr. Los Angeles Welfare Dept., 1986—. Pres. Gardena (Calif.) Hotline, 1971-72, Gardena Swimteam Parents, 1978-79; elder Presbyn. Ch., Gardena, 1987—; active Torrance (Calif.) Civic Chorale, 1989—.

WEED, RONALD DE VERN, engineering consulting company executive; b. Indian Valley, Idaho, Sept. 1, 1931; s. David Clinton and Grace Elizabeth (Lavendar) W.; m. Doris Jean Hohener, Nov. 15, 1953; children: Geraldine Gayle, Thomas De Vern, Cheryl Ann. BSChemE, U. So. Calif., 1957; MS in Chem. Engring., U. Wash., 1962; LLB, La Salle U., Chgo., 1975; postgrad., Century U., Beverly Hills, Calif., 1979—. Registered profl. engr., Washington, Calif. Devel. engr. GE Co., Richland, Washington, 1957-65, Battelle N.W. Labs., Richland, 1965-68; oper. plant engr. NIPAK, Inc., Kerens, Tex., 1968-72; aux. systems task engr. Babcock & Wilcox Co., Lynchburg, Va., 1972-74; materials and welding engr. Bechtel Group Cos., San Francisco, 1974-85; cons. engr. Cygna Energy Svcs., Walnut Creek, Calif., 1985-91; with inter city fund Cygna Energy Svcs., Oakland, Calif., 1991-94; corrosion engr. Gen. Physics Corp., Oakland, 1994—; sr. environ. engr. Jacobs Engring. Group. Contbr. rsch. reports, papers and chpts. in books; patentee in field. With U.S. Army, 1951-53. Mem. Am. Inst. Chem. Engrs., Am. Welding Soc., Nat. Assn. Corrosion Engrs. (cert., sect. vice chmn. and chmn. 1962-68). Home and Office: 74 Sharon St Bay Point CA 94565-1527

WEED, RONALD LEAMING, radiation safety consultant, educator; b. Portland, Oreg., Jan. 23, 1942; s. Robert Leaming Weed and Rosa Clara (Stricker) Thomson; m. Marguerite Elizabeth Cronin, 1970 (div. 1984); 1 child, Ronald Leaming. BS, U. Oreg., 1966, MEd, 1977; MEd, Our Lady of Lake Coll., San Antonio, 1982; MA, Incarnate Word Coll., San Antonio, 1980; postgrad., Tex. A & M U., U. Autonowa Tawanlysas. Cert. secondary tchr. and high sch. counselor, Tex., Ill., Wash., Mont.; cert. X-ray physicist, Ill., Md. Calif., N.C., Ohio. Instr. of English, Def. Lang. Inst., Lackland AFB, Tex., 1974-76; instr. X-ray physics Acad. Health Scis., Ft. Sam Houston, Tex., 1976-80; health physicist USAF Occupational and Environ. Health Lab., 1980-83, USAF Sch. Radiation Scis., 1983-85, Scott Med. Ctr., Scott AFB, Ill., 1985-89; med. physicist Mallinckrodt Med. Inst., St. Louis, 1990-92; pres. Radiation Safety Consultation, Belleville, Ill., 1992-94; instr. ESL, Psychology Columbia Basin Coll., Pasco, Wash., 1994-96, instr. prevocat. ESL, vocat. ESL,, 1997—; disaster preparedness officer Fed. Emergency Mgmt. Agy.-City of St. Louis, 1991-93; instr. Columbia Basin Coll., 1993, 94, 95-96, radiation chemistry designer, instr. Inventor X-ray source to table measure, 1971. Vol. Habitat for Humanity, East St. Louis, Ill., 1991-93, Ostuncalco, Guatemala, 1992; site guide Cahokia Mounds Archaeol. Site, Caseyville, Ill., 1992. With USAF, 1980-89, lt. col. USAFR, 1995. Mem. Health Physics Soc. (plenary), Am. Coll. Radiology, Am. Coll. Med. Physics. Episcopalian. Office: Columbia Basin Coll 2600 N 20th Ave Pasco WA 99301-3379

WEEKS, LIONEL EDWARDS, orthopedic surgeon; b. Rockville Ctr., N.Y., Jan. 19, 1947; m. Sue Jensen, 1973; childen: Edward Jesse, Lionel Tyler. AB magna cum laude, Williams Coll., 1968; MD, Columbia U., 1973. Diplomate Am. Bd. Orthop. Surgery, Am. Bd. Emergency Medicine. Pvt. practice emergency medicine Wasatch Emergency Physicians, Salt Lake City, Utah, 1975-82; pvt. practice orthop. surgery Orthop. Specialty Hosp., Salt Lake City, 1985—; clin. instr. orthop. surgery U. Utah Sch. of Medicine, Salt Lake City, 1986-91, clin. asst. prof., 1991—; chmn. shoulder guidelines com. Utah State Indsl. Commn., 1994-95. Fellow Am. Acad. Orthop. Surgeons; mem. Western Orthop. Assn., Arthroscopy Assn. N. Am., Internat. Coll. Surgeons, N.Y. Orthop. Hops. Alumni Assn. Home: 1485 Alta Cir Salt Lake City UT 84103 Office: Orthop Specialty Hosp 5848 S 300 E Salt Lake City UT 84107-6121

WEEKS, ROBERT LEE, electronic engineer, program manager; b. Woonsocket, R.I., Mar. 8, 1957; s. Joseph Bernard and Claire Lorraine (Jolicoeur) W.; m. Christine Ann Bentley; children: Barbara Ann, Christopher Lee. BSEE, U. Ariz., 1985, postgrad., 1987; MBA, U. Phoenix, 1996. Laborer ASARCO Mine Inc., Sahuarita, Ariz., 1979-82; test engr. EMI and TEMPEST br. U.S. Army Electronic Proving Ground, Ft. Huachuca, Ariz., 1985-88, chief EMI and TEMPEST br., 1988-95; chief electromagnetics br. U.S. Army Electronic Proving Ground, Ft. Huachuca, 1995-96, mgr. R&D program, 1996—; mem. MIL-STD-461 Joint Working Group, 1989-94; mem. DOD and industry E3 standards com. Dept. Def., 1994—. Bd. dirs. Bristol Park Neighborhood Assn., Tucson, 1994—; vol. YMCA, 1994—. With USMC, 1975-79. Mem. IEEE (named Engr. of Yr. local chpt. 1994), Electromagnetic Compatibility Soc. of IEEE, Nat. Assn. Radio and Telecomms. Engrs. (cert. electromagnetic compatibility engr.). Democrat. Roman Catholic. Office: US Army Electronic Proving Ground STEWS-EPG-TE Fort Huachuca AZ 85613

WEEKS, ROGER WOLCOTT, JR., retired German and Russian language educator; b. Boston, Mar. 31, 1930; s. Roger Wolcott and Kara (Stanley) W.; m. Lore Marianne Apfel, Jan. 26, 1955; children: Kara, Tanya. BA in German cum laude, U. Mass., 1959, MA in German, 1962; MA in Russian, U. Colo., 1967. Instr. German and Russian, U. Mass., Amherst, 1962-63; asst. prof. U. Denver, 1963-67; assoc. prof. So. Oreg. State Coll., Ashland, 1967-92; ret., 1992. Author: Reading Between the Lines, 1992. With USAF, 1951-55. Republican. Presbyterian. Home: 1107 Paradise Ln Ashland OR 97520-3527

WEEKS, WILFORD FRANK, retired geophysics educator, glaciologist; b. Champaign, Ill., Jan. 8, 1929; married; 2 children. BS, U. Ill., 1951, MS, 1953; PhD in Geology, U. Chgo., 1956. Geologist mineral deposits br. U.S. Geol. Survey, 1952-55; glaciologist USAF Cambridge Research Ctr., 1955-57; asst. prof. Washington U., St. Louis, 1957-62; adj. prof. earth scis. Dartmouth Coll., Hanover, N.H., 1962-85; glaciologist Cold Regions Rsch. and Engring. Lab., Hanover, 1962-89; chief scientist Alaska Synthetic Aperture Radar Facility, Fairbanks, 1986-93; prof. geophysics Geophys. Inst. U. Alaska, Fairbanks, 1986-96; cons. in field, 1996—; vis. prof. Inst. Low Temperature Sci. Hokkaido U., Sapporo, Japan, 1973; chair Arctic marine sci. USN Postgrad. Sch., Monterey, Calif., 1978-79; mem. earth sys. sci. com. NASA, Washington, 1984-87; advisor U.S. Arctic Rsch. Commn., divsn. polar programs NSF, Washington, 1987-88; chmn. NAS Com. on Cooperation with Russia in Ice Mechanics, 1991-92; mem. environ. task force MEDEA Cons. Group, 1992—. Capt. USAF, 1955-57. Recipient Emil Usibelli Prize for Rsch., 1996. Fellow Arctic Inst. N.Am., Am. Geophys. Union; mem. NAE, Internat. Glaciological Soc. (v.p. 1969-72, pres. 1973-75, Seligman Crystal award 1989). Home and Office: 6533 SW 34th Ave Portland OR 97201-1077

WEEKS, WILLIAM RAWLE, JR., oil company executive; b. Denver, Oct. 23, 1920; s. William Rawle Sr. and Besse Elizabeth (Griffith) W.; m. June Suzanne Stephens, Jan. 22, 1944 (div. 1980); children: Stephen R., Tacy A. Weeks Hahn. BA, Stanford U., 1943. With book prodn. divsn. Stanford U. Press, 1948-49; advt. exec. Palo Alto, Calif., 1949-50; with CIA, 1951—; gen. ptnr. Weeks, Brewer & Assocs., 1971; CEO Fort Collins Consol. Royalties, Inc., Cheyenne, Wyo., 1983—. Author: Knock and Wait Awhile, 1957 (Edgar Allan Poe award 1958, Commonwealth award 1958). Nat. press and media advance man Muskie Vice Presdl. Campaign, 1968. 2nd lt. U.S. Army, 1943-46. Mem. Nat. Press Club, Denver Petroleum Club. Home: Apt 8C 1201 Williams St Denver CO 80218 Office: Fort Collins Consol Royalties Inc 1508 Stillwater Ave Cheyenne WY 82009

WEEMS, MARY ANN, business owner; b. Carlsbad, N.Mex., June 12, 1948; d. Myer and Nadine Lolita (Miller) Rosenberg; div. 1993; children: Elizabeth Nadine, Brian Eli. BS in Art cum laude, William Woods Coll., 1970. Cert. tchr., Mo., Tex. Tchr. art Lubbock (Tex.) Pub. Sch., 1970-71; profl. artist Albuquerque, 1972-77; owner Weems Galleries & Framing, Albuquerque, 1981—, Weems Artfest, Albuquerque, 1982—, Weems Gallery - Old Town, Albuquerque, 1994—; bd. dirs. N.Mex. Arts and Crafts Fair, Albuquerque, 1972-76, Rio Grande Arts and Crafts Fair, 1974-77. Mem. Albuquerque Conv. and Visitors Bur., 1981—, bd. dirs., 1990-92; loan fund mem. West Corp., Albuquerque, 1992-95; bd. dirs. Albuquerque Mus., 1986-88. Named one of Women on the Move YWCA, 1996, 10 Top Smart, Savvy, Successful Albuquerque Women's Mag., 1997; named #1 Fine Arts and Crafts Fair in N.Mex. Harris List, 1996. Mem. Internat. Festivals and Events Assn. (Pinnacle award 1996), S.W. Festivals and Events Assn., Albuquerque C. of C., Albuquerque Gallery Assn. (pres. 1984-86). Jewish. Office: Weems Galleries and Framing 2801 M Eubank NE Albuquerque NM 87112

WEESE, BRUCE ERIC, pharmaceutical industry lobbyist; b. Chewelah, Wash., Mar. 22, 1942; s. Harry M. and Roberta B. (Carman) W.; m. Elaine M. Smith, June 18, 1962 (div. July 1972); children: Sandra G., Michael D.; m. Vera B. Reed, Mar. 22, 1975; stepchildren: Kevin E. Bayron, Kelly M. Bayron. BA in Edn., Ea. Wash. State U., Cheney, 1964; MBA, Pepperdine U., 1981. Tchr. Grant Joint Union High Sch. Dist., Sacramento, 1964-70; pharm. sales McNeil Labs., San Jose, Calif., 1970-77, Adria Labs., San Francisco, 1977-83, Serono Labs., San Francisco, 1983-84, Boehringer Ingelheim, Santa Rosa, Calif., 1984-91; mgr. govt. affairs (lobbyist) for western states Boehringer Ingelheim, 1991—. Bd. dirs. Russian River Health Ctr., Guerneville, Calif., 1994-95. Mem. United Anglers, Sequoia Paddlers, Santa Rosa Sailing Club, Sierra Club. Democrat. Home: 20303 NE 226th Cir Battle Ground WA 98604-4943 Office: Boehringer Ingelheim PO Box 368 Ridgefield CT 06877-0368

WEESE, WILLIAM CURTIS, physician; b. Chgo., Dec. 13, 1944. BS with distinction, U. Mich., 1965; MD, U. Chgo., 1969. Diplomate Nat. Bd. Med. Examiners, Am. Bd. Internal Medicine, specialty bd. pulmonary diseases. Intern U. Iowa Hosps., 1969-70, resident in internal medicine, 1970-72; fellow in pulmonary diseases Mass. Gen. Hosp., Boston, 1972-74, asst. in medicine, 1974-75; instr. medicine Harvard Med. Sch., Boston, 1974-75; pvt. practice chest diseases Phoenix, 1975—; chmn. dept. internal medicine St. Joseph's Hosp., Phoenix, 1983-87; med. dir. St. Joe's Preferred Choice Health Plan, Phoenix, 1990—; mem. exec. com. St. Joseph's Hosp., Phoenix, 1983-86, 90-92; med. advisor Social Security Adminstrn. Health and Human Svcs. Dept., Phoenix, 1979—. Fellow ACP, Am. Coll. Chest Physicians; mem. AMA, Ariz. Med. Assn., Ariz. Thoracic Soc. (pres. 1984-86), Maricopa County Med. Soc., Osler Club, Am. Lung Assn., Am. Thoracic Soc., Am. Coll. Health Care Execs., Am. Coll. Physicians Execs., Med. History Club Ariz. (pres. 1977-80), Ariz. Lung Assn. (bd. dirs. 1984—, pres. bd. 1990-92). Office: 375 E Virginia Ave Ste C Phoenix AZ 85004-1202

WEGELIN, JACOB ANDREAS, statistician; b. Eugene, Oreg., Dec. 14, 1954; s. Christof Andreas and Caroline (Locke) W. BA, BS, U. Wash., 1986, MS, 1989. With Shiloh Youth Revival Ctrs., Inc., Eugene, 1971-76, Eugene Hotel, 1976-78; deckhand Alaska Fishing Industry, 1978-79; tech. writer, editor IBM Corp., San Jose, Poughkeepsie, N.Y., 1985-86; cook, deckhand, bull cook Alaska Boat Co., Wards Cove Packing Co., 1991-93; instr. MathSoft, Seattle, 1995; statistician U. Wash., Seattle, 1996—. Recipient Pres.'s medal U. Wash., 1986; NSF fellow, 1986-89. Mem. Am. Statis. Assn., Phi Beta Kappa. Office: Dept Stats Univ Wash Seattle WA 98195

WEGENER, DON EDWARD, pharmacist, retired military officer; b. St. Louis, Feb. 16, 1942; s. Earl Carl Sr. and Irma Emily Ida (Struebing) W. BS, St. Louis Coll. Pharmacy, 1965. Registered pharmacist, Mo., Tex., Wash. Commd. 2d lt. USAF, 1967, advanced through grades to maj., 1978, ret., 1987. Vol., relief pharmacist ARC. Lutheran. Home: 11321 N Post St Spokane WA 99218-2689

WEGGE, LEON LOUIS FRANÇOIS, economics educator; b. Breendonk, Antwerp, Belgium, June 9, 1933; came to U.S., 1959; s. Petrus Maria and Alberta (De Maeyer) W.; m. Beate Maria Teipel, Nov. 22, 1962; children: Simone, Robert, Elizabeth. B in Thomistical Philosophy, Cath. U. Louvain, Belgium, 1957, Licentiate in Econ. Sci., 1958; PhD in Indsl. Econs., MIT, 1963. Assoc. lectr. U. New S. Wales, Kensington, Australia, 1963-66; prof. econs. U. Calif., Davis, 1966—; vis. prof. U. Bonn, Fed. Republic Germany, 1980-81. Assoc. editor Jour. Internat. Econs., 1971-84; contbr. articles to profl. jours. Rsch. fellow Ctr. for Ops. Rsch. and Econometrics, 1972-73, fellow The Netherlands Inst. for Advanced Study, 1987-88. Mem. Econometric Soc., Am. Statistical Assn. Roman Catholic. Home: 26320 County Rd # 98 Davis CA 95616 Office: U Calif Davis Dept Econs Davis CA 95616

WEGNER, DARLENE JOY, civic worker, event coordinator; b. Pasadena, Calif., May 2, 1953; d. Glenn Raymond and Evelyn Pryor (Ingram) Thornton; m. Robert Culbertson, July 25, 1975 (div. May 1977); m. Karl James, June 21, 1986; 1 child, Heather Joy. Student, East L.A. Jr. Coll., 1971-72, Chaffey Coll., Rancho Cucamonga, Calif., 1995. Exec. sec. Wlls Fargo Bank, Rosemead, Calif., 1972-76; adminstrv. sec. Ford Aerospace, Pasadena, 1977-78; sales sec. A&F Sales Engring., Pasadena, 1979-84; sr. sec. Xerox Med., Pasadena, 1984-89; cmty. activist Ontario (Calif.) City Hall, 1991-92; vice chmn. Concerned Citizens Commn. on Pornography and Obscenity, Ontario, 1992-93; project dir. Inland Empire Prayer Gathering Nat. Day of Prayer, Ontario, 1993-94; office adminstr. Prayer Command Post, Ontario, 1995-96; adminstrv. svcs. dir. Inland Empire Secretarial Svcs., Ontario, 1996—. Author: Beauty Instead of Ashes, 1994; freelance writer. Republican. Mem. Community Ch.

WEGNER, SAMUEL JOSEPH, museum executive; b. Twin Falls, Idaho, Aug. 27, 1952; s. Albert Henry and Eleanor Esther (Wright) W.; m. Linda

Louise Talley, May 27, 1972; children: Ethan, Elena. BA, U. Ariz., 1973; MA, U. Idaho, 1975. Curator Mansion Mus.-Oglebay Inst., Wheeling, W.Va., 1975-76; curator of edn. State Hist. Soc. Wis., Madison, 1976-78; asst. supt. Region I Mo. Dept. Nat. Resources, Brookfield, 1978-85; dir. ops. So. Oregon Hist. Soc., Jacksonville, Oreg., 1985-87; exec. dir. So. Oregon Hist. Soc., Medford, Oreg., 1987-96; dep. exec. dir. Jamestown-Yorktown Found., Williamsburg, Va., 1996—; mem. Nat. Adv. Com. Common Agenda for History Mus., 1990-92, Nat. Adv. Com. Phila. Documentation Project for Common Agenda, 1989-91; chmn. Region 11 Am. Assn. State and Local History Awards Program, 1989-90, chmn. Oregon State chpt., 1987-88; chmn. Western Region Assn. Living History Farms and Agrl. Mus., 1986-87; mem. Am. Assn. Mus. Ad Hoc Com. for Hist. Sites and Mus. in Pks., 1984-85. Mem. adv. com. Medford (Oreg.) Vis. and Conv. Bur., 1988-96; bd. dirs. Oreg. Trail Coordinating Coun., 1994-96, So. Oreg. Visitors Assn., 1995-96; bd. dirs., coord. Applegate Trail Coalition, 1993-96; mem. Jacksonville Transp. Com., 1993-95. Mem. Am. Assn. Mus., Nat. Trust for Hist. Preservation, Oreg. Mus. Assn., Rotary. Office: Jamestown-Yorktown Found PO Box 1607 Williamsburg VA 23187-1607

WEH, ALLEN EDWARD, airline executive; b. Salem, Oreg., Nov. 17, 1942; s. Edward and Harriet Ann (Hicklin) W.; m. Rebecca Ann Roberton, July 5, 1968; children: Deborah Susan, Ashley Elizabeth, Brian Roberton. BS, U. N.Mex., 1966, MA, 1973. Asst. to chief adminstrv. officer Bank N.Mex., Albuquerque, 1973; pres. N.Mex. Airways, Inc., Albuquerque, 1974; dep. dir. N.Mex. Indochina Refugee Program, Santa Fe, 1975-76; dir. pub. affairs UNC Mining & Milling Co., Albuquerque, 1977-79; pres., CEO, CSI, Inc., Albuquerque, 1979—. Mem. steering com. Colin McMillan for lt. gov., Albuquerque, 1982; bd. dirs. N.Mex. Symphony Orgh., Albuquerque Conv. and Visitors Bur., 1982; mem. Albuquerque Police Adv. Bd., 1977-78; treas., bd. dirs. Polit. Action Com., Albuquerque, 1982. Capt. USMC, 1966-71, Vietnam; col. USMCR, 1971-90, Col. USMC, 1990-91, Persian Gulf, 1992-93, Somalia. Decorated Bronze Star, Purple Heart with two gold stars, Meritorious Svc. medal with gold star, Air medal. Mem. Marine Corps Res. Officers Assn. (life, bd. dirs. 1973, 86), Res. Officers Assn. U.S. (life), SCV (life), Mil. Order Stars and Bars (life). Republican. Episcopalian. Home: 6722 Rio Grande Blvd NW Albuquerque NM 87107-6330 Office: CSI Inc 3700 Rio Grande Blvd NW Albuquerque NM 87107-3042

WEHR, WESLEY CONRAD, museum curator; b. Everett, Wash., Apr. 17, 1929; s. Conrad John and Ingeborg (Hall) W. BA, U. Washington, 1951, MA, 1953. Affiliate curator paleontology Burke Mus. U. Wash., Seattle, 1976—; cons. Stonerose Interpretive Ctr., Republic, Wash., 1990—; guest curator Cheney Cowles Mus., Spokane, 1987, 88, State Capitol Mus., Olympia, Wash., 1986, Frye Art Mus., Seattle, 1984. Mem. Internat. Soc. Paleontology, Botanical Soc. Am., U. Wash. Pres. Club, U. Wash. Deans Club. Democrat. Home: PO Box 45221 Seattle WA 98145-0221 Office: Burke Mus U Wash Seattle WA 98195

WEHRLI, JOHN ERICH, biotechnology executive; b. Bogota, Colombia, Dec. 1, 1963; came to U.S., 1969; s. Werner Freiderich and Graciela Wehrli; m. Vicki Lee Burnett, Aug. 18, 1991; children: Sophia Cristina, Sarina Darlene. BS summa cum laude in Mgmt. and Econs., Golden Gate U., 1993; Tax cert., Foothill Coll., 1994; postgrad., U. Calif., San Francisco, 1994—, U. Calif., Berkeley, 1995—. Analytical chemist dept. Chem. Analysis Syva Diagnostics Co., 1985-87; robotics specialist dept. Automation Tech. Syntex Rsch. Inc., 1987-89, rsch. chemist Inst. Pharm. Scis., dept. Pharm. Chemistry, 1987-91, sr. sci. analyst programmer, sys. mgr. Rsch. Info. Sys., 1991-93, sys. analyst, sr. sys. mgr., 1993-94; part-time fin. cons. assoc. Shearson Lehman Bros., San Francisco, 1989; v.p. Precision Instrument Design Inc., Tahoe City, Calif., 1989-96; legal intern patent and tech. licensing Lawrence Berkeley Nat. Lab., 1995-96; dir. Raptorgraphics Lawrence Berkeley Nat. Lab., Mountain View, Calif., 1995—; pres. Wehrli Tech. Cons., Mountain View, Calif., 1995-96; legal intern Cooley Godward LLP, 1996—; v.p. bus. devel. and intellectual property NaviCyte Inc., Reno, 1996—. Contbr. articles to profl. jours. Enterprise scholar Golden Gate U., 1992, Kanze scholar, 1993, Univ. Honors scholar, 1993, Pres.'s scholar Foothill Coll., 1993. Mem. AAAS, ABA (sci. and tech. sect.), Am. Chem. Soc. (chem. info. and computer scis. sect.), Assn. Univ. Tech. Mgrs., Licensing Execs. Soc., Am. Intellectual Property Law Assn., N.Y. Acad. Scis., Phi Alpha Delta. Home: 1879 Springer Rd Apt B Mountain View CA 94040-4052 Office: NaviCyte Inc Reno NV 89501

WEIBEL, CATHY DENISE, entertainer; b. Mountain View, Calif., May 29, 1965; d. Richard A. and Marylyn J. (Wickliffe) Brugh; m. Neal O. Weibel, June 24, 1984; children: Aimee, Katie, Ryan. Entertainer Most Unique, Brookdale, Calif., 1992-95, A Magic Touch, San Jose, Calif., 1996—. Author: (poetry) The Choice, 1991, The Commission, 1992; (children's book) Dousing the Flame, 1990. Office: 5220 Alum Rock Ave San Jose CA 95127

WEIDNER, MARK, environmental research executive; b. 1952. MS in Analytical Chemistry, Purdue U., 1976. With Mich. State U., East Lansing, 1976-78; instr. Finnigan Corp., San Jose, Calif., 1978-80; sr. chemist Metro Lab., Seattle, 1980-85; now pres., treas. Analytical Resources, Inc., Seattle, 1985—. Office: Analytical Resources Inc 333 9th Ave N Seattle WA 98109-5122*

WEIGAND, WILLIAM KEITH, bishop; b. Bend, Oreg., May 23, 1937. Ed., Mt. Angel Sem., St. Benedict, Oreg., St. Edward's Sem. and St. Thomas Sem., Kenmore, Wash. Bishop Diocese Salt Lake City, 1980-93, Diocese Sacramento, 1993—; Ordained priest Roman Cath. Ch., 1963. Office: See of Sacramento 2110 Broadway Sacramento CA 95818-2518*

WEIGEL, JAMES JOHN, real estate developer, consultant; b. Denver, Colo., May 11, 1957; s. Jacob J. and Pauline R. (Armstrong) W.; m. Beverly S. Whorton, Sept. 25, 1983; children: Shannon, David, Tyson. BA in Econ., U. Colo., 1979; MBA, U. Denver, 1983. Commercal loan officer United Bank of Denver, 1979-81; fin. counselor Asset Mgmt. Group, Rolling Hills Estates, Calif., 1982-84; v.p., comml. loans Comml. Fed. Sav., Denver, 1984-87; v.p., real estate Colo. Nat. Bank, Denver, 1987-92; exec. v.p., COO Pride Mark Homes, Westminster, Colo., 1992—. Bd. dirs. Adams County Sch. Dist. 12, Northglen, Colo., 1994—, Home Builders Assn., Denver, 1989-90. Mem. Northglen/Thornton Rotary. Home: 960 E 133d Dr Thornton CO 80241 Office: 8791 Wolff Ct Westminster CO 80030

WEIGEL, RICHARD GEORGE, psychologist, educator; b. St. Louis, Feb. 23, 1937; s. George D. and Irene K. (Bretz) W.; children: Paul K., Laura K. BA, DePauw U., 1959; MA, U. Mo., Columbia, 1962, PhD in Psychology, 1968. Diplomate in clin. psychology Am. bd. Profl. Psychology; lic. psychologist Colo., Ill., Utah. Counselor/asst. prof. psychology Oreg. State U., Corvallis, 1964-67, acting dir. Counseling Ctr., 1967; asst. prof. to prof. and chmn. counseling psychology program Colo. State U., Ft. Collins, 1967-78; sr. cons. psychologist Rohrer, Hibler & Replogle, Inc., Denver, 1978-90, mgr., 1981-86; dir. and adj. prof. psychology Student Counseling Ctr., Ill. State U., Normal, 1990-92; dir. Counseling Ctr. U. Utah, Salt Lake City, 1992—, clin. prof. psychology, ednl. psychology and psychiatry, 1992—, asst. v.p. student devel., 1996-97, interim v.p. for student affairs, 1997—; pvt. practice psychology, Ft. Collins, 1970-78; adj. prof. Denver U. Sch. Profl. Psychology, 1977-78, Counseling Psychology Program, Ctr. for Spl. and Advanced Programs of U. No. Colo., Greeley, 1975-78, vis. assoc. prof. counseling psychology program, summer 1975; lectr. continuing edn. for nurses Poudre Valley Meml. Hosp., Ft. Collins, 1975; selection psychologist Peace Corps, 1973-74; asst. prof. psychology divsn. continuing edn. Oreg. State Sys. Higher Edn., Salem, 1965; ind. practice marriage counseling, Corvallis, Oreg., 1965-67; clin. psychologist Mo. Tng. Sch. for Boys, summer 1964; instr. psychology U. Mo., Columbia, 1963-64; counselor Counseling Svc., Stephens Coll., Columbia, 1963-64, Univ. Testing and Counseling Svc., U. Mo., Columbia, 1961-62; instr. psychology, resident advisor George Williams Coll., Lake Geneva, Wis., summer 1961; tchg./rsch. asst. psychology U. Mo., 1960-61; rsch. asst. Purdue U., West Lafayette, Ind., 1960; VA clin. psychology trainee Indpls., 1959-60; vis. scientist/lectr. APA, Drury Coll., 1974; lectr. in field; condr. workshops in field; v.p. Bd. Psychologist Examiners State of Colo., 1973-76. Assoc. editor Cons. Psychology Jour.: Practice and rsch., 1991-93, editl. bd., 1990—; editl. bd. Jour. Coll. Student Devel., 1970-73, 92—, Profl. Psychology: Rsch. and Practice, 1990-92; reviewer Jour. Counseling Psychology, 1994, 95, Counseling Psychologist, 1994, 95, 96, Jour. Cons. and Clin. Psychology, 1977; editl. cons. Wadsworth-Brooks/Cole Pub. Co., 1974-78, Univ. Park Press, 1976; contbr. numerous articles to profl. jours.; co-author: Innovative Psychological Therapies, 1975, Innovative Medical-Psychiatric Therapies, 1976. Bd. dirs. Mental Health Assn., Benton County, Oreg., 1966-67; mem. Soc. Indiana Pioneers, 1990—; mem. profl. adv. bd. Denver U. Sch. Profl. Psychology, 1976-78. NIMH grantee, 1977-82, Colo. State U. grantee, 1976-77, Oreg. State U. grantee, 1965-66, 66-67; Paul Harris fellow Rotary, 1981-86. Fellow APA (task force on revision of accreditation criteria 1977-78, vis. scientist 1974, divsn. cons. psychology pres.-elect 1995-96, pres. 1996-97, sec. 1993-95, exec. com. 1990-93, com. fellows 1989-93, chair 1991-93, program com. 1990, counseling psychology divsn. awards com. 1993-95, edn. and tng. com. 1975-78, 91-93, coll. counseling interest group 1991—, clin. psychology divsn., group psychology and group psychotherapy divsn. com. on fellows 1991-93, 95—, chair 1992-93), Am. Psychol. Soc.; mem. AAUP, Assn. Univ. and Coll. Counseling Ctr. Dirs. (governing bd. 1993-95), Rocky Mountain Psychol. Assn. (pres. 1973-74, treas. 1971-72, Disting. Svc. award 1987), Rsch. Consortium of Counseling and Psychol. Svcs. in Higher Edn. (bd. dirs. 1993-95), Internat. Assn. Counseling Svcs. (site visitor 1991-95), Am. Coll. Pers. Assn., Utah Psychol. Assn., Colo. State Bd. Psychologist Examiners (vice chmn. 1974-76, del. to Am. Assn. State Psychology Bds. 1976), Coun. of Counseling Psychology Tng. Programs (bd. dirs. 1974-79, liaison to Am. Assn. State Psychology Bds. 1979), Newcomen Soc. U.S., Sigma Xi, Psi Chi, Phi Gamma Delta, Phi Mu Alpha. Office: University of Utah 208 Park Bldg Salt Lake City UT 84112

WEIGEND, GUIDO GUSTAV, geographer, educator; b. Zeltweg, Austria, Jan. 2, 1920; came to U.S., 1939, naturalized, 1943; s. Gustav F. and Paula (Sorgo) W.; m. Areta Kelble, June 26, 1947 (dec. 1993); children: Nina, Cynthia, Kenneth. B.S., U. Chgo., 1942, M.S., 1946, Ph.D., 1949. With OSS, 1943-45; with mil. intelligence U.S. War Dept., 1946; instr. geography U. Ill., Chgo., 1946-47; instr. then asst. prof. geography Beloit Coll., 1947-49; asst. prof. geography Rutgers U., 1949-51, assoc. prof., 1951-57, prof., 1957-76, acting dept. chmn., 1951-52, chmn. dept., 1953-67, assoc. dean, 1972-76; dean Coll. Liberal Arts, Prof. geography Ariz. State U., Tempe, 1976-84, prof. geography, 1976-89; ret., 1989; Fulbright lectr. U. Barcelona, 1960-61; vis. prof. geography Columbia U., 1963-67, NYU, 1967, U. Colo., summer 1968, U. Hawaii, summer 1969; liaison rep. Rutgers U. to UN, 1950-52; invited by Chinese Acad. Scis. to visit minority areas in Chinese Cent. Asia, 1988; mem. U.S. nat. com. Internat. Geog. Union, 1951-58, 61-65; chmn. Conf. on Polit. and Social Geography, 1968-69. Author articles, monographs, bulls. for profl. jours.; contbr.: (4th edit.) A Geography of Europe, 1977; geog. editor-in-chief: Odyssey World Atlas, 1966. Bd. adjustment Franklin Twp., N.J., 1959; mem. Highland Park (N.J.) Bd. Edn., 1973-75, v.p., 1975; mem. Ariz. Coun. on Humanities and Pub. Policy, 1976-80; vice chmn. Phoenix Com. on Fgn. Rels., 1976-79, chmn., 1979-81; mem. exec. com. Fedn. Pub. Programs in Humanities, 1977-82; bd. dirs. Coun. Colls. Arts and Scis., 1980-83, Phoenix Chamber Music Soc., 1995—; commr. N. Cen. Assn. Colls. and Schs., 1976-80, bd. dirs. commn. on instns. of higher edn., 1980-83. Research fellow Office Naval Research, 1952-55, Rutgers Research Council, 1970-71; grantee Social Sci. Research Council, 1956, Ford Found., 1966, Am. Philos. Soc., 1970-71, German Acad. Exchange Service, 1984; Fulbright travel grantee Netherlands, 1970-71. Mem. Assn. Am. Geographers (chmn. N.Y. Met. divsn. 1955-56, editl. bd. 1955-59, mem. coun. 1965-66, chmn. N.Y.-N.J. divsn. 1965-66), Am. Geog. Soc., Phoenix Chamber Mus. Soc. (bd. dirs. 1995—), Sigma Xi (pres. Ariz. State U. chpt. 1989-91). Home: 2094 E Golf Ave Tempe AZ 85282-4046 Office: Ariz State U Dept Geography Tempe AZ 85287

WEIGHTMAN, ESTHER LYNN, emergency trauma nurse; b. Tawas City, Mich., June 13, 1966; d. Garrie Lee and Naomi Ruth (Atwood) Schneller; m. Robert Thomas Weightman, Dec. 31, 1996. BS in Christian Secondary Edn., Ozark Bible Inst. & Coll., Neosho, Mo., 1988; BSN, Ind. Wesleyan U., Marion, 1991; MS in Cmty. Health Nursing, U. Colo. Health Scis. Ctr., Denver, 1995. RN, Colo.; CEN; cert. ACLS, pediatric advanced life support, trauma nurse core course; cert. type E cert. Colo. Dept. Edn. Staff nurse emergency dept. Marion Gen. Hosp., 1991-92, Penrose-St. Francis Healthcare Sys., Colorado Springs, Colo., 1992-95; staff nurse registry QS Nurses Corp., Colorado Springs, 1992—; staff devel. nurse 302d ASTS-USAFR, Peterson AFB, Colo., 1994—; mentor various healthcare instrnl. facilities, 1991—; vol. tchr. health classes Knowledge is Power, Red Cross Shelter, Colorado Springs, 1995-96. Mem. orch. Living Springs Worship Centre, 1993—. Mem. Emergency Nurses Assn., Res. Officers Assn., Sigma Theta Tau.

WEIGHTMAN, JUDY MAE, lawyer; b. New Eagle, Pa., May 22, 1941; d. Morris and Ruth (Gutstadt) Epstein; children: Wayne, Randall, Darrell. BS in English, California U. of Pa., 1970; MA in Am. Studies, U. Hawaii, 1975; JD, U. Hawaii, 1981. Bar: Hawaii 1981. Tchr. Fairfax County Sch. (Va.), 1968-72, Hawaii Pub. Schs., Honolulu, 1973-75; lectr. Kapiolani Community Coll., Honolulu, 1975-76; instr. Olympic Community Coll., Pearl Harbor, Hawaii, 1975-77; lectr. Hawaii Pacific Coll., Honolulu, 1977-78; law clk. to atty. gen. Hawaii & Case, Kay & Lynch, Davis & Levin, 1979-81, to chief judge Intermediate Ct. Appeals State of Hawaii, 1981-82; dep. pub. defender Office of Pub. Defender, 1982-84; staff atty. Dept. Commerce & Consumer Affairs, State of Hawaii 1984-86; pres., bd. dirs. Am. Beltwrap Corp., 1986—; asst. prof. law, dir. pre-admission program, asst. prof. Richardson Sch. Law, U. Hawaii, 1987—, faculty senator; faculty senate exec. com. U. Hawaii Manoa. Author: Days of Remembrance: Hawaii Witnesses to the Holocaust; producer (documentary) The Panel: The First Exchange, Profile of An Aja Soldier, Profile of a Holocaust Survivor; prodr., dir. From Hawaii to The Holocaust: A Shared Moment in History; patentee in field; mem. Richardson Law Rev., 1979-81. Mem. neighborhood bd. No. 25 City and County Honolulu, 1976-77; vol. Legal Aid Soc., Honolulu, 1977-78; bd. dirs. Jewish Fedn., Protection and Advocacy Agy.; parent rep. Wheeler Intermediate Adv. Coun., Honolulu, 1975-77; trustee Carl K. Mirikitani Meml. Scholarship Fund, Arts Coun. Hawaii; membership dir. ACLU, 1977-78, bd. dirs., Hawaii, 1988—, treas. Amicus; founder Hawaii Holocaust Project; trustee Jewish Fedn. Hawaii. Community scholar, Honolulu, 1980; Internat. Rels. grant Chaminade U., 1976; recipient Hawaii Filmmakers award Hawaii Internat. Film Festival, 1993, Golden Eagle award CINE, 1995, Silver Apple Nat. Edn. Film & Video Festival, 1995, Bronze World medal N.Y. Festivals, 1996, CINDY Bronze medal, 1996, Lifetime Achievement award Jewish Fedn. Hawaii, Kansha award 442 Vets. Club. Mem. ABA, Afro-Am. Lawyers Assn. (bd. trustee), Hawaii Women Lawyers, Assn. Trial Lawyers Am., Hawaii State Bar Assn., Am. Judicature Soc., Richardson Sch. Law Alumni Assn. (alumni rep. 1981-82), Advocates for Pub. Interest Law, U. Hawaii Senate Faculty (senator), Phi Delta Phi (v.p. 1980-81), Hadassah Club, Women's Guild Club. Democrat. Jewish. Office: U Hawaii William S Richardson Sch Law 2515 Dole St Honolulu HI 96822-2328

WEIGLE, WILLIAM OLIVER, immunologist, educator; b. Monaca, Pa., Apr. 28, 1927; s. Oliver James and Caroline Ellen (Alsing) W.; m. Kathryn May Lotz, Sept. 4, 1948 (div. 1980); children—William James, Cynthia Kay; m. Carole G. Romball, Sept. 24, 1983. B.S., U. Pitts., 1950, M.S., 1951, Ph.D., 1956. Research assoc. pathology U. Pitts., 1955-58, asst. prof. immunochemistry, 1959-61; assoc. div. exptl. pathology Scripps Rsch. Inst., La Jolla, Calif., 1961-62, assoc. mem. div., 1962-63; mem. dept. exptl. pathology Scripps Rsch. Inst., La Jolla, 1963-74, mem. dept. immunopathology, 1974-82, chmn. dept. immunopathology, 1980-82, mem., vice chmn. dept. immunology, 1982-85, mem. dept. immunology, 1982—, chmn. dept. immunology, 1985-87; adj. prof. biology U. Calif., San Diego; McLaughlin vis. prof. U. Tex., 1977; mem. adv. bd. Immunetech Pharms., San Diego, 1988—; cons. in field. Author: Natural and Acquired Immunologic Unresponsiveness, 1967; assoc. editor: Clin. and Exptl. Immunology, 1972-79; Jour. Exptl. Medicine, 1974-84; Immunochemistry 1964-71; Procs. Soc. Exptl. Biology and Medicine, 1967-72; Jour. Immunology, 1967-71; Infection and Immunity, 1969-86, Aging: Immunology and Infectious Disease, 1987—; sect. editor: Jour. Immunology, 1971-75; editorial bd.: Contemporary Topics in Immunobiology, 1971-93; Cellular Immunology, 1984—; contbr. articles to profl. jours. Emeritus Coun. of the Trustees, Lovelace Inst., Albuquerque, 1996—. Pub. Health Research fellow, Nat. Inst. Neurol. Diseases and Blindness, 1956-59; NIH sr. research fellow, 1959-61, Research Career award, 1962. Mem. Am. Assn. Immunologists, Am. Soc. Exptl. Pathology (Parke Davis award 1967), Am. Soc. Microbiology, N.Y. Acad. Scis., Am. Assn. Pathologists, Soc. Exptl. Biology and Medicine. Home: 688 Via De La Valle Solana Beach CA 92075-2461 Office: Scripps Rsch Inst Dept Immunology IMM9 10666 N Torrey Pines Rd La Jolla CA 92037-1027

WEIGNER, BRENT JAMES, secondary education educator; b. Pratt, Kans., Aug. 19, 1949; s. Doyle Dean and Elizabeth (Hanger) W.; m. Sue Ellen Weber Hume, Mar. 30, 1985; children: Russell John Hume, Scott William Hume. BA, U. No. Colo., 1972; MEd, U. Wyo., 1977, PhD, 1984. Counselor, coach Olympia Sport Village, Upson, Wyo., summer 1968; dir. youth sports F.E. Warren AFB, Cheyenne, summers 1973, 74; instr. geography Laramie County Community Coll., Cheyenne, 1974-75; tchr. social sci. McCormick Jr. High Sch., Cheyenne, 1975—, Laramie County Sch. Dist. 1, Cheyenne, 1975—; head social studies dept. McCormick Jr. High Sch., 1987—; curriculum adv. coun. chmn. Laramie County Sch. Dist. No. 1, 1988-89; lectr. ednl. methods U. Wyo., 1989, mem. clin. faculty, 1992-94; nat. chmn. Jr. Olympic cross-country com. AAU, Indpls., 1980-81; pres. Wyo. Athletic Congress, 1981-87; tchr. cons. Nat. Geog. Soc. Geography Inst., summer 1991; bd. dirs. Shadow Mountain Lodge, Aspen, Colo., 1992-93, United Med. Ctr. of Wyo. Found., 1995—. Fgn. exch. student U. Munich, 1971-72; head coach Cheyenne Track Club, 1976—, pres., 1980; deacon 1st Christian Ch., Cheyenne, 1987-90, elder, 1991-93; rep. candidate gen. election Wyo. Legis., 1991. Named Wyo. U.S. West Outstanding Tchr., 1989, Wyo. Coun. for the Social Studies K-8 Tchr. of Yr., 1994-95, Jr. High Coach of Yr., Wyo. Coaches Assn., 1996; fellow Taft Found., 1976, Earthwatch-Hearst fellow, Punta Allen, Mex., summer 1987, Christa McAuliffe fellow, 1991-92, Wyo. Christa Mcauliffe Selection Com., 1994, 95; Fulbright grantee, Jerusalem, summer 1984; Fulbright scholar Ghana and Senegal, 1990; People-to-People Internat. Ambassador to Vietnam, 1993; recipient Masons of Wyo. Disting. Tchr. award 1994. Mem. ASCD, NEA, Nat. Network for Ednl. Renewal, Nat. Coun. Social Studies, Nat. Coun. Geog. Edn., Dominican Rep. Nat. Coun. for Geog. Edn. (Cram scholarship 1992), Wyo. Geog. Alliance (steering com.), Cheyenne Tchrs. Edn. Assn. (govtl. rels. com., instrn. and profl. devel. com.), U. No. Colo. Alumni Assn., Cheyenne C. of C., Wyo. Heritage Soc., Wyo. Edn. Assn. (World Book Ency. classroom rsch. project cons. 1976—, accountability task force 1989-90), Fulbright Alumni Assn. (life), U. Wyo. Alumni Assn. (life), Cheyenne Sunrise, Lions (bd. dirs. Cheyenne 1987, pres. 1995-96, 1st v.p. 1993-94, Melvin Jones Fellowship, 1995), Phi Delta Kappa (life, bd. dirs. Cheyenne 1989—, v.p., edn. award for rsch. 1990, pres. 1992-93, ednl. found. rep. 1993-94, area 4-D coord. 1994-95, Gerald Read Internat. Seminar scholar 1994; mem. outstanding doctoral dissertation com. 1994, 96). Home: 402 W 31st St Cheyenne WY 82001-2578 Office: McCormick Jr HS 6000 Education Dr Cheyenne WY 82009-3991

WEIHAUPT, JOHN GEORGE, geosciences educator, scientist, university administrator; b. La Crosse, Wis., Mar. 5, 1930; s. John George and Gladys Mae (Ash) W.; m. Audrey Mae Reis, Jan. 28, 1961. Student, St. Norbert Coll., De Pere, Wis., 1948-49; BS, U. Wis., 1952, MS, 1953; MS, U. Wis.-Milw., 1971; PhD, U. Wis., 1973. Exploration geologist Am. Smelting & Refining Co., Nfld., 1953, Anaconda Co., Chile, S.Am., 1956-57; seismologist United Geophys. Corp., 1958; geophysicist Arctic Inst. N.Am., Antarctica, 1958-60, Geophys. and Polar Research Center, U. Wis., Antarctica, 1960-63; dir. participating Coll. and Univ. program, chmn. dept. phys. and biol. sci. U.S. Armed Forces Inst., Dept. Def., 1963-73; assoc. dean for acad. affairs Sch. Sci., Ind. U.-Purdue U., Indpls., 1973-78; prof. geology Sch. Sci., Ind. U.-Purdue U., 1973-78; asst. dean (Grad. Sch., prof. geoscis. Purdue U.), 1975-78; prof. geology, assoc. acad. v.p., dean grad. studies and research, v.p. Univ. Research Found., San Jose (Calif.) State U., 1978-82; vice chancellor for acad. affairs U. Colo., Denver, 1982-86, prof. geoscis., 1987—; Sci. cons., mem. sci. adv. bd. Holt Reinhart and Winston, Inc., 1967—; sci. editor, cons. McGraw-Hill Co., 1966—; hon. lectr. U. Wis., 1963-73; geol. cons., 1968—; editorial cons. John Wiley & Sons, 1968; editorial adv. bd. Dushkin Pub. Group, 1971—. Author: Exploration of the Oceans: An Introduction to Oceanography; mem. editorial bd. Internat. Jour. Interdisciplinary Cycle Research, Leiden; co-discoverer USARP Mountain Range (Arctic Inst. Mountain Range), in Victoria Land, Antarctica, 1960; discoverer Wilkes Land Meteorite Crater, Antarctic. Mem. Capital Community Citizens Assn.; mem. Madison Transp. Study Com., Found. for Internat. Energy Research and Tng.; U.S. com. for UN Univ.; mem. sci. council Internat. Center for Interdisciplinary Cycle Research; mem. Internat. Awareness and Leadership Council; mem. governing bd. Moss Landing Marine Labs.; bd. dirs. San Jose State U. Found. Served as 1st lt. AUS, 1953-55, Korea. Mt. Weihaupt in Antarctica named for him, 1966; recipient Madisonian medal for outstanding community service, 1973; Outstanding Cote Meml. award, 1974; Antarctic medal, 1968. Fellow Geol. Soc. Am., Explorers Club; mem. Antarctican Soc., Nat. Sci. Tchrs. Assn., Am. Geophys. Union, Internat. Council Corr. Edu., Soc. Am. Mil. Engrs., Wis. Alumni Assn., Soc. Study Biol. Rhythms, Internat. Soc. for Chronobiology, Marine Tech. Soc., AAAS, Univ. Indsl. Adv. Council, Am. Council on Edn., Expdn. Polaire France (hon.), Found. for Study Cycles, Assn. Am. Geographers, Nat. Council Univ. Research Adminstrs., Soc. Research Adminstrs., Man-Environ. Communication Center, Internat. Union Geol. Scis., Internat. Geog. Union, Internat. Soc. Study Time, Community Council Pub. TV, Internat. Platform Assn., Ind., Midwest assns. grad. schs., Western Assn. Grad. Schs., Council Grad. Schs. in U.S., Wis. Alumni Assn. of San Francisco, Kiwanis, Carmel Racquet Club (Rinconada), The Ridge at Hiwan (Evergreen, Colo., pres. 1991-93). Home: 23906 Currant Dr Golden CO 80401-9243 Office: U Colo Campus Box 172 PO Box 173364 Denver CO 80204-5310

WEIL, LOUIS ARTHUR, III, newspaper publishing executive; b. Grand Rapids, Mich., Mar. 14, 1941; s. Louis Arthur, Jr. and Kathryn (Halligan) W.; m. Mary Elizabeth Buckingham, Sept. 7, 1963 (div. June 1977); children: Scott Arthur, Christopher Davison, Timothy Buckingham; m. Daryl Hopkins Goss, Jan. 26, 1980. B.A. in English, Ind. U., 1963; DHL (hon.), Mercy Coll., Grand Valley State U. Various positions Times Herald, Port Huron, Mich., 1966-68; personnel dir., pub. Journal and Courier, Lafayette, Ind., 1968-73; gen. mgr., pub. Gannett Westchester Rockland Newspapers, White Plains, N.Y., 1973-74, pres., gen. mgr., 1974-77, pres., pub., 1977-79; v.p. devel. Gannett Co., Inc., N.Y.C., 1979-83, sr. v.p. planning and devel., 1982-86; chmn., pub. Gannett Westchester Rockland Newspapers, White Plains, 1984-86; pres. The Detroit News, 1986-89, pub., 1987-89; U.S. pub. Time Mag., 1989-91; pub., chief exec. officer, exec. v.p. Ariz. Republic, Phoenix Gazette, Ariz. Bus. Gazette, 1991-96; pres., CEO Central Newspapers, Inc., Phoenix, 1996—; bd. dirs. Ctrl. Newspapers, Inc., Prudential. Chmn. membership Trustee Found. for Am. Comm.; bd. trustees, adv. bd. Ariz. Cancer Ctr. at U. Ariz.; chmn. adv. bd. Kids Voting USA; bd. dirs. Ariz. Cmty. Found., Ariz. Cities in Schs., Ind. U. Found.; campaign chmn. Valley of the Sun United Way, 1992; past chmn. Greater Phoenix Leadership; past pres. bd. trustees Phoenix Art Mus. With USN. Office: Phoenix Newspapers Inc 200 E Van Buren St Phoenix AZ 85004-2227*

WEIL, PETER HENRY, lawyer; b. N.Y.C., Nov. 20, 1933; s. Frank L. and Henrietta Amelia (Simons) W.; m. Helen Fay Kolodkin, Dec. 18, 1960; children: Karen W. Markus, Frank L. BA cum laude, Princeton U., 1954; LLB cum laude, Harvard U., 1957. Bar: N.Y. 1957, U.S. Dist. Cts. (so. and ea. dists.) N.Y. 1972. Assoc. Weil, Gotshal & Manges, N.Y.C., 1958-62; from assoc. to ptnr. Kaye Scholer, N.Y.C., 1962-95, ret., 1995; lectr. SMU Inst. on Comml. Financing, 1985-94, Banking Law Inst., 1987-89. Author: Asset Based Lending: An Introductory Guide to Secured Financing, P.L.I., 1989, 3d edit., 1996. Fellow Am. Coll. of Commercial Fin. Lawyers; former chmn. N.Y. bd. overseers, former bd. govs. Hebrew Union Coll., Jewish Inst. Religion, Cin., N.Y.C., Los Angeles, Jerusalem. With U.S. Army 1957-58. Mem. Ringwood Golden Master Volleyball Team, U.S. Nat. Champions, 1983. Mem. ABA, Assn. of Bar of City of N.Y. (banking law com. 1975-78).

WEILAND, I. HYMAN, psychiatrist; b. Cin., Sept. 17, 1921; s. Jonah and Goldie (Ginsburg) W.; m. Ruth Kissa Mirsky, Feb. 2, 1946 (div. 1969); children: Sally Ann, Arthur Ronald, Nancy Cottrell; m. Sue Davis, Sept. 14, 1970; children: Elizabeth Anne Bauer, Jonah David, Sharon Anne. BS, U. Cin., 1943, MD, 1946; postgrad. in Psychoanalysis, Phila. Psychoanlytic Inst., 1959-62; PhD, So. Calif. Psychoanlytic Inst., 1971. Diplomate Am. Bd. Psychiatry and Neurology. Intern So. Pacific Gen. Hosp. (now Harkness Hosp.), San Francisco, 1946-47; from asst. resident to resident dept. pscyhiatry Coll. Medicine, U. Cin., 1947-49; sr. resident dept. psychiatry, fellow child guidance home U. Cin., 1949-51; assoc. clin prof. child and gen. psychiatry Sch. Medicine UCLA, 1967-79; clin. prof. dept. psychiatry Sch. Medicine UCLA., 1979—; assoc. instr. So. Calif. Psychoanalytic Inst.,

Beverly Hills, Calif., 1976-84; instr. So. Calif. Psychoanalytic Inst., Beverly Hills, 1984—; pvt. practice psychiatry L.A., 1972—; instr. Sch. Social Work, U. Louisville, 1949-51, dept. psychiatry U. Cin., 1951, dept. psychiatry Coll. Medicine U. Wash., Seattle, 1951-55, dept. psychiatry Sch. Medicine U. Pa., Phila., 1957-62; dir. psychiatry Pinel Found. Hosp., Seattle, 1951-55, San Fernando Guild Guidance Clinic, L.A., 1961-71, San Fernando Valley Cmty. Health Ctr., L.A., 1967-71; cons. in child psychiatry Seattle Children's Home, 1951-55; asst. dir. children's unit Ea. Pa. Psychiatric Inst., Phila., 1967-62, others. Contbr. numerous articles to profl. jours.; presenter many confs. and convs. profl. groups. Mem. select com. on psychiatric care and evaluation, sponsored by Dept. Defense, Am. Psychiat. Assn., NIMH, Cmty. Adv. Bd., KOST radio; bd. dirs. Grad. Ctr. for Child Devel. and Psychotherapy, 1981-90, chmn. 1983-86, sec.-treas., 1986-88; adolescent med. dir. dept. psychiatry, Northridge Hosp., 1987—. Lt. cmmdr. US Navy, 1955-56. Grantee: NIMH, 1959-61, 63-68, 64-71, 65-67, 67-74, L.A. County Dept. Mental Health, 1964-71. Fellow Am. Psychiat. Assn. (life, commn. on childhood and adolescence), Am. Orhtopsychiat. Assn. (life), Acad. Child and Adolescent Psychiatry (life); mem. So. Calif. Psychiatric Soc. (task force on allied mental health workers, pvt. practice com.), So. Calif. Soc. for Child and Adolescent Psychiatry, So. Calif. Psychoanalytic Soc., So. Calif. Psychoanalytic Inst. Home and Office: 18531 Roscoe Blvd Ste 211 Northridge CA 91325

WEILER, DOROTHY ESSER, librarian; b. Hartford, Wis., Feb. 21, 1914; d. Henry Hugo and Agatha Christina (Dopp) Esser; A.B. in Fgn. Langs., Wash. State U., 1935; B.A.L., Grad. Library Sch., U. Wash., 1936; postgrad. U. Ariz., 1956-57, Ariz. State U., 1957-58, Grad. Sch. Librarianship, U. Denver, 1971; m. Henry C. Weiler, Aug. 30, 1937; children—Robert William, Kurt Walter. Tchr.-librarian Roosevelt Elem. Schs., Dist. #66, Phoenix, 1956-59; extension librarian Ariz. Dept. Library and Archives, Phoenix, 1959-67; library dir. City of Tempe (Ariz.), 1967-79; assoc. prof., dept. library sci. Ariz. State U., 1968; vis. faculty Mesa Community Coll., 1980-84. Mem. public relations com. United Fund; treas. Desert Samaritan Med. Ctr. Aux., 1981, v.p. community relations Hosp., 1982, vol. asst. chaplain, 1988—, pastoral care vol. Named Ariz. Librarian of Yr., 1971; recipient Silver Book award Library Binding Inst., 1963. Mem. Tempe Hist. Soc., Ariz. Pioneers Hist. Soc., Am. Radio Relay League, Am. Bus. Women's Assn., ALA, Southwestern Library Assn., Ariz. State Libr. Assn. (pres. 1973-74), Ariz. Libr. Pioneer. Roman Catholic. Clubs: Our Lady of Mt. Carmel Ladies' Sodality, Soroptimist Internat. Founder, editor Roadrunner, Tumbling Tumbleweed; contbr. articles to mags. Home: 1605 E Southern Ave Tempe AZ 85282-5610

WEILL, SAMUEL, JR., automobile company executive; b. Rochester, N.Y., Dec. 22, 1916; s. Samuel and Bertha (Stein) W.; student U. Buffalo, 1934-35; m. Mercedes Weil, May 20, 1939 (div. Aug. 1943); children: Rita and Eric (twins); m. Cléanthe Kimball Carr, Aug. 12, 1960 (div. 1982); m. Jacqueline Natalie Bateman, Jan. 5, 1983. Co-owner, Brayton Air Coll., St. Louis, 1937-42; assoc. editor, advt. mgr., bus. mgr. Road and Track Mag., Los Angeles, 1951-53; pres. Volkswagen Pacific, Inc., Culver City, Calif., 1953-73, Porsche Audi Pacific, Culver City, 1953-73; chmn. bd. Minto Internat., Inc., London; v.p. fin. Chieftain Oil Co., Ojai, Calif. Recipient Tom May award Jewish Hosp. and Research Center, 1971. Served with USAAF, 1943-45. Home: 305 Palomar Rd Ojai CA 93023-2432 Office: Chieftain Oil Co 214 W Aliso St Ojai CA 93023-2502 *Try to find a position that can utilitze whatever knowledge and abilities you have. Learn all you can about that company and its workings and then work as hard as you can, giving more than is expected of you, much more, but not more than you can capably handle.*

WEIMER, DAWN, sculptor; b. Denver, June 11, 1943; d. Morton Weil and Elsie Ione (Gudgel) Griswold; m. Thomas Eugene Weimer, June 14, 1964; 1 child, Heath. Executed bronzes for City of Westminister, Colo., 1996, City of Fort Collins, Colo., 1996-97, City of Loveland, Colo., 1996-97, City of Greeley, Colo., 1996-97; represented in permanent collections Lockheed-Martin Corp., Bethesda, Md., Express Pers. Internat. Hdqs., Oklahoma City, Okla., Bliss Industries Inc. Internat. Hdqs., Ponca City, Okla., Am. Quarter Horse Mus., Amarillo, Tex.; one-person shows include Bank One, Loveland, 1997. Recipient Best of Show, First Place award Draft Horse Classic, 1996, Philip Isenberg award Pen and Brush Sculpture Exhibit, 1994, Anna Hyatt Huntington award Am. Artists Pro League, 1993. Mem. Nat. Sculpture Soc., Catharine Lorillard Wolfe Art Club (Leila Gardin Sawyer award 1992), We. Art Assn., We. Heritage Artists. Office: Western Dawn Studio 1125 Centennial Rd Fort Collins CO 80525

WEINBERG, ALVIN HOWARD, engineer; b. Buffalo, N.Y., June 30, 1956; s. Sidney Roger and Evelyn (Miller) W.; m. Lisa Prechter, Nov. 1, 1986; children: Alyson Rae, Nash Devereau. BE, Vanderbilt U., 1978; MS, Drexel U., 1981. Engrng. mgr. Cordis Corp., Miami, Fla., 1981-87, Pacesetter, Inc., Sylmar, Calif., 1987—. Patentee in field; contbr. articles to profl. jours. Mem. Internat. Soc. for Hybrid Microelectronics (Tech. Achivement award, 1991), Internat. Electronics Packaging Soc., ASM Internat., IEEE. Home: 11859 Maple Crest St Moorpark CA 93021-3171 Office: Pacesetter Inc 15900 Valley View Ct Sylmar CA 91342-3577

WEINBERG, BERND, management scientist and educator; b. Chgo., Jan. 30, 1940; s. Berthold and Freda (Gramms) W.; children: John, Katherine, Mark. BA, SUNY, Fredonia, 1961; MA, Ind. U., 1963, PhD, 1965. Instr. Ind. U. Schs. Medicine and Dentistry, Indpls., 1964-66, 68-71, asst. prof., 1968-71, assoc. prof., 1971-74; rsch. fellow NIH, Bethesda, Md., 1966-68, 71-74; assoc. prof. Purdue U., West Lafayette, Ind., 1974-76; prof. Purdue Rsch. Found., West Lafayette, 1976-87; assoc. dir. div. sponsored programs Office of Patents and Copyrights, West Lafayette, 1985-87; dir. instnl. rels. Rsch. Corp. Technologiges, Inc., Tucson, 1987—. Author: Readings in Speech Following Total LAryngectormy, 1980, (with D. Shedd) Approaches to Surgical Prosthetic Speech Rehabilitation, 1980, (with I. Meitus) Diagnosis in Speech-Language Pathology, 1983; contbr. over 75 articles to profl. jours., 15 chprs. to books; patentee in field. Recipient Disting. Alumni award SUNY-Fredonia, 1981. Fellow Am. Speech/Lang. and Hearing Assn. (cert.); mem. Acoustical Soc. Am., Assn. Univ. Tech. Mgrs. Home: 4950 N Apache Hills Trl Tucson AZ 85715-5909 Office: Rsch Corp Technologies Inc 101 N Wilmot Rd Ste 600 Tucson AZ 85711-3361

WEINBERGER, FRANK, information management consultant; b. Chgo., Sept. 18, 1926; s. Rudolph and Elaine (Kellner) W.; m. Beatrice Natalie Fixler, June 27, 1953; children: Alan J., Bruce I. BSEE, Ill. Inst. Tech., Chgo., 1951; MBA, Northwestern U., 1959; DBA, U.S. Internat. U., San Diego, 1996. Registered profl. engr., Ill, Calif. Engr. Admiral Corp., Chgo., 1951-53; sr. engr. Cook Rsch., Chgo., 1953-59; mem. tech. staff Rockwell Internat., Downey, Calif., 1959-80, info. systems advisor, 1980-95; info. mgmt. cons., 1995—. Pres. Temple Israel, Long Beach, Calif., 1985-87, bd. dirs. 1973-85. With USN, 1944-46. Mem. Assn. for Computer Machinery. Democrat. Jewish. Home and Office: 3231 Yellowtail Dr Los Alamitos CA 90720-5253 *Don't ask "what can I do?" Instead, survey the needs, prepare the information, and give your best recommendation.*

WEINBERGER, MARTIN ANDREW, computer company executive; b. Santa Monica, Calif., Sept. 9, 1962; s. Tibor Weinberger and Katalin Klara (Winkler) Avedissian. BSEE, UCLA, 1984; postgrad., U. So. Calif. Microsoft cert. sys. engr.; Microsoft cert. product specialist; digital level II engr.; sun expert level 1000 engr.; cert. Microsoft solutions program mem. digital equipment corp. network product bus. unit level II engr. With Northrop Electronics, Hawthorne, Calif., 1985-87; sr. engr. data systems divsn. Litton Industries, Van Nuys, Calif., 1987-90; prin. Genesis Software Applications, Santa Monica, 1990—, Peerless Systems Corp., Manhattan Beach, Calif., 1997—; cons. Microsoft, IBM, Digital Equipment Corp., Compaq, others. Developer: (software) MediSec. Democrat. Office: Genesis Software Applications 2118 Wilshire Blvd Ste 753 Santa Monica CA 90403-5784

WEINER, DORA B., medical humanities educator; b. Furth, Germany, 1924; d. Ernest and Emma (Metzger) Bierer; m. Herbert Weiner, 1953; children—Timothy, Richard, Antony. Baccalaureat, U. Paris, 1941; B.A. magna cum laude, Smith Coll., 1945; M.A., Columbia U., 1946, Ph.D., 1951. Lectr. gen. studies Columbia U., N.Y.C., 1949-50, instr., 1950-52, vis. lectr. Tchrs. Coll., 1962-63; instr. Barnard Coll., 1952-56; fellow in history of medicine Johns Hopkins U., Balt., 1956-57; mem. faculty dept. social sci. Sarah Lawrence Coll., 1958-62; asst. prof. history Manhattanville Coll., 1964-65, assoc. prof., 1966-78, prof., 1978-82; adj. prof. med. humanities UCLA Sch. Medicine, Los Angeles, 1982—, prof., 1987—, prof. history, 1997; cons. and lectr. in field. Author: Raspail: Scientist and Reformer, 1968; The Clinical Training of Doctors: An Essay of 1793, 1980, The Citizen-Patient in Revolutionary and Imperial Paris, 1993; editor: Jacques Tenon's Memoirs of Paris Hospitals, 1995; co-editor: From Parnassus; Essays in Honor of Jacques Barzun, 1976, The World of Dr. Francisco Hernández, 1997; contbr. chpts. to books, articles to profl. jours. Grantee numerous profl. and ednl. instns. Mem. Am. Hist. Assn. (nominating com. 1979-82, Leo Gershoy award com. 1985-88), AAUP, Am. Assn. History Medicine (past mem. numerous coms.), Soc. 18th Century Studies, Soc. for French Hist. Studies (exec. com. 1978-81), History of Sci. Soc., Acad. Sci., Inscriptions Belles Letters (Toulouse, France). Office: UCLA 12-138 Ctr Health Scis Los Angeles CA 90024

WEINER, KATHRYN ANN, medical association administrator, special education educator; b. Denver, July 21, 1949; d. Jerry E. and Mildred G. (Jenson) Padgett; m. Richard S. Weiner, Aug. 25, 1985; 1 child, Rebecca. BA, Ariz. State U., 1971, MA, 1976; PhD, Walden U., 1993. Cert. basic elem., LH specialist, adminstrn. and supervision, resource specialist. Program specialist Stanislaus County Dept. Edn., Modesto, Calif.; coord. spl. edn. Modesto (Calif.) City Schs.; exec. dir. Am. Acad. of Pain Mgmt., Modesto; supr. spl. edn. Modesto (Calif.) City Schs.; founder, assoc. dir. Am. Acad. Pain Mgmt., Sonora, Calif. Mem. Assn. Calif. Sch. Adminstrs. (dir.), Soroptimist Internat. (pres.), Mental Health Adv. Bd. (chair), Children's Svcs. Com. (chair). Office: Am Acad Pain Mgmt 13947 Mono Way # A Sonora CA 95370-2807

WEINER, NORMAN, pharmacology educator; b. Rochester, N.Y., July 13, 1928; m. Diana Elaine Weiner, 1955; children: Steven, David, Jeffrey, Gareth, Eric. BS, U. Mich., 1949; MD, Harvard U., 1953. Diplomate Am. Bd. Med. Examiners. Intern 2d and 4th Harvard Med. Svc., Boston City Hosp., 1953-54; rsch. med. officer USAF, 1954-56; instr. dept. pharmacology-biochemistry Sch. of Aviation Medicine, San Antonio, 1954-56; from instr. to asst. prof. Harvard Med. Sch., Boston, 1956-67; prof. pharmacology U. Colo. Health Sci. Ctr., Denver, 1967—, disting. prof., 1989, chmn. dept. pharmacology, 1967-87; vis. prof. U. Calif., Berkeley, 1973-76; interim dean U. Colo. Sch. Medicine, 1983-84; Allan D. Bass lectr. sch. medicine Vanderbilt U., Nashville, 1983, divsn. v.p. Abbott Labs., Abbott Park, Ill., 1985-87; Pfizer lectr. Tex. Coll. Osteo. Medicine, Ft. Worth, 1985; disting. prof. UCHSC, 1989. Editor: Drugs and the Developing Brain, 1974, Structure and Function of Monoamine Enzymes, 1977, Regulation and Function of Monoamine Enzymes, 1981, Neuronal and Extraneuronal Events in Autonomic Pharmacology, 1984. Recipient Rsch. Career Devel. award USP HS, 1963, Kaiser Permanente award, 1974, 81, Otto Krayer award Am. Soc. Pharmacology and Exptl. Therapeutics, 1985; Spl. fellow USPHS, London, 1961-62; Disting. Volwiler Rsch. fellow Abbott Labs., 1988; Norman Weiner Festschrift, 1993; Julius Axelrod medal for outstadning scholarship in catecholamine rsch., 1993. Mem. AAAS, Am. Soc. for Pharmacology and Exptl. Therapeutics (Otto Krayer award 1985), N.Y. Acad. Scis., Assn. Med. Sch. Pharmacology, Am. Soc. Neurochemistry, Western Pharmacology Soc., Am. Coll. Neuropsychopharmacology, Soc. Neurosci., Biochem. Soc., Internat. Brain Rsch. Orgn., Internat. Soc. Neurochemistry, Rsch. Soc. on Alcoholism, Phi Beta Kappa, Sigma Xi, Alpha Omega Alpha, Phi Eta Sigma, Phi Lambda Upsilon, Phi Kappa Phi. Office: U Colo Health Sci Ctr Pharmacology Dept 4200 E 9th Ave Denver CO 80220-3706

WEINER, PETER H., lawyer; b. N.Y.C., July 10, 1944. BA, Harvard U., 1966; MSc, London Sch. Econs., 1967; LLB, Yale U., 1970. Bar: Calif. 1971. With Heller, Ehrman, White & McAuliffe, San Francisco. Mem. Phi Beta Kappa. Office: Heller Ehrman White & McAuliffe 333 Bush St San Francisco CA 94104-2806

WEINER, SANDRA SAMUEL, critical care nurse, nursing consultant; b. N.Y.C., Jan. 12, 1947; d. Herbert A. and Ruth (Wallerstein) Samuel; m. Neil D. Weiner, June 15, 1969 (div. June 1980); 1 child, Jaime Michelle. BS in Nursing, SUNY, Buffalo, 1968; cert. in critical care, Golden West Coll., 1982; postgrad. UCLA, U. West L.A. Sch. of Law, 1992. RN, Pa., Calif. Staff nurse N.Y. Hosp.-Cornell Med. Ctr., 1968-69; head nurse med.-surg. nursing Abington (Pa.) Hosp., 1969; assoc. prof. Sch. Nursing, U. Pa., Phila., 1970; instr. nursing Coll. of Med. Assts., Long Beach, Calif., 1971-72; surg. staff nurse Med. Ctr. of Tarzana, Calif., 1978-79, Cedar-Sinai Med. Ctr., L.A., 1979-81; supr. recovery room Beverly Hills Med. Ctr., L.A., 1981-92; Post Anesthesia Care Unit nurse Westside Hosp., 1992-96, Midway Hosp., Beverly Hills, Calif., 1996—; med. cons. RJA & Assocs., Beverly Hills, Calif., 1984-92; instr. CPR, L.A., 1986-95. Mem. women's aux. Ctr. Theater Group Vols., L.A., 1986—, Maple Ctr., Beverly Hills, 1987-96. Mem. Am. Nursing Assn., Am. Soc. Post-Anesthesia Nursing, Am. Assn. Critical Care Nurses, Heart and Lung Assn., Post Anesthesia Nurses Assn., U.S. Ski Assn. Democrat. Jewish. Avocations: skiing, aerobics, travel, theater, ballet. Home: 12633 Moorpark St Studio City CA 91604-4537

WEINER-HEUSCHKEL, SYDELL, theater educator; b. N.Y.C., Feb. 18, 1947; d. Milton A. and Janet (Kay) Horowitz; children: Jason, Emily; m. Rex Heuschkel, Sept. 3, 1992. BA, SUNY, Binghamton, 1968; MA, Calif. State U., L.A., 1974; MS in Counseling, Calif. State U., Dominguez Hills, 1996; PhD, NYU, 1986; postgrad. in acting, Yale U., 1968-70; MS in Counseling, Calif. State U., Dominguez Hills, 1996. Prof. theater arts, chmn. dept., dir. honors program Calif. State U. Dominguez Hills, Carson, 1984—; guest lectr. Calif. Inst. Arts, 1988. Appeared in play Vikings, Grove Shakespeare Festival, 1988; dir. Plaza Suite, Brea (Calif.) Civic Theatre, 1982, Gypsy, Carson Civic Light Opera, 1990, Same Time Next Year, Muckehthaler, 1987, Slow Dance on the Killing Ground, Alternative Repertory Theatre, 1989; co-author: School and Community Theater Problems: A Handbook for Survival, 1978, (software) Public Speaking, 1991; contbr. Am. Jour. Psychotherapy, Jour. Clin. Psychology, 1997. Yale U. fellow, 1969; recipient Lyle Gibson Disting. Tchr. award, 1989. Mem. Screen Actors Guild, Am. Fedn. TV and Radio Artists, Calif. State U. Women's Coun. (treas. 1989-91), Phi Kappa Phi.

WEINGARTEN, SAUL MYER, lawyer; b. Los Angeles, Dec. 19, 1921; s. Louis and Lillian Dorothy (Alter) W.; m. Miriam Ellen Moore, Jan. 21, 1949; children: David, Steven, Lawrence, Bruce. AA, Antelope Valley Coll., 1940; AB, UCLA, 1942; cert., Cornell U., 1943; JD, U. Southern Calif., 1949. Prin. Saul M. Weingarten, Inc., Seaside, Calif., 1954—; pres, CEO Quaestor Inc., Seaside, Calif., 1995—, also bd. dirs.; atty. City of Gonzales, Calif., 1954-74, City of Seaside, 1955-70; gen. counsel Redevel. Agy., Seaside, 1955-76, Security Nat. Bank, Monterey, Calif., 1968-74; bd. dirs., exec. com. Frontier Bank, Cheyenne, Wyo., 1984—, Mariposa Hall Inc., 1989—. Author: Practice Compendium, 1950; contbr. articles to profl. jours. Del. Internat. Union of Local Authorities, Brussels, Belgium, 1963, 73; candidate state legislature Dem. Com., Monterey County, 1958; counsel Monterey Peninsula Mus. of Art, Inc., 1972-80; gen. counsel Monterey County Symphony Assn., Carmel, Calif., 1974—, Mountain Plains Edn. Project, Glasgow, Mont., 1975-81; chmn. fund raising ARC, Monterey, 1964; chmn., bd. dirs. fund raising United Way, Monterey, 1962-63; pres., bd. dirs. Alliance on Aging, Monterey, 1968-82; bd. dirs. Family Svc. Agy., Monterey, 1958-66, Monterey County Cultural Coun., 1986—, Clark Found., 1982—; dir., mem. exec. com. Monterey Bay Performing Arts Ctr., 1990. Served to commdr. USN, 1942-46, 50-54, Korea. Grad. fellow Coro Found., 1949-50. Mem. Calif. Bar Assn., Monterey County Bar Assn., Monterey County Trial Lawyers Assn., Rotary (pres. 1970-71, 82-83), Commonwealth Club, Meadowbrook Club. Jewish. Home: 4135 Crest Rd Pebble Beach CA 93953-3008 Office: 1123 Fremont Blvd Seaside CA 93955-5759

WEINMAN, GLENN ALAN, lawyer; b. N.Y.C., Dec. 9, 1955; s. Seymour and Iris Rhoda (Bergman) W. BA in Polit. Sci., UCLA, 1978; JD, U. So. Calif., 1981. Bar: Calif. 1981. Assoc. counsel Mitsui Mfrs. Bank, Los Angeles, 1981-83; assoc. McKenna, Conner & Cuneo, Los Angeles, 1983-85, Stroock, Stroock & Lavan, Los Angeles, 1985-87; sr. counsel Buchalter, Nemer, Fields & Younger, Los Angeles, 1987-91; ptnr. Keck, Mahin & Cate, 1991-93; sr. v.p., gen. counsel Western Internat. Media Corp., L.A., 1993-96; gen. counsel Guess?, Inc., L.A., 1996—. Mem. ABA (corp. banking and bus. law sect., com. on savs. instns., com. on banking law corp. counsel sect.), Calif. Bar Assn. (bus. law sect., com. fin. instns. 1989-91, com. consumer svcs. 1991-94), L.A. County Bar Assn. (corp. legal depts. sect., bus. and corps. law sect., subcom. on fin. instns.), Calif. Fashion Assn. (legal com. 1997—), Am. Apparel Mfgs. Assn. (legal com. 1997—), Legion Lex., U. So. Calif. Law Alumni Assn., Phi Alpha Delta. Office: Guess? Inc 1444 S Alameda St Los Angeles CA 90021

WEINMAN, ROBERTA SUE, marketing and financial communications consultant; b. Bennington, Vt., Sept. 22, 1945. BA, U. Calif., Berkeley, 1967; MA, Stanford U., 1975, MLA, 1994; MBA, Pepperdine U., 1982. Tech. editor SRI Internat., Menlo Park, Calif.; adminstr. consumer affairs Fed. Home Loan Bank, San Francisco, 1977-79; legal research asst. Townsend and Townsend, San Francisco, 1979-80; ind. cons. mktg. and fin. comm., 1981—. Editor, writer, developer various mktg., pub. relations and fin. documents, primarily for high-tech. industry. Home and Office: 27560 Altamont Rd Los Altos Hills CA 94022

WEINMANN, ROBERT LEWIS, neurologist; b. Newark, Aug. 21, 1935; s. Isadore and Etta (Silverman) W.; m. Diana Weinmann, Dec. 13, 1980 (dec. Dec. 1989); children: Paul, Chris, Dana, Paige. BA, Yale U., 1957; MD, Stanford U., 1962. Diplomate Am. Bd. of EEG and Neurophysiology, v.p.; diplomate Am. Acad. Pain Mgmt., Am. Bd. Forensic Medicine. Intern Pacific Presbyn. Med. Ctr., San Francisco, 1962-63; resident in neurology Stanford U. Hosp., 1963-66, chief resident, 1965-66; pvt. practice San Jose, Calif., 1969—; former clin. instr. neurology, Stanford (Calif.) U. Chmn. editl. bd. Clin. EEG Jour.; mem. editl. bd. Jour. Am. Acad. Pain Mgmt.; formerly mem. editl. bd. Clin. Evoked Potentials Jour.; contbr. articles to various publs. Capt. M.C., U.S. Army, 1966-68, Japan. Award recipient State of R.I., Santa Clara County Med. Soc., Epilepsy Soc., other orgns.; fellow Univ. Paris, 1957-58. Union of Am. Physicians and Dentists (pres. 1990—, bd. dirs. 1972—, pres. Calif. fedn. 1990—). Office: Union Am Physicians & Dentists 1330 Broadway Ste 730 Oakland CA 94612-2506

WEINREB, ROBERT NEAL, ophthalmologist, educator; b. N.Y.C., Nov. 23, 1949; s. David and Ruth (Kramer) W. S.B., MIT; M.D., Harvard U., 1975. Diplomate Am. Bd. Ophthalmology. Resident in ophthalmology U. Calif.-San Francisco, 1976-80, fellow in glaucoma, 1981; mem. faculty U. Calif.-San Diego, La Jolla, 1984—, prof. ophthalmology, 1984—, vice chair, 1984—, chief glaucoma div., 1984—. Chief editor Focus on Glaucoma, 1986—; assoc. editor Jour. Glaucoma, 1992—; editor Invest Ophthalmol. Vis. Sci., 1996, Arch Ophthalmol. Recipient Hogan prize U. Calif.-San Francisco, 1981, Alcon prize Alcon Rsch. Inst., 1983, 92. Fellow Am. Acad. Ophthalmology (Honor award 1986, Sr. Honor award 1996); mem. Internat. Soc. Eye Rsch., Assn. Rsch. in Vision and Ophthalmology (Helmholtz award 1979). Office: U Calif San Diego Glaucoma Ctr and Rsch Labs 9415 Campus Point Dr La Jolla CA 92093

WEINRICH, JAMES DONALD, psychobiologist, educator; b. Cleve., July 2, 1950; s. Albert James and Helen (Lautz) W. AB, Princeton U., 1972; PhD, Harvard U., 1976. Postdoctoral fellow, then instr. Johns Hopkins U., Balt., 1980-82; rsch. assoc., then asst. rsch. prof. psychiatry Boston U., 1983-87; asst. rsch. psychobiologist, project mgr. U. Calif., San Diego, 1987-89, asst. rsch. psychobiologist, ctr. mgr., 1989-91, sr. investigator sexology, 1991-93, prin. investigator sexology project, 1994—; bd. dirs. Found. Sci. Study of Sexuality, Mt. Vernon, Iowa. Author: Sexual Landscapes, 1987; co-editor: Homosexuality: Social, Psychological and Biological Issues, 1982, Homosexuality: Research Implications for Public Policy, 1991; cons. editor Jour. of Sex Rsch., 1997—. Mem. Internat. Acad. Sex Rsch., Soc. for Sci. Study of Sex (Hugo Beigel award 1987), Am. Coll. Sexologists (cert.), Phi Beta Kappa. Office: Univ Calif San Diego 2760 5th Ave Ste 200 San Diego CA 92103-6325

WEINSHIENK, ZITA LEESON, federal judge; b. St. Paul, Apr. 3, 1933; d. Louis and Ada (Dubov) Leeson; m. Hubert Troy Weinshienk, July 8, 1956 (dec. 1983); children: Edith Blair, Kay Anne, Darcy Jill; m. James N. Schaffner, Nov. 15, 1986. Student, U. Colo., 1952-53; BA magna cum laude, U. Ariz., 1955; JD cum laude, Harvard U., 1958; Fulbright grantee, U. Copenhagen, Denmark, 1959; LHD (hon.), Loretto Heights Coll., 1985; LLD (hon.), U. Denver, 1990. Bar: Colo. 1959. Probation counselor, legal adviser, referee Denver Juvenile Ct., 1959-64; judge Denver Mcpl. Ct., 1964-65, Denver County Ct., 1965-71, Denver Dist. Ct., 1972-79, U.S. Dist. Ct. Colo., Denver, 1979—. Precinct committeewoman Denver Democratic Com., 1963-64; bd. dirs. Crime Stoppers. Named one of 100 Women in Touch with Our Time Harper's Bazaar Mag., 1971, Woman of Yr., Denver Bus. and Profl. Women, 1969; recipient Women Helping Women award Soroptimist Internat. of Denver, 1983, Hanna G. Solomon award Nat. Coun. Jewish Women, Denver, 1986. Fellow Colo. Bar Found., Am. Bar Found.; mem. ABA, Denver Bar Assn., Colo. Bar Assn., Nat. Conf. Fed. Trial Judges (exec. com.), Dist. Judges' Assn. of 10th Cir. (past pres.), Colo. Women's Bar Assn., Fed. Judges Assn., Denver Crime Stoppers Inc. (bd.dirs.), Devner LWV, Women's Forum Colo., Harvard Law Sch. Assn., Phi Beta Kappa, Phi Kappa Phi, Order of Coif (hon. Colo. chpt.). Office: US Dist Ct US Courthouse Rm C-418 1929 Stout St Denver CO 80294-0001

WEINSTEIN, NORMAN CHARLES, writer; b. Phila., Jan. 26, 1948; s. Emanuel Weinstein and Gertrude (Zamarin) Shaffer; m. Julie Jane Hall. BA, Bard Coll., 1969; MA in Tchg., SUNY, New Paltz, 1975. Instr. SUNY, New Paltz, 1971-73, Boise (Idaho) Sr. Ctr., 1981-85, Boise State U., 1981-93; music reviewer Christian Sci. Monitor Radio, 1996—. Author: Gertrude Stein and the Literature of Modern Consciousness, 1970, (poetry) Nigredo, 1982, A Night in Tunisia, 1992. Recipient Deems Taylor award ASCAP, 1989. Mem. NARAS, African Studies Assn., Ctr. for Black Music Rsch. (assoc.). Home: 730 E Bannock St Boise ID 83712-6409

WEINSTEIN, RACHEL, clown; b. Edmonton, Alta., Can., Jan. 30, 1912; came to U.S., 1952; d. Samuel and Rebecca (Rabinovich) Caplan; m. Sam Weinstein, June 1952 (div. 1962); 1 child, Lee Gray. *Rachel Weinstein's parents operated a trading post in tiny Weldon, Saskatchewan, where she lived until age 20. Her pioneer spirit was developed bathing in melted snow, having river ice hauled 15 miles for drinking water, lighting with oil and gas lamps, using an outhouse, and having only a cellar for refrigeration, as temperatures swung from -60 degrees to 100 degrees Fahrenheit. She worked in her parents' store every day after school, and twelve-hour shifts after graduating. They sold groceries and dry-goods (jeans were $2.95 a pair!), and traded for the products of farmers and trappers. These versatile experiences laid the foundation for her skills in retail merchandising, management, and accounting which served her throughout her life.* Cert. Completion, Prince Albert Bus. Coll., Sask., 1941; Master Clown Cert., Lane C.C., Eugene, Oreg., 1992; studied with clown Frosty Little, 1997. Founder, mgr. Strand Shoe Store, Prince Albert, 1932-41; chief window display decorator Hudson's Bay Co., Victoria, B.C., Can., 1942-45; founder Dominion Paint Co., Victoria, B.C., Can., 1945-52; owner, mgr. Rachel Weinstein Bus. and Tax Cons. Svc., Eugene, 1962-85, Rachel Weinstein Vita and Resume Svc., Eugene, 1962-85; entertainer Tango the Clown, Eugene, 1985—. Editor/pub.: Cow Creek Valley Memories, 1971, Genealogy of Mrs. Chatt, 1975. Recipient Gov. Gen.'s medal Province of Sask., 1926, Outstanding Achievement Commendation, Prince Albert Bus. Coll., 1941. Mem. AAI Investors, World Clown Assn., Rental Owner's Assn. Office: PO Box 1722 Eugene OR 97440

WEINSTEIN, STEVEN SAMUEL, marketing executive; b. N.Y.C., May 18, 1942; s. Jack Sidney and Fannie (Reiss) W.; m. Judith Ruhlman, Dec. 15, 1968; children: Rachel, Brian. BS, Rensselaer Poly. Inst., 1964; PhD, U. N.H., 1969; MBA, U. Conn., 1975. Product mgr. Becton-Dickinson Co., Cockeysville, Md., 1973-77; mktg. mgr. Tex. Instruments Corp., Lubbock, 1977-83; v.p. mktg. Spectravideo Inc., N.Y.C., 1983-84; pres. Databar Corp., Eden Prairie, Minn., 1984-85; mktg. cons. S.S. Weinstein & Assocs., Wayzata, Minn., 1985-87; v.p. mktg. Micro Display Systems, Inc., Hastings, Minn., 1987-89, Jr. Achievement Inc., Colorado Springs, Colo., 1989—; instr. Coll. St. Thomas, St. Paul, 1985—. Little League coach, Lubbock, 1978-80; bd. mem. Shaareth Israel Temple, Lubbock, 1981-82. Jewish. Home: 2225 Angelbluff Ct Colorado Springs CO 80919-3847

WEINSTOCK, HAROLD, lawyer; b. Stamford, Conn., Nov. 30, 1925; s. Elias and Sarah (Singer) W.; m. Barbara Lans, Aug. 27, 1950; children—Nathaniel, Michael, Philip. B.S. magna cum laude, N.Y. U., 1947; J.D., Harvard, 1950. Bar: Conn. bar 1950, Ill. bar 1950, Calif. bar 1958. Atty. SEC, Washington, 1950-52, IRS, 1952-56; tax atty. Hunt Foods & Industries, Inc., Los Angeles, 1956-58; pvt. practice Beverly Hills, Calif., 1958-71, Los Angeles, 1971—; mem. Weinstock, Manion, Reisman, Shore & Neumann (and predecessor firms), 1958—; Lectr. extension div., estate planning courses U. Calif. at Los Angeles, 1959—; estate planning and taxation courses Calif. Continuing Edn. of the Bar, 1960—. Author: Planning An Estate, 4th edit., 1995; contbr. articles to profl. publs. Nat. trustee Union Am. Hebrew Congregations, 1976-79; bd. trustees Jewish Cmty. Found., L.A.; adv. bd. Estate Planning Inst. UCLE Law Sch., 1979-92, NYU Inst. on Fed. Taxation, 1986-95. Mem. ABA, Calif. Bar Assn., Beverly Hills Bar Assn. (chmn. probate and trusts com. 1967-68), Los Angeles Bar Assn., Beverly Hills Estate Planning Council (pres. 1968-69), Estate Counselors Forum of Los Angeles (pres. 1963-64). Jewish (pres. temple 1974-76). Office: Weinstock Manion 1888 Century Park E Los Angeles CA 90067-1702

WEINSTOCK, RONALD JAY, research and development company executive; b. L.A., Mar. 14, 1960; s. Howard Frank and Anne Carol (Schneider) W.; m. Sigrid Lipsett, June 11, 1988; children: Rachel, Brent. Student, U. Calif., San Diego, 1978-80, U. Calif., Santa Barbara, 1980-81. CEO Magnetic Resonance Diagnostics Corp., Thousand Oaks, Calif., 1989—; vice chmn. Magnetic Resonance Rsch. Soc., Tokyo, 1991—; lectr. in field. Co-developer Magnetic Resonance Analyzer; contbr. articles to profl. jours. CPR instr. Am. Heart Assn., Beverly Hills, 1981; EMT, UCLA, 1980; chmn. police dept. disaster response team City of Thousand Oaks, 1995—.

WEIR, ALEXANDER, JR., utility consultant, inventor; b. Crossett, Ark., Dec. 19, 1922; s. Alexander and Mary Eloise (Field) W.; m. Florence Forschner, Dec. 28, 1946; children: Alexander III, Carol Jean, Bruce Richard. BSChemE, U. Ark., 1943; MChemE, Poly Inst. Bklyn., 1946; PhD, U. Mich., 1954; cert., U. So. Calif. Grad. Sch. Bus. Adminstrn., 1968. Chem. engr. Am. Cyanamid Co., Stamford Rsch. Labs., 1943-47; with U. Mich., 1948-58; rsch. assoc., project supr. Engring. Research Inst., U. Mich., 1948-57; lectr. chem. and metall. engring. dept. U. Mich., 1954-56, asst. prof., 1956-58; cons. Ramo-Woolridge Corp., L.A., 1956-57; mem. tech. staff, sect. head, asst. mgr. Ramo-Wooldridge Corp., Los Angeles, 1957-60, incharge Atlas Missile Captive test program, 1956-60; tech. adv. to pres. Northrop Corp., Beverly Hills, Calif., 1960-70; prin. scientist for air quality So. Calif. Edison Co., Los Angeles, 1970-76, mgr. chem. systems research and devel., 1976-86, chief research scientist, 1986-88; utility cons. Playa Del Rey, Calif., 1988—; rep. Am. Rocket Soc. to Detroit Nuclear Council, 1954-57; chmn. session on chem. reactions Nuclear Sci. and Engring. Congress, Cleve., 1955; U.S. del. AGARD (NATO) Combustion Colloquium, Liege, Belgium, 1955; Western U.S. rep. task force on environ. research and devel. goals Electric Research Council, 1971; electric utility advisor Electric Power Research Inst., 1974-78, 84-87; industry advisor Dept. Chemistry and Biochemistry Calif. State U., Los Angeles, 1981-88. Author: Two and Three Dimensional Flow of Air through Square-Edged Sonic Orifices, 1954; (with R.B. Morrison and T.C. Anderson) Notes on Combustion, 1955, also tech. papers; inventor acid rain prevention device used in 5 states. Sea scout leader, Greenwich, Conn., 1944-48, Marina del Rey, Calif., 1965-70; bd. govs., past pres. Civic Union Playa del Rey, chmn. sch., police and fire, nominating, civil def., army liaison coms.; mem. Senate, Westchester YMCA, chmn. Dads sponsoring com., active fundraising; chmn. nominating com. Paseo del Rey Sch. PTA, 1961; mem. L.A. Mayors Cmty. Adv. Com.; asst. chmn. advancement com., merit badge dean Cantinella dist. L.A. Area coun. Boy Scouts Am. Recipient Nat. Rsch. Coun. Flue Gas Desulfurization Industrials Scale Reliability award NAS, 1975, Power Environ. Achievement award EPA, 1980, Excellence in Sulfur Dioxide Control award EPA, 1985. Mem. AICE, Am. Geophys. Union, Navy League U.S. (v.p. Palos Verdes Peninsula coun. 1961-62), N.Y. Acad. Scis., Sci. Rsch. Soc. Am., Am. Chem. Soc., U.S. Power Squadron, St. Andrew Soc. So. Calif., Clan Macnachtan Assn., Clan Buchanan Soc. Am., Betty Washington Lewis Soc. of Children of Am. Revolution (past pres.), Ark. Soc. of Children of Am. Revolution (past pres.), Santa Monica Yacht Club, Sigma Xi, Phi Kappa Phi, Phi Lambda Upsilon, Alpha Chi Sigma, Lambda Chi Alpha. Office: 8229 Billowvista Dr Playa Del Rey CA 90293-7807

WEIR, JIM DALE, small business owner; b. Phoenix, Feb. 2, 1956; s. Jim Earl and Laverne Alice (Mahan) W.; m. Myra Yvonne Anglin, July 19, 1980; children: Justin, Kevin, Amanda, Jordan. Student, Phoenix Coll., 1978; BS, Grand Canyon Coll., 1980. Owner Quality S Mfg., Phoenix, 1980—. Vol. Tempe (Ariz.) Ch. of the Nazarene, 1987-89, Latin Am. Ch. of the Nazarene, Phoenix, 1988-89. Recipient Key of City award Phoenix, 1987, Fast Growth award Inc. mag., 1988. Republican. Home: PO Box 23910 Phoenix AZ 85063-3910

WEIS, EDMUND BERNARD, JR., orthopaedist, educator, engineer, lawyer; b. Bismarck, N.D., Aug. 4, 1931; s. Edmund Bernard and Margaret Catherine (Rickert) W.; m. Annette Mary Fernandes, Nov. 19, 1972; children: John Paul, Giselle Anne, Susan Ellen, Melanie Elizabeth, Edmund Bernard III, Bronwyn Kristen. Attended, U. Utah, 1949-52; grad., U. Notre Dame, 1953; MD, U. Colo., 1957; MS in Bioengring., Drexel Inst. Tech., 1962; doctoral candidate, Ohio State U., 1968-71; JD, Newport U., 1994. Diplomate Am. Bd. Orthopaedic Surgery; Bar: Calif. 1994. Intern Good Samaritan Hosp., Phoenix, 1957-58; chief vibration and impact br. mercury astronaut crew selection Aerospace Med. Rsch. Labs., Wright-Patterson AFB, Ohio, 1958-66; resident in orthopaedics Ohio State U., Columbus, 1968-71; amputations tng. Dept. Vet. Affairs, Grossinger, N.Y., 1985; pedicle screw fixation tng. Cleve. Rsch. Inst., 1987; thermography tng. Acad. Neuromuscular Thermography, L.A., 1989; surg. lasers tng. Loma Linda (Calif.) U., 1992; rsch. med. officer USAF, Wright-Patterson AFB, Ohio, 1966-68; mem. staff Ohio Vets. Oupatient Ctr., Columbus, 1974-76, N.D. Vets. Hosp., Fargo, 1976-79; mem. staff VA Hosp., Omaha, 1979-85, acting chief rehab., 1983-85; mem. staff, chief orthopaedics VA Hosp., Loma Linda, 1985—; mem. staff Loma Linda Cmty. Hosp., 1985—, chief orthopaedics, 1989-90; mem. staff Loma Linda U. Med. Ctr., 1985—, Redlands (Calif.) Cmty. Hosp., 1986-94, San Bernardino (Calif.) Cmty. Hosp., 1990—, Moreno Valley (Calif.) Hosp., 1992-94, San Gorgonio Meml. Hosp., Banning, Calif., 1993-94; instr. to asst. prof. orthopaedics Ohio State U., 1971-76; assoc. prof. U. N.D., Grand Forks, 1976-79, asst. dean, 1977-79; prof. Creighton U., Omaha, 1979-85; clin. prof. Loam Linda U., 1985—; bioengring. cons. Cox Coronary Heart Inst., Dayton, Ohio, 1962-66, Battelle Meml. Inst., Columbus, 1970-76; orthopaedics cons. Grand Forks AFB Hosp., 1976-79, Ehrling-Berquist AFB Hosp., Omaha, 1979-84, Jour. Bone and Joint Surgery, Waltham, Mass., 1980—; com. mem. Am. Acad. Orthopaedics Emergency Svcs. Contbr. numerous articles to profl. jours.; inventor sonic surg. tool; patentee method and sys. for control of a powered prosthesis. Maj. USAF, Wright-Patterson AFB, 1957-66. Recipient R & D award USAF, 1966, Rsch. award Dept. Vet. Affairs, 1988, U.S. Svc. award, 30 Yr. pin, Jerry L. Pettis Vets. Hosp., 1993; rsch. fellow NIH, 1969-71, travelling fellow Am. Orthopaedics Assn., 1971. Fellow Am. Acad. Orthopaedic Surgeons (Rsch. and Edn. Found. award 1969), Am. Coll. Legal Medicine; mem. AMA, Orthopaedic Rsch. Soc., San Bernardino County Med. Soc., Calif. Med. Soc., Nat. Assn. Vet. Physicians, N.Am. Spine Soc., Phi Rho Sigma. Home: 30555 7th Ave Redlands CA 92374-7619 Office: 1800 Western Ave Ste 300 San Bernardino CA 92411-1354

WEISBROD, KEN (JOSEPH LOUIS WEISBROD), marketing professional; b. Los Angeles, July 31, 1957; s. Louis Isadore and Dolores Joan (Adamczyk) W.; m. Kary Lin Shirley, Jan. 25, 1992; children: Katherine Irene, Benjamin Joseph. Cert., Gemological Inst. Am, 1988. Jewelry designer House of Time Jewelers, Granada Hills, Calif., 1968-79; pres. Ken Weisbrod Prodns., Inc., Chatsworth, Calif., 1979-85; v.p. The Ramolap Co., Chatsworth, 1985—; dir. prodn. Katherine's of Broadway Market, Chatsworth, 1987—. Designer jewelry for numerous art exhibits, 1969-75. Mem. Greater L.A. Zoo Assn., Publ. Prodn. Club So. Calif. Democrat. Roman Catholic. Office: Ramolap Co PO Box 5359 Chatsworth CA 91313-5359

WEISBURD, HARRY NOAH, artist, educator; b. N.Y.C., Feb. 18, 1938; m. Guang Xin, Mar. 10, 1990; 1 child, Jing-Lin. Cert., Parsons Sch. Design, N.Y.C., 1959; student, San Francisco Art Inst., 1963; BFA, Calif. Coll. Arts & Crafts, 1965, MFA, 1966. Prof. art U. Conn., Storrs, 1966-71, Westfield (Mass.) State Coll., 1971-78; art instr. DeYoung Mus. Art, San Francisco, 1981; head Ctr. for the Visual Arts, Oakland, 1984-87. Work exhibited in numerous group exhbns., one-person shows, art galleries and pvt. collections; selected for representation on ACI-Art Comm. Internat., CD-ROM, 1996; contbr. articles to mags. With USAR, 1958-64. Recipient Purchase award North Bay Artists Assn., Benecia, Calif., 1963, Ford Found. grant Calif. Coll. Arts and Crafts, Oakland, 1964, Faculty grants for exptl. film making and sculpture U. Conn., Storrs, 1966-71. Mem. Coll. Art Assn. Home: PO Box 10036 Oakland CA 94610-0036

WEISENBURGER, THEODORE MAURICE, judge, poet, educator, writer; b. Tuttle, N.D., May 12, 1930; s. John and Emily (Rosenau) W.; children: Sam, Jennifer, Emily, Todd, Daniel, Dwight, Holly, Michael, Paul, Peter; m. Maylyne Chu, Sept. 19, 1985; 1 child, Irene. BA, U. N.D., 1952, LLB, 1956, JD, 1969; BFT, Am. Grad. Sch. Internat. Mgmt., Phoenix, 1957. Bar: N.D. 1963, U.S. Dist. Ct. N.D. 1963. County judge, tchr. Benson County, Minnewaukan, N.D., 1968-75, Walsh County, Grafton, N.D., 1975-87; tribal judge Devils Lake Sioux, Ft. Totten, N.D., 1968-84, Turtle Mountain Chippewa, Belcourt, N.D., 1974-87; U.S. magistrate U.S. Dist. Ct., Minnewaukan, 1972-75; Justice of the Peace pro tem Maricopa County, Ariz., 1988-92; instr. Rio Salado C.C., 1992—; tchr. in Ethiopia, 1958-59. 1st lt. U.S. Army, 1952-54. Author: Poetry and Other Poems, 1991. Recipient Humanitarian award U.S. Cath. Conf., 1978, 82, Right to Know award Sigma Delta Chi, 1980, Spirit of Am. award U.S. Conf. Bishops, 1982. Home: 4353 E Libby Phoenix AZ 85032-1647

WEISKOPF, KIM ROBERT, television producer, writer; b. N.Y.C., Apr. 10, 1947; s. Robert Jerome and Eileen May (Ito) W.; m. Jo Ellen Erwin Legendre, May 17, 1980; 1 child, Kathleen. BA in English Lit., San Francisco State U., 1969. Story editor, writer TV show Good Times, Hollywood, Calif., 1977; exec. script cons., writer TV show Three's Company, L.A., 1979-80; prodr., writer TV show 9 to 5, L.A., 1981; exec. prodr., writer TV show What's Happening Now, Burbank, Calif., 1985-87; prodr., writer TV show Full House, Culver City, Calif., 1988-91; supervising prodr., writer TV show Rachel Gunn, R.N., Hollywood, 1992-93; supervising/co-exec. prodr., writer TV show Married...With Children, Columbia TV, Culver City and Hollywood, 1994-96; exec. prodr., writer TV show Malcolm & Eddie, Tri-Star TV, Culver City, 1996—; co-exec. prodr., writer TV show Sister, Sister Paramount, Hollywood, Calif., 1997.

WEISMAN, ADAM MARK, clinical psychologist; b. N.Y.C., Jan. 7, 1959; s. Nelson N. and Selma Cecilia (Winthrop) W. BA in Drama, BS in Psychology, U. Wash., 1982; MA, Kent (Ohio) State U., 1987, PhD, 1991. Lic. psychologist, Calif., Mich., Wash. Psychology asst. Akron (Ohio) Child Guidance Ctr., 1987-88; psychology intern Henry Ford Hosp., Detroit, 1989-90; instr. Kent State U., 1986-89; psychologist asst. Summit County Courthouse, Akron, 1988-90; outreach therapist Neighborhood Svc. Orgn., Detroit, 1990-92; postdoctoral sr. fellow in forensic psychology U. So. Calif., L.A., 1992-94, clin. asst. prof. psychiatry, 1992—; adj. prof. psychology Pepperdine U., Malibu, Calif., 1994—; staff psychologist Parole Clinic Dept. of Corrections, L.A., 1993—; cons. psychologist Patton (Calif.) State Hosp., 1992-94; cons. L.A. Adult Protective Svcs., 1995—; mem. psychiat.-psychol. panel adult, mental health and juvenile Superior Ct., L.A., 1995—, U.S. Dist. Ct., 1995—. Bd. dirs., comm. adv. bd. L.A. Police Dept., 1995-97; bd. dirs., pres. Franklin Hills Residents Assn., L.A., 1994—. Recipient Outstanding Civic Svc. award City of L.A., 4th Coun. Dist., 1996. Mem. APA, Wash. State Psychol. Assn., Nat. Register Health Sci. Providers in Psychology, Forensic Mental Health Assn. Calif., Soc. Behavioral Medicine, Am. Acad. Forensic Scis., Am. Psychosomatic Soc., Calif. Coalition on Sex Offending, Calif. Psychol. Assn., Sex Offenders Roundtable of L.A., Homicide Rsch. Working Group, Psi Upsilon. Jewish. Office: PO Box 29366 Los Angeles CA 90029-0366

WEISMAN, MARTIN JEROME, manufacturing company executive; b. N.Y.C., Aug. 22, 1930; s. Lewis E. and Estelle (Scherer) W.; m. Sherrie Cohen, Jan. 27, 1952; children: Jane Dory, Andrea Sue, Amy Ellen. B in Chem. Engring., N.Y.U., 1951. Sr. chem. engr. Ideal Toy Corp., Hollis, N.Y., 1951-57; research chemist Chesebrough-Ponds, Stamford, Conn., 1957-62; mgr. nail products lab. Max Factor and Co., Hollywood, Calif., 1962-81; v.p., tech. dir. Sher-Mar Cosmetics div. Weisman Industries, Inc., Canoga Park, Calif., 1981—. Patentee in field. Mem. Soc. Cosmetic Chemists, Los Angeles Soc. Coatings Tech., Am. Chem. Soc. Office: Sher-Mar Cosmetics 8755 Remmet Ave Canoga Park CA 91304-1519

WEISMAN, PAUL HOWARD, lawyer; b. Los Angeles, Oct. 14, 1957; s. Albert L. and Rose J. (Zimman) W.; m. Allison L. Minas, Oct. 19, 1985. BA cum laude, U. Calif., Davis, 1979; JD, Loyola U., Los Angeles, 1982. Bar: Calif. 1982. Tax atty. legis. and regulations div. office of chief counsel Dept. of Treasury IRS, Washington, 1982-83; tax atty. dist. counsel/office of chief counsel Dept. of Treasury IRS, L.A., 1983-87; tax atty. Law Offices of Paul H. Weisman, L.A., 1987—; registered players contract rep. Nat. Football League Players Assn. Co-author BNA Tax Mgmt. Portfolio 404 2d Federal Tax Collection Procedure, publs. in field. Participant vol. Income Tax Assistance, L.A., 1981-83. Mem. San Fernando Valley Bar Assn., Beverly Hills Bar Assn. (co-chmn. tax ct. prose program). Republican.

WEISS, HERBERT KLEMM, retired aeronautical engineer; b. Lawrence, Mass., June 22, 1917; s. Herbert Julius and Louise (Klemm) W.; m. Ethel Celesta Giltner, May 14, 1945 (dec.); children: Janet Elaine, Jack Klemm (dec.). B.S., MIT, 1937, M.S., 1938. Engr. U.S. Army Arty. Bds., Ft. Monroe, Va, 1938-42, Camp Davis, N.C., 1942-44, Ft. Bliss, Tex., 1944-46; chief WPN Systems Lab., Ballistic Research Labs., Aberdeen Proving Grounds, Md, 1946-53; chief WPN systems analysis dept. Northrop Aircraft Corp., 1953-58; mgr. advanced systems devel. mil. systems planning aeronutronic div. Ford Motor Co., Newport Beach, Calif., 1958-61; group dir., plans devel. and analysis Aerospace Corp., El Segundo, Calif., 1961-65; sr. scientist Litton Industries, Van Nuys, Calif., 1965-82; cons. mil. systems analysis, 1982-90; Mem. Sci. Adv. Bd. USAF, 1959-63, sci. adv. panel U.S. Army, 1965-74, sci. adv. commn. Army Ball Research Labs., 1973-77; advisor Pres.'s Commn. Law Enforcement and Adminstrn. Justice, 1966; cons. Office Dir. Def., Research and Engring., 1954-64. Contbr. articles to profl. jours. Patentee in field. Recipient Commendation for meritorious civilian service USAF, 1964, cert. appreciation U.S. Army, 1976. Fellow AAAS, AIAA (assoc.); mem. IEEE, Ops. Research Soc. Am. Republican. Presbyterian. Club: Cosmos. Home: PO Box 2668 Palos Verdes Peninsula CA 90274-8668 *The difference between having something to do and having to do something is a pain in the neck. Anything worth doing takes more doing than it is worth except for the fun of it.*

WEISS, IRWIN KEVIN, pediatrician, educator; b. Bklyn., Nov. 13, 1961; married; 3 children. BA magna cum laude, Yeshiva U., 1982, MD Albert Einstein Coll. Medicine, 1986. Diplomate Am. Bd. Pediatrics, sub bd. pediatric critical care medicine, Nat. Bd. Med. Examiners. Intern. in Pediatrics North Shore U. Hosp. Cornell U. Med. Coll., Manhasset, N.Y., 1986-87; resident in Pediatrics North Shore U. Hosp., clin. assoc. Cornell U. Hosp., Manhasset, 1987-89; fellow Pediatric Critical Care The N.Y. Hosp. Cornell U. Med. Ctr., N.Y.C., 1989-92; asst. prof. Pediatrics divsn. Critical Care UCLA Med. Ctr., L.A., 1992—. Contbr. articles to profl. jours. Mem. AMA, Am. Acad. Pediatrics, Soc. Critical Care Medicine, N.Y. Soc. Pediatric Critical Care Medicine. Office: UCLA Med Ctr 10833 Le Conte Ave Los Angeles CA 90035

WEISS, LAWRENCE J., broadcast executive; b. Cleve., Apr. 3, 1948; s. William S. and Esther (Sidelman) W. BBA, Ohio U., 1970. Cert. HIV test counselor, Calif. Agent William Morris Agy., N.Y.C., 1970-75; personal mgr., literary rep. The Shukat Co., Ltd., N.Y.C., 1975-90; personnel mgr., literary rep. Artist Circle Entertainment, L.A., 1990-96; exec. dir., writer, devel. Universal TV, Universal City, Calif., 1996—. Counselor HIV test Valley Cmty. Clinic, N. Hollywood, Calif., 1993—. Capt. U.S. Army, 1970-76. Office: Universal TV 100 Universal City Plz Universal City CA 91608

WEISS, LOREN ELLIOT, lawyer, law educator; b. Cleve., Sept. 28, 1947; s. Harry and Gertrude (Rapport) W.; m. Gina Dalton. BA with honors, UCLA, 1969; JD cum laude, U. San Diego, 1972. Bar: Calif. 1972, U.S. Dist. Ct. (so. dist.) Calif. 1972, Utah 1983, U.S. Dist. Ct. (cen. dist.) Calif. 1983, U.S. Dist. Ct. Utah 1983, U.S. Ct. Appeals (9th cir.) 1972, U.S. Ct. Appeals (10th cir.) 1986. With various law firms, San Diego, 1972-80; owner, gen. mgr. Mid-Mountain Lodge, Park City, Utah, 1980-83; pvt. practice, Salt Lake City, 1983-89, 93—; of counsel Purser, Okazaki & Berrett, Salt Lake City, 1989-93; prin. Weiss Berrett Loyd Petty, Salt Lake City, 1996—; mem. Utah Com. Bar Examiners, Salt Lake City, 1989-93; mem. ann. meeting com. Utah State Bar, 1985-91, chmn., 1994-95; liaison, panel atty. rep. U.S. Jud. Conf.Com. on Defender Svc., 1992-95; mem. mandatory cont. legal edn. bd. Utah Judicial Conf., 1995—. Contbr. articles to legal jours. Trustee Utah Trout Found., Salt Lake City, 1988—. Mem. FBA, Calif. Bar Assn., Utah Bar Assn., Nat. Assn. Criminal Def. Lawyers (co-chmn. continuing legal edn. com. 1992-93, co-chair indigent svcs. com. 1994-95), Utah Assn. Criminal Def. Lawyers (pres. 1993), Am. Bd. Trial Advocates. Office: 170 S Main St Ste 1100 Salt Lake City UT 84101

WEISS, MARTIN HARVEY, neurosurgeon, educator; b. Newark, Feb. 2, 1939; s. Max and Rae W.; m. R. Debora Rosenthal, Aug. 20, 1961; children: Brad, Jessica, Elisabeth. AB magna cum laude, Dartmouth Coll., 1960, BMS, 1961; MD, Cornell U., 1963. Diplomate Am. Bd. Neurol. Surgery (bd. dirs. 1983-89, vice chmn. 1987-88, chmn. 1988-89). Intern Univ. Hosps., Cleve., 1963-64; resident in neurosurgery Univ. Hosps., 1966-70; sr. instr. to asst. prof. neurosurgery Case Western Res. U., 1970-73; asso. prof. neurosurgery U. So. Calif., 1973-76. prof., 1976-78, prof., chmn. dept., 1978—; chmn. neurology B study sect. NIH; mem. residency rev. com. for neurosurgery Accreditation Commn. for Grad. Med. Edn., 1989—, vice chmn., 1991-93, chmn., 1993-95, mem. appeals coun. in neurosurgery, 1995—; Courville lectr. Loma Linda U. Sch. Medicine, 1989; Edgar Kahn vis. prof. U. Mich., 1987; W. James Gardner lectr. Cleve. Clinic, 1993; Edwin Boldrey vis. prof. U. Calif., San Francisco, 1994; hon. guest San Francisco Neurol. Soc., 1994, Australian Neurosurg. Soc., 1996; Arthur Ward vis. prof. U. Wash., 1988; John Raff vis. prof. U. Oreg., 1995; Afrox traveling prof. South African Congress Neurol. Surgeons, 1989; Loyal Davis lectr. Northwestern U., 1990; vis. prof. U. Melbourne, 1996, U. Sydney, 1996. Author: Pituitary Diseases, 1980; editor-in-chief Clin. Neurosurgery, 1980-83; assoc. editor Bull. L.A. Neurol. Socs., 1976-81, Jour. Clin. Neurosci., 1981—; mem. editl. bd. Neurosurgery, 1979-84, Neurol. Rsch., 1980—, Jour. Neurosurgery, 1987—, chmn., 1995—, assoc. editor, 1996. Served to capt. USAR, 1964-66. Spl. fellow in neurosurgery NIH, 1969-70; recipient Jamieson medal Australasian Neurosurg. Soc., 1996. Mem. ACS (adv. coun. neurosurgery 1985-88), Soc. Neurol. Surgeons, Neurosurg. Soc. Am., Am. Acad. Neurol. Surgery (exec. com. 1988-89, v.p. 1992-93), Rsch. Soc. Neurol. Surgeons, Am. Assn. Neurol. Surgeons (bd. dirs. 1988-91, sec. 1994-97), Congress Neurol. Surgeons (v.p. 1982-83), Western Neurosurg. Soc., Neurosurg. Forum, So. Calif. Neurosurg. Soc. (pres. 1983-84), Phi Beta Kappa, Alpha Omega Alpha. Home: 357 Georgian Rd La Canada-Flintridge CA 91011-3520 Office: 1200 N State St Los Angeles CA 90033-4525

WEISS-CORNWELL, AMY, interior designer; b. Mpls., Dec. 8, 1950; d. August Carl and Margaret Amelia (Wittman) Weiss; m. Dan Cornwell, July 31, 1995; 1 child, Emma Elizabeth. AA in Home Econs., Cerritos Coll.; student, Long Beach State U., Santa Ana Jr. Coll. Asst. to interior designer Pati Pfahler Designs, Canoga Park, Calif., 1974-75; interior designer B.A. Interiors, Fullerton, Calif., 1976-78, Birns Cos., Rancho Mirage, Calif., 1978-79, Carole Eichen Interiors, Fullerton, 1981, Sears, Roebuck and Co., Alhambra, Calif., 1982-84; staff interior designer Assoc. Design Studios, Costa Mesa, Calif., 1979-81; sr. corp. designer, mgr. design studio Barratt Am., Irvine, Calif., 1984-88; owner Amy Weiss Designs, Coronado, Calif., 1988—; designer in residence San Diego Design Ctr., 1990-94. Mem. Am. Soc. Interior Designers (Globe-Guilders steering com. 1989-92, chmn. Christmas party, co-chmn. Christmas on Prado 1989, 89, designer for ASID showcase house 1992, 93), Bldg. Industry Assn. (sales and mktg. coun. awards com. 1993, mem. sales and mktg. coun. 1986-88, mem. home builders coun. 1994, 2d place M.A.M.E. award 1987, 1st place M.A.M.E. award 1986, 2d place S.A.M. award 1987), Building Industry Assn. Remodeler's Coun., Nat. Kitchen and Bath Assn., Coronado C. of C., Coronado Rotary; participant in Pacific Design Ctr. Designer on Call program, L.A.. Coronado Cays Yacht Club. Home and Office: Amy Weiss Designs 10 Admiralty Cross Coronado CA 92118-3202

WEISSENBUEHLER, WAYNE, former bishop, pastor. Bishop of Rocky Mountain Evang. Luth. Ch. in Am., Denver, 1993; pastor Bethany Luth. Ch., Englewood, Colo., 1993—. Office: Bethany Luth Ch 4500 E Hampton Englewood CO 80110*

WEITZ, SUE D., academic administrator; b. Coeur D'Alene, Idaho, Oct. 16, 1948; d. Donald and Larraine (Kiefer) W.; m. Greg Intinarelli, Nov. 25, 1984; children: Derek, Lauran, Marcus. BA cum laude, Albertson's Coll. Idaho, 1971, MEd, 1975; postgrad., Ind. U., 1979-81; PhD, Gonzaga U., 1990. Coord. student activities, then asst. dean students Coll. Idaho, Caldwell, 1971-73, dean student life, 1974-76; assoc. dean students U. Cen. Ark., 1976-78; v.p. student affairs St. Mary-of-the-Woods (Ind.) Coll., 1978-81; dean of students Gonzaga U., Spokane, Wash., 1981-87, v.p. student life, 1987—; cons. Seattle U., 1989; evaluator Commn. on Colls., Seattle, 1990. Contbr. to profl. publs. Mem. Nat. Assn. Student Pers. Adminstrs. (nat. chairperson 1995), N.W. Assn. Coll. and Univ. Housing Officers, Nat. Assn. Coll. Activities, N.W. Coll. Pers. Assn. Office: Gonzaga Univ 502 E Boone Ave Spokane WA 99258-1774

WEITZE, WILLIAM FREDERICK, mechanical engineer; b. Westwood, N.J., May 4, 1960; s. Joseph Harry and May Elizabeth Weitze; m. Sylvia Bankston Garcia, June 1, 1985 (div. Nov. 1991); m. Terri Lee Cotter, March 1, 1996. BS in Mech. Engring., Rutgers U., 1982; MS in Mech. Engring., U. Calif., Berkeley, 1985. Lic. profl. engr., Calif. Program engr. GE Nuclear Energy, San Jose, Calif., 1982-85, engr., 1985-91, sr. engr., 1991—; cons. Engring. Cons. Svcs., San Jose, 1990—. Editor newsletter Silicon Valley Engring. Coun., 1991-92; contbr. articles to popular publs. Mem. ASME (treas., Santa Clara Valley 1990-91, sec. 1991-92, vice chmn. 1992-93, chmn. 1993-94, editor newsletter, 1988-90, 95-96). Office: GE Nuclear Energy 175 Curtner Ave M/C 747 San Jose CA 95125-1014

WEITZEL, JOHN QUINN, bishop; b. Chgo., May 10, 1928; s. Carl Joseph and Patricia (Quinn) W. BA, Maryknoll (N.Y.) Sem., 1951, M of Religious Edn., 1953; PMD, Harvard U. Ordained priest Roman Cath. Ch., 1955. With ednl. devel. Cath. Fgn. Mission Soc. of Am., Maryknoll, 1955-63, nat. dir. vocations for Maryknoll, dir. devel. dept. and info. services, 1963-72, mem. gen. council, 1972-78; asst. parish priest Cath. Ch., Western Samoa, 1979-81, pastor, vicar gen., 1981-86; consecrated bishop, 1986; bishop Cath. Ch., Am. Samoa, 1986—. Office: Diocese Samoa-Pago Pago Fatuoaiga PO Box 596 Pago Pago AS 96799-0596

WELCH, BOBBY O'NEAL, dean; b. Brunswick, Ga., Sept. 26, 1937; s. Thomas Joseph and Inez (Gibbs) W.; m. Margaret Ann Sias, Oct. 1, 1960; children: Linda Ailieen, Carol Ann. BBA, U. Miami, 1961; MS in Sys. Mgmt., U. So. Calif., L.A., 1968; PhD in Mgmt. and Adminstrn., Walden U., 1994. Commd. 2d lt. USAF, 1961, advanced through grades to lt. col., 1975, ret., 1982; tech. staff Logicon, Ft. Walton Beach, Fla., 1985-88; sr. contract adminstr. Logicon, San Pedro, Calif., 1988-91, Intermetrics, Inc., Huntington Beach, Calif., 1991-92; pres., CEO Harbour Corp., Laguna Hills, Calif., 1992-93; dean Sch. Bus. and Mgmt. West Coast U., L.A., 1989—; dean Coll. Bus. and Mgmt. So. Calif U., Santa Anna, 1996—, dean Coll. Tech., 1996—; v.p. Nat. Contract Mgmt. Assn., Huntington Beach, 1989-91. V.p. Village Pk. Homeowners Assn., Irvine, 1990-91, pres., 1991-92. Decorated Air medal, Bronze Star. Mem. Air Force Assn., mem. Qualitative Rsch. Cons. Assn. Republican. Methodist. Home: 118 Sequoia Tree Ln Irvine CA 92612-2228

WELCH, MICHAEL DENNIS, university official; b. Modesto, Calif., Jan. 18, 1947; s. Virgil W. and Shirlee (Sutphin) W.; m. Susan Shaffer, June 24, 1975; children: Kathryn S., Christopher M., Anna M. BA in History, La Verne Coll., 1968; MS in Sch. Counseling, U. La Verne, 1972; EdD in Higher Edn. Adminstrn., Brigham Young U., 1983. Deferred giving counselor McPherson (Kans.) Coll., 1972-74; dir. admissions and fin. aid U. La Verne, Calif., 1974-85, dir. devel., 1985-90; assoc. dir. ann. fund Duke U., Durham, N.C., 1990-94; asst. vice chancellor for ann. giving and alumni advancement Pepperdine U., Malibu, Calif., 1994—. Office: Pepperdine U 24255 Pacific Coast Hwy Malibu CA 90263

WELCH, RICHARD LEROY, personal improvement company executive; b. Lincoln, Nebr., Oct. 15, 1939; s. Raymond Nathanial and Helen Lila (Ludwig) W.; m. Donna Lee Gysegem, Nov. 3, 1991; children: Terri L. Flowerday, Julie A. Kuhl; 1 stepchild, Shannon Panzo. Student, U. Nebr., 1958-59. Agt. Gurantee Mut. Life, Lincoln, Nebr., 1960-61; agt., mgr. Mut. of Omaha, 1962-68; gen. agt. Loyal Protective Life, Omaha, 1969-70; mgr. Mut. Benefit Life, Dallas, 1971-73; br. mgr. Great West Life, San Jose, Calif., 1973-74; pres. Internat. Speedreading Inst., Phoenix, 1975-80; founder, pres. Educom, Inc./Subliminal Dynamics, Aurora, Colo., 1980—; mem. adv. bd. Great West Life, San Jose, 1973; pres. bd. dirs. Internat. Speedreading Inst., Phoenix, 1975-80, Subliminal Dynamics, Inc., San Jose, 1980-93, Educom, Inc., Aurora, 1993—. Author: Brain Management, 1996. Mem. Shriners, Masons (32d degree). Democrat. Office: Educom Inc dba Subliminal Dynamics 14700 E Kentucky Dr Ste 535 Aurora CO 80012

WELCHERT, STEVEN JOSEPH, public affairs consultant; b. Davenport, Iowa, June 16, 1956; s. Richard Marshall and Norma Jean (Waters) W.; m. Kathleen Ann Agnitsch, June 13, 1981; children: Sarah Elizabeth, Matthew Joseph. BGS, U. Iowa, 1979. Nat. field staff Ted Kennedy for President, 1979-80; polit. dir. Lucero for U.S. Senate, Denver, 1984; legis. dir. for Gov. Richard Lamm, Denver, 1984-87, sr. edn. advisor for, 1985-87; issues dir. for Mayor Federico Peña, Denver, 1987; v.p. Bonham/Shlenker & Assocs., Denver, 1988-90; pres. The Welchert Co., Denver, 1990—; staff chmn. Nat. Govs. Assn., Washington and Denver, 1986; on-air analyst Sta. KMGH-TV, Denver, 1987-94; Wis. dir. Gore for Pres., Milw., 1988; floor whip Dem. Nat. Platform Com., 1988; dir. Western Hemisphere Trade and Commerce Forum Hosting Trade Mins. and Bus. Leaders, 1995. Writer radio series Ind. Thinking, 1987-88. Advisor Cultural Facilities Dist., Denver, 1988; bd. dirs. Citizens for Denver's Future, 1989-90; mem. Denver Baseball Commn., 1986-89, also chmn. govt. com., Rocky Mt. chpt. Am. Ireland Fund. Named Rising Leader for 90's Colo. Bus. Mag., 1990. Mem. Am. Assn. Polit. Cons. (Pollie awards 1st pl. Best Free Media, 2d pl. Print Graphics and Collateral Material 1995). Democrat. Roman Catholic. Office: The Welchert Co 1525 Market St # 200 Denver CO 80202-1607

WELK, RICHARD ANDREW, plastic surgeon; b. Aug. 9, 1956. BS, U. Mich., 1977, MD, 1981. Diplomate Am. Bd. Surgery, Am. Bd. Plastic Surgery. Resident gen. surgery Grand Rapids, Mich., 1981-86; resident plastic surgery U. Calif., Irvine, 1986-88; plastic surgeon pvt. practice, Kirkland, Wash., 1988-91, Polyclinic, Seattle, 1991—. Mem. Am. Soc. Plastic & Reconstructive Surgery, Am. Soc. Aesthetic Plastic Surgery, Wash. State Med. Assn., Wash. Soc. Plastic Surgeons (pres. 1995-96). Office: Polyclinic 1145 Broadway Seattle WA 98122-4201

WELLER, DEBRA ANNE, elementary educator; b. New Orleans, Feb. 4, 1954; d. James Garretson and Elizabeth Gene (Blakely) Hyatt; m. Bruce Weller, June 15, 1974; children: Jenny, Todd. AA in Art, St. Petersburg Jr. Coll., 1974; BA in Art Edn., Glassboro State Coll., 1983; MS in Curriculum and Instrn., Nat. U., 1991. Cert. tchr. Profl. storyteller Mission Viejo, Calif., 1980—; tchr. Capistrano Unified Sch. Dist., San Juan Capistrano, Calif., 1989—; edn. dir. South Coast Storytellers Guild, Costa Mesa, Calif., 1990—; workshop presenter Orange County Dept. Edn., Costa Mesa, 1991—, Imagination Celebration, Irvine, Calif., 1993—. Author: (pamphlet) Image-U-Telling Clubs, 1995. Sec. Mission Viejo Cultural Com., 1995—. Cultural Arts grantee Dana Point (Calif.) Cultural Commn., 1993. Mem. NEA, Nat. Storytelling Assn. (Pacific region liaison), Calif. Tchrs. Assn., Calif. Kindergarten Assn. Mormon. Home: 27676 Bahamonde Mission Viejo CA 92692

WELLES, JOHN GALT, museum director; b. Orange, N.J., Aug. 24, 1925; s. Paul and Elizabeth Ash (Galt) W.; m. Barbara Lee Chrisman, Sept. 15, 1951; children: Virginia Chrisman, Deborah Galt, Barton Jeffery, Holly Page. BE, Yale U., 1946; MBA, U. Pa., 1949; LHD (hon.) U. Denver, 1994. Test engr. Gen. Electric Co., Lynn, Mass., 1947; labor relations staff New Departure div. Gen Motors Corp., Bristol, Conn., 1949-51; mem. staff Mountain States Employers Coun., Denver, 1952-55; head indsl. econs. div. U. Denver Research Inst., Denver, 1956-74; v.p. planning and devel. Colo. Sch. Mines, Golden, 1974-83; regional adminstr. EPA, Denver, 1983-87; exec. dir. Denver Mus. Natural History, 1987-94, exec. dir. emeritus, 1994—. Sr. cons. Secretariat, UN Conf. Human Environment, Geneva, 1971-72; cons. Bus. Internat., S.A., Geneva, 1972; trustee Tax Free Fund of Colo., N.Y., 1987—, Denver Pub. Libr. Friends Found., 1996—; mem. Rocky Mountain regional adv. bd. Inst. Internat. Edn., 1996—; exec. com. Denver Com. on Fgn. Rels., 1987—; bd. dirs Gulf of Maine Found., 1995—; chmn. Colo. Front Range Project, Denver, 1979-80. Contbr. articles to profl. jours., newspapers. Recipient Disting. Svc. award Denver Regional Coun. Govts., 1980, Barnes award EPA, 1987. Mem. AAAS, Am. Assn. Museums (ethics commn. 1991-94, v.p. 1992-95), Sustainable Futures Soc. (nat. adv. bd. 1994—), Met. Denver Exec. Club (pres. 1967-68), World Future Soc., Univ. Club (Denver) Denver Athletic Club, Tau Beta Pi, Blue Key. Republican. Episcopalian.

WELLES, MELINDA FASSETT, artist, educator; b. Palo Alto, Calif., Jan. 4, 1943; d. George Edward and Barbara Helena (Todd) W. Student, San Francisco Inst. Art, 1959-60, U. Oreg., 1960-62; BA in Fine Arts, UCLA, 1964, MA in Spl. Edn., 1971, PhD in Ednl. Psychology, 1976; student fine arts and illustration Art Ctr. Coll. Design, 1977-80. Cert. ednl. psychologist, Calif. Asst. prof. Calif. State U., Northridge, 1979-82; assoc. prof. curriculum, teaching and spl. edn. U. So. Calif., L.A., 1980-89; prof. liberal studies Art Ctr. Coll. Design, 1978—; mem. acad. faculty Pasadena City Coll., 1973-79, Otis Coll. Art and Design, L.A., 1986—, UCLA Extension, 1980-84, Coll. Devel. Studies, L.A., 1978-87, El Camino C.C., Redondo Beach, Calif., 1982-86; cons. spl. edn.; pub. adminstrn. analyst UCLA Spl. Edn. Rsch. Program, 1973-76; exec. dir. Atwater Park Ctr. Disabled Children, L.A., 1976-78; coord. Pacific Oaks Coll. in svc. programs for L.A. Unified Schs., Pasadena, 1978-81; mem. Southwest Blue Book, The Blue Ribbon, Friends of Robinson Gardens, Freedom's Found. at Valley Forge; bd. dirs. The Mannequins, Costume Coun. L.A. County Mus. of Art., Assistance League of So. Calif. Author: Calif. Dept. Edn. Tech. Reports, 1972-76; editor: Teaching Special Students in the Mainstream, 1981, Educating Special Learners, 1986, 88, Teaching Students with Learning Problems, 1988, Exceptional Children and Youth, 1989, Left Brain Right Brain, 1997; group shows include: San Francisco Inst. Art, 1960, U. Hawaii, 1978, Barnsdall Gallery, L.A., 1979, 80; represented in various pvt. collections. HEW fellow, 1971-72; grantee Calif. Dept. Edn., 1975-76, Calif. Dept. Health, 1978. Mem. Am. Psych. Assn., Calif. Learning Disabilities Assn., Am. Council Learning Disabilities, Calif. Scholarship Fedn. (life), Alpha Chi Omega. Office: 700 Levering Ave Apt 1 Los Angeles CA 90024-2795

WELLING, GENE B., dentist; b. Salt Lake City; s. Lawrence Darrel and Anne Bertha (Bowring) W.; m. Carol Lee Reynolds, Sept. 9, 1957; children: Bart Darrel, Miquolyn Welling Smith, Steven Gene, Nathan Hal. BS, U. Utah, 1960; DDS, Coll. Physicians & Surgeons, 1962. Dentist pvt. practice, Eureka, Calif. Pres. Boy Scouts Am., Redwood Coun., 1982; bishop LDS Ch., Sale Lake City, 1963-65, Eureka, 1975-77, state pres., 1966-75. Fellow Internat. Coll. Dentists, Peirra Fauehard Acad.; mem. ADA (reference com. 1992-95), Calif. Dental Assn.(sec. 1994-96, v.p., 1997-98), LDS Acad. Dentists, Psi Omega. Republican. Home: 2232 Wood St Eureka CA 95501-4755 Office: 3142 Harrison Ave Eureka CA 95503-5638

WELLISCH, WILLIAM JEREMIAH, social psychology educator; b. Vienna, Austria, July 3, 1938; came to U.S., 1940; s. Max and Zelda (Schanser) W.; m. Geraldine Eve Miller (dec. Feb. 1970); children: Garth Kevin, Miriam Rhoda; m. Claudine Abbey Truman, Sept. 5, 1971; children: Rebecca Colleen, Marcus Joshua, Gabriel Jason. MA in Sociology, U. Mo., 1965, PhD in Sociology, 1968. Researcher urbanization Hemispheric Consultants, Columbia, Mo., 1968-69; cons. to local govt. ofcl. on L.Am. Bicultural Consultants, Inc., Denver, 1969-70; prof. Red Rocks Coll., Lakewood, Colo., 1970-76, 77—. Author: Bi-Cultural Development, 1971, Honduras: A Study in Sub-Development, 1978. Mem. citizen's adv. bd. Sta. KCFR Pub. Radio, Denver, 1989—. Republican. Mem. Unification Ch. Home: 2325 Clay St Denver CO 80211-5123 Office: Red Rocks CC 13300 W 6th Ave Golden CO 80401-5357

WELLIVER, CHARLES HAROLD, hospital administrator; b. Wichita, Kans., Feb. 14, 1945; married. BA, Wichita State U., 1972; MHA, U. Mo., 1974. Asst. dir. St. Luke's Hosp., Kansas City, 1974-79, assoc. dir., 1979-80; adminstr. Spelman Meml. Hosp., Smithville, Mo., 1980-82; sr. adminstr., COO Good Samaritan Med. Ctr., Phoenix, 1982-86, v.p., CEO, 1989—; v.p., CEO Thunderbird Samaritan Hosp., Glendale, Ariz., 1986-89. Office: Good Samaritan Regional Med Ctr 1441 N 12th St Phoenix AZ 85006-2837*

WELLMAN, MARIAN THOMPSON, financial planner; b. Belvidere, Ill., Sept. 8, 1948; d. Avery and Elizabeth (McGuigan) Thompson; m. Mr. Wellman, June 24, 1972 (div. Aug. 1993); chldren: Andrew, Paul. BME, U. Colo., Boulder, 1971; MBA, U. Colo., Denver, 1983. Enrolled agt.; cert. fin. planner. Personal fin. planner, 1983—. Mem. legacy com. Am. Cancer Soc., Denver; mem. adv. com. Multiple Sclerosis Soc., Denver; bd. dirs. Prevent Blindness Colo., Denver, 1994-95. Mem. Denver Athletic Club, mem. Rotary. Republican. Home: 8231 S Tamarac St Englewood CO 80112 Office: Wellman Fin Cons 7535 E Hampden Ste 101 Denver CO 80231

WELLS, CHRISTINE LOUISE, physical education educator; b. Buffalo, N.Y., Mar. 22, 1938; d. Harold Edward and Edythe Adelina (Burton) W. BS in Edn., U. Mich., 1959; MS, Smith Coll., 1964; PhD, Pa. State U., 1969. Phys. edn. tchr. Grosse Pointe (Mich.) Pub. Schs., 1959-62; instr. Smith Coll., Northampton, Mass., 1962-66; NDEA scholar Pa. State U., University Park, 1969-72; asst. prof. Dalhousie U., Halifax, N.S., Can., 1969-72; NIH postdoctoral fellow U. Calif., Santa Barbara, 1971-73; assoc. prof. Temple U., Phila., 1973-76; assoc. prof. Ariz. State U., Tempe, 1976-80, prof., 1980—; Lorraine C. Snell vis. prof. Northeastern U., Boston, 1984; mem. adv. bd. Rodale Press, Emmaus, Pa., The Women's Sports Found., Eisenhower Park, N.Y., 1992—; presenter more than 100 papers in field, 1970—; cons. U.S. Olympic Physiology Com., 1982-86, Granville Corp., 1982, Whittle Corp., 1986-91; mem. adv. bd. Internat. Dance-Exercise Assn., 1982-90, Melpomene Inst. Women's Health Rsch., 1983—, Nat. Inst. Fitness and Sport, 1985-91. Author: Women, Sport and Performance: A Physiological Perspective, 1985, 2d edit., 1991, (with E.M. Haymes) Environment and Human Performance, 1986, (with others) Research and Practice in Physical Education, 1977, Female Endurance Athletes, 1986, Physical Activity and Human Well-Being, 1986, Future Directions in Exercise and Sport Science Research, 1989; mem. editorial bd. Cycling Sci., 1990-94, Women in Sport and Phys. Activity Jour., 1990—, biol. rev. editor; mem. adv. bd. Walking Mag., 1987—, Time-Life Fitness Series, 1987, Moxie, 1989-90, Living Fit Mag., 1993—, Fit Pregnancy Mag., 1993—, Bicycling Mag., 1987—, Runner's World, 1987—; contbr. articles to profl. jours., chpts. to books; jour. reviewer in field. Alumni fellow Pa. State U., 1984; recipient Wonder Woman Found. award 1982, Women's Sport Found. Individual Contbn. to Women's Sports award 1983, Disting. Alumna award U. Mich., 1994. Fellow AAHPERD, Rsch. Consortium, (chmn. position statements 1976-77, pres. 1978-79, exec. v.p. search com. 1986, alliance scholar com. chair 1988-89), Am. Coll. Sports Medicine (trustee 1979-92, v.p. for edn. 1982-84, chmn. meetings evaluation 1976-77; pres. S.W. chpt. 1989-90, chmn. student breakfast 1984, position statements com. 1984, Citation award 1995, S.W. Chpt. Recognition award 1996); mem. Ariz. State Assn. of Health, Phys. Edn. and Recreation, Am. Acad. Kinesiology and Phys. Edn. (membership com. chairperson 1986-87, 93-94, program com. 1988-89), Mountaineers' Inc. (pres. 1995—), Sigma Xi, Phi Lambda Theta, Phi Sigma. Office: Ariz State U Dept Exercise Sci Phys Edn Tempe AZ 85287-0404

WELLS, DAVID PATRICK, career officer; b. Ravenna, Ohio, July 15, 1965; s. Douglas Charles and Margaret Ann (Whited) W.; m. Laura Marie Masi, Aug. 3, 1991; children: Erin Marie, Megan Elizabeth. BS in Aerospace Engring., U.S. Naval Acad., 1988; MS in Elec. Engring., Naval Postgrad. Sch., 1994. Commd. 2d lt. USMC, 1988; advanced through grades to capt. USMC, 1993; comm. officer Comm. Co. 3d Marine divsn., Okinawa, Japan, 1989-90, 9th Comm. Bn., Camp Pendleton, Calif., 1990-92; tactical data network officer Marine Corps. Tactical Sys. Support Activity, Camp Pendleton, 1994—. Mem. IEEE, Civil Air Patrol (Amelia Earhart award 1982), Armed Forces Comm. Electronics Assn., Marine Corps. Assn., Eta Kappa Nu. Republican. Roman Catholic. Office: Marine Corps Tactical Sys Support Activity Box 555171 Camp Pendleton CA 92055

WELLS, MERLE WILLIAM, historian, state archivist; b. Lethbridge, Alta., Can., Dec. 1, 1918; s. Norman Danby and Minnie Muir (Huckett) W.; student Boise Jr. Coll., 1937-39; A.B., Coll. Idaho, 1941, L.H.D. (hon.), 1981; M.A., U. Calif., 1947, Ph.D., 1950; L.H.D., U. Idaho, 1990. Instr. history Coll. Idaho, Caldwell, 1942-46; assoc. prof. history Alliance Coll., Cambridge Springs, Pa., 1950-56, 58, dean students, 1955-56; cons. historian Idaho Hist. Soc., Boise, 1956-58, historian and archivist, 1959—; hist. preservation officer, archivist State of Idaho, Boise, 1968-86. Treas., So. Idaho Migrant Ministry, 1960-64, chmn., 1964-67; nat. migrant adv. com. Nat. Council Chs., 1964-67, gen. bd. Idaho council, 1967-75; bd. dirs. Idaho State Employees Credit Union, 1964-67, treas., 1966-67; mem. Idaho Commn. Arts and Humanities, 1966-67; mem. Idaho Lewis and Clark Trail Commn., 1968-70, 84-88; mem. Idaho Bicentennial Commn., 1971-76; bd. dirs. Sawtooth Interpretive Assn., 1972—, dept. history United Presbyn. Ch., 1978-84; v.p. Idaho Zool. Soc., 1982-84, bd. dirs., 1984-94, treas., 1988-90, historian, 1990—. State Hist. Preservation Officers (dir. 1976-81, chmn. Western states council on geog. names 1982-83), Am. Hist. Assn., Western History Assn. (council 1973-76), AAUP, Am. Assn. State and Local History (council 1973-77), Soc. Am. Archivists, Assn. Idaho Historians (pres., 1994), others. Author: Anti-Mormonism in Idaho, 1978, Boise: An Illustrated History, 1982, Gold Camps and Silver Cities, 1984, Idaho: Gem of the Mountains, 1985. Office: Idaho State Hist Soc 210 Main St Boise ID 83702-7264 *Those of us in government positions need to focus upon helping people: when reviewing projects that may be harmful, we should help make them acceptable, rather than simply express opposition or reject them.*

WELLS, RICHARD H., gaming research executive; b. Stillwater, Okla., June 24, 1940; s. James R. and Edna Ruth (McKnight) W.; m. Peggy P. Puyear, Aug. 7, 1988; children: Shanley Renne, Richard Carlyle, Amy Luru. BS in Gen. Bus., Okla. State U., 1964; postgrad. sys. dynamics, MIT, 1985-86. Sr. fin. analyst Conoco, Houston, 1964-69; v.p. planning Union Planters Nat. Bank, Memphis, 1969-75; v.p. fin. planning Inn devel. Holiday Inns, Memphis, 1975-78, v.p. corp. adminstrn., 1979-80; sr. v.p. planning-adminstrn. Harrah's, Reno, 1980-86; v.p. Bally's Casino Hotels, Reno, 1986-90; co-owner Pennington & Assocs., Reno, 1990—; founder, owner Casino Player Count Svc., Reno, 1990—; founder, pres. Wells Gaming Rsch., Reno, Nev., 1995—. Mem. Reno Downtown Redevel. Com., 1983-84, Reno Task Force for Econ. Diversification, 1984, Nev. Gov.'s Econ. Adv. Com., 1983-84, Reno-Sparks Conv. Authority Rsch. Coun., 1990; chmn. Washoe Med. Found. Project Mgmt. Group, 1990; mem. dir. Econ. Devel. Authority Western Nev., 1992-96. Served with U.S. Army, 1958-61. Mem. Reno C. of C. (dir. 1983-84), Fin. Execs. Inst. (pres. 1974-75). Home: PO Box 3781 Reno NV 89505-3781

WELLS, ROGER STANLEY, software engineer; b. Seattle, Apr. 13, 1949; s. Stanley A. and Margaret W. BA, Whitman Coll., 1971; postgrad., U. Tex., Austin, 1973-74; BS, Oreg. State U., 1977. Software evaluation engr. Tektronix, Beaverton, Oreg., 1979-83; computer engr. Aramco, Dhahran, Saudi Arabia, 1983-84; software engr. Conrac Corp., Clackamas, Oreg., 1984-85, Duarte, Calif., 1985; software analyst Lundy Fin. Systems, San Dimas, Calif., 1986-89; contract software analyst for various orgns. Seattle, 1989-92; software engr. Illuminet (formerly U.S. Intelco. Networks), Olympia, Wash., 1993—. Bd. dirs. The Sci. Fiction Mus., Salem, Oreg., 1993—; co-founder, bd. dirs., pres. Oreg. Sci. Fiction Conv., 1979-81. Mem. IEEE, Am. Philatelic Soc., Nat. Assn. Parliamentarians, Am. Inst. Parliamentarians (chpt. v.p. 1996-97), Nat. Assn. Parliamentarians, Portland Sci. Fiction Soc., N.W. Sci. Fiction Soc., Internat. Platform Assn., Mensa, Assn. Computing Machinery, L.A. Sci. Fantasy Soc., Melbourne (Australia) Sci. Fiction Club, Toastmasters Internat. (pres. 1980, v.p. edn. 1994-95, area gov. 1994-95, dist. 32 parliamentarian 1996-97). Home: 4820 Yelm Hwy SE Apt B-102 Lacey WA 98503-4903

WELLS, WILLIAM ADRAIN, non-profit executive; b. San Antonio, Jan. 16, 1951; s. Jarold Adrain and Sarah Ferne (Cain) W. BA, Trinity U., San Antonio, 1972; MA, 1974; cert. in History, Woodbrooke Coll., U.K., 1976. Instr. Trinity U., San Antonio, 1972-76; nat. dir. Programs Rsch. Epilepsy Found. Am., Washington, 1978-81; nat. dir. Planning and Evalulation Fund Raising Am. Heart Assn., Dallas, 1981-83; exec. dir. Am. Heart Assn., Washington, 1983-86; exec. v.p. Am. Heart Assn., L.A., 1986-88, Childrens Hosp. Found., L.A., 1989-92; exec. dir. Ctr. for Living, L.A., 1992-93; v.p. Weingart Ctr. Assn., L.A., 1993—; adv. coun. George Washington U., 1980-81; exec. com. Calif. Biomedical Rsch. Found., Berkeley, Calif., 1986-88; founding assoc. Lymphoma Rsch. Found., L.A., 1991-92; bd. dirs. Am. Heart Assn., Hollywood, Calif., 1991-92. Author, producer: (video series) New Directions in Rehabilitation, 1980; author: Epilepsy Research, 1981, Prentice-Hall Fund Raising Sries, 1984. Ofcl. participant Jeunesse-Carnegie Hall, N.Y.C., 1980; mem. Rotary L.A., 1986-89; com. mem. L.A. Com. Nat. Inst. Health Centennial, 1987; city commn. Ethical Standards, L.A. Social Svcs., 1990. Mem. Nat. Soc. Fund Raising Execs. Republican. Home: 913 Dolores Rd Altadena CA 91001-1740

WELLS-HENDERSON, RONALD JOHN, investment counselor; b. Shanghai, Jan. 28, 1934; s. William Noel and Sylvia Mary (Gowen) Wells-H.; m. Kathleen Louise McDonnell, Sept. 14, 1957; children—Anne, John. B.A., U. Wash., 1955; M.B.A., Northwestern U., 1957. Chartered fin. analyst. Security analyst Continental Bank, Chgo., 1957-59; fin. analyst Boeing Co., Seattle; trust investment mgr. Seattle Trust, 1970-80; prin. KAS Investment Cons., Seattle, 1980—. Treas., Civil Affairs Assn., 1975-79; curator-treas. Seattle King County Mil. History Soc., 1978-80. Contbr. articles to profl. jours. Mem. Seattle Art Mus., Bellevue Art Mus., 1957—. Served to lt. col. USAR, 1955-83. Gazzam Found. scholar, 1952-55. Mem. Seattle Soc. Fin. Analysts, Inst. Chartered Fin. Analysts, Assn. for Investment Mgmt. and Rsch., Washington Water Trails Assn. Episcopalian. Home: 13005 SE 46th St Bellevue WA 98006-2042 Office: KAS Investment Cons PO Box 5617 Bellevue WA 98006-0117

WELSCH, SUZANNE CAROL, mathematics educator; b. Chgo., Nov. 23, 1941; d. James Dumont Seiler and Lotta May Marjorie (Grayson) Langford; m. Ralph Kelley Ungermann, Mar. 31, 1962 (div. Mar. 1980); children: Annette Carol, Scott Kelley; m. John Henry Welsch, Jan. 2, 1981; children: James Henry, Lee William. AA in Math., Ventura Coll., 1962; BA in Stats., U. Calif., Berkeley, 1964; MA in Math., U. Calif., Irvine, 1972. Computer programmer N.Am. Space & Info. Systems, Downey, Calif., 1964-65; biostatistician U. Calif., Irvine, 1969-73; owner, mgr. Ungermann Assocs., developers Logcap software, Los Altos, 1972-80; prof. math., stats. and computers Sierra Nevada Coll., Incline Village, Nev., 1983—; chmn. sci. dept. Sierra Nevada Coll., Incline Village, 1989—; founder, owner, mgr. Zilog, Los Altos, Calif., 1974; cons. Long Beach Heart Assn., 1972-75. Contbr. articles to profl. jours. Neighborhood chmn., bd. dirs., coun., treas., leader Girl Scouts U.S., 1971—, treas., Reno, 1985-86; bd. dirs. Nev. State Odyssey of the Mind. Recipient appreciation pin Sierra Nevada coun. Girl Scouts U.S.A., 1986. Mem. AAUW (state bd. dirs.), Math. Assn. Am., Am. Statis. Assn., Nat. Coun. Tchrs. Math., Assn. Women in Math., Nat. Assn. Advisors for Health Professions, Consortium of Math. Programs, Nev. Assn. for Gifted, U. Calif. Alumni Assn. Home: 680 Saddlehorn Dr Incline Village NV 89451-8500 Office: Sierra Nevada Coll 800 College Dr Incline Village NV 89451-9114

WELSH, JOHN BERESFORD, JR., lawyer; b. Seattle, Feb. 16, 1940; s. John B. and Rowena Morgan (Custer) W. Student U. Hawaii, 1960, Georgetown U., 1960; BA, U. Wash., 1962, LLB, 1965. Bar: Wash. 1965. Staff counsel Joint Com. on Govtl. Cooperation, 1965-66; asst. atty. gen. Dept. Labor and Industries, 1966-67; atty. Legis. Coun., acting as counsel to Pub. Health Com., Labor Com., Pub. Employees Collective Bargaining Com., Com. on State Instns. and Youth Devel., State of Wash., 1967-73; sr. counsel Wash. Ho. of Reps., counsel to Ho. Com. on Social and Health Svcs., Olympia, 1973-86; counsel Ho. Com. Human Svcs., 1987-91, 93-95, Ho. Com. on Health Care, 1987—, Ho. Com. on Trade and Econ. Devel., 1995—, Joint Select Com. on Nurse Delegation, 1995—, Joint Select Com. on Oral Health, 1996; legal cons. Gov's. Planning Commn. Vocat. Rehab., 1968, Gov.'s Commn. on Youth Involvement, 1969; envoy from Gov. Wash. to investiture of Prince of Wales, London, 1969; faculty Nat. Conf. State Legislatures, Denver, 1977, New Orleans, 1977, San Francisco, 1984, Orlando, Fla., 1985, Denver 1986, Kansas City, Mo., 1987, Washington, 1988, Indpls., 1989, Seattle, 1990, Ft. Lauderdale, Fla., 1991, Albuquerque, 1992, Boston, 1994, San Antonio, 1995, mem. steering com., 1986-90, legis. issues com., 1986—, Coun. on Licensure, Enforcement and Regulation, 1984, 86-90, 87-88, Coun. of State Govts. com. on suggested state legis., 1988—, sub. com. scope and agenda, 1988-95. Hon. prof. health adminstrn. Eastern Wash. U., 1982. Mem. Wash. Bar Assn., Govtl. Lawyers Assn., Nat. Health Lawyers Assn., Soc. des Amis du Musee de l'Armee, Paris, English Speaking Union, La Societe Napoleonienne, Medals Soc. Am., Sons of Union Veterans of the Civil War, Custer Battlefield Hist. & Mus. Assn., 8th Army Air Force Hist. Assn., Napoleonic Assn Am., Northwest Hist. Assn., Friends of Willie & Joe, Phi Delta Phi. Office: Wash Ho Reps PO Box 40600 Olympia WA 98504

WELSH, JOHN RICHARD, state official; b. Neillsville, Wis., May 27, 1938; s. Francis Richard and Bernice Margaret (Schneider) W.; m. Carol Kay Ableidinger, Sept. 30, 1961; children: Tony, Becky, Cathy, Michael, Chelley. BBA, Loyola U., Chgo., 1977; MEd, No. Ariz. State U., 1996. Benefit mgr. George F. Brown & Sons, Chgo., 1968-69, Marsh & McLennon, Chgo., 1969-71; adminstrv. mgr. Kemper Ins. Group, Long Grove, Ill., 1971-73; benefits mgr. 1st Nat. Bank of Chgo., 1973-79, The Arizona Bank, Phoenix, 1979-81; cons. Phoenix, 1981-84; benefits mgr., arbitrator Frontier Airlines, Inc., Denver, 1984-85; benefits mgr. Dept. Adminstrn., State of Ariz., Phoenix, 1985-91; retirement officer, seminar facilitator Ariz. State Retirement Sys., Phoenix, 1991—; team leader, benefits adv. Total Quality Mgmt. Ariz. State Retirement System, Phoenix, 1995. High sch. football ofcl. Ariz. Interscholastic Assn., Phoenix, 1980-93; football coach Portage Park Sports, Chgo., 1969-79, baseball coach, 1969-79; basketball coach K.C., Durand, Wis., 1966-68. With USN, 1956-59. Mem. Nat. Assn. for Pre-Retirement Edn., Loyola U. Alumni Assn. (Phoenix chpt.), Notre Dame Club of Phoenix, Bellaire Men's Golf Assn. Roman Catholic. Home: 4141 W Hayward Ave Phoenix AZ 85051-5751 Office: Ariz State Retirement Sys 3300 N Central Ave Phoenix AZ 85012-2501

WELSH, MARY MCANAW, educator, family mediator; b. Cameron, Mo., Dec. 7, 1920; d. Francis Louis and Mary Matilda (Moore) McA.; m. Alvin F. Welsh, Feb. 10, 1944 (dec.); children: Mary Celia, Clinton F., M. Ann. AB, U. Kans., 1942; MA, Seton Hall U., 1960; EdD, Columbia U., 1971. Reporter, Hutchinson (Kans.) News Herald, 1942-43; house editor Worthington Pump & Machine Corp., Harrison, N.J., 1943-44; tchr., housemaster, coordinator Summit (N.J.) Pub. Schs., 1960-68; prof. family studies N.Mex. State U., Las Cruces, 1972-85; adj. faculty dept. family practice Tex. Tech. Regional Acad. Health Ctr., El Paso, 1978-82, Family Mediation Practice, Las Cruces, 1986—. Mem. AAUW (pres. N.Mex. 1981-83), N.Mex. Council Women's Orgn. (founder, chmn. 1982-83), Delta Kappa Gamma, Kappa Alpha Theta. Democrat. Roman Catholic. Author: A Good Family is Hard to Found, 1972; Parent, Child and Sex, 1970; contbr. articles to profl. jours.; writer, presenter home econs. and family study series KRWG-TV, 1974; moderator TV series The Changing Family in N.Mex./LWV, 1976. Home and Office: University Park 4150 Tesota Dr Las Cruces NM 88011

WELSH, ROBERT NEVILLE, broadcasting executive; b. Dayton, Ohio, Apr. 26, 1961; s. James Carter Welsh and Mary Dee (Neville) Kubiak. BS, U. Fla., 1983. On-air host WUFT-FM Radio, Gainesville, Fla., 1981-83; announcer WRUF-FM Radio, Gainesville, 1982-83; account exec. WMFM-Radio, Gainesville, 1983-84, WOGX-TV, Ocala, Fla., 1984-89, WCJB-TV, Gainesville, 1989-92, KGMB-TV, Honolulu, 1992—. Dir. pub. rels. Big Bros./Big Sisters, Gainesville, 1986-91. Mem. Gainesville Advt. Fedn. (v.p. 1988-92), U.S. Golf Assn. Episcopalian. Office: KGMB-TV 1534 Kapiolani Blvd Honolulu HI 69814

WELSH, WILLIAM DANIEL, family practitioner; b. Balt., May 18, 1950; s. Joseph Leo and Bessie Mary (Tangires) W.; m. Loraine Lynn Barkhaus, July 11, 1985; children: Sean William, Ryan Daniel. Student, Johns Hopkins U., 1971; BS in Biology cum laude, Fairleigh Dickinson U., 1972; DO, Coll. Osteo. Medicine-Surgery, Des Moines, 1975. Diplomate Am. Bd. Osteo. Family Practitioners. Intern Martin Place Hosp., Madison Heights, Mich., 1975-76, resident in internal medicine, 1976-77; pvt. practice, Detroit, 1976-79, Whittier, Calif., 1979—; instr. ACLS, L.A., 1980-92; dir. Family Asthma Forum, L.A., 1982-88; bd. dirs. Whittier Hosp. Med. Ctr., 1981, vice chief staff, 1982-84, med. dir. family asthma forum, 1979-88, med. dir. Summit Place alcohol treatment program, 1983-88; med. dir. Mirada Hills Rehab. Hosp., La Mirada, Calif., 1980-88; former clin. preceptor Coll. Osteo. Med. Pacific, Pomona, Calif., clin. assoc. prof. internal medicine; mem. dept. family practice, physician rev. com. Friendly Hills Regional Med. Ctr., La Habra, Calif.; mem. staff Presbyn. Intercmty. Hosp., Whittier. Participant Calif. Beach Clean Up Day, 1996. Mem. Am. Osteo. Assn., Am. Coll. Osteo. Family Physicians (bd. cert.), Am. Acad. Antiaging Medicine, Osteo. Physicians and Surgeons Calif. Home: 16871 Marina Bay Dr Huntington Beach CA 92649-2913 Office: Friendly Hills HealthCare Network Network 12291 Washington Blvd Whittier CA 90606

WELSOME, EILEEN, journalist; b. N.Y.C., Mar. 12, 1951; d. Richard H. and Jane M. (Garity) W.; m. James R. Martin, Aug. 3, 1983. BJ with honors, U. Tex., 1980. Reporter Beaumont (Tex.) Enterprise, 1980-82, San Antonio Light, 1982-83, San Antonio Express-News, 1983-86, Albuquerque Tribune, 1987-94. Recipient Clarion award, 1989, News Reporting award Nat. Headliners, 1989, John Hancock award, 1991, Mng. Editors Pub. Svc. award AP, 1991, 94, Roy Howard award 1994, James Aronson award, 1994, Gold Medal award Investigative Reporters and Editors, 1994, Sigma Delta Chi award, 1994, Investigative Reporting award Nat. Headliners, 1994, Selden Ring award, 1994, Heywood Broun award, 1994, George Polk award, 1994, Sidney Hillman Found. award, 1994, Pulitzer Prize for nat. reporting, 1994; John S. Knight fellow Stanford U., 1991-92.

WELTER, LINDA ALLAIRE, development executive; b. Bayonne, N.J., Aug. 11, 1949; d. Godfrey Adolf and Grace Elizabeth (Buss) W. BA in Philosophy and Polit. Sci., Drew U., 1971, postgrad., 1972-73; postgrad., Harvard U., 1985; MBA, Boston Coll., 1987. Development asst. Harvard U., Cambridge, Mass., 1980-83, development assoc., 1983-85, dir. class and area programs, 1985-86, sr. development officer, 1986-87; from capital campaign dir. to asst. v.p. for resources Wellesley (Mass.) Coll., 1987-93; v.p., gen. mgr. for development ops. ARC, Washington, 1993-94; dir. major gifts U. Calif., Berkeley, 1994—; instr. Stonehill Coll., Easton, Mass.; lectr. Northeastern U., Boston; cons. Vassar Coll.; fundraising cons. Dimock Comty. Health Ctr., Boston, 1992. Vol. co-chair fundraising Ruah; mem. capital campaign com. Fenway Cmty. Health Ctr.; vol. Nat. Network on Women as Philanthropists. Mem. Women in Development (bd. dirs., chair city svc. project), Coun. for Advancement and Support of Edn. (teaching faculty 1985—), Women in Philanthropy. Address: 116 W Willow Grove Ave Philadelphia PA 19118 Office: U Calif Univ Rels 2440 Bancroft Way Berkeley CA 94720-4201

WELTON, CHARLES EPHRAIM, lawyer; b. Cloquet, Minn., June 23, 1947; s. Eugene Frances and Evelyn Esther (Koski) W.; m. Nancy Jean Sanda, July 19, 1969, (div.); children: Spencer Sanda, Marshall Eugene. BA, Macalester Coll., 1969; postgrad., U. Minn., 1969-70; JD, U. Denver, 1974. Bar: Colo. 1974, U.S. Dist. Ct. Colo. 1974, U.S. Supreme Ct. 1979, U.S. Ct. Appeals (10th cir.) 1980. Assoc. Davidovich & Assocs., and predecessor firm, Denver, 1974-77, Charles Welton and Assocs., Denver, 1978-80, 1984-88; ptnr. Davidovich & Welton, Denver, 1981-84, OSM Properties, Denver, 1982—; prin. Charles Welton, P.C. and predecessor firms, 1988—; grievance com., panelist, arbitrator Colo. Supreme Ct., 1996—; adj. prof. Inst. Advanced Legal Studies U. Denver, 1991—; lectr. in field. Author of instructional materials; author study; contbr. articles to profl. jours. Sch. pres. PTSA, Denver, 1983-84; coach Colo. Jr. Soccer League, 1980-85; coach Odessey of the Mind (formerly Olympics of the Mind), 1986-88; bd. dirs. Virginia Vale Swim Club, officer, 1989-91, Pioneer Jr. Hockey Assn., 1990-92. Served alt. mil. duty Denver Gen. Hosp., 1970-72. Mem. Denver Bar Assn. (facilitator bench/bar retreat 1995, 96, legal fee arbitration com.), Colo. Bar Assn. (legal fee arbitration com.), Assn. Trial Lawyers Am., Colo. Trial Lawyers Assn. (bd. dirs. 1985-90, chmn. seminar com. 1986-88, exec. com. 1987-88, legis. com. 1988-94, case assistance com. 1995—), Am. Bldg. a Lasting Earth (founder), Exec. Ventures Group of Am. Leadership Forum (adv. bd. 1987-90). Democrat. Lutheran. Home: 680 Vista Ln Lakewood CO 80215-6037 Office: Old Smith Mansion 1751 Gilpin St Denver CO 80218-1205

WELTY, JOHN DONALD, academic administrator; b. Amboy, Ill., Aug. 24, 1944; s. John Donald and Doris (Donnelly) W.; m. Sharon Welty; children: Anne, Elisabeth. B.S., Western Ill. U., 1965; M.A., Mich. State U., 1967; Ed.D., Ind. U., 1974. Asst. v.p. for student affairs SW State U., Marshall, Minn., 1973-74; dir. residences SUNY-Albany, 1974-77, assoc. dean for student affairs, 1977-80; v.p. for student and univ. affairs Indiana U. of Pa., 1980-84, pres., 1984-91; pres. Calif. State U., Fresno, 1991—; lectr. in field. Contbr. articles to profl. jours. Chmn. Small Bus. Incubator of Indiana, 1985-91; bd. dirs. Open Door Crises and Counseling Ctr., Indiana, Big Bros./Big Sisters, Indiana, 1980-84. Recipient Chancellor's award SUNY, 1977. Mem. Fresno Bus. Coun., Fresno Econ. Devel. Commn., Sunnyside Country Club. Roman Catholic. Lodge: Rotary. Office: Calif State U 5241 S Maple Ave Fresno CA 93725-9739

WELTZIEN, O(LIVER) ALAN, English educator, researcher; b. Seattle, Oct. 27, 1952; s. Robert Taylor and Lorraine Cushing (Boos) W.; m. Elizabeth Margaret Mory, May 14, 1977 (div. June 1991); 1 child, Alec M.; m. Lynn Petty Myer, June 6, 1992; children: Melinda Myer, Joel R. AB, whitman Coll., 1974; MA, U. Va., 1975, PhD, 1982. Asst. prof. Ferrum (Va.) Coll., 1980-86, assoc. prof., 1986-91; prof. Western Mont. Coll. of U. of Mont., Dillon, 1991—; mem. spkrs. bur. Mont. Com. for Humanities, 1993—. Recipient Cheatham fellowship Ferrum Coll., 1991, Fulbright fellowship Coun. for Internat. Exch. of Scholars, USIA, U. Gdansk, Poland, 1989-90. Mem. Nat. Coun. Tchrs. of English, Western Lit. Assn., Phi Beta Kappa. Office: Western Mont Coll Univ Mont 710 S Atlantic St Dillon MT 59725-3511

WEMPLE, JAMES ROBERT, psychotherapist; b. Hardin, Mont., May 31, 1943; s. Charles Clifford and Lillian Louise (Smith) W.; m. Sarah Ann House, May 7, 1983; children: Brian Matthew, Laura Ashley. BA, U. Mont., 1966, MA, 1970, postgrad., 1970-71; PhD, Wash. State U., 1979. Diplomate Am. Acad. Pain Mgmt. Tchr., coach Custer County High Sch., Miles City, Mont., 1966-67; sch. psychologist Missoula, Mont., 1970-71; grad. asst. U. Mont., Missoula, 1970-71; dir. counseling Medicine Hat (Alberta) Coll., Canada, 1971-73; counselor Lethbridge (Alberta) C.C., 1973-76; head resident Wash. State U., Pullman, 1976-79; mental health specialist Missoula Rehab., 1979-82; clin. mental health counselor Missoula, 1982—. With U.S. Army, 1960-69, Korea. Fellow Am. Bd. Med. Psychotherapists; mem. Am. Psychol. Assn., Soc. for Clin. and Exptl. Hypnosis, Am. Soc. for Clin. Hypnosis, Internat. Soc. for Hypnosis, Nat. Acad. Cert. Clin. Mental Health Counselors, Soc. for Personality Assessment, AACD, Phi Kappa Phi. Home: 2410 Clydesdale Ln Missoula MT 59804-9297 Office: 255 B West Front St Missoula MT 59802

WEN, CHAUR SHYONG, chemical engineer; b. Kaohsiung, Taiwan, Mar. 15, 1947; came to U.S., 1972; s. I-chun and Pien (Kuo) W.; m. Limei C. Wen, July 4, 1972; children: Kenneth C., Katherine T. BS in Chem. Engring., Cheng Kung U., 1969, MS in Chem. Engring., 1971; MS in Environ. Health, U. Cin., 1974; PhD in Chem. Engring., U. So. Calif., L.A., 1976. Cert. environ. health profl. Rsch. asst. Kettering Labb., Cin., 1972-73; rsch. asst./rsch. assoc. dept. chem. engring. U. So. Calif., 1973-77; rsch. engr. to sr. rsch. engr. Gulf Rsch. and Devel. Co., Pitts., 1977-86; sr. devel. engr. to prin. engr. Solar Turbines, Inc., San Diego, Calif., 1986—. Patentee in field; contbr. articles to profl. jours. and books. Mem. Am. Chem. Soc., Am. Inst. Chem. Engring., Sigma Xi, Phi Tau Phi. Home: 13036 Candela Pl San Diego CA 92130-1800 Office: Solar Turbines Inc PO Box 85376 2200 Pacific Hwy San Diego CA 92101-1745

WENDEL, JEANNE LAURETTA, economics educator; b. Cleve., May 24, 1951; d. Charles William and Patricia (O'Reilly) Seelbach; 1 child, Nathan. BA in Econs. and History summa cum laude, Rice U., 1973; PhD in Econs., So. Meth. U., 1977. Economist Fed. Res. Bank, Dallas, 1977; asst. prof. Miami U., Oxford, Ohio, 1977-80; economist Sverdrup & Parcel, St. Louis, 1980-83; instr. U. Louisville, Bellarmine Coll., 1983-85; assoc. prof. U. Nev., Reno, 1985—; quality improvement advisor Washoe Med. Ctr., Reno, 1993—; cons. Bur. Bus. and Econ. Rsch. Projects. Contbr. articles to profl. jours. Home: 1720 Rockhaven Dr Reno NV 89511-8663 Office: U Nev Coll Bus Dept Econs Reno NV 89557

WENDEL, O. THEODORE, JR., university chancellor; b. Phila., Mar. 21, 1948; s. Otto Theodore and Elmira Robinson (Bricker) W.; m. Jessie Self, Dec. 27, 1969 (div. June 1986); 1 child, Laura Prentiss; m. Janet Kay Canole, July 11, 1987; 1 child, Sarah Ann. BA, St. Andrews Presbyn. Coll., Laurinburg, N.C., 1969; MS, Wake Forest U., 1973, PhD, 1974. Instr. Bowman Gray Sch. Medicine, Winston-Salem, 1975-78, asst. prof., 1978-79; asst. prof. Kirksville (Mo.) Coll. Osteo. Medicine, 1979-83, assoc. prof., 1983-86; assoc. prof. Coll. of Osteo. Medicine of Pacific, Pomona, Calif., 1986-92, prof. pharmacology, 1992—, asst. dean med. edn., 1987-89, dean allied health professions, 1989-95, v.p. instl. planning and assessment, 1992-95; chancellor Western U. Health Scis., Chico, Calif., 1995—; lectr. in field. Contbr. numerous articles and abstracts to profl. jours.; author: Basic Concepts in Health and Disease: The Musculoskeletal System, Vol. III, 1977; author microcomputer software: Principles of Pharmacology, 1984, Nutrition and Pregnancy, 1986, You and Your Baby, 1986. Recipient A.T. Still Staff Award for Excellence in Tchg., 1983; USPHS Rsch. fellow, 1975; N.C. Heart Assn. Rsch. Award grantee, 1976, 78; Grantee office of Naval Rsch., 1978-79, USPHS, 1978-79, 78-81, 87-88, 90-94, Am. Osteo. Assn., 1982-84, Parke-Davis Pharm. Co., 1984-85, Mo. Dept. Social Svcs., 1984-85. Mem. Am. Soc. for Pharmacology and Exptl. Therapeutics, Western Pharmacology Soc., N.C. Soc. for Neuroscis., Am. Heart Assn., Generalists in Med. Edn., Am. Ednl. Rsch. Assn., Am. Soc. of Health Educators and Tchrs., Am. Assn. Colls. of Pharmacy, Am. Acad. Physician Assts. (assoc.), Am. Assn. Colls. of Pharmacy. Office: Western U Health Scis 1400 W 3d St Ste 106 Chico CA 95928

WENDER, DEBORAH ELIZABETH, policy consultant, social worker; b. Sacramento, June 30, 1954; d. Joseph Andrew Sr. and Caroline Elizabeth (Wulff) Wender; adopted children: Alexander Darius Andrew, Zodie Miriam Caroline. AA, American River Coll., Sacramento, 1974; BA, Calif. State U., Sacramento, 1980, MSW, 1988. Counselor coord. Sacramento Women's Ctr., 1980-81, rape crisis project dir., 1981-84; program coord. Rape Prevention Edn. Program, U. Calif., Davis, 1984-87; criminal justice specialist Calif. Office Criminal Justice Planning, Sacramento, 1988-89; assoc. health program advisor Office of AIDS Calif. Dept. Health Svcs., Sacramento, 1989-91, pub. health social work cons. maternal and child health, 1991-93, assoc. govtl. program analyst Medi-Cal Eligibility, 1993-95; social svcs. consultant III Child Welfare Svcs. Bur. Calif. Dept. Social Svcs., 1995—; contract social worker Family Connections Adoptions, 1995—. Bd. dirs. Child Sexual Abuse Treatment Ctr., Yolo County, Woodland, Calif., 1984-86, WomanKind Health Clinic, Sacramento, 1984-86; bd. dirs. Sacramento Women's Ctr., 1987-91, bd. pres. 1989-91. Democrat. Home: 8649 Glenroy Way Sacramento CA 95826-1743

WENDLAND, CLAIRE, nursing administrator, geriatrics nurse; b. Havre, Mont., July 5, 1952; d. Sam W. and W. Inez (Dent) Berge; m. John Wendland, Sept. 20, 1975; children: Erin Mariah, Jared Keefe. ADN, No. Mont. Coll., 1973, BSN, 1993. RN, Mont. Staff nurse II pediatric unit Mont. Deaconess Med. Ctr., Great Falls, 1973-75; supr. staff nurse Lutheran Home of the Good Shepherd, Havre, 1985-87, dir. insvc. edn., 1987-88, DON, 1989-94, adminstr., 1993-94; cmty. programs coord. No. Mont. Hosp., Havre, 1995—. Mem. Evang. Luth. Ch. Am. Mem. Mont. Dirs. Long Term Care, Mont. Health Care Assn., Mont. Gerentol. Soc., Nat. League Nursing.

WENDLANDT, WENDY ANN, political organizer; b. Portland, Dec. 7, 1961; d. James R. and Elizabeth A. (Burnham) W.; m. Lawrence Eason, Apr. 22, 1989. BA, Whitman Coll., 1983. Exec. dir. Wash. Pub. Interest Rsch. Group, Seattle, 1986-89; grants dir. The Fund for Pub. Interest Rsch., Boston, 1989-90; polit. dir. The State Pub. Interest Rsch. Group, L.A., 1990—; bd. dirs. Wash. Pub. Interest Rsch. Group, L.A. Bd. pres. Earth Day 2000, L.A., 1990—; bd. trustee Green Century Funds, L.A., 1991—. Recipient Young Alumni award Whitman Coll., Walla Walla, Wash., 1995. Home: 1512 Harvard St Apt 1 Santa Monica CA 90404-3534 Office: The StatePIRGs 11965 Venice Blvd Ste 408 Los Angeles CA 90066

WENDLE, KEVIN, computer company executive. News producer WABC-TV, N.Y.C.; founding pres., COO Quincy Jones Entertainment; exec, v.p. Fox Entertainment Group; founder CNET: The Computer Network. Office: Computer Network 150 Chestnut St San Francisco CA 94111

WENDRUCK, LOUIS, publisher, television personality, consultant; b. Hollywood, Calif., Apr. 8, 1957; s. Albert and Anna (Goldberger) W. BA in Commerce, McGill U., 1977; BA in Biology, Occidental Coll., L.A., 1978; MBA, Pepperdine U., 1985. Sys. analyst/computer programmer cons. L.A., 1978-86; ind. pub., owner Fan Club Pub., West Hollywood, Calif., 1986—; pres., pub. club newsletter for The Dark Shadows Fan Club, The Munsters and the Addams Family Fan Club, The Girl Groups 60's Rock 'n Roll Fan Club, The Gay Airline and Travel Club, The Mil. and Police Uniform Assn. Office: Fan Club Publishing PO Box 69A04 Dept WW West Hollywood CA 90069

WENDT, STEVEN WILLIAM, business educator; b. Rockford, Ill., Sept. 18, 1948; s. Roy W. Wendt and Betty Lou (Phillips) Wendt Oser. AAS, Clark County Community Coll., North Las Vegas, Nev., 1982; BS, U. Nev., 1985, MBA, 1987. Cert. vocat. adult educator, Nev. Electronics tech. engr. Rockford Automation, Inc., 1972-74; owner, operator S.W. Ltd., Rockford, 1972-76, S.W. Enterprises, Henderson, Nev., 1977—; instr. electronics Nev. Gaming Sch., Las Vegas, 1977-83; gen. mgr., corp. sec. treas. Customs by Peter Schell, Las Vegas, 1977-83; field engr. Bell & Howell Mailmobile Ops. div., Zeeland, Mich., 1982-90; instr. bus. U. Nev., Las Vegas, 1985—; dir. Wing Fong & Family Microcomputer Labs. Coll. Bus. and Econs. U. Nev., 1990—; sr. arbitrator Better Bus. Bur., Las Vegas, 1982—; bus. cons. Small Bus. Devel. Ctr., Las Vegas, 1985—; incorporator, v.p. Info. Sys., Warren, Mich., 1990-91; fin. officer, gen. ptnr. Obsidian Pub. Press, Henderson, Nev., 1991-96; mem. faculty senate U. Nev., 1993-96; bd. dirs. Gem Crafters Inc., Warren. Author: Intro to Microcomputers, For Future PC Experts, 1992. Treas. U. Nev. Grad. Student Assn, 1986-87. Served with USN, 1967-71. Recipient Cert. Appreciation UNICEF, 1984. Mem. IEEE, Computer Soc., Assn. Info. Systems, Fin. Mgmt. Assn. (Nat. Honor Soc. 1985), Strategic Gaming Soc., U. Nev. Computer User Group (exec. com., chair stds. com.), U. Nev. Alumni Assn., Am. Legion, VFW (life), Phi Lambda Alpha. Home: 1325 Chestnut St Henderson NV 89015-4208 Office: U Nev 4505 S Maryland Pky Las Vegas NV 89154-9900

WENICK, DEAN, photographer; b. Washington, Aug. 20, 1967; s. Harvey and Linda Joyce (Ewing) W. BA, Saint Lawrence Univ., 1989. Freelance photographer Seattle, 1991—; owner Terrapin Transit, Boston, 1991-92; pres. Kiliwear, Seattle, 1995—. Author (photo-essay) Fellowship, 1994. Mem. adv. bd. Youth in Focus, Seattle, 1996—. Mem. Nat. Press Photographer's Assn., Am. Soc. Media Photographers. Home and Office: PO Box 20283 Seattle WA 98102-1283

WENIGER-PHELPS, NANCY ANN, media specialist, photographer; b. Kingman, Kans., Sept. 4, 1948; d. Watson and Reva Jo (Schlup) W. BA in Phys. Edn., Ottawa (Kans.) U., 1970; MA in LS, U. Denver, 1980. Cert. K-12 media specialist, secondary phys. edn. tchr., Ariz. Phys. edn. tchr. Grand Junction (Colo.) Sch. Dist., 1970-73; dist. mgr. World Book Ency., 1973-74; personal sec. Younger Bail Bond Svc., Grand Junction, 1974-76; media specialist K-12, phys. edn. tchr. Kingman (Kans.) Unified Sch. Dist., 1976-78, Ovid (Colo.) Sch. Dist., 1980-82, Sargeant Sch. Dist., Monte Vista, Colo., 1982-84, Antonito Sch. Dist., Ovid, Colo., 1984-85; photographer's asst. Bill Westenberg Photography, Alamosa, Colo., 1985-86; sch. media specialist Window Rick (Ariz.) Unified Sch. Dist., 1986-96; profl. photographer; trainer adult and student storytellers; head dist. lib. computer program. Author: Photographic Uses in the Library; exhibited in group shows Gallup (N.Mex.) Gallery, 1989, Window Rock Elem. Sch., 1989, Sunflower Shop, Wichita, Kans. 1989-90, 96-97, also Alamosa, Colo., 1985-87, 1st Nat. Bank, Kingman, Fernley (Nev.) Phys. Therapy, 1993. Mem. AAHPERD, ALA, Am. Fedn. Tchrs., Ariz. Fedn. Tchrs., Window Rock Fedn. Tchrs., Ariz. Edn. Media Assn., Assoc. Photographers Internat. Ariz. Edn. Assn., Alpha Delta Kappa. Home: 3070 Farm Dist Rd Fernley NV 89408

WENN, DEREK JAY, entrepreneur; b. New Orleans, Aug. 8, 1956; s. Julian George Jr. and Jane Marilyn (Canone) W.; m. Karen Kunz, Sept. 4, 1986; children: Jared Ian, Colton Ryan, Jamie Lauren. BA in Arts, Humanities and Architecture, U. Southwestern La., 1981. Architect, developer Tom Isbell Devel., Lafayette, La., 1980-82; vol. missionary LDS Ch., Washington, 1982-85; archtl. designer Walker, Lee, Halander Architects, Provo, Utah, 1985-87; mktg. cons. The McKinley Inst., Orem, Utah, 1987-89; dealer consumer affairs mgr. Rick Warner Nissan, Salt Lake City, 1989-90; rsch. and mktg. dir. Hayes Bros. Buick, Jeep, Eagle, Salt Lake City, 1990-95; prin., owner D. Wenn & Co. Devel., Salt Lake City, 1986—; ptnr. Target Market Rsch., Sandy, Utah, 1991—; owner Alta West Distbg., Draper, Utah, 1994—, PoBoys LLC Restaurant, Salt Lake City, 1995—. Elder LDS Ch., 1983—. Mem. AIA, Pi Kappa Alpha. Office: Alta West 11675 Brisbane Dr Sandy UT 84094-5696

WENNIK, ROBERTA SCHWARTZ, dietitian; b. San Francisco, June 12, 1948; d. Ernest and Annette Louise (Lamdan) Schwartz; m. Lawrence Paul Wennik, Oct. 24, 1971; children: Deborah, Shari. BA in Interior Design, U. Calif., Berkeley, 1970; MS in Nutrition, U. Wash., 1991. Registered dietician. Interior designer Interiors and Textiles Corp., Burlingame, Calif., 1970-72; cons. dietitian, owner HealthPro, Edmonds, Wash., 1991—; tchr. Edmonds C.C., Lynnwood, Wash., 1993—. Author: Drawing the Line on Fat and Cholesterol, 1992, Beyond Food Labels, 1996; patentee in field; contbr. articles to popular mags. Spkr. om nutrition issues civic and women's groups, 1993—. Scholarship U. Wash., 1988. Mem. Am. Dietetic Assn., Wash. State Dietetic Assn., Greater Seattle Dietetic Assn., Sports, Cardiovascular and Wellness Nutritionists. Office: HealthPro PO Box 83 Lynnwood WA 98046-0083

WENTWORTH, THEODORE SUMNER, lawyer; b. Bklyn., July 18, 1938; s. Theodore Sumner and Alice Ruth (Wortmann) W.; AA, Am. River Coll., 1958; JD, U. Calif., Hastings, 1962; m. Sharon Linelle Arkush, 1965 (dec. 1987); children: Christina Linn, Kathryn Allison; m. Diana Webb von Welanetz, 1989; 1 stepchild, Lexi von Welanetz. Bar: Calif. 1963, U.S. Dist. Ct. (no., ctrl. dists.) Calif., U.S. Ct. Appeals (9th cir.), U.S. Supreme Ct.; cert. civil trial specialist; diplomate Nat. Bd. Trial Advocacy; assoc. Am. Bd. Trial Advocates. Assoc. Adams, Hunt & Martin, Santa Ana, Calif., 1963-66; ptnr. Hunt, Liljestrom & Wentworth, Santa Ana, 1967-77; pres. Solabs Corp.; chmn. bd., exec. v.p. Plant Warehouse, Inc., Hawaii, 1974-82; prin. Law Offices of Theodore S. Wentworth, specializing in personal injury, product liability, profl. malpractice, bus. fraud, fire loss litigation, human rights issues, Newport Beach and Temecula, Calif.; judge pro tem Superior Ct. Attys. Panel, Harbor Mcpl. Ct.; owner Eagles Ridge Ranch, Temecula, 1977—. Pres., bd. dirs. Santa Ana-Tustin Community Chest, 1972; v.p., trustee South Orange County United Way, 1973-75; pres. Orange County Fedn. Funds, 1972-73; bd. dirs. Orange County Mental Health Assn. Mem. ABA, Am. Bd. Trial Advocates (assoc.), State Bar Calif., Orange County Bar Assn. (dir. 1972-76), Am. Trial Lawyers Assn., Calif. Trial Lawyers Assn. (bd. govs. 1968-70), Orange County Trial Lawyers Assn. (pres. 1967-68), Lawyer-Pilots Bar Assn., Aircraft Owners and Pilots Assn., Bahia Corinthian Yacht Club, Balboa Bay Club, Corsair Yacht Club, The Center Club, Pacific Club, Newport. Research in vedic prins., natural law, quantum physics and mechanics. Office: 4631 Teller Ave Ste 100 Newport Beach CA 92660-8105 also: Wells Fargo Bank Bldg 41530 Enterprise Cir S Temecula CA 92590-4816

WENTZ, CATHERINE JANE, elementary education educator; b. Boise, Idaho, Aug. 11, 1948; d. Frank Paul and Litha Zella (Langer) W. BA, Boise State U., 1970, MA, 1975. Tchr. 2d grade Longfellow Sch., Boise, 1970-72, Taft Elem. Sch., Boise, 1972-84; tchr. 1st grade Cole Elem. Sch., Boise, 1984-87, Garfield Elem. Sch., Boise, 1987-92, Horizon Elem. Sch., Boise, 1992—; instr. Spalding Edn. Found., Boise, 1980—. Active Horizon PTO. Mem. NEA, Idaho Coun. Internat. Reading Assn., Boise Edn. Assn., Idaho Edn. Assn., Orton Dyslexia Soc., Alpha Delta Kappa. Home: 2063 E Lochmeadow Ct Meridian ID 83642-5789 Office: Horizon Elem Sch 730 N Mitchell St Boise ID 83704-9783

WENTZ, CHRISTOPHER JAMES, state agency administrator; b. St. Louis, Apr. 28, 1955; s. Walter William and Mary Elenor (Wamser) W.; m. Christine Marie Schulte, Oct. 13, 1978; children: Ashley Kristen, Ryan Christine. BS in Biology, S.W. Mo. State U., Springfield, 1977. Technician Century Geophys. Corp., Tulsa, Okla., 1978-80; energy cons., policy analyst State of N.Mex. Energy Dept., Santa Fe, 1980—. N.Mex. rep. Western Interstate Energy Bd., Denver, 1983—, Western Govs. Assn., Denver, 1989—, Interstate Oil and Gas Compact Commn., Oklahoma City, 1984-90; pres. Friends of the Corrales (N.Mex.) Libr., 1994-96. Home: PO Box 2174 Corrales NM 87048 Office: NMex Radioactive Waste Task Force 2040 Pacheco St Santa Fe NM 87505

WENTZ, JEFFREY LEE, information systems consultant; b. Philippi, W.Va., Nov. 29, 1956; s. William Henry and Edith Marie (McBee) W. AS in Data Processing, BS in Acctg., Fairmont (W.Va.) State Coll., 1978. Programmer/analyst U.S. Dept. Energy, Morgantown, W.Va., 1978-79; analyst Middle South Svcs., New Orleans, 1979-81; sr. analyst Bank of Am., San Francisco, 1981-83; pres., cons. Wentz Cons. Inc., San Francisco, 1983—. Office: Wentz Consulting Inc 1378 34th Ave San Francisco CA 94122-1309

WERBACH, MELVYN ROY, physician, writer; b. N.Y.C., Nov. 11, 1940; s. Samuel and Martha (Robbins) W.; m. Gail Beth Leibsohn, June 20, 1967; children: Kevin, Adam. BA, Columbia Coll., N.Y.C., 1962; MD, Tufts U., Boston, 1966. Diplomate Am. Bd. Psychiatry and Neurology. Intern VA Hosp., Bklyn., 1966-67; resident in psychiatry Cedars-Sinai Med. Ctr., L.A., 1969-71; dir. psychol. svcs., clin. biofeedback UCLA Hosp. and Clinics, 1976-80; pres. Third Line Press, 1986—; asst. clin. prof. Sch. Medicine, UCLA, 1978—; mem. nutritional adv. bd. Cancer Treatment Ctrs. Am., 1989-93; mem. adv. com. The Dead Sea Confs., Israel, 1990—; mem. adv. bd. Longevity Rsch. Ctr., 1996—. Author: Third Line Medicine, 1986, Nutritional Influences on Illness, 1987, 2d edit., 1993, Nutritional Influences on Mental Illness, 1991, Healing Through Nutrition, 1993; co-author: Botanical Influences on Illness, 1994, Foundations of Nutritional Medicine, 1997; mem. editl. bd. Jour. of Nutritional Medicine, 1993—, Health News and Rev., 1991—, Jour. Optimal Nutrition, 1993—, Alt. Medicine Digest, 1994—; mem. internat. adv. bd. Jour. Bodywork and Movement Therapics, 1996—; mem. adv. bd. HealthWorld Online, 1996—; mem. med. adv. bd. Let's Live Mag., 1989-93; columnist Internat. Jour. Alt. and Complementary Medicine, 1992—, Townsend Letter for Doctors, 1993—, Australian Jour. Nutrition and Environ. Medicine, 1994—, Jour. Orthomolekulare Medizin, 1997—; mem. panel What Doctors Don't Tell You, 1993—; contbr. articles to med. jours. Mem. Am. Coll. Nutrition, Biofeedback Soc. Calif. (hon. life mem., pres. 1977, Cert. Honor 1985), Australian Coll. Nutritional and Environ. Medicine (hon.).

WERDEGAR, KATHRYN MICKLE, judge; b. San Francisco; d. Benjamin Christie and Kathryn Marie (Clark) Mickle; m. David Werdegar; children: Maurice Clark, Matthew Mickle. Student, Wellesley Coll., 1954-55; AB with honors, U. Calif., Berkeley, 1957; JD with distinction, George Washington U., 1962; JD, U. Calif., Berkeley, 1990. Bar: Calif. 1964, U.S. Dist. Ct. (no. dist.) Calif. 1964, U.S. Ct. Appeals (9th cir.) 1964, Calif. Supreme Ct. 1964. Legal asst. civil rights divsn. U.S. Dept. Justice, Washington, 1962-63; cons. Calif. Study Commn. on Mental Retardation, 1963-64; assoc. U. Calif. Ctr. for Study of Law and Soc., Berkeley, 1965-67; spl. cons. State Dept. Mental Hygiene, 1967-68; cons. Calif. Coll. Trial Judges, 1968-71; atty., head criminal divsn. Calif. Continuing Edn. of Bar, 1971-78; assoc. dean acad. and student affairs, assoc. prof. Sch. Law, U. San Francisco, 1978-81; sr. staff atty. Calif. 1st Dist. Ct. Appeal, 1981-85, Calif. Supreme Ct., 1985-91; assoc. justice Calif. 1st Dist. Ct. Appeal, 1991-94, Calif. Supreme Ct., San Francisco, 1994—. Author: Benchbook: Misdemeanor Procedure, 1971, Misdemeanor Procedure Benchbook, 1975, 83; contbr. California Continuing Education of the Bar books; editor: California Criminal Law Practice series, 1972, California Uninsured Motorist Practice, 1973, I California Civil Procedure Before Trial, 1977. Recipient Charles Glover award George Washington U., J. William Fulbright award for disting. pub. svc. George Washington U. Law Sch. Alumni Assn., award of excellence Calif. Alumni Assn., also 5 Am. Jurisprudence awards. Mem. Nat. Assn. Women Judges, Calif. Judges Assn., Nev./Calif. Women Judges Assn., Boalt Hall Alumni Assn. (bd. dirs.), Order of the Coif. Office: Calif Supreme Court South Tower 303 2nd St San Francisco CA 94107-1366

WERNER, E. LOUIS, JR., lawyer, retired insurance company executive; m. Sandra M. Johnston; children: E. Louis III, Eric R., Matthew J. BA, Princeton U., 1949; BS, Washington U., St. Louis, 1950, LLB, 1952, JD, 1952. Bar: Mo. 1952, U.S. Ct. Mil. Appeals 1963, U.S. Supreme Ct. 1963; CPCU 1957; lic. pilot single, multi-engine and instrument ratings. Exec. v.p. TOR Mgmt., Shawnee Mission, Kans.; mng. ptnr. Dukes Deux Leasing Co., Scottsdale, Ariz.; dir. ABC Moving and Storage Co., Inc., Phoenix; v.p. devel. Phoenix (Ariz.) Country Day Sch.; chmn. emeritus, dir. Insurers Svc. Corp., Briarcliff Manor, N.Y.; bd. dirs. The Antigua Group, Inc., Scottsdale; bd. dirs. The Antigua Group, Scottsdale, Ariz. Trustee Scottsdale Meml. Health Found., Valley Presbyn. Found., San Francisco Theol. Sem.; mem. Fiesta Bowl Com., Tempe, Ariz.; bd. dirs. Playgoers of St. Louis, Inc., Rossman Sch., St. Louis; former deacon, trustee, ruling elder Ladue Chapel, St. Louis; ruling elder Valley Presbyn. Ch., Paradise Valley, Ariz.; magistrate judge Town of Paradise Valley, Ariz.; mng. dir. dirs. FBI Citizens Acad. Mem. Fed. Bar Assn., Mo. Bar Assn., St. Louis Bar Assn., Mo. Athletic Club, USPGA (assoc.), Assn. Corp. Growth (Ariz. chpt.), Am. Soc. CPCU, Aircraft Owners and Pilots Assn., Econ. Club of Phoenix, Paradise Valley Country Club, Forest Highlands Golf Club, Desert Mtn. Golf Club, Desert Highland Golf Club. Home: 5715 N Cameldale Way Paradise Valley AZ 85253 Office: 6900 E Camelback Rd Ste 700 Scottsdale AZ 85251-2443

WERNER, MARLIN SPIKE, speech pathologist and audiologist; b. Portland, Maine, Aug. 15, 1927; s. Leonard Matthews and Margaret (Steele) W.; m. Caroline Emma Paul, Dec. 23, 1985; children: Leo Hart, Joseph Hart. BA in Sociology and Social Work, U. Mo., 1950; ScM in Audiology and Speech Pathology, Johns Hopkins U., 1957; PhD in Speech and Hearing Sci., Ohio State U., 1966. Lic. in audiology, hearing aid dispensing, speech pathology, Hawaii; lic. in audiology and speech pathology, Calif. Audiologist/speech pathologist, dir. Speech and Hearing Ctr. Asheville (N.C.) Orthopedic Hosp., 1960-64; assoc. prof. speech pathology and audiology We. Carolina U., Cullowhee, N.C., 1965-69; assoc. prof. speech pathology, audiology and speech sci. Fed. City Coll. (now U. D.C.), Washington, 1969-73; pres. Friends of Nepal's Hearing Handicapped, Oakland, Calif., 1979-84; audiologist, speech pathologist pvt. practice, Oakland and Lafayette, Calif., 1973-85; pvt. practice Lafayette, 1985-87; pvt. practice speech pathology and audiology Hilo, Hawaii, 1987—; speech and hearing cons. VA Hosp., Oteen, N.C., 1960-64; clin. cons. Speech and Hearing Clinic, Asheville Orthopedic Hosp., 1966-67; lectr., presenter in field. Contbr. articles to profl. jours.; contbr. to Ency. Brit., Am. Heritage Book of Natural Wonders, others. Mem. hearing impaired svcs. task force State of Hawaii Dept. Health, 1987-88; mem. Hawaii County Mayor's Com. for Persons with Disabilities, 1988-94; adv. bd. Salvation Army, 1992; bd. dirs. Hawaii chpt. Am. Arthritis Found.; past pres. Big Island Safety Assn.; mem. Hawaii Gov.'s Bd. Hearing Aid Dealers and Fitters; mem. adv. com., pres. Older Adult Resource Ctr., Laney Coll., Oakland, Calif.; v.p. Hawaii Speleol. Survey; chmn. Hawaii Grotto of Nat. Speleol. Soc., others; mem. adv. bd. Hilo Bay Clinics. MCH fellow Johns Hopkins U., 1954, Pub. Health fellow Ohio State U., 1964. Fellow Nat. Speleological Soc.; mem. AAAS, Am. Speech and Hearing Assn., Acoustical Soc. Am., Calif. Speech and Hearing Assn., Calif. Writers Club (bd. dirs., past pres.), Hawaii Speech/Lang. Hearing Assn. Home: PO Box 11509 Hilo HI 96721-6509 Office: 400 Hualani St Ste 191-a Hilo HI 96720-4378

WERNER, RICHARD ALLEN, retired entomologist; b. Reading, Pa., Feb. 20, 1936; s. Roy M. and Hazel (Rightmeyer) W.; m. Patricia Thomas, Aug. 25, 1973; children: Sarah T., Luke O. BS in Forestry, Pa. State U., 1958, BS in Entomology, 1960; MS in Entomology, U. Md., 1966; PhD in Entomology, N.C. State U., 1971. Forester Forest Svc., USDA, Roseberg, Oreg., 1957-60; rsch. entomologist Forest Svc., USDA, Juneau, Alaska, 1960-64; insect toxicologist Forest Svc., USDA, Research Triangle Park, N.C., 1965-74; rsch. entomologist Forest Svc., USDA, Fairbanks, Alaska, 1974-85, project leader, 1985-91, chief rsch. entomologist, 1991-96; ret., 1996; adj. prof. U. Alaska, Fairbanks, 1980—; prin. rsch. assoc. Inst. Arctic Biology, U. Alaska, 1985—. Author: Insects and Diseases of Alaskan Forests, 1980, 2d edit. 1985. Counselor Boy Scouts Am., Fairbanks, 1989—. Mem. Entomol. Soc. Am., Soc. Am. Foresters, sa. Entomol. Soc., Entomol. Soc. Can., Chem. Ecology Soc. Am., Western Forest Insect Wk. Conf. (sec.-treas. 1980-82), N. Am. Forest Insect Wk. Conf. (steering com. 1989-91).

WERNER, ROGER HARRY, archaeologist; b. N.Y.C., Nov. 11, 1950; s. Harry Emile and Rena (Roode) W.; m. Kathleen Diane Engdahl, Feb. 20, 1982; children: Meryl Lauren, Sarah Melise, Jeremy Marshall; 1 stepchild, Amber Fawn. BA, Belknap Coll., 1973; MA, Sonoma State U., Rohnert Park, Calif., 1982. Curatorial aide Anthro. Lab. Sonoma State Coll., 1975-76, curatorial asst., 1976-77, staff archaeologist, 1977-80; staff archaeologist Planning Dept., Lake County, Calif., 1977; cir. riding archaeologist western region Nat. Park Service, Tucson, Ariz., 1978; prin. investigator ASI Cartography and Geog. Info. Sys., Stockton, Calif., 1979—; pres. Cmty. Wide Web of Stockton, 1995—; cons. Calif. Indian Legal Svcs., Ukiah, 1977, Geothermal Rsch. Impact Projection Study, Lakeport, Calif., 1977—, Delta Net Comms., Stockton, Calif., 1995—; instr. Ya-Ka-Ana Indian Ednl. Ctr., Santa Rosa, Calif., 1978-79; lead archaeologist No. Calif., WESTEC Svcs., Inc., San Diego, 1979-81; adj. prof. U. Puget Sound, summer 1995. Sec. Colonial Hts. PTA, 1983-84, 2d v.p., 1985-86, historian, 1986-87, v.p., 1987-88; cons., instr. Clovis Adult Sch., 1984-85; instr. U. Pacific Lifelong Learning Ctr., 1987—, San Joaquin Delta Coll., 1990—, Calif. State U., Fresno, 1992—; bd. dirs. Valley Mountain Regional Ctr., 1987-88, treas., 1988-89, v.p., 1989-90, pres.-elect, 1990-91, pres., 1991-92; bd. trustees Stockton Chorale, treas., 1992-93, youth chorale rep., 1993-94; active Spl. Olympics, Stockton, Calif. Anthropology dept. research grantee, Sonoma State U., 1980. Mem. Geol. Soc. Am., Soc. for Am. Archaeologists, Great Basin Anthropol. Conf., Soc. for Calif. Archaeology, Soc. Profl. Archaeologists, Soc. for Hist. Archeology, Assn. for Retarded Citizens, Am. Soc. Photogrammetry and Remote Sensing, Urban Regional Info. Systems Assn., Bay Automated Mapping Assn., Kiwanis. Democrat. Lodge: Kiwanis (Stockton). Home: 1117 Aberdeen Ave Stockton CA 95209-2625 Office: ASI Cartography & GIS 8026 Lorraine Ave Ste 218 Stockton CA 95210-4224

WERNER, ROY ANTHONY, aerospace executive; b. Alexandria, Va., June 30, 1944; s. William Frederick and Mary Audrey (Barksdale) W.; m. Paula Ann Privett, June 8, 1969; children: Kelly Rene, Brent Alastair. BA, U. Cen. Fla., 1970; MPhil, Oxford U., 1973; MBA, Claremont (Calif.) Grad. Sch., 1986. Reporter St. Petersburg (Fla.) Times, 1968-69; assoc. dir. White House Conf. on Youth, 1970-71; exec. sec. Oxford Strategic Studies Group, 1971-73; internat. officer Fed. Energy Adminstrn., 1973-74; mem. legis. staff U.S. Senate, Washington, 1974-79; prin. dept. asst. Sec. of The Army, Washington, 1979-81; dir. policy rsch. Northrop Corp., L.A., 1982-83, spl. asst. to sr. v.p., mktg. to mgr. program planning and analysis electronics system divsn., 1989-94, sr. internat. bus. advisor, 1994; mgr. Asia and Pacific programs Northrop Internat. Aircraft, Inc., Hawthorne, Calif., 1995-96; dir. bus. devel. Northrop Grumman Internat., Inc., 1996—; chmn. U.S. delegation/polit. com. Atlantic Treaty Assn. Meeting, Brussels, 1989, mem. U.S. delegation, Paris, 1990, Athens, 1993, others; staff dir. East Asian and Pacific Affairs subcom. U.S. Sentate Fgn. Rels. Com., 1977-79; mem. Atlantic Coun. of U.S., 1985—; speaker Pacific Parliamentary Caucus, numerous acad. confs. in U.S. and East Asia. Editorial bd. Global Affairs, 1982-86; contbr. numerous articles to profl. jours./publs. Pres. Irvine (Calaif.) Boys and Girls Club, 1990-92, v.p., 1989-90, bd. dirs., 1987—; treas. Irvine Temp. Housing, 1988-91, bd. dirs., 1986-91; chmn. Irvine Fin. Commn., 1986-89; mem. fin. com. Irvine Barclay Theatre, 1989-95; chmn. Oxford U. L.A. Phonathon, 1995; nat. rep. Oriel Coll. Oxford Devel. Trust, 1994—; chmn. fin. com. Outreach Univ. United Meth. Ch., Irvine, 1989-90, also others; corp. sec. Irvine Housing Opportunities, 1988-89, pres., 1993-96; bd. dirs. Harbor Area Boys and Girls Club. Recipient Disting. Alumnus award U. Ctrl. Fla. Alumni Assn., Orlando, 1982, Outstanding Civilian Svc. medal Dept. Army, 1981, Fed. Energy Adminstr., 1974; sr. rsch. fellow Atlantic Coun. of the U.S., 1988-89. Mem. Am. Fgn. Svc. Assn., Am. Def. Preparedness Com. Methodist. Home: 1 Moonray Irvine CA 97270

WERNER, WILLIAM ARNO, architect; b. San Francisco, Dec. 11, 1937; s. William Arno and Sophie (Menutis) W.; m. Wendy Rolston Wilson, Feb. 3, 1963 (div. Jan. 1983); 1 child, Christa Nichol. BA with honors, Yale U., 1959, BArch, 1962, MArch, 1963. Drafter Serge Chermayeff, Paul Rudolph and Charles Brewer, New Haven, 1961-63; project designer Johnson, Poole & Storm, San Francisco, 1963-64; project designer Leo S. Wou & Assocs., Honolulu, 1965-66, v.p. of design, 1971-72; project architect John Tatom Assocs., Honolulu, 1965-66; sr. designer Skidmore, Owings & Merrill, San Francisco, 1968-71, assoc./project architect, 1972-76; prin. W.A. Werner Assocs., San Francisco, 1976-80; ptnr. Werner & Sullivan, San Francisco, 1980—; mem. planning commn. City of Sausalito, Calif.; bd. govs. Yale U., New Haven; visitorship in architecture U. Auckland Found., New Zealand, 1994. Prin. works include Alameda Mcpl. Credit Union, Lane Pub. Co., Menlo Park, Calif., Pacific Data Images, Mountain View, Calif., Saga Corp., Menlo Park, Tiffany & Co., Union Square, San Francisco, Somerset Collection, Troy, Mich., Touche Ross & Co., Oakland, U.S. Post Office, San Francisco, (renovations) Fed. Express Co., San Francisco, KD's Grog N' Grocery, San Francisco, Jessie Street. Substation, San Francisco, Lakeside Tower Health Ctr./Mt. Zion Hosp., Qantas Bldg, San Francisco, Women's Care, San Francisco, Moon Residence, Dillon Beach, Calif., Shenkar Residence, San Francisco, Tacker Residence, Denver, Lasky Residence, San Francisco, Starring Residence, San Francisco, Whitehead Residence, Monte Rio, Calif., various laboratories, theatres and rsch. facilities, urban design. Recipient Progressive Architecture Design award Jessie St. Substation, 1980, DuPont Co. Design award Touche Ross & Co., 1983, award of Excellence Woodwork Inst. of Calif., 1989, USPS/NEA Nat. Honor award for Design Excellence, 1990, Tucker Design Excellence award Bldg. Stone Inst., Tiffany & Co., 1992. Mem. AIA (San Francisco chpt.), Found. for San Francisco's Architectural Heritage (hon.). Home: 213 Richardson St Sausalito CA 94965-2422 Office: Werner & Sullivan 207 Powell St Ste 800 San Francisco CA 94102

WERTH, ROGER ALAN, photojournalist; b. Portland, Oreg., Apr. 17, 1957; s. Dean Erwin and Patricia Ann (Loehner) W.; m. Belinda Marie Campbell, Sept. 6, 1985 (Apr. 1991); 1 child, Shardé Marie. BS, Oreg. State U., 1980. Intern in photography The Daily News, Longview, Wash., 1978, part-time photojournalist, 1978, photojournalist, 1978-79, photo editor, photojournalist, 1979—. Photographer cover Time Mag., 1980. Recipient Pulitzer prize for photos of eruption of Mt. St. Helens, 1981. Mem. Nat. Press Photographers Assn. Office: The Daily News 770 11th St PO Box 189 Longview WA 98632

WERTHEIMER, ROBERT E., paper company executive; b. 1928; married. BSME, U. Wash., 1950; MBA, Harvard U., 1952. With Longview (Wash.) Fibre Co., 1952—, package engr., 1955-59, asst. mgr. container ops., 1959-60, asst. mgr. container sales, 1960-63, v.p. container sales West, 1963-75, v.p. prodn., 1975, group v.p. containers, now exec. v.p., dir. Office: Longview Fibre Co 120 Montgomery St Ste 2200 San Francisco CA 94104-4325 Office: Longview Fiber Co Longview WA 98632*

WERTS, JOSEPHINE STARR, artist; b. Osage, Iowa, Aug. 5, 1903; d. William Jessie and Edna Lavinia (Wheeland) Starr; m. Leo Robert Werts, June 15, 1929 (div. 1947); 1 child, Barbara Werts Blatt. BA in Phys. Edn., Iowa State Tchrs. Coll., 1926; postgrad., Art Inst. Chgo., 1945, 46, U. Chgo., 1945, 46; MA in Fine Arts, U. So. Calif., 1961. One-woman shows include Cambria (Calif.) Coast Gallery, Ten Directions Gallery, Baywood Park, Calif., San Luis Obispo (Calif.) Art Ctr.; group shows include San Luis Obispo Art Ctr., U. So. Calif., Oakland (Calif.) Art Mus., Pasadena (Calif.) Art Mus., M.H. de Young Meml. Mus., San Francisco, Richmond (Calif.) Art Mus., Otis Art Inst., L.A., Long Beach (Calif.) Mus. Art, La Jolla (Calif.) Art Ctr., Ten Directions Gallery, Baywood Park, Calif., 1994, Kings County Art Ctr., Hanford, Calif., 1995, Paso Robles (Calif.) Art Ctr., 1996; represented in permanent collections Va. Mus. Fine Arts, Richmond, U. So. Calif. Fisher Gallery, also pvt. collections. Recipient award Palos Verdes Community Arts Assn., 1954, 57. Mem. Nat. Watercolor Soc. (bd. dirs. 1965, corr. sec. 1965, D'Arches award 1969), Watercolor U.S.A. Honor Soc. (Jurors award 1990), Ctrl. Coast Printmakers Soc., San Luis Art Assn. Democrat. Home and Studio: 2050 Emmons Rd Cambria CA 93428-4510

WERTZ, GARY RANDALL, secondary education educator, counselor; b. Lewistown, Pa., Feb. 19, 1959; s. Harold Ira and Beverly Arlene (Miller) W.; m. Iris Christine Holloway, Sept. 26, 1981; children: Christopher, Joss, Morgan, Cord. BS in Wildlife, Fisheries Mgmt., U. Idaho, 1982; MEd in Gen. and Sch. Counseling, Coll. Idaho, 1991. Cert. tchr., Idaho. Tchr., football coach, counselor O'Leary Jr. H.S., Twin Falls, Idaho, 1984-85; football coach, driver edn. instr. Cambridge (Idaho) Schs., 1985—; dir. Natural Helpers, Cambridge, 1988—; mem. bd. dirs. Adams Co. Child Abuse Prevention Team, Council, Idaho, 1994—. singer Cambridge Cmty. Choir, Cambridge, 1986—, Treasure Valley Cmty. Choir, Ontario, Oreg., 1988—; bishop Jesus Christ Latter-Day Saints, Cambridge, 1992—. Mem. Idaho Sch. Counselors Assn.

WESCOAT, KYLE BURLEY, finance executive; b. New Kensington, Pa., Oct. 24, 1951; s. Corydon Frank and Jean (Burley) W. BS, Drexel U., 1974; MBA in Fin., U. Mich., 1976. Fin. planner Occidental Petroleum, L.A., 1977-81; fin. mgr. Memorex Corp., Santa Clara, Calif., 1981-84; v.p. fin., chief fin. officer ICN Biomedicals Inc., Costa Mesa, Calif., 1984-86, Tenn. Chem. Co., Atlanta, 1986-88, Mobex Corp., Anaheim, Calif., 1988-90, Prestige Leather Creations, Vernon, Calif., 1990-94, Shirmar Corp., Montebello, Calif., 1994-95; with Vans, Inc., 1996—. Mem. Fin. Execs. Inst., Newport Beach Athletic Club. Presbyterian. Home: 315 9th St Huntington Beach CA 92648-4634 Office: Vans Inc 15700 Shoemaker Rd Santa Fe Springs CA 92865-3101

WESLEY, VIRGINIA ANNE, real estate property manager; b. Seattle, Apr. 29, 1951; d. Albert William and Mary Louise (Heusser) W. BA in Speech, U. Hawaii, Hilo, 1978. Cert. property mgr. Mgr. office, traffic Sta. KIPA-Radio, Hilo, 1972-74; reporter West Hawaii Today, Kailua-Kona, Hawaii, 1974; mgr. office U. Hawaii, Hilo, 1975-78; dir. property mgmt. First City Equities, Seattle, 1978-88, Winvest Devel. Corp., Seattle, 1988-89; with Quadrant Corp, Bellevue, Wash., 1992—; instr. Bellevue (Wash.) Community Coll., 1982-85. Bd. dirs. Mayor's Small Bus. Task Force, Seattle, 1981-83, 1st Hill Improvement Assn., Seattle, 1982—; active Goodwill Games, Seattle, 1990, Kauri Investments, Ltd., Seattle, 1991-92. Mem. Inst. Real Estate Mgmt., Internat. Coun. Shopping Ctrs., Comml. Real Estate Women, Women's Bus. Exch., Seattle-King County Bd. Realtors, Big Island Press Club, Phi Kappa Phi. Home: 906 Lake Washington Blvd S Seattle WA 98144-3314

WESSLER, MELVIN DEAN, farmer, rancher; b. Dodge City, Kan., Feb. 11, 1932; s. Oscar Lewis and Clara (Reiss) W.; grad. high sch.; m. Laura Ethel Arbuthnot, Aug. 23, 1951; children: Monty Dean, Charla Cay, Virgil Lewis. Farmer-rancher, Springfield, Colo., 1950—; dir., sec. bd. Springfield Co-op. Sales Co., 1964-80, pres. bd., 1980—. Pres., Arkansas Valley Co-op. Council, SE Colo. Area, 1965-87, Colo. Co-op. Council, 1969-72, v.p. 1974, sec. 1980-86; community com. chmn. Baca County, Agr. Stablzn. and Conservation Svc., Springfield, 1961-73, 79—, vice chmn. Baca County Com., 1980-90; mem. spl. com. on grain mktg. Far-Mar-Co.; mem. adv. bd. Denver Bapt. Bible Coll., 1984-89; chmn., bd. dirs. Springfield Cemetery Bd., 1985—; apptd. spl. com. Farmland Industries spl. project Tomorrow, 1987—. Recipient The Colo. Cooperator award The Colo. Coop Coun., 1990. Mem. Colo. Cattlemen's Assn., Colo. Wheat Growers Assn., Southeast Farm Bus. Assn. (bd. dirs. 1991-95), Big Rock Grange (treas. 1964-76, master 1976-82), Southwest Kans. Farm Bus. Assn. (dir. 1996—). Address: 18363 County Road Pp Springfield CO 81073-9210

WEST, BILLY GENE, public relations executive; b. Richmond, Ind., Nov. 22, 1946; s. Billy D. and Jean C. (Cox) W. AA, Cerritos Coll., 1966; BA, U. So. Calif., 1969; MA, U. Minn., 1971. Salesman, Marina Art Products, L.A., 1967-73; v.p. Am. Telecon Network, Dallas, 1974-77; gen. mgr. Phoenix Publs., Houston, 1977-78; pres. San Dark, Inc., San Francisco, 1978-82; gen. ptnr. Billy West & Assocs., 1982—; pres. V.G. Prodns., 1983—; chief exec. officer Westmarking, San Francisco, 1989— ; exec. dir. Young Ams. for Freedom, Minn. and Wis., 1970-72; pres. S.F.P.A., San Francisco, 1982-83. Mem. Assn. MBA Execs. Mem. Am. Ref. Ch.

WEST, CYNTHYA THOMAS, municipal agency administrator; b. Massillon, Ohio, Sept. 12, 1947; d. Anthony Frank and Beverly Elaine Thomas; m. William Alan West, Oct. 13 1985. BS, Kent (Ohio) State U., 1969. Purchasing agt. Masoneilan/Dresser, Houston, 1981-85; purchasing supr. commodity and svcs. contracts Purchasing and Transp., Orange County Gen. Svcs. Agy., Santa Ana, Calif., 1985-93; purchasing supr. City of Costa Mesa, Calif., 1993—; dir. County of Orange Vendor Products Fair, 1991. Assisted in restoration of the Hist. Orange County Courthouse, Santa Ana, 1985-87; negotiated contract for design and devel. of mus. exhibit gallery, 1988; assisted in preparing Rancho Del Rio, Calif. for Visit from Pres. George Bush, 1989; negotiated helicopter contracts Airborne Law Enforcement Svcs., 1995, 96, 97; mem. Friends of Costa Mesa Libr., Friends of San Juan Capistrano Libr. Mem. Nat. Inst. Govtl. Purchasing (membership chair 1992, bd. dirs. Calif. chpt. 1993, cert. profl. pub. buyer), Nat. Assn. Purchasing Mgmt., Purchasing Mgmt. Assn. Houston (co-chmn. pub. rels. com. 1984-85), Purchasing Mgmt. Assn. Orange County (chmn. planning com. 1988), Calif. Assn. Pub. Purchasing Officers (Orange County group chair 1995, 96, chair conf. registration com. 1986), Friends of South Coast Repertory and Orange County Performing Arts Ctr. Office: City of Costa Mesa Purchasing Divsn 77 Fair Dr Costa Mesa CA 92626-6520

WEST, EDWARD ALAN, graphics communications executive; b. L.A., Dec. 25, 1928; s. Albert Reginald and Gladys Delia (White) W.; m. Sonya Lea Smith, Jan. 2, 1983; children: Troy A., Tamara L.; stepchildren: Debra, Chris, Donna. A.A., Fullerton Coll., 1966; student, Cerrotos Coll., 1957, UCLA, 1966-67. Circulation mgr. Huntington Park (Calif.) Signal Newspaper, 1946-52; newspaper web pressman Long Beach (Calif.) Press Telegram, 1955-62; gravure web pressman Gravure West, Los Angeles, 1966-67; sales engr. Halm Jet Press, Glen Head, N.Y., 1968-70; salesman Polychrome Corp., Glen Head, 1970-74; supr. reprographics Fluor Engring & Construction, Irvine, Calif., 1974-81; dir. reprographics Fluor Arabia, Dhahran, Saudi Arabia, 1981-85, Press Telegram, Long Beach, 1986—; printing advisor Saddleback C.C., Mission Viejo, Calif., 1979, 80. Author: How to Paste up For Graphic Reproduction, 1967. Sgt. USMC, 1952-55, Korea. Mem. In-Plant Printing Assn. (cert. graphics comm. mgr. 1977, editor newsletter 1977, pres. Orange County chpt. 1979-80, Internat. Man of Yr. award 1980), 1st Marine Divsn. Assn. (life), VFW (life), Am. Legion, Internat. Assn. Legions of Honor (emeritus), Western Shrine Assn. (comdr. 1996-97), Masons, Shriners (life, pres. South Coast club 1991, editor blue and gold unit Legion of Honor El Bekal Temple 1989-92, comdr. Legion of Honor 1992, Shriner of Yr. award 1994), KT (life), Internat. High Twelve #500 (Capistrano pres. 1995, 96). Presbyterian. Home: 198 Monarch Bay Dr Dana Point CA 92629-3437 Office: 604 Pine Ave Long Beach CA 90844-0003 *Personal philosophy: With God's help anything is possible.*

WEST, HUGH STERLING, aircraft leasing company executive; b. Kansas City, Kans., Apr. 5, 1930; s. Gilbert Eugene and Dorothy (Johnson) W.; BS, U. Va., 1952; BS in Aero., U. Md., 1959; grad. U.S. Naval Test Pilot Sch., 1959; m. Willa Alden Reed, Jan. 16, 1954; children: Karen, Phillip, Susan. Commd. 2d lt. U.S. Marine Corps., 1948, advanced through grades to maj., 1961; exptl. flight test pilot, U.S. Naval Air Test Center, Patuxent River, Md.; resigned, 1961; program mgr. Boeing Aircraft Co., Seattle and Phila., 1961-66, dir. airworthiness, comml. airplane divsn., 1969-71; dir. aircraft sales Am. Airlines, Tulsa, 1971-76; v.p. equipment mgmt. GATX Leasing Corp., San Francisco, 1976-80; v.p. tech., partner Polaris Aircraft Leasing Corp., San Francisco, 1980-85; v.p., co-founder U.S. Airlease, Inc. divsn. Ford Motor Co., 1986-96, ret., 1996; pres. Hugh S. West & Assocs., Comml. Aircraft Cons. Mem. Soc. Exptl. Test Pilots, Army Navy Country Club. Republican. Episcopalian. Home and Office: 387 Darrell Rd Hillsborough CA 94010-6763

WEST, JACK HENRY, petroleum geologist; b. Washington, Apr. 7, 1934; s. John Henry and Zola Faye (West) Pigg; m. Bonnie Lou Ruger, Apr. 1, 1961; children: Trent John, Todd Kenneth. BS in Geology, U. Oreg., 1957, MS, 1961. Cert. petroleum geologist. Geologist Texaco Inc., L.A and Bakersfield, Calif., 1961-72; asst. dist. devel. geologist Texaco Inc., L.A., 1972-78; geologist Oxy Petroleum Inc., Bakersfield, 1978-80, div. geologist, 1980-83; exploitation mgr. Oxy U.S.A. Inc./Cities Svc. Oil and Gas, Bakersfield, 1983-89; sr. petroleum advisor WZI Inc., Bakersfield, 1990-92, petroleum cons., 1993—. Active Beyond War, Bakersfield, 1983-90. Mem. Am. Assn. Petroleum Geologists (pres. Pacific sect. 1988-89, adv. coun. 1992-94, sec. divsn. profl. affairs 1995—), San Joaquin Geol. Soc. (pres. 1984-85), Alfa Romeo Owners Club. Republican. Methodist.

WEST, JAMES STUART, small business owner; b. Modesto, Calif., Jan. 22, 1935; s. Donald Hayden and Ruby Edith (Garrison) W.; m. Sandra Lee Hedman, June 7, 1958 (div.); m. Jessie Lee Dunn, May 23, 1973; children: Jason sTephan, Janet Lynn. AA, Menlo Jr. Coll., Menlo Park, Calif., 1955; student, Kans. State U., 1957-58. V.p. J.S. West & Co., Modesto, Calif., 1958—. Bd. dirs., sec.-treas. Delta Blood Bank, Stockton, Calif., 1972—; bd. dirs., vice-chmn. Modesto C. of C., 1980-89 (Disting. Svc. award 1989). Recipient Good Egg of Yr. award Annual Good Egg Breakfast Com., 1992. Mem. Calif. Egg Com. (bd. dirs. 1985-92, pres. 1992-95), Pacific Egg and Poultry Assn. (bd. dirs. 1984-92, pres. 1992, 93), Am. Egg Bd. (bd. dirs. 1989—, treas. 95—, chmn. 1997—), Rotary (pres. Modesto club 1979-80, Paul Harris fellow 1977). Republican. Home: 224 Patricia Ln Modesto CA 95354-0262

WEST, JERRY ALAN, professional basketball team executive; b. Chelyan, W.Va., May 28, 1938; s. Howard Stewart and Cecil Sue (Creasey) W.; m. Martha Jane Kane, May, 1960 (div. 1977); children: David, Michael, Mark; m. Karen Christine Bua, May 28, 1978; 1 son, Ryan. BS, W.Va. Coll.; LHD (hon.), W.Va. Wesleyan Coll. Mem. Los Angeles Lakers, Nat. Basketball Assn., 1960-74, coach, 1976-79, spl. cons., 1979-82, gen. mgr., 1982-94; exec. v.p. basketball operations L. A. Lakers, 1994—; mem. first team Nat. Basketball Assn. All-Star Team, 1962-67, 70-73, mem. second team, 1968, 69; mem. NBA champion L.A. Lakers, 1972. Author: (with William Libby) Mr. Clutch: The Jerry West Story, 1969. Capt. U.S. Olympic Basketball Team, 1960; named Most Valuable Player NBA Playoff, 1969, All-Star Game Most Valuable Player, 1972; named to Naismith Meml. Basketball Hall of Fame, 1979, NBA Hall of Fame, 1980; mem. NBA 35th Anniversary All-Time Team, 1980; named NBA Exec. of Yr. Sporting News, 1994-95. Office: LA Lakers 3900 W Manchester Blvd PO Box 10 Inglewood CA 90305*

WEST, LINDA LEA, administrator; b. Sparta, Wis., Oct. 5, 1943; d. Larry C. and Florance M. (Haskell) Lomax; m. Thomas C. West, Aug. 29, 1964; children: Timothy C., Daniel H., Deborah R. AB magna cum laude, Occidential Coll., 1965; MLS, UCLA, 1966. Cert. profl. adminstrv. svcs.; cert. tchr. Calif. Libr. young adult L.A. Pub. Libr., 1966-67; libr. edn., psychology Humbolt State Coll. Libr., Arcata, Calif., 1967-68; reference libr. Monterey (Calif.) Bay Area Coop. Libr., 1969-70; instr. Hacienda La Puente & El Monte (Calif.) Adult Edn., 1976-78; instr., curriculum writer Indochinese RAP, Hacienda La Puente (Calif.) Sch. Dist., 1978-81, coord. refugee project, 1981-88; instr. adult edn. UCLA Extension, 1988—; resource tchr. Baldwin Park (Calif.) Adult Sch., 1988-90; archives mgr. Outreach & Tech. Assistance Network Hacienda La Puente Sch. Dist., 1990-94; asst. dir. Outreach and Tech. Asst. Network, Sacramento County Office of Edn., Sacramento, 1994—; cons. in field. Comtbr. articles to profl. jours. Jr. troop leader Girl Scouts Am., West Covina, Calif., 1985-88. Mem. ALA, AAUW, Am. Assn. Adult Continuing Edn., Am. Vocat. Assn., Calif. Tchrs. English to Speakers Other Langs. (asst. adult level chmn. 1985-86, adult level chmn. 1986-87), Calif. Coun. Adult Edn., Calif. Libr. Assn., Tchrs. English to Speakers Other Langs., Phi Beta Kappa, Beta Phi Mu, Phi Alpha Theta. Democrat. Episcopalian. Home: 912 S Coral Tree Dr West Covina CA 91791-3330 Office: Sacramento County Office Edn 9738 Lincoln Village Dr Sacramento CA 95827-3399

WEST, MADELINE FLORENCE, elementary education educator; b. San Francisco, Mar. 10, 1944; d. John Victor Hughes and Daisy Elizabeth (Darling) Irwin; m. Victor Vance West, Mar. 27, 1965; children: Amanda Elizabeth West Sutter, Aaron Frederick. BA, La Sierra Coll., Riverside, Calif., 1966; MA, Loma Linda U., Riverside, 1982. Tchr. Alvord Unified Sch. Dist., Riverside, 1966-71, 78—, sci. coord., 1992-96, learning facilitator, 1993-96, textbook selection rep., 1994—. Author: The Constitutional Convention of 1787: The Delegates in Profile, 1987 (mentor award 1987), Women Who Made a Difference, 1988 (mentor award 1988). Mem. World Affairs Coun., Riverside, 1983-92. Recipient mentor tchr. award Alvord Unified Sch. Dist., 1987, 88, Tchr. of Yr. award S. Christa McAuliffe Sch., Riverside, 1988, outstanding contbns. award Inland Empire Calif. chpt. International Reading Assn., 1988. Mem. NEA (rep. 1992-96, del. 1994). Home: 5611 Peacock Ln Riverside CA 92505-3140 Office: S Christa McAuliffe Elem Sch 4100 Golden Ave Riverside CA 92505-3403

WEST, NATALIE ELSA, lawyer; b. Greenwich, Conn., Mar. 11, 1947. AB, Smith Coll., 1968; JD, U. Calif., Berkeley, 1973. Bar: Calif. 1974. Counsel Calif. Fair Polit. Practices Commn., Sacramento, 1975-79; city atty. City of Berkeley, Calif., 1980-85, City of Novato, Calif., 1985-92, City of Brentwood, Calif., 1994—; gen. counsel Livermore-Amador Valley Water Mgmt. Agy., 1996—; shareholder McDonough, Holland & Allen, Oakland, Calif., 1991—. Pres. city attys. dept. League of Calif. Cities, 1986-87, bd. dirs., 1995—. Mem. State Bar Calif., Alameda County Bar Assn. Office: McDonough Holland & Allen 1999 Harrison St Ste 1300 Oakland CA 94612-3517

WEST, ROBERT JOHNSON, state agency administrator; b. Pensacola, Fla., Apr. 13, 1939; s. Ernest Reid and May Rose (Johnson) W.; m. Catherine Brooke VanValkenburgh, Jan. 26, 1983; children: Matthew, Van, Hadleigh. BA, Stanford U., 1961, MBA, 1970. Appraiser Union Bank, L.A., 1962-68; joint venture mgr. William Lyon Co., Inc., Newport Beach, Calif., 1970-73; owner West Assocs., Newport Beach, Calif., 85, 90-92; prin. Tarantella & Co., Newport Beach, 1985-90; cons. The World Bank, Washington, 1993-96; dir. Office of Real Estate Appraisers, State of Calif., Sacramento, 1992—. Contbr. articles to profl. jours. Mem. planning commn. City of Irvine, Calif., 1972-73, mem. city coun., 1973-75; mem. assessment appeals bd. County of Orange, Santa Ana, Calif., 1977-85. Mem. Am. Soc. Appraisers (L.A. chpt. pres. 1987, regional gov. 1991-92, real property com. 1986—, accredited appraiser). Republican. Lutheran. Home: 2681 Latham Dr Sacramento CA 95864 Office: Office of Real Estate Appraisers State of California 1225 R St Sacramento CA 95814

WEST, ROBERT SUMNER, surgeon; b. Bowman, N.D., Nov. 20, 1935; s. Elmer and Minnie (DeBode) W.; m. Martha W. Hopkins, Mar. 23, 1957; children: Stephen, Christopher, Anna Marie, Catherine, Sarah. BA, U. N.D., 1957, BS in Medicine, 1959; MD, Harvard U., 1961. Diplomate Am. Bd. Surgery. Intern U.S. Naval Hosp., Chelsea, Mass., 1961-62; resident in surgery U. Vt. Med. Ctr. Hosp., 1965-69; pvt. practice Coeur d'Alene, Idaho, 1969—; coroner Kootenai County, Coeur d'Alene, 1984—. Trustee, pres. Coeur d'Alene Sch. Dist. 271 Bd. Edn., 1973-77. Lt. M.C., USN, 1960-65. Fellow ACS (pres. Idaho chpt. 1985, gov. at large); mem. Idaho Med. Assn. (pres. 1989-90, trustee), Kiwanis. Republican. Methodist. Office: 920 W Ironwood Dr Coeur D Alene ID 83814-2643

WEST, STERLING GAYLORD, physician; b. St. Petersburg, Fla., Aug. 4, 1950; s. Curtis Gaylord and Patricia (Bottome) W.; m. Brenda Sue White, June 20, 1972; children: Dace Nichole, Matthew Sterling. Grad., U.S. Mil. Acad., 1972; MD, Emory U., 1976. Diplomate Nat. Bd. Med. Examiners, Am. Bd. Internal Medicine, subspecialty rheumatology. Commd. 2d lt. U.S. Army, 1972, advanced through grades to col., 1992; intern, resident Fitzsimons Army Med. Ctr., Denver, 1976-79, chief resident in medicine, 1979; fellowship rheumatology Walter Reed Army Med. Ctr., Washington, 1979-81; chief rheumatology, fellowship program dir. Fitzsimmons Army Med. Ctr., 1981-94; cons. in rheumatology to U.S. Army Surgeon Gen., 1991-94; prof. of medicine and rheumatology fellowship program dir. U. Colo. Health Scis. Ctr., Denver, 1995—. Assoc. editor Arthritis and Rheumatism, 1995—; contbr. articles to profl. jours. Col. U.S. Army, 1972-95. Recipient Legion of Merit; Sr. fellow rsch. Merck, Sharp and Dohme, 1981; recipient AMSUS Philip Hench award, 1983; rsch. grantee Rocky Mountain chpt. Arthritis Found., Denver, 1994. Fellow Am. Coll. Rheumatology, Am. Coll. Physicians (laureate award 1995); mem. AMA, Rocky Mtn. Rheumatism Assn., Alpha Omega Alpha. Office: U Colo Health Sci Ctr 4200 E 9th Ave # B115 Denver CO 80220-3706

WEST, TONY, state official; b. Phoenix, Ariz., Oct. 29, 1937; m. Margaret O'Malley, 1962; 3 children: William A., III, John Patrick, Stephen Michael. BS, Ariz. State Univ., 1961. Formerly pres., chief exec. officer Shenendoah Ranches; Ariz. state rep., 1973-82, former Ariz. state senator, dist. 18, now Ariz. state treas. Mem. Ariz. Club (formerly pres.), Ariz. Found. for Handicapped (pres.), John C. Lincoln Hosp. Found. Republican. Office: Office of the State Treas 1700 W Washington St Phoenix AZ 85007-2812*

WESTBERG, PATRICIA ANN, community health nurse; b. Norfolk, Va., Aug. 8, 1958; d. Patrick Lawrence and Bernadette Marian (Shatalsky) Sullivan; m. Robert Joe Westberg, June 11, 1978; children: Jennifer Lynn, Christine Marie. Assoc., Grossmont Coll., El Cajon, Calif., 1979; BS in Nursing with High Distinction, George Mason U., Fairfax, Va., 1991; postgrad., San Diego State Univ., 1996—. RN, Va., Calif.; cert. BLS, ACLS, Calif. Clin. nurse IV, ortho. Nat. Naval Med. Ctr., Bethesda, Md., 1989-92; cmty. health/infection control nurse Br. Med. Clinic Naval Shipyard, Mare Island, Calif., 1992-93; supr. Miramar Family Practice Clinic, Walnut, Calif., 1995-96; acting charge nurse, team leader/mgr.; patient controlled anesthesia task force ortho Nat. Naval Med. Ctr., Bethesda, Md., 1991-92; infection control policy com. Br. Med. Clinic Naval Shipyard, Mare Island, 1992-93. Fund raiser chmn. St. Basil's Sch., Vallejo, 1994-95. Mem. Mare Island Officers' Wives Club (pres. 1994-95, civilian of the quater, 1993, letter of commendation, 1993), Sigma Theta Tau, Alpha Chi. Republican. Roman Catholic. Home: PO Box 3070 1167 Westhaven Dr Trinidad CA 95570

WESTBO, LEONARD ARCHIBALD, JR., electronics engineer; b. Tacoma, Wash., Dec. 4, 1931; s. Leonard Archibald and Agnes (Martinson) W.; B.A. in Gen. Studies, U. Wash., 1958. Electronics engr. FAA, Seattle Air Route Traffic Control Center, Auburn, Wash., 1961-72; asst. br. chief electronics engring. br. 13th Coast Guard Dist., Seattle, 1972-82. Served with USCG, 1951-54, 1958-61. Registered profl. engr., Wash. Mem. Aircraft Owners and Pilots Assn., IEEE, Am. Radio Relay League. Home and Office: 10528 SE 323rd St Auburn WA 98092-4734

WESTBROOK, G. JAY, hospice nurse, grief counselor; b. N.Y.C., Apr. 23, 1947; s. Albert Joseph and Mary Paula (Purnell) W.; m. Nancy Morgan, May 1, 1970. BS, U. So. Calif., 1980, MS, 1984; Diploma, Los Angeles County Med. Ctr., 1993. RN, Calif.; lic. nursing home adminstr., Calif.; cert. in applied geriatric mental health. Gerontologist, cons. dir. profl. svcs. Angeles Home Health Care, Inc., 1984-85; asst. dir. product devel. ElderMed divsn. HealthWest, 1985-86; gerontologist, adminstr.-in-tng. ARA Living Ctrs., Inc., 1986-87; assoc. rsch. dir., dir. info. svcs. Shriners Hosp., 1987-89; dir., sr. counselor The Resource Ctr. divsn. Health Care Delivery Svcs., 1990-91; adminstr., respite coord. Bonnie Brae Convalescent Hosp., 1991-92; clin. nurse U. So. Calif./Los Angeles County Med. Ctr., 1994-95; fellow and gerontologist UCLA/U. So. Calif. Long Term Care Gerontology Ctr., 1983—; pvt. counselor in grief recovery, 1983—; clin. hospice nurse, edn. dir., clin. coord. Coordinated Home Hospice, 1995—; cons. Alzheimer's Assn., Ariz. Gov.'s Adv. Coun. on Aging, Rancho Los Amigos Med. Ctr., L.A., City of Hope Med. Ctr., Kaiser Permanente Hosps., Penn State Sch. Medicine, U. So. Calif. Sch. Medicine, others. Numerous TV interviews. Mem. Am. Pain Soc., Am. Soc. Pain Mgmt. Nurses, Assn. for Deth Edn. and Counseling, Gerontol. Soc. Am., Nat. Hospice Assn., Am. Pub. Health Assn., Am. Soc. onAging, Gerontol. Nursing Assn., Nat. Cancer Pain Initiative, others. Home: 17216 Saticoy St Ste 306 Van Nuys CA 91406-1603

WESTBROOK, T. L., bishop. Bishop of Wash. Ch. of God in Christ, Spanaway. Office: Ch of God in Christ 1256 176th St Spanaway WA 98402*

WESTBY, JEROME BRAMBLE, II, editor; b. Janesville, Wis., Sept. 2, 1949; s. Jerome Bramble and Patricia Jane (Dearborn) W.; m. Cheryl Maureen Victor, Dec. 20, 1975; children: Spencer Dearborn, Abigail Jane. Student, Beloit (Wis.) Coll., 1972. Co-founder, asst. mng. dir. New Am. Theater, Rockford, Ill., 1972-73; salesman Chambers and Owen, Janesville, 1974; law clk. Eisenberg and Kletzke, Milw., 1975-76; sales rep. Goodyear Pub. Co., Santa Monica, Calif., 1976-78, mktg. mgr., 1978-79, mktg. dir., 1980-81; acquisitions editor Scott, Foresman & Co., Glenview, Ill., 1982-83, West Pub. Co., St. Paul, 1983—. Editor: Inquiry into Physics, 1987, 2d edit., 1991, 3rd edit., 1995, Chemistry for Today, 1987, 2nd edit., 1994, 3rd edit., 1997, Human Heredity, 1988, 2d edit., 1991, 3rd edit., 1995, 4th edit., 1997, Human Physiology, 1989, 2nd edit., 1993, 3rd edit., 1997, Historical Geology, 1989, 2nd edit., 1993, In Quest of The Universe, 1991, 2nd edit., 1994, Human Biology, 1991, 2nd edit., 1995, Physical Geology, 1992, 2nd edit., 1995, The Changing Earth, 1994, 2nd edit., 1997, An Invitation to Computer Science, 1995, Introduction to Computer Science with

C , 1996, Biology, 1996, Environmental Science, 1996. Active Conejo Valley Adoptive Families; vol. United Fund. Named Editor of Yr. West Pub. Co., 1988, 89, 92, 96. Mem. Am. Assn. Pubs., Soc. Am. Baseball Researchers, Smithsonian Inst., Sierra Club. Home: 1124 Hendrix Ave Thousand Oaks CA 91360-3647

WESTCOTT, BRIAN JOHN, manufacturing executive; b. Rexford, N.Y., June 19, 1957; s. John Campbell and Norma (Cornell) W.; m. Andrea Belrose, Apr. 23, 1988; children: Sarah Katharine, Paul Brian. BS, Lehigh U., 1979; MS, Stanford U., 1980, PhD, 1987. Engr. Combustion Engring., Windsor, Conn., 1980-81; rsch. engr. Gen. Electric Corp. Rsch., Niskayuna, N.Y., 1981-83; rsch. fellow Stanford (Calif.) Grad. Sch. Bus., 1987-88; mgr. Gen. Electric Corp. Mgmt., Bridgeport, Conn., 1988-89; prin. A.T. Kearney Tech. Inc., Redwood City, Calif., 1989—; chief exec. officer Westt, Inc., Menlo Park, Calif., 1990—. Author: (with others) Paradox and Transformation, 1988; contbr. articles to profl. jours.; inventor, patentee in field. Mem. Menlo Park Vitality Task Force, 1993-94. Recipient Tech 500 award Westt, Inc., 1996; postdoctoral rsch. fellow Stanford U. Grad. Sch. Bus., 1987, 88; rsch. fellow Electric Power Rsch., Stanford, 1983-87. Mem. ASME, Soc. Mfg. Engrs. Office: Westt Inc 1090 O'Brien Dr Menlo Park CA 94025-1407

WESTCOTT, JAY YOUNG, pulmonary and critical care medicine educator; b. Phila., Jan. 5, 1953; m. Jamie L. English, June 14, 1989; children: Claire, Jay. BS in Biology, SUNY, Albany, 1975; PhD in Biology, Purdue U., 1981. Teaching asst. Purdue U., West Lafayette, Ind., 1976-77, grad. asst., 1977-81; postdoctoral fellow pharmacology dept. U. Colo. Health Sci. Ctr., Denver, 1981-85; instr. dept. medicine Cardiovasc. Pulmonary Rsch. Lab. U. Colo. Health Scis. Ctr., Denver, 1986-88, asst. prof. divsn. Pulmonary Critical Care Medicine, 1988-95, assoc. prof. divsn. pulmonary and crit. care medicine, 1995-96; with Nat. Jewish Ctr. for Immunology and Respiratory Medicine, 1996—. Contbr. articles to sci. jours., chpts. to books. Grantee NIH, 1977-80, NIH, 1988-95, Abbott Labs., 1992-93; fellow Nat. Inst. on Alcohol Abuse and Alcoholism, 1982-84, rsch. fellow Am. Lung Assn., 1987-89. Mem. Am. Thoracic Soc. Home: 2211 Vine St Denver CO 80205-5651 Office: Nat Jewish Ctr Immunol/Resp Medicine Dept Medicine 1400 Jackson St Denver CO 80206

WESTENDORF, ELAINE SUSAN, social worker; b. Beruit, Lebanon, Jan. 7, 1956; came to U.S., 1957; d. Glen Albert and Barbara (Redlick) L. AA, Fresno City Coll., 1979; BA in Psychology, U. Calif., Santa Cruz, 1981; MSW, San Francisco State U., 1985. Cert. coll. instr., coll. counselor. Intern Star Lodge Drug and Alcohol Treatment Ctr., Scotts Valley, Calif., 1983; with employees assistance program NASA, Moffett Field, Calif., 1983-84; psychiat. social worker intern Cath. Social Services Children's Counseling Ctr., Santa Clara, Calif., 1984, Kaiser Permanente-Psychiatry, Redwood City, Calif., 1984-85; psychiat. social worker San Benito County Mental Health, Hollister, Calif., 1985-88, San Benito County Schs., Hollister, 1985-88, Personal Performance Coms., Mountain View, Calif., 1988-90; pvt. practice, 1990—; cons. San Benito County Schs., 1985-88. Mem. Nat. Assn. Social Workers, Assn. Clin. Social Workers. Democrat. Home: 1089 Belvedere Ln San Jose CA 95129 Office: 1475 Saratoga Ave Ste 220 San Jose CA 95129-4959

WESTENSKOW, SUSAN R., school administrator; b. Preston, Idaho, Mar. 13, 1949; d. Ray W. and Madge (Hiatt) Ransbottom; m. James L. Westenskow, Sept. 29, 1972; children: Ryan, Jamie, Kelly. BS, Utah State U., 1974. Dir. St. Benedict's Found., Ogden, Utah, 1988-89; dir. comty. rels. Weber County Schs., Ogden, 1989—. Mem. bus. advocacy com. Utah Ctr. for Families in Edn., 1992—; bd. dirs. Child Abuse Prevention Coun., No. Utah, 1991—, United Way of No. Utah, 1994—; commr. Utah Gov.'s Commn. for Women and Families, chair, 1991—; mem. Jr. League Ogden, pres., 1982—. Recipient Spirit of Am. Woman award Your Cmty. Connection, (formerly YWCA), 1994. Fellow Ogden Leadership Acad. (chair 1990—); mem. Women in Bus. (chair exec. com. 1988—), Nat. Sch. Pub. Rels. Assn. (pres. Utah chpt. 1989—), Nat. Assn. Ptnrs. in Edn., Ogden/Weber C. of C. (bd. dirs. 1996—), Rotary Club Ogden (treas.). Office: Weber County Schs 5320 S Adams Ave Ogden UT 84405

WESTERDAHL, JOHN BRIAN, nutritionist, health educator; b. Tucson, Dec. 3, 1954; s. Jay E. and Margaret (Meyer) W.; m. Doris Mui Lian Tan, Nov. 18, 1989. AA, Orange Coast Coll., 1977; BS, Pacific Union Coll., 1979; MPH, Loma Linda U., 1981. Registered dietitian; chartered herbalist; cert. nutrition specialist. Nutritionist, health educator Castle Med. Ctr., Kailua, Hawaii, 1981-84, health promotion coord., 1984-87, asst. dir. health promotion, 1987-88, dir. health promotion, 1988-89; dir. nutrition and health rsch. Health Sci., Santa Barbara, Calif., 1989-90; sr. nutritionist, project mgr. Shaklee Corp., San Francisco, 1990-96; dir. nutrition Dr. McDougall's Right Foods, Inc., S. San Francisco, 1996—; mem. faculty staff, dir. continuing edn. Am. Acad. Nutrition, 1996—; talk show host Nutrition and You, Sta. KGU Radio, Honolulu, 1983-89; nutrition com. mem. Hawaii div. Am. Heart Assn., Honolulu, 1984-87; mem. nutrition study group Govs. Conf. Health Promotion and Disease Prevention for Hawaii, 1985. Editor: Nourish Mag., 1995-96; nutrition editor: Veggie Life Mag., 1995—. Mem. AAAS, Am. Coll. Sports Medicine, Am. Dietetic Assn. (Calif. coord. vegetarian nutrition practice group), Am. Nutritionists Assn., Am. Coll. Nutrition, Soc. for Nutrition Edn., Nat. Wellness Assn., Nutrition Today Soc., Am. Soc. Pharmacognosy, Inst. Food Technologists, Hawaii Nutrition Coun. (v.p. 1983-86,m pres.-elect 1988-89, pres. 1989), Hawaii Dietetic Assn., Calif. Dietetic Assn., N.Y. Acad. Scis., Seventh-day Adventist Dietetic Assn., several other profl. assns. Republican. Seventh-day Adventist. Office: Dr McDougall's Right Foods 101 Utah Ave South San Francisco CA 94080 Personal philosophy: "Beloved, I wish above all things that thou mayest prosper and be in health, even as thy soul prospereth." 3 John 2.

WESTERMAN, JOHN HAROLD, health administrator; b. Mpls., July 24, 1933; s. Harold V. and Kay S. Westerman; children: James, Laura (dec.), Eric, Peter. B.S., U. Minn., 1954, B.B.A., 1958, M.H.A., 1960. Asst. adminstr., sr. instr. U. Rochester (N.Y.) Med. Center, 1961-64; research assoc. Sci. Planning Office, U. Minn., Mpls., 1964-66; assoc. prof. pub. health, gen. dir. hosps. and clinics, coordinator health systems research and devel. Sci. Planning Office, U. Minn. (Office Vice pres.), 1967-82; pres. Allegheny Health, Edn. and Research Corp., 1982-85, Allegheny Gen. Hosp., Allegheny Diagnostic Services, Inc., Allegheny Singer Research Corp.; chief exec. officer Allegheny Health Services, Inc.; pres., chief exec. officer Hosp. of the Good Samaritan, Los Angeles, 1985-92; interim pres. Assn. of Univ. Programs in Health Adminstrn., Arlington, Va., 1993; CEO Hilo (Hawaii) Med. Ctr., 1993—; acting CEO Hawaii Health Sys. Corp., 1996—; mem. bd. Minn. Blue Cross-Blue Shield, 1972-78; mem. bd. commrs. Joint Commn. Accreditation Hosps., Chgo., 1976-82; pres., mem. bd. Minn. Bd. Health, 1972-78; mem. clin. research adv. com. NIH, 1976-80; accrediting mem. Commn. Edn. for Health Services Adminstrn., 1977; mem. adv. panel on multi-instnl. arrangements Am. Hosp. Assn., 1977-83; mem. Nat. End Stage Renal Disease Planning Com., 1980-81; pres. Consortium for Study Univ. Hosps., 1980-81; mem. Vol. Hosp. Am., 1983-85, Premier Health Alliance, 1988-92; chmn. Big Island Health Consortium, 1994. Author articles in field; mem. editl. bd. Jour. Med. Edn., 1972-78, Health Care Mgmt. Rev, 1979-82, Frontiers of Health Svcs. Mgmt., 1992-95. Served with USAF, 1955-58. Recipient Distinguished Service award. Democrat. Episcopalian. Office: Hawaii Health Sys Corp 688 Kinoole St Ste 121 Hilo HI 96720

WESTGARD, JOYCE VICTORIA SUZANNE, education educator; b. Butte, Mont., June 30, 1951; d. Blake E. and Martha (Wernham) Westgard; children: Suzanne, Karen, Denise. BS, Mont. State U., 1973, MEd, 1981, EdD, 1989. Cert. tchr., Mont., Wash. Lab. asst. chemistry dept. Mont. State U., Bozeman, 1969-73, lab. instr., 1972, 85, lab. technician State Soils Lab.; adult edn. instr. Bozeman Sch. Dist., 1976-85; workshop instr. Mont. Edn. Assn. State Conv., Expanding your Horizons, 1984-88; ins. instr. staff Bozeman Sch. Dist., 1988-88; tchr. Bozeman Jr. High Sch., 1973-88; prof. St. Martin's Coll., Lacey, Wash., 1988—, dir. continuing edn., 1988-90, dir. MEd program, divsn. 90-93, dean edn. divsn., 1993—; cons. to sch. dists.; grant reader U.S. Dept. Edn. Jour. referee Nat. Coun. Tchrs. Math.: Arithmetic Tchr., 1989—, Internat. Soc. Tech. in Edn. Math./sci. grantee Eisenhower Found., 1993, 95, 96. Mem. ASCD, Nat. Coun. Tchrs. Math. (presenter regional and nat. confs.), Wash. State Math Coun. Office: St Martins Coll Edn Divsn Lacey WA 98503

WESTIN, HELEN TILDA, writer, songwriter; b. Laporte, Minn., Oct. 14, 1918; d. Theodore Olsen and Hannah Christina (Pedersen) Granvold; m. Kermit Wallace Westin, Oct. 25, 1936; 1 child, Gail Westin Ochiai. Sec. LaSalle Mgmt. Co., Detroit, 1946-50; acct. State of Oreg., Salem, 1953-54. Author: Introducing the Song Sheet, 1976; creator game Song Twisters, 1988; composer various songs; publ. Keiko's Song, 1997; contbr. numerous articles to Nat. Sheet Music Soc. Mem. City Roses Sheet Music Club (charter). Home: 912 NE 113th Ave Portland OR 97220

WESTLAKE, RENEE ELYSE, music educator; b. San Pedro, Calif., Mar. 27, 1954; d. Ernest Elbon Barker and Mary Louise (Shannon) Shriver; m. Stuart Lovitt Westlake, Mar. 16, 1974; children: Tobi Lynn, Kaci Marie. BA, Mont. State U., 1976, MEd, 1987. Music educator Bozeman (Mont.) Pub. Sch., 1976—; flutist Bozeman Symphony Orch., 1974—, Bozeman Flute and Harp Ensemble, Bozeman, 1987—; founder, coord. Longfellow Percussion Ensemble, Bozeman, 1986-92, Bozeman High Flute Choir, Bozeman, 1988-96, Bozeman H.S. Flute Choir, 1988—. Composer (elem. musical) Longfellow, 1981, Love & Harmony, 1991, Emily, 1993; contbr. articles to profl. jours. Dir. 1st Presbyn. Choir, Bozeman, 1976-79, Grand Ave. Ch. Choir, Bozeman, 1979-81; elder Grand Ave. Christian Ch., Bozeman, 1980—; guest spkr. Grand Ave. Ch., Bozeman, 1988—. Recipient Centennial Alumni award Mont. State U., Bozeman, 1993; named Outstanding Young Women of Am., 1982. Mem. Nat. Fedn. Music Adjudicators Assn., Mont. Gen. Music Tchrs. Assn. (editor 1982-84, pres. 1984-86), Mont. Music Educators Assn. (pres. 1996-97), Mont. Bandmasters, Bozeman Friends of Music (faculty bd. 1980—). Democrat. Home: 2900 Love Ln Bozeman MT 59718-9730 Office: Bozeman Pub Schs 515 W Main St Bozeman MT 59718-3466

WESTON, EDWARD, art dealer, consultant; b. N.Y.C., Feb. 25, 1925; s. Joseph and Mona Weston; m. Ann Jean Gould, May 4, 1974; children: Jon Marc, Cari Alyn Rene. News editor Sta. WMCA, N.Y.C., 1940-41; announcer news dept. Sta. WSAV, Savannah, Ga., 1941-43; newscaster, disc jockey Sta. WNOX, Knoxville, Tenn., 1943-45; program dir. Sta. WXLH, Okinawa, Japan, 1945-47; newscaster, announcer Sta. WAVZ, New Haven, 1947-48; program dir. Sta. WCCC, Hartford, Conn., 1948-49; asst. gen. mgr. Sta. WCPO AM-FM-TV, Cin., 1949-59; pres., gen. mgr. Sta. WZIP, Cin., 1959-61; pres. Weston Entertainment, Northridge, Calif., 1961—, Edward Weston Fine Art; exec. v.p. Hollywood Archives Collectible Ltd.; chmn. bd. Fulton J. Sheen Communications; pres. Inspirational Programs, Inc., 1983—, Weston Editions, 1970—, Marilyn Monroe Editions, 1975—. Producer TV/video cassettes Life Is Worth Living; PBS TV series How to Paint with Elke Sommer, 1984. Founder Cin. Summer Playhouse, 1950. Served with U.S. Army, 1945-46. Recipient Outstanding News Coverage award Variety mag., 1949, Outstanding Sta. Ops. award Variety mag., 1950, Best Programming award Nat. Assn. Radio TV Broadcasters, 1951. Mem. Nat. Franchise Assn. (founder). Home: 10511 Andora Ave Chatsworth CA 91311-2004 Office: Weston Entertainment 19355 Business Center Dr Northridge CA 91324-3503

WESTON, JANE SARA, plastic surgeon, educator; b. Oceanside, N.Y., May 21, 1952; m. Jan K. Horn; 1 child, Jonathan Spencer Horn. MD, Stanford U., 1975-79. Diplomate Am. Bd. Plastic Surgery. Resident gen. surgery Sch. Medicine Stanford (Calif.) U., 1979-82, resident plastic surgery Sch. Medicine, 1982-83; fellow craniofacial surgery Hopital des Enfants Malades, Paris, 1983-84; plastic surgeon Kaiser Permanente Med. Group, San Jose, Calif., 1985-90; pvt. practice Palo Alto, Calif., 1990—; plastic surgeon Stanford U. Med. Sch., 1994—. Active Leadership Palo Alto, 1993. Fellow ACS; mem. Am. Soc. Plastic and Reconstructive Surgeons (chair women plastic surgeons com. 1993-96). Office: 750 Welch Rd Ste 321 Palo Alto CA 94304-1510

WESTON, JIM, protective services official. Chief of police Reno. Office: 455 E 2d St Reno NV 89505

WESTON, JOHN FREDERICK, business educator, consultant; b. Ft. Wayne, Ind., Feb. 6, 1916; s. David Thomas and Bertha (Schwartz) W.; children: Kenneth F., Byron L., Ellen J. B.A., U. Chgo., 1937, M.B.A., 1943, Ph.D., 1948. Instr. U. Chgo. Sch. Bus., 1940-42, asst. prof., 1947-48; prof. The Anderson Sch. UCLA, 1949—; Cordner prof. The Anderson Sch., 1981-94, prof. emeritus recalled The Anderson Sch., 1986—, dir. rsch. program in competition and bus. policy, 1969—, dir. Ctr. for Managerial Econs. and Pub. Policy, 1983-86; econ. cons. to pres. Am. Bankers Assn., 1945-46; disting. lecture series U. Okla., 1967, U. Utah, 1972, Miss. State U., 1972, Miami State U., 1975. Author: Scope and Methodology of Finance, 1966, International Managerial Finance, 1972, Impact of Large Firms on U.S. Economy, 1973, Financial Theory and Corporate Policy, 1979, 2d edit., 1983, 3d edit., 1988, Mergers, Restructuring and Corporate Control, 1990, Managerial Finance, 9th edit, 1992; assoc. editor: Jour. of Finance, 1948-55; mem. editorial bd., 1957-59; editorial bd. Bus. Econs., Jour. Fin. Rsch., Managerial and Decision Econs.; manuscript referee Am. Econ. Rev., Rev. of Econs. and Statistics, Engring. Economist, Bus. Econs., Fin. Mgmt. Bd. dirs. Bunker Hill Fund. Served with Ordnance Dept. AUS, 1943-45. Recipient Abramson Scroll award Bus. Econs., 1989-94; McKinsey Found. grantee, 1965-68; GE grantee, 1967; Ford Found. Faculty Rsch. fellow, 1961-62. Fellow Nat. Assn. Bus. Economists; mem. Am. Finance Assn. (pres. 1966, adv. bd. 1967-71), Am. Econ. Assn., Western Econ. Assn. (pres. 1962), Econometric Soc., Am. Statis. Assn., Royal Econ. Soc., Fin. Analysts Soc., Fin. Mgmt. Assn. (pres. 1979-80). Home: 258 Tavistock Ave Los Angeles CA 90049-3229 Office: UCLA Anderson Sch Los Angeles CA 90095-1481

WESTON, SANDRA, jewelry designer; b. N.Y.C., Sept. 27, 1949; d. Moses Soloman and Sally May (Gelbman) Fradkin; m. Kenneth Allen Weston, Aug. 9, 1969 (div. Oct. 1981); m. Barry Clyde Lipton, Oct. 17, 1981. Grad. high sch., East Meadow, N.Y. Bookkeeper Coachman Restaurant, N.Y.C., 1967-69; salesperson Fortunoff's Silver Dept., Westbury, N.Y., 1970; designer, salesperson jewelry Weston Studio, Winter Park, Fla., 1972-79; asst. mgr. Design Sphere, Niwot, Colo., 1980-81; mgr. Imperial Jewelers, San Rafael, Calif., 1982-83, Quintessence Gemstones & Jewelry, San Francisco, 1983-84; jewelry designer Weston Designs, Novato, Calif., 1984—; instr. Yoga, 1981—. Recipient 2d prize Crafts, Roslyn, N.Y., 1974, Honarable Mention Indialantic, Fla., 1974, 75, Equal Merit award Drawing Room, Sarasota, Fla., 1974, Honorable Mention, West Palm Beach, Fla., 1974, 1st pl. Martello Gallery, Key West, Fla., 1975, Merit award Mt. Dora, Fla., 1975, 1st pl. Young Artists Expo, Cleaarwater, Fla., 1975, Best Display Fun and Sun Art Show, Clearwater, 1976, Honorable Mention Fun and Sun Art Show, 1976, 1st prize Maurice Podell Art Show, Long Branch, N.J., 1976, Best Display-Ringling Mus. Crafts, 1977, 2d pl. Pompano Beach Art Show, 1978, Best in Jewelry-St. Augustine Art Show, 1978. Office: PO Box 2023 Novato CA 94948-2023

WESTPHAL, RUTH LILLY, educational audiovisual company executive, author, publisher; b. Glendale, Calif., July 27, 1931; d. Glen R. and Margaret E. (John) Lilly; m. H. Frederick Westphal, June 25, 1953. B.A. in Edn., UCLA, 1953; M.A. in Instructional System Tech., Chapman Coll., 1968. Cert. tchr. Calif. Tchr. pub. schs., Los Angeles, Glendale, Whittier, Calif., 1953-65; instuctional systems analyst Litton Industries, Anaheim, Calif., 1965-67; dir. devel. Trainex Corp., Garden Grove, Calif., 1967-69; owner, pres. Concept Media, Inc., Irvine, Calif., 1969—; pres. Westphal Pub., Irvine, 1980—. Co-founder Friends of City Library, LaHabra, Calif., 1960-65; mem. Los Angeles County Mus. Art, 1975—, Laguna Beach Mus. Art, 1979-96, Orange County Mus. of Art, 1996—, Nautical Heritage Soc. Dana Point, Calif. 1982—. Author, editor numerous ednl. filmstrip, video programs, CD ROM. Author: Plein Air Painters of California: The Southland, 1982 (Western Books award 1982), Plein Air Painters of California: The North, 1986 (Western Books award 1986), American Scene Painting: California, 1930s and 1940s, 1991. Recipient numerous awards Info. Film Producers Am., Internat. Film and TV Festival N.Y., Chgo. Film Festival, Am. Jour. Nursing Media Festival, Author Recognition award U. Calif., 1983. Mem. Nat. Audiovisual Assn., Assn. Media Producers. Avocations: Art history. Office: Concept Media Inc 2493 Du Bridge Ave Irvine CA 92606-5022

WETENKAMP, HERBERT DELOS, JR., publisher; b. Santa Monica, Calif., June 22, 1954; s. Herbert Delos Sr. and Roberta Joan (Hilliard) W. BA in Comms./Journalism, Calif. State U., Fullerton, 1988. Newspaper reporter/photographer News-Times, Orange County, Calif., 1976; mng. editor Bicycle Dealers Showcase Mag., Santa Ana, Calif., 1977-80, pub., 1980-81; co-prodr. Interbike Expo, Mission Viejo, Calif., 1981-85; pres., founder Info Net Pub., San Clemente, Calif., 1985—, Info Net Rep. Svcs., Dana Point, Calif., 1985—. Editor, pub. 7 books, 1995—; columnist Bicycle Retailer and Industry News, 1994—; contbr. articles to mags. Bd. dirs. San Clemente Hist. Soc., 1993—, co-pres., 1995-96; pres. Pendleton Coast Natural History Assn., San Clemente, 1995—. Named Citizen of the Day, San Clemente Sun-Post, 1988. Mem. Am. Polit. Items Collectors, Soc. Profl. Journalists (Best Deadline News Story 1976), Pubs. Mktg. Assn. Republican. Home: PO Box 3789 San Clemente CA 92674 Office: Info Net Pub Ste C 34188 Coast Hwy Dana Point CA 92629

WETHERWAX, GEORGIA LEE (PEG WETHERWAX), elementary education educator; b. St. Louis, Oct. 7, 1931; d. Kenneth Alden and Frances Marie (Cuming) Smith; m. Alfred R. Wetherwax, Oct. 7, 1950; children: C. Todd, Steven, Karen, Kent. BA in Elem. Edn., Calif. State U., L.A., 1955, MA in Elem. Adminstrn., 1966. Tchr. Burbank (Calif.) Unified Schs., 1955-56; tchr., vice prin. L.A. Unified Sch. Dist., 1957-68, master tchr., profl. expert, 1983-86, bi-lingual tchr., 1987-91; tchr., vice prin. Mammoth Unified Sch. Dist., Mammoth Lakes, Calif., 1969-79; asst. supt., prin. K-8, tchr. Middletown (Calif.) Unified Sch. Dist., 1979-83, ret., 1991; curriculum devel. specialist Calibre Industries, L.A., 1986-87; CEO Creative Curriculums, Sacramento, Calif., 1989—. Author: Careful Mathematics Lesson Plans, 1986. Faculty Women's scholar L.A. City Coll., William Snyder scholar Calif. State U. L.A.; grantee L.A. Ednl. Partnership. Mem. Pi Lambda Theta (treas. L.A. chpt.), Delta Kappa Gamma. Home and Office: 7412 Sunwest Ln Sacramento CA 95828-6241

WETZEL, JODI (JOY LYNN WETZEL), history and women's studies educator; b. Salt Lake City, Apr. 5, 1943; d. Richard Coulam and Margaret Elaine (Openshaw) Wood; m. David Nevin Wetzel, June 12, 1967; children: Meredith (dec.), Richard Rawlins. BA in English, U. Utah, 1965, MA in English, 1967; PhD in Am. Studies, U. Minn., 1977. Instr. Am. studies and family social sci. U. Minn., 1973-77, asst. prof. Am. studies and women's studies, 1977-79, asst. to dir. Minn. Women's Ctr., 1973-75, asst. dir., 1975-79; dir. Women's Resource Ctrs. U. Denver, 1980-84, mem. adj. faculty history, 1981-84, dir. Am. studies program, dir. Women's Inst., 1983-84; dir. Women in Curriculum U. Maine, 1985-86, mem. coop. faculty sociology, social work and human devel., 1986; dir. Inst. Women's Studies and Svcs. Met. State Coll. Denver, 1986—, assoc. prof. history, 1986-89, prof. history, 1990—; speaker, presenter, cons. in field; vis. prof. Am. studies U. Colo., 1985. Co-author: Women's Studies: Thinking Women, 1993; co-editor: Readings Toward Composition, 2d edit., 1969; contbr. articles to profl. pubs. Del. at-large Nat. Women's Meeting, Houston, 1977; bd. dirs. Rocky Mountain Women's Inst., 1981-84; treas. Colo. Women's Agenda, 1987-91. U. Utah Dept. English fellow, 1967; U. Minn. fellow, 1978-79; grantee NEH, 1973, NSF, 1981-83, Carnegie Corp., 1988; named to Outstanding Young Women of Am., 1979. Mem. Am. Hist. Assn., Nat. Assn. Women in Edn. (Hilda A. Davis Ednl. Leadership award 1996, Sr. Scholar 1996), Am. Assn. for Higher Edn., Am. Studies Assn., Nat. Women's Studies Assn., Golden Key Nat. Honor Soc. (hon.), Alpha Lambda Delta, Phi Kappa Phi. Office: Met State Coll Denver Campus Box 36 PO Box 173362 Denver CO 80217-3362

WEXLER, RALPH MARTIN, physician, consultant; b. Texarkana, Tex., July 8, 1924; s. Max Herman and Marguerite Hortense (Goldstein) W.; m. Miriam Ruth Miller, July 1, 1948; children: Marcie Naomi, Edi Ann, Susan Beth. BS, La. State U., 1947; MD, U. Tex., Dallas, 1952. Cert. ABFP 1970, 79, 86,. Intern Denver Gen. Hosp., 1952-53; residence surgery Menorah Med. Ctr., Kansas City, Mo., 1953-54; pvt. practice in medicine Pueblo, Colo., 1954-78; area med. dir. AT&T, Denver, 1978-89; cons. Clinicare, Denver, 1990-94, Rose Med. Ctr., Denver, 1994—; sec./treas. Rocky Mountain Acad. Occupl. Medicine, Denver, 1986-93. Pres. Pueblo Kiwanis Club, 1967. Maj. U.S. Army, 1955-64. Recipient Meritorious Svc. award Emergency Tech. Assn. of Colo., 1976. Fellow Am. Coll. Occupl. and Environ. Medicine (chmn. internat. occupl. medicine sect. 1992-94, coun. chmn. 1993—, Presdl. award 1996), Am. Acad. Family Physicians, Royal Soc. Medicine; mem. Al Kaly Shrine. Democrat. Jewish. Home and Office: 111 Emerson St # 1643 Denver CO 80218

WEYAND, FREDERICK CARLTON, retired military officer; b. Arbuckle, Calif., Sept. 15, 1916; s. Frederick C. W. and Velma Semans (Weyand); m. Lora Arline Langhart, Sept. 20, 1940; children: Carolyn Ann, Robert Carlton, Nancy Diane. A.B., U. Calif.-Berkeley, 1939; LL.D. (hon), U. Akron, 1975. Officer U.S. Army, advanced to gen. chief of staff, 1940-76; sr. v.p. First Hawaiian Bank, Honolulu, 1976-82; trustee Estate of S.M. Damon, Honolulu, 1982—; bd. dirs. First Hawaiian, Inc., Ltd., First Hawaiian Bank, First Hawaiian Credit Corp. Chmn. ARC, Honolulu, 1982, Hawaiian Open golf Tourney, 1981-82. Decorated D.S.C. U.S. Army, 1967, D.S.M. Army (3), Dept. Def. (1), 1966-76, other U.S. and fgn. mil. decorations. Mem. Am. Def. Preparedness Assn., Assn. U.S. Army, U.S. Strategic Inst. (v.p. 1976—), USAF Assn. Lutheran. Clubs: Waialae Country. Lodge: Masons. Home: 2121 Ala Wai Blvd Ph 1 Honolulu HI 96815-2211 Office: SM Damon Estate 999 Bishop St 28th Fl Honolulu HI 96813

WEYERHAEUSER, GEORGE HUNT, forest products company executive; b. Seattle, July 8, 1926; s. John Philip and Helen (Walker) W.; m. Wendy Wagner, July 10, 1948; children: Virginia Lee, George Hunt, Susan W., Phyllis A., David M., Merrill W. BS with honors in Indsl. Engring., Yale U., 1949. With Weyerhaeuser Co., Tacoma, 1949—, successively mill foreman, br. mgr., 1949-56, v.p., 1957-66, exec. v.p., 1966-88, pres., chief exec. officer, 1988, chmn. bd., chief exec. officer, 1988-91, chmn. bd., past CEO, also bd. dirs.; bd. dirs. Boeing Co., SAFECO Corp., Chevron Corp.; mem. Bus. Coun., Bus. Roundtable, Wash. State Bus. Roundtable. Office: Weyerhaeuser Fin Svcs CH 5B Tacoma WA 98477-0001*

WEYGAND, LEROY CHARLES, service executive; b. Webster Park, Ill., May 17, 1926; s. Xaver William and Marie Caroline (Hoffert) W.; BA in Sociology cum laude, U. Md., 1964; m. Helen V. Bishop, Aug. 28, 1977; children: Linda M. Weygand Vance (dec.), Leroy Charles, Cynthia R., Janine P. Enlisted in U.S. Army, 1944, commd. 2d lt., 1950, advanced through grades to lt. col., 1966; service in Korea, 1950; chief phys. security U.S. Army, 1965-70; ret., 1970; pres. Weygand Security Cons. Srvcs., Anaheim, Calif., 1970—, W & W Devel. Corp., 1979—; security dir. Jefferies Banknote Co., 1972-78; pres. Kern County Taxpayers Assn., 1986—; dir. Mind Psi-Biotics, Inc. Bd. dirs. Nat. Assn. Control Narcotics and Dangerous Drugs. Decorated Legion of Merit. Mem. Am. Soc. Indsl. Security. Contbr. articles profl. jours. Patentee office equipment locking device. Home: 12110 Backdrop Ct Bakersfield CA 93306-9707 Office: Kern County Taxpayers Assn 1415 18th St Ste 407 Bakersfield CA 93301-4442

WEYL, NATHANIEL, writer; b. N.Y.C., July 20, 1910; s. Walter Edward and Bertha Nevin (Poole) W.; m. Sylvia Castleton, Mar. 15, 1935 (dec. Nov. 1987); children: Walter Castleton, Jonathan Vanderpoel; m. Marcelle Cowan, Dec. 3, 1988. BS, Columbia Coll., 1931; postgrad., London Sch. Econs., 1931-32, Columbia U., 1932-33. Economist Agrl. Adjustment Adminstrn., Washington, 1933-35, Fed. Res. Bd., Washington, 1940-41, Bd. Econ. Welfare, Washington, 1941-43, Dept. Commerce, Washington, 1945-47; reporter N.Y. Post, N.Y.C., 1937-38; pres. Internat. Found. Gifted Children, Boca Raton, Fla., 1964-75. Author: Red Star Over Cuba, 1960;, The Geography of American Achievement, 1989, (poetry) Sarpedon, 1993. Program dir. Unitarian Ch. of Ojai, Calif., 1995—. With U.S. Army, 1943-45, ETO. Decorated Bronze Star. Mem. Am. Mensa (vice chmn. 1967-69), Phi Beta Kappa. Home and Office: 1402 White Oak Cir Ojai CA 93023

WEYMAN, STEVEN ALOYSIUS, military officer; b. Fort Thomas, Ky., May 31, 1957; s. Edward Joseph Weyman and Carol Jean (Steffen) Jackson; m. Kathleen Anne Bradford, June 2, 1990; 1 child, Jennifer Elizabeth. BS, No. Ky. U., 1978; MS, Naval Postgrad. Sch., 1988. Commd. 2d lt. U.S. Army, 1978, advanced through grades to lt. col., 1995; bn. signal officer 8th Engr. Bn., 1st Cav. Divsn., Ft. Hood, Tex., 1979-81, 2nd M.I. Bn., Pirmasens, Germany, 1982-85; co. comdr. B Co., 307th M.I. Bn., Ludwigsburg, Germany, 1985-86; signal combat devel. project officer Combined Arms Command, Ft. Leavenworth, Kans., 1988-91; bn. exec. officer 123rd Signal Bn., 3rd Inf. Divsn., Kitzingen, Germany, 1992-94; asst. divsn. signal officer 3rd Inf. Divsn., Wuerzburg, Germany, 1994-95; operational readiness evaluation team chief 5th U.S. Army (West), Ft. Lewis, Wash., 1995—. Mem. U.S. Signal Corps Assn. (Bronze Order of Mercury 1995), Armed Forces Comm. Electronics Assn. Home: 717 Shannon St Steilacoom WA 98388-3607

WHALEN, CATHRYN ANN, reading specialist; b. Catskill, N.Y., Dec. 7, 1946; d. Kenneth Edward and Hazel Florence (Reynolds) Jones; m. Richard Thomas Whalen, Mar. 9, 1968; children: Jennifer Maureen, Timothy Thomas, Allison Elizabeth. BS, SUNY, Oswego, 1968; MA, U. Colo., Denver, 1988. Cert. tchr. elem. edn. and reading, Colo. Tchr. multiply handicaped BOCES, Fairport, N.Y., 1970-71, 74-79, 80-81; Title I tchr. Littleton (Colo.) Schs., 1984-86; tchr. reading/6th grade Cherry Creek Schs., Englewood, Colo., 1986—. Religious edn. tchr. St. Thomas More Ch., Englewood, 1985-86, 90-91. Mem. ASCD, Internat. Reading Assn. (presenter Colo. Coun.). Democrat. Roman Catholic. Home: 8248 S Albion St Littleton CO 80122

WHALEN, MARGARET CAVANAGH, retired secondary school educator; b. Des Moines, Iowa, Mar. 9, 1913; d. Thomas J. and Ann Lenore (Paul) Cavanagh; m. George Hubert Whalen, Aug. 3, 1946; children: Michael T., Ann Whalen Carrillo, George Patrick (dec.), Cheryl. BS in Commerce, St. Teresa Coll., Winona, Minn., 1935. Head bus. dept. St. Augustine High Sch., Austin, Minn., 1935-36, Parochial High Sch., Caledonia, Minn., 1936-37; clk., typist U.S. Govt., Dept. Socicl Security, Des Moines, 1937-38; county investigator for old age asst., aid to blind Marion County, Knoxville, Iowa, 1938; hydro dept. U.S. Weather Bur. Regional Office, Iowa City, Kansas City, Mo., 1939-42; head bills/warrants dept. IRS, Des Moines, 1942-46; substitute tchr. Los Gatos High Sch., Calif., 1961-65, Saratoga High Sch., Calif., 1961-65. Vol. Girl Scouts U.S.A., Boy Scouts Am., Saratoga, Calif., 1957-62; poll insp. Santa Clara County Regional Voters, Saratoga; precinct insp. Saratoga for Santa Clara County Registrar of Voters; organizer, vol. Saratoga Area Sr. Coord. Coun., 1979—; Eucharistic minister, lector, commentator Sacred Heart Ch., Saratoga, 1986—; charter pres. Oz chpt. Children's Home Soc. Calif., Saratoga; mem. Sacred Heart Women's Club, Our Lady of Los Gatos # 197 Young Ladies Inst. Recipient Papal Bronze medal for Pub. Rels. Nat. Coun. Cath. Women, Saratoga, 1958, Merit award Friends of Saratoga Librs., 1975—, Merit award Saratoga Area Sr. Coord. Coun., 1981. Mem. AAUW (corr. sec. Los Gatos-Saratoga br., chmn. social arts, bridge, hospitality, Friday Matinee sect., book rev. sect.), Saratoga Hist. Found., Alumnae Assn. St. Theresa Coll., Montalvo Assn., Saratoga Foothill Club. Democrat. Roman Catholic. Home: 14140 Victor Pl Saratoga CA 95070-5425

WHALEY, JAMES C., architect; b. Missoula, Mont., Mar. 23, 1953; s. Matthew L. and Eloise M. (Reichenberger) W.; m. Janet Marie Brooke, Aug. 12, 1982; children: Christopher Marvin, Justin Ignatius Mathew, Basil James. BArch, Mont. State U., 1976. Registered arch., Mont. Chief Design and Constrn. Bur. Mont. Architecture and Engring. Divsn., Helena; panel mem. AAA, Salt Lake City, 1973; mem. ICBO, Whittier, Calif., 1992. mem. Helena Bd. Adjustments, 1987—; ADA coord. City of Helena, 1992-95; active Nat. Ski Patrol, 1984—. Recipient Environ. Excellence award EPA,, Helena, 1976. Mem. AIA, Archtl. Soc. Helena (pres. 1991-93). Office: Architecture and Engring Divsn 1520 E 6th Ave Helena MT 59620

WHALEY, ROBERT HAMILTON, judge; m. Lucinda schilling; 1 child. BA, Princeton U., 1965; JD, Emory U., 1968. Litigator land and natural resources divsn. Dept. Justice, 1969-71; asst. U.S. atty. U.S. Dist. Wash. (ea. dist.), 1971-72; assoc. Winston & Cashatt, Spokane, Wash., 1972-76; ptnr. Winston & Cashatt, 1976—; judge Spokane County Superior Ct., 1992-95, U.S. Dist. Ct., Spokane, 1995—. Office: US Dist Ct Wash PO Box 283 920 Riverside Ave W 7th Fl Spokane WA 99210

WHALIN, W. TERRY, author, editor; b. Huntington, W.Va., Aug. 12, 1953; s. Wallace Eugene and Rose Terry (Estill) W.; children: Jonathan David, Timothy Benjamin; m. Christine Elizabeth Johnson, May 3, 1995. BA, Ind. U., 1975; cert., Multnomah Sch. of Bible, 1977; MA, U. Tex., Arlington, 1984. Linguist Wycliffe Bible Translators, Huntington Beach, Calif., 1975-85, mng. editor In Other Words, 1985-93; assoc. editor Decision mag. Billy Graham Evangelistic Assn., Mpls., 1993-94; CEO, pres. Whalin & Assocs., Colorado Springs, Colo., 1994—. Author: When I Grow Up, 1992, Never Too Busy, 1993, A Strange Place to Sing, 1994, Chuck Colson, 1994, Today's Heroes Series, 1994, The Brave But Gentle Shepherd, 1996, Samuel Morris, Heroes of the Faith series, 1997, Sojourner Truth Heroes of the Faith Series, 1997, Luis Palau, Men of Faith Series, 1996, Billy Sunday, 1996, John Perkins, 1996, Today's Heroes Series, 1996, co-author: One Bright Shining Path, 1993, Ayachcho Para Cristo, 1995, Bottom-Line Faith, Ten Characteristics of Committed Christians, 1995, Let the Walls Fall Down, 1996, The World at Your Door, 1997, Seven Paths to Purity, 1997; ghostwriter books: Men Seeking Christ, 1994, Freedom From Addiction, 1996; contbr. articles to profl. publs. and mags. Treas. Evangelical Press Assn., Earlysville, Va., 1992-94. Mem. Evangelical Press Assn., Am. Soc. Journalists and Authors, Soc. Children's Book Writers and Illustrators. Republican. Office: #C-368 445 E Cheyenne Mtn Blvd Colorado Springs CO 80906-4570

WHARTON, HUGH DAVIS, III, lawyer, judge; b. Buffalo, June 1, 1940; s. Hugh Davis and Helen Bricka (McAuliffe) W.; m. Patricia Granville Ditton, June 20, 1964 (div. Apr. 1982); children: Jennifer Wharton, Gregory Paul, Michael David. BA, Princeton U., 1961; JD, Yale U., 1964. Bar: Alaska 1965, Colo. 1965, Calif. 1969. Asst. atty. gen. State of Alaska, Juneau, 1964-65; chief law clk. to Judge Doyle, U.S. Dist. Ct., Denver, 1965-66; field rep. U.S. OEO, Office of Pres., Kansas City, Mo., 1966-67; field rep. U.S. OEO, Office of Pres., San Francisco, 1967-69, dep. regional atty. Western region, 1969-71, regional atty., 1971-73; city atty. City of Livermore, Calif., 1973-74; regional atty. Western region U.S. Dept. Energy, San Francisco, 1974-80; pvt. practice, San Francisco, 1980—; adminstrv. law judge City and County of San Francisco, 1984—. Pres. Golden Gate Bus. Assn., San Francisco, 1989-92; mem. bd. dirs. United Way of the Bay Area, 1989—; candidate for supr. City and County of San Francisco, 1982, 84, candidate for muni judge, 1988; mem. vol. bd. dirs. San Francisco Gen. Hosp., 1983-88; pres. Diamond Hts. Cmty. Assn., San Francisco, 1987-90. Recipient John W. Gardner Disting. Leadership award United Way, 1992. Mem. State Bar of Calif., Bay Area Lawyers for Individual Freedom. Democrat. Episcopalian.

WHARTON, THOMAS WILLIAM, mining executive; b. St. Louis, Nov. 20, 1943; s. Thomas William and Elaine Margaret (Bassett) w.; divorced; children: Thomas William, Christopher John. BSc in Econs., U. Mo., 1967; M in Health Adminstrn., U. Ottawa, Ont., Can., 1978. Asst. to exec. dir. Ottawa Civic Hosp., 1978-80; exec. dir. Caribou Meml. Hosp., Williams Lake, B.C., Can., 1980-83; dir. clinic and rehab. services Workers' Compensation Bd., Vancouver, B.C., 1983-89; dir. Conquistador Gold Mines, Vancouver, 1989—; pres. Diagnostic and Health Cons., Vancouver, 1989—; dir. Citrine Holdings, Ltd., Vancouver, B.C., Can., 1994—; bd. dirs. Corona Goldfields, Inc., Vancouver, USV Telemanagement, Inc., Vancouver, Leopardus Resources, Inc., Vancouver. Recipient Founder award Cariboo Musical Soc., 1983; named Lord of the Manors of Wharton and Kirkby Stephen (Eng.), 1991.

WHATCOTT, MARSHA RASMUSSEN, elementary education educator; b. Fillmore, Utah, Mar. 29, 1941; d. William Hans and Evangelyn (Robison) Rasmussen; m. Robert LaGrand Whatcott, Sept. 14, 1961; children: Sherry, Cindy, Jay Robert, Justin William. Assoc., So. Utah State U., 1962; BS, Brigham Young U., 1968. Cert. tchr. early childhood, Utah. Tchr. 1st grade Provost Elem. Sch., Provo, Utah, 1968-84, kindergarten tchr., 1984-91, tchr. 3d grade, 1991—; music specialist Provost Elem., 1984-87, 91-92, 93-94, art specialist, 1984-85, math. specialist, 1988-89, sci. specialist, 1994-95, 96, 97; del. Utah Edn. Assn., 1989-90; bldg. rep. Provo Edn. Assn., 1993-94, 94-95. Mem. polit. action com. Provo Sch. Dist., 1982, 90, mem. profl. devel. com. Bonniville Uniserve (Provo, Alpine and Nebo Sch. Dist.), 1994-95. Recipient Millard County Utah PTA scholarship, 1959-62, Golden Apple award Provo City PTA, 1984, Recognition Disting. Svc. in Edn. award Utah State Legis., 1992; named Outstanding Educator in Utah Legis. Dist. # 64, 1992. Mem. Utah Edn. Assn. (del. 1989-90), Provo Edn. Assn. (bldg. rep. 1993-94, 94-95), Bonneville Uniserve (profl. devel. com.). Mem. LDS Ch. Office: Provost Elem Sch 629 S 1000 E Provo UT 84606-5204

WHEATLEY, MELVIN ERNEST, JR., retired bishop; b. Lewisville, Pa., May 7, 1915; s. Melvin Ernest and Gertrude Elizabeth (Mitchell) W.; m. Lucile Elizabeth Maris, June 15, 1939; children: Paul Melvin, James Maris, John Sherwood. AB magna cum laude, Am. U., 1936, DD, 1958; BD summa cum laude, Drew U., 1939; DD, U. of Pacific, 1948. Ordained to ministry Meth. Ch., 1939. Pastor area Meth. ch., Lincoln, Del., 1939-41; assoc. pastor First Meth. Ch., Fresno, Calif., 1941-43; pastor Centenary Meth. Ch., Modesto, Calif., 1943-46, Cen. Meth. Ch., Stockton, Calif., 1946-54, Westwood Meth. Ch., L.A., 1954-72; bishop Denver Area, 1972-84, ret., 1984; instr. philosophy Modesto Jr. Coll., 1944; summer session instr. Hebrew-Christian heritage U. of Pacific; instr. Homiletics U. So. Calif., So. Calif. Sch. Theology, Clarement; lectr. St. Luke's Lectures, Houston, 1966; mem. Bd. of Ch. and Soc., Commn. on Status and Role of Women, United Meth. Ch., 1976-84; condr. European Christian Heritage tour, 1961, Alaska and Hawaii Missions, 1952, 54. Author: Going His Way, 1957, Our Man and the Church, 1968, The Power of Worship, 1970, Family Ministries Manual, 1970, Christmas Is for Celebrating, 1977; contbr. articles to profl. jours. Chmn. Community Rels. Conf. So. Calif., 1966-69; pres. So. Calif.-Ariz. Conf. Bd. Edn., 1960-68; hon. trustee Iliff Sch. Theology; hon. dir., active mem. Parents and Friends of Lesbians and Gays, 1980—. Recipient Disting. Alumnus award Am. U., 1979, Ball award Meth. Fedn. Social Action, 1984, Prophetic Leadership award The Consultation on Homosexuality, Tolerance and Roman Cath. Theology, 1985, Human Rights award Universal Fellowship of Met. Community Congregations, 1985. Home: 859A Ronda Mendoza Laguna Hills CA 92653-5940

WHEATON, ALICE ALSHULER, secretary; b. Burbank, Calif., Mar. 20, 1920; d. Elmore and Anzy Jeanette (Richards) Wheaton; m. Robert Edward Alshuler, Sept. 19, 1942 (div. 1972); children: John Robert, Katherine Dennis. BA in Edn., UCLA, 1942. Cert. profl. sec. Owner, dir. The Fitness Studio, Washington, 1974-85; staff asst. Pres. Coun. Phys. Fitness and Sports, Washington, 1980-89; coord. Fed. Inter Agy. Health Fitness Coun., Washington, 1986-89; expert advisor U.S. Office Pers. Mgmt., Washington, 1986-89; sec. Pala Mesa Village Homes Assn., 1994-96; cons. Pres. Coun. Phys. Fitness and Sports. Editor: The Federal FitKit-Guidelines for Federal Agencies, 1988. Recipient Gold Key award L.A. Area United Way, 1966. Mem. Profl. Secs. Internat. (pres. Palomar chpt. 1993-95), UCLA Gold Shield Hon. (pres.), UCLA Alumni Assn. (v.p., Disting. Com. Svc. award 1968), San Diego Hist. Soc., North County Kappa Kappa Gamma Alumnae Assn. (pres. 1995—). Republican. Episcopalian.

WHEELAND, DALE N., physician; b. Tucson, Mar. 17, 1953; s. George P. and Buelah M. (Mitchell) W.; m. Christine Ridenour, July 4, 1981; children: Katherine Janelle, Elyse Nicole. BS cum laude, U. Ariz., 1975, MS, 1979; DO, Kirksville Coll. Osteo., 1983. Physician pvt. practice, Tucson, 1984—. Office: Foothills Family Practice 1601 W Ina Rd Tucson AZ 85704-1977

WHEELER, CARL COVERT, mathematics educator; b. Geneva, N.Y., Sept. 7, 1932. AB, Hamilton Coll., 1953; MA in Liberal Studies, Wesleyan U., 1970. Tchr., adminstr. Mid-Pacific Inst., Honolulu, 1956-58, 61-85, chair maths. dept., tchr., 1987—; admissions officer Hamilton Coll., Clinton, N.Y., 1958-61; tchr. Punahou Sch., Honolulu, 1985-87; mem. Math. Edn. Leadership Network, Washington, 1990—; tchg. fellow Ctr. for Excellence in Edn., San Diego, 1990; cons. Coll. Bd., Ednl. Testing Svcs. With U.S. Army, 1954-56. Woodrow Wilson Found. fellow, 1985; grantee NSF; Tandy Tech. scholar, 1991; recipient Presdl. award, 1990. Mem. Nat. Coun. Tchrs. Math. (v.p. 1986-88), Oahu Maths. League (pres. 1990-93), Nat. Coun. Suprs. Math., Math. Assn. Am., Hawaii State Math. Coalition, Coun. Presdl. Awardees in Math. Office: Mid Pacific Inst 2445 Kaala St Honolulu HI 96822-2204

WHEELER, GERALDINE HARTSHORN, historian; b. Pomona, Calif., Feb. 5, 1919; d. Albion True and Beatrice Osa (Barnes) Hartshorn; m. Lloyd Franklyn Wheeler, Dec. 2, 1938 (dec. Mar. 1996); children: Russell Lloyd, Robert Gerald. AA, Santa Barbara (Calif.) C.C., 1950's. Co-owner Atheling's, Santa Barbara, Calif., 1971-76, Pomona, 1976-90; chmn. bd. trustees Atheling Heritage Trust, Claremont, Calif., 1994—. Pub., editor (mag.) Atheling's, 1974-75; pub. editor (newsletter) Grand Priory of America Order of St. Lazarus, 1974-86; editor, founder St. Margaret's Jour., 1975—. Vol. PTA, Fontana and Santa Barbara, 1945-60; active Hist. Soc. Pomona Valley, 1950—; mem. various coms. and choir First Congl. Ch., Santa Barbara, 1952-72; leader Cub Scouts Am., Santa Barbara, 1953-56; grey lady unit chmn. Santa Barbara chpt.-ARC, 1958-62; women's project bd. v.p., activities chmn., active various coms. Santa Barbara Hist. Soc., 1960-74; exec. sec. 1960 Nixon for Pres. Campaign, Santa Barbara, 1960; mem. spkrs. bur. Nixon for Gov. Campaign, Santa Barbara, 1962; mem. Rep. state ctrl. com. State of Calif., 1962-64; blitz chmn. Rockefeller for Pres. Campaign, Santa Barbara, 1964; coord. vol. svcs. Office of Civil Def., City of Santa Barbara, 1965-76; coord. tv series on earthquakes Sta. KEYT, Office of Civil Def., Santa Barbara, 1968; bd. dirs. Calif. Ctrl. Coast Area, U.S.O., 1968-76, treas. bd., 1970-76; active Friends of the Claremont Pub. Libr., 1996—; supporter Vis. Nurses and Hospice Assn., 1994—; others. Recipient Cert. of Merit, Santa Barbara Jr. Coll., 1954-55. Mem. Nat. Soc. DAR (Mission Canyon chpt. regent 1967-69, state chmn. schs. 1970-72, Claremont chpt. regent 1987-89), Nat. Soc. Daus. of Founders and Patriots of Am. (life, Calif. state registrar 1972-74, Calif. state v.p. 1974-76, So. Calif. chpt. pres. 1975-78, nat. councillor 1987-90, Cert. of Award 1977), Huguenot Soc. Calif. (state chaplain 1970-78, state v.p. 1978-82, La Rochelle chpt. pres. 1982-83), Soc. Mayflower Descs. in the State Calif., Soc. State Gov.'s Commendation award 1992), Women Descs. of the Ancient and Honorable Artillery Co.-Calif. Ct. (life, nat. soc. bylaws chmn. 1988, nat. chaplain 1989-92), Hereditary Order of Descs. of Colonial Govs. (life, dep. gov. gen. 1973-79), The Colonial Dames Am. (2nd v.p. chpt. V, 1978-82, aux. chmn. L.A., Pasadena, 1978-82, founder L.A., Pasadena chpt. XX, 1982, pres, 1988-91), Daus. of Colonial Wars in Calif. Soc. (Calif. state registrar, 1972-74), Nat. Soc. Magna Charta Dames (life, regent So. Calif. divsn., 1972-79), Soc. Descs. of the Most Noble Order of the Garter (life), Sovereign Colonial Soc. Ams. Royal Descent (life), Plantagenet Soc. (life), Colonial Order of the Crown (life), Calif. Soc. Dames of the Court of Honor, Guild of St. Margaret of Scotland (founder, serene grand dame life, 1975—), Nat. Soc. New Eng. Women, Nat. Soc. Descs. of Early Quakers (founding nat. clerk life, 1980—), Order of Ams. of Armorial Ancestry (life), Associated Daus. of Early Am. Witches (life, treas. gen., 1987-89), Order of the Crown of Charlemagne in the U.S. Am. (life), Nat. Soc. Ams. of Royal Descent (life), Nat. Gavel Soc. (life), Pomona Ebell, Shakespeare Club Pomona Valley (com. treas., 1980—), Mil. and Hospitaller Order of St. Lazarus of Jerusalem (officer companion 1971, commander, 1977, dame of grace, 1979). Republican. Home: 1047 E Baseline Rd Claremont CA 91711-1577

WHEELER, HELEN RIPPIER, writer, educator, consultant. BA, Barnard Coll., 1950; MS, Columbia U., 1951; MA, U. Chgo., 1954; PhD, Columbia U., 1964. Media adminstr. Chgo. City Colls., 1958-62; Latin Am. coord. Columbia U. Librs., N.Y.C., 1962-64; assoc. prof. La. State U., Baton Rouge, 1971-73; cons. Womanhood Media, Berkeley, Calif., 1973—; vis. lectr. U. Calif., Berkeley, 1978-87; cons. U. Hawaii Community Coll. System. Author: Womanhood Media, 1972, The Bibliographic Instruction Course Handbook, 1988, Getting Published in Women's Studies, 1989, Women & Aging: A Guide to Literature, 1997; contbr. chpts. to books, articles to profl. jours, scripting for instructional media. Presdl. appointee Comm. on Status of Women, Internat. Rels. Com.; subcom. mem. Sexist Subject-Heads; caucus mem. Nat. Women's Studies Assn.; mem. City of Berkeley Commn. on Aging. Mem. ALA, NOW (chpt. founder), Josei to Toshokan No Tameno Network, Women's Inst. for Freedom of Press. Democrat. Address: 1909 Cedar St # 303 Berkeley CA 94709-2036

WHEELER, LARRY RICHARD, accountant; b. Greybull, Wyo., Nov. 30, 1940; s. Richard F. and Olive B. (Fredrickson) W.; m. Marjorie A. Frady, Dec. 20, 1961; m. Patricia C. Marturano, Dec. 3, 1977; children: Anthony, Richard, Teresa, Kara. BS, U. Wyo., 1965. CPA, Colo. Staff acct. H. Greger CPA, Ft. Collins, Colo., 1965-66, sr. acct. Lester Draney & Wickham, Colorado Springs, Colo., 1966-67; acct., controller/treas., J.D. Adams Co., Colorado Springs, 1967-74; ptnr. Wheeler Pierce & Hurd, Inc., Colorado Springs, 1974-80; gen. mgr., v.p. Schneebeck's, Inc., Colorado Springs, 1980-81; prin. L.R. Wheeler & Co., P.C., Colorado Springs, 1981-94; pres. Wheeler & Gilmartin Assocs., P.C., Colorado Springs, 1994—, L.R. Wheeler & Co., P.C., 1995; dir. Schneebeck's Industries, Williams Printing,

Inc., Pathfinder Tech., Inc. Mem. U.S. Taekwondo Union; bd. dirs. Domestic Violence Prevention Ctr. Paul Stock Found. grantee, 1962. Mem. Nat. Assn. Cert. Valuation Analysts, Am. Inst. CPA's, Colo. Soc. CPA's (map. com.), Colo. Litigation Support Group. Office: 317 E San Rafael St Colorado Springs CO 80903-2405 *Personal philosophy: Success comes from good judgment good judgment comes from experience experience comes from bad judgment.*

WHEELER, MALCOLM EDWARD, lawyer, law educator; b. Berkeley, Calif., Nov. 29, 1944; s. Malcolm Ross and Frances Dolores (Kane) W.; m. Donna Marie Stambaugh, July 21, 1981; children: Jessica Ross, M. Connor. SB, MIT, 1966; JD, Stanford U., 1969. Bar: Calif. 1970, Colo. 1992, U.S. Dist. Ct (cen. dist.) Calif. 1970, U.S. Ct. Appeals (9th cir.) 1970, U.S. Ct. Appeals (10th cir.) 1973, U.S. Dist. Ct. (no., so., ea. and cen. dists.) Calif. 1975, U.S. Ct. Appeals (11th cir.) 1987, U.S. Ct. Appeals (D.C. cir.) 1987, U.S. Supreme Ct. 1976, U.S. Ct. Appeals (3d cir.) 1989, (4th cir.) 1992. Assoc. Howard, Prim, Smith, Rice & Downs, San Francisco, 1969-71; assoc. prof. law U. Kans., Lawrence, 1971-74; assoc. Hughes Hubbard & Reed, Los Angeles, 1974-77, ptnr., 1977-81, 83-85, cons., 1981-83; ptnr. Skadden, Arps, Slate, Meagher & Flom, Los Angeles, 1985-91; dir. Parcel, Mauro, Hultin & Spaanstra P.C., Denver, 1991—; vis. prof. U. Iowa, 1978, prof., 1979; prof. U. Kans., Lawrence, 1981-83; chief counsel U.S. Senate Select Com. to Study Law Enforcement Undercover Activities, Washington, 1982-83. Mem. editorial bd. Jour. Products Liability, 1984—; bd. editors Fed. Litigation Guide Reporter, 1986—; contbr. articles to profl. jours. Mem. ABA, Calif. Bar Assn., Colo. Bar Assn., Am. Law Inst. Office: Parcel Mauro Hultin & Spaanstra PC 1801 California St Denver CO 80202-2658

WHEELER, RALPH (MOON), state senator, pharmacist; b. American Falls, Idaho, Aug. 10, 1932; s. Ralph Merrill and Monne Mary (Zemo) W.; m. Patricia J. Howard (dec.); children: Vickie D., Michael M., Jodi L.; m. Ann F. Reed, June 19, 1965; children: Clark R., Ryan M. BS, Idaho State U., 1954. Registered pharmacist. Owner Rockland Pharmacy, 1960-88, part-time staff, 1988—; pres. Assn. Idaho Cities, Boise, 1971-72, Idaho State Pharmaceutical Assn., 1979-80. Pres. Lion's Club, American Falls, 1962; rep. State Legis. Boise, Idaho, 1972-76; county commr. Power County, American Falls, 1982-94; senator State of Idaho, 1994—, vice chair health & welfare com. Named Pharmacist of Yr., Idaho Pharmaceutical Assn., 1972. Republican. Roman Catholic. Home: 659 Gifford Ave American Falls ID 83211-1315

WHEELER, ROBERT ROSS, medical director; b. Milw., Sept. 12, 1949; s. Ross W. and Mary Lou Wheeler. AB with honors, U. Calif., Berkeley, 1972; MD, U. Calif., San Francisco, 1976. Resident U. Calif., San Francisco, 1979; physician internal medicine pvt. practice, Cottage Grove, Oreg., 1981-92; med. dir. Lane Individual Practice Assn., Eugene, Oreg., 1992—. Author: (software) OHP Linefinder, 1994. Med. advisor Ambulence Svc., Cottage Grove, 1983-92. Mem. AAAS, Am. Coll. Physician Execs., Am. Coll. Physicians, Internat. Soc. Tech. Assessment, Soc. Med. Decisionmaking, Phi Beta Kappa. Office: Lane Individual Practice Assn 1200 Executive Pkwy Ste 200 Eugene OR 97401-2191

WHEELER, STEVEN M., lawyer; b. Evanston, Ill., Jan. 5, 1949. AB, Pricneton U., 1971; JD with distinction, Cornell U., 1974. Bar: Ariz. 1974. Mem. Snell & Wilmer, Phoenix. Mng. editor Cornell Law Review, 1973-74; contbr. articles to profl. jours. Mem. ABA, Order Coif, Phi Kappa Phi. Office: Snell & Wilmer 1 Arizona Ctr Phoenix AZ 85004-0001

WHEELON, ALBERT DEWELL, physicist; b. Moline, Ill., Jan. 18, 1929; s. Orville Albert and Alice Geltz (Dewell) W.; m. Nancy Helen Hermanson, Feb. 28, 1953 (dec. May 1980); children—Elizabeth Anne, Cynthia Helen; m. Cicely J. Evans, Feb. 4, 1984. B.Sc., Stanford U., 1949; Ph.D., Mass. Inst. Tech., 1952. Teaching fellow, then rsch. assoc. physics MIT, Boston, 1949-52; with Douglas Aircraft Co., 1952-53, Ramo-Wooldridge Corp., 1953-62; dep. dir. sci. and tech. CIA, Washington, 1962-66; with Hughes Aircraft Co., L.A., 1966-88, chmn., chief exec. officer, 1987-88; vis. prof. MIT, 1989; mem. Def. Sci. Bd., 1968-76; mem. Pres.'s Fgn. Intelligence, 1983-88; mem. Presdl. Commn. on Space Shuttle Challenger Accident, 1986; trustee Aerospace Corp., 1990-93, Calif. Inst. Tech., Rand Corp. Author 30 papers on radiowave propagation and guidance systems. Recipient R.V. Jones Intelligence award, 1994. Fellow IEEE, AIAA (Von Karman medal 1986, Goddard Astronautics award 1997); mem. NAE, Am. Phys. Soc., Sigma Chi. Republican. Episcopalian. Address: 181 Sheffield Dr Montecito CA 93108-2242

WHELCHEL, SANDRA JANE, writer; b. Denver, May 31, 1944; d. Ralph Earl and Janette Isabelle (March) Everitt; m. Andrew Jackson Whelchel, June 27, 1965; children: Andrew Jackson, Anita Earlyn. BA in Elem. Edn., U. No. Colo., 1966; postgrad. Pepperdine Coll., 1971, UCLA, 1971. Elem. tchr. Douglas County Schs., Castle Rock, Colo., 1966-68, El Monte (Calif.) schs., 1968-72; br. librarian Douglas County Libraries, Parker, Colo., 1973-78; zone writer Denver Post, 1979-81; reporter The Express newspapers, Castle Rock, 1979-81; history columnist Parker Trail newspapers, 1985-93; columnist Gothic Jour. 1994; writing tchr. Aurora Parks and Recreation, 1985-91; writing instr. Arapahoe C.C., 1991—; exec. dir. Nat. Writers Assn., 1991—, literary agt., 1996—; editor Authorship mag., 1992—; lit. agent NWLA 1996—; contbr. short stories and articles to various publs. including: Genre Sampler, Writer's World, Writer's Open Forum, Writer's Jour., Reunions, Fresno Bee, Ancestry Newsletter, Empire mag., Calif. Horse Rev., Host mag., Jack and Jill, Child Life, Children's Digest, Peak to Peak mag.; author (non-fiction books): Your Air Force Academy, 1982, A Guide to the U.S. Air Force Acad., 1990, Parker, Colorado: A Folk History, 1990, The Beginning Writer's Writing Book, 1996, A Folk History of Parker and Hilltop, 1996; (coloring books): A Day at the Cave, 1985, A Day in Blue, 1984, Pro Rodeo Hall of Champions and Museum of the American Cowboy, 1985, Pikes Peak Country, 1986, Mile High Denver, 1987; co-author: The Register, 1989; lectr. on writing and history. Mem. Colo. Author's League, Nat. Writers Club (treas. Denver Metro chpt. 1985-86,, v.p. membership 1987, sec. 1990, bd. dirs. 1990-91, pres. 1990-91, v.p. programs 1992), Parker Area Hist. Soc. (pres. 1987, 88, 89). *Personal philosophy: Tenacity and perseverance are keys to success. Optimism and self-belief open the door. The goals achieved through these elements are the most thrilling and savory.*

WHIDDEN, MARY BESS, English language educator; b. San Angelo, Tex., Aug. 14, 1936; d. James Edgar and Bess (Mullican) W. BA, U. Tex., 1957, PhD, 1965; MA, U. N.C., 1959. Rsch. assoc. U. Tex., Austin, 1956-58, spl. instr., 1962-63; asst. prof. English, U. N.Mex., Albuquerque, 1963-71, assoc. prof., 1971-95, prof., 1995—; bd. dirs. N.Mex. Endowment for Humanities, Albuquerque, 1987-93. Author: Provincial Matters, 1985; co-editor: Staging Howells, 1994; contbr. essays to various publs. Recipient Disting. Svc. award N.Mex. Endowment for Humanities, 1993; Woodrow Wilson fellow, 1958-59, 61, Univ. fellow U. Tex., 1960-61. Mem. MLA, NAACP. Democrat. Home: 421 Richmond Dr SE Albuquerque NM 87106-2241 Office: U NMex Dept English Humanities Bldg Albuquerque NM 87131

WHIDDON, CAROL PRICE, writer, editor, consultant; b. Gadsden, Ala., Nov. 18, 1947; d. Curtis Ray and Vivian (Dooly) Price; m. John Earl Caulking, Jan. 18, 1969 (div. July 1987); m. Ronald Alton Whiddon, Apr. 13, 1988. Student, McNeese State U., 1966-68; BA in English, George Mason U., 1984. Flute instr. Lake Charles, La., 1966-68; flutist Lake Charles Civic Symphony, 1966-69, Beaumont (Tex.) Symphony, 1967-68; freelance editor The Washington Lit. Rev., 1983-84, ARC Hdqrs., Washington, 1984; writer, editor Jaycor, Vienna, Va., 1985-87; writer, editor Jaycor, Albuquerque, 1987-90, publs. mgr., 1990-91; writer, editor Proteus Corp., Albuquerque, 1991-92; owner Whiddon Editorial Svcs., Albuquerque, 1989—; mem. S.W. Writer's Workshop, 1991—. Co-author: The Spirit That Wants Me: A New Mexico Anthology, 1991; contbr. various articles to Albuquerque Woman and mil. dependent pubs. in Fed. Rpublic Germany. Bd. dirs. Channel 27-Pub. Access TV, 1991-93, exec. bd. sec., 1992, v.p., 1993; dep. mgr. Fed. Women's Program, Ansbach, Fed. Republic Germany, 1980-81; pres. Ansbach German-Am. Club, 1980-82; sec. Am. Women's Activities, Fed. Republic Germany, 1980-81, chairwoman, 1981-82. Recipient cert. of appreciation from Am. amb. to Germany Arthur T. Burns, 1982, medal of appreciation from comdr. 1st Armored Div., Ansbach, Germany, 1982. Mem. NAFE, Women in Comm. (newsletter editor 1989-90, 91-92, 94-95, v.p. 1990-91, pres.-elect 1992-93, pres. 1993-94, chair programs com. Nat. Profl. Conf. 1994, sr. mem. 1994), Soc. Tech. Comm. (membership dir. 1993-94), Nat. Assn. Desktop Pubs., Am. Mktg. Assn., Greater Albuquerque C. of C., N.Mex. Cactus Soc. (historian 1989-94, sec. 1991, newsletter editor 1992—, various show ribbons 1989-91). Republican. Home: 1129 Turner Dr NE Albuquerque NM 87123-1917

WHIMBEY, ARTHUR EMIL, writer; b. New York, Sept. 18, 1940. BA in Psychology, U. Miami, 1961; PhD, Purdue U., 1964. Asst. prof. psychology U. Ill., Urbana, 1965-67; from asst. to assoc. prof. psychology Calif. State U., Hayward, 1967-71; sr. postdoctoral fellow NIMH Inst. Human Learning, Berkeley, Calif., 1971-72; assoc. prof. psychology Dillard U., 1974-75; dir. rsch. CUE project Bowling Green State U., 1976-77, coord. math. and comm. labs. devel. edn. program, 1977-78; acad. support specialist Bethune-Cookman Coll., 1983; reading specialist Miami-Dade Pub. Schs., 1988; adj. prof. math. CCNY, fall, 1978; vis. prof. math. dept. Xavier U., spring, 1979; cons. Ventures in Edn., Coll. Bd., N.J. State Dept. Edn.; assoc. editor On TRAC Text Reconstrn. Across the Curriculum Newsletter, 1993—; speaker in field. Author: Intelligence Can Be Taught, 1973, Analytical Reading and Reasoning, 2d edit., 1989; (with M.J. Linden) Analytical Writing and Thinking: Facing the Tests, 1990; (with J. Lochhead) Problem Solving & Comprehension, 1991; (with others) Thinking Through Math Word Problems, 1990, Keys to Quick Writing Skills: Sentence Combining and Text Reconstruction, 1992, Blueprint for Educational Change: Improving Reasoning, Literacies, and Science Achievement, 1993; contbr. articles to profl. jours. Resident scholar CCNY, 1978, Clark Coll., 1980-82. Home and Office: 3920 Avalon Rd NW Albuquerque NM 87105-1814

WHINERY, LINDA SHAW, psychotherapist, police consultant; b. Phoenix, Feb. 12, 1949; d. William John and Barbara (Bairstow) Shaw; m. Marvin R. Whinery, Apr. 22, 1978 (dec. Apr. 1987); children: Michael William, Laura Shaw, Barbara Frances. BS in Rehab., U. Ariz., 1972; MS in Counseling, Calif. State U., Long Beach, 1979. Cert. tchr. spl. edn., Calif. Rehab. counselor Rehab. Inst. Easter Seals, Orange, Calif., 1976-80; dir. juvenile divsn. Cypress (Calif.) Police Dept., 1989—; psychotherapist in pvt. practice Tucson, 1990—; guest lectr. chapman Coll., Calif., Ariz. State U., Tempe. Democrat. Home: 7321 E Wikieup Cir Tucson AZ 85750

WHISTLER, BRADLEY JAMES, state government official; b. Juneau, Alaska, Mar. 22, 1958; s. Robert Leo and Beverly Jean Whistler; m. Laurie Susan Kildow, June 14, 1980 (div. Aug. 1994); children: Kelly Anne, Brian Robert. BA, Western Wash. U., Bellingham, 1980; DMD, Oreg. Health Scis. U., Portland, 1984. Tax examiner Alaska Dept. Revenue, Juneau, 1984-86, tax specialist, 1986-88; rsch. analyst Alaska Dept. Health & Social Svcs., Juneau, 1988-90, health planner, 1990-93, health planner, state dental dir., 1993—. Author: Alaska Department of Health and Social Services Database Directory, 1989, 1990 Alaska Hospital Survey, 1991; author, editor: Health Alaskans 2000, 1994; editor: Meeting the Challenge, 1994. Bd. dirs. Alaska Rural Health Ctr., Fairbanks, 1995—. Mem. Am. Pub. Health Assn., Am. Health Planners Assn., Assn. State and Territorial Dental Dirs., Am. Assn. Pub. Health Dentistry, Alaska Pub. Health Assn. (pres. 1994—, exec. bd., Short Term Svc. award 1995), Alaska Health Educators Consortium. Home: PO Box 32936 Juneau AK 99803-2936 Office: Alaska Dept Health & Social Svcs PO Box 110611 Juneau AK 99811-0611

WHITACRE, JOHN, apparel executive; b. 1953. Student, U. Wash. With Nordstrom Inc., 1976—; co-chmn. Nordstrom Inc., Seattle, 1995—. Office: Nordstrom Inc 1501 5th Ave Seattle WA 98101-1603*

WHITAKER, MORRIS DUANE, university administrator; b. Pocatello, Idaho, Apr. 4, 1940; s. Mirl William and Ada Belle (Bruesch) W.; m. Marguerite Fae Benson, Sept. 3, 1963; children: Jacqueline, Cynthia, Angela, Carolyn, Melinda, James, William, Christina. BS in Econs., Utah State U., 1965, MS in Econs., 1966; PhD in Agrl. Econs., Purdue U., 1970. Asst. prof. econs. Utah State U., Logan, 1970-75, assoc. prof. econs., 1976-83, prof. econs., 1983—; co-dir. planning Bolivian Ministry of Agr., La Paz, 1973-76; dep. exec. dir. Bd. for Internat. Food and Agrl. Devel., Washington, 1978-82; sr. advisor, adminstr. U.S. AID, Washington, 1981-82, policy advisor agr. programs, Quito, Ecuador, 1987-90, cons. on Asia, Near East, Latin Am., 1971-90; dir. internat. programs Utah State U., Logan, 1982-87, 90—. Author: Status of Bolivian Agriculture, 1975, Agricultural Development in Bangladesh, 1984, Agriculture and Economic Survival/Ecuador, 1990; contbr. articles to profl. jours. Com. mem. sch. bd. Cotopaxi Acad., Quito, 1987-90; asst. scoutmaster troop 240 Boy Scouts Am., Quito, 1987-90; mem. U.S. Presidential Task Force in Agr. to Ecuador, 1984; bd. dirs. LDS Charities, 1986—. Mem. Am. Agrl. Econs. Assn., Consortium for Internat. Devel. (bd. trustees). Republican. LDS. Office: Utah State U Internat Programs Logan UT 84322-9500

WHITCHURCH, CHARLES AUGUSTUS, art gallery owner, humanities educator; b. Long Beach, Calif., Sept. 29, 1940; s. Charles Augustus and Frances Elizabeth (White) W.; m. Michèle Elizabeth Cartier, Aug. 17, 1968 (div. 1977); 1 child, Gialisa Elizabeth; m. Mary Susan Ornelas, Jan. 28, 1984; 1 child, Marisa Tatiana. BA in History, Santa Clara U., Irvine, 1962; MA in Comparative Lit., U. Calif., Irvine, 1970. Cert. grad. secondary teaching credential. Asst. ops. officer United Calif. Bank, Inglewood, 1965-66; tchr. English Laguna Beach (Calif.) High Sch., 1966-68; teaching assoc., fellow U. Calif., Irvine, 1968-70; prof. lit. and humanities Golden West Coll., Huntington Beach, Calif., 1971—; owner, dir. Charles Whitchurch Fine Arts, Huntington Beach, Calif., 1978—; cons. Pyo Gallery, Seoul, Dem. Peoples Rep. Korea, 1989-90, Gordon Gallery, Santa Monica, Calif., 1989-96; judge, spkr. in field. Exec. editor Art Views, 1997; author mus. catalogues; contbr. articles to profl. jours. Founding mem., mem. adv. coun. Modern Mus. Art, Santa Ana, Calif., 1987-92. NEA grantee; named One of Outstanding Young Men Am., 1977. Mem. Nat. Coun. Tchrs. English, Art Dealers Assn. of Calif. (bd. dirs. 1988—, sec. 1988-90, pres. 1990-92), Huntington Beach Art Assn. (founding mem. 1990), Robert Gumbiner Found. for the Arts (bd. dirs. 1994-95), Found. Creative Arts (bd. dirs. 1996—), The Libra Group (pres. 1994-95), Santa Clara Alumni Assn., Alpha Sigma Nu, Phi Sigma Tau.

WHITE, ALVIN MURRAY, mathematics educator, consultant; b. N.Y.C., N.Y., June 21, 1925; s. Max and Beatrice White; m. Myra Goldstein, Dec. 4, 1946; children: Louis, Michael. BA, Columbia U., 1949; MA, UCLA, 1951; PhD, Stanford U., 1961. Acting instr. Stanford (Calif.) U., 1950-54; asst. prof. U. Santa Clara, Calif., 1954-61; postdoctoral fellow U. Wis., Madison, 1961-62; prof. Harvey Mudd Coll., Claremont, Calif., 1962—; vis. scholar MIT, 1975; initiator-facilitator humanistic math. network of over 2000 mathematicians worldwide; cons. coop. learning tutorial program Claremont Unified Sch. Dist. Author: Interdisciplinary Teaching, 1981; pub., editor: Humanistic Mathematics Network Jour.; contbr. articles to profl. jours. Served with USN, 1943-46, PTO. Grantee Fund for Improvement of Post-secondary Edn., Exxon Found. Mem. Am. Math. Soc., Math. Assn. Am., Nat. Coun. Tchrs. Math., Profl. Organizational Developers Network, Fedn. Am. Scientists, AAUP, Sigma Xi. Office: Harvey Mudd Coll 1250 N Dartmouth Ave Claremont CA 91711

WHITE, ANTHONY ROY, JR., composer, educator; b. Lakeport, Calif., Jan. 14, 1949; s. Anthony Roy White, Sr. and Merrie (Haynes) Wilkinson; m. Karen Jean Lamb, Dec. 21, 1980; 1 child, Jesse Solomon Sheibley. BA in Anthropology, Calif. State U., Sacramento, 1972, MA in Edn., 1982. Instr. in devel. edn. Clark College, Vancouver, Wash., 1990—. Composer: variety of commissioned chamber and concert works, 1989—; composer, author, producer, dir. (musical dance drama) In the Wound, 1996. Faculty senator Assn. Higher Edn. NEA, Washington Edn. Assn., Clark Coll., Vancouver, !993-95. Recipient Artist Trust Music fellowship Wash. State Arts Commn., NEA, 1995. Mem. ASCAP, NEA, Nat. Coun. Tchrs. of English, Artist Trust of Wash.

WHITE, BETTY, actress, comedienne; b. Oak Park, Ill., Jan. 17, 1922; m. Allen Ludden, 1963 (dec.). Student pub. schs., Beverly Hills, Calif. Appearances on radio shows This Is Your FBI, Blondie, The Great Gildersleeve; actress: (TV series) including Hollywood on Television, The Betty White Show, 1954-58, Life With Elizabeth, 1953-55, A Date With The Angels, 1957-58, The Pet Set, 1971, Mary Tyler Moore Show, 1974-77, The Betty White Show, 1977, The Golden Girls, 1985-92 (Emmy award for best actress 1986), The Golden Palace, 1992-93, Maybe This Time, 1995—; (TV miniseries) The Best Place to be, 1979, The Gossip Columnist, 1980, (film) Advise and Consent, 1962; guest appearances on other programs; summer stock appearances Guys and Dolls, Take Me Along, The King and I, Who Was That Lady?, Critic's Choice, Bells are Ringing. Recipient Emmy award NATAS, 1975, 76, 86; L.A. Area Emmy award, 1952. Mem. AFTRA, Am. Humane Assn., Greater L.A. Zoo Assn. (dir.). Office: care William Morris Agy care Tony Fantozzi 151 S El Camino Dr Beverly Hills CA 90212-2704*

WHITE, BONNIE YVONNE, management consultant, educator; b. Long Beach, Calif., Sept. 4, 1940; d. William Albert and Helen Iris (Harbaugh) W. BS, Brigham Young U., 1962, MS, 1965, EdD in Ednl. Adminstrn., 1976, postgrad. Harvard U., 1987. Tchr., Wilson High Sch., Long Beach, Calif., 1962-63; grad. asst. Brigham Young U., Provo, Utah, 1963-65; instr., dir. West Valley Coll., Saratoga, Calif., 1965-76; instr., evening adminstr. Mission Coll., Santa Clara, Calif., 1976-80; dean gen. edn. Mendocino Coll., Ukiah, Calif., 1980-85; dean instrn. Porterville (Calif.) Coll., 1985-89, dean adminstrv. svc., 1989-93; rsch. assoc. SAGE Rsch. Internat., Orem, Utah, 1975—. Del. Tulare County Ctrl. Com. Rep. Party, 1993-94; pres. community adv. bd. Calif. Conservation Corps, 1989-93; v.p. Porterville Community Concerts, 1990-94; bd. dirs. United Way North Bay, Santa Rosa, Calif., 1980-85, St. Vincent de Paul, 1993-97; mem. Calif. Commn. on Basic Skills, 1987-89, Calif. Commn. on Athletics, 1987-90. Mem. AAUW, Faculty Assn. Calif. Community Colls., Calif., Coun. Fine Arts Deans, Assn. Calif. Community Coll. Adminstrs. Assn. Calif. Community Coll. Adminstrs. Liberal Arts, Zonta (intern), Soroptimists (intern). Republican. Mormon.

WHITE, BRITTAN ROMEO, manufacturing company executive; b. N.Y.C., Feb. 13, 1936; s. Brittan R. and Matilda H. (Baumann) W.; m. Esther D. Friederich, Aug. 25, 1958 (dec. May 1981); children: Cynthia E., Brittan R. VII; m. Peggy A. Lee, Aug. 30, 1990. BSChemE, Drexel U., 1958; MBA, Lehigh U., 1967; JD, Loyola U., Los Angeles, 1974; MA, Pepperdine U., 1985. Bar: Calif., U.S. Dist. Ct. Calif.; registered profl. engr., Calif. Process engr. Air Reduction Co., Bound Brook, N.J., 1958-64; area supr. J.T. Baker Chem. Co., Phillipsburg, N.J., 1964-66; asst. plant mgr. Gamma Chem. Co., Great Meadows, N.J., 1966-69; plant mgr. Maquite Corp., Elizabeth, N.J., 1969-70; purchasing mgr. Atlantic Richfield Co., Los Angeles, 1970-79; dir. mfg. Imperial Oil, Los Angeles, 1979-82; mgr. chem. mgmt. program Hughes Aircraft Co., Los Angeles, 1982-94; pres. The Crawford Group, 1994—; bd. dirs. Diversified Resource Devel. Inc., Los Angeles, 1979—; seminar moderator and speaker Energy Conservation Seminars, 1979-83. Editor Rottweiler Rev., 1979-81; chief award judge Chem. Processing mag., 1976, 78, 80; contbr. articles to profl. jours. Vice chmn. Bd. Zoning and Adjustment, Flemington, N.J., 1970-72; pres. bd. dirs. Homeowners' Assn., Palm Springs, Calif., 1983-90. Capt. C.E., U.S. Army, 1958-60, res., 1960-68. Mem. ABA, Am. Inst. Chem. Engrs., Am. Chem. Soc., Mensa, Psi Chi. Republican. Lodge: Elks. Home: 1091 Pine Country Ct Prescott AZ 86303 Office: The Crawford Group PO Box 3020 Prescott AZ 86302

WHITE, CECIL RAY, librarian, consultant; b. Hammond, Ind., Oct. 15, 1937; s. Cecil Valentine and Vesta Ivern (Bradley) W.; m. Frances Ann Gee, Dec. 23, 1960 (div. 1987); children—Timothy Wayne, Stephen Patrick. B.S. in Edn., So. Ill. U., 1959; cert. in Czech., Syracuse, U., 1961; M. Div., Southwestern Bapt. Sem., 1969; M.L.S., N. Tex. State U., 1970, Ph.D., 1984. Librarian, Herrin High Sch. (Ill.), 1964-66; acting reference librarian Southwestern Sem., Ft. Worth, 1968-70, asst. librarian, 1970-80; head librarian Golden Gate Bapt. Sem., Mill Valley, Calif., 1980-88; head librarian West Oahu Coll., Pearl City, Hawaii, 1988-89; dir. spl. projects North State Coop. Library System, Yreka, Calif., 1989-90; dir. library St. Patrick's Sem., Menlo Park, Calif., 1990—; library cons. Hist. Commn., So. Bapt. Conv., Nashville, 1983-84, Internat. Bapt. Sem., Prague, Czech Republic, 1996; mem. Thesaurus Com., 1974-84; mem. adv. bd. Cath. Periodical and Lit. Index, 1995—. Bd. dirs. Hope and Help Ctr., 1986-88, vice chmn. 1987-88; libr. cons. Internat. Bapt. Theol. Sem., Prague, 1996. With USAF, 1960-64. Lilly Found. grantee Am. Theol. Library Assn., 1969. Mem. Am. Theol. Library Assn. (coord. consultation svc. 1973-78, program planning com. 1985-88, chmn., 1986-88), Nat. Assn. Profs. Hebrew (archivist 1985—), ALA, Assn. Coll. and Rsch. Librarians, Cath. Libr. Assn., Phi Kappa Phi, Beta Phi Mu. Democrat. Baptist. Home: 40509 Ambar Pl Fremont CA 94539 Office: St Patricks Sem 320 Middlefield Rd Menlo Park CA 94025 *Personal philosophy: Except for the gift of life and faith, the best gift that has been given to me, and which I can give, is the unique gift of oneself in friendship. No one else can give it, and it cannot be bought at any price.*

WHITE, CHARLES OLDS, aeronautical engineer; b. Beirut, Apr. 2, 1931; s. Frank Laurence and Dorothy Alice (Olds) W.; m. Mary Carolyn Liechty, Sept. 3, 1955; children—Charles Cameron, Bruce Blair. B.S. in Aero. Engring., MIT, 1953, M.S., 1954. Aero. engr. Douglas Aircraft Long Beach, 1954-60, aero. engr. Ford Aerospace & Communication Corp., Calif., 1960-79, sr. engr. specialist, 1979-80, staff office of gen. mgr. DIVAD div., 1980-81, tech. mgr. DIVAD Fuzes, 1981-82, supr. design and analysis DIVAD div., 1982-85; tech. mgr. Advanced Ordnance Programs, 1985-87, PREDATOR Missile, 1987-90, cons. 1990-93; engring. tech. prin. Aerojet Corp., 1993-94; tech. prin. OCSW Ammunition Olin Ordinance, 1994-97, cons., 1997—. Mem. AIAA, Nat. Mgmt. Assn., Am. Aviation Hist. Soc., Sigma Gamma Tau. Republican. Presbyterian. Clubs: Masters Swimming, Newport Beach Tennis. Contbr. articles to profl. jours.

WHITE, CLAYTON M., science educator, environmental consultant; b. Afton, N.Y., Apr. 19, 1936; s. Mondell and Reita (Thurman) W.; m. Merle Tanner, Mar. 19, 1959; children: Craig, Kelly, Tod, Kip, Jana. AB in Zoology, U. Utah, 1963, PhD in Zoology, 1968. Instr. U. Kans., Lawrence, 1965-66; rsch. fellow Cornell U., Ithaca, N.Y., 1968-70; from asst. prof. to assoc. prof. Brigham Young U., Provo, Utah, 1970-78, prof., 1978—; cons. U.S. AEC, Amchitka Island, Alaska, 1969-73, U.S. Fish and Wildlife Svc., Anchorage, 1973-75, Exxon, Inc., USA, Prince William Sound, Alaska, 1989-92; vertebrate ecologist U.S. ERDA, Washington, 1975-76. Contbr. articles to profl. jours. Elected mem. Am. Ornithologists' Union. Democrat. Mem. LDS Ch. Home: 1146 S 300 W Orem UT 84058 Office: Brigham Young U Dept Zoology Provo UT 84602

WHITE, DANNY LEVIUS, counselor, consultant, educator; b. Temple, Tex., Oct. 9, 1956; s. Chester Allen and Elizabeth (Jimmerson) W.; m. Phemonia Lyvette Miller, July 23, 1988; 1 child, Amadi Najuma. AA, Mesa (Ariz.) Community Coll., 1976; BA, Ottawa (Kans.) U., 1982; postgrad., Chapman Coll., 1989-90; MEd magna cum laude, No. Ariz. U., 1993. Clinician V Phoenix South Mental Health, 1982-85; therapist I Ariz. Dept. of Correction, Tucson, 1985-87; cons. Tucson Urban League, 1987-88; counselor, assessment specialist Pima County Atty.'s Office, Tucson, 1988-96; pres., CEO Family Matters Counseling and Cons. Svcs., Tucson, 1996—; adj. faculty Pima C.C., 1993-95; mem. com. So. Ariz. Task Force Against Domestic Violence, Tucson, 1989—, outreach coord., Day of Unity chmn., 1993, 94, 95; psychology assoc. II minor's unit Ariz. Dept Corrections, 1996. Dem. precinct committeeman, Tucson, 1988-92; del. 1988 Nat. Dem. Conv.; dep. registrar Pima & Maricopa County Recorders Office, Phoenix and Tucson, 1983-90; mem. citizens adv. coun. Phoenix Elem. Sch. Dist. 1, 1983-85; chair radiothon membership drive com. Tucson chpt. NAACP, 1990-93, chair health fair drive, 1992-93; pres. bd. dirs. P.A.S.A.R., Tucson, 1989-91; booster Spl. Olympics, 1980-90; spl. friend Ariz. Children's Home Foster Care, 1990; implemented Will to Win and Stay In Sch. drive programs, 1987-91; vol., blooddrive coord. United Blood Svcs., Phoenix, 1983-87. Named Outstanding West Campus Adj. Faculty Mem., Pima C.C., 1994-95; recipient Robert L. Horn Outstanding Cmty. Svc. award NAACP, 1996. Mem. United Parent and Youth League Inc. (pres. bd. dirs. 1984-85), Gov.'s Alliance Against Drugs (bd. dirs. 1989-91), Omega Psi Phi (named Man of Yr. Ariz. chpts. 1983, 85, 92, pres. Tucson grad. chpt. 1991-95), Delta Alpha Alpha. Home: PO Box 1135 Tucson AZ 85702-1135

WHITE, DAVID OLDS, researcher, former educator; b. Fenton, Mich., Dec. 18, 1921; s. Harold Bancroft and Doris Caroline (Olds) W.; m. Janice Ethel Russell, Sept. 17, 1923; children: John Russell, David Olds Jr., Benjamin Hill. BA, Amherst Coll., 1943; MS, U. Mass., 1950; PhD, U. Oreg., 1970. Tchr. human physiology Defiance (Ohio) Coll., summer 1950; sci. tchr. Roosevelt Jr. High Sch., Eugene, Oreg., 1951-52; prin. Glide (Oreg.) High Sch., 1952-56; tchr. Munich Am. Elem. Sch., 1957-69; prin. Wurzburg (Fed. Republic Germany) Am. High Sch., 1959-60, Wertheim (Fed. Republic

Germany) Am. Elem. Sch., 1960-61; tchr. Dash Point Elem. Sch., Tacoma, 1961-63, Eugene (Oreg.) Pub. Schs., 1963-81; internat. rschr. in field. Contbr. articles to profl. publs.; patentee electronic model airplane. Staff sgt. U.S. Army, 1942-45, PTO. Fulbright grantee, 1956-57, 72-73. Mem. NEA, Fulbright Alumni Assn., Phi Delta Kappa. Home: 4544 Fox Hollow Rd Eugene OR 97405-3904

WHITE, DEEDEE, human services executive; b. Fayetteville, N.C., June 30, 1947; d. Justin Smith and Dorothy Taylor (Spears) W. BA in Biology, U. N.C., Greensboro, 1969; MA in Internat. Rels., U. San Diego, 1990. Asst. v.p. Sci. Applications Internat. Corp., San Diego, 1977-1996; v.p. MAXIMUS, 1996—. Republican. Home and Office: 3154 Bremerton Pl La Jolla CA 92037-2211

WHITE, DON WILLIAM, banker; b. Santa Rita, N.Mex., June 27, 1942; s. Thomas Melvin and Barbara (Smith) W.; m. Jacqueline Diane Bufkin, June 12, 1965; children: Don William Jr., David Wayne. BBA, Western N.Mex. U., 1974, MBA, 1977. Field acct. Stearns Roger Corp., Denver, 1967-70; controller, adminstrv. mgr. USNR Mining and Minerals Inc., Silver City, N.Mex., 1970-72; devel. specialist County of Grant, Silver City, 1973-77; divisional controller Molycorp. Inc., Taos, N.Mex., 1977-78; mgr. project adminstrn. Kennecott Minerals Co., Hurley, N.Mex., 1978-83; sr. v.p. Sunwest Bank Grant County, Silver City, N.Mex., 1983-84, exec. v.p., 1984-85, pres., chief exec. officer, 1985—; bd. dirs. Bank of Grant County. Bd. dirs. Sunwest Bank of Grant County, Silver City/Grant County Econ. Devel., 1983—; councilman Town of Silver City, 1977; chmn. Dems. for Senator Pete Domenici, 1986; pres. Gila Regional Med. Found., 1989-92; pres. SWNM Econ. Devel. Corp., 1984—; trustee Indian Hills Bapt. Ch., 1988-89; chmn. State of N.Mex. Small Bus. Adv. Coun.; vice chmn. vocat. edn. adv. com. Western N.Mex. U., 1989; mem. Silver Schs.-Sch./Bus. Partnership Coun. Named Outstanding Vol., Silver City/Grant County Econ. Devel., 1987, 94, FFA, 1985. Mem. Am. Bankers Assn., N.Mex. Bankers Assn., Bank Adminstrn. Inst., Assn. Commerce and Industry (bd. dirs. 1988-91), N.Mex. Mining Assn. (assoc.), Rotary (past pres., dist. gov. rep.). Office: Sunwest Bank of Grant County 1203 N Hudson St Silver City NM 88061-5519

WHITE, DONALD HARVEY, physics educator emeritus; b. Berkeley, Calif., Apr. 30, 1931; s. Harvey Elliott and Adeline White; m. Beverly Evalina Jones, Aug. 8, 1953; children: Jeri, Brett, Holly, Scott, Erin. AB, U. Calif., Berkeley, 1953; PhD, Cornell U., 1960. Rsch. physicist Lawrence Livermore (Calif.) Nat. Lab., 1960-71, cons., 1971-90; prof. physics Western Oreg. U., Monmouth, 1971-95; ret.; vis. rsch. scientist Inst. Laue-Langevin, Grenoble, France, 1977-78, 84-85, 91-92. Author: (with others) Physics, an Experimental Science, 1968, Physics and Music, 1980. Pres. Monmouth-Independence Cmty. Arts, 1983. DuPont scholar, 1958; Minna-Heineman Found. fellow, Hannover, Fed. Republic Germany, 1977. Mem. Am. Phys. Soc., Am. Assn. Physics Tchrs. (pres. Oreg. sect. 1974-75), Oreg. Acad. Sci. (pres. 1979-80), Phi Kappa Phi (pres. West Oreg. chpt. 1989-90). Democrat. Presbyterian. Home: 411 S Walnut Dr Monmouth OR 97361-1948

WHITE, EMMET, JR., retirement community administrator; b. Newark, Oct. 18, 1946; s. Emmet Sr. and June (Howlett) W.; m. Betty Orr, June 7, 1970; children: Benjamin, Suzanne, George. BA, Lafayette Coll., 1968; JD, Coll. of William and Mary, 1971. Bar: Hawaii 1972; cert. nursing home adminstr., Hawaii. Law ptnr. Mau & White AAL, Honolulu, 1975-83, White & Tom AAL, Honolulu, 1983-95; CEO, adminstr. Arcadia Retirement Residence, Honolulu, 1996—. Bd. trustees Ctrl. Union Ch., Honolulu, 1980-84, chmn. 1983-84, moderator, 1987. Col. USAR, 1968-94. Mem. Hawaii Bar Assn., Hawaii Long Term Care Assn. Office: Arcadia Retirement Residence 1434 Punahou St Honolulu HI 96822

WHITE, ERIC MILTON, optometrist; b. Chgo., Sept. 6, 1959; s. Milton George and Nancy Grace (Williams) W.; m. Lorie Ann Fitch, June 27, 1981; children: Tyler, Cameron, Samuel. BA in Physiol. Psychology, U. Calif., San Diego, 1982; BS in Visual Sci., So. Calif. Coll. Optometry, Fullerton, 1984, DO, 1986. Ptnr. DM Rasmussen OD Inc., San Diego, 1986-89; optometrist in pvt. practice San Diego, 1989—; cons. Am. Indian Health Svcs., Lions Optometric Clinic of San Diego, Sharp Hosp. Sr. Citizens Health Ctr., Am. Contact Lenses Adv. Bd., Allergan Medicare Alliance Task Force Com., Tryuson Sys., Dicon Sys., others; lectr., rschr., presenter in field. Contbr. numerous articles to profl. jours. Bd. dirs. So. Calif. chpt. Prevent Blindness Am., 1992—, v.p., 1993-94, pres.-elect, 1994—; active Boy Scouts Am.; chmn. stewardship com. First Christian Ch. of El Cajon, 1993-95, trustee, 1993-95; mem. Wesley Jessen Adv. Bd., 1996-97. Recipient Appreciation award Nat. Soc. to Prevent Blindness, 1985, 95, Vol. of Yr., United Way/Combined Health Agys., 1995. Mem. Am. Optometric Assn. (Young OD of Yr. 1995), Am. Optometric Found., Sports Vision Assn. Am., Calif. Optometric Assn., So. Calif. Coll. Optometry Alumni Assn. (life), San Diego Optometric Soc., Nat. Eagle Scout Assn. (life). Republican. Home: 1625 Hollow Pl El Cajon CA 92019-3718 Office: Mission Village Med Ctr 2202 Ruffin Rd Ste L San Diego CA 92123

WHITE, GARY RICHARD, electrical engineer; b. Detroit, Nov. 15, 1962; s. Thomas Richard and Davene (Reynolds) W. BS in Elec. Engring., Wayne State U., 1986. Electronics engr. U.S. Army Info. Sys. Engring. Command, Ft. Belvoir, Va., 1987-88, Ft. Shafter, Hawaii, 1988-92; elec. worker U.S. Navy Pub. Works Ctr., Pearl Harbor, Hawaii, 1992-96; plant operator helper U.S. Navy Pub. Works Ctr., Pearl Harbor, 1996—. Mem. IEEE, NRA, Nat. Soc. Profl. Engrs., Assn. Computing Machinery, Nat. Republican Senatorial Com., Am. Assn. Individual Investors, Am. Mgmt. Assn. Office: PO Box 19055 Honolulu HI 96817

WHITE, GAYLE CLAY, aerospace company executive; b. Wyandotte, Mich., Sept. 28, 1944; s. John Leonard and Irene Francis (Clay) W.; m. Sharon Wong, June 8, 1968; children: Lai Jean, Quinn Yee. BBA, Ea. Mich. U., 1967; MBA, Utah State U., 1971; MPA, Auburn U., 1976; postgrad., Nova U., 1985—. Computer system analyst USAF Logistics Command, Odgen, Utah, 1967-71, U.S.-Can. Mil. Officer Exec., Ottawa, Ont., 1971-73; mgr. software devel. USAF Data System Design Ctr., Montgomery, Ala., 1973-77; data base adminstr. Supreme Hdqrs. Allied Powers Europe, Casteau, Belgium, 1977-81; mgr. software configuration System Integration Office, Colorado Springs, Colo., 1981-83; mgr. computer ops. N.Am. Aerospace Def. Command, Colorado Springs, 1983-84; dir. ops. 6 Missile Warning Squadron, Space Command, Cape Cod, Mass., 1984-86, comdr., 1986-87; mgr. program devel. Rockwell Internat., Colorado Springs, 1987-96; mgr. bus. devel. The Boeing Co., Colorado Springs, 1996—; mem. faculty computer sci. and bus. Regis U., Colorado Springs, 1981—. Treas. Christian Ctr. Ch., Colorado Springs, 1989-95; v.p. European Parents, Tchrs. and Students Assn., 1979-81. Recipient Mil.-Civilian Rels. award Otis Civilian Adv. Coun., 1987, awarded cert. Data Processing Mgmt. Assn., 1973. Mem. Armed Forces Comm. Electronics Assn., Inst. Nav. (treas. Rocky Mountain sect. 1996—), Global Positioning Sys. Internat. Assn., Air Force Assn., SHAPE Officers Assn., Nat. Security Indsl. Assn. (bd. dirs. Rocky Mountain chpt. 1990—, vice chmn. space com. ctrl. region 1996—), Christian Businessmen's Assn., Lynmar Racquet Club, Alpha Kappa Psi. Republican. Office: Boeing Ste 134 1250 Academy Park Loop Colorado Springs CO 80910-3708

WHITE, GEOFFREY MILES, anthropologist; b. Bridgeport, Conn., Nov. 11, 1949; s. Stephen Theodore and Marjorie Elizabeth (Richardson) W.; m. Nancy Ann Montgomery, June 17, 1978; 1 child, Michael Geoffrey. BA in Sociology and Anthropology, Princeton U., 1971; PhD in Anthropology, U. Calif. San Diego, La Jolla, 1978. Rsch. assoc. East-West Ctr., Honolulu, 1978-92, sr. fellow, 1992—, dir. cultural studies, 1992-95. Author: Identity Through History, 1991; co-author: Island Encounters, 1990; co-editor: The Pacific Theater, 1989 (award 1992), New Directions in Psychological Anthropology, 1992; editl. bd. The Contemporary Pacific, 1987—, Ethos: Jour. of the Soc. for Psychological Anthropology, 1990—. Recipient Masayoshi Ohira Meml. Book prize, Japan, 1992; Intrepretive Rsch. Project grantee NEH, 1987-89, Summer Seminar dir. NEH, 1991, 93, 95, 97; Rsch. grantee Wenner-Gren Found., N.Y. Mem. Am. Anthropol. Assn. (Stirling award 1978), Am. Ethnol. Soc., Soc. for Psychol. Anthropology (bd. dirs. 1988-90). Office: East-West Ctr 1601 East West Rd Honolulu HI 96848-1601

WHITE, JANE SEE, journalist; b. St. Louis, Aug. 26, 1950; d. Robert Mitchell and Barbara Whitney (Spurgeon) W.; 1 child, Laura Mitchell. BA in History and Am. Studies, Hollins Coll., 1972. Reporter Roanoke (Va.) Times, 1972-73, Kansas City (Mo.) City Star, 1973-76, AP, N.Y.C., Hartford, 1976-78; spl. writer AP, N.Y.C., 1978-81; sr. writer, chief news and bur., chief profl. div. Med. Econs. Mag., Oradell, N.J., 1981-87; dep. city editor, city editor Roanoke Times World News, 1987-91; asst. metro. editor Phoenix Gazette, 1991-93; asst. city editor Ariz. Rep., Phoenix, 1993, features editor, 1993-95; asst. mng. editor adminstrn. Ariz. Rep. and Phoenix Gazette, Pheonix, 1995-96; staff devel. and tng. editor Ariz. Rep. & Phoenix Gazette, 1996-97; freelance journalist Phoenix, 1997—. Editor: Medical Practice Management, 1985; contbr. articles to profl. jurs. Home: 7143 N 15th Pl Phoenix AZ 85020-5416 Office: Ariz Rep PO Box 2243 Phoenix AZ 85002-2243

WHITE, JOY MIEKO, communications executive; b. Yokohama, Japan, May 1, 1951; came to U.S., 1951; d. Frank Deforest and Wanda Mieko Mellen; m. George William White, June 5, 1948; 1 child, Karen. BA in Comms., Calif. State U., Fullerton, 1974, tchg. cert., 1977; cert. bus. mgmt., Orange Coast Coll., 1981; cert. teaching, Cmty. Coll., 1990. Cert. secondary tchr., Calif. Secondary tchr. Anaheim (Calif.) Union H.S. Dist., 1977-80; tech. writer Pertec Computer Corp., Irvine, Calif., 1980-81; supr. large sys. disvn. Burroughs, Mission Viejo, Calif., 1981-83; mgr. Lockheed divsn. CalComp, Anaheim, 1983-86; owner, pres. Communicator's Connection, Irvine, Calif., 1986-90; pres. Info Team, Inc., 1989—; mem. adj. faculty, coord. tech. comm. program Golden West Coll., Huntington Beach, Calif., 1987-90; instr. U. Calif., Irvine, 1987-89, Calif. State U., Fullerton, 1988-91; condr. numerous workshops, profl. presentations, 1982—; sec. Santa Ana Dist. chpt. U.S. SBA Assn. for Minority-Owned Bus., 1991-96. Active Performing Arts, Costa Mesa, 1986—; troop leader Girl Scouts U.S., 1995—, life mem., 1994—. Fellow Soc. Tech. Comm. (internat. assoc., sr., Orange County chpt. 1987, Mem. of Yr.); mem. NAFE, Soc. Profl. Journalists, Women in Comms. (pres. Orange County Profl. chpt. 1989-90), Nat. Assn. Women Bus. Owners, Rembrandts Wine Club (Yorba Linda), Girl Scouts U.S. (life). Democrat. Home: 21651 Vintage Way Lake Forest CA 92630-5760 Office: 22365 El Toro Rd # 265 Lake Forest CA 92630-5053

WHITE, KATHLEEN MERRITT, geologist; b. Long Beach, Calif., Nov. 19, 1921; d. Edward Clendenning and Gladys Alice (Merritt) White; m. Alexander Kennedy Baird IV, Oct. 1, 1965 (dec. 1985); children: Pamela Roberts, Peter Madlem, Stephen Madlem, Mari Afify. Attended, Sch. Boston Mus. Fine Arts, 1939-40, Art Students League, 1940-42; BS in Geology, Pomona Coll., 1962; MS in Geochemistry, Claremont Grad. Sch., 1964. Rsch. asst. geology Pomona Coll., Claremont, Calif., 1962-66, rsch. assoc. geology, 1966-75; cons. geology Claremont, Calif., 1975-77; sr. scientist Jet Propulsion Lab./NASA, Pasadena, 1977-79, mem. tech. staff, 1979-86; ind. rschr. Claremont, 1986—; owner Kittie Tales, Claremont, 1992—. Contbr. Geosat Report, 1986; contbr. articles to profl. jours.; author, illustrator children's books. Grantee NASA, 1984, 85; Pomona Coll. scholar, 1963. Fellow Am. Geophys. Union; mem. Geol. Soc. Am. (invited paper 1994), Pomona Coll. Alumni Assn. Republican. Home: 265 W 11th St Claremont CA 91711-3804

WHITE, KENTON STOWELL, writer, publisher; b. Long Beach, Calif., July 9, 1933; s. Ernest Euliel (Ballenger) W.; m. Elizabeth Mills Laurenson, June 22, 1957; 1 child, Corey Ross. BA, U. Calif., Berkeley, 1955, MLS, 1964. Cert. secondary tchr., Calif. Tchr. English Alameda (Calif.) High Sch., 1958-60, San Lorenzo (Calif.) High Sch., 1960-61; libr. intern Alameda County, Fremont, Calif., 1962-63; ref. libr. San Bernardino (Calif.) Pub. Libr., 1964-65; audio visual coord. Inland Libr. System, San Bernardino, 1966-69; asst. city libr. Huntington Beach (Calif.) Pub. Libr., 1969-74; pub., v.p. Lightning Pubs., Fullerton, Calif., 1992; pub. North Hills Pub. Co., Costa Mesa, Calif., 1994-96; seminar instr. Learning Tree U., Learning Annex; mem. Costa Mesa Libr. Svcs. Com., 1996—. Author: Buying America Back, 1988, Winning the Peace, 1992, How to Publish Your Short, Long Fiction, How to Publish Your Poetry; Avisson Book of Contests for Fiction Writer; columnist San Diego Rev. Campaign dir. Ron Pattison for City Coun., Huntington Beach, 1975-76; Dem. cand. for Congress, 40th Dist., Calif., 1983-84; mem. com. Costa Mesa (Calif.) Libr. Svcs., 1996—; pres. Neighborhood Watch, Huntington Beach, 1975-76. Mem. Exch. Club (pres. Huntington Beach club 1975-76). Democrat. Avocations: economic philosophy, writing. Home and Office: 2824 Shantar Dr Costa Mesa CA 92626-3539

WHITE, LORAY BETTY, public relations executive, writer, actress, producer; b. Houston, Nov. 27, 1934; d. Harold White and Joyce Mae (Jenkins) Mills; m. Sammy Davis Jr., 1957 (div. 1958); 1 child, Deborah R. DeHart. Student, UCLA, 1948-50, 90-91, Nichiren Shoshu Acad., 1988-92; AA in Bus., Sayer Bus. Sch., 1970; study div. mem. dept. L.A., Soka U., Japan, 1970-86. Editor entertainment writer L.A. Community New, 1970-81; exec. sec. guest rels. KNBC Prodns., Burbank, Calif., 1969-75; security specialist Xerox X10 Think Tank, L.A., 1975-80; exec. asst. Ralph Powell & Assocs., L.A., 1980-82; pres., owner, producer LBW & Assocs. Pub. Rels., L.A., 1980—; owner, producer, writer, host TV prodn. co. Pub. Pub. Rels., L.A., 1987—; dir., producer L.B.W. Prodn. "Yesterday, Today, Tomorrow, L.A., 1981—. Actress (film) Ten Commandments, 1956, (Broadway) Joy Ride; appeared in the following endorsements including Budweiser Beer, Old Gold Cigarettes, Salem Cigarettes, TV commls. including Cheer, Puffs Tissue, Coca Cola, Buffern, others; entertainment editor L.A. Community News, 1970-73; writer (column) Balance News, 1980-82. Vol. ARC, 1995; mem. Habitat for Humanity Internat. Recipient award ARC, 1955, 84, Cert. of Honor, Internat. Orgn. Soka Gakkai Internat. of Japan, Cmty. Vols. of Am. award, 1994; named Performer of Yr. Cardella Demillo, 1976-77. Mem. ARC (planning, mktg., prodn. event com. 1995), UCLA Alumni Assn., Lupus Found. Am. (So. Calif. chpt.), Nat. Fedn. Blind, Myohoji-Hokkeko Internat., Libr. of Congress Assocs. (charter). Buddhist. *Accepting challenges in life is a choice. The choice is always yours. I've chosen never to give up-to always give my best, to constantly keep a growing and open mind. To remember to strengthen and reinforce the quality of my integrity no matter what- be a winner to yourself.*

WHITE, LYLA LEE, religious organization administrator; b. Watsonville, Calif., Apr. 20, 1940; d. Lyle Verne Loehr and Marjorie (Rhoades) Smith; m. J. Melville White, Sept. 7, 1962 (Jan. 1987); children: Erinn Kathleen, Michael Christopher. BA in English and History, Warner Pacific Coll.; postgrad., Pepperdine U. Tchr. of English Crescenta Valley High Sch./Glendale (Calif.) C.C., 1964-74; v.p. Mel White Prodns., 1964-84; editor Harper and Row Pubbs., 1983-86; dir. devel. All Saints Ch., Pasadena, Calif., 1986-94; dir. devel. and pub. rels. Grace Cathedral, San Francisco, 1994-96; dir. devel. The Pasadena Playhouse-The State Theater of Calif., 1996—. Co-author: In the Presence of Mine Enemies, 1973, Tested by Fire, 1976. Mem. Leadership Calif., 1993—; fundraising cons., conf. spkr., San Francisco, 1990—. Mem. LWV, Nat. Assn. Fundraising Execs., San Francisco Planned Giving Round Table, Pasadena Rotary, San Francisco City Club. Office: Pasadena Playhouse State Theater of Calif 39 S El Molino Pasadena CA 91101

WHITE, MATTHEW, family practice physician; b. Phila., May 21, 1941; s. Frank and Minerva (Shiffmann) W.; m. Kristina J. Johnson, Aug. 15, 1978. AB in Chemistry, Temple U., 1963; MD, Jefferson Med. Coll., 1967. Diplomate Am. Bd. Family Practice. Commd. lt. USN, 1967, advanced through grades to comdr., 1975; intern U.S. Naval Hosp., Newport, R.I., 1967-68; resident U.S. Naval Hosp., Jacksonville, Fla., 1968-70; family practice medicine USN, Japan, 1970-73, Bremerton, Wash., 1973-77; family practice medicine Sand Pt. Naval Air Sta., Seattle, 1977-78; resigned USN, 1978; family practice medicine Tacoma, 1978—; mem. active staff, bd. dirs., exec. com. Franciscan Health System-West; active staff St. Clare Hosp.; pres. med. staff Lakewood Hosp., 1989-90. Mem. utilization rev. com. Georgian House Nursing Home, Meadow Park Nursing Home, Lakewood Health Care N.H. Fellow Am. Acad. Family Practice; mem. AMA (nat., state and county chpts.). Republican. Jewish. Office: #304 11311 Bridgeport Way SW Tacoma WA 98499

WHITE, MICHAEL LEE, executive producer, writer; b. Rochester, Minn., Aug. 2, 1967; s. Floyd Leroy and Yvonne Cecile (Jarrett) W.; m. Tatyana Nayda, Sept. 17, 1996. Student, U. Ariz., 1984-85. Glazier Sunset Glass & Mirror, Tucson, 1980-84; assoc. astronomer Flandrau Planetarium, Tucson, 1984-85; owner W.A.V. Enterprises, Hemet, Calif., 1985-88; programming cons. TMJ Stations, Temecula, Calif., 1988-91; exec.producer, writer Nine Star-Domestic, Hemet, 1989-95; news/program dir. Buffalo Comms., San Jacinto, Calif., 1992, gen. mgr., 1993; co-owner Mail Depot, Hemet, 1993-97, Aeropig Systems, Hemet, 1995—; co-owner, producer, writer Misha Prodns., Hemet, 1995—. Editor Hemet Valley Bull. Bd. List, 1990-96, Tucson Bull. Bd. List, 1987-96; contbr., author: Computer Phone Book, 1986; author screenplay Summer Breeze, 1996, Summer Breeze: The Series, 1997. Founder, spokesperson Pro-Am. Found., Tucson, 1985—, internat. pres., 1986-88, 92; pres. Tucson Jr. Civitan, 1982-83. Republican. Lutheran. Home: 3030 W Acacia H-103 Hemet CA 92545 Office: Aeropig Systems 3007 W Florida Ave # 106 Hemet CA 92545

WHITE, PAUL VERLIN, electronics marketing executive; b. Sioux Falls, S.D., Apr. 12, 1941; s. Verlin J.A. and Dorothy M. (Bates) W.; m. Judi Maureen Greene, July 3, 1965; children—Paul H., Sean M. B.S.E.E., Ariz. State U., 1964. Quality engr. mil. div. Motorola, Scottsdale, Ariz., 1962-65, dist. sales mgr. semicondr. div., Los Angeles, 1965-71, mgr. hi-rel mktg., Mesa, Ariz., 1971-74, mktg. mgr., Phoenix, 1974-75, dir. mktg. power products, 1976-82, v.p., dir. mktg. discrete and spl. technologies group, 1982-95, mem. adv. council to bd. dirs., 1984; v.p. dir. mktg. Analog I/C divsn., 1995—., Bd. dirs. Grace Community Ch., Tempe, 1983-96, treas., 1984—, Wildlife for Tomorrow Ariz. Game and Fish Dept., 1992—. . Author articles in field. Mem. Motorola PAC, 1983—. Phoenix Coll. scholar, 1962. Mem. Am. Mktg. Assn. (award 1978). Republican. Home: 2062 E Malibu Dr Tempe AZ 85282-5966 Office: Motorola Inc 2100 E Elliott Scottsdale AZ 85254

WHITE, RAYMOND, health facility administrator. BS in Microbiology, U. Oreg., 1965; PhD in Microbiology, MIT, 1971; postdoctoral study, Stanford U. Assoc. prof. Microbiology Dept. U. Mass. Sch. Medicine, Worcester, 1978-80; assoc. prof. Cellular, Viral & Molecular Biology U. Utah Sch. Medicine, Salt Lake City, 1980-84; investigator Howard Hughes Med. Inst. U. Utah, 1980-94; co-chair Human Genetics Dept. U. Utah Sch. Medicine, 1984-94, dir. Huntsman Cancer Inst., 1994—, chmn. Dept. Oncological Scis., 1994—. Recipient Rosenthal Found. award Am. Assn. Cancer Rsch., Charles S. Mott prize for Cancer Rsch. Gen. Motors Found., Nat. Med. Rsch. award Nat. Health Coun., Allan award for Cancer Rsch. Am. Soc. Human Genetics, Friedrich von Recklinghausen award Nat. Neurofibromatosis Found., Lewis S. Rosenstiel award for Disting. Work in Med. Scis. Brandeis U. Mem. NAS. Office: Huntsman Cancer Inst Bldg 533 Ste 7410 U Utah Sch Medicine Salt Lake City UT 84112

WHITE, RAYMOND EDWIN, JR., astronomer, educator, researcher; b. Freeport, Ill., May 6, 1933; s. Raymond Edwin White and Beatrice Ellen (Rahn) Stone; m. Ruby Elaine Fisk, Oct. 16, 1956; children: Raymond Edwin III, Kathleen M., Kevin D. BS, U. Ill., 1955, PhD in Astronomy, 1967. Instr. astronomy U. Ariz., Tucson, 1964-65, asst. prof. astronomy, 1965-71, lectr. astronomy, 1972-81, assoc. prof. astronomy, 1981-93, prof. astronomy, 1993—, disting. prof., 1995—; program officer astronomy NSF, Washington, 1971-72; astronomer Dunsink Observatory, Dublin, Ireland, 1996-97; vis. lectr. Trinity Coll., Dublin, 1996-97. Editor: Observational Astrophysics, 1992; editor Astronomy Quar. jour., 1989-91; North Am. editor Vistas in Astronomy jour., 1992-97. 1st lt. U.S. Army, 1955-58. Fulbright scholar Dublin Inst., 1996-97. Fellow AAAS, Royal Astron. Soc.; mem. Am. Astron. Soc., Am. Assn. Physics Tchrs., Math Assn. Am., Internat. Astron. Union, Sigma Xi. Office: Univ Ariz Steward Observatory Tucson AZ 85721 also: Dunsink Observatory, Castleknock, Dublin 15, Ireland

WHITE, RICHARD WEDDINGTON, JR., writer, editor; b. San Francisco, Aug. 21, 1936; s. Richard Weddington Sr. and Virginia Elizabeth (Goodyear) W.; m. Kay Cleveland, Jan. 26, 1957; children: Karen Debs, David King. AA in Premed., UCLA, 1956; AB in Sociology with honors, U. Calif., Berkeley, 1958, MA in Sociology, 1964. Mgmt. intern U.S. Dept. Labor, Washington, 1960, 64; job corps planner Pres.'s Task Force on War Against Poverty, Washington, 1964-65; chief govtl. rels., chief field ops. U.S. Office Econ. Oppty., San Francisco, 1965-81; strategic planning cons., chief Alameda County Svcs. United Way of the Bay Area, San Francisco, 1981-83; econ. editor, COO Inst. for Contemporary Studies, San Francisco, 1983-86; freelance, writer, editor, program mgr. World Without War Coun., Berkeley, 1986—; vis. lectr. Sch. Social Welfare U. Calif., Berkeley, 1987-93; owner, mgr. bed and breakfast. Editor: The Farm Fiasco, 1986; author: Rude Awakenings: What the Homeless Crisis Tells Us, 1992; contbr. articles to profl. publs. Trustee, chair policy rev. com., chair appeals com. United Way of the Bay Area, 1971-83; mem. exec. com. San Francisco Great Books Coun., 1991—; organizer interracial event Allen Temple Bapt. Ch., Lafayette-Orinda Presbyn. Ch., 1997. Grantee H&L Bradley Found., 1988, Earhart Found., 1988. Fellow James Madison Found. (sr.), Inst. for Self Governance. Republican. Home: 501 Santa Barbara Rd Berkeley CA 94707 Office: World Without War Coun 1730 MLK Way Berkeley CA 94707

WHITE, RICK, congressman. Mem. 105th Congress dist. 1. Republican. Office: 116 Cannon Ho Office Bldg Washington DC 20515

WHITE, ROBERT C., air transportation executive; b. 1943. Student, Wake Forest U., 1961-65. With Procter & Gamble, Columbus, Ohio, 1971-73; asst. dir. Shreveport (La.) Airport Authority, 1973-75; airport mgr. Gainesville (Fla.) Regional Airport, 1975-78; dep. dir. aviation Jacksonville (Fla.) Port Authority, 1978-80; exec. dir. Peninsula Airport Commn., Newport News, Va., 1980-82; dir./cons. Lockheed Air Terminal, Burbank, Calif., 1982—; exec. dir. Reno Tahoe Internat. Airport, 1988—. With USN, 1966-71. Office: Reno Tahoe Internat Airport PO Box 12490 Reno NV 89510-2490*

WHITE, ROBERT GORDON, research director, biology educator; b. Lithgow, NSW, Australia, Jan. 17, 1938; s. Richard Robert and Francis Elsie (Schubert) W.; m. Sandra Elizabeth Ferrier, Dec. 9, 1961 (dec. May 1995); children: Robert Ian, Andrew Douglas. B. in Agrl. Sci., Melbourne U., Australia, 1962; M in Rural Sci./Physiology, U. New Eng., Australia, 1968, PhD, 1974. Rsch. asst. Melbourne U., 1962-63; demonstrator U. New Eng., Armidale, Australia, 1963-66, teaching fellow, 1966-69; asst. prof. zoophysiology and nutrition Inst. Arctic Biology, U. Alaska, Fairbanks, 1970-75; assoc. prof. U. Alaska, Fairbanks, 1975-81, prof., 1981—; acting dir. Inst. Arctic Biology, U. Alaska, Fairbanks, 1985, 92, dir., 1993—; dir. Large Animal Rsch. Sta., 1979—. Co-editor: (with Hudson) Bioenergetics of Wild Herbivores, 1985; editor: (proceedings, with Klein, Keller) First International Muskox Symposium, 1984 (proceedings, with Luick, Lent, Klein) First International Reindeer and Caribou Symposium, 1975; editorial bd.: Rangifer/Biol. Papers U. Alaska; contbr. over 100 papers to profl. jours. Pipe major Fairbanks Red Hackle Pipe Band, 1975-90; pres. Fairbanks Nordic Ski Club, 1973-75. NATO Rsch. fellow, Trondheim, Norway, 1975-76. Fellow AAAS (Alaska chmn. 1985, 94), Arctic Inst. N.Am.; mem. Am. Physiol. Soc., Wildlife Soc., Am. Soc. Mammologists, Australasian Soc. Willdlife Mgmt., Australian Soc. Animal Prodn., Australian Soc. Biochemistry and Molecular Biology, Sigma Xi. Office: U Alaska Inst Arctic Biology Fairbanks AK 99775

WHITE, ROBERT RANKIN, writer and historian, hydrologist; b. Houston, Feb. 8, 1942; s. Rankin Jones and Eleanor Margaret (White) W. BA in Geology, U. Tex., 1964; MS in Hydrology, U. Ariz., 1971; PhD in Am. studies, U. N.Mex., 1993. Hydrologist Tex. Water Devel. Bd., Austin, 1972-74; hydrologist U.S. Geol. Survey, Las Cruces, N.Mex., 1974-78, Santa Fe, 1978-80, Albuquerque, 1980-89; writer, historian Albuquerque, 1989—; mem. planning bd. N.Mex. Art History Conf., Taos, N.Mex., 1987—. Author: The Lithographs and Etchings of E. Martin Hennings, 1978, The Taos Soc. of Artists, 1983; co-author: Pioneer Artists of Taos, 1983, Bert Geer Phillips and The Taos Art Colony, 1994; contbr. articles to profl. jours. Bd. dirs. Friends of U. N.Mex. Librs., Albuquerque, 1984-90. With U.S. Army, 1965-68. Mem. NRA (life), Hist. Soc. N.Mex. (pres. 1991-93), N.Mex. Book League (pres. 1994, exec. dir. 1996—), Taos County Hist. Soc. Episcopalian. Home and Office: 1409 Las Lomas Rd NE Albuquerque NM 87106-4529

WHITE, ROBERT STEPHEN, physics educator; b. Ellsworth, Kans., Dec. 28, 1920; s. Byron F. and Sebina (Leighty) W.; m. Freda Marie Bridgewater, Aug. 30, 1942; children: Nancy Lynn, Margaret Diane, John Stephen, David

Bruce. AB, Southwestern Coll., 1942, DSc hon., 1971; MS, U. Ill., 1943; PhD, U. Calif., Berkeley, 1951. Physicist Lawrence Radiation Lab., Berkeley, Livermore, Calif., 1948-61; head dept. particles and fields Space Physics Lab. Aerospace Corp., El Segundo, Calif., 1962-67; physics prof. U. Calif., Riverside, 1967-92, dir. Inst. Geophysics and Planetary Physics, 1967-92, chmn. dept. physics, 1970-73, prof. emeritus physics dept., rsch. physicist, 1992—; lectr. U. Calif., Berkeley, 1953-54, 57-59. Author: Space Physics, 1970; contbr. articles to profl. jours. Officer USNR, 1944-46. Sr. Postdoctoral fellow NSF, 1961-62; grantee NASA, NSF, USAF, numerous others. Fellow AAAS, Am. Phys. Soc. (exec. com. 1972-74); mem. AAUP, Am. Geophys. Union, Am. Astron. Soc. Home: 5225 Austin Rd Santa Barbara CA 93111-2905 Office: U Calif Inst Geophysics & Planetary Physics Riverside CA 92521

WHITE, ROBERTA LEE, comptroller; b. Denver, Sept. 18, 1946; d. Harold Tindall and Araminta (Campbell) Bangs; m. Lewis Paul White, Jr., Jan. 23, 1973 (div. Sept. 1974). BA cum laude, Linfield Coll., 1976; postgrad., Lewis and Clark Coll. Lic. tax preparer, Oreg. Office mgr. Multnomah County Auditor, Portland, Oreg., 1977-81; rsch. asst. Dan Goldy and Assocs., Portland, 1981-83; regional asst. Vocat. Rehab., Eugene, Oreg., 1983-85; internal auditor Multnomah County, Portland, 1985-89; cons. Portland, 1989-91; fin. analyst City of Portland, 1991-93; comptroller Wordsmith Svcs., Portland, 1993—; mem. Com. for Implementation of the ADA, Portland, 1991-93. Treas. Mary Wendy Roberts for Sec. of State, Portland, 1992, Re-Elect Mary Wendy Roberts, Portland, 1990, Elect Hank Miggins Com., 1994; mem. Oreg. Women's Polit. Caucus, Portland, 1982-85, City Club, Portland, 1978-81. Democrat. Mem. Disciples of Christ. Home: 1620 NE Irving Apt 80 Portland OR 97232 Office: The Marchbanks Agy Inc 6355 SE Tibbetts Portland OR 97206

WHITE, RONALD CEDRIC, JR., religion educator; b. Mpls., May 22, 1939; s. Ronald Cedric and Evelyn Ann (Pearson) W.; m. Sherrie Rosalind Derrick, June 18, 1964 (div. Nov. 1988); children: Melissa Gale White Clawson, Bradley Derrick; m. Cynthia Conger, Nov. 23, 1991. BA, UCLA, 1961; MDiv, Princeton Theol. Sem., 1964; MA, Princeton U., 1970, PhD, 1972. Ordained to ministry Presbyn. Ch., 1964. Min. First Presbyn. Ch., Colorado Springs, Colo., 1964-68; lectr. history Colo. Coll., Colorado Springs, 1965-66; chaplain, asst. prof. Am. studies Rider Coll., Lawrenceville, N.J., 1972-74; chaplain, assoc. prof. religion Whitworth Coll., Spokane, Wash., 1974-80, assoc. prof., chair dept. religion and philosophy, 1980-81; lectr. in ch. history, dir. continuing edn. Princeton (N.J.) Theol. Sem., 1981-88; rsch. scholar The Huntington Libr., San Marino, Calif., 1988-95; Presby. Eccles. prof. Fuller Theol. Sem., Pasadena, Calif., 1988-92; lectr. in history UCLA, 1991-95; v.p. acad. affairs, dean of the sem., prof. ch. history San Francisco Theol. Sem., 1995—; vis. prof. ch. history San Francisco Sem./Grad. Theol. Union, San Anselmo/Berkelry, Calif., 1979;. Author: The Social Gospel: Religion and Reform in Changing America, 1976, Liberty and Justice for All, 1990; editor, author: American Christianity: A Case Approach,1986, An Unsettled Arena: Religion and the Bill of Rights, 1990. Founding dir. Martin Luther King Edn. Fund, Colorado Springs, 1968; trustee Spokane Peace and Justice Ctr., Spokane, 1976-80, Wesley-Westminster Found., Princeton U., 1984-86. World Coun. Chs. scholar Lincoln Theol. Coll., Eng., 1966-67; Ford Found. fellow, 1970-72; Haynes-Huntington fellow; Lilly Endowment scholar, 1992-94. Mem. Am. Hist. Assn., Am. Soc. Ch. History, Orgn. Am. Historians, Assn. of Case Teaching (bd. dirs.). Democrat. Home: 79 Bolines Ave San Anselmo CA 94960

WHITE, STANLEY ARCHIBALD, research electrical engineer; b. Providence, Sept. 25, 1931; s. Clarence Archibald White and Lou Ella (Givens) Arford; m. Edda Maria Castaño-Benitez, June 6, 1956; children: Dianne, Stanley Jr., Paul, John. BSEE, Purdue U., 1957, MSEE, 1959, PhD, 1965. Registered profl. engr., Ind., Calif. Engr. Rockwell Internat., Anaheim, Calif., 1959-68, mgr., 1968-84, sr. scientist, 1984-90; pres. Signal Processing and Controls Engrng. Corp., 1990—; adj. prof. elec. engrng. U. Calif., 1984—; cons. and lectr. in field; bd. dirs. Asilomar Signals, Systems and Computers Conf. Corp. Publisher, composer music; contbr. chpts. to books; articles to profl. jours.; patentee in field. With USAF, 1951-55. Fellow N.Am. Aviation Sci. Engrng., 1963-65; recipient Disting. Lectr. award Nat. Electronics Conf., Chgo., 1973, Engr. of Yr. award Orange County (Calif.) Engrng. Coun., 1984, Engr. of Yr. award Rockwell Internat., 1985, Leonardo Da Vinci Medallion, 1986, Sci. Achievement award, 1987, Disting. Engrng. Alumnus award Purdue U., 1988, Meritorious Inventor's award Rockwell Internat. Corp., 1989, Outstanding Elec. Engr. award Purdue U., 1992. Fellow AAAS, AIAA, IEEE (Centennial medalist chair of ICASSP and ISCAS, Signal Processing Soc. disting. lect. and founding chmn. L.A. coun. chpt., Circuits and Sys. Soc. Tech. Achievement award 1996), Inst. for Advancement Engrng., N.Y. Acad. Scis.; mem. Choral Condrs. Guild and Saddleback Master Chorale; mem. Air Force Assn. (life), Am. Legion (life), Sigma Xi (founding pres. Orange County chpt.), Eta Kappa Nu (disting. fellow, internat. dir. emeritus), Tau Beta Pi. Home: 433 E Avenida Cordoba San Clemente CA 92672-2350

WHITE, TIM DALE, minister; b. LaGrands, Oreg., June 29, 1955; s. Dale Vernon and Elizabeth Jane (Saunders) W.; m. Jackie Ann Svangren, Dec. 18, 1974; children: Betsie, Roman, Becca. MDiv, Western Evang. Sem., Portland, Oreg., 1984; postgrad., Eastern Wash. U., Cheney. Ordained to ministry Evangelical Ch., 1978. Youth pastor Cathedral of the Desert, Richland, Wash., 1974-84; founding pastor Wash. Cathedral, Redmond, 1984-96. Author: To Dreamers Long Forgotten, 1991. Mem. Chs. United in Global Mission, Garden Grove, Calif., 1992-96. Office: Wash Cathedral 12300 Woodinville Redmond Rd NE Redmond WA 98052

WHITE, VICTOR DEA, airport management executive; b. Ft. Worth, Tex., Mar. 16, 1951; s. Victor George and Louise Emily (Roach) W.; m. Denise Sue Bonzo, Sept. 3, 1977; children: Kathy, Tiffany, Daniel. BS in Bus. and Transportation with honors, St. Louis U., 1974. Airport mgmt. intern St. Louis Internat. Airport, 1974-75; airport mgmt. cons. Landrum & Brown, Cinn., 1975-77; airport duty mgr. Dallas/Ft. Worth Internat. Airport, 1977-81; exec. dir Waukegan (Ill.) Port Authority, 1981-83; dir. airports City of Midland (Tex.)/Odessa, 1983-90; dep. dir. airports Salt Lake City Airport Authority, 1990—; pres. U.S. Airport Svcs. Corp., Salt Lake City, 1983—, Bedford Industries Corp., Ft. Worth, 1977—. Author: Small Hub Airport Management, 1985. Chmn. Midland/Odessa Interant. Task Force, 1986-90, Mayor's Transp. Task Force 1991-95, Mayor's Americans with Disabilities Task Force 1991-94, Internat. Airport Rescue/Firefighting Acad. 1986-89, Internat. Airport Facilities Conf. 1993; mem. The Midland Com., 1986-90. Alpha Sigma Nu scholar, 1974, Alpha Chi scholar, 1974. Mem. Am. Assn. Airport Execs (pres. Northwest chpt. 1993-95, Southcentral chpt. 1988-90), Midland C. of C. (chmn. aviation task force 1986—). Republican. Roman Catholic. Office: Salt Lake City Internat Airport AMF Box 22084 776 N Terminal Dr Salt Lake City UT 84122*

WHITE, W. ROBIN, author; b. Kodaikanal, Madras, India, July 12, 1928; came to U.S., 1944; s. Emmons Eaton and Ruth Esther (Parker) W.; m. Marian Lucille Biesterfield, Feb. 3, 1948 (dec. Mar. 1983); children: Christopher, Parker, Shelley. BA, Yale U., 1950; MA, Calif. State Poly. U., 1991. Instr. writers program UCLA, 1985-93; lectr. Calif. State Poly. U., Pomona, 1985-93; exec. officer Calif. State Regional Ctrs., Ukiah, Calif., 1973-79. Author: Elephant Hill, 1959 (Harper prize), House of Many Rooms, 1958, Men and Angels, 1961, Foreign Soil, 1962, All in Favor Say No, 1964, His Own Kind, 1967, Be Not Afraid, 1972, The Special Child, 1978, The Troll of Crazy Mule Camp, 1979, Moses the Man, 1981, The Winning Writer, 1997, Studies in the Art of Self-Expression, 1997; anthologies include: Best American Stories, O. Henry Prize Stories, Best Modern Short Stories, Seventeen's Stories, others; contbr. numerous mags. including Harper's, The New Yorker, New York Times, L.A. Times, Harper's Bazaar, Saturday Evening Post, Ladies' Home Jour., Seventeen, Nat. Wildlife, Mademoiselle, The Reporter; author poetry (Poetry award 1993, 94, 95); editor-in-chief Per/Se Internat. Quar., 1965-69; fiction editor UCLA West/Word, 1989-90. Class rep. Kodai-Woodstock Found., 1986—; elder Presbyn. Session, Claremont, Calif., 1988-91; mem. libr. commn. Pasadena Presbyn. Ch., 1996—. Recipient Disting. Achievement award Ednl. Press Assn., 1974, North Coast Regional Ctr., Ukiah, 1978; Bread Loaf fellow Middlebury Coll., 1956, Stegner fellow Stanford U., 1956-57. Mem. Calif. State Poetry Soc., Authors Guild. Democrat. Presbyterian. Home: 1940 Fletcher Ave South Pasadena CA 91030

WHITEHEAD, ARDELLE COLEMAN, advertising and public relations executive; b. Carrollton, Ohio, May 13, 1917; d. James David and Gilsie Dale (Hendricks) Coleman. BS, Wittenberg U., 1938. Account exec. Steve Hannagan Assocs., N.Y.C., 1946-52; dir. publicity Fieldcrest Mills, Inc., N.Y.C., 1952-55; account and pub. rels. exec. Calkins & Holden, N.Y.C., 1956-59; creative dir. Leslie Advt. Agy., Greenville, S.C., 1960-62; dir. advt. Lanz Originals, Los Angeles, 1962-64; account exec., copywriter, consumer affairs specialist Jennings & Thompson, Phoenix, 1965-73; mgr. pub. communications Valley Nat. Bank, Phoenix, 1974-75; pres. The Whiteheads, Inc., Phoenix, 1976-96. Author: (pamphlets) How to Be a Client, 1979, Advertising Isn't Everything, 1981; contbr. articles to various Phoenix and regional art mags. Recipient Lulu award Los Angeles Advt. Women, 1974; named Adperson of Yr. Ad II of Phoenix, 1978. Mem. Pub. Relations Soc. (Percy award 1985), Women in Communications (Woman of Achievement award for west region 1981), Phoenix Advt. Club (hon. life mem.).

WHITEHEAD, PAUL LEON, physician; b. Salt Lake City, May 23, 1936; s. Rolland N. and Marva B. (Bullock) W.; m. Marilyn Davis, Sept. 5, 1964; children: Anne, Paul D., Kathryn, Emily. BS, U. Utah, 1957, MD, 1960. Diplomate Am. Bd. Psychiatry and Neurology-Psychiatry (examiner child and adolescent psychiatry 1976—, examiner gen. psychiatry 1994—), Am. Bd. Psychiatry and Neurology-Child Psychiatry. Pvt. practice of child, adolescent and adult psychiatry, 1967—; clin. prof. psychiatry U. Utah Coll. Medicine, 1977—; pub. affairs rep. Utah Psychiat. Assn., 1977-89, 91-93; psychiat. cons. Salt Lake Alliance for the Mentally Ill, 1991—; active med. staff Primary Children's Med. Ctr., 1967—, dir. children's psychiat. ctr., 1967-75, chmn. dept. child psychiatry, 1975-81, chmn. human subjects com., 1978-81; cons. child psychiatry Utah State Divsn. Health, 1968-80, Wyo. State Hosp., 1976-77; cons. Children's Ctr. Group Home, Salt Lake City, 1968-69; chmn. adv. coun. children's svcs. Utah State Divsn. Mental Health, 1968-73; mem. Utah State Mental Health Task Force, 1969-71; mem. adv. bd. Salt Lake City Cmty. Mental Health Ctr., 1971-75; courtesy med. staff St. Mark's Hosp., LDS Hosp.; chmn. Norman S. Anderson, M.D. award Fund bd., 1993-95; del. Intermountain Acad. of Child and Adolescent Psychiatry to Assembly of Regional Orgns., Am. Acad. of Child and Adolescent Psychiatry, 1987-91; psychiat. admissions rev. com. to advise Utah State Legis., 1989-90; med. dir. CPC Olympus View Hosp., Salt Lake city, 1986-88; instr. psychiatry coll. medicine U. Utah, 1969-70, asst. prof., 1970-76, dir. divsn. child and adolescent psychiatry, 1977-78; mem. med. evaluation com. St. Mark's Hosp., 1985, chmn. libr. com., 1986; mem. Spl. Rev. Task Force Valley Mental Health, 1988-89; presenter in field. Contbr. numerous articles to profl. jours. Gen. Med. Officer USAF, 1961-63. Ford Early Admissions scholarship, 1953-57; recipient Norman S. Anderson, MD award, 1989. Fellow Am. Psychiat. Assn., Am. Acad. Child and Adolescent Psychiatry (continuing edn. com. 1977-90); mem. AMA, Utah State Med. Assn. (dangerous drugs com. 1971-75, del. ho. dels. 1975-79, legis. com. 1976-77, bd. dirs. acad. continuing med. edn. 1978-84, chmn. psychiat. sect. ann. sci. meeting 1987), Salt Lake County Med. Soc., Utah Psychiat. Assn. (pres. 1977-78), Intermountain Acad. Child and Adolescent Psychiatry (pres. 1969-70), Alpha Omega Alpha (pres. 1959-60), Phi Beta Kappa. Office: Paul L Whitehead MD & Assocs 1580 E 3900 S Ste 200 Salt Lake City UT 84124-1567

WHITEHILL, JULES LEONARD, surgeon, educator; b. N.Y.C., Mar. 7, 1912; s. Karl and Jenny (Abrahams) W.; m. Muriel Jeannette Berry, Sept. 21, 1943 (dec.); children: Jonathan Robert (dec.), David Carl Evan, Jules Leonard II (dec.). BS magna cum laude, CCNY, 1931; MD, NYU, 1935. Diplomate Am. Bd. Surgery. Intern, resident, fellow Mt. Sinai Hosp., N.Y.C., 1935-40; assoc. Dr. John Garlock, Dr. Leon Ginzburg, N.Y.C., 1940-42; pvt. practice surgery, chief of surgery Pima County Hosp., Tucson, 1946-60; prof., chair dept. surgery Chgo. Med. Sch., 1960-70, prof. emeritus, 1970—; chief of surgery, med. dir. Mt. Sinai Med. Ctr., Chgo.; cons. in field San Diego, 1970—; trustee Chapman Coll., Orange, Calif., 1971-76; chmn. bd. dirs. World Campus Afloat, Orange, 1971-76; bd. visitors, steering com. exec. bd. U. Calif. San Diego Med. Sch., 1996—; vis. prof. surgery U. Zagreb, Yugoslavia, 1969; chmn. bd., pres. Equidyne Systems Inc., 1996—. Col. USAF, 1941—, Africa, Italy, France, 3rd gen. hosp. comdr. gen. surg. team 5th Aux. Surg. Group. Stroock scholar, N.Y. Regents scholar; Gallatin fellow NYU; Jules Leonard Whitehill chair in surgery named in his honor NYU; recipient citation Surgeon Gen. USAF. Fellow Am. Coll. Surgeons; mem. N.Y. Acad. Sci., Chgo. Surg. Soc., AMA, Internat. Coll. Surgeons (regent, bd. govs.), Royal Soc. Medicine (England), Phi Beta Kappa, Alpha Omega Alpha. Home: 5238 Renaissance Ave San Diego CA 92122-5602

WHITENER, PHILIP CHARLES, aeronautical engineer, consultant; b. Keokuk, Iowa, July 9, 1920; s. Henry Carroll and Katherine Ethel (Graham) W.; m. Joy Carrie Page, Oct. 9, 1943; children: David A., Barbara C., Wendy R., Dixie K. BSME, U. N.Mex., 1941. Ordained to elder Presbyn. Ch., 1956. Engr. Boeing Airplane Co., Seattle, 1941-47, supr. wind tunnel model design, 1947-57, project engr. B-52 flight test, 1957-62, engrng. mgr. Fresh I hydrofoil, 1962-65, configurator supersonic transport, 1965-70, with preliminary design advanced concepts, 1970-83, ret., 1983; pres., chief engr. Alpha-Dyne Corp., Bainbridge Island, Wash., 1983—. Inventee in field. Organizer Trinity Ch., Burien, Wash., 1962, Highline Reformed Presbyn., Burien, 1970, Liberty Bay Presbyn., Poulsbo, Wash., 1978; pres. Whitener Family Found., Bainbridge Island, 1979; bd. dirs. Mcpl. League of Bainbridge, 1993—, v.p., 1994, pres., 1996; pres. Mcpl. League Found., 1994—. Republican. Home: 5955 NE Battle Point Dr Bainbridge Island WA 98110

WHITESIDE, CAROL GORDON, state official, former mayor; b. Chgo., Dec. 15, 1942; d. Paul George and Helen Louise (Barre) G.; m. John Gregory Whiteside, Aug. 15, 1964; children: Brian Paul, Derek James. BA, U. Calif., Davis, 1964. Pers. mgr. Emporium Capwell Co., Santa Rosa, 1964-67; pers. asst. Levi Strauss & Co., San Francisco, 1967-69; project leader Interdatum, San Francisco, 1983-88; with City Coun. Modesto, 1983-87; mayor City of Modesto, 1987-91; asst. sec. for intergovtl. rels. The Resources Agy., State of Calif., Sacramento, 1991-93; dir. intergovtl. affairs Gov.'s Office, Sacramento, 1993—. Trustee Modesto City Schs., 1979-83; nat. pres. Rep. Mayors and Local Ofcls., 1990. Named Outstanding Woman of Yr. Women's Commn., Stanislaus County, Calif., 1988, Woman of Yr., 27th Assembly Dist., 1991; Toll fellow Coun. of State Govts., 1996. Republican. Lutheran. Office: Governor's Office 1400 10th St Sacramento CA 95814-5502

WHITESIDE, LOWELL STANLEY, seismologist; b. Trinidad, Colo., Jan. 7, 1946; s. Paul Edward and Carrie Belle (Burgess) W. BS, Hamline U., 1968; postgrad., Oswego State U. of N.Y., 1970-72; MS, U. Nebr., 1985; postgrad., Ga. Inst. of Tech., 1986-88, U. Colo., 1990-94. Instr. U.S. Peace Corps, Mhlume, Swaziland, 1968-71; rsch. assoc. CIRES, U. Colo., Boulder, 1988-90; geophysicist in charge of internat. earthquake data base NOAA, Nat. Geophys. Data Ctr., Boulder, 1990—; vis. rschr. Nuclear and Geol. Scis. Inst., Wellington, New Zealand, 1997. Scoutmaster Boy Scouts Am., St. Paul, Lincoln, Nebr., 1968-80, camp counselor, 1968-76. Recipient Eagle Scout award Boy Scouts Am., 1968, NGDC/DOAA Customer Svc. award, 1995. Mem. AAAS (chmn. 1986-87, vice chmn. 1985-86, Geology-Geography, Rocky Mountain sect., Outstanding Articles Referee 1992, Best Student Paper award 1984, 85), Seismol. Soc. of Am., Am. Geophys. Union, Sierra Club, Planetary Soc. Presbyterian. Home: PO Box 3141 Eldorado Springs CO 80025-3141 Office: NOAA/NGDC/NESOIS 325 Broadway St Boulder CO 80303-3337

WHITE-VONDRAN, MARY-ELLEN, retired stockbroker; b. East Cleveland, Ohio, Aug. 21, 1938; d. Thomas Patrick and Rita Ellen (Langdon) White; m. Gary L. Vondran, Sr., Nov. 25, 1961; children: Patrick Michael, Gary Lee Jr. BA, Notre Dame Coll., South Euclid, Ohio, 1960; postgrad., John Carroll U., 1960, U. Mass., 1961, U. S.C., 1969, San Jose State U., 1971-75, U. Santa Clara, Calif., 1972, Stanford U., 1989; MSL, Peninsula U., Mountain View, Calif., 1994; Intern Program in Legal Field, DeAnza Coll., Calif., 1996-97. Cert. life secondary tchr., Calif.; lic. NASD series 7, 18 & 63 broker. Tchr. Cleve. Sch. Dist., 1960-61, East Hartford (Conn.) Sch. Dist., 1961-62, San Francisco Bay Area Sch. Dist., 1970-75; life and disability agt. Travelers Ins. Co. and BMA Ins. Co., San Jose, Calif., 1975-77; stockbroker Reynolds, Bache, Shearson, Palo Alto, Calif., 1977-78, Schwab & Co., San Francisco, 1980; adminstr. pension and profit Crocker Nat. Bank, San Francisco, 1980-82; stockbroker Calif. Fed./Invest Co., San Francisco, 1982-83; head trader, br. mgr. Rose & Co., San Francisco, 1983-84; ret., 1984; tchr. citizenship for fgn. born adult community edn. Fremont Union High Sch. Dist., Sunnyvale, Calif., 1988—. Author: Jo Mora-Renaissance Man, 1973, Visit of Imperial Russian Navy to San Francisco, 1974, John Franklin Miller, 1974, 1905 Quail Meadow Road. Sec. Quota Internat., Los Altos, Calif., 1987; constn. chairperson LWV, Los Altos, 1985—, lectr. speakers bur. 1987, moderator, co-producer TV/Cable programs; precinct capt. 1988 & 90 Elections, Los Altos; appointee ad hoc com. for transp. of mobility impaired Santa Clara County, 1988; vol. tchr. English in Action; usher lively arts Stanford U.; mem. tele com. Peninsula Dem. Coalition; active Internat. Vis. Com., Palo Alto, People for Accessible Health Care, Women in History Mus., Calif. History Ctr., Cupertino, Palo Alto Neighbors Abroad. Recipient Valley Cable Recognition award, 1988. Mem. AAUW, ACLU, NOW (speakers bur. coord.), World Affairs Forum, Women in History Assn., The Great War Soc., Am. Assn. Retired Persons, Older Women's League, Los Altos Women in Bus., Women's Internat. League for Peace & Freedom, Irish Cultural Soc., Commonwealth Club (steering com., program com. Palo Alto/Midpeninsula chpt.), Kenna Club. Democrat. Roman Catholic. *Personal philosophy: Live life fully! Do everything that you want - if you can!.*

WHITFORD, JOSEPH P., lawyer; b. N.Y.C., Apr. 30, 1950. BA, Union Coll., 1972; JD, Syracuse U., 1975; LLM in Taxation, George Washington U., 1978. Bar: N.Y. 1976, D.C. 1977, Wash. 1979. Staff atty. divsn. corp. fin. SEC, Washington, 1975-78; assoc. Foster, Pepper & Shefelman, Seattle, 1978-83, ptnr., 1983—; chmn. bd. dirs. MIT Forum on the Northwest, 1992-93. Office: Foster Pepper & Shefelman 1111 3rd Ave Fl 34 Seattle WA 98101-3207

WHITING, ARTHUR MILTON, diversified company executive; b. St. Johns, Ariz., 1928. With Kaibab Industries, chmn., chief exec. officer; formerly bd. dir. Western Savs. & Loan, Western Fin. Corp. Office: Kaibab Industries 4602 E Thomas Rd Phoenix AZ 85018-7710

WHITLEY, DAVID SCOTT, archaeologist; b. Williams AFB, Ariz., Mar. 5, 1953; s. Edgar Duer and Yvonne Roca (Wightman) W.; m. Tamara Katherine Koteles, Feb. 13, 1987; 1 child, Carmen. AB in Anthrop. & Geog. (magna cum laude), U. Calif., 1976, MA in Geography, 1979, PhD in Anthropology, 1982. Soc. Profl. Archeology. Chief archeologist Inst. Archeology UCLA, L.A., 1983-87; rsch. fellow Archeology Dept. U. Witwatersrand, Johannesburg, S. Africa, 1987-89; pres. W&S Cons., Simi Valley, Calif., 1989—; U.S. rep. internat. com. rock art Internat. Coun. Monuments and Sites, 1992—, exec. com., 1997-99. Author: A Guide to Rock Art Sites: Southern California and Southern Nevada, 1996, L'Art des chamanes: art rupestre en Californie, 1997; editor: archeological monographs; contbr. articles to profl. jours. Prehistoric Archeologist, State of Calif. Hist. Resources Commn., 1986-87; mem. rsch. adv. com. Chauvet Cave, France, 1996—. Recipient post doctoral fellowship, Assn. for Field Archeology, 1983, tech. specialist grant, U.S. Aid, 1986. Fellow Am. Anthrop. Assn.; mem. Soc. Am. Archeology, SAR, Sons of the Indian Wars, Mayflower Soc. Home: 447 3rd St Fillmore CA 93015-1413 Office: W&S Consultants 2422 Stinson St Simi Valley CA 93065

WHITLOW, DONNA MAE, daycare and primary school administrator; b. Buffalo, S.D., May 23, 1933; d. Carl Axel and Esther Johanna (Wickman) Magnuson; married, June 13, 1953; children: Debra Diane Reasy, Cathleen Denise Corallo, Lisa Mae. Diploma, Eugene Bible Coll., 1956; BA in Religious Edn., Internat. Seminary, 1985, MA, 1986. Corp. sec. various orgns., 1953-56; asst. registrar, prof. child edn. Calif. Open Bible Inst., Pasadena, 1956-57; dir. religious edn. and music, sec. to gen. bd. Jamaica Open Bible Inst., 1958-59; dir. religious edn. and music, sec. to gen. bd.. prof. on staff, bus. mgr. Trinidad Open Bible Inst., 1960-65; asst. to full-charge bookkeeper Jennings Strouss Law Firm, 1966-68; dir. religious edn. and music., mem. gen. bd., assoc. pastor Biltmore Bible Ch., Phoenix, Ariz., 1967-93; founder, dir. Biltmore Bible Day Care & Kindergarten, Phoenix, 1977—; founder bible schs. in South Africa, Argentina, Ctrl. Am., Europe, Caribbean, Singapore. Author: How To Start a Daycare in the Local Church, 1986. Republican. Home: 2144 E Lamar Rd Phoenix AZ 85016-1147 Office: Biltmore Bible Ch 3330 E Camelback Rd Phoenix AZ 85018-2310

WHITMAN, KATHY VELMA ROSE (ELK WOMAN WHITMAN), artist, sculptor, jeweler, painter, educator; b. Bismarck, N.D., Aug. 12, 1952; d. Carl Jr. and Edith Geneva (Lykken) W.; m. Robert Paul Luger, Feb. 21, 1971 (div. Jan. 1982); children: Shannon, Lakota, Cannupa, Palani; m. Dean P. Fox (div. 1985); 1 child, Otgadahe. Student, Standing Rock C.C., Ft. Yates, N.D., 1973-74, Sinte Gleska Coll., Rosebud, S.D., 1975-77, U. S.D., 1977, Ariz. State U., 1992-93. Instr. art Sinte Gleska Coll., 1975-77, Standing Rock C.C., 1977-78; co-mgr. Four Bears Motor Lodge, New Town, N.D., 1981-82; store owner Nux-Baga Lodge, New Town, 1982-85; artist-in-residence N.D. Coun. on Arts, Bismarck, 1983-84, bd. dirs., 1985; artist-in-residence Evanston Twp. H.S., Ill., 1996; cultural cons. movie prodn., Phoenix, Ariz., 1994. One woman shows include Mus. of Am. Indian, N.Y.C., 1983, Charleroi Internat. Fair, Belgium, 1984, Heard Mus., Phoenix, 1987-92, Phoenix Gallery, Nurnburg, Germany, 1990-96, Lovena Ohl Gallery, Phoenix, 1990-94, Phoenix Gallery, Coeur d'Alene, Idaho, 1992, Turquoise Tortoise Gallery, Tubac, Ariz., 1992-93, Yah-ta-hey Gallery, New London, Conn., 1992-93, Silver Sun Gallery, Santa Fe, N.Mex., 1992-96, Tribal Expessions Gallery, Arlington Heights, Ill., 1994-96, others; represented in permanent collections at Mus. of the Am. Indian, N.Y.C., Mesa (Ariz.) C.C. Bd. dirs. Ft. Berthold C.C., New Town, 1983-85; pres. Cannonball (N.D.) Pow-Wow Com., 1978; parent rep. Head Start, Ft. Yates, 1974. Recipient best craftsman spl. award Bullock's Indian Arts and Crafts, 1986, best of fine arts award No. Plains Tribal Arts, Sioux Falls, S.D., 1988, best of show award Pasadena Western Relic and Native Am. Show, 1991, 2 1st place awards Santa Fe Indian Market, 1993, 2 2nd place awards, 1994, 2 3rd place awards, 1994, 74th Ann. SWAIA Santa Fe Indian Mkt. 1st place award, 1995, 2d place award, 1995, 2 3rd place awards, 1995, 2 Honorable Mentions in sculpture N.Mex. State Fair, 1996. Mem. Indian Arts and Crafts Assn., S.W. Assn. on Indian Affairs (life, 1st and 2nd place awards Santa Fe Indian Market 1995, 2 3rd place awards 1995, 1st place and 2nd place awards Santa Fe Indian Market 1996). Home and Studio: 2717 E Victor Hugo Ave Phoenix AZ 85032

WHITMAN, SCOTT RANDY, computer scientist; b. Balt., Oct. 11, 1961; s. J. Martin and Adrienne Frances (Ableman) W.; m. Carol. Ann Mattioli, Dec. 27, 1991. BS, Carnegie-Mellon U., 1983; MS, Ohio State U., 1987, PhD, 1991. Applications engr. Evans & Sutherland C.C., Phila., 1983-85; graphics programmer Cranston-Csuri Prodns., Columbus, Ohio, 1985; grad. teaching asst. Ohio State Computer Sci., Columbus, Ohio, 1985-86, Ohio State Supercomputer Ctr., Columbus, Ohio, 1986-90; researcher Lawrence Livermore Lab., Livermore, Calif., 1991-93; mem. tech. staff David Sarnoff Rsch. Ctr., Princeton, N.J., 1993-94; PATP visualization scientist Cray Rsch., Pasadena, Calif., 1994-97; MTS Equator Techs., Seattle, 1997—; invited spkr. HPCGV Conf., 1995, Bilkent Graphics Conf., 1993, Paragraph Conf., 1990, Aizu (Japan) Internat. Symposium on Parallel Algorithms/Arch. Synthesis; vis. lectr. UCLA, 1996—. Author: Multiprocessor Methods for Computer Graphics Rendering, 1992; contbr. articles to profl. jours. Senator CMU Student Senate, Pitts., 1982. Mem. IEEE Computer Soc., Assn. Computing Machinery. Home: 500 N Rosemead Blvd Apt 1 Pasadena CA 91107-2115 Office: Equator Techs 520 Pike St Ste 900 Seattle WA 98119

WHITMORE, DONALD CLARK, retired engineer; b. Seattle, Sept. 15, 1932; s. Floyd Robinson and Lois Mildred (Clark) W.; m. Alice Elinor Winter, Jan. 8, 1955; children: Catherine Ruth, William Owen, Matthew Clark, Nancy Lynn, Peggy Ann, Stuart John. BS, U. Wash., 1955. Prin. engr. The Boeing Co., Seattle, 1955-87, ret., 1987; developer, owner mobile home pk., Auburn, Wash., 1979—. Author: Towards Security, 1983, (monograph) SDI Software Feasibility, 1990, Characterization of the Nuclear Proliferation Threat, 1993, Rationale for Nuclear Disarmament, 1995. Activist for arms control, Auburn, Wash., 1962—; chmn. Seattle Coun. Orgns. for Internat. Affairs, 1973, Auburn Citizens for Schs., 1975; v.p. Boeing Employees Good Neighbor Fund, Seattle, 1977, Spl. Svc. award, 1977; bd. dirs. 8th Congl. Dist. Sane/Freeze, 1992—; pres., founder Third Millennium

Found., 1994—. Home and Office: 16202 SE Lake Moneysmith Rd Auburn WA 98092-5274

WHITNEY, DAVID CLAY, business educator, consultant, writer; b. Astoria, Oreg., May 30, 1937; s. Rolla Vernon and Barbara (Clay) W.; m. Kathleen Donnelley, 1956 (div. 1963); children: David Jr., Sandra, Sara; m. Zelda Gifford, 1967 (div. 1973); m. Emily Jane Williams, 1992. BS in Chemistry, San Diego State U., 1959; PhD in Chemistry, U. Calif., Berkeley, 1963. Cert. data processor, cert. data educator. Acting asst. prof. U. Calif., Davis, 1962-63; chemist, mathematician Shell Devel. Corp., Emeryville, Calif., 1963-72; dir. computer services Systems Applications, Inc., San Rafael, Calif., 1973-77; prof. Coll. Bus. San Frandico State U., 1977—; info. systems cons. numerous cos., 1977—; textbook reviewer numerous pubs., 1979—. Author: Instructors' Guides to Understanding Fortran, 1977, 83, 87, Understanding Fortran, 1984, 88, BASIC, 1988, 89, 95. Mem. Assn. Computing Machinery, Data Processing Mgmt. Assn., Soc. Data Educators, Mensa. Home: 1501 S Norfolk St San Mateo CA 94401-3605 Office: San Francisco State U Coll of Bus San Francisco CA 94132

WHITNEY, JANE, foreign service officer; b. Champaign, Ill., July 15, 1941; d. Robert F. and Mussette (Cary) W. BA, Beloit Coll., 1963; CD, U. Aix, Marseille, France, 1962. Joined Fgn. Service, U.S. Dept. State, 1965, vice consul, Saigon, Vietnam, 1966-68, career counselor, 1968-70, spl. asst. Office of Dir. Gen., 1970-72, consul, Stuttgart, Fed. Republic Germany, 1972-74, Ankara, Turkey, 1974-76, spl. asst. Office of Asst. Sec. for Consular Affairs, 1976-77, mem. Bd. Examiners Fgn. Service, 1977-78, 79-81, consul, Munich, Germany, 1978-79, Buenos Aires, Argentina, 1981-82, ethics officer Office of Legal Adviser, 1982-85, advisor Office of Asst. Sec. for Diplomatic Security, 1985-86, dep. prin. officer, consul, Stuttgart, 1986-90, prin. officer, consul gen., Perth, Australia, 1990-91. Recipient awards U.S. Dept. State, 1968, 70, 81, 85, 87, 90. Mem. Presbyterian Ch.

WHITNEY, LISA VANDERSLUIS, technology professional; b. Oak Ridge, Tenn., Mar. 3, 1960; d. Kenneth Leory and Joan (Harvie) VanderSluis; m. David John Whitney, June 3, 1995. BA in Computer Sci./Bus. Adminstrn., U. Tenn., 1982; MS in Computer Sci., Rensselaer Poly. Inst., 1992; MBA, U. Wash., 1997. Computer scientist, computer programmer/analyst Naval Underwater Sys. Ctr., Newport, R.I., 1983-87; project computer programmer analyst Tech. Applications, Inc., New London, Conn., 1987-92; sr. programmer analyst Cray Rsch. Inc., Eagan, Minn., 1992-93; software engr., new tech. specialist Sterling Software, NASA Ames Rsch. Ctr., Moffett Field, Calif., 1993-95. Contbr. articles to profl. jours. Home: 1825 NE 58th St Seattle WA 98105-2440

WHITNEY, NATALIE WHITE, primary school educator; b. Pasadena, Calif., Mar. 26, 1917; d. Walter Patton and Natalie May (Brokaw) White; m. John Parker Whitney, Mar. 17, 1943 (dec. July 1969); children: John Parker, Jr., Sarah Carpenter. Student, Univ. Ariz., 1936-38, Claremont Coll., 1940-43; BA, Whittier Coll., 1940. Kindergarten primary tchr. credential, Calif. Asst. dir. M.B. Eyer Nursery Sch., Scripps Coll., Claremont, 1940-43; dir. kindergarten Westridge Sch. Girls, Pasadena, 1943-45; tchr. kindergarten Oak Grove Sch. Dist., San Jose, Calif., 1971-73, 73-86, primary tchr., 1973—. Author: Pumpkins, 1996 (also Spanish edit. Calabazas 1996), The Tiny Dot, 1996 (also Spanish edit. El puntito 1996). Gray Lady, ARC, Pasadena, 1943; sponsor Ford Country Day Sch., Los Altos, Calif., 1955-58, Children's Country Sch. (name now Hillbrook Sch.), Los Gatos, Calif., 1958-64, Youth Sci. Mus., San Jose, 1971-86; den mother Boy Scouts Am., Los Altos, 1956-58; mem. women's aux. San Jose Symphony, 1963; asst. gift shop Alexian Bros. Hosp. League, 1965. Recipient Merit award ARC, 1951. Mem. Mayflower Soc. (life), Valle Monte League (sustaining), Los Altos Hunt Club (resident), Kappa Kappa Gamma. Republican. Episcopalian. Home: 15785 Alta Vista Way San Jose CA 95127-1702

WHITNEY, RODGER FRANKLIN, university housing director; b. Dallas, Feb. 2, 1948; s. Roger Albert and Genevieve Mae (Mohr) W. Cert. higher studies, U. Lausanne, Switzerland, 1970; BA, So. Meth. U., 1971, M Liberal Arts, 1973; EdD, Harvard U., 1978. Dir. upperclass residences So. Meth. U., Dallas, 1971-73, mem. faculty, 1973-75; dir. Mohr Chevrolet Edn. Found., Dallas, 1975-77; dir. North Park East, Raymond D. Nasher Co., Dallas, 1977-79; dir. Stanford Housing Ctr., asst. dean student affairs Stanford (Calif.) U., 1979-91, assoc. dir. housing and dining, 1991—; dir. Camp Grady Spruce, YMCA, Dallas, 1971-76, bd. dirs., 1976-80. Bd. dirs. Kentfield Commons, Redwood City, Calif., 1989-91. Mem. APPA, Assn. Coll. and Univ. Housing Officers, Harvard Club San Francisco, Phi Beta Kappa. Home: 861 Whitehall Ln Redwood City CA 94061-3685 Office: Stanford U Housing Ops 565 Cowell Ln Stanford CA 94305-8512

WHITNEY, STAN, marriage and family therapist; b. Wellsboro, Pa., Jan. 15, 1935; m. Ida G. Shoop, Dec. 29, 1960 (div. Jan. 1984); children: Rebecca Whitney Jones, Mark Daniel; m. Gloria Leon LeFleur, Jan. 30, 1988. BS, Bob Jones U., Greenville, S.C., 1961, MA, 1962; PhD, San Antonio Theol. Sem., St. Paul, 1989. Diplomate Am. Bd. Cert. Managed Care Providers. Pastoral counselor various area chs., Ottawa, Ill., 1964-74; bus. cons. Rental Real Estate Co., Ottawa, 1974-87; pastoral counselor various area chs., Las Vegas, Nev., 1987-92; founder, clin. dir. Hope Counseling Inc., Bullhead City, Ariz., 1992—; exec. bd. and cons. Blasingame Found., Dallas, 1987—. Fellow Am. Acad. Clin. Sexologists; mem. Am. Counseling Assn., Am. Assn. Christian Counselors, Am. Acad. Clin. Family Therapists. Office: Hope Counseling Inc PO Box 1068 Bullhead City AZ 86430-1068

WHITNEY, STEVEN, writer, producer; b. Chgo., Oct. 14, 1946; s. Lambert M. and Kathryn (Erickson) Ochsenschlager. BFA, So. Meth. U., 1967; postgrad., Harvard U., 1967-68. Writer, producer Vineland Prodns., Studio City, Calif.; crime reporter New York Times, 1971-76, freelance writer and screenwriter, 1977—; pres. Vineland Prodn., 1988—. Author: (fiction) Singled Out, 1978, (non-fiction) It's Your Body, 1980; writer TV series Against The Law, 1990, movie Night Hunt, 1993. Sponsor several children Children Internat., Share Am., Save the Children. Served with U.S. Army, 1968-70. Office: Vineland Prodns Inc 11054 Ventura Blvd # 261 Studio City CA 91604

WHITSEL, RICHARD HARRY, biologist, entomologist; b. Denver, Feb. 23, 1931; s. Richard Elstun and Edith Muriel (Harry) W.; children by previous marriages: Russell David, Robert Alan, Michael Dale, Steven Deane. BA, U. Calif., Berkeley, 1954; MA, San Jose State Coll., 1962. Sr. rsch. biologist San Mateo County Mosquito Abatement Dist., Burlingame, Calif., 1959-72; environ. program mgr., chief of watershed mgmt., chief of planning Calif. Regional Water Quality Control Bd., Oakland, 1972—; mem. grad. faculty water resource mgmt. U. San Francisco, 1987-89. Served with Med. Service Corps, U.S. Army, 1954-56. Mem. Entomol. Soc. Am., Entomol. Soc. Wash., Am. Mosquito Control Assn., Calif. Alumni Assn., The Benjamin Ide Wheeler Soc., Nat. Parks and Conservation Assn. (life), Sierra Club. Democrat. Episcopalian. Contbr. articles to profl. jours. Home: 4331 Blenheim Way Concord CA 94521-4258 Office: Calif Regional Water Quality Control Bd 2101 Webster St Oakland CA 94612-3027 *Any success that I have achieved probalby is the result of my fortune to have been exposed to some outstanding educators and scientists as well as being somewhat imaginative by nature. Working with young professional people keeps me young in spirit and seems to renew my enthusiasm in whatever I do.*

WHITSITT, ROBERT JAMES, professional basketball team executive; b. Madison, Wis., Jan. 10, 1956; s. Raymond Earl and Dolores June (Smith) W.; m. Jan Leslie Sundberg; children: Lillian Ashley, Sean James. BS, U. Wis., Stevens Point, 1977; MA, Ohio State U., 1978. Intern Indiana Pacers, Inpls., 1978, bus. tickets mgr., 1979, dir. bus. affairs and promotions, 1980, asst. gen. mgr., 1981-82; v.p. mktg. Kansas City (Mo.) Kings, 1982-84, v.p., asst. gen. mgr., 1984-85; v.p., asst. gen. mgr. Sacramento Kings, 1985-86; pres. Seattle Supersonics, 1986—. Mem. Nat. Basketball Assn. (alternate gov., mem. competition and rules com.). Republican. Lutheran. Lodge: Rotary. Office: Portland Trailblazers One Center Court Portland OR 97227

WHITSON, ANGIE, artist; b. San Jose, Calif.; d. Joseph and Francis (Chiaremonte) Noto; m. Claude Loren Whitson, May 11, 1932; children: Gregory, Jeffrey. Cert. art tchr. Cartoonist Warner Ctr. News, 1987—. Principle works include bronze busts sculptures of Ernie Kovacs, Joyce Hall, Leanard Goldenson for TV Arts and Scis.; exhibiter Art-A-Fair, Laguna Beach, Calif., 1976—. Mem. So. Calif. chpt. Mus. Women in Arts. Mem. Rotayr Club Woodland Hills.

WHITSON, WILLIAM WALLACE, foundation administrator, retired military officer; b. San Antonio, Dec. 3, 1926; m. Mary Heywood Vance, May 30, 1956 (div.); children: William Jr., Christina, Shawn, Andrew, Robert; m. Judith Whitson, Dec. 31, 1984. BS, U.S. Mil. Acad., West Point, N.Y., 1948; PhD, Tufts U., 1958. Commd. 2d lt. U.S. Army, 1948; advanced through grades to col. U.S. Army, Intelligence Br., 1970; ret., 1970; analyst Rand Corp., Washington, 1970-74; dir. policy divsn. BDM Corp., Washington, 1974-75; chief fgn. affairs Nat. Def. Libr. Congress, Washington, 1975-80; dir. Calif. Emergency Earthquake Task Force, Sacramento, 1980-82; pres. CIM Assocs., Tiburon, Calif., 1982-97; exec. sec. Found. for Inner Peace, Tiburon, Calif., 1988—. Author: Chinese High Command, 1976, Doing Business with China, 1978. Vice chmn. bd. Calif. Inst. Integral Studies, San Francisco, 1989-94; mem. bd. Inst. Noetic Scis., Sausalito, Calif., 1981-94. Decorated (twice) Legion of Merit. Home and Office: CIM Assocs 6 Venado Dr Tiburon CA 94920-1626

WHITTAKER, GARY IRWIN, health science association administrator; b. Granite City, Ill., Jan. 24, 1949; s. Granville Dwight and Nadine Dorothy (Frohardt) W.; m. Jayme Roberta Nielson, Mar 28, 1981 (div. Dec. 1989); m. Barbara Ann Boland, July 7, 1995. BA, U. Tex. El Paso, 1973; MA, Webster U., 1976; PhD, Inst. Scis. Houston, 1994; MHS, U. Denver, 1997. Sr. human resources specialist OPM, Denver, 1984-85; real estate broker Whittaker & Assocs., Boulder, Colo., 1985-86; sr. program analyst OCHAMPUS, Aurora, Colo., 1986-89; project mgr. Dept. Interior, Lakewood, Colo., 1989-92; program dir. Dept. Transp., Washington, 1992-93; dir. mktg. and pub. affairs OCHAMPUS, Aurora, 1993—; bd. dirs. Boland Consulting, Inc., Denver, Inst. Scis. et de Tech. Ouest Africaine, Houston. Mem. Am. Coll. Healthcare Execs. (diplomate), Colo. Healthcare Sys. Soc. (charter), Pi Sigma Alpha. Home: 1001 E Dakota Ave Denver CO 80209 Office: OCHAMPUS Tricare Support Office Aurora CO 80045-6900

WHITTAKER, SUE MCGHEE, music educator, pianist; b. Chgo., Feb. 17, 1942; d. Chester O. and Bevie Faye (Smith) McGhee; m. Jerry Roy Whittaker, Aug. 9, 1968; children: Judd, Eric, Holly. BME, Roosevelt U., Chgo., 1965, MM, 1966; DMA, U. Ariz., 1996. Faculty Lee Coll., Cleveland, Tenn., 1965-68; gen. music tchr. Madison Sch. Dist., Phoenix, 1969-72; faculty Ariz. Coll. of the Bible, Phoenix, 1983-92; founding dir. North Valley Sch. of the Arts, Scottsdale, Ariz., 1995—. Guest soloist (as part of 2-piano team Whittaker and Ross) Mesa Symphony, Scottsdale Symphony, Phoenix Symphony, others; accompanist Phoenix Little Theatre, Masterworks Chorale, Met. Opera auditions, Scottsdale Symphony Chorale. Named to Outstanding Young Women of Am., 1967. Mem. Music Educators Nat. Conf., Music Tchrs. Nat. Assn., Nat. Conf. Piano Pedagogy (mem. rsch. com. 1988—), Ariz. State Music Tchrs. Assn. (adjudicator 1980—). Republican. Home: 15009 N 93d Way Scottsdale AZ 85260

WHITTENBURG, RUSSELL THOMAS, finance executive; b. Ponca City, Okla., Jan. 23, 1957; s. William Robert and Jerry Lee (Mullins) W.; m. Barbara Rose Billard, Sept. 17, 1983; children: Jocelyn Rose, Jamie Lee. BSME, U. Tex., 1978; MBA, Harvard U., 1980. From sr. planning analyst to fin. dir. Atlantic Richfield Co., L.A., 1980-86; engagement leader Boston Consulting Group, L.A., 1986-90; chief fin. officer, agribus. Roll Internat. Corp., L.A., 1990—. Bd. dirs. Westside Food Bank; chmn. fin. com. 1st United Meth. Ch., Santa Monica, Calif.; v.p. Rotary, Santa Monica. Home: 409 18th St Santa Monica CA 90402-2429 Office: Roll Internat Corp 11444 W Olympic Blvd Los Angeles CA 90064

WHITTIER, MONTE RAY, lawyer; b. Pocatello, Idaho, June 28, 1955; s. Raymond Max and Marjorie Lucille (Pea) W.; m. Denise Womack, May 29, 1982; children: Jason Dennis, Sarah Michell, Sadie Mckenzie. BS in Acctg., U. Utah, 1976; JD, U. Idaho, 1978. Bar: U.S. Dist. Ct. Idaho, 1979, U.S. Supreme Ct. 1985, U.S. Tax Ct. 1989, U.S. Ct. Appeals (9th cir.) 1991, Idaho, 1979. Ptnr., shareholder Whittier & Souza, Pocatello, 1979-89; head pub. defender 6th jud. dist. State Idaho, 1989-95; shareholder, mng. atty. Whittier, Souza & Naftz, Pocatello, 1989-97, head pub. defender, 1989-95; asst. gen. counsel Maleleuca, Inc., Pocatello, 1997—. Vol. Internat. Spl. Olympics, South Bend, Ind., 1987, Mpls., 1991; mem. Magistrate Commn. 6th Jud. Dist., Pocatello, 1989-91; bd. dirs. Bannock Baseball, Inc., 1996—. Mem. ATLA, Idaho Trial Lawyers Assn. (bd. dirs. 6th Jud. Dist. Pro Bono award 1994), Civitan (pres. Bannock chpt. 1983-84, bd. dirs. 1981-87, 92-93, lt. gov. Intermountain chpt. 1986-87, Outstanding Pres. award 1984, Outstanding Svc. award 1982-83, 86-88, 91), Rotary. Office: Maleleuca Inc PO Box 4833 3910 S Yellowstone Hwy Idaho Falls ID 83402

WHITTINGHAM, CHARLES EDWARD, thoroughbred race horse owner and trainer; b. San Diego, Apr. 13, 1913; s. Edward and Ellen (Taylor) W.; m. Peggy Boone, Oct. 12, 1944; children: Michael Charles, Charlene. T-rainer thoroughbred horses, Calif., 1930-42; asst. trainer Luro Pub. Stable, N.Y., 1945-49; owner, trainer Whittingham Pub. Stable, Sierra Madre, Calif., 1949—; winner Ky. Derby with Ferdinand, 1986, with Sunday Silence, 1989. Mem. Rep. Senatorial Inner-Circle, Washington, 1983—, nat. advisor bd. Am. Security Council, Washington, 1976—; campaigner mem. Rep. Nat. Com., Washington, 1976—. Served to master sgt. USMC, 1942-45, PTO. Recipient Eclipse awards Thoroughbred Race Track Assn./Daily Racing Form/Nat. Turf Writers Assn., 1971, 82, 89; named to Nat. Racing Hall of Fame, 1974, Brietbard Hall of Fame/Hall of Champions, San Diego, 1993. Mem. Horsemens Benevolent & Protective Assn. (v.p 1976—). Republican. Roman Catholic. Home: 88 Lowell Ave Sierra Madre CA 91024-2510 Office: Charles Whittingham Inc 19 Suffolk Ave Ste E Sierra Madre CA 91024-2556*

WHYTE, ROBERT ANDREW, art curator, writer; b. L.A., Jan. 27, 1931; s. James Syme and Mary Josephine (Turner) W. AA, Orange Coast Coll., 1950; BA in History of Art, UCLA, 1958; MA in History of Art, U. Calif., Berkeley, 1965. Dir. edn. San Francisco Mus. Modern Art, 1967-87; exec. dir. Mus. Italo-Americano, San Francisco, 1987-92; curator Mus. Italo Americano, San Francisco, 1992—; lectr. San Francisco State U., 1986-87. Sgt. USAF, 1951-55. Mem. Am. Assn. Mus. (curators com. 1994—, edn. com. 1976-87). Office: Mus Italo Americano Ft Mason Ctr San Francisco CA 94123

WHYTE, RONALD M., federal judge; b. 1942. BA in Math., Wesleyan U., 1964; JD, U. So. Calif., 1967. Bar: Calif. 1967, U.S. Dist. Ct. (no. dist.) Calif. 1967, U.S. Dist. Ct. (cen. dist.) Calif. 1968, U.S. Ct. Appeals (9th cir.) 1986. Assoc. Hoge, Fenton Jones & Appel, Inc., San Jose, Calif., 1971-77, mem., 1977-89; judge Superior Ct. State of Calif., 1989-92, U.S. Dist. Ct. (no. dist.) Calif., San Jose, 1992—; judge pro-tempore Superior Ct. Calif., 1977-89; lectr. Calif. Continuing Edn. of Bar, Rutter Group, Santa Clara Bar Assn., State Bar Calif.; legal counsel Santa CLara County Bar Assn., 1986-89; mem. county select com. Criminal Conflicts Program, 1988. Bd. trustees Santa Clara County Bar Assn., 1978-79, 84-85. Lt. Judge Advocate Gen.'s Corps, USNR, 1968-71. Recipient Judge of Yr. award Santa Clara County Trial Lawyers Assn., 1992, Am. Jurisprudence award. Mem. Calif. Judges Assn., Assn. Bus. Trial Lawyers (bd. govs. 1991-93), Santa Clara Inn of Ct. (exec. com. 1993—), San Francisco Bay area Intellectual Property Inn of Ct. (exec. com. 1994—). Office: US Courthouse 280 S 1st St Rm 4156 San Jose CA 95113-3002

WICHTERMAN, JAMES ALBERT, management consulting executive; b. Columbus, Ohio, Feb. 7, 1940; s. Paul Herbert and Geraldine Ester (James) W.; m. Sue Redd Ross, Dec. 21, 1963 (div. Dec. 1982); children: William Paul, Eric John; m. Deborah Ann Brown, June 4, 1983. BS in Bus. Adminstrn., Ohio State U., 1961. Product mgr. Procter & Gamble, Cin., 1961-69; v.p. mktg. Cunard Line, N.Y.C.; v.p. mktg./sales Cudahy Foods Co., Phoenix; sr. v.p. Patchen Brownfeld Advt., Phoenix; staff cons. Mgmt. Action Programs, Sherman Oaks, Calif., 1990-94; CEO, pres. Mgmt. Action Programs, Phoenix, 1994—, bd. dirs., 1993—. Mem. Phoenix Rotary 100, 1994—. 1st lt. USAF, 1962-66, Korea. Office: Mgmt Action Programs 4747 N 7th St Ste 302 Phoenix AZ 85014-5816

WICKER, ALLAN WERT, psychology educator; b. Elk Falls, Kans., Aug. 10, 1941; s. Lester Allen and Hazel Katherine (Clum) W.; m. Kathleen O'Brien, Feb. 5, 1973; 1 child, David Allan. BA, U. Kans., 1963, MA, 1965, PhD, 1967. Asst. prof. psychology U. Wis., Milw., 1967-69, U. Ill., Urbana, 1969-71; assoc. then prof. psychology Claremont (Calif.) Grad. Sch., 1971—. Author: Introduction to Ecological Psychology, 1979; contbr. articles to profl.jours., chpts. to books. Rsch. grantee NIMH, 1968-72, NSF, 1972-76, Haynes Found., 1985-87; Fulbright sr. lectr. Coun. for Internat. Exchange of Scholars, Zimbabwe, 1989, Ghana, 1993, Malaysia, 1997. Fellow Am. Psychol. Assn.; mem. Acad. Mgmt., African Studies Assn. Office: Claremont Grad Sch Ctr Orgnl and Behavioral Sci 130 E 9th St Claremont CA 91711-5907

WICKIZER, CINDY LOUISE, elementary school educator; b. Pitts., Dec. 12, 1946; d. Charles Sr. and Gloria Geraldine (Cassidy) Zimmerman; m. Leon Leonard Wickizer, Mar. 21, 1971; 1 child, Charlyn Michelle. BS, Oreg. State U., 1968. Tchr. Enumclaw (Wash.) Sch. Dist., 1968—. Mem. NEA, Wash. Edn. Assn., Enumclaw Edn. Assn., Buckley C. of C., Wash. Contract Loggers Assn., Am. Rabbit Breeders Assn. (judge, chmn. scholarship found. 1986-87, pres. 1988-94, 96—, dist. dir. 1994-96, Disting. Svc. award 1987), Wash. State Rabbit Breeders Assn. (life, Pres.'s award 1983, 94, sec., dir., v.p. 1995—), Vancouver Island Rabbit Breeders Assn., Wash. State Rabbit and Cavy Shows Inc. (sec. 1994—), Evergreen Rabbit Assn. (sec., v.p., pres.), Alpha Gamma Delta. Home: 26513 112th St E Buckley WA 98321-9258

WICKIZER, MARY ALICE See BURGESS, MARY ALICE

WICKLUND, LEE ARTHUR, school superintendent; b. Ft. Atkinson, Wis., Aug. 10, 1938; s. Verner F. and Ellen V. (Anderson) W.; m. Georganne Emilie Trumbull, June 27, 1964; children: Eric Trumbull, Lance Frederick. AA, Wright Jr. Coll., Chgo., 1958; BEd, Chgo. Tchrs. Coll., 1961; MEd, Loyola U., Chgo., 1964; DEd, U. Oreg., 1969. Cert. supt./prin., Oreg., Ill., Wis., Minn. Elem./secondary/adult edn. tchr., asst. prin. Chgo. Bd. Edn., 1961-67; rsch. asst. U. Oreg., Eugene, 1967-69; dir. lab. sch., asst. prof. Idaho State U., Pocatello, 1969-71; R&D specialist N.W. Regional Edn. Lab., Portland, Oreg., 1971-72; assoc. prof., ednl. adminstr. U. Wis., Superior, 1972-75; dir. curriculum and instrn. North Bend (Oreg.) Sch. Dist., 1975-89; assoc. supt. Mercer Island (Wash.) Sch. Dist., 1989-92; supt. Riverdale Sch. Dist., Portland, 1992-94; supt. in residence N.W. Regional Ednl. Lab., Portland, 1994—; chmn. Oreg. State Textbook Commn., Salem, 1981-87; sr. fellow Inst. for Devel. of Edn. Activities, Kettering, Ohio, 1977—; past chair Inter-Luth. Commn. for Continuing Edn., Tacoma, 1982-89. Chair budget com. North Bay Rural Fire Dist., North Bend, 1984-89; mem. adv. com. South Slough Natural Estuarine Rex., Coos Bay, Oreg., 1984-90; sec. exec. com. United Way of S.W. Oreg., Coos Bay, 1978-83; mem. exec. com. Music Enrichment Assn., Coos Bay, 1977-81; trustee Lake Oswego (Oreg.) Libr. Bd., 1993-95; bd. dirs. Slingerland Inst., vice chmn., 1989-94. Served to sgt. Ill. Air N.G., 1956-65. Mem. Am. Assn. Sch. Adminstrs., Conf. Oreg. Sch. Adminstrs. (prep. and licensure com. 1994—), Lake Oswego Rotary (pres.), Alumni Soc. Coll. Edn. U. Oreg. Lutheran. Home: 16860 Lakeridge Dr Lake Oswego OR 97034-6819 Office: NW Regional Ednl Lab 101 SW Main St Ste 500 Portland OR 97204-3213

WICKSTRAND, ALAN KEITH, service executive; b. Portland, Oreg., Nov. 3, 1953; s. Arthur Theodore and Eleanor Florence (Tucker) W.; m. Georgene Mae Cowles, June 12, 1976; children: Philip Arthur, Emily Anne, Laura Jayne. Student, Mt. Hood Coll., 1972-74. Janitor, supr. br. mgr., v.p. ops. Mchts. Bldg. Maintenance, Portland, 1973-79; owner, mgr. New Life Cleaning Systems, Portland, 1979-90; dist. mgr. Century Cleaning, Portland, 1990-94; pres. Follow Through Cleaning, Inc., Portland, 1994—. Mem. Bldg. Maintenance Assn. Am. (bd. dirs. 1985-89), Bldg. Svc. Contractors Assn. Internat., Internat. Exec. Housekeepers Assn. Republican. Baptist.

WICKWIRE, PATRICIA JOANNE NELLOR, psychologist, educator; b. Sioux City, Iowa; d. William McKinley and Clara Rose (Pautsch) Nellor; m. Robert James Wickwire, Sept. 7, 1957; 1 child, William James. BA cum laude, U. No. Iowa, 1951; MA, U. Iowa, 1959; PhD, U. Tex., Austin, 1971; postgrad. U. So. Calif., UCLA, Calif. State U., Long Beach, 1951-66. Tchr., Ricketts Ind. Schs., Iowa, 1946-48; tchr., counselor Waverly-Shell Rock Ind. Schs., Iowa, 1951-55; reading cons., head dormitory counselor U. Iowa, Iowa City, 1955-57; tchr., sch. psychologist, adminstr. S. Bay Union High Sch. Dist., Redondo Beach, Calif., 1962-82, dir. student svcs. and spl. edn.; cons. mgmt. and edn.; pres. Nellor Wickwire Group, 1981—; mem. exec. bd. Calif. Interagency Mental Health Coun., 1968-72, Beach Cities Symphony Assn., 1970-82; chmn. Friends of Dominguez Hills (Calif.), 1981-85. Lic. ednl. psychologist, marriage, family and child counselor, Calif.; pres. Calif. Women's Caucus, 1993-95. Mem. APA, AAUW (exec. bd., chpt. pres. 1962-72), Nat. Career Devel. Assn. (media chair 1992—), Am. Assn. Career Edn. (pres. 1991—), L.A. County Dirs. Pupil Svcs. (chmn. 1974-79), L.A. County Personnel and Guidance Assn. (pres. 1977-78), Assn. Calif. Sch. Adminstrs. (dir. 1977-81), L.A. County SW Bd. Dist. Adminstrs. for Spl. Edn. (chmn. 1976-81), Calif. Assn. Sch. Psychologists (bd. dirs. 1981-83), Am. Assn. Sch. Adminstrs., Calif. Assn. for Measurement and Evaluation in Guidance (dir. 1981, pres. 1984-85), ACA (chmn. Coun. Newsletter Editors 1989-91, mem. com. on women 1989-92, mem. com. on rsch. and knowledge, 1994—, chmn. 1995—, chmn. 1996—), Assn. Measurement and Eval. in Guidance (Western regional editor 1985-87, conv. chair 1986, editor 1987-90, exec. bd. dirs. 1987-91), Calif. Assn. Counseling and Devel. (exec. bd. 1984—, pres. 1988-89, jour. editor 1990—), Internat. Career Assn. Network (chair 1985—), Pi Lambda Theta, Alpha Phi Gamma, Psi Chi, Kappa Delta Pi, Sigma Alpha Iota. Contbr. articles in field to profl. jours. Office: The Nellor Wickwire Group 2900 Amby Pl Hermosa Beach CA 90254-2216

WIDAMAN, GREGORY ALAN, financial executive, accountant; b. St. Louis, Oct. 4, 1955; s. Raymond Paul Sr. and Louise Agnes (Urschler) W. BS in Bus. Econs. cum laude, Trinity U., 1978. CPA, Tex. Sr. auditor Arthur Andersen & Co., Houston, 1978-82; sr. cons. Price Waterhouse, Houston, 1983-85; fin. advisor to segment pres. Teledyne, Inc., Century City, Calif., 1985-95; sr. mgr. ops. planning for consumer products ABC Broadcasting/TV The Walt Disney Co., Burbank, Calif., 1995—; cons. Arthur Andersen & Co., Price Waterhouse, Teledyne, Walt Disney Co. Mem. AICPAs, Calif. Soc. CPAs, Christian Bus. Mens com. of U.S.A., World Affairs Coun., MIT/Calif. Tech. Enterprise Forum. Republican. Home: 1416 S Barrington Ave # 4 Los Angeles CA 90025-2363 Office: The Walt Disney Co 500 S Buena Vista St Burbank CA 91521-0001

WIDENER, MARY LEE, social services executive; b. Schaal, Alaska, July 6, 1938; d. Mert and Johnnie (Newton) Thomas; m. Warren Widener Sr., Apr. 4, 1959; children: Warren Jr., Michael, Stephen. Diploma, Heald Bus. Coll., 1956; Pub. Adminstrn. Program, U. San Francisco Sch. Profl. Studies, 1978; Hon. Doctor of Laws, John F. Kennedy U., 1979. Adminstrv. asst. to exec. v.p. U. Calif., Berkeley, 1959-69, office mgr. gifts and endowments, 1959-69; urban programming coord. Fed. Home Loan Bank, Washington, 1972-73; housing cons. Ford Found., N.Y.C., 1973-74; exec. dir. Oakland (Calif.) NHS, 1973-76; program cons. Urban Reinvestment Task Force, Washington, 1974-76; exec. v.p. Neighborhood Housing Svcs., Oakland, 1976—, pres., CEO; chmn. bd. dirs. Fed. Home Loan Bank, San Francisco, 1994—; bd. dirs. PMI Group , San Francisco, 1995—. Author: (with others) Housing America, 1993. Trustee San Francisco Found; adv. bd. PEW Partnership for Civic Change, Phila.; former dir. KQED, San Francisco; former state chair Calif. Dem. Ctrl. Com., San Francisco; former mem. U.S. Senate Housing Task Force, Washington, Commn. on Homelessness, Oakland. Recipient award Nat. Coalition of 100 Black Women, N.Y., 1989, San Francisco LWV, 1996. Democratic. Methodist. Office: Neighborhood Housing Svc Am Inc 1970 Broadway Ste 470 Oakland CA 94612

WIDMANN, GLENN ROGER, electrical engineer; b. Newark, Jan. 8, 1957; s. Elmer and Ellen (Eccles) W. BSEE, Rutgers U., 1979; MSEE, Purdue U., 1981, PhDEE, 1988. Engr. N.J. Bell Telephone Co., Hopelawn, 1979; instr. Purdue U., West Lafayette, Ind., 1979-81, 83-88; prof. elec. engring. Colo. State U., Ft. Collins, 1988-91; engr. Hughes Aircraft Co., Canoga Park, Calif., 1980-83; scientist, project mgr., automotive controls engring. dir. GM Hughes Electronics Corp., Canoga Park, Calif., 1991-94; sr. sci. automotive elecs. devel. dir. Hughes Rsch. Labs. GM Hughes Electronics Corp., Malibu, Calif., 1994-96; dept. mgr. Hughes Rsch. Labs., Malibu, 1996—; cons. Bur.

Reclamation, Denver, 1989, Benjamin Cummings Pub. Co., Ft. Collins, 1989; mem. program com. Internat. Symposium Robotics and Mfg., Santa Fe, N.Mex., 1991—. Contbr. articles to tech. jours.; patentee in robotics field. Recipient presentation award Am. Controls Conf., 1990. Mem. IEEE, Soc. Automotive Engrs., Tau Beta Pi, Eta Kappa Nu. Home: 3370 Crestwater Ct Apt 2011 Rochester Hills MN 48309 Office: Hughes Aircraft Co Hughes Rsch Labs MS RL 71 3011 Malibu Canyon Rd Malibu CA 90265

WIEBE, J. E. N., province official. Lt. gov. Govt. Saskatchewan, Regina, Can. Office: Office of the Lieutenant Gov Govt House 4607 Dewdney Ave, Regina, SK Canada S4P 3V7

WIEBE, JOHN CLEMENT, school director; b. Ootacamund, India, Aug. 17, 1930; s. John Abraham and Viola (Bergthold) Wiebe; m. Carol Hiebert, Dec. 30, 1954; children: Wendell Wiebe-Powell, Roland Philipp, Evelyn Wiebe-Anderson, Rebecca Wiebe-Freed. AB, Tabor Coll., 1953; MA, Kans. State U. Tchr. South Humboldt Unified Dist., Miranda, Calif., 1960-65; tchr., adminstr. Kodaikanal (India) Internat. Sch., 1968-78; tchr., facilitator ARAMCO Schs., Abqaiq, Saudi Arabia, 1978-83; dir., developer Lincoln Internat. Sch., Kampala, Uganda, 1984-86; dir. archeology ICRISAT, Pattaancheru, India, 1972-73; coach, activity dir., 1960-86; mgmt. com. Kodaikanal Internat. Sch., 1974-78; facilitator environ. edn. ARAMCO, Saudi Arabia, 1978-83; dir., developer Lincoln Internat. Sch., Kampala, 1984-86,. Cartoonist, illustrator various publs., 1953-70; contbr. articles to profl. jours., newspapers, sport manuals, 1968—. Founder, sec. Kodaikanal Conservation Coun., 1969-75; charter mem., organizer Westhaven (Calif.) Com. Devel. Coun., 1992—. Mem. Sierra Club (exec. com. North Group Redwood chpt. 1988-89, 94—). Mem. Mennonite Ch. Home: 1026 Westhaven Dr S Trinidad CA 95570-9731

WIEBELHAUS, PAMELA SUE, school administrator, educator; b. Stanley, Wis., May 28, 1952; d. Wilbur Leroy and Marjorie Jean (Bernse) Thorne; m. Mark Robert Wiebelhaus, Apr. 27, 1985; 1 child, Sarah Jean. AS in Nursing, No. Ariz. U., 1973, BS in Gen. Home Econs., 1974. R.N. Ariz., Colo; cert. post secondary vocat. tchr., Colo. Nurse Flagstaff (Ariz.) Community Hosp., 1973-75, Children's Hosp., Denver, 1975, St. Joseph's Hosp., Denver, 1980; office nurse, surg. asst. OB-Gyn Assocs., P.C., Aurora, Colo., 1975-78; nursing coordinator perinatal services Community Hosp. Smaritan Health, Phoenix, 1978-79; nurse, mem. personnel pool Good Samaritan Hosp., Phoenix, 1979-80, J. Bains, MD, Phoenix, 1979-80; file clk. Pharm. Card Systems, Inc., Phoenix, 1979-80; office nurse S. Eisenbaum, MD, Aurora, Colo., 1980; instr., coordinator med. office program T.H. Pickens Tech. Ctr., Aurora (Colo.) Pub. Schs., 1980—; med. supr. healthfair sites, Denver, 1982-85; mem. adv. com. Emily Griffith Opportunity Sch., Denver, 1984-90; mem. survey team North Ctrl. Bd. Edn., 1985, Colo. Bd. Edn., Denver, 1987; book reviewer proposal and new edit. ins. text-reference book W.B. Saunders, 1992—; chair adv. com. Media Ctr., Pickens Tech., 1995—. Acad. scholar No. Ariz. U., 1970, nat. def. grantee, 1970-74; PTA and Elks Club scholar, 1970. Mem. Am. Assn. Med. Assts. (cert.; membership chmn. Capitol chpt. Colo. Soc. 1981). Lutheran.

WIECHEC, DONALD, photographer; b. Phila., Jan. 28, 1943; s. Frank and Kathryn (Reinhart) W.; m. Betty Wiechec, Aug. 27, 1966. BA, U. Pitts., 1966; MFA, NYU, 1970. Asst. to program dir. Corp. for Pub. Broadcasting, N.Y.C., 1968-70; filmmaker, photographer Herman Miller, Inc., Zeeland, Mich., 1970-73; supervising producer Sandy Co., Detroit, 1974; documentary filmmaker Agoura Hills, Calif., 1975-86, photographer, 1987—. Exhibited photographs in numerous shows including purchase of portfolio for permanent exhibit Bibliotheque Nationale, France, 1992, Smithsonian Instn., 1981, High Mus. Art, Atlanta, 1970. Bd. dirs. Santa Monica (Calif.) Mountains Parkland Assn., 1986-87; mem. planning adv. com. City of Agoura Hills, 1982; del. Las Virgenes Homeowners Fedn., 1983-87. Capt. USMC, 1965-68. Grantee Sierra Club, 1970; recipient 2d prize Columbus Film Festival, 1970, Award of Excellence, 1972. Mem. DAV (life). Home and Office: 4039 Liberty Canyon Rd Agoura Hills CA 91301-3550

WIEDEN, DAN G., advertising executive; b. 1945. With Georgia-Pacific Corp., Portland, Oreg., 1967-72; free-lance writer, 1972-78; with McCann-Erickson, Portland, 1978-80, William Cain, Portland, 1980-82; pres. Wieden & Kennedy, Portland, 1982—. Office: Wieden & Kennedy Inc 320 SW Washington St Portland OR 97204-2640*

WIEDERHOLT, WIGBERT C., neurologist, educator; b. Germany, Apr. 22, 1931; came to U.S., 1956, naturalized, 1966; m. Carl and Anna-Maria (Hoffmann) W.; student (Med. Sch. scholar), U. Berlin, 1952-53; M.D., U. Freiburg, 1955; M.S., U. Minn., 1965; children—Sven, Karen, Kristin. Intern in Ob-Gyn, Schleswig (W. Ger.) City Hosp., 1955-56; rotating intern Sacred Heart Hosp., Spokane, Wash., 1956-57; resident in medicine Cleve. Clinic, 1957-58, 60-62, U.S. Army Hosp., Frankfurt, W. Ger., 1958-59; resident in neurology Mayo Clinic, Rochester, Minn., 1962-65; assoc. prof. medicine, dir. clin. neurophysiology Ohio State U. Med. Sch., Columbus, 1966-72; prof. neurosci. U. Calif. Med. Sch., San Diego, 1972—, neurologist-in-chief, 1973-83, chmn. dept. and group in neurosci. 1978-83, 90-93; chief neurology VA Hosp., San Diego, 1972-79. Fulbright scholar, 1956-58. Diplomate Am. Bd. Psychiatry and Neurology. Fellow Am. Acad. Neurology (S. Weir Mitchell award 1956); mem. Internat. Brain Research Orgn., Am. Assn. EEG and Electrodiagnosis (sec.-treas. 1971-76, pres. 1977-78), AAAS, Soc. for Neurosci., Am. Neurol. Assn., Am. EGG Soc., Western EEG Soc., Calif. Neurol. Soc., San Diego Neurol. Soc., N.Y. Acad. Scis., AMA, Calif. Med. Assn., San Diego County Med. Soc. Club: La Jolla Tennis. Contbr. numerous articles to med. jours. Home: 1001 Genter St Apt 10B La Jolla CA 92037-5527 Office: Univ Calif at San Diego Dept Neurosci 0624 9500 Gilman Dr La Jolla CA 92093-5003

WIEDERRICK, ROBERT, museum director. Pres. Lemhi County Hist. Mus., Salmon, Idaho. Office: Lemhi County Hist Mus 210 Main PO Box 645 Salmon ID 83467

WIEDLE, GARY EUGENE, real estate management company executive; b. San Antonio, July 28, 1944; s. Eugene Wiley and Melba Frances (Keeney) W.; m. Regena Zokosky, July 7, 1977 (div. June 1983); children: Ana Lauren, Aric Brandt. AA, Coll. of the Desert, Palm Desert, Calif., 1975; BA, Calif. State U., Long Beach, 1967; MA, U. So. Calif., 1973. Lic. real estate broker, Calif.; cert. profl. community assn. mgr. Adminstrv. asst. City of Inglewood, Calif., 1967-68, asst. city mgr., 1970-74; exec. dir. Coachella Valley Assn. of Govts., Palm Desert, 1974-84; mgr. The Springs Country Club, Rancho Mirage, Calif., 1984-87; prof. polit. sci. Coll of the Desert, Palm Desert, 1987-90; owner Fortune West Mgmt., Palm Desert, 1990—; cons. polit. orgns., bus. and community groups, Riverside County, Calif., 1984—. State comdr. DAV, Dept. Calif., 1982. 1st lt. U.S. Army, 1968-70, Vietnam. Decorated Bronze Star for valor, Purple Heart, Commendation of valor. Mem. Am. Inst. Cert. Planners (cert. planner), Cmty. Assns. Inst. (pres. 1986-89), Calif. Assn. Cmty. Mgrs., Real Estate Educators Cert. Inst., Bd. Realtors Palm Desert, Am. Planning Assn., Western Govtl. Rsch. Assn., Gideons Internat. Republican. Lutheran. Home: 82-362 Gable Dr Indio CA 92201-7439 Office: Fortune West Mgmt GE Wiedle Co 73-900 El Paseo Rear Palm Desert CA 92260-4336

WIELE, PATRICIA GIORDANO, interior decorator; b. Houston, Aug. 29, 1947; d. Conrad Joseph and Ellen Patricia (Condon) Schoppe; m. Natale Joseph Giordano, Apr. 17, 1971 (dec. Sept. 1989); children: Keith Joseph, Michael David, Ryan Peter, Todd Christopher; m. Fred J. Wiele, Jan. 16, 1994; stepchildren: Robin, Scott, Brian, Craig, Suzanne. Student, U. Houston, 1965-67, NYU, 1969. Prin. Patricia S. Giordano Interiors, Ridgefield, Conn., 1975-94, Patricia G. Wiele Interiors, Los Gatos, Calif., 1994—; pub. speaker various floral design and horticulture workshops. Bd. dirs. Family and Children's Aid, Inc., Danbury, Conn., 1976-78, program and rev. and nominating coms., 1978, head pub. rels. com., 1978-79, pres. aux., 1976-79; v.p. Twin Homeowner's Assn., Ridgefield, Conn., 1978-79, chmn., founder area beautification, 1978; pres. East Ridge Mid. Sch. PTO, 1988-89, PTA, 1991-92. Recipient award of Excellence Fed. Garden Clubs Conn., 1984, Tricolor award Nat. Council State Garden Clubs, 1984, Aboreal award Nat. Council State Garden Clubs, 1984, Hort. Excellence award Nat. Council State Garden Clubs, 1984. Mem. Allied Bd. Trade, Caudatowa Garden Club (v.p. 1987-89, 90-91, pres. 1991-93). Republican. Roman Catholic.

WIEMAN, DAVID LAWRENCE, retired transportation executive; b. L.A., Oct. 8, 1925; s. Donald Simpson and Helene Edelweiss (Franke) W.; m. Virginia Mae Thomas, Sept. 8, 1956; 1 child, Lori Lynn Vasquez. BS in Engring., UCLA, 1950. Registered civil engr. Civil engr. Divsn. Hwys., San Bernardino, Calif., 1950-65; rsch. mgr. Divsn. Hwys., Sacramento, 1965-67, legis. rep., 1967-69; dept. head Caltrans, Sacramento, 1969-76; dist. dir. Caltrans, Stockton, Calif., 1976-82; divsn. chief Caltrans, Sacramento, 1982-90; pres. D. L. Wieman & Assocs., Sacramento, 1990-96; chair, program mgr. Caltrans, Sacramento, 1985-90, coun. chair R&D com., 1983-89. Mem., bd. dirs. Calif. Transp. Found., Sacramento, 1995. Lt. USNR, 1946-66. Recipient Resolution of Commendation, Calif. Legislature, 1990, Letter of Commendation, Calif. gov., 1990, Letter of Commendation, Pres. Bush, 1990, Congl. Record, Rep. Vic Fazio, 1990. Fellow ASCE; mem. Ret. Officers Assn. Home: 7439 Mooncrest Way Sacramento CA 95831-4045

WIEMER, ROBERT ERNEST, film and television producer, writer, director; b. Highland Park, Mich., Jan. 30, 1938; s. Carl Ernest and Marion (Israelian) W.; m. Rhea Dale McGeath, June 14, 1958; children: Robert Marshall, Rhea Whitney. BA, Ohio Wesleyan U., 1959. Ind. producer, 1956-60; dir. documentary ops. WCBS-TV, N.Y.C., 1964-67; ind. producer of television, theatrical and bus. films N.Y.C., 1967-72; exec. producer motion pictures and TV, ITT, N.Y.C., 1973-84; pres. subs. Blue Marble Co., Inc., Telemontage, Inc., Alphaventure Music, Inc., Betaventure Music, Inc. ITT, 1973-84; founder, chmn., chief exec. officer Tigerfilm, Inc., 1984—; chmn., bd. dirs. Golden Tiger Pictures, Hollywood, Calif., 1988—; pres, CEO Tuxedo Pictures Corp., Hollywood, Calif., 1993—. Writer, prodr., dir.: (feature films) My Seventeenth Summer, Witch's Sister, Do Me a Favor, Anna to the Infinite Power, Somewhere, Tomorrow, Night Train to Kathmandu; exec. prodr.: (children's TV series) Big Blue Marble (Emmy and Peabody awards); dir. (TV episodes) seaQuest DSV, Star Trek: The Next Generation, Deep Space Nine, The Adventures of Superboy; composer (country-western ballad) Tell Me What To Do. Recipient CINE award, 1974, 76, 77, 79, 81, Emmy award, 1978. Mem. NATAS, ASCAP, Info. Film Producers Assn. (Outstanding Producer award), Nat. Assn. TV Programming Execs., Am. Women in Radio and TV, N.J. Broadcasters Assn., Dirs. Guild Am. Office: Golden Tiger Pictures 3896 Ruskin St Las Vegas NV 89117-1097

WIENER, VALERIE, communications consultant, state senator; b. Las Vegas, Nev., Oct. 30, 1948; d. Louis Isaac Wiener and Tui Ava Knight. BJ, U. Mo., 1971, MA, 1972; MA, U. Ill., Springfield, 1974; postgrad., McGeorge Sch. Law, 1976-79. Producer TV show "Checkpoint" Sta. KOMU-TV, Columbia, Mo., 1972-73; v.p., owner Broadcast Assocs., Inc., Las Vegas, 1972-86; pub. affairs dir. First Ill. Cable TV, Springfield, 1973-74; editor Ill. State Register, Springfield, 1973-74; producer and talent "Nevada Realities" Sta. KLVX-TV, Las Vegas, 1974-75; account exec. Sta. KBMI (now KFMS), Las Vegas, 1975-79; nat. traffic dir. six radio stas., Las Vegas, Albuquerque and El Paso, Tex., 1979-80; exec. v.p., gen. mgr. Stas. KXKS and KKJY, Albuquerque, 1980-81; exec. adminstr. Stas. KSET AM/FM, KVEG, KFMS and KKJY, 1981-83; press sec. U.S. Congressman Harry Reid, Washington, 1983-87; adminstrv. asst Friends for Harry Reid, Nev., 1986; press sec. U.S. Senator Harry Reid, Washington, 1987-88; owner Wiener Comm. Group, Las Vegas, 1988—; senator State of Nev., 1996-. Author: Power Communications: Positioning Yourself for High Visibility (Fortune Book Club main selection 1994), Gang Free: Friendship Choices for Today's Youth, 1995; contbg. writer The Pacesetter, ASAE's Comm. News. Sponsor Futures for Children, Las Vegas, Albuquerque, El Paso, 1979-83; mem. El Paso Exec. Women's Coun., 1981-83; mem. VIP bd. Easter Seals, El Paso, 1982; media chmn. Gov.'s Coun. Small Bus., 1989-93, Clark Coun. Sch. Dist. and Bus. Cmty. PAYBAC Spkrs. and Partnership Programs, 1989—; med. dir. 1990 Conf. on Women, Gov. of Nev.; media chmn. Congl. Awards Coun., 1989-93; vice chmn. Gov.'s Commn. on Postsecondary Edn., 1992-96; bd. dirs. BBB So. Nev. Named Outstanding Vol., United Way, El Paso, 1983, SBA Nev. Small Bus. Media Adv. of Yr., 1992; recipient Woman of Achievement in Media award, 1992, Outstanding Achievement award Nat. Fedn. Press Women, 1991, Disting. Leader award Nat. Assn. for Cmty. Leadership, 1993, over 106 other comm. awards. Mem. Nev. Press Women (numerous 1st place media awards 1990—), Nat. Spkrs. Assn., Nat. Assn. Women Bus. Owners (media chmn., nat. rep. So. Nev. 1990-91, Nev. Adv. of Yr. award 1992), Dem. Press Secs. Assn., El Paso Assn. Radio Stas., U.S. Senate Staff Club, Las Vegas C. of C. (Circle of Excellence award 1993), Soc. Profl. Journalists. Democrat. Office: 1500 Foremaster Ln Ste 2 Las Vegas NV 89101-1103

WIERSEMA, HAROLD LEROY, aerospace engineer; b. Erie, Ill., Sept. 17, 1919; s. Clarence John and Tena (Griede) W.; m. Joanne Kearney, Mar. 19, 1955; children: Roger Kent, Marilyn Tena. BS, U. Ill., 1949. Aerospace engr. Space Div. Rockwell Internat., Downey, Calif., 1953-78; sr. spl. engr. Boeing Mil. Airplane Co., Wichita, Kans., 1978-86; aerospace engr., avionics cons. Long Beach, Calif., 1986-94. Com. chmn. Boy Scouts Am., Lynwood, Calif., 1968-70; pres. Compton (Calif.) Pacific Little League, 1966-69; deacon Presbyn. Ch., Southgate, Calif., 1965-70. Col. USAF, World War II, Korea. Decorated D.F.C., Air medal (5); recipient Mach Buster award N.Am. Aviation, Edwards AFB, 1963, Order of Arrow, Boy Scouts Am., 1967. Mem. IEEE (life), U.S. Air Force Assn., 388th Bomb Group/8th Air Force Assn. (life), Nat. Geog. Soc., UCLA Alumni Assn., Shriners. Democrat. Presbyterian. Home: 5451 Jonesboro Way Buena Park CA 90621-1615

WIES, BARBARA, editor, publisher; b. Dec. 5, 1939; m. Norman W. Bassett. BA, U. Conn., 1961; student, New Sch. for Social Rsch., 1961-62. Product devel. Fearn Soya, Melrose Park, Ill., 1973-75; product devel. Modern Products, Milw., 1973-75; editor, pub. Bestways Mag., Carson City, Nev., 1977-89; pub. The Healthy Gourmet Newsletter, 1989-91, Fine Wine-Good Food Newsletter, 1991—; publicity dir. Nev. Artists Assn., 1994—; owner Gualala (Calif.) Galleries, 1989-90; owner, operator cooking sch. Greensboro N.C. 1969-73; instr. Very Spl. Arts Nev., 1997. Author: Natural Cooking, 1968, Wok and Tempura, 1969, Japanese Home Cooking, 1970, The Wok, 1971, Super Soy, 1973, The Health Gourmet, 1981, International Healthy Gourmet, 1982; one-woman show paintings Dolphin Gallery, Gualala, Calif., 1990, River Gallery, Reno, 1994; 2 women show 1992, 94, 96, Dolphin Gallery, Calif., 1994, solo exhbn. Nev. Artists Assn. Gallery, 1993, 95, 96, 97; featured artist Nev. State Libr., 1996, West Nev. C.C., 1996, art show judge, 1997; restaurant critic Reno Gazette Jour., 1995—. Recipient First Place adult fiction Nev. State Lit. Co., 1995. Mem. Nat. League Am. Pen Women (chair 1st ann. lit. competition Reno br., chairperson 1st Nat. Lit. award), Inst. Food Technologists, Pastel Soc. of the West Coast, Inst. Am. Culinary Profls.

WIESNER, ERHARD, management consultant, realtor; b. Giersdorf, Germany, Sept. 22, 1943; came to U.S., 1969; s. Herbert A. and Margarete C. Wiesner; children: Erik Michael, Martin Andreas. BS, Tech. U., Hannover, Fed. Republic Germany, 1964; Diplom-Kaufmann degree, Georgia Augusta U., Goettingen, Fed. Republic Germany, 1969; MBA, Columbia U., 1970. Asst. prof. mktg. Georgia Augusta U., 1969; sr. cons. Quickborner Team, Inc., Hamburg, Fed. Republic Germany, 1970-72, ptnr., 1972-86; v.p. Quickborner Team, Inc., Millburn, N.J., 1972-78; pres. Plan-Consult, Inc., Evergreen-Hiwan, Colo., 1978—; realtor Coldwell Banker, Evergreen, Colo., 1997—; lectr., various orgns.; cons. in field. Contbr. articles to profl. jours. Bd. dirs. Hiwan Golf Club Homeowners' Assn.; active Boys Scouts Am. Fellow, Columbia U. German Acad. Exchange program (DAAD), Bonn, Fed. Republic Germany, 1969, 70; grantee German Acad. Exchange program, 1969-70. Mem. Nat. Assn. Realtors, Colo. Assn. Realtors, Evergreen-Conifer Assn. Realtors. Home: 2641 S Pinehurst Dr Evergreen CO 80439-8909 Office: 1291 Bergen Pkwy Evergreen CO 80439

WIEST, WILLIAM MARVIN, education educator, psychologist; b. Loveland, Colo., May 8, 1933; s. William Walter and Katherine Elizabeth (Buxman) W.; m. Thelma Lee Bartel, Aug. 18, 1955; children: William Albert, Suzanne Kay, Cynthia May. BA in Psychology summa cum laude, Tabor Coll., 1955; MA, U. Kans., 1957; PhD, U. Calif., Berkeley, 1962. Rsch. asst. psychol. ecology U. Kans., 1955-57; rsch. asst. measurement cooperative behavior in dyads U. Calif., Berkeley, 1958-59; from asst. to assoc. prof. Reed Coll., Portland, Oreg., 1961-74, prof., 1974-95, prof. emeritus, 1995—; adj. investigator Ctr. Health Rsch., Portland, 1985—; project coord. WHO, Geneva, 1976-84; fgn. travel leader Assiniboine Travel, Winnipeg, Man., Can., 1990-91, Willamette Internat. Travel, Portland, 1993-95; lectr. Fgn. Travel Club, Portland, 1990, 94; vis. scientist Oceanic Inst., Waimanalo, Hawaii, 1967-68; chmn. dept. psychology Reed Coll., Portland, 1973-75, 86; social sci. adv. com. Population Resource Ctr., N.Y.C., 1978—; vis. investigator Health Svcs. Rsch. Ctr., Portland, 1975-76, cons. 1976-80; com. protection human subjects Kaiser Permanente Med. Care Program, Portland, 1978-81; cons. WHO, 1980-81, U.S. Dept. Energy, 1980-83; mem. panel population study sect. HHS. Consulting editor Population and Environment, 1981—; jour. referee Health Psychology, Jour. Social Biology, Jour. Personality and Social Psychology, Memory and Cognition; contbr. articles to profl. jours. Sloan Found. Faculty Rsch. fellow, 1972-73, NSF fellow, 1975-76, USPSH fellow U. Calif., 1957-58, Woodrow Wilson Found. fellow U. Calif., 1960-61. Mem. AAAS, APHA, Am. Hist. Soc. Germans from Russia (conv. spkr. 1991, 97), Germans from Russia Heritage Soc., Am. Psychol. Assn., Population Assn. Am., Phi Beta Kappa, Sigma Xi. Home: 5009 SE 46th Ave Portland OR 97206-5048 Office: Reed Coll Psych Dept SE Woodstock Blvd Portland OR 97202

WIGGINS, CHARLES EDWARD, judge; b. El Monte, Calif., Dec. 3, 1927; s. Louis J. and Margaret E. (Fanning) W.; m. Yvonne L. Boots, Dec. 30, 1946 (dec. Sept. 1971); children: Steven L., Scott D.; m. Betty J. Koontz, July 12, 1972. B.S., U. So. Calif., 1953, LL.B., 1956; LL.D. (hon.) Ohio Wesleyan, 1975, Han Yang. U., Seoul, Korea, 1976. Bar: Calif. 1957, D.C. 1978. Lawyer, Wood & Wiggins, El Monte, Calif., 1956-66, Musick, Peeler & Garrett, Los Angeles, 1979-81, Pierson, Ball & Dowd, Washington, 1982-84, Pillsbury, Madison & Sutro, San Francisco, 1984; mem. 90-95th congresses from 25th and 39th Calif. Dists.; judge U.S. Ct. Appeals 9th Circuit, 1984—. Mayor City of El Monte, Calif., 1964-66; mem. Planning Commn. City of El Monte, 1956-60; mem. Commn. on Bicentennial of U.S. Constitution, 1985—, mem. standing com. on rules of practice and procedure, 1987—. Served to 1st lt. U.S. Army, 1945-48, 50-52, Korea. Mem. ABA, State Bar Calif., D.C. Bar Assn. Republican. Lodge: Lions.

WIGGINS, JAMES JOSEPH, family practice physician; b. Pasadena, Calif., Apr. 12, 1960; s. John Lawson and Rita Angela (Cassidy) W. BS, Rutgers U., 1989; DO, Phila. Coll. Osteo. Medicine, 1994. Diplomate Am. Acad. Family Physicians. Chief resident U. Calif.-Davis/Stockton Family Practice Residency Program; osteopath San Joaquin Gen. Hosp., Stockton, Calif., 1994—. Mem. Am. Osteopath. Assn. Home: 2009 Rosemarie Ln Apt 277 Stockton CA 95207-7800 Office: San Joaquin Gen Hosp PO Box 1020 Stockton CA 95201

WIGGINS, KIM DOUGLAS, artist, art dealer; b. Roswell, N.Mex., Apr. 8, 1959; s. Walton Wray Wiggins and Barbara Jo (Chesser) Ortega; m. Mary Allison Raney, Sept. 4, 1977 (div. May 1984); children: Rebekah, Mona; m. Cynthia Meredith, Sept. 29, 1985 (div. Oct. 1994); m. Maria C. Trujillo, June 17, 1995; children: Gianna Josiah, Elisha Douglas. Student, Ea. N.Mex. U., Roswell, 1977, 83-84, San Antonio Coll., 1978-79, Ind. Bapt. Coll., Dallas, 1982-83, Santa Fe Inst. Fine Art, 1989, Rhema C.B.S., Tulsa, 1997. Dir. Clarke-Wiggins Fine Art, Palm Springs, Calif., 1986-89; owner, mgr. Wiggins Fine Art, Santa Fe, 1989-93, Wiggins Studio, Roswell, 1991—; owner Print & Promise, Roswell, 1996—; cons. Mus. N.Mex., Santa Fe, 1992—, Cline Fine Art, Santa Fe, 1993—. One man shows at Altermann Morris Galleries, Houston, Dallas, 1992-97; exhibited in group shows Pa. Acad. Fine Art, Phila., 1992-96, M.H. DeYoung Mus., San Francisco, 1993-96; represented in permanent collections Mus. of N.Mex., Anschutz Collection, Denver; editor: K. Douglas Wiggins: Sense of Spirit, 1993. Mem. Internat. Platform Assn., Soc. Am. Impressionists, Coun. for Art of West, Gladney Ctr., Assurance Home. Republican. Home: 6 El Arco Iris Roswell NM 88201 Studio: Altermann & Morris Galleries 225 Canyon Rd Santa Fe NM 87501

WIGGLESWORTH, DAVID CUNNINGHAM, business and management consultant; b. Passaic, N.J., Sept. 23, 1927; s. Walter Frederick and Janet (Cunningham) W.; m. Rita Dominguez, Mar. 15, 1956 (dec.); children: Mitchell Murray, Marc David, Miles Frederick, Janet Rose; m. Gayle Coates, Aug. 1, 1981; 1 child, Danielle. BA, Occidental Coll., 1950, MA, 1953; postgrad. U. de las Ams., 1954-56; PhD, U. East Fla., 1957; LHD (hon.), Arubaanse Handels Academie, 1969. Dir., Spoken English Inst., Mexico City, also lectr. Mexico City Coll., 1954-56; headmaster Harding Acad., Glendale, Calif., also lectr. Citrus Jr. Coll., 1956-58; dir. Burma-Am. Inst., Rangoon, 1958-60; project dir. Washington Ednl. Rsch. Assocs., Washington, Conakry, Guinea, Benghazi, Libya, Carbondale, Ill., 1960-64; mng. editor linguistics div. T. Y. Crowell Pub. Co., N.Y.C., 1964-66; dir. linguistic studies Behavioral Rsch. Labs., Palo Alto, Calif., 1966-67; pres. D.C.W. Rsch. Assocs. Internat., Foster City, Calif., 1967—. Author: PI/LT-Programmed Instruction/Language Teaching, 1967, Career Education, 1976, ASTD in China, 1981, Resources for Workforce Diversity, 1993; contbr. articles to profl. publs.; mem. editorial bd. Vision/Action; mem. editorial rev. bd. Human Resource Devel. Quar. Trustee, City U. L.A.; bd. dirs. Cmty. Career Edn. Ctr., San Mateo, Calif., 1996—; mem. adv. bd. Martin Luther King Reading Acad., L.A., Internat. Ctr. Cultural Ergonomics, 1990—; mem. tng. systems design and prodn. program adv. bd. U. Calif.-Santa Cruz; U.S. rep. Internat. Com. Human Resources Devel., Kuwait, 1990—; ordained minister Universal Life Ch., 1969. Served with U.S. Army, 1945-46, 52-54. Mem. Am. Mgmt. Assn., Orgn. Devel. Network, Am. Soc. Tng. and Devel. (bd. dirs. internat. div., named Practitioner of Yr. 1988), Internat. Fedn. Tng. and Devel. Organs. (task force), Soc. Internat. Edn. Tng. and Rsch., 1st World Congress Internat. Orgn. Devel., Orgn. Devel. Forum, Peninsula Orgn. Devel. Support, Mideast Am. Bus. Conf., World Future Soc., Peninsula Exec. Club (Los Altos), SEDUMEX (Mexico City), Benghazi Sailing Club, Orient Club (Rangoon), Arctic Brotherhood (Skagway, Alaska). Office: DCW Rsch Assocs Internat PO Box 4400 San Mateo CA 94404-0400

WIGHTMAN, THOMAS VALENTINE, rancher, researcher; b. Sacramento, Oct. 7, 1921; s. Thomas Valentine and Pearl Mae (Cutbirth) W.; m. Lan Do Wightman. Student, U. Calif., Berkeley, 1945-46; B of Animal Husbandry, U. Calif., Davis, 1949; student, Cal. Poly. Inst., 1949-50. Jr. aircraft mechanic SAD (War Dept.), Sacramento, Calif., 1940-42; rancher Wightman Ranch, Elk Grove, Calif., 1950-59; machinest Craig Ship-Bldg. Co., Long Beach, Calif., 1959-70; rancher Wightman Ranch, Austin, Nev., 1970-88; dir. Wightman Found., Sacramento, 1988—. Dir. med. rsch. Staff sgt. U.S. Army, 1942-45. Recipient scholarship U.S. Fed. Govt., 1945-50. Fellow NRA, VFW, U. Calif. Alumni Assn., U. Calif. Davis Alumni Assn., Bowles Hall Assn.; mem. Confederate Air Force, The Oxford Club. Republican. Home and Office: Wightman Found 2130 51st St Apt 129 Sacramento CA 95817

WIGTON, CHESTER MAHLON, family physician; b. Pueblo, Colo., Jan. 12, 1928; s. Washington Irving and Bessie Marie (Ramsey) W.; m. Marjorie Chanak, Aug. 29, 1953 (dec. Jan. 1981); children: Robin, Renee, Kent, Lance, Bruce, Scott; m. Anita Kay Nelson, July 4, 1993; children: Sallie Michelle Short, Sadie Kay Short. BS cum laude, Colo. Coll., 1950; MD, U. Colo., Denver, 1954. Diplomate Am. Bd. Family Practice. Intern Swedish Hosp., Seattle, 1954-55; pvt. practice family medicine, Durango, Colo., 1957—; emeritus active Med. Mercy Hosp., Durango, 1990—, v.p. staff, 1970-73; med. dir. Hacienda Nursing Home, Bloomfield, N.Mex., 1992-95. Pres. CAMP Inc., Durango, 1970, CEOW Inc., Durango, 1964; treas. Tamarron Owners Assn. Bd., Durango, 1986-95; sec. Durango Sch. Bd., 1969-73; dir. San Juan Devel., Durango, 1971. Lt. (j.g.) USPHS, 1955-57; sec. Cmty. Hosp. Bd., Durango, 1986-92. Fellow Am. Acad. Family Practice, Electra Lake Sporting Club (pres. 1982-85), Delta Epsilon, Sigma Nu, Nu Sigma Nu. Republican. Presbyterian. Home: 151 Riverview Dr Durango CO 81301 Office: 3575 Main Ave Durango CO 81301-4028

WIKER, STEVEN FORRESTER, industrial engineering educator; b. Alhambra, Calif., Sept. 29, 1952; s. Bruce Forrester and Joan (Centers) W.; m. Jody Louise Wiker, Jan. 24, 1976; children: Douglas Forrester, James McCallum. BS in Physiology, U. Calif., Davis, 1975; MS in Biol. Scis., Washington U., 1981; MS in Indsl. Engring., U. Mich., 1982, PhD in Indsl. Engring., 1986. Rsch. project officer USCG, Washington, 1976-79; rsch. asst. U. Mich., Ann Arbor, 1979-86; rsch. engr. Naval Ocean Systems Ctr. Lab., Kailua, Hawaii, 1986-87, Naval Ocean Systems Ctr., San Diego, 1987-88; asst. prof. indsl. engring. U. Wis., Madison, 1988-93, head indsl. ergonomics rsch. lab., 1989-93; assoc. prof.dept. environ. health U. Wash., Seattle, 1993; assoc. prof. Dept. Environ. Health, U. Wash., Seattle, 1993—; dir. Ergonomic Design inst., Seattle, 1996—; dir. Ergonomic Design Inst., Redmond, Wash., 199—; sr. rsch. engr. James Miller Engring., Inc., Ann Arbor, 1981-88; dirs. telerobotics lab. Wis. Ctr. for Space Automation and Robotics, 1991-93. Contbr. articles to profl. jours. Comdr. USCGR, 1976—. Recipient Achievement medal USCG, 1988, 92, Humanitarian Svc. medal, 1993; fellow Ford Motor Co., Detroit, 1983-86; grantee Nat. Inst. Occupational Safety and Health, Washington, 1979-84, NASA, Ctrs. for Disease Control. Mem. Am. Soc. Safety Engrs., Inst. Indsl. Engrs., Internat. Soc. Biomechs., Aerospace Med. Soc., Human Factors Soc., Res. Officers Assn., N.Y. Acad. Scis., Sigma Xi, Alpha Pi Mu. Office: Ergonomic Design Inst 14150 NE 20th St # 375 Bellevue WA 98007 also: Ergonomic Design Inst 8353 160th Ave NE Redmond WA 98052

WIKSTROM, FRANCIS M., lawyer; b. Missoula, Mont., Aug. 20, 1949. BS summa cum laude, Weber State Coll., 1971; JD, Yale U., 1974. Bar: Utah 1974, U.S. Supreme Ct. 1980. Asst. U.S. atty. U.S. Dist. Ct. Utah, 1979-80, U.S. atty., 1981; mem. Parsons Behle & Latimer, Salt Lake City; adj. prof. coll. law U. Utah, 1986-89; mem. adv. com. on rules civil procedure Utah Supreme Ct; mem. Appellate Cts. Judicial Nominating Com., 1991—. Mem. ABA, Fed. Bar Assn. (adv. com.), Salt Lake County Bar Assn. (v.p. exec. com.), Am. Inns Ct. II (master bench 1989). Office: Parsons Behle & Latimer PO Box 11898 One Utah Ctr 201 S Main St Ste 1800 Salt Lake City UT 84111-2218

WILBUR, ROBERT L., biologist, science editor; b. Phila., Mar. 11, 1942; s. Nelson C. and Theodora (Linn) W.; m. Brenda Fritsche, Sept. 22, 1962; children: Robert Todd B., Nelson F. BS in Zoology, N.C. State U., Raleigh, 1965, MS, 1967. Cert. fisheries biologist. Biologist Fla. Game and Fish Commn., Eustis, Fla., 1967-74, Ariz. Gamd and Fish Dept., Phoenix, 1974-76; biologist, editor Alaska Dept. Fish and Game, Juneau, 1976—. Contbr. articles to profl. jours. Mem. several citizens adv. coms., Juneau, 1976—; organized Norway Point Neighborhood Assn., 1983—. Mem. Coun. Biology Editors (style manual commn. 1995—), Am. Fisheries Soc., Soc. Scholarly Pub. Home: 1441 Glacier Hwy Juneau AK 99801-7804

WILCK, CARL THOMAS, public relations executive; b. Quantico, Va., May 26, 1933; s. Carl and Glennie Alma (Jones) W.; m. Tommie England, June 16, 1961 (dec. Sept. 1985); m. Nadine Bagley Henry, May 21, 1989; 1 child, Jacqueline Leigh Henry. AA, Santa Monica Coll., 1955; BA in Polit. Sci., UCLA, 1957. Pres. Thomas Wilck Assocs., L.A., 1960-70, chmn., pres.; asst. adminstr. SBA, Washington, 1971; dep. chmn. Rep. Nat. Com., Washington, 1972-73; v.p. pub. affairs Irvine Co., Newport Beach, Calif., 1973-85; pres. Thomas Wilck Assocs., Orange County, 1985-95; ptnr. Nelson Comm. Group, Irvine, Calif., 1995—. Bd. chmn. Coro Found., L.A., 1982-83. Sgt. USMC, 1950-52, PTO. Mem. Fellow Pub. Rels. Soc. Am. (Silver Anvil award 1964, 77); mem. CORO Found. (bd. dirs.), Orange County C. of C., Chmn., 1993. Republican. Presbyterian. Office: Nelson Comm Group 18401 Von Karman Ave Ste 120 Irvine CA 92715

WILCOCK, JOHN, television producer, writer, editor; b. Sheffield, Eng., Aug. 4, 1927; s. Richard Barker Wilcock and Edith Clara Gambling; divorced. Grad. high sch., Halifax, Eng. Reporter Sheffield Telegraph, 1944-48, The Daily Mail, London, 1948-50, The Daily Mirror, London, 1950-52, Liberty mag., Saturday Night mag., Toronto, Ont., Can., 1952-54; asst. travel editor N.Y. Times, N.Y.C., 1957-60; producer The John and Joanna Show Wait a Minute!, N.Y.C., L.A., 1980—. Author: The Village Square, 1957, Magical and Mystical Sites, 1977, Occult Guide to South America, 1978, Traveling in Venezuela, 1978, The Book of Days, 1996; travel books about Greece, India, Japan, California, Texas, Italy, Vancouver, Las Vegas, Mexico and Seattle, 1960-95; West Coast editor Insight Guides; columnist Montecito Jour. Home: 814 Robinson Rd Topanga CA 90290-3627

WILCOX, CHARLES STEVEN, pharmacology research institute director; b. June 21, 1955. BS, U. So. Calif., 1978, MPA, 1979, MBA, 1982, PhD, 1989. Spanish/English tutor Joint Ednl. Project U. So. Calif., 1976; legis. analyst Am. Petroleum Inst., Washington, 1977; asst. policy analyst Office of Planning and Rsch. Gov.'s Office, State of Calif., Sacramento, 1978; rsch. adminstr. psychopharmacology unit U. Calif., Irvine, 1978-79, adminstrv. analyst psychopharmacology unit, 1979-81; exec. dir. Psychopharmacology Rsch. Assocs., Inc., Irvine, Calif., 1981-84, Pharmacology Rsch. Inst., Long Beach, Calif., 1984—; mktg. rsch., pharm. rsch. and personnel mgmt. cons. Contbr. articles to profl. jours. Vol. L.A. and Orange County Alzheimer's Assn. Speakers Bur., L.A. Mem. ASPA (life), Soc. for Clin. Trials, Regulatory Affairs Profls. Soc., Internat. Personnel Mgmt. Assn., Am. Soc. Clin. Psychopharmacology, Assocs. of Clin. Pharmacology (cert.), Pi Alpha Alpha. Home: 177 Bay Shore Ave Long Beach CA 90803-3452 Office: 1000 Dove St Ste 200 Newport Beach CA 92660-2814

WILCOX, DAVID CORNELL, ballet company director; b. L.A., May 7, 1951; s. Robert Carlos and Eileen Germaine (Babcock) W.; m. Tami Hirabayashi, Nov. 8, 1989; 1 child, Nicole Marie. Soloist Heidelberg (Germany) Ballet, 1971-72, Nuremberg (Germany) Ballet, 1973-74, Berlin (Germany) Ballet, 1975-78; founder, dir. L.A. Classical Ballet (founded as Long Beach Ballet), Long Beach, Calif., 1981—; dir. Ballet Arts Ctr., Long Beach, 1981—; asst. prof. Calif. State U., Long Beach, 1984-88; guest faculty Columbia (S.C.) City Ballet, 1991-92. Choreographer various ballets. Mem. Royal Acad. Dancing (assoc.), Dance USA. Home: 2630 Faust Ave Long Beach CA 90815-1336 Office: L A Classical Ballet 1122 E Wardlow Rd Long Beach CA 90807-4726

WILCOX, JOHN P., publishing executive. Pub. Ventura (Calif.) County Star. Office: Ventura County Star 5250 Ralston St Ventura CA 93003

WILCOX, MICHAEL JOHN, vision systems researcher, medical educator; b. Detroit, Mar. 20, 1948; s. Fred Edwin and LaVergne Elizabeth (Anderson) W.; m. Claudie Nicole Zamet, June 26, 1980; children: Christopher, Marc. BS, Purdue U., 1971, MS, 1976, PhD, 1980. Teaching asst. Purdue U., West Lafayette, Ind., 1972-74, rsch. assoc., 1974-80; postdoctoral fellow Fogarty Internat. Ctr., Bethesda, Md., 1980-82; chercheur associé Centre Nat. de la Recherche Scientifique, Marseille, France, 1982-83; chercheur boursié Fondation de la Recherche Medicale, Paris, 1983-84, Delduca Found., Marseille, 1984-85; asst. prof. U. P.R., Mayaguez, 1984-86, U. So. Calif., L.A., 1987-89; staff scientist Doheny Eye Inst., L.A., 1986-89; rsch. asst. prof. U. N.Mex., Albuquerque, 1989-96, assoc. prof., 1996—; cons. Allergan Pharms., Irvine, Calif., 1986-89, Kirtland AFB, Albuquerque, 1990—; co-founder Interdisciplinary Computational Sys. Group, Albuquerque, 1993-95; pres. Hyperacuity Sys. Author chpts. and articles. Leader Boy Scouts Am., Albuquerque, 1989-92. NIH grantee, 1985-90; Office of Naval Rsch. grantee, 1989—. Mem. AAAS, IEEE, Assn. for Rsch. in Vision and Ophthalmology, N.Y. Acad. Scis., Am. Soc. for Cell Biology, Internat. Neural Network Soc. Office: U NMex Dept Anatomy Albuquerque NM 87131-5211

WILCOX, RHODA DAVIS, elementary education educator; b. Boyero, Colo., Nov. 4, 1918; d. Harold Francis and Louise Wilhelmina (Wilfert) Davis; m. Kenneth Edward Wilcox, Nov. 1945 (div. 1952); 1 child, Michele Ann. BA in Elem. Edn., U. No. Colo., 1941; postgrad., Colo. Coll., 1955-65. Life cert. tchr., Colo. Elem. tchr. Fruita (Colo.) Pub. Sch., 1938-40, Boise, Idaho, 1940-42; sec. civil service USAF, Ogden, Utah, 1942-43, Colorado Springs, Colo., 1943-44; sec. civil service hdqtrs. command USAF, Panama Canal Zone; sec. Tech. Libr., Eglin Field, Fla., 1945-46; elem. tchr. Colorado Springs Sch. Dist. 11, 1952-82, mem. curriculum devel. com., 1968-69; lectr. civic, profl. and edn. groups, Colo.; judge for Excellence in Literacy Coldwell Bankers Sch. Dist. 11, Colo. Coun. Internat. Reading. Assn. Author: Man on the Iron Horse, 1959, Colorado Slim and His Spectacklers, 1964, (with Jean Pierpoint) Changing Colorado (Social Studies), 1968-69, The Founding Fathers and Their Friends in Denver Posse of the Westerners Brand Bank, 1971, The Bells of Manitou, 1973, (with Len Froisland) In the Footsteps of the Founder, 1993. Mem. hist. adv. bd. State Colo., Denver, 1976; mem. Garden of the Gods master plan rev. com. City of Colorado Springs, 1987—; mem. cemetery adv. bd. City of Colorado Springs, 1988-91; mem. adv. bd. centennial com., 1971; mem. steering com. Spirit of Palmer Festival, 1986; judge Nat. Hist. Day, U. Colo., Colorado Springs, and Colo. Coll., Colorado Springs; hon. trustee Palmer Found., 1986—; mem. Am. the Beautiful Centennial Celebrations, Inc., 1992-93; active Friends of the Garden of the Gods, Friends of Winfield Scott Stratton, Friends of the Libr. Named Tchr. of the Yr., Colorado Springs Sch. Dist. 11, 1968. Mem. AAUW (Woman of Yr. 1987), Colo. Ret. Educators Assn., Colorado Springs Ret. Educators Assn., Helen Hunt Jackson Commemorative Coun., Women's Ednl. Soc. Colo. Coll. Home: 1620 E Cache La Poudre St Colorado Springs CO 80909-4612

WILCOX, ROBERT KALLEEN, journalist; b. Indpls., July 21, 1943; s. Jacob Guire and Agnes Louise (Kalleen) W.; m. Begoña de Amezola, June 1, 1970; children: Robert, Amaya Begoña. BS in Journalism, U. Fla., 1966. Reporter, editor Miami (Fla.) News, 1967-72; freelance author, 1972—. Author: The Mysterious Deaths at Ann Arbor, 1977, Shroud, 1977, Fatal Glimpse, 1981, Japan's Secret War, 1985, 2d edit., 1995, Scream of Eagles: The True Story of Top Gun, 1990, Wings of Fury, 1997; (film, TV) Simon and Simon, 1985, God's Order, 1986, Frank's Place, 1987, Legend, 1994; writer TV pilots; staff story editor Famous Teddy Z, 1988-89, The New WKRP in Cin., 1990-93; contbr. numerous mags. With USAF, 1967-72. Recipient William Randolph Hearst award Gainesville Sun, 1967, Cine Golden Eagle award, 1981, 82, Gold medal Venice Internat. Film Festival, 1982, Supple Meml. award Religious Newswriters Assn., 1970. Mem. Author's Guild, Writer's Guild Am. West. Home and Office: 4064 Woodman Cyn Sherman Oaks CA 91423-4739

WILCZEK, JOHN FRANKLIN, history educator; b. San Francisco, Jan. 9, 1929; s. Leonard Matthew and Teresa Edith (Silvey) W.; m. Kuniko Akabane, Nov. 14, 1966; 1 child, Mary Theresa Shepherd. BA in History with honors, U. Calif., Berkeley, 1952; MA, U. Calif., 1953; PhD, Pacific Western U., Encino, Calif., 1978. Cert. secondary tchr., Calif. Instr. history and polit. sci. City Coll. San Francisco, 1956-94, instr. history of Japan, 1995; tchr. Japan History part-time City Coll. of San Francisco, 1996—; instr. Kobe (Japan) Women's Coll., 1979-81; instr. Seido Lang. Inst., Kobe, 1979-81; sec.-treas. Tokyo TV Broadcasting Corp., San Francisco, 1975—. Author: The Teaching of Japanese History on the Community College Level, 1978. Sgt. U.S. Army, 1953-55. Mem. U. Calif. Alumni Assn. Republican. Roman Catholic. Home: 5 Windsor Dr Daly City CA 94015-3257 Office: City Coll of San Francisco 50 Phelan Ave San Francisco CA 94112-1821

WILDE, DAVID, publisher, writer, biographer; b. Hereford, Nov. 12, 1944; s. Elizabeth Lillian (Price-Slawson) W. Diploma, Kneller Hall, London, 1965; pvt. mus. studies with Carmello Pace, Malta, 1964-68; student, Cardiff (Wales) Coll. Music, 1970-71; diploma in art, Open U., Leicester, Eng., 1980; student, Lancaster (Eng.) U., 1980-81, U. N.Mex., 1984. With BBC Radio, Eng., 1975-79; resident mem. wind ensemble Loughborough (Eng.) U., 1976-79; oil field worker Bawden Drilling Western Oceanic Inc., North Sea, Scotland, 1983-84; tutor U. N.Mex., Albuquerque, 1986-88, tchr. dept. continuing edn., 1989-90; musician/composer Civic Orch., Albuquerque, 1988-89; legal rschr. Wilde & Sprague, Albuquerque, 1988-90; pub., author Wilde Pub., Albuquerque, 1989—; clerical officer Severn-Trent Water, Eng., 1972-74, Social Security, Eng., 1983; rschr. Ctr. Southwest Rsch. U. N.Mex., 1994-97. Author: The Spirit That Wants Me, 1989, In the South: The Five Year Diary of a Journey Across America, 1991, Route 66: The Five Year Diary of a Journey Across America, 1991, Wildeland: Prose, 1992, North Sea Saga, 1960s: Opera of Oil, 1993, Desert Meditations: A Fairy Tale of New Mexico, 1993, Black Innocence: The Immigrant, 1993, Poems, People, Places: Travels on My Own, 1994, Basic Horn Technique: Studies for the French Horn, 1994, The Life and Times of Cdr. E.C. Zeke Cortez, USNR, 1996, (with others) La Puerta: A Doorway Into the Academy, 1997; contbr. to National Library of Poetry, 1996; editor 6 books; actor Geronimo prodn. Turner Network TV, 1993; extra various prodns., 1969-84. Rschr. SRIC, Albuquerque, 1989-96; cons. N.Mex. Bd. Appraisers, Albuquerque, 1989-90. Roman Catholic. Office: 105 Stanford Dr SE Albuquerque NM 87106-3537 also: Wilde Pub PO Box 4581 Albuquerque NM 87196-4581

WILDE, JAMES L., lawyer; b. Provo, Utah, May 27, 1940. BS, Brigham Young U., 1965; JD, Columbia U., 1968. Bar: Utah 1968. Mem. Ray, Quinney & Nebeker, Provo. Mem. ABA, Utah State Bar, Am. Inn Ct. I (master bench), Blue Key, Pi Sigma Alpha. Office: Ray Quinney & Nebeker 210 First Security Bank Bldg 92 N University Ave Provo UT 84601-4420

WILDER, JAMES D., geology and mining administrator; b. Wheelersburg, Ohio, June 25, 1935; s. Theodore Roosevelt and Gladys (Crabtree) W.; children: Jaymie Deanna, Julie Lynne. Graduated high sch., Wheelersburg. Lic. real estate agt., Ohio. Real estate agt. Portsmouth, Ohio; mgr. comml. pilots, fixed base operator Scioto County Airport, Ohio; mgr. and part owner sporting goods store, Portsmouth; cons. geologist Paradise, Calif., 1973-81; pres. Mining Cons., Inc., Paradise, 1981-84; dir. geology and devel. Para-Butte Mining, Inc., Paradise, 1984-88, pres., 1988-90, pres., chief exec. officer, 1990—. Served with U.S. Army, 1956-57. Home and Office: Para-Butte Mining Inc PO Box 564 Paradise CA 95967-0564

WILDER, JENNIFER ROSE, interior designer; b. Washington, Nov. 23, 1944; d. Winfield Scott and Blanche Irene (Taylor) Wilder; m. Scott Harris Smith, 1973 (div. 1987); children: Jason W., Adam S., Molly L., Whitney W. AA, Colo. Woman's Coll., Denver, 1965, BA, 1967. Interior designer Jamaica St. Interiors, Aurora, Colo., 1969-71; mgr./interior designer Interior Systems, Denver, 1971-73; owner/interior designer Jennifer Smith Designs, Denver, 1973-85, Inside Image Ltd., Castle Rock, Colo., 1985-86; interior designer Greenbaum Home Furnishings, Bellevue, Wash., 1986-94; mgr., interior designer Westbay Interiors, Gig Harbor, Wash., 1994—; instr. Tacoma C.C., Gig Harbor, Wash., 1995—. Recipient Design for Better Living award Am. Wood Coun., Seattle, 1987, Silver Mame awards Master Bldrs. Assn., 1992, 1st place Internat. Design Competition, Shintaku Daiwa, Hokaido, Japan,1 992. Mem. Am. Soc. Interior Design (allied mem.). Office: Westbay Interiors 5790 Soundview Dr Gig Harbor WA 98335-2042

WILDERMUTH, RONALD E., public relations professional; married; two children. BA in Internat. Rels. and Sociology, St. Ambrose Coll.; MS in Pub. Rels. with honors, Am. U.; MS in Naval Sci., Naval War Coll.; honor. grad., U. Okla. Commd. ensign USN, 1968, advanced through grades to capt., 1992; line officer USS Catamount, Comphibron 5, 1968-71; pub. rels. for Navy recruiting USN, 1971-75, pub. rels. staff Office of Info. dept., 1975-78; pub. rels. officer U.S. European Command, 1978-81; student Naval War Coll., Newport, R.I., 1981-82; dep. dir. pub. rels. U.S. Atlantic Command, Norfolk, Va., 1982-84; pub. rels. advisor Joint Chiefs of Staff, 1984-86; pub. rels. dir. Naval Air Forces, Pacific Fleet, 1986-88; pub. rels. advisor Gen. Schwarzkopf, 1989-92; dir. corp. rels. The Parsons Corp., Pasadena, Calif., 1992—; spokesman, pub. rels. counselor, speech writer in field, 1984-91. Active Feline Conservation Ctr., Greater Pasadena Bus. Ptnrs., Pasadena NOW; bd. dirs., mem. exec. com. Pasadena-Foothill br. L.A. Urban League. Decorated two Meritorious Svc. medals Dept. Def., two Meritorious Svc. medals USN, Personal Achievement medal USN, Legion of Merit medal Gen. H. Norman Schwarzkopf; recipient Accolades award for cmty. svc., Easter Seals Appreciation award for cmty. svc., Navy League Appreciation award for cmty. svc., Armed Forces YMCA Appreciation award for cmty. svc., others. Mem. Pub. Rels. Soc. Am., Am. Mktg. Assn., L.A. C. of C., Pasadena C. of C. (bd. dirs., mem. exec. com.), U.S. C. of C. Office: The Parsons Corp 100 W Walnut St Pasadena CA 91124-0001

WILDIN, MAURICE WILBERT, mechanical engineering educator; b. Hutchinson, Kans., June 24, 1935; s. John Frederick and Mildred Minerva (Dawson) W.; m. Mary Ann Brovan Christiansen, Aug. 9, 1958; children: Molly, Mildred. AA, Hutchinson Jr. Coll., 1955; BSME, U. Kans., 1958; MSME, Purdue U., 1959, PhD, 1963. Grad. asst. and instr. mech. engring. Purdue U., West Lafayette, Ind., 1958-61; from asst. prof. to assoc. prof. mech. engring. U. N.Mex., Albuquerque, 1961—, prof., 1973, dept. chair, 1968-73; mem. tech. staff Sandia Nat. Labs., Albuquerque, 1984-85; cons. several domestic and fgn. firms on stratified thermal storage, 1985—. Contbr. articles to profl. jours. Fellow ASHRAE; mem. ASME, Am. Solar Energy Soc. Office: U NMex Dept Mech Engring Albuquerque NM 87131

WILENSKY, HAROLD L., political science and industrial relations educator; b. New Rochelle, N.Y., Mar. 3, 1923; s. Joseph and Mary Jane (Wainsten) W.; children: Stephen David, Michael Alan, Daniel Lewis. Student, Goddard Coll., 1940-42; AB, Antioch Coll., 1947; MA, U. Chgo., 1949, PhD, 1955. Asst. prof. sociology U. Chgo., 1951-53, asst. prof. indsl. relations, 1953-54; asst. prof. sociology U. Mich., Ann Arbor, 1954-57, assoc. prof., 1957-61, prof., 1961-62; prof. U. Calif., Berkeley, 1963-82, prof. polit. sci., 1982—, research sociologist Inst. Indsl. Relations, 1963—, project dir. Inst. Internat. Studies, 1970-90; project dir. Ctr. for German and European Studies, Berkeley, 1994—; mem. research career awards com. Nat. Inst. Mental Health, 1964-67; cons. in field. Author: Industrial Relations: A Guide to Reading and Research, 1954, Intellectuals in Labor Unions: Organizational Pressures on Professional Roles, 1956, Organizational Intelligence: Knowledge and Policy in Government and Industry, 1967, The Welfare State and Equality: Structural and Ideological Roots of Public Expenditures, 1975, The New Corporatism, Centralization, and the Welfare State, 1976, (with C.N. Lebeaux) Industrial Society and Social Welfare, 1965, (with others) Comparative Social Policy, 1985, (with L. Turner) Democratic Corporatism and Policy Linkages, 1987; editor: (with C. Arensberg and others) Research in Industrial Human Relations, 1957, (with P.F. Lazarsfeld and W. H. Sewell) The Uses of Sociology, 1967; contbr. articles to profl. jours. Recipient aux. award Social Sci. Rsch. Coun., 1962, Book award McKinsey Found., 1967; fellow Ctr. for Advanced Study in Behavioral Scis., 1956-57, 62-63, German Marshall Fund, 1978-79; Harry A. Millis rsch. awardee U. Chgo., 1950-51. Fellow AAAS; mem. AAUP, Internat. Sociol. Assn., Internat. Polit. Sci. Assn., Indsl. Relations Research Assn. (exec. com. 1965-68), Soc. for Study Social Problems (chmn. editorial com.), Am. Polit. Sci. Assn., Am. Sociol. Assn. (exec. council 1969-72, chmn. com. on info. tech. and privacy 1970-72), Council European Studies (steering com. 1980-83). Democrat. Jewish. Office: U Calif Dept Polit Sci 210 Barrows Hall Berkeley CA 94720-1951

WILES, LISA GILMAN, accountant; b. San Bernardino, Calif., Nov. 28, 1956; d. Richard Francis and Judith Elizabeth (Stolba) Gilman; m. Christopher Clause Wiles, June 29, 1990; 1 child, Charles Gilman. Student, Pierce Coll., 1974-75; AA, Butte Coll., 1977; BA, U. Mont., 1979. Acct. Dobbins, DeGuire & Tucker, Missoula, Mont., 1977-80, Nev. Power Co., Las Vegas, 1980-81, Pine, Bratton & McMorrow, Ventura, Calif., 1981-84; pvt. practice acct. West Hills, Calif., 1984—. Chairperson Jr. League L.A., 1991—; exec. com., chair budget and fin. com. Friends of Queen of Angels Hollywood Presbyn. Med. Ctr., L.A., 1994—. Mem. Jonathan Club. Office: 23535 Windom St West Hills CA 91304

WILEY, BONNIE JEAN, journalism educator; b. Portland, Oreg.; d. Myron Eugene and Bonnie Jean (Galliher) W. BA, U. Wash., 1948; MS, Columbia U., 1957; PhD, So. Ill. U., 1965. Mng. editor Yakima (Wash.) Morning Herald; reporter, photographer Portland Oregonian; feature writer Seattle Times; war correspondent PTO AP; western feature editor AP, San Francisco; reporter Yakima Daily Republic; journalism tchr. U. Wash., Seattle, Cen. Wash. U., Ellensburg, U. Hawaii, Honolulu; mem. grad. faculty Bangkok U., Thailand, 1991; mem. faculty journalism program U. Hawaii, Honolulu, 1992—; Adminstr. Am. Samoa Coll., Pago Pago; news features advisor Xinhua News Agy., Beijing, Yunnan Normal U., Kumming, China, 1995. Mem. Women in Communications (Hawaii Headliner award 1985, Nat. Headliner award 1990), Theta Sigma Phi. Home: 1434 Punahou St Apt 1212 Honolulu HI 96822-4748

WILEY, MATTHEW FORREST, real estate broker; b. Richmond, Va., July 21, 1960. BSBA, San Diego State U., 1982. Comml. real estate broker Frost Trinen Ptnrs., Costa Mesa, Calif., 1982-89, Security Pacific Frost Trinen, Costa Mesa, 1989-92, The Street Co., Newport Beach, Calif., 1992-94, Travers Realty Corp., Newport Beach, 1994—. Office: Travers Realty Corp Ste 1210 4675 MacArthur Ct Newport Beach CA 92660

WILHELM, ROBERT OSCAR, lawyer, civil engineer, developer; b. Balt., July 7, 1918; s. Clarence Oscar and Agnes Virginia (Grimm) W.; m. Grace Sanborn Luckie, Apr. 4, 1959. B.S. in Civil Engring., Ga. Tech. Inst., 1947, M.S.I.M., 1948; J.D., Stanford U., 1951. Bar: Calif. 1952, U.S. Supreme Ct. Mem. Wilhelm, Thompson, Wentholt and Gibbs, Redwood City, Calif., 1952—; gen. counsel Bay Counties Gen. Contractors; pvt. practice civil engring., Redwood City, 1952—; pres. Bay Counties Builders Escrow, Inc., 1972-88. With C.E., AUS, 1942-46. Mem. Bay Counties Civil Engrs. (pres. 1957), Peninsula Builders Exchange (pres. 1958-71, dir.), Calif. State Builders Exchange (treas. 1971), Del Mesa Carmel Comm. Assn. (bd. dirs. 1977—). Clubs: Mason, Odd Fellows, Eagle, Elks. Author: The Manual of Procedures for the Construction Industry, 1971, Manual of Procedures and Form Book for Construction Industry, 9th edit., 1995; columnist Law and You in Daily Pacific Builder, 1955—; author: Construction Law for Contractors, Architects and Engineers. Home: 134 Del Mesa Carmel Carmel CA 93923-7950 Office: 600 Allerton St Redwood City CA 94063-1504

WILHITE, WILSON CECIL, JR., anesthesiology educator; b. Birmingham, Ala., Apr. 19, 1935; s. Wilson Cecil and Lorraine (Gibbs) W.; m. Patricia Sewell, Aug. 13, 1957; children: Jennifer Lee, Tiffany Willhite Lynch. BA, Samford U., 1956; MD, U. Ala., 1960. Diplomate Am. Bd. Anesthesiology. Intern U. Miami, Fla., 1960-61; resident in anesthesiology Wilford Hall USAF Med. Ctr., San Antonio, 1962-64; chmn. dept. anesthesiology Carraway Meth. Med. Ctr., Birmingham, 1966-82, pres. med. staff, 1975-77; vice chmn. dept. anesthesiology Bapt. Med. Ctr.-Montclair, Birmingham, 1982-83, chmn. dept., 1983-87; attending anesthesiologist Phenix Med. Park Hosp., Phenix City, Ala., 1987-89; prof. U. Tex. Med. Sch., Houston, 1989-91; prof. dept. anesthesiology UCLA Sch. Medicine, 1991-97; prof. anesthesiology U. Tex., Houston, 1997—; nat. lectr. in field. Hon. dep. sheriff Jefferson County (Ala.) Sheriff's Dept., 1971—. Capt. M.C., USAF, 1961-66. Named Outstanding Clin. Instr. Dept. Anesthesiology, U. Tex. Med. Sch., 1990, 91. Fellow Am. Coll. Anesthesiologists; mem. Am. Soc. Anesthesiologists (bd. dirs. dist. 9 1971-80 asst. treas. 1980-85, treas. 1985-91, 1st v.p. 1991-92, pres. elect 1993, pres. 1994), So. Med. Assn., Internat. Anesthesia Rsch. Soc., Soc. Cardiovascular Anesthesiologists, Calif. Soc. Anesthesiologists (ex officio mem. bd. dirs. and ho. of dels. 1991-92), Am. Soc. Post Anesthesia Nurses (hon. life), Ala. Post Anesthesia Nurses Assn. (hon. life). Republican. Baptist. Home: PO Box 190 Daphne AL 36526

WILK, DIANE LILLIAN, architect, educator; b. L.A., July 14, 1955; d. Stefan Piotr and Wanda Helen (Harasimowicz) W. BS in Architecture, U. So. Calif., 1977; MArch, Yale U., 1981; postgrad., Stanford U., 1981-82. Registered architect, Calif., Colo.; cert. Nat. Coun. Archtl. Registration Bds. Project designer Daniel, Mann, Johnson & Mendenhall, L.A., 1981, Boyd Jenks Architect, Palo Alto, Calif., 1982-84; project arch. HED Architects, Redwood City, Calif., 1984-86; assoc. prof. architecture U. Colo., Denver, 1986—, assoc. dir. architecture program, 1991-92. Author: Historic Denver Guides, 1995; contbg. author: The Avant Garde and The Landscape, 1991; editor: Avant Garde; contbr. articles to profl. jours. Cellist Redwood Symphony, Redwood City, 1982-85. Recipient faculty rsch. award U. Colo. Sch. Architecture, 1988, 92; grantee Graham Found., 1989. Mem. AIA, Soc. Archtl. Historians, Tau Sigma Delta (award student chpt. 1990), Alpha Rho Chi, Alpha Lambda Delta. Office: U Colo Campus Box 126 PO Box 173364 Denver CO 80217-3364

WILKENING, LAUREL LYNN, academic administrator, planetary scientist; b. Richland, Wash., Nov. 23, 1944; d. Marvin Hubert and Ruby Alma (Barks) W.; m. Godfrey Theodore Sill, May 18, 1974. BA, Reed Coll., Portland, Oreg., 1966; PhD, U. Calif., San Diego, 1970; DSc (hon.), U. Ariz., 1996. Asst. prof. to assoc. prof. U. Ariz., Tucson, 1973-80, dir. Lunar and Planetary Lab., head planetary scis., 1981-83, vice provost, prof. planetary scis., 1983-85, v.p. rsch., dean Grad. Coll., 1985-88; div. scientist NASA Hdqrs., Washington, 1980; prof. geol scis., adj. prof. astronomy, provost U. Washington, Seattle, 1988-93; prof. earth system sci., chancellor U. Calif., Irvine, 1993—; dir. Seagate Tech., Inc., 1993—, Rsch. Corp., 1991—; vice chmn. Nat. Commn. on Space, Washington, 1984-86, Adv. Com. on the Future of U.S. Space Program, 1990-91; chair Space Policy Adv. Bd., Nat. Space Coun., 1991-92; co-chmn. primitive bodies mission study team NASA/European Space Agy., 1984-85; chmn. com. rendezvous sci. working group NASA, 1983-85; mem. panel on internat. cooperation and competition in space Congl. Office Tech. Assessment, 1982-83; trustee NASULGC, 1994-97, UCAR, 1988-89, 97—, Reed Coll., 1992—. Author: (monograph) Particle Track Studies and the Origin of Gas-Rich Meteorites, 1971; editor: Comets, 1982. U. Calif. Regents fellow, 1966-67; NASA trainee, 1967-70. Fellow Meteoritical Soc. (councilor 1976-80), Am. Assn. Advanced Sci.; mem. Am. Astron. Soc. (chmn. div. planetary scis. 1984-85), Am. Geophys. Union,

AAAS, Planetary Soc. (dir. 1994—), Phi Beta Kappa. Democrat. Office: U Calif Chancellors Office 501 Adminstrn Bldg Irvine CA 92697-1900

WILKENS, STEVE, software marketing and sales executive; b. Burbank, Calif., Nov. 14, 1962; s. Martin Allen and Eileen Elizabeth (Jacobson) W.; m. Georgia Jean Lalonde, Dec. 31, 1987; children: Andrea, Stefani. BA in Mgmt., St. Mary's Coll. of Calif., Moraga, 1995. Account exec. Dean Witter, San Francisco; sales mgr. WPS/IBM, Houston; regional sales mgr. The McCosker Corp., San Ramon, Calif.; terr. mgr. Aldon Computer Corp., Oakland, Calif.; regional sales mgr. Smith Dennis & Gaylord, Santa Clara, Calif. Sgt. U.S. Army, 1981-85. Decorated Army Commendation medal. Mem. NASD, Am. Fgn. Legion, 82d Airborne Assn. Methodist.

WILKES, SHAR (JOAN CHARLENE WILKES), elementary education educator; b. Chgo., July 15, 1951; d. Marcus and Hattie (Ehrich) Wexman; 1 child, McKinnon. Student, U. Okla., 1973, U. Wyo., 1975—. Rsch. dirs., exhibit designer Nicolaysen Art Mus.-Children's Ctr., Casper, Wyo., 1984-85; tchr. Natrona County Sch. Dist. 1, Casper, Wyo., 1974-96; reading specialist Southridge Elem. Sch., 1995—; enrichment coord. Paradise Valley Elem. Sch., 1993-94; co-coord. Children's Health Fair/Body Works Healthfair, Ptnrs. in Edn., Paradise Valley Elem. Sch./Wyo. Med. Ctr. and Blue Envelope, 1994. Author: Fantastic Phonics Food Factory. Dem. candidate Wyo. State Legis., 1986, 88; edn. chair United Way, Casper, 1988; chairperson Very Spl. Arts Festival, 1988, March of Dimes, 1989; grants person Casper Symphony, 1990; NCSD coord. Bear Trap Meadow Blue Grass Festival, 1995, 96. Mem. NEA, LWV, Coun. Exceptional Children, Nat. Coun. Edn. Assn., Wyo. Edn. Assn., Natrona County Sch. Dist. # 1 (spelling bee coord.), Soroptimist (charter), Phi Delta Kappa (exec. bd. 1988-90), Delta Kappa Gamma. Home: 4353 Coffman Ct Casper WY 82604

WILKINSON, FRANCES CATHERINE, librarian, educator; b. Lake Charles, La., July 20, 1955; d. Derrell Fred and Catherine Frances (O'Toole) W.; div.; 1 child, Katrina Frances. BA in Communication with distinction, U. N.Mex., 1982, MPA, 1987; MLS, U. Ariz., 1990. Mktg. rsch. auditor Mktg. Rsch. N.Mex., Albuquerque, 1973-78; freelance photographer, 1974-75; libr. supr. gen. libr. U. N.Mex., Albuquerque, 1978-89, libr., asst. dept. head, 1989-90, libr., dept. head, 1990—; cons., trainer ergonomics univs. and govt. agys. across U.S., 1986—; bd. dirs. Friends of U. N.Mex. Librs., Aubuquerque, 1991-94; mediator Mediation Alliance, 1991-94. Contbr. articles to profl. jours.; author, editor books. Counselor, advocate Albuquerque Rape Crisis Ctr., 1981-84. Mem. ALA (mem. com. 1990—), N.Am. Serials Interest Group (mem. exec. bd. 1997—), N.Mex. Libr. Assn., N.Mex. Preservation Alliance, (vice chair 1995-96), Phi Kappa Phi (chpt. treas. 1991-92, chpt. pres. 1992-94), Pi Alpha Alpha. Home: PO Box 8102 Albuquerque NM 87198-8102 Office: U NMex Gen Libr Acquisitions and Serials Dept Albuquerque NM 87131

WILKINSON, JOAN KRISTINE, nurse, pediatric clinical specialist; b. Rochester, Minn., June 15, 1953; d. A. Ray and Ruth Audrey (Wegwart) Kubly; m. Robert Morris Wilkinson, June 14, 1975; children: Michael Robert, Kathryn Ann. BS in Nursing, U. Wis., 1975; MS, U. Colo., 1986. RN, clin. nurse specialist. Team leader Mendota Mental Health Inst., Madison, Wis., 1975-76; care leader Boulder (Colo.) Psychiat. Inst., 1976-78; pub. health nurse, head nurse Rocky Mountain Poison Ctr., Denver, 1978-83; research teaching asst. U. Colo. Health Scis. Ctr., Denver, 1986-87. Disaster nurse ARC, Boulder, 1976—; participant community service United Way, Denver, 1981-84; vol. nurse Channel 9 Health Fair, Boulder, 1983. Fellow U. Colo. Health Scis. Ctr., 1986; recipient Recognition cert. ARC, Madison, 1978, Gold award United Way, Denver, 1981, Outstanding Citizen award Boulder, 1990, Torch award for outstanding leader Girl Scouts, 1995. Mem. Colo. Nurses Assn. (dist. 12 scholar 1983-86), Am. Nurses Assn., World Health Assn., Sigma Tau Theta. Lutheran. Home: 1195 Hancock Dr Boulder CO 80303-1101 Office: Denver Vis Nurse Assn 3801 E Florida Ave Ste 800 Denver CO 80210-2545

WILLARD, GARCIA LOU, artist; b. Huntington, W.Va., Apr. 15, 1943; d. Harry Lee and Laura Lillian (Riley) Hall; m. Victor Percy Young, Sept. 2, 1972 (dec. Mar. 1980); m. Roger Lee Willard, Aug. 22, 1988. Student, Marshall U., 1978-83, W.Va. U., 1993, U. N.D., 1994-95. Owner, pres. Young's Fine Art, Huntington, 1975-85, Dyna Line, Wheeling, W.Va., 1980-85; instr. pastel and drawing Oglebay Mus.'s Stifel Fine Art Ctr., Wheeling, 1984-87; instr. pastel and portraiture Ohio U., Athens, 1987; owner, operator Outlines, Phoenix, Ariz., 1988-91; contbg. artist Sonoran Gallery, Phoenix, 1993—; mem. adv. bd. Profl. Art League, St. Clairsville, Ohio, 1984-85; lectr. and exhbn. juror various art orgns., Ohio, W.Va., Pa., 1987-88; art cons. Journey's End Designs, Wheeling, 1987. One woman shows include: Delf-Norona Mus., Moundsville, W. Va., Ariel Gallery, N.Y.C., Sonoran Gallery, Phoenix; Group shows include: Pen & Brush Club, N.Y.C., 1988, Hermitage Found. Mus., Va., 1988; contbr., illustrator: (book) Dr. Horton on African Art, 1985. Advisor Ariz. Fine Arts Commn., Phoenix, 1989-92. Recipient Best of Show award Delf-Norona Mus., 1985, Molly Guion award for graphics Catharine Lorillard Wolfe Art Club, 1988, Douglas Pickering Carnegie Mellon award, 1986. Fellow Am. Artists Profl. League (Pastel award 1988); mem. Pastel Soc. Am. (artist mem., A & M design award, 1988), Acad. Artists Assn. (artist mem., award for pastel portrait 1989), Degas Pastel Soc. (artist mem., M. Grumbacher award for excellence 1988), Nat. Drawing Assn., Art Assn. Harrisburg (artist mem.). Republican. Home: 16215C North 37th Dr Phoenix AZ 85023 Office: Sonoran Gallery 16215 N 37th Dr Phoenix AZ 85023

WILLARD, H(ARRISON) ROBERT, electrical engineer; b. Seattle, May 31, 1933; s. Harrison Eugene and Florence Linea (Chelquist) W.; BSEE, U. Wash., 1955, MSEE, 1957, PhD, 1971. Staff assoc. Boeing Sci. Research Labs., Seattle, 1959-64; rsch. assoc. U. Wash., 1968-72, sr. engr. and rsch. prof. applied physics lab., 1972-81; sr. engr. Boeing Aerospace Co., Seattle, 1981-84; dir. instrumentation and engring. MetriCor Inc. (previously Tech. Dynamics, Inc.), 1984—. Served with AUS, 1957-59. Lic. profl. engr., Wash. Mem. IEEE, Am. Geophys. Union, Phi Beta Kappa, Sigma Xi, Tau Beta Pi. Contbr. articles to tech. jours. Patentee in field. Office: 17525 NE 67th Ct Redmond WA 98052-4939

WILLARDSON, ROBERT KENT, physicist, manufacturing technology executive; b. Gunnison, Utah, July 11, 1923; s. Anthony Robert and Alice Eva (Pierce) W.; m. Beth Marie Bennett, Sept. 12, 1947; children: Amanda Marie Ballou, Elizabeth Ann Engar, Jennie Lynette. B.S. in Physics, Brigham Young U., 1949; M.S. in Solid State Physics, Iowa State U., 1951. Asst. chief phys. chemistry div. Battelle Meml. Inst., Columbus, Ohio, 1951-60; chief scientist, gen. mgr. electronic materials div. Bell & Howell Co., Pasadena, Calif., 1960-72; pres. Electronic Materials Corp., Pasadena, 1973; sales mgr., sr. scientist Cominco Am. Inc., Spokane, Wash., 1973-82; pres. Willardson Cons., Spokane, 1982-84; pres., dir. Cryscon Techs. Inc., Phoenix, 1984-87; tech. dir. EniChem Ams., Inc., Phoenix, 1988-91; pres. Willardson Cons., 1991—. Editor: Compound Semiconductors, 1962; Semiconductors and Semimetals, 58 vols., 1966—. Served as sgt. USAF, 1942-46. Mem. Am. Phys. Soc., IEEE (sr., chmn. San Gabriel chpt. 1967-68), Am. Chem. Soc., Electrochem. Soc. Democrat. Mormon. Home: 12722 East Spokane WA 99216-0327

WILLBANKS, ROGER PAUL, publishing and book distributing company executive; b. Denver, Nov. 25, 1934; s. Edward James and Ada Gladys (Davis) W.; m. Beverly Rae Masters, June 16, 1957; children: Wendy Lee, Roger Craig. B.S., U. Denver, 1957, M.B.A., 1965. Economist, bus. writer, bus. forecaster Mountain States Tel. Co., Denver, 1959-66; dir. pub. relations Denver Bd. Water Commrs., 1967-70; pres. Royal Publs. Inc., Denver, 1971—, Nutri-Books Corp., Denver, 1971—, Inter-Sports Book and Video, 1986—. Editor Denver Water News, 1967-70, Mountain States Bus., 1962-66. Mem. Gov. of Colo.'s Revenue Forecasting Com., 1963-66. Served with U.S. Army, 1957-58. Recipient Pub. Rels. award Am. Water Works Assn., 1970, Leadership award Nat. Inst. of Nutritional Edn., 1989, Medal of Freedom, U.S. Senate, 1994. Mem. Am. Booksellers Assn., Nat. Nutritional Foods Assn., Pub. Rels. Soc. Am. (charter mem. health sect.), Denver C. of C., SAR. Republican. Lutheran. Clubs: Columbine Country, Denver Press, Auburn Cord Duesenberg, Rolls Royce Owners, Classic Car of Am., Denver U. Chancellor's Soc., Ferrari. Address: Royal Publs Inc PO Box 5793 Denver CO 80217-5793

WILLER, KENNETH HENRY, library director; b. Buffalo, N.Y., May 24, 1954; s. Harold and Ruth (Kroll) W. BA, SUNY, Buffalo, 1977, MLS, 1984. Audiovisual technician Sunbird Teleproductions, Williamsville, N.Y., 1978; acct. exec. Beam-Cast, Inc., Buffalo, 1979-81; sales and mktg. rep. Wine Merchants, Ltd., Buffalo, 1981-82; asst. to head of circulation SUNYAB Health Scis. Libr., Buffalo, 1983-84; asst. slide libr. Albright-Knox Art Gallery, Buffalo, 1984; reference/media libr. Medaille Coll., Buffalo, 1984-85; med. info. svcs. coord. L.I. Libr. Resources Coun., Inc., Stony Brook, N.Y., 1985-87; libr. United Hosp. Fund N.Y., N.Y.C., 1987-90; libr., cons. Tech. Engring. Libr., Lockheed Missile and Space Co., Sunnyvale, Calif., 1990; dir. Med. Resource Facility Los Gatos, Calif., 1990—. Host, producer: (cable TV show) Here's To Your Health!, 1991—. Pub. speaker local healthcare support groups, Santa Clara Valley, Calif., 1992—. Mem. Am. Libr. Assn., Med. Libr. Assn., Spl. Libr. Assn. Office: Med Resource Fclt Los Gatos 815 Pollard Rd Los Gatos CA 95030-1438

WILLEY, ROBERT BRUCE, biology educator; b. Long Branch, N.J., Sept. 15, 1930; s. Walter Howard and Helen Cecilia (Baerman) W.; m. Ruth Hutchinson Lippitt, Jan. 14, 1956. BA magna cum laude, Montclair State Tchrs. Coll., N.J., 1952; MA, Harvard U., 1956, PhD, 1959. Tchr. biology West Orange (N.J.) Sr. H.S., 1952-54; from asst. prof. to assoc. prof. biology Ripon (Wis.) Coll., 1959-65; assoc. prof. biol. scis. U. Ill., Chgo., 1965-95, emeritus, 1995—; trustee Rocky Mountain Biol. Lab., Crested Butte, Colo., 1962-87, v.p. 1972-75, pres. 1976-84, sci. adv. bd., 1988—. Contbg. author books in field; contbr. article to ency., 1986; contbr. articles to profl. jours. Recipient Pres.'s Stewardship award The Nature Conservancy, 1988, Robert and Ruth Willey Lab. dedication, Rocky Mountain Biol. Lab., 1988, grants NSF, 1965-68, 71-74. Mem. Am. Soc. Naturalists, Animal Behavior Soc., Soc. Conservation Biology, Sigma Xi. Office: Rocky Mt Biol Lab PO Box 519 Crested Butte CO 81224

WILLHITE, CALVIN CAMPBELL, toxicologist; b. Salt Lake City, Apr. 27, 1952; s. Jed Butler and Carol (Campbell) W. BS, Utah State U., 1974, MS, 1977; PhD, Dartmouth Coll., 1980. Toxicologist USDA, Berkeley, Calif., 1980-85, State of Calif., Berkeley, 1985—; adj. assoc. prof. toxicol. Utah State U., 1984-94; mem. data safety rev. bd. Johns Hopkins Sch. Medicine, 1996—; mem. Calif./OSHA Gen. Industry Safety Order/Lead in Constrn. PEL Adv. Bd., 1994, 96. Mem. editl. bd. Toxicology and Applied Pharmacology, 1989—; editor N.Y. Acad. Scis., 1993, Toxicology, 1996—, Jour. Toxicological Environ. Health, 1996—; contbr. articles on birth defects to profl. jours. Nat. Inst. Child Health and Human Devel. grantee, 1985, 89, 92, March of Dimes Birth Defects Found. grantee, 1987-91, Hoffmann LaRoche grantee, 1992-94, Chem. Mfg. Assn., Nat. Ctr. Toxicol. Rsch., 1996. Mem. Soc. Toxicology (mem. program com. 1995—, Frank R. Blood award 1986), Teratology Soc. (chair pub. affairs), Am. Conf. Govt. Ind. Hygienists (vice-chair TLV com.), Internat. Occupl. Hygiene Assoc. Democrat. Mem. United Ch. of Christ. Home: 2863 Sanderling Dr Fremont CA 94555-1368 Office: State Calif 700 Heinz Ave Berkeley CA 94710-2721

WILLIAMS, ANGELITA SOPHIA, acquisitions negotiator; b. San Antonio, Apr. 2, 1964; d. Herbert Jr. and Ligaya Williams. BA in Sociel Sci., U. Calif., Berkeley, 1987; MBA, Calif. Poly. State U., 1991. Asst. store mgr., purchasing asst., advt. coord. Cost Plus Imports, Oakland, Calif., 1987-89; lab. asst. mgr. Calif. Poly. State U., San Luis Obispo, 1990-91; intern KSBY Action News/NBC News, San Luis Obispo, 1990-91; sr. buyer, contractor adminstr. IBM, San Jose, Calif., 1991-94; acquisition negotiator Bank of Am. NT & SA, Concord, Calif., 1994—. Asst. campaign mgr. Dist. 28 Assembly, San Jose, 1993-94; vol. March of Dimes, 1995—. Mem. NAFE, Oakland SPCA, Commonwealth Club (San Francisco).

WILLIAMS, ARTHUR COZAD, broadcasting executive; b. Forty Fort, Pa., Feb. 12, 1926; s. John Bedford and Emily Irene (Poyck) W.; m. Ann Cale Bragan, Oct. 1, 1955; children: Emily Williams Van Hoorickx, Douglas, Craig. Student, Wilkes U., 1943-44; B.A. cum laude, U. So. Calif., 1949. With Kaiser Aluminum, 1949, Sta. KPMC, 1950-51; v.p., mgr. KFBK and KFBK-FM Radio Stas., Sacramento, 1951-80; with public relations dept. Sacramento Bee, McClatchy Newspapers, 1981-86; dir.-treas. Norkal Opportunities, Inc.; pres. Sacramento Bee Credit Union. Served with AUS, 1944-46. Mem. Sigma Delta Chi. Clubs: Rotary, Sutter, Valley Hi Country, Masons, Shriners. Home: 1209 Nevis Ct Sacramento CA 95822-2532 Office: 1125 Brownwyk Dr Sacramento CA 95822-1028

WILLIAMS, BEN FRANKLIN, JR., mayor, lawyer; b. El Paso, Tex., Aug. 12, 1929; s. Ben Franklin and Dorothy (Whitaker) W.; m. Daisy Federighi, June 2, 1951; children: Elizabeth Lee, Diane Marie, Katherine Ann, Benjamin Franklin III. BA, U. Ariz., 1951, JD, 1956. Bar: Ariz. 1956. With Bd. Immigration Appeals, Dept. Justice, 1957, ICC, 1959; pvt. practice Tucson, Ariz., 1956—; city atty. Douglas and Tombstone, 1962; atty. Mexican consul, 1960; mayor of Douglas, 1980-88; bd. dirs. Ariz. Pub. Service Co., Univ. Med. Ctr. Corp. Pres. Ariz. League Cities and Towns, pres. Douglas Sch. Bd., 1963, 69, 70; mem. bd. Ariz. Dept. Econ. Planning and Devel.; bd. dirs. Ariz.-Mex. Commn., Ariz. Acad. (Town Hall), Merabank & Ariz. Pub. Service Co.; ward committeeman Douglas Republican Com., 1962. Served to 1st lt. AUS, 1951-53. Mem. ABA, Internat. Bar Assn., Ariz. Bar Assn. (treas. 1963), Cochise County Bar Assn. (pres. 1959), Pima County Bar Assn., Am. Judicature Soc., U. Ariz. Law Coll. Assn. (dir.), Ariz. Hist. Soc. (dir.), Sigma Nu, Phi Delta Phi, Blue Key. Episcopalian. Lodge: Elks. Home: 6555 N St Andrews Dr Tucson AZ 85718-2615 Office: 3773 E Broadway Blvd Tucson AZ 85716-5409

WILLIAMS, BERYLE LOU, writer, photographer; b. Grafton, Iowa, July 13, 1930; d. Ezra and Maybelle E. (Thompson) Wood; m. William Vincent Williams, Sept. 6, 1953; children: Michael Alan, Donald Paul, Blythe Anne, Jeffrey Brian. Student, Cornell Coll., Mt. Vernon, Iowa, 1950-53, Hamline U., 1980-82. Admissions sec. Cornell Coll., 1953-54; clk. Prudential Ins. Co., Denver, 1954-55; office mgr. Am. Water Resources Assn., Mpls., 1974-79, Zack Johnson & Assocs., St. Paul, 1979-83; conversational English tchr. Beijing U., 1983-84; book rev. editor, columnist Minn. Women's Press, St. Paul, 1984-91; freelance writer, photographer Estes Park, Colo., 1992—; mem. awards com. The Loft, Mpls., 1984-87; guest poet, critic various orgns., schs., 1969—. Contbr. poems to anthologies: Women Poets of the Twin Cities, 1975, Border Crossings, 1984, Mixed Voices, 1991, Atomic Ghost, 1995. Asst. coord. Poetry Under the Arch. program Hamline U., St. Paul, 1974-81; vol. tchr. St. Paul Pub. Schs., 1970-73; v.p. St. Anthony Park Arts Forum, St. Paul, 1979-82; Danforth assoc. Danforth Found., St. Louis, 1965-78; bd. dirs. Minn. Literature, St. Paul, 1982-89. Recipient Fellowship for Writers award Minn. State Arts Bd., 1976, 1st pl. poetry award AAUW, 1980, 82, featured poet Women's Art Registry of Minn. Jour., 1981. Mem. Friends of Estes Park Libr., Inc., Art Ctr. of Estes Park, Estes Park Prose Writers (founder), Estes Park Poets (founder). Home: 2035 Uplands Cir Estes Park CO 80517

WILLIAMS, CAROLE ANN, cytotechnologist; b. Duquesne, Pa., Apr. 14, 1934; d. Theodore Wylie and Dorothy Belle (Mehrmann) Williams; BS, Chatham Coll., 1956; postgrad. Case-Western Res. U., 1956-57; MS Calif. State U., 1989. Cytotechnologist, Clin. Path. Lab. of Paul Gross, Pitts., 1957-59; chief cytotechnologist, teaching supr. Presbyn. U. Hosp., Pitts., 1959-63; staff Pathology Lab. of Drs. Armanini & Wegner, Stockton, Calif., 1964; chief cytotechnologist, teaching supr. Hosp. of Good Samaritan, Los Angeles, 1964-89; dir. cytotechnology tng. program UCLA Med. Ctr., 1989—; conductor workshops in field. Mem. Am. Soc. Clin. Pathologists (cytotech. exam. com. bd. registry 1978-84, mem. bd. govs. 1990-95), Calif. Assn. Cytotechnologists (pres. 1967-68, 72-73), Internat. Acad. Cytology, Am. Soc. Cytopathology (Technologist of Yr. award 1981). Republican. Presbyterian. Home: 2460 Stoner Ave Los Angeles CA 90064-1326 Office: 10833 Le Conte Ave Los Angeles CA 90024-1602

WILLIAMS, CHARLES D., bishop. Bishop of Alaska Ch. of God in Christ, Anchorage. Office: Ch of God in Christ 2212 Vanderbilt Cir Anchorage AK 99504

WILLIAMS, CHARLES JUDSON, lawyer; b. Sam Mateo, Calif., Nov. 23, 1930; s. John Augustus and Edith (Babcock) W.; children: Patrick, Victoria, Apphia. AB, U. Calif.-Berkeley, 1952, LLB, 1955. Bar: Calif. 1955, U.S. Supreme Ct. 1970. Assoc. Kirkbride, Wilson, Harzfeld & Wallace San Mateo County, Calif. 1956-59; sole practice Solano County, Calif., 1959-64, Martinez, Calif., 1964—, Benicia, Calif. 1981-88; city atty. Pleasant Hill, Calif., 1962-80, Yountville, Calif., 1965-68, Benicia, 1968-76, 80-82, Lafayette, Calif. 1968—, Moraga, Calif., 1974-92, Danville, Calif., 1982-88, Pittsburg, Calif., 1984-93, Orinda, Calif., 1985-97; lectr. Calif. Continuing Edn. Bar 1964-65, U. Calif. Extension 1974-76, John F. Kennedy U. Sch. Law 1966-69; spl. counsel to various Calif. cities; legal advisor Alaska Legis. Council 1959-61; advisor Alaska sup. ct. 1960-61; advisor on revision Alaska statues 1960-62; atty. Pleasant Hill Redevel. Agy. 1978-82; sec., bd. dirs. Vintage Savs. & Loan Assn., Napa County, Calif., 1974-82; bd. dirs. 23d Agrl. Dist. Assn., Contra Costa County, 1968-70. Author: California Code Comments to West's Annotated California Codes, 3 vols. 1965, West's California Code Forms, Commercial, 2 vols., 1965, West's California Government Code Forms, 3 vols., 1971, supplement to California Zoning Practice, 1978, 80, 82, 84, 85, 87, 89, 91, 92, 94, 95, 96, 97; contbr. articles to legal jours. Mem. ABA, Calif. Bar Assn., Contra Costa County Bar Assn., Mt. Diablo Bar Assn. Office: 1320 Arnold Dr Ste 160 Martinez CA 94553-6537

WILLIAMS, CHRISTIE LEE, journalist; b. La Chapelle, Orleans, France, Jan. 1, 1967; came to U.S., 1967; m. Dominic Castro, Feb. 29, 1992. BA in Journalism, U. Hawaii, Manoa, 1997. Media analyst Intrastate Comm., Honolulu, 1994; copy editor Honolulu Star-Bull., 1994, Honolulu Advertiser, 1995—; news dir., exec. prodr. KTUH-FM, Honolulu, 1995—. Mem. Soc. Profl. Journalists (chpt. pres. 1992—), Asian Am. Journalists Assn., Investigative Reporters and editors, Radio and TV News Dirs. Assn.

WILLIAMS, CLARENCE, protective services official; b. Shreveport, La., Oct. 1, 1945; s. Leonard and Hearlean (Willis) W.; m. Mary K. Mannings, Nov. 30, 1974 (div. 1982); 1 child, Makala Deloris; m. Paulette Maria Guyton, Nov. 9, 1991; children: Kevin Michael, Maleah Requal. Student, So. U., 1963-64, Seattle C.C., 1968. Aerospace mechanic Boeing Aircraft Co., Seattle, 1965-68; fire fighter Seattle Fire Dept., 1968-76, engr., driver, 1976-82, emergency med. tech., 1976—, lt., 1982—; accreditation inspector Nat. Fire Protection Assn., Quincy, Mass., 1990—; cons. Pryor McClendon Counts Investment Bankers, 1993. Chmn. bd. trustees Mt. Zion Bapt. Ch., Seattle, 1992—; active Leadership Tomorrow, Seattle, 1986—, N.W. Conf. Black Pub. Ofcls., Wash., 1980—. With Wash. NG, 1965-71. Named one of Outstanding Young Men Am., 1978, 81, Most Outstanding Fire Fighter in State of Wash. Wash. State Jaycees, 1979; recognized for furthering cause of human rights UN Assn. U.S.A., 1979. Mem. Internat. Assn. Black Profl. Fire Fighters (pres. 1984-88), NAACP (membership com. 1976), Seattle Urban League (scholarship com. 1978), Seattle Black Fire Fighters Assn. (pres. 1968), So. U. Alumni Assn. Democrat. Office: Internat Assn Black Profl Fire Fighters PO Box 22005 Seattle WA 98122-0005

WILLIAMS, DAVID ALEXANDER, pilot; b. Helena, Mont., May 29, 1939; s. Daniel samuel and Dorothy (Alexander) W.; m. Jacquoline anders, Feb. 14, 1964 (div. Mar. 1988); children: Daniel Alexander, Darryl Jackson. BA, U. So. Calif., L.A., 1962. Lic. airline transport pilot, FAA. Commd. ensign USNR, 1963, advanced through grades to capt., 1985; tng. and test pilot McDonnell Douglas Corp., Long Beach, Calif., 1980-87, chief pilot, 1987—; mem. internat. adv. com. Flight Safety Found., Washington, 1987—; mem. windshear tng. aid task force FAA/industry, Washington, 1985-87; mem. CFIT tng. com. Flight Safety Found./FAA, 1992-96. Author: Turbulence Education and Training Aid FAA/Industry, 1996-97. Mem. Naval Res. Assn., catalina Conservancy. Republican. Home: 436 N Bellflower Blvd Unit 311 Long Beach CA 90814-2008 Office: McDonnell Douglas Corp 1MC94-12 3855 N Lakewood Blvd # Imc94-12 Long Beach CA 90846-0003

WILLIAMS, DAVID MICHAEL, manufacturing executive; b. Bklyn., Feb. 25, 1936; s. Robert Irving and Patricia Margaret (Flanagan) W.; m. Carol Bultmann, Nov. 13, 1965; children: Mark, Jennifer. Cert., NYU, Ctr. for Safety Engring., Manhattan, N.Y., 1960. Mgr. various mfrs., 1956-79; pres. D.M. Williams, Inc., Livermore, Calif., 1979—; cons. various mfrs., 1979—. Candidate for Gov., Calif., 1990; candidate for Congress, Calif., 1986, 88, 89, 92, 94, 96; active Rep. Ctrl. Com., Calif., 1987-88. Cole grantee NYU, 1960. Mem. Inst. Packaging Profls. (bd. dirs. no. Calif. chpt., 1982-85, chmn. 1985-86), ASTM, Mensa (founder interest group 1983-86). Roman Catholic. Office: 1560 Kingsport Ave Livermore CA 94550-6149

WILLIAMS, DAVID WELFORD, federal judge; b. Atlanta, Mar. 20, 1910; s. William W. and Maude (Lee) W.; m. Ouida Maie White, June 11, 1939; children: David Welford, Vaughn Charles. A.A., Los Angeles Jr. Coll., 1932; A.B., UCLA, 1934; LL.B., U. So. Calif., 1937. Bar: Calif. 1937. Practiced in Los Angeles, 1937-55; judge Mcpl. Ct., Los Angeles, 1956-62, Superior Ct., Los Angeles, 1962-69, U.S. Dist. Ct. (cen. dist.) Calif., Los Angeles, 1969—; now sr. judge U.S. Dist. Ct. (cen. dist.) Calif.; judge Los Angeles County Grand Jury, 1965. Recipient Russwurm award Nat. Assn. Newspapers, 1958; Profl. Achievement award UCLA Alumni Assn., 1966. Office: US Dist Ct 255 E Temple St Rm 7100 Los Angeles CA 90012-3334

WILLIAMS, DAY ROBERT, lawyer; b. Fresno, Calif., June 2, 1954; s. Rene Harold and Maurine Anne (Elliot) W.; m. Robin Alyss McKee, Aug. 11, 1993; 1 stepchild, Alyss Evans; 1 child, Nathanael Day. BA in English Lit., Reed Coll., Portland, Oreg., 1976; JD, U. Ariz., 1991. Bar: Nev. 1991. Law clk. Pima Savs. & Loan, Tucson, 1989-91; law clk. to Justice of Nev. Supreme Ct., Carson City, 1992; legal rschr. Carson City, 1993, pvt. practice law, 1993—; freelance photographer, Conn., N.Y., Nev., 1976-85. Editor and pub. Daylight newsletter, 1991-95; author: (book of poetry) Daybreak, 1986, (novel) Gambling With Death, 1995. Exec. com. Friends of Pyramid Lake, Reno, Nev., 1991-93; mem. Leadership Reno, 1987; donator of photographs Nev. Hist. Soc.; mem. Parable Prodns. Vineyard Christian Community. U. Ariz. Grad. Christian fellow, 1990-91. Mem. State Bar Nev. (mem. No. Nev. Fee Dispute Com.). Republican. Office: 204 N Minnesota St Carson City NV 89703-4151

WILLIAMS, DEREK, JR., pharmaceutical professional; b. Ft. Rucker, Ala., June 25, 1958; s. Derek W. Sr. and Carol E. (Kaufman) W.; m. Penny L. Bradly, Apr. 22, 1991; children: Jason Brian, Courtney Elizabeth. AS, U. Nev., 1981; BA, U. Colo., 1984; MA, U. Nev., 1986; postgrad., Pepperdine U. Rsch. asst. U. Nev., Reno, 1984-86; surgical counselor St. Lukes Hosp., Denver, 1987-89; pub. health advisor Ctrs. for Disease Control, Atlanta, 1989-91; clin. rsch. assoc. Amgen, Inc., Thousand Oaks, Calif., 1991-92, regulatory affairs specialist, 1992-97; mgr. regulatory affairs SangStat Med. Corp., Menlo Park, Calif., 1997—. Named Outstanding Young Men of Am., 1989-90. Mem. Assocs. Clin. Pharmacology, Regulatory Affairs Profls. Soc. Internat. Aids Soc., Am. Pub. Health Assn., Drug Info. Assn., Brit. Inst. Regulatory Affairs. Office: SangStat Med Corp 1505 Adams Dr Menlo Park CA 94025

WILLIAMS, ELIZABETH YAHN, author, lecturer, lawyer; b. Columbus, Ohio, July 20, 1942; d. Wilbert Henry and Elizabeth Dulson (Brophy) Yahn. BA cum laude, Loyola Marymount U., 1964; secondary tchg. credential, UCLA, 1965; JD, Loyola U., 1971. Cert. tchr. h.s. and jr. coll. law, English and history. Writer West Covina, Calif., 1964—; designer West Covina, 1966-68; tchr. jr./sr. h.s. L.A. City Schs., Santa Monica, Calif., 1964-65, La Puente (Calif.) H.S. Dist., 1965-67; legal intern, lawyer Garvey, Ingram, Baker & Uhler, Covina, Calif., 1969-72; lawyer, corp. counsel Avco Fin. Svcs., Inc., Newport Beach, Calif., 1972-74; sole practitioner and arbitrator Santa Ana, Calif., 1974-80, Newport Beach, 1980-87; mem. faculty continuing edn. State Bar of Calif., 1979; adj. prof. Western State U. Sch. Law, Fullerton, Calif., 1980; mem. fed. cts. com. Calif. State Bar, San Francisco, 1977-80. Author: (1-act plays) Acting-Out Acts, 1990, Grading Graciela, 1992, Boundaries in the Dirt, 1993; author, lyricist: (1-act children's musical) Peter and the Worry Wrens, 1995; editor: The Music of Poetry, 1997; contbr. articles to profl. jours.; panelist TV show Action Now, 1971; interviewee TV show Women, 1987; scriptwriter, dir. TV show Four/Four, 1994, (3-act adaptation) Saved in Sedona, 1995; scriptwriter, prodr., host TV show Guidelights to Success, 1996. Mem. alumni bd. Loyola-Marymount U., L.A., 1980-84; mem. adv. bd. Rancho Santiago Coll., Santa Ana, 1983-84; spkr. Commn. on Status on Women, Santa Ana, 1979. Recipient Editor's Choice award Nat. Libr. of Poetry, 1995-96, Telly award finalist, 1996; grantee Ford Found., 1964-65; French scholar Ohio State U., 1959, acad. scholar Loyola-Marymount U., 1960-64. Mem. Calif. Women Lawyers (co-founder, life, bd. dirs. 1975-76), Orange County Bar Assn.

(faculty Orange County Coll. Trial Advocacy 1982, chmn. human and individual rights com. 1974-75, comml. law and bankruptcy com. 1978-79, corp. and bus. law sect. 1980-81), So. Calif. Book Writers and Illustrators, Magee Park Poets, Phi Delta Delta, Phi Alpha Delta, Phi Theta Kappa (most disting. hon. life mem.). Office: PO Box 146 San Luis Rey CA 92068-0146

WILLIAMS, EMILY JEAN, dietitian, medical researcher; b. Indpls., July 18, 1928; d. Emil Charles and Vera Pearl (White) Rinsch; m. Donald Eugene Williams, Feb. 21, 1953; children: Donald Eugene, Ronald Owen. BS in Dietetics, Ind. U., 1950, MS, 1979, Dr.Med. Scis., 1983. Registered dietitian. Dietetic intern U. Mich., 1951; therapeutic dietitian Ind. U., 1952-53; asst. prof. Ind. U.-South Bend, 1980, 81, grad. teaching asst., 1978-80; clin. assoc. Ind. U. Med. Ctr., Indpls., 1984-92 ; therapeutic dietitian Desert Hosp., Palm Springs, Calif., 1965-66, 70-71, reviewer Diabetes Care and Edn. Practice Group Jour., 1985—; panel moderator Am. Dietetic Assn., New Orleans, 1985; lectr. in field. Author: Diabetes Care and Education Practice Group Newsletter, 1985. Contbr. articles to profl. jours. Pres. Western Art Coun. Palm Springs Desert Mus., 1993-95; chair mus. svc. coun. Desert Mus., 1994-95. Named Outstanding Mem., Alpha Xi Delta. Mem. DAR, Am. Dietetic Assn., Calif. Dietetic Assn., Am. Diabetes Assn. (profl. sect., hon. mem. cmty. blood bank bd. 1996-97), Palm Springs Hist. Soc., Coachella Valley Panhellenic Club (pres. 1970-71), Palm Springs Woman's Club (v.p.), P.E.O., Pi Lambda Theta. Republican. Avocation: needlepoint. Home: 38-681 E Bogert Trl Palm Springs CA 92264-9651

WILLIAMS, HAROLD MARVIN, foundation official, former government official, former university dean, former corporate executive; b. Phila., Jan. 5, 1928; s. Louis W. and Sophie (Fox) W.; m. Nancy Englander; children: Ralph A., Susan J., Derek M. AB, UCLA, 1946; JD, Harvard U., 1949; postgrad. U. So. Calif. Grad. Sch. Law, 1955-56; DHL (hon.), Johns Hopkins U., 1987. Bar: Calif. 1950; practiced in Los Angeles, 1950, 53-55; with Hunt Foods and Industries, Inc., Los Angeles, 1955-68, v.p. 1958-60, exec. v.p., 1960-68, pres., 1968; gen., mgr. Hunt-Wesson Foods, 1964-66, pres., 1966-68; chmn. finance com. Norton Simon, Inc., 1968-70, chmn. bd., 1969-70, dir., 1959-77; dir. Times-Mirror Corp., SunAmerica, Calif. Endowment; prof. mgmt., dean Grad. Sch. Mgmt., UCLA, 1970-77; pres., dir. Special Investments & Securities Inc., 1961-66; chmn. SEC, Washington, 1977-81; pres., chief exec. officer J. Paul Getty Trust, 1981—; regent U. Calif., 1983-94. Mem. Commn. for Econ. Devel. State of Calif., 1973-77; energy coordinator City of Los Angeles, 1973-74; public mem. Nat. Advt. Review Bd., 1971-75; co-chmn. Public Commn. on Los Angeles County Govt.; mem. Coun. on Fgn. Rels., Com. for Econ. Devel.; commn. to rev. Master Plan for Higher Edn., State of Calif., 1985-87; co-chair Calif. Citizens Commn. Higher Edn.; trustee Nat. Humanities Ctr., 1987-93; dir. Ethics Resource Ctr.; mem. Pres.' Com. on Arts and Humantities; mem. Commn. on the Acad. Presidency. Served as 1st lt. AUS, 1950- 53. Mem. State Bar Calif. Office: J Paul Getty Trust 1200 Getty Ctr Dr # 400 Los Angeles CA 90049

WILLIAMS, HARRIETTE FLOWERS, retired school system administrator, educational consultant; b. L.A., July 18, 1930; d. Orlando and Virginia (Carter) Flowers; m. Irvin F. Williams, Apr. 9, 1960; children: Lorin Finley, Lori Virginia. BS, UCLA, 1952, EdD, (HEW fellow), 1973; MA, Calif. State U., L.A., 1956. Tchr. L.A. Unified Sch. Dist., 1952-59, counselor, 1954-59, psychometrist, 1958-62, faculty chmn., 1956-57, student activities coord., 1955-59, leader insts. and workshops, 1952-76, dir. counseling, 1960-65, supr. Title I programs Elem. Secondary Edn. Act, 1965-68, asst. prin., 1968-76, prin., 1976-82, dir. instrn. sr. high sch. div., 1982-85, adminstr. ops., 1985-92; field svc. rep. Assn. Calif. Sch. Adminstrs., Culver City, Calif., 1992—; asst. dir. HEW project for high sch. adminstrn. UCLA, 1971-72; adj. prof. in Masters in Sch. Adminstrn. program Pepperdine U., L.A., 1974-78; ednl. cons. Teach for Am., 1991-94; L.A. County commr. Children and Family Commn.; 1996—. Recipient Sojourner Truth award Nat. Assn. Negro Bus. and Profl. Women's Clubs, L.A., 1968, Life Membership Svc. award L.A. PTA, 1972-75, L.A. Mayor's Golden Apple award for ednl. excellence. Mem. Assn. of Adminstrs. of L.A. (pres. region 16), Assn. Calif. Sch. Adminstrs. (state chmn. urban affairs com. 1985-88, region pres. 1989-90), Nat. Assn. Secondary Sch. Prins., Sr. High Sch. Asst. Prins. Assn. of L.A. (bd. dirs. 1974-76, sponsor 1985—), Sr. High Sch. Prins. Orgn., Nat. Coun. of Negro Women (life mem.), Lullaby Guild of Children's Home Soc. L.A. (pres. 1987-89), UCLA Gold Shield (1st v.p. 1994-96), L.A. PTA, NAACP, Urban League, Inglewood-Pacific cpt. Links Inc. (sec. 1984-86, treas. 1987-89), Jack and Jill of Am., Inc. (pres. L.A. chpt. 1980-82), UCLA Alumni Assn. (bd. dir., 1979-83, v.p. 1992-94, Excellence in the Cmty. award, 1996), Wilfandel (pres. 1994—), Delta Sigma Theta (pres. L.A. chpt. 1964-66, regional dir. 1968-72, nat. committeewoman 1966-94), Pi Lambda Theta, Kappa Delta Pi, Delta Kappa Gamma (treas. 1991-94). Baptist.

WILLIAMS, HARRY EDWARD, management consultant; b. Oak Park, Ill., July 20, 1925; s. Harry E. and Mary E.; m. Jean Horner; 1 child, Jeanne. Student, West Coast U., Los Angeles, 1958-60; BS in Engring., Calif. Coast Coll., Santa Ana, 1975; MA, Calif. Coast Coll., 1975; PhD, Golden State U., Los Angeles, 1981. Registered profl. engr., Calif. Mgr. Parker Aircraft Co., Los Angeles, 1958-60, Leach Corp., Los Angeles, 1968-69, Litton, Data Systems, Van Nuys, Calif., 1969-72; dir. Electronic Memories, Hawthorne, Calif., 1972-78, Magnavox Co., Torrance, Calif., 1978-80; v.p. Stacoswitch Inc., Costa Mesa, Calif., 1981-87; mgmt. cons., Westminster, Calif., 1987—; cons. in field. Contbr. articles to profl. jours. With USAF, 1943-46. Recipient Mgr. of the Yr. award Soc. for Advancement of Mgmt., 1984, Phil Carroll award for outstanding contbns. in field of ops. mgmt., 1985, Profl. Mgr. citation, 1984. Fellow Internat. Acad. Edn. Republican. Methodist.

WILLIAMS, HEATHER PAULINE, secondary education educator; b. Pocatello, Idaho, Jan. 25, 1972; d. John Ralph Hayes and Kathleen Goicoechea; m. Travis Thayne Williams, Sept. 8, 1990. AA, Coll. So. Idaho, Twin Falls, 1993; BS, Idaho State U., 1995. Rocky Mountain regional sec. NIRA, Idaho, 1993-96; sec. to gen. mgr. Nat. Finals Rodeo, Twin Falls, 1993-96; tchr. Gooding (Idaho) H.S.

WILLIAMS, HOWARD RUSSELL, lawyer, educator; b. Evansville, Ind., Sept. 26, 1915; s. Clyde Alfred and Grace (Preston) W.; m. Virginia Merle Thompson, Nov. 3, 1942; 1 son, Frederick S.T. AB, Washington U., St. Louis, 1937; LLB, Columbia U., 1940. Bar: N.Y. 1941. With firm Root, Clark, Buckner & Ballantine, N.Y.C., 1940-41; prof. law, asst. dean U. Tex. Law Sch., Austin, 1946-51; prof. law Columbia U. Law Sch., N.Y.C., 1951-63; Dwight prof. Columbia Law Sch., 1959-63; prof. law Stanford U., 1963-85, Stella W. and Ira S. Lillick prof., 1968-82, prof. emeritus, 1982, Robert E. Paradise prof. natural resources, 1983-85, prof. emeritus, 1985—; Oil and gas cons. President's Materials Policy Commn., 1951; mem. Calif. Law Revision Commn., 1971-79, vice chmn., 1976-77, chmn., 1978-79. Author or co-author: Cases on Property, 1954, Cases on Oil and Gas, 1956, 5th edit., 1987, Decedents' Estates and Trusts, 1968, Future Interests, 1970, Oil and Gas Law, 8 vols., 1959-64 (with ann. supplements/rev. 1964-95), abridged edit., 1973, Manual of Oil and Gas Terms, 1957, 9th edit., 1994. Bd. regents Berkeley Bapt. Divinity Sch., 1966-67; trustee Rocky Mountain Mineral Law Found., 1964-66, 68-85. With U.S. Army, 1941-46. Recipient Clyde O. Martz Tchg. award Rocky Mountain Mineral Law Found., 1994. Mem. Phi Beta Kappa. Democrat. Home: 360 Everett Ave Apt 4B Palo Alto CA 94301-1422 Office: Stanford U Sch Law Nathan Abbott Way Stanford CA 94305

WILLIAMS, HOWARD WALTER, aerospace engineer, executive; b. Evansville, Ind., Oct. 18, 1937; s. Walter Charles and Marie Louise (Bollinger) W.; m. Phyllis Ann Scofield, May 4, 1956 (div. Sept. 1970); m. Marilee Sharon Mulvane, Oct. 30, 1970; children: Deborah, Steven, Kevin, Glenn, Lori, Michele. AA, Pasadena City Coll., 1956; BSME, Calif. State U., Los Angeles, 1967; BSBA, U. San Francisco, 1978; PhD in Comml. Sci. (hon.), London Inst. Applied Rsch., 1992. Turbojet, rocket engr. Aerojet-Gen. Corp., Azusa, Calif., 1956-59, infrared sensor engr., 1959-60, rocket, torpedo engr., 1960-66; power, propulsion mgr. propulsion divsn. Aerojet-Gen. Corp., Sacramento, 1967-73, high speed ship systems mgr., 1974-78, combustion, power mgr., rocket engine and energy mktg. mgr., 1979-89, dir. strategic planning, 1989-94; program mgr. Pratt & Whitney Space Propulsion Ops., San Jose, Calif., 1995—. Author: (with others) Heat Exchangers, 1980, Industrial Heat Exchangers, 1985, History of Liquid Rocket Engine Development in the U.S., 1992, History of Aerojet, 1997; co-inventor Closed Cycle Power System, 1969. Recipient Energy Innovation award U.S. Dept. Energy, 1985. Mem. AIAA (sr., Best Paper 1966), Am. Soc. Metals (organizing dir. indsl. heat exch. confs. 1985). *Personal philosophy: I hope to be as good a parent and grandparent as mine have been.*

WILLIAMS, ISABEL MAFNAS, systems engineer, computer consultant; b. Austin, Tex., Sept. 21, 1965; d. Juan Crisostomo and Isabel (Iglesias) Mafnas; m. Dereck S. Williams, June 10, 1995. BA in Statistics, U. Calif., Berkeley, 1987; postgrad., Chabot Coll., 1989-91, Merritt Coll., 1991-92. Stats. tutor, stats. reader U. Calif., Berkeley, 1986-87; stats. reader U. Calif. Extension, Berkeley, 1987-89; instrnl. asst. II Chabot Coll., Hayward, 1988-92, computer lab. specialist, 1992-96; systems engr. MDL Info. Systems, Inc., San Leandro, Calif., 1996—; tchr. computers Eureka!-Girls Inc., San Leandro, 1993-96. Author: (Software user's guide) Academic Session Time Keeper, 1990, 91, 92, 94, 96. Recipient Newspaper Carrier scholarship Gannett Found., Inc., Guam, 1983, Gannett Spl. scholarship Gannett Found., Inc., Guam, 1983. Office: MDL Info Systems Inc 14600 Catalina St San Leandro CA 94577

WILLIAMS, J. D., state controller; b. Malad, Idaho; m. Rosemary Zaugg; 4 daus. MPA, Brigham Young U.; JD, Am. Univ. Bar: Idaho, D.C., several fed. cts.; cert. govt. fin. mgr. Apptd. law clk. D.C. Ct. Appeals; dep. Idaho Atty. Gen. Boise; lawyer Preston, Idaho; mayor City of Preston; appt. auditor State of Idaho, Boise, 1989-94, elected controller, 1994—; mem. Info. Tech. Res. Coun., Idaho. Past mem. Idaho Law Enforcement Planning Commn., past chmn. Idaho Youth Commn.; past chmn. Preston Sch. Dist. Excellence in Edn. com.; past mem. Idaho Water Resource Bd. Nat. Assn. State Comptrollers (pres.), Nat. Assn. State Auditors, Comptrollers and Treasurers (exec. com.). Office: Office of State Controller State Capital Boise ID 83720-0001

WILLIAMS, JACK JEFF, realtor, retired executive administrator; b. Cushing, Okla., July 28, 1936; s. Jeff Davis and Pauline Vera (Meyers) W.; m. Mary Ann Hill, June 1, 1957; children: Janet Lee Williams Charlin, Jeff Brian. BA in Econs., U. Calif., Dominguez Hills, 1974. Lic. real estate sales, Calif. Exec. adminstr. TRW Space & Electronics, Redondo Beach, Calif.; realtor Moore & Assocs. Hermosa Bch. (Top ten agent); cons. Delta Airlines, Atlanta, Aerospace Corp., El Segundo, Calif., Amdahl Corp., Santa Clara, Calif., Continental Airlines, L.A. Author, editor: Meyers from Moyers, 1996. Mem. TRW Retirees Assn. (v.p. 1997), Torrance Rose Float Assn. (bd. dirs. 1996, v.p., 1997), South Bay Genealogy Soc., Snow Valley Ski Club (coord.), Masons (sr. deacon 1993). Republican. Baptist. Home: 5216 Emerald St Torrance CA 90503-2724 Office: Moore & Assocs Realtors 2615 Pacific Coast Hwy #100 Hermosa Beach CA 90274

WILLIAMS, JAMES CALHOUN, history educator, public historian, consultant; b. San Francisco, Sept. 24, 1942; s. Otho Clinton and Elizabeth Helene (Giffen) W.; 1 child, Lisa Anet. BA in History, U. Oregon, 1964; MA in History, San Jose State U., 1970; PhD in Pub. History, U. Calif., Santa Barbara, 1984. Cert. tchr., Calif.; registered profl. historian. Tchr. Campbell (Calif.) Union H.S., 1968-71; prof. Gavilan Coll., Gilroy, Calif., 1971-85; exec. dir. Calif. History Ctr. & Found. De Anza Coll., Cupertino, Calif., 1985-93; prof. De Anza Coll., Cupertino, 1985—; cons. Pacific Gas and Elec., San Francisco, 1978—, So. Calif. Edison, Rosewood, Calif., 1978—. Author: (book) Energy and the Making of Modern Calif., 1997; contbr. 44 articles to hist. jours. including Calif. Hist., Am. Heritage of Inventions and Tech., IEEE Tech. and Soc. Mag., So. Calif. quarterly and many others; project dir. and author (exhibition) By The Sweat of Thy Brow, Cupertino, Calif., 1989 (award for Interpretation, Calif. Hist. Soc. 1989), project dir., curator 6 other exhibits Cupertino, Calif., 1986-91. Recipient Rockefeller Found. scholarship for grad. studies U. Calif., San Bernardino, 1976-77, Merit aware Sourisseau Acad., San Jose, Calif., 1984. Mem. Soc. for Hist. of Tech. (treas. 1992—), Nat. Coun. on Pub. History (bd. dirs. 1988-91), Orgn. Am. Historians, Am. Hist. Assn., Calif. Coun. for Promotion of History (pres. 1982-85, exec. sec. 1985-94, award of Distinction 1985, award for Disting. Svc. 1995), Calif. Hist. Soc. (bd. dirs. 1989-92). Home: 1130 Delynn Way San Jose CA 95125-3619 Office: De Anza Coll History Dept 21250 Stevens Creek Blvd Cupertino CA 95014

WILLIAMS, JEANNE, writer; b. Elkhart, Kans., Apr. 10, 1930; d. Guy Edwin and Louella Isabel (Salmon) Kreie; m. Gene F. Williams, Jan. 18, 1949 (div. 1968); children: Michael Williams, Kristian Williams; m. John Creasey, 1970 (div. 1973); m. Robert Joseph Morse, Feb. 13, 1981. Student, U. Okla. Author: Beasts with Music, 1967, Bride of Thunder, 1978, The Cave Dreamers, 1983, Daughter of the Sword, 1979, Harvest of Fury, 1981, The Heaven Sword, 1985, A Lady Bought with Rifles, 1976, Lady of No Man's Land, 1988, A Mating of Hawks, 1983, No Roof but Heaven, 1990, River Guns, 1962, So Many Kingdoms, 1986, Texas Pride, 1987, The Valiant Women, 1980, A Woman Clothed in Sun, 1977, Home Mountain, 1990, Island Harp, 1991, The Longest Road, 1993, Daughter of the Storm, 1994, The Unplowed Sky, 1994, Home Station, 1995, Wind Water, 1997, (novels as Megan Castell) The Queen of a Lonely Country, 1980, (novels as Jeanne Crecy) The Evil Among Us, 1975, Hands of Terror, 1972, The Lightning Tree, 1973, My Face Beneath the Stone, 1975, The Night Hunter, 1982, The Winter Keeper, 1975, (novels as Jeanne Foster) Deborah Leigh, 1981, Eden Richards, 1982, Women of the Three Worlds, 1984, (novels as Kristin Michaels) Enchanted Journey, 1977, Enchanted Twilight, 1976, Magic Side of the Moon, 1979, Make Believe Love, 1977, Song of the Heart, 1977, A Special Kind of Love, 1976, To Begin With Love, 1975, Voyage to Love, 1977, (novels as Deirdre Rowan) Dragon's Mount, 1973, Ravensgate, 1977, Shadow of the Volcano, 1975, Silver Wood, 1973, Time of the Burning Mask, 1976, (books for young adults) The Confederate Fiddle, 1962, rev. edit. 1995, Coyote Winter, 1966, Freedom Trail, 1973, The Horsetalker, 1961, Mission to Mexico, 1958, New Medicine, 1972 (new edit. 1994), Oh! Susanna, 1963, Oil Patch Partners, 1967, Promise of Tomorrow, 1959, Tame the Wild Stallion, 1957, To Buy a Dream, 1958, Trails of Tears, 1972 (new edit. 1993), Winter Wheat, 1975. Bd. dirs. Internat. Soc. for Animal Rights, Clark's Summit, 1982-86, Defenders of Wildlife, Washington, 1988-90; vol. EMT, Portal, Ariz., 1986—. Mem. Western Writers Am. (pres. 1974-75, Levi Strauss Golden Saddleman 1962, Spur award Best Novel of the West 1981, 91, Best Western Juvenile 1962, 74), Tex. Inst. of Letters, Authors Guild. Democrat. Unitarian. Home: Cave Creek Canyon Rd Portal AZ 85632

WILLIAMS, JEFFREY D., counselor; b. Dallas, Jan. 7, 1970; s. Paul Roger and Susan Carol (Barnett) W.; m. Allison Lynne Applegate, Aug. 28, 1993. BS, Houston Bapt. U., 1994; MA, Denver Sem., 1996. Counselor Kanakuk Kamps Inc., Branson, Mo., 1990-92; coll. pastor Tallowood Bapt. Ch., Houston, 1992-94; jr. high dir. Cherry Creek Presbyn. Ch., Denver, 1994-95; counselor Shelterwood, Denver, 1996—; mem. Houston Area Bapt. Student Unions, 1994. Mem. Young Reps., Waco, Tex., 1990; bd. dirs. Cherry Creek Drug Awareness Bd., Denver, 1995. Mem. Am. Counseling Assn., Assn. Christian Counselors.

WILLIAMS, JOHN CHARLES, II, data processing executive; b. Dayton, Ohio, Jan. 29, 1955; s. John Charles and Frances Jerline (McKean) W.; m. Diane Catherine Busch, Feb. 11, 1978; 1 child, Tabitha Anne. Programmer Kino Starr, Tucson, 1977-78, City of Boise (Idaho), 1978; data processing mgr. Nat. Assn. Ind. Businesses, Inc., Boise, 1978-79; chief exec. officer Williams Rsch. Assoc., Boise, 1979-80, MRW Data Systems, Inc., Tucson, 1981-82, Computer Security, Tucson, 1983-86, Modern Magic, Tucson, 1986-88; tech. support dir. Program Sources, Inc., Tucson, 1988—; chief exec. officer Cactus Explosives Corp., 1989-90, Systems Cons. Assocs., Tucson, 1990—; sr. systems analyst Desert Diamond Casino, 1994—. Area coord. Kolbe For Congress Campaign, Tucson, 1984; Ariz. Rep. State Committeeman, 1986—; mem. Ariz. Sonora Desert Mus., Tucson, 1983—. Republican. Home: PO Box 26164 Tucson AZ 85726-6164

WILLIAMS, JOHN CHRISTOPHER RICHARD, bishop; b. Sale, Cheshire, Eng., May 22, 1936; arrived in Can., 1960; s. Frank Harold and Ceridwen Roberts (Hughes) W.; m. Rona Macrae Aitken, Mar. 18, 1964; children: Andrew David, Judith Ann. BA in Commerce, Manchester U., Eng., 1958; diploma in theology, Cranmer Hall, Durham, Eng., 1960; DD, Emmanuel St. Chad Coll., Saskatoon, Can., 1997. Ordained deacon Anglican Ch. of Can., 1960, priest, 1962. Missionary in charge Anglican Ch. Can., Sugluk, Que., Can., 1961-72, Cape Dorset, N.W.T., Can., 1972-75, Baker Lake, N.W.T., 1975-78; archdeacon of the Keewatin Anglican Ch. Can., 1975-87; rector Holy Trinity Anglican Ch. Can., Yellowknife, N.W.T., 1978-87; bishop suffagan Diocese of the Arctic, Can., 1987-90, diocesan bishop, 1990—; trustee Can. Churchman, Anglican Ch. Can., 1976-82, mem. nat. exec. com., 1976-79, 92-95. Coord., trans. into Eskimo Inukkitut New Testament, 1992.

WILLIAMS, JOHN JAMES, JR., architect; b. Denver, July 13, 1949; s. John James and Virginia Lee (Thompson) W.; m. Mary Serene Morck, July 29, 1972. BArch, U. Colo., 1974. Registered architect, Colo., Calif., Idaho, Va., Utah, Nev. Project architect Gensler Assoc. Architects, Denver, 1976, Heinzman Assoc. Architects, Boulder, Colo., 1977, EZTH Architects, Boulder, 1978-79; prin. Knudson/Williams PC, Boulder, 1980-82, Faber, Williams & Brown, Boulder, 1982-86, John Williams & Assocs., Denver, 1986—; panel chmn. U. Colo. World Affairs Conf.; vis. faculty U. Colo. Sch. Architecture and Planning, Coll. Environ. Design, 1986-91. Author (with others) State of Colorado architect licensing law, 1986. Commr. Downtown Boulder Mall Commn., 1985-88; bd. dirs. U. Colo. Fairway Club, 1986-88; mem. Gov's. Natural Hazard Mitigation Coun., State of Colo., 1990. Recipient Teaching Honorarium, U. Colo. Coll. Architecture and Planning, 1977, 78, 79, 80, 88, Excellence in Design and Planning award City of Boulder, 1981, 82, Citation for Excellenc, WOOD Inc., 1982, 93, Disting. Profl. Svc. award Coll. Environ. Design U. Colo., 1988. Mem. AIA (sec. 1988, bd. dirs. Colo. North chpt. 1985-86, chair Colo. govtl. affairs com., Design award 1993, pres. 1990, v.p. 1989, sec. 1987, sec. Colo. chpt. 1988, ednl. fund Fisher I traveling scholar 1988, state design conf. chair 1991, North chpt. Design award 1993), Architects and Planners of Boulder (v.p. 1982), Nat. Coun. Architect Registration Bd., Nat. Golf Found. (sponsor), Kappa Sigma (chpt. pres. 1970). Home: 1031 Turnberry Cir Louisville CO 80027-9594 Office: John Williams and Assocs 821 17th St Ste 502 Denver CO 80202-3018

WILLIAMS, JOYCE MARILYN, artist, business owner; b. Waterbury, Conn., Sept. 12, 1933; d. Carl Vosburgh and Arline Dorothy (Cummings) Miller; m. Ralph Gray, Apr. 8, 1949 (div. 1955); children: Diane Leslie, Jerri Joyce-Gray; m. Charles Edward Williams, July 24, 1958; 1 child, Carol Lea. Grad. h.s., San Mateo, Calif., 1950. Pres., owner JC Enterprises, Phoenix, Ariz., 1993—; art instr. Sta. KHIZ-TV, Victorville, Calif., 1995; judge fine art San Bernardino County Fair, Victorville, 1995. Author: (instrn. books) Painting Portraits, 1994, Painting Horses, 1995; author, artist: (videos) Painting Portraits, 1993, Painting Horses, Wildlife, 1995. Recipient numerous 1st pl. awards various art shows, 1985-95. Mem. High Desert Art League, High Desert GD (editor newsletter 1992-95). Office: JC Enterprises PO Box 82815 Phoenix AZ 85071-2815

WILLIAMS, KENNETH A., food service executive; b. Coeur d'Alene, Idaho, July 16, 1936; s. Lyle Ernest Williams and Helen Violet DesChamp; (div.); children: Ronda, Kelly, Lisa, Scott. BA, Wash. State U., 1960. Asst. v.p., supr. Szabo Food Svc., Seattle, 1960-69; pres. Food Mgmt. Control, Seattle, 1969-95; CEO, chmn. Food Mgmt. Corp., Seattle, 1995—. Office: Food Mgmt Corp 21400 Pacific Hwy S Seattle WA 98198

WILLIAMS, KENNETH JAMES, retired county official; b. Eureka, Calif., Apr. 28, 1924; s. E. J. and Thelma (Hall) W.; student Humboldt State Coll., 1942-43; B.S., U. Oreg., 1949, M.Ed., 1952; m. Mary Patricia Warring, Sept. 3, 1949; children—James Clayton, Susan May, Christopher Kenneth. Engaged as mountain triangulation observer with U.S. Coast and Geodetic Survey, 1942; instr. bus. and geography Boise (Idaho) Jr. Coll., 1949-51; tchr. Prospect High Sch., 1952-54; prin. Oakland (Oreg.) High Sch., 1954-58; supt. prin. Coburg Public Schs., 1958-64; supt. Yoncalla (Oreg.) Public Schs., 1964-66, Amity (Oreg.) Public Schs., 1966-72; adminstr. Yamhill County, McMinnville, Oreg., 1974-85; cons., 1985—; county liaison officer Land and Water Conservation Fund, 1977-85. Dist. lay leader Oreg.-Idaho ann. conf. United Methodist Ch., 1968-80, bd. dirs. western dist. Ch. Extension Soc., 1976; mem. Mid-Willamette Manpower Council, 1974-85; bd. dirs. Lafayette Noble Homes, 1970-72; mem. adv. com. local budget law sect. State of Oreg. Served with AUS, 1943-46. Decorated Purple Heart. Mem. NEA, Oreg. Edn. Assn., Oreg. Assn. Secondary Prins., Nat. Assn. Secondary Prins., AAUP, Oreg., Am. Assn. Sch. Adminstrs., Assn. Supervision and Curriculum Devel., Nat. Sch. Pub. Relations Assn., Phi Delta Kappa. Mason (Shriner), Lion. Home: 21801 SE Webfoot Rd Dayton OR 97114-8832

WILLIAMS, LEE DWAIN, lawyer; b. Enid, Okla., Sept. 2, 1950; s. Lawrence and Wilma Jean (Richards) W. BA Polit. Sci., U. Calif., Santa Barbara, 1974; postgrad., U. Calif., 1974; JD, UCLA, 1977. Bar: Calif. 1977, U.S. Dist. Ct. (cen. dist.) Calif. 1977. Assoc. Irell & Manella, L.A., 1977-79, Riordan & McKinzie (formerly Riordan, Caps, Carbone & McKinzie), L.A., 1979-84; prin. Law Offices of Lee D. Williams, L.A., 1984-88; ptnr. Williams & Kilkowski, L.A., 1988—; bd. dirs. RJS Enterprises, Inc., Monrovia, Calif., 1987-96. Vol. atty. Pub. Counsel, La., 1978-80; trustee Children's Inst. Internat., L.A., 1981—, v.p., 1982-83, treas., 1995—. Mem. Calif. State Bar. Democrat. Office: Fox Plaza 2121 Avenue of the Stars 22d Fl Los Angeles CA 90067

WILLIAMS, LEONA RAE, lingerie shop owner, consultant; b. Fairfield, Nebr., July 1, 1928; d. Melton M. and Helga D. (Sorensen) Brown; m. Eugene F. Williams, June 6, 1946; 1 child, Dennis D. Grad. high sch., Fairfield. Owner Alice Rae Apparel Shop, Tucson, 1953-96, second location, 1967-96, Green Valley, Ariz., 1976-93, Sun City, Ariz., 1979-96; ret., 1996; cons. in field. Sponsor Distributive Edn. Program, 1978-82; coord. fashion shows Am. Cancer Soc., Tucson, 1987, 88, 89. Mem. Exec. Women's Internat. Assn. (chpt. pres. 1994), Mchts. Assn. (pres. 1987-89), Soroptomists, C. of C. Better Bus. Bur. Republican. Baptist. *Personal philosophy: We can be what we want to be with dedicated hard work, time, determination working with professionalism at all times.*

WILLIAMS, LESLIE BEALL, elementary education educator; b. Berkeley, Calif., Apr. 27, 1948; d. Jim Henry and Dorothy Loris (Smith) Beall; m. Robert Alan Williams, Feb. 20, 1970; children: Robert Alan, Jr., Erin Elizabeth. BA, Calif. State U., Hayward, 1970; Calif. credential K-12, U. Calif., Irvine, 1985. Spl. reading tchr. Anderson Elem., Newport Beach, Calif., 1985-87, Mariner's Elem., Newport Beach, 1987-89; tchr. Prospect Elem., Orange, Calif., 1989-91; tchr. Panorama Elem., Santa Ana, Calif., 1991—, Pentathlon coach, 1996—; curriculum coun. Orange Unified Sch. Dist., 1994—; internat. spkr. seminar Vision and Learning in the Classroom, 1994. Usher South Coast Repatory Theater, Costa Mesa, Calif., 1996. Recipient Hon. Svc. award Calif. PTA, 1996. Mem. ASCD, Internat. Reading Assn., Orange County Reading Assn., Calif. Educators Assn., Smithsonian Inst., World Wildlife Fund. Home: 308 Robinhood Ln Costa Mesa CA 92627 Office: Panorama Elem 10512 Crawford Canyon Rd Santa Ana CA 92705-1418

WILLIAMS, MARION LESTER, government official; b. Abilene, Tex., Dec. 1, 1933; s. Martin Lester and Eddie Faye (Wilson) W.; m. Johnnie Dell Ellinger, Dec. 14, 1957; children: Tammy Dawn Cole, Pamela DeAnn Ritterbush. BS, Tex. A&M U., 1956; MS, U. N.Mex., 1967; PhD, Okla. State U., 1971. Test engr. Sandia Nat. Labs., Albuquerque, 1959-61; weapons sys. engr. Naval Weapons Evaluation Facility, Albuquerque, 1961-66; ops. rsch. analyst Joint Chiefs of Staff/Joint Task Force II, Albuquerque, 1966-68; chief reliability div. Field Command DNA, Albuquerque, 1969-71; prin. scientist SHAPE Tech. Ctr., The Hague, Netherlands, 1971-74; chief tech. advisor HQ AF Test & Evaluation Ctr., Albuquerque, 1974-81; chief scientist HQ AF Operational Test & Evaluation Ctr., Albuquerque, 1981-89; tech. dir. HQ AF Operational Test & Evaluation Ctr., 1989—; vis. adv. com. Okla. State U., Stillwater, 1988—; adv. com. U. N.Mex., Albuquerque, 1985—. Editor T&E Tech. Jour., 1987—; contbr. articles to profl. jours. Sci. advisor N.Mex. Sci. & Tech. Oversigh Com., Albuquerque, 1988; bd. advisors U. N.Mex. Cancer Ctr., 1987—; bd. dirs. Contact Albuquerque, 1986-87. 1st lt. USAF 1956-59. Recipient Presdl. Rank award, 1987, 92. Fellow Mil. Ops. Rsch. Soc. (pres. 1982-83, bd. dirs. 1976-81, Wanner award 1991), Internat. Test & Evaluation Ctr. (bd. dirs. 1984-86, 88-90, v.p. 1990, pres. 1992-93), Ops. Rsch. Soc. Am., Tau Beta Pi, Phi Eta Sigma, Alpha Pi Mu, Sigma Tau, Kappa Mu Epsilon. Democrat. Baptist. Home: 1416

Stagecoach Ln SE Albuquerque NM 87123-4429 Office: HQ AF Operational Test Ctr Kirtland AFB Albuquerque NM 87117-7001

WILLIAMS, MARK TULLY, foundation executive; b. Bishop, Calif., Jan. 20, 1948; s. Paul Jacob Williams and Gertrude Margaret (Melsheimer) W.; m. Paula Marie Fink, June 20, 1970 (div. 1980); 1 child, Joshua Glen; m. Melinda Kay Bell, Aug. 14, 1982; children: Brian, Mark. BA magna cum laude, Pacific Union Coll., 1970; MDiv cum laude, Andrews U. SDA Theol. Sem., 1973; MA in Health Sys. Mgmt., Webster U., 1987. Pastor, tchr. Seventh-Day Adventist Ch., 1970-80; editor, publisher The Bldg. and Real Estate Jour., Hemet, Calif., 1980-83; asst. adminstr. Anacapa Adventist Hosp., 1983-85; v.p. mktg. and devel. Boulder (Colo.) Meml. Hosp., 1985-89; v.p. devel. San Antonio Cmty. Hosp., Upland, Calif., 1989-90; pres., CEO Riverside (Calif.) Cmty. Hosp. Found., 1990—; ptnr. Philanthropic Mgmt. Group. Bd. dirs. Vol. Ctr. of Riverside. mem. Nat. Assn. for Healthcare Philanthropy (cert. mem.), Riverside Rotary Club (bd. dirs.), La Sierra U. Sch. of Bus. and Mgmt. (adv. coun.), So. Calif. Assn. for Hosp. Devel., Nat. Soc. of Fund Raising Execs. Republican. Office: Riverside Cmty Hosp Found 4445 Magnolia Ave # A Riverside CA 92501-4135

WILLIAMS, MICHAEL ANTHONY, lawyer; b. Mandan, N.D., Sept. 14, 1932; s. Melvin Douglas and Lucille Ann (Gavin) W.; m. Marjorie Ann Harrer, Aug. 25, 1962 (div. 1989); children: Ann Margaret, Douglas Raymond, David Michael; m. Dorothy Ruth Hand, 1989. B.A., Coll. of St. Thomas, 1954; LL.B., Harvard U., 1959. Bar: Colo. 1959, N.D. 1959, U.S. Dist. Ct. Colo. 1959, U.S. Ct. Appeals (10th cir.) 1959, U.S. Supreme Ct. 1967. Assoc. Sherman & Howard and predecessor Dawson, Nagel, Sherman & Howard, Denver, 1959-65, ptnr., 1965-91; pres. Williams, Youle & Koenigs, P.C., Denver, 1991—. Served as 1st lt. USAF, 1955-57. Mem. Am. Coll. Trial Lawyers, Am. Bd. Trial Advs., Colo. Bar Found., Am. Law Inst., ABA, Colo. Bar Assn., Denver Bar Assn., Arapahoe County Bar Assn. Office: Williams Youle & Koenigs PC 1200 17th St Ste 1420 Denver CO 80202-5835

WILLIAMS, MICHAEL WAYNE, public policy analyst, researcher; b. Savannah, Ga., Sept. 27, 1950; s. Lyle Wayne and Pearl Beryl (Burr) W.; m. Marie Hoa Tho, Aug. 16, 1975; children: Steven Andrew, Stephanie Ann. BA, Am. U., 1971; MPA, George Washington U., 1980. Commd. ensign U.S. Navy, 1973, advanced through grades to lt. comdr., 1983, naval intelligence officer, 1973-93, ret., 1993; v.p. ops. Brightstar, Inc., North Brunswick, N.J., 1993-94; ptnr. Cochise Oil Co., Naples, Fla., 1993—; coun. rep. City of San Diego, 1995—; dir. bus. devel. Arabian Gulf Cons., Escondido, Calif., 1995—. Author, editor: Photo Reconnaissance Tactical Manual, 1976; author: (screenplay) The Green Cloak, 1993. Mem. ctr. com. Hillsborough County Rep. Party, Tampa, Fla., 1993-94; mem. candidate recruitment com. San Diego County Rep. Party, 1995—; asst. scoutmaster Boy Scouts Am., Tampa, 1993-94. Decorated Bronze Star. Mem. Ret. Officers Assn., Assn. Former Intelligence Officers, World Affairs Coun. San Diego, Navy League. Lutheran. Home: 27 Bridgetown Bnd Coronado CA 92118-3260 Office: City Coun Dist 2 City Adminstrn Bldg 202 C St San Diego CA 92101-4806

WILLIAMS, MIKEL H., judge. Chief magistrate judge Boise. Office: US Dist Ct Idaho Fed Bldg US Courthouse 550 W Fort St MSC 040 Boise ID 83724

WILLIAMS, NANCY ELLEN-WEBB, social services administrator; b. Quincy, Ill., Aug. 1; d. Charles and Garnet Naomi (Davis) Webb; m. Jesse B. Williams, Apr. 11, 1959; children: Cynthia L. Williams Clay, Troy Andrea Williams Redic, Bernard Peter. BA, Quincy Coll., 1957; postgrad., Tenn. A&I U., 1961; M Pub. Adminstrn., U. Nev., Las Vegas, 1977; LHD (hon.), U. Humanistic Studies, 1986. Cert. peace officer, Nev. (chmn. Standards and Tng. Com., 1978-81); cert. social worker. Tchr. Shelby County Tng. Sch., Memphis, 1957-61; dep. probation officer Clark County Juvenile Ct., Las Vegas, 1961-66, supervising probation officer, 1966-74, dir. probation services, 1974-80, dir. intake admissions, 1980-81, dir. Child Haven, 1989—; mem. Nev. Crime Commn., 1970-81. Author: When We Were Colored, 1986, Dinah's Pain and Other Poems of the Black Life Experience, 1988, Them Gospel Songs, 1989, The Soul Side: Big Mama Remembers, 1996; contbr. poetry to various mags. Mem. exec. com. Clark County Econ. Opportunity Bd., Las Vegas, 1963-71; chmn. So. Nev. Task Force on Corrections, 1974-81; mem. Gov.'s Com. on Justice Standards and Goals, 1979-81; bd. dirs. U. Humanistic Studies, Las Vegas, 1984—. Recipient Friend of Golden Gloves award Golden Gloves Regional Bd., 1981, Tribute to Black Women award U. Nev., Las Vegas, 1984, Commr.'s award HHS, 1991, Folklore mini-grant Nev. Coun. of the Arts, 1992. Fellow Am. Acad. Neurol. and Orthopedic Surgeons (assoc.); mem. AAUW, Nat. Council Juvenile Ct. Judges, Nat. Writers Assn. Democrat. Office: Flamingo Pecos Plaza 3430 E Flamingo Rd Ste 210 Las Vegas NV 89121-5064

WILLIAMS, PAT, former congressman; b. Helena, Mont., Oct. 30, 1937; m. Carol Griffith, 1965; children: Griff, Erin, Whitney. Student, U. Mont., 1956-57, William Jewell U.; BA, U. Denver, 1961; postgrad., Western Mont. Coll.; LLD (hon.), Carroll Coll., Montana Coll. of Mineral Sci. and Tech. Mem. Mont. Ho. of Reps., 1967, 69; exec. dir. Hubert Humphrey Presdl. campaign, Mont., 1968; exec. asst. to U.S. Rep. John Melcher, 1969-71; mem. Gov.'s Employment and Tng. Council, 1972-78, Mont. Legis. Reapportionment Commn., 1973; co-chmn. Jimmy Carter Presdl. campaign, Mont., 1976; mem. 96th-102nd Congresses from 1st Mont. dist., 1979-97; sr. fellow Ctr. Rocky Mountain West U. Mont., Missoula, 1997—; ranking mem. postsecondary edn. subcom. Coordinator Mont. Family Edn. Program, 1971-78. Served with U.S. Army, 1960-61; Served with Army N.G., 1962-69. Mem. Mont. Fedn. Tchrs. Democrat. Lodge: Elks. Home: 907 Beckwith Missoula MT 59801 Office: U Montana Ctr Rocky Mountain West Missoula MT 59801*

WILLIAMS, PHILIP ANTHONY, engineering executive. Student, Long Beach City Coll., 1978-91. Advanced tng. cert. Comm. Workers Am., 1979; Digital Network Automatic Switch cert. LARSE Corp., Sunnyvale, Calif., 1983; cert. income tax preparer Am. Schs., 1992; cert. comty. alcohol and drug abuse tng. City of Long Beach, 1995. Electrician Naval Post Grad. Sch., Monterey, Calif., 1972-73; electrician helper Long Beach (Calif.) Naval Shipyard, 1977; equipment maintainer GTE, Thousand Oaks, Calif., 1978-81; engr. III GTE, Thousand Oaks, 1981-83, sr. engr., 1983-86, staff engr., 1986—. Contbr. articles to profl. jours.; inventor Bupger Dog. Founder, CEO Mentor 2000; participant Long Beach Leadership Program; bd. mem. Long Beach Midnight Basketball League; vol. United Way-Greater L.A./Harbor Area, Calif. Police Summer Games, Long Beach, Sr. Olympics, Long Beach. With U.S. Army, 1969-76. Mem. VFW, Am. Legion, Vietnam Vets. Am. Home and Office: 140 E Scott St Long Beach CA 90805

WILLIAMS, RANDY LEE, special education educator; b. Downey, Calif., Dec. 30, 1947; s. Leland Harold and Valerie Clara (Herman) W.; m. Betty Fry Williams, Mar. 10, 1977; children: Lee Timothy, Maileen. BA in Psychology, Pomona Coll., Claremont, Calif., 1970; MA in Clin. Psychology, Western Mich. U., 1973; PhD in Devel. and Child Psychology, U. Kans., 1976. Home and sch. therapist Multicap Ctr., Kalamazoo, 1971-73; dist. advisor, coord. R&D, assoc. dir. Follow Through program Project Follow Through, U. Kans., Lawrence, 1973-79; dir. comm. disorders Gonzaga U., Spokane, Wash., 1981-85, asst. prof. spl. edn., 1979-83, assoc. prof. spl. edn., 1983-87, prof. spl. edn., 1987—, pres. faculty assembly, 1991-92; adj. asst. prof. human devel. U. Kans., Lawrence, 1977-79; cons. in field; presenter at confs. Assoc. editor: Education and Treatment of Children, 1983-86; guest editor, reviewer various jours.; contbr. articles to profl. jours. Mem. Mayor's Com. on Handicapped, Spokane, 1982-84; cons., vol. various sch. and cmty. activities. Mem. N.W. Assn. Behavior Analysis (conf. chair 1990-91, pres.-elect 1996), Assn. Behavior Analysis, Coun. for Exceptional Children, Assn. Direct Instrn., Assn. Retarded Citizens, Parent Tchr. Student Assn. Office: Gonzaga U Dept Spl Edn Ad Box 25 Spokane WA 99258

WILLIAMS, RAY RALPH, advisory engineer; b. Blackfoot, Idaho, Aug. 6, 1935; s. Millard William Roberts and Ardell Lydia Evans; m. Beverly Boyce, June 17, 1957; children: Serena Ardell, Steven Ray, David Tim, Travis Ralph, Brannon Dean. BA in Econs. and Bus., Chapman U., 1975; MS in Sys. Mgmt., U. So. Calif., 1979; B in Indsl. Tech., U. Idaho, 1987. Cert. quality engr.; cert. quality auditor. Master chief petty officer USN, 1974-77; tech. asst. to corp. quality mgr. San Diego Gas and Electric, 1977-79; sr. project engr. Exxon Nuc. Idaho, Idaho Falls, Ind., 1979-82; start up mgr. Union Electric-Callaway Nuclear Power Plant, Fulton, Mo., 1982-84; start up engr. Ill. Power, Clinton, 1984-85; sr. engr. Rockwell Corp., Idaho Falls, 1985-89; staff engr. EG&G Idaho Corp., Idaho Falls, 1989-94, chmn. quality assn., 1992-93; advisory engr. Lockheed Martin Idaho Tech., Idaho Falls, 1994—. With USN, 1974-77. Decorated Submarine Patrol pin USN; recipient Navy Achievment medals. Mem. VFW, Am. Soc. Quality (chmn. sect. 1992-93, scholarship chair 1994-96), Am. Nuc. Soc., Navy Res. Assn., Am. Legion. Republican. Mem. LDS Ch. Home: 4190 E 460 N Rigby ID 83442 Office: Lockheed Martin Idaho Technologies Dept Packaging and Transp PO Box 1625 Idaho Falls ID 83415-4105

WILLIAMS, RICHARD STANLEY, chemistry educator; b. Kodiak, Alaska, Oct. 27, 1951; s. Bobby Lebe and Shirley Ann (Tweten) W.; m. Jennifer C.-Y. Kao, June 30, 1990. BA, Rice U., 1974; MS, U. Calif., Berkeley, 1976, PhD, 1978. Mem. tech. staff AT&T Bell Labs., Murray Hill, N.J., 1978-80; asst. prof. chemistry UCLA, 1980-84, assoc. prof., 1984-86, prof., 1986—, vice chmn. dept. chemistry, 1991-94; prin. lab. scientist, dir. basic rsch. dept. Hewlett-Packard Labs., 1995—. Mem. editorial bd. Chem. Physics Letters Sci. Jour., 1986-93, Jour. of Materials Rsch., 1988-92, Accounts of Chem. Rsch., 1995—; contbr. articles to profl. jours. Fellow NSF, 1974-77, Alfred P. Sloan Found., 1984-86; Camille and Henry Dreyfus Found. scholar, 1983-88. Mem. AAAS, Am. Chem. Soc., Am. Phys. Soc., Am. Vacuum Soc., Materials Research Soc., Alpha Chi Sigma (Glenn T. Seaborg award 1984, Herbert Newby McCoy award 1989). Office: Hewlett Packard Labs 3500 Deer Creek Rd MS U-12 Palo Alto CA 94304

WILLIAMS, ROBERT STONE, protective services official; b. Mathews, Va., Jan. 22, 1952; s. Charles H. and Anne (Stone) W.; m. Danielle Williams, July 1987. AAS, Rowan Tech. Inst., 1972; BS in Fire Protection and Safety Engring., Okla. State U., 1975, MBA, 1976. Adminstrv. specialist Oklahoma City Fire Dept., 1977-79; dep. fire chief Clovis Fire Dept., N.Mex., 1979-82; fire chief Billings Fire Dept., Mont., 1982-88; fire chief City of Spokane, Wash., 1988—. Mem. Wash. State Bldg. Code Coun., 1989-94; bd. dirs. Salvation Army, Billings, 1984-85, Am. Heart Assn., Clovis, N.Mex., 1980-82; chmn. Internat. Fire Code Inst., 1993-94, 94-95, mem., 1990—. Named Fireperson Yr. Billings Downtown Exchange Club, 1988. Mem. Western Fire Chiefs Assn. (1st v.p. 1984-85, pres. 1985-86), Internat. Assn. Fire Chiefs, Nat. Fire Protection Assn., Curry County Jaycees (v.p. 1981-82, Jaycee of Yr. 1982), Billings Jaycees (bd. dirs. 1983-87, v.p. community devel. 1985, Outstanding Jaycee 1983, Disting. Service award 1985), Mont. Jaycees (treas. 1986-87, speak-up program mgr. 1986-87, Outstanding Young Montanan award 1985-86). Roman Catholic. Office: Spokane Fire Dept 44 W Riverside Ave Spokane WA 99201-0114*

WILLIAMS, RONALD LEE, pharmacologist; b. Koleen, Ind., June 26, 1936; s. Marion Raymond and Doris May (Lynch) W.; m. Sondra Sue Cobb, June 7, 1957; children: Robin Lee, Christopher P., David R., Jonathan V. BS, Butler U., 1959, MS, 1961; PhD, Tulane U., 1964. Registered pharmacist, Colo. From instr. to assoc. prof. pharmacology La. State U., New Orleans, 1964-84, assoc. prof. medicine, 1978-84, ret., 1984; asst. dir. Dept. of Corrections Hosp. Pharmacy, Canon City, Colo., 1986-93; with Canon Pharmacy, Canon City, Colo., 1994-95; with pharmacy svc. VA Med. Ctr., Ft. Lyon, Colo., 1996—; expert adv. panel renal drugs U.S. Pharmacopeia Drug Info., 1981-85; cons. in field. Editorial bd. jour. Pharmacology, 1979; reviewer jour. Pharmaceutical Sci., 1976; contbr. articles to profl. jours. La. Heart Assn. grantee, 1964, 66. Mem. Am. Soc. Pharmacology, N.Y. Acad. Sci., Fedn. Am. Soc. Exptl. Biology, So. Colo. Soc. Hosp. Pharm. Assn., Sigma Xi, Rho Chi. Republican. Baptist.

WILLIAMS, RONALD OSCAR, systems engineer; b. Denver, May 10, 1940; s. Oscar H. and Evelyn (Johnson) W. BS in Applied Math., U. Colo. Coll. Engring., 1964, postgrad. U. Colo., U. Denver, George Washington U. Computer programmer Apollo Systems dept., missile and space divsn. Gen. Electric Co., Kennedy Space Ctr., Fla., 1965-67, Manned Spacecraft Ctr., Houston, 1967-68; computer programmer U. Colo., Boulder, 1968-73; computer programmer analyst def. systems divsn. System Devel. Corp. for NORAD, Colorado Springs, 1974-75; engr. def. systems and command-and-info. systems Martin Marietta Aerospace, Denver, 1976-80; systems engr. space and comm. group, def. info. systems divsn. Hughes Aircraft Co., Aurora, Colo., 1980-89; rsch. analyst, 1990—. Vol. fireman Clear Lake City (Tex.) Fire Dept., 1968; officer Boulder Emergency Squad, 1969-76, rescue squadman, 1969-76, liaison to cadets, 1971, pers. officer, 1971-76, exec. bd., 1971-76, award of merit, 1971, 72, emergency med. technician 1973—; spl. police officer Boulder Police Dept., 1970-75; spl. dep. sheriff Boulder County Sheriff's Dept., 1970-71; nat. adv. bd. Am. Security Coun., 1979-91, Coalition of Peace through Strength, 1979-91. Served with USMCR, 1958-66. Decorated Organized Res. medal; recipient Cost Improvement Program award Hughes Aircraft Co., 1982, Systems Improvement award, 1982, Top Cost Improvement Program award, 1983. Mem. AAAS, AIAA (sr.), Math. Assn. Am., Am. Math. Soc., Soc. Indsl. and Applied Math., Math. Study Unit of the Am. Topical Assn., Armed Forces Comm. and Electronics Assn., Assn. Old Crows, Am. Def. Preparedness Assn., Marine Corps Assn., Air Force Assn., U.S. Naval Inst., Nat. Geog. Soc., Smithsonian Instn., Soc. Amateur Radio Astronomers, Met. Opera Guild, Colo. Hist. Soc., Hist. Denver, Inc., Historic Boulder, Inc., Hawaiian Hist. Soc., Denver Botanic Gardens, Denver Mus. Natural History, Denver Zool. Found., Inc., Mensa. Lutheran.

WILLIAMS, RUTH LEE, clinical social worker; b. Dallas, June 24, 1944; d. Carl Woodley and Nancy Ruth (Gardner) W. BA, So. Meth. U., 1966; M Sci.in Social Work, U. Tex., Austin, 1969. Milieu coordinator Starr Commonwealth, Albion, Mich., 1969-73; clin. social worker Katherine Hamilton Mental Health Care, Terre Haute, Ind., 1973-74; clin. social worker, supr. Pikes Peak Mental Health Ctr., Colorado Springs, Colo., 1974-78; pvt. practice social work Colorado Springs, 1978—; pres. Hearthstone Inn, Inc., Colorado Springs, 1978—; practitioner Jin Shin Jyutsu, Colorado Springs, 1978—; pres., v.p. bd. dirs. Premier Care (formerly Colorado Springs Mental Health Care Providers Inc.), 1986-87, chmn. quality assurance com., 1987-89, v.p. bd. dirs., 1992-93; bd. dirs. Beth Haven, Inc. Author, editor: From the Kitchen of The Hearthstone Inn, 1981, 2d rev. edit., 1986, 3d rev. edit., 1992. Mem. Am. Bd. Examiners in Clin. Social Work (charter mem., cert.), Colo. Soc. Clin. Social Work (editor 1976), Nat. Assn. Soc. Workers (diplomate), Nat. Bd. Social Work Examiners (cert.), Nat. Assn. Ind. Innkeepers, So. Meth. U. Alumni Assn. (life). Home: 11555 Howells Rd Colorado Springs CO 80908-3735 Office: 536 E Uintah St Colorado Springs CO 80903-2515

WILLIAMS, SALLY, landscape designer; b. Kansas City, Mo., June 30, 1955; d. Douglas John and Margaret Ann (Paul) Williams; m. Siegfried Peter Duray-Bito, June 16, 1984; children: Cassie, Alana. BA, Metro State Coll., Denver, 1979. Bus. mgr. Muse, Denver, 1985-87; exec. dir. Colo. Fedn. of the Arts, Denver, 1987-88; owner Perennial Garden Planning, Littleton, Colo., 1992—. Advanced master gardener Arapahoe County Ext. Svc., Littleton, 1985-96. Home and Office: Perennial Garden Planning 5000 Aspen Dr Littleton CO 80123

WILLIAMS, STEPHEN, anthropologist, educator; b. Mpls., Aug. 28, 1926; s. Clyde Garfield and Lois (Simmons) W.; m. Eunice Ford, Jan. 6, 1962; children: Stephen John, Timothy. BA, Yale U., 1949, PhD, 1954; MA, U. Mich., 1950; MA (hon.), Harvard, 1962. Asst. anthropology dept. Peabody Mus., Yale U., 1950-52; mem. faculty Harvard U., Cambridge, Mass., 1958—, prof. anthropology, 1967-72, Peabody prof., 1972-93, prof. emeritus, 1993—, chmn. dept., 1967-69; rsch. fellow Peabody Mus., Harvard U., Cambridge, Mass., 1954-57, mem. staff, 1954—, dir. mus., 1967-77; curator N.Am. Archaeology, 1962-93, hon. curator 1993—; dir. rsch. of Peabody Mus.'s Lower Miss. Survey, 1958-93. Author books and articles on N.Am. archaeology and "Fantastic" archaeology. Home: 1017 Foothills Trl Santa Fe NM 87505-4537 Office: PO Box 22354 Santa Fe NM 87502-2354

WILLIAMS, STUART VANCE, real estate executive; b. Bloomington, Ind., Aug. 5, 1960; s. Walter and Jacqueline (Block) W.; m. Lucy Keenan, Sept. 5, 1993. BA, Claremont McKenna Coll., Calif., 1982; MBA, Harvard U., 1986. Nat. accounts officer Lloyds Bank calif., L.A., 1982-84; asst. project mgr. Pacific Realty, Dallas, 1985; prin. The Norman Co., Seattle, 1986-92; prin., co-founder Pacific Real Estate Ptnrs., Bellevue, Wash., 1993—. Bd. dirs. Alki Found., Seattle, 1992-94, North End Jewish Cmty. Ctr., Seattle, 1994—; campaign vol. Rice for Mayor, Congress, Seattle, 1989, 91. Mem. Claremont McKenna Coll. Alumni Assn. (bd. dirs. 1988-90), Rotary. Home: 6820 Phinney Ave N Seattle WA 98103-5238 Office: Pacific Real Estate Ptnrs 1975 112th Ave NE Ste 201 Bellevue WA 98004-2942

WILLIAMS, WALTER BAKER, mortgage banker; b. Seattle, May 12, 1921; s. William Walter and Anna Leland (Baker) W.; m. Marie Davis Wilson, July 6, 1945; children: Kathryn Williams-Mullins, Marcia Frances Williams Swanson, Bruce Wilson, Wendy Susan. BA, U. Wash., 1943; JD, Harvard U., 1948. With Bogle & Gates, Seattle, 1948-63, ptnr., 1960-63; pres. Continental Inc., Seattle, 1963-91, chmn., 1991—; bd. dirs. United Graphics Inc., Seattle, 1973-86, Fed. Nat. Mortgage Assn., 1976-77; chmn. Continental Savings Bank, 1991—. Rep. Wash. State Ho. of Reps., Olympia, 1961-63; sen. Wash. State Senate, Olympia, 1963-71; chmn. Econ. Devel. Council of Puget Sound, Seattle, 1981-82; pres. Japan-Am. Soc. of Seattle, 1971-72; chmn. Woodland Park Zoo Commn., Seattle, 1984-85. Served to capt. USMC, 1942-46, PTO. Recipient Brotherhood Citation, NCCJ, Seattle, 1980, First Citizen award Seattle-King County Assn. Realtors, 1997. Mem. Mortgage Bankers Assn. Am. (pres. 1973-74), Wash. Mortgage Bankers Assn. (pres. 1971), Fed. Home Loan Mortgage Corp. (adv. com.), Wash. Savs. League (bd. dirs., chmn. 1991-92), Rotary (pres. local club 1984-85), Rainier Club Seattle (pres. 1987-88). Republican. Congregationalist. Office: Continental Inc 2000 Two Union Sq Seattle WA 98101

WILLIAMS, WALTER DAVID, aerospace executive, consultant; b. Chgo., July 22, 1931; s. Walter William and Theresa Barbara (Gilman) W.; m. Joan Haven Armstrong, Oct. 22, 1960; children: Latham Lloyd, Clayton Chapell, William Haven. BS, Ohio U., 1951; MBA, Harvard U., 1955; MS, MIT, 1972. Supr. fin. policy and systems Hughes Aircraft Co., Culver City, Calif., 1955-57; staff mem. Rand Corp. and SDC, Santa Monica, Calif., 1957-60; mgr. adminstrn. and fin. Microwave Div. TRW Inc., Canoga Park, Calif., 1960-63; exec. asst. Space Labs. Northrop Corp., Hawthorne, Calif., 1963-66; fin. mgr. comml. group Aircraft Div. Northrop Corp., Hawthorne, Calif., 1966-72; dir. internat. plans Northrop Corp., L.A., 1972-74, dir. internat. mkt. devel., 1974-77, exec. dir. internat., 1977-93; pres. Williams Internat. Assocs., L.A., 1994—; export advisor U.S. Sec. Commerce, Washington, 1986—. Author (study/lect. series) Internat. Def. Mktg., 1982. Dir. KCET Men's Coun., L.A., 1970; pres. Westwood Rep. Club, L.A., 1970; assoc. mem. Rep. State Ctrl. Com., Calif., 1968; div. chmn. Rep. Ctrl. Com., L.A. County, 1968. Served to capt. U.S. Army, 1951-53. Recipient fellowship Alfred P. Sloan Found., 1971-72. Mem. AIAA, Soc. Sloan Fellows, MIT Club, Harvard Bus. Sch. Assn., Newcomen Soc., Chaine des Rotisseurs, L.A. Country Club, Harvard Club, Soc. Bacchus Am., Delta Sigma Pi, Pi Kappa Alpha. Office: Williams Internat Assocs PO Box 491178 Los Angeles CA 90049-9178

WILLIAMS, WILLIAM ARNOLD, agronomy educator; b. Johnson City, N.Y., Aug. 2, 1922; s. William Truesdall and Nellie Viola (Tompkins) W.; m. Madeline Patricia Moore, Nov. 27, 1943; children—David, Kathleen, Andrew. B.S., Cornell U., 1947, M.S., 1948, Ph.D., 1951. Prof. emeritus U. Calif., Davis, 1993—. Editor agr. sect. McGraw-Hill Ency. Sci. & Tech.; contbr. articles to profl. jours. Mem. Nat. Alliance for Mentally Ill. Served to lt. U.S. Army, 1943-46. Grantee NSF, 1965-82, Kellogg Found., 1963-67; Fulbright scholar, Australia, 1960, Rockefeller Found. scholar, Costa Rica, 1966. Fellow AAAS, Am. Soc. Agronomy, Crop Sci. Soc. Am.; mem. Soil Sci. Soc. Am., Soc. Range Mgmt., Am. Statis. Assn., Assn. for Tropical Biology, Fedn. Am. Scientists, Am. Math Soc. Democrat. Home: 718 Oeste Dr Davis CA 95616-3531 Office: Univ California Dept Agronomy And Rang Davis CA 95616

WILLIAMS, WILLIAM COREY, theology educator, consultant; b. Wilkes-Barre, Pa., July 12, 1937; s. Edward Douglas and Elizabeth Irene (Schooley) W.; m. Alma Simmenroth Williams, June 27, 1959; 1 child, Linda. Diploma in Ministerial Studies, NE Bible Inst., 1962; BA in Bibl. Studies, Cen. Bible Coll., 1963, MA in Religion, 1964; MA in Hebrew and Near Ea. Studies, NYU, 1966, PhD in Hebrew Lang. and Lit., 1975; postgrad., Hebrew U., 1977-78, Inst. Holyland Studies, 1986. Ref. libr. Hebraic section Libr. of Congress, Washington, 1967-69; prof. Old Testament So. Calif. Coll., Costa Mesa, 1969—; adj. prof. Old Testament Melodyland Sch. Theology, Anaheim, Calif., 1975-77; vis. prof. Old Testament Fuller Theol. Sem., Pasadena, Calif., 1978-81, 84, Asian Theol. Ctr. for Evangelism and Missions, Singapore and Sabah, E. Malaysia, 1985, Continental Bible Coll., Saint Pieters-Leeuw, Belgium, 1985, Mattersey Bible Coll., Eng., 1985, Inst. Holy Land Studies, Jerusalem, 1986, Regent U., 1994; transl. cons. and reviser New Am. Std. Bible, 1969-94; transl. cons. The New Internat. Version, 1975-76, New Century Version, 1991, The New Living Translation, 1992-95, New Internat. Version, Reader's Version, 1993-94; transl. cons. and editor Internat. Children's Version, 1985-86. Author: (books, tapes) Hebrew I: A Study Guide, 1986, Hebrew II: A Study Guide, 1986; contbr. articles to International Standard Bible Encyclopedia, New International Dictionary of Old Testment Theology and Evangelical Dictionary of Biblical Theology; contbr. articles to profl. jours.; contbr. notes to Spirit Filled Life Study Bible. Nat. Def. Fgn. Lang. fellow NYU, 1964-67; Alumni scholar N.E. Bible Inst., 1960-61; NEH fellow, summer 1992. Mem. Soc. Bibl. Lit., Evang. Theol. Soc. (exec. office 1974-77), Am. Acad. Religion, Nat. Assn. Profs. of Hebrew, Inst. Bibl. Rsch., The Lockman Found. (hon. mem. bd. dirs. 1992-94, mem. editorial bd. 1974-94). Home: 1817 Peninsula Pl Costa Mesa CA 92627-4591 Office: So Calif Coll 55 Fair Dr Costa Mesa CA 92626-6520

WILLIAMS, WILLIAM JAMES, public administration educator. AB, Morehouse Coll., 1956; MPA, NYU, 1958; D. Pub. Adminstrn., U. So. Calif., L.A., 1966. Various positions, 1958-68; dir. Ctr. for Social Action Shaw U., U. So. Calif., 1968-74; employee rels. bd. mediator City of L.A., County of L.A., 1974; lectr. Golden Gate U., San Francisco, 1974-75; vis. prof. Howard U., Washington, 1975-76; personnel cons. Libr. of Congress, Washington, 1976; lectr. Long Beach (Calif.) State U., 1976; asst. prof. U. So. Calif. Sch. Pub. Adminstrn., L.A., 1968-73, assoc. prof., 1974-80, prof., 1980—; cons. Port Authority of N.Y., 1970, HEW, 1972, Calif. State Legis., 1961-62; program cons. Fenley Consultants, L.A., 1966; mem. CBS and ABC Program on Social Conflict and change, 1970-71. Author: General Semantics and the Social Sciences, 1972, Uncommon Sense and Dimensional Awareness, 1973, Epistemics, 1975, Selections from Semantic Behavior and Decision Making, 1975, Semantic Behavior and Decision Making, 1973, The Miracle of Abduction, 1985; contbr. articles to profl. jours. Mem. Pub. Personnel Assn., Am. Humanist Soc., Am. Soc. Pub. Adminstrn., Internat. Soc. for Gen. Semantics, Am. Polit. Sci. Assn., Soc. Equal Employment Consultants, Inst. for Gen. Semantics, Am. Assn. Univ. Profs., Am. Acad. Polit. and Social Sci., AAAS, Am. Fedn. Radio and TV Artists.

WILLIAMS, WILLIE, protective services official; b. 1943; m. Evelina; children: Lisa, Willie Jr., Eric. AS, Phila. Coll. Textiles and Sci., 1982; postgrad., St. Joseph U., 1991. Police officer City of Phila., 1964-72, police detective, 1972-74, police sgt., 1974-76, police lt. juvenile aid div., 1976-83, police capt. 22nd and 23rd dists., 1984-86, police inspector, head tng. bur., civil affairs div., North police div., 1986-88, dep. commr. adminstrn., 1988, police commr., 1988-92; chief of police L.A. Police Dept., 1992—; lecture, instr. Temple U., Univ. Pa., Univ. Del. Former scoutmaster Boy Scouts Am.; mem. Pa. Juvenile Officers' Assn., Southeastern Pa. Chiefs of Police, West Angeles Ch. of God in Christ; past bd. dirs. Rebuild L.A. Mem. Nat. Orgn. Black Law Enforcement Execs. (past nat. pres.), Internat. Assn. Chiefs of Police, Alpha Sigma Lambda. Office: Office of Police Chief 150 N Los Angeles St Los Angeles CA 90012-3309*

WILLIAMS-LABAGH, BARBARA J., elementary educator; b. San Francisco, Jan. 17, 1944; d. Robert Joseph and Jean Elizabeth (Morgan) Williams; m. Paul Steele Labagh, May 30, 1970; children: Christine Ann, Brian Steele. BA, Dominican Coll., 1966; tchg. cert., Calif. State U., San Jose, 1967; MPA with 1st honors, Coll. Notre Dame, Belmont, Calif., 1996. Cert. lang. devel. specialist. Classroom tchr. grades 5-8 Jefferson Elem. Sch. Dist., Daly City, Calif., 1967-74; classroom tchr. grade 5 St. Catherine's Sch., Burlingame, Calif., 1987-89; classroom tchr. grades 5 and 6 Ravenswood City Sch. Dist., East Palo Alto, Calif., 1991-93; classroom tchr. grade 2 Hillsborough (Calif.) City Sch. Dist., 1994—; mem. leadership sch. Bay Area Sch. Reform Collaborative, San Mateo-Bay Area; mem. multicultural festival com. West Hills Sch., 1995; mem. dist. bilingual edn. com. and lang. arts com. Com. chair Jr. League San Francisco; officer, chair, bd. dirs. Little Children's Aid Aux., San Francisco; chair Dominican Coll. Alumni, San Francisco; v.p., bd. dirs. Med. Mission Sister Aux., Hillsborough. Recipient 2 mini grants Hillsborough Sch. Found., 1996; Smart Schs. Tech. grantee, 1996.. Mem. AAUW (bd. dirs.), ASCD, NEA, Calif. Assn. for Gifted, Calif. Tchrs. Assn. (negotiating coun.), Hillsborough Tchrs. Assn., Delta Sigma Upsilon. Republican. Roman Catholic. Home: 520 Fordham Rd San Mateo CA 94402-2245 Office: West Hillsborough Sch 376 Barbara Way Hillsborough CA 94010-6760

WILLIAMS-LOHMAR, JUDITH ANN, technical and engineering services company executive; b. Lancaster, Calif., Aug. 10, 1954; d. Robert Melvin Williams and Cora Lee (Clemow) Williams Campbell. AA, Ventura Coll., 1979; BA in Communications, U. Wash., 1982. Editor NOAA, Seattle, 1982; liaison asst. Naval Ship Weapon Systems Engring. Sta., Washington, 1983; mgmt. analyst Triton Assocs., Inc., 1983-84; program mgr. Tech. Applications, Inc., Alexandria, Va., 1984-86; logistics analyst Value Systems Engring. Corp., Alexandria, 1986-87; tng. analyst Designers & Planners, Inc., Arlington, Va., 1987; prin. Ind. Profl. Writers & Assoc., Alexandria, 1987-88; sr. logistician Support Mgmt. Svcs., Inc., Oxnard, Calif., 1989-91; sys. engr. GE Govt. Svcs., Oxnard, 1991-92, Martin Marietta Svcs., Inc., Oxnard, 1993-94, Lockheed Martin Svcs., Oxnard, Calif., 1995—. Author newsletter articles, 1986-88. Mem. Soc. Naval Architects and Marine Engrs. (assoc. dir. 1987-88), Navy League U.S. (dir. pub. affairs 1986-87, mng. editor newsletter 1986), Soc. Logistics Engrs., Ventura County Writers' Club. Christian.

WILLIAMSON, DAVID HENRY, data processing professional; b. Ogden, Utah, Aug. 21, 1952; s. Arthur Williamson; m. Kathleen Price, May 20, 1972 (dec. July 1974); children: Arthur Larry, Tiffany; m. Cindy Ann Singleton, Feb. 21, 1976. BS, Weber State Coll., 1981. Computer operator Envirtech, Salt Lake City, 1974-75, control clk., 1975-76, programmer, 1977-80; programmer State of Utah Office of Edn., Salt Lake City, 1981-83, database analyst, 1984—. With USN, 1971-74. Mem. Software AG Rocky Moutain West User Group (pres. 1989-92). Mem. LDS Ch. Office: Utah State Office of Edn 250 E 500 S Salt Lake City UT 84111-3204

WILLIAMSON, EDWIN LEE, wardrobe and costume consultant; b. Downey, Calif., Dec. 2, 1947; s. Cecil Earnest and Edwina Louise (Tedie) W. AA, L.A. City Coll., 1967-70; BA in Theater and Music Edn., 1971, MA in Theater and Music Edn., 1973; student, U. So. Calif., 1971-73. Wardrobe master Ice Capades, 1973-76; mem. wardrobe dept. Paramount Studios, 1976-78, Disney Studios, 1978-81; freelance wardrobe and costume cons., L.A., 1981—; spl. events coord. Wet Internat. Appeared as Michael in original mus. Peter Pan. Mem. adv. bd. Halfway House and AIDS Hospsice, Valley Presbyn. Hosp.; founder West Coast Singers L.A., Inner City Athletic Union L.A.; founding mem. Gay Mens Chorus, Gt. Am. Yankee Freedom Band L.A., L.A. Gay and Lesbian Community Ctr.; hon. mem. bd. dirs. U. So. Calif. Idylwild Sch. Music and Arts.; bd. dirs. One Christopher St. West; founding vol. Gay Community Svc. Ctr.; emperor Imperial Ct. of San Fernando Valley. Scholar U. So. Calif., 1971-73; nominee Tony award Best Supporting Actor in musical Happy Time. Mem. SAG, AFTRA, Wardrobe Union, Masons. Lutheran. Home and Office: 4741 Elmwood Ave Apt 4 Los Angeles CA 90004-3135

WILLIAMSON, GEORGE EUGENE, lawyer; b. Danville, Ill., Nov. 2, 1946; s. Eugene Victor and Marie Elaine (Rekau) W.; m. Diana F. Williamson, July 18, 1981; 1 child, Lance Eugene. BS in Material Sci. Engring., Purdue U., 1974; JD, U. West L.A., 1982. Bar: Calif. 1982. Chief metallurgist, asst. tech. dir., lab. supr. Harrison Steel casting Co., Attic, Ind., 1974-79; law clk. Ronald P. Slates, A Profl. Corp., L.A., 1980-82; trial atty. Staplewton & Stapleton, Lawndale, Calif., 1982-85, Rogers & Hartley, A Law Corp., Huntington Beach, Calif., 1985-88; assoc. R.W. Harlan & Assocs., Newport Beach, Calif., 1988-91; sr. trial atty. Law Offices of Alexander Gelman, Fountain Valley, Calif., 1991-92, Koester, Brislin & Gelman, Santa Ana, Calif., 1992—. With U.S. Army, 1966-69. Mem. State Bar of Calif., Orange County Bar Assn., Assn. of So. Calif. Def. Counsel. Republican. Office: Andresen & James # 900 425 Market St San Francisco CA 94119

WILLIAMSON, JOHN, computer game producer; b. El Paso, Tex., Feb. 21, 1963; s. John Gilbert and Lucille Loraine (Summer) W. BS in Psychology, Tex. A&M U., 1985, MS in Psychology, 1990. VR rschr. Tex. A&M U., College Station, 1990-93, USAF, San Antonio, 1993, U. Wash., Seattle, 1993-94, Revco, Hawthorne, N.Y., 1994-95; video prodr. Virtual: O, Seattle, 1995-96; video game prodr. Zombie, Seattle, 1996—. Contbr. articles to profl. publs. Rsch. grantee USAF, 1993, U.S. Dept. Energy, 1994, Boeing, 1996, Wash. State, 1996. Home: 9811 Ravenna Ave NE Seattle WA 98115

WILLIAMSON, LAIRD, stage director, actor; b. Chgo., Dec. 13, 1937; s. Walter B. and Florence M. (Hemwell) W. B.S. in Speech, Northwestern U., 1960; M.F.A. in Drama, U. Tex., 1965. Dir. Am. Conservatory Theatre, San Francisco, 1974—; stage dir. A Christmas Carol, 1976-81, The Matchmaker (tour of Soviet Union), 1976, A Month in the Country, 1978, The Visit, 1979, Pantagleize, 1980, Sunday in the Park, 1986, End of the World, 1988, Imaginary Invalid, 1990, Machinal, 1997; dir. Oreg. Shakespearean Festival, Ashland, 1972-74, Western Opera Theatre, San Francisco, 1976-77, Theater Fest, Santa Maria, Calif., 1971-84, Denver Theater Ctr., 1981, Bklyn. Acad. Music, 1981, Denver Ctr. Theatre Co., 1985-97, Seattle Repertory Theatre, 1990, Old Globe Theatre, San Diego, 1977, 92, 94; artistic dir. Theater Fest, Solvang, Calif., 1981-83, Intiman Theatre, 1986, 88, Seattle Repertory Theatre, 1990, Berkeley Shakespeare Festival, 1990, Guthrie Theatre, 1991, 93, The Shakespeare Theatre, Washington, 1995, 96; actor in Othello, 1973, Twelfth Night, 1974, Cyrano, 1974, Enrico IV, 1977, Judas, 1978, Hamlet, 1979, The Bacchae, 1981. Mem. Soc. Stage Dirs. Actors Equity Assn., Screen Actors Guild.

WILLIAMSON, SAMUEL CHRIS, research ecologist; b. New Braunfels, Tex., Nov. 1, 1946; s. Jens Christian Jr. and Dorothy Marie (Marbach) W.; m. Kathryn Laverne Rutherford, Dec. 28, 1971; children: James Ray, Mark Travis. MS, Tex. Arts and Industries U., 1973; PhD, Colo. State U., 1983. Stats. programmer Tex. Parks and Wildlife Dept., Austin, 1973-77; computer specialist U.S. Fish and Wildlife Svc., Ft. Collins, Colo., 1980-82, rsch. ecologist, 1982-93; rsch. ecologist Nat. Biol. Svc., Ft. Collins, Colo., 1993-96, U.S. Geol. Survey, Ft. Collins, Colo., 1996—; statis. cons. U. Wyo., Baidoa, Somalia, 1988, LGL Alaska Rsch., Inc., Anchorage, 1991; mem. adv. bd. EPA, Las Vegas, Nev., 1989-90; participant confs. and symposia. Contbr. articles to profl. jours., chpt. to manual. With U.S. Army, 1968-70, Vietnam. Decorated Bronze Star medal; scholar Caesar Kleberg Wildlife Found., 1971-73. Mem. Ecol. Soc. Am., Am. Statis. Assn., Am. Fisheries Soc., Range Soc., Wildlife Soc. Office: US Geol Survey 4512 McMurry Ave Fort Collins CO 80525-3400

WILLIS, CHARLES DUBOIS, neuropsychiatrist, writer; b. N.Y.C., Dec. 30, 1925; s. William Charles and Alma Anna (Lazear) W.; m. Shirley Mae Clarke, Jan. 28, 1951; children: Carol, Nancy, John, Sarah, James. BA in Religion, Atlantic Union Coll., 1949; MD, Loma Linda U., 1955. Diplomate Am. Bd. Psychiatry and Neurology. Intern Orange (Calif.) County Hosp.; resident in psychiatry Met. State Hosp., Norwalk, Calif., 1956, 57-60; resident in neurology U. Calif. Med. Ctr., San Francisco, 1966-68; pres. Ancient World Found., Pinedale, Calif., 1990—; staff psychiatrist Dept. Corrections, Corcoran, Calif., 1983—; leader Mt. Ararat Expdns., 1983, 84, 86, 88. Author: End of Days=1971-2001, 1973. Capt. U.S. Army Med. Corps, 1957-60. Republican. Office: Ancient World Found PO Box 3118 Fresno CA 93650-3118

WILLIS, CLIFFORD LEON, geologist; b. Chanute, Kans., Feb. 20, 1913; s. Arthur Edward and Flossie Duckworth (Fouts) W.; m. Serreta Margaret Thiel, Aug. 21, 1947 (dec.); 1 child, David Gerard. BS in Mining Engring., U. Kans., 1939; PhD, U. Wash., 1950. Geophysicist The Carter Oil Co. (Exxon), Tulsa, 1939-42; instr. U. Wash., Seattle, 1946-50, asst. prof., 1950-54; cons. geologist Harza Engring. Co., Chgo., 1952-54, 80-82, chief geologist, 1954-57, assoc. and chief geologist, 1957-67, v.p., chief geologist, 1967-80; pvt. practice cons. geologist Tucson, Ariz., 1982—; cons. on major dam projects in Iran, Iraq, Pakistan, Greece, Turkey, Ethiopia, Argentina, Venezuela, Colombia, Honduras, El Salvador, Iceland, U.S. Lt. USCG, 1942-46. Recipient Haworth Disting. Alumnus award U. Kans., 1963. Fellow Geol. Soc. Am., Geol. Soc. London; mem. Am. Assn. Petroleum Geologists, Soc. Mining, Metallurgy and Exploration Inc., Assn. Engring. Geologists, Sigma Xi, Tau Beta Pi, Sigma Tau, Theta Tau. Republican. Roman Catholic. Home: 4795 E Quail Creek Dr Tucson AZ 85718-2630

WILLIS, DAWN LOUISE, paralegal, small business owner; b. Johnstown, Pa., Sept. 11, 1959; d. Kenneth William and Dawn Louise (Joseph) Hagins; m. Marc Anthony Ross, Nov. 30, 1984 (div.); m. Jerry Wayne Willis, Dec. 16, 1989 (div.). Grad. high sch., Sacramento, Calif. Legal sec. Wilcoxen & Callahan, Sacramento, 1979-87, paralegal asst., 1987-88; legal adminstr. Law Office Jack Vetter, Sacramento, 1989—; owner, mgr. Your Girl Friday Secretarial and Legal Support Svcs., Sacramento, 1991—; ind. distributor Herbalife, 1997—. Vol. ARC, 1985. Mem. Assn. Legal Adminstrs., Consumer Attys. of Calif., Sacramento Legal Secs. Assn. Republican. Lutheran. Office: Law Office Jack Vetter 928 2nd St Ste 300 Sacramento CA 95814-2201

WILLIS, EDWARD OLIVER, management consultant, state official; b. St. Louis, Apr. 6, 1948; s. George Washington and Mary (Fantroy) W.; m. Jennifer Linnea Johnson, June 17, 1972 (div. Dec. 1991); children: Linnea, Eric; m. Linda Diane Clark, Aug. 8, 1992. AA, Am. River Coll., Sacramento, 1972; BS in BA, Calif. State U., Sacramento, 1974; MBA in Mgmt., Golden Gate U., San Francisco, 1978. Divsn. ops. supr., casualty claims investigator Allstate Ins. Co., Menlo Park, Sacramento, 1974-75; budget analyst Dept. Fin., State of Calif., Sacramento, 1975-77; assoc. govtl. program analyst Dept. Health, Medi-Cal Procurement Project, State of Calif., Sacramento, 1977-78; chief fiscal br. solid waste mgmt. bd. State of Calif., Sacramento, 1978-79, mgr. adminstrv. svcs. state lands commn., 1979-80, asst. to assoc. supt. pub. instrn. dept. edn., 1980-82, dep. dir. adminstrn. dept. fish and game, 1982-90, acting adminstr. office of oil spill prevention and response, 1990-92, dep. dir. adminstrn. dept. developmental svcs., 1992-93, dep. dir. adminstrv. svcs. program dept. toxic substances, 1993-94, asst. sec. policy devel. Calif. Environ. Protection Agy., 1994-95, chief dep. dir. Calif. Conservation Corps, 1995—; owner, prin. cons. WW Assocs., 1994—; part-time instr. Cosumnes River Coll., Sacramento, 1980-83. Author: Business Employment Equity Plan, 1994. Vol. United Way Campaign, United Negro Coll. Fund, Sacramento Children's Home, YMCA; 1st v.p. Nat. Black Child Devel. Inst., Sacramento, 1981-82; chmn. Black Adv. Com. to State Pers. Bd., 1984-85; mem. St. Francis of Assisi Sch. Bd., Sacrammento, 1996—, pres., 1991-93; bd. trustees Black Advocates in State Svc., 1992; bd. dirs. Nat. Forum for Black Pub. Adminstrs., Washington, 1993—, pres., 1991-93, 1st v.p. 1990-91); Little League coach, 1996—. With USAF, 1966-70. Decorated Air medals (4). Mem. Nat. Forum for Black Pub. Adminstrs. (Sacramento chpt. bd. dirs. 1993—, 1st v.p. 1990-91, pres. 1991-93), Am. Soc. Pub. Adminstrn. (Pub. Adminstr. of the Yr.). Home: 9046 Headwind Ct Fair Oaks CA 91696 Office: Conservation Corps State of California 1719 24th St Sacramento CA 95826

WILLIS, HAROLD WENDT, SR., real estate developer; b. Marion, Ala., Oct. 7, 1927; s. Robert James and Della (Wendt) W.; student Loma Linda U., 1950, various courses San Bernardino Valley Coll.; m. Patsy Gay Bacon, Aug. 2, 1947 (div. Jan. 1975); children: Harold Wendt II, Timothy Gay, April Ann, Brian Tad, Suzanne Gail; m. Vernette Jacobson Osborne, Mar. 30, 1980 (div. 1984); m. Ofelia Alvarez, Sept. 23, 1984; children: Ryan Robert, Samantha Ofelia. Ptnr., Victoria Guernsey, San Bernardino, Calif., 1950-63, co-pres., 1963-74, pres., 1974—; owner Quik-Save, 9th & Waterman shopping ctr., 1966—, Ninth and Waterman Shopping Ctr., San Bernardino, 1969—; pres. Energy Delivery Systems, Food and Fuel, Inc. San Bernardino City water commr., 1965—, pres. bd. water commrs., 1994—. Bd. councillors Loma Linda (Calif.) U., 1968-85, pres., 1971-74; mem. So. Calif. Strider's Relay Team (set indoor Am. record in 4x800 1992, set distance medley relay U.S. and World record for 60 yr. old 1992). Served as officer U.S. Mcht. Marine, 1945-46. Mem. Calif. Dairy Industries Assn. (pres. 1963, 64), Liga Internat. (2d v.p. 1978, pres. 1982, 83). Seventh-day Adventist (deacon 1950-67). Lic. pvt. pilot; rated multi engr. in 601 P aerostar. Office: PO Box 5607 San Bernardino CA 92412-5607

WILLIS, PAUL JONATHAN, English language educator; b. Fullerton, Calif., Nov. 8, 1955; s. David Lee and Earline Louise (Fleischman) W.; m. Sharon Gail Leitzel, Aug. 25, 1979; children: Jonathan David, Johanna Leitzel. BA in Biblical Studies, Wheaton Coll., 1977; MA in English, Washington State U., 1980, PhD in English, 1985. Wilderness guide Sierra Treks, Bridgeport, Calif., 1974—; English instr. Whitworth Coll., Spokane, Wash., 1981-85; asst. prof. English Houghton (N.Y.) Coll., 1985-88; assoc. prof. English Westmont Coll., Santa Barbara, Calif., 1988—. Author: No Clock in the Forest, 1991, The Stolen River, 1992 (award Christianity Today 1993). Mem. MLA, Assn. Study of Lit. and Environment, So. Calif. C.S. Lewis Soc., Conf. on Christianity and Lit., Sierra Club (chair wilderness com. 1983-84), Wilderness Soc. Democrat. Mem. Evangelical Covenant Ch. Office: Westmont Coll 955 La Paz Rd Santa Barbara CA 93108-1023

WILLIS, SELENE LOWE, electrical engineer, software consultant; b. Birmingham, Ala., Mar. 4, 1958; d. Lewis Russell and Bernice (Wilson) Lowe; m. André Maurice Willis, June 12, 1987. BSEE, Tuskegee (Ala.) U., 1980; postgrad. in Computer Programing, UCLA, 1993-94; student, U. So. Calif., 1996. Component engr. Hughes Aircraft Corp., El Segundo, Calif., 1980-82; reliability and lead engr. Aero Jet Electro Systems Corp., Azusa, Calif., 1982-84; sr. component engr. Rockwell Internat. Corp., Anaheim, Calif., 1984, Gen. Data Comm. Corp., Danbury, Conn., 1984-85; design engr. Lockheed Missile & Space Co., Sunnyvale, Calif., 1985-86; property mgr. Penmar Mgmt. Co., L.A., 1987-88; aircraft mechanic McDonnell Douglas Corp., Long Beach, 1989-93; Unix system adminstrn. Santa Cruz Ops., 1994; mem. tech. staff Space Applications Corp., El Segundo, Calif., 1995-96; bus. ops. mgr., cons. New Start, Santa Monica, Calif., 1995; software developer Nat. Advancement Corp., 1995-96; entrepreneur Datatronics, 1996—; exec. v.p., owner DataTronics, L.A., 1996—; software engr. Jet Propulsion Lab, Pasadena, Calif., 1996, network engr., application engr., 1996—; cons., software designer Kern & Wooley, attys., Westwood, Calif., 1995; software developer Nat. Advancement Corp., Santa Ana, Calif., 1995—. Vol. Mercy Hosp. and Children's Hosp., Birmingham, 1972-74; mrm. L.A. Gospel Messengers, 1982-84, West Angeles Ch. of God and Christ, L.A., 1990; cons., mgr. bus. ops. New Start/Santa Monica (Calif.) Bay Area Drug Abuse Coun., 1995. Scholar Bell Labs., 1976-80, UCLA, 1994. Mem. IEEE, ASME, Aerospace and Aircraft Engrs., So. Calif. Profl. Engring. Assn., Tuskegee U. Alumni Assn., UCLA Alumni Assn. (scholarship and adv. com.), Eta Kappa Nu. Mem. Christian Ch.

WILLKENS, ROBERT F., interist, rheumatologist; b. N.Y.C., July 1, 1927; s. Robert Albert and Christine (Lehreider) W.; m. Marjory Elaine Thompson, June 24, 1950; children: Garen, Holly, Rebecca, Matthew. BS in Biology, Antioch Coll., Yellow Springs, Ohio, 1950; MD, U. Rochester, 1954. Diplomate Am. Bd. Internal Medicine; lic. physician, Wash. Intern in medicine King County Hosp., Seattle, 1954-55, asst. resident in medicine, 1955-57, chief resident in medicine, 1958-59; rsch. fellow in arthritis Columbia Presbyn. Med. Ctr., N.Y.C., 1957-58; pvt. practice Seattle, 1959—; clin. instr. medicine (arthritis) U. Wash., Seattle, 1959-61, clin. asst. prof., 1961-66, clin. assoc. prof., 1966-73, clin. prof. medicine (arthritis), 1973—; pres. med. staff King County Hosp., Seattle, 1964-65; staff Harborview Med. Ctr., Seattle, Univ. Wash. Hosp., Seattle, Swedish Hosp. Med. Ctr., Seattle; chmn. Wash. State Bd. Med. Examiners, 1975-77p; trustee Northwest Pub. Co., 1973-75; mem. physician adv. panel Harrington Arthritis Rsch. Ctr., Phoenix, 1982-88; mem. med. sch. admissions com. U. Wash., 1981-84. Assoc. editor Bull. of King County Med. Soc., 1963-68, editor, 1969-70; editor Primary Care rheumatology, 1990-93; reviewer Jour. Rheumatology, 1979—, Annals of Internal Medicine, 1980—; editl. bd. Rheumatic Therapies, 1983-88, Clin. Aspects of Autoimmunity, 1986-88, Arthritis and rheumatism, 1989-92; contbr. articles to profl. jours. Western Wash. chpt. chmn., bd. dirs. The Arthritis Found., 1969-73; mem. Gov.'s Coun. on Aging, 1968-71; exec. bd. A Contemporary Theater, 1963-80, pres. exec. bd., 1964-66, mem. adv. coun., 1980—; bd. dirs. Pike Place Mkt. Found., 1982-92; mem. alumni coun. U. Rochester Sch. Medicine and dentistry, 1982-85; vice chmn. King County Arts Commn., 1986-87, commr., 1984-87. 2d lt. U.S. Army, 1945-47. Recipient Disting. Svc. award Arthritis Found., 1969, Nat. Vol. Svc. citation, 1986, R.H. Williams Superior Leadership award in medicine Seattle Acad. Internal Medicine, 1990; Mead Johnson Postgrad. scholar ACP, 1958-59; travel grantee Am. rheumatism Assn., 1965, 67. Master Am. Coll. Rheumatology (mem. edn. coun. 1987-90, program com. 1990, mktg. and comm. com. 1989-92, others); fellow Am. Coll. Medicine; mem. ACP, Am. Fedn. Clin. Rsch., Am. rheumatism Assn. (mem. conjoint clinics com. 1969—, diagnostic and therapeutic com. 1970-71, program com. 1982, 83, 84, 85, 90, vice chmn. edn. coun. 1986-88, chmn. liaison subcom. 1988), North Pacific Soc. Internal Medicine, Northwest Rheumatism Assn. (v.p. 1970-71, pres. 1972-74), King County Med. Soc. (chmn. program com. 1969-71), Seattle Arthritis assn. (pres. 1967-69). Home: 1307 Willard Ave W Seattle WA 98119 Office: 1229 Madison St #1490 Seattle WA 98119

WILLMS, ARTHUR HENRY, gas executive; b. Namaka, Alta., Can., Oct. 28, 1939; m. June Gladstone, 1961; children: Tara Nicole, Jordan Peter. BEd in Math., U. Calgary, Alta., Can., 1965, BA in Math., 1967, MA in Econs., 1970. Pub. sch. teacher Strathmore, Alta., 1961-63, Calgary Pub. Sch. Bd., 1965-67; lectr. in econs. U. Calgary, 1969-70; exec. v.p., chief operating officer pipeline div. Westcoast Transmission Co. Ltd., Vancouver, B.C., 1971—; also bd. dirs.; bd. dirs. Westcoast Petroleum Ltd., Pacific Northern Gas Ltd., Foothills Pipe Lines Ltd. Mem. Canadian Gas Assn. (bd. dirs. 1983). Clubs: Vancouver, Hollyburn Country. Office: Westcoast Transmission Co Ltd, 1333 W Georgia St, Vancouver, BC Canada V6E 3K9*

WILLMS, CAROL COX, elementary education educator, audiologist; b. Nyack, N.Y., Dec. 2, 1945; d. John Walter Cox and Selina Jane (Gorton) Cox Eshleman; m. Raymond Harry Willms, June 17, 1978; children: Sue Ann, Kate Christine. BA in Speech Pathology and Audiology, San Diego State U., 1974, MA in Audiology, 1976; tchg. cert., U. No. Colo., 1988. Cert. elem. edn.; cert. clin. competence in audiology, Am. Speech and Hearing Assn. Audiologist U. Calif. Med. Ctr., San Diego, 1976-77, Klamath Speech and Hearing Ctr., Klamath Falls, Oreg., 1977-80; clin. supr. in audiology Sacramento State U., 1981-83; audiologist Sutter Hearing and Speech Ctr., Sacramento, 1981-83, So. Colo. Clinic, Pueblo, 1983-85; clin. supr. in audiology U. No. Colo., Greeley, 1986-87; tchr. 6th grade Lasley Elem. Sch., Lakewood, Colo., 1989—. Mem. Alameda Area Mgmt. Team, Lakewood, 1994-95, Multicultural Response Team, Lakewood, 1995-96. Sgt. U.S. Army, 1964-67. Mem. Internat. Reading Assn. (Colo. coun.).

WILLNER, JAY R., consulting company executive; b. Aurora, Ill., Sept. 22, 1924; s. Charles R. and Ida (Winer) W.; m. Suzanne Wehmann, July 17, 1958; 1 child, Adam. Student, UCLA, 1946-48; BS, MIT, 1950; MBA, Rutgers U., 1959. Researcher Andrew Brown Co., Los Angeles, 1950-52; tech. salesman Glidden Co., Los Angeles, 1952-54; market researcher Roger Williams Inc., N.Y.C., 1954-59; sr. market analyst Calif. Chem. Co., San Francisco, 1959-63; mgr. planning chem. coatings div. Mobil Chem. Co., N.Y.C., 1963-68; pres. WEH Corp., San Francisco, 1968—; lectr. U. Calif., Berkeley, 1962—; adj. faculty U. San Francisco, 1977—; U.S. corr. German mag. Farbe & Lack. Contbg. editor Jour. Protective Coatings and Linings; editor The WEH Report. Supporter San Francisco Mus. of Modern Art. 2d lt. A.C., AUS, 1943-46. Mem. Am. Chem. Soc. (steel structures painting coun.), San Francisco Comml. Club, Chemists Club (N.Y.C.), MIT Club No. Calif. Home: 700 Presidio Ave San Francisco CA 94115 Office: WEH Corp PO Box 470038 San Francisco CA 94147-0038

WILLOUGHBY, JAMES RUSSELL, artist; b. Toronto, Ohio, Apr. 22, 1928; s. Russell Lee and Edna Gertrude (McKeown) W.; m. Dorothy M. Ponder, Sept. 12, 1952 (div. 1958); children: Jim Jr., David; m. Susan N. Boettjer, Nov. 28, 1980. AA, Pasadena City Coll., 1951; postgrad., Art Ctr. Sch. Mem. staff Chrysler Corp., Maywood, Calif., 1951-57; adminstrv. asst., tech. artist Ramo-Wooldridge, El Segundo, Calif., 1957-59; adminstr. asst. Space Tech. Labs., El Segundo, 1959-61; intelligence analyst Aerospace Corp., El Segundo, 1961-65; freelancer Calif., 1965-72, Filmation Studios, Reseda, Calif., 1972-82, various orgns., 1982—; storyboard designer Hanna-Barbera, Disney Studios, 1987-90. Author, illustrator: Cowboy Country Cartoons, 1988, Birds of the Southwest, 1997; co-author, illustrator: Cowboy Cartoon Cookbook, 1990, Cactus County, 1992, Sharlot Hall Coloring Book, 1994, Cowboy Cartoons: Quick on the Draw, 1996, A Dude's Guide to the West, 1996; illustrator: Cowpies Ain't No Dish You Take To The County Fair, 1997. Mem. Nat. Cartoonist Soc., Westerners Internat., Prescott Corral. Home: 1407 Sierra Vista Dr Prescott AZ 86303-4545

WILLOUGHBY, STUART CARROLL, contractor; b. Tucson, Mar. 19, 1951; s. Stuart Carroll and Margeret Ann (Thornton) W.; m. Beth Anne Willoughby; children: Julie Ann, Aimee Sue, Scott Tyler, John Christopher, Jeremy Luke. Student, U. Ariz., 1970-74, U. Ariz., 1973. Owner Willcox (Ariz.) Realty and Constrn. Co., 1974-75, Willoughby Constrn. and Devel. Corp., Tucson, 1975—; owner, broker Red Baron Realtors, Inc., Tucson, 1978—; owner Willoughby Plumbing Corp., Tucson, 1985—, Sunshine Solar Co., Tucson, 1980—. Leader 4H Club. Mem. So. Ariz. Home Builders Assn. (bd. dirs. 1978—, life dir., Bd. Mem. of Yr. award 1981, honored PAC com. 1985, 86, 87), Tucson Bd. Realtors, Nat. Assn. of Home Builders (Life Spike award 1980). Republican. Home: 7979 S Camino Loma Alta Tucson AZ 85747-9372

WILLOUGHBY, SUSAN NELL, museum director; b. Flint, Mich., Dec. 3, 1941; d. Arthur Francis and Fay R. (Randolph) Boettjer; m. Joe Stuard, June 29, 1961 (div. 1977); children: Sherri B. Carlsberg, Nick Stuard; m. James R. Willoughby Sr., Nov. 28, 1980. Grad. h.s., Glendale, Calif. Pers. dir. Kaufman & Broad Home Sys., L.A., 1971-72; dir. adminstrv. svcs. Carlsberg Corp., Santa Monica, Calif., 1972-85; dir. Phippen Mus., Prescott, Ariz., 1987-88, 91—; chair Prescott Mus. Coalition, 1993-94; program chair Prescott Art Docents, 1988-90. Co-author: Cowboy Country Cookbook, 1990—, Cactus Country, 1993. Sheriff Westerners Corral, Prescott, 1992. Mem. Am. Assn. of Mus., Ariz. Assn. of Mus., Mus. Educators of Ctrl. Ariz., Western Registrars Com., Westerners Internat. (Heads Up award 1993). Republican. Office: Phippen Mus 4701 Hwy 89 North Prescott AZ 86301

WILLRICH, MASON, executive, consultant; b. L.A., 1933; m. Patricia Rowe, June 11, 1960 (dec. July 1996); children: Christopher, Stephen, Michael, Katharine. BA magna cum laude, Yale U., 1954; JD, U. Calif., Berkeley, 1960. Atty. Pillsbury Madison and Sutro, San Francisco, 1960-62; asst. gen. coun. U.S. Arms Control and Disarmament Agy., 1962-65; assoc. prof. law U. Va., 1965-68, prof. law, 1968-75, John Stennis prof. law, 1975-79; dir. internat. rels. Rockefeller Found., N.Y.C., 1976-79; v.p. Pacific Gas & Electric, San Francisco, 1979-84, sr. v.p., 1984-88, exec. v.p., 1988-89; CEO, pres. PG&E Enterprises, San Francisco, 1989-94; exec. Pacific Gas and Electric Co., San Francisco, 1979-94; chmn. EnergyWorks, 1995—; prin. Nth Power Technologies, Inc., 1996—; cons., 1994—. Author: Non-Proliferation Treaty, 1969, Global Politics of Nuclear Energy, 1971, (with T.B. Taylor) Nuclear Theft, 1974, Administration of Energy Shortages, 1976 (with R.K. Lester) Radioactive Waste Management and Regulation, 1977. Trustee, past chmn. World Affairs Coun. No. Calif.; pres. Midland Sch.; dir. Resources for the Future, Atlantic Coun. Guggenheim Meml. fellow, 1973. Mem. Phi Beta Kappa, Order of Coif. Office: PO Box 50907 Palo Alto CA 94303-0673

WILLS, DONALD ALLISON, lawyer; b. Phoenix, May 3, 1946; s. William Donald Wills and Mary Polly Alice (Ernst) Burdick; m. Joy Charlene Martin, Sept. 14, 1969; children: Eric Donald, Warren Bradley. BS, Calif. Poly. State U., 1968; JD, U. West L.A., 1978; postgrad., Sch. of Theology of Claremont, 1993—. Bar: Calif. 1978. Assoc. atty. Bralley, Bentley & Dickinson, L.A., Pasadena, 1978-81; ptnr. Bralley, Bentley & Wills, Pasadena, 1981-82; owner Law Offices Donald A. Wills, Arcadia, South Pasadena, 1982-86; owner, ptnr. Wills & Rifkin, South Pasadena, 1986-88; owner Law Offices Donald A. Wills, South Pasadena, 1988-92; owner, ptnr. Wills & Griepp, South Pasadena, 1992-93; owner, ptnr. Wills & Kliger, South Pasadena, 1993—, Pasadena, 1994—; adj. prof. Pasadena (Calif.) C.C., 1983-87, U. West L.A. Sch. of Law, 1988; instr. Ins. Edn. Assn., 1986-91; dir. Calif. State Bar Workers' Compensation Exec. Com., San Francisco, 1989-91. Transp. com. mem. City of South Pasadena, 1989-91; fin. dir. South Pasadena Tournament of Roses Assn., 1990-93. Capt. U.S. Army, 1969-72, West Berlin. Mem. L.A. County Bar Assn. (dir. Workers' Compensation sect. 1991-94), State of Calif. Divsn. Indsl. Rels. (judge pro-tem Workers' Compensation Appeals bd. 1988—), Workers' Compensation Def. Attys. Assn., Calif. Self Ins. Assn., So. Calif. Coun. of Self-Insurers, Oneonta Club (dir. 1989-92, Lyons/Adams award 1991-92). Republican. Office: Wills & Kliger 547 S Marengo Ave Pasadena CA 91101-3114

WILLS, JOHN ELLIOT, JR., history educator, writer; b. Urbana, Ill., Aug. 8, 1936; s. John Elliot and George Anne (Hicks) W.; m. Carolin Connell, July 19, 1958; children: Catherine, Christopher John, Jeffrey David, Joanne, Lucinda. BA in Philosophy, U. Ill., 1956; MA in East Asian Studies, Harvard U., 1960, PhD in History and Far Ea. Langs., 1967. History instr. Stanford (Calif.) U., 1964-65; history instr. U. So. Calif., L.A., 1965-67, asst. prof., 1967-72, assoc. prof., 1972-84, prof., 1984—, acting chair East Asian Langs. and Cultures, 1987-89; dir. East Asian Studies Ctr. USC-UCLA Joint East Asian Studies Ctr., L.A., 1990-94; rsch. abroad in The Netherlands, Taiwan, China, Japan, Macao, Philippines, Indonesia, India, Italy, Spain, Portugal, Eng. Author: Pepper, Guns, and Parleys: The Dutch East India Company and China, 1662-1681, 1974, Embassies and Illusions: Dutch and Portuguese Envoys to K'ang-hsi, 1666-1687, 1984, Mountain of Fame: Portraits in Chinese History, 1994; co-editor: (with Jonathan D. Spence) From Ming to Ch'ing: Conquest, Region, and Continuity in Seventeeth-Century China, 1979; contbr. articles to profl. jours. Grantee Nat. Acad. Scis., 1985, Am. Coun. Learned Soc., 1979-80; Younger Humanist fellow NEH, 1972-73. Mem. Assn. for Asian Studies, Am. Hist. Assn., Phi Beta Kappa, Phi Kappa Phi (Recognition award 1986, 95). Office: U So Calif Dept History Los Angeles CA 90089-0034

WILLSON, DAVID ALLEN, reference librarian, writer; b. Seattle, June 30, 1942; s. Robert Richard and Alice Hansine (Aspen) W.; m. Penelope Poeschl, Dec. 13, 1972 (div. Mar. 1986); children: Mungo Park, Darcy Monroe; m. Michele Geraldine DeBruyne, Mar. 8, 1986; children: Joaquin Sandoval, Alice Maria. BA, U. Wash., 1964, MLS, 1970. Reference libr. Green River C.C., Auburn, Wash., 1970—; archivist Joe Hooper Collection of Vietnam War Lit. at Green River C.C., 1987—. Author: (novels) REMF Diary, 1988, The REMF Returns, 1992, In the Army Now, 1995; co-editor: (bibliography) Vietnam War Literature, 1996. With U.S. Army, 1966-67. Recipient Disting. Faculty award Puget Power, 1996. Mem. Popular Culture Assn., Vietnam Vets. Am. Democrat. Lutheran. Home: 23630 201st Ave SE Maple Valley WA 98038 Office: Green River CC 12401 SE 320th St Auburn WA 98092

WILLSON, GEORGE BIGELOW, civil engineer, consultant; b. Douglas, Wyo., May 12, 1929; s. Eugene P. and Marie V. (Lipe) W.; m. Lois Ann Goodman, Dec. 21, 1959; children: John A., Carol A. Phifer. BS in Civil Engring., U. Wyo., 1951, MS, 1963. Registered profl. engr., Wyo. Project engr. mcpl. engring. projects J.T. Banner and Assocs., Laramie, Wyo., 1956-58; tchr., rschr. gen. and agrl. engring. U. Wyo., Laramie, 1958-65; rschr. on agrl. and mcpl. waste mgmt. ARS, USDA, Md., 1966-87; cons. composting tech. and organic waste recycling, prin. George B. Willson Assocs., Laurel, Md., 1988-93, Loveland, Colo., 1993—; facilitator workshops and seminars; cons. on numerous projects. Contbg. author: On-Farm Composting Handbook, 1992; mem. editorial bd. BioCycle Jour. of Waste Recycling; contbr. numerous articles to profl. jours. Recipient Md. Gov.'s citation, 1982, other awards. Mem. Am. Soc. Agrl. Engrs., Water Environment Fedn. (Thomas R. Camp medal 1992). Home: 1535 Park Dr Loveland CO 80538-4285 Office: George B Willson Assocs Ste 103 407 N Lincoln Ave Loveland CO 80537

WILLSTATTER, ALFRED, retired army officer; b. Landsberg, Germany, Oct. 17, 1925; came to U.S., 1938; s. Louis M. and Lucia (Cahn) W.; m. Edith R. Klabunde, Dec. 24, 1955; children: Kurt, Karl, Steve. BA, U. Minn., 1951. Commd. 2d lt. U.S. Army, 1949, advanced through grades to lt. col., 1966; ret., 1979; owner, operator Twin Plunges, Ashland, Oreg., 1966-77; fraud investigator L.A. County Charities, 1957-66. Coun. mem. City of Ashland, 1969-72, chmn., 1971; bd. dirs. Rogue Valley Transit Dist., Medford, Oreg., 1975—, original chmn., vice chmn.; vol. probation officer Project Misdemeanant, Medford, 1969—; vol., arbitrator BBB, Portland, Oreg., 1985—; mem. Rogue Valley Internat./Medford Airport Adv. Com., 1995—; mem. Oreg. State Bar Disciplinary Bd., 1996—. Recipient Cert. of Svc. Project Misdemeanant, 1992; named Outstanding Bd. Mem. Spl. Dists., 1991. Mem. Nat. CIC Assn., Spl. Dist. of Oreg. Assn. (budget com. 1993). Home: 128 Central Ave Ashland OR 97520-1715

WILMOWSKI, WENDY ANN, feature film and television production executive; b. Elmhurst, Ill., Dec. 10, 1962; d. Edward Joseph and Mary Ann Wilmowski. BA in Theology magna cum laude, Franciscan U. Steubenville, 1984, BA in Communications magna cum laude, 1984. Comml. dir., videographer Community Video Svcs., Dallas, summer 1983, 84; dir. statewide communications Ariz. Dept. Corrections, Phoenix, 1985-86; producer, dir., writer LUMEN 2000, Dallas, 1986-88; owner, exec. producer InnerVision Prodns. Internat., L.A., 1988-95; pres. feature film and TV prodn. EO Prodns. Internat., Santa Monica Studios, Calif., 1995—; internat. cons., bd. dirs. LUMEN 2000-Brazil, Sao Paulo, 1988-89; internat. producer, bd. dirs., cons. LOGO Media-The Netherlands, Hilversum, 1989-91; cons. South Am., Innervision Prodns. Internat., the Netherlands, 1988-92. Prodr., dir. (TV documentary) Evangelization 2000, 1987, (TV series) LUMEN 2000, 1989-91 (award European Film Inst. 1991); prodr., dir., writer (TV documentary) The Church in India, 1990; photographer The Manna Mag., 1990; video asst. (film short) The Champion, 1992; line prodr. (feature film) The Conspiracy, 1992; prodn. coord. (film short) The Champion, 1992; prodr. (film short) Serial Killer, 1992; exec. prodr. (TV documentary) Williams Syndrome: A Highly Musical Species, 1996 (Crystal Heart award, CINE Golden Eagle award, Silver award Worldfest, Charleston); exec. prodr., (feature film) Goldilocks and the Three Bears, 1995; prodr., dir., writer (TV documentary) . . .and then there is hope, 1996. Recipient Alumni Citizen award U. Steubenville, 1996. Mem. Acad. TV Aarts and Scis. Republican. Roman Catholic. Office: EO Prodns Internat Inc 3025 W Olympic Blvd Santa Monica CA 90404

WILNER, PAUL ANDREW, journalist; b. N.Y.C., Feb. 12, 1950; s. Norman and Sylvia (Rubenstein) W.; m. Alyson Paula Bromberg, June 3, 1980; children: Anne Charlotte, Daniel Joseph. Student, U. Calif., Berkeley, 1968; BA, CUNY, 1976. Copy clk. N.Y. Times, 1976-80; reporter L.A. Herald Examiner, 1980-85; mng. editor Hollywood Reporter, L.A., 1985-87; asst. mng. editor features San Francisco Examiner, 1987—; sr. instr. U. So. Calif., L.A., 1983-85. Author: (poetry) Serious Business, The Paris Rev., 1977. Office: SF Examiner Mag 110 5th St San Francisco CA 94103-2918

WILSHIRE, HOWARD GORDON, research geologist; b. Shawnee, Okla., Aug. 19, 1926; s. Leslie Maynard and Mae Pearl (Craig) W.; m. Jane Ellen Nielson, June 1, 1984; children: Ruth, Paul, David. BA, U. Okla., 1952; PhD, U. Calif., 1956. Lectr. U. Sydney, 1956-60; rsch. fellow Australian Nat. U., Canberra, Australia, 1960-61; geologist U.S. Geol. Survey, Menlo Park, Calif., 1961—; mem. panel on surface processes Nat. Rsch. Coun.; cons. Pres.'s Coun. on Environ. Quality, Washington, 1979. Author, editor: Environmental Effects of Offroad Vehicles, 1983; contbr. numerous articles to profl. jours. Pres. Com. for Green Foothills, Palo Alto, 1981-82; bd. dirs. Desert Protective Coun., Palm Springs, Calif., 1988-90; v.p. Pub. Employees for Environ. Responsibility, Washington, 1994. Recipient Meritorious Svc. award Dept. of Interior, 1988. Fellow AAAS, Geol. Soc. of Am. (com. on environ. and pub. policy); Am. Geophys. Union. Home: 1348 Isabelle Ave Mountain View CA 94040-3038 Office: US Geological Survey 345 Middlefield Rd # MS/975 Menlo Park CA 94025-3561

WILSON, ARCHIE FREDRIC, medical educator; b. L.A., May 7, 1931; s. Louis H. and Ruth (Kert) W.; m. Tamar Braverman, Feb. 11, 1937; children: Lee A., Daniel B. BA, UCLA, 1953, PhD, 1967; MD, U. Calif., San Francisco, 1957. Intern L.A. County Gen. Hosp., 1957-58; resident U. Calif., San Francisco, 1958-61; fellow in chest disease dept. medicine UCLA, 1966-67, asst. prof., 1967-70; asst. prof. U. Calif., Irvine, 1970-73, assoc. prof., 1973-79, prof., 1979—. Editor: Pulmonary Function Test: Interpretation, 1986; contbr. articles to profl. jours. Bd. mem. Am. Lung Assn., Orange County, 1970-90, Am. Heart Assn., Calif., 1990—. Capt. USMC, 1961-63. Mem. Am. Fedn. Clin. Rsch., Western Soc. Clin. Investigation. Office: Univ Calif 101 The City Dr S Orange CA 92868-3201

WILSON, BERNARD JOHN, protective services official; b. Preston, England, Jan. 19, 1953; came to U.S., 1954; s. William Joseph and Jenny Josephine (Bowman) W.; m. Diane Louise Peat, Feb. 12, 1977; children: Victoria, Nicholas, Stephen. B in Sci. and Law, Valley U., 1978. Aviation line chief Great Atlantic/Pacific Aeroplane Co., Van Nuys, Calif., 1973-74; crime prevention asst. L.A. Police Dept., 1975-77, sta. officer, 1977-79; from airport police officer to airport police capt. L.A. Airport Police, 1979-88, airport police capt., 1988—. Author: Airport Policing in the U.S., 1989, Specialized Law Enforcement, 1995. Officer cadet program Civil Air Patrol, Calif., 1972-74, 75-90, commdr. squadron, 1974-75; sub-deacon Orthodox Ch. Am., 1991. Recipient Meritorious Svc. award Civil Air Patrol, 1984, Calif. Commendation medal Calif. Nat. Guard, 1992. Republican. Office: LA Airport Police 6320 W 96th St Los Angeles CA 90045

WILSON, BETTY, mayor. Mayor City of Santa Fe Springs, Calif. Office: City of Santa Fe Springs 11710 Telegraph Rd Santa Fe Springs CA 90670

WILSON, BLENDA JACQUELINE, academic administrator; b. Woodbridge, N.J., Jan. 28, 1941; d. Horace and Margaret (Brogsdale) Wilson; m. Louis Fair Jr. AB, Cedar Crest Coll., 1962; AM, Seton Hall U., 1965; PhD, Boston Coll., 1979; DHL (hon.), Cedar Crest Coll., 1987, Loretto Heights Coll., 1988, Colo. Tech. Coll., 1988, U. Detroit, 1989; LLD (hon.), Rutgers U., 1989, Ea. Mich. U., 1990, Cambridge Coll., 1991, Schoolcraft Coll., 1992. Tchr. Woodbridge Twp. Pub. Schs., 1962-66; exec. dir. Middlesex County Econ. Opportunity Corp., New Brunswick, N.J., 1966-69; exec. asst. to pres. Rutgers U., New Brunswick, N.J., 1969-72; sr. assoc. dean Grad. Sch. Edn. Harvard U., Cambridge, Mass., 1972-82; v.p. effective sector mgmt. Ind. Sector, Washington, 1982-84; exec. dir. Colo. Commn. Higher Edn., Denver, 1984-88; chancellor and prof. pub. adminstrn. & edn. U. Mich., Dearborn, 1988-92; pres. Calif. State U., Northridge, 1992—; Am. del. U.S./U.K. Dialogue About Quality Judgments in Higher Edn.; adv. bd. Mich. Consolidated Gas Co., Stanford Inst. Higher Edn. Rsch., U. So. Col. Dist. 60 Nat. Alliance, Nat. Ctr. for Rsch. to Improve Postsecondary Teaching and Learning, 1988-90; bd. dirs. Alpha Capital Mgmt.; mem. higher edn. colloquium Am. Coun. Edn., vis. com. Divsn. Continuing Edn. in Faculty of Arts & Scis., Harvard Coll., Pew Forum on K-12 Edn. Reform in U.S. Dir. U. Detroit Jesuit High Sch., Northridge Hosp. Med. Ctr., Arab Cmty. Ctr. for Econ. and Social Svcs., Union Bank, J. Paul Getty Trust, James Irvine Found., Internat. Found. Edn. and Self-Help, Achievement Coun., L.A.; dir., vice chair Met. Affairs Corp.; exec. bd. Detroit area coun. Boy Scouts Am.; bd. dirs. Commonwealth Fund, Henry Ford Hosp.-Fairlane Ctr., Henry Ford Health System, Met. Ctr. for High Tech., United Way Southeastern Mich.; mem. Nat. Coalition 100 Black Women, Detroit, Race Rels. Coun. Met. Detroit, Women & Founds., Greater Detroit Interfaith Round Table NCCJ, Adv. Bd. Valley Cultural Ctr., Woodland Hills; trustee assoc. Boston Coll.; trustee emeritus Cambridge Coll.; trustee emeritus, bd. dirs. Found. Ctr.; trustee Henry Ford Mus. & Greenfield Village, Sammy Davis Jr. Nat. Liver Inst. Mem. AAUW, Assn. Governing Bds. (adv. coun. of pres.'s), Edn. Commn. of the States (student minority task force), Am. Assn. Higher Edn. (chair-elect), Am. Assn. State Colls. & Univs. (com. on policies & purposes, acad. leadership fellows selection com.), Assn. Black Profls. and Adminstrs., Assn. Black Women in Higher Edn., Women Execs. State Govt., Internat. Women's Forum, Mich. Women's Forum, Women's Econ. Club Detroit, Econ. Club, Rotary. Office: Calif State Univ Office of President 18111 Nordhoff St Northridge CA 91330-0001

WILSON, BRANDON LAINE, writer, advertising and public relations consultant, explorer; b. Sewickley, Pa., Oct. 2, 1953; s. Edgar C. and Mary Beth (Tuttle) W.; m. Cheryl Ann Keefe, June 23, 1989. BA, U. N.C., 1973; Cert. Am. Acad. Dramatic Arts, 1974. actor stage mgr., lighting, Red Barn Theatre, Little Patriot Theatre, Pittsburgh, 1969-70, actor, Carolina Playmakers, Chapel Hill, 1971-73, Asst. acct. exec. Hill & Knowlton Pub. Rels., Pitts., 1973; dir. video Seattle Repertory Theatre/2d Stage Theatre, 1975-76; asst. dir., videographer pub. Broadcasting Network, Chapel Hill, 1976-77, wrote 7 long-format videos for Sheraton Hotels Hawaii, Japan, wrote and produce numerous TV comml.; dir. advt. and TV Prodn. N.Am. Films, Eugene, Oreg., 1977-79; gen. mgr. Boulder Community Coops., 1980-81; pub. info. officer, asst. to mayor City of Barrow, Alaska, 1981-82; dir. advt. and promotion Anchorage Conv. and Visitors Bur., Anchorage, 1983-85; mgr. mktg. communications GTE, Honolulu, 1986-87; v.p., sr. copywriter, producer Peck, Sims, Mueller Advt. (NW Ayer affiliate), Honolulu, 1987-89; pres., creative dir. Wilson & Assoc., Inc., Hawaii, 1987—, pres. Brandon Wilson Lit. Svcs., 1991—. Author: Dead Men Don't Leave Tips - A Couple's Trans-African Odyssey, 1991, Yak Butter Blues, 1994; prin. works (TV) include The General Assembly Today, 1976-77, (films) Sasquatch, Mystery of the Sacred Shroud, Buffalo Rider; (Theatre) L'Histoire du Soldat Benito Cereno made for TV, One Flew over the Cuckoo's Nest, Street Car Named Desire, Suddenly Last Summer, Rose Tattoo, Typist and the Tiger, Star Spangled Girl, Everything in the Garden, Period of Adjustment, Any Wednesday, The Great Soc.; contbr. articles to nat. mags. and newspapers. Named Eagle Scout Boy Scouts Am., one of Exceptionally Able Youth, 1970, Literary award U. Pitts., 1970, one of Outstanding Young Men in Am., 1986, Men of Achievement award U.K., 1987, 93, Dict. of Internat. Biography, U.K., 1993; recipient Order of the Arrow, two Ike Pono Gold awards Internat. TV Assn., 6 creative advt. awards. Mem. (accreditation) PRSA, Soc. of Friends, Mensa, Internat. Campaign for Tibet, Amnesty Internat. Journeyed length of Africa overland (Ceuta to Cape Town), 1990; half of first western couple to hike Himalayas from Lhasa, Tibet to Kathmandu, Nepal, 1992; climbed Mt. Nyragongo, Zaire, Mt. Kilimanjaro, Tanzania, Mt. Olympus, Greece, Mt. Everest Base Camp, Tibet, Mt Miyajima, Japan, Crough Patrick, Ireland, Te Rua Manga, Rarotonga, Mt. Zeus, Greece; rafted down the Zambezi River; tracked mountain gorillas in Zaire; journeyed overland across C.Am.; explored Eastern Europe, 1989; hiked Alps and Tyrennes, 1996.

WILSON, CARL ARTHUR, real estate broker; b. Manhasset, N.Y., Sept. 29, 1947; s. Archie and Florence (Hefner) W.; divorced; children: Melissa Starr, Clay Alan. Student UCLA, 1966-68, 70-71. Tournament bridge dir. North Hollywood (Calif.) Bridge Club, 1967-68, 70-71; computer operator IBM, L.A., 1967-68, 70-71; bus. devel. mgr. Walker & Lee Real Estate, Anaheim, Calif., 1972-76; v.p. sales and mktg. The Estes Co., Phoenix, 1976-82, Continental Homes Inc., 1982-84; pres. Roadrunner Homes Corp., Phoenix, 1984-86, Lexington Homes, Inc., 1986, Barrington Homes, 1986-90; gen. mgr. Starr Homes, 1991—, pres., 1996—; pres. Offsite Utilities, Inc., 1992—; adv. dir. Liberty Bank. Mem. Glendale (Ariz.) Citizens Bond Coun., 1986-87, Ariz. Housing Study Commn., 1988-89, Valley Leadership, 1988—; pres.'s coun. Am. Grad. Sch. Internat. Mgmt., 1985-89; vice-chmn. Glendale Planning and Zoning Commn., 1986-87, chmn., 1987-91; mem. bd. trustees Valley of Sun United Way, 1987-92, chmn. com. Community Problem Solving and Fund Distbn., 1988-89; mem. City of Glendale RTC Task Force, 1990, Maricopa County Citizens Jud. Reform Com., 1990-92, Maricopa County Citizens Jud. Adv. Coun., 1990-91; co-founder, bd. dirs. Leadership West, Inc., 1993-94; mem. Maricopa County Trial Ct. Appointment Commn., 1993—. Mem. Nat. Assn. Homebuilders (bd. dirs. 1985-93, nat. rep. Ariz. 1990-92), Cen. Ariz. Homebuilders Assn. (adv. com. 1979-82, treas. 1986, sec. 1987, v.p. 1987-89, chmn. 1989-90, bd. dirs. 1985—, life dir. 1994—); mem. bd. adjustments City of Glendale, 1976-81, chmn., 1980-81, mem. bond coun., 1981-82; mem. real estate edn. adv. coun. State Bd. Community Coll., 1981-82; precinct committeeman, dep. registrar, 1980-81. With U.S. Army, 1968-70. Mem. Glendale C. of C. (dir. 1980-83, 89-91), Sales and Mktg. Coun. (chmn. edn. com. 1980, chmn. coun. 1981-82, Mame grand award 1981). Home: PO Box 39985 Phoenix AZ 85069-0985 Office: Starr Homes Inc Offsite Utilities Inc 2432 W Peoria Ave Ste 1190 Phoenix AZ 85029-4736

WILSON, CARTER, writer, educator; b. Washington, Dec. 27, 1947; s. George and Harriet W.; life partner, Reynolds S. Martinez, Oct. 29, 1977. BA, Harvard Coll., 1963; MA, Syracuse U., 1966. Lectr. Stanford U., Calif., 1965-66; Briggs-Copeland lectr. Harvard U., Cambridge, Mass., 1966-69; from lectr. to asst. prof. Tufts U., Medford, Mass., 1969-72; from asst. prof. to prof. U. Calif., Santa Cruz, 1972—. Author: Crazy February, 1966, I Have Fought the Good Fight, 1967, (children's book) On Firm Ice, 1969, A Green Tree and a Dry Tree, 1972, Treasures on Earth, 1981, Hidden in the Blood, 1995, contbr. (films) The Times of Harvy Milk, 1983, Common Threads, 1989, Where Are We? A Trip Across America. Recipient achievement award Assn. Gay & Lesbian Artists, 1984, Ruth Benedict prize Soc. Lesbian and Gay Anthropologists, 1996. Office: U Calif College 8 Steno Pool Santa Cruz CA 95064

WILSON, CHARLES E., air industry service executive; b. 1941. With White Motor Co. & Fresno (Calif.) Truck Ctr., 1962-77; pres. Exec. Wings, Fresno, 1977-87; now pres. Corp. Aircraft Inc., Fresno, 1987—. Office: Corp Aircraft Inc 4885 E Shields Ave Fresno CA 93726-6420*

WILSON, CHARLES ZACHARY, JR., newspaper publisher; b. Greenwood, Miss., Apr. 21, 1929; s. Charles Zachary and Ora Lee (Means) W.; m. Doris J. Wilson, Aug. 18, 1951 (dec. Nov. 1974); children: Charles III, Joyce Lynne, Joanne Catherine, Gary Thomas, Jonathan Keith; m. Kelly Freeman, Apr. 21, 1986; children: Amanda Fox, Walter Bremond. BS in Econs., U. Ill., 1952, PhD in Econs. and Stats., 1956. Asst. to v.p. Commonwealth Edison Co., Chgo., 1956-59; asst. prof. econs. De Paul U., Chgo., 1959-61; assoc. prof. bus. SUNY, Binghamton, 1961-67, prof. econs. and bus., 1967-68; prof. mgmt. and edn. UCLA, 1968-84, vice chancellor acad. programs, 1985-87; CEO, pub., pres. Cen. News-Wave Publs., L.A., 1987—; pres. Czand Assocs., Pacific Palisades, Calif., 1994—; mem. adv. council Fed. Res. Bank, San Francisco, 1986-88, 2001 com. Office of Mayor of Los Angeles, 1986-89. Author: Organizational Decision-Making, 1967; contbr. articles on bus. to jours. Bd. dirs. Los Angeles County Mus. Art, 1972-84; com. on Los Angeles City Revenue, 1975-76, United Nations Assn. panel for advancement of U. and Japan Relations, N.Y.C. 1972-74; chmn. Mayor's task force on Africa, 1979-82. Fellow John Hay Whitney, U. Ill., 1955-56, Ford Found., 1960-61, 81-82, 84, Am. Council of Edn., UCLA, 1967-68, Aspen Inst. for Human Studies; named one of Young Men of Yr., Jaycees, 1965. Mem. AAAS, Am. Econ. Assn., Nat. Newspaper Pub. Assn., Am. Mgmt. Assn., Alpha Phi Alpha (pres., pledgemaster 1952-54), Phi Kappa Phi, Order of Artus (pres.). Home: 1053 Tellem Dr Pacific Palisades CA 90272-2243 Office: Cen Newspaper Publs 2621 W 54th St Los Angeles CA 90043-2614

WILSON, DARRYL B(ABE), teacher, writer; b. Fall River Mills, Calif., Nov. 21, 1939; s. Herman Ira Wilson and Laura (Larillard) Carmony; m. Donna Lee Griffith (div.); children: Sonny, Lance, Erik, Cory; life ptnr. Danell Rene Garcia (dec.); children: Theodoro, Seterro (twins). BA, U. Calif., Davis, 1992; MA, U. Ariz., 1994, postgrad., 1995—. With Am. Indian Lang. Devel. Inst. U. Ariz., Tucson, 1994—; tchr. Lawrence Intermediate Sch., Yaqui Reservation, Ariz., 1995. Author: Wellen Auf Dem Meer Der Zeit, 1974, The Sound of Rattles and Clappers, 1993, Wilma Mankiller, Principal Chief of the Cherokee Nation, 1995; co-author: (with Lois Hogle) Voices from the Earth, 1997; contbg. author: (short story anthologies) Earth Song, Sky Spirits, 1993, Coming to Light, 1994, Native American Oral Traditions, Collaboration and Interpretation, The California Reader; contbr. articles to profl. jours.; co-editor: Dear Christopher, 1993. With USMC, 1957-61. Grantee Fund for Folk Cuolture, 1993, SEVA, 1993; fellow Ford Found., 1994. Home and Office: 249 E Drachman Tucson AZ 85705

WILSON, DAVID ALLEN, political science educator, economic development consultant; b. Rockford, Ill., May 1, 1926; s. Allen C. and Margaret (McKay) W.; m. Marie Mannes; children: Elizabeth, Stephen; m. Belle Lifson Cole, Jan. 1, 1989. BA, U. Toledo, 1948; PhD, Cornell U., 1960. Prof. UCLA, 1959—; pres. The PMR Group, Westwood, Calif., 1988—; cons. The Rand Corp., Santa Monica, Calif., 1963-68, Aid U.S. Ops. Mission Thailand, Bangkok, 1968-71, Dept. Def./Office Sec. Def., Washington, 1982-86. Author: Politics In Thailand, 1961, United States and Future of Thailand, 1970; editor: Universities And Military, 1988; co-editor: Future of State University, 1986. Ford Found. fellow, 1955-58. Fellow AAAS; mem. Am. Pol. Sci. Assn. Office: UCLA Dept Polit Sci Los Angeles CA 90024

WILSON, DAVID JEAN, ophthalmologist; b. Houston, July 24, 1955; s. Joseph William and Mary Catherine (Fitter) W.; m. Nancy Reva Greene, July 17, 1982; children: Reid, Eric, Claire. BS in Chemistry, Stanford U., 1977; MD, Baylor Coll. of Medicine, 1981. Diplomate Am. Bd. Ophthalmology. Resident in ophthalmology Oreg. Health Scis. U., Portland, 1981-85; fellow ophthalmic pathology Wilmer Eye Inst. Johns Hopkins U., Balt., 1985-87; fellow retina vitreous Ophthalmic Cons. of Boston Harvard U., 1987-88; asst. prof. ophthalmology Oreg. Health Scis. U., Portland, 1988-93, assoc. prof. ophthalmology, 1993—. Office: Casey Eye Inst 3375 SW Terwilliger Blvd Portland OR 97201-4146

WILSON, DONNA MAE, foreign language educator, administrator; b. Columbus, Ohio, Feb. 25, 1947; d. Everett John and Hazel Margaret (Bruck) Palmer; m. Steven L. Wilson, Nov. 16, 1968. BA, Ohio State U., 1973, MA, 1976; postgrad studies, U. Wash., Seattle Pacific U., 1980-93; cert., U. Salamanca, Spain, 1985. Tchg. assoc. Ohio State U., Columbus, 1974-76; lectr. U. Wash., Seattle, 1977-78; grants officer Seattle U., 1978-82; adj. prof. Shoreline Coll., Seattle, 1982-84; coord. fgn. langs., prof. Spanish Bellevue (Wash.) Coll., 1984-87; prof. Spanish Highline Coll., Des Moines, Wash., 1987—, chair fgn. lang. dept., 1990-94; chair arts and humanities Highline Coll., Des Moines, 1994—; bd. dirs. Wash. C.C.s, Olympia, 1991—; spkr. at lang. orgns., confs. regional and nat., 1985—. Editor: (book) Fronteras: En Contacto, 1992-93; (jours.) Modern Lang. Jour., 1991, 92, 94, 96, 97, Hispania, 1993, 95; text editor D. C. Heath and Co., Harcourt, Brace and Jovanovich, Houghton Mifflin, Prentice Hall; contbr. articles to profl. jours., chpt. to book. Recipient cert. of excellence Phi Theta Kappa, 1990, Pathfinder award Phi Beta Kappa, 1995; fellowshp grant Coun. Internat. Edn. Exchange, Santiago, Chile, 1992. Mem. Am. Assn. Tchrs. of Spanish (v.p. Wash.), Am. Coun. Tchrs. of Fgn. Langs. (cert. oral proficiency), Assn. Dept of Fgn. Langs. (exec. bd. 1994—), Pacific N.W. Coun. Fgn. Langs., 1986—, Nat. Assn. Fgn. Lang. Suprs., Sigma Delta Mu. (nat. exec. sec. 1992—). Home: 8720 229th Pl SW Edmonds WA 98026-8438 Office: Highline Coll 240th & Pacific Hwy S Des Moines WA 98198

WILSON, ELEANOR MCELROY, county official; b. Lancaster, Pa., Sept. 10, 1938; d. Hartford Ford and Jane Ann (Bowker) McElroy; m. Frank Eugene Wilson, July 17, 1976 (dec. Jan. 1980). AA, Monterey Peninsula Jr. Coll., Monterey, Calif., 1959; BA in Edn., San Jose State U., 1963; MA in Bus. Adminstrn./Mgmt., Webster U., St. Louis, 1981; MA in Internat. Rels., Salve Regina Coll., Newport, R.I., 1990; MA in Nat. Security/Strategic Studies, Naval War Coll., Newport, 1991. Sec. Geo. Dovolis Real Estate, Monterey, 1957-59; legal sec. Thompson & Thompson Attys., Monterey, 1959-61; legal asst., supr. Thompson J. Hudson, Atty., Monterey, 1963-68; legal asst. Thompsopn J. Hudson, Atty., Monterey, 1972-74. Mem. Orange County Grand Jury, Superior Ct., Santa Ana, Calif., 1982-83; citizen mem. Orange County Parole Bd., Santa ana, 1993-96; mem., chair Orange County Juvenile Justice Commn., Orange, 1992—. Col. USMCR, 1968—. Decorated Meritorious Svc. medal, Navy Commendation medal, others. Mem. Marine Corps Hist. Found. (bd. dirs.), Marine Corps Aviation Assn. (bd. dirs.), Linda Sloan Mundy Found. (bd. dirs.). Republican. Episcopalian. Home: 22476 Alcudia Mission Viejo CA 92692-1157

WILSON, EMILY MARIE, sales executive; b. Aberdeen, Wash., Mar. 24, 1951; d. Charles Robert and Alice Adele (Robinson) W.; m. Michael A. Rich, July 1, 1976. Student, U. Puget Sound, 1969-71, Austro-Am. Inst., Vienna, 1971; BA in Polit. Sci., U. Wash., 1973. U.S. sales mgr. Clairol, Inc., Seattle, 1975-81, sales rep. N.W. Wash., drug-mass mdse. div., 1975-77, sales rep. Met. Seattle, 1977-78, dist. mgr. sales western Wash., 1978-81; trainer territorial sales reps., mgr. dist. dollar sales, and dist. sales mgr. of Wash., Oreg., Idaho and Mont., Clorox, Inc., Seattle, 1981-82, assoc. regional mgr. Western div. spl. markets, 1982-83; regional mgr. Olympic Stain Co., Bellevue, Wash., 1983-86; dir. sales Inscape Products The Weyerhauser Co., Tacoma, 1986-88; dir. ops. Wildland Journeys, Seattle, 1988-89; Traveller World Wide Explorations, 1989—; sales mgr. Adventures Abroad, Seattle, 1990-92; owner Emily Unltd. Organizational Svcs. and Mgmt., 1992—. Mem. Transcendental Meditation Soc., Oreg. Hist. Soc., Sons and Daus. of Oreg. Pioneers, Pioneer Assn. Wash., Seattle Hist. Soc., Sidha of the Age of Enlightenment World Govt. Assn., Grad. Sci. of Creative Intelligence, Women's Profl. Managerial Network. Office: 4417 54th Ave NE Seattle WA 98105-4942 *Personal philosophy: One can never consent to creep, when one feels the impulse to soar!.*

WILSON, FRANK HENRY, electrical engineer; b. Dinuba, Calif., Dec. 4, 1935; s. Frank Henry and Lurene (Copley) W.; m. Carol B. Greening, Mar. 28, 1964; children: Frank, Scott E. BS, Oreg. State U., 1957. Electronic engr. Varian Assoc., Palo Alto, Calif., 1960-61, Stanford U. Med. Sch., Palo Alto, 1961-68, U. Calif. Med. Sch., Davis, 1968-77, Litronix, Cupertino, Calif., 1978-81, Quantel, Santa Clara, Calif., 1981-87, Heraeus Lasersonics,

Milpitas, Calif., 1987-91, Continuum Electro-Optics, Santa Clara, Calif., 1992-96. 1st lt. Signal Corps U.S. Army, 1958-60. Mem. IEEE. Home: 3826 Nathan Way Palo Alto CA 94303-4519

WILSON, GARY THOMAS, engineering executive; b. Pitts., Sept. 26, 1961; s. Charles Zachary and Doris Jean (Thomas) W.; m. Georgiann E. Wilson, Dec. 31, 1994. AB, Dartmouth Coll., 1983, BEEE, 1984; MSEE, Calif. State U., Long Beach, 1992; postgrad., UCLA, 1993—. Elec. engr. AiResearch, Man., Garrett, Torrance, Calif., 1983; sr. mem. tech. staff TRW Space & Electronics Group, Redondo Beach, Calif., 1984-93; v.p. of R&D CZAND Assocs., L.A., 1993—; rsch. asst. UCLA Flight System Rsch. Ctr., Westwood, Calif., 1994-96; sr. staff engr. payload syss. Hughes Space & Comms., 1996—; cons. CZAND Assocs., L.A., 1985-93; instr. electronics UCLA Smarts Program. Tutor math. and sci. TRW Bootstrap, Redondo Beach, 1991-93. Recipient Meritorious Svc. award United Negro Coll. Fund, 1989; TRW master's fellow, doctoral incentive fellow Calif. State U., 1993. Mem. IEEE, Nat. Soc. Black Engrs. (pres. Dartmouth chpt. 1982-83), Dartmouth Soc. Engrs.

WILSON, HERSCHEL MANUEL (PETE WILSON), retired journalism educator; b. Candler, N.C., July 17, 1930; s. Shuford Arnold and Ida Camilla (Landreth) W.; m. Ruby Jean Herring, Aug. 10, 1952. AB in Journalism, San Diego State U., 1956; MS in Journalism, Ohio U., Athens, 1959; postgrad., U. So. Calif., 1966-70. Reporter, copy editor, picture editor The San Diego Union, 1955-58; reporter, wire editor Long Beach (Calif.) Ind., 1959-65; prof. journalism Calif. State U., Northridge, 1965-71; fgn. desk copy editor L.A. Times, 1966-71; prof. and former chmn. journalism Humboldt State U., Arcata, Calif., 1971-91; ret., 1991; cons. KVIQ-TV News Dept., Eureka, Calif., 1985-87. Contbr. articles to profl. jours. Publicity dir. Simi Valley (Calif.) Fair Housing Coun., 1967; bd. dirs., publicity dir. NAACP, Eureka, Calif., 1978-80. Journalist with USN, 1948-52, Korea. Named Nat. Outstanding Advisor, Theta Sigma Phi, 1970. Mem. Soc. Profl. Journalists. (named Disting. Campus Advisor 1982), San Fernando Valley Press Club (v.p. 1969-70), Beau Pre Men's Golf Club (McKinleyville, Calif., pub. rels. dir., treas. 1978). Democrat. Methodist. Home: 115 Bent Creek Ranch Rd Asheville NC 28806-9521

WILSON, IAN ROBERT, food company executive; b. Pietermaritzburg, South Africa, Sept. 22, 1929; s. Brian J. and Edna C. W.; m. Susan Diana Lasch, Jan. 14, 1970; children: Timothy Robert, Christopher James, Diana Louise, Jason Luke. B.Commerce, U. Natal, South Africa, 1952; postgrad., Harvard U. Bus. Sch., 1968. With Coca-Cola Export Corp., Johannesburg, South Africa, 1956-74; mgr. Coca-Cola Export Corp., 1969-72, v.p., regional mgr., 1972-73, area mgr., 1973; pres., chief exec. officer Coca-Cola Ltd., Toronto, Ont., Can., 1974-76; chmn. bd., dir. Coca-Cola Ltd., 1976-81; exec. v.p. Coca-Cola Co., Atlanta, 1976-79; vice chmn. Coca-Cola Co., 1979-81, pres. Pacific group; dir. Coca-Cola Export Corp., Atlanta, 1976-81; pres., chief exec. officer, dir. Castle & Cooke, Inc., San Francisco, 1983-84, Wyndham Foods, Inc., 1985-89; chmn. bd., chief exec. officer Windmill Corp., San Francisco, 1989-94; mng. ptnr. Dartford Partnership and Induna Ptnrs., San Francisco, 1993—; also bd. dirs. Dartford Partnership and Induna Ptnrs.; bd. dirs. Novell Inc., Golden State Foods, Inc., Egoli Ptnrs., New Age Beverages Ltd., U.S./Asean Coun., East-West Ctr.; chmn. bd. dirs. Windy Hill Pet Foods, Van de Kamp Inc. and MBW Foods Inc. Mem. Church of Eng. Clubs: Durban Country and Johannesburg Country, Inanda Hunt and Polo, Atlantic Salmon, San Francisco Golf, Pacific Union, Burlingame Country. Home: 945 Green St San Francisco CA 94133-3639 Office: Dartford Partnership 801 Montgomery St Ste 400 San Francisco CA 94133-5164

WILSON, J. R., editor, writer, publisher; b. Oklahoma City, Oct. 5, 1949; s. Ralph Clayton and Wilma (Melton) W. B of Journalism, U. Mo., 1971; bus. postgrad., Calif. State U., Long Beach, 1981-83. Reporter Springfield (Mo.) Daily News, 1970, Okla. Jour., Oklahoma City, 1971; bur. mgr. UPI, Tulsa, 1972-75; regional staff editor UPI, Atlanta, 1976-79; mgr. external rels. McDonnell Douglas Astronautics Co., Huntington Beach, Calif., 1980-83; mgr. pub. rels. Cubic Corp., San Diego, 1983-85; pres. Calif. Sun Stoppers Inc., El Cajon, Calif., 1986-87; contbg. editor ComputorEdge Mag., San Diego, 1987—; North Am. Aerospace editor Jane's Info. Group, Irvine, Calif., 1988-92; mng. editor Today's Officer, L.A., 1992-93; pres. Pollax Pub., Irvine, Calif., 1994—; mem. organizing bd. Aviation/Space Writers Assn. convs., San Diego, 1987; pub. rels. chmn. Winter conv. of Industry/Govt. on Nat. Def., Costa Mesa, Calif., 1984; nat. rep., Atlanta chmn. contract drafting com. Wire Svc. Guild, Atlanta, N.Y.C., 1978-79. Author: Position Paper Requirements for a Manned Space Station, 1983 (AIAA L.A. Sect. Svc. award), Bury Me Not on the Lone Freeway, 1994, One If By Congress, Two If By White House, 1995; freelance writer, syndicated mag. column Monch Media, Washington, 1986, Interavia Aerospace Bus. and Tech., Asian Aerospace, Mil. and Aerospace Electronics, Flight Internat., Internat. Def. Rev., Jane's Airport Rev., Armed Forces Jour., Aerospace Am., Signal, Air Letter; editor AeroWeb, Def. Web, CompuWeb; editor Def. and Security Rev., 1997, 98; co-pub. electronic version DSR97 Online. Bd. dirs. Clairemont Town Coun., San Diego, 1986-87; adv. bd. Orange County Community Airport Coun., 1981-83; pub. rels com. Orange County chpt. ARC, 1980-83; adv. coun. Orange County Transit Dist., 1981-83. Mem. Soc. Aerospace Comm., Internet Developers Assn., HTML Writers Guild, Aviation/Space Writers Assn., Soc. Profl. Journalists, Am. Mensa (Atlanta v.p. 1978-79), World Affairs Coun. Orange County. Republican. Office: Pollux Pub 2030 Main St Ste 1300 Irvine CA 92614

WILSON, JAMES BRIAN, English as a second language educator; b. Ventura, Calif., Aug. 14, 1961; s. Arthur James and Patricia (Fottrell) W. BA in French, U. Calif., Irvine, 1983, tchr. ESL cert., 1994; MA in Comparative Lit., Calif. State U., Fullerton, 1992. Tchr. ESL, Claremont H.S., Huntington Beach, Calif., 1994; instr. adult basic edn.-ESL, Pasadena (Calif.) City Coll. Cmty. Edn. Ctr., 1994-96; instr. ESL, Mt. San Antonio Coll., Walnut, Calif., 1994—; lectr. ESL, Pasadena City Coll., 1996—. Tutor South Coast Literacy Coun., Irvine, 1993-94. Mem. TESOL, Calif. Tchrs. English to Spkrs. Other Langs., Orange County Guitar Circle.

WILSON, JAMES CRAIG, state welfare administrator; b. Salt Lake City, Dec. 4, 1941; s. George Law and Mary Irene (Thornton) W.; m. Eileen Jewell, Sept. 4, 1964; children—Aaron, David, Trevor, Bonnie, Robert, Angela. B.A., U. Idaho, 1967, M.A., 1970. Adminstr. div. welfare Idaho Dept. Health and Welfare, Boise, 1973-78; supr. program specialists Health Care Fin. Adminstrn., Seattle, 1978-80; dep. adminstr. Oreg. Adult and Family Services Div., Salem, 1980-84, dep. adminstr. Sr. and Disabled Services Div., 1984-91, adminstr., 1991-95; dept. dir. Idaho Dept. Health and Welfare, 1995—. NSF fellow, 1967. Mem. Phi Beta Kappa, Phi Kappa Phi, Phi Theta Kappa, Phi Gamma Mu. Mormon. Home: 11342 West Dallan Ct Boise ID 83713 Office: Idaho Dept Health and Welfare PO Box 83720 Boise ID 83720-0036

WILSON, JAY, tapestry weaver; b. Clarksburg, W.Va., May 21, 1947; s. William Hall Wilson and Elizabeth Wamsley. BArch, Auburn U., 1971. Archtl. designer Architects Hawaii, Honolulu, 1972-75; pvt. practice Honolulu, Hawaii, 1976—. Represented in pvt., corp. and pub. collections in Hawaii, on U.S. mainland and Can.; exhibited in numerous juried & invitational art exhbns., 1972—, including solo exhbn. at Contemporary Arts Ctr., Honolulu, 1980, 3 tapestries with juried exhibit Artists of Hawaii, Honolulu Acad. Arts, 1987, 1 tapestry at 25th Anniversary exhbn. of State Found. on Culture and Arts, Contemporary Mus., Honolulu, 1990; commns. include State Found. Culture and Arts, 1995, 96. Named Master Artist State Found. Culture and Arts; featured in art and craft publs. Mem. Hawaii Craftsmen, Am. Tapestry Alliance, Internat. Tapestry Network, Handweaver's Guild Am. (award of merit 1989). Home and Office: 3155 Nahenahe Pl Kihei HI 96753-9314

WILSON, JOHN FRANCIS, educational administrator; b. Springfield, Mo., Nov. 4, 1937; s. Frederick Marion and Jesse Ferrel (Latimer) W.; m. L. Claudette Faulk, June 9, 1961; children: Laura, Amy, Emily. BA, Harding U., Searcy, Ark., 1959; MA, Harding U., Memphis, 1961; PhD, U. Iowa, 1967. Dir. Christian Student Ctr., Springfield, 1959-73; prof. religious studies S.W. Mo. State U., Springfield, 1961-83; prof. of religion, dean Seaver Coll. Arts, Letters and Scis. Pepperdine U., Malibu, Calif., 1983—. Author: Religion: A Preface, 1982, 2d edit., 1989; co-author: Discovering the Bible, 1986, Excavations at Capernaum, 1989; contbr. articles, revs. to profl. publs. Mem. Archaeol. Inst. Am., Am. Schs. of Oriental Rsch., Soc. Bib. Lit., Am. Numismatic Soc., Am. Coun. Acad. Deans. Mem. Ch. of Christ. Office: Pepperdine U Seaver Coll 24255 Pacific Coast Hwy Malibu CA 90263-0001

WILSON, JOHN PASLEY, law educator; b. Newark, Apr. 7, 1933; s. Richard Henry and Susan Agnes (Pasley) W.; m. Elizabeth Ann Reed, Sept 10, 1955; children: David Cables, John, Jr., Cicely Reed. AB, Princeton U., 1955; LLB, Harvard U., 1962. Bar: N.J. 1962, U.S. Dist. Ct. N.J. 1962, Mass. 1963, U.S. Dist. Ct. Mass. 1963. Budget examiner Exec. Office of Pres., Bur. of Budget, Washington, 1955-56; assoc. Riker, Danzig, Scherer & Brown, Newark, 1962-63; asst. dean Harvard U. Law Sch., Cambridge, Mass., 1963-67; assoc. dean Boston U. Law Sch., 1968-82; dean Golden Gate U. Sch. Law, San Francisco, 1982-88, prof., 1988—; vis. prof. dept. health policy and mgmt. Harvard U., 1988; cons. Nat. Commn. for the Protection of Human Subjects of Biomed. and Behavioral Rsch.; mem. Mass. Gov's. Commn. on Civil and Legal Rights of Developmentally Disabled; former chmn. adv. com. Ctr for Community Legal Edn., San Francisco, now mem. Author: The Rights of Adolescents in the Mental Health System. Contbr. chpts. to books, articles to profl. jours. Bd. dirs. Greater Boston Legal Svcs., Chewonki Found.; mem. Health Facilities Appeals Bd., Commonwealth of Mass.; assoc. mem. Democratic Town Com., Concord; chmn. Bd. Assessors, Concord; bd. overseers Boston Hosp. for Women, past chmn. med. affairs com.; past mem. instl. rev. bd. Calif. Pacific Hosp., San Francisco. Served to lt. (j.g.) USNR, 1956-59. NIMH grantee, 1973. Mem. Nat. Assn. Securities Dealers (arbitrator). Office: Golden Gate U Sch Law 536 Mission St San Francisco CA 94105-2921

WILSON, JOHNNY LEE, editor-in-chief; b. Santa Maria, Calif., Oct. 20, 1950; s. John Henry and Bobbie Lou (Henson) W.; m. Susan Lynne Leavelle, Aug. 28, 1970; children: Jennifer Lynne, Jonathan Lee. BA, Calif. Bapt. Coll., Riverside, 1972; MDiv, Golden Gate Bapt. Seminary, Mill Valley, Calif., 1975; ThM, So. Bapt. Theol. Seminary, Louisville, 1978, PhD, 1981. Pastor Rollingwood Bapt. Ch., San Pablo, Calif., 1974-75, Temple Bapt. Ch., Sacramento, Calif., 1975-77, Hermosa-Redondo Beach (Calif.) Ministries, 1981-82, Immanuel. Bapt. Ch., La Puente, Calif., 1982-86; asst. editor Computer Gaming World, Anaheim, Calif., 1986-89, editor, 1989-94; editor-in-chief Computer Gaming World, San Francisco, 1993-95; pres. and prof. of Old Testament Calif. Korean Bapt. Seminary, Walnut, 1990-93; adj. prof. O.T. studies So. Calif. Ctr., Garden Grove, Calif., 1981-86; mem. com. Software Pub. Assn. Ratings Group, Washington, 1994; mem. adv. coun. Recreation Software Adv. Coun., 1995; bd. govs. Acd. Interactive Arts and Scis., 1995. Author: The Sim City Planning Commission Handbook, 1990, The Sim Earth Bible, 1991; co-author: The Mercer Dictionary of Bible, 1990, Sid Meier's Civilization: Rome on 640K A Day, 1992. Named to Outstanding Young Men of Am., Jaycees, Ala., 1977, Best Software Reviewer, Software Pubs. Assn., Washington, 1990. Home: 1328 Pearl St Alameda CA 94501-4714 Office: Ziff-Davis Pub 135 Main St Fl 14 San Francisco CA 94105-1812

WILSON, JOHNNY LEE, secondary school educator; b. Norfolk, Va., May 1, 1959; s. Thomas H. and Dolly S. (Stefko) W.; m. Tami Lu Nichols, Oct. 20, 1959 (div. Apr. 1993); 1 child, Nickolas A. BS, Ohio State U., 1995. Cert. secondary English tchr., Ohio, Colo. Clk. Nationwide Ins. Co., Columbus, Ohio, 1980-90; English tchr. Alameda H.S., Jefferson County Pub. Schs., Golden, Colo., 1996—. With Ohio Army NG, 1980-86, cpl., 1990-96. Zuck scholar, 1993-94, Seeley scholar, 1994-96, Durfey scholar, 1994-96. Mem. NEA, Colo. Edn. Assn., Jefferson County Edn. Assn., Soc. Profl. Journalists, Golden Key Nat. Honor Soc. Republican. Home: 222 S Carr St # 303 Lakewood CO 80226

WILSON, KEITH CHARLES, retired English educator, poet, short story writer; b. Clovis, N. Mex., Dec. 26, 1927; s. Earl Charles and Marjorie Valentine (Edwards) W.; m. Lorna Heloise Brigham, Feb. 15, 1958; children: Lorna Kathleen, Kristin Mavournin, Kevin O'Keith, Kerrin Noel. BS in Engring., U.S. Naval Acad., 1950; MA in English, U. N. Mex., 1958. Staff mem. Sandia Corp., Albuquerque, 1958-60; instr. English U. Ariz., Tucson, 1960-65; from asst. prof. to full prof. N. Mex. State U., Las Cruces, 1965-86; vis. poet U. Kansas, Utah State U., U. Sibiu, Romania, Cluj-Napoca, Romania; vis. dir. workshops U. N. Mex., Bowling Green State U., SUNY, Cortland, Utah State U., Banff Art Ctr., Can. and others; cons. to Coordinating Coun. for Literary Mags., 1972-74, for NEA to Voice of Am., 1975; master poet N. Mex. Poetry in the Schs. Program. Author: (books of poetry) Sketches for a New Mexico Hill Town, 1967, II Sequences, 1967, The Old Car, 1967, Graves Registry and Other Poems, 1969 (Lamont prize runner-up), Homestead, 1969, Rocks, 1971, The Shadow of Our Bones, 1971, The Old Man and Others: Some Faces for America, 1971, Psalms for Various Voices, Midwatch, Thantog: Songs of a Jaguar Priest, 1977, The Shaman Deer, 1977, While Dancing Feet Shatter the Earth, 1977 (Nat. Book award nominee), Desert Cenote, 1978, The Streets of San Miguel, 1979, Retablos, 1981, Stone Roses: Poems from Transylvania, 1983, Lovesongs and Mandalas, 1984, Lion's Gate: Selected Poems, 1963-86, 1988, The Winds of Pentecost, 1991, Graves Registry, 1992 (nominated for Nat. Book award, Critics Circle award, Western States Art Found. Book award, P.E.N., West Book award), The Way of the Dove, 1994, Warrior's Song and Other Poems, 1996; poems have been translated into Spanish, Polish, Japanese, Romanian, Hungarian, German and Indonesian. Lt. USN, 1950-54, Korea. Recipient D.H. Lawrence fellowship U. N. Mex., 1971, Creative Writing fellowship Nat. Endowment for the Arts, Washington, 1974-75, Fulbright-Hays fellowship, Romania, 1974-75; grantee P.E.N., Am. Ctr., N.Y.C., 1971. Mem. Rio Grane Inst. Democrat. Episcopalian. Home: 1500 S Locust St Las Cruces NM 88001

WILSON, KENNETH ALLEN, educator; b. Somerset, Pa., May 5, 1951; s. Richard Burdine and Thelma Jean (Stahl) W.; m. Nancy Lee Commins, May 25, 1984; 1 child, Alexander Saul Commins Wilson. BA, Mich. State U., 1974; MAT, Antioch U., 1975; CAS, Harvard U., 1980. Cert. tchr., N.Mex., Mass. Tchr. sci. and social studies Ramah Navajo Sch. Bd., Pine Hill, N.Mex., 1975-78; tchr. math. Window Rock Sch. Dist., Ft. Defiance, Ariz., 1978-79; rsch. asst. Harvard Grad. Sch. Edn., Cambridge, Mass., 1979-80; tchr. math. and sci. Belmont (Mass.) Pub. Schs., 1980-81; curriculum developer Am. Indian Upward Bound Program, Boulder, Colo., 1981-82; assoc. dir. sci. fairs project Am. Indian Sci. and Engring. Soc., Boulder, 1982-83; assoc. dir. Am. Indian Upward Bound, Boulder, 1983-86, dir., 1986-88; assoc. dir. pre-coll. ops. U. Colo., Boulder, 1988-89, asst. dir. for instructional svcs., 1989—. Contbr. articles to profl. jours. Bd. dirs. Sta. KGNU Cmty. Radio, Boulder, 1985-90; facilitator Louisville (Colo.) Resource Conservation Adv. Bd., 1994—; alt. mem. Boulder County Waste Recycling and Composting Authority, 1996—; precinct chair Boulder County Dems., 1996—. Recipient numerous fed. grants related to Native Am. edn. and creating ednl. opportunities for low income, first-generation coll. students; Nat. Merit scholar, 1969. Mem. Assoc. Spl. Programs in Region Eight, Nat. Assn. Devel. Educators. Office: U Colo Campus Box 107 Boulder CO 80309

WILSON, MATTHEW FREDERICK, newspaper editor; b. San Francisco, May 10, 1956; s. Kenneth E. and Verna Lee (Hunter) W. BA in Philosophy, U. Calif., Berkeley, 1978. Copy person San Francisco Chronicle, summers 1975, 76, 77, copy editor, 1978-82, editorial systems coord., 1982-84; budget analyst San Francisco Newspaper Agy., 1984085; asst. news editor San Francisco Chronicle, 1985-87, asst. to exec. editor, 1987-88, mng. editor, 1988-95, exec. editor, 1995—. Mem. Am. Soc. Newspaper Editors, AP Mng. Editors, Calif. Soc. Newspaper Editors. Office: San Francisco Chronicle 901 Mission St San Francisco CA 94103-2988

WILSON, MELVIN EDMOND, civil engineer; b. Bremerton, Wash., Aug. 3, 1935; s. Edmond Curt and Madeline Rose (Deal) W.; m. Deanna May Stevens, Nov. 22, 1957 (div. Mar. 1971); children: Kathleen, Debra Wilson Frank. BSCE, U. Wash., 1957, MSCE, 1958. Registered profl. engr., Wash. Asst. civil engr. City of Seattle, 1958-60, assoc. civil engr., 1960-64, sr. civil engr., 1964-66, supervising civil engr., 1966-75, sr. civil engr., 1975-77, mgr. X, 1977-88; owner Wilson Cons. Svcs., Seattle, 1988-89; transp. sys. dir. City of Renton, Wash., 1989-96, ret., 1996; owner Mel Wilson Photographer, Seattle, 1975-84. Contbr. reports to profl. jours. Rep. Renton transp. work group King County (Wash.) Growth Mgmt. Policy Com.; rep. Renton tech. adv. com. South County Area Transp. Bd., King County, 1992-96, developer svc. policy (adopted by Puget Sound Govtl. Conf.) to encourage travel by transit. successfuly led effort to make Renton first suburban city to receive direct transit svc. under Met. King County Plan, 1994. Mem. ASCE, Am. Pub. Works Assn., Inst. Transp. Engrs., Tau Beta Pi, Sigma Xi.

WILSON, MICHAEL GREGG, film producer, writer; b. N.Y.C., Jan. 21, 1942; s. Lewis Gilbert Wilson and Dana (Natol) Broccoli; m. Coila Jane Hurley; children: David, Gregg. BS, Harvey Mudd Coll., 1963; JD, Stanford U., 1966. Bar: D.C., Calif., N.Y. Legal advisor FAA-DOT, Washington, 1966-67; assoc. Surrey, Karasik, Gould, Green, Washington, 1967-71; ptnr. Surrey and Morse, Washington and N.Y.C., 1971-74; legal advisor Eon Prodns., London, 1974-78, producer, mng. dir., 1978—. Writer/prodr.: For Your Eyes Only, 1981, Octopussy, 1983, View to a Kill, 1985, The Living Daylights, 1987, Licence to Kill, 1989; prodr.: Goldeneye, 1995; author: Pictorialism in California, Getty Museum, 1994.

WILSON, MIRIAM GEISENDORFER, retired physician, educator; b. Yakima, Wash., Dec. 3, 1922; d. Emil and Frances Geisendorfer; m. Howard G. Wilson, June 21, 1947; children—Claire, Paula, Geoffrey, Nicola, Marla. B.S., U. Wash., Seattle, 1944, M.S., 1945; M.D., U. Calif., San Francisco, 1950. Mem. faculty U. So. Calif. Sch. Medicine, L.A., 1965—, prof. pediatrics, 1969—. Office: U So Calif Med Ctr 1129 N State St Rm 1G24 Los Angeles CA 90033-1069

WILSON, MYRON ROBERT, JR., retired psychiatrist; b. Helena, Mont., Sept. 21, 1932; s. Myron Robert Sr. and Constance Ernestine (Bultman) W. BA, Stanford U., 1954, MD, 1957. Diplomate Am. Bd. Psychiatry and Neurology. Dir. adolescent psychiatry Mayo Clinc, Rochester, Minn., 1965-71; pres. and psychiatrist in chief Wilson Ctr., Faribault, Minn., 1971-86; ret., 1986; chmn. Wilson Ctr., 1986-90; ret., 1990; assoc. clin. prof. psychiatry UCLA, 1985—. Contbr. articles to profl. jours. Chmn., chief exec. officer C.B. Wilson Found., L.A., 1986—; mem. bd. dirs. Pasadena Symphony Orchestra Assn., Calif., 1987. Served to lt. comdr., 1958-60. Fellow Mayo Grad. Sch. Medicine, Rochester, 1960-65. Fellow Am. Psychiat. Assn., Am. Soc. for Adolescent Psychiatry, Internat. Soc. for Adolescent Psychiatry (founder, treas. 1985-88, sec. 1985-88, treas. 1988-92); mem. Soc. Sigma Xi (Mayo Found. chpt.). Episcopalian. Office: Wilson Found 8033 W Sunset Blvd # 4019 West Hollywood CA 90046-2427

WILSON, PATRICIA POPLAR, electrical manufacturing company executive; b. Chgo., Sept. 20, 1931; d. George and Leona (O'Brien) Poplar; BS U. Wash., 1966, MA 1967, PhD 1980; m. Chester Goodwin Wilson, Jan. 30, 1960; children: Susan Spadafora, Chester Wilson. Instr., U. Wash., Seattle, 1967-74; women's editor Nor'westing Mag., Seattle, 1969—; pres. Wilson & Assos. N.W. Inc., Seattle, 1974—; v.p. N.W. Mfg. & Supply, Inc., 1977-87, pres., 1987—; pres. Trydor Sales Alberta Ltd., Can. Mem. Electric League, N.W. Mfg. & Supply. Episcopalian. Club: Seattle Yacht. Author: Household Equipment, Guide to Surplus Equipment. Contbr. articles to profl. jours. Office: 4045 7th Ave S Seattle WA 98108-5240

WILSON, PETE, governor of California; b. Lake Forest, Ill., Aug. 23, 1933; s. James Boone and Margaret (Callaghan) W.; m. Betty Robertson (div.); m. Gayle Edlund, May 29, 1983. B.A. in English Lit., Yale U., 1955; J.D., U. Calif., Berkeley, 1962; LL.D., Grove City Coll., 1983, U. Calif., San Diego, 1983, U. San Diego, 1984. Bar: Calif. 1962. Mem. Calif. Legislature, Sacramento, 1966-71; mayor City of San Diego, 1971-83; U.S. Senator from Calif., 1983-91; gov. State of Calif., 1991—. Trustee Conservation Found.; mem. exec. bd. San Diego County council Boy Scouts Am.; hon. trustee So. Calif. Council Soviet Jews; adv. mem. Urban Land Inst., 1985-86; founding dir. Retinitis Pigmentosa Internat.; hon. dir. Alzheimer's Family Ctr., Inc., 1985; hon. bd. dirs. Shakespeare-San Francisco, 1985. Recipient Golden Bulldog award, 1984, 85, 86, Guardian of Small Bus. award, 1984, Cuauhtemoc plaque for disting. svc. to farm workers in Calif., 1991, Julius award for outstanding pub. leadership U. So. Calif., 1992, award of appreciation Nat. Head Start, 1992; named Legislator of Yr., League Calif. Cities, 1985, Man of Yr. N.G. Assn. Calif., 1986, Man of Yr. citation U. Calif. Boalt Hall, 1986; ROTC scholar Yale U., 1951-55. Mem. Nat. Mil. Family Assn. (adv. bd.), Phi Delta Phi, Zeta Psi. Republican. Episcopalian. Office: State Capitol Office Of Governor Sacramento CA 95814*

WILSON, PETER TRIMBLE, fisheries development consultant. Cons. Global Ocean Cons., Inc., 1982—; cons. Societe Nouvelle Conserveries du Senegal, 1990, Kosrae State, 1991—, Dept. Agriculture, 1989, Mankoadze and Pioneer, 1988, Asian devel. Bank, 1988, Seychelles Tuna Cannery, 1988, Cannery Devel. Plan, Indonesia, 1992, Papua New Guinea Tuna Cannery Devel. Plan, 1993, Republic of Maldiver, 1984-89, Maurituer, 1994, Maui Pacific Ctr., 1993, 94, 95, Pacific Ocean Rsch. Found., 1994, 95, 96. Contbr. numerous articles to profl. jours. Office: Global Ocean Consultants Inc 1130 Mano Dr # A Kula HI 96790-9500

WILSON, RICHARD RANDOLPH, lawyer; b. Pasadena, Calif., Apr. 14, 1950; s. Robert James and Phyllis Jean (Blackman) W.; m. Catherine Goodhugh Stevens, Oct. 11, 1980; children: Thomas Randolph, Charles Stevens. BA cum laude, Yale U., 1971; JD, U. Wash., 1976. Bar: Wash. 1976, U.S. Dist. Ct. (we. dist.) Wash. 1976, U.S. Ct. Appeals (9th cir.) 1977. Assoc. Hillis, Phillips, Cairncross, Clark & Martin, Seattle, 1976-81, ptnr., 1981-84; ptnr. Hillis, Cairncross, Clark & Martin, Seattle, 1984-87; ptnr. Hillis Clark Martin & Peterson, Seattle, 1987—, chmn. land use and environ. group; bd. dirs. Quality Child Care Svcs., Inc., Seattle, Plymouth Housing Group, Seattle; mem. legal com. Bldg. Industry Assn. Wash.; lectr. various bar assns., 1980—. Contbr. articles to profl. jours. Mem. Seattle Mayor's Kidsplace Adv. Task Force, Seattle, 1985; chmn. class agts. Yale U. Alumni Fund, New Haven, 1985-87, class agt., 1971—, mem. class coun., 1991-96, mem. Western Wash. exec. com. Yale capital campaign, vice chmn. leadership gifts com. Yale 25th reunion, 1995-96; mem., vice chmn. Medina (Wash.) Planning Commn., 1990-92; chmn. capital campaign Plymouth Congrl. Ch., Seattle, 1995. Mem. ABA, Wash. State Bar Assn. (dir. environ. and land use law sect. 1985-88), Seattle-King County Bar Assn., Kingsley Trust Assn. (pres. 1996-98), Yale Assn. of Western Wash. Congregationalist. Home: 2305 86th Ave NE Bellevue WA 98004-2416 Office: Hillis Clark Martin & Peterson 1221 2nd Ave Ste 500 Seattle WA 98101-2925 *Notable cases include: Barrie vs. Kitsap County, 1980; Sore vs. Snohomish County, 1983; Conv. Ctr. Coalition vs. City of Seattle, 1986; Orion Corp. vs. State, 1987, Cougar Mountain Assocs. vs. King County, 1988.*

WILSON, ROBERT LLEWELLYN, clinical psychologist, educator; b. Cleveland, Tenn., Oct. 11, 1954; s. Robert Anderson and Louise Bell (Bible) W.; m. Belen Austria, June 22, 1996. BA, U. Tenn., 1976; MS, Auburn U., 1980, PhD, 1988. Lic. psychologist, Calif.; cert. profl. healthcare quality. Staff psychologist Fed. Bur. Prisons, Pleasanton, Calif., 1988-89, chief of psychology, 1989-90; assoc. chief mental health VA Med. Clinic, Martinez, 1990—; clin. instr. psychiatry U. Calif.-Sch. Medicine, Davis, 1990—; external cons. Readjustment Counseling Ctr., Concord, Calif., 1993—; trainer quality improvement VA, No. Calif., 1994—, mem. nat. facilitation com., Cleve., 1995—; faculty mem. Bayer Inst. Comm., New Haven, 1996—. Mem. social com. Gateview Homeowners, Albany, Calif., 1996—. Named one of Outstanding Young Men Am., 1983, 88. Mem. Mensa Internat., Calif. Psychol. Assn. Democrat. Home: 555 Pierce St # 1009 Albany CA 94706 Office: VA NCHCS 150 Muir Rd Martinez CA 94553

WILSON, ROBERT MCCLAIN, plastic surgeon, educator; b. Cornwall, N.Y., Dec. 6, 1942; s. James Van Gorder and Isabel Mae (Steele) W.; m. Dorothea Louise Figge; children: Michael McClain, Sara Malia. MD, U. Colo., Denver, 1968. Diplomate Am. Bd. Surgery, Am. Bd. Plastic Surgery. Commd. U.S. Army, 1967, advanced through ranks to Col., 1993; intern Tripler Army Med. Ctr., Honolulu, 1968-69, resident gen. surgery, 1970-74; resident orthopaedic surgery Martin Army Hosp., Ft. Benning, Ga., 1969-70; resident plastic surgery Walter Reed Army Med. Ctr., Washington, 1974-76, asst. chief plastic surgery svcs., 1976-78; chief plastic surgery svcs. Landstuhl Army Regional Med. Ctr., Germany, 1978-81, 90-93, 1996—; chief plastic surgery svcs. Fitzsimons Army Med. Ctr., Aurora, Colo., 1993-96; plastic surgeon Wenatchee (Wash.) Valley Clinic, 1981-90. Fellow ACS; mem. AMA, Am. Soc. Plastic Surgeons, Assn. Mil. Surgeons of U.S. Luth. Home: Adam Müller Strasse #9, 66894 Gerhardsbrunn Germany Office: Landstuhl Regional Med Ctr CMR 402 Box 734 APO AE 09180-3460

WILSON, ROBERT MICHAEL ALAN, writer; b. Jamestown, N.Y., June 19, 1944; s. Harry Garfield and Hazel Virginia (Groscost) W.; m. Ursula Lieselotte Frank, May 14, 1987; 1 child, Jeffrey Aryan. BS, Calif. State U., 1974; MPA, U. So. Calif., 1976; JD, Western State U., 1983. Deputy sheriff L.A. County Sheriff's Dept., 1968-92; traffic safety advocate San Bernardino (Calif.) Police Dept., 1992-94; free-lance writer, Moreno Valley, Calif., 1992—. Author: Bad Wimpfen, 1994, Nolocaust, 1995, The Only Good Indian. . ., 1996. Creator, mgr. 999 Run for Abused Kids, Industry, Calif., 1988-91; creator, chmn. Grocery Bag Essay Contest Against Drugs, Moreno Valley, 1991—. Sgt. USAF, 1964-67. Recipient award of merit Calif. Peace Officers Assn., 1991, Disting. Svc. award Nat. Commn. Against Drunk Drivers, Washington, 1991. Mem. Masons (Hiram award 1992), Shriners. Republican. Home: 10837 Cloud Haven Dr Moreno Valley CA 92557-4211

WILSON, ROBIN SCOTT, university president, writer; b. Columbus, Ohio, Sept. 19, 1928; s. John Harold and Helen Louise (Walker) W.; m. Patricia Ann Van Kirk, Jan. 20, 1951; children: Kelpie, Leslie, Kari, Andrew. B.A., Ohio State U., 1950; M.A., U. Ill., 1951, Ph.D., 1959. Fgn. intelligence officer CIA, Washington, 1959-67; prof. English Clarion State Coll., (Pa.), 1967-70; assoc. dir. Com. Instnl. Cooperation, Evanston, Ill., 1970-77; assoc. provost instrn. Ohio State U., Columbus, 1977-80; univ. pres. Calif. State U., Chico, 1980-93, pres. emeritus, 1993—. Author: Those Who Can, 1973, Death By Degrees, 1995, Paragons, 1996; short stories, criticism, articles on edn. Lt. USN, 1953-57. Mem. AAAS, Phi Kappa Phi.

WILSON, SHARON ROSE, educator, researcher; b. Denver, May 13, 1941; d. John William Wilson and Rose Schlagel; m. Roger Lloyd Brown, May 5, 1973; 1 child, Stephen Roger Wilson-Brown. BA, Colo. State Coll., 1963; MA, Purdue U., 1967; PhD in Eng., U. Wis., 1976. Cert. secondary edn., Colo. Teaching asst. Purdue U., West Lafayette, Ind., 1963-65, U. Wis., Madison, 1965-70; instr. U. Northern Colo., Greeley, 1970-73, asst. prof., 1974-78, assoc. prof., 1978-84, prof. eng., women's studies, 1985—; vis. humanist Boulder County Women's Resources Ctr., 1980; speaker and lectr. in field. Author: Margaret Atwood's Fairy-Tale Sexual Politics, 1993, The Self-Conscious Narrator and His Twentieth-Century Faces, 1976; co-editor: Approaches to Teaching Atwood's The Handmaid's Tale and Other Works, 1996; contbr. articles to profl. jours. Founding mem. local Nat. Orgn. for Women, 1982; women's issues chairperson League of Women Voters, Longmont, 1978-85; founding co-pres. Margaret Atwood Soc., 1983-88. Recipient numerous rsch. grants. Mem. MLA (organizer of spl. sessions 1980, 85, 88), Colo. Seminars (adv. bd. 1980—, coord. of program), Colo. Women's Studies Assn. (conf. coord. 1977), Margaret Laurence Soc., Samuel Beckett Soc. (charter), Doris Lessing Soc., Internat. Assn. Fantastic in the Arts, Assn. for Canadian Studies in the U.S., Popular Culture Assn., Pacific Ctrl. Canadian Studies Network, Western Canadian Studies Assn., Rocky Mountain MLA. Office: U Northern Colo Eng Dept Greeley CO 80639

WILSON, STAN LE ROY, mass communications educator, county official; b. Orange, Calif., May 24, 1935. AA, Modesto Jr. Coll., 1955; BA, Calif. State U., Fresno, 1958; MA, Calif. State U., Stanislaus, 1966; EdD, U. So. Calif., 1973. Newspaper reporter, editor Turlock Daily Jour., 1957-60; news reporter KYNO-Fresno, 1960-61; asst. to exec. dean Calif. State U., Stanislaus, 1961-66, part-time prof. journalism and radio-TV, 1961-65; lectr. in mass comm. Calif. State U., Fullerton, 1975-76; prof. mass comm. Coll. of the Desert, Palm Desert, Calif., 1967-95, chmn. dept. comm., 1975-81; mem. Riverside County (Calif.) Bd. Suprs., 1995—; mem. acad. adv. bd. telecomm. course WGBH-TV, Boston, 1989-90; pub. rels. cons. Medic-Alert Found., 1963-64; speaker in field. Author: Mass Media/Mass Culture: An Introduction, 4th edit., 1997; contbr. articles to profl. publs. Mem. Palm Desert City Coun., 1977-95; mayor City of Palm Desert, 1980-82, 88-89, 93-94; mem. Palm Desert Planning Commn., 1974-77, chmn., 1975-77; mem. Riverside County Transp. Commn., 1980-97, chmn., 1982-83, 86-87; Riverside Cities and County rep. bd. dirs., South Coast Air Quality Mgmt. Dist., 1988—; chmn. adminstrv. com., 1988-91, chmn. mobile source commn.; vice chmn. Riverside County Mayors' and Councilmen's Conf., 1986-87; adv. bd. Chapman Coll. Residence Ctr., 1982-88; bd. dirs. Coachella Valley Counseling, 1982-93, pres., 1989-90; bd. dirs. Valley Partnership, 1992-95. Named Outstanding Journalism Educator, Calif. Newspaper Pubs. Assn., 1978, Outstanding Cmty. Leader, Coll. of Desert Alumni Assn., 1987, Journalism Hall of Fame, 1995; recipient Outstanding Cmty. Svc. award Palm Desert C. of C., 1995. Mem. Coachella Valley Assn. Govts. (exec. bd. 1979-84, 88-89, 93—, chmn. energy and environ. com. 1983-84), Am. Legion, Coachella Valley Mex. Am. C. of C., Assn. for Edn. in Journalism and Mass Comm. (nat. adv. bd. 1987-88), Soc. Profl. Journalists (charter sec. Desert chpt. 1976-77), Nat. C.C. Journalism Assn. (pres. 19979-80). Office: County of Riverside 46200 Oasis St Ste 318 Indio CA 92201-5964

WILSON, STEPHEN JAY, psychiatrist, consultant; b. Syracuse, N.Y., Aug. 23, 1940; s. Louis L. and Esther A. (Alderman) W.; children from previous marriage: Leigh, Eric; m. Anne Nadel, Aug. 26, 1986. BA, Cornell U., 1961; MD, SUNY, Syracuse, 1965. Diplomate Am. Bd. Psychiat. and Neurology. Intern Med. Coll. of Va. Hosps., Richmond, 1965-66; resident in psychiat. Neuropsychiat. Inst. U. Mich., Ann Arbor, 1969-72; UCLA legal psychiat. fellow, 1972-73; pvt. practice psychiat. Tarzana, Calif., 1973—; cons. Vista Del Mar Child Care Svc., L.A., 1974-75, Tarzana Psychiat. Hosp., 1974-75, L.A. Unified Sch. Dist., 1983-85, L.A. Superior Ct. Adult Criminal Psychiat. Evaluations, 1985—, Children of Our Future Group Home, 1990-95, Passageway Group Home, 1990-95, Pioneer Boys Ranch, Newhall, Calif., 1982—, Walden Environ., Mission Hills, Calif., 1988-96, Stirling Acad., Reseda, Calif., 1989—, Pain Care Ctr. Van Nuys, Calif. Valley Presbyn. Hosp., 1988—, Dr.'s Co. Malpractice Revs., 1992—; cons., psychiat. evaluator L.A. Juvenile Ct., 1983—, L.A. Superior Ct. Family Law Sect., 1974—, Ventura Family Law Sect., 1988—; cons. pvt. industry issues mgmt. and devel., 1982—; instr. dept. cmty. medicine SUNY Upstate Med. Ctr., Syracuse, 1968-69; clin. asst. prof. dept. psychiat. Neuropsychiat. Inst. UCLA, 1973-86, Calif. Sch. Profl. Psychology, L.A., 1975-78; med. dir. Western Ctr. for Emotionally Handicapped, Tarzana, 1972-73, staff psychiatrist Calif. Dept. Corrections Parole Outpatient Clinic, L.A., 1972-73; pres. med. staff Van Nuys Hosp., 1976-78, v.p. med. staff, 1990-91, mem. exec. com., 1976-80, mem. utilization rev. com., 1985-92, chmn. com. impaired physicians, 1978-80, med. dir. adolescent program, 1985-89, dir. cmty. rels., 1989-91; mem. med. exec. com. Woodview Calabasas Hosp., Calif., 1976-78, 80-82; agreed med. examiner, ind. med. examiner Calif. Workers' Compensation Appeals Bd., 1979—; expert witness L.A. and Ventura County Superior Cts., 1982—; expert, lectr. in field; dir. behavioral scis. ALTA Health Strategies, 1990-91, psychiat. reviewer, 1990—; mem. quality assurance com. Los Robles Regional Med. Ctr., Thousand Oaks, Calif., 1989-94, mem. emergency room com., 1987-88; hosp. affiliations include Pine Grove Hosp., West Hills, Calif., 1989-92, Los Robles Regional Med. Ctr., 1987—, Simi Valley (Calif.) Adventist Hosp., 1988-89, Westlake Cmty. Hosp., Westlake Village, Calif., 1985-91, Valley Hosp. Med. Ctr., Van Nuys, 1983-86, Tarzana Med. Ctr., 1981—, Northridge (Calif.) Hosp., 1979-90, Valley Presbyn. Hosp., 1973-74, 1988-97, Woodview-Calabasas Hosp., 1973-84, Van Nuys Psychiat. Hosp., 1973-90. Contbr. articles to profl. jours. Physician Free People's Clin., Ann Arbor, 1969-72, Goose Lake Rock Festival, Ann Arbor, 1969; bd. dirs. San Fernando Valley Cmty. Mental Health Ctr., Northridge, 1974-76, mem. profl. adv. coun. 1976-77; mem. drug, alcohol and tobacco adv. com. Las Virgenes Sch. Dist., 1990-92. Peace Corps. physician USPHS, 1966-68. Recipient Achievement award for meritorious svc. Guyana Lions Club, 1968. Mem. Am. Psychiat. Assn., So. Calif. Psychiat. Soc. (drug abuse and alcoholism com. 1973-75, peer rev. com. 1982-91), So. Calif. Soc. Adolescent Psychiat., Am. Acad. Psychiat. and the Law (So. Calif. chpt.). Office: 18370 Burbank Blvd Ste 503 Tarzana CA 91356-2804

WILSON, STEPHEN VICTOR, federal judge; b. N.Y.C., Mar. 26, 1942; s. Harry and Rae (Ross) W. B.A. in Econs., Lehigh U., 1963; J.D., Bklyn. Law Sch., 1967; LL.M., George Washington U., 1973. Bars: N.Y. 1967, D.C. 1971, Calif. 1972, U.S. Ct. Appeals (9th cir.) U.S. Dist. Ct. (so., cen. and no. dists.) Calif. Trial atty. Tax div. U.S. Dept. Justice, 1968-71; asst. U.S. atty., L.A., 1971-77, chief spl. prosecutions, 1973-77; ptnr. Hochman, Salkin & Deroy, Beverly Hills, Calif., from 1977; judge U.S. Dist. Ct. (cen. dist.) Calif., L.A., 1985—; adj. prof. law Loyola U. Law Sch., 1976-79; U.S. Dept. State rep. to govt. W.Ger. on 20th anniversary of Marshall Plan, 1967; del. jud. conf. U.S. Ct. Appeals (9th cir.), 1982-86. Recipient Spl. Commendation award U.S. Dept. Justice, 1977. Mem. ABA, L.A. County Bar Assn., Beverly Hills Bar Assn. (chmn. criminal law com.), Fed. Bar Assn. Jewish. Contbr. articles to profl. jours. Home: 9100 Wilshire Blvd Beverly Hills CA 90212-3415 Office: US Dist Ct 312 N Spring St Los Angeles CA 90012-4701

WILSON, TERESA ANN, maternal/newborn nurse; b. Iowa City, Sept. 1, 1950; d. Robert Reginald and Patricia Mary (McMahon) W. B of Gen. Studies, U. Iowa, 1972, BSN, 1983; MS in Maternal Newborn Nursing, U. Ariz., 1990. RN, Ariz., Iowa. Staff nurse maternity ward U. Iowa Hosps./Clinics, Iowa City, 1983-85; nurse level III Carondelet St. Joseph's Hosp., Tucson, 1985-94; clin. mgr. labor delivery recovery postpartum Carondelet St. Mary's Hosp., Tucson, 1994-96, nurse level IV, 1997—; instr. childbirth and parenting Carondelet St. Joseph's Hosp., Tucson, 1986-93; project dir., rsch. specialist U. Ariz. Coll. Nursing, Tucson, 1991-92, clin. instr., 1993; nurse level III, Tucson Med. Ctr., 1992-94; cons. Ariz. Dept. Health Svcs., Office of Women & Children's Health, 1996—. Mem. cmty. svcs. com. So. Ariz. March of Dimes, 1990-96, cmty. adv. bd. The Parent Connection Inc., 1992-96; health educator El Rio Health Ctr., Tucson, 1992-95; adv. bd. trainer Woman to Woman Cmty. Prenatal Action Team, 1994—. Mem. Pima County Health Mothers Health Babies Coalition (sec. 1991-96), Assn. Women's Health, Obstetrics and Neonatal Nursing (chpt. coord. 1991-94), Tucson-Almaty Health Care Coalition, Sigma Theta Tau. Office: Carondelet St Mary's Hosp 1601 W Saint Marys Rd Tucson AZ 85745-2623

WILSON, THEODORE HENRY, retired electronics company executive, aerospace engineer; b. Eufaula, Okla., Apr. 23, 1940; s. Theodore V. and Maggie E. (Buie) W.; m. Barbara Ann Tassara, May 16, 1958 (div. 1982); children: Debbie Marie, Nita Leigh, Wilson Axten, Pamela Ann, Brenda Louise, Theodore Henry II, Thomas John; m. Colleen Fagan, Jan. 1, 1983 (div. 1987); m. Karen L. Lerohl, Sept. 26, 1987 (div. 1997); m. Sandra Rivadeneira, Mar. 27, 1997. BSME, U. Calif., Berkeley, 1962; MSME, U. So. Calif., 1964, MBA, 1970, MSBA, 1971. Sr. rsch. engr. N.Am. Aviation Co. div. Rockwell Internat., Downey, Calif., 1962-65; propulsion analyst, supr. div. applied tech. TRW, Redondo Beach, Calif., 1965-67, mem. devel. staff systems group, 1967-71; sr. fin. analyst worldwide automotive dept. TRW, Cleve., 1971-72; contr. systems and energy group TRW, Redondo Beach, 1972-79; dir. fin. control equipment group TRW, Cleve., 1979-82, v.p. fin. control indsl. and energy group, 1982-85; mem. space and def. group TRW, Redondo Beach, 1985-93, ret., 1993; lectr., mem. com. acctg. curriculum UCLA Extension, 1974-79. Mem. Fin. Execs. Inst. (com. govt. bus.), Machinery and Allied Products Inst. (govt. contracts coun.), Nat. Contract Mgmt. Assn. (bd. advisors), Aerospace Industries Assn. (procurement and fin. coun.), UCLA Chancellors Assocs., Tau Beta Pi, Beta Gamma Sigma, Pi Tau Sigma. Republican. Home: 3617 Via La Selva Palos Verdes Peninsula CA 90274-1115

WILSON, VINCENT LEE, geneticist, toxicologist, educator; b. Kentfield, Calif., Dec. 4, 1950; s. Thomas H. Wilson and Elizabeth I. Vincent; married; 2 children. BS in Chemistry, Sonoma State Coll., 1973; MS in Phys. Chemistry, U. Calif., Davis, 1976; PhD in Pharmacology and Toxicology, Oreg. State U., 1980. Cert. clin. lab. dir. in genetic testing svcs., N.Y. Postdoctoral fellow U. So. Calif. Comprehensive Cancer Ctr. and Childrens Hosp., L.A., 1980-82; sr. staff fellow Nat. Cancer Inst./NIH, Bethesda, Md., 1982-88; dir. molecular genetics/oncology The Children's Hosp., Denver, 1988-94; affiliate faculty Colo. State U., Ft. Collins, 1994—; assoc. prof. U. Colo. Sch. Medicine, Denver, 1989-95; vis. assoc. prof. La. State U., Baton Rouge, 1994-95, assoc. prof., Claiborne chair environ. toxicology, 1995—; cons. BioServe Biotechs. Ltd., Laurel, Md., 1994—; chmn. molecular genetics com. Mountain States Regional Genetic Svcs. Network, Denver, 1991-93; mem. ad hoc subcom. on genetics and ins. Gov.'s Commn. on Life and the Law, Denver, 1993. Contbr. numerous articles to profl. jours. Recipient numerous grants in field. Mem. AAAS, Am. Chem. Soc., Am. Assn. for Cancer Rsch., Am. Soc. for Cell Biology, Am. Soc. for Human Genetics, Environment Mutagenesis Soc., Sigma Xi, Phi Kappa Phi, Rho Chi. Home: 3435 W 101st Pl Westminster CO 80030-6753

WILSON, WARREN BINGHAM, artist, art educator; b. Farmington, Utah, Nov. 4, 1920; s. Alma L. and Pearl E. (Bingham) W.; B.S. in Edn., Utah State U., 1943; M.F.A., U Iowa, 1949; m. Donna Myrle VanWagenen, Dec. 22, 1948 (dec. May 1996); children—Vaughn Warren, Michael Alma, Annette, Pauline, Douglas George, Craig Aaron, Robert Kevin. Asst. prof. art Utah State U., Logan, 1949-54; vis. instr. Salt Lake Art Center, Utah, 1952-53; prof. art and edn. Brigham Young U., Provo, Utah, 1954-83; ret., 1983 vis. lectr. ceramics U. Calif., Davis, 1968; fellow in residence Huntington Hartford Found., Pacific Palisades, Calif., 1960-61; vis. instr. Pioneer Crafthouse, Salt Lake City, 1969-70; one-man shows of paintings and/or sculpture include: Salt Lake Art Center, 1951, Yakima Valley Coll., 1962, UCLA, 1962, Mont. State U., Bozeman, 1963, Stanford U., 1963, Wash. State U., Pullman, 1964, Central Wash. State Coll., Ellensburg, 1964, Nev. So. U., Las Vegas, 1967, Ricks Coll., Rexburg, Idaho, 1976, 80, Brigham Young U., Provo, Utah, 1970, 75, 79, 82, retrospective retirement exhbn. of sculpture, ceramics and paintings, 1983; group shows include: Denver Art Mus., 1951, Colorado Springs (Colo.) Fine Arts Center, 1951, Santa Fe Art Mus., 1953, Madison Sq. Gardens, N.Y.C., 1958, Wichita Art Center, 1960, Ceramic Conjunction Invitational, Glendale, Calif., 1973; represented in permanent collections: Utah State Inst. Fine Arts Salt Lake City, Utah State U., Logan, Utah State Fair Assn., Utah Dixie Coll., St. George, Coll. So. Utah, Cedar City, Brigham Young U., also numerous pvt. collections. Asst. dist. commr. Boy Scouts Am., 1975-80; counselor in Ward Bishopric, Ch. of Jesus Christ of Latter-day Saints, 1981-83; scoutmaster, 1954-75; served L.D.S. Mission, Nauvoo, Ill., 1984-85. Served with USAAF, 1943-46. Recipient Am. Craftsman Council merit award, 1964; Silver Beaver award Boy Scouts Am. Republican. Home: 1000 Briar Ave Provo UT 84604-2868

WILSON, WESLEY M., retired lawyer, writer; b. Mangum, Okla., June 21, 1927; s. Frank Henry and Fern (McCool) W.; m. Marjorie Helen Montague, Sept. 7, 1957; children: Larry Arthur, Bruce Alan. BS, Ill. Inst. Tech., Chgo., 1952; MBA, U. Chgo., 1954; JD, U. Wash., 1960. Bar: Wash., 1960. With AT&T Long Lines, Chgo., 1948-50; equipment engr. Western Elec. Co., Chgo., 1952-54; pers. asst., pers. dir. West Coast Telephone Co., Everett, Wash., 1954-57; atty. NLRB, Seattle, 1960-69; labor rels. atty. Wilson & Lofland, Yakima, Wash., 1970-85; part-time mgmt. cons. Donworth & Assocs., Seattle, 1957-58; instr. pers. rels. U. Wash., Seattle, 1958; instr. labor rels. City U., Yakima, 1980-84. Author: Labor Law Handbook and 10 supplements, 1963, 68-85, The Labor Relations Primer, 1973, Know Your Job Rights, 1976, Countries and Cultures of the World, Then and Now, (3 vols.), 1997, Five Languages Made Simpler, French, Italian, English, Spanish, German, 1997. With U.S. Merchant Marines, 1945-46, U.S. Army, 1946-48. Mem. Wash. State Bar Assn., Yakima County Bar Assn. (pres. 1984-85). Home: 3300 Carpenter Rd SE Olympia WA 98503

WILSON, W(ILLIAM) DANIEL, language professional educator; b. Sedalia, Mo., Dec. 3, 1950; children: Adrian, Marguerite. AB, Shimer Coll., 1973; MA, Cornell U., 1976, PhD, 1978. Asst. prof. U. Toronto, Can., 1978-79; asst. prof., postdoctoral rschr. McGill U., Montreal, Que., Can., 1979-83; asst. prof., assoc. prof. dept. German U. Calif. Berkeley, 1983-93, prof., 1993—. Author: Narrative Strategy of Wieland's Don Sylvio, 1981, Humanitaet und Kreuzzugsideologie, 1983, Geheimraete gegen Geheimbuende, 1991; co-editor: Impure Reason: Dialectic of Enlightenment, 1993. Mem. MLA (exec. com. divsn. 18th century German lit. 1993—), Am. Assn. Tchrs. German, Am. Soc. 18th Century Studies, Goethe Soc. Weimar, Goethe Soc. N.Am., German Soc. 18th Century Studies, German Studies Assn., Lessing Soc. (Biberach prize 1979, mem. editl. bd. 1986—). Office: Dept German Univ Calif Berkeley CA 94720-3243

WILSON, WILLIAM J., construction executive. Northwestern U., Evanston, Ill., 1972, Northwestern U., Evanston, Ill., 1974. Pres. Dillingham Constrn. Co., Honolulu, Hawaii, 1974—. Office: Dillingham Constr Corp PO Box 4088 Honolulu HI 96812-4088*

WILTERMOOD, KELLY ANN, artist, marketing consultant; b. Boise, May 20, 1994; d. Warren James and Denise Louise (Jones) Peterson; m. Michael Curtis Wiltermood, May 20, 1994; children: Kyle, Savannah, Kelsey, Calvin. BS in Bus. Mgmt., U. Wash., 1984; MFA, Brigham Young U., 1986. Sales specialist Exxecs, Oakland, Calif., 1986-91; mktg. v.p. Waterpack, Lindon, Utah, 1991—. Exhbns. include Salt Lake City Fine Arts Gallery, 1986, Silver Gallery, Seattle, 1992. Chmn. Columbia Basin Edn. Coun., Moses Lake, Wash., 1994—; mem. Young Republicans, Provo, Utah, 1981-86; campaign mgr. Karl Snow for State Sen. Rep. Party, Provo, 1984; vice-chair Deaconess Med. Ctr. Found., 1994—; troop leader Am. Grand Couler chpt. Girl Scouts U.S.A., 1994—. 1st lt. USCG, 1981-84. Named Young Artist of the Yr. Utah Valley Fine Arts Assn., 1986, Marketer of the Yr. Utah State Marketers Assn., 1989. Mem. Rotary Internat. Republican. Mem. LDS Ch.

WILTON, PETER CAMPBELL, marketing educator; b. Adelaide, S.A., Australia, Jan. 28, 1951; came to U.S., 1975; s. Murray and Kathleen (Ratcliffe) W. B in Commerce with hons., U. New South Wales, Sydney, 1972; PhD in Mgmt., Purdue U., 1979. Product mgr. Colgate Palmolive, Sydney, 1973-75; mktg. prof. U. Calif., Berkeley, 1979-87, 92—; COO Myer Pacific Corp., Melbourne, Australia, 1987-90; sr. assoc. Melbourne U., 1990, Sir Donald Hibberd lectr., 1991; vis. fellow Griffith U., Brisbane, Australia, 1982; vis. assoc. prof. Duke U., Durham, N.C., 1985-86; pres., dir. Applied Mktg. Analysis, Inc., Wilmington, Del., 1987—, Orbis Assocs., San Francisco, 1992—. Contbr. articles to profl. jours. Recipient Mktg. Rsch. Soc. Australia prize, 1973; Australian Govt. fellow, 1975-79; grantee NSF, 1981, 84. Mem. Assn. Pub. Opinion Rsch. (officer 1985), Am. Mktg. Assn. (officer 1982-84), Australian-Am. C. of C. (dir. 1993-95).

WIMMER, GEORGE ALBERT, chiropractor, consultant; b. Ogden, Utah, Sept. 3, 1918; s. Charles Warren and Neta Hortense (Benson) W.; m. Fern Bernice Holley, Oct. 19, 1942; children: Holly Kay, Michael Warren, Connie Louise, Douglas Max, Debra. BS, Weber State Coll., 1980; D Chiropractic, Tex. Chiropractic Coll., 1948, Philosopher of Chiropractic cum laude, 1948. Cook Bob's Bar-b-que, Ogden, 1935-36; night watchman Hill AFB, Ogden, 1941; assoc. Turley Chiropractic Clinic, San Antonio, 1948-50, Wheeler Chiropractic Ctr., Ogden, 1952-59; chiropractor Ogden, 1959-86; sr. cons., assoc. mem. Wimmer Chiropractic Ctr., Ogden, 1986—. Contbr. articles to profl. jours. Pres. Five Pts. Lions Club, Ogden, 1956; v.p. Lake Bonneville Coun., Boy Scouts Am., Ogden, 1957; pres. Ogden (Utah) City Sch. Bd. With USAF, 1941-45. Named Father of Yr., Ogden (Utah) City Coun., 1964. Mem. Lewis Peak Lions Club (bd. dirs., pres. 1990, Pres.'s award 1990). Republican. LDS Ch. Home: 1246 S 775 E Ogden UT 84404-5826

WINCHELL, RICHARD G., urban planning educator, consultant; b. Waverly, Iowa, Aug. 16, 1949; s. Clark D. and Minnie F. (Eckhoff) W.; m. Susan M. Mitchell, Mar. 21, 1990; children: Matthew James, Anne Elizabeth. BA in Sociology and Philosophy, Wartburg Coll., 1971; M of Urban and Regional Planning, U. Colo., Denver, 1972; PhD, Ariz. State U., Tempe, 1982. Cert. planner. Asst. planner City of Huntington Beach, Calif., 1972-73; assoc. planner City of Scottsdale (Ariz.) Long Range Planning, 1973-74; planner Schoneberger, Straub, Florence Assoc. Architects, Phoenix, 1974-75; planning dir. Ft. McDowell (Ariz.) Yavapai Indian Community, 1975-80; dir. Native Am. pub. adminstrn. prog. Ctr. for Pub. Affairs, Ariz. State U., Tempe, 1978-80; asst. prof. geography West Ga. Coll., Carrollton, 1982-86; assoc. prof. urban and regional planning Ea. Wash. U., Cheney, Wash., 1986-93, prof. urban and regional planning, 1993—; mem., vice chair Spokane Housing Authority, 1993—; chair Inland Empire Planner's Assn., 1990-91. Contbg. author: Geography in America, 1992, Human Geography in North America, 1996; co-editor: Planning American Indian Lands, 1997; contbr. articles to profl. jours. Co-founder, bd. dirs. Habitat for Humanity Spokane, 1987-90. Office: Dept Urban and Regional Planning Ea Wash U Cheney WA 99004

WINCHELL, ROBERT ALLEN, government agency administrator, accountant; b. Ft. Monmouth, N.J., Oct. 28, 1945; s. Robert Winslow Winchell; B.A., U. Calif., Santa Barbara, 1967; M.B.A., U. Pa., 1969. CPA, Calif. Air Force Audit Agy., El Segundo, Calif., 1972-73; accountant Scholefield, Bellanca & Co., W. Los Angeles, 1974-75, So. Calif. Gas Co., Los Angeles, 1975-76; auditor Def. Contract Audit Agy., Dept. Def., Los Angeles, 1976-86, supervisory auditor, 1986-96; ret., 1996. Served with AUS, 1969-71; Vietnam. Decorated Bronze Star. Mem. Assn. Govt. Accountants, Am. Inst. C.P.A.'s, Alpha Kappa Psi. Republican. Presbyterian. Club: Los Angeles Country. Home: 2008 California Ave Santa Monica CA 90403-4506

WINCHESTER, ED, protective services official. Chief of police Fresno, Calif. Office: 2326 Fresno St Fresno CA 93721

WINDER, DAVID KENT, federal judge; b. Salt Lake City, June 8, 1932; s. Edwin Kent and Alma Eliza (Cannon) W.; m. Pamela Martin, June 24, 1955; children: Ann, Kay, James. BA, U. Utah, 1955; LLB, Stanford U., 1958. Bar: Utah 1958, Calif. 1958. Assoc. firm Clyde, Mecham & Pratt Salt Lake City, 1958-66; law clk. to chief justice Utah Supreme Ct., 1958-59; dep. county atty. Salt Lake County, 1959-63; chief dep. dist. atty., 1965-66; asst. U.S. atty. Salt Lake City, 1963-65; partner firm Strong & Hanni, Salt Lake City, 1966-77; judge State of Utah Dist. Ct., Salt Lake City, 1977-79; U.S. Dist. judge Utah, 1979-93, chief U.S. Dist. judge, 1993-97; examiner Utah Bar Examiners, 1975-79, chmn., 1977-79. Served with USAF, 1951-52. Mem. Am. Bd. Trial Advocates, Utah State Bar (Judge of Yr. award 1978), Salt Lake County Bar Assn., Calif. State Bar. Democrat. Office: US Dist Ct 235 US Courthouse 350 S Main St Salt Lake City UT 84101-2106

WINDHAM, EDWARD JAMES, bank executive, leasing company executive; b. Salt Lake City, Dec. 13, 1950; s. James Rudolph and Margaret Ann (Griffith) W.; m. Marilyn Ann Kenyon, Mar. 27, 1973 (div. May 1996); children: Ian James (dec.), Kendra Ann. Student, U. Calif., San Diego, 1969-70, 72-74. Cert. mortgage credit examiner HUD; accredited residential originator. Salesman Bonanza Properties, Tustin, Calif., 1976; loan officer Medallion Mortgage, Santa Cruz, Calif., 1976-80; sr. loan officer Cen. Pacific Mortgage, Santa Cruz, 1980-83, v.p., 1983-86; ptnr. Winn Leasing Co., Santa Cruz, 1983-90; v.p. Community West Mortgage, 1986-89, Central Pacific Mortgage, Citrus Heights, Calif., 1989-95; trainer GMAC Mortgage, 1995—; cons. Sr. Nat. Trainer, Contour Inc., San Jose, Calif., 1983-85. Pres. Evergreen Estates Homeowners Assn., Soquel, Calif., 1983-85; treas. Sacramento/Placer chpt. MADD. No. Calif. State champion #3 Nat. Age Group award Am. Bicycle Assn., 1991. Mem. Nat. Assn. Rev. Appraisers and Rev. Underwriters (sr., cert.), Mortgage Bankers Assn. (Willis Bryant scholar 1994), Mensa, Intertel. Republican. Lodge: Masons (master Santa Cruz 1987). Home: PO Box 1087 Truckee CA 96160 Office: GMAC Mortgage 1406 Highland Ave Melbourne FL 32935-6519

WINDHAM, TIMOTHY RAY, healthcare executive; b. Jackson, Miss., Oct. 11, 1963; s. Albert S. and Olivia J. (Ray) W.; m. Susan Charlene Carroll, Feb. 16, 1985. BBA, Millsaps Coll., Jackson, Miss., 1983; postgrad., Loyola Law Sch., L.A., 1994—. Area sales mgr. McRae's Dept. Stores, Vicksburg, Miss., 1987-90; store mgr. S and K Menswear, Jackson, 1990-91; gen. mgr. Abbey Healthcare, L.A., 1991-93; regional account exec. Supercare Healthcare, Industry, Calif., 1993-94; account mgr. Nat. Med. Care, L.A., 1994—. Dist. commr. Boy Scouts Am., 1971—; founding mem. Miss. Indian Cultural Soc., Jackson, 1981—. Recipient Am. Jurisprudence award Bancroft Whitney, 1996. Mem. ABA, ATLA, Calif. Assn. Health Svcs. at Home (adv. com. 1991—), Healthcare Sales Profls. Libertarian. Home: 360 E Essex St Glendora CA 91740 Office: National Medical Care 70 Daisey Ave Pasadena CA 91107

WINDSOR, WILLIAM EARL, consulting engineer, sales representative; b. Evansville, Ind., Jan. 24, 1927; s. Charles H. and Lora E. (Archey) W.; divorced; children: Kim, William, Robert. Student, Purdue U., 1946-50. Field engr. Philco Corp., Phila., 1950-53, Europe, Africa, Arabia; studio ops. engr. Sta. WFBM, Indpls., 1953-55; field engr. RCA Svc. Co., Cherry Hill, N.J., 1955-56; audio facilities engr. ABC, N.Y.C., 1956-62; rsch. engr. Fine Recording, Inc., N.Y.C., 1962-66; chief engr. A & R Recording, Inc., N.Y.C., 1966-68; chief engr., corp. sec. DB Audio Corp., N.Y.C., 1968-70; pres. Studio Cons., Inc., N.Y.C., 1970-72; sr. v.p., v.p., gen. mgr. Quad Eight Electronics-Quad Eight/Westrex, San Fernando, Calif., 1972-85; sr. mktg. exec. Mitsubishi Pro Audio Group, San Fernando, Calif., 1985-89; pres., CEO Quad Eight Electronics, Inc., Valencia, Calif., 1989-90; ind. cons., Valencia, 1991—. Inventor monitor mixer for multitrack audio consoles, 1967, update function for audio console automation, 1973; designer of new architecture for film scoring and film re-recording sound mixing consoles, 1974. Served with USNR, 1945-50. Fellow Audio Engring. Soc. (chmn. N.Y. sect. 1970); mem. Soc. Motion Picture & TV Engrs. Home and Office: 23112 Yvette Ln Valencia CA 91355-3060

WINDY BOY, ALVIN JOHN, SR., tribal councilman; b. Harlem, Mont., May 3, 1951; s. John Sr. and Katherine (First Raised) W.B.; m. Darlene Athena Elliott (dec. Sept. 1995); children: John (dec.), Jaycene, Alvin Jr., Big Wind, Naomi, Eldon. Diploma, Box Elder H.S. Rancher Rocky Boy, Mont., 1957—; tribal councilman Chippewa-Cree Tribe, Rocky Boy, Mont., 1988—; inspector State Brand Office, Helena, Mont.; dancer, 1952-88. Mem. Mont./Wyo. Area Indian Health Bd., Billings, Mont., 1988—, chmn., 1992—; chmn. Rocky Boy Health Bd., 1988—. Recipient Integrity Honor Leadership award Chippewa-Cree Tribe, 1995, Outstanding Performance in Agrl. Devel. award Indian Agrl. Coun., 1995. Mem. Mont./Wyo. Stockgrowers Assn. (sec. 1990-96). Democrat. Office: Chippewa Cree Tribe RR # 1 Box 544 Box Elder MT 59521

WINEBERG, HOWARD, research director; b. N.Y.C., Aug. 30, 1955; s. Moe and Ruth (Blinder) W. BA, Bowling Green (Ohio) State U., 1977, MA, 1980; PhD, Johns Hopkins U., 1985. Demographer Indian Nations Coun. of Govts., Tulsa, 1985; asst. dir. Population Rsch. Ctr., prof. urban studies and planning Portland (Oreg.) State U., 1986—; co-founder Oreg. Demographic Group, Portland, 1990; Oreg. rep. to Fed.-State Coop. Program for Population Estimates, 1986—; mem. steering com. Fed.-State Coop. Program for Population Estimates, 1994—. Author: Do All Trails Lead to Oregon? Population Estimates for Oregon 1980-90, 91, 92, 93, 94, 95, 96; contbr. articles to profl. jours. Johns Hopkins U. fellow, 1980-82; Children's Svcs. Commn., grantee, 1989. Mem. Internat. Soc. for Philos. Enquiry, Population Assn. Am., Population Reference Bur., Soc. for Study of Social Biology, So. Demographic Assn., Oreg. Acad. Sci., Internat. Platform Assn. Office: Portland State U Population Rsch Ctr 1604 SW 10th Ave Portland OR 97201

WINEMAN, PAUL RAYMOND, JR., contract negotiator; b. Hollywood, Calif., Oct. 22, 1936; s. Paul R. and Frances Neale (Dienst) W.; m. Eleanore Connelly, Dec. 15, 1968 (div. Nov. 7, 1971). BA in Comm., U. Wash., 1958; MA in Arab Studies, Am. U. Beirut, 1967. Regional dir. Avco Corp., Beirut, 1969-73, United Tech., Inc., Beirut, 1973-77; pres. P.R. Wineman and Assoc., L.A., 1977—. Capt. U.S. Army, 1958-65. Mem. Rotary. Home and Office: 4267 Marina City Dr Unit 1108 Marina Del Rey CA 90292-5812

WINFIELD, ARMAND GORDON, international plastics consultant, educator; b. Chgo., Dec. 28, 1919; grad. Newark Acad. 1937; BS, Franklin and Marshall Coll., 1941; postgrad. U. N.Mex., 1941, State U. Iowa, 1944, Washington U., St. Louis, 1948-50; m. Lillian Tsukea Kubota, June 8, 1951 (dec. Dec. 1965); m. Barbara Jane La Barge, July 23, 1966 (dec. May 1992). Undergrad. tchg. fellow Franklin and Marshall Coll., 1939-41; owner Winfield Fine Art in Jewelry, N.Y.C., 1945-48; rsch. dir. Hanley Plastics Co. divsn. Wallace Pencil Co., St. Louis, 1955-57; plastic cons. engr. DeBell & Richardson, Inc., Hazardville, Conn., 1957-64; exec. v.p. Crystopal Ltd., Hazardville, Conn., 1963-64; pres., CEO Armand G. Winfield Inc., Santa Fe, 1963-93; rsch. prof. mech. engring., dir. Tng. and Rsch. Inst. for Plastics, U. N.Mex., Albuquerque, 1993—; mem. faculty Harris Tchrs. Coll., 1950, dept. Engring. Washington U., St. Louis, 1956, Yale U., 1960-61; adviser USIA on plastics show to tour USSR, 1960-61; chmn. SPR Traveling Exhibition: Plastics-A New Dimension in Bldg., 1960-62; vis. critic in plastics Sch. Architecture, CCNY, 1968-69; plastics cons. indsl. design dept., faculty Pratt Inst., Bklyn., 1964-70, instr. prodn. methods, 1968-70; lectr. U. Hartford, U. Kans., 1970, U. Ariz., 1978, Calif. Poly. State U., 1980, numerous others; adj. prof. plastics engring. U. Lowell (Mass.), 1978-81; spkr. Acoplásticos conf., Cartagena, Colombia, 1986; conceived and directed the building of 13 installations at the N.Y. Worlds Fair, 1962-63; U. N.Mex. del., paper presenter XVIII Pacific Sci. Congress, Beijing, 1995; trustee Plastics Inst. Am., Lowell, Mass., 1996—. Mem. Vol. in Tech. Assistance, 1983—; bd. dir. Santa Fe Crime Stoppers, 1980-94, chmn., 1986, 87, carnival chmn., 1983, 84. U.S. State Dept. Am. Specialist grantee to USSR, 1961, UNIDO grantee, 1968-69, 1971; recipient Santa Fe Crime Stoppers award, 1980-94, 94. UNIDO expert in newer fibers and composites, India, 1977, cons. glass fibers and composites, Colombia, 1979. Fellow Plastics and Rubber Inst. (Eng., 1970); mem. Soc. Advancement Materials and Process Engring. (chpt. chmn. 1986, 87, 94, 95, 96, 97, editor newsletter 1987, 94, 95, special status hon. sr. mem. life, 1994), Soc. Plastics Engrs. (pres. Western New Eng. sect. 1963-64, v.p. N.Y. sect. 1968-69, chmn. regional tech. conf. 1967, historian ann. tech. conf. 1968), Soc. Plastic Industry, Plastics Pioneers Assn. Author: The Alexian Brothers, 1951; The Merchants Exchange of St. Louis, 1953, Plastics For Architects, Artists and Interior Designers, 1961, 100 Years Young, 1968, Inventors Handbook, 1990; also chpts. in books, monthly column in Display World Mag., 1965-68, Designer Mag., 1971-72, Museum Scope, 1976-77; spl. exhibitions at The Smithsonian Inst., Washington, 1988—, Cooper Hewitt, N.Y.C., 1993, Mus. Sci. and Industry, London, 1994, Franklin & Marshall Coll. Mus., 1996; numerous articles on plastics; patentee of mass-producible process for embedding specimens in acrylics; patentee in the field. Office: U NM Sch Engring TRIP 109 Pine St NE Albuquerque NM 87106-4553

WING, JANET ELEANOR SWEEDYK BENDT, nuclear scientist; b. Detroit, Oct. 12, 1925; d. Jack and Florence C. (Springman) Sweedyk; m. Philip J. Bendt, Sept. 4, 1948 (div. Jan. 1972); children: Karen Ann Bendt Sox, Paul Philip, Barbara Jean Bendt Medlin, LindaSue Bendt Garner; m. G. Milton Wing, Aug. 26, 1972 (div. Jan. 1987). BSEE with distinction, Wayne State U., 1947; MA in Physics, Columbia U., 1950; postgrad., U. Oreg., 1966-67, U. N.Mex., 1968-71. Research engr. Gen. Motors Corp., Detroit, 1944-48; physicist, mathematician Manhattan Project Columbia U., N.Y.C., 1950-51; mem. research staff Los Alamos (N.Mex.) Nat. Lab, 1951-57, 68-94; retired; project leader Los Alamos (N.Mex.) Nat. Lab, 1976-81, asst. group leader, 1980-84, assoc. group leader, 1985-89. Bd. dirs., treas. Esperanza Shelter, Santa Fe, N. Mex., 1984—. Mem. Am. Nuclear Soc., AAAS, Women in Sci. and Engring., Los Alamos Women in Sci., Sigma Xi, Tau Beta Pi.

WING, ROGER, management consultant; b. N.Y.C., May 26, 1945; s. John A. and Norma M. (LeBlanc) W.; m. Judith A. King, June 7, 1963 (div. 1980); m. Peggy J. McFall, Aug. 27, 1983; children: Roger, Karin, Nicole, Sean, Nathan, Alexandra. BBA, Cleve. State U., 1972, MBA, 1975. Supr. Am. Greetings Co., Brooklyn, Ohio, 1969-74; dir. Revco D.S. Inc., Twinsburg, Ohio, 1974-78; mgr. Hughes Aircraft Co., Los Angeles, 1978-79; sr. dir., v.p. Continental Airlines, Los Angeles, 1979-81; dir., practice leader Coopers & LyBrand, Los Angeles, 1981-83; pres. Huntington Cons. Group, Huntington Beach, Calif., 1983—; prof. Cleve. State U., 1977-78. Named Systems Man of Yr., Assn. Systems Mgmt., 1978. Office: The Huntington Cons Group 8531 Topside Cir Huntington Beach CA 92646-2117

WINGARD, DIANA KAY, financial services executive; b. Indepedence, Mo., Apr. 2, 1955. Lic. real estate sales assoc., Calif. Loan processor Dirs. Mortgage, Inc., Van Nuys, Calif., 1985-86; asst. br. mgr. builder/tract divsn. Dirs. Mortgage Loan Corp., Van Nuys, Calif., 1990-91; supr. builder/processing divsn. Dynesty Mortgage, Inc., Van Nuys, 1986-88; asst. v.p., dir. residential lending builder & tract divsn. Windtree Mortgage Co., Sherman Oaks, Calif., 1988-90; pres., CEO Profl. Contract Svcs., Sherman Oaks, 1990—. spkr. at confs. in field. Mem. Assn. Profl. Mortgage Women, Calif. Assn. Mortgage Brokers, Mortgage Brokers Assn. Am., Am. Entrepreneur Soc. Office: Profl Contract Svcs 14542 Ventura Blvd Ste 200 Sherman Oaks CA 91403-5512

WINGATE, MARCEL EDWARD, speech educator; b. New Castle, Pa., Feb. 27, 1923; s. Morton Harvey and Elizabeth (Martin) Wingett; m. Elaine C. Kayser, June 8, 1948 (div. July 1968); children: Nancy, Amy, Jennifer; m. Cicely Anne Johnston, June 7, 1969; children: Marcel Richard, Cicely Anna Marie. BA, Grinnell (Iowa) Coll., 1948; MA, U. Wash., 1952, PhD, 1956. Lic. psychologist, Wash., N.Y. Psychologist Childrens Hosp., Seattle, 1953-57, Wash. State C.P. Ctr., Seattle, 1954-57; asst. prof. U. Wash., Seattle, 1957-65, assoc. prof., 1965-68; prof. SUNY, Buffalo, 1968-73, U. Ariz., Tucson, 1973-75; prof. speech, hearing sci. Wash. State U., Pullman, 1975—; cons. psychologist St. Mary's Hosp., Lewiston, N.Y., 1969-73; internationally recognized expert on stuttering. Author: Stuttering: Theory and Treatment, 1976, Structure of Stuttering, 1988; assoc. editor Jour. Speech/Hearing Disorders, 1966-73; editorial cons. Jour. Speech/Hearing Rsch., 1974-80; editorial bd. Jour. Fluency Disorders, 1974—; contbr. articles to profl. jours., chpts. to books. With U.S. Army, 1942-45, ETO. Fellow Am. Speech and Hearing Assn. Home: RR 2 Box 102 Pullman WA 99163-9605 Office: Wash State U Speech and Hearing Sci Pullman WA 99164-2420

WINMILL, B. LYNN, judge; m. Judy Winmill; 3 children. BA, Idaho State U.; JD, Harvard U. Atty. Holland and Hart, Denver; trial lawyer Hawley, Troxell, Ennis and Hawley, Pocatello, Idaho; judge Idaho Sixth Jud. Dist. Ct., Pocatello, Idaho, 1987—. Office: US Dist Ct Idaho 6th Fl 550 W Fort St MCS 040 Boise ID 83724

WINN, H. RICHARD, surgeon; b. Chester, Pa., 1947. MD, U. Pa., 1968; BA, Princeton U., 1964. Diplomate Am Bd. Neurological Surgeons. Intern U. Hosp., Cleve., 1968-69, resident surgery, 1969-70; resident neurolog. surgery U. Hosp. Va., Charlottesville, 1970-74; neurol. surgeon U. Wash. Hosp., Seattle, 1983—; prof., chmn. neurol. surgery U. Wash., Seattle, 1983—; dir. Am. Bd. Neurol. Surgery. Founding editor Neurosurgical Clinics of North Amercia; mem. editl. bd. Jour. Neurosurgery, Am. Jour. Physiology, Am. Jour. Surgery. Fellow AAAS, Soc. Brit. Neurol. Surgeons (hon.); mem. AMA, Coll. Neurol. Surgery, Am. Assn. Neurol. Surgeons. Office: U Wash Dept Neurosurg 325 9th Ave # 359766 Seattle WA 98104-2420

WINN, ROBERT CHARLES, retired military officer, aeronautical engineer, consultant; b. Chgo., Sept. 4, 1945; s. Bart James and Dorothy Eleanor (Smith) W.; m. Kathleen Nowak, Aug. 3, 1968; children: Eric Michael, Kara Michelle. BSME, U. Ill., 1968, MSME, 1969; PhD in Mech. Engring., Colo. State U., 1982. Registered profl. engr., Colo. Enlisted USAF, 1969, advanced through grades to lt. col., 1991; instr. pilot 14 student squad USAF, Columbus AFB, Mo., 1970-74; instr. pilot 61 Tactical Airlift Squad USAF, Little Rock AFB, 1974-76; asst. prof. dept. aeronautics USAF Acad., Colorado Springs, Colo., 1976-79, assoc. prof., 1982-90; chief scientist USAF European Office of Aerospace R&D, London, 1986-88; prof. USAF Acad., 1988-91; adj. prof. Colo. Tech. Coll., 1991—; cons. Colorado Springs, 1991-94; sr. cons. Engring. Sys., Inc., Colorado Springs, 1994—. Contbr. articles to profl. jours. Mem. AIAA (assoc. fellow, vice chmn. Rocky Mountain sect. 1985, sec. 1984, mem. terrestrial energy systems nat. tech. com. 1984-91, dep. dir. energy conversion 1989—). Roman Catholic. Office: 4775 Centennial Blvd Ste 106 Colorado Springs CO 80919-3309

WINNER, CHERIE LYNN, journalist, author; b. Salt Lake City, Sept. 16, 1955; d. Vernon Max and Helen Elizabeth Olsen; m. Robert William Winner, May 21, 1987 (dec. Aug. 1993). BS in Zoology, Ohio State U., 1977, MS in Zoology, 1980, PhD in Zoology, 1982. Postdoctoral rschr. Baylor Coll. Medicine, Houston, 1982-83, Washington U. Med. Sch., St. Louis, 1983-85; asst. prof. dept. zoology Miami U., Oxford, Ohio, 1985-90; reporter Casper (Wyo.) Star-Tribune, 1996. Author: (children's books) Salamanders, 1993 (Outstanding Sci. trade Book for Children 1993-94), Coyotes, 1995 (Outstanding Sci. Trade Book for Children 1995-96), The Sunflower Family, 1996 (Outstanding Sci. Trade Book for Children 1996-97); contbr. numerous articles to profl. jours. Sec., newsletter editor Sierra Club-Snowy Range Group, Laramie, Wyo., 1994-96. Recipient Grad. Tchg. award Ohio State U., 1982, Grad. Leadership award, 1982; NIH postdoctoral fellow, 1984-85. Mem. Am. Soc. Journalists and Authors, Soc. Children's Book Writers and Illustrators.

WINNER, KARIN, newspaper editor. Editor San Diego Union-Tribune. Office: Copley Press Inc 350 Camino De La Reina San Diego CA 92108-3003

WINNICK, KAREN B., writer; b. Bklyn., June 28, 1946; d. Sandy and Mimi (Sclar) Binkoff; m. Gary Winnick, Dec. 24, 1972; children: Adam, Alex, Matthew. BFA, Syracuse U., 1968. Author, illustrator (picture book) Mr. Lincoln's Whiskers, 1996, Sandro's Dolphin, 1980, Patch and the Strings, 1977. Bd. libr. overseers mem. Tufts U., 1994—; mem. adv. bd. Simon Weisenthal Book Award, 1996. Mem. Soc. Children's Book Writers.

WINOGRAD, MORLEY ALEC, sales executive; b. Detroit, Nov. 12, 1942; s. Daniel and Lillian Winograd; m. Roberta H. Leib, Sept. 29, 1942; children: Lesley, Randy, Jennifer. BBA, U. Mich., 1963. Sec.-treas. Danby's Stores For Men, Inc., Detroit, 1964-72; chmn. Mich. Dem. Party, Lansing, 1973-79; dist. mgr. Mich. Bell Telephone Co., Detroit, 1980-82; br. mgr. AT&T, Southfield, Mich., 1983-89; pres. AT&T V.S.E., Cin., 1990-91; sales v.p. AT&T, L.A., 1992—; faculty mem. Sch. for Managing, Assn. for Quality and Participation, Mystic, Conn., 1995—. Co-author: Taking Control: Politics in the Information Age, 1996. Bd. mem. Greater L.A. World Trade Ctr., Long Beach, Calif., 1993—; pres., sec. Assn. State Dem. Chmn., Washington, 1979-80; mem. Dem. Nat. Com., Washington, 1980-92; mem. exec. com. Calif. Dem. Leadership Coun., San Francisco, 1993—; chmn. Tech. for Results in Elem. Edn., L.A., 1995—; treas. Inst. for New California. Mem. Asian Bus. League So. Calif. (adv. bd. 1994—), Calif. Hispanic C. of C. (adv. bd. 1993—), L.A. County Office Edn. Tech. for Learning Initiative (exec. coun. 1995—). Jewish. Home: 2165 Canyon Rd Arcadia CA 91006-1506 Office: AT&T 1000 Corporate Center Dr Monterey Park CA 91754-7600

WINSKILL, ROBERT WALLACE, manufacturing executive; b. Tacoma, Oct. 30, 1925; s. Edward Francis William and Margaret Eyre (Myers) W. BA, Coll. Puget Sound, Tacoma, 1947. Field rep. Ray Burner Co., San Francisco, 1954-57, nat. sales mgr., 1960-69; v.p. sales Western Boiler Co., L.A., 1957-60; gen. sales mgr. Ray Burner Co., San Francisco, 1973-82; v.p., chief exec. officer Orr & Sembower, Inc., Middletown, Pa., 1969-73; pres. Combustion Systems Assocs., Inc., Mill Valley, Calif., 1982—; bd. dirs. Sino-Am. Boiler Engring. Co., Shanghai, China, S. T. Johnson Co., Oakland, Calif. Contbr. articles to profl. jours.; columnist Marin Scope, Mill Valley Harold, 1991—. With U.S. Army, 1943-44. Mem. ASME, Olympic Club (San Francisco), Rotary. Office: Combustion Systems Assocs Inc PO Box 749 Mill Valley CA 94942-0749

WINSLEY, SHIRLEY J., state legislator, insurance agent; b. Fosston, Minn., June 9, 1934; d. Nordin Marvel Miller and Helga Christine Sorby; m. Gordon Perry Winsley, July 19, 1952; children: Alan, Nancy. ABS, Tacoma C.C., 1970; BA, Pacific Luth., 1971. Mem. legis. staff Wash. Senate, Olympia, 1971-75; appraiser Pierce County Assessor, Tacoma, 1971-75; mem. Wash. Ho. of Reps., Olympia, 1974, 77-92; exec. dir. Lakewood (Wash.) Chamber, 1975-76; mem. Wash. Senate, 1993—; ins. agent, family counselor New Tacoma Cemetary & Funeral Home, 1996—. Republican. Lutheran. Home: 1109 Garden Cir Fircrest WA 98466

WINSLOW, BETTE KILLINGSWORTH, dance studio owner; b. Springfield, Mo., Dec. 10, 1919; d. Troy Kenwood andWinifred Elizabeth (Reed) Killingsworth; m. Kenelm Crawford Winslow, Sept. 5, 1947; children: Katherine, Jeanette, Kenelm, Elizabeth, Priscilla. Student, Christian Coll., 1937-39, Perry Mansfield Theater Arts Camp, summer 1938; studied with, George Balanchine, 1939-41, Pierre Vladimiroff, Anatole O'Boukhoff, Anatole Vilzak, Ludmila Shollar, Muriel Stuart, Jack Stanley, Jose Fernandez, Doris Humphrey, Jose Limon, Martha Graham, Nimura. Dancer Vogue Ballet, Rodeo, Vernon Youman Concert Revue, Met. Opera Ballet, N.Y.C., Boston and Can., 1939-44; program dir. overseas clubs ARC, New Guinea, Philippines and Korea, 1944-47; owner dance studios, pvt. tchr. dance Hermon, N.Y., Ishpeming, Mich., and Taos, N.Mex., 1947—; dir. Dance Taos summer workshops, 1986—. Choreographer numerous dance prodns., original ballets. Recipient Disting. Alumni award Columbia Coll., 1996. Home: PO Box 927 El Prado NM 87529 Office: PO Box 425 Taos NM 87571

WINSLOW, DAVID ALLEN, chaplain, naval officer; b. Dexter, Iowa, July 12, 1944; s. Franklin E. and Inez Maude (McPherson) W.; m. Frances Lavinia Edwards, June 6, 1970; children: Frances, David. BA, Bethany Nazarene Coll., 1968; MDiv, Drew U., 1971, STM, 1973. Ordained to ministry United Meth. Ch., 1969; cert. FEMA instr. Clergyman, 1969—; assoc. minister All Sts. Episcopal. Ch., Millington, N.J., 1969-70; asst. minister Marble Collegiate Ch., N.Y.C., 1970-71; min. No. N.J. Conf., 1971-75; joined chaplain corps USN, 1974, advanced through grades to lt. comdr., 1980, ret., 1995; exec. dir. Marina Ministries, 1995—. Author: The Utmost for the Highest, 1993, Epiphany: God Still Speaks, 1994, Be Thou My Vision, 1994, Evening Prayers At Sea, 1995, Wiseman Still Adore Him, 1995, God's Power At Work, 1996; (with Walsh) A Year of Promise: Meditations, 1995, editor: The Road to Bethlehem: Advent, 1993, Preparation for Resurrecton: Lent, 1994, God's Promise: Advent, 1994, The Way of the Cross: Lent, 1995; contbr. articles to profl. jours. Bd. dirs. disaster svcs. and family svcs. ARC, Santa Ana, Calif., 1988-91, Child Abuse Prevention Ctr., Orange, Calif., 1990-91; bd. dirs. Santa Clara County Coun. Chs., 1993-94, del., 1995—; bd. dirs. The Salvation Army Adult Rehab. Ctr. Adv. Coun., San Jose, Calif; bd. dirs. disaster svcs. ARC, Santa Clara Valley chpt., San Jose, 1995—. Mem. ACA, USN League (hon.), Sunrise Exch. Club (chaplain 1989-91), Dick Richards Breakfast Club (chaplain 1988-91), Masons (charter), Shriners, Scottish Rite. Home: 20405 Via Volante Cupertino CA 95014-6318

WINSLOW, NORMAN ELDON, business executive; b. Oakland, Calif., Apr. 4, 1938; s. Merton Conrad and Roberta Eilene (Drennen) W.; m. Betty June Cady, Jan. 14, 1962 (div. Aug. 1971); 1 child, Todd Kenelm; m. Ilene Ruth Jackson, Feb. 3, 1979. BS, Fresno (Calif.) State U., 1959. Asst. mgr. Proctors Jewelers, Fresno, 1959-62; from agt. to dist. mgr. Allstate Ins. Co., Fresno, 1962-69; ins. agt. Fidelity Union Life Ins., Dallas, 1969-71; dist. and zone mgr. The Southland Corp., Dallas, 1971-78; owner Ser-Vis-Etc., Goleta, Calif., 1978—. Pub./editor FranchiserviceNews; author: Hands in Your Pockets, 1992; contbr. numerous articles to profl. jours. With USAFNG, 1961-67. Mem. Nat. Coalition of Assn. of 7-11 Franchises (affiliate, mem. adv. bd. Glendale, Calif. chpt. 1984-90), Am. Arbitration Assn. (expert witness/cons. Calif. superior cts.). Republican. Methodist. Home: 1179 N Patterson Ave Santa Barbara CA 93117-1813 Office: Ser-Vis-Etc PO Box 8276 Goleta CA 93118-2276

WINSLOW, PHILIP CHARLES, agriculturist, marketing consultant; b. Carthage, Ind., Jan. 13, 1924; s. William Howard and Ione (Morris) W.; m. Arlis Brown, Oct. 6, 1951; children: Mark, Jay, Julie. BS, Purdue U., 1948. Successively dist. mgr., regional product mgr., asst. div. sales mgr., div. sales mgr., nat. product mgr., nat. mktg. mgr. Ralston Purina Co., 1950-1970; v.p. mktg. Namolco, Inc., Willow Grove, Pa., 1971-84; dir. mktg. Liquid Products Divsn. Cargill, Inc., Willow Grove, 1984-85; nat. mktg. cons. Cargill, Inc., Mpls., 1986-88; v.p. The Montgomery Group, Huntingdon, Tenn., 1989—; pres., dir. Winslow Farms, Inc., Carthage, 1982—. Sgt. U.S. Army, 1948-50. Mem. Am. Feed Industry Assn. (com. chmn. 1975-76, com. sec. 1982-83), Big 10 Club Phila. (pres. 1981), Shadowridge Golf Club (sec.-treas. 1992, pres. 1993, bd. govs. 1993-94), Purdue Club Phila. (v.p. 1982-83, pres. 1983-86), Purdue Club San Diego. Republican. Lutheran. Home and Office: 1305 La Salle Ct Vista CA 92083-8945 *Personal philosophy: Respected people accomplish respectable results.*

WINSLOW, WARDELL V., writer, editor; b. San Francisco, May 19, 1927; s. Edward Taber and Roberta (Jennings) W.; m. Marilyn Mills, Apr. 5, 1953 (div. Apr. 1979); children: Lynne Mary, Wendy Ann, Edward Taber, Mary Southern Winslow Hanson; m. Holly Haste, June 23, 1979; stepchildren: Holly Anne Thuman, Carol Lynn Thuman, Teresa Thuman Bunnage. BS in Journalism, Naval Sci., U. Colo., 1948; postgrad., Stanford U., 1950-52. Reporter Palo Alto (Calif.) Times, 1948-52, reporter politics, 1954-58, assoc. editor, 1959-79; congl. fellow Am. Polit. Sci. Assn., Washington, 1958-59; editl. page editor Peninsula Times Tribune, Palo Alto, 1979-81, mng. editor, 1981-84; prin. Ward Winslow Writing, Palo Alto, 1985—. Prin. author: Palo Alto: A Centennial History, 1993; author: Pages From a Palo Alto Editor's Scrapbook, 1994; editor: The Making of Silicon Valley: A 100-Year Renaissance, 1996; developmental editor/agt.: California Divorce Handbook, 1990, 3d edit., 1995. Lt. (j.g.) USNR, 1952-54. Mem. Nat. Conf. Editl. Writers (membership chmn. 1969-72), Soc. of Profl. Journalists (No. Calif. chpt. past pres.). Episcopalian. Home and Office: 193 Hemlock Ct Palo Alto CA 94306-4623

WINSOR, DAVID JOHN, cost consultant; b. Duluth, Minn., May 27, 1947; s. Alphonse Joseph and Sylvia Mae (Petrich) W.; m. Linda Kay Sanders, Dec. 22, 1968 (div. Mar. 1974). BA in Bus., U. Puget Sound, 1978; M of Mech. Engring., Pacific Western U., 1979. Jr. engr. J.P. Head Mech., Inc., Richland, Wash., 1965-67; estimator, project engr. Subs. of Howard S. Wright Co., Seattle, 1972-75; sr. estimator Massart Co., Seattle, 1975-76; project mgr. Univ. Mechanical, Portland, Oreg., 1976; cons. Kent, Wash., 1976-79; owner Leasair, Federal Way, Wash., 1978-83; pres., owner Expertise Engring. & Cons., Inc., Bellevue, Wash., 1979-82, 90—; cons. Winsor & Co., Walnut Creek, Calif., 1983—; cons. NASA, Mountain View, Calif., 1986, Lockheed Missile & Space, Sunnyvale, Calif., 1984-87, The Boeing Co., Seattle, 1979-82. Author: (with others) Current Construction Costs, 1987, 88, 89, Construction Materials Inventory Systems, 1973, 74, Construction Inflation Trends, 1975, 76, 77, 78, 79, 80, 81, Construction Claims and Prevention, 1981, 82. Served to sgt. USAF, 1967-71. Mem. Jaycees (state dir. 1972-73, state chmn. 1973-74). Republican. Roman Catholic.

WINSTON, HAYDN, lawyer; b. Doncaster, Yorkshire, Eng., Feb. 27, 1958; s. Joseph H. and Anita M. (Jones) W.; m. Pamela Dee Walters, May 20, 1986; 1 child, Meredith S. BS in Geology, U. So. Colo., Pueblo, 1984; JD with honors, U. Wyo., Laramie, 1989. Bar: Calif., Colo., U.S. Dist. Ct. Colo., U.S. Dist. Ct. (so. dist.) Calif. Assoc. Best, Best & Krieger, Riverside, Calif., 1989-92; assoc. Leavenworth & Lockhead, Glenwood Springs, Colo., 1992-94; pres. Haydn Winston, P.C., Glenwood Springs, 1994—; v.p. 9th Jud. Dist. Bar Assn., Glenwood Springs, 1993—. Editor: Law Rev. (land and water law rev.), 1986-89. Mem. Colo. Bar Assn., Colo. Trial Lawyers Assn. Office: Haydn Winston PC 214 8th St Ste 209 Glenwood Springs CO 81601-3312

WINTER, DONALD CHRISTOPHER, computer systems architect; b. Hull, Eng., Feb. 23, 1944; came to U.S., 1966; s. Henry and Ethel (Bradley) W.; m. Christine Alice Kopp, June 6, 1969; 1 child, Henry Christopher. BSc with honors, U. Southampton, Eng., 1965; MS, U. Cin., 1970. Engr. Avco Electronics, Cin., 1966-70, Xerox Electro-optical sys., Pasadena, Calif., 1970-83; sys. engr. Xerox Spl. Info. Sys., Pasadena, 1983-93; solutions architect Xerox Integrated Sys., Pasadena, 1993; sys. architect Xerox Printing Sys., El Segundo, Calif., 1994—. Mem. IEEE, Assn. for Computing Machinery, Instn. of Elec. Engrs. (assoc.), Mensa.

WINTER, RICHARD SAMUEL, JR., computer training company owner, writer; b. Denver, Mar. 17, 1958; s. Richard Samuel and Jerryl Dene (Gano) W.; m. Karen Annette Hansen, May 27, 1989. Student, Griffith U., Brisbane, Australia, 1979; BA in Internat. Environment, Colo. Coll., 1981; MA in Pub. Adminstrn., U. Colo., Denver, 1989. Range aide U.S. Forest Svc., Desert Exptl. Station, Utah, 1976-77; pub. health investigator, lab. technician Denver Health Dept., 1982-84; projects mgr. Colo. Statesman, Denver, 1984-85; editor Mile Hi Prep, Denver, 1985; fin. analyst Pan Am. World Airways, N.Y.C., 1985-88; sr. ptnr., owner PRW, Denver, 1988—; pres. info. systems Trainers, Denver, 1994. Co-author, revisor: MicroRef Quick Reference Bd. Lotus 1-2-3 Rel. 3.0, 1990, MicroRef Quick Reference Gd. Lotus 1-2-3 Rel. 2.2, 1990, Que Q&A QueCards, 1991, Que 123 Release 2.3 QuickStart, 1991, Que 123 Release 2.4 QuickStart, 1992, Que Look Your Best with Excel, 1992, Que Excel for Windows Sure Steps, 1993, Que Using Lotus 123 Release 4, 1994, Que Using Excel 5, 1994, Que Using Microsoft Office, 1994, Que Using Microsoft Office 95, 1995, Que Special Edition Using Microsoft Office Professional for Windows 95, 1996, Que Special Edition Using Microsoft Office 97 Professional, 1997, Que Microsoft Access 97 Quick Reference Guide, 1997. Chmn. N.Y. Victims for Victims, N.Y.C., 1986-87; bd. dirs. Colo. Common Cause, Denver, 1984-85; steering com. Voter Registration "Motor Voter" Amendment, Denver, 1983-84; pres. Broadway Commons Homeowners Assn., Denver, 1982-84; pres. Info. Systems Trainers, 1994, bd. dirs. 1990-96. Recipient Vigil Honor, Order of the Arrow, 1976, Disting. Svc. award Info. Sys. Trainers, 1996. Mem. Phi Beta Kappa, Alpha Lambda Delta.

WINTERLIN, WRAY LAVERN, environmental chemist emeritus, educator; b. Sioux City, Iowa, July 20, 1930; s. William and Nettie (Larson) W.; m. Arlene Fay Harper, Nov. 15, 1929; children: Jerry and Larry (twins), Dwight. Student, Morningside Coll., 1948-50, Iowa State U., 1950-51; BS, U. Nebr., 1955, MS, 1956. Jr. chemist Calif. Dept. Water Resources, Sacramento, 1958-59; staff rsch. assoc., exptl. sta. specialist U. Calif., Davis, 1959-79, lectr., environ. chemist, 1979—, dir. pesticide residue and trace analysis lab., 1965-84, acting chmn. dept. environ. toxicology, 1972; instr. workshops Nat. Inst. Environ. Health Scis., Cairo, Egypt, 1982. Contbr. to numerous profl. publs. With U.S. Army, 1951-53, Korea. Grantee numerous fed. and state agys., indsl. orgns. Mem. AAAS, Am. Chem. Soc., Sigma Xi, Gamma Sigma Delta. Republican.

WINTERMAN, CRAIG L., lawyer; b. Denver, Oct. 29, 1950. BS, U. Oreg., 1973; JD, Southwestern U., 1976. Bar: Calif. 1977, U.S. Dist. Ct. (cen. dist.) Calif. 1977, U.S. Dist. Ct. (so. and no. dists.) Calif. 1980, U.S. Ct. Appeals (9th cir.) 1980, U.S. Supreme Ct. 1980. Ptnr. Herzfeld & Rubin, L.A. Mem. State Bar Calif., Assn. So. Calif. Def. Counsel, Assn. Advancement Auto. Medicine. Office: Herzfeld & Rubin 1925 Century Park E Los Angeles CA 90067-2701

WINTER-NEIGHBORS, GWEN CAROLE, special education educator, art educator; b. Greenville, S.C., July 14, 1938; d. James Edward and Evelyn (Lee) Walters; m. David M. Winter Jr., Aug., 1963 (dec. Feb. 1982); children: Robin Carole Winter, Charles G. McCuen, Dustin Winter TeBrugge; m. Thomas Frederick Neighbors, Mar. 24, 1989. BA in Edn. & Art, Furman U., 1960, MA in Psychology, 1967; cert. in guidance/pers., Clemson U., 1981; EdD in Youth & Mid. Childhood Edn., Nova Southeastern U., 1988; postgrad., U. S.C., Spartanburg, 1981-89; cert. clear specialist instruction, Calif. State U., Northridge, 1991; art edn. cert., Calif. State U., L.A., 1990—; postgrad., Glendale U., 1996—. Cert. tchr. art, elem. edn., psychology, secondary guidance, S.C. Tchr. 7th grade Greenville Jr. H.S., 1960-63; art tchr. Wade Hampton H.S., Greenville, 1963-67; prin. adult edn. Woodmont H.S., Piedmont, S.C., 1983-85, Mauldin H.S., Greenville and Mauldin, S.C., 1981; tchr. ednl. psychology edn. dept. Allen U., Columbia, S.C., 1969; activity therapist edn. dept. S.C. Dept. of Corrections, Columbia, 1973-76; art specialist gifted edn. Westcliffe Elem. Sch., Greenville, 1976-89; tchr. self-contained spl. day class Elysian Heights Elem. Sch., Echo Park and L.A., Calif., 1989-91; art tchr. medh. drawing Sch. Dist. Greenville County Blue Ridge Mid. Sch., Greer, S.C., 1991-95; participant nat. conf. U.S. Dept. Edn./So. Bell, Columbia, 1989; com. mem. nat. exec. com. Nova Southeastern U., 1988-89. Illustrator: Mozart Book, 1988; author: (drama) Let's Sing a Song About America, 1988 (1st pl. Nat. Music award 1990). Life mem. Rep. Presdl. Task Force, 1970—; mem. voter registration com. Lexington County Rep. Party, 1970-80; grand jury participant 13th Jud. Ct. Sys., Greenville, 1987-88, guardian ad litem, 1988-89. Tchr. Incentive grantee Sch. Dist. Greenville County, 1986-88, Project Earth grantee Bell South, 1988-89, 94-95, Edn. Improvement Act/Nat. Dissimination Network grantee S.C. State Dept. Edn., 1987-88, Targett 2,000 Arts in Curricular grantee S.C. Dept. Edn., 1994-95, Alliance grantee Bus. Cmty. Greenville, 1992-95, Greer Art Rsch. grantee, 1993-94, S.C. Govs. Sch. Study grantee, 1994, Edn. Improvement Act Competitive Tchr. grantee S.C. Dept. Edn., 1994-95, Alliance Grand grant, 1995-96. Mem. NEA, ABA (student orgn.), Nat. Art Edn. Assn., Nat. Mus. Women in Arts, S.C. Arts Alliance, S.C. Art Edn. Assn., Phi Delta Kappa (com. mem. 1976-90), Upstate IBM-PC Users Group. Baptist/Lutheran. Home: 26 Charterhouse Ave Piedmont SC 29673-9139 Office: Neighbors Enterprises 3075 Foothill Blvd Unit 138 La Crescenta CA 91214-2742

WINTERS, PAUL ANDREW, editor; b. San Diego, Apr. 3, 1965; s. Robert James and Alma (Chavannes) W. BA, UCLA, 1988; MA, U. Calif., Davis, 1991. Editl. asst. oral history program UCLA, 1988-89; asst. editor Getty Art History Info. Program, Santa Monica, Calif., 1989; tchg. asst. U. Calif., Davis, 1989-91; editor Greenhaven Press, San Diego, 1993—. Editor: Crime and Criminals: Opposing Viewpoints, 1994 (Books for the Teen Age citation N.Y. Pub. Libr. 1995), Islam: Opposing Viewpoints, 1995, Gambling, 1995, Interventionism, 1995, Policing the Police, 1995, America's Victims: Opposing Viewpoints, 1996, Race Relations: Opposing Viewpoints, 1996, Hate Crimes, 1996, Urban Terrorism, 1996, The Media and Politics, 1996, Voting Behavior, 1996. Home: 4186 Madison Ave San Diego CA 92116

WINTERS, RICHARD KEITH, social services administrator; b. Salt Lake City, Sept. 11, 1931; s. Elwood Grant and Elizabeth Louise (Bennett) W.; m. Mary Janet Nebeker, Dec. 22, 1953; children: Richard Jr., Steven, Katherine, Elizabeth, David, Sidney. Ann. BS in Polit. Sci., U. Utah, 1954. Credit mgr. Western Steel Co., Salt Lake City, 1956-61; exec. v.p. Bennetts, Salt Lake City, 1961-81; land developer Edge of Eden, Laketown, Utah, 1981-88; owner, mgr. Cedars & Shade Campground, St. Charles, Idaho, 1981—; exec. dir. Cmty. Svcs. Coun., Salt Lake City, 1988—. Mem. citizens adv. bd. Salt Lake Detention Ctr., 1987-93; bd. dirs. Bd. Juvenile Justice & Delinquency Prevention, Salt Lake City, 1990-92; bd. dirs. Utah Bd. Youth Correction, Salt Lake City, 1992—, chmn., 1992-96. With U.S. Army, 1954-56. Mem. Sons of Utah Pioneers (life). Republican. Mem. LDS Ch.

WINTHROP, JOHN, business executive; b. Salt Lake City, Apr. 20, 1947; m. Marilyn MacDonald, May 17, 1975; children: Grant Gordon, Clayton Hanford. AB cum laude, Yale U., 1969; JD magna cum laude, U. Tex., 1972. Bar: Calif. 1972. Law clk. 9th cir. U.S. Ct. Appeals, L.A., 1972-73; conseil juridique Coudert Freres, Paris, 1973-75; v.p. gen. counsel MacDonald Group, Ltd., L.A., 1976-82; pres., CEO MacDonald Mgmt. Corp. and MacDonald Group Ltd., L.A., 1982-86; pres., chief exec. officer MacDonald Corp. (gen. contractors), L.A., 1982-86; chmn., CEO Comstock Mgmt. Co., L.A., 1986—; pres., CEO Winthrop Investment Properties, Los Angeles, 1986—; CEO Veritas Imports, L.A., 1995—; bd. dirs. Plus Prods., Tiger's Milk Prods., Irvine, Calif., 1977-80. Bd. dirs., sec. L.A. Sheriff's Dept. Found.; bd. dirs. L.A. Opera. Mem. Calif. Bus. Properties Assn. (mem. bd. advisors 1981-87), Internat. Coun. Shopping Ctrs., Nat. Eagle Scout Assn. (life), French-Am. C. of C. (bd. dirs. 1982-87), Urban Land Inst., Nat. Realty Bd., Regency Club, Yale Club N.Y., Calif. Club, The Beach Club, Elizabethan Club. Republican. Office: Comstock Mgmt Co Penthouse 9460 Wilshire Blvd Beverly Hills CA 90212

WINTHROP, KENNETH RAY, insurance executive; b. N.Y.C., Dec. 29, 1950; s. Ralph and Lore (Bruck) W.; m. Sharon Swinnich, 1976 (div. 1978); m. Diane Louise Denney, June 27, 1981; children: Alyssa Louise, Matthew Lawrence, Andrew Lee. BA in English, SUNY, Buffalo, 1972. Agt. Northwestern Mut. Life Ins., Woodland Hills, Calif., 1975-78, Nat. Life of Vermont, L.A., 1978-93; mgr. Mass Mut., L.A., 1993-97, agt., 1997—. Mem. Mass Mut. Leaders Club; referee Am. Youth Soccer Orgn., L.A., 1996. Mem. Million Dollar Round Table, Mass. Mut. Leaders Club. Home: 7609 W 83rd St Playa Del Rey CA 90293-7979 Office: 4601 Wilshire Blvd Fl 3 Los Angeles CA 90010-3880

WINZELER, JUDITH KAY, foundation administrator; b. Canton, Ohio, Dec. 17, 1942; d. Charles and Pauline Doris (Werstler) Wenzlawski; m. Robert Lee Winzeler, Nov. 4, 1961; children: Elizabeth Ann, Alice Louise Winzeler Smith. BA, U. Nev., 1971, MA, 1981. Instr. anthropology Western Nev. C.C., Reno, 1976-77; program developer Nev. Humanities Com., Reno, 1977-78, asst. dir., 1978-80, assoc. dir., 1980-84, exec. dir., 1984—; panelist NEH, 1991; mem. Hilliard Found. Com., Reno, 1984—; mem. program com. Fedn. of State Humanities Couns., Washington, 1989; mem. selections com. Grace A. Griffen Chair in History, Reno, 1992. Mem. Nev. Commn. on Bicentennial of U.S. Constn., 1985-91; pres. Luth. Ch. of Good Shepherd, Reno, 1987-89; mem. nominating com. Evang. Luth. Ch. Am., Sierra Synod, Oakland, Calif., 1991-94; bd. dirs., officer Reno/Sparks Metro Min., Reno, 1987—; active Nev. Hist. Soc., Nev. State Mus., Nev. Mus. Art, Western Folklife Ctr., Friends of Washoe County Libr. Mem. Asian Pacific Assn. of No. Nev., Sierra Art Found., Reno Rotary Club, Nev. Corral, Westerners Internat. Home: 1579 Belford Rd Reno NV 89509-3907 Office: Nev Humanities Com 1034 N Sierra St Reno NV 89503-3721

WIRKKALA, JOHN LESTER, software company executive; b. Wadena, Minn., Sept. 25, 1947; s. Rueben Richard and Virginia Grace (Plank) W.; m. Connie Lee Cardarelle (div.); children: Scott, Todd; m. Lynn Diane Braund, Feb. 14, 1984; children: Scott, Seth, Shawn. AS in Electronic Tech., Brown Inst., 1982. Acct. La Maur Inc., Mpls., 1969-72, regional sales mgr., 1976-78; controller Nat. Beauty Supply, Mpls., 1972-76; store mgr. Schaak Electronics, Mpls., 1980-82; divsn. mgr. Mktg. Link, Denver, 1982-85; owner, operator Computer Systems Cons., Aurora, Colo., 1985-87; v.p. sales and mktg. Mgmt. Info. Support, Lakewood, Colo., 1987-89; sales mgr. Foothills Software Inc., Littleton, Colo., 1989-93; ops. mgr. Data Packaging Corp., Denver, 1993-95; pres. Practical Bus. Concepts, Aurora, Colo., 1995—. Contbr. articles to profl. jours. and mags.; speaker at seimnars and industry trade shows. With U.S. Army, 1966-69, Vietnam. Mem. VFW (quartermaster post # 6331 1993-94). Home and Office: 11211 Wynona Ct Westminster CO 80030-7811

WIRT, SHERWOOD ELIOT, writer, minister; b. Oakland, Calif., Mar. 12, 1911; s. Loyal Lincoln and Harriet Eliot (Benton) W.; m. Helen Winola Wells, July 2, 1940 (dec. Sept. 1986); 1 child, Alexander Wells; m. Ruth Evelyn Love, Aug. 29, 1987. BA, U. Calif., Berkeley, 1932; BD, Pacific Sch. Religion, Berkeley, 1943; PhD, Edinburgh (Scotland) U., 1951. Ordained to ministry, 1943. Pastor 1st Congl. Ch., Collinsville, Conn., 1943-44, Knox Presbyn Ch., Berkeley, 1951-55, Hillside Presbyn. Ch., Oakland, Calif., 1955-59; editor Decision mag. Billy Graham Evangelistic Assn., 1959-76; min. to students U. Wash., 1946-49. Author 26 books including Crusade at the Golden Gate, 1959, Not Me, God, 1966, Social Conscience of the Evangelical, 1968, Translation, Confessions of Augustine, 1971, Jesus Power, 1972, Topical Encyclopedia of Living Quotations, 1974, Afterglow, 1975, A Thirst for God, 1980, The Doomsday Connection, 1986, The Making of a Writer, 1987, Jesus, Man of Joy, 1991, The Book of Joy, 1994, Billy, 1997; editor 7 books. Pres. San Diego Gilbert and Sullivan Soc., 1980-81; scoutmaster Boy Scouts Am., 1936. Capt. USAAF, 1944-46. Recipient Freedom of Valley Forge Found. award, 1968; named Hon. Col., State of Tenn. Mem. Associated Ch. Press (life), Evang. Press Assn. (life, pres. 1969-71), San Diego County Christian Writers Guild (founder/convener 1977-96), Theta Chi, Sigma Delta Chi. Republican. Home: 14140 Mazatlan Ct Poway CA 92064-3964

WIRTZ, DAVID REINER, enologist; b. Hillsboro, Oreg., May 22, 1952; s. Reiner Shogren and Mary Ellen (Greip) W.; m. Mary Lois Wirtz, Oct. 28, 1978; 1 child, Thatcher. BS, Portland State U., 1976. Cellar master Coury Vineyards, Forest Grove, Oreg., 1971-77; wine maker Rueter Hill Vineyards, Forest Grove, 1977-80; instr. Clackamas Coll., Oregon City, 1980-84; wine grower Writz Vineyards, Forest Grove, 1966—; cons. Oreg. Wine Industry, 1980—; mem. adv. bd. Viticulture and Winemaking, Clackamas Coll., Oregon City, 1980-84. Author: Wheels of Time, 1992. Mem. Am. Soc. Enologists, Sons and Daus. of Oreg. Pioneers, Am. Truck Hist. Soc. (historian 1988-93), Pacific N.W. Truck Mus., Antique Truck Club of Am., N.W. Car Collectors, Oreg. Winegrowers Assn. Home: 49690 NW Hillside Rd Forest Grove OR 97116-7631

WISE, JANET ANN, college official; b. Detroit, Aug. 8, 1953; d. Donald Price and Phyllis (Licht) W.; m. Peter Anthony Eisenklam, Oct. 16, 1976 (div. Aug. 1982); m. Edward Henry Moreno, Mar. 31, 1984; 1 child, Talia. Student, U. N.Mex., 1971-73; BA in English, Coll. of Santa Fe, 1989. Editl. asst., writer The New Mexican, Santa Fe, 1975-77; press asst., press sec. Office of Gov. N.Mex., Santa Fe, 1979-82; dir. pub. rels. City of Santa Fe, 1983-84, Coll. of Santa Fe, 1984—. Bd. dirs. Santa Fe Bus. Bur., 1984-87, Santa Fe Girl's Club, 1986-89. Recipient Exemplary Performance award Office Gov. of N.Mex., Santa Fe., 1981, 3 Grand awards for publs. Coun. for Advancement and Support of Edn., 1993-95. Mem. Pub. Rels. Soc. Am., N.Mex. Press Women, Santa Fe Media Assn. (pres. 1989-91). Democrat. Unitarian. Home: 7 Conchas Ct Santa Fe NM 87505-8803 Office: Coll of Santa Fe 1600 Saint Michaels Dr Santa Fe NM 87505-7615 *Personal philosophy: I try to go out on a limb - put myself, my career, on the line every day. Otherwise, I'm not really growing or achieving to my fullest potential.*

WISE, JOSEPH STEPHEN, secondary education educator, artist; b. Seattle, Nov. 26, 1939; s. Prentice Lafayette and Norma Fay (Freeman) W.; m. Virginia Mae Linstrom, Nov. 15, 1960 (div. Oct. 1961); 1 child, Tristan Marie; m. Jeanne Marie Avila, Aug. 27, 1977; 1 child, Marilyn Jeanette. BS in Edn., Ind. U., 1963; MA in Art, San Jose State U., 1966. Cert. kindergarten through jr. coll. tchr., Calif. Art tchr. Studebaker Mid. Sch., South Bend, Ind., 1963, Meany Mid. Sch., Seattle, 1963-64, Santa Venetia Mid. Sch., San Rafael, Calif., 1967-68; tchr. art, phys. edn., English, social studies Steinbeck Mid. Sch., San Jose, Calif., 1968-95; tchr. English, art Gunderson H.S., San Jose, 1995—. One-man shows include Bingham Gallery, San Jose, 1987, Cabrillo Jr. Coll. Gallery, Santa Cruz, Calif., 1973, Mankato (Minn.) State Coll. Union, 1972, Stanford U. Internat. Ctr., Palo Alto, Calif., 1969, Los Robles Gallery, Palo Alto, 1970, Wash. State Coll. Union Gallery, Idaho State Coll. Union Gallery, Moscow, Idaho, San Jose State U. Union Art Gallery, 1971, Triton Mus., San Jose; exhibited in group shows at Mus. Art, San Francisco, 1967, Owens Corning Fiberglas Corp., Santa Clara, Calif., 1972, Pavilion Gallery, Los Gatos, Calif., Discovery Gallery, San Jose, Ages Gallery, San Jose, 1986, Greenleaf Gallery, Saratoga, Calif. 1979-83, Los Gatos Art Mus., 1990-96; represented in permanent collections at IBM Corp., San Jose, Amdahl Corp., Sunnyvale, Calif., Owens Corning Fiberglas Corp., Calvary Cmty. Ch., San Jose, Mankato State Coll., San Jose Pub. Libr., De Saisset Mus., Santa Clara, San Jose Mus. Art, Dunn Instruments, San Francisco, St. John's Episcopal Ch., Capitola, Calif.; represented in numerous pvt. collections. Republican. Home: 4383 Glenmont Dr San Jose CA 95136-1747

WISE, KATHRYN ANN, middle school educator; b. Mpls., Aug. 2, 1957; d. Joseph F. Doyle and Doris Ann (Scheller) Hume; m. Eddy Lee Wise, May 13, 1978; children: Benjamin Lee, Kimberly Ann. BS in Edn., Black Hills State U., 1978, MS in Curriculum and Devel., 1993. Cert. tchr., Wyo. Tchr. Worland (Wyo.) Mid. Sch., 1980—; tchr. night classes Northwest Coll., Powell, Wyo., 1991—. Mem. Wyo. Edn. Assn., Wyo. Ednl. Computing Consortium. Home: 300 S 23d St Worland WY 82401 Office: Worland Mid Sch 1200 Culbertson Ave Worland WY 82401

WISE, WOODROW WILSON, JR., small business owner; b. Alexandria, Va., Mar. 9, 1938; s. Woodrow Wilson Sr. and Helen (Peverill) W.; m. Barbara Jean Hatton, Oct. 6, 1956 (div. 1975); m. Sandra Kay Habitz, Dec. 17, 1983; children: Anthony P., Laura J. Gen. mgr. Alexandria (Va.) Amusement Corp., 1956-73; curator Harold Lloyd Estate, Beverly Hills, Calif., 1973-75; pres. Discount Video Tapes, Inc., Burbank, Calif., 1975—. Office: Discount Video Tapes Inc PO Box 7122 833 "A" N Hollywood Way Burbank CA 91510

WISEMAN, JAY DONALD, photographer, mechanical designer and contractor; b. Salt Lake City, Dec. 23, 1952; s. Donald Thomas and Reva (Stewart) W.; m. Barbara Helen Taylor, June 25, 1977; children: Jill Reva, Steve Jay. Ed. Utah State U., Logan, U. Utah. Cert. profl. photographer. Pvt. practice photography; owner, pres. JB&W Corp. Recipient Grand prize Utah State Fair, 1986, Kodak Crystal for Photographic Excellence, 1986, 87, Master of Photography degree, 1989, Best of Show award, 1991-92; Profl. Photographer Mag. cover photo, 1988; numerous photos inducted for permanent collection Internat. Photographic Hall of Fame, 1989; photo named one of World's Greatest, Kodak, 1987-88; 2 photos named among World's Best, Walt Disney World and Profl. Phototgraphers Assn., 1988, 2 prints tied for Best of Show award RMPPA Regional contest, 1991; recipient Gold Medallion award Best in Show (world wide). Mem. Profl. Photographers Assn. Am. (one of top 10 scores internat. photo contest), Rocky Mountain Profl. Photographers (Best of Show, highest score ever 1987, Master Photographer of Yr. 1991, Ct. of Honour 1981-91), Inter-Mountain Profl. Photographers Assn. (Master's Trophy Best of Show 1982, 86, 88, Photographer of Yr. award 1986, Ct. of Honour 1981-91), Photographers Soc. Am (Best of Show award Utah chpt. 1986). Latter Day Saints. Represented in Salt Lake City Internat. Airport permanent photo exhibit, various traveling loan collections, U.S. and Europe, 1988, loan collection Epcot Ctr., 1988-91; photographs published numerous profl. jours.

WISEMAN, T. JAN, association executive; b. Prairie du Chien, Wis., Mar. 26, 1941; s. C. Edward and Gertrude Jeanette (Roth) W. Journalism BS, U. Wis., 1964; MS in Edn., No. Ill. U., 1968, CAS, 1979. Editor Rockford (Ill.) Register Republic, 1963; tchr. sci. and math. Pearl City (Ill.) H.S., 1964-65; tchr. journalism Rock Falls (Ill.) H.S., 1965-66; tchr. journalism and English Glenbrook North H.S., Northbrook, Ill., 1966-68; dean comm. edn. Kishwaukee Coll., Malta, Ill., 1968-79; staff v.p., dir. edn. and mktg. Nat. Assn. Realtors, Chgo., 1979-82; exec. v.p. Soc. Farm Mgrs. and Rural Appraisers, Denver, 1982-85, Profl. Ins. Agts. of Colo., Denver, 1985-90, Apt. Assn. Met. Denver, 1990—; pres. Profl. Devel. Inst., Denver, 1981—, Apt. Solutions Cybermall, Denver, 1996, Sr. On-Line Solutions, Denver, 1996, Bus. Solutions Cybermall, Denver, 1996. Author: Creative Communications, 1971, 74; editor: Taxidermy Techniques, 1976; contbr. articles to profl. jours. Mem. exec. com., chmn. tng., Goodwill Industries, Denver, 1994—; cofounder Cmty. Environment Assn., Shabbona, Ill., 1975-79; com. mem. Rocky Mountain Mutual Housing Assn., Denver, 1996. Named Nat. Exec. of Yr., Nat. Apt. Assn., Washington, 1994; recipient Innovation in Pub. and Pvt. Partnerships award, Denver Regional Coun. Govts., 1996. Mem. Journalism Edn. Assn. (pres. 1973-75, Carl Towley award 1976), Internat. Assn. Cmty. Educators (charter), Colo. Soc. Assn. Execs. (bd. mem. 1994-96, Pres.'s award 1992, Exec. of Yr. 1995). Office: Apartment Assn of Metro Denver 650 S Cherry St Ste 635 Denver CO 80222-1808

WISENER, MAUREEN MAYDEN, public relations, marketing executive; b. Hialeah, Fla., Apr. 17, 1961; d. Harry and Joyce Adele (Christensen) Mayden; m. Charles (Chuck) Richard Wisener, June 3, 1984; children: Jeffrey Stewart, Keith Nathaniel. BA, So. Coll. Seventh Day Adventists, 1984; MS in Mass Comm., San Diego State U., 1997. Pub. rels. asst. Park Ridge Hosp., Fletcher, N.C., 1984-86; pers. receptionist Fla. Hosp., Orlando, 1986-87; mktg. asst. San Joaquin Cmty. Hosp., Bakersfield, Calif., 1987-89; assoc. dir. mktg., comms. Paradise Valley Hosp., San Diego, 1989—. Contbr. articles to Adventist Review. Mem. Internat. Assn. Bus. Communicators (newsletter editor, 1990-91, v.p. San Diego chpt. 1991-92), Am. Mktg. Assn., Soc. for Health Strategy and Mgmt. Devel., Acad. for Health Svcs. Mktg., Pub. Rels. Soc. Am., Health Care Communicators San Diego (pres. 1996). Republican. Office: Paradise Valley Hosp 2400 E 4th St National City CA 91950-2026

WISHINGRAD, RICHARD JOEL, retail executive; b. Calif., May 15, 1958. Student, U. Calif., Santa Barbara, 1976-77, UCLA, 1978, 80, 83,89; AA in Psychology, L.A. Valley Coll., Van Nuys, 1994. Playground supr. Burbank Blvd Elem. Sch., North Hollywood, Calif., 1980; tchg. asst. Pacific Palasides (Calif.) Elem. Sch., 1983, Circle Nursery Schs., San Fernando Valley, Calif., 1985; pres. Utopia Enterprises, Van Nuys, 1990—; program asst. Mens Gym Office, Van Nuys, 1995-96. Author: A Positive Account of Life's Potential Destiny, 1986. Democrat. Jewish. Home: 5050 Sepulveda Blvd Apt 222 Sherman Oaks CA 91403-1523

WISMER, PATRICIA ANN, secondary education educator; b. York, Pa., Mar. 23, 1936; d. John Bernhardt and Frances Elizabeth Loreen Marie (Fry) Feiser; m. Lawrence Howard Wismer, Aug. 4, 1961. BA in English, Mt. Holyoke Coll., 1958; MA in Speech/Drama, U. Wis., 1960; postgrad., U. Oreg., 1962, Calif. State U., Chico, 1963-64, U. So. Calif., 1973-74. Tchr., co-dir. drama program William Penn Sr. High Sch., York, 1960-61; instr. English, dir. drama York Jr. Coll., 1961-62; assoc. church editor San Francisco Examiner, 1962-63; reporter, publicist News Bur. Calif. State U., Chico, 1963-64; chmn. English Dept. Chico Sr. H.S., 1966-96; mentor tchr. Chico Sr. High Sch., Chico Unified Sch. Dist., 1983-93; judge writing awards Nat. Coun. Tchr. English, 1970—; cons. No. Calif. Writing Project, 1977—; curriculum cons., freelance writer and photographer, 1996—. Mem. Educators for Social Responsibility, Calif. Assn. for Gifted, Upper Calif. Coun. Tchrs. English (bd. dirs. 1966-85, pres. 1970-71), Calif. Assn. Tchrs. English, Nat. Coun. Tchrs. English, NEA, Calif. Tchrs. Assn., Chico Unified Tchrs. Assn. Democrat. Lutheran. Home: 623 Arcadian Ave Chico CA 95926-4504 Office: PO Box 1250 Cannon Beach OR 97110-1250

WISNIEWSKI, STEPHEN ADAM, professional football player; b. Rutland, Vt., Apr. 7, 1967. Student, Pa. State U. Offensive guard L.A. Raiders, 1989—. Named All-Pro Team Guard by Sporting News, 1990-93, Coll. All-Am. Team, 1987, 88. Office: L A Raiders 332 Center St El Segundo CA 90245-4047*

WITEMEYER, HUGH HAZEN, English language educator; b. Flint, Mich., June 10, 1939; s. Benton Diehl and Dorothy June (Hazen) W.; m. Sharon Kay Bristol Dec. 28, 1967 (div. Sept. 1980); 1 child, Hazen Allison; m. Barbara Ellen Watkins, Aug. 21, 1987. BA, U. Mich., 1961, Oxford U., 1963; PhD, Princeton U., 1966. Asst. prof. English U. Calif., Berkeley, 1966-73; assoc. prof. English U. N.Mex., Albuquerque, 1973-79, prof. English, 1979—; bd. govs. N.Mex. D.H. Lawrence Festival, Santa Fe, 1979-80; selection com. Marshall Scholarships, San Francisco, 1977-80. Author: Poetry of Ezra Pound 1908-1920, 1969, George Eliot and the Visual Arts, 1979; editor: William Carlos Williams and James Laughlin: Selected Letters, 1989; co-editor: W.B. Yeats, Letters to the New Island, 1989; mem. editorial bd. George Eliot/George Henry Lewes Rev., 1992—. Fulbright fellow, 1984, 89, NEH fellow, 1977, ACLS fellow, 1971-72. Mem. AAUP (pres. campus chpt. 1995—), MLA, PEN N.Mex., George Eliot Fellowship, Ezra Pound Soc. (pres. 1972—), Soc. for Textual Scholarship. Office: Dept English U NMex Albuquerque NM 87131

WITH, GERDA BECKER, artist; b. Hamburg, Germany, Mar. 4, 1910; came to U.S., 1939; d. Ludwig and Martha (De Bruycker) Becker; m. Karl E. With, July 17, 1939 (dec. Dec. 1980); children: Christopher B., Nela W. Dwyer. M in Decorative Arts, Charlottenburg, Berlin, 1938. One woman shows include Otis Art Inst., Mus. St. Barbara, also pvt. galleries throughout Europe and U.S., 1958—; illustrator: (book) The Man Who Stole the Word "Beautiful", 1991, others. Home: 3045 Kelton Ave Los Angeles CA 90034-3021

WITHERELL, ELIZABETH HALL, scholarly editor; b. Columbus, Ohio, Aug. 15, 1948; d. Donivan Lester and Elizabeth Jane (Mason) Hall; m. Michael Stewart Witherell, Dec. 27, 1969. BA, U. Mich., 1969; MA, U. Wis., 1972, PhD, 1979. Editor writings of Henry David Thoreau Princeton (N.J.) U., 1975-80, editor-in-chief writings of Henry David Thoreau, 1980-83; editor-in-chief writings of Henry David Thoreau U. Calif., Santa Barbara, 1983—; bd. dirs. Mark Twain Project, Berkeley; mem. adv. bd. Am.: History and Life, Santa Barbara, 1991-93, 93-95. Editor: Henry David Thoreau, A Week on the Concord and Merrimack Rivers, 1980, Henry David Thoreau, Journal 1:1837-44, 1981. NEH grantee, 1980-87, 89-97, summer stipend, 1988. Mem. MLA (mem. com. on scholarly edits. 1981-85, 93-96), ALA, Thoreau Soc. (bd. dirs. 1993-96, pres. 1996—), Assn. Documentary Editing (pres. 1992-93), Soc. Am. Archivists. Office: Univ Calif Davidson Libr Santa Barbara CA 93106-9010

WITHERS, HUBERT RODNEY, radiotherapist, radiobiologist, educator; b. Queensland, Australia, Sept. 21, 1932; came to the U.S., 1966; s. Hubert and Gertrude Ethel (Tremayne) W.; m. Janet Macfie, Oct. 9, 1959; 1 child, Genevieve. MBBS, U. Queensland, Brisbane, Australia, 1956; PhD, U. London, 1965, DSc, 1982. Bd. cert. Ednl. Coun. for Fgn. Med. Grads. Intern Royal Brisbane (Australia) and Associated Hosps., 1957; resident in radiotherapy and pathology Queensland Radium Inst. and Royal Brisbane (Australia) Hosp., 1958-63; Univ. Queensland Gaggin fellow Gray Lab., Mt. Vernon Hosp., Northwood, Middlesex, Eng., 1963-65, Royal Brisbane (Australia) Hosp., 1966; radiotherapist Prince of Wales Hosp., Randwick, Sydney, Australia, 1966; vis. rsch. scientist Lab. Physiology, Nat. Cancer Inst., Bethesda, Md., 1966-68; assoc. prof. radiotherapy sect. exptl. radiotherapy U. Tex. Sys. Cancer Ctr. M.D. Anderson Hosp. & Tumor Inst., Houston, 1968-71; prof. radiotherapy, chief sect. exptl. radiotherapy U. Tex. Sys. Cancer Ctr. M.D. Anderson Hsop. & Tumor Inst., Houston, 1971-80; prof. dir. exptl. radiation oncology dept. radiation oncology UCLA, 1980-89, prof., vice-chair dir. exptl. radiation oncology dept. radiation oncology, 1991-94, Am. Cancer Soc. Clin. Rsch. prof. dept. radiation oncology, 1992—, interim dir. Jonsson Comprehensive Cancer Ctr., 1994-95, chmn. radiation oncology, 1994—; assoc. grad. faculty U. Tex., Grad. Sch. Biomed. Scis, Houston, 1969-73, mem. grad. faculty, 1973-80; prof. dept. radiotherapy Med. Sch., U. Tex. Health Sci. Ctr., Houston, U. Tex. Med. Sch., Houston, 1975-80; prof., dir. Inst. Oncology, The Prince of Wales Hosp., U. NSW, Sydney, Australia, 1989-91; mem. com. mortality mil. pers. present-at-atmosphere tests of nuclear weapons Inst. Medicine, 1993-94; mem. radiation effects rsch. bd. NRC, 1993—; mem. com. neutron dose reporting Internat. Commn. Radiation Units and Measurements, 1982—, mem. report com. clin. dosimetry for neutrons, 1993—; mem. task force non-stochastic effects radiation Internat. Com. Radiation Protection, 1980-84, mem. com. 1, 1993—; mem. radiobiology com. Radiation Therapy Oncology Group, 1979—, mem. dose-time com., 1980-89, mem. gastroenterology com., 1982-89; mem. edn. bd. Royal Australian Coll. Radiology, 1989-91; mem. cancer rsch. coord. com. U. Calif., 1991-97, mem. standing curriculum com. UCLA biomed. physics grad. program, 1993—; cons. exptl. radiotherapy U. Tex. System Cancer Ctr., 1980—. Mem. Am. editl. bd.: Internat. Jour. Radiat. Oncol. Biol. Phys., 1982-89, 91—, internat. editl. bd., 1989-91; cons. editor: The European Jour. Cancer, 1990-95; editl. bd. dirs.: Endocurietherapy/Hyperthermia Oncology, 1991—, Radiation Oncology Investigations, 1992—; assoc. editor: Cancer Rsch., 1993-94, editl. bd. 1995-97. Mem. Kettering selection com. Gen. Motors Cancer Rsch. Found., 1988-89, chmn., 1989, awards assembly, 1990-94. Recipient Medicine prize Polish Acad. Sci., 1989, Second H.S. Kaplan Disting. Scientist award Internat.

Assn. for Radiation Rsch., 1991, Gray medal Internat. Commn. Radiation Units, 1995U.S. Dept. Energy Fermi award 1997, Am. Radium Soc. Janeway medal, 1994, A,/ Soc. Therapeutic Radiology, Oncolody Gold medal, 1991, Radiation Rsch. Soc. Failla award, 1988); named Gilbert H. Fletcher lectr. U. Tex. Sys. Cancer Ctr., 1989, Clifford Ash lectr. Ont. Cancer Inst., Princess Margaret Hosp., 1987, Erskine lectr. Radiol. Soc. N.Am., 1988, Ruvelson lectr. U. Minn., 1988, Milford Schultz lectr. Mass. Gen. Hosp., 1989, Del Regato Found. lectr. Hahnemann U., 1990, Bruce Cain Meml. lectr. New Zealand Soc. Oncology, 1990, others. Fellow Royal Australasian Coll. Radiologists (bd. cert.), Am. Coll. Radiology (bd. cert. therapeutic radiology, adv. com. patterns of care study 1988—, radiation oncology advisory group 1993-97, others), Am. Radium Soc. (mem. and credential c om. 1986-89, 93-94, treas. 1993-94, pres.-elect 1995-96, pres. 1996-97, others), Am. Soc. Therapeutic Radiology and Oncology (awards com. 1993, publs. com. 1993-97, vice chair Publs. Commn., 1996-98, keynote address 1990, , others); mem. Nat. Cancer Inst. (various ad-hoc rev. coms. 1970—, radiation sudy sect. 1971-75, cons. U.S.-Japan Coop. Study high LET Radiotherapy 1975-77, cancer rsch. emphasis grant rev. com. 1976, clin. cancer ctr. rev. com. 1976-79, toxicology working group 1977-78, reviewer outstanding investigator grants 1984-93, bd. sci. counselors, 1986-88), Nat. Cancer Inst. Can. (adv. com. rsch. 1992-95), Pacific N.W. Radiol. Soc. (hon.), Tex. Radiol. Soc. (hon.), So. Calif. Radiation Oncology Soc. (sec., treas., 1992-94, pres. 1996-97), European Soc. Therapeutic Radiology an d Oncology (hon.), Polish Oncology Soc. (hon.) Austrian Radiation Oncology Soc. (hon.), Phila. Roentgen Ray Soc. (hon.), Radiation Rsch. Soc. (pres. 1982-83, honors and awards com. 1988-84, ad hoc com. funds utilization 1987-89, adv. com. Radiation Rsch. Jour., 1988—). Office: UCLA Med Ctr 10833 Le Conte Ave Los Angeles CA 90095-1714

WITKIN, JOEL-PETER, photographer; b. Bklyn., Sept. 13, 1939; s. Max and Mary (Pellegrino) W.; m. Cynthia Jean Bency, June 30, 1978; one child, Kersen Ahanu. B.F.A., Cooper Union, 1974; M.F.A., U. N.Mex., 1986; student (fellow), Columbia U., 1973-74. Artist in residence Zerybthia Rome, Italy, summer 1996; represented by Pace/McGill, N.Y.C., Fraenkel Gallery, San Francisco, Baudion Lebon Gallery, Paris; lectr. Am. Acad. Rome. Exhibited in Projects Studio One, N.Y.C., 1980, Galerie Texbraun, Paris, 1982, Kansas Ctiy Art Inst., 1983, Stedelijk Mus., Amsterdam, 1983, Fraenkel Gallery, 1983-84, 87, 91, 93, 95, 97, Pace Wilden-Stein MacGill Gallery, N.Y.C., 1983, 84, 87, 89, 91, 93, 95, 97, San Francisco Mus. Modern Art, 1985, Bklyn. Mus., 1986, Galerie Baudoin Lebon, Paris, 1987, 89, 91, 95, Centro de Arte Reina Sofia Mus., Madrid, 1988, Palais de Tokyo, Paris, 1989, Fahey/Klein Gallery, L.A., 1987, 89, 91, 97, Mus. Modern Art, Haifa, Israel, 1991, Photo Picture Space Gallery, Osaka, Japan, 1993, Guggenheim Mus., N.Y.C., 1995, Interkamera, Prague, 1995, Il Castello de Rivoli Mus., Turin, 1995, Encontros de Fotografia, Colombia, Portugal, 1996, Rencontres de la Photographie, Arles, France, 1996, Taipei Photo Gallery, Taiwan; group shows: Mus. Moder Art, N.Y.C., 1959, San Francisco Mus. Moder Art, 1981, Whitney Biennial, 1985, Palais de Tokyo, Paris, 1986, La Phorographie Contemporaine en France, 1996, Foto Masson, Goteberg, Sweden, 1997; represented in permanent collections, Mus. Modern Art, N.Y.C., San Francisco Mus. Modern Art, 1980, Nat. Gallery Art, Washington, Victoria and Albert Mus., London, George Eastman House, N.Y., The Getty Collection, Moder Museet, Stockholm, Sweden, Whitney Mus., N.Y.C., The Guggenheim Mus., N.Y.C., Tokyo Met. Mus. Photography; subject of monographs: Joel-Peter Witkin, 1985, 88-89, 91, 93, 95-96; editor: Masterpieces of Medical Photography, 1987, Harms Way, 1994; artist residency, Rome, 1996. Served with U.S. Army, 1961-64. Decorated Chevalier Des Arts et de Letters (France), 1990, The Augustus Saint Gaudens medal The Cooper Union, 1996; recipient Disting. Alumni award The Cooper Union, 1986, Internat. Ctr. Photography award, 1988; Ford Found. grantee, 1977, 78, Nat. Endowment in Photography grantee, 1980, 81, 86, 92. Address: 1707 Five Points Rd SW Albuquerque NM 87105-3017 *My need is to understand existence. That need becomes art when it reaches into the extreme limit of the possible.*

WITKIN, SUSAN BETH, broadcast journalist, reporter; b. Denver, June 10, 1959; d. Bernard Theodore and Sharon Elaine (Ginsberg) W. BA in Communications Arts, Fort Lewis Coll., 1982. Anchor, gen. assignment reporter Sta. KBCO-FM/KADE-AM, Boulder, Colo., 1982-83; asst. news dir. Sta. KSPN-FM/TV, Aspen, Colo., 1983-84, Sta. KIUP/KRSJ-FM, Durango, Colo., 1984-85; anchor, gen. assignment reporter Sta. KOA, Denver, 1985-90; anchor, reporter Sta. KGO ABC/Capital Cities, San Francisco, 1990-94. Producer, reporter series on st. gangs Nothing To Do, No Place To Go, 1986 (1st place gen. reporting category Soc. Profl. Jours., 2nd place feature category AP). Bd. dirs. Allied Jewish Fedn. Women's Div., Denver, 1987-89, March of Dimes, San Francisco, 1991—. Named one of Outstanding Young Women of Am., 1987; recipient 2d Pl. award Spl. Report Saudi Arabia AP, 1990, 1st Place award L.A. Riot Coverage, 1992, 1st Place award RTNDA, 1992. Mem. AFTRA, AP, Bus. Profl. Women's Orgn., Soc. Profl. Jours. Democrat.

WITMEYER, RICHARD JAMES, health products executive; b. Bethlehem, Pa., Nov. 28, 1948; s. John Robert and Dora Clarene (Braswell) W.; m. Sally Lynne Godshall, June 7, 1975; children: Flynn Godshall, Catherine Rose. BSChemE, Lehigh U., 1970, MSChemE, 1973; PhD in Materials Engring., N.C. State U., 1978; MBA, Ga. State U., 1985. Jr. process engr. Cities Svc. Corp., Trenton, N.J., 1970-71; process engr. Nat. Starch and Chem. Corp., Plainfield, N.J., 1973-74; rsch. scientist Kimberly-Clark Corp., Neenah (Wis.) and Roswell, Ga., 1977-87; mgr. mktg. Burlington Precision Fabrics Group, Greensboro, N.C., 1987-88; mgr. R&D James River Corp., Greenville, S.C., 1988-90; v.p. sci. affairs London Internat. U.S. Holdings, Regent Hosp. Products Ltd., Greenville, 1990-92; v.p. tech. affairs Standard Textile Co., Cin., 1992-95, Safeskin Corp., San Diego, 1995—; bd. dirs. Bio Barrier Inc., Denver; affiliate mem. Am. Soc. Hosp. Ctrl. Svc. Pers., Atlanta, 1985-87; co. rep. Assn. for the Nonwovens and Disposables Assn., N.y.C., 1987-88. Mem. ASTM (co. rep. 1990-92), Am. Mgmt. Assn., Health Industries Mfg. Assn. (adv. bd. 1991-92), Soc. Plastics Engrs., Assn. for Advancement of Med. Instrumentation, Am. Soc. for Quality Control.

WITT, CATHERINE LEWIS, neonatal nurse practitioner, writer; b. Burlington, Iowa, Nov. 21, 1957; d. Rodney Darrell and Neola Ann (Wharton) Lewis; m. John Robert Witt, Mar. 31, 1984; children: Jeffrey Lewis, Jennifer Diane. BSN, U. No. Colo., 1980; MSN, U. Colo., 1987. Cert. neonatal nurse practitioner. Staff nurse St. Joseph's Hosp., Denver, 1980-85; neonatal nurse practitioner Denver Children's Hosp., 1986-88; coord. neonatal nurse practitioner and neonatal transport Presbyn.-St. Luke's Med. Ctr., Denver, 1988—. Column editor Neonatal Network; contbr. chpts. to books. Troop leader Girl Scouts U.S. Mem. Nat. Assn. Neonatal Nurses (co-chair program com. 1992-94, bd. dirs., dir.-at-large 1997—), Nat. Cert. Corp. (test. com. 1994-96). Democrat. Episcopalian. Home: 17586 E Dickinson Pl Aurora CO 80013 Office: Presbyn-St Luke's Med Ctr 1719 E 19th Ave Denver CO 80218-1235

WITT, JUDITH ANNE, elementary education educator; b. Danville, Ill., Mar. 8, 1949; d. Dale Norman and Ruby Lou (Stonecipher) Shideler; m. Robert Witt, Feb. 24, 1970; children: Eric, Sean, Ryan. BA, U. Ariz., 1971; MA, U.S. Internat. U., San Diego, 1990; EdS, Point Loma Nazarene Coll., 1993. Tchr. Ovid-Elsie (Mich.) Schs., 1971-73; tchr., coord. gifted and talented edn. Poway (Calif.) Unified Sch. Dist., 1987-91; tchr., dist. gifted and talented coord. Ramona (Calif.) Unified Sch. Dist., 1991-95; dist. GATE coord. Castro Valley (Calif.) Unified Sch. Dist., 1995—; presenter local sch. and dist. insvc. days, state and nat. confs.; Calif. mentor tchr. learning styles. Active community orgns. Mem. ASCD, Calif. Assn. for Gifted (regional bd. rep.), Phi Delta Kappa (newsletter editor, exec. bd.).

WITTE, ROBERT ALAN, electrical engineer, writer; b. Ft. Wayne, Ind.; m. Joyce Dianne Selking, May 28, 1978; children: Sara, Rachel. BSEE, Purdue U., 1978; MSEE, Colo. State U., 1981. R & D project mgr. Hewlett-Packard Co., Colorado Springs, Colo., 1990-95, R & D sect. mgr., 1995—; adj. prof. Colo. Tech. U., Colorado Springs, 1992-94. Author: Spectrum and Network Measurements, 1991, Electronic Test Instruments, 1993; patentee anti-alias filtering apparatus. Mem. IEEE (sr.), Eta Kappa Nu, Tau Beta Pi. Office: Hewlett-Packard Co 1900 Garden of Gods Rd Colorado Springs CO 80901

WITTENSTEIN, GEORGE JUERGEN, surgeon, educator; b. Tubingen, Germany, Apr. 26, 1919; s. Oskar Juergen and Elisabeth (Vollmoeller) W.; m. Elisabeth Hartert, Apr. 26, 1947 (dec. Jan. 1966); m. Christel J. Bejenke, July 1, 1966; children: E. Deirdre, Nemone E., W. Andreas, Catharina J. MD, U. Munich, 1944; MSc in Surgery, U. Colo., 1956, MD, 1956. Diplomate Am. Bd. Surgery and Thoracic Surgery. Instr. U. Colo. Sch. Medicine, Denver, 1953-60; instr., clin. asst., then prof. UCLA Sch. Medicine, 1964-73, prof. surgery, 1974-90, prof. surgery emeritus, 1990—; chmn. dept. surgery Olive View Med. Ctr., Sylmar, Calif., 1974-90; pvt. practice surgery Santa Barbara, Calif., 1989—; vis. prof. at various European med. sch., 1958—. Contbr. sci. articles to profl. publs. Bd. dirs. Friends of U. Calif.-Santa Barbara Libr., 1965-75; trustee Santa Barbara Mus. Art, 1968-75. Boettcher Found. scholar, 1955. Home: 4004 Cuervo Ave Santa Barbara CA 93110-2412

WITTER, WENDELL WINSHIP, financial executive, retired; b. Berkeley, Calif., Oct. 16, 1910; s. George Franklin Jr. and Mary Ann (Carter) W.; m. Florence Corder, Oct. 18, 1935 (div. Oct. 1973); 1 child, Wendelyn; m. Janet Hutchinson Alexander, Dec. 12, 1973 (dec. 1977); m. Evelyn Grinter Harkins Gooding, Mar. 26, 1978. BA, U. Calif., Berkeley, 1932; Diploma, Investment Bankers Inst., Wharton Bus. Sch., 1955. Salesman Dean Witter & Co., San Francisco, 1933-50, ptnr., 1950-68, exec. v.p., 1968-76; cons. Dean Witter, Reynolds, Inc., San Francisco, 1976-82, retired cons., 1982—. Past Regent U. Calif., 1969-70; mem. Coordinating Coun. Higher Edn., Calif., 1970-71; trustee State Univs., Long Beach, Calif., 1971-79; past bd. dirs. San Francisco Symphony, ARC Golden Gate Chpt., Met. YMCA, Grace Cathedral, Better Bus. Bur. Lt. col. Army Air Force, 1941-46. Mem. San Francisco Bond Club (pres. 1955), Assn. of Stock Exch. Firms (pres. 1962), Investment Bankers Assn. Am. (pres. 1965), U. Calif. Alumni Assn. (pres. 1969-70), Berkeley Fellows, Pacific Union Club, San Francisco Golf Club, Bohemian Club, Zeta Psi. Republican. Episcopalian. Home: 1400 Geary Blvd Apt 2109 San Francisco CA 94109-6572 Office: PO Box 7597 101 California St San Francisco CA 94120

WITTERS, ROBERT DALE, chemist, educator; b. Cheyenne, Wyo., May 2, 1929; s. Alva Oscar and Vera Leona Witters; m. Brenda M. Marlow, Dec. 13, 1987. BA in Chemistry, U. Colo., 1951; PhD of Phys. Chemistry, Mont. State U., 1964. Chemist duPont, Parlin, N.J., 1951-53; asst. prof. SUNY, Plattsburgh, 1959-60, 61-62, Mont. State U., Bozeman, 1962-63; postdoctoral fellow Harvey Mudd Calif., Claremont, 1964-65; from asst. prof. to prof. Colo. Sch. Mines, Golden, 1965-95. With U.S. Army, 1953-55. Recipient Outstanding Tchg. award Amoco Found., 1972-73, 76-77. Mem. Am. Chem. Soc., Am. Crystallographic Assn., Sigma Xi, Alpha Chi Sigma. Office: Colo Sch Mines Golden CO 80401

WITTMANN, OTTO, art museum executive; b. Kansas City, Mo., Sept. 1, 1911; s. Otto and Beatrice Knox (Billingsley) W.; m. Margaret Carlisle Hill, June 9, 1945; children: William Hill, John Carlisle. Student, Country Day Sch., Kansas City; AB, Harvard U., 1933; postgrad., 1937-38, postgrad. Carnegie scholar, summer 1937; LLD, U. Toledo; DFA, Hillsdale Coll., Bowling Green State U., U. Mich., Kenyon Coll., Skidmore Coll. Curator prints Nelson Gallery Art, Kansas City, 1933-37; instr. history of art Emerson Sch., Boston, 1937-38; curator Hyde Collection, Glens Falls, N.Y., 1938-41; instr. history of art Skidmore Coll., Saratoga Springs, N.Y., 1938-41; asst. dir. Portland (Oreg.) Mus. Art, 1941; assoc. dir. Toledo Mus. Art, 1946-59, trustee, 1958—, dir., 1959-76, dir. emeritus, 1977—; v.p., cons., art advisor, 1977—; trustee, cons. Los Angeles County Mus. Art, 1977-78; vice chmn., trustee, cons. J. Paul Getty Trust, 1977—; organizer exhbns. art activities Am. museums USIA, 1953-55; editl. cons. Gazette des Beaux Arts; vice chmn. Nat. Collection Fine Arts Commn.; bd. dirs. Toledo Trust Co.; cons. Clark Art Inst., 1990—. Editl. chmn. Toledo Mus. Catalogue of European Paintings and Guide to Collections; writer numerous museum catalogues, profl. articles. Founding mem. Nat. Coun. Arts; mem. mus. panel NEH; chmn. adv. panel Nat. Found. Arts and Humanities; mem. art adv. panel IRS; mem. nat. arts accessions com. U.S. embassies; mem. U.S.-ICOM Nat. Com.; former sec. gen. com. pour Musées du Verre, ICOM; founding mem. Ohio Arts Coun.; sponsor Nat. Trust Sch., Attingham, Shropshire, Eng. Maj. AUS, USAAF, OSS, 1941-46. Decorated officer Legion of Honor, France, officer Order Orange Nassau, Netherlands, comdr. Arts and Letters France; comdr. Order of Merit Italy). Fellow Museums Assn. (Eng.); mem. Intermus. Conservation Assn. (pres. 1955-56, trustee), Harvard Soc. Contemporary Art (co-dir. 1931-33), Assn. Art Mus. Dirs. (pres. 1961-62, 71-72), Am. Assn. Museums (former v.p., Disting. Service to Mus. award 1987), Coll. Art Assn., Archeol. Inst. Am., Internat. Inst. for Conservation of Hist. and Artistic Works, Soc. Archtl. Historians, Verien der Freunde Antiker Kunst, Am. Soc. French Legion Honneur, Alliance Francaise de Toledo (trustee), Phi Kappa Phi. Episcopalian (vestryman). Clubs: Traveller's (London); Century Assn. (N.Y.C.); Toledo, Harvard (pres. 1956-57), Rotary (pres. 1963-64). Home: 300 Hot Springs Rd Apt 163 Montecito CA 93108-2065 Office: J Paul Getty Trust Ste 400 1200 Getty Center Dr Los Angeles CA 90049-1681

WITWER, JEFFREY GARTH, marketing executive; b. Elkhart, Ind., July 18, 1944. BSME, Northwestern U., 1966; MSME, U. Calif., Berkeley, 1967, PhD in Mech. Engring., 1971; MBA, Golden Gate U., 1982. Registered profl. engr., Calif. Asst. prof. Sch. Aerospace, Mech. and Nuclear Engring. U. Okla., Norman, 1972-74; with SRI Internat., Menlo Park, Calif., 1974-78, 79-81; ASME Congl. fellow Com. on Interstate and Fgn. Commerce, U.S. Ho. of Reps., Washington, 1978-79; mktg. and mgmt. cons. Strategies Unltd., Mountain View, Calif., 1981-84; from mgr. bus. and mktg. devel. to dir. draftstation programs GE Calma, Milpitas, Calif., 1984-87; from mgr. MCAE major accounts/bus. devel. to dir. internat. mktg. Silicon Graphics, Mountain View, 1987-91; v.p. mktg. and bus. devel. Centric Engring. Systems, Palo Alto, Calif., 1991-93; v.p. internat. ops. Knowledge Revolution, San Mateo, Calif., 1994—. Bd. dirs. Jr. Achievement Santa Clara County. Recipient Ralph Teetor award Soc. Automotive Engrs., 1992; named Sports Car Club Am. Class Champion, 1991. Mem. ASME. Home: 27030 Elena Rd Los Altos CA 94022-3346 Office: Knowledge Revolution 66 Bovet Rd Ste 200 San Mateo CA 94402-3127

WIZARD, BRIAN, publisher, author; b. Newburyport, Mass., June 24, 1949; s. Russell and Ruth (Hidden) Willard. BA, Sonoma (Calif.) State U., 1976; D of Metaphysics, Universal Life Ch., 1997. Ordained to ministry Universal Life Ch., 1997. Pvt. practice as jeweler, sculptor and craftsman Calif., 1974-79; Wallowa, Oreg., 1991—; prin. The Starquill Pub., Port Douglas, Queensland, Australia, 1981-86; owner Starquill Internat., Wallowa, Oreg. Author: (novels) Permission to Kill, 1985, Shindara, 1987, Heaven on Earth, 1990, Coming of Age, 1990, Permission to Live, 1992, Pollution IV, 1993, Back in the World, 1995, (short stories) Tropical Pair, 1986, Metempsychosis, 1988 (In Search of) The Silver Lining, 1994, The Moon Whistling By on a Cloud, 1994, (The Princess of the) Wildflowers, 1995, Mushroom Magic, 1996; contbr. to Smithsonian Inst.'s The Vietnam War Generation; contbr. to SpaceArc; prodr. (video documentaries) Thunderhawks, 1987, Swift Action Newsteam, Tope Creek Lookout, 1995; songwriter, prodr. (cassette) Brian Wizard Sings for His Supper, 1989 (cert. of achievement Billboard 1993); songwriter, singer, prodr. (music videos) (I Don't Want) Permission to Kill, 1989, Busker's Theme Song, Living in North Queensland, Circus Act, Hitch Hiking Man, Self-Portrait, The Love We Share Will Never End, 1994, Never Met a Girl Like You, Folk-Rock Opera: A Cover Story: After That Ugly Saloon Incident. Renovator hist. landmark The Tope Creek Lookout (Skyship); sponsor Adopt A Hwy., 1995; min. Universal Life Ch. With U.S. Army, 1967-70. Decorated Air medals (26), Aviator Flight Wings; recipient Cert. of Appreciation, Pres. Richard M. Nixon. Mem. Vietnam Helicopter Crewmember Assn., 145th Combat Aviation Bn. Assn., Vietnam Combat Vets. Assn., Vietnam Vets. Am., Vietnam Vets. Australia Assn. Office: PO Box 42 Wallowa OR 97885-0042 *Vietnam combat veteran Brian Wizard upgraded his combat experience to creative insight. He turns his inner visions into expressive art with the same gusto developed as a crew member of the historical assault helicopter Pollution IV. His art work is wide ranging and top quality. He can write a good story, compose a catchy tune, produce amazing videos, and make outrageous sculptures and jewelry. Brian Wizard is a turn-of-the-millennium artist/author who has locked and loaded his mind with clear and concise thoughts.*

WLODARSKI, ROBERT JAMES, archaeologist; b. L.A., July 17, 1948; s. Matthew Bill and Henrietta Barbara (Rokita) W.; m. Linda Marie Porfilio, Oct. 19, 1974 (div. Aug. 14, 1985); m. Anne Walker Powell, Nov. 22, 1990. AA, Fullerton (Calif.) Jr. Coll., 1968; BA, Calif. State U., Northridge, 1971, 72, MA, 1975. Clk. Fullerton Jr. Coll. Bookstore, 1967-68; archaeol. asst. UCLA Archaeol. Survey, Westwood, Calif., 1973-74; staff archaeologist Calif. State U., Northridge, 1974-78; archaeol. asst. Greenwood & Assocs., Pacific Palisades, Calif., 1973-83; archaeol. project leader Calif. Dept. Transp., L.A., 1983-85; pres. H.E.A.R.T., Calabasas, Calif., 1978—, Mayan Moon Prodns., Calabasas, 1988—; tech. cons. Ironwood Prodns., L.A., 1985. Author: Out of Mind, 1989; co-author 6 screenplays: The Crawling Eye, Illusion, No Innocents, Shattered Secrets, Cool Change, Cities of Stone; co-author: A Guide to the Haunted Queen Mary and Haunted Catalina, The Haunted Alamo, The Haunted Whaley House; contbr. articles to profl. jours. Recipient Spl. Archaeol. Recognition, Candelaria Am. Indian Coun., Oxnard, 1988. Mem. Soc. Profl. Archaeologists, Calif. Com. for Promotion of History. Democrat. Roman Catholic. Home and Office: 8701 Lava Pl West Hills CA 91304-2126

WNUCK, KENNETH LLOYD, software engineer; b. Yonkers, N.Y., July 6, 1957; s. Adolph Lloyd and Grace (Evjen) W. BS, SUNY, Stony Brook, 1979; MS, Poly. U. N.Y., 1985. Rsch. scientist Revlon Health Care Group, Tuckahoe, N.Y., 1979-81, CIBA-Geigy Corp., Ardsley, N.Y., 1981-85; tech. staff AT&T Bell Lab., Denver, 1985—; pres. KJ Custom Software; cons. in field. Contbr. articles to profl. jours. Mem. IEEE. Home: 11632 W 75th Cir Arvada CO 80005-5336 Office: AT&T Bell Labs 11900 Pecos St Denver CO 80234-2703

WOERNER, ROBERT EUGENE, federal agency administrator, editor; b. Cadillac, Mich., Sept. 23, 1947; s. William Reginald and Ellen Hazel (Van Zoeren) W. BA in English, Grand Valley State U., 1969. Logistics coord. Colo. Outward Bound, 1979-80; writer, editor Bur. of Land Mgmt., U.S. Dept. Interior, Grand Junction, Colo., 1977-78, Elko, Nev., 1980-82, Craig, Colo., 1982-84, Denver, 1984—; free-lance writer, Buena Vista, Colo., 1976-77; mem. computer tech. adv. bd. Warren Tech, Golden, Colo., 1994—. Newsletter editor Urban Peak, Denver, 1989-95. Vol. Craig Hosp., Englewood, Colo., 1994. Capt. USAF, 1970-76. Honors scholar Grand Valley State U., 1966-69. Mem. Electronic Dreams, So. Utah Wilderness Alliance. Office: Bur Land Mgmt RS-150C PO Box 25047 Denver CO 80225

WOESSNER, FREDERICK T., composer, pianist; b. Teaneck, N.J., July 23, 1935; s. Fred and Bertha W.; m. Lise, Feb. 14, 1960 (div. 1973); children: Betty, Allison. Student, Peabody Conservatory of Music, Balt., 1960-61; MBA, NYU, 1968; MA, Calif. State U., Los Angeles, 1975; pvt. study with, David Diamond, Charles Haubiel, Albert Harris. Owner Al-Fre-Bett Music, Los Angeles, 1980—. Composer (for orch.) Nursery Song, Variations on an Irish Air, Reflections for Strings, Fanfare for Winds, String Quartet, Concerto for piano improvisations and orch., Secret Gospels (Cantata), Sonic studies for Piano I Elegy for Trumpet and Winds, (music for films) Sky Bandits, Gunbus, Pale Horse, Pale Rider, The Curb Your Appetite Diet, Centerfold, (title music for TV) Actors Forum, (for stage) From Berlin to Broadway, Oh Atlantis, Kurt, Lil Nell, Another Town, Victorian Atmospheres; composer and pianist, album-film/video, Vincent Moreaux, His Finest Hour In My Forest Cathedral, Songs from the Sea; rec. artist Sonic Arts and Repertoire Records. Pres. bd. dirs. Inst. for Recording and Multimedia Arts; mem. bd. govs.Music and the Arts Found. of Am., Inc.; dir. West Coast Musical Theatre Lab. Mem. ASCAP, Nat. Acad. Recording Arts and Scis., Dramatists Guild, Soc. Composers and Lyricists, Am. Fedn. Musicians, Am. Soc. Music Arrangers and Composers (treas. 1978—), Composers and Arrangers Found. Am. (sec.). Democrat. Office: Al-Fre-Bett Music PO Box 45 Los Angeles CA 90078-0045

WOGSLAND, JAMES WILLARD, retired heavy machinery manufacturing executive; b. Devils Lake, N.D., Apr. 17, 1931; s. Melvin LeRoy and Mable Bertina (Paulson) W.; m. Marlene Claudia Clark, June 1957; children: Karen Lynn, Steven James. BA in Econs., U. Minn., 1957. Various positions fin. dept. Caterpillar Tractor Co., Peoria, Ill., 1957-64, treas., 1976-81; mgr. fin. Caterpillar Overseas S.A., Geneva, 1965-70, sec.-treas., 1970-76; dir.-pres. Caterpillar Brasil S.A., São Paulo, 1981-87; exec. v.p. Caterpillar, Inc., Peoria, 198-90, also bd. dirs., vice-chmn., 1990-95; bd. dirs. Cipsco, Inc., Springfield, Ill. Mem. adv. bd. St. Francis Hosp., Peoria, 1987-95; bd. dirs. Peoria Area Cmty. Found., 1986-92; trustee Eureka Coll., 1987-95. Sgt. USAF, 1951-55. Mem. Hayden Lake Golf and Country Club. Republican. Presbyterian. Home: 9675 Easy St Hayden Lake ID 83835-9526

WOHL, ARMAND JEFFREY, cardiologist; b. Phila., Dec. 11, 1946; s. Herman Lewis and Selma (Paul) W.; m. Marylouise Katherine Giangrossi, Sept. 4, 1977; children: Michael Adam, Todd David. Student, Temple U., 1967; MD, Hahnemann U., 1971. Intern Bexar County Hosp., San Antonio, 1971-72; resident in internal medicine Parkland Hosp., Dallas, 1972-74; fellow in cardiology U. Tex. Southwestern Med. Ctr., Dallas, 1974-76; chief of cardiology USAF Hosp. Elmendorf, Anchorage, 1976-78; chief cardiologist Riverside (Calif.) Med. Clin., 1978-79; cardiologist Grossmont Cardiology Med. Group, La Mesa, Calif., 1980-84; pvt. practice, La Mesa, 1985—; chief of cardiology Grossmont Hosp., La Mesa, 1988-90; asst. clin. prof. Sch. Medicine. U. Calif., San Diego, 1990—. Contbr. articles to profl. jours. Bd. dirs. Grossmont Healthcare Dist., 1995—, San Diego County chpt. Am. Heart Assn., 1981-87. Maj. USAF, 1976-78. Fellow Am. Coll. Cardiology (councilor Calif. chpt. 1991—), Am. Coll. Physicians, Coun. on Clin. Cardiology. Office: 5565 Grossmont Center Dr La Mesa CA 91942-3020 *Personal philosophy: Work hard, respect others, enjoy life.*

WOHL, CHARLES MARTIN, business development executive; b. Cambridge, Mass., June 12, 1959; s. Martin and Ann Hedges (Findley) W.; m. Martha Ellen Fleming, Apr. 30, 1988; children: Amelia Ann, Diana Catherine. BA, Calif. State U., Long Beach, 1981; BS, U. So. Calif., L.A., 1985, MS, 1985. Project engr. Hughes Aircraft Co., El Segundo, Calif., 1979-85; project mgr. Northrop Corp., Hawthorne, Calif., 1985-89; sr. product mgr. Magnavox Electronics, Torrance, Calif., 1989-94; cons. Group L, Newport Beach, Calif., 1994-96; gen. mgr., ptnr. Significant Improvements, Long Beach, 1991—; program mgr. Rockwell Internat., Calif., 1996—. Dist. commrs. Boy Scouts Am., Long Beach, 1987-88, asst. scoutmaster, 1979-86. Mem. Alamitos Bay Yacht Club, Snipe Class Internat. Racing Assn. (dist. gov. 1986-89). Methodist.

WOHLETZ, LEONARD RALPH, soil scientist, consultant; b. Nekoma, N.D., Oct. 22, 1909; s. Frank and Anna (Keifer) W.; m. Jane Geisendorfer, Sept. 1, 1935; children: Mary Jane, Leonard Ralph Jr., Elizabeth Ann, Catherine Ellen, Margaret Lee. BS, U. Calif., Berkeley, 1931, MS, 1933. Jr. soil expert USDA Soil Erosion Svc., Santa Paula, Calif., 1934; asst. regional chief soil surveys USDA Soil Conservation Svc., Santa Paula, 1935; asst. regional chief soil surveys USDA Soil Conservation Svc., Berkeley, 1939-42, soil survey supr., 1942-45, state soil scientist, 1945-68, asst. to state conservationist, 1969-71; cons. soil scientist Berkeley, 1973—. Author: Survey Guide, 1948; contbr. articles to profl. publs. including Know Calif. Land, Soils and Land Use Planning, Planning by Foresight and Hindsight. Mem. Waste Mgmt. Commn., Berkeley, 1981; chmn. com. Rep. for Congress, 8th Dist. Calif., 1980; pres. State and Berkeley Rep. Assembly, 1985—. Recipient Soil Conservationist of Yr., Calif. Wildlife Fedn., 1967. Mem. Soil and Water Conservation Soc. (chmn. organic waste mgmt. com. 1973—, sect. pres., Dist. Svc. award, charter and life mem., Disting. Svc. award 1971, Outstanding Svc. award 1983), Soil Sci. Soc. Am. (emeritus), Internat. Soc. Soil Sci., Profl. Soil Sci. Assn. Calif., Commonwealth Club Calif., San Francisco Farmers Club. Roman Catholic. Home: 510 Vincente Ave Berkeley CA 94707-1522

WOIKE, LYNNE ANN, computer scientist; b. Torrance, Calif., Oct. 20, 1960; d. Stephen J. and Virginia (Ursich) Shane; m. Thomas W. Woike, Feb. 13, 1988; 1 child, Karla. BSc in Computer Sci., Calif. State U., Dominguez Hills, 1994. Computer cons. Unocal Oil Co., Wilmington, Calif., 1992-94; x-window/motif software developer Logican Inc., San Pedro, Calif., 1994-95; reticle engr. TRW, Inc., Redondo Beach, Calif., 1982-88, product data mgmt. database adminstr., 1995—, chmn. product data mgmt. change control bd., 1995—. Mem. IEEE, IEEE Computer Sci., Assn. for Computing Machinery (chmn. student chpt. 1993-94), Calif. State U. Sci. Soc. (computer sci. rep. 1993—). Office: TRW Inc One Space Park S/2157 Redondo Beach CA 90278

WOJTYLA, WALTER HAASE, artist; b. Chgo., Feb. 10, 1933; s. Louis Walter and Helen Julia (Haase) W.; m. Susan Virginia Leonard, Sept. 2, 1967 (div.); 1 child, Anthony Lewis. BFA, U. Ill., 1956; MFA, U. Cin., 1967. Solo exhbns. include San Diego Art Inst., 1992, 93; group exhbns. include Spanish Village Art Ctr., San Diego, 1991, La Jolla (Calif.) Art Exhbn. 1991, San Diego-Tijuana Yokohama Art Exch., 1992, The Paladion, San Diego, 1994, others; works collected at Mus. of Contemporary Art, San Diego, 1993; contbr. to profl. publs.; (TV documentary) Artists-in-Residence, San Diego, 1983. Mem. San Diego Art Guild. Home: 2102 C St San Diego CA 92102-1835

WOLANER, ROBIN PEGGY, internet and magazine publisher; b. Queens, N.Y., May 6, 1954; d. David H. and Harriet (Radlow) W.; m. Steven J. Castleman, 1992; 1 child, Terry David. BS in Indsl. and Labor Rels., Cornell U., 1975. Sr. editor Viva Mag., N.Y.C., 1975-76; editor Impact Mag., N.Y.C., 1976-77; circulation mgr. Runner's World Mag., Mountain View, Calif., 1977-79; cons. Ladd Assocs., San Francisco, 1979-80; gen. mgr. Mother Jones Mag., San Francisco, 1980-81, pub., 1981-85; founder, pub. Parenting Mag., San Francisco, 1985-91, pres., 1991-92; v.p. Time Pub. Ventures, 1990-96; pres., CEO Sunset Pub. Corp., 1992-95; chmn. Online Ptnrs. LLC, 1997—. Bd. dirs. Med. Self Care Inc., 1996—, Ifusion Com. LLC, 1996—. Jewish. Office: 2240 Hyde St San Francisco CA 94109

WOLBERS, HARRY LAWRENCE, engineering psychologist; b. L.A., Jan. 29, 1926; s. Harry Lawrence and Edith Christine (Nordeen) W.; m. Mary Lou Jordan Call, Feb. 18, 1972; children: Harry L., Richard C., Leslie A., Suzanne M. BS, Calif. Inst. Tech., 1946; MA, U. So. Calif., L.A., 1949, PhD, 1955. Lic. psychologist Calif. V.p. Psychol. Svcs., Inc., L.A., 1948-54; chief systems rsch. Douglas Aircraft Co., El Segundo, Calif., 1954-63; chief program engr. space systems Douglas Aircraft Co., Santa Monica, Huntington Beach, 1963-74; chief systems engr. advanced space systems McDonnell Douglas Astronautics Co., Huntington Beach, Calif., 1974-85; adj. prof. dept. indsl. and systems engring. U. So. Calif., L.A., 1954-85; dep. dir. flight crew systems McDonnell Douglas Space Systems Co., Huntington Beach, 1985-91; ret.; mem. USAF Sci. Adv. Bd., Washington, 1991-96; cons. NASA, Washington, 1988—. Contbr. articles to profl. jours. Lt. (j.g.) USN, 1943-47; ATO; PTO. Decorated Meritorious Civilian Svc. medal, 1995, Recipient Engring. Merit award San Fernando Valley Engrs. Coun., Calif., 1988. Fellow Human Factors and Ergonomics Soc. (Orange County chpt. pres. 1989); mem. APA (divsn. applied exptl. and engring. psychology), Soc. Indsl. and Orgnl. Psychologists, Sigma Xi, Psi Chi.

WOLD, DAVID C., bishop. Bishop of Southwestern Wash. Evang. Luth. Ch. in Am., Tacoma. Office: Synod of Southwestern Washington 420 121st St S Tacoma WA 98444-5218*

WOLF, ALFRED, rabbi; b. Eberbach, Germany, Oct. 7, 1915; came to U.S., 1935, naturalized, 1941; s. Hermann and Regina (Levy) W.; m. Miriam Jean Office, June 16, 1940; children: David B., Judith C. (dec.), Dan L. BA, U. Cin., 1937; MHL, Hebrew Union Coll., 1941; DD, 1966; PhD, U. So. Calif., 1961; DHL, U. Judaism, 1987, Loyola Marymount U., 1990. Ordained rabbi, 1941. Rabbi Temple Emanuel, Dothan, Ala., 1941-46; S.E. regional dir. Union Am. Hebrew Congregations, 1944-46; Western regional dir. Union Am. Hebrew Congregations, Los Angeles, 1946-49; rabbi Wilshire Blvd. Temple Los Angeles, 1949-85, rabbi emeritus, 1985—; dir. Skirball Inst. on Am. Values of Am. Jewish Com., 1985-95; founding dir., 1996—; lectr. U. So. Calif., 1955-69, Hebrew Union Coll., Jewish Inst. Religion, Calif., 1963-65, 74; lectr. religion Seven Seas div. Chapman Coll., 1967; adj. prof. theology Loyola U. Los Angeles, 1967-74; lectr. sociology Calif. State U., Los Angeles, 1977; co-chair First Nationwide Conf. for Cath. Jewish and Protestant seminaries, Chgo., 1993. Author: (with Joseph Gaer) Our Jewish Heritage, 1957, (with Monsignor Royale M. Vadakin) Journey Of Discovery - A Resource Manual for Catholic-Jewish Dialogue, 1989; editor Teaching About World Religions: A Teacher's Supplement, 1991. Mem. camp commn. adminstrv. com. Camp Hess Kramer, 1951—; mem. L.A. Com. on Human Rels., 1956-72, mem. exec. bd., 1960—, chmn., 1964-66, hon. mem., 1972—; pres. Anytown U.S.A., 1964-66; mem. United Way Planning Coun. Bd., chmn., 1974-78; mem. youth adv. com. NCCJ, 1968-72, exec. bd., 1972-93; founding pres. Interreligious Coun. So. Calif., 1970-72; chmn. clergy adv. com. L.A. Sch. Dist., 1971-81; chmn. Nat. Workshop on Christian-Jewish Rels., 1978; bd. govs. Hebrew Union Coll., bd. alumni overseers, 1972—; mem. L.A. 2000 Com., 1986-89, The 2000 Partnership, 1989-95, Berlin Sister City Com., L.A., 1987-89; bd. dirs. Jewish Fedn. Coun., 1978-85, bd. govs., 1985—; bd. dirs. Jewish Family Svc. L.A., sec., 1978-80. Recipient Samuel Kaminker award as Jewish educator of year Western Assn. Temple Educators, 1965, John Anson Ford Human Relations award County Commn. on Human Relations, 1972, 90, Harry Hollzer Meml. award Los Angeles Jewish Fedn. Council, 1978, Volpert Community Service award, 1986, Community Service award United Way of Los Angeles, 1980, Leadership award Los Angeles Bd. Edn., 1981, Service to Edn. award Associated Adminstrs. Los Angeles, 1983, Pub. Service award Jewish Chautauqua Soc., 1986, N.Am. Interfaith Leadership award Nat. Workshop for Christian-Jewish Rels., 1990. Mem. Bd. Rabbis So. Calif. (pres.), Am. Jewish Com. (exec. com. Los Angeles chpt., Max Bay Meml. award 1986), Central Conf. Am. Rabbis (exec. bd., mem. commn. on Jewish edn. 1970-72, treas. 1975-79, chmn. interreligious activities com. 1975-79, hon. mem. 1991—), Pacific Assn. Reform Rabbis (pres.), So. Calif. Assn. Liberal Rabbis (pres.), Synagogue Council Am. (mem. com. interreligious affairs), Alumni Assn. Hebrew Union Coll.-Jewish Inst. Religion, Town Hall, Los Angeles World Affairs Council, U. So. Calif. Alumni Assn. Home: 3389 Ley Dr Los Angeles CA 90027-1315 Office: Skirball Inst on Am Values 635 S Harvard Blvd Ste 214 Los Angeles CA 90005-2586

WOLF, ARTHUR HENRY, museum administrator; b. New Rockford, N.D., June 18, 1953; s. Louis Irwin and Vivian Joyce (Grinde) W.; m. Holly M. Chaffee, Oct. 18, 1984. BA in Anthropology, U. Nebr., 1975; MA, U. Ariz., 1977. Lab. asst., acting curator anthropology U. Nebr. State Mus., Lincoln, 1973-75; rsch. asst. Ariz. State Mus., Tucson, 1975-77; curator of collections Sch. Am. Rsch., Santa Fe, N.Mex., 1977-79; dir. Millcent Rogers Mus., Taos, N.Mex., 1979-87, Nev. State Mus. and Hist. Soc., Las Vegas, 1988-92, Mus. of Rockies, Bozeman, Mont., 1992-96; pres. High Desert Mus., Bend, Oreg., 1996—; speaker in field; cons. Pueblos of Zuni, Picuris, San Ildefonso and Taos. Contbr. articles and revs. to profl. jours. Trustee Kokopelli Archeol. Rsch. Fund, Bozeman, 1992-96; active Mont. Ambs. Recipient Young Alumnus award U. Nebr. Lincoln, 1990. Mem. Am. Assn. Mus. (bd. dirs. 1994—, vis. com. roster 1989—, vice chair 1996-97), Rotary, Assn. Sci. Mus. Dirs. Home: 110 NW Wau St Bend OR 97701 Office: Mus of Rockies Montana State U Bozeman MT 59717 also: High Desert Mus 59800 S Hwy 97 Bend OR 97702

WOLF, CHARLES, JR., economist, educator; b. N.Y.C., Aug. 1, 1924; s. Charles and Rosalie W.; m. Theresa van de Wint, Mar. 1, 1947; children: Charles Theodore, Timothy van de Wint. B.S., Harvard U., 1943, M.P.A., 1948, Ph.D. in Econs., 1949. Economist, fgn. service officer U.S. Dept. State, 1945-47, 49-53; mem. faculty Cornell U., 1953-54, U. Calif., Berkeley, 1954-55; sr. economist The Rand Corp., Santa Monica, Calif., 1955-67, head econs. dept., 1967-81; dean The Rand Grad. Sch., 1970—, sr. economist, 1981—, corp. fellow in internat. econs., 1996—; sr. fellow Hoover Inst., 1988—; bd. dirs. Fundamental Investors Fund, Capital Income Builder Fund, Am. Capital Fund, Capital World Growth Fund; mem. adv. com. UCLA Clin. Scholars Program; lectr. econs. UCLA, 1960-72; mem. adv. bd. grad. sch. pub. policy Carnegie-Mellon U., 1992—. Author: The Costs and Benefits of the Soviet Empire, 1986, Markets or Governments: Choosing Between Imperfect Alternatives, 1988, 93, (with others) The Impoverished Superpower: Perestroika and the Soviet Military Burden, 1990, Linking Economic Policy and Foreign Policy, 1991, Promoting Democracy and Free Markets in Eastern Europe, 1992, Defense Conversion and Economic Reform in Russia and Ukraine, 1994, Long-Term Economic and Military Hands: The United States and Asia, 1994-2015; contbr. articles to profl. jours. Mem. Assn. for Public Policy Analysis and Mgmt. (pres. 1980-81), Am. Econs. Assn., Econometric Soc., Coun. on Fgn. Rels., Internat. Inst. Strategic Studies London. Clubs: Cosmos (Washington); Riviera Tennis (Los Angeles); Harvard (N.Y.). Office: RAND Grad Sch Policy Studies 1700 Main St Santa Monica CA 90401-3208

WOLF, CYNTHIA TRIBELHORN, librarian, library educator; b. Denver, Dec. 12, 1945; d. John Baltazar and Margaret (Kern) Tribelhorn; m. H.Y. Rassam, Mar. 21, 1969 (div. Jan. 1988); children: Najma C., Yousuf J.; adopted children: Leonard Joseph Lucero, Lakota E. Rassam-Lucero. BA, Colo. State U., 1970; MLS, U. Denver, 1985. Cert. permanent profl. librarian, N.Mex. Elem. tchr. Sacred Heart Sch., Farmington, N.Mex., 1973-78; asst. prof. library sci. edn. U. N.Mex., Albuquerque, 1985-90, dir. libr. sci. edn. divsn., 1989-90; pres. Info. Acquisitions, Albuquerque, 1990—; libr. dir. Southwestern Coll., Santa Fe, 1992-94; mem. youth resources Rio Grande Valley Libr. Sys., Albuquerque, 1994—; fine arts resource person for gifted edn. Farmington Pub. Schs., 1979-83; speaker Unofficial Mentorships & Market Research, 1992—. Mem. Farmington Planning and Zoning Commn., 1980-81; bd. dirs. Farmington Mus. Assn., 1983-84; pres. Farmington Symphony League, 1978. Mem. ALA, N.Mex. Library Assn., LWV (bd. dirs. Farmington, 1972-74, 75, pres.). Office: Rio Grande Valley Libr Sys Albuquerque NM 87000

WOLF, DOROTHY JOAN, poet; b. Cannon, Del., July 9, 1934; d. Floyd Henry Wilson and Catherine M. Robert Wolf; div.; 3 children. AA, Canada C.C., Redwood City, Calif., 1982; BA, San Francisco State U., 1984; post-grad., Calif. State U., Dominguez Hills, 1992. Cert. tchr., Calif.; cert. nurse asst., Calif. Tchr. Monterey County H.S., 1991—. Author: Earth These Are Your Children, 1991, Mothers of Russia and Other Essays, A Delightful Place, 1994, A Forest is a Cathedral, 1995. Home: PO Box 5424 Carmel CA 93921-5424

WOLF, DOUGLAS JEFFREY, lawyer; b. Merced, Calif., June 19, 1953; s. Stanley William and Phyllis (Donner) W.; m. Vicki Lynn Fields, July 8, 1979; children: Joshua Michael, Carly Suzanne, Jordan Matthew. AB, U. Calif., Davis, 1974; JD, Southwestern U., Los Angeles, 1977. Bar: U.S. Dist. Ct. (cen. dist.), U.S. Ct. of Appeals (9th cir.). Criminal justice planner San Mateo County Criminal Justice Council, Burlingame, Calif., 1972-74; law clk. Friedman and Cone, Los Angeles, 1974-79; pvt. practice Los Angeles, 1979-82, Woodland Hills, Calif., 1982—. Pres. The Cheryl Fields Found. for Victims, L.A., 1984; bd. dirs. Adam Walsh Child Resource Ctr., Orange, Calif., 1986; bd. dirs. Mothers Against Sexual Abuse, Temple Aliyah; adv. bd. Vis. Nurses Assn., Van Nuys, Calif. Mem. Calif. State Bar, San Fernando Valley Bar Assn., Los Angeles County Bar Assn. Democrat. Jewish.

WOLF, G. VAN VELSOR, JR., lawyer; b. Balt., Feb. 19, 1944; s. G. Van Velsor and Alice Roberts (Kimberly) W.; m. Ann Holmes Kavanagh, May 19, 1984; children: George Van Velsor III, Timothy Kavanagh (dec.), Christopher Kavanagh, Elisabeth Huxley. BA, Yale U., 1966; JD, Vanderbilt U., 1973. Bar: N.Y. 1974, Ariz. 1982, U.S. Dist. Ct. (so. dist.) N.Y. 1974, U.S. Dist. Ct. Ariz. 1982, U.S. Ct. Appeals (2d cir.) 1974, U.S. Ct. Appeals (9th cir.) 1982. Agrl. advisor U.S. Peace Corps, Tanzania and Kenya, 1966-70; assoc. Milbank, Tweed, Hadley & McCloy, N.Y.C., 1973-75; vis. lectr. law Airlangga U., Surabaya, Indonesia, 1975-76, U. Ariz. 1990, Vanderbilt U., 1991, U. Md., 1994, Ariz. State U., 1995; editor in chief Environ. Law Reporter, Washington, 1976-81; cons. Nat. Trust for Historic Preservation, Washington, 1981; assoc. Lewis & Roca, Phoenix, 1981-84, ptnr., 1984-91; ptnr. Snell & Wilmer, Phoenix, 1991—. Bd. dirs. Ariz. div. Am. Cancer Soc., 1985-96, sec. 1990-92, vice chmn. 1992-94, chmn., 1994-96; bd. dirs. S.W. divsn. Am. Cancer Soc., 1996—, chmn., 1996—. Editor: Toxic Substances Control, 1980; contbr. articles to profl. jours. Bd. dirs. Phoenix Little Theater, 1983-90, chmn., 1986-88. Mem. ABA (vice chmn. SONREEL commn. state and regional environ. coop.), Assn. Bar City N.Y., Ariz. State Bar Assn. (coun. environ. & nat. res. law sect. 1988-93, chmn. 1991-92), Maricopa County Bar Assn., Ariz. Acad., Union Club (N.Y.C.), Univ. Club (Phoenix), Phoenix Country Club. Office: Snell & Wilmer 1 Arizona Ctr Phoenix AZ 85004-0001

WOLF, HANS ABRAHAM, retired pharmaceutical company executive; b. Frankfurt, Fed. Republic Germany, June 27, 1928; came to U.S., 1936, naturalized, 1944; s. Franz Benjamin and Ilse (Nathan) W.; m. Elizabeth J. Bassett, Aug. 2, 1958; children: Heidi Elizabeth, Rebecca Anne, Deborah Wolf Streeter, Andrew Robert. AB magna cum laude, Harvard U., 1949, MBA, 1955; PhB, Oxford U., 1951. Math instr. Tutoring Sch., 1946-47; statis. research Nat. Bur. Econ. Research, N.Y.C., 1948-49; researcher Georgetown U., 1951-52; confidential aide Office Dir. Mut. Security, Washington, 1952; analyst Ford Motor div. Ford Motor Co., Dearborn, Mich., summer 1954; foreman prodn. M&C Nuclear Inc., Attleboro, Mass., 1955-57; asst. supt. prodn. Metals & Controls Corp., Attleboro, 1957-59, mgr. product dept., 1959-62, controller, 1962-67; asst. v.p., controller materials and services group Tex. Instruments Inc., Dallas, 1967-69, treas., v.p., 1969-75; v.p. fin., chief fin. officer Syntex Corp., Palo Alto, Calif., 1975-78, exec. v.p., 1978-86, vice chmn., chief adminstrv. officer, 1986-92, vice chmn., 1992-93, also bd. dirs., 1986-93; bd. dirs. Clean Sites, Inc., Alexandria, Va., Tab Products Co., Palo Alto, Calif., chmn., 1995—; bd. dirs. Network Equipment Techs., Redwood City, Calif., chmn., 1996—; bd. dirs. Satellite Dialysis Ctrs., Inc., Redwood City, Hyal Pharms., Mississauga, Ont. Author: Motivation Research—A New Aid to Understanding Your Markets, 1955. Mem. Norton (Mass.) Sch. Bd., 1959-62, chmn., 1961-62; pres., bd. dirs. Urban League Greater Dallas, 1971-74; bd. dirs. Dallas Health Planning Coun., mem. community adv. com., 1973-75; bd. dirs., pres. Children's Health Coun. of the Mid Peninsula; cubmaster Boy Scouts Am., 1976-78; elder United Ch. Christ, 1970-73, vice chmn. gen. bd., 1970-71, moderator, 1978-80; trustee Pacific Sch. Religion, 1986-94, chmn., 1990-94; trustee World Affairs Coun. San Francisco, 1986-92, 94—; dir. Tech Mus. San Jose. With USAF, 1952-53. Mem. Am. Mgmt. Assn. (planning council fin. div. 1970-76), Phi Beta Kappa.

WOLF, HARRY, retired dean and educator; b. Alameda, Calif., Dec. 26, 1922; s. Morris J. and Regina (Fischer) W.; m. Doris Zena Rackow, Feb. 15, 1947; children: Stephen F., Bernard N., Rebecca J. BA, U. Calif., Berkeley, 1947, MA, 1951. Salary and wage analyst Dept. of the Navy, San Francisco, 1947-57; chief salary adminstrn. U.S. Atomic Energy Commn., Washington, 1957-62; pers. dir. U.S. Atomic Energy Commn., Berkeley, 1962-66, 72-77; dir. Exec. Seminar Ctr., U.S. Civil Svc. Commn., Berkeley, 1966-72; prof. Golden Gate U., San Francisco, 1965-87, dean pub. adminstrn., 1987-90; ret., 1990; pers. cons. Exec. Mgmt. Svcs., Inc., Washington, 1977-82; chair county civil svc. revision bd. Contra Costa County, Calif., 1980. Contbr. articles to profl. jours. Master sgt. U.S. Army, 1943-46. Recipient Bay Area Outstanding Contbr. award ASPA, 1983, Disting. Svc. award Golden Gate U., 1990. Mem. Nat. Assn. Ret. Fed. Employees (state pub. rels. chair 1995—). Democrat. Jewish. Home: 669 Montezuma Ct Walnut Creek CA 94598-2913

WOLF, JOHN ARTHUR, JR., urologist; b. Yakima, Wash., Feb. 8, 1933; s. John Arthur and Annie Laurie (Hutson) W.; m. Dorothy Ann Kemp, June 25, 1960; children: Stephanie Ann Nerne, John Arthur IV, Robert Kemp. BS in Zoology, U. Wash., 1957, MD, 1961. Diplomate Am. Bd. Urology. Resident in urology U. Wash. Hosps., Seattle, 1961-66; instr. dept. surgery U. Wash., Seattle, clin. asst. prof. dept. urology; pvt. practice Yakima; physician II DSHS, Divsn. DD, State of Wash., Yakima, physician III, med. dir. Contbr. articles to profl. jours. Bd. dirs. ARC, Yakima. With USNR, 1950-53. Mem. N.W. Urol. Assn. (pres. 1978-79). Office: State of Washington DSHS DDD 609 Speyers Rd Selah WA 98942

WOLF, LAWRENCE JOSEPH, mechanical engineering educator; b. St. Louis, Aug. 10, 1938; s. Vincent F. and Clara A. (Holtkamp) W.; m. Barbara Ann Bieber, Aug. 12, 1961; children: Theresa, Carl, Lawrence V. AA, Harris Tchrs. Coll., 1959; BSME, Washington U., St. Louis, 1961, MS, 1962, DSc, 1971. Registered profl. engr., Tex., Mo., Ind., Ill. Engr. Monsanto Corp., St. Louis, 1962-63; design engr. McDonnell Douglas, St. Louis, 1963-64; from instr. to assoc. prof. to dept. head St. Louis C.C.-Florissnat Valley, 1964-72, assoc. dean, 1975-78; assoc. prof. U. Petroleum and Minerals, Dhahran, Saudi Arabia, 1972-74; dean instrn. Wentworth Inst., Boston, 1974-75; dept. head Purdue U.-Calumet, Hammond, Ind., 1978-80; dean tech. U. Houston, from 1980; pres., prof. Oreg. Inst. of Tech., Klamath Falls, 1991—; cons. engr. Nooter Corp., St. Louis, 1965-72; guest scientist Brookhaven Nat. Lab. and Superconducting Supercollider Lab., 1989—; founder Tex. Assn. Schs. Engring. Tech.; bd. dirs. United Way of Klamath Falls, Cascades East Area Health Edn. Ctr. Author: Understanding Structures...A Parallel Approach to Statics and Strength of Materials; editor Jour. Engring. Tech., 1983-87; contbr. 40 articles to profl. jours. Leader Webelos Boy Scouts Am., Houston; chmn. Sesquicentennial Cannon Com., Houston, 1986; bd. dirs. Klamath County United Way; founder, chmn. Cascades-East Health Edn. Ctr. Served with U.S. Army, 1956-57. Recipient Fellow Members awd., Am. Soc. for Engineering Education, 1992. Fellow Accrediting Bd. Engring. and Tech. (TAC chmn.); mem. ASME, Am. Soc. Engring. Edn. (div. chmn., James H. McGraw award 1987), Soc. Mfg. Engrs. Office: Oreg Inst Tech Office of Pres 3201 Campus Dr Klamath Falls OR 97601-8801*

WOLF, PATRICIA B., museum director. Dir., exec. dir. Anchorage Mus. History and Art. Office: Anchorage Mus History and Art 121 W 7th Ave Anchorage AK 99501

WOLF-CHASE, GRACE ANNAMARIE, astronomer, astrophysicist; b. N.Y.C., Dec. 12, 1957; d. Franz and Ruth Anna (Schnabel) Wolf; m. Dennis Arthur Chase, Apr. 25, 1994; children: Jaclyn Ruth Chase, Dennis Rolf Chase, Jason Arthur Chase. AB, Cornell U., 1981; PhD, U. Ariz., 1992. Undergrad. rsch./teaching asst. Cornell U., Ithaca, N.Y., 1980-81; grad. rsch./teaching asst. U. Ariz., Tucson, 1981-86; telescope operator Nat. Radio Astronomy Obs., Kitt Peak, Ariz., 1986-90; instr. astronomy lab. U. Ariz., Tucson, 1990-91; lectr. astronomy U. Nev., Las Vegas, 1993; postdoctoral fellow NASA/Ames Rsch. Ctr., Moffett Field, Calif., 1994-96, U. Calif., Riverside, Calif., 1996—; pub. lectr. Flandrau Sci. Ctr., U. Ariz., Tucson, 1990-92; lectr. astronomy camp Steward Obs., Tucson, 1991-92; presenter in field. Contbr. articles to conf. procs. and sci. jours. including Astron. Jour., Astrophys. Jour. Letters, Bull. of the Am. Astron. Soc., CO: 25 Years of Millimeter-wave Spectroscopy; book rev. to Nature mag. Nat. Rsch. Coun. fellow NAS, 1994-95. Nat. Rsch. Coun. fellow NAS, 1994-96, Pres.'s fellow U. Calif., 1996—. Mem. Am. Astron. Soc. Office: U Calif Dept Physics Riverside CA 92521

WOLFE, BRIAN AUGUSTUS, sales executive, small business owner; b. Mexico City, Nov. 23, 1946; came to U.S., 1947; s. Steward Augustus and Vivia Idalene (Fouts) W.; m. Holly Joyce Gilhart, Dec. 29, 1981; 1 child, Derek Augustus. BSME, Tex. A&M U., 1968. Project engr. Tex. Power & Light Co., Dallas, 1968-72; service engr. Babcock & Wilcox, Chgo., 1972-74; sales engr., New Eng. dist. Babcock & Wilcox, Boston, 1974-79; area mgr., Far East, internat. bus. Babcock & Wilcox, Barberton, Ohio, 1979-81; dist. sales mgr. Babcock & Wilcox, Sheridan, Colo., 1981—; owner Grease Beast South Metroplex, Lakewood, Colo., 1996—. Mem. Rocky Mountain Elec. League (bd. dirs. 1988—, v.p. 1990-91, pres.-elect 1991-92, pres. 1992-93). Home: 7285 W Vassar Ave Denver CO 80227-3303 Office: Unit G-3 3535 S Platte River Dr Sheridan CO 80110

WOLFE, BURTON H., non-profit organization executive; b. Washington, Sept. 2, 1932; s. Simon and Gertrude (Hinkle) W.; m. Sandra Sue Smith, Jan. 22, 1962 (div. Nov. 1966); children: James Burton, Brendan Simon. BA, George Washington U., 1954. Reporter/editor Stars & Stripes, Darmstadt, Germany, 1955-56; reporter/feature writer Burlington (Vt.) Free Press, 1956-57, Internat. News Svc., San Francisco, 1957-58; editor/pub. The Californian, San Francisco, 1960-62; pub. rels. writer B'nai B'rith, Washington, 1963; pub. editor AFSCME, AFL-CIO, Washington, 1964-65; writer/editor Civic Edn. Svc., Washington, 1965-66; founder, dir. Homosapiens Ednl. and Legal Project, San Francisco, 1986—; lectr. in field. Author: The Hippies, 1968, Hitler and the Nazis, 1970, The Devil and Dr. Noxin, 1973, Pileup on Death Row, 1973, The Devil's Avenger: A Biography of Anton Szandor Lavey, 1974; contbr. numerous articles to profl. jours.; contbr. San Francisco Bay Guardian. Sgt. U.S. Army, 1954-56. Recipient Newswriting award AP, 1956-57, Journalism award Cath. Press Assn., 1960, 70, Writing award Bar Assn. Calif., 1975. Mem. Am. Legion, Elks, Phi Beta Kappa. 01. Office: 1095 Market St #814 San Francisco CA 94103-1631

WOLFE, CAMERON WITHGOT, JR., lawyer; b. Oakland, Calif., July 7, 1939; s. Cameron W. and Jean (Brown) W.; m. Frances Evelyn Bishopric, Sept. 2, 1964; children: Brent Everett, Julie Frances, Karen Jean. AB, U. Calif.-Berkeley, 1961, JD, 1964. Bar: Calif. 1965, U.S. Dist. Ct. (no. dist.) Calif. 1965, U.S. Ct. Appeals (9th cir.) 1965, U.S. Tax Ct. 1966, U.S. Ct. Claims 1977, U.S. Ct. Appeals (3d cir.) 1980, U.S. Ct. Appeals (fed. cir.) 1983, U.S. Supreme Ct. 1986 . Assoc., then ptnr. Orrick, Herrington & Sutcliffe, San Francisco, 1964—; bd. dirs. Crowley Maritime Corp.; mem. steering com. Western Pension Conf. Pres. League to Save Lake Tahoe, 1979, 80; chmn. League to Save Lake Tahoe Charitable Trust, 1966-91, Piedmont Ednl. Fund Campaign, 1982-83; pres. Piedmont Ednl. Found., 1986-90; bd. dirs. Yosemite Fund., 1993—. Served with U.S. Army, 1957, with USAR, 1957-65. Mem. ABA (mem. taxation com.), Calif. State Bar, San Francisco Bar Assn., Order of Coif, Phi Beta Kappa. Clubs: Pacific Union (San Francisco); Claremont Country (Oakland, Calif.). Home: 59 Lakeview Ave Piedmont CA 94611-3514 Office: Orrick Herrington & Sutcliffe 400 Sansome St San Francisco CA 94111-3308

WOLFE, CLIFFORD EUGENE, architect, writer; b. Harrington, Wash., Mar. 26, 1906; s. Delwin Lindsley and Luella Grace (Cox) W.; m. Frances Lillian Parkes, Sept. 12, 1936 (dec.); children: Gretchen Yvonne Wolfe Mason, Eric Von; m. Mary Theye Worthen. A.B. in Architecture, U. Calif.-Berkeley, 1933. Registered architect, Calif. Assoc. architect John Knox Ballantine, Architect, San Francisco, 1933-42; supervising architect, prodn. engr. G.W. Williams Co. Contractors, Burlingame, Calif., 1942-44; state-wide coord. med. schs. and health ctrs. office archs. and engrs. U. Calif.-Berkeley, San Francisco and Los Angeles, 1944-52; sec. council on hosp. planning Am. Hosp. Assn., Chgo., 1952-59; dir. planning dept. Office of York & Sawyer, Architects, N.Y.C., 1959-74; prin. Clifford E. Wolfe, AIA-E, Oakland, Calif., 1974-88; ret.; assoc. designer State of Calif. Commn. for Golden Gate Internat. Exposition, San Francisco, 1938-39; cons. Fed. Hosp. Council, Washington, 1954-60; mem. Pres.'s Conf. on Occupational Safety, Washington, 1955; rsch. architect Hosp Rsch. and Ednl. Trust, Chgo., 1957-59; instr. hosp. planning Columbia U., N.Y.C., 1961-73. Author, editor manuals on hosp. planning, engring. and safety, 1954-58. Author: Ballad of Humphrey The Humpback Whale, 1985; contbr. poetry to Tecolote Anthology, 1983, The Ina Coolbrith Circle, 1985, 87, 89, 91, 93, 95 (Grand prize Ina Coolbrith award 1986, Cleone Montgomery award 1990), Islandia, 1986, Tidings, 1989, Calif. Fedn. Chaparral Poets (pres. Tecolote chpt. 1982-86, 91-95). Hosp. planning research grantee USPHS, 1956. Mem. AIA (chmn. honor awards com. Chgo. chpt. 1958-59, chmn. activities com. N.Y. chpt. 1972-74, mem. emeritus East Bay chpt. 1974—). Address: 3900 Harrison St Apt 306 Oakland CA 94611-4525

WOLFE, GARY JOHN, foundation administrator, wildlife biologist; b. Georgetown, Tex., Mar. 29, 1949; s. Ervin Wright and Faye Margaret (Houston) W.; m. Rita May Boulton, Aug. 30, 1980. BS in Biology, U. N.Mex., 1971, BA in Chemistry, 1971; MS in Wildlife Biology, Colo. State U., 1974, PhD in Wildlife Biology, 1985. Park ranger Nat. Park Svc., Mt. Rainier Nat. Park, Wash., 1968-71, Big Bend Nat. Park, Tex., 1972; wildlife biologist Vermejo Park Corp., Raton, N.Mex., 1974-81, v.p., gen. mgr., 1981-86; field dir. Rocky Mountain Elk Found., Ft. Collins, Colo., 1986-88; group mgr. field ops. Rocky Mountain Elk Found., Missoula, Mont., 1988-93, exec. v.p., COO, 1993—; bd. dirs. Range Edn. Inst., Reno. Contbr. articles to prof. jours. Mem. Mt. Jumbo steering com., Missoula, 1995-96, Open Space Stewardship subcom., Missoula, 1996. Recipient Disting. Svc. award Ducks Unlimited, 1983. Mem. Nat. Wildlife Fedn. (life), Nat. Eagle Scout Assn., The Wildlife Soc. (cert. wildlife biologist, wildlife administr. award N.W. sect. 1991), Trout Unlimited, N.Mex. Wildlife Fedn. (life, conservationist of yr. award 1978), Rocky Mountain Elk Found. (life). Office: Rocky Mountain Elk Found PO Box 8249 Missoula MT 59802

WOLFE, WILLIAM CARL, JR., interest rate risk management consultant; b. Wadsworth, Ohio, Aug. 26, 1964; s. William Carl and Maja (Birgardt) W. BA in Math. and Econs., New Coll., 1986; MBA in Internat. Fin./Mgmt. Info. Svcs., Emory U., 1990. Mktg. support staff IBM, Sarasota, Fla., 1985; asst. mgr. Bennigan's Restaurant, Sarasota, Fla., 1986-88; rsch. assoc. Fed. Res. Bank, Atlanta, 1989; asst. treas. Next Computer, Redwood City, Calif., 1990-93, Conner Peripherals, San Jose, Calif., 1993-94; sr. cons. interest rate risk mgmt. Risk Mgmt. Techs., Berkeley, Calif., 1994-95; first v.p. asset/liability mgmt. Gt. Western Bank, Chatsworth, Calif., 1995—. Home: 13 Concho Ln Bell Canyon CA 91307

WOLFE, WILLIAM JEROME, librarian, English language educator; b. Chgo., Feb. 24, 1927; s. Fred Wiley and Helen Dorothea (Lovaas) W.; m. ViviAnn Lundin O'Connell, June 25, 1960 (div. 1962); 1 child, Lund. *Son Lund, Navy veteran and graduate of the University of Arizona, is a computer programmer. Father Fred Wolfe, World War II U.S. Army veteran, worked in the Railway Mail Service 1920-61 and practiced law in Chicago 1927-61. Grandparents Ludvig Lovaas (cabinetmaker) and Anna Anderson emigrated from Norway in 1888. Grandfather Alfred Wolfe, graduate of Tri-State Normal College, taught school in Kosciusko County, Indiana, 1897-1930. Great-grandfather James Wiley, from Ohio, served in the Union Army at the Battle of Shiloh. Great-great-grandfather Garret Wolfe served in the Pennsylvania militia during the American Revolution.* AB, U. Chgo., 1948; BA, Roosevelt U., Chgo., 1953; MEd, Chgo. State U., 1963; AA with high honors, Pima C.C., 1992; BA in Art magna cum laude, U. Ariz., 1994. Tchr. English John Marshall High Sch., Chgo., 1956-60; libr. Safford Jr. High Sch., Tucson, Ariz., 1961-71, Santa Rita High Sch., Tucson, 1971-75, Tucson High Sch., 1975-87; tutor Eastside Ctr., Tucson Adult Lit. Vols., 1988—, supr., 1993—. Co-founder Tucson Classic Guitar Soc., 1969-72; docent U. Ariz. Mus. Art, Tucson, 1989—; mem. adv. bd. U. Ariz. Sch. Music, 1995—; singer U. Ariz. Collegium Musicum, 1981-96, Sons of Orpheus Men's Chorus, Lane Justus Chorale. With U.S. Army, 1945-46, ETO. Mem. Sons of Norway, U. Ariz. Pres. Club, U. Ariz. Hon. Fellows Soc., Nat. Assn. Scholars, Assn. Lit. Scholars and Critics, Amnesty Internat., Human Life Found., Norsemen's Fedn., Phi Kappa Phi. Republican. Mem. Ch. of Christ Scientist. Home: 8460 E Rosewood Tucson AZ 85710 *Through every turn of events, an always reliable and inspiring way to make a pleasing composition out of life consists in joyous thankfulness to the Creator for the love of family, wise counsel of teachers, and kind encouragement of friends.*

WOLFF, BRIAN RICHARD, metal manufacturing company executive; b. L.A., Dec. 11, 1955; s. Arthur Richard and Dorothy Virginia (Johnson) W.; divorced; children: Ashley Rachael, Taryn Nicole. BSBA, Calif. State U., Chico, 1980; postgrad., U. Phoenix, 1990—. Registered counseling practitioner, Calif., 1996, guidance practitioner, Calif., 1996; ordained min. Progressive Universal Life Ch., 1996. Sales rep. Federated Metals Corp./ASARCO, Long Beach, Calif., 1980-82, dist. sales mgr., 1983-84; sales mgr. Copper Alloys Corp., Beverly Hills, Calif., 1982-83; dir. mktg. Federarted-Fry Metals/Cookson, Long Beach, Industry and Paramount, Calif., 1984-87; regional sales mgr. Colonial Metals Co., L.A., 1987-91; nat. sales mgr. Calif. Metal X/Metal Briquetting Co., L.A., 1991-93; sales engr. Ervin Industries, Inc., Ann Arbor, Mich., 1993-95; sales mgr. Southbay Bronze, San Jose, Calif., 1996—; tech. sales mgr. GSP Metals & Chems. Co., 1987-91; cons. sales Calif. Metal Exch., L.A., 1987-91, Atlas Pacific Inc., Bloomington, Calif., 1993—; sales mgr. Southbay Bronze, San Jose, Calif., 1996—; dealer Mason Shoe Co., 1996—. Mem. citizens adv. com. on bus. Calif. Legis., 1983; ordained min. Universal Life, 1996. Mem. Non Ferrous Founders Soc., Am. Foundrymen Soc., Calif. Cast Metals Assn., Steel Structures Painting Coun., Am. Electroplaters Soc., Soc. Die Cast Engrs., NRA. Republican. Presbyterian.

WOLFF, JOEL HENRY, human resources engineer; b. New Rochelle, N.Y., Oct. 29, 1966; s. s. Richard Eugene and Elise Leonora (Wolff) A. BA, U. Nev. at Las Vegas, 1991; JD, Gonzaga U., 1995. Computer operator Sun Teleguide, Henderson, Nev., 1987-90; engring. aide Wojcik Engring., Las Vegas, 1989-90; computer cons. Ax Med. Interfaces, Las Vegas, 1990-91; programmer Biosoft, Las Vegas, 1991-92; rule 9 legal intern, 1994-95, univ. legal assistance, 1994; computer cons., sys. analyst Wolff Legal Engines, 1995—. Named Eagle Scout Boy Scouts Am., 1984. Mem. ASCE (sec. student chpt. 1986-87), ABA (Law Student Divsn., 1992—), Internat. Law Soc. of Gonazaga Univ., Nat. Eagle Scout Assn., Phi Alpha Delta, Sigma Nu. Home: 2724 E Cape Hope Way Las Vegas NV 89121

WOLFF, MARK ROBERT, elementary and secondary education educator; b. North Hollywood, Calif., Jan. 5, 1961; s. Hanns and Elke (Lohmayr) W. AA, L.A. Pierce Coll., Woodland Hills, Calif., 1983; BA in History, Calif. State U., Northridge, 1987. Elem., jr. and sr. high sch. tchr. L.A. Unified Sch. Dist. Author and editor: The Illustrated Math Book on Animal Cules, 1992. Home: 8703 Ranchito Ave Panorama City CA 91402-3315

WOLFGANG, BONNIE ARLENE, musician, bassoonist; b. Caribou, Maine, Sept. 29, 1944; d. Ralph Edison and Arlene Alta (Obetz) W.; m. Eugene Alexander Pridonoff, July 3, 1965 (div. Sept. 1977); children: George Randall, Anton Alexander, Stephan Eugene. MusB, Curtis Inst. Music, Phila., 1967. Soloist Phila. Orch., 1966; soloist with various orchs. U.S., Cen. Am., 1966-75; prin. bassoonist Phoenix Symphony, 1976—, with Woodwind Quintet, 1986—. Home: 9448 N 106th St Scottsdale AZ 85258-6056*

WOLFLE, DAEL LEE, public affairs educator; b. Puyallup, Wash., Mar. 5, 1906; s. David H. and Elizabeth (Pauly) W.; m. Helen Morrill, Dec. 28, 1929 (dec. July 1988); children: Janet Helen (Mrs. Wilhelm G. Christophersen), Lee Morrill, John Morrill. B.S., U. Wash., 1927, M.S., 1928; postgrad., U. Chgo., summers 1929, 30; Ph.D., Ohio State U., 1931, D.Sc., 1957; D.Sc., Drexel U., 1956, Western Mich. U., 1960. Instr. psychology Ohio State U., 1929-32; prof. psychology U. Miss., 1932-36; examiner in biol. scis. U. Chgo., 1936-39, asst. prof. psychology, 1938-43, assoc. prof., 1943-45; on leave for war work with Signal Corps, 1941-43; with OSRD, 1944-45; exec. sec. Am. Psychol. Assn., 1946-50; dir. commn. on human resources and advanced tng. Assoc. Research Councils, 1950-54; exec. officer AAAS, 1954-70; editor Sci., 1955, pub., 1955-70; prof. pub. affairs U. Wash., Seattle, 1970-76; prof. emeritus U. Wash., 1976—; mem. sci. adv. bd. USAF, 1953-57; mem. def. sci. bd. Dept. Def., 1957-61; mem. adv. council on mental health NIMH, 1960-64; mem. nat. adv. health council USPHS, 1965-66; mem. commn. on human resources NRC, 1974-78; mem. adv. bd. Geophys. Inst., Fairbanks, Alaska., 1970-93, chmn. adv. bd., 1972-81. Author: Factor Analysis to 1940, 1941, Science and Public Policy 1959, The Uses of Talent, 1971, The Home of Science, 1972, Renewing a Scientific Society, 1989; editor: America's Resources of Specialized Talent, 1954. Trustee Russell Sage Found., 1961-78, Pacific Sci. Cent. Found., 1962-80, Biol. Scis. Curriculum Study, 1980-85; chmn. bd. J. McK. Cattell Fund, 1962-82. Named Alumnus Summa Laude Dignatus, U. Wash., 1979. Mem. AAAS, (pres. Pacific divsn. 1991-92, exec. com. 1990—), AAUP, APA, Am. Acad. Arts and Scis. (exec. com. western sect. 1985-92), Sigma Xi. Home: 4545 Sand Point Way NE Apt 805 Seattle WA 98105-3926 Office: U Wash Box 353055 Grad Sch Pub Affairs Seattle WA 98195-3055

WOLFLEY, VERN ALVIN, dentist; b. Etna, Wyo., Aug. 4, 1912; s. Rudolf E. and Eliza (Neuenschwander) W.; m. Bernice Michaelson, June 12, 1936; children: Norda Beth Wolfley Brimley, Vern A. Jr., Paul R., Carol Jo Wolfley Bennett. BS, U. Wyo., 1934; BS in Dentistry and DDS, U. Nebr., 1947. Farm mgmt. specialist USDA, 1934-43; placement officer War Relocation Authority, 1943; pvt. practice, Idaho Falls, Idaho, 1947-57, Phoenix, 1957—. Pres. Ariz. Children's Soc., Phoenix, 1960-61. With AUS, 1943; 1st lt. USAF, 1954. Mem. ADA (life), Ariz. Dental Assn. (life), Idaho Falls Dental Soc. (pres. 1949-50), Upper Snake River Dental Soc. (pres. 1955-56), Am. Soc. Dentistry for Children (life), Acad. Gen. Dentistry, Internat. Assn. Orthodontics (life), Am. Assn. Functional Orthodontists (charter), Fedn. Dentaire Internat., Cen. Ariz. Dist. Dental Soc. (life), Am. Legion, Lions (v.p. 1956), Omicron Kappa Upsilon, Alpha Zeta. Republican. Mem. LDS Ch. Home: 7819 W Banff Ln Peoria AZ 85381 Office: 2837 W Northern Ave Phoenix AZ 85051-6646 *Personal philosophy: Do not depend entirely on the arm of flesh for your knowledge, but on He who organized the Earth and put it into orbit. Ask and you shall receive, knock and it shall be opened unto you.*

WOLFSBERG, MAX, chemist, educator; b. Hamburg, Germany, May 28, 1928; came to U.S., 1939, naturalized, 1945; s. Gustav and Ida (Engelmann) W.; m. Marilyn Lorraine Fleischer, June 23, 1957; 1 dau., Tyra Gwendolen. A.B., Washington U., St. Louis, 1948, Ph.D., 1951. Asso. chemist Brookhaven Nat. Lab., Upton, N.Y., 1951-54; chemist Brookhaven Nat. Lab., 1954-63, sr. chemist, 1963-69; prof. chemistry SUNY, Stony Brook, 1966-69; vis. prof. chemistry Ind. U., Bloomington, 1965, Cornell U., Ithaca, N.Y., 1963; prof. chemistry U. Calif., Irvine, 1969—, chmn. dept., 1974-80; Deutsche Forschungs Gemeinschaft guest prof. U. Ulm, Fed. Republic Germany, 1986; Forchheimer vis. prof. Hebrew U., 1993. Assoc. editor: Jour. Chem. Physics, 1968-70; editor: Comments on Chemical Physics, 1986-89; mem. editorial bd. Isotopenpraxis, 1987—; contbr. articles to profl. jours. AEC fellow, 1950-51; NSF sr. postdoctoral fellow, 1958-59; Alexander von Humboldt awardee, 1977, reinvitations 1982, 93. Mem. Am. Chem. Soc., Phi Beta Kappa, Sigma Xi. Jewish. Home: 4533 Gorham Dr Corona Del Mar CA 92625-3111 Office: U Calif Dept Chemistry Irvine CA 92717

WOLFSCHMIDT, WILLI See FLINT, WILLIS WOLFSCHMIDT

WOLFSON, MURRAY, economics educator; b. N.Y.C., Sept. 14, 1927; s. William and Bertha (Finkelstein) W.; m. Betty Ann Goessel, July 21, 1950; children: Paul G., Susan D., Deborah R. BS, CCNY, 1948; MS, U. Wis., 1951, PhD, 1964; postgrad., Marquette U., 1958-59. Cert. secondary tchr., Wis., Mich. Tchr. math. Montrose (Mich.) High Sch., 1959-61; instr. econs. Thornton Jr. Coll., Harvey, Ill., 1961-63; prof. Oreg. State U., Corvallis, 1963-86, Calif. State U., Fullerton, 1986—; vis. prof. numerous univs., including Ahamdu Bello U., Zaria, Nigeria, U. Canterbury, Christchurch, New Zealand, U. Wis., Milw., Marquette U., Milw., U. Durham, Eng., U. Oreg., U. So. Calif., Haifa (Israel) U., U. Adelaide, Australia; Fulbright specialist lectr., Japan, 1976-77, Tokyo U., Hitotsubashi U., Waseda U., Keio U.; docent Groningen U., The Netherlands; vis. fellow history of ideas unit Australian Nat. U., Sofia U., 1993-94; adj. prof. U. Calif., Irvine, 1986—; others. Author: A Reappraisal of Marxian Economics, 1968, (transl. into Japanese and Portuguese), Karl Marx, 1971, Spanish transl., 1977, A Textbook of Economics: Structure, Activities, Issues, 1978, Marx: Economist, Philosopher, Jew, 1982, Japanese transl., 1987, Economic Activities: Microeconomics, 1989, rev. edit., 1991, Essays on the Cold War, 1992, Computer Laboratory Manual, 1997, (with Vincent Buranelli) In the Long Run We Are All Dead, A Macroeconomics Murder Mystery, 1983, 2d edit., 1989; also numerous articles. Adv. bd. Yale U. Civic Edn. Project. With USN, 1945-46. Scholar N.Y. Bd. Regents, 1943; staff devel. fellow Oreg. State U., 1976; travel grantee Am. Coun. Learned Socs., 1979; recipient 1st nat. prize for excellence in teachng coll. econs. Joint Coun. on Econ. Edn., 1970. Mem. AAUP (chpt. pres. 1983-84), Am. Econ. Assn., Hist. of Econs. Soc., Peace Sci. Soc., Def. Econs. Assn., Western Econs. Assn., Peace Sci. Soc. (pres.). Home: 2022 Via Mariposa E # D Laguna Hills CA 92653-2247

WOLIN, MERLE LINDA, journalist, consultant; b. Cheyenne, Wyo., Jan. 1, 1948; d. Morris Aaron and Helen (Sobol) W. AA, Pine Manor Coll., 1968; BA, U. Calif., Berkeley, 1970. Co-founder, philanthropic cons. Pacific Change, San Francisco, 1971-73; mem editorial staff City Mag., San Francisco, 1974-75; co-founder, assoc. pub. Mother Jones mag., San Francisco, 1973-74; freelance writer N.Y Times, L.A. Times, People, 1976-79; Latin affairs writer L.A. Herald Examiner, 1979-82; nat. Latin affairs writer Wall Street Journal, L.A., 1982-83; correspondent Latin Am. L.A. Herald Examiner, Mexico City, 1983-86; freelance journalist Life, Premier Mag., The New Republic, 1986-95; tv. news feature producer BBC, Fox TV., 1991-95, ABC News, CBS News, 1991-95; show prodr. CNBC Asia Network, 1995—. Recipient Mark Twain prize, regional prize AP, 1981, Journalism Atrium award U. Ga. 1981, econ. understanding award Dartmouth Coll., 1981, disting. writing award Hearst Newspapers, 1981, Paul Tobenkin Meml. award Columbia U., 1982, Robert F. Kennedy award, 1982, best investigative reporting award, L.A. Press Club, 1982, best fgn. press writing award, 1985, Clarence Darrow award ACLU, 1982, Unity award Lincoln U. Mo., 1982. Mem. Writers Guild Am., PEN Internat. (Gold Pen award for meritorious achievement, 1982).

WOLINSKY, LEO C., newspaper editor. BA in Journalism, U. So. Calif., 1972. Journalist, 1972—; staff writer L.A. Times, 1977-86, dep. chief Sacramento bur., 1987-89, city editor, 1990, Calif. polit. editor, 1991, metro editor, 1994—. Office: Los Angeles Times Times Mirror Sq Los Angeles CA 90053

WOLINSKY, RICHARD BARRY, writer; b. N.Y.C., July 10, 1950; s. Melvin Wolinsky and Judith Sally (Weisberg) Green. BA, SUNY, Binghampton, 1971; MA, The New Sch. for Social Rsch., 1975. Asst. publicity dir. KPFA-FM, Berkeley, Calif., 1977; pub. dir. KPFA-FM, 1978, editor folio program guide, 1978-92; editor Alonzo Mag. Alonzo Printing, Hayward, Calif., 1993—; freelance editor, writer, 1977—; host Probabilities KPFA, 1977—, Broadway Madness, 1991—, Cover to Cover, 1995—. Office: PO Box 1173 El Cerrito CA 94530-1173

WOLK, BRUCE ALAN, law educator; b. Bklyn., Mar. 2, 1946; s. Morton and Gertrude W.; m. Lois Gloria Krepliak, June 22, 1968; children: Adam, Daniel. BS, Antioch Coll., 1968; MS, Stanford U., 1972; JD, Harvard U., 1975. Bar: D.C. 1975. Assoc. Hogan & Hartson, Washington, 1975-78; prof. U. Calif. Sch. Law, Davis, 1978—, acting dean, 1990-91, dean, 1993—. Danforth Found. fellow, 1970-74, NSF fellow, 1970-72, Fulbright sr. research fellow, 1985-86. Mem. ABA, Am. Law Inst. Office: U Calif Sch Law King Hall Univ of Cal-Davis Davis CA 95616-5201

WOLK, MARTIN, electronic engineer, physicist; b. Long Branch, N.J., Jan. 13, 1930; s. Michael and Tillie (Barron) W.; 1 child, Brett Martin. BS, George Washington U., 1957, MS, 1968; PhD, U. N.Mex., 1973. Physicist Naval Ordnance Lab., White Oak, Md., 1957-59, Nat. Oceanic and Atmospheric Adminstrn., Suitland, Md., 1959-66; solid state physicist Night Vision Lab., Fort Belvoir, Va., 1967-69; rsch. asst. U. N.Mex., Albuquerque, 1969-73; electronics engr. Washington Navy Yard, 1976-83, TRW, Inc., Redondo Beach, Calif., 1983-84; physicist Metrology Engring. Ctr., Pomona, Calif., 1984-85; electronics engr. Naval Aviation Depot North Island, San Diego, 1985—; cons. Marine Corps Logistics Base, Barstow, Calif., 1985—, Naval Weapons Station, Fallbrook, Calif., 1987-89, Naval Weapons Support Ctr., Crane, Ind., 1989—. Contbr. articles to Jour. Quantitative Spectroscopy and Radiative Transfer, Monthly Weather Rev., Proceedings of SPIE, Procs. of EUROPTO. Cpl. U.S. Army, 1946-49, Japan. Mem. IEEE, Soc. Photo-Optical Instrumentation Engring., European Optical Soc., Sigma Pi Sigma, Sigma Tau. Home: 740 Eastshore Ter Chula Vista CA 91913-2421

WOLKOWITZ, EDWARD MARVIN, mayor; b. Kassal, Germany, Mar. 11, 1949; married. BA in Polit. Sci. San Fernando, Valley State Coll., 1970, BA in History, 1971; JD cum laude, Southwestern U. Sch. Law, 1975; LLM, U. Mich., 1976. Assoc. atty. Robinson Diamant Brill Profl. Corp., L.A., 1976-81, atty., 1981—; mem. City Coun. Culver City, 1994—; mayor City of Culver City, 1996—; adj. prof. law Southwestern U. Sch. Law, 1979-91; bd. dirs. L.A. Bankruptcy Forum, pres., 1990-91; bd. dirs. Calif. Bankruptcy Forum; vice-chmn. Culver City Redevel. Agy., 1994—. Contbr. articles to profl. jours. Trustee Southwestern U. Sch. Law, 1989-94. Office: Office of Mayor 9770 Culver Blvd Culver City CA 90230

WOLKOWITZ, OWEN MARK, physician, psychiatrist, researcher; b. Washington, Oct. 3, 1952; s. Gabriel Wolkowitz and Mandzia (Wroclawska) Wolkowitz-Murik; m. Janet Anne Negley, Sept. 9, 1984. BA, NYU, 1974; MD, U. Md., 1979. Diplomate Am. Bd. Psychiatry and Neurology. Intern in psychiatry Stanford (Calif.) U. Med. Ctr., 1979-80, resident in psychiatry, 1980-82, chief resident in psychiatry, 1983; med. staff fellow NIMH, Bethesda, Md., 1983-86; attending psychiatrist, assoc. prof., rschr. U. Calif., San Francisco, 1986—, staff psychiatrist, team leader Adult Inpatient Svcs., 1991-95; dir. Adult Psychopharmacology Clinic, San Francisco, 1995—; mem. dean's award com. U. Calif., San Francisco, 1986-93, mem. student rsch. fellowship com., 1986-87, mem. residency tng. objective com., 1986-87; jour. reviewer Archives of Gen. Psychiatry, Biol. Psychiatry, Gen. Hosp. Psychiatry, Hosp. & Cmty. Psychiatry, Jour. Clin. Psychopharmacology, Jour. Nervous & Mental Disease, Jour. Neurosci., Jour. Psychiat. Rsch., Psychiatry Rsch., Psychosomatics, Schizophrenia Bull., Schizophrenia Rsch., Western Jour. Medicine; mem. behavioral scis. rev. bd. VA, 1988, 90, rsch. adv. group, 1993; mem. adv. bd. for clin. investigation Western Jour. Medicine, 1993; mem. steering com. Napa State Hosp., 1988-95. Contbr. more than 100 articles to profl. jours. Recipient Young Rschr. Neurosci. award Calif. Assn. for the Mentally Ill, 1989, Stanley award Nat. Assn. for the Mentally Ill, 1993, Young Investigator award Nat. Alliance for Rsch. on Schizo and Effective Disorder, 1989, established investigator award Nat. Alliance for Rsch. in Schizo and Affective Disorder, 1995; grantee S. Henderson Fund, 1988-90, Biomed. Rsch. Support, 1989-91, 93, AIDS Clin. Rsch. Ctr., 1990-91, NIMH, 1987-93, Scottish Rite Found., 1993-95, Stanley Found., 1993-95. Mem. AAAS, Am. Psychiat. Assn. (session chmn. ann. meeting 1993), Psychiat. Rsch. Soc., Soc. for Biol. Psychiatry, Am. Soc. Clin. Psychopharmacology, Internat. Soc. for Psycho-Neuro-Endocrinology (Carl P. Richter prize 1992), Collegium Internationale Neuropsychopharmacoligicum, World Fedn. Socs. Biol. Psychiatry, West Coast Coll. Biol. Psychiatry (consensus conf. on benzodiazepine regulation 1993—), No. Calif. Psychiat. Soc., Psi Chi. Office: U Calif/Dept Psychiatry Langley Porter Psychiat 401 Parnassus Ave # F0984 San Francisco CA 94122-2720

WOLLENBERG, DAVID ARTHUR, real estate developer; b. Longview, Wash., Aug. 6, 1947; s. Richard Peter and Leone Bonney; m. Katrina Moulton, Aug. 30, 1975 (div.); children: Andrew Richard, Blake Endicott. BA, Brown U., 1969; MBA, Stanford U., 1973. Front office mgr. Caneel Bay Plantation, St. John, V.I., 1969-71; adminstrn. asst. AMFAC Communities-Hawaii, Honolulu, 1973-77; exec. v.p. The Cortana Corp., Palo Alto, Calif., 1977-83, pres., 1983—; dir. Longview Fibre Co., Wash. 1979—. Bd. dirs. Peninsula Ctr. for Blind, Palo Alto, 1984-90; bd. dirs. Christmas in April, Mid-Peninsula, 1992, pres., 1994-95, treas., 1995-96, sec., 1996-97. Mem. Outrigger Canoe Club (Honolulu), Menlo Circus Club, Palo Alto Club. Republican. Office: The Cortana Corp 800 El Camino Real Ste 175 Menlo Park CA 94025-4808

WOLLENBERG, RICHARD PETER, paper manufacturing company executive; b. Juneau, Alaska, Aug. 1, 1915; s. Harry L. and Gertrude (Arnstein) W.; m. Leone Bonney, Dec. 22, 1940; children: Kenneth Roger, David Arthur, Keith Kermit, Richard Harry, Carol Lynne. BSME, U. Calif., Berkeley, 1936; MBA, Harvard U., 1938; grad., Army Indsl. Coll., 1941; D in Pub. Affairs (hon.), U. Puget Sound, 1977. Prodn. control Bethlehem Ship, Quincy, Mass., 1938-39; with Longview (Wash.) Fibre Co., 1939—, safety engr., asst. chief engr., chief engr., mgr. container operations, 1951-57, v.p., 1953-57, v.p. ops., 1957-60, exec. v.p., 1960-69, pres., 1969-78, pres., chief exec. officer, 1978-85, pres., chief exec. officer, chmn. bd., 1985—, also bd. dirs.; mem. Wash. State Council for Postsecondary Edn., 1969-79, chmn., 1970-73; mem. western adv. bd. Allendale Ins. Bassoonist SW Washington Symphony. Trustee Reed Coll., Portland, 1962—, chmn. bd. 1982-90. Served to lt. col. USAAF, 1941-45. Recipient Alumni Achievement award Harvard U., 1994. Mem. NAM (bd. dirs. 1981-86), Pacific Coast Assn. Pulp and Paper Mfrs. (pres. 1981-92), Inst. Paper Sci. and Tech. (trustee), Wash. State Roundtable, Crabbe Huson (bd. dirs.). Home: 1632 Kessler Blvd Longview WA 98632-3633 Office: Longview Fibre Co PO Box 606 Longview WA 98632-7391*

WOLLINS, DAVID H., lawyer; b. N.Y.C., Nov. 1, 1952; s. Donald J. Wollins and Constance Joy Graham; m. Leslie Bjerg Lilly, Apr. 1, 1989; 1 child, Alexander Bjerg Lilly W. BS in Fin. and Mktg., U. Pa., 1974; JD, New Eng. Sch. Law, 1978. Bar: N.Y. 1979, U.S. Dist. Ct. (ea. and so. dists.) N.Y. 1989, U.S. Dist. Ct. Colo., U.S. Ct. Appeals (10th cir.) 1986, U.S. Ct. Appeals (fed., D.C. and 2d cirs.) 1990, U.S. Ct. Claims 1983, U.S. Supreme Ct. 1994. Pres. Nature's Way Recycling Co., Boston, 1974-75; summer assoc. Phillips, Nizer, Benjamin, Krim & Ballon, N.Y.C., 1976-77, assoc., 1978-86; of counsel Cortez and Friedman, P.C., Englewood, Colo., 1986-87; mem. firm, co-head litigation dept. Brenman, Raskin, Friedlob & Tenenbaum, P.C., Denver, 1987-91; shareholder, head litigation dept. McGeady Sisneros & Wollins, P.C., Denver, 1991-95; spl. counsel Jonathan J. Hellman & Assoc., P.C., Englewood, Colo., 1995-96; shareholder Wollins, Hellman & Green, Denver, 1996—; pro bono atty., City N.Y., 1978-86. Author short stories and numerous poems. Mem. ABA, N.Y. Bar Assn., Colo. Bar Assn., Denver Bar Assn. Home: 311 Bannock St # C Denver CO 80223-1103 Office: Wollins Hellman & Green Ste 620-S 720 S Colorado Blvd Denver CO 80222

WOLLMAN RUSOFF, JANE SUSAN, journalist, writer; b. N.Y.C., Oct. 15, 1942; d. Charles Saul and Fay Wollman; m. Garry B. Rusoff, Nov. 9, 1991. Student, Hunter Coll., 1963-65. Accredited film journalist Motion Picture Assn. Am. Publicity asst. Am. Internat. Pictures, N.Y.C., 1961-62, 63-64, L.A., 1962-63; writer, editor London Express Features, N.Y.C., 1964-69; editor home electronics Merchandising Mag., N.Y.C., 1974-77, Chgo., 1977-79; freelance electronics writer N.Y.C., 1979-85, freelance entertainment writer, 1985-91; freelance entertainment writer L.A., 1991—; stringer N.Y. Times, L.A., 1996—. Author: Computer Workplace: Ergonomic Design for Computing at Home, 1985; co-author: (with Steve Allen) How to Be Funny, 1987; contbr. articles to Washington Post, L.A. Times Syndicate, Good Housekeeping, USA Today. Mem. Soc. Profl. Journalists, Deadline Club.

WOLPE, CLAIRE FOX, civic worker, psychotherapist; b. N.Y.C., June 24, 1909; d. David and Pauline (Hirsch) Fox; A.B., Mills Coll., 1930; M.A., U. So. Calif., 1936, M.S.W., 1965; Ph.D., Marquette U., 1970; postgrad. Smith Coll., summer 1931, Columbia U., summer 1963, U. Mexico City, summer 1964; m. Arthur S. Wolpe, Dec. 25, 1932 (dec. Mar. 1962); children—Ruth (Mrs. Roy Rose), Sheri (Mrs. Jerome Langer). Student advisor Jewish student orgn. UCLA, 1931-33; with Travelers Aid, Los Angeles, 1934; med. social work Los Angeles County Gen. Hosp., 1934-38; with USPHS, 1938; social worker Los Angeles County Health Dept., 1938-39; psychiat. social worker Gateways Psychiat. Hosp. and Mental Health Center, Los Angeles, 1962-63, 65-66, ret. 1996; exec. dir. Bay Cities Mental Health Center, Los Angeles, 1966-68; supr. Airport Marina Counseling Service; pvt. practice. Mem. Mayors Com. on Civil Def. 1950-52, Wilshire Coordinating Council, 1954-58; leader Girl Scouts U.S.A., 1954-58; mem. regional bd. NCCJ, 1951-55. Bd. dirs. So. Calif. Mental Health Assn., 1955-58, Los Angeles chpt. A.R.C., 1951-53, Community Relations Conf. So. Calif., 1950-60, Los Angeles Jewish Fedn. Council, 1952-58, B'nai B'rith Anti-Defamation League, 1973—, Hillel Assn., 1973—. Fellow Soc. Clin. Social Workers, Am. Assn. Orthopsychiatry; mem. Nat. Assn. Social Workers, Psychotherapy Assn. So. Calif. (dir. 1967—, pres.-elect 1984), Calif. Marriage, Family and Child Counseling Assn., Group Psychotherapy Assn. So. Calif. (tribute award 1989), Am. Group Psychotherapy Assn., Los Angeles Transactional Analysis Soc. (sec.-treas. 1966-68), Psi Chi. Jewish religion. Mem. B'nai B'rith Women. Home and Office: 234 S Orange Dr Los Angeles CA 90036-3011

WOLSEY, THOMAS DEVERE, middle school educator; b. Salt Lake City, Mar. 6, 1962; d. T. Mark and Lynn Wolsey. BS, So. Utah State Coll., 1986; MA in Ednl. Adminstrn., Calif. State U., San Bernardino, 1990. Cert. tchr., Utah; mid. sch. endorsement, reading, English tchr., adminstrv. svcs., Calif. Tchr. adult edn., tchr. English San Bernardino City Unified Sch. Dist., 1986-89; ESL tutor Alpine Sch. Dist., American Fork, Utah, 1981-84; tchr. U.S. History and English Lake Elsinore (Calif.) Unified Sch. Dist., 1989—; adj. faculty sch. of edn. and human svcs./reading methodology Nat. Univ., 1995—. Mem. Nat. Coun. Tchrs. English, Internat. Reading Assn., Lake Elsinore Tchrs. Assn. (pres. 1996—). Home: 31996 Corte Ruiz Temecula CA 92592-3621 Office: Elsinore Mid Sch 1203 W Graham Ave Lake Elsinore CA 92530

WOLTERBEEK, MARC WILLIAM, English language educator; b. San Francisco, July 7, 1951; s. Robert Daniel Wolterbeek and Mary Bella (Chiapetta) Muse; m. Kim Silveira, Dec. 11, 1951; 1 child, Marc William Jr. BA, U. Calif., Berkeley, 1972, MA, 1974, PhD, 1984. Cert. C.C. instr., Calif. English instr. Contra Costa Coll., San Pablo, Calif., 1974-85, Napa (Calif.) Coll., 1975-82, Chabot Coll., Hayward, Calif., 1984-85; tchg. asst. French dept. U. Calif., Berkeley, 1980-81, tchg. asst. comparative lit. dept., 1982-83, acting instr. comparative lit., 1983-84; lectr. English Calif. State U., Hayward, 1984-85, U. of the Pacific, Stockton, Calif., 1985-87; assoc. prof., head English dept. Coll. of Notre Dame, Belmont, Calif., 1987—. Author: Comic Tales of the Middle Ages, 1991; contbr. articles to profl. publs. Chair, judge poetry contest San Mateo (Calif.) County Fair, 1990-94; chair 4th Ann. Jack London Writers' Conf., Belmont, 1992. Mem. Philol. Assn. of Pacific Coast (sec. session on medieval lit. 1994—), Pacific Coast Writing Ctrs. Assn. (pres. 1991-92). Office: Coll of Notre Dame 1500 Ralston Ave Belmont CA 94002-1908

WOLTERS, CHRISTOPHER FREDERICK, performing company executive; b. Oceanside, Calif., Dec. 27, 1959; s. Gerald Frederick and Charlene Ann (Peters) W.; m. Jill Annette Posey, July 24, 1982 (div. Dec. 12, 1989). BA in Psychology, U. Calif., Santa Cruz; postgrad. in edn., Ariz. State U. Dir. Evening of One Acts The Moore Theater, 1977-78; learning asst. kindergarten De La Veaga Elem. Sch., Santa Cruz, 1983; coach and instr. Santa Cruz Gymnastics Ctr., 1982-84; performing arts specialist City of Sacramento, 1984-86; expressive arts coord. Sacramento Children's Home, 1986-87; achievement specialist Cruddas Family Home, 1987-89; performing arts cons. Santa Cruz City Sch. Dist., 1992-94; program asst. U. Calif., Santa Cruz, 1989—; artistic dir. Life in Motion Musical Theatre Co., Inc., Santa Cruz, 1982—; creative arts cons. Santa Cruz City Sch. Dist., 1983—, Sacramento City Schs., 1984-87, Davis City Schs., 1984-87, Yolo County, 1984-87, San Diego Sch. Dist., 1991-92, Pajaro Valley Sch. Dist., 1994-95; instr. U. Calif.-Davis Exptl. Coll., 1986; Spectra artist Cultural Coun. Santa Cruz, 1996-97. Editor The Children's Musical Theatre News, 1991—; rec. artist: I Heard the Children Say, 1991, Soup of Stone, 1992, Jack and the Beanstalk, 1992, Sarah and Her Brother, 1992; live radio performer KUSP Radio, Santa Cruz; choreographer GATE Dance Concerts, Santa Cruz; profl. dancer Pamela Trokansky Dance Theatre, 1986-87; contbr. articles to jours.; author children's plays and musicals including: Soup of Stone, 1984, Aladdin, 1985, Jack and the Beanstalk, 1986, Substitute Blues, 1994, Revenge of the Sub, 1995, Sarah and Her Brother, 1991, Soup of the Day, 1996, Giant Friends, 1997, others. Vol. Santa Cruz AIDS Project, 1992—; dir./children's musical fund-raiser Santa Cruz Natural History Assn., 1994. Schs. Plus Found. grantee, 1988, 92, 93, Title VII Fund grantee, 1994, Cultural Coun. Santa Cruz County grantee, 1996-97, Stocker Family Found. grantee, 1996. Mem. No. Calif. Songwriters Assn. (Award for Best Song/ Performance 1989), Broadcast Music Inc., Santa Cruz Performing Arts Alliance. Office: Life in Motion Children Mus PO Box 267 Santa Cruz CA 95061-0267

WOLVERTON, TERRY L(YNN), writer, consultant; b. Cocoa Beach, Fla., Aug. 23, 1954; d. Donald E. Wolverton and Ruth L. Miller Tackabery; life ptnr. Susan M. Silton. PhB, Grand Valley State U., Allendale, Mich., 1977. Dir. The Woman's Bldg., L.A., 1977-89; mgmt. cons. Consult'Her, L.A., 1982—; creative writing instr. L.A. Gay and Lesbian Ctr., 1988—; bd. dirs. The Woman's Bldg., 1982-86, 96—; mem. adv. bd. L.A. Poetry Festival, 1990—, The Fringe Festival, L.A., 1987-88. Author: (novel) Bailey's Beads, 1996, (poetry collection) Black Slip, 1992; editor (anthology series) His, 1995, 97, Hers, 1995, 97, (anthologies) Indivisible, 1991, Blood Whispers: L.A. Writers on AIDS, vol. 1, 1991, vol. 2, 1994. Mem. pub. policy com. Calif. Confedn. of the Arts, Sacramento, 1986-88. Recipient Lesbian Rights award So. Calif. Women for Understanding, 1986, Vesta award in lit. The Woman's Bldg., 1991, Movers and Shakers award for Women Writers, So. Calif. Libr. for Social Studies and Rsch., 1995, Lesbian and Bisexual Woman Active in Cmty. Empowerment award L.A. Gay and Lesbian Ctr., 1997, Harvey Milk award Christopher St. West Assn., 1997. Mem. PEN Ctr. USA West.

WOLVINGTON, WINSTON WARREN, retired judge; b. Denver, July 10, 1923; s. William Thomas and Bessie Maude (Roberts) W.; m. Shirley Anne Vail, Sept. 9, 1944; children: Gloria, Judith, Donald, Glenn. JD, U. Mich., 1948; BA, Oberlin (Ohio) Coll., 1949. Bar: Colo. 1949. Assoc. Wolvington & Wormwood, Denver, 1949-54, ptnr., 1954-73; dist. judge State of Colo., Golden, 1973-89, sr. judge, 1989-94; retired, 1994. Mem. ABA, Am. Judicature Soc., Colo. Bar Assn., Colo. Judicature Soc., 1st Judicial Bar Assn. (pres., v.p.). Democrat. Home: 1391 S Winston Dr Golden CO 80401-8040

WOLZINGER, RENAH, medical products executive, music company executive; b. Culver City, Calif., Aug. 8, 1964; d. Ezekiel Joseph and Sheila Gene Joseph Wolzinger; m. Keith Wolzinger, Mar. 25, 1990; children: Rebecca Sheryl, Michelle. BS, U. Calif., San Diego, 1987. Bioengr. VA Med. Ctr., La Jolla, Calif., 1986-87; rsch. engr. Kendall McGaw, Irvine, Calif., 1987-88; staff engr. Baxter Healthcare, Irvine, 1988-93; v.p. Catheter Protection Sys., Huntinton Beach, Calif., 1993—; pres. Wolzinger Prodns., Huntinton Beach, 1995—. Inventor: Protective Pouch. Mem. ASCAP (writer). Home and Office: 5901 Midway Dr Huntington Beach CA 92648

WOMACK, THOMAS HOUSTON, manufacturing company executive; b. Gallatin, Tenn., June 22, 1940; s. Thomas Houston and Jessie (Eckel) W.; Linda Walker Womack, July 20, 1963 (div. Dec. 1989); children: Britton Ryan, Kelley Elizabeth; m. Pamela Ann Reed, Apr. 20, 1991. BSME, Tenn. Tech. U., Cookeville, 1963. Project engr. U.S. Gypsum Co., Jacksonville, Fla., 1963-65; project mgr. Maxwell House Div. Gen. Foods Corp., Jacksonville, 1965-68; mfg. mgr. Maxwell House Div. Gen. Foods Corp., Hoboken, N.J., 1968-71, div. ops. planning mgr., 1971-73; industry sales mgr. J.R. Schneider Co., Tiburon, Calif., 1973-79; pres., CEO Womack Internat., Inc., Novato, Calif., 1979—; pres. Ceramic Microlight Technologies, LLC, Novato, Calif., 1995—; pres., CEO WestAmerica Precisiion Machinery Co., 1997—. Holder 5 U.S. patents. Mem. Soc. Tribologists and Lubrication Engrs., Am. Filtration Soc., Soc. Mfg. Engrs., Am. Soc. Chem. Engrs. Office: Womack Internat Inc 105 Digital Dr Novato CA 94949-5703

WONDER, JOHN PAUL, educator; b. Long Beach, Calif., July 29, 1921; s. John Paul and Etta (Jones) W.; m. Jane Josephine Walder, Dec. 22, 1946; children: John Walder, Peter Charles. A.B., Stanford U., 1943, A.M., 1948, Ph.D., 1952; Exchange scholar, Universidad Central, Madrid, 1950-51. Grad. fellow Stanford, 1946-50; instr., asst. prof. Spanish U. Ariz., 1951-56; dir. Binational Center, Belo Horizonte, Brazil; with USIA, also Rio de Janeiro and Port-au-Prince, Haiti, 1956-62; asst. prof. Los Angeles State Coll., 1962-63; prof. Spanish U. Pacific, Stockton, Calif., 1963-91; chmn. dept. modern langs. U. Pacific, 1964-75; dir. Center for Internat. Programs, 1979-82. Author: (with Aurelio M. Espinosa, Jr.) Gramática Analítica, 1976; assoc. editor: (theoretical linguistics) Hispania, 1979-89. Served as 1st lt., arty. M.I. AUS, 1943-46, ETO. Mem. Alpha Tau Omega. Home: 660 W Euclid Ave Stockton CA 95204-1819

WONDERS, WILLIAM CLARE, geography educator; b. Toronto, Apr. 22, 1924; s. George Clarence and Ann Mary (Bell) W.; m. Lillian Paradise Johnson, June 2, 1951; children—Karen Elizabeth, Jennifer Anne, Glen William. B.A. with honors, Victoria Coll., U. Toronto, 1946; M.A., Syracuse U., 1948; Ph.D., U. Toronto, 1951; Fil. Dr. h.c., Uppsala U., 1981. Teaching asst. dept. geography Syracuse U., 1946-48; lectr. dept. geography U. Toronto, 1948-53; asst. prof. geography dept. polit. economy U. Alta., 1953-55, assoc. prof. geography, 1955-57, prof., head dept. geography, 1957-67, prof. dept. geography, 1967-87, Univ. prof., 1983—, prof. emeritus, 1987—; vis. prof. geography U. B.C., 1954, U. Okla., 1965-66, St. Mary's U., 1977, U. Victoria, 1989, J.F. Kennedy Inst., Free U. Berlin, 1990; guest prof. Inst. Geography, Uppsala (Sweden) U., 1962-63; rsch. fellow in Geography U. Aberdeen, Scotland, 1970-71, 78; vis. fellow in Can. Studies, U. Edinburgh, Scotland, 1987. Author: Looking at Maps, 1960, The Sawdust Fusiliers, 1991, Norden and Canada-A Geographer's Perspective, 1992, Alaska Highway Explorer, 1994; (with T. Drinkwater et al) Atlas of Alberta, 1969, (with J.C. Muller et al) Junior Atlas of Alberta, 1979; contbr., editor: Canada's Changing North, 1971, The North, 1972, The Arctic Circle, 1976, Knowing the North, 1988; contbr. articles to jours. and encys., chpts. to books. Mem. Nat. Adv. Com. on Geog. Rsch., 1965-69; chmn. Boreal Inst. No. Studies, 1960-62; mem. Can. Permanent Com. on Geog. Names, 1981-94, Alta. Hist. Sites Bd., 1978-83, vice chmn., 1982-83; mem. policy bd. Can. Plains Rsch. Centre, U. Regina (Sask.), 1975-86; mem. adv. bd. Royal Tyrrell Mus. Paleontology, 1984-89; bd. dirs. The Muttart Found., 1986-93, 95—, v.p., 1991-93, mem., 1991—. NSF sr. fgn. scientist fellow, 1965-66; Canada Council leave fellow, 1969-70, 77-78; Nuffield Found. fellow, 1970-71. Fellow Arctic Inst. N.Am., Royal Soc. Can., Royal Can. Geog. Soc.; mem. Can. Assn. Geographers (past pres.), Royal Scottish Geog. Soc., Can. Assn. Scottish Studies (councillor 1974-77), Scottish Soc. No. Studies, Champlain Soc. (councillor 1981-86), Sigma Xi, Gamma Theta Upsilon.

WONG, ALEXANDER SHIH-WEI, electrical engineer; b. Lawrence, Kans., Apr. 26, 1966; s. Sheh and Eugenia J.K. Wong. BS in Computer Engring., U. Ill., 1987; MSEE, U. Calif., Berkeley, 1989, PhD in Elec. Engring., 1992. Customer engr. GE, Research Triangle Park, N.C., 1985; sr. tech. assoc. AT&T Bell Labs., Murray Hill, N.J., 1986; engr. Lawrence Livermore (Calif.) Lab., 1987-88; cons. Motorola Corp., Mesa, Ariz., 1989; sr. CAD engr. Intel Corp., Santa Clara, Calif., 1992-93, staff CAD engr., 1994—; chmn. tech. CAD wafer subcom. CAD Framework Initiative, Austin Tex., 1989—. Editor CAD Framework Initiative wafer TCAD, 1992. Mem. IEEE, Phi Kappa Phi, Tau Beta Pi, Eta Kappa Nu. Republican. Office: Intel Corp 2200 Mission College Blvd Santa Clara CA 95054-1537

WONG, ASTRIA WOR, cosmetic business consultant; b. Hong Kong, Oct. 23, 1949; came to U.S., 1970; B in Vocat. Edn., Calif. State U., Long Beach, 1976. Cert. coll. tchr. (life), Calif. West coast sales trainer Revlon Inc., N.Y.C, 1975-82; nat. tng. dir. diReniel Internat., Palm Springs, Calif., 1982; dir. Beauty Cons. Service Agy., Long Beach, Calif., 1983—; pres. Boutique Astria, Scottsdale, Ariz., 1994—. Author: The Art of Femininity, 1971; editor (newsletter) So. Calif. Cosmetic, 1983-86. Chair Cmty. Involvement Paradise Rep. Woman's Club. Named Salesperson of Yr., Revlon, Inc., N.Y.C., 1978. Mem. So. Calif. Cosmetic Assn. (correspondence sec. 1982—), Women's Coun., Cosmetologist Tchr. Assn., Bus. and Profl. (ind. devel. chair.), Fashion Group Internat. Republican. Office: Beauty Cons Service Agy 7121 E 1st Ave Scottsdale AZ 85251-4305

WONG, BERNARD P., anthropologist; b. China, Feb. 12, 1941; came to U.S., 1969; s. Maurice S. and Theresa S. (Chau) W.; m. Rosemarie Deist, Apr. 14, 1973; children: Veronica, Alexandra. BA, Berchmans Coll., Quezon City, Philippines, 1966; post grad., Ateneo de Manila, Philippines, 1968; MA, U. Wis., 1971, PhD, 1974. Asst. prof. U. Wis., Anthropology Dept., Janesville, 1974-81, assoc. prof., 1981-86; assoc prof. San Francisco State U., Anthropology Dept., 1986-88, prof., 1988—; dir. San Francisco State U., Ctr. Urban Anthropology, 1988—, chair anthropology dept., 1990-94. Author: A Chinese American Community, 1979, Chinatown, 1982, Patronage Brokerage, 1988, Ethnicity and Entrepreneurship, 1997; editor: Bridge: An Asian American Perspective, 1978-80; contbr. articles to profl. jours. Coun. mem. Gov's. Asian Adv. Coun. Wis., 1983-86. Fellow; Am. Anthrop. Assn., Soc. Applied Anthropology; mem. Am. Ethnological Soc., Soc. Urban Anthopology, Soc. Anthropology Work, Chinese Hist. Soc. Am. (bd. dirs.). Office: San Francisco State Univ Dept of Anthropology 1600 Holloway Ave San Francisco CA 94132-1722

WONG, CHOY-LING, interior designer; b. Hong Kong, Nov. 25, 1949; arrived in U.S., 1996.; d. Teh-Chung Wang; m. Francis Michael Wong, Feb. 9, 1975; children: Shelby, Kenton. BFA in Environ. Design, BA in Art, U. Hawaii, 1973. Graphics/mapping artist Hawaii, 1972-73; asst. Lanai Urban Planning Project, Hawaii, 1973; interior designer C.S. Wo & Sons, Inc., Honolulu, 1973-83; pres. Choy-Ling Wong, Inc., Honolulu, 1984—, Furniture Catalog Libr., Honolulu, 1986—. Contbr. articles to profl. jours. Active Hist. Hawaii Preservation Parade, Honolulu, 1985-88. Recipient Design awards Bldg. Industry Assn., 1990, Cert. of Appreciation, U. Hawaii, 1990, Outstanding Vol. award First Lady of Hawaii, 1990. Mem. Am. Soc. Interior Designers (profl., participant showhouse 1978, 80, 82, 85, 87, Sunday snoop, 1988, 91-94, Presdl. citations 1993, 94), Assn. Chinese Univ. Women, U. Hawaii Internat. Students Alumni Assn. (charter), U. Hawaii Sch. Architecture Alumni Assn. (bd. dirs. 1993-95). Office: Choy-Ling Wong Inc 931 Hausten St Honolulu HI 96826-3000

WONG, FAY SHIEN, writer; b. Palo Alto, Calif., Nov. 7, 1949; d. Kam Hong and Yo Tsin (Chow) W.; m. K. Greene, 1984; 1 child, Chow-Chow. AA, Foothill U., 1969; BA, San Jose State U., 1975. Author Doubleday, N.Y.C.; screen writer Warner Brothers, Calif.; song writer MCA, Giffen Records, Calif. Author poetry and short stories; author: (by A. Lane) The Story of Three Scoundrels, 1989. Republican. Roman Catholic.

WONG, GWENDOLYN NGIT HOW JIM, bank executive; b. Chgo., Oct. 9, 1952; d. Vernon K. S. and Yun Soong (Chock) Jim; m. Carey R. Wong, Nov. 10, 1979; children: Jacquelyn C., Brandon R. BEd in Secondary Math., U. Hawaii, 1974; MA in Secondary Math., Columbia U., 1975; postgrad., St. John's U., N.Y.C., 1975-77; MBA, U. San Francisco, 1979. Tng. and devel. analyst and instr. Chase Manhattan Bank, N.Y.C., 1975-77; human resources profl. Crocker Nat. Bank, San Francisco, 1978-82, with credit rev. dept. contrs. divsn., 1982-85; comml. lender Calif. middle market Wells Fargo Bank/Crocker Nat. Bank, Palo Alto and San Mateo, Calif., 1985-88; mgr. credit dept. San Francisco (Calif.) internat. br. Algemene Bank Nederland N.V., 1988-90; sr. v.p., mgr. credit control and rsch. The Indsl. Bank of Japan, Ltd. San Francisco (Calif.) Agy., 1990—. Treas. United Way of Bay Area; bd. dirs. United Nonprofits Ops., San Francisco Bay coun. Girl Scouts, v.p., legis. liaison, coun. trainer, internat. applicants selection com., chair Tri-City Assn., 1991-92, troop leader; bd. dirs. San Francisco Sch. Vols.; chair, founding bd. dirs. Multicultural Initiative, 1991—; mem. US/ China Women's Issues Conf. & NGO Forum, Beijing, White House Briefing, Interagy. Coun. Women. Mem. AAUW (nat. LAF com., San Mateo br., bd. dirs. 1989-90, 94—, v.p. program, newsletter editor, cmty. programs com., chair couples gourmet interest group, others), Fin. Women's Assn., Assn. Jr. Leagues Internat. Inc. (1st v.p., exec. com. 1993-95, bd. dirs. 1992-95), Jr. League San Francisco, Inc. (adv. mem. bd. dirs. 1992-95, treas. 1990-91, exec. com., bd. dirs. 1990-91, endowment fund com. 1992, others).

WONG, ING LIONG, nephrologist; b. Sibu, Malaysia, Feb. 16, 1945; came to the U.S., 1971; s. Tiong Keng and Kieu Hung (Su) W.; m. Chu Fong, Nov. 8, 1969; children: Yu-Tian, Yu-Tung, Adrienne. BS, U. Manitoba, 1969, MD, 1971. Diplomate Am. Bd. Internal Medicine. Intern U. So. Calif. Med. Ctr., L.A., 1971-72; resident in internal medicine VA Hosp., Long Beach, Calif., 1972-74; nephrology fellowship UCI and affiliated hosps., 1974-76; asst. clin. prof. U. Calif., Irvine, 1979—; pres. Alamitos Renal-Med. Group Inc., Los Alamitos, Calif., 1978—, Hemotech, Inc., Los Alamitos, 1979—; med. dir. Norwalk (Calif.) Dialysis Ctr., 1991—, Lakewood Dialysis Ctr., Calif., 1995—; chmn. dept. medicine Bellwood Gen. Hosp., Bellflower, Calif., 1996; chmn. governing bd. Clin. United Dialysis Ctr., Long Beach, Calif., 1996—. Founding mem. Chinese Ams. United for Self-Empowerment, L.A., 1994. Mem. ACP, Am. Soc. Nephrology, Internat. Soc. Nephrology. Democrat. Office: Alamitos Renal Med Group 3801 Katella Ave Los Alamitos CA 90720-3338

WONG, IVAN GYNMUN, seismologist; b. Portland, Oreg., Feb. 23, 1948; s. Edward P. and Elizabeth K. (Lee) W.; m. Laly B. Flores, Oct. 22, 1988; children: Matthew W., Scott G. BS in Physics, Oreg. State U., 1970; BS in Geology, Portland (Oreg.) State U., 1972; M.S. in Geophysics, U. Utah, 1976. Phys. sci. technician/geologist U.S. Army Corps of Engrs., Portland, Oreg., 1967-72; seismol. field asst. U.S. Geol. Survey, Salt Lake City, 1974-75; rsch. asst. U. Utah, Salt Lake City, 1974-75, U. Calif., Berkeley, 1975-76; v.p./sr. seismologist Woodward-Clyde Fed. Svcs., Oakland, Calif., 1976—; rsch. assoc. Ariz. Earthquake Info. Ctr., Northern Ariz. U., Flagstaff, 1986—; seismology instr. Calif. Acad. Scis., San Francisco, 1989—; cons. to several U.S. govt. agys. including Dept. Energy and U.S. Bur. Reclamation; rev. and adv. panels, U.S. Geol. Survey, various locations, 1991—; invited spkr., guest lectr. various profl. orgns., 1982—. Contbr. 140 papers and abstracts to profl. jours. Staff sgt. USMCR, 1970-79. Recipient 4 rsch. grants Nat. Earthquake Hazards Reduction Program, U.S. Geol. Survey, 1986-96. Mem. Am. Geophys. Union, Geol. Soc. Am., Seismol. Soc. Am., Earthquake Engring. Rsch. Inst., Internat. Soc. Rock Mechanics. Office: Woodward-Clyde Fed Svcs 500 12th St Ste 100 Oakland CA 94607-4010

WONG, JAMES BOK, economist, engineer, technologist; b. Canton, China, Dec. 9, 1922; came to U.S., 1938, naturalized, 1962; s. Gen Ham and Chen (Yee) W.; m. Wai Ping Lim, Aug. 3, 1946; children: John, Jane Doris, Julia Ann. BS in Agr., U. Md., 1949, BS in Chem. Engring., 1950; MS, U. Ill., 1951, PhD, 1954. Rsch. asst. U. Ill., Champaign-Urbana, 1950-53; chem. engr. Standard Oil of Ind., Whiting, 1953-55; process design engr., rsch. engr. Shell Devel. Co., Emeryville, Calif., 1955-61; sr. planning engr., prin. planning engr. Chem. Plastics Group, Dart Industries, Inc. (formerly Rexall Drug & Chem. Co.), L.A., 1961-66, supr. planning and econs., 1966-67, mgr. long range planning and econs., 1967, chief economist, 1967-72, dir. econs. and ops. analysis, 1972-78, dir. internat. techs., 1978-81; pres. James B. Wong Assocs., L.A., 1981—; chmn. bd. dirs. United Pacific Bank, 1988—; tech. cons. various corps. Contbr. articles to profl. jours. Bd. dirs., pres. Chinese Am. Citizens Alliance Found.; mem. Asian Am. Edn. Commn., 1971-81. Served with USAAF, 1943-46. Recipient Los Angeles Outstanding Vol. Service award, 1977. Mem. Am. Inst. Chem. Engrs., Am. Chem. Soc., VFW (vice comdr. 1959), Commodores (named to exec. order 1982), Sigma Xi, Tau Beta Pi, Phi Kappa Phi, Pi Mu Epsilon, Phi Lambda Upsilon, Phi Eta Sigma. Home: 2460 Venus Dr Los Angeles CA 90046-1646 *Personal philisophy: A man's reputation is his most prized possession.*

WONG, JANET SIU, writer; b. L.A., Sept. 30, 1962; d. Roger and Joyce Wong; m. Glenn Schroeder; 1 child, Andrew. BA, UCLA, 1983; JD, Yale U., 1987. Lawyer L.A., 1987-91; writer Medina, Wash., 1991—. Author: Good Luck Gold, 1994, A Suitcase of Seaweed, 1996. Office: 8245 NE 8th St Medina WA 98039

WONG, JEFFREY YUN CHUNG, radiation oncologist, medical researcher; b. Honolulu, Nov. 5, 1955; s. Tom Kam Yee and Rose Ah Moy (Chun) W.; m. Julia Kyoko Yoshikawa, Oct. 17, 1987; 1 child, Marisa Midori. BS in Biology, Stanford U., 1977; MD, Johns Hopkins U., 1981. Diplomate in radiation oncology Am. Bd. Radiology. Intern Harbor-UCLA Med. Ctr., Torrance, 1981-82; resident U. Calif., San Francisco, 1982-85; staff physician City of Hope Med. Ctr., Duarte, Calif., 1985—. Contbr. articles to profl. jours. Am. Cancer Soc. clin. fellow, 1984. Mem. Am. Soc. Therapeutic Radiology and Oncology, Am. Soc. Clin. Oncology, Soc. Nuclear Medicine, Radiation Rsch. Soc., Phi Beta Kappa.

WONG, KENNETH LEE, software engineer, import executive, consultant; b. L.A., Aug. 15, 1947; s. George Yut and Yue Sam (Lee) W.; m. Betty (Louie) Wong, June 29, 1975; children: Bradford Keith, Karen Beth. BS in Engring., UCLA, 1969, MS in Engring., 1972, postgrad., 1972-73, 76-78. Cert. community coll. instr., Calif. Engring. aide Singer Librascope, Glendale, Calif., 1972-73; computer system design engr. Air Force Avionics Lab., Wright-Patterson AFB, Ohio, 1973-75; mem. tech. staff Hughes Aircraft Co., various cities, Calif., 1976-78, 79-81, TRW Def. and Space Systems Group, Redondo Beach, Calif., 1975-76, 78-79; engring. specialist Northrop Corp., Hawthorne, Calif., 1981-84; mem. tech. staff Jet Propulsion Lab., Pasadena, Calif., 1984-87; software cons. EG&G Spl. Projects, Las Vegas, Nev., 1987, AT&T Bell Labs., Warren, N.J., 1987-88, Westinghouse Electric Corp., Linthicom, Md., 1988, E Systems, Inc., Greenville, Tex., 1988-89; prin. Wong Soft Works, L.A., 1987—; pres. Oriental Silk Co., L.A., 1989—. Author tech. reports. 1st lt. USAF, 1973-75. Mem. AIAA, IEEE, Assn. Computing Machinery, Upsilon Pi Epsilon. Republican. Home: 3385 Mclaughlin Ave Los Angeles CA 90066-2004 Office: Oriental Silk Co 8377 Beverly Blvd Los Angeles CA 90048-2633

WONG, KIN-PING, university dean, biotechnology researcher, company executive, educator, science administrator; b. Guangzhou, China, Aug. 14, 1941; s. Kwok-Keung and Yuan-Kwan (Loo) W.; m. Anna S.K. Koo, Sept. 16, 1968; children: Voon-Chung Wong, Ming-Chung Wong. BS, U. Calif., Berkeley, 1964; PhD, Purdue U., 1968. Postdoctoral fellow Duke U., Durham, N.C., 1968-70; asst. and assoc. prof. chemistry U. South Fla., Tampa, 1970-75; vis. scientist Max Planck Inst. Molecular Genetics, Berlin, 1972; vis. prof. U. Uppsala, Sweden, 1975; assoc. and prof. biochemistry U. Kans., Kansas City, 1975-83, dean grad. studies, 1980-83; vis. prof. biochemistry U. Tokyo, 1979; program dir. of biophysics NSF, Washington, 1982-83; sci. dean, prof. Calif. State U., Fresno, 1983—; mng. dir., CEO Hong Kong Inst. Biotechnology, 1992-93; founder, chmn., pres., CEO RiboGene Inc., Menlo Pk., Calif., 1989-91; vis. prof. biochemistry Stanford U. Med. Ctr., summer 1985; adj. prof. medicine U. Calif. San Francisco Med. Sch., 1986—; adj. prof. biochemistry and biophysics, U. Calif., San Francisco, 1987—; mem. U.S. Govt. Interagency Com. on Radiation, Washington, 1982-83; gov. Moss Landing (Calif.) Marine Labs., 1983—; cons. HHS, Washington, 1985—; trustee U. Calif., San Francisco, Fresno 1986—; mem. rev. panel NSF; mem. sci. expert panel Calif. Commn. Tchr. Credentialing. Contbr. over 50 research articles to prof. jours.; 32 pub. research abstracts; author various keynote speeches, convocation lectures. Chmn. sci. com. Fresno Met. Mus., 1983-85; co-chmn. planning com. Cen. Calif. Biomed. Rsch. Inst., Fresno, 1987—; co-chmn. multicultural coun. Clovis Unified Sch. Dist., 1988-90. Recipient cancer research grants and awards, Damon Runyan Fund, Milheim Found., Am. Cancer Soc., Eli Lilly Corp., Research Corps., Am. Heart Assn., 1980-81; grantee HHS, 1986-89, Nat. Inst. Heart Lung and Blood, 1972-87, Nat. Inst. Gen. Med. Scis., 1972-80; research career devel. awardee NIH, 1972-75; sr. research fellow European Molecular Biology Orgn., 1975; NSF summer rsch. professorship Stanford U., 1985; Laval Research award in innovative scis. and tech. Calif. State U., Fresno, 1985; scholarship Pepperdine U. presdl. and key exec. program, 1986-88; Calif. Sea grant Dept. Commerce, 1987-90. Fellow Royal Soc. Chemistry, Am. Inst. Chemists; mem. Am. Soc. Biol. Chemistry (membership com. 1983-86), AAAS, Biophys. Soc., Am. Chem. Soc., Sigma Xi. Office: Calif State U Sch Natural Sci Fresno CA 93740-0090

WONG, LINDA L., surgeon; b. Portland, Oreg., June 14, 1960; d. Livingston M.F. and Rose K.L. Wong. BS in Biology, Stanford U., 1982; MD, U. Calif., Irvine, 1986. Diplomate Am. Bd. Gen. Surgery; lic. physician, Calif., Hawaii. Rschr. dept. urology Stanford (Calif.) U. Med. Ctr., 1980-81; rschr. Cardiovascular Rsch. Lab. Queen's Med. Ctr., Honolulu, 1980-82; rschr. dept. surgery U. Calif.-Irvine, Orange, 1984-86; rschr. dept. surgery Cedars-Sinai Med. Ctr., L.A., 1987-88, gen. surgery resident, 1986-91; transplant fellow liver, kidney, pancreas Calif. Pacific Med. Ctr. Transplant Svcs., San Francisco, 1991-92; dir. liver transplant program St. Francis Med. Ctr., Honolulu, 1993—; asst. prof. surgery U. Hawaii Sch. Medicine, Honolulu, 1993—; gen. transplant surgeon Surg. Assocs., Inc., Honolulu, 1993—; lectr., presenter various orgns. and confs. Contbr. articles to profl. jours. Recipient Pacific Health Rsch. Inst. Scholarship, 1980, Zimmerman Found. Rsch. Scholarship, 1981, Leo Rigler award for excellence in surgery, 1988, 90, 91. Fellow ACS; mem. AMA, Hawaii Med. Assn., Am. Soc. Artificial Internal Organs, Soc. Organ Sharing, Am. Assn. Study of Liver Diseases, Transplantation Soc., Western Assn. Transplant Surgeons. Office: Surg Assocs Inc 1329 Lusitana St Ste 709 Honolulu HI 96813-2434

WONG, MAI-LON, public school assistant principal; b. Phoenix, Dec. 15, 1957; d. James and Willie Mae (Eng) Tang; m. Eddy Wong, May 28, 1977; children: Jarrett, Steven. BA in Edn., Ariz. State U., 1979, MA in Edn., 1985; EdD, Nova Southeastern U., 1996. Tchr. Peoria Unified Sch. Dist., Glendale, Ariz., 1979-89; tchr./facilitator gifted and Chpt. 1 programs Phoenix Union H.S. Dist., Phoenix, 1991-95; asst. prin. Scottsdale (Ariz.) Unified Pub. Sch. Dist., 1995—. Mary Catherine Ellwein Dissertation award finalist, 1995 (dissertation presenter Uppsala, Sweden, 1996). Mem. Am. Ednl. Rsch. Assn., Assn. Supervision and Curriculum Devel., Phi Delta Kappa. Baptist. Office: Anasazi Elem Sch 11130 E Cholla St Scottsdale AZ 85259

WONG, NANCY L., dermatologist; b. Chung King, China, Aug. 23, 1943; came to U.S., 1947; d. YinPao Harry and Alice Wang; m. Robert Lipshutz; children: Seth, Alison, David. BS magna cum laude, Pa. State U., 1963; MS in Physics, Columbia U., 1965; MD, Jefferson Med. Coll., Phila., 1971. Diplomate Am. Bd. Dermatology. Intern Wilmington Med. Ctr., 1972; resident Jackson Meml. Hosp., Miami, Mount Sinai Med. Ctr., Miami, 1977; pvt. practice Palo Alto, Calif., 1987—. Woodrow Wilson fellow 1963-64, NSF fellow, 1963-64, AEC fellow, 1963-64. Fellow Am. Acad. Dermatology. Office: 1101 Welch Rd Ste C6 Palo Alto CA 94301

WONG, NATHAN DONALD, medicine and epidemiology educator; b. Downey, Calif., Apr. 18, 1961; s. Donald Wah and Mew Lun (Hee) W. BA, Pomona Coll., 1983; MPH, Yale U., 1985, PhD, 1987. Lectr. in medicine Yale U., New Haven, 1987; asst. prof. U. Calif., Irvine, 1988-94, assoc. prof., 1994—, dir. preventive cardiology, dept. medicine, 1991—; assoc. adj. prof. dept. epidemiology UCLA, 1996—; pres., CEO Profl. Rsch. Inst. for Design and Evaluation, Inc., Dana Point, Calif., 1994—; prin. investigator Antihypertensive Lipid-Lowering to Prevent Heart Attack Trial and other lipid and cardiovascular prevention trials, 1994—; co-prin. investigator Women's Health Initiative, 1995—; numerous presentations and seminars in field; mem. Prevention 2000 Com., Calif. Dept. Health Svcs., 1995—; mem. adv. com. Cardiovascular Diseases Outreach, Resources and Epidemiology Program, 1995—; interviewed for various publs. and programs, including ABC Eyewitness News, L.A. Times, Orange County Register, CBS News This Morning, Spring Fgn. News Svc., USA Today, N.Y. Times, others; profl. cons. Montebello Schs. Phys. Assessment Program, 1989, Tobacco Resistance Activity Program, Pomona Unified Sch. Dist., 1990-94; Cordis-Webster, Baldwin Park, 1992—, Univ. Heart Imaging, 1994, PacifiCare Wellness Co., Cypress, Calif., 1994-96. Contbr. articles to profl. jours. mem. Calif. Senate Hearing Panel on Youth Phys. Edn. and Fitness, 1991; mem. Women's Health Initiative Cmty. Adv. Bd., U. Calif., Irvine, 1994—, vol. Coll. Medicine Health Fair, 1995; vol. Anaheim Sr. Health Fair, 1995; mem. health adv. coun. KOCE 50 TV, 1995. Fellow Am. Coll. Cardiology, Am. Heart Assn. Coun. on Epidemiology and Prevention; mem. Cardiovascular Disease Prevention Coalition. Office: U Calif Dept Medicine C240

MedSci I Irvine CA 92697 Office: Kaiser Permanente Dept Rsch and Evaluation 100 S Los Robles 2d Fl Pasadena CA 91101

WONG, OTTO, epidemiologist; b. Canton, China, Nov. 14, 1947; came to U.S., 1967, naturalized, 1976; m. Betty Yeung, Feb. 14, 1970; children: Elaine, Jonathan. BS, U. Ariz., 1970; MS, Carnegie Mellon U., 1972; MS, U. Pitts., 1973, ScD, 1975. Cert. epidemiologist, Am. Coll. Epidemiology, 1982. USPHS fellow U. Pitts., 1972-75; asst. prof. epidemiology Georgetown U. Med. Sch., 1975-78; mgr. epidemiology Equitable Environ. Health Inc., Rockville, Md., 1977-78; dir. epidemiology Tabershaw Occupational Med. Assocs., Rockville, 1978-80; dir. occupational rsch. Biometric Rsch. Inst., Washington, 1980-81; exec. v.p., chief epidemiologist, ENSR Health Scis., Alameda, Calif., 1981-90; chief epidemologist, pres. Applied Health Scis., San Mateo, Calif., 1991—; adj. prof. epidemiology and biostats. Tulane U. Med. Ctr., New Orleans; vis. prof. epidemiology and occupl. health Nat. Def. Med. Ctr., Taipei, Taiwan; cons. WHO, Nat. Cancer Inst., Nat. Inst. Occupl. Safety and Health, Occupl. Safety and Health Adminstrn., Nat. Heart, Lung and Blood Inst., Internat. Agy. for Rsch. on Cancer, U.S. EPA, Ford Motors Co., Gen. Electric, Mobil, Chevron, Union Carbide, Fairfax Hosp., Agy. for Toxic Substances and Disease Registry, Va. U. Ariz. scholar, 1967-68. Fellow Am. Coll. Epidemiology, Human Biology Council; mem. Am. Pub. Health Assn., Biometric Soc., Soc. Epidemiologic Rsch., Phi Beta Kappa, Pi Mu Epsilon. Republican. Contbr. articles to profl. jours. Office: Applied Health Scis PO Box 2078 181 Second Ave Ste 628 San Mateo CA 94401

WONG, PHILLIP ALLEN, osteopathic physician; b. Oakland, Calif., Dec. 8, 1956; s. Timothy Him and Lillian (Lee) W.; m. Lisa Perreault, Apr. 30, 1983; children: Ashley, Heather. BS in Microbiology and Chemistry, No. Ariz. U., 1979; DO, Kirksville Coll. Osteo. Med., 1983. Intern Kirksville Osteo. Health Ctr., 1983-84; staff family physician USAF, Kirtland AFB, N.Mex., 1984-87; CEO, pvt. practice Albuquerque, 1987—. Capt. USAF, 1984-87. Mem. Am. Acad. Osteopathy (bd. cert. in osteo. manipulative medicine), Am. Osteo. Assn., Am. Coll. Osteo. Family Physicians (bd. cert. family practice), N.Mex. Osteo. Med. Assn. (bd. mem.), Ariz. Acad. Osteopathy (bd. mem.), Cranial Acad. (bd. cert. in cranial in the osteo. field). Office: 10211 Montgomery Blvd NE Ste A Albuquerque NM 87111-3604

WONG, REBECCA KIMMAE, mathematics educator, consultant; b. San Francisco, Apr. 4, 1959; d. Wing On and Lucille Lorraine (Chan) Chong; m. Wesley Robert Wong, Aug. 14, 1982; children: Nathaniel, Allison. BA in Maths. and Psychology, U. Calif., Santa Barbara, 1981; MSin Teaching Maths., Santa Clara (Calif.) U., 1990. Cert. maths. tchr., Calif. Tchr. Independence High Sch., San Jose, Calif., 1982-92, chpt. I resource tchr., 1984-87; instr. Evergreen Valley Coll., San Jose, 1992-94, West Valley Coll., Saratoga, Calif., 1994—; coord. univ. and coll. opportunity program Independence High Sch., San Jose, 1988-90, chair maths. dept., 1989—; cons. in field. U. Calif. scholar, 1977-81. Mem. Nat. Coun. Tchrs. of Maths., Internat. Assn. for the Study of Cooperation in Edn., Math. Assn. Am., Phi Beta Kappa. Roman Catholic.

WONG, SAMUEL, conductor; b. Hong Kong, Apr. 12, 1962; m. Hae-Young Ham, Oct. 27, 1991. AB, Harvard U., 1984, MD, 1988. Music dir. N.Y. Youth Symphony, N.Y.C., 1988-93, Ann Arbor (Mich.) Symphony, 1992—; asst. conductor N.Y. Philharm., N.Y.C., 1990-94; music dir. Honolulu Symphony, 1996—; internat. guest conductor various orchs., in Montreal, Toronto, Vancouver, Seattle, Oreg., New Orleans, Hong Kong, Singapore, Brussels, Budapest, Israel, Mex., and New Zealand; guest conductor Japan Philharm., Tokyo, KBS Orch., Seoul. Operas conducted include The Barber of Seville, Madame Butterfly, Rigoletto; author: Heartbeat, a Life in Music and Medicine, 1997. Office: Honolulu Symphony Orchestra 677 Ala Moana Blvd Ste 615 Honolulu HI 96813

WONG, SUN YET, engineering consultant; b. Honolulu, Dec. 6, 1932; s. Chip Tong and Shiu Inn (Chang) W.; m. Janet Siu Hung Lau; children: Cathleen, Bryan, Jonathan. BS in Civil Engring. with honors, U. Hawaii, 1954; MS in Civil Engring., Yale U., 1955. Engr. N.Am. Aviation, Downey, Calif., 1955-58; mem. tech. staff Ramo Woolridge Space Tech. Labs., Redondo Beach, Calif., 1958-64; exec. v.p., treas., tech. dir. Mechanics Rsch. Inc., El Segundo, Calif., 1964-77; treas. System Devel. Corp., Santa Monica, Calif., 1977-79; chmn. bd., pres., treas. Applied Rsch. Inc., El Segundo, 1979-81; ind. cons. Rolling Hills Estates, Calif., 1981—; cons. Acurex, Mountain View, Calif., 1983, Ampex, Redwood City, Calif., 1991, Applied Tech., Mountain View, 1983-85, Astron, Mountain View, 1983-85, E Systems, Garland, Tex., 1986-93, Electromech. Systems Inc., Anaheim, Calif., 1984, Hughes, El Segundo, 1992, 94, 96—, Intercon, Cerritos, Calif., 1982-84, J.H. Wiggins Co., Redondo Beach, 1982-84, Kodak Datatape, Pasadena, Calif., 1989, Lion Engring., Rancho Palos Verdes, Calif., 1994—, Measurement Analysis Corp., Torrance, Calif., 1984-96, MRJ, Fairfax, Va., 1984, Odectics, Anaheim, 1990, Swales & Assocs., Beltsville, Md., 1992-93, Statis. Scis., Inc., Beverly Hills, Calif., 1986, Tompkins and Assocs., Torrance, 1984—, TRW, Redondo Beach, 1984; dir. Lion Engring. Home and Office: 7 Club View Ln Rolling Hills Estates CA 90274

WONG, WALLACE, medical supplies company executive, real estate investor; b. Honolulu, July 13, 1941; s. Jack Yung Hung and Theresa (Goo) W.; m. Amy Ju, June 17, 1963; children: Chris, Bradley, Jeffery. Student, UCLA, 1960-63. Chmn., pres. South Bay Coll., Hawthorne, Calif., 1965-86; chmn. Santa Barbara (Calif.) Bus. Coll., 1975—; gen. ptnr. W B Co., Redondo Beach, Calif., 1982—; CEO Cal Am. Med. Supplies, Rancho Santa Margarita, Calif., 1986-96, Cal Am. Exports, Inc., Rancho Santa Margarita, 1986-96, Pacific Am. Group, Rancho Santa Margarita, 1991-96; chmn., CEO Alpine, Inc., Rancho Santa Margarita, Calif., 1993-96; pres. Bayside Properties, Rancho Santa Margarita, 1993—; bd. dirs. Metrobank, L.A. FFF Enterprises; chmn. bd. 1st Ind. Fin. Group., Rancho Santa Margarita, 1994—; chmn. Affinity Fin. Corp., 1996—. Acting sec. of state State of Calif., Sacramento, 1982; founding mem. Opera Pacific, Orange County, Calif., 1985; mem. Hist. and Cultural Found., Orange County, 1986; v.p. Orange County Chinese Cultural Club, Orange County, 1985. Named for Spirit of Enterprise Resolution, Hist. & Cultural Found., Orange Country, 1987; recipient resolution City of Hawthorne, 1973. Mem. Westren Accred Schs. & Colls. (v.p. 1978-79), Magic Castle (life), Singapore Club. Office: Bayside Properties 23042 Arroyo Vis Rancho Santa Margarita CA 92688-2604

WONG, WALTER FOO, county official; b. San Francisco, Apr. 11, 1930; s. Harry Yee and Grace (Won) W. AA, Hartnell Coll., 1952; BS, U. Calif., Berkeley, 1955; MPH, U. Hawaii, 1968. Registered sanitarian, Calif. Sanitarian Stanislaus County Health Dept., Modesto, Calif., 1955-56; sanitarian Monterey County Health Dept., Salinas, Calif., 1956-67, sr. sanitarian, 1968-69, supervising sanitarian, 1969-70, dir. environ. health, 1971—; sec. Monterey County Solid Waste Mgmt. Com., 1976—, Monterey County Hazardous Waste Mgmt. Com., 1987—; coord. Monterey County Genetic Engring. Rev. Com., 1987—; mem. Monterey County Genetic Engring. Experiment Permit Rev. Panel, 1995; mem. Monterey County Hazardous Materials Response Task Force, 1988—; mem. tech. adv. com. Monterey Peninsula Water Mgmt. Dist., 1985—, Monterey Regional Water Pollution Control Agy., 1985—; chmn. task force Monterey Regional Wastewater Reclamation Study for Agr., EPA and State of Calif. Chmn. Salinas Bicentennial Internat. Day Celebration, 1974, Pollution Clean-up Com. of Fort Ord Task Force, 1992; mem. Calif. Bare Closure Environ. adv. com., 1993. Mem. Calif. Conf. Dirs. Environ. Health (pres. 1982-83), Assn. Environ. Health Adminstrs. (pres. 1982-83), Salinas C. of C. (Mem. of Yr. award 1971), U. Calif. Berkeley Alumni Assn., U. Hawaii Alumni Assn. (Disting. Alumni award 1992), Monterey County Hist. Soc. (pres. 1995-96), Ethnic Cultural Coun. (chmn. 1995). Republican. Presbyterian. Home: 234 Cherry Dr Salinas CA 93901-2807 Office: Monterey County Health Dept 1270 Natividad Rd Rm 301 Salinas CA 93906-3122

WONG, WAYNE D., nutritionist; b. San Francisco, May 13, 1950; s. Chaney Noon and La Dean Maryan (Mah) W. m. Betty Lee, Oct. 16, 1977; children: Michael Gabriel, Elizabeth Catherine, Whitney Forbes, Ellesse Florence. BS in Dietetic Adminstrn., U. Calif., Berkeley, 1972; MS in Sch. Bus. Mgmt., Pepperdine U., 1976; student, Nikon Sch. Photography, San Francisco, 1969. Cert. Food Svc. Dir., Calif. Community Coll. tchr.; Registered Dietitian, Sch. Bus. Official, Benefit specialist. Food svc. worker, lab. asst. U. Calif., Berkeley, 1968-69, 70-71; mgmt. intern Mich. State U., East Lansing, 1970; dietetic intern Milw. Pub. Schs., 1972-73; food svc. cons. Trader Vic's, San Francisco, 1973; dir. food svcs. Bakersfield (Calif.) City Sch. Dist., 1973—; instr. Bakersfield Coll., 1978—; cons. Wong, R.D., Bakersfield, 1978—; registered Benefit Specialist Investors Retirement Mgmt., Carpenteria, Calif., 1988—; mem. nat. child nutrition adv. coun. USDA, Washington, 1977-79; 1st v.p. Ptnrs. in Nutrition Coop., Lancaster, Calif., 1988-90; food svc. edn. task force Calif. Dept. Edn., Sacramento, 1979—; project coord. nutrition edn. and tng. exemplary program adoption grant Bakersfield City Sch. Dist., 1982; project dir. basic skills, basic foods course, curriculum and recipe devel. grant Calif. Dept. Edn., 1985, cons. tchg. course, 1985-88; mem. adv. coun. Calif. State U. Long Beach Child Nutrition Program Mgmt. Tng. Ctr., 1991; mem. Sch. Nutrition Adv. Coun., Bakersfield, 1990—; graphics and tech. writing cons. Cal-Pro-Net Ctr., Fresno City Coll., 1995—; program panelist Ptnrs. Nutrition Coop., Am. Sch. Food Svc. Assn., Ann. Nat. Conf., 1995. Author: Food Service Equipment-How Long Should It Last?, 1985; co-author (videotape) Bettermade Plastics, 1991, Recycle: Save Earth's Resources Now; programmer Food Svc. Pers. Database, 1988, Dishmachine Labor and Energy Matrix, 1991; contbr. articles to profl. jours. BBQ fund-raiser co-chmn. Citizens for Yes on Measure B, Bakersfield, 1989; legis. com. Child Nutrition Facilities Act 1975, Sacramento, 1973-76; expert witness State Senate Select Subcom. on Nutrition and Human Needs, Sacramento, 1973; asst. troop leader Boy Scouts Am., Troop 219, San Francisco, 1965-67; participant Chinese Family Life Study U. Calif., Berkeley; dir. polystyrene recycling project Bakersfield City Sch. Dist., 1990; team leader Healthy Kids, Healthy Calif. program Calif. Dept. Edn., 1985-87; sponsor Christian Broadcasting Network Satellite Comms. Ctr., 1978; world vision sponsor India Cmty. Devel. Program, 1974-92; guitarist Canyon Hills Assembly of God Ch. Orch., 1996—. Recipient Leadership award Calif. State Dept. Edn., 1987, Outstanding Sch. Lunch Program award USDA, 1989; 1st pl. Calif. Sch. Food Svc. Assn. Country Cook-off, 1983, 84; Toto Wizard nominee Sabatasso Foods, 1985, Best Practice award USDA, 1992. Mem. Am. Dietetic Assn. (Young Dietitian of Yr. 1976), Am. Sch. Food Svc. Assn. (child nutrition mktg. bike ride 1991, Cycle Across Am. for Child Nutrition and Fitness 1993), Am. Running and Fitness Assn., Calif. Assn. Sch. Bus. Ofcls. (photographer 1985, food svc. R&D chmn. 1985-87, recognition 1987, food and nutrition R&D com. 1984), Calif. Sch. Food Svc. Assn. (edn. tng. chmn. 1975-76, wellness awareness bike ride 1990-91, child nutrition bike ride 1991, 1st pl. photo contest 1993, cover photographer assn. jour. Poppyseeds 1992), Sports and Cardiovasc. Nutritionists, Kern County Sch. Food Svc. Assn. (pres. 1987-90, Golden Poppy award 1990), Kern Wheelmen (v.p. 1992), Hour of Power Sparrows Club, Pi Alpha Phi, Omicron Nu. Republican. Baptist. Home: 4901 University Ave Bakersfield CA 93306-1773

WONG, WILLIAM SHEH, librarian; s. Po and Te-i (Liao) W.; m. Eugenia J.K. Shih, June 27, 1964; 1 child, Alexander. BA, Taiwan Normal U., 1956; MA, Meiji U., 1960, George Peabody Coll., 1963; PhD, Northwestern U., 1971. Cataloger U. N.H., Durham, 1963-64; asst. East Asian libr. U. Kans., Lawrence, 1964-67; curator East Asian collection Northwestern U., Evanston, Ill., 1967-70; chief bibliographer Loyola U. Libr., Chgo., 1970-71; East Asian libr., assoc. prof. U. Minn., Mpls., 1971-78; Asian libr., prof. libr. adminstrn. U. Ill., Urbana, 1978-90; East Asian libr. U. Calif., Irvine, 1990—. Contbr. profl. publ. Coun. Libr. Resources fellow, 1977-78, Fulbright rsch. fellow, 1984-85; grantee William and Flora Hewlett Found., Chiang Ching-Kuo Found. Mem. ALA, Am. Assn. Chinese Studies, Internat. Assn. Orientalist Librs. (sec., treas. 1983-86, 86-90, pres. 1993-97), Assn. Asian Studies. Home: 23 Zola Ct Irvine CA 92612-4061 Office: U Calif Libr PO Box 19557 Irvine CA 92623-9557

WONG-DIAZ, FRANCISCO RAIMUNDO, lawyer, educator; b. Havana, Cuba, Oct. 29, 1944; came to U.S., Nov. 1961; s. Juan and Teresa (Diaz de Villegas) Wong; 1 child, Richard Alan. BA with honors, No. Mich. U., 1963; MA with highest honors, U. Detroit, 1967; PhD, MA, U. Mich., 1974; JD, U. Calif.-Berkeley, 1976. Bar: Calif. 1980, U.S. Dist. Ct. (no. dist.) Calif. 1990, Fla. 1987. Asst. prof. San Francisco State U., 1977; vis. scholar U. Calif. Berkeley Sch. Bus., Berkeley, 1983-84; prof. City Coll. San Francisco, 1975—, dept. chmn., 1978-85; rsch. atty. Marin Superior Ct., 1980-81; ct. arbitrator Marin Mcpl. Ct., 1985; solo practice, Kentfield, Calif., 1980—; assoc. dean Miami-Dade Coll., 1986; dir. Cutcliffe Consulting, Inc., Hawthorne, LaFamila Ctr., Inc., San Rafael, Calif., 1980-85, Small Bus. Inst., Kentfield, 1982-86; cons. ICC Internat., San Francisco, 1980-82. Bd. editors Indsl. Relations Law Jour., 1975-76; mem. editl. bd. California Lawyer, 1991-93; lector St. Sebastian's Ch., 1984—, Parish Coun., 1995. Diplomat-scholar U.S. Dept. State, Washington, 1976; Horace C. Rackham fellow U. Mich., 1970, Summer fellow U. Calif., Berkeley, 1995, Nat. Security Law Ctr. U. Va., 1996. Mem. Am. Polit. Sci. Assn., Latino Ednl. Assn. (treas. 1985), Cuban Am. Nat. Coun., World Affairs Coun. (seminar leader San Francisco 1980). Roman Catholic. Club: Commonwealth. *Personal philosophy: "This is what Yahueh asks of you, only this: to act justly, to love tenderly and to walk humbly with your God" Micah 6:8.*

WOO, RAYMOND, aerospace engineer; b. Tokyo, Nov. 22, 1949; came to U.S., Sept. 7, 1966; s. Eric Dee and Alice Chi-Hua (Chang) W. BS in Engring., UCLA, 1972, MS in Engring., 1975; Engr., U. So. Calif., 1988. Tech. staff Rockwell Internat., Downey and El Segundo, Calif., 1975-78, TRW (Aerospace), Redondo Beach, Calif., 1978-82, Logicon (Aerospace), San Pedro, Calif., 1982-84; tech. staff, engr. Jet Propulsion Lab., Pasadena, Calif., 1984-87; dept. staff, engr. TRW (Aerospace), Redondo Beach, Calif., 1988-89; electronics engr. Naval Air Warfare Ctr. USN, China Lake, Calif., 1989—. Contbr. article to profl. jour. Dept. scholar UCLA Sch. Engring., 1971. Mem. AIAA, IEEE (China Lake (Calif.) exec. com. 1971—). Republican. Baptist. Home: 1301 S Atlantic Blvd No 118 Monterey Park CA 91754 Office: Naval Air Warfare Ctr Code Sec 471260D China Lake CA 93555

WOO, TIMOTHY DAVID, JR., lawyer; b. Hilo, Hawaii, Oct. 30, 1944; s. Timothy David and Evelyn Momi (Goo) W.; m. Donna May Lee, Aug. 2, 1948; 1 child, Tiffany Wing Yan. BA, Northwestern U., 1967; MBA, Golden Gate U., 1968; JD, U. Calif., 1971. Bar: U.S. Supreme Ct. Hawaii, Calif. Assoc. atty. Evans, Jackson & Kennedy, Sacramento, 1973-74; asst. U.S. atty. U.S. Dept. Justice, Honolulu, 1974-78; ptnr. Chang & Woo, Attys., Honolulu, 1978-80; law clerk to Judge Philip C. Wilkins U. S. Dist. Cts., Sacramento, 1971-73; asst. clerk of the senate Hawaii State Senate, Honolulu, 1979-82, clerk of the senate, 1982-96. Mem. Waialae County Club. Democrat. Office: 733 Bishop St Ste 2530 Honolulu HI 96813

WOO, VERNON YING-TSAI, lawyer, real estate developer; b. Honolulu, Aug. 7, 1942; s. William Shu-Bin and Hilda Woo; m. Arlene Gay Ischar, Feb. 14, 1971; children: Christopher Shu-Bin, Lia Gay. BA, U. Hawaii, 1964, MA, 1966; JD, Harvard U., 1969. Pres. Woo Kessner Duca & Maki, Honolulu, 1972-87; pvt. practice law Honolulu, 1987—; judge per diem Honolulu Dist. Ct., 1978-84, 95—. Bd. dirs. Boys and Girls Club of Honolulu,. 1985—, pres., 1990-92. Mem. ABA, Hawaii Bar Assn., Honolulu Bd. Realtors, Pacific Club. Home: 2070 Kalawahine Pl Honolulu HI 96822-2518 Office: 1019 Waimanu St Ste 205 Honolulu HI 96814-3409

WOOD, DANIEL BRIAN, educational consultant; b. Roseburg, Oreg., Mar. 5, 1960; s. Jack Livingston and E. June (Gamble) W. BS, U. Oreg., 1982, MS, 1985, PhD, 1989. Cert. folklore and ethnic studies. Fare policy analyst Lane Transit Dist., Eugene, Oreg., 1984-85; asst. to dean for internships Univ. Oreg., Eugene, 1987-88; rsch. analyst Oreg. System Higher Edn., Eugene, 1988; pvt. practice, ednl. rsch. Eugene, 1988—; co-designer, coauthor statewide exam. and analysis of transfer student performance in Oreg. higher edn.; manuscript reviewer for refereed jours.; vis. asst. prof., rsch. assoc. U. Miss., 1992-93; active Statewide Task Force on Transfer Followup, 1987-88. Reviewer Internat. Jour. Intercultural Rels., 1995—; contbr. articles to profl. jours. Mem. Am. Soc. Pub. Adminstrn., Oreg. Sect. Pub. Adminstrn. Edn., Pi Lambda Theta (pres.), Phi Delta Kappa. Home and Office: 122 E Howard Ave Eugene OR 97404-2617

WOOD, DAVID BRUCE, naturopathic physician; b. Fayetteville, N.C., Jan. 21, 1954; s. Marvin James and Rachel Elenor (Thom) W.; m. Wendy Ann McKiernan, Aug. 1974 (div. Aug. 1976); m. Cheryl Lynn Garbarino, Aug. 17, 1980. BS in Microbiology, U. Wash., 1977; D in Naturopathic Medicine, Bastyr U., Seattle, 1983. Pres., co-founder Trinity Family Health Clinic, Inc., P.S., Edmonds, Wash., 1984—; Spkr. local and nat. TV programs. Singer Sound of Praise Choir, Overlake Christian Ch., Kirkland, Wash., 1987-92; narrator Easter Pagent, 1989; mem. Cedar Park Assembly of God, Bothel, Wash. Mem. Am. Assn. Nutritional Cons., Nat. Health Fedn., Am. Assn. Naturopathic Physicians, Wash. Assn. Naturopathic Physicians (trustee, exec. bd. 1989-92). Home: 13721 Cascadian Way Everett WA 98208-7345 Office: Trinity Family Health Clinic Inc PS 7614 195th St SW Edmonds WA 98026-6260

WOOD, DAVID DUANE, clinical psychologist, marriage and family counselor; b. Pasadena, Calif., Feb. 22, 1950; s. Robert Andrew and Carolyn Irene (Cartier) W.; m. Laurel Beth Roska, Sept. 23, 1973; 1 child, Daniel Cody. Student, U. Bergen, Norway, 1971-72; BA in Psychology with high honors, U. Calif., Santa Barbara, 1973; MA in Clin. Psychology, U. Utah, 1980, PhD in Clin. Psychology, 1985. Lic. psychologist, Calif.; lic. marriage, family and child counselor, Calif. Rsch. tech. Psychophysiology Rsch. Lab. Camarillo (Calif.) Neuropsychiatric Inst. Rsch. Ctr. Camarillo State Hosp., 1970-71, rsch. asst. behavior analysis and modification project, 1972-73, rsch. asst. hosp. improvement project, 1973-74; psychology trainee II pilot alcohol drug abuse treatment unit Salt Lake VA Med. Ctr., 1974-75, psychology trainee III behavior modification unit and day hosp., 1975-76, intern medicine and neurology, 1977-78; instr. dept. psychology divsn. continuing edn. U. Utah, 1979-81; postdoctoral fellow behavioral pediatrics Sch. Medicine U. Md., Balt., 1983-85; psychologist mental health program Turning Point, Visalia, 1985-86; clin. dir. Visalia Children's Svcs. Clinic Tulare County Youth Mental Health Svcs. Consortium, 1986-89, consulting chief psychologist, 1989-90, consulting psychologist, 1990—; consulting psychologist Tulare County Dept. Mental Health, 1993—; mem. med. staff Charter Behavioral Health Care Systems Hosp., Visalia, 1994-95; therapist Behavioral Pediatric Clinic U. Md. Sch. Medicine, 1983-85; clinician, cons. Balt. youth health project City of Balt. Health Dept., 1983-85; cons. Lyndhurst Elem. Sch., Balt. City Sch. Dist., 1983-85; cons. James L. Kernan Hosp., Balt., 1984-85; mem. adj. faculty Calif. State U., Fresno, 1987-88, U. San Francisco, 1987, Calif. Sch. Profl. Psychology, Fresno, 1989; rep. med. staff, community governing bd. Mill Creek Hosp., Visalia, 1993-94; mem. med. staff Cedar Vista Hosp., Fresno, 1989—, Mill Creek Hosp., 1990-94; textbook reviewer Holt, Rinehart & Winston; presenter in field. Contbr. chpts. to Evaluation of Behavioral Programs in Cmommunity, Residential and School Settings, 1974, International Handbook of Behavior Modification and Therapy, 1982, 2d edit., 1990; ad hoc editorial cons. Behavior Therapy, Behavioral Assessment, Jour. Adolescent Health Care, Jour. Consulting and Clin. Psychology, Jour. Devel. and Behavioral Pediatrics, Pediatrics, Psychotherapy Bulletin; contbr. articles to profl. jours. Cons. behavior counseling Ventura County Dept. Social Welfare, Calif., 1974, behavioral contracting workshop dist. 2 Juvenile Ct., State of Utah, 1976; program dir. Sports Camp Salt Lake Jewish Community Ctr., Salt Lake City, 1975; program cons. behavioral intervention outpatient chronic schizophrenic program Salt Lake Community Mental Health Ctr., Salt Lake City, 1977; sub. house parent, clin. cons. Child Abuse Intervention/Family Support Ctr., Salt Lake City, 1978-81; lectr. sch. health Balt. City Schs., 1985; cons. venereal disease control program Dept. Health and Mental Hygiene, State of Md., 1985, Tulare County Dept. Mental Health, 1986-87, Visalia Unified Sch. Dist., 1987. Recipient Outstanding Mental Health Advocate award Calif. Mental Health Advocates for Children & Youth, 1989; grantee Calif. Dept. Mental Health/Tulare County Mental Health Calif., 1988—. Mem. APA, Calif. State Psychol. Assn., Soc. for Behavioral Pediatrics, Assn. Advancement Psychology, Assn. Advancement Behavior Therapy, Sigma Xi. Office: 5343 W Hillsdale Visalia CA 93291-5143

WOOD, DONALD FRANK, transportation educator, consultant; b. Waukesha, Wis., Feb. 22, 1935; s. Frank Blaine and Uilah (Mathson) W.; m. Doreen Johnson, July 5, 1968; children: Frank, Tamara. BA, U. Wis., 1957, MA, 1958; PhD, Harvard U., 1970. Transp. planner State of Wis., Madison, 1960-70; prof. San Francisco State U., 1970—. Author: El Camino, 1982, (with others) Motorized Fire Apparatus of the West, 1991, Contemporary Transportation, 1996, Contemporary Logistics, 1996, American Volunteer Fire Trucks, 1993, Commercial Trucks, 1993, International Logistics, 1994, Wreckers & Tow Trucks, 1995, Logging Trucks, 1996, Big City Fire Trucks, 1997; contbr. Ency. Britannica. 2d lt. U.S. Army, 1958. Mem. Coun. of Logistics Mgmt. (chpt. pres. 1975-76), Transp. Rsch. Forum (chpt. pres. 1974), Am. Truck Hist. Soc. Presbyterian. Home: 321 Riviera Cir Larkspur CA 94939-1508 Office: San Francisco State U. Coll Bus San Francisco CA 94132

WOOD, DONALD NEAL, educator in media, author; b. Chgo., Sept. 20, 1934; s. Claude Obern and Mary Elmira (Neal) W.; m. Marie Ann Vayo, June 9, 1956; children: Bridget Louise, Brian Hamilton. BA, Earlham Coll., 1956; MA, U. Mich., 1958, PhD, 1963. Cert. tchr. secondary schs., profl. adminstrs. cert. Elem. and secondary tchr. Economy (Ind.) Twp Schs, 1956-57; speech instr. Westminister Coll., New Wilmington, Pa., 1958-59; program coord. Nat. Ednl. TV and Radio Ctr., N.Y.C., 1959-60; area coord. Midwest Program on Airborne TV Instrn., Lafayette, Ind., 1960-63; asst. prof. speech, TV San Diego State U., 1963-65; dir. ednl. TV Hawaii Dept Edn., Honolulu, 1965-70; prof. radio-TV-film Calif. State U., Northridge, 1970—. Author: (books) Educational Telecommunications, 1977, Designing the Effective Message, 1989, 96, Post Intellectualism and the Decline of Democracy, 1996; (textbook) Mass Media and the Individual, 1983; co-author: (textbook) Television Production, Disciplines and Techniques, 1978, 95. Bd. dirs. Monte Nido Valley Property Owners Assn., Calabasas, Calif., 1971-72, 73-74, 86-87; mem. Malibu (Calif.) Creek Docents, 1977—, pres. 1977-78. Recipient Broadcast Preceptor award San Francisco State U., 1978, Disting. Tchg. award Calif. State U. Northridge, 1995; grantee Calif State U. Fund for Innovation, 1971. Mem. Broadcast Edn. Assn. Office: Calif State U Northridge Dept Radio-TV-Film Northridge CA 91330

WOOD, FERGUS JAMES, geophysicist, consultant; b. London, Ont., Can., May 13, 1917; came to U.S., 1924, naturalized, 1932; s. Louis Aubrey and Dora Isabel (Elson) W.; student U. Oreg., 1934-36; AB, U. Calif., Berkeley, 1938, postgrad., 1938-39; postgrad. U. Chgo., 1939-40, U. Mich., 1940-42, Calif. Inst. Tech., 1946; m. Doris M. Hack, Sept. 14, 1946; children: Kathryn Celeste Wood Madden, Bonnie Patricia Wood Ward. Teaching asst. U. Mich., 1940-42; instr. in physics and astronomy Pasadena City Coll., 1946-48, John Muir Coll., 1948-49; asst. prof. physics U. Md., 1949-50; assoc. physicist Johns Hopkins U. Applied Physics Lab., 1950-55; sci. editor Ency. Americana, N.Y.C., 1955-60; aero. and space rsch. scientist, sci. asst. to dir. Office Space Flight Programs, Hdqrs., NASA, Washington, 1960-61; program dir. fgn. sci. info. NSF, Washington, 1961-62; phys. scientist, chief sci. and tech. info. staff U.S. Coast and Geodetic Survey, Rockville, Md., 1962-66, phys. scientist Office of Dir., 1967-73, rsch. assoc. Office of Dir., 1973-77, Nat. Ocean Svc.; cons. tidal dynamics, Bonita, Calif., 1978—; mem. Am. Geophys. Union, ICSU-UNESCO Internat. Geol. Correlation Project 274, Working Group #1-Crescendo Events in Coastal Environments, Past and Future (The Millennium Project), 1988—. Capt. USAAF, 1942-46. Recipient Spl. Achievement award Dept. Commerce, NOAA, 1970, 74, 76, 77. Mem. Sigma Pi Sigma, Pi Mu Epsilon, Delta Phi Alpha. Democrat. Presbyterian. Author: The Strategic Role of Perigean Spring Tides in Nautical History and North American Coastal Flooding, 1635-1976, 1978; Tidal Dynamics: Coastal Flooding, and Cycles of Gravitational Force, 1986, Synergetic Gravitational Forces in Tides and the Solar System, 2 vols., 1997; contbr. numerous articles to encys., reference sources, profl. jours.; writer, tech. dir. documentary film: Pathfinders from the Stars, 1967; editor-in-chief: The Prince William Sound, Alaska, Earthquake of 1964 and Aftershocks, vols. 1-2A and sci. coordinator vols. 2B, 2C and 3, 1966-69. Home: 3103 Casa Bonita Dr Bonita CA 91902-1735

WOOD, GERALD WAYNE, electrical engineer; b. Lubbock, Tex., June 6, 1956; s. Glendon Waldo and Nelive Ruth (Parker) W. BSEE, Tex. Tech. U., 1979, MSEE, 1984. Engr.-in-tng. Staff mem. BDM Internat., Albuquerque, 1984-89; staff engr. Voss Scientific, Albuquerque, 1989-90; engr. EG&G Mgmt. Systems, Inc., Albuquerque, 1990—. Mem. AAAS, IEEE. Home: 7709 Ranchwood Dr NW Albuquerque NM 87120-4026 Office: EG&G Mgmt Sys Inc 2501 Yale Blvd SE Ste 102 Albuquerque NM 87106-4200

WOOD, GLADYS BLANCHE, retired secondary education educator, journalist; b. Sanborn, N.D., Aug. 12, 1921; d. Charles Kershaw and Mina Blanche (Kee) Crowther; m. Newell Edwin Wood, June 13, 1943 (dec. 1990); children: Terry N., Lani, Brian R., Kevin C.; m. F.L. Stutzman, Nov. 30,

1991. BA in Journalism, U. Minn., 1943; MA in Mass Comm., San Jose State U., 1972. Cert. secondary tchr., Calif. Reporter St. Paul Pioneer-Dispatch, 1943-45; editor J.C. Penney Co., N.Y.C., 1945-46; tchr. English and journalism Willow Glen H.S., San Jose, Calif., 1968-87; freelance writer, photographer, 1947—; cons. in field. Named Secondary Journalism Tchr. of Yr. Calif. Newpaper Pubs. Assn., 1977. Mem. AAUW, Soc. Profl. Journalists, Journalism Edn. Assn., Calif. Tchrs. English, Calif. Ret. Tchrs. Assn., Women in Comm., Santa Clara County Med. Assn. Aux., Friends of Libr., Delta Kappa Gamma, Alpha Omicron Pi. Republican. Methodist. Home: 14161 Douglass Ln Saratoga CA 95070-5535

WOOD, JAMES LESLIE, sociology educator; b. Aug. 30, 1941. BA in Sociology, U. Calif., Berkeley, 1963, postgrad., MA in Sociology, 1966, PhD in Sociology, 1973. Asst. prof. San Francisco State U., summer 1972; instr. in sociology Holy Names Coll., 1971-73; lectr. in sociology U. Calif., Riverside, 1973-75; lectr. in sociology San Diego State U., 1975-76, asst. prof. sociology, 1976-78, assoc. prof. sociology, 1978-81, prof. sociology, 1981—, chmn. sociology, 1991—; SDSU mem. Promotions com., Executive com., Curriculum Com., Methodology com., Syposium com., Post-Tenure review com. (chair), San Diego Poll com., Personnel com., Rsch. Human Subjects com., Applied Social Rsch. Group com., Reappointment Tenure com. (chair), Master's essay com., Graduate com., Master's Degree theory and Methodology Exam com., Colloquium com., Teaching Eval. com.; lectr. in field; resident scholar U. London, Goldsmiths' Coll., 1984. Author: The Sources of American Student Activism, 1974, (co-author) Sociology: Traditional and Radical Perspectives, Adapted for the United Kingdom, 1982, Social Movements: Development, Participation and Dynamics, 1982, 3d printing, 1985, Sociology: Traditional and Radical Perspectives, 2d edit., 1990; author: (monographs) Political Consciousness and Student Activism, New Left Ideology: Its Dimensions and Development, 1975, Aging in America; works presented at profl. organizations; contbr. articles to profl. jours.; chpts. to books in field. U. Calif. grantee, 1969, 73-74, 75, San Diego State U. grantee, 1976, 79, 81, 82, 88, 83, 85, 90, 96. Mem. Am. Sociol. Assn. (collective behavior and social movements sect., polit. sociology sect.), Internat. Soc. Polit. Psychology, Pacific Sociol. Assn., Soc. for the Study of Social Problems, Calif. Sociol. Assn., Phi Beta Delta, Alpha Kappa Delta. Office: San Diego State U Dept of Sociology 5300 Campanile Dr San Diego CA 92115-1338

WOOD, JAMES MICHAEL, lawyer; b. Oakland, Calif., Mar. 22, 1948; s. Donald James and Helen Winifred (Reiman) W.; div.; children: Nathan, Sarah, Ruth. BA, St. Mary's Coll., 1970; JD, U. San Francisco, 1973. Bar: Calif. 1973, U.S. Dist. Ct. (no., cen. and so. dists.) Calif. 1973. Rsch. atty. Alameda County Superior Ct., Oakland, 1973-76; ptnr. Crosby, Heafey, Roach & May, Oakland, 1976—; presenter at profl. confs. Contbr. articles to profl. jours. Chair alumni-faculty devel. fund St. Mary's Coll. Alumni Bd. Dirs., 1990-94. Mem. ABA (litigation sect., health law litigation com., litigation products liability com.), Assn. Trial Lawyers Am. (assoc.), State Bar Calif., Calif. Trial Lawyers Assn. (assoc.), No. Calif. Assn. Def. Counsel, Alameda County Bar Assn., Def. Rsch. and Trial Lawyers Assn., Am. Acad. Hosp. Attys., Am. Soc. Pharmacy Law, Nat. Health Lawyers Assn., Drug Info. Assn. Office: Crosby Heafey Roach & May 1999 Harrison St Oakland CA 94612-3517

WOOD, JEANNINE KAY, state official; b. Dalton, Nebr., Apr. 22, 1944; d. Grover L. and Elsie M. (Winkelman) Sanders; m. Charles S. Wood, Dec. 7, 1968; children: Craig C., Wendi L. Wood Armstrong. Exec. sec. Idaho Hosp. Assn., Boise, 1966-71; com. sec. Idaho State Senate, Boise, 1976-81, jour. clk., 1981-85, asst. to sec. of senate, 1991-95, sec. of senate, 1991—; pvt. practice typing svc. Boise, 1979-86. Mem. Am. Soc. Legis. Clks. and Secs. Methodist. Home: 3505 S Linder Meridian ID 83642 Office: Idaho State Capitol PO Box 83720 Boise ID 83720-0081

WOOD, JOHN MORTIMER, retired aerospace executive, aeronautical engineer; b. New Orleans, July 7, 1934; s. John Mortimer Sr. and Annie Jeff (Gates) W.; m. Bonnie Ann Blanchette, June 6, 1958 (div. Oct. 1977); m. Barbara Lee Butler, Aug. 12, 1978; 1 child, Mark Douglas. BA in Aero. Engring., U. Tex., 1957. Project engr. Gen. Dynamics/Convair, San Diego, 1957-58, Rocket Power, Inc., Mesa, Ariz., 1961-64; sales mgr. S.E. region Rocket Power, Inc., Huntsville, Ala., 1964-67; dir. mktg. Quantic Industries, San Carlos, Calif., 1967-70; sr. mktg. mgr. Talley Industries of Ariz., Mesa, 1970-77; dir. mktg. Universal Propulsion Co., Inc., Phoenix, 1977-85, v.p. mktg., 1985-91, v.p. contract mgmt., 1992-94, v.p. mktg., 1994-96, ret., 1997. 1st lt. USAF, 1958-61. Mem. Am. Def. Preparedness Assn., Assn. for Unmanned Vehicle Sytsems, Tech. Mktg. Soc. of Am., Survival and Flight Equipment Assn. Republican. Home: 111 W Canterbury Ln Phoenix AZ 85023-6252

WOOD, KENNETH ARTHUR, retired newspaper editor, writer; b. Hastings, Sussex, Eng., Feb. 25, 1926; came to U.S., 1965; s. Arthur Charles and Ellen Mary (Cox) W.; m. Hilda Muriel Harloe, Sept. 13, 1952. Educated in Eng. Editor Stamp Collector newspaper Van Dahl Publs., Albany, Oreg., 1968-80, editor emeritus, 1980—. Author (ency.) This Is Philately, 1982, (atlas) Where in the World, 1983, Basic Philately, 1984, Post Dates, 1985, Modern World, 1987; author several hundred articles and columns published in the U.K. and U.S.A., 1960—. Served with Brit. Army WW II. Recipient Disting. Philatelist award Northwest Fedn. Stamp Clubs, 1974, Phoenix award Ariz. State Philatelic Hall of Fame, 1979, Disting. Philatelist award Am. Topical Assn., 1979. Fellow Royal Philatelic Soc. (London); mem. Am. Philatelic Soc. (Luff award 1987, Hall of Fame Writers Unit, 1984).

WOOD, LARRY (MARY LAIRD), journalist, author, university educator, public relations executive, environmental consultant; b. Sandpoint, Idaho; d. Edward Hayes and Alice (McNeel) Small; children: Mary, Marcia, Barry. BA summa cum laude, U. Wash., 1939, MA summa cum laude, with highest honors, 1940; postgrad., Stanford U., 1941-42, U. Calif., Berkeley, 1946-47; cert. in photography, U. Calif., Berkeley, 1971; postgrad. journalism, U. Wis., 1971-72, U. Minn., 1971-72, U. Ga., 1972-73; postgrad. in art, architecture and marine biology, U. Calif., Santa Cruz, 1974-76, Stanford Hopkins Marine Sta., Santa Cruz, 1977-80. Lifetime secondary and jr. coll. teaching cert., Wash., Calif. Feature writer and columnist Oakland Tribune and San Francisco Chronicle, Calif., 1939—; archtl. and environ. feature and travel writer and columnist San Jose (Calif.) Mercury News (Knight Ridder), 1972-90; teaching fellow Stanford U., 1940-43; dir. pub. rels. 2-counties, 53-parks East Bay Regional Park Dist., No. Calif., 1948-68; pres. Larry Wood Pub. Rels., 1946—; pub. rels. dir. Calif. Children's Home Soc., 1947-58; prof. (tenure) pub. rels., mag. writing, journalism, investigative reporting San Diego State U., 1974, 75; disting. vis. prof. journalism San Jose State U., 1976; assoc. prof. journalism Calif. State U., Hayward, 1978; prof. sci. and environ. journalism U. Calif. Berkeley Ext. grad. divsn., 1979—; press del. nat. convs. Am. Geophys. Union Internat. Conf., 1986—, AAAS, 1989—, Nat. Park Svc. VIP Press Tour, Yellowstone after the fire, 1989—, Nat. Assn. Sci. Writers, 1989—, George Washington U./Am. Assn. Neurol. Surgeons Sci. Writers Conf., 1990, Am. Inst. Biol. Scis. Conf., 1990, Nat. Conf. Sci. Writers, Am. Heart Assn., 1995, Internat. Cardiologists Symposium for Med./Sci. Writers, 1995, Annenberg Program Electronic Media Symposium, Washington, 1995; EPA del. to USSR and Ea. Europe; expert witness on edn., pub. rels., journalism and copyright; cons. sci. writers interne project Stanford U., 1989—; spl. media guest Sigma Xi, 1990—; mem. numerous spl. press corps; selected White House Spl. Media, 1993—; selected mem. Duke U. 14th Ann. Sci. Reporters Conf., 1995; internat. press guest Can. Consulate Gen. Dateline Can., 1995—, French Govt. Tourist Office, 1996—, Ministerio delle Risorse Agricole Alimentari e Forestali and Assocs. Conf., 1995; appeared in TV documentary Larry Wood Covers Visit of Queen Elizabeth II. Contbr. over 5,000 articles on various topics for newspapers, nat. mags., nat. and internat. newspaper syndicates including L.A. Times-Mirror Syndicate, Washington Post, Phila. Inquirer, Chgo. Tribune, Miami Herald, Oakland Tribune, Seattle Times, San Francisco Chronicle, Parade, San Jose Mercury News (Nat. Headliner award), Christian Sci. Monitor, L.A. Times/Christian Monitor Worldwide News Syndicate, Washington Post, Phila. Inquirer, Hawaiian Airlines In Paradise and other in-flight mags., MonitoRadio, Sports Illus., Life, Mechanix Illus., Popular Mechanics, Parents (contbg. editor), House Beautiful, Am. Home (awards 1988, 89), Archl. Digest, Better Homes and Gardens, Sunset, Architectural Digest, National Geographic World, Travel & Leisure, Chevron USA/Odyssey (Calif. Pub.'s award 1984), Xerox Edn. Publs., Europe's Linguapress, PSA Mag., Off Duty, Oceans, Sea Frontiers, AAA Westways, AAA Motorland, Travelin', others. Significant works include home and garden columnist and editor, 5-part series Pacific Coast Ports, 5-part series Railroads of the West, series Immigration, Youth Gangs, Endangered Species, Calif. Lighthouse Chain, Lighthouses of the World, Pacific Coast Wetlands, Elkhorn Slough Nat. Estuarine Res., Ebey's Landing Nat. Hist. Island Res., Calif. Water Wars, BLM's Adopt a Horse Program, Mt. St. Helen's Eruption, Oreg's Covered Bridges, Loma Prieta Earthquake, Oakland Firestorm, Missing Children, Calif. Prison Reform, Columbia Alaska's Receding Glacier, Calif. Underwater Parks, and many others; author: Wonderful U.S.A.: A State-by-State Guide to Its Natural Resources, 1989; co-author over 21 books including: McGraw-Hill English for Social Living, 1944, Fawcett Boating Books, 1956-66, Fodor's San Francisco, Fodor's California, 1982-89, Charles Merrill Focus on Life Science, Focus on Physical Science, Focus on Earth Science, 1983, 87, Earth Science, 1987; contbr. Earth Science 1987; 8 works selected for use by Europe's Woltors-Nordoff-Longman English Language Texts, U.K., Netherlands, 1988; author: (with others) anthology West Winds, 1989; reviewer Charles Merrill texts, 1983-84; book reviewer Profl. Communicator, 1987—; selected writings in permanent collections Oakland Pub. Libr., U. Wash. Main Libr.; environ. works included in Dept. Edn. State of Md. textbook; contbr., author Journalism Quar.; author script PBS/AAA America series, 1992; contbg. editor: Parents. Nat. chmn. travel writing contest for U.S. univ. journalism students Assn. for Edn. in Journalism/Soc. Am. Travel Writers, 1979-83; judge writing contest for Nat. Assn. Real Estate Editors, 1982—; press del. 1st Internat. Symposium Volcanism and Aviation Safety, 1991, Coun. for Advancement of Sci. Writing, 1977—, Rockefeller Media Seminar Feeding the World-Protecting the Earth, 1992, Global Conf. on Mercury as Pollutant, 1992, Earth Summit Global Forum, Rio de Janeiro, 1992; invited Nat. Park Svc. Nat. Conf. Sci. Writers, 1985, Postmaster Gen.'s 1992 Stamps, 1991, Internat. Geophys. Union Conf., 1982—, The Conf. Bd., 1995, Corp. Comm. Conf., Calif. Inst. Tech.'s Media and Sci. Seminar, 1995—, EPA and Dept. Energy Tech. Conf., 1992, Am. Soc. Photogrammetry and Remote Sensing Internat. Conv. Mapping Global change, 1992, N.Y. Mus. Modern Art Matisse Retrospective Press Rev., 1992, celebration 150th anniversary Oreg. Trail, 1993, Coun. Advancement Sci. Writing, 1993-96, Sigma Xi Nat. Conf., 1988-96, Nat. Sci. Writers Confs., 1996, PRSA Travel and Tourism Conf., 1993—, Internat. Conf. Environment, 1994, 95, Quality Life Europe, Prague, 1994, Calif. Sesquicentennial, 1996, 14th Ann. Sci. Writers Conf., 1996, Picasso Retrospective, 1996, many others; mem. Gov.'s Conf. Tourism N.C., 1993, 94, 95, Calif., 1976—, Fla., 1987—; press guest 14 U.S. states and 12 fgn. countries' Depts. Tourism, 1986—. Recipient numerous awards, honors, citations, speaking engagements, including induction into Broadway Hall of Fame, U. Wash., 1984, Broadway Disting. Alumnus award, 1995; citations for environ. writing Nat. Park Svc., U.S. Forest Svc., Bur. Land Mgmt., Oakland Mus. Assn., Oakland C. of C., Chevron USA, USN plaque and citation, best mag. articles citation Calif. Pubs. Assn., 1984; co-recipient award for best Sunday newspaper mag. Nat. Headliners, citation for archtl. features Oakland Mus., 1983; honoree for achievements in journalism Nat. Mortar Bd., 1988, 89; selected as one of 10 V.I.P. press for Yellowstone Nat. Park field trip on "Let Burn" rsch., 1989; named one of Calif.'s top 40 contemporary authors for writings on Calif. underwater parks, 1989, nat. honoree Social Issues Resources Series, 1987; invited V.I.P. press, spl. press guest numerous events worldwide. Mem. Am. Bd. Forensic Examiners, Calif. Acad. Scis., San Francisco Press Club, Nat. Press Club, Pub. Rels. Soc. Am. (charter mem. travel, tourism, environment and edn. divs.), Nat. Sch. Pub. Rels. Assn., Environ. Cons. N.Am., Am. Assn. Edn. in Journalism and Comm. (exec. bd. nat. mag. div. 1978, panel chmn. 1979, 80, author Journalism Quar. jour.), Women in Comm. (nat. bd. officer 1975-77, book reviewer Prof. Communicator), Soc. Profl. Journalists (nat. bd. for hist. sites 1980—), Nat. Press Photographers Assn. (hon. life, cons. Bay Area interne project 1989—, honoree 1995), Investigative Reporters and Editors (charter), Bay Area Advt. and Mktg. Assn., Nat. Assn. Sci. Writers, Calif. Writers Club (state bd., Berkeley bd. 1989—, honoree ann. conv. Asilomar, Calif. 1990), Am. Assn. Med. Writers, Internat. Assn. Bus. Communicators, Soc. Environ. Journalists (charter), Am. Film Inst., Am. Heritage Found. (citation 1986, 87, 88), Soc. Am. Travel Writers, Internat. Oceanographic Found., Oceanic Soc., Calif. Acad. Environ. News Writers, Seattle Advt. and Sales Club (former officer), Nature Conservancy, Smithsonian Audubon Soc., Nat. Wildlife Fedn., Nat. Parks and Conservation Assn., Calif. State Parks Found., Calif. Environ. Leadership Roundtable, Fine Arts Mus., San Francisco, Seattle Jr. Advt. Club (charter), U. Wash. Comm. Alumni (Sch. Comm. alumni, life, charter mem. ocean scis. alumni, Disting. Alumni 1987), U. Calif., Berkeley Alumni (life, v.p., scholarship chmn. 1975-81), Stanford Alumni (life), Mortar Board Alumnae Assn. (life, honoree 1988, 89), Am. Mgmt. Assn., Nat. Soc. Environ. Journalists (charter), Calif. Environ. Leadership Roundtable, Phi Beta Kappa (v.p., bd. dirs. Calif. Alumni Assn., statewide chmn. scholarship awards 1975-81), Purple and Gold Soc. (planning com., charter, 1995—), Pi Lambda Theta, Theta Sigma Phi. Home: Piedmont Pines 6161 Castle Dr Oakland CA 94611-2737 *A creed I follow is Ralph Waldo Emerson's statement: "Nothing great was ever achieved without enthusiasm."*

WOOD, LINCOLN JACKSON, aerospace engineer; b. Lyons, N.Y., Sept. 30, 1947; s. William Hulbert and Sarah Brock (Strumsky) W. BS with distinction, Cornell U., 1968; MS in Aeronautics and Astronautics, Stanford U., 1969, PhD, 1972. Staff engr. Hughes Aircraft Co., El Segundo, Calif., 1974-77; mem. tech. staff Jet Propulsion Lab. Calif. Inst. Tech., Pasadena, 1977-81, tech. group supr. Jet Propulsion Lab., 1981-89, tech. mgr., 1989-91, dep. tech. section mgr., 1991—; Bechtel instr. engring. Calif. Inst. Tech., Pasadena, 1972-74, lectr. in systems engring., 1975-76, vis. asst. prof., 1976-78, vis. assoc. prof., 1978-84; cons. in field. Contbr. articles on space navigation and optimal control theory to profl. jours. Bd. dirs. Boys Republic, Chino, Calif., 1991. Assoc. fellow AIAA (tech. com. on astrodynamics 1985-86, chmn. 1986-88, assoc. editor Jour. Guidance, Control and Dynamics 1983-89); sr. mem. Am. Astro. Soc. (space flight mechanics com. 1980—, chmn. 1993-95, assoc. editor Jour. of Astro. Scis. 1980-83, gen. chmn. AAS/AIAA Space Flight Mechanics Meeting, 1993), IEEE (sr. mem.), AAAS, Los Solteros (pres. 1991), Sigma Xi. Office: Jet Propulsion Lab 4800 Oak Grove Drive Mail Stop 301-125L Pasadena CA 91109

WOOD, LINDA MAY, librarian; b. Fort Dodge, Iowa, Nov. 6, 1942; d. John Albert and Beth Ida (Riggs) Wiley; m. C. James Wood, Sept. 15, 1964 (div. Oct. 1984). BA, Portland State U., 1964; M in Librarianship, U. Wash., 1965. Reference libr. Multnomah County Libr., Portland, Oreg., 1965-67, br. libr., 1967-72, adminstrv. asst. to libr., 1972-73, asst. libr., asst. dir., 1973-77; asst. city libr. L.A. Pub. Libr., 1977-80; libr. dir. Riverside (Calif.) City and County Pub. Libr., 1980-91; county libr. Alameda County Libr., Fremont, Calif., 1991—; adminstrv. coun. mem. Bay Area Libr. and Info. Svcs., Oakland, Calif., 1991—. Chair combined charities campaign County of Alameda, Oakland, 1992; bd. dirs. Inland AIDS Project, Riverside, Calif., 1990-91; vol. United Way of Inland Valleys, Riverside, 1986-87, Bicentennial Competition on the Constitution, 36th Congl. Dist., Colton, Calif., 1988-90. Mem. ALA (CLA chpt. councilor 1992-95), Calif. Libr. Assn. (pres. 1985, exec. com., ALA chpt. councilor 1992-95), Calif. County Librs. Assn. (pres. 1984), League of Calif. Cities (cmty. svcs. policy com. 1985-90), OCLC Users Coun. (Pacific Network del. 1986-89). Democrat. Avocations: folk dancing, opera, reading. Office: Alameda County Libr 2450 Stevenson Blvd Fremont CA 94538-2326*

WOOD, MARCUS ANDREW, lawyer; b. Mobile, Ala., Jan. 18, 1947; s. George Franklin and Helen Eugenia (Fletcher) W.; m. Sandra Lee Pellonari, July 25, 1971; children: Edward Alan, Melinda Janel. BA cum laude, Vanderbilt U., 1969; JD, Yale U., 1974. Bar: Oreg. 1974, U.S. Dist. Ct. Oreg. 1974, U.S. Ct. Appeals (9th cir.) 1982. Assoc., then ptnr. Rives, Bonihadi & Smith, Portland, Oreg., 1974-78; ptnr. Stoel Rives LLP and predecessor firms, Portland, 1974—. Pres., bd. dirs. Indochinese Refugee Ctr., Portland, 1980, Pacific Ballet Theatre, Portland, 1986-87; bd. dirs. Outside In, Portland, 1989—. Lt. USNR, 1969-71. Mem. ABA, Phi Beta Kappa. Home: 9300 NW Finzer Ct Portland OR 97229 Office: Stoel Rives 900 SW 5th Ave Ste 2300 Portland OR 97204-1232

WOOD, NANCY C., author; b. Trenton, N.J., June 20, 1936; d. Harold W. and Eleanor C. (Green) Clopp; m. Myron Wood, Mar. 1, 1962 (div. Oct. 1969); children: Karin Cannon, Chris, Kate Lynch, India. Student, Bucknell U., 1954-56. Author: The King of Liberty Bend, 1976, The Last Five Dollar Baby, 1976, The Man Who Gave Thunder to Earth, 1977, (poetry) Hollering Sun, 1972, Many Winters, 1974, War Cry on a Prayer Feather, 1979, Spirit Walker, 1993, Dancing Moons, 1995, Shaman's Circle, 1996, (children's books) Little Wrangler, 1966, The Girl Who Loved Coyotes, 1995, (photography) Colorado: Big Mountain Country, 1969, In This Proud Land: America 1935-43 As Seen in the FSA Photographs, 1974, The Grass Roots People, 1978, Heartland: The FSA in New Mexico 1934-43, 1989, Taos Pueblo, 1989, The Serpent's Tongue, 1997, Wild Love, 1997. Democrat. Home: Box 6990 Santa Fe NM 87502

WOOD, NATHANIEL FAY, editor, writer, public relations consultant; b. Worcester, Mass., June 23, 1919; s. Henry Fletcher and Edith (Fay) W.; m. Eleanor Norton, Dec. 19, 1945; children: Gary Nathaniel, Janet Ann. BS in Journalism, Bus. Adminstrn., Syracuse U., 1946. Editor, writer various publs., various cities, 1946-51; mng. editor Butane-Propane News, L.A., 1951-52; editor Western Metalworking Mag., L.A., 1952-62; western editorial mgr. Penton Pub. Co. Cleve., L.A., 1962-71; editor Orange County Illustrated, Orange County Bus., Newport Beach, Calif., 1971-72; western editor Hitchcock Pub., L.A., 1972-75; co-owner, mgr. Norton-Wood Pub. Rels. Svcs., Pasadena, Calif., 1975—; editorial dir. Security World, SDM and SCA Mags., Culver City, Calif., 1975-80; mgr. trade show Cahners Pub. and Expo Group, L.A., 1979-82; sr. editor Alarm Installer Dealer Mag., L.A., 1982-89; editor CNC West Mag., Westminster and Pasadena, Calif., 1982—. Freelance indsl. writer miscellaneous bus. pubs. Organizer Willkie Presdl. Campaign, Syracuse, N.Y., 1940; advisor various GOP campaigns, L.A., Washington, 1940-96; charter mem. Rep. Nat. Com., 1995, delegate-at-large GOP conv., 1996, mem. Pres.' Club, 1996, 97, convention guest, 1996; nat. adv. bd. Am. Security Coun.; donor L.A. Civic Light Opera and Ctr. Theatre Group; mem., donor L.A. Mus. Art, 1989—; founding mem. Western Heritage Mus., L.A., 1989—; active Met. Opera Guild, Colonial Williamsburg Found., Mus. Natural History L.A. 2nd lt. U.S. Army, 1943-45, PTO. Decorated Purple Heart; recipient Silver, Bronze and Gold medals for Editorial Excellence Gov. of Calif., 1959, 60, 62. Mem. Am. Legion, Am. Film Inst., Scabbard and Blade, L.A. World Affairs Coun., Smithsonian Instn., The Nat. Air and Space Soc., Soc. Profl. Journalists, Alpha Epsilon Rho, Tau Theta Upsilon. Home and Office: 1430 Tropical Ave Pasadena CA 91107-1623

WOOD, NICOLA, artist; b. Gt. Crosby, Lancashire, Eng., Oct. 18, 1936; d. John Wood and Eva Wood Heyes; m. Theodore Cartan, Mar. 25, 1965 (dec. 1972); m. Emmet Baxter June 11, 1981 (dec. 1994). Diploma with 1st class honors, Manchester (Eng.) Coll. Art, 1959, Royal Coll. Art, London, 1960; postgrad. degree, Parsons Sch. Design, N.Y.C., 1963. Freelance textile designer, 1959-84; graphic designer N.Y.C., 1960-63; wallpaper designer Rasch Tapeten Fabric, Osnabruck, Germany, 1965-84; lectr. Farnham (Eng.) Coll. Art, 1975, Ctrl. Coll. Art, London, 1976-78, Claremont (Calif.) Coll., 1992-93, 95. Represented in permanent collections Sherry Frumkin Gallery, Santa Monica, Calif., Bruce Lewin Gallery, N.Y.C., O.K. Harris/David Klein Art Gallery, Detroit; group shows include Jerry Silverman Gallery, L.A., 1987, Pebble Beach Concours d'Elegance, Carmel, Calif., 1987-95, Lancaster (Calif.) Mus., 1988, Butler Inst., Ohio, 1988, Harrahs Mus., Las Vegas, 1989, Krasle Art Ctr., Mich., 1991, The Automobile in Art Gallery, Long Beach, Calif., 1992, Bakersfield (Calif.) Mus. Art, 1994, Peterson Automotive Mus., L.A., 1994, Chalmers Gallery, Tustin, Calif., 1996, Automotive Fine Art Soc., Pebble Beach, Carmel, Calif., 1996. Work auctioned for charity Pebble Beach Concourse d'Elegance. Proctor Meml. Travel scholar, 1959, Fulbright scholar, 1960, Am. Travel scholar Royal Coll. Art, 1960; recipient Excellence award Pebble Beach Concours d'Elegance, 1992, Peter Helk award, 1993, Raymond E. Holland award, 1993. Mem. Automotive Fine Art Soc. Studio: 1728 S Bedford St Los Angeles CA 90035-4321

WOOD, RAYMUND FRANCIS, retired librarian; b. London, Nov. 9, 1911; came to U.S., 1924; s. George S. and Ida A. (Lawes) W.; m. Margaret Ann Peed, Feb. 26, 1943; children: Paul George, Gregory Leo, David Joseph. AB, St. Mary's U., Balt., 1931; MA, Gonzaga U., 1939; PhD, UCLA, 1949; MS in Libr. Sci., U. So. Calif., L.A., 1950. Instr. English U. Santa Clara (Calif.), 1939-41; rehab. officer VA, L.A., 1946-48; reference libr. Fresno (Calif.) State Coll., 1950-66; prof. libr. sci. UCLA, L.A., 1966-77, prof. emeritus, 1977—, from asst. dean to assoc. dean Grad. Sch. Libr. & Info. Sci., 1970-77. Author: California's Agua Fria, 1952, Life and Death of Peter Lebec, 1954, The Saints of the California Landscape, 1987; co-author: Librarian and Laureate: Ina Coolbrith of California, 1973, many others. Vol. driver ARC, Van Nuys, Calif., 1977—; pres. Friends of the Encino/Tarzana Br. Libr., Tarzana, Calif., 1977-80, Jedediah Smith Soc., Stockton, Calif., 1987-90, knight comdr. Order of St. Gregory, 1994. With U.S. Army, 1942-46, ETO. Travel grantee Am. Book Found., 1964, Del Amo Found., 1974. Mem. ALA (book reviewer 1974—), Calif. Libr. Assn. (many offices), Mariposa County Hist. Assn. (life), Oral History Assn. (life), Fresno County Hist. Soc. (editor 1959-66), Westerners L.A. Corral (editor of Brand Book 1982). Democrat. Byzantine Catholic. Home: 18052 Rosita St Encino CA 91316-4217

WOOD, ROBERT CHARLES, financial consultant; b. Chgo., Apr. 8, 1956; s. Roy Edward and Mildred Lucille (Jones) W.; m. Jennifer Jo Briggs, Oct. 1984; children: Jacqueline Jones, Reagan Keith. BA in History, BBA in Real Estate, So. Meth. U., 1979, JD, 1982. Bar: Tex. 1983. Appraiser McClellan-Massey, Dallas, 1977-79; researcher, acquisitions officer Amstar Fin. Corp., Dallas, 1979-80; prin. Robert Wood Cons., Dallas, 1981—; cons. Plan Mktg. Cos., 1983-84; pvt. practice law, Dallas, 1983-84; gen. counsel Diversified Benefits, Inc., Dallas, 1984-86; nat. accts. mgr. L. omas & Nettleton Real Estate Group, Dallas, 1987-88; sr. pension cons., prin. Eppler, Guerin &Turner, 1988-93; chmn. adv. coun. on devel. Medisend, 1991; nat. consulting coord. fin. advisors coun., v.p. Callan Assocs., San Francisco, 1994-95; atty. at law, 1995—. Author: Electionomics: How the Money Managers View the Election, 1992, After the Congress Vote: How the Managers See Things Now, 1993; mem. So. Meth. U. Law Rev., 1981-82; contbr. articles to profl. publs. Bd. dirs. Am. Cancer Soc., Dallas unit, 1982-87, mem. spl. events com., 1986-87, crusade com., 1987-88, corp. devel. bd. chmn. 1989—. Mem. Tex. Bar Assn., Phila. Bar Assn., Phi Gamma Delta.

WOOD, ROBERT EARLE, artist, educator; b. Gardena, Calif., Feb. 4, 1926; s. Earle Charlton and Ruth Marie (Stewart) W.; m. Jane E. Clark, Dec. 14, 1975. BA, Pomona Coll., 1950; MFA, Claremont Grad. Sch., 1952. Dir. Robert E. Wood Ann. Summer Sch. of Painting, 1961-94; instr. U. Minn., Otis Art Inst., L.A., Scripps Coll., Claremont, Calif., Claremont Grad. Sch., Riverside (Calif.) Art Ctr., Rex Brandt Summer Sch., Corona del Mar, Calif.; presenter many workshops. One-man shows include Reinike Gallery, Atlanta, Stary/Sheets Gallery, Irvine, Calif., Huntsman Galleries, Aspen, Colo., Challis Galleries, Laguna Beach, Calif., The Gallery, Burlingame, Calif., A Gallery, Palm Desert, Calif., Beretich Gallery, Claremont, Calif., Galeria Blu Di Prussia, Naples, Italy; Gallery Eight, Claremont, Zachary Waller Gallery, La Cienega, Calif., The Jones Gallery, La Jolla, Calif, others; contbr. articles to profl. jours. Recipient Exhbn. award Nat. Acad. Design, 1993, Nat. Watercolor Soc., 1958, 63, 64, 68, 70, 73, 76, Am. Watercolo Soc., 1969, 71, 78, 81, 82, 83, 85, 87, Silver medal 1982, High Winds medal 1985, exhbn. award Watercolor U.S.A., 1963, 66, 72, Rocky Mountain Nat. Watermedia Exhbn., 1974, 78, 86, Watercolor West, 1970, 71, 72, 73, 74, 75, 76, 77, Nat. Orange Show, Calif., 1961, 64, 67, 70, 73, 76, 79, many others. Home and Office: 1321 Arroyo Cres Redlands CA 92373-6507

WOOD, ROBERT WARREN, lawyer; b. Des Moines, July 5, 1955; s. Merle Warren and Cecily Ann (Sherk) W.; m. Beatrice Wood, Aug. 4, 1979; 1 child, Bryce Mercedes. Student, U. Sheffield, Eng., 1975-76; AB, Humboldt State U., 1976; JD, U. Chgo., 1979. Bar: Ariz. 1979, Calif. 1980, U.S. Tax Ct. 1980, N.Y. 1989, D.C. 1993. Assoc. Jennings, Strouss, Phoenix, 1979-80, McCutchen, Doyle, San Francisco, 1980-82, Broad, Khourie, San Francisco, 1982-85; assoc. Steefel, Levitt & Weiss, San Francisco, 1985-87, ptnr., 1987-91; ptnr. Bancroft & McAlister, San Francisco, 1991-93; prin. Robert W. Wood, P.C., San Francisco, 1993—; instr. in law U. Calif. San Francisco, 1981-82. Author: Taxation of Corporate Liquidations: A Complete Planning Guide, 1987, The Executive's Complete Guide to Business Taxes, 1989, Corporate Taxation: Complete Planning and Practice Guide, 1989, S Corporations, 1990, The Ultimate Tax Planning Guide for Growing Companies, 1991, Taxation of Damage Awards and Settlement Payments, 1991, Tax Strategies in Hiring, Retaining and

Terminating Employees, 1991, The Home Office Tax Guide, 1991; (with others) California Closely Held Corporations: Tax Planning and Practice Guide, 1987, Legal Guide to Independent Contractor Status, 1992, Home Office Money & Tax Guide, 1992, Tax Aspects of Settlements and Judgements, 1993; editor-in-chief The M & A Tax Report; mem. editorial bd. Real Estate Tax Digest, The Practical Accoutant. Mem. Calif. Bd. Legal Specialization (cert. specialist taxation), Internat. Platform Assn., Bohemian Club, Internat. Order of St. Hubert. Republican. Office: 235 Montgomery St Ste 972 San Francisco CA 94104-2902

WOOD, STUART KEE, retired engineering manager; b. Dallas, Mar. 8, 1925; s. William Henry and Harriet (Kee) Wood; m. Loris V. Poock, May 17, 1951 (dec. June 1990); children: Linda S. Kuehl, Thomas N., Richard D.; m. Lois H. Morton, Nov. 25, 1994. BS in Aero. Engring., Tex. A&M U., 1949. Aircraft sheet metal worker USAF SAC, Kelly Field, San Antonio, Tex., 1942-45; structural design engr. B-52, 367-80, KC-135, 707 Airplanes Boeing, Seattle and Renton, Wash., 1949-55; thrust reverser design engr. 707 and 747 Airplanes Boeing, Renton, 1955-66; supr. thrust reverser group 747 Airplane Boeing, Everett, Wash., 1966-69; supr. rsch. basic engine noise 727 airplane FAA, NASA, 1969-74; supr. jetfoil propulsion Jetfoil Hydrofoil Boeing, Renton, 1974-75; supr. rsch. basic engine performance loss JT9D Pratt & Whitney, 1975-79; supr. propulsion systems 757 Airplane Boeing, Renton, 1979-90; supr., propulsion systems thrust reverser 737, 747, 757, 767 Boeing, Kent, Wash., 1990-94, ret., 1994. Patentee in field. Recipient Ed Wells award AIAA, N.W. chpt., Bellevue, Wash., 1992. Republican. Presbyterian. Home: 3831 46th Ave SW Seattle WA 98116-3723

WOOD, THOMAS COWAN, physician; b. Denver, Oct. 4, 1938; s. Gerald Cowan and Virginia Elizabeth (Sevier) W.; m. Kathryn Louise Francis, June 12, 1964 (div. Mar. 1993); children: Karen, Robert, Paul. BA, Dartmouth Coll., 1960; postgrad., Denver U., 1961; MD, U. Colo., 1965. Intern Letterman Gen. Hosp., San Francisco, 1965-66; resident U. Wash., Seattle, 1968-70, fellowship in nephrology, 1970-71; pvt. practice Anchorage, 1971—; md. dir. Alaska Kidney Ctr., Anchorage, 1973-94; chief of medicine Providence Hosp., 1982, LifeAlaska, 1992—, N.W. Organ Procurement Agy., Seattle, 1985-96. Initiator, tchr. Paramedic Sys., Anchorage, 1972-76; initiator Alaska Kidney Found., Anchorage, 1973. With U.S. Army, 1965-68. Fellow ACP (gov. 1985-89); mem. Renal Physicians Assn. (state leader 1985—), N.W. Renal Soc., Alaska State Med. Assn., Anchorage Med. Soc. Mem. Internat. Soc. Nephrology, Am. Soc. Nephrology. Office: Providence Med Office Bldg #55 3340 Providence Dr Ste 551 Anchorage AK 99508-4643

WOOD, THOMAS EUGENE, nonprofit organization executive; b. San Bernardino, Calif., Sept. 25, 1946; s. Horace Edward and Mary Jane (Hubbs) W. BA, U. Calif., Berkeley, 1969, PhD, 1975. Exec. dir. Calif. Assn. of scholars, Berkeley, 1992—. Author: Mandukya Upanisad and the Aganna Sastra, 1990, Mind Only, 1991, Nagarjunian Disputations, 1994. Proponent and co-author Calif. Civil Rights Initiative. Ford Found. fellow, 1969-71. Mem. Am. Philos. Assn. Republican. Office: California Assn of Scholars 1730 Martin Luther King Jr Way Berkeley CA 94709-2140

WOOD, WILLIS BOWNE, JR., utility holding company executive; b. Kansas City, Mo., Sept. 15, 1934; s. Willis Bowne Sr. and Mina (Henderson) W.; m. Dixie Gravel, Aug. 31, 1955; children: Bradley, William, Josh. BS in Petroleum Engring., U. Tulsa, 1957; grad. advanced mgmt. program, Harvard U., 1983; JD (hon.), Pepperdine U., 1996. With So. Calif. Gas Co., L.A., 1960-74, from v.p. to sr. v.p., 1975-80, exec. v.p., 1983-84; pres., CEO Pacific Lighting Gas Supply Co., L.A., 1981-83; from sr. v.p. to chmn., pres., CEO Pacific Enterprises, L.A., 1984-93, chmn., CEO, 1993—; bd. dirs. Gt. Western Fin. Corp., Gt. Western Bank, L.A.; dir. Automobile Club So. Calif.; trustee U. So. Calif.; bd. visitors Rand Grad. Sch. Trustee, vice-chmn. Harvey Mudd Coll., Claremont, Calif., 1984—; trustee Calif. Med. Ctr. Found., L.A., 1983—, past chmn.; trustee, past pres. S.W. Mus., L.A., 1983—; bd. dirs. L.A. World Affairs Coun.; dir., past chmn. bus. coun. for Sustainable Energy Future, 1994—; dir. Pacific Coun. for Internat. Affairs. Recipient Disting. Alumni U. Tulsa, 1995. Mem. Soc. Petroleum Energy Engrs., Am. Gas Assn., Pacific Coast Gas Assn. (past bd. dirs.), Pacific Energy Assn., Calif. Bus. Roundtable, Calif. State C. of C. (bd. dirs.), Nat. Assn. of Mfrs. (bd. dirs.), Hacienda Golf CLub, Ctr. Club, Calif. Club. Republican. Office: Pacific Enterprises 633 E 5th St Ste 5400 Los Angeles CA 90013-2109

WOODARD, ALVA ABE, business consultant; b. Roy, N.Mex., June 28, 1928; s. Joseph Benjamin and Emma Lurania (Watkins) W.; m. Esther Josepha Kaufmann, Apr. 5, 1947 (div. Sept. 1991); children: Nannette, Gregory, Loreen, Arne, Mark, Kevin, Steven, Curtis, Marlee, Julie, Michelle; m. Margaret Adele Evenson, Oct. 1, 1994. Student, Kinman Bus. U., 1948-49, Whitworth Coll., 1956, Wash. State U., 1953-54. Sec.-treas., dir. Green Top Dairy Farms, Inc., Clarkston, Wash., 1948-52; v.p., treas., sec., dir. ASC Industries, Inc. (subs. Gifford-Hill and Co.), Spokane, Wash., 1953-75; dir. Guenther Irrigation, Inc., Pasco, Wash., 1966-71; mng. dir. Irrigation Rental, Inc., Pasco, 1968-75, Rain Chief Irrigation Co., Grand Island, Nebr., 1968-75; sec., dir. Keeling Supply Co., Little Rock, 1969-72; pres., dir. Renters, Inc., Salt Lake City, 1971-75, Woodard Western Corp., Spokane, 1976-86, Woodard Industries, Inc., Auburn, Wash., 1987-90; cons. Woodard Assocs., Spokane, Wash., 1985—; pres., dir. TFI Industries, inc., Post Falls, Idaho, 1989-90; v.p., sec., treas., dir. Trans-Force, Inc., Post Falls, 1989-90, TFI Computer Scis., Inc., Post Falls, 1989-90. Newman Lake (Wash.) Rep. precinct committeeman, 1964-80; Spokane County del. Wash. Rep. Conv., 1968-80. Mem. Adminstrv. Mgmt. Soc. (bd. dirs. 1966-68), Optimists. Home and Office: 921 E 39th Ave Spokane WA 99203-3034

WOODARD, DOROTHY MARIE, insurance broker; b. Houston, Feb. 7, 1932; d. Gerald Edgar and Bessie Katherine (Crain) Floeck; student N.Mex. State U., 1950; m. Jack W. Woodard; June 19, 1950 (dec.); m. Norman W. Libby, July 19, 1982 (dec. Dec. 1991). Ptnr. Western Oil Co., Tucumcari, N.Mex., 1950—; owner, mgr. Woodard & Co., Las Cruces, N.Mex., 1959-67; agt., dist. mgr. United Nations Ins. Co., Denver, 1968-74; agt. Western Nat. Life Ins. Co., Amarillo, Tex., 1976—. Exec. dir. Tucumcari Indsl. Commn., 1979—; dir. Bravo Dome Study Com., 1979—; owner Libby Cattle Co., Libby Ranch Co.; regional bd. dirs. N.Mex., Eastern Plains Council Govts., 1979—. Mem. NAFE, Tucumcari C. of C., Mesa Country Club. Home: PO Box 823 Tucumcari NM 88401-0823 *Personal philosophy: A never ending search and quest for knowledge, through participation and understanding.*

WOODARD, JOHN A., artist, art educator; b. Seattle, Oct. 10, 1949; s. Ralph and Edna (McElven) W.; m. Martha Monroe Haygood, Dec. 29, 1976. BFA, U. Wash., 1975. Art instr. Associated Students U. of Wash. Exptl. Coll., Seattle, 1975—; pvt. art instr. Seattle; instr. drawing Vashon Visual Arts; instr. drawing, painting King County Parks Dept. One man exhbns. include U. Unitarian Gallery, Vashon Allied Arts; group exhbns. include Magnolia Art Fair (award), The Down Under, Whale Fest 1990, Kirkland Arts and Crafts Fair, Bellevue Arts and Crafts Fair, Husted Gallery, Linda Hodges, Everett Waterfron Show (award). Mem. Seattle Art Mus., Artist Trust, Vashon (Wash.) Allied Arts. Home: 11619 SW Cove Rd Vashon WA 98070 Studio: 18875 103rd SW Vashon WA 98070

WOODARD, JOHN HENRY, quality control professional; b. Alameda, Calif., Mar. 25, 1948; s. Charles A. and Louise E. (Fick) W.; m. Nancy L. Smith, Apr. 8, 1972; 1 child, Victoria A. BA in Psychology, Calif. State Coll., Hayward, 1970. Quality control supr. Hunt Wesson Foods, Hayward, Calif., 1969-75; quality control mgr. Hunt Wesson Foods, Davis, Calif., 1975-92; quality control and bulk paste mgr. Hunt Wesson Foods, Davis, 1992—. Mem. Woodland (Calif.) Davis Rail Study, 1993-94. Mem. Inst. Food Technologists, Alpha Phi Omega (historian, treas., pres.). Republican. Episcopalian. Home: 614 Ashley Ave Woodland CA 95695-3671 Office: Hunt Wesson Foods 1111 E Covell Blvd Davis CA 95616-1209

WOODARD, LARRY L., college official; b. Lebanon, Oreg., Apr. 16, 1936; s. Hugh Frank and Ima Ellen (Bilyeu) W.; m. Bette Jeanette Brown, Aug. 10, 1956; children: Perry, Craig, Stacy. BS in Forestry, Oreg. State U., 1957. Forester Bur. of Land Mgmt., Oreg., 1957-69, Washington, 1969-72; dist. mgr. Bur. of Land Mgmt., Coeur d'Alene, Idaho, 1972-76; assoc. state dir. Bur. of Land Mgmt., Boise, Idaho, 1976-78, Santa Fe, 1978-82, Boise, 1982-86; state dir. Bur. of Land Mgmt., Santa Fe, 1987-93; dir. devel. Boise Bible Coll., 1993—. Author: A to Z, The Biography of Arthur Zimmerman, 1988, Before the First Wave, 1994. Bd. dirs. Boise Bible Coll., 1977-87; trustee N.Mex. Nature Conservancy, 1987-90. Recipient Disting. Svc. award U.S. Dept. Interior, 1986, Sec.'s Stewardship award U.S. Dept. Interior, 1989, Pres.'s Meritorious Exec. award, 1991. Republican. Home: PO Box 365 Meridian ID 83680-0365 Office: Boise Bible Coll 8695 Marigold St Boise ID 83714-1220

WOODBURY, JAMES ROBERTS, electronics consultant; b. Hollywood, Calif., May 24, 1931; s. Walter Edgar Woodbury and Gladys Rose Rockwell (Roberts) Woodbury Abberley; m. Joyce Elaine Albaugh, June 27, 1953; children: Jennifer Lynne, Neal Walter, Elaine Dorothy. BSc in Electronics and Aero. Engring., Brown U., 1953; MSEE, Stanford U., 1962, MS in Math., 1964. Mem. tech. staff Bell Telephone Labs., Whippany, N.J., 1953-56, TRW (formerly Ramo Wooldridge), L.A., 1956-59; rsch. engr. SRI Internat., Menlo Park, Calif., 1959-76; mem. tech. staff Phillips (formerly Signetics), Mountain View, Calif., 1976-81, Fairchild Semi Conductor, Mountain View, 1981-84; sr. mem. tech. staff MTel (formerly M/A Com Linkabit), San Diego, 1984-87; sr. design engr. Hughes Network Systems, San Diego, 1987-93; cons. Woodbury Electronics Cons., San Diego, 1993—. Mem. IEEE, Tau Beta Pi. Baptist. Home and Office: Woodbury Electronics Cons 11745 Avenida Sivrita San Diego CA 92128-4525

WOODBURY, LAEL JAY, theater educator; b. Fairview, Idaho, July 3, 1927; s. Raymond A. and Wanda (Dawson) W.; m. Margaret Lillian Swenson, Dec. 19, 1949; children: Carolyn Inez (Mrs. Donald Hancock), Shannon Margaret (Mrs. Michael J. Busenbark), Jordan Ray, Lexon Dan. BS, Utah State U., 1952; MA, Brigham Young U., 1953; PhD (Univ. fellow), U. Ill., 1954. Teaching asst. U. Ill., 1953; assoc. prof. Brigham Young U., 1954-61; guest prof. Colo. State Coll., 1962; asst. prof. Bowling Green State U., 1961-62; asso. prof. U. Iowa, 1962-65; producer Ledges Playhouse, Lansing, Mich., 1963-65; prof. speech and dramatics, chmn. dept. Brigham Young U., 1966-70, assoc. dean Coll. Fine Arts and Communications, 1969-73, dean Coll. Fine Arts and Communications, 1973-82; vis. lectr. abroad; bd. dirs. Eagle Systems Internat.; bd. dir. workshop Fedn. for Asian Cultural Promotion, Republic of China; dir. European study tour. Author: Play Production Handbook, 1959, Mormon Arts, vol. 1, 1972, Mosaic Theatre, 1976, also articles, original dramas; profl. actor PBS and feature films. Chmn. gen. bd. drama com. Young Men's Mut. Improvement Assn., 1958-61; bd. dirs. Repertory Dance Theatre; bd. dirs., vice-chmn. ctrl. Utah ARC; chmn. Utah Alliance for Arts Edn.; mem. adv. coun. Utah Arts Festival; missionary LDS Ch., N.Y.C., 1994. With USN, 1942-46. Recipient Creative Arts award Brigham Young U., 1971, Disting. Alumni award, 1975, Tchr. of Yr. award, 1988, Excellence in Rsch. award, 1992, Disting. Svc. award, 1992. Mem. Rocky Mountain Theatre Conf. (past pres.), Am. Theatre Assn. (chmn. nat. com. royalties 1972—, mem. fin. com. 1982—), NW Assn. Univs. and Colls. (accrediting officer), Am. Theatre Assn. (v.p. Univ. and Coll. Theatre Assn.), Theta Alpha Phi, Phi Kappa Phi. Home: 1303 Locust Ln Provo UT 84604-3651

WOODBURY, MARDA LIGGETT, librarian, writer; b. N.Y.C., Sept. 20, 1925; d. Walter W. and Edith E. (Fleischer) Liggett; m. Philip J. Evans, Sept. 1948 (div. 1950); 1 child, Mark W. Evans; m. Mark Lee Woodbury, 1956 (div. 1969); children: Brian, Heather. Student, Bklyn. Coll., 1942-44; BA in Chemistry and Polit. Sci., Bard Coll., 1946; BS in L.S., Columbia U., 1948; postgrad., U. Calif., Berkeley, 1955-56, 60-61, MJ, 1005. Cert. tchr. Libr. various spl., med. and pub. librs., San Francisco, 1946-60, Coll. Pk. High Sch., Mt. Diablo, Calif., 1962-67; elem. sch. libr. Oakland and Berkeley, Calif., 1967-69; libr. dir. Far West Lab. Ednl. Rsch. & Devel., San Francisco, 1969-73; libr., editor Gifted Resource Ctr., San Mateo, Calif., 1973-75; libr. cons. Rsch. Ventures, Berkeley, Calif., 1975—; libr. dir. Life Chiropractic Coll., San Lorenzo, Calif., 1980-95. Author: A Guide to Sources of Educational Information, 1976, 2d edit., 1982, Selecting Instructional Materials, 1978, Selecting Materials for Instruction, Vol. I: Issues and Policies, 1979, Vol. II: Media and the Curriculum, 1980, Vol. III: Subject Areas and Implementation, 1980, Childhood Information Resources, 1985 (Outstanding Ref. Work, Assn. Ref. Librs. 1985), Youth Information Resources, 1987; mem. editorial bd. Ref. Libr., 1980-95. Mem. Med. Libr. Assn. (editor Chiropractic Librs. 1990-92). Home: 145 Monte Cresta Ave # 402 Oakland CA 94611

WOODEN, JOHN ROBERT, former basketball coach; b. Martinsville, Ind., Oct. 14, 1910; s. Joshua Hugh and Roxie (Rothrock) W.; m. Nellie C. Riley, Aug. 8, 1932; children: Nancy Anne, James Hugh. B.S., Purdue U., 1932; M.S., Ind. State U., 1947. Athletic dir., basketball and baseball coach Ind. State Tchrs. Coll., 1946-48; head basketball coach UCLA, 1948-75; lectr. to colls., coaches, business. Author: Practical Modern Basketball, 1966, They Call Me Coach, 1972; Contbr. articles to profl. jours. Served to lt. USNR, 1943-46. Named All-Am. basketball player Purdue U., 1930-32, Coll. Basketball Player of Yr., 1932, to All-Time All-Am. Team Helms Athletic Found., 1943, Nat. Basketball Hall of Fame, Springfield (Mass.) Coll., as player, 1960, as coach, 1970, Ind. State Baksetball Hall of Fame, 1962, Calif. Father of Yr., 1964, 75, Coach of Yr. U.S. Basketball Writers Assn., 1964, 67, 69, 70, 72, 73, Sportsman of Yr. Sports Illustrated, 1973, GTE Acad. All-Am., 1994; recipient Whitney Young award Urban League, 1973, 1st ann. Velvet Covered Brick award Layman's Leadership Inst., 1974, 1st ann. Dr. James Naismith Peachbasket award, 1974, medal of excellence Bellarmine Coll., 1985, Sportslike Pathfinder award to Hoosier with extraordinary svc. on behalf of Am. youth, 1993, GET All Am. Acad. Hall of Fame, 1994, 40 for the Age award Sports Illustrated, 1994, the 1st Frank G. Wells Disney award for role model to youth, 1995, Disting. Am. award Pres. Reagan, 1995, Svc. to Mankind award Lexington Theol. Sem., 1995, NCAA Theodore Roosevelt Sportsman award, 1995. *I have tried to live the philosophy of my personal definition of success which I formulated in the middle thirties shortly after I entered the teaching profession. Not being satisfied that success was merely the accumulation of material possessions or the attainment of a position of power or prestige, I chose to define success as "peace of mind which can be attained only through the self-satisfaction that comes from knowing you did your best to become the best that you are capable of becoming."*

WOODHULL, JOHN RICHARD, electronics company executive; b. LaJolla, Calif., Nov. 5, 1933; s. John Richard Woodhull and Mary Louise (Fahey) Hostetler; m. Barbara Adams; children: Elizabeth A., John A. BS in Engring. Physics, U. Colo., 1957, MS in Applied Math., 1960. Engr. Space Tech. Labs. (now TRW Systems), Redondo Beach, Calif., 1960-63; mgr., engr. Northrop Corp., Hawthorne, Calif., 1964; mem. tech. staff Logicon, Inc., San Pedro, Calif., 1964-69, pres., chief exec. officer, Torrance, Calif., 1969—, also bd. dirs.; instr. physics U. Colo., 1959-60; bd. dirs. 1st Fed. Fin. Corp. Bd. mgrs. San Pedro (Calif.) and Peninsula YMCA; bd. dirs. Los Angeles YMCA, 1985—, Sunrise Med., Torrance, 1986—. With USN, 1956-59. Mem. Chief Execs.' Orgn., World Bus. Coun., Nat. Indsl. Security Assn. (bd. dirs. 1986—). Avocations: sailboat racing, tennis, skiing. Office: Logicon Inc 3701 Skypark Dr Ste 200 Torrance CA 90505-4712*

WOODHULL, PATRICIA ANN, artist; b. Gary, Ind., Nov. 24, 1924; d. John Joseph and Georgia Mildred (Voorhis) Harding; m. Bradley Allen Woodhull, May 8, 1948; children: Leslie, Marcia, Clarisse. BS in Clothing Design, Purdue U., 1946; life teaching credential, Calif. State U., Fullerton, 1978. Social worker County Dept. Lake County and Bartholomew County, Gary and Columbus, Ind., 1946-50; home demonstrator Pub. Svc. Co. Ind., Columbus, 1950-53; substitute tchr. Fullerton (Calif.) H.S. Dist., 1968-73; children's art and drama tchr. Fullerton Cmty. Svcs., 1973-85; children's pvt. art tchr. Fullerton, 1990-93; art tchr. Montessori Sch., Fullerton, 1990-91; art/drama tchr. creative arts program Fullerton Pub. Schs., 1972-89; founder, dir. Players Improv Theatre Group, Fullerton, Calif. One woman shows include Fullerton City Libr., 1992, William Carlos Gallery, Fullerton , 1992, 93, Whittier (Calif.) City Hall, 1993, Muckinthaler Ctr., Fullerton, 1993, Brookhurst Ctr., Anaheim, 1993, Whitier Libr. Show, 1994, L.A. Mcpl. Art Gallery, 1996, Orlando Gallery, 1996, Laguna Art Inst., 1996; exhibited in group shows at Whittier Art Gallery, 1991, Hillcrest Art Show, Creative Arts Ctr., Burbank, Calif., 1991, Bidge Gallery City Hall, L.A., 1992, The Art Store, Fullerton, 1992, Women Painters West, 1993, New England Fine Arts Inst., Boston, 1993; represented in pvt. collections. Recipient Spl. award Orange County Fair, Costa Mesa (Calif.) County Fair, 1985; 3rd pl. award Hillcrest Whittier (Calif.) Show, 1990, 2nd award West Coast Collage Show, Lancaster, Calif., 1989, Evelyn Nunn Miller award Women Painters West, Torrance, Calif., 1994. Mem. Nat. League Am. Pen Women (pres. Orange County 1993), Women Painters West, Pan Hellenic Orange County (pres. 1994), Alpha Chi Omega (pres. local chpt. 1993). Republican. Home: 1519 Harmony Ln Fullerton CA 92831-2015

WOODMAN, DIANE, media specialist; b. Pullman, Wash., Oct. 26, 1950; d. Donald Glover Davis and Beverly Gene (Burden) Melior; m. Daniel William Woodman, Oct. 4, 1969 (div. Feb. 1977). BA in Edn., Ea. Wash. U., 1975; MEd, Gonzaga U., 1990. Cert. tchr. K-12, Wash. Tchr. kindergarten East Valley Sch. Dist. 361, Spokane, Wash., 1975-80, reading specialist Chpt. I., 1980-81, elem. libr., media specialist, 1982—, site based mgr., 1996—; computer salesperson Spokane, 1981-82. Vol. Habitat for Humanity, Spokane, 1996; mem. Hanford Action League, Spokane, 1990. Mem. ALA, ASCD, AAUW, Nat. Edn. Assn., Assn. Curriculum Devel., East Valley Edn., Assn. (pres. 1980-81), Phi Delta Kappa (sec. 1992), Wash. Edn. Assn., Wash. Assn. Curriculum Devel. Democrat. Roman Catholic. Home: 14114 S Marshall Rd Valleyford WA 99036

WOODRING, MARGARET DALEY, architect, planner; b. N.Y.C., Mar. 29, 1933; d. Joseph Michael and Mary (Barron) Daley; m. Francis Woodring, Oct. 25, 1954 (div. 1962); m. Robert Bell, Dec. 20, 1971 (dec.); children: Ward, Lissa, Gabrielle, Phaedra. Student, NYU, 1959-60; BArch, Columbia U., 1966; MArch, Princeton U., 1971. Registered architect; cert. planner. Architect, planner various firms, N.Y.C.; environ. design specialist Rutgers U., New Brunswick, N.J., 1966-68; programming cons. Davis & Brody, N.Y.C., 1968-71; planning cons. William H. Liskamm, San Francisco, 1971-74; mgr. planning Met. Transp. Commn., Oakland, Calif., 1974-81; dir. Internat. Program for Housing and Urban Devel. Ofcls. Ctr. for Environ. Design Rsch. U. Calif., Berkeley, 1981-89; prin. Woodring & Assocs., San Rafael, Calif., 1989—; adj. lectr. dept. architecture U. Calif., Berkeley, 1974-84; founder New Horizons Savs. Assn., San Rafael, 1977-79; cons. U.S. Agy. for Internat. Devel., Washington, 1981-89; mem. jury Nat. Endowment Arts, others. Chair Bicentennial Com., San Rafael, 1976; bd. dirs. Displaced Homemakers Ctr., Oakland, 1981-84; pres. Environ Design Found., San Francisco, 1984-90. William Kinne Travel fellow Columbia U., 1965-66; Richard King Mellon fellow Princeton U., 1968-70. Mem. AIA (chair urban design com. San Francisco chpt. 1980-81), Am. Inst. Cert. Planners, Urban Land Inst., Soc. for Internat. Devel. (pres. San Francisco chpt. 1980-83), World Affairs Coun., Internat. World Congress on Land Policy. Home: 226 Magnolia Ave San Rafael CA 94901-2244 Office: Woodring & Assocs 938 B St San Rafael CA 94901-3005

WOODRUFF, FAY, paleoceanographer, geological researcher; b. Boston, Jan. 23, 1944; d. Lorande Mitchell and Anne (Fay) W.; m. Alexander Whitehill Clowes, May 20, 1972 (div. Oct. 1974); m. Robert G. Douglas, Jan. 27, 1980; children: Ellen, Katerina. RN, Mass. Gen. Hosp. Sch. Nursing, Boston, 1966; BA, Boston U., 1971; MS, U. So. Calif., 1979. Rsch. assoc. U. So. Calif., L.A., 1978-81, rsch. faculty, 1981-96; keynote spkr. 4th Internat. Symposium on Benthic Foraminifera, Sendai, Japan, 1990. Contbg. author: Geological Society of America Memoir, 1985; contbr. articles to profl. jours. Life mem. The Nature Conservancy, Washington, 1992; bd. dirs. Friends of Friendship Park, 1995-97. NSF grantee, 1986-94. Mem. Am. Geophys. Union, Geol. Soc. Am., Internat Union Geol. Scis. (internat. commn. on stratigraphy, subcommn. on Neogene stratigraphy 1991-97), Soc. Woman Geographers (sec. So. Calif. chpt. 1990-96), Soc. Econ. Paleontologists and Mineralogists (sec., editor N.Am. Micropaleontology sect. 1988-90), Oceanography Soc., Sigma Xi. Office: U So Calif Dept Geol Scis Los Angeles CA 90089-0740

WOODRUFF, JAMES ROBERT, engineer; b. Akron, Ohio, Oct. 13, 1929; s. James Henry and Grace Eunice (Titus) W.; m. Mary Arlene Pancharian, Dec. 20, 1959; children: Katherine Arlene Waite, Mary Lucinda Ruefenacht, James Thomas. BA in Phys. Sci., Chapman U., 1951. Aerospace technologist NASA Ames Rsch. Ctr., Sunnyvale, Calif., 1959-75; engr. Systron Donner, Concord, Calif., 1975-88; rsch. specialist Allied Signal, Redmond, Wash., 1988—. With USN, 1951-55. Mem. AAAS, IEEE. Home: 7910 146th Ave NE Redmond WA 98052-4169 Office: Allied Signal 15001 NE 36th St Redmond WA 98052-5317

WOODRUFF, VIRGINIA, broadcast journalist, writer; b. Morrisville, Pa.; d. Edwin Nichols and Louise (Meredith) W.; m. Raymond F. Beagle Jr. (div.); m. Albert Plaut II (div.); 1 child, Elise Meredith. Student, Rutgers U. News corr. Sta. WNEW-TV Metromedia, N.Y.C., 1967; nat., internat. critic-at-large Mut. Broadcasting System, 1968-75; lectr. Leigh Bur., 1969-71; byline columnist N.Y. Daily Mirror, N.Y.C., 1970-71; first Arts critic Teleprompter and Group W Cable TV, 1977-84; host/producer The First Nighter N.Y. Times Primetime Cable Highlight program, 1977-84; pres., chief exec. officer Starpower, Inc., 1984-91; affiliate news corr. ABC Radio Network, N.Y.C., 1984-86; pres. Promarket People Inc., 1991-93; S.W. contbg. corr. Am. in the Morning, First Light, Mut. Broadcasting System, 1992; S.W. freelance corr. Voice of Am., USIA, 1992—; perennial critic Off-Off Broadway Short Play Festival, N.Y.C., 1984—; was 1st Woman on 10 O'Clock News, WNEW-TV, 1967. Contbg. feature writer Vis a Vis mag., 1988-91. Mem. celebrity panel Arthritis Telethon, N.Y.C., 1976. Selected episodes of First Nighter program in archives N.Y. Pub. Libr., Billy Rose Theatre Collection, Rodgers and Hammerstein Collection, Performing Arts Rsch.Ctr. Mem. Drama Desk. Presbyterian. Clubs: National Arts, Dutch Treat.

WOODS, ALMA JEAN, elementary educator; b. Pueblo, Colo., Aug. 26, 1937; d. Melvin Leroy and Lillian Roberta (Ullrich) W. Assoc., Pueblo (Colo.) Jr. Coll., 1958; BA, Western State Coll., Gunnison, Colo., 1960; MA, U. No. Colo., Greeley, 1964. Lic. elem. educator. Elem. tchr. Sch. Dist. 60, Pueblo, 1960-93; travel-cultural spkr., educator So. Colo. Sch., Colorado Springs. Bd. dirs. YWCA, 1996—, Pueblo 2010 Recreation and Leisure Task Force, 1996—; vol. to patients Sangre de Cristo Hospice, Pueblo, 1994—; historic docent Rosemount Mus. Mem. Colo. Ret. Educators, Ark. Valley Audubon, Pueblo YWCA Internat. Club, Alpha Delta Kappa (chpt. pres. 1982-84). Democrat. Methodist. Home: 124 W 22nd St Pueblo CO 81003-2520

WOODS, (MARY) ANNIE, writer, educator; b. Lubbock, Tex., Sept. 15, 1952; d. Denton Bishop Woods and JoAn (Franklin) Stewart; m. Josef V. Tornick, Oct. 28, 1990. BA in English, U. Tex., 1974; MA in Creative Writing, U. Tex., Odessa, 1976; postgrad., Southwestern Coll., 1995. Freelance journalist, 1987—; pub. info. dir., mem. adj. faculty No. N.Mex. C.C., Espanola, 1990-94; mem. adj. faculty in English Santa Fe C.C., 1994—; editor ArtJob Western States Arts Fedn., Santa Fe, 1994—. Author: (novella) Journeys To Places Out of Bounds (Discovery award Recursos de Santa Fe 1996); contbr. articles to mags. and newspapers; author numerous poems. Ptnr. Santa Fe Creatives. Recipient 1st Pl. award N.Mex. Press Assn., 1989; Writing Residency grantee Vt. Studio Ctr., 1997.

WOODS, BOBBY JOE, transportation executive; b. Frederick, Okla., June 20, 1935; s. Vivin Richard and Mattie Marie (Malone); divorced; children: Donald B., Kathryn M., David R., Lynda J. Student U. Calif., Berkeley, 1955-56; AA, Phoenix Coll., 1955; student, Glendale (Ariz.) Coll., 1968, 75. Pres. Southwest Prorate Inc., Phoenix, 1967-95, TCAB Registration Cons., Inc., 1993—; office mgr. Menke Transp., Phoenix, 1967-68; dist. exec. Boy Scouts Am., Phoenix, 1968-76; pres. Facing E's Enterprises, Inc., Yarnell, Ariz., 1991—. Commr. Boy Scouts Am., Ariz., N.Mex. Mem. Profl. Trucking Svcs. Assn. (pres. 1989-90), Lions Club (dist. gov. 1992-93, zone chmn. 1983-84, dep. dist. gov. 1984-85, lt. gov. 1991-92, dist. sight and hearing chmn. 1985-91, Sight and Hearing Found. state hearing chmn. 1985-89). Republican. Home: 918 W Cochise Dr Phoenix AZ 85021-2343 Office: TCAB Registration Cons Inc 2045 W Glendale Ave Phoenix AZ 85021-7841

WOODS, CYNDY JONES, junior high educator, researcher; b. Phoenix, Oct. 26, 1954; d. Glenn Billy and Helen Marie (Harrison) Jones; m. Clifford R. Woods, Apr. 3, 1975; children: Sean, Kathleen, Connor. AA in English, St. John's Coll., 1974; BA in English, Ariz. State U., 1992, M in Secondary Edn., 1994. Cert. secondary tchr., c.c. instr., Ariz. Tchr. grades 6-8 John R. Davis Sch., Phoenix, 1993, Thomas J. Pappas Sch., Phoenix, 1994—; tchr. Glendale C.C., 1997—; adj. faculty English and lit. Rio Salado C.C., 1995—, Glendale C.C., 1997—; treas. Martin Luther Sch. Bd., Phoenix, 1985-89;

presenter in field. Contbr. poetry to anthologies Dance on the Horizons, 1993, The Sound of Poetry: Best Poems of 1995, Across the Universe, 1996; contbr. articles to profl. jours. Mem. St. Francis Xavier Sch. Bd., Phoenix, 1995; v.p. City/County Child Care Bd., Phoenix, 1988-92; youth group advisor Mt. Calvary Luth. Ch., Phoenix, 1988-96; mem. SRP Ednl. Adv. Coun., 1996—; mem. Maricopa County Juvenile Cmty. Justice Com., 1997—. Mem. Ariz. Edn. Assn., Brophy Coll. Prep. Mother's Guild, Xavier Coll. Prep. Mother's Guild. Democrat. Home: PO Box 27575 Phoenix AZ 85061 Office: Thomas J Pappas Sch 355 N 6th Ave Phoenix AZ 85003

WOODS, DONALD PETER, real estate executive, marketing professional; b. Seneca Falls, N.Y., Oct. 14, 1911; s. James Henry and Isabell Teresa (McDonald) W.; m. June 17, 1935; children: Donald Peter Jr., Richard, Terrence, Lynn, Thomas. PhB, Niagara U., Niagara Falls, N.Y., 1933; postgrad., Bklyn. Law Sch., 1933-36. Law clk. N.Y. State Ins. Dept., N.Y.C., 1933-36; title examiner Abstract Title and Mortgage, Rochester, N.Y., 1936-38; title officer Monroe Abstract & Title, Rochester, 1938-43; pres., chief exec. officer D.P. Woods, Inc., Rochester, 1945-54, Don Woods Realty, Phoenix, 1954-82; assoc. v.p. Colliers Internat., Phoenix, 1982—. Lt. USNR, 1943-45, PTO. Mem. Cert. Real Estate Appraisal, Internat. Coun. of Shopping Ctrs., Ariz. Club, Camelback Racquet Club (pres. Phoenix chpt. 1959—), Phi Delta Phi. Republican. Roman Catholic. Home: 5301 E Palomino Rd Phoenix AZ 85018-1911 Office: Colliers Internat 3636 N Central Ave Ste 600 Phoenix AZ 85012-1935 *Personal philosophy: Be patient with the faults of others recalling your own imperfections.*

WOODS, GRANT, state attorney general; m. Marlene Galán; children: Austin, Lauren, Cole, Dylan. Grad., Occidental Coll., Ariz. State Coll., 1979. Atty. gen. Ariz., 1990—. Founder Mesa Boys and Girls Club. Office: Atty Gen Office 1275 W Washington St Phoenix AZ 85007-2926

WOODS, GURDON GRANT, sculptor; b. Savannah, Ga., Apr. 15, 1915; s. Frederick L. and Marion (Skinner) W. Student, Art Student's League N.Y.C., 1936-39, Bklyn. Mus. Sch., 1945-46; Ph.D. (hon.), Coll. San Francisco Art Inst., 1966. exec. dir. San Francisco Art Inst., 1955-64; dir. Calif. Sch. Fine Arts, 1955-65; prof. Adlai E. Stevenson Coll., U. Calif. at Santa Cruz, 1966-74; dir. Otis Art Inst., Los Angeles, 1974-77; asst. dir. Los Angeles County Mus. Natural History, 1977-80; Sculptor mem. San Francisco Art Commn., 1954-56; mem. Santa Cruz County Art Commn., Regional Arts Council of Bay Area. Exhibited: N.A.D., 1948, 49, San Francisco Art Assn. anns., 1952-54, Denver Mus. Anns., 1952, 53, Whitney Mus. Ann., 1953, Sao Paulo Biennial, 1955, Bolles Gallery San Francisco, 1969, 70, 72, L.A. Mcpl. Gallery, 1977, San Jose Inst. Contemporary Art (Calif.), Washington Project for the Arts retrospective, 1968-85, Washington, 1985, Retrospective Art Mus. Santa Cruz County, Calif., 1987, d.p. Fong Gallery, 1993, 94, Michael Angelo Gallery, Santa Cruz, 1995; commns. include: cast concrete reliefs and steel fountain, IBM Ctr., San Jose, Calif., fountain, Paul Masson Winery, Saratoga, Calif., McGraw Hill Pubs. (now Birkenstock), Novato, Calif.; work in permanent collection Oakland (Calif.) Mus.; papers in Archives of Am. Art, Smithsonian Instn., Washington. Recipient citation N.Y.C., 1948; prize N.A.D., 1949; Chapelbrook Found. research grantee, 1965-66; Sequoia Fund grantee, 1967; Research grantee Creative Arts Inst., U. Calif., 1968; grantee Carnegie Corp., 1968-69. Mem. Artists Equity Assn (pres. No. Calif. chpt. 1950-52, nat. dir. 1952-55). Address: 133 Seascape Ridge Dr Aptos CA 95003-5890

WOODS, JAMES C., museum director. Dir. Herrett Ctr. Arts and Sci. and Faulkner Planetarium, Twin Falls, Idaho. Office: Coll Southern Idaho Herrett Ctr Arts and Sci 315 Falls Ave Twin Falls ID 83303

WOODS, ROBERT OCTAVIUS, aerospace engineer; b. Evanston, Ill., Feb. 17, 1933; s. Robert and Anna Margaret (Welch) W.; m. Judith Charlene Neese, Dec. 27, 1965; children: Lisa Ann, Robert David. BS in Engring., Princeton U., 1962, MS in Engring., 1964, MA, 1965, PhD, 1967. Registered profl. engr., Pa., N.Mex. From draftsman to profl. engr. Allstates Engring. Co., Trenton, N.J., 1950-60; sr. mem. tech. staff Sandia Nat. Labs., Albuquerque, 1967—. Contbr. articles to profl. jours.; patentee in field. Fellow Ford Found., 1963, NSF, 1965. Fellow Brit. Interplanetary Soc., ASME (ASME/AAAS congl. sci. fellow 1991-92); mem. AAAS, Am. Phys. Soc., Albuquerque Soaring Club (v.p. 1972-74), Princeton Club (pres. 1976-91), Sigma Xi, Tau Beta Pi (Eminent Engr. award 1978). Republican. Presbyterian. Home: 7513 Harwood Ave NE Albuquerque NM 87110-1479 Office: Sandia Nat Labs 9671 Albuquerque NM 87185

WOODS, RONALD EARL, foreign policy educator; b. Detroit, Oct. 10, 1938; s. Earl L. and Marie C. (Banasiak) W.; m. Judith M. Wishner, Dec. 26, 1959; children: Lisa Anne, Christina L. BS in Fgn. Svc., Georgetown U., 1961. Dir. No. Europe Dept. of State, Washington, 1976-79; polit. mil. counselor U.S. Embassy, Madrid, 1979-82; dep. amb. U.S. Embassy, Oslo, 1982-85, Brussels, 1985-89; min. U.S. Embassy, London, 1989-92; affiliate prof. U. Wash., Seattle, 1992—; exec. dir. World Affairs Coun., Seattle, 1993-96; U.S. fgn. svc. officer Dept. State, Paris, Rome, Cairo, 1961-71; consul gen. U.S. Consulate Gen., Strasbourg, France, 1971-74; staff dir. Sec. of State H.A. Kissinger, Washington, 1974-75. Home: 4527 52nd Ave S Seattle WA 98118-1501 Office: U Wash Henry M Jackson Sch Internat Studies Box 353650 Seattle WA 98195-3650

WOODS, TRUDY ANN OLSON, gallery director; b. Mason City, Iowa, Mar. 14, 1946; d. Arnold E. and Audrey A. (Makeever) Olson; m. Michael G. Woods, June 15, 1969. BA, Grinnell (Iowa) Coll., 1968; MA in Tchg., Northwestern U., Evanston, Ill., 1969. Tchr. Highland Park (Ill.) Sch. Dist., 1968-69, Moreno Valley High Sch., Sunnymead, Calif., 1970-72, McNary High Sch., Salem, Oreg., 1974-76, Hoquiam (Wash.) High Sch., 1976-78; tchr. Lower Columbia Coll., Longview, Wash., 1988-89, art gallery dir., 1991—; artist, owner Woods Pottery, 1979—; founder, treas. Broadway Gallery, Longview, 1982—. Bd. dirs., pres. LWV of Grays Harbor, Aberdeen, Wash., 1978-81, LWV of Cowlitz County, Longview, Wash., 1981-97. Mem. Oreg. Potters Assn. Office: Art Gallery Lower Columbia Coll 1600 Maple St Longview WA 98632-3907

WOODS, WINTON D., law educator; b. Balt., Jan. 11, 1938; s. W.D. and Nancy N. W.; m. Barbara Lewis; children: Tad, Adam, Brooke, Lindsy, Jessica. AB Econ./Gov., Ind. U., 1961, JD with distinction, 1965. Bar: Ind., Ariz.; U.S. Supreme Ct. Law clk. U.S. Dist. Ct. (no. dist.) Calif., Sacramento, 1965-67; prof. law U. Ariz., Tucson, 1967—; reporter U.S. Dist. Ariz. Civil Justice Reform Act Com., 1992—; pres. Law Office Computing, Inc., 1990—; dir. Courtroom of the Future Project, U. Ariz., 1993—. Contbr. articles to profl. jours; author: The Lawyers Computer Book, 1990. Mem. bio-ethics com. UMC, Tucson, 1984-96. Recipient Fulbright award, 1979, Educator of Yr. award Internat. Comm. Industry Assn., 1996-97; fellow NEH, 1972, Nat. Inst. for Dispute Resolution, 1982. Mem. ABA, Ariz. State Bar Assn. Jewish. Office: U Ariz Coll of Law U Ariz Tucson AZ 85721

WOODSIDE, GEORGE ROBERT, computer software developer; b. Meadville, Pa., Oct. 29, 1949; s. William Clinton and Bernadette Lorena (Greene) W.; m. Diane Claire Hickenlooper, June 14, 1980 (div. 1996). Grad. h.s., Fairview, Pa. Program GE Co., Erie, Pa., 1967-69; programmer-analyst Lovell Mfg. Co., Erie, 1969-70; mgr. data processing Eriez Mfg. Co., Erie, 1970-74; owner Woodside-Benson Assocs., Fairview, Pa., 1974-78; prin. mem. tech. staff Transaction Tech. Inc. (now Citicorp/TTI), Santa Monica, Calif., 1978-92; owner GRW Sys. and Programming, Gardnerville, Nev., 1993—. Contbr. articles to mags.; developer software to detect and eliminate computer viruses. Mem. IEEE. Office: 1590 Lombardy Rd Gardnerville NV 89410-5633

WOODWARD, DEAN ALLEN, state agency administrator; b. Denver, Feb. 1, 1942; m. Marsha Faye Hendricks; children: Kelly Marie, Timothy D., Lindsay J. BS in Psychology, Colo. State U., 1963; MDiv in Theology and Psychology, Iliff Sch. Theology, Denver, 1972. Ordained to ministry United Meth. Ch., 1974. Sr. pastor Torrington (Wyo.) United Meth. Ch., 1978-80; cons. Denver, 1980-82; mgr. appeals Colo. Medicaid Program, Denver, 1982-85; mgr. physician svcs. Colo. Medicaid Program, 1985-92, mgr. policy and benefits, 1992-94; dir. office legis. affairs Colo. Dept. Health Care Policy and Financing, Denver, 1994—. Mem. Gov.'s Children's Cabinet, Denver, 1995—, Colo. Inter-Agy. Coordinating Coun., Denver, 1992—, Infant Immunization Adv. Coun., Denver, 1993—; mem. task force on child health Piton Found., Denver, 1994; mem. steering com. Robert Wood Johnson Found. "Making the Grade", Denver, 1994—; commr. Colo. Life and Law Commn., Denver, 1992—; chair bd. dirs. Parkhill Children's Ctr., Denver, 1990; bd. dirs. Greater Parkhill Cmty. Inc., Denver, 1992; trustee Parkhill United Meth. Ch., 1992—; vice chair bd. dirs. Linkages Inc., 1990; mem. adv. coun. Baby Care/Kids Care Program, 1991-93; area dir. UN Study Seminars, 1985-87. Recipient Children's Health and Welfare award Am. Acad. Pediat., Denver, 1992, commendation Gov. Colo., Denver, 1983, State Judge and Coach award Colo. Odyssey of the Mind, Denver, 1987-91. Democrat. Office: Health Care Policy and Financing 1575 Sherman St Ste 820 Denver CO 80203

WOODWARD, JAMES FRANCIS, humanities educator; b. Chgo., Sept. 17, 1946; s. Harry Herbert and Mary Winifred (O'Brien) W.; m. Julia Ann Gerber Woodward, June 3, 1978; 1 child, Katherine Julia. BA, Carleton Coll., Northfield, Minn., 1968; PhD, U. Tex., 1977. Asst. prof. U. Wis., LaCrosse, 1976-79, Coll. Charleston, S.C., 1980-81, Memphis State U., 1981-83; Mellon postdoctoral fellow in philosophy Calif. Inst. Technol., Pasadena, 1983-85; asst. prof. Caltech, Pasadena, 1986-88, assoc. prof., 1988-92, prof., 1992—, exec. officer Humanities, 1992-95. Contbr. articles to profl. jours. Fellow Mellon Postdoctoral Caltech, 1983-85; grantee Nat. Sci. Found., 1994-95. Mem. Philosophy of Sci. Assn. Home: 694 S Oakland Ave Pasadena CA 91106-3797 Office: Calif Inst Tech Mail Code 228-77 Pasadena CA 91125

WOODWARD, JOHN RUSSELL, motion picture production executive; b. San Diego, July 10, 1951; s. Melvin C. and Dora M. (Rorabaugh) W. BA in Visual Arts, U. Calif., San Diego, 1973; MA in Cinema Prodn., U. So. Calif., 1978. V.p. prodn. World Wide Motion Pictures Corp., 1982—. Asst. prodr. The Manitou, 1977; 1st asst. dir. Mortuary, 1981, They're Playing with Fire, 1983, Prime Risk, 1984, Winners Take All, 1986, Kidnapped, 1986, Slam Dance, 1986, Honor Betrayed, 1986, The Hidden, 1987, New Monkees, 1987, Bad Dreams, 1987, Night Angel, 1988, Disorganized Crime, 1988, UHF, 1988, the Horror Show, 1988, Fear, 1989, Tremors, 1989, Young Guns II, 1990, Shattered, 1990, Tales from the Crypt, 1990, Two-Fisted Tales, 1990, Buries Alive, 1990, Dream On, 1991, Strays, 1991, Universal Soldier, 1991, An Army of One, 1992, The Vanishing, 1992, Ghost in the Machine, 1992, The Shawshank Redemption, 1993, City Slickers II, 1993, Breach of Conduct, 1994, The Craft, 1995, Broken Arrow, 1995, The Rich Man's Wife, 1995, Gattaca, 1996, Liar, Liar, 1996, Wild Things, 1997; location mgr. Star Chamber, 1982, To Be or Not to Be, 1983, Flashdance, 1983, Two of a Kind, 1983, Touch and Go, 1984, Explorers, 1984, Sweet Dreams, 1985, The Long Shot, 1985, The Running Men, 1985, A Different Affair, 1985, Walk Like a Man, 1986.

WOODWARD, KESLER EDWARD, artist, educator; b. Aiken, S.C., Oct. 7, 1951; s. Norman Edward and Bebe Helen (Kneece) W.; m. Marianna Boaz, May 15, 1971. BA, Davidson Coll., 1973; MFA, Idaho State U., 1977. Curator temporary exhibits Alaska State Mus., Juneau, 1977-78; artistic dir. Visual Arts Ctr. Alaska, Anchorage, 1978-79; curator visual arts Alaska State Mus., 1979-81; asst. prof. art U. Alaska, Fairbanks, 1981-88, assoc. prof., 1989-96, prof., 1996—, chair dept. art, 1995—, chair divsn. arts and comm., 1996—; gallery dir. U. Alaska Fine Arts Gallery, 1982—; dir. fine arts and humanities project Inst. on Can., Dartmouth Coll., Hanover, N.H., 1988-91, vis. rsch. fellow, 1988-91; acad. affiliate U. Alaska Mus., 1991—; workshop instr. U. Alaska Mus., others.; bd. dirs. Western States Arts Found, 1987-88; council mem. Alaska State Council on Arts, 1983-88; mem. adv. panel Visual Arts Ctr., Anchorage, 1979-92, Alaska Pub. Art Adv. Panel, 1979—. One-man exhbns. include Alaska State Mus., 1985, U. Alaska Mus., 1985, 91, Davidson Coll. Art Gallery, 1986, Anchorage Fine Arts Mus., 1983, 91, U. Ala., Huntsville, 1990, Anderson (S.C.) Art Ctr., 1994; exhbn. juror; author: Sydney Laurence, Painter of the North, 1990, Painting in the North, 1993, A Sense of Wonder: Art in Alaska, 1995. Alaska State Council Arts fellow, 1981. Mem. Mus. Alaska, Anchorage Fine Arts Mus. Assn., Coll. Art Assn., Friends of U. Alaska Mus. Lutheran. Home: PO Box 82211 Fairbanks AK 99708-2211 Office: U Alaska Art Dept Fairbanks AK 99701

WOODWARD, TIM JOSEPH, writer, journalist; b. Boise, Idaho, Oct. 17, 1946; s. Bertram Francis and Marguerite Ellen (O'Leary) W.; m. Sheila Diane Ryan, June 12, 1971; children: Andrea, Jennifer, Mark. BA, U. Idaho, 1971. Columnist, reporter The Idaho Statesman, Boise, 1971—. Author: Shirttail Journalist, 1980, McCracker Takes a Vacation, 1984, Tiger on the Road: The Life of Vardis Fisher, 1989 (Idaho Book of the Yr. 1990), Is Idaho in Iowa?, 1982. Mem. Boise Visions com. City of Boise, 1988. Recipient MADD Citizenship award Mothers Against Drunk Driving, 1984, Historic Preservation Orchid award Idaho Hist. Soc., 1995, also numerous awards including AP. Mem. Soc. Profl. Journalists (awards), Idaho Press Club (awards). Roman Catholic. Office: The Idaho Statesman PO Box 40 Boise ID 83707

WOODWORTH, STEPHEN DAVIS, business and financial consultant, investment banker; b. Stillwater, Okla., Nov. 4, 1945; s. Stanley Davis and Elizabeth (Webb) W.; m. Robin Woodworth; children: Lisa Alexander, Ashley Ives. BA, Claremont McKenna Coll., 1967; MBA, Calif. Lutheran U., 1975; grad. Mgmt. Policy Inst., U. So. Calif., 1981. Div. mgr. Security Pacific Bank, L.A., 1970-86; pres. Channel Island Equities, Oxnard, Calif., 1988—; chmn. Cen. Coast MIT Enterprise Forum, Santa Barbara, Calif., 1992-94; moderator The White House Conf. on Small Bus., 1995; exec. com., dir. World Affairs Coun. of Ventura County, 1995—; dir. Greater Oxnard Econ. Devel. Corp., 1996—, Santa Barbara chpt. Am. Inst. Wine and Food; instr. fin. and banking Calif. Luth. U., 1978-79; active Calif. CPA Edn. Found., 1996; mem. adv. bd. Hanson Lab Furniture Ind., Inc., Newbury Park, Calif., 1995-96; co-founder Calif. Family Bus. Inst., 1996. Contbr. articles to profl. jours. Chmn. Alliance for the Arts, Thousand Oaks, Calif., 1988-95. Ret. Lt. Col. U.S. Army Res., 1970-96, Korea. Recipient Outstanding Alumnus Calif. Lutheran U., 1986. Mem. Res. Officers Assn. of the U.S., Ventura County Econ. Devel. Assn., Tower Club, Santa Barbara Vintners Assn., James Beard Found., Santa Maria Valley Econs. Devel. Asn., Marine Meml. Club, Spanish Hills Country Club. Republican. Roman Catholic. Home: 163 Stanislaus Ave Ventura CA 93004-1172 Office: Channel Islands Equities 300 E Esplanade Dr Ste 900 Oxnard CA 93030-1251

WOOLF, MICHAEL E., lawyer; b. Phoenix, Mar. 17, 1949. BS, Ariz. State U., 1971, JD cum laude, 1974. Bar: ariz. 1974. Ptnr. O'Connor, Cavanagh, Anderson, Killingsworth & Beshears, P.A., Phoenix. Mem. ABA, Maricopa County Bar Assn., State Bar Ariz. Office: O'Connor Cavanagh Anderson Killingsworth & Beshears PA 1 E Camelback Rd Ste 1100 Phoenix AZ 85012-1656

WOOLF-SCOTT, HELENE LYDA, real estate developer; b. N.Y.C., Apr. 2, 1938; d. Harry and Eleanor (Wolfson) Burke; m. William Woolf, Aug. 17, 1958 (div. 1982); 1 child, Gina Karen; m. Walter Scott Jr., May 1, 1987. BA, NYU, 1959. Lic. real estate agt. Calif. Realtor Wright & Co., Los Altos, Calif., 1974-80; v.p. Munsey Devel. Corp., Los Altos, Calif., 1978—; v.p. McKeon, Scott, Woolf & Assocs., 1982-84; pres. GKW Enterprises, Inc. 1978—, Scott, Woolf & Assocs., 1984—; bd. dirs. Mulford, Moreland, Scott & Assocs., San Jose. Mem. Los Altos Bd. Realtors, Am. Mgmt. Assn., Nat. Trust for Historic Preservation, Nat. Assn. Realtors, Calif. Assn. Realtors. Democrat. Home: 564 Santa Rita Ave Palo Alto CA 94301-4035 Office: Scott Woolf & Assocs Ste V 4546 El Camino Real Los Altos CA 94022

WOOLLEY, DONNA PEARL, timber and lumber company executive; b. Drain, Oreg., Jan. 3, 1926; d. Chester A. and Mona B. (Cheever) Rydell; m. Harold Woolley, Dec. 27, 1952 (dec. Sept. 1970); children: Daniel, Debra, Donald. Diploma, Drain High Sch. Sec. No. Life Ins. Co., Eugene, Oreg., 1943-44; sec., bookkeeper D & W Lumber Co., Sutherlin, Oreg., 1944, Woolley Logging Co. & Earl Harris Lumber Co., Drain, 1944-70; pres. Woolley Logging Co., 1970—, Smith River Lumber Co., 1970—, Mt. Baldy Mill, 1970-81, Drain Plywood Co., 1970-81, Woolley Enterprises, Inc., Drain, 1973—, Eagle's View Mgmt. Co., Inc., Eugene, 1981—. Bd. dirs. Oreg. Cmty. Found., Portland, Oreg., 1990—, Wildlife Safari, Winston, Oreg., 1986; trustee emeritus U. Oreg. Found., Eugene, 1979—; trustee Linfield Coll. Found., McMinnville, Oreg., 1990—; v.p. Oreg. Trail coun. Boy Scouts Am., Eugene, 1981—; exec. dir. World Forestry Ctr., Portland, 1991—. Recipient Pioneer award U. Oreg., 1982, Econ. and Social Devel. award Soroptimist Club, 1991. Mem. Oreg. Women's Forum, Pacific Internat. Trapshooting Assn., Amateur Trapshooting Assn., Eugene C. of C. (bd. dirs. 1989-92), Arlington Club, Town Club (bd. dirs., pres.), Sunnydale Grange, Cottage Grove/Eugene Rod & Gun Club. Republican. Office: Eagle's View Mgmt Co Inc 1399 Franklin Blvd Eugene OR 97403-1979

WOOLLIAMS, KEITH RICHARD, arboretum and botanical garden director; b. Chester, Eng., July 17, 1940; s. Gordon Frank and Margaret Caroline W.; m. Akiko Narita, Apr. 11, 1969; children: Frank Hiromi, Angela Misako. Grad., Celyn Agrl. and Hort. Inst., North Wales, 1955; student, U. Liverpool, various horticultural insts., 1956-59; Kew Cert., Royal Bot. Gardens, Kew, U.K., 1963. Cert. Horticulture Union Cheshire and Lancs. Insts., 1955, Royal Hort. Soc., 1956, 57, 58, Nat. Cert. Horticulture, 1958, Cert. Arboriculture, 1962. Supt. field sta. U. London Queen Mary Coll., Brentwood, Essex, Eng., 1963-65; horticulturist Horizons Ltd., Bermuda, 1965-67; dept. forests, supt. botanic gardens Papua, New Guinea, 1967-68; instr. Eng. staff indsl. cos., Japan, 1968-71; supt., horticulturist Nat. Tropical Bot. Garden, Kauai, Hawaii, 1971-74; horticulturist Waimea Arboretum and Botanical Garden, Haleiwa, Hawaii, 1974-80, dir., 1980—; mem. Pacific islands plant recovery coordinating com. U.S. Fish and Wildlife Svc., 1993—; mem. Hawaii Rare Plant Restoration Group, 1991—. Contbr. articles to profl. jours., New Royal Hort. Soc. Dictionary of Gardening, 1992. Field assoc. botany Bishop Mus., Honolulu, 1981—; bd. dirs. Friends of Honolulu Bot. Gardens, 1980-96; v.p., founder Waimea Arboretum Found., 1977—; bd. dirs. Condominium Estate, Wahiawa, Hawaii, 1990—. Mem. Am. Assn. Botanical Gardens and Arboreta, Am. Hort. Soc., Hawaii Audubon Soc., Hawaiian Botanical Soc. (pres. 1979), Internat. Assn. Plant Taxonomists, Royal Hort. Soc., Kew Guild. Office: Waimea Arboretum & Bot Garden 59-864 Kamehameha Hwy Haleiwa HI 96712-9406*

WOOLSEY, LYNN, congresswoman; b. Seattle, Nov. 3, 1937. BA, U. San Francisco, 1980. Mem. 103rd-104th Congresses from 6th Calif. dist., 1993—; mem. Ho. Reps. coms. on budget, & econ. & ednl. opportunity. Office: US House of Reps 439 Cannon Bldg Washington DC 20515-0003*

WOOLSEY, ROY BLAKENEY, electronics company executive; b. Norfolk, Va., June 12, 1945; s. Roy B. and Louise Stookey (Jones) W.; m. Patricia Bernadine Elkins, Apr. 17, 1988. Student, Calif. Inst. Tech., 1962-64; BS with distinction, Stanford U., 1966, MS, 1967, PhD, 1970. Sr. physicist Tech. for Communications Internat., Mountain View, Calif., 1970-75; mgr. radio direction finding systems Tech. for Communications Internat., Mountain View, 1975-80, program mgr., 1980-83, dir. strategic systems, 1983-88, dir. research and devel., 1988-91, v.p. engring., 1991-92; v.p. programs Tech. for Communications Internat., Sunnyvale, Calif., 1992—; bd. dirs. Merit Software Corp., Menlo Park, 1990-96. Author: (with others) Applications of Artificial Intelligence to Command and Control Systems, 1988, Antenna Engineering Handbook, 1993; contbr. articles to profl. jours. Active YMCA, Palo Alto, Calif., Los Altos Hills com. rels. com., 1994—. Fellow NSF, 1966-70. Mem. AFCEA, Stanford Club, Sequoia Yacht Club, Sigma Xi, Phi Beta Kappa. Republican. Presbyterian. Home: 26649 Snell Ln Los Altos CA 94022-2039 Office: Tech for Communications Internat 222 Caspian Dr Sunnyvale CA 94089-1014 *Personal philosophy: Life is short but as full as one makes it, so one should work hard and play hard at a variety of endeavors.*

WOOSLEY, ANNE I., cultural organization administrator. Dir. The Amerind Found., Inc., Dragoon, Ariz. Office: The Amerind Found Inc PO Box 400 200 N Amerind Rd Dragoon AZ 85609

WOOSLEY, JOAN LOUISE, university registrar; b. Altadena, Calif., Dec. 8, 1951; d. Louis Leo and Vivian Viola (Kitchen) Vitali; children: Brian Cole, Bradley Christopher. BA in Child Devel., Calif. State U., L.A., 1973, MA in Spl. Edn., 1980. Credentialed elem. tchr. Asst. to admissions officer Calif. State U., L.A., 1982-86, admissions officer, 1986-89, univ. registrar, 1989—. Mem. Am. Assn. Collegiate Registrars and Admissions Officers, Student Info Systems Users (presenter), Pacific Assn. Collegiate Registrars and Admissions Officers, Phi Kappa Phi. Office: Calif State U LA 5151 State University Dr Los Angeles CA 90032

WOOTEN, FREDERICK (OLIVER), applied science educator; b. Linwood, Pa., May 16, 1928; s. Frederick Alexander and Martha Emma (Guild) W.; m. Jane Watson MacPherson, Aug. 30, 1952; children: Donald, Bartley. BS in Chemistry, MIT, 1950; PhD in Chemistry, U. Del., 1955. Sr. scientist Lawrence Livermore (Calif.) Lab., 1957-72; prof. applied sci. U. Calif., Davis, 1972—, chmn. designated emphasis in computational sci., 1989—; vis. prof. physics Drexel U., Phila., 1964, Chalmers Tech. H.S., Goteborg, Sweden, 1967-68, Heriot-Watt U., Edinburgh, Scotland, 1979, Trinity Coll., Dublin, Ireland, 1986, Mich. State U., East Lansing, 1993, Boston U., 1996; vis. scholar in math. U. Mass., Amherst, 1991; staff physicist All-Am. Engring. Co., Wilmington, Del., 1955-57; chmn. applied sci. U. Calif., Davis, 1973-93, chmn. designated emphasis in computational sci., 1989—; cons. in field. Author: Optical Properties of Solids, 1972. Mem. AAAS, Am. Phys. Soc., N.Y. Acad. Scis., Sigma Xi. Home: 2328 Alameda Diablo Diablo CA 94528 Office: Univ Calif Dept Applied Sci Davis CA 95616

WOOTEN, MICHAEL ERIC, marine officer; b. San Diego, June 12, 1959; s. James Willis and Elease (Lewis) W.; m. D'Andrea Michele Wilson, Feb. 1, 1988; children: John Michael Christopher, Sarah Mary Elizabeth. AA, DeKalb C.C., 1981; BA in Psychology, Chapman U., 1987; MA in Leadership and Orgnl. Mgmt., Norwich U., 1996; postgrad., Naval Postgrad. Sch., 1996—. Cert. tower operator. Air traffic controller Hdqs. & Hdqs. Squadron, Tustin, Calif., 1983-86; commd. 2nd lt. USMC, 1987, advanced through grades to maj., 1997; officer student, 1987-88; asst. supply officer Second Maintenance Battalion, Camp LeJeune, N.C., 1988-89; supply officer Second Landing Support Battalion, Camp LeJeune, N.C., 1989-90; protocol officer Marine Corps Logistics Base, Albany, Ga., 1990; asst. br. head Mgmt. Br. Integrated Logistics Support, Albany, Ga., 1990-91; aide-de-camp Marine Corps Logistics Base, Albany, Ga., 1991-92; logistics officer Hdqs. Battalion, Albany, Ga., 1992-93; supply officer First sLight Anti Aircraft Missile Battalion, Yuma, Ariz., 1993-96; student Naval Postgrad. Sch., 1996—; nonresident dir. Navy Mut. Aid Assn., Arlington, Va., 1994. Recipient Navy Commendation medal. Mem. Nat. Naval Officer Assn., NAACP, Toastmasters Internat., Masons, Phi Beta Sigma. Episcopalian. Home: 595 Michelson Rd # B Monterey CA 93940-6223 Office: Capt M E Wooten Naval Postgrad Sch 2 University Cir SGC #TBA Monterey CA 93943-5000

WORKMAN, LARRY JOE, natural resources interpreter, photographer-writer; b. Franklin, Ind., Oct. 24, 1947; s. Jack Lee and Martha Louise (Schroer) W.; m. Janet Marie Manzer, Aug. 1, 1981; children: Sarah Louise, David Nathaniel. BS in Agr., Purdue U., 1970. Reforestation forester U.S. Peace Corps, Makalle, Tigre, Ethiopia, 1970-73; rehab. forester Quinault Indian Nation, Taholah, Wash., 1974-78; natural resources interpreter Quinault Indian Nation, Taholah, 1978—; active interpretive ctr. proposal Quinault Indian Nation, Taholah, 1995—, mem. employee benefit com., 1992-96. Co-author: Portrait of Our Land, 1978, Land of the Quinault, 1990 (WPA award 1991, Nat. Fedn. Press Women award 1991); editor Quinault Natural Resources mag., 1980-96 (WPA awards 1982-96); photographer, writer ann. Quinault Indian Nation Calendar, 1979—. Hist. rsch. mini-grantee Nat. Fedn. Press Women, 1994. Mem. Wash. Press Assn. (sec. 1992-94, v.p. 1994-95, pres. 1995—, Superior Performance award 1986, Torchbearer award 1991, Communicator of Achievement 1995). Office: Quinault Indian Nation PO Box 189 Taholah WA 98587

WORKMAN, NORMAN ALLAN, accountant, graphic arts consultant; b. Boston, Apr. 20, 1918; s. William Horace and Estelle Emily (Hanlon) W.; m. Harriet Patricia Banfield, Aug. 1, 1946; children: Stephen, Mark, Brian, Patricia. Student, Coll. William and Mary, 1938-39; BS in Econs. magna cum laude, Bowdoin Coll., 1941. CPA, Oreg. Staff acct. Lybrand Ross Bros. & Montgomery, Boston, 1941-43, Whitfield Stratford & Co., Portland, Oreg., 1946-51; ptnr. Workman, Shephard & Co., CPAs, Portland, 1951-60; sole practitioner Portland, 1961—. Newsletter columnist Good Impressions,

1993—. Chmn. bd. Sylvan Sch., Portland, 1956-57; pres. Doernbecher Children's Hosp. Found., Portland, 1963-85, Bowdoin Club Oreg., Portland, 1963—; trustee Oreg. Episcopal Schs., Portland, 1974-76. Lt. (j.g.) Supply Corps, USNR, 1944-46. Mem. AICPA, Inst. Mgmt. Accts. (pres. Portland chpt. 1954-55), Oreg. Soc. CPA's, Pacific Printing and Imaging Assn., Arlington Club, Multnomah Athletic Club, Phi Beta Kappa. Home: 4381 SW Fairview Blvd Portland OR 97221-2709 Office: 1750 SW Skyline Blvd Portland OR 97221-2533

WORKMAN, TIMATHEA SHAYS, production company executive; b. San Diego, May 25, 1961; d. E. Michael and Nancy (Shurmon) Shays; m. Lyle D. Workman, Jr., June 25, 1989. BA in English, Principia Coll., Elsah, Ill., 1983; postgrad., Calif. State U., Sacramento, 1989, Northwestern U., 1990. Project mgr. Artists & Friends, San Francisco, 1983-84, Bill Graham Presents, San Francisco, 1984-85, ILM, Lucasfilm, San Rafael, Calif., 1985-86; tchr. Sacramento H.S., 1988-89; dean, tchr. Marin Acad., San Rafael, 1986-96; ptnr. Green Bean Prodns., Hollywood, Calif., 1993—. Contbr. articles to profl. jours. E.E. Ford Found. fellow, 1994.

WORRELL, CYNTHIA CELESTE, school nurse; b. Des Moines, Feb. 13, 1948; d. Ralph E. and Mary (Nading) W.; children: Steven F. Durand II, Sonya R. Bellson. BSN, Ariz. State U., 1977, MS, 1983; postgrad. in law, Newport U.; PhD student in Health Svcs., Walden U. RN, Ariz. Adminstrv. nurse mgr. Humana Hosp.; charge nurse med./surg. floor Humana Hosp. Desert Valley, Phoenix; staff nurse Staff Builders, Phoenix; sch. nurse Creighton Sch. Dist., Phoenix, 1978-81, Scottsdale Sch. Dist., 1986—; instr. nursing dept. U. Phoenix, 1990—; mem. comprehensive sch. health essential skills adv. com. Ariz. Dept. Edn. Allstate Found. scholar. Mem. NEA, Am. Holistic Nurses Assn. (cert.), Ariz. Sch. Nurses Assn., Sch. Nurse Orgn. Ariz. (del.), Ariz. Edn. Assn., Scottsdale Edn. Assn. (exec. bd.), Inst. Noetic Scis.

WORRELL, RICHARD VERNON, orthopedic surgeon, college dean; b. Bklyn., June 4, 1931; s. John Elmer and Elaine (Callender) W.; BA, NYU, 1952; MD, Meharry Med. Coll., 1958; m. Audrey Frances Martiny, June 14, 1958; children: Philip Vernon, Amy Elizabeth. Intern Meharry Med. Coll., Nashville, 1958-59; resident gen. surgery Mercy-Douglass Hosp., Phila., 1960-61; resident orthopedic surgery State U. N.Y. Buffalo Sch. Medicine Affiliated Hosps., 1961-64; resident in orthopedic pathology Temple U. Med. Ctr., Phila., 1966-67; pvt. practice orthopedic surgery, Phila., 1964-68; asst. prof. acting head div. orthopedic surgery U. Conn. Sch. Medicine 1968-70; attending orthopedic surgeon E.J. Meyer Meml. Hosp., Buffalo, Millard Fillmore Hosp., Buffalo, VA Hosp., Buffalo, Buffalo State Hosp.; clin. instr. orthopedic surgery SUNY, Buffalo, 1970-74; chief orthopedic surgery VA Hosp., Newington, Conn., 1974-80; asst. prof. surgery (orthopedics) U. Conn. Sch. Medicine, 1974-77, assoc. prof., 1977-83, asst. dean student affairs, 1980-83; prof. clin. surgery SUNY Downstate Med. Ctr., Bklyn., 1983-86; dir. orthopedic surgery Brookdale Hosp. Med. Ctr., Bklyn., 1983-86; prof. of orthopedics U. N.Mex. Sch. of Medicine, 1986—, prof., vice chmn. dept. orthopaedics, 1997—; dir. orthopedic oncology U. N.Mex. Med. Ctr., 1987—; mem. med. staff U. N.Mex. Cancer Ctr., 1987—; chief orthopedic surgery VA Med. Ctr., Albuquerque, 1987—; cons. in orthopedic surgery Newington (Conn.) Children's Hosp., 1968-70; mem. sickle cell disease adv. com. NIH, 1982-86. Bd. dirs. Big Bros. Greater Hartford. Served to capt. M.C., U.S. Army Res., 1962-69. Diplomate Am. Bd. Orthopedic Surgery, Nat. Bd. Med. Examiners. Fellow ACS, Am. Acad. Orthopedic Surgeons, Royal Soc. Medicine, London; mem. AMA, Am. Orthopaedic Assn., Am. Soc. Clin. Pathologists, Orthopedic Rsch. Soc., Internat. Soc. Orthopedic Surgery and Traumatology, N.Mex. Soc. Clin. Oncology, Internat. Fedn. Surg. Colls. (assoc.), Alpha Omega Alpha. Office: U NMex Sch Medicine Albuquerque NM 87131-5296

WORTH, RICHARD CARLETON, gallery owner; b. L.A., Feb. 18, 1932; s. Clarence Walter and eleanor Louise (Boyle) W.; m. Susan Oliver, Dec. 15, 1956 (div. Jan. 1974); children: John Richard, Sharon Harte Worth Jones; m. Diane Gardner, Nov. 25, 1978. BA, UCLA, 1955; MC, Ariz. State U., 1972. Account supr. Ayer/Jorgensen/MacDonald, L.A., 1961-70; v.p. Barnes Assocs., Phoenix, 1972-74; dir. pub. rels. Motorola, Scottsdale, Ariz., 1974-82; self-employed cons. Scottsdale, 1983-87; mgr. mktg. Regional Pub. Transp. Authority, Phoenix, 1987-89; self-employed cons. Phoenix, 1990-95; owner Carleton Connection, Phoenix, 1995—; adj. faculty U. Phoenix, 1991—. Contbr. articles to profl. jours. Facilitator Phoenix Futures, 1988-89. Comdr. USNR, ret. Republican. Episcopalian. Home: 5132 N 35th St Phoenix AZ 85018

WORTH, VONNE NOELL, newspaper publisher, editor, writer, disability rights activist; b. Dayton, Ohio, Jan. 5, 1950; d. William Dewey Worth and Donna Jean (Clay) Klammer; m. Harry Louderback Young Jr., Mar. 25, 1984 (dec. Dec. 1987). BA in English, Transylvania U., 1972; BA in Journalism, Seattle U., 1986. Proofreader The Kernel, U. Ky. newspaper, 1973, staff writer, 1974-75; fiction editor Amanuensis, U. Ky. lit. mag., 1975-76; freelance writer Lexington (Ky.) Herald-Leader, 1975-76; reporter The Univ. News, Kansas City, Mo., 1978; editorial page editor, reporter, copy editor The Spectator, Seattle, 1985-86; reporter Flaherty Newspapers, Seattle, 1986-87; freelance writer Diversity, Seattle, 1993; founder, editor, pub. Different TIMES, Seattle, 1987—; speaker in field. Bd. dirs. Girl Scouts Totem Coun., 1993-95, co-chair diversity team; mem. choir St. Mark's Episcopal Cathedral, 1993—; chair spl. ministries commn. St. George's Episcopal Ch., 1992-93; pres. Seattle Disabled Businesswomen's Network, 1990-92. Episcopalian. Home and Office: 201 NW 39th St Apt 206 Seattle WA 98107-4953

WORTHEY, CAROL, composer; b. Worcester, Mass., Mar. 1, 1943; d. Bernard Krieger and Edith Lilian (Cramer) Symonds; m. Eugene Worthey III, June 1969 (div. 1980); 1 child, Megan; m. Raymond Edward Korns, Sept. 21, 1980. BA in Music Composition, Columbia U., 1965; grad., Dick Grove Sch. Music., L.A., 1979; grad. filmscoring prog., UCLA, 1978; music studies with Darius Milhaud, Walter Piston, Elliot Carter, Vincent Persichetti, Grant Beglarian, Karl Korte, Otto Luening, Eddy Lawrence Manson, Dick Grove; studied, RISD, 1948-54, Columbia U., 1965. Sr. composer, arranger Celebrity Ctr. Internat. Choir, Hollywood, Calif., 1985—. Composer, arranger The Hollywood Chorale; composer ballets Athena, 1963, The Barren, 1965, piano works performed in France, Italy, Germany, Canada, U.S., Eng. by Mario Feninger, 1992, Pastorale, performed in Mex., 1994, Neighborhood of the Heart, 1994, (choir) Unquenchable Light, 1993, (film score) The Special Visitor, 1992; compositions performed at Aspen Music Festival, 1963, Carnegie Hall, 1954, Dorothy Chandler Pavilion, 1986-89; appeared as singer-songwriter L.A. Songwriter's Showcase, 1977; arranger Merv Griffin Show, 1981, The Night Before Christmas, L.A. Children's Theater, 1988-91, Capistrano Valley Symphony, 1994, Very Old Merry Old Christmas, Dorothy Chandler Pavilion, 1994, Judge, 1994; (CD) David Arkenstone Return of the Guardian, 1996; composer, lyricist, librettist full-length musical The Envelope Please, 1988; author: Treasury of Holiday Music, 1992, (poems) The Lonely Wanderer Comes Home, 1994; art work exhibited RISD, 1952, Folk and Art Mus., L.A., 1975, 1st Internat. Art Exhibit Celebrity Ctr. Pavilion, 1992; cable tv show: Neighborhood of the Heart, 1995, 96. Vol. performer various childcare ctrs., old folks homes, etc.; judge Composer's Competition, Inner City Cultural Ctr., 1995, 96. Recipient Silver Poet award World of Poetry, 1987, 2nd place winner, 1st BarComposers and Songwriters Competition for "Fanfare for Joy & Wedding March", 1990, Golden Poet award World of Poetry, 1992. Mem. Nat. Assn. Composers, USA, Broadcast Music Inc., Nat. Acad. Songwriters, Songwriters and Composers Assn., Toastmasters Internat. (Competent Toastmaster 1996), Film Adv. Bd. Jewish.

WOTRUBA, DAVID LAWRENCE, marriage and family therapist; b. Bremerton, Wash., July 1, 1942; s. Joe Lawrence Cook and Louise (Powell) Smith; m. Diane Gayle Mason, Mar. 21, 1986; 1 child, Elizabeth Louise Cook. BS, U. Wash., 1967; MS, Seattle Pacific U., 1995; postgrad., Saybrook Inst., 1995—. Registered counselor, Wash.; lic. pharmacist, Wash., Calif., Hawaii. Pharmacist, 1967—; family therapist Cath. Cmty. Svc., Bremerton, Wash., 1994—; cert. mediator Dispute Resolution Ctr., Bremerton, 1988-92; faculty mem. Inst. Reality Therapy, 1992—. Registered lobbyist, Hawaii, 1975-76. Mem. ACA, Am. Assn. Marriage and Family Therapists, Am. Pharm. Assn., Hawaii Pharmacists Assn. (pres. 1975-76). Home: 13133 Central Valley Rd NW Poulsbo WA 98370-8105

WOTT, JOHN ARTHUR, arboretum and botanical garden executive, horticulture educator; b. Fremont, Ohio, Apr. 10, 1939; s. Arthur Otto Louis and Esther Wilhelmina (Werth) W.; children: Christopher, Timothy, Holly. BS, Ohio State U., 1961; MS, Cornell U., 1966, PhD, 1968. Mem. staff Ohio State Coop. Extension Svc., Bowling Green, 1961-64; rsch. asst. Cornel U., Ithaca, N.Y., 1964-68; prof. Purdue U., West Lafayette, Ind., 1968-81; prof. Ctr. Urban Horticulture U. Wash., Seattle, 1981—; assoc. dir. Ctr. Urban Horticulture U. Wash., Seattle, 1990-93; dir. arboreta Washington Park Arboretum, Seattle, 1993—. Contbr. numerous papers to profl. jours. Mem. Am. Soc. Horticultural Sci. (com. chmn. 1967-82), Am. Assn. Botanic Gardens and Arboreta, Internat. Plant Propagators Soc. (pres. 1984, sec.-treas. 1985—). Office: Washington Park Arboretum U Wash Box 358010 Seattle WA 98195-8010

WOTTON, ROBERT H., JR., small business owner; b. Renton, Wash., Nov. 14, 1963; s. Robert H. and Ruth E. (Hart) W. BA, U. Puget Sound, 1986. Adminstrv. intern Sec. of State, Olympia, Wash., 1986; mgr. Red Wing Shoe Store, Silverdale, Wash., 1987-88, The Shoe Hutch, Corvallis, Oreg., 1988-89; owner Wotton's of Shelton, Wash., 1990—; mem. adj. faculty Olympic Coll., Shelton, 1995—; pres. Western Ind. Shoe Enterprises, 1993-94; vice chair Wash. delegation White House Conf. Small Bus., 1995. Chmn. Mason County Rep. Party, Shelton, 1991-94, state commetteeman, 1994-96; chmn. Mason Dist. Boy Scouts, Shelton, 1987; chmn., co-founder Shelton-Talsi Latvia Sister City Project, Shelton, 1991—; mem. adv. bd. Shelton Vocat. Edn., mktg. chair, 1991-93, chmn. bd. dirs., 1995—; founder Edn. First, 1993—. Named Eagle Scout Boy Scouts Am., 1981, Dist. award of Merit, 1987. Mem. Shelton Lions Club (pres. 1995-96), Shelton-Mason County C. of C., Evergreen Apparel Guild. Republican. Methodist. Office: Wotton's of Shelton 331 W Railroad Ave Shelton WA 98584-3542

WOYSKI, MARGARET SKILLMAN, retired geology educator; b. West Chester, Pa., July 26, 1921; d. Willis Rowland and Clara Louise (Howson) Skillman; m. Mark M. Woyski, June 19, 1948; children: Nancy Elizabeth, William Bruno, Ronald David, Wendelin Jane. BA in Chemistry, Wellesley (Mass.) Coll., 1943; MS in Geology, U. Minn., 1945, PhD in Geology, 1946. Geologist Mo. Geol. Survey and Water Resources, Rolla, 1946-48; instr. U. Wis., Madison, 1948-52; lectr. Calif. State U., Long Beach, 1963-67; lectr. to prof. Calif. State U., Fullerton, 1966-91, assoc. dean Sch. Natural Sci. and Math., 1981-91, emeritus prof., 1991—. Contbr. articles to profl. jours.; author lab. manuals; editor guidebooks. Fellow Geol. Soc. Am. (program chmn. 1982); mem. South Coast Geol. Soc. (hon. pres. 1974), Mineral Soc. Am. Home: 1843 Kashlan Rd La Habra CA 90631-8423

WOYTOWITZ, PETER JOHN, mechanical engineer; b. Balt., Nov. 9, 1953; s. Peter John and Anna Mae (Zink) W.; m. Cristina Guevarra, Oct. 12, 1985; children: Christopher John, Phillip Charles. BSME, U. Md., 1976; MS in Engring., Santa Clara U., 1980; degree of engr., Stanford U., 1985; PhD, Santa Clara U., 1993. Registered profl. engr. Calif. Stress engr. Boeing Comml. Airplane Co., Seattle, 1977-78; engr. rsch. & devel. Ford Aerospace and Communications Corp., Palo Alto, Calif., 1978-83; sr. engr. Anamet Labs., Inc., San Carlos, Calif., 1983-85; sr. mech. engr. Failure Analysis Assocs., Menlo Park, Calif., 1985-93; v.p., prin. engr. Engring. Mechanics Tech., San Jose, Calif., 1993—; lectr. San Jose State U., 1985-88, 93—, Santa Clara (Calif.) U., 1993—; book reviewer McGraw-Hill, 1993; jour. reviewer Mechanism & Machine Theory, 1993. Co-author: Optimization of Structural Systems, 1991. Mem. ASME (v.p. student chpt. 1975), AIAA, Am. Acad. Mechs., Pi Tau Sigma. Roman Catholic. Home: 318 Farley St Mountain View CA 94043-4422 Office: Engring Mechanics Tech 4340 Stevens Creek Blvd Ste 166 San Jose CA 95129-1147

WOZNIAK, JOYCE MARIE, sales executive; b. Detroit, Aug. 3, 1955; d. Edmund Frank and Bernice (Liske) W. BA, Mich. State U., 1976; MA, Nat. U., San Diego, 1988; postgrad., U.S. Internat. U., 1989-90. Probation officer San Diego County Probation, 1979-81; prodn. engr. Tuesday Prodns., Inc., San Diego, 1981-85; nat. sales mgr. Advance Rec. Products, San Diego, 1986-88; acct. exec. Joyce Enterprises, San Diego, 1986-95; sales exec. Audio-Video Supply Inc., San Diego, 1988—. Producer (video) Loving Yourself, 1987, southwest cable access program, 1986-95; registered marriage, family and child counselor-intern, Calif., 1989. Active Zool. Soc. San Diego. Mem. NAFE, Art Glass Assn. So. Calif., Calif. Assn. Marriage and Family Therapists, Internat. TV Assn. (treas. San Diego chpt. 1990-91), Nat. Acad. TV Arts and Scis.

WRACKER, BRIAN D., art educator; b. Oberlin, Ohio, Sept. 26, 1966; s. Donald Gene and Thelma Jean (Kannenberg) W. BFA n Graphic Design, Winthrop U., 1991; postgrad., Sierra Nev. Coll. Home: PO Box 1291 Crystal Bay NV 89402-1291

WRIGHT, BERNARD, artist; b. Pitts., Feb. 23, 1938; s. Garfield and Emma (Jefferson) W.; m. Corrine Westley, Mar. 7, 1964; 1 son, Jeffrey. Student Otis Art Inst., Los Angeles, 1969-70, Los Angeles Trade Tech. Coll., 1971-73. Exhibited traveling art show Moscow, Baku, Leningrad, Alma Alta, USSR, European capitals, 1966, Los Angeles City Hall Rotunda Gallery, 1967, Calif. Lutheran Coll., Thousand Oaks, 1967, Alley Gallery, Beverly Hills, 1968, Florenz Art Gallery, Los Angeles, 1969, San Diego Mus., 1969, Phillip E. Freed Gallery of Fine Arts, Chgo., 1969, Art West Gallery, Los Angeles, 1973, N.J. State Mus., Trenton, Detroit Inst. Arts, Mich., 1974, U. So. Calif., Calif. Mus. Sci. and Industry, 1974, City Art Mus., St. Louis, 1976, N.Y.C. Pub. Library, 1977, Pitts. City Hall Rotunda, 1982, The Mus. of African Am. Art, Los Angeles, 1982, Main Bridge Art Gallery, Los Angeles City Hall, 1983; represented in pvt. and pub. collections including Howard U., Library of Congress. collections past pres. co-founder Wright's & Westley Prodns., furniture and garment designers. Cited by U.S. Rep. Cardiss Collins, Ill., 1978, state senator Bill Greene, Calif, 1981, Mayor Richard S. Callguiri, Pitts., 1981, Mayor Coleman A. Young, Detroit, 1981, Mayor Tom Bradley, Los Angeles. bd. supr. Kenneth Hahn, Los Angeles, 1981; active community involvement Sta. KHJ-TV, 1982. Mem. Art West Assn. (bd. dirs.). Contbr. articles to profl. jours. Home: PO Box 76169 Los Angeles CA 90076-0169

WRIGHT, C. T. ENUS, former college administrator; b. Social Circle, Ga., Oct. 4, 1942; s. George and Carrie Mae (Enus) W.; m. Mary Stephens, Aug. 9, 1974. B.S., Fort Valley State U. (Ga.), 1964; M.A., Atlanta U., 1967; Ph.D., Boston U., 1977. Tchr., Ga. Pub. Schs., Social Circle, 1965-67; mem. faculty Morris Brown Coll., Atlanta, 1967-73, div. chmn., 1973-77; program dir., asst. provost Eastern Wash. U., Cheney, 1977-81; v.p. academic affairs Talladega Coll. (Ala.), 1981-82; pres. Cheyney U. Pa., Cheyney, 1982-85; v.p. and provost Fla. Meml. Coll., 1985-89; exec. dir. Internat. Found. and Coord. African-African Am. Summit, 1989—; cons. and lectr. in field. Author: (booklet) The History of Black Historical Mythology, 1980; contbr. articles to profl. jours. Commnr., Wash. Pub. Broadcasting, Olympia, 1980-84; exec. com. Boy Scouts Am., Phila., 1982—. Human Relations scholar, 1969, Nat. Teaching fellow Boston U., 1971. Mem. Am. Assn. Colls. and Univs. (coms. 1982—), Am. Hist. Assn. (coms. 1970—), Assn. Study Afro-Am. Life & History (coms. 1965—), Nat. Assn. Equal Opportunity in Higher Edn. (coms. 1982—), NEA (coms. 1965—). Am. Baptist. Clubs: Lions (Cheyney, Wash. (v.p. 1979-81)); Tuscan; Atlanta Constitution. Office: Intl Found 5122 E Shea Blvd Apt 2098 Scottsdale AZ 85254-4679

WRIGHT, CAMERON HARROLD GREENE, electrical engineer; b. Quincy, Mass., Jan. 21, 1956; s. Frederick Herman Greene and Dorothy Louise (Harrold) W.; m. Robin Michele Rawlings, May 14, 1988. BSEE summa cum laude, La. Tech. U., 1983; MSEE, Purdue U., 1988; PhD, U. Tex., 1996. Registered profl. engr., Calif. Commd. 2d lt. USAF, 1983, advanced through grades to major, 1995; avionics design engr. USAF Avionics Lab., Wright-Patterson AFB, Ohio, 1983-86; divsn. chief space test range space divsn. USAF, L.A. AFB, 1988-90, dir. advanced satellite systems, 1990-91; instr. elec. engring. USAF Acad., Colorado Springs, 1991-93, asst. prof., 1996—; mem. exec. com. Nat. Aerospace and Electronics Conf., Dayton, Ohio, 1983-86; bd. dirs. Rocky Mountain Bioengring. Symposium. Contbr. articles to profl. jours.; reviewer profl. jours.; co-author, editor: An Introduction to Electrical Engineering, 1994. Coord. tech. career motivation Dayton Sch. Dist., 1983-86; speaker engring. careers Colorado Springs Middle Sch., 1991-93; vol. computer/network cons. Project Transitions Hospice, Austin, Tex., 1995-96. Mem. IEEE (sr.), Air Force Assn. (life, dir. L.A. Young Astronaut program 1988-91, Officer of Yr. 1991), Am. Soc. for Engring. Edn. Office: Dept Elec Engring 2354 Fairchild Dr Ste 2F6 U S A F Academy CO 80840

WRIGHT, CAROLE YVONNE, chiropractor; b. Long Beach, Calif., July 12, 1932; d. Paul Burt and Mary Leoan (Staley) Fickes; 1 child, Morgan Michelle. D. Chiropractic, Palmer Coll., Davenport, Iowa, 1976. Instr. Palmer Coll., 1975-76; dir., owner Wright Chiropractic Clinic, Rocklin, Calif., 1978-88, Woodland, Calif., 1980-81; co-owner Ft. Sutter Chiropractic Clinic, Sacramento, 1985-89; owner Wright Chiropractic Health Ctr., Sacramento, 1989—, Capitol Chiropractic, Sacramento, 1993—; cons. in field; lectr., speaker on radio and TV programs, at seminars. Contbr. articles to profl. jours. Co-chmn. Harold Michaels for Congress campaign, Alameda, Calif., 1972; dist. dir. 14th Congl. Dist., 1983—. Mem. Internat. Chiropractic Assn. Calif. (bd. dirs. 1978-81, pres. 1983-85), Palmer Coll. Alumni Assn. (Calif. state pres. 1981-83), Rocklin C. of C. (bd. dirs. 1979-81). Republican. Avocations: reading, travel. Home: 1404 Stonebridge Way Roseville CA 95661-5456

WRIGHT, CHARLES LEE, information systems consultant; b. Dalton, Ga., Dec. 18, 1949; s. Charlie William and Catherine Christine (Quarles) W.; children: Charles Lee, Christina. AA in Bus., Dalton Jr. Coll., 1971; BS in Bus., U. Tenn., Chattanooga, 1977; also numerous IBM classes on various machines and systems;. Trainee Ludlow Carpets, Dalton, 1971, EDP supr., 1971-73, EDP mgr., 1973-77; ops. mgr. Walter Carpet Mills, Industry, Calif., 1977-80; ptnr., cons. TCT Systems, San Dimas, Calif., 1978-92; ptnr., CEO Williams, Wright and Assocs., Upland, Calif., 1978-92; dir. ops. Roland Corp., U.S., 1993—. Served as sgt. U.S. Army, 1969-71; Vietnam, Cambodia. Decorated Bronze Star, Army Commendation medal with oak leaf and oak leaf cluster, Air medal. Mem. Data Processing Mgmt. Assn., Am. Mgmt. Assn., Small Systems User Group, COMMON. Home and Office: 3708 Palamino Place Ontario CA 91761-5107 *Personal philosophy: Efficient work and dedication to detail is the key to success.*

WRIGHT, CHATT GRANDISON, academic administrator; b. San Mateo, Calif., Sept. 17, 1941; s. Virgil Tandy and Louise (Jeschien) W.; children from previous marriage: Stephen Brook, Jon David, Shelley Adams; m. Janice Teply, Nov. 28, 1993. Student, U. Calif., Berkeley, 1960-62; BA in Polit. Sci., U. Calif., Davis, 1964; MA in Econs., U. Hawaii, 1968. Instr. econs. U. Hawaii, Honolulu, 1968-70; mgr. corp. planning Telecheck Internat., Inc., Honolulu, 1969-70; economist State of Hawaii, Honolulu, 1970-71; adminstr. manpower City & County of Honolulu, 1971-72; bus. adminstr., dean. Hawaii Pacific U., Honolulu, 1972-74, v.p., 1974-76, pres., 1976—. Mem. City and County of Honolulu Manpower Area Planning Commn., 1976-82; mem. Mayor's Salary Commn. City of County of Honolulu, 1977-80; mem. Honolulu City Ethics Commn., 1978-84; em. City and County of Honolulu Labor Market Adv. Coun., 1982-84; bd. dirs. Hawaii Econ. Devel. Corp., 1980-84; trustee Queen's Med. Ctr., Honolulu, 1986-92, Honolulu Armed Svcs. YMCA, 1984-86, Hawaii Maritime Ctr., 1990-92; chmn. bd. trustees Hist. Hawaii Found., 1995-96, mem., 1990-96; mem. adv. bd. Cancer Rsch. Ctr. Hawaii, 1987; trustee St. Andrew's Priory Sch., 1994—; bd. dirs. Hawaii Visitors Bur., 1995—; mem. adv. bd. HCEE, 1996—; bd. dirs. Downtown Improvement Assn., 1988-96, Outrigger Duke Kahanamoku Found., 1996—, Hawaii Opera Theatre, 1997—; mem. Hawaii Execs. Coun., 1996—; bd. govs. Hawaii Med. Libr., 1989-92; mem. adv. bd. Aloha coun. Boy Scouts Am., 1991—; trustee Molokai Gen. Hosp., 1991-92. With USN, 1967-80. Recipient Pioneer award Pioneer Fed. Savs. Bank, 1982. Mem. Am. Assn. Higher Edn., Assn. Governing Bds. Univs. and Colls., Japan-Am. Soc. Honolulu, Social Sci. Assn., Nat. Assn. Intercollegiate Athletics (vice chair NAIA coun. of pres. 1994, mem. NAIA coun. of pres. 1985—), Hawaii Joint Coun. Econ. Edn. (bd. dirs. 1982-88), Western Coll. Assn. (exec. com. 1989-92), Hawaii Assn. Ind. Colls. and Univs. (chmn. 1986), Hawaii C. of C., Sales and Mktg. Execs. Club Honolulu, Outrigger Canoe Club, Pacific Club (Honolulu), Plaza Club (bd. govs. 1992—), Oahu Country Club, Waialae Country Club, Rotary (Paul Harris fellow 1986). Republican. Episcopalian. Office: Hawaii Pacific U Office Pres 1166 Fort Street Mall Honolulu HI 96813-2708 also: Hawaii Pacific Univ Gallery 1164 Bishop St Honolulu HI 96813

WRIGHT, CONNIE SUE, special education educator; b. Nampa, Idaho, Aug. 26, 1943; d. Ruel Andrew and Renabel Carol (Graham) Farwell; m. Roger R. Wright, July 5, 1968; 1 child, Jodi C. BA, N.W. Nazarene Coll., 1967; MA in Spl. Edn., Boise State U., 1990. Cert. elem. tchr. grades kindergarten through 8th, cert. spl. edn. tchr. grades kindergarten through 12th, Idaho. Tchr. 3rd and 4th grades Vallivue Sch. Dist. 139, Caldwell, Idaho, 1967-69; tchr. 2nd grade Nampa Sch. Dist. 131, 1969-70; tchr. 3rd grade Caldwell Sch. Dist. 132, 1970-73; tchr. spl. edn. grades kindergarten through 3rd Hubbard Elem. Sch., Kuna (Idaho) Joint Sch. Dist. 3, 1985-92; tchr. adolescents CPC Intermountain Hosp. of Boise, 1992-93; tchr. spl. edn. Pioneer Elem. Sch., Meridian, Idaho, 1993—; mem. Internat. Edn. Conf. Between Russia and U.S., 1994. Libr. Horizon's Reading Coun., 1990-91. Named Tchr. Yr. Pioneer Elem. Sch., 1994-95. Mem. Coun. for Exceptional Children, Coun. for Learning Disabilities, Internat. Reading Assn. (Idaho coun.), Delta Kappa Gamma Soc. Internat. (Omicron chpt.).

WRIGHT, DANIEL ROBERT, educational administrator; b. Madison, Wis., July 1, 1958; s. Norman William and Bertha Ellen (Miller) W.; m. Grace del Carmen Gonzalez, June 30, 1984; 1 child, Miller Alexander. BS, U. Wis., 1981; MA, Calif. State U., 1992; postgrad., U. Pacific, Stockton, Calif., 1995—. Cert. tchr., adminstr., Calif. Tchr. Am./Nicaraguan Sch., Managua, Nicaragua, 1983-85, Cotulla (Tex.) Ind. Sch. Dist., 1985-86, Kennedy (Tex.) Ind. Sch. Dist., 1986-88, Valle Lindo Elem. Sch. Dist., El Monte, Calif., 1988-93; asst. prin. Stockton (Calif.) Unified Sch. Dist., 1993—. Mem. Valle Lindo Tchr. Assn., (pres. elect 1990-91, pres. 1991-93), Phi Delta Kappa (treas. U. Pacific chpt. 1996—). Democrat. Roman Catholic. Home: 808 Garner Ln Stockton CA 95207-4809 Office: Stockton Unified Sch Dist Hamilton Middle Sch 2245 E 11th St Stockton CA 95206-3606

WRIGHT, EDWARD N., political science educator; b. Chillicothe, Ohio, Mar. 20, 1945; s. Herbert Wright and Martha A. (Boden) Grant; m. June Claire Goodwin, Apr. 26, 1969; children: Edward II, Robert E., Benjamin J. BS in Polit. Sci. and Econs. with highest honors, U. So. Miss., Hattiesburg, 1971, MA in Polit. Sci., 1973; PhD in Govt., Georgetown U., 1985. Commd. 2d lt. USAF, 1965, advanced through the grades to lt. col, 1990; politico miltary affairs officer Project Peace Hawk, U.S. Air Force, Alkhabar, Saudi Arabia, 1977-78; staff analyst Office of Sec. of Defense, Washington, 1978-79; instr. polit. sci. USAF Acad., Colorado Springs, Colo., 1979-80; rsch. assoc. Carnegie Endowment for Internat. Peace, Washington, 1980-81; assoc. prof. polit. sci. USAF Acad., Colorado Springs, Colo., 1983-87; spl. asst. to the Atty. Gen., U.S. Dept. Justice, Washington, 1987-88; assoc. prof. polit. sci. USAF Acad., Colorado Springs, Colo., 1988-90; prof. pub. adminstrn. Grad Sch. of Pub. Affairs, U. Colo., Colorado Springs, Colo., 1990-91; assoc. prof. polit. sci. U. So. Colo., Pueblo, Colo., 1991—; assoc. provost U. Soc. Colo., 1995—; mem. nat. advisory coun. Ctr. for Study of the Presidency, N.Y.C., 1990—. Editor: (book) American Defense Policy, 1990. V.p. Rocky Mt. Coun. Boy's Scouts of Am., Pueblo, Colo., 1992-94; mem. 2010 commn. Comm. of Pueblo Strategic Plan, Pueblo, 1994-96; mem. state bd. agrl. Colo. State Govt., 1994-95. Mem. Am. Polit. Sci. Assn., Western Polit. Sci. Assn., Phi Kappa Phi, Phi Sigma Alpha, Omicron Delta Kappa. Republican. Roman Catholic. Home: 457 W Hahns Peak Ave Pueblo West CO 81007-2860 Office: U So Colo Office of the Provost 2200 Bonforte Blvd Pueblo CO 81001-4901

WRIGHT, ERIC R., physician assistant; b. Fremont, Mich., Apr. 8, 1952; s. Owen Aaron and Ethlyn Emily (Crandall) W.; m. Teresa Christine Harrison, May 3, 1979; 1 child, Natalie Ann. Grad., Hackley Hosp. Sch. Radiol.Tech, Muskegon, Mich., 1975; AS in Physician Assisting with honors, Kettering (Ohio) Coll. Med.Art, 1984. Diplomate Colo. Bd. Med. Examiners; cert. graphoanalyst. Physician asst. Peak Nine Med. Ctr./Family & Emergency Med. Assocs., Breckenridge, Colo., 1984-85, Richard Wageman, M.D., Monument, Colo., 1985-86, Dennis Caldwell, M.D., Colorado Springs, Colo., 1986-88, Sheldon Ravin, D.O., Skyway Family Practice, Colorado Springs, 1988-90, The People's Clinic, Boulder, Colo., 1990-95, Columbine Family Practice Ctr., Loveland, Colo., 1991-93, Alpine Ear, Nose and Throat, Ft. Collins, Colo., 1993—. Author: Acute Mountain Sickness, 1988, PA Protocols: A Guidebook, 1992. Mem. Internat. Graphoanalysis Soc.,

Am. Registry of Radiologic Technologists, Beaven-Black Student Soc. Physician Assts. (v.p. 1982-83), Am. Acad. Physician Assts., Colo. Assn. Physician Assts. (membership chmn. 1990-92), Soc. Physician Assts. in Otolaryngology. SDA. Home: 3411 N Douglas Loveland CO 80538-2574

WRIGHT, FRANCES JANE, educational psychologist; b. Los Angeles, Dec. 22, 1943; d. step-father John David and Evelyn Jane (Dale) Brinegar. BA, Long Beach State U., 1965, secondary tchr. cert., 1966; MA, Brigham Young U., 1968, EdD, 1980; postgrad. U. Nev., 1970, U. Utah, 1972-73; postdoctoral Utah State U., 1985-86. Cert. tchr., adminstr. Utah. Asst. dir. Teenpost Project, San Pedro, Calif., 1966; caseworker Los Angeles County, 1966-67; self-care inservice dir. Utah State Tng. Sch., American Fork, Utah, 1968, vocat. project designer, 1968; tchr. mentally handicapped Santa Ana Unified Schs., Calif., 1968-69; state specialist intellectually handicapped State Office Edn., Salt Lake City, 1969-70; vocat. counselor Manpower, Salt Lake City, 1970-71; tchr. severely handicapped Davis County Schs., Farmington, Utah, 1971-73, diagnostician, 1973-74, resource elem. tchr., 1974-78; instr. Brigham Young U., Salt Lake City, 1976-83; resource tchr. jr. high Davis County Schs., Farmington, 1978-90; ednl. cons., Murray, Utah, 1973-90; chief ednl. diagnostician Ctr. for Evaluation of Learning and Devel., Layton, Utah, 1989-90; clin. dir. assessment and observation program Idaho Youth Ranch, 1990-95, clin. dir. intake program, 1992-94, supr. family preservation svc./aftercare teams, 1993-95, co-ranch treatment dir. and placement officer, 1995; cons. juvenile correctional dist. 5, 1996—; clin. cons. Magic Hot Springs Youth Camp, 1996-97; mem. cmty. accountability bd. McNeil Assn., 1996—; lectr. in field. Author curriculums in spl. edn.; contbr. articles to profl. jours. Named Profl. of Yr., Utah Assn. for Children with Learning Disabilities, 1985. Mem. Assn. Children/Adults with Learning Disabilities (del. 1979-85, 87, nat. nominating com. 1985-86, nat. bd. dirs. 1988-91), Utah Assn. Children/Adults with Learning Disabilities (exec. bd. 1978-84, profl. adv. bd. 1985-90, coord. LDA orgn. Idaho 1991—), Coun. Exceptional Children (div. learning disabilities, ednl. diagnostics, behavioral disorders), Coun. Learning Disabilities, ASCD (regional adv.), Windstar Found., Nat. Wildlife Found., World Wildlife Fedn., Best Friends Animal Sanctuary, Cousteau Soc., Nat. Assn. Sch. Adminstrs. Democrat. Mormon. Lodge: Job's Daughters. Avocations: geneology research, horseback riding, sketching, crafts, reading. Home: 2176 Julie Ln Twin Falls ID 83301 Office: Youth Ctr Juvenile Corrections 2469 Wright Ave Twin Falls ID 83301-7972 *Personal philosophy: I dream of the day when man will value man and his surrounding world.*

WRIGHT, FREDERICK HERMAN GREENE, II, computer systems engineer; b. Quincy, Mass., Feb. 23, 1952; s. Frederick Herman Greene and Dorothy Louise (Harrold) W. Student, MIT, 1968-69. Test and measurement technician The Foxboro (Mass.) Co., 1968; hardware and software designer MIT Project MAC, Cambridge, Mass., 1969, Info. Internat., Brookline, Mass., 1969, Stanford Artificial Intelligence Lab, Palo Alto, Calif., 1971-73, Systems Concepts, San Francisco, 1970, 73-74, 1976-90; hardware and software designer, then pres. Resource One, San Francisco, 1974-76; pvt. cons. San Rafael, Calif., 1991—; computer cons. Langley-Porter Neuropsychiatric Inst., San Francisco, 1976. Membership chmn. Pacific Soaring Coun., San Francisco, 1983-85, bd. dirs., 1984-85; active Mayflower Cmty. Chorus, 1993—. Recipient Gold Soaring Badge Fed. Aeronautique Internat., 1983. Mem. Digital Equipment Corp. Users Soc., Bay Area Soaring Assn. Home and Office: 251 C St San Rafael CA 94901-4916

WRIGHT, GEORGE THADDEUS, humanities educator; b. S.I., N.Y., Dec. 17, 1925; s. George Thaddeus and Tekla Alida (Anderson) W.; m. Jerry Honeywell, Apr. 28, 1955. A.B., Columbia, 1946, M.A., 1947; student, U. Geneva, Switzerland, 1947-48; Ph.D. (Dr. Benjamin P. Wall meml. fellow 1955-56), U. Calif. at Berkeley, 1957. Lectr. English U. Calif. at Berkeley, 1956-57; instr., then asst. prof. U. Ky., 1957-60; asst. prof. San Francisco State Coll., 1960-61; assoc. prof. U. Tenn., 1961-68; prof. English U. Minn., Mpls., 1968-89, Regents' prof., 1989-93, prof. emeritus, 1993—, chmn. dept. English, 1974-77; Fulbright lectr. Am. lit. U. d'Aix Marseille, France, 1964-66, U. Thessaloniki, Greece, 1977-78. Author: The Poet in the Poem: The Personae of Eliot, Yeats and Pound, 1960, W.H. Auden, 1969, rev. edit., 1981, Shakespeare's Metrical Art, 1988, paperback edit., 1991; also articles, poems.; Editor: Seven American Literary Stylists from Poe to Mailer, 1973. Served with U.S. Army, 1944-46. NEH stipend, 1981; Guggenheim fellow, 1981-82; NEH fellow, 1984-85. Mem. Shakespeare Assn. Am., MLA (William Riley Parker prize 1974, 81), Phi Kappa Phi. Home: 2617 W Crown King Dr Tucson AZ 85741-2569

WRIGHT, GEORGIA SOMMERS, educator, video producer; b. St. Paul, Minn., Jan. 23, 1937; d. Ben and Mary (Crosby) Sommers; m. David Herndon Wright, July 14, 1967; 1 child, Elizabeth. BA, Swarthmore Coll., 1959; MA, Columbia U., 1961, PhD, 1966; MBA, U. Calif., Berkeley, 1981. Vis. lectr U. Minn., Mpls., 1962, 64; vis. lectr U. Calif., Berkeley, 1966-67, Davis, 1967-68; asst. prof. Mills Coll., Oakland, Calif., 1968-76; vis. assoc. prof. Stanford (Calif.) U.; co-dir. Limestone Sculpture Provenance Project, 1995—. Dir., prod. 2 edn. videos; contbr. articles to profl. jours. Grantee NEH, 1993-94; named Chevalier in the Order of Academic Palms, Govt. of France, 1989. Mem. Nat. Coalition of Ind. Scholars (editor 1986-93), Inst. for Hist. Study (pres. 1985-87, 1995—). Home: 105 Vicente Rd Berkeley CA 94705-1605

WRIGHT, GORDON BROOKS, musician, conductor, educator; b. Bklyn., Dec. 31, 1934; s. Harry Wesley and Helen Philomena (Brooks) W.; m. Inga-Lisa Myrin Wright, June 13, 1958 (div. 1979); children: Karin-Ellen Sturla, Charles-Eric, Daniel Brooks. MusB, Coll. Wooster, 1957; MA, U. Wis., 1961; postgrad., Salzburg Mozarteum, 1972, Loma Linda U., 1979; studied with, René Leibowitz, Carl Melles, Wilfred Pelletier, Herbert Blomstedt, Hans Swarowsky. Founder, music dir. Wis. Chamber Orch., 1960-69; music dir. Fairbanks (Alaska) Symphony Orch., 1969-89; prof. music Univ. Alaska, Fairbanks, 1969-89, prof. emeritus, 1989—; founder, music dir. Arctic Chamber Orch., Fairbanks, 1970-89; exec. dir. The Reznicek Soc., Indian, Alaska, 1982—. Guest condr. Philharmonia Hungarica, Philomusica London, Norwegian Radio Orch., Orch. St. Luke's, Anchorage Symphony Orch., Musashino Orch., Tokyo, Tohoku Orch., Sendai, Japan; composer: Suite of Netherlands Dances, 1965, Six Alaskan Tone Poems, 1974, Symphony in Ursa Major, 1979 (Legis. award 1979), 1984 Overture, Scott Joplin Suite, 1987, Toccata Festiva, 1992; columnist Alaska Advocate. Founder, bd. dirs. No. Alaska Environ. Ctr., Fairbanks, 1971-78. Served as pvt. AUS, 1957-59. Mem. Am. Musicol. Soc., Royal Musical Assn., Am. Symphony Orch. League, Condr.'s Guild, Arturo Toscanini Soc., Am. Fedn. Musicians, Royal Mus. Assn., Sierra Club (lchmn. Fairbanks Group 1969-71), Friends of Earth-Alaska (bd. dirs. 1978—), Wilderness Soc., Audubon Soc., Alaska Conservation Soc. (editor Rev. 1971-78), Ctr. for Alaskan Coastal Studies (bd. dirs. 1982—). Home: HC 52 Box 8899 Indian AK 99540-9604

WRIGHT, JAMES BARON, electrical engineer; b. San Francisco, Sept. 17, 1933; s. George Baron and Louise Henerette (Vallee) Boyd; m. Judith Clarice Gehring, May 25, 1962; children: Peter Baron, Erich Paul, John Conrad. BSEE, U. Calif., Berkeley, 1958. Engr. elec. design divsn. Sandia Labs., Livermore, Calif., 1958-60, engr. W55 project engring. divsn., 1960-61, engr. electronic support divsn., AF&F designer, 1961-63, engr. preliminary analysis divsn., 1963-64, lead elec. engr. Pebbles/W68 devel. team, 1964-69, supr. nuclear safety divsn., 1969-71, supr. preliminary design div., 1971-74, supr. B77/B83 elec. sys. div., 1974-82, mgr. solar ctrl. receiver dept., 1982-85, mgr. W89 program sys. devel. dept., 1985-92, dir. Calif. Weapon Sys. Engring. Ctr., 1992—. With USN, 1950-54. Mem. IEEE. Home: 2141 Hampton Rd Livermore CA 94550-6509 Office: Sandia National Labs Ctr 2200 MS9005 Box 969 Livermore CA 94551-0969

WRIGHT, JEFF, minister, non-profit religious administrator; b. Jan. 15, 1960; s. James Lee and Mary E. (Shelton) W.; m. Debra Yvonne Thesman, June 6, 1981; children: Bethany Nicole, Jordan Nicholas. BA, Tabor Coll., Hillsboro, Kans., 1981; postgrad., Kans. State U., 1981-83; Ctrl. Bapt. Theol. Sem., 1983; MDiv, Mennonite Brethren Bibl. Sem., Fresno, Calif., 1986; MBA, Grad. Theol. Found., Donaldson, Ind., 1995. Ordained to ministry, Gen. Conf. Mennonite Ch., 1989. Pastoral intern Fairlawn Mennonite Brethren Ch., Topeka, Kans., 1981-83; youth pastor Zion Mennonite Brethren Ch., Dinuba, Calif., 1983-85; assoc. minister Meml. United Meth. Ch., Clovis, Calif., 1985-86; pastor First Mennonite Ch., Upland, Calif., 1986-89; founding pastor Peace Mennonite Fellowship, Rancho Cucamonga, Calif., 1989-92; coord. Pacific S.W. Mennonite Conf., Downey, Calif., 1992-95; dir. ministry devel. Shalom Ministries, Inc., Downey, 1992—; area minister Pacific S.W. Mennonite Conf., 1995—. Author column Youth Guide, 1990-94. Bd. dirs. Urban Health Care Ctr., Inglewood, Calif., 1993-96, Shalom Homes, Inc., Glendora, Calif., 1987-95, Peace and Justice Ctr. of Pomona Valley, La Verne, Calif., 1993-95; mem. Commn. on Edn., Gen. Conf. Mennonite Ch., Newton, Kans., 1992—, chmn., 1995—. Mem. Christian Mgmt. Assn., Nat. Network of Youth Ministries, Mennonite Econ. Devel. Assocs., Christian Community Devel. Assocs., Religious Conf. Mgmt. Assn. Democrat. Office: Shalom Ministries Inc 11821 Old River School Rd Downey CA 90241-4625

WRIGHT, JOHN MACNAIR, JR., retired army officer; b. L.A., Apr. 14, 1916; s. John MacNair and Ella (Stradley) W.; m. Helene Tribit, June 28, 1940; children: John MacNair III, Richard Kenneth. B.S., U.S. Mil. Acad., 1940; grad., Airborne Sch., 1947, Strategic Intelligence Sch., 1948; advanced course, Inf. Sch., 1951, Command and Gen. Staff Coll., 1953; M.B.A., U. So. Calif., 1956; grad., Army Logistics Mgmt. Sch., 1957, Advanced Mgmt. Program, U. Pitts., 1959, Nat. War Coll., 1961, Army Aviation Sch., 1965; M.S. in Internat. Affairs, George Washington U., 1973. Enlisted U.S. Army, 1935, comd. 2d. lt., 1940, advanced through grades to lt. gen., 1970; comdr. Battery Wright Corregidor, P.I., 1942; with intelligence div. War Dept. Gen. Staff, 1946-48; mil. attache Am. embassy, Paraguay, 1948-50; bn. comdr. 508th Airborne Regtl. Combat Team, 1951-52; asst. chief of staff for pers. 7th Inf. Div., Korea, 1953, asst. chief staff logistics, 1954; assigned office U.S. Army Chief of Staff, 1956-60; chief staff 8th Inf. Div., 1961-62, asst. chief staff plans and ops. 7th Corps, 1962-63, asst. chief staff plans and ops. 7th Army, 1963-64, asst. div. comdr. 11th Air Assault Div., 1964-65; asst. div. comdr. 1st Cav. Div. (Airmobile) Vietnam, 1965-66; assigned office asst. Chief Staff Force Devel., 1966-67; comdg. gen. U.S. Army Inf. Ctr., 1967-69; comdt. U.S. Army Inf. Sch., 1967-69; comdg. gen. 101st Airborne Div. (Airmobile), Vietnam, 1969-70; controller of the Army Washington, 1970-72; ret., 1973. Dir. R&D Boy Scouts Am., 1973, nat. dir. program, 1974-77, nat. dir. program support, 1977-78; nat. dir. exploring, 1978-81, mem. nat. exploring com., 1981—; pres. Chattahoochee (Ga.) coun. Boy Scouts Am., 1968-69, mem. exec. bd. region 5, 1967-69; mem. nat. coun., 1964-73; tech. adviser Vietnamese Boy Scout Assn., 1965-66; Regent for Life Nat. Eagle Scout Assn., 1988—; exploring chmn. five nations dist. Calif. Inland Empire Coun., 1992—. Decorated D.S.M. with 2 oak leaf clusters, Silver Star with oak leaf cluster, Legion of Merit with oak leaf cluster, D.F.C., Bronze Star with oak leaf cluster, Air medal with 59 oak leaf clusters, Army Commendation medal, Prisoner of War medal, Purple Heart with oak leaf cluster, Combat Inf. badge, Master Parachutist, Sr. Army Aviator, numerous area and campaign ribbons, fgn. decorations; recipient Silver Beaver award Boy Scouts Am., 1961, Silver Antelope award, 1969, Distinguished Eagle Scout award, 1971, Disting. Svc. award Founders and Patriots Am., 1988, Freedoms Found. at Valley Forge Hon. medal, 1992; elected Army Aviation Hall of Fame, 1986. Mem. Assn. U.S. Army, Army Aviation Assn. Am. (pres. 1974-76), 101st Airborne Divsn. Assn., 1st Cavalry Divsn. Assn., SAR (pres. Tex. Soc. 1987-88, pres. Inland Empire chpt. 1992-93, Silver Good Citizenship medal 1984, 87, Meritorious Svc. medal 1986, Patriot, Liberty and Gold Good Citizenship medals 1988), Ret. Officers Assn., West Point Soc., Mil. Order World Wars (Patrick Henry award 1986, 90, comdr. Dallas chpt. 1985-86, vice comdr. dept. ctrl. Calif. 1991-92, comdr. Inland Empire chpt. 1992-93), Nat. Gavel Soc., Nat. Order Founders and Patriots of Am. (sec.-gen. 1986-88, gov. gen. 1988-90, councillor gen. Calif. Soc. 1990-95), Soc. Descendants of Colonial Clergy, Flagon and Tchr. Soc., Soc. Colonial Wars (lt. gov. Calif. soc. 1992—, gov. 1997-98), Sons of the Revolution in State of Calif. (pres. 1993-94), Soc. War of 1812 (dist. dep. pres. gen. 1991—, v.p. Calif. soc. 1993-94, pres. 1994-95), Nat. Huguenot Soc., Soc. Sons and Daus. of Pilgrims, Order Ams. Armorial Ancestry, Soc. Descendents Founders of Hartford, Old Plymouth Colony Descendents, Mil. Order of the Loyal Legion of the U.S., Mil. Order Fgn. Wars of the U.S. (pres. Calif. Soc. 1996-97), Hereditary Order of First Families of Mass., Masons, Shriners, Sojourner, Phi Kappa Phi, Beta Gamma Sigma, Alpha Kappa Psi. Home: 21227 George Brown Ave Riverside CA 92518-2880

WRIGHT, MARY R., state park superintendent; b. Hartford, Conn., Jan. 12, 1949; d. J. William and Eileen J. (Walsh) Bigoness; m. Roy C. Gunter III, June 24, 1972 (div. Feb. 1988); m. Kenneth Ross Wright, Dec. 1, 1988. BA, Marquette U., 1970; MS, U. Mo., 1972. Prgram analyst State Calif. Dept. Health, Sacramento, 1972-76; tng. ctr. dir. State Calif. Dept. Parks and Recreation, Pacific Grove, 1976-81; visitor svcs. mgr. State Calif. Dept. Parks and Recreation, Monterey, 1981-83, Monterey dist. supr., 1983-92, dep. dir., 1992-93; Monterey dist. supt. Calif. Dept. Parks and Recreation, 1993—; hist. preservation commr. City of Monterey, 1984-92. Bd. dirs. Big Sur Health Ctr., 1993—; bd. govs. Santa Lucia Conservancy, 1995—. Office: Monterey Dist Calif State Parks 2211 Garden Rd Monterey CA 93940-5317*

WRIGHT, MICHAEL RAGSDALE, artist, educator; b. La Grande, Oreg., Jan. 26, 1944; s. Thomas Wright and Chris (Rieden) Wu; m. Jo-Ann Morgan, Aug. 14, 1993; 1 child, Marcy Jean. BFA in Painting and Drawing, U. Wash., 1970, BA in European History, 1970. Instr. Shoreline Coll., Seattle, 1969-70, Cabrillo Coll. Cmty. Edn., Santa Cruz, Calif., 1974-80, U. Calif. Extension, Santa Cruz, 1978-81, U. Calif. Kresge Coll., Santa Cruz, 1979, Foothill Coll., Los Altos Hills, Calif., 1980-81, DeAnza Coll., Cupertino, Calif., 1980-82, Santa Cruz County Cultural Coun., Santa Cruz, 1980-90, West Valley Coll., Saratoga, Calif., 1978-84, Rancho Santago Coll., Santa Ana, Calif., 1985-89, Otis Coll. Art and Design, L.A., 1986-95, Performing Tree, L.A., 1986-95, Calif. State U., L.A., 1988-94, L.A. H.S. For the Arts, 1989-95, Crossroads Sch. For the Arts and Scis., Santa Monica, 1989-95, Mt. San Antonio Coll., Walnut, Calif., 1994-95, L.A. CountyMus. Art, L.A.; bd. dirs. Downtown Artists Devel. Assn., L.A., 1995—; mem. resource com. Cultural Action Plan for Santa Cruz County, 1979; dir., curator The Gallery Santa Cruz Public Library, 1978-79; arts commr. first dist. Santa Cruz County, 1978-82; spokesperson Artists Coalition Convention Ctr. Expansion Project, 1987-88; arts specialist Santa Cruz County Cultural Coun., 1980-90; mem. bd. dirs. Artists Equity of L.A., 1989-90; mem. adv. coun. L.A. H.S. for the Arts, 1991-95; arts educator L.A. County Mus. of Art, 1988-95; gallery dir. Sam Francis Gallery Crossroads Sch. for Arts and Scis., Santa Monica, 1989-95; guest artist, vis. artist numerous orgns. One person exhbns. include First Interstate Bank, Brentwood, Calif., 1994-95, Cerro Coso Coll. Fine Arts Gallery, Ridgecrest, Calif., 1993, The Wilshire Hobart Bldg., L.A., 1992, Buena Park City Coun. Chambers Gallery, Buena Park, Calif., 1991, numerous others; group exhbns. include Curator Mus. of Contemporary Art, L.A., Downey (Calif.) Mus. Art, 1995, Mt. San Antonio Coll. Art Gallery, Walnut, Calif., 1995, Cheekwood Mus. Art, Nashville, 1994, The Conejo Valley Art Mus., Thousand Oaks, Calif., 1994, L.A. Mcpl. Art Gallery, 1994, San Francis Gallery, Crossroads Sch. for Arts & Scis., Santa Monica, 1994, Pres's. Gallery No. Aberdeen State U., S.D., 1994, Univ. Art Gallery Calif. State U., Chico, 1994, Mt. San Antonio Coll. Art Gallery, Walnut, 1994, Downtown Artists Devel. Assn., L.A., 1993, La Grand Gallery Loyola Marymount U., Joslyn Fine Arts Ctr., Torrance, Calif., 1995, Cafe, N.Y.C., 1995, L.A. Conv. Ctr., 1995, numerous others; also numerous public works, Calif.; contbr. articles to jours. in field. Recipient Cultural Affairs grant The City of L.A., 1990, Otis Parsons award Otis Art Inst. Parsons Sch. Design, 1990. Mem. Coll. Art Assn. Am., Calif. Art Edn. Assn., L.A. Mural Conservancy. Office: M Ragsdale Wright Studios 2021 S Alameda St Ste 10 Los Angeles CA 90058-1036

WRIGHT, PAUL KENNETH, mechanical engineering educator; b. Watford, Eng., Aug. 24, 1947; came to U.S., 1979; s. Kenneth Browett and Violet Anne (Woodland) W.; m. Frances June Ody, Oct. 24, 1970 (div. June 1984); children: Samuel, Joseph, Thomas; m. Terry Lee Naylor Schuster, Jan. 1, 1996; stepchildren: Jesse, Jennifer. BSc, U. Birmingham, Eng., 1968, MSc, 1970, PhD, 1971. Engr. dept. sci. and indsl. rsch. U. Auckland, New Zealand, 1972-75, sr. lectr., 1975-78; rsch. assoc. Cambridge (Eng.) U., 1978; prof. Carnegie Mellon U., Pitts., 1979-87, NYU, N.Y.C., 1987-91, U. Calif., Berkeley, 1991—; dir., prin. Berkeley (Calif.) Mfg. Group, 1991—; mem. mfg. studies bd. Nat. Rsch. Coun., Washington, 1988—, mem. com. on info. tech. mfg., 1991—. Author: Manufacturing Intelligence, 1988; contbr. articles to profl. jours. Recipient Bursary award Royal Soc., London, 1978. Mem. ASME (Blackall award 1984), N.Am. Mfg. Rsch. Inst., Am. Computing. Mem. Ch. of England. Home: 2 Hillcrest Ct Berkeley CA 94705 Office: U Calif Hearst Ave Berkeley CA 94720

WRIGHT, RICHARD OSCAR, III, pathologist, educator; b. La Junta, Colo., Aug. 9, 1944; s. Richard O. Sr. and Frances R. (Curtiss) W.; m. Bernale Trout, May 31, 1969; children: Lauren Diane, Richard O. IV. BS in Biology, Midwestern State U., 1966; MS in Biology, U. Houston, 1968; DO, U. Health Sci., 1972. Cert. anatomic pathology and lab. medicine Am. Osteo. Bd. Pathology. Sr. attending pathologist Normandy Met. Hosps., St. Louis, 1977-81; sr. attending pathologist Phoenix (Ariz.) Gen. Hosps., 1981-97, dir. med. edn., 1989-92, 96—; clin. asst. prof. pathology Coll. Osteo. Medicine, Pomona, Calif., 1985—; dir. labs., chmn. dept. John C. Lincoln Hosp., Deer Valley, 1997—; dir. med. edn., chmn. dept. pathology, dir. labs. John C. Lincoln Hosp., Deer Valley, Ariz., 1997—; clin. instr. pathology Ohio U. Coll. Osteo. Medicine, Athens, 1976-77; clin. asst. prof. pathology Kirksville (Mo.) Coll. Osteo. Medicine, 1985-87; vis. lectr. pathology New Eng. Coll. Osteo. Medicine, Biddeford, Maine, 1989-92; cons. pathologist Phoenix (Ariz.) Indian Med. Ctr., 1992-94; adv. bd. Inter Soc. Coun. Pathology, Chgo., 1992—. Active Ariz. Rep. Party, Phoenix, Rep. Nat. Coun., Washington; precinctman Dist. 18 Maricopa County, Ariz., 1996, Madison Heights Precinct, 1996; chmn. bd. trustees Phoenix (Ariz.) Gen. Hosp., 1994-95; ex-occicio, trustee, 1995-97; trustee John C. Lincoln Found., 1997—; mem. found. adv. coun. Lincoln Health Found.-Phoenix Gen. Hosp. Osteo. Endowment Fund. Recipient Mead-Johnson award Nat. Osteo. Assn., 1975. Fellow Am. Osteo. Coll. Pathologists (pres. 1989-90, bd. govs. 1984-91), Coll. Pathologists, Coll. Am. Pathologists, Am. Soc. Clin. Pathologists; mem. Ariz. Osteo. Med. Assn. (del. dist. 2 ho. of dels.), Ariz. Soc. Pathologists, Century Club Alumni Assn., AAAS, Alpha Phi Omega, Rho Sigma Chi, Psi Sigma Alpha. Presbyterian. Office: Anatomic Pathology Assoc 19829 N 27th Ave Phoenix AZ 85027-4001

WRIGHT, ROSALIE MULLER, magazine and newspaper editor; b. Newark, June 20, 1942; d. Charles and Angela (Fortunata) Muller; m. Lynn Wright, Jan. 13, 1962; children: James Anthony Meador, Geoffrey Shepard. BA in English, Temple U., 1965. Mng. editor Suburban Life mag., Orange, N.J., 1960-62; assoc. editor Phila. mag., 1962-64, mng. editor, 1969-73; founding editor Womensports mag., San Mateo, Calif., 1973-75; editor scene sect. San Francisco Examiner, 1975-77; exec. editor New West mag., San Francisco and Beverly Hills, Calif., 1977-81; features and Sunday editor San Francisco Chronicle, 1981-87, asst. mng. editor features, 1987-96; v.p. and editor-in-chief Sunset Mag, Menlo Park, Calif., 1996—; tchr. mag. writing U. Calif., Berkeley, 1975-76; participant pub. procedures course Stanford U., 1977-79; chmn. mag. judges at conf. Coun. Advancement and Support of Edn., 1980, judge, 1984. Contbr. numerous mag. articles, critiques, revs., Compton's Ency. Mem. Am. Assn. Sunday and Feature Editors (treas. 1984, sec. 1985, 1st v.p. 1986, pres. 1987), Am. Newspaper Pubs. Assn. (pub. task force on minorities in newspaper bus. 1988-89, Chronicle minority recruiter 1987-94), Internat. Women's Forum, Women's Forum West (bd. dirs. 1993—, sec. 1994), Western Pub. Assn., Am. Soc. Mag. Editors. Office: Sunset Magazine 80 Willow Rd Menlo Park CA 94025 *Keep a sharp eye out for talent, recognize it and reward it, and everyone profits.*

WRIGHT, SHARON, mayor. Mayor City of Santa Rosa, Calif. Office: 100 Santa Rosa Ave Rm 10 Santa Rosa CA 95404

WRIGHT, THEODORE OTIS, forensic engineer; b. Gillette, Wyo., Jan. 17, 1921; s. James Otis and Gladys Mary (Marquiss) W.; m. Phyllis Mae Reeves, June 21, 1942 (div. 1968); children: Mary Suzanne, Theodore Otis Jr., Barbara Joan; m. Edith Marjorie Jewett, May 22, 1968; children: Marjorie Jane, Elizabeth Carter. BSEE, U. Ill., 1951, MS in Engring., 1952; post-grad., Air Command and Staff Coll., 1956-57, UCLA, 1958. Registered profl. engr. Wash. 2d lt. U.S. Air Force, 1942-65, advanced through grades to lt. col., 1957, ret., 1965; dep. for engring. Titan SPO, USAF Sys. Command, L.A., 1957-65; rsch. engr. The Boeing Co., Seattle, 1965-81; pres. The Pretzelwich, Inc., Seattle, 1981—; cons., forensic engr. in pvt. practice Bellevue, Wash., 1988—; adj. prof. U. Wash., Greenriver Jr. Coll., both 1967-68. Contbr. articles to nat. and internat. profl. jours. Decorated Purple Heart, Air medal. Mem. NSPE (v.p. western region 1985-87), ASTM (com. E-43 metric practice 1988—), Nat. Coun. Weights and Measures, Wash. Soc. Profl. Engrs. (state pres. 1981-82, Disting. Svc. award 1980, Engr. of Yr. 1996, Columbia award 1996), U.S. Metric Assn. (life, cert. advanced metrication speciallist), Am. Nat. Metric Coun. (bd. dirs. 1978-94), Air Force Assn. (charter life, state pres. 1974-76, 90-91, Jimmy Doolittle fellow 1975), Order of Daedalians (life), Eta Kappa Nu, Pi Mu Epsilon, Tau Beta Pi. Democrat. Presbyterian. Home: 141 140th Pl NE Bellevue WA 98007-6939

WRIGHT, TIM EUGENE, packaging development executive; b. Weed, N.Mex., Oct. 13, 1943; s. Clyde Everett and Juanita Delores (Barrett) W.; m. Nancy Ann Ausenbaugh, Oct. 2, 1965 (div. 1975); 1 child, Ramsey Jordan. Diploma, Dayton Art Inst., 1967, M.F.A., U. Idaho, 1969. Designer, Lawson Mfg. Co., Troy, Idaho, 1968-70, Boise Cascade, Burley, Idaho, 1970-72; project coord. Boise Cascade, Golden, Colo., 1972-76, product devel. mgr., Wallula, Wash., 1976-84; mng. ptnr. Matrix Applications Co., Pasco, Wash., 1984—. Patentee folding carton, spacer for rolls, collapsible pallet. Recipient Silver award for packaging, 1978. Mem. Inst. Packaging Profls., Western Packaging Assn. (bd. dirs., past pres. Columbia chpt.), Soc. Plastics Engrs., TAPPI. Office: Matrix Applications Co PO Box 3668 Pasco WA 99302-3668

WROLSTAD, HELEN LOUISE, interior designer, business owner; b. Portland, Oreg., Aug. 2, 1931; d. J. Sanford and Annette (Robins) Wrolstad; m. Glen Edward Dillon, Dec. 27, 1953 (div. Apr. 1976); children: Eric Edward, Karl Douglas, Nancy Sue. BS, Oreg. State U., 1953. Tchr. Millbrae (Calif.) H.S., 1953-54, Martinez (Calif.) H.S., 1954-57, Skagit Valley Coll., Mt. Vernon, Wash., 1970; shop-at-home design cons. Meier & Frank, Portland, 1976-86; owner interior design bus. Portland, 1987—; interior designer St. Luke Luth. Ch. Bldg. Projects, 1978, 88; interior designer Home in St. of Dreams Show, Portland, 1981. Photograph printed in Marine Biology Textbook, 1971; exhibited in Creative Stitchery Profl. Art Show, 1968. Pres. AAUW, Anacortes, Wash., 1970, PTA, Anacortes, 1971; co-chmn. Sch. Bond Drive, Anacortes, 1974; Sunday Sch. Supt. Anacortes Luth. Recipient 1981 Best Kitchen award Portland St. of Dreams Homebuilders; named Woman of Distinction in Design and Architecture, Columbia River Girl Scouts Coun., 1994. Mem. Am. Soc. Interior Designers (profl. mem.), Oreg. Remodelers Assn., Portland Art Mus., Oreg. Hist. Soc. (designer Kitchen of the 90's, 1992), Sons of Norway Lodge, Bergfreunde Ski Club, Kappa Alpha Theta Alumni, Kappa Alpha Theta, Phi Kappa Phi, Omicron Nu. Lutheran.

WU, ELLEN YUNG-HUA, pharmacology research scientist; b. Georgetown, Penang, Malaysia, Apr. 15, 1961; came to U.S., 1966; d. Sinmin and Betty (Chang) W. BA, St. Olaf Coll., 1983; PhD, U. Calif., San Francisco, 1988. Rsch. scientist Calif. Inst. for Med. Rsch.-Calif. Parkinson's Found., San Jose, 1989-91; sr. toxicologist Parametrix, Inc., Kirkland, Wash., 1991-93; rsch. scientist Agouron Pharms., Inc., San Diego, 1993-96; sr. scientist Agouron Pharms. Inc., San Diego, 1996—. Co-author book chpts.: MPTP: A Neurotoxin Producing a Parkinsonian Syndrome, 1986, Progress in Catecholamine Research, Part B: Central Aspects, 1988, Zenobiotics Metabolism and Disposition: Proceedings of the 2nd International ISSX Symposium, Kobe, Japan, 1989, Molecular Basis of Neurological Disorders and their Treatment, 1991, Neurotoxins and Neurodegenerative Diseases, 1992; contbr. articles to profl. jours. NSF grad. fellow, 1984-87. Mem. Internat. Soc. for Study of Xenobiotics, Am. Assn. Pharm. Scientists, Soc. Toxicology. Democrat. Lutheran. Office: Agouron Pharms Inc 3565 General Atomics Ct San Diego CA 92121-1122

WU, HUNG-HSI, mathematician, educator; b. Hong Kong, May 25, 1940; came to U.S., 1956; s. Tsao-Chih and Mary Tsun (Ouyang) W.; m. Charlotte Lee, July 1967; m. Kuniko Weltin, Aug. 9, 1976; 1 child, Colin Weltin-Wu. AB, Columbia Coll., 1961; PhD, MIT, 1963. Rsch. assoc. MIT, Cambridge, 1963-64; mem. Inst. for Advanced Study, Princeton, N.J., 1964-65; from asst. prof. to assoc. prof. U. Calif., Berkeley, 1965-73, prof., 1973—. Author: The Bochner Technique in Differential Geometry, 1988; co-author: (with R.K. Sachs) General Relativity for Mathematicians, 1977.

WU, QINGYUN, Chinese language and literature educator; b. Zhengding, China, Aug. 28, 1950; came to U.S., 1985; d. Ming and Xuejin (Zhao) W.; m. Yulong Jin, Jan. 23, 1979 (div.); 1 child, Lin Jin. BA in English, Kaifeng (China) Normal U., 1975; Diploma in English, Ctrl. London Poly., 1978; MA in English, So. Ill. U., 1987; PhD in Comparative Lit., Pa. State U., 1991. Lectr. English Zhengzhou (China) U., 1978-85; grad. lectr. Chinese Pa. State U., State College, 1987-91, coord. for Chinese Summer Intensive Lang. Inst., 1990-91; asst. prof. Chinese Calif. State U., L.A., 1991—, dir. Chinese Studies Ctr., 1991—. Author: (novel) Clouds and Rain: A China-to-America Memoir, 1994, (criticism) Female Rule in Chinese and English Literary Utopias, 1995 (Choice Outstanding Acad. Book 1996), others; translator: (novel) Remote Country of Women, 1994. Recipient Bayard award Pa. State U., 1991, Acad. Merit prize for translation, 1986; Brit. Coun. fellow, 1976-77; Calif. State U. grantee, 1991-92, 94-95, 96—. Fellow Asian Rsch. Ctr. (Hong Kong); mem. MLA, Assn. Asian Studies, Soc. for Utopian Studies. Home: 1233 Hartview Ave La Puente CA 91744-2328 Office: Calif State U 5151 State University Dr Los Angeles CA 90032

WU, RAO-HSIEN RAY, engineering consultant; b. Tai-Chung, Taiwan, July 9, 1963; came to U.S., 1970; s. I-Chen and Hsiao-Hua (Huang) W. BSME, U. Calif., Berkeley, 1986. Frame layout designer Peterbilt Motors, Newark, Calif., 1987-89; engring. aide Lockheed Aeronautics, Burbank, Calif., 1989-90; tech. staff II Hughes Missiles, Canoga Park, Calif., 1990-91, Hughes Space and Comm., El Segundo, Calif., 1991-94; cons. Allied Signal, Torrance, Calif., 1995—. Mem. Highland Club (life), Calif. Alumni Assn. (life). Republican.

WU, ROBERT CHUNG YUNG, space sciences educator; b. Kao-hsiung, Taiwan, Republic of China, Oct. 16, 1943; came to U.S., 1969; s. Liang-Cheng and Grace (Huang) W.; m. Grace S.J. Lee, June 20, 1970; children: David, John, Michael. MS, U. Ill., 1970, PhD, 1973. Postdoctoral fellow U. Iowa, Iowa City, 1976-77; postdoctoral fellow U. So. Calif., L.A., 1973-75, rsch. scientist, 1977-78, asst. rsch. prof., 1978-88, assoc. rsch. prof., 1988-94; rsch. prof., 1995—; cons. Rockwell Internat., L.A., 1984, Jet Propulsion Lab., Pasadena, 1985, 89. Contbr. articles to Jour. Chem. Physics, Jour. Geophys. Rsch., Optical Communs., Applied Physics B, Jour. Quantitative Spectroscopy and Radiative Transfer, Jour. Planetary Space Sci. Mem. Am. Geophys. Union, Optical Soc. Am., Am. Astronomy Soc. (divsn. planetary scis.). Office: U So Calif Space Scis Ctr Los Angeles CA 90089

WU, RU-SHAN, geophysicist; b. XingYang, Henan, China, Dec. 9, 1938; came to U.S., 1993; s. Yue Ren Wu and Song Zhen Zhang; children: Xili, Hui-han. BSc in Physics, North-Western Univ., Sian, China, 1962; PhD in Geophysics, MIT, 1984. Rsch. asst. Inst. Geophysical Prospecting, Min. Geology, Peking, China, 1962-65; rsch. scientist Inst. Geophysical Prospecting, Min. Geology, Peking, 1966-77, sr. rsch. scientist, 1977-78; asst. rsch. physicist Univ. Calif., Santa Cruz, 1986, assoc. rsch. geophysicist, 1987-88, 90-95; rsch. geophysicist Inst. Tectonics, Univ. Calif., Santa Cruz, 1995—; assoc. rsch. geophysicist Inst. Geophysics, Chinese Acad. Scis., Beijing, 1988-89, rsch. geophysicist, 1989-90; vis. sci. MIT, Cambridge, 1978-80, postdoc. assoc., 1984-85; vis. sci. Nat. Rsch. Ctr. Disaster Prevention, Tsukuba, Japan, 1988-89; cons. exploration rsch. Arco Oil and Gas Co., 1988-92; vis. prof. Fed. Univ. Bahia, Salvador, Brazil, 1990-91, Karlsruhe (Germany) Univ., 1992. Guest editor Jour. Pure Applied Geophysics, 1987-88; mem. editl. bd. Acta Geophysica Sinica; contbr. over 70 articles to profl. publs. Recipient Cert. of Merit, Nat. Conf. Sci. Tech. China, 1977. Fellow Chinese Geophys. Assn.; mem. Am. Geophy. Union, Soc. Exploration Geophys., Seismol. Soc. Am., Internat. Assn. Seismology Physics Earth Interior (mem. com. heterogeneity). Office: Inst Tectonics Univ Calif Santa Cruz 1156 High St Santa Cruz CA 95064

WU, SHU-LIN SHARON, animation educator; b. Taipei, Taiwan, Nov. 22, 1961; came to U.S., 1988; d. Kuo-chu and Kuei-Yin (Wang) W.;. BE in Social Edn., Nat. Taiwan Normal U., Taipei, 1985; MA in Telecomm. and Film, San Diego State U., 1993; MFA, Calif. Inst. Arts, Valencia, 1996. Coord. animation showcase dept. telecomm. and film San Diego State U., 1993, instr. dept. telecomm. and film, 1993, lectr. dept. telecomm. and film, 1994—; instr. dept. character animation Calif. Inst. of the Arts, 1996—. Director: (animated film) The Ephemeral, 1992 (2nd prize animation, Festival Internat. de Video do Algarve, Portugal 1993, Eagle award Coun. Internat. Nontheatrical Events, Washington 1993); (16 mm films) Them, 1993, Beyond Water and Ink, 1994, Stampede, 1996; one person show at Pacific Beach, Calif., 1993. Home: 118 N Lamer St Apt D Burbank CA 91506-2330

WU-CHU, STELLA CHWENYEA, nutritionist, consultant; b. Kaohsiung, Taiwan, Sept. 22, 1952; came to U.S., 1976; d. Jin-Shoui and Sue-Tuan (Ling) Wu; children: Christine, Whitney. BS, Fu-Jen Cath. U., Taiwan, 1974; MA, San Francisco State U., 1979. Registered dietitian. Intership U. Calif., Berkeley, 1978; food svc. supr. Calif. Surgery Hosp., Oakland, 1979-80; nutritionist, cons. Solano Napa Agy. on Aging, Vallejo, Calif., 1980—; nutrition cons. Marin County Div. of Aging, San Rafael, Calif., 1981—; nutritionist San Francisco Commn. on Aging, 1990-95, nutrition cons., 1995—; nutritional advisor Veggie Life Mag., Walnut Creek, Calif., 1993, Salt Free Cooking Made Easy. Chief editor quar. publ. Taiwanese Assn. publ., 1991-94. Cmty. liaison East Bay Taiwanese Assn., Walnut Creek, 1992-93; v.p. No. Calif. Formosan Fedn., 1993; dist. supportive com. chair United Meth. Women, 1995-97, Bayview dist. social actions mission coord., 1997—. Mem. Am. Dietetic Assn., Am. Pub. Health Assn., Jacob Inst. of Women's Health, Nat. Assn. Nutrition and Aging Svcs., Formosan Assn. for Pub. Affairs. Home: 6400 Christie Ave # 1312 Emeryville CA 94608 Office: San Francisco Commn Aging 25 Van Ness Ave Ste 650 San Francisco CA 94102-6033

WUDL, FRED, chemistry educator; b. Cochabamba, Bolivia, Jan. 8, 1941; came to U.S., 1958; s. Robert and Bertha (Schorr) W.; m. Linda Raimondo, Sept. 2, 1967. BS, UCLA, 1964, PhD, 1967. Postdoctoral rsch. fellow Harvard U., 1967-68; asst. prof. dept. chemistry SUNY, Buffalo, 1968-72; mem. tech. staff AT&T Bell Labs., Murray Hill, N.J., 1972-82; prof. chemistry and materials U. Calif., Santa Barbara, 1982—. Recipient arthur C. Cope scholar award Am. Chem. Soc., 1993, Award for Chemistry of Materials, 1996, Natta medal Italian Chem. Soc., 1994, Wheland medal U. Chgo., 1994. Fellow AAAS. Office: U Calif Dept Chemistry Santa Barbara CA 93106

WULFSON, MICHELLE ELISE, artist; b. Boston, Apr. 3, 1972; d. Howard David and Carol Alexandra (Gordon) W. BFA, Syracuse U., 1993. Asst. art dept. Walt Disney Pictures, Burbank, Calif., 1992; comic book colorist Electric Crayon, Santa Monica, Calif., 1994-96, Motown Comics, L.A., 1996; graphics designer 20th Century Fox Newscorp Internet, L.A., 1995-96; graphics cons. Pacific Bell Interactive Media, Pasadena, Calif., 1996; comic book colorist Scholastic Books, N.Y.C., 1996—.

WUNDERMAN-COOPER, RUTH ANN, mortgage loan broker; b. Camden, N.J., Nov. 1, 1952; d. Abraham Abad Perez and Santina Maria (Fanara) Wunderman; m. Steven Mark Gottlieb, Nov. 29, 1981 (div. June 1986); children: Gregory Steven Gottlieb, Randall Douglas Gottlieb; m. Donald Edward Cooper, June 6, 1987; children: Santina Nicole Cooper, Alexander James Cooper. AA in Gen. Studies, L.A. Pierce Coll., 1974; BS in Bus. Adminstrn., Calif. State U., 1977. Lic. real estate mortgage broker Calif. Comml. loan officer Union Bank, L.A., 1977-78; life and disability agent Northwestern Mut. Life Ins. Co., Woodland Hills, Calif., 1978-81; pension design & adminstrn. Integrated Resources, Encino, Calif., 1981-82; exec. v.p. venture capital Densmore Devel. Corp., Encino, 1982-88; CFO, prin. East Coast Health Orgn., Balt., 1986-87; first rate fin., 1992-94; real estate loan cons. Five Star Fin., Inc., Westlake Village, Calif., 1993-95; mortgage broker, owner The Mortgage Source, Westlake Village, 1995—. Adv. coun. bd. Conejo Valley Unifed Sch. Dist. 1994—, PTA vol., 1993, scholarship selection com., classroom vol., 1993—; Career Day Spkr., 1995, Fund Run participant, 1994-95, mem. at large adv. bd.-exec. bd., 1997—; Think Day chair Brownie Troop #509, 1995, 96; 1st v.p. Friends of Thousand Oaks Libr., 1995—, pres., 1997—; founder, Friends of the Thousand Oaks Book Endowment Fund, 1995, chaired Afternoon Tea in the Libr., 1996, Xochimok program, 1996, membership v.p., 1993-95, Rabbit Tales newsletter editor, 1990-93, Conejo Valley Days Strawberry Shortcake Booth chair, 1991, various other coms.; chair youth groups Thousand Oaks Libr. Restoration Com.; mentor Colina & Sequoia Mid. Schs., 1994; AVID program mentor Redwood, 1996. Recipient Spl. Vol. Salute award United Way. Mem. Calif. Assn. Mortgage Brokers, Assn. Profl. Mortgage Women, AAUW (Thousand Oaks br., v.p. legal advocacy fund 1997—, br. treas. 1994—, edn. found. v.p. 1993-94, market scrip fund-raising chair 1992-93, children's theatre vol. 1994, creative options vol. 1992-96, Mathews Mgmt. forum 1995-96, math./sci. conf. presenter 1995, 96, summer youth cultural program 1995, 96, women's history project 1995-96, Named Gift Honoree award 1995). Office: The Mortgage Source 2659 Townsgate Rd Ste 101 Westlake Village CA 91361-2797

WURM, CHARLES RICHARD, environmentalist; b. San Francisco, May 5, 1954; s. James Francis and Lois Melba (Carpenter) W.; m. Teh-Jung Yang, Nov. 13, 1993. Hazardous materials mgmt., U. Calif. Santa Cruz, 1992, health and safety, 1993, advanced. environ. mgmt., 1996; environ. studies, Chadwick U., 1996. Registered environ. assessor. Engr. Monolithic Memories, 1980-84; equipment engr. Amdahl Corp., 1984-85; sys. engr. The Semi Group, 1985-87; equipment specialist Siliconix Corp., 1987-88; equipment specialist, environ. mgr. Orbit Semiconductor, Inc., 1988—. Author: A Collection of Short Stories, 1989, American Dream, 1993. Mem. Am. Chem. Soc., Nat. Safety Coun., Toastmasters Internat. Home: 25515 Soquel San Jose Rd Los Gatos CA 95030

WYATT, BRETT MICHAEL, secondary school educator; b. Toledo, Dec. 31, 1958; s. Warren Dale and Jacqueline Elizabeth (Angelides) W.; m. Nancy Elizabeth Colby, June 19, 1993; 1 child, Adrian. BA in Geography, Calif. State U., San Bernardino, 1981; MA in Geography, U. Calif., Davis, 1985. Elem. tchr. Sacramento City Unified Sch. Dist., 1987-89, tech. resource tchr., 1989-91; ednl. cons. IBM, Sacramento, 1989-92; asst. editor Computers in the Schs., Reno, Nev., 1991-93; computer tchr. Washoe County Schs., Reno, 1993—. Author: Jewish Settlement in Sacramento, 1987; prodr.: (video) Sacramento Educational Cable Consortium, 1991, 92; contbr. articles to profl. jours. Advisor Tech. Preparation Com., Sacramento, 1991; founding dir. Nev. Schs. Network, Reno, 1992; advisor WCSD Internet Task Force, Reno, 1994—; archivist Temple B'hai Israel, Sacramento, 1986-87; computer technician vol. Ptnrs. in Edn., Sparks, Nev., 1994—. Named Vol. of the Yr., Ptnrs. in Edn., Sparks, 1995; recipient award for outstanding ednl. video Sacramento Ednl. Cable Consortium, 1991, 92. Democrat. Home: 3077 Coverdale Dr Sparks NV 89434

WYATT, EDITH ELIZABETH, elementary education educator; b. San Diego, Aug. 13, 1914; d. Jesse Wellington and Elizabeth (Fultz) Carne; m. Lee Ora Wyatt, Mar. 30, 1947 (dec. Jan. 1966); children: Glenn Stanley (dec.), David Allen. BA, San Diego State U., 1936. Elem. tchr. Nat. Sch. Dist., National City, Calif., 1938-76. Sec. San Diego County Parks Soc., 1986—; librarian Congl. Ch. Women's Fellowship, Chula Vista, Calif., 1980—; active Boy Scouts Am, 1959—. Recipient Who award San Diego County Tchrs. Assn., 1968, Silver Fawn award Boy Scouts Am. Mem. AAUW (sec. 1978-80, pub. rels. 1985—), Calif. Ret. Tchrs. Assn. (scholarship com. 1985-90, 92-95, treas. South Shores divsn. 1996—), Starlite Hiking Club (sec.-treas. 1979—). Home: 165 E Millan St Chula Vista CA 91910-6255

WYATT, PERICLES, food service executive; b. London, Aug. 22, 1963; came to U.S., 1981; s. Woodrow Lyle Wyatt and Moorea (Hastings) Black. Mgr. restaurant Guard House, Gladwyne, Pa., 1988-92, Monterey (Calif.) Plz. Hotel, 1992-94; owner restaurant Crossroads Cafe, Carmel, Calif., 1994-96, Wyatt's Steakhouse, Prunedale, Calif., 1995—. Named Best Bus. in Prunedale, C. of C., 1995, Best Restaurant North Monterey County, 1997. Office: Wyatt's Steakhouse 17870 Moro Rd Prunedale CA 93907

WYATT, SUSAN MELINDA CLOUGH, career counselor, human resource development specialist; b. Ft. Worth, Feb. 6, 1943; d. Forrest Weldon and Mildred (Wyatt) Clough; m. David W. McClintock, Dec. 29, 1968 (div. Mar. 1987); children: Lesley Karen, Nathan Crane. BA in Polit. Sci., Whittier Coll., 1965; MA in Lit., Sci., and Arts, U. Mich., 1966; MAT in Secondary Edn., Antioch-Putney Grad. Sch. Edn., 1968; PhD in Human Resource Devel. and Counseling, Columbia Pacific U., 1992. Nat. cert. counselor, nat. cert. career counselor. Research asst. U. Mich., Ann Arbor, 1969-70; fgn. service sec., researcher U.S. Dept. State, Sanaa, Yemen, Washington, 1966-68, 70-72; English tchr. U. Jordan, Amman, 1972-74; cons. various orgns. Washington, 1974-78; personnel officer U.S. Dept. State, Washington, 1978-82; pvt. practice cons., trainer Rome, Ga., 1982-84; dir. career services The Women's Ctr., Raleigh, N.C., 1985-86; dir. edn. Hospice of N.C., Raleigh, 1986; placement counselor N.C. State U., Raleigh, 1987-92; group therapist Duke Alcoholism and Addictions Program, 1992-93; pvt. practice, Raleigh, Albuquerque ,1985—; career mgmt. cons. Rights Assocs., 1991—. Recipient Mentor of Distinction award Women in Bus. Adv. Coun., 1988; Woodrow Wilson vis. fellow, 1978-82, Nathaniel Hill Rsch. award, Am. Soc. Tng. and Devel., 1990, Career Devel. Assn., New Mex. Southwest Writers Assn., Human Resource Mgmt. Assn. Mem. Am. Counseling Assn. Democrat.

WYCKOFF, J. B., international economic development consultant; b. Russell, Kans., Sept. 21, 1932; s. Christian Cornelius and Frances Naomi (Bratton) W.; m. Winnefred Lee Johnson, June 12, 1955; children: Gary Reid, Lori Jean, Douglas Kent. AA, Taft (Calif.) Jr. Coll., 1951; BS, Oreg. State U., 1953, MS, 1957; PhD, Wash. State U., 1963. Asst. prof. agrl. econs. Wash. State U., Pullman, 1957-63; mktg. mgr. Am. Sheep Prodrs. Coun., Denver, 1963-64; assoc. prof. agrl. econs., head dept. U. Nev., Reno, 1964-66; prof., head dept. U. Mass., Amherst, 1966-71, U. Hawaii, Honolulu, 1986-88; prof., ext. coord. Oreg. State U., Corvallis, 1971-83; project assoc. Harvard U. Inst. Internat. Devel., Cambridge, Mass., 1982-86; internat. econ. devel. cons., Sun City West, Ariz., 1988—; co-dir. food sec. rsch. project So. Africa Devel. Commn., Mich. State U., Harare, Zimbabwe, 1990-92. Editor 6 books, including Food Security in Southern Africa; contbr. over 150 articles on applied econs. to profl. jours. Bd. dirs. Western Maricopa Coalition, Glendale, Ariz., 1995—; mem. water com. Property Owners and Residents Assn., Sun City West, 1996—; mem. adv. bd. Gov.'s N.W. Valley Water Resources. With U.S. Army, 1953-55. Rsch. grantee USDA, Malhenn County Oreg., Pierce County, Wash.. Consortium for Internat. Devel., among others, 1958-81, Office Water Res. Res., 1964-81, Resources for Future, 1968-69. Mem. Am. Agrl. Econs. Assn. (bd. dirs.), Am. Water Resources Assn. (charter), Internat. Assn. Agrl. Econs. (chmn. U.S. coun. 1979-82), Internat. Agrl. Trade Rsch. Consortium, Western Agrl. Econs. Assn. (vice chmn., editor 1966-67), Northeastern Agrl. Econs. Coun. (chmn. 1969-70). Home and Office: 13406 W Stardust Blvd Sun City West AZ 85375

WYCOFF, CHARLES COLEMAN, retired anesthesiologist; b. Glazier, Tex., Sept. 2, 1918; s. James Garfield and Ada Sharpe (Braden) W.; m. Gene Marie Henry, May 16, 1942; children: Michelle, Geoffrey, Brian, Roger, Daniel, Norman, Irene, Teresa. AB, U. Calif., Berkeley, 1941; MD, U. Calif., San Francisco, 1943. Diplomate Am. Bd. Anesthesiology. Founder The Wycoff Group of Anesthesiology, San Francisco, 1947-53; chief of anesthesia St. Joseph's Hosp., San Francisco, 1947-52, organizer residency tng. program in anesthesiology, 1950; organizer residency tng. program in anesthesiology San Francisco County Hosp., 1954, chief anesthesia, 1953-54; practice anesthesiology, tchr. Presbyn. Med. Ctr., N.Y.C., 1955-63; asst. prof. anesthesiology Columbia U., N.Y.C., 1955-63; clin. practice anesthesiology St. Francis Meml. Hosp., San Francisco, 1963-84. Producer, dir. films on regional anesthesia; contbr. articles to sci. jours. Scoutmaster Boy Scouts Am., San Francisco, 1953-55. Capt. M.C., U.S. Army, 1945-47. Mem. Alumni Faculty Assn. Sch. Medicine U. Calif.-San Francisco (councilor-at-large 1979-80). Democrat. Home: 394 Cross St Napa CA 94559-3840

WYCOFF, ROBERT E., petroleum company executive; b. Tulsa, 1930; married. B.S.M.E., Stanford U., 1952, M.S.M.E., 1953. With Atlantic Richfield Co., L.A., 1953—, various engring. and mgmt. positions, 1957-70, mgr. western region Internat. div., 1971-73, v.p., resident mgr. Alaska region N.Am. Producing div., 1973-74, corp. planning v.p., 1974-77, sr. v.p. planning and fin., 1977-80, exec. v.p., 1980-84, chief corp. officer, 1984, vice chmn., 1985, pres. emeritus, 1986-93, also dir.; chmn. Lyondell Petrochem. Co., Houston. Mem. ASME, Am. Petroleum Inst. Office: Atlantic Richfield Co PO Box 2579 515 S Flower St Los Angeles CA 90071*

WYDEN, RON, senator; b. Wichita, Kans., May 3, 1949; s. Peter and Edith W.; m. Laurie Oseran, Sept. 5, 1978; 1 child, Adam David. Student, U. Santa Barbara, 1967-69; A.B. with distinction, Stanford U., 1971; J.D., U. Oreg., 1974. Campaign aide Senator Wayne Morse, 1972, 74; co-founder, co-dir. Oreg. Gray Panthers, 1974-80; dir. Oreg. Legal Services for Elderly, 1977-79; instr. gerontology U. Oreg., 1976, U. Portland, 1980, Portland State U., 1979; mem. 97th-104th Congresses from 3d Oreg. dist., Washington, D.C., 1981-96; U.S. Senator from Oreg., 1996—. Recipient Service to Oreg. Consumers award Oreg. Consumers League, 1978, Citizen of Yr. award Oreg. Assn. Social Workers, 1979, Significant Service award Multnomah County Area Agy. on Aging, 1980; named Young Man of Yr. Oreg. Jr. C. of C., 1980. Mem. Am. Bar Assn., Iowa Bar Assn. Democrat. Jewish. Office: 259 Russell Senate Bldg Washington DC 20510

WYDICK, JUDITH BRANDLI JAMES, volunteer; b. Eldon, Mo., Aug. 14, 1937; d. William Bruce and Helen Bertha (Wiemer) James; m. Richard Crews Wydick, Aug. 26, 1961; children: William Bruce, Derrick Cameron. Student, Univ. Colo., 1955-57; BS in Edn., Univ. Mo., 1959, MA in Eng., 1960. Cert. secondary tchr., Mo., Calif. Tchr. English Oakland (Calif.) Tech. H.S., 1960-61, Awalt H.S., Mountain View, Calif., 1961-62. Author: Preparing for College, 1982-89, Mad Capers, 1993-94. Organizer Univ. Farm Circle, Davis, Calif., 1972-77, 83, pres. 1976-77; pres., organizer Lawyers Wives Yolo County, Davis, 1973-75; pres., bd. dirs. Pence Art Gallery, Davis, 1979-81; pres., chair adv. coun. Jr. H.S. PTA, Davis, 1980-82; co-chair fundraising Yolo County Mental Health Assn., Davis, 1981; organizer Davis H.S. Madrigal Choir, 1983-85, pres. PTA, 1984-85; full-time organizer Internat. House-Davis, 1981—, pres., 1985-87, 89-91, bd. dirs., 1984-94; mem. Calif. State Bd. Food and Agr., 1992-94. Recipient Madrigal Parent award Davis H.S., 1985, PTA Honorary Svc. award, 1985; named Citizen of Yr., City of Davis, 1986. Episcopalian. Home: 2620 Corona Dr Davis CA 95616

WYLE, EWART HERBERT, clergyman; b. London, Sept. 12, 1904; s. Edwin and Alice Louise (Durman) W.; B.A., U. Louisville, 1930; B.D., Lexington Theol. Sem., 1933; postgrad. Louisville Presbyn. Theol. Sem., Temple U., 1933-35; D.D., Tex. Christian U., 1953; m. Prudence Harper, June 12, 1959; 1 son, Ewart Herbert. Ordained to ministry Christian Ch., 1935; pastor First Ch., Palestine, Tex., 1935-37, First Ch., Birmingham, Ala., 1937-41, First Ch., Tyler, Tex., 1944-54, Country Club Ch., Kansas City, Mo., 1954-59; minister Torrey Pines Ch., La Jolla, Calif., 1959-79, minister emeritus, 1979—. Bd. dirs. Scripps Meml. Hosp., pres., 1980-81. Served as chaplain, maj., AUS, 1941-44. Mem. Mil. Order World Wars, Am. Legion, Tau Kappa Epsilon, Pi Kappa Delta. Clubs: Masons (32 deg.), Shriners, Rotary, LaJolla Beach and Tennis. Home: 8850 N La Jolla Scenic Dr La Jolla CA 92037-1608

WYLE, FREDERICK S., lawyer; b. Berlin, Germany, May 9, 1928; came to U.S., 1939, naturalized, 1944; s. Norbert and Malwina (Mauer) W.; m. Katinka Franz, June 29, 1969; children: Susan Kim, Christopher Anthony, Katherine Anne. B.A. magna cum laude, Harvard U., 1951, LL.B., 1954. Bar: Mass. 1954, Calif. 1955, N.Y. 1958. Teaching fellow Harvard Law Sch., 1954-55; law clk. U.S. Dist. Ct., No. Dist. Calif., 1955-57; assoc. firm Paul, Weiss, Rifkind, Wharton & Garrison, N.Y.C., 1957-58; pvt. practice San Francisco, 1958-62; spl. asst. def. rep. U.S. del. to NATO, Paris, 1962-63; mem. Policy Planning Council, Dept. State, Washington, 1963-65; dep. asst. sec. def. for European and NATO affairs Dept. Def., Washington, 1966-69; v.p. devel., gen. counsel Schroders, Inc., N.Y.C., 1969-71; atty., cons. Schroders, Inc., 1971-72; chief exec. officer Saturday Rev. Industries, Inc., San Francisco, 1972-76; individual practice law San Francisco, 1976—; internat. counsel to Fed. States Micronesia, 1974-82; cons. Rand Corp., Dept. of Def., Nuclear Regulatory Commn.; trustee in bankruptcy, receiver various corps since 1974. Contbr. to: Ency. Brit, 1972, also articles in profl. publs., newspapers. Served with AUS, 1946-47. Mem. World Affairs Coun., Internat. Inst. Strategic Studies, Phi Beta Kappa. Office: 28th Flr 3 Embarcadero Ctr San Francisco CA 94111-4066

WYLIE, KAREN ELIZABETH, local government official; b. Midway Island, Hawaii, Dec. 20, 1965; d. Gary Owen and Judith Ann (Stevens) Sauer; m. Steven Ware Wylie, June 26, 1993. BA in Sports Sci., U. Denver, 1986; MPA, San Diego State U., 1987. Adminstrv., adminstrv. svcs. City of Coronado, Calif., 1988-89; mgmt. analyst City Mgr.'s Office City of Carlsbad, Calif., 1989-91; mgmt. analyst Housing & Redevel. Dept. City of Carlsbad, Calif., 1991-93; adminstrv. analyst comml. devel. City of Burbank, Calif., 1993, adminstrv. officer comml. devel., 1993—. Mem. Mcpl. Mgmt. Assts. So. Calif. (bd. dirs., regional chair 1991-92, regional liaison 1992-93, v.p. 1993-94), Internat. City Mgrs. Assn., League Calif. Cities (employee rels. policy com. 1994-95, housing, cmty. and econ. devel. policy com. 1995-96). Home: 710 E Fairmount Rd Burbank CA 91501-1712 Office: City of Burbank 275 E Olive Ave Burbank CA 91502

WYLIE, RICHARD THORNTON, aerospace engineer; b. Long Beach, Calif., July 11, 1956; s. Howard Hance and Marcella Dart (Metcalf) W. BS, Calif. State Poly. U., Pomona, 1978; MS, U. Calif., Berkeley, 1979. Registered profl. engr., Calif. Engr. Aerocraft Heat Treating, Paramount, Calif., 1991-94, TRW, Inc., Redondo Beach, Calif., 1980-91, 94—. Vol. tutor TRW Bootstrap, 1981—. Mem. Mensa (scholarship chmn. Harbor area 1995—). Home: 1005 Kornblum Ave Torrance CA 90503

WYLLIE, PETER JOHN, geologist, educator; b. London, Feb. 8, 1930; came to U.S., 1961; s. George William and Beatrice Gladys (Weaver) W.; m. Frances Rosemary Blair, June 9, 1956; children: Andrew, Elizabeth (dec.), Lisa, John. B.Sc. in Geology and Physics, U. St. Andrews, Scotland, 1952, B.Sc. with 1st class honours in Geology, 1955, Ph.D. in Geology, 1958, D.Sc. (hon.), 1974. Glaciologist Brit. W. Greenland Expdn., 1950; geologist Brit. N. Greenland Expdn., 1952-54; asst. lectr. geology U. St. Andrews, 1955-56; research asst. geochemistry Pa. State U., State College, 1956-58, asst. prof. geochemistry, 1958-59, asso. prof. petrology, 1961-65, acting head, dept. geochemistry mineralogy, 1962-63; research fellow chemistry Leeds (Eng.) U., 1959-60, lectr. exptl. petrology, 1960-61; prof. petrology geochemistry U. Chgo., 1965-77, Homer J. Livingston prof., 1978-83, chmn. dept. geophys. scis., 1979-82, master phys. scis. collegiate div., asso. dean coll., asso. dean phys. scis. div., 1972-73; chmn. div. geol. and planetary scis. Calif. Inst. Tech., Pasadena, 1983-87, prof. geology, 1987—; chmn. commn. exptl. petrology high pressures temperatures Internat. Union Geol. Scis.; mem. adv. panel earth scis. NSF, 1975-78, chmn. adv. com. earth scis. div., 1979-82; mem. U.S. Nat. Com. on Geology, 1978-82; mem. U.S. Nat. Com. Internat. Union Geodesy and Geophysics, 1980-84, U.S. Nat. Com. Geochemistry, 1981-84; chmn. com. on objectives in solid-earth scis. NRC, 1988-93; hon. prof. China U. Geoscis., Beijing, 1996. Author: The Dynamic Earth, 1971, The Way the Earth Works, 1976; editor: Ultramafic and Related Rocks, 1967; chmn. editorial & writing com. Solid-Earth Sciences and Society, 1993; editor Jour. Geology, 1967-83; editor-in-chief Minerals Rocks (monograph series), 1967—. Served with RAF, 1948-49. Heavyweight boxing champion RAF Scotland, 1949; recipient Polar medal H.M. Queen Elizabeth, Eng., 1954; Quantrell award, 1979; Wollaston medal Geol. Soc. London, 1982, Abraham-Gottlob-Werner-Medaille German Mineral. Soc., 1987. Fellow Am. Acad. Arts and Sci., Royal Soc. London, Edinburgh Geol. Soc. (corr.), Mineral Soc. Am. (pres. 1977-78, award 1965), Am. Acad. Scis. (fgn. assoc.), Am. Geophys. Union, Indian Geophys. Union (fgn.), Nat. Acad. Sci. India (fgn.), Russian Acad. Scis. (fgn.), Russian Mineral. Soc. (fgn., hon.), Indian Nat. Sci. Acad. (fgn.), Academia Europaea (fgn.), Geol. Soc. Am.; mem. Mineral. Soc. Gt. Britain and Ireland (hon.), Internat. Mineral Assn. (2d v.p. 1978-82, 1st v.p. 1982-86, pres. 1986-90), Internat. Union of Geodesy and Geophysics (v.p. 1991-95, pres. 1995-99), Chinese Acad. Scis. (fgn. mem.). Office: Calif Inst Tech Geol Planetary Scis 17 # 25 Pasadena CA 91125

WYMAN, MAX MCDONALD, real estate broker, spatial technologies scientist; b. Hutchinson, Kans., July 19, 1957; parents Donald Max and Betty (Petrie) W. BS in Astronautics, USAF Acad., 1979; MS in Bldg. Design, Ariz. State U., 1991, PhD in Econ. Geography, 1994. Pilot USAF, 1979-86; broker Wyman Real Estate, Tempe, Ariz., 1986—; scientist Ariz. State U., Tempe, 1994—; cons. Local Tech. Assistance Program, Idaho, Ariz., Wash., 1995-96. Contbr. articles to profl. jours. Capt. USAF, 1975-86. Office: Ariz State U PO Box 876306 Tempe AZ 85287-6306

WYNAR, BOHDAN STEPHEN, librarian, author, editor; b. Lviv, Ukraine, Sept. 7, 1926; came to U.S., 1950, naturalized, 1957; s. John I. and Euphrosina (Doryk) W.; m. Olha Yarema, Nov. 23, 1992; children: Taras, Michael, Roxolana, Yarynka. Diplom-Volkswirt Econs., U. Munich, Germany, 1949, Ph.D., 1950; M.A., U. Denver, 1958. Methods analyst, statistician Tramco Corp., Cleve., 1951-53; freelance journalist Societ Econs., Cleve., 1954-56; adminstrv. asst. U. Denver Librs., 1958-59, head tech. svcs. div., 1959-62; assoc. prof. Sch. Librarianship, U. Denver, 1962-66; dir. div. libr. edn. State U. Coll., Geneseo, N.Y., 1966-67; dean Sch. Libr. Sci. State U. Coll., Geneseo; prof. State U. Coll., 1967-69; pres. Libraries Unlimited Inc., 1969—. Author: Soviet Light Industry, 1956, Economic Colonialism, 1958, Ukrainian Industry, 1964, Introduction to Bibliography and Reference Work, 4th edit, 1967, Introduction to Cataloging and Classification, 8th edit, 1992, Major Writings on Soviet Economy, 1966, Library Acquisitions, 2d edit, 1971, Research Methods in Library Science, 1971, Economic Thought in Kievan Rus', 1974; co-author: Comprehensive Bibliography of Cataloging and Classification, 2 vols., 1973, Ukraine: A Bibliographic Guide to English Language Publications, 1990; editor Ukrainian Quar., 1953-58, Preliminary Checklist of Colorado Bibliography, 1963, Studies in Librarianship, 1963-66, Research Studies in Library Science, 1970—, Best Reference Books, 3d edit., 1985, 4th edit., 1992, Colorado Bibliography, 1980; gen. editor: American Reference Books Ann., 1969—; editor: ARBA Guide to Subject Encyclopedias and Dictionaries, 1985, ARBA Guide To Biographical Dictionaries, Reference Books in Paperback, An Annotated Guide, 2d edit., 1976, 3rd edit., 1991, Dictionary of Am. Library Biography, 1978, Ukraine-A Bibliographic Guide to English-Language Publications, 1990, International Writings of Bohdan S. Wynar 1949-1992, 1993, Recommended Reference Books for Medium-Sized and Small Libraries, 1981—; co-editor, contbr. Ency. Ukraine, 1955—;editor Library Sci. Ann., 1984-90. Bd. dirs., mem. exec. bd. ZAREVO, Inc. Mem. ALA (pres. Ukrainian Congress com. br., Denver 1976), Colo. Library Assn., N.Y. Library Assn., Am. Assn. Advancement Slavic Studies (pres. Ukrainian Research Found. 1976-90), AAUP, Ukranian Hist. Assn. (exec. bd.), Sevčenko Societe Scientifique (Paris), Ukrainian Acad. Arts and Scis. (N.Y.C.). Office: Librs Unltd Inc 6931 S Yosemite St Englewood CO 80112-1415

WYNKOOP-GREEN, DEBRA RENEE, health facility administrator; b. Sacramento, July 10, 1955; d. Daniel Woodbury and Edna Mae (Brammer) Wynkoop; m. Wayne Barnes, Dec. 18, 1975 (div. Oct. 1985); children: Patrick Barnes, Brett Barnes; m. David Jack Green, Nov. 15, 1986 (dec. Jan. 1997); stepchildren: Jeff Green, Rebecca Green, Karen Green. BS in Recreation Edn., Brigham Young U., 1975; MPA, U. Utah, 1990. Lic. therapeutic recreational specialist, Utah. Asst. mgr. Knight Adjustment Bur., Provo, Utah, 1974-76; recreational therapist Phillips Nursing Home, Provo, 1976-77; recreational therapist Utah State Tng. Sch., American Fork, Utah, 1977-82, qualified mental retardation profl., 1982-89; OBRA coord. Divsn. Svcs. for People with Disabilities, Salt Lake City, 1989-90; dir. planning and program devel. Utah Dept. Human Svcs., Salt Lake City, 1990-92; dir. Bur. Health Facility Licensure Utah Dept. Health, Salt Lake City, 1992—; mem. adv. bd. U. Utah, Salt Lake City, 1994—. Fellow Am. Assn. Mental Retardation (consulting editor 1994-98, bd. mem.-at-large 1994-96, spkr. pro-tem 1992-93, Cert. Appreciation 1994); mem. Nat. Assn. Regulatory Adminstrs., Assn. Health Survey Agys., Utah Pub. Health Assn. (conf. planning com. 1994—). Home: 2785 E Commonwealth Ave Salt Lake City UT 84109 Office: Utah State Dept Health Box 142853 Salt Lake City UT 84114-2853

WYNN, ROBERT E., retired career officer, electronics executive; b. Dallas, Jan. 31, 1942; s. Wendell W. and Thelma (Smart) W.; m. Lavenia K. Davis, Mar. 25, 1972; children: Leslie, Lauren. Bachelors degree, West Point, 1964; MEE, U. Tenn., 1971. Commd. 2d lt. U.S. Army, 1964, advanced through grades to commdg. gen., 1990; chief comm. Ops. Divsn. 5th Signal Command, Heidelberg, Germany, 1979-81; chief of staff 5th Signal Command, Worms, Germany, 1984-85; chief plans and programs, dep. chief staff Ops. and Plans DCS for OPS and PLANS, Washington, 1981-84; comdr. 2d Signal Brigade, Mannheim, Germany, 1986-88, U.S. Army Info. Systems Command/Tng. Doctrine Command, Ft. Monroe, Va., 1988-90; commdg. gen. 7th Signal Command, Ft. Ritchie, Md., 1990-92, U.S. Army Info. Systems Engring. Command, Ft. Huachuca, Ariz., 1992—; ret., 1995; mgr. C3 sys. Raytheon E-Systems Inc., Richardson, Tex., 1995—. Decorated Bronze Star, Legion of Merit, Silver Order of Mercury. Mem. Assn. U.S. Army Assn. Grads. (life), Armed Forces Comm. and Electronics Assn. (life, bd. dirs.), Sky Soldier (life, 173d airborne brigade), Signal Corps Regiment (life). Home: 703 Laredo Cir Allen TX 75002-5444

WYNN, ROBERT RAYMOND, engineer, consultant; b. Omaha, Mar. 4, 1929; s. Horace Oscar and Yvonne Cecil (Witters) W.; m. Joann Elizabeth Swicegood, June 28, 1974; children: Kay, William, Frederick, Andrew, Emma, Lawrence, Robert. Diploma in Nuclear Engring., Capitol Radio Engring. Inst., 1964; BSEE, Pacific Internat. Coll. Arts and Scis., 1964; AA in Bus. Adminstrn., Allen Hancock Coll., 1969; MSEE, Pacific Internat. Coll. Arts and Scis., 1971; MSMS, West Coast U., 1975, ASCS, 1985; BSCS, U. State of N.Y., 1985. Registered profl. engr., Calif. Meteorologist United Air Lines, Calif., 1949-53; engring. planner Aircraft Tools Inc., Inglewood, Calif., 1953-55; field service engr. N. Am. Aviation, Inglewood, Calif., 1955-59; R&D engr. Carstedt Research Inc., N. Long Beach, Calif., 1959-60; test engr. Martin Marrietta Corp., Vandenburg AFB, Calif., 1960-64; project engr. Fed. Electric Corp., Vandenburg AFB, Calif., 1965-69; systems engr. Aeronutronic Ford Corp., Pasadena, Calif., 1970-75; MTS Jet Propulsion Lab., Pasadena, Calif., 1975-83; engring. mgr. Space Com., Redondo Beach, Calif., 1983-84; engring. specialist Boeing Service Inc., Pasadena, 1984-86; cons., mem. tech. staff Jet Propulsion Lab., Pasadena, 1986—; instr. computer sci. and CAD, Jet Propulsion Lab., 1980-82. With USAAF, 1946. Mem. Calif. Soc. Profl. Engrs., Exptl. Aircraft Assn. (pres. Lompoc chpt. 1968), W. Coast U. Alumni Assn. Democrat. Home: PO Box 26316 Prescott Valley AZ 86312-6316 Office: Jet Propulsion Lab 4800 Oak Grove Dr Pasadena CA 91109-8001

WYNNE, LESLEY BIRD, computer engineer; b. Rome, N.Y., Nov. 10, 1963; d. Richard Andrew and Suzanne (Van Auken) Bird; m. John Marshall Wynne, Sept. 20, 1996. BSEE, U. of the Pacific, Stockton, Calif., 1986; MSEE, U. Calif., Santa Barbara, 1990. Student engr. IBM Corp., San Jose, Calif., 1984-85; electronic design engr. Delco Electronics, Goleta, Calif., 1986-90; computer engr. Apple Computer, Cupertino, Calif., 1990—. Scholarship Soc. Women Engrs., 1984. Mem. IEEE, Eta Kappa Mu. Home: 1088 W Remington Dr Sunnyvale CA 94087 Office: Apple Computer 20705 Valley Green Dr Cupertino CA 95014-1703

WYSS, JUDITH ANN, artist; b. Spokane, Wash., Jan. 19, 1938; d. Maurice Landon and Catherine Evangeline (Deemy) Thomson; m. Loren L. Wyss, June 9, 1962; children: Emily Alison, Jennifer Ann, Isabel Jean, Edmund John. BA in English, San Francisco State U., 1961; BFA in Drawing, Mus. Art Sch., Portland, Oreg., 1981. Mem. Inkling Printmaking Studio, Portland, 1982-86, Blackfish Co-operative Gallery, Portland, 1992—, Graystone Gallery, Portland, 1984-92, Troy Co-operative Studios, Portland, 1981—. Exhibited in Oreg., Wash., and Eng. Past pres. and sec. Cmty. Music Ctr., Portland, 1975—, Alumni and Friends of PNCA, Portland, 1982-94; mem. bd. govs. Pacific Northwest Coll. of Art, Portland, 1993—; mem. awards/fellowships Adv. Coun. Literary Arts, 1991—; bd. dirs. Burdock/Burn Art Resource; sec., v.p. Wyss Found. Award for Best Unbuilt Chair, Table, Lamp & Chair, Portland, 1988; participant-juried show Oreg. Biennial/Portland Art Mus., 1985. Mem. Artists' Equity, Met. Art's Com. Per-Cent for Art Coms., Tri-Met Art (adv. com. 1993—), Oreg. Cello Soc. Democrat. Presbyterian. Home: 3028 SE Crystal Springs Blvd Portland OR 97202-8561 Office: Troy Studios 221 SE 11th Ave Portland OR 97214-1355

XANTHEAS, SOTIRIS STAVROS, chemist, researcher; b. Athens, Greece, June 20, 1961; came to U.S., 1984; s. Stavros S. and Effie (Beneas) X.; m. Maria A. Hadjos, July 7, 1990; 1 child, Effie. Diploma in chem. engring., Nat. Tech. U. of Athens, 1984; PhD in Phys. Chemistry, Iowa State U., 1990. Nat. coll. and univ. assn. for sci. postdoctoral fellow Pacific N.W. Lab., U.S. Dept. Energy, Richland, Wash., 1990-92; sr. rsch. scientist Batelle Pacific N.W. Nat. Lab., Richland, 1992—. Contbr. articles to sci. jours. Sci. and Rsch. scholar Austrian Fed. Ministry, 1984. Mem. Am. Chem. Soc., Am. Phys. Soc., Alpha Chi Sigma. Christian Orthodox. Office: Molecular Sci Rsch Ctr PO Box 999 Richland WA 99352

XIONG, JEAN Z., artist, consultant; b. Beijing, China, Nov. 1, 1953; came to U.S., 1983.; d. Xian-Li and Zhang Yao (Zhu) Xiong; m. Charles C. Feng, Apr. 12, 1989. Grad., Shu Zhou (China) Inst., 1977; MFA, Acad Art Coll., San Francisco, 1986. Freelance artist/instr. Beijing, 1978-81; design artist First Impressions Advt., Reno, 1986; computer artist Visual Dynamics, San Francisco, 1988-89, Mediagenic, Menlo Park, 1989-91; leader artist Tecmagik Inc., Redwood City, Calif., 1992-94; computer artist Electronic Arts, San Mateo, Calif., 1995—; cons. entertainment software devel., Calif., 1991-92, 94-95; artist Electronic Arts, San Mateo, 1995—. One-woman shows San Francisco, 1984, 85, Monterey, Calif., 1984; exhbns. in Hong Kong, China, 1979, 80, 81. Recipient prize of Excellence Nat. Youth Artist Assn., 1980, Artist Assn., Hong Kong, 1981; scholar Acad. Art Coll., 1983-86. Mem. Mus. Modern Art, Tradtional Chinese Inst. (Beijing). Office: 2000 De Anza Blvd San Mateo CA 94402-3915

YACK, PATRICK ASHLEY, editor; b. Little Rock, Oct. 25, 1951; s. Leo Patrick and Sarah Ann (Dew) Y.; m. Susan Marie Courtney, June 7, 1980; children: Alexander Ryan, Kendall Elizabeth. BFA, So. Meth. U., 1974. Staff asst. U.S. Rep. Alan Steelman, Washington, 1975-76; press aide U.S. Senator Charles Percy, Chgo., 1977-78; reporter Fla. Times-Union, Jacksonville, 1979-80; regional reporter Fla. Times-Union, Atlanta, 1981-82; reporter The Denver Post, 1983-85, Washington bur. chief, 1985-87; nat. editor Atlanta Constitution, 1987-89; mng. editor The Register-Guard, Eugene, Oreg., 1989-94; editor News & Record, Greensboro, N.C., 1994—. Mem. Am. Soc. Newspaper Editors, AP Mng. Editors Assn.

YACOB, YOSEF, lawyer, economist; b. Dire Dawa, Harar, Ethiopia, Nov. 12, 1947; s. Yacob and Egziaraya (Osman) Zanios; m. Betsy Ann Boynton; children: Sarah Ann, Matthew Yosef, Ezra Yosef, Jarred Yosef, Rachel Helen. BA, Linfield Coll., 1971; JD, Lewis and ClarkU., 1974. Bar: Oreg. 1975, U.S. Dist. Ct. Oreg. 1979, U.S. Ct. Appeals (9th cir.) 1980. Rschr. criminal justice State of Oreg., Salem, 1974, sr. administrv. analyst, 1974-76; adjudications specialist, legal counsel, law enforcement coun. Office of the Gov. State of Oregon, Salem, 1976-78; chief administrv. law judge State of Oregon, Milwaukie, 1978-83, dir. hearings, appeals, 1982-84; mng. atty. Hyatt Legal Services, Clakamas, Oreg., 1984-86; pres., sr. ptnr. Yacob & Assocs. P.C., Clackamas, 1986-93; dir. gen. for legal affairs, gen. counsel Ministry of Fgn. Affairs, Govt. of Ethiopia, 1993—. Co-author: Evaluation of Multowmah County District Attorney's High Impact Project, 1978. Home: 6885 SW Montgomery Way Wilsonville OR 97070-6739 Office: Yacob & Assocs PC Northwest Legal Svcs 6885 SW Montgomery Way Wilsonville OR 97070-6739

YAFFE, JAMES, author; b. Chgo., Mar. 31, 1927; s. Samuel and Florence (Scheinman) Y.; m. Elaine Gordon, Mar. 1, 1964; children: Deborah Ann, Rebecca Elizabeth, Gideon Daniel. Grad., Fieldston Sch., 1944; B.A. summa cum laude, Yale U., 1948. Prof. Colo. Coll., Colo. Springs, 1968—; dir. gen. studies Colo. Coll., 1981—. Author: Poor Cousin Evelyn, 1951, The Good-for-Nothing, 1953, What's the Big Hurry?, 1954, Nothing But the Night, 1959, Mister Margolies, 1962, Nobody Does You Any Favors, 1966, The American Jews, 1968, The Voyage of the Franz Joseph, 1970, So Sue Me!, 1972, Saul and Morris, Worlds Apart, 1982, A Nice Murder for Mom, 1988, Mom Meets Her Maker, 1990, Mom Doth Murder Sleep, 1991, Mom Among the Liars, 1992, My Mother the Detective, 1997; play The Deadly Game, 1960, (with Jerome Weidman) Ivory Tower, 1967, Cliffhanger, 1985; also TV plays, stories, essays, revs. Served with USNR, 1945-46. Recipient Nat. Arts Found award, 1968. Mem. P.E.N., Authors League, Writers Guild of Am., Dramatists Guild, A.A.U.P., Mystery Writers of Am., Phi Beta Kappa. Jewish. Club: Elizabethan (Yale). Address: 1215 N Cascade Ave Colorado Springs CO 80903-2303 Office: Colo Coll Off Dir Gen Studies Colorado Springs CO 80903

YAGER, JOEL, psychiatry educator; b. Bronx, N.Y., June 27, 1941; s. Edward and Natalie (Schwartzman) Y.; m. Eileen Danies, Oct. 8, 1964; children: Jonathan Eric, Alison Rachel. BS, CCNY, 1961; MD, Albert Einstein Coll. Medicine, 1965. Diplomate Am. Bd. Psychiatry and Neurology. Asst. prof. psychiatry U. Calif., San Diego, 1971-73; asst. prof. psychiatry U. Calif., L.A., 1988-95, assoc. prof. psychiatry, 1988-95, prof., 1988—, prof. emeritus, 1995—; prof. psychiatry, vice chair edn. U. N.Mex., Albuquerque, 1995—; assoc. chair for edn. dept. psychiatry West L.A. VA, 1973-91, U. Calif. Neuropsychiat. Inst., L.A., 1991-95. Editor: Teaching Psychiatry and Behavioral Science, 1982, The Future of Psychiatry as a Medical Specialty, 1989, Special Problems in Managing Eating Disorders, 1991. Maj. U.S. Army, 1969-71. Recipient Joseph B. Goldberger award in clin. nutrition AMA, 1989, ANAD award Nat. Assn. for Anorexia Nervosa and Related Disorders, 1991. Fellow Am. Psychiat. Assn. (chair coun. on med. edn. and career devel. 1988-89, Vestermark award 1996), Am. Assn. Dirs. Psychiat. Residency Tng. (pres. 1979-80). Office: U N Mex Dept Psychiatry 2400 Tucker NE Albuquerque NM 87131-5326

YAKE, WILLIAM ELLSWORTH, environmental scientist, poet; b. Spokane, Wash., Mar. 9, 1947; s. William Albert and Barbara (Ellsworth) Y. BS in Zoology, Wash. State U., Pullman, 1969, MS in Environ. Sci., 1972, MS in Environ. Engring., 1977. Investigator Spokane County Air Pollution Control Authority, Spokane, 1973-77; head ambient and compliance monitoring sect. Wash. State Dept. Ecology, Olympia, 1977-87, head toxics investigation sect., 1987-93, sr. scientist, 1993—; mem. Puget Sound Rsch. Coun., 1986-89; mem. Lake Roosevelt Sci. Adv. Bd., 1992-95. Author: Confluence, 1995; sponsor, designer Wash. State Pesticide Monitoring Program, 1990. Bd. dirs., treas. Olympia Poetry Network, 1993—, Olympia Zen Ctr., 1995-96. Mem. Wash. Poets Assn., Phi Beta Kappa. Home: 4032 Green Cove St NW Olympia WA 98502 Office: Wash State Dept Ecology Box 47760 Olympia WA 98504

YAKICH, DAVID ELI, international sales executive; b. Denver, May 31, 1957; s. Eli and Josephine (Goodnough) Y. Jr.; m. Carrie Elizabeth. BS, Colo. State U., 1979; postgrad., U. Minn., 1980-82; BA, U. Colo., 1984. Geophys. tech. Amoco Prodn. Corp., Denver, 1980-81; cons. geophycist Lear Petroleum, Denver, 1982-84; computer svc. mgr. Daniel Geophys., Denver, 1984-87; nat. sales mgr. Graphics Info. Inc., Denver, 1987-89; area mgr. Far East Auto-trol Tech., Denver, 1989-91; v.p. sales and support GeoGraphix Inc., Denver, 1991; dir. internat. sales Visual Numerics Inc., 1992-93; Japan mktg. mgr. Xilinx, Inc., Boulder, Colo., 1994—; computer cons. Daniel Geophysical, Denver, 1983. Mem. Soc. Exploration Geophysics, Denver C. of C. Republican. Roman Catholic. *Personal philosphy: Success is founded in your attitude. Remain positive and you can succeed.*

YALAM, ARNOLD ROBERT, allergist, immunologist, consultant; b. N.Y.C., Apr. 1, 1940; s. Herman and Sylvia (Taber) Y.; m. Carol Ann Strocker, June 16, 1964; children: John, Matthew. AB, Johns Hopkins U., 1960; MD, U. Md., Balt., 1964. Diplomate Am. Bd. Internal Medicine, Am. Bd. Allergy and Immunology. Intern Jackson Meml. Hosp., Miami, Fla., 1964-65; resident in internal medicine SUNY Downstate Med. Ctr., Bklyn., 1965-67; fellow Scripps Clinic and Rsch. Found., La Jolla, Calif., 1967-68; cons. allergist and immunologist San Diego, 1970—. Maj. US Army, 1968-70. Fellow Am. Acad. Allergy and Immunoloy; mem. Am. Soc. Addiction Medicine (cert.), San Diego Allergy Soc. Office: 8929 University Center Ln San Diego CA 92122-1006

YAMADA, STEPHEN KINICHI, lawyer, real estate developer; b. Honolulu, July 19, 1946; s. Harold Kiyoshi and Frances Sadako (Uchida) Y.; m. Amy M. Chiemi, Apr. 23, 1965 (div.); 1 child, Tammy Lynn; m. Kwi Nam Kim, Nov. 18, 1984. BA, U. Hawaii, 1968; JD, U. Calif., San Francisco, 1971. Bar: Hawaii 1972, U.S. Dist. Ct. Hawaii 1972, U.S. Ct. Appeals (9th cir.) 1992; lic. real estate broker. Dep. atty. gen. State of Hawaii, Honolulu, 1971-74; pvt. practice law Honolulu, 1974—, pvt. practice real estate, 1975—; real estate developer, 1996; instr. Chaminade U., Honolulu, 1975, owner Sky Sch. Real Estate, Honolulu, 1976. Mem. exploring com. Boy Scouts Am., Honolulu, 1974; second vice chmn. 7th Dem. Dist., Honolulu, 1978. Fellow Hawaii Trial Lawyers Assn.; mem. ABA, Assn. Trial Lawyers Am., Hawaii Jaycees (state legal counsel 1976), Rotary. Democrat. Office: 820 Mililani St Ste 700 Honolulu HI 96813-2937

YAMADA, TOMOKIYO TOM, advertising executive; b. Seattle, May 8, 1924; s. Toyojiro and Toku (Fukumoto) Y.; m. Miye Yamagishi, June 5, 1948; children: Mark, Ann Ellen, Grant. B in Design, U. Mich., 1950. Cert. tchr., Mich. Art dir. J. Walter Thompson, Detroit, 1950-53, San Francisco, 1954-60; art group supr. J. Walter Thompson, N.Y.C., 1960-65; v.p., creative dir. J. Walter Thompson, Tokyo, 1965-74; v.p., sr. art dir. J. Walter Thompson, N.Y.C., 1974-77; sr. v.p., design dir. J. Walter Thompson, San Francisco, 1978-91; exec. dir. world identity program J. Walter Thompson, San Francisco, N.Y.C., 1990-91; creative cons. Compass Group, Oakland, Calif., 1991—; instr. Golden Gate Coll., San Francisco, 1957. Contbr.: Designing Education in Values, 1958, Japan's Market and Foreign Business, 1971. Cons. Med. Edn. for South African Blacks, Washington, 1989-93, Japanese Am. Soc. East Bay, 1987-92. Recipient Silver award Clio, 1977, Andy award Advt. Club N.Y., 1982; named Best of Show San Francisco Ad Club, 1981. Mem. Oakland Asian Cultural Ctr., Oakland Art Mus., Berkeley Hist. Soc. Office: Compass Group 801 Franklin St Apt 603 Oakland CA 94607-4233

YAMAGATA, LESLIE CRAIG, realty specialist; b. Sacramento, Calif., Aug. 15, 1961; s. Mitsuru and Dorothy Tsuyumi (Toyota) Y. BA in History magna cum laude, San Diego State U., 1984; postgrad., Calif. State U., Sacramento, 1983-86. Exec. intern State of Calif., Sacramento, 1979; asst. field coach, 1980; life ins. analyst CalFarm Life Ins. Co., Sacramento, 1988-90, life/annuity specialist, 1989-90; contract specialist intern Gen. Svcs. Adminstrn., San Francisco, 1990-92, contract specialist, 1993-96, contracting officer, 1993-96. Mem. Japanese-Am. Citizens League, San Francisco, 1990, Very Spl. Arts Calif., 1991, Commonwealth Club San Francisco, 1992, World Affairs Coun., 1996, Federal Asian Pacific Am. Coun., 1997. Mem. Am. Mgmt. Assn., Nat. Contract Mgmt. Assn. (cert. assoc. contracts mgr., cert. profl. contracts mgr.), Fed. Mgrs. Assn., Nat. Forensic League, Profl. Mgrs. Assn., San Diego State U. Alumni Assn., Phi Alpha Theta, Phi Beta Kappa.

YAMAGUCHI, MICHAEL JOSEPH, prosecutor. Bar: Calif. 1978. U.S. atty. U.S. Dept. Justice, San Francisco, 1980—. Office: US Attys Office Box 36055 450 Golden Gate Ave San Francisco CA 94102*

YAMAKAWA, DAVID KIYOSHI, JR., lawyer; b. San Francisco, Jan. 25, 1936; s. David Kiyoshi and Shizu (Negishi) Y. BS, U. Calif., Berkeley, 1958, JD, 1963. Bar: Calif. 1964, U.S. Supreme Ct. 1970. Prin. Law Offices of David K. Yamakawa Jr., San Francisco, 1964—; dep. dir. Cmty. Action Agy., San Francisco, 1968-69; dir. City Demonstration Agy., San Francisco, 1969-70; mem. adv. coun. Calif. Senate Subcom. on the Disabled, 1982-83, Ctr. for Mental Health Svcs., Substance Abuse and Mental Health Svcs. Adminstrn. U.S. Dept. Health and Human Svcs., 1995—; chmn. cmty. residential treatment system adv. com. Calif. Dept. Mental Health, 1980-85, San Francisco Human Rights Commn., 1977-80; pres. Legal Assistance to the Elderly, 1981-83; 2d v.p. Nat. Conf. Social Welfare, 1983—; v.p. Region IX, Nat. Mental Health Assn., 1981-83; vice-chmn. Mt. Zion Hosp. and Med. Ctr., 1986-88; bd. dirs. United Neighborhood Ctrs. of Am., 1977-83, ARC Bay Area, 1988-91, Goldman Inst. on Aging, 1993—, v.p., 1994-96, vice-chmn., 1996—; bd. trustees Mt. Zion Med. Ctr., U. Calif., San Francisco, 1993—; chmn. bd. trustees United Way Bay Area, 1983-85; chief fin. officer Action for Nature, Inc., 1987—; v.p. Friends of Legal Assistance to the Elderly, 1984—; bd. dirs. Ind. Sector, 1986-92, Friends of the San Francisco Human Rights Commn., 1980—, CFO, 1980-85, vice chmn., 1985-94, CFO, 1994—, La Madre de los Pobres, 1982—, v.p., 1994—, Nat. Concilio Am., 1987—, Legal Coun., 1996—, Hispanic Community Found. of the Bay Area, 1989—, legal coun., 1989—; bd. dirs. Non-Profit Svcs., Inc., 1987—, sec., 1987-90, chmn., 1990—; pres. Coun. Internat. Programs, San Francisco, 1987-89, pres. Internat. Inst. of San Francisco, 1990-93; mem. citizens adv. com. San Francisco Hotel Tax Fund Grants for the Arts Program, 1991—. Recipient John B. Williams Outstanding Planning and Agy. Rels. vol. award United Way of the Bay Area, 1980, Mortimer Fleishhacker Jr. Outstanding Vol. award United Way, 1985, Spl. Recognition award Legal Assistance to the Elderly, 1983, Commendation award Bd. Suprs. City and County of San Francisco, 1983, cert. Honor, 1985, San Francisco Found. award, 1985, 1st Mental Health Awareness award Mental Health Assn. San Francisco, 1990; David Yamakawa Day proclaimed in San Francisco, 1985. Mem. ABA (Liberty Bell award 1986). Office: 582 Market St Ste 410 San Francisco CA 94104-5305

YAMAMOTO, AARON I., film editor; b. Lihue, Hawaii, Oct. 27, 1965; s. George and Lily (Hamamura) Y. BA, U. So. Calif., 1989, MA, 1996. Asst. film editor PGFW Prodns., Hollywood, Calif., 1993-94, Disney Prodns., Burbank, Calif., 1995, Universal/MCA Studios, Universal City, Calif., 1996-97; editl. cons. U. So. Calif. Sch. Cinema and TV, L.A., 1995-96; pres. Silversword Entertainment, L.A., 1994—. Asst. editor: (post-prodn. film) No Easy Way, 1994, Tom and Huck, 1995, Dragonheart, 1996, Daylight, 1996, Kull The Conqueror, 1997. Recipient Student Acad. award Acad. Motion Picture Arts and Scis., 1989. Mem. Editor's Guild (local 776).

YAMAMOTO, MICHAEL TORU, journalist; b. San Francisco, July 9, 1960; s. Harry Naoto and Noriko (Yoshitomi) Y.; m. Marianne Chin, Oct. 9, 1993. BA Psychology, San Francisco State U., 1981, BA Journalism, 1981. Editor San Francisco State U. Phoenix, 1980; news editor Hayward (Calif.) Daily Rev., 1979-80, Long Beach (Calif.) Press-Telegram, 1981; nat. desk editor L.A. Times, 1981-85; night news editor L.A. Times, Washington, 1986-87, investigative projects editor, 1988; dep. city editor San Francisco Chronicle, 1989-92, exec. projects editor, 1993, city editor, 1993-95; mng. editor news CNET, San Francisco, 1996—; adj. prof. Am. U., Washington, 1987, Calif. State U. at Northridge, Calif., 1984-85; vis. faculty mem. Am. Press Inst., Reston, Va., 1994, Poynter Inst. for Media Studies, St. Petersburg, Fla., 1995, San Francisco Unified Sch. Dist., 1994; fellow Coro Found., San Francisco, 1990-91. Recipient Dow Jones Newspaper Fund scholarship, Princeton, N.J., 1980. Mem. Asian Am. Journalism Assn., White House Corr. Assn., Soc. Profl. Journalists., World Affairs Coun. Office: CNET 150 Chestnut St San Francisco CA 94111

YAMANI, ELAINE REIKO, computer-peripheral company executive; b. Ogden, Utah, Apr. 2, 1945; d. Joe and Chieko (Kato) Yamani; m. Victor G. Sugihara, Aug. 10, 1970 (div. June 1973); 1 dau., Jo Ann Renae. B.S. in English and Psychology, Weber State U., 1965, A.A., 1967; M in Human Resource Mgmt., U. Utah, 1975-79. Personnel generalist Weber State U., Odgen, Utah, 1973-78; personnel specialist Cutter Lab., Ogden, 1978-81; human resource mgr. Iomega, Ogden, 1981-83, compensation and benefits mgr., 1983-85; dir. human resources Cericor Inc., 1983; personnel mgr., Hewlett-Packard, 1983—. Mem. Utah Personnel Assn. (pres. 1988), No. Utah Personnel Assn. (pres. 1980-81).

YAMAOKA, SEIGEN HARUO, bishop; b. Fresno, Calif., Aug. 21, 1934; s. Haruichi and Rika (Ogawa) Y.; m. Shigeko Masuyama, Apr. 3, 1966; children—Jennifer Sae, Stacy Emi. B.A., Calif. State U.-Fresno, 1956; M.A., Ryukoku U., Kyoto, Japan, 1961; M.R.E., Pacific Sch. Religion, Berkeley, Calif., 1969, D.Min., 1979. Ordained to ministry Buddhist Chs. Am., 1961. Minister Oakland Buddhist Ch., Calif., 1964-71; registrar Inst. Buddhist Studies, Berkeley, 1969-71, lectr., mem. Curriculum com., 1969-81, pres., 1981—; minister Stockton Buddhist Temple, Calif., 1971-81; treas. No. Calif. Radio Ministry, 1975-76; cons. ethnic studies Stockton Unifed Sch. Dist., 1974-76; chmn. Buddhist Chs. Am. Ministers Assn., 1979-81; bishop Buddhist Chs. Am., San Francisco, 1981-97; resident min. Oakland Buddhist Ch., 1997—; English sec. Ministerial Assn., 1972-75; assoc. in doctrinal studies Hokyo, Kyoto, 1974; mem. Bd. Buddhist Edn., 1975; vice chmn. No. Calif. Ministers Assn., 1976; mem. rsch. com. Buddhist Chs. Am., San Francisco, 1970-79; trustee Numata Ctr. for Buddhist Translation and Research, Buddhist Dharma Kyokai Soc. of Am. Author: Compassion in Encounter, 1970, Teaching and Practice Jodo Shinshu, 1974, Jodo Shinshu: Religion of Human Experience, 1976, Meditation-Gut-Enlightenment... Way of Hara, 1976, Awakening of Gratitude in Dying, 1978; editor, advisor, writer: Dharma School Teachers Guide, 1979. World advisor Thanksgiving Sq., Dallas; eccleseastical endorsing agt. for Buddhists chaplains Dept. of Def. Mem. Japan Karate Fedn., Shinshu Acad. Soc., San Francisco-Japanese Am. Citizens League, Calif. State U.-Fresno Alumni Assn., Pacific Sch. Religion Alumni Assn., Internat. Assn. Shin Buddhist Studies, Internat. Translation Ctr. Kyoto, Hongwanji Bishops Council Kyoto. Home: 14981 Portofino Cir San Leandro CA 94578-1872 Office: Oakland Buddhist Ch 825 Jackson St Oakland CA 94607-4723

YAMASHITA, FRANCIS ISAMI, judge; b. Hilo, Hawaii, May 14, 1949; s. Yuji and Sadako (Hirayama) Y.; m. Alexa D. M. Fujise, Feb. 26, 1983. BA, Pacific U., 1971; JD, U. Chgo., 1974. Bar: Hawaii 1974. Law clk. 1st Cir. Ct., Hawaii, 1975-76; dep. pros. atty. City/County of Honolulu, 1976-79, 82-87; assoc. Ikazaki, Devens, Lo, Youth & Nakano, Honolulu, 1979-82; dist. judge State of Hawaii, Honolulu, 1987-92, U.S. magistrate judge, 1992—. Office: US Dist Ct of Hawaii Box 50122 300 Ala Moana Blvd Honolulu HI 96850

YAMASHITA, JOHN HIROSHI, engineer; b. Tachikawa, Japan, Dec. 9, 1958; s. Saburo and Ruth Nobuko (Tokuhisa) Y. B of Mech. Engring., U. Wash., 1980. Engr., stress analysis Boeing Comml. Airplane Co., Seattle, 1981-88. Republican. Presbyterian.

YAN, CHONG CHAO, pharmacology, toxicology and nutrition researcher; b. Qing Jiang, Jiangsu, China, Oct. 16, 1963; came to the U.S., 1993; s. Mao Liang Yan and Gui Ying Ding; m. Yun Sun, July 28, 1988; 1 child, Jenny. BSc, Nanjing (China) Med. Coll., 1985; MS, Chinese Acad. Preventive Med., Beijing, 1988, MD/PhD, 1992. Rsch. fellow dept. metabolism and pathol. biochemistry Inst. Superiore di Sanità, Rome, 1990-92; rsch. fellow dept. gastroenterology U. Modena, Italy, 1992-93; rsch. assoc. dept. pharmacology U. Ariz., Tucson, 1993-95, asst. sci. investigator dept. pharmacology, 1995—; rschr. Chinese Acad. Preventive Medicine, Beijing, 1985-90; rschr. Nutrition Inst. Internat., Inc., 1996—; dir. Nutrition Inst. Internat., Inc., 1996—. Contbr. articles to profl. jours. Mem. Internat. Soc. Toxinology, Soc. Exptl. Biology and Medicine, Soc. Toxicology. Office: Univ Ariz Dept Pharmacology Tucson AZ 85724-1969

YAN, PEI-YANG, electrical engineer; b. Tianjin, People's Republic of China, July 18, 1957; came to U.S., 1981; d. Zhi-Da and De-Qiu (Yu) Y.; m. Xiao-Chun Mu, June 2, 1984; children: Wendy Mu, Kevin Mu. MS in Physics, Wayne State U., 1983; PhD in Elec. Engring., Pa. State U., 1988. Sr. staff engr. Intel Corp., Santa Clara, Calif., 1988—. Cotnbr. articles to profl. jours. including, Phys. Rev., IEEE Jour. Quantum Electronics, Jour. Optical Soc. Am., Optical Engring., and Jour. Photopolymer Sci. and Tech. Mem. Internat. Soc. Optical Engring., Optical Soc. Am. Office: Intel Corp PO Box 58119 Santa Clara CA 95052-8119

YAN, QIAO, neurobiologist; b. Shanghai, People's Republic of China, Dec. 20, 1955; came to U.S., 1983; s. Weinian and Ji Chang (Xia) Y.; m. Lilian Huacong Jiang, July 14, 1985; children: Heather H., Iris H., Johathan H. BSc, Fudan U., Shanghai, China, 1982; PhD, Washington U., St. Louis, 1989. Postdoctoral fellow in devel. biology Genentech, Inc., San Francisco, 1989-90; rsch. scientist I dept. neurobiology Amgen, Inc., Thousand Oaks, Calif., 1990-93, rsch. scientist II dept. neurobiology, 1993—; vis. scientist dept. of CNS rsch. FIDIA Rsch. Labs., Pardova, Italy, 1989. Contbr. chpts. to books and articles to profl. jours. Olin Med. fellow Washington U., 1987. Mem. Soc. for Neurosci., Internat. Brain Rsch. Orgn. Home: 1840 Marview Dr Thousand Oaks CA 91362-1846 Office: Amgen Inc 1840 De Havilland Dr Thousand Oaks CA 91320-1701

YANDELL, GEORGE WILSON, physician, psychiatrist; b. Greenwood, Miss., Mar. 30, 1924; s. George Wilson Sr. and Beatrice (Parsons) Y.; m. Margaret Ann King, Sept. 24, 1950; children: Brian Stuart, Lynn, Paul Reid, George W. III, Bruce Parsons. BA, U. Calif., Berkeley, 1943; MD, U. Rochester, 1947. Diplomate Am. Bd. Psychiatry and Neurology, Psychiatry and Child Psychiatry. Intern Evanston (Ill.) Hosp. Assn., 1947-48; rotating resident Seaside Meml. Hosp., Long Beach, Calif., 1948-49; resident in psychiatry Fairfield State Hosp., Newtown, Conn., 1953-54, Phila. Gen. Hosp., 1954-55; NIMH fellow in child psychiatry Langley Porter Psychiat. Inst., U. Calif. Med. Ctr., San Francisco, 1955-57; asst. clin. prof., supervising psychiatrist children's svc. U. Calif., San Francisco, 1957-68; lectr., asst. rsch. educator U. Calif., Berkeley, 1968-82; sr. psychiatrist Calif. Med. Facility Dept. of Corrections, Vacaville, Calif., 1981-83; pvt. practice psychiatry Orinda, Calif., 1957-93; ret.; psychiat. cons. Adolescent Treatment Ctrs., Inc., Oakland, Calif., 1992—. Contbr. articles to profl. jours. Pres., Orinda, Lafayette, Moraga Coun. Civic Unity, Contra Costa County, Calif., 1964-65. With USPHS, 1951-53. Fellow Am. Psychiat. Assn. (life), Am. Orthopsychiat. Assn. (life), Am. Acad. Child and Adolescent Psychiatry (life); mem. Calif. Med. Assn., Alameda-Contra Costa Med. Assn., No. Calif. Psychiat. Soc. (chmn. awards com. 1983-88), East Bay Psychiat. Assn. (pres. 1982-83), No. Calif. Regional Orgn. Child and Adolescent Psychiatry.

YANG, ANAND ALAN, history educator; b. Shantineketan, India, Jan. 12, 1949; came to U.S., 1966; s. Yun Yuan and Heng (Lo) Y. BA, Swarthmore Coll., 1970; PhD, U. Va., 1976. Instr. Sweet Briar (Va.) Coll., 1975; asst. prof. U. Utah, Salt Lake City, 1975-81, assoc. prof., 1981-92, prof., 1992—, chair dept. history, 1989-94. Author: The Limited Raj, 1989; editor: Crime and Criminality in British India, 1986; editor Jour. Asian Studies, 1995—. Mem. nat. bd. Reportory Dance Theater, Salt Lake City, 1985—; bd. dirs. Chinese Cmty Action, Salt Lake City, 1977—, Asian Assn. Utah, Salt Lake City, 1980-82, Wimmer & Wimmer Dance Co., Salt Lake City, 1979-80. Fulbright Hays scholar, 1994—; Travel to Collections grantee NEH, 1990, Bernadotte E. Schmitt grantee, Am. Hist. Assn., 1988-89; ACLS/SSRC grantee, 1985. Mem. Am. Hist. Assn. (profl. divsn. 1991-93, program com. 1986-87, 94-95), Assn. Asian Studies (asst. editor 1993-94, bd. dirs. 1991-92, 95—, coun. confs. 1989-92), World History Assn., Phi Alpha Theta. Office: U Utah Dept History 211 Carlson Hall Salt Lake City UT 84112-1127

YANG, DAVID CHIE-HWA, business administration educator; b. Taiwan, Republic of China, Nov. 7, 1954; came to U.S., 1977; s. Wen-Shen and Chin-Huei (Lee) Y. BA, Nat. Taiwan U., Taipei, 1977; MBA, U. Calif., Berkeley, 1979; PhD, Columbia U., 1985. Prof., faculty dir. China-focused MBA program U. Hawaii, Honolulu, 1985—; rsch. assoc. Acctg. Rsch. Ctr. Grad. Sch. Bus. Columbia U., N.Y.C., 1981-84; vis. prof. Beijing (People's Republic of China) Inst. Chem. Engring. Mgmt., 1988-89; cons. to China Nat. Chem. Constrn. Corp., 1990, 91, CIEC CPAs, Shanghai Acad. Social Scis. CPAs, China; past tchr. Peking U., Nat. Taiwan U. Author: Modern Western Financial Management, 1992, The Association Between SFAS 33 Information and Bond Ratings, 1985; co-author: FASB Statement 33 Data Bank Users Manual, 1985, FASB Statement 36 Data Bank Users Manual, 1985. Recipient Title VI Grant U.S. Dept. Edn., 1987, curriculum devel. grant Coopers S. Lybrand Found, N.Y.C., 1987, ednl. improvement fund award U. Hawaii, 1987. Mem. Inst. Mgmt. Accts., Am. Acctg. Assn., Inst. of Internal Auditors, EDP Auditors Assn., Chinese Acctg. Profs. Assn. N.Am. (pres.-elect), Inst. Mgmt. Accts. (v.p. Hawaii chpt.), Beta Gamma Sigma, Beta Alpha Psi (Outstanding Prof. 1989, 91, 92, Dennis Ching 1st Interstate Bank Meml. Teaching award 1993). Office: U Hawaii Coll Bus Adminstrn 2404 Maile Way Honolulu HI 96822

YANG, HENRY CHANG-LIEN, oncology educator, physician; b. Shanghai, China, Oct. 7, 1947; came to U.S., 1955; s. Li-Ching and Ling-Ta (Ling) Y. BA, Johns Hopkins U., 1968; MD, U. Pa., 1972; MTS, Boston U., 1983. Diplomate Am. Bd. Internal Medicine, Hematology, Med. Oncology. Asst. prof. Medicine U. Mass., Worcester, 1975-78, Tufts U., Boston, 1978-83; vis. lectr. in Pharmacology Harvard Med. Sch., Dana-Farber Cancer Inst., Boston, 1984-86; asst. prof. Medicine UCLA, 1986-92, assoc. prof. Medicine, 1992—; dir. outpatient oncology svcs. Harbor Med. Ctr. UCLA, Torrance, Calif., 1992—; dir. hemophilia rsch. lab. Meml. Hosp., Worcester, 1975-78; med. dir. South Cove Cmty. Health Ctr., Boston, 1978-82; mem. adv. com. Boston Area Health Edn. Ctr., Boston, 1979-80, adv. com. on health promotion Med. Found., Boston, 1980-82; cons. in med. oncology Magan Med. Clinic, Covina, Calif., 1991—. Contbr. articles to profl. jours. Vol. physician Sage Meml. Hosp., Ganado, Ariz., 1976; participant Mini-White House Conf. on the Asian-Am. Elderly, 1981; mem. Citizens Rev. com. United Way, Boston, 1984-86; bd. dirs. Pacific-Ackworth Sch. Found., Temple City, Calif., 1989-91. Johns Hopkins U. scholar, 1964-68. Fellow ACP; mem. Am. Soc. Clin. Oncology, Phi Beta Kappa. Home: 1618 Harper Ave Redondo Beach CA 90278-2725 Office: Divsn Med Oncology Harbor UCLA Med Ctr 1000 W Carson St Torrance CA 90502-2004

YANG, HENRY T., university chancellor, educator; b. Chungking, China, Nov. 29, 1940; s. Chen Pei and Wei Gen Yang; m. Dilling Tsui, Sept. 2, 1966; children: Maria, Martha. BSCE, Nat. Taiwan U., 1962; MSCE, W.Va. U., 1965; PhD, Cornell U., 1968; D honoris causa, Purdue U., 1996. Rsch. engr. Gilbert Assocs., Reading, Pa., 1968-69; asst. prof. Sch. Aeros. and Astronautics, Purdue U., West Lafayette, Ind., 1969-72, assoc. prof., 1972-76, prof., 1976-94, Neil A. Armstrong Disting. prof., 1988-94, sch. head, 1979-84; dean engring. Purdue U., 1984-94; chancellor U. Calif., Santa Barbara, 1994—; mem. sci. adv. bd. USAF, 1985-89; mem. aero. adv. com. NASA, 1985-89; mem. engring. adv. com. NSF, 1988-91; mem. mechanics bd. visitors ONR, 1990-93; mem. def. mfg. bd. DOD, 1988-89, def. sci. bd., 1989-91; mem. acad. adv. bd. Nat. Acad. Engring., 1991-94; mem. tech. adv. com. Pratt & Whitney, 1993-95; bd. dirs. Allied Signal; mem. Naval Rsch. Adv. Com., 1996—. Recipient 12 Best Tchg. awards Purdue U., 1971-94, Centennial medal Am. Soc. Engring. Edn., 1993. Fellow AIAA, ASEE; mem. NAE, Academia Sinica. Home: University Calif University House Santa Barbara CA 93106 Office: U California Chancellors Office Santa Barbara CA 93106

YANG, HSIN-MING, immunologist; b. Taipei, Taiwan, Dec. 2, 1952; came to U.S., 1980; s. Sze Piao and Yun-Huan (Chang) Y.; m. Yeasing Yeh, June 28, 1980; children: Elaine, Albert. BS, Nat. Taiwan U., 1976, MS, 1983; PhD, U. Wash., 1985. Rsch. assoc. Tri-Svc. Gen. Hosp., Taipei, 1979-80; fellow Scripps Clinic and Rsch. Found., La Jolla, Calif., 1986-88, sr. rsch. assoc., 1988-90; asst. prof. U. Nebr. Med. Ctr., Omaha, 1990-91; sr. rsch. scientist Pacific Biotech, Inc., San Diego, 1991-95; mgr. Scantibodies Lab., Inc., Santee, Calif., 1995—; lectr. Yun-Pei Coll. Med. Tech., Shinchiu, Taiwan, 1979-80. Contbr. articles to profl. jours., chpt. to book; inventor in field; patentee on analyte detection device including a hydrophobic barrier for improved fluid flow. Joseph Drown Found. fellow, 1986, Nat. Cancer Ctr. fellow, 1987-88. Mem. Am. Assn. for Cancer Rsch., Am. Assn. Clin. Chemistry, N.Y. Acad. Scis. Office: Scantibodies Lab Inc 9336 Abraham Way Santee CA 92071

YANG, I-YEN, internist, acupuncturist; b. Tokyo, Mar. 25, 1940; s. Ji Yin and Tatsue (Ko Ike) Y.; m. Bi Fang Liu, Jan. 4, 1968; children: Tso-Ming, Hsin Hung. MD, Nat. Taiwan U., 1966. Diplomate Am. Bd. Internal Medicine, Am. Bd. Hematology, Am. Bd. Med. Oncology, Am. Bd. Allergy and Immunology. Resident in internal medicine Grace Hosp., Detroit, 1968-71; fellow in hematology and med. oncology Cleve. Clinic, 1971-73; pvt. practice, Richland, Wash., 1973—; mem. adv. coun. acupuncture and oriental medicine Bastyr U., Seattle, 1994—. Co-author: East & West—Acupuncture An Alternate to Suffering, 1994; co-founder Vineyard Quar., poetry mag., Taipei, Taiwan, 1964. Pres. Benton County (Wash.) chpt. Am. Cancer Soc., 1974-76; co-founder Tri-City (Wash.) Chinese Christian Ch., 1975; pres. Tri-City Chinese Lang. Sch., 1976; founder Found. Acupuncture Rsch. and Edn., Richland, 1995—. Mem. The Am. Soc. of Contemporary Medicine and Surgery. Office: The Acupoint 1110 Goethals Dr Richland WA 99352-3304

YANG, SAMUEL CHI-AN, software engineer; b. Taipei, Taiwan, June 21, 1956; s. Chia Shan and Yuen Chen (Tsui) Y.; m. Connie Wong, June 21, 1992. BA in Biology and Computer Sci., U. Pa., 1979; MS in Computer Sci., Rensselaer Polytech. Inst., 1984. Data base analyst AT&T, Piscataway, N.J., 1979-82; programmer IBM, Poughkeepsie, N.Y., 1982, 83; software engr. Xerox Corp., El Segundo, Calif., 1984-95, CyberMedia Inc., Santa Monica, Calif., 1996—; researcher in genetic algorithms and artificial life, UCLA, 1987-96. Mem. Mensa, IEEE, Pi Mu Epsilon. Democrat. Office: 3000 Ocean Park Ste 2001 Santa Monica CA 90405

YANG, SHIGUANG, parasitologist, educator; b. Ma'anshan, Anhui, China, Nov. 21, 1954; came to U.S., 1986; s. Guilin and Xiufang Zhu; m. Chunwei Du, Jan. 30, 1984; children: Hongfei, Annie, Aohua. DVM, Anhui Agrl. U., 1981; MS, Nanjing Agrl. U., Jiangsu, China, 1984; PhD, Purdue U., 1989. Grad. rsch. asst. Nanjing Agrl. U., 1982-84, instr., 1985; grad. rsch. asst. Purdue U., West Lafayette, Ind., 1986-89; postdoctoral rsch. assoc. U. Wyo., Laramie, 1989-91; rsch. asst. prof. Utah State U., Logan, 1991-95, rsch. assoc. prof., 1996—. Contbr. articles to sci. jours. Grantee Utah State U., NIH, AWWARF. Mem. AAAS, Am. Soc. Parasitologists. Home: 1747 E 1550 North St Logan UT 84341 Office: Utah State U ADVS Dept UMC 5600 Logan UT 84322

YANG, XINJIAN (SAM YANG), environmental engineer; b. Changde, Peoples Republic of China, Nov. 15, 1954; came to the U.S., 1988; s. Taochu and Pei Hua (Fu) Y.; m. Shui Bing, Feb. 4, 1982; 1 child, Yanfei. BS, Xiangtan U., 1981; MS in Engring., U. Cin., 1991. Asst. lectr. Xiangtan (Peoples Republic of China) U., 1982-86, lectr., 1986-87; rsch. scholar U. Cambridge, England, 1987-88; rsch. asst. U. Cin., 1988-91; sr. engr. process and devel. Noell Inc., Long Beach, Calif., 1991-96; sr. project engr. Mitsubishi Heavy Industries Am. Inc., 1997—. Contbr. articles to profl. jours. Hon. rsch. fellow Salford U., 1987-88, Chinese Ednl. Commn. fellow, 1985. Mem. Air and Waste Mgmt. Assn., So. Calif. EPA. Home: 12001 Cherry St Los Alamitos CA 90720-4171 Office: Mitsubishi Heavy Industries Am Inc 660 Newport Center Dr Ste 1000 Newport Beach CA 92660

YANKEE, ALAN LEE, composer; b. Dallas, Oreg., Feb. 14, 1954; s. Gale and Freda Lee (Loyd) Y.; m. Melanie Martha Cobb, June 13, 1977; 1 child, Matthew Kenton. BA in Music, U. Calif., Riverside, 1980; M Music Composition, U. Redlands, Calif., 1985. Musician Stan Kenton Orch., L.A., 1975-78; composer Air Force Band of Golden West, March AFB, Calif., 1979-94; entertainment cons. Legacy Artists, Palm Desert, Calif., 1994—; band leader Al Yankee Orch., Palm Springs, Calif., 1980—; music contractor McCallum Theater, Palm Desert, Calif., 1990—; educator Riverside (Calif.) C.C., 1985—; composer, arranger Warner Bros. Publs., Miami, 1993—. Band leader, performer: (compact discs) Al Yankee Conducting, 1990, Bermuda Triangle, 1994, Somewhere ... in a Dream, 1996; composer; StealthFanfare, 1988; Golden Anniversary Composition Commn. Interlochen (Mich.) Arts Acad., 1979; compositions commd. Stan Kenton Orch., 1977; arrangement commd. Count Basie Orch., 1978. 1st sgt. Air Force Band of Golden West, March AFB, Calif., 1992-94. Master sgt. USAF, 1979-94. Decorated Meritorious Svc. medal. Mem. Nat. Assn. Rec. Arts and Scis., Am. Soc. Music Arrangers and Composers, Internat. Assn. Jazz Educators, Am. Fedn. Musicians. Democrat. Office: Legacy Artists 73101 Us Highway 111 Palm Desert CA 92260-3900

YAO, LAWRENCE, radiologist; b. Chgo., June 23, 1959; s. John and Eleanor Yao. BA, Brown U., 1981, MD, 1985. Diplomate Am. Bd. Radiology, Nat. Bd. Med. Examiners. Med. intern Miriam Hosp., Brown U., Providence, 1985-86; radiology resident Albany (N.Y.) Med. Ctr. Hosp., 1986-90; fellow musculoskeletal imaging dept. radiol. scis. UCLA Ctr. for the Health Scis., 1990-91, asst. prof. dept. radiol. scis., 1991—. Reviewer Radiology, 1993—; mem. editorial bd. Radiology, 1996—; contbr. numerous articles to profl. jours. Home: 11044 Ophir Dr Apt 601 Los Angeles CA 90024-2003 Office: Dept Radiol Scis Ste 165-45 200 UCLA Medical Plz Los Angeles CA 90095

YAO, MENG-CHAO, molecular geneticist; b. Taipei, Taiwan, Mar. 21, 1949; s. Da-Liang and Shing (Huang) Y.; m. Ching-Ho Chang, Nov. 8, 1974; 1 child, Kairu. BS, Nat. Taiwan U., 1971; PhD, U. Rochester, 1975. Postdoctoral assoc. Yale U., New Haven, Conn., 1975-78; asst. prof. Washington U., St. Louis, 1978-84, assoc. prof., 1984-86; mem. Fred Hutchinson Cancer Rsch. Ctr., Seattle, Wash., 1986—; affil. prof. U. Wash., 1988—; rev. bd. Jour. Eukanyotic Microbiology, 1991-95. Editl. bd. Jour. Protozoology, 1989-91, Molecular Cell Biology, 1997—; contbr. articles to profl. jours. Recipient career devel. award NIH, Bethesda, Md., 1983, rsch. grantee NIH, NSF. Mem. AAAS, Am. Assn. Cell Biology, Soc. Chinese Bioscientist in Am. Home: 3724 Cascadia Ave S Seattle WA 98144-7220 Office: Fred Hutchinson Cancer Rsch 1124 Columbia St Seattle WA 98104-2015

YAP, FRANK, JR., lawyer; b. Honolulu, 1945. JD, U. San Diego, 1971. Bar: Hawaii 1971, U.S. Ct. Appeals (9th cir.) 1974, U.S. Supreme Ct. 1975. Ptnr. Hoe, Yap & Sugimoto, Honolulu, 1980-91; chmn. Labor and Indsl. Rels. Appeals Bd., Honolulu, 1991—. Lt. col. USAR, ret. Office: Labor Appeals Bd 830 Punchbowl St Ste 404 Honolulu HI 96813

YARBER, MARY LAINE, secondary school educator, writer; b. San Diego, Nov. 5, 1963; d. Robert Earl and Mary Roberta (Winzerling) Y. BA in Anthropology, UCLA, 1995; cert. in tchg., San Diego State U., 1987; MA, Smith Coll., 1996. Cert. English tchr., Calif. Literature tchr. Santa Monica (Calif.) H.S., 1988—; edn. columnist L.A. Times, 1990-94; freelance writer, 1994—; English tchr. Northampton Summer Sch.-Smith Coll., Northampton, Mass., summer 1994, 96. Co-author: Reviewing Basic Grammar, 3d edit., 1993, 4th edit., 1996; contbr. poetry, short fiction to mags. Vol. The Ctr. women's svcs. orgn., L.A. Mem. AAUW, Northampton Hist. Soc., Friends of Smith Coll. Libr. Office: Santa Monica HS 601 Pico Blvd Santa Monica CA 90405

YARBER, ROBERT EARL, writer, retired educator; b. St. Louis, Sept. 28, 1929; s. Earl Yarber and Dorothy Anastasia Dwyer; m. Mary Roberta Winzerling, Nov. 27, 1952; children: Robert D., Charles C., Mary L. BA, McKendree Coll., 1951; MA, St. Louis U., 1953; postgrad., Exeter Coll. Oxford U., 1969. Prof. Mesa Coll., San Diego, 1963-89. Author: Writing for College, 1995, Reviewing Basic Grammar, 1996; contbr. articles to textbooks, revs., articles to profl. jours. Democrat. Roman Catholic. Home: 4125 Rochester Rd San Diego CA 92116

YARYAN, RUBY BELL, psychologist; b. Toledo, Apr. 28, 1938; d. John Sturges and Susan (Bell) Y.; m. John Frederick Buenz, Jr., Dec. 15, 1962 (div. 1968). AB, Stanford U., 1960; PhD, U. London, 1968. Lic. clin. psychologist; diplomate Am. Bd. Psychology. Rsch. dir., univ. radio and tv U. Calif., San Francisco, 1968-70; dir. delinquency coun. U.S. Dep. Justice, Washington, 1970-73; evaluation dir. Office of Criminal Justice Planning, Sacramento, Calif., 1973-76; CAO project mgr. San Diego (Calif.) County, 1977-92; dir. devel. svcs. Childhelp USA, Woodland Hills, Calif., 1992-94; rsch. coord. Neuropsychiat. Inst. and Hosp. UCLA, 1986-87; exec. dir. Centinela Child Guidance Clinic, Inglewood, Calif., 1987-89; clin. dir. Nat. Found. Emotionally Handicapped, North Hills, Calif., 1990-93; pvt. practice Beverly Hills, Calif., 1973—; psychologist Sr. Psychology Svcs., North L.A. County, 1994—; cons. White House Conf. Children, Washington, 1970; mem. Nat. Adv. Com. Criminal Justice Standards and Goals, Washington, 1973; clin. affiliation UCLA Med. Ctr. Contbr. articles to profl. jours.; chpts. to books and monographs in field. Chair Human Svcs. Commn., City of West Hollywood, Calif., 1986; first vice-chair United Way/Western Region, L.A., 1988; mem. planning-allocations-rsch. coun. United Way, San Diego, 1980-82. Grantee numerous fed., state and local govt. orgns. Mem. Am. Psychol. Assn., Western Psychol. Assn., Calif. Psychol. Assn., Am. Orthopsychiat. Assn., Am. Profl. Soc. on Abuse of Children, Phi Beta Kappa. Episcopalian. Office: 337 S Beverly Dr Ste 107 Beverly Hills CA 90212-4307

YASNYI, ALLAN DAVID, communications company executive; b. New Orleans, June 22, 1942; s. Ben Z. and Bertha R. (Michalove) Y.; BBA, Tulane U., 1964; m. Susan K. Manders; children: Benjamin Charles, Evelyn Judith, Brian Mallut. Free-lance exec. producer, producer, writer, actor and designer for TV, motion picture and theatre, 1961-73; producer, performer The Second City; dir. fin. and adminstrn. Quinn Martin Prodns., Hollywood, Calif., 1973-76, v.p. fin., 1976-77, exec. v.p. fin. and corp. planning, 1977; vice chmn., CEO QM Prodns., Beverly Hills, Calif., 1977-78, chmn. bd., CEO, 1978-80; pres., CEO The Synapse Communications Group, Inc., 1981—; exec. dir., adj. prof. U. So. Calif. Entertainment Tech. Ctr., 1994—; participant IC IS Forum, 1990-95; exec. prodr. first live broadcast combining Intelsat, Intersputnik, The Voice of Am., and The Moscow World Radio Svc., 1990; resource guest Aspen Inst. Exec. Seminars, 1990; chmn. bd. dirs. Found. of Global Broadcasting, Washington, 1987-93. Trustee Hollywood Arts Coun., 1980-83; exec. v.p., trustee Hollywood Hist. Trust, 1981-91; bd. dirs. Internat. Ctr. for Intergative Studies, N.Y.C., 1988-92; bd. dirs. Asthma and Allergy Foun. Am., 1981-85. Logistical combat officer U.S. Army, 1964-66, Viet Nam. Named to Tulane U. Hall of Fame. Mem. Acad. TV Arts and Scis., Inst. Noetic Scis., Hollywood Radio and TV Soc., Hollywood C. of C. (dir., vice-chmn. 1978-93), Screen Actors Guild, Assn. Transpersonal Psychology (keynote speaker 1988). Office: 4132 Fulton Ave Sherman Oaks CA 91423-4340

YASSIN, ROBERT ALAN, museum administrator, curator; b. Malden, Mass., May 22, 1941; s. Harold Benjamin and Florence Gertrude (Hoffman) Y.; m. Marilyn Kramer, June 9, 1963; children: Fredric Giles, Aaron David. BA (Rufus Choate scholar), Dartmouth Coll., 1962; postgrad., Boston U., 1962-63; M.A., U. Mich., 1965, postgrad. (Samuel H. Kress Found. fellow), 1968-70, Ph.D. candidate, 1970; postgrad (Ford Found. fellow), Yale U., 1966-68. Asst. to dir. Mus. Art U. Mich., 1965-66, asst. dir., 1970-72, asso. dir., 1972-73, acting dir., 1973, instr. dept. history of art, 1970-73; co-dir. Joint Program in Mus. Tng., 1970-73; chief curator Indpls. Mus. Art, 1973-75, 87-89, acting dir., 1975, dir., 1975-89; exec. dir. Tucson Mus. Art, 1990—; adj. prof. Herron Sch. Art Ind. U./Purdue U., 1975-89. Contbr. to mus. publications. Mem. Ariz. Hist. Soc., Ariz. Mus. Assn., Tucson Mus. Assn., Tucson Arts Coalition., Tucson Downtown Adv. Coun. Mem. Am. Assn. Mus. (bd. dirs. Internat. Coun. Mus. 1986-89), Assn. Art Mus. Dirs., Coll. Art Assn. Am., Intermus. Conservation Assn. (chmn. exec. com. 1977-78), Tucson C. of C. (cultural affairs com., econ. devel. com.), Nat. Trust Historic Preservation, Rotary. Jewish. Home: 3900 N Calle Casita Tucson AZ 85718-7204 Office: Tucson Mus Art 140 N Main Ave Tucson AZ 85701-8218

YATCHAK, MICHAEL GERARD, electrical engineer; b. Wakefield, Mich., July 3, 1951; s. Roman C. and Mary A. (Zorich) Y.; separated; 1 child, Rika M. BSEE, Mich. State U., 1974. Assoc. engr. Eagle Signal, Davenport, Iowa, 1974-76; engr. computer lab. Mich. State U., East Lansing, 1977-84; sr. engr. Martin Marietta Corp., Denver, 1984-86; sr. engr. McDonnell Douglas Corp., Huntington Beach, Calif., 1986-92, mgr., 1992-93, prin. engr., 1993—. Mem. IEEE. Roman Catholic.

YATES, ALBERT CARL, academic administrator, chemistry educator; b. Memphis, Sept. 29, 1941; s. John Frank and Sadie L. (Shell) Y.; m. Ann Young; children: Steven, Stephanie, Aerin Alessandra, Sara Elizabeth. B.S., Memphis State U., 1965; Ph.D., Ind. U., 1968. Research assoc. U. So. Calif., Los Angeles, 1968-69; prof. chemistry Ind. U., Bloomington, 1969-74; v.p. research, grad. dean U. Cin., 1974-81; exec. v.p., provost, prof. chemistry Washington State U., Pullman, 1981-90; pres. Colo. State U., Fort Collins, 1990—; chancellor Colo. State U. System, Fort Collins, 1990—; mem. grad. record exam. bd. Princeton (N.J.) U., 1977-80, undergrad. assessment program council, 1977-81; cons. NRC, 1975-82, Office End., HEW, 1978-80; mem. exec. council acad. affairs NASULGC, 1983-87, ACE, 1983-87,, nat adv. council gen. med. scis. NIH, 1987—. Contbr.: research articles to Jour. Chem. Physics; research articles to Phys. Rev.; research articles to Jour. Physics, Phys. Rev. Letters, Chem. Physics Letters. Served with USN, 1959-62. Recipient univ. and State honors and awards. Mem. Am. Phys. Soc., Am. Chem. Soc., AAAS, Nat. Assn. State Univs. and Land Grant Colls. (mem. exec. council academic affairs), Am. Council Edn. (mem. exec. com. academic affairs), Sigma Xi, Phi Lambda Upsilon. Home: 1744 Hillside Dr Fort Collins CO 80524-1965 Office: Colo State U 102 Administration Bldg Fort Collins CO 80523*

YATES, GARY, mayor. Mayor City of San Mateo, 1996—. Office: 330 W 20th Ave San Mateo CA 94403

YATES, JERE EUGENE, business educator, management consultant; b. Memphis, Apr. 4, 1941; s. Emmett Eugene and Naomi Christine (Whitfield) Y.; m. Carolyn Kay Hall, June 8, 1962; children: Camille, Kevin, Brian. BA, Harding U., 1963, MTh, MA, 1966; PhD, Boston U., 1968. Instr. Harding U., Searcy, Ark., 1967-69; prof. bus. Pepperdine U., Malibu, Calif., 1969—; cons. Hughes Aircraft Co., L.A., 1973—, Allied-Signal Corp., North Hollywood, Calif., 1985-90, Pacific Physican Svcs., 1988-96, Med Ptnrs./ Mullikin, 1996—. Author: Managing Stress, 1979 (membership book award, 1979); contbr. articles to profl. jours. Mem. AAUP, Acad. Mgmt., UCP/ Spastic Children's Found. (bd. dirs., exec. com.), Orgnl. Behavior Teaching Soc., North Ranch Country Club. Republican. Mem. Ch. of Christ. Office: Pepperdine U Business Dept 24255 Pacific Coast Hwy Malibu CA 90263-0001

YATES, KEITH LAMAR, retired insurance company executive; b. Bozeman, Mont., Oct. 29, 1927; s. Thomas Bryan and Altha (Norris) Y.; m. Dolores Hensel, Aug. 30, 1948; children: Thomas A., Molly Yates McIntosh, Richard A., Nancy Yates Sands, Penny Dannielle Yates, Pamela Yates Beeler. BA, Eastern Wash. State U., 1953. Salesman Ancient Order United Workmen, Spokane, Wash., 1952-53, sales mgr., 1953-56, corp. sec., 1956-73;

corp. sec. Neighbors of Woodcraft, Portland, Oreg., 1973-89, pres., 1989-92; ret., 1992. Author: Life of Willie Willey, 1966, The Fogarty Years, 1972, History of The Woodcraft Home, 1975, An Enduring Heritage, 1992. Pres. Wash. State Christian Mens Fellowship, Seattle, 1965-67; pres. Met. Area Assn. Christian Chs., 1981-83; mem. regional bd. Christian Chs. Oreg., 1990-94. Command sgt.-maj., ret., 1987; served with USN, USAF, USANG, 1946-87. Mem. Wash. State Frat. Cong., (cert. Commendation 1969, sec. 1957-68, pres., mem. exec. bd., chmn. conv. program advt. com. 1960-73), Oreg. State Frat. Cong. (Outstanding Frat. 1975-76, Spl. Appreciation award 1984, Frat. Family of Yr. 1986, sec. 1975-87, pres., mem. exec. bd. 1974—), Nat. Fraternal Congress Am. (conv. arrangement com. 1964, 90, publicity com. 1964, 65, 68, 90, credentials com. 1970, 77, 78, pres. press & pub. rels. sec. 1971-72, pub. rels. com. 1971-73, chmn. 1972, co-chmn. press and pub. rels. frat. seminar 1972, frat. monitor com. 1974-75, mem. com. 1975-76, family life com. 1978-80, constitution com. 1980, pres. state frat. congs. sec. 1981-82, historian 1987—, Washington County's Disting. Patriot, 1988), Portland Ins. Acctg. and Statis. Soc. Assn. Records Mgrs. and Adminstrs. (Oreg. chpt.), Portland C. of C., Wash. Ins. Coun., Wash. Claims Assn., Seattle Underwriting Assn. Home: 29860 SW Buckhaven Rd Hillsboro OR 97123-8821

YATES, LINDA GAYLE, school counselor, consultant; b. Everett, Wash.; d. Burle Vayle Ingraham and Mildred Kathryn (Safstrom) Sinnott; m. Lonnie Michael Hart, June 8, 1963 (div. May 1970); children: Chris Q., B.J., Wendy D. Hart Lubash; m. Larry Bruce Yates, Aug. 23, 1977. BA, Sangamon State U., Springfield, Ill., 1973, MA, 1973; MA, Colo. State U., 1974. Cert. counselor. Cons., tchr. psychodrama Sangamon State U., 1972-73; cons. Colo. State U., Ft. Collins, 1974; dir. vocat. curriculum Wash. State Office Pub. Instrn., Cheney, 1974-75; coord. Speedy Familiarization Project fed. program, Spokane, Wash., 1979; writer, vocat. curriculum Wash. State Vocat. Edn., Cheney, 1980; Stephen min. trainer First Presbyn. Ch., Spokane, 1993-96; sch. counselor Spokane Sch. Dist., 1978—; cons., tchr. (self-esteem, suicide) Wash. State C.Cs., 1975—; adv. bd. Morning Star Boys Ranch, Spokane, 1990—; tchr. educator bias awareness/equity, Spokane; peer mediator, trainer Spokane schs. Author ednl. materials Colo. State U., Wash. State Office Instrn.; author career ednl. materials, Spokane Sch. Dist. Deacon, TLC leader, Stephen min., trainer Stephen mins. 1st Presbyn. Ch., Spokane, 1994—; vol. YWCA, cmty. mental health, Martin Luther King Ctr., Spokane, 1994—. Mem. Am. Vocat. Assn. (life), Suicide Prevention Task Force, Inland Empire Pers. and Guidance Assn. (pres.), Wash. State Univ. Cougar Club (bd. mem. 1994-96), Chapultepec Investment Club (pres. 1978-96). Presbyterian. Office: Spokane Sch Dist Chase Middle Sch 4747 E 37th Ave Spokane WA 99223-1206

YATES, STEVEN A., artist, curator; b. Chgo., Nov. 14, 1949; s. Thomas A. and Phyllis E. (Wilson) Y.; m. Lynne A. Smith, Aug. 5, 1972; children: Kelsey Victoria, Mackenzie Phyllis. BFA, U. Nebr., 1972; MA, U. N.Mex., 1975, DFA, 1978. Curatorial asst. Sheldon Meml. Art Gallery, 1972-73; U. Art Mus., U. N.Mex., 1973-75; faculty dept. art Claremont (Calif.) Coll. and Pomona, 1976; part-time faculty, U. N.Mex., Albuquerque, 1976-79; assoc. adj. prof. art and art history U. N.Mex.; curator prints, drawings and photographs, Mus. of N.Mex., Santa Fe, 1980-84, curator of photography Mus. Fine Arts, 1985—; frequent lectr. in sculpture and photography; guest artist Tamarind Inst., Albuquerque, 1988. One-man shows include: Sheldon Meml. Art Gallery, Lincoln, Nebr., 1978, Humboldt State U., Arcata, Calif., 1986, Northlight Gallery, Tempe, Ariz., 1988; group shows include: San Francisco Mus. Modern Art, 1980, 81, 84, 86, Sheldon Meml. Art Gallery, 1982-83, Light Factory, Charlotte, N.C., 1983, U. Denver, 1984, Jonson Gallery, U. N.Mex., 1985, Visions: New Mexico Contemporary Photographers at U. N.Mex., 1987; represented in permanent collections: San Francisco Mus. Modern Art, Sheldon Art Gallery, Mint Mus., Art Mus. U. N.Mex. Editor: The Essential Landscape, The New Mexico Photographic Survey, 1985; guest editor spl. issue Contemporary Photography, 1987, El Palacio, 1987. Ford Found. fellow, 1977, Nat. Endowment Arts fellow, 1980; recipient Vreeland award U. Nebraska, 1972, Outstanding Alumni Achievement award U. Nebraska, 1994; Sr. Fulbright Scholars award USSR, 1991, Russian Federation, 1995.

YAU, KEVIN KAM-CHING, astronomer; b. Hong Kong, July 11, 1959; came to U.S., 1992; s. Ching-Fat and Ping-Kiu (Leung) Y.; m. Florence Wai-Chung Liu, Aug. 22, 1987; children: Stephanie, Cherrymay. BS in Physics, U. Liverpool, Eng., 1982; MS in Astrophysics, U. Durham, Eng., 1984, PhD in Astronomy, 1988. Sr. rsch. asst. U. Durham, 1987-92; postdoctoral fellow Jet Propulsion Lab., Pasadena, Calif., 1992-94, mem. tech. staff, 1994—. Co-author: Halley's Comet in History, 1985; contbr. articles to profl. jours. Rsch. scholar U. Durham, 1984-87; awardee Victor Nadarov Fund, Royal Astron. Soc., 1983. Fellow Royal Astron. Soc.; mem. Internat. Astron. Union, Am. Astron. Soc. Office: Jet Propulsion Lab MS 230-101 4800 Oak Grove Dr Pasadena CA 91109-8001

YBARRA, KATHRYN WATROUS, systems engineer; b. Middletown, Conn., Aug. 7, 1943; d. Claude Philip Jr. and C. Lyle (Crook) Watrous; m. Norman L. Adams (div.); children: Cynthia Anne Leonard, Suzette Mae Gross, Daniel Joseph Adams; m. Raul M. Ybarra, Dec. 11, 1976; stepchildren: Esther Ingram, Yolanda Ybarra, Lisa Ybarra. BA in Computer Sci., U. Tex., 1985. Scientific programmer Tracor, Inc., Austin, 1978-86; tech. staff engr. Honeywell, Inc. Comml. Avionics, Phoenix, 1986—. Mem. Friends of Phoenix Libr., v.p. Juniper chpt., 1996-97. Mem. RTCA (spl. com. # 147, Traffic Alert and Collision Avoidance Sys. II, chair requirements working group 1991—, leadership citation 1995), IEEE Computer Soc. Roman Catholic. Home: 3360 W Phelps Rd Phoenix AZ 85023

YEAGER, DAVID CLARK, product designer, education specialist; b. Hinsdale, Ill., July 1, 1951; s. William Frances and Helen Gerrity (Clark) Y.; m. Tina Alden, Jan. 4, 1974; 1 child, Christopher Alden. BA, U. Colo., 1975. Cert. tchr., Colo. Tchr. Boulder (Colo.) Valley Schs., 1976-86, ednl. cons., 1986-90; aide to Gov. Romer State of Colo., Denver, 1990-91; devel. dir. Boulder Valley Schs. and Colo. Partnership for Ednl. Renewal, 1991-94; ednl. product designer InGenius, Englewood, Colo., 1994-95; writer, edn. cons. children's museums, 1995—; cons. Va. Commonwealth U., Richmond, 1990, 91; coord. Am. Coun. Learned Socs. Elem. and Secondary Curriculum Devel. Project, 1992—. Author several math. books; film reviewer McArthur Found., 1989; contbr. articles to profl. jours. Active Safehouse for Children, Boulder County, 1994. Recipient numerous grants. Home and Office: 3745 Birchwood Dr Boulder CO 80304-1423

YEARLEY, DOUGLAS CAIN, mining and manufacturing company executive; b. Oak Park, Ill., Jan. 7, 1936; s. Bernard Cain and Mary Kenny (Howard) Y.; m. Elizabeth Anne Dunbar, Feb. 8, 1958; children: Sandra, Douglas Jr., Peter, Andrew. BMetE, Cornell U., 1958; postgrad., Harvard U., 1968. Engr. welding Gen. Dynamics, Groton, Conn., 1958-60; dir. rsch., project engr. Phelps Dodge Copper Products, Elizabeth, N.J., 1960-68; mgr. ops. Phelps Dodge Internat. Co., N.Y.C., 1968-71; v.p. ops. Phelps Dodge Tube Co., L.A., 1971-73; exec. v.p. Phelps Dodge Cable and Wire Co., Yonkers, N.Y., 1973-75; pres. Phelps Dodge Brass Co., Lyndhurst, N.J., 1975-79; pres. Phelps Dodge Sales Co., N.Y.C., 1979-82, v.p. mktg., 1979-82; sr. v.p. Phelps Dodge Corp., N.Y.C., 1982-87, exec. v.p., 1987-89, chmn., CEO, 1989-91; chmn., pres., CEO Phelps Dodge Corp., Phoenix, 1991—, also bd. dirs.; bd. dirs. USX Corp., Pitts., J.P. Morgan and Co., Inc. and Morgan Guaranty Trust Co., N.Y.C., Lockheed Martin Corp., Calabasas, Calif., So. Peru Copper Co. Mem. Ariz. Econs. Coun., 1989—, Conf. Bd., 1989—; bd. dirs. Am. Grad. Sch. Internat. Mgmt., 1990-92, Phoenix Symphony, 1988-94; chmn. Arts Coalition, 1989-90; trustee Phoenix Art Mus., 1994—. Mem. Nat. Elec. Mfrs. Assn. (bd. dirs. 1983-92), Internat. Copper Assn. (bd. dirs. 1987—, chmn. 1990—), Am. Mining Congress (vice chmn.), Nat. Mining Assn. (chmn.), Copper Devel. Assn. (chmn. 1989-93, dir. 1993—), Nat. Assn. Mfrs. (bd. dirs. 1988-94), Bus. Roundtable, Bus. Coun., Skyu Club, Echo Lake Country Club, Paradise Valley Country Club, Ariz. Club, Blind Brook Country Club. Republican. Congregationalist. Home: 8201 N Via De Lago Scottsdale AZ 85258-4215 Office: Phelps Dodge Corp 2600 N Central Ave Phoenix AZ 85004-3050*

YEAW, MARION ESTHER, retired nurse; b. Chgo., June 13, 1926; d. Clarence Yates and Olga Sophia (Gorling) Y. BSN, U. Mich., 1949; MEd, Mills Coll., Oakland, Calif., 1965. Cert. tchr. in nursing, Calif. Staff nurse U. Mich. Hosp., Ann Arbor, 1949-51; instr. pediatric nursing Kaiser Found. Sch. Nursing, Oakland, 1951-76, 1976-78; instr. pediatric nursing Contra Costa Community Coll., San Pablo, Calif., 1976-78, Merritt C.C., Oakland, Calif.; dir. staff devel. Waters Edge Inc., Alameda, Calif., 1978-89; retired, 1989. Mem. AAUW, LWV, Bus. and Profl. Women's Club (Woman of Achievement award 1988), Alumnae Assn. U. Mich. Sch. Nursing, Mills Coll. Alumni Assn. Lutheran. Home: 1601 Broadway # 6 Alameda CA 94501-3050

YEE, ALFRED ALPHONSE, structural engineer, consultant; b. Honolulu, Aug. 5, 1925; s. Yun Sau and Kam Ngo (Lum) Y.; m. Janice Ching (div.); children: Lailan, Mark, Eric, Malcolm, Ian; m. Elizabeth Wong, June 24, 1975; children: Suling, Trevor, I'Ling. BSCE, Rose Hulman Inst. Tech., 1948, Dr. of Engring. (hon.), 1976; MEng in Structures, Yale U., 1949. Registered profl. engr., Hawaii, Calif., Guam, Fla., Tex., Minn., Ohio., Northern Mariana Islands. With civil engring. dept. Dept. Pub. Works, Terr. of Hawaii, Honolulu, 1949-51; structural engr. 14th Naval Dist., Pearl Harbor, Hawaii, 1951-54; pvt. practice structural engring. cons. Honolulu, 1954-55; structural engring. cons. Park & Yee Ltd., Honolulu, 1955-60; pres. Alfred A. Yee & Assocs. Inc., Honolulu, 1960-82; v.p., tech. adminstr. Alfred. A. Yee div. Leo A. Daly, Honolulu, 1982-89; pres. Applied Tech. Corp., Honolulu, 1984—. Patentee in concrete tech., land and sea structures; contbr. articles to profl. jours. Served with U.S. Army, 1946-47. Named Engr. of Yr., Hawaii Soc. Profl. Engrs., 1969, one of Men Who Made Marks in 1970, Honolulu, 1970. Fellow Yale Engring. Assn., PCI; mem. Nat. Acad. Engring., Prestressed Concrete Inst. (Martin P. Korn award 1965), NSPE, Soc. Naval Architects and Marine Engrs., Fla. Engring. Soc., Internat. Assn. Bridge and Structural Engring., Post-Tensioning Inst., ASCE (hon.), Am. Concrete Inst. (hon.). Office: 1441 Kapiolani Blvd Ste 810 Honolulu HI 96814-4404

YEE, DARLENE, gerontological health educator; b. N.Y.C., Sept. 19, 1958; d. Jimmy Tow and Yuen Hing (Chin) Y. BA in Biology, Barnard Coll., 1980; MS in Gerontology, Coll. New Rochelle, 1981; MS in Health Edn., Columbia U., 1984, EdD in Health Edn., 1985. Cert. Nat. Commn. Health Edn. Asst. dir. biology lab. Barnard Coll., N.Y.C., 1980-83; rsch. assoc, safety rsch. and edn. project Columbia U. Tchrs. Coll., N.Y.C., 1983-85; asst. prof. health and phys. edn. York Coll., N.Y.C., 1985-88; cons. Transp. Rsch. Bd., NAS, Washington, 1987, N.Y. State Dept. Edn., Albany, 1987, U.S. Dept. Edn., Washington, 1991; assoc. prof. clin. gerontology, health edn. and promotion U. Tex. Med. Br., Galveston, 1988-90; assoc. prof. health edn. San Francisco State U., 1990-93; prof. health edn., 1994-95; dir., prof. gerontology San Francisco State U., 1995—. Contbr. articles to profl. jours. Mem. Am. Coll. Health Care Adminstrs., Gerontol. Soc. Am., Am. Soc. on Aging, Assn. for Advancement Health Edn., Nat. Coun. on Aging, Sigma Xi. Home: 40 Meadow Park Cir Belmont CA 94002-2947 Office: San Francisco State U Gerontology Programs 20 Tapia Dr San Francisco CA 94132-1717

YEE, KANE SHEE-GONG, mathematician, electrical engineer; b. Canton, Kwangtung, China, Mar. 26, 1934; came to U.S., 1951; s. Wing Dye Yee and Check Wah Fong; m. Maxine Big-Shung Fong, Aug. 19, 1962; children: Audrey, Albert. BS, U. Calif., Berkeley, 1957, MS in Elec. Engring., 1958, PhD in Applied Math., 1963. Scientist, mathematician Lawrence Livermore Nat. Lab., Livermore, Calif., 1964-87; assoc. prof. math. U. Fla., Gainesville, 1966-68; prof. math. and elec. engring. Kans. State U., Manhattan, 1968-84; cons. sr. scientist Lockheed Missiles and Space Co., Sunnyvale, Calif., 1987—; advisor NSF, Washington, 1989-92. Originator finite difference time domain method in numerical solution of Maxwell's equations; frequent reviewer for IEEE Jours., 1968—; author more than 30 tech. papers. Recipient scholarships and fellowships. Mem. IEEE. Democrat. Home: 23350 Toyonita Rd Los Altos CA 94024-6525

YEE, KEITH PHILIP, accountant; b. Luton, Eng., Apr. 26, 1958; came to the U.S., 1985; m. Ginny Sung, Feb. 9, 1985; children: Ashley, Brittany. BA in Acctg. with honors, Exeter (Eng.) U., 1979. CPA, Calif. Audit sr. Ernst & Whinney, London, 1979-83; investigation supr. Ernst & Whinney, Hong Kong, 1983-85; audit mgr. Ernst & Whinney, Memphis, 1985-86; audit sr. mgr. Ernst & Young, San Francisco, 1986-91; internat. resident Ernst & Young, 1991-93; audit sr. mgr. Ernst & Young, San Francisco, 1993-95, Price Waterhouse, San Jose, Calif., 1995—. Vice chmn. adv. coun. for svcs. to srs. Salvation Army, San Francisco, 1989. Grad. leadership San Francisco program San Francisco C. of C., 1990. Fellow Inst. Chartered Accts. in Eng. and Wales; mem. AICPA, Asian Am. CPAs (mem. adv. bd. 1994-95), Calif. Soc. CPAs, Inst. for Internat. Edn. (student programs com. 1990-95), San Francisco C. of C. (internat. bus. devel. com. 1993-95), Asian Am. Mfrs. Assn., Churchill Club. Office: Price Waterhouse 150 Almaden Blvd Ste 1200 San Jose CA 95113-2009

YEE, STEPHEN, airport executive. Adminstrv. asst. health dept. City of L.A., 1958-63, sr. adminstrv. asst. dept. airports, 1963-72, fed. aid coord., 1972-75, project mgr., 2d level roadway and terminal improvements, airport facilities planner, 1975-83, staff asst. to bd. airport commrs., 1983-85, airport mgr. L.A. Internat. Airport, 1985—. Office: Los Angeles Intl Airport Los Angeles Dept of Airports 1 World Way Los Angeles CA 90045-5803*

YEGEN, PETER, JR., insurance and real estate executive; b. Billings, Mont., July 12, 1896; s. Peter and Margaret (Trepp) Y.; grad. Inst. Dr. Schmidt., St. Gall, Switzerland, 1913; student U. Wis., 1915-17; m. Zellah Wilson Cardwell, Mar. 27, 1918; children—Peter, III, Edward Cardwell. Ins., real estate bus. as Peter Yegen, Jr., Billings, 1919—; pres. Yellowstone Ditch Co., 1935—, Arnold Drain Repair, 1955-70. Pres., Shiloh Drainage Dist., 1942—, Arnold Drainage Dist., 1965—; chmn. Urban Renewal, 1962-63. Chmn., Yellowstone County Tb Soc., 1948; chmn. Salvation Army Adv. Bd., 1949-66, hon. life mem., 1966—; chmn., pres. Yellowstone Mus. Bd., 1956—. Served to 2d lt. F.A., U.S. Army, 1918. Named hon. state fire marshall, hon. chief Billings Fire Dept.; mem. Nat. Cowboy Hall of Fame; 1st co-recipient with Zellah Realtors ann. Peter Yegen, Jr. award for outstanding community service, 1976; named Agri-Bus. Man of Yr., N. Internat. Livestock Expn., 1978. Mem. Billings Bd. Insurors (life, pres. 1936), Hartford Jonathan Trumbull Assn., Billings Bd. Realtors (life mem., pres. 1937), Mont. Assn. Realtors (life mem., pres. 1948-49, realtor emeritus), Mont. Assn. Ins. Agts. (life, pres. 1940-41), Pioneers of Eastern Mont. and their Sons and Daus. (pres. 1953, sec. 1960-81), Yellowstone Hist. Soc. (life, pres. 1960), Westerners Internat., Mont. Pioneer and Classic Auto Club, Mus. Assn. Mont. (pres. 1967-69), Am. Legion (life, comdr. 1933, comdr. emeritus 1977), Mont. Stockgrowers Assn., Range Riders. Episcopalian. Mason (life, past master, Shriner). Clubs: Saddle (pres. 1939, 41, 43), Yellowstone Corral, Goggles and Dusters, Yellowstone Country (pres. 1952-54), Kiwanis (life, pres. 1947, lt. gov. 1958, Kiwanian of Yr. 1979). Home: 306 N 30th St Billings MT 59101-1249 Office: Yellowstone County Museum PO Box 959 Billings MT 59103*

YEGGE, ROBERT BERNARD, lawyer, college dean emeritus, educator; b. Denver, June 17, 1934; s. Ronald Van Kirk and Fairy (Hill) Y. A.B. magna cum laude, Princeton U., 1956; M.A. in Sociology, U. Denver, 1958, J.D., 1959. Bar: Colo. 1959, D.C. 1978. Ptnr. Yegge, Hall and Evans, Denver, 1959-78; with Harding Shultz & Downs successor to Nelson and Harding, 1979—; prof. U. Denver Coll. Law, 1965—, dean, 1965-77, dean emeritus, 1977—; asst. to pres. Denver Post, 1971-75; v.p., exec. dir. Nat. Ctr. Preventive Law, 1986-91. Author: Colorado Negotiable Instruments Law, 1960, Some Goals; Some Tasks, 1965, The American Lawyer: 1976, 1966, New Careers in Law, 1969, The Law Graduate, 1972, Tomorrow's Lawyer: A Shortage and Challenge, 1974, Declaration of Independence for Legal Education, 1976. Mng. trustee Denver Ctr. for Performing Arts, 1972-75; chmn. Colo. Coun. Arts and Humanities, 1968-80, chmn. emeritus, 1980—; mem. scholar selection com. Henry Luce Found., 1975—; Active nat. and local A.R.C., chmn. Denver region, 1985-88; trustee Denver Symphony Soc., Inst. of Ct. Mgmt., Denver Dumb Friends League, 1992—, Met. Denver Legal Aid Soc., 1994—, Colo. Acad.; trustee, vice chmn. Nat. Assembly State Arts Agys.; vice chmn. Mexican-Am. Legal Edn. and Def. Fund, 1970-76. Recipient Disting. Svc. award Denver Jr. C. of C., 1965; Harrison Tweed award Am. Assn. Continuing Edn. Adminstrs., 1985, Alumni Faculty award U. Denver, 1993. Mem. Law and Soc. Assn. (life, pres. 1965-70), ABA (chmn. lawyers conf. 1987-88, chmn. accreditation commn. for legal assistant programs 1980-90, standing com. legal assts. 1987-92, standing com. delivery legal svcs. 1992-95, com. on Gavel award 1995—, del. to jud. adminstrn. coun. 1989-95, Robert B. Yegge award 1996), Colo. Bar Assn. (bd. govs. 1965-77), Denver Bar Assn., D.C. Bar Assn., Am. Law Inst., Am. Judicature Soc. (bd. dirs. 1968-72, 75-85, Herbert Harley award 1985), Am. Acad. Polit. and Social Sci., Am. Sociol. Soc., Assn. Am. Law Schs., Order St. Ives, Phi Beta Kappa, Beta Theta Pi, Phi Delta Phi, Alpha Kappa Delta, Omicron Delta Kappa. Home: 3472 S Race St Englewood CO 80110-3138 Office: Harding Shultz & Downs 1200 17th St Ste 1950 Denver CO 80202-5835

YEGIAN, RICHARD, real estate executive. BSME, Harvey Mudd Coll., 1985; MCE, MBA, Northwestern U., 1986. Co-founder Admiral Devel. Co., Burbank, Calif., 1986—; pres., CEO Admiral Realty, Glendale, Calif., 1989—. Mem. Mensa. Office: Admiral Realty 100 N Brand Blvd 2d Fl Glendale CA 91203-2614

YEH, PAUL PAO, electrical and electronics engineer, educator; b. Sung Yang, Chekiang, China, Mar. 25, 1927; came to U.S., 1956, naturalized, 1963; s. Tsung Shan and Shu Huan (Mao) Y.; m. Beverley Pamela Eng, May 15, 1952; children: Judith Elaine, Paul Edmond, Richard Alvin, Ronald Timothy, Cheryl Chuan-Hang. Student, Nat. Cen. U., Nanking, China, 1946-49; BSEE, U. Toronto (Ont., Can.), 1951; MSEE, U. Pa., 1960, PhD, 1966. Registered profl. engr., Ont. Design engr. Can. Gen. Electric Co., Toronto, 1951-56; asst. prof. SUNY, Binghamton, 1956-57; sr. engr. H.K. Porter, ITE & Kuhlman, Phila. and Detroit, 1957-61; assoc. prof. N.J. Inst. Tech., Newark, 1961-66; supr. rsch. and devel. N.Am. Rockwell, Anaheim, Calif., 1966-70; sr. R&D engr. Lockheed Advanced Devel. Co., Burbank, Calif., 1970-72, 78-89; mem. tech. staff The Aerospace Corp., El Segundo, Calif., 1972-78; chief scientist Advanced Systems Rsch., Pasadena, Calif., 1989—; cons. Consol. Edison Co., N.Y.C., 1963-64, Pub. Svc. Elec. and Gas Co. N.J., 1965-66, Zhejiang Sci. and Tech. Exch. Ctr. with Fgn. Countries, 1995—; sr. lectr. State U. Calif., Long Beach, 1967-73; vis. prof. Chung Shan Inst. Sci. and Tech., 1989-92, Tsinghua U., 1993—, S.E. U., 1994—, Zhejiang U., 1994—; cons. prof. Northwestern Poly. U., 1993—, Shanghai U., 1994—; hon. prof. Beijing U. Aeros. and Astronautics, 1993—, Zhejiang U. Sci. and Tech., 1994—; rschr. power sys. design and control, 1951-66; investigator R&D Stealth tech. electronic warfare, avionics, IR/EO Tech, nuclear hardening, anti-submarine warfare. Recipient Achievement award for anti-submarine warfare/magnetic anomaly detection sys. Lockheed Corp. Mem. IEEE (sr., life), Nat. Mgmt. Assn. (life), Am. Def. Preparedness Assn., Assn. Old Crows, Chinese Am. Engring./Sci. Assn. So. Calif. (pres. 1969-71), Nat. Ctrl. U. Alumni Assn. (pres. 1977), Nat. Security Indsl. Assn., Beijing Assn. for Sci. and Tech. Exchs. with Fgn. Countries, (hon. dir.), Assn. Profl. Engrs. of Ont., N.Y. Acad. Scis., Air Force Assn., Zhejiang Assn. for Sci. and Tech. Exchs. with Fgn. Countries (advisor), Armed Forces Comms. and Electronics Assn., U.S. Naval Inst., Assn. U.S. Army. Republican. Presbyterian. Home: 5555 Via De Campo Yorba Linda CA 92887-4916 Office: Advanced Systems Rsch Inc 33 S Catalina Ave Ste 202 Pasadena CA 91106-2426

YEN, DUEN HSI, corporate executive, physicist; b. Nyack, N.Y., Apr. 24, 1949; s. Ernest Chu and Louise (Loo) Y.; m. Linda Leiko Takai, June 22, 1989. BS in Physics, Rensselaer Polytech. Inst., 1971; MA in Biophysics, Johns Hopkins U., 1974; MSEE, U. Vt., 1978. Mem. tech. staff Bell Telephone Labs., Holmdel, N.J., 1978-83; pres. Multipath Systems, Inc., Honolulu, 1984—; Violinist Oahu Civic Orch. Inventor noise detector, electronic travel aids for blind; contbr. articles to profl. jours. Small Bus. Innovation Rsch. grantee, NSF grantee 1984, Nat. Eye Inst. grantee 1988, 89, 91. Mem. Acoustical Soc. Am., Audio Engring. Soc., Sigma Pi Sigma. Home: 1255 Nuuanu Ave Apt 2315E Honolulu HI 96817-4012

YEN, TEH FU, civil and environmental engineering educator; b. Kun-Ming, China, Jan. 9, 1927; came to U.S., 1949; s. Kwang Pu and Ren (Liu) Y.; m. Shiao-Ping Siao, May 30, 1959. BS, Cen. China U., 1947; MS, W.Va. U., 1953; PhD, Va. Poly. Inst. and State U., 1956; hon. doctoral degree, Pepperdine U., 1982, Internat. U. Dubna, Russia, 1996. Sr. research chemist Good Yr. Tire & Rubber Co., Akron, 1955-59; fellow Mellon Inst., Pitts., 1959-65; sr. fellow Carnegie-Mellon U., Pitts., 1965-68; assoc. prof. Calif. State U., Los Angeles, 1968-69; assoc. prof. U. So. Calif., 1969-80, prof. civil engring. and environ. engring., 1980—; hon. prof. Shanghai U. Sci. and Tech., 1986, U. Petroleum, Beijing, 1987, Daqing Petroleum Inst., 1992; cons. Universal Oil Products, 1968-76, Chevron Oil Field Rsch. Co., 1968-75, Finnigan Corp., 1976-77, GE, 1977-80, United Techs., 1978-79, TRW Inc., 1982-83, Exxon, 1981-82, DuPont, 1985-88, Min. Petroleum, Beijing, 1982—, Biogas Rsch. Inst.-UN, Chengdu, 1991. Author numerous tech. books; contbr. articles to profl. jours. Recipient Disting. Svc. award Tau Beta Pi, 1974, Imperial Crown Gold medal, Iran, 1976, Achievement award Chinese Engring. and Sci. Assocs. So. Calif., 1977, award Phi Kappa Phi, 1982, Outstanding Contbn. honor Pi Epsilon Tau, 1984, Svc. award Republic of Honduras, 1989, award in Petroleum Chem. Am. Chem. Soc., 1994, Kapitsa Gold medal Russian Fedn., 1995. Fellow Royal Chem. Soc., Inst. Petroleum, Am. Inst. Chemists; mem. Am. Chem. Soc. (bd. dirs. 1993, councillor, founder and chmn. geochemistry divsn. 1979-81, Chinese Acad. Scis. (standing com.), Acad. Scis. Russian Fedn. (academician, fgn. mem.). Home: 2378 Morslay Rd Altadena CA 91001-2716 Office: U So Calif University Park KAP 224A Los Angeles CA 90089

YEN, WEN-HSIUNG, language professional educator; b. Tainan, Taiwan, June 26, 1934; came to U.S., 1969; m. Yuan-yuan Yen, Jan. 6, 1961; children: Tin-ju, Tin-jen, Tin-Tao. BA, Nat. Taiwan Normal U., 1960; MA, UCLA, 1971, postgrad., 1995. Instr. Taiwan Provincial Taichung Tchr. Coll., 1961-62; prof. Chinese Culture U., Taipei, 1964-69; lectr. West L.A. C.C., 1978-82; founder Chinese Culture Sch. L.A., 1976—; grad. tchg. asst. U. Md., 1982-83; instr. L.A. City Coll., 1983—, Calif. State U. L.A., 1984—, Pasadena City Coll., 1989—; prof. Chinese Santa Monica (Calif.) Coll., 1986—, Calif. State U. Northridge, 1986—; founder Wen Yen Piano Studio, 1972—; founder, dir. Chinese Mus. Orch. So. Calif., 1974—. Musical compositions include: Collection of Works by Mr. Yen, 1969; recordings: Art Songs and Chinese Folk Songs, 1982; author: Taiwan Folk Songs, 1967, vol. 2, 1969, A Dictionary of Chinese Music and Musicians, 1967, A Collection of Wen-hsiung Yen's Songs, 1968, vol. 2, 1987, Achievement and Methodology for Comparative Musicology, 1968; transl. Chinese Musical Culture and Folk Songs, 1989; organizer concerts and conductor. Mem. Chinese-Am. Musicians Assn. So. Calif., Chinese Choral Soc. So. Calif. (music dir.), Soc. Ethnomusicology, Coll. Music Soc., Internat. Coun. Traditional Music, Soc. Asian Music, Alumni Assn. Chinese Culture U. in USA, Taiwan Benevolent Assn. Am. (bd. dirs.), Taiwan Benevolent Assn. Calif. (bd. dirs., v.p. 1986, pres. 1987-89), Chinese Am. PTA So. Calif. (supr. 1985—). Office: Chinese Culture Sch 482 Los Altos Ave Arcadia CA 91007

YENER, MUZZ, civil engineer, educator; b. Iskenderun, Turkey, June 30, 1947; s. Celal and Rahmiye (Koraltan) Y.; m. Barbara Ann Valovage, Dec. 14, 1980; children: Devren Adem, Alden Efrem, Erin Esra, Suzan Nora. BCE, NYU, 1969, MS, 1971; PhD, Cornell U., 1979. Design engr. Herbert Fleisher Assocs., N.Y.C., 1970; teaching asst., rsch. assoc. Cornell U., Ithaca, N.Y., 1974-80; design engr. Turkish Army Engring. Corps., 1976; supervising engr. Dalsar Corp., Turkey, 1977; asst. prof. Purdue U., West Lafayette Ind., 1980-86; prof. civil engring. Utah State U., 1986—; cons. Served with Turkish Army, 1976. Recipient govt. grants for coll. edn., 1966-72. Mem. ASCE, Am. Concrete Inst., Sigma Xi, Chi Epsilon. Author: Dynamics of Bridge Structures, 1984; contbr. articles to profl. jours. Office: Utah State U Dept Civil Engring Logan UT 84322

YEOMANS, RUSSELL ALLEN, lawyer, translator; b. Vancouver, B.C., Can., May 13, 1944; came to U.S., 1951; s. Douglas Allen and Mabel Jean (Maguire) Y.; m. Minako Hara, July 7, 1981; children: Megumi Kay, Ken Douglas. BA, U. Calif., Berkeley, 1966, postgrad.; LLB, U. Ottawa, Ont., Can., 1985; LLM, U. Wash., 1986; postgrad., Hiroshima (Japan) U., York U., Toronto, 1990-92. Bar: N.Y. 1988, Calif. 1992; called to Ont. bar, 1991. Mem. rsch. dept. Japan External Trade Orgn., San Francisco, 1967-69; translator Sec. State, Ottawa, Ont., 1971-73, 84-85; head fgn. trade dept. Tanaka Shoji, Hiroshima, Japan, 1973-76; head tchr. Brit. Japan, Tokyo, 1977-81; fgn. law cons. Tokyo Aoyama Law Office, 1986-88; assoc. Baker & McKenzie, Toronto, 1989-91, L.A., 1991-92; pvt. practice, Rancho Palos Verdes, Calif., 1992-93; ptnr. Sanders and Yeomans, Torrance, Calif., 1993-94; pvt. practice Rancho Palos Verdes, Calif., 1994—; legal adv. Seicho-No-Ie Internat. Hdqs., Tokyo. With USN, 1961-65. Mem. N.Y. State Bar Assn., York Bar Assn., Law Soc. Upper Can., C. of C., Indonesian Bus.

Soc., U. Calif. Berkeley Alumni Assn., U. Wash. Law Alumni Assn., Tokyo Can. Club (v.p., pres. 1987-89). Home: 6746 Los Verdes Dr Palos Verdes Peninsula CA 90275-5528 Office: PO Box 3214 Palos Verdes Peninsula CA 90274-9214

YEP, LAURENCE MICHAEL, author; b. San Francisco, June 14, 1948; s. Thomas Kim and Franche (Lee) Y. B.A., U. Calif., Santa Cruz, 1970; Ph.D., SUNY, Buffalo, 1975. Tchr. San Jose (Calif.) City Coll., part-time 1975-76, Foothill Coll., Mountain View, Calif., 1975, U. Calif., Berkeley, 1987-89; writer in residence U. Calif., Santa Barbara, 1990; Book-of-the-Month writing fellow, 1970; teaching fellow SUNY, Buffalo, 1970-73, research fellow, 1973-74. Author sci. fiction stories, children's stories, 1968—: Sweetwater, 1973, Dragonwings (Newbery Honor Book award ALA 1976, Children's Book award Internat. Reading Assn. 1976), (Carter G. Woodson award Nat. Council Social Studies 1976), 1975, Child of the Owl, 1977, Seademons, 1977, Sea Glass, (Commonwealth Club lit. award 1979), 1979, Kind Hearts and Gentle Monsters, 1982, The Mark Twain Murders, 1982, Dragon of the Lost Sea, 1982, Liar, Liar, 1983, Tom Sawyer Fires, 1984, Dragon Steel, 1985, Mountain Light, 1985, Shadow Lord, 1985, Monster Makers, Inc., 1986, Curse of the Squirrel, 1987, The Rainbow People, 1989; author one-act plays Pay the Chinaman, 1987, FairyBones, 1987, Dragon Cauldron, 1991, The Lost Garden, 1991, The Star Fisher, 1991 (Christopher award 1992, W.Va. Literary award 1995), Tongues of Jade, 1991, theatrical adaption of Dragonwings, 1991, Dragon War, 1992, American Dragons, 1992, also editor, Butterfly Boy, 1993, Dragon's Gate, (Newbery Honor Book award ALA 1994), 1993, The Ghost Fox, 1993, The Man Who Tricked a Ghost, 1993 (Am. Book award 1995), The Shell Woman and the King, 1993, The Boy Who Swallowed Snakes, 1994, The Junior Thunder Lord, 1994, The Tiger Woman, 1994, Thief of Hearts, 1995, Ribbons, 1996, Goblin Pearls, 1996, The Khan's Daughter, 1996. Literature fellow Nat. Endowment for Arts, 1990. Address: 921 Populus Pl Sunnyvale CA 94086-9050

YESTADT, JAMES FRANCIS, music director, conductor; b. Harrisburg, Pa., Nov. 24, 1921; s. Frederic John and Emelie Josephine (Speer) Y.; m. Victoria Ann Turco; children: Gregory James, Frederic John II, James Francis Jr. MusB, Lebanon Valley Conservatory Music, Pa., 1947; MA in Music, Columbia U., 1952; postgrad., New Sch. Music, Pa.; cert. in performance, Lucerne (Switzerland) Conservatory, 1962. Assoc. music prof. Xavier U., New Orleans, 1947-58; music dir., condr. New Orleans Summer Pops, 1954-58; resident condr. New Orleans Philharm. Symphony Orch., 1960-63; condr., dir. Transylvania Symphony Orch., Brevard, N.C., 1963-66; music dir., condr. Mobile (Ala.) Symphony Orch., 1965-71, Opera Mobile; dir. orchestral studies U. So. Miss., Hattiesburg, 1971-76; music dir., condr. Baton Rouge Symphony Orch., 1976-82; dir. orchestral studies La. State U., Baton Rouge, 1976-88; music dir., condr. Sun Cities Symphony Orch., Sun City, Ariz., 1988—; gen. dir., condr. Mobile Opera Co., 1966-82; guest condr. Jackson (Miss.) Symphony Orch., 1986, Zurich Radio Orch., numerous festivals, U.S., Europe. Numerous TV appearances and radio shows;. Served with U.S. Army, 1942-46, ETO. Mem. Music Educators Nat. Conf. (Performance award 1984), Coll. Music Soc., Am. Symphony Orch. League. Office: Sun Cities Symphony Orch Assn PO Box 1417 Sun City AZ 85372-1417

YETTO, JOHN HENRY, corporation president; b. N.Y.C., Apr. 25, 1928; s. Michael and Josephine (Sofo) Y.; m. Nancy A. Cagliostro, June 9, 1957; children: Sheryl, Kay, Michelle. BSChemE, CCNY, 1950, Bklyn. Poly., 1951; postgrad., Rutgers U., 1952. Devel. engr. Materials Lab. N.Y. Naval Shipyard, Bklyn., 1951-52; process engr. Bakelite Co., Div. UCC, Bound Brook, N.J., 1953-57; asst. plant engr. Revlon, Inc., Passaic, N.J., 1957-59; dept. mgr. Aerojet, Inc., Sacramento, Calif., 1959-71; pres. Systemedics, Sacramento, Calif., 1971-85, Proserv, Inc., Sacramento, Calif., 1975—. Chmn. YMCA Bd. of Mgrs., San Juan, Sacramento, Calif., 1964; pres. C. of C., Fair Oaks, Sacramento, 1984; pres. Rotary Club of Fair Oaks, 1982; pres. Fairway Pines Homeowners Assn., 1989—, Sunrise Knolls Townhouse Owners' Assn., 1995. 1st lt. USAF, 1952-53.

YGLESIAS, KENNETH DALE, college president; b. Tampa, Fla., Feb. 3, 1946; s. Jose and Julia (Quintero) Y.; m. Donna Carmen Belli, Nov., 1977. BA, U. South Fla., 1969; MA, Western Carolina U., 1973; EdD, U. So. Calif., 1977. Cert. tchr., Calif., Fla. Tchr., coach pub. schs., Tampa, 1969-73; tchr., dept. chmn. Am. Sch. Madrid, 1973-76; fgn. svc. officer USIA, Washington and Tel Aviv, 1977-79; assoc. prof. Pepperdine U., L.A., 1979-83; prof., dir. El Camino Coll., Torrance, Calif., 1981-83; adminstrv. dean Coastline Coll., Fountain Valley, Calif., 1983-88; v.p. Coast C.C. Dist., Costa Mesa, Calif., 1988-95; pres. Golden West Coll., Huntington Beach, Calif., 1995—. Contbr. articles to profl. jours. Bd. dirs. C.C.'s for Internat. Devel., 1988-94, Orange County Marine Inst., Costa Mesa, 1990-93, United Way Orange County, Santa Ana, Calif., 1991-94. Mem. Am. Assn. for Higher Edn. (Hispanic caucus), Assn. Calif. C.C. Adminstrs., Phi Delta Kappa. Democrat. Roman Catholic. Office: Golden West Coll PO Box 2748 Huntington Beach CA 92647-2748

YGUADO, ALEX ROCCO, economics educator; b. Lackawanna, N.Y., Jan. 17, 1939; s. Manuel and Rose (Barrillio) Y.; m. Patricia Ann Rieker; children: Gary Alexander, Melissa Rose, Charissa Ann. BA, San Fernando State Coll., Northridge, 1968; MA, Calif. State U., Northridge, 1970; MS, U. So. Calif., 1972. Contractor Los Angeles, 1962-69; instr. Calif. Poly. State U., San Luis Obispo, 1969-70, U. So. Calif., Los Angeles, 1970-74; prof. econs. L.A. Mission Coll., San Fernando, Calif., 1975—, acad. senate pres., 1992-93, cluster chair profl. studies, 1993—; cons. Community Service Orgn., Los Angeles, 1969-71. Author: Principles of Economics, 1978; contbr. chpts. to books. Served with U.S. Army, 1957-60. Recipient: Blue Ribbon landscape design City of Albuquerque, 1962, Cert. Appreciation Los Angeles Mission Coll., 1978; Fulbright scholar, 1986-87. Mem. Calif. Small Bus. Assn. Democrat. Roman Catholic. Clubs: Newman (Los Angeles), Sierra Retreat (Malibu, sponsor). Home: 30960 Romero Canyon Rd Castaic CA 91384-3449 Office: LA Mission Coll 13356 Eldridge Ave Sylmar CA 91342-3200

YIM, SOLOMON CHIK-SING, civil engineering educator, consultant; b. Hong Kong, Sept. 11, 1952; came to U.S., 1972; s. Fuk-Ching and San-Chan (Leung) Y.; m. Lenore S. Hata, Aug. 27, 1983; children: Rachel L., Joshua A. BSCE, Rice U., 1976; MSCE, U. Calif., Berkeley, 1977, MA in Math., 1981, PhD in Civil Engring., 1983. Registered profl. engr., Oreg. Rsch. asst. U. Calif., 1976-83, vis. lectr., 1983-84, vis. assoc. prof., 1993-94; sr. rsch. engr. Exxon Prodn. Rsch. Co., Houston, 1984-87; asst. prof. civil engring. Oreg. State U., Corvallis, 1987-91, assoc. prof., 1991-97, prof., 1997—; cons. engr., 1977—; mem. ship structures com. NRC, 1990-96; mem. grad. fellowship com. in sci. and engring. Dept. Def., 1989-96; sr. vis. scientist Norwegian Coun. for Sci. and Indsl. Rsch., Trondheim, 1994. Fellow Office Naval Rsch., 1989-91; sr. faculty rsch. fellow USN, 1993. Mem. ASCE (publ. com. 1993-96, editl. bd. 1996—), ASME, Soc. Naval Architecture and Marine Engrs., Internation Soc. Offshore and Polar Engrs. (charter, conf. tech. program com. 1992—). Office: Oreg State U Apperson Hall 202 Corvallis OR 97331

YIN, GERALD ZHEYAO, technology and business executive; b. Beijing, Jan. 29, 1944; came to U.S., 1980; s. Huaixing and Halumi Yin; m. Junling June Yen; 1 child, John Chengjian. BS in Chem. Physics, U. Sci. & Tech. China, Beijing, 1967; postgrad., Beijing U., 1978-80; PhD in Chemistry, UCLA, 1984. Process engr. Lanzhou Oil Refinery, Lanzhou, People's Republic of China, 1967-73; mgr. research staff Chinese Acad. Sciences, Lanzhou, 1973-78; sr. process engr. Intel Corp. Santa Clara TD, Santa Clara, Calif., 1984-86; mgr., staff engr. Lam Rsch. Corp., Rsch. & Devel., Fremont, Calif., 1986-91; mng. dir., v.p. Applied Materials, Inc., Santa Clara, Calif., 1991—; v.p., chief tech. officer Etch Bus. Group; gen. mgr. Silicon Etch divsn. Etch Bus. Group. Author: Introducing Orthogonal Design to Semiconductor Industry, 1985; inventor Rainbow oxide etcher, 200mm enhanced Electron Cyclotron Resonance reactor, High Density plasma source for Dielectric Etch (IPS) and Decoupled Plasma Source and reactors for Conductor Etches (DPS). Recipient Nat. Acad. award People's Republic of China, 1979, Nat. Acad. Invention award, People's Republic of China, 1980. Mem. Electrochem. Soc., Am. Chem. Soc., Am. Vacuum Soc., Silicon Valley Chinese Engring. Assn. (founder, first pres.). Office: Applied Materials Inc 3320 Scott Blvd # 1114 Santa Clara CA 95054-3101

YINGLING, ROBERT GRANVILLE, JR., accountant; b. Lakewood, Ohio, Nov. 8, 1940; s. Robert Granville and Natalie (Phillips) Y.; m. Linda Kay Patterson, Mar. 30, 1968; 1 child, Michael Philip. AB in Polit. Sci., U. Mo., 1963; postgrad., U. Ariz., 1966-67, Portland State U., 1971-73. CPA, Oreg.; cert. govt. fin. mgr. Mgmt. trainee Mich. Nat. Bank, Flint, 1963-65; comml. note teller First Nat. Bank Ariz., Tucson, 1965-67; spl. asst. Travelers Ins. Cos., Phoenix, then Portland, Oreg., 1967-70; chief acct. Am. Guaranty Life Ins. Co., Portland, 1970-73; supr. Peat, Marwick, Mitchell & Co., Portland, 1973-79; ptnr. Dietrich, Bye, Griffin & Youel, Portland, 1979-84; prin. Isler, Collins & McAdams, Portland, 1984-85; owner, acct. R.G. Yingling Jr., CPA, Portland, 1985—; adj. asst. prof., U. Portland, 1988. Treas. Portland Amateur Hockey Assn., 1977-78; mem. exec. bd. Columbia Pacific coun. Boy Scouts Am., 1980—, asst. treas., 1986-87, treas. 1988-91, dist. chmn. Mt. View, 1991; bd. dirs. Artist Repertory Theatre, Inc., 1992-96, St. Andrew Legal Clinic, Inc., 1992—, treas.; dir., treas. Mt. Hood Repertory Theatre, 1997—. Recipient Silver Beaver award, Boy Scouts Am., 1986. Mem. AICPA, Oreg. Soc. CPAs, Inst. Mgmt. Accts. (nat. dir. 1985-87), Assn. Govt. Accts. (nat. v.p. 1983), Nat. Conf. CPA Practitioners, Rotary.

YNDA, MARY LOU, artist, educator; b. Los Angeles, Apr. 4, 1936; d. Ernest Pastor Ynda and Mary Estella (Ruiz) Zapotocky, m. Gary Lynn Coleman, Sept. 1, 1956 (div. Feb. 1983); children: Debra Lynn, Lisa Annette, David Gary; m. Miles Ciletti, May 25, 1991. Student, Immaculate Heart Coll., Los Angeles, 1973-79; AA in Fine Arts, Los Angeles City Coll., 1976; BA, Calif. State U., L.A., 1993. Instr. Fashion Inst. Design, L.A., 1980-81; tchr. art to disabled First St. Gallery, Claremont, Calif., 1991-94; tchr. art Tierra Del Sol Found., Sunland, Calif., 1995-96. Exhibited in group shows at Double Rocking G Gallery, L.A., 1983, Improv Theater West, West Hollywood, Calif., 1983, Exposition Gallery Calif. State U., L.A., 1983, L.A. Art Core Gallery, 1985, Poly. Tech. Sch., Pasadena, Calif., 1986, Bad Eye Gallery, L.A., 1987, Art in the Hall VI West Hollywood City Hall, 1989, Echo Park Gallery, L.A., 1991, Art N Barbee Gallery, 1992, A Celebration of City Life, 1993, DADA Show-Downtown Lives, L.A., 1994, 96, Spirit Exhbn. for Women's Caucus for Art, Santa Ana, Calif., 1995; designer Spoken Word CD Long Days and Monster Nights, 1994; contbg. author poetry Spoken Word Voices of the Angels, 1982; book rev. Yesterday and Tomorrow: California Women Artists, 1989. Archetypes and Contemporary Images in The Hispanic World. The City of Lancaster Mus./Art Gallery, Lancaster Calif. Mem. Women's Caucus for Art. Democrat.

YOCAM, DELBERT WAYNE, software products company executive; b. Long Beach, Calif., Dec. 24, 1943; s. Royal Delbert and Mary Rose (Gross) Y.; m. Janet McVeigh, June 13, 1965; children—Eric Wayne, Christian Jeremy, Elizabeth Janelle. B.A. in Bus. Adminstrn., Calif. State U.-Fullerton, 1966; M.B.A., Calif. State U., Long Beach, 1971. Mktg.-supply changeover coordinator Automotive Assembly div. Ford Motor Co., Dearborn, Mich., 1966-72; prodn. control mgr. Control Data Corp., Hawthorne, Calif., 1972-74; prodn. and material control mgr. Bourns Inc., Riverside, Calif., 1974-76; corp. material mgr. Computer Automation Inc., Irvine, Calif., 1976-78; prodn. planning mgr. central staff Cannon Electric div. ITT, World hdqrs., Santa Ana, Calif., 1978-79; exec. v.p., COO Apple Computer, Inc., Cupertino, Calif., 1979-91; pres., COO, dir. Textronix Inc., Wilsonville, Oreg., 1992-95; chmn., CEO Borland Internat., Inc., Scotts Valley, Calif., 1996—; ,em. faculty Cypress Coll., Calif., 1972-79; bd. dirs. Adobe Sys Inc., Mountain View, Calif., 1991—, Oracle Corp., Redwood Shores, Calif., 1992-97, AST Rsch., Inc., Irvine, Calif., 1992-95, Integrated Measurement Sys. Inc., Beaverton, Oreg., 1995-97, Castelle, Inc., Santa Clara, Calif., 1995-96, Sapiens Internat. Corp., 1995—, Boomtown, Inc., Verdi, Nev., 1995—, Raster Graphics, Inc., San Jose, Calif., 1995—, Xircom, Inc., Thousand Oaks, Calif., 1996—; vice chmn. Tech. Ctr. Innovation, San Jose, Calif., 1989-90. Mem. Am. Electronics Assn. (nat. bd. dirs. 1988-89), Control Data Corp. Mgmt. Assn. (co-founder 1974), L.A. County Heart Assn. (active 1966).

YOCHEM, BARBARA JUNE, sales executive, lecturer; b. Knox, Ind., Aug. 22, 1945; d. Harley Albert and Rosie (King) Runyan; m. Donald A. Yochem (div. 1979); 1 child, Morgan Lee; m. Don Heard, Dec. 12, 1987. Grad. high school, Knox, Ind., 1963. Sales rep. Hunter Woodworks, Carson, Calif., 1979-84, sales mgr., 1984-87; sales rep. Comml. Lumber and Pallet, Industry, Calif., 1987-92; owner By By Prodns., Glendora, Calif., 1976—. Author: Barbara Yochem's Inner Shooting; contbr. articles to profl. jours. Head coach NRA Jr. Olympic Shooting Camp, 1989-94; foster parent, 1992-94. Recipient U.S. Bronze medal U.S. Olympic Com., 1976, World Bronze medal U.S. Olympic Com., 1980; nominated Calif. Trapshooting Hall of Fame, 1994. Address: By Prodns PO Box 7363 Mesa AZ 58216

YODER, MARIANNE ELOISE, software developer, consultant; b. Phoenix, Ariz.; d. William Amber and Maryanne King; m. William Ernest Yoder, Dec. 26, 1977. BSN, U. San Francisco, 1972; MS, U. Ariz., 1982, PhD, 1989. RN, Ariz. Nurse U.S. Navy, 1971-80, 91; grad. teaching asst. U. Ariz., Tucson, 1980-82; faculty U. Ariz., Carson City, Nev., 1982-85; grad. rsch. assoc. U. Ariz., Tucson, 1985-90; faculty, dir. coll. health profl. Computer Learning Ctr. No. Ariz. U., Flagstaff, Ariz., 1990-92; software developer, 1992-96, Carson City, Nev., 1996—; chair Ariz. state commn. nursing rsch., 1992-96; chair of PILOT group, Assn. Devel. of Computer-Based Instructional Systems, Columbus, Ohio, 1990-92. Author: Software Integration Plan Introduction to Nursing Diagnosis, 1992, 2nd edit., 1993, contbg. author: Computer Applications in Nursing Education and Practice, 1993; contbr. articles to profl. jours. Vol. Flagstaff Pub. Libr., 1993-96. Recipient Pioneer in Nursing Edn. Informatics award Nurse Educator's Microworld & Fuld, 1994, Meritorious Tchg. Asst. award U. Ariz. Found., 1987. Mem. NLN (exec. bd. 1993-97), N.Y. Acad. of Scis., WEB Soc., Sigma Xi, Sigma Theta Tau (treas. 1970-71), Pi Lambda Theta. Home and Office: 631 Roundup Rd Carson City NV 89701-7615

YOHE, ROBERT MICHAEL, archaeologist, researcher; b. Loma Linda, Calif., Aug. 12, 1958; s. Robert Eugene Michael Yohe and Marylyn Jane Britton; m. Belinda Joy Sharp, Oct. 21, 1978. BA, Calif. State U., 1983; MA, U. Calif., Riverside, 1990, PhD, 1992. Staff archaeologist Archaeol. Rsch. Unit, Riverside, 1984-90; asst. dir. Cultural Resource Facility Calif. State U., Bakersfield, 1990-92, dir. Cultural Resource Facility, 1992-93; state archaeologist Idaho State Hist. Soc., Boise, 1993—, dep. state hist. preservation officer, 1993-96, interim state hist. preservation officer, 1996—; dir. Archaeol. Survey Idaho, Boise, 1993—; vice chmn. Resource Adv. Coun. (Bur. Land Mgmt.), Boise, 1995—; adj. asst. prof. anthropology Boise State U., 1993—. Contbg. author: (coll. textbook) Archaeological Laboratory Methods, 1996; editor: (monograph series) Monographs in Idaho Archaeology and Ethnology, 1996; sr. author: (book) Archaeological Investigations at Breakfast Canyon, Death Valley, Calif., 1996. Recipient Extraordinary Svc. award Gt. Basin Found., 1985; Humanities Rsch. grantee U. Calif., 1987. Mem. Soc. Am. Archaeology, Soc. Hist. Archaeology, Idaho Archaeol. Soc., Soc. Calif. Archaeology, Soc. Archaeol. Sci., Soc. Profl. Archeologists. Home: 2601 Helen St Boise ID 83705 Office: Idaho State Hist Soc 210 Main Boise ID 83702

YOKLEY, RICHARD CLARENCE, fire department administrator; b. San Diego, Dec. 29, 1942; s. Clarence Ralph and Dorothy Junese (Sackman) Y.; m. Jean Elizabeth Liddle, July 25, 1964; children: Richard Clarence II, Karin Denise Yokley Dillard. Student, San Diego City Coll., 1967; AS, Miramar Coll., 1975; student, London Fire Brig. Tng. Acad., 1994, Fire Svc. Coll., Eng., 1994. Cert. fire officer, fire instr., Calif. Disc jockey Sta. KSDS-FM, San Diego, 1966-67; bldg. engr. Consolidated Systems, Inc., San Diego, 1968-72; with Bonita-Sunnyside Fire Dept., Calif., 1972—; ops. chief Bonita-Sunnyside Fire Dept., 1991-93, maintenance officer, 1993—; med. technician Hartson Ambulance, San Diego, 1978-80, Bay Gen. Hosp. (now Scripps Hosp.), Chula Vista, Calif., 1980-83, EMT-D Sea World of San Diego, 1997—; chmn. South Bay Emergency Med. Svc., 1988. Contbr. articles to jours., newspapers and mags. Asst. curator Firehouse Mus., San Diego, 1972-89, docent, 1990-93; scoutmaster troop 874 Boy Scouts Am., Bonita, Calif., 1978-79. With USAF, 1962-66. Recipient Heroism and Community Svc. award Firehouse Mag., N.Y.C., 1987, Star News Salutes award Chula Vista Star News, 1987, Golden Svc. award San Diego County Credit Union, 1988. Mem. Internat. Assn. Firefighters (pres. local chpt. 1981-82), Calif. State Firefighters Assn. (dep. dir. so. divsn. 1994—), Calif. Fire Mechanics, San Diego County Fire Prevention Officers (v.p. 1984, pres. 1985), Bonita Bus. and Profl. Assn. (bd. dirs. 1991-93, Historian award 1987), Fire Mark Cir. of the Ams. (dir. 1994—), Smokey Bear Collectors Assn. (co-founder, dir. 1995—), South Bay Commn., Bonita Hist. Mus. (co-founder 1986), Sport Chalet Dive Club (v.p. 1991). Republican. Methodist. Office: Bonita-Sunnyside Fire Dept 4900 Bonita Rd Bonita CA 91902-1725

YOMTOV, MICHELLE RENE, journalist; b. Galveston, Tex., Mar. 24, 1948; m. Joseph Yomtov. MA, Rice U., 1970. Counselor Houston Coun. for Retarded Children, 1970-73; tchr., counselor Willowbrook Hosp., Staten Island, N.Y., 1973-76; forensic Journalist, freelance journalist and legal rsch., emphasis on neo Nazi activity in police agencies, 1976—, investigator of neo-Nazi and white supremacist subversive groups in U.S. Author: (children's book) Something Strange Called Depression, 1996; author of poetry. Mem., investigator Citizen Commn. on Human Rights, L.A., 1995—, Adv. for reform in state mental hospitals. Named Educator of Yr., Calif. Coun. on Depression, 1992. Democrat. Jewish. Home: 3361 Perlita Ave Los Angeles CA 90039 Office: 321 S Beverly Dr Ste A Beverly Hills CA 90212-4303

YOOL, GEORGE RICHARD, consultant; b. Orange, Calif., Apr. 16, 1969; s. George Malcolm and Norma Susan (Cravey) Follette; m. Megan Tiffaney Jacksen, June 6, 1991; children: Thor Alexander, Logan Anthony. BS in Criminal Justice, No. Ariz. U., Flagstaff, 1993, MEd in Ednl. Leadership, 1995. Cons. dir. Cons. Unltd., Apache Junction, Ariz., 1988—; co-founder Barbarian Corp., 1996. Author: The Blue Rose/Silence, 1986 (1st pl. art contest 1986), Silent Dreams, 1992, The Writer's Cookbook, 1992, An Introduction to Zen Thought, 1993, Classic of Ethic, 1994; co-author: Handbook for Humanizing Higher Education, 1995; creator, author: (discovery) Problem Solving Using Paradology, 1995, Integrated Theory of Learning and Development, 1995; author, discover: (book, presentation, discovery) Mensonnomy: A New Unified Cosmology, 1994; inventor: Virtual Keyboard, 1995. Recipient grad. scholarship No. Ariz. U., Flagstaff, 1995. Mem. Ariz. Grad. Student Assn. (del. 1995), Students and Tchrs. Instrnl. Needs Group (pres. 1995—), Grad. Student Assn. No. Ariz. U. (v.p. 1995). Home: 2060 S Val Vista Apache Junction AZ 85219 Office: Cons Unltd 2060 S Val Vista Apache Junction AZ 85219

YOON, JI-WON, virology, immunology and diabetes educator, research administrator; b. Kang-Jin, Chonnam, Korea, Mar. 28, 1939; came to U.S., 1965; s. Baek-In and Duck-Soon (Lee) Y.; m. Chungja Rhim, Aug. 17, 1968; children: John W., James W. MS, U. Conn., 1971, PhD, 1973. Sr. investigator NIH, Bethesda, Md., 1978-84; prof., chief div. virology U. Calgary, Alta., Can., 1984—, prof., assoc. dir. diabetes rsch. ctr., 1985-90, prof., dir. diabetes rsch. ctr., 1990—; mem. edit. bd. Annual Review Advances Present Rsch. Animal Diabetes, 1990—, Diabetes Rsch. Clin. Practice, 1989—; scientific coord. 10th Internat. Workshop on Immunology Diabetes, Jerusalem, 1989-90; sr. investigator NIH, 1976-84. Contbg. author: Current Topics in Microbiology and Immunology, 1990, Autoimmunity and Pathogenesis of Diabetes, 1990; contbr. articles to New England Jour. Medicine, Jour. Virology, Sci., Nature, The Lancet, Jour. Diabetes. Rsch. fellow Sloan Kettering Cancer Inst., 1973-74, Staff fellow, Sr. Staff fellow NIH, 1974-76, 76-78; recipient NIH Dir. award, 1984, Heritage Med. Scientist award, Alberta Heritage Found. Med. Rsch., 1984, Lectrship. award, 3d Asian Symposium Childhood Diabetes, 1989, 8th Annual Meeting Childhood Diabetes, Osaka, Japan, 1990, 9th Korean/Can. Heritage award, 1989. Mem. Am. Soc. Immunologists, Am. Diabetes Assn., Am. Soc. Microbiology, N.Y. Acad. Sci., Soc. Virology, Internat. Diabetes Fedn. Baptist. Home: 206 Edgeview Dr NW, Calgary, AB Canada T3A 4W9 Office: Julia McFarlane Diabetes Rsch Ctr, 3330 Hospital Dr NW, Calgary, AB Canada T2N 4N1

YORK, GARY ALAN, lawyer; b. Glendale, Calif., Aug. 29, 1943; m. Lois York, 1987; 1 child, Jonathan Alan. BA, Pomona Coll., 1965; LLB, Stanford U., 1968. Bar: Calif. 1969. Ptnr. Dewey Ballantine, L.A., 1985-95, Buchalter, Nemer, Fields & Younger, L.A., 1995—; instr. law sch. UCLA, 1968-69. Bd. editors Stanford Law review, 1966-68. Mem. ABA (chmn. real estate fin. com., real property probate and trust sect. 1987-89, chmn. usury com. 1992-93), L.A. County Bar Assn. (chmn. real estate fin. sect. 1993-96), State Bar of Calif., Am. Coll. Real Estate Lawyers. Office: Buchalter Nemer Fields & Younger 601 S Figueroa St Los Angeles CA 90017-5704

YORK, THEODORE ROBERT, consulting company executive; b. Mitchel Field, N.Y., May 4, 1926; s. Theodore and Helen (Zierak) Y.; m. Clara Kiefer, Jan. 3, 1952; children: Theodore R. II, Sharon L., Scott K., Krista A. Jarman. BS, U.S. Mil. Acad., 1950; MBA, George Washington U., 1964; MPA, Nat. U., 1984. Commd. 2d lt. USAF, 1950, advanced through grades to col., 1970, ret., 1974; pres. T. R. York Cons., Fairfax, Va., 1974-79, T. R. Cons., San Diego, 1979-85, ULTRAPLECS Intelligent Bldgs., Sandy, Utah, 1991—; dir. Software Productivity Consortium, Herndon, Va., 1985-90. Mem. Loudoun County Rep. Com., Leesburg, Va., 1990-91. Decorated DFC, Air medal (5), Meritorius Svc. medal, Joint Svcs. Commendation medal, Air Force Commendation medal (5). Mem. Internat. Facilities Mgmt. Assn., Intelligent Bldgs. Inst. (advisor), Instituto Mexicana Del Edificios Intelegente (hon.), Office Planners and Users Group, Shriners, Masons. Office: ULTRAPLECS Intelligent Bldg 1289 S Bluff View Dr Sandy UT 84092-5922 *Success is measured in terms of help from others. I believe in building a team to manage any project. Always use the word "we" and forget the word "I" when addressing a successful project and loyalty will follow.*

YORK, WALTER ALLEN, photographer; b. Knoxville, Tenn., Aug. 7, 1938; s. James Claude and Mary Louise (Sherrill) Y.; m. Victoria Ann Mix, June 1967 (div.); 1 child, Shannon Michelle; m. Bettye June Kiser, Dec. 27, 1986. AA, Hiwassee Coll., 1959; BFA, Art Ctr. Coll. of Design, Pasadena, Calif., 1982. Freelance photographer L.A., 1971—. Mentor Pasadena City Schs., 1994—; judge Nat. CableAce Awards, 1993, 94, 95, 96. With USAF, 1960-61. Mem. Am. Soc. Lighting Designers, Siggraph, Sigma Phi Epsilon (life), UCLA Alumni Assn. (life).

YOSHIDA, AKIRA, biochemist; b. Okayama, Japan, May 10, 1924; came to U.S., 1961; s. Isao and Etsu (Kagawa) Y.; m. Michiko Suzuki, Nov. 10, 1954; 1 child, Emmy. MSc, U. Tokyo, 1947, DSc, 1954. Assoc. prof. U. Tokyo, 1952-60; sr. rsch. fellow U. Pa., Phila., 1960-63; rsch. scientist NIH, Bethesda, Md., 1963-65; rsch. prof. U. Wash., Seattle, 1965-72; dir. dept. biochem. genetics City of Hope Med. Ctr., Duarte, Calif., 1972—. Contbr. over 300 articles to profl. jours. Rockefeller Found. scholar, 1955-56; recipient Merit award Japanese Soc. Human Genetics, 1980, Achievement award City of Hope, 1981, Merit Grant award NIH, 1988. Mem. AAAS, Am. Soc. Biol. Chemists, Am. Soc. Human Genetics (assoc. editor), Am. Soc. Hematology, N.Y. Acad. Scis. Home: 2140 Pinecrest Dr Altadena CA 91001-2121 Office: City of Hope Beckman Inst 1450 Duarte Rd Duarte CA 91010-3011

YOSHIDA, KAREN KAMIJO CATEEL, public relations professional; b. Honolulu, Sept. 18, 1964; d. William Francis and Masako (Kamijo) Cateel. BSBA in Mktg., Hawaii Pacific Coll., 1989. Jour. editorial asst. Univ. Press, U. Hawaii, Honolulu, 1983; customer svc. rep. GTE Hawaiian Tel, Honolulu, 1988; account coord. Ogilvy & Mather Hawaii, Honolulu, 1989; pub. rels. asst. McCormick Communications, Honolulu, 1989-90; account dir. Joyce Timpson & Assocs., Honolulu, 1989-90; mgr. communications and pub. rels. Hawaii State Bar Assn., Honolulu, 1990—; tchr. spl. edn. Kahi Mohala Sch., 1994—; mng. mag. editor, dir. membership benefits Hawaii State Bar Assn., 1990—; mem. Pub. Radio Community Adv. Bd., 1993; instr. Honolulu C.C., 1993. Vol. Easter Seal Soc., Hawaiian Humane Soc., Lanakila Elem. Sch. State contest winner Exec. Women's Internat., 1982. Mem. Sons. and Daus. 442nd RCT (newsletter and membership coms. 1993), Hawaii Pacific U. Alumni Assn. (comm. com. 1993). Home: 94-217 Lumiaina Pl # A202 Waipahu HI 96797-5010 Office: Kahi Mohala School 91-2301 Fort Weaver Rd Ewa Beach HI 96706-3602

YOSHIDA, KOSAKU, quantitative methods educator; b. Tokyo, July 23, 1938; s. Sakujiro and Shizu (Arita) Y.; m. Chizu Matsuda, Oct. 30, 1977; 1 child, Kayo. BA in Commerce, Waseda U., Tokyo, 1962; MS in Bus. Adminstrn., U. Mont., 1968; PhD in Bus. Adminstrn., NYU, 1975. Asst. prof. Calif. State U., Dominquez Hills, 1975-79, assoc. prof., 1979-84, prof., 1984—; cons. in quality mgmt., 1987—. Author: Elementary Statistics,

1989; contbr. articles to profl. jours. Productivity commr. City of L.A., 1988-92. Mem. Decision Scis. Inst., Am. Statis. Assn., Inst. for Ops. Rsch. and the Mgmt. Scis., Am. Soc. for Quality Control. Office: Calif State U Sch Mgmt Dominguez Hls Carson CA 90747

YOSHIMOTO, CEDRIC MITSUO, physician; b. Kansas City, Mo., Aug. 22, 1951; s. Mitsuru and Annie Nakami (Koga) Y.; 1 child, Walden Emil Bjorn. AB, U. Calif., Berkeley, 1972; MD, U. Hawaii, 1977; DTM&H, London Sch., 1990; MPH, U. Hawaii, 1993. Integrated Flexible resident U. Hawaii, Honolulu, 1977-78; staff physician Tumutumu Hosp., Karatina, Kenya, 1979-80; locum tenans physician Kalihi-Palama Clinic, Honolulu, 1982; cons. Hawaii State Dept. of Health, Honolulu, 1983-91; staff physician Waianae Coast Comprehensive Health Ctr., 1983—; cons. U.S. Fish and Wildlife Svc., Honolulu, 1990—; preceptor Hawaii Dept. of Health, Waianae, 1991-92; cons. Ebeye Hosp., Marshall Islands, 1992; cons. Health Care Orgn. for Africa, The Gambia, 1994; asst. clin. prof. Dept. Family Practice and Cmty. Health, John A. Burns Sch. Medicine, U. Hawaii, Honolulu, 1992—, asst. clin. prof. dept. pub. health sci. Sch. Pub. Health, 1994—. Mem. Amnesty Internat., Honolulu, 1983. Fellow Am. Acad. of Family Physicians, Royal Soc. of Tropical Medicine and Hygiene; mem. Am. Soc. of Tropical Medicine and Hygiene, Physicians for Social Responsibility, Wilderness Med. Soc., Sierra Club (instr., cons. 1990—, outing leader, 1990—). Office: Waianae Coast Comprehensive Health Ctr 86-260 Farrington Hwy Waianae HI 96792-3128

YOSHIMOTO, HIROKO, art educator, artist; b. Kobe, Japan, Apr. 23, 1943; came to U.S., 1958; d. Akira and Teiko Yoshimoto. BA with highest honors, UCLA, 1965, MA with highest honors, 1967. Cert. tchr., Calif. Freelance designer Addison-Wesley Pub. Co., 1967-68; graphic designer Zamparelli Graphics, Los Angeles, 1968; with IBM Japan, Tokyo, 1968-70; instr. studio art Ventura (Calif.) Coll., 1970—; instr. Santa Ana (Calif.) Coll., 1970; pres. Studio 83, Ventura, 1983-85, 92-93. One-woman shows include Ventura County Mus. of History and Art, 1978, Gallery 932, Ventura, 1982 New Media Gallery at Ventura Coll., 1989, Tokyo Mcpl. Art Space, 1994, Osaka Contemporary Art Ctr., 1994; exhibited in group shows at Grandview Gallery, L.A., L.A. Artcore Gallery, 1984, 86, L.A. County Mus. Art Rental Gallery, 1987, 92, Ventura County Mus. History and Art, 1997; represented by L.A. County Mus. of Art Rental and Sales Gallery; art dir. (video tapes) Art and Anatomy, 1989, Sumi-e and Western Watercolor, 1989. Recipient Outstanding Faculty Recognition award Ventura Coll. Acad. Senate, 1990. Mem. Am. Fedn. Tchrs., Ventura Art Assn., Asian Am. Women Artists Assn. Democrat. Home: 352 Lupine Way Ventura CA 93001-2221 Office: Ventura Coll 4667 Telegraph Rd Ventura CA 93003-3872

YOSHIZUMI, DONALD TETSURO, dentist; b. Honolulu, Feb. 18, 1930; s. Richard Kiyoshi and Hatsue (Tanouye) Y.; BS, U. Hawaii, 1952; DDS, U. Mo., 1960, MS, 1963; m. Barbara Fujiko Iwashita, June 25, 1955; children: Beth Ann E., Cara Leigh S., Erin Yuri. Clin. instr. U. Mo. Sch. Dentistry, Kansas City, 1960-63; pvt. practice, Santa Clara, Calif., 1963-70, San Jose, Calif., 1970—. With USAF, 1952-56. Mem. Am. Dental Assn., Calif. Dental Assn., Santa Clara County Dental Soc., Omicron Kappa Upsilon, Delta Sigma Delta. Contbr. articles to profl. jours. Home: 5054 Parkfield Ave San Jose CA 95129-3225 Office: 2011 Forest Ave San Jose CA 95128-4813

YOUKHARIBACHE, PHILIPPE BIJIN, pharmaceutical software company executive; b. Paris, Sept. 16, 1955; came to U.S., 1986; s. Amedée Mehdi and Alberte Marie (Baldelli) Y. MS in Phys. Chemistry, U. Paris, Orsay, 1976; PhD in Phys. Sci., U. Paris, 1986. Researcher Ecole Poly., Palaiseau, France, 1978-86; postdoctoral fellow Columbia U., N.Y.C., 1986-87; mgr. Polygen (Europe) Ltd., Paris, 1987-88; dir. product planning Biosym Techs. Inc., San Diego, 1988-90, project dir., 1991-95; pres. InPharmatics Corp., San Diego, 1995—; cons. in field. Mem. AAAS, IEEE, Assn. for Computing Machinery, Biophys. Soc., Protein Soc., Molecular Graphics Soc., Am. Chem. Soc. Office: InPharmatics Corp 7960 Silverton Ave Ste 202 San Diego CA 92126-6345

YOUNG, ANNA LUCIA, communications professional; b. Boise, Idaho, Feb. 13, 1960; m. H. Fred Young II, Aug. 25, 1990. BS in Computer Sci., Nat. U., 1985; MA in Psychology, U.S. Internat. U., 1993, PhD in Indsl./Orgnl. Psychology, 1997. Cert. in stress mgmt. edn., Biofeedback Cert. Inst. Am. Programmer analyst Courseware, Inc., San Diego, 1983-84, Computer Scis. Corp., San Diego, 1984-85; software engr. II Sys. Engring. Assoc., San Diego, 1985-86; sr. programmer analyst Home Fed. Bank, San Diego, 1986-88, exec. info. specialist, 1988-91; orgnl. devel. sys. cons. Cox Comm., San Diego, 1991—. Recipient Appreciation cert. 1st Supervisorial Dist. of County of San Diego, 1994. Mem. APA, ACA, Calif. Psychol. Assn., Psi Chi.

YOUNG, BETTYE JEANNE, retired secondary education educator; b. Chgo., Nov. 2, 1929; d. Frank M. Forbish and Mary Bernice (Phillips) Lunde; m. Dale Eugene Young, July 22, 1950; 1 child, Debra Jeanne. AA, Vallejo Jr. Coll., 1964; BA in History, Dominican Coll., 1968. Tchr. North Star Elem., Anchorage, 1968-78; tchr. Inlet View Elem., Anchorage, 1978-82, tchr.-in-charge, 1979-82; tchr. Ctrl. Jr. High Sch., Anchorage, 1982—, chair social studies dept., 1994-95; vol. tchr. reading and math. Anacortes Elem. Sch., 1997—; chairperson N.W. Accreditation for Ctrl. Jr. High Sch., 1983; mem. Supt.'s Apprasal Com., Anchorage, 1983-85, Anchorage Sch. Dist.'s Talent Bank, 1979-93, Social Studies Curriculum Com., 1979-93, exec. bd. State Coun. Social Studies, 1990-92; chair social study dept. Ctrl. Jr. H.S., 1994—, established youth ct. Author: Thematic Approach to U.S. History, 1989 (Merit award Alaska State Dept.), Immigration Unit for U.S. History, 1988 (Merit award Alaska State Dept.), others in field. Voter registrar, Anchorage, 1984; del. Rep. Caucus, Fairbanks, Alaska, 1984; facilitator marriage seminars, Anchorage, 1989-90; mem. Ch. choir, music dept., Anchorage, 1978-93; mem. adv. bd. Law Related Edn., Anchorage, 1993-94; bd. dirs. Alaska Jr. Coll., 1993-94; vol. reading and math. tchr. elem. schs.; vol. Anacortes Aux. Patrol Police, 1995—. Named Tchr. of Month Anchorage Sch. Dist., 1981; recipient Jr. Achievement Appreciation award, Project Bus., 1987-92, Support of Social Studies award, Alaska Dept. Edn., 1991, 92; grantee Law Related Edn. Fed. Govt., ABA, 1990-94. Mem. NEA, Anchorage Edn. Assn. (chair instrnl. profl. devel. 1984-85), Anchorage Area Social Studies Coun. (sec. 1983-84, v.p. 1988-90, pres. 1990-92), Nat. Coun. Social Studies, Alaska Coun. Social Studies (secondary tch. of the yr. 1991), Phi Delta Kappa (Cook Inlet chpt., v.p. 1990-92), Delta Kappa Gamma. Home: 3909 W 6th St Anacortes WA 98221-1295 Office: Ctrl Jr High Sch 1405 E St Anchorage AK 99501-5047

YOUNG, BONNIE DARLINE, primary school educator; b. Gorden, Nebr., Oct. 14, 1944; d. Raymond Franklin and Mildred Gladys (Gotheridge) Denison; m. Lester R. Young, Sept. 5, 1965; children: Tamara, Kelby, Kadee. BS in Elem. Edn., Kans. State U., 1968. Cert. tchr., Colo., Kans., Mo. Tchr. Geary County Schs., Junction City, Kans., 1968-69, Cherry County Schs., Merriman, Nebr., 1969-70, U.S. Army, Fed. Republic Germany, 1970-73, Smith Acad., Lakewood, Colo., 1985-88, Gilpin Grammar Sch., Denver, 1988-91, Jefferson County Pub. Schs., 1991—. Republican. Nazarene. Office: PO Box 5190 Arvada CO 80005

YOUNG, C. CLIFTON, judge; b. Nov. 7, 1922, Lovelock, Nev.; m. Jane Young. BA, U. Nev., 1943; LLB, Harvard U., 1949. Bar: Nev. 1949, U.S. Dist. Ct. Nev. 1950, U.S. Supreme Ct. 1955. Justice Nev. Supreme Ct., Carson City, 1985—, chief justice, 1989-90. Office: Nev Supreme Ct 201 S Carson St Carson City NV 89701

YOUNG, CHARLES EDWARD, university chancellor; b. San Bernardino, Calif., Dec. 30, 1931; s. Clayton Charles and Eula May (Walters) Y. AA, San Bernardino Coll., 1954; AB, U. Calif., Riverside, 1955; MA, UCLA, 1957, PhD, 1960; DHL (hon.), U. Judaism, L.A., 1969. Congl. fellow Washington, 1958-59; adminstrv. analyst Office of the Pres., U. Calif., Berkeley, 1959-60; asst. prof. polit. sci. U. Calif., Davis, 1960; asst. prof. polit. sci. UCLA, 1960-66, assoc. prof., 1966-69, prof., 1969—, asst. to chancellor, 1960-62, asst. chancellor, 1962-63, vice chancellor, adminstrn., 1963-68, chancellor, 1968—; bd. dirs. Intel Corp., Acad. TV Arts and Sci. Found.; cons. Peace Corps., 1961-62, Ford Found. on Latin Am. Activities, 1964-66; mem. bd. govs. L.A. Met. Project. Mem. Knight Found. Commn. on Intercollegiate Athletics, Calif. Coun. on Sci. and Tech., Town Hall of Calif., Carnegie Comm. Task Force on Sci. and Tech. and the States, Pacific Coun. on Internat. Policy, NCAA Pres.'s Commn., Coun. for Govt.-Univ.-Industry Rsch. Roundtable and the Nat. Rsch. Coun. Adv. Bd.-Issues in Sci. and Tech., Nat. Com. on U.S.-China Rels., chancellor's assocs. UCLA, coun. trustees L.A. Ednl. Alliance for Restructuring Now; past chair. Assn. Am. Univs., Nat. Assn. State Univs. and Land-Grant Colls.; past co-chair Calif. Campus Compact; mem. adminstrv. bd. Internat. Assn. Univs.; bd. govs. Found. Internat. Exchange Sci. and Cultural Info. by Telecom., The Theatre Group Inc.; v.p. Young Musicians Found.; bd. dirs. L.A. Internat. Visitors Coun., Greater L.A. Energy Coalition, L.A. World Affairs Coun.; trustee UCLA Found. With USAF, 1951-52. Named Young Man of Year Westwood Jr. C. of C., 1962; recipient Inter-Am. U. Cooperaton award Inter-Am. Orgn. Higher Edn., Neil H. Jacoby Internat. award UCLA Student Ctr., 1987, Edward A. Dickson Alumnus of Yr. award UCLA Alumni Assn., 1994, Disting. Svc. award U. Calif. Riverside Alumni Assn., 1996, Treasure of L.A. award L.A. Ctrl. City Assn., 1996, Albert Schweitzer Leadership award Hugh O'Brien Youth Found., 1996; hon. fellow UCLA Coll. Letters and Sci., 1996. Fellow AAAS. Office: UCLA Office of Chancellor 405 Hilgard Ave Los Angeles CA 90024-1301

YOUNG, CONNIE SUE, public affairs specialist; b. Oxnard, Calif.. BS in Psychology with honors, Colo. State U., 1977; MA in Journalism, U. Colo., 1987. Adminstrv. officer Divsn. Mental Health, Denver, 1980-86; asst. dir. mktg. Bethesda Hosp., Denver, 1986; writer U. Colo., Boulder, 1987; pub. rels. cons. Boulder, 1987-88; pub. info. specialist Colo. Divsn. Wildlife, Denver, 1988-93; pub. affairs specialist U.S. Fish and Wildlife Svc., Lakewood, Colo., 1993—; cons. pub. rels., mktg. Denver Film Soc., 1996—. Contbr. articles to profl. jours. Recipient 2nd Pl. award print media advt. Nat. Fedn. Press Women, 1990. Mem. Pub. Rels. Soc. Am. (Silver Pick award Colo. chpt. 1994), Alliance Francaise, World Trade Ctr., Inst. Internat. Edn., Mensa, Phi Beta Kappa. Office: US Fish & Wildlife Svc 134 Union Blvd Ste 440 Lakewood CO 80228-1807

YOUNG, DANIEL EDWIN, principal; b. Akron, Ohio; s. Eugene E. and Allys M. (Holmes) Y. BS in Edn., No. Ariz. U., 1969, MA in Edn., 1972; postgrad., Ariz. State U., 1993—. Cert. elem., jr. high, high sch., prin., supt., supr., spl. edn., social studies, elem. grades K-8. Tchr. Cross Categorical Spl. Edn., Flagstaff, Ariz., 1969-71, Emotionally Handicapped Jr. High, Mesa, Ariz., 1971-73; tchr., cons. spl. edn., emotionally handicapped, trainable mentally handicapped, Mesa, 1973-74; asst. prin. C. D. Poston Jr. High Sch., Mesa, 1974-78; prin. D. Mac Arthur Elem. Sch., Mesa, 1978-81, J. J. Rhodes Jr. High Sch., 1981-85, V.E. Johnson Elem. Sch., 1986-90, W.S. Porter Elem. Sch., 1991-96, Barbara Bush Elem. Sch., Mesa, 1996—; cofaciliator conf. and workshop ASU and No. Ariz. U., 1978—; north ctrl. evaluation chair North Ctrl. Accreditation-Tucson, 1980—; on-site visitor nat. blue ribbon panelist U.S. Dept. Edn., Washington, 1984—; workshop cons. State Dept Edn.; co-facilitator to Ariz. Dept. Edn. Principal's Acad.; negotiations facilitator. Author: Guidelines to Supervising Student Teachers, 1972. Named Prin. of Leadership, Nat. Sch. Safety Ctr., 1990, Ariz. Top Ten Elem. Sch. Adminstr., 1990. Mem. Ariz. ASCD (Excellence in Supervision award 1990), Nat. Assn. Elem. Adminstrs./Prins., Mesa Assn. for Sch. Adminstrs., Phi Delta Kappa, Maricopa County Sheriff Posse (life mem.). Office: B Bush Elem Sch 4924 E Ingram Mesa AZ 85205

YOUNG, DAVID VERN, surgeon; b. Bryan, Tex., May 5, 1949; s. LeVern Benjamin and Mary Frances (Smith) Y.; m. Neta Ann Hendricks; children: Sarah, John. BA, Calif. Bapt. Coll., 1969; MD, U. Calif., San Francisco, 1973. Diplomate Am. Bd. Surgery. Rotating intern Valley Med. Ctr./U. Calif. San Francisco, Fresno, Calif., 1973-74, resident in surgery, 1974-78; missionary surgeon Jiblah Bapt. Hosp., Yemen, 1979-81, 83-85, Ajloun Bapt. Hosp., Jordan, 1981-82; postgrad. fellow in surgery VA Hosp., Fresno, 1982-83; pvt. practice surgery Fresno, 1985—; chair dept. surgery Fresno Cmty. Hosp., 1990, v.p. med. staff, 1991; pres. med. staff Cmty. Hosps. of Ctrl. Calif., Fresno, 1992; exec. com. Fresno Cmty. and Com. Hosp. Ctrl. Calif., 1989-94; pres. Comty. Surg. Group, 1996—. Contbr. articles to profl. jours. Organizer, mem. Christian Health Care Network, Fresno, 1989—; deacon Harvard Terr. Bapt. Ch., Fresno, 1985-90; mem. leadership team Cmty. Bible Ch., Fresno, 1993-95. Named Alumnus of Yr., Calif. Bapt. Coll., 1989. Fellow ACS; mem. Calif. Med. Assn., Christian Med./Dental Soc. Republican. Office: 110 N Valeria St Ste 401 Fresno CA 93701-2168

YOUNG, DONALD ALLEN, writer, consultant; b. Columbus, Ohio, June 11, 1931; s. Clyde Allen and Helen Edith (Johnston) Y.; m. Rosemary Buchholz, Feb. 26, 1955 (div. Nov. 1976); children: Kent Allen, Kelly Ann; m. Marjorie Claire Shapiro, Aug. 20, 1977; stepchildren: Jo Alene, Andrea Lynn, Beth Ellen. Student, Ohio State U., 1949-51, Columbia Coll., 1952, North Cen. Coll., Naperville, Ill., 1956, Coll. DuPage, 1978. Editor various newspapers, mags., Detroit, Chgo., Columbus, 1946-63, 1973-74, 1978-79; v.p. Frydenlund Assocs., Chgo., 1963; pub. relations mgr. info. systems div. Gen. Electric Co., Phoenix, 1963-70; publs. dir. Data Processing Mgmt. Assn., Park Ridge, Ill., 1970-72; pub. relations mgr. Addressograph-Multigraph Corp., Arlington Heights, Ill., 1975-76; acct. exec. John Ripley & Assocs., Glenview, Ill., 1977-78; editorial dir. Radiology/Nuclear Medicine mag., Des Plaines, Ill., 1979-81; pres. Young Byrum Inc., Hinsdale, Ill., 1982-83; writer, consultant Tucson, 1983—; cons. various companies, 1973—; sports reporter, Copley newspapers, 1975-83; mem. adv. council Oakton Community Coll., 1970-75. Author: Principles of Automatic Data Processing, 1965, Data Processing, 1967, Rate Yourself as a Manager, 1985, Nobody Gets Rich Working for Somebody Else, 1987, 2d edit., 1993, Rate Your Executive Potential, 1988, If They Can...You Can, 1989, The Entrepreneurial Family, 1990, How to Export, 1990, Women in Balance, 1991, Sleep Disorders: America's Hidden Nightmare, 1992, Small Business Troubleshooter, 1994, Crime Wave: America Needs a New Get-Tough Policy, 1996, Popcorn Publications, 1996, Adventure Guide to Southern California, 1997. Arbitrator Better Bus. Bur., Tucson, 1987-92; docent Ariz. Sonora Desert Mus., 1988-92. With USAF, 1952-56. Recipient Jesse Neal awards Assn. of Bus. Pub., 1959, 61, Silver Anvil award Pub. Rels. Soc. of Am., 1976. Mem. Publicity Club of Chgo. (pres. 1978-79). Soc. Southwestern Authors (pres. 1992), Glen Ellyn (Ill.) Jaycees (bd. dirs., SPOKE award 1959, Outstanding Jaycee 1960), Young Reps. Club (v.p. 1960). Home: 4866 N Territory Loop Tucson AZ 85750-5948

YOUNG, DONALD E., congressman; b. Meridian, Calif., June 9, 1933; m. Lula Fredson; children—Joni, Dawn. AA, Yuba Jr. Coll., 1952; BA ., Chico (Calif.) State Coll., 1958. Former educator, river boat capt.; mem. Fort Yukon City Council, 6 years, mayor, 4 years; mem. Alaska Ho. of Reps., 1966-70, Alaska Senate, 1970-73, 93rd-104th Congresses from Alaska, 1973—; mem. transp. & infrastructure com., chmn. resources com. With U.S. Army, 1955-57. Republican. Episcopalian. Office: US House of Representatives 2111 Rayburn Bldg Ofc B Washington DC 20515-0005

YOUNG, ERNEST, park administrator. Park ranger Puukahola Nat. Hist. Site, Kamuela, Hawaii. Office: PO Box # 44340 Kamuela HI 96743

YOUNG, HENRY, executive director. Exec. dir. Dance Aspen, Inc., Colo. Office: Dance Aspen Inc PO Box 8745 Aspen CO 81612*

YOUNG, HOWARD THOMAS, foreign language educator; b. Cumberland, Md., Mar. 24, 1926; s. Samuel Phillip and Sarah Emmaline (Frederick) Y.; m. Carol Osborne, Oct. 5, 1949 (div. 1966); children—Laurie Margaret, Jennifer Anne; m. Jennifer Bunker, July 15, 1966 (div. 1980); m. Edra Lee Airheart, May 23, 1981; 1 child, Timothy Howard. B.S. summa cum laude, Columbia U., 1950, M.A., 1952, Ph.D., 1954. Lectr. Columbia U., N.Y.C., 1950-54; asst. prof. Romance langs. Pomona Coll., Claremont, Calif., 1954-60; assoc. prof. Pomona Coll., Claremont, 1960-66, Smith prof. Romance langs., 1966—; vis. prof. Middlebury Program in Spain, Madrid, 1986-87, U. Zaragoza, 1967-68; chief reader Spanish AP Ednl. Testing Service, Princeton, 1975-78, chmn. Spanish lang. devel. commn., 1976-79; mem. fgn. lang. adv. commn. Coll. Bd., N.Y.C., 1980-83; mem. West Coast selection commn. Mellon Fellowships for Humanities, Princeton, 1984-86, European selection com., 1987, 90. Author: The Victorious Expression, 1964, Juan Ramón Jiménez, 1967, The Line in the Margin, 1980; editor: T.S. Eliot and Hispanic Modernity, 1995; contbr. numerous articles and book revs. to profl. jours. Dir. NEH summer seminar for Sch. tchrs., 1993. Served with USNR, 1944-46, ETO. Fellow Del Amo Found., 1960-61, NEH, 1975, 89-90; Fulbright fellow; 1967-68; Rockefeller Study Ctr. scholar, 1976. Mem. MLA, Assn. Tchrs. Spanish and Portuguese, Am. Comparative Lit. Assn., Acad. Am. Poets, Assn. Lit. Scholars and Critics. Home: 447 W Redlands Ave Claremont CA 91711-1638 Office: Pomona Coll Modern Romance Dept 550 Harvard Ave Claremont CA 91711-6380

YOUNG, J. LOWELL, soil chemist, biologist; b. Perry, Utah, Dec. 13, 1925; s. I.A. and Elzada (Nelson) Y.; m. Ruth Ann Jones, Sept. 15, 1950; children: Gordon, LoAnn, Colene, Kathryn. BS, Brigham Young U., 1953; PhD, Ohio State U., 1956. Rsch. asst. Ohio Agrl. Expt. Sta., Columbus, 1953-56, postdoctoral fellow, 1956-57; chemist Agrl. Research Service USDA, Corvallis, Oreg., 1957-64, rsch. chemist, 1964-78; asst. prof. Oreg. State U., Corvallis, 1957-63, assoc. prof., 1963-78, prof. soil sci., 1978-90, Courtesy prof. soil sci., 1990—; rsch. chemist Horticultural Crops Rsch. Unit USDA, Corvallis, 1978-88; collaborator Horticultural Crops Rsch. Unit U.S. Dept. Agrl., Corvallis, 1988-91. Contbr. articles to profl jours. Served with USAAF, 1944-46. Mem. AAAS, Am. Inst. Soil Sci. Soc., Internat. Humic Substances Soc., Soil Sci. Soc. of Am. (officer 1972-75, assoc. editor jour. 1975-80), Am. Soc. Agronomy (officer western 1966-72), Western Soc. Soil Sci. (officer 1966-71), Inst. for Alternative Agrl. Office: Oreg State U Crops & Soil Sci Dept Corvallis OR 97331

YOUNG, JOAN CRAWFORD, advertising executive; b. Hobbs, N.Mex., July 30, 1931; d. William Bill and Ora Maydelle (Boone) Crawford; m. Herchelle B. Young, Nov. 23, 1971 (div.). BA, Hardin Simmons U., 1952; postgrad. Tex. Tech. U., 1953-54. Reporter, Lubbock (Tex.) Avalanche-Jour., 1952-54; promotion dir. Sta. KCBD-TV, Lubbock, 1954-62; account exec. Ward Hicks Advt., Albuquerque, 1962-70; v.p. Mellekas & Assocs., Advt., Albuquerque, 1970-78; pres. J. Young Advt., Albuquerque, 1978—. Bd. dirs. N.Mex. Symphony Orch., 1970-73, United Way of Greater Albuquerque, 1985-89; bd. trustees N.Mex. Children's Found., 1994-96. Recipient Silver medal N.Mex. Advt. Fedn., 1977. Mem. N.Mex. Advt. Fedn. (bd. dirs. 1975-76), Am. Advt. Fedn., Greater Albuquerque C. of C. (bd. dirs. 1984), Albuquerque Petroleum Club (membership chmn. 1992-93, bd. dirs. 1993—, sec. 1994-95, v.p. 1995-97, pres. 1997—). Republican. Author: (with Louise Allen and Audre Lipscomb) Radio and TV Continuity Writing, 1962. Office: 1638 Tierra Del Rio NW Albuquerque NM 87107

YOUNG, JOHN ALAN, electronics company executive; b. Nampa, Idaho, Apr. 24, 1932; s. Lloyd Arthur and Karen Eliza (Miller) Y.; m. Rosemary Murray, Aug. 1, 1954; children: Gregory, Peter, Diana. BSEE, Oreg. State U., 1953; MBA, Stanford U., 1958. Various mktg. and fin. positions Hewlett Packard Co. Inc., Palo Alto, Calif., 1958-63, gen. mgr. microwave divsn., 1963-68, v.p. electronic products group, 1968-74, exec. v.p., 1974-77, COO, 1977-78, pres., 1977-92, CEO, 1978-92; ret., 1992; bd. dirs. Wells Fargo Bank, Wells Fargo and Co., Chevron Corp., SmithKline Beecham Plc. Affymetrix, Inc., Shaman Pharms. Inc., Ciphergen, Novell, Inc.; chmn. Smart Valley, Inc., Lucent Technologies. Chmn. ann. fund Stanford U., 1966-73, nat. chmn. corp. gifts, 1973-77, mem. adv. coun. Grad. Sch. Bus., 1967-73, 75-80, Univ. trustee, 1977-87; bd. dirs. Mid-Peninsula Urban Coalition, 1971-80, co-chmn., 1983-85; chmn. Pres.'s Commn. on Indsl. Competitiveness, 1983-85, Nat. Jr. Achievement, 1983-84; pres. Found. for Malcolm Baldrige Nat. Quality Award; mem. Adv. Com. on Trade Policy and Negotiations, 1988-92. With USAF, 1954-56. Mem. Nat. Acad. Engring., Coun. on Competitiveness (founder, founding chair computer systems policy project 1986), Bus. Coun. (co-chair pres. com. of adcisors on sci. & tech. 1993—).

YOUNG, JOHN BYRON, retired lawyer; b. Bakersfield, Calif., Aug. 10, 1913; s. Lewis James and Gertrude Lorraine (Clark) Y.; m. Helen Beryl Stone, Dec. 26, 1937; children: Sally Jean, Patricia Helen, Lucia Robin. BA, UCLA, 1934; LLB, U. Calif., Berkeley, 1937. Pvt. practice law Hargreaves & Young, later Young Wooldridge, Bakersfield, 1937-40; dep. county counsel County of Kern, Bakersfield, 1940-42; dep. rationing atty. U.S. OPA, Bakersfield and Fresno, Calif., 1942; ptnr. firm Young Wooldridge and predecessors, Bakersfield, 1946-78, assoc. law firm, 1978-91; bd. dirs., legal counsel Kern County Water Assn., Bakersfield, 1953-76. Mem., chmn. Kern County Com. Sch. Dist. Orgn., Bakersfield, 1950s and 60s; mem. Estate Planning Coun. of Bakersfield, 1960-76, pres., 1965-66. Capt. JAGC, U.S. Army, 1943-46. Mem. Kern County Bar Assn. (prs. 1948, Bench and Bar award 1978). Home: 13387 Barbados Way Del Mar CA 92014-3501 Office: Young Wooldridge 1800 30th St 4th Fl Bakersfield CA 93301-5298

YOUNG, JON NATHAN, archaeologist; b. Hibbing, Minn., May 30, 1938; s. Robert Nathan Young and Mary Elizabeth (Barrows) Roy; m. Karen Sue Johnson, June 5, 1961 (div. May 1980); children: Shawn Nathan, Kevin Leigh; m. Tucker Heitman, June 18, 1988 (div. Apr. 1996). BA magna cum laude, U. Ariz., 1960, PhD, 1967; MA, U. Ky., 1962. Archeologist Nat. Park Svc. Southwest Archeol. Ctr., Globe and Tucson, Ariz., 1967-75; exec., camp dir. YMCA of Metro. Tucson, 1976-77; asst. dir. Kit Carson Meml. Found., Taos, N.Mex., 1978; co-dir. Las Palomas de Taos, 1979; archeologist Nat. Forest Svc., Carson Nat. Forest, Taos, 1980—; exec. order cons. U.S. Sec. Interior, 1973-75. Author: The Salado Culture in Southwestern Prehistory, 1967; co-author: Excavation of Mound 7, 1981, First-Day Road Log in Tectonic Development of the Southern Sangre de Cristo Mountains, 1990. Advisor Boy Scouts Am.; active YMCA White Rag Soc.; mem. Kit Carson Hist. Mus. Grantee NEH, 1978; Ariz. Wilson Found., NSF, Ky. Rsch. Found. fellow, 1960-62; Baird Found., Bausch and Lomb, Elks; recipient cert. merit USDA, 1987, 89. Fellow AAAS, Am. Anthrop. Assn., Explorers Club, Royal Anthrop. Inst.; mem. Current Anthropology (assoc.), Ariz. Archaeol. and Hist. Soc., Ariz. Hist. Soc., Ctr. Anthropol. Studies, Coun. on Am.'s Mil. Past, Friends of Taos Pub. Libr., Kit Carson Hist. Mus., New Mex. Heritage Preservation Alliance, Soc. Hist. Archaeology, Soc. Am. Archaeology, Harwood Found., Millicent Rogers Mus., Taos Archaeol. Soc., Taos County Hist. Soc. (bd. dirs.), Sigma Xi, Phi Beta Kappa, Alpha Kappa Delta, Phi Kappa Phi, Delta Chi. Home: PO Box 2207 Taos NM 87571-2207 Office: Nat Forest Svc Suprs Office 208 Cruz Alta Rd Taos NM 87571-5983

YOUNG, JOYCE HENRY, adult education educator, consultant; b. Oak Park, Ill., July 3, 1930; d. Jesse Martin and Adelina Patti (Gillander) H.; m. James Edward Young, Apr. 26, 1958; children: Richard Allen, Patti Ann. BA, Calif. State U., Fresno, 1951; MA, Northwestern U., 1952; EdD, U. So. Calif., 1986. Tchr. Glencoe (Ill.) Pub. Schs., 1952-53, Hayward (Calif.) Schs., 1953-59, Honolulu Dept. Edn., 1969-83, Kamehameha Schs., Honolulu, 1987; instr. Hawaii Pacific Coll., Honolulu, 1987, Honolulu Community Coll., 1988, Chaminade U., Honolulu, 1990, Kansai Gaidai Hawaii Coll., 1991-93, U. Hawaii, Manoa, 1994—; cons. Computer Lab., Honolulu, 1988. Mem. AAUW, Am. Ednl. Rsch. Assn., Educom, Delta Epsilon, Kappa Delta Pi, Pi Lambda Theta. Democrat. Presbyterian.

YOUNG, LESTER REX, engineering company administrator; b. Marion, Ind., Aug. 26, 1946; s. Harold Leroy and Willow Marie (May) Y.; m. Bonnie Darline Denison, Sept. 5, 1965; children: Tamara Lynn, Kelby Gene, Kadee Lynn. BSEE, Kans. State U., 1969; MBA, Wichita State U., 1979. Reg. engr. Colo., Kans., Ohio, Mont., Utah, La. Plant engr. Beech Aircraft Corp., Wichita, Kans., 1973-75; asst. to v.p. mfg. Beech Aircraft Corp., Wichita, 1975-77; sr. project mgr. Smith & Boucher, Inc., Overland Park, Kans., 1977-80; dir. engring. R.M. Henning, Inc., New Philadelphia, Ohio, 1980-82; mgr. indsl. engring. Williams Internat., Ogden, Utah, 1982-84; mgr. plant engring. Sundstrand Corp., Denver, 1984-86; pres. ECS Engrs. Inc., Arvada, Colo., 1986-90; dir. bus. devel. Morrison Knudsen Corp., Denver, 1990-96; v.p. western region R&R Internat., Inc., Denver, 1996—; cons. Compliance Recycling Industires, Denver, 1984-87. Author: (reference manuals) Selection of Reverse Osmosis for Boiler Applications, 1987, Applications for Enzyme Activated Carbon, 1989, Integrated Refinery Waste Management, 1992. Capt. U.S. Army, 1969-73, Europe. Republican. Nazarene. Office: R&R Internat 3333 Quebec St Ste 7800 Denver CO 80207

YOUNG, LIH-JIUAN SHIAU (LILY YOUNG), environmental and utility industries consultant; b. Taiwan, Republic of China, Mar. 3, 1951; d. Jia-Jen and Yeh-Horn (Shieh) Shiau; m. Masefield J. Young, Apr. 9, 1976; 1 child, Jason S. BS in Nutrition, U. Chinese Culture, Taipei, 1973, MS in Nutrition, 1975; MS in Biochemistry, Duquesne U., 1978, PhD in Phys. Chemistry, 1982. Assoc. rsch. chemist Food Industry R&D Inst., Taiwan, 1975-76; post-doctoral rsch. assoc. Scripps Clinic and Rsch. Found., San Diego, 1984-85, U. Calif., San Diego, 1985-86; R&D lab. mgr. Foster Wheeler Devel. Co., San Diego, 1986-1996; cons. Englewood, Colo., 1996—; sci., math. instr.

Accelerated Schs., 1997—. Contbr. articles to profl. jours. Active San Diego Chinese Hist. Soc. Mem. Am. Chem. Soc.

YOUNG, LOWELL SUNG-YI, medical administrator, educator; b. Honolulu, Dec. 5, 1938. AB, Princeton U., 1960; MD, Harvard U., 1964. Di;omate Am. Bd. Internal Medicine with subspecialty in infectious diseases. Intern, jr. asst. resident, sr. asst. resident med. divsn. Bellevue Hosp. and Meml. Hosp., N.Y.C., 1964-67; fellow in medicine Cornell U. Med. Coll., 1965-67; epidemic intelligence officer bacterial diseases br. Nat. Communicable Disease Ctr., Atlanta, 1967-69, chief spl. pathogens sect., 1968-69; spl. postdoctoral rsch. fellow Nat. Inst. Allergy and Infectious Diseases, 1969-70; rsch. fellow in medicine Meml. Hosp./Cornell U. Med. Coll., 1969-70; clin. asst. physicisn infectious disease svc. dept. medicine Meml. Hosp., 1970-72, assoc. dir. microbiology lab., 1971-72; instr. in medicine Cornell U. Med. Coll., 1970-72; asst. clinician Sloan-Ketterin Inst. for Cancer Rsch., 1971-72; adj. prof. pharmacy U. of Pacific, San Francisco, 1989—; mem. microbiology and invectious diseases adv. com. Nat. Inst. Allergy and Infectious Diseases, 1981-85, mem. allergy and immunology rsch. com., 1975-79; mem. staff Calif. Pacific Med. Ctr., Mt. Zion Hosp. and Med. Ctr., U. Calif., San Francisco; mem. sci. adv. bd. Am. Found. for AIDS Rsch. Mem. editl. bd. Infection, Infectious Diseases in Clin. Practice, Diagnostic Microbiology and Infectious Diseases, Antomicrobial Agts. and Chemotherapy, Infection and Immunity; contbr. numerous articles to profl. jours., chpts. to books. Recipient Alexander D. Langmuir prize Epidemic Intelligence Svc., 1970, Garrod medal Brit. Soc., 1992. Fellow ACP (mem. med. self-assessment com.), Infectious Diseases Soc. Am. (councillor 1983-85); mem. Am. Soc. for Clin. Investigation, Am. Fedn. for Clin. Rsch., Am. Soc. for Microbiology, Western Soc. for Clin. Rsch., Internat. Immunocompromised Host Soc., Brit. Soc. Antimicrobial Chemotherapy. Office: Calif Pacific Med Ctr Kuzell Inst 2200 Webster St Ste 305 San Francisco CA 94115-1821

YOUNG, MARILYN RAE, former school system adminstrative secretary, mayor; b. Muskegon, Mich., Dec. 29, 1934; d. Albert Henry Cribley and Mildred Ida (Johnson) Raby; m. Peter John Young, May 21, 1955; children: Pamela Lynn Young-Walker, Lane Allen. Grad. high sch., Calumet City, Ill., 1952. Dep. pub. fiduciary Yuma County, Ariz., 1979-83; adminstrv. sec. Yuma Sch. Dist. One, 1983-95; councilman City of Yuma, 1990-93, mayor, 1993—. Pres. bd. dirs. Behavioral Health Svcs. of Yuma, 1979-90; vice chmn. Yuma Planning and Zoning Commn., 1985-89; v.p. bd. dirs. Children's Village, Yuma, 1983-89; lay leader Trinity United Meth. Ch., 1986-95; grad. Yuma Leadership Inc., 1985, treas. bd. dirs., 1986-89; participant Ariz. Women's Town Hall, 1989, various Yuma County Town Halls, 1987-93; adv. bd. mem. Friends of KAWC; chmn. Yuma Pub. Safety Police Bd., 1990—, Yuma Fire Pub. Safety Bd., 1990—, Yuma Youth Leadership Com., 1991-95; mem. allocation panel United Way, 1991-93; charter mem. Friends of Roxaboxen; active H.S. Ad Hoc Com., 1991-97; exec. bd. mem. Yuma Met. Planning Orgn., 1990—, Western Ariz. Coun. of Govts., 1990—; corp. bd. dirs. Greater Yuma Econ. Devel., 1990-95; hon. chmn. Yuma County San Luis Rio Colo. Commn., 1990—; mem. Nat. League of Cities FAIR Com., 1990—, FAIR steering com., 1997—, Binational Border Health Task Force, 1990—, resolution com. League of Ariz. Cities and Towns, 1990—, mem. com. U.S. Conf. of Mayors, 1990—. Mem. Yuma County C. of C. (mem. mil. affairs com. 1988-90). Home: 1288 W 18th St Yuma AZ 85364-5313 Office: City of Yuma 180 W 1st St Yuma AZ 85364-1407

YOUNG, MARY JANE, American studies and folklore educator; b. Apollo, Pa., Oct. 25, 1950; d. Floyd Clark and Lillian Grace (Deemer) Y. BA, St. John's Coll., 1973; MA, U. Pa., 1978, PhD, 1982. Math. tchr. Severn Sch., Severna Park, Md., 1973-75; asst. dir. admissions St. John's Coll., Annapolis, Md., 1975-76; rsch. asst. U. Pa., Phila., 1976-79, teaching fellow dept. folklore, 1979-80, lectr. dept. folklore, 1979-82; asst. prof. folklore ctr. U. Tex., Austin, 1982-87; assoc. prof. Am. studies, Regents lectr. U. N.Mex., Albuquerque, 1987—; cons. Tribal Mus. Com., Zuni, N.Mex., 1980—. Author: Signs from the Ancestors, 1988; editorial bd. Jour. of the Am. Studies Assn. Tex., 1988—, Archaeoastronomy, bull. for Ctr. for Archaeoastronomy, 1979—; contbr. articles to profl. jours. Fellow Roothbert Found., 1976-79, dissertation fellow AAUW, 1981-82; recipient rsch. assistantship Smithsonian Inst., 1978. Office: U NMex Dept Am Studies 305 Ortega Rd NW Albuquerque NM 87114-1501

YOUNG, MICHAEL EDWARD, composer, music educator; b. San Francisco, June 25, 1939; s. John Davis and Mary Katherine (Polese) Y. BA in Music, U. Wash., 1964, MA in Music, 1966. Organist First Presbyn. Ch., Seattle, 1961-65, St. Paul's Episcopal Ch., Seattle, 1966-70; instr. music Cornish Sch. Allied Arts, Seattle, 1966-70; organist Sts. Peter and Paul Ch., Vancouver, B.C., 1970-74, Cathedral of Our Lady of Lourdes, Spokane, Wash., 1979-83, Messiah Luth. Ch., Spokane, 1988-92; asst. to assoc. prof. music Whitworth Coll., Spokane, 1976—. Composer: Season's Song for Baritone and Piano, 1992, Give Glory, All Creation for Trumpet, Choir and Organ, 1991, A Mountain Symphony for Orchestra, 1987-88, Mountain Sketches, Set 5, 1988, Set 9 for piano, 1994, String Quartet No. 2, 1986, Northwest Images Horn, Cello, Piano, 1981, Serenade to the Mountains for orch., 1995. With U.S. Army, 1957-60. Mem. Am. Guild Organists (assoc.; 25th Creative Ann award 1983), Christian Fellowship of Art Music Composers, Glacier Mountaineering Soc. (charter mem.), Alpine Club of Canada. Orthodox. Office: Whitworth Collge Station 1701 Spokane WA 99251

YOUNG, ROBERT ALLEN, architectural engineer; b. Portland, Maine, Sept. 18, 1956; s. Raymond William and Marilyn Manola (Stilphen) Y.; m. Deborah Lee Gagnon, July 19, 1980. BS in Civil Engring., U. Maine, 1978; MS in Archtl. Engring., Pa. State U., 1984; MBA, U. Mich., 1991; MS in Historic Preservation, Ea. Mich. U., 1992. Registered profl. engr., Mich. Grad. asst. Pa. State U., University Park, 1979-80; sr. engr. Albert Kahn Assocs., Inc., Detroit, 1980-85, Blount Engrs. Inc., Detroit, 1985-87; project engr. energy cost avoidance project U. Mich., Ann Arbor, 1987-93; cons. Workplace Edn. Assocs., Canton, Mich., 1989—; adj. instr. coll. architecture and urban planning U. Mich., 1989-91; asst. prof. Grad. Sch. Architecture, U. Utah, 1993—, dir. hist. preservation program, 1995—. Contbr. articles to Nat. Soc. Archtl. Engrs. Times, 1991—. Councilman Christ the King Ch., Livonia, Mich., 1983-86, co-chmn. youth com., 1983-85, chmn. fin. com., 1985-86, renovations/access com., 1989-91). Mem. ASHRAE (gov. 1987-89, sec. 1989-91, v.p. 1991-92, pres.-elect 1992-93, pres. Detroit chpt. 1993), Nat. Soc. Archtl. Engrs. (founding state dir. 1991-93), NSPE (Mathcounts com. 1984-91), Assn. Energy Engrs., Nat. Trust for Hist. Preservation Forum, Salt Lake City Historic Landmarks Commn., Phi Kappa Phi.

YOUNG, ROBERT EDWARD, computer company executive; b. L.A., Nov. 28, 1943; s. David and Sue (Wise) Y. Student, E. Los Angeles Coll., 1973, Santa Monica Coll., 1975; BA, UCLA, 1978. Cert. securities analyst N.Y. Inst. Fin., 1972. Computer operator Rocketdyne Corp., Canoga Park, Calif., 1963-65; computer ops. supr. Hughes Aircraft Corp., El Segundo, Calif., 1965-67; with investment securities dept. Smith, Tilton & Co., Inc., Santa Ana, Calif., 1967-70, Morton Seidel & Co., Inc., L.A., 1970-78; sales mgr. of comml. interior constrn. NICO Constrn. Co., Inc., L.A., 1978-80; sales mgr. Strauss Constrn. Co., Inc., L.A., 1981-82; v.p., instl. investment officer FCA Asset Mgmt./Am. Savs., Los Angeles, 1982-87; pres., chief exec. officer Avalon Fin. Group, Inc., Los Angeles, 1988-90; prin. Robert Young & Co., 1991—; bd. dirs. RESA Prodns. 1973-80, Edu Care, L.A., 1981-90, ASC Edn. Svcs. Inc., L.A., chmn. fin. com.; mktg. cons. Shehata Enterprises, L.A., 1978-79; sales tng. cons. Versailles Gallery, L.A., Schwartz Constrn., L.A., 1982; cons. PC Etcetera, L.A., 1990-91. Photographer: prin. works include Man at Work or Play UN, Geneva, 1976, Cat of Yr. photo, 1977, Photomontage U. So. Calif. Early Childhood Edn. Ctr., 1977; producer weekly pub. affairs prog. for family fin. planning sta. KPOL Radio, 1974, Stocks and Bonds Show KWHY-TV, 1975-78, MacRadio show, Am. Radio Network, 1989, WinRadio Show, 1990, MacWin Radio, 1991-93. Fin. cons. Hofheinz Fund, Houston, 1988. Served with USCGR, 1964-70. Mem. Archtl. Hist. Soc. (life mem. So. Calif. chpt.), Reel Sports Club, Masons, Marina Venice Yacht Club. Home: 4531 Don Arturo Pl Los Angeles CA 90008-2803 Office: Robert Young & Co 8306 Wilshire Blvd Ste 499 Beverly Hills CA 90211-2382

YOUNG, ROGER CARL, computer company executive; b. Clayton, Mo., Mar. 21, 1932; s. Gerald Lee Young and Bertha Augusta (Schlottach) McCulloh; m. Nadine Fay Basch, Apr. 27, 1952; children: Julia Allyn, David Ford. Student, Washington U., St. Louis, 1956-57, U. Calif., Berkeley, 1957-60, Contra Costa Coll., 1970. V.p. and div. mgr. Crocker Nat. Bank, San Francisco, 1967-75; nat. accts. mgr. Wang Labs., San Francisco, 1975-78; industry cons. Fortune 500, 1978-81; pres. ComTrak, Richmond, Calif., 1981-83; dir. mktg. Delphi Systems, Inc., Westlake Village, Calif., 1983-89; regional sales mgr. Applied Systems, Inc., Chgo., 1991-92; pres. YOUNG Tech., Vacaville, Calif., 1992—. Served with USAF, 1951-55. Mem. Data Processing Mgmt. Assn. (cert., bd. dirs., sec. San Francisco chpt. 1965-67), Am. Contract Bridge League (life master 1959), Green Tree Golf Club. Republican. Home and Office: 779 Arbor Oaks Dr Vacaville CA 95687-5252 *Personal philosophy: "If you don't use your own head, someone else will use it for you."*

YOUNG, ROSABEL RIBARES, neurologist; b. Laredo, Tex., June 1, 1960; d. Arthur and Rosario Ribares; m. Anthony O. Young, Nov. 25, 1984. AB, U. Chgo., 1982, MS in Pharmacology and Physiology, 1984; MD, U. Ill., 1987. Diplomate Am. Bd. Psychiatry and Neurology, Am. Bd. Neurophysiology; cert. Am. Bd. Electrodiagnostic Medicine, Am. Bd. Clin. Neurophysiology. Intern in neurology The Nat. Hosp., London, 1987; intern in internal medicine UCLA-Wadsworth VA Med. Ctr., 1987-88; resident in neurology Ctr. for Health Scis., UCLA, 1988-91; neurologist CIGNA Health Care, L.A., 1991-94; fellow neurophysiology EEG, EMG Harbor-UCLA Med. Ctr., 1994—; attending neurologist UCLA Neurology Clinic; chair edn. com. CIGNA Health Care, L.A., 1993—, cons. pharmacy and therapeutics, 1991—, mem. instnl. rev. bd., 1991—; dir. Doctors-to-Schs. Sci. Advisors Program, Chgo. and L.A., 1989—. Contbr. articles to profl. jours. judge advisor L.A. County Schs., 1990—; judge and awards contbr. Calif. State Sci. Fair, L.A., 1992—. Rsch. fellow Pharm. Mfrs. Assn., UCLA, 1984-85, NIH, 1983, Epilepsy Found. Am., 1984; Nat. Med. fellow, 1983, 85; Bertram Richardson Internat. Studies scholar, 1987, Joseph K. Narat Found. scholar, 1985, MacArthur Found. scholar, 1982-86, Becker-Warburg Found. scholar, 1978-82, Joseph Blazek scholar, 1980-81, Ill. Gen. Assembly scholar, 1984-85, 85-86; recipient Chgo. Edmondson Rsch. award, 1981. Mem. AMA (Leadership in Cmty. Svc. award 1989, 90, RPS resource com. rep. to AMA ho. dels. 1989-90), Am. Electroencephalographers Soc., Am. Assn. Electrodiagnostic Medicine, Am. Acad. Neurology (legis. affairs com., subcom. on edn. of non-neurologists, chair Neurosci. Prize com., chair comms. and liaison com.), Calif. Med. Assn., L.A. County Med. Assn., L.A. Soc. for Neurol. Scis. Office: 2700 Neilson Way Ste 1130 Santa Monica CA 90405

YOUNG, SCOTT THOMAS, business management educator; b. Oak Park, Ill., Dec. 28, 1949; s. Thomas Menzies and Grace (Butler) Y.; m. Teresa M. Foskey, Jan. 2, 1981; children: Reginald, Galen. BA, U. Ga., 1974; MBA, Ga. Coll., 1982; PhD, Ga. State U., 1987. Prof. U. Utah, Salt Lake City, 1987—, chmn. mgmt. dept., 1994-97; mgmt. cons. to numerous orgns., 1987—; lectr., speaker, cons. on ops., quality and project mgmt. Author: Managing Global Operations; contbr. numerous articles to profl. jours. Founder MITSI Awards. With U.S. Army, 1971-73. Decorated Commendation medal; grantee Nat. Assn. Purchasing Mgmt., 1986. Mem. Decision Sci. Inst., Acad. Mgmt., Prodn. and Ops. Mgmt. Soc. Office: U Utah David Eccles Sch Bus Salt Lake City UT 84112

YOUNG, STEVEN, professional football player; b. Salt Lake City, Oct. 11, 1961. JD, Brigham Young, 1993. With L.A. Express, USFL, 1984-85, Tampa Bay Buccaneers, 1985-87; quarterback San Francisco 49ers, 1987—. Davey O'Brien Award, 1983, All-America team quarterback, The Sporting News, 1983; Named NFL's Top-rated quarterback, 1991, named NFL MVP The Sporting News, 1992, NFL All-Pro team quarterback, The Sporting News, 1992, Superbowl MVP, 1994. Office: San Francisco 49ers 4949 Centennial Blvd Santa Clara CA 95054-1229*

YOUNG, VIRGIL M., education educator; b. Santa Rosa, Calif., Sept. 24, 1936; s. Virgil M. and Vesta May (Huyett) Williams; stepson Louis H. Young; m. Katherine Ann Young, Dec. 20, 1964; 1 child, Susan Annette. BS, U. Idaho, 1958, EdD, 1967. Cert. advanced secondary sch., sch. supt., Idaho. Tchr. Moscow (Idaho) Sch. Dist.; adminstrv. asst. to supt. Coeur d'Alene (Idaho) Sch. Dist.; prof. emeritus Boise (Idaho) State U. Author: (elem., jr. high textbook) The Story of Idaho, 3 editions; co-author: The Story of the Idaho Guide and Resource Book, 1993. Capt. USAR. Mem. N.W. Assn. Tchr. Educators (past pres.), Idaho Assn. Colls. Tchr. Edn. (past pres.), Phi Delta Kappa (past pres.).

YOUNG, ZORA ORAL, psychiatrist; b. Baytown, Tex., Nov. 30, 1922; s. Zora Oral Sr. and Kathryn (Litzler) Y.; m. Mary Ella Young (div.); children: Richard, Jame, John; m. Rosemary Ruth Young, Oct. 18, 1980. BS, U. Ariz., 1947; MD, U. So. Calif., 1952. Diplomate Am. Bd. Psychiatry and Neurology. Intern Santa Fe Coast Lines Hosp., L.A., 1950-51; resident Langley Porter Neuropsychiat. Inst., San Francisco, 1951-54; med. dir. No. Nev. Child and Adolescent Svcs., Reno, 1980—. Office: Childrens Behavioral Svc 2655 Enterprise Rd Reno NV 89512-1666

YOUNGQUIST, ANDREW LANCE, construction executive; b. Newport Beach, Calif., Nov. 30, 1940; s. Vincent R. and Elizabeth (Tebbs) Y.; children: Bill, Jennifer; m. Linda Kay, May 17, 1980. Student, Orange Coast Coll. Pres. Decco Constrn., Orange, Calif., 1970-78; v.p. Capitol Systems, Newport Beach, 1976-77; with Saffell & McAdam, Irvine, Calif., 1977-79; pres. MBK Constrn., Ltd., Irvine, 1979-96. Dir. Girl Scout Coun., Orange Empire, Girl Scouts U.S., 1991; bd. mem. Orange County Together. Mem. Nat. Assn. Indsl. Office Pks., Internat. Coun. Shopping Ctrs., Associated Gen. Contractors (bd. mem. Orange County dist.), Bldg. Industry Assn., Balboa Bay Club, Pacific Anglers. Republican. Home: 1851 Braemer Way Newport Beach CA 92660-3724*

YOUNGQUIST, WALTER LEWELLYN, consulting geologist; b. Mpls., May 5, 1921; s. Walter Raymond and Selma Regina (Knock) Y.; m. Elizabeth Salome Pearson, Dec. 11, 1943; children: John, Karen, Louise, Robert. BA, Gustavus Adolphus Coll., St. Peter, Minn., 1942; MSc, U. Iowa, 1943, PhD, 1948. Registered profl. geologist, Oreg. Jr. geologist U.S. Geol. Survey, 1943-44; rsch. assoc. U. Iowa, Iowa City, 1945-48; asst. prof. geology U. Idaho, Moscow, 1948-51; sr. geologist Internat. Petroleum Co., Talara, Peru, 1951-54; prof. geology U. Kans., Lawrence, 1954-57, U. Oreg., Eugene, 1957-66; cons. geologist Minerals dept. Exxon Corp., Houston, 1968-73; geothermal cons. Eugene Water & Electric Bd., 1973-92; ind. cons. Eugene, 1992—. Author: Investing in Natural Resources, 1980, Mineral Resources and the Destinies of Nations, 1990, GeoDestinies, 1997; co-author: Ordovician Cephalopod Fauna of Baffin Island, 1954. Ensign, USNR, 1944-45. Recipient Lowden Prize in Geology, U. Iowa, 1943. Fellow AAAS, Geol. Soc. Am.; mem. Am. Assn. Petroleum Geologists, Geothermal Resources Coun., N.W. Energy Assn., N.Y. Acad. Scis. Lutheran. Office: PO Box 5501 Eugene OR 97405-0501

YOUNGS, JACK MARVIN, cost engineer; b. Bklyn., May 2, 1941; s. Jack William and Virginia May (Clark) Y.; B in Engring., CCNY, 1964; MBA, San Diego State U., 1973; m. Alexandra Marie Robertson, Oct. 31, 1964; 1 child, Christine Marie. Mass properties engr. Gen. Dynamics Corp., San Diego, 1964-68, rsch. engr., 1968-69, sr. rsch. engr., 1969-80, sr. cost devel. engr., 1980-81, cost devel. engring. specialist, 1981-95; prin. estimator Martin Marietta Astronautics, 1994-95; estimating adminstr. Lockheed Martin Astronautics, 1995-96; prin., owner Youngs Group, 1996—. Dist. dir. Scripps Ranch Civic Assn., 1976-79; pres. Scripps Ranch Swim Team, 1980-82; dir., 1986-87; judge Greater San Diego Sci. and Engring. Fair, 1981-92. Mem. Princeton U. Parents Assn. Recipient 5th place award World Body Surfing Championships, 1987, 6th place award, 1988. Mem. AIAA, N.Y. Acad. Scis., Alumni Assn. CUNY, Bklyn. Tech. H.S. Alumni Assn., Inst. Cost Analysis (cert., charter mem., treas. Greater San Diego chpt. 1986-90), Soc. Cost Estimating and Analysis (cert. cost estimator/analyst, pres. San Diego chpt. 1990-91), Internat. Soc. Parametric Analysts (bd. dirs. San Diego chpt. 1987-90), Nat. Mgmt. Assn. (space systems divsn. charter mem. 1985, award of honor Convair chpt. 1975), Assn. MBA Execs., San Diego State U. Bus. Alumni Assn. (charter mem. 1986), Convair Alumni Assn., Scripps Ranch Swim and Racquet Club (dir. 1977-80, treas. 1978-79, pres. 1979-80), Beta Gamma Sigma, Chi Epsilon, Sigma Iota Epsilon. Lutheran. Research in life cycle costing and econ. analysis. Office: 11461 Tribuna Ave San Diego CA 92131-1907

YOUNT, CHARLES ROBERT, electrical and computer engineer; b. Hickory, N.C., Jan. 9, 1965; s. Charles Ivo and Thelma Gay (Lane) Y.; m. Sharron Lynn Stevens, Oct. 19, 1991; children: Danielle Christine, Sydney Ann. BS in Computer Engring., N.C. State U., 1987; MS in Elec. and Computer Engring., Carnegie Mellon U., 1990, PhD in Elec. and Computer Engring., 1993. Free-lance computer programmer Hickory, N.C., 1982-85; with personal comm. products dept. IBM, Research Triangle Park, N.C., 1984; with transmission tech. dept. IBM, Research Triangle Park, 1985, with material and logistics support dept., 1986, with Very Large-Scale Integration application design dept., 1986-87, 87-88; with Advanced Tech. Ctr. Boeing Computer Svcs., Bellevue, Wash., 1989-90; head software engr. Omniview, Inc., Pitts., 1992; sr. software engr. Inter-Nat. Rsch. Inst., San Diego, 1993-95; sr. design engr. Intel Corp., Folsom, Calif., 1995—; tchg. asst. Carnegie Mellon U., Pitts., 1988, 89, guest lectr. Carnegie BOSCH Inst., 1991, seminar instr. Pa. Jr. Acad. Sci., 1991. Contbr. articles to profl. jours. Bd. dirs. United Campus Ministry of Pitts., corp. treas., 1992-93; adult edn. coord. Pine Run United Meth. Ch., 1993. Mem. IEEE, IEEE Computer Soc., IEEE Reliability Soc., Assn. Computing Machinery (spl. interest group in design automation), Phi Kappa Phi, Eta Kappa Nu, Tau Beta Pi (rec. sec. 1986-87). Home: 1062 Uplands Dr El Dorado Hills CA 95762-3822

YOUNT, DAVID EUGENE, physicist, educator; b. Prescott, Ariz., June 5, 1935; s. Robert Ephram and Jeannette Francis (Judson) Y.; m. Christel Marlene Notz, Feb. 22, 1975; children—Laura Christine, Gregory Gordon, Steffen Jurgen Robert, Sonja Kate Jeannette. B.S. in Physics, Calif. Inst. Tech., 1957; M.S. in Physics, Stanford U., 1959, Ph.D. in Physics, 1963. Instr. Princeton U., 1962-63, asst. prof. physics, 1963-64, Minn. Mining and Mfg. fellow, 1963; NSF postdoctoral fellow U. Paris, Orsay, France, 1964-65; rsch. assoc. Stanford Linear Accelerator Ctr. Stanford U., 1965-69; assoc. prof. U. Hawaii, 1969-73, prof., 1973—, chmn. dept. physics and astronomy, 1979-85, acting asst. v.p. for acad. affairs, 1985-86, v.p. rsch. and grad. edn., 1986-95. Author: Who Runs the University: The Politics of Higher Education in Hawaii, 1985-92, 96. Mem. Am. Phys. Soc., Undersea and Hyperbaric Med. Soc., Am. Chem. Soc., U.S. Tennis Assn., Sigma Xi. Republican. Lutheran. Home: 5468 Opihi St Honolulu HI 96821-1924 Office: U Hawaii 2505 Correa Rd Honolulu HI 96822-2219 *Actualizing my potential is the central theme of my life. I have the potential to work, to play, to learn, to love, to teach, and to understand. These are not conscious goals so much as forces which motivate my behavior. I work very hard, not for success, but because fulfillment requires an effort. I try to be honest, not as a goal, but because dishonesty interferes with learning, loving, teaching and understanding. I enjoy children, not because I'm an affectionate adult, but because I see that we are involved in the same process.*

YOUNT, GEORGE STUART, paper company executive; b. L.A., Mar. 4, 1949; s. Stanley George and Agnes (Pratt) Y.; m. Geraldine Marie Silvio, July 18, 1970; children: Trisha Marie, Christopher George. Postgrad., Harvard U., 1983-86. Mgmt. trainee Fortifiber Corp., L.A., 1969-71, asst. to v.p. ops., 1971-75, adminstrv. v.p., treas., sec., 1975-85, exec. v.p., sec., cfo, dir., 1985-90, chmn., cfo, 1991—; pres., dir. Fonzia Corp., 1993—; bd. dirs. Stanwall Corp., pres., 1989—; bd. dirs. Thompson & Co. Ins. Svcs., Pasadena, Calif., 1996—; past pres. Hollister Ranch Cattle Coop., Gaviota, Calif., 1986-88; bd. dirs. Consol. Media Corp., Pasadena, Calif., Electrocel Tech. Sys., Santa Fe Springs, Calif. Team leader L.A. United Way, 1981-86; bd. dirs. Big Bros. Greater L.A., 1984-87, L.A. coun. Boy Scouts Am., 1992—; mem. Young Pres. Orgn., 1991, forum moderator, 1993-95, chpt. forum officer, 1997—. Mem. Am. Paper Inst. (dir. 1993—, splty. coaters and extrusion sect. 1990—), Nat. Assn. Corp. Dirs., Harvard Bus. Club So. Calif., Harvard Owner/Pres. Mgmt. Program Club, Jonathan Club (L.A.), Rotary (bd. dirs. L.A. club 1992-94), Internat. Wine and Food Soc. Office: Fortifiber Corp 1001 Tahoe Blvd Incline Village NV 89451-9309

YOUNT, PHILIP RICHARD, insurance company executive; b. Hartwick, Iowa, Feb. 7, 1937; s. Fred Austin and Katherine Elizabeth (Gross) Y.; m. Mary Maxine White, June 3, 1956 (div. Jan. 1989); children: Jo Ann Yount Pearson, Mary Beth Yount King, Douglas Alan; m. Donna Mae Eki, Sept. 4, 1989; stepchildren: Maile Hitomi Solis, Gabriella Chiharu Solis, Ayala Masayo Solis. BA magna cum laude, Parsons Coll., 1959. CPCU; cert. computer profl.; assoc. in mgmt. Staff acct., instr. Grinnell (Iowa) Coll., 1959-60; from acct. to pres. and chief exec. officer Grinnell Mut. Reins. Co., 1960-91; v.p., sec., treas. Grange Mut. Ins. Co., Tigard, Oreg., 1992—, sr. v.p., 1996—; pres., bd. dirs. Big M Agy., Inc., Grinnell, 1983-91, Grinnell Realty, Inc., 1985-91; bd. dirs. Grinnell Life Ins. Co., 1985-91, pres., 1985-89. Pres. pk. bd. City of Grinnell, 1972-78; pres., founder Grinnell Cmty. Taxpayers Assn., 1974-78; pres., bd. dirs. Greater Poweshiek Cmty. Found., Grinnell, 1988-92, GMG Found., Grinnell, 1989-91; bd. dirs. Grinnell Gen. Hosp., 1989-92, Beaverton Edn. Found., 1996—; mem. strategic planning com. Tigard Pub. Libr., 1996. Recipient Meritorious Svc. award Nat. Assn. Mut. Insurers, 1989. Fellow Life Mgmt. Inst.; mem. CPCU Soc., Ins. Inst. Am., Data Processing Mgmt. Assn., Toastmasters, Grante (chpt. treas. and exec. com. mem. 1993—), Chi Beta Chi, Phi Kappa Phi. Office: Grange Mut Ins Co PO Box 230969 7105 SW Varns St Tigard OR 97281-0969

YOUSEF, FATHI SALAAMA, communication studies educator, management consultant; b. Cairo, Jan. 2, 1934; came to U.S., 1968, naturalized, 1973; s. Salaama and Rose (Tadros) Y.; m. Marjan El-Faizy Lowies, Jun. 24, 1994. B.A., Ain Shams U., Cairo, 1955; M.A., U. Minn., 1970, Ph.D., 1972. Service ctr. supt. Shell Oil Co., Cairo, 1955-61; indsl., mgmt. tng. instr. ARAMCO, Dhahran, Saudi Arabia, 1961-68; teaching assoc. U.-Minn., Mpls., 1968-72; speech communication prof. Calif. State U.-Long Beach, 1972—; with orgn. and indsl. engring. dept. ARAMCO, 1978-80. Grantee NSF, 1981, 82, 83. Mem. Am. Mgmt. Assn., Internat. Communication Assn., AAUP, Am. Soc. Tng. and Devel., Soc. Cross-Cultural Research, Speech Communication Assn., Internat. Soc. Intercultural Edn., Tng. and Research, World Communication Assn., Western States Communication Assn., Assn. Egyptian Am. Scholars. Democrat. Co-author: An Introduction to Intercultural Communication, 1975, 85; contbr. articles to profl. jours. Office: Calif State U Dept Speech Communication Long Beach CA 90840

YOUSEF, MARJAN, gerontologist, psychology educator; b. Amsterdam, The Netherlands, Apr. 10, 1945; came to the U.S., 1966; d. Theodorus Antonius Johannus and Johanna Maria (ter Beek) Lowies; m. Fathi S. Yousef, June 24, 1994; children: Monique El-Faizy, Robert El-Faizy. RN, Wilhelmina Gasthuis, 1966; BA, U. Calif., Irvine, 1987, MA, 1993. Grad. rsch. asst. dept. phys. medicine and rehab. U. Calif., 1988-93; adj. prof. Concordia U., Irvine, Calif., 1991-95; rsch. coord. Dept. Phys. Medicine & Rehab. U. Calif., Irvine Med. Ctr., 1995—. Author articles in psychology and gerontology. Ombudsman Orange County Coun. on Aging, Irvine, 1987-88; vol. Hospice Orange County, Santa Ana, 1979-80. Mem. Gerontol. Soc. Am., Am. Psychol. Assn., Phi Eta Sigma. Office: UCI Med Ctr 101 The City Dr Bldg 53 Rt 81 Orange CA 92868

YU, CHONG HO, educational researcher; b. Hong Kong, Aug. 9, 1963. BS in Mass Comm., BA in Art, Bemidji State U., 1989; cert. in profl. photography, N.Y. Inst. Profl. Photography, 1991; advanced cert. in liberal studies in philosophy, Hamline U., 1993; M Human Rels., U. Okla., 1992, MEd in Ednl. Psychology, 1993; PhD in Measurement of Stats., Ariz. State U., 1995. Cert. in computer programming; cert. Novell engr. Sales mgr. Youth Lit. Book Co., Hong Kong, 1985-86; rsch. asst. human rels. U. Okla., Norman, 1990-92, rsch. asst. rsch. bur., 1992-94; faculty assoc. Ariz. State U., Tempe, 1994—, computer site supr., 1995-96, mgmt. rsch. analyst, 1996—; presenter in field. Columnist Macau Daily News, 1986—, Tin Tin Daily News, 1987, Ming Pao Daily News, Olive, others. Mem. APA, Am. Ednl. Rsch. Assn., Am. Statis. Assn., Assn. Computing Machinery, Assn. Ednl. Commn. and Tech., Psychometric Soc. Office: Ariz State U Divsn Data Adminstrn/Analys Admin B-Wing B302 Tempe AZ 85287-1203

YU, KITSON SZEWAI, computer science educator; b. Toishan, Kwangtung, China, Apr. 4, 1950; came to U.S., 1969; s. Ho Yee and Yin Sang (Chan) Y.; m. Mabel Griseldis Wong, July 15, 1972; 1 child, Robin Roberta Emily. BS, Troy State U., 1974, MS, 1977, BS, 1980. Cert. systems profl.; cert. data processing educator. V.p. Troy (Ala.) Computer Ctr., 1976-81; computer instr. Tory State U., 1980-81, Linn Benton Community Coll., Albany, Oreg., 1981—; dir. real estate program Linn Benton Community Coll., 1985—; mng. broker Kitson Realty, Corvallis, Oreg., 1975—. Vice pres. econ. devel. Daleville C. of C., Ala., 1976; dir. Corvallis Youth Symphony, 1990-93. Mem. Data Processing Mgmt. Assn. (bd. dirs. at large 1982-93, v.p. 1984-85, pres. 1985-86), Greater Albany Rotary (treas.

1985—), Corvallis Multiple Listing Exch. (bd. dirs. 1990-94), Gamma Beta Phi. Home: 2768 NW Wintergreen Pl Corvallis OR 97330-3550 Office: Linn Benton C C 6500 Pacific Blvd SW Albany OR 97321-3755 *Personal philosophy: Ask, when appropriate; Aid, when appreciated.*

YU, ROGER HONG, physics educator; b. Shanghai, China, Apr. 19, 1960; came to U.S., 1987; s. Rei Qian and Wei-Zen (Zhang) Y.; m. Ting Shi, Sept. 8, 1990; children: William S., John S. BS, Shanghai U. Sci. & Tech., 1982; MS, U. Mo., 1987; PhD, Mont. State U., 1990. Lectr. physics Shanghai U. Sci., 1982-85; teaching asst. U. Mo., Kansas City, 1985-86, rsch. asst., 1986-87; teaching asst. Mont. State U., Bozeman, 1987-88, rsch. asst., 1988-90; prof. physics Ctrl. Wash. U., Ellensburg, 1990—, dist. prof. rsch., chmn. dept. physics, 1997—. Contbr. articles to profl. jours.; referee Phys. Rev. B. Mem. Am. Phys. Soc., Acoustic Soc. Am., Coun. Undergrad. Rsch., Associated Western Univs. (rsch. and edn. com.). Office: Ctrl Wash U Dept Physics Ellensburg WA 98926

YUAN, ROBIN TSU-WANG, plastic surgeon; b. Boston, July 2, 1954; s. Robert Hsun-Piao and Grace I. (Chen) Y. AB, Harvard U., 1974, MD, 1978. Diplomate Am. Bd. Plastic Surgery. Resident in gen. surgery UCLA Med. Ctr., 1978-80, Cedars-Sinai Med. Ctr., L.A., 1980-81, 83-84; resident in plastic surgery U. Miami (Fla.)-Jackson Meml. Hosp., 1985-87; pvt. practice L.A., 1987—; clin. instr. div. plastic surgery UCLA, 1987—; vice-chief div. plastic surgery Cedars-Sinai Med. Ctr., L.A., 1991—; pres., chief exec. officer, founder Family of Independent Reconstructive Surgery Teams (F.I.R.S.T.), 1990—. Author: Cheer Up...You're Only Half Dead!, Reflections at Mid-Life, 1996; contbr. numerous articles to med. jours. Mem. Am. Soc. Plastic and Reconstructive Surgery, Am. Cleft Palate Assn., Calif. Med. Assn. (del.), L.A. County Med. Assn. (bd. govs. dist. 1), Phi Lambda (co-mgr. 1991—). Office: 150 N Robertson Blvd Ste 315 Beverly Hills CA 90211-2145

YUAN, SHAO-YUEN, management consultant; b. Shanghai, China, July 30, 1929; came to U.S., 1947; m. Cecilia X. Zhou, Nov. 30, 1989; children: Chris, Mark. BSChemE, Ill. Inst. Tech., 1950; MSChemE, U. Louisville, 1951. Rsch. engr. E.I. DuPont De Nemours Co., Phila., 1951-56; sr. rsch. engr. Chevron Rsch. Co., Richmond, Calif., 1956-69; regional exec. Chevron Rsch. Co., San Francisco, 1977-84; plant mgr. Chevron Chem. Co., Anaheim, Calif., 1966-69; sr. engring. assoc. Chevron Chem. Co., San Francisco, 1969-77; country mgr. Chevron Overseas Petroleum, Ltd., Beijing, 1984-89; licensing exec. Chevron Rsch. & Tech. Co., Richmond, Calif., 1989-92; prin. Yuan & Assocs., San Rafael, Calif., 1992—. Contbr. articles to profl. jours.; patentee in field. V.p. Am. C. of C. in China, Bejing, 1987, pres., 1988. AIChe, Am. Chem. Soc., Commonwealth Club Calif. Office: Yuan & Assocs 70 Heritage Dr San Rafael CA 94901-8308

YUAN TSEH LEE, chemistry educator; b. Hsinchu, Taiwan, China, Nov. 29, 1936; came to U.S., 1962, naturalized, 1974; s. Tsefan and Pei (Tasi) L.; m. Bernice Wu, June 28, 1963; children: Ted, Sidney, Charlotte. BS, Nat. Taiwan U., 1959; MS, Nat. Tsinghua U., Taiwan, 1961; PhD, U. Calif., Berkeley, 1965. From asst. prof. to prof. chemistry U. Chgo., 1968-74; prof. emeritus U. Calif., Berkeley, 1974—, also former prin. investigator Lawrence Berkeley Lab. Contbr. numerous articles on chem. physics to profl. jours. Recipient Nobel Prize in Chemistry, 1986, Ernest O. Lawrence award Dept. Energy, 1981, Nat. Medal of Sci., 1986, 90, Peter Debye award for Phys. Chemistry, 1986; fellow Alfred P. Sloan, 1969-71, John Simon Guggenheim, 1976-77; Camille and Henry Dreyfus Found. Tchr. scholar, 1971-74, Harrison Howe award, 1983. Fellow Am. Phys. Soc.; mem. NAS, AAAS, Am. Acad. Arts and Scis., Am. Chem. Soc. Office: U Calif Dept Chemistry Berkeley CA 94720*

YUEN, ANDY TAK SING, electronics executive; b. Wanchai, Hong Kong, Aug. 26, 1952; came to U.S., 1984; s. Yan Chong and Chi Oi (Tse) Y.; m. Kathy Man Kwan Chan, Jan. 29, 1983; children Lambert Hann Shi, Robin Hann Lang. Higher Cert. in Elec. Engring., Hong Kong Poly., 1975; Diploma in Bus. Mgmt., Hong Kong Bapt. Coll., 1976; Diploma in Exec. Devel., Chinese U., Hong Kong, 1981; MBA, Chui Hai Coll., Hong Kong, 1981; PhD in Bus. Mgmt., Calif. Coast U., 1987. Supervising engr. Teledyne Semiconductor Ltd., Kowloon, Hong Kong, 1976-79; ops. mgr. Microsemi (Hong Kong) Ltd., Kowloon, 1979-81, gen. mgr., 1981-84; corp. mgr. Microsemi Corp., Santa Ana, Calif., 1984-89, corp. v.p., 1989—; corp. dir. Semcon Electronics Pvt. Ltd., Bombay, 1984—. Author (books): Can Quality Circles Bring the Breakthrough to Hong Kong Industrial Management, 1982, Harnessing Japanese Quality Circles in Hong Kong, 1987. Fellow Inst. Sales and Mktg. Mgmt., Brit. Inst. Mgmt., Inst. Elec. and Electronics Inc. Engrs. Office: Microsemi Corp PO Box 26890 Santa Ana CA 92799-6890

YUEN, RICHARD JOSEPH, university dean; b. San Francisco, Mar. 1, 1956; s. Joseph Edward Yuen and Nancy Louie; m. Mabel Sikmei Teng, Dec. 10, 1983; children: Tania, Leticia. BA in Sociology/BA in Asian Am. Studies, U. Calif., Berkeley, 1978; MA in Social Work Edn., San Francisco State U., 1983. Rare book handler John Howell Books, San Francisco, 1973-82; supr. youth svcs. Oakland (Calif.) Chinese Cmty. Coun., 1982-84, supr. adult vocat., 1984-86; acad. counselor City Coll. of San Francisco, 1986-89; asst. dean of students Stanford (Calif.) U., 1989—, dir. Asian Am. Activities Ctr., 1989—. Founding mem. Asian Pacific Student Union, U. Calif., Berkeley, 1978, Nat. Coalition for Redress and Reparations, San Francisco, 1980, Asian Pacific Dem. Club, Oakland, 1985. Recipient Dir.'s award Black Cmty. Svcs. Ctr., Stanford, 1992, Dedicated Svc. award Stanford U. Nikkei, 1993; Children, Youth and Family fellow Frederick Burke Found., San Francisco, 1980; named one of 500 most influential Asian Ams., Ave. Mag., 1996—. Mem. Asian Pacific Ams. in Higher Edn., Nat. Assn. of Student Pers. Adminstrs., Orgn. Chinese Ams., Chinese for Affirmative Action, Asian Staff Forum-Stanford (chair 1989-95), Kappa Delta Phi (Outstanding Svc. award 1994). Democrat. Roman Catholic. Office: Stanford University Old Union Clubhouse Stanford CA 94305-3064

YUNKER, CONRAD ERHARDT, biologist; b. Matawan, N.J., Dec. 22, 1927; s. Conrad Erhardt and Helen (Merrill) Y.; m. Samira Louise Abozeid, 1958; children: Conrad Erhardt, Dina L., Samira E., Lawrence O. BS, U. Md., 1952, MS, 1954, PhD, 1958. Asst. prof. Dept. Zoology, U. Md., College Pk., 1958-59; rsch. entomologist Canada Agriculture, Ottawa, 1960; scientist NIH, USPHS, Canal Zone, Panama, 1960-62; scientist dir. Rocky Mtn. Lab., NIH, USPHS, Hamilton, Mont., 1962-82; prof. Dept. Vet. Microbiology, Wash. State U., Pullman, 1982-85; rsch. prof. Dept. Infectious Diseases, U. Fla., Gainesville, 1985-92; rsch. fellow Vet. Rsch. Inst., Onderstepoort, Rep. South Africa, 1992-95; dir. Tickconsult, Port Ludlow, Wash., 1995—; cons. in field; adj. prof. U. Idaho, Moscow, 1982-85; chief-of-party USAID/Zimbabwe/Heartwater Rsch. Project, Harare, 1985-91; affiliated prof. dept. zoology U. Mont., Missoula, 1971-75. Editor: Arboviruses in Arthropod Cells in Vitro, 1987; author: Guide to the Families of Mites, 1958; contbr. numerous articles to profl. jours. Officer B.P.O. Elks, Hamilton, 1964-67. With USN, 1947-48. Recipient Acarology award Ohio State U., 1972, Sigrid Juselius award, 1975. Fellow AAAS; mem. Am. Soc. Parasitologists (emeritus), Am. Soc. Tropical Med. Hygiene, Entomol. Soc. Am. Address: Tickconsult 230 Pioneer Dr Port Ludlow WA 98365

YURIST, SVETLAN JOSEPH, mechanical engineer; b. Kharkov, USSR, Nov. 20, 1931; came to U.S., 1979, naturalized, 1985; s. Joseph A. and Rosalia S. (Zoilman) Y.; m. Imma Lea Erlikh, Oct. 11, 1960; 1 child, Eugene. M.S. in Mech. Engring. with honors, Poly. Inst., Odessa, USSR, 1954. Engr. designer Welding Equipment Plant, Novaya Utka, USSR, 1954-56; sr. tech. engr. Heavy Duty Automotive Crane Plant, Odessa, 1956-60, asst. chief matallugist, 1971-78; supr. research lab. Inst. Spl. Methods in Foundry Industry, Odessa, 1960-66, project engr. sci. research, 1966-71; engr. designer Teledyne Cast Product, Pomona, Calif., 1979-81; sr. mech. engr. Walt Elliot Disney Enterprises, Glendale, Calif., 1981-83; foundry liaison engr. Pacific Pumps div. Dresser Industries, Inc., Huntington Park, Calif., 1984-86; casting engr. Superior Industries Internat., Inc., Van Nuys, Calif., 1986-89; mech. engr. TAMCO Steel, Rancho Cucamonga, Calif., 1989-96. Recipient award for design of automatic lines for casting electric motor parts USSR Ministry Machine Bldg. and Handtools Mfr., 1966, for equipment for permanent mold casting All Union Exhbn. of Nat. Econ. Achievements, 1966-70. Mem. Am. Foundrymen's Soc. Contbr. reports, articles to collections All Union Confs. Spl. Methods in Foundry, USSR; USSR patentee permanent mold casting. Home: 184 W Armstrong Dr Claremont CA 91711-1701

YUSE-MILLER, MARY ADONNA, dietitian, holistic nutrition therapist; b. Walla Walla, Wash., Mar. 3, 1960; d. Francis Theodore and Adonna Helen (Nuxoll) Yuse; m. Keith Michael Miller, Oct. 13, 1990; stepchildren: Seth, Dustin. BS in Food and Nutrition, Ea. Wash. U., 1982; postgrad., Portland State U., 1987-90. Lic. dietitian, Oreg. Clin. dietitian Ctrl. Wash. Hosp., Wenatche, 1983; asst. food svc. mgr. Rogue Valley Manor, Medford, Oreg., 1984-86; nutrition specialist Area Agy. on Aging, Yreka, Calif., 1986-87; field mgr. Nutrition Svcs. Portland (Oreg.) Pub. Schs., 1987-90; cons. dietitian Beverly Enterprises, Portland, 1990-94; pres., founder Mary's Holistic Nutrition Therapy, Carlton, Oreg., 1994—; freelance model, 1992—; yoga instr. Chemetaka C.C., McMinnville, 1994—; cookbook reviewer Vegetarian Jour., 1993. Author: Yoga-Fitness, 1994; editor newspaper G St. Sentinel, 1972. Recipient Wo-He-Lo medallion award Camp Fire, 1978, Quadrathon Woman's Winner Graham's Rowing Shells, 1987, Woman'w winner McMinnville Triathlon, 1989. Mem. Am. Dietetic Assn. (registered, vegetarian nutrition practice group 1991—), Oreg. Dietetic Assn., Toastmasters Internat. (pres., v.p., pub. rels., sec., area gov. Newberg chpt. 1986-96). Roman Catholic. Office: Mary's Holistic Nutrition Therapy 10800 Modaffari Rd Carlton OR 97111

ZABELSKY, WILLIAM JOHN, choral and band director; b. Homestead, Pa., May 2, 1954; s. William John Sr. and Elizabeth Jean (Tisza) Z.; m. Leslie Jane Sloan, June 11, 1977; children: Jennifer Ann, Amy Elizabeth, Sarah Jane. BS in Music Edn., Duquesne U., 1976. Cert. music tchr. Substitute tchr. Pitts. Area Schs., 1976-79; gen. music tchr. Gardnerville (Nev.) Elem. Sch., 1979-85; band and choir dir. Douglas High Sch., Minden, Nev., 1985—. Rep. presdl. inaugural parade, Nev., 1989; chmn. Nev. All-state Choir, 1997. Mem. NEA, Am. Choral Dirs. Assn., Music Educators Nat. Conf., Nat. Band Assn., Nev. Music Educators Assn. (v.p. 1989-91, pres. 1991-93), Douglas County Profl. Edn. Assn. (pres. 1981-84, 85-87, 90-91, 94-96), Phi Mu Alpha. Democrat. Roman Catholic. Office: Douglas High Sch PO Box 1888 Minden NV 89423-1888

ZABINSKY, ZELDA BARBARA, operations researcher, industrial engineering educator; b. Tonawanda, N.Y., Oct. 31, 1955; d. Joseph Marvin and Helen Phyllis (Kava) Z.; m. John Clinton Palmer, July 15, 1979; children: Rebecca Ann Zabinsky, Aaron Zeff Palmer. BS, U. Puget Sound, Tacoma, 1977; MS, U. Mich., 1984, PhD, 1985. Tutor math. U. Puget Sound, 1975-77; programmer, analyst Nat. Marine Fisheries, Seattle, 1977, Boeing Computer Svcs., Seattle, 1977-78; sr. systems analyst Vector Rsch. Inc., Ann Arbor, Mich., 1980-84; asst. prof. indsl. engring. U. Wash., Seattle, 1985-93, assoc. prof. indsl. engring., 1993—, affiliated assoc. prof. mech. engring., 1993—, affiliated assoc. prof. civil engring., 1996—; cons. Boeing Corp., Seattle, 1987, Numerical Methods, Inc., Seattle, 1989-90, METRO, Seattle, 1992. Contbr. articles to tech. jours. Mem. faculty adv. bd. Women in Engring., U. Wash., 1990—. Recipient E. Goman Math. award, 1977, Rsch. Initiation award NSF, 1992-95; Howarth-Thompson scholar, 1973-77; Benton fellow, 1983-84; rsch. grantee NSF, NASA-Langley, FAA, Nat. Forest Svc., NATO, Boeing, 1985—. Mem. Ops. Rsch. Soc. Am., Inst. Indsl. Engrs. (sr.), Math. Programming Soc., Mortar Board, Phi Kappa Phi. Jewish. Office: U Wash Box 352650 Seattle WA 98195

ZABRISKIE, ROBERT, performing arts association administrator, data processing manager; b. Monroe, Utah, July 22, 1929; s. John Peter and Violet (Harding) Z.; m. Betty Ross, Feb. 2, 1952 (div.); m. Beverly Young, Oct. 16, 1970; children: Michael, Christie, Lara. BA in Music, Brigham Young U., 1953. Missionary Ch. of Jesus Christ of Latter Day Saints, Germany, 1957-60; owner Utah Conv. Svc., Salt Lake City, 1961-63; stockbroker G.L. Jones and Assocs., Salt Lake City, 1963-74; data processing mgr. Utah Dept. Transp., Salt Lake City, 1974—; founder, dir. Salt Lake Opera Theatre, 1978—; adj. prof. Westminster Coll., Salt Lake City, 1989—. condr. Murray Intermtn. Symphony, 1987—, operas and musicals including Pagliacci, Faust, Madame Butterfly, Rigoletto, The Mikado and My Fair Lady, The King & I; dir. La Boheme, The Mikado, Suor Angelica, Il Tabarro, Gianni Schicchi, Lucia di Lammermoor, Tales of Hoffman, Verdi Requiem, Brahms Requiem, Turandot, Puccini. Mem. Mormon Tabernacle Choir. Tech. sgt. USAF, 1951-55. Home and Office: Salt Lake Opera Theatre Am Towers 807-S 44 W Broadway Salt Lake City UT 84101-3201

ZABSKY, JOHN MITCHELL, engineering executive; b. Joplin, Mo., Apr. 18, 1933; s. Joseph Anthony and Joan (Lucas) Z. AS, Joplin Jr. Coll., 1953; BSME, U. Mo., 1956; MSME, U. Kans., 1965. Profl. engr., Mo. System engr. Bendix KCD, Kansas City, Mo., 1958-62; rsch. engr. Rocketdyne, Neosho, Mo., 1962-65, Boeing Co., Huntsville, Ala., 1965-66; prin. rsch. engr., scientist Honeywell Inc., St. Paul, 1966-71; chief engr. Pressure Tank & Pipe Fabrication Co., Nashville, 1971-72, Engring. for Industry, Danville, Va., 1972-73; area mgr. fluid machinery Dresser Adv. Tech. Ctr., Irvine, Calif., 1973-85; v.p. ops. ATI, Laguna Niguel, Calif., 1985-93; pres. Cytoprobe, San Diego, 1993-94, v.p. ops., 1994-95; cons. Oral Care Products, L.A., 1990-92, Kleenair Sys., Inc., Irvine, Calif., 1995—. Patentee in field. Pres. Mpls.-St. Paul Singletons, 1969-72. Mem. AIAA, ASME, Mo. Soc. Profl. Engrs., Soc. Mfg. Engrs. Home: 3640C S Main St Santa Ana CA 92707-5720

ZACHARIAS, RICHARD ALLEN, electrical engineer; b. Fresno, Calif., Dec. 3, 1953; s. John Henry and Georgia Margaret (Botts) Z.; m. Janice Anne Carter, Aug. 24, 1974; children: Eric, Nicole, Laura, Nathan, Karen. BSEE, U. of the Pacific, 1977; MSEE, U. So. Calif., 1979. Radio person, sta. engr. KSTN/AM, KUOP/FM, Stockton, Calif., 1972-74; engr. Concord (Calif.) Naval Weapons Sta., 1974-79; tech. staff mem. Hughes Aircraft Co., El Segundo, Calif., 1977-79; sect. leader L.L.N.L., Livermore, Calif., 1979—. Soccer referee Manteca (Calif.) Area Soccer League, 1987-92. Named Disting. alumni U. of the Pacific Engring., 1980. Republican. LDS. Office: Lawrence Livermore Nat Lab Mail Code L-495 7000 East Ave Livermore CA 94550

ZACHER, VALERIE IRENE, interior designer; b. Woodland, Calif., Dec. 12, 1942; d. Albert Richard and Laura Ruth (Mast) Z.; m. William Robert Wallace, June 14, 1964 (div. Oct. 1968); 1 child, Jason Zachery Wallace. BA in Polit. Sci., Stanford U., 1964; AS in Interior Design, West Valley Coll., 1982; cert. TESL, U. Calif. Santa Cruz, Santa Clara, 1994. Owner, operator Artefactorage, Fresno, Calif., 1968-77; owner, designer Viz a Viz, Los Gatos, Calif., 1978-82; facilities project mgr. Nat. Semiconductor, Santa Clara, Calif., 1982-85; project supr. Mervyns, Hayward, Calif., 1985-86; interior designer, project mgr. Charles Schwab & Co., San Francisco, 1986-87; small bus. advisor US Peace Corps, Gaborone, Botswana, 1987-89, Swedish Coop. Ctr., Gaborone, 1989-90; English tchr. YCC Am. Club, Yokohama, Japan, 1992-93; interior design cons. Los Gatos, 1993—; design/facilities cons. Octel Comm. Corp., Milpitas, Calif., 1994—; interior designer Am. Cancer Soc. Designers Showcase, 1994, 95, 96. Mem. Internat. Facilities Mgrs. Assn. Home and Office: 16721 Madrone Ave Los Gatos CA 95030-4120

ZACK, JAMES G(ORDON), JR., construction claims executive, consultant; b. Springfield, Mass., Sept. 6, 1946; s. James Gordon and Marione Mildred (Langevin) Z.; m. Yvonne Eileen Beezley, Oct. 26, 1970; children: Jennifer Yvonne, Stacy Rebecca, James William, Trevor David. AB in Polit. Sci., Assumption Coll., 1968; MPA, U. S.C., 1975. Dir. budgets and grants adminstrn. S.C. Dept. Health and Environ. Control, Columbia, 1972-78; mgr. constrn. contracts group CH2M Hill, Inc., Milw., 1978-85; mgr. scheduling and claims dept. CH2M Hill, Inc., L.A., 1986-95; mng. dir. constrn. claims and litigation support svcs. High-Point Rendel, L.A., 1995—; cons. EPA, 1977-88; reviewer Engring. Mgmt. Jour., 1987—; expert witness on constrn. litigation; lectr. profl. devel. seminars. Contbr. articles to profl. jours. Commr. Pacifica dist. Boy Scouts Am., 1987-94, scoutmaster, 1994—; mem. Calif. Compact Com., Huntington Beach, 1988-92. Mem. ASCE, Am. Assn. Cost Engrs., Project Mgmt. Inst., Constrn. Mgmt. Assn. Am., Am. Arbitration Assn.,. Methodist. Home: 9531 Netherway Dr Huntington Beach CA 92646-6051 Office: High Point Univ Tower 4199 Campus Dr Ste 60C Irvine CA 92715

ZACK, TERESA ISON, civil engineer; b. Ft. Campbell, Ky., Aug. 30, 1950; d. Venon Harrison and Frances Lorene (Jarvis) Ison; m. Richard Clark Zack, July 7, 1973 (div. June 1994). BS in Edn., U. Ga., 1972; BSCE, Fresno State U., 1982. Registered profl. engr., Calif. Tchr. Rockdale County H.S., Conyers, Ga., 1973-75; engring. technician Zack & Assocs., Tulare, Calif., 1975-80; asst. civil engr. Conlan Engring., Tulare, 1983-85; asst. civil engr. City of Hanford, Calif., 1985-88, asst. city engr., 1988, city engr., 1988—. Mem. ASCE, Am. Pub. Works Assn., Internat. Transp. Engrs., Hanford Jaycees (charter), Kiwanis, Beta Sigma Phi. Office: Hanford Pub Works Dept 900 S 10th Ave Hanford CA 93230

ZAFFARONI, ALEJANDRO C., biochemist, medical research company executive; b. Montevideo, Uruguay, Feb. 27, 1923; came to U.S., 1944; s. Carlos and Luisa (Alfaro) Z.; m. Lyda Russomanno, July 5, 1946; children—Alejandro A., Elisa. B., U. Montevideo, 1943; Ph.D. in Biochemistry, U. Rochester, 1949; Doctorate (hon.), U. Republic, Montevideo, 1983; M.Divinity, Cen. Bapt. Seminary, 1987. Dir. biochem. research Syntex S.A., Mexico City, 1951-54, v.p., dir. research, 1954-56; exec. v.p., dir. Syntex Corp., Palo Alto, Calif., 1956-68; pres. Syntex Labs. Inc., Palo Alto, Calif., 1962-68, Syntex Research, Palo Alto, Calif., 1962-68; founder, co-chmn. ALZA Corp., Palo Alto, Calif., 1968—, also CEO; founder, mem. policy bd. and exec. com. DNAX Research Inst. of Molecular and Cellular Biology, Inc., Palo Alto, Calif., 1980—, chmn., 1980-82; founder, chmn., chief exec. officer Affymax, N.V., Palo Alto, 1989—; chmn. Internat. Psoriasis Research Found., Palo Alto; incorporator Neuroscis. Research Found. MIT, Brookline, Mass.; bd. govs. Weizmann Inst. Sci., Rehovot, Israel; mem. pharm. panel of com. on tech. and internat. econs. and trade issues Nat. Acad. Engring. Office of Fgn. Sec. and Assembly of Engring., Washington; hon. prof. biochemistry Nat. U. Mex., 1957, U. Montevideo, 1959. Contbr. numerous articles to profl. jours.; patentee in field. Recipient Barren medal Barren Found., Chgo., 1974; Pres.'s award Weizmann Inst. Sci., 1978; Chem. Pioneer award Am. Inst. Chemists, Inc., 1979, National Medal of Technology, 1995. Fellow Am. Acad. Arts and Scis., Am. Pharm. Assn.; mem. AAAS, Am. Chem. Soc., Am. Found. Pharm. Edn., Am. Inst. Chemists, Inc., Am. Soc. Biol. Chemists, Inc., Am. Soc. Microbiology, Am. Soc. Pharmacology and Exptl. Therapeutics, Biomed. Engring. Soc., Calif. Pharmacists Assn., Internat. Pharm. Fedn., Internat. Soc. Chronobiology, Internat. Soc. Study of Biol. Rhythms, Soc. Exptl. Biology and Medicine, Sociedad Mexicana de Nutricion y Endocrinologia, Biochem. Soc. Eng., Endocrine Soc., Internat. Soc. Research in Biology of Reproduction, N.Y. Acad. Scis., Christian Legal Soc. (Mo. bd. dirs. 1973—), Tau Kappa Epsilon (internat. pres. 1953-57). *

ZAGON, LAURIE, artist, writer, color consultant; b. N.Y.C., Feb. 4, 1950; d. Jerome and Janet (Rabinowitz) Z.; m. Joseph Sorrentino, Dec. 21, 1991. BFA, Md. Inst. Coll. Art, 1971; MFA, Syracuse U., 1973. Asst. prof. Art CUNY, N.Y.C., 1973-87; color cons. Fieldcrest/Cannon, N.Y.C., 1987-88; nat. speaker Am. Soc. Interior Designers, Washington, 1993—; color, art therapist, Flagstaff, Ariz., 1996, Big Brothers/Big Sisters No. Ariz., 1996. Illustrator (book) It's Never Too Late to Have a Happy Childhood, 1989; one-woman shows include The Nat. Arts Club, N.Y.C., 1989, Gallery 1757, Laguna Beach, Calif., 1991; group exhibits include John Szoke Gallery, N.Y.C., Helio Galleries, N.Y.C., CUNY Abstract Show of Shanghai, China, 1986, L.A. Mcpl. Gallery, 1993, Phoenix Airport Galleries, 1996; co-author: Power of Color, 1995. Color/art therapist for AIDS Children, L.A. Children's Hosp., 1994—; color/art therapist for recovering addicts Capo by the Sea, Dana Point, Calif., 1991, Martin Luther Hosp., Anaheim, 1990; active painting workshops for the terminally ill, 1995-97. Home and Office: 1107 Fair Oaks Ave # 147 South Pasadena CA 91030-3311

ZAHARIA, ERIC STAFFORD, developmental disabilities program administrator; b. Pomona, Calif., Aug. 24, 1948; s. Edgar A. and Dorothy (Stafford) Z.; m. Caryle Koentz, Dec. 23, 1967; children: Tye W., Tieg A. BA, Pomona Coll., 1970; MEd, U. Ariz.-Tucson, 1973; PhD, George Peabody Coll., 1978; postgrad., Govt. Execs. Inst. U. N.C., Chapel Hill, 1981. Mental retardation worker Ariz. Tng. Program, Tucson, 1970-71, unit dir., 1971-73; dir. residential svcs. Willmar State Hosp., (Minn.), 1973-76; rsch. asst. Inst. on Mental Retardation and Intellectual Devel., Nashville, 1976-78; dir. mental retardation program svcs. Dept. Mental Health/Mental Retardation, State of Tenn., Nashville, 1978-79; dir. Caswell Ctr., Kinston, N.C., 1979-86; program adminstr. Colo. Div. of Devel. Disabilities, Denver, 1986-90; dir. Utah divsn. Svcs. for People with Disabilities, Salt Lake City, 1990-95; ind. cons. Park City, Utah, 1995—; mem. adj. faculty East Carolina U., Greenville, 1979-86; bd. dirs. Neuse Enterprises Inc., Kinston. Chmn. Big Bros./Sisters Kinston Inc., 1980-83; mem. N.C. Coalition for Community Svc., 1982-85. Mem. Am. Assn. Mental Retardation, Nat. Assn. Supts., Pub. Residential Facilities, Assn. Retarded Citizens, Kinston C. of C. (bd. dirs. 1983-86). Home: 8010 Juniper Dr Park City UT 84060-5370 Office: 120 N 200 W Salt Lake City UT 84103-1550

ZAIDI, EMILY LOUISE, retired elementary school educator; b. Hoquiam, Wash., Apr. 20, 1924; d. Burdick Newton and Emily Caroline (Williams) Johnston; m. M. Baqar Abbas Zaidi, June 12, 1949 (dec. Dec. 1983). BA in Edn. and Social Studies, Ea. Wash. State U., 1948; MEd, U. Wash., 1964, EdD, 1974. Tchr. 4th grade Hoquiam Schs., 1948-49; tchr. grades 5-6 Lake Washington Sch. Dist., Kirkland, Wash., 1949-51; tchr. grades 2-3 Port Angeles (Wash.) Schs., 1951-54; tchr. grade 2 Seattle Schs., 1954-55; tchr., reading specialist Northshore sch. Dist., Bothell, Wash., 1955-69, Sacramento City Schs., 1969-87; ret.; mem. Calif. State Instructional Materials Panel, Sacramento, 1975. Mem. Sacramento Opera Assn., 1986—, Sacramento Ballet Assn., 1987—, Sacramento Symphony Assn., 1985—. Fulbright Commn. Exchange Tchr., 1961-62. Mem. Reading Club, Comstock Club. Democrat. Home: 4230 N River Way Sacramento CA 95864-6055

ZAIDI, IQBAL MEHDI, biochemist, scientist; b. Bijnor, India, June 30, 1957; s. Iqbal Haider and Habib (Zehra) Z.; m. Nuzhat Shikoh, Jan. 2, 1993; 1 child, Shan Zehra. BS in Chemistry with honors, Aligarh M. U., 1976, MS in Biochemistry, 1978, PhD in Biochemistry, 1984. Cert. in radiation. Rsch. fellow Indsl. Toxicology Rsch. Ctr., Lucknow, India, 1979-83; rsch. affiliate N.Y. State Health Dept., Albany, 1984-91; scientist Applied Biosystems div. Perkin Elmer Corp., Foster City, Calif., 1991—. Contbr. articles to profl. jours. Mem. AAAS, Am. Chem. Soc. (biochem. tech. div. 1992—), Shia Assn. Bay Area, N.Y. Acad. Scis. Office: Perkin Elmer Corp Applied Biosystems Divsn 850 Lincoln Centre Dr Foster City CA 94404-1128

ZAJAC, JOHN, semiconductor equipment company executive; b. N.Y.C., July 21, 1946; s. John Andrew and Catherine (Canepa) Z.; m. Vera Barbagallo, Jan. 13, 1973; children: Jennifer, Michelle. AAS, NYU, 1966; BEE, U. Ky., 1968. Project engr. B.C.D. Computing, N.Y.C., 1968-70; v.p. Beacon Systems, Commack, N.Y., 1970-73, E.T. Systems, Santa Clara, Calif., 1973-77; v.p. research and devel. Eaton Corp., Sunnyvale, Calif., 1977-81; pres. Semitech/Gen. Signal, Los Gatos, Calif., 1981-83; mgr. advanced product div. Tegal/Motorola Inc., Novato, Calif., 1983-86; v.p. research and devel. U.S.A. Inc., San Jose, Calif., 1986-94; mgr. continuous improvement program Mattson Tech., Fremont, Calif., 1994—. Author: Delicate Balance, 1988; holder of 19 patents in field; guest TV and radio. Office: Mattson Tech 3550 W Warren Ave Fremont CA 94538

ZAKARAUSKAS, PIERRE, physicist, educator; b. Amos, Que., Can., Dec. 25, 1958; s. Joseph and Réjeanne (Latreille) Z. BSc, U Que., 1980; PhD, U. B.C., Vancouver, 1984. Def. scientist Def. Rsch. Establishment Atlantic, Dartmouth, N.S., 1984-86, Def. Rsch. Establishment Pacific, Victoria, B.C., 1986-95; rsch. assoc. dept. psychology U. B.C., 1988-93, asst. prof. dept. ophthalmology, 1993—. Contbr. articles and referee to profl. jours. including Jour. Acoustical Soc. Am., IEEE Transaction on Signal Processing, Neural Network for Ocean Engring., IEEE Proceedings, Hearing Res., Phys. Rev. D. Mem. Acoustical Soc. Am., Can. Acoustical Assn. Home: 3325 W 2d Ave, Vancouver, BC Canada V6R 1H9 Office: U BC Dept Ophthalmology, 2550 Willow St, Vancouver, BC Canada V5Z 3N9

ZAKIAN, MICHAEL, museum director. Dir. Frederick R. Weisman Mus. Art, Malibu, Calif., 1994—. Office: Pepperdine U Mus Art 24255 Pacific Coast Hwy Malibu CA 90263

ZALESKI, BRIAN WILLIAM, chiropractor; b. Trenton, N.J., Oct. 27, 1962; s. Joseph Rudolph and Roseline (Moore) Z.; m. Petra Gertrude Tucker, Apr. 10, 1983; children: Natasha Reneé, Tatyana Amber. Student, Def. Lang. Inst., Monterey, Calif., 1980-81; BS, Palmer Coll., 1992, D of Chiropractic, 1992. Indsl. disability evaluator, Calif.; qualified med. evaluator, Calif. Grad. rschr. Palmer Coll. of Chiropractice, Davenport, Iowa, 1991-92; chiropractor Peninsula Spinal Care, Daly City, Calif., 1992; chiropractor Creekside Family Chiropractic, Vacaville, Calif., 1992—, Suisun City, Calif., 1996—; prin. investigator, presenter Internat. Conf. on Spinal Manipulation, 1992. Editor Napa Solano Chiropractor, 1996—. Baseball umpire Iowa High Schs., Davenport, 1989-92, Men's Sr. League, Davenport, 1989-91, No. Calif. Umpires Assn., San Mateo, Calif., 1992; mem. adv. bd. Solano Serve Our Srs. Recipient scholarship Internat. Chiropractors Assn., 1989, 90, Cecil M. Grogan scholarship Palmer Internat. Alumni Assn., 1991, Alma Nielsen scholarship Internat. Chiropractors Assn. Aux., 1991, Student Rsch. grant Palmer Coll. Chiropractic, 1992; named to Dean's List, 1991-92. Mem. Internat. Chiropractors Assn. (coun. on chiropractic pediatrics), Calif. Chiropractic Assn. (net masters com., ins. rels. com., webmaster home pages sect.), Assn. for History of Chiropractic, Palmer Internat. Alumni Assn., Napa/Solano Chiropractic Soc. (pres., editor), Masons, Delta Sigma Chi, Chi Rho Theta. Republican. Office: Creekside Family Chiropractic 3000 Alamo Dr Ste 108 Vacaville CA 95687-6345 also: Creekside Family Chiropractic 411 Main St Ste C Suisun City CA 94585

ZALESKI, HALINA MARIA, animal scientist; b. Marlborough, Eng., June 24, 1950; came to the U.S., 1992; d. Witold Andrzej and Ludmila Anne (Kwiatkowska) Z.; m. Christopher Ernest Mewhort, June 15, 1973; children: Celka Z., Lisa Z. BSc, U. Sask., Saskatoon, Sask., Can., 1974; PhD, Guelph (Ont., Can.) U., 1992. Rsch. asst. U. Sask., Saskatoon, 1972-75; owner, mgr. Self-Reliance and Hard Struggle Coop. Farm Ltd., Sonningdale, Sask., 1973-85; farm mgr. V&V Livestock, Naicam, Sask., 1985-89; rsch. assoc. U. Ill., Urbana-Champaign, 1992-93; asst. specialist U. Hawaii, Honolulu, 1993—. Contbr. articles to profl. jours. Dir. Fedn. Prodn. Coops., Swift Current, Sask., 1976-81, Can. Lacombe (Alta.) Swine Breeders Assn., 1980-81, Swine Improvement Svcs. Coop., Melfort, Sask., 1981-86; pres. Sask. Lacombe Swine Breeders Assn., Regina, 1981-82. Soden fellow U. Guelph, 1990, Williams fellow, postgrad. scholar Natural Scis. and Enging. Rsch. Coun., 1990, 91; rsch. grantee Gov.'s Agrl. Coordinating Com., Honolulu, 1993, 95, Agriculture Devel. Am. Pacific, Honolulu, 1996. Mem. Am. Soc. Animal Sci., Soc. for Study of Reproduction, Ctr. for the Study of Animal Welfare, Agrl. Inst. Can. Office: Univ Hawaii Dept Animal Scis 1800 E West Rd Honolulu HI 96822-2318

ZALLE, PAUL MARTIN, financial services company executive; b. L.A., Aug. 13, 1945; s. Morris D. and Esther M. (Kahn) Z.; m. Judith Ann Willen, Mar. 31, 1968; children: Melissa Elise, Michael Brandon. BSBA, Calif. State. U., Northridge, 1968; postgrad. in acctg., Calif. State U., L.A., 1969-71. Cert. internal auditor, cert. info. sys. auditor, cert. fraud examiner. Sr. acct. Cohen & Cohen, CPA's, L.A., 1968-72; mgr. auditing Carte Blanche Corp., L.A., 1973-77; regional audit mgr. Avco. Corp., Newport Beach, Calif., 1978-82; regional dir. auditing Textron Corp., Irvine, Calif., 1983-86; v.p. auditing Avco Fin. Svcs., Inc., Irvine, 1987--; cons. to pres. Bus. Spltys., Inc., Newport Beach, Calif., 1986—; cons. to chmn. Imperial Thrift & Loan Assn., Burbank, Calif., 1987-93. Contbr. articles to profl. publs. Family advisor prosthetic program for handicapped UCLA, 1975--. Mem. Am. Fin. Svcs. Assn. (nat. audit com. 1985—, chmn. 1990-92, 95-97), Inst. Internal Auditors (editor, advisor 1980—, hon. svc. award 1983, bd. govs. Orange County chpt. 1990—), EDP Auditors Assn., Orange County Pvt. Investment Club. Democrat. Jewish. Home: 30 Ocean Vis Newport Beach CA 92660-6224 Office: Avco Fin Svcs Inc 17770 Cartwright Rd Irvine CA 92714

ZALTA, EDWARD, otorhinolaryngologist, physician; b. Houston, Mar. 2, 1930; s. Nouri Louis and Marie Zahde (Lizmi) Z.; m. Carolyn Mary Gordon, Oct. 8, 1971; 1 child, Ryan David; children by previous marriage: Nouri Allan, Lori Ann, Barry Thomas, Marci Louise. BS, Tulane U., 1952, MD, 1956. Diplomate Am. Bd. Quality Assurance and Utilization Rev. Physicians. Intern Brooke Army Hosp., San Antonio, 1956-57; resident in otolaryngology U.S. Army Hosp., Ft. Campbell, Ky., 1957-60; practice medicine specializing in otolaryngology Glendora, West Covina and San Dimas, Calif., 1960-82; ENT cons. City of Hope Med. Ctr., 1961-76; mem. staff Foothill Presbyn.; past pres. L.A. Found. Community Svc., L.A. Poison Info. Ctr., So. Calif. Physicians Coun., Inc.; founder, chmn. bd. dirs. CAPP CARE, INC.; founder Inter-Hosp. Coun. Continuing Med. Edn.; mem. bd. trustees U.S. Pharmacopeial Convention, Inc. Author: (with others) Medicine and Your Money; mem. editorial staff Managed Care Outlook, AAPPO Jour., Med. Interface; mem. editl. adv. bd. Inside Medicaid Managed Care, Disease Management News; contbr. articles to profl. jours. Pres. bd. govs. Glendora Unified Sch. Dist., 1965-71; mem. Calif. Cancer Adv. Coun., 1967-71, Commn. of Californias, L.A. County Commn. on Economy and Efficiency. Served to capt. M.C. AUS, 1957-60. Recipient Award of Merit Order St. Lazarus, 1981. Mem. AMA, Calif. Med. Assn., Am. Acad. Otolaryngology, Am. Coun. Otolaryngology, Am. Assn. Preferred Provider Orgns. (past pres.), Am. Coll. Med. Quality, L.A. County Med. Assn. (pres. 1980-81), Kappa Nu, Phi Delta Epsilon, Glendora CountryClub, Centurion Club, Sea Bluff Beach and Racquet Club; Center Club (Costa Mesa, Calif.), Pacific Golf Club (San Juan, Capistrano). Republican. Jewish. Home: 3 Morning Dove Laguna Niguel CA 92677-5331 Office: West Tower 4000 Macarthur Blvd Ste 10000 Newport Beach CA 92660-2526

ZALUTSKY, MORTON HERMAN, lawyer; b. Schenectady, Mar. 8, 1935; s. Albert and Gertrude (Daffner) Z.; m. Audrey Englebardt, June 16, 1957; children: Jane, Diane, Samuel. BA, Yale U., 1957; JD, U. Chgo., 1960. Bar: Oreg. 1961. Law clk. to presiding judge Oreg. Supreme Ct., 1960-61; assoc. Hart, Davidson, Veazie & Hanlon, 1961-63, Veatch & Lovett, 1963-64, Morrison, Bailey, Dunn, Cohen & Miller, 1964-69; prin. Morton H. Zalutsky, P.C., 1970-76; ptnr. Dahl, Zalutsky, Nichols & Hinson, 1977-79, Zalutsky & Klarquist, P.C., Portland, Oreg., 1980-85, Zalutsky, Klarquist & Johnson, Inc., Portland, 1985-94; Zalutsky & Klarquist, P.C., Portland, 1994—; instr. Portland State U., 1961-64, Northwestern Sch. of Law, 1969-70; assoc. prof. U. Miami Law Sch.; lectr. Practising Law Inst., 1971—, Oreg. State Bar Continuing Legal Edn. Program, 1970, Am. Law Inst.-ABA Continuing Legal Edn. Program, 1973—, 34th, 37th NYU ann. insts. fed. taxation, So. Fed. Tax Inst., U. Miami Inst. Estate Planning, Southwestern Legal Found., Internat. Found. Employee Benefit Plans, numerous other profl. orgns.; dir. A-E-F-C Pension Plan, 1994—. Author: (with others) The Professional Corporation in Oregon, 1970, 82; contbg. author: The Dentist and the Law, 3d edit.; editor-in-chief (retirement plans) Matthew Bender's Federal Tax Service, 1987—; contbr. to numerous publs. in field. Mem. vis. com. U. Chgo. Law Sch. Mem. ABA (vice chair profl. svcs. 1987-89, mem. coun. tax sect. 1987-89, spl. coord. 1980-85), Am. Law Inst., Am. Bar Retirement Assn. (trustee, bd. dirs., vice chair 1990-91, chair 1991-92), Multnomah County Bar Assn., Am. Tax Lawyers (charter mem.), Oreg. Estate Planning Coun. Jewish. Home: 3118 SW Fairmount Blvd Portland OR 97201-1466 Office: 215 SW Washington St Fl 3D Portland OR 97204-2636

ZAMBETTI, DENIS EGAN, product specialist; b. Riverdale, N.Y., Oct. 18, 1953; s. Emil John and Teresa Veronica (McSherry) Z. BS, U.S. Mil. Acad., 1977; MBA, Golden Gate U., 1985; grad., Command and Gen. Staff Coll., 1993. Commd. 2d lt. U.S. Army, 1977, advanced through ranks to capt., 1977-81, resigned, 1985; platoon leader B Co. 2d/22d Inf., Wiesbaden, Fed. Republic Germany, 1977-78, mortar platoon leader, 1978-79, exec. officer, 1979-80; communications and electronics officer HHC Co. 2d/22d Inf., Wiesbaden, 1980-81; morale support fund custodian U.S. Mil. Command Activity Group, Bad Kreuznach, Fed. Republic Germany, 1981-82; equal opportunity staff officer HQ Presidio of San Francisco, 1982-83, chief reserve pay, 1983-85; peninsula area mgr. Beringer Wines/Wineworld, San Francisco, 1985-87; nat. accts. mgr. SW region Beringer Wines/Wineworld, Mission Viejo, Calif., 1987—; v.p. product devel. IQUEST Bus. Devel., Santa Clara, Calif., 1988—; nat. accts. mgr. Sutter Home Winery, 1988-92; mgr. sales Union Camp Corp., Stockton, Calif., 1992-95; bulk specialist Union Camp Corp., Hanford, Calif., 1995—. Lt. comdr. USAR, 1996. Named One of Outstanding Young Men of Am. Jaycees, 1983. Mem. Knights of the Vine, West Point Soc. of Bay Area (bd. govs. 1982-85), West Point Soc. Orange County (admissions rep. 1987—, mil. liaison officer 1991—). Democrat. Roman Catholic. Home: 4843 Kimberly Common Livermore CA 94550-7707

ZANETTA, JOSEPH MICHAEL, university administrator, lawyer; b. Jamestown, N.Y., Apr. 26, 1953; s. Joseph A. and Freda (Felanzo) Z.; m. Ellen L. Leggett, June 2, 1979; 1 child, Samuel Leggett Zanetta. BS, Cornell U., 1975, JD, 1978. Bar: N.Y. 1980. Mem. Hartley & Fessenden, Attys., Jamestown, 1978-79; devel. officer Cornell U., Ithaca, N.Y., 1979-82; assoc. dir. maj. gifts Tufts U., Medford, Mass., 1982-83; dir. devel. Belmont Hill Sch., Belmont, Mass., 1983-86; exec. dir. external affairs Sch. Bus. Administrn. U. So. Calif., L.A., 1986-93; v.p. advancement Whittier (Calif.) Coll., 1993—; chmn. Pasadena Enterprise Ctr. Sec.-treas. Lord Found. of Calif., L.A., 1988-93. Mem. Coun. for Advancement and Support of Edn. (chair nat. confs. 1990, 92), Univ. Club of L.A. (bd. dirs. 1991—), Phi Kappa Phi (bd. dirs. 1991—). Roman Catholic. Home: 391 S Parkwood Ave Pasadena CA 91107-5037 Office: Whittier College 13406 Philadelphia St Whittier CA 90601-4446

ZAREM, HARVEY ALAN, plastic surgeon; b. Savannah, Ga., Feb. 13, 1932; s. Harry A. and Rose (Gold) Z.; m. Beth McCanghey, July 11, 1981; children: Harold, Allison, Melissa, Kathryn, Michael, Robert. BA, Yale U., 1953; MD, Columbia U., 1957. Diplomate Am. Bd. Surgery, Am. Bd. Plastic Surgery; lic. physician, Md., Ill., Calif. Intern Johns Hopkins Hosp., Balt., 1957-58, resident in plastic surgery, 1964-66; rsch. fellow Peter Bent Brigham Hosp., Boston, 1958-59, asst. resident in surgery, 1959-61; resident in surgery then chief resident Boston City Hosp., 1961-63; postdoctoral fellow NYU, N.Y.C., 1963-64; from asst. prof. to assoc. prof. surgery U. Chgo., 1966-73; prof. surgery U. Calif., L.A., 1973-87, prof. emeritus, 1987—; mem. med. staff Pacific Surgicenter, Santa Monica, Calif., 1987—; physician Sepulveda (Calif.) VA Hosp., 1974—; mem. med. staff St. Johns Hosp., Santa Monica, Calif., 1987—, Santa Monica Hosp., 1988—; vis. prof. So. Ill. U., 1983, Lackaland AFB, 1986, Creighton U., 1987, Comesa, Milan, 1989, Baylor Coll. Medicine, 1990; Kazanjian vis. prof. Mass. Gen. Hosp., 1986, 88; cons. and presenter in field. Contbr. numerous articles to profl. jours. Grantee NIH, 1964-75, NIH, 1967-72, Sheldon and Carol Appel Family Found., 1982—, Chantal Pharms., 1983-84, Mentor Corp./Heyer-Schulte Products, 1985—, Michael Jackson Burn Found., 1986-87. Fellow ACS; mem. AMA, Am. Soc. Plastic Reconstructive Sugeons, Inc., Am. Burn Assn., Am. Cleft Palat Assn., Am. Assn. Plastic Surgeons, Am. Soc. Aesthetic Plastic Surgery, Am. Assn. Hand Surgery, Am. Assn. Surgery of Trauma, Calif. Med. Asssn., Calif. Soc. Plastic Surgeons, New Eng. Soc. Plastic Surgeons (hon.), L.A. Cunty Med. Assn., Johns Hopkins Med. and Surg. Soc., Plastic Surgery Rsch. Coun., Soc. Head and Neck Surgeons (sr.), Soc. U. Surgeons, N.W. Soc. Plastic Surgeons (hon.), others. Office: Pacific Surgicenter 1301 20th St Ste 470 Santa Monica CA 90404-2054

ZEAMER, RICHARD JERE, engineer, executive; b. Orange, N.J., May 13, 1921; s. Jay and Margery Lilly (Herman) Z.; m. Jean Catherine Hellens, July 8, 1944 (div. 1966); children: Audrie Dagna, Richard Warwick, Geoffrey Hellens; m. Theresa Elizabeth Taborsky, Mar. 27, 1969; children: Emily Elizabeth, Charlotte Anne. BSME, MIT, 1943, MSCE, 1948; PhD in Mech. Enging., U. Utah, 1975. Registered profl. engr., Utah. Civil engr. Morton C. Tuttle, Boston, 1949-53; process design engr. Nekoosa Edwards Paper Co., Port Edwards, Wis., 1953-55; process engr. W.Va. Pulp and Paper Co., Luke, Md., 1955-60; rocket engr., supr. Allegany Ballistics Lab., Rocket Ctr., W.Va., 1960-65; enging. supr. Hercules Powder Co., Magna, Utah, 1965-69; engr. structures, heat, flow, combustion & failure analysis Hercules Rocket Plant, Magna, 1969-83; project enging. mgr. Hercules Aerospace Div., Magna, 1983-89; pres., mgr. Applied Sci. Assocs., Salt Lake City, 1989—; chmn. policy studies UN Assn. Utah, 1990—; project leader world problem analyses, 1990—. Contbr. papers, articles, reports to profl. publs. Judge sci. fair, Salt Lake County, Utah, 1985—; chmn. citizens policy panel Utah chpt. UN Assn., U.S.A., N.Y.C., 1990—; mem. Utah State Hist. Soc., Salt Lake City, 1968-91, Mil. History Soc. Utah, Salt Lake City, 1990—. 1st lt. U.S. Army, 1943-46. Recipient commendation for presentation on world population problem Utah's Forum on Global Environ., 1992. Fellow AIAA (astronautics assoc.); mem. Cons. Engrs. Coun. Utah (article award 1992), League Utah Writers, Wasatch Mountain Club (hike leader 1987—). Home and Office: Applied Sci Assocs 843 13th Ave Salt Lake City UT 84103-3327

ZEHR, NORMAN ROBERT, association administrator; b. Niagara Falls, N.Y., May 19, 1930; s. George Andrew and Ina Kate (Morrell) Z.; Engr. of Mines, Colo. Sch. Mines, 1952, M.S., 1956; m. Janet Hutchinson, Apr. 24, 1976; children—Jeanette Ann, Leslie. Sales trainee Ingersoll-Rand Co., N.Y.C., 1955-56, sales engr., Lima, Peru, 1956-64, regional mgr. mining and constrn. sales, Lima, Peru and N.Y.C., 1964-68, gen. sales mgr. Latin Am., N.Y.C., 1968-69, gen. mgr. Latin Am. ops., N.Y.C., 1969-71, v.p. Ingersoll Rand Internat., Woodcliff Lake, N.J., 1971-72, pres., 1972-83, , v.p. Ingersoll-Rand Co., 1975-83; exec. dir. Colo. Sch. Mines Alumni Assn., 1984-95, ret. 1995. Served with AUS, 1952-54. Recipient Colo. Sch. Mines Disting. Achievement medal, 1977. Mem. AIME, Scabbard and Blade, Nat. Soc. Pershing Rifles, Mining Club , Sigma Nu.

ZEIGER, ROBERT S., allergist; b. Bklyn., July 31, 1942; s. Murray and Mildred (Oransky) Z.; m. Karen P. Zeiger, June 25, 1967; children: Joanna, Laurie. BA with honors, Tulane U., 1963; MD, PhD, SUNY, Bklyn., 1969. Diplomate Am. Bd. Pediatrics, Am. Bd. Allergy-Immunology. Intern pediatrics Harriet Lane Johns Hopkins Hosp., Balt., 1969-70; staff assoc. NIH, Bethesda, Md., 1970-72; resident pediatrics Boston Children's Hosp., 1972-73, allergy fellow, 1973-75; instr. Harvard Med. Sch., Boston, 1975-76; chief of allergy Kaiser Permanente, San Diego, 1976—; clin. assoc. prof. U. Calif., San Diego, 1980-87, clin. prof., 1987—. Editorial bd. Family Practice Survey, 1983-85, Jour. Allergy Clin. Immunology, 1985-91, Pediatric Allergy Immunology Jour., 1990—; author: Nasal Manifestations of Systemic Diseases, 1990; contbr. articles to profl. jours. Lt. comdr. USPHS, 1970-72. Phizer Honor scholar Phizer Corp., 1967-69, Charles A. Janeway scholar Harvard U., 1975; Hood Found. grantee, 1975-77. Fellow Am. Acad. Pediatrics, Am. Acad. Allergy Clin. Immunology (Travel award 1975), Phi Beta Kappa, Alpha Omega Alpha. Democrat. Office: So Calif Permanente Med Group 7060 Clairemont Mesa Blvd San Diego CA 92111-1003

ZEILINGER, ELNA RAE, elementary educator, gifted-talented education educator; b. Tempe, Ariz., Mar. 24, 1937; d. Clayborn Eddie and Ruby Elna (Laird) Simpson; m. Philip Thomas Zeilinger, June 13, 1970; children: Shari, Chris. BA in Edn., Ariz. State U., 1958, MA in Edn., 1966, EdS, 1980. Bookkeeper First Nat. Bank of Tempe, 1955-56; with registrar's office Ariz. State U., 1956-58; piano tchr., recreation dir. City of Tempe; tchr. Thew Sch., Tempe, 1958-61; elem. tchr. Mitchell Sch., Tempe, 1962-74, intern prin., 1976, personnel intern, 1977; specialist gifted edn. Tempe Elem. Schs., Tempe, 1977-86; elem. tchr. Holdeman Sch., Tempe, 1986-89; tchr. grades 1-12 and adult reading, lang. arts, English Zeilinger Tutoring Svc., 1991—; grad. asst. edn. adminstrn., Iota Workshop coordinator Ariz. State U., 1978; presenter Ariz. Gifted Conf., 1978-81; condr. survey of gifted programs, 1980; reporter public relations Tempe Sch. Dist., 1978-80, Access com. for gifted programs, 1981-83. Author: Leadership Role of the Principal in Gifted Programs: A Handbook, 1980; Classified Personnel Handbook, 1977, also reports, monographs and paintings. Mem. Tempe Hist. Assn., liaison, 1975; mem. Tempe Art League; mem. freedom train com. Ariz. Bicentennial Commn., 1975-76; bd. dirs. Maple Property Owners Assn., 1994—; storyteller Tempe Hist. Mus., 1997—. Named Outstanding Leader in Elem. and Secondary Schs., 1976' Ariz. Cattle Growers scholar, 1954-55; Elks scholar, 1954-55; recipient Judges award Tempe Art League, 1970, Best of Show, Scottsdale Art League, 1976. Democrat. Congregationalist.

ZEILINGER, PHILIP THOMAS, aeronautical engineer; b. David City, Nebr., Feb. 13, 1940; s. Thomas Leroy and Sylvia Dorothy Zeilinger; m. Elna Rae Simpson, June 13, 1970; children: Shari, Chris. AS, Wentworth Mil. Acad., Lexington, Mo., 1959; BSME, Kans. U., 1962. Estimator, engr. Reynolds Electronics and Enging. Co., El Paso, Tex., 1966-68; accessories coord. ITI Garrett, Phoenix, 1974-79, cntrl. access engr., 1968—, controls coord. ITEC, 1983-84, integrated support specialist ITEC, 1984-86, mgr. systems software light helo turbine enging. co. div., 1986-91, FAA designated engr. rep. engine div., 1991—; chmn. Light Helicopter Turbine Engine Company Computer Aided Acquistion and Logistics Working Group. V.p. Indsl. Devel. Authority, Tempe, Ariz., 1979-84; pres. Univ. Royal Garden Homes Assn., Tempe, 1984-90. 1st lt. U.S. Army, 1962-66. Recipient Vol. Svc. award City of Tempe, 1984, Grand Cross of Color, Internat. Order of Rainbow Girls, 1978. Mem. AIAA, Aircraft Owners and Pilots Assn., Explt. Aircraft Assn. (v.p. chpt. 228 1974-79), Masons (master 1990-92, chmn. statewide picnic 1992, Mason of the Yr. 1992). Democrat. Unitarian. Home: 760 N Sycamore Pl Chandler AZ 85224-6925 Office: 111 S 34th St Phoenix AZ 85034-2802

ZEITLER, BILL LORENZ, aviation engineer; b. Columbus, Ohio, July 14, 1920; s. Walter Andrew and Naomi Lee (Limes) Z.; BSCE, Calif. State U., Long Beach, 1965; m. Betty Eileen Thomas, Nov. 8, 1942; children: Eddie, Naomi Lawrence. Cert. vocat. tchr., Calif. Loftsman, Curtiss Wright Corp., Columbus, 1941-45, 46-50; linesman Lockheed Corp., Burbank, Calif., 1945-46; linesman N.Am. Rockwell (and predecessor firms), Inglewood, Calif., 1950-58, airframe designer, 1958-62, supr. enging. coll. unit, 1962-65, project engr. life scis., health care delivery systems, 1965-68, project dir. health care delivery systems, Princeton, W.Va., 1968-69, mem. tech. staff, Downey, Calif., 1950-85; project engr. space shuttle design, 1971-75, shuttle alignment and mating, 1975-77, space shuttle design support extra vehicular stowage and testing, 1978-85; ret., 1985; mem. Space Shuttle Speakers Bur. Instr. 55 Alive-mature driving classes; former pres. Big Bear Valley Sr. Citizens; mem. Annual Mayor's Prayer Breakfast Com.; chairperson Living Forest Task Force, Friends of Moonridge Zoo; bd. dir. Sr. Center. Mem. AIAA, Nat. Space Inst., Nat. Geog. Soc., Smith Instn. Assocs., Rockwell Mgmt. Club, Toastmasters, Kiwanis, Big Bear Mcpl. Water Dist. Citizens Adv. Com., Erwin Lake Home Owners Assoc.

ZEITLIN, GERALD MARK, electrical engineer; b. Phila., May 7, 1937; s. David Edward and Charlotte (Freedman) Z.; m. Frances Loretta Scherr, May 17, 1983 (div. 1988). BEE, Cornell U., 1960; MSEE, U. Colo., 1969. Electronic engr. Nat. Security Agy., Ft. Meade, Md., 1962-64, Westinghouse Georesearch Lab., Boulder, Colo., 1966-69; owner Sunrise Books, Estes Park, Colo., 1969-71; asst. research computer sci. U. Calif., San Francisco, 1972-78; assoc. devel. engr. U. Calif., Berkeley, 1978-82; sr. systems engr. EEG Systems Lab., San Francisco, 1982-86; computer cons., expert systems design Pacific Bell, San Francisco, 1986-87; mgr. microcomputer security Pacific Bell, San Ramon, Calif., 1987-89; dir. Alliance for Innovation tech. devel. ctr., Scottsdale, Ariz., 1990-91; pres. Centauri Secure Computing, Scottsdale, 1990; computer security cons. Bedford Cons., San Francisco, 1991; owner, operator Mono Communications, Oakland, Calif., 1991—; also bd. dirs. Mono Communications, Lee Vining and Oakland, Calif. Contbr. articles to profl. jours. Served to 1st lt. U.S. Army, 1960-62. Summer Faculty fellow NASA-Am. Soc. Engring. Edn., Ames Research Ctr., 1981. Mem. IEEE, Civil Air Patrol. Jewish. *Personal philosophy: It's a learning experience.*

ZEITLIN, HARRY LEON, artist, rabbi, educator; b. Denver, Apr. 29, 1952; s. Cecil and Sandra (Rothenberg) Z.; m. Beth Leslie Ackerman, Aug. 20, 1984; children: Naomi, Avital, Yael, Aaron. BA, Yale U., 1974. Ordained rabbi, 1996. Novelist N.Y.C., Denver, Bloomingt, 1974-76; journalist, photographer Newfoundland, Can., 1976; artist L.A., Jerusalem, Seattle, 1976—; instr. Talmud and Jewish Thought, Congregation Beth Shalom, Seattle, 1996—; instr. photography Evergreen Sch., Seattle, 1996—. One-man exhibitions include Colo. Photographic Art Cen., Denver, 1979, Am. Cultural Ctr., Jerusalem, 1986, Bezalel Acad. Art, Jerusalem, 1986, Bertha Urdang Gallery, N.Y.C., 1988, 91, Henry Art Gallery, Seattle, 1991, Silver Image Gallery, Seattle, 1991, 93, C.G. Jung Inst. Chgo., 1994, Goldwasser & Wilkinson, San Francisco, 1996, Anigrafix, Jerusalem, 1996-97;; group shows include Susan Spiritus Gallery, Newport Beach, Ca., 1980, West Colo. Gallery, Pasadena, 1981, White Bird Gallery, Portland, 1993 and others. Founder Young Israel of Santa Monica, 1981, Congregation Zechut Avotainu, Seattle, 1993. Mem. Seattle Art Mus., Friends of Photography, Am. soc. Media Photographers. Jewish. Office: Art is the Spiritual 5508 35th Ave NE Seattle WA 98105-2312

ZEITLIN, MARILYN AUDREY, museum director; b. Newark, July 14, 1941; d. Sidney M. and Theresa Feigenblatt) Litchfield; widowed; children: Charles C. Sweedler, Milo Sweedler. Student, Vanderbilt U., 1963-65; AB in Humanities, Harvard U., 1966, MA in Teaching of English, 1967; postgrad., Cornell U., 1971-74. Dir. Ctr. Gallery, Bucknell U., Lewisburg, Pa., 1975-78; Freedman Gallery, Albright Coll., Reading, Pa., 1978-81, Anderson Gallery, Va. Commonwealth U., Richmond, 1981-87; curator, acting co-dir. Contemporary Arts Mus., Houston, 1987-90; exec. dir. Washington Projects for the Arts, 1990-92; dir. Univ. Art Mus., Ariz. State U., Tempe, 1992—; juror Dallas Mus. of Arts, McKnight Awards, Mpls.; grant evaluator IMS; grant evaluator, panelist NEH; lectr., cons. in field. Editor, contbr. essays to art publs. Bd. dirs. Cultural Alliance Washington; curator, commr. for U.S. for 1995 Venice Biennale. Samuel H. Kress fellow, 1972-73. Mem. Assn. Coll. and Univ. Mus. and Galleries (v.p. 1986-88), Am. Assn. Mus., Coll. Art Assn. (U.S. commr. Venice Biennale 1995). Office: Ariz State U Art Mus PO Box 872911 Tempe AZ 85287-2911

ZEITLIN, MAURICE, sociology educator, author; b. Detroit, Feb. 24, 1935; s. Albert J. and Rose (Goldberg) Z.; m. Marilyn Geller, Mar. 1, 1959; children: Michelle, Carla, Erica. BA cum laude, Wayne State U., 1957; MA, U. Calif., Berkeley, 1960, PhD, 1964. Instr. anthropology and sociology Princeton (N.J.) U., 1961-64, research assoc. Ctr. Internat. Studies, 1962-64; asst. prof. sociology U. Wis.-Madison, 1964-67, assoc. prof., 1967-70, prof., 1970-77, dir. Ctr. Social Orgn., 1974-76; prof. sociology UCLA, 1977—, also research assoc. Inst. Indsl. Relations; vis. prof. polit. sci. and sociology Hebrew U., Jerusalem, 1971-72. Author: (with R. Scheer) Cuba: An American Tragedy, 1963, 1964, Revolutionary Politics and the Cuban Working Class, 1967, 1970, The Civil Wars in Chile, 1984, (with R.E. Ratcliff) Landlords and Capitalists, 1988, The Large Corporation and Contemporary Classes, 1989; (with J. Stepan-Norris) Talking Union, 1996; Latin Am. editor Ramparts mag., 1967-73; editor-in-chief: Political Power and Social Theory, 1980-90; mem. editorial adv. bd. The Progressive mag., 1985-96; editor: (with J. Petras) Latin America: Reform or Revolution?, 1968, American Society, Inc., 1970, 1977, Father Camilo Torres: Revolutionary Writings, 1972, Classes, Class Conflict, and the State, 1980, How Mighty a Force?, 1983, Insurgent Workers: The Origins of Industrial Unionism, 1987. Chmn. Madison Citizens for a Vote on Vietnam, 1967-68; chmn. Am. Com. for Chile, 1973-75; mem. exec. bd. U.S. Com. for Justice to Latin Am. Polit. Prisoners, 1977-84; mem. exec. com. Calif. Campaign for Econ. Democracy, 1983-86. Ford Found. fellow, 1965-67, 70-71; Guggenheim fellow, 1981-82; NSF grantee, 1981, 82; recipient Project Censored award Top Censored Story, 1981; named to Ten Best Censored list, 1978. Mem. Am. Sociol. Assn. (governing council 1977-80, Disting. Contbn. Scholarship award in Pol. Sociology 1992, 96). Internat. Sociol. Assn. (editorial bd. 1977-81), Latin Am. Studies Assn., Orgn. Am. Historians. Democrat. Jewish. *Personal philosophy: "If I am not for myself who will be? and when I am for myself, what am I?" Hillel, the Elder.*

ZEKMAN, TERRI MARGARET, graphic designer; b. Chgo., Sept. 13, 1950; d. Theodore Nathan and Lois (Bernstein) Z.; m. Alan Daniels, Apr. 12, 1980; children: Jesse Logan, Dakota Caitlin. BFA, Washington U., St. Louis, 1971; postgrad, Art Inst. Chgo., 1974-75. Graphic designer (on retainer) greeting cards and related products Recycled Paper Products Co., Chgo., 1970—, Jillson Roberts, Inc., Calif.; apprenticed graphic designer Helmuth, Obata & Kassabaum, St. Louis, 1970-71; graphic designer Container Corp., Chgo., 1971; graphic designer, art dir., photographer Cuerden Advt. Design, Denver, 1971-74; art dir. D'Arcy, McManus & Masius Advt., Chgo., 1975-76; freelance graphic designer Chgo., 1976-77; art dir. Garfield Linn Advt., Chgo., 1977-78; graphic designer Keiser Design Group, Van Noy & Co., Los Angeles, 1978-79; owner and operator graphic design studio Los Angeles, 1979—. Recipient cert. of merit St. Louis Outdoor Poster Contest, 1970, Denver Art Dirs. Club, 1973.

ZELEZNY, WILLIAM FRANCIS, retired physical chemist; b. Rollins, Mont., Sept. 5, 1918; s. Joseph Matthew and Birdie Estelle (Loder) Z.; m. Virginia Lee Scarcliff, Sept. 14, 1949. BS in Chemistry, Mont. State Coll., 1940; MS in Metallurgy, Mont. Sch. Mines, 1941; PhD in Phys. Chemistry, State U. Iowa, 1951. Scientist NACA, Cleve., 1951-54; metallurgist div. indsl. research Wash. State Coll., Pullman, 1954-57; scientist atomic energy div. Phillips Petroleum Co., Idaho Falls, Id., 1957-66, Idaho Nuclear Corp., Idaho Falls, 1966-70; mem. staff Los Alamos (N.Mex.) Nat. Lab., 1970-80; instr. metallurgy State U. Iowa, Iowa City, 1948-49; asst. prof. metallurgy Wash. State Coll., 1956-57; instr. U. Idaho, Idaho Falls, 1960-68. Contbr. articles to profl. jours.; patentee in field. Served with AUS, 1944-46. Mem. Am. Chem. Soc. (sec. N.Mex. sect. 1978-79), Microbeam Analysis Soc., Am. Soc. Metals, The Minerals, Metals & Materials Soc., Sigma Xi, Alpha Chi Sigma. Democrat. Methodist. Home: PO Box 37 Rollins MT 59931-0037

ZELLER, KATHARINE MARGRET, physician; b. Portland, Oreg., May 21, 1957; d. Herbert Arnold and Margret Katharine (Zwald) Z.; m. David

Walker Hill, May 2, 1987. BA, Linfield Coll., 1979; MD, Oreg. Health Scis. U., 1985. Intern Case We. Reserve U., Cleve.; resident Oreg. Health Scis. U., Portland; gen. internist Northwest Internal Medicine now Primary Care Assocs., Portland, 1988—. Vol. Neighborhood Health Clinic, Portland, 1987—. Mem. AMA, Soc. Gen. Internal Medicine, Am. Med. Women's Assn., Oreg. Med. Assn., Multnomah County Med. Soc., Alpha Omega Alpha. Home: 4720 SW Dosch Park Ln Portland OR 97201-1284 Office: Primary Care Assocs 2222 NW Lovejoy St Ste 315 Portland OR 97210-5101

ZELON, LAURIE DEE, lawyer; b. Durham, N.C., Nov. 15, 1952; d. Irving and Doris Miriam (Baker) Z.; m. David L. George, Dec. 30, 1979; children: Jeremy, Daniel. BA in English with distinction, Cornell U., 1974; JD, Harvard U., 1977. Bar: Calif. 1977, U.S. Ct. Appeals (9th cir.) 1978, U.S. Supreme Ct. 1989. Assoc. Beardsley, Hufstedler & Kemble, L.A., 1977-81; assoc. Hufstedler, Miller, Carlson & Beardsley, L.A., 1981-82, ptnr., 1983-88; ptnr. Hufstedler, Miller, Kaus & Beardsley, L.A., 1988-90, Hufstedler, Kaus & Ettinger, L.A., 1990-91, Morrison & Foerster, L.A., 1991—; mem. Calif. Assembly, 1993—. Editor-in-chief: Harvard Civil Rights-Civil Liberties Law Rev., 1976-77; contbg. author: West's California Literary Forms: Civil Procedure Before Trial, 1996. Vol. atty. ACLU of So. Calif., L.A., 1977—; bd. dirs. N.Y. Civil Liberties Union, 1973-74. Mem. ABA (chmn. young lawyers divsn. pro bono project 1981-83, delivery and pro bono projects com. 1983-85, subgrant competition-subgrant monitoring project 1985-86, chair standing com. on lawyers pub. svc. responsibility 1987-90, chair law firm pro bono project 1989-91, standing com. legal aid and indigent defendants 1991—, chair 1993—), Calif. Bar Assn. (bd. dirs. appellate project 1995—, chair commn. on access to justice 1997), L.A. County Bar Assn. (trustee 1989-91, v.p. 1992-93, sr. v.p. 1993-94, pres.-elect 1994-95, pres. 1995-96, fed. cts. and practices com. 1984-93, vice chmn. 1987-88, chmn. 1988-89, chmn. judiciary com. 1991-92, chair real estate litigation subsect. 1991-92), Women Lawyers Assn. L.A., Calif. Women Lawyers Assn. Democrat. Office: Morrison & Foerster 555 W 5th St Ste 3500 Los Angeles CA 90013-1080

ZELUS, PAUL ROBERT, education researcher; b. Chgo., May 28, 1947; s. Robert J. and Olga C. (Antonacci) Z.; m. Kathryn E. Rehorst, Jan. 15, 1972; children: Jason P., Aaron M. BA, Loyola U., Chgo., 1969, MA, 1972; PhD, Northwestern U., 1975. Asst. prof. sociology SUNY, Geneseo, 1972-79; assoc. prof. sociology Capital U., Columbus, Ohio, 1979-83; asst. prof. sociology Idaho State U., Pocatello, 1983-88, dir. Ctr. for Bus. Rsch., 1988—; prin. cons. Zelus Assocs., Pocatello, 1995—. Co-author: I Just Went to Work: J.R. Simplot and His Business Career, 1995. Bd. dirs. Greater Pocetello C. of C., 1994-96, Idaho Rural Devel. Coun., Boise, 1995. Fellow Gerontol. Soc. Am.; mem. Rotary Internat. Lutheran. Office: Ctr for Bus Rsch 1651 Alvin Ricken Dr Pocatello ID 83201-2727

ZEMAN, VALERIE DENISE, home economics educator; b. Sacramento, Calif., Nov. 6, 1959; d. Richard Gerald and Nina Irene (Henman) Sheley; children: Paul Richard, Katherine Elizabeth Joy. BA in Home Econs., Calif. State U., Sacramento, 1990. Cert. tchr. Sec./bookkeeper George's Pest Control, Chico, Calif., 1976-78; dispatcher Suburban Airporter, Bellevue, Wash., 1978-80; systems analyst Energy Sci. Corp., Bellevue, Wash., 1980-84; customer svc. rep. Proctor and Gamble, Sacramento, Calif., 1984-91; tchr. Elk Grove (Calif.) Unified Sch. Dist., 1994—. Office: Samuel Jackman Middle Sch 7925 Kentwac Dr Sacramento CA 95823

ZEMEL, NORMAN PAUL, orthopedic surgeon; b. Bklyn., Oct. 15, 1939; s. Nathan M. and Mary (Sklarevsky) Z.; m. Mary P. Kane. BSN, Rutgers U., 1961; MD, Thomas Jefferson Med. Sch., 1965. Bd. cert. orthopaedic surgery with added qualification in hand surgery Am. Bd. Orthopaedic Surgery. Orthopaedic surgery resident Northwestern U., Chgo., 1969-73; hand surgery fellow Boyes Hand Fellowship, L.A., 1973-74; hand surgery physician Boyes, Stark, Ashworth, L.A., 1974-88, Kerlan-Jobe Orthopaedic Clinic, Inglewood, Calif., 1989—; clin. assoc. prof. dept. orthopaedics U. So. Calif. Sch. Medicine, L.A., 1977—. Contbr. chpts. to books and articles to profl. jours. Lt. USNR, 1966-68, Vietnam. Mem. ACS, Am. Acad. Orthopaedic Surgery (bd. councilors), Am. Soc. for Surgery of the Hand, Western Orthopaedic Assn. (pres. L.A. chpt. 1993-94), Soc. Internat. de Orthopedique et de Traumatologie. Office: Kerlan-Jobe Orthopaedic Clinic 501 E Hardy St Ste 300 Inglewood CA 90301-4026

ZEMP, KERRY LLOYD, oil company executive; b. Oxford, Eng., May 1, 1954; came to U.S., 1954; s. Lloyd J. and Betty (Marshall) Z.; m. Lois Erika Hamm, Apr. 5, 1986; children: Lauren Elizabeth, Eric Andrew. BSChemE, U. Okla., 1977; MBA, U. Denver, 1989. Registered profl. engr., Calif. Petroleum engr. Amoco, Liberal, Kans., 1977-80, Ogle Petroleum, Santa Barbara, Calif., 1980-83; sr. engr. Union Pacific Resources Co., Denver, 1983-89, Bechtel Petroleum, Bakersfield, Calif., 1990-91; v.p., COO Gotland Oil, Inc., Bakersfield, 1991—. Mem. Friends of the Gleaners, Bakersfield, 1994—; mem. organizing com. Cmty. Energy Night, Bakersfield, 1996. Mem. Soc. Profl. Engrs., Calif. Ind. Petroleum Assn. (bd. dirs. 1994—), Am. Petroleum Inst. (bd. dirs. 1996—), Calif. Gas Producers Coop. Assn. (bd. dirs. 1996—). Home: 504 Brightwood St Bakersfield CA 93312 Office: Gotland Oil Inc 1400 Eastern Dr #142 Bakersfield CA 93309

ZENEV, IRENE LOUISE, museum curator; b. Albuquerque, Nov. 18, 1948; d. Stanley D. and Louise Marie (Risler) Z.; 1 child, Carson M. Bell. BA, U. N.Mex., 1971. Dir. Umpqua Valley Arts Assn., Roseburg, Oreg., 1978-82; edn. coord. Douglas County Mus., Roseburg, 1985-86, curator history, 1986—; editor Dispatch newsletter Oreg. Mus. Assn., 1995—; publs. rschr. Oreg. Mus. Assn., Portland, 1989-92. Reviewer The Roseburg News-Review, 1989-93. Chmn. Douglas County Oreg. Trail Sesquicentennial Celebration Com., 1991-93; mem. Oreg. Coun. for Humanities, 1997—. Mem. Nat. Assn. for Mus. Exhbn. (Oreg. State rep. 1995—), Registrar's Com. Western Region (Oreg. state rep. 1995—).

ZENKER, CARYL H, marketing professional; b. N.Y.C., Jan. 29, 1961; d. Norman Seymour and Marjorie Helen (Bernstein) Z.; m. Michael Lewis McKenzie, July 22, 1989; 1 child, Noah Wyatt. BA, Evergreen State Coll., Olympia, Wash., 1984. Cert. fundraiser, Univ. Wash. Program coord. Wash. State Centennial Com., Olympia, 1984-89; mktg. cons. City of Tacoma, Wash., 1991-92; membership coord. Seattle Art Mus., 1992; mktg. and devel. dir. Tacoma Art Mus., 1993—. Mem. steering com. Zoobillee, Port Defiance Zoo and Aquarium, Tacoma, 1995-96. Mem. Rotary. Office: Tacoma Art Mus 1123 Pacific Ave Tacoma WA 98402-4303

ZEPEDA, SUSAN GHOZEIL, county official; b. N.Y.C., Aug. 8, 1946; d. Harry S. and Anne (Golden) Kantor; m. Isaac Ghozeil, Jan. 29, 1967 (div. Oct. 1979); children: Daniel Jacob, Adam Leo; m. Fernando Zepeda, Jan. 2, 1983; children: Paloma Andrea, Sofia Elisa. BA, Brown U., 1967; MA, U. Ariz., 1971, postgrad., 1971-75; PhD, Internat. Coll., 1985. Rsch. assoc. div. bus. and econ. rsch. U. Ariz., Tucson, 1971-73, rsch. assoc. Coll. Medicine, 1975-76; assoc. dir. Pima Alcoholism Consortium, Tucson, 1976-79, exec. dir., 1979-80; dep. dir. pub. health Orange County Health Care Agy., Santa Ana, Calif., 1980-89; dir. policy, planning Orange County Health Care Agy., Santa Ana, 1989-90; dir. pub. fin. Orange County, 1990-92; dir. San Luis Obispo County Health Agy., 1993—; cons. Tucson Sch. Dist. No. 1, 1973-75, U.S. Dept. Labor, Washington, 1976-79, Indian Health Svc., Rockville, Md., 1984-85; ptnr. Zepeda Assocs., Fullerton, Calif., 1987-93; presenter confs. Mem. Fullerton Planning Commn., 1984-91, chmn., 1990-91; mem. Calif. Task Force on Comparable Worth, 1984-85, Calif. Dist. Appeal Bd. No. 510, L.A., 1986—. Recipient Woman of Achievement award Orange County Bd. Suprs., 1988, Disting. Achievement awards Nat. Assn. Counties, 1985, 86, 87, 89. Mem. APHA, County Health Execs. Assn. Calif. (exec. com.), Ctrl. Coast Hosp. Coun. (chair 1996), County Alcohol Program Adminstrs. Assn. Calif. (v.p. 1983, pres. 1984-85), Rotary (San Luis Obispo de Tolosa). Home: 109 Cerro Romauldo San Luis Obispo CA 93405-1274 Office: San Luis Obispo County Health Agy 2191 Johnson Ave San Luis Obispo CA 93401-4534

ZERAH, AARON, minister, author; b. N.Y.C., Dec. 6, 1951; Joseph and Bronia (Fiszer) Krause; m. Madhuri Peterson, July 30, 1996. Cert. in massage therapy, Rocky Mountain Healing Arts Inst., 1976; BA in Interfaith Minstry, New Sem., N.Y.C., 1989, M in Divine Wisdom, 1993. Mgr. J & J Produce, Long Beach, N.Y., 1970-74; owner Down to Earth, Boulder, Colo., 1974-82; pvt. practice tchr. Boulder, 1983-86; CEO J & J Produce, Inc., Oceano, Calif., 1986-89, New Leaf Foods, Santa Cruz, Calif., 1989-92; dir. Interfaith Sem., Santa Cruz, 1994—; chair Interfaith Sem., Santa Cruz, 1995—; tchr. Inst. Transpersonal Psychology, Palo Alto, Calif. Author: From Heaven to Earth: Spiritual Living in a Market-Oriented World, 1996; columnist San Jose Mercury News; contbr. articles to periodicals and internet mags. Mem. adv. bd. Food for All, Redlands, Calif., 1987-95, United Religions Initiative, San Francisco, 1996—; chair Celebrating The Spirit: Towards A Global Ethic, 1993-95, Santa Cruz Faith in Action Project, 1996—. Mem. Assn. Interfaith Mins. Home and Office: 136 Swift St Santa Cruz CA 95060

ZERBE, RICHARD OLIS, JR., public affairs educator; b. Nitro, W.Va., Oct. 2, 1938; s. Richard Olis and Fanny Hammond (Carter) Z.; m. Evelyn A. Ashe Benoit, June 1966 (div. 1970); 1 child, Robert Riley; m. E. Diane Husband, June 24, 1971; 1 child, Richard Alexander. AB in Polit. Sci., U. Okla.; PhD in Econs., Duke U., 1969. Lectr. Marshall U., 1964-66; asst. prof. York U., 1966-69; rsch. fellow law and econs. U. Chgo., 1969-71; assoc. prof. econs. Roosevelt U., 1971-76; rsch. assoc. dept. econs. U. Chgo., 1972-76; prof. Grad. Sch. Pub. Affairs U. Wash., Seattle, 1981—, acting dir. program in mgmt. of tech., 1976-77, adj. prof. dept. econs., 1990, adj. prof. civil engring., 1980-92, adj. prof. Sch. Law, 1992—; Gether Inst. invitee; scholar in residence Am. Bar Found.; fellow law and econs. U. Chgo., 1969-71; bd. econ. advisors to econs. com. ABA, antitrust sect.; cons. FTC; scholar in residence Am. Bar Found., 1971-72, affiliated scholar, 1972-74; vis. assoc. prof. econs. Northwestern U., 1972-76; vis. rsch. scholar FTC, Washington, 1989; cons. Novell Corp., Jones, Day, McDonald Hogue andBayless, Mann and Simon, Abloni and Foster, City of Seattle Legal Dept., Perkins Coie, others. Sr. editor Jour. Rsch. in Law and Econs.; author: (with K. Croke) Urban Transportation and the Environment: The Cost-Effectiveness Approach, 1975; (with D. Dively) Benefit Cost Analysis in Theory and Practive, 1994; contbr. articles to profl. jours., chpt. to books; referee Jour. Polit Economy, Am. Econ. Rev., Jour. Law and Econs., Econ. Inquiry. Commr. Regional Taxicab Comm.; cubmaster pack 9 Boy Scouts Am. Olinfellow Yale Law Sch., 1990; sea grantee, 1977-78, Ford Found. grantee, 1969, Ont. Dept. Pub. Health rsch. grantee, 1968, Rand Rsch. grantee, 1994; recipient Rsch. award Nat. Bureau of Econ. Rsch., 1978. Mem. ABA (assoc.), Am. Law and Econs. Assn. (bd. dirs. 1990-94), Am. Econ. Assn., Law and Soc. Assn., Western Econs. Assn. (exec. com. 1994-99). Home: 939 21st Ave E Seattle WA 98112-3510 Office: U Wash Grad Sch Pub Affairs Box 353055 Seattle WA 98195

ZERETZKE, FREDERICK FRANK H., artist, educator; b. Milw., July 4, 1919; s. Herman and Hertha Hildegarde (Riebow) Z.; m. Marian Louise Elfers, Dec. 7, 1942; children: Frederick J., David L., Mary J., John E. Student, Milw. Art Inst., 1938-39, Layton Sch. of Art, Milw., 1940-41, Rockford (Ill.) Coll., 1947. Art tchr. Burpee Art Gallery, Rockford, Ill., 1946-48; mural artist People's Real Estate Agy., Rockford, 1958, Grace Luth. Ch., Loves Park, Ill., 1960, Sweden House, Rockford, 1972; artist oil meml. young girl First United Presbyn. Ch., Greeley, Colo., 1963; mural artist Linos, Rockford, 1974; art tchr. pvt. studio, Rockford, Ill., 1968-78; art. tchr. pvt. studio, Burlington, Wash., 1978—; artist and tchr. art in nat. def. Camp Callan, San Diego, 1942-43, Rock Valley Coll., Rockford, Ill., 1970-77, Skagit Valley Coll., Mt. Vernon, Wash., 1978-80; water color instr. Daniel Smith Art, Seattle, 1994, 95. Exhibited in Z Studio, Burlington, Vt., Departures Gallery, Anacortes, Wash., 1996; also group shows in art galleries, Wis., Calif., Wash., Ill., Elements Gallery, Bellingham, Wash., 1988-90, Fox Glove Art Gallery, Mt. Vernon, Wash., 1989—, Twisted Willow Gallery, Mt. Vernon, 1993—, Arts and Frame Gallerie, Canyon Lake, Calif., 1993, Arts Coun. Snohomish County, Everett, Wash., 1993; executed mural in Hadamar, Germany, 1945, Lino's Italian REstaurant, Rockford, Ill.; pvt. collections include Joseph Stroyan 1978-91, North Whidbey Inn, Oak Harbor, Wash., Kenney Fellers 1990-95 Timbers Restaurant, Sedro-Woolley, Wash., Pastor Karsten Baalson 1983-95. Sec. Loves Park (Ill.) Zoning Bd., 1949-56; mem. Skagit Human Rights Task Force to Protect Fundamental Human Rights Guaranteed in Constitution of U.S., 1996. With U.S. Army, 1941-45, ETO. Scholar Milw. Art Inst., 1939, Layton Sch. Art, 1940; awarded commission for design for Swedish Tour of Sveas Soner Chorus of Rockford, 1965; named Artist of Yr. Winnebago County, 1974. Mem. Tamaroa Water Color Soc. Rockford (hon. lifetime, founder, pres. 1964), Skagit Art Assn. (pres. 1987-88). Mem. Unitarian Ch. Home: 722 Peterson Rd Burlington WA 98233-2656

ZERNIAL, SUSAN CAROL, education educator; b. L.A., July 2, 1948; d. Gus Edward and Gladys Elizabeth (Hale) Z. BA, Calif. State U., Long Beach, 1973; MA, Calif. State U., 1975; EdD, U. San Francisco, 1992. Cert secondary and elementary tchr.; libr. credential. Libr. Clovis (Calif.) Unified Schs., 1975-78; media specialist Anaheim (Calif.) Union High Sch. Dist., 1975; libr. Benicia (Calif.) Unified Sch. Dist., 1978-80; tchr. Atascadero (Calif.) Unified Schs., 1985-93; adj. prof. Edn. Adams State Coll., Alamosa, Colo., 1993—; acquisitions editor Librs. Unltd./Tchrs. Ideas Press, Englewood, Colo. Recipient Scholarship, Calif. Assn. Sch. Librs., 1974. Mem. ASCD, Am. Rsch. Assn., Phi Delta Kappa. Home: 8547 E Arapahoe Rd # J-152 Englewood CO 80112-1430

ZERNOW, LOUIS, physicist; b. N.Y.C., Dec. 27, 1916; s. Meyer and Lena (Fradkin) Z.; m. Edith Hazel Weinstein, Nov. 2, 1940; children: Lenore R., Elaine, Melvin R., Richard H. BChemE, Cooper Union Inst. Tech., 1938; PhD in Physics, Johns Hopkins U., 1953. Chief detonation physics br. Ballistic Rsch. Lab., Aberdeen Proving Ground, Md., 1940-55; mgr. ordnance rsch. div. Aerojet Gen. Corp., Downey, Calif., 1955-63; pres. Shock Hydrodynamics Inc., Sherman Oaks, Calif., 1963-67, Shock Hydrodynamics div. Whittaker Corp., N. Hollywood, Calif., 1967-81, Zernow Tech. Svcs. Inc., San Dimas, Calif., 1981—. Contbr. over 200 tech. reports to Dept. Def. agys.; 6 patents in field. Recipient Meritorious Civilian Svc. award U.S. Army Ballistic Rsch. Lab., 1945. Mem. AIME, Am. Phys. Soc., Accoustical Soc. Am., Am. Soc. for Metals, Am. Def. Preparedness Assn. (exec. bd. ballistics div. 1973—, Outstanding Leadership award 1987), Internat. Ballistics Com. Home: 1103 E Mountain View Ave Glendora CA 91741-3165 Office: Zernow Tech Svcs Inc 425 W Bonita Ave San Dimas CA 91773-2541

ZERZAN, CHARLES JOSEPH, JR., gastroenterologist; b. Portland, Oreg., Dec. 1, 1921; s. Charles Joseph and Margaret Cecelia (Mahony) Z.; BA, Wilamette U., 1948; MD, Marquette U., 1951; m. Joan Margaret Kathan, Feb. 7, 1948; children: Charles Joseph, Michael, Kathryn, Paul, Joan, Margaret, Terrance, Phillip, Thomas, Rose, Kevin, Gregory. Commd. 2d. lt., U.S. Army, 1940, advanced through grades to capt., 1945, ret., 1946, re-enlisted, 1951, advanced through grades to lt. col., M.C., 1965; intern Madigan Gen. Hosp., Ft. Lewis, Wash., 1951-52; resident in internal medicine Letterman Gen. Hosp., San Francisco, 1953-56, Walter Reed Gen. Hosp., Washington, 1960-61; chief of medicine Rodriquez Army Hosp., 1957-60, U.S. Army Hosp., Fort Gordon, Calif., 1962-65; chief gastroenterology Fitzsimmons Gen. Hosp., Denver, 1965-66; chief profl. services U.S. Army Hosp., Ft. Carson, Colo., 1967-68; dir. continuing med. edn. U. Oreg., Portland, 1968-73; ptnr. Permanente Clinic, Portland, 1973—; assoc. clin. prof. medicine U. Oreg., 1973—; individual practice medicine, specializing in gastroenterology, Portland, 1968-92; staff Northwest Permanente, P.C., ret., 1996, dir., 1980-83. Mem. Portland Com. Fgn. Rels., 1986—, bd. dirs., 1994—. Decorated Legion of Merit, Army Commendation medal with oak leaf cluster; Meritorious Alumnus award Oreg. Health Scis. U., 1990. Diplomate Am. Bd. Internal Medicine. Fellow A.C.P.; mem. Am. Gastroenterol. Assn., Oreg. Med. Assn. (del. Clackamas County), Ret. Officers Assn. Republican. Roman Catholic. Home and Office: 6364 SE Mcnary Rd Portland OR 97267-5119

ZETTERMAN, POLLY DAVIS, secondary school educator; b. Amityville, N.Y., June 21, 1944; d. Thomas Wilson and Clara (Robinson) Davis; m. V. Robert Zetterman II, Aug. 4, 1971. BS in Edn., Shippensburg (Pa.) State Coll., 1965; MA in Speech, U. Denver, 1967. Cert. secondary tchr., Colo. Tchr. lang. arts and math. Adams County Sch. Dist. 50, Westminster, Colo., 1967-97, bd. dirs. Fed. Credit Union, 1985-95; Named Tchr. Who Makes a Difference, Sta. KCNC-TV, Denver, 1987. Mem. Nat. Coun. Tchrs. English, Nat. Coun. Tchrs. Math. Home: 7131 Pierce St Arvada CO 80003-3607 Office: Adams County Sch Dist 50 4476 W 68th Ave Westminster CO 80030-5856

ZGOURIDES, GEORGE DEAN, psychology educator; b. Houston, May 21, 1961; s. Ted John and Katherine Louise (Palios) Z. BA, Rice U., 1982, MusM, 1985; MA, Trinity U., San Antonio, 1986; Psychology D, Pacific U., Forest Grove, Oreg., 1989. Lic. clin. psychologist, Tex., Ariz. Resident in psychology Tualatin Valley Mental Health Ctr., Portland, Oreg., 1989-90; instr. Pacific U., 1989-90; asst. prof. U. Portland, 1990—; pastoral resident U. Portland, 1991—. Author: Don't Let Them Psych You Out!, 1993, Human Sexuality, 1996; co-author: Anxiety Disorders, 1991; contbr. articles to profl. jours.; composer 2 orch. poeces (premiers 1985, 89), also numerous classical and liturgical works, 1983—. pastoral resident U. Portland, 1991—; asst. pastor Portsmouth Trinity Luth. Ch., 1996—. Will Rice fellow Rice U., 1982; scholar Am. Hellenic Progressive Assn., 1987. Mem. Coun. Tchrs. Undergrad. Psychology, Am. Assn. Christian Counselors. Office: U Portland Dept Psychology 5000 N Willamette Blvd Portland OR 97203-5743

ZHANG, XIAO-FENG, power system engineer, researcher; b. Sichuan, Peoples Republic of China, Aug. 8, 1951; came to U.S., 1988; d. Yong-Qing and Lan (Li) Z.; m. Paul McEntire, June 22, 1996; 1 child, John. BS in EE, Taiyuan Engring. Inst., Shanxi, 1976; MS in EE, Electric Power Rsch. Inst., 1983. Power engr. Jinchong Dist. Power Bur., Shanxi, 1976-80; power system engr. EPRI, Beijing, 1983-88, Systems Control, Palo Alto, Calif., 1988-89; sr. power engr. Empros Systems Internat., Plymouth, Minn., 1989-93; cons. Pacific Gas & Elec. Co., San Ramon, Calif., 1993-94; sr. engr. ABB Systems Control, Santa Clara, Calif., 1995—. Contbr. articles to profl. jours. Recipient 1st prize EPRI of China, 1985, 2d prize Ministry of Electric Power, Beijing, 1986, 3d prize Chinese Nat. Com., 1987. Mem. Power Engring. Soc. IEEE (sr.), Computer Soc. IEEE. Home: 1523 Johnson Ave San Jose CA 95129-4714 Office: ABB Systems Control 2550 Walsh Ave Santa Clara CA 95051-1315

ZHANG, ZHEN, electrical engineer; b. Beijing, Dec. 6, 1945; came to U.S., 1982; s. Liyan and Jingxin (Zhu) Z.; m. Xiaolu Zhang, Oct. 1, 1977; 1 child Ruonan (Nancy). B in Math., Nankai U., Tianjin, China, 1969, M in Math., 1980; PhD in Applied Math., Cornell U., 1984; Habilitation in Math., Bielefeld (Germany) U., 1988. Lectr. Nankai U., Taiinjin, 1981-82; rsch. assoc. Cornell U., Ithaca, N.Y., 1984-85, Stanford U., Palo Alto, Calif., 1985, Bielefeld U., 1986-88; asst. prof. U. So. Calif., L.A., 1988-92, assoc. prof., 1992-96, prof., 1996—. Contbr. articles to profl. jours. Rsch. grantee NSF, 1989—. Mem. IEEE (sr. mem.). Home: 19329 Red Hawk Rd Walnut CA 91789-4229 Office: Univ So Calif EEB 508 Los Angeles CA 90089-2565

ZHAO, LI, fine arts company executive, teacher, consultant; b. Tianjin, China, Mar. 16, 1958; came to U.S., 1984; d. Robert Yunnian Chao and Qizhen Cao; m. Shiyi Zhang, Aug., 1984 (div. 1987); m. Kenneth Lloyd Schoolland, Aug. 8, 1988 (div. 1994); 1 child, Kenli Dulcinea. BA, Foreign Lang. Inst., Tianjin, China, 1983; MA, U. Minn., 1987; Mgmt. Sci. (Japanese), Japan-Am. Inst. Mgmt. Sci., Honolulu, 1988; MS in Japanes Bus. Study, Chaminade U., Honolulu, 1988. Steel mill worker Guang Xi, China, 1969-78; tchr. Liu-Zhou Steel Mill High Sch., Guang Xi, 1978; translator, researcher China Dept. Transp., Beijing, 1983-84; teaching asst. U. Minn., Mpls., 1985-87; intern trainee Tobu Dept. Store, Tokyo, Japan, 1988; pres. Schoolland Internat., 1988—; sales mgr. trainee Duty Free Shops, Honolulu, 1989-92; gen. mgr. Double-Eye Hawaii, Honolulu, 1989-92, 1989—; gen. mgr. Tianjin Victor Entertainment Co. Ltd., Tianjin, China, 1994—. Editor: (newsletters) Double-Eye News, 1989-92, Libertarian Party Hawaii News, 1991-93. Chmn. membership com. U.S.-China People's Friendship Assn., 1988-89; mem. legis. com. Small Bus. Hawaii; bd. dirs. Libertarian Party Hawaii, 1992. Recipient Model Citizen award Mpls. Police Dept., 1992; named Outstanding Grad. Student, U. Minn., 1992. Mem. Am. Mktg. Assn. (bd. dirs.), Am. Soc. Interior Designers, Sales and Mktg. Execs. of Honolulu, Honolulu Japanese C. of C. (chair com.), Honolulu Acad. Art, Japan-Am. Assn. Hawaii, Assn. Hawaii Artists (corr. sec.), Chinese C. of C. Honolulu.

ZHAO, TIEMIN, electrical engineer; b. Beijing, June 1, 1963; came to U.S., 1988; s. Yunfei Zhao and Jinqing Liu; m. Shuye Lily Huan, Jan. 19, 1988; children; Michael H., Thomas S. BS in Microelectronics, Peking U., Beijing, 1985, MS in Microelectronics, 1988; PhD in Elec. Engring., Stanford U., 1994. Instr. Stone Group Corp., Beijing, 1987-88; device engr. Cypress Semicondr., San Jose, Calif., 1991-92; vis. rschr. Matsu Shita Electric, Osaka, Japan, 1992; sr. engr. Xilinx, San Jose, 1994-96, Actel, Sunnyvale, Calif., 1997—. Inventor in field. Outstanding student scholar Peking U., 1981-84; rsch. fellow Cypress Semicondr., 1990-94. Mem. IEEE, AAAS.

ZHENG, QIANG, research scientist; b. Beijing, Jan. 27, 1961; s. Chang-Qiu and Wen-Ze (Li) Z.; m. Lui Yuen, Mar. 11, 1994. BS in Physics, Beijing U., 1983; MS in Physics, Academia Sinica, Beijing, 1986; PhD in Physics, Temple U., 1989. Postdoctoral fellow Stanford (Calif.) U., 1989-90; rsch. assoc. Boston U., 1990-92; sr. scientist Scios Nova Inc., Balt., 1992-94, Mountain View, Calif., 1994—. Office: Scios Nova Inc 820 W Maude Ave Sunnyvale CA 94086-2910

ZHOU, CHIPING, mathematician, educator; b. Shanghai, People's Republic of China, Jan. 21, 1957; s. Xingui Zhou and Qi Zhu; m. Xiaoyu He, June 22, 1986; children: Kevin K., Brandon K. BS, Fudan U., Shanghai, 1983, MS, 1986; PhD, U. Hawaii, 1990. Asst. prof. Fudan U., Shanghai, 1986; lectr. Chaminade U., Honolulu, 1990; asst. prof. U. Hawaii, Honolulu, 1990-. Author: Some Problems for Elliptic and Hyperbolic Equations, 1986, Maximum Principles and Liouville Theorems for Elliptic Partial Differential Equations, 1991; contbr. articles to profl. jours. Recipient rsch. fellowship Rsch. Corp. of U. Hawaii, 1989. Mem. Am. Math. Soc., Math. Assn. Am. Office: U Hawaii - HCC Math Dept 874 Dillingham Honolulu HI 96817

ZHU, JUN, mathematics educator; b. Suzhou, Jiangsu, People's Republic of China, June 13, 1957; arrived in Can, 1989; s. Chengyan and Ronghua (Jiang) Z.; m. Yunfang Xu, Jan. 1, 1985; 1 child, Chenchong. Student, Suzhou U., 1982. Tchr. Suzhou (Peoples Republic of China) U., 1982-89; researcher U. B.C., Vancouver, 1989—. Contbr. articles to profl. jours. Office: U BC Dept Math, 1984 Math Rd, Vancouver, BC Canada V6T 1Z2

ZICK, LESTER GEORGE, actor, systems consultant; b. Sumter, S.C., Jan. 6, 1944; s. William Henry and Frances (Fauntleroy) Z. BS, U.S. Naval Acad., 1966. Commd. ensign USN, 1966, assigned to Vietnam,, 1966-68; resigned, 1968; systems programmer Internat. Harvester, Broadview, Ill., 1968-73; systems cons. Atlantic Richfield, L.A., 1973-80; self-employed theoretical physicist, L.A., 1980-90, actor,, 1990—; systems cons. Data Products, Woodland Hills, Calif., 1985. Author: Theory of Predication, 1982, Metaphysics of Matter, 1987; appeared in movies Line of Fire: The Moris Dees Story, 1992, Never Forget, 1992. Mem. AFTRA.

ZIEGAUS, ALAN JAMES, public relations executive; b. Bremerton, Wash., May 8, 1948; s. Alan Moon and Dorothy (Lamont) Z.; m. Constance Jean Carver, 1972; children: Jennifer, Ashley. BJ, San Diego State U., 1970. Staff writer San Diego Tribune, 1972-77; exec. asst. San Diego City Council, 1977-78; v.p. Gable Agy., San Diego, 1978-80; pres. Stoorza, Ziegaus & Metzger, San Diego, 1980—. Mem. planning com. County San Diego, 1980-82; mem. sewage task force City of San Diego, 1986-88, civil svc. com., 1992—; trustee armed forces YMCA, San Diego, 1984—. Recipient Best Investigative Series award AP, 1975. Mem. San Diego Press Club (Best News Story award 1973). Home: 12351 Brassica St San Diego CA 92129-4127 Office: Stoorza Ziegaus & Metzger 225 Broadway 18th Flr San Diego CA 92101-5018*

ZIEHLER, TONY JOSEPH, insurance agent; b. Anderson, Ind., June 20, 1936; s. Joseph Anthony and Julie Ann (Kette) Z.; m. Alice Mae Pattison, Apr. 2, 1956 (div. 1972); children: Susan Z. Brown, Kathryn Z. Dwyer, Jane Z. Bee, Patricia Z. Koty, Michael; m. Barbara Buys Wood, Feb. 28, 1981; stepchildren: David Wayne Wood, Brent Douglas Wood. BSBA, U. Ariz., 1958. CLU. Prin. Ziehler Ins. Group, LLC, Tucson, 1958—. Employee edn. chmn. So. Ariz. Div. Am. Cancer Soc.; co-chmn. Medic-Alert Found., Pima County, Ariz.; chmn. Tucson Festival Soc.; mem. Salpointe High Sch. Found., others. Recipient William Wisdom award U. Ariz., Tucson, 1958. Mem. Greater Tucson Assn. Life Underwriters (pres. 1963-64, Agt. of Yr. 1975), Ariz. Assn. Life Underwriters (pres. 1970-71, Agt. of Yr. 1980), So. Ariz. CLU Soc. (pres. 1968-69), Salvation Army (pres. adv. bd. 1984-85),

Univ. of Ariz. Found. (mem. planned giving com.), Rotary, (com. chmn.), Tucson Conquistadores (pres. 1985-86), Los Charros del Desierto, Golden Key Soc., MIllion Dollar Round Table, others. Republican. Home: 6000 E Calle De Vita Tucson AZ 85750-1957 Office: 6420 E Broadway Blvd Ste B102 Tucson AZ 85710-3536

ZIELINSKI, MELISSA L., museum director. BS, Coll. William an Mary, 1978; MS, N.C. State U., 1983. Park svc. ranger, interpreter Cape Hatteras Nat. Seashore, Buxton, N.C., 1980, 81; exhibits intern N.C. Mus. Natural Scis., Raleigh, 1980-81, 81-82, asst. curator pub. programs, 1984-92; vol. svcs. coord. N.C. State U., 1981-82, 82-83, lab. instr. vertebrate zoology lab., 1983; naturalist Durant Nature Park Raleigh (N.C.) Parks and Recreation Dept., 1983-84; mus. educator Humboldt State U. Natural History Mus., Arcata, Calif., 1992-93, dir., 1993—. Co-author, editor, illustrator vertebrate zoology lab. text, 1983-84. Sch. edn. program dir. Friends of the Dunes The Nature Conservancy, Arcata, Calif., 1993-94, mem. Mem. Am. Mus. Natural History, Nat. Assn. Interpretation, Nat. Marine Educators Assn., Guild of Natural Sci. Illustrators, Nat. Audubon Soc. Home: 2699 Pleasant Ave Eureka CA 95503 Office: Humboldt State U Natural History Mus 1315 G St Arcata CA 95521

ZIELINSKI, PATRICIA ANNE, women's health nurse; b. Berwick, Pa., Aug. 2, 1954; d. John B. and Wilma A. (Weil) Z. BSN, Ea. Wash. State U., 1976; MN, U. Wash., 1985. Cert. high-risk perinatal RN, ANA. Staff RN obstetrics March AFB (Calif.) Regional Hosp., 1977-80, Stevens Meml. Hosp., Edmonds, Wash., 1980-86; clin. staff RN med.-surg. 50th Gen. Hosp. Reserves, Seattle, 1980-86; asst. head nurse labor and delivery Madigan Army Med. Ctr., Ft. Lewis, Wash., 1986-88; asst. head nurse post partum Madigan Army Med. Ctr., Ft. Lewis, 1988; asst. head nurse obstetrics Bassett Army Community Hosp., Ft. Wainwright, Alaska, 1988-90, 91; nursing supr. and emergency rm. staff Bassett Army Community Hosp., Ft. Wainwright, 1990-91; staff RN obstetrics Samaritan Hosp., Moses Lake, Wash., 1991—; mem. standards com. Madigan Army Med. Ctr., Ft. Lewis, 1986-87, quality assurance com., 1987-88; edn. com. U.S. Army, Ft. Wainwright, 1988-91. Tutor Literacy Coun., Fairbanks, Alaska, 1990-91. Capt. USAF, 1977-80, U.S. Army, 1986-91. Recipient Army Svc. ribbon , Seattle, 1982, Army Achievement medal, Seattle, 1984, Army Commendation medal, Ft. Wainwright, 1991, Overseas Svc. ribbon, Ft. Wainwright, 1991, Nat. Def. Svc. medal, Ft. Wainwright, 1991. Mem. United Staff Nurses Union UFCW, Assn. Women's Health, Obstetric and Neonatal Nurses, Intercollegiate Ctr. for Nursing Edn. Alumni Assn., U. Wash. Alumni Assn., Smithsonian Instn. Jewish.

ZIELKE, PATRICK MICHAEL, aerospace company executive; b. San Antonio, Dec. 4, 1945; s. Albert J. and Ruth Grace (Crissey) Z.; m. Patriaia Ann Krikorian, Dec. 30, 1966; 1 child, Christopher Patrick. BS in Physics, Wayne State U., 1967; MBA, U. Phoenix, 1991. Engr. Boeing Aircraft, Seattle, 1967-69; lead engr. Beech Aircraft, Wichita, 1969-73; project engr. Grumman Corp., Cleve., 1973-74; engring. mgr. Crescent Metal Products, Cleve., 1974-75; pres. Almont Insulation, Gunnison, Colo., 1975-82; program mgr. GE, Moffett Field, Calif., 1982-86; dir. tech. svcs. Thiokol Corp., Ogden, Utah, 1986—; cons. in pvt. practice, Willard, Utah, 1986-93. Fundraiser Make-A-Wish Found., Ogden, 1993; mem. allocation com. United Way, Ogden, 1993, Corinth, Miss., 1994; mem. Almont Vol. Fire Dept., 1975-82. Roman Catholic. Home: 906 E 3400 N Ogden UT 84414 Office: Thiokol Corp PO Box 707 Brigham City UT 84302

ZIEMANN, G. PATRICK, bishop; b. Pasadena, Calif., Sept. 13, 1941. Attended, St. John's Coll. and St. John's Sem., Camarillo, Calif., Mt. St. Mary's Coll., L.A. Ordained priest Roman Cath., 1967. Titular bishop, aux. bishop Diocese Santa Rosa, Obba, 1986-92; bishop Diocese Santa Rosa, Santa Rosa, Calif., 1992—. Office: Chancery Office PO Box 1297 547 B St Santa Rosa CA 95401*

ZIERATH, MARILYN JEAN, adult medical, surgical and pediatrics nurse; b. Centralia, Wash., Jan. 24, 1942; d. Lloyd and Lolita Jeneva (Francis) Reese; m. David William Zierath, Dec. 1963; children: Carolyn, Robert, Michael. Diploma in nursing, Tacoma Gen. Hosp., 1964; BSN, U. Puget Sound, 1965; MS in Nursing, Calif. State U., Fresno, 1975. RN, Wash.; cert. in enterostomal therapy; advanced nurse practitioner. Instr. nursing Calif. State U., Fresno, 1973-75; nursing supr. med.-surg. Good Samaritan Hosp., Puyallup, Wash., 1977; clin. instr. Pacific Luth. U., Tacoma, 1977-79; med.-surg. clin. specialist, enterostomal therapy nurse Tacoma Gen. Hosp., 1979-92, nurse oper. rm., 1992-95; enterostomal therapy nurse Quad-C, Tacoma Terrace, Wash., 1995, Wash. State Nurses Assn., Seattle, 1995-96; with Frank Tobey Jones Retirement Estates, Tacoma, 1996—. Contbr. articles to nursing jours. Mem. ANA (cert. med.-surg. clni. nurse specialist), Wound, Ostomy and Continence Nurses, Assn. Enterostomal Therapy Nurses, Wash. State Nurses Assn., Puget Sound Enterostomal Nurses, Clin. Nurse Specialists Puget Sound, Phi Kappa Phi, Alpha Phi. Office: Tacoma Terrace Health Care Ctr 3625 E B St Tacoma WA 98404-1524

ZIERNICKI, RICHARD MIECZYSLAW, engineering firm executive; b. Krakow, Poland, Feb. 3, 1950; came to U.S., 1981; m. Mila Kristine Czarnecka, Apr. 1, 1952; children: Maciek, Daniel. BS in Mech. Design, U. Mining and Metallurgy, Krakow, 1973, MS in Mech. Engring., 1975, PhD in Tech. Sci. cum laude, 1979. Registered profl. engr., Colo., Calif., Tex. and Wyo. Asst. prof. engring. Inst. Vibrations and Acoustics, Krakow, 1975-80; mgr. rsch. and devel. Inst. Tech., Krakow, 1980-81; mgr. mech. engring. Over-Lowe Co., Denver, 1981-84; sr. cons., pres., chmn., CEO Knott Lab., Denver, 1984—; presenter, lectr. in field at internat. tech. confs. in U.S., Europe, and South Am; spkr. Johns Hopkins U., Balt., Tech. Inst., Vienna, Austria, U. Denver. Contbr. articles to profl. jours.; patentee in field. NSF grantee. Mem. ASME, NSPE, Soc. Automotive Engrs., Soc. for Exptl. Stress Analysis, Robotic Internat. Soc. Mfg. Engrs., Profl. Engrs. Colo., Nat. Assn. Profl. Accident Reconstruction Specialists, Nat. Forensic Ctr., Nat. Acad. Forensic Engrs. Home: 5751 S Beech Ct Greenwood Village CO 80121 Office: Knott Lab Inc 2727 W 2nd Ave Denver CO 80219-1605

ZIEVE, SHERRIE LEE, writer, realtor; b. Sebring, Fla., Jan. 29, 1945; d. Joseph F. and Dorothy (Rudasill) Bradley; m. Richard Zieve (dec. Mar. 1989). Student, Fullerton Coll., 1975, Skadron Coll., 1978. Sales mgr. C.D.I., L.A., 1980-81; nat. acct. exec. Gen. Electric ICS, Compton, Calif., 1981-83; voice mail cons. Compath, North Hollywood, Calif., 1983-85; CEO Voice-Link Express, North Hollywood, Calif., 1985-88; acct. mgr. Fujitsu, L.A., 1988-93; realtor Prudential Hooten/Stahl, Albuquerque, 1996—; multi-state mktg. mgr. Pacific Tel., L.A. Author: The Scattering, 1996, Cloudwalker, 1996, Journey, 1994. Mem. S.W. Writers Workshop. Republican. Office: Prudential Hooten Stahl 11000-B Spain Rd NE Albuquerque NM 87111

ZIFERSTEIN, ISIDORE, psychoanalyst, educator, consultant; b. Klinkowitz, Bessarabia, Russia, Aug. 10, 1909; came to U.S., 1920; s. Samuel David and Anna (Russler) Z.; m. Barbara Shapiro, June 21, 1935; children: D. Gail, J. Dan. BA, Columbia U., 1931, MD, 1935; PhD, So. Calif. Psychoanalytic Inst, 1977. Intern Jewish Hosp. of Bklyn., N.Y., 1935-37; staff psychiatrist Mt. Pleasant (Iowa) State Hosp., 1937-41; chief resident psychiatrist Psychiat. Inst. of Grasslands Hosp. of Westchester County, Valhalla, N.Y., 1941-44; pvt. practice, psychoanalysis and psychiatry N.Y.C., 1944-47, L.A., 1947—; mem. faculty So. Calif. Psychoanalytic Inst., L.A., 1951-70, mem. bd. trustees, 1953-57, mem. edn. com., 1953-57; cons. L.A. (Calif.) Psychiat. Svcs., 1954-63; researcher The Psychiat. & Psychosomatic Rsch. Inst., Mt. Sinai Hosp., L.A., 1955-65; assoc. clin. prof. of psychiatry Univ. So. Calif., L.A., 1960-64, Univ. Calif., L.A., 1970-77; rsch. cons. Postgrad. Ctr. for Mental Health, N.Y.C., 1962-75; attending staff dept. psychiatry Cedars-Sinai Med. Ctr., L.A., 1975—; psychiat. cons. Iowa State Penitentiary, Ft. Madison; lectr. on transcultural psychiatry, group psychotherapy and group dynamics UCLA, U. Calif., Berkeley, USC, U. Wash., Willamette Coll., Eugene, Oreg., U. Oreg., U. B.C., U. Md., U. Wis., U. Judaism, U. Mex., Wayne State U., U. Pitts., Chgo. Med. Coll., Ctr. for Study of Democratic Instns., U. Leningrad, Bekhterev Psychoneurol. Rsch. Inst., Leningrad, BBC, San Francisco State Coll., others. Contbr. over 65 articles to Am. Jour. Psychiatry, Am. Jour. Orthopsychiatry, Internat. Jour. Group Psychotherapy, Praxis Der Kinderpsychologie Und Kinderpsychiatrie, and others. Bd. dirs. Viewer-Sponsored TV Found., L.A., 1960, Nat. Assn. for Better Broadcasting, L.A., 1962-75, ACLU So. Calif. chpt., L.A., 1962-77; pres. Peace Edn. Coun., Pasadena, Calif., 1960; del. to state conv. Calif. Dem. Coun., Sacramento, 1960; mem. del. to Soviet Union, Promoting Enduring Peace, New Haven, 1959; participant Conf. of Scientists for Peace, Oslo, Norway, 1962; del. to "Pacem in Terris" Convocation, SANE, N.Y.C., 1963, mem. nat. bd., 1970-74, and many others. Recipient Pulitzer scholarship award Pulitzer Found., N.Y.C., 1927, Green Prize for Outstanding scholarship Columbia Coll., N.Y.C., 1930, Peace award Women for Legis. Action, L.A., 1962, grant for rsch. in transcultural psychiatry Founds. Fund for Rsch. in Psychiatry, New Haven, 1963, grant for continuing rsch. in transcultural psychiatry NIMH, Bethesda, Md., 1969, Pawlowski Peace Prize, Pawlowski Peace Found., Inc., Wakefield, Mass., 1974. Fellow Am. Psychiat. Assn. (life, fellowship medal 1970), AAAS (life); mem. AMA (life), Am. Psychoanalytic Assn. (life, cert. in psychoanalysis by bd. profl. standards), Internat. Psychoanalytical Assn., World Fedn. for Mental Health, Westside Jewish Culture Club (lectr.), Physicians for Social Responsibility, Sierra Club, Nat. Wildlife Fedn., Environ. Def. Fund, Common Cause, MADD, Phi Beta Kappa. Democrat. Jewish. Office: 3150 E Tropicana Ave # C351 Las Vegas NV 89121-7315

ZIGMAN, PAUL EDMOND, environmental consultant, executive; b. L.A., Mar. 10, 1924; s. Fernand and Rose (Orlijan) Z.; m. children: Andrea, Eric. BS in Chemistry, UCLA, 1948. Supr., applied research U.S. Naval Radiol. Def. Lab., San Francisco, 1949-59, head tech. mgmt. office, 1961-69; supr., analytical chemistry Atomics Internat., Canoga Park, Calif., 1960-61; pres. Environ. Sci. Assocs., San Francisco, 1969-94, chmn., bd. dirs, 1969—. Contbr. articles to profl. jours. Served as pvt. U.S. Army, 1943. Recipient USN Meritorious Civilian Service award, 1968. Mem. Am. Chem. Soc., Nat. Assn. Environ. Profls. (v.p. 1977), Assn. Environ. Profls. (pres. 1974-76) (Outstanding Service award 1977, Cert. Appreciation 1984). Home: 2311 Crystal Downs Ct Oxnard CA 93030-7755

ZIL, JOHN STEPHEN, psychiatrist, physiologist; b. Chgo., Oct. 8, 1947; s. Stephen Vincent and Marillyn Charlotte (Jackson) Zilius; 1 child, Charlene-Elena. BS magna cum laude, U. Redlands, 1969; MD, U. Calif., San Diego, 1973; MPH, Yale U., 1977; JD with honors, Jefferson Coll., 1985. Intern, resident in psychiatry and neurology U. Ariz., 1973-75; fellow in psychiatry, advanced fellow in social and community psychiatry, Yale community cons. to Conn. State Dept. Corrections, Yale U., 1975-77, instr. psychiatry and physiology, 1976-77; instr. physiology U. Mass., 1976-77; acting unit chief Inpatient and Day Hosp. Conn. Mental Health Ctr., Yale-New Haven Hosp. Inc., 1975-76, unit chief, 1976-77; asst. prof. psychiatry U. Calif., San Francisco, 1977-82, assoc. prof. psychiatry and medicine, 1982-86, vice-chmn. dept. psychiatry, 1983-86; adj. prof. Calif. State U., 1985-87; assoc. prof. bioengring. U. Calif., Berkely and San Francisco, 1982-92, clin. faculty, Davis, 1991—; chief psychiatry and neurology VA Med. Ctr., Calif., 1977-86, prin. investigator Sleep Rsch. & Physiology Lab., 1980-86; dir. dept. psychiatry and neurology U. Calif.-San Francisco, Fresno-Cen. San Joaquin Valley Med. Edn. Program and Affiliated Hosps. and Clinics, 1983-86; chief psychiatrist State of Calif. Dept. Corrections cen. office, 1986—; chmn. State of Calif. Inter-Agy. Tech. Adv. com. on Mentally Ill Inmates & Parolees, 1986-92; mem. med. adv. com. Calif. State Personnel Bd., 1986-95; appointed councillor Calif. State Mental Health Plan, 1988-93; cons. Nat. Inst. Corrections, 1992-94; invited faculty contbr. and editor Am. Coll. Psychiatrist's Resident in Tng. Exam., 1981-86. Author: The Case of the Sleepwalking Rapist, 1992, Mentally Disordered Criminal Offenders, 5 vols., 1989, reprinted, 1991, Suicide Prevention Handbook, 3 edits.; contbg. author: The Measurement Mandate: On the Road to Performance Improvement in Health Care, 1993; assoc. editor Corrective and Social Psychiatry Jour., 1978—, referee, 1980—, reviewer, 1981—; contbr. articles in field to profl. jours. Nat. Merit scholar, 1965; recipient Nat. Recognition award Bank of Am., 1965, Julian Lee Roberts award U. Redlands, 1969, Kendall award Internat. Symposium in Biochemistry Research, 1970, Campus-Wide Profl. Achievement award U. Calif., 1992, Career Achievement award U. Redlands, 1994. Fellow Royal Soc. Health, Am. Assn. Social Psychiatry; mem. Am. Assn. Mental Health Profls. in Corrections (nat. pres. 1978—), Calif. Scholarship Fedn. (past pres.), AAUP, Am. Psychiat. Assn., Nat. Council on Crime and Delinquency, Am. Pub. Health Assn., Delta Alpha, Alpha Epsilon Delta. Office: PO Box 163359 Sacramento CA 95816-9359

ZILLY, THOMAS SAMUEL, federal judge; b. Detroit, Jan. 1, 1935; s. George Samuel and Bernice M. (McWhinney) Z.; divorced; children: John, Peter, Paul, Luke; m. Jane Greller Noland, Oct. 8, 1988; stepchildren: Allison Noland, Jennifer Noland. BA, U. Mich., 1956; LLD, Cornell U., 1962. Bar: Wash. 1962, U.S. Ct. Appeals (9th cir.) 1962, U.S. Supreme Ct. 1976. Ptnr. Lane, Powell, Moss & Miller, Seattle, 1962-88; judge U.S. Dist. Ct. (we. dist.) Wash., Seattle, 1988—; judge pro tem Seattle Mcpl. Ct., 1972-80. Contbr. articles to profl. jours. Mem. Cen. Area Sch. Council, Seattle, 1969-70; scoutmaster Thunderbird Dist. council Boy Scouts Am. Seattle, 1976-84; bd. dirs. East Madison YMCA. Served to lt. (j.g.) USN, 1956-59. Recipient Tuahku Dist. Service to Youth award Boy Scouts Am., 1983. Mem. ABA, Wash. State Bar Assn., Seattle-King County Bar Assn. (treas. 1979-80, trustee 1980-83, sec. 1983-84, 2d v.p. 1984-85, 1st v.p. 1985-86, pres. 1986-87). Office: US Dist Ct 410 US Courthouse 1010 5th Ave Seattle WA 98104-1130

ZIMA, GORDON EVERETT, metallurgist; b. Mason City, Iowa, June 20, 1920; s. Albert Gordon and Agnes Elisabeth (Nolan) Z.; m. Phyllis Anne Main, July 10, 1942; children: Marguerite, Antonia, Paula. AB, Stanford U., 1942; MS, Calif. Inst. Tech., 1952, PhD, 1956. Sr. rsch. engr. Jet Propulsion Lab., Pasadena, Calif., 1946-50; sect. head propulsion Naval Ordnance Test Sta., Pasadena, 1950-55; sr. rsch. metallurgist Internat. Nickel Co., Bayonne, N.J., 1956-58; sr. rsch. specialist GE Hanford Atomic Products, Richland, Wash., 1958-62, Boeing Nuclear Power Divsn., Seattle, 1962-63; sr. rsch. engr. Lawrence Radiation Lab., Livermore, Calif., 1963-70; sr. devel. engr. Battelle Pacific NW Lab., Richland, 1974-83. Patentee on classified materials; contbr. articles to tech. jours including Am. Soc. Metals, Powder Metallurgy, Metal Progress of Am. Soc. Metallurgists. Author: (young readers book) Sun Birds and Evergreens, 1996. 1st lt. U.S. Army Air Corps, 1942-46 PTO. Mem. Sigma Xi, Phi Lamda Upsilon. Home: 2265 Humboldt St Los Osos CA 93402-2326

ZIMAN, RONALD BERT, physician, researcher, consultant; b. Chgo., Oct. 20, 1948. MD, Washington U., St. Louis, 1973. Diplomate Am. Bd. Psychiatry & Neurology, Am. Bd. Internal Medicine. Rotating medicine intern Harbor Gen. Hosp., Torrance, Calif., 1973-74; medicine intern UCLA, Wadsworth, Va., 1974-75, neurology resident, 1975-78; pres. Northridge (Calif.) Neurol. Ctr., 1979—; med. dir. electrophysiology Northridge Hosp. Med. Ctr., 1983—; med. dir. care program Granada Hills. (Calif.) Community Hosp., 1986—, bd. dirs., 1989—, vice chair bd. dirs., 1994—; bd. dirs. L.A. chpt. Nat. Parkinson Found., Pacific region Multiple Sclerosis Assn. of Am.; assoc. clin. prof. neurology & dentistry UCLA, 1993—, clin. faculty exec. com., 1993—. Recipient Lange Med. Book award Lange Publs., 1973. Fellow ACP, Am. Acad. Neurology, Am. EEG Soc., Royal Soc. Medicine, Multiple Sclerosis Assn. Am. (chair healthcare regional bd. 1996—). Office: Northridge Neurol Ctr 18433 Roscoe Blvd Ste 210 Northridge CA 91325-4197

ZIMKAS, CHARLES PATRICK, JR., space foundation director; b. Scranton, Pa., Sept. 8, 1940; s. Charles Zimkas Sr. and Margaret (Bakunas) Sullick; m. Ursula Frediel Marten; children: Robert L., Uwe F., Michael P., Brian David. Enlisted USAF, advanced through grades to chief master sgt., 1958; dep. chief of staff, personnel adminstrv. div. Aerospace Def. Command, Colorado Springs, Colo., 1971-74; exec. to dep. chief of staff personnel Aerospace Def. Command, Colorado Springs, 1975-80; chief of adminstrn. Air Forces Iceland, Keflavik, 1974-75; first sr. enlisted advisor USAF Space Command, Colorado Springs, 1980-84; ret., 1984; dir. regional devel. Noncommissioned Officers Assn., San Antonio, 1984-86; dir. ops. U.S. Space Found., Colorado Springs, 1986—. Named Air Force Outstanding Airman of Yr., 1978; recipient Air Force Legion Merit. Mem. Noncommd. Officers Assn. (bd. dirs. 1978-84, chmn. bd. dirs. 1982-84, Order of Sword award 1978, Excalibur award 1979), Air Force Assn. (pres. Lance P. Sijan chpt., medal of merit 1990, 94, exceptional svc. award 1996). Home: 729 Drew Dr Colorado Springs CO 80911-2606 Office: US Space Found 2860 S Circle Dr Ste 2301 Colorado Springs CO 80906-4107

ZIMMER, DONALD WILLIAM, coach professional athletics, former professional baseball manager; b. Cin., Jan. 17, 1931; s. Harold Lesley and Lorraine Bertha (Ernst) Z.; m. Jean Carol Bauerle, Aug. 16, 1951; children: Thomas Jeffrey, Donna Jean. Student pub. schs., Cin. Baseball player Dodger Farm Clubs, 1949-54, Bklyn. Dodgers, 1954-57, Los Angeles Dodgers, 1958-59, Chgo. Cubs, 1960-61, N.Y. Mets, 1962, Cin. Reds, 1962, Los Angeles Dodgers, 1963, Washington Senators, 1963-65, Toei Flyers, Tokyo, 1966; mgr. Cin. Reds Farm Clubs, Knoxville and Buffalo, 1967, Indpls., 1968; mgr. San Diego Padre Farm Clubs, Key West, Fla., 1969, Padre Farm Club, Salt Lake City, 1970; coach Montreal Expos, Que., Can., 1971; mgr. San Diego Padres, 1972-73; coach Boston Red Sox, 1974-76, mgr., 1976-80; mgr. Tex. Rangers, 1981-82; coach N.Y. Yankees, 1983, 86, 96—, Chgo. Cubs, 1984, 85, 86, San Francisco Giants, 1987; mgr. Chgo. Cubs, 1988-91; coach Boston Red Sox, 1992, Colo. Rockies, Denver, 1993-95; mem. minor league All-Star Teams, Hornell, N.Y., 1950, Elmira, N.Y., 1951, Mobile, Ala., 1952, St. Paul, 1953; player World Series teams 1955, 56, 59, coach 1975, 96. Recipient Bill Stern award NBC, 1949; named St. Paul Rookie of Yr., 1953; mem. All Star Team, 1961, 78, 81, 90; named Nat. League Mgr. of Yr. 1989. Mem. Profl. Baseball Players Am. (life), Old Time Ball Players Wis. Office: care NY Yankees Yankees Stadium Bronx NY 10451

ZIMMERER, KATHY LOUISE, university art gallery director; b. Whittier, Calif., Dec. 9, 1951. BA cum laude, U. Calif., Berkeley, 1974; MA, Williams Coll., 1976. From tour guide to curatorial asst. Sterling and Francine Clark Inst., Williamstown, Mass., 1975-76; spl. asst. dept. modern art L.A. County Mus. Art, 1976-77; mus. edn. fellow Fine Arts Mus. San Francisco, 1977-78; dir. coll. art gallery SUNY, New Paltz, 1978-80; cons. in field, 1980-81; dir. univ. art gallery Calif. State U., Dominguez Hills, 1982—. Mem. Internat. Assn. Art Critics, Art Table. Office: Univ Art Gallery Calif State U 1000 E Victoria St Carson CA 90747-0001

ZIMMERMAN, HAROLD SAMUEL, retired state senator, newspaper editor and publisher, state administrator; b. Valley City, N.D., June 1, 1923; s. Samuel Alwin and Lulu (Wylie) Z.; m. Julianne Williams, Sept. 12, 1946; children—Karen, Steven, Judi Jean (dec.). B.A., U. Wash., 1947. News editor Sedro-Woolley (Wash.) Courier-Times, 1947-50; editor, pub. Advocate, Castle Rock, Wash., 1950-57; pub. Post-Record, Camas, Wash., 1957-80; assoc. pub., columnist, 1980; assoc. pub., columnist, dir. Eagle Publs., Camas, 1980-88. Mem. Wash. Ho. of Reps., 1967-80; mem. Wash. Senate, 1981-88, Wash. State Environ. Hearings Bd., Lacey, 1988-93. Served with USAAF, 1943-46. Mem. Grange, Sigma Delta Chi, Sigma Chi. Republican. United Methodist. Clubs: Lions, Kiwanis.

ZIMMERMAN, KATHERINE LOUISE, hypnotherapist; b. L.A., Sept. 4, 1946; d. Rollin Murray Dorsey and Mary Carol (Schricker) Stickler; m. Paul Williams, July 6, 1969 (div. May 30, 1985); children: Jennifer Williams, Ryan Williams. Student in Liberal Arts, Ventura Coll., 1966. Cert. hypnotherapist, Am. Coun. Hypnotist Examiners. Hypnotherapist Davis, Calif., 1989—; adminstrv. asst. UC Davis, 1981-96; spkr. Spkrs. Network, Davis, 1990—. Author: Self Hypnosis Training, 1994, Self Esteem/Stress Red, 1995, Hypnotherapy Scripts, Vol.1, 1995, Vol. 2, 1996, The Business of Hypnotherapy, 1996.

ZIMMERMAN, LYDIA, retired public health nurse; b. McMinnville, Oreg., Jan. 12, 1929; d. Frederick H. and Anna Katarina (Beisel) Koch; m. Howard C. Zimmerman, July 14, 1956; children: Sylvia, Angela, Joan, Garth. Diploma in nursing, Emanuel Hosp. Sch. Nursing, Portland, Oreg., 1949; BSN, U. Wash., 1953; cert. sch. nurse practitioner, UCLA, 1977. RN, Calif.; cert. pub. health nurse; cert. family life educator, sch. nurse. Asst. supr., head nurse surg. Emanuel Hosp., Portland, Oreg., 1949-50; coll. nurse Linfield Coll., McMinnville, Oreg., 1951-52; public health nurse I, sch. nurse, counselor high sch. Lane County Health Dept., Eugene, Oreg., 1953-57, staff nurse, asst. supr. maternal-child, mental health, 1958-63; public health nurse Lucas County Health Dept., Toledo, Ohio, 1967-69; private nurse Shafter, Calif., 1972-74; sch. nurse Rosedale Sch. Dist., Bakersfield, Calif., 1974-76, Beardsley Sch. Dist., Bakersfield, Calif., 1974-80, Panama-Buena Vista Union Sch. Dist., Bakersfield, Calif., 1974-96; ret., 1996; lctr. Bakersfield Coll., Calif. State Coll., Bakersfield. Mem. APHA, NEA, AAUW, Am. Acad. Nurse Practitioners, Calif. Tchrs. Assn., Nat. Assn. Sch. Nurses (Calif. rep. 1986-87, 87-88), Calif. Sch. Nurses Orgn., Kern County Sch. Nurses Orgn. (co-founder, pres. 1981-83, 91-92), Sex Info. and Edn. Coun. U.S., Nat. Coun. on Family Rels., Ctr. Sci. in Pub. Interest, Calif. Assn. Neurologically Handicapped Children, Assn. Children with Learning Disabilities, Learning Disabilities Assn. Am. (co-founder, pres. Kern County chpt. 1972-74, 76-78, 88-96, past pres., program chairperson 1997), Am. Hist. Soc. Germans from Russia, Sigma Theta Tau Internat. Congregationalist.

ZIMMERMAN, MICHAEL DAVID, state supreme court chief justice; b. Chgo., Oct. 21, 1943; s. Elizabeth Porter; m. Lynne Mariani (dec. 1994); children: Evangeline Albright, Alessandra Mariani, Morgan Elisabeth. BS, U. Utah, 1966, JD, 1969. Bar: Calif. 1971, Utah 1978. Law clk. to Chief Justice Warren Earl Burger U.S. Supreme Ct., Washington, 1969-70; assoc. O'Melveny & Myers, L.A., 1970-76; assoc. prof. law U. Utah, 1976-78, adj. prof. law, 1978-84, 89—; of counsel Kruse, Landa, Zimmerman & Maycock, Salt Lake City, 1978-80; spl. counsel Gov. of Utah, Salt Lake City, 1978-80; ptnr. Watkiss & Campbell, Salt Lake City, 1980-84; assoc. justice Supreme Ct. Utah, Salt Lake City, 1984-93, chief justice, 1994—; co-moderator Justice Soc. Program of Snowbird Inst. for Arts and Humanities, 1991, 92; moderator, Tanner lecture panel dept. philosophy U. Utah, 1994—; faculty Judging Sci. Program Duke U., 1992; bd. dirs. Conf. of Chief Justices, 1995—. Note editor: Utah Law Rev., 1968-69; contbr. numerous articles to legal publs. Mem. Project 2000, Coalition for Utah's Future, 1985-96; trustee Hubert and Eliza B. Phibard Found., Rowland-Hall St. Mark's Sch. Named Utah State Bar Appellate Ct. Judge of Yr., 1988; recipient Excellence in Ethics award, Ctr. for Study of Ethics, 1994; participant Justice and Soc. Program of Aspen Inst. for Humanistic Studies, 1988, co-moderator, 1989; Awareness Day Found. fellow. Fellow Am. Bar Found.; mem. ABA (faculty mem. judges' seminar 1993), Am. Law Inst., Utah Bar Assn., Salt Lake County Bar Assn., Jud. Conf. U.S. (adv. com. civil rules 1985-91), Utah Jud. Coun. (supreme ct. rep. 1986-91), chair 1994—, Utah Constnl. Revisions Commn., Snowbird Inst. for Arts and Humanities (bd. dirs., 1989—), Am. Inns of Ct. VII, Am. Judicature Soc. (bd. dirs. 1995—), Order of Coif, Phi Kappa Phi. Office: Utah Supreme Ct 332 State Capitol Building Salt Lake City UT 84114-1202*

ZIMMERMAN, RICHARD ORIN, safety engineer; b. Newberg, Oreg., Mar. 2, 1956; s. Orin Frank and Eva Josephine (Schumann) Z.; m. Susan Scharn, Aug. 27, 1977; children: Andrea J., Chad O. BS, Oreg. State U., 1977, MS, 1978; EdD, Wash. State U., 1988. Cert. safety profl., accident investigator. Grad. teaching asst. Oreg. State U., Corvallis, 1977-78; safety coord. Iowa Beef Processors, Inc., Pasco, Wash., 1978-80; fire and safety engr. Westinghouse Hanford Co., Richland, Wash., 1980-88; mgr. emergency preparedness Westinghouse Savannah River Co., Aiken, S.C., 1989-91; mgr. indsl. hygiene Westinghouse Hanford Co., Richland, Wash., 1991-94, sr. prin. scientist, 1995-96; safety mgr. Babcock & Wilcox Hanford Co., Richland, 1996—; adj. prof. Ctrl. Wash. U.; mem. steering com. trade emergency preparedness spl. interest group U.S. Dept. Energy, Washington, 1988-91; speaker nat. confs., 1981—. Instr. ARC, Kennewick, Wash., 1978-85, Am. Heart Assn., Richland, 1978-85; mem. Tri-City Tech. Coun., Richland, 1983-85. Recipient outstanding svc. award Oreg. Vocat. Indsl. Clubs Am., 1977, outstanding vol. award ARC, 1983. Mem. Am. Soc. Safety Engrs. (prof., sect. chmn. 1983-85, chpt. pres. 1989, regional oper. com. 1989-91). Republican. Roman Catholic. Home: 220 Orchard Way Richland WA 99352-9659 Office: Babcock & Wilcox Hanford PO Box 1200 N2-57 Richland WA 99352-1200

ZIMMERMAN, STEPHEN, marketing executive. Pres., CEO Paria Group, Orem, Utah. Office: Paria Group Central Park East 1815 South State St Ste 4000 Orem UT 84097*

ZIMMERMAN, WILLIAM IRVING, lawyer; b. Miami Beach, Fla., Dec. 10, 1952; s. S. Robert Zimmerman and Shirley (Munroe) Neivert; m. Felicia Jo French, children: William, Jason, Cyrina, Hunter. BA, Wesleyan U., 1974; JD, U. Miami, 1978. Bar: Fla. 1978, Hawaii 1991. Lawyer William I. Zimmerman Atty. at Law, Pompano Beach, Fla., 1978-90, Captain Cook,

Hawaii, 1991-93; lawyer Van Pernis, Smith & Vancil, Kailua-Kona, Hawaii, 1993—; dir. Families in Transition, Kailua-Kona, Hawaii, 1994-95. Pro bono counsel Protect Kohanaiki Ohana, 1991-92; officer, dir. Green Alert, Kailua-Kona, 1992-93; pro bono atty. Hui Hee Nalu o Kona, 1992-94. Named in Am. Leading Lawyers, 1993-94; recipient Cert. Outstanding Excellence, Families in Transition, 1994-95. Mem. Lymans Surf Classic (atty. 1992-94), Ocean Awareness and Preservation. Home and Office: PO Box 266 Captain Cook HI 96704-0266

ZIMMERMANN, GERHARDT, conductor; b. Van Wert, Ohio, June 22, 1945; s. Ervin and Ethel Jane (Allen) Z.; m. Sharon Marie Reher, Mar. 17, 1974; children: Anna Marie, Peter Karl Irum. MusB, Bowling Green State U.; MFA, U. Iowa; student, with James Dixon, Leopold Sipe, Flora Contino, Richard Lert. Tchr. in Genoa (Ohio) Pub. Schs., 1967-70; condr. orch. Augustana Coll., Rock Island, Ill., 1971-72; music dir. Clinton (Iowa) Symphony Orch., 1971-72; asst. prof. music, condr. orchs. Western Ill. U., Macomb, 1972-74; asst. condr. St. Louis Symphony Orch., 1974-78, assoc. condr., 1978-82; music dir., condr. St. Louis Youth Orch., 1975-82, Canton Symphony Orch., 1980—, N.C. Symphony Orch., Raleigh, 1982—; guest condr. Recipient 2d Prize Georg Solti Conducting Competition 1973. Mem. Am. Symphony Orch. League, Nat. Acad. Rec. Arts and Scis., Phi Mu Alpha Sinfonia. Office: NC Symphony Orch Meml Auditorium PO Box 28026 Raleigh NC 27611-8026*

ZIMMERMANN, JOHN PAUL, plastic surgeon; b. Milw., Mar. 9, 1945; s. Paul August and Edith Josephine (Tutsch) Z.; m. Bianca Maria Schaldach, June 13, 1970; cbildren: Veronica, Jean-Paul. BS in Biology, Chemistry, Marquette U., 1966; MD, Med. Coll. Wis., 1970. Diplomate Am Bd. Plastic Surgery. Internship surgery Stanford U. Sch. of Medicine, Calif., 1970-71, residency in gen. surgery, plastic & reconstructive surgery, 1974-79; flight surgeon USAF, 1971-73; fellowship head & neck surgery Roswell Park Meml. Cancer Inst., Buffalo, N.Y., 1977; pvt. practice Napa, Calif., 1979—; dir. Aesthetic Surgery Ctr. of Napa Valley, Calif., 1993—; clinical asst. prof. of plastic surgery Stanford U. Sch. of Medicine, Calif., 1993—; bd. dirs. Interplast, Palo Alto, Calif. (pres., bd. dirs. 1991-94, chmn. bd. dirs. 1994-95). Mem. Am. Soc. Plastic & Reconstructive Surgeons, Am. Soc. Aesthetic Plastic Surgeons, Lipoplasty Soc., Calif. Soc. Plastic Surgeons (bd. dirs.), Calif. Med. Assn., Napa County Med. Assn. Republican. Roman Catholic. Office: 3344 Villa Ln Ste 10 Napa CA 94558

ZIMMERMANN, LAURA KRISTINE, psychology educator; b. Charlotte, N.C., Dec. 12, 1968; d. G. Floyd and Janet (Snow) Z. BA cum laude in Psychology, Emory U., 1990, BA in Religion, 1990; MS in Developmental Psychology, U. N.Mex., 1993. Teaching assoc., asst. U. N.Mex., Albuquerque, 1991—; rsch. coord., clin. asst. Wesley Woods Geriatric Hosp., Atlanta, 1990-91; rsch. asst. Emory U., Atlanta, 1990-91, student computing instr., 1991, computer lab. cons., 1991. Mem. Soc. for Rsch. in Child Devel. Republican. Methodist. Office: U NMex Psychology Dept Logan Hall Albuquerque NM 87131

ZIMRING, STUART DAVID, lawyer; b. L.A., Dec. 12, 1946; s. Martin and Sylvia (Robinson) Z.; m. Eve Axelrad, Aug. 24, 1969 (div. 1981); m. Carol Grenert, May 24, 1981; children: Wendy Lynn Grenert, Joseph Noah, Matthew Kevin Grenert, Dov Shimon. BA in U.S. History, UCLA, 1968, JD, 1971. Bar: Calif. 1972, U.S. Dist. Ct. (cen. dist.) Calif. 1972, U.S. Dist. Ct. (no. dist.) Calif. 1984; U.S. Supreme Ct., 1994; cert. specialist in estate planning, probate and trust law. Assoc. Law Offices Leonard Smith, Beverly Hills, Calif., 1971-73; ptnr. Law Offices Smith & Zimring, Beverly Hills, Calif., 1973-76; assoc. Levin & Ballin, North Hollywood, Calif., 1976-77; prin. Levin, Ballin, Plotkin, Zimring & Goffin, A.P.C., North Hollywood, 1978-91, Law Offices Stuart D. Zimring, North Hollywood, 1991—; lectr. Los Angeles Valley Coll., Van Nuys, Calif., 1974-82. Author: Inter Vivos Trust Trustees Operating Manual, 1994, Lending to Inter Vivos Trusts—A Guide for Bankers and Their Counsel, 1995, Durable Powers of Attorney for Health Care—A Practical Approach to an Intimate Document, 1995, Reverse Mortgages—An Update, 1996. Bd. dirs. Bet Tzedek, Jewish Legal Svcs., L.A., 1975-88, chmn. legal svcs. com., 1978-82; bd. dirs. Brandeis-Bardin Inst., Simi Valley, Calif., 1976-80; bd. dirs. Bur. Jewish Edn., L.A., 1973-88, chmn. com. on parent and family edn., 1985-87; trustee Adat Ari El Synagogue, L.A., 1982—; bd. dirs. Orgn. for the Needs of the Elderly, 1994, 1st v.p. 1995-97, pres., 1997—. Recipient Circle award Juvenile Justice Connection Project, L.A., 1989, Wiley W. Manuel award for pro bono legal svcs., 1994, 95, 96. Mem. State Bar Calif., San Fernando Valley Bar Assn. (trustee 1979-86), Nat. Acad. Elder Law Attys. (pres. So. Calif. chpt., chair nat. tech. com.). Democrat. Office: 12650 Riverside Dr North Hollywood CA 91607

ZINK, MELISSA ELLIS, artist; b. Kansas City, Mo., June 9, 1932; d. Everett Elgin and Margaret Iola (Logan) Ellis; m. William Morgan Howell, Dec. 20, 1952 (div. 1973); 1 child, Mallery Logan Howell Downs; m. Nelson John Zink, June 23, 1975. Student, Swarthmore Coll., 1950-53, U. Chgo., 1953, Kansas City (Mo.) Art Inst., 1959-60. One-person shows include Bellas Artes, N.Y.C., 1992, U. Colo., Boulder, 1993, The Parks Gallery, Taos, N.Mex., 1994, Roswell Mus., 1996; works appeared in groups shows including Munson Gallery, Santa Fe, 1993, J. Cacciola Galleries, N.Y.C., 1993, Santa Fe Mus., 1993; represented in permanent collections Santa Fe (N.Mex.) Mus., Albuquerque (N.Mex.) Mus., The Harwood Found., Taos, The Old Jail Found., Albany, Tex., Roswell Mus. Mem. Nat. Sculpture Soc.

ZINK, STEVEN DOUGLAS, academic administrator, dean; b. Salem, Ind., Aug. 30, 1954; s. Victor I. and Anita P. (Clark) Z.; m. Lois C. Bowers, May 17, 1975; children: Joel, Ryan. BS, Ind. State U., 1974; MA, U. Wis., Madison, 1975; MLS, La. State U., 1979; PhD, Nova Southeastern U., 1991. Documents libr. The Coll. of Wooster (Ohio), 1979-80; head govt. publs. U. Nev., Reno, 1980-85, dir. pub. svcs., 1985-93, dean, 1993—, assoc. v.p. info. resources and tech., 1995—; sr. ptnr., editl. info. svcs. Depository Libr. Coun. U.S. Pub. Printer, Washington, 1982-85. Author (book) United States Government Publications Catalogs, 1981, 1988, Guide to the Presidential Advisory Commissions, 1987; co-editor (book) Government Documents and Microforms, 1984; editor in chief Jour. Govt. Info., 1984—; contbr. articles to profl. jours. Mem. ALA, Am. Soc. Info. Sci., Assn. Computing Machinery, Assn. for Bibliography of History, Soc. for Fed. History. Home: 160 Gooseberry Dr Reno NV 89523-9610 Office: U Nev MS 322 Reno NV 89557

ZINK, STEVEN MARTIN, software engineer; b. Bronx, N.Y., May 30, 1946; s. Robert and Florence Blanche (Katz) Z. BS in Math. and Humanities, MIT, 1968. Instr. math. and physics Maine Maritime Acad., Castine, 1968-69; math. tchr. Sharon (Mass.) Jr. High Sch., 1969-70; systems analyst John Hancock Ins., Boston, 1970-73; software devel. engr. Control Data, Sunnyvale, Calif., 1973-75, Hewlett Packard, Cupertino, Calif., 1975-90; sr. software devel. engr. Tandem Computers, Cupertino, 1990-92, mgr. quality initiatives, 1992-93; software engring. cons. Silicon Graphics, Mountain View, Calif., 1994—; software cons. Systems Ptnrs., Orinda, Calif, 1994; librettist (with composer Randol Bass) In Praise of Music, 1994; coun. mem. comm. South Bay Eckankar, Cupertino, 1990-93. Author: (poetry) At Days End, 1994. Facilitator, vol. ARIS Project, Campbell, Calif., 1987-92; team capt. Walk for AIDS, Cupertino, 1992; pres., treas. Eastridge Townhouse Homeowners Assn., San Jose, Calif., 1979-80. Mem. Coun. for Continuous Improvement, Barbary Coast Boating Club, Alumni Assn. MIT, Alumni Assn. Bronx High Sch., Calif. Satsang Soc. Inc. (communications dir. 1992-93). Mem. Green Party. Mem. Eckankar Ch. Home: 24 Trillium Ln San Carlos CA 94070-1525

ZINKE, SALLY GRIFFITHS, geophysicist, consultant; b. St. Louis, Aug. 30, 1951; d. John William II and Ada Dorothy (Agnew) Griffiths; m. Val Philip Zinke, June 23, 1984; 1 child, Allyson Marie. BS in Geology and Geophysics, U. Wis., 1973; MS in Geophysics, Pa. State U., 1979; MBA, U. Denver, 1987. Registered profl. geologist, Wyo. Sr. exploration geologist Mobil Oil Corp., Denver, 1973-80, sr. prodn. geologist, 1980-81; regional geophysicist Pan Can. Petroleum Co., Denver, 1981-89; rsch. assoc. Bureau Econ. Geology U. Tex., Austin, 1989-90; sr. dist. geophysicist Pacific Enterprises Oil Co., Denver, 1990-91; ind. geophys. cons. Denver, 1991—. Bd. dirs. Parent's Day Out, Denver, 1994—. Mem. Am. Assn. Petroleum Geologists (del. 1980—), Denver Geophys. Soc. (treas. 1987, v.p. 1988, pres. 1989), Denver Internat. Petroleum Assn., Rocky Mountain Assn. Geologists, Soc. Exploration Geophysicists (gen. chmn. ann. meeting 1996, sec., treas. 1992-93, fin. com. 1992-94, chmn. policy and procedures com. 1994-96, chmn. profl. affairs com. 1990-92, coun. 1988-91, constitution and bylaws com. 1989-92). Home and Office: 3060 Oak St Denver CO 80215-7176

ZINMAN, DAVID, coductor; b. Bklyn., 1936. Grad., Oberlin Conservatory; LHD (hon.), U. Minn.; postgrad., Boston Symphony's Tanglewood Music Ctr. Music dir., condr. Balt. Symphony Orch.; guest condr. London Symphony Orch., 1963, Phila. Orch., 1967, Hollywood Bowl, Mostly Mozart, Ravinia, Tanglewood music festivals, Berlin Philharm., Royal Philharm., others; artistic dir. Minn. Orch. Viennese Sommerfest, 1994-96; music dir., chief condr. Aurich Tonhalle Orch., 1995; music dir. Rochester Philharm., Rotterdam Philharm., Netherlands Chamber Orch., Aspen Music Festival, 1997, Aspen Music Sch., 1997. Recordings include (with Balt. Symphony) The New York Album, 1994, (2 Grammy awards), (with London Sinfonietta) Henryk górecki's Symphony No. 3, (with Christian Zacharias) Mozart Piano Concdertos, (with Berlin Radio Symphony) The Jungle Book (Gramophone award 1994), Metropolis Symphony, others; programmar, condr. numerous radio stas. including Pub. Radio Internat. Recipient 3 Grammy awards, 1990, 2 Grand Prix Disque awards, 2 Edison prizes, Deutsche Schallplatten Preis award. Office: Aspen Chamber Symphony 2 Music Sch Rd Aspen CO 81611*

ZINSER, ELISABETH ANN, academic administrator; b. Meadville, Pa., Feb. 20, 1940; d. Merle and Fae Zinser. BS, Stanford U., 1964; MS, U. Calif., San Francisco, 1966, MIT, 1982; PhD, U. Calif., Berkeley, 1972. Nurse VA Hosp., Palo Alto, Calif., 1964-65, San Francisco, 1969-70; instr. Sch. Nursing U. Calif., San Francisco, 1966-69; pre-doctoral fellow Nat. Inst. Health, Edn. and Welfare, 1971-72; adminstr. Sch. Medicine U. Wash., Seattle, 1972-75, Coun. Higher Edn., State of Ky., 1975-77; prof., dean. Coll. Nursing U. N.D., Grand Forks, 1977-83; vice chancellor acad. affairs U. N.C., Greensboro, 1983-89; pres. Gallaudet U., Washington, 1988, U. Idaho, Moscow, 1989-95; chancellor U. Ky., Lexington, 1995—; bd. dirs. Am. Coun. Edn., Washington; cons. Boeing Aircraft Co., Seattle; chmn. commn. on outreach and tech. transfer; bd. dirs. Nat. Assn. State Univs. and Land Grant Colls. Primary author: (with others) Contemporary Issues in Higher Education, 1985, Higher Education Research, 1988. Bd. dirs. Humana Hosp., Greensboro, 1986-88; v.p., bd. dirs. Ea. Music Festival, Greensboro, 1987-89; trustee N.C. Coun. Econ. Edn., 1985-89, Greensboro Day Sch., 1987-89. Leadership fellow Bush Found., 1981-82. Mem. Am. Assn. Higher Edn., Assn. Am. Colls. (Coun. Liberal Learning), Am. Assn. Univ. Adminstrs., AAUP, AAUW, Pi Lambda Theta, Sigma Theta Tau. Office: U Ky 111 Adminstrn Bldg Lexington KY 40506-0032*

ZIPF, TERI M., poet, medical librarian, researcher; b. Mpls., Dec. 15, 1954. BA in English, Walla Walla Coll., 1993. Paralegal Evergreen Legal Svcs., Seattle, 1980-85; tchg. asst. Walla Walla (Wash.) Sch. Dist. 140, 1985-908; instr. Walla Walla Coll., College Place, Wash., 1993-96, Walla Walla C.C., 1993-96; rschr. Coffey Comm., Walla Walla, 1996—. Organizer Walla Walla Poetry Party, 1991—. scholar Fishtrap Writer's Conf., 1991; fellow Fishtrap Writer's Conf., 1992; Lit. fellow Wash. Artist Trust, 1993. Home: 115 Natches St Walla Walla WA 99362 Office: Coffey Comm 1505 Business One Cir Walla Walla WA 99362

ZITO, MICHAEL ANTHONY, advertising and graphic design typesetting company owner; b. San Diego, Feb. 25, 1957; s. Richard and Margaret Jane (Greggs) Z. Student, El Paso C.C., 1976-77, Grossmont Coll., 1977-78. Emergency med. technician E&E Ambulance Svc., Colorado Springs, Colo., 1972-73; psychiat. technician Alvarado Hosp., San Diego, 1975-78; surg. technician, orderly Eisenhower Osteopathic Hosp., Colorado Springs, 1973-75; mktg. mgr. Calif. Dept. Forestry Fire Fighters, San Diego, 1978-79; mktg. rep. Mort Fin. Svcs., San Diego, 1980-81, Mil.-Civil Svc. Yellow Pages, San Diego, 1983-84; nuclear technician San Onofre (Calif.) Nuclear Power Plant, 1982-83; mktg. rep. Stas. XPRS, XHRM, KMLO, 1982-84; pres. Discount Yellow Pages, San Diego, 1984-87, 3-D Advt. Graphics and Typesetting Co., San Diego, 1987—; nat. coord. Robbins Rsch. Internat., La Jolla, Calif., 1993-94. Actor TV documentary and movies, San Diego, 1987 (award Nat. Movie Arts Festival and Movies 1988). Instr. YMCA/USO, 1971-72. Recipient award Nat. Movie Arts Festival, 1988. Roman Catholic.

ZIVELONGHI, KURT DANIEL, artist, painter; b. Barstow, Calif., Oct. 3, 1960; s. Vincent Otto and Beverly Dean (Schwind) Z. Student, Pasadena (Calif.) City Coll., 1984-85, Art Students League, N.Y.C., 1988-89; BFA, Art Ctr. Coll. of Design, 1993. Mgr. Foothill Airplane Washing Svc., Claremont, Calif., 1980-82; sales rep. Valley Group Fin. Svc., Claremont, 1986-88; loan rep. Pacific Group Funding, Claremont, 1989-90; self employed fine artist Alhambra, Calif., 1990—. One man show at Coll. of Design Art Ctr., Pasadena, Calif., 1993, two man show at Flux Gallery, Eagle Rock, Calif., 1993, group show at Art Students League, N.Y.C., 1989. Mem. Ctr. for the Study of Popular Culture, Century City, Calif., 1994. Mem. Am. Soc. Portrait Artists. Representative: Local Colors 16624 Marquez Ave Pacific Palisades CA 90272 Representative: The Print Merchants Pacific Design Ctr 8687 Melrose Ave West Hollywood CA 90069

ZLAKET, THOMAS A., judge; b. May 30, 1941. AB in Polit. Sci., U. Notre Dame, 1962; LLB, U. Ariz., 1965. Bar: Ariz. 1965, U.S. Dist. Ct. Ariz. 1967, U.S. Ct. Appeals (9th cir.) 1969, Calif. 1976. Atty. Lesher Scruggs Rucker Kimble & Lindamood, Tucson, 1965-68, Maud & Zlaket, 1968-70, Estes Browning Maud and Zlaket, 1970-73, Slutes Estes Zlaket Sakrison & Wasley, 1973-82, Zlaket & Zlaket, 1982-92; judge pro tempore Pima County (Ariz.) Superior Ct., 1983—; justice Ariz. Supreme Ct., 1992, vice chief justice, 1996, chief justice, 1997. Fellow Am. Coll. Trial Lawyers, Am. Bar Found., Ariz. Bar Found.; mem. ABA, Pima County Bar Assn., Am. Bd. Trial Advocates, Ariz. Coll. Trial Advocacy, U. Ariz. Law Coll. Assn., Ariz. Law Rev. Assn. Office: Office of Supreme Ct 1501 W Washington Phoenix AZ 85007

ZOBEL, JAN ARLEEN, tax consultant; b. San Francisco, Feb. 8, 1947; d. Jerome Fremont and Louise Maxine (Purwin) Z. BA, Whittier Coll., 1968; MA, U. Chgo., 1970. Tchr. Chgo. Pub. Schs., 1969-70, San Francisco Pub. Schs., 1971-78; editor, pub. People's Yellow Pages, San Francisco, 1971-81; pvt. practice tax cons. San Francisco, Oakland, 1978—; tchr. community coll. dist., San Francisco, 1986—; tax lectr. U. Hawaii, 1989—, U. Calif., San Francisco State U., Marin C.C. Author: Minding Her Own Business: The Self-Employed Woman's Guide to Taxes and Recordkeeping, 1997; editor People's Yellow Pages, 1971-81 (cert. of honor San Francisco Bd. Suprs. 1974), Where the Child Things Are, 1977-80. Com. mem. Bay Area Career Women's Fund. Named Acct. Adv. of Yr., SBA, 1987; presented Key to City of Buffalo, 1970. Mem. Nat. Assn. Enrolled Agts., Calif. Assn. Enrolled Agts., Nat. Assn. Tax Preparers, Bay Area Career Women. Home: 3045 Holyrood Dr Oakland CA 94611-2541 Office: 1197 Valencia St San Francisco CA 94110-3026

ZOBEL, LOUISE PURWIN, author, educator, lecturer, writing consultant; b. Laredo, Tex., Jan. 10, 1922; d. Leo Max and Ethel Catherine (Levy) Purwin; m. Jerome Fremont Zobel, Nov. 14, 1943; children: Lenore Zobel Harris, Janice A., Robert E., Audrey Zobel Dollinger. BA cum laude, Stanford U., 1943, MA, 1976. Cert. adult edn. and community coll. tchr., Calif. Freelance mag. writer and author Palo Alto, Calif., 1942—; writer, editor, broadcastor UP Bur., San Francisco, 1943; lectr. on writing, history, travel No. Calif., 1964—; lectr., educator U. Calif. campuses, other colls. and univs., 1969—; writing cons. to pvt. clients, 1969—; editorial asst. Assn. Coll. Unions Internat., Palo Alto, 1972-73; acting asst. prof. journalism San Jose State U., 1976; keynote speaker, seminar leader, prin. speaker at nat. confs.; cruise/shipboard enrichment lectr. and presenter of travel slide programs; coord. TV shows; TV personality. Author: (books) The Travel Writer's Handbook, 1980, (paperback), 1982, 83, 84, 85, rev. edits., 1992, 94, 97; author, narrator (90 minute cassette) Let's Have Fun in Japan, 1982; contbr. articles to anthologies, nat. mags. and newspapers; writer advertorials. Bd. dirs., publicity chair Friends of Palo Alto Libr., 1985—; officer Santa Clara County Med. Aux., Esther Clark Aux., others; past pres. PTA. Recipient award for excellence in journalism Sigma Delta Chi, 1943, awards Writers Digest, 1967-95, Armed Forces Writers League, 1972, Nat. Writers Club, 1976, All Nippon Airways and Japanese Nat. Tourist Orgn., 1997. Mem. Am. Soc. Journalists and Authors, Travel Journalists Guild, Internat. Food, Wine and Travel Writers Assn., Pacific Asia Travel Assn., Calif. Writers Club (v.p. 1988-89), AAUW (v.p. 1955-57, Nat. writing award 1969), Stanford Alumni Assn., Phi Beta Kappa. Home and Office: 23350 Sereno Ct Unit 30 Cupertino CA 95014-6543

ZOBELL, CHARLES W., newspaper managing editor; b. Provo, Utah, Mar. 17, 1950; m. Marilyn M. Earl, May 5, 1978; children: David, Rebecca. BA in Comm., Brigham Young U., 1974. Reporter Las Vegas Rev.-Jour., 1975-78; dir. Office Intergovtl. Rels. City of Las Vegas, 1978-80; city editor Las Vegas Rev.-Jour., 1980-92, mng. editor, 1992—. Vol. rep. Mormon Ch., Argentina, 2 yrs. Office: Las Vegas Review-Journal PO Box 70 1111 W Bonanza Rd Las Vegas NV 89125-0070

ZODL, JOSEPH ARTHUR, international trade executive, consultant; b. Hackensack, N.J., Aug. 13, 1948; s. Joseph Frank and Edna Josephine (Hokanson) Z. BA in Polit. Sci., Fordham Coll., 1970; MA in Polit. Sci., New Sch. for Social Rsch., N.Y.C., 1991. Lic. customs broker U.S. Treasury Dept. Export mgr. Savage Universal Corp., Tempe, Ariz., 1984-93; corp. transp. mgr. Nat. Media Corp., Phoenix, 1993—; adj. instr. internat. bus. Rio Salado C.C., 1989—, Keller Grad. Sch. Bus., 1995—, Scottsdale C.C., 1996—. Author: Export-Import: Everything You and Your Company Need To Know To Compete in World Markets, 1992, rev., 1995; contbr. articles to profl. jours. Vice chmn. Legis. Dist. 20 Dems., 1978-80, chmn., 1980-82; mem. Ariz. State Dem. Com., 1978-89; cand. Ariz. Ho. Reps., 1986. Named Eagle Scout, Boy Scouts Am., 1966. Mem. Am. Polit. Sci. Assn., Ariz. World Trade Ctr., Internat. Transp. Mgmt. Assn. (dir. 1990-91), Phoenix Traffic Club, Phoenix Customs Brokers Assn., Delta Nu Alpha (pres. 1980-81, Ariz. Transp. Man of Yr. 1980), Alpha Phi Omega. Roman Catholic.

ZOECKLER, LINDA KAY, librarian art historian; b. Chgo., Ill., Dec. 11, 1946; d. Harold David and Catherine (Welch) Davies; m. John Carr Zoeckler, Mar. 17, 1967. BA in Art History cum laude, U. Calif., Riverside, 1970, M in Art History, 1976; M in Lib. and Info. Sci., UCLA, 1985. Art cataloguer, bibliographer U. Calif., Riverside, 1969-81; head of lib. Otis Art Inst., L.A., 1981-83; curator of collections Edward Dean Mus., Cherry Valley, Calif., 1984-85; head tech. info. ctr. Singer Librascope Corp., Glendale, Calif., 1985-88; head art reference lib. Huntington Lib. Art Collections and Bot. Gardens, San Marino, Calif., 1988—; adj. prof. art Golden West Coll., Huntington Beach., Calif., 1989—; vice chair Art Librs. Soc. N.Am., So. Calif. chpt., 1993-94; mem. rsch. com. Art Librs. Soc.-N.Am., 1993-94. Contrb. article to profl. jour., chpt. to book Art, Artifact and Architecture Law, 1996. Honorable mention Gerd Muehsam award ARLIS/NA, 1985. Mem. Coll. Art Assn. Episcopalian. Home: 23227 Forest Canyon Dr Diamond Bar CA 91765-3018 Office: Huntington Lib Art Collections Bot Gardens 1151 Oxford Rd San Marino CA 91108

ZOELLNER, ROBERT WILLIAM, chemistry educator; b. Marshfield, Wis., May 30, 1956; s. Willard Rudolph and Marie Martha (Prihoda) Z.; m. Barbara Moore, Feb. 5, 1983; children: Joan Moore, Thaddeus Barak. BS, St. Norbert Coll., De Pere, Wis., 1978; PhD, Kans. State U., 1983. Postdoctoral assoc. Cornell U., Ithaca, N.Y., 1983-84; vis. scientist U. Aix-Marseille (France) III, 1984-85; asst. prof. No. Ariz. U., Flagstaff, 1986-92, assoc. prof., 1992—; sabbatical assoc. Istituto per lo Studio della Stereochimica Consiglio Nazionale delle Ricerche, 1994-95. Mem. Am. Chem. Soc., Internat. Coun. on Main Group Chemistry, N.Y. Acad. Scis., Wis. Acad. Sci., Arts and Letters, Sigma Xi, Alpha Chi Sigma, Phi Lambda Upsilon. Office: No Ariz U Dept Chemistry PO Box 5698 Flagstaff AZ 86011-5698

ZOHNER, STEVEN K., environmental scientist; b. Driggs, Idaho, June 8, 1953; s. LaVar Orin and Shirley Elizabeth (Kempton) Z.; m. Marivene Amelia List, Apr. 26, 1977; children: Suzanne, Nathan, Julie, Audrey. AS with high honors, Ricks Coll., 1976; BSmagna cum laude, Brigham Young U., 1978, student, 1978-79, MS magna cum laude, 1982; grad., Dept. Energy/Westinghouse Sch. Environ. Excellence, Idaho, 1992. Rsch. chemist Brigham Young U., Provo, Utah, 1978-81; plant chemist Martin Marietta, Lemington, Utah, 1981-82; engr. prodn. dept. Exxon Nuclear Idaho, Idaho Falls, 1982-85; sr. engr. tech. dept. Westinghouse Idaho Nuclear, Idaho Falls, 1985-91, sr. scientist environ. dept., 1991-94; sr. scientist environ. safety & health dept. Lockheed Idaho Tech. Co., Idaho Falls, 1994—; staff scientist environ. characterization Lockheed Martin Idaho Technologies, 1994—; calculator Idaho Nat. Engring. Lab. toxic air emissions, SARA Title III emissions, Clean Air Act chem. emissions and radioactive emissions under 40 CFR NESHAP for Dept. of Energy facilities; cons. EG&G Idaho, Idaho Falls, 1986, Fernald Nuclear Facility, Cin., 1991. Inventor decontamination solution (Recognition award 1990). Lay minister Ch. Jesus Christ Latter Day Sts., Stockholm, 1972-74, ward clerk, 1985—, computer specialist, 1995—; active Boy Scouts Am., Idaho Falls, 1982—, PTO, Idaho Falls, 1986—. Mem. Am. Chem. Soc., Phi Kappa Phi. Republican. Home: 1042 Grizzly Ave Idaho Falls ID 83402-3822 Office: Lockheed Martin Idaho Techs MS-3428 PO Box 1625 Idaho Falls ID 83415-3428

ZOLTAN, ELIZABETH, psychology educator, consultant; b. Cherry Hill, N.J., Dec. 18, 1957; d. Ivan Nicholas and Olga (Riabov) Z.; m. Robert L. Caret, June 13, 1993; children: Katalyn, Kellen; stepchildren: Colin, Katherine. BA, Johns Hopkins U., 1980, MA, 1980, PhD, 1983. Asst. prof. dept. psychology Towson (Md.) State U., 1982-89, asst. dean, 1989-91, assoc. prof., 1989-95, assoc. dean, 1991-95; assoc. prof. San Jose (Ca.) State U., 1995-97; dean bus. and social scis. Foothill Coll., Los Altos Hills, Calif., 1997—; cons. GTE Lab., Waltham, Mass., 1982-83, Acer Am., San Jose, 1995—, University On-Line, Alexandria, Va., 1995—; prin. investigator Army Rsch. Office, Research Triangle Park, N.C., 1986; cons. NASA/AMES, Mountain View, Calif., 1996—. Contbr. articles to profl. jours. NASA Summer Faculty fellow Greenbelt, Md., 1985, 86. Mem. Human Factors Ergonomics Soc. Home: 18026 Saratoga Los Gatos Rd Monte Sereno CA 95030-4227 Office: Foothill Coll Divsn Bus and Social Scis Los Altos CA 94022

ZONE, JANINE DENISE, elementary education educator; b. L.A., Sept. 15, 1953; d. Michael and Mildred (Heischuber) Z. AA, L.A. City Coll., 1975; diploma in Lang. Studies, U. Vienna, Austria, 1977; BA in Art History, UCLA, 1979. Multiple subject credential profl., Calif. Tchr. Alexandria Ave. Sch. L.A. Unified Sch. Dist., 1986—; bd. dirs. Jr. Arts Ctr.-Barnsdall Art Pk., L.A., 1988—; mem. adv. bd. Cotsen Art Fellowship, L.A., 1985—; coord. visual arts L.A. Unified Sch. Dist. Festivals of Achievement, 1987-88; participant Vassar Coll. Inst. for Publishing Children's Books, 1994; mem. instrnl. leadership team LEARN, 1995—. Author: David Hockney Is Coming to the Jr. Arts Center, 1988; artist, author: (gallery installations) The Teacher's Press, 1987—. Vol. outreach educator, fund raiser U.S. Com. for UNICEF, L.A., 1986-96; precinct leader Dem. Nat. Com.; conf. participant Children's Def. Fund, Washington, 1993. Recipient Award of Appreciation, Hollywood Arts Coun., L.A. Children's Mus. Mem. United Tchrs. Home: 3941 Veselich Ave Apt 151 Los Angeles CA 90039-1436 Office: Alexandria Avenue Sch 4211 Oakwood Ave Los Angeles CA 90004-3214

ZONGOLOWICZ, HELEN MICHAELINE, education and psychology educator; b. Kenosha, Wis., July 22, 1936; d. Edmund S. and Helen (Ostrowski) Z.; EdB, Dominican Coll., 1966; MA, Cardinal Stritch Coll., 1973; EdD, U. No. Colo., 1977. Tchr. elem. schs. Kenosha, 1956-58, Center Line, Mich., 1958-59, Taft, Calif., 1960-61, Lake Wales, Fla., 1962-63, Albuquerque, 1963-65; tchr., asst. prin. St. Mary's Sch., Taft, 1965-69; asst. sch. supt. Diocese of Fresno, Calif., 1969-70; tchr. primary grades Greasewood Boarding Sch., Ganado, Ariz., 1970-72, coord. spl. projects, 1972-75, liaison to parent adv. coun., 1972-75, tchr. supr., 1972-76; ednl. specialist Ft. Defiance Agy., Navajo Area, Ariz., 1974-75, ednl. diagnostician, 1979-80; asst. prof. Auburn (Ala.) U., 1977-79; asst. prof. U. N.Mex.-Gallup, 1981-94, prof. edn. and psychology, 1994—, dir. child care ctr.; prin. Chuska Sch., 1980-93; chair dept. psychology/edn. CDA dir., 1995—; vis. prof. U. Colo., 1976; mem. N.Mex. State Articulation Task Force, 1994—. Recipient Spl. Achievement award U.S. Dept. Interior, 1971, 73, Points of Light award, 1990, Superior Performance award, 1982, Achievement award Navajo Nation, 1993; named Prin. of Yr. Bur. of Indian Affairs, 1990; named Prin. of Yr. Navajo Area Sch. Bd. Assn., 1991. Mem. AAUW, Nat. Assn. Edn. of Young Children, Nat. Staff Devel. Coun., Am. Assn. Mental Deficiency, Assn. for Supervision and Curriculum Devel., Coun. for Exceptional Children, Coun. for Basic Edn., Am. Ednl. Rsch. Assn., NAFE, Internat.

Reading Assn., Assn. for Children with Learning Disabilities Nat. Coun. Tchrs. of English., Assn. Childhood Edn. Internat., Kappa Delta Pi, Phi Delta Kappa. Address: 604 Mckee Dr Gallup NM 87301-4830 *Personal philosophy: I believe that each person has within themselves the potential for success. It is up to each of us to cultivate that potential within ourselves and others. Children, who are our future, must be active learners who will learn best when education is whole, real and relevant.*

ZORITCH, GEORGE, dance educator, choreographer; b. Moscow, June 6, 1917; came to U.S., 1935; s. Serge and Helen (Grunke) Z. Diploma Lady Deterding's Russian Sch., Paris, 1933. Mem. Ida Rubinstein Ballet Co., Paris, 1933-34, Pavlova's Co., West Indies, Australia, India, Egypt and Eng., 1934-35, Col. de Basil's Ballet Russe de Monte-Carlo, U.S.A., S. Am., Europe, 1936-38; soloist Denham Ballet Russe de Monte-Carlo, U.S.A., Can., S. Am., Europe, 1938-42; prof., mem. dance faculty com. fine arts U. Ariz., 1973-87; actor, dancer plays, musicals, concert tours, Broadway and throughout U.S., S. Am., Europe, 1943-50: actor 17 movies in Hollywood, Calif. and Rome; premier danseur noble Grand Ballet du Marquis de Cuevas, Europe, Africa, S.Am., 1951-57, Denham Ballet Russe de Monte Carlo, U.S.A., 1957-62; founder George Zoritch Sch. Classical Ballet, West Hollywood, Calif., 1963-73; fine arts prof., mem. com. on dance, U. Ariz., Tucson, 1973-87, ret.; freelance engagements, 1973—. Editor records: George Zoritch for Classical Ballet, 1962-65. Recipient Key to Jacksonville (Fla.) Mayor Hans G. Tantzler Jr., 1968, The Bolshoi Theatre Medallion of Merit award IV Internat. Ballet Competition-Moscow, 1981, Ariz. Dance Treasures award Ariz. Dance Arts Alliance and Ariz. State U. Dept. Dance, 1992, Merit award Acad. of Choreographic Sch. A. Vaganova, 1993, Vaslav Nijinsky Medallion of Merit award The Consulate Gen. of Republic of Poland, 1994, Diaghilev House Silver Medallion of Merit award Sixth Dance Competition of Paris, 1994; named Amb. San Antonio World Hemisphere, 1968. Mem. Ariz. Dance Arts Alliance (hon. life mem.), Phoenix Ballet Guild (hon. mem.), Nat. Soc. Arts and Letters (Medallion of Merit award Valley of Sun chpt. 1990).

ZORNES, MILFORD, artist; b. Camargo, Okla., Jan. 25, 1908; s. James Francis and Clara Delphine (Lindsay) Z.; m. Gloria Codd, 1935; 1 son, Franz Milford; m. Patricia Mary Palmer, Nov. 8, 1942; 1 dau., Maria Patricia. Student, Otis Art Inst., Los Angeles, 1929, Pomona Coll., 1930-34. Instr. art Pomona Coll., 1946-50; art dir. Vortox and Padua Hills Theatre, Claremont, 1954-66. Exhibited, Calif. Watercolor Soc., Met. Mus., Am. Watercolor Soc., Corcoran Gallery, Bklyn. Mus., Denver Mus., Cleve. Mus., L.A. Mus., Brooks Gallery, London, Bombay Art Assn., Chgo. Art Inst., Butler Mus., Gallery Modern Masters, Washington, Santa Barbara (Calif.) Mus., Cin. Mus., Laguna (Calif.) Art Gallery, Oklahoma City Mus., Springville (Utah) Mus.; represented in permanent collections at L.A. Mus., White House Collection, Met. Mus., Pentagon Bldg., Butler Mus., UCLA, Nat. Acad., San Diego Mus., L.A. County Fair, Home Savs. and Loan Assn., L.A., Corcoran Gallery, Washington; mem. art com., Nat. Orange Show, San Bernardino, Calif., 1963-65; author: A Journey to Nicaragua, 1977, The California Style: California Watercolor Artists, 1925-1955, 1985; subject of book by Gordon McClelland: Milford Zornes, Hillcrest Press, 1991. Served with U.S. Army, 1943-45, CBI. RecipientPaul Prescott Barrow award Pomona Coll., 1987, David Prescott Burrows award, 1991, A Most Disting. Citizen award So. Utah State Coll., 1988, Am. Artist Achievement award Am. Artist Mag., 1994. Mem. NAD, Am. Watercolor Soc., Southwestern Watercolor Soc., Watercolor West, Nat. Watercolor Soc., Utah Watercolor Soc. Address: PO Box 176 Orderville UT 84758-0176 *It has been my effort in life to have awareness: not to have all knowledge because no one can encompass all knowledge; not to have only wealth or only success, because there is no dimension of completeness of wealth or success; not to achieve complete goodness, because goodness and right are relative; not to enjoy the epitomy in taste because taste is a gratification of self alone; but rather to seek and achieve understanding of relative values and a concept of the completeness of life. With this as my effort and my inner goal, I find success within the areas of my limited abilities, my meager knowledge, and my frail grasp of the infinite.*

ZUBER, WILLIAM FREDERICK, thoracic and vascular surgeon; b. New Orleans, Dec. 30, 1932; s. Frederick and Bertie B. (Seale) Z.; m. Norma Burns Keen, Sept. 27,1958; children: William Frederick, Michael Craig, Kimberly, Karen. MD, Tulane U., 1956. Diplomate Am. Bd. Surgery with subspecialty in thoracic and vascular surgery. Teaching fellow Temple U., Phila., 1963-64; asst. prof. U. So. Calif., L.A., 1967-82; pvt. practice Ventura, Calif.; cons. Ventura County Med. Ctr., 1966—, chief surgery, 1973, 83-84, chief of staff, 1986-87; chief surgery Cmty. Meml. Hosp., Ventura, 1977, 85, 93, chief of staff, 1979. Contbr. articles to profl. jours. Pres. Am. Heart Assn., Ventura, 1972. Capt. M.C. U.S. Army, 1959-61. Mem. ACS, Internat. Cardiovascular Soc., Soc. Thoracic Surgeons, So. Calif. Vascular Surg. Soc. Office: 2856 Cabrillo Dr Ste 201 Ventura CA 93003-2819

ZUCCA, GARY JOSEPH, educator; b. Hermosa Beach, Calif., June 14, 1938; s. Joseph Guido and Dorothy Francis (McMellon) Z.; m. Carol Patterson, Apr. 6, 1968; children: Matthew, Anthony. BS, U. So. Calif., 1961; MA, U. Okla., 1979; PhD, U. Fla., 1984. Commd. ensign U.S. Navy, 1961, advanced through grades to lt. comdr., ret., 1981; asst. prof. Nat. U., Sacramento, 1986-93; dean Nat. U., San Diego, 1993-95; asst. prof. Nat. U., L.A., 1995—. Patroller, Nat. Ski Patrol, 1989—. Home: 7830 Airola Rd PO Box 438 Vallecito CA 95251 Office: Nat U 9920 La Cienega Blvd Inglewood CA

ZUCCARELLI, ANTHONY JOSEPH, molecular biology and biochemistry educator; b. N.Y.C., Aug. 11, 1944; m. Sharron Adele Ames; children: Cara N., A. Alexandar. BS in Bacteriology, Cornell U., 1966; MS in Microbiology with honors, Loma Linda U., 1968; PhD in Biophysics, Calif. Inst. Tech., 1974; postdoctoral studies in molecular biology, U. Konstanz, Fed. Republic Germany, 1974-76. Asst. prof. grad. sch. biology Loma Linda (Calif.) U., 1976-80, assoc. prof. microbiology sch. medicine, 1980-91; prof. microbiology Sch. Medicine, 1991—; assoc. mem. grad. faculty biology program Loma Linda (Calif.) U., 1982—, mem. grad. faculty microbiology program, 1982—, mem. grad. faculty biochemistry program, 1986—, asst. dir. med. scientist program, grad. coord., 1989-91, dir. med. scientist program, grad. coord., 1991—; mem. Ctr. for Molecular Biology and Gene Therapy, 1994—; grad. student rsch. mentor, chmn., mem. numerous coms. including mem. sch. medicine basic sci. course coords. com., 1987—, sch. medicine basic sci. faculty coun., 1987—, acad. rev. com., 1987-96, med. scientist curriculum com., 1989—, microbiology dept. faculty search com., 1988—, grad. sch. coun. Loma Linda U.; instr. microbial genetics, molecular biology Nat. Med. Sch. Rev., 1987-96; outside reviewer grant applications NSF, 1977-78, 81-82; reviewer NIH Small Bus. Innovative Rsch. Grants, 1994, 95. Contbr. articles to profl. jours. Fellow NSF, 1968-71, Am. Cancer Soc., 1974-76; trainee NIH, 1971-74; recipient First Prize for Sci. Exhibit award Macpherson Soc., 1989, Basic Sci. Student-Faculty Rsch. award, 1990, 96; grantee Loma Linda U., 1977, 78, 79, 81, 82, 83, 85, 86, 87, 90, 95. Mem. Am. Soc. Microbiology, Am. Soc. Advancement Sci., Am. Soc. Biotechnology, Am. Chem. Soc., N.Y. Acad. Scis., Sigma Xi. Mem. Seventh Day Adventist Ch. Office: Loma Linda U AH115 Dept Microbiol/Molec Genet Loma Linda CA 92350

ZUCKER, ALFRED JOHN, English educator, academic adminstrator; b. Hartford, Sept. 25, 1940; s. Samuel and Rose (Zucker) Z.; AA, L.A. Valley Coll., 1960; AB in English, UCLA, 1962, AB in Speech, MA in English, 1962, MA in Speech, 1963, PhD, 1966, postgrad., UCLA, U. So. Calif., Harvard U.; m. Sallie Lea Friedheim, Dec. 25, 1966; children—Mary Anne, John James, Jr., James Patrick, Patrick Jonathan, Anne-Marie Kathleen, Kathleen Mary. Lectr. English, Los Angeles City Coll., 1963-68; prof. English, philosophy, chmn. div. humanities Los Angeles Southwest Coll., 1968-72, chmn. English dept., 1972-74, asst. dean instruction, 1974—; prof. English El Camino Coll., 1985—; prof. English L.A. Valley Coll., 1989—. Mem. Los Angeles Coll. Dist. Senate, 1969—. Mem. Los Angeles Coll. Tchrs. Assn. (dir.), Calif. Jr. Coll. Assn., Calif. Tchrs. Assn., AAUP, World Affairs Coun., Mensa, Phi Beta Kappa, Phi Delta Kappa (pres. U. Calif. at Los Angeles chpt. 1966-67, v.p. 1967-68), Tau Alpha Epsilon. Lodge: KC. Contbr. articles to profl. jours. Office: 5800 Fulton Ave Van Nuys CA 91401-4062

ZUCKSCHWERDT, OTTO SALVATORE, counselor, substance abuse specialist, chaplain; b. N.Y.C., Aug. 16, 1947; s. Kenneth and Jennis Z.; m. Carole Jalanti, Apr. 28, 1968 (div. 1994); children: Christina Z. Brown, Julie; m. Vickey Lee Zuckschwerdt, June 4, 1994. AA, Muskegon C.C., 1977; BS in Bibl. Studies, Lee Coll., Cleveland, Tenn., 1980; PhD, DLitt. in Counseling, Evangel Christian U., Monroe, La., 1990; MEd in Counseling and Guidance, Albertson Coll. Idaho, Caldwell, 1987; PhD in Clin. Psychology, Calif. Coast U., Santa Anna. Nat. cert. counselor and master addictions counselor Nat. Bd. Cert. Counselors; lic. profl. counselor, psychologist extended provider, driving under influence and substance abuse evaluator, Idaho; cert. clin. supr., drug and alcohol counselor Bd. Alcoholism Drug Counselor's Cert., Inc.; internat. cert. substance abuse specialist Internat. Cert. Reciprocity Consortium and other Drug Abuse, Inc.; ordained min. Internat. Ministerial Fellowship, 1994. Youth svc. coord. Port of Hope, Nampa, Idaho, 1982-87; coord. Big Bros. and Big Sisters, Nampa, Idaho, 1985-87; staff psychologist Idaho Child Protection, Caldwell, 1988-89; resource officer Canyon County Sheriff Dept., Caldwell, 1989-94; sr. counselor, CAFS dir. New Life Counseling Ctr., Boise, Idaho, 1989-94; sr. counselor Rice Clinic, Boise, Idaho, 1994—; clinician and youth counselor Challenge, Inc., Boise, Idaho, 1994—; chaplain Full Gospel Chaplain Commn.; sr. counselor, dir. children and family svcs., Boise, 1989-94; dual diagnosis counselor and youth clinician Challenge, Inc., 1994—; owern Northwerdt Psychol. Svcs., 1996—; pastor Assemblies of God and Ch. of Brethren, throughout U.S., 1970-92. Contbr. articles on Christian living to various jours.; developer various youth svcs. programs. Chaplain, lt. col. USAF CAP, Caldwell, 1985—; co-founder Marine Christian Cadet Corps, N.Y.C., 1966; chief chaplain St. Joseph County Sheriff Dept., Centerville, Mich., 1975-78; developer, promoter Dial-A-Blessing Ministries, 1980&; mem. Idaho Gov.'s Commn. for Youth, 1993-94, Idaho Crime Commn. Mem. ACA, Law Enforcement Alliance Am., Internat. Assn. for Addictions and Offender Counselors. Home: 134 Poplar St Nampa ID 83651

ZUETEL, KENNETH ROY, JR., lawyer; b. L.A., Apr. 5, 1954; s. Kenneth Roy Sr. and Adelle Francis (Avant) Z.; m. Cheryl Kay Morse, May 29, 1976; children: Bryan, Jarid, Christopher, Lauren. BA, San Diego State U., 1974; JD, U. San Diego, 1978. Bar: Calif. 1978 U.S. Ct. Appeals (9th cir.) 1979, U.S. Dist. Ct. (ctrl. dist.) Calif. 1979, U.S. Dist. Ct. (so. and no. dists.) Calif. 1980, U.S. Dist. Ct. (ea. dist.) 1981. Clk. to fed. Judge Martin Pence U.S. Dist. Ct. Hawaii, Honolulu, 1978-79; assoc. litigation Buchalter, Nemer, L.A., 1979-83, Thelen, Marrin, L.A., 1983-88; ptnr. Zuetel & Cahill, Pasadena, Calif., 1988—; superior ct. arbitrator L.A. Superior Ct., 1982-90, superior ct. settlement officer, 1988-93; judge pro temp L.A. Mcpl. Ct., 1983—, L.A. Superior Ct., 1989—; guest lectr. Loyola U. Sch. Law, 1986—; CEB lectr. Author: Civil Procedure Before Trial, 1992; cons. editor: Cal. Civ. Proc., 1992; contbr. articles to profl. jours. Recipient Recognition award L.A. (Calif.) Bd. Suprs., 1988. Mem. State Bar Calif. (mem. adv. com. continuing edn. 1985-88, trial practice subcom. 1985-88, disciplinary examiner 1986), Los Angeles County Bar Assn. (chair trial atty. project 1982-83, mem. L.A. del. conf. of dels. 1986—, chair L.A. del. conf. of dels. 1995, exec. com. barristers 1984-88, superior ct. com. 1985-88, civil practice com. 1992-94, exec. com. litigation sect. 1989-90), Pasadena Bar Assn., Inns of Ct. (barrister L.A. chpt. 1991-92), Phi Beta Kappa, Phi Kappa Phi, Phi Alpha Theta, Pi Sigma Alpha. Republican. Presbyterian. Home: 567 Willow Springs Ln Glendora CA 91741-2974 Office: Zuetel & Cahill 180 S Lake Ave Ste 540 Pasadena CA 91101-2619

ZUNKER, RICHARD E., insurance company executive; b. 1938. BS, U. Wis., 1964. With Employers Ins. Wausau, Wis., 1964-69, Northwestern Nat. Investors Life, 1969-75; with Safeco Life Ins. Co., Seattle, 1975—, pres., also bd. dirs. With U.S. Army, 1956-58. Office: Safeco Life Ins Co PO Box 34690 Seattle WA 98124-1690*

ZUSCHLAG, NANCY LYNN, environmental educator; b. Montclair, N.J., Dec. 12, 1954; d. Irving Djalmar and Carmen (Delgrippo) Z.; m. Jeffrey Jon Miller, Sept. 21, 1991. BA in Biology cum laude, Coe Coll., 1977; MA in Biology, U. Kans., 1982. Regional conservation educator and coord. Mo. Conservation Dept., Jefferson City, 1982-84; coord. sch. programs Denver Mus. Natural History, 1986-87; program dir. dept. natural resources and environ. edn. Coop. Ext. Colo. State U., Golden, 1988—; instr. environ. educator Mus. Natural History, U. Kans., Lawrence, 1976-82, assoc. pub. edn. dept. , 1986-89; lectr. William Woods Coll., 1982-84; mem. study, rsch. rev. group Canary Islands, 1985; cons. Kongskilde Field Study Edn. Ctr., Soro, Denmark, 1985; bd. dirs. Foothills Nature Ctr., Boulder, Colo., 1987-89; assoc. zool. Denver Mus. Natural History, 1988; cons. and educator Mus. Zool., U. Copenhagen, 1984-85, 95-96. Author, editor: Back to Ancient Egypt, 1987; (with others) Science - Natur/Teknik, Assessment and Learning Studies and Educational Theory Curriculum, Vol. 22, 1995; editor: (with others) Contributions to Vertebrate Ecology and Systematic; a Tribute to Henry S. Fitch, 1983; contbr. articles to profl. jours. state edn. coord. Colo. Earth Day is Every Day campaign, Boulder, 1990; bd. dirs. Colo. Found. Agr., Denver, 1992-95, mem. edn. bd., 1993; facilitator and presenter UN Program Youth in the Environment, U. Colo., Boulder, 1993; chair environ. and natural resources future's task force com., Colo. State U. Coop. Ext., 1993; mem. nat. natural resources and eviron. mgmt. support team coop. states, rsch. ext. edn. sys., USDA, 1993-96; mem. synthesis team and original document writing team, Colo. Environ. Edn. Master Plan, 1994; mem. state steering com. Denver Urban Resources Partnership, 1994—, Denver Youth Naturally Project, 1995. Recipient N.J. award AUW, County Achievement award Nat. Assn. Counties, 1989, Environ. Scholar award USEPA, 1990, region 8 Outstanding Women's Contbns. in Environ. Edn. award, 1992, Nat. Environ. Coun. award, 1992, 94, Celebrate Colo. Environ. Leadership award Colo. State Gov., 1993; scholar Coe Coll., 1973-74; Virginia Harkness-Sawtelle Found. scholar Coe Coll. and U. Kans., 1976-78; Fulbright scholar U. Copenhagen Zool. Mus., 1984-85, Fulbright scholar assoc. Royal Danish Sch. Edn., 1995-96. Mem. Am. Assn. Biol. Scis., Nat. Wildlife Fedn. (mem. steering com. Naturlink 1993), North Am. Assn. Environ. Edn., Alliance Environ. Edn., Nat. Assn. Interpreters, Am. Arachnological Assn., Colo. Alliance Environ. Edn. (bd. dirs. 1988-92, pres. 1990-91, adv. bd. 1997), Colo. Assn. Tchrs., Fulbright Alumni Soc., Phi Sigma, Epsilon Sigma Phi (State Early Career Excellence award 1990). Office: Colo State U Coop Ext 15200 W 6th Ave Golden CO 80401-5018

ZWAHLEN, FRED CASPER, JR., journalism educator; b. Portland, Oreg., Nov. 11, 1924; s. Fred and Katherine (Meyer) Z.; m. Grace Eleanor DeMoss, June 24, 1959; children: Molly, Skip. BA, Oreg. State U., 1949; MA, Stanford U., 1952. Reporter San Francisco News, 1949-50; acting editor Stanford Alumni Rev., Palo Alto, Calif., 1950; successively instr. journalism, news bur. asst., prof. journalism, chmn. journalism dept. Oreg. State U., Corvallis, 1950-91, prof. emeritus, 1991—; Swiss tour guide, 1991—; corres. Portland Oregonian, 1950-67. Author: (with others) Handbook of Photography, 1984. Coord. E.E. Wilson Scholarship Fund, 1964—; active budget com. Corvallis Sch. Dist., 1979. Recipient Achievement award Sch. Journalism U. Oregon, 1988. Mem. Assn. for Edn. in Journalism and Mass Communications (conv. chmn. 1983, pres.' award 1988), Oreg. Newspaper Pubs. Assn. (bd. dirs. 1980-85, student loan fund named in his honor 1988), Soc. Profl. Journalists (nat. svc. citation 1988), Corvallis Country Club, Shriners, Masons, Elks, Moose, Eagles, Delta Tau Delta. Republican. Presbyterian. Home: 240 SW 7th St Corvallis OR 97333-4551 Office: Oreg State U Dept Student Activities Corvallis OR 97331

ZWICK, BARRY STANLEY, newspaper editor, speechwriter; b. Cleve., July 21, 1942; s. Alvin Albert and Selma Davidovna (Makofsky) Z.; m. Roberta Joan Yaffe, Mar. 11, 1972; children: Natasha Yvette, Alexander Anatol. BA in Journalism, Ohio State U., 1963; MS in Journalism, Columbia U., 1965. Copy editor Phila. Inquirer, 1964; night news editor Detroit Free Press, 1965-67; West Coast editor L.A. Times/Washington Post News Svc, 1967-77; makeup editor L.A. Times, 1978—; adj. prof. U. So. Calif., L.A., 1975-77. Author: Hollywood Tanning Secrets, 1980. NEH profl. journalism fellow Stanford U., 1977-78. Jewish. Office: LA Times Times Mirror Sq Los Angeles CA 90012

ZYROFF, ELLEN SLOTOROFF, information scientist, classicist, educator; b. Atlantic City, N.J., Aug. 1, 1946; d. Joseph George and Sylvia Beverly (Roth) Slotoroff; m. Jack Zyroff, June 21, 1970; children: Dena Rachel, David Aaron. AB, Barnard Coll., 1968; MA, The Johns Hopkins U., 1969, PhD, 1971; MS, Columbia U., 1973. Instr. The Johns Hopkins U., Balt., 1970-71, Yeshiva U., N.Y.C., 1971-72, Bklyn Coll., 1971-72; libr., instr. U. Calif., 1979, 81, 91, San Diego State U., 1981-85, 94; prof. San Diego Mesa Coll., 1981—; dir. The Reference Desk Rsch. Svcs., La Jolla, Calif., 1983—; prin. libr. San Diego County Libr., 1985—; v.p. Archaeol. Soc. Am., Balt., 1970-71. Author: The Author's Apostrophe in Epic from Homer Through Lucan, 1971, Cooperative Library Instruction for Maximum Benefit, 1989; contbr. articles to profl. jours. Pres. Women's Am. ORT, San Diego, 1979-81. Mem. ALA (chair divsn. coms. 1982—), Am. Philol. Assn., Calif. Libr. Assn. (elected to assembly 1993-95, 96—), Am. Soc. Info. Sci., Am. Classical League, Libr. Congress Cataloging in Publ. Adv. Group, Toastmasters, Beta Phi Mu. Office: PO Box 12122 La Jolla CA 92039-2122

Professional Index

AGRICULTURE

UNITED STATES

ARIZONA

Paradise Valley
Twist, Robert Lanphier *farmer, rancher, cattleman*

Phoenix
Ramos, Christina Sierra *natural resource specialist*

Tucson
Anderson, Raymond Eugene *land revegetation specialist*
Thacker, Gary William *agricultural extension agent*

CALIFORNIA

Anaheim
Guajardo, Elisa *educator*

Bakersfield
Hershey, John C. *retired rancher*

Dixon
Timm, Olin Henry *animal breeder, farmer*

Hanford
Hall, Richard Dennis *agribusiness and international trade writer*

La Jolla
Foxley, William Coleman *cattleman*

Morro Bay
MacElvaine, William Stephen *rancher, consultant*

Oxnard
Hansen, J. Woodford *agricultural products supplier*

Pacific Palisades
Jennings, Marcella Grady *rancher, investor*

Sacramento
Wightman, Thomas Valentine *rancher, researcher*

Salinas
Merrill, Thomas M. *produce executive*

San Diego
Caughlin, Stephenie Jane *organic farmer*

San Luis Obispo
McCorkle, Robert Ellsworth *agribusiness educator*

Sanger
Hackett, Ralph *agricultural products supplier*

Shingletown
Denny, James Clifton *tree farm administrator, forestry consultant*

Sierra Madre
Whittingham, Charles Edward *thoroughbred race horse owner and trainer*

Sonoma
Cooke, Charles Maynard *vineyardist, business executive*

Trinity Center
Hartman, Ruth Gayle *rancher*

West Hollywood
Harting, Trip *equine trainer*

COLORADO

Denver
McFarlane, Willis McKee *buffalo company executive*

Greeley
McKee, Byron Duncan *livestock broker*
Oppelt, Norman Theodore *park researcher, retired psychology educator*

Kersey
Guttersen, Michael *rancher, investor*

Springfield
Wessler, Melvin Dean *farmer, rancher*

HAWAII

Pearl City
Hoshmand, Ahmad Reza *agricultural and resources economist*

IDAHO

Boise
Johnson, Ronald Douglas *business executive*

MONTANA

Choteau
De Bruycker, Lloyd Henry *rancher, feedlot operator*

Drummond
Gilman, June Isabelle Brander *rancher*

Miles City
Fraser, Mac Robert (Rob Fraser) *livestock auction owner, auctioneer*

Polson
Marchi, Jon *cattle rancher, former investment brokerage executive*

Pony
Anderson, Richard Ernest *agribusiness development executive, rancher*

Savage
Thiessen, Dwight Everett *farmer*

Utica
Stevenson, Sarah Schoales *rancher, business owner*

NEVADA

Yerington
Scatena, Lorraine Borba *rancher, women's rights advocate*

NEW MEXICO

Bernalillo
Langley, Rocky D. *agricultural business executive*

Clovis
Jones, Robbie Rene *farmer*

OREGON

Corvallis
Ripple, William John *forestry researcher, educator*

Forest Grove
Wirtz, David Reiner *enologist*

Grants Pass
Miller, Richard Alan *agricultural consultant, hypnotherapist*

Lake Oswego
Green, Daniel Fred *forester*

WASHINGTON

Kirkland
Holden, Fred Stephen *industrial tree farmer*

Toppenish
Hefflinger, LeRoy Arthur *agricultural manager*

Waldron
Thorson, Margaret Helen *farmer, librarian*

Yakima
Grandy, Jay Franklin *fruit processing executive*

WYOMING

Aladdin
Brunson, Mabel (Dipper) *researcher*

Douglas
Sanford, Leroy Leonard *rancher*

Fort Laramie
Hageman, James C. *rancher*

Lander
Raynolds, David Robert *buffalo breeder, author*

Wheatland
Bunker, John Birkbeck *cattle rancher, retired sugar company executive*

ADDRESS UNPUBLISHED

Hanley, Joan Corette *vineyard owner*
Hansen, Clifford Peter *rancher, former governor and senator*
Kontny, Vincent L. *rancher, engineering executive*
Stanley, Marlyse Reed *horse breeder*

ARCHITECTURE AND DESIGN

UNITED STATES

ALASKA

Anchorage
Maynard, Kenneth Douglas *architect*

Eagle River
Brooks, Stuart Dale *building consultant*

ARIZONA

Bisbee
Bogatay, Todd Cunningham *architect*

Carefree
Robbins, Conrad W. *naval architect*

Paradise Valley
Blumer, Harry Maynard *architect*

Phoenix
DeBartolo, Jack, Jr. *architect*
Elmore, James Walter *architect, retired university dean*
Ham, Stephanie Ann *interior architect*
Schiffner, Charles Robert *architect*

Scottsdale
Ball, Donald Edmon *architect*
Hooker, Jo *interior designer*
Rutes, Walter Alan *architect*

Tempe
Brandt, Beverly Kay *design educator*
Cutler, Lorraine Masters *interior designer, facilities manager*
Kenyon, David Lloyd *architect, architectural firm executive*
Klien, Wolfgang Josef *architect*
Thums, Charles William *designer, consultant*

Tucson
Dinsmore, Philip Wade *architect*
Wallach, Leslie Rothaus *architect*

CALIFORNIA

Agoura
Bechelian, Lisa *interior designer*

Bakersfield
McAlister, Michael Hillis *architect*

Belvedere
Gale, Daniel Bailey *architect*

Berkeley
Brocchini, Ronald Gene *architect*
Burger, Edmund Ganes *architect*
Burk, Gary Maurice *health care facility planner*

Beverly Hills
Blakeley, James Edward, III *interior designer*

Bolinas
Carpenter, Arthur Espenet *furniture designer*

Burbank
Naidorf, Louis Murray *architect*

Burlingame
Tanzi, Carol Anne *interior designer*

Carmichael
Hummel, Fred Ernest *architect*

Chula Vista
Quisenberry, Robert Max *architect, industrial designer*

Coronado
Weiss-Cornwell, Amy *interior designer*

Costa Mesa
Renne, Janice Lynn *interior designer*

Culver City
Korney, Ellen Lemer *interior designer*
Moss, Eric Owen *architect*

Dillon Beach
Caddy, Edmund H.H., Jr. *architect*

El Cerrito
Hand, Harland Julius *garden designer, consultant, retired educator*

Encino
Rance, Quentin E. *interior designer*

Fresno
Pings, Anthony Claude *architect*
Putman, Robert Dean *golf course architect*

Glen Ellen
Rockrise, George Thomas *architect*

Glendale
Colby, Barbara Diane *interior designer, consultant*
Stanfill, Latayne Colvett *non-fiction writer*

Healdsburg
Disrud, Carol Ann *interior designer*

Huntington Beach
Lans, Carl Gustav *architect, economist*

Irvine
Dorius, Kermit Parrish *architect*
Kraemer, Kenneth Leo *architect, urban planner, educator*

La Jolla
Brandt, Maryclare *interior designer, educator*

Laguna Niguel
Robinson, Theodore Gould *golf course architect*

Los Angeles
Adams, William Wesley, III *architect*
Axon, Donald Carlton *architect*
Holzbog, Thomas Jerald *architect, planner*
Krag, Olga *interior designer*
Maltzan, Michael Thomas *architect*
Moe, Stanley Allen *architect, consultant*
Murdoch, Paul Allan *architect*
Nahmias, Victor Jay *architect*
Neutra, Dion *architect*
Phelps, Barton Chase *architect, educator*
Shinday, Manny Shrawan *architect*
Thoman, John Everett *architect, mediator*
Verger, Morris David *architect, planner*

Los Gatos
Zacher, Valerie Irene *interior designer*

Manhattan Beach
Blanton, John Arthur *architect*

Marina Del Rey
Crockett, Robert York *architect*

Mill Valley
D'Amico, Michael *architect, urban planner*

Montrose
Greenlaw, Roger Lee *interior designer*

Morgan Hill
Halopoff, William Evon *industrial designer, consultant*

Mountain View
Kobza, Dennis Jerome *architect*

Napa
Davidow, Sheldon M. *consulting firm and insurance executive*
Ianziti, Adelbert John *industrial designer*

Newport Beach
Bauer, Jay S. *architect*

Oakland
Nicol, Robert Duncan *architect*
Wolfe, Clifford Eugene *architect, writer*

Orange
Mason, Naomi Ann *interior designer*

Oxnard
O'Connell, Hugh Mellen, Jr. *retired architect*

Palm Desert
Chambers, Milton Warren *architect*

Palm Springs
Broderick, Harold Christian *interior designer*

Pasadena
Goei, Bernard Thwan-Poo (Bert Goei) *architectural and engineering firm executive*
Kohlhase, Charles Emile, Jr. *mission architect*
Thomas, Joseph Fleshman *architect*

Placerville
Eaton, Marybeth Brendon *interior designer*

Pomona
Lyle, John Tillman *landscape architecture educator*

Redondo Beach
Shellhorn, Ruth Patricia *landscape architect*

Redwood City
Morrison, Murdo Donald *architect*

Sacramento
Dahlin, Dennis John *landscape architect*
Hallenbeck, Harry C. *architect*
Lionakis, George *architect*

Muller, David Webster *architectural designer*
Wasserman, Barry L(ee) *architect*

San Diego
Holl, Walter John *architect, interior designer*
Paderewski, Clarence Joseph *architect*
Stepner, Michael Jay *architect*

San Francisco
Brown, Joseph E. *landscape architecture executive*
Budzinski, James Edward *interior designer*
Bull, Henrik Helkand *architect*
Costa, Walter Henry *architect*
Del Campo, Martin Bernardelli *architect*
Dodge, Peter Hampton *architect*
Field, John Louis *architect*
Johnson, David Mitchell *architect, artist*
Judd, Bruce Diven *architect*
Keenan, Robert *architect*
Kriken, John Lund *architect*
MacDonald, Donald William *architect*
Matas, Myra Dorothea *interior architect and designer, kitchen and bath designer*
Minar, Paul G. *design consultant*
Raeber, John Arthur *architect, construction specifier consultant*
Rockwell, Burton Lowe *architect*
Turnbull, William, Jr. *architect*
Werner, William Arno *architect*

San Jose
Tanaka, Richard Koichi, Jr. *architect, planner*

San Luis Obispo
Fraser, Bruce Douglas, Jr. *architect, artist*
Tickell, William Earl *architect, educator*

San Marcos
Eichman, Patricia *interior designer*

San Marino
Man, Lawrence Kong *architect*

San Mateo
Castleberry, Arline Alrick *architect*
Sadilek, Vladimir *architect*

San Rafael
Badgley, John Roy *architect*
Clark, Charles Sutter *interior designer*
Thompson, Peter L. H. *golf course architect*
Woodring, Margaret Daley *architect, planner*

Santa Barbara
Kruger, Kenneth Charles *architect*

Santa Clara
Dyer, Kecia Carole *interior designer*

Santa Monica
Eizenberg, Julie *architect*
Gehry, Frank Owen *architect*
Koning, Hendrik *architect*

Santa Rosa
Gilger, Paul Douglass *architect*
Sohm, Irene Maxine *interior designer*

Somerset
Setzekorn, William David *retired architect, consultant, author*

South Pasadena
Girvigian, Raymond *architect*

Tarzana
Smith, Mark Lee *architect*

Torrance
Ryniker, Bruce Walter Durland *industrial designer, manufacturing executive*

Venice
Baldon, Cleo *interior designer*

Ventura
Okuma, Albert Akira, Jr. *architect*
Ruebe, Bambi Lynn *interior, environmental designer*

Villa Park
Buffington, Linda Brice *interior designer*

Visalia
Heidbreder, Gail *architect, educator*

Walnut Creek
Kuechle, Roland Koerner *architect*

West Hollywood
Luckman, Charles *architect*

COLORADO

Aspen
Alstrom, Sven Erik *architect*
Ensign, Donald H. *landscape architect*

Aurora
Hynek, Frederick James *architect*

Boulder
Hoffman, Charles Fenno, III *architect*

Colorado Springs
Phibbs, Harry Albert *interior designer, professional speaker, lecturer*

Denver
Anderson, John David *architect*
Brownson, Jacques Calmon *architect*
Cowley, Gerald Dean *architect*
Falkenberg, William Stevens *architect, contractor*
Fuller, Robert Kenneth *architect, urban designer*
Nagel, Jerome Kaub *architect*
Sharkey, Richard David *product designer, architect, musician*

Wilk, Diane Lillian *architect, educator*
Williams, John James, Jr. *architect*

Englewood
Eccles, Matthew Alan *golf course and landscape architect*
Stead, Timothy *architect*

Grand Junction
Morris, Rusty Lee *architectural consulting firm executive*

Littleton
Williams, Sally *landscape designer*

Vail
Nelson, Nevin Mary *interior designer*
Vosbeck, Robert Randall *architect*

HAWAII

Hanalei
Schaller, Matthew Fite *architect*

Honolulu
Ayer, David Clay *architect*
Botsai, Elmer Eugene *architect, educator, former university dean*
Ferraro, Joseph James *architect*
Hamada, Duane Takumi *architect*
Vidal, Alejandro Legaspi *architect*
Wong, Choy-Ling *interior designer*

Kaneohe
Fisette, Scott Michael *golf course designer*
Jackson, Jane W. *interior designer*

IDAHO

Boise
Shneider, Jeffrey A. *architect*
Turney, Steven Craig *architect*

Sun Valley
Bryant, Woodrow Wesley *architect*
McLaughlin, James Daniel *architect*

MONTANA

Bozeman
DeHaas, John Neff, Jr. *retired architecture educator*

Great Falls
Hoiland, Andrew Calvin *architect*

Helena
Whaley, James C. *architect*

Livingston
Russell, Carina Boehm *interior designer*

NEVADA

Las Vegas
Thomas, Roger Parry *interior designer, art consultant*

NEW MEXICO

Albuquerque
Campbell, C(harles) Robert *architect*
Davis, Bruce Warren *architect*
Hakim, Besim Selim *architecture and urban design educator, researcher*
Sabatini, William Quinn *architect*
Smith, Jean *interior design firm executive*

Farmington
Freimuth, William Richard *architect*

Santa Fe
Leon, Bruno *architect, educator*

OREGON

Eugene
Matthews, Kevin Michael *architecture educator, researcher*

Grants Pass
Oliver, Leon Eugene *building and development designer, consultant*

Medford
Skelton, Douglas H. *architect*

Newport
Gordon, Walter *architect*

Portland
Hacker, Thomas Owen *architect*
Kilbourn, Lee Ferris *architect, specifications writer*
Ritz, Richard Ellison *architect, architectural historian, writer*
Scott, George Larkham, IV *architect*

Sunriver
Sawyer, Gerald *interior designer*

UTAH

Orem
Jacobson, Gordon R. *architect*

Provo
Gifford, Lisa Bonnie *interior designer*

Salt Lake City
Beall, Burtch W., Jr. *architect*

WASHINGTON

Auburn
Keimig, Alan Charles *architect*

Bellingham
Christensen, David Earl *architect*

Bothell
Browne, Gretchen Lynn *interior designer*
Sakkal, Mamoun *architect, interior designer*

Edmonds
Petersen, Aimee Bernice *interior designer, artist, landscape designer*

Everett
Arbogast, Genevieve L. *interior designer*
King, Indle Gifford *industrial designer, educator*

Gig Harbor
Flom, Robert Michael *interior designer*
Wilder, Jennifer Rose *interior designer*

Hansville
Griffin, DeWitt James *architect, real estate developer*

Kirkland
Mitchell, Joseph Patrick *architect*
Steinmann, John Colburn *architect*

Mount Vernon
Hall, David Ramsay *architect*
Klein, Henry *architect*

Ocean Shores
Morgan, Audrey *architect*

Olympia
Moffett, Frank Cardwell *architect, civil engineer, real estate developer*
Thomas-John, Yvonne Maree *artist, interior designer*

Redmond
Sowder, Robert Robertson *architect*

Renton
Brown, Shirley Kern (Peggy Brown) *interior designer*

Seattle
Buursma, William F. *architect*
Cichanski, Gerald *golf course architect*
Hastings, L(ois) Jane *architect, educator*
Jones, Johnpaul *architect*
Klontz, James Mathias *architect*
Kolb, Keith Robert *architect, educator*
Meyer, C. Richard *architect*
Miles, Don Clifford *architect*
Morse, John Moore *architect, planner*

Spokane
Stone, Michael David *landscape architect*

Tacoma
Bowman, Michael O. *interior designer*
Harris, James Martin *architect*

Underwood
Delehanty, Michael Patrick *sail designer*

Vancouver
Graffis, Julie Anne *entrepreneur, interior designer*

CANADA

ALBERTA

Edmonton
Manasc, Vivian *architect, consultant*

BRITISH COLUMBIA

Vancouver
Oberlander, Cornelia Hahn *landscape architect*
Patkau, John *architect*
Patkau, Patricia *architect, architecture educator*

SASKATCHEWAN

Saskatoon
Henry, Keith Douglas *architect*

ADDRESS UNPUBLISHED

Alexander, Christopher *architecture educator*
Bilezikjian, Edward Andrew *architect*
Blair, Frederick David *interior designer*
Carey, Audrey Lane *interior designer, motivational speaker, educator*
Chao, James Min-Tzu *architect*
Cowee, John Widmer, Jr. *architecture company executive*
Crowther, Richard Layton *architect, consultant, researcher, author, lecturer*
Deal, Lynn Hoffmann *interior designer*
Dobbel, Rodger Francis *interior designer*
Ely, Marica McCann *interior designer*
Funte-Radford, Deidrea Lea *interior designer, consultant*
Gerou, Phillip Howard *architect*
Harding, Teresa J. *interior designer*
Hooper, Roger Fellowes *architect, retired*
Jones, Jeffrey Dean *interior designer*
Lamona, Thomas Adrian *consulting engineer*
McGraw, Susan Catherine *interior designer*
Peters, Robert Woolsey *architect*

Salazar, Luis Adolfo *architect*
Sande, Barbara *interior decorating consultant*
Sullivan, Robert Scott *architect, graphic designer*
Sutton, Marcella French *interior designer*
Tomasi, Donald Charles *architect*
Wiele, Patricia Giordano *interior decorator*
Wrolstad, Helen Louise *interior designer, business owner*

ARTS: LITERARY. *See also* **COMMUNICATIONS MEDIA.**

UNITED STATES

ALASKA

Anchorage
Cowell, Fuller A. *publisher*
Molinari, Carol V. *writer, investment company executive, educator*
Strohmeyer, John *writer, former editor*
Thomas, Lowell, Jr. *author, lecturer, former lieutenant governor, former state senator*
Warden, Patricia Starratt *writer, actress, composer*

Arctic Village
Tritt, Lincoln C. *writer, educator, musician*

Fairbanks
Kremers, Carolyn Sue *writer, musician, educator*

Palmer
Grady, David P. *freelance writer, retired air force sergeant*

Tok
Blasor-Bernhardt, Donna Jo *screenwriter, poet, author, photographer*

ARIZONA

Bowie
Burke, Ruth *writer*

Camp Verde
Hilbers, Betty Gaylor *poet*

Carefree
Ripley, Robert Elliott *author, psychologist, training film producer*

Chinle
Browne, Vee F. *writer*

Flagstaff
Cline, Platt Herrick *author*

Glendale
Perkins, Wendy Frances *author, speaker*

Phoenix
Chorlton, David *writer*
Duyck, Kathleen Marie *poet, musician, retired social worker*
Ellison, Cyril Lee *literary agent, publisher*
Fontenot, Marshall Wayne *literary agent, author*
McNulty, Francis Robert *writer, graphic artist*

Portal
Williams, Jeanne *writer*

Sedona
Prather, Richard Scott *author*
Thorne, Kate Ruland *writer, publisher, editor*

Sun City West
Ault, Phillip Halliday *author, editor*

Tempe
Nolle, Richard *writer, astrological consultant*
Raby, William Louis *author*

Tucson
Elkington, Sandra Louise *writer*
Hallett, Jane Martin *writer, educator*
Hawke, Simon Nicholas *writer, educator*
Ingalls, Jeremy *poet, educator*
King, Harry Alden *author*
Leydet, François Guillaume *writer*
Warren, Bacil Benjamin *writer, publisher*

Yuma
Desmond, Leif *writer*

ARKANSAS

Fayetteville
Jones, Douglas Clyde *author*

CALIFORNIA

Antioch
Chu, Valentin Yuan-ling *author*

Apple Valley
Nolan, Ruth Marie *writer*

Arcadia
Kenvin, Roger Lee *writer, retired English educator*
Sloane, Beverly LeBov *writer, consultant*

Belmont
Hedden, Thomas Dexter *translator*
Morris, Bruce Dorian *technical writer, literary historian, educator*

Berkeley
Diamond, Sara Rose *writer, sociologist, lecturer*
Harrison, Helen Herre *writer, volunteer, advocate*
Masson, Jeffrey Moussaieff *writer*
Milosz, Czeslaw *poet, author, educator*
Mudge, Jean McClure *writer, filmmaker*
O'Brien, Mark David *poet, journalist*
Singh, Rashmi Sharma *writer*
Soto, Gary *poet, educator*
Temko, Allan Bernard *writer*
Wheeler, Helen Rippier *writer, educator, consultant*
White, Richard Weddington, Jr. *writer, editor*

Beverly Hills
Basichis, Gordon Allen *author, screenwriter*
Belknap, Maria Ann *writer*
Davenport, Robert Ralsey *writer*
McGee, Rex Alan *motion picture screenwriter*
Reiner, Annie *writer, psychotherapist*
Silverman, Treva *writer, producer, consultant*

Bishop
Kelley, William *author, screenwriter*

Camarillo
Alexander, John Charles *editor, writer*
Stewart, Sharon Diane *writer*

Canoga Park
Alexander, Sue *writer*
McAuley, Milton Kenneth *author, book publisher*

Carlsbad
Johnson, Carolyn Everall *poet, secondary school educator*

Carmel
Shapiro, Stephen George *screenwriter, photographer*
Wolf, Dorothy Joan *poet*

Carmichael
Goodin, Evelyn Marie *writer*

Carson
Davidson, Mark *writer, educator*

Chico
Dorman, N.B. *writer*

Chino Hills
Sanders, Nancy Ida *writer*

Chula Vista
Trujillo, Teófilo-Carlos *writer, publisher, history educator*

Claremont
Dolence, Michael G. *writer, consultant, educator*
Tilden, Wesley Roderick *author, retired computer programmer*
Wachtel, Albert *writer, educator*

Concord
Albrecht, Donna G. *author*

Corte Madera
Long, Theodore Dixon *writer, investor*

Costa Mesa
Black, Alan *author*
White, Kenton Stowell *writer, publisher*

Covina
More, Blake *writer, poet*
Phillips, Jill Meta *novelist, critic, astrologer*

Cromberg
Kolb, Ken Lloyd *writer*

Culver City
Binder, Bettye B. *author, lecturer*

Cupertino
Zobel, Louise Purwin *author, educator, lecturer, writing consultant*

Cypress
Edmonds, Ivy Gordon *writer*

Del Mar
Smith, Robert Hamil *author, fund raiser*

Duncans Mills
Schuett, Stacey Lynn *writer, illustrator*

El Cerrito
Wolinsky, Richard Barry *writer*

El Segundo
Halloran, James Vincent, III *technical writer*

Escondido
Aplon, Roger Laurence *poet*

Felton
McMillan, Joan *poet*

Fresno
Petrochilos, Elizabeth A. *writer, publisher*
Wayne, Kyra Petrovskaya *writer*

Fullerton
Conway, James F. *writer, counselor, minister*

Georgetown
Lengyel, Cornel Adam (Cornel Adam) *author*

Gualala
Alinder, Mary Street *writer, lecturer*

Hesperia
Du Lac, Lois Arline *writer*

Hillsborough
Atwood, Mary Sanford *writer*

Hollywood
Shurtleff, C. Michael *writer*

Idyllwild
Schneider, Paul *writer, retired*

Irvine
Brueske, Charlotte *poet, composer*
Marx, Wesley *writer, environmental educator*
Ryan, Allyn Cauagas *author, educator*

Kensington
Nathan, Leonard Edward *writer, educator*

La Jolla
Freilicher, Melvyn Stanley *writer, educator*
Havis, Allan Stuart *playwright, theatre educator*

Lake Forest
McPeak, William John *science and technical author, consultant*
Stern, Matthew Arnold *technical writer*

Landers
Landers, Vernette Trosper *writer, educator, association executive*

Lodi
Schulz, Laura Janet *retired writer, secretary*

Long Beach
Datsko, Tina Michelle *writer, producer*
Dawson, Frances Emily *poet, nurse*

Los Angeles
Allen, Miriam Marx *writer*
Bayless, Raymond *writer, artist, parapsychologist*
Carlip, Hillary *author, screenwriter*
Chetwynd, Lionel *screenwriter, producer, director*
Engelbach, David Charles *scriptwriter, television producer*
Good, Edith Elissa *writer*
Hotz, Robert Lee *science writer, editor*
Kenner, Ronald W. *writer, editor*
Kraft, Scott Wallace *writer, actor*
Larbalestrier, Deborah Elizabeth *writer*
Maicor, Linda A. *writer, researcher*
Messerli, Douglas *author, publisher*
Mooser, Stephen *author*
Patterson, Agnes Stark *author*
Rhoads, Rick *writer, editor*
Steinbrecher, Edwin Charles *writer, film executive producer*
Thomas, Shirley *author, educator, business executive*

Malibu
McCall, Elizabeth Kaye *columnist, consultant*

Mendocino
Shep, Robert Lee *editor, publisher, textile book researcher*

Menlo Park
Dorset, Phyllis Flanders *technical writer, editor*
Phillips, Jeffrey Richard *magazine writer*

Mill Valley
Haspiel, George Sidney *writer, illustrator*
Swan, James Albert *environmental psychologist, writer, actor*

Moreno Valley
Wilson, Robert Michael Alan *writer*

Newcastle
Madril, Lee Ann *writer*

Newport Beach
Burke, Doug *author, inventor*

North Hollywood
Kuter, Kay E. *writer, actor*

Oakland
Berlak, Harold *writer, educator, consultant*
Grzanka, Leonard Gerald *writer, consultant*
Narell, Irena *freelance writer, history educator*
Solomon, Norman *author, columnist*

Oceanside
Bengelsdorf, Irving Swem *science writer, consultant*
Humphrey, Phyllis A. *writer*

Ojai
Weyl, Nathaniel *writer*

Orange
DeCarlo, Angela Rocco *writer, journalist*
Lindskoog, Kathryn Ann *writer, educator*

Orinda
Berens, E. Ann *writer, mental health and youth advocate*

Pacific Grove
O'Shaughnessy, Ellen Cassels *writer*

Palm Springs
Jamison, Warren *writer, lecturer, publisher, literary agent*
Racina, Thom (Thomas Frank Raucina) *television writer, editor*
Shaeffer, Claire Brightwell *writer, educator*

Palo Alto
Drexler, Kim Eric *researcher, author*
Shoemaker, Dorothy Hays *technical writer*
Wachtel, Alan Larry *writer, transportation consultant*
Winslow, Wardell V. *writer, editor*

Palomar Mountain
Day, Richard Somers *author, editorial consultant, video producer*

Palos Verdes Peninsula
Stockwell, Shelley Lessin *writer, hypnotherapist, television personality*

Pasadena
Alwan, Ameen *writing educator*
Arrieta, Marcia *poet, editor, publishing executive, educator*
Holbrook, Sally Davis *author*
Rasmussen, R. Kent *writer*

Penngrove
Chadwick, Cydney Marie *writer, art projects executive*

Petaluma
Pronzini, Bill John (William Pronzini) *author*

Poway
Wirt, Sherwood Eliot *writer, minister*

Rancho Mirage
Olderman, Murray *columnist, cartoonist*

Rancho Palos Verdes
Kent, Lisa *writer*

Rancho Santa Fe
Simon, William Leonard *film and television writer and producer, author*
Sommer-Bodenburg, Angela *author, artist*

Riverside
Simon, Maurya *poet, educator*

Rohnert Park
Haslam, Gerald William *writer, educator*

Sacramento
Blackwell, Charles Curtis *writer, visual artist*
Foley, Louise Munro *writer*
Hauck, Dennis William *writer*

Salinas
Canada, Stephen Andrew *writer*

San Anselmo
Torbet, Laura *author, artist, graphic designer*

San Bernardino
Brown, James Michael *writer, educator*
Hansen, Anne Katherine *poet, retired elementary education educator*

San Diego
Broening, Elise Hedwig *writer*
Hart, Anne *author*
Koski, Donna Faith *poet*
March, Marion D. *writer, astrologer, consultant*
Prescott, Lawrence Malcolm *medical and health science writer*
Self, Susan Carolyn *technical writer*
Skwara, Erich Wolfgang *novelist, poet, educator, literary critic*
Yarber, Robert Earl *writer, retired educator*

San Francisco
Allen, Bruce John *writer, activist*
Anderson, Walter Truett *author*
Boutilier, Nancy W. *writer, secondary English educator*
Bowman, Alison Frances *writer*
Chadwick, Whitney *writer, art historian, educator*
Corkery, Paul Jerome *author, editor*
Cousineau, Philip Robert *writer, filmmaker*
Ferris, Russell James, II *freelance writer*
Field, Carol Hart *writer, journalist, foreign correspondent*
Graham, Toni *writer*
Hopkins, Lee Wallace *writer*
Krasney, Martin *writer, organization executive, educator*
Livingston, Myran Jay *film writer, film director, film producer*
Lustgarten, Celia Sophie *freelance consultant, writer*
Montney, Marvin Richard *writer, poet, playwright*
O'Connor, Sheila Anne *freelance writer*
Pantaleo, Jack *playwright, composer, social worker*
Paul, Don *writer, musician*
Polanco, Rosana Lim *grant writer*
Quick, William Thomas *author, consultant*
Reinhardt, Richard Warren *writer*
Shepard, Robert Ethan *literary agent*
Taylor, Sabrena Ann *author, visual artist*
Wayburn, Peggy (Cornelia Elliott Wayburn) *author, editor*

San Jose
Fitzgerald, Tim K. *writer*
Loventhal, Milton *writer, playwright, lyricist*
Rosemire, Adeline Louise *writer, publisher*
Scharlach, Bernice Sherman *writer, lecturer*

San Luis Obispo
Bunge, Russell Kenneth *writer, poet, editor*
Sachs, Robert Michael *author*

San Luis Rey
Williams, Elizabeth Yahn *author, lecturer, lawyer*

San Marcos
Sauer, David Andrew *writer, computer consultant*

San Mateo
Hearle, Kevin James *poet, educator*
Korn, Walter *writer*

San Rafael
Henry, Marie Elaine *poet*
Turner, William Weyand *author*

Santa Ana
Hanson, Bonnie Blanche *author, artist*
Paul, Florence Joseph *writer*

Santa Barbara
Bock, Russell Samuel *author*
Branch, Taylor *writer*
Carrel, Annette Felder *writer*
Easton, Robert (Olney) *author, environmentalist*
Gibbs, Wolcott, Jr. *writer, editor*
Jackson, Beverley Joy Jacobson *columnist, lecturer*

Santa Clara
Simmons, Janet Bryant *writer, publisher*

Santa Cruz
Sward, Robert Stuart *author*
Wilson, Carter *writer, educator*

Santa Monica
Casty, Alan Howard *author, retired humanities educator*
Courtney, Mary E. *writer, editor*
Halliwell, Betty Mary *writer*

Santa Rosa
Frazer, Lance William *writer*

Santa Ynez
Walker, Burton Leith *engineering writer, psychotherapist*

Sausalito
Follett, Carolyn Brown *poet, artist*

Sherman Oaks
MacMullen, Douglas Burgoyne *writer, editor, retired army officer, publisher*
Schilling, Vivian *novelist, screenwriter and actress*

Simi Valley
Bolton, Martha O. *writer*

Sonoma
Delaplane, Susan Aven *writer, poet*

South Pasadena
White, W. Robin *author*

Studio City
Whitney, Steven *writer, producer*

Sun Valley
Casey, Paul Arnold *writer, composer, photographer*

Sunnyvale
Yep, Laurence Michael *author*

Topanga
Grossman, Arnold Joseph *writer, producer*
Kelly, Beth *writer, songwriter*

Tracy
Smith, Heather Kay *freelance writer*

Turlock
Schmidt, Arnold Anthony *writer*

Universal City
Chang, Cindy *writer*

Valencia
Meeks, Christopher Nelson *writer*

Van Nuys
Coen, Dana *playwright, TV and film scriptwriter*
Fanning, Don Brian *poet, computer services consultant*
Mahon, Tom *novelist, insurance analyst*

Venice
Padilla, Mario René *literature educator, writer, actor*

Ventura
Barrett, Ethel *juvenile fiction writer*
King, Elizabeth Ann *writer*

Victorville
Bowers, Bonnie Jean *writer*

Vista
Beversdorf, Anne Elizabeth *author, astrologer, educator*

Walnut Creek
Pollock, Robert A. *author*
Ruppenthal, Karl M. *author, educator*

West Covina
Menefee, Gerald Robert *writer, management consultant*

West Hills
Katz, Illana Paulette *writer*

Westminster
Amato, Carol Joy *writer, anthropologist*

Whittier
Caro, Evelyn Inga Rouse *writer*

Yucca Valley
Van Hise, James Nicholas *writer, editor*

COLORADO

Aurora
Bower, Donald Edward *author*

Boulder
Dorn, Edward Merton *poet, educator*
Jason, Debra Ann *copywriter*
Martinez, Jose Rafael *writer, educator*
Moore, George Barnard *poet, educator*

Colorado Springs
Ball, Jennifer Leigh *writer, editor*
Golden, Donald Michael *writer, inventor*
Hicks, David Earl *author, inventor*
Leasure, Robert Ellis *writer, photographer*
Rhodes, Daisy Chun *writer, researcher*
Vosevich, Kathi Ann *technical writer and editor, scholar*
Whalin, W. Terry *author, editor*
Yaffe, James *author*

Conifer
Kalla, Alec Karl *writer, rancher*

Denver
Delffs, Dudley J. *writer, educator*
Dyman, Jenni L. *author*
Hagman, Jean Cassels *museum publisher, writer*
Kasper, Catherine Louise *poet, editor*
Mead, Beverly Mirium Anderson *author, educator*
Sheldon Epstein, Vivian *author, publisher*

Estes Park
Williams, Beryle Lou *writer, photographer*

Fort Collins
Mark, Maxine Catherine Schlieker *writer*

Glade Park
Tipton, James Sherwood *poet, beekeeper*

Golden
Eber, Kevin *science writer*

Ignacio
Mattey, Angela Marie *author, psychic, educator*

Louisville
Dumke, Nicolette Marie *author, food allergy consultant*
Roth-Nelson, Stephanie Faye *technical writer, trainer*

Pueblo
Sidebottom, David Kirk *writer, former engineer*

Salida
Quillen, Edward Kenneth, III *freelance writer, columnist*

Trinidad
Tamez, Lorraine Diane *writer, nurse*

Vail
Knight, Constance Bracken *writer, realtor, corporate executive*

DISTRICT OF COLUMBIA

Washington
Cavnar, Samuel Melmon *author, publisher, activist*

HAWAII

Hilo
Tummons, Lois Patricia *writer, editor*

Honolulu
Arbeit, Wendy Sue *writer*

Kaneohe
Shiroma, Gladys Akiko *children's book author, retired educator*

Lanai City
Black, Anderson Duane *writer, business consultant*

Puunene
Santos, Barbara Ann *writer, public relations executive*

IDAHO

Boise
Jones, Josephine A. *poet*
Russell, Carl Lloyd *technical writer*
Sadler, Norma J. *educator, writer*
Weinstein, Norman Charles *writer*
Woodward, Tim Joseph *journalist*

Wilder
Olsen, Helen May *author*

MASSACHUSETTS

Boston
Headding, Lillian Susan (Sally Headding) *writer, forensic clairvoyant*

MONTANA

Billings
Scherer, Bonnie Lou *writer*

Great Falls
Rimel, Linda June *writer*

Hamilton
Monday, Mark James Albert *author*

Kalispell
Coleman, J.D. *author*

Livingston
Clarke, Urana *writer, musician, educator*

Mc Leod
Hjortsberg, William Reinhold *author*

NEVADA

Henderson
Brown, David Gerard *author, actor, air trafic controller*
Ruettiger, Daniel Eugene (Rudy Ruettiger) *author, speaker*

Las Vegas
Caro, Mike *writer, editor, publisher*

Eikenberry, Arthur Raymond *writer, service executive, researcher*
King, Gary Curtis *author, lecturer*
Latimer, Heather *writer*
Palmer, Lynne *writer, astrologer*

Reno
Stratton, Bruce Cornwall *writer, landscape photographer, publisher*

Sparks
Grady, Sean Michael *writer*

NEW JERSEY

Manahawkin
Aurner, Robert Ray *author, corporate executive*

NEW MEXICO

Albuquerque
Durant, Penny Lynne Raife *author, educator*
Giles, Jana Maria *writer, editor*
Grammer, Maurine Parker *educator, writer, appraiser*
Gregory, George Ann *writer, Native American education consultant*
Miller, Michael *literary arts researcher, writer*
Moore, Todd Allen *poet*
Morris, David Brown *writer*
Pflock, Karl Tomlinson *writer, researcher*
Whiddon, Carol Price *writer, editor, consultant*
Whimbey, Arthur Emil *writer*
Zieve, Sherrie Lee *writer, realtor*

Aztec
Kent, Mollie *writer, publishing executive, editor*

Clovis
True, Dan James *writer, photographer*

Corrales
Page, Jake (James K. Page, Jr.) *writer, editor*

Deming
Carson, Harry Glenn, II *writer, editor, retired educator*

Espanola
Shymkus, Harold *author*

Las Cruces
Medoff, Mark Howard *playwright, screenwriter, novelist*
Seton, Julie Anne *technical writer*

Peralta
Glass, Timothy Faron Kit *writer, screenwriter, small business owner*

Ranchos De Taos
Dickey, Robert Preston *author, educator, poet*
Lackey, Marcia Ann *writer*

Santa Fe
Bergé, Carol *author*
Berne, Stanley *author*
Cast, Patricia Wynne *writer, former nun, executive secretary*
Ensana, Joel Anthony *writer*
Gallenkamp, Charles *writer*
Gildzen, Alex *writer*
Hanson, Cappy Love *writer, musician, singer, composer*
Harter, Penny *poet, English educator*
Hice, Michael *editor, marketing professional*
Knight, Carol Bell *author, lecturer, clergyperson*
Lamb, Elizabeth Searle *freelance writer, poet*
Tarn, Nathaniel *poet, translator, educator*
Vernon, Gayle (Lumari) *psychic consultant, author, publisher*
Wood, Nancy C. *author*

Taos
Hemp, Christine Elizabeth *poet, educator*
Spring-Moore, Michele Lea *poet*

NEW YORK

New York
Burland, Brian Berkeley *novelist, poet, painter, scenarist*
Kluger, Steve *writer, scriptwriter*
Nicosia, Gerald Martin *author, freelance writer*
Salter, James *writer*

Sunnyside
Wallmann, Jeffrey Miner *author*

OREGON

Applegate
Pursglove, Laurence A. *technical writer, computer quality tester*

Ashland
Jackson, Elizabeth Riddle *writer, translator, educator*

Boring
Gentry, Jeanne Louise *lecturer, writer*

Cave Junction
Karczewski, Raymond Ronald *writer, philosopher*

Coos Bay
Reynolds, David Kent *writer, educator*

Eugene
Ailor, Karen Tana *marketing writer, proposal consultant*
Allen, Gloria Lindsay *interpreter, translator, publisher*

Kannenberg, Ida Marguerite *writer*

Grants Pass
Clinton, Robert Emmett (Fritter Clinton) *writer*
Stafford, Patrick Purcell *poet, writer, management consultant*

Gresham
Larson, Elsie J. *writer*

Hillsboro
Cornish, Linda Sowa Young *children's books author and illustrator, educator*

Newberg
Herman, George Adam *writer*

Newport
Kennedy, Richard Jerome *writer*

Otis
King, Frank William *writer*

Pleasant Hill
Kesey, Ken *writer*

Portland
Castro, Diana Maria *writer*
DePrez, Daniel Robert *writer*
Hillis, Rick *writer, educator*
Larson, Wanda Z(ackovich) *writer, poet*
Milholland, David Marion *writer, editor*
Tuska, Jon *author, publisher*
Westin, Helen Tilda *writer, songwriter*

Roseburg
Cox, Clarice R. *writer*

Salem
Eriksen, Kent Roger *author, inventor*
Marsh, Katherine Cynthia *writer, journalist, poet*

Springfield
Kelso, Mary Jean *author*

Tillamook
Griffin, Dorsey *author*

TEXAS

Dallas
Phillips, Betty Lou (Elizabeth Louise Phillips) *author, interior designer*

UTAH

Provo
Hart, Edward LeRoy *poet, educator*

Salt Lake City
Becher, Stuart Lorenz *writer, planetarium show producer*
Bowes, Florence (Mrs. William David Bowes) *writer*
Ghiselin, Brewster *author, English language educator emeritus*
Hall, Charles McAllister *writer*
Lee, Bellavance *writer, publishing executive*

Springville
Hickman, Craig Ronald *author*

WASHINGTON

Bellevue
Dickerson, Eugenie Ann *writer, journalist*
Habbestad, Kathryn Louise *writer*

Bellingham
Skinner, Knute Rumsey *poet, English educator*

Bremerton
Hanf, James Alphonso *poet, government official*

Ellensburg
Bowen, Byron Rolland *writer, educator*
Paul, Virginia O. *writer, administrator*

Federal Way
Scott, Otto *writer*
Sonnenfeld, Sandi *writer*

Goldendale
Holmes, Dorothy Sparhawk *writer, retired nurse*

Issaquah
Trask, Robert Chauncey Riley *author, lecturer, foundation executive*

Kent
Raymond, Eugene Thomas *technical writer, retired aircraft engineer*

Lynnwood
Bear, Gregory Dale *writer, illustrator*

Manson
Hackenmiller, Thomas Raymond *writer, publisher*

Medina
Wong, Janet Siu *writer*

Mercer Island
Porad, Francine Joy *poet, painter*

Normandy Park
Clifford, Walter Howard *TV production consultant, author*

Oysterville
Holoway, Susan E. *writer*

Port Angeles
Volenski, Anthony Alexander *poet*

Redmond
Thompson, Joyce Marie *writer*

Seattle
Barkey, Brenda *technical writer, publications manager*
Kunkel, Georgie Myrtia *writer, retired school counselor*
Loeb, Paul Rogat *writer, lecturer*
O'Mahony, Timothy Kieran *writer*
Robb, Candace *novelist*
Sonenberg, Maya *writer, educator*
Sprague, Dale Joseph *writer*
Wason, Betty (Elizabeth Wason) *author*

Spokane
Smith, Lester LeRoy *poet*

Tacoma
Douglas, Robert Owen *writer*
Marre, Diana Katherine *author, theater educator*

Walla Walla
Zipf, Teri M. *poet, medical librarian, researcher*

WYOMING

Casper
Gunderson, Mary Alice *writer, educator*

Jackson
Thomasma, Kenneth Ray *author, storyteller*

Laramie
Boresi, Arthur Peter *author, educator*

Moose
Schreier, Carl Alan *writer, publisher*

MEXICO

Mexico City
Mansell, Catherine *writer, editor, economist*

ADDRESS UNPUBLISHED

Alkana, Louis David *writer, editor*
Askew, Dennis Lee *poet*
Baird, Alan C. *screenwriter*
Baker, Lucinda *novelist, short story writer*
Barnes, Joanna *author, actress*
Bassman, Theda Rita *writer*
Blair, Sandy Jean *author, publisher*
Bourrie, Sally Ruth *writer*
Buckstein, Caryl Sue *writer*
Campbell, Addison James, Jr. *writer*
Char, Carlene *writer, publisher, editor*
Christina, Greta *book and film critic, writer, editor*
Claes, Gayla Christine *writer, editorial consultant*
Cobb, Sharon Yvonne *screenwriter*
Codye, Corinn *writer, editor*
Cogan, Karen Elizabeth *author, educator*
Collins, Jenni Jean *writer*
Cook, Gloria Jean *writer*
Cossitt, Helen *poet*
Crisman Carlson, Ruth Marie *writer*
Curtiss, A.B. *writer*
Davidson, Idelle *writer*
Delaney, DJ *freelance writer, clergywoman*
Dighton, Stephen Dorian *writer, retired nurse*
Druffel, Ann Bernice *researcher, writer*
Elfman, Eric *writer*
Elliott, Corinne Adelaide *retired copywriter*
Exton, Inez Pauline *writer, apparel designer*
Ford, Victoria *author, educator*
Fritz, Ethel Mae Hendrickson *writer*
Fuchs, Thomas *writer*
Grant, John Barnard *writer*
Green, Joey *writer*
Gross, Catherine Mary (Kate Gross) *writer, educator*
Hall, Liza Forster *writer, artist*
Hamit, Francis Granger *freelance writer*
Hardy, Bridget McColl *screenwriter*
Harshman, Virginia Robinson *writer, historical researcher*
Heim, Victoria Lynne *writer*
Herbert, Mary Katherine Atwell *freelance writer*
Hessler, Douglas Scott *screenwriter*
Hughes, Marvis Jocelyn *poet, photographer*
Hummer-Sharpe, Elizabeth Anastasia *genealogist, writer*
Humphries, Stephen Edward *writer*
Isbell, Harold M(ax) *writer, investor*
Jacobs, Wilbur Ripley *writer, history educator*
Janos, Leo Herbert *writer*
Jenks, Tom *writer*
Kass, Jerome Allan *writer*
Katzen, Mollie *writer, artist*
Kearse, David Grier *stage and screen writer, journalist*
Kellerman, Faye Marder *novelist, dentist*
Kessler, Stephen James *writer, editor*
Kimbrell, Grady Ned *author, educator*
Krouse, Erika Dawn *technical writer*
Kyd, Marilyn Gratton *writer, editor*
Lambert, William Jesse, III *writer*
Lane, Linda Patricia *scriptwriter*
Lawrence, Jerome *playwright, director, educator*
Lenard, Lisa H. *writer, educator*
Levine, Philip *poet, educator*
Lightwood, Carol Wilson *writer*
Livo, Norma Joan *writer*
Lloyd, David Nigel *song writer, poet, performer*
London, Adele *poet*
Luhn, Robert Kent *writer, magazine editor*
Madsen, Susan Arrington *writer*
McDade, Donna Marie *writer*
McMillan, Terry L. *writer, educator*
Mitchell, Laura Remson *public policy analyst, writer*
Morang, Diane Judy *writer, television producer, business entrepreneur*
Morris, Richard Ward *author*
Morse, Flo *writer*
Oates, Catherine Anne *writer, editor*
Orenstein, Peggy Jo *writer, editor*

Ossana, Diana Lynn *screenwriter, author*
Overby, Paul *writer, political analyst*
Paul, Paula Griffith *writer*
Peters, Barbara Humbird *writer, editor*
Prescott, Richard Chambers *writer*
Price, Lew Paxton *writer, engineer*
Rider, Fae B. *writer*
Rising, Catharine Clarke *author*
Rogers, Michael Alan *writer*
Romans, Elizabeth Anne *writer, artist*
Rosenberg, Jane *author, illustrator*
Ross, Jonathan *director, writer, producer*
Sarana, Shiree *writer*
Schenkkan, Robert Frederic *writer, actor*
Schuck, Joyce Haber *author*
Sears, Steven Lee *screenwriter, consultant*
Sharpe, Wenonah Finch *writer, educator, editor*
Shore, David Lincoln *author*
Simmons, Ted Conrad *writer*
Snow, Marina Sexton *author*
Soland, Lisa Ann (Elizabeth Soland) *playwright, actress*
Soler, Dona Katherine *poet, artist, educator, metaphysical counselor, researcher, writer, political activist*
Solomon, Dorothy Jeanne Allred *writer, communications executive*
Spada, James *author, publisher*
Spiegel, Marcia Cohn *writer*
Spies, Karen Bornemann *writer, education consultant*
Stano, Mary Gerardine *writer, tax accountant*
Steelsmith, Mary Joanne *playwright, actress*
Stone, Arlene *writer*
Stone, Sandra *writer, artist*
Stonecypher, David Daniel *writer, retired psychiatrist and ophthalmologist*
Storey, Isabel Nagy *writer, television producer*
Tobias, Sheila *writer, educator*
Ulam, Françoise *retired freelance writer, editor*
Whelchel, Sandra Jane *writer*
Wilson, Brandon Laine *writer, advertising and public relations consultant, explorer*
Winnick, Karen B. *writer*
Wolverton, Terry L(ynn) *writer, consultant*
Wong, Fay Shien *writer*
Woods, (Mary) Annie *writer, educator*

ARTS: PERFORMING

UNITED STATES

ALASKA

Indian
Wright, Gordon Brooks *musician, conductor, educator*

ARIZONA

Flagstaff
Aurand, Charles Henry, Jr. *music educator*
Lev, Leora *cinema educator, arts journalist*

Glendale
Neff, John *recording engineer, producer*
Reed, Lynda Bernal *video producer, writer*

Mesa
Mason, Marshall W. *theater director*

Phoenix
Aschaffenburg, Walter Eugene *composer, music educator*
Cohen, Warren *musician, writer*
Nijinsky, Tamara *actress, puppeteer, author, librarian, educator*
Shaw, Lillie Marie King *vocalist*
Uthoff, Michael *dancer, choreographer, artistic director*

Scottsdale
Pizzuto, Michael Julian *pianist, entertainer*
Whittaker, Sue McGhee *music educator, pianist*
Wolfgang, Bonnie Arlene *musician, bassoonist*

Sedona
Gregory, James *actor*
Griffin, (Alva) Jean *entertainer*

Sun City
Yestadt, James Francis *music director, conductor*

Teec Nos Pos
Smith, Mark Edward *music educator*

Tempe
Lombardi, Eugene Patsy *orchestra conductor, violinist, educator, recording artist*
Reber, William Francis *music educator, conductor*
Saldaña, Johnny *theater educator, researcher*

Tucson
Armstrong, R(obert) Dean *entertainer*
Brault, Margueritte Bryan *theatre organization administrator*
Cook, Gary Dennis *music educator, administrator*
Hanson, George *music director, conductor*
Malmgren, René Louise *educational theater administrator*
Puente, Tito Anthony *orchestra leader, composer, arranger*
Roe, Charles Richard *baritone*
Seaman, Arlene Anna *musician, educator*
Severinsen, Doc (Carl H. Severinsen) *conductor, musician*

CALIFORNIA

Antioch
Adams, Liliana Osses *music performer, harpist*

Apple Valley
Beller, Gerald Stephen *professional magician, former insurance company executive*

Aptos
Penny, Steve *media producer, speaker*
Swenson, Kathleen Susan *music and art educator*

Bakersfield
Mason, Jeffrey Daniel *theater educator*

Balboa
Cole, Verla Faye *music educator*

Benicia
Allen, Rick (Frederick Allen Klycinski) *magician, advertising and publicity consultant*
Cummings, Barton *musician*

Berkeley
Adams, Julian *writer, retired educator*
Kleiman, Vivian Abbe *filmmaker*

Beverly Hills
Becks, Ronald Arthur *film producer*
Brokaw, Norman Robert *talent agency executive*
Chritton, George A. *film producer*
Farley, Bill Thomas *entertainment industry executive*
Foch, Nina *actress, creative consultant, educator, director*
Foster, Lawrence *concert and opera conductor*
Fradis, Anatoly Adolf *film producer*
Greenberg, Barry Michael *talent executive*
Griffin, Merv Edward *former entertainer, television producer, entrepreneur*
Harvey, Simon *actor, writer*
Jordan, Glenn *director*
Kantor, Igo *film and television producer*
Khaiat, Laurent E. *producer, films*
Kravitz, Lenny *singer, guitarist*
Linkletter, Arthur Gordon *radio and television broadcaster*
Lynn, Jonathan Adam *director, writer, actor*
Martinson, Constance Frye *television program hostess, producer*
Matovich, Mitchel Joseph, Jr. *motion picture producer, executive*
Mischer, Donald Leo *television director and producer*
Nichols, Mike *stage and film director*
Rafkin, Alan *television and film director*
Turturro, John *actor*
Uffner, Beth M. *television and film agent*
Uzielli, Alessandro Ford *movie producer*
Vintas, Gustav *actor, psychiatrist*
White, Betty *actress, comedienne*

Burbank
Berg, Dave *television producer, writer*
Ernst, Donald William *producer*
Ett, Alan Paul *composer*
Glenn, Jonathan Philip *post production producer, editor, consultant*
McGee, Anastasia Guiniviere *visual effects coordinator*
Sprosty, Joseph Patrick *weapons specialist, producer, writer, consultant*
Tatum, Thomas Deskins *film and television producer, director*

Calabasas
Albrecht, Joie *television and film producer, director, writer*

Carmel
Suttle, Clark *performing company executive*

Chico
Pate, Susan Lee Hargrave *theater arts educator, choreographer*

City Of Commerce
DeLorenzo, George Oliver *production company executive, artist, writer, publisher*

Claremont
Baker, Israel *musician, music educator*
Doty, Horace Jay, Jr. *theater administrator, arts consultant*

Costa Mesa
Craft, Brian Thomas *stand-up comedian, embetterment consultant*

Culver City
Stark, Ray *motion picture producer*

Del Mar
Curl, James Michael *special events producer, manager*

Encinitas
McNeil, Dee Dee *singer, songwriter*

Escondido
Freedman, Robert Allen *arts executive*

Fremont
Powell, Steven Donald *carpenter, inventor*

Fresno
Harvey, Raymond Curtis *conductor*
Speace, Oscar Kimbrough *television producer and director, writer*

Fullerton
Linahon, James Joseph *music educator, musician*
Stedman, William Preston *music educator*

Glendale
Grillo, Leo *actor, photographer, animal rescuer*
Rabe, Elizabeth Rozina *hair stylist, horse breeder*

Glendora
Peters, Joseph Donald *filmmaker*

Hemet
Bible, Frances Lillian *mezzo-soprano, educator*
White, Michael Lee *executive producer, writer*

Hidden Hills
Andrews, Ralph Herrick *television producer*

Hollywood
Levy, Dena Christine *television producer, director*
Schwartz, Harriette Jeanne *television operations company executive*

Irvine
Murata, Margaret Kimiko *music educator*
Ruyter, Nancy Lee Chalfa *dance educator*

Joshua Tree
Styles, Beverly *entertainer*

La Crescenta
James, Mark William *camera operator*

La Jolla
Corrigan, Mary Kathryn *theater educator*
Gall, Sally Moore *librettist, poet, scholar*
Reynolds, Roger Lee *composer*

Lake Hughes
La Mont-Wells, Tawana Faye *camera operator, video director*

Lakewood
Robbins, Daniel Charles *music educator*

Littlerock
Caston, Jonathon Craig *talk radio producer, engineer*

Long Beach
Wilcox, David Cornell *ballet company director*

Los Angeles
Autry, Gene (Orvon Gene Autry) *actor, entertainer, broadcasting executive, baseball team executive*
Banner, Bob *television producer, director*
Barker, Robert William *television personality*
Barkin, Elaine Radoff *composer, music educator*
Bell, Lee Phillip *television personality, television producer*
Benson, Francis M. *production engineer, radio producer*
Bezemer, Cal Gene *composer*
Bialosky, Marshall Howard *composer*
Blankenburg, Heinz Horst *vocalist, director*
Brosnan, Peter Lawrence *documentary filmmaker*
Burrows, James *television and motion picture director, producer*
Busch, Anita M. *journalist*
Bymel, Suzan Yvette *talent manager, film producer*
Caffey, H. David *music educator*
Calman, Craig David *writer, actor, director*
Carnicke, Sharon Marie *drama educator, theatre specialist and director*
Carr, Adrian Walter *film director, editor*
Conner, Lindsay Andrew *screenwriter, producer*
Davidson, Gordon *theatrical producer, director*
Dumas, William Joseph *filmmaker*
DuMont, James Kelton, Jr. *actor, producer*
Fleischmann, Ernest Martin *music administrator*
Glick, Samuel David *entertainment and communications executive, shop owner*
Goussé, Maggie *actress*
Halpern, Leon (Hal Perrin) *composer*
Healy, Kieran John Patrick *lighting designer, consultant*
Hemion, Dwight Arlington *television producer, director*
Hemmings, Peter William *orchestra and opera administrator*
Hicklin, Ronald Lee *music production company executive*
Hiller, Arthur *motion picture director*
Howe, John Thomas *film director, educator*
Hunt, Peter Roger *film director, writer, editor*
Jackson, Isaiah *conductor*
Kahan, Sheldon Jeremiah *musician, singer*
Kaplan, Martin Harold *writer, producer*
Klauss, Kenneth Karl *composer, educator*
Lew, Joycelyne Mae *actress*
Lewitzky, Bella *choreographer*
London, Andrew Barry *film editor*
Maldonado, Gregory Matthew *music director, educator*
Manwiller, Debi *casting director*
Mc Coy, Frank Milton *concert pianist, educator, lecturer*
Michelson, Sonia *music educator, author*
Quinn, Maura Kathleen *television producer*
Reale, Paul Vincent *composer, music educator*
Richmond, Rocsan *television and video producer, director, publicist, actress, inventor*
Salzman, David Elliot *entertainment industry executive*
Saphier, Peter F. *film producer*
Schock, Anthony *entertainment executive*
Schwartzman, Arnold Martin *film director, graphic designer*
Sherman, Eric *director, writer, educator*
Smight, Alec Dow *film editor, consultant*
Stanfill, Shelton G. *performing arts administrator*
Steel, Dawn *motion picture producer*
Stevenson, Robert Murrell *music educator*
Strader, James Harlow, IV *entertainment executive, financial consultant*
Termini, Olga Ascher *music educator*
VanDevere, Christian *fashion model, writer*
Warner, Paul Wellman *film and theater director, educator*
Williamson, Edwin Lee *wardrobe and costume consultant*
Woessner, Frederick T. *composer, pianist*

Malibu
Georgopoulos, Dean Elias *film producer, real estate developer*
Page, Richard Edward *entertainment company executive, business owner*

Marina Del Rey
Bergmann, Peter Jay *television director and producer, educator*
Chomsky, Marvin J. *director*
Webb, Roy *television producer, writer*

Menlo Park
Baez, Joan Chandos *folk singer*

Monrovia
Del Vecchio, Dawn Marie *theater manager*

Montrose
Twitchell, Theodore Grant *music educator and composer*

Mountain Center
De Forest, Edgar Lester *actor, poet, educator*

Newport Beach
Cano, Larry Raymond *film maker*

North Hollywood
Balmuth, Bernard Allen *retired film editor*
Epcar, Richard Michael *actor, writer, director*
Levin, Alvin Irving *composer*

Northridge
Hafer, John Richard *musician*

Novato
Valentino, Stephen Eric (Il Conté Valentino) *production and entertainment company executive, actor, singer*

Oakland
Blank, Carla Maria *performance director, author*
Davis, John Jeffrey *musician*
DeFazio, Lynette Stevens *dancer, choreographer, educator, chiropractor, author, actress, musician*
Paine, Herbert *ballet administrator*
Randle, Ellen Eugenia Foster *opera and classical singer, educator*

Ojai
Starcevich, John (John Stark) *producer, writer*

Orange
Bradac, Thomas Frank *theater educator*

Orinda
Jekowsky, Barry *conductor, music director*

Pacific Palisades
Nachmanovitch, Stephen *violinist, composer, author and educator*
Walsh, Thomas Francis, Jr. *producer, writer, director*

Palm Desert
Yankee, Alan Lee *composer*

Palmdale
Luther, Amanda Lisa *producer*
Nuse, Deland Lynn *film director, writer, producer*

Pasadena
Adams, Elaine *art agent, publicist*

Pebble Beach
Klevan, Robert Bruce *music educator*

Porterville
Hensley, David Lawrence *music educator*

Rancho Cucamonga
Robertson, Carey Jane *musician, educator*

Redondo Beach
Reed, John E. *producer, consultant*

Redwood City
Vieira, Robert *composer*

Riverside
Adams, Byron *composer, conductor*

Sacramento
Gawthrop, Daphne Wood *performing company executive*

San Anselmo
Farr, David Donald *musician, educator, administrator*

San Bruno
Hansen, Julia *music educator*

San Carlos
Alvares, Joel G. *songwriter, recording artist*

San Diego
Angelo, Sandra McFall *television and video producer, writer*
Elaine, Karen *musician, educator*
Price, Betty Jeanne *choirchime soloist, writer*
Scheide, Kathleen Ellen *music educator, musician*

San Francisco
Bergen, Christopher Brooke *opera company administrator, translator, editor*
De Coteau, Denis *music director, conductor*
Eilenberg, Lawrence Ira *theater educator, artistic director*
George, Vance *conductor*
Getty, Gordon Peter *composer, philanthropist*
King, Alonzo *artistic director, choreographer*
Marinacci, Teresa Denise *theater director*
Pastreich, Peter *orchestra executive director*
Peterson, Wayne Turner *composer, pianist*
Schechter, Joel *magazine editor, writer, educator*
Talbot, Stephen H. *television producer, writer*
Thomas, Michael Tilson *performing company executive*
Tomasson, Helgi *dancer, choreographer, dance company executive*

San Jose
Grin, Leonid *conductor*
Weibel, Cathy Denise *entertainer*

San Mateo
Leong, Carol Jean *electrologist*

San Pedro
Fritzsche, Kathleen (Dragonfire Fritzsche) *performing arts educator*

San Rafael
Lucas, George W., Jr. *film director, producer, screenwriter*
Sheldon, Gary *conductor, music director*

Santa Ana
Isaacson, Gene Lester *fine arts educator*
St. Clair, Carl *conductor, music director*
Spisto, Louis G. *performing company executive*
Sudbeck, Robert Francis *music educator, philosophy educator*

Santa Barbara
Ben-Dor, Giséle *conductor, musician*
Potter, Robert Alonzo *dramatic art educator*
Wayland, Newton Hart *conductor*

Santa Clarita
Powell, Mel *composer*

Santa Cruz
Wolters, Christopher Frederick *performing company executive*

Santa Monica
Angel, Steven *musician*
Angier, Joseph *television producer, writer*
Avshalomov, David *conductor, composer*
Black, Noel Anthony *television and film director*
Jason, Sonya *recording artist*
Kalb, Benjamin Stuart *television producer, director*
Kaplan, Mike *film and video producer, director, and distributor, marketing executive*
Nemo, Gina *actress, producer, photographer, recording executive*
Nord, Richard *film editor*
Plone, Allen L. *media company executive, writer, game designer*
Schroeder, William Robert *actor, graphic designer, linguist*
Simons, Annette *performing company executive*
Webber, Peggy McClory *actress, director, producer*
Wilmowski, Wendy Ann *feature film and television production executive*

Sherman Oaks
Graham, Steven Piddington *entertainment production company executive*
Howard, Joseph B. (Joe Howard) *actor*
Peterson, Lowell *cinematographer*
Sutter, Diane *television executive*
Tesh, John *television talk show host*

Simi Valley
Akiyama, Carol Lynn *motion picture industry executive*
Brock, James Wilson *drama educator, playwright, researcher*

Stockton
Coburn, Robert James *music educator, composer*
Jennings, Charles Raymond *music educator, bands director*
Roche, Catherine Mary *music educator*
Tregle, Linda Marie *dance educator*

Studio City
Bergen, Polly *actress*
Cockrell, Frank Boyd, II *film production company executive*

Sunset Beach
Bettis, John Gregory *songwriter*

Sylmar
Foster, Dudley Edwards, Jr. *musician, educator*

Tarzana
LaPage, Roger *film producer*

Topanga
Wilcock, John *television producer, writer, editor*

Turlock
Klein, James Mikel *music educator*

Universal City
Devin, Richard *film industry executive*

Upper Lake
Scobey, Jan (Jeannette Marie Scobey) *jazz musician, store owner, author*

Val Verde
Goren, Bruce Neal *technical administrator*

Valencia
Millar, Michael William *trombonist*
Simmons, Ann Lorraine *actor*

Valley Village
Toussaint, Christopher Andre *video producer, director, writer*

Van Nuys
Allen, Stephen Valentine Patrick William *television comedian, author, pianist, songwriter*
Kazle, Elynmarie *producer*
Morgan, Lanny *musician*

Venice
Danciger, Matthew Allen *producer*
Furman, Will *film producer, director, cinematographer, writer*

West Hills
Peirson, George Ewell *film producer, art director, educator*

West Hollywood
Alenikov, Vladimir *motion picture director and writer*
Harper, Robert *actor*
Seeman, Brian *actor, writer, comedian*

Sherman, Robert B(ernard) *composer, lyricist, screenwriter*

Whittier
Korf, Leonard Lee *theater arts educator*

Yorba Linda
Herold, Ralph Elliott *motion picture arts educator*

COLORADO

Arvada
Finton, Kenneth Harper *writer, producer, publishing executive, literary agent*

Aspen
Harth, Robert James *music festival executive*
Young, Henry *executive director*
Zinman, David *coductor*

Boulder
Bernstein, Giora *artistic director*
Blake, Bambi Reva *international fine artist*
Boydston, James Christopher *composer*
Brakhage, James Stanley *filmmaker, educator*
Duckworth, Guy *musician, educator*
Fink, Robert Russell *music theorist, former university dean*
Hayes, Deborah *musicology educator, college administrator*
Kuchar, Theodore *conductor, academic administrator, musician*
Sarson, John Christopher *television producer, director, writer*
Spanier, Nancy Louise *artistic director, educator, choreographer*
Symons, James Martin *theater and dance educator*
Tolliver-Palma, Calvin Eugene *violist, instructor, performer*

Castle Rock
McVicar, Heather Lyn *actress*

Cherry Hills Village
Stapleton, Katharine Hall (Katie Stapleton) *food broadcaster, author*

Colorado Springs
Bergman, Yaacov *performing company executive*

Denver
Ceci, Jesse Arthur *violinist*
Folger, William Montraville *actor, journalist*
Fredmann, Martin *ballet artistic director, educator, choreographer*
Moulton-Gertig, Suzanne Carey LeRoy *musician, educator*
Robinson, Cleo Parker *artistic director*
Schwartz, Cherie Anne Karo *storyteller, writer*

El Jebel
Rowe, Henry Theodore, Jr. (Ted Rowe) *industrial video producer, director*

Estes Park
Bridges, Douglas M. *musician, small business owner*

Glenwood Springs
Callier, Cecile *writer, actress*

Grand Junction
Gustafson, Kirk *performing company executive*

Littleton
Fortna, Valerié Annette *dance and performing company owner, instructor*

Pueblo
Park, Dale Lee *stand-up comedian, author*

Salida
Barnes, Robert James *cosmetologist*

Sterling
Kuebler, Richard Arthur *theater educator, consultant*

FLORIDA

North Palm Beach
Hayman, Richard Warren Joseph *conductor*

HAWAII

Captain Cook
Link, Matthew Richard *video producer*

Ewa Beach
Kea, Jonathan Guy *instrumental music educator*

Honolulu
Baker, Kent Alfred *broadcasting company executive*
Engle, Robert Irwin *music educator, musician, composer, writer*
Furst, Dan (Daniel Christopher Furst, III) *producer, writer, actor*
Harvey, Arthur Wallace *music educator*
Kelin, Daniel Allen, II *theater director, writer, storyteller*
Smith, Barbara Barnard *music educator*
Wong, Samuel *conductor*

Wailuku
French, James L. *performing company executive*

Waimanalo
Dougherty, Michael *writer, filmmaker*

IDAHO

Boise
Ogle, James *performing company executive*

Idaho Falls
LoPiccolo, John *conductor, music director*

Pocatello
George, Thom Ritter *conductor, music educator, composer*

Sandpoint
Kramer, Remi Thomas *film director*

Twin Falls
Halsell, George Kay *music educator*
Tario, Terry C(harles) *broadcasting executive*

MONTANA

Bozeman
Savery, Matthew *music conductor, director, educator*
Westlake, Renee Elyse *music educator*

Great Falls
Johnson, Gordon James *artistic director, conductor*

Missoula
Marquand, Ian MacDonald *television producer*

NEBRASKA

Lincoln
Hu, Yong-Yan *performing company executive*

Omaha
Johnson, James David *concert pianist, organist, educator*

NEVADA

Carson City
Bugli, David *conductor*

Henderson
Nelson, Darryl Allan *television cameraman*

Las Vegas
Capelle, Madelene Carole *opera singer, educator, music therapist*
Castro, Joseph Armand *music director, pianist, composer, orchestrator*
Fuller, Dolores Agnes *songwriter, actress*
Gordon, Lonny Joseph *choreographer, dance and fine arts educator*
Leibovit, Arnold L. *film producer, director*
Mitchell, Guy *singer, entertainer, actor*
Sulich, Vassili *artistic director*
Wiemer, Robert Ernest *film and television producer, writer, director*

Reno
Daniels, Ronald Dale *conductor*

NEW MEXICO

Albuquerque
Ellingboe, Bradley Ross *musician, educator*

Las Cruces
Pinnow, Timothy Dayne *theater educator, fight choreographer*

Santa Fe
Baustian, Robert Frederick *conductor*
Crosby, John O'Hea *conductor, opera manager*
Jackson, Sally *location casting director*
Reggio, Godfrey *film director*

NEW YORK

New York
Alcantara, Theo *conductor*
Falletta, Jo Ann *musician*
Fryer, Robert Sherwood *theatrical producer*
Johanos, Donald *orchestra conductor*
Koenig, James William *opera singer, writer*
Nagano, Kent George *conductor*
Penn, Arthur Hiller *film and theatre producer*
Sedares, James L. *conductor*
Talmi, Yoav *conductor, composer*
Tilson Thomas, Michael *symphony conductor*

NORTH CAROLINA

Raleigh
Zimmermann, Gerhardt *conductor*

OREGON

Ashland
Hirschfeld, Gerald Joseph *cinematographer*
Shaw, Arthur E. *conductor*

Eugene
Bailey, Exine Margaret Anderson *soprano, educator*
Benson, Joan *musician, music educator*
Bergquist, Peter (Ed P. Jr.) *music educator emeritus*
Harth-Bedoya, Miguel *conductor*
Riley, Grannan *performing company executive*
Weinstein, Rachel *clown*

Lake Oswego
Edwards, Andrew *arts administrator*

Medford
DuMond, Mark Douglas *film and television producer*
Shinn, Duane K. *music publisher*
Tevis, Barry Lee *television producer, marketing executive*

Portland
Cole-McCullough, Daniel *music educator, conductor, clinician*
DePreist, James Anderson *conductor*
Huggett, Monica *performing company executive*
Leyden, Norman *conductor*
Stone, Desireé Naomi *artistic director, film producer and director*

Roseburg
Ferguson, John Franklin *music educator*

Talent
O'Rourke, Michael *artistic director*

UTAH

Cedar City
Cook, Douglas Neilson *theater educator, producer, artistic director*

Orem
Hansen, Brett James *music educator*

Provo
Pratt, Rosalie Rebollo *harpist, educator*
Threlfall, Timothy Allen *theater arts educator, director*
Woodbury, Lael Jay *theater educator*

Saint George
Belnap, Norma Lee Madsen *musician*

Salem
Hahn, Joan Christensen *retired drama educator, travel agent*

Salt Lake City
Andrews, Donald L. *performing arts company executive*
Hart, John *artistic director*
Johnson, Mary Perrine *musician, educator*
Miller, Kuby Susie *dance and modeling school owner*
Silverstein, Joseph Harry *conductor, musician*
Wallace, William *composer, educator*
Zabriskie, Robert *performing arts association administrator, data processing manager*

Sandy
Rice, Stuart Evan *music educator*

VERMONT

Burlington
Tamarkin, Kate *conductor*

VIRGINIA

Norfolk
Allen, Russell Plowman *opera company executive*

WASHINGTON

Auburn
Overholt, Miles Harvard *cable television consultant*

Bainbridge Island
Moyemont, Terry Walter *video producer, videographer*

Bellevue
Hilbert, Stephanie Mayer *actress, director, producer*

Bellingham
Larner, Daniel M. *theater educator, playwright, author*

Bremerton
Rickerson, Jean Marie *video producer, journalist, photographer*

College Place
Spring, Glenn Ernest *composer*

Everett
Waldron, Richard Frederick *musician, educator*

Gig Harbor
Ramsey, Jerry Virgil *educator, financial planner, radio broadcaster*

Issaquah
Hunt, Robert William *theatrical producer, data processing consultant*

Lynnwood
Krause, Thomas Evans *record promotion consultant*

Marysville
Philpott, Larry La Fayette *horn player*

Mercer Island
Francis, Carolyn Rae *music educator, musician, author, publisher*

Poulsbo
Moody, Kate Ladd *composer, music educator*

Seattle
Anang, Kofi *artistic director, educator, dancer*
Forbes, David Craig *musician*
Graber, Jonathan Schultz *musician, music educator*
Ireland, Barbara Alice *film producer, director, writer*
Jenkins, Speight *opera company executive, writer*
Jensen, Helen *musical artists management company executive*
Nishitani, Martha *dancer*
Nolte, Scott Lloyd *artistic director, actor*
Russell, Francia *ballet director, educator*
Rutter, Deborah Frances *orchestra administrator*

Ryder, Hal *theater educator, director*
Sateren, Terry *theater technical production*
Shroyer, Roberta Wayman *music educator*
Stowell, Kent *ballet director*
Tsutakawa, Deems Akihiko *musician, composer, record producer*

Spokane
Bray, R(obert) Bruce *music educator*
Pugh, Kyle Mitchell, Jr. *musician, retired music educator*
Young, Michael Edward *composer, music educator*

Woodinville
McGowan, Mitchell Joseph *director, actor, stage manager*

WYOMING

Rock Springs
Proctor, Vincent P. *music educator*

CANADA

ALBERTA

Calgary
Epton, Gregg *performing company executive*
Graf, Hans *conductor*
LaHay, David George Michael *ballet company director*

Edmonton
Archer, Violet Balestreri *music educator, composer, pianist, organist, percussionist, adjudicator*

BRITISH COLUMBIA

Vancouver
Washburn, Jon *artistic director*

ONTARIO

Hamilton
Brott, Boris *orchestra conductor*

Toronto
Beckwith, John *musician, composer, educator*

MEXICO

Mexico City
Batiz, Enrique *pianist, conductor*

ENGLAND

London
Salonen, Esa-Pekka *conductor*

ISRAEL

Tel Aviv
Mehta, Zubin *conductor, musician*

ADDRESS UNPUBLISHED

ackerman, Bettye Louise (Mrs. Sam Jaffe) *actress*
adelson, Merv Lee *entertainment and communication industry executive*
aguiar, William, Jr. *music and dance critic*
alberts, David *artistic director, mime*
aldag, Richard Jeffrey *composer*
baerwald, Susan Grad *television broadcasting executive producer*
behlmer, Rudy H., Jr. *director, writer, film educator*
bergen, Candice *actress, writer, photojournalist*
berman, Sanford Solomon *motion picture sound designer, composer, arranger, artist*
bogart, Rebecca A. *musician, educator*
Campobasso, Craig *casting director*
Canin, Stuart Victor *violinist*
Carr, Paul Wallace *actor*
Carroll, Pat *actress*
Cohen, Ellis Avrum *producer, writer*
Collard, Lorraine Fullmer *music educator*
Cunningham, Ron *choreographer, artistic director*
Curry, Jane Kathleen *theater educator*
Debus, Eleanor Viola *retired business management company executive*
Decchario, Tony Houston *symphony orchestra executive*
D'Elia, William Vincent *film director*
Elikann, Lawrence S. (Larry Elikann) *television and film director*
Faroudja, Philippe Yves *television director*
Favre, June Marie *actress, singer*
Flood, James Tyrrell *broadcasting executive*
Foley, Mary Kathleen *theater arts educator*
Frankish, Brian Edward *film producer, director*
Goddard, James Russell *producer, writer, actor*
Goldstein, William M. *composer, producer*
Great, Don Charles *composer, music company executive*
Guttentag, William Sidney *television producer, writer, director*
Guttman, Irving Allen *opera stage director*
Hanket, Arthur Anthony *actor, marketing and sales analyst, consultant*
Hansen, Christine Merri *music educator*
Harper, Richard Henry *film producer, director*
Harris, Harry H. *television director*
Hartman, Phil Edward *actor*
Hartman, Terry A. *filmmaker*
Hawkins, Roberta Rosenthal *theater educator*
Henderson, Scott *jazz guitarist*
Hislop, Kare Elizabeth *music director, educator*
Huning, Deborah Gray *actress, dancer, audiologist, photographer, video producer-editor*
Iacangelo, Peter August *actor*
Issari, M(ohammad) Ali *film producer, educator, consultant*
Janis, Sharon Leah *film and television editor and producer, author*
Kaylan, Howard Lawrence *musical entertainer, composer*
Kennedy, Orin *film company executive*
Kerr, Forrest David *actor, writer, producer*
Kyriakopoulos, Steve George *song writer*
Lamppu, Judy Sonia *composer, writer*
Little, Loren Everton *musician, ophthalmologist*
Lobanov-Rostovsky, Oleg *arts association executive*
Lucas, Beth Anne *television producer*
Main, Robert Gail *communications educator, training consultant, television and film producer, former army officer*
Mansouri, Lotfollah (Lotfi Mansouri) *opera stage director, administrator*
Matthau, Charles Marcus *film director*
McClain, Richard Stan *cinematographer*
Medina, Javier Michael *musician, entertainer*
Megalos, Bill *film director*
Myerson, Alan *director, film and television writer*
Neary, Patricia Elinor *ballet director*
Numano, Allen Stanislaus Motoyuki *musician, writer*
O'Brien, Jack George *artistic director*
Pimble, Toni *artistic director, choreographer, educator*
Porter, Richard Kane *audio engineer, consultant*
Quick, John Antony *film and video producer*
Rain, Rhonda L. *performing arts executive, counselor, educator*
Russo, Vincent Barney *music educator*
Salvatore, Richard John *cinematographer, company executive*
Sandrich, Jay H. *television director*
Schwarz, Gerard *conductor, musician*
Simpson, Dave *radio producer*
Sisemore, Claudia *educational films and videos producer, director*
Smith, Carter Blakemore *broadcaster*
Smith, Irby Jay *film producer*
Soh, John Junggwon *film editor, producer*
Solow, Herbert Franklin *film producer, writer*
Spier, Luise Emma *film editor, director*
Steinberg, Russell *composer*
Summers, Cathleen Ann *film producer*
Sutherland, Bruce *composer, pianist, music educator*
Symmes, Daniel Leslie *three-dimensional technology executive, producer, director*
Tarbuck, Barbara Joan *actor*
Taylor, Guy Watson *symphonic conductor*
Timmons, William Milton *producer, freelance writer, retired cinema arts educator, publisher, film maker*
Tokofsky, Jerry Herbert *film producer*
Topilow, Carl S. *conductor*
Uchitel, Neil *composer*
von, Dennis *actor, producer*
Weiner-Heuschkel, Sydell *theater educator*
Weiskopf, Kim Robert *television producer, writer*
White, Anthony Roy, Jr. *composer, educator*
Williamson, Laird *stage director, actor*
Wilson, Michael Gregg *film producer, writer*
Worthey, Carol *composer*
Yamamoto, Aaron I. *film editor*
Zhao, Li *fine arts company executive, teacher, consultant*
Zick, Lester George *actor, systems consultant*
Zoritch, George *dance educator*

ARTS: VISUAL

UNITED STATES

ALASKA

Anchorage
Sexton Atkins, Jan *artist*
Shadrach, (Martha) Jean Hawkins *artist*
Tuckey, John Davison *artist, commercial photographer*

Cordova
Bugbee-Jackson, Joan *sculptor*

Dutch Harbor
Sloan, Patrice S. *artist*

Fairbanks
Chin, Wanda Won *graphics designer*
Fejes, Claire *artist, writer*
Maginnis, Tara Michele *costume designer, educator*
Mollett, David L. *artist*
Woodward, Kesler Edward *artist, educator*

Juneau
DeRoux, Daniel Grady *artist*

Ketchikan
McDermott, David (John) *artist, writer, photographer*

ARIZONA

Apache Junction
Coe, Anne Elizabeth *artist*

Bisbee
Stiles, Knute *artist*

Carefree
Peterson, Susan Harnly *artist, writer*

Chandler
Matus, Nancy Louise *artist*

Cornville
Waddell, John Henry *sculptor*

Eagar
McCain, Buck *artist*

Flagstaff
Salsig, Doyen *photographer, photography studio owner*

Glendale
Golubic, Theodore Roy *sculptor, designer, inventor*

Gold Canyon
Braig, Betty *artist, educator*

Green Valley
Easton, Roger David *art history educator*
Nasvik-Dennison, Anna *artist*

Lake Montezuma
Burkee, Irvin *artist*

Mesa
Kaida, Tamarra *art and photography educator*

Paradise Valley
Heller, Jules *artist, writer, educator*
Maxey, Diane Meadows *artist*

Peoria
Di Giacinto, Sharon *artist, educator*

Phoenix
Haas, Thomas L. *artist, art gallery owner*
Lawes, Patricia Jean *art educator*
Nisula, Larry William *artist*
Schaumburg, Donald Roland *art educator, ceramic artist*
Schmieder, Carl *jeweler*
Whitman, Kathy Velma Rose (Elk Woman Whitman) *artist, sculptor, jeweler, painter, educator*
Willard, Garcia Lou *artist*
Williams, Joyce Marilyn *artist, business owner*

Prescott
Dunham, Bandhu Scott *glass artist, author*
Dusard, Jay *photographer*
Willoughby, James Russell *artist*

Scottsdale
Afsary, Cyrus *artist*
Fratt, Dorothy *artist*
Kleppe, Shirley R. Klein *artist*
Lang, Margo Terzian *artist*
Lehrman, Lewis Barrett *artist, writer*
Rosenthal, Charles Louis *artist, educator*
Simmons, Julie Lutz *artist*
Van Dusen, Peter *artist*

Sedona
DeMille, Leslie Benjamin *artist*
Jennerjahn, Warren P. *artist, educator*
Powell, Marlys Kaye *artist*
Ware, Peggy Jenkins *photographer, writer, artist, dancer*

Tempe
Kinney, Raleigh Earl *artist*
Pile, James William *artist educator*

Tucson
Bissell, Cynthia L. *artist*
Bloomfield, Suzanne *artist*
Bredlow, Thomas Gayle *metals designer, craftsman*
Denniston, Douglas *artist, educator*
Flint, Willis Wolfschmidt (Willi Wolfschmidt) *artist*
Geoffrion, Moira Marti *artist, educator*
Goodman, Mary A. *photographer*
Harbart, Gertrude Carol *artist, educator*
Johnson, Ciri Diane *graphic design firm owner*
Mathews, Elden Clair *art instructor, sculptor, painter*
Quiróz, Alfred James *art educator, artist, lecturer*
Root, Nile *photographer, educator*
Sauer, Anne Katherine *glass blower, artist, educator*
Schaffer, Richard Enos *artist, registrar*
Teiwes, Helga *photographer*

CALIFORNIA

Acampo
Eger, Marilyn Rae *artist*

Agoura Hills
Wiechec, Donald *photographer*

Altadena
Bockus, Herman William, Jr. *artist, educator, writer*
Green, David Oliver, Jr. *sculptor, designer*

Anaheim
Nelipovich, Sandra Grassi *artist*

Angwin
Seyle, Robert Harley *artist, educator*

Aptos
Howe, Susan Leone *artist, printmaker, design consultant*
Schy, Gay *artist, investor*
Woods, Gurdon Grant *sculptor*

Arcadia
Danziger, Louis *graphic designer, educator*
Ensign, Donald Dale *art director*

Arcata
Anderson, William Thomas *art educator, artist*
Hess, Ivan Edward *set designer, educator*
Land-Weber, Ellen *photography educator*

Aromas
Nutzle, Futzie (Bruce John Kleinsmith) *artist, author, cartoonist*

Auburn
Blaney, Suzanne Avery *artist*
Schulzke, Margot Seymour *artist, educator*

Avalon
Burns, Denise Ruth *artist*

Azusa
Tarkington, Dickey Edward *artist, educator*

Bakersfield
Hackman, Vida Bernice *artist*

Baldwin Park
Phillips, Donna Rose *production artist, writer*

Belmont
Harris, David Jack *artist, painter, educator*
Pava, Esther Shub *artist, educator*

Benicia
Shannonhouse, Sandra Lynne Riddell *sculptor*

Berkeley
Cantor, Rusty Sumner *artist*
Edwards, John David *artist*
Felter, June Marie *artist*
Genn, Nancy *artist*
Hack, Elizabeth *artist*
Hartman, Robert Leroy *artist, educator*
Healy, Anne *sculptor*
Hoare, Tyler James *sculptor*
McNamara, John Stephen *artist, educator*
Moore, Frank James *artist, educator*
Olmsted, Suzanne M. *photographer*
Sussman, Wendy Rodriguez *artist, educator*

Beverly Hills
Potter, Stephen Arnold *production designer*
Ringwald, Lydia Elaine *artist, poet*
Shishim, Francis G. *artist, performer*

Big Bear Lake
Essman, Robert Norvel *artist, graphic designer*

Bodega
Hedrick, Wally Bill *artist*

Brentwood
Peters, William Frank *art educator*

Burbank
Merrill, Thomas St. John *medical photographer*
Wu, Shu-Lin Sharon *animation educator*

Burlingame
Voelker, Elizabeth Anne *artist*

Calistoga
Nechis, Barbara *artist*

Cambria
Harden, Marvin *artist, educator*
Werts, Josephine Starr *artist*

Canoga Park
Rosenfeld, Sarena Margaret *artist*

Capistrano Beach
Clark, Timothy John *artist, educator*

Carmel
Jacobs, Ralph, Jr. *artist*
Kennedy, John Edward *art dealer, appraiser, curator*
Skalagard, Hans Martin *artist*

Carmel Valley
Corser, Kira Dorothy Carrillo *photographic artist*
Sands, Sharon Louise *graphic design executive, art publisher, artist*

Carmichael
Sahs, Majorie Jane *art educator*
Smith, Sylvia Sue *artist, sculptor*

Castro Valley
Erwin, Frances Suzanne *artist*
Soldahl-Hertzog, Nan *architectural illustrator, artist*

Chatsworth
Luebtow, John Gilbert *artist*

Chula Vista
Cannon-Wilson, Margaret Elizabeth *art educator, artist*
Gilliam, Elizabeth M. *illustrator, printmaker, poet*

Claremont
Benjamin, Karl Stanley *art educator*
Leabhart, Thomas Glenn *art educator, performer*
Macko, Nancy *artist, educator*
Pinkel, Sheila Mae *artist, photographer, educator*

Concord
Tackitt, James William *graphic arts and photography educator, genealogical researcher*

Coronado
Hubbard, Donald *marine artist, writer*

Costa Mesa
Muller, Jerome Kenneth *photographer, art director, editor*

Culver City
Apple, Jacqueline B. (Jacki Apple) *artist, writer, educator*

Cypress
Bloom, Julian *artist, editor*
George, Patricia Byrne *artist*

Daggett
Bailey, Katherine Christine *artist, writer*

Daly City
Kennedy, Gwendolyn Debra *film animator, parapsychologist, artist, play and film writer*
Leong, Lam-Po (Lanbo Liang) *artist, educator*

Dana Point
Collins, Robert Wayne *photographer, public speaker*
Hodara, Eden *artist*
Strand, Sally Lee (Sally Strand Ellis) *artist, educator*

Desert Hot Springs
Hall, Anthony R. *photographer*

Diamond Springs
Tarbet, Urania Christy *artist, writer*

Emeryville
Grafton, Frederick Wellington *artist*
Jones, David *artist*
Marcus, Aaron *graphic artist*

Encinitas
Breslaw, Cathy Lee *artist, graphic designer, educator*
Budek, Allin Alla *artist*
Perine, Robert Heath *artist, writer*

Encino
Baciu, Michael *photographer*
Knoll, William Lee *animation director*
LaCom, Wayne Carl *artist, writer*

Eureka
Marak, Louis Bernard, Jr. *art educator*

Fair Oaks
Potter, George Kenneth *artist*

Fillmore
Timmons, Terry Lee *photographer, educator*

Flintridge
Hammerbeck, Wanda Lee *artist*

Fresno
Gullickson, Norman Anthony *graphic designer, educator*
Stuart, Dorothy Mae *artist*

Fullerton
Corsi, Sandro *artist, educator*
Macaray, Lawrence Richard *art educator*
Woodhull, Patricia Ann *artist*

Garden Grove
Bell, Melodie Elizabeth *artist, massage therapist*

Gilroy
Decker, Bo *artist*

Glendale
Gill, Gene *artist*
Kagan, Martin I. *arts administrator*
Lebejoara, Ovidiu *artist*
Sweet, Harvey *theatric, scenic and lighting designer*

Goleta
Argent, Philip *artist, educator*
Gabrielson, Walter Oscar *artist*

Greenbrae
Blatt, Morton Bernard *medical illustrator*

Hawthorne
Palmer, Charles Ray *retired graphics specialist, investor*

Hayward
Jordahl, Geir Arild *photographer, educator*
Jordahl, Kathleen Patricia (Kate Jordahl) *photographer, educator*
Knight, Andrew Kong *visual artist, educator*

Huntington Beach
Berry, Kim Lauren *artist*
Moyer, Linda Lee *artist, educator*

Irvine
Berryhill, Georgia Gene *graphic designer, educator*
Giannulli, Mossimo *designer, apparel business executive*
Kingman, Dong *artist, educator*
Varo, Marton-Geza *sculptor*

Kelseyville
Fletcher, Leland Vernon *artist*

La Canada Flintridge
Drees, Elaine Hnath *artist and educator*

La Jolla
Fredman, Faiya Rubenstein *artist*
Imana, Jorge Garron *artist*
Low, Mary Louise (Molly Low) *documentary photographer*
Silva, Ernest R. *visual arts educator, artist*

La Mirada
Feldman, Roger Lawrence *artist, educator*

La Puente
Collins, Dick *artist*

Lafayette
Beaumont, Mona *artist*
Kapp, Eleanor Jeanne *impressionistic artist, writer, researcher*
Shurtleff, Akiko Aoyagi *artist, consultant*

Laguna Beach
Blacketer, James Richard *artist*
Darrow, Paul Gardner *painter, printmaker, cartoonist, illustrator*

Laguna Hills
Walker, Virginia L. *art educator*

Laguna Niguel
Apt, Charles *artist*
Pierce, Hilda (Hilda Herta Harmel) *painter*

Lakewood
Barton, Billie Jo *artist, educator*

Lancaster
Coleman-Levy, Jack Robin *photographic laboratory design consultant*

Larkspur
Frances, Harriette (Harriette Sherana) *painter, printmaker, consultant*

Lompoc
Solberg, Morten Edward *artist*

Long Beach
Braunstein, Terry Malikin *artist*
Nielsen, Pamela Jeanne *artist, writer*
Sanchez-H., Jose *fine arts educator, producer, director, media consultant*

Los Angeles
Amdur, Judith Devorah *artist, cook*
Anderegg, Ronald Henry *artist*
Anderson, Isabel *artist, educator*
Asano, Hisako *fine arts educator*
Bachenheimer, Beth Adair *artist, educator*
Boyett, Joan Reynolds *arts administrator*
Burke, Kristin Marie *costume designer*
Cassell, Beverly Anne *artist, art association executive*
Di XX Miglia, Gabriella *artist, conservationist*
Doolin, James Lawrence *artist, educator*
Ewing, Edgar Louis *artist, educator*
Fedors, Paul Edward *architectural lighting designer*
Goins, Ronald L. *art director*
Hamilton, Patricia Rose *artist's agent*
Janowski, Karyn Ann *artist*
Karabay, Adnan Sami *artist*
Kienholz, Lyn Shearer *international arts projects coordinator*
Korelov, Nikolai *artist*
Kory, Michael A. *3D computer animator*
Lang, Wendy Frances *artist, photographer*
Lark, Raymond *artist, art scholar*
Leeson, Thomas Aubert *painter*
Lem, Richard Douglas *painter*
Manolakas, Stanton Peter *watercolor artist*
McAuley, Skeet *artist*
Miller, Harriet Sanders *art center director*
Odel, Franklin David *photography educator, publisher*
Outterbridge, John Wilfred *artist, art administrator*
Scott, James Michael *artist, filmmaker*
Simon, Steven Adam *sculptor, educator*
Smith, Alexis *artist, educator*
Stone, George *artist, art educator*
Turner, Nancy Elizabeth *artist, designer*
Welles, Melinda Fassett *artist, educator*
With, Gerda Becker *artist*
Wood, Nicola *artist*
Wright, Bernard *artist*
Wright, Michael Ragsdale *artist, educator*

Los Banos
Peterson, Stanley Lee *artist*

Los Osos
Dorland, Frank Norton *artist, educator*

Malibu
Almond, Joan Harwood Elkins *photographer*
Bowman, Bruce *art educator, writer, artist*

Manhattan Beach
Millar, Robert *artist*

Marina Del Rey
Lange, Gerald William *book artist, typographer*

Mariposa
Rogers, Earl Leslie *artist, educator*

Mckinleyville
Berry, Glenn *artist, educator*

Mendocino
de la Fuente, Lawrence Edward *artist*

Menlo Park
Mayes, Sharon Suzette *sculptor, educator*

Merced
LeCocq, Karen Elizabeth *artist*

Mill Valley
Baruch, Ruth-Marion Evelyn *photographer, writer*
Meader, Jonathan Grant (Kythe Ascian) *artist*

Millbrae
Dawdy, Faye Marie Catania *photographer, lecturer*

Mission Hills
Jones, John Harding *photographer*

Monterey
Gilpin, Henry Edmund, III *photographer, educator*

Montrose
Handford, Jack *fashion education consultant*

Moraga
Schmaltz, Roy Edgar, Jr. *artist, art educator*

Morgan Hill
Freimark, Robert (Bob Freimark) *artist*

Mount Shasta
Saint-Marie, Mary Sheila *artist, writer, educator*

Napa
Kravjansky, Mikulas *artist*

North Hollywood
Brommer, Gerald Frederick *artist, writer*
Powell, Stephanie *visual effects director, supervisor*

Northridge
Weatherup, Wendy Gaines *graphic designer, writer*
Weston, Edward *art dealer, consultant*

Novato
Weston, Sandra *jewelry designer*

Oakhurst
Cantwell, Christopher William *artist*

Oakland
Alba, Benny *artist*
Beasley, Bruce Miller *sculptor*
Bowen-Forbes, Jorge Courtney *artist, author, poet*
Dickinson, Eleanor Creekmore *artist, educator*
Donahue, Philip Richard *artist, educator*
Gonzalez, Arthur Padilla *artist, educator*
Hardy, David Whittaker, III *artist, educator*
Harper, Rob March *artist, educator*
Kagemoto, Patricia Jow (Pat Jow) *artist, printmaker*
Levine, Marilyn Anne *artist*
Tait, William Henderson *artist*
Weisburd, Harry Noah *artist, educator*

Occidental
Chester, Elfi *artist*

Oceanside
Boutell Moonier, Sylvia *artist*
Sarkisian, Pamela Outlaw *artist*

Ojai
McIntosh, Gregory Stephen *artist*

Orange
Felisky, Barbara Rosbe *artist*

Orange Cove
Paris, Vreda *artist, educator*

Orinda
Epperson, Stella Marie *artist*

Oroville
Rugenstein, Robert Wayne *clothing designer*

Pacific Palisades
Zivelonghi, Kurt Daniel *artist, painter*

Pacifica
Brooks-Korn, Lynne Vivian *artist*
Torlakson, James Daniel *artist*

Palm Desert
Bell, Helen Lavin *artist*
Kaufman, Charlotte King *artist, retired educational administrator*

Palo Alto
Chu, Christopher Kar Fai *graphic designer*
Eisenstat, Benjamin *artist*
Kiser, Stephen *artist, educator*
McCluskey, Lois Thornhill *photographer*
Rich, Lesley Mosher *artist*

Pasadena
Goldstein, Debbe *art history educator*
Marrow, Marva Jan *photographer, writer, video and multimedia producer*
Mesquita, Rosalyn Anaya *artist, educator*
Pashgian, Margaret Helen *artist*
Sakoguchi, Ben *artist, art educator*
Savedra, Jeannine Evangeline *art educator, artist*

Petaluma
Fuller-McChesney, Mary Ellen *sculptor, writer, publisher*

Phelan
Erwin, Joan Lenore *artist, educator*

Pinole
Gerbracht, Robert Thomas (Bob Gerbracht) *painter, educator*

Placentia
Nettleship, William Allan *sculptor*

Pleasant Hill
Greenley, Carol Jean *graphics designer, music educator, photographer*

Poway
Dohm, Rodger Matthew *painter, sculpter*

Redlands
Wood, Robert Earle *artist, educator*

Redondo Beach
Brett-Elspas, Janis Ellen *fashion designer, public relations executive*

Richmond
Huckeby, Karen Marie *graphic arts executive*

Riverside
Jones, Amelia Gwen *art history educator, curator*
Medel, Rebecca Rosalie *artist*

Running Springs
Gordon, Steven Eric *animator, designer*

Sacramento
Cosgrove, James *artist, industrial designer*
Drachnik, Catherine Meldyn *art therapist, artist*
LaPena, Frank Raymond *art educator*
McCullough, Gayle Jean *graphic artist, publisher*
Merta, Paul James *cartoonist, photographer, engineer, restaurateur, real estate developer*
Moment, Joan *artist, educator*
Thomas, Laura Marlene *artist, private antique dealer*

Salinas
Kirby, Thomas Paul *artist*
Smith, Gary Thomas *fine arts educator, curator*

San Bernardino
Warehall, William Donald *art educator*

San Clemente
Lopina, Louise Carol *artist*

San Diego
Barone, Angela Maria *artist, researcher*
Braley, Jean (J. McNeil Sargent) *artist, educator*
Doll, Linda A. *artist, educator*
Farmer, Janene Elizabeth *artist, educator*
Jung, Kwan Yee *artist*
Jung, Yee Wah *artist*
Lauer, Stefanie Dorothea *painter, writer*
Lebadang *artist*
Mandolf, Judy *artist*
Markarian, Alexia Mitrus *artist*
Nyiri, Joseph Anton *sculptor, art educator*
Penney, Roger Lee *artist*
Sargent, J. McNeil *artist, art educator*
Sorby, J(oseph) Richard *artist, educator*
Sowinski, Stanislaus Joseph *artist, retired naval officer*
Wojtyla, Walter Haase *artist*

San Francisco
Adams, Mark *artist*
Babcock, Jo *artist, educator*
Beall, Dennis Ray *artist, educator*
Bechtle, Robert Alan *artist, educator*
Brooke, Pegan Struthers *artist, art educator*
Bryce, Mark Adams *artist, painter*
Chin, Sue Soone Marian (Suchin Chin) *conceptual artist, portraitist, photographer, community affair activist*
DeSoto, Lewis Damien *art educator*
Dreibelbis, Ellen Roberts *artist*
Gerzso, Gunther *painter, graphic artist*
Helder, David Ernest *artist, educator*
Hendricks, Mark Kenneth *animator, artist*
Hershman, Lynn Lester *artist*
Kehlmann, Robert *artist, critic*
Komater, Christopher John *artist*
Komenich, Kim *photographer*
Krempel, Ralf Hugo Bernhard *author, artist, art gallery owner*
Lemkhin, Mikhail *photographer, journalist*
Lew, Weyman *artist*
Lupper, Edward *artist*
Martin, Fred *artist, college administrator*
Maxim, David Nicholas *artist*
Mick, Neil Michael *artist, educator*
Oropallo, Deborah *artist, educator*
Phill, Daniel Stouffer *artist*
Phillips, Thomas Embert *artist*
Piccolo, Richard Andrew *artist, educator*
Preble, Patricia Joan *visual artist, writer*
Raciti, Cherie *artist*
Rascón, Armando *artist*
Roloff, John Scott *artist, art educator*
Sassone, Marco Massimo *artist*
Schmalz, Charles Joseph *artist, photographer, creative consultant*
Shaw, Richard Blake *artist, art educator*
Southard, James Bruce *lecturer, painter*
Stermer, Dugald Robert *designer, illustrator, writer, consultant*
Sultan, Larry *photographer*
Taylor, Sandra Ortiz *artist, educator*
Villa, Carlos Pedro *artist, activist, educator*

San Jose
Ellner, Michael William *art educator*
French, Stephen Warren *art educator, university official*
Gussin, Clark Louis *multimedia graphic designer, fine artist*
Johnson, Gwenavere Anelisa *artist*
Lopez, Angelo Cayas *freelance illustrator*
Perrotto, Glen Rogers *artist, teacher*
Suggs, Patricia Ann *artist*
Thurston, Jacqueline Beverly *art educator*
Verbiest, Claire Schroeven *artist*

San Leandro
Waldron, Vanis Roy *artist, educator*

San Luis Obispo
Dickerson, Colleen Bernice Patton *artist, educator*

San Mateo
Chester, Sharon Rose *photographer, natural history educator*
Huxley, Mary Atsuko *artist*
Xiong, Jean Z. *artist, consultant*

San Pedro
Strasen, Barbara Elaine *artist, educator*

Santa Barbara
Brown, Gary Hugh *artist, art educator*
Dorra, Henri *art historian, educator*
Eguchi, Yasu *artist*
Gottlieb, Jane Drew *artist*
Nideffer, Robert Foster *artist, educator*
Wallin, Lawrence Bier *artist*

Santa Clara
Hernandez, Sam *sculptor, educator*
Hofstetter, Jane Robinson *artist, educator*

Santa Cruz
Bartlett Abood, Kathleen Gene *artist, educator*
Lanting, Frans Marten *photographer, writer*
Martin, Linde Benison *artist, interior designer*
Massaro, Karen Thuesen *artist*
Rydell, Amnell Roy *artist, landscape architect*
Stolpe, Daniel Owen *artist, printmaking educator*
Summers, Carol *artist*

Santa Monica
Barth, Uta *artist, educator*
Cheng, Carl Fu Kang *artist*
Chu, Julia Nee *artist*
Fellows, Alice Combs *artist*
Fukuhara, Henry *artist, educator*
Hopkins, Glenn Ernest *artist, educator*
Mitchell, Kathleen Ann *illustrator, graphic designer*
Mitchell, Robin *artist, educator*
Posner, Judith Lois *art dealer*

Santa Rosa
Cohen, Mark Jeffrey *cartoonist agent*
Mancusi, Timothy John *artist, illustrator*
Monk, Diana Charla *artist, stable owner*
Rider, Jane Louise *artist, educator*
Thistlethwaite, Aline M. *artist*

Santa Ynez
Bornell, Cecil Jean *computer graphics designer, small business owner*

Saratoga
Sherwood, Patricia Waring *artist, educator*

Sausalito
Holmes, Robert Edward *photographer*
Kuhlman, Walter Egel *artist, educator*

Sebastopol
Stanford, Ginny Crouch *painter*

Sepulveda
Field, Jeffrey Frederic *designer*

Sherman Oaks
Carl, Joan Strauss *sculptor, painter*
Corrie, Richard Wayne *lighting designer, artist, musician*
Shersher, Zinovy Israil *artist*
Studley, Helen Ormson *artist, poet, writer, designer*

Simi Valley
Shawn, Eric *software and consumer products company executive*

Solana Beach
Beck-von-Peccoz, Stephen George Wolfgang *artist*

Somis
Kehoe, Vincent Jeffré-Roux *photographer, author, cosmetic company executive*

Sonoma
Anderson, Gunnar Donald *artist*
Shannon, Jonathan J. *artist*

Sonora
Price, Joe (Allen) *artist, former educator*

South Lake Tahoe
Darvas, Endre Peter *artist*

South Pasadena
Zagon, Laurie *artist, writer, color consultant*

Stinson Beach
Chapline, Claudia Beechum *artist, art dealer*

Stockton
Miller, Carl Vosburgh *artist*
Oak, Claire Morisset *artist, educator*

Studio City
Manders, Susan Kay *artist*

Sunnyvale
Holt, Steven Hamilton Skov *industrial designer, educator*

Sylmar
Scheib, Gerald Paul *fine art educator, jeweler, metalsmith*

Temecula
Bouchard, Paul Eugene *artist*

Thousand Oaks
Heyer, Carol Ann *illustrator*
Villegas, Richard Junipero *artist*

Tiburon
Carlson, Kay Marie *artist, educator*

Trinidad
Simmons, Ned Lee *landscape artist, art dealer, consultant*

Upper Lake
Twitchell, Kent *mural artist*

Vacaville
Ford, John T., Jr. *art, film and video educator*

Valencia
Fiskin, Judith Anne *artist, educator*
Lawson, Thomas *artist*
Meyers, Randal Curtis *sculptor*

Vallejo
Bullock, James Benbow *sculptor*

Valley Center
Nelson-Rodriguez, Catherine Lynn *artist, writer, American Indian basket weaver*

Van Nuys
Corinblit, Nita Green *artist, educator*
Graham, Roger John *photography and journalism educator*
Penny, Aubrey John *painter, sculptor*
Sandel, Randye Noreen *artist*

Venice
Adams, Lisa Kay *artist*
Chipman, Jack *artist*
Eversley, Frederick John *sculptor, engineer*

Ventura
Radley, Gregory Norman *custom furniture maker, educator*
Yoshimoto, Hiroko *art educator, artist*

Victorville
Grogan, Suzann Jeanette-Wyman *artist*

Vista
Simmons, Cleda-Marie *artist*

Walnut
Owen, Carol Thompson *artist, educator*

Walnut Creek
Neacsu, Maria *artist*

Watsonville
Hansen, Elizabeth Jean *appraiser, author*

West Covina
Shiershke, Nancy Fay *artist, property manager*

West Hills
Duzy, Merrilyn Jeanne *artist, educator*

Woodland
Nye, Gene Warren *art educator*

Woodland Hills
Reed, Harold Ervin *artist, educator*

Woodside
Gallaway, Marthine S. *artist*

Yreka
Fiock, Shari Lee *design entrepreneur, researcher*

COLORADO

Aspen
Appleoff, Sandra S. *artist, educator*

Aurora
Hickman, Grace Marguerite *artist*

Boulder
Bierman, Sandra L. *artist*
Donovan-Johnson, D. J. *artist, educator*
Dowden, Anne Ophelia *botanical illustrator, writer*
Iris (Silverstein), Bonnie *artist, writer, educator*
Matthews, Eugene Edward *artist*
Stevens, Janet *illustrator*
Yeager, David Clark *product designer, education specialist*

Colorado Springs
Budd, Barbara Tews *sculptor*
Fox, Gwen *artist, educator*
Goehring, Kenneth *artist*
Lee, Kang S. *artist, educator*

Denver
Carter, Melvin Whitsett (Mel Carter) *artist, educator*
Cole, Jean Anne *artist*
DeMaree, Betty *artist, educator*
Enright, Cynthia Lee *illustrator*
Kaplan, Sandra Lee *artist*
Nesheim, Dennis Warren *art educator, artist, writer, instructional materials producer*
Norman, John Barstow, Jr. *designer, educator*
Ragland, Bob *artist, educator*
Speer, Andrew Kevin *art educator*
Thompson, Richard Craig *artist*

Dolores
Wagner, Richard *artist*

Durango
Reber, Mick *artist, educator*

Elizabeth
Kaplinski, Buffalo *artist*

Englewood
Burrows, E. Michael *art educator, artist*
Lamb, Darlis Carol *sculptor*
Walter, Patricia Ann *graphic designer*

Evergreen
Desrochers, Jeri Kilzer *artist*

Fort Collins
Jacobs, Peter Alan *artist, educator*
Risbeck, Philip Edward *graphic designer*
Weimer, Dawn *sculptor*

Greeley
Ursyn, Anna Z. *computer graphics artist, educator*

Lakewood
Binkley, Joan Vivian (Jody Binkley) *artist, educator, gallery owner*
Denton, Patry Redding *artist, educator*
Navratil, Greg Allan *artist*

Larkspur
Bierbaum, Janith Marie *artist*

Littleton
Barnes, Cloyd Ray *sculptor, retired engineer*
Valderrama, Alexander Stanley *graphic designer*

Longmont
King, Jane Louise *artist*
Kirk, Janet Brown *artist, educator, art gallery owner*

Louisville
Qualley, Charles Albert *fine arts educator*

Northglenn
Lancaster, Kimberly Meiron (KC Lancaster) *artist*

Pagosa Springs
Mion, Pierre Riccardo *artist, illustrator*

Pueblo
Wands, Robert James *art educator*

Salida
Miller, Marian Lofton *artist, musician*
Ragan, Susan Swartz *art educator*

Snowmass Village
Beeman, Malinda Mary *artist, program administrator*

Telluride
Smith, Samuel David *artist, educator*

Westcliffe
Merfeld, Gerald Lydon *artist*

HAWAII

Haiku
Cost, James Peter *artist*

Hilo
Miyamoto, Wayne Akira *painter, printmaker, educator*

Honolulu
Amor, Simeon, Jr. *photographer*
Betts, Barbara Stoke *artist, educator*
Bushnell, Kenneth Wayne *artist, educator*
Chang, Rodney Eiu Joon *artist, dentist*
Gilbert-Bushnell, Helen Odell *artist, art educator*
Guthrie, Edgar King *artist*
Morita, John Takami *artist*
Pedesky, Geraldine Golick *design project professional*
Scott, Kenneth Craig *artist*
Uhl, Philip Edward *marine artist*

Kapaau
Jankowski, Theodore Andrew *artist*

Kauai
Kahn, Martin Jerome *art gallery owner*

Kihei
Wilson, Jay *tapestry weaver*

Lahaina
Killingsworth, Kathleen Nola *artist, photographer, company executive*
Sato, Tadashi *artist*

Lihue
Lai, Waihang *art educator*

Makawao
Kratka, Ilene *artist, sculptor*

IDAHO

Lewiston
Scott, Linda Byrne *artist*

Weiser
Hough, Michael James *sculptor, educator*

Yellow Pine
Auth, Robert Ralph *art educator*

INDIANA

Purdue University
Bannatyne, Mark William McKenzie *technical graphics educator*

MASSACHUSETTS

Concord
Masi, Robin *artist, humanities educator*

MISSOURI

Kansas City
Bransby, Eric James *muralist, educator*

MONTANA

Belgrade
Dolan, James Wilson *sculptor*

Billings
Deschner, Jane Waggoner *collage artist, public relations consultant*
Pomeroy, Lyndon Fayne *sculptor*

Browning
Scriver, Robert Macfie *sculptor*

Helena
Breth, Charles Andrew *artist*
Cleary, Shirley Jean *artist, illustrator*

Kalispell
Abbrescia, Joseph Leonard *artist, educator*
von Krenner, Hana R. *artist*
von Krenner, Walther G. *artist, writer, art consultant and appraiser*

Livingston
Chatham, Russell *landscape artist*

Missoula
Morin, Paula Marie Yvette (Maryan Morin) *photographer, artist, photo researcher*
Rippon, Thomas Michael *art educator, artist*

NEVADA

Carson City
Alcorn, Karen Zefting Hogan *artist, art educator, analyst*

Crystal Bay
Wracker, Brian D. *art educator*

Elko
Sweetwater, Sarah Alice *art educator*

Fallon
Stevenson, Patricia Kennard *artist, journalist*

Henderson
Goldblatt, Hal Michael *photographer, accountant*
Hara-Isa, Nancy Jeanne *graphic designer*
Turner, Florence Frances *ceramist*

Las Vegas
Holder, Thomas Jay *art educator*

Lesnick, Stephen William *artist*
Newquist, Donald Stewart *designer, technical director, consultant*

Reno
Harder, Kelsie T. *artist, educator*
Newberg, Dorothy Beck (Mrs. William C. Newberg) *portrait artist*
Waddell, Theodore *painter*

NEW MEXICO

Albuquerque
Adams, Clinton *artist, historian*
Antreasian, Garo Zareh *artist, lithographer, art educator*
Barrow, Thomas Francis *artist, educator*
Barry, Steve *sculptor, educator*
Cia, Manuel Lopez *artist*
Coleman, Barbara McReynolds *artist*
Dunn, Dennis Steven *artist, illustrator*
Easley, Loyce Anna *painter*
Hahn, Betty *artist, photographer, educator*
Hammersley, Frederick Harold *artist*
Humphries, Sandra Lee Forger *artist, teacher*
Keating, David *photographer*
Lafferton, Mackie V. (Makki V. Lafferton) *artist*
Multhaup, Merrel Keyes *artist*
Nelson, Mary Carroll *artist, author*
Ramirez, Joel Tito *artist*
Robb, Peggy Hight *artist, educator*
Terry, Martin Michael *visual artist, art therapist*
Townsend, Alvin Neal *artist*
Witkin, Joel-Peter *photographer*

Angel Fire
Shanhouse, Bill *sculptor, educator*

Anthony
Porter, L(awrence) B(enjamin) *artist*

Arroyo Hondo
Ferguson-Huntington, Kathleen Elizabeth *artist, educator*

Corrales
Eaton, Pauline *artist*
Leis, Marietta Patricia *artist*
Townsend, Storm Diana *sculptor*

Dixon
Saxe, Mark Ian *artist*

Galisteo
Merrick, Nicholas Gregory *photographer*

Gallup
Cattaneo, Jacquelyn Annette Kammerer *artist, educator*
Roberts, Kenneth Richard *artist, educator*

Jemez Springs
Bennett, Noël *artist, author*

Las Cruces
Ritter, Sallie *painter, sculptor*

Lincoln
Waterhouse, Russell Rutledge *artist, painter*

Los Alamos
Finney, Henry Christopher *artist, educator, writer*
Sarracino, Margaret C. *artist*

Ranchos De Taos
Koehler, James *tapestry artist*

Rio Rancho
Warder, William *artist*

Rociada
Reed, Carol Louise *designer*

Roswell
Avery, Keith Willette *artist, educator*
Hallenbeck, Pomona Juanita *artist*
Wiggins, Kim Douglas *artist, art dealer*

San Patricio
Meigs, John Liggett *artist*

Santa Fe
Allen, Page Randolph *artist*
Bass, David Loren *artist*
Bauer, Betsy (Bauer Elizabeth) *artist*
Clift, William Brooks, III *photographer*
Dechert, Peter *photographer, writer, foundation adminstrator*
Dominguez, Eddie *artist*
Fangor, Voy *painter*
Hartford, Jane Davis *textile artist*
Henrickson, Paul Robert *artist*
Hensley, Jackson Morey *artist*
Mhaffey, Merrill Dean *artist*
Mitchell, Mary McElwain *art therapist art educator*
Orduno, Robert Daniel *artist, painter, sculptor*
Shubart, Dorothy Louise Tepfer *artist, educator*
Sonnenberg, Frances *sculptor, educator*
Steinke, Bettina *artist*
Sturgen, Winston *photographer, printmaker, artist*

Taos
Bell, Larry Stuart *artist*
Harmon, Cliff F. *artist*
Lerner, Alexandria Sandra *artist*
Macpherson, Kevin Dan *artist*
Martin, Agnes *artist*
Ray, Robert Donald *artist*
Scott, Doug *sculptor*
Vigil, Veloy Joseph *artist*

Tesuque
Novak, Joe *artist*

Tijeras
Sweet, Mary French *artist*

NEW YORK

New York
Brown, Christopher *artist*

OREGON

Applegate
Boyle, (Charles) Keith *artist, educator*

Ashland
Anderson, Arthur Lee *sculptor, writer*
Hay, Richard Laurence *theater scenic designer*

Bandon
Lindquist, Louis William *artist, writer*

Bend
Acosta, Cristina Pilar *artist*

Brookings
Johnson, Richard Vernon *artist, educator*
Lang, Norma Ellen *art educator*

Cannon Beach
Greaver, Harry *artist*

Dayton
Gilhooly, David James, III *artist*

Eugene
Buckner, Matthew Eric *sculptor*
Fenstermacher, Cathleen Irene Field *art dealer, secondary education educator*
Hoy, Harold Henry *artist*
O'Connell, Kenneth Robert *artist, animator, educator*

Hillsboro
Hurley, Bruce Palmer *artist*

Jacksonville
Bennett, Eugene Peart *artist*

Lake Oswego
DaVinci, Ushana Maraldo *multimedia artist, environmental designer*

Medford
Puckett, Richard Edward *artist, consultant, retired recreation executive*

Newberg
Keith, Pauline Mary *artist, illustrator, writer*

Pendleton
Harper, Gloria Janet *artist, educator*

Portland
Ace, Katherine *artist*
Baker, Allison Paige *photographer, musician, educator*
Borgeson, Bet *artist*
Canfield, James *art director*
Clodfelter, Richard Doyle *artist*
Cooke, Judy *artist, educator*
Gimbolo, Aleksei Frank Charles *artist, philosopher, author*
Montone, Kenneth Alan *art director, creative director, consultant*
Pander, Hendrik Pieter (Henk Pander) *artist*
Ramsby, Mark Delivan *lighting designer and consultant*
Waddingham, John Alfred *artist, journalist*
Wyss, Judith Ann *artist*

Prineville
Kolding, Laura Alice *artist, educator*

Salem
Forgue, Kerry Jo *artist, educator*
Pierre, Joseph Horace, Jr. *commercial artist*

Sheridan
Turner, Ralph James *artist*

Sisters
Bennett, Paul Alan *artist, educator*

Springfield
Gurdjian, Annette Ovsanna *artist*

White City
Johnson, Morgan Burton *artist, writer*

TEXAS

Laredo
Knapp, Thomas Edwin *sculptor, painter*

UTAH

Ivins
Riggs, Francis Porter *sculptor*

Monroe
Kirby, Orville Edward *potter, painter, sculptor*

Orderville
Zornes, Milford *artist*

Park City
Pierce, Diane Jean *artist*

Provo
Barsch, Wulf Erich *artist, educator*
Linn, David Edward *artist*
Wilson, Warren Bingham *artist, art educator*

Salt Lake City
Goldstein, Barbara Joan *sculptor*

Smithfield
Rasmuson, Brent (Jacobsen) *photographer, graphic artist*

Vernal
Harrison, Garth Trevier *artist, retired social worker*

WASHINGTON

Anacortes
Bergner, Lanny Michael *sculptor*
Mc Cracken, Philip Trafton *sculptor*
Osborne, Leo Ewell *artist*

Bainbridge Island
Carlson, Robert Michael *artist*

Battle Ground
Hansen, James Lee *sculptor*

Bellevue
Warsinke, Norman George *interior designer, sculptor*

Bellingham
Johnston, Thomas Alix *artist, educator*

Burlington
Zeretzke, Frederick Frank H. *artist, educator*

Ellensburg
Parker-Fairbanks, Dixie *artist*

Everett
Krahn, Thomas Frank *photographer*

Goldendale
Musgrave, Lee *artist, museum administrator*

Longview
Werth, Roger Alan *photojournalist*

Mercer Island
Steinhardt, Henry *photographer*

North Bend
Kaplan, Donna Elaine *artist, educator*

North Seattle
Spafford, Michael Charles *artist*

Ocean Park
Lee, Martha *artist, writer*

Olalla
Kimura, Joan Alexandra *artist, educator*

Olga
Trogdon, Dorothy Weber *interior designer*

Olympia
Davis, Steven Arthur *photographer, educator*
Fitzgerald, Betty Jo *artist, educator*

Palouse
Duffy, Irene Karen *artist*

Pullman
Coates, Ross Alexander *art educator*
Lee, Paul Pak-hing *artist, educator*
Watts, Christopher John *artist, educator*

Puyallup
Chalk, Earl Milton *retired art director*

Quincy
Dal Porto, Danna S. *art educator, artist*

Redmond
Scharf, Barry W. *artist, educator*

Richland
Fraser, Frederick Ewart *art educator*

Seattle
Allen, Judith Syma *art educator, artist*
Berger, Paul Eric *artist, photographer*
Bruch, Barbara Rae *artist, educator*
Dailey, Michael Dennis *painter, educator*
Du Pen, Everett George *sculptor, educator*
Gardiner, T(homas) Michael *artist*
Garvens, Ellen Jo *art educator, artist*
Guzak, Karen Jean Wahlstrom *artist*
Hanan, Laura Molen *artist*
Hu, Mary Lee *artist, educator*
Huchthausen, David Richard *sculptor, real estate developer*
Kucera, Gregory Michael *art dealer*
Pawula, Kenneth John *artist, educator*
Ross, Sueellen *artist*
Santucci, Selene Marie *artist, educator*
Segan, Kenneth Akiva *artist, educator*
Simpson, Lewis Cole (Buster Simpson) *artist*
Tanzi, Ronald Thomas *artist, educator*
Theobald, Gillian Lee *artist*
Washington, James Winston, Jr. *artist, sculptor*
Wenick, Dean *photographer*
Zeitlin, Harry Leon *artist, rabbi, educator*

Spokane
Flahavin, Marian Joan *artist*
Miller, Wendy Franklund *artist*

Tacoma
Colby, Bill *artist*
Guilmet, Glenda Jean *artist*

Vancouver
Maurice, Alfred Paul *educator, artist*

Vashon
Woodard, John A. *artist, art educator*

Walla Walla
Meitzler, Neil *artist*

Woodland
Feston, Edath Anne *artist*

WYOMING

Casper
Seeger, Sondra Joan *artist*

Centennial
Russin, Robert Isaiah *sculptor, educator*

Cheyenne
Craft, Robbie Wright *artist*
Moore, Mary French (Muffy Moore) *potter, community activist*

Cody
Jackson, Harry Andrew *artist*
Patrick, Lucille Nichols *artist, rancher*

Gillette
Omang, Bonita Ella *artist*

Laramie
Reif, (Frank) David *artist, educator*

CANADA

ALBERTA

Calgary
Esler, John Kenneth *artist*

Edmonton
Jungkind, Walter *design educator, writer, consultant*

BRITISH COLUMBIA

Duncan
Hughes, Edward John *artist*

Vancouver
Smolarek, Waldemar *artist, printmaker*

Victoria
Harvey, Donald *artist, educator*

SASKATCHEWAN

Saskatoon
Bornstein, Eli *artist, sculptor*

SPAIN

Seville
Sanchez, Leonedes Monarrize Worthington (Duke de Leonedes) *fashion designer*

ADDRESS UNPUBLISHED

Abraham, Carol Jeanne *artist, photography educator*
Ancona, George E. *photographer, film producer, author*
Astaire, Carol Anne Taylor *artist, educator*
Aust, Carol Peterson *artist, educator*
Balet, Jan *artist*
Baxter, Carol Cairns *fiber artist*
Beckmann, Robert Owen *artist*
Benton, Fletcher *sculptor*
Blankenship, Julie Renee *artist, educator*
Blinder, Janet *art dealer*
Boboia, Horia *artist, educator*
Bowen, Maria Antonia *artist*
Brodie, Howard *artist*
Brown, Theophilus *artist*
Buckner, Kay Lamoreux *artist*
Bush, Maria Westy *artist, educator*
Cabot, Hugh, III *painter, sculptor*
Calzolari, Elaine *sculptor*
Campbell, Demarest Lindsay *artist, designer, writer*
Chabot, Aurore *artist, educator*
Cheney, Galen Walcott *artist*
Cogan, John Dennis *artist*
Cooper, Susan *artist*
Cowell, Ernest Saul *lighting designer, consultant*
Cox, Pat *artist*
Cretara, Domenic Anthony *artist, educator*
Dagodag, Melissa Kerry *product design company executive*
Dahl, Bren Bennington *photo retoucher*
Davey, Patricia Aileen *poet, artist, writer*
Davidson, Jeannie *costume designer*
de Caro, Marc Clement *artist, designer*
DeLoyht-Arendt, Mary I. *artist*
Demaree, Suzette English *artist, photographer*
Dickau, Keith Michael (Mike Dickau) *artist, secondary school educator*
Dill, Laddie John *artist*
Drooyan, John Neal *visual artist, photographer, fine artist*
Eis, Joel David *scenic and lighting designer*
Ettenberg, Frank Joseph *artist*
Fahey-Cameron, Robin *artist, photographer*
Farnham, Mary Glade Siemer *artist*
Farrar, Elaine Willardson *artist*
Ferreira, Armando Thomas *sculptor, educator*
Flower, Renée Beville *artist*
Fritz, Charles John *artist*
Garrison, Gene Kirby *artist, writer, photographer*
Gause, Charles Marvin *artist*
Gifford, Leslie Jane *artist, writer, educator*
Goodwill, Margaret Jane *artist*
Gregory, Eleanor Anne *artist, educator*
Grim, Ellen Townsend *artist, retired art educator*
Groat, Jenny Hunter (LaVida June Groat) *painter, artist, choreographer, writer, curator, reviewer*
Gurwitz-Hall, Barbara Ann *artist*
Guthrie, Timothy Sean *art educator, artist*
Haley, Sally Fulton *artist*
Heilman, Marlin Grant *photographer*
Hendrix, Jill E. *artist*
Hertel, Howard Jay *photographer*
Hillman, Leilani Gené *artist, gallery owner*
Hirondelle, Anne Elizabeth *ceramic artist*
Hodges, Judith Anne *artist, art educator*
Holbrook, Peter Greene *artist*
Jimenez, Luis Alfonso, Jr. *sculptor*
Johnson, Douglas Walter *artist*
Jones, Claire Burtchaell *artist*
Jones, Thomas William *artist*
Katona, Robert Roy *artist, sculptor*
Kiskadden, Robert Morgan *artist, educator*
Klein, M(ary) A(lice) *fiber artist*
Klotz, Suzanne Ruth *artist*
Kramer, James Joseph *artist, painter*
Kuhn, Robert Frederick (Bob Kuhn) *artist, illustrator*
Langager, Craig T. *artist*
Lefranc, Margaret (Margaret Schoonover) *artist, illustrator, editor, writer*
Leventhal-Stern, Barbara Lynn *artist, marriage and family counselor*
Lindsay, Carol Frances Stockton *art specialist*
Lisnek, Margaret Debbeler *artist, educator*
Liu, Katherine Chang *artist, art educator*
Lo, Waituck *artist*
Lord, Carolyn Marie *artist*
Maher, Jan *artist, educator*
Maree, Wendy *painter, sculptor*
McCracken, John Harvey *painter, sculptor*
McMillan, Stephen Walker *artist*
Milant, Jean Robert *art dealer*
Miller, Barbara Darlene *art educator*
Miller, Philip Gray *artist*
Minami, Robert Yoshio *artist, graphic designer*
Mouffe, David H. *woodworker, sculptor*
Nadel, Ann Honig *sculptor, educator*
Nemiroff, Maxine Celia *art educator, gallery owner, consultant*
Newton, Barbara Bess *artist, educator*
Nguyen-Ely, Darlene *sculptor*
Nilles, Darrell LeRad *artist, inventor, architect*
Noble, Helen Bonner *artist*
O'Kiersey, Patrick M. *artist, company executive*
Ord, Linda Banks *artist*
Osmar, Nils Arnold *visual artist*
Parker, Wilma Joan *artist*
Partlow, Marianne Fairbank *artist, consultant, curator*
Patterson, Marion Louise *photographer, educator*
Penn, Barbara A(nne) *artist, educator*
Phillips, B. Kelly L. *sculptor*
Phillips, Billy Saxton *artist, designer, painter*
Pomeroy, Mary Barnas *artist, illustrator, writer*
Preston, Astrid *artist*
Quigley, Richard Lawrence *artist, educator*
Roberts, Holly Lynn *artist*
Root, Doris Smiley *portrait artist*
Ross, Molly Owings *gold and silversmith, jewelry designer, small business owner*
Ryan, Jodell *fine artist*
Schutte, Dorothy Anne *art educator*
Simmons, Christopher Laird *graphic designer, art director*
Skirvin, William David *artist, art director*
Sorensen, Jean *artist*
Soto, Thomas De *photographer*
Steel, Kuniko June *retired artist*
Steffian, Emily Enders *artist*
Stevens, Ann L. Hense *art educator, artist*
Stevens, Michael Keith *artist*
Strawn, Evelyn Rae *artist*
Swig, Roselyne Chroman *art advisor*
Taylor, Ann *artist*
Taylor, Elouise Christine *artist*
Thomson, Valerie *artist*
Travis, Lucinda Louise *display designer, writer, editor*
Turner, Bonese Collins *artist, educator*
Underwood, Martha Jane Menke *artist, educator*
Vaccarino, Robin *artist*
Villa, Theodore B. *artist, educator*
Walker, Debra *artist*
Walker, Edward Donald (Rusty Walker) *artist, educator*
Whitson, Angie *artist*
Wiltermood, Kelly Ann *artist, marketing consultant*
Wiseman, Jay Donald *photographer, mechanical contractor, designer*
Wulfson, Michelle Elise *artist*
Yates, Steven A. *artist, curator*
Ynda, Mary Lou *artist, educator*
York, Walter Allen *photographer*
Zekman, Terri Margaret *graphic designer*
Zink, Melissa Ellis *artist*

ASSOCIATIONS AND ORGANIZATIONS. *See also* specific fields.

UNITED STATES

ALASKA

Anchorage
Jones, Jewel *social services administrator*
Jones, Mark Logan *educational association executive, educator*
Marcey, Jean LaVerne *educational association administrator*
O'Regan, Deborah *association executive, lawyer*
Thrasher, Kara Scott *art association director*

Fairbanks
Thomas, Joseph James, Jr. *trade association administrator*

Nome
McCoy, Douglas Michael *social services administrator, clergyman*

ARIZONA

Dewey
Burch, Mary Lou *organization consultant, housing advocate*

Dragoon
Woosley, Anne I. *cultural organization administrator*

Florence
Wallace, Brenda Ann *human service community planner*

Mesa
Duncan, H(oward) Daniels *social welfare administrator*

Phoenix
Baldwin, Rhonda *state health services administrator*
Hays, E. Earl *youth organization administrator*
Hoyt, Diana Vaughn *fundraising executive*
Orton, Mary C. *nonprofit administrator*
Rodriguez, Leonard *foundation administrator*
Smith, Stuart Robert *foundation executive*

Scottsdale
Carney, Richard Edgar *foundation executive*
Ferree, John Newton, Jr. *fundraising specialist, consultant*
O'Meara, Sara *nonprofit organization executive*

Sierra Vista
Morrow, Bruce William *educational administrator, business executive, consultant*

Tempe
Moeller, D(ouglas) Joe *development professional*
Sullivan-Boyle, Kathleen Marie *association executive*

Tucson
Ahumada, Martin Miguel *education association administrator*
McConkey, Max *association executive*
Pack, Phoebe Katherine Finley *civic worker*
Powers, Stephen *educational researcher, consultant*
Roberts, Vern Edward *sport association executive*
Ross, Mary Caslin *educational/academic administrator*
Sickel, Joan Sottilare *foundation administrator*

Wickenburg
Lahey, Carolyn Baker *foundation administrator, realtor*

CALIFORNIA

Alamo
Hardy, Lois Lynn *educational training company executive*

Altadena
Griswold, Martha Kerfoot *social worker*
Wells, William Adrain *non-profit executive*

Arcadia
Day-Gowder, Patricia Joan *association executive, consultant*

Atherton
King, Jane Cudlip Coblentz *volunteer educator*

Bakersfield
Stanley, Forrest Edwin *fundraiser, university program director*

Berkeley
Chew, Linda Lee *fundraising management executive*
Gee, Marguerite *nonprofit organization administrator*
Welter, Linda Allaire *development executive*
Wood, Thomas Eugene *nonprofit organization executive*

Beverly Hills
Brenner, Esther Lerner *fundraiser*

Brea
Tamura, Cary Kaoru *fundraiser*

Burbank
Angele, Alfred Robert *police labor union executive*

Burlingame
Costa, John Anthony *social services administrator*

Canoga Park
Lederer, Marion Irvine *cultural administrator*

Carlsbad
Liddicoat, Richard Thomas, Jr. *professional society administrator*
Parker, Alan Dale *financial development executive*

Carmel
Chester, Lynne *foundation executive, artist*
Criley, Richard Lawrence *retired advocate*

Chico
Burks, Rocky Alan *social services executive, consultant*

Chula Vista
Gilstrap, Linda Lee *fundraising executive*

Citrus Heights
Leisey, Donald Eugene *educational materials company executive, educator*

Claremont
Pendleton, Othniel Alsop *fundraiser, clergyman*
Warder, Michael Young *think tank executive*

Concord
Brown, Linda Louise *trade association executive, communication consultant*

Culver City
Imlay, Gordon Lake *development consultant*
Netzel, Paul Arthur *fundraising management executive, consultant*

Daly City
Civitello-Joy, Linda Joan *association executive*

Davis
Hays, Myrna Grace *educational association administrator, fashion consultant*
Wydick, Judith Brandli James *volunteer*

Fontana
Cory, Rolland Wayne *business administrator*

Foster City
Carter, William Gerald *non-profit corporation executive*

Glendora
Schiele, Paul Ellsworth, Jr. *educational business owner, writer*

Hayward
Archuleta, Keith Anthony *arts administrator, consultant, educational administrator*
Evanoff, Mark Evan *advocate*

Hermosa Beach
Ulep, Lei Ann Estampador *political campaign manager*

Hollister
Schiffner, Joan Lessing *consultant*

Kentfield
Blum, Joan Kurley *fundraising executive*

Laguna Beach
Pinto, Michael Jack *philanthropist, therapist, educator*

Lemon Cove
Mullen, Rod Gorden *nonprofit organization executive*

Lodi
Nusz, Phyllis Jane *fundraising consultant, meeting planner*

Long Beach
Brown, Lester B. *social work educator*

Los Altos
Farber, Geraldine Ossman *civic worker*

Los Angeles
Banks, Melissa Richardson *fund raising professional*
Bonowitz, Abraham Jacob *human rights activist*
Caldwell-Portenier, Patty Jean Grosskopf *advocate, educator*
Cosman, Mark Goodrich *association administrator, author*
Fox, Joel David *political association executive*
Gottlieb, Leonard *foundation administrator*
Harris, Barbara Hull (Mrs. F. Chandler Harris) *social agency administrator*
Headlee, Rolland Dockeray *professional society administrator*
Hirsch, Daniel Oren *public policy organization executive*
Hubbs, Donald Harvey *foundation executive*
Lindley, F(rancis) Haynes, Jr. *foundation president, lawyer*
Mack, J. Curtis, II *civic organization administrator*
Marrow, Deborah *foundation executive, art historian*
Meyer, Roger Allen *higher education fund raising executive*
Millman, Paul Richard *fundraiser*
O'Daniel, Damon Mark *government relations administrator*
Reagan, Nancy Davis (Anne Francis Robbins) *volunteer, wife of former President of United States*
Reisler, Raymond Frank *foundation administrator*
Schaffer, Jeffrey Lee *nonprofit organization executive*
Schine, Wendy Wachtell *foundation administrator*
Smith, Peggy Anne *fundraising executive*
Snowhook, Ann Laferty *social services administrator*
Walton, Brian *labor union executive*
Watkins, Sydney Lynn *sports administrator*
Wendlandt, Wendy Ann *political organizer*
Williams, Harold Marvin *foundation official*
Wolpe, Claire Fox *retired civic worker, psychotherapist*

Los Gatos
Rowe, Randy Roland *nonprofit organization executive, consultant*

Manhattan Beach
Devitt-Grasso, Pauline Virginia *civic volunteer, nurse*

Marina Del Rey
Stebbins, Gregory Kellogg *foundation executive, chairman*

Menlo Park
Fairbank, Jane Davenport *editor, civic worker*
Morrison, James Ian *research institute executive*
Pallotti, Marianne Marguerite *foundation administrator*

Modesto
Richardson, Ernest Ray (Rocky Richardson) *housing program supervisor*

Moffett Field
Scott, Donald Michael *educational association administrator, educator*

Morongo Valley
Lindley, Judith Morland *cat registry administrator*

Mountain View
Michalko, James Paul *library association administrator*

Murrieta
Hurst, Raymond Thomas *special education facility administrator, educator*

Nevada City
Hudson, Lee (Arlene Hudson) *environmental activist*

Newport Beach
Ford, Michael Q. *not-for-profit association administrator*
Greenfield, James M. *fund raiser*
Poole, Thomas Richard *endowment campaign director, fund raising counsel*

North Hollywood
Grasso, Mary Ann *theater association executive*

Novato
Raphael, Tamar Amita *development director*

Oakland
Borchardt, Marilyn *development administrator*
Dozier, Flora Grace *civil and human rights activist, entrepreneur*
Misner, Charlotte Blanche Ruckman *community organization administrator*
Oberti, Sylvia Marie Antoinette *rehabilitation counselor and administrator, career advisor, textile consultant*
Smith, Jeffrey Alan *international educator*
Widener, Mary Lee *social services executive*

Oakley
Tomiska, Cora Lorena *civic worker*

Orange
Tavoularis, Katherine Efy *political organization coordinator*

Orinda
Fisher, Robert M. *foundation administrator, university administrator*

Palm Desert
O'Rourke, Joan B. Doty Werthman *educational administrator*

Palm Springs
Hearst, Rosalie *philanthropist, foundation executive*

Palo Alto
Lovell, Howell, Jr. *non profit organization executive*

Pasadena
King, Rheta Baron *disability management consultant*
Staehle, Robert L. *foundation executive*

Redwood City
Spangler, Nita Reifschneider *volunteer*

Richmond
Cohen, Andrew Neal *activist, writer, scientist*

Riverside
Williams, Mark Tully *foundation executive*

Rolling Hills Estates
King, Lea Ann *community volunteer and leader*

Sacramento
Bartosik, Norbert John *state fair association executive*
Hayward, Fredric Mark *social reformer*
Larsen, Kenneth Marshall *art and human services advocate, consultant*
Meyer, Rachel Abijah *foundation director, artist, theorist, poet*
Naglestad, Frederic Allen *legislative advocate*
Oberlink, James Richard *environmental association executive, lawyer*

Salinas
Leaver, Betty Lou *educational administrator, writer*

San Anselmo
Lundeen, Ronald Arthur *theology educator*

San Bernardino
Arnquist, Jeanette Green *charitable foundation administrator, activist*
Traynor, Gary Edward *association administrator*

San Bruno
Eckert, Steven Paul *social services administrator*

San Diego
Beattie, Geraldine Alice (Geri Beattie) *advocate*
Blair, Steven Douglas *development director*
Boersma, Lawrence Allan *animal welfare administrator*
Brown, James Cooke *nonprofit organization administrator, game and language inventor, educational administrator, writer*
Carleson, Robert Bazil *public policy consultant, corporation executive*
Clarke, Evelyn Woodman *volunteer*
Downey, Paul Scott *social services administrator*
Gallison, H(arold) Bailey, Sr. *youth agency administrator, public relations and marketing consultant*
Hinsvark, Don George *social services agency professional*
Kelly, Brett *fundraiser*
Lane, Gloria Julian *foundation administrator*
Lovelace, Susan Ellen *professional society administrator*
Mone, Louis Carmen *clinical social worker*
Steiner, Maureen *political organization worker*

San Francisco
Ahn, Tina Marie *development executive*
Canales, James Earl, Jr. *foundation administrator*
Collins, Dennis Arthur *foundation executive*
Eastham, Thomas *foundation administrator*
Evankovich, George Joseph *labor union administrator*
Fitch, Jack *association executive*
Gordon, Gloria Kathleen *business association executive, magazine editor*
Grose, Andrew Peter *foundation executive*
Grundberg, Andy *cultural organization administrator*
Hasenkamp, Bruce Henry *foundation executive*
Hickman, Maxine Viola *social services administrator*
Jacobs, John Howard *professional society administrator*
Lord, Mia W. *world peace and disarmament activist*

Madson, David John *fundraising executive*
McCuaig, Ian Carruthers *fundraising consultant*
McIntyre, Robert Wheeler *conservation organization executive*
Mikuriya, Mary Jane *educational agency administrator*
Olmstead-Rose, Lester Morton *social welfare administrator*
Pettey, Janice Gow *fund raising executive non profit organization*
Pollack, Betty Gillespie *health care executive*
Rodrigues, Michelle Beachly *association executive*
Salazar, Wayne Hardy *arts and social services administrator*
Wolfe, Burton H. *non-profit organization executive*

San Jose
Bennett, Charles Turner *social welfare administrator*
Dargis, Jean Anthony *retired voluntary health agency executive*
Lind, Terrie Lee *social services administrator*
Orton, Eva Dorothy *volunteer*
Torrisi, Ralph Joseph *labor union executive*
Westendorf, Elaine Susan *social worker*

San Luis Obispo
Jamieson, James Bradshaw *foundation administrator*

San Mateo
Diehr, David Bruce *social service administrator*
Hongo, Florence Makita *educational association administrator*
Postel, Mitchell Paul *association administrator*

San Pedro
Gammell, Gloria Ruffner *professional association administrator*

San Rafael
Bobb, Richard Allen *non-profit executive*
Hill, Nathan Scott *educator, writer, cultural consultant*

Santa Barbara
Bailey, Marsha Ann *association executive*
Golden, Nancy McAleer *fundraising consultant*
Mc Coy, Lois Clark *emergency services executive, retired county official, magazine editor*
Redick, Kevin James *cultural organization administrator*
Schlosser, Thea Sussanne *advocate, association executive*
Shreeve, Susanna Seelye *educational planning facilitator*

Santa Fe Springs
Silverman, Dale Karen *association administrator, educator*

Santa Monica
Carstens, Diane Yvonne *retirement housing consultant*
Davis, Paul Kensil *strategic planner*
Fredricks, Shirley Jean *foundation director, consultant*

Santa Rosa
Harris, David Joel *foundation executive*

Sherman Oaks
Barron, Tiana Luisa *foundation developer, fundraiser, educator*
Marckwardt, Harold Thomas *association executive*

Simi Valley
Bumgardner, Larry G. *foundation administrator, law and political science educator*

Sonora
Coffill, Marjorie Louise *civic leader*

Stanford
Mahoney, Ann Dickinson *fundraiser*

Stockton
Blodgett, Elsie Grace *association executive*

Studio City
Barrett, Dorothy *performing arts administrator*

Sylmar
Branch, Anne Heather *fund raiser*

Tiburon
Cook, Lyle Edwards *retired fund raising executive, consultant*
Whitson, William Wallace *foundation administrator, retired military officer*

Truckee
Johnston, Bernard Fox *foundation executive*

Valley Center
Fry, Eva Margaret *volunteer worker*

Visalia
Keenan, Robert Joseph *trade association executive*

Walnut
Chaney, G. P. Russ *trade association administrator*

Watsonville
Cane, William Earl *nonprofit organization executive*

West Hollywood
Hoffenblum, Allan Ernest *political consultant*

Woodside
Patterson, Francine G. P. *foundation administrator*

COLORADO

Aurora
Fish, Ruby Mae Bertram (Mrs. Frederick Goodrich Fish) *civic worker*

Boulder
Cross, Christopher S. *fundraising executive*
Eberl, Patricia Jo *professional society administrator, editor*
Neinas, Charles Merrill *athletic association executive*
Secunda, David Abraham *trade association executive director*

Broomfield
Belk, John Blanton *educational and cultural organization executive*

Colorado Springs
Killian, George Ernest *educational association administrator*
Loux, Gordon Dale *organization executive*
MacLeod, Richard Patrick *foundation administrator*
Miller, Zoya Dickins (Mrs. Hilliard Eve Miller, Jr.) *civic worker*
Prensner, Steven R. *nonprofit organization executive*

Denver
Blish, Eugene Sylvester *trade association administrator*
Brown, Jody Touchton *arts and sciences organization administrator*
Bryan, A(lonzo) J(ay) *service club official*
Cole, George William *foundation administrator*
Daley, Richard Halbert *foundation executive*
Dinner, Marie Bernice *social services program administrator*
Eisenman, Athena Joyce *association administrator*
Futch, Marguerite Elizabeth *not-for-profit organization executive*
Gloss, Lawrence Robert *fundraising executive*
Knighton, Gwendolyn Layvonee *advocate*
Loeup, Kong *cultural organization administrator*
Low, Merry Cook *civic worker*
Proctor, Bettina Rea *fish and wildlife organization administrator*
Raughton, Jimmie Leonard *educational foundation administrator, urban planner*
Smith, Andrea Jean *professional association executive*
Wiseman, T. Jan *association executive*

Englewood
Bendel, Adrienne Antink *association manager, writer*
Reese, Monte Nelson *agricultural association executive*

Fort Collins
Adams, Frank Stewart *family service agency director, bishop/pastor*
Cummings, Sharon Sue *state extension service youth specialist*

Grand Junction
McCarthy, Mary Frances *hospital foundation administrator*

Greeley
Schrenk, Gary Dale *foundation executive*

Greenwood Village
Walker, Eljana M. du Vall *civic worker*

Littleton
Mergl, Betty Mae *senior center executive director*

Snowmass
Lovins, L. Hunter *public policy institute executive*

U S A F Academy
Coppock, Richard Miles *nonprofit association administrator*

CONNECTICUT

Ridgefield
Weese, Bruce Eric *pharmaceutical industry lobbyist*

DISTRICT OF COLUMBIA

Washington
Uehling, Barbara Staner *educational administrator*

HAWAII

Hawaii National Park
Nicholson, Marilyn Lee *arts administrator*

Honolulu
Blackfield, Cecilia Malik *civic volunteer, educator*
Botti, Richard Charles *association executive*
Furuyama, Renee Harue *association executive*
Kahikina, Michael Puamamo *social services administrator, state legislator*
McCall, Stephen Shawn *philanthropist*
Mirikitani, John Masa *foundation administrator*
Olmsted, Ronald David *foundation executive, consultant*
Schoenke, Marilyn Leilani *foundation administrator*
Sheridan, Mary Stoebe *social worker*
White, Emmet, Jr. *retirement community administrator*

Kapaa
Atkins, William Theodore *community volunteer, retired insurance executive*

Lihue
Lenthall, Judith Faith *non-profit corporation administrator*
Pironti, Lavonne De Laere *developer, fundraiser*

Paauilo
Sinnex, Ceil *nonprofit foundation founder, newsletter publisher*

IDAHO

Boise
Guerber, Stephen Craig *historical society director*

Hennessey, Alice Elizabeth *community foundation executive*

Moscow
Samaniego, Pamela Susan *organization administrator*

Orofino
Reynolds, Ron L. *foundation administrator, fundraising consultant*

ILLINOIS

Vernon Hills
Michalik, John James *legal educational association executive*

MONTANA

Billings
Sample, Joseph Scanlon *foundation executive*

Bozeman
Sanddal, Nels Dodge *foundation executive, consultant*

Great Falls
Ebbinga, Crystalle Yvonne *social services administrator*
Mulvaney, Janelle Williams *development professional*

Harrison
Jackson, Peter Vorious, III *retired association executive*

Helena
Langley, Pamela Jane *association executive*

Missoula
Amundson, Eva Donalda *civic worker*
Kemmis, Daniel Orra *cultural organization administrator, author*
Klaphake, Ronald Lawrence *non-profit executive*
Wolfe, Gary John *foundation administrator, wildlife biologist*

NEVADA

Carson City
Ayres, Janice Ruth *social service executive*

Ely
Rajala, Karen Rae *economic and community development administrator*

Henderson
Freyd, William Pattinson *fund raising executive, consultant*

Las Vegas
Anderson, Marsha Kobre *educational administrator*
Chinn-Hechter, Mamie May *nonprofit organization executive*
Deacon, Maxine Shirley *grant writer, fundraiser*
Horner, Lee *foundation executive, speaker, consultant, computer specialist*
Lowman, Mary Bethena Hemphill (Mrs. Zelvin D. Lowman) *civic worker, realtor*
Martin, Myron Gregory *foundation administrator*
Williams, Nancy Ellen-Webb *social services administrator*

Minden
Jackson, John Jay *clergyman, denomination administrator*

North Las Vegas
Gallardo-Salguero, Helen Christine *social welfare specialist*

Pahrump
Hersman, Marion Frank *professional administrator, lawyer*

Reno
Leipper, Diane Louise *association administrator*
Winzeler, Judith Kay *foundation administrator*

NEW MEXICO

Albuquerque
Cole, Terri Lynn *organization administrator*
Reynalds, Jeremy Graham *rescue mission administrator*
Roberts, Dennis William *trade association administrator*

Angel Fire
Dillon, Robert Morton *retired association executive, architectural consultant*

Farmington
Mathers, Margaret *charitable agency consultant, political activist, newspaper editor*

Santa Fe
Charles, Cheryl *non-profit executive, business owner*
Seemann, Charles Henry, Jr. *folklorist, cultural organization administrator*

Taos
Scott, Aurélia Carmelita *non-profit organization executive, writer*

OHIO

Columbus
Fordham, Marilyn Monroe *fraternal organization administrator*

OREGON

Bandon
Millard, Esther Lound *foundation administrator, educator*

Eugene
Hale, Dean Edward *social services administrator*
Wood, Daniel Brian *educational consultant*

Gladstone
St. Clair, Shane Scott *communications and international health specialist*

Grants Pass
Boling, Judy Atwood *civic worker*

Junction City
Humphry, Derek *association executive*

Lake Oswego
Miller, Barbara Stallcup *development consultant*

Lincoln City
Campbell, Cindy Irene *social service administrator*

Portland
Anderson, Bruce E. *association executive*
Beaird, Steven Edward *fundraising professional*
Bloch, Ernest, II *foundation administrator*
Bruce, John Allen *foundation executive, educator*
Orloff, Chet *cultural organization administrator*
Pine, William Charles *foundation executive*
Rianda, David Noel *medical foundation administrator*
Rooks, Charles S. *foundation administrator*
Schultz, James Michael *nonprofit marketing administrator*

Redmond
Johnson, Elizabeth Hill *foundation administrator*

Salem
Barnett, Kerry Evan *state business administrator*

UTAH

Bountiful
Pedersen, Gaylen *genealogy organization administrator*

Cedar City
Weaver, Max Kimball *social worker, consultant*

Ogden
Littleton, Gaye Darlene *nonprofit executive director*
Pappas, Leah Aglaia *civic worker, political consultant, educator*
Westenskow, Susan R. *school administrator*

Provo
Hulterstrom, William E. *foundation executive*
Lee, Blaine Nelson *executive consultant, educator, author*

Salt Lake City
Christensen, Michael E. *foundation administrator*
Cofield, Philip Thomas *educational association administrator*
Dolcourt, Joyce Linda *social service administrator*
Oswald, Delmont Richard *humanities organization executive, writer*

VIRGINIA

Alexandria
Pastin, Mark Joseph *executive consultant, association executive*

WASHINGTON

Auburn
Piraino, Ann Mae *seminar trainer, leader, vocational counselor*

Bainbridge Island
Rosner, Robert Allan *advocate*

Battle Ground
Fineran, Diana Lou *association administrator*

Bellevue
Arnold, Ronald Henri *nonprofit organization executive, consultant*
Kiest, Alan Scott *social services administrator*

Blaine
James, Herb Mark (Jay James) *foundation and insurance executive, free trade consultant*

Centralia
Olson, Steven Stanley *social service executive*

Edmonds
Thyden, James Eskel *diplomat, educator*

Everett
Corkran, John Rogerson *fundraising executive*

Olympia
Bellon-Fisher, Linda Sue *cultural organization administrator*
Gray, Donovan Michael *cultural development specialist*
Hernandez, Carrol *social services administrator*

Redmond
Andrew, Jane Hayes *nonprofit organization executive*

Seattle
Arthur, William Lynn *environmental foundation administrator*
Hirstel, Robert *labor relations consultant*

Koehler, Christopher Joseph *non-profit company executive, consultant*
Mathis, Teresa Gale *association executive*
Ray, Marianne Yurasko *social services administrator*
Sayward, Jenny *cultural organization executive*
Thompson, Dwight Alan *vocational rehabilitation expert*

Spokane
Falkner, James George *foundation executive*
Murphy, Mary Ann *human services administrator*
Rowe, Marjorie Douglas *retired social services administrator*
Wagner, Teresa Ann *handwriting analyst*

Tacoma
Gillmore, Richard Duane *nonprofit association director*
Zenker, Caryl H *marketing professional*

Vancouver
Anderson, Ford A., II (Drew Anderson) *foundation executive*
Smith, Sam Corry *retired foundation executive, consultant*

Washougal
McIntyre-Ragusa, Mary Maureen *social services consultant*

Woodinville
Manevich, Leonard A. *cultural organization administrator, composer*

Yakima
Nelson, Bryan H(erbert) *non-profit agency administrator*

WYOMING

Cody
Coe, Margaret Louise Shaw *community service volunteer*

Jackson
Symmons, Clare Payne *foundation administrator*

Laramie
Freeman, John Francis *foundation executive*
Hanson, Mary Louise *retired social services administrator*
Powers, Judith Kay *educational administrator, English educator*

CANADA

ALBERTA

Medicine Hat
Sorensen, Elizabeth Julia *cultural administrator*

BRITISH COLUMBIA

Vancouver
Saywell, William George Gabriel *foundation administrator*

ADDRESS UNPUBLISHED

Anderson, Ned, Sr. *Apache tribal chairman*
Barone, Janine Mason *foundation administrator*
Bashore, Irene Saras *research institute administrator*
Black, Karen L. *not-for-profit administrator, social worker, advocate*
Blum, Joanne Lee *development executive, educator*
Carrell, Heather Demaris *foundation executive*
Cilek, Jeffrey Robert *nonprofit executive*
Conran, James Michael *consumer advocate, public policy consultant*
Cooper, Minna Louise Morgan (Bobbie Cooper) *volunteer*
Eastman, Francesca Marlene *volunteer, art historian*
Edmunds, Kristine Ann *public administrator*
Eliot, Theodore Lyman, Jr. *international consultant*
Fiedler, Bobbi *community agency director, former congresswoman*
Hansen, Michael Joseph *association executive, writing educator*
Ikeda, Tsuguo (Ike Ikeda) *social services center administrator, consultant*
Klopfleisch, Stephanie Squance *social services agency administrator*
Loucks, Nancy J. *association executive*
Mack, Charles Daniel, III *labor union executive*
MacMillan, Kip Van Metre *foundation executive*
McCall, Franceen Kay *social services administrator*
Migden, Chester L. *professional society administrator*
Morgan, Kat C. *political activist*
Peck, Robert David *educational foundation administrator*
Ramo, Virginia M. Smith *civic worker*
Ramsey, Douglas Arthur *foundation executive*
Richards, Morris Dick *social work administrator, educator*
Ritchie, Steven John *foundation administrator, fundraising consultant*
Robbins, John *foundation executive, writer*
Robison, William Thomas *retired trade association executive*
Schiff Bernard, Ellie *political and nonprofit fundraiser*
Shuman, Thomas Alan *correctional operations executive, consultant*
Siri, Jean Brandenburg *citizen advocate*
Steiner, Roberta Pearl *not-for-profit foundation administrator*
Stewart, Paul Anthony, II *association executive, author*
Stout, Elizabeth West *foundation administrator*
Swain, Nola V. *foundation administrator, marketing professional*
Terrill, W(allace) Andrew *international security analyst*
Uhde, Larry Jackson *joint apprentice administrator*

Weddle, Judith Ann *social services administrator*
Wegner, Darlene Joy *civic worker, event coordinator*
Winters, Richard Keith *social services administrator*
Zehr, Norman Robert *association administrator*

ATHLETICS

UNITED STATES

ALABAMA

Mobile
Jackson, Bo (Vincent Edward Jackson) *professional baseball, former football player*

ARIZONA

Phoenix
Ainge, Danny Ray *professional basketball coach*
Barkley, Charles Wade *professional basketball player*
Bidwill, William V. *professional football executive*
Colangelo, Jerry John *professional basketball team executive*
Fitzsimmons, (Lowell) Cotton *professional basketball executive, broadcaster, former coach*
Geddis, Scott Winfield *physical education educator*
Johnson, Kevin Maurice *professional basketball player*
Jones, Lucia Jean *physical education educator*
Starks, Rosalyn June *physical education and health educator*
Tobin, Vince *football coach*
Van Arsdale, Dick *basketball team executive*

Tempe
Wells, Christine Louise *physical education educator*

Tucson
Kearney, Joseph Laurence *retired athletic conference administrator*
Olson, Lute *university athletic coach*

CALIFORNIA

Agoura Hills
Patano, Patricia Ann *health and fitness professional, marketing and public relations specialist*

Alameda
Gossett, Jeffrey Alan *professional football player*
Herrera, John *professional football team executive*

Anaheim
Lachemann, Marcel *professional baseball manager*
Stark, Milton Dale *sports association executive*

Bellaire
Levy, Louis *chess master*

Berkeley
Owens, Billy Don *martial arts educator*

Beverly Hills
Shoemaker, Bill (William Lee Shoemaker) *retired jockey, horse trainer*

Camarillo
Griffith Joyner, Florence DeLorez *track and field athlete*

Clovis
Mort, Gary Steven *physical education educator*

Coronado
Axelson, Joseph Allen *professional athletics executive, publisher*

Danville
Behring, Kenneth E. *professional sports team owner*

El Cajon
Addis, Thomas Homer, III *professional golfer*

El Segundo
Brown, Timothy Donell *professional football player*
Davis, Allen *professional football team executive*
Wisniewski, Stephen Adam *professional football player*

Inglewood
Harris, Del William *professional basketball coach*
Johnson, Earvin (Magic Johnson) *professional sports team executive, former professional basketball coach*
O'Neal, Shaquille Rashaun *professional basketball player*
Sharman, William *professional basketball team executive*
West, Jerry Alan *professional basketball team executive*

Irvine
Farrell, Dennis *sports association executive*

Los Angeles
Barnett, Michael *sports agent, business manager*
Barretta-Keyser, Jolie *professional athletics coach, author*
Barry, Brent Robert *professional basketball player*
Baylor, Elgin Gay *professional basketball executive*
Chamberlain, Wilton Norman *retired professional basketball player*
Claire, Fred *professional baseball team executive*
Fitch, Bill *professional basketball coach*
Lasorda, Thomas Charles (Tommy Lasorda) *professional baseball team manager*
O'Malley, Peter *professional baseball club executive*
Piazza, Michael Joseph *professional baseball player*

Malibu
Louganis, Greg E. *former Olympic athlete, actor*

Manhattan Beach
Kamin, Aviva *sports association administrator*

Menlo Park
Walsh, William *former football coach*

Napa
Miller, John Laurence *professional golfer*

Oakland
Cohan, Christopher *professional sports team executive*
McGwire, Mark David *professional baseball player*
Mullin, Chris(topher) Paul *professional basketball player*
Sprewell, Latrell Fontaine *professional basketball player*
Twardzik, Dave *manager professional athletics*

Oceanside
Lomeli, Refugio (Jesse Lomeli) *athletics educator*

Palm Springs
Jumonville, Felix Joseph, Jr. *physical education educator, realtor*

Pomona
Stromer, Priscilla (Perky Stromer) *physical education educator*

Sacramento
Benner, Rick *professional basketball team executive*
Fortunato, Joanne Alba *athletic director*
Richmond, Mitchell James *professional basketball player*
Thomas, Jim *professional basketball team executive*

San Bernardino
Rizzo, Terry Lee *physical education educator*

San Diego
Gilbride, Kevin *professional football coach*
Glass, Luis T.P. *retired tennis professional*
Gwynn, Anthony Keith (Tony Gwynn) *professional baseball player*
Seau, Junior (Tiana Seau, Jr.) *professional football player*
Spanos, Alexander Gus *professional football team executive*

San Francisco
Beck, Rodney Roy *professional baseball player*
Bonds, Barry Lamar *professional baseball player*
Gray, Lawrence Clifton, Jr. *physical education educator*
Magowan, Peter Alden *professional baseball team executive, grocery chain executive*
Mays, Willie Howard, Jr. (Say Hey Kid) *former professional baseball player*
McGee, William Dean (Willie McGee) *professional baseball player*

San Luis Obispo
Buccola, Victor Allan *physical education educator, sports association executive*

Santa Clara
Hanks, Merton Edward *professional football player*
Mariucci, Steve *coach professional and college football*
McDonald, Tim *professional football player*
Rice, Jerry Lee *professional football player*
Young, Steven *professional football player*

Santa Cruz
Holiday, Linda Freya *educator, school administrator*

Sausalito
Casals, Rosemary *professional tennis player*

Sherman Oaks
Hamilton, Scott Scovell *professional figure skater, former Olympic athlete*

Stanford
Van Derveer, Tara *university athletic coach*

Sunnyvale
Cognata, Joseph Anthony *football commissioner*

Walnut Creek
Hallock, C. Wiles, Jr. *athletic official*
Hansen, Thomas Carter *college athletics conference commissioner*

Westminster
Treadway-Dillmon, Linda Lee *athletic trainer, actress*

COLORADO

Alamosa
Layton, Terry Wayne *college basketball coach*

Colorado Springs
Badger, Sandra Rae *health and physical education educator*
Evans, Janet *Olympic swimmer*
Groebli, Werner Fritz (Mr. Frick) *professional ice skater, realtor*
Schultz, Richard Dale *national athletic organizations executive*

Denver
Baylor, Don Edward *professional baseball manager*
Galarraga, Andres Jose *professional baseball player*
Gebhard, Bob *professional baseball executive*
Swift, William Charles *professional baseball player, Olympic athlete*

Englewood
Craw, Nicholas Wesson *motor sports association executive*
Elway, John Albert *professional football player*
Perry, Michael Dean *professional football player*
Shanahan, Mike *professional football coach*
Sharpe, Shannon *professional football player*

Littleton
Garvin, Peter Graham *golf industry executive, business educator*

Strasburg
Straub, Richard Neal *coach*

CONNECTICUT

Bristol
Abdul-Jabbar, Kareem (Lewis Ferdinand Alcindor) *retired professional basketball player, sports commentator*

FLORIDA

Gainesville
Lopez, Andy *university athletic coach*

ILLINOIS

Moline
Carls, Judith Marie *physical education educator, golf coach*

MARYLAND

Baltimore
Davis, Eric Keith *former professional baseball player*

Landover
Bickerstaff, Bernard Tyrone, Sr. *professional basketball team coach*

MICHIGAN

Auburn Hills
Thorpe, Otis Henry *professional basketball player*

MISSOURI

Saint Louis
Eckersley, Dennis Lee *professional baseball player*
Frontiere, Georgia *professional football team executive*

MONTANA

Billings
Hahn, Woody *sports association executive*

Great Falls
McKinnon, Robert Scott *swimming educator*

NEVADA

Las Vegas
Holmes, David Leo *recreation and leisure educator*
Schneiter, George Malan *golf professional, development company executive*

NEW MEXICO

Albuquerque
Unser, Al *professional auto racer*

Las Cruces
Dudenhoeffer, Frances Tomlin *physical education educator*

NEW YORK

Bronx
Zimmer, Donald William *coach professional athletics, former professional baseball manager*

OHIO

Youngstown
DeBartolo, Edward John, Jr. *professional football team owner, real estate developer*

OREGON

Eugene
Decker Slaney, Mary Teresa *Olympic athlete*

Portland
Carlesimo, P. J. (Peter J. Carlesimo) *former college basketball coach, professional basketball coach*
Glickman, Harry *professional basketball team executive*
Kolde, Bert *professional basketball team executive*
Wallo, Steven F. *physical education and athletics director*
Whitsitt, Robert James *professional basketball team executive*

RHODE ISLAND

Kingston
Harrick, Jim *university athletic coach*

TEXAS

Austin
Garrido, Augie *university athletic coach*

Houston
Drexler, Clyde *professional basketball player*

UTAH

Cedar City
Morrison, Craig Somerville *physical education educator*

Park City
Kelly, Thomas J. *sports association executive*

Salt Lake City
Howells, R. Tim *professional sports team executive*
Layden, Francis Patrick (Frank Layden) *professional basketball team executive, former coach*
Malone, Karl *professional basketball player*
Miller, Larry H. *professional sports team executive, automobile dealer*
Richardson, Glenn Earl *health education educator*
Sloan, Jerry (Gerald Eugene Sloan) *professional basketball coach*
Stockton, John Houston *professional basketball player*

WASHINGTON

Kirkland
Erickson, Dennis *professional football coach, former university football coach*

Seattle
Ackerley, Barry *professional basketball team executive, communications company executive*
Ellis, John W. *professional baseball team executive, utility company executive*
Griffey, Ken, Jr. (George Kenneth Griffey, Jr.) *professional baseball player*
Johnson, Randall David (Randy Johnson) *professional baseball player*
Karl, George *professional basketball coach*
Martinez, Edgar *professional baseball player*
Payton, Gary Dwayne *professional basketball player*
Piniella, Louis Victor *professional baseball team manager*
Walker, Walter Frederick *professional basketball team executive*

Spokane
Moe, Orville Leroy *racetrack executive*

CANADA

ALBERTA

Calgary
Hay, William Charles *professional hockey team executive*
Risebrough, Doug *professional hockey team executive*

Edmonton
Sather, Glen Cameron *professional hockey team executive, coach*

BRITISH COLUMBIA

Vancouver
Bure, Pavel *professional hockey player*
Griffiths, Arthur R. *professional hockey team executive*
Jackson, Stu *professional sports team executive, former university basketball coach*

QUEBEC

Montreal
Damphousse, Vincent *professional hockey player*
King, W. David *professional hockey coach*

ADDRESS UNPUBLISHED

Banks, Ernest (Ernie Banks) *retired professional baseball player*
Benes, Andrew Charles *professional baseball player*
Burkett, John David *professional baseball player*
Haag, Carrie H. *former sports association executive*
Hall, J. Tillman *physical education educator, administrator, writer*
Harding, F(red) Victor *fitness consultant*
Herzog, Whitey (Dorrel Norman Elvert Herzog) *former professional baseball team executive*
Kemp, Shawn T. *professional basketball player*
Kent, Betty Dickinson *horsemanship educator*
Landovsky, Rosemary Reid *figure skating school director, coach*
Lindsey, D. Ruth *physical education educator*
McIntyre, Guy Maurice *professional football player*
McVay, John Edward *professional football club executive*
Ross, Robert Joseph *head professional football coach*
Schrempf, Detlef *professional basketball player*
Wooden, John Robert *former basketball coach*

BUSINESS. *See* **FINANCE; INDUSTRY.**

COMMUNICATIONS. *See* **COMMUNICATIONS MEDIA; INDUSTRY: SERVICE.**

COMMUNICATIONS MEDIA. *See also* **ARTS: LITERARY.**

UNITED STATES

ALASKA

Anchorage
Atwood, Robert Bruce *publisher*
Carter, Susie Gloria *publisher, editor, television and radio personality*
Crawford, Sarah Carter (Sally Crawford) *broadcast executive*
Dougherty, Patrick *editor*
Hill, Erik Bryan *newspaper photographer*
Lindauer, John Howard, II *newspaper publisher*
Pollock, Kent *editor*
Tobin, William Joseph *newspaper editor*

Fairbanks
Berry, Kathryn Allen *editor in chief science publication*
Cole, Dermot Matthew *newspaper columnist, historian*
Hatch, Kelley Marie *journalist, television news anchor, writer*
Massey, Paul J. *newspaper publisher*
Mitchell, Susan E. *editor, desktop publisher*
Nafpliotis, Cindy Herman *editor, publisher*
Pickett, Anna Margaret *newspaper editor*

Glennallen
Smelcer, John E. *publishing company executive*

Homer
Beach, Geo *journalist, poet*

Juneau
Hall, Booker Teleferio *broadcaster*

Seward
Leary, Lory Diane Mary B. *publishing executive*

ARIZONA

Bisbee
Eppele, David Louis *columnist, author*
Rubin, Bruce I. *newspaper editor, geologist*

Casa Grande
Grimes, James Cahill *publishing executive, advertising executive*
Kramer, Donovan Mershon, Sr. *newspaper publisher*

Chandler
Keaton, Susan Camille *editor*

Flagstaff
Aitchison, Stewart Wayne *photojournalist*
Hammond, Howard David *retired botanist and editor*
Siegmund, Mark Alan *editor, publisher, business consultant*

Green Valley
Lasch, Robert *former journalist*

Mesa
Gorder, Cheryl Marie *book publisher*

Phoenix
Benson, Stephen R. *editorial cartoonist*
Early, Robert Joseph *magazine editor*
Edens, Gary Denton *broadcasting executive*
Floyd, Barbara Irene *newspaper editor-in-chief*
Genrich, Mark L. *newspaper editorial writer, columnist*
Godwin, Mary Jo *editor, librarian consultant*
Grafe, Warren Blair *cable television executive*
Gruver, William Rand, II *journalist, educator*
Johnson, Pam *newspaper editor*
Kaiser, Robert Blair *journalist*
Leach, John F. *newspaper editor, journalism educator*
Murian, Richard Miller *book company executive*
Perkes, Kim Sue Lia *journalist*
Perlman, Janet *indexer*
Roth, Richard Wayne *media consultant*
Schatt, Paul *newspaper editor*
Smith, Greg Bruce *journalist*
Stahl, Richard G. C. *journalist, editor*
Steckler, Phyllis Betty *publishing company executive*
Weil, Louis Arthur, III *newspaper publishing executive*
White, Jane See *journalist*

Prescott
Anderson, Parker Lynn *editorial columnist, playwright*
Kimball, Richard Wilson *reporter, copy editor*

Scottsdale
Bowie, Herbert Hughes, Jr. *magazine editor, publisher, writer*
Fox, Kenneth L. *retired newspaper editor, writer*
Frischknecht, Lee Conrad *retired broadcasting executive*
Gates, Sheldon Wilbur *publishing executive*
Reidy, Richard Robert *publishing company executive*
Smyth, Bernard John *retired newspaper editor*
Walsh, Mason *retired newspaperman*

Sedona
Chicorel, Marietta Eva *publisher*
Edwards, F(loyd) Kenneth *journalist, educator, management consultant, marketing executive*
Sasmor, James Cecil *publishing representative, educator*

Tempe
Douglas, Michael *publishing executive*
Koppes, Steven Nelson *public information officer, science writer*
Milner, Joe W. *journalism educator*
Rankin, William Parkman *communications educator, former publishing company executive*

Tucson
Annerino, John Joseph *photojournalist, author*
Buel, Bobbie Jo *editor*
Copenhaver, Larry James *journalist*
Foran, Kevin Richard *television station executive*
Hatfield, Charles Donald *newspaper executive*
Hutchinson, Charles Smith, Jr. *book publisher*
Martin, June Johnson Caldwell *journalist*
Meehan, Eileen R. *communications educator*
Neal, James Madison, Jr. *retired editor and educator*
Reel, James *music critic, writer*
Roos, Nestor Robert *consultant*
Weber, Samuel *editor, retired*
Young, Donald Allen *writer, consultant*

Yuma
Watson, Larry Sullivan *editor, educator*

CALIFORNIA

Agoura Hills
Chagall, David *journalist, author*
Teresi, Joseph *publishing executive*

Albany
Elkus, Jonathan Britton *music publisher, music educator*

Alhambra
Duke, Donald Norman *publisher*

Alpine
Greenberg, Byron Stanley *newspaper and business executive, consultant*

Antioch
Jawad, Said Tayeb (Said Tayeb Djawad) *political commentator, writer*

Auburn
Renner, Jeannette Irene (Jay Renner) *publishing executive*

Avila Beach
Kamm, Herbert *journalist*

Bakersfield
Beene, Richard Stuart *editor*
Jenner, Mike *newspaper editor*

Belvedere
Lake, David S. *publisher, lawyer*

Berkeley
Bagdikian, Ben Haig *journalist, emeritus university educator*
Benet, Carol Ann *journalist, career counselor, teacher*
Brodsky, Bart Lou *publisher*
Brooke, Tal (Robert Taliaferro) *company executive, author*
Drechsel, Edwin Jared *retired magazine editor*
Lesser, Wendy *literary magazine editor, writer, consultant*
Lubenow, Gerald Charles *journalist*
Perera, Victor Haim *journalism educator, writer*
Salski, Andrzej M. *journalist, editor*
Weber, David Ollier *writer*

Beverly Hills
Bland, Janeese Myra *editor*
Farhat, Carol S. *motion picture company executive*
Filosa, Gary Fairmont Randolph V., II *multimedia executive, financier*
Iafrate, Gerald Carl *motion picture company executive, lawyer*
Levy, David *broadcasting executive*
Lond, Harley Weldon *editor, publisher*
McClafferty, William Mark *film company executive*
Schneider, Charles I. *newspaper executive*
Stambler, Irwin *publishing executive*
Yomtov, Michelle Rene *journalist*

Brea
Coniglio, John Vincent *publishing company executive, acquisitions editor*

Burbank
Bierman, Jack Victor *magazine editor, publisher*
Brogliatti, Barbara Spencer *television and motion picture executive*
Chiolis, Mark Joseph *television executive*
Disney, Roy Edward *broadcasting company executive*
Eisner, Michael Dammann *entertainment company executive*

Camino
Miller, Carole Ann Lyons *editor, publisher, marketing specialist*

Canoga Park
Birenbaum, Marc Allen *editor, writer*
Bloomfield, Masse *publishing executive, writer*
Destler, Dave M. *publisher, editor, journalist*

Carmel
Koeppel, Gary Merle *publisher, art dealer, writer, marketing consultant*
Mollman, John Peter *book publisher, consultant electronic publishing*

Chico
Langevin, Michael Peter *publisher, author*
Paton, Scott Madison *publisher*

Chula Vista
Blankfort, Lowell Arnold *newspaper publisher*
Pasqua, Thomas Mario, Jr. *journalism educator*

Cobb
Kandanes, Andrew *recording industry executive, percussionist*

Concord
Anderberg, Roy Anthony *journalist*
MacDonald, Angus *writer, editor*

Cool
Toren, Robert *photojournalist*

Corona Del Mar
Michaels, Patrick Francis *broadcasting company executive*

Costa Mesa
Beck, Martin *journalist*

Cupertino
Lim, Kenneth Ting *interactive multimedia analyst*

Dana Point
Hawk, Steve J. *magazine editor*
Wetenkamp, Herbert Delos, Jr. *publisher*

Davis
Anderson, Lorraine Pearl *writer, editor*
Motley, Michael Tilden *communication educator*

Del Mar
Faludi, Susan C. *journalist, scholarly writer*
Kaye, Peter Frederic *television editor*

El Centro
Kent, Gaylon Mark *broadcasting executive, reporter*
Lokey, Frank Marion, Jr. *broadcast executive, consultant*

Encinitas
Newman, Katharine Dealy *author, consultant*

Eureka
Lollich, Leslie Norlene *journalist, educator*
Shepard, William Wayne *editor*

Fair Oaks
Douglas, Marion Joan *proofreader, editor, labor negotiator*

Fairfax
Codoni, Frederick Peter *editor*

Fall River Mills
Caldwell, Walter Edward *editor, small business owner*

Fallbrook
Johnston, Betty *editor*

Foster City
Alvarez, Robert Smyth *editor, publisher*

Frazier Park
Nelson, Harry *journalist, medical writer*

Fremont
Rockstroh, Dennis John *journalist*

Fresno
Bochin, Hal William *speech communication educator*
Hart, Russ Allen *telecommunications educator*
Mettee, Stephen Blake *publishing executive*
Moyer, J. Keith *newspaper editor*
Rehart, Burton Schyler *journalism educator, freelance writer*

Fullerton
Lewandoski, Robert Henry *editor, publisher*

Happy Camp
Brown, Barbara Black *publishing company executive*

Hayward
Hammerback, John Clark *communications educator*
Roberts, Timothy Wynell *journalist*

Hollywood
Kirschenman, Karl Aaron *editor*
Miller, Brian Alan *television production executive*
Murphy, Philip Edward *broadcast executive*
Ogden, Steven Kevin *recording industry executive, producer*
Sarley, John G. *broadcast executive, writer*
Svetlik, John Anthony *entertainment company executive*

Huntington Beach
De Massa, Jessie G. *media specialist*
Frye, Judith Eleen Minor *editor*

Indio
Ellis, Lee *publisher, editor*
Wilson, Stan Le Roy *mass communications educator, county official*

Irvine
Madera, Marie Louise *magazine publishing executive*
Segal, D. Robert *publishing and broadcast company executive*
Wilson, J. R. *editor, writer, publisher*

La Canada
Paniccia, Patricia Lynn *television news reporter, lawyer*

La Habra
Maxwell, Donald Stanley *publishing executive*
Oliver, Joyce Anne *journalist, editorial consultant, columnist*

La Jolla
Christopher, L. Carol *communication researcher, freelance writer*
Copley, Helen Kinney *newspaper publisher*
Hornaday, Aline Grandier *publisher, independent scholar*
McGilvery, Laurence *book publisher, dealer*
Schudson, Michael Steven *communications educator*

La Mesa
Raftery, Miriam Genser *writer, columnist*

Lafayette
Stewart, Leslie Mueller *editor, writer*

Lake Elsinore
Corral, Jeanie Beleyn *journalist, school board administrator*

Lake Isabella
Gohlke, Josh Randall *journalist*

Linden
Smith, Donald Richard *editor, publisher*

Loma Linda
Bell, Denise Louise *newspaper reporter, photographer, librarian*

Long Beach
Archbold, Richard *newspaper editor*
Crutchfield, James N. *publishing executive*
Ellis, Harriette Rothstein *editor, writer*
Sadowski, Richard J. *publishing executive*

Los Altos
Miller, Ronald Grant *journalist*

Los Angeles
Arnold, David *film company executive*
Askin, Richard Henry, Jr. *entertainment company executive*
Bart, Peter Benton *newspaper editor, film producer, novelist*
Benty, Cameron Todd *magazine editor*
Borin, Boris Michaylovitch *writer, publisher*
Brockman, Kevin Michael *broadcast network executive*
Cate, Benjamin Wilson Upton *journalist*
Coffey, C. Shelby, III *newspaper editor*
Cordova, Jeanne Robert *publisher, journalist, activist*
Corrick, David Lawrence *radio producer, editor, journalist*
Crippens, David Lee *broadcast executive*
Day, Anthony *newspaper writer*
Del Olmo, Frank *newspaper editor*
Delugach, Albert Lawrence *journalist*
de Passe, Suzanne *record company executive*
Dolan, Mary Anne *journalist, columnist*
Dreyfuss, John Alan *journalist*
Dwyre, William Patrick *journalist, public speaker*
Firstenberg, Jean Picker *film institute executive*
Flanigan, James J(oseph) *journalist*
Fromson, Murray *journalism educator*
Furlong, Thomas Castle *newspaper editor*
Garza, Oscar *newspaper editor*
Gray, Thomas Stephen *newspaper editor*
Green, Marc Edward *editor*
Groves, Martha *newspaper writer*
Hamilton, Walter Nicholas *newspaper reporter, editor*
Hammond, Teena Gay *editor*
Harris, John Carson *editor*
Hart, John Lewis (Johnny Hart) *cartoonist*
Hines, William Everett *publisher, producer, cinematographer, writer*
Hudson, Christopher John *publisher*
Jampol, Jeffrey *music industry executive*
Jarmon, Lawrence *developmental communications educator*
Knittle, William Joseph, Jr. *media executive, psychologist, religious leader, management and marketing consultant*
Kraft, Scott Corey *correspondent*
Laventhol, David Abram *newspaper editor*
Loehwing, Rudi Charles, Jr. *publicist, marketing, advertising, internet, commerce, radio broadcasting executive, journalist*
Mack, Donald *publisher*
Maltin, Leonard *television commentator, writer*
Mann, Wesley F. *newspaper editor*
Margulies, Lee *newspaper editor*
Maslin, Harry *recording industry executive, producer*
Morgan, Dirck *broadcast journalist*
Murray, James Patrick *newspaper columnist*
O'Neil, W. Scott *publishing executive*
Parks, Michael Christopher *journalist*
Pearlman, Nancy Sue *environmental broadcaster*
Perenchio, Andrew Jerrold *film and television executive*
Peters, Kevin Casey *interactive multimedia producer*
Petersen, Robert E. *publisher*
Phillips, Geneva Ficker *editor*
Porterfield, Andrew Maurice *journalist*
Rense, Paige *editor, publishing company executive*
Richmond, Ray S(am) *journalist*
Scott, Kelly *newspaper editor*
Shaw, David Lyle *journalist, author*
Smith, Lane Jeffrey *automotive journalist, technical consultant*
Sturken, Marita Louise *communications educator, writer, critic*
Trembly, Cristy *television executive*
Wilson, Charles Zachary, Jr. *newspaper publisher*
Wolinsky, Leo C. *newspaper editor*
Zwick, Barry Stanley *newspaper editor, speechwriter*

Los Gatos
Goss, Eileen Abel *editor*
Lee, Edmund *photojournalist*
Monday, Jon Ellis *music publishing company executive*

Malibu
Blakemore, Paul Henry, Jr. *retired publishing executive*
Klevit, Alan Barre *publishing executive, motivational speaker, writer*

Manhattan Beach
Mecoy, Laura Hope *reporter*

PROFESSIONAL INDEX 831 COMMUNICATIONS MEDIA

Marina
Grenfell, Gloria Ross *freelance journalist*

Marina Del Rey
Görg, Alan Kent *media company executive, writer, filmmaker*

Menlo Park
Wright, Rosalie Muller *magazine and newspaper editor*

Mill Valley
Butler, Katy (Katherine Anne Butler) *editor, freelance writer*
Cushing, Richard Gollé *journalist*
Daigon, Ruth *editor, poet*
Leslie, Jacques Robert, Jr. *journalist*
McNamara, Kay Copeland *publishing executive*
McNamara, Stephen *newspaper executive*

Modesto
LaMont, Sanders Hickey *journalist*
Vasche, Mark *editor*

Montara
Tyler-Parker, Sydney Billig *publishing executive, author, educational consultant*

Monterey
Gotshall, Cordia Ann *publishing company executive, distributing executive*

Mountain View
Bottoms, David Timothy *editor, journalist*

Newport Beach
Bryant, Thomas Lee *magazine editor*
Reisman, Richard S. *publisher*
Snow, Alan Albert *publisher*
Van Mols, Brian *publishing executive*

Nicasio
Hopkin, John Barton *publisher, editor*

North Hollywood
Koran, Dennis Howard *publisher*
Loper, James Leaders *broadcasting executive*

Northridge
Wood, Donald Neal *educator in media, author*

Oakland
Bernhard, Peter *publishing executive*
Conway, Nancy Ann *editor*
Dailey, Garrett Clark *publisher, lawyer*
Davis, Sterling Evan *television executive*
Erlich, Reese William *journalist*
Kelso, David William *fine arts publishing executive, artist*
Lavoie, Steven Paul *writer, librarian*
Powell, Lane Alan *editor*
Torrez, Naomi Elizabeth *editor, librarian*
Wood, Larry (Mary Laird) *journalist, author, university educator, public relations executive, environmental consultant*

Ontario
Ferguson, Michael Roger *newspaper executive*

Orange
Fletcher, James Allen *video company executive*

Oxnard
Morgan, Gary B. *journalism educator*

Pacific Palisades
Bernheimer, Martin *music critic*
Fine, Cynthia Mizer *producer interactive media*
Hadges, Thomas Richard *media consultant*

Palm Desert
Godfrey, Alden Newell *communications educator*

Palm Springs
Browning, Norma Lee (Mrs. Russell Joyner Ogg) *journalist*
Mann, Zane Boyd *editor, publisher*

Palo Alto
Hamilton, David Mike *publishing company executive*
McNeil, John Stuart *publisher*
Rusk, Lauren *editor, educator*

Paradise
Swanson, Carolyn Rae *news reporter, counselor*

Pasadena
Carey, Keith Grant *editor, publishing executive*
Hopkins, Philip Joseph *journalist, editor*
Hurt, Arlen Lee *editor, retired public school principal*
Ozminkowski, Mariusz *journalist, educator*
Spector, Phil *record company executive*
Wood, Nathaniel Fay *editor, writer, public relations consultant*

Pebble Beach
Neswitz, Margye Fulgham *newspaper columnist*

Point Reyes Station
Austen, Hallie Iglehart *author*
Mitchell, David Vokes *editor, publisher*

Portola Valley
Garsh, Thomas Burton *publisher*

Rancho Palos Verdes
Hillinger, Charles *journalist, writer*

Rancho Santa Fe
McNally, Connie Benson *editor, publisher, antiques dealer*

Rancho Santa Margarita
Abanes, Richard James *freelance journalist, religion writer*
Miller, Elliot Ivan *editor*

Redding
Walsh, Madge Richardson *editor, writer*

Redondo Beach
Sparlin, Julie Angela *magazine editor*

Richmond
Doyle, William Thomas *retired newspaper editor*

Ridgecrest
Roberts, Jerry Bill *publishing company executive*

Rio Linda
Wall, Karen Elisabeth *editor*

Riverside
Holley, Jack K. *journalist*
Locke, Francis Philbrick *retired editorial writer*
McQuern, Marcia Alice *newspaper publishing executive*
Opotowsky, Maurice Leon *newspaper editor*

Sacramento
Baltake, Joe *film critic*
Block, Alvin Gilbert *journal editor*
Blum, Deborah *reporter*
Bottel, Helen Alfea *columnist, writer*
Endicott, William F. *journalist*
Giacomo, Gary Christopher *magazine editor, journalist*
Grossman, Marc Richard *media consultant*
Jones, James Edward *editor, publisher*
Jones, Mark Alan *broadcast technician*
Knudson, Thomas Jeffery *journalist*
Lundstrom, Marjie *newspaper editor*
McClatchy, James B. *editor, newspaper publisher*
Moore, William James *newspaper editor*
Prine, Stephen Brent *publisher*
Rodriguez, Rick *newspaper managing editor*
Swatt, Stephen Benton *communications executive, consultant*
Williams, Arthur Cozad *broadcasting executive*

Salinas
Duncan, James Richard *systems administrator*

San Andreas
Hoeper, George William, Jr. *editor*

San Bernardino
Burgess, Mary Alice (Mary Alice Wickizer) *publisher*
Fairley Raney, Rebecca *journalist*
Johnson, Brooks *publishing executive*

San Carlos
Barnard, William Calvert *retired news service executive*
Jones, Georgia Ann *publisher*

San Clemente
Dinkel, John George *magazine editor*
Singer, Kurt Deutsch *news commentator, author, publisher*
Stallknecht-Roberts, Clois Freda *publisher, publicist*

San Diego
Bennett, Ronald Thomas *photojournalist*
Blom, Jeffrey Lewis *publishing executive*
Freedman, Jonathan Borwick *journalist, author, lecturer*
Hall, TennieBee M. *editor*
Hosler, Laddie *editor*
Kaufman, Julian Mortimer *broadcasting company executive, consultant*
Kopp, Harriet Green *communication specialist*
Krulak, Victor Harold *newspaper executive*
Majkut, Paul Theodore *newspaper editor*
Martin, David Arthur *magazine editor, writer*
Mc Kinnon, Clinton D. *editor, former congressman*
Mickelson, Sig *broadcasting executive, educator*
Morgan, Neil *author, newspaper editor, lecturer, columnist*
Petrillo, Lisa Marie *newspaper reporter*
Pfeiffer, John William *publisher, management consultant*
Phillips, Frank Sigmund *business executive*
Ristine, Jeffrey Alan *reporter*
Simms, Maria Kay *publishing and computer services executive*
Steen, Paul Joseph *retired broadcasting executive*
Steward, Hal David *correspondent*
Vandiver, Linton Mitchell, II *publisher*
Warren, Gerald Lee *retired newspaper editor*
Winner, Karin *newspaper editor*
Winters, Paul Andrew *editor*

San Francisco
Barnum, Alexander Stone *journalist*
Berger, Arthur Asa *broadcast communication educator*
Blakey, Scott Chaloner *journalist, writer*
Bloomfield, Arthur John *music critic, food writer*
Caine, Carolyn Moore *activist, publishing executive, author, consultant*
Carlisle, Daniel James *announcer*
Carroll, Jon *newspaper columnist*
Chimsky, Mark Evan *editorial executive*
Close, Sandy *journalist*
Cole, David Macaulay *editor, publisher, consultant, writer*
Dopps, Carola Froukina Sophia *advertising media consultant*
Duscha, Julius Carl *journalist*
Eastwood, Susan *medical scientific editor*
German, William *newspaper editor*
Getto, Michael Hutson *communications consultant*
Hartgraves, Jeffrey Burton *editor*
Hearst, William Randolph, III *newspaper publisher*
Heuring, Wayne Robert *newspaper journalist*
Hill, Greg *newspaper bureau chief*
Horrigan, Theresa Marie *publishing executive*
Hudson, Heather Elizabeth *telecommunications educator, consultant, lawyer*
Jenkins, Bruce *sportswriter*
Johns, Roy (Bud Johns) *publisher, author*
Junker, Howard Henry *periodical editor*
Kayfetz, Victor Joel *writer, editor, translator*
Klein, Marc S. *newspaper editor and publisher*
Knee, Richard Alan *journalist*
Lara, Adair *columnist, writer*
Lefevre, Greg *bureau chief*
Lewis, Andrea Elen *editor*
Louie, David A. *television journalist*
Martin, Michael *publisher*
Moor, Anthony James *reporter*
Morgan, Michael Brewster *publishing company executive*
Musser, George S. *editor, astronomer*
Muto, Sheila Nobuko *journalist*
O'Reilly, Sean Joseph *editor*
Pimentel, Benjamin Impelido *journalist*
Rice, Jonathan C. *retired educational television executive*
Rogoff, Alice Elizabeth *writer, editor*
Rosenheim, Daniel Edward *journalist, television news director*
Saunders, Debra J. *columnist*
Schwarz, Glenn Vernon *editor*
Spander, Art *sportswriter*
Strupp, Joseph P. *reporter*
Taylor, Belinda Carey *magazine editor, writer*
Tullis, Paul Rowan *journalist*
Vande Berg, Marsha Joan *journalist, columnist, author*
Wilner, Paul Andrew *journalist*
Wilson, Johnny Lee *editor-in-chief*
Wilson, Matthew Frederick *newspaper editor*
Wolaner, Robin Peggy *internet and magazine publisher*
Yamamoto, Michael Toru *journalist*

San Jose
Carey, Peter Kevin *reporter*
Edmonds, Charles Henry *publisher*
Eng, Sherri Lynn *newspaper reporter*
Frymer, Murry *columnist, theater critic, critic-at-large*
Geracie, Michael Louis, Jr. (Bud Geracie) *journalist*
Ingle, Robert D. *newspaper editor, newspaper executive*
Pulcrano, Dan Michael *newspaper and online services executive*
Richards, Evelyn Jean *journalist*
Rubinfien, Elisabeth Sepora *journalist*
Singh, Loren Chan *technical writing specialist*
Sumrall, Harry *journalist*
Trounstine, Philip J. *editor, journalist*

San Luis Obispo
Busselen, Steven Carroll *journalist, editor*
Carr, Peter Emile *publisher*
Shea, B(arbara) Christine *communications educator, consultant*

San Mateo
Golding, George Earl *journalist*
Motoyama, Catherine Tomoko *communications educator*

San Pedro
Ackerman, Susan Moon *editor*

San Rafael
Sansweet, Stephen Jay *journalist, author, marketing executive*

Santa Ana
Cheverton, Richard E. *newspaper editor*
Katz, Tonnie *newspaper editor*
Rosenberg, Donald Lee *magazine publisher*
Slone, Ernie L. *journalist*

Santa Barbara
Brown, J'Amy Maroney *journalist, media relations consultant, investor*
Gibney, Frank Bray *publisher, editor, writer, foundation executive*
Poynter, Daniel Frank *publisher*
Tapper, Joan Judith *magazine editor*
Witherell, Elizabeth Hall *scholarly editor*

Santa Clara
Charles, Mary Louise *newspaper columnist, photographer, editor*

Santa Clarita
Adams, Jack *film company executive, screenwriter, producer, educator*

Santa Maria
Miller, Ken C. *editor*

Santa Monica
Lane, James Frederick, IV *publishing executive*
Palmatier, Malcolm Arthur *editor, consultant*
Renetzky, Alvin *publisher*
Rozenfeld, Kim David *television company executive and producer*
van Allen, Philip Andrew *multimedia production company executive, educator*

Santa Rosa
Mower, Melissa Bee *magazine editor, writer*
Parman, Michael J. *publishing executive*
Swofford, Robert Lee *newspaper editor, journalist*

Saugus
Pasternak, Bill *amateur radio newswriter*

Seal Beach
Blanning, William Andrew *media specialist*

Sherman Oaks
Davidson, Bill (William John Davidson) *entertainment journalist, author*
Wilcox, Robert Kalleen *journalist*
Yasnyi, Allan David *media communications executive*

Sierra Madre
Dewey, Donald William *magazine publisher, editor, writer*

Sonoma
Lynch, Robert Montgomery *newspaper publisher*

Soquel
Thacker, Netha Lynn *editor*

Stanford
Andreopoulos, Spyros George *writer*
Chaffee, Steven Henry *communication educator*
Maharidge, Dale Dimitro *journalist, educator*
Much, Kathleen *editor*
Risser, James Vaulx, Jr. *journalist, educator*
Salisbury, David Francis *newspaper, television science writer*

Stockton
Kraus, Joe *editor and publisher, writer*
Kroeger, Terry J. *newspaper publisher*

Studio City
Gordon, Robert William *editor*
Kumagai, Stacey *broadcast executive*

Summerland
Cannon, Louis Simeon *journalist, author*

Tarzana
Brook, Winston Rollins *retired audio-video design consultant*

Temecula
Crider, Jeffrey John *journalist*
Kindred, Ramona Genith *publishing company executive, management consultant*

Thousand Oaks
Westby, Jerome Bramble, II *editor*

Torrance
Adelsman, (Harriette) Jean *newspaper editor*
Box, James M. *newspaper editor*
Trousdale, Stephen Richard *newspaper editor*
Wafer, Thomas J., Jr. *newspaper publisher*

Union City
Funston, Gary Stephen *publishing and advertising executive*

Universal City
Geffen, David *recording company executive, producer*
Horowitz, Zachary I. *entertainment company executive*
Wasserman, Lew R. *film, recording and publishing company executive*
Weiss, Lawrence J. *broadcast executive*

Vallejo
Applin, George Stewart *journalist*

Van Nuys
Front, Theodore *music publishing company executive*

Ventura
Gallagher, Tim *editor, newspaper*
Howry, Joe *newspaper editor*
Moran, Rita Jane *music, drama, restaurant critic, travel writer*
Wilcox, John P. *publishing executive*

Victorville
Barsky, Martin *editor, publisher*

Vista
Klungness, Elizabeth Jane *publisher, writer, retired accountant*

Walnut Creek
Armstrong, John *newspaper editor*
Borenstein, Daniel Asa *newspaper political editor*

Watsonville
Stickler, John Cobb *publisher, journalist, author*

West Hollywood
Wendruck, Louis *publisher, television personality, consultant*

Westlake Village
Artof, Susan Dale *publisher, writer, psychology educator*

Westminster
Milligan, Ronald Edgar *journalist*

Whittier
Dannenbaum, Robert Marcus *publisher, editor*
Tisbert, Stephen James *recording industry executive*

Wilton
Harrison, George Harry, III (Hank Harrison) *publishing executive, author*

Woodland Hills
Anastasi, Michael Anton *journalist*
DeWitt, Barbara Jane *journalist*
Shuster, Fred Todd *journalist, commentator*

Yosemite National Park
Nash, K(im) Alan *public information executive*

Yreka
Smith, Vin *sports editor, business owner, novelist*

Yucaipa
Phillips, Anna *publisher, editor-in-chief newspaper*

COLORADO

Aspen
Hayes, Mary Eshbaugh *newspaper editor*

Boulder
Brink, Glen Arthur *publisher, wholesaler*
Hauser, Gerard Alan *communication educator*
Holloway, Debra Linn *humanities educator*
Horii, Naomi *editor*
Quint, Bert *journalist*
Shafran, Michael Wayne *editor*

Broomfield
Marrs, Roy Alonzo *magazine editor, educator*

Colorado Springs
Mansfield, Roger Leo *astronomy and space publisher*

Sommers, Karen Rose *editor, writer*
Stewart, Wayne M. *newspaper editor*

Denver
Ballentine, Lee Kenney *writer, publishing company executive*
Barbour, Alton Bradford *human communication studies educator*
Bates, James Robert *newspaper editor*
Burdick, Robert W. *newspaper editor*
Carlson, Robert Ernest *freelance writer, architect, lecturer*
Dallas, Sandra *correspondent, writer*
Dance, Francis Esburn Xavier *communication educator*
Dobbs, Gregory Allan *journalist*
Doyle, Alfreda Carrol *publisher, writer*
Dubroff, Henry Allen *newspaper editor*
Haselbush, Ruth Beeler *retired newspaper editor*
Hirschfeld, A. Barry *printing executive*
Kerver, Thomas Joseph *editor, consultant*
Krichels, Ted *public television station executive*
May, Clifford Daniel *newspaper editor, journalist*
McGowan, Joseph Anthony, Jr. *news executive*
McKibben, Ryan Timothy *newspaper executive*
Price, Kathleen McCormick *book editor, writer*
Strutton, Larry D. *newspaper executive*
Temple, John *publishing executive*
Willbanks, Roger Paul *publishing and book distributing company executive*

Durango
Ballantine, Morley Cowles (Mrs. Arthur Atwood Ballantine) *newspaper editor*
Hansen, Leonard Joseph *author, journalist, marketing consultant*

Estes Park
Asbury, Timothy Edward *editor*

Fort Collins
MacLauchlin, Robert Kerwin *communications artist, educator*

Golden
Baron, Charlotte Foehner *publishing executive*
Baron, Robert Charles *publishing executive*
Jamieson Nichols, Jill *journalist*

Granby
Johnson, William Potter *newspaper publisher*

Grand Junction
Reed, Kristen King *broadcast sales manager*

Greeley
Roberts, David Lowell *journalist*

Idaho Springs
Kelley, Louanna Elaine *newspaper columnist, researcher*

Lake George
Glover, Paula Ellen *journalist*

Lakewood
Kelly, Ryan Joseph *newspaper editor, writer, pilot*

Littleton
Keogh, Heidi Helen Dake *publishing executive*
Rothman, Paul Alan *publisher*

Longmont
Davis, Donald Alan *author, news correspondent, lecturer*
Hibler, Jude Ann *photojournalist*

Manitou Springs
James, George LeRoy *broadcasting executive*

Masonville
Hammond, Alan David *public speaker*

Mc Coy
Hastings, Merrill George, Jr. *publisher, marketing consultant*

Pueblo
Gregory, Leonard *publishing executive*
Noblit, Betty Jean *publishing technician*
Rawlings, Robert Hoag *newspaper publisher*

Rifle
Runck, Roger John *editor*

Salida
Shovald, Arlene Elizabeth *newspaper reporter*

Silverton
Denious, Jon Parks *publishing executive*
Denious, Sharon Marie *publisher*

DISTRICT OF COLUMBIA

Washington
Fenwick, James H(enry) *editor*
Herman, Andrea Maxine *newspaper editor*
Johnson, John H. *publisher, consumer products executive, chairman*

HAWAII

Haleiwa
Austen, Shelli *radio news anchor, consultant*

Honolulu
Chaplin, George *newspaper editor*
Flanagan, John Michael *editor, publisher*
Frankel, Charles Edward *retired newspaperman, journalism educator*
Fuller, Lawrence Robert *newspaper publisher*
Jellinek, Roger *editor*
Kamemoto, Garett Hiroshi *reporter*
Kim, Joung-Im *communication educator, consultant*
Novick, Stuart Allan *publishing executive*
Parma, Florence Virginia *magazine editor*
Rexner, Romulus *publishing executive*
Roth, Michael James *magazine publisher*
Shapiro, David *newspaper editor*
Simonds, John Edward *newspaper editor*
Twigg-Smith, Thurston *newspaper publisher*
Welsh, Robert Neville *broadcasting executive*
Wiley, Bonnie Jean *journalism educator*

Kailua
Mudd, Michael Edward *communications educator*

Kaneohe
McGlaughlin, Thomas Howard *publisher, retired naval officer*

Wailuku
Martin, Doris Ellen *publisher, management consultant*

IDAHO

Boise
Baker, Karen *newspaper editor*
Costa, John A. *newspaper editor*
Meals, Pamela F. *publishing executive*

Caldwell
Gipson, Gordon *publishing company executive*

Kamiah
St. Peter, Jeffrey F. *publishing executive, consultant*

Moscow
Anderson, Clifton Einar *writer, communications consultant*
Haarsager, Sandra Lynn *author, communications educator*

Pocatello
Morrison, Joy South *journalist*
Reedy, Penelope Michal *publisher, writer*

Rupert
Barborka, Clifford Joseph, III *broadcaster, marketing consultant*

Sandpoint
Bowne, Martha Hoke *publishing consultant*

ILLINOIS

Chicago
Rice, Linda Johnson *publishing executive*

Normal
Mc Knight, William Warren, Jr. *publisher*

MONTANA

Anaconda
Crockford, William Richard, II *newspaper editor*

Bigfork
Blumberg, Nathan(iel) Bernard *journalist, educator, writer and publisher*

Billings
Larsen, Kimbert E. *journalist*
Schile, Wayne *newspaper publishing executive*
Svee, Gary Duane *newspaper editor, author, journalist*

Bozeman
O'Donnell, Victoria J. *communications educator*

Conrad
Traxler, Buck *newspaper editor*

Great Falls
Newhouse, Eric *newspaper editor*

Havre
Gallus, Charles Joseph *journalist*

Helena
Korson, Gerald Michael *newspaper editor*
Malcolm, Andrew Hogarth *journalist, writer*
Sullivan, Leslie Noelle *editor-in-chief*

Kalispell
Ruder, Melvin Harvey *retired newspaper editor*

Livingston
Sullivan, John Charles *journalist, editor, publisher*

Whitefish
James, Marion Ray *magazine founder, editor*

NEVADA

Carson City
Christensen, Jon Allan *journalist*

Fernley
Weniger-Phelps, Nancy Ann *media specialist, photographer*

Henderson
Furimsky, Stephen, Jr. *freelance writer*
Martin, Donald Walter *author, publisher*

Incline Village
Scheller, Erin Linn *publishing company executive*

Las Vegas
Castaldi, Gwen *journalist*
Engstrom, Erika Julie *communications educator*
Frederick, Sherman *publishing executive*
Magliocco, Peter Anthony *editor, writer*
Mitchell, Thomas *journal editor*
Rossin, Herbert Yale *television producer*
Zobell, Charles W. *newspaper managing editor*

Reno
Bushee, Ward *newspaper editor*
Clark-Jackson, Susan *publishing executive*
Cunning, Tonia *newspaper managing editor*
Kosich, Dorothy Yvonne *editor, general manager, journalist*
Puckett, Martha Louise *publishing company executive*
Sheeran, Angela Maureen *information specialist*

NEW MEXICO

Albuquerque
Dahl, Donald Douglas *newswriter*
Davidson, Juli *creativity consultant*
Goldston, Barbara M. Harral *editor*
Guthrie, Patricia Sue *newspaper reporter, free-lance writer*
Hadas, Elizabeth Chamberlayne *publisher*
Johnson, Robert Hersel *journalist*
Lang, Thompson Hughes *publishing company executive*
Mc Million, John Macon *retired newspaper publisher*
Wilde, David *publisher, writer, biographer*

Deming
Lind, Lynn Hunter *reporter*

Las Cruces
Dickinson, James Gordon *editor*
Harris, Linda Gradyne *publishing executive*
Hastings, Nancy Peters *editor, publisher*
Merrick, Beverly Childers *journalism, communications educator*

Las Vegas
Trujillo, Arthur Benjamin *journalism educator*

Los Alamos
Mendius, Patricia Dodd Winter *editor, educator, writer*

Santa Fe
Atkinson, John Christopher *magazine editor, critic, writer*
Bowman, Jon Robert *editor, film critic*
Forsdale, (Chalmers) Louis *education and communication educator*
Friedenberg, Walter Drew *journalist*
Mc Kinney, Robert Moody *newspaper editor and publisher*
Moyes, Terence E. *publishing executive*
Ott, Robert William *publishing executive, corporate trainer, author*
Stieber, Tamar *journalist*
Teters, Charlene (Joun) *editor*

NEW YORK

Farmingdale
Steckler, Larry *publisher, editor, author*

NORTH CAROLINA

Asheville
Wilson, Herschel Manuel (Pete Wilson) *retired journalism educator*

OREGON

Baker City
Brinton, Byron Charles *publishing executive, editor*

Beaverton
Challem, Jack Joseph *health, advertising/public relations writer*
Sanford, David Roy *journalist, educator*

Bend
Bagwell, Steven Kent *newspaper editor*
Hill, Geoffrey William *publisher*

Brookings
Kocher, Charles Rodney *journalist*

Coquille
Taylor, George Frederick *newspaper publisher, editor*

Corvallis
Zwahlen, Fred Casper, Jr. *journalism educator*

Eugene
Baker, Bridget Downey *newspaper executive*
Baker, Edwin Moody *retired newspaper publisher*
Calvert, Leonard James *editor, writer*
Franklin, Jon Daniel *writer, journalist, educator*
Hildenbrand, Donald Gerald *editor*
Lee, Michael Eric *editor, designer*
Lemert, James Bolton *journalist, educator*
McGlone, David Anthony Joseph *publishing executive*
Robinson, Donald Wallace *journalist*
Sherriffs, Ronald Everett *communication and film educator*
Toké, Arun Narayan *editor, educator, electrical engineer*
Tykeson, Donald Erwin *broadcasting executive*

Florence
Serra, Robert Emmett *newspaper editor*

Gleneden Beach
Marks, Arnold *journalist*

Lake Oswego
Helbock, Richard William *editor, publisher*

Madras
Matheny, Susan Kay *news editor*

Medford
Taylor, Gregory Hobbs *publisher*
Twitchell, Cleveland Edwards *journalist, writer*

Newberg
Dan, Barbara Griffin *publisher, editor, author*

Newport
O'Donnell, Leslie Ann *newspaper editor*

Portland
Abel, Richard Eugene *book publishing consultant*
Bhatia, Peter K. *editor, journalist*
Broderick, Michael Joseph *radio news director*
Crabbs, Roger Alan *publisher, consultant, small business owner, educator*
Franks, Thomas Allen *editorial cartoonist*
Freiser, Helen *editor*
Graves, Earl William, Jr. *journalist*
Johnston, Richard C. *newspaper editor*
Johnston, Virginia Evelyn *editor*
Larson, Lars Kristopher *broadcast executive*
Loomis, James Arthur *broadcast technician, newsletter editor*
Mak, Stanley Ming *radio broadcasting management executive*
Mapes, Jeffrey Robert *journalist*
Murphy, Francis Seward *journalist*
Rowe, David Alan *magazine publisher*
Rowe, Sandra Mims *newspaper editor*
Sterling, Donald Justus, Jr. *retired newspaper editor*
Stickel, Frederick A. *publisher*

Rhododendron
Cole, Sherrie *communications technician*

Saint Helens
Parsons-Petersen, Pamela Anne *publishing executive*

Salem
Bentley, Sara *newspaper publishing executive*
Bergel, Peter Robin *editor*
Frank, Gerald Wendel *civic leader,journalist*
Mainwaring, William Lewis *publishing company executive, author*
Martin, Jim *copy editor, writer*
Merriman, Edward Franklin *journalist*
Wallace, Julia Diane *newspaper editor*

Tigard
Clark, Earl Ernest *publisher*
Nokes, John Richard *retired newspaper editor, author*

Wallowa
Wizard, Brian *publisher, author*

SOUTH DAKOTA

Sioux Falls
Garson, Arnold Hugh *newspaper publisher*

UTAH

Bountiful
Meitzler, Leland Keith *executive editor*

Ogden
Larson, Brent T. *broadcasting executive*
Marino, Mike *newspaper editor*
Thornburg, Ron *newspaper editor*
Trundle, W(infield) Scott *publishing executive newspaper*

Provo
Egan, Kathryn Smoot *communications educator*
Hatch, Steven Graham *publishing company executive*
Sanchez, Sheila Leonor *journalist*
Tata, Giovanni *publishing executive*

Saint George
Skinner, E. Morgan, Jr. *broadcast executive*

Salt Lake City
Anderson, Arthur Salzner *publishing company executive, marketing executive*
Bauman, Joseph Matthew *journalist, author*
Brady, Rodney Howard *broadcast company executive, holding company executive, former college president, former government official*
Brown, Carolyn Smith *communications educator, consultant*
Chase, Randal Stuart *communication educator, consultant*
Evensen, Jay Douglas *newspaper editor*
Fehr, J. Will *newspaper editor*
Harrie, Daniel Andrew *newspaper reporter*
Hatch, George Clinton *television executive*
Lustica, Katherine Grace *publisher, artist, marketing consultant*
Lythgoe, Dennis Leo *newspaper columnist*
Mortimer, William James *newspaper publisher*
Murphy, Miriam Brinton *editor, writer*
Newell, Clayton *media professional, writer*
Paulsen, Vivian *magazine editor*
Smith, Donald E. *broadcast engineer, manager*
Todd, Jay Marlyn *editor*
Trapp, Gerald Bernard *journalist*

West Jordan
Carter, Paul Edward *publishing company executive*

VERMONT

Saint Johnsbury
Mandelstein, Paul Stanley *book publishing executive*

WASHINGTON

Bellingham
Doerper, John Erwin *publisher, editor*

Bothell
Ferraiuolo, Perucci DiAndrea *journalist*

Centralia
MacCracken, Gordon Stuart *columnist, wire editor*

Edmonds
Owen, John *retired newspaper editor*

Lynnwood
Araki, Takaharu *editor, mineralogist, crystallographer, consultant*

Olympia
Howard, David Hal *journalist*
McClelland, Kamilla Kuroda *news reporter, proofreader, book agent*

Oroville
DeVon, Gary Albert *newspaper editor*

Port Orchard
Bonsell, Thomas Allen *journalist, publisher*

Port Townsend
Buhler, Jill Lorie *editor, writer*
Rollins, Louis Arthur *editor*

Redmond
Lamb, Ronald Alfred *editor*
Riddell, Jacqueline Anne *computer company executive*

Renton
Gifford, Arthur Roy *publishing executive*

Roy
Pledger, Leland James (Lee Pledger) *publisher, travel writer*

Seattle
Alexander, J.D. *publishing executive*
Anderson, Ross *columnist*
Arends, Jack *journalist*
Blethen, Frank A. *newspaper publisher*
Boardman, David *newspaper editor*
Buckner, Philip Franklin *newspaper publisher*
Bunting, Kenneth Freeman *newspaper editor*
Cochran, Wendell *science editor*
Crumb, Robert *cartoonist*
Dietrich, William Alan *reporter*
Fancher, Michael Reilly *newspaper editor, newspaper publishing executive*
Fitzgerald, Waverly *publishing executive*
Fluke, Lyla Schram (Mrs. John M. Fluke) *publisher*
Gold, Jerome *publisher, novelist*
Gormèzano, Keith Stephen *arbitrator*
Gouldthorpe, Kenneth Alfred Percival *publisher, state official*
Gwinn, Mary Ann *newspaper reporter*
Hargreaves, Mathew D. *printer, publishing executive*
Hawthorne, Nan Louise *publisher, internet resources consultant, trainer*
Henkel, Cathy *newspaper sports editor*
Hills, Regina J. *journalist*
Hobart, Willis Lee *editor*
Johnson, P. Anna *publishing executive*
Johnson, Wayne Eaton *writer, editor, former drama critic*
Keith, Kathryn Marie *editor, systems operator*
Kelly, Carolyn Sue *newspaper executive*
MacLeod, Alex *newspaper editor*
Nalder, Eric Christopher *investigative reporter*
Ng, Assunta *newspaper publisher*
Parks, Michael James *publisher, editor*
Payne, Ancil Horace *retired broadcasting executive*
Rathe, Karen Marie *editor*
Read, Thomas A. *editor, retired*
Rozen, Leland Allen *newspaper publishing executive*
Steele, Cynthia *literary critic, translator, educator*
Szeto, Hung *publisher*
Turner, Wallace L. *reporter*
Voorhees, John Lloyd *columnist*
Worth, Vonne Noell *newspaper publisher, editor, writer, disability rights activist*

Snohomish
Frohnen, Richard Gene *journalism educator*

Spokane
Blewett, Stephen Douglas *journalism educator, public relations consultant*
Cowles, William Stacey *publisher*
Grant, Thomas Arthur *television journalist*
Gray, Alfred Orren *journalism educator, communications specialist*
Peck, Christopher *editor*

Tacoma
Gilbert, Ben W. *retired newspaper editor*
Mottram, Robert Hugh *journalist*
Shipman, Keith Bryan *sportscaster*
Warren, Dale Andrew *publishing company executive*

Vancouver
Campbell, Scott *newspaper publishing company executive*
Geisinger, Pamela Susan *editor*
Power, Margaret Rae (Margo Power) *publisher*
Wagner, Diane Masters *newspaper editor*

Vashon
Mann, Claud Prentiss, Jr. *retired television journalist, real estate agent*

Woodinville
Margeson, Douglas William *reporter*

WYOMING

Casper
Levendosky, Charles Leonard *journalist, poet*

Cheyenne
Occhipinti, Carl Joseph *retired broadcasting executive*
Schliske, Rosalind Routt *journalism educator, journalist*

Glendo
Curtis, Nancy Nell *publisher, rancher*

Jackson
Ninneman, Thomas George *broadcast educator*

Laramie
Roten, Robert Charles *newspaper reporter, movie critic, columnist*

Yellowstone National Park
Schullery, Paul David *editor, writer, consultant*

CANADA

ALBERTA

Edmonton
Hughes, Linda J. *newspaper publisher*
Stanway, Paul William *newspaper editor*

ONTARIO

Toronto
Cruickshank, John Douglas *newspaper editor*

ENGLAND

London
Hinton, Leslie Frank *media executive*

ADDRESS UNPUBLISHED

Ainsworth, Harriet Crawford *journalist, public relations consultant*
Allen, Donald Merriam *editor, publisher*
Baltz, Antone Edward, III *journalist, writer*
Barnhurst, Christine Louise *broadcast executive*
Barry, Rick (Richard Francis Dennis Barry, III) *sportscaster, retired professional basketball player, marketing professional*
Baumann, Michelle Renae *editor, writer*
Benn, Julie Eve Arend *writer, communications specialist*
Berke, Judie *publisher, editor*
Blackstock, Joseph Robinson *newspaper editor*
Bradley, Jean Eleanor *newspaper executive, public relations consultant*
Byrne-Dempsey, Cecelia *journalist*
Cairns, Diane Patricia *motion picture executive*
Calvano-Smith, Rita *journalist, small business owner*
Capell, Cydney Lynn *editor*
Carey, Margaret Theresa Logan *newspaper education consultant*
Cheshire, William Polk *retired newspaper columnist*
Collins, Amy Denise *reporter*
Cooper, Jon Hugh *public television executive*
Cullen, Robert John *publishing executive, financial consultant*
Curtin, David Stephen *newswriter*
Draznin, Jules Nathan *journalism and public relations educator, consultant*
Everingham, Harry Towner *editor, publisher*
Ewell, Miranda Juan *journalist*
Farkas, Judi G. *film studio executive*
Fistell, Ira J. *newspaper editor, radio and television personality*
Fraser, Laura Jane *journalist*
Hedler, Kenneth Bruce *journalist*
Helford, Paul Quinn *communications educator, academic administrator*
Herdeck, Donald Elmer *publishing executive, retired humanities educator*
Hill, Steven John *journalist, educator*
Holzberlein, Kurt W. *news director*
Hudson Pomije, Maura Ann *editor*
Hunter, Scott Warren *journalist*
Jacobs, Joanne Lee *journalist*
Johnson, Frank Edward *former newspaper editor*
Kounalakis, Markos *foreign correspondent*
Lee, Robert W(illiam) *journalist, researcher*
Love, Laurie Miller *science editor*
Lush, Pamela Grace Meine *international publishing company executive*
Madsen, William Marshall *media specialist*
Maestas, Amy *journalist*
Manheim, Thomas L. *public affairs officer*
Marshall, Ronald E. *media and communications educator*
McCulloch, Frank Walter, Jr. *editor*
Medavoy, Mike *motion picture company executive*
Melendez, James Patrick *editor*
Morton, George Thomas *reporter*
Moskowitz, Robert Arthur *publishing executive*
Nichols, Carl Michael *interactive media executive*
Nish, Albert Raymond, Jr. *retired newspaper editor*
Noeth, Louise Ann *journalist*
Pedersen, Kim Aasberg *newsletter publisher, video producer*
Perry, Tekla Shelestak *editor, writer*
Peterson, Kevin Bruce *newspaper editor, publishing executive*
Piller, Charles Leon *journalist*
Pudney, Gary Laurence *television executive*
Radke, Linda Foster *publishing consultant*
Rhodes, Gerald Lee *writer*
Riggs, George E. *newspaper publishing executive*
Roberts, Jerry (Gerald Keith Roberts) *film critic, writer*
Robinson, Frank Robert *radio station executive*
Ryan, Cathrine Smith *publisher*
Sapsowitz, Sidney H. *entertainment and media company executive*
Smith, Chester *broadcasting executive*
Smith, Martin Bernhard *journalist*
Smith, Steven A. *newspaper editor*
Spitaleri, Vernon Rosario *newspaper publisher*
Sullivan, Patricia *journalist*
Taylor-Pickell, Lavonne Troy *editor*
Traylor, William Robert *publisher*
Tynes, John Cowan *publisher, writer*
Vaden-Neuenschwander, Sherry Mae *broadcaster, poet*
Vandenberg, Peter Ray *magazine publisher*
Vaughn, Michael James *arts critic, poet*
Vree, Dale *editor*
Weaver, Howard C. *newspaper executive*
Webber, Marilyn Aspen Kay *writer*
Weber, Mark Edward *editor, historian*
Welsome, Eileen *journalist*
Wies, Barbara *editor, publisher*
Williams, Christie Lee *journalist*
Winner, Cherie Lynn *journalist, author*
Witkin, Susan Beth *broadcast journalist, reporter*
Wolin, Merle Linda *journalist, consultant*
Wollman Rusoff, Jane Susan *journalist, writer*
Wood, Kenneth Arthur *retired newspaper editor, writer*
Woodruff, Virginia *broadcast journalist, writer*
Woodward, John Russell *motion picture production executive*
Yack, Patrick Ashley *editor*

EDUCATION. For postsecondary education, *See also* specific fields.

UNITED STATES

ALASKA

Anchorage
Behrend, Donald Fraser *university administrator*
Brunstad, Michael Lewis *elementary education educator*
Collins, Michael Paul *secondary school educator, earth science educator, consultant*
Fahl, Charles Byron *college dean*
Gillam, David Allen *elementary school educator*
Gorsuch, Edward Lee *chancellor*
Matsui, Dorothy Nobuko *elementary education educator*
Oesting, Susan Carolyn *education counselor*
Skladal, Elizabeth Lee *elementary school educator*
Young, Bettye Jeanne *retired secondary education educator*

Fairbanks
Abels, Michael Alan *university administrator*
Burch, Barbara Jean *special education educator*
Komisar, Jerome Bertram *university administrator*
Meritt, Patricia Anne *early childhood specialist*
Schlegel, James M. *educational administrator*
Wadlow, Joan Krueger *academic administrator*

Juneau
Romesburg, Kerry D. *state education administrator*

Kodiak
Griffin, Elaine Burks *secondary school educator*

Nome
Dunaway, Samantha Jo *secondary school educator*

North Pole
Kilbourn, Aldean Gae *secondary educator*

Old Harbor
O'Brien, Annmarie *education educator*

Tuntutuliak
Daniel, Barbara Ann *elementary and secondary education educator*

Unalaska
Newell, Doni Leonard *elementary school principal*

Wasilla
Burton, Marie Dinie *principal*
Milne, James David *educator*
Moore, Toni F. *elementary education educator*

ARIZONA

Apache Junction
Michelich, Joanna Kurdeka *college dean*

Arizona City
Donovan, Willard Patrick *retired elementary education educator*

Avondale
Huffman, Thomas Patrick *secondary education educator*
Thompson, Bonnie Ransa *secondary educator, chemistry educator*

Buckeye
Palmer, Marsha Kay *special services administrator*

Chandler
Barnard, Annette Williamson *elementary school educator*
Paloian, Renata Diana *elementary art educator, writer*

Chinle
Best, Dana Jo *primary school educator*
Reed, Leonard Newton *secondary school educator*

Flagstaff
Hatch, Lynda Sylvia *education educator*
Ratzlaff, Vernon Paul *elementary education educator, consultant*
Reyhner, Jon Allan *education educator*

Fort Huachuca
Adams, Frank *education specialist*

Fountain Hills
Humes, Charles Warren *counselor educator*

Glendale
Barrett, Darrell Gene *secondary education educator*
Deans, Penny Candace *business educator*
Edwards, Vicki Ann *elementary school assistant principal*
Field, Earl Lyle *dean, education educator*
Horner, Jennie Linn *retired educational administrator, nurse*
Louk, Donna Pat *elementary education educator, music educator*
Shuck, Lola Mae *retired elementary school educator*
Throp, George Lawrence *secondary education educator, mathematics educator*
Voris, William *academic administrator emeritus*

Globe
Scholl, Glen *principal*

Green Valley
Carpenter, John Everett *retired principal, educational consultant*

Kingman
McAfee, Susan Jacqueline *educator*
Roddy, David Bruce *college program director*

Lake Havasu City
Rheinish, Robert Kent *university administrator*
Schmoker, Michael James *educator, writer, journalist*

Litchfield Park
Asadi, Robert Samir *high school principal*

Many Farms
Hamilton, Jimmy Ray *secondary education educator*

Mesa
Bydalek, David Allen *educator*
Colbert, George Clifford *college administrator*
Hinde, Elizabeth Rose *elementary education educator*
Kleemann, Gary Lewis *university official*
Malcolm, Richard Ward *academic administrator, consultant*
Mead, Linda McCullough *secondary education educator*
Ramirez, Janice L. *assistant school superintendent*
Young, Daniel Edwin *principal*

Morristown
Rosehnal, Mary Ann *educational administrator*

Page
Hart, Marian Griffith *retired reading educator*
Tsinigine, Allen *educator*

Paradise Valley
Hendrickson, Robert J. *educational administrator*
Morris, Bonnie S. *education director*

Peoria
Jenkins, Carol Anne *educator*

Phoenix
Ambrose, Janine Lee *primary school educator*
Barela, Bertha Cicci *elementary education educator, artist*
Brawley, Edward Allan *academic administrator*
Buehler, Marilyn Kay Hasz *secondary education educator*
Cain, Robert Joseph *elementary school educator*
Cloyd, Sandra Gomez *bilingual educator*
Culnon, Sharon Darlene *reading specialist, special education educator*
Davis, Colleen Teresa *elementary education educator, reading educator*
Durham, Fleta Evelyn *educator, community volunteer*
Gibbs, William Harold *university administrator*
Gibson, Treva Kay *university official*
Hughes, Robert Edward *elementary education educator*
Hutchinson, Ann *development director*
Kuhn, Holly Hunt *elementary education educator*
Linderman, William Earl *elementary school educator, writer*
Losh, Charles Lawrence *vocational education administrator*
Meddles, Sharon Diane Gunstream *school counselor*
Minor, Willie *college dean*
Richardson, Judy McEwen *education administrator, consultant, cartoonist*
Whitlow, Donna Mae *daycare and primary school administrator*
Woods, Cindy Jones *junior high educator, researcher*

Picacho
Batina, Kimberly Jeanne *elementary education educator*

Pima
DeWitt, Charles Neil *educational administrator*

Prescott
Baca, Sherry Ann *secondary school educator*
Beaumont, Roderick Fraser *education consultant*
Halvorson, Mary Ellen *education educator, writer*
Pielstick, Clayton Dean *academic administrator*
Smith, Margaret Linn *retired educator, writer*

Prescott Valley
Peoples, Esther Lorraine *elementary education educator*

Roll
Jorajuria, Elsie Jean *elementary education educator*

San Manuel
Hawk, Dawn Davah *secondary education educator*
Lemley, Diane Claire Beers *principal*

Scottsdale
Churchill, William DeLee *retired education educator, psychologist*
Cianfarano, Sam Anthony, Jr. *principal, educator*
Lynch, Wanda Folgert *secondary education educator*
Phillips, Wanda Charity *secondary education educator, writer*
Smith, Stacy Arlene *educational management administrator*
Tubbs, Janet Carolyn *educational consultant*
Wong, Mai-Lon *public school assistant principal*
Wright, C. T. Enus *former university president*

Sedona
Goldberg, Melvyn *retired educator*

Shonto
Haviland, Marlita Christine *elementary school educator*

Somerton
Reed, Frank Vern *principal*

Sun Lakes
Anderson, Stuart Anton *education consultant, educator*
Johnson, Marian Ilene *education educator*

Tempe
Coor, Lattie Finch *university president*
Forsyth, Ben Ralph *academic administrator, medical educator*
Haggerson, Nelson Lionel, Jr. *education educator*
Ingle, Mary Svetz *preschool educator*
Lunsford, Jack William *government relations director*
Marsh, Roberta Reynolds *elementary education educator, consultant*
Pijawka, K. David *environmental educator, researcher*
Richardson, Richard Colby, Jr. *higher education educator, researcher*
Saunders, Karen Estelle *secondary school educator*
Simmons, Howard Lee *education educator*
Thompson, Anna Blanche *retired educator*
Wallen, Carl *education educator*
Yu, Chong Ho *educational researcher*

Tucson
Baker, Robert Kerry *college administrator, author, editor*
Benton, Eugene Alfred *assistant superintendent schools*
Bjorhovde, Patricia Ordonez *university development director*
Bounds, M. Betsy *educational administrator, consultant*
Chamberlin, Gordon Robert *secondary education educator*
Cutrone, Lawrence Gary *school system administrator, consultant, writer*
Dyer-Raffler, Joy Ann *special education diagnostician, educator*
Evans, Arthur Haines, Jr. *educational and organizational consultant*
Garcia, Juan Ramon *historian, educator*
Giorgi, Peter Bonnard *educator*
Hawk, Floyd Russell *secondary school educator*
Heins, Marilyn *college dean, pediatrics educator, author*
Humphrey, John Julius *university program director, historian, writer*
Johnson, Christopher Gardner *technology educator*
Leavitt, Jerome Edward *childhood educator*
Levin, John Stewart *education educator*
Pacheco, Manuel Trinidad *academic administrator*
Padilla, Elsa Norma *school system administrator*
Padró, Fernando Francisco *history and education educator, administrator*
Sander, Eugene George *vice provost, dean*
Starr, Melvin Lee *counselor*
Triffet, Terry *college dean*
Ungar, Lisa Elaine *school counselor, education educator*
Watson, Alvin, Jr. *educational administrator*
White, Danny Levius *counselor, consultant, educator*
Wilson, Darryl B(abe) *teacher, writer*

Vail
Wallach-Levy, Wendee Esther *secondary school educator*

Winslow
Black, Trudy Rae Letts *education educator*

Yuma
Rivera, Jaime Arturo *secondary education educator*
Robinson, Laura Ann *elementary education educator*
Young, Marilyn Rae *former school system adminstrative secretary, mayor*

CALIFORNIA

Agoura
Forman, Judith Avis *educator*

Alameda
Carter, Roberta Eccleston *therapist, counselor*
Fonzeno, Gregory Michael *principal*
Hooke, Michael Peter *secondary education educator*
Sakamoto, Katsuyuki *college chancellor, psychology educator*
Smith, Carol Louise *elementary school director*

Albany
Chook, Edward Kongyen *university official, disaster medicine educator*

Altadena
Montanez, Mary Ann Chavez *vocational rehabilitation counselor, writer, producer*

Anaheim
Grose, Elinor Ruth *retired elementary education educator*
Jackson, David Robert *school system administrator*

Apple Valley
Flinn, Janice Cecilia *secondary school educator, administrator*

Aptos
Hirsch, Bette G(ross) *college administrator, foreign language educator*

Arcadia
Soriano, Debbie Ann *educator*

Arcata
McCrone, Alistair William *university president*

Avenal
Barr, Maurice Alan *elementary education educator*

Azusa
Gray, Paul Wesley *university dean*

Bakersfield
Arciniega, Tomas Abel *university president*
Fallon, Robert Kyle *university administrator*
Hess, Helen Elizabeth *retired secondary school educator, musician*
Hodash, Bob (Robert A. Hodash) *educational program specialist*
Neumann, Herman Ernest *elementary and special education educator*
Peterson, Pamela Carmelle *principal, educator*
Skillin, Therese Jeno *elementary school educator*

Bellflower
Saldaña, Matthew Arnold *principal, academic administrator*

Ben Lomond
Sikora, James Robert *educational business consultant*

Benicia
Garrop, Barbara Ann *elementary education educator*

Berkeley
Cross, Kathryn Patricia *education educator*
Geist, Karin Ruth Tammeus Mcphail *secondary education educator, realtor, musician*
Johnson, Mary Katherine *elementary education educator*
Lilly, Luella Jean *academic administrator*
Peterson, Andrea Lenore *law educator*
Ralston, Lenore Dale *academic policy and program analyst*
Rice, Robert Arnot *school administrator*
Tien, Chang-Lin *chancellor*

Beverly Hills
Van De Kamp, Andrea Louise *academic administrator*

Blythe
Thomas, Marcella Elaine *elementary education educator*

Bonita
Barnard, Arlene *retired secondary education educator*

Boulder Creek
Billings, Judith Diane *elementary education educator*

Buena Park
Turkus-Workman, Carol Ann *educator*

Burbank
Stokes, Gordon Arthur *educational company executive, author*
Walters, Kenneth C. *retired educator*

Camarillo
El Shami, Patricia Ann *elementary school tutor*

Campbell
Mirk, Judy Ann *elementary educator*

Campo
Charles, Blanche *retired elementary education educator*
Jermini, Ellen *educational administrator, philosopher*

Canoga Park
Andreassian, Ellie E. *private school educator, educational administrator*

Canyon Lake
Knight, Vick, Jr. (Ralph Knight) *dean, education educator, counselor*

Carlsbad
Gardner, David Chambers *education educator, psychologist, business executive, author*

Carmel
Longman, Anne Strickland *special education educator, consultant*

Carmichael
Green, Marjorie Joan *elementary education educator*
Marmaduke, Arthur Sandford *educational administrator*

Carson
Detweiler, Robert Chester *university president, historian*

Castro Valley
Parris, Anne Witmer *secondary education educator, writer*

Chatsworth
Miller, Robert Steven *secondary school educator*

Chico
Esteban, Manuel Antonio *university administrator, educator*
Robinson, Beulah Lobdell *educator*
Shadd, Vicki Marie Nagos *secondary education educator*
Wendel, O. Theodore, Jr. *university chancellor*

Chino
Alpert, Dolores Esther *secondary education educator*

Chula Vista
Livziey, James Gerald *secondary school educator*
Maggi, Gayle J.B. *secondary school educator*
Wyatt, Edith Elizabeth *elementary education educator*

Claremont
Alexander, John David, Jr. *college administrator*
Bekavac, Nancy Yavor *academic administrator, lawyer*
Chiu, Rebecca Oi-Mui *elementary education educator*
Douglass, Enid Hart *educational program director*
Faranda, John Paul *college administrator*
Gerard, Neil Barry *educator*
Maguire, John David *academic administrator, educator, writer*
Pitts, Sadie Turner *retired educator*
Platt, Joseph Beaven *former college president*
Riggs, Henry Earle *academic administrator, engineering management educator*
Stark, Jack Lee *academic administrator*
Taulbee, Amy Louise *college administrator*

Clovis
Bitters, Conrad Lee *biological sciences educator*

Colton
Dybowski, Douglas Eugene *education educator, economist*
Naugle, Charlotte June *principal, educator*

Concord
Langley, Michael Douglas *secondary education educator*
Thall, Richard Vincent *school system administrator*

Corona
Clark, Nanci *elementary education educator*

Coronado
Heap, Suzanne Rundio *elementary school educator*

Costa Mesa
Hansen, Sally Jo *school system coordinator*

Covina
Sweger, Glenda Lee *educator*

Culver City
Kamm, Jacqueline Ann *elementary reading specialist*
Maxwell-Brogdon, Florence Morency *school administrator, educational adviser*
Parsons, Adrienne Mary *principal*

Cupertino
Garvey, Kelly Ann *secondary education educator*
Reza, Jacquelyn Valerie *counselor, consultant*

Cypress
Hall, Georgianna Lee *special education educator*

Danville
Penner-Sekera, Cynthia Dawn *secondary education educator*

Davis
Bittlingmayer, George *educator*
Denison, Michael Steven *education educator*
Hawke, Deborah Sue *academic counselor*
Hendrix, Louise Butts *retired educator, author*
Springer, Sally Pearl *university administrator*
Vanderhoef, Larry Neil *academic administrator*

Delano
Lucas, Stephanie Heune *elementary education educator*

Diamond Bar
Domeño, Eugene Timothy *elementary education educator, principal*

Downey
De Lorca, Luis E. *educational administrator, educator, speaker*
Gogolin, Marilyn Tompkins *educational administrator, language pathologist*
Thompson, Rena Louise *elementary education educator*

Dunlap
Gair, Kevin Lindsey *learning director*

El Cajon
Bell, Kimberly Jeanne *secondary school and adult education educator*
Palafox, Mari Lee *private school educator*
Thomas, Esther Merlene *elementary education educator*

El Centro
Kussman, Eleanor (Ellie Kussman) *retired educational superintendent*

El Cerrito
Herzberg, Dorothy Crews *middle school educator*

El Monte
Deaver, Sharon Mae *special education educator*

Elk Grove
Landon, JoJene Babbitt *special education educator*
Sparks, Jack Norman *college dean*

Encinitas
Galiley, C. Jerome *secondary education educator*

Encino
Blair, Mary B. *education educator*

Escondido
Gilkeson, Jerrell Estle *principal*

Eureka
Kandus, Richard Jay *adult education educator*
Ksicinski, Joyce Mary *education specialist*

Fair Oaks
Lemke, Herman Ernest Frederick, Jr. *retired elementary education educator, consultant*

Fontana
Donica, Cheryl Marie *elementary education educator*

Forestville
Kielsmeier, Catherine Jane *school system administrator*

Fortuna
Fisher, Bruce David *elementary school educator*

Foster City
Berman, Daniel K(atzel) *educational consultant, university official*

Fremont
Cormier, Evelyn M. *educator*
Lapiroff, Jerry *secondary school educator*

Fresno
Coleman, Donald Gene *education educator*
Keen, Derl Walter *child development educator*
Nickel, Rosalie Jean *reading specialist*
Tanner, David Earl *education educator*
Welty, John Donald *academic administrator*
Wong, Kin-Ping *university dean, biotechnology researcher, company executive, educator, science administrator*

Fullerton
Baker, Kathleen Ann *student services counselor*
Barchi, Barbara Ann *education educator*
Barnes, Carol Pardon *education educator*
Fellow, Anthony Raymond *communications educator*
Goodman, Joel Harry, Jr. *university administrator*
Gordon, Milton Andrew *academic administrator*
Pullen, Rick Darwin *dean*
Snider, Jane Ann *elementary school educator*

Garden Grove
Dublin, Stephen Louis *secondary school educator, singer, musician*
Ibasitas, Jan Wong *special education educator*

Glendale
Case, Lee Owen, Jr. *retired academic administrator*
DeVincintis, Lani *adult educator*
Empey, Donald Warne *educational administrator*
Leeds-Horwitz, Susan Beth *school system administrator, speech-language pathology educator*
Levine, Benjamin Jacob *secondary education educator*

Glendora
Graziani, Roger Daniel *secondary school educator*
Lindly, Douglas Dean *elementary school educator, administrator*

Granada Hills
Klinger, Paul Anthony *educational therapist, administrator*

Granite Bay
Mallo, Annmarie *elementary educator*

Hacienda Heights
Mallen, Mary A. *secondary school science educator*

Hanford
Bartel, Arthur Gabriel *educational administrator, city official*

Hayward
Gin, Hal Gabriel *university administrator*
Lambert, Linda Lou *educator*
Laycock, Mary Chappell *gifted and talented education educator, consultant*
McCune, Ellis E. *retired university system chief administrator, higher education consultant*
Rees, Norma S. *academic administrator*

Hillsborough
Hower, Donna Wilson *elementary education educator*
Williams-Labagh, Barbara J. *elementary educator*

Hollister
Allen, Harold Jim *secondary school English educator*
Turpin, Calvin Coolidge *retired university administrator, educator*

Huntington Beach
Davidson-Shepard, Gay *secondary education educator*
Yglesias, Kenneth Dale *college president*

Huntington Park
Veis, Fred Alan *special education educator*

Idyllwild
Crowell, Samuel M., Jr. *education educator*

Indian Wells
Trotter, F(rederick) Thomas *retired academic administrator*

Indio
Houghton, Robert Charles *secondary education educator*

Inglewood
Crump, Gloria Jean *elementary and adult educator*
Guzy, Marguerita Linnes *secondary education educator*
Logan, Lynda Dianne *elementary education educator*
Moghadam, Amir *consultant, educational administrator*
Zucca, Gary Joseph *educator*

Inyokern
Norris, Lois Ann *elementary school educator*

Irvine
Beach, Christopher John *American literary arts educator*
Garretson, Steven Michael *elementary education educator*
Hudson, Katherine Lee *education association executive*
Kleeman, Nancy Gray Ervin *special education educator*
Peltason, Jack Walter *former university president, educator*
Welch, Bobby O'Neal *dean*
Wilkening, Laurel Lynn *academic administrator, planetary scientist*

Kerman
Fischle, Daniel Karl *school system administrator*

La Canada Flintridge
Lamson, Robert Woodrow *retired school system administrator*

PROFESSIONAL INDEX 835 EDUCATION

La Crescenta
Winter-Neighbors, Gwen Carole *special education educator, art educator*

La Jolla
Caserio, Marjorie Constance *academic administrator*
Lee, Jerry Carlton *university administrator*
Mitry, Darryl Joseph *educator, writer, strategic advisor*

La Mesa
Anderson, Kathryn Corinn *counselor, educator*
Black, Eileen Mary *elementary school educator*
Guest, Ratima L. *educator, counselor*
Tarson, Herbert Harvey *university administrator emeritus*

La Verne
Coray, Jeffrey Warren *assistant principal, instructor*

Lafayette
Quincy, Alpha Ellen Beers *school board executive*

Laguna Niguel
Munsell, Joni Anne *middle school educator*
Offen, Ronald Charles *school librarian*

Lake Elsinore
Wolsey, Thomas DeVere *middle school educator*

Lakewood
Bogdan, James Thomas *secondary education educator, electronics researcher and developer*

Lancaster
Bohannon, Linda Sue *special education educator*
Schneider, Elaine Fogel *special education educator, consultant*

Larkspur
Schatzman, Susan *adult education educator*

Lawndale
Davis, Jeffrey Alan *secondary school educator, coach*

Lebec
Shelby, Tim Otto *secondary education educator*

Lemon Grove
Mott, June Marjorie *school system administrator*

Livermore
Daniel, Helen Anderson *secondary education educator, psychotherapist, intern*
Hiskes, Dolores G. *educator*
Lucas, Linda Lucille *dean*
Roshong, Dee Ann Daniels *dean, educator*

Lodi
Alberti, Del Joseph *school system administrator*
Bishop-Graham, Barbara *secondary school educator, journalist*

Loma Linda
Johnston, Patricia Kathleen *college dean*

Lomita
Malm, Royce Elliott *secondary education educator*

Lompoc
Brown, Donald Ray *school system administrator*
Duke, Pamela Ruth *reading specialist*
Maxwell, Marilyn Julia *elementary education educator*

Long Beach
Armstrong, Joanna *education educator*
Baca, Hilda Sue *primary education educator*
Blazey, Michael Alan *educator*
Creason, Paul Joseph *college administrator*
Feldman, Stephen *university president*
Hobgood, E(arl) Wade *college dean*
Ley, David Chanpannha *secondary education educator*
Lunderville, Gerald Paul *bilingual education educator*
Maxson, Robert C. *university president*
Munitz, Barry *university administrator, English literature educator, business consultant*
Reichard, Gary Warren *university administrator, history educator*
Stewart, Gail Benita *alumni development director, editor*

Los Altos
Camous, Louise Michelle *secondary education educator, sister*
Gonzales, Richard Robert *academic administrator*
Keller, James Warren *college administrator*
Puder, Janice *special education educator*

Los Angeles
Albert, Sidney Paul *philosophy educator*
Allums, Henriene *elementary education educator*
Ansley, Julia Ette *elementary school educator, consultant, poet, writer*
Best, Gary Allen *special education educator*
Burman, Sheila Flexer Zola *special education educator*
Cavanaugh, Michael Arthur *education administrator, retired sociologist*
Cohen, Arthur M. *education educator*
Darmstaetter, Jay Eugene *secondary education educator*
Dunham, Anne *educational institute director*
Ecklund, Judith Louise *academic administrator*
Gilbert, Richard Keith *education educator, researcher*
Gothold, Stuart E. *school system administrator, educator*
Harris, F. Chandler *retired university administrator*
Harvey, James Gerald *educational counselor, consultant*
Hickey, Lynn Zwerg *visual and performing arts school coordinator*
Kennelly, Sister Karen Margaret *college administrator*
Lee, Dorothy Wong *secondary art educator*
Leveque, Thomas Joseph *elementary school educator, writer*
Lim, Larry Kay *university official*
Littleton, C(ovington) Scott *anthropology educator, consultant*
Lucente, Rosemary Dolores *educational administrator*
Marlin, Robert Matthew *secondary school educator*
McDonough, Patricia Marie *education educator*
Money, Ruth Rowntree *child development specialist, consultant*
Moore, Donald Walter *academic administrator, school librarian*
Moran, Thomas Harry *academic administrator*
Mull, Jocelyn Bethe *school administrator*
Parks, Debora Ann *principal*
Polon, Linda Beth *elementary school educator, writer, illustrator*
Redding-Lowder, Christine Arnita *elementary education educator*
Rodes, David Stuart *college program director*
Rosser, James Milton *academic administrator*
Sample, Steven Browning *university executive*
Simon, Sheila Sandra *special education educator, administrator*
Slaughter, John Brooks *university administrator*
Steinberg, Warren Linnington *principal*
Stevens, Gerald D. *secondary education educator, consultant*
Taylor, Leigh Herbert *college dean*
Taylor, Velma Jean *elementary education educator*
Ungar, Roselva May *primary and elementary educator*
Utterback, David *financial aid counselor*
Woosley, Joan Louise *university registrar*
Young, Charles Edward *university chancellor*
Zone, Janine Denise *elementary education educator*

Madera
Rozario, Gwendolyn Michelle *educator*

Malibu
Luft, Herbert *history educator, former dean*
Mollner, Frederick Richard *director publications, graphic designer*
Welch, Michael Dennis *university official*

Manhattan Beach
Brooks, Edward Howard *college administrator*

Marina
Livermore, Donald Raymond *elementary/secondary education educator, library media specialist, educational/technology consultant*

Marysville
DeVore, Marilyn Ruth *education educator, consultant*

Menifee
Tausig, Michael Robert *college administrator, higher education planning consultant*

Merced
Delgado, Theresa Michelle *middle school educator*

Milpitas
Leonardi, Rosarius Roy *special education educator*

Mineral
Hoofard, Jane Mahan Decker *elementary education educator*

Miramonte
Dike, Kenneth P. *elementary school educator, principal*

Mission Viejo
O'Banion, Terry Underwood *academic administrator, consultant*
Weller, Debra Anne *elementary educator*

Modesto
Price, Robert William *school superintendent, consultant*

Monrovia
Ladner, Alan Robert *secondary school educator*

Montebello
Dible, Rose Harpe McFee *special education educator*
Kolbeck, Sister Ann Lawrence *school principal*

Monterey
Di Girolamo, Rosina E. *education educator*
Oder, Broeck Newton *school emergency management consultant*

Monterey Park
Choyke, George Raymond *safety educator, consultant*
Meysenburg, Mary Ann *principal*

Moorpark
Buxton, Marion West *middle school education educator*

Moreno Valley
McMurty, Judy Jean *school counselor*
Tworek, Richard Kenneth *dean*

Mountain View
Cicora, Mary Angela *researcher, author*
Craig, Joan Carmen *secondary school educator, drama teacher*

Napa
Moore, William Joseph *retired educator*
Rada, Alexander *university official*

North Hollywood
Chang, Wung *researcher, lecturer, business advisor*

Northridge
Brotman, Carol Eileen *adult education educator, advocate*
Falk, Heinrich Richard *theater and humanities educator*
Wilson, Blenda Jacqueline *academic administrator*

Norwalk
Matsuura, Kenneth Ray *counselor, articulation officer*

Oakland
Atkinson, Richard Chatham *university president*
Caulfield, Carlota *education educator*
Fries, Lita Linda *school system administrator*
Gantt, Barry *secondary school educator*
Griego, Elizabeth Brownlee *college dean*
Holmgren, Janet L *college president*
Lawrence, Gary Sheldon *academic administrator*
Roberts, William Lawrence, Jr. *education researcher, statistician*

Oceanside
Coate, Lester Edwin *university administrator*

Ontario
Morton, Laurel Anne *elementary education educator*

Orange
Garcia-Razanskas, Ada Ann *educator*
Shukla, Pradip Kantilal *academic administrator, educator, consultant*
Stelling, E. Edmund *educator*

Oroville
Rasmussen, Mike Joseph *academic administrator*

Oxnard
DeGrazia-Sanders, John Joseph *headmaster*

Pacific Grove
Eadie, Margaret L. *educational and career consultant*
Wangberg, Elaine Gregory *university administrator*

Palm Springs
Aikens, Donald Thomas *educational administrator, consultant*
Gill, Jo Anne Martha *middle school educator*
Hartman, Rosemary Jane *special education educator*
Owings, Thalia Kelley *elementary school educator*
Satcher, Clement Michael *special education educator*
Schreiman, Howard Leslie *special education educator*
Stewart, Lucille Marie *special education coordinator*

Palmdale
Faulk, Betty Price *elementary school educator*

Palo Alto
Attig, John Clare *secondary education educator, consultant*
Bolitho, Louise Greer *educational administrator, consultant*
Gong, Mamie Poggio *elementary education educator*
Haertel, Geneva DiLuzio *educational researcher*
Liddell, Barbara Anne *school administrator*

Palos Verdes Estates
Hara, Tadao *educational administrator*

Palos Verdes Peninsula
Baxter, Betty Carpenter *educational administrator*
Copeland, Phillips Jerome *former university administrator, former air force officer*
Gaines, Jerry Lee *secondary education educator*
Miller, Francie Loraditch *college counselor*

Panorama City
Wolff, Mark Robert *elementary and secondary education educator*

Parlier
Rodriguez, Angelina *primary school educator*

Pasadena
Almore-Randle, Allie Louise *special education educator*
Brown, David R. *academic administrator*
Coghill, Davis Garold *secondary school educator*
Everhart, Thomas Eugene *academic administrator, engineering educator*
Levy, David Steven *college administrator*
Siemon-Burgeson, Marilyn M. *education administrator*

Pebble Beach
Roth, Frederic Hull, Jr. *secondary education educator*

Piedmont
Marinelly, Ralph *retired secondary education educator*

Pinole
Baum, Ralph Werner *primary education educator*
Grogan, Stanley Joseph *educational consultant*

Placentia
Sexson, Stephen Bruce *educational writer, educator*

Playa Del Rey
Hite, Janet Sue *elementary education educator*

Pleasant Hill
Lundgren, Susan Elaine *counselor, educator*

Pleasanton
Aladeen, Lary Joe *secondary school educator*

Pomona
Amaya, Patricia Mojarro *elementary education educator*
Ambrose, William Wright, Jr. *college dean, accounting educator, tax researcher*
Bullock, Molly *retired elementary education educator*
Callaway, Linda Marie *special education educator*
Demery, Dorothy Jean *secondary school educator*
Gugelchuk, Gary Michael *academic administrator*
Kawai, Ernest Gordon *higher education director*
Lawrence, William, Jr. *elementary education educator*
Markham, Reed B. *education educator, consultant*
Schmitt, Catherine Laura *academic career counselor*
Suzuki, Bob H. *university president*

Portola Valley
Cody, Frank Joseph *secondary school administrator, teacher education educator*
Oscarson, Kathleen Dale *writing assessment coordinator, educator*

Poway
Vitti, Anthony Mark *secondary education educator*

Rancho Palos Verdes
Schach, Barbara Jean *elementary education educator*

Red Bluff
Kennedy, James William, Jr. (Sarge Kennedy) *special education administrator, consultant*

Redlands
Appleton, James Robert *university president, educator*
Barnes, A. Keith *management educator*
Healy, Daniel Thomas *secondary education educator*
Jennings, Irmengard Katharina *academic administrator*
Ritchie, C(laude) Alen *secondary education educator, tax preparer*

Redondo Beach
Barrie, Joan Parker *elementary school educator*
Fix, Tobie Lynn *special education educator*
Mahrenholtz, Dayla Dianne *elementary school principal*

Redway
Branzei-Velasquez, Sylvia Carol *secondary education educator*

Reseda
Moss, Debra Lee *special education educator*

Rialto
Bauza, Christine Diane *special education educator*
Johnson, Ruth Floyd *university educator, consultant*
Straight, James Wesley *secondary education educator*

Ridgecrest
Matulef, Gizelle Terese *secondary education educator*
Metty, Michael Pierre *college dean*

Riverside
Allen, William Merle *university administrator, museum director*
Diamond, Richard *secondary education educator*
Doyle, Michael James *educator, organist*
D'Souza, Edward John *educational administrator*
Dutton, Jo Sargent *education educator, researcher, consultant*
Lacy, Carolyn Jean *elementary education educator, secondary education educator*
Leo, Louis Joseph *university administrator*
Malcolm, Joan Edwards *principal, elementary education educator*
Peterson, Leroy *retired secondary education educator*
Prosser, Michael Joseph *community college staff member*
Reardon, James Louis *education educator, consultant*
Thomas, Sylvia Ann *community college dean*
West, Madeline Florence *elementary education educator*

Rohnert Park
Arminana, Ruben *university president, educator*
Swanson, Anne Barrett *dean*

Rosemead
Hansen, Robert Dennis *educational administrator*

Roseville
Ferguson, Britt Tatman *educator*

Ross
Matan, Lillian Kathleen *educator, designer*

Rowland Heights
Park, Jong Hwan *educational company executive*

Sacramento
DeNardo, Gerald Louis *academic director*
Foster, Stanley Kenneth *adult education educator, real estate appraiser*
Gerth, Donald Rogers *university president*
Gridley, George Thomas *dean*
Grimes, Pamela Rae *elementary school educator*
Kellough, Richard Dean *educator*
Konold, Elizabeth Kay *university administrator*
Lasley, Mona Carol *elementary education educator, consultant*
Lawrence, Paul Frederic *educational consultant*
McKim, Harriet Megchelsen *education educator*
Mendy, Sharon Lee *vocational educator*
Reed-Graham, Lois L. *administrator, secondary education educator*
Riles, Wilson Camanza *educational consultant*
Shoemaker, Cameron David James *dean, educator*
Steinhaus, Patricia *university administrator*
Stuart, David R. *academic administrator*
West, Linda Lea *administrator*
Wetherwax, Georgia Lee (Peg Wetherwax) *elementary education educator*
Zaidi, Emily Louise *retired elementary school educator*

Salinas
Trujillo, Michael Joseph *elementary school principal*

San Bernardino
Butler, Arthur Maurice *university administrator*
DiPaolo, Patricia Ann *reading specialist*
Evans, Anthony Howard *university president*
Handleman, Martin Ian *music teacher*
Kaisershot, Edward Joseph *elementary education educator, coach*

San Diego
Alexander, Deborah Sims *public administration educator*
Berrian, James Edwin *biology teacher*
Carleton, Mary Ruth *dean, consultant*
Clement, Betty Waidlich *literacy educator, consultant*
Clifton, Mark Stephen *administrator*
Day, Thomas Brennock *university president*
Donley, Dennis Lee *school librarian*
Eisemann, Kurt *director computer center, mathematics educator*
Fay, Helyn *college counselor*
Heath, Berthann Jones *education administrator*

Hoye, Walter Brisco *retired college administrator*
Lomeli, Marta *elementary education educator*
Maurer, Lawrence Michael *acting school administrator, educator*
Oviatt, Larry Andrew *retired secondary school educator*
Reynolds, Hallie Bellah *elementary education educator*
Shearer, Rick Leland *academic administrator*
Till, Franklin L. *school system administrator*
Weber, Stephen Lewis *university president*

San Dimas
Cameron, Judith Lynne *secondary education educator, hypnotherapist*
Sutton, Parker Forest *principal*

San Fernando
Behnke, Donna Beth *counselor*

San Francisco
Albino, Judith E.N. *university president*
Barney, Susan Leslie *academic administrator*
Buidang, George (Hada Buidang) *educator, administrator, consultant, writer*
Corrigan, Robert Anthony *academic administrator*
Counelis, James Steve *education educator*
Davis, James Wesley *university program administrator, artist, writer, composer*
Elia, John Patrick *health education and psychology educator*
Essa, Lisa Beth *elementary education educator*
Haro, Roberto Pedro *university official, education educator*
Hasan, Mahmood Ul *secondary school educator*
Krevans, Julius Richard *university administrator, physician*
O'Neill, Michael *academic administrator*
Pierce, Deborah Mary *educational administrator*
Pinsky, Charlotte Lee (Cherie Pinsky) *academic administrator*
Robertson, Merle Greene *art historian, academic administrator*
Runyon, Steven Crowell *academic administrator, communications educator*
Schlegel, John Peter *academic administrator*
Stephens, Elisa *art college president, lawyer*
Tahmassian, Ara Zarneh *university director*
Ury, Claude Max *educational consultant, book reviewer*

San Jose
Caret, Robert Laurent *university president*
Duncan, Gloria Celestine *elementary educator*
Hernandez, Frank *university educator, federal agency administrator, educator*
Liehr, Robert Joseph *private school educator*
Mazur, Meredith Margie Handley *reading educator*
Merriam, Janet Pamela *special education educator*
Pflughaupt, Jane Ramsey *secondary school educator*
Sanders, Adrian Lionel *educational consultant*
Swan, Joe B. *retired journalism educator, emeritus*
Tiedt, Iris McClellan *emeritus university dean*
Whitney, Natalie White *primary school educator*
Wise, Joseph Stephen *secondary education educator, artist*

San Lorenzo
Perry, Lori *preschool educator*
Schultz, Frederik Emil *academic administrator*

San Luis Obispo
Baker, Warren J(oseph) *university president*
Dalton, Linda Catherine *university administrator*
Maas, Donald Kenneth *education educator, consultant*

San Marino
Footman, Gordon Elliott *educational administrator*

San Mateo
Bonnell, William Charles *secondary education educator*
Patnode, Darwin Nicholas *academic administrator, professional parliamentarian*

San Pedro
Matich, Matthew P. *secondary school English educator*

San Rafael
Blum, Arthur Marvin *academic administrator*
Cloud, James Merle *university and hospital administrator, learning specialist*

Santa Ana
Davis, Lenard Eugene *middle school education educator*
Kato, Terri Emi *special education educator*
Vail, Michael George *academic director*
Verhaegen, Terri Lynn Foy *middle school educator*
Williams, Leslie Beall *elementary education educator*

Santa Barbara
Allaway, William Harris *retired university official*
Cirone, William Joseph *school superintendent*
Hengstler, Dennis Dean *university program director*
O'Dowd, Donald Davy *retired university president*
Tettegah, Sharon Yvonne *education educator*
Yang, Henry T. *university chancellor, educator*

Santa Clara
Abdaljabbar, Abdalhameed A. *educational administrator*
Harrison, Wendy Jane Merrill *university official*
Locatelli, Paul Leo *university administrator*
Nordmeyer, Mary Betsy *vocational educator*

Santa Clarita
Doran, Carter *academic administrator*
Lavine, Steven David *academic administrator*
Schwartz, Betty Barsha *secondary education educator, writer, artist*
Volpe, Eileen Rae *special education educator*

Santa Cruz
Davis, Geraldine Sampson *special education educator*
Silver, Roberta Frances (Bobbi Silver) *special education educator, writer*

Santa Monica
Dickerson, Joe Bernard *principal, educator*
Lord, John William *educational materials developer, writer*
Yarber, Mary Laine *secondary school educator, writer*

Santa Rosa
Karas, Gene Arthur *secondary education educator*
Moore, Arlene Joy *elementary school educator*

Santee
Deckard, Steve Wayne *science educator*

Saratoga
Houston, Elizabeth Reece Manasco *correctional education consultant*
Whalen, Margaret Cavanagh *retired secondary school educator*
Wood, Gladys Blanche *retired secondary education educator, journalist*

Seal Beach
Melton, Cheryl Ann *educator, small business owner*

Seaside
Wall, Janet E. *assessment, testing and evaluation professional*

Selma
Jura, Debra Dowell *bilingual educator*

Sherman Oaks
Cauley, Linda Marilyn *high school counselor*
Fortuna, Anthony Frank *educator, consultant*
O'Neill, Sallie Boyd *educator, business owner, sculptor*

Simi Valley
Bullock, Donald Wayne *elementary education educator, educational computing consultant*
Jackson, Thirston Henry, Jr. *retired adult education educator*

Solana Beach
DeMarco-Dennis, Eleanor (Poppy DeMarco-Dennis) *elementary education educator, community activist*

Sonoma
Hobart, Billie *education educator, consultant*

South Gate
Cluxton, Joanne Genevieve *elementary school educator*
Lee, Kerry Youngae *school program director*

South Lake Tahoe
Grutter, Judith Appley *career counselor*

South Pasadena
Sato, Irving Shigeo *education consultant*

Stanford
Bridges, Edwin Maxwell *education educator*
McClanahan, Clarence Edward *university official*
Raisian, John *university institute director, economist*
Spence, Andrew Michael *dean, finance educator*
Strena, Robert Victor *retired university research laboratory manager*
Strober, Myra Hoffenberg *education educator, consultant*
Whitney, Rodger Franklin *university housing director*
Yuen, Richard Joseph *university dean*

Stinson Beach
Metz, Mary Seawell *university dean, retired college president*

Stockton
Jantzen, J(ohn) Marc *retired education educator*
Klinger, Wayne Julius *secondary education educator*
Peters, Rita *university administrator*
Wright, Daniel Robert *educational administrator*

Suisun City
Bishop, Carol Ward *dean*
Blood, Peggy A. *college administrator*
Kirkorian, Donald George *college official, management consultant*

Sun Valley
Cinnamon, William, III *elementary and special education educator*
Mayhue, Richard Lee *dean, pastor, writer*

Sunland
Epley, Thelma Mae Childers *retired gifted and talented education educator*

Sunnyvale
Caleca, John Edward *secondary education educator*
Passantino, Heather Ann *special education educator*

Sylmar
Lisalda, Sylvia Ann *primary education educator*

Tarzana
Cattando-Held, Donna *school director*

Temple City
Matsuda, Stanley Kazuhiro *secondary education educator*

Thermal
Lynn, Nanne Joyce *educator*

Thousand Oaks
Cipriano, Patricia Ann *secondary education educator, consultant*
Dunkel, Peter Carl *university administrator*
Tennant, Mary Jo *secondary education educator*

Trinidad
Lundeen, Samuel Edward *elementary education educator*
Wiebe, John Clement *school director*

Tujunga
Mayer, George Roy *educator*

Turlock
Ratto, Carolyn Elizabeth *educator*
Volk, Greg T. *secondary education educator*

Tustin
Gray, Sandra Rae *retired secondary school educator*
Greene, Wendy Segal *special education educator*

Union City
Nacario, Robert John *educational administrator*

Valencia
Hugo, Joan Lyall *academic administrator, art critic, curator*
Joseph, Michele Beth *special education educator, educational therapist*
Looney, Claudia Arlene *academic administrator*

Vallejo
Bonham, Charlie Leonard *college official*

Van Nuys
Altshiller, Arthur Leonard *secondary education educator*
Meier, Robert John *secondary education educator*

Ventura
Evans, James Handel *university administrator, architect, educator*
Lawson, William Harold *college dean, labor economist*

Visalia
Goulart, Janell Ann *elementary education educator*

Vista
Castle, Alfred *administrator*
Palmer, William Earl *private school educator*

Walnut
Kaiser, Sue *school administrator*

Walnut Creek
Wolf, Harry *retired dean and educator*

West Hollywood
Lewis, Ian David *special education educator*

Westlake Village
Doerr, Patricia Marian *elementary and special education educator*
Snyder, Carole Marie *parochial school educator*

Westminster
Hill, Debra Lee *school counselor, educator*

Whittier
Drake, E Maylon *academic administrator*
Shackelford, Anastasia Marie *secondary school educator*
Tunison, Elizabeth Lamb *education educator*
Walner, William Dennis *school system administrator*
Zanetta, Joseph Michael *university administrator, lawyer*

Yorba Linda
Lunde, Dolores Benitez *retired secondary education educator*
Sternitzke-Holub, Ann *elementary school educator*

Yuba City
Higdon, Bernice Cowan *retired elementary education educator*
Perry, Phillip Edmund *middle school educator*

Yucaipa
Gomez, Louis Salazar *college president*
Jones, Richard Arthur *retired community college president, educator*

Yucca Valley
Walker, Michael Maurice *secondary education educator*

COLORADO

Alamosa
Frazee, John Patric *academic administrator, English educator*

Arvada
Hammond-Blessing, DiAnn A. *elementary education educator*
Johnson, Tina *elementary education educator*
Rusch, Pamela Jean *middle school educator*
Young, Bonnie Darline *primary school educator*

Aurora
Fain, Karen Kellogg *retired history and geography educator*
Hartenbach, David Lawrence *school system administrator*
McBride, Carol Ann *visual arts educator*
Verniero, Joan Evans *special education educator*
Walker, Joyce Marie *secondary school educator*
Weber-Shadrick, Dorothy Jo *management consultant*

Bayfield
Hunt-Jenkins, Lori Evelyn *education educator*

Boulder
Buechner, John C. *academic administrator*
Carroll, Stephen Graham *university communications administrator, writer*
Domenico, Frances Ann *school counselor*
Healy, James Bruce *cooking school administrator, writer*
House, Mary Donna *dean*
Malmgren, Dick *retired school principal, educator*
Maresh, Nancy Mae *educational entrepreneur*
McWilliams, Spencer Albert *academic administrator*
Park, Roderic Bruce *academic administrator*
Saltzman, Joanne Ellen *cooking school administrator*
Snyder, Sherry Ann *university administrator*

Vigil, Daniel Agustin *academic administrator*
Wilson, Kenneth Allen *educator*

Brighton
Capillupo, Jean Nady *public school administrator, educator*

Broomfield
Di Martini, Stacy Jean *elementary education educator*
Ekey, Carrie Rae *elementary education educator*
Little, Mark Douglas *secondary school educator*

Calhan
Henderson, Freda LaVerne *elementary education educator*

Canon City
Baumann, Ernst Frederick *college president*
Perrin, Cynthia Suzanne *secondary education educator*

Cheyenne Wells
Palmer, Rayetta J. *technology coordinator, educator*

Colorado Springs
Bowden, Randall Glen *academic administrator*
Grady, Dolores Anne *academic administrator, educator, consultant*
Guy, Mildred Dorothy *retired secondary school educator*
Paris, Edward Marvin *education administrator*
Shade, Linda Bunnell *university chancellor*
Snyder, Beverly Ann *counselor, educator, therapist*
Wilcox, Rhoda Davis *elementary education educator*

Craig
Bilodeau, Gene Paul *student services administrator, counselor*

Creede
Carter, Shirley Raedelle *retired elementary school educator*

Denver
Billig, Shelley Hirschl *educational research and training consultant*
Black, Lavonne Patricia *special education educator*
DePew, Marie Kathryn *retired secondary school educator*
Emmet, Thomas Addis, Jr. *college administrator, consultant*
Fielden, C. Franklin, III *early childhood education consultant*
Fulkerson, William Measey, Jr. *college president*
Goodchild, Lester Francis *higher education educator*
Hill, Kathleen Lois *performing art school executive*
Jeffryes, Mark Allen *elementary school educator, administrator*
Lane, Peggy Lee *educator*
Lees, Fred Arthur *middle school educator, retired*
Linenbrink, Cecilia *educator*
Lofthouse, Russ Wilbert *school administrator*
McCall, Laura *education educator, writer*
Miller, Clara Burr *education educator*
Mornes, Amber J. Bishop *consultant, computer software trainer, analyst*
Parsell, Roger Edmund *retired educator, civic worker*
Ritchie, Daniel Lee *academic administrator*
Rothenberg, Harvey David *educational administrator*
Roy, Lisa Rai *education program administrator*
Ryman, Ruth (Stacie) Marie *primary education educator*
Tucker, James Raymond *primary education educator*

Durango
Candelaria, Angie Mary *special education educator*
Jones, Joel Mackey *college president*

Ellicott
Fuller, Janice Marie *secondary school educator*

Englewood
Dawson, Eugene Ellsworth *university president emeritus*
Gibson, Elisabeth Jane *principal*
Leo, Mary Gaye *school administrator*
Morgan, Glen *college official*
Nelson, Barbara Louise *secondary education educator*
Zernial, Susan Carol *education educator*

Estes Park
Johnson, Carol Lynn *secondary school counselor*

Fort Collins
Cook, Dierdre Ruth Goorman *school administrator, secondary education educator*
Crabtree, Loren William *dean, history educator*
Fotsch, Dan Robert *elementary education educator*
Freeman, David M. *educator*
Green, Ronnie David *education educator*
Jaros, Dean *university official*
Mason, Carolyn S. *career coordinator*
Thomas, Laura Hebenstreit *English educator*
Treaster, Melba Mauck *education consultant*
Yates, Albert Carl *academic administrator, chemistry educator*

Fruita
Boughton, Irene *elementary education educator*

Golden
Klug, John Joseph *secondary education educator, director of dramatics*
Perry-Crumrine, Lori Frances *special education educator, administrator*
Tomczyk, Theodore Clayton *secondary education educator*
Zuschlag, Nancy Lynn *environmental educator*

Grand Junction
Moberly, Linden Emery *educational administrator*
Thomas, Richard McKennon, II *college administrator*

Greeley
Drake, Lucius Charles, Jr. *school administrator, university consultant, educator*
Eldridge, Roger Gilbert, Jr. *education educator*

Green, Vickie Lee *gifted and talented, music educator*
Guest, Linda Sand *education educator*
Lujan, Herman D. *academic administrator*
Lynch, Robert Michael *university administrator*
Smythe, Valerie Ann *special education educator*
Stewart, Betty Jean *secondary school educator*

Gunnison
Venturo, Frank A. *academic affairs administrator, communications educator*

Gypsum
Kershner, Ivan Harry *principal*

Idalia
Norby-Loud, Marie Barbara *secondary education educator*

Iliff
Nichols, Lee Ann *library media specialist*

Keystone
Chopyak-Minor, Christine Marie *school administrator, educator*

Lakewood
Abbott, Truman Cleveland *school administrator*
Addison, John Robert *counselor*
Forrest, Kenton Harvey *middle school educator, historian*
Marlatt, Dorothy Barbara *university dean*
Perito, Joseph Gerald, Jr. *educator, musician, counselor, consultant*
Reed, Joan-Marie *special education educator*
Wilson, Johnny Lee *secondary school educator*

Lamar
Baer, Cynthia Lynn *adult education educator*

Littleton
Bush, Stanley Giltner *secondary school educator*
Connell, Elizabeth Ann *elementary school educator*
Feist, Edward Joseph *secondary education educator*
Lening, Janice Allen *physical education educator*
Miller, Kathryn Louise *elementary school educator*
Suarez, Elisabeth Clemence *secondary mathematics educator*
Wallisch, Carolyn E. *principal*
Whalen, Cathryn Ann *reading specialist*

Parker
Nelson, Paula Morrison Bronson *educator*

Pueblo
Shirley, Robert Clark *retired university president, strategic planning consultant, educator*
Vest, Rosemarie Lynn Torres *secondary school educator*
Woods, Alma Jean *elementary educator*

Pueblo West
Lightell, Kenneth Ray *education educator*

Rangely
Mullen, Robert Charles *school system administrator*

Sheridan
Bosworth, Bruce Leighton *school administrator, educator, consultant*

Sheridan Lake
Shields, Joseph David *secondary school educator, guidance counselor*

Sterling
Hunter, Frank A. *secondary education educator*

Superior
Hatfield, Samuel Fay, Jr. *educator, small business owner*

Westminster
Eaves, Stephen Douglas *educator, vocational administrator*
Hartman, Susan P(atrice) *adult education administrator*
Judson, Cheryl Jean *college administrator, management consultant*
Zetterman, Polly Davis *secondary school educator*

Wheat Ridge
Seahorn, Janet Jane *educational researcher*

Yuma
Pfalmer, Charles Elden *secondary school educator*

DISTRICT OF COLUMBIA

Washington
Stein, Paul E. *superintendent*

HAWAII

Hickam AFB
Peterson, Edwin Cuthbert *adult education educator, counselor, educational administrator*

Hilo
Best, Mary Lani *university program coordinator*
Hartle-Schutte, David *elementary school educator*

Honolulu
Armstrong, Sara Jo *elementary school educator*
Blumhardt, Jon Howard *college official*
Bogart, Louise Berry *education educator*
Bopp, Thomas Theodore *university administrator, chemistry educator*
Hunt, John Joseph *educational specialist*
Kaiser-Botsai, Sharon Kay *early chilhood educator*
Karelitz, Raymond *secondary school educator and writer*
Keith, Kent Marsteller *academic administrator, corporate executive, government official, lawyer*
Masters, Elaine *educator, writer*
Metz, James Robert *secondary education educator*
Meyer, Robert Allen *human resource management educator*
Pacific, Joseph Nicholas, Jr. *educator*
Pickens, Alexander Legrand *education educator*
Ramler, Siegfried *educator*
Souza, Joan of Arc *educational administrator*
Tune, Suelyn Ching *secondary education educator*
Wright, Chatt Grandison *academic administrator*

Kailua
Elsbury, Michelle Lynn *elementary educator*
Masagatani, Ernesta *retired school superintendent*

Kailua Kona
Diama, Benjamin *retired educator, artist, composer, writer*

Kaneohe
Schimmelfennig, Ladona Beth *special education educator*

Pahoa
Mathis-Gamber, Kathleen Anne *special education educator*
Rodgers, Marilyn Carol *special education educator*

Pearl City
Lee, Kenneth *secondary education educator*
Rhinelander, Esther Richard *secondary school educator*
Tokuno, Kenneth Alan *college dean*

Waipahu
Casey, James Leroy *curriculum director*
Stevens, Muriel Kauimaeole Lee *elementary educator*

IDAHO

Bancroft
Larsen, Aileen *principal*
Pristupa, David William *secondary education educator*

Blackfoot
Patton, Anne Jewell *elementary school counselor*

Boise
Andrus, Cecil Dale *academic administrator*
Baird, Donald Robert *secondary school educator*
Cook, Sharon Evonne *university official*
Ellis-Vant, Karen McGee *special education educator, consultant*
Greear, Michael Allyn *employment counselor and consultant*
Griffin, Gloria Jean *elementary school educator*
Griffin, Sylvia Gail *reading specialist*
Kaupins, Gundars Egons *education educator*
Maloof, Giles Wilson *academic administrator, educator, author*
Morse, Christienne *counselor*
Prinzing, Daniel Lee *secondary education educator*
Ruch, Charles P. *academic administrator*
Wentz, Catherine Jane *elementary education educator*
Woodard, Larry L. *college official*

Caldwell
Hendren, Robert Lee, Jr. *academic administrator*
Sloviaczek-Smyser, Melinda *counselor*

Carey
Hauck, Joann Rae *secondary education educator*

Coeur D Alene
Dunnigan, Mary Ann *former educational administrator*
Hosack, Kathleen Elizabeth *counselor, arts consultant, artist*
Laferriere, Gail Karen *college administrator*

Eagle
Knudsen, Linda *special education educator*

Kellogg
Haller, Ann Cordwell *secondary school educator*

Lewiston
Duley, Charlotte Dudley *vocational counselor*
Harris, Bernice Lee *educator*

Meridian
Babcock, Dale Arlan *school psychologist, counselor*
Rutan, Douglas Edwin *administrator*

Moscow
Atwood, Roy Alden *academic administrator, communications educator*
Hoover, Robert Allan *university president*

Mountain Home
Graves, Karen Lee *high school counselor*
Krueger, Candice Jae *assistant principal*

Mountain Home AFB
Borchert, Warren Frank *elementary education educator*

Nampa
Hopkins, Martha Jane *education educator*
Riley, John Eckel *retired academic administrator*

Pocatello
Bowen, Richard Lee *academic administrator, political science educator*
Croker, Robert Ernest *vocational and human resource development educator*
Davis, E. E. (Gene Davis) *educational administrator*
Griffing, Barry L. *school system administrator*
Lawson, Jonathan Nevin *academic administrator*
Zelus, Paul Robert *education researcher*

Post Falls
Ketchum, Robert George *college administrator*
Mikles, Chris *secondary school educator*

Saint Anthony
Blower, John Gregory *special education educator*

Sandpoint
Rigas, Anthony Leon *univerity department director*

Shelley
Thompson, Sandra Jane *secondary school educator*

Twin Falls
Anderson, Marilyn Nelle *elementary education educator, librarian, counselor*
Geren, Laurie Hewitt *educator*

Wallace
Paroni, Genevieve Marie Swick *retired secondary education educator*

INDIANA

South Bend
Perrin, Kenneth Lynn *university chancellor*

KENTUCKY

Lexington
Zinser, Elisabeth Ann *academic administrator*

MICHIGAN

Maple City
Morris, Donald Arthur Adams *college president*

MINNESOTA

Saint Paul
Kerschner, Lee R(onald) *academic administrator, political science educator*

MISSISSIPPI

Jackson
Tidball, Lee Falk *elementary education educator*

MISSOURI

Florissant
Johnson, Mary Elizabeth *retired elementary education educator*

MONTANA

Belt
Anderson, Harold Sterling *elementary school educator*

Bigfork
Keller, Barbara Lynn *special education educator, reading teacher*
Lamar, Sharon Ann *special and gifted education educator, consultant*

Billings
Abbott, Patti Marie *middle school educator*
Bryngelson, Jim *educational administrator*
May, Michael Wayne *technical school executive*
McDaniel, Susan Roberta *academic administrator*

Bozeman
Carparelli, Peter Louis *education educator*
Malone, Michael Peter *academic administrator, historian*
Monaco, Paul *academic administrator, educator, artist, writer*

Butte
Lawson, Michael Lee *educator*
Sherrill, Barbara Ann Buker *elementary school educator*

Great Falls
Cooper, B. Lee *university administrator, author, history educator*

Havre
Daehling, William A. *academic administrator*
Lanier, William Joseph *college program director*

Helena
Crofts, Richard A. *academic administrator*
Dorrance, Debra Ann *secondary school educator*
Lockyer, Kathleen Lois *high school principal*
Noonan, Edward James *student activity director*

Kalispell
Ford, Alice Havens *primary school educator*

Missoula
Barnett, Mary Louise *elementary education educator*
Dennison, George Marshel *academic administrator*

Superior
Tull, Steven Gerald *secondary education educator*

Victor
Stewart, JoAnne *secondary school educator*

NEVADA

Battle Mountain
Dahl, Richard L. *elementary school educator*

Boulder City
Holmes, BarbaraAnn Krajkoski *secondary education educator*

Carson City
Hull, Dennis Jacques *counselor*
Wadman, William Wood, III *educational director, technical research executive, consulting company executive*

Fallon
Dwyer, Doris Dawn *adult education educator*

Hawthorne
Graham, Lois Charlotte *retired educator*

Incline Village
Peterson, Vance Tullin *academic administrator, educator*

Las Vegas
Andersen, Dale Gordon *academic administrator*
Brooks, Shelley *middle school educator*
Carroll, Rossye O'Neal *college administrator*
Cloud, Barbara Lee *adult education educator*
Dax, Betty Joyce *primary education educator*
Gaspar, Anna Louise *retired elementary school teacher, consultant*
Hair, Kittie Ellen *secondary educator*
Harter, Carol Clancey *university president, English language educator*
Kassouf, Esther Kay *middle school education educator*
Moore, Richard *academic administrator*
Opfer, Neil David *construction educator, consultant*
Ozi, Elizabeth *private school administrator*
Sullivan, Debra Kae *elementary education educator*

Mc Gill
Soliday, Michael David *secondary school and special educator*

Minden
Zabelsky, William John *choral and band director*

North Las Vegas
Jacks, Roger Larry *secondary education educator*
Watson, Rebecca M. *elementary school educator*

Reno
Crowley, Joseph Neil *university president, political science educator*
Dupree, Marsha Anne *academic administrator*
Graham, Margaret Katherine *secondary school educator*
Jarvis, Richard S. *academic administrator*
Kaylor, Andrea Lynn *secondary school counselor*
Lord, Jacklynn Jean *student services representative*
McKay, Alice Vitalich *academic administrator*
Salls, Jennifer Jo *secondary school educator*
Walen, Joanne Michele *secondary education educator, consultant*
Zink, Steven Douglas *academic administrator, dean*

Sparks
Wyatt, Brett Michael *secondary school educator*

Tonopah
Norcross, Catherine Belle *elementary education educator*

NEW MEXICO

Alamogordo
Lee, Joli Fay Eaton *elementary education educator*
McFadin, Helen Lozetta *retired elementary education educator*

Albuquerque
Bass, Martha Postlethwaite *high school principal*
Caplan, Edwin Harvey *university dean, accounting educator*
Donovan, Leslie Ann *honors division educator, consultant*
Elkins, Hollis *secondary education educator*
Howard, Jane Osburn *educator*
Lassen, Betty Jane *educator*
Lattman, Laurence Harold *retired academic administrator*
Peck, Richard Earl *academic administrator, playwright, novelist*
Peniston, Lorraine Carol *special education educator, therapeutic recreation specialist*
Polding, Brian Earl *assistant dean*
Reed, Alan Barry *university executive, consultant, investor*
Steckley, Richard Allan, Sr. *secondary school educator*
Stuart, Cynthia Morgan *university administrator*
Swayze, Margaret Ann *elementary education educator*
Van Why, Rebecca Rivera *retired guidance counselor*
Vigil, Michael J. *school system administrator*

Artesia
Gallegos, José Esquipula *adult education educator*
Horner, Elaine Evelyn *secondary education educator*

Carlsbad
Gossett, Janine Lee *middle school educator*

Casa Blanca
Ortiz, Diana M. *curriculum coordinator*

Chacon
Vásquez, Ben L. *school guidance counselor*

Clovis
Ingram, Peggy Joyce *secondary education educator*
King, Teresa Howard *special education educator, consultant*
Richards, Rosalie Anne *community college administrator*

Farmington
Matthews, Marilyn Ann *college development director*
Salazar, Kimberly D'Nae *secondary educator*

Gallup
Miller, Elizabeth Heidbreder *dean instruction*
Swain, Melinda Susan *elementary education educator*
Zongolowicz, Helen Michaeline *education and psychology educator*

Grants
Marquez, Martina Zenaida *elementary education educator*
Ward, Katherine Marie *school system administrator*

Hobbs
Hart, Pamela June *educator*
Smith, T. Wayne *education director, rodeo announcer, rancher*

Kirtland
Robbins, Heather Lee *special education educator*

Las Cruces
Boykin, William Edward *principal*
Pelking, Marian Virginia *early childhood educator*
Sharp, George Lawrence *counselor*
Thayer, Michael J. *secondary education educator*

Las Vegas
Schufle, Joseph Albert *retired chemistry educator, writer*

Los Alamos
Nekimken, Judy Marie *secondary school educator*
Ramirez, Carlos B. *college administrator*
Seidel, Tammy Sue *secondary education educator*

Rio Rancho
Foesch, Gloria Bogart *elementary school educator*
Weber, Alois Hughes *principal*

Ruidoso
Stover, Carolyn Nadine *middle school educator*

San Cristobal
Namba, Kathryn Elizabeth *elementary educator*

Santa Fe
Harcourt, Robert Neff *educational administrator, journalist*
Pond, Wallace Kimball *education educator*
Wise, Janet Ann *college official*

Santa Teresa
Clement, Shirley George *educational services executive*

Shiprock
Hill, Melodie Anne *special education educator*

Silver City
French, Laurence Armand *social science educator, psychology educator*
Moses-Foley, Judith Ann *special education educator*

Socorro
Lopez, Daniel Heraldo *academic administrator*
Saiz, Bernard R. *principal*

Taos
Martin, Kena Sue *educator*
Martinez, Augustine P. *academic administrator*

Tohatchi
Crowe, Beverly Ann *middle school educator*
Hansen, Harold B., Jr. *elementary school educator*

Vaughn
Maes, Pat Julian *secondary education educator*

NEW YORK

New York
Fitch, Noel Riley *writer, educator*

Potsdam
Ratliff, Gerald Lee *dean, speech and theater educator*

NORTH CAROLINA

Clemmons
Cahill, Eileen Mary *secondary education educator*

OHIO

Crestline
Maddy, Janet Marie *retired educator, dean of students*

OREGON

Ashland
Brown, James Chandler *college administrator*

Beaverton
Branscomb Harmon, Hazel Marie *training specialist, consultant*
Chaney, Victor Harvey *secondary education educator, historical dramatist*
Duncan, Richard Fredrick, Jr. *secondary education educator, travel consultant*

Bend
Hart-Schulz, Tabitha Bernier *alternative education educator*

Cannon Beach
Wismer, Patricia Ann *secondary education educator*

Cave Junction
Maxcy, Lawrence Stahl *education administrator*

Corvallis
Bruce, Robert Kirk *college administrator*
Burke, Michael John *dean, academic programs director*
Byrne, John Vincent *higher education consultant*
Harding, Anna Kristine *education educator*
Healey, Deborah Lynn *education administrator*
Johnson, Duane P. *academic administrator*
Thielges, Bart Arthur *university adminstrator*
Verts, Lita Jeanne *university administrator*

Cottage Grove
Miller, Joanne Louise *middle school educator*
Rasmussen, Ellen L. *secondary school educator*

Dayton
Purcell, Kevin Brown *elementary school principal*

Eugene
Barr, Sue *secondary education educator*
Bartlett, Thomas Alva *educational administrator*
Carnine, Douglas Wayne *education educator, author*
Cox, Joseph William *academic administrator*
Daener, Pamela Hill *university budget officer*
Frohnmayer, David Braden *university president*
Katz, Steven Joseph *school counselor*
McDonald, Penny S(ue) *educational administrator*

Forest Grove
Hosley, Edward Howard *career development organization executive*
Moeller, Bonnie Jean *elementary school educator*
Rogers, Donna Arlene *counselor*

Glendale
Shepard, Brandon Wesley *secondary education educator*

Grants Pass
Christensen, James Arthur *middle school educator*

Gresham
Kuney, Gary Wallace *elementary school educator, real estate agent*

Hillsboro
Parich, Beatrice Ann *secondary school educator*

Jacksonville
Lowe, Barbara Annette *elementary education educator*

Klamath Falls
Crawford, Marcella *migrant bilingual resource educator*
Warner, Linda Marie *elementary education educator*

Lake Oswego
Meltebeke, Renette *career counselor*
Shaff, Beverly Gerard *educational administrator*

Madras
Hillis, Stephen Kendall *secondary education educator*

Mcminnville
Edwards, Wayne A. *school administrator, religious studies educator*
Howland, Peter McKinnon *academic administrator*
Pemberton, Cindy Lee A. *physical education educator*

Merrill
Porter, Roberta Ann *counselor, educator, school system administrator*

Monmouth
Gallimore, Laurene Elizabeth *education educator*
Link-Jobe, Jannice Louise *education educator*

Murphy
Hugle, Linda Jane *gifted and talented educator*

Myrtle Creek
Hull, Tom Allan *mechanics educator*

Newberg
Stevens, Edward Franklin *college president*

Newport
Fitzpatrick, Al W. *educator*

North Bend
de Sá e Silva, Elizabeth Anne *secondary school educator*

Portland
Bennett, Charles Leon *vocational and graphic arts educator*
Braun, Stephen Baker *academic administrator*
Campbell, William Joseph *academic director*
Darling, Lynda Karen *secondary education educator*
Edwards, Peter John *secondary education educator, historic preservation consultant, coach*
Fan, Lee Siu *business executive and vocational training program administrator*
Franklin, Dolores Roberts *elementary education educator*
Hall, James Byron *college provost, author*
Henry, Samuel Dudley *educator*
Kreinberg, Penelope Pettit *counselor*
Lawrence, Sally Clark *academic administrator*
Lenderman, Joanie *elementary education educator*
Leupp, Edythe Peterson *retired education educator, administrator*
Newman, Sharon Ann *principal*
Ramaley, Judith Aitken *academic administrator, endocrinologist*
Ricks, Mary F(rances) *academic administrator, anthropologist*
Seliner, Barbara Ann *elementary education educator*
Wicklund, Lee Arthur *school superintendent*
Wiest, William Marvin *education educator, psychologist*
Wineberg, Howard *research director*

Roseburg
Bowser, M. Gayl *special education coordinator*
Johnson, Doris Ann *educational administrator*
Tilson, Daniel *elementary education educator*

Saint Benedict
Tehrani, Diane Hawke *English as a second language educator*

Salem
Beranek, David John *educational administrator, educator*
Hudson, Jerry E. *university president*
Janota, Debilyn Marie *school principal*
Kearns, Homer H. *school system administrator*

Sandy
Thies, Lynn Wapinski *elementary education educator*

The Dalles
Conklin, Thomas Ray *secondary education educator*

Warrenton
Thompson, Linda Lee *educational consultant*

Yachats
Robeck, Mildred Coen *educator, writer*

Yamhill
Close, Beverly Jean *secondary education educator*

TEXAS

Austin
Brewer, Thomas Bowman *retired university president*

Fort Stockton
Dixon, Danny André *secondary education educator, minister*

Mcallen
Cowart, Bill F(rank) *academic administrator*

San Antonio
Ledvorowski, Thomas Edmund *secondary education educator*

UTAH

American Fork
Swenson, Shirley Ruth *elementary education educator*

Cedar City
Ferguson, Maxel Jarrel *education educator*
Sherratt, Gerald Robert *university president*
Stauffer, Gregory L. *program director*
Thompson, Georgia Beth *university department administrator*

Delta
Arnoldson, Earl Randon *educator*

Farmington
Flygare, Kathleen Tiffeni *elementary education educator, piano educator*

Layton
Rawlins, Jan *educator*

Logan
Gay, Charles W., Jr. *academic administrator*
Hunsaker, Scott Leslie *gifted and talented education educator*
Jeppesen, M. K. *university administrator*
Whitaker, Morris Duane *university administrator*

Magna
McDonough, Karel Joy *secondary education educator, musician*

Ogden
Alexander, Robb Smith, Jr. *academic program director*
DeFrain, Dennis Allen *education director, retired army officer*
Graff, Darrell Jay *physiology educator*
Jolovich-Motes, Sondra Lea *principal*
Protzman, Grant Dale *university administrator, state legislator*
Thompson, Paul Harold *university president*
Thorpe, Patricia Watts *secondary education educator*

Orem
Bowman, Naoma Susann *elementary school educator*

Payson
Allred, Gary Dane *secondary education educator*

Provo
Allred, Ruel Acord *education educator*
Bateman, Merrill Joseph *university president*
Huber, Clayton Shirl *university dean*
Keele, Alan Frank *adult education educator*
Randall, Earl Vance *educational leadership educator, consultant*
Todd, Sally McClay *gifted and special education educator, psychologist*
Whatcott, Marsha Rasmussen *elementary education educator*

Salt Lake City
Bennion, John Warren *urban education educator*
Hardy-Valdez-Woodward, Nancy Greaves *educational administrator*
Makowski, Heidi Michelle *academic program director*
Matsen, John Martin *academic administrator, pathologist*
Matthews, Patricia Deneise *special education educator*
McIntyre, Jerilyn Sue *academic administrator*
Miller, William Charles *college dean, architect*
Morris, Sylvia Marie *university official*
Newell, L. Jackson *education educator*
Peterson, Chase N. *university president*
Pickering, AvaJane *specialized education facility executive*
Rockwood, Linn Roy *retired recreation executive, educator*
Smith, J(ames) Scott *elementary education educator*
Stock, Peggy A(nn) *college president, educator*
Thatcher, Blythe Darlyn *assistant principal*
Trujillo, Augustine *university administrator*

Sandy
Beckman, Patty Zoe *special education educator, consultant*
Liddle, Jacqueline S. *secondary education educator*
Sabey, J(ohn) Wayne *academic administrator, consultant*
Volpe, Ellen Marie *middle school educator*

Tooele
Lawrence, Stephen Lee *elementary school principal, mechanic*

VIRGINIA

Arlington
Hill, Donald Wain *education accreditation commission executive*

WASHINGTON

Amboy
Herzog, Colleen Diane *special education educator*

Arlington
Landry, William Francis *counselor, teacher*

Auburn
Eaton, Edgar Eugene *educator, writer*

Bellevue
Bergstrom, Marianne Elisabeth *program coordinator, special education educator*
Clark, Richard Walter *education consultant*
Meilleur, Cynthia Clark *school system administrator*
Rice, Kay Diane *elementary education educator, consultant*
St. George, Laura M. *middle school educator*

Bellingham
Becker, Michael Kelleher *university administrator, consultant*
Guelker-Cone, Michael Alfred *elementary education educator*
Morse, Karen Williams *academic administrator*
Mortimer, Kenneth P. *academic administrator*
Pierce, George Adams *university administrator, educator*

Bickleton
Matsen, Brynn Marie *elementary school educator, consultant*

Bothell
Banks, Cherry Ann McGee *education educator*
Pizzorno, Joseph Egidio, Jr. *college president*

Buckley
Wickizer, Cindy Louise *elementary school educator*

Camas
Aldrich, Willard Maxwell *retired college president and educator*

Centralia
Kirk, Henry Port *academic administrator*

Chimacum
Hollenbeck, Dorothy Rose *special education educator*

Clarkston
Johnson, Maryann Elaine *educational administrator*

Darrington
Laster, Martin *school superintendent*

Edmonds
Tyllia, Frank Michael *principal*

Ellensburg
Jones, Gail Kathleen *educational administrator*
Nelson, Ivory Vance *academic administrator*

Everett
Callaghan, Mary Anne *secondary school educator*
Hundley, Ronnie *academic administrator*
Thunder, Spencer K. *retired elementary school principal*

Federal Way
Martin, Gwendolyn Elaine *school librarian*

Gig Harbor
Minnerly, Robert Ward *retired headmaster*

Goldendale
Nygaard, Mary Payne *primary school education*

Issaquah
Newbill, Karen Margaret *elementary school educator, education educator*

Kennewick
Fontana, Sharon Marie *early childhood education educator*

Kent
Hickey, Shirley Louise Cowin *elementary education educator*

Lacey
Simmons, Kelley Lynn *mental health counselor, administrator*
Westgard, Joyce Victoria Suzanne *education educator*

Lakewood
Elisara, Cheryl Denise *educator*
Holmes, Sandra Faye *elementary school educator*
Oakes, DuWayne Earl *retired principal*

Lakewood Center
Jones, Stanley Belmont *counselor*

Leavenworth
Wadlington, William Jewell *principal, secondary education educator*

Lynnwood
Ransons, Ellen Frances *high school administrator*

Mount Vernon
Bogensberger, Joan Helen Hess *school administrator, consultant*
Bunge, Robert Alexander, Jr. *educational administrator*

Naches
Glover, Marie Elizabeth *special education educator, speech pathologist*

Nespelem
Edwards, Sheri Rae *elementary education educator*

Oak Harbor
Carlstrom, R. William *retired special education educator*

Odessa
Pitts, Michael Duane *secondary education educator*

Olympia
Averill, Ronald Henry *political science educator, retired military officer*
Jervis, Jane Lise *college official, science historian*
Lambert, Kathy L. *elementary educator, legislator*
Mauer, Charles M. *elementary school educator*
Walter, Jacqueline Jo *elementary educator*

Omak
Best, Susan Kimberly *gifted education educator*

Prosser
Boyle, Steven Leonard *secondary school educator*

Pullman
Nelson, Douglas Michael *school system administrator, educator*
Rennebohm Franz, Kristi *primary education educator*
Richards, Glenice DeBique *education educator*
Smith, Robert Victor *university administrator*
Smith, Samuel Howard *academic administrator, plant pathologist*

Renton
Lockridge, Alice Ann *secondary education educator*
Schoenrock, Cheri Michelle *elementary education educator*

Richland
Haler, Lawrence Eugene *technology educator, councilman*

Seattle
Banks, James Albert *educational research director, educator*
Bassett, Edward Powers *university official*
Cesaro, Wayne Robert *maritime technology educator*
Chan, Anthony Bernard *university administrator, educator, filmmaker*
Coulter, John Arthur *academic administrator*
Counsell, Ann Berner *academic administrator*
DeForeest, Joanne Marie *educator*
Dobel, J. Patrick *dean, educator*
Drew, Jody Lynne *secondary education educator*
El-Moslimany, Ann Paxton *paleoecologist, educator, writer*
Fischer, Mary E. *special education educator*
Gardiner, John Jacob *leadership studies educator*
Halferty, Frank Joseph *middle school music educator*
Hampton, Shelley Lynn *hearing impaired educator*
Koerber, Linda René Gwéns *educator, counselor*
Mailer, Kathleen *university dean*
Omenn, Gilbert Stanley *university dean, physician*
Pritchard, Jackie Lee *information center manager*
Schulte, Henry Gustave *college administrator*
Siegel, Shepherd *education administrator*
Stringer, William Jeremy *academic administrator*
Tschernisch, Sergei P. *academic administrator*

Snohomish
Meister, John Edward, Jr. *consultant, technical educator, systems analyst*

Spokane
Baker, Danial Edwin *director, consultant, pharmacy educator*
Barnes, Steve James *elementary education educator*
Breshears, Guy Ruben *social studies educator, researcher*
Sladich, Harry Hamill *university administrator*
Waters, J. Kevin *university administrator, educator*
Weitz, Sue D. *academic administrator*
Williams, Randy Lee *special education educator*

Springdale
Morrell, June Elizabeth *elementary educator*

Stanwood
Sams, H. Leon *principal*

Steilacoom
Curtis, Joan Corfield *retired college administrator*

Tacoma
Baldassin, Michael Robert *secondary school educator*
Edwards, Lisa Simone *technical college educator*
King, Gundar Julian *retired university dean*
Lewis, Jan Patricia *education educator*
Maloney, Patsy Loretta *university official, nursing educator*
Murray, Lynnette R. *elementary education educator*
Reisberg, Leon Elton *education educator*

Toppenish
Jensen, Cherryl Kay *college public relations director*
Ross, Kathleen Anne *academic administrator*

University Place
Clark, Susan Patrick *secondary English educator*

Valleyford
Woodman, Diane *media specialist*

Vancouver
Felde, Kristin Linn *primary education educator*
Fulton, Richard Delbert *dean*
McGee, Linda Jeanne Danner *school counselor*
Ovens, Mari Camille *school system administrator, dietitian*

Walla Walla
Cronin, Thomas Edward *academic administrator*

Wenatchee
Krebs, Sherry Lynn *elementary education educator*

West Richland
Galliher, Nancy Lynn *elementary education educator*

Yakima
Eng, Joan Louise *special education educator*

WYOMING

Buffalo
Urruty, Katherine Jean *secondary school educator*

Casper
Wilkes, Shar (Joan Charlene Wilkes) *elementary education educator*

Centennial
Houston, Jane Hunt *retired educator*

Cheyenne
McDowell, Sherrie Lorraine *secondary education educator*
Rice, Wallace William *secondary education educator*
Richardson, Earl Wilson *elementary education educator*
Robertson, Susan Joyce Coe *special education educator*
Weigner, Brent James *secondary education educator*

Cody
Fees, Nancy Fardelius *special education educator*

Lander
van Barselaar, Leslie Frances *private school director*

Laramie
Baker, David L. *university administrator*
Baldwin, Hugh John *dean*
Booth, Mark Warren *university dean*
Darnall, Roberta Morrow *academic administrator*
Forster, Bruce Alexander *dean*
Meyer, Joseph B. *academic administrator, former state attorney general*
Roark, Terry Paul *academic administrator, physicist*
Schmitt, Diana Mae *elementary education educator*
Simpson, Peter Kooi *university official*

Rock Springs
Kathka, David Arlin *director educational services*

Torrington
Johnson, Linda Dunlavy *principal*

Wheatland
Morrison, Samuel Ferris *secondary school educator*

Worland
Wise, Kathryn Ann *middle school educator*

TERRITORIES OF THE UNITED STATES

NORTHERN MARIANA ISLANDS

Saipan
Okawa, Antonia Camacho *primary school educator*

CANADA

ALBERTA

Calgary
Samuels, Barbara Ann *university administrator, planner, educator, information architect*

Edmonton
Horowitz, Myer *retired university president, education educator*
Schwabe, Marcus Christopher *alumni affairs director*

Grande Prairie
Harper, Donald Calvin *dean*

Lethbridge
Tennant, Howard Edward *university president, management educator*

BRITISH COLUMBIA

Vancouver
Webber, William Alexander *university administrator, physician*

ADDRESS UNPUBLISHED

Abraham, Willard *special education educator*
Akana, Keith Kalani *elementary education educator, consultant*
Anderson, Carol Ruth *secondary school educator*
Anderson, Iris Anita *retired secondary education educator*
Archuleta, Walter R. *educational consultant, language educator*
Armstrong, Lloyd, Jr. *university official, physics educator*
Ataie, Judith Garrett *middle school educator*
Bachtel, Ann Elizabeth *educational consultant*
Baker, C. B. *retired day care director, organizer, communicator*
Barville, Rebecca Penelope *elementary school educator*
Bassett, Carol Ann *journalism educator, freelance and writer, producer*
Beamon, Ruby T. *elementary education educator*
Beck, Karen Portsche *elementary education educator*
Bennett, Brenda G. *secondary school counselor, mathematics educator*
Berry, Mary Douglas Poindexter *university official*
Beyersdorf, Marguerite Mulloy *educator*
Bindschadler, Brian Charles *gifted and talented education educator, writer*
Black, David R. *superintendent*
Bloom, John W. *counselor, educator*
Blummer, Kathleen Ann *counselor*
Borchers, Mary Amelia *middle school educator*
Brawner, Sharon Lee *bilingual education educator, researcher*
Casper, Gerhard *academic administrator, law educator*
Castruita, Rudy *school system administrator*
Chi, Bernadette Sun *educational administrator*
Christensen, Caroline *vocational educator*
Clough, Sheryl Anne *secondary school educator, poet*
Cocks, J. Fraser, III *educator*
Cole, Verna Jo *educator*
Cooke, Thomas Paul *education educator*
Copenhaver, Brian Paul *university administrator, historian*
Cortlund, Joan Marie *educator*
Darke, Charles Bruce *academic administrator, dentist*
Day, Charlotte Ellen *education administrator*
De Long, Katharine *retired secondary education educator*
Derucher, Kenneth Noel *university dean*
Dexter, Dallas-Lee *education administrator*
Dey, Carol Ruth *secondary education educator*
DiSalle, Michael Danny *secondary education educator*
Duplessis, Audrey Joseph *school system administrator*
Edwards, Ardis Lavonne Quam *retired elementary education educator*
Fair, Marcia Jeanne Hixson *retired educational administrator*
Faverty, Patrick William *principal*
Fetters, Doris Ann *retired secondary education educator*
Fleming, Jane Williams *retired educator, author*
Frost, Everett Lloyd *academic administrator*
Gaggiano, Andrea Jean *secondary education educator*
Galli, John Ronald *academic administrator, physics educator*
Giblett, Phylis Lee Walz *middle school educator, information specialist*
Gray, Richard Moss *retired college president*
Gronli, John Victor *college administrator, minister*
Hamlin, Beverly *gifted education educator*
Hansen, Nancy C. Urdahl *special education educator*
Haynes, Michael Scott, Sr. *resource specialist*
Hensley, Dorothy Sue *elementary educator*
Holtkamp, Susan Charlotte *elementary education educator*
Hughes, Eugene Morgan *university president*
Jerrytone, Samuel Joseph *trade school executive*
Jimmink, Glenda Lee *retired elementary school educator*
Johnson, Sylvia Sue *university administrator, educator*
Johnson, Warren Lyle *secondary education educator*
Johnson, William Theodore *school system administrator*
Kamstra, Bettye Maurice *secondary education educator*
Kasberger-Mahoney, Elvera A. *educational administrator*
Keiper, Marilyn Morrison *elementary education educator*
Kilmer, Joseph Charles *secondary school educator*
Kimbrough, Lorelei *elementary education educator*
Kirk, Rea Helene (Rea Helene Glazer) *special education educator*
Knapp, Lonnie Troy *elementary education educator*
Kolb, Dorothy Gong *elementary education educator*
Kormondy, Edward John *university official, biology educator*
Kravetz, nathan *educator, author*
Kuhn, Ronald Greg *education corporation executive*
Kuttner, Donna Holberg *health education specialist*
Ledbury, Diana Gretchen *adult education educator*
Legington, Gloria R. *middle school educator*
Leister-Campbell, Betty Ann *special education educator*
Lindegren, Jack Kenneth *elementary and secondary education educator*
Lipschutz, Marian Shaw *secondary education educator, writer*
Lockart, Barbetta *counselor, jeweler, artwear designer, artist*
Lundgren, Leonard, III *retired secondary education educator*
Martzen, Barbara Aileen *retired teacher*
Matera, Frances Lorine *elementary educator*
Mattison, Rose Elaine Bacote *elementary and secondary education educator*
McAdams, Charles Michael *academic administrator*
McCulloh, Regina Theresa *elementary school educator, writer*
McEvoy-Jamil, Patricia Ann *English language educator*
McLean, Amy C. *secondary school educator*
Meyer, Robert Lee *secondary education educator*
Miller, Richard Franklin *educational consultant, researcher*
Monroe, Sidni McCluer *special education educator*
Munroe, Mary Hills *preschool and daycare operator*
Nakamoto, Carolyn Matsue *principal*
Nixon, Nora *educational director*
Oldham, Elaine Dorothea *retired elementary and middle school educator*
Oliveira, Mary Joyce *middle school education educator*
O'Malley, Thomas Patrick *academic administrator*
Pardue, Karen Reiko *elementary education educator*
Perry, Josephine *secondary education educator, writer*
Perry, Joyce Fitzwilliam *secondary school educator*
Perry, Raymond Carver *education educator*
Potts, Sandra Dell *elementary education educator*
Prince, Deborah Ann *academic counselor*
Profaizer, Josephine E. *elementary education educator*
Ransel, Sandra Lee *academic administrator*
Ray, Paula Dickerson *elementary education educator*
Reed-Jackson, Leona Mae *educational administrator*
Rice-Dietrich, Therese Ann *elementary education educator*
Richardson, Elsie Helen *retired elementary education educator*
Rife, Mary Lou *school counselor*
Ritchie, Anne *educational administrator*
Roberts, Patricia Lee *education educator*
Robinson, Carmen Delores *educator*
Rohrer, Jane Carolyn *gifted education specialist, administrator, consultant*
Rose, Faye Schuman *retired university department director communications*
Ross, Janine *elementary education educator*
Roth, Evelyn Austin *elementary school educator*
Sanchez, Gilbert *retired academic administrator, microbiologist, researcher*
Scholl, Allan Henry *retired school system administrator, education consultant*
Schultz, Jared C. *vocational counselor, therapist*
Sciaroni, Linda Gillingham *high school educator*
Scudero, Leslie Jeannine *preschool teacher*
Sestini, Virgil Andrew *secondary education educator*
Shagam, Marvin Hückel-Berri *private school educator*
Silvius, Donald Joe *educational consultant*
Siverts, Sharon Ann *academic administrator*
Skaggs, Bebe Rebecca Patten *college dean, clergywoman*
Snow, W. Sterling *secondary education educator, retired sports coach*
Stacy, Bill Wayne *academic administrator*
Steinberg, Joan Emily *retired middle school educator*
Stoneberg, Connie *educational administrator*
Szelenyi, Ivan *educator*
Szenasi, Gail *educational administrator*
Tarbi, William Rheinlander *secondary education educator, curriculum consultant, educational technology researcher*
Terada, Alice Masae *retired elementary school teacher, writer*
Thrift, William Boyd *retired lecturer*
Tonjes, Marian Jeannette Benton *education educator*
Trujillo, Lucy Ann *elementary education counselor and educator*
Wallen, Lina Hambali *educator, consultant*
Wertz, Gary Randall *secondary education educator, counselor*
Wiebelhaus, Pamela Sue *school administrator, educator*
Williams, Harriette Flowers *retired school system administrator, educational consultant*
Williams, Heather Pauline *secondary education educator*
Willms, Carol Cox *elementary education educator, audiologist*
Wilson, Robin Scott *university president, writer*
Witt, Judith Anne *elementary education educator*
Workman, Timathea Shays *production company executive*
Wright, Connie Sue *special education educator*
Wyatt, Susan Melinda Clough *career counselor, human resource development specialist*
Young, Joyce Henry *adult education educator, consultant*
Young, Virgil M. *education educator*
Zeilinger, Elna Rae *elementary educator, gifted-talented education educator*

ENGINEERING

UNITED STATES

ALASKA

Anchorage
Baker, Grant Cody *civil engineering educator*
Jumao-as, Alex Baronda *civil engineer*
Pressley, James Ray *electrical engineer*
Thomas, Howard Paul *civil engineer, consultant*

Copper Center
Ashby, Randall Fawcett *engineering company executive, lodge operator*

Fairbanks
Bennett, Fred Lawrence *engineering educator*

Juneau
Hansen, Ronald Gregory *civil engineer*

ARIZONA

Chandler
Fordemwalt, James Newton *microelectronics engineering educator, consultant*
Kreutel, Randall William, Jr. *electrical engineer*
Meieran, Eugene Stuart *material scientist*
Myers, Gregory Edwin *aerospace engineer*

Flagstaff
Damon, James Christian *communications engineer*

Fort Huachuca
Weeks, Robert Lee *electronic engineer, program manager*

Gilbert
Cook, Peter Gifford *communications engineer*

Glendale
Harris, Warren Lynn *development engineer*
Landrum, Larry James *computer engineer*

Litchfield Park
Heermans, John Michael *electrical, chemical engineer*

Mesa
Eldridge, Terrance Foy *avionics engineer*

Scaven, Gregory Joseph *chemical engineer*
Stemple, Alan Douglas *aerospace engineer*

Paradise Valley
Swan, Peter Alfred *systems engineer*

Phoenix
Bachus, Benson Floyd *mechanical engineer, consultant*
Blevins, Willard Ahart *electrical engineer*
Cazier, Barry James *electrical engineer, software developer*
Chisholm, Tom Shepherd *environmental engineer*
Cicioni, Walter William *traffic engineer*
Ehst, Eric Richard *aerospace engineer*
Fullmer, Steven Mark *systems engineer*
Hamilton, Darden Cole *flight test engineer*
Jorgensen, Gordon David *engineering company executive*
McGhay, Jon Davies *engineer*
McGuire, Gerard Joseph *engineering executive*
Nishioka, Teruo (Ted Nishioka) *electrical engineer*
Sarsam, Mumtaz Bashir *bridge engineer*
Thomas, Harold William *avionics systems engineer, flight instructor*
Watson, Harold George *engineering executive, mechanical engineer*
Ybarra, Kathryn Watrous *systems engineer*
Zeilinger, Philip Thomas *aeronautical engineer*

San Manuel
Courtright, Morris *electrical engineer and educator*

Scottsdale
Bodensieck, Ernest Justus *mechanical engineer*
Cunningham, Larrie John *retired engineering executive, arbitrator*
Diaz, Michael Anthony *electrical engineer, software engineer*
Eckelman, Richard Joel *engineering specialist*
Geyer, David Warren *aerospace scientist, software engineer*
Gookin, Thomas Allen Jaudon *civil engineer*
Kiehn, Mogens Hans *aviation engineer, consultant*
Leeland, Steven Brian *electronics engineer*
Miller, Kevin Lane *software engineer/architect, consultant*
Newman, Marc Alan *electrical engineer*
Pemberton, Randall Grant *industrial engineer*
Ragland, Samuel Connelly *industrial engineer, management consultant*
Roberts, Peter Christopher Tudor *engineering executive*

Sedona
Silvern, Leonard Charles *retired engineering executive*

Sun City
Vander Molen, Jack Jacobus *engineering executive, consultant*

Sun Lakes
Richardson, Robert Carleton *engineering consultant*

Tempe
Ferreira, Jay Michael *mechanical engineer*
Kaufman, Irving *retired engineering educator*
Laananen, David Horton *mechanical engineer, educator*
Moor, William Chattle *industrial engineering educator*
Ostler, David Val *engineering executive*
Singhal, Avinash Chandra *engineering administrator, educator*
Tychowski, Christopher Roman *engineer*

Tucson
Arnell, Walter James William *mechanical engineering educator, consultant*
Brooks, Donald Lee *civil engineering and scientific consulting firm executive*
Bryan, Gordon Redman, Jr. *nuclear power engineering consultant*
Coates, Wayne Evan *agricultural engineer*
Collins, Charles Arthur, III *mechanical engineer*
Cuello, Joel L. *biosystems engineer, educator*
Fasel, Hermann F. *aerospace and mechanical engineering educator*
Gill, Rebecca LaLosh *aerospace engineer*
Hall, Richard Lee *engineering manager*
Jones, Roger Clyde *retired electrical engineering educator*
Kececioglu, Dimitri Basil *reliability engineering educator, consultant*
Kerwin, William James *electrical engineering educator, consultant*
Kulatilake, Pinnaduwa H.S.W. *mining and geological engineering educator*
Levinson, David W. *engineering educator, consultant*
Marefat, Michael M. *electrical and computer engineering educator*
Mitcheli, Robert Campbell *nuclear consultant*
Petersen, Margaret Sara *civil engineering consultant, retired civil engineering educator*
Rubendall, Richard Arthur *civil engineer*
Slack, Donald Carl *agricultural engineer, educator*
Szilagyi, Miklos Nicholas *electrical and computer engineering educator*
Tellington, Wentworth Jordan *engineer*
Tucker, Roy Anthony *electro-optical instrumentation engineer, consultant*

Vail
Hunnicutt, Robert William *engineer*

CALIFORNIA

Agoura Hills
Hokana, Gregory Howard *engineering executive*

Alpine
Roberts, Dwight Loren *engineering consultant*

Alta Loma
Bordner, Gregory Wilson *chemical engineer*

Altadena
Edgar, Herman Burton *aerospace engineer, managment and tax consultant*

Anaheim
Franklin, Cheryl Jean *engineer, author*
Kimme, Ernest Godfrey *communications engineer*
Watson, Oliver Lee, III *aerospace engineering manager*

Antioch
Davis, Stanford Evol *civil engineer*

Aptos
Herman, James Jerome *electronics engineer, lawyer*

Arcadia
Broderick, Donald Leland *electronics engineer*
Massier, Paul Ferdinand *mechanical engineer*

Arcata
Chaney, Ronald Claire *environmental engineering educator, consultant*

Atherton
Morel-Seytoux, Hubert Jean *civil engineer, educator*

Auburn
Perilloux, Bruce Edgar *optical engineer*

Bay Point
Weed, Ronald De Vern *engineering consulting company executive*

Belmont
Hollis, Mary Frances *aerospace educator*

Berkeley
Cairns, Elton James *chemical engineering educator*
Frenklach, Michael Yehoshua *mechanial engineering educator*
Koshland, Catherine Preston *mechanical engineer, educator*
Kuh, Ernest Shiu-Jen *electrical engineering educator*
Laitone, Edmund Victor *mechanical engineer*
Lewis, Edwin Reynolds *biomedical engineering educator*
Mote, Clayton Daniel, Jr. *mechanical engineer, educator, administrator*
Prausnitz, John Michael *chemical engineer, educator*
Schlueter, Erika Manriquez *civil engineer research scientist*
Smith, Otto J. M. *electrical engineering educator*
Susskind, Charles *engineering educator, author, publishing executive*
Tomizuka, Masayoshi *mechanical engineering educator, researcher*
Wright, Paul Kenneth *mechanical engineering educator*

Boron
Potrovitza, Nicholas Pompei *mechanical engineer, solar energy researcher*

Buena Park
Wiersema, Harold LeRoy *aerospace engineer*

Burbank
Halpert, Leslie Dean *engineering executive*
Strain, John Thomas *electronics engineer*

Calabasas
Chiang, Albert Chin-Liang *electrical engineer*

Camarillo
Lam, Cheung-Wei *electrical engineer*
MacDonald, Norval (Woodrow) *safety engineer*
Parker, Theodore Clifford *electronics engineer*

Cambria
DuFresne, Armand Frederick *retired management and engineering consultant*

Campbell
Schmitt, Richard George *industrial engineer*

Canoga Park
Fuller, Paul Norman *retired aerospace executive*
Kivenson, Gilbert *engineering consultant, patent agent*
Ng, Choon Meng *design engineer, consultant*
Olson, Paul S. *nuclear engineer*
Vinson, Connie Sue *aerospace engineer*

Capitola
Barna, Arpad Alex *electrical engineering consultant*

Carlsbad
Pantos, William Pantazes *mechanical engineer, consultant*

Castro Valley
Heckman, Richard Ainsworth *chemical engineer*

Cayucos
Theurer, Byron W. *aerospace engineer, business owner*

Cerritos
Jones, Cleon Boyd *research engineer*

Chatsworth
Levine, Arnold Milton *retired electrical engineer, documentary filmmaker*

China Lake
Woo, Raymond *aerospace engineer*

Chula Vista
Rusconi, Louis Joseph *marine engineer*
Wolk, Martin *electronic engineer, physicist*

Claremont
Dym, Clive Lionel *engineering educator*
Phillips, John Richard *engineering educator*
Shore, John James, III *materials and environmental engineering consultant*
Sparling, Rebecca Hall *retired materials engineer, energy consultant*
Tanenbaum, Basil Samuel *engineering educator*
Yurist, Svetlan Joseph *mechanical engineer*

Concord
Middleton, Michael John *civil engineer*

Copperopolis
Frantzen, John Joseph *chemical engineer, scientist, inventor*

Corona
Blanche, Joe Advincula *aerospace engineer, consultant, educator*
Jungren, Jon Erik *civil engineer*
Tillman, Joseph Nathaniel *engineering executive*

Coronado
Crilly, Eugene Richard *engineering consultant*

Corralitos
Short, Harold Ashby *imaging engineer*

Costa Mesa
Buchtel, Michael Eugene *optical mechanical engineer*
Carpenter, Frank Charles, Jr. *retired electronics engineer*

Crockett
Leporiere, Ralph Dennis *quality engineer*

Cupertino
Dhuey, Michael Joseph *computer engineer*
Franson, C(arl) Irvin *aerospace material and process engineer, educator*
Jung, Henry Hung *mechanical engineer*
Lee, Ho John *electrical engineer*
Wynne, Lesley Bird *computer engineer*

Dana Point
Kaplan, Ozer Benjamin *environmental health specialist, consultant*

Danville
Karpenko, Victor Nicholas *mechanical engineer*

Davis
Copley, John Duane *civil engineer*
Diemer, William David *retired engineer, research analyst*
Gates, Bruce Clark *chemical engineer, educator*
Hull, Maury Lane *mechanical engineering educator*
Larock, Bruce Edward *civil engineering educator*

Downey
Baumann, Theodore Robert *aerospace engineer, consultant, army officer*
Grooms, Henry Randall *civil engineer*
Nash, Richard Eugene *aerospace engineer*
Nguyen, Han Van *mechanical engineer*
Nichols, Mark Edward *engineer*
Silverman, Steven Lee *aeronautical engineer*

Edwards
Garcia, Andrew B. *chemical engineer*
Hamlin, Edmund Martin, Jr. *engineering manager*

El Cajon
Summers, Stanley Eugene *mechanical engineer*

El Dorado Hills
Huppert, Merle Cecil *mechanical engineer*
Yount, Charles Robert *electrical and computer engineer*

El Macero
Guyer, J. Paul *civil engineer, architect, consultant*

El Segundo
Bauer, Jerome Leo, Jr. *chemical engineer*
Chang, I-Shih *aerospace engineer*
Daughaday, Douglas Robert *computer engineer*
Lantz, Norman Foster *electrical engineer*
Lotrick, Joseph *aeronautical engineer*
Mackey, Wayne Allison *electrical engineer*
Mathur, Ashok *telecommunications engineer, educator, researcher*
Mitchell, John Noyes, Jr. *electrical engineer*
Mo, Roger Shih-Yah *electronics engineering manager*

El Sobrante
Bloom, Rose Ellen Giehl *engineer*

Escondido
Fraitag, Leonard Alan *project and manufacturing engineer*
Ghandhi, Sorab Khushro *electrical engineering educator*

Fair Oaks
Agerbek, Sven *mechanical engineer*
Smiley, Robert William *industrial engineer*

Folsom
Simonsen, Richard Severin *retired aerospace engineer*

Fountain Valley
Tu, John *engineering executive*

Fremont
Bush, Mary Elizabeth *mechanical engineer*
Gupta, Praveen *engineering executive, software engineer*
Hill, John Earl *mechanical engineer*

Fresno
Huffman, David George *electrical engineer*

Fullerton
Tehrani, Fleur Taher *electrical engineer, educator, researcher*
Tuazon, Jesus Ocampo *electrical engineer, educator, consultant*

Glendale
Knoop, Vern Thomas *civil engineer, consultant*
Stemmer, Jay John *safety engineer, consultant*
Vilnrotter, Victor Alpár *research engineer*

Glendora
Haile, Benjamin Carroll, Jr. *retired chemical and mechanical engineer*

Hanford
Zack, Teresa Ison *civil engineer*

Hawthorne
Pi, Wen-Yi Shih *aircraft company engineer, researcher*
Turner, David Winburn *aerospace engineer*

Hercules
Emmanuel, Jorge Agustin *chemical engineer, environmental consultant*
Heffelfinger, David Mark *optical engineer*

Huntington Beach
Badzey, Peter Gyula Gusztav *aerospace engineer*
Hildebrant, Andy McClellan *retired electrical engineer*
Stillman, Alfred William, Jr. *design and support engineer*

Idyllwild
Peters, Cal Anthony *engineer*

Irvine
Boczkaj, Boleslaw Franciszek *electrical engineer, consultant*
Davis, Richard Ernest *engineer*
Jacobs, Henry Stephen *computer engineer*
Kinsman, Robert Preston *biomedical plastics engineer*
Korb, Robert William *former materials and processes engineer*
McCraw, Leslie G. *engineering and construction company executive*
Minot, Mark Morton *engineering executive*
Orme, Melissa Emily *mechanical engineering educator*
Pluta, Stanley John *manufacturing project engineer*
Sheldon, Mark Scott *research engineer*
Sklansky, Jack *electrical and computer engineering educator, researcher*
Werner, Roy Anthony *aerospace executive*

La Canada Flintridge
Price, Humphrey Wallace *aerospace engineer*

La Jolla
Elkan, Charles Peter *engineer educator*
Rudolph, Walter Paul *engineering research company executive*
Schmid-Schoenbein, Geert Wilfried *biomedical engineer, educator*
Skalak, Richard *engineering mechanics educator, researcher*

La Mesa
Threlkeld, Steven Wayne *civil engineer*

Lafayette
Krueger, Robert Edward *manufacturing executive, mechanical engineer*
Peirano, Lawrence Edward *civil engineer*

Laguna Beach
Bushman, Edwin Francis Arthur *engineer, plastics consultant, rancher*
Kramarsic, Roman Joseph *engineering consultant*
Nathanson, Theodore Herzl *aeronautical engineer, architect*

Laguna Niguel
Born, Robert Heywood *consulting civil engineer*

Lake Forest
Duringer, Jacob Clyde *project engineer, researcher*
Sheehy, Jerome Joseph *electrical engineer*

Lakeport
Anderson, Terry Marlene *civil engineer*

Lancaster
Bjuring, Göran Lennart *engineering executive*
Figueiredo, Hubert Fernandes *aerospace engineer*

Livermore
Cassens, Nicholas, Jr. *ceramics engineer*
Dalder, Edward Neil Cliff *materials engineer*
Hauber, Janet Elaine *mechanical engineer*
Johnson, Roy Ragnar *electrical engineer*
Sebasco, Salvador Monastra *safety engineer*
Sengupta, Sailes Kumar *engineering researcher, statistical consultant*
Twogood, Richard Edward *electrical engineer*
Wright, James Baron *electrical engineer*
Zacharias, Richard Allen *electrical engineer*

Lomita
Balcom, Orville *engineer*

Lompoc
Means, James Andrew *engineer*

Long Beach
Appleberry, Walter Thomas *aerospace engineering project executive*
Brent, Paul Leslie *mechanical engineering educator*
Elliott, John Gregory *aerospace design engineer*
Jager, Merle LeRoy *aerospace engineer*
Kumar, Rajendra *electrical engineering educator*
Pugay, Jeffrey Ibanez *mechanical engineer*
Raiklen, Harold *aerospace engineering consultant*
Thorn, James Douglas *safety engineer*
Valla, Robert *aeronautical engineer, aerodynamicist*
Vassberg, John Charles *aerospace engineer*
Williams, Philip Anthony *engineering executive*

Los Altos
Bergrun, Norman Riley *aerospace executive*
Hecker, Michael Hanns Louis *electrical engineer, speech scientist*
Sharpe, Roland Leonard *engineering company executive, earthquake and structural engineering consultant*

Los Angeles
Bittenbender, Brad James *environmental safety and health administrator*
Buffington, Gary Lee Roy *safety standards engineer, construction executive*
Cross, Glenn Laban *engineering executive, development planner*

Ferro, Robert Joseph electronics engineer, researcher
Fitzsimmons, Jeffrey Lynn astronautical engineer, military officer
Friedmann, Peretz Peter aerospace engineer, educator
Hahn, Hong Thomas mechanical engineering educator
Huang, Sung-cheng electrical engineering educator
James, William Langford aerospace engineer
Kelly, Robert Edward engineer, educator
Klehn, Henry, Jr. engineering company executive
Kumar, Anil nuclear engineer
Leal, George D. engineering company executive
Li, Victor On-Kwok electrical engineering educator
Lynn, Katherine Lyn quality engineer, chemist
Marmarelis, Vasilis Zissis engineering educator, author, consultant
Marsh, Frank Raymond engineering technical writer, artist
Meecham, William Coryell engineering educator
Meyer, Rudolf X. engineering educator, retired space technology executive
Newman, Richard engineering executive
Peplinski, Daniel Raymond project engineer
Philpott, Lindsey civil engineer, researcher, educator
Portenier, Walter James aerospace engineer
Ramo, Simon engineering executive
Udwadia, Firdaus Erach engineering educator, consultant
Urena-Alexiades, Jose Luis electrical engineer
Yen, Teh Fu civil and environmental engineering educator
Zhang, Zhen electrical engineer

Los Gatos
Breitels, Barbara Renee engineer

Malibu
Hooper, Catherine Evelyn senior development engineer
Widmann, Glenn Roger electrical engineer

Marysville
Klein, Stephen Paul engineering and mathematics educator
Lanphier, Scott Matthew transportation engineer

Mcclellan AFB
Frank, Christopher Lynd mechanical engineer
Walser, Milton Wesley (Buddy Walser) systems engineer

Menlo Park
Edson, William Alden electrical engineer
Milanfar, Peyman research engineer
Nell, Janine Marie metallurgical and materials engineer
Ross, Bernard engineering consultant, educator
Schnebly, F(rancis) David aerospace and electronics company executive
Shelton, Robert Charles electrical engineer

Milpitas
Costa, Vincenzo Francesco engineer
Dennison, Ronald Walton engineer
McDonald, Mark Douglas electrical engineer
Mian, Guo electrical engineer
Wang, Huai-Liang William mechanical engineer

Mission Viejo
Ljubicic Drozdowski, Miladin Peter consulting engineer
Pohl, John Henning chemical engineer, consultant
Subramanian, Sundaram electronics engineer

Moffett Field
Goldstein, Howard Edward chemical engineer
Rogers, Stuart Eames aerospace engineer

Monrovia
Pray, Ralph Emerson metallurgical engineer

Montebello
Danupatampa, Ekachai electrical engineer

Monterey
Ball, Robert Edwin engineering educator
Newberry, Conrad Floyde aerospace engineering educator
Vitale, Robert Louis electrical engineer

Moorpark
Bahn, Gilbert Schuyler retired mechanical engineer, researcher

Moraga
Chua, Constantino Pina electrical and instrument engineer, consultant

Morgan Hill
Sailor, J. Douglas engineering consultant

Mountain View
Fujitani, Martin Tomio software quality engineer
Huang, Sungrung Ron engineer
Papamarcos, Mark Stanley electronic design automation consultant
Savage, Thomas Warren engineering manager

Newport Beach
Kraus, John Walter former aerospace engineering company executive
Parks, Fredrick Scott systems engineer
Sharbaugh, W(illiam) James plastics engineer, consultant
Yang, Xinjian (Sam Yang) environmental engineer

Norco
Lu, Guiyang electrical engineer

North Hollywood
Kaplan, Martin Nathan electrical and electronic engineer

Northridge
Bekir, Nagwa Esmat electrical engineer, educator, consultant
Costea, Ileana civil engineer, educator, consultant, researcher
Epstein, Melvin engineering educator
Rengarajan, Sembiam Rajagopal electrical engineering educator, researcher, consultant

Oak View
Hanchett, William A. Barton mechanical engineer, designer

Oakland
Elliott, Jon Frederick environmental consultant, educator, lawyer
Kint, Arne Tonis industrial engineer, mechanical engineer
Liang, Junxiang aeronautics and astronautics engineer, educator
Musihin, Konstantin K. electrical engineer
Swaminathan, Venkates Vadakanchery electrical engineer, software company executive
Veltfort, Theodore Ernst electrical engineer, physicist

Oceanside
Clark, Arthur Bryan engineer

Orange
Fisk, Edward Ray civil engineer, author, educator
Toeppe, William Joseph, Jr. retired aerospace engineer
Vasudevan, Ramaswami engineering consultant
Vice, Charles Loren electromechanical engineer

Orinda
Calderwood, Neil Moody retired telephone traffic engineer, consultant

Oxnard
Harrower, Thomas Murray electro-mechanical design engineer
Lust, Peter, Jr. microwave engineer, consultant

Palm Desert
Smith, Walter J. engineering consultant

Palmdale
Baker, Richard W. structural and architectural engineer
Moule, William Nelson electrical engineer
Olmstead, Richard Gale, Jr. engineering manager

Palo Alto
Adapa, Rambabu electrical engineer
Aitken, Robert Campbell engineer
Bjeletich, John George metallurgical engineer
Geng, Hwai-yu manufacturing engineer, plant manager
Szczerba, Victor Bogdan electrical engineer, sales engineer
Thuery, Jacques H.A. space industry engineer
Wilson, Frank Henry electrical engineer

Palos Verdes Estates
Abbott, Anton Dwight aerospace engineer
Aro, Glenn Scott environmental and safety executive

Palos Verdes Peninsula
Denke, Paul Herman aircraft engineer
Frassinelli, Guido Joseph retired aerospace engineer
Lowi, Alvin, Jr. mechanical engineer, consultant
Weiss, Herbert Klemm retired aeronautical engineer

Pasadena
Barrett, Robert Mitchell electrical engineer
Craymer, Loring Goddard engineer
Farr, Donald Eugene engineering scientist
Hall, William E. engineering and construction company executive
Hemann, Raymond Glenn research company executive
Holmgren, Richard S., Jr. environmental engineering executive
Jennings, Paul Christian civil engineering educator, academic administrator
Kayalar, Selahattin electrical engineer
Knowles, James Kenyon applied mechanics educator
McCloud, Paul Duane chemical engineer
Miller, James Kay aerospace engineer
Monacos, Steve Perry electrical engineer
Nguyen, Tien Manh communications systems engineer
Otoshi, Tom Yasuo electrical engineer, consultant
Perez, Reinaldo Joseph electrical engineer
Poon, Peter Tin-Yau engineer, physicist
Presecan, Nicholas Lee civil, environmental engineer, consultant
Sayano, Reizo Ray electrochemical engineer
Schober, Robert Charles electrical engineer
Sims, Robert Reynold civil engineer
Stelzried, Charles Thomas engineer
Tolaney, Murli environmental engineering executive
Trussell, R(obert) Rhodes environmental engineer
Wood, Lincoln Jackson aerospace engineer
Wynn, Robert Raymond engineer, consultant
Yeh, Paul Pao electrical and electronics engineer, educator

Pico Rivera
Banuk, Ronald Edward mechanical engineer
Peavey, Charles Carman engineering executive

Piedmont
Schell, Farrel Loy transportation engineer

Pismo Beach
Parker, Roy Alfred transportation engineer, planner

Placerville
Burnett, Eric Stephen environmental consultant
Morrin, Thomas Harvey engineering research company executive

Playa Del Rey
Tai, Frank aerospace engineering consultant

Pleasant Hill
Hopkins, Robert Arthur retired industrial engineer

Pleasanton
Chou, Tai-Yu electrical engineer
Meany, David William civil engineer

Point Mugu
South, Matthew Todd aerospace engineer

Pomona
Armstrong, Bruce Irving mechanical engineer
Kauser, Fazal Bakhsh aerospace engineer, educator

Teague, Lavette Cox, Jr. systems educator, consultant

Port Hueneme
Rosenbluth, Murray Joseph chemical engineer

Rancho Mirage
Copperman, William H. value engineer, consultant
Kramer, Gordon mechanical engineer

Rancho Palos Verdes
Serafini, Victor Renato aerospace engineer

Redondo Beach
Buchta, Edmund engineering executive
Chazen, Melvin Leonard chemical engineer
Cohen, Clarence Budd aerospace engineer
Hughes, James Arthur electrical engineer
Sackheim, Robert Lewis aerospace engineer, educator
Subramanya, Shiva aerospace systems engineer

Redwood City
Bertrand, Keith Jay electrical engineer

Reseda
Cornog, Robert Alden engineering consultant

Ridgecrest
Pearson, John mechanical engineer

Riverside
Allan, David R. safety engineer
Beni, Gerardo electrical and computer engineering educator, robotics scientist
Mathaudhu, Sukhdev Singh mechanical engineer
Mohanty, Binayak Prasad hydrologist, environmental engineer

Rohnert Park
Lord, Harold Wilbur electrical engineer, electronics consultant
Pugliese, John David mechanical engineer, consultant, programmer

Rolling Hills Estates
Diaz-Zubieta, Agustin nuclear engineer, executive
Wong, Sun Yet engineering consultant

Sacramento
Bailey, Thomas Everett engineering company executive
Carleone, Joseph aerospace and defense company executive
Cavigli, Henry James petroleum engineer
Collins, William Leroy telecommunications engineer
Diaz-Flores, Hebert De Jesus scientist, engineer, consultant, manager
Forsyth, Raymond Arthur civil engineer
Khandekar, Shekhar Dinkar electrical engineer
Lathi, Bhagawandas Pannalal electrical engineering educator
Peck, Raymond Charles, Sr. driver and traffic safety research specialist
Simeroth, Dean Conrad chemical engineer
Tovar, Nicholas Mario mechanical engineer

Salinas
Layton, Donald Merrill aeronautics educator

San Bernardino
Bauer, Steven Michael cost containment engineer
French, Kirby Allan transportation engineer, computer programmer

San Carlos
Symons, Robert Spencer electronics engineer
Zink, Steven Martin software engineer

San Clemente
Cramer, Eugene Norman nuclear power engineer, computer educator
White, Stanley Archibald research electrical engineer

San Diego
Anderson, Karl Richard aerospace engineer, consultant
Burke, Arthur Thomas engineering consultant
Chapelle, Gregory Philippe electronics engineer, researcher
Chiles, Wilton Richardson electrical engineer
Coleman, Dale Lynn electrical engineer
Crook, Sean Paul aerospace systems program manager
Doliber, Darrel Lee design engineer, consultant, laboratory manager
Fernandez, Fernando Lawrence research company executive, aeronautical engineer
Gray, Gavin Campbell, II computer information engineer, computer consultant
Gross, Jeffrey software engineer
Hall, Harold Robert retired computer engineer
Hanna, Nabil biomedical engineer
Hanson, Wendy Karen chemical engineer
Hills, Linda Launey advisory systems engineer
Hoffman, Robert James retired electronics engineer
Hoyt, Jack Wallace engineering educator
Huang, Chien Chang electrical engineer
Inoue, Michael Shigeru industrial engineer, electrical engineer
Kropotoff, George Alex civil engineer
Lee, Long Chi electrical engineering and chemistry educator
Maynard, John Herbert electronics engineer
McLeod, John Hugh, Jr. mechanical and electrical engineer
Moroz, Andrew chemical engineer
Paget, John Arthur mechanical engineer
Powell, Robert Francis manufacturing engineer
Ruther, Christine L. biomedical engineer
Schaefer, Michael Jude industrial control systems engineer
Schryver, Bruce John safety engineer
Taylor, John O'Mara engineer
Tom, Lawrence engineering executive
Wen, Chaur Shyong chemical engineer
Woodbury, James Roberts electronics consultant
Youngs, Jack Marvin cost engineer

San Dimas
Lau, Henry mechanical engineer, consultant

San Fernando
Bridges, Robert McSteen mechanical engineer

San Francisco
Bechtel, Riley Peart engineering company executive
Bechtel, Stephen Davison, Jr. engineering company executive
Brodsky, E. Jason audio engineer
Coté, Ralph Warren, Jr. mining engineer, nuclear engineer
Hamburger, Ronald Owen structural engineering executive
Laubscher, Roderick engineering company executive
Lolli, Andrew Ralph industrial engineer, retired army officer
Luft, Rene Wilfred civil engineer
Mattern, Douglas James electronics reliability engineer
Park, U. Young nuclear engineer
Shushkewich, Kenneth Wayne structural engineer
Smith, Bernard Joseph Connolly civil engineer
Taussig, Robert Trimble engineering executive
Vreeland, Robert Wilder electronics engineer

San Jose
Bordelon, Scott Lee computer systems engineer
Chandramouli, Ramamurti electrical engineer
Contos, Paul Anthony engineer, investment consultant
Dix, Gary Errol engineering executive
Ferrante, John Anthony engineering consultant
Hasser, Christopher John electrical engineer
Henry, William Rader mechanical engineering consultant
Hodgson, Gregory Bernard software systems architect
Huang, Francis Fu-Tse mechanical engineering educator
Israel, Paul Neal computer design engineer, author
Lehane, Andrew Desmond civil engineer
Morimoto, Carl Noboru computer system engineer, crystallographer
Parruck, Bidyut electrical engineer
Prasad, Jayasimha Swamy electrical engineer
Shaw, Charles Alden engineering executive
Weitze, William Frederick mechanical engineer
Woytowitz, Peter John mechanical engineer

San Lorenzo
Thompson, Lyle Eugene electrical engineer

San Luis Obispo
Cummings, Russell Mark aerospace engineer, educator
Hoffmann, Jon Arnold aeronautical engineer, educator

San Marcos
Jeffredo, John Victor aerospace engineer, manufacturing company executive, inventor
Maggay, Isidore, III engineering executive, food processing engineer

San Pedro
Birkenbach, Adam Stephen engineer
Ellis, George Edwin, Jr. chemical engineer
Heck, Thomas S. civil engineer, management consultant

San Rafael
Godfrey, Douglas tribologist, consultant
Taylor, Irving mechanical engineer, consultant
Wright, Frederick Herman Greene, II computer systems engineer

San Ramon
Christensen, Thomas Craig engineering executive
Leonte, Dinu Ioan software engineer

Santa Ana
Do, Tai Huu mechanical engineer
Johnson, F. Michael electrical and automation systems professional
Loarie, John Adams engineer
Zabsky, John Mitchell engineering executive

Santa Barbara
Bernstein, Robert David design engineer
Crispin, James Hewes engineering and construction company executive
Frederic, Brad engineering company executive
Gilbert, Paul Thomas chemical development engineer
Kluge, Arthur J. engineering company executive
Mitra, Sanjit Kumar electrical and computer engineering educator
Swalley, Robert Farrell structural engineer, consultant

Santa Clara
Aguinsky, Richard Daniel software and electronics engineer
Barker, Nancie Lynne engineer
Falgiano, Victor Joseph electrical engineer, consultant
Kaneda, David Ken electrical engineering company executive
Mohr, Siegfried Heinrich mechanical and optical engineer
Nee, Christopher Chi-Huang computer software engineer
Pease, Robert Allen electrical engineer
Ran, Xiaonong research and development engineer
Wong, Alexander Shih-Wei electrical engineer
Yan, Pei-Yang electrical engineer
Yin, Gerald Zheyao technology and business executive
Zhang, Xiao-Feng power system engineer, researcher

Santa Clarita
Abbott, John Rodger electrical engineer
Granlund, Thomas Arthur engineering executive, consultant

Santa Cruz
Pister, Karl Stark engineering educator

Santa Monica
Horn, Kenneth Porter aeronautical/astronautical engineering administrator
Kayton, Myron engineering company executive
Mc Guire, Michael John environmental engineering executive
Thomas, Frank Joseph nuclear engineer

Santa Rosa
Cortelyou, Robert J(ohn) *civil engineer*
Solomon, Susanna *electrical engineer, novelist*

Saratoga
Brown, Paul Fremont *aerospace engineer, educator*

Sausalito
Green, Joanta Hermion *electrical engineer*

Seal Beach
Cummings, Darold Bernard *aircraft engineer*
Harsha, Philip Thomas *aerospace engineer*

Sebastopol
Norman, Arnold McCallum, Jr. *engineer*

Simi Valley
Ahsan, Omar Faruk *computer engineer, manager, consultant*

Sonora
Walasek, Otto Frank *chemical engineer, biochemist, photographer*

South Pasadena
Glad, Dain Sturgis *retired aerospace engineer, consultant*

Stanford
Goodman, Joseph Wilfred *electrical engineering educator*
Madix, Robert James *chemical engineer, educator*
Miller, Daniel James *systems engineer*
Nelson, Drew Vernon *mechanical engineering educator*
Ott, Wayne Robert *environmental engineer*

Sugarloaf
Kind, Anne Wilson *engineer*

Sunnyvale
Antweiler, Dennis Francis *mechanical engineer*
Forester, John *cycling transportation engineer*
Ghosh, Abhijit *electrical engineer*
Goslow, Robert Henry *consulting mechanical, aeronautical and forensic engineer*
Laurance, Mark Rodney *applications engineer, entrepreneur*
Ma, Fengchow Clarence *agricultural engineering consultant*
Miller, Joseph Arthur *manufacturing engineer, educator, consultant*
Nagasamy, Vijay *mechanical and aerospace engineer*
Pearce, Hugh Morris *engineering executive*
Pugmire, Gregg Thomas *optical engineer*
Robbins, James Edward *electrical engineer*
Sankar, Subramanian Vaidya *aerospace engineer*
Schubert, Ronald Hayward *retired aerospace engineer*
Swanson, Richard Marker *electrical engineering company executive*
Watson, David Colquitt *electrical engineer, educator*

Sylmar
Kroll, Mark William *electrical engineer*
Madni, Asad Mohamed *engineering executive*
Weinberg, Alvin Howard *engineer*

Temecula
Petersen, Vernon Leroy *communications and engineering corporations executive*

Thousand Oaks
Deisenroth, Clinton Wilbur *electrical engineer*
Smith, Michael Robert *electro-optical engineer, physicist*

Torrance
Das, Subhendu *electrical engineer*
Deibel, Farrell Lee *aerospace engineer*
Flagg, Robert Finch *research aerospace engineer*
Gran, Robert *engineering company executive*
Malinowski, Walter William *manufacturing engineer*
Mazzolini, James William *engineering administrator*
Opfell, John Burton *chemical engineer, educator*
Sorstokke, Susan Eileen *systems engineer*
Wylie, Richard Thornton *aerospace engineer*

Tracy
Nelson, Kenneth Arthur *electrical engineer*

Tustin
Dorneman, Robert Wayne *manufacturing engineer*

Ukiah
Eschenbach, Richard Corey *mechanical engineer*

Upland
Schwarz, Joseph Richard *engineering manager*

Valencia
Windsor, William Earl *consulting engineer, sales representative*

Vallejo
Hudak, Paul Alexander *retired engineer*

Van Nuys
Freiberg, Robert Jerry *physicist, engineer, technology administrator*
Lagasse, Bruce Kenneth *structural engineer*
Milan, John Maurice *engineering executive*
Schultz, Kenneth W. *engineering executive*

Vandenberg AFB
Stevens, Thomas Edward *aerospace engineer*

Ventura
Matley, Benvenuto Gilbert (Ben Matley) *computer engineer, educator, consultant*

Victorville
Lagomarsini, George Caesar *engineering and mathematics educator, consultant*

Walnut
Caudron, John Armand *forensic engineer, technical forensic investigator*

Walnut Creek
Barnett, David Hughes *software engineer, information technology architect*
Burgarino, Anthony Emanuel *environmental engineer, consultant*
Van Maerssen, Otto L. *aerospace engineer, consulting firm executive*

Weed
Kyle, Chester Richard *mechanical engineer*

Westminster
Armstrong, Gene Lee *systems engineering consultant, retired aerospace company executive*

Whittier
Hartling, Earle Charles *environmental engineer*

Woodland Hills
Brozowski, Laura Adrienne *mechanical engineer*
Higginbotham, Lloyd William *mechanical engineer*
Meeks, Crawford Russell, Jr. *mechanical engineer*
Portney, Joseph Nathaniel *aerospace executive*

Woodside
Frank, Victor Robert *electrical engineer*

COLORADO

Arvada
Bailly, Julie Ann *manufacturing engineer*
Brooks, Dennis Eugene *electrician*
Fuhrman, Kendall Nelson *software engineer*
Loomis, Christopher Knapp *metallurgical engineer*

Aurora
Schwartz, Lawrence *aeronautical engineer*

Boulder
Breddan, Joe *systems engineering consultant*
Burr, John Charles *software engineer*
Chow, Chuen-Yen *engineering educator*
Gardner, Homer Jay *electrical engineer*
Kompala, Dhinakar Sathyanathan *chemical engineering educator, biochemical engineering researcher*
Shang, Er-Chang *acoustician*
Sture, Stein *civil engineering educator*
Tary, John Joseph *engineer, consultant*
Waters, M. Bruce *engineering technician*

Colorado Springs
Adnet, Jacques Jim Pierre *astronautical and electrical engineer, consultant*
Carroll, David Todd *computer engineer*
Ferguson, Jackson Robert, Jr. *astronautical engineer*
Hutchens, John Gregory *engineering and management consultant*
Jacobsmeyer, Jay Michael *electrical engineer*
James, Wayne Edward *electrical engineer*
McKenzie, Richard Elvin *aerospace engineer*
Wainionpaa, John William *computer equipment company executive*
Watts, Oliver Edward *engineering consultancy company executive*
White, Gayle Clay *aerospace company executive*
Witte, Robert Alan *electrical engineer, writer*

Conifer
Powers, Edwin Malvin *consulting engineer*

Denver
Bogart, Frank Jeffrey *system and product planning engineer*
Colvis, John Paris *aerospace engineer, mathematician, scientist*
Devitt, John Lawrence *consulting engineer*
Fay, Richard James *mechanical engineer*
Ferguson, Lloyd Elbert *manufacturing engineer*
Mehring, Clinton Warren *engineering executive*
Riese, Arthur Carl *environmental engineering company executive, consultant*
Shapiro, Alison Esther *software engineer*
Stephens, Larry Dean *engineer*
Young, Lester Rex *engineering company administrator*
Ziernicki, Richard Mieczyslaw *engineering firm executive*

Durango
Langoni, Richard Allen *civil engineer*

Englewood
Bingham, Paris Edward, Jr. *electrical engineer, computer consultant*
Skaar, Daniel (Leif) *engineering executive*
Tirman, Valentin Woldemar, Jr. *engineering executive and educator*

Fort Collins
Criswell, Marvin Eugene *civil engineering educator, consultant*
Mesloh, Warren Henry *civil and environmental engineer*

Glenwood Springs
Violette, Glenn Phillip *construction engineer*

Golden
Ansell, George Stephen *metallurgical engineering educator, academic administrator*
Arent, Douglas Jay *electrical engineer*
Ayler, Maynard Franklin *mining engineer*
Clausen, Bret Mark *industrial hygienist, safety professional*
Davenport, Roger Lee *research engineer*
Ervin, Patrick Franklin *nuclear engineer*
Gupta, Bimleshwar Prasad *mechanical engineer, manager*
Patino, Hugo *food science research engineer*
Salamon, Miklos Dezso Gyorgy *mining engineer, educator*

Grand Junction
Gardner, Arthur Speedie *engineering executive*
Rybak, James Patrick *engineering educator*

Greeley
Rames, Douglas Dwight *civil engineer*

Greenwood Village
Peterson, Ralph R. *engineering executive*
Wallace, William Arthur, Jr. *environmental engineering executive*

Lafayette
Hutchison, James Donald *retired engineer, historian*

Lakewood
Lu, Paul Haihsing *mining engineer, geotechnical consultant*

Littleton
Ballard, Jack Stokes *engineering educator*
Brychel, Rudolph Myron *engineer, consultant*
Moger, Colette Ann *planning engineer*
Montgomery, Robert Louis *chemical engineer*
Paredes, Bert (Norbert Paredes) *computer systems engineer*
Paynter, Howard Lager *mechanical engineer, educator, consultant*
Tom, Creighton Harvey *aerospace engineer, consultant*

Longmont
Rueckert, Ronald Frank *engineering executive*

Louisville
Donze, Jerry Lynn *electrical engineer*
Harney, Francis Paul *mechanical engineer, consultant*

Loveland
Sleeper, Andrew Duke *electrical engineer, statistician*
Taylor, Marian Alecia *manufacturing development engineer*
Willson, George Bigelow *civil engineer, consultant*

Parker
Teller, Marc Joel *computer systems engineer, consulting researcher*

Pueblo West
Giffin, Walter Charles *retired industrial engineer, educator, consultant*

U S A F Academy
Wright, Cameron Harrold Greene *electrical engineer*

Westminster
Dalesio, Wesley Charles *former aerospace educator*

Wheat Ridge
Gulman, Paul James *engineer*
Scherich, Erwin Thomas *civil engineer, consultant*

HAWAII

Hilo
Peterson, Gerald Joseph *aerospace executive, consultant*

Honolulu
Brock, James Melmuth *engineer, futurist*
Holmes-Smith, David Michael *computer engineer, consultant, priest, dean*
Mizokami, Iris Chieko *mechanical engineer*
Saxena, Narendra K. *marine research educator*
White, Gary Richard *electrical engineer*
Yee, Alfred Alphonse *structural engineer, consultant*

Kailua
Tetreault, Mark David *nuclear engineer and financial planner*

Kapolei
Sakamoto, Norman Lloyd *civil engineer*

Makawao
Lester, John James Nathaniel, II (Sean Lester) *engineer, environmental analyst, human rights activist*

IDAHO

Boise
Allen, Jeffrey Douglas *engineering manager*
Nuttall, Michael Lee *engineer, educator*
Sandhu, Gurtej Singh *engineer, researcher*

Idaho Falls
Crepeau, John Christian *mechanical engineer*
Dahl, Christian Adam *engineer*
Daniher, John M. *retired engineer*
Epstein, Jonathan Stone *engineering executive*
Greenwade, Lance Eric *scientific visualization specialist, mathematician*
Kerr, Thomas Andrew *advisory engineer, scientist*
Mortensen, Glen Albert *chemical engineer*
Singleterry, Robert Clay, Jr. *nuclear engineer*
Stevens, John Gerald *nuclear engineer*
Williams, Ray Ralph *advisory engineer*

Moscow
Jacobsen, Richard T. *mechanical engineering educator*
Johnson, Brian Keith *electrical engineering educator*

Pocatello
Bennion, John Stradling *engineering educator, consultant*

Rigby
Peterson, Erle Vidaillet *retired metallurgical engineer*

ILLINOIS

Rockford
Vincenti-Brown, Crispin Rufus William *engineering executive*

INDIANA

Fort Wayne
Fairchild, James Leroy *systems engineer*
Joffe, Benjamin *mechanical engineer*

LOUISIANA

Monroe
Khan, Khalid Saifullah *engineering executive*

MONTANA

Bozeman
McLeod, Bruce Royal *electrical engineering educator, consultant*

Helena
Johnson, David Sellie *civil engineer*
Johnson, Qulan Adrian *software engineer*

Missoula
Rice, Steven Dale *electronics educator*
Thistle, Harold William, Jr. *engineer*

NEVADA

Carson City
Hughes, Robert Merrill *control system engineer*
James, Daryl Norman *environmental engineer*

Fallon
Kelley, Harold Edward *metallurgical engineer*

Las Vegas
Broca, Laurent Antoine *aerospace scientist*
Brown, Marc M. *civil engineer*
Grace, John William *retired electrical company executive*
Mavady, Kaykham *electrical engineer, drafting*
Peng, Zhong *electrical engineer*
Ramos, Albert A. *electrical engineer*
Richey, Marvin E(lden) *electrical engineer, administrator*
Schwichtenberg, Daryl Robert *drilling engineer*
Wolff, Joel Henry *human resources engineer*

Minden
Bently, Donald Emery *electrical engineer*

Reno
Daemen, Jaak Joseph K. *mining and geotechnical engineering educator*
Danko, George *engineering educator*
Lee, David DeWitt *industrial hygienist*

Silver City
Bloyd, Stephen Roy *environmental manager, educator, consultant*

Sparks
Byrd, Ronald Dallas *civil engineer*

Verdi
Kmetovicz, Ronald Eugene *new product development educator, engineer, writer*

Winnemucca
Bhaduri, Rahul Sankar *metallurgical engineer*

NEW MEXICO

Albuquerque
Allard, Thurman J. *electrical engineer*
Blouin, Scott E. *engineering company executive*
Brown, James Randall *mechanical engineer*
Byrne, Raymond Harry *electrical engineer, educator*
Chua, Koon Meng *civil engineering educator*
Clark, Arthur Joseph, Jr. *retired mechanical and electrical engineer*
Cooper, Susan Carol *environmental, safety and health professional*
Craig, James Norman *communications engineer, Internet consultant*
Dorato, Peter *electrical and computer engineering educator*
Doughty, John Robert *mechanical engineer, college president*
Eaton, George Wesley, Jr. *petroleum engineer, oil company executive*
Emlen, Warren Metz *electronics engineer, consultant*
Gross, Joel Edward *consultant, safety and security executive*
Gruchalla, Michael Emeric *electronics engineer*
Haddad, Edward Raouf *civil engineer, consultant*
Johnson, Daniel Leon *aeronautical engineer*
Johnson, Jeffrey Paul *systems engineer*
Kelly, Brian Matthew *industrial hygienist*
Orman, John Leo *software engineer, writer*
Plamondon, Maynard Alfred *civil engineer*
Plough, Charles Tobias, Jr. *retired electronics engineering executive*
Prindle, Robert William *civil and geotechnical engineer*
Prinja, Anil Kant *nuclear engineering educator*
Reed, Ray Paul *engineering mechanics measurement consultant*
Robinett, Rush Daleth, III *robotics research manager*
Sharp, Robert Lee *aerospace engineering consultant, test pilot*
Wildin, Maurice Wilbert *mechanical engineering educator*
Wood, Gerald Wayne *electrical engineer*
Woods, Robert Octavius *aerospace engineer*

Belen
Toliver, Lee *mechanical engineer*

Carlsbad
Wayman, Cooper Harry *environmental legal counsel*

Farmington
Caldwell, John Winston, III *petroleum engineer*

Finch, Thomas Wesley *corrosion engineer*
Garretson, Owen Loren *petroleum engineer*
Rollstin, Gary Raymond *electrical engineer*

Holman
Bagley, Fenton Lloyd *mechanical engineer*

Kirtland AFB
Baum, Carl Edward *electromagnetic theorist*

Los Alamos
Doss, James Daniel *electrical engineer, writer*
McDonald, Thomas Edwin, Jr. *electrical engineer*
Sicilian, James Michael *research engineer*

Mayhill
Carter, Joy Eaton *electrical engineer, consultant*

Santa Fe
Davidson, James Madison, III *engineer, technical manager*
Tenison, John Hughes *civil engineer, retired military officer*
Turney, Thomas Charles *civil engineer*

Silver City
La Fleur, Walter J. *engineering executive*

White Sands Missile Range
Arthur, Paul Keith *electronic engineer*
Begert, Matthew *engineering company official*
Kestner, Robert Richard, II *engineering psychologist*

OREGON

Ashland
Berkman, James L. *bicycle builder, publisher*

Beaverton
Chartier, Vernon Lee *electrical engineer*
Davis, Stanford Melvin *engineering executive, publishing consultant*
Getreu, Ian E(dwin) *electronics engineer*

Corvallis
Forbes, Leonard *engineering educator*
Huber, Wayne Charles *engineering educator*
Rapier, Pascal Moran *chemical engineer, physicist*
Yim, Solomon Chik-Sing *civil engineering educator, consultant*

Eugene
Goodson, John Earl *civil engineering executive*
Martin, John Stewart *software engineer*
Richards, James William *electromechanical engineer*

Hillsboro
Abel, Mark Jeffrey *electrical engineer, communications researcher*
Kahn, Kevin Comerford *software engineering executive*
Li, Zhi *process engineer*

Klamath Falls
Buchanan, Walter Woolwine *electrical engineer, educator and administrator*
Wolf, Lawrence Joseph *mechanical engineering educator*

Lake Oswego
Kovtynovich, Dan *civil engineer*

Medford
Horton, Lawrence Stanley *electrical engineer, apartment developer*

Portland
Antoch, Zdenek Vincent *electrical engineering educator*
Becker, Bruce Douglas *mechanical engineer*
Cassidy, Richard Arthur *environmental engineer*
Chrzanowska-Jeske, Malgorzata Ewa *electrical engineering educator, consultant*
Cook, Steven Donald *electrical engineer*
Forsberg, Charles Alton *computer, infosystems engineer*
Grappe, Harold Hugo *civil engineer*
Kocaoglu, Dundar F. *engineering management educator, industrial and civil engineer*
Li, Fu *electrical engineering educator, editor*
McCoy, Eugene Lynn *civil engineer*
Perkowski, Marek Andrzej *electrical engineering educator*
Pham, Kinh Dinh *electrical engineer, educator, administrator*
Pierzchala, Edmund *electronics engineer*

Redmond
Rychetsky, Steve *civil and environmental engineer, consultant*

Roseburg
Amnéus, John Sigfrid *retired research mechanical engineer*

Salem
Butts, Edward Perry *civil engineer, environmental consultant*
Dixon, Robert Gene *manufacturing engineering educator, mechanical engineering company executive*

Tualatin
Webster, Merlyn Hugh, Jr. *manufacturing engineer, information systems consultant*

Wilsonville
Knierim, Robert Valentine *electrical engineer, consultant*

TEXAS

Humble
Fortney, Thomas Kent *cost and petroleum engineer, management consultant*

UTAH

Bingham Canyon
Callender, Jonathan Ferris *environmental engineer, consultant*

Brigham City
Krejci, Robert Henry *aerospace engineer*
Webster, Ronald Lewis *structural engineer*

Fort Duchesne
Cameron, Charles Henry *petroleum engineer*

Hurricane
Cummins, Nancyellen Heckeroth *electronics engineer*

Kaysville
Calder, Robert Mac *aerospace engineer*

Logan
Peralta, Richard Carl *groundwater engineer*
Stevens, David King *civil engineer, educator*
Yener, Muzz *civil engineer, educator*

Murray
Volberg, Herman William *electronics engineer, consultant*

Ogden
Davidson, Thomas Ferguson *chemical engineer*
Hagen, Kirk Dee *mechanical engineer, educator*
Ritchey, Harold W. *retired chemical engineer*

Orem
Nordgren, William Bennett *engineering executive*

Salt Lake City
Anderson, Charles Ross *civil engineer*
Anderson, Robert Ernest *safety engineer, consultant*
Bhayani, Kiran Lilachand *environmental engineer, programs manager*
Crawford, Kevan Charles *nuclear engineer, educator*
De Vries, Kenneth Lawrence *mechanical engineer, educator*
Gandhi, Om Parkash *electrical engineer*
Gill, Ajit Singh *civil engineer*
Gutzman, Philip Charles *aerospace executive, logistician*
Hereth, Lyle George *electrical engineering technologist*
Hogan, Mervin Booth *mechanical engineer, educator*
Judd, Thomas Eli *electrical engineer*
Lee, James Norman *bioengineering researcher, educator*
Loggins, William Conley *industrial engineer*
Mitlin, Vladimir Solomon *chemical engineer, researcher*
Zeamer, Richard Jere *engineer, executive*

South Jordan
Brinkerhoff, Lorin C. *nuclear engineer, management and safety consultant*

West Valley City
Bertoch, Richard Keith *electrical engineer, consultant*

VERMONT

Waterbury Center
Howsmon, Alan Johnston *consulting engineer*

VIRGINIA

Afton
Anderson, Donald Norton, Jr. *retired electrical engineer*

WASHINGTON

Auburn
Duhnke, Robert Emmet, Jr. *retired aerospace engineer*
Westbo, Leonard Archibald, Jr. *electronics engineer, educator*
Whitmore, Donald Clark *retired engineer*

Bainbridge Island
Kincheloe, William Robertson, Jr. *electrical engineering educator*
Whitener, Philip Charles *aeronautical engineer, consultant*

Bellevue
Erickson, Virginia Bemmels *chemical engineer*
Hibbard, Richard Paul *industrial ventilation consultant, lecturer*
Liang, Jeffrey Der-Shing *retired electrical engineer, civil worker, diplomat*
Parks, Donald Lee *mechanical engineer, human factors engineer*
Wiker, Steven Forrester *industrial engineering educator*
Wright, Theodore Otis *forensic engineer*

Bellingham
Albrecht, Albert Pearson *electronics engineer, consultant*
Johnstone, Kenneth Ernest *electronics and business consultant*

Bothell
Blackburn, John Lewis *consulting engineering executive*
Cao, Thai-Hai *industrial engineer*
Piroozmandi, Farid *mechanical engineer*
Sengupta, Mritunjoy *mining engineer, educator*
Slawiatynsky, Marion Michael *biomedical electronics engineer, software consultant*

Bremerton
Joseph, James Edward *engineering technician*

Camas
Prouty, Alan Leslie *environmental engineer*

Edmonds
Peckol, James Kenneth *consulting engineer*

Federal Way
Studebaker, Irving Glen *mining engineering consultant*

Kelso
Vincent, Steve *environmental engineer*

Kennewick
Henager, Charles Henry *civil engineer*

Kirkland
Boxleitner, Warren James *electrical engineer, researcher*
Evans, Robert Vincent *engineering executive*

Manchester
Miner, Robert Frederick *consulting engineer*

Mercer Island
Bridgforth, Robert Moore, Jr. *aerospace engineer*
Walker, Robert Eugene *aerospace engineer*

Moses Lake
Silver, Barnard Joseph Stewart *mechanical and chemical engineer, consultant, inventor*

Mukilteo
Bohn, Dennis Allen *electrical engineer, executive*

Olympia
Nichols, James Raymond, Jr. *civil engineer*
Saari, Albin Toivo *electronics engineer*
Schmidt, John Wesley *engineer, environmental scientist*

Pullman
Petersen, James Niels *chemical engineering educator*

Puyallup
Pontsler, Donald N. *electrical engineer*

Redmond
Anderson, Patrick Lee *electrical/electronics engineer*
Lane, James F. *software engineer*
Oh, Seho *research engineer*
Willard, H(arrison) Robert *electrical engineer*
Woodruff, James Robert *engineer*

Richland
Andre, James P. *nuclear engineer*
Daniels, Frederick Thomas *reactor engineer*
Liu, Yosen *nuclear engineer*
Pillay, Gautam *chemical engineer, electrochemist*
Piper, Lloyd Llewellyn, II *engineer, government/service industry executive*
Schwinkendorf, Kevin Neil *nuclear engineer*
Trent, Donald Stephen *thermo fluids engineer*
Zimmerman, Richard Orin *safety engineer*

Seattle
Allen, Gary King *aerospace advance development engineer*
Bates, Dwight Lee *mechanical engineer*
Choi, Jai Joon *scientist, researcher, educator*
Davis, Terry Lee *communications and control systems engineer*
Drinkard, Terrell DeWayne *aeronautical engineer*
Gartz, Paul Ebner *systems engineer*
Haralick, Robert Martin *electrical engineering educator*
Hom, Richard Yee *research engineer*
Juhlin, Nils Frederick *engineering company executive, consultant*
Kim, Yongmin *electrical engineering educator*
Kinnison, Harry Austin *transportation engineer*
Levinson, Mark *retired engineering educator*
Martin, Thomas Henry, Jr. *water resource engineer, software writer*
Morris, David John *mining engineer, consultant, mining executive*
Olson, Ronald Charles *aerospace executive*
Oman, Henry *retired electrical engineer, engineering executive*
Raecker, Jeffrey Scott *aerospace engineer*
Robinson, Ronald Howard *aeronautical engineer*
Rudolph, Thomas Keith *aerospace engineer*
Savrun, Ender *engineering executive, researcher, engineer*
Somani, Arun Kumar *electrical engineer, educator*
Tencer, Allan Fred *mechanical engineer, medical educator*
Tweney, George Harrison *aeronautical engineer*
Weidner, Mark *environmental research executive*
Wood, Stuart Kee *retired engineering manager*

South Bend
Heinz, Roney Allen *civil engineering consultant*

Spokane
Maus, John Andrew *computer systems engineer*
Nandagopal, Mallur R. *engineer*

Woodinville
Lanter, Sean Keith *software engineer*
McGavin, Jock Campbell *airframe design engineer*

Woodland
Mairose, Paul Timothy *mechanical engineer, consultant*

Yakima
Brown, Randy Lee *systems engineer*

WYOMING

Casper
Hinchey, Bruce Alan *environmental engineering company executive*

Gillette
Sharp, Pamela Ann *quality assurance engineer*

Green River
Schwartz, John Charles *chemical engineer*

Laramie
Stewart, Larry Ray *engineer, financial director, quality consultant*

Powell
Hecht, Scott James *mechanical engineering executive*

Riverton
Pursel, Harold Max, Sr. *mining, civil and architectural engineer*

CANADA

ALBERTA

Calgary
Kentfield, John Alan *mechanical engineering educator*

Edmonton
Morgenstern, Norbert Rubin *civil engineering educator*

BRITISH COLUMBIA

Burnaby
Saif, Mehrdad *electrical engineering educator*

ADDRESS UNPUBLISHED

Artingstall, Thomas *electrical and mechanical engineer*
Avakian, James Lawrence *engineering executive*
Barnes-Roberts, Philip Irwin *engineer*
Beck, John Roland *environmental consultant*
Bertin, John Joseph *aeronautical engineer, educator, researcher*
Bowman, David Winslow *mechanical engineer*
Brown, Ronald Malcolm *engineering corporation executive*
Burlingham, Aragon *aerospace engineer*
Carter, Peter Lenn *electrical engineer*
Chance, Kenneth Donald *engineer*
Cline, Bryan M. *manufacturing manager*
Coble, Hugh Kenneth *engineering and construction company executive*
Constant, Clinton *chemical engineer, consultant*
Cooper, Austin Morris *chemist, chemical engineer, consultant, researcher*
Davis, Roswita Beate *architectural engineer*
Dietz, Patricia Ann *engineering administrator*
Divine, Theodore Emry *electrical engineer*
Dodd, Joe David *safety engineer, consultant*
Donges, Samuel Arnold *process control engineer*
Ellington, James Willard *mechanical design engineer, retired*
Field, Charles William *metallurgical engineer, small business owner, consultant*
Ford, Oral Ivan (Van Ford) *engineering consultant*
Fritcher, Earl Edwin *civil engineer, consultant*
Goetzel, Claus Guenter *metallurgical engineer*
Gorenberg, Norman Bernard *aeronautical engineer, consultant, retired*
Groenier, James Scott *civil engineer*
Haag, Ken Lee *civil engineer, management consultant*
Harris, Martin Stephen *aerospace engineering executive*
Hejhall, Roy Charles *electrical engineer*
Herbert, Robert Norman *engineering company executive*
Herriott, David Neil *aerospace engineer*
Hetfeld, Elizabeth Ann *industrial engineer*
Hollmann, Martin *aircraft design engineer*
Holton, William Chester *engineer, consultant*
Hood, Paul *reservoir engineer*
Johnson, Stewart Willard *civil engineer*
Kahn, Irwin William *industrial engineer*
Kersey, Terry L(ee) *astronautical engineer*
Ketchum, Milo Smith *civil engineer*
Koltai, Stephen Miklos *mechanical engineer, consultant, economist, writer, educator*
Liu, Young King *biomedical engineering educator*
Lutze, Robert Stephen *engineering director*
MacDonough, Robert Howard *retired consulting engineer*
Magnabosco, Louis Mario *chemical engineer, researcher, consultant*
Matthews, Shaw Hall, III *reliability engineer*
Matthiesen, David Karl *netware engineer*
McClellan, Robert Edward *civil engineer*
Meinel, Marjorie Pettit *optical engineer*
Mulvihill, Peter James *fire protection engineer*
Muri, John Imre *mechanical engineer*
Nyman, David Harold *retired nuclear engineer*
Nyquist, Michael S. *civil engineer*
Parker, William Elbridge *consulting civil engineer*
Peters, Douglas Cameron *mining engineer, geologist*
Pezeshki, Kambiz A. *metallurgical engineer*
Remer, Donald Sherwood *engineering economist, cost estimator, educator*
Richardson, Jean McGlenn *retired civil engineer*
Robkin, Maurice Abraham *nuclear engineer, educator*
Rokke, Donald Leif *aerospace engineer, mechanical engineer*
Schimmel, Walter P. *aerospace engineer, educator*
Schoeppel, John Frederick *mechanical and electrical engineer, consultant*
Seldner, Betty Jane *environmental engineer, consultant, aerospace company executive*
Sheaffer, Richard Allen *electrical engineer*
Sheh, Robert Bardhyl *environmental management company executive*
Sitnyakovsky, Roman Emmanuil *scientist, writer, inventor, translator*
Siyan, Karanjit Saint Germain Singh *software engineer*
Snyder, Kelly Ann *engineering company administrator*
Spencer, Tamar Lish *aerospace engineer*
Stiglich, Jacob John, Jr. *engineering consultant*
Sweeney, James D. *computer engineer*
Tetelbaum, Solomon David *research engineer*
Toupin, Edward Bernard *engineer, mathematician and computer scientist*
Tyler, Steven Anthony *mechanical engineer*
Vobejda, William Frank *aerospace engineer*
Ward, Patrick Stanley *applications engineer*

White, Charles Olds *aeronautical engineer*
Williams, Howard Walter *aerospace engineer, executive*
Williams, Ronald Oscar *systems engineer*
Williams-Lohmar, Judith Ann *technical and engineering services company executive*
Willis, Selene Lowe *electrical engineer, software consultant*
Wilson, Gary Thomas *engineering executive*
Wilson, Melvin Edmond *civil engineer*
Wing, Janet Eleanor Sweedyk Bendt *nuclear scientist*
Wu, Rao-Hsien Ray *engineering consultant*
Yamashita, John Hiroshi *engineer*
Yatchak, Michael Gerard *electrical engineer*
Young, Robert Allen *architectural engineer*
Zeitler, Bill Lorenz *aviation engineer*
Zeitlin, Gerald Mark *electrical engineer*
Zhao, Tiemin *electrical engineer*

FINANCE: BANKING SERVICES. *See also* FINANCE: INVESTMENT SERVICES.

UNITED STATES

ALASKA

Anchorage
Harris, Roger J. *mortgage company executive, entrepreneur*
Mehner, William Michel *real estate executive*
Rasmuson, Elmer Edwin *banker, former mayor*
Reed, Frank Metcalf *bank executive*

ARIZONA

Gilbert
Duran, Michael Carl *bank executive*

Phoenix
Fisher, Daniel Russell *banker, lawyer*
Houseworth, Richard Court *banker*
Wallace, Kenneth Alan *investor*

Prescott
Moore, Elizabeth Jane *banker*

Scottsdale
Carpenter, Peter Rockefeller *bank executive*

Tucson
Ross, Mark L. *mortgage broker*
Sniezek, Patrick William *real estate loan officer*

CALIFORNIA

Beverly Hills
Delvoye, Jacques Victor *bank executive*

Chatsworth
Montgomery, James Fischer *savings and loan association executive*

Corona Del Mar
Ripper, Rita Jo (Jody Ripper) *strategic planner, researcher*

Costa Mesa
Medina, Daniel Andrew *corporate development executive*

Crestline
Holloway, Cindy *mortgage company executive*

Davis
Morgan, Charles Edward Phillip *bank executive*

Encino
Feria, Kenneth Peter *mortgage banker*

Fairfax
Delaney, Marion Patricia *bank executive*

Fallbrook
David, Ward S. *bank officer, retired federal agency executive*

Glendale
Trafton, Stephen J. *bank executive*

Glendora
Mestad, Orville Laverne *bank executive*

Grass Valley
Apple, Daniel Bryce *finance company executive, financial planner*

Huntington Beach
MacCauley, Hugh Bournonville *banker*

Irvine
Kuhn, Robert Lawrence *investment banker, corporate financier, strategist, author, educator*

Irwindale
Rinehart, Charles R. *savings and loan association executive*

Laguna Hills
Pelton, Harold Marcel *mortgage broker*

Long Beach
Keller, J(ames) Wesley *credit union executive*

Los Altos
Ilstad, Geir Are *venture capitalist*

Los Angeles
Lombardi, Phillip Ernest *banker*
McLarnan, Donald Edward *banker, corporation executive*
Riordan, George Nickerson *investment banker*
Van Asperen, Morris Earl *banker*

Monterey
Spitler, Lee William *banker*

Monterey Park
Crawford, Philip Stanley *bank executive*

Oakland
Sandler, Herbert M. *savings and loan association executive*
Sandler, Marion Osher *savings and loan association executive*

Orange
Floyd, Brett Alden *mortgage banker*

Pebble Beach
Burkett, William Andrew *banker*

Piedmont
Hoover, Robert Cleary *retired bank executive*

Playa Del Rey
Blomquist, Carl Arthur *medical and trust company executive, insurance executive*

Pomona
Wagemann, Douglas Gerald *banker*

Rancho Cucamonga
Horton, Michael L. *mortgage company executive, publishing executive*

Sacramento
Waller, Larry Gene *mortgage banking executive*

San Dimas
Sawyer, Nelson Baldwin, Jr. *credit union executive*

San Francisco
Braasch, Barbara Lynn *banker*
Coulter, David A. *bank executive*
Dinkelspiel, Paul Gaines *investment banking and public financial consultant*
Dorfman, Paul Michael *bank executive*
Eckersley, Norman Chadwick *banker*
Gillette, Frankie Jacobs *retired savings and loan executive, social worker, government administrator*
Hazen, Paul Mandeville *banker*
Oliver, John Edward *bank training consultant*
Rosenberg, Richard Morris *banker*

San Jose
Myer, Warren Hitesh *mortgage broker, internet advertising executive*

San Luis Obispo
Carr, Roxanne Marie *mortgage company executive*

San Mateo
Douglass, Donald Robert *banker*

San Rafael
Riley, Brian M. *banker*

Santa Monica
Mortensen, William S. *banking executive*
Uberstine, Mitchell Neil *bank executive*

Sherman Oaks
Wingard, Diana Kay *financial services executive*

Turlock
Wallström, Wesley Donald *bank executive*

Westlake Village
Wunderman-Cooper, Ruth Ann *mortgage loan broker*

Woodland Hills
Masline, Richard Charles *financial executive*

COLORADO

Denver
Davidson, John Robert (Jay) *banking executive*
Grant, William West, III *banker*
Levinson, Shauna T. *financial services executive*

Englewood
Corboy, James McNally *investment banker*
Hoffmann, Wayne Thomas *financial services executive*

Greeley
Smith, Jack Lee *bank executive*

FLORIDA

Melbourne
Windham, Edward James *bank executive, leasing company executive*

HAWAII

Honolulu
Dods, Walter Arthur, Jr. *bank executive*
Hoag, John Arthur *retired bank executive*
Johnson, Lawrence M. *banker*
Keir, Gerald Janes *banker*
Stephenson, Herman Howard *retired banker*

IDAHO

Eagle
Tschacher, Darell Ray *mortgage banking executive*

MONTANA

Billings
Posey, F. Bruce *mortgage banker*

NEVADA

Hawthorne
Kennedy, Christopher Robbins *credit union executive*

Henderson
Gonyea, Bruce Edward *mortgage company executive*

Las Vegas
Donohue, Christopher A. *banker*
Hoefer, Gregory Allen *banker*
Jackson, Wilfried *banker*
Thomas, Keith Vern *bank executive*

NEW MEXICO

Albuquerque
Constantineau, Constance Juliette *retired banker*
Frost, W. Gregory *mortgage company executive*

Santa Fe
Duncan, James Herbert Cavanaugh, Sr. *banker*

Silver City
White, Don William *banker*

NEW YORK

New York
Newman, Frank Neil *bank executive*

OREGON

Eugene
Drennan, Michael Eldon *banker*

Portland
Jensen, Edmund Paul *bank holding company executive*

UTAH

Ogden
Draper, Richard N. *banker*
Manning, Donna *banker*

Orem
Millstead, Susan *mortgage loan officer*

Salt Lake City
Eccles, Spencer Fox *banker*
Lamborn, W. John *bank executive*
Simmons, Roy William *banker*
Studdert, Stephen Mark *investment banker*

WASHINGTON

Oak Harbor
Piercy, Gordon Clayton *bank executive*

Seattle
Campbell, Robert Hedgcock *investment banker*
Satterlee, T(homas) Michael *mortgage broker*
Taifel, Roman S. *mortgage company executive*
Williams, Walter Baker *mortgage banker*

Sequim
Laube, Roger Gustav *retired trust officer, financial consultant*

Spokane
Jones, D. Michael *banker*

Tacoma
Harlow, Steven Michael *banker*

Walla Walla
Oliver, Dan David *banker*

WYOMING

Cheyenne
Knight, Robert Edward *banker*

Rock Springs
Hay, John Woods, Jr. *retired banker*

ADDRESS UNPUBLISHED

Birnbaum, Stevan Allen *investment company executive*
Clark, Raymond Oakes *banker*
Clemons, Steve Alan *mortgage company executive, insurance company executive*
Coleman, Lewis Waldo *bank executive*
Fielding, Harold Preston *bank executive*
Iles, Eileen Marie *bank executive, controller*
Lankford, Duane Gail *investment banker, mountaineer*
Taylor, Kathryn Lee *bank officer*
Wong, Gwendolyn Ngit How Jim *bank executive*

FINANCE: FINANCIAL SERVICES

UNITED STATES

ALASKA

Anchorage
Illk, Serena Pearl *accountant*
Price, Margaret Ruth *financial services company executive*
Rose, David Allan *investment manager*
Rylander, Robert Allan *financial service executive*

Juneau
Campbell, Brad Lee *financial executive*

Wrangell
Prophet, Todd Elliott *financial executive*

ARIZONA

Douglas
Stickney, Philip Michael *accountant, educator*

Eagar
Saunders, James Harwood *accountant*

Gilbert
Larson, Dorothy Ann *business educator*

Glendale
Ricks, David Artel *business educator, editor*

Mc Neal
Smith, Clifford Neal *business educator, writer*

Mesa
Markey, Thomas Adam *financial officer*

Peoria
Molinsky, Bert *tax consultant*

Phoenix
Barnes, Stephen Paul *financial planner*
Burg, Jerome Stuart *financial planning consultant*
Hardy, Gary Wayne *financial planner*
Jungbluth, Connie Carlson *tax manager*
Khan, Ahmed Mohiuddin *finance, insurance executive*
Linxwiler, Louis Major, Jr. *retired finance company executive*
Pfeiffer, Geoffrey E. *financial company executive*
Schabow, John William *accountant*
Scozzari, Albert *portfolio manager*
Veit, William Arthur *financial planner*

Scottsdale
Rogers, William Cordell *financial executive*

Sun City
Cortright, Inga Ann *accountant*
Feldman, Allan Jay *financial planner, stockbroker*
Roberts, Anna Ruth *financial consultant*

Sun City West
Abels, Robert Frederick *tax consultant*

Tempe
Brooke, Edna Mae *retired business educator*
Ger, Shaw-Shyong *accountant*
Happel, Stephen Kent *business educator, dean*
Kaufman, Herbert Mark *finance educator*
Oakes, Thomas Chapas *financal analyst*

Tucson
Allardice, Linda Marie *controller, financial executive*
Burke, Patrick George *financial executive*
Couture, Richard Edmund *tax auditor*
Dubow, Susan Diane *financial consultant*
Nixon, Robert Obey, Sr. *business educator*
Norvelle, Joan Wilson *forensic accountant, educator, consultant*
Schulman, Elizabeth Weiner *financial consultant*
Weinberg, Bernd *management scientist and educator*

CALIFORNIA

Alameda
Taveggia, Thomas Charles *management educator*

Anaheim
Barbas, Jeffrey Lawrence *finance company executive*

Arcadia
Overell, William Lawrence *finance executive*

Bakersfield
Bacon, Leonard Anthony *accounting educator*

Bell Canyon
Wolfe, William Carl, Jr. *interest rate risk management consultant*

Belvedere Tiburon
Cook, Robert Donald *financial service executive*

Berkeley
Balderston, Frederick Emery *business administration educator, university dean*
Blume, James Beryl *financial advisor*
Bucklin, Louis Pierre *business educator, consultant*

Beverly Hills
Matzdorff, James Arthur *investment banker, financier*
Taggart, Sondra *financial planner*
Tsung, Christine Chai-yi *financial executive, treasurer*

Buena Park
Kristy, James E. *financial management consultant*

Burbank
Berman, Geoffrey Louis *credit manager*
Gold, Stanley P. *diversified investments executive*
Morris, Janet Eloise *controller, poet*
Thornton, Cameron Mitchell *financial planner*
Widaman, Gregory Alan *financial executive, accountant*

Camarillo
Smith, David Michael *financial planner*

Carlsbad
Peasland, Bruce Randall *financial executive*

Carmel
Steele, Charles Glen *retired accountant*

Cathedral City
Konwin, Thor Warner *financial executive*

Cerritos
Ayloush, Cynthia Marie *financial executive*

Chatsworth
Maher, John Francis *financial executive*

Chico
O'Neill, Michael Foy *business educator*
Van Auken, Stuart *marketing educator*

Claremont
Christian, Suzanne Hall *financial planner*

Concord
Gregory, Leslie Finlayson *tax accountant, financial consultant, realtor*
Hollingsworth, Margaret Camille *financial services administrator, consultant*
Lhotka, Sidney Bruno *tax accountant*

Costa Mesa
Curtis, Gary Lynn *accountant*
Kolanoski, Thomas Edwin *financial company executive*
Shackleton, Robert James *accounting executive*

Crestline
Carter, Larry Vince *financial planner*

Culver City
Abarbanell, Gayola Havens *financial planner*
Richardson, John Edmon *marketing educator*

Cypress
Freedman, Gail *financial analyst*

Davis
Tsai, Chih-Ling *management educator*

Diamond Bar
DeLlamas, Lloyd Richard *government financial consultant*

Duarte
Fayad, Mike Samih *financial analyst*

El Segundo
Curran, Michael Harvey *finance executive*

Emeryville
Chason, Lloyd Ralph *corporate educator*

Encino
Fuld, Steven Alan *financial advisor, insurance specialist*

Escondido
Strong, James Thompson *management, security, human resources consultant*

Foster City
Holbrook, Richard L. *investment manager*
MacNaughton, Angus Athole *finance company executive*

Fountain Valley
Penderghast, Thomas Frederick *business educator*

Fremont
Jensen, Paul Edward Tyson *business educator, consultant*

Garden Grove
Norsby, Kimberly Lyn *tax specialist, consultant*

Glendale
Katzbeck, Karen Lynn *accounting executive*
Tookey, Robert Clarence *consulting actuary*
Tripoli, Masumi Hiroyasu *financial consultant and diplomat*

Harbor City
Lee, Grace Tze *controller*

Hawthorne
Ford, Alyson *accountant*

Hayward
Kam, Vernon Tam Siu *accounting educator*

Hemet
Rowe, Mary Sue *accounting executive*

Inglewood
Lewis, Janie Carol *tax preparer, accounting consultant*

Irvine
Zalle, Paul Martin *financial services company executive*

La Habra
Schoppa, Elroy *accountant, financial planner*

La Jolla
Bradley, Wade Harlow *acquisitions specialist*
Purdy, Kevin M. *estate planner*

La Mesa
Bailey, Brenda Marie *accountant*

La Mirada
Schreiber, Carl William *financial analyst*

Laguna Beach
Indiek, Victor Henry *finance corporation executive*

Laguna Niguel
Duong, Nghiem Duc *estate planner*

Lake Sherwood
Pollak, Norman L. *retired accountant*

Lodi
Sullivan, Janice E. *accountant*

Long Beach
Harlow, Charles Vendale, Jr. *finance educator, consultant*
Lewis, Ralph Jay, III *management and human resources educator*
Valek, Bernard Michael *accounting executive*

Los Altos
Sanchez, Marla Rena *finance director*

Los Angeles
Allison, Laird Burl *business educator*
Anderson, Kenneth Jeffery *family financial planner, accountant, lawyer*
Bennis, Warren Gameliel *business administration educator, author, consultant*
Bookman, Mark Andrew *business educator, consultant*
Broad, Eli *financial services executive*
Chan, David Ronald *tax specialist*
Chase, Richard Barth *operations management educator*
Chavez, Albert Blas *financial executive*
Fisher, Robert John *business educator*
Gillis, Nelson Scott *financial executive*
Goldberg, Harvey *financial executive*
Gooch, Lawrence Boyd *accounting executive*
Greenwood, Richard M. *finance company executive, bank executive*
Lin, Thomas Wen-shyoung *accounting educator, researcher, consultant*
Meloan, Taylor Wells *marketing educator*
Moffatt, Robert Henry *accountant, publisher, writer, consultant*
Morrow, Winston Vaughan *financial executive*
Ross, Stan *accounting firm executive*
Roth, Gary Neal *accountant*
Siegel, David Aaron *accountant*
Slouber, James Kirk *accountant*
Stewart, David Wayne *marketing educator, psychologist, consultant*
Tanaka, Togo W(illiam) *retired real estate and financial executive*
Urban, Jeffrey C. *financial analyst, portfolio manager*
Vogel, Nadine Orsoff *estate planner*
Walendowski, George Jerry *accounting educator*
Weston, John Frederick *business educator, consultant*
Whittenburg, Russell Thomas *finance executive*

Los Osos
Gonzalez, Elizabeth Farr *accountant, management consultant*

Malibu
Yates, Jere Eugene *business educator, management consultant*

Manhattan Beach
Anderson, Charles Michael *accountant*

Menlo Park
Langdon, Paul Russell *retired accountant*
Schleh, Edward Carl *business analyst*
Taylor, Henry Stuart *financial consultant*
Timmins, James Donald *venture capitalist*

Mill Valley
Ware, David Joseph *financial consultant*

Mission Viejo
Rodrigues, Mark *financial executive, manpower consultant*

Modesto
Sargent, Diana Rhea *corporate executive*

Montebello
Orr, Stanley Chi-Hung *financial executive*

Monterey Park
Lin, Lawrence Shuh Liang *accountant*
Tseng, Felix Hing-Fai *accountant*

Moraga
Coleman, Henry James, Jr. *management educator, consultant*

Napa
Schunke, Hildegard Heidel *accountant*

Newbury Park
Kocen, Lorraine Ayral *accountant*

Newport Beach
Randolph, Steven *insurance and estate planner*
Tracy, James Jared, Jr. *accountant, law firm administrator*

Northridge
Lehtihalme, Larry (Lauri) K. *financial planner*
Ruley, Stanley Eugene *cost analyst*

Oakland
Barlow, William Pusey, Jr. *accountant*
Lee, Jong Hyuk *accountant*
Lemmons, Gregory Bertram, Sr. *accountant*
Randisi, Elaine Marie *accountant, educator*
Schwyn, Charles Edward *accountant*

Oceanside
Taverna, Rodney Elward *financial services company executive*

Orange
Caporaso, Karen Denise *financial planner*
Ruiz, Luis Rafael *investment and financial planning consultant*

Oxnard
Woodworth, Stephen Davis *business and financial consultant, investment banker*

Palo Alto
Herrick, Tracy Grant *fiduciary*

Palos Verdes Peninsula
Barab, Marvin *financial consultant*

Pasadena
Axelson, Charles Frederic *retired accounting educator*
Caldwell, William Mackay, III *business executive*
Fisk, Irwin Wesley *financial investigator*

Petaluma
Sedlander, John Wingate *controller*

Pleasanton
Vandenberghe, Ronald Gustave *accountant, real estate developer*

Poway
Tello, Donna *tax strategist*

Rancho Mirage
Fulton, Norman Robert *consumer credit manager*

Rancho Palos Verdes
Fox, Jack *financial service executive*
Hughs, Mary Geraldine *accountant, social service specialist*
Manning, Christopher Ashley *finance educator*

Richmond
Brown, Alan Whittaker *accountant*
McKeever, Mike Pierce *economics and business educator*

Riverside
Harrison, Ethel Mae *financial executive*
Smith, Anita Bingham *accountant, tax preparer*

Sacramento
Doria, Robin Galian *financial consultant*
Kiehn, Ruben Lewis *construction cost estimator*
Putney, Mary Engler *federal auditor*
Ramey, Felicenne Houston *business educator*

Salinas
Stevens, Wilbur Hunt *accountant*

San Carlos
Franklin, Albert Brent *financial consultant*

San Clemente
Petruzzi, Christopher Robert *business educator, consultant*

San Diego
Disney, Michael George *financial services executive*
Gee, Roger Allan *accounting educator, writer*
Schechter, Clifford *financial executive, lawyer*
Sledge, Reginald Leon *regulatory compliance analyst*
Stambaugh, Larry G. *finance executive*
Tennent, Valentine Leslie *accountant*

San Francisco
Ahuruonye, Hyacinth Chidi *accountant, consultant*
Entriken, Robert Kersey *management educator*
Fracchia, Charles Anthony *investment advisor, educator*
Gruber, George Michael *accountant, business management and financial systems consultant*
Hallstrom, Robert Chris *government actuary*
Herringer, Frank Casper *diversified financial services company executive*
Jimenez, Josephine Santos *portfolio manager*
Kahn, Paul Markham *actuary*
Kuhns, Craig Shaffer *business educator*
Kupferman, David Jan *accountant, internet and multimedia consultant*
Lee, Pamela Anne *accountant, business analyst*
Maginn, Stephen Arthur *financial company executive*
Mayer, Patricia Jayne *financial officer, management accountant*
Mumford, Christopher Greene *corporate financial executive*
Olshen, Abraham Charles *actuarial consultant*
O'Toole, James Joseph *business educator*
Palmer, William Joseph *accountant*
Ramos, Charles Joseph (Joe Ramos) *financial consultant*
Sciammas, Jacques Daniel *financial services executive, controller*
Tarlson, Nick Glenn *financial advisor*
Trone, Donald Burnell *investment company executive*
Uri, George Wolfsohn *accountant*
Whitney, David Clay *business educator, consultant, writer*
Witter, Wendell Winship *financial executive, retired*
Zobel, Jan Arleen *tax consultant*

San Jose
Delucchi, George Paul *accountant*
Kertz, Marsha Helene *accountant, educator*
Morrison, William Fosdick *business educator, retired electrical company executive*
Rutherford, Reid *finance company executive*
Simons, Roger Mayfield *tax specialist*
Smith, David Eugene *business administration educator*
Wahler, Dennis Daniel *business studies educator, administrator*
Yee, Keith Philip *accountant*

San Mateo
Hopkins, Cecilia Ann *business educator*
Johnson, Charles Bartlett *mutual fund executive*
Johnson, Rupert Harris *finance company executive*
Lamson, Kristin Anne *finance company executive*

San Rafael
Lieberman, Anne Marie *financial executive*

Santa Ana
Greytak, Lee Joseph *lender services and real estate company executive*
Pratt, Paul Bernard *financial services executive*
Schulte, Mary Ann *finance executive*
Terence, Frank *financial executive*

Santa Barbara
Myerson, Raymond King *investment counseling company executive*

Santa Clara
Beebe, Naomi Marie *financial consultant, accountant*

Santa Fe Springs
Wescoat, Kyle Burley *finance executive*

Santa Monica
Rath, Stephen Charles *controller*
Rizzo, Michael Anthony *contract manager, baseball coach*
Sidhu, Victor S. *investment executive*
Taylor, Nigel Brian *financial planner*

Santa Rosa
Adolph, Mary Rosenquist *financial company executive*
Dado, Arnold Emmett *financial and insurance consultant*
Root, Charles Joseph, Jr. *finance executive, consultant*

Sherman Oaks
Rich, Gareth Edward *financial planner*

Sonoma
Abramowitz, Margaret Fitch *accountant, tax specialist*

South Lake Tahoe
Diamond, Stephen Earle Michael *investor, consultant, inventor*

Stanford
Serbein, Oscar Nicholas *business educator, consultant*

Stockton
Ballot, Michael Harvey *business administration educator, consultant*
Couvillion, Kenneth Paul *accountant*
Goldstrand, Dennis Joseph *business and estate planning executive*
Meyers, Andrew George *accountant*

Sun City
Smith, Jack Daryl *accountant, travel company executive*

Tahoe City
Siedenburg, Carrie *program manager*

Tarzana
Krivis, Scott Alan *accountant, limousine company executive*

Thousand Oaks
Allen, David Harlow *business educator, consultant*
Detterman, Robert Linwood *financial planner*

Torrance
Kramer, Alexander Gottlieb *financial director*
Pettersen, Thomas Morgan *accountant, computer company executive*

Tulare
Joseph, Judy *business administration and health educator*

Vallejo
Feil, Linda Mae *tax preparer*

Ventura
Cammalleri, Joseph Anthony *financial planner, retired air force officer*

Visalia
Neeley, James K. *credit agency executive*

Vista
Helmuth, Philip Alan *tax consultant*
Muscio, Richard J. *accountant*

Walnut Creek
Coit, R. Ken *financial planner*
Fridley, Saundra Lynn *internal audit executive*
Hamilton, Allen Philip *financial advisor*
Morrow, Sharon R. *financial advisor*

West Covina
Barnwell, David R. *financial and computer systems analyst programmer*

West Hills
Wiles, Lisa Gilman *accountant*

West Hollywood
Kathol, Anthony Louis *finance executive*
Santillan, Antonio *financial company executive*

Westlake Village
Cucina, Vincent Robert *retired financial consultant*

Westminster
Smith, William Hugh, Sr. *retired audit manager, consultant*
Strutzel, J(od) C(hristopher) *escrow company executive*

Whittier
Maxwell, Raymond Roger *accountant*

Willits
Akins, George Charles *accountant*

Woodbridge
Thames, Carroll Thomas *financial consultant*

Woodland Hills
Babayans, Emil *financial planner*
La Vine, Mark Leslie *financial advisor*

Woodside
Isaacson, Robert Louis *investment company executive*

COLORADO

Arvada
Hancock, N(ewell) Les(lie) *accountant*
Laidig, Eldon Lindley *financial planner*
Wambolt, Thomas Eugene *financial consultant*

Aurora
McColl, Carol Ann *financial executive, educator*

Boulder
Alpers, John Hardesty, Jr. *financial planning executive*
Richardson, Donn Charles *business and marketing educator*
Stanton, William John, Jr. *marketing educator, author*
Walker, Linda Ann *financial planner*

Broomfield
Affleck, Julie Karleen *accountant*

Colorado Springs
Bressan, Robert R. *accountant*
Homan, Ralph William *finance company executive*
Leonard, George Edmund *real estate, bank, and consulting executive*
Wheeler, Larry Richard *accountant*

Denver
Barber, Larry Eugene *financial planner*
Bennett, Barbara Esther *accountant, tax professional*
Clark, Suzanne *accountant*
Cook, Albert Thomas Thornton, Jr. *financial advisor*
Delk, Richard Allen *accountant, financial consultant*
Gillis, Paul Leonard *accountant*
Hall, Richard Murray, Jr. *finance executive, consultant*
Johnson, J. V. *financial analyst*
Karras, Donald George *tax administrator*
Lincoln, Alexander, III *financier, lawyer, private investor*
Shannon, Patrick Kavanaugh *finance manager*
Steele, William Arthur *financial analyst, public utilities executive*
Theis, Joan C. *accountant*
Wellman, Marian Thompson *financial planner*

Englewood
Anderson, Peggy Rees *accountant*
Bergmann, Michael Dean *financial services company executive*
Bondi, Bert Roger *accountant, financial planner*
Forcey, Stephen Eugene *controller, systems analyst*
Hagman, Richard Harlan *financial advisor*
Lager, Douglas Roy *property tax consultant*
Schumacher, Mark Allen *accountant*
Shannon, Richard Stoll, III *financial executive*
Sprincz, Keith Steven *financial services company professional*

Fort Collins
Ewing, Jack Robert *accountant*
Kinnison, Robert Wheelock *retired accountant*
Thomas, Jeanette Mae *accountant*
Tucker, Mary Linda *management educator, consultant*

Greenwood Village
Barnard, Rollin Dwight *retired financial executive*

Lakewood
Keller, Shirley Inez *accountant*

Littleton
Bass, Charles Morris *financial and systems consultant*
Newell, Michael Stephen *finance company executive, international finance, security-protection consultant*

Niwot
Sliker, Todd Richard *accountant, lawyer*

Wheat Ridge
Leino, Deanna Rose *business educator*

CONNECTICUT

Norwalk
Mueller, Gerhard G(ottlob) *financial accounting standard setter*

HAWAII

Honolulu
Betts, James William, Jr. *financial analyst*
Hook, Ralph Clifford, Jr. *business educator*
Kam, Thomas Kwock Yung *accountant educator*
Ng, Wing Chiu *accountant, computer software consultant, educator, activist*
Palia, Aspy Phiroze *marketing educator, researcher, consultant*
Sterrett, James Melville *accountant, business consultant*

Kihei
Bonfield, Andrew Joseph *tax practitioner*

IDAHO

Boise
Gray, Lonna Irene *indemnity fund executive*
Hedrick, Wallace Edward *lottery executive*
Mock, Stanley Clyde *financial planner, investment advisor*
Porter, Barbara Reidhaar *accounting executive*

Caldwell
Allen, Edward Raymond *retired business educator, accountant*

Idaho Falls
Riddoch, Hilda Johnson *accountant*

Pocatello
Green, David Leroy *accountant*
Morgan, Richard Thomas *accountant, county official*

LOUISIANA

Lafayette
Castellini, Patricia Bennett *business management educator*

MASSACHUSETTS

Chestnut Hill
Goldstein, Michael Aaron *finance educator*

MONTANA

Billings
Allen, Donald Wayne *accountant, educator*
Elser, Danny Ray *financial planner*
Piltz, Anthony Robert *accounting educator, consultant*

Cut Bank
McCormick, Betty Leonora *accountant*

Great Falls
Christiaens, Chris (Bernard Francis Christiaens) *financial analyst, state senator*

Kalispell
Barrett, John Charles *accountant, financial advisor*

Stevensville
Laing-Malcolmson, Sally Anne *enrolled tax agent, tax consultant*

Troy
Sherman, Signe Lidfeldt *portfolio manager, former research chemist*

NEBRASKA

Omaha
Drummer, Donald Raymond *financial services executive*

NEVADA

Carson City
Larson, Gerald Lee *auditor*
Reid, Belmont Mervyn *brokerage house executive*

Incline Village
Diederich, J(ohn) William *financial consultant*

Las Vegas
Carroll, Jeremiah Patrick, II *auditor*
Henley, Preston vanFleet *former banker, financial consultant*
Hobbs, Guy Stephen *financial executive*
Rodgers, Steven Edward *tax practitioner, educator*
Schweinfurth, Scott David *accountant*
Shindler, Jack Thomas *finance company executive, lawyer*
Wendt, Steven William *business educator*

Sparks
Vandergriff, Christina Rai *controller*

NEW MEXICO

Albuquerque
Chavez, Ronald Joseph *business educator, chamber of commerce executive*
Kroll, Paul Benedict *auditor*
Mitchell, Lindell Marvin *financial planner*
Royle, Anthony William *accountant*

Edgewood
Shields, Deborah Joanne *accounting technician*

Las Cruces
Bell, M. Joy Miller *financial planner, real estate broker*
Kriegel, Arlyn Alvin *accounting company executive*

Los Alamos
Ogburn, Gregory Allen *accountant*

Santa Fe
Montoya, Paul Anthony *accountant*

Silver City
Hamlin, Don Auer *financial executive*

OREGON

Ashland
Chatfield, Michael *accounting educator*

Beaverton
Larsen, Janice Casey *financial analyst*

Clackamas
Luchterhand, Ralph Edward *financial advisor*

Eugene
Hamren, Nancy Van Brasch *bookkeeper*
Lindholm, Richard Theodore *economics and finance educator*

Lake Oswego
Mylnechuk, Larry Herbert *financial executive*
Stojanik, Kathryn Ann *accounting manager*

Madras
Brooks, Marian *retired comptroller and credit manager*

Portland
Cato, Robert George *financial company manager*
Dow, Mary Alexis *auditor*
Epperson, Eric Robert *financial executive, film producer*
Kondrasuk, Jack N. (John Kondrasuk) *business educator*
Krahmer, Donald L., Jr. *financial services company executive*
Stewart, Marlene Metzger *financial planning practitioner, insurance agent*
Weber, George Richard *financial consultant, writer*
White, Roberta Lee *comptroller*
Workman, Norman Allan *accountant, graphic arts consultant*

Salem
Lew, Donald Evan *accountant*

UTAH

Brigham City
Billingsley, Laron Kent *financial planner*

Logan
Brackner, James Walter *accounting educator, consultant*

Salt Lake City
Creer, James Read *financial officer*
Johnson, Auston G. *auditor*
Snell, Ned Colwell *financial planner*

Sandy
Mitchell, David Campbell *inventor, corporate executive*

WASHINGTON

Bellingham
Ross, Steven Charles *business administration educator, consultant*

Chelan
Lundberg, Larry Thomas *business executive*

Cheney
Drummond, Marshall Edward *business educator, university administrator*

Lynnwood
Cotton, Kathleen Laura *financial planner*

Mount Vernon
Gaston, Margaret Anne *retired business educator*

Mountlake Terrace
Rapp, Nina Beatrice *financial company executive*

Olympia
Christensen, Robert Wayne, Jr. *financial and leasing company executive*
Myers, Sharon Diane *auditor*

Pullman
Stem, Donald Edward, Jr. *marketing educator, researcher*

Redmond
Gierlasinski, Kathy Lynn *accountant*

Richland
Craven, William Donald *internal auditor, consultant*

Seattle
Collett, Robert Lee *financial company executive*
DeJarnatt, George Lee *financial executive, business owner*
Dively, Dwight Douglas *finance director*
Erickson, Gary Michael *business and management educator*
Evans, Richard Lloyd *financial services company executive*
Feiss, George James, III *financial services company executive*
Gaskill, Herbert Leo *accountant, engineer*
Gorans, Gerald Elmer *accountant*
Johnson, Janice Susan Gallik *finance executive*
Kaminski, Charles Anthony *portfolio manager*
Kasama, Hideto Peter *accountant, advisor, real estate consultant*
Lane, Thomas James *business analyst, investment consultant*
Millett, Blaine William *sales and marketing executive*
Pitts, Barbara Towle *accountant, painter*
Taafe, Peter James *financial consultant*
van der Werff, Terry Jay *management consultant, professional speaker, futurist*

Sequim
Walker, Raymond Francis *business and financial consulting company executive*

Spokane
Burton, Robert Lyle *accounting firm executive*
Teets, Walter Ralph *accounting educator*

Tacoma
Nichols, Robin Ann *accountant*

WYOMING

Afton
Hunsaker, Floyd B. *accountant*

Cheyenne
Case, Rocky Ceciel *finance company executive*
Ferrari, David Guy *auditor*
Price, Keith Glenn *accountant*

Green River
Thoman, Mary E. *business and marketing educator rancher*

Rock Springs
Schumacher, Jon Walter *accountant, educator*

Sheridan
Ryan, Michael Louis *controller*

CANADA

ALBERTA

Calgary
Webber, Patrick Neil *diversified financial services company executive*

BRITISH COLUMBIA

Powell River
Carsten, Arlene Desmet *financial executive*

Salt Spring Island
Kandler, Joseph Rudolph *financial executive*

SASKATCHEWAN

Saskatoon
Deng, Shengliang *marketing educator*
Irvine, Vernon Bruce *accounting educator, administrator*

HONG KONG

Hong Kong
Kwong, Alvin Lin-Pik *financial controller*

ADDRESS UNPUBLISHED

Allen, Bonnie Lynn *pension actuary*
Atcheson, Sue Hart *business educator*
Bagnull, Gary Lynn *accountant*
Barton, Ann Elizabeth *retired financial executive*
Belluomini, Frank Stephen *accountant*
Bishop, Betty Josephine *financial consultant, expert witness*
Boxer, Alan Lee *accountant*
Branson, Harley Kenneth *finance executive, motion picture producer*
Brennan, Ciaran Brendan *independent oil producer, real estate developer*
Burns, Mary Ferris *finance executive*
Cain, Patricia Jean *accountant*
Chen, Nai-Fu *finance educator*
Darany, Michael Anthony *financial executive*
Davis, Robert H. *financial executive, arbitrator, mediator, educator*
Dunlap, James Riley, Sr. *former financial executive, credit manager*
Fagerberg, Dixon, Jr. *retired accountant, weather observer*
Gabriel, Rennie *financial planner*
Galbreath, James Howard *portfolio manager*
Henne, Andrea Rudnitsky *business educator*
Hickson, Ernest Charles *financial executive*
Hoffman, George Bernard *estate planner*
Hutner, Herbert L. *financial consultant, lawyer*
Kaufman, Charles David *controller*
Larizadeh, M(ohammed) R(eza) *business educator*
Martin, Preston *financial services executive*
Miller, Robert Stevens, Jr. *finance professional*
Nelson, Albert Louis, III *finance executive*
Norton, Karen Ann *accountant*
Oldshue, Paul Frederick *financial executive*
Ong, Ernest Grant *auditor, researcher, accountant*
Ortega, Cynthia *financial analyst*
Pefley, Norman Gordon *financial analyst*
Pellone, David Thomas *financial executive*
Pick, James Block *management and sociology educator*
Ray, Richard Stanley *accountant*
Roller, David Isaac *financial services company executive*
Schulz, Marianne *accountant*
Segel, Karen Lynn Joseph *accountant, taxation specialist, lawyer*
Steward, Patricia Ann Rupert *real estate executive, management consultant*
Stralser, Steven Michael *marketing educator, consultant*
Tanouye, Marian Natsuko *accountant*
Tyson, Eric *personal finance writer, finance counselor*
Udvar-Hazy, Steven F. *leasing company financial executive*
VanAtta, Merry Janice *accountant*
Wachbrit, Jill Barrett *accountant, tax specialist*
Wain, Christopher Henry Fairfax Moresby *actuary, insurance and investment consultant*
Wood, Robert Charles *financial consultant*
Yingling, Robert Granville, Jr. *accountant*

FINANCE: INSURANCE

UNITED STATES

ALASKA

Anchorage
Trevithick, Ronald James *underwriter*

ARIZONA

Phoenix
Fugiel, Frank Paul *insurance company executive*
Healy, Barbara Anne *insurance company executive, financial planner*
Redmon, Bob Glen *insurance company executive*
Shcolnik, Robert Milton *insurance company executive*

Scottsdale
Prisbrey, Rex Prince *retired insurance agent, underwriter, consultant*
Sager, Donald Allen *insurance company executive*

Tucson
Ziehler, Tony Joseph *insurance agent*

CALIFORNIA

Agoura Hills
Koff, Robert Louis *insurance executive*

Beverly Hills
Mehdizadeh, Parviz *insurance company executive*

Brea
Spiegel, Ronald Stuart *insurance company executive*

Camarillo
Halperin, Kristine Briggs *insurance sales and marketing professional*

Carlsbad
Haney, Robert Locke *retired insurance company executive*

Chatsworth
Blomstrom, Bruce A. *healthcare executive*

Costa Mesa
Palmer, Gilbert Charles *insurance company executive*

Dana Point
Lang, George Frank *insurance executive, consultant, lawyer*

Encino
Surrell, Kevin Joel *insurance company official*

Escondido
Harker, Robert Twaites *retired insurance executive, archaeology educator*

Eureka
Kaiser, James Russell *insurance agent, retired police officer*

Gustine
Carlsen, Janet Haws *insurance company owner, mayor*

La Mesa
Schlador, Paul Raymond, Jr. *insurance agent*

Los Angeles
Davis, David Richard *business succession consultant*
Holden, William Willard *insurance executive*
Inman, James Russell *claims consultant*
Johnson, E. Eric *insurance executive*
Milgrim, Darrow A. *insurance broker, recreation consultant*
Rinsch, Charles Emil *insurance company executive*
Winthrop, Kenneth Ray *insurance executive*

Monterey Park
Lim, Sally-Jane *insurance consultant*

Newport Beach
Cosgrove, Cameron *insurance executive*
Fries, Arthur Lawrence *life health insurance broker, disability claim consultant*
Gerken, Walter Bland *insurance company executive*

Novato
Grove, Douglas David *insurance company executive*

Oakland
Ching, Eric San Hing *health care and insurance administrator*

Orange
Boynton, Donald Arthur *retired title insurance company executive*

Pasadena
Christensen, Donn Wayne *insurance executive*

Pismo Beach
Brisbin, Robert Edward *insurance agency executive*

Poway
Churchill, David Brian *claims services executive, lawyer*

Sacramento
Basconcillo, Lindy *insurance and financial services company executive*
Keeley, Michael Glenn *risk management analyst*

San Diego
Fuhlrodt, Norman Theodore *retired insurance executive*
Keller, Susan Agnes *insurance executive*
Rotter, Paul Talbott *retired insurance executive*

San Francisco
Clark, Edgar Sanderford *insurance broker, consultant*
Enfield, D(onald) Michael *insurance executive*

San Jose
Jackson, Patrick Joseph *insurance executive*

San Mateo
MacCorkle, Emmett Wallace, III *insurance agent*

San Pedro
Roberts, James Lewis, Jr. *insurance executive*

Santa Ana
Johnson, Joan Bray *insurance company consultant*

Santa Rosa
Farrell, Thomas Joseph *insurance company executive, consultant*

Sherman Oaks
Erickson, Richard Beau *life insurance company executive*

Thousand Oaks
Gregory, Calvin *insurance service executive*

Torrance
Mavros, Glenn Scott *insurance agency executive*

Tustin
Evans, Thomas Edgar, Jr. *title insurance agency executive*

Vacaville
Norling, Lloyd Iver *insurance agency owner*

Westlake Village
Kleban, Cheryl Christine *insurance company executive*

Woodside
Freitas, Antoinette Juni *insurance company executive*

COLORADO

Aurora
Kruger, Paul Robert *insurance broker*

Colorado Springs
Volpe, Richard Gerard *insurance accounts executive, consultant*

Denver
Axley, Hartman *underwriter*
Gundzik, Michael John *health insurance executive*
Hopkins, James Clarence *insurance company executive*
Kelly, Jerome Bernard *insurance company executive*

Englewood
Hardy, Wayne Russell *insurance broker*
Manley, Richard Walter *insurance executive*

Fort Collins
Schendel, Winfried George *insurance company executive*

Littleton
Moore, Dan Sterling *insurance executive, sales trainer*

Pueblo
Kelly, William Bret *insurance executive*

HAWAII

Honolulu
Hu, Joseph Kai Ming *insurance company executive*
Kanehiro, Kenneth Kenji *insurance educator, risk analyst, consultant*
Matthews, Norman Sherwood, Jr. *insurance company executive*
Metcalf, Wayne C. *insurance commissioner*
Okada, Ronald Masaki *insurance agent*
Ronsman, Wayne John *insurance company executive*

IDAHO

Nampa
Heidt, Raymond Joseph *insurance company executive*
Reed, William Glen *retired insurance agency executive*

Twin Falls
Lewis, Frederick Thomas *insurance company executive*

MONTANA

Billings
Yegen, Peter, Jr. *insurance and real estate executive*

NEVADA

Carson City
Marangi, Vito Anthony, Sr. *claim administrator*

NEW MEXICO

Albuquerque
Bauer, Lynton G. *insurance company executive*
Parsley, Steven Dwayne *title company executive*
Rotherham, Larry Charles *insurance executive*
Wainio, Mark Ernest *insurance company consultant*

Deming
Levine, Michael Joseph *insurance company executive*

Tucumcari
Woodard, Dorothy Marie *insurance broker*

OREGON

Hillsboro
Yates, Keith Lamar *retired insurance company executive*

Lake Oswego
Atwood, Kelly Palmer *insurance agency executive*

Medford
Dvorak, Ray P. *insurance company official*

Salem
Rasmussen, Neil Woodland *insurance agent*

Tigard
Yount, Philip Richard *insurance company executive*

Tualatin
Chambers, Lois Irene *insurance automation consultant*

Waldport
Ginter, Carol(yn) Augusta Romtvedt *retired bond underwriter*

West Linn
Dunstan, Larry Kenneth *insurance company executive*

UTAH

Pleasant Grove
Gross, Bruce Leon *financial services representative*

Salt Lake City
Allen, Roy Verl *life insurance company executive*
Elliott, Ross Cox *insurance company executive*
Engar, Richard Charles *insurance executive, dentist, educator*
Larkin, Dixon F. *state insurance commissioner*
Leary, G. Edward *state finance commissioner*
Riley, Larry William *agency executive, insurance agent*

Sandy
Macumber, John Paul *insurance company executive*

WASHINGTON

Auburn
Colburn, Gene Lewis *insurance and industrial consultant*

Bellevue
Eigsti, Roger Harry *insurance company executive*
McCaw, Bruce R. *insurance executive*

Bellingham
Fullmer, Donald Kitchen *insurance executive*

Bremerton
Varga, Steven Carl *reinsurance company executive, consultant*

Kennewick
Stevens, Henry August *insurance agent, educator*

Kirkland
McDonald, Joseph Lee *insurance broker*

Mountlake Terrace
English, Donald Marvin *loss control representative*

Olympia
Schoengarth, R(obert) Scott *life insurance company executive*
Senn, Deborah *insurance commisioner*

Seattle
Duckworth, Tara Ann *insurance company executive*
Johnson, Mildred Grace Mash *investment company executive*
Kibble, Edward Bruce *insurance-investment advisory company executive*
Sausser, Gail Dianne *insurance broker*
Zunker, Richard E. *insurance company executive*

Spokane
Garrett, Paul Edgar *insurance executive, writer*

WYOMING

Glenrock
Bennington, Leslie Orville, Jr. *insurance agent*

ADDRESS UNPUBLISHED

Bovey, Terry Robinson *insurance executive*
Clemens, Charles Joseph *insurance agent*
Dackow, Orest Taras *insurance company executive*
Fibiger, John Andrew *life insurance company executive*
Hinds, Edward Dee *insurance and investment professional, financial planner*
Ipsen, Grant Ruel *insurance and investments professional*
Merk, Elizabeth Thole *sales representative*
Morris, Edward J(ames), Jr. *insurance agent, small business owner*
Porter, Dixie Lee *insurance executive, consultant*
Preuss, Gregory Edward *insurance association manager*
Stenberg, Stephen Joseph *risk manager, retail store manager*

FINANCE: INVESTMENT SERVICES

UNITED STATES

ALASKA

Anchorage
Hickel, Walter Joseph *investment firm executive, forum administrator*

ARIZONA

Mesa
Tennison, William Ray, Jr. *financial planner, stockbroker, resort owner*

Phoenix
Jones, Donald Ray *entrepreneur*
Salmonson, Marty Lee *stockbroker, consulting engineer*
Scarbrough, Ernest Earl *stockbroker, financial planner*
Tribble, Richard Walter *brokerage executive*

Scottsdale
Luke, David Kevin *investment company executive*

Sierra Vista
Hasney, Christopher William *retired investment company executive, educator*

Vail
Maierhauser, Joseph George *entrepreneur*

Yuma
Stuart, Gerard William, Jr. *investment company executive, city official*

CALIFORNIA

Alamo
Morgan, Joe Leonard *investment company executive, former professional baseball player*

Arcadia
Berkus, David William *venture capitalist*

Bermuda Dunes
Myers, William Elliott *investment company executive*

Beverly Hills
Dawson, Derek *investment company executive*
Evans, Louise *investor, retired psychologist, philanthropist*
Gambrell, Thomas Ross *investor, retired physician, surgeon*
Israel, Richard Stanley *investment banker*
Skromeda, Steve *investment company executive*
Winthrop, John *business executive*

Camarillo
Sullivan, Michael Evan *investment and management company executive*

Carmel
Jordan, Edward George *business investor, former college president, former railroad executive*
Sweeney, Joseph W., III *investment executive*

Cedarpines Park
Carter, Larry Alexander *brokerage firm executive*

Chico
Houx, Mary Anne *investments executive*

Coronado
Smith, Albert Cromwell, Jr. *investments consultant*

Costa Mesa
Kiang, Assumpta (Amy Kiang) *brokerage house executive*

Covina
Colley, Janet Scritsmier *investment consultant*

Cupertino
Horn, Christian Friedrich *venture capital company executive*
Markkula, A. C., Jr. *entrepreneur, computer company executive*
Perkins, Thomas James *venture capital company executive*

Dixon
Molina, Rafael Antonio *investment company executive*

Escondido
Allen, Donald Vail *investment executive, author, concert pianist*

Gardena
Ishimatsu, Eiji *investment company executive*

Glendale
Kinney, Paul William *investment company executive*

Granada Hills
Silliman, Brian Allen *commodities trader*

Hollywood
Marshall, Conrad Joseph *entrepreneur*

Irvine
Burns, Donald Snow *registered investment advisor, financial and business consultant*
Le Bon, Douglas Kent *investment manager*

La Crescenta
Koonce, John Peter *investment company executive*

La Jolla
Stone, Donald D. *investment and sales executive*

Long Beach
Augerbright, Pamela Jean *entrepreneur*

Los Angeles
Bernstein, Arthur Harold *venture capital executive*
Davis, Jack *securities dealer*
DeBard, Roger *investment executive*
Egan, Susan Chan *security analyst*
Emmeluth, Bruce Palmer *investment banker, venture capitalist*
Gordy, Berry *entrepreneur, record company executive, motion picture executive*
Greenberg, Stuart S. *investment banker*
Mann, Nancy Louise (Nancy Louise Robbins) *entrepreneur*
Nilles, John Mathias (Jack Nilles) *futurist*
Ogle, Edward Proctor, Jr. *investment counseling executive*
Perry, Donald Lester, II *venture capitalist*
Shanahan, R. Michael *securities dealer*
Weary, Thomas Martin *investment company executive*

Malibu
Ortiz, Geoffrey *stock broker, retirement planning specialist*

Menlo Park
Lucas, Donald Leo *private investor*
Roberts, George R. *investment banking company executive*

Napa
Strock, David Randolph *brokerage house executive*

Newport Beach
Thorp, Edward Oakley *investment management company executive*

Northridge
Lauter, James Donald *retired stockbroker*

Oakland
Alford, Joan Franz *entrepreneur*
Swaney, Thomas Robbins *venture capitalist*

Oceanside
Rosier, David Lewis *investment banker*

Orinda
Bach, Martin Wayne *stockbroker, owner antique clock stores*

Oxnard
Caplan, David Leon *brokerage house executive*

Palo Alto
Cirigliano, John J(oseph) *investment company executive*

Pasadena
Arnott, Robert Douglas *investment company executive*
Gold, Michael Nathan *investment banker, management consultant*
Liebau, Frederic Jack, Jr. *investment manager*

Placentia
Frank, Judith Ann (Jann Frank) *entrepreneur, small business owner*

Rancho Santa Fe
Polster, Leonard H. *investment company executive*

Riverside
Rosenzweig, Herbert Stephen *stockbroker*

Ross
Rosenbaum, Michael Francis *securities dealer*

San Diego
Ensign, Paulette *entrepreneur*
Gengor, Virginia Anderson *financial planning executive, educator*
Martinez, John Stanley *entrepreneur*
Nourse, Thomas Miller *consulting company executive*

San Francisco
Bass, Audrey *commodities trader*
Dellas, Robert Dennis *investment banker*
Greber, Robert Martin *financial investments executive*
Guilfoyle, Bill *securities executive*
Gund, George, III *financier, professional sports team executive*
Hagenbuch, John Jacob *investment banker*
Halliday, John Meech *investment company executive*
Hambrecht, William R. *venture capitalist*
Harris, Bob *investment company executive*
Hellman, F(rederick) Warren *investment advisor*
Hsu, Charles *venture capitalist*
Mc Kee, Allen Page *investment company executive*
Pottruck, David Steven *brokerage house executive*
Redo, David Lucien *investment company executive*
Rosner, Robert Mendel *securities analyst*
Schwab, Charles R. *brokerage house executive*
Smelick, Robert Malcolm *investment bank executive*
Stupski, Lawrence J. *investment company executive*
Vallee, Jacques Fabrice *venture capitalist*

San Jose
Goetz, George David *small business owner*
Hall, Robert Emmett, Jr. *investment banker, realtor*

San Leandro
Pansky, Emil John *entrepreneur*

San Marcos
Stillman, Howard Neil *investment analyst, consultant, writer*

Santa Clara
Lynch, Charles Allen *investment executive, corporate director*

Santa Monica
D'Angelo, Victoria Scott *entrepreneur, writer*

Santa Rosa
Cooper, Annette Carlesta *entrepreneur*

Stanford
Marotta, George Raymond *money manager*

Tarzana
Smuckler, Harvey Glasgow *financial consultant*

Templeton
Guenther, Robert Stanley, II *investment and property executive*

Thousand Oaks
Horton, Kenneth *investor*

Vallejo
Muhammad, Khaleedah *entrepreneur, sales and marketing consultant, community activist*

Walnut Creek
Cervantez, Gil Lawrence *venture capital company executive*

West Covina
Tuck, Edward Fenton *business consultant, venture capitalist*

West Sacramento
Lipscomb, Jeffrey Jon *fund specialist, insurance agent*

Westlake Village
Fredericks, Ward Arthur *venture capitalist, food industry consultant*
Valentine, Gene C. *securities dealer*

COLORADO

Aurora
Ericson, Mark Frederick *investment analyst*

Denver
Heitler, Bruce F. *entrepreneur*
Kelly, Thomas Lloyd, II *investment firm executive*
Leraaen, Allen Keith *financial executive*
Martin, Deric Kriston *securities broker*
Wagner, Judith Buck *investment firm executive*

Englewood
Larkin, Edward Colby *securities analyst, financial services company executive*
Van Loucks, Mark Louis *venture capitalist, business advisor*

Grand Junction
Skogen, Haven Sherman *investment company executive*

Placerville
Kickert, Juliana Arlene *private investor*
Monferrato, Angela Maria *entrepreneur, investor, writer, designer*

Vail
Graves, Richard Tracy *stockbroker, professional golfer*

HAWAII

Honolulu
Behnke, Richard Frederick *investment banking executive*

Kailua
Amos, Wally *entrepreneur*

IDAHO

Boise
Ballantyne, James Henry, IV *investor, developer*

Mountain Home
Bergh, David Morgan *entrepreneur*

MONTANA

Bozeman
Gorman, Brian Dean *investment professional*

Missoula
Liston, Albert Morris *investor, political science educator*

NEVADA

Carson City
Hoskins, Thomas Richard, Jr. *corporate securities agent*

Glenbrook
Jabara, Michael Dean *investment banker*

Las Vegas
Holland, Robert Debnam, Sr. *investment company executive*
Stock, Lincoln Frederick *stockbroker*

Reno
Newberg, William Charles *stock and real estate broker, automotive engineer*

NEW MEXICO

Alamogordo
Green, Francis William *investment consultant, former missile scientist*

Albuquerque
Edenfield, T(homas) Keen, Jr. *music publishing and real estate investor*
Huffman, Nona Gay *financial consultant, retirement planning specialist*

Santa Fe
Dreisbach, John Gustave *investment banker*
Goldberg, Fredric I. *investment management company executive*
Schuyler, Robert Len *investment company executive*

Taos
Lipscomb, Anna Rose Feeny *entrepreneur, arts organizer, fundraiser*

OREGON

Chiloquin
Reed, David George *entrepreneur*

Depoe Bay
Fish, Barbara Joan *investor, small business owner*

Medford
Hennion, Carolyn Laird (Lyn Hennion) *investment executive*

Portland
Hay, Andrew Mackenzie *merchant banking and commodities company executive*
Rutherford, William Drake *investment executive, lawyer*

Salem
Monroe, Cecil R. *securities trader*

TEXAS

San Antonio
Kehl, Randall Herman *investment company executive, consultant*

UTAH

Salt Lake City
Wallace, Matthew Walker *entrepreneur*

Sandy
Wenn, Derek Jay *entrepreneur*

WASHINGTON

Bellevue
Arnold, Robert Lloyd *investment broker*
Jones, John Wesley *entrepreneur*
Ryles, Gerald Fay *private investor, business executive*
Wells-Henderson, Ronald John *investment counselor*

Seattle
Anches, Jerry *investment company executive*
Nelson, Allen F. *investor relations and proxy solicitation company executive*
Paup, Martin Arnold *real estate and securities investor*

Vancouver
Bilbruck, Daniel Wayne *investment company executive*

WYOMING

Cowley
Henderson, James Harold *entrepreneur, business executive, financial planner*

Jackson
Hirschfield, Alan J. *entrepreneur*

Wilson
Chrystie, Thomas Ludlow *investor*

CANADA

ALBERTA

Edmonton
Pocklington, Peter H. *business executive*

BRITISH COLUMBIA

Vancouver
Lyons, Terrence Allan *merchant banking, investment company executive*

Ang, Paul Thienchai *entrepreneur, international business consultant*
Black, Richard Bruce *business executive, consultant*
Browning, Jesse Harrison *entrepreneur*
Carter, Robert Spencer *private investor*
Cockrum, William Monroe, III *investment banker, consultant, educator*
Coleman, Leon Horn *real estate investor, factor*
Fitzgerald, John Charles, Jr. *investment banker*
Friedlander, Charles Douglas *investment company executive, space consultant*
Gelpi, Michael Anthony *entrepreneur*
Greene, Frank Sullivan, Jr. *investment management executive*
Groezinger, Leland Becker, Jr. *investment professional*
Howard, James Webb *investment banker, lawyer, engineer*
Marks, Leonard, Jr. *retired corporate executive*
Marler, Larry John *private investor*
Morgenroth, Earl Eugene *entrepreneur*
Roberts, Kenneth Melvin *investment advisor*
Robinson, Annettmarie *entrepreneur*
Stanfill, Dennis Carothers *business executive*
Svikhart, Edwin Gladdin *investment banker*
Washburn, Dorothy A. *entrepreneur*
White-Vondran, Mary-Ellen *retired stockbroker*

FINANCE: REAL ESTATE

UNITED STATES

ALASKA

Anchorage
Faulkner, Sewell Ford *real estate executive*

ARIZONA

Bullhead City
Jones, Vernon Quentin *surveyor*

Cottonwood
Izzo, Mary Alice *real estate broker*

Flagstaff
Hull, Tod Christopher *environmental consultant*

Mesa
Bell, Daniel Carroll *realtor, community association, ranch and land manager*
Kegley, Joseph Edward *realtor*
McCollum, Alvin August *real estate company executive*

Phoenix
Clements, John Robert *real estate professional*
Donaldson, Wilburn Lester *property management corporation executive*
Jarnagin, David Richard *real estate appraiser, real estate executive*
Mee, Joy Anne *city planning executive*
Schrader, William P. *organization executive, farmer*
Wilson, Carl Arthur *real estate broker, contractor*
Woods, Donald Peter *real estate executive, marketing professional*

Prescott
Martinez, Anthony Joseph *real estate appraiser*

Scottsdale
Bertiger, Karen Lee *real estate broker, asset manager, consultant*
Lennox, Gloria (Gloria Demeree) *real estate executive*
Lutin, David Louis *real estate development and finance consultant*

Sun City
Meade, Kenneth John *realty company owner, broker*

Tucson
Acton, William John *real estate appraiser and consultant*
Bodinson, Holt *conservationist*
Longan, George Baker, III *real estate executive*
Swihart, H. Gregg *real estate company executive*
Taylor, William Malcolm *environmentalist, educator*

CALIFORNIA

Agoura Hills
Kaplan, Donald Sheldon *real estate developer and rehabilitator, property management company executive*

Apple Valley
Ledford, Gary Alan *real estate developer*

Berkeley
Arazi, Lorri Rosenberg *realtor*
Grimes, Ruth Elaine *city planner*
Tinker, Irene *city and regional planning educator, women's studies educator*
Wachs, Martin *urban planning educator*

Beverly Hills
Nguyen, Edward Duy *real estate financier*
Shank, Thom Lewis *real estate executive, entertainment consultant, author*
Tamkin, Curtis Sloane *real estate development company executive*

Big Sur
Cross, Robert Louis *realtor, land use planner, writer*
Owings, Margaret Wentworth *conservationist, artist*

Coronado
Stames, William Alexander *realtor, cost management executive*

Salt Lake City
Sperry, Edmund Lynn *real estate broker*

WASHINGTON

Arlington
Miller, Gene Frederick *land use planner*

Bellevue
Williams, Stuart Vance *real estate executive*

Bellingham
Friedman, Mitch Alan *conservation biologist*

Cheney
Winchell, Richard G. *urban planning educator, consultant*

Friday Harbor
Padve, Martha Bertonneau *urban planning and arts consultant, fundraiser*

Lacey
Deatherage, Leo Jackson, Jr. *real estate developer, construction consultant*

Lynnwood
Edwards, Kirk Lewis *real estate company executive*

Olympia
Stewart, Jeffree Robert *environmental planner, artist*

Puyallup
DeBock, Ronald Gene *real estate company executive*

Redmond
Doman, Margaret Horn *land use planning consultant, civic official*

Rollingbay
Morris, Donald Charles *real estate developer*

Seattle
Dillard, Marilyn Dianne *property manager*
Downey, Heather Anne *property manager*
Fisher, Kurt Andrew *real estate broker*
Fouts, Gordon Philip *real estate consultant*
Gerrodette, Charles Everett *real estate company executive, consultant*
Hoffman, David Wayne, III *real esate appraiser*
McKinnon, James Buckner *real estate sales executive, writer, researcher*
Sander, Susan Berry *environmental planning engineering corporation executive*
Sasaki, Tsutomu (Tom Sasaki) *real estate company executive, international trading company executive, consultant*
Stevens, Clyde Benjamin, Jr. *property manager, retired naval officer*
Wesley, Virginia Anne *real estate property manager*

Taholah
Cardwell, Michael Richard *land use planner*

WYOMING

Rawlins
Pedersen, Martin Albert *consulting land surveyor*

CANADA

ALBERTA

Calgary
Milavsky, Harold Phillip *real estate executive*

BRITISH COLUMBIA

Vancouver
Goldberg, Michael Arthur *land policy and planning educator*

ADDRESS UNPUBLISHED

Craig, Michael Scott *real estate executive, pharmacologist*
Dickey, Robert Marvin (Rick Dickey) *property manager*
Disick, Renée *real estate broker, real estate securities broker*
Edwards, Clarence Jerome *environmental services administrator*
Foley, Daniel Edmund *real estate development executive*
Holness, Allan DeLano, Jr. *real estate developer*
Holway, James Michael *regional planner, state agency administrator*
Hufschmidt, Maynard Michael *resources planning educator*
Jungbluth, Kirk E. *real estate appraiser, mortgage banking executive*
Karakey, Sherry JoAnne *financial and real estate investment company executive, interior designer*
Kiefer, Robert Harry *real estate broker*
Kohn, Robert Samuel, Jr. *real estate investment consultant*
Kredlo, Thomas Andrew *real estate appraiser*
Latini, Henry Peter *real estate management executive*
Mann, Clarence Charles *real estate company official*
Meyer, Daniel Kramer *real estate executive*
Montague, Sidney James *real estate developer*
Nakahata, Tadaka *retired consulting engineer, land surveyor*
Ownbey, Lenore F. Daly *real estate investment specialist*
Richman, Marvin Jordan *real estate developer, investor, educator*
Steblay, Craig Douglas *real estate executive, entrepreneur*
Stern, John Louis *real estate development and management executive*
Wadsworth, Jacqueline Dorèt *private investor*
Yamagata, Leslie Craig *realty specialist*

GOVERNMENT: AGENCY ADMINISTRATION

UNITED STATES

ALASKA

Anchorage
Lindbeck, Stephen Emanuel *state agency administrator*
Lyou, John Christian *corrections services administrator*
Nolan, James Michael *fire chief*
Salerno, Christopher *air quality specialist*
Spaman, Morgan Patrick *fire and safety specialist*
Udland, Duane S. *protective services official*

Fairbanks
Davis, Charles Lee *fire marshal*
Moody, Brent *protective services official*

Juneau
Burke, Marianne King *state agency administrator, financial executive*
George, Dean Curtis *state insurance agency administrator*
Kirkpatrick, Willis F. *state banking and securities administrator*
Larson, Paul Roman *state agency administrator*

Nome
Korenek, Stephen Duane *state agency official*

ARIZONA

Flagstaff
Madden, Edward P. *protective services official*
Schoner, Steven Ronald *park ranger*

Gilbert
Dees, Fred J. *protective services official*

Glendale
Dobrotka, David A. *protective services official*
Goforth, Nathan Dan *police officer*

Mesa
Jarvie, Lars N. *protective services official*

Peoria
Strope, Michael Lee *protective services official*

Phoenix
Bishop, C. Diane *state agency administrator, educator*
Brunacini, Alan Vincent *fire chief*
Cohen, Charles Robert *state agency administrator*
Garrett, Dennis Andrew *police official*
Nielson, Theo Gilbert *law enforcement official, university official*
Travous, Kenneth E. *state agency administrator*

Scottsdale
Heidingsfield, Michael J. *protective services official*
Hill, Robert Martin *police detective, consultant, lecturer*

Tempe
Pies, Ronald E. *city official*

Tucson
Done, Robert Stacy *criminal investigation specialist, consultant*
Lehner, Gregory Michael *federal agency administrator*

CALIFORNIA

Alta Loma
Rivera, George *private investigator, consultant*

Anaheim
Bowman, Jeffrey R. *protective services official*
Gaston, Randall Wallace *police chief*

Bakersfield
Brummer, Steven E. *police chief*

Benicia
von Studnitz, Gilbert Alfred *state official*

Berkeley
Butler, Daschel E. *protective services official*

Bishop
Dodge, Douglas Stuart *federal agency administrator*

Bonita
Yokley, Richard Clarence *fire department administrator*

Burbank
Chaffee, James Albert *protective services official*
Newsham, David P. *protective services official*

Capo Beach
Ely-Chaitlin, Marc Eric *government official*

Castro Valley
Palmer, James Daniel *inspector*

Corona
Cleghorn, John H. *protective services official*

Coronado
Hutchins, Jeffrey Carlton *protective services official*

Costa Mesa
Snowden, David L. *protective services official*

East Palo Alto
Lima, Samuel Mendonca *probation officer, martial arts instructor*

El Centro
Steensgaard, Anthony Harvey *federal agent*

El Monte
Clayton, Wayne Charles *protective services official, educator*
George, Leslie Earl *protective services official*

Escondido
Stein, Michael P. *protective services official*

Folsom
Renfro, Leonard Earl, II *retired protective services professional*

Fremont
Jackson, Keith Douglas *police captain*
Steckler, Craig Theodore *law enforcement official*

Fresno
Winchester, Ed *protective services official*

Fullerton
McKinley, Patrick *protective services official*

Galt
Keller, Michael Crosley *correctional facilities official*

Garden Grove
Sherrard, Raymond Henry *retired government official*

Glendale
Anthony, James *protective services official*

Hollister
Rodriguez, Carlos *fire chief*

Indio
Hare, Paul DeHaven *public safety director*

Long Beach
Jeffery, James Nels *protective services official*
Luman, Robert M. *protective services official*
Omel, Harold *protective services official*

Los Angeles
Bangs, John Wesley, III *law enforcement administrator*
Fisher, Barry Alan Joel *protective services official*
Grobeson, Mitchell *protective services official*
Morten, Ralph Edward *police officer, bomb technician*
Williams, Willie *protective services official*
Wilson, Bernard John *protective services official*

Malibu
Edmiston, Joseph Tasker *state official*

Modesto
Jefferson, Paul *police chief*

Moraga
Laye, John E(dward) *contingency planning and disaster recovery consulting executive*

Oakland
Ewell, P. Lamont *fire department chief*
Samuels, Joseph, Jr. *police chief*

Ontario
Bernard, Alexander *airport police official*

Palm Springs
Borders, Karen Lynn *police officer*

Pasadena
Schander, Mary Lea *police official*

Placerville
Palmieri, Rodney August *state agency administrator, pharmacist*

Redlands
Enslow, Mel Dennis *fire chief*

Richmond
Lansdowne, William M. *police chief*

Riverside
Fortier, Ken *police chief*

Rocklin
Ha, Chong Wan *state government executive*

Roseville
Simms, Thomas Haskell *police chief*

Sacramento
Archer, Mary Jane *state agency administrator*
Berte, Marjorie Marie *state agency administrator*
Burroughs, James Travis *state agency administrator*
Coleman, Ronny Jack *fire chief*
Drown, Eugene Ardent *federal agency administrator*
Dunaway, Margaret Ann (Maggie Dunaway) *state agency administrator, consultant*
Dunlap, John Daniel, III *state agency administrator*
Gentry, James William *retired state official*
Mayberg, Stephen W. *state agency administrator*
McDowell, Marion *state agency director*
McLennan, Geoffrey Thomas *state agency real estate executive*
Pettite, William Clinton *public affairs consultant*
Strock, James Martin *state agency administrator, lawyer, conservationist*
West, Robert Johnson *state agency administrator*

San Bernardino
Farmer, Wesley Steven *police officer*

San Diego
Sanders, Jerry *protective services official*

San Francisco
Axtell, Keith Elton *federal agency administrator*
Buddress, Loren A.N. *state agency administrator*
Green, Katherine Elizabeth *federal agency administrator*
Lau, Fred H. *protective services official*
Tognetti, Gene *protective services official, consulta*

San Jose
Cobarruviaz, Louis A. *protective services official*

Santa Ana
Walters, Paul *protective services official*

Santa Maria
Roadarmel, Stanley Bruce *federal government offic*

Santa Monica
Brucker, Connie *police officer, consultant*
Madara, Thomas Albert *retired federal agency administrator*
Winchell, Robert Allen *retired government agency administrator, accountant*

Shingle Springs
Guay, Gordon Hay *postal service executive, marketing educator, consultant*

Sonora
Efford, Michael Robert *police administrator, educator*

South San Francisco
Opitz, Bernard Francis, Jr. *postal service administrator*

Stockton
Chavez, Edward *police chief*
Gillis, William Gareth *fire protection official*
Jackson, Jewel *state youth authority executive*

West Covina
Mitchell, Serette Elizabeth *law enforcement official*

Westlake Village
Rogge, Richard Daniel *former government executiv security consultant, investigator*

Willits
McGill, Lamont Edmond *fire and explosion investigator, educator*

Yuba City
Doscher, Richard John *protective services official*
Eden, Edward Frank *probation officer*

COLORADO

Aurora
Barnes, Raymond Edward *fire department official*
Mitterer, Bruce Alan *government agency administrator*
Vincent, Verne Saint *protective services official*

Boulder
Koby, Thomas *protective services official*

Colorado Springs
Kramer, Lorne C. *protective services official*
Linebaugh, David Eugene *fire marshal*
Navarro, Manuel *protective services official*

Denver
Barrett, Tom *state agency administrator*
Berger, John Milton *state agency administrator*
Gonzales, Richard L. *fire department chief*
Jameson, Patricia Marian *government agency administrator*
Logan, James Scott, Sr. *emergency analyst*
Michaud, David L. *protective services official*
Smith, Waldo Gregorius *former government official*
Woerner, Robert Eugene *federal agency administrator, editor*
Woodward, Dean Allen *state agency administrator*

Fort Carson
Trenary, Ralph Hiram, III *federal agency administrator, human resources manager*

Golden
Kirschner, Bruce Herbert *federal official, political science educator*
Olson, Marian Katherine *emergency management executive, consultant, publisher*

Lakewood
Johnston, Charles *protective services official*
Miller, Neil Allen *police agent*
Young, Connie Sue *public affairs specialist*

Littleton
Hayes, Roger Matthew *deputy sheriff*

Vail
McGee, Michael Jay *fire marshal, educator*

HAWAII

Hilo
Carvalho, Wayne G. *protective services official*

Honolulu
Devaney, Donald Everett *law enforcement official*
Eberhart, Erika Lee *government agency official*
Kudo, Emiko Iwashita *former state official*
Nakashima, Mitsugi *state agency administrator*
Roseberry, Edwin Southall *state agency administrator*
Seely, Marilyn Ruth *state agency administrator*

Kaneohe
Ikeda, Moss Marcus Masanobu *retired state education official, lecturer, consultant*

Wailuku
Tagomori, Howard H. *protective services official*

IDAHO

Boise
Alcorn, James M. *state insurance administrator*
Cory, Wallace Newell *state official, civil engineer*
Heitman, Gregory Erwin *state official*
McCambridge, Dennis *marshal*
Paulson, Larry A. *protective services official*
Peterson, Eileen M. *state agency administrator*
Sargeant, Roy *state agency administrator*
Turner, Hal Wesley *state agency administrator*
Wood, Jeannine Kay *state official*

Meridian
Becar, Michael Noel *protective services official*

Spalding
Walker, Franklin Curtis *national park administrator*

MARYLAND

Bethesda
Varmus, Harold Eliot *government health institutes administrator, educator*

MONTANA

Billings
Ballard, Lorren Lee *fire protection official*
Ward, David Charles *police chief*

Helena
Anderson, Dan *state agency administrator*
Rude, Maureen Joy *state agency administrator*

NEVADA

Henderson
Perkins, Richard Dale *police official, state legislator*

Las Vegas
Chevers, Wilda Anita Yarde *probation officer*
Goynes, Byron Anthony *state agency administrator*
Klein, Freda *retired state agency administrator*
Lally, Norma Ross *federal agency administrator, retired*
Martin, Michael Albert *protective services official, poet*

Reno
Weston, Jim *protective services official*

NEW MEXICO

Albuquerque
Cole, Leon Monroe *retired government administrator*
Maestas, Alex Walter *state agency clerk*
Manz, Bruno Julius *retired government agency executive*
Marsh, William David *government operations executive*
Martinez, Stephanie Roberta *state agency administrator*
Williams, Marion Lester *government official*

Las Cruces
True, Virgil *retired government official*

Rio Rancho
Dorn, James Martin *school safety coordinator*

Santa Fe
Callaghan, John W. *state agency administrator*
Garcia, Dennis R. *state agency administrator*
Guambaña, Teodoro I. *government executive*
Hart, Darrel Gene *government agency administrator, consultant*
McHenry, Patricia Rose *state agency administrator*
Mitio, John, III *state agency administrator*
Padilla, Donald Lorenzo *state records manager, consultant*
Saurman, Andrew (Skip Saurman) *state agency executive*
Verant, William J. *state agency administrator*
Wentz, Christopher James *state agency administrator*

OREGON

Medford
Cole, Richard George *public administrator*

Portland
Belille, Ronald *safety and security coordinator*
DeHart, Douglas Alan *state agency executive*
Erickson, Pamela Sue *state agency administrator*
Thorne, Mike *state agency administrator*

Salem
Chandler, Al Bart *state agency administrator*
DeLuca, Peter *state agency administrator, lawyer*
Dunn, Kimberly Ann *state agency administrator, archaeologist*
Kast, Barry *state agency administrator*
Myers, Walter E. *protective services official*
Osborne, Rebecca J. *state agency administrator*

TEXAS

Floresville
Robenson, James Melford *protective services official*

UTAH

Provo
Cooper, Gregory M. *protective services official*

Salt Lake City
Alden, Meredith *state agency administrator*
Flint, Lou Jean *state education official*
Gold, Rick L. *federal government executive*

WASHINGTON

Aberdeen
Caster, Ronald Lynn *fire chief*

Fairchild AFB
Sveen, James E. *state official*

Olympia
Bley, John L. *state agency administrator*
Marsh, Dennis Charles *state agency official*
Robertson, Eric Eugene *state trooper*
Shanks, Bernard D. *state official*

Renton
Barker, Mitchell Frederick *former government public relations official*
Berkley, Robert John *federal agency professional*

Richland
Dunigan, Paul Francis Xavier, Jr. *federal agency administrator*

Seattle
Harding, Jim *state agency executive, energy policy specialist*
Harris, Claude *fire department chief*
Peddy, Julie Ann *federal agent*
Stamper, Norman H. *police chief*
Williams, Clarence *protective services official*

Spokane
Dashiell, G. Ronald *marshal*
Mangan, Terence Joseph *police chief*
Williams, Robert Stone *protective services official*

Tacoma
Hansen, Sharon M. *state agency administrator, policy analyst*

Vancouver
Howsley, Richard Thornton *lawyer, regional government administrator*

Walla Walla
Andring, Ronald Paul *protective services official*

WYOMING

Casper
Reed, James Earl *fire department commander*

Cheyenne
Catchpole, Judy *state agency administrator*
Hittle, George F. *state agency administrator*
Patton, Marilyn Janice *state agency administrator*

Gillette
Oedekoven, Byron Frank *protective services official*

Jackson
Daily, John G. *protective services official*

Laramie
Devine, Michael J. *history center director, history educator*

Rock Springs
Simpson, Linda Anne *retired police detective, municipal official*

CANADA

SASKATCHEWAN

Regina
Gordon, Hugh Sangster, Jr. *fire services administrator*

ADDRESS UNPUBLISHED

Adams, Howard *state agency administrator*
Clark, Thomas Ryan *retired federal agency executive, business and technical consultant*
Gordon, Peter Lowell *immigration administrator*
Hayes, Gladys Lucille Allen *state community care official, poet, writer*
Hedrick, Basil Calvin *state agency administrator, ethnohistorian, educator, museum and multicultural institutions consultant*
Heyman, Ira Michael *federal agency administrator, museum executive, law educator*
Johnson, Rodney Dale *law enforcement officer, photographer*
Kelley, Kevin Patrick *security, safety, risk management administrator*
Kornelly, Irene Louise *state government affairs consultant*
Le, Diana Lynn *county worker*
Nyquist, Maurice Otto *government agency administrator and scientist*
Patino, Isidro Frank *law enforcement educator*
Reistroffer, Jeff Paul *fire management supervisor, electronics technician*
Rieder, Richard Walter *federal government official*
Ritchie, Catherine D. *correctional officer, deputy marshal*
Shanahan, Michael George *police officer*
Silva, Robert Owen *retired protective service official*
Waggener, Theryn Lee *law enforcement professional*

GOVERNMENT: EXECUTIVE ADMINISTRATION

UNITED STATES

ALASKA

Fairbanks
Hayes, James C. *mayor*
Smith, Robert London *commissioner, retired air force officer, political scientist, educator*

Juneau
Botelho, Bruce Manuel *state official, mayor*
Knowles, Tony *governor*
Twomley, Bruce Clarke *commissioner, lawyer*
Ulmer, Frances Ann *state official*
Wanie, Don *state government official*
Whistler, Bradley James *state government official*

Kodiak
Selby, Jerome M. *mayor*

Seward
Murphy, Linda S. *city official*

ARIZONA

Chandler
Tibshraeny, Jay *mayor*

Florence
Griffis, Stanley Douglas *county manager*

Gilbert
Carrico, Donald Jefferson *public transit system manager*

Glendale
Scruggs, Elaine M. *mayor*

Mesa
Brown, Wayne J. *mayor*

Page
Jentzsch, Richard Allen *city manager*

Peoria
Forgia, Ken *mayor*

Phoenix
Arauz, Carlos Gaspar *city official*
Christensen, Bradford William *state official*
Cordova, Alexander M. *city clerk*
Curcio, Christopher Frank *city official*
Eaton, David E. *city administrator*
Griffiths, Marian E. (Mimi Griffiths) *government administrator*
Hull, Jane Dee *state official, former state legislator*
McClennen, Miriam J. *former state official*
Miel, Vicky Ann *municipal government executive*
Miner, John Edward *city manager*
Rimsza, Skip *mayor*
Symington, J. Fife, III *governor*
Vanderheiden, Richard Thomas *government official, lawyer*
Welsh, John Richard *state official*
West, Tony *state official*
Woods, Grant *state attorney general*

Prescott
Daly, Paul Sylvester *mayor, retired academic administrator*

Scottsdale
Campana, Sam Kathryn *mayor*
Dobronski, Mark William *state government official*
Warnas, Joseph John *municipal official*

Tucson
Crawford, Michael *city council*
Dicochea, Alfred Quijada *municipal executive*
Hutchinson, Edward Paul *city official*
Ibarra, Jose *city council*
Leal, Steve *city council*
Marcus, Janet *city council*
McKasson, Molly Elizabeth *city council*
Miller, ELizabeth Rodriguez *city manager*
Miller, George *mayor*
Scott, Shirley *city council*
Williams, Ben Franklin, Jr. *mayor, lawyer*

CALIFORNIA

Anaheim
Daly, Tom *mayor*
Hill, Harry David *city official, human resources professional*

Atascadero
Cherry, Brady Dean *municipal government official*

Azusa
Alexander, Stephen J. *mayor*

Bakersfield
Franey, Philip David *county treasurer, tax collector*
Plane, Fredrick Alan *county official*
Price, Robert O. *mayor*

Baldwin Park
Vargas, Fidel A. *mayor*

Bell
Jansser, Rolls *mayor*

Benicia
Lee, Richard Carl *government official*

Berkeley
Feinland, Marsha *municipal official*

Hamilton, Randy Haskell *city manager*
McClatchy, Kate *political candidate*

Burbank
Wylie, Karen Elizabeth *local government official*

Cerritos
Hu, Grace *mayor*

Chino
Ulloa, Eunice *mayor*

Chula Vista
Horton, Shirley *mayor*

Clovis
Armstrong, Harry *mayor*

Colton
Gaytan, Karl E. *mayor*

Compton
Bradley, Omar *mayor*

Concord
Rosas, Lou *mayor*

Corona
Stein, Karen *mayor*

Coronado
Hostler, Charles Warren *international affairs consultant*

Costa Mesa
Buffa, Peter *mayor*
West, Cynthya Thomas *municipal agency administrator*

Covina
Sarver, Linda *mayor*

Culver City
Gourley, Steven *mayor*
Wolkowitz, Edward Marvin *mayor*

Cupertino
Bautista, John *mayor, lawyer*

Cypress
Kelly, Christine Elise *city planner*

Daly City
Klatt, Carol *mayor*

Dana Point
Connors, John Michael *retired city official*

Diamond Bar
Huffs, Bob *mayor*

Downey
Lawrence, Joyce L. *mayor*

El Cajon
Pollock, Richard Edwin *former county administrator*

El Monte
Wallach, Patricia *mayor*

Encinitas
Davis, John *mayor*

Escondido
Hollins, Sid *mayor*

Fair Oaks
Nichols, John Roger *county official*

Fairfield
Hammond, Chuck *mayor*

Fall River Mills
Reed, Eva Silver Star *chieftain*

Fontana
Eshleman, David *mayor*

Fremont
Morrison, Gus (Angus Hugh Morrison) *mayor, engineer*

Fresno
Patterson, James *mayor*

Fullerton
Norby, Christopher *mayor*
Sa, Julie *restaurant chain owner, former mayor*

Garden Grove
Broadwater, Bruce A. *mayor*

Hawthorne
Guidi, Larry Michael *mayor*

Hayward
Cooper, Roberta *mayor*

Hesperia
James, Rosemarie *mayor*

Huntington Beach
Bauer, Ralph H. *mayor*

Huntington Park
Jackson, Tom *mayor*

Indio
Birbeck, Stephen Anthony *city official*

Inglewood
Vincent, Edward *mayor*

Irvine
Vander Dussen, Sheri Tulley *city official*
Ward, Michael *mayor*

Livermore
Brown, Cathie *city official*

Lodi
Pennino, Phil *mayor*
Sieglack, Jack Alan *mayor*
Warner, David P. *council member*

Long Beach
Levi, Herbert A. *deputy city manager, consultant*

Los Angeles
Flores, Fernando E. *diplomat, publisher*
Kawasaki, Lillian Yuriko *city general manager environmental affairs*
Lake, Molly Anne *state official*
Lynch, Timothy Bruce *city adminstrator*
Reagan, Ronald Wilson *former President of United States*
Riordan, Richard J. *mayor*

Lynwood
Richards, Paul H., II *mayor*

Merced
Bernasconi, Richard *mayor*

Mill Valley
Davis, Linda Jacobs *municipal official*

Mission Viejo
Wilson, Eleanor McElroy *county official*

Modesto
Lang, Richard Arthur *mayor, educator*

Monterey
Wright, Mary R. *state park superintendent*

Monterey Park
Smith, Betty Denny *county official, administrator, fashion executive*

Mountain View
Kleitman, Joseph *mayor*

Napa
Battisti, Paul Oreste *county supervisor*

Norwalk
Brennan, Judith *mayor*
Drant, Sandra Elizabeth *court reporter, educator*

Oakland
Harris, Elihu Mason *mayor*
Jackson, Rogernald Douglas *county tax collector*
Jennings, Judith Madrone *city official*

Oceanside
Lyon, Richard *mayor, retired naval officer*

Ontario
Skropos, Gus James *mayor*

Orange
Coontz, Joanne *mayor*

Oxnard
Lopez, Manuel M. *mayor*

Palm Springs
Kleindienst, William *mayor*
Parrish, Jeanne Elaine *former mayor, city councilwoman, former health services administrator, nurse*

Palmdale
Ledford, James C., Jr. *mayor*

Palo Alto
Fleming, June Helena *city manager*
Huber, Joseph H. *mayor*

Pasadena
Hawkey, Philip A. *city manager*
Paparian, William M. *mayor*

Paso Robles
Surber, Russell Jay *retired foreign service officer*

Pico Rivera
Chavez, John *mayor*

Pleasanton
Tarver, Ben *mayor*

Pomona
Cortez, Eddie *mayor*

Rancho Cucamonga
Alexander, William *mayor*

Rancho Mirage
Ford, Gerald Rudolph, Jr. *former President of United States*

Redding
McGeorge, David *mayor*

Redlands
Hanson, Gerald Warner *retired county official*
Larson, Swen *mayor*

Redondo Beach
Parton, Brad *mayor*

Redwood City
Franklin, Robert Charles *probation officer*
Hartnett, Jim *mayor*

Rialto
Longville, John *mayor*

Richmond
Corbin, Rosemary Mac Gowan *mayor*

Riverside
Downs, Keith David *county official*
Loveridge, Ronald O. *mayor*

Rosemead
Clark, Margaret *mayor*

Sacramento
Black, Richard *government adminstrator*
Brooks, John Scott *county official*
Cozad, Lyman Howard *city manager*
Davis, Gray *lieutenant governor*
Dunnett, Dennis George *state official*
Fong, Matthew Kipling *state official*
Grissom, Lee Alan *state official*
Hovious, Gregory Paul *municipal contract officer, contract consultant*
Lapsley, Robert Charles *state official*
Lungren, Daniel Edward *state attorney general*
Nelson, Alan Curtis *government official, lawyer*
Peck, Ellie Enriquez *retired state administrator*
Pernell, Robert *municipal official*
Quackenbush, Chuck *insurance commissioner*
Serna, Joe, Jr. *mayor*
Thompson, C. Michael *state official*
Tubbs, William Reid, Jr. *public service administrator*
Walston, Roderick Eugene *state government official*
Whiteside, Carol Gordon *state official, former mayor*
Wilson, Pete *governor of California*

Salinas
Mora, David Richard *city manager*
Styles, Alan *mayor*
Wong, Walter Foo *county official*

San Bernardino
Lenz, Philip Joseph *municipal administrator*
Minor, Tom *mayor*
Stark, S. Daniel, Jr. *convention and visitors bureau executive*

San Diego
Bernstein, Sandra Marie *county official*
Bliesner, James Douglas *municipal/county official, consultant*
Golding, Susan *mayor*
Lipke, James Scott *municipal official*
McDade, J. Michael *port commissioner*
Roberts, Ron *county board supervisor*
Van Deventer, Jess *municipal official*

San Francisco
Brown, Willie Lewis, Jr. *mayor, former state legislator, lawyer*
Hewitt, Conrad W. *state superintendant of banks*
Taylor, John Lockhart *city official*

San Gabriel
Paules, Paul Michael *city manager*

San Jose
Hammer, Susan W. *mayor*
McHugh, Peter *mayor*

San Leandro
Corbett, Ellen M. *mayor*

San Luis Obispo
Blakely, David Albert *county supervisor*
Zepeda, Susan Ghozeil *county official*

San Mateo
Yates, Gary *mayor*

San Pedro
Main, Betty Jo *management analyst*

San Rafael
Jindrich, Ervin James *municipal government official*

Sanger
Haddix, Charles E. *legislative and regulatory consultant*

Santa Ana
Pulido, Miguel *mayor*

Santa Barbara
Conklin, Hal (Harold Conklin) *mayor*

Santa Clara
Nadler, Judy *mayor*

Santa Clarita
Boyer, Carl, III *mayor, city official, secondary education educator*

Santa Fe Springs
Wilson, Betty *mayor*

Santa Maria
Maldonado, Abel *mayor*

Santa Monica
de La Vega, Dianne Winifred DeMarinis (Mrs. Jorge de La Vega) *government official*
O'Connor, Pam *mayor*
Rice, Donald Blessing *business executive, former secretary of air force*

Santa Rosa
Duffy, Barbara Jean *county official, librarian, education consultant, publisher*
Wright, Sharon *mayor*

Santee
Dale, Jack E. *mayor*

Saratoga
Peacock, Harry Richard *city manager*

South Gate
Garcia, Jerry *mayor*
Mosby, Dorothea Susan *municipal official*

South San Francisco
Drago, Jack *mayor*

Stanford
Shultz, George Pratt *former government executive, economics educator*

Stockton
Podesto, Gary *mayor*
Simas, Edward Alfred *chairman county board supervisors*

Sunnyvale
Crabill, Linda Jean *municipal government official*
Parker, Robin *mayor*

Thousand Oaks
Fox, Andrew P. *mayor*

Torrance
Geissert, Katy *mayor*
Hardison, Dee *mayor*

Tustin
Potts, James *mayor*

Ukiah
Beltrami, Albert Peter *state commissioner*

Union City
Green, Mark *mayor*
Lewis, Mark Earldon *city manager*

Upland
Nolan, Robert R. *mayor*

Vacaville
Fleming, David A. *mayor*

Vallejo
Exlin, Gloria *mayor*

Ventura
Smith, Bill *city manager*
Tingstrom, Jack *mayor*

Visalia
Vivier, Mary Louise *mayor*

Vista
McClellan, Gloria *mayor*

Walnut Creek
Regalia, Gwen *mayor*

West Covina
Manners, Nancy *retired mayor*

Whittier
Sullens, Michael *mayor*

Woodland
Kaplan, Douglas Allen *county official*

Yorba Linda
Gullixson, John *mayor*

Yuba City
Mitnick, Scott W. *municipal administrator*

COLORADO

Aurora
Tauer, Paul E. *mayor, educator*

Bayfield
Giller, Edward Bonfoy *retired government official, retired air force officer*

Boulder
Callen, Lon Edward *county official*
Trembour, Fred William *foreign service officer, metallurgist*

Colorado Springs
Isaac, Robert Michael *past mayor*

Denver
Brown, Keith Lapham *retired ambassador*
Buckley, Vikki *state official*
Dedio, Patricia Ann *city/county official*
Ehnes, Jack *state insurance commissioner*
Farley, Robert Day *metropolitan planning official*
Folkerson, R. *commissioner*
Hackworth, Theodore James, Jr. *city official*
Howlett, John David *government relations*
Huyghebaert, James E. *state official*
Mauro, Richard Joseph, Jr. *government official*
Minger, Terrell John *public administration institute executive*
Norton, Gale A. *state attorney general*
Owens, Bill *state treasurer*
Romer, Roy R. *governor*
Solin, David Michael *state official*
Webb, Wellington E. *mayor*

Fort Collins
Azari, Ann *mayor*

Grand Junction
Achen, Mark Kennedy *city manager*

Greeley
Jordan, Loyd Edward *county sheriff*
Nelson, LaVern C. *mayor*

Lakewood
Morton, Linda *mayor*

Littleton
Cismaru, Pat Klein *municipal official*

Longmont
Stoecker, Leona *mayor*

Loveland
Chen, Eve Ying Vong *city official*

Pueblo
Kastelic, Fay Barr *city official*
Occhiato, Michael Anthony *city official*

Sterling
Gustafson, Randall Lee *city manager*

Thornton
Carpenter, Margaret Wilson *mayor*

Westminster
Heil, Nancy *mayor*

DISTRICT OF COLUMBIA

Washington
Peña, Federico Fabian *federal official*
Reilly, William Kane *former government official, educator, lawyer, conservationist*

HAWAII

Honolulu
Bronster, Margery S *attorney general*
Cayetano, Benjamin Jerome *governor, former state senator and representative*
Hao, Lawrence Kaholo *state official, clinical hypnotherapist*
Harris, Jeremy *mayor*
Hirono, Mazie Keiko *state official*
Marks, Robert Arthur *lawyer, attorney general*
Pai, Gregory Gi Yong *public utilities official*
Wakatsuki, Lynn Y. *commissioner*

Lihue
Kusaka, Maryanne W. *mayor*

Wailuku
Lingle, Linda Crockett *mayor*

IDAHO

Boise
Batt, Philip E. *governor*
Benham, James H. *state official*
Cenarrusa, Pete T. *secretary of state*
Coles, Brent *mayor*
Edwards, Lydia Justice *state official*
Gee, Gavin M. *state government official*
Otter, Clement Leroy *lieutenant governor*
Peterson, Martin Lynn *public administrator*
Williams, J. D. *state controller*
Wilson, James Craig *human services administrator*

Coeur D Alene
Taggart, Tom *county administrator*

Pocatello
Angstadt, Peter J. *mayor*

Salmon
Sloan, Lanny Gene *municipal official*

MONTANA

Billings
Larsen, Richard Lee *former mayor and city manager, business, municipal and labor relations consultant, arbitrator*

Box Elder
Windy Boy, Alvin John, Sr. *tribal councilman*

Bozeman
Petersen, Gerald Michael *city official*

Fairfield
Graf, Ervin Donald *municipal administrator*

Great Falls
Deming, Robert Jackson *mayor*

Helena
Cooney, Mike *state official*
Hutchinson, Donald Wilson *state commissioner of financial institutions*
Mazurek, Joseph P. *state attorney general, former state legislator*
McCarthy, Colleen *mayor*
O'Keefe, Mark David *state official*
Racicot, Marc F. *governor*
Schwinden, Ted *former governor of Montana*
Taylor, Dennis Merrill *state official*

Superior
Schneider, Brenda Laureen *town official*

NEVADA

Carson City
Berkich, John *city manager*
Del Papa, Frankie Sue *state attorney general*
Heller, Dean *state official*
Krolicki, Brian Keith *state official*
Masayko, Ray *mayor*
Miller, Robert Joseph *governor, lawyer*
Molasky, Alice *state insurance commissioner*
Seale, Robert L. *state treasurer*
Walshaw, L. Scott *commissioner*

Henderson
Groesbeck, Robert A. *mayor*
King, Robert Eugene *economic development consultant*

Las Vegas
Brown, Lawrence Leonard, III *city official*
Hammargren, Lonnie *lieutenant governor*
Jones, Jan Laverty *mayor*
Park, James Edward, Sr. *former city administrator, materials management consultant*
Vandever, Judith Ann *county official*

North Las Vegas
Seastrand, James Kent *mayor*

Reno
Balentine, John L. *county official*
Griffin, Jeff *mayor*
Wagner, Sue Ellen *former state official*

Sparks
Breslow, Bruce *mayor*

NEW MEXICO

Albuquerque
Grossetete, Ginger Lee *retired gerontology administrator, consultant*
Harden, Clinton Dewey, Jr. *restaurant owner, state official*
Haulenbeek, Robert Bogle, Jr. *government official*
Hughes, Herbert Howard *public administrator*

Las Cruces
Shepard, Earl Alden *retired government official*
Smith, Ruben *mayor*

Roswell
Jennings, Thomas E. *mayor*

Santa Fe
Bradley, Walter D. *lieutenant governor, real estate broker*
Dossey, Donna Marie *state official*
Gonzales, Stephanie *state official*
Jaramillo, Debbie *mayor*
Johnson, Gary Earl *governor*
Montoya, Michael A. *state treasurer, accountant*
Spath, Charles Emmett *state official*
Udall, Thomas *state attorney general*
Valdez, Joseph Vincent, II *state government information management executive*

OREGON

Beaverton
Drake, Rob *mayor*

Dayton
Williams, Kenneth James *retired county official*

Eugene
Bascom, Ruth F. *former mayor*
Torrey, James D. *mayor, communications executive, consultant*

Hillsboro
Kneese, George Vernon *city manager*

Lake Oswego
Campbell, Colin Herald *former mayor*

Medford
Harvey, Ellen Mae *county official*

Portland
Church, Lorene Kemmerer *retired government official*
Katz, Vera *mayor, former college administrator, state legislator*
Moose, Charles A. *state official*
Stein, Beverly *chairperson county board supervisors*

Salem
Hill, Jim *state official*
Keisling, Phillip Andrew *state official*
Kitzhaber, John Albert *governor, physician, former state senator*
Kulongoski, Theodore R. *state supreme court justice*
McMurdo, C(harles) Gregory *state official*
Myers, William Hardy *attorney general*

UTAH

Midvale
Brown, Melvin R. *state legislator*

Ogden
Haun, David Harding *government official*
Parker, Wayne Charles *municipal finance official*
Schow, Terry D. *state official*

Saint George
Sizemore, Kenneth Lee *county official*

Salt Lake City
Alter, Edward T. *state treasurer*
Brockert, John Earl *state official*
Corradini, Deedee *mayor*
Dixon, Katie Loosle *county official*
Foxley, Cecelia Harrison *commissioner*
Graham, Jan *state attorney general*
Johnson, Frank *retired state official, educator*
Leavitt, Michael Okerlund *governor, insurance executive*
Walker, Olene S. *lieutenant governor*

Sandy
Duerksen, Nick Alan *public administrator*

Tooele
Ewing, Dennis D. *county clerk, realtor*

WASHINGTON

Bellevue
Smith, Ron *mayor*

Bellingham
Asmundson, Mark *mayor*

Dayton
McFarland, Jon Weldon *retired county commissioner*

Everett
Vaughn, Kathy *municipal official*

Oak Harbor
Nevins, Keith Patrick *municipal consultant*

Olympia
Godfrey, Patrick Lewis *state government official*
Hagens, William Joseph *state official, public health educator*
Jacobs, Bob *mayor*
Locke, Gary *governor*
Mowat, Greg Thomas *state official*
Munro, Ralph Davies *state government official*
Murphy, Michael Joseph *county official*
Owen, Bradley Scott *lieutenant governor*
Pritchard, Joel *state lieutenant governor*

Pullman
Halvorson, Alfred Rubin *retired mayor, consultant, education educator*

Renton
Lowry, Mike *former governor, former congressman*

Seattle
Chandler, Bridgett Ann *municipal government policy advisor*
Gardner, Booth *governor*
O'Neill, Maureen Anne *city administrator, arts administrator*
Rice, Norman B. *mayor*
Skidmore, Donald Earl, Jr. *government official*
Smith, Le Roi Matthew-Pierre, III *municipal administrator*
Voget, Jane J. *city official, lawyer*

Sequim
Huston, Harriette Irene Otwell (Ree Huston) *retired county official*

Spokane
Geraghty, John Vincent *mayor*
Hasson, Steven J. *chairman board of county commissioners*
Lenzi, Jerry C. *state official*

Sumas
Hemry, Larry Harold *former federal agency official, writer*

Tacoma
Vlasak, Walter Raymond *state official, management development consultant*

WYOMING

Casper
Dixon, Kathleen B. *mayor*

Cheyenne
Geringer, James E. *governor*
Hendrickson, L. Bruce *state banking commissioner*
McBride, John P. *state insurance commissioner*
Ohman, Diana J. *state official, former school system administrator*
Pando, Leo *mayor*
Rubald, Terry Ellen *state official*
Smith, Stanford Sidney *state treasurer*

Gillette
Darrington, John Charles *city administrator*

Rock Springs
Rickabaugh, Michael Paul *city official*

TERRITORIES OF THE UNITED STATES

AMERICAN SAMOA

Pago Pago
Lutali, A. P. *governor of American Samoa*

FEDERATED STATES OF MICRONESIA

Pohnpei
Eu, March Fong *ambassador, former California state official*

CANADA

ALBERTA

Calgary
Duerr, Alfred *mayor*

BRITISH COLUMBIA

Richmond
Halsey-Brandt, Greg *mayor*

Vancouver
Campbell, Gordon Muir *mayor*

SASKATCHEWAN

Regina
Archer, Douglas Robert *mayor, insurance services executive*
Romanow, Roy John *provincial government official, barrister, solicitor*
Wiebe, J. E. N. *province official*

Saskatoon
Blakeney, Allan Emrys *Canadian government official, lawyer*
Dayday, Henry *mayor*
Hewitt, William James *municipal official*

YUKON TERRITORY

Whitehorse
Phelps, Willard *Canadian government official*

ADDRESS UNPUBLISHED

Allen, Edgar Burns *records management professional*
Anderson, Dee *government relations and management consultant*
Bruns, Judson Leroy, III *diplomat*
Coghill, John Bruce *former state official*
Dodd, Deborah Jane *military contracting officer*
Eckles, Paul David *city manager*
Gregoire, Christine O. *state attorney general*
Harcourt, Michael Franklin *retired premier of Province of British Columbia, lawyer, educator*
Hett, Joan Margaret *civic administrator*
McGinnis, Deborah Cheryl *county official*
Monfils-Clark, Maud Ellen *analyst*
Neff, Francine Irving (Mrs. Edward John Neff) *former federal government official*
Posey, James Madison *commissioner*
Rich, David Barry *city official, auditor, accountant, entertainer*
Ritter, Russell Joseph *mayor, college official*
Rudin, Anne Noto *former mayor, nurse*
Schoettler, Gail Sinton *state official*
Tarkowski, Larry Michael *municipal official*
Thomas, Brian Gordon *municipal finance executive*
Whitney, Jane *foreign service officer*
Williams, William James *public administration educator*

GOVERNMENT: LEGISLATIVE ADMINISTRATION

UNITED STATES

ALASKA

Anchorage
Sturgulewski, Arliss *state senator*

Fairbanks
Davies, John Norman *state legislator*

Homer
Phillips, Gail *state legislator*

Juneau
Hensley, William Lynn (Willie Hensley) *state senator, corporate executive*
Kelly, Timothy Donahue *state senator*

Wasilla
Kohring, Vic *state legislator, construction company executive*

ARIZONA

Glendale
Brewer, Janice Kay *state legislator, property and investment firm executive*

Phoenix
Aguirre, Linda G. *state legislator*
Burchfield, Don R. *counselor, youth services administrator*
Daniels, Lori S. *state legislator, insurance agent*
Eberhart, David L. *state legislator*
Hamilton, Arthur Markell *state legislator*
Kennedy, Sandra Denise *state representative*
Killian, Mark *state legislator*
Patterson, Tom C. *state legislator*
Preble, Lou-Ann M. *state legislator*

Tucson
Richardson, Elaine *state legislator*

Waddell
Turner, Warren Austin *state legislator*

Window Rock
Henderson, James, Jr. *senator*

Yuma
McLendon, Robert *state legislator*

CALIFORNIA

Garden Grove
Dornan, Robert Kenneth *former congressman*

Glendale
Moorhead, Carlos J. *former congressman*

Hayward
Sweeney, Michael *state representative*

Lodi
Land, Keith *councilman*
Mann, Stephen J. *councilman*

Los Altos
Thurber, Emily Forrest *political consultant*

Newport Beach
Badham, Robert E. *former congressman*
Cox, Christopher *congressman*

Sacramento
Alpert, Deirdre Whittleton *state legislator*
Brown, Valerie *state legislator*
Detwiler, Peter Murray *legislative consultant, educator*
Hammond, Lauren Rochelle *senate consultant*
Holmes, Robert Eugene *state legislative consultant, journalist*
Jones, William Leon *state legislator, rancher*
Napolitano, Grace F. *state legislator*

San Francisco
Brandon, Michael James *legislative aide*

COLORADO

Denver
Allen, Deborah Colleen *state legislator*
Bishop, Tilman Malcolm *state senator, retired college administrator*
Kopel, Gerald Henry *retired state legislator*
Kurtz, Karl Theodore *government executive*
Meiklejohn, Alvin J., Jr. *state senator, lawyer, accountant*
Morrison, Marcy *state legislator*

Greeley
Brown, Hank *former senator*

DISTRICT OF COLUMBIA

Washington
Abercrombie, Neil *congressman*
Akaka, Daniel Kahikina *senator*
Allard, A. Wayne *senator, veterinarian*
Baucus, Max S. *senator*
Becerra, Xavier *congressman, lawyer*
Bennett, Robert F. *senator*
Berman, Howard Lawrence *congressman*
Bilbray, Brian P. *congressman*
Bingaman, Jeff *senator*
Boxer, Barbara *senator*
Brown, George Edward, Jr. *congressman*
Brown, Marta Macias *legislative staff member, executive assistant*
Bryan, Richard H. *senator*
Burns, Conrad Ray *senator*
Calvert, Ken *congressman*
Campbell, Ben Nighthorse *senator*
Campbell, Thomas J. *congressman, law educator*
Cannon, Christopher B. *congressman*
Chenoweth, Helen *congresswoman*
Condit, Gary A. *congressman*
Craig, Larry Edwin *senator*
Crapo, Michael Dean *congressman, lawyer*
Cubin, Barbara Lynn *congresswoman, former state legislator, public relations consultant*
Cunningham, Randy *congressman*
DeFazio, Peter A. *congressman*
Degette, Diana *congresswoman*
Dellums, Ronald V. *congressman*
Dicks, Norman De Valois *congressman*
Dixon, Julian Carey *congressman*
Domenici, Pete (Vichi Domenici) *senator*
Dooley, Calvin Millard *congressman*
Doolittle, John Taylor *congressman*
Dreier, David Timothy *congressman*
Dunn, Jennifer Blackburn *congresswoman*
Ensign, John E. *congressman*
Enzi, Michael Bradley *senator, accountant*
Eshoo, Anna Georges *congresswoman*
Farr, Sam *congressman*
Fazio, Vic *congressman*
Feinstein, Dianne *senator*
Filner, Bob *congressman*
Furse, Elizabeth *congresswoman, small business owner*
Gibbons, Jim *congressman*
Gorton, Slade *senator*
Hansen, James V. *senator*
Harman, Jane Frank *congresswoman, lawyer*
Hastings, Richard (Doc Hastings) *congressman*
Hayworth, John David, Jr. *congressman, sportscaster, commentator, broadcaster*
Hefley, Joel M. *congressman*
Herger, Wally W. *congressman*
Hill, Rick Allan *congressman*
Hooley, Darlene *congresswoman, county commissioner*
Horn, (John) Stephen *congressman, political science educator*
Inouye, Daniel Ken *senator*
Kempthorne, Dirk Arthur *senator*
Kim, Jay *congressman*
Kolbe, James Thomas *congressman*
Kyl, Jon *senator*
Lantos, Thomas Peter *congressman*
Lewis, Jerry *congressman*
Lofgren, Zoe *congresswoman*
Martinez, Matthew Gilbert *congressman*
Matsui, Robert Takeo *congressman*
McCain, John Sidney, III *senator*
McDermott, James A. *congressman, psychiatrist*
McInnis, Scott Steve *congressman, lawyer*
McKeon, Howard P. (Buck McKeon) *congressman, former mayor*
Merrill, Cook *congressman*
Metcalf, Jack *congressman, retired state senator*
Millender-McDonald, Juanita *congresswoman, former school system administrator*
Miller, George *congressman*
Mink, Patsy Takemoto *congresswoman*
Murkowski, Frank Hughes *senator*
Murray, Patty *senator*
Nethercutt, George Rector, Jr. *congressman, lawyer*
Orton, William H. (Bill Orton) *former congressman, lawyer*
Packard, Ronald *congressman*
Packwood, Bob *retired senator*
Pastor, Ed *congressman*
Pelosi, Nancy *congresswoman*
Pombo, Richard *congressman, rancher, farmer*
Quigley, Kevin *state senator*

Radanovich, George P. *congressman*
Riggs, Frank *congressman*
Rohrabacher, Dana *congressman*
Roybal-Allard, Lucille *congresswoman*
Royce, Edward R. (Ed Royce) *congressman*
Salmon, Matt *congressman*
Sanchez, Loretta *congresswoman*
Schaefer, Dan L. *congressman*
Schaffer, Robert *congressman*
Schiff, Steven Harvey *congressman, lawyer*
Schroeder, Patricia Scott (Mrs. James White Schroeder) *former congresswoman*
Shadegg, John B. *congressman*
Skaggs, David E. *congressman*
Skeen, Joseph Richard *congressman*
Smith, David Adam *congressman*
Smith, Linda A. *congresswoman, former state legislator*
Stark, Fortney Hillman (Pete Stark) *congressman*
Stevens, Theodore Fulton *senator*
Stump, Bob *congressman*
Thomas, Craig *senator*
Thomas, William Marshall *congressman*
Torres, Esteban Edward *congressman, business executive*
Vucanovich, Barbara Farrell *former congresswoman*
Waters, Maxine *congresswoman*
Waxman, Henry Arnold *congressman*
White, Rick *congressman*
Woolsey, Lynn *congresswoman*
Wyden, Ron *senator*
Young, Donald E. *congressman*

HAWAII

Honolulu
Baker, Rosalyn Hester *state legislator*
Fasi, Frank Francis *state senator*
Kobayashi, Ann H. *state legislator*
Tanaka, Joe Sueo *state legislator*

Kaneohe
Beirne, Danielle Ululani *former state legislator*

IDAHO

American Falls
Wheeler, Ralph (Moon) *state senator, pharmacist*

Boise
Ahrens, Pamela *state legislator*
Black, Pete *state legislator, educator*
McLaughlin, Marguerite P. *state senator, logging company executive*
Stone, Ruby Rocker *state legislator*

Coeur D Alene
Reed, Mary Lou *state legislator*

MARYLAND

Chevy Chase
Beilenson, Anthony Charles *former congressman*

MONTANA

Helena
Bartlett, Sue *state legislator*
Estrada, Sharon Kay *state senator*
Hargrove, Don *state senator*
Masolo, Gay Ann *state legislator*
Swanson, Emily *state legislator*

Miles City
Bergman, Ellen Marie *state legislator*

Missoula
Williams, Pat *former congressman*

NEVADA

Carson City
O'Connell, Mary Ann *state senator, business owner*
Tiffany, Sandra L. *state legislator*
Titus, Alice Cestandina (Dina Titus) *state legislator*

Sparks
Washington, Mauriece E. *senator*

Yerington
Dini, Joseph Edward, Jr. *state legislator*

NEW MEXICO

Albuquerque
Hall, Lois Riggs *former state senator, former symphony orchestra administrator*
Riley, Ann J. *state legislator, technology specialist*

Hobbs
Reagan, Gary Don *state legislator, lawyer*

Los Alamos
Wallace, Jeannette Owens *state legislator*

Santa Fe
Nava, Cynthia D. *state legislator*

NEW YORK

New York
Richardson, William Blaine *former congressman*

OREGON

Beaverton
Strobeck, Ken L. *state legislator, healthcare organization executive*

Bend
Cooley, Wes *former congressman*

Cascade Locks
Montgomery, Robert Lemuel *state legislator*

Medford
Smith, Robert F. *congressman*

Portland
Blumenauer, Earl *congressman*
Hatfield, Mark O. *former senator*

Salem
Brown, Kate *state legislator*
Bunn, James Lee *congressman*
Oakley, Carolyn Le *state legislator, small business owner*

Scio
Hayden, Cedric L. *state legislator, dentist*

UTAH

Bountiful
Burningham, Kim Richard *former state legislator*

Corinne
Ferry, Miles Yeoman *state official*

Hooper
Hull, Joseph L. *state senator*

Layton
Barlow, Haven J. *state legislator, realtor*

Moroni
Blackham, Leonard Moyle *state senator*

Orem
Peterson, Craig A. *state senator*

Provo
Tanner, Jordan *state legislator*
Valentine, John Lester *state legislator, lawyer*

Salt Lake City
Buhler, David L. *senator, institute director*
Howe, Bryant Richard *legislative staff member*
Overson, Brent C. *municipal official, former state senator*
Shepherd, Karen *former congresswoman*

Tooele
Mantes, George *state senator*

Tremonton
Kerr, Kleon Harding *former state senator, educator*

West Bountiful
Beattie, Lane *state senator*

VIRGINIA

Alexandria
Kopetski, Mike *former congressman*

Fairfax Station
Baker, William P. (Bill Baker) *former congressman*

WASHINGTON

Fircrest
Winsley, Shirley J. *state legislator, insurance agent*

Gig Harbor
McMahan, Lois Grace *state representative*

Olympia
Ballard, Clyde *state legislator*
Hatfield, Brian Allen *state legislator*
Kohl, Jeanne Elizabeth *state senator, sociologist, educator*
Long, Jeanine Hundley *state legislator*
Neeld, Michael Earl *legislative staff administrator*
Thomas, Brian Chester *state legislator, engineer*
Veloria, Velma Rosete *state legislator*

Puyallup
Tate, Randall J. (Randy Tate) *former congressman*

Ritzville
Schoesler, Mark Gerald *state legislator, farmer*

WYOMING

Gillette
Gilbertz, Larry E. *state legislator, entrepreneur*

CANADA

ALBERTA

Edmonton
Klein, Ralph *premier of Alberta*

ADDRESS UNPUBLISHED

Arnold, Sheila *former state legislator*

Bilbray, James Hubert *former congressman, lawyer, consultant*
Bono, Sonny Salvatore *congressman, singer, composer, former mayor*
Britti, Julie McGregor *communications director*
Cantwell, Maria E. *congresswoman*
Cunningham, George *senator*
De Concini, Dennis *former senator, lawyer*
Gallegly, Elton William *congressman*
Gillham, Grant David *political consultant*
Hansen, James Vear *congressman*
Hatch, Orrin Grant *senator*
Hickey, Winifred E(spy) *former state senator, social worker*
Hunter, Duncan Lee *congressman*
Ikeda, Donna Rika *former state senator*
Pascoe, Patricia Hill *state senator, writer*
Pettis-Roberson, Shirley McCumber *former congresswoman*
Reid, Harry *senator*
Seastrand, Andrea H. *former congresswoman*
Simpson, Alan Kooi *former senator*
Sorensen, Sheila *state senator*
Zimmerman, Harold Samuel *retired state senator, state administrator, newspaper executive*

HEALTHCARE: DENTISTRY

UNITED STATES

ARIZONA

Chandler
Crouthamel, David Wayne *oral and maxillofacial surgeon*

Flagstaff
Ririe, Craig Martin *periodontist*

Phoenix
Fournier, Donald Frederick *dentist*
Wolfley, Vern Alvin *dentist*

Prescott
Lange, Gary David *periodontist*

Tucson
Davis, Richard Calhoun *dentist*

CALIFORNIA

Arcadia
Gamboa, George Charles *oral surgeon, educator*

Arcata
Hise, Mark Allen *dentist*

Burlingame
Donlon, William Christopher *maxillofacial surgeon, educator, author, editor*
Truta, Marianne Patricia *oral and maxillofacial surgeon, educator, author*

Carmel
Kim, Han Pyong *dentist, researcher*

Citrus Heights
Tse, Kelvin Anthony *dentist*

Claremont
Valdez, Arnold *dentist, lawyer*

Concord
Chiappone, Robert Carl *orthodontist*

Downey
Duncker, Michael Charles *dentist*

Eureka
Welling, Gene B. *dentist*

Fresno
Fairchild, Richard Palmer *dental technician*

Highland
Percy, Robert Wayne *dentist*

La Mesa
Johnson, Peter Fink *prosthodontist, educator, consultant*

La Verne
Huigens, Daniel Dean *dentist*

Larkspur
Danielson, Gordon Douglas *dentist*

Long Beach
Domondon, Oscar *dentist*
Gehring, George Joseph, Jr. *dentist*

Los Angeles
Evans, Caswell Alves, Jr. *dentist*

Manteca
Tonn, Elverne Meryl *pediatric dentist, dental benefits consultant*

Modesto
Boyd, J. Michael *dentist*

Newport Beach
DeFreece, Gerald Arlington *retired dentist, orthodontist*

Northridge
Logan, Lee Robert *orthodontist*

Orange
Martin, Michael Lee *orthotist*

San Diego
Barsan, Richard Emil *oral and maxillofacial surgeon*

San Francisco
Greenspan, John S. *dentistry educator, educator and administrator*
Khosla, Ved Mitter *oral and maxillofacial surgeon, educator*
Rouda, Robert E. *dentist*

San Jose
Higgins, James Bradley *dentist*
Tanno, Ronald Louis *dentist*
Yoshizumi, Donald Tetsuro *dentist*

San Mateo
Wasserman, Bruce Arlen *dentist, mail order company executive*

Sunnyvale
Eng, Roger Steven Choi *dentist, educator*

Vacaville
Dedeaux, Paul J. *orthodontist*

Whittier
Lowe, Oariona *dentist*

COLORADO

Boulder
Schaffer, Joel Lance *dentist*

Denver
Patterson, Daniel William *dentist*

Englewood
Simpson, Robert Houser *orthodontist*

U S A F Academy
Linehan, Allan Douglas *prosthodontist*

HAWAII

Honolulu
George, Peter T. *orthodontist*

Pearl City
Sue, Alan Kwai Keong *dentist*

IDAHO

Boise
Pickett, Hal Gene *prosthodontist*

MONTANA

Hardin
MacClean, Walter Lee *dentist*

NEVADA

Reno
Waltz, Marcus Ernest *retired prosthodontist*

OREGON

Portland
Rosenthal, John David *dentist*

Tualatin
Barnett, Baron Gale *prosthodontist*

UTAH

Ogden
Thompson, Elbert Orson *retired dentist, consultant*

WASHINGTON

Bellevue
Carlson, Curtis Eugene *orthodontist, periodontist*

Seattle
Seely, Dona Marlene *orthodontist*

Spokane
Foster, Ruth Mary *dental association administrator*
Kolsrud, Henry Gerald *dentist*

WYOMING

Casper
Keim, Michael Ray *dentist*

Laramie
Devin, Jerry Preston *orthodontist*

HEALTHCARE: HEALTH SERVICES

UNITED STATES

ALASKA

Anchorage
Erickson, Merlyn K. *anesthesia nurse*

Gier, Karan Hancock *counseling psychologist*
Henderson-Dixon, Karen Sue *psychologist*
Jordan, Marianne Wallace *nursing administrator, educator*
Risley, Todd Robert *psychologist, educator*

Fairbanks
Brody, Bonnie *clinical social worker*

Juneau
Johnson, Mark Steven *community health facility administrator*
Renfro, Michael *human services administrator*

Kodiak
Ackley, Marjorie Rose *health educator*

Kotzebue
Harris, Jan C. *health care administrator*

ARIZONA

Bisbee
Behney, Charles Augustus, Jr. *veterinarian*

Bullhead City
Whitney, Stan *marriage and family therapist*

Casa Grande
McGillicuddy, Joan Marie *psychotherapist, consultant*

Chandler
Graham, Anita Louise *correctional and community health nurse*

Cottonwood
Peck, Donald Harvey *chiropractor*

Flagstaff
Maxwell, Mary Susanna *psychology educator*

Fountain Hills
Block, M. Juliann McCarthy *school psychologist*

Glendale
Cassidy, Barry Allen *physician assistant, clinical medical ethicist*
Schmitz, Donna Jean *critical care nurse, nurse administrator*

Hereford
Klein, Perry Andrew *counselor*

Mesa
Beck, Jerome Joseph *health care administrator, biomedical technologist*
Boyd, Leona Potter *retired social worker*
Hoefle, Karen Marie *hospice executive*
Linton, Marigold L. *psychology educator*
Nagle, Robert David *therapist, educator, author*
Schroeter, Vernon Walter *chiropractor*
Warble, Bonnie Cheryl *massage therapist, holistic educator*

Nogales
Honaker, Charles Ray *health facility administrator*

Paradise Valley
McKinley, Joseph Warner *health science facility executive*

Parker
Helminiak, Clare *public health service officer*

Phoenix
Benach, Sharon Ann *physician assistant*
Bertsch, Brenda R. *flight nurse*
Binnie, Nancy Catherine *retired nurse, educator*
Blair, Virginia Frey *public health service officer*
Boone, Birthe Schnohr *nurse practitioner*
Chan, Michael Chiu-Hon *chiropractor*
Chard, Carolyn Dobbs *physical therapist*
Cheifetz, Lorna Gale *psychologist*
Grimes, Mary Anne *nurse*
Hartnell, Agnes E. *dietitian, educator*
Lyon, William James *psychotherapist, sociologist*
Manning-Weber, Claudia Joy *medical radiography administrator, consultant*
McWhorter, Ruth Alice *counselor, marriage and family therapist*
Mitchell, Wayne Lee *health care administrator*
Neman, Edward Louis, III *hospital administrator*
Packman, Vicki Sue *human services assessment analyst*
Richardson, Kenneth T., Jr. *psychotherapist, consultant, educator, author*
Richardson, Mary Lou *psychotherapist*
Roe, William Thomas *psychology educator, researcher*
Schwartz, Arthur Solomon *research psychologist*
Seiler, Steven Lawrence *health facility administrator*
Shah, Bhailal Morarji *pharmacist*
Sieperman, Kathleen Louise *nurse*
Todd, William Michael *counselor, educator*
Van Halderen, Laurel Lynn *dietitian*
Welliver, Charles Harold *hospital administrator*

Pima
Shafer, James Albert *health care administrator*

Prescott
Goodman, Gwendolyn Ann *nursing educator*
Markham, Richard Glover *research executive*

Safford
Carpenter, Jeannine Nuttall *nurse*

Scottsdale
Cohen, Stephen Mitchell *optometrist*
Ellensohn, Karol Kaye *psychotherapist*
Garrett, Abigail *health facility administrator, nutritionist*
Kizziar, Janet Wright *psychologist, author, lecturer*
McKelvey, Tanya Hope *histocompatibility technologist*
Pitcher, Helen Ione *healthcare services administrator, retired*
St. Clair, Barbara Louise *healthcare facility administrator*
Shannon, Bernard Joseph *optometrist, vision care company executive*
Troxell-Gurka, Mary Theresa (Terry Troxell-Gurka) *geriatrics services professional*

Sedona
Catterton, Marianne Rose *occupational therapist*
Rothschild, Helene *marriage/family therapist and author*

Sonoita
Scott, William Coryell *medical executive*

Sun City West
Mc Donald, Barbara Ann *psychotherapist*

Tempe
Case, Patricia Sullivan *mental health counselor, educator*
Gazley, Jef *psychotherapist*
Guinouard, Donald Edgar *psychologist*
Gustavson, Joan Ellen Carlson *psychologist*
Mason, Terence K. *critical care nurse*
Stone, Gregory Orville *cognitive psychology educator*
Uttal, William R(eichenstein) *psychology and engineering educator, research scientist*

Thatcher
Heaton, Debbie Ann *mental health services worker*

Tucson
Allen, John Jeffrey Beck *psychology educator*
Andersen, Luba *electrologist, electropigmentologist*
Avolio, Wendy Freedman *speech and language pathologist*
Beach, Lee Roy *psychologist, educator*
Blue, James Guthrie *veterinarian*
Dobson, Margaret Velma *experimental psychologist, educator*
Harris, Emma Earl *nursing home executive*
Horan, Mary Ann Theresa *nurse*
Kirk, Samuel Alexander *psychologist, educator*
Kmet, Rebecca Eugenia Patterson *pharmacist*
Lauver, Edith Barbour *nonprofit organization administrator*
McCabe, Monica Jane *oncological nurse*
Rumler, Diana Gale *geriatrics nurse*
Sampliner, Linda Hodes *psychologist, consultant*
Schussel, Alan Lewis *rehabilitation counselor*
Shropshire, Donald Gray *hospital executive*
Smith, David Wayne *psychologist, educator*
Whinery, Linda Shaw *psychotherapist, police consultant*
Wilson, Teresa Ann *maternal/newborn nurse*

Whiteriver
Baken, Terry Lee *mental health services professional*
Murphey, Margaret Janice *marriage and family therapist*

Yuma
McCarthy-Tucker, Sherri Nevada *psychology educator, consultant, researcher, writer*

CALIFORNIA

Agoura Hills
Merchant, Roland Samuel, Sr. *hospital administrator, educator*

Alameda
Boyer, Ford Sylvester *relationship consultant*
Yeaw, Marion Esther *retired nurse*

Albany
Mohrdick, Eunice Marie *nurse, consultant, health educator*

Alhambra
Bortell, Linda Lee *clinical psychologist*

Aliso Viejo
Bridges, Kathleen Erickson *communication disorders specialist*

Alta Loma
Guyan, Cheryl Ann *nurse*

Arcadia
Anderson, Holly Geis *women's health facility administrator, commentator, educator*
Razor, Beatrice Ramirez (Betty Razor) *enterostomal therapy nurse, educator, consultant*
Sloane, Robert Malcolm *healthcare consultant*

Atherton
Trimble, Donna Denise *counselor*

Bakersfield
Hamann, Janet M. *educational psychology educator*
McMillan, Leonard David *family life specialist, consultant, lecturer*
Murillo, Velda Jean *social worker, counselor*
Watkins, Judith Ann *nurse administrator*
Wong, Wayne D. *nutritionist*

Belmont
Post, Gerald Steven *veterinarian*
Schreiber, Andrew *psychotherapist*

Berkeley
Baumrind, Diana *research psychologist*
Day, Lucille Lang *health facility administrator, educator, author*
Enoch, Jay Martin *vision scientist, educator*
Harris, Michael Gene *optometrist, educator, lawyer*
Hill, Lorie Elizabeth *psychotherapist*
Lazarus, Richard Stanley *psychology educator*
Little, Lawrence Alan *health facility administrator*
Maslach, Christina *psychology educator*
Morgan, Meredith Walter *optometrist, retired educator*
Poe, Lenora Madison *psychotherapist and author*
Rosenzweig, Mark Richard *psychology educator*
Segal, Steven Paul *social work educator*
Singer, Rosalind Ruth *retired public health educator*
Tutashinda, Abd Karim Kweli (Brian P. Altheimer) *chiropractic physician, educator*

Beverly Hills
Aguilera, Donna Conant *psychologist, researcher*
Dreifuss-Kattan, Esther *psychoanalyst, art therapy educator*
Marcus, Donald Morton *psychoanalyst*
Mindell, Earl Lawrence *nutritionist, author*
Mojas, Kathleen Marie *psychologist*
Phillips, Debora R. *psychotherapist*
Yaryan, Ruby Bell *psychologist*

Bieber
Jones, James David *health care executive*

Brea
Dyer, Alice Mildred *psychotherapist*

Burlingame
Pemberton, Bobette Marie (Harman) *nursing administrator*

Canoga Park
Taylor, Edna Jane *employment program representative*

Capitola
Crawford, George Truett *health facility executive*

Carlsbad
Anshel, Jeffrey Robert *optometrist*
Mahan, Brad Haver *mental health services professional, artist*
Sullivan, Linda Ann *psychologist, researcher*

Carmel
Elmstrom, George P. *optometrist, writer*
Reese, William Albert, III *psychologist*

Carmichael
Edgar, Marilyn Ruth *counselor*

Carpinteria
Lipinski, Barbara Janina *psychotherapist, psychology educator*

Carson
Alexander-King, Pearl Coqueece *nurse*
Palmer, Beverly Blazey *psychologist, educator*

Castro Valley
Bennett, Shoshana Stein *post partum counselor, consultant, lecturer*
Lin, Doris Bishyng *optometrist*

Cathedral City
Flood, Sheila Theresa *physical therapist*

Cedar Ridge
Bruno, Judyth Ann *chiropractor*

Chatsworth
Boswell, Dan Alan *health maintenance organization executive, health care consultant*
Hart, Bonita Ellen *registered dietitian analyst*
Shore, Diana Kay *nutritionist*
Stephenson, Irene Hamlen *biorhythm analyst, consultant, editor, educator*

Chico
Brislain, Judy Ann *psychologist*
Clarke, Michael William *substance abuse professional, psychotherapist*
Silliman, Kathryn *nutrition educator*

Chowchilla
Cook, Beverly Lavonne *medical administrator*
Von Prince, Kilulu Magdalena *occupational therapist, sculptor*

Chula Vista
Kemery, William Elsworth *psychotherapist, hypnotherapist*
Schorr, Martin Mark *forensic psychologist, educator, writer*

Citrus Heights
Barth, Sharon Lynn *nurse*

Claremont
Berger, Dale Edmund *psychologist, educator*
Hartford, Margaret Elizabeth (Betty Hartford) *social work educator, gerontologist, writer*
Kopp, Claire Joan Bernstein *psychologist, educator*
Wicker, Allan Wert *psychology educator*

Colton
Osburn, Melvin L. *psychotherapist, realtor*

Compton
Thompson, Darlene *vocational nurse*

Concord
Clark, Beverly Wyone *nutritionist*

Corona
Mintz, Dena Marlene *optometrist*

Corona Del Mar
Davis, Arthur David *psychology educator, musician*

Costa Mesa
Crinella, Francis Michael *neuropsychologist, science foundation director*
Klein, (Mary) Eleanor *retired clinical social worker*

Culver City
Davidson, Valerie LaVergne *institute administrator*
Edwards, Marie Babare *psychologist*
Smith, Martin Ronald *psychotherapist, consultant*

Cupertino
Lounsberry, Joyce Beverly *occupational health consultant*

Cypress
Friess, Donna Lewis *psychology educator, writer*

Dana Point
Bullick, Karen Faye *dietitian*

Danville
Nothern, Marjorie Carol *nursing administrator*

Davis
Hawkes, Glenn Rogers *psychology educator*
Ilkiw, Janet Elizabeth *veterinary science educator*
McBride, Linda Carroll *psychologist*
Owings, Donald Henry *psychology educator*
Shaver, Phillip Robert *psychologist, educator*

Del Mar
Moeller, Scott Russell *psychologist*

Downey
Duling, Jean M. Hart *clinical social worker*

Dublin
Ingram, Judith Elizabeth *counselor*

El Cajon
Brown, Marilynne Joyce *emergency nurse*
Schenk, Susan Kirkpatrick *geriatric psychiatry nurse, educator, consultant*
Spaegel, Charles (Louis S.J. Spiegel) *psychology educator*

El Cerrito
Conti, Isabella *psychologist, consultant*
Cooper, William Clark *physician*
Schilling, Janet Naomi *nutritionist, consultant*

El Dorado Hills
Lowe, Claudia Marie *childbirth assistant*

Elk Grove
Weagraff, Patrick James *psychologist, educator*

Encino
Bekey, Shirley White *psychotherapist*
Gould, Catherine Anne *clinical psychologist*
House-Hendrick, Karen Sue *nursing consultant*
Shapiro, Sumner Leroy *psychoanalyst*
Vogel, Susan Carol *nursing administrator*

Escondido
Damsbo, Ann Marie *psychologist*

Fairfax
Neuharth, Daniel J., II *psychotherapist*

Fairfield
Datta, Purna Chandra *clinical psychologist, educator*

Fontana
Beckner, Ardis Stern *nutrition specialist, educator*

Foster City
Nugent, Denise Smith *holistic nurse*

Fremont
Allen, Jacquelyn May *school psychologist, consultant*
Loarie, Thomas Merritt *healthcare executive*
Reeves, Carla Marianne *women's health, nurse midwife*
Sahatjian, Manik *nurse, psychologist*

Fresno
Coe, William Charles *psychology educator*
Ezaki-Yamaguchi, Joyce Yayoi *renal dietitian*
Huddleston, Forest Willis *mental healing counselor*
Lippmann, Bruce Allan *rehabilitative services professional*
Pankratz, Robert Lee *psychologist*
Rusch, Patricia Hull *dietitian*
Ryan, Charlotte Muriel *oncology nurse*
Schroeder, Rita Molthen *retired chiropractor*
Simonian, Debra Lyn *dietitian, educator*

Fullerton
Downie, Pamela *psychologist*
Grimley, Cynthia Patrizi *rehabilitation consultant, special education educator*
Kaisch, Kenneth Burton *psychologist, priest*

Glendale
Hughes, Margaret Jane *nurse*

Goleta
Smith, Thomas Harry *counselor*

Granada Hills
Pappas, Maria Eleni *nurse*

Guerneville
Grassa, Rosemarie Lucia *massage therapist*

Hayward
Kahn, Arlene Judy Miller *nurse, educator*

Healdsburg
McGinnis, Michael Patrick *psychotherapist*

Hemet
Gagneja, Gurcharan Lol *health facility administrator*
Hernandez, Lillian A. *health facility administrator*
Lawrence, Paula Denise *physical therapist*
Minnie, Mary Virginia *social worker, educator*

Hermosa Beach
Wickwire, Patricia Joanne Nellor *psychologist, educator*

Huntington Beach
Carey, Shirley Anne *nursing consultant*
Jenkins, Geni Louise Evans *home health nurse*
Kanode, Carolyn Kerrigan *school nurse, pediatric nurse practitioner*
Martin, Wilfred Wesley Finny *psychologist, property owner and manager*
Olsen, Greg Scott *chiropractor*

Inglewood
Miller, Donna Jean *nursing educator*

Irvine
Ryan, Julie Mae *optometrist, educator, researcher*
Shafranske, Edward Paul *psychologist, educator*

Kenwood
Podboy, John Watts *clinical, forensic psychologist*

La Jolla
Anderson, Norman Henry *psychology educator, researcher*
Cain, William Stanley *psychologist, educator*
Castleman, Breaux Ballard *health management company executive*
Coburn, Marjorie Foster *psychologist, educator*
Fontaine, Deborah Ann *geriatrics nurse practitioner*
Mandler, George *psychologist*
Martin, Joy Anne *clinical psychologist, consultant*
Meltzoff, Julian *psychologist*
Pratt, George Janes, Jr. *psychologist, author*
Randolph, Harry Franklin, III *health facility administrator, physician assistant*
Ruggeri, Zaverio Marcello *medical researcher*
Spinweber, Cheryl Lynn *research psychologist*
White, Deedee *human services executive*

La Mesa
Walther, Leslie Rae *nurse administrator*

La Mirada
Chen, Susie *nursing educator*

Lafayette
Cotton, Barbara Lynn *correctional health systems management consultant*
Giragossiantz, Roxana *nursing administrator*

Laguna Beach
Banuelos, Betty Lou *rehabilitation nurse*
Luck, Kenneth Leverett *healthcare executive, author*

Laguna Hills
Nader, Kathleen Olympia *psychotherapist, consultant in childhood trauma*

Laguna Niguel
de Beixedon, S(usan) Yvette *psychologist*
Freeland, Darryl Creighton *psychologist, educator*

Lakewood
Walton, Linda Gail *nursing administrator*

Larkspur
Saxton, Lloyd *psychologist, author*
Selandia, Elizabeth *acupuncturist, Oriental medicine physician*

Lodi
Bernhoft, Franklin Otto *psychotherapist, psychologist*

Loma Linda
Betancourt, Hector Mainhard *psychology scientist, educator*
Bullock, Weldon Kimball *health facility administrator, pathologist, pathology educator*
Smith, Gerald Kenneth *rehabilitation nurse*
Snyder, John Joseph *optometrist*

Lompoc
Redding-Stewart, Deborah Lynn *psychologist*

Long Beach
Brault, G(ayle) Lorain *healthcare executive*
Carlton-Adams, Dana Georgia Marie Anne *psychotherapist*
Ferreri, Michael Victor *optometrist*
Gunderson, Bernice Blower *retired nurse, genealogy researcher*
Hall, Phyllis Charlene *therapist, counselor*
Kingore, Edith Louise *retired geriatrics and rehabilitation nurse*
Kohn, Gerhard *psychologist, educator*
Mullins, Ruth Gladys *pediatrics nurse*
Ratliff, Leigh Ann *pharmacist*

Los Alamitos
Anderson, Mitchell *chiropractor*

Los Angeles
Abramson, Paul Richard *psychologist, educator*
Anastasia, Paula Jean *oncological nurse*
Ash, Lawrence Robert *public health educator, administrator*
Baron, Melvin Farrell *pharmacy educator*
Blitz-Weisz, Sally *speech pathologist*
Bourque, Linda Anne Brookover *public health educator*
Bowman, Gary Martin *social worker*
Brooks, Scott David *health facility administrator*
Brown, Gay West *school psychologist*
Butterworth, Robert Roman *psychologist, researcher, media therapist*
Chen, Peter Wei-Teh *mental health services administrator*
Cohn, Daniel Howard *laboratory director*
Collins, Michael David *environmental health educator, developmental toxicologist*
Donaldson, Mary Kendrick *nurse*
Everette, Mable Louise *nutrition educator*
Frankel, Frederick David *psychologist*
Friedman, Russell Peter *grief recovery educator, restaurant manager*
Gilman, John Joseph *research scientist*
Goldberg, Herb *psychologist, educator*
Gross, Sharon Ruth *forensic psychologist, researcher*
Holt, Susan Lynne *mental health counselor*
Horowitz, Ben *medical center executive*
Horton, Gwendolyn *nursing educator emeritus*
Hummel, Joseph William *hospital administrator*
Ilanit, Tamar *psychologist*
Johns, Karen Louise *nurse, psychotherapist*
Johnson, Leonidas Alexander *optometrist, minister*
Katchur, Marlene Martha *nursing administrator*
Kronenberg, Jacalyn (Jacki Kronenberg) *nurse administrator*
Leckart, Bruce *psychologist*
Lopez-Navarro, Eduardo Luis *family therapist*
McCarthy, William James *research psychologist, consultant, psychology educator*
McRae, Marion Eleanor *critical care nurse*
Meduski, Jerzy Wincenty *nutritionist, biochemist*
Miller, Eric Nathan *neuropsychologist*

Morales, Cynthia Torres *clinical psychologist, consultant*
Neville-Harris, Alice Almeda (Alice Almeda Ahna) *retired critical care nurse*
Parham, Linda Diane *occupational therapist, researcher, educator*
Scanlon, Deralee Rose *dietitian, educator, author*
Serafine, Mary Louise *psychologist, educator, lawyer*
Silberman, Irwin Alan *public health physician*
Sokolov, Jacque Jenning *health care executive, nuclear cardiologist*
Solomon, Rhonda Hope *school and educational psychologist*
Soo Hoo, Wayne Edward *orthopedic trauma clinical nurse specialist*
Stevens, Eleanor Sandra *home health care professional*
Stone, Norman Michael *psychologist*
Strack, Stephen Naylor *psychologist*
Terzian, Shohig Garine Sherry *mental health facility administrator*
Thompson, Judith Kastrup *nursing researcher*
van Dam, Heiman *psychoanalyst*
Ver Steeg, Donna Lorraine Frank *nurse, sociologist, educator*
Watkins, Gloria Thomas *health care worker*
Watson, Sharon Gitin *psychologist, executive*
Weisman, Adam Mark *clinical psychologist*
Williams, Carole Ann *cytotechnologist*

Los Gatos
Asher, James John *psychology educator*
Vieira, Linda Marie *endoscopy technician*

Marina Del Rey
Heisser-Metoyer, Patricia *psychologist, organizational consultant*
Thro, Broydrick (Elaine Thro) *science and psychology educator*

Mariposa
Bryant, Carol Lee *public health educator, psychotherapist, consultant*

Martinez
Wilson, Robert Llewellyn *clinical psychologist, educator*

Marysville
Myers, Elmer *psychiatric social worker*

Menlo Park
Clair, Theodore Nat *educational psychologist*
Pike, Nancy Ann *pediatric cardiothoracic surgery nurse*

Mentone
Molnar, Joseph *retired clinical social worker*

Merced
Valencia-Castillo, Maribel *social worker*

Mission Hills
Stevens, Serita Deborah Mendelson *psychiatric and forensic nurse, writer*

Mission Viejo
Sendrowski, David Peter *optometrist*
Sikand, Geeta *dietitian*

Modesto
Berry, John Charles *psychologist*
Freeman, Leslie Jean *neuropsychologist, researcher*
Lipomi, Michael Joseph *health facility administrator*
Moe, Andrew Irving *veterinarian*

Montecito
Bell, Donald William *experimental psychologist*

Monterey
Caldwell, Joni *psychology educator, small business owner*
Finnberg, Elaine Agnes *psychologist, editor*
Marra, Thomas *psychologist, health facility administrator*

Monterey Park
Chan, Daniel Siu-Kwong *psychologist*

Moreno Valley
Gull, Paula Mae *renal transplant coordinator, nephrology nurse, medical-sugical nurse*

Mount Shasta
Heller, Joseph *health professional*
Mariner, William Martin *chiropractor*

Mountain View
Alameda, Russell Raymond, Jr. *radiologic technologist*
Hayes, Susan Wylie *non-profit medical organization executive*
Heaney, Dorothy Phelps *nurse, nursing administrator*
Kanchier, Carole *psychologist*

Napa
Lee, Margaret Anne *social worker, psychotherapist*
Sedlock, Joy *psychiatric social worker*

Newhall
Bratspis, Ned David *marriage and family therapist*

Newport Beach
Green, Melanie Jane *speech-language pathologist*
Hansen, Mark H. *retired speech pathologist, consultant*
Stephens, Michael Dean *hospital administrator*
Wilcox, Charles Steven *pharmacology research institute director*

North Hollywood
Jaeger, Sharon Ann *chiropractor*

Northridge
Reagan, Janet Thompson *psychologist, educator*

Oakland
Beeson, Montel Eileen *human services administrator, gerontologist*

Caulfield, W. Harry *health care industry executive, physician*
Crawford, Charlotte Joanne *psychologist, psychoanalyst, psychological anthropologist*
Duprat, Jo Ann *pediatric rehabilitation nurse, consultant*
Gaál, Violetta *retired social worker, massage therapist*
Gardner, Robert Alexander *career counselor, career management consultant*
Hodson, Christine Ann *psychologist*
Ko, Kathleen Lim *health administrator*
Lusby, Grace Irene *infection control nurse practitioner*
Nebelkopf, Ethan *psychologist*

Oceanside
Fyler, Patricia Ann *legal nurse consultant, small business owner*
Harbord, Anne Marie *consulting dietetics company executive*
Hertweck, E. Romayne *psychology educator*

Ojai
Noriega, Dorothy Lorraine *nursing educator*

Orange
Brown, Lillian Eriksen *retired nursing administrator, consultant*
Schlose, William Timothy *health care executive*
Yousef, Marjan *gerontologist, psychology educator*

Oroville
Shelton, Joel Edward *clinical psychologist*

Oxnard
Dimitriadis, Andre C. *health care executive*

Palm Springs
Boyajian, Timothy Edward *public health officer, educator, consultant*
Loya, Ranaldo *senior physician assistant*
Williams, Emily Jean *dietician, medical researcher*

Palmdale
Ellsworth, Richard German *psychologist*
Kinzell, La Moyne B. *school health services administrator, educator*

Palo Alto
Bodin, Arthur M. *clinical psychologist*
Cásarez-Levison, Rosa *psychologist*
Ferrell, Mark Stephen *flight nurse*
Gordon, Marc Stewart *pharmacist, scientist*
Hammett, Benjamin Cowles *psychologist*
Kelsey, Edith Jeanine *psychotherapist, consultant*
O'Leary, Stephanie Smith *occupational therapist, educational therapist*
Saldich, Anne Rawley *counseling psychologist*
Silverthorn, Lee James *clinical psychology*
Skeff, Kelley Michael *health facility administrator*
Turgel, Stuart Charles *hospital administrator*
Ward-Shaw, Sheila Theresa *nurse*

Panorama City
Henrickson, Mark *social worker, priest*

Pasadena
Helander, Terrill Webb *educational psychologist*
Horner, Althea Jane *psychologist*
Messenger, Ron J. *health facility administrator*
Sharp, Sharon Lee *gerontology nurse*

Paso Robles
Rocha, Marilyn Eva *clinical psychologist*

Pebble Beach
Ohanian, Edward *psychologist*

Petaluma
Nussinow, Jill Anne *nutritionist*

Pico Rivera
Brotman, Richard Dennis *counselor*

Pleasant Hill
Richard, Robert Carter *psychologist*

Pleasanton
Arterburn, James David *health care executive*
Carter, Raymond (Beau) *healthcare association executive*
Eddleman, Janie Ann *nurse*
Klein, Louis *physical therapist*

Pomona
Garrity, Rodman Fox *psychologist, educator*

Port Hueneme
Starr, Ruby *counselor*

Rancho Mirage
Deiter, Newton Elliott *clinical psychologist*
Doi, Lois *psychiatric social worker*
Ford, Betty Bloomer (Elizabeth Ford) *health facility executive, wife of former President of United States*
Kiser, Roberta Katherine *medical administrator, education educator*
Overby, Monessa Mary *clinical supervisor, counselor*

Rancho Palos Verdes
Keenan, Retha Ellen Vornholt *retired nursing educator*

Redding
Mongold, Michael Ray *psychologist*
Skrocki, Edmund Stanley, II *health fair promoter, executive*

Redlands
Grames, George Miller *human services administrator, physician*

Redwood City
Rothhammer, Craig Robert *social worker, consultant*

Richmond
Terrill, Karen Stapleton *retired medical planning consultant*

Riverside
Burgess, Curt *psychologist, computer scientist, educator*
Chang, Sylvia Tan *health facility administrator, educator*
Ham, Gary Martin *psychologist*
Petrinovich, Lewis F. *psychology educator*

Rocklin
Hardy, William Taylor *psychologist, educator*

Rohnert Park
Criswell, Eleanor Camp *psychologist*

Rosemead
Gibson, Frances *nurse*

Roseville
Wright, Carole Yvonne *chiropractor*

Sacramento
Cerezo, Abraham Johnson *marriage and family counselor*
Chapman, Loring *psychology educator, neuroscientist*
Childress, Dori Elizabeth *nursing consultant*
Dauner, C. Duane *health facility administrator*
Farrell, Francine Annette *psychotherapist, educator, author*
Harris, Wilson *psychiatrist, research scientist*
Kalish, Nancy *psychology educator, writer*
Kelley, Lisa Stone *public guardian, conservator*
Krebs, Nina Boyd *psychologist*
Papathakis, Peggy Callaghan *registered dietitian*
Patnoe, Shelley Elizabeth *psychologist, writer*
Piert, Edwyna Patrice *child care worker*
Rapoza, Glenn Roberts *vocational rehabilitation counselor, teacher*
Roberts, Paul Dale *health services administrator*
Sato-Viacrucis, Kiyo *nurse, inventor, entrepreneur, consultant*
Seid, Melinda Joy *health and safety studies educator*
von Friederichs-Fitzwater, Marlene Marie *health communication educator*

Salinas
Eifler, Carl Frederick *retired psychologist*

San Bernardino
Brown-Stigger, Alberta Mae *nurse*
Godager, Jane Ann *social worker*
Maul, Terry Lee *psychologist, educator*
Tacal, Jose Vega, Jr. *public health official, veterinarian*
Timmreck, Thomas C. *health sciences and health administration educator*
Tinker, Judy Marie Northrop *nutritionist, musician*
Turpin, Joseph Ovila *counselor, educator*

San Bruno
Ebersole, Priscilla Pier *mental health nurse, geriatric nurse*

San Diego
Callahan, LeeAnn Lucille *psychologist*
Colling, Kenneth Frank *hospital administrator*
Conte, Julie Villa *nurse, administrator*
Cooper, James Melvin *healthcare executive, consultant*
Duester, Karen Christensen *nutritionist, food industry executive*
Edwards, Darrel *psychologist*
Heuschele, Werner Paul *veterinary researcher*
Kalla, Kristin Anne *genetic counselor*
Kent, Theodore Charles *psychologist*
Lewis, Shirley Jeane *psychology educator*
McGuigan, Frank Joseph *psychologist, educator*
Melese-d'Hospital, Patrick Yves *veterinarian, ethologist*
Murray, Colette Morgan *healthcare executive, fundraising consultant*
Rickler, Martin *human services agency administrator*
Riegel, Barbara J. *nursing educator, clinical researcher, editor*
Sabatella, Elizabeth Maria *clinical therapist, educator, mental health facility administrator*
Shanahan, Teresa Ann *therapist*
Smith, Raymond Edward *retired health care administrator*
Thomas, Verneda Estella *retired perfusionist*
Thompson, Mari Hildenbrand *medical staff services executive*
Vaughn, Billy Eldridge *psychology educator, publisher*
Walker, Carolyn Louise *nursing researcher, educator*
White, Eric Milton *optometrist*

San Francisco
Auerback, Sandra Jean *social worker*
Backlund, Michael Anders *clinical psychologist, priest*
Calvin, Allen David *psychologist, educator*
Chin, Jennifer Young *public health educator*
Colling, Catharine Mary *nurse, hospital administrator*
Collins, Fuji *mental health professional*
Cordes, Fauno Lancaster *retired nuclear medicine technologist*
De Cecco, John Paul *psychology and human sexuality educator, author*
Fleischmann, Nancy Norton *medical research technician, educator*
Gee, Debbie *ophthalmologic nurse*
Henkin, William Asher *psychotherapist*
Howatt, Sister Helen Clare *human services director, former college library director*
Krippner, Stanley Curtis *psychologist*
Luxenberg, Jay S. *medical facility administrator*
Mannino, J. Davis *psychotherapist*
Norbeck, Jane S. *nursing educator*
Phillips, Kathryn Ann *health services researcher*
Rankin, Jimmie R. *neuroscience nurse*
Rosales, Suzanne Marie *hospital coordinator*
Webel, Charles Peter *human science and psychology educator*
Wu-Chu, Stella Chwenyea *nutritionist, consultant*
Yee, Darlene *gerontological health educator*
Young, Lowell Sung-yi *medical administrator, educator*

San Jose
Cedoline, Anthony John *psychologist*
Connolly, Phyllis Marie *nursing educator, clinical specialist*
Cunnane, Patricia S. *medical facility administrator*
Fisher, Terri Lynn *intensive care nurse*
Jordan, James Douglas, Jr. *chemical dependency consultant*
McEntee, James Patrick, Sr. *human relations executive*
Osborne, Thomas Jefferson *chiropractor*
Siberts, Dawn Anne *dietitian*
Storz, Donna Marie *clinical dietitian*
Supan, Richard Matthew *health facility administrator*

San Luis Obispo
Smith, Joey Spauls *mental health nurse, biofeedback therapist, bodyworker, hypnotist*

San Mateo
Richens, Muriel Whittaker *AIDS therapist, counselor and educator*

San Pablo
Daniels, Lydia M. *health care administrator*

San Rafael
Best-Martini, Elizabeth M. *recreation therapist*
Friesecke, Raymond Francis *health company executive*
Tosti, Donald Thomas *psychologist, consultant*

Santa Ana
Cerullo, Rudy Michael, II *psychology, theology educator, minister*
Daniel, Ramon, Jr. *psychologist, consultant, bilingual educator*
DiLuigi, Ronald Richard *health care agency executive*
Oberstein, Marydale *geriatric specialist*
Rockoff, Sheila G. *nursing and health facility administrator, nursing and health occupations educator*

Santa Barbara
Asche, Elizabeth Hill *retired public health nurse*
Barbakow, Jeffrey *health facility administrator*
Campbell, Charles Curtis *healthcare consultant*
Focht, Michael Harrison *health care industry executive*
Kendler, Howard H(arvard) *psychologist, educator*
Löwen, Petra Elisabeth *social worker*
Narayanamurti, Venkatesh *research administrator*
Painter, Joel H. *psychologist*
Sherman, Alan Robert *psychologist, educator*
Singer, Janice Gail *psychotherapist, consultant*

Santa Cruz
Domhoff, George William *psychology and sociology educator*
Hilyard, David Franklin *optician*

Santa Monica
Gellert, Michael John *psychotherapist*
Lamm, Jule David *optometrist*
Nizze, Judith Anne *physician assistant*
Russell, Marlou *psychologist*
Sandford, Paul Allan *biomedical laboratory director, biochemist*
Veit, Clairice Gene Tipton *measurement psychologist*

Santa Rosa
Cornett, Donna J. *counselor, alcohol moderation administrator*
Lewis, Marion Elizabeth *social worker*
Searight, Mary Dell (Mrs. Paul James Searight) *nursing educator*

Sausalito
Seymour, Richard Burt *health educator*

Seal Beach
Saravo, Anne Cobble *clinical psychologist, mental health consultant*
Stillwell, Kathleen Ann Swanger *healthcare consultant*

Selma
Arnsberger, Bradley Kirk *family nurse practitioner, physician assistant*

Sepulveda
Burton, Paul Floyd *social worker*

Sherman Oaks
Tucker, Annabelle Doris *medical device company executive*

South San Francisco
Becker, Anne Margaret *neonatal nurse*
Westerdahl, John Brian *nutritionist, health educator*

Stanford
Bardas, Sandra Leigh *pharmacist*
Heeger, David J. *psychology educator*
Pelletier, Kenneth R. *behavioral physician, educator, author*

Stockton
Hutchison, Loyal Dwayne *pharmacist*
Maslow, Richard Emanuel *psychology consultant*
Ross, Sandra K. *critical care nurse*

Studio City
Herrman, Marcia Kutz *child development specialist*
Weiner, Sandra Samuel *critical care nurse, nursing consultant*

Suisun City
Maher, Christine Rita *emergency room nurse, sexual assault specialist*

Sunnyvale
Cohen, D. Ashley *clinical neuropsychologist*

Sunset Beach
Austin, James Albert *healthcare executive, obstetrician-gynecologist*

Taft
Brewer, Lia Harper *marriage and family therapist*

Tarzana
Rinsch, Maryann Elizabeth *occupational therapist*

Thousand Oaks
Conant, David Arthur *architectural acoustician, educator, consultant*
Emerson, Alton Calvin *physical therapist*
Schiltz, Karen Loraine *neuopsychologist, educator, consultant*

Tiburon
Harary, Keith *psychologist*

Torrance
Culton, Paul Melvin *retired counselor, educator, interpreter*
Lemkin, Pamela Ayleen *health facility administrator, oncological nurse, consultant*
Medley, Nancy May *nurse*
Prell, Joel James *medical group administrator*
Todd, Frances Eileen *pediatrics nurse*

Trinidad
Westberg, Patricia Ann *community health nurse*

Ukiah
Nugent, Constance Marie Julie *health facility administrator*

Union City
Glueck, Mary A. *psychiatric and mental health nurse, administrator*

Upland
Rice, Sharon Margaret *clinical psychologist*

Vacaville
Dailey, Dawn Elaine *public health service official*
Zaleski, Brian William *chiropractor*

Van Nuys
Marei, Ibrahim *medical technologist*
Rieger, Elaine June *nursing administrator*
Westbrook, G. Jay *hospice nurse, grief counselor*

Vandenberg AFB
Reinhardt, Linda Lou *medical and surgical nurse*

Ventura
Bircher, Andrea Ursula *psychiatric mental health nurse, educator, clinical nurse specialist*

Visalia
Caldwell, Marcia Diane *nurse*
Fortier, Dana Suzanne *psychotherapist*
Wood, David Duane *clinical psychologist, marriage and family counselor*

Walnut
Martin, George *psychologist, educator*

West Covina
Adams, Sarah Virginia *family counselor*
Franden, Blanche M. *nursing educator*

West Hills
Cheney, Anna Marie *medical, surgical nurse*

West Hollywood
Dery, Gabriel *optometrist*
des Sagettes, Christiane Guillermin *pharmacist, biologist*

Whittier
Johnson, Ruth Eileen *dietician, researcher, home economics educator*

Woodland
Butler, Patricia Lacky *mental health nurse, educator, consultant*
Clement, Katherine Robinson *social worker*
Stormont, Clyde Junior *laboratory company executive*

Woodland Hills
Blanchard, William Henry *psychologist*
Holley, Elizabeth Shelby *educational therapist*

Yountville
Jones, Thomas Robert *social worker*

Yucaipa
Marks, Sharon Lea *primary school educator, nurse*

COLORADO

Aurora
Fedak, Barbara Kingry *technical center administrator*
Oster, Cynthia Ann *critical care nurse*
Starr, Nancy Barber *pediatric nurse practitioner*
Vessels, Kevin Daryl *mental health clinician, inventor*
Whittaker, Gary Irwin *health science association administrator*

Boulder
Blechman, Elaine Ann *psychology educator*
Chan, Peter Wing Kwong *pharmacist*
Copeland, Poppy Carlson *psychotherapist*
Davidson, Alice Ware *nurse, educator*
Good, Janet Lois *occupational health nurse*
Harvey, O.J. *retired psychology educator*
Holdsworth, Janet Nott *women's health nurse*
Jacobson, Jacob G. *psychoanalyst*
Kelley, Bruce Dutton *pharmacist*
Rogers, Richard Gregory *sociology educator*
Sutton, Philip D(ietrich) *psychologist*

Brighton
Fair, Rodney Dale *optometrist*

Broomfield
Lybarger, Marjorie Kathryn *nurse*

Vlosky, Mark Alan *psychologist*
Von Star, Brenda Lee *primary care family nurse practitioner*

Buena Vista
Herb, Edmund Michael *optometrist, educator*

Canon City
Hubbell, Robert Newell *psychologist*

Colorado Springs
Baker, Dennis Michael *counselor, retired law enforcement officer*
Cameron, Paul Drummond *research facility administrator*
Cumber, Sherry G. *psychotherapist, research consultant*
Katz, Jeanne Lyn *counselor, educator*
Moorhouse, Mary Frances *rehabilitation nurse*
Olson, Kenneth Paul *rehabilitation counselor*
Plunkett, Michael C. *psychotherapist*
Potterat, John James *public health officer, researcher*
Shockney, Edwin Allen *psychotherapist, healthcare consultant*
Williams, Ruth Lee *clinical social worker*

Cortez
Meredith, Richard Stephen *psycotherapist, educator*
Selzer, Stephen Rashaw *healthcare administrator*

Denver
Barton, Phoebe Lindsey *healthcare educator*
Bawmann, Brad Craig *health facility administrator*
Burnett, Elizabeth (Betsy Burnett) *counselor*
Cada, Ronald Lee *laboratory administrator, consultant*
Carroll, Kim Marie *nurse*
Cohn, David Leslie *health facility executive*
Dirks, Jerald Frederick *psychotherapist*
Gonzalez, Jesus Manuel *hospital program administrator*
Hami, Lisa Suzanne *laboratory supervisor, medical technologist*
Hand, Dale L. *pharmacist*
Jennett, Shirley Shimmick *home care management executive, nurse*
Jordan, Karin Balten-Babkowski *health facility administrator*
Lefly, Dianne Louise *research psychologist*
Mastrini, Jane Reed *social worker, consultant*
McBurney, Linda Lee *health facility administrator*
Miller, Jill Marie *psychoanalyst*
Nicol, Noreen Heer *nursing administrator, dermatology nurse practitioner, educator*
Parker, Catherine Susanne *psychotherapist*
Plummer, Ora Beatrice *nursing educator, trainer*
Rael, Henry Sylvester *retired health administrator, financial and management consultant*
Rizzi, Teresa Marie *bilingual speech and language pathologist*
Sawyer, Joy Roulier *counselor*
Selkin, James *psychologist*
Shepard, Thomas Akers *physician assistant*
Valdez, Jesse Najera *psychologist*
Watson, Mary Ann *psychologist, educator*
Wilkinson, Joan Kristine *nurse, pediatric clinical specialist*
Witt, Catherine Lewis *neonatal nurse practitioner, writer*

Englewood
Higgins, Ellen M. *physician assistant*

Evergreen
Dawrant, Stacey Beth *dietitian*
Jones, Ann Akridge *construction company executive*

Fort Carson
Boylan, Michelle Marie Obie *medical surgical nurse*

Fort Collins
Hu, Edna Gertrude Fenske *pediatrics nurse*
Schatz, Mona Claire Struhsaker *social worker, educator, consultant, researcher*
Smith, Mary Olivia *veterinary medicine educator*
Smith, Nina Maria *mental health nurse, administrator, consultant*

Fort Lupton
Stevenson, James Ralph *school psychologist, author*

Glenwood Springs
Reinisch, Nancy Rae *therapist, consultant*

Golden
Boyd-Verquer, Robyn Gayle *medical technologist, executive*
Wellisch, William Jeremiah *social psychology educator*

Grand Junction
Graves, Thomas Dayle *psychology educator*
Miller, Jessica Lynn *psychologist, educator, researcher*

Greeley
Baldo, Tracy Dee Bostwick *counselor, educator*
Engle, Cindy *medical transcriptionist*
Falcon, Patricia *nursing educator*
Gritts, Gerald Lee *home health nurse, AIDS care nurse, AIDS educator*
Hart, Milford E. *psychotherapist, counselor*
Hyslop, Rosann Ross *psychotherapist, educator*
Linde, Lucille Mae (Jacobson) *motor-perceptual specialist*
Rhodes, Jess Lynn *counselor*

Greenwood Village
Schulz, Justin William *psychologist, management consultant*

Hugo
Kruse, Katharine Ann *women's health nurse*
Robinson, Mary Susan *nurse administrator*

La Junta
Strong, Mayda Nel *psychologist, educator*

Lakewood
Cambio, Irma Darlene *nursing consultant*
Mouskos, Andreas Alexander *psychotherapist*

Lamar
Gamble, Barbara Jean *dietitian and consultant*

Littleton
Hitchens, David William *purchasing and health materials management consultant*

Longmont
Dalke, John David *family therapist*
Hutchinson, Debra Ann *school psychologist*

Louisville
Schmidt, Carol Suzanne *hospital administrator*
Shively, Merrick Lee *pharmaceutical scientist, consultant*

Loveland
Goldsmith, Margaret Mabel *critical care nurse*

Manitou Springs
Trentalange, John Joseph *counselor, educator*

Monument
Ahlgren, Aleda Joan *nursing administrator, career officer*

Parker
Haas, Bradley Dean *pharmacy director, clinical pharmacist, consultant*
Lembeck, James Peter *nutritionist, consultant*

Pueblo
Hawkins, Robert Lee *health facility administrator*
Kulkosky, Paul Joseph *psychology educator*
Parker, Marsha L. *nutrition services director*
VanSell, Sharon Lee *nursing administrator, nursing educator, researcher, obstetrical and psychiatric clinical nurse*
Vega, Jose Guadalupe *neuropsychologist, clinical director*

Thornton
Hendren, Debra Mae *critical care nurse*

Wheat Ridge
LaMendola, Walter Franklin *human services, information technology consultant*
Rogers, Andrea Maria *medical administrator*

Yuma
Hertneky, Randy Lee *optometrist*

GEORGIA

Richmond Hill
McCormack, Dennis K. *clinical psychologist*

HAWAII

Hanalei
Snyder, Francine *psychotherapist, registered nurse, writer*

Hilo
Werner, Marlin Spike *speech pathologist and audiologist*
Westerman, John Harold *health administrator*

Honolulu
Annon, Jack Dorcey Stafford *forensic and criminal psychologist, detective*
Ardolf, Deborah Ann *speech pathologist*
Bitterman, Morton Edward *psychologist, educator*
Coach, Marlene Evonne *clinical social worker*
Corsini, Raymond Joseph *psychologist*
Fischer, Joel *social work educator*
Flannelly, Kevin J. *psychologist, research analyst*
Flannelly, Laura T. *mental health nurse, nursing educator, researcher*
Fullmer, Daniel Warren *psychologist, educator, retired*
Gormley, Francis Xavier, Jr. *social worker*
Kadohiro, Jane Kay *diabetes nurse educator, consultant*
Katz, Alan Roy *public health educator*
Loh, Edith Kwok-Yuen *oncology nurse, health education specialist*
Lum, Jean Loui Jin *nurse educator*
Martin, Jamal *public health scientist, researcher*
Moccia, Mary Kathryn *social worker*
Shotwell, Cherrie Leigh *speech and language pathologist*
Wang, Weiqun *cancer researcher, biochemist*

Kailua
Ditzler, Ann Marie *nutritionist benefit contract analyst*
Lee, James Gyeong-Jin *health facility administrator*

Kaneohe
Lange-Otsuka, Patricia Ann *nursing educator*
Spezzano, Charles Lee *seminar leader, lecturer, trainer, writer*

Lahaina
Vonderheid, Arda Elizabeth *nursing administrator*

Mililani
Kiley, Thomas *rehabilitation counselor*
Kiyota, Heide Pauline *clinical psychologist*

Wailuku
Friedman, George Jay *psychologist*

Waipahu
Kuwabara, Dennis Matsuichi *optometrist*

IDAHO

Boise
Baker, Marshall Manfred *health facility administrator*
Blonshine, Sheena Kay *medical, surgical nurse*

Brown, Christopher Patrick *health care administrator, educator*
Frye, Todd Michael *counselor*
Harper, Anthony *counselor, singer*
Jackson, Dawna Darlene *mental health counselor, educator*
Jones, Kenneth Merle *rehabilitation services professional*
Simpson, C. Dene *clinical neuropsychologist, psychophysiologist*
Thomas, Laura Faler *nutrition educator*
Townsend, Sandra Lynnette *nurse*

Burley
King, Janet Felland *family nurse practitioner*

Driggs
Lusser, Carole Anne *nurse*

Emmett
Satchwell, Chris Albert *dental group executive*

Idaho Falls
Croft, Richard Todd *psychotherapist*

Kimberly
Maschek, Roger Alan *counselor*

Lewiston
Phillips, James Robert *psychologist*

Moscow
Gordon, Sallie Elizabeth *psychologist, educator*

Nampa
Denney, Doris Elaine *pharmacist*
Doner, John Roland *hospital administrator*
Zuckschwerdt, Otto Salvatore *counselor, substance abuse specialist, chaplain*

Payette
Bragg, Darrell Brent *nutritionist, consultant*

Pocatello
Crockett-Maillet, Ginny Lou *obstetrician/gynecologist nurse practitioner*
Heyneman, Nicholas Ernest *psychologist*

Post Falls
Hamman, Steven Roger *vocational rehabilitation specialist*

Twin Falls
Nielson, Thomas Allen *mental health company executive*
Wright, Frances Jane *educational psychologist*

KANSAS

Kansas City
Lemire, David Stephen *school psychologist, educator*

KENTUCKY

Louisville
Sims, Darcie Dittberner *grief management specialist, psychotherapist, clinical hypnotherapist*

MINNESOTA

Minneapolis
Farr, Leonard Alfred *hospital administrator*

MONTANA

Billings
Furukawa, Dean Kelii *psychotherapist*
Martinez, Virginia Marcelina *dietitian*

Bozeman
Christopher, John Chambers *counseling psychology educator*
Gray, Philip Howard *retired psychologist, educator*

Circle
Good-Brown, Sue Ann *nurse, small business owner*

Glendive
Bruno, Peter Jackson *counselor, consultant, pastor*

Havre
DonTigny, Richard Louis *physical therapist*

Helena
Anderson, Daniel David *health care executive*
Venzke, Ray Frank *psychotherapist*

Missoula
Watkins, John Goodrich *psychologist, educator*
Wemple, James Robert *psychotherapist*

Poplar
Gabrielson, Shirley Gail *nurse*

NEVADA

Carson City
Brandenburg, Carlos Henry *clinical psychologist*
Roelke, Ada (Knock-Leveen) *psychotherapist*

East Ely
Alderman, Minnis Amelia *psychologist, educator, small business owner*

Ely
Edelstein, Rose Marie *nurse educator, medical-legal consultant*

Hawthorne
Sortland, Trudith Ann *speech and language therapist, educator*

Henderson
Byleckie, Scott Andrew, Sr. *health facility coordinator*
Justiss, Barbara Harris *hospital foundation executive*

Incline Village
Ullmann, Leonard Paul *psychologist, educator, author, artist*

Las Vegas
Beglinger, Susan Marie *marriage and family therapist, rehabilitation counselor*
Benbow, Richard Addison *psychologist*
Brighton, Joan Kathleen *psychologist*
Close, Jack Dean, Sr. *physical therapist*
Cunningham, Eleanor Elizabeth *nurse*
DiOrio, Robert Joseph *psychotherapist, consultant*
Een, Miriam Blackham *dietitian*
Emerson, Shirley *counseling educator*
Francis, Timothy Duane *chiropractor*
Gilchrist, Ann Roundey *medical/surgical nurse*
Goldstein, Steven Edward *psychologist*
Herron, Gayle Ann *mental health consultant, psychotherapist, health facility administrator*
Israel, Joan *social worker*
Jagodzinski, Ruth Clark *nursing administrator*
Kowalski, Susan Dolores *critical care nurse, educator*
Law, Flora Elizabeth (Libby Law) *retired community health and pediatrics nurse*
Leake, Brenda Gail *enterostomal therapist nurse practitioner*
Michel, Mary Ann Kedzuf *nursing educator*
Pearson, Robert Allen *optometrist*
Roy, Raymond Albert, Jr. *pharmacist*
Salman, Jenan Al-Yazdi *pharmacist, small business owner*
Silva, Ladon Gay *dietitian*
Smith, Mary B. *medical and surgical nurse*
Talbot, Steven Richards *vascular technologist, consultant, writer*
Van Noy, Terry Willard *health care executive*
Ziferstein, Isidore *psychoanalyst, educator, consultant*

Lovelock
Ellis-Ogborn, Francesca Angela *mental health counselor and clinic administrator*

Reno
Cummings, Nicholas Andrew *psychologist*
Martines, Karen Louise *hospital administrator, nurse*
Tearnan, Blake Hoesley *psychologist*

NEW MEXICO

Albuquerque
Adams, Mary Elizabeth *counselor, psychotherapist, writer*
Allman, James Kirk *physician's assistant*
Andrade, Joseph J., III *counselor, educator*
Hadley, Jane Francis *family nurse practitioner*
Harris, Richard Jerome *psychology educator*
Howe, Debra Ann *therapist*
Johnson, William Hugh, Jr. *hospital administrator*
Magnussen, Max Gene *psychologist*
Manzitto, Arthur Sebastian *nursing and hospital administrator*
Moody, Patricia Ann *psychiatric nurse, artist*
Olson, Lenora Mary *health facility administrator, epidemiologist*
Rodriguez, William Joseph *vocational counselor, mental health professional*
Romero, Olivia Dolores *counselor*
Sanderlin, Terry Keith *counselor*
Zimmermann, Laura Kristine *psychology educator*

Anthony
Romer, Ann Elizabeth *school psychologist*

Bernalillo
Gellert-Ross, Julie Charen *psychotherapist*
Koski, Charlene Weber *social worker*

Carlsbad
Moore, Bobbie Fay *geriatrics nurse practitioner, nurse administrator*

Chama
Black, Kay Cherene *clinical nurse specialist*

Clovis
Rehorn, Lois M(arie) *nursing administrator*

Corrales
Adams, James Frederick *psychologist, educational administrator*

Farmington
MacCallum, (Edythe) Lorene *pharmacist*

Gallup
Fuhs, Terry Lynn *emergency room nurse, educator*

Las Cruces
Emerson, Brenda Ann *radiology and emergency nurse*
Kutinac, John George, Jr. *psychologist*
McElyea, Ulysses, Jr. *veterinarian*
Oderkirk, Wendell W. *nursing educator*
Welsh, Mary McAnaw *family mediator, educator*

Los Alamos
Martz, Carol Ann *career and organization development specialist*
Thompson, Lois Jean Heidke Ore *psychologist*

Placitas
Simpson, Gary Lavern *public health medical executive*

Rio Rancho
Hollingsworth, Meredith Beaton *enterostomal therapy clinical nurse specialist*

Roswell
Allen, Janice Faye Clement *nursing administrator*
Johnston, Mary Ellen *nursing educator*
MacKellar, Keith Robert *hospital administrator*

Ruidoso
Ernest, Dorothetta P. *health facility administrator, critical care nurse*

Santa Fe
Davis, Genevieve Anna *clinical counselor, marriage and family therapist*
Gallaher, Frederick Blake *public health specialist*
King, Ro *psychotherapist, educator*
Kudza, Sarah Marie *human services administrator*
Melnick, Alice Jean (AJ Melnick) *counselor*
Perry, Elisabeth Scherf *psychologist*
Phipps, Claude Raymond *research scientist*
Ruybalid, Louis Arthur *social worker, community development consultant*

Taos
Pasternack, Robert Harry *school psychologist*

Truth Or Consequences
Rush, Domenica Marie *health facilities administrator*

OREGON

Albany
Chowning, Orr-Lyda Brown *dietitian*
Cochran, Carol Louise *home care manager, nurse*
Saboe, LaVerne Alden, Jr. *chiropractor, author, educator*

Beaverton
Mersereau, Susan S. *clinical psychologist*

Brookings
Cross, Lynda Lee *health facility administrator, nurse*

Carlton
Yuse-Miller, Mary Adonna *dietitian, holistic nutrition therapist*

Chiloquin
Mead, Terry Eileen *clinic administrator, consultant*

Corvallis
Gillis, John Simon *psychologist, educator*
Hall, Jean Ann *veterinarian, educator*

Dexter
Myhre, Kathleen Randi *nurse*

Eugene
Camp, Delpha Jeanne *counselor*
Dresser, Jack William *research psychologist*
DuShane, Phyllis Miller *nurse*
Lechnyr, Ronald Joseph *psychologist*
Phelps, Kathryn Annette *mental health counseling executive, consultant*
Slovic, Stewart Paul *psychologist*
Smith, Lee R. (Colleen Smith) *family therapist, political breast cancer activist*
Sundberg, Norman Dale *psychology educator*
Watson, Mary Ellen *ophthalmic technologist*

Florence
Corless, Dorothy Alice *nurse educator*

Forest Grove
Gibby-Smith, Barbara *psychologist, nurse*

Hermiston
Brunk, Patrick Charles Roy *mental health professional, counselor*

Klamath Falls
Klepper, Carol Herdman *mental health therapist*

La Grande
Monahan, Rita Short *nursing educator*

Lake Oswego
Silbert, Amy Foxman *clinical art therapist*

Lebanon
Pearson, Dennis Lee *optometrist*

Medford
Linn, Carole Anne *dietitian*
Smith, Douglas G. *optometrist*

Newberg
Kleiner, Kathleen Allen *psychology educator*

Oregon City
Lareau, Virginia Ruth *counselor*

Portland
Baker, Timothy Alan *healthcare administrator, educator, consultant*
Baldwin-Halvorsen, Lisa Rogene *community health and critical care nurse*
Busch, Ann Marie Herbage *medical/surgical clinical nurse specialist*
Campbell, Kristine Koetting *pediatric nurse, administrator*
Edwards, Julie Diane *maternity and staff nurse*
Goldfarb, Timothy Moore *hospital administrator*
Hanks, Susan Budlong *physical therapist*
Hartnett, Kathleen Camblin *counselor*
Heart, Tracy *psychotherapist, counselor, facilitator*
Johnson, Jim Charles *clinical psychologist*
Kafoury, Ann Graham *psychotherapist*
Maynard, Glenn C. *healthcare administrator, counselor*
McDaniel, Rickey David *senior living executive*
McDonald, Robert Wayne *cardiac sonographer*
Meighan, Stuart Spence *hospital consultant, internist, writer*
Miller, Sonja Glaaser *social worker*
Pickett-Trudell, Catherine *family therapist*
Rondorf-Klym, LouAnn M. *clinical investigator, nurse*
Ross, Frances Margaret *medical technologist, artist*

Shaw, Richard Scott *mental health therapist, educator*
Shireman, Joan Foster *social work educator*
Ward, Michael Dean *marriage and family therapist, minister*
Zgourides, George Dean *psychology educator*

Saint Helens
Van Horn, O. Frank *retired counselor, consultant*

Salem
Callahan, Marilyn Joy *social worker*
Crockett, Ronald Michael *chiropractor*
Edge, James Edward *health care administrator*
Fisher, William G.E. *nursing home owner and operator, state senator*
Fore, Ann *counselor, educator, country dance instructor*

Tigard
McKeen, Edwin Clifford *psychologist*

Tualatin
Tyler, Darlene Jasmer *dietitian*

White City
Moore, Charles August, Jr. *psychologist*

Williams
Morrison, Michelle Williams *nursing educator, administrator, author*

PENNSYLVANIA

North Hills
Rollosson, Matthew Paul *neuroscience nurse*

UTAH

Bountiful
MacKay, Dewey Calder *health facility executive, retired physician*
Rowland, Ruth Gailey *retired hospital official*
Sims, Daniel Allen *veterinarian*

Clearfield
Ashmead, Harve DeWayne *nutritionist, executive, educator*

Holladay
Reinkoester, Robert William, Jr. *critical care nurse*

Kaysville
Ashmead, Allez Morrill *speech, hearing, and language pathologist, orofacial myologist, consultant*

Logan
Eldredge, Garth Melvin *rehabilitation counseling educator*
Hendricks, Deloy G. *nutrition educator*

Ogden
Best, Angela Kaye *dietitian*
Palmer, Kim Michaele *mental health counselor, consultant*
Parker, LeAnne *nursing educator, nurse practitioner*
Wimmer, George Albert *chiropractor, consultant*

Orem
Sauter, Gail Louise *speech pathologist*

Provo
Bergin, Allen Eric *clinical psychologist, educator*
Daniels, Philip Bliss *psychology educator*
Hancock, Eugene Merrill *dietitian*
Kelly, Emma Jane *veterinarian*
Parent, Edward Alphonse *psychologist, consultant, publishing company executive*

Salt Lake City
Benjamin, Lorna Smith *psychologist*
Giles, Gerald Lynn *psychology,learning enhancement,computer educator*
Good, Rebecca Mae Wertman *learning and behavior disorder counselor, grief and loss counselor, hospice nurse*
Goodey, Ila Marie *psychologist*
Grabarz, Donald Francis *pharmacist*
Gunnell, Dale Ray *hospital administrator*
Johnson, Lynn Douglas *psychologist*
Jorgensen, Lou Ann Birkbeck *social worker*
Kelen, Joyce Arlene *social worker*
Lee, Glenn Richard *medical administrator, educator*
Lindsay, Elena Margaret *nurse*
Martineau, Holly Low *dietitian*
Morris, Elizabeth Treat *physical therapist*
Perkins, Nancy Ann *nurse*
Plaas, Kristina Maria *neonatal nurse specialist*
Reeves, Bruce *social worker*
Sinclair, Sara Voris *health facility administrator, nurse*
Skidmore, Rex Austin *social work educator*
Wall, David Elliott *substance abuse specialist*
Ward, R(obert) Scott *physical therapist*
Weigel, Richard George *psychologist, educator*
White, Raymond *health facility administrator*
Wynkoop-Green, Debra Renee *health facility administrator*
Zaharia, Eric Stafford *developmental disabilities program administrator*

Sandy
Gomez, Laura Marie *mental health therapist*
Jones, Galen Ray *physician assistant*
Smith, Willard Grant *psychologist*

VIRGINIA

Falls Church
Braun, Stephen Hughes *psychologist*

WASHINGTON

Auburn
Ketchersid, Wayne Lester, Jr. *medical technologist*

Bellevue
Akutagawa, Donald *psychologist, educator*
Gosslee, Mary June *chiropractor*
Knoepfler, Gayle Stewart *sex therapist*
Lipkin, Mary Castleman Davis (Mrs. Arthur Bennett Lipkin) *retired psychiatric social worker*

Bellingham
Johnson, Jennifer Lucky *psychotherapist*
Nugent, Frank Anthony *psychology educator*

Chehalis
Burrows, Robert Paul *optometrist*

Cheney
Gerber, Sanford Edwin *audiologist*

Clarkston
Holt, Vonnie *counselor, educator*
Ramsden, Norma La Vonne Huber *nurse*

Concrete
Mincin, Karl John *nutritionist, educator*

Edmonds
Carle, Harry Lloyd *social worker, career development specialist*
Hillerstrom, Per Roger *psychotherapist*

Everett
O'Connell, Michael Alexander *social worker*
Sandahl, Bonnie Beardsley *pediatric nurse practitioner, clinical nurse specialist, nurse manager*

Everson
McGulpin, Elizabeth Jane *nurse*

Federal Way
Bolaños, Mary Catherine *infection control coordinator*

Friday Harbor
MacGinitie, Walter Harold *psychologist*

Gig Harbor
Larson, Maureen Inez *rehabilitation consultant*
Nash, Clarice Aldine Hayes *family nurse practitioner, critical care nurse*

Issaquah
Cernak, Keith Patrick *health care and financial consultant*

Kent
Slagle, Marjorie Witman *occupational health program manager, educator*

Kingston
Stengele, Brian Joel *mental health nurse*

Kirkland
Look, Janet K. *psychologist*

Lake Forest Park
Calas, Napoleon Evans *medical laboratory administrator*

Lakewood
Monk, Gordon Ray *recreation therapist*

Leavenworth
Bergren, Helen Duffey *retired nurse*
Smith, Carin A. *veterinarian, writer*

Lynnwood
Wennik, Roberta Schwartz *dietitian*

Medical Lake
Taylor, Eldon *psychologist researcher*

Napavine
Morgan-Fadness, Corrina May *staff charge nurse*

Oak Harbor
Miller, Robert Scott *mental health administrator, social worker*

Olympia
Boruchowitz, Stephen Alan *health policy analyst*
Coolen, Phyllis R. *community health nurse*
Inverso, Marlene Joy *optometrist*
Langer, Stephen Marc *clinical psychologist*
Reilly, Robert Joseph *counselor*
Shkurkin, Ekaterina Vladimirovna (Katia Shkurkin) *social worker*

Poulsbo
Wotruba, David Lawrence *marriage and family therapist*

Pullman
Baugh, Bradford Hamilton *occupational and environmental health advisor*
Chermak, Gail Donna *audiologist, speech and hearing sciences educator*

Puyallup
Veatch, John William *Reiki educator, educational administrator*
Walize, Reuben Thompson, III *health research administrator*

Redmond
Sasenick, Joseph Anthony *health care company executive*

Richland
Henry, Michael Fitzroy *psychotherapist*

Seattle
Adams, Julie Karen *clinical psychologist*
Blissitt, Patricia Ann *nurse*
Boomer, Deborah Lynn *counselor, educator*
Carlson, Margaret Eileen (Peggy Carlson) *counselor, hypnotherapist*
Day, Robert Winsor *cancer research administrator*
Dear, Ronald Bruce *social work educator*
DesRoches, Brian *psychotherapist, organizational systems consultant*
Freeman, Ion Chalmers *health provider*
Golston, Joan Carol *psychotherapist*
Horton, John Michael *psychoanalyst*
Kolbeson, Marilyn Hopf *holistic practioner, educator, artist, retired organization and management consultant*
Larson, Eric Hugh *public health scientist*
Lewis, Frances Marcus *nursing educator*
Liang, Louise Linda *medical group executive, pediatrician*
MacDonald, Don *psychotherapist, educator*
Meltzoff, Andrew N. *psychologist, educator*
Portuesi, Donna Rae *psychotherapist, consultant*
Thompson, Arlene Rita *nursing educator*
Voigt, Lynda Fay *cancer researcher, former nurse*

Sequim
Mc Hugh, Margaret Ann Gloe *psychologist*

Shoreline
Treseler, Kathleen Morrison *retired nursing educator*

Spokane
Jaeger-Keenan, Geralyn Marie *medical/surgical and women's health nurse*
Lindenbauer, Leo Kennith *chiropractor*
Paulsen, Richard Wallace *counselor*
Paulsen, Susan Steenbakkers *counselor*
Rice, Michael John *psychiatric mental health nurse*
Robinson, Herbert Henry, III *educator, psychotherapist*
Vaux, Dora Louise *sperm bank official, consultant*
Wegener, Don Edward *pharmacist, retired military officer*
Yates, Linda Gayle *school counselor, consultant*

Tacoma
Ernst, John Allan *clinical neuropsychologist*
Ingram, Artonyon S. *mental health professional, therapist*
Mohler, Georgia Ann *geriatrics nurse practitioner*
Reim, Ruthann *career and personal counselor, corporate trainer*
Schauss, Alexander George *psychologist, researcher*
Smith, Leo Gilbert *hospital administrator*
Zierath, Marilyn Jean *adult medical, surgical and pediatrics nurse*

Vancouver
Archer, Barbara Louise *hospital administrator, nursing consultant*
Gantz, Nancy Rollins *nursing administrator, consultant*
Lollar, Katherine Louise *social worker, therapist*
Nelson, Robert Earl *mental health counselor*
Simontacchi, Carol Nadine *nutritionist, retail store executive*
Simpson, Carolyn Marie *critical care nurse*

Wenatchee
Lehinger, Susan Elizabeth *school psychologist*

Yakima
Catts, Lois May *critical care nurse specialist*
McCown, Linda Jean *medical technology educator*
Simonson, Susan Kay *hospital administrator*
Tanner, Patricia Ruth *gerontology nurse*

WYOMING

Basin
Kennette, Jennie Laura Fakes *medical and surgical nurse*

Casper
Johnson, Raymond Bruce *medical educator*
Killean, Catherine Louise *psychotherapist, psychiatric nursing specialist*

Cheyenne
Hardway, James Edward *vocational and rehabilitative specialist*
Hirst, Wilma Elizabeth *psychologist*

Green River
Thompson, Josie *nurse*

Hanna
Turner, Lillian Erna *nurse*

Laramie
Berger, Bonnie G. *sport psychologist, educator*
Meuli, Mindy Denise *clinical dietitian*
Pine, Lois Ann Hasenkamp *nurse*
Schroeder, Cheryl Ann *health and educational consultant*

Newcastle
Lane, Patricia Baumgartner *medical office manager*

Pinedale
Margo, Kenneth Craig *counselor*

Powell
Brophy, Dennis Richard *psychology and philosophy educator*

Rock Springs
O'Jack, Helen Margaret *clinical social worker*

Saratoga
Collamer, Sonja Mae Soreide *veterinary facility administrator*

Sheridan
Roth, Steven D. *mental health counselor*

Wilson
Breitenbach, Mary Louise McGraw *psychologist, chemical dependency counselor*

Worland
Munsterteiger, Kay Diane *speech and language pathologist*

CANADA

ALBERTA

Calgary
Lafleur, Karen Jamie *psychologist*
Meyers, Marlene O. *hospital administrator*

Edmonton
Fields, Anthony Lindsay Austin *health facility administrator, oncologist, educator*
Hislop, Mervyn Warren *health advocate administrator, psychologist*

BRITISH COLUMBIA

Vancouver
Splane, Richard Beverley *social work educator*

SASKATCHEWAN

Saskatoon
Belovanoff, Olga *retired health care facility administrator*
Randhawa, Bikkar Singh *psychologist, educator*

SINGAPORE

Henderson Industrial Park
Shima, Larry Mitsuru *health facility administrator*

ZAMBIA

Mumbwa
Hansen, Florence Marie Congiolosi (Mrs. James S. Hansen) *social worker*

ADDRESS UNPUBLISHED

Altstock, Marsha Marie *pediatrics nurse*
Ancoli-Israel, Sonia *psychologist, researcher*
Anderson, Dorothy Fisher *social worker, psychotherapist*
Anderson, Elizabeth Anne *psychologist*
Andress, Cathy *psychologist, educator*
Babao, Donna Marie *community health, psychiatric nurse, educator*
Baker, Ginger Lee *oncological and cardiac nurse*
Baldridge, Thad Clifton Walker *psychotherapist, consultant*
Belles, Donald Arnold *pastoral therapist, mental health counselor*
Belmont, Larry Miller *health association executive*
Berner, Judith *mental health nurse*
Bjorklund, Janet Vinsen *speech pathologist*
Blacher, Joan Helen *psychotherapist, educator*
Boles, Thomas Lee *medical technician*
Boone, Karen *nutritionist, oriental medicine physician*
Bower, Debby Rae *nursing administrator*
Brame, Marillyn A. *hypnotherapist*
Bridge, Sherry *clinical dietitian*
Burton, Kathleen T. *mental health professional*
Callison, Nancy Fowler *nurse administrator*
Calvert, Patricia Viola *dietitian*
Carden, Thom(as) Ray *psychologist*
Carlsen, Mary Baird *clinical psychologist*
Caspers, Corlyn Marie *adult nurse practitioner*
Chiverton, Lorraine Morgan *developmental specialist*
Clecak, Dvera Vivian Bozman *psychotherapist*
Coleman, Arlene Florence *nurse practitioner*
Condry, Robert Stewart *retired hospital administrator*
Connelly, Cynthia Donaldson *nursing scientist*
Conner, Natalie Ann *community health nurse specialist*
Connolly, David Kevin *healthcare executive, consultant, educator*
Cook, Todd McClure *health care executive*
Craig, Carol Mills *marriage, family and child counselor*
Custer, Constance M. *critical care nurse, surgical nurse*
Davis, Alphonse *health facility administrator, special education counselor*
Davis, Pamela Ann *women and childrens health education manager*
Dempsey, Barbara Matthea *medical, surgical and critical care nurse*
De Roest, Jan M. *mental health counselor*
Diedrick, Geraldine Rose *retired nurse*
Dolan, June Ann *health facility administrator*
Dunning, Kenneth Owen *mental health counselor*
Dusserre-Farrell, Michelle *dietitian, gymnastics coach*
Erdman, Terri Sue *pediatric and neonatal nurse, consultant*
Fifer, Linda Sue *speech pathologist, interior designer*
Fletcher, J. Sue *health educator*
Forest, Eva Brown *nurse, supervisor and paralegal*
Fryer, Gladys Constance *retired physician, medical director, educator*
Garvey, Evelyn Jewel *retired mental health nurse*
Gengler, Sue Wong *health educator*
Gerry, Debra Prue *psychotherapist*
Giles, Walter Edmund *alcohol and drug treatment executive*
Govan, Gladys Vernita Mosley *retired critical care and medical/surgical nurse*
Grant, Richard Earl *medical and legal consultant*
Grasso, Monica Marie *home health nurse*
Gray, Rhea Collette *mental health counselor*
Green, Beth Ingber *intuitive practitioner, counselor, musician, composer*
Grimm, Larry Leon *psychologist*
Haining, Jeane *psychologist*
Hanni, Geraldine Marie *therapist*
Hardy, Beth Benita *nurse*
Harris, Anthony Joseph *physical therapist*
Hartzell, Irene Janofsky *psychologist*
Healy, Sonya Ainslie *health facility administrator*
Held, Nancy B. *perinatal nurse, lactation consultant*
Henneman, Stephen Charles *counselor*
Hickcox, Leslie Kay *health educator, consultant, counselor*
Higgins, Ruth Ann *social worker, family therapist*
Hofmann, Paul Bernard *health care consultant*
Hollie, Gladys Miriam *nurse*
Hughes, W. James *optometrist*
Hyatt, Laura *healthcare company executive*
Jacobs, Arthur Dietrich *educator, researcher, health services executive*
Jankovitz, Joseph Edward *psychologist, educator, nurse*
Juarez, Maretta Liya Calimpong *social worker*
Kaiser, Nina Irene *health facility administrator*
Keiser, Megan Marie *neuroscience nurse specialist*
Kellam, Norma Dawn *medical, surgical nurse*
Kepner, Jane Ellen *psychotherapist, educator, minister*
Lagerberg, Randall Erland *mental health specialist*
Lee, Aldora G. *social psychologist*
Leigh, Vincenta M. *health administrator*
Lerit, Delia Tumulak *school nurse*
Lewis, Nancy Patricia *speech and language pathologist*
Lewis, Robert Turner *retired psychologist*
Lewis Mill, Barbara Jean *psychologist*
Lilly-Hersley, Jane Anne Feeley *nursing researcher*
Linden, Molly Kathleen *nursing administrator, educator*
Logan, Glenn Raymond *mental health professional, counselor*
Loughman, William Doster *retired lab director*
Maroon, Mickey *clinical social worker*
Marshall, Donald Thomas *medical technologist*
Mayer, Patricia Lynn Sorci *mental health nurse, educator*
Maynard, E. Rose *retired school health services coordinator*
McClane, Angela Dawn *marriage, family and child counselor*
McComb, Ronald Graeme *rolfer*
McDougall, Jacquelyn Marie Horan *therapist*
McGregor, Darren James *counselor, researcher*
Mehlman, Benjamin *psychologist, educator*
Meyer, Harry Martin, Jr. *retired health science facility administrator*
Meyer, Roberta *mediator, communication consultant*
Mikel, Thomas Kelly, Jr. *laboratory administrator*
Mitchell, Geneva Brooke *retired hypnotherapist*
Moffatt, Hugh McCulloch, Jr. *hospital administrator, physical therapist*
Mosqueira, Charlotte Marianne *dietitian*
Muico-Mercurio, Luisa *critical care nurse*
Nakagawa, Allen Donald *radiologic technologist*
Nordel, Patricia A. Olmstead *medical/surgical, critical care, and obstetrical nurse*
Parker, Joyce Steinfeld *social worker*
Parks, Richard Keith *clinical social worker*
Peters, Shirley Ann *pediatrics nurse*
Petow, Joan Claudia *orthopedic nurse*
Pettit, Ghery DeWitt *retired veterinary medicine educator*
Phillips, Deborah Delores *adolescent therapist*
Pilcher, Ellen Louise *rehabilitation counselor*
Porter, Marie Ann *neonatal nurse, labor and delivery nurse*
Preszler, Sharon Marie *psychiatric home health nurse*
Rathmell, Sandra Lee *women's health nurse*
Reisch, Michael Stewart *social work educator*
Riley, Dorothy Elaine *nursing executive*
Risley-Curtiss, Christina *social worker, educator*
Rodriguez, Margaret Louise *crisis intervention counselor, community debriefer and trainer*
Romanos, Nabil Elias *business development manager*
Ropchan, Rebecca G. *nursing administrator*
Rose, Joan Marie *medical-surgical nurse*
Rose, Mason H., IV *psychoanalyst*
Sanders, Augusta Swann *retired nurse*
Schwartz, Stephen Wayne *critical care, emergency and recovery room nurse*
Shapiro, Yanina *psychology educator*
Sherwin, Noel V. *psychologist, educator*
Sievers, Ann Elisabeth Furiel *clinical nurse specialist in otolaryngology*
Simms, Maria Ester *health services administrator*
Skarda, Richard Joseph *clinical social worker*
Smith, Arthur, Jr. *pharmacist, pharmacy company executive*
Smith, Jeffry Alan *health administrator, physician, consultant*
Solomon, Julius Oscar Lee *pharmacist, hypnotherapist*
Stein, Ellyn Beth *mental health services professional*
Stezoski-Rodriguez, Lorise Ann *critical care nurse, educator*
Stickles, Bonnie Jean *nurse*
Suber, Robin Hall *former medical and surgical nurse*
Swan, Anna *school nurse*
Thomassen, Pauline F. *medical and surgical nurse*
Thomson, Grace Marie *nurse, minister*
Tyler, Gail Madeleine *nurse*
Uhrich, Richard Beckley *hospital executive, physician*
Violet, Woodrow Wilson, Jr. *retired chiropractor*
Voelker, Margaret Irene (Meg Voelker) *gerontology, medical, surgical nurse*
Wallerstein, Judith Saretsky *divorce and family researcher*
Webster, John Kingsley Ohl, II *health administrator, rehabilitation manager*
Weightman, Esther Lynn *emergency trauma nurse*
Wendland, Claire *nursing administrator, geriatrics nurse*
Williams, Jeffrey D. *counselor*
Wolbers, Harry Lawrence *engineering psychologist*
Worrell, Cynthia Celeste *school nurse*
Zielinski, Patricia Anne *women's health nurse*
Zimmerman, Katherine Louise *hypnotherapist*
Zimmerman, Lydia *retired public health nurse*

HEALTHCARE: MEDICINE

UNITED STATES

ALABAMA

Daphne
Wilhite, Wilson Cecil, Jr. *anesthesiology educator*

ALASKA

Anchorage
Chen, Barbara Marie anesthesiologist
Mala, Theodore Anthony physician, consultant
Wald, Robert David psychiatrist
Wood, Thomas Cowan physician

Fairbanks
Hutchison, Richard Louis plastic surgeon
Parry, Richard Gittings plastic and reconstructive surgeon, writer

Juneau
Robinson, David B. psychiatrist

Ketchikan
Johnson, David Ellsworth pediatrician, medical educator

Nome
Swenson, Michael David internist

ARIZONA

Apache Junction
Borik, Anne osteopath

Casa Grande
Hopple, Janet Lynette medical technologist

Cottonwood
Davis, Linda Ann anesthesiologist, physician

Flagstaff
Giesecke, Mark Ernst psychiatrist

Gilbert
Labovitz, Earl A. allergist

Litchfield Park
Nitz, Gary Lee psychiatrist

Mesa
Boren, Kenneth Ray endocrinologist
Bunchman, Herbert Harry, II plastic surgeon
Fiorino, John Wayne podiatrist
Rogers, Philo Alan osteopath
Thompson, Ronald MacKinnon family physician, artist, writer
Verschoor, John, IV physician assistant

Paradise Valley
Campbell, Barbara Ann podiatrist
Hudak, Thomas Michael plastic surgeon
Polson, Donald Allan surgeon

Peoria
Kastrul, Jerome Joe geriatrician

Phoenix
Ansel, Lee surgeon
Bankoff, Peter Rosner anesthesiologist
Bloemker, E. Fredrick physician, ophthalmologist
Borel, James David anesthesiologist
Bull, John Carraway, Jr. plastic surgeon
Burstein, Alvin C. physician
Butler, Byron Clinton obstetrician, gynecologist
Bybee, Paul Ralph psychiatrist
Callison, James R. plastic surgeon
Casano, Salvatore Frank physician
Charlton, John Kipp pediatrician
Clifford, Nathan Joseph cardiologist
Fife, Terry D. neurologist
Friedland, Jack Arthur plastic surgeon
Goldansky, Alvin Ephraim physician
Goldberg, Morris internist
Goldenthal, Nathan David physician
Haddad, Farid Sami educator
Harris, Benjamin Keith rheumatologist
Hendin, Barry Allen physician
Holman, Paul David plastic surgeon
Jacobson, Albert Dale pediatrician, accountant
Kail, Konrad physician
Karpman, Robert Ronald orthopedic surgeon
Koep, Lawrence James surgeon
Kuivinen, Ned Allan pathologist
Laufer, Nathan cardiologist
Lee, Gilbert Brooks retired ophthalmology engineer
Lorenzen, Robert Frederick ophthalmologist
Singer, Jeffrey Alan surgeon
Stern, Stanley psychiatrist
Steward, Lester Howard addictiologist, academic administrator
Strong, David Warren urologist
Swafford, Leslie Eugene physician assistant, consultant
Tafur, Mario Humberto psychiatrist
Tour, Robert Louis ophthalmologist
Vu, Eric Tin neurobiologist, researcher
Weese, William Curtis physician
Wright, Richard Oscar, III pathologist, educator

Prescott
Schwartz, Dale Lewis physician

Scottsdale
Adler, Charles Howard neurologist
Callies, Quinton Carl allergist
Cawley, Leo Patrick pathologist, immunologist
DeHaven, Kenneth Le Moyne retired physician
D'Luzansky, James Joseph urologist, nephrologist
Friederich, Mary Anna gynecology and obstetrics consultant, retired
Friedman, Jay Scott internist
Friedman, Shelly Arnold cosmetic surgeon
Irons, George Benton plastic surgeon
Kjellberg, Betty J. association administrator
Lewis, John Christopher allergist
Offenkrantz, William Charles psychiatrist
Reece, Thomas Howard physician
Starr, Phillip Henry psychiatrist, educator
Wareing, Thomas Hightower cardiothoracic surgeon, educator

Sedona
Hawkins, David Ramon psychiatrist, writer, researcher

Sun City
De La Pava, Daniel plastic surgeon

Sun City West
Anderson, Roger Banks retired surgeon
Calderwood, William Arthur physician
Forbes, Kenneth Albert Faucher urological surgeon

Tempe
Anand, Suresh Chandra physician
Levin, Hal Alan psychiatrist

Tucson
Abrams, Herbert Kerman physician, educator
Ahern, Geoffrey Lawrence behavioral neurologist
Alberts, David Samuel physician, pharmacologist, educator
Ben-Asher, M. David physician
Berg, Robert Allen pediatrician, educator
Binkiewicz, Anna I.S. pediatrician
Dommisse, John Vlok nutritional, metabolic physician, psychiatrist
Epstein, Norman Richard internist
Giesser, Barbara Susan neurologist, educator
Goldfarb, Robert Paul neurological surgeon
Graham, Anna Regina pathologist, educator
Harris, David Thomas immunology educator
Hess, Richard Neal plastic surgeon
Johnson, Kenneth Russell medical educator
Justice, James Walcott physician, research scientist
Kaszniak, Alfred Wayne neuropsychologist
Ketchel, Steven J. internist
Kischer, Clayton Ward embryologist, educator
Kittredge, John Russell physician
Lam, Kit Sang medical educator
Lopez, Ana Maria medical educator, physician
Martin, Loren Winston physician
Misiaszek, John J. psychiatrist
Otto, Charles Wilson anesthesiologist, educator
Palmer, Craig M. anesthesiologist, educator
Pike, Steven occupational health physician
Ricke, P. Scott obstetrician, gynecologist
Salmon, Sydney Elias medical educator, director
Sampliner, Richard Evan physician
Schilling, Jolyon David vascular and general surgeon
Shimm, David Stuart medical educator
Sutherland, John Campbell pathologist, educator
Toff, Howard David psychiatrist
Wheeland, Dale N. physician
Yan, Chong Chao pharmacology, toxicology and nutrition researcher

Yuma
Replogle, Stephen Patrick osteopath, health facility administrator

CALIFORNIA

Agoura Hills
Bleiberg, Leon William surgical podiatrist

Alameda
Sharp, Jean Harriet retired physician and surgeon, antique dealer

Anaheim
Sweet, Thomas Ira physician

Arcadia
Mouchizadeh, Joseph urologist

Atherton
Ritter, Henry, Jr. physician

Auburn
Hanowell, Ernest Goddin physician

Avila Beach
Gritter, Gordon William psychiatrist

Bakersfield
Betancourt, Nellie physician
Grabski, Daniel Alexis psychiatrist
Prunes-Carrillo, Fernando plastic surgeon, educator
Rice, Frances Mae pediatrician

Baldwin Park
Blitz, Ira Allen obstetrician-gynecologist

Barstow
Sutterby, Larry Quentin internist

Bellflower
Ho, Wan Chuen plastic surgeon
Nguyen Trung, B. plastic surgeon

Berkeley
Ames, Richard Galyon epidemiologist
Caetano, Raul psychiatrist, educator
Grossman, Seymour retired gastroenterologist
Kaye, Brian Randall rheumatologist, educator
Oken, Richard Leslie pediatrician
Patterson, Lloyd Clifford psychiatrist
Poor, Clarence Alexander retired physician
Rutherford, George Williams, III preventive medicine physician
Seitz, Walter Stanley cardiovascular research consultant
Sheen, Portia Yunn-ling retired physician

Beverly Hills
Bierman, Howard Richard physician
Cambre, Athleo Louis, Jr. plastic surgeon
Catz, Boris endocrinologist, educator
Dennis, Karen Marie plastic surgeon
Fein, William ophthalmologist
Goodman, Mark Paul physician
Gordon, Martin Neil pulmonologist
Groth, Michael Joseph oculoplastic surgeon
Havivi, Abraham psychiatrist
Klein, Arnold William dermatologist
Kravitz, Hilard L(eonard) physician
Kreitenberg, Arthur orthopedic surgeon, consultant
Labiner, Gerald Wilk physician, medical educator
Marshak, Harry physician, plastic surgeon
Osman, Marvin Phillip psychiatrist and psychoanalyst
Reed, Enid neuropsychologist
Rodman, Francis Robert psychoanalyst, writer
Sanford, Robert Stanley physician, urologist
Seiff, Stephen S. ophthalmologist
Semel, George Herbert plastic surgeon
Sones, Leon Isaac psychiatrist
Yuan, Robin Tsu-Wang plastic surgeon

Balboa Island
Robinson, Hurley surgeon

Borrego Springs
Strong, John Oliver plastic surgeon, educator

Boulder Creek
Piazza, Duane Eugene biomedical researcher

Brawley
Jaquith, George Oakes ophthalmologist

Burlingame
Beattie, George Chapin orthopedic surgeon

Camp Pendleton
Bohman, Harold Ray surgeon
Edwards, Bruce George ophthalmologist, naval officer

Campbell
Schwartz, Steven Michael cardiothoracic surgeon

Capo Beach
Roemer, Edward Pier neurologist

Carmel Valley
Chapman, Robert Galbraith retired hematologist, administrator

Castro Valley
Fernandes, Dionisio A. physician

Century City
Spirt, Mitchell Jeffrey internist, gastroenterologist, medical consultant

Cerritos
Gulasekaram, Balasubramaniam psychiatrist, educator

Chatsworth
Hage, Stephen John radiology administrator, consultant

Chula Vista
Cardona-Loya, Octavio plastic surgeon
Rosenburg, Jeffrey Michael cardiovascular and thoracic surgeon

Claremont
Johnson, Jerome Linné cardiologist

Clovis
Terrell, Howard Bruce psychiatrist

Corona
Shaffer, Audrey Jeanne medical records administrator, educator

Costa Mesa
Albertson Owens, Shirley A. psychology educator, researcher
Coulter, Christopher Harvey physician, healthcare executive
Sharp, Laurence Newton diagnostic company executive

Covina
Schneider, Calvin physician
Takei, Toshihisa otolaryngologist

Daly City
Shaw, Richard Eugene cardiovascular researcher

Dana Point
Kaufman, Edward Redding psychiatrist, educator

Danville
Bunkis, Juris plastic surgeon

Davis
Hance, Anthony James retired pharmacologist, educator
Kass, Philip Howard epidemiology educator
Lazarus, Gerald Sylvan physician, university dean
Schaefer, Saul cardiologist

Deer Park
Hodgkin, John E. pulmonologist

Del Mar
Lesko, Ronald Michael osteopathic physician

Downey
Burger, Emil Ferdinand allergist, medical group executive
Gong, Henry, Jr. physician, researcher
Shapiro, Richard Stanley physician

Duarte
Comings, David Edward physician, medical genetics scientist

East Los Angeles
Leach, Gary Edward urologist, educator

El Cajon
Turk, Robert Louis radiologist

Emeryville
Waller, Kirsten Orlette epidemiologist

Encinitas
Au, Melinda L. osteopathic family practice physician
Hill, David Michael cardiologist
Humber, Philip Richard plastic surgeon
Jaffe, Charles J. allergist
Rummerfield, Philip Sheridan medical physicist

Encino
Colvard, D. Michael ophthalmologist, consultant, educator
Hochman, John Ira psychiatrist

Escondido
Spencer, Mary Josephine pediatrician

Fair Oaks
Hendry, John Easton, III physician, surgeon

Fairfield
Martin, Clyde Verne psychiatrist
Munn, William Charles, II psychiatrist

Folsom
Desai, Asha allergist

Fontana
Mirante, Kathleen Marie cardiologist
Resch, Charlotte Susanna plastic surgeon

Fortuna
Jutila, George Armas surgeon

Fountain Valley
Leport, Peter Cary surgeon

Fremont
Heine, John Parker urologist, medical administrator

Fresno
Allshouse, Michael James pediatric surgeon
Askren, Carl Colwell plastic surgeon
Chandler, Bruce Frederick internist
Connor, Paul Lyle medical librarian
Edmonds, Harvey Lawrence neurologist
Glassheim, Jeffrey Wayne allergist, immunologist, pediatrician
Knapp, Donald Eugene gastroenterologist
Tschang, Tai-Po pathologist
Willis, Charles Dubois neuropsychiatrist, writer
Young, David Vern surgeon

Garden Grove
Boyce, James Daniel ophthalmologist

Gilroy
Grisez, James Louis physician, plastic surgeon

Glendale
Dent, Ernest DuBose, Jr. pathologist
Hall, Josephine Weissman obstetrician/gynecologist

Glendora
Lasko, Allen Howard pharmacist

Graeagle
Dewey, Richard Ryder retired internist, educator

Harbor City
Ackerson, Bradley Kent physician
Kwan, Benjamin Ching Kee ophthalmologist

Hayward
Hung, Sammy T. physician

Hemet
Galletta, Joseph Leo physician

Huntington Beach
Appelbaum, Bruce David physician
Solmer, Richard surgeon

Indian Wells
Carter, Paul Richard physician

Inglewood
Kasamatsu, Robert Ken podiatric physician, surgeon, educator
Sukov, Richard Joel radiologist
Zemel, Norman Paul orthopedic surgeon

Irvine
Connolly, John Earle surgeon, educator
Gwon, Arlene ophthalmologist
Matory, W(illiam) Earle, Jr. plastic surgeon, educator
Myers, Rhonda Jan allergist
Wong, Nathan Donald medicine and epidemiology educator

La Canada Flintridge
Byrne, George Melvin physician

La Crescenta
Riccardi, Vincent Michael pediatrician, researcher, educator, entrepreneur

La Jolla
Backus, Varda Peller psychiatrist
Brems, John Joseph surgeon
Covell, Ruth Marie medical educator, medical school administrator
Diamant, Joel Charles internist
Foster, Chris B. otolaryngologist
Freeman, William Roseman ophthalmologist
Gerber, Michael Lewis surgeon
Goldman, Mitchel Paul dermatologist
Hamburger, Robert N. pediatrics educator, consultant
Hench, Philip Kahler physician
Herwig, Karl Robert physician
Hofmann, Alan Frederick biomedical educator, researcher
Hostetler, Karl Yoder internist, endocrinologist, educator
Jaffer, Adrian Michael physician
Jorgensen, Judith Ann psychiatrist
Keeney, Edmund Ludlow physician
Lewis, Carson McLaughl retired plastic surgeon
Masouredis, Serafeim Panagiotis pathologist, educator
Mathews, Kenneth Pine physician, educator
Miller, Stephen Herschel surgery educator
Peebles, Carol Lynn immunology researcher
Pockros, Paul Joseph gastroenterologist
Rearden, Carole Ann clinical pathologist, educator

Reid, Robert Tilden *medical association administrator, internist*
Rights, Clyde Siewers *obstetrician and gynecologist*
Roberts, Anne Christine *interventional radiologist, educator*
Rosenblatt, Allan D. *psychiatrist*
Rudolph, Ross *surgeon, researcher, educator*
Saltz, Lori Hodgson *plastic surgeon*
Schneider, Gerald L. *plastic surgeon*
Sherman, Linda Arlene *immunologist*
Shively, Harold Hastings, Jr. *cardiologist*
Singer, Robert *plastic surgeon*
Tan, Eng Meng *immunologist, rheumatologist, biomedical scientist*
Teirstein, Paul Shepherd *physician, health facility administrator*
Traynor-Kaplan, Alexis Elaine *biomedical researcher*
Utne, John Richard *retired radiation oncologist*
Walker, Richard Hugh *orthopaedic surgeon*
Weigle, William Oliver *immunologist, educator*
Weinreb, Robert Neal *opthalmologist, educator*
Wiederholt, Wigbert C. *neurologist, educator*

La Mesa
Wohl, Armand Jeffrey *cardiologist*

La Puente
Good, William Zev *physician*

Laguna Hills
Askin, Jerald Mark *podiatrist*
Kirshbaum, Jack D. *pathologist*
Rhyne, Dennis Alfred *orthopedic surgeon*

Laguna Niguel
Strenger, George *surgeon*

Lake Forest
Larsen, Robert Ray *healthcare executive, surgeon*

Lakewood
Tong, Richard Dare *anesthesiologist*

Lancaster
Manning, John Joseph *physician, healthcare administrator*

Larkspur
Denkler, Keith Alan *surgeon*

Loma Linda
Adey, William Ross *physician*
Aloia, Roland Craig *scientist, administrator, educator*
Behrens, Berel Lyn *physician, academic administrator*
Bull, Brian Stanley *pathology educator, medical consultant, business executive*
Coggin, Charlotte Joan *cardiologist, educator*
Condon, Stanley Charles *gastroenterologist*
Houchin, Kenneth Wayne *ophthalmologist, neuro-opthalmologist, educator*
Llaurado, Josep G. *nuclear medicine physician, scientist*
Orr, Robert David *clinical ethicist, educator, physician*
Stilson, Walter Leslie *radiologist, educator*

Long Beach
Adams, H. Richard *physiatrist*
Anderson, Garry Michael *diagnostic radiologist*
Berke, Irving *obstetrician-gynecologist, military officer*
Bolton, Leon Leslie *plastic surgeon*
Burke, Donald Warren *anesthesiologist*
Cohen, Manley *gastroenterologist*
Fagan, Frederic *neurosurgeon*
Gaspar, Max Raymond *surgeon*
Hickman, Donn Michael *plastic surgeon*
Honning, Bengt Eugene *chiropractic physician, consultant, biochemist*
Horowitz, Jed H. *plastic surgeon, reconstructive surgeon*
Kwaan, Jack Hau Ming *retired physician*
Leidl, Peter Janos *internist*
Looney, Gerald Lee *medical educator, administrator*
Macer, George Armen, Jr. *orthopedic hand surgeon*
Mills, Don Harper *pathology and psychiatry educator, lawyer*
Parker, Lawrence Neil *medical educator*
Pineda, Anselmo *neurosurgery educator*
Schoendorf, Judson Raymond *allergist*

Los Alamitos
Wong, Ing Liong *nephrologist*

Los Angeles
Ahn, Samuel Seunghae *vascular surgeon, researcher, consultant*
Alkana, Ronald Lee *neuropsychopharmacologist, psychobiologist*
Amstutz, Harlan Cabot *orthopaedic surgeon*
Anderson, Kathryn Duncan *surgeon*
Archie, Carol Louise *obstetrician and gynecologist, educator*
Aronowitz, Joel Alan *plastic and reconstructive surgeon*
Ashley, Sharon Anita *pediatric anesthesiologist*
Bailey, Julia Nancy *epidemiologist*
Bao, Joseph Yue-Se *orthopaedist, microsurgeon, educator*
Barbers, Richard George *physician, educator*
Barker, Wiley Franklin *surgeon, educator*
Barnes, Peter Francis *physician, researcher, medical educator*
Batzdorf, Ulrich *neurosurgeon, educator*
Beart, Robert W., Jr. *surgeon, educator*
Becker, Donald Paul *surgeon, neurosurgeon*
Belzberg, Howard *critical care physician, educator*
Bernstein, Sol *cardiologist, educator*
Bodey, Bela *immunomorphologist*
Braunstein, Glenn David *physician, educator*
Brickman, Harry Russell *psychiatrist, psychoanalytic institute dean*
Buck, Francis Scott *pathologist, educator*
Burgess, Wes *neuropsychiatrist, psychopharmacologist*
Campese, Vito Michele *nephrologist*
Chandor, Stebbins Bryant *pathologist*
Cherkas, Marshall S. *psychiatrist, psychoanalyst*
Cherry, James Donald *physician*
Chopra, Inder Jit *physician, endocrinologist*
Cicciarelli, James Carl *immunology educator*
Comar, Kanwar Dave *surgeon*
Cook, Ian Ainsworth *psychiatrist, researcher, educator*
Cote, Richard James *pathologist, researcher*
Danoff, Dudley Seth *surgeon, urologist*
Dee, Anthony James *psychiatrist*
De Shazo, Billy W. *physician, plastic surgeon*
Dixit, Vivek *biomedical scientist, medical educator*
Drinkwater, Davis Clapp, Jr. *surgeon, educator*
Edgerton, Bradford Wheatly *plastic surgeon*
Eilber, Frederick Richard *surgeon*
Engel, Jerome, Jr. *neurologist, neuroscientist, educator*
Figlin, Robert Alan *physician, hematologist, oncologist*
Fisher, Mark Jay *neurologist, neuroscientist, educator*
Forrester, James Stuart *cardiologist, medical educator*
Fuerst, David Jonathan *ophthalmologist, educator*
Fyfe, Alistair Ian *cardiologist, scientist, educator*
Gallik, Donna Marie *cardiologist*
Gambino, Jerome James *nuclear medicine educator*
Geffner, David Lewis *endocrinologist*
Giannotta, Steven Louis *neurosurgery educator*
Godzik, Cathleen A. *orthopaedic surgeon, hand surgeon, educator*
Goldsmith, Jonathan Charles *hematologist, internist*
Graham, John Mathewson *pediatrician, medical geneticist*
Green, Michael Foster *neuropsychologist, educator*
Grody, Wayne William *physician*
Gunn, Michela Faith *psychiatrist*
Hagen, Jeffrey August *thoracic surgeon*
Halbert, Ronald Joel *preventive medicine physician, educator*
Heckenlively, John Robert *ophthalmology educator*
Hines, Melissa *neuroscientist, psychologist*
Hirsch, Anthony T. *physician*
Hoang, Duc Van *theoretical pathologist, educator*
Holland, Gary Norman *ophthalmologist, educator*
Hsiao, Chie-Fang *neuroscientist*
Hurvitz, S. Allan *thoracic and cardiovascular surgeon*
Jacobson, Edwin James *medical educator*
Johnson, Richard Greene *physician, psychiatrist, psychoanalyst*
Jones, Neil Ford *surgeon*
Kalmansohn, Robert Bruce *physician, consultant, lecturer*
Kato, Norman Scott *cardiac surgeon, educational administrator*
Katz, Roger *pediatrician, educator*
Kerman, Barry Martin *ophthalmologist, educator*
Kilburn, Kaye Hatch *medical educator*
Kinney, Brian Maltbie *plastic surgeon*
Kramer, Barry Alan *psychiatrist*
Kruger, Lawrence *neuroscientist*
Lamb, H. Richard *psychiatry educator*
Landing, Benjamin Harrison *pathologist, educator*
Lavretsky, Helen *geriatric psychiatrist, researcher*
Lawrence, Sanford Hull *physician, immunochemist*
Leavitt, Maimon *psychiatrist*
Lin, Henry C. *gastroenterologist, researcher*
Liu, Don *ophthalmologist, medical researcher*
Lubman, Richard Levi *physician, educator, research scientist*
Mabee, John Richard *physician assistant, educator*
Machleder, Herbert Ivan *surgeon, educator*
Madlang, Rodolfo Mojica *urologic surgeon*
Maguen, Ezra *ophthalmologist, researcher*
Mahour, Gholam Hossein *pediatric surgeon, educator*
Maloney, Robert Keller *ophthalmologist, medical educator*
Mark, Rufus James *physician, educator*
Martin, Neil Alfred *neurosurgeon*
Martin, Paul *hepatologist, medical educator*
Martinez, Miguel Acevedo *urologist, consultant, lecturer*
Miles, Samuel Israel *psychiatrist, educator*
Miller, Timothy Alden *plastic and reconstructive surgeon*
Monke, J. Victor *psychiatrist, health services administrator*
Mower, William Rex *medical educator, researcher*
Nathwani, Bharat Narottam *pathologist, consultant*
Neinstein, Lawrence Steven *physician, educator*
Newman, Anita Nadine *surgeon*
Nuwer, Marc Roman *neuroscientist, physician*
Oizumi, Jun *pediatrician, geneticist*
Parker, John William *pathology educator, investigator*
Parker, Robert George *radiation oncology educator, academic administrator*
Paulson, Richard John *obstetrician, gynecologist, educator*
Penny, Robert *pediatrician, educator, researcher*
Pi, Edmond Hsin-Tung *psychiatry educator*
Rachelefsky, Gary S. *medical educator*
Read, Stephen L. *physician, psychiatrist*
Reynolds, Charles Patrick *pediatric oncologist, researcher*
Rimoin, David Lawrence *physician, geneticist*
Roven, Alfred Nathan *surgeon*
Rudkin, George Henry *plastic surgeon*
Saad, Mohammed Fathy *medical educator*
Sadun, Alfredo Arrigo *neuro-ophthalmologist, scientist, educator*
Sartini, Richard Lee *retired internist*
Sattin, Albert *psychiatry and neuropharmacology educator*
Schmid, Ingrid *medical researcher*
Schneider, Edward Lewis *medicine educator, research administrator*
Schwartz, Lawrence Jay *ophthalmologist*
Shechter, Pagiel *physician, internist, nephrologist*
Sherman, Randolph *plastic and reconstructive surgeon, educator*
Siegel, Sheldon C. *physician*
Siegel, Stuart Elliott *physician, pediatrics educator, cancer researcher*
Sigman, Melvin Monroe *psychiatrist*
Silverman, Jeffrey Michael *radiologist*
So, George J. K. *radiologist, researcher*
Stein, Herbert I. *internist, educator*
Sullivan, Stuart Francis *anesthesiologist, educator*
Terz, Jose Juan *physician, surgical educator*
Titus, Edward Depue *psychiatrist, administrator*
Tourtellotte, Wallace William *neurologist*
Tranquada, Robert Ernest *medical educator, physician*
Tuch, Richard Howard *psychoanalyst, psychiatrist*
Van Der Meulen, Joseph Pierre *neurologist*
van Leeuwen, Kato *psychiatrist*
Vierling, John Moore *physician*
Villablanca, Jaime Rolando *medical scientist, educator*
Wagner, Willis Harcourt *vascular surgeon*
Wallace, Daniel Jeffrey *rheumatologist*
Wallach, Howard Frederic *psychiatrist*
Waltzer, Kenneth Brian *physician, marketing consultant*
Weiner, Dora B. *medical humanities educator*
Weiss, Irwin Kevin *pediatrician, educator*
Weiss, Martin Harvey *neurosurgeon, educator*
Wilson, Miriam Geisendorfer *retired physician, educator*
Withers, Hubert Rodney *radiotherapist, radiobiologist, educator*
Yao, Lawrence *radiologist*

Los Gatos
Naughten, Robert Norman *pediatrician*

Los Osos
Allison, Ralph Brewster *psychiatrist*

Malibu
Morgenstern, Leon *surgeon*

Martinez
McKnight, Lenore Ravin *child psychiatrist*
Swislocki, Arthur L. M. *physician, internist*

Mendocino
Lobue, Ange Joseph *psychiatrist, author*

Menlo Park
Jaffe, Ross Allan *physician*
Kaplan, Jonathan *psychiatrist, educator*
Kovachy, Edward Miklos, Jr. *psychiatrist*

Merced
Maytum, Harry Rodell *retired physician*

Mill Valley
Deikman, Arthur J. *psychiatrist*

Milpitas
Chiu, Peter Yee-Chew *physician*

Mission Hills
Tram, Kenneth Khai Kt *internist*

Mission Viejo
Caliendo, Theodore Joseph *pediatrician, neonatalogist*

Modesto
Carroll, Wallace B. *allergist, immunologist*
Jacisin, John James *psychiatrist*
Tan, Joo Sim *medical officer*

Monterey
Lehr, Jeffrey Marvin *immunologist, allergist*

Monterey Park
Chang, Jonathan Lee *orthopedist*

Mountain View
Beaver, William Lawrence *retired scientist, consultant*
Goldring, Stanley Donald *medical instrument designer*
Lowen, Robert Marshall *plastic surgeon*
Warren, Richard Wayne *obstetrician, gynecologist*

Napa
Price, John James, Jr. *retired orthopaedic surgeon, forensic reporter*
Wycoff, Charles Coleman *retired anesthesiologist*
Zimmermann, John Paul *plastic surgeon*

National City
Morgan, Jacob Richard *cardiologist*

Newport Beach
Brown, John Vincent *gynecologic oncologist*
Chiu, John Tang *physician*
Zalta, Edward *otorhinolaryngologist, physician*

North Hollywood
Adelson, Leonard Joseph *physician*

Northridge
Alexander, John M. *physician*
Weiland, I. Hyman *psychiatrist*
Ziman, Ronald Bert *physician, researcher, consultant*

Norwalk
Vo, Huu Dinh *pediatrician, educator*

Novato
Franklin, Robert Blair *cardiologist*

Oakland
Cody, Patricia Herbert *health educator*
Donegan, Elizabeth Ann *anesthesiologist*
Eisenberg, Ronald Lee *radiologist*
Friedman, Gary David *epidemiologist, research facility administrator*
Kao, Lily Ching-Chiung *neonatologist*
Killebrew, Ellen Jane (Mrs. Edward S. Graves) *cardiologist*
Klatsky, Arthur Louis *cardiologist, epidemiologist*
Lee, Michael Anthony *cardiologist, electrophysiologist*
Ng, Lawrence Ming-Loy *pediatric cardiologist*
Schoen, Edgar Jacob *pediatrician, pediatric endocrinologist*
Weinmann, Robert Lewis *neurologist*

Oceanside
Curtin, Thomas Lee *ophthalmologist*
Folkerth, Theodore Leon *cardiovascular surgeon, educator*

Olympic Valley
Hsu, Shu-Dean *hematologist, oncologist*

Orange
Armentrout, Steven Alexander *oncologist*
Chishti, Nadeem Ahmad *physician*
Fowler, Glenn W. *pediatric neurologist*
Furnas, David William *plastic surgeon*
Gislason, Irving Lee *psychiatry educator*
Goettsche, Denise Stallings *physician*
MacArthur, Carol Jeanne *pediatric otolaryngology educator*
Manetta, Alberto *gynecologic oncologist*
Newman, Richard Stephen *pathology educator*
Rowen, Marshall *radiologist*
Thompson, William Benbow, Jr. *obstetrician, gynecologist, educator*
Trivedi, Narendra Shantilal *physician, educator, researcher*
Waters, Jonathon Hale *anesthesiologist*
Wilson, Archie Fredric *medical educator*

Oxnard
Niesluchowski, Witold S. *cardiovascular and thoracic surgeon*

Pacific Palisades
Barritt, Clay Franklin *psychiatrist, educator*
Claes, Daniel John *physician*
Love, Susan Margaret *surgeon, educator, medical administrator*

Palm Springs
Grayman, Glen *emergency medicine physician*

Palo Alto
Adamson, Geoffrey David *reproductive endocrinologist, surgeon*
Blessing-Moore, Joann Catherine *physician*
Buck, Louise Bryden *psychiatrist*
Charlton, Randolph Seville *psychiatrist, educator*
Dalessandri, Kathie Marie *surgeon*
Dennery, Phyllis Armelle *pediatrician, educator*
Ebi, Kristie Lee *epidemiologist, consultant*
Fann, James Ilin *cardiothoracic surgeon*
Gendzel, Ivan Bennett *psychiatrist, educator*
Gupta, Suneel Kumar *pharmacologist*
Harkonen, Wesley Scott *physician*
Harris, Robert Francis *psychoanalyst, psychiatrist*
Jamplis, Robert Warren *surgeon, medical foundation executive*
Kabalin, John Nicholas *urologist*
Kundu, Smriti Kana *biomedical scientist*
Lane, William Kenneth *physician*
Lepore, Vincent Donald, Jr. *plastic surgeon*
Link, Michael Paul *pediatrics educator*
Lobel, Charles Irving *physician*
Lunde, Donald Theodore *physician*
Pirofsky, Harvey *psychiatrist*
Rosenthal, Alan Jay *psychiatry educator*
Segre, Eugene Joseph *drug development consultant, physician*
Thom, David Hinton *family physician, medical educator*
Tinklenberg, Jared Ray *psychiatrist, researcher*
Weston, Jane Sara *plastic surgeon, educator*
Wong, Nancy L. *dermatologist*

Palos Verdes Peninsula
Chandraratna, Premindra Anthony N. *physician*
Thomas, Claudewell Sidney *psychiatry educator*

Panorama City
Bass, Harold Neal *pediatrician, medical geneticist*
Pollack, Alan Myron *physician*
Sue, Michael Alvin *physician*

Paramount
Cohn, Lawrence Steven *physician, educator*

Pasadena
Barnard, William Marion *psychiatrist*
Carroll, Robert Lloyd *orthopaedic surgeon*
Glovsky, Myron Michael *medical educator*
Helsper, James T. *surgical oncologist, researcher, educator*
Morgan, Stanley Charles *plastic and reconstructive surgeon*
Phelan, Jeffrey Patrick *obstetrician, gynecologist, lawyer*
Pitts, Ferris Newcomb *physician, psychiatry educator*
Procci, Warren R. *psychiatrist*
Riffenburgh, Ralph Sidney *ophthalmologist*

Piedmont
Sharpton, Thomas *physician*

Placentia
Dana, Hugh Richard *internist, educator*

Placerville
Bonser, Quentin *retired surgeon*

Pleasanton
Anastasiou, Mary M. *pediatrician*
Hisaka, Eric Toru *plastic surgeon*
Iverson, Ronald E. *plastic surgeon*

Pomona
Leslie, Robert Andrew *physician*
Rebhun, Joseph *allergist, immunologist, medical educator*
Routman, Burton Norman *medical educator*

Portola Valley
Fogarty, Thomas James *surgery educator*

Poway
Venn-Watson, Patricia *psychiatrist*

Rancho Mirage
Cone, Lawrence Arthur *research medicine educator*
Le Winn, Laurence Rynes *plastic & reconstructive surgeon*

Rancho Palos Verdes
Askren, Misha *physician*

Redding
Campbell, Patrick Milton *internist, educator*
Renard, Ronald Lee *allergist*
Shadish, William R. *plastic surgeon, retired*

Redlands
Haddad, Wisam Boulos *surgeon*
Richardson, A(rthur) Leslie *former medical group consultant*
Skoog, William Arthur *retired oncologist*
Smith, Dunbar Wallace *retired physician, clergyman*

Wang, Colleen Iona *medical association administrator, writer*

Riverside
Hatton, Glenn Irwin *neuroscientist, educator*
Hiler, Emerson Gard *psychiatrist*
Jukkola, George Duane *obstetrician, gynecologist*
Jung, Timothy Tae Kun *otolaryngologist*
Lau, Kam Yung *physician, educator*
Linaweaver, Walter Ellsworth, Jr. *physician*
Schwartz, Louis *radiologist*
Seyfert, Howard Bentley, Jr. *podiatrist*
Shoji, Hiromu *orthopedic surgeon, educator*
Sparks, Dale Boyd *allergist, health facility administrator*

Rolling Hills Estates
Bellis, Carroll Joseph *surgeon*

Sacramento
Achtel, Robert Andrew *pediatric cardiologist*
Boylan, Richard John *psycologist hypnotherapist, researcher, behavioral scientist*
Evrigenis, John Basil *obstetrician-gynecologist*
Garcia, Gordon Stanley *physician*
Greenspan, Adam *radiologist, educator*
Ichelson, David Leon *physician*
Laslett, Lawrence J. *physician, educator*
Lilla, James A. *plastic surgeon*
Lim, Alan Young *plastic surgeon*
Lippold, Roland Will *surgeon*
Nagy, Stephen Mears, Jr. *physician, allergist*
Reiber, Gregory Duane *forensic pathologist*
Rosenthal, Seth Allan *radiologist, oncologist*
Shapero, Harris Joel *pediatrician*
Sharma, Arjun Dutta *cardiologist*
Strauch, Harold Benjamin *orthopaedic surgeon*
Tung, Prabhas *plastic surgeon*
Tupin, Joe Paul *psychiatry educator*
Zil, John Stephen *psychiatrist, physiologist*

Salinas
Ginsburg, Jerry Hugh *physician, health facility administrator*
Kellogg, Donald Ray *surgeon, plastic surgeon*
Kellogg, George William *psychiatrist*
Leighton, Henry Alexander *physician, consultant*
Rudo, Neil Dennis *surgeon*

San Bernardino
Gorenberg, Alan Eugene *physician*
Kuehn, Klaus Karl Albert *ophthalmologist*
Levister, Ernest Clayton, Jr. *physician*
Prendergast, Thomas John, Jr. *physician, epidemiologist*
Smith, Roger Alexander *surgeon*
Weis, Edmund Bernard, Jr. *orthopaedist, educator, engineer, lawyer*

San Bruno
Bradley, Charles William *podiatrist, educator*
Kaplan, Jerrold Marvin *internist*

San Carlos
Ellis, Eldon Eugene *surgeon*

San Clemente
Kim, Edward William *ophthalmic surgeon*

San Diego
Ambrose, Jayaseelan *cardiovascular physician*
Bejar, Ezra *pharmacologist, biology educator*
Benirschke, Kurt *pathologist, educator*
Brookler, Harry Aaron *retired physician*
Buchbinder, Maurice *cardiologist*
Davidson, Terence Mark *surgery educator, otolaryngologist*
Deftos, Leonard John *medical scientist and educator, jurist*
Dziewanowska, Zofia Elizabeth *neuropsychiatrist, pharmaceutical executive, researcher, educator*
Elliott, Gladden V. *retired radiologist*
Gillin, John Christian *psychiatrist*
Goldman, Leon *dermatologist, laser surgeon*
Goldzband, Melvin George *psychiatrist*
Gruber, Andras *physician, researcher*
Haroun, Ansar M. *forensic psychiatrist*
Holmes, Ralph Edward *plastic surgeon*
Horner, Anthony Adam *pediatrician, educator*
Intriere, Anthony Donald *physician*
Iragui-Madoz, Vicente J. *neurologist, neurosciences educator*
Jablecki, Charles K. *clinical neurologist*
Jacobs, Irvin Herbert *physician, social services consultant*
Kaweski, Susan *plastic surgeon, naval officer*
Kruggel, John Louis *plastic surgeon*
Lamberti, John Joseph *cardiovascular surgeon*
Lane, John Gerhart *orthopedic surgeon*
Lavine, Joel Edward *physician, medical educator*
Levy, Jerome *dermatologist, retired naval officer*
Liu, Fu-Tong *allergist, biomedical researcher, dermatologist*
Moore, Robert Horton *physician*
Moossa, A. R. *surgery educator*
O'Leary, Michael Joseph *surgeon, neurotologist*
Oliphant, Charles Romig *physician*
Parsons, C. Lowell *surgery educator*
Parthemore, Jacqueline G. *physician, educator*
Petersen, Thomas Se Tienne *orthopedic surgeon*
Pitt, William Alexander *cardiologist*
Sartoris, David John *radiologist*
Schmidt, Joseph David *urologist*
Schulman, Paul Stuart *radiologist*
Selzer, Kenneth A. *neurologist, editor*
Shin, Sung Sik *pathologist, educator, researcher*
Shirer, Bruce Edward *pathologist*
Smith, Richard Alan *neurologist, medical association administrator*
Stevens, John Joseph *physician*
Wallace, Helen Margaret *physician, educator*
Wallace, Mark Raymond *physician*
Wasserman, Stephen Ira *physician, educator*
Whitehill, Jules Leonard *surgeon, educator*
Yalam, Arnold Robert *allergist, immunologist, consultant*
Zeiger, Robert S. *allergist*

San Francisco
Abrams, Gary Mitchell *neurologist, educator*
Ai, Everett *ophthalmologist*
Aminoff, Michael Jeffrey *medical educator*
Anthony, James Peter *plastic surgeon, educator*
Arsham, Gary *medical educator*
Augustyn, Damian Henry *gastroenterologist*
Bikle, Daniel David *research physician*
Bishop, John Michael *biomedical research scientist, educator*
Brown, Donald Malcolm *plastic surgeon*
Cahan, Robert Barmach *psychiatrist, educator*
Capozzi, Angelo *surgeon*
Caputo, Gary Richard *radiology educator*
Cheitlin, Melvin Donald *physician, educator*
Cline, Carolyn Joan *plastic and reconstructive surgeon*
Darney, Philip Dempsey *gynecologist, educator*
Duh, Quan-Yang *surgeon*
Epstein, Ervin Harold, Jr. *dermatologist, educator, researcher*
Erskine, John Morse *surgeon*
Fishman, Robert Allen *neurologist, educator*
Frick, Oscar Lionel *physician, educator*
German, Donald Frederick *physician*
Gibbs, Patricia Hellman *physician*
Goldman, Lee *physician, educator, researcher*
Gooding, Gretchen Ann Wagner *physician, educator*
Gottfried, Eugene Leslie *physician, educator*
Greenberg, Roger L. *plastic and reconstructive surgeon*
Grimes, Orville Frank *surgery educator*
Halvorsen, Robert Alfred, Jr. *radiologist, educator*
Harris, Jeffrey Saul *physician executive*
Hentz, Vincent R. *surgeon*
Herbert, Chesley C. *psychiatrist, educator*
Hering, William Marshall *medical organization executive*
Higashida, Randall Takeo *radiologist, neurosurgeon, medical educator*
Hinman, Frank, Jr. *urologist, educator*
Hoffman, William Yanes *plastic surgeon*
Horton, Jonathan Charles *neuroscientist, neuro-ophthalmologist*
Hwang, David Genpai *ophthalmologist, educator*
Ikeda, Clyde Junichi *plastic and reconstructive surgeon*
Israel, Mark A. *pediatrics and neurological surgery educator*
Jaume, Juan Carlos *physician, educator*
Katzung, Bertram George *pharmacologist*
Kiefer, Renata Gertrud *pediatrician, epidemiologist, economist, international health consultant*
Kimmich, Robert André *psychiatrist*
Kline, Howard Jay *cardiologist*
Kramer, Steven G. *ophthalmologist*
Leoung, Gifford S. *physician*
Levin, Alan Scott *pathologist, allergist, immunologist, lawyer*
Levin, Barry Sherwin *physician*
Levy, Leonard Alvin *podiatric medicine educator, college president*
Lewis, Rose *plastic surgeon*
Lidofsky, Steven David *medical educator*
Lowe, Rolland Choy *surgeon*
Martin, Joseph Boyd *neurologist, educator*
Mason, Dean Towle *cardiologist*
Massie, Barry Michael *cardiologist*
McAninch, Jack Weldon *urological surgeon, educator*
Murray, John Frederic *physician, educator*
Mustacchi, Piero *physician, educator*
Ochitill, Herbert Nolan *psychiatrist, educator*
Paiement, Guy Darius *orthopedic surgeon, educator*
Palmer, Robert Fields *neurosurgeon, educator*
Parer, Julian Thomas *obstetrics and gynecology educator*
Polites, Demetri John *psychiatrist*
Presti, Joseph Charles, Jr. *urologist*
Reus, Victor I. *psychiatry educator, hospital administrator*
Ristow, Brunno *plastic surgeon*
Roe, Benson Bertheau *surgeon, educator*
Rosenthal, Philip *gastroenterologist*
Schatz, Howard *ophthalmologist*
Schiller, Nelson Benjamin *physician, cardiologist*
Schmid, Rudi (Rudolf Schmid) *internist, educator, academic administrator*
Scholten, Paul *obstetrician, gynecologist, educator*
Scotton, Bruce Warren *psychiatrist, educator*
Seebach, Lydia Marie *physician*
Shapiro, Larry Jay *pediatrician, scientist, educator*
Shumate, Charles Albert *retired dermatologist*
Silverman, Norman Henry *cardiologist, educator*
Skolnikoff, Alan Zachary *psychiatrist*
Smith, David Elvin *physician*
Snyder, John David *pediatric gastroenterologist, epidemiologist*
Sokolow, Maurice *physician, educator*
Stamper, Robert Lewis *ophthalmologist, educator*
Steinman, John Francis *psychiatrist*
Szabo, Zoltan *medical science educator, medical institute director*
Trigiano, Lucien Lewis *physician*
Wallerstein, Ralph Oliver *physician*
Wayburn, Edgar *internist, environmentalist*
Wolkowitz, Owen Mark *physician, psychiatrist, researcher*

San Gabriel
Chen, John Calvin *child and adolescent psychiatrist*

San Jose
Avakoff, Joseph Carnegie *medical and legal consultant*
Boldrey, Edwin Eastland *retinal surgeon, educator*
Cobb, Luther Fuson *surgeon, educator*
Hovey, Leslie Morris *plastic surgeon, educator*
Isaacson, Joseph Morris *rheumatologist*
Joshi, Janardan Shantilal *surgeon*
Lippe, Philipp Maria *physician, surgeon, neurosurgeon, educator, administrator*
Malish, David Marc *physician*
Mallison, Robert Andrew *neurologist*
Mayo, Cesar M. *neurologist*
Multz, Carter Victor *rheumatologist*
Nelson, Randall Erland *surgeon*
Nguyen, Thinh Van *physician*
Shatney, Clayton Henry *surgeon*
Stevens, David Alec *medical educator*
Sullivan, John Harvey *ophthalmologist, plastic surgeon*

San Juan Capistrano
Fisher, Delbert Arthur *physician, educator*

San Marcos
Billing, Ronald James *immunologist, researcher*

San Mateo
Adams, Robert Monroe *retired dermatologist, educator*
Bell, Leo S. *retired physician*
Chapman, Alger Baldwin, III *pediatrician, researcher*
Marcus, Hubert C. *ophthalmologist*
Meyerowitz, Basil Ralph *surgeon*
Van Kirk, John Ellsworth *cardiologist*
von Doepp, Christian Ernest *psychiatrist*
Wong, Otto *epidemiologist*

San Pablo
Drager, Sharon B. *vascular surgeon*

San Rafael
Benzler, Bruce C. *healthcare executive*
Danse, Ilene Homnick Raisfeld *physician, educator, toxicologist*
Hicks, Philip Stanley *psychiatrist*
Meecham, William James *ophthalmologist*

San Ramon
Litman, Robert Barry *physician, author, television and radio commentator*

Santa Barbara
Aijian, Haig Schuyler *pathologist, educator*
Clark, Ramona Richli *radiologist*
Cumes, David M. *urologist*
Ellis, Eugene Joseph *cardiologist*
Formby, Bent Clark *immunologist*
Klakeg, Clayton Harold *cardiologist*
Kohn, Roger Alan *surgeon*
Liebhaber, Myron I. *allergist*
MacArthur, John Reed *physician*
Mathews, Barbara Edith *gynecologist*
Patterson, Donald Scott *psychiatrist*
Rockwell, Don Arthur *psychiatrist*
Wittenstein, George Juergen *surgeon, educator*

Santa Clara
Gale, Arnold David *pediatric neurologist, consultant*

Santa Cruz
Kwan, Marcus R. *surgeon*
Magid, Gail Avrum *neurosurgeon, neurosurgery educator*
Pletsch, Marie Eleanor *plastic surgeon*
Schwartz, Arthur Alan *surgeon*

Santa Monica
Bohn, Paul Bradley *psychiatrist, psychoanalyst*
Carr, Ruth Margaret *plastic surgeon*
Dollinger, Malin Roy *physician, author*
Feinstein, Beverly *psychiatrist, psychoanalyst*
Fogelson, David Leslie *psychiatrist, educator*
Frey, Harvey Stuart *radiologist, law student*
Galton, Elizabeth *psychiatrist, psychoanalyst*
Giuliano, Armando Elario *surgical oncologist, educator, author*
Hoefflin, Steven M. *plastic surgeon*
Hurvitz, James S. *plastic surgeon*
Kawamoto, Henry K. *plastic surgeon*
Landau, Joseph White *dermatologist*
McGuire, Michael Francis *plastic and reconstructive surgeon*
Mitchell, Thomas Soren *urologist*
Nelson, Ronald John *cardiothoracic surgeon, educator*
Pearson, Warren Thomas *surgeon*
Pollis, Richard P. *orthopedic surgeon*
Resnick, Jeffrey I. *plastic surgeon*
Thompson, Dennis Peters *plastic surgeon*
Wasserman, Martin Stephen *psychiatrist, psychoanalyst, child psychiatrist*
Young, Rosabel Ribares *neurologist*
Zarem, Harvey Alan *plastic surgeon*

Santa Paula
Deutsch, Gary Michael *internist*

Santa Rosa
Bauman, Martin Harold *psychiatrist, therapist*
Canales, Francisco Luis *hand surgeon*
Leissring, John Cother *pathologist*
Leuty, Gerald Johnston *osteopathic physician and surgeon*
Trucker, Albert *plastic surgeon*

Santee
Yang, Hsin-Ming *immunologist*

Sausalito
Arieff, Allen Ives *physician*

Seal Beach
Carlin, Jean Effal *physician, psychiatrist, psychologist*

Sebastopol
Delgado, Roger Rodriguez *surgeon, educator*

Sepulveda
Nishimura, Robert Neal *physician, medical educator, researcher*
Wasterlain, Claude Guy *neurologist*

Sherman Oaks
Stein, Karl N. *plastic and reconstructive surgeon*

Somis
Cho, Sung-Nei Charles *physician*

Sonora
Weiner, Kathryn Ann *medical association administrator, special education educator*

South San Francisco
Curd, John Gary *physician, scientist*

Stanford
Bensch, Klaus George *pathology educator*
Bergeron, Paul Phillip *internist*
Blumenkranz, Mark Scott *surgeon, researcher, educator*
Brodsky, Jay Barry *medical educator*
Dafoe, Donald Cameron *surgeon, educator*
Fee, Willard Edward, Jr. *otolaryngologist*
Hubert, Helen Betty *epidemiologist*
Hui, Kenneth Chi-Wan *surgeon*
Jadvar, Hossein *physician, biomedical engineer*
Klima, Roger R. *physiatrist*
McGuire, Joseph Smith *physician*
Miller, David Craig *cardiovascular surgeon*
Moss, Richard B. *pediatrician*
Reitz, Bruce Arnold *cardiac surgeon, educator*
Spiegel, David *psychiatrist*
Terris, David James *head and neck surgeon, researc scientist*
Vistnes, Lars M. *plastic surgeon*

Stockton
Chapnick, Robert Ian *physician*
Wiggins, James Joseph *family practice physician*

Studio City
Shekhar, Stephen S. *obstetrician, gynecologist*

Sylmar
Chernof, Bruce *internist, educator*
Morrow, Mark Jay *neurologist, educator*
Munro, Malcolm Gordon *obstetrician, gynecologist, educator*
Tully, Susan Balsley *pediatrician, educator*

Tarzana
Wilson, Stephen Jay *psychiatrist, consultant*

Tehachapi
Melsheimer, Harold *obstetrician, gynecologist*

Temecula
Gill, Becky Lorette *addictionist, psychiatrist*

Templeton
Abernathy, Shields B. *allergist, immunologist, internist*
Carey, James C., Jr. *plastic surgeon*
Peterson, Richard Allan *pediatrician*

Thousand Oaks
Klein, Jeffrey Howard *oncologist, internist*
Merrin, James Steven *internist*

Torrance
Anderson, Thomas Leif *physician, researcher*
Booker, James Avery, Jr. *surgeon*
Canalis, Rinaldo Fernando *surgeon, educator, researcher*
Casaburi, Richard *respiratory and critical care physician*
Emmanouilides, George Christos *physician, educator*
Goldberg, Mark Arthur *neurologist*
Kitano, Masami *neurologist*
Krout, Boyd Merrill *psychiatrist*
Leake, Rosemary Dobson *physician*
Tabrisky, Joseph *radiologist, educator*
Wan, Yu-Jui Yvonne *educator, scientist*
Yang, Henry Chang-Lien *oncology educator, physician*

Turlock
Maurer, John Irving *psychiatrist*

Vallejo
Charney, Philip *dermatologist*

Van Nuys
Handel, Neal *plastic surgeon, researcher*
Jaivin, Jonathan Steven *orthopedic surgeon*
Kirschner, Melvin Henry *physician*

Ventura
Abul-Haj, Suleiman Kahil *pathologist*
Armstrong, Dale P. *plastic surgeon*
Goldie, William David *neurologist, educator*
Lindsay, Donald Gene *retired dermatologist, educator, writer*
Shakman, Robert Allan *public health physician*
Zuber, William Frederick *thoracic and vascular surgeon*

Visalia
Riegel, Byron William *ophthalmologist*

Volcano
Prout, Ralph Eugene *physician*

Walnut Creek
Farr, Lee Edward *nuclear medicine physician*
Jervis, William Horace, Jr. *plastic and reconstructive surgeon*
Kang, Isamu Yong *nuclear medicine physician*
Wassermann, Franz Walther *physician*

Watsonville
Alfaro, Felix Benjamin *physician*
Stubblefield, James Irvin *emergency medicine physician, health facility administrator*

West Covina
Lee, Lily Shiny *medical consultant*
Pollak, Erich Walter *surgeon, educator*
Singh, Rajesh Kumar *psychiatrist*

West Hollywood
Wilson, Myron Robert, Jr. *retired psychiatrist*

Westlake Village
Kottler, Dennis Bruce *physician*

Whittier
Arcadi, John Albert *urologist*
Arenowitz, Albert Harold *psychiatrist*
Hilde, Reuben Lynn *plastic surgeon*
Prickett, David Clinton *physician*
Welsh, William Daniel *family practitioner,*

Windsor
Dahmer, Joan Marie *physician*

Woodland Hills
Herdeg, Howard Brian *physician*

Yuba City
Lefever, Eric Bruce *anesthesiologist*

COLORADO

Aspen
Evans, William Thomas *physician*

Oden, Robert Rudolph *surgeon*

Aurora
Burgess, David Bruce *pediatrician*

Boulder
Bock, S. Allan *physician, educator*
Garmany, George Parker *neurologist*
Plazak, Dean James *physician, psychiatrist*
Warner, Richard *psychiatrist*

Colorado Springs
Anderson, Paul Nathaniel *oncologist, educator*
Barley, Leonard Vaughn *physician*
Biggers, Robert David *urologist, nutritionist*
Du Bois, David D. *plastic surgeon*
Gorab, Lawrence Ned *urologist*
Nathan, Robert A. *allergist, educator*
Rose, Cynthia *psychiatrist*
Sciotto, Cosimo Gino *pathologist, hematopathologist*
Stein, Gerald S. *psychiatrist*
Todd, Harold Wade *association executive, retired air force officer*

Crested Butte
Lyons, Stephen H. *medical educator*

Denver
Adler, Charles Spencer *psychiatrist*
Aikawa, Jerry Kazuo *physician, educator*
Barber, Patricia Louise *clinical specialist*
Bateman, Jane Bronwyn *ophthalmology educator*
Baum, Kenneth Francis *medical educator, physician*
Bearman, Scott Irvin *internist, educator*
Bies, Roger David *cardiologist*
Brown, William Carroll *plastic surgeon, microsurgeon*
Bunn, Paul A., Jr. *oncologist, educator*
Carson, Stanley David *cardiothoracic surgeon*
Cherington, Michael *neurologist, educator*
Chessick, Cheryl Ann *psychiatrist*
Cochran, John Howard *plastic and reconstructive surgeon*
Collier, David Harris *rheumatologist*
Conger, John D. *vascular physiologist, nephrologist*
Espey, William Malloneé *psychiatrist*
Filley, Christopher Mark *neurologist*
Freed, Curt Richard *pharmacology educator*
Gabow, Patricia Anne *internist*
Gelfand, Erwin William *immunologist*
Golitz, Loren Eugene *dermatologist, pathologist, clinical administrator, educator*
Harken, Alden Hood *surgeon, thoracic surgeon*
Hartford, Charles Edward *surgeon*
Hathaway, William Ellison *pediatrics educator*
Hoehn, Robert J. *plastic surgeon, educator*
Huang, Linda Chen *plastic surgeon*
Hutchison, David Easton *surgeon, educator*
Iseman, Michael Dee *medical educator*
Kamada, Alan Katsuki *pharmacology educator*
Kappy, Michael Steven *pediatrics educator*
Kassan, Stuart S. *rheumatologist*
Khoo, Robert E.H. *colon and rectal surgeon*
Kluck, Clarence Joseph *physician*
La Rosa, Francisco Guillermo *pathologist, researcher, educator*
Litvak, John *neurosurgeon*
Logan, John Landiss *physician*
Lubeck, Marvin Jay *ophthalmologist*
Mackin, Glenn Alexander *neurologist*
Mayerson, Peter *psychiatrist, educator*
McGregor, James Allan *obstetrician, gynecologist*
McIlvaine, William Brown, Jr. *pediatric anesthesiologist*
Merenstein, Gerald Burton *pediatrician, educator*
Metzner, Jeffrey Lee *psychiatrist, educator*
Miller, Robert David *forensic psychiatrist*
Nelson, Nancy Eleanor *pediatrician, educator*
Niermeyer, Susan *medical educator*
Parsons, Polly Elsbeth *internist*
Payea, Norman Philip, II *plastic surgeon, lawyer*
Pomerantz, Marvin *thoracic surgeon*
Reiter, Michael Jay *cardiologist educator*
Rhine, Mark Woodforde *psychiatrist, psychoanalyst*
Rymer Davis, Carol Ann *radiologist*
Sanders, Richard Jeremiah *vascular surgeon, medical educator*
Schooley, Robert T. *medical educator*
Schwarz, I. Gene *psychiatry educator*
Singleton, John Weir *gastroenterology educator, consultant*
Stienmier, Richard Harold *pathologist*
Talbott, Richard David *physician*
Washington, Reginald Louis *pediatric cardiologist*
Weatherley-White, Roy Christopher Anthony *surgeon, consultant*
Weiner, Norman *pharmacology educator*
West, Sterling Gaylord *physician*
Westcott, Jay Young *pulmonary and critical care medicine educator*
Wexler, Ralph Martin *physician, consultant*

Durango
Grossman, Richard *obstetrician/gynecologist*
Wigton, Chester Mahlon *family physician*

Englewood
Aarestad, Norman O. *radiologist*
Arenberg, Irving Kaufman *ear surgeon, educator*
Burks, Jack Sheldon *neurologist*
Greenhut, Saul Ephriam *biomedical researcher, engineer*
Hatfield, Wendell Benton *physician*
Kapelovitz, Leonard Herman *psychiatrist*
Kovarik, Joseph Lewis *surgeon*

Estes Park
Baker, Robert N. *neurologist*

Fort Carson
Beitz, Richard Theodore, Jr. *family physician, acute care physician*
Lewey, Scot Michael *gastroenterologist, army officer*

Fort Collins
Dennis, David Tappen *epidemiologist*
Dudek, F. Edward *educator*
Lee, Robert Edward *medical educator, researcher*

Fort Garland
Leighninger, David Scott *cardiovascular surgeon*

Golden
Christensen, Robert Wayne *oral maxillofacial surgeon, minister*

Grand Junction
Brandon, Gary Kent *physician, health facility administrator*
Janson, Richard Anthony *plastic surgeon*
Virgilio, Joanne *oncologist, hematologist*

Greeley
Cook, Donald E. *pediatrician*
Jaouen, Richard Matthie *plastic surgeon*

Littleton
Forstot, S. Lance *ophthalmologist*
Garfein, Arthur Douglas *psychiatrist, psychoanalyst*
Glasco, Donald Glee *psychiatrist*
Hammerly, Milt *physician*
Palmer, Madelyn Stewart Silver *family practice physician*

Loveland
Wright, Eric R. *physician assistant*

Pueblo
Lewallen, William M., Jr. *ophthalmologist*
Mou, Thomas William *physician, medical educator and consultant*

Silverthorne
Rutherford, Robert Barry *surgeon*

Vail
Chow, Franklin Szu-Chien *obstetrician, gynecologist*

Wheat Ridge
Brown, Steven Brien *radiologist*
Jones, Arthur Francis *surgeon*

HAWAII

Ewa Beach
Neudorf, Howard Fred *family physician*

Hilo
Taniguchi, Tokuso *surgeon*

Honolulu
Batzer, Gabrielle Bemis *physician, psychiatrist*
Brady, Stephen R.P.K. *physician*
Camara, Jorge de Guzman *ophthalmologist, educator*
Chee, Percival Hon Yin *ophthalmologist*
Chock, Clifford Yet-Chong *family practice physician*
Chung, Chin Sik *genetic epidemiologist*
Cordts, Paul Roger *surgeon*
Diamond, Milton *anatomy and reproductive biology educator*
Edwards, John Wesley, Jr. *urologist*
Goldstein, Sir Norman *dermatologist*
Goodhue, William Walter, Jr. *pathologist, military officer, medical educator*
Hay-Roe, Victor *plastic surgeon*
Hundahl, Scott Alfred *oncologic surgeon*
Ishii, Clyde Hideo *plastic surgeon*
Kane, Thomas Jay, III *orthopaedic surgeon, educator*
Kaye, Michael Duncan *physician, gastroenterologist, consultant*
Lee, Yeu-Tsu Margaret *surgeon, educator*
Lewis, Philip Christie *psychiatrist*
McCarthy, Laurence James *physician, pathologist*
Meagher, Michael *medical radiologist*
Moreira, Allan *urologist*
Moreno-Cabral, Carlos Eduardo *cardiac surgeon*
Oda, Yoshio *physician, internist*
Oishi, Calvin Shizuo *orthopedic surgeon*
Pang, Herbert George *ophthalmologist*
Paperny, David Mark N. *pediatrician*
Parsa, Fereydoun Don *plastic surgeon*
Salzman, Keith Lawrence *family practice physician, military officer*
Stevens, Stephen Edward *psychiatrist*
Sugiki, Shigemi *ophthalmologist, educator*
Terminella, Luigi *critical care physician, educator*
Wong, Linda L. *surgeon*

Kamuela
Bracher, George *radiologist*

Koloa
Donohugh, Donald Lee *physician*

Lahaina
Ard, James George *family physician*

Pahoa
Domizio, Dan *physician assistant, consultant*

Waialua
DeLuze, James Robert *physician*

Waianae
Kakugawa, Terri Etsumi *osteopath*
Yoshimoto, Cedric Mitsuo *physician*

Waikoloa
Copman, Louis *radiologist*

Wailuku
Savona, Michael Richard *physician*

IDAHO

Boise
Benavides, Mary Kathleen *anesthesiologist, nutritional consultant*
Khatain, Kenneth George *psychiatrist, former air force officer*
Moss, Stanley W. *orthopedic surgeon*
Pressman, Scott Hughes *ophthalmologist*
Priest, Marshall Franklin, III *cardiologist*

Coeur D Alene
West, Robert Sumner *surgeon*

Idaho Falls
Moore, Elaine Ann *medical technologist*

Lewiston
Majure, Joyce Arlene *surgeon*
Thorne, Gary Marvin *surgeon*

Moscow
De Santis, Mark Edward *anatomist, neuroscientist and educator*

Nampa
Botimer, Allen Ray *retired surgeon, retirement center owner*

Pocatello
Heilman, June E. *general surgeon*
Hunt, Winslow Robert *psychiatrist*
Maloff, Stephen Martin *plastic surgeon*

Priest River
Freibott, George August *physician, chemist, priest*
Hayden, James Walworth *emergency physician, medical director*

Sun Valley
Fairman, Dan S. *internist*

ILLINOIS

Galena
Scheuring, Richard Anthony *physician*

INDIANA

Indianapolis
Brandt, Ira Kive *pediatrician, medical geneticist*

MONTANA

Billings
Glenn, Guy Charles *pathologist*
Kohler, William Curtis *sleep specialist, neurologist*
Rich, Joseph David *psychiatrist*

Butte
Baggenstos, Pius A. *neurosurgeon*

Great Falls
O'Connor, John Edward *physician*
Rohrer, David Arnold *surgeon*

Havre
Reynolds, Stuart Arnold *surgeon*

Helena
Foster, Michael Lewis *hospital administration, state senator*
Reynolds, James Francis, Jr. *physician*

Kalispell
Milheim, Stephen George *surgeon*

Miles City
Rauh, J. Randall *physician*

Missoula
Diettert, Gerald Allen *cardiologist*
Hoell, Noel Laramie *psychiatrist*
McLaughlin, Dixie Goeres *medical humanities administrator*
Murray, Donald Eugene *plasic surgeon*

NEVADA

Carson City
Meyer, Roger Paul *physician*
Walls, Joseph Patrick *orthopaedic surgeon*

Elko
Tyburczy, John Adrian *surgeon*

Henderson
Perel, Michael Joseph *dermatologist, inventor*

Las Vegas
Abu-Samrah, Sameer Abdallah *internist*
Bandt, Paul Douglas *physician*
Barger, James Daniel *physician*
Canada, William H. *plastic surgeon*
Capanna, Albert Howard *neurosurgeon, neuroscientist*
Davidson, Joel *surgeon*
Fennel, Peter J., Sr. *retired anesthesiologist*
Garry, Stacey Lynne *pathologist*
Harrison, William Orville *physician*
Kurlinski, John Parker *physician*
Mackey, Maureen Elise *rehabilitation medicine physician*
Matheis, Lawrence Paul *association executive, public health consultant*
Moritz, Timothy Bovie *psychiatrist*
Perer, Marvin A. *gastroenterologist*
Petty, Leonora Kathleen *psychiatrist*
Records, Raymond Edwin *ophthalmologist*
Speck, Eugene Lewis *internist*
Stone, William Gene *psychiatrist*

Reno
Ascensáo, Joáo Luis Afonso *physician, researcher*
Gerow, Lynn Burdette, Jr. *psychiatrist*
Jackson, Michael Vincent *physician, medical educator*
Krumpe, Peter E. *medical educator*
Lloyd, William Judd, Jr. *obstetrician, gynecoloist*
MacKintosh, Frederick Roy *oncologist*
Rahe, Richard Henry *psychiatrist, educator*
Shapiro, Leonard *immunologist, allergist*
Young, Zora Oral *psychiatrist*

NEW MEXICO

Alamogordo
Ashdown, Franklin Donald *physician, composer*
Jackson, Gary Lynn *osteopath, internist, pulmonologist*
Lindley, Norman Dale *physician*

Albuquerque
Abrums, John Denise *internist*
Arora, Sanjeev *gastroenterology educator*
Baack, Bret Rolyn *plastic surgeon*
Barton, Larry Lumir *mircobiology educator, consultant*
Boyd, John Franklin *orthopaedic surgeon*
Brya, William John *anesthesiologist*
Frank, Alan *retired psychiatry educator*
Goss, Jerome Eldon *cardiologist*
Graham, Susan Brandt *gynecologist, anthropologist*
Harvie, Keith William *orthopaedic surgeon*
Hudson, Patrick A. *plastic surgeon*
Irani, Mehraboon S. *pathologist*
Janis, Kenneth M. *physician*
Lindeman, Robert Dean *medical educator, researcher, consultant*
Ottensmeyer, David Joseph *healthcare consultant, retired neurosurgeon*
Papile, Lucille Ann *pediatrician, educator*
Reyes, Edward *pharmacology educator*
Saland, Linda Carol *anatomy educator*
Sherman, Frederick Charles *orthopedic surgeon*
Stevenson, James Richard *radiologist, lawyer*
Summers, William Koopmans *neuropsychiatrist, researcher*
Wong, Phillip Allen *osteopathic physician*
Worrell, Richard Vernon *orthopedic surgeon, educator, academic administrator*
Yager, Joel *psychiatry educator*

Clovis
Goodwin, Martin Brune *radiologist*

Gallup
Kayate, Ethel Mae *physician assistant*

Hobbs
Lee, Wayland Sherrod *otolaryngologist*
Stone, William Coy *surgeon*

Las Cruces
Jacobs, Kent Frederick *dermatologist*

Las Vegas
Stoltze, David Albert *physician*

Los Alamos
Wadstrom, Ann Kennedy *retired anesthesiologist*

Rio Rancho
Mendez, C. Beatriz *obstetrician, gynecologist*

Rodeo
Scholes, Robert Thornton *allergist, research administrator*

Santa Fe
Saltzman, Beth Melanie *medical librarian*
Seedman, Susan Ann *surgeon*
Stennis, William *psychiatrist, educator*
Tashjian, Levon Donald *psychiatrist*

NEW YORK

New York
Gebbie, Kristine Moore *health science educator, health official*

OREGON

Albany
Crow, Kenneth Arthur *pathologist*

Ashland
Kirschner, Richard Michael *naturopathic physician, speaker, author*

Astoria
Wayne, Robert *surgeon*

Athena
Mengis, Chris Ludwig *retired internist*

Cave Junction
Robinson, Arthur Brouhard *scientist, educator*

Coos Bay
Collins, Harold Theodore *urologist*

Corvallis
Hafner-Eaton, Chris *health services researcher, educator*

Eugene
Balz, James B. *surgeon*
Dreyer, Thomas Morgan *plastic surgeon*
Flanagan, Latham, Jr. *surgeon*
Nissel, Martin *radiologist, consultant*
Schroeder, Donald J. *orthopedic surgeon*
Simmons, Geoffrey Stuart *physician*
Starr, Grier Forsythe *retired pathologist*
Teal, Donald F. *physician, surgeon*
Wheeler, Robert Ross *medical director*

Lake Oswego
Stark, Allen Lytton *psychiatrist, educator*

Lebanon
Girod, Frank Paul *retired surgeon*

Medford
Dibb, Charles Robert *physician, educator*
Luther, Robert Chester *psychiatrist, consultant*

Ontario
Tyler, Donald Earl *urologist*

Portland
Barker, Alan Freund *internist*
Benson, John Alexander, Jr. *physician, educator*
Berthelsdorf, Siegfried *psychiatrist*
Bonafede, R. Peter *rheumatologist*
Breda, Michael Alexander *surgeon*
Breen, Roy Eugene *physician*
Brummett, Robert Eddie *pharmacology educator*
Buist, Neil Robertson MacKenzie *medical educator, medical administrator*
Campbell, Robert Allen *pediatrician*
Casey, Daniel E. *psychiatrist, educator*
Collins, Michael Sean *obstetrician and gynecologist, educator*
Crawshaw, Ralph *psychiatrist*
Duell, Paul Barton *internist, endocrinologist, educator*
Duncan, Elmore Edward *psychiatrist*
Geist, Howard J. *orthopedic surgeon*
Goldberg, Linn *physician*
Janzen, Timothy Paul *family practice physician*
Johnson, Martin Clifton *physician*
Labby, Daniel Harvey *medical educator, psychiatry educator*
LaFranchi, Stephen Henry *pediatric endocrinologist, educator, researcher*
Layman, Charles Donald *plastic surgeon*
Leonard, Hubert Arnold *neurologist*
McClung, Michael Roy *physician, medical educator, researcher*
Morrison, John Carl *ophthalmologist, educator*
Mozena, John Daniel *podiatrist*
Palmer, Earl A. *ophthalmologist, educator*
Prendergast, William John *ophthalmologist*
Rosenbaum, Richard Barry *neurologist*
Rosenfeld, Ron Gershon *pediatrics educator*
Schmidt, Waldemar Adrian *pathologist, educator*
Seres, Joel Leonard *neurosurgeon*
Seyfer, Alan Eric *surgeon*
Sheppard, Brett C. *surgeon*
Sklovsky, Robert Joel *naturopath, pharmacist, educator*
Stalnaker, John Hulbert *physician*
Stevens, Jeffrey S. *chief of nuclear medicine*
Swan, Kenneth Carl *surgeon*
Szeto, Erik K. *family practice physician*
Takahashi, Gary Wayne *internist, hematologist, oncologist*
Toffler, William Louis *medical educator*
Van Buskirk, Edmund Michael *ophthalmologist*
Vea, Henry Walter *radiologist, nuclear medicine specialist*
Veverka, Michael J. *diagnostic radiologist*
Wilson, David Jean *ophthalmologist*
Zeller, Katharine Margret *physician*
Zerzan, Charles Joseph, Jr. *gastroenterologist*

Roseburg
Donahoo, Stanley Ellsworth *orthopedic surgeon*
Tan, Alfonso O. *internist*

Salem
Cozart, Rebecca Lydia *medical association executive*

Silverton
Centerwall, Willard Raymond *physician*
Watson, Milton Russell *retired surgeon*

Wilsonville
Bernard, Richard Montgomery *physician*

PENNSYLVANIA

Philadelphia
Tannen, Richard Laurence *medical educator, nephrologist*

UTAH

Logan
Wade, Kenneth Alan *physician assistant*

Ogden
Galassie, John Perry *medical supervisor*

Salt Lake City
Aldous, Richard Allen *ophthalmologist*
Anderson, Richard Lee *ophthalmologist, educator*
Bauer, A(ugust) Robert, Jr. *surgeon, educator*
Brandon, Kathryn Elizabeth Beck *pediatrician*
Brinton, Gregory S. *ophthalmologist, educator*
Christensen, Brent J. *surgeon*
Dayton, Merril Taylor *gastrointestinal surgeon*
Evanega, George Ronald *medical company executive*
Gilbert, Edward Michael *cardiology educator*
Goates, Delbert Tolton *child psychiatrist*
Harvey, Stewart Clyde *retired pharmacologist, educator*
Jacobson, Jay Andrew *physician*
Kanner, Richard Elliot *physician, educator*
Lewis, Edward C. *plastic surgeon*
Mamalis, Nick *ophthalmologist, researcher*
Middleton, Anthony Wayne, Jr. *urologist, educator*
Middleton, Richard George *urologist, educator*
Milley, John Ross *neonatologist, educator*
Morris, Stephen Eugene *surgery educator*
Petersen, Finn Bo *oncologist, educator*
Petersen, Marta Jean *dermatologist, educator*
Petersen, Phil Brent *psychiatrist, educator*
Rallison, Marvin L. *pediatrician, educator*
Schricker, J. Louis, Jr. *neurosurgeon*
Siegler, Richard Louis *pediatric nephrologist, educator*
Smith, Eileen Pazderka *dermatologist*
Stanford, Joseph Barney *medical educator, physician*
Stromquist, Don Leonard *rheumatologist*
Thomas, David Snow *plastic surgeon*
Weeks, Lionel Edwards *orthopedic surgeon*
Whitehead, Paul Leon *physician*

WASHINGTON

Bellevue
Dunn, Jeffrey Edward *neurologist*
Gofman, John David *physician, ophthalmologist*
Hackett, Carol Ann Hedden *physician*
Simonowitz, David Alan *surgeon*
Vath, Raymond Eugene *psychiatrist, educator*

Bellingham
Howe, Warren Billings *physician*
James, Helen Ann *plastic surgeon*

Bothell
Ross, Amy Ann *experimental pathologist*

Bremerton
Ringler, Robert Lloyd, Jr. *family practice physician, naval officer*

Chelan
Carlton, Thomas Grant *psychiatrist*

Clarkston
Chinchinian, Harry *pathologist, educator*

Edmonds
Crone, Richard Allan *cardiologist, educator*
Kim, Sang U. *gastroenterologist*
Wood, David Bruce *naturopathic physician*

Everett
Beegle, Earl Dennis *family physician*

Fircrest
Martin, Robert Joseph *dermatologist*
Torgenrud, Terry Wayne *pediatrician*

Hansville
Strahilevitz, Meir *inventor, researcher, psychiatry educator*

Issaquah
Maguire, Yu Ping *cell biologist, medical scientist*

Kent
Dorman, Thomas Alfred *internist, orthopaedist*

Kirkland
Dundas, Dennis Franklin *plastic surgeon*

Longview
Kenagy, John Warner *surgeon*
Kirkpatrick, Richard Alan *internist*
Sandstrom, Robert Edward *physician, pathologist*

Madigan Hospital
Ulnick, Keith Mitchell *physician, health care administrator*

Maple Valley
Grosskopf, Barry *psychiatrist, consultant*

Moses Lake
Leadbetter, Mark Renton, Jr. *orthopedic surgeon*

Mount Vernon
Peterson, Laurence Robert *pathologist*

Mountlake Terrace
Imamura, Eugene Hachiro *osteopathic physician, surgeon*

Olympia
Fisher, Nancy Louise *pediatrician, medical geneticist, former nurse*
Flemming, Stanley Lalit Kumar *family practice physician, mayor, state legislator*
Hayes, Maxine Delores *physician*
Smith, Sherwood Paul *plastic surgeon*

Pasco
Rose, Ray Vincent *surgeon*

Pullman
Sclar, David Alexander *medical policy educator*

Redmond
Louie, Ronald Richard *pediatric hematologist, oncologist, educator*

Richland
Yang, I-Yen *internist, acupuncturist*

Seattle
Altman, Leonard Charles *physician*
Artru, Alan Arthur *anesthesiologist, educator*
Berger, Richard Eugene *urologist, educator*
Bredfeldt, James Edward *gastroenterologist, hepatologist*
Broudy, Virginia Constance *hematologist, educator*
Brown, Thomas Joseph *immunologist*
Bursten, Stuart Lowell *physician, biochemist*
Chatard, Peter Ralph Noel Jr. *aesthetic plastic surgeon*
Chen, Leway *cardiologist*
Clarren, Sterling Keith *pediatrician*
Clowes, Alexander Whitehill *surgeon, educator*
Dailey, David Kevin *psychiatrist*
DeAndrea, Gary Anthony *neurologist*
Dewhurst, Timothy Andrew *clinical cardiologist, researcher*
Domino, Karen Barbara *anesthesiology educator*
Downey, Daniel Lee *plastic surgeon*
Engrav, Loren Henry *plastic surgeon*
Furst, Daniel Eric *medical educator*
Garnett, Daniel Joseph *surgeon*
Geiduschek, Jeremy Mark *pediatric anesthesiologist*
Giedt, Walvin Roland *epidemiologist, educator*
Gloyd, Stephen Stewart *physician, educator, health facility administrator*
Greene, Martin Lee *internist*
Han, Mao-Tang *surgeon, researcher*
Hargiss, James Leonard *ophthalmologist*
Hudgins, Louanne *pediatrician, educator*
Johnson, Lloyd P. *surgeon, educator*
Kalina, Robert Edward *physician, educator*
Kowdley, Kris V. *gastroenterologist, hepatologist, educator*
Kozarek, Richard Anthony *gastroenterologist, educator*
Kraft, George Howard *physician, educator*
Krohn, Kenneth Albert *radiology educator*
Langman, Alan Wayne *physician*
Leininger, Chris J. *physician*
Linker, David Thor *cardiologist*
Mangham, Charles Adley, Sr. *psychiatrist, psychoanalyst*
Mannik, Mart *medical educator*
Marks, William H. *organ transplant program director, pharmacologist, pharmacognosist, and director for laboratory transplantation biology*
May, Eugene Frank *neuro-ophthalmologist*
Mehlum, David L. *otolaryngologist*
Mills, Richard Pence *ophthalmologist*
Mitchell, Michael Ernst *pediatric urologist, educator*
Mohai, Peter *internist, educator*
Nelson, James Alonzo *radiologist, educator*
Neppe, Vernon Michael *neuropsychiatrist, author, educator*
Ochs, Hans Dieter *pediatrics educator*
Orcutt, James Craig *ophthalmologist*
Paauw, Douglas Stephen *medical educator, primary care physician*
Pagon, Roberta Anderson *pediatrics educator*
Pellegrini, Carlos Alberto *surgeon, educator*
Pious, Donald A. *medical educator*
Plorde, James Joseph *physician, educator*
Pritchett, James W. *orthopaedic surgeon, educator*
Reif, Mary Ellen *neurologist*
Ries, Richard Kirkland *psychiatrist*
Rivara, Frederick Peter *pediatrician, educator*
Rutledge, Joe *pathologist, scientist*
Sale, George Edgar *physician*
Sarnat, Harvey Barry *pediatric neurology educator*
Schimmelbusch, Werner Helmut *psychiatrist*
Schwartz, Michael Warren *physician investigator*
Scott, John Carlyle *gynecologist, oncologist*
Spoerl, Otto Heinrich *psychiatrist, educator*
Staheli, Lynn Taylor *pediatric orthopedist, educator*
Stevenson, James Geoffrey *pediatrician and cardiologist*
Tapper, David *pediatric surgeon*
Tenney, William Frank *pediatrician*
Thomas, Edward Donnall *physician, researcher*
Toomey, Hugh Edward *orthopedist, surgeon*
Veith, Richard Charles *geriatric psychiatrist, educator*
Vincenzi, Frank Foster *pharmacology educator*
Welk, Richard Andrew *plastic surgeon*
Willkens, Robert F. *interist, rheumatologist*
Winn, H. Richard *surgeon*

Selah
Wolf, John Arthur, Jr. *urologist*

Shoreline
Hondl, Edeltraud A. *retired psychiatrist*

Silverdale
Walcott, William Oliver *family practice physician*

Spokane
Dittman, William Albert, Sr. *hematologist*
Gibson, Melvin Roy *pharmacognosy educator*
James, Norman John *plastic and reconstructive hand surgeon*
Lovell, Tim P. *orthopedic surgeon*
Luna, Gregory Kevin *surgeon*

Tacoma
Cheah, Keong-Chye *psychiatrist*
Chen, Stephen Shau-tsi *psychiatrist, physiologist*
Flick, Gervase Mead *surgeon*
Hinson, Roger Mack *physician*
Irish, Thomas Judson *plastic surgeon*
Nazaire, Michel Harry *physician*
Rawlings, James Scott *neonatologist*
Thrasher, James Brantley *surgeon*
Verhey, Joseph William *psychiatrist, educator*
White, Matthew *family practice physician*

Vancouver
Hall, Madelyn Gael Priebe *medical librarian*

Walla Walla
Simon, Richard DeLoe, Jr. *internist*

Wellpinit
Riley, Richard Leon *psychiatrist, consultant*

Wenatchee
Knecht, Ben Harrold *surgeon*
Sorom, Terry Allen *ophthalmic surgeon*

Woodinville
Lipton, Judith Eve *psychiatrist*

Yakima
Cleary, Sean Fulton *radiation oncologist*
Newstead, Robert Richard *urologist*

WYOMING

Buffalo
Watkins, Eugene Leonard *surgeon, educator*

Casper
Cole, Malvin *neurologist, educator*
Frary, Timothy Neil *physician assistant*

Cheyenne
Flick, William Fredrick *surgeon*
Malm, Ronald Lee *physician*
Merrell, Arthur Nelson *psychiatrist*

Gillette
Naramore, James Joseph *family practice physician, educator*

Powell
Cooperman, Oliver B(urton) *psychiatrist*

Rock Springs
Guicheteau, John Edward *internist, respiratory therapy physician*

Sheridan
Batty, Hugh Kenworthy *physician*

Story
Hoadley, Joseph E. *retired physician*

MILITARY ADDRESSES OF THE UNITED STATES

EUROPE

APO
Wilson, Robert McClain *plastic surgeon, educator*

CANADA

ALBERTA

Calgary
Leung, Alexander Kwok-Chu *pediatrician educator*

Edmonton
Dewhurst, William George *psychiatrist, educator, research director*

BRITISH COLUMBIA

Vancouver
Simons, Richard Keith *medical educator*

West Vancouver
Knauff, Hans Georg *physician, educator*

ADDRESS UNPUBLISHED

Aagaard, Earla Gardner *retired psychiatrist*
Altman, Adele Rosenhain *radiologist*
Angel, Armando Carlos *rheumatologist, internist*
Angelov, George Angel *pediatrician, anatomist, teratologist*
Atkinson, Roland Moore *psychiatrist*
Bachicha, Joseph Alfred *obstetrician, gynecologist, educator*
Beach, William Brown *psychiatrist, educator*
Bell, Douglas Scott *internist*
Bergin, Colleen Joan *medical educator*
Boddie, Lewis Franklin *obstetrics and gynecology educator*
Brehove, Theresa M. *physician*
Brewer, Timothy Francis, III *retired cardiologist*
Bruggeman, Lewis LeRoy *radiologist*
Bussey, George Davis *psychiatrist*
Compton, Allan *psychoanalyst, researcher*
Cozen, Lewis *orthopedic surgeon*
Culver, Larry G. *medical research executive*
Deyo, Richard Alden *medical educator*
Douglass, John Michael *internist*
Erickson, Russell John *pediatrician*
Fineman, Jo Ann Booze *psychiatrist, psychoanalyst*
Foster, Lawrence Hunt, Jr. *physician, plastic surgeon*
Friedman, Emanuel *physician, educator*
Garvey, Justine Spring *immunochemistry educator, biology educator*
Geis, John Richard *plastic surgeon*
Giem, Ross Nye, Jr. *surgeon*
Gottschalk, Adele M. *surgeon*
Graham, James Herbert *dermatologist*
Greene, Laurence Whitridge, Jr. *surgical educator*
Greenhouse, Lynn *physician*
Halliday, William Ross *retired physician, speleologist, writer*
Hamilton, Thomas Percy *preventive medicine physician, military officer*
Hansen, Lowell Howard *physician*
Heiner, Douglas Cragun *pediatrician, educator*
Howard, Mark W. *surgeon*
Jackman, Jay M. *psychiatrist*
James, Freburn Leroy *pathologist, retired*
Kanner, Steven Brian *immunologist*
Karpilow, Craig *physician*
Kaunitz, Jonathan Davidson *physician*
Kendall, Harry Ovid *internist*
Kern, Donald Michael *internist*
Knauss, Thomas Alvin *pediatric neurologist*
Kornfeld, Peter *internist*
Kost, Gerald Joseph *physician, scientist*
Krippaehne, Marion Carolyn *physician*
Levin, Jack *physician, educator, biomedical investigator*
Levy, Wayne David *psychiatrist*
Lewis, Sandra Jean *cardiologist*
Lieberman, Carole Ilene *media psychiatrist, commentator, consultant*
Major, Carol Ann *perinatologist, obstetrician/gynecologist*
Mandac, Benjamin Reyes *pediatric rehabilitation physician*
Metzner, Richard Joel *psychiatrist, psychopharmacologist, educator*
Meyer, Greg Charles *psychiatrist*
Minard, Eugene Watkins *consulting forensic psychiatrist*
Mutafova-Yambolieva, Violeta Nikolova *pharmacologist*
Nelson, Scott Haviland *psychiatrist, administrator*
Nelson, William Rankin *surgeon, educator*
Nora, James Jackson *physician, author, educator*
Norton, Steven David *immunologist, researcher*
Oates, Joyce Marie *psychiatrist*
Pardue, A. Michael *plastic and reconstructive surgeon*
Philipp, John Joseph *family physician, managed care consultant*
Pomeroy, Kent Lytle *physical medicine and rehabilitation physician*
Popp, Dale D. *orthopedic surgeon*
Rasgon, Barry Mitchell *otolaryngologist*
Reichman, Ronald Peter *medical educator*
Renson, Jean Felix *psychiatry educator*
Ringel, Steven Peter *neurology educator*
Roberts, Alan Silverman *orthopedic surgeon*
Schneck, Stuart Austin *retired neurologist, educator*
Scrimshaw, George Currie *retired plastic surgeon*
Seidel, James Stephen *pediatrician, educator*
Silverberg, Stuart Owen *obstetrician, gynecologist*
Stone, James Robert *surgeon*

Stoney, Ronald J. vascular surgeon, educator
Storek, Jan hematologist, oncologist, researcher
Taranta, Angelo (Visca) physician, educator
Tavoularis, Marjorie Osterwise psychiatrist
Theodosakis, Jason J. physician
Thurmond, Amy Suzanne physician, radiologist, educator
Turner, William Joseph retired psychiatrist
Turrill, Fred Lovejoy surgeon
Uman, Stephen Jonas physician
Van Brunt, Edmund Ewing physician
Vetto, John Tyson surgeon, educator
Vogelsang, Philip John pathologist
Watring, Watson Glenn gynecologic oncologist, educator
Webb, Eric Seth physician
Werbach, Melvyn Roy physician, writer
Williams, Ronald Lee pharmacologist
Wong, Jeffrey Yun Chung radiation oncologist, medical researcher
Yandell, George Wilson physician, psychiatrist

HUMANITIES: LIBERAL STUDIES

UNITED STATES

ALASKA

Anchorage
Bunde, Con communication educator, state legislator
Stuart, Laurie K. English language educator, court transcriber

Barrow
MacLean, Edna Ahgeak language educator, researcher

Fairbanks
Falk, Marvin William historian, bibliographer

Juneau
Ruotsala, James Alfred historian, writer

Valdez
Clifton, Dorothy I. historian, inn proprietor

ARIZONA

Apache Junction
Ransom, Evelyn Naill language educator, linguist

Davis-Monthan AFB
Miller, Charles Wallace historian, environmental geologist

Flagstaff
Marcus, Karen Melissa foreign language educator

Glendale
Quirós-Winemiller, Bel language educator
Tuman, Walter Vladimir Russian language educator, researcher

Green Valley
Brewington, Arthur William retired English language educator
Elliott, Jeanne Bate retired English educator, writer

Lake Havasu City
Brydon, Ruth Vickery history educator

Mesa
Cárdenas, Antonio Contreras foreign language educator
Cervantes, James Valentine English language educator

Peoria
Bergmann, Fredrick Louis English language educator, theater historian

Phoenix
Cristiano, Marilyn Jean speech communication educator
Kohi, Susan bilingual educator, translator
Kupel, Douglas Edward historian
Maimon, Elaine Plaskow English educator, university provost
Rister, Gene Arnold humanities educator
Socwell, Margaret Gertrude Osborn Harris reading and language arts educator, consultant
Tompkins, Cynthia Margarita women's studies educator

Prescott
Moses, Elbert Raymond, Jr. speech and dramatic arts educator

Scottsdale
Gwinn, Mary Dolores philosopher, author, speaker
Mousseux, Renate language educator

Snowflake
Hiatt, Holly Marlane history educator

Surprise
Clark, Lloyd historian, educator

Tempe
Bjork, Robert Eric language professional educator
Carlson, Ronald Frank educator, fiction writer
Doebler, Bettie Anne language educator, researcher, writer
Hendrickson, William Lee French language educator

Tucson
Adamson, H. Douglas English language educator
Aiken, Susan Hardy English language educator
Allbaugh, Mary Ellen reading educator
Arrieta, Olivia humanities educator
Austin, John Norman classics educator
Beck, Jonathan P. French language educator
Birkinbine, John, II philatelist
Canfield, J(ohn) Douglas English language educator
Chisholm, David Hollister German studies educator
Classen, Albrecht German language educator
Dahood, Roger English literature educator
Eaton, Richard Maxwell history educator
Enos, Theresa English educator, editor
Evers, Lawrence Joseph English language educator
Foley, Peter Wilhelm Christian humanities educator, researcher, translator
Furlow, Mary Beverley English language educator
Goldman, Alvin Ira philosopher, educator
Hogle, Jerrold Edwin English language educator
Karimi, Simin linguist, educator
Kellogg, Frederick historian, educator
Kleese, William Carl genealogy research consultant
Kovach, Thomas Allen educator
Martinez, Oscar Jaquez educator, author
Monk, Janice Jones women's studies researcher, university program administrator
Moore, Alison Lynn English educator, author
Negley, Floyd Rollin genealogist, retired army officer and civilian military employee
Parry, Ellwood Comly, III art history educator
Schechter, Roberta Lynne English educator
Schulz, Renate Adele German studies and second language acquisition educator
Tao, Chia-lin Pao humanities educator
Wearing, J.P. English language educator
Wright, George Thaddeus humanities educator

Winslow
Kaliher, Michael Dennis historian, book seller

CALIFORNIA

Alhambra
Nielsen, David Edward history and physical education educator

Anaheim
Borges, Stephany Patricia English language educator

Aptos
Kiehl, Kathleen Suzanne English language educator

Arcadia
Yen, Wen-Hsiung language professional educator

Azusa
Glyer, Diana Pavlac English language educator

Bakersfield
Boyd, William Harland historian
Kegley, Jacquelyn Ann philosophy educator
Schmidt, Joanne (Josephine Anne Schmidt) language educator

Bellflower
Hastings, Elisa Kipp English language educator

Belmont
Wolterbeek, Marc William English language educator

Berkeley
Adelman, Janet Ann English literature educator
Anderson, William Scovil classics educator
Baas, Jacquelynn art historian, museum administrator
Barish, Jonas A. English educator
Bloom, Robert language professional educator
Booth, Stephen Walter English language educator
Brinner, William Michael Near Eastern studies educator
Falk, Candace Serena historian, biographer, documentary editor
Faulhaber, Charles Bailey Spanish language educator, librarian
Feldman, Gerald Donald history educator
Friedman, Donald M. English language educator
Heinze, Ruth-Inge Asian studies educator, researcher, writer
Hollinger, David Albert historian, educator
Jay, Martin Evan historian, educator
Johnson, David George Chinese history educator
Larson, James Lee Scandinavian languages educator
Mace, Susan Lidgate comparative literature educator, researcher
Mazurek, Stephen Jerome foreign language educator
Nagler, Michael Nicholas classics and comparative literature educator
Partridge, Loren Wayne art historian, educator
Richmond, Hugh Macrae English language educator
Rosenmeyer, Thomas Gustav retired classics educator, researcher
Shannon, Thomas Frederic German language educator
Stern, David Gerald philosophy educator
Ting, Pang-Hsin linguistics educator
Wilson, W(illiam) Daniel language professional educator
Wright, Georgia Sommers educator, video producer

Beverly Hills
Kravitz, Ellen King musicologist, educator

Big Bear City
Hewitt, Jerene Cline English language educator

Calexico
Shumaker, Jeanette Roberts English language educator

Carmel
Feisthamel, Judy language educator, interpreter, translator
McGlynn, Betty Hoag art historian

Carson
Butler, Peter, Jr. retired educator
Grenier, Judson A., Jr. history educator

Claremont
Ackerman, Gerald Martin art historian, consultant
Davis, Nathaniel humanities educator
Elsbree, Langdon English language educator
Fossum, Robert H(eyerdahl) retired English literature educator
Neumann, Harry philosophy educator
Niven, William John historian, educator
Rolle, Myra Moss (Myra E. Moss) philosophy educator, author, translator
Roth, John King philosopher, educator
Wheeler, Geraldine Hartshorn historian
Young, Howard Thomas foreign language educator

Cool
Sheridan, George Groh English and history educator

Corte Madera
Layman, Richard Dean historian, editor

Costa Mesa
Prout, Carl Wesley history educator

Covina
Straw, Ellen Katrina English educator, writer

Culver City
Forman, Joel Jon numismatic appraiser

Cupertino
Dunbar, Maurice Victor English language educator
Melendy, Howard Brett historian, educator
Tice, Bradley Scott humanities educator
Williams, James Calhoun history educator, public historian, consultant

Davis
Alarcón, Francisco Xavier poet, educator
Fishman, Stanley Jerome (Jerry Fishman) retired English language educator
Gilbert, Sandra M. English language educator, writer
Howard, Seymour
Manoliu-Manea, Maria linguist
Osborn, Marijane English language professional/educator
Tinney, Thomas Milton, Sr. genealogical research specialist
Torrance, Robert Mitchell comparative literature educator

Downey
Petrovich, Peter Yurosh English and foreign language educator, writer

El Cerrito
Kuo, Ping-chia historian, educator
Ma, L. Eve Armentrout lawyer, nonprofit administrator, historical consultant

Eureka
Peterson, Gary Taylor English educator

Fallbrook
Burns, Louis Francis retired history educator

Fremont
Ortiz, Beverly Ruth ethnographic consultant

Fresno
Chang, Hsu Hsin (Sidney H. Chang) history educator
Clifton, Michael Edward English language educator
Genini, Ronald Walter history educator, historian
Kouymjian, Dickran art historian, Orientalist, educator

Fullerton
Dick, Tessa Busby English educator
Hardy, Blaine Carmon history educator
Hobson, Wayne K. humanities educator
Loewy, Dana English educator, translator
Orr, John Christopher English language educator

Glendale
DeGrassi, Leonard Rene art historian, educator

Guerneville
Johnston, Andrea Ruth writer, educator

Hayward
Reichman, Henry Frederick history educator

Huntington Beach
Boyer, Nancy Gail language educator

Irvine
Clark, Michael Phillip English educator
Hufbauer, Karl George historian of science
Key, Mary Ritchie (Mrs. Audley E. Patton) linguist, author, educator
Nester, Robbi Lynne Kellman writing and literature educator
Norris, Margot Christa English language educator
O'Brien, Patricia Ann history educator
Toliver, Harold Earl language professional, English

Kingsburg
Garrigus, Charles Byford retired literature educator

La Jolla
Allison, Henry Edward philosophy educator
Friedman, Richard Elliott Hebrew and literature educator
McDonald, Marianne classicist
Miyoshi, Masao English literature educator, writer

La Mirada
Buchanan, Paul William English language educator
Rambo, Elizabeth Louise English literature educator

Long Beach
Alkana, Linda Kelly history educator
Beebe, Sandra E. retired English language educator, artist, writer
Lau, Beth English language educator
Polakoff, Keith Ian historian, university administrator
Sater, William Frederick history educator, writer
Tang, Paul Chi Lung philosophy educator
Yousef, Fathi Salaama communication studies educator, management consultant

Los Angeles
Allen, Paula Gunn English educator
Alpers, Edward Alter history educator
Bahr, Diana Meyers humanities educator
Bahr, Ehrhard German language educator
Baldwin, Peter history educator
Barber, Elizabeth Jane Wayland archeology and linguistics educator, researcher
Berst, Charles Ashton English educator
Brier, Peter A. English literature educator
Burns, Robert Ignatius historian, educator, clergyman
Cherkin, Adina interpreter, translator
Cheung, King-Kok English language educator
Cortinez, Veronica literature educator
De Jong-Hawley, Cherie reading and language arts educator
Dumitrescu, Domnita Spanish language educator, researcher
Dyck, Andrew Roy philologist, educator
Eckert, Geraldine Gonzales language professional, educator, entrepreneur
Eggebroten, Anne Marie literature educator
Ehret, Christopher Paul history and linguistics educator
Frank, Peter Solomon art critic, curator
Gómez, Ricardo Juan philosophy educator
Harrison, Thomas Joseph Italian and comparative literature educator
Hundley, Norris Cecil, Jr. history educator
Kemp, Anthony Maynard English educator
Kirsner, Robert Shneider Dutch and Afrikaans educator
Klein, Snira L(ubovsky) Hebrew language and literature educator
Krance, Charles Andrew literature educator
Li, David Leiwei English and Asian American studies educator
Mellor, Ronald John history educator
Miles, Richard Robert art historian, writer
Peditto, Christopher Natale humanities, English and communications educator
Plann, Susan Joan linguist, foreign language educator
Sarris, Greg Native American educator
Schutz, John Adolph historian, educator, former university dean
See, Carolyn English language educator, novelist, book critic
Sellin, Paul Roland retired English literature educator
Shaw, Stanford J. history educator
Shideler, Ross Patrick foreign language and comparative literature educator, author, translator, poet
Sonnenfeld, Albert French language and comparative literature educator, food historian
Steele, Timothy Reid English language educator, poet
Stern, Anita Enkel English language educator
Wills, John Elliot, Jr. history educator, writer
Wu, Qingyun Chinese language and literature educator

Los Gatos
Rogers, Franklin Robert former language educator, writer
Tinsley, Barbara Sher historian, educator, writer

Los Olivos
Norris, James Leo "Jim" historian, editor, publisher

Marysville
Moorman, Lawrence Alan humanities educator

Merced
Elliott, Gordon Jefferson English language educator

Midway City
McCawley, William Dale, II ethnohistorian, author, corporate accountant

Millbrae
Palmer, Patricia Ann Texter English language educator

Montclair
Haage, Robert Mitchell retired history educator, organization leader

Monterey
Kennedy-Minott, Rodney international relations educator, former ambassador
Shropshire, Helen Mae historian

Moorpark
Hall, Elton A. philosophy educator

Moreno Valley
Kari, Daven Michael religion educator

Northridge
Broesamle, John Joseph history educator
Flores, William Vincent Latin American studies educator
Larson, Gale Kjelshus English language educator, consultant
Lothrop, Gloria Ricci educator
Peters, John U. English language educator
Watson, Julia women's studies and liberal studies educator

Novato
Uhalley, Stephen, Jr. history educator

Oakland
Cai, Xing Yi art historian, educator
Walkup, Kathleen Ann English language educator

Orange
Flores, Yolanda literature educator
Krug, Donna Rebecca Dondes history educator, small business owner

Oxnard
Hill, Alice Lorraine history, genealogy and social researcher, educator

Pacific Grove
Elinson, Henry David artist, language educator

Palos Verdes Peninsula
Thomas, Pearl Elizabeth English educator

Pasadena
Kevles, Daniel Jerome history educator, writer
Woodward, James Francis humanities educator

Placentia
Nettleship, Lois Ellen *history educator*

Pleasant Hill
Rawls, James Jabus *history educator*

Pomona
Cook, Stanley Joseph *English language educator, poet*
Jacobsen, Michael Anthony *art historian, educator*
Morsberger, Robert Eustis *English language educator*

Poway
Terry, Patricia A. *literature educator*

Rancho Palos Verdes
Sun, Teresa Chi-Ching *foreign languages educator*

Redlands
Bricker, Lauren Weiss *historian*
Stuart, Robert Lee *English language educator*

Rialto
Walker, Jeanne Claire *retired English educator, writer*

Riverside
Bensick, Carol Marie *English literature educator*
Daviau, Donald George *foreign language educator*
Decker, Catherine Helen *English language educator*
Dunn, Robert Paul *English language educator*
Grimm, Reinhold *humanities educator*
Kollitz, Janice Arlene *English literature educator, freelance writer*
Loveless, Edna Maye *English language educator*
Snyder, Henry Leonard *history educator, bibliographer*

Rocklin
Dickson, David Douglas *humanities educator*

Rohnert Park
Martinez, Elizabeth Coonrod *Spanish language educator*

Sacramento
Bankowsky, Richard James *English educator*
Carr, Gerald Francis *German educator*
Meindl, Robert James *English language educator*
Nesbitt, Paul Edward *historian, author, educator*
Reed, Nancy Boyd *English language and elementary education educator*

San Anselmo
Ocker, Christopher Michael *historian, educator*

San Bernardino
Ruml, Treadwell *English language educator*

San Diego
Baker, James Rupert *English educator*
Butler, Gerald Joseph *English and comparative literature educator*
Cain, Seymour *historian, philosopher and writer*
Chamberlin, Eugene Keith *historian, educator*
González-Trujillo, César Augusto *Chicano studies educator, writer*
Gross, George Clayburn *English language educator*
Huggins, Earl McClure *English language educator*
Kehler, Dorothea Faith *English educator*
Kennedy, Rick Alan *history educator*
Peterson, Richard Hermann *history educator, retired*
Starr, Raymond G. *history educator*
Vanderwood, Paul Joseph *history educator*
Velasquez, Ana Maria *languages educator*

San Francisco
Batchelor, Karen Lee *English language educator*
Compton, James Vincent *retired history educator*
Cornford, Adam Francis *literature and writing educator, poet*
Costa-Zalessow, Natalia *foreign language educator*
Gleason, Elisabeth Gregorich *history educator*
Hadreas, Peter James *philosophy educator*
Landar, Herbert Jay *linguistics educator, author*
Langton, Daniel Joseph *English, writing educator, poet*
Marmysz, John Alexander *philosophy educator, consultant*
Nakayama, Randall Shige *English language educator*
Needleman, Jacob *philosophy educator, writer*
Schlesinger, Norma H. *art historian, writer*
Turks, Victor Leonard *English language educator*
Wilczek, John Franklin *history educator*

San Jose
Maio, Samuel Joseph *English language and literature educator*
Sabalius, Romey *foreign language and literature educator*

San Luis Obispo
Duffy, Bernard Karl *educator*
Estes, Angela M. *English language educator*
Gish, Robert Franklin *English language educator, writer*

San Marcos
Christman, Albert Bernard *historian*
Gowen, Brent Darrell *English educator, writer*
Gundersen, Joan Rezner *historian, educator*
Tanner, John Douglas, Jr. *history educator, writer*
Watts, Jill Marie *history educator*

San Mateo
Petit, Susan Yount *French educator*

San Rafael
Dougherty, (Mary) Patricia *history educator*

Santa Barbara
Bliss, Lee *English language educator*
Brownlee, Wilson Elliot, Jr. *history educator*
Duffy, Andrew Enda *language educator*
Hansen, Robert Gunnard *philatelist*
Hoffmeister, Gerhart *German language educator*
Lim, Shirley Geok Lin *English language educator, author*
Moir, Alfred Kummer *art history educator*
Rickels, Laurence Arthur *foreign language educator*
Willis, Paul Jonathan *English language educator*

Santa Clara
Mori, Maryellen Toman *language educator, translator, literature educator*
Pierson, Peter O'Malley *history educator*

Santa Cruz
Berkhofer, Robert Frederick, Jr. *history educator*
Cioc, Mark *history educator*
Lieberman, Fredric *ethnomusicologist, educator*
Suckiel, Ellen Kappy *philosophy educator*

Santa Monica
Kotansky, Roy D. *ancient languages, religion and culture educator*
Schipper, Merle *art historian and critic, exhibition curator*

Santa Rosa
Gorris, Wendy Kathleen *English language educator*

Simi Valley
Lee, Nancy Jane McCleary *American studies educator*

Spring Valley
Clark, John DeWitt *retired fine arts educator, sculptor*

Stanford
Carson, Clayborne *history educator*
Castle, Terry Jacqueline *English language educator*
Duus, Peter *history educator*
Guerard, Albert Joseph *retired modern literature educator, author*
Lohnes, Walter F. W. *German language and literature educator*
Offen, Karen Marie *historian, educator*
Perry, John Richard *philosophy educator*
Ruotolo, Lucio Peter *English language educator*
Steidle, Edward *humanities educator*
Stone, Wilfred H. *English educator, writer*
Traugott, Elizabeth Closs *linguistics educator and researcher*

Stockton
Lutz, Reinhart *English language educator, writer*
Rogers, William Darrow *history educator*
Ward, Barry John *historian*
Wonder, John Paul *educator*

Truckee
Sylvester, June Gladden *English literature educator*

Ukiah
Lohrli, Anne *retired English educator, author*

Union City
Cobos, Josè Manuel *Spanish language educator*

Van Nuys
Ross, Kelley Lee, II *philosophy educator, politician*
Zucker, Alfred John *English educator, academic administrator*

Walnut
Dibell, Marta Lee *foreign language educator*

Woodland Hills
Pickard, Dean *philosophy and humanities educator*

COLORADO

Boulder
Baena, Julio *Spanish language and literature educator*
Barchilon, Jacques *foreign language educator, researcher, writer*
Colwell, James Lee *humanities educator*
Del Caro, Adrian *German language and literature educator*
Farago, Claire J. *art historian, educator*
Jamieson, Dale Walter *philosophy and biology educator*
Jordan, Isolde Jahncke *Spanish and Portuguese language educator*
Maier, Edward Karl *foreign language educator*
Main, Gloria Lund *history educator*
Menn, Lise *linguistics educator*
Moulakis, Athanasios *philosopher, educator*
Schütrumpf, Eckart Ernst *classical languages and philosophy educator*

Colorado Springs
Blackburn, Alexander Lambert *author, English literature educator*
Bryson, Dorothy Printup *retired educator*
Newmiller, William Ernest *English educator*

Denver
Black, Robert Clifford, III *history educator*
Chapman, Gerald Wester *educator*
Espenlaub, Margo Linn *women's studies educator*
Fleck, Richard Francis *English language educator, writer*
Porter, Donna Jean *genealogist*
Ronning, Charlotte Jean *foreign language educator*
Storey, Brit Allan *historian*
Templin, John Alton *historical theology educator, minister*
Wetzel, Jodi (Joy Lynn Wetzel) *history and women's studies educator*

Fort Collins
Berwanger, Eugene Harley *history educator*
Keane, Kevin Patrick *philosopher, consultant*
Knight, Thomas Joseph *history educator*
Tremblay, William Andrew *English language educator*

Golden
Kubias, Craig Owen *philosophy educator*
Quirke, Terence Thomas, Jr. *genealogist, retired geologist*

Grand Junction
Fay, Abbott Eastman *history educator*

Greeley
Arneson, Patricia Ann *speech communication educator*
Wilson, Sharon Rose *educator, researcher*

Lakewood
Joy, Carla Marie *history educator*

Littleton
Champney, Linda Lucas *reading educator*
Dolan, Patrick Thomas *English educator*
Elrick, Billy Lee *English language educator*

Pueblo
Farwell, Hermon Waldo, Jr. *parliamentarian, educator, former speech communication educator*
Sheidley, William Edwards *English language educator*
Taylor, Cynthia Hinkel *English literature educator*
Vorpagel, Wilbur Charles *historical consultant*

Sterling
Christian, Roland Carl (Bud Christian) *retired English and speech communications educator*

HAWAII

Honolulu
Aung-Thwin, Michael Arthur *history educator*
Ball, Robert Jerome *classics educator*
Chandler, Paul Michael *Spanish and Portuguese educator, homeless advocate*
Chapman, William Ryan *history educator*
Fujita, James Hiroshi *history educator*
Hoffmann, Kathryn Ann *humanities educator*
Howes, William Craig *English educator*
La Luzerne-Oi, Sally Ann *humanities educator*
Moody, Raymond Albert *foreign language educator*
Moore, Willis Henry Allphin *history and geography educator*
Nagtalon-Miller, Helen Rosete *humanities educator*
Newby, Idus Atwell *historian, educator*
Onopa, Robert Lawrence *English language educator*
Pagotto, Louise *English language educator*
Wayne, Valerie *English language educator*

Keaau
Bailey, Charles-James Nice *linguistics educator*

Pahala
Cuddihy, Geraldine Noriko *English educator*

Pearl City
Roberts, Norman Frank *English composition and linguistics educator*

IDAHO

Blackfoot
McBurney, Constance C. *foreign language educator*

Boise
Lovin, Hugh Taylor *history educator*
Maguire, James Henry *English language educator*
Neil, J. Meredith *historian*
Nguyen, King Xuan *language educator*
Odahl, Charles M. *history and languages educator*
Wells, Merle William *historian, state archivist*

Moscow
Harris, Robert Dalton *history educator, researcher, writer*
Schwantes, Carlos Arnaldo *history educator, consultant*

Pocatello
Van Pelt, Tamise Jo *English educator*

MINNESOTA

Saint Paul
Stephenson, Scot Alan *English educator*

MONTANA

Bozeman
Allard, James Willard, Jr. *philosophy educator*
Mentzer, Raymond A. *history educator*

Columbia Falls
McKay, Kathryn Lee *historian*

Dillon
Weltzien, O(liver) Alan *English educator, researcher*

Helena
Cockhill, Brian Edward *historical society executive*

Missoula
Bier, Jesse *literature educator*
Brenner, Gerry *English educator*
Charbonneau, Joanne Adrienne *literature and humanities educator*
Elliott, Deni *ethics educator*
Flores, Dan Louie *history educator*
Lauren, Paul Gordon *history educator*
Schwaller, John Frederick *historian*

NEVADA

Las Vegas
Abramson, Albert *television historian, consultant*
Barnes, H. Lee *English and creative writing educator, writer*
Bellver, Catherine Gullo *foreign language educator*
Buechler, Ralph Wolfgang *German language and literature educator*
Hudgins, Christopher Chapman *English educator*
Lang-Peralta, Linda Ann *English language educator*
McCafferty, Steven Garth *English educator*
McComb, Karla Joann *foreign language educator, curriculum administrator, consultant*
Strauss, Paul Edward *English language educator*
Walton, (Delvy) Craig *philosopher, educator*

North Las Vegas
Beachley, DeAnna Eileen *history educator*
Green, Michael Scott *history educator, consultant, columnist*
Miller, Eleanor *English language and literature educator*
Schmitt, Paul John *history and geography educator*

Reno
Branch, Michael Paul *humanities educator*
Brown, Richard Elwood *educator*
Ronald, Ann *English literature educator*
Simonian, Lane Peter *history educator*

NEW MEXICO

Albuquerque
Bybee, Joan Lea *linguistics educator*
DePalo, William Anthony, Jr. *Latin American studies educator*
Feller, Daniel M. *history educator*
Gatlin, Karen Christensen *English language educato*
Hannan, Barbara Ellon *philosophy educator, lawyer*
Himmerich y Valencia, Robert Theron *historian, farmer*
Joost-Gaugier, Christiane Louise *art history educato*
Kutvirt, Duda Chytilova (Ruzena) *scientific translator*
Lind, Levi Robert *classics educator, author*
Peña, Juan José *interpreter*
Rabinowitz, Howard Neil *history educator*
Whidden, Mary Bess *English language educator*
White, Robert Rankin *writer and historian, hydrologist*
Witemeyer, Hugh Hazen *English language educator*
Young, Mary Jane *American studies and folklore educator*

Las Cruces
Matray, James Irving *history educator*
Newman, Edgar Leon *historian, educator*
Wilson, Keith Charles *retired English educator, poet, short story writer*

Las Vegas
Croxton, Dorothy Audrey Simpson *speech educator*

Los Lunas
Field, Susan Lee *English educator*

Portales
Oldknow, Antony *English educator, writer, publishe*

Santa Fe
Maehl, William Henry *historian, university administrator, educational consultant*
Pesic, Peter Dragan *liberal arts educator*

NEW YORK

Buffalo
Riepe, Dale Maurice *philosopher, writer, illustrator, educator, Asian art dealer*

NORTH CAROLINA

Durham
Güzeldere, Güven *philosophy and cognitive educator, computer science consultant*

OHIO

Oxford
Pletsch, Carl Erich *history educator*

Wooster
Glasgow, Janis Marilyn *foreign language educator*

OREGON

Ashland
Weeks, Roger Wolcott, Jr. *retired German and Russian language educator*

Bend
Donohue, Stacey Lee *English language educator*

Corvallis
King, David Burnett *history educator*
Rudinsky, Norma Leigh *English language educator, translator*
Sarasohn, Lisa Tunick *history educator*

Eugene
Albert-Galtier, Alexandre *language educator*
Roth, Leland Martin *art and architecture educator*
White, David Olds *researcher, former educator*

Forest Grove
Steele, Michael Rhoads *humanities and peace studies educator, writer*

Mcminnville
Ericksen, Kenneth Jerrold *English literature educator*
Mc Kaughan, Howard Paul *linguistics educator*

Medford
Hamilton, Jay Martin *genealogist, author*
La Lande, Jeffrey Max *historian*

Monmouth
Ferté, Thomas Lee *literature and writing educator, poet, editor*
Harding, Carol Elaine *English language educator*
Soldati, Joseph Aurthur *language and literature educator*
Strand, Cheryl Marie *Spanish language, literature educator*

Netarts
Hartman-Irwin, Mary Frances *retired language professional*

North Bend
Shepard, Robert Carlton *English language educator*

Portland
Beckham, Stephen Dow *history educator*
Ferrua, Pietro Michele Stefano *foreign language educator, writer*
Greco, Gina Lyn *French language and literature educator*
Harris, Frederick Philip *retired philosophy educator*
Henning, Martha Louise *English language educator*
Kimbrell, Leonard Buell *retired art history educator, art appraiser*
Manchester, Arthur Herschell *English and foreign language educator*
Nguyen, Joseph Kim Quy *foreign language educator*
Sacks, David Harris *historian, humanities educator*
Schmidt, Stanley Eugene *retired speech educator*

Salem
Trueblood, Paul Graham *retired English educator, author, editor*

Tolovana Park
Muñoz-Sandoval, Ana F. *Language educator*

Waldport
Harrison, Ruth Feuerborn *retired literature and writing educator*

SOUTH CAROLINA

Columbia
Stetler, Charles Edward *English language educator*

UTAH

Hurricane
Christensen, Steven J. *foreign language educator*

Logan
Butler, Anne M. *history educator*
Crumbley, Paul James *English language educator*
Lye, William Frank *history educator*

Ogden
Burton, Thomas Roghaar *English language educator*
Dohrer, Gary Ray *English language educator*
Laff, Ned Scott *English educator, university administrator*

Provo
Cracroft, Richard Holton *English literature educator*
Hatch, Gary Layne *English educator, writer*
Lyon, James Karl *German language educator*
Paxman, David Brockbank *English literature educator*
Skousen, Royal Jon *linguist*

Saint George
Compton, Merlin David *Spanish language educator*

Salt Lake City
Arrington, Harriet Ann *historian, women's biographer, writer*
Eakle, Arlene Haslam *genealogist*
Garrett, Don James *philosophy educator*
Hibbard, Charles Gustin *historian*
Justesen, Elaine Toomer *genealogist*
Olpin, Robert Spencer *art history educator*
Sanderson, Cathy Ann *histotechnician, researcher*
Yang, Anand Alan *history educator*

WASHINGTON

Bellevue
Kananen, Marvin John *English educator, author*

Bellingham
Fiero, Petra Schug *language professional educator*
Gallay, Alan *history educator*
Johnson, Ellwood Gerd *English language educator*
Purtill, Richard Lawrence *philosopher, writer*

Cheney
Kaufman, Judith Diane *English language educator, consultant*
Smith, Grant William *English language educator, civic fundraiser*
Urcia, Ingeborg *English language educator*

Des Moines
Wilson, Donna Mae *foreign language educator, administrator*

Edmonds
Leblon, Jean Marcel *retired French language educator, consultant*

Ellensburg
Cadello, James Peter *philosopher, educator*
Dunning, William Vance *fine arts educator*
Powell, Joseph Edward *English language educator*

Kirkland
Francis, Mark Edwin *literature educator*

Lacey
Edwards, Margaret H. *English as second language instructor*

Longview
LeMonds, James Edward, Jr. *English language educator*

Medina
Opperman, Hal N. *art historian*

Olympia
Beck, Gordon Eugene *art history educator, consultant*
Chang, Sheng-Tai *English language educator*
Daugherty, Leo *literature and language educator*

Port Angeles
de Broux, Peggy C. *English educator, French educator, publisher*

Pullman
Ashby, Darrel LeRoy *history educator*
Burbick, Joan *English educator*
Frykman, George Axel *history educator, researcher*
McLeod, Susan Margaret *English language educator*
Swan, Susan Linda *history educator*
Wingate, Marcel Edward *speech educator*

Seattle
Abrams, Robert Edward *English educator*
Bachar, Gregory Paul *English educator, editor*
Bacharach, Jere L. *history educator, academic administrator*
Berman, Morris *historian, author*
Bozarth, George S. *historian, musicologist, pianist*
Brand, Gerhard *retired English educator*
Bultmann, William Arnold *historian*
Burt, Eugene Clinton *art historian, library director*
Canaday, Nicholas *retired English educator*
Clauss, James Joseph *classics educator*
Hertling, Gunter Helmut *Germanics educator*
Jones, Edward Louis *historian, educator*
Layton, Marilyn Smith *English language educator*
Long, Mark Chistopher *english educator*
Moore, Ronald Melville *Philosophy educator*
Moss, Melody Ann *history educator, researcher*
Oldknow, Constantina W. *art historian*
Rorabaugh, William Joseph *historian*
Sokoloff, Naomi Beryl *Hebrew language and literature educator*
VanArsdel, Rosemary Thorstenson *English studies educator*
van den Berg, Sara Jane *English educator*
Waluconis, Carl Joseph *English language educator, humanities educator*

Sedro Woolley
Hinckley, Ted C. *historian, educator, writer*

Spokane
Bona, Mary Jo *English educator*
Carlson, Nancy Lee *English language educator*
Carriker, Robert Charles *history educator*
Stackelberg, John Roderick *history educator*

Tacoma
Barnett, Suzanne Wilson *history educator*
Collier, Richard Bangs *philosopher, foundation executive*
Jensen, Mark Kevin *foreign language educator*
Krieger, William Carl *English language educator*
Sloane, Sarah Jane *English educator*

Walla Walla
Stratton, Jon *philosophy educator*

WYOMING

Casper
Demorest, Margaret Orahood *humanities educator*

Laramie
Bantjes, Adrian Alexander *history educator*
Frye, Susan Caroline *English literature educator*
Kohler, Eric Dave *history educator*
Moore, William Howard *history educator, writer*
Nye, Eric William *English language and literature educator*
Roberts, Philip John *history educator, editor*

Riverton
Rogalski, Chester Harry, Jr. *English language and literature educator*

Rock Springs
Taylor, Lee Roger, Jr. *English language educator*

Sheridan
Aguirre-Batty, Mercedes *Spanish and English language and literature educator*

CANADA

ALBERTA

Calgary
Izzo, Herbert John *language and linguistics educator, researcher*
Mc Kenna, Marian Cecilia *historian*

Edmonton
Lynn, Richard John *Chinese language and literature educator*

BRITISH COLUMBIA

Burnaby
Kitchen, John Martin *historian, educator*

Vancouver
Batts, Michael Stanley *German language educator*

ADDRESS UNPUBLISHED

Abraham, Claude Kurt *language educator*
Adams, Harlene Carolyn *speech communications educator*
Alcosser, Sandra *English language educator*
Aubrey, James Reynolds *English educator*
Broadley, Hugh T. *art history educator*
Brody, Jacob Jerome *art history educator*
Bush, Sarah Lillian *historian*
Caldwell, Howard Bryant *English language educator*

Cassel, Susie Lan *literature educator*
Cohen, Henry *historian, retired educator*
Cully, Suzanne María *modern language educator*
Del Purgatorio, Karen Francine *English educator*
Donelson, Kenneth LaVern *English language educator*
Drake, Jessica *dialect and speech coach*
Fleck, Jade Carlson *literature educator, nurse*
Fleck, Stephen Harlan *French language educator*
Frusetta, James Walter *historian, researcher*
Gardner, Barbara Rogers *humanities educator*
Garza, Deborah Jane *bilingual education educator*
Ghymn, Esther Mikyung *English educator, writer*
Goldstein, Marcia *historian, educator, law office administrator*
Hamp-Lyons, Liz *language educator, consultant*
Hansen, Carol Louise *English language educator*
Hanson-Smith, Elizabeth *English language educator, computer consultant*
Huchel, Frederick M. *historian, writer, consultant, speaker*
Hungerford, Edward Arthur *humanities professional educator*
Hutchinson, Joseph Candler *retired foreign language educator*
Ingham, Charles Andrew *English language educator*
Jonsson-Devillers, Edith *foreign language educator*
Kaplan, Robert B. *linguistics educator, consultant, researcher*
Lewis, Norman *English language educator, writer*
Lingenfelter, Andrea D. *translator, writer*
Lobach, Melissa Renee *English language educator*
Maehl, William Harvey *historian, educator*
Matthews, Glenna Christine *historian*
Miller, Robert Ryal *history educator*
Niedzielski, Henri Zygmunt *French and English language educator*
Nix, Nancy Jean *librarian, designer*
Nye, Mary Jo *historian, humanities educator*
Özkaragöz, Inci Zühra *linguist*
Pace, R(alph) Wayne *organizational leadership educator*
Parlante, Diane Goullard *interpreter, translator*
Pearson, Velvet D. *English and composition educator*
Peterson, Barbara Ann Bennett *history educator, television personality*
Porter, James B. *hieroglyphic specialist*
Porter, Marsha Kay *Language professional and educator, English*
Porter, Richard Ernest *speech educator, author*
Raymond, C. Elizabeth *history educator*
Riasanovsky, Nicholas Valentine *historian, educator*
Smith, Susan Lee *history educator*
Sprowl, Dale Rae *English educator*
Thiroux, Emily Lofton *English educator, theater director*
Topik, Steven Curtis *history educator*
Walters, David Wayne *history and government educator, tennis coach*
Weber, Eugen *historian, educator, author*
Wilson, James Brian *English as a second language educator*

HUMANITIES: LIBRARIES

UNITED STATES

ALASKA

Anchorage
Parham, Robert Bruce *archivist*

Juneau
Smith, George Vinal *librarian*

ARIZONA

Ajo
Anderson, John Thomas *librarian, historian*

Avondale
Gillen, Katherine Elizabeth *librarian*

Bullhead City
Huelsbeck, Julie Marie *librarian*

Camp Verde
Hazekamp, Phyllis Wanda Alberts *library director*

Chino Valley
Rothlisberg, Allen Peter *librarian, educator, deacon*

Dewey
Beck, Doris Olson *library media director*

Mesa
Anderson, Herschel Vincent *librarian*

Phoenix
Fox, Frances Juanice *retired librarian, educator*
Norman, Nita Vegamora *librarian, educator, storyteller*

Scottsdale
Biglin, Karen Eileen *library director*
Dalton, Phyllis Irene *library consultant*

Tempe
Borovansky, Vladimir Theodore *librarian*
Maynard, Michael *librarian*
Metros, Mary Teresa *librarian*
Weiler, Dorothy Esser *librarian*

Tucson
Anderson, Rachael Keller *library administrator*
Grams, Theodore Carl William *librarian, educator*
Hurt, Charlie Deuel, III *library school director, educator*
Irwin, Mildred Lorine Warrick *library consultant, civic worker*
Renaud, Robert (Edwin) *librarian*
Wolfe, William Jerome *librarian, English language educator*

CALIFORNIA

Alhambra
Harnsberger, Therese Coscarelli *librarian*

Altadena
Tema, William John *librarian*

Auburn
Sanborn, Dorothy Chappell *retired librarian*

Bakersfield
Duquette, Diane Rhea *library director*

Berkeley
Hanff, Peter Edward *librarian, bibliographer*
Levin, Marc Alan *librarian*
Minudri, Regina Ursula *library director, consultant*
Purat, Jacek *library director*
Spohrer, James Henry *librarian, consultant*

Carlsbad
Kennedy, Charlene Farrington *librarian*

Chula Vista
Vess, Ronald Wayne *librarian*

Coalinga
Anthony, Kay Carroll *librarian*

Culver City
Chow, Judy *library science and information sciences educator*

Cupertino
Fletcher, Homer Lee *librarian*

El Centro
Gotti, Margaret Lynn *library administrator*

Encino
Stover, Mark Edwin *librarian*
Wood, Raymund Francis *retired librarian*

Fremont
Wood, Linda May *librarian*

Fresno
Kallenberg, John Kenneth *librarian*

Granada Hills
Stump, D. Michael *librarian*

Hayward
Ramsdell, Kristin Romeis *librarian, researcher*

Hollywood
Baer, D(avid) Richard *film archive administrator*

Huntington Beach
Halvorsen, Jan La Rayne *library services manager*
Hayden, Ron L. *library director*

Inglewood
Alaniz, Miguel José Castañeda *library director*

Irvine
Laird, Wilbur David, Jr. *bookseller, editor*
Wong, William Sheh *librarian*

Jamestown
Ward, Dennis Francis *librarian*

La Jolla
Mirsky, Phyllis Simon *librarian*

La Mesa
Freeland, Robert Frederick *retired librarian*

Livermore
Love, Sandra Rae *information specialist*

Long Beach
Lathrop, Ann *librarian, educator*

Los Angeles
Barlow, Deborah Lynn *librarian*
Fry, Stephen Michael *music librarian*
Helgeson, Duane Marcellus *retired librarian*
Kent, Susan Goldberg *library director, consultant*
O'Brian, Bonnie Jean *library services supervisor*
Sutherland, Michael Cruise *librarian*

Los Gatos
Willer, Kenneth Henry *library director*

Manteca
Hunt, Charles Amoes *librarian*

Menlo Park
Josephine, Helen Bowden *librarian*
White, Cecil Ray *librarian, consultant*

Mission Hills
Weber, Francis Joseph *archivist, museum director*

Modesto
Kreissman, Starrett *librarian*

Monterey
Reneker, Maxine Hohman *librarian*

Mountain View
Anderson, Barbara Elaine *information specialist, librarian*

Oakland
Bibel, Barbara Mita *librarian*
MacKay, Nancy *librarian, archivist*
Spencer, Dorothy Ann *library director, consultant*
Woodbury, Marda Liggett *librarian, writer*

Orange
Miller, Jean Ruth *librarian*

Palmdale
Moore, Everett LeRoy *library administrator*

Palo Alto
Van Velzer, Verna Jean *retired research librarian*

Pasadena
Bluth, John Frederick *archivist, oral historian*
Buck, Anne Marie *library director, consultant*
Gordon, Helen Wilcox *church librarian*

Pleasant Hill
Gold, Anne Marie *library director*

Redlands
Canterbury, Leslie John *librarian*
Musmann, Klaus *librarian*

Sacramento
Killian, Richard M. *library director*
Liberty, John Joseph *librarian*

San Clemente
Stafford-Mann, Patricia Ann *library and textbook consultant, writer*

San Diego
Ling, David Chang *international book dealer*
Sannwald, William Walter *librarian*

San Francisco
Aldrich, Michael Ray *library curator, health educator*
Cline, Fred Albert, Jr. *retired librarian, conservationist*
Dowlin, Kenneth Everett *librarian*
Eliassen, Meredith Morgan *librarian, archivist, writer*
Shadwick, VirginiaAnn Greer *librarian*

San Jose
Bratman, David Stephen *librarian*
Crowe, Edith Louise *librarian*

San Luis Obispo
Reynolds, Brian Arthur *library director*

San Marcos
Allison, Terry Lane *librarian*

San Marino
Thorpe, James *humanities researcher*
Zoeckler, Linda Kay *librarian art historian*

Santa Ana
Adams, John M. *library director*
Brown, Stephanie Cecile *librarian, writer*

Santa Clara
Hopkinson, Shirley Lois *library science educator*

Santa Monica
Levin, Barry Raymond *rare book dealer*

Seaside
Hogan, Eddy *library director*

Sebastopol
Sabsay, David *library consultant*

Sierra Madre
Duran, Margaret Adelaide Proctor *librarian*

Simi Valley
Vitt, Lisa Osburn *archivist*

Stanford
Fortson, Judith Lee *library administrator*

Stockton
Harrison, Isom *librarian*

Thousand Oaks
Brogden, Stephen Richard *library administrator*

Turlock
Parker, John Carlyle *retired librarian and archivist, editor*

Valencia
Hanft, Margie Evelyn *librarian*

Ventura
Adeniran, Dixie Darlene *library administrator*

Westminster
Gylseth, Doris (Lillian) Hanson *retired librarian*

Whittier
Topjon, Ann Johnson *librarian*

COLORADO

Colorado Springs
Budington, William Stone *retired librarian*
Chen, Lynn Chia-Ling *librarian*
Fritts, Mary Madelyn (Mary Bahr) *librarian, writer*
Jones-Eddy, Julie Margaret *librarian*
Sheridan, John Brian *librarian*

Denver
Ahern, Arleen Fleming *retired librarian*
Ashton, Rick James *librarian*
Kroll, James Xavier *librarian*
Schafer, Gerald Lewis *librarian*

Englewood
Wynar, Bohdan Stephen *librarian, author, editor*

Fort Collins
Ernest, Douglas Jerome *librarian*

Golden
Mathews, Anne Jones *consultant, library educator and administrator*

Grand Junction
Bragdon, Lynn Lyon *library administrator*

Lakewood
Knott, William Alan *library director, library management and building consultant*

Leadville
McCain, Nancy Schloerke *library director*

Pueblo
Bates, Charles Emerson *library administrator*

Trinidad
Murphy, Sara Jo *library director*

HAWAII

Fort Shafter
Hanusey, Richard Dmytro *library director*

Honolulu
Eldredge, Jeffrey Robert Carleton *librarian*
Kane, Bartholomew Aloysius *state librarian*
King, Charles Lynn *librarian*
Lee, Pali Jae (Polly Jae Stead Lee) *retired librarian, writer*
Masuchika, Glenn Norio *librarian, university official, book reviewer*
Spencer, Caroline *library director*

IDAHO

Boise
Bolles, Charles Avery *librarian*

Moscow
Jankowska, Maria Anna *librarian*

MASSACHUSETTS

Boston
Margolis, Bernard Allen *library administrator*

MINNESOTA

Rochester
Key, Jack Dayton *librarian*

MISSOURI

Saint Peters
Michel, Victor James, Jr. *retired librarian*

MONTANA

Billings
Cochran, William Michael *librarian*

Helena
Fitzpatrick, Lois Ann *library administrator*
Schlesinger, Deborah Lee *librarian*

NEVADA

Las Vegas
Batson, Darrell Lynn *librarian, consultant*
Gordon, Lee Diane *librarian*
Hunsberger, Charles Wesley *library consultant*
Ortiz, Diane Thorman *librarian, management analyst*
Richardson, Jane *librarian*
Smith, Thomas James *reference librarian*
Walker, Gwendolyn Kaye *librarian assistant, small business owner*

Pahrump
Karpisek, Marian Ellen *librarian*

NEW MEXICO

Albuquerque
Freeman, Patricia Elizabeth *library and education specialist*
Sabatini, Joseph David *librarian*
Snell, Patricia Poldervaart *librarian, consultant*
Wilkinson, Frances Catherine *librarian, educator*
Wolf, Cynthia Tribelhorn *librarian, library educator*

Gallup
Fellin, Octavia Antoinette *retired librarian*

Las Cruces
Dresp, Donald Francis *retired library director*
Townley, Charles Thomas *librarian, educator*

Los Alamos
Sayre, Edward Charles *librarian*

Roswell
Long, Betty Jean *library director*
McLaren, M(alcom) Bruce *library director*

NORTH CAROLINA

Raleigh
Osegueda, Laura Margaret *librarian*

OKLAHOMA

Tulsa
Saferite, Linda Lee *library director*

OREGON

Albany
House, Edward Briley, Jr. *librarian*

Ashland
Gaulke, Mary Florence *library administrator*

Astoria
Foster, Michael William *librarian*

Coquille
DePlois, Molly *library director*

Eugene
Edwards, Ralph M. *librarian*
Hildebrand, Carol Ilene *librarian*

Gresham
Pierik, Marilyn Anne *librarian*

Helix
Mitchell, Martha L. *library director*

Ontario
Edwards, Dale Leon *library director*

Portland
Browne, Joseph Peter *retired librarian*
Cooper, Ginnie *library director*
Eshelman, William Robert *librarian, editor*

Roseburg
Reenstjerna, Frederick Roberts *librarian, writer*

Salem
Hill, Daniel Webb *retired reference librarian*
Kenyon, Carleton Weller *librarian*
Phelps, Becky June *school library professional*

Veneta
Buck, G. Wendell *library director*

Wilsonville
Turner, Stephen Wayne *library director*

UTAH

Logan
Anderson, Janet Alm *librarian*
Heister, Carla Gayle *library director*

Ogden
Ayer, Carol Anne *librarian*

Orem
Hall, Blaine Hill *retired librarian*

Provo
Smith, Nathan McKay *library and information sciences educator*

Salt Lake City
Mogren, Paul Andrew *librarian*
Partridge, Cathleen Flanagan *library director*

WASHINGTON

Auburn
Willson, David Allen *reference librarian, writer*

Bellevue
Mutschler, Herbert Frederick *retired librarian*

Edmonds
Betz-Zall, Jonathan Richard *librarian*

Ellensburg
Johnson, Leona Mindell *librarian, educator*

Ferndale
Harris, Kevin Michael *library manager, investigative specialist*

Kennewick
Vickery, Byrdean Eyvonne Hughes (Mrs. Charles Everett Vickery, Jr.) *retired library services administrator*

Lacey
Smith, Donald Evans *library consultant*

Renton
Telban, Ethel *librarian*

Seattle
Abendroth, Kathi Judkins *archivist*
Bishop, Virginia Wakeman *retired librarian and humanities educator*
Blase, Nancy Gross *librarian*
Greggs, Elizabeth May Bushnell (Mrs. Raymond John Greggs) *retired librarian*
Haines, Irene Lois *librarian*
Hiatt, Peter *library studies educator*
Jennerich, Elaine *librarian*
Stroup, Elizabeth Faye *librarian*

Spokane
Burr, Robert Lyndon *information services specialist*

Tacoma
Crisman, Mary Frances Borden *librarian*

Toppenish
Veomett, Colleen Michelle *librarian*

Vancouver
Hammer, Sharon Arlene *library director*

Walla Walla
Haley, Anne Elizabeth *library director*

Yakima
Weber, Joan L. *library director*

WYOMING

Casper
Boughton, Lesley D. *library director*

Cheyenne
Johnson, Wayne Harold *librarian, county official*
Osborn, Lucie P. *library director*

Sundance
Collier, Gaydell Maier *library director, writer, rancher*

CANADA

ALBERTA

Calgary
Meek, Gerry *library director*

Edmonton
McDougall, Donald Blake *retired government official, librarian*

BRITISH COLUMBIA

North Vancouver
Ellis, Sarah Elizabeth *librarian*

Vancouver
Aalto, Madeleine *library director*

ADDRESS UNPUBLISHED

Anderson, Barbara Louise *retired library director*
Bullard, Sharon Welch *librarian*
Curley, Elmer Frank *librarian*
Dixon, Ann Renee *librarian, writer*
Dutton, Pauline Mae *fine arts librarian*
Gould, Martha Bernice *retired librarian*
Gregor, Dorothy Deborah *librarian*
Lowell, Waverly B. *archivist*
Nelson, Helen Martha *retired library director*
Rafael, Ruth Kelson *archivist, librarian, consultant*
Silvia, Raymond Alan *librarian*
Tower, Kathleen Ruth *librarian, consultant*
Waugh, Kathleen Mary *archivist*

HUMANITIES: MUSEUMS

UNITED STATES

ALASKA

Anchorage
Spencer, Ted *museum director*
Wolf, Patricia B. *museum director*

Fairbanks
Jonaitis, Aldona Claire *museum administrator, art historian*

Juneau
Kato, Bruce *curator*

ARIZONA

Bisbee
Gustavson, Carrie *museum director*

Chandler
Baudoin, James *museum director*

Flagstaff
Eide, Joel S. *museum director*
Fox, Michael J. *museum director*

Grand Canyon
Arnberger, Robert *museum administrator*
Richard, Carolyn Lee *curator, park ranger, fire fighter*

Mesa
Mead, Tray C. *museum director*

Phoenix
Ballinger, James K. *art museum executive*
Grinell, Sheila *museum director*
Johnson, Mary *museum director*
Keane, Melissa *museum director*
Lidman, Roger Wayne *museum director*
Myers, Cindy L. *museum director*
Sullivan, Martin Edward *museum director*
Worth, Richard Carleton *gallery owner*

Prescott
Willoughby, Susan Nell *museum director*

Tempe
Zeitlin, Marilyn Audrey *museum director*

Tucson
Bermingham, Peter *museum director*
Brown, Don *museum director*
Hancocks, David Morgan *museum director, architect*
Krakel, Dean *museum administrator, consultant, historian*
Yassin, Robert Alan *museum administrator, curator*

Yuma
Reid, Megan Beth *museum administrator*

CALIFORNIA

Arcata
Zielinski, Melissa L. *museum director*

Bakersfield
Enriquez, Carola Rupert *museum director*
Meyer, Charles G. *museum director*

Berkeley
Barr, Cheryl B. *curator*

Beverly Hills
Berman, Jerome *museum director, curator*

Caliente
de Fonville, Paul Bliss *historic organization administrator*

Carmel
Cost, BettyJo (BettyJo Cost-Hansen) *art gallery executive, agent, print distributor*

Carmel Valley
Heimann, Janet Barbara *volunteer trail consultant*

Carson
Zimmerer, Kathy Louise *university art gallery director*

Costa Mesa
Botello, Troy James *arts administrator, counselor*
Korzec, Patricia Ann *museum administrator*
Labbe, Armand Joseph *museum curator, anthropologist*

Fresno
Sobey, Edwin J. C. *museum director, oceanographer, consultant*

Fullerton
McGee, Mike James *gallery director, writer*

Irvine
Botwinick, Michael *museum director*

La Jolla
Beebe, Mary Livingstone *curator*

Long Beach
Glenn, Constance White *art museum director, educator, consultant*
Nelson, Harold Bernhard *museum director*

Los Angeles
Beal, Graham William John *museum director*
Beggs, Vincent *museum director*
Cohen, Daniel Morris *museum administrator, marine biology researcher*
Fontenote-Jamerson, Belinda *museum director*
Gluckman, Dale Carolyn *art museum curator*
Henderson, Jai *museum director*
Hess, Catherine Mary *museum curator*
Hirano, Irene Ann Yasutake *museum director*
Holo, Selma Reuben *museum director, educator*
Hopkins, Henry Tyler *museum director, art educator*
Kaye, Carole *museum director and curator*
Koshalek, Richard *museum director, consultant*
Kuwayama, George *curator*
Naef, Weston John *museum curator*
Nottage, James H. *museum administrator, curator, historian*
Powell, James Lawrence *museum director*
Rich, Andrea Louise *museum executive*
Rudolph, Jeffrey N. *museum director*
Stooker, Hendrik Cornelis *curator, gallery director*
Wittmann, Otto *art museum executive*

Malibu
Zakian, Michael *museum director*

Monterey
Penwell, Donna Carol *museum director*

Newport Beach
Gaiber, Maxine Diane *museum education director*

Northridge
Lewis, Louise Miller *gallery director, art history educator*

Novato
Schaufel, Shirley *museum director, curator*

Oakland
Caldwell, Carey Teresa *museum curator*
Hayes, E. Hope *museum director*
Joans, Barbara *museum director*
Power, Dennis Michael *museum director*
Reuther, Ronald Theodore *museum director*

Orinda
Dorn, Virginia Alice *art gallery director*

Pacific Grove
Bailey, Stephen Fairchild *museum director and curator, ornithologist*

Redding
Becker, Stephen Arnold *museum executive*

Riverside
Esparza, Richard R. *museum director*
Green, Jonathan William *museum administrator and educator, artist, author*
Warren, Katherine Virginia *art gallery director*

Sacramento
Ball, Jacqueline *park administrator*
Gray, Walter P., III *museum director, consultant*
Mette, Joe *museum director*
Pond, Bill *museum executive, director*

San Diego
Brezzo, Steven Louis *museum director*
DiMattio, Terry *historic site administrator*
Longenecker, Martha W. *museum director*
Navarro, Edward *historic site administrator*
Ollman, Arthur Lee *museum director, photographer*
Petersen, Martin Eugene *museum curator*
Scott, Mary Louise *educator, writer*
Stofflet, Mary Kirk *museum curator, writer*

San Francisco
Austerer-Williams, Eleonore *art gallery owner, director*
Delacote, Goery *museum director*
Griggs, Theresa *historic site administrator*
McKeon, Elaine *museum administrator*
Miko, Leslie *museum administrator*
Nash, Steven Alan *museum curator, art historian*
O'Neill, Brian *landmark administrator*
Parker, Harry S., III *art museum administrator*
Sano, Emily J. *museum director*
Smith, James Weldon *museum director*
Whyte, Robert Andrew *art curator, writer*

San Jose
Burkhart, Sandra Marie *art gallery director*
Callan, Josi Irene *museum director*
Gordon, Peter Howard *museum curator*

San Marino
Wark, Robert Rodger *art curator*

Santa Ana
Keller, Peter Charles *museum director, mineralogist*

Santa Barbara
Karpeles, David *museum director*

Santa Clara
Schapp, Rebecca Maria *museum director*

Santa Monica
Walsh, John *museum director*

Sausalito
Elliott, James Heyer *retired university art museum curator, fine arts consultant*

Stanford
Ratliff, William Elmore *curator, researcher*

Ukiah
Lee, Lila June *historical society officer, library director*

Venice
Davis, Kimberly B. *art gallery director*

Watsonville
Hernandez, Jo Farb *museum curator, consultant*

Wilmington
O'Brien, Marge Ett *museum administrator*

Yosemite National Park
Bates, Craig Dana *curator, ethnographer, government official*
Forgang, David M. *museum curator*

Yucaipa
Griesemer, Allan David *retired museum director*

Yucca Valley
DeMersman, James Richard *museum director*

COLORADO

Boulder
Danilov, Victor Joseph *museum management program director, consultant, writer, educator*
Meier, Thomas Joseph *museum director, author*

Colorado Springs
Conway, Wallace Xavier, Sr. *retired curator*
Hoge, Robert Wilson *museum curator*
Riggs, William G(erry) *art gallery director, museum studies educator*

Denver
Conn, Richard George *retired art museum curator*
Harrison, Carole Alberta *museum curator, restaurateur, civic worker*
Maytham, Thomas Northrup *art and museum consultant*

Evergreen
Lang, Brian Joseph *museum curator*

Pueblo
Henning, William Thomas *museum director*

HAWAII

Honokaa
Loewenhardt, Joseph H. *museum director*

Honolulu
Duckworth, Walter Donald *museum executive, entomologist*
Ellis, George Richard *museum administrator*
Gray, Harvey *museum director*
Klobe, Tom *art gallery director*
Sendzikas, Aldona Marija *museum curator*

Kalaupapa
Alexander, Dean *museum director*

Kaneohe
Lagoria, Georgianna Marie *curator, writer, editor, visual art consultant*

Lawai
Klein, William McKinley Jr. *museum director*

Lihue
Lovell, Carol *museum director*

Puunene
Kubota, Gaylord *museum director*

Schofield Barracks
Fairfull, Thomas McDonald *museum director*

IDAHO

Boise
O'Leary, Dennis *museum director*
Swanson, Kenneth J. *museum administrator*

Coeur D Alene
Dahlgren, Dorothy *museum director*

Pocatello
Jackson, Allen Keith *museum administrator*

Salmon
Wiederrick, Robert *museum director*

Twin Falls
Woods, James C. *museum director*

MARYLAND

Saint Marys City
Matelic, Candace Tangorra *museum studies educator, consultant, museum director*

MONTANA

Billings
Moss, Lynda Bourque *museum director*
Towe, A. Ruth *museum director*

Bozeman
Wolf, Arthur Henry *museum administrator*

Butte
Thompson, John *museum director*

Crow Agency
Deernose, Kitty *museum curator*
Ditmanson, Dennis L. *national monument administrator*

Dillon
Horst, Randy *museum director*
Mastandrea, Eva *museum education educator*

Missoula
Brown, Robert Munro *museum director*
Millin, Laura Jeanne *museum director*

NEVADA

Baker
Mills, Becky *park administrator*

Boulder City
Ferraro, Robert *museum president*

Elko
Seymour, Lisa *museum director*

Las Vegas
Lewis, Oli Parepa *curator*
Naegle, Shirl R. *museum director*
Schefcik, Jerry Allen *art gallery administrator, university official*

North Las Vegas
Gillespie, Marilyn *museum administrator*

Reno
Feinhandler, Edward Sanford *writer, photographer, art dealer, sports mentor, consultant, educator*
Spencer, Howard DaLee *art museum curator*

NEW MEXICO

Alamogordo
Starkey, Don J. *museum director*

Albuquerque
Bawden, Garth Lawry *museum director*
Martinez, Ray *museum director*
Moore, James C. *museum director*
Smartt, Richard A. *museum director*

Santa Fe
Ashman, Stuart *museum director*
Cerny, Charlene Ann *museum director*
Chávez, Thomas Esteban *curator*
Conley, Zeb Bristol *art gallery director*
DiMaio, Virginia Sue *gallery owner*
Livesay, Thomas Andrew *museum administrator, lecturer*

OREGON

Ashland
Kramer, George H. *historic preservation consultant*
Lamb, Philip *museum administrator*

Klamath Falls
Favell, Eugene Hunter *museum director*

Portland
Eichinger, Marilynne H. *museum administrator*
Gilkey, Gordon Waverly *curator, artist*
Lacrosse, Patrick *museum administrator*
Russo, Laura *gallery director*

Schnitzer, Arlene Director *art dealer*

UTAH

Salt Lake City
Kohler, Dolores Marie *gallery owner*
Leonard, Glen M. *museum administrator*
Sanguinetti, Eugene Frank *art museum administrator, educator*

VIRGINIA

Williamsburg
Wegner, Samuel Joseph *museum executive*

WASHINGTON

Bellevue
Douglas, Diane Miriam *museum director*
Trubner, Henry *museum curator*
Warren, James Ronald *retired museum director, author, columnist*

Bellingham
Clark-Langager, Sarah Ann *curator, director, university official*

Longview
Woods, Trudy Ann Olson *gallery director*

Seattle
Herschensohn, Michael J. *museum administrator*
Neill, Mary Gardner *museum administrator*
Wehr, Wesley Conrad *museum curator*

Spokane
Walsdorf, Donald P. *art show producer, gallery director*

Tacoma
Paulson, Dennis Roy *museum director, biology educator, curator*

Yakima
Baule, John Alvin *museum director, consultant*

WYOMING

Casper
Mobley, Karen Ruth *art gallery director*

Rock Springs
Chadey, Henry F. *museum director*

CANADA

ALBERTA

Calgary
Janes, Robert Roy *museum executive, archaeologist*

Drumheller
Naylor, Bruce Gordon *museum director*

BRITISH COLUMBIA

Victoria
Barkley, William Donald *museum executive director*
Finlay, James Campbell *retired museum director*

ADDRESS UNPUBLISHED

Bacigalupa, Andrea *art gallery owner, writer, artist*
Douglass, Amy Anita *museum director*
Glad, Suzanne Lockley *retired museum director*
Harvey, Virginia Isham *curator, fiber artist*
Hodson, Sara Suzanne *manuscripts curator*
Mason, James Albert *museum director, former university dean*
Mayfield, Signe *curator of exhibitions*
McDonnell, Jeanne Farr *museum director*
Pal, Pratapaditya *museum curator*
Perrot, Paul Norman *museum director*
Shimoda, Jerry Yasutaka *retired national historic park superintendent*
Stuart, Joseph Martin *art museum administrator*
Welles, John Galt *retired museum director*
Whitchurch, Charles Augustus *art gallery owner, humanities educator*
Zenev, Irene Louise *museum curator*

INDUSTRY: MANUFACTURING. See also FINANCE: FINANCIAL SERVICES.

UNITED STATES

ALASKA

Anchorage
DeLoach, Robert Edgar *corporate executive*
Doran, Vincent James *steel fabricating company consultant*
Easley, George Washington *construction executive*

Juneau
Lauber, Mignon Diane *food processing company executive*
Mallott, Byron Ivar *holding corporation executive*
Smith, Charles Anthony *businessman*

ARIZONA

Glendale
Lopez, Steven Richard *small business owner, consultant*

Mesa
Brier, James Roy *airplane manufacturing company official*
DeRosa, Francis Dominic *chemical company executive*
Frisk, Jack Eugene *recreational vehicle manufacturing company executive*

Phoenix
Francisco, Wayne M(arkland) *automotive executive*
Kopp, David Eugene *manufacturing company executive*
Locher, Walter *agricultural products company*
Mardian, Daniel *construction company director*
Norris, John Steven *healthcare company executive*
Platt, James Robert *business executive*
Schaffer, James Richard *aerospace company executive*
Thompson, Herbert Ernest *tool and die company executive*
Van Horssen, Charles Arden *manufacturing executive*
Whiting, Arthur Milton *diversified company executive*

Prescott
White, Brittan Romeo *manufacturing company executive*

Sahuarita
Walden, Richard Keith *agri-business executive*

Scottsdale
Breeden, Townsend Dean *electronics company executive, consultant*
Farrar, James Paul *electronics company official*
Malohn, Donald A. *manufacturing executive, retired*
Wong, Astria Wor *cosmetic business consultant*

Sedona
Bolton, Robert Floyd *construction executive*

Sun City
Moore, William Cullen *retired electronics company executive*

Tempe
Brumbaugh, Kevin James *electronics executive*
Penley, Larry Edward *management educator*

Tolleson
Etchart, Mike *agricultural products company executive*
Rousseau, David *agricultural products executive*
Rousseau, Will *agricultural products executive*

Tucson
Acker, Loren Calvin *medical instrument company executive*
Prichard, Merrill E. *business executive*
Sundt, Harry Wilson *construction company executive*
Willoughby, Stuart Carroll *contractor*

Yuma
Curtis, Michael *food products executive*

CALIFORNIA

Alhambra
Fried, Elaine June *business executive*
Hovsepian, Abraham *metal products executive*

Aliso Viejo
Baumgartner, Anton Edward *automotive sales professional*

Anaheim
Price, Richard Taft, Jr. *manufacturing company executive*
Valdez, James Gerald *automotive aftermarket executive*

Arcadia
Dodds, Dale Irvin *chemicals executive*
Plessner, Gerald Maurice *business executive*

Atherton
Hogan, Clarence Lester *retired electronics executive*

Bakersfield
Barker, Douglas P. *food products executive*
Evans, Berne, III *food products company executive*
Grimm, Bob *food products executive*
Grimm, Rod *food products executive*

Benicia
Lipsky, Ian David *contracting executive*

Beverly Hills
Casey, Joseph T. *corporate executive*
dePaolis, Potito Umberto *food company executive*
Hoch, Orion Lindel *corporate executive*
Schoenfeld, Lawrence Jon *jewelry manufacturing company executive, travel industry consultant*
Singleton, Henry Earl *industrialist*

Brawley
Colace, Joseph J. *agricultural products company executive*
Colace, William M. *food products executive*

Buena Park
Parker, Larry Lee *electronics company executive, consultant*

Burbank
Altschul, David Edwin *record company executive, lawyer*
Beymer, Dale Allen *manufacturing executive*

Burlingame
Hepler, Kenneth Russel *manufacturing executive*

Calabasas
Cohen, William *construction executive*
Lipchik, Harold *company executive*
Sperber, Burton S. *construction executive*

Camarillo
Gill, David *food products executive*
Gill, Steven *food products executive*

Canoga Park
Weisman, Martin Jerome *manufacturing company executive*

Carlsbad
Crooke, Stanley Thomas *pharmaceutical company executive*
Garruto, Michelle Bartok *cosmetic company executive*

Castroville
Boutonnet, Edward *food products executive*
Tottino, Leslie *food products executive*

Chatsworth
Morris, Henry Madison, III *software manufacturing executive, minister*

Chico
Mooney, Steve *food products executive*

Chino
Goodman, Lindsey Alan *furniture manufacturing executive, architect*

Chula Vista
Manary, Richard Deane *manufacturing executive*

City Of Industry
Scritsmier, Jerome Lorenzo *manufacturing company executive*

Clovis
Tatham, William R. *vintner*

Compton
Golleher, George *food company executive*

Concord
Thompson, Jeremiah Beiseker *international medical business executive*

Corona Del Mar
Hochschild, Richard *medical instruments executive, researcher*

Costa Mesa
Brady, John Patrick, Jr. *electronics educator, consultant*
Hazewinkel, Van *manufacturing executive*

Cupertino
Amelio, Gilbert Frank *electronics company executive*
Mathias, Leslie Michael *electronic manufacturing company executive*
Peltzer, Douglas Lea *semiconductor device manufacturing company executive*

Cypress
Barman, Robert John *home electronics company executive*
Dorn, Marian Margaret *educator, sports management administrator*

Danville
Mariani, Mark A. *food products executive*

Delano
Caratan, Anton G. *food products executive*
Caratan, George *food products executive*
Pandol, Jack J. *food products executive*
Pandol, Matt *food products executive*

Duarte
Bres, Philip Wayne *automotive executive*

Edison
Giumarra, George, Jr. *vintner*

El Segundo
Amerman, John W. *toy company executive*

Emeryville
Nady, John *electronics company executive*

Encinitas
Friedman, Paul *food products executive*

Encino
Davenport, Alfred Larue, Jr. *manufacturing company executive*

Firebaugh
Perez, Mark *food products executive*
Perez, Thomas *food products executive*

Fontana
De Tomaso, Ernest Pat *general building contractor, developer*

Foster City
Sletten, Kenneth G. *construction executive*

Fowler
Bedrosian, James Kenneth *food products executive*

Fremont
Zajac, John *semiconductor equipment company executive*

Fresno
Baloian, Edward *food products executive*
Baloian, Timothy *food products executive*
Burford, Richard S. *agricultural products executive*
Donaldson, George Burney *chemical company executive*
Emigh, Mike *agricultural products company executive*
Freeman, Richard J. *medical products financial executive*

Fullerton
Gustin, David Joseph *food products executive*

Gardena
Kanner, Edwin Benjamin *electrical manufacturing company executive*
Salesky, William Jeffrey *manufacturing company executive*

Glendale
Raval, Ruchika *regulatory affairs specialist*

Gold River
Harper, Robert Levell *pharmaceutical company executive*

Goleta
Baxter, Dan *manufacturing executive*

Gonzales
Silva, Ed *food products executive*
Silva, Evelyn *food products executive*

Greenfield
Munoz, John Joseph *retired transportation company executive*

Gridley
Tanimoto, George *agricultural executive, farmer*

Guadalupe
Murphy, Tim *food products executive*
Tompkins, Nick *agricultural products executive*

Hawthorne
Roberts, George Christopher *manufacturing executive*

Hayward
Banister, James Henry, Jr. *manufacturing company executive, consultant*
Gallo, Joseph E. *vintner*
Minzner, Dean Frederick *aviation company executive*

Healdsburg
Long, Zelma Reed *winery administrator, winemaker*

Hesperia
Butcher, Jack Robert (Jack Risin) *manufacturing executive*

Huntington Beach
Joseph, Ezekiel (Ed Joseph) *manufacturing company executive*
Thomas-Cote, Nancy Denece *office products manufacturing company executive*
Wolzinger, Renah *medical products executive, music company executive*

Irvine
Basler, Richard Alan *biomedical instruments manufacturer*
Copeland, Lawrence R. *construction company executive*
Haggerty, Charles A. *electronics executive*
Herbert, Gavin Shearer *health care products company executive*
Ruttencutter, Brian Boyle *manufacturing company executive*
Shepherd, William C. *pharmaceutical company executive*
Stricklin, Guy Michael *construction company executive*
Thornton, Robert Lee *aircraft manufacturing company executive*
Zack, James G(ordon), Jr. *construction claims executive, consultant*

Ivanhoe
Meling, Eric M. *food executive*

King City
Giudici, Francis *food products executive*

La Canada Flintridge
Spencer, Herbert Ward, III *air pollution control manufacturing company executive*

La Crescenta
Crites, Richard Ray *international franchising company executive*

La Jolla
Koplin, Donald Leroy *health products executive, consumer advocate*

La Mesa
Bourke, Lyle James *electronics company executive, small business owner*
Reiff, Theodore Curtis *construction executive*

Lafayette
Shurtleff, William Roy *food products executive*

Lebec
Haskell, Donald *agricultural products executive*

Livermore
Kerner, Robert Fred *packaging company executive*

Livingston
Shamgochian, Theron *food products executive*

Lodi
Elkins, Carl *food products executive*
Mettler, Leeman *food executive*

Long Beach
Bos, John Arthur *aircraft manufacturing executive*
Crane, Steven *financial company executive*
McGihon, Michael Edwin *sheet metal manufacturing executive*
McGuire, James Charles *aircraft company executive*
Reid, Wallace Leo *manufacturing executive*

Los Altos
Albin, Randy Clark *record company executive*
Kao, Cheng Chi *electronics executive*

Los Angeles
Berger, Robert Sydney *paper company executive*
Borneman, John Paul *pharmaceutical executive*
Dalton, James Edward *aerospace executive, retired air force officer*
Gerstell, A. Frederick *aggregates and asphalt and concrete manufacturing executive*
Handschumacher, Albert Gustave *retired corporate executive*
Hourizadeh, Arash *espresso manufacturing company executive, physician*
Irani, Ray R. *oil and gas and chemical company executive*
Johnson, Keith Liddell *chemical company executive*
Jones, Jerve Maldwyn *construction company executive*
Karatz, Bruce E. *business executive*
Meyers, Theda Maria *textile company executive*
Nakra, Naresh Kumar *food products executive*
Perkins, William Clinton *company executive*
Preston, Martha Sue *pharmaceutical company executive*

Los Gatos
Nitz, Frederic William *electronics company executive*

Madera
Pierre, Phil *food products executive*

Marina Del Rey
Brown, Anthony B. *aerospace executive*

Menlo Park
Bremser, George, Jr. *electronics company executive*
Cook, Paul M. *technology company executive*
Fergason, James L. *optical company executive*
Westcott, Brian John *manufacturing executive*
Williams, Derek, Jr. *pharmaceutical professional*

Merced
Bianchi, Richard *food products executive*

Mill Valley
Winskill, Robert Wallace *manufacturing executive*

Milpitas
Berkley, Stephen Mark *computer peripherals manufacturing company executive*
Roddick, David Bruce *construction company executive*

Mission Viejo
Gilbert, Heather Campbell *manufacturing company executive*
McDonnel, William George *chemical instrumentation executive*
Sheridan, George Edward *manufacturing company executive*

Montebello
Meeker, Arlene Dorothy Hallin (Mrs. William Maurice Meeker) *manufacturing company executive*

Mountain View
Cusumano, James Anthony *chemical company executive, former recording artist*
Levy, Ricardo Benjamin *chemical company executive*
Nydam, Ronald Daniel *manufacturing executive*

Murrieta
Spangler, Lorna Carrie *pharmacy technician*

Napa
Graves, David William *winery executive*
Massey, Lawrence Martin *manufacturing executive*
Mondavi, Robert Michael *vintner*

Newport Beach
Bolen, Michael D. *construction executive*
Chihorek, John Paul *electronics company executive*
Jones, Roger Wayne *electronics executive*
Laidlaw, Victor D. *construction executive*
Rogers, Robert Reed *manufacturing company executive*
Youngquist, Andrew Lance *construction executive*

Northridge
Toole, Floyd Edward *manufacturing company executive*

Novato
Fedrick, C. Richard *food products executive*
Womack, Thomas Houston *manufacturing company executive*

Oakland
Sullivan, G. Craig *household products executive*

Oceano
Donovan, Dennis *agricultural products executive*

Oceanside
Garruto, John Anthony *cosmetics executive*

Ojai
Weill, Samuel, Jr. *automobile company executive*

Oxnard
Boskovich, George, Jr. *food products executive*
Duda, Luther *food products executive*
Hansen, Margaret *food executive*
Poole, Henry Joe, Jr. *business executive*

Palo Alto
Chow, Winston *engineering research executive*
Hewlett, William (Redington) *manufacturing company executive, electrical engineer*
Kincaid, Judith Wells *electronics company executive*
Kung, Frank F. C. *medical products executive*
Mario, Ernest *pharmaceutical company executive*

O'Rourke, J. Tracy manufacturing company executive
Platt, Lewis Emmett electronics company executive
Saldich, Robert Joseph electronics company executive
Smith, Pamela Iris consulting company executive

Palos Verdes Peninsula
Pfund, Edward Theodore, Jr. electronics company executive
Thomas, Hayward manufacturing company executive
Wilson, Theodore Henry retired electronics company executive, aerospace engineer

Pasadena
Falick, Abraham Johnson printing company executive
Jenkins, Royal Gregory manufacturing executive
Miller, Charles Daly self-adhesive materials company executive
Neal, Philip Mark diversified manufacturing executive
Watson, Noel G. construction executive
Windham, Timothy Ray healthcare executive

Paso Robles
Carter, Paul Edward contractor, construction company executive

Pleasanton
Pugliese, Vincent Joseph Alfred manufacturing executive
Stager, Donald K. construction company executive

Pomona
Puckett, Paul David electronics company executive

Poway
Aschenbrenner, Frank Aloysious former diversified manufacturing company executive

Rancho Cordova
Gebhart, John E., III health products company executive

Rancho Mirage
Foster, David Ramsey soap company executive

Rancho Santa Fe
Jordan, Charles Morrell retired automotive designer

Rancho Santa Margarita
Wong, Wallace medical supplies company executive, real estate investor

Redondo Beach
Dockstader, Jack Lee electronics executive
Kagiwada, Reynold Shigeru advanced technology manager
Sabin, Jack Charles engineering and construction firm executive

Redwood City
Ellison, Lawrence J. computer software company executive
Hegedus, John S. medical products executive
Howe, Lee Martin electronics marketing executive, army officer
Muratore, Marilyn Ann contractor
Sagar, Mahendrakumar Pitamber pharmaceutical company executive
Wang, Chen Chi electronics company and real estate and finance company and investment services and international trade executive

Reedley
Surabian, Dennis G. food products executive

Riverside
Crean, John C. housing and recreational vehicles manufacturing company executive
Kummer, Glenn F. manufactured housing executive
Morgan, Dan L. manufacturing company executive
Reeder, Samuel Kenneth analytical laboratory executive
Smith, Elden Leroy recreational vehicle company executive

Sacramento
Boekhoudt-Cannon, Gloria Lydia business education educator

Salinas
Carr, Noel food products executive
Drever, Mark food products executive
Esquivel, Joe G. food products executive
Esquivel, Mary agricultural products company executive
Gheen, Betty M. food products executive
Lugg, James R. agricultural products executive
Mills, Basil E. food products executive
Mills, Roger E. food products executive
Nunes, Frank R., Jr. food products executive
Nunes, Thomas P. food products executive
Taylor, Steven Bruce agriculture company executive

San Bruno
Agresti, Jack Joseph construction company executive

San Clemente
Cate, Floyd Mills electronic components executive

San Diego
Blumberg, Robert Lee manufacturing executive
Canter, Barry Mitchell electronics specialist, musician
Carver, Juanita Ash plastic company executive
Childs, John David computer hardware and services company executive
Cobianchi, Thomas Theodore engineering and marketing executive, educator
Garcia, Stephanie Brown aerospace company pricing manager
Gordon, Bradley B. pharmaceutical research executive
Henig, Suzanne medical biological research company executive
Jahn, E. Mark research specialist
Jones, Ronald H. computer information systems executive
Keith, Norman Thomas aerospace company administrator
Luby, Charles Strong company executive
Tidwell, Geoffrey Morgan medical company executive

San Francisco
Clark, James H. electronics executive
Clark, Richard Ward food industry executive, consultant
Grubb, David H. construction company president
Haas, Robert Douglas apparel manufacturing company executive
James, George Barker, II apparel industry executive
Kaune, James Edward ship repair company executive, former naval officer
Kreitzberg, Fred Charles construction management company executive
Nicholson, William Joseph forest products company executive
Pulido, Mark A. pharmaceutical and cosmetics company executive
Satre, Rodrick Iverson environmental consultant, business developer
Tusher, Thomas William retired apparel company executive
Wertheimer, Robert E. paper company executive
Wilson, Ian Robert food company executive

San Jacinto
Minor, Larry J. food products executive

San Jose
Benzing, David Warren semiconductor equipment company executive
Hill, Anna Marie manufacturing executive
Jacobson, Raymond Earl electronics company entrepreneur and executive
Koriat, Raphael manufacturing company executive
Schroeder, William John electronics executive

San Leandro
Aidells, Bruce food products executive

San Lorenzo
Downey, James Edgar manufacturing executive

San Luis Obispo
Sullivan, Thomas James retired manufacturing company executive

San Marcos
Andersen, Robert health products business executive
Blackburn, Charles Edward manufacturing executive
Page, Leslie Andrew disinfectant manufacturing company executive

San Mateo
Aadahl, Jorg business executive
Besse, Robert Gale food technologist
Grammater, Rudolf Dimitri retired construction executive
Horwitz, David Larry pharmaceuticals company executive, researcher, educator

Sanger
Albertson, David food products executive
Chooljian, Leo food products executive
Chooljian, Mehran food products executive

Santa Ana
Ramsay, Mackay food executive
Yuen, Andy Tak Sing electronics executive

Santa Clara
Baird, Mellon Campbell, Jr. electronics industry executive
Craigie, Earle James manufacturing consultant
Dunlap, F. Thomas, Jr. electronics company executive, engineer, lawyer
Grove, Andrew S. electronics company executive
Hallin, Karl-Eliv Johann industrial process control company executive
House, David L. electronics components company executive
Moore, Gordon E. electronics company executive
Parikh, Anjan electronics company executive

Santa Cruz
Marks, Peter Amasa technical consulting firm administrator

Santa Maria
Ardantz, Henri agricultural products executive
Ferini, Robert Pat agricultural products company executive

Santa Monica
Deckert, Harlan Kennedy, Jr. manufacturing company official
Goldaper, Gabriele Gay clothing executive, consultant
Marsden, Eugene Dennis, Sr. bleacher seating manufacturing executive
O'Gara, Barbara Ann soap company executive

Santa Paula
Dillard, Michael L. food products company executive

Santa Rosa
Jackson, Jess S. vintner
Scott, Peter, Jr. vintner
Stolte, Charles Albert company executive

Seal Beach
Beall, Donald Ray multi-industry high-technology company executive

Sebastopol
Sugrue, Donal food products executive

Sherman Oaks
Oakes, Robert Gibson retired electronics company executive, management consultant

Solana Beach
Daniels, James Arthur electronics sales company executive

Sonoma
Sasaki, Y. Tito business services company executive

Stockton
Corkern, Robert J. agricultural products company executive
Guardino, Sal food executive

Sun Valley
Kamins, Philip E. diversified manufacturing company executive

Sunnyvale
Fairweather, Edwin Arthur electronics company executive
Hemmes, Paul Richard, Jr. health products executive
Kempf, Martine voice control device manufacturing company executive
Lewis, John Clark, Jr. manufacturing company executive
Sanders, Walter Jeremiah, III electronics company executive
Woolsey, Roy Blakeney electronics company executive

Tarzana
Broadhurst, Norman Neil foods company executive

Temecula
Roemmele, Brian Karl internet and electronics and publishing and financial and real estate executive
Traner, Norman food products executive

Thermal
Kitagawa, Joe food products executive
Kitagawa, Kiyoko food products executive

Thousand Oaks
Binder, Gordon M. health and medical products executive
Lee, Lily Kiang scientific research company executive
Pope, Edward John Andrew corporate executive, consultant

Torrance
El-Bayoumy, Lotfi E. engineering executive
Lee, James King technology corporation executive
Mann, Michael Martin electronics company executive
Woodhull, John Richard electronics company executive

Tracy
Esformes, Joseph agricultural products company executive
Esformes, Nathan food products executive

Turlock
Arias, Joe agricultural products company executive

Ukiah
McAllister, (Ronald) Eric pharmaceutical executive, physician

Upland
Porrero, Henry, Jr. construction company executive
Raymond, Lloyd Wilson machinery company executive

Vacaville
Castro, David Alexander construction executive

Walnut Creek
Aronson, Bradley Alan construction management company executive
Palmer, Vincent Allan construction company consultant

Watsonville
Capurro, Frank L. food products executive
Costanzo, Patrick M. constuction executive
Solari, R. C. heavy construction company executive
Watts, David H. construction company executive

West Hills
Krive, Irwin new products development company executive

Westlake Village
DeLorenzo, David A. food products executive

Woodside
Gates, Milo Sedgwick retired construction company executive
Skieller, Christian manufacturing executive

Yorba Linda
Forth, Kevin Bernard beverage distributing industry consultant

Yountville
Farver, Ed vintner

Yuba City
Giacolini, Earl L. agricultural products company executive

COLORADO

Arvada
Holden, George Fredric brewing company executive, policy specialist, author, professional speaker

Aspen
Hansen, Steven Alan custom builder

Boulder
Johnston, David Ritchey construction company executive
Malone, Michael William electronics executive, software engineer
Siegel, Mo J. beverage company executive
Szostak, Edward Walter, Jr. pharmaceutical company executive

Colorado Springs
Robinson, Ronald Alan manufacturing executive
Varoglu, Mary wholesale distribution executive

Denver
Bennett, James P. construction executive
Clark, Walter W. construction executive
Gates, Charles Cassius rubber company executive
Hohner, Kenneth Dwayne retired fodder company executive
Johnson, James Gibson, Jr. community recycling specialist
Onofrio, Joe Frederick, III piano company executive
Shreve, Theodore Norris construction company executive

Englewood
Baldwin, Brian Eugene medical devices manufacturing company executive
Bauer, Randy Mark management training firm executive
Bowlen, Patrick Dennis holding company executive, lawyer, professional sports team executive
Bui, Tuan Sy biomedical company executive, researcher
Routson, Clell Dennis manufacturing company executive
Runice, Robert E. retired corporate executive

Golden
Coors, Peter Hanson beverage company executive
Coors, William K. brewery executive
Henthorne, Jason Fitzgerald explosives consultant

Greeley
Carrico, Stephen J. construction company executive
Morgensen, Jerry Lynn construction company executive

Highlands Ranch
Breuer, Werner Alfred retired plastics company executive

Lakewood
Heath, Gary Brian manufacturing firm executive, engineer
Rosa, Fredric David construction company executive

Littleton
Gertz, David Lee homebuilding company executive
Heath, Edward V. rubber company executive

Longmont
Hahn, Yubong electro-optics company executive
Hall, Kathryn O'Neil photographic company official

Monument
Karasa, Norman Lukas home builder, developer, geologist

Rocky Ford
Holder, J. Hal food products executive

Wellington
Grant, Lewis O. agricultural products executive, meteorology educator

CONNECTICUT

Fairfield
Krueger, Kurt Edward appliance manufacturing company official

GEORGIA

Marietta
Richards, Joe McCall chemical company executive

Roswell
Boley, Dennis Lynn construction company executive

HAWAII

Captain Cook
Vidgen, Rick food products executive

Honolulu
Andrasick, James Stephen agribusiness company executive
Buyers, John William Amerman agribusiness and specialty foods company executive
Couch, John Charles diversified company executive
Osada, Stan construction executive
Schnack, Gayle Hemingway Jepson (Mrs. Harold Clifford Schnack) corporate executive
Usui, Leslie Raymond clothing executive
Wilson, William J. construction executive
Yen, Duen Hsi corporate executive, physicist

Kahului
Marrs, Linda Diane manufacturing executive
Meyer, Paul J. food products executive
Viglione, Eugene Lawrence automotive executive

Kailua Kona
Rule, Roger Collins builder, developer, publisher

Kaumakani
Kennett, E. Alan agricultural products executive

Keaau
Cole, Lecil agricultural products company executive

IDAHO

Boise
Appleton, Steven R. electronics executive
Fery, John Bruce forest products company executive
Harad, George Jay manufacturing company executive
Sullivan, James Kirk forest products company executive

Hayden Lake
Wogsland, James Willard *retired heavy machinery manufacturing executive*

Post Falls
Jacklin, Doyle *food products executive*
Jacklin, Duane *agricultural products executive*

Salmon
Snook, Quinton *construction company executive*

ILLINOIS

Deerfield
Gast, Nancy Lou *chemical company executive*

KENTUCKY

Erlanger
Cuneo, Dennis Clifford *automotive company executive*

MARYLAND

Gaithersburg
Couse, R. D. *construction company executive*

MISSOURI

Saint Louis
McDonnell, John Finney *aerospace and aircraft manufacturing company executive*

MONTANA

Butte
Tuck, Michael Ray *technical services executive*

Deer Lodge
Baehr, Robert E. *electrical contractor*

Helena
Warren, Christopher Charles *electronics executive*

NEVADA

Carson City
Burns, Dan W. *manufacturing company executive*

Fallon
Tedford, Jack Nowlan, III *construction executive, small business owner*

Hawthorne
Stahl, Louise W. *defense company executive*

Incline Village
Marguleas, Howard P. *agricultural products executive*
Yount, George Stuart *paper company executive*

Las Vegas
Bernard, Thelma Rene *property management professional*
Le Fave, Gene Marion *polymer amd chemical company executive*
Nicoletti, William Walter *pharmaceutical company executive*
Strahan, Julia Celestine *electronics company executive*

Reno
Graham, Denis David *company executive*
Mahin, Glenda Gordon *product development specialist, hydrologist*

Sparks
Kramer, Gordon Edward *manufacturing executive*
Root, William Dixon *construction company executive*

NEW JERSEY

East Hanover
Knight, Frank James *pharmaceutical marketing professional*

NEW MEXICO

Alamogordo
Linde, Gary J. *goldsmith*

Albuquerque
Riley, Peter Christopher *aeronautics company official*
Thomas, Douglas Graham *technology company executive, communications consultant*
Winfield, Armand Gordon *international plastics consultant, educator*

Farmington
Webb, Marlo L. *automobile executive, banking executive*

Rio Rancho
Dougherty, Rae Ann *semiconductor manufacturing company executive*

Roswell
Armstrong, Billie Bert *retired highway contractor*

Santa Fe
Bearwald, Jean Haynes *company executive*
Odell, John H. *construction company executive*
Robinson, Charles Wesley *energy company executive*
Spraitz, Stephen Michael *ceramic tile contractor*

NEW YORK

New York
Wachner, Linda Joy *apparel marketing and manufacturing executive*

OREGON

Beaverton
Donahue, Richard King *athletic apparel executive, lawyer*
Hayes, Delbert J. *athletic company executive*
Knight, Philip H(ampson) *shoe manufacturing company executive*

Bend
Babcock, Walter Christian, Jr. *membrane company executive*

Eugene
Chaney, James Alan *construction company executive*
Woolley, Donna Pearl *timber and lumber company executive*

Hermiston
Betz, Richard *agricultural products executive*

Hood River
Garcia, David *agricultural products executive*
Girardelli, Ronald K. *food products executive*

La Pine
Mirrasoul, Robin Stuart *first aid safety products executive*

Medford
Hannum, Gerald Luther (Lou Hannum) *retired tire manufacturing company official*

Milwaukie
Moffitt, Kevin David *food products executive*

Oregon City
Abbott, Robert Carl *management company executive*

Portland
Eberwein, Barton Douglas *construction company executive, consultant*
Egerter, John *information services executive*
Jones, Alan C. *grocery company executive*
Leineweber, Peter Anthony *forest products company executive*
Nagel, Stanley Blair *retired construction and investment executive*
Pamplin, Robert Boisseau, Jr. *agricultural company executive, minister, writer*
Parsons, J. A. *paper and wood products company executive*
Rogel, Steven R. *paper company executive*
Russell, Marjorie Rose *manufacturing company executive*
Sheldon, Christopher Charles *food products executive*
Steinfeld, Ray, Jr. *food products executive*
Stott, James Charles *chemical company executive*
Stott, Peter Walter *forest products company executive*
Swindells, William, Jr. *lumber and paper company executive*
Walker, Daphine Broadhead *construction executive*
Watkins, Charles Reynolds *medical equipment company executive*

Wilsonville
Kimberley, A. G. *industrial products factory representative, management executive*
Meyer, Jerome J. *diversified technology company executive*

TEXAS

Dallas
Roach, John D. C. *manufacturing company executive*

Houston
Ferguson, E. Robert *construction and engineering company executive*

San Antonio
Faley, Robert Lawrence *instruments company executive*

UTAH

Holladay
Stout, Gary Francis *inventor, entrepreneur*

Ogden
Garrison, U. Edwin *military, space and defense products manufacturing company executive*
Klepinger, John William *trailer manufacturing company executive*
Parson, Scott W. *construction company executive*

Provo
Rosen, David Allen *manufacturing executive*

Salt Lake City
Clark, Jeffrey Raphiel *research and development company executive*
Cook, Merrill A. *explosives company executive*
Frank, Thomas *design, construction and management executive*
Frary, Richard Spencer *international consulting company executive*
Huntsman, Jon M. *chemical company executive*
Nelson, Jim *chemicals executive*
Patel, Dinesh C. *business executive*

Sandy
Robbins, Charles Dudley, III *manufacturing executive*

West Jordan
Bland, Dorothy Ann *construction executive, real estate agent*

WASHINGTON

Bainbridge Island
Blumenthal, Richard Cary *construction executive, consultant*

Bellevue
Hovind, David J. *manufacturing company executive*
Meeker, Milton Shy *manufacturing company executive*
Morie, G. Glen *manufacturing company executive, corporate lawyer*
Pigott, Charles McGee *transportation equipment manufacturing executive*
Pigott, Mark C. *automotive executive*

Bellingham
Bestwick, Warren William *retired construction company executive*
Krmpotich, Frank Zvonko *fiberglass company executive, consultant*

Bothell
Dern, Christopher M. *construction executive*

Brewster
Chapman, George J. *agricultural products executive*
Thomas, Dalton *food products executive*

Eastsound
Anders, William Alison *aerospace and defense manufacturing executive*

Federal Way
Creighton, John W., Jr. *forest products company executive*

Kirkland
Biggs, Thomas Wylie *chemical company executive*
Ross, Alvin *manufacturing executive*

Longview
Wollenberg, Richard Peter *paper manufacturing company executive*

Outlook
Monson, Arvid *food products executive*

Pasco
Wright, Tim Eugene *packaging development executive*

Prosser
Brulotte, Bennett *agricultural products executive*

Pullman
Frigon, Judith Ann *electronics executive, office systems consultant*

Puyallup
Stover, Miles Ronald *manufacturing executive*

Redmond
Huck, Larry Ralph *manufacturers representative, sales consultant*

Seattle
Balint, Joseph Philip *medical products executive*
Bookkey, Gerald C. *agricultural products executive*
Braithwaite, Walt Waldiman *aircraft manufacturing company executive*
King, Robert Leonard *warehousing executive*
Mennella, Vincent Alfred *automotive manufacturing and airplane company executive*
Shrontz, Frank Anderson *airplane manufacturing executive*
Stumbles, James Rubidge Washington *multinational service company executive*
Tanaka, T. *health and medical products executive*
Whitacre, John *apparel executive*
Wilson, Patricia Poplar *electrical manufacturing company executive*

Tacoma
Carlson, Frederick Paul *electronics executive*
Sutherland, Douglass B. *former mayor, tent and awning company executive*
Tash, Graham Andrew, Jr. *automobile retail company executive*
Weyerhaeuser, George Hunt *forest products company executive*

Vancouver
Ritchie, Eric Robert David *manufacturing executive*

Wapato
Buntain, Jeannine *agricultural products executive*
Doty, Everett *food products executive*

Wenatchee
Birdsall, Brian *food products executive*
Chandler, Allen *food products executive*

Woodland
Brown, Alan Johnson *chemicals executive*

Yakima
Sims, Bernard *food products executive*

CANADA

ALBERTA

Calgary
Southern, Ronald D. *diversified corporation executive*

SASKATCHEWAN

Regina
Phillips, Roger *steel company executive*

TAIWAN

Hsinchu
Chang, Kuang-Yeh *microelectronics technologist*

ADDRESS UNPUBLISHED

Azarnoff, Daniel Lester *pharmaceutical company consultant*
Baker, Charles DeWitt *research and development company executive*
Barca, George Gino *winery executive, finanial investor*
Bennett, Paul Grover *agribusiness executive*
Boehm, Paul Eugene *health medical products executive, pharmacist*
Bruce, Norman Richard *manufacturing executive*
Buck, Linda Dee *recruiting company executive*
Buell, Thomas Allan *retired lumber company executive*
Campbell, Richard Alden *electronics company executive*
Castberg, Eileen Sue *construction company owner*
Chaykin, Robert Leroy *manufacturing and marketing executive*
Cupery, Robert Rink *manufacturing executive*
Davis, Darrell L. *automotive executive*
Dempsey, David A. *company official, small business owner*
Diener, Royce *corporate director, retired healthcare services company executive*
Dobelis, George *manufacturing company executive*
Eissmann, Walter James *consulting company executive*
Fatzinger, James A. S. *construction educator, estimator*
Gardner, Clyde Edward *health care executive, consultant, educator*
Gassman, Victor Alan *cosmetics executive*
Geisert, Otto *food products executive*
Goldberg, Lee Winicki *furniture company executive*
Gorman, Bruce Charles *health care executive*
Gorman, Michael Stephen *construction executive*
Grass, George Mitchell, IV *pharmaceutical executive*
Hansen, Donald Curtis *retired manufacturing executive*
Hartwick, Thomas Stanley *technical management consultant*
Harvey, Joseph Emmett *construction executive*
Jacobson, Stuart Neil *biotechnology company executive, consultant*
Kostrikin, Marybeth Elaine *excavating company executive*
Lentes, David Eugene *corporate executive*
Madden, Richard Blaine *forest products executive*
Malson, Rex Richard *drug and health care corporation executive*
Marrington, Bernard Harvey *retired automotive company executive*
Mason, Frank Henry, III *automobile company executive, leasing company executive*
McCann, Jack Arland *former construction and mining equipment company executive, consultant*
Miller, David Wayne *construction inspector, coordinator*
Moens, David Brian *manufacturing company executive*
Morita, Toshiyasu *technical manager*
Munera, Gerard Emmanuel *manufacturing company executive*
Mutch, James Donald *herbal pharmacist*
Nestor, John Joseph, Jr. *pharmaceutical executive*
Pettigrew, Steven Lee *healthcare management consultant*
Putnam, J. O. *construction executive*
Richardson, Thomas Andrew *business executive, educator*
Rymar, Julian W. *manufacturing company executive*
Scheid-Raymond, Linda Anne *property management professional*
Schilling, Dean William *manufacturing executive*
Smith, James Alexander *metal processing executive*
Soll, Larry *retired pharmaceutical executive*
Stamper, Malcolm Theodore *aerospace company executive*
Stern, Arthur Paul *electronics company executive, electrical engineer*
Wagner, John Lee *food products executive*
Warner, Walter Duke *corporate executive*
Witmeyer, Richard James *health products executive*
Wolf, Hans Abraham *retired pharmaceutical company executive*
Wolff, Brian Richard *metal manufacturing company executive*
Young, John Alan *electronics company executive*

INDUSTRY: SERVICE

UNITED STATES

ALASKA

Anchorage
Gottstein, Barnard Jacob *retail and wholesale food company executive, real estate executive*
Holman, Karen Marie *purchasing agent*
Porcaro, Michael Francis *advertising agency executive*
Schmitt, Nancy Cain *public and corporate relations executive, writer*
Schneibel, Vicki Darlene *public relations administrator*

Fairbanks
Thompson, Daniel Emerson *vending machine service company*

Juneau
Elton, Kim Steven *state legislator, pollster*

PROFESSIONAL INDEX 873 INDUSTRY: SERVICE

Ketchikan
Kraft, Richard Joe *sales executive*

ARIZONA

Apache Junction
Steckbauer, James J. *technical assessment professional*
Yool, George Richard *consultant*

Benson
Collmer, Russell Cravener *data processing executive, educator*

Chandler
Barrett, Craig R. *computer company executive*
Brunello-McCay, Rosanne *sales executive*
Steinbuchel, Maximilian Frederick *program manager*

Cortaro
Fossland, Joeann Jones *professional speaker, personal coach*

Flagstaff
Bolin, Richard Luddington *industrial development consultant*

Glendale
Baum, Phyllis Gardner *travel management consultant*
Copen, Melvyn Robert *management educator, university administrator*
Shimek, John Anton *legal investigation business owner, educator*

Globe
Lee, Joyce Ann *administrative assistant*

Green Valley
Green, Paul Cecil *management consultant*

Mayer
Davis, Scott Milton *information systems professional*

Mesa
McDonald, Thomas Robert *materials technologist, consultant, business owner*

Paradise Valley
Denning, Michael Marion *computer company executive*
Kahn, Earl Lester *market research executive*
Swanson, Robert Killen *management consultant*

Peoria
Saunders, James *management and training consultant*

Phoenix
Adams, Ann Elizabeth *corporate communications executive, lawyer*
Alsaker, Robert John *information systems specialist*
Bellus, Ronald Joseph *marketing and communications executive*
Booth, John Louis *service executive*
Brown, Bart A., Jr. *consumer products company executive*
Brown, James Carrington, III (Bing Brown) *public relations and communications executive*
Buscha, Ralph Victor *security firm executive*
Collins, Dane H. *marketing executive*
DeMichele, Barbara Joan *public relations executive*
DeWall-Owens, Karen Marie *marketing consultant*
DuMoulin, Diana Cristaudo *marketing professional*
English, Philip Stephen *sales executive*
Evans, Handel E. *marketing professional*
Evans, Ronald Allen *lodging chain executive*
Gall, Donald Alan *data processing executive*
Grier, James Edward *hotel company executive, lawyer*
Landis, Richard Preston *corporate executive*
Last, Dianna Linn Schneider *marketing company executive*
Lemon, Leslie Gene *consumer services company executive*
Pavlik, Michael *management consultant*
Simpson, Charles Robert *marketing professional*
Simunich, Mary Elizabeth Hedrick (Mrs. William A. Simunich) *public relations executive*
Snell, Richard *holding company executive*
Stewart, Sally *public relations practitioner*
Subach, James Alan *infosystems company executive, consultant*
Teets, John William *retired diversifed company executive*
Turner, William Cochrane *international management consultant*
Wade, Michael Stephen *management consultant*
Wichterman, James Albert *management consulting executive*

Prescott
Mayol, Richard Thomas *advertising executive, political consultant*
Palmer, Robert Arthur *private investigator*

Scottsdale
Adams, Robert Granville *marketing professional*
Blinder, Martin S. *business consultant, art dealer*
Boone, Earle Marion *business executive*
Comfort, Clifton C. *management consultant*
Doglione, Arthur George *data processing executive*
Joaquim, Richard Ralph *hotel executive*
O'Donnell, William Thomas *management consultant*
Pavlik, Nancy *convention services executive*
Perry, David Niles *public relations executive*
Polkinghorne, Patricia Ann *hotel executive*
Quigley, Jerome Harold *management consultant*
Randau, Karen Lynette *public relations executive*
Russell, Jay D. *marketing executive*
White, Paul Verlin *electronics marketing executive*

Sedona
Braman, Donald William *public relations consultant*

Sierra Vista
Reynolds, John Curby *sales representative*

Sun City
Riley, Marilyn Gledhill *communications executive*

Sun City West
Suttles, Virginia Grant *advertising executive*

Tempe
Dunbar, Richard Paul *sales manager*
Edmunds, Holly Brook *market research consultant*
Goldstein, Mark Alan *information science and research company executive, consultant*
Guinouard, Philip Andre *restaurant executive*
Herbert, Christopher Jay *marketing professional, management consultant*
Huntsman, Edward Loyd *business consultant, marketing executive*
Sackton, Frank Joseph *public affairs educator*

Tucson
Auslander, Steven Lawrence *advertising executive, newspaper editor*
Cox, William Larry *astrologer, educator*
Emerine, Stephen Edward *communications executive*
Paley, Alfred Irving *value engineering and consulting company executive, lecturer*
Rose, Hugh *management consultant*
Sarlat, Gladys *public relations consultant*
Sohnen-Moe, Cherie Marilyn *business consultant*
Williams, John Charles, II *data processing executive*

Wickenburg
Kardinal, Royce Ann *hotel executive*

Yuma
Hilgert, Arnie D. *management educator*
Swearingin, Kevin Brian *human resources administrator*

CALIFORNIA

Agoura Hills
Powers, J. D., III *marketing executive*
Schmidt, Frank Broaker *executive recruiter*

Alameda
Billings, Thomas Neal *computer and publishing executive, management consultant*

Alamo
Crocker, Kenneth Franklin *data processing consultant*

Alta Loma
Anderson, Jack Joe *communications and multimedia training consultant*

Altadena
Fairbanks, Mary Kathleen *data analyst, researcher*

Anaheim
Jackson, Samuel John *scuba diving industry executive*
Kallay, Michael Frank, II *medical devices company official*
Keller, Kent Eugene *advertising and public relations executive*
Noorda, Raymond J. *computer software company executive*
Roark, Susan Pamela *advertising executive, publisher*
Sorenson, Sandra Louise *merchandising manager*

Apple Valley
Yochem, Barbara June *sales executive, lecturer*

Arroyo Grande
Pfeiffer, Gerald G. *human resources specialist*

Atherton
Lowry, Larry Lorn *management consulting company executive*

Atwater
DeVoe, Kenneth Nickolas *food service executive, mayor*

Auberry
Ninkovich, Thomas *owner research firm, consultant*

Avila Beach
McLaren, Archie Campbell, Jr. *marketing executive*

Bakersfield
Weygand, Leroy Charles *service executive*

Berkeley
Criswell, Kimberly Ann *public relations executive*
Marcant, Christophe *company executive*

Beverly Hills
Carlson, Gary Lee *public relations executive, director, producer*
Falk, Bradley Davis *information services executive*
Gleason, Douglas Renwick *marketing professional*
Hilton, Barron *hotel executive*
Levine, Michael *public relations executive, author*
Ratliff, James Conway *hotel executive*
Royer, Victor Henry *marketing consultant, author*
Warren, Lisa Lynne *telecommunications executive*
Young, Robert Edward *computer company executive*

Brea
Burgess, Stephen Andrew *company executive*
Herzing, Alfred Roy *computer executive*
Powell, Keith Peter *marketing professional, small business owner*

Buena Park
Thomas, David Stanley *sales executive*
Underwood, Thomas Woodbrook *communications company executive*

Burbank
Brankovich, Mark J. *restaurateur*
Korkunis, Tony William *consumer products executive*
McElwee, Jeanette Gaye *management and philanthropic consultant*
Tyler, Richard R. *marketing executive*

Burlingame
Riach, Douglas Alexander *marketing and sales executive, retired military officer*

Camarillo
Crombach, Danita Lynn *communications professional*

Cambria
Morse, Richard Jay *human resources and organizational development consultant, manufacturers' representative company executive*

Campbell
Panec, Donald John *marketing executive*

Cardiff By The Sea
Karr, Marie Aline Christensen *executive*

Carlsbad
Chereskin, Valerie Lee *marketing professional*
De La Cruz, Jennifer Lyn *marketing and finance executive*
McKay, Michael Joseph *religious educational products developer, theologian*
Moore, Terry Wayne *high technology venture management consultant*
Voigt, John Louis *advertising and marketing executive*

Carmel
Allan, Robert Moffat, Jr. *corporate executive, educator*
Creighton, John Wallis, Jr. *consultant, author, former management educator*
Louvau, Gordon Ernest *management consultant, educator*

Cerritos
Morlock, Walter O'Malley *marketing professional*
Rice, Barbara Pollak *advertising and marketing executive*

Chatsworth
Bartling, Judd Quenton *research corporation executive*
Nwasike, Chike Okechukwu *computer industry executive, engineering and computer consultant*
Sklar, Louise Margaret *service executive*
Weisbrod, Ken (Joseph Louis Weisbrod) *marketing professional*

Chico
Heinze, David C. *business administration educator*

Citrus Heights
Bickmore, Edward Clifton, Jr. *risk management consulting executive*

Claremont
Farnum, Nancy Alyson *communications executive*

Concord
Jones, Gregory Taylor *human resources risk manager*
Leighton, Peter Elliott *marketing executive*
Martin, William Baxter *business owner*
Padget, John E. *management consultant*
Travers, Judith Lynnette *human resources executive*

Corona Del Mar
Terrell, A. John *business organization, management and telecommunications consultant*

Coronado
Walker, Richard Allen *multimedia computing executive, consultant*

Costa Mesa
Bereznay, Frank M. *information systems specialist*
Damsky, Robert Philip *communications executive*
Florey, Jerry Jay *management consultant*

Crescent City
Hight, Harold Philip *retired security company executive*

Culver City
Dutt, Birendra *research specialist*
Hankins, Hesterly G., III *computer systems analyst, inventor, educator*

Cupertino
Baab, Carlton *advertising executive*
Brill, Yvonne Theresa *marketing research company executive, consultant*
Flynn, Ralph Melvin, Jr. *sales executive, marketing consultant*
Fox, Lorraine Susan *marketing professional*
Kvamme, Mark D. *marketing professional*
Mattathil, George Paul *communications specialist, consultant*
Suiter, Thomas *advertising executive*

Daly City
Elleby, Gail *management consultant*
Rubin, Jonathan *government relations consultant*

Dana Point
Mardian, Robert Charles, Jr. *restaurateur*

Danville
da Roza, Victoria Cecilia *human resources administrator*
Donnally, Patrick Andrew *quality management consultant*
Gorman, Russell William *marketing executive, consultant*
Randolph, Kevin H. *marketing executive*

Davis
Woodard, John Henry *quality control professional*

Del Mar
Wadia, Maneck Sorabji *management consultant, writer*

Diamond Bar
Olson, Earle Oliver *marketing and sales executie, consultant*

Duarte
Hand, Heather Denise *human resources executive, educator*

El Cerrito
Addison, Alonzo Church *multimedia communications executive, educator, consultant*

El Segundo
Armstrong, Wallace Dowan, Jr. *data processor*
Autolitano, Astrid *consumer products executive*
Barad, Jill Elikann *toy company executive*
Cordner, Tom *advertising executive*
Gilbert, Scott *advertising executive*
Katz, Lew *advertising executive*
Mehlman, Lon Douglas *information systems specialist*
Sloan, Michael Dana *information systems specialist*

Elk Grove
Bundesen, Faye Stimers *investment and management company owner, educator*
Mark, Arthur *information systems specialist*
Ray-Sims, Deborah *marketing analyst*

Encinitas
Deuble, John L., Jr. *environmental science and engineering services consultant*

Escondido
Daniels, Richard Martin *marketing communications company executive*
Duncan, Ralph Miller *contract management specialist*
Sampson, Richard Arnim *security professional*

Fair Oaks
Marigold, Lawrence Lee *international energy consultant*
Nolan, Mark Gregory *advertising executive*

Fallbrook
Cralley, Lester Vincent *retired industrial hygienist, editor*

Fontana
Hood, Edward *data processing executive*

Fort Bragg
Galli, Darrell Joseph *management consultant*

Foster City
Pratt, John William *sales representative*

Fountain Valley
Lonegan, Thomas Lee *retired restaurant corporation executive*

Fremont
Brooks, Samuel Everett *purchasing agent*

French Camp
Hoberg, Michael Dean *management analyst, educator*

Fresno
Hardison, Roy Lewis *marketing professional*
Pinkerton, Richard LaDoyt *management educator*
Shmavonian, Gerald S. *entertainment executive*

Fullerton
Smythe, Ted Curtis *communications educator*

Gardena
Allison, William Robert *company executive*

Glen Ellen
Kath, Vikki *public relations coordinator, writer*

Glendale
Dohring, Doug *marketing executive*
Dohring, Laurie *marketing executive*
Horton, Kathryn Lynne *marketing executive*
Misa, Kenneth Franklin *management consultant*

Granada Hills
Shoemaker, Harold Lloyd *infosystem specialist*

Grass Valley
Hutcherson, Christopher Alfred *marketing and recruiting and educational consultant*

Half Moon Bay
Fennell, Diane Marie *marketing executive, process engineer*
Hinthorn, Micky Terzagian *volunteer, retired*
Kinsman, Robert Warren *emergency management consultant*

Hawthorne
Perry, James Gregory *sales and marketing executive*

Hayward
Mackin, Terrence Christian *infosystems consultant*

Healdsburg
Canfield, Grant Wellington, Jr. *management consultant*

Hemet
Coad, Dennis L. *marketing executive, management consultant*
Mosley, Cynthia Lisa *marketing professional*

Hermosa Beach
Le Veque, Matthew Kurt *public affairs and marketing consultant*

Hillsborough
West, Hugh Sterling *aircraft leasing company executive*

Hollywood
Duhart, Lawrence Albert *auralist*
Lempert, Philip *advertising executive, author, consumerologist, syndicated columnist, broadcast journalist*

Huntington Beach
Carino, Linda Susan *business consultant*
Lopata, Martin Barry *executive*
Viccaro, James Richard *marketing executive*
Wing, Roger *management consultant*

Inglewood
Lee, Louis, II *security services company executive*
Leiweke, Timothy *sales executive, marketing professional*

Irvine
Colino, Richard Ralph *communications consultant*
Colucci, Chuck Roger *management consultant*
Kuhl, Ronald Webster *marketing executive*
Lee, Robert Erich *information technology consultant*
Maybay, Duane Charles *recycling systems executive*
Moon, William Lawrence *sales representative*
Pape, Barbara Karen *administrative assistant*
Schuetz, John Michael *sales executive*
Seller, Gregory Erol *marketing executive, writer*
Stanton, Lewis Harris *software company executive*
von Tilsit, Heidemarie *information management specialist*
Westphal, Ruth Lilly *educational audio-visual company executive, author, publisher*
Wilck, Carl Thomas *public relations executive*

Irwindale
Dostourian, Dick *computer systems executive*

La Canada
Bernabe, Gretta Marie Domingo *company officer*

La Habra
Hatai, Thomas Henry *international marketing professional*

La Jolla
Barrett, Larry Leon *housing and dining services administrator*
Deal, Luisa *management consultant, trainer, speaker, former elementary school educator*
Fricke, Martin Paul *science company executive*
Muniain, Javier P. *computer company executive, physicist, researcher*
Reed, James Anthony *hotel industry executive, consultant*

La Mirada
Campbell, Douglas L. *communications company executive, consultant*

La Puente
Ogden, Jean Lucille *sales executive*

Laguna Beach
Hafey, Edward Earl Joseph *precision tool company executive*
Smith, Patricia Jacquline *marketing executive*
Taylor, James Walter *marketing consultant*

Laguna Hills
Pearson, Thomas Carleton *management executive*
Schulz, Raymond Alexander *medical marketing professional, consultant*
Thomas, Jeffery Michael *sales executive*

Laguna Niguel
Gamal, Irwin Bert *management consultant*
Kursewicz, Lee Z. *marketing consultant*

Lake Arrowhead
Bauer, Ralph Leroy *business executive*

Lake Elsinore
Medina, Ramon M. *housing professional, consultant*

Lake Forest
White, Joy Mieko *communications executive*

Lancaster
Hutchins, James Leigh *quality assurance professional*

Larkspur
Finkelstein, James Arthur *management consultant*

Laton
Vargas, Al Garcia *building contractor*

Lee Vining
McQuilkin, Geoffrey James *communications director*

Livermore
Clark, Woodrow Wilson, Jr. *strategic planner*
Kalb, Ronald Gary *public relations executive*
Rippe, Lynn E. *contract administrator*
Williams, David Michael *manufacturing executive*
Zambetti, Denis Egan *product specialist*

Loma Linda
Huff, Dale Eugene *retired environmental services executive*
Maurice, Don *personal care industry executive*

Long Beach
Aldrich, David Lawrence *public relations executive*
Chesser, Steven Bruce *public relations executive*
Johnson, William Harry *international management consultant*
Le, Nguyen Minh *computer company executive*
McClain, Samuel Albert *marketing professional*
Metzger, Vernon Arthur *management educator, consultant*
Scholnick, Joseph B. *public relations executive, journalist*
Simon, Renee Blatt *communications executive*
Smith, Keith Larue *research company executive*
Sosoka, John Richard *consulting firm executive, engineer*
Vejsicky, Cathleen Lynn *management executive, educator*
West, Edward Alan *graphics communications executive*

Los Alamitos
Kidde, John Edgar *food company executive*
Weinberger, Frank *information management consultant*

Los Altos
Doby, Karen Elaine *data processing company executive*
Poonja, Mohamed *business reorganization, financial and management consultant*
Weinman, Roberta Sue *marketing and financial communications consultant*

Los Angeles
Armstrong, C. Michael *computer business executive*
Bakeman, Carol Ann *administrative services manager, singer*
Barrett, Stephen DeYoe *marketing executive*
Berk, Karen M. *marketing and communications professional*
Berman, Saul Jay *strategic consultant*
Calvo, Debra Lee Goff *public relations executive*
Campbell, Carolyn Margret *communications consultant*
Cho, Dean Deuk *computer company executive*
Djujich, David B. *computer software company executive*
Dorfman, Steven David *electronics company executive*
Duke, William Edward *public affairs executive*
Edwards, William H., Sr. *retired hotel corporation executive*
Einstein, Clifford Jay *advertising executive*
Ferraro, Douglas Gene *executive*
Ferry, Richard Michael *executive search firm executive*
Fishman, Arnie *marketing executive, consultant, film producer*
Florence, Verena Magdalena *business and computer consultant*
Funk, Susan E. *management consultant*
Garland, G(arfield) Garrett *sales executive, golf professional*
Georgesco, Victor *printing company executive*
Goldstein, Norton Maurice (Goldy Norton) *public relations consultant*
Greene, Alvin *service company executive, management consultant*
Grossman, Dorothea G. *consulting services administrator, poet*
Harris, Godfrey *public policy consultant*
Hartsough, Gayla Anne Kraetsch *management consultant*
Hofert, Jack *consulting company executive, lawyer*
Hotchkiss, Vivian Evelyn *employment agency executive*
Katz, Jerry Paul *corporate executive*
Kessler, Robert Allen *data processing executive*
Krinsky, Ira Walter *executive search consultant*
Laba, Marvin *management consultant*
Lamonica, John *food executive*
Lee, James Jui-Chang *public relations executive*
Leibert, Richard William *special events producer*
LeMaster, Susan M. *communications executive, writer*
Livdahl, Roger C. *wine appraiser*
LoBaugh, Leslie E., Jr. *holding company executive, corporate lawyer*
McArthur, John D. *communications executive*
Morris, Brian *advertising executive*
Nava, Yolanda Margot *public relations and communications consultant*
Otto, Joseph Clair *information systems educator*
Ovitz, Michael S. *communications executive*
Patel, Chandra Kumar Naranbhai *communications company executive, educator, researcher*
Patterson, Russell Alfred *business valuation consultant*
Paura, Catherine *marketing professional*
Peden, Lynn Ellen *marketing executive*
Pekar, Peter, Jr. *business professional*
Ranftl, Robert Matthew *management consulting company executive*
Reiner, James Anthony *marketing executive*
Roeschlaub, Jean Marian Clinton *restaurant chain executive*
Rucker, Thomas Douglas *purchasing executive*
Sackman, Dave *marketing executive*
Schwartz, Arthur Allen *trade show producer*
Shiffman, Leslie Brown *management executive*
Shonk, Albert Davenport, Jr. *advertising executive*
Spofford, Robert Houston *advertising agency executive*
Stauber, Brandon Frederick *consultant information technology and communications*
Stern, James Coper *sales executive*
Stoltz, Eric Michael *public relations executive*
Stretch, Shirley Marie *marketing executive*
Sylvester, Richard Russell *economist, management executive*
Taylor, Richard W. *public relations executive*
Van Remmen, Roger *management consultant*
Wade, Michael Robert Alexander *marketing specialist*
Webster, Jeffery Norman *technology policy analyst*

Los Gatos
Bederka, Stephen Edward *management consultant*
Maas, Joan Louise *training and development consultant*

Los Osos
Maddy, Donald Lee *computer company executive, software developer*

Mammoth Lakes
Buchanan, Lee Ann *public relations executive*

Manhattan Beach
Deutsch, Barry Joseph *management development company executive*
Trager, Russell Harlan *advertising consultant*

Marina Del Rey
Holland, Robin Jean *personnel company executive*
Lott, Davis Newton *advertising agency executive, publisher*

Menlo Park
Creswell, Donald Creston *management consultant*
Dolgow, Allan Bentley *consulting company executive*
Fried, Louis Lester *information technology and management consultant*
Kornfeld, Judith R. *product marketing consultant*
Kurtzig, Sandra L. *software company executive*
Sommers, William Paul *management consultant, think tank executive*
Straubel, John Frederick *public relations and advertising executive*

Mill Valley
Baker, Malcolm *marketing executive*

Millbrae
Mank, Edward Warren *marketing professional*

Milpitas
Corrigan, Wilfred J. *data processing and computer company executive*
De Smidt, Frank Joseph *communications executive*
Sobeck, Gerald Robert *quality assurance professional, professional baseball scout*

Mission Viejo
Corey, Jo Ann *senior management analyst*
Dillon, Francis Patrick *human resources executive, management and sales consultant*
Harder, Wendy Wetzel *communications executive*
Ross, Renae Lynn *marketing professional*

Modesto
Cofer, Berdette Henry *public management consulting company executive*

Moffett Field
Baldwin, Betty Jo *computer specialist*
Waller, Peter William *public affairs executive*

Montebello
Norkin, Mark Mitchell *sales executive*

Monterey
Cutino, Bert Paul *chef, restaurant owner*
Reierson, Lawrence Edward *organizational development consultant, executive*

Monterey Park
Kwong, Daniel Wai-Kin *business consultant, educator, songwriter, poet*
Winograd, Morley Alec *sales executive*

Montrose
Sanders, David Clyde *management and marketing consultant*

Moreno Valley
Cowan, James Cornelius *security firm executive*

Morgan Hill
Sall, Jeni P. *marketing executive*

Mountain View
Akeley, Kurt Barton *computer graphics company executive, engineer*
Benrey, Jeff Michael *marketing professional*
Castor, Jon Stuart *management consultant*
Cook, Robert P., II *business development executive*
de Urioste, George Adolfo, IV *software company executive*
Herbert, Kenneth George *management consultant*
Kwong, Donald *purchasing agent, consultant*
Lee, Murlin E. *program manager*
Mc Nealy, Scott *computer company executive*
Rondell, Thomas *public relations consultant, marketing communications consultant*
Rulifson, Johns Frederick *computer company executive, computer scientist*
Shah, Girish Popatlal *data processing services company executive*
Thapa, Mukund Narain-Dhami *software company executive*

Napa
Buchanan, Teri Bailey *communications executive*
Gelven, Michael Paul *marketing executive*
LaRocque, Marilyn Ross Onderdonk *writer, public relations consultant*

National City
Wisener, Maureen Mayden *public relations, marketing executive*

Newbury Park
Heldt, Jean-Paul *management consultant*

Newhall
Heekin, Valerie Anne *telecommunications technician*

Newport Beach
Allumbaugh, Byron *retired grocery company executive*
Bullis, Michael A. *hotel executive*
de Garcia, Lucia *marketing professional*
Gellman, Gloria Gae Seeburger Schick *marketing professional*
Lawson, Thomas Cheney *fraud examiner*
McCue, Dennis Michael *management consultant*
Melrose, Albert Joseph *investor relations professional*

Newport Coast
Mitchell, Herbert Eugene *management consultant, marketing specialist*

Oakland
Dunn, David Cameron *entrepreneur, business executive*
Hoffman, George Alan *consulting company executive*
Howard, Bradford Reuel *travel company executive*
Kriskovich, Joe *human resources specialist*
Misner, Gervase Arthur *personnel analyst*
Potash, Stephen Jon *international public relations practitioner*
Yamada, Tomokiyo Tom *advertising executive*

Oceanside
McDonald, John Peter *management and technology consultant*

Ontario
Hawley, Nanci Elizabeth *public relations and communications professional*
Kahn, Mario Santamaria *international marketing executive*
Wright, Charles Lee *information systems consultant*

Orange
LaGreen, Alan Lennart *public relations executive, radio personality*
Maier, John Mark *organizational leadership educator*
McNeil, David James *communications executive, marketing consultant*

Orinda
Somerset, Harold Richard *retired business executive*

Oxnard
Snasdell, Susan Kathleen *computer company executive*
Zigman, Paul Edmond *environmental consultant, executive*

Pacific Palisades
Kalis, Murray *advertising agency executive, writer*
Perse, Aria Leon *international business advanced technologies executive*

Palm Desert
Kern, Paul Alfred *advertising company executive, research consultant, realtor*

Palm Springs
Richard, Brenda G. *administrative professional*
Seale, Robert McMillan *office services company executive*
Vivian, Linda Bradt *sales and public relations executive*

Palo Alto
Adler, Richard Paul *technology consultant, writer*
Allen, Louis Alexander *management consultant*
Carter, Janice Joene *telecommunications executive*
Curry, William Sims *procurement executive*
Eleccion, Marcelino *marketing executive, computer engineer, programmer, editor, writer, lecturer, artist*
Kirk, Carmen Zetler *data processing executive*
Lawrence-Forrest, Lori Louise *restaurateur*
Seethaler, William Charles *international business executive, consultant*
Willrich, Mason *executive, consultant*

Palos Verdes Peninsula
Covington, Francis A. *marketing executive*
Marlett, De Otis Loring *retired management consultant*

Pasadena
Berger, Jay Vari *executive recruiter*
Caine, Stephen Howard *data processing executive*
Dixon, Diane Brooks *communications executive*
Drutchas, Gerrick Gilbert *investigator*
Griesche, Robert Price *hospital purchasing executive*
Jarvis, Steven L. *technology director*
Jasnow, Edward Jay *subcontracts manager*
Kaplan, Gary *executive recruiter*
Langdell, Tim *software company executive*
Little, Paul Edward *communications executive, city official*
Lugg, Marlene Martha *health information systems specialist, health planner*
Mangum, William *management consulting company executive*
Pattie, Steven Norris *advertising executive, artist, author*
Soloway, Jay Stephen *consulting firm executive*
Strick, Ruth Cochran *career counselor*
Wildermuth, Ronald E. *public relations professional*

Paso Robles
Boxer, Jerome Harvey *computer and management consultant, vintner, accountant*

Pebble Beach
Harvie, J. Jason *administrative aide, private secretary*

Pescadero
Crawford, James Barclay *management consultant, travel writer*

Petaluma
Daniel, Gary Wayne *communications and music industry executive*

Pico Rivera
Luevano, Fred, Jr. *computer systems executive*
Rapier, Stephen Michael *marketing executive*

Placerville
Hemsley, David Lee *computer company executive*

Playa Del Rey
Rich, Susan Abby *efficiency consultant*

Pleasant Hill
Munch, William David *information systems consultant*
Newkirk, Raymond Leslie *management consultant*

Pleasanton
Burd, Steve *food service executive*
Lykins, Jay Arnold *economic development director*
Petrone, Joseph Anthony *business consultant, writer*
Stout-Pierce, Susan *clinical specialist*

Point Reyes Station
Harvey, Gregory Alan *microcomputer technology educator, consultant*

Pomona
Kapoor, Sandra A. *restaurant management educator*

Port Hueneme
Cobb, Roy Lampkin, Jr. *computer sciences corporation executive*
Haddad, Edmonde Alex *public affairs executive*
Hedvig, Michael Elliott *management consultant*

Porter Ranch
Rothenberg, Marcy Miroff *public relations consultant*

Poway
Berger, Newell James, Jr. *security professional*

Prunedale
Wyatt, Pericles *food service executive*

Rancho Cordova
Hope, Gerri Danette *telecommunications management executive*

Rancho Cucamonga
DiTommaso, Karl Joseph *business executive*
Southard, Burton M. *political and public affairs consultant*

Rancho La Costa
Handel, William Keating *advertising and sales executive*

Rancho Palos Verdes
Rubenstein, Leonard Samuel *communications executive, ceramist, painter, sculptor, photographer*
Savage, Terry Richard *information systems executive*
Semos, William *management consultant, educator*

Rancho Santa Fe
Baker, Charles Lynn *management consultant*
Gruenwald, George Henry *new products development management consultant*
Schirra, Walter Marty, Jr. *business consultant, former astronaut*

Rancho Santa Margarita
Kidde, Andrew Judson *sales executive, consultant*

Red Bluff
Bates, Deborah Filbeck *career counselor*

Redwood City
Bertman, Roger Bruce *management executive*
Bertram, Jack Renard *information systems company executive*
Gagarin, Dennis Paul *advertising agency executive*
Henley, Jeffrey O. *restaurant executive*
Miller, Anne Kathleen *training company executive, technical marketing consultant*
Rohde, James Vincent *software systems company executive*

Redwood Shores
Hrut, Christopher Boleslaw *sales and marketing executive*

Reseda
Leahy, T. Liam *marketing and management consultant*

Riverside
Gordon, Jerry Arthur *family services organization administrator*
Taylor, Lyndon Elmer *planning and development consultant*
Walker, Moira Kaye *sales executive*

Rocklin
Gans, Dennis Joseph *information technology specialist*

Sacramento
Anderson, Michael Kenneth *marketing professional*
Briscoe, Agatha Donatto *data processing executive, instructor*
Collings, Charles LeRoy *supermarket executive*
Davies, William Ralph *service executive*
Fear, David Lane *employee benefit consultant*
Hunt, Dennis *public relations executive*
Kidd, Reuben Proctor *management engineer*
Kline, Fred Walter *retired communications company executive*
McElroy, Leo Francis *communications consultant, journalist*
Willis, Edward Oliver *management consultant, state official*

Saint Helena
Posert, Harvey Peres *public relations professional*

Salinas
Jeffries, Russell Morden *communications company official*

San Carlos
Eby, Michael John *marketing research and technology consultant*
Fleishman, Alan Michael *marketing consultant*
Walrad, Charlene Chuck *management consultant*

San Clemente
Anderson, Michael Robert *marketing representative*
Sullivan, Shawn E. *marketing and sales professional*

San Diego
Adams, Loretta *marketing executive*
Adamson, Robert Michael Knaggs *spiritual teacher, whole body wellness and health restoration specialist*
Barr, Robert Edward *computer company executive*
Bryan, John Rodney *management consultant*
Cady, Joseph Howard *management consultant*
Deffley, Mark Garon *environmental purchasing executive*
De Sio, Anthony William *communications executive*
DiRuscio, Lawrence William *advertising executive*
Downs, Kathleen Joan *purchasing supervisor*
Evans, John Joseph *management consultant*
Galbraith, Nanette Elaine Gerks *forensic and management sciences company executive*
Gilbertson, Oswald Irving *marketing executive*
Goodall, Jackson Wallace, Jr. *restaurant company executive*
Gunter, Emily Diane *communications executive, marketing professional*
Hale, David Fredrick *health care company executive*
Hall, Myrna Anne *marketing professional, development professional*
Harris, James Michael *sales executive*
Hays, Diana Joyce Watkins *consumer products company executive*
Johnson, Michael Edward *communication consultant, magician*
Kilmer, Maurice Douglas *marketing executive*
Krejci, Robert Harry *non-profit organizations development consultant*

Kunkel, Scott William *strategic management and entrepreneurship educator*
MacCracken, Peter James *marketing executive, communications executive*
Marchetti, Karen J. *advertising executive*
Mitchell, Thomas Edward, Jr. *communications cabling executive*
Mosteller, James Wilbur, III *data processing executive*
Murray, Robert Michael *telecommunications executive*
Nugent, Robert J., Jr. *fast food company executive*
O'Leary, John Joseph *security firm executive*
Oolie, Darlene *advertising executive*
Ortiz, Antonio Ignacio *public relations executive*
Province, Sharon G. *research and development executive*
Ronci, Curtis Lee *marketing professional*
Samaras, Thomas Theodore *management system specialist, author, researcher*
Schlesinger, Robert Jackson *business administration educator*
Shirley, John Jeffery *management information systems executive*
Short, Jay Milton *biotechnology company executive*
Slade-Lundy, Bettie B. *retired electronics professional*
Stoorza Gill, Gail *corporate professional*
Theis, James Edward *pastry chef, interior designer*
Tompane, Mary Beth *management consultant*
Vallbona, Marisa *public relations counselor*
Youkharibache, Philippe Bijin *pharmaceutical software company executive*
Ziegaus, Alan James *public relations executive*

San Francisco
Bancel, Marilyn *fund raising management consultant*
Barnett, Lester A. *advertising executive*
Beene, M. Melanie *arts management consultant*
Bernstein, Gerald William *management consultant, researcher*
Bigony, F. Randall *leasing company executive*
Butenhoff, Susan *public relations executive*
Carr-Ruffino, Norma *management educator*
Cavanagh, John Charles *advertising agency executive*
Colton, Roy Charles *management consultant*
Corcoran, John *advertising executive*
Edgar, James Macmillan, Jr. *management consultant*
Faron, Fay Cheryl *private investigator, writer*
Gehb, Michael *public relations executive*
Gesner, Bruce David *consulting company executive*
Glinsky, Simon *management consultant*
Goldberg, Fred Sellmann *advertising executive*
Goodby, Jeffrey *advertising agency executive*
Gross, Richard Philip *retired business executive*
Haas, Peter E., Sr. *company executive*
Halsey, Minor *computer company executive*
Henderson, Nancy Grace *marketing and technical documentation executive*
Holding, Carol Pierson *brand positioning consultant*
Jennings, Nancy Patricia *publications and communications executive*
Jones, J. Gilbert *research consultant*
Jones, Stanton William *management consultant*
Kielarowski, Henry Edward *marketing executive*
Klammer, Joseph Francis *management consultant*
Landis, Richard Gordon *retired food company executive*
Loden, D. John *advertising executive*
Marshall, Scott *advertising agency executive*
Massaro, Mike *advertising executive*
Meyer, Keith John *marketing professional*
Miller, Phoebe Amelia *marketing professional*
Muegge, Lyn *advertising executive*
Murphy, Catherine Maria *public affairs consultant*
Oppel, Andrew John *computer systems consultant*
O'Rourke, Dennis *advertising executive*
Pascale, Antonina Susanna *marketing professional, writer*
Pivnicka, Barbara Milliken *marketing executive*
Pollack, Jeffrey Lee *restaurateur*
Probert, Colin *advertising executive*
Pryor, Lois Marie *management consultant*
Riney, Hal Patrick *advertising executive*
Russell, Carol Ann *personnel service company executive*
Saunders, Sharon *media director*
Silverstein, Richard *advertising agency executive*
Staub, Anita (Anita Kilpatrick) *management analyst, educator*
Tarter, Blodwen *marketing and information technology executive*
Thompson, Gary W. *public relations executive*
Tonini, Leon Richard *sales professional*
Torme, Margaret Anne *public relations executive, communications consultant*
Warrick, Brooke *marketing executive*
Wendle, Kevin *computer company executive*
Wentz, Jeffrey Lee *information systems consultant*
Willner, Jay R. *consulting company executive*

San Gabriel
Ramirez, Ralph Roy *management consultant*

San Jose
Ashford, Robert Louis *computer professional*
Beverett, Andrew Jackson *marketing executive*
Botkin, Monty Lane *computer company executive*
Bunn, Charles Nixon *strategic business planning consultant*
Cayne, Douglas Andrew *computer company executive*
Chinery, James Patrick *marketing professional*
Chung, Heon Hwa *research and development executive*
Connor, Gary Edward *manufacturing company marketing executive*
Dietz, Russell Scott *communications company executive*
Franson, Paul Oscar, III *public relations executive*
Harkins, Craig *management consultant*
Harrus, Alain Simon *marketing professional*
Highlander, Richard William *communications executive*
Hutcheson, Jerry Dee *market research company executive*
Jordan, Thomas Vincent *advertising educator, consultant*
Mizer, Richard Anthony *technology company executive*
Nguyen, Lam Duc *business executive, consultant*
Nguyen, Thomas *computer executive*
Orr, Gregory Thomas *restaurant manager, business studies educator*
Ostrom, Philip Gardner *computer company executive*
Smith, Charles Richard *high technology marketing executive*

San Luis Obispo
Vanderspek, Peter George *management consultant, writer*

San Marino
Babcock, Catherine Marly *public relations executive*

San Mateo
Helfert, Erich Anton *management consultant, author, educator*
Larkin, Nelle Jean *computer programmer, analyst*
Nazzaro, David Alfred *sales executive*
Wigglesworth, David Cunningham *business and management consultant*
Witwer, Jeffrey Garth *marketing executive*

San Rafael
Marmann, Sigrid *software development company executive*
Prowell, Anne Durfee *marketing consultant, writer*
Thompson, John William *international management consultant*
Yuan, Shao-Yuen *management consultant*

San Ramon
Gardner, Nord Arling *management consultant administrator*
Moore, Justin Edward *data processing executive*
Warren, Sandra Lyn *quality assurance professional*

Santa Ana
Boynton, William Lewis *electronic manufacturing company official*
Holtz, Joseph Norman *marketing executive*
Lesly, Craig Edwards *marketing professional*
McFarlane, William John *software development company executive*

Santa Barbara
Amory, Thomas Carhart *management consultant*
Emmons, Robert John *corporate executive*
Hanley, Kevin Lance *maintenance manager*

Santa Clara
Carter, Dennis Lee *marketing professional*
Desrosier, James Norman *marketing executive*
Menkin, Christopher (Kit Menkin) *leasing company executive*
Rudolph, Ronald Alvin *human resources executive*
Vincent, David Ridgely *management consulting executive*

Santa Cruz
Giddings, Debra Lynn *marketing executive, computer consultant*
Phanes, Margaret Astrid *trainer, visual designer*
Swartz, Ray *data processing executive*

Santa Fe Springs
Hammond, Judy McLain *business services executive*
Ittner, Perry Martin *sales and marketing consultant*

Santa Monica
Bachrach, Charles Lewis *advertising agency executive*
Corrigan, Gerald F. *executive search consultant*
Field, Edward C. *research executive*
Fraser, Renee *advertising executive*
Jones, Penn Holter *advertising executive*
Lucas, James Bruno *public relations consultant*
McCreary, Lori L. *entertainment business executive*
Mullen, William Kemp, Jr. *contract management executive*
Nathanson, Joseph S. *media relations company executive*
Naulin, John Arthur *entertainment company executive*
Postaer, Larry *advertising executive*
Ryan, Jane Frances *corporate communications executive*
Seymour, Jeffrey Alan *governmental relations consultant*
Uretz, Michael Albert *health and fitness executive*
Weinberger, Martin Andrew *computer company executive*

Santa Rosa
Christopher, Linda Ellen *consultant, association executive*
Furen, Shirley Ann *marketing professional*
Howard, Victor *management consultant*

Saugus
Hauenstein, Donald Herbert, Jr. *computer company executive*

Sausalito
Delaney, Michael Ben *publisher, marketing executive, consultant*

Scotts Valley
Brough, Bruce Alvin *public relations and communications executive*
Delear, Richard Henry *personnel consultant*
Shugart, Alan F. *electronic computing equipment company executive*

Seal Beach
Burge, Willard, Jr. *software company executive*
Thompson, Craig Snover *corporate communications executive*

Shell Beach
Barca, Kathleen *marketing executive*

Sherman Oaks
Best, Barbara *personal manager, publicist*
Peters, Claire Leila *public relations, advertising executive*

Sierra Madre
MacGillivray, MaryAnn Leverone *marketing professional*

Signal Hill
Jarman, Donald Ray *retired public relations professional, minister*

Simi Valley
Jakubanis, Beth *advertising executive*

Solana Beach
Friedmann, Lynne Timpani *public relations consultant, writer*
Jebens, Arthur Bertram *management consultant, lawyer*

Sonora
Mathias, Betty Jane *communications and community affairs consultant, writer, editor, lecturer*

South Pasadena
Keller-Hom, Kimberly S. *marketing professional, researcher, editor*
Lowe, Richard Gerald, Jr. *computer programming manager*

South San Francisco
Lewis, Jason Alvert, Jr. *communications executive*

Spring Valley
Hoff, Bernadine Ryan *management consultant*

Stanford
Hellyer, Constance Anne *communications executive, writer*
Karabela, Leda *public relations and fund raising executive*
Miller, William Frederick *research company executive, educator, business consultant*

Stockton
Hackley, Carol Ann *public relations educator, consultant*

Studio City
Chambers, Clytia Montllor *public relations consultant*
Richman, Anthony E. *textile rental industry association executive*

Sun City
Bavardo, Patricia Carol *marketing executive, author*

Sunnyvale
Byers, Charles Frederick *public relations executive, marketing executive*
Charlton, (James) Paul(ett Jr.) *information systems architect*
Climo, Robert Shipley *public relations executive*
Clinton, John Philip Martin *communications executive*
Krich, Kenneth L. *computer dealer executive*

Taft
Smith, Lee L. *hotel executive*

Talmage
Adams, Donald Elwin *cultural and organization development consultant*

Tehachapi
Smith-Thompson, Patricia Ann *public relations consultant, educator*

Temecula
Buzbee, John D., Jr. *sales executive*
Coram, David James *marketing professional*

Thousand Oaks
Cobb, Shirley Ann *public relations specialist*
Guggenheim, Suzanne *company executive*
Lark, M. Ann *management consultant, strategic planner, naturalist*
Noonan, Daniel Christopher *consultant*

Toluca Lake
Mracky, Ronald Sydney *marketing and promotion executive, travel consultant*

Torrance
Brown, Jeffrey Charles *rental company executive*
Carey, Kathryn Ann *advertising and public relations executive, consultant*
Herendeen, David Louis *software company executive*
Hoyt, Leeza Lee *public relations and advertising firm executive*
Kasari, Leonard Samuel *quality control professional, concrete consultant*
Ko, Denny R. S. *research & development executive*
McQuillin, Richard Ross *management consultant*

Tracy
Green, Brian Gerald *marketing executive*

Tustin
Ding, Mae Lon *employee compensation consultant*
Jay, David Jakubowicz *management consultant*
Jensen, Carolyn Jean *public relations executive*
LeBow, Bennett S. *communications executive*
Rigdon, Judy Anne *business administrator*

Twentynine Palms
Fultz, Philip Nathaniel *management analyst*

Ukiah
Eversole, Walter Robert *funeral director*

Union City
Ingram, Robert M. *communications company executive*

Upland
Deppisch, Paul Vincent *data communications executive*
Ward, Michael Alan *public information consultant*

Vacaville
Young, Roger Carl *computer company executive*

Van Nuys
Bick, Israel *collectables and memorabilia company executive*
Josephs, Alice Ruth *retired executive secretary*

Venice
Chiat, Jay *advertising agency executive*
King, Frederic *health services management executive, educator*

Villa Park
Britton, Thomas Warren, Jr. *management consultant*

Walnut Creek
Baumann, Frederick *retired management consultant*
Garlough, William Glenn *marketing executive*
Leftwich, James Stephen *management consultant*
Maslin, Harvey Lawrence *staffing service company executive*
Moore, John D. *management consultant*
Vitrac, Jean-Jacques Charles *international marketing consultant*

West Covina
Musich, Robert Lorin *motivational speaker*

West Hollywood
Holt, Dennis F. *media buying company executive*

Westlake Village
Catrambone, Eugene Dominic *public relations consultant*
Murdock, David H. *diversified company executive*
Pickman, Phillip *management consultant*

Whittier
Kennedy, Charles John *marketing company executive*

Woodland Hills
Lee, Elizabeth Anne *marketing executive*
Maeda, J. A. *data processing executive*
Parrott, Dennis Beecher *sales executive*
Reynolds, Edward Evan, Jr. *information systems consultant*

Yorba Linda
Tuttle, Frank Douglas *marketing executive*

Yucca Valley
Clay, Sean Cochrane *software development company executive*

COLORADO

Allenspark
Newman, Dean Gordon *business consultant*

Arvada
Hulse, Ralph Robert *management consultant*
Pennington, Arthur Stewart *systems consultant*

Aurora
Brunell, David H. *information systems manager*
Hadsall, Debra June *business service and consulting executive*
Harlan, Raymond Carter *communication executive*
Pohlman, David Lawrence *training systems consultant*
Reitan, Harold Theodore *management consultant*
Welch, Richard LeRoy *personal improvement company executive*

Boulder
Bryson, Gary Spath *cable television and telephone company executive*
Fisher, Joseph Stewart *management consultant*
Hart, Michael John *environmental management*
Jerritts, Stephen G. *computer company executive*
Li Dessau, Kathryn Dairoh *product manager*
Marshall, James Kenneth *academic administrator*

Breckenridge
Sbragia, Gary W. *communications company executive*

Broomfield
Cole, Lee Arthur *new product development executive*
Johnson, Holly Rouillard *public relations executive*
Livesay, Valorie Ann *security analyst*

Castle Rock
Danner, Paul Kruger, III *telecommunications executive*

Colorado Springs
Bayne, Kim Miklofsky *marketing communications and public relations professional, consultant, author*
Deiotte, Charles Edward *computer software company executive*
Ford, James Carlton *human resources executive*
Fortune, James Michael *marketing executive*
Guthrie, David Neal *marketing executive*
Hurley, Rebecca Johnson *marketing professional*
Korsten, Mary Ann *subcontract administrator, buyer*
Ledbetter, Logan Scott *management consultant*
Lewis, Sheila Muriel O'Neil *retired communications management specialist*
Loux, Jonathan Dale *business development consultant*
McDevitt, John Alfred *program manager, military officer, retired*
Midkiff, Donald Wayne *program manager*
Mills, Sherry Rae *training and conference planning*
Pool, Timothy Kevin *facilities management consultant*
Robinson, Richard Gary *management consultant, accountant*
Sandoval, Isabelle Medina *human resources specialist*
Starr, James Edward *logistics management executive*
Vickerman, Paula Marie *marketing professional, consultant*
Weinstein, Steven Samuel *marketing executive*

Delta
Vanderheyden, Mirna-Mar *resort management and services executive*

Denver
Avrin, David Lawrence *public relations executive, legislative liason, vocalist*
Ayers, Rendall Paul *public relations consultant*
Clinch, Nicholas Bayard, III *business executive*
Cooper, Larry S. *cleaning network executive, textile consultant*
Cotherman, Audrey Mathews *management and policy consultant, administrator*
Dolsen, David Horton *mortician*
Greenberg, Pamela Thayer *public policy specialist*
Hamrick, Joseph Eugene, Jr. *information services specialist*
Harris, Howard Jeffrey *marketing and printing company executive*
Hartman, Diane Lawrence *communication professional*
Heck, Gary L. *security management company executive*
Henry, David Allen *advertising executive*
Hobbs, Stephen Craig *management consultant*
Hughes, Bradley Richard *business executive*
Johnston, Gwinavere Adams *public relations consultant*
Kennel, James Otto *marketing professional*
Kurtz, Maxine *personnel consultant, lawyer*
Lybarger, John Steven *business development consultant, trainer*
Marcus, Jeffrey Howard *electronic security system company executive*
Martin, Robert Burton *management and marketing consultant*
McLean, Robin Jennifer *marketing, advertising professional*
Muftic, Felicia Anne Boillot *consumer relations professional*
Murdock, Pamela Ervilla *travel and advertising company executive*
Murray, James Alan *urban and environmental consultant, investor*
Neu, Carl Herbert, Jr. *management consultant*
Owen, William Frederick *engineering and management consultant*
Peck, George Holmes *public relations executive*
Price, Harvey Raymond *safety, environmental health services administrator*
Primavera, Dianne I. *customer service representative administrator*
Robinson, Lisa Hertz *public relations consultant*
Servoss, Marcus Edward *public relations executive*
Shuler, Sally Ann Smith *telecommunications, computer services and software company executive*
Sundel, Harvey H. *marketing research analyst and consultant*
Thomas, Michael Steven *software company executive*
Wall Hofer, Marjorie Selma *career specialist, consultant*
Welchert, Steven Joseph *public affairs consultant*

Englewood
Ament, Jonathan Jay *governmental affairs specialist*
Ames, A. Gary *communications company executive*
Bowlin, Gregory Lee *marketing professional*
Cooper, Steven Jon *healthcare management consultant, educator*
Daniels, C. Eugene *owner executive search company*
Greenagel, Debra *travel agency executive*
Harding, Wayne Edward, III *software company executive, accountant*
Joffe, Barbara Lynne *computer project manager*
Kail, Joseph Gerard *communications sales and marketing executive*
Kuhn, Donald Marshall *marketing professional*
Lake, Stanley James *security consulting company executive, motel chain executive, locksmith*
Mahadev, Rajesh *strategic marketing professional*
Nelson, Thomas Wilfred *computer network company executive*
Reisinger, George Lambert *management consultant*
Rounds, Donald Michael *public relations executive*
Slater, Shelley *communications executive*

Estes Park
Thomas, David Timothy *marketing professional*

Evergreen
Rodolff, Dale Ward *sales executive, consultant*
Wiesner, Erhard *management consultant, realtor*

Fort Collins
Fletcher, Charles R. *public affairs specialist*
Gilmore, Timothy Jonathan *executive recruiter, paralegal*
Hinz, Shirley Sorensen *administrative secretary*
Newlin, Douglas Randal *learning products engineer*

Franktown
Smith, James Micheal *marketing executive*

Fraser
Hibbs, John David *software executive, engineer, business owner*

Golden
Chandramouli, Srinivasan (Chandra Chandramouli) *management and systems consultant*
Kuehn, JoDee Stahlecker *information technology consultant*
Nelson, Frances Patricia *food service executive*
Stroh, Gary Roland *development company executive*

Grand Junction
Freeman, Neil *accounting and computer consulting firm executive*

Greeley
Mader, Douglas Paul *quality engineering manager*
Miller, Diane Wilmarth *human resources director*

Greenwood Village
Shaddock, Paul Franklin, Sr. *human resources director*

Lakewood
Allen, Sam Raymond *organization development specialist*
Richards, Robert Charles *management consultant*
Shoe, Stephen Charles *marketing professional*
Walton, Roger Alan *public relations executive, mediator, writer*

Littleton
Allen, Gordon Kelley *communications company executive*
Hopping, William Russell *hospitality industry consultant and appraiser*
Schoeppel, Cynthia Louise *human resource executive*
Snyder, John Millard *recreation resources executive, educator*

Longmont
Anderson, Michael George *marketing and advertising executive*
Burns, Michael Edward *technology company executive*
Nevling, Harry Reed *health care human resources executive*

Louisville
Amalfitano, Andrew Michael *advisory reliability manager*
Ferguson, Gary L. *public relations executive*

Palmer Lake
Guller, Todd Jaime *marketing and communications executive*

Parker
Pastore, Thomas Michael *telecommunications sales executive*

Sheridan
Wolfe, Brian Augustus *sales executive, small business owner*

Silverthorne
Schaffer, Thomas Ray *water and wastewater management executive*

Steamboat Springs
Guettich, Bruce Michael *sporting goods company executive*
Van Baak, Anthony Edward *resort executive*

Sterling
Jones, Daniel Lee *software development company executive*

Telluride
Hadley, Paul Burrest, Jr. (Tabbit Hadley) *chef services manager, photographer*

Thornton
Clanton, Paul David, Jr. *management information systems director*

Westminster
Wirkkala, John Lester *software company executive*

Winter Park
Hamilton, Penny Rafferty *research executive, writer, educator*

DISTRICT OF COLUMBIA

Washington
Fuller, Edwin Daniel *hotel executive*

FLORIDA

Shalimar
Kelly, Kathleen Suzanne *marketing professional*

HAWAII

Aiea
Lenhart, James Robert *sales manager, food service administrator*

Ewa Beach
Yoshida, Karen Kamijo Cateel *public relations professional*

Fort Shafter
Maruoka, Jo Ann Elizabeth *information systems manager*

Honolulu
Bossert, Philip Joseph *information systems executive*
Devenot, David Charles *human resource executive*
Dougherty, Raleigh Gordon *manufacturing representative*
Kampfer, John Brennan *data processing administrator*
Klink, Paul Leo *business executive*
Lee, Lorrin L. *marketing executive, architect, designer, author, speaker*
Miyamoto, Craig Toyoki *public relations executive*
Rogers, Dwane Leslie *management consultant*
Shirai, Scott *communications executive*
Simpson, Andrea Lynn *energy communications executive*
Singer, Hersh *marketing executive*
Yang, David Chie-Hwa *business administration educator*

Kailua
Grimmer, Beverley Sue *consumer products executive*
Torraca, Louis A., Jr. *retired public relations executive*

Kailua Kona
Causey, Gill Terry *recreation company executive*

Kamuela
Plum, Thomas Schunior *software company executive*

Kihei
Christman, Helen Dorothy Nelson *resort executive*

Kula
Rohlfing, Frederick William *travel company executive, political consultant, retired judge*

IDAHO

American Falls
Newlin, L. Max *parks and recreation director*

Boise
Burke, Larry Dryden *public relations administrator*
Faltin, Bruce Charles *hotel executive*
Fiedler, John Amberg *marketing scientist*
Harrison, Anthony Robert *public relations executive*
Hayes, Robert B. *communications executive*
Luthy, John Frederick *management consultant*
Mortensen, Richard Harold *data processing executive*
Saldin, Thomas R. *consumer products company executive, corporate lawyer*
Wall, Judith Lindley *data entry professional*

Eagle
Gerber, Lloyd M. *business consultant*

Hailey
Crofts, Mary Austin *parks and recreation director*

Idaho Falls
Gregory, Nelson Bruce *motel owner, retired naval officer*
Hoopes, Sidney Lou *marketing consultant, educational association administrator*
Stosich, Davidjohn *company executive*

Moscow
Olsen, Nayantara Marietta *human resources executive, marketing consultant*

Plummer
Matheson, Donna Jane *communications executive, editor*

Sandpoint
Malcolm, Richard Douglas, Jr. *resort administrator*

MICHIGAN

Bloomfield Hills
Adams, Charles Francis *advertising and real estate executive*

MONTANA

Billings
Cull, Chris Alan *operations executive*
Leroy, Norbert Ghislain *management and financial consultant*
Tooley, Charles Frederick *communications executive, consultant*

Butte
Ouellette, Debra Lee *administrative assistant, policy and procedure consultant*

Columbia Falls
Thomas, Steve D. *infosystem specialist*

Helena
Waterman, Mignon Redfield *public relations executive, state legislator*

Kalispell
Daly, Carol Lynn *economic policy center executive*

NEVADA

Carson City
Beecher, Earl William *marketing professional*
Downey, Michael Dean *interactive distance education coordinator*
Powers, Jeffrey *business executive, speaker*

Henderson
Bradford, Craig Snow *corporate executive*
Head, Samuel *management consultant*
Henry, Philip Lawrence *marketing professional*
Smyth, Cornelius Edmonston *retired hotel executive*

Las Vegas
Belport, Stanley Curtis *computer professional*
Bennett, William Gordon *casino executive*
Boyle, Carolyn Moore *public relations executive, marketing professional*
Collis, Kay Lynn *professional beauty consultant*
Cummings, Leslie Edwards *hospitality management educator*
Dickinson, Scott Ward *printing company executive*
Hechter, Marc Steven *management consultant*
Koon, Ray Harold *management and security consultant*
Mataseje, Veronica Julia *sales executive*
Pringle, Thomas Hivick *sales executive*
Rowe, Carl Osborn *business consultant*
Shipper, Todd Jeffrey *communications executive*
Shively, Judith Carolyn (Judy Shively) *office assistant, contract administrator*
Wiener, Valerie *communications consultant, state senator*

North Las Vegas
Folden, Norman C. (Skip Folden) *information systems executive, consultant*

Pahrump
Taylor, Mary Elizabeth *retired recreation administrator, retired dietitian*

Reno
Ford, Victoria *public relations executive*
Howard, Christopher Philip *business consultant*
Johnson, Richard Karl *hospitality company executive*
Putnam, Howard Dean *speaker, writer, former airline executive*
Reed, Michael Raybren *government affairs consulting executive*
Wells, Richard H. *gaming research executive*

Sparks
Adams, Ken R. *gaming analyst, consultant, historian*

Zephyr Cove
Amico, Charles William *management consultant*
Langlois, Donna Lee *educational executive consultant*

NEW MEXICO

Albuquerque
Geary, David Leslie *communications executive, educator, consultant*
Golden, Julius *advertising and public relations executive, lobbyist, investor*
Hale, Bruce Donald *retired marketing professional*
Horner, Harry Charles, Jr. *sales executive, theatrical and film consultant*
Ivester, Vicky Jo *sales professional*
Keyler, Robert Gordon *material handling company executive*
Kircher, Anne Catherine *communications consultant*
Leach, Richard Maxwell, Jr. (Max Leach, Jr.) *corporate professional*
Myers, Carol McClary *retired sales administrator, editor*
Ofte, Donald *retired environmental executive, consultant*
Oppedahl, Phillip Edward *computer company executive*
Ortiz, Kathleen Lucille *travel consultant*
O'Toole, Robert John, II *telemarketing consultant*
Smith, Katherine Theresa *human resources specialist, small business owner*
Tolman, Ruth *personal care industry executive*
Tope, Dwight Harold *retired management consultant*
Young, Joan Crawford *advertising executive*

Belen
Caldwell, Thomas Michael *facilities director*

Corrales
Moody, Helen F. *training and consulting company executive, writer*

Holloman AFB
Molander, Glenn M. *human resources executive*

Los Alamos
Greene Lloyd, Nancy Ellen *infosystems specialist, physicist*

Sandia Park
Greenwell, Ronald Everett *communications executive*

Santa Fe
Taylor, Beverly Lacy *stringed instrument restorer, classical guitarist*

Tesuque
Poedtke, Carl Henry George, Jr. *management consultant*

Tijeras
Sholtis, Joseph Arnold, Jr. *business owner, nuclear and aerospace engineer*

White Sands Missile Range
Starkweather, Frederick Thomas *data processing executive*

NEW YORK

New York
Craig, Sandra Kay *sales executive*
Sprague, Peter Julian *software company executive, lecturer*

OKLAHOMA

Midwest City
Unverrich, Lena Shirley *contracting and purchasing executive*

OREGON

Beaverton
Niskanen, Paul McCord *travel company executive*
Rupp, Jean Louise *communications executive, author*

Canby
Flinn, Roberta Jeanne *management, computer applications consultant*

Corvallis
Hill, Philip Richardson *management consultant*
Shaeumin, Minaya *claims representative*
Sullivan, Anita Christine *piano tuner*

Eugene
Chambers, Carolyn Silva *communications company executive*
Gale, Maradel Krummel *public policy and management educator, consultant*
Hendrix, Timothy Dale *highway construction company manager*
Miner, John Burnham *industrial relations educator, writer*

Gleneden Beach
Parker, Edwin Burke *communications executive*

Hillsboro
Masi, Edward A. *computer company executive*

Klamath Falls
Hartman, Gloria Jean *janitorial executive*

Lake Oswego
Hall, David Bicknell *marketing company executive*
Hick, Kenneth William *business executive*
Maldonado, Jennifer Ann *special events and marketing executive*

Mcminnville
Holst, Wendell *marketing professional, consultant, writer*
Naylor-Jackson, Jerry *public relations consultant, retired, entertainer*

Milwaukie
Moys, Jack J. *sales and advertising executive*

Mosier
Hoffman, Donald James *management consultant*

Newberg
Ecklund, Carl David *security services executive*

Otis
Haralson, Linda Jane *communications executive*

Pendleton
Bedford, Amy Aldrich *public relations executive, corporation secretary*

Portland
Boynton, Robert Granville *computer systems analyst*
Bruechert, Beverly Ann *sales executive, recording artist, pianist*
Butler, Leslie Ann *advertising executive, portrait artist, writer*
Cornyn, John Eugene, III *management consultant*
Day, L. B. *management consultant*
Deal, Terry Dean *marketing executive*
Edstrom, Pam *public relations executive*
Griggs, Gail *marketing executive*
Linstone, Harold Adrian *management and systems science educator*
Mangin, René-Marc *management consultant, systems scientist*
Martin, Lucy Z. *public relations executive*
Middlewood, Martin Eugene *technical communications specialist, writer, consultant*
Robbins, Jeanette Lee *sales and manufacturing executive*
Rotzien, Frederick William, III *marketing executive*
Sackett, Timothy David *information systems specialist*
Schoppe, James Henry *printing company executive, retired*
Scott, Patricia Jean *educational telecommunications administrator*
Thenell, Janice Catherine *public relations director, educator*
Waggener, Melissa *public relations executive*
Wieden, Dan G. *advertising executive*

Roseburg
Parkinson, Thomas Brian *marketing executive*
Plunkett, Marvin Wayne *data processing company executive*

Salem
Alves, Carol Ann *office assistant*
Baker, Edwin Stuart *retired computer consultant*
Hands, Elizabeth S. (Elizabeth S. Geltz) *nutrition analysis software company executive*
Miles, Dennis Gordon *public affairs executive, consultant*
Nelson, David Samuel *public relations executive*

Scappoose
Trudel, John Davis *management consultant*

Tigard
Michelet, John Jacob, Jr. *advertising agency executive, screenplay writer*

Tualatin
Peters, Robert Wayne *direct mail and catalog sales specialist*

Veneta
Warner, Thomas Martin *advertising executive*

Warm Springs
Watlamet, Aurolyn Renee *casino management professional*

Wilsonville
Barker, Gordon *consumer products company executive*
Kehoe, James William, Jr. *marketing manager*

PENNSYLVANIA

Wilkes Barre
Van Stekelenburg, Mark *food service executive*

TENNESSEE

Nashville
Kephart, Floyd W. *corporate strategist*

UTAH

Cedar City
Smith, Raymond William *management consultant*

Farmington
Freed, Peter Quentin *amusement park executive*

Heber City
McLean, Hugh Angus *management consultant*

Midvale
Richardson, Alfred *food service executive, consultant*

Murray
Alba, Felix *industrial computer systems company executive*

Orem
Morey, Robert Hardy *communications executive*
Sawyer, Thomas Edgar *management consultant*
Zimmerman, Stephen *marketing executive*

Pleasant View
Nelsen, Kevin Kirk *contracts and proposals executive*

Provo
Clark, Loyal Frances *public affairs specialist*
Hart, David Kirkwood *management educator, consultant*
Herrera, Shirley Mae *personnel and security executive*
Hutchison, Merrill Dean *recreation facility professional*
Newell, Gregory John *international business advisor*
Soter, Nicholas Gregory *advertising agency executive*

Saint George
Bowler, Lewis J. *communications executive*
Petersen, Mark L. *public relations executive*

Salt Lake City
Burkle, Ronald *consumer products company executive*
Campbell, Stewart Clawson *retired sales executive, artist*
Daniels, Mark Cornwall *sales executive*
Davis, Gene *public relations professional, state legislator*
Davis, Loyd Evan *defense industry marketing professional*
Hansen, Kent *public relations professional, consultant*
Howell, Scott Newell *computer company executive, state legislator*
Johnson, Kenneth Louis *education marketing specialist*
Kitto, Franklin Curtis *computer systems specialist*
Lund, Victor L. *retail food company executive*
Maher, David L. *drug store company executive*
Mills, Carol Margaret *business consultant, public relations consultant*
Olsen, Rodney Wayne *business development manager, technical consultant*
Phillips, Ted Ray *advertising agency executive*
Scott, Howard Winfield, Jr. *temporary help services company executive*
Steiner, Richard Russell *linen supply company executive*
Young, Scott Thomas *business management educator*

Sandy
York, Theodore Robert *consulting company executive*

WASHINGTON

Anacortes
Spaulding, John Pierson *public relations executive, marine consultant*

Auburn
Howard, George Harmon *management consultant*

Bellevue
Allen, Paul *computer executive, professional sports team owner*
Bates, Charles Walter *human resources executive, lawyer, internal auditor*
Dayton, Douglas Emory *computer marketing consultant*
Dulaney, Mary Elaina *public relations executive*
Dykstra, David Charles *management executive, consultant, accountant, author, educator*
Johnson, Gary Kent *management education company executive*
Kevane, Raymond A. *career consultant, management consultant*
O'Byrne, Michael *management consultant*
Ruiz, Anthony *organizational development consultant, educator*
Vander Houwen, Boyd A. *marketing and management executive*

Burlington
Herbaugh, Roger Duane *computer and software company executive*

Edmonds
Sankovich, Joseph Bernard *cemetery management consultant*

Federal Way
Muzyka-McGuire, Amy *marketing professional, nutrition consultant*

Fox Island
Tillman, Peggy Louise (Peggy Louise Larson) *human factors and ergonomics company executive*

Friday Harbor
Acheson, Alice Brewen *publicist*

Gig Harbor
Holmberg, Branton Kieth *management consultant*

Granger
Phillips, Robert Ward *advertising executive*

Hoquiam
Brinton, Richard Kirk *marketing executive*

Issaquah
Harris, Patricia Carol *business executive, consultant*

Kent
Cheung, John B. *research and development executive*

Kirkland
McCaw, Craig O. *communications executive*
Rosenberg, Jeanette L. *personal business advisor, speaker*

Lacey
Breytspraak, John, Jr. *management consultant*

Littlerock
Gunderson, Cleon Henry *management consultant corporation executive*

Loon Lake
Ranck, John Stevens *human resources executive, consultant*

Lynnwood
Hoerner, Michael Duane *beauty salon executive*

Malaga
Nanto, Roxanna Lynn *marketing professional, management consusltant*

Maple Valley
Jordan, Michael Aytch *accounts manager*

Mercer Island
Alvord, David Michael *marketing and sales executive*

Oak Harbor
Meaux, Alan Douglas *facilities technician, sculptor*

Olympia
Adkins, Ben Frank *management and engineering consultant*
Calkins, Bruce Edgar *computer company executive*
Marcelynas, Richard Chadwick *management consultant*
Ogden, Valeria Juan *management consultant, state representative*
Petersen, Donald Felix *consultant*

Poulsbo
Seteroff, Sviatoslav Steve *management and logistics company executive*

Puyallup
Ruff, Lorraine Marie *public relations executive*

Redmond
Addams, Robert Jean *finance executive*
Beer, Joseph Ernest *telecommunications manager*
Butler-Thomas, Jannette Sue *human resources professional*
Dumas, Bob Alan *marketing executive*
Gates, William Henry, III *software company executive*
Gilmore, A. Douglas *retail sales executive*

Renton
Jones, Stanley R. *government contracts business consultant*

Richland
Eckard, Roy Conrad (Connie Eckard) *communications consultant, writer, editor*
Schwier, Edward George *company executive*
Stoll, Leonard Peter *business consultant*
Towner, Larry Edwin *consulting company executive*

Ridgefield
Rusunen, Robert Lee *purchasing manager*

Seattle
Barron, MaryAnn *public relations executive*
Beetham, Stanley Williams *international management consultant*
Bianco, James A. *research and development executive*
Brandmeir, Christopher Lee *hospitality and food service consultant*
Bryant, Arthur Steven *public relations executive*
Buck, Gene *graphics company executive, satirist, historian*
Carter, C. Craig *sales consultant*
Chang, Taiping *marketing executive, magazine publisher*
DuBois, Patricia LaVonne *retail mobile electronics company executive*
Duryee, David Anthony *management consultant*
Elgin, Ron Alan *advertising executive*
Feinberg, David Allen *computer software executive*
Gist, Marilyn Elaine *organizational behavior and human resource management educator*
Grover, Stuart Ralph *management consultant*
Harrison, William Craig *computer company executive*
Holmes, Christopher *public relations executive*
Hurlow, Randal Thomas *communications executive*
Imre, John VanArsdale *quality improvement consultant*
Kane, Karen Marie *public affairs consultant*
Kaperick, John Anthony *information specialist*
Kelly, Dennis Ray *sales executive*
Leale, Olivia Mason *import marketing company executive*
MacDonald, Andrew Stephen *management consulting firm executive*
Miyata, Keijiro *culinary arts educator*
O'Leary, Thomas Howard *resources executive*
Palmer, Hollis Marie *public relations executive*
Patten, Richard E. *personnel company owner*
Porad, Laurie Jo *jewelry company official*
Ray, Sankar *opto-electric device and communication network research and development administrator*
Scafe, Lincoln Robert, Jr. *retired sales executive*
Southwell, Phyllis Arlene *medical transcriptionist*
Williams, Kenneth A. *food service executive*
Wilson, Emily Marie *sales executive*

Spokane
Ballinger, Charles Kenneth *information specialist*
Glatzer, Robert Anthony *marketing and sales executive*
Higgins, Shaun O'Leary *media executive*
Hixon, Robin Ray *food service executive, writer*
Nicolai, Eugene Ralph *public relations consultant, editor, writer*
Olson, William Thomas *business executive, educator, management consultant*
Storey, Francis Harold *business consultant, retired bank executive*
Tsutakawa, Edward Masao *management consultant*
Woodard, Alva Abe *business consultant*

Tacoma
Hudson, Edward Voyle *linen supply company executive*
Knudson, Melvin Robert *management consultant, business executive*
Licens, Lila Louise *administrative assistant*
Lonergan, Michael Henry *development administrator, journalist*
Metsker, Thomas Charles *map company executive*
Robinson, Richard Allen, Jr. *human resources development trainer, consultant*
Taylor, Peter van Voorhees *advertising and public relations consultant*

Tonasket
Vawter, Donald *retired workers compensation administrator, personnel management consultant*

Walla Walla
Potts, Charles Aaron *management executive, writer*

Wenatchee
Montague, Gary Leslie *newspaper advertising executive*

Yakima
Jongeward, George Ronald *retired systems analyst*
Myers, Elizabeth Rouse *management consultant*
Vujovic, Mary Jane *education and employment training planner*

WYOMING

Cheyenne
Miller, Monica Jeanne *public relations administrator*

Laramie
Armintrout, Edward Gilbert *human resources executive*
Hanly, Jeri Ryan *computer science educator*
Hashimoto, Lloyd Ken *communications executive*

Mills
Kennerknecht, Richard Eugene *marketing executive*

Riverton
Hudson, Gary Michael *corporate executive*

Sheridan
Taylor, Judith Ann *marketing and sales executive*

CANADA

ALBERTA

Banff
Frey, Gerrard Rupert (Gary Frey) *management executive*

Calgary
Berg, Kenneth Lloyd *purchasing agent, writer, historian, educator*

BRITISH COLUMBIA

Vancouver
Anglesio, Franco J. *hotel executive*
Chu, Allen Yum-Ching *automation company executive, systems consultant*

ADDRESS UNPUBLISHED
Akbarian, Shah-Rokh *management consultant*
Alden, Susan Jane *technical writing/multimedia agency executive*
Ambrose, Thomas Cleary *communications executive*
Anderson, Mark Robert *data processing executive, biochemist*
Bailey, John Arthur *management consultant*
Baker, Marjorie Neuman *information broker*
Bauer, Charles Edward *microelectronics consultant*
Beck, Timothy Daniel *human resources specialist, consultant*
Bloom, Michael Eugene *consulting executive*
Blount, Kerry Andrew *defense analyst*
Borda, Richard Joseph *management consultant*
Braden, George Walter, II (Lord of Carrigaline) *company executive*
Brennen, Stephen Alfred *international business consultant*
Brown, Harry Parker, Jr. (Butch Brown) *program manager*
Brun, Margaret Ann Charlene *semiconductor industry buyer, planner*
Buell, James Richard, Jr. *investment management company executive*
Burgoin, Catherine Ann *management, personnel consultant*
Burney, Victoria Kalgaard *business consultant, civic worker*
Cain, Shannon Margaret *fundraising executive*
Calhoun, John Joseph *advertising executive*
Camper, John Saxton *public relations and marketing executive*
Carpenter, James Farlin *press secretary*
Carter, David MacCormick *marketing professional*
Chamberlain, William Edwin, Jr. *management consultant*
Chesney, Susan Talmadge *human resources specialist, technical writer*
Chin, Janet Sau-Ying *data processing executive, consultant*
Christy, Thomas Patrick *human resources executive, educator*
Clark, Joyce Lavonne *receptionist*
Clevenger, Mark Thomas *communications executive, writer*
Collett, Merrill Judson *management consultant*
Collings, Celeste Louise (Shorty Vassalli) *marketing executive, professional artist*
Conto, Aristides *advertising agency executive*
Cotter, John Catlin *marketing consultant*
Cotter, Lawrence Raffety *management consultant*
Crum, Robert M. *business management executive*
Cruse, Denton W. *marketing and advertising executive, consultant*
Culberson, Gary Michael *hotel manager*
Damaschino, Ann Toothman *development consultant*
Davis, Beatrice *management consultant*
Day, Janine *marketing specialist, insurance agent*
d'Heilly, Louis Paul *marketing executive*
Dickerson, Cynthia Rowe *marketing firm executive, consultant*
Dietz, Janis Camille *sales executive, educator*
Dolich, Andrew Bruce *sports marketing executive*
D'Onofrio, Mary Ann *medical transcription company executive*

Dossett, Lawrence Sherman *professional services company official*
Eddy, David Maxon *health policy and management administrator*
Ellis, Robert Harry *retired television executive, university administrator*
Elsberry, Susan Davise *computer-aided manufacturing engineer*
Eltringham, Thomas James Gyger *telecommunications professional*
Ennis, Thomas Michael *management consultant*
Erb, Richard Louis Lundin *resort and hotel executive*
Evans, Deborah Lynne *private investigator, writer*
Farrell, William Edgar *sales executive, infosystems specialist, management consultant*
Fassel, Diane Mary *organizational consultant*
Fetter, William Allan *computer graphics executive*
Finnigan, Dennis Michael *management consultant*
Fischer, Zoe Ann *real estate and property marketing company executive, consultant*
Flagg, Norman Lee *retired advertising executive*
Frappia, Linda Ann *management executive*
Frost, Sterling Newell *arbitrator, mediator, management consultant*
Fujita, Beverly Yumi *advertising copywriter*
Gerwick-Brodeur, Madeline Carol *marketing and timing professional*
Gibson, Denice Yvonne *telecommunications, networking and computer executive*
Goffe, Randal Antonio *administrator*
Gooding, Barbara K. *marketing executive, consultant, author*
Gordon, Judith *communications consultant, writer*
Gottlieb, Alan Merril *advertising, fundraising and broadcasting executive, writer*
Grace, Kay Sprinkel *management consultant*
Grant, John Carrington *advertising executive*
Graziano, Joseph A. *computer company executive*
Green, James Craig *retired data systems company executive*
Greene, Richard Boyd, Jr. *marketing and sales executive*
Griggs, Emma *management executive*
Grindal, Mary Ann *sales professional*
Grody, Mark Stephen *public relations executive*
Hale, Violet Elaine *inventor, retired food service executive*
Hamilton, Jody Ann *personal manager, film producer*
Harlan, Kathleen T. (Kay Harlan) *business consultant, professional speaker and seminar leader*
Hausdorfer, Gary Lee *management consultant*
Heeger, Jack Jay *public relations consultant*
Helmke, Beate Helen *administrator*
Hemphill, William Alfred, III *marketing executive*
Herbert, Carol Sellers *farming executive, lawyer*
Hochschild, Carroll Shepherd *medical equipment and computer company executive, educator*
Holland, Henry Norman *marketing consultant*
Hoover, William R(ay) *computer service company executive*
Jay, Roy *corporate executive*
Jones, Gayle Clausse *secretary*
Jones, Gerre Lyle *marketing and public relations consultant*
Jordan, Jeffrey Guy *marketing and marketing research consultant*
Karalis, John Peter *computer company executive, lawyer*
Kasulka, Larry Herman *management consultant*
Katemopoulos, Mildred Josephine *executive secretary*
Kelleher, Richard Cornelius *marketing and communications executive*
Kemmer, Michelle Marie *music merchandiser, bookkeeper*
Kennedy, Debra Joyce *marketing professional*
Kilpatrick, Frank Stanton *management consultant, producer*
Koelmel, Lorna Lee *data processing executive*
Kurimsky, Carol Gray *marketing executive*
Lampert, Eleanor Verna *retired human resources specialist*
Lee, Kai-Fu *computer company executive*
Lee, W. Bruce *management consultant*
Leger, Richard Roubine *public relations executive, writer*
Levitt, Irene Hansen *sales associate, writer, artist*
Lininger, Schuyler White *hotelier*
Locher, Marianne *marketing professional*
Loven, Charles John *human resource executive*
Macon, Carol Ann Gloeckler *micro-computer data base management company executive*
Malphurs, Roger Edward *biomedical marketing executive*
Maltin, Freda *retired university administrator*
Matthew, Lyn *sales and marketing executive consultant*
McDowell, Marcia Ann *security professional*
McInnis, Susan Musé *corporate communications specialist*
McKinney, John Gage *purchasing agent, writer*
McVeigh-Pettigrew, Sharon Christine *communications consultant*
Merrow, William Woodrow *management consultant*
Milanovich, Norma JoAnne *training company executive, occupational educator*
Miller, Diane Doris *executive search consultant*
Missett, Kathryn McAndrew *public relations expert*
Monda, Marilyn *quality improvement consultant*
Moore, Matthew Emerson *environmental program planning management specialist*
Morgan, Ronald William *sales executive*
Muttart, Susan Chambless *corporate communications manager*
Myhren, Trygve Edward *communications company executive*
Nachman, Richard Joseph *management training executive*
Nason, Dolores Irene *computer company executive, counselor, eucharistic minister*
Nelson, Margaret Rose *tourism executive*
Ollander-Krane, Jason Eric *management consultant*
Olson, Kenneth Harvey *computer company executive*
Ortiz, James George *data information services company executive*
Parenti, Kathy Ann *sales professional*
Peavy, Frank *management consultant*
Pfaff-Harris, Kristina Lee *management and computer consultant*
Philippi, Ervin William *mortician*
Pratt, Ronald Franklin *public relations executive*
Probasco, Dale Richard *management consultant*
Przybyla, Leon Hugh, Jr. *sales executive*
Railsback, Sherrie L. *adoption search and reunion consultant*
Rayner, Steven Robert *management consultant*

Richards, Kenneth Edwin *management consultant*
Robinson, Herbert William *corporate executive, economist*
Rodrigues, Alfred Benjamin Kameeiamoku *marketing consultant*
Roiz, Myriam *foreign trade marketing executive*
Roller, Susan Lorrayne *industrial communications specialist, consultant*
Saunders, Brian Keith *consulting company executive*
Scaglione, Cecil Frank *marketing executive, publisher*
Schultze, Ernst Eugene *marketing communications executive*
Shank, Bryan Leigh *marketing executive*
Shirley, Michael James *ski area executive*
Simpson, Bob G. *retired quality assurance professional*
Smith, Garry Lee *marketing manager*
Smith, Thomas Winston *cotton marketing executive*
Sommers, Shari Catherine *management executive*
Sooter, Will James *executive search consultant*
Spellman, Douglas Toby *advertising executive*
Spikes, Rozelia Katherine *speaker, consultant, author, poet*
Spoor, James Edward *human resources executive, entrepreneur*
Springer, Gerald William *sales executive*
Terry, Richard Frank *data transcriber*
Thornsley, Randall G. *management consultant*
Tipton, Gary Lee *retired services company executive*
Togerson, John Dennis *computer software company executive, retired*
Underwood, Ralph Edward *computer systems engineer*
Vallerand, Philippe Georges *sales executive*
von Linsowe, Marina Dorothy *information systems consultant*
Wadley, M. Richard *consumer products executive*
Wagner, Richard *business executive, former baseball team executive*
Walsh, Michael Joseph *security director*
West, Billy Gene *public relations executive*
Wheaton, Alice Alshuler *secretary*
White, Bonnie Yvonne *management consultant, educator*
White, Loray Betty *public relations executive, writer, actress, producer*
Whitehead, Ardelle Coleman *advertising and public relations executive*
Wickstrand, Alan Keith *service executive*
Wilkens, Steve *software marketing and sales executive*
Williams, Angelita Sophia *acquisitions negotiator*
Williams, Harry Edward *management consultant*
Wilton, Peter Campbell *marketing educator*
Winsor, David John *cost consultant*
Wohl, Charles Martin *business development executive*
Wozniak, Joyce Marie *sales executive*
Yakich, David Eli *international sales executive*
Yamani, Elaine Reiko *computer peripheral company executive*
Yetto, John Henry *corporation president*
Yocam, Delbert Wayne *software products company executive*
Young, Anna Lucia *communications professional*
Zito, Michael Anthony *advertising and graphic design typesetting company owner*

INDUSTRY: TRADE

UNITED STATES

ALASKA

Anchorage
Vandergriff, Jerry Dodson *retired computer store executive*

Denali National Park
Swenson, Richard Allen *business owner, animal trainer*

Juneau
Anderson, Terry Drew *small business owner*

ARIZONA

Glendale
Covington, B(athild) June *business owner, advocate*

Phoenix
Antioco, John F. *convenience store chain executive*
Weir, Jim Dale *small business owner*

Scottsdale
Boat, Ronald Allen *business executive*
Swenson, Susan Ann *engineering recruiting company executive*

Sun City
Thompson, Betty Jane *small business owner*

Winslow
Graham, Alice Virginia *small business owner, civic worker*

CALIFORNIA

Arcadia
Stangeland, Roger Earl *retail chain store executive*

Beverly Hills
Orenstein, (Ian) Michael *philatelic dealer, columnist*

Burbank
Wise, Woodrow Wilson, Jr. *small business owner*

Cerritos
Webb, Lewis M. *retail executive*

Concord
Mackie, Richard Allen *small business owner, publishing company executive*

Culver City
Byrd, Marc Robert *florist*

Danville
Ritchey, Samuel Donley, Jr. *retired retail store executive*

El Segundo
Pickett, Michael D. *computer hardware and software distributor*

Emeryville
Weaver, Velather Edwards *small business owner*

Encino
Vigdor, James Scott *distribution executive*

Glendora
O'Hagan, William Gordon *state agency administrator*

Goleta
Winslow, Norman Eldon *business executive*

Half Moon Bay
Hoffman, Gary Allan *retail executive, human resource consultant*

La Crescenta
Graw, LeRoy Harry *purchasing-contract management company executive*

Lancaster
Harris, Carol Sue *small business owner*

Loomis
Keyston, Stephani Ann *small business owner*

Los Angeles
Dailey, Victoria Keilus *antiquarian bookseller, writer*
Dawes, Wallace Ernest *small business owner*
Hawley, Philip Metschan *retired retail executive, consultant*
Kanavalov, Maria Jose *small business owner*

Modesto
Cahill, Lawrence Glenn, Jr. *investigation firm owner*
West, James Stuart *small business owner*

Newark
Ferber, Norman Alan *retail executive*

Newport Beach
Rosten, David Bruce *international investment advisor*
Sweet, Cheryl Ann *small business owner*

Oak View
Revoyr, Jack Ronald *trademark licensing consultant, writer*

Oakland
Spitzer, Matthew L. *retail store executive*

Orange
Underwood, Vernon O., Jr. *grocery stores executive*

Orinda
Hendler, Rosemary Nielsen *business owner, computer artist*

Pasadena
Cappello, Eve *international keynote speaker, training specialist*
Hecht, Harold Michael *retail executive*

Pleasant Hill
Dolan, Maryanne McLorn *small business owner, writer, educator, lecturer*

Porterville
Swindler, Stephen Francis *distribution company executive*

Riverside
Najjar, Tamara Litchfield *mail order business owner*

San Bernardino
Sagmeister, Edward Frank *business owner, hospitality industry executive, civic official, retired consultant, fund raiser, career officer*

San Diego
Monaco, Dick Steven *mail order vendor*
Saito, Frank Kiyoji *import-export firm executive*

San Francisco
Drexler, Millard S. *retail executive*
Fisher, Donald G. *casual apparel chain stores executive*
Jensen, Jakki Renee *retail company executive*
Seelenfreund, Alan *distribution company executive*
Seifel, Elizabeth Margaret *business owner*
Ullman, Myron Edward, III *retail executive*

San Jacinto
Howard, Jo Ann *business owner*

San Jose
Pan, William Jiawei *import and export company executive, consultant*

San Rafael
Koetser, David *export company executive*

Santa Ana
Fitzgerald, Robert Lynn *small business owner*
Shahin, Thomas John *dry cleaning wholesale supply company executive*

Santa Maria
Baker-Lievanos, Nina Gillson *jewelry store executive*

Santa Monica
Sigoloff, Sanford Charles *retail executive*

Santa Paula
Anderson, William *retail company executive, business education educator*

Sherman Oaks
Wishingrad, Richard Joel *retail executive*

Thousand Oaks
Knight, Jeffrey Richard *small business owner*

Vernon
Lynch, Martin Andrew *retail company executive*

Walnut Creek
Long, Robert Merrill *retail drug company executive*

Watsonville
Pye, David Thomas *retail company executive*

West Sacramento
Teel, Joyce *supermarket and drugstore retail executive*

Westminster
Edwards, Charles Richard *retired printing equipment and supplies company executive*

COLORADO

Arvada
Pracko, Bernard Francis, II *artist, business owner*

Aurora
Magalnick, Elliott Ben *retail medical supply company executive*
Reynolds, Robert Harrison *retired export company executive*

Castle Rock
Sjostrom, Joan Sevier *travel consultant*

Colorado Springs
Carson, Elizabeth Lorraine Neal *small business owner, civilian military employee*

Denver
Cashman, Michael Richard *small business owner*
Cheris, Elaine Gayle Ingram *business owner*
Newberry, Elizabeth Carter *greenhouse and floral company owner*
Oakes, Terry Louis *retail clothing store executive*
Tutt, Margaret Honnen *retail store owner*

Littleton
Bowe, Roger Lee *small business owner*

Loveland
Rodman, Alpine Clarence *arts and crafts company executive*
Rodman, Sue Arlene *wholesale Indian crafts company executive, artist, consultant*

Morrison
Graham, Pamela Smith *distributing company executive, artist*

Pueblo
Pisciotta, Samuel James *small business owner*

HAWAII

Hanalei
Vogel, Richard Wiedemann *business owner, ichthyodynamicist, educator*

Honolulu
Lee, Candie Ching Wah *retail executive*
Nakabayashi, Nicholas Takateru *retired retail executive*
Tong, Yiming *import company executive, accountant*

Kailua Kona
Luizzi, Ronald *wholesale distribution executive*

Waipahu
Matsui, Jiro *importer, wholesaler, small business owner*

IDAHO

Boise
McCain, Warren Earl *retired supermarket company executive*
Michael, Gary G. *retail supermarket and drug chain executive*
Shaver, Carl Hutchens *retail executive*

Meridian
Sorenson, Rick J. (Richard John Sorenson, Jr.) *import company executive, artist, educator*

MONTANA

Butte
Pavlovich, Robert J. *small business owner, state legislator*

NEVADA

Las Vegas
Miller, Virginia Lee *business owner*

NEW HAMPSHIRE

Rye Beach
Nord, Harold Emil, Jr. *small business owner, consultant*

NEW MEXICO

Albuquerque
Phillips, Larry Duane *gemologist, appraiser*
Weems, Mary Ann *business owner*

Taos
Winslow, Bette Killingsworth *dance studio owner*

OREGON

Applegate
Pursglove, Betty Merle *small business owner, technical writer, quality assurance tester*

Ashland
Kellar, William Owen *business owner, writer*

Bend
Nosler, Robert Amos *sports company executive*

Days Creek
Lassesen, Catherine Avery Clay *small business owner, manager, trainer*

Eugene
Gillespie, Penny Hannig *business owner*

Klamath Falls
Pastega, Richard Louis *retail specialist*

Medford
Stong, John Elliott *retail electronic company executive*

Myrtle Creek
Shirtcliff, John Delzell *business owner, oil jobber*

Oregon City
Danielson, Craig *wholesale grocery corporation executive*

Pacific City
Hampton, Carolyn Seeba *small business owner, minister*

Portland
Greenstein, Merle Edward *import and export company executive*
Meluso, John, Jr. *small business owner*
Miller, Robert G. *retail company executive*
Watkinson, W. Grant *distribution company executive*

Salem
Benson, Steven Donald *shop owner, sheet metal mechanic, author*
Robertson, Marian Ella (Marian Ella Hall) *small business owner, handwriting analyst*

South Beach
Aldrich, Daniel Eugene *small business owner*

Wilsonville
Straus, Leonard Hirsch *retail company executive*

TEXAS

Dallas
Hume, Darrel J. *retail executive*

UTAH

Heber City
Day, Gerald W. *wholesale grocery company executive*

Provo
Feller, Wilford Carter *jewelry retailer, manufacturing company executive*

Saint George
Day, John Denton *retired company executive, cattle and horse rancher, trainer, wrangler, actor*

Salt Lake City
Cragun, Calvin *business owner*
Hayes, G. Jerry *automobile dealer executive*
Miller, Lorraine *business owner*
Tanner, William Coats, Jr. *business owner*

WASHINGTON

Bellingham
Olsen, Mark Norman *small business owner*

Buckley
Christensen, Doris Ann *antique dealer, researcher, writer*

Ellensburg
Shults, Mary J. *retail store owner*

Issaquah
Brotman, Jeffrey H. *variety stores executive*
Sinegal, James D. *variety store wholesale business executive*

Lynnwood
Stocking, Sherl Dee *retail executive*

Seattle
Denniston, Martha Kent *business owner, author*
Fix, Wilbur James *department store executive*
McMillan, John A. *retail executive*
Mizrahi, Yves *retail executive*
Nordstrom, Bruce A. *department store executive*
Nordstrom, John N. *department store executive*
Read, Charles Raymond, Sr. *business executive*
Stearns, Susan Tracey *lighting design company executive, lawyer*

Williamson, John *computer game producer*

Shelton
Wotton, Robert H., Jr. *small business owner*

Spokane
Leighton, Jack Richard *small business owner, former educator*
Sines, Randy Dwain *business executive*

Yakima
Newland, Ruth Laura *small business owner*

WYOMING

Douglas
Harrop, Diane Glaser *shop owner, mayor*

ADDRESS UNPUBLISHED

Adler, Shelley *barber, poet*
Busch, Joyce Ida *small business owner*
Cavnar, Margaret Mary (Peggy Cavnar) *business executive, former state legislator, nurse, consultant*
Debenham, Ray Gene *electric supply company executive*
Decker, Richard Kelsey *equipment distribution company executive*
Edwards, Patricia Burr *small business owner, counselor, consultant*
Galvao, Louis Alberto *import and export corporation executive, consultant*
Green, Cyril Kenneth *retired retail company executive*
Hackworth, Mark Steven *chemical company executive*
Kassner, Jay Edward *small business owner*
Martini, Robert Edward *wholesale pharmaceutical and medical supplies company executive*
McCall, Susan Elizabeth *small business owner*
Metz, Steven William *small business owner*
Moss, Jack *print shop executive, textile chemist, consultant*
Nicolas, Kenneth Lee *international financial business executive*
Parks, Richard Cameron *outdoor sports professional, small business owner*
Phillips, Darrell *retail executive*
Reichel, John Kento *small business owner, writer*
Rizzolo, Robert Steven *small business owner*
Vandertuin, Victoria Elva *book seller*
Williams, Leona Rae *lingerie shop owner, consultant*
Winter, Richard Samuel, Jr. *computer training company owner, writer*
Zodl, Joseph Arthur *international trade executive, consultant*

INDUSTRY: TRANSPORTATION

UNITED STATES

ALASKA

Anchorage
Silverstein, Steven B. *railroad executive*

ARIZONA

Bullhead City
Hicks, Norm *airport operations executive*

Hayden
Jacobson, Lowell Steven (Jake Jacobson) *railroad executive*

Litchfield Park
Cox, Gary Evans *aerospace company official, consultant*

Phoenix
Amoako, James Kwaku *transportation services executive, financial analyst*
Aybar, Charles Anton *aviation executive*
Berthof, Neilson Allan, Jr. *aviation executive*
Wood, John Mortimer *retired aerospace executive, aeronautical engineer*
Woods, Bobby Joe *transportation executive*

Scottsdale
Hess, Robert, Jr. *ambulance service executive*

Tucson
Burg, Walter A. *airport terminal executive*
Mercker, Mary Alice *aviation school administrator*
Smith, Gordon Eugene *pilot*

ARKANSAS

Harrison
Garrison, F. Sheridan *transportation executive*

CALIFORNIA

Bayside
Pierce, Lester Laurin *aviation consultant*

Borrego Springs
Scannell, William Edward *aerospace company executive, consultant, psychologist*

Burbank
Volk, Robert Harkins *aviations company executive*

Calabasas
Caren, Robert Poston *aerospace company executive*

Camarillo
Dunkle, William Earl *pilot, airline executive, retired*
McConnel, Richard Appleton *aerospace company official*

Chatsworth
Butler, Viggo M. *airport terminal executive*

Corona Del Mar
Tether, Anthony John *aerospace executive*

Costa Mesa
Schooley, O. B. *commercial airport executive*

Edwards
Smolka, James William *aerospace research pilot*

El Segundo
Miller, Gary Douglas *aerospace company executive*

Fremont
Smith, Bernald Stephen *retired airline pilot, aviation consultant*

Gilroy
Borton, George Robert *airline captain*

Hermosa Beach
Kokalj, James Edward *retired aerospace administrator*

Huntington Beach
Richman, David William *aerospace executive*

La Canada Flintridge
Stratton, John Maclean *air transport company executive*

Long Beach
Anderson, Gerald Verne *retired aerospace company executive*
Moss, Elizabeth Lucille (Betty Moss) *transportation company executive*
Williams, David Alexander *pilot*

Los Altos
Stefanki, John X. *airline pilot*

Los Angeles
Ajer, Randolf E. *airport terminal executive*
Anderson, Roy A. *aerospace company executive*
Coln, William Alexander, III *pilot*
Kresa, Kent *aerospace executive*
Mishkin, Marjorie Wong *aviation and marketing consultant*
Moore, Walter Dengel *rapid transit system professional*
Williams, Walter David *aerospace executive, consultant*
Yee, Stephen *airport executive*

Menlo Park
O'Brien, Raymond Francis *transportation executive*

Mission Viejo
LaRosa, Gianni *aerospace industry administrator*

Newport Beach
Penso, Pierpaolo *ship repair company executive*

Oakland
Reynolds, Kathleen Diane Foy (K.D.F. Reynolds) *transportation executive*

Palmdale
Nardi, William Anthony *aerospace executive, consultant*

Palo Alto
Moffitt, Donald Eugene *transportation company executive*

Palos Verdes Estates
Smith, Stephen Randolph *aerospace executive*

Palos Verdes Peninsula
Slusser, Robert Wyman *aerospace company executive*

Redwood City
Waller, Stephen *air transportation executive*

Sacramento
Engel, Thomas P. *airport executive*
Wieman, David Lawrence *retired transportation executive*

San Francisco
Anschutz, Philip F. *transportation executive*
Hickerson, Glenn Lindsey *leasing company executive*
Kahn, Linda McClure *maritime industry executive*
Tulis, Ronald Lee *airport consultant*
Wood, Donald Frank *transportation educator, consultant*

San Jose
Steiling, Daniel Paul *railroad conductor*
Verlot, Frank Oscar *aerospace executive*

San Mateo
Trabitz, Eugene Leonard *aerospace company executive*

South San Francisco
Scherer, Phil *airport terminal executive*

Stockton
Biddle, Donald Ray *aerospace company executive*
DeAngelis, Dan *transportation executive*

Sunnyvale
Davis, Michael Chase *aerospace industry executive, consultant, retired naval officer*
Finnie, C(larence) Herbert (Herb Finnie) *aerospace company executive*
Stapleton, Beverly Cooper *aerospace company executive*

Stough, Stephen Alan *aerospace and railroad company executive*

Torrance
Vampola, Alfred Ludvik *aerospace consultant*

Van Nuys
Stender, Charles Frederick *test pilot*

Villa Park
Thomas, Mitchell, Jr. *aerospace company executive*

Walnut Creek
DeBoer, David James *transportation executive*

Woodland Hills
Richards, Benness Melvin *airline pilot*

COLORADO

Arvada
Eaves, Sally Ann *logistics specialist, research administrator*

Aspen
Edwards, H. Boyd *air transportation executive*

Aurora
Minnich, Joseph Edward *tourist railway consultant*

Cherry Hills Village
Claussen, Bonnie Addison, II *aerospace company executive*

Colorado Springs
Brown, Alison K. *aeronautics company executive*
Eller, Thomas Julian *computer company executive, astronautical engineer*
Kahn, Seymour *air transportation executive*

Denver
Boulware, Richard Stark *airport administrator*
Boyd, Dawn Andrea Williams *airline official, artist*
Burgess, Larry Lee *aerospace executive*
DeLong, James Clifford *air transportation executive*
Rokosz, Richard Eugene *aerospace manager*

Grand Junction
Buescher, Bernard *air transportation executive*
Buescher, Louis *airport service executive*

Littleton
Bragg, Albert Forsey *retired airline captain*

DISTRICT OF COLUMBIA

Washington
Mineta, Norman Yoshio *aerospace transportation exescutive, former congressman*

FLORIDA

Dania
Vecci, Raymond Joseph *airline industry consultant*

GEORGIA

LaGrange
Brown, Thomas Adams *aviation executive*

HAWAII

Honolulu
Miyamoto, Owen *transportation consultant*
Olsen, Phillip Buck *corporate pilot, retired educator*
Pfeiffer, Robert John *business executive*

Kilauea
Fairechild, Diana *airline passenger activist, writer, speaker*

IDAHO

Boise
DeVilbiss, Jonathan Frederick *aircraft sales engineer*

Idaho Falls
Thorsen, James Hugh *aviation director*

NEVADA

Las Vegas
Di Palma, Joseph Alphonse *airline company executive, lawyer*

Reno
White, Robert C. *air transportation executive*

NEW MEXICO

Albuquerque
Weh, Allen Edward *airline executive*

Farmington
Anderson, Mark Eugene *specialized truck driver, safety inspector*

Roswell
Hammond, Joseph Carroll, III *flight service specialist, genealogist*

OREGON

Mcminnville
Lane, Larry K. *air industry service executive*

Portland
Cheston, Michael Galloway *airport executive*

UTAH

Bountiful
Clement, Walter Hough *retired railroad executive*

Brigham City
Pflug, Andrew Knox *aerospace company executive*
Zielke, Patrick Michael *aerospace company executive*

Salt Lake City
Bouley, Joseph Richard *pilot*
Fox, L. Robert *transportation and management consultant*
White, Victor Dea *airport management executive*

WASHINGTON

Auburn
Hartmann, Steven Martin *freight company executive*

Bainbridge Island
Cioc, Charles Gregory *information systems executive*

Federal Way
Stober, Mason Frederick, Jr. *retired air traffic control educator*

Medina
Waldmann, Raymond John *aerospace executive*

Seattle
Brazier, Robert G. *transportation executive*
Cella, John J. *freight company executive*
Chittick, Arden Boone *steamship agency executive*
Clarkson, Lawrence William *airplane company executive*
Cline, Robert Stanley *air freight company executive*
Condit, Philip Murray *aerospace executive, engineer*
Elliott, Jeanne Marie Koreltz *transportation executive*
Fowler, John Robert *airline executive*
Miller, Paige *port executive*
Strombom, Cathy Jean *transportation planner, consultant*

Spanaway
Loete, Steven Donald *pilot*

Sumner
Goodman, William Lee *commercial pilot*

Tacoma
Slater, Don Austin *shipyard executive, consultant*

MILITARY ADDRESSES OF THE UNITED STATES

EUROPE

APO
Kinsler, Bruce Whitney *air traffic controller, consultant, air traffic control engineer, air defense engineer*

CANADA

ALBERTA

Calgary
Jenkins, Kevin J. *airline company executive*
McCaig, Jeffrey James *transportation company executive*
Paquette, Richard *airport executive*

ONTARIO

Toronto
Turpen, Louis A. *airport terminal executive*

ADDRESS UNPUBLISHED

Boldon, Allifee *aerospace company executive*
Cassidy, Donald Lawrence *former aerospace company executive*
Cook, Stephen Champlin *retired shipping company executive*
Crowder, Richard Morgan *pilot*
Dutton, Angela Lois *trucking industry executive*
Freitag, Peter Roy *transportation specialist*
Gray, Richard Arden *transportation executive*
Kerbs, Wayne Allan *transportation executive*
Langs, Ted Charles *aerospace company executive*
Reihel, Ronald Ernest *pilot*
Stepp, William Edward *retired military operations analyst*
Tucker, Joel Lawrence *aviation company executive*
Walling, Douglas Dean *retired airline pilot*
Webb, Richard L. *air industry service executive*

INDUSTRY: UTILITIES, ENERGY, RESOURCES

UNITED STATES

ALASKA

Anchorage
Hopkins, Stephen Davis *mining company executive*
Luttrell, Eric Martin *oil company executive*
Shultz, Delray Franklin *oil company executive*

Nikiski
Bumbaugh, Robert Warren, Sr. *oil industry executive*

ARIZONA

Buckeye
Burton, Edward Lewis *industrial procedures and training consultant, educator*

Cave Creek
LeNeau, Thomas Ervin *gas company executive*

Phoenix
Hagerdon, Kathy Ann (Kay Hagerdon) *electric power industry executive*
Yearley, Douglas Cain *mining and manufacturing company executive*

Prescott
Bennett, Kenneth R. *oil company executive, school board executive*

Tempe
Clevenger, Jeffrey Griswold *mining company executive*

Tucson
Davis, James Luther *retired utilities executive, lawyer*
Peeler, Stuart Thorne *petroleum industry executive and independent oil operator*
Pillar, Charles Littlefield *retired mining consultant*

CALIFORNIA

Alamo
Shiffer, James David *retired utility executive*

Anaheim
Fenton, Donald Mason *retired oil company executive*

Bakersfield
Zemp, Kerry Lloyd *oil company executive*

Beverly Hills
Brann, Alton Joseph *oil field services executive*

Brea
Stegemeier, Richard Joseph *oil company executive*

Camarillo
MacAlister, Robert Stuart *oil company executive*

Carmel
Loper, D. Roger *retired oil company executive*
Mills, Robert Charters *retired oil company executive*

Costa Mesa
Dougherty, Michael Joseph *oil company executive*

El Segundo
Beach, Roger C. *oil company executive*

Fresno
Wilson, Charles E. *air industry service executive*

Fullerton
Sadruddin, Moe *oil company executive, consultant*

Los Altos
Sun, Bill Kawo-Hwa *energy consulting company executive*

Los Angeles
Bowlin, Michael Ray *oil company executive*
Chazen, Stephen I. *oil company executive*
Davis, Marvin *petroleum company executive, entrepreneur*
Foley, John V. *water company executive*
Homek, Peter Edward *gas company executive*
Jonker, Peter Emile *gas company executive*
McIntyre, Robert Malcolm *utility company executive*
Wood, Willis Bowne, Jr. *utility holding company executive*
Wycoff, Robert E. *petroleum company executive*

Manteca
Talmage, Kenneth Kellogg *business executive*

Martinez
Meyer, Jarold Alan *oil company research executive*

Monterey Park
Montag, David Moses *telecommunications company executive*

Newhall
Nelson, Warren James, III *oil company executive, accountant*

Palo Alto
Mattice, Jack Shafer *electric power research manager*

Palos Verdes Estates
Christie, Hans Frederick *retired utility company subsidiaries executive, consultant*

Placentia
Douglas, Donald Wills, Jr. *energy executive*

Playa Del Rey
Weir, Alexander, Jr. *utility consultant, inventor*

Rosemead
Bryson, John E. *utilities company executive*
Rosenblum, Richard Mark *utility executive*

San Clemente
Clark, Earnest Hubert, Jr. *tool company executive*

San Diego
Russel, Richard Allen *telecommunications consultant, aerospace engineer, nuclear engineer, electrical engineer, retired naval officer*
Sifferman, Thomas Raymond *speciality chemical researcher*

San Dimas
Brown, Marian Van de Water *utilities executive*

San Francisco
Bonney, John Dennis *retired oil company executive*
Carter, George Kent *oil company executive*
Clarke, Richard Alan *electric and gas utility company executive, lawyer*
Derr, Kenneth T. *oil company executive*
Ginn, Sam L. *telephone company executive*
Johnstone, Clint *electric power industry executive*
Keller, George Matthew *retired oil company executive*
Littlefield, Edmund Wattis *mining company executive*
Mallen, Michael Paul *telephone company executive*
Maneatis, George A. *retired utility company executive*
Millard, Derek *industrial organizational development consultant*
Quigley, Philip J. *telecommunications industry executive*
Skinner, Stanley Thayer *utility company executive, lawyer*
Sproul, John Allan *retired public utility executive*
Sullivan, James N. *fuel company executive*

Santa Monica
Hearne, John Q. *telecommunications executive*

Stanford
Huckabee, Phyllis *gas industry professional*

Templeton
Gandsey, Louis John *petroleum and environmental consultant*

Van Nuys
Fisher, Earl Monty *utilities executive*

COLORADO

Arvada
McFadden, Michael J. *utilities industry consultant*

Boulder
Adams, Linda Alcorn *telecommunications policy professional*
Kirkman, Roy C. *mining executive*
Schwartz, John Benjamin *telecommunications and real estate executive*

Cherry Hills Village
Steinhauser, John Stuart (Jack Steinhauser) *oil company executive*

Colorado Springs
Bauman, Walter Joseph *telecommunication company executive*

Denver
Cevenini, Roberto Mauro *gas and oil industry executive, educator, author, athlete, inventor, consultant, speaker*
Fryt, Monte Stanislaus *petroleum company executive, speaker, advisor*
Pepper, John Roy *oil and gas executive*
Stewart, Gary Crawford *oil company executive*
Taylor, Leslie George *mining and financial company executive*
Toenjes, Joni Elizabeth *gas and oil consultant, researcher*

Durango
Thurston, William Richardson *oil and gas industry executive, geologist*

Englewood
Le, Khanh Tuong *utility executive*
Malone, John C. *telecommunications executive*
McCormick, Richard *telecommunications company executive*
Ward, Milton Hawkins *mining company executive*

Evergreen
McEldowney, Roland Conant *gold mining company executive*

Golden
Coakley, William Thomas *utilities executive*

Grand Junction
Pforzheimer, Harry, Jr. *oil consultant*

Lakewood
Hall, Larry D. *energy company executive, lawyer*

Littleton
Haley, John David *petroleum consulting company executive*
VanderLinden, Camilla Denice Dunn *telecommunications industry manager*

HAWAII

Honolulu
Amioka, Wallace Shuzo *retired petroleum company executive*
Bates, George E. *oil industry executive*
Clarke, Robert F. *utilities company executive*

IDAHO

Idaho Falls
Newman, Stanley Ray *oil refining company executive*

Mountain Home
Hiddleston, Ronal Eugene *drilling and pump company executive*

MICHIGAN

Jackson
Buckman, Frederick W. *gas utility executive*

MONTANA

Billings
Holm, Darrell Vaughn *oil company consultant*
Nance, Robert Lewis *oil company executive*

Butte
Bishop, Robert Charles *architect, metals and minerals company executive*

NEVADA

Fallon
Sanwick, James Arthur *mining executive*

Las Vegas
Garcia-Borras, Thomas *oil company executive*
Guinn, Kenny C. *utility company executive*

Reno
Busig, Rick Harold *mining executive*
Doyle, Michael Joseph *mining executive*

Sparks
Hines, Garold Paul *utilities executive*

NEW MEXICO

Albuquerque
Giron, Rick *adminstrative services manager*

Artesia
Owens, B. Raydean *retired oil company field service executive*

Farmington
Macaluso, Frank Augustus *oil company executive*

Hobbs
Garey, Donald Lee *pipeline and oil company executive*

Roswell
Robinson, Mark Leighton *oil company executive, petroleum geologist, horse farm owner*

Santa Fe
Shepard, Robert Henry *retired oil company executive*

OREGON

Aloha
Jones, Charles J. *consultant*

Bend
Miller, William Elwood *mining company executive*

Neskowin
Sifford, Benton Alexander, III *energy consultant*

Portland
Bacon, Vicky Lee *lighting services executive*
Cohen, Joyce E. *utilities executive, former state senator, investment executive*
Frisbee, Don Calvin *retired utilities executive*
McCall, William Calder *oil and chemical company executive*
Reiten, Richard G. *natural gas industry executive*

UTAH

Salt Lake City
Cash, R. D. *natural gas and oil executive*
Schmitt, Gary A. *energy company director*

Vernal
Covington, Robert Edward *mining executive, geologist*

WASHINGTON

Bellevue
Weaver, William Schildecker *electric power industry executive*

Seattle
Smith, Andrew Vaughn *telephone company executive*

WYOMING

Casper
Smith, Dick Martin *oil field service company executive, owner*

Cheyenne
Weeks, William Rawle, Jr. *oil company executive*

CANADA

ALBERTA

Calgary
Furnival, George Mitchell *petroleum and mining consultant*
MacNeill, Brian F. *oil and natural gas company executive*
Maier, Gerald James *natural gas transmission and marketing company executive*
McIntyre, Norman F. *petroleum industry executive*
Mc Kee, John Angus *oil company executive*
Shultz, C. E. (Chuck Schultz) *exploration and production company executive*

BRITISH COLUMBIA

Vancouver
Phelps, Michael Everett Joseph *energy company executive*
Willms, Arthur Henry *gas executive*

West Vancouver
Kloepfer, Clarence Victor *oil company executive*

ADDRESS UNPUBLISHED

Abram, John Charles *energy consultant, retired*
Ataie, Ata Jennati *oil products marketing executive*
Bending, David Alexander Glen *mining executive, geoscientist*
Binder, James Kauffman *computer consultant*
Cashatt, Charles Alvin *retired hydro-electric power generation company executive*
Cliff, Ronald Laird *energy company executive*
Counsil, William Glenn *electric utility executive*
Engel, Linda Jeanne *mining executive*
Fisher, David Carl *telecommunications company executive*
Gigliotti, Richard Joseph *nuclear security executive*
Greenberg, Arnold Elihu *water quality specialist*
Hesse, Christian August *mining and underground construction consultant*
Holmes, Michael *oil and gas consultant*
Isautier, Bernard François *business executive*
Krempel, Roger Ernest *public works management consultant*
Land, Kenneth Dean *test and balance agency executive, energy and environmental consultant*
McCready, Kenneth Frank *past electric utility executive*
Ormasa, John *retired utility executive, lawyer*
Osterhoff, James Marvin *retired telecommunications company executive*
Trusler, James Hall *oil company research and development technician*
Wharton, Thomas William *mining executive*

LAW: JUDICIAL ADMINISTRATION

UNITED STATES

ALASKA

Anchorage
Branson, Albert Harold (Harry Branson) *magistrate judge, educator*
Compton, Allen T. *state supreme court justice*
Eastaugh, Robert L. *judge*
Fabe, Dana Anderson *federal judge*
Holland, H. Russel *federal judge*
Singleton, James Keith *federal judge*

Fairbanks
Kleinfeld, Andrew Jay *federal judge*

ARIZONA

Phoenix
Canby, William Cameron, Jr. *federal judge*
Carroll, Earl Hamblin *federal judge*
Feldman, Stanley George *state supreme court justice*
Martone, Frederick J. *judge*
McNamee, Stephen M. *federal judge*
Moeller, James *state supreme court justice*
Rosenblatt, Paul Gerhardt *federal judge*
Schroeder, Mary Murphy *federal judge*
Strand, Roger Gordon *federal judge*
Weisenburger, Theodore Maurice *judge, poet, educator, writer*
Zlaket, Thomas A. *judge*

Tucson
Bilby, Richard Mansfield *federal judge*
Browning, William Docker *federal judge*
Roll, John McCarthy *judge*

CALIFORNIA

Berkeley
Ogg, Wilson Reid *lawyer, poet, retired judge, lyricist, curator, publisher, educator, philospher, social scientist, parapsychologist*

Downey
Emerson, (Virgil) Leon *retired judge*

Tucker, Marcus Othello *judge*

Fresno
Coyle, Robert Everett *federal judge*
Wanger, Oliver Winston *federal judge*

Los Angeles
Ahart, Alan M. *judge*
Alarcon, Arthur Lawrence *federal judge*
Armstrong, Orville *judge*
Baird, Lourdes G. *federal judge*
Bufford, Samuel Lawrence *federal judge*
Byrne, William Matthew, Jr. *federal judge*
Curry, Daniel Arthur *superior court judge*
Davies, John G. *federal judge*
Fischer, Dale Susan *judge*
Fleming, Macklin *judge, author*
Gembacz, Gilbert Thaddeus *judge*
Hatter, Terry Julius, Jr. *federal judge*
Hupp, Harry L. *federal judge*
Ideman, James M. *federal judge*
Jaffe, F. Filmore *judge*
Keller, William D. *federal judge*
Kenyon, David V. *federal judge*
Letts, J. Spencer *federal judge*
Lew, Ronald S. W. *federal judge*
Marshall, Consuelo Bland *federal judge*
Norris, William Albert *federal judge*
Pfaelzer, Mariana R. *federal judge*
Rafeedie, Edward *federal judge*
Rea, William J. *federal judge*
Real, Manuel Lawrence *federal judge*
Takasugi, Robert Mitsuhiro *federal judge*
Tevrizian, Dickran M., Jr. *federal judge*
Wardlaw, Kim A.M. *judge*
Williams, David Welford *federal judge*
Wilson, Stephen Victor *federal judge*

Manhattan Beach
Chettle, A(lvin) B(asil), Jr. *lawyer, educator*

Moraga
Harrington, Charles Lee *retired judge*

Oakland
Armstrong, Saundra Brown *federal judge*
Cline, Wilson Ettason *retired administrative law judge*
Jensen, D. Lowell *federal judge, lawyer, government official*

Pasadena
Boochever, Robert *federal judge*
Fernandez, Ferdinand Francis *federal judge*
Hall, Cynthia Holcomb *federal judge*
Hogoboom, William Perry *judge, arbitrator, mediator*
Kozinski, Alex *federal judge*
Nelson, Dorothy Wright (Mrs. James F. Nelson) *federal judge*
Rymer, Pamela Ann *federal judge*
Tashima, Atsushi Wallace *federal judge*

Redwood City
Harrington, Walter Howard, Jr. *judge*

Richmond
Herron, Ellen Patricia *retired judge*

Sacramento
Burrell, Garland E., Jr. *federal judge*
Garcia, Edward J. *federal judge*
Karlton, Lawrence K. *federal judge*
Levi, David F. *federal judge*
Schwabe, Peter Alexander, Jr. *judge*
Shubb, William Barnet *federal judge*

San Diego
Adler, Louise DeCarl *bankruptcy judge*
Brewster, Rudi Milton *federal judge*
Gilliam, Earl B. *federal judge*
Gonzalez, Irma Elsa *federal judge*
Huff, Marilyn L. *federal judge*
Keep, Judith N. *federal judge*
Lewis, Gerald Jorgensen *judge*
McKee, Roger Curtis *federal magistrate judge*
Orfield, Adrienne Adams *judge*
Parker, Larry Benson *judge*
Thompson, David Renwick *federal judge*
Thompson, Gordon, Jr. *federal judge*
Wallace, J. Clifford *federal judge*

San Francisco
Baxter, Marvin Ray *state supreme court judge*
Brennan, Joan Stevenson *federal judge*
Brown, Janice Rogers *state judge*
Browning, James Robert *federal judge*
Carlson, Thomas E. *judge*
Chesney, Maxine M. *judge*
Chin, Ming *judge*
George, Ronald M. *judge*
Henderson, Thelton Eugene *federal judge*
Jarvis, Donald Bertram *judge*
Kennard, Joyce L. *judge*
Legge, Charles Alexander *federal judge*
Lynch, Eugene F. *federal judge*
Mosk, Stanley *state supreme court justice*
Noonan, John T., Jr. *federal judge, legal educator*
Patel, Marilyn Hall *federal judge*
Poole, Cecil F. *circuit court judge*
Schwarzer, William W *federal judge*
Walker, Vaughn R. *federal judge*
Werdegar, Kathryn Mickle *judge*

San Jose
Aguilar, Robert P. *federal judge*
Ware, James W. *federal judge*
Whyte, Ronald M. *federal judge*

San Marino
Mortimer, Wendell Reed, Jr. *superior court judge*

Santa Ana
Barr, James Norman *federal judge*
McLaughlin, Linda Lee Hodge *federal judge*
Rylaarsdam, William F. *judge*
Stotler, Alicemarie Huber *judge*
Taylor, Gary L. *federal judge*

Santa Monica
Vega, Benjamin Urbizo *retired judge*

Studio City
Lasarow, William Julius *retired federal judge*

Susanville
Bradbury, Stephen Douglas *judge, rancher*

Woodland Hills
Lax, Kathleen Thompson *federal judge*
Mund, Geraldine *bankruptcy judge*
Pregerson, Harry *federal judge*

COLORADO

Brighton
Bruner, Cindy Hull *judge*

Denver
Babcock, Lewis Thornton *federal judge*
Brooks, Sidney B. *judge*
Brumbaugh, Roland John *federal judge*
Ebel, David M. *federal judge*
Felter, Edwin Lester, Jr. *judge, agency administrator*
Hobbs, Gregory J., Jr. *judge*
Kirshbaum, Howard M. *arbiter, judge*
Kourlis, Rebecca Love *judge*
Lohr, George E. *state supreme court justice*
Matsch, Richard P. *judge*
Miller, Walker David *judge*
Mullarkey, Mary J. *state supreme court justice*
Nottingham, Edward Willis, Jr. *federal judge*
Porfilio, John Carbone *federal judge*
Rovira, Luis Dario *state supreme court justice*
Satter, Raymond Nathan *judge*
Schlatter, O. Edward *judge*
Sparr, Daniel Beattie *federal judge*
Swihart, Steven Taylor *judge*
Vollack, Anthony F. *state supreme court justice*
Weinshienk, Zita Leeson *federal judge*

Englewood
Erickson, William Hurt *retired state supreme court justice*

Golden
Rodgers, Frederic Barker *judge*
Wolvington, Winston Warren *retired judge*

HAWAII

Honolulu
Choy, Herbert Young Cho *judge*
Ezra, David A. *federal judge*
Gilmor, Helen W. *judge*
Kay, Alan Cooke *federal judge*
King, Samuel Pailthorpe *federal judge*
Klein, Robert Gordon *judge*
Levinson, Steven H. *judge*
Lum, Herman Tsui Fai *retired state supreme court chief justice*
Moon, Ronald T. Y. *state supreme court chief justice*
Nakayama, Paula Aiko *justice*
Pence, Martin *federal judge*
Ramil, Mario R. *judge*
Soong, Melvin Kaipoleimanu *circuit court judge*
Watanabe, Corinne Kaoru Amemiya *lawyer, judge, state official*
Yamashita, Francis Isami *judge*

IDAHO

Boise
Boyle, Larry Monroe *federal judge*
Callister, Marion Jones *federal judge*
Hagan, Alfred Chris *federal judge*
Johnson, Byron Jerald *state supreme court judge*
Lodge, Edward James *federal judge*
McDevitt, Charles Francis *state supreme court justice*
Nelson, Thomas G. *federal judge*
Pappas, Jim D. *judge*
Silak, Cathy R. *judge*
Trott, Stephen Spangler *federal judge, musician*
Williams, Mikel H. *judge*
Winmill, B. Lynn *judge*

KANSAS

Lawrence
Tacha, Deanell Reece *federal judge*

MONTANA

Billings
Shanstrom, Jack D. *federal judge*

Great Falls
Hatfield, Paul Gerhart *federal judge, lawyer*

Helena
Gray, Karla Marie *state supreme court justice*
Harrison, John Conway *state supreme court justice*
Hunt, William E., Sr. *state supreme court justice*
Leaphart, W. William *judge*
Lovell, Charles C. *federal judge*
McDonough, Russell Charles *retired state supreme court justice*
Nelson, James C *justice*
Regnier, James *state supreme court justice*
Trieweiler, Terry Nicholas *justice*
Turnage, Jean A. *state supreme court chief justice*

NEVADA

Carson City
Rose, Robert E(dgar) *state supreme court justice*
Springer, Charles Edward *state supreme court justice*
Young, C. Clifton *judge*

Las Vegas
George, Lloyd D. *federal judge*
Hunt, Roger Lee *judge*

Johnston, Robert Jake *federal magistrate judge*
Pro, Philip Martin *judge*

Reno
Brunetti, Melvin T. *federal judge*
Hagen, David W. *judge*
Hug, Procter Ralph, Jr. *federal judge*
McKibben, Howard D. *federal judge*
Reed, Edward Cornelius, Jr. *federal judge*

NEW MEXICO

Albuquerque
Conway, John E. *federal judge*
Hansen, Curtis LeRoy *federal judge*
Parker, James Aubrey *federal judge*
Ransom, Richard Edward *retired state supreme court justice*

Las Cruces
Apodaca, Rudy Samuel *judge*
Bratton, Howard Calvin *federal judge*

Roswell
Baldock, Bobby Ray *federal judge*

Santa Fe
Baca, Joseph Francis *state supreme court justice*
Campos, Santiago E. *federal judge*
Franchini, Gene Edward *state supreme court chief justice*
Frost, Stanley *retired judge*
Kelly, Paul Joseph, Jr. *federal judge*
Minzner, Pamela B. *judge*
Serna, Patricio *state judge*

OREGON

Eugene
Coffin, Thomas M. *federal magistrate judge*
Hogan, Michael R(obert) *judge*
Radcliffe, Albert E. *judge*

Portland
Frye, Helen Jackson *judge*
Jones, Robert Edward *federal judge*
Leavy, Edward *federal judge*
Marsh, Malcolm F. *federal judge*
O'Scannlain, Diarmuid Fionntain *federal judge*
Panner, Owen M. *federal judge*
Redden, James Anthony *federal judge*
Unis, Richard L. *state supreme court justice*

Salem
Carson, Wallace Preston, Jr. *state supreme court chief justice*
Durham, Robert Donald, Jr. *judge*
Fadeley, Edward Norman *state supreme court justice*
Graber, Susan P. *judge*
Peterson, Edwin J. *retired supreme court justice, law educator*
Van Hoomissen, George Albert *state supreme court justice*

UTAH

Provo
Harding, Ray Murray, Jr. *judge*

Salt Lake City
Anderson, Stephen Hale *federal judge*
Benson, Dee Vance *federal judge*
Campbell, Marilyn B. *judge*
Clark, Glen Edward *judge*
Durham, Christine Meaders *state supreme court justice*
Greene, John Thomas *judge*
Hall, Gordon R. *retired state supreme court chief justice*
Howe, Richard Cuddy *state supreme court justice*
Jenkins, Bruce Sterling *federal judge*
McKay, Monroe Gunn *federal judge*
Murphy, Michael R. *federal judge*
Russon, Leonard H. *judge*
Sam, David *federal judge*
Stewart, Isaac Daniel, Jr. *judge*
Winder, David Kent *federal judge*
Zimmerman, Michael David *state supreme court chief justice*

WASHINGTON

Olympia
Alexander, Gerry L. *justice*
Dolliver, James Morgan *state supreme court justice*
Durham, Barbara *state supreme court justice*
Guy, Richard P. *state supreme court justice*
Harrison, William Alan *judge, arbitrator*
Johnson, Charles William *justice*
Sanders, Richard Browning *state supreme court justice*
Smith, Charles Z. *state supreme court justice*

Seattle
Beezer, Robert Renaut *federal judge*
Coughenour, John Clare *federal judge*
Dimmick, Carolyn Reaber *federal judge*
Dwyer, William L. *federal judge*
Farris, Jerome *federal judge*
Fletcher, Betty B. *federal judge*
Mc Govern, Walter T. *federal judge*
Overstreet, Hon. Karen A. *federal bankruptcy judge*
Rothstein, Barbara Jacobs *federal judge*
Zilly, Thomas Samuel *federal judge*

Spokane
Imbrogno, Cynthia *judge*
Nielsen, William Fremming *federal judge*
Quackenbush, Justin Lowe *federal judge*
Van Sickle, Frederick L. *federal judge*
Whaley, Robert Hamilton *judge*

Tacoma
Bryan, Robert J. *federal judge*

Yakima
McDonald, Alan Angus *federal judge*
Suko, Lonny Ray *judge*

WYOMING

Cheyenne
Brimmer, Clarence Addison *federal judge*
Brorby, Wade *federal judge*
Cardine, Godfrey Joseph *state supreme court justice*
Golden, Michael *state supreme court justice*
Johnson, Alan Bond *federal judge*
Lehman, Larry L. *judge*
Macy, Richard J. *state judge*
Schrader, Robert Wesley *judge*
Taylor, William Al *judge*
Thomas, Richard Van *state supreme court justice*
Urbigkit, Walter C., Jr. *state supreme court chief justice*

Green River
Marty, Lawrence A. *magistrate*

TERRITORIES OF THE UNITED STATES

GUAM

Dededo
Diaz, Ramon Valero *retired judge*

NORTHERN MARIANA ISLANDS

Saipan
Dela Cruz, Jose Santos *retired state supreme court chief justice*

CANADA

ALBERTA

Edmonton
Fraser, Catherine Anne *Canadian chief justice*

SASKATCHEWAN

Regina
Bayda, Edward Dmytro *judge*

ADDRESS UNPUBLISHED

Bistline, Stephen *retired state supreme court justice*
Boulden, Judith Ann *federal judge*
Burke, Edmond Wayne *retired judge*
Case, Charles G., II *federal bankruptcy judge*
Finesilver, Sherman Glenn *retired federal judge*
Fisher, Ann L. *pro tem judge*
Ghareeb, Donald L. *judge*
Gillette, W. Michael *judge*
Hayek, Carolyn Jean *retired judge*
Jones, Charles E. *state chief justice*
Linde, Hans Arthur *state supreme court justice*
Madsen, Barbara A *judge*
Matthews, Warren Wayne *state supreme court justice*
Montgomery, Seth David *retired state supreme court chief justice*
Moore, Daniel Alton, Jr. *retired state supreme court justice*
Reinhardt, Stephen Roy *federal judge*
Schroeder, Gerald F. *judge*
Scott, Gregory Kellam *state supreme court justice*
Shearing, Miriam *justice*
Smith, Fern M. *federal judge*
Talmadge, Philip Albert *judge, former state senator*
Trout, Linda Copple *judge*
Utter, Robert French *retired state supreme court justice*
Weber, Fred J. *retired state supreme court justice*
Wiggins, Charles Edward *federal judge*

LAW: LAW PRACTICE AND ADMINISTRATION

UNITED STATES

ALASKA

Anchorage
Anderson, Kathleen Gay *mediator, hearing officer, arbitrator, educator*
Bundy, Robert C. *prosecutor*
Cantor, James Elliot *lawyer*
Hayes, George Nicholas *lawyer*
Hughes, Mary Katherine *lawyer*
Linxwiler, James David *lawyer*
Oesting, David W. *lawyer*
Owens, Robert Patrick *lawyer*
Reeves, James N. *lawyer*
Ross, Wayne Anthony *lawyer*
Senungetuk, Vivian Ruth *lawyer*
Taylor, Deborah Ann *paralegal*

Fairbanks
Rice, Julian Casavant *lawyer*

Juneau
Cole, Charles Edward *lawyer, former state attorney general*

Kodiak
Jamin, Matthew Daniel *lawyer, magistrate judge*

ARIZONA

Flagstaff
Bertoldo, Joseph Ramon *lawyer*
Cowser, Danny Lee *lawyer, mental health specialist*

Mesa
Cameron, Janice Carol *legal regulatory administrator*
Le Clair, Douglas Marvin *lawyer, educator*

Paradise Valley
Houseworth, Laura Jennings *lawyer*

Peoria
Moshier, Mary Baluk *patent lawyer*

Phoenix
Allen, Robert Eugene Barton *lawyer*
Barclay, Steven Calder *lawyer*
Bauman, Frederick Carl *lawyer*
Beggs, Harry Mark *lawyer*
Breecher-Breen, Sheila Rae *lawyer*
Brown, Jack Edward *lawyer*
Chanen, Steven Robert *lawyer*
Comus, Louis Francis, Jr. *lawyer*
Condo, James Robert *lawyer*
Coppersmith, Sam *lawyer*
Corson, Kimball Jay *lawyer*
Craig, Stephen Wright *lawyer*
Cronin, Larry V. *lawyer, pro tempore judge*
Dawson, John Joseph *lawyer*
Denea, Michael Philip *lawyer, minister of music*
Derdenger, Patrick *lawyer*
Derouin, James G. *lawyer*
Dunipace, Ian Douglas *lawyer*
Everett, James Joseph *lawyer*
Gaines, Francis Pendleton, III *lawyer*
Gallagher, Michael L. *lawyer*
Gilbert, Donald R. *lawyer*
Gladner, Marc Stefan *lawyer*
Hammond, Larry Austin *lawyer*
Hay, John Leonard *lawyer*
Hicks, Bethany Gribben *lawyer, commissioner*
Hienton, James Robert *lawyer*
Hirsch, Steven A. *lawyer*
Holden, Michael John *lawyer*
Howard, Lucia Fakonas *lawyer*
James, Charles E., Jr. *lawyer*
Jirauch, Charles W. *lawyer*
King, Jack A. *lawyer*
Klausner, Jack Daniel *lawyer*
Klein, R. Kent *lawyer*
Knoller, Guy David *lawyer*
Koester, Berthold Karl *lawyer, retired honorary consul, educator*
Kreutzberg, David W. *lawyer*
Lacey, Henry Bernard *lawyer*
Leonard, Jeffrey S. *lawyer*
Lindholm, Donald Wayne *lawyer*
Lundin, John E. *lawyer*
MacDonnell, Philip J. *lawyer*
Madden, Paul Robert *lawyer*
Marks, Merton Eleazer *lawyer*
McDaniel, Joseph Chandler *lawyer*
McRae, Hamilton Eugene, III *lawyer*
Meschkow, Jordan Mark *lawyer*
Meyers, Howard Craig *lawyer*
Meyerson, Bruce Elliot *lawyer*
Miller, Eleanor Louise *lawyer*
Mousel, Craig Lawrence *lawyer*
Napolitano, Janet Ann *prosecutor*
Olson, Robert Howard *lawyer*
Platt, Warren E. *lawyer*
Price, Charles Steven *lawyer*
Richards, Charles Franklin, Jr. *lawyer*
Rose, Scott A. *lawyer*
Sherk, Kenneth John *lawyer*
Silverman, Alan H. *lawyer*
Smith, Susan Kimsey *lawyer*
Smock, Timothy Robert *lawyer*
Stahl, Louis A. *lawyer*
Sterbach, Charles Robert *lawyer*
Sterns, Patricia Margaret *lawyer, consultant*
Storey, Norman C. *lawyer*
Tancer, Shoshana B. *lawyer, business educator*
Thompson, Terence William *lawyer*
Thumma, Samuel Anderson *lawyer*
Udall, Calvin Hunt *lawyer*
Ulrich, Paul Graham *lawyer, author, publisher, editor*
Walker, Richard K. *lawyer*
Wheeler, Steven M. *lawyer*
Wolf, G. Van Velsor, Jr. *lawyer*
Woolf, Michael E. *lawyer*

Prescott
Gose, Richard Vernie *lawyer*

Scottsdale
Barbee, Joe Ed *lawyer*
Basinger, Richard Lee *lawyer*
Lisa, Isabelle O'Neill *law firm administrator, mergers and acquisitions executive*
Mybeck, Richard Raymond *lawyer*
Sears, Alan Edward *lawyer*
Swartz, Melvin Jay *lawyer, author*
Werner, E. Louis, Jr. *lawyer, retired insurance company executive*

Sedona
Gliege, John Gerhardt *lawyer*

Sun City
Davidson, Robert Lee, III *retired lawyer, author, consultant*
Hauer, James Albert *lawyer*
Treece, James Lyle *lawyer*

Sun City West
Gillen, Arthur Fitzpatrick *retired lawyer*

Tempe
Evans, Lawrence Jack, Jr. *lawyer*
Furnish, Dale Beck *law educator*
Spritzer, Ralph Simon *lawyer, educator*
Vanderpoel, James Robert *lawyer*

Tucson
Boswell, Susan G. *lawyer*
D'Antonio, James Joseph *lawyer*
Hyams, Harold *lawyer*
Levitan, Roger Stanley *lawyer*
Meehan, Michael Joseph *lawyer*

Robinson, Bernard Leo *retired lawyer*
Simmons, Sarah R. *lawyer*
Woods, Winton D. *law educator*

Yuma
Hossler, David Joseph *lawyer, educator*

CALIFORNIA

Altadena
Coulter, George Prothro *retired lawyer, real estate executive*

Anaheim
McFarlane, Richard Alan *lawyer*
Miller, Jeremy Matthew *lawyer, legal educator*

Atascadero
Dashjian, Michael Bryan *lawyer*

Auburn
Henry, Karen Hawley *lawyer*
Lyon, Bruce Arnold *lawyer, educator*

Bakersfield
Farr, G(ardner) Neil *lawyer*
Kind, Kenneth Wayne *lawyer, real estate broker*
Martin, George Francis *lawyer*
Young, John Byron *retired lawyer*

Berkeley
Buxbaum, Richard M. *law educator, lawyer*
Concepción, David Alden *arbitrator, educator*
Feller, David E. *law educator, arbitrator*
Goldsmith, Donald William *lawyer, astronomer, writer*
Hetland, John Robert *lawyer, educator*
Kay, Herma Hill *law educator*
Reilley, Kathleen Patricia *lawyer*
Scheiber, Harry N. *law educator*
Van Winkle, Wesley Andrew *lawyer, educator*

Beverly Hills
Bordy, Michael Jeffrey *lawyer*
Dickerson, William Roy *lawyer*
Florence, Kenneth James *lawyer*
Franzen, Don Erik *lawyer*
Haile, Lawrence Barclay *lawyer*
Horwin, Leonard *lawyer*
Jessup, W. Edgar, Jr. *lawyer*
Nicholas, Frederick M. *lawyer*
Ramer, Bruce M. *lawyer*
Rosky, Burton Seymour *lawyer*
Schiff, Gunther Hans *lawyer*
Shacter, David Mervyn *lawyer*
Shire, Harold Raymond *law educator, author, social scientist*
Thompson, Richard Dickson *lawyer*
Wainess, Marcia Watson *legal management consultant*

Bishop
Buchanan, James Douglas *lawyer*

Brea
Lounsbury, Steven Richard *lawyer*
Pearson, April Virginia *lawyer*

Burbank
Litvack, Sanford Martin *lawyer*

Burlingame
Demanes, Floyd A. *lawyer, arbitrator, mediator, consultant*
Narayan, Beverly Elaine *lawyer*
Peel, Fred Welch, Jr. *law educator, writer*

Carmichael
Halpenny, Diana Doris *lawyer*

Chico
Morgan, James Frederick *lawyer, educator*

Chula Vista
Santee, Dale William *lawyer, air force officer*

Coalinga
Frame, Ted Ronald *lawyer*

Concord
Orlebeke, William Ronald *lawyer*

Corte Madera
Gordon, Robert Eugene *lawyer*

Costa Mesa
Oderman, Jeffrey M. *lawyer*
Shallenberger, Garvin F. *lawyer*
Stone, Samuel Beckner *lawyer*
Tennyson, Peter Joseph *lawyer*

Culver City
von Kalinowski, Julian Onesime *lawyer*

Cupertino
Maddux, Parker Ahrens *lawyer*

Cypress
Olschwang, Alan Paul *lawyer*

Davis
Oakley, John Bilyeu *law educator, lawyer, judicial consultant*
Wolk, Bruce Alan *law educator*

Diamond Bar
Ofner, William Bernard *lawyer*

El Centro
Albertson, Jack Aaron Paul *prosecutor*

El Cerrito
Garbarino, Joseph William *labor arbitrator, economics and business educator*

El Segundo
Gambaro, Ernest Umberto *lawyer, consultant*
Grundtisch, Jeffery Lynn *lawyer, medical and environmental consultant*

Elverta
Betts, Barbara Lang (Mrs. Bert A. Betts) *lawyer, rancher, realtor*

Emeryville
Dezurick, Paul A. *lawyer*

Encino
Kaufman, Albert I. *lawyer*
Kuklin, Jeffrey Peter *lawyer, talent agency executive*
Smith, Selma Moidel *lawyer, composer*

Fairfield
Honeychurch, Denis Arthur *lawyer*
Moore, Marianna Gay *law librarian, consultant*

Fresno
Ewell, A. Ben, Jr. *lawyer, businessman*

Fullerton
Ackerman, Richard Charles *lawyer, state legislator*
Bakken, Gordon Morris *law educator*
Everett, Pamela Irene *legal management company executive, educator*
Frizell, Samuel *law educator*
Moerbeek, Stanley Leonard *lawyer*
Ruby, Charles Leroy *law educator, lawyer, civic leader*

Gilroy
Jacobs, Bruce Marrin *lawyer*

Glendale
Ball, James Herington *lawyer*
Boukidis, Constantine Michael *lawyer*
Cayse, Phyllis *federal mediator*
MacDonald, Kirk Stewart *lawyer*
Martinetti, Ronald Anthony *lawyer*
Stack, Kevin J. *lawyer*

Hayward
Smith, John Kerwin *lawyer*

Indio
Edwards, William Joseph *lawyer, educator*

Irvine
Hilker, Walter Robert, Jr. *lawyer*
Hobart, Jean Adrian *lawyer*
Puzder, Andrew F. *lawyer*
Specter, Richard Bruce *lawyer*
Toledano, James *lawyer*
Umberg, Thomas John *lawyer*

Kernville
Hix, Phyllis Marie *lawyer*

La Habra
Kent, Jeffrey Donald *lawyer*

La Jolla
Karlen, Peter Hurd *lawyer, writer*

Lancaster
Berg, Hans Fredrik *lawyer*

Larkspur
Greenberg, Myron Silver *lawyer*
Maier, Peter Klaus *law educator, investment adviser*
Marker, Marc Linthacum *lawyer, investor*

Loma Linda
Chang, Janice May *lawyer, law educator, naturopath, psychologist*

Long Beach
Johnson, Philip Leslie *lawyer*
Roberts, James Donzil *lawyer*
Russell, Thomas Arthur *lawyer*
Stolpman, Thomas Gerard *lawyer*
Taylor, Reese Hale, Jr. *lawyer, former government administrator*

Los Angeles
Abrams, Norman *law educator, university administrator*
Adler, Erwin Ellery *lawyer*
Adler, Michael I. *lawyer*
Adler, Sara *arbitrator*
Antin, Michael *lawyer*
Argue, John Clifford *lawyer*
Ballsun, Kathryn Ann *lawyer*
Bardach, Sheldon Gilbert *lawyer*
Barnes, (Benjamin Warren) Grant *lawyer, poet*
Basile, Paul Louis, Jr. *lawyer*
Bauman, Stephen Adrian *lawyer*
Bell, Wayne Steven *lawyer*
Belleville, Philip Frederick *lawyer*
Berman, Myles Lee *lawyer*
Bice, Scott Haas *lawyer, educator*
Biederman, Donald Ellis *lawyer*
Bierstedt, Peter Richard *lawyer, entertainment industry consultant*
Bonner, Robert Cleve *lawyer*
Boxer, Lester *lawyer*
Bradford, David Paul *judicial assistant*
Brassell, Roselyn Strauss *lawyer*
Brian, Brad D. *lawyer*
Burdge, Richard James, Jr. *lawyer*
Carrey, Neil *lawyer, educator*
Castro, Leonard Edward *lawyer*
Chiate, Kenneth Reed *lawyer*
Chin, Kelvin Henry *legal association executive, mediator, consultant*
Clark, R. Bradbury *lawyer*
Cleary, William Joseph, Jr. *lawyer*
Cole, William L. *lawyer*
Collins, Michael K. *lawyer*
Davis, J. Alan *lawyer, producer, writer*
Decker, Richard Jeffrey *lawyer*
Demoff, Marvin Alan *lawyer*
Diamond, Stanley Jay *lawyer*
Dinel, Richard Henry *lawyer*
Douglas, Joel Bruce *lawyer*
Downey, William J., III *lawyer*
Field, Morton Richard *lawyer*
Fisher, Raymond Corley *lawyer*
Follick, Edwin Duane *law educator, chiropractic physician*
Franceschi, Ernest Joseph, Jr. *lawyer*
Friedman, Alan E. *lawyer*
Gallo, Jon Joseph *lawyer*
Galton, Stephen Harold *lawyer*
Gebb, Sheldon Alexander *lawyer*
Gilbert, Robert Wolfe *lawyer*
Gitt, Cynthia E. *lawyer*
Goodman, Max A. *lawyer, educator*
Gordon, David Eliot *lawyer*
Gould, Julian Saul *lawyer*
Graubart, Jeffrey Lowell *entertainment lawyer*
Gray, Jan Charles *lawyer, business owner*
Greaves, John Allen *lawyer*
Green, Kenneth Norton *lawyer, law educator*
Green, William Porter *lawyer*
Grosz, Philip J. *lawyer*
Hahn, Elliott Julius *lawyer*
Handzlik, Jan Lawrence *lawyer*
Hayes, Byron Jackson, Jr. *lawyer*
Hayes, Steven Lee *lawyer*
Hedlund, Paul James *lawyer*
Heller, Philip *lawyer*
Heyck, Theodore Daly *lawyer*
Howard, Edward Paxson, IV *law center executive*
Howard, Nancy E. *lawyer*
Hsieh, Stewart *lawyer*
Iamele, Richard Thomas *law librarian*
Jacobs, Randall Brian *lawyer*
Jansen, Allan W. *lawyer*
Johnson, Willie Dan *lawyer*
Jordan, Robert Leon *lawyer, educator*
Kamine, Bernard Samuel *lawyer*
Kaplowitz, Karen (Jill) *lawyer*
Kim, Mark Christopher *prosecutor*
Kupperman, Henry John *lawyer*
Lambert, Thomas P. *lawyer*
Lashley, Lenore Clarisse *lawyer*
Lauchengco, Jose Yujuico, Jr. *lawyer*
Lavin, Laurence Michael *lawyer*
Le Sage, Bernard E. *lawyer*
Levine, C. Bruce *lawyer*
Lurvey, Ira Harold *lawyer*
Manatt, Charles Taylor *lawyer*
Manella, Nora M. *prosecutor*
Marcus, Stephen Howard *lawyer*
Marshall, Arthur K. *lawyer, judge, arbitrator, educator, writer*
Matsunaga, Geoffrey Dean *lawyer*
May, Lawrence Edward *lawyer*
McLaughlin, Joseph Mailey *lawyer*
McLurkin, Thomas Cornelius, Jr. *lawyer*
Meyer, Michael Edwin *lawyer*
Millard, Neal Steven *lawyer*
Miller, Mona Joy Deutsch *lawyer*
Miller, O'Malley Murray *lawyer*
Mintz, Marshall Gary *lawyer*
Miyoshi, David Masao *lawyer, international investment consultant*
Moloney, Stephen Michael *lawyer*
Morgenthaler, Alisa Marie *lawyer*
Moyer, Craig Alan *lawyer*
Muhlbach, Robert Arthur *lawyer*
Newman, Michael Rodney *lawyer*
Nibley, Robert Ricks *retired lawyer*
Noble, Richard Lloyd *lawyer*
O'Leary, Prentice L. *lawyer*
Palmer, Robert L. *lawyer*
Pascotto, Alvaro *lawyer*
Pasich, Kirk Alan *lawyer*
Pieper, Darold D. *lawyer*
Polley, Terry Lee *lawyer*
Pollock, John Phleger *lawyer*
Pope, Alexander H. *lawyer, former county official*
Porter, Verna Louise *lawyer*
Pugsley, Robert Adrian *legal educator*
Rae, Matthew Sanderson, Jr. *lawyer*
Renwick, Edward S. *lawyer*
Richardson, Arthur Wilhelm *lawyer*
Robertson, Hugh Duff *lawyer*
Rolin, Christopher E(rnest) *lawyer*
Roney, John Harvey *lawyer, consultant*
Rosendahl, Roger Wayne *lawyer*
Rosenthal, Sol *lawyer*
Rothman, Michael Judah *lawyer*
Rutter, Marshall Anthony *lawyer*
Sacks, Robert Neil *lawyer*
Schmidt, Karl A. *lawyer*
Selvin, Peter Sam *lawyer*
Shartin, Stacy D. *lawyer*
Sherwood, Allen Joseph *lawyer*
Silbergeld, Arthur F. *lawyer*
Simmons, Richard J. *lawyer*
Sinclitico, Dennis J. *lawyer*
Smith, Gregory R. *lawyer*
Sorrentino, Joseph Nicholas *prosecutor*
Spivak, Joel A. *lawyer*
Stashower, Arthur L. *lawyer*
Tackowiak, Bruce Joseph *lawyer*
Tan, William Lew *lawyer*
Taylor, Minna *lawyer*
Thornton, Charles Victor *lawyer*
Thorpe, Douglas L. *lawyer*
Tinsley, Walton Eugene *lawyer*
Valenzuela, Manuel Anthony, Jr. *lawyer*
Valner, Rudy *lawyer*
Van de Kamp, John Kalar *lawyer*
Weinman, Glenn Alan *lawyer*
Weinstock, Harold *lawyer*
Williams, Lee Dwain *lawyer*
Winterman, Craig L. *lawyer*
York, Gary Alan *lawyer*
Zelon, Laurie Dee *lawyer*

Los Gatos
Seligmann, William Robert *lawyer, author*

Malibu
Darraby, Jessica L. *lawyer, educator, writer*

Marina Del Rey
Davis, Donald G(lenn) *lawyer*
Wineman, Paul Raymond, Jr. *contract negotiator*

Martinez
Williams, Charles Judson *lawyer*

Menlo Park
Dyer, Charles Arnold *lawyer*
Kirk, Cassius Lamb, Jr. *lawyer, investor*
Sauers, William Dale *lawyer, playwright*

Mill Valley
Nemir, Donald Philip *lawyer*

Newport Beach
Barclay, John Allen *lawyer*
Caldwell, Courtney Lynn *lawyer, real estate consultant*
Clark, Thomas P., Jr. *lawyer*
Damon, James Graham *lawyer*
Mortensen, Arvid LeGrande *lawyer*
Saltarelli, Thomas Richard *lawyer*
Schnapp, Roger Herbert *lawyer*
Wentworth, Theodore Sumner *lawyer*

North Hollywood
Harwick, Maurice *lawyer*
Kreger, Melvin Joseph *lawyer*
Zimring, Stuart David *lawyer*

Novato
Obninsky, Victor Peter *lawyer*

Oakland
Allen, Jeffrey Michael *lawyer*
Burnison, Boyd Edward *lawyer*
Johnson, Kenneth F. *lawyer*
Leslie, Robert Lorne *lawyer*
McCarthy, Steven M. *lawyer*
Thompson Stanley, Trina *lawyer*
Wallis, Eric G. *lawyer*
West, Natalie Elsa *lawyer*
Wood, James Michael *lawyer*

Oceanside
Richards, Gerald Thomas *lawyer, consultant*

Orange
Bennett, William Perry *lawyer*
Parker, Charles Edward *retired lawyer*

Orinda
Brookes, Valentine *retired lawyer*
Perez, Richard Lee *lawyer*

Oroville
Chapman, Joyce Eileen *law educator, administrator*

Oxnard
O'Hearn, Michael John *lawyer*

Pacific Palisades
Flattery, Thomas Long *lawyer, legal administrator*
Nothmann, Rudolf S. *legal researcher*
Verrone, Patric Miller *lawyer, writer*

Palm Desert
Gribow, Dale Seward *lawyer, business executive*
Spirtos, Nicholas George *lawyer, financial company executive*

Palm Springs
FitzGerald, John Edward, III *lawyer*
Sarner, Harvey *lawyer*

Palo Alto
Anderson, Matthew L. *lawyer*
Benton, Lee F. *lawyer*
Brigham, Samuel Townsend Jack, III *lawyer*
Herbst, David W. *lawyer*
Jackson, Cynthia L. *lawyer*
Marquis, Matthew Elliot *lawyer*
Massey, Henry P., Jr. *lawyer*
Nycum, Susan Hubbell *lawyer*
Rinsky, Arthur C. *lawyer*
Smith, Glenn A. *lawyer*
Taylor, Barry E. *lawyer*

Palos Verdes Estates
Toftness, Cecil Gillman *lawyer, consultant*

Palos Verdes Peninsula
Yeomans, Russell Allen *lawyer, translator*

Pasadena
Ammirato, Vincent Anthony *lawyer*
Armour, George Porter *lawyer*
Cahill, Richard Frederick *lawyer*
Cranston, Howard Stephen *lawyer, management consultant*
Hunt, Gordon *lawyer*
Mosher, Sally Ekenberg *lawyer*
Tanner, Dee Boshard *retired lawyer*
Wills, Donald Allison *lawyer*
Zuetel, Kenneth Roy, Jr. *lawyer*

Pleasanton
Scott, G. Judson, Jr. *lawyer*
Staley, John Fredric *lawyer*

Pomona
Anderson, William J. *lawyer*

Rancho Cordova
Lynch, Robert Berger *lawyer*

Rancho Mirage
Goldie, Ray Robert *lawyer*

Rancho Santa Fe
Freeberg, Eric O. *lawyer, real estate developer*

Rancho Santa Margarita
Black, William Rea *lawyer*

Redding
Ragland, Carroll Ann *law educator, judicial officer*

Redlands
Ely, Northcutt *lawyer*

Redondo Beach
Hachmeister, John H. *lawyer, educator, mediator*
Martin, Robert Michael *lawyer*

Redwood City
Heuman, Donna Rena *lawyer*
Inama, Christopher Roy *lawyer, educator*
Silvestri, Philip Salvatore *lawyer*
Wilhelm, Robert Oscar *lawyer, civil engineer, developer*

Rio Linda
Lebrato, Mary Theresa *lawyer, psychologist*

Riverside
Bergman, Daniel Charles *county official, lawyer, environmental manager*
Darling, Scott Edward *lawyer*
Marlatt, Michael James *lawyer*

Rolling Hills
Rumbaugh, Charles Earl *lawyer, arbitrator/mediator*

Roseville
Heisler, Bradley Paul *lawyer*
Robbins, Stephen J. M. *lawyer*

Sacramento
Albert-Sheridan, Lenore LuAnn *legal research fellow, business owner*
Blake, D. Steven *lawyer*
Bobrow, Susan Lukin *lawyer*
Brookman, Anthony Raymond *lawyer*
Burton, Randall James *lawyer*
Callahan, Gary Brent *lawyer*
Callahan, Ronald *federal investigator, historian*
Callison, Russell James *lawyer*
Carrel, Marc Lovis *lawyer, legislative policy consultant*
Collentine, John Thomas *arbitrator, public art consultant*
Collins, Robert D. *lawyer, consultant*
Dignan, Mary *lawyer*
Janigian, Bruce Jasper *lawyer, educator*
Jarrett, Ronald Douglas *lawyer, nurse*
Kolkey, Daniel Miles *lawyer*
Lee, Adam Sidney *lawyer*
Lesch, Barry M. *lawyer*
Micheli, Christopher Michael *lawyer*
Miller, Suzanne Marie *law librarian, educator*
Perschbacher, Debra Bassett *lawyer*
Root, Gerald Edward *courts resource manager*
Roseme, Sharon Day *lawyer*
Stevens, Charles J. *prosecutor*
Taylor, Walter Wallace *lawyer*
Waks, Dennis Stanford *lawyer*
Willis, Dawn Louise *paralegal, small business owner*

San Bernardino
Eskin, Barry Sanford *court investigator*

San Diego
Bacino, Birger Greg *lawyer*
Bersin, Alan Douglas *prosecutor, lawyer*
Boggs, William S. *lawyer*
Buzunis, Constantine Dino *lawyer*
Campbell, Arthur Waldron *lawyer, educator*
Cannon, Gary Curtis *lawyer, publishing executive*
Carter, Nancy Carol *legal educator, law librarian*
Chatroo, Arthur Jay *lawyer*
Cox, Kim Carroll *lawyer, broadcaster*
Estep, Arthur Lee *lawyer*
Frasch, Brian Bernard *lawyer*
Guinn, Stanley Willis *lawyer*
Guinn, Susan Lee *lawyer*
Hofflund, Paul *lawyer*
Lathrop, Mitchell Lee *lawyer*
McClellan, Craig Rene *lawyer*
Paupp, Terrence Edward *legal research associate, educator*
Peters, Richard *lawyer*
Preston, David Raymond *lawyer*
Root, George L., Jr. *lawyer*
Ross, Terry D. *lawyer*
Schoville, Dennis A(rnold) *lawyer*
Shepersky, Mimi *probate examiner*
Shippey, Sandra Lee *lawyer*
Slomanson, William Reed *law educator, legal writer*
Von Passenheim, John B. *lawyer*
Weaver, Michael James *lawyer*

San Dimas
Abner, Eddie Lee *lawyer*

San Francisco
Adams, Philip *lawyer*
Alderman, William Fields *lawyer*
Alexander, Robert C. *lawyer*
Allen, Jose R. *lawyer*
Arbuthnot, Robert Murray *lawyer*
Baker, Michael J. *lawyer*
Barber, James P. *lawyer*
Baxter, Ralph H., Jr. *lawyer*
Berning, Paul Wilson *lawyer*
Bertain, G(eorge) Joseph, Jr. *lawyer*
Bookin, Daniel Henry *lawyer*
Booth, Forrest *lawyer*
Boven, Douglas George *lawyer*
Bridgman, Richard Darrell *lawyer*
Briscoe, John *lawyer*
Burden, James Ewers *lawyer*
Bushnell, Roderick Paul *lawyer*
Campisi, Dominic John *lawyer*
Cannon, Christopher John *lawyer*
Coombe, George William, Jr. *lawyer, retired banker*
Daggett, Robert Sherman *lawyer*
Davies, Paul Lewis, Jr. *retired lawyer*
Davis, Roger Lewis *lawyer*
Donnici, Peter Joseph *lawyer, law educator, consultant*
Drozd, Leon Frank, Jr. *lawyer*
Dryden, Robert Eugene *lawyer*
Dunne, Kevin Joseph *lawyer*
Edwards, Priscilla Ann *litigation support business owner*
Fergus, Gary Scott *lawyer*
Fleisher, Steven M. *lawyer*
Freud, Nicholas S. *lawyer*
Friedman, Robert Eric *lawyer*
Gillmar, Stanley Frank *lawyer*
Goetzl, Thomas Maxwell *law educator, consultant*
Guggenhime, Richard Johnson *lawyer*
Haas, Raymond P. *lawyer*
Hall, Paul J. *lawyer*
Hendrick, James T. *lawyer*
Hesketh, Thomas A.E. *lawyer, arbitrator*
Hilton, Stanley Goumas *lawyer, educator, writer*
Hing, Lawrence Stewart *lawyer, management consultant*
Hisert, George A. *lawyer*
Hone, Michael Curran *law educator, venture capitalist*
Howe, Drayton Ford, Jr. *lawyer*
Hunt, James L. *lawyer*
Hurabiell, John Philip, Sr. *lawyer*
Hyman, Harvey Andrew *lawyer*

Innes, Kenneth Frederick, III *lawyer*
Jones, J. Sorton *lawyer*
Keane, Peter Gerald *lawyer, educator, broadcaster*
Kelly, J. Michael *lawyer*
Kleinberg, James P. *lawyer*
Lawton, Larry David *lawyer*
Lee, John Jin *lawyer*
Logan, Peter B. *lawyer*
Lopes, James Louis *lawyer*
Mandel, Martin Louis *lawyer*
Mattes, Martin Anthony *lawyer*
Mesina, Dennis G. *lawyer*
Miles, Donald F. *lawyer*
Miller, Gregory Keith *corporate lawyer*
Morrissey, John Carroll *lawyer*
Mosk, Susan Hines *lawyer*
Neiman, Tanya Marie *legal association administrator*
Parker, Harold Allen *lawyer, real estate executive*
Peritore, Laura *law librarian*
Philipsborn, John Timothy *lawyer, author*
Pickett, Donn Philip *lawyer*
Preuss, Charles F. *lawyer*
Raven, Robert Dunbar *lawyer*
Reding, John A. *lawyer*
Reese, John Robert *lawyer*
Richardson, Daniel Ralph *lawyer*
Riley, William L. *lawyer*
Rogan, Richard A. *lawyer*
Roman, Stan G. *lawyer*
Roosevelt, Michael A. *lawyer*
Rosch, John Thomas *lawyer*
Rossmann, Antonio *lawyer, educator*
Saxe, Steven Louis *lawyer*
Schaffer, Jeffrey L. *lawyer*
Scholick, Gary P. *lawyer*
Seabolt, Richard L. *lawyer*
Seavey, William Arthur *lawyer, vintner*
Sevier, Ernest Youle *lawyer*
Shiffman, Michael A. *lawyer*
Sibley, Peter Edward *lawyer*
Silk, Thomas *lawyer*
Siniscalco, Gary Richard *lawyer*
Smegal, Thomas Frank, Jr. *lawyer*
Smith, Thorn McClellan *lawyer*
Soberon, Presentacion Zablan *state bar administrator*
Sochynsky, Yaroslav *lawyer*
Sorensen, Linda *lawyer*
Staring, Graydon Shaw *lawyer*
Stuppi, Craig *lawyer*
Sullivan, James Patrick *lawyer*
Thompson, Robert Charles *lawyer*
Tobin, James Michael *lawyer*
Traynor, J. Michael *lawyer*
Weber, Arnold I. *lawyer*
Weiner, Peter H. *lawyer*
Williamson, George Eugene *lawyer*
Wilson, John Pasley *law educator*
Wolfe, Cameron Withgot, Jr. *lawyer*
Wood, Robert Warren *lawyer*
Wyle, Frederick S. *lawyer*
Yamaguchi, Michael Joseph *prosecutor*
Yamakawa, David Kiyoshi, Jr. *lawyer*

San Jose
Alexander, Katharine Violet *lawyer*
Alexander, Richard *lawyer*
Anderson, Edward Virgil *lawyer*
Cummins, Charles Fitch, Jr. *lawyer*
Denver, Thomas H.R. *lawyer*
Gonzales, Daniel S. *lawyer*
Katzman, Richard Alan *lawyer, judicial arbitrator*
King, Ellen McGinty *lawyer*
Kraw, George Martin *lawyer, essayist*
Laskin, Barbara Virginia *legal association administrator*
Manayan, Henry C. *corporate executive, mayor*
McManis, James *lawyer*
Mogensen, Eric *lawyer*
Nopar, Alan Scott *lawyer*
Ruby, Allen Joel *lawyer*
Stutzman, Thomas Chase, Sr. *lawyer*

San Leandro
Newacheck, David John *lawyer*

San Marino
Arkenberg, Jerome Stephen *law and history researcher*

San Mateo
Dworkin, Michael Leonard *lawyer*
Kenney, William Fitzgerald *lawyer*
Lorenz, Brian *lawyer*
Monaco, Daniel Joseph *lawyer*

San Rafael
Drexler, Kenneth *lawyer*
Roth, Hadden Wing *lawyer*
Townsend, Russell Henry *lawyer*

San Ramon
Davis, John Albert *lawyer*

Santa Ana
Andres, Eugen Charles *lawyer*
Blaine, Dorothea Constance Ragetté *lawyer*
Chambers, Gary Lee *lawyer*
Dillard, John Martin *lawyer, pilot*
Fay-Schmidt, Patricia Ann *paralegal*
Harley, Robison Dooling, Jr. *lawyer, educator*
Mei, Tom Y. K. *lawyer*
Schiff, Laurie *lawyer*

Santa Barbara
Ah-Tye, Kirk Thomas *lawyer*
Bauer, Marvin Agather *lawyer*
Cappello, A. Barry *lawyer*
Gaines, Howard Clarke *retired lawyer*
McGinnes, James Marc *lawyer, lecturer*
Nelson, Sonja Bea *paralegal*
Nolte, John Michael *lawyer, consultant*
Perloff, Jean Marcosson *lawyer*
Reed, Frank Fremont, II *retired lawyer*
Stirling, Clark Tillman *lawyer*

Santa Clara
Blawie, James Louis *law educator*
Kaner, Cem *lawyer, computer software consultant*

Santa Clarita
Kotler, Richard Lee *lawyer*

Santa Cruz
Atchison, Rodney Raymond *lawyer, arbitrator*

Santa Maria
Montandon, Arther Ronald *municipal lawyer*

Santa Monica
Hirsch, Richard G. *lawyer*
Kanner, Gideon *lawyer*
Le Berthon, Adam *lawyer*
Loo, Thomas S. *lawyer*
Ringler, Jerome Lawrence *lawyer*

Santa Rosa
Lanahan, Daniel Joseph *lawyer*
Meechan, Rick James *lawyer*

Santee
Parker, Marilyn Adele *paralegal*

Saratoga
Adams, Jo-Ann Marie *lawyer*

Seaside
Weingarten, Saul Myer *lawyer*

Sherman Oaks
Joyce, Stephen Michael *lawyer*
Luna, Barbara Carole *expert witness, accountant, appraiser*
Reznik, Benjamin Menachem *lawyer*

Solana Beach
Upp, Robert Dean *lawyer*

Stanford
Bagley, Constance Elizabeth *lawyer, educator*
Brest, Paul A. *law educator*
Friedman, Lawrence M. *law educator*
Sofaer, Abraham David *lawyer, legal advisor, federal judge, legal educator*
Williams, Howard Russell *lawyer, educator*

Studio City
Miller, Charles Maurice *lawyer*

Sunnyvale
Donnally, Robert Andrew *lawyer*

Temecula
Thompson, James Avery, Jr. *legal intern*
Thompson, Susannah Elizabeth *lawyer*

Thousand Oaks
Anderson, Stanley Edward, Jr. *lawyer*
Trover, Ellen Lloyd *lawyer*

Torrance
Cohen, Seymour I. *lawyer*
Petillon, Lee Ritchey *lawyer*
Smith, Michael Cordon *lawyer*
Van Emburgh, Joanne *lawyer*

Universal City
Peter, Arnold Philimon *lawyer*

Van Nuys
Arabian, Armand *arbitrator, mediator, lawyer*
Boyd, Harry Dalton *lawyer, former insurance company executive*

Ventura
Bride, Robert Fairbanks *lawyer*
Clabaugh, Elmer Eugene, Jr. *lawyer*
Gartner, Harold Henry, III *lawyer*

Visalia
Crowe, John T. *lawyer*
Hart, Timothy Ray *lawyer, dean*
Smukler, Kim Bennett *lawyer*

Vista
Patrick, Wendy Lynn *lawyer*
Rigby, Amanda Young *paralegal firm executive*

Walnut Creek
Miller, Eugene H. *lawyer*
Newmark, Milton Maxwell *lawyer*

West Hollywood
Finstad, Suzanne Elaine *writer, laywer, producer*
Golden, Renée Wayne *lawyer*

Westlake Village
Stuehrmann, Raymond Louis *lawyer*

Westminster
Foster Vargas, Kathleen Diane *legal administrator*

Windsor
Greiner, Robert Philip *lawyer, real estate broker*

Woodland Hills
Even, Randolph M. *lawyer*
Geiser, Thomas Christopher *lawyer*

Woodside
Martin, Joseph, Jr. *retired lawyer, former ambassador*

COLORADO

Arvada
Guinn, Linda Ann *lawyer*

Aspen
Consor, Jennette Estelle *lawyer, consultant and fundraiser*
McGrath, J. Nicholas *lawyer*

Aurora
Kaplan, Marc J. *lawyer*
Seybert, Janet Rose *lawyer, military officer*

Boulder
Dubofsky, Jean Eberhart *lawyer, former state supreme court justice*
Gamm, Gordon Julius *lawyer*

Miller, Jonathan Lewis *lawyer, computer consultant*
Porzak, Glenn E. *lawyer*
Purvis, John Anderson *lawyer*

Colorado Springs
Adams, Deborah Rowland *lawyer*
Campbell, Frederick Hollister *lawyer, historian*
Evans, Paul Vernon *lawyer*
Rowan, Ronald Thomas *lawyer*
Salley, George Henry, III *lawyer*

Commerce City
Trujillo, Lorenzo A. *lawyer, educator*

Denver
Abramovitz, Michael John *lawyer*
Allen, Stephanie West *mediator, workplace entertainment company owner*
Archibold, John Ewing *lawyer, consultant*
Arundel, James D. *lawyer*
Ash, Walter Brinker *lawyer*
Atlass, Theodore Bruce *lawyer, educator*
Bader, Gerald Louis, Jr. *lawyer*
Bolocofsky, David N. *lawyer, psychology educator*
Bolton, Bradford L. *court clerk*
Breeskin, Michael Wayne *lawyer*
Bronesky, Joseph J. *lawyer*
Bruno, Harold Robinson, III *lawyer*
Carrigan, Jim R. *arbitrator, mediator, retired federal judge*
Commander, Eugene R. *lawyer*
Conover, Frederic King *lawyer*
Cox, William Vaughan *lawyer*
Daniel, Wiley Y. *lawyer*
De Gette, Diana Louise *lawyer, state legislator*
de Marino, Thomas John *lawyer*
Dolan, Brian Thomas *lawyer*
Donder, Pauline Veronica *legal secretary, library page*
Dowdle, Patrick Dennis *lawyer*
Edwards, Daniel Walden *lawyer*
Eklund, Carl Andrew *lawyer*
Erisman, Frank *lawyer*
Finegan, Cole *lawyer*
Gehres, James *lawyer*
Grissom, Garth Clyde *lawyer*
Gustus, Stacey A. *legal secretary*
Harris, Dale Ray *lawyer*
Hodges, Joseph Gilluly, Jr. *lawyer*
Houtsma, Peter C. *lawyer*
Irwin, R. Robert *lawyer*
Johnson, Robert Leland *lawyer*
Jones, Peter F. *lawyer*
Kahn, Edwin S. *lawyer*
Keatinge, Robert Reed *lawyer*
Krendl, Cathy Stricklin *lawyer*
Lerman, Eileen R. *lawyer*
Linn, Todd Alexander *lawyer*
Lutz, John Shafroth *lawyer*
Marquess, Lawrence Wade *lawyer*
Mauro, Richard Frank *lawyer, investment manager*
McKendree, John W. *lawyer*
McLain, William Allen *lawyer*
Meyer, Frederick G. *lawyer*
Murane, William Edward *lawyer*
Nelson, John Gustaf *lawyer*
O'Brien, Kevin E. *lawyer*
Otten, Arthur Edward, Jr. *lawyer, corporate executive*
Parcel, Randy Lynn *lawyer*
Peloquin, Louis Omer *lawyer*
Polumbus, Gary M. *lawyer*
Pringle, Edward E. *legal educator, former state supreme court chief justice*
Rich, Ben Arthur *lawyer, educator*
Rich, Robert Stephen *lawyer*
Ritsema, Fredric A. *lawyer*
Ruppert, John Lawrence *lawyer*
Sattler, Bruce Weimer *lawyer*
Sayre, John Marshall *lawyer, former government official*
Schmidt, Diana Gail *paralegal*
Schmidt, L(ail) William, Jr. *lawyer*
Schroeder, Merrie Jo *law librarian*
Scott, Peter Bryan *lawyer*
Seifert, Stephen Wayne *lawyer*
Steefel, David Simon *lawyer*
Syke, Cameron John *lawyer*
Taylor, T. Raber *lawyer*
Tisdale, Douglas Michael *lawyer*
Ulrich, Theodore Albert *lawyer*
Watson, William D. *lawyer*
Welton, Charles Ephraim *lawyer*
Wheeler, Malcolm Edward *lawyer, law educator*
Williams, Michael Anthony *lawyer*
Wollins, David H. *lawyer*
Yegge, Robert Bernard *lawyer, college dean emeritus, educator*

Eads
Marsh, Richard Alan *lawyer*

Englewood
Harris, Robert W. *lawyer*
Karr, David Dean *lawyer*
Karstaedt, Arthur R., III *lawyer*
Nixon, Scott Sherman *lawyer*
Poe, Robert Alan *lawyer*
Smead, Burton Armstrong, Jr. *lawyer, retired*
Steinhauser, John William *lawyer*
Wagner, David James *lawyer*

Fort Collins
Gamlin, John Paschall *lawyer*
Gandy, H. Conway *lawyer, state official*
Rogers, Garth Winfield *lawyer*

Frisco
Helmer, David Alan *lawyer*

Glenwood Springs
Winston, Haydn *lawyer*

Golden
Cassidy, Samuel H. *lawyer, lieutenant governor, state legislator*
Phillipson, Donald E. *lawyer*

Grand Junction
Mayberry, Herbert Sylvester *lawyer*

Greeley
Conway, Rebecca Ann Koppes *lawyer*
Kerr, Robert James *mediator, educational consultant*

Greenwood Village
Katz, Michael Jeffery *lawyer*

Lakewood
Guyton, Samuel Percy *retired lawyer*

Longmont
Martin, Ralph Michael (Rick Martin) *patent lawyer, marketing consultant*

Manassa
Garcia, Castelar Medardo *lawyer*

Parker
Greenberg, Morton Paul *lawyer, consultant, insurance broker, underwriter*

Pueblo
Farley, Thomas T. *lawyer*
Geisel, Henry Jules *lawyer*
O'Conner, Loretta Rae *lawyer*

Pueblo West
McHardy, John Alexander *lawyer*

Silverton
Padrick, Kevin D. *lawyer*

DISTRICT OF COLUMBIA

Washington
Foley, Thomas Stephen *lawyer, former speaker House of Representatives*
Katz, John W. *lawyer, state official*
McClure, James A. *lawyer, retired senator*
Ryan, Frederick Joseph, Jr. *lawyer, public official*

HAWAII

Captain Cook
Zimmerman, William Irving *lawyer*

Honolulu
Alm, Steve *prosecutor*
Bloede, Victor Carl *lawyer, academic executive*
Boas, Frank *lawyer*
Boggs, Steven Eugene *lawyer*
Chuck, Walter G(oonsun) *lawyer*
Cowan, Stuart Marshall *lawyer*
Crumpton, Charles Whitmarsh *lawyer*
Dang, Marvin S. C. *lawyer*
Deaver, Phillip Lester *lawyer*
Devlin, Patricia *lawyer*
Dezzani, David John *lawyer*
Donahoe, Peter Aloysius *lawyer*
Dreher, Nicholas C. *lawyer*
Fukumoto, Leslie Satsuki *lawyer*
Gebbia Pinetti, Karen Marie *lawyer, educator*
Gelber, Don Jeffrey *lawyer*
Geshell, Richard Steven *lawyer*
Hazlett, Mark A. *lawyer*
Jaffe, Edward A. *lawyer*
Kawachika, James Akio *lawyer*
Lacy, John R. *lawyer*
Lilly, Michael Alexander *lawyer, author*
Lombardi, Dennis M. *lawyer*
Ma, Alan Wai-Chuen *lawyer*
Mau-Shimizu, Patricia Ann *lawyer*
Miller, Clifford Joel *lawyer*
Morry, G. Richard *lawyer*
Morse, Jack Craig *lawyer*
Reinke, Stefan Michael *lawyer*
Starshak, James L. *lawyer*
Taylor, Carroll Stribling *lawyer*
Umebayashi, Clyde Satoru *lawyer*
Weightman, Judy Mae *lawyer*
Woo, Timothy David, Jr. *lawyer*
Woo, Vernon Ying-Tsai *lawyer, real estate developer*
Yamada, Stephen Kinichi *lawyer, real estate developer*
Yap, Frank, Jr. *lawyer*

Kailua Kona
Martin, William Charles *lawyer*

Kihei
Burns, Richard Gordon *retired lawyer, writer, consultant*

Paia
Richman, Joel Eser *lawyer, mediator, arbitrator*

Wailuku
Krueger, James *lawyer*
Luna, B. Martin *lawyer*

IDAHO

Boise
Hamlin, Susan Elizabeth *lawyer, educator*
Klein, Edith Miller *lawyer, former state senator*
Lance, Alan George *lawyer, legislator, attorney general*
McGown, John, Jr. *lawyer*
Meyer, Christopher Hawkins *lawyer*
Minnich, Diane Kay *state bar executive*
Richardson, Betty H. *prosecutor*
Risch, James E. *lawyer*

Caldwell
Kerrick, David Ellsworth *lawyer*

Idaho Falls
Whittier, Monte Ray *lawyer*

Lewiston
Tait, John Reid *lawyer*

Pocatello
Nye, W. Marcus W. *lawyer*

Twin Falls
Hohnhorst, John Charles *lawyer*

MISSOURI

Saint Louis
Needham, Carol Ann *lawyer, educator*

MONTANA

Billings
Addy, John Kelly *lawyer*
Gannett, Damon L. *lawyer*
Matteucci, Sherry Scheel *lawyer*
Thompson, James William *lawyer*

Butte
Krueger, Kurt Donn *lawyer*

Great Falls
Baker, Lynn Dale *lawyer, educator*
Speer, John Elmer *freelance paralegal, reporter*

Missoula
Bowman, Jean Louise *lawyer, civic worker*

NEVADA

Carson City
Maupin, Bill *associate justice*
Rodefer, Jeffrey Robert *lawyer, prosecutor*
Williams, Day Robert *lawyer*

Elko
Vaughan, Robert Oren *lawyer*

Las Vegas
Blouke, Milton Baker *lawyer*
Cardinalli, Marc Patrick *lawyer*
Chesnut, Carol Fitting *lawyer*
Galane, Morton Robert *lawyer*
Goodwin, John Robert *law educator, author*
Gray, Patricia Joyce *court administrator*
Han, Ittah *lawyer, political economist, high technology and financial strategist, computer engineer*
Hilbrecht, Norman Ty *lawyer*
Hill, Judith Deegan *lawyer*
Kennedy, Dennis L. *lawyer*
Larsen, Paul Edward *lawyer*
Nohrden, Patrick Thomas *lawyer*
Singer, Michael Howard *lawyer*
Smallwood, Betty *lawyer*
Sobelle, Richard E. *lawyer*
Solomon, Mark A. *lawyer*

Reno
Barkley, Thierry Vincent *lawyer*
Denham, Rena Belle *lawyer, educator*
Hill, Earl McColl *lawyer*
Richards, Paul A. *lawyer*

NEW MEXICO

Albuquerque
Addis, Richard Barton *lawyer*
Aurbach, Robert Michael *lawyer, consultant, photographer*
Beach, Arthur O'Neal *lawyer*
Farmer, Terry D(wayne) *lawyer*
Harman, Wallace Patrick *lawyer*
Kelly, John J. *prosecutor*
Messinger, J. Henry *lawyer*
Miller, Ranne B. *lawyer*
Rezler, Julius *labor arbitrator*
Schoen, Stevan Jay *lawyer*
Schuler, Alison Kay *lawyer*
Stephenson, Barbera Wertz *lawyer*
Thornton, J. Duke *lawyer*
Throckmorton, Rex Denton *lawyer*
Vigil, Douglas Elliott *lawyer*
Walker, Roger Alfred *lawyer*

Deming
Sherman, Frederick Hood *lawyer*

Farmington
Gurley, Curtis R. *lawyer*
Morgan, Jack M. *lawyer*

Hobbs
Stout, Lowell *lawyer*

Las Cruces
Lutz, William Lan *lawyer*
Palacios, Pedro Pablo *lawyer*

Ruidoso
Thomsen, David Allen *lawyer*

Santa Fe
Bluestone, Stuart Michael *lawyer*
Brannen, Jeffrey Richard *lawyer*
Burton, John Paul (Jack Burton) *lawyer*
Carpenter, Richard Norris *lawyer*
Mellow, Judith Elizabeth *lawyer*
Moll, Deborah Adelaide *lawyer*
Schwarz, Michael *lawyer*
Shaw, Mark Howard *lawyer, business owner, entrepreneur*

Taos
Manzanares, Dennis *lawyer*

Tijeras
Berry, Dawn Bradley *lawyer, writer*

OHIO

Canfield
Goldberg, Martin Stanford *lawyer*

OREGON

Albany
Boatner, James William *trial court administrator*

Ashland
Turner, Garrison F. *lawyer*

Cannon Beach
Hillestad, Charles Andrew *lawyer*

Eugene
Dugan, Marianne Guenevere *lawyer*
Henner, Martin E. *arbitrator, mediator*
Scoles, Eugene Francis *law educator, lawyer*

Lincoln City
Elliott, Scott *lawyer*

Mcminnville
Hansen, Bernt Allan *lawyer*

Milwaukie
Anderson, Mark Alexander *lawyer*

Ontario
Rader, Diane Cecile *lawyer*

Pendleton
Bloom, Stephen Michael *lawyer, judge*
Kottkamp, John Harlan *lawyer*

Portland
Abravanel, Allan Ray *lawyer*
Achterman, Gail Louise *lawyer*
Bakkensen, John Reser *lawyer*
Balmer, Thomas Ancil *lawyer*
Berger, Leland Roger *lawyer*
Brown, David W. *lawyer*
Campbell, James, VII *patent lawyer*
Canaday, Richard A. *lawyer*
Dailey, Dianne K. *lawyer*
Druckman, Jeffrey Julius *lawyer*
Eakin, Margaretta Morgan *lawyer*
Edwards, Richard Alan *lawyer*
English, Stephen F. *lawyer*
Fell, James F. *lawyer*
Foster, Mark Edward *lawyer, consultant, international lobbyist*
Frank, Stephen Richard *lawyer*
Grossmann, Ronald Stanyer *lawyer*
Hammer, Susan M. *lawyer*
Harrell, Gary Paul *lawyer*
Helmer, M. Christie *lawyer*
Houseworth, Steven Michael *court counselor*
Hunt, Steven Bruce *law educator*
Hurd, Paul Gemmill *lawyer*
Hyatt, Dan Richard *lawyer*
Jarvis, Peter R. *lawyer*
Jolles, Bernard *lawyer*
Josselson, Frank *lawyer*
Kamin, Scott Allan *lawyer*
Kennedy, Jack Leland *lawyer*
Knoll, James Lewis *lawyer*
Lewis, Charles S., III *lawyer*
Livingston, Louis Bayer *lawyer*
Luedtke, Roger A. *lawyer*
Lusky, John A. *lawyer*
Matarazzo, Harris Starr *lawyer*
Moore, Thomas Scott *lawyer*
Nicolai, Thomas R. *lawyer*
Palmer, Thomas Philip *lawyer*
Purcell, John F. *lawyer*
Ragen, Douglas M. *lawyer*
Rawlinson, Dennis Patrick *lawyer*
Rosen, Steven O. *lawyer*
Schuster, Philip Frederick, II *lawyer, writer*
Shellan, Ronald A. *lawyer*
Sokol, Jan D. *lawyer*
Tomlinson, William M. *lawyer*
Wood, Marcus Andrew *lawyer*
Zalutsky, Morton Herman *lawyer*

Salem
Bulkley, Robert De Groff, Jr. *lawyer*
Ferris, Evelyn Scott *lawyer*
Nafziger, James Albert Richmond *law educator*

Wilsonville
Yacob, Yosef *lawyer, economist*

TEXAS

Houston
Fried, Gil Ben *lawyer, educator, expert witness*

UTAH

Brigham City
McCullough, Edward Eugene *patent agent, inventor*

Logan
Hillyard, Lyle William *lawyer*
Honaker, Jimmie Joe *lawyer, ecologist*

Magna
Gardner, Ray Dean, Jr. *lawyer*

Manti
Petersen, Benton Lauritz *paralegal*

Midvale
Nash, William Kelly *lawyer*

Ogden
Kaufman, Steven Michael *lawyer*
Mecham, Glenn Jefferson *lawyer, mayor*
Richards, Richard *lawyer, political consultant*
Sullivan, Kevin Patrick *lawyer*
Warner, Frank Shrake *lawyer*

Orem
Abbott, Charles Favour, Jr. *lawyer*

Park City
Kennicott, James W. *lawyer*

Provo
Sutterfield, Kevin James *lawyer, consultant*
Wilde, James L. *lawyer*

Saint George
Gallian, Russell Joseph *lawyer*

Salt Lake City
Anderson, Robert Monte *lawyer*
Balthaser, Anita Young *legal assistant*
Barker, Ronald C. *lawyer*
Broadbent, Berne Steven *lawyer*
Callister, Louis Henry, Jr. *lawyer*
Clark, Scott H. *lawyer*
Colessides, Nick John *lawyer*
Cornaby, Kay Sterling *lawyer, former state senator*
Curtis, LeGrand R., Jr. *lawyer*
Detton, David K. *lawyer*
Felt, Paul Schenk *lawyer*
Gaufin, Samuel Oliver *lawyer*
Gessel, David Clyde *lawyer*
Holbrook, James Russell *lawyer*
Hunt, George Andrew *lawyer*
Kimball, Spencer Levan *lawyer, educator*
Leta, David Edward *lawyer*
Livsey, Herbert C. *lawyer*
Madsen, Francis Armstrong, Jr. *investor, lawyer, consultant*
Matsumori, Douglas *lawyer*
McCoy, Harry E., II *lawyer*
Melich, Mitchell *retired lawyer*
Mills, Lawrence *lawyer, business and transportation consultant*
Mooney, Jerome Henri *lawyer*
Ockey, Ronald J. *lawyer*
Rasmussen, Thomas Val, Jr. *lawyer, small business owner*
Smith, Janet Hugie *lawyer*
Teitelbaum, Lee E. *law educator*
Vincent, Mark Kent *lawyer*
Wangsgard, Chris Prince *lawyer*
Weiss, Loren Elliot *lawyer, law educator*
Wikstrom, Francis M. *lawyer*

Sandy
Bush, Rex Curtis *lawyer*

Snowbird
Gardiner, Lester Raymond, Jr. *lawyer*

Vernal
Judd, Dennis L. *lawyer*

WASHINGTON

Bainbridge Island
Otorowski, Christopher Lee *lawyer*

Bellevue
Boespflug, John F., Jr. *lawyer*
Sebris, Robert, Jr. *lawyer*

Bellingham
Packer, Mark Barry *lawyer, financial consultant, foundation official*
Raas, Daniel Alan *lawyer*

Everett
Bowden, George Newton *lawyer*

Hoquiam
Kessler, Keith Leon *lawyer*

Mount Vernon
Moser, C. Thomas *lawyer*

Olympia
Allen, Robert Mark *lawyer*
Tytler, Morton Maynard *lawyer, retired state assistant attorney general*
Walker, Francis Joseph *lawyer*
Welsh, John Beresford, Jr. *lawyer*
Wilson, Wesley M. *retired lawyer, writer*

Port Orchard
Shiers, Frank Abram *lawyer*

Pullman
Michaelis, Karen Lauree *law educator*

Redmond
Burt, Thomas William *lawyer*

Renton
Barber, Mark Edward *lawyer*

Richland
Barr, Carlos Harvey *lawyer*

Seattle
Alkire, John D. *lawyer*
Andreasen, Steven W. *lawyer*
Bergstedt, Anders Spencer *lawyer*
Blais, Robert Howard *lawyer*
Bodi, F. Lorraine *lawyer*
Bradley, Mark Charles *defender*
Bringman, Joseph Edward *lawyer*
Cornell, Kenneth Lee *lawyer*
Cross, Bruce Michael *lawyer*
Cullen, Jack Joseph *lawyer*
Cunningham, Joel Dean *lawyer*
Cutler, Philip Edgerton *lawyer*
Dalton, Thomas George *paralegal, social worker, legal consultant*
DeVore, Paul Cameron *lawyer*
Diamond, Josef *lawyer*
Diggs, Bradley C. *lawyer*
Dolan, Andrew Kevin *lawyer*
Freedman, Bart Joseph *lawyer*
Glover, Karen E. *lawyer*
Goeltz, Thomas A. *lawyer*
Graybeal, Lynne Elizabeth *lawyer*
Gunter, Robert L. *lawyer*
Guy, Andrew A. *lawyer*
Haggard, Joel Edward *lawyer*
Hansen, Wayne W. *lawyer*
Hanson, William Lewis *lawyer*
Hecht, Irene Margret *lawyer*
Hermsen, James R. *lawyer*

Holtan, Ramer B., Jr. *lawyer*
Hopp, Richard A. *lawyer*
Huff, Gary D. *lawyer*
Jackson, Dillon Edward *lawyer*
Jaffe, Robert S. *lawyer*
Kaplan, Barry Martin *lawyer*
Katz, Charles J., Jr. *lawyer*
Keegan, John E. *lawyer*
Kellogg, Kenyon P. *lawyer*
Kelly, Kevin Francis *lawyer*
Linn, Brian James *lawyer*
Loftus, Thomas Daniel *lawyer*
Lopez, Carl A. Taylor *lawyer*
Marshall, David Stanley *lawyer*
McKay, John *lawyer*
Mines, Michael *lawyer*
Moore, James R. *lawyer*
Mussehl, Robert Clarence *lawyer*
Nellermoe, Leslie Carol *lawyer*
Niemi, Janice *lawyer, former state legislator*
Noble, Phillip D. *lawyer*
Oles, Stuart Gregory *lawyer*
Olver, Michael Lynn *lawyer*
Oyer, Sarah Elizabeth *lawyer*
Palmer, Douglas S., Jr. *lawyer*
Perey, Ron *lawyer*
Peterson, Ronald Arthur *business law educator*
Pettigrew, Edward W. *lawyer*
Pym, Bruce Michael *lawyer*
Rosen, Jon Howard *lawyer*
Schneider, Harry H., Jr. *lawyer*
Steers, George W. *lawyer*
Steinberg, Jack *lawyer*
Stoebuck, William Brees *law educator*
Strichartz, James Leonard *lawyer*
Sussman, Neil A. *lawyer*
Tallman, Richard C. *lawyer*
Thorne, David W. *lawyer*
Veblen, John Elvidge *lawyer*
Vestal, Josephine Burnet *lawyer*
Wagner, Patricia Hamm *lawyer*
Wagoner, David Everett *lawyer*
Walter, Michael Charles *lawyer*
Wechsler, Mary Heyrman *lawyer*
Whitford, Joseph P. *lawyer*
Wilson, Richard Randolph *lawyer*

Spokane
Connelly, James P. *prosecutor*
Harbaugh, Daniel Paul *lawyer*
Weatherhead, Leslie R. *lawyer*

Tacoma
Barcus, Benjamin Franklin *lawyer*
Chiappinelli, Eric Andrew *law educator*
Frohmader, Frederick Oliver *lawyer*
George, Nicholas *criminal defense lawyer, entrepreneur*
Holt, William E. *lawyer*
Pearson, Claude Meredith *legal consultant*
Rudnick, Rebecca Sophie *lawyer, educator*
Sterbick, Peter Lawrence *lawyer*
Thompson, Ronald Edward *lawyer*

Vancouver
Dodds, Michael Bruce *lawyer*

Yakima
Larson, Paul Martin *lawyer*

WYOMING

Casper
Combs, W(illiam) Henry, III *lawyer*
Durham, Harry Blaine, III *lawyer*
Hjelmstad, William David *lawyer*
Lowe, Robert Stanley *lawyer*

Cheyenne
Freudenthal, David D. *prosecutor*
Hanes, John Grier *lawyer, state legislator*
Hathaway, Stanley Knapp *lawyer*
Hill, William U. *lawyer, prosecutor*
Palma, Jack D. *lawyer*
Scorsine, John Magnus *lawyer*

Cody
Kepler, Charles George *lawyer*

Glenrock
Bunn, Dorothy Irons *court reporter*

Jackson
Schuster, Robert Parks *lawyer*

Laramie
Smith, Thomas Shore *lawyer*

Wheatland
Hunkins, Raymond Breedlove *lawyer, rancher*

CANADA

ALBERTA

Athabasca
Rodnunsky, Sidney *lawyer, educator*

Calgary
Lougheed, Peter *lawyer, former Canadian official*

BRITISH COLUMBIA

Richmond
Colton, Sterling Don *lawyer, business executive, missionary*

SASKATCHEWAN

Regina
Shirkey, Ronald Earl *lawyer*

ADDRESS UNPUBLISHED

Aaron, Roy Henry *lawyer, arbitrator, business consultant*
Atkinson, Sheridan Earle *lawyer*
Baker, Patricia (Jean) *lawyer, mediator*
Bateman, David Alfred *lawyer*
Baughn, Alfred Fairhurst *lawyer*
Berry, Robert Worth *lawyer, educator, retired army officer*
Blizinsky, Marlin Joel *lawyer*
Bondi, Harry Gene *lawyer*
Bouvier, Marshall Andre *lawyer*
Brechbill, Susan Reynolds *lawyer, educator*
Brundin, Brian Jon *lawyer*
Canoff, Karen Huston *lawyer*
Carmack, Mildred Jean *retired lawyer*
Christian, Ann Seger *lawyer*
Cologne, Gordon Bennett *lawyer*
Criscuolo, Wendy Laura *lawyer, interior design consultant*
Culp, Gordon Calvin *retired lawyer*
Davis, Wanda Rose *lawyer*
Essig, Christine Cay *paralegal*
Evrensel, Arthur *lawyer*
Ferguson, Jack Lee *retired lawyer*
Fernandez, Dennis Sunga *lawyer, electrical engineer, entrepreneur*
Fortner, Hueston Gilmore *lawyer, writer, composer*
Foster, Judith Christine *lawyer, writer*
Gardner, Cathy Anne *defender*
Gold, Harold *retired lawyer, accountant*
Gomez, David Frederick *lawyer*
Grajewski, Julian *law librarian, educator*
Gustavson, Mark Steven *lawyer*
Hanzlik, Rayburn DeMara *lawyer*
Harriman, John Howland *lawyer*
Hart, Howard Franklin *lawyer*
Hawes, Sue *lawyer*
Heppe, Karol Virginia *lawyer, educator*
Hitchcock, Vernon Thomas *farmer, lawyer*
Howard, John Wayne *lawyer*
Hybl, William Joseph *lawyer, foundation executive*
Jallins, Richard David *lawyer*
Jeffrey, John Orval *lawyer*
Jorgensen, Erik Holger *lawyer*
June, Roy Ethiel *lawyer*
Katkin, Ken *lawyer*
Keister, Jean Clare *lawyer*
Kippur, Merrie Margolin *lawyer*
Kleinberg, Judith G. *lawyer, children's advocate*
Kolodny, Stephen Arthur *lawyer*
Kramer, Melany Beth *lawyer*
Levinson, Kenneth Lee *lawyer*
Levy, David *lawyer, insurance company executive*
Lightstone, Ronald *lawyer*
Lowe, James Allen *lawyer*
Maloney, John William *lawyer*
Marks, Stanley Jacob *lawyer, historian, lecturer, author*
Millard, Malcolm Stuart *retired lawyer*
Mugridge, David Raymond *lawyer*
Newman, Carol L. *lawyer*
Orloff, Neil *lawyer*
Ously, Pamela Darlene *legal assistant*
Paulus, Norma Jean Petersen *lawyer, state school system administrator*
Pereyra-Suarez, Charles Albert *lawyer*
Peterson, Howard Cooper *lawyer, accountant*
Protigal, Stanley Nathan *lawyer*
Rosen, Martin Jack *lawyer*
Scheidenhelm, Richard Joy *lawyer, legal historian, writer*
Schild, Raymond Douglas *lawyer*
Schlei, Norbert Anthony *lawyer*
Schor, Suzi *lawyer, psychologist*
Schuele, Donna Clare *lawyer, educator*
Shambaugh, Stephen Ward *lawyer*
Skratek, Sylvia Paulette *mediator, arbitrator, dispute systems designer*
Spivey, Roberta Lee *paralegal, community counselor*
Tanaka, Jeannie E. *lawyer*
Tapia, Arthur Albert *lawyer*
Taylor, James William *lawyer*
Taylor, Ruth Anne *lawyer*
Tolentino, Casimiro Urbano *lawyer*
Torkildson, Raymond Maynard *lawyer*
Treloar, Harriette Ellen *lawyer*
Walker, John Sumpter, Jr. *lawyer*
Wallace, John Barry *lawyer*
Weil, Peter Henry *lawyer*
Weisman, Paul Howard *lawyer*
Wharton, Hugh Davis, III *lawyer, judge*
Wolf, Douglas Jeffrey *lawyer*
Wong-Diaz, Francisco Raimundo *lawyer, educator*

MEDICINE. *See* HEALTHCARE: MEDICINE.

MILITARY

UNITED STATES

ALASKA

Anchorage
Overly, Frederick Dean *civilian military employee, entrepreneur*
Schnell, Roger Thomas *retired military officer, state official*

ARIZONA

Fort Huachuca
Tyler, Cecilia K. *army officer*

Mesa
Boyd, Edward Hascal *retired military officer*
Kiesecker, Robert *retired military officer, educator*

Phoenix
Beltrán, Anthony Natalicio *military non-commissioned officer, deacon*
Graf, Gary Lynn *career officer*

Scottsdale
Coffinger, Maralin Katharyne *retired air force officer, consultant*

Tucson
Guice, John Thompson *retired air force officer*
Huber, Linda Ruth *non-commissioned officer*
Nikides, Bill *military officer*
Rutter, George B., Jr. *career officer*

Yuma
Hudson, John Irvin *retired marine officer*

CALIFORNIA

Arroyo Grande
Oseguera, Palma Marie *marine corps officer, reservist*

Camp Pendleton
Turlip, James Douglas *career officer*
Wells, David Patrick *career officer*

China Lake
Lundstrom, Mary Meyer *naval contracts technician, educator*

Claremont
VavRosky, Mark James *career officer, educator*

Coronado
Rizza, Joseph Padula *naval officer, former president maritime academy*
Robinson, David Brooks *retired naval officer*

Edwards
Bertapelle, Allen Louis *air force officer, flight test engineer*
Major, Karl Burce *air force officer*

Folsom
Meigel, David Walter *military officer, retired musician*

La Jolla
Greer, Howard Earl *former naval officer*

Laguna Hills
Faw, Duane Leslie *retired military officer, law educator, lay worker, author*

Lompoc
Walker, Duncan Edward *retired air force officer*

Mcclellan AFB
Tucker, Pierce Edward *air force officer*

Monterey
Giordano, Angela Maria *military officer*
Hoivik, Thomas Harry *military educator, international consultant*
Matthews, David Fort *military weapon system acquisition specialist*
Wooten, Michael Eric *marine officer*

Napa
Smith, Robert Bruce *former security consultant, retired army officer*

Oceanside
Key, Jack Rollin *contracting officer*

Pebble Beach
Fergusson, Robert George *retired army officer*

Pleasanton
Petersen, Norman William *naval officer, engineering facility administrator*

Port Hueneme
Balk, David Michael *career officer, marine engineer, aquanaut*

Riverside
Mc Cormac, Weston Arthur *retired educator and army officer*
Wright, John MacNair, Jr. *retired army officer*

Sacramento
Mills, Timothy Ignatius *logistics officer, East-Asian culture consultant*

San Carlos
Schumacher, Henry Jerold *former career officer, business executive*

San Diego
Cheney, Stephen Allen *career officer, foreign policy analyst*
Everett, Hobart Ray, Jr. *engineer, naval officer, consultant, researcher, inventor*
Hull, Roger Kermit *naval officer*
Snyder, David Allen *naval officer, surgeon*
Stakelum, Richard Allen *naval officer*
Vaughan, Mark Bass *naval officer*

Santa Ana
Izac, Suzette Marie *retired air force officer*

Santa Clarita
Tilton, Ronald William *naval officer*

Santa Maria
Everhart, Leon Eugene *retired air force officer*

Santa Rosa
Andriano-Moore, Richard Graf *naval officer*

Seaside
Gales, Samuel Joel *retired civilian military employee, counselor*

South Dos Palos
Hirohata, Derek Kazuyoshi *air force reserve officer*

Travis AFB
Eberle, Michael Lee *air force officer*

COLORADO

Aurora
Dawes, Douglas Charles *retired military officer*

Boulder
Stone, John Helms, Jr. *admiralty advisor*

Cheyenne Mountain AFB
Bailey, Paul Leroy *career officer*

Colorado Springs
Allery, Kenneth Edward *air force officer*
Bowen, Clotilde Dent *retired army officer, psychiatrist*
Brooks, Timothy Joe *career military officer*
Forgan, David Waller *retired air force officer*
Keen, Ronald Lee *career officer*
Kracht, Theodore Andrew *air force officer*
Mitchell, John Henderson *retired army officer, management consultant*
Mooney, William Oliver *retired military officer, corporation executive*
Schaeffer, Reiner Horst *air force officer, retired librarian, foreign language professional*
Winn, Robert Charles *retired military officer, aeronautical engineer, consultant*

Englewood
Nuce, Madonna Marie *military officer*
Thompson, Robert Frank, Jr. *career officer*

Fort Carson
Granger, Jeff Roland *military personnel specialist*

Fort Collins
Roberts, Archibald Edward *retired army officer, author*
Schmidt, Mark David *military officer*

Littleton
Kinder, Ralph Eugene *military officer*

Monument
Erving, Claude Moore, Jr. *military career officer, pilot*

Peterson AFB
Boylan, Steven Arthur *career officer*

U S A F Academy
Becker, John David *career officer, philosophy educator*
Fariss, Laurence Alan *air force officer, pilot*
Giletti, Gregory Paul *military officer*

FLORIDA

Eglin AFB
Seligman, Jay Arnold *military officer, social worker*

HAWAII

Honolulu
Hays, Ronald Jackson *naval officer*
Roberson, Kelley Cleve *army officer*
Weyand, Frederick Carlton *retired military officer*

Schofield Barracks
Davis, Mark Dehlen *military officer*

MONTANA

Great Falls
Jimenez, Walter Anthony *air force officer*
Loftin, Orrin Keith *retired officer, poet, actor*

NEBRASKA

Lincoln
Heng, Stanley Mark *national guard officer*

Offutt AFB
Luckett, Byron Edward, Jr. *air force chaplain*

NEVADA

Boulder City
Heinlein, Oscar Allen *former air force officer*

Henderson
Creech, Wilbur Lyman *retired military officer*

NEW MEXICO

Albuquerque
Erck, Walter W. *air force officer*
Kather, Gerhard *retired air force base administrator*

Cedar Crest
Sheppard, Jack W. *retired air force officer*

Cerrillos
Goodwin, Samuel McClure *officer*

Roswell
Miller, Nelson Alvin *retired army officer, public affairs administrator*

NEW YORK

Canajoharie
MacFarland, Christopher John *military officer*

OHIO

Fairborn
Ingham, Edward A. *career officer*

OREGON

Ashland
Willstatter, Alfred *retired army officer*

Portland
Blackwell, Garland Wayne *retired military officer*

TEXAS

Allen
Wynn, Robert E. *retired career officer, electronics executive*

UTAH

American Fork
Baum, Kerry Robert *retired military officer*

Brigham City
Fife, Dennis Jensen *military officer, chemistry educator*

Hill AFB
Lohman, Arthur Grover *civilian military employee*

Salt Lake City
Askew, Eldon Wayne *army officer, biochemist, researcher, educator*

WASHINGTON

Everett
Van Eaton, Errol Hay *career officer*

Fort Lewis
Vos, Thomas James *career officer, criminal investigator*

Lynnwood
Jenes, Theodore George, Jr. *retired military officer*

Oak Harbor
Fragola, Albert Thomas *retired army officer*

Olympia
March, George Patrick *retired naval officer*

Prosser
Hill, Dale Richard *military officer*

Renton
Norris, William Scott *retired career officer, automotive educator*

Seattle
Belec, Marguerite Elizabeth *naval officer*

Steilacoom
Weyman, Steven Aloysius *military officer*

Whidbey Island Naval Air
All, William Hamilton, IV *military officer*

MILITARY ADDRESSES OF THE UNITED STATES

EUROPE

FPO
Civilikas, Robert George *naval officer*

ADDRESS UNPUBLISHED

Bridges, Roy Dubard, Jr. *career officer*
Brooks, James Sprague *retired national guard officer*
Bruggemeyer, Mark Edward *career officer*
Carter, William George, III *army officer*
DiCocco, Marc *air force officer, flight test engineer*
Evans, Marsha Johnson *naval officer*
Ferguson, Michael Gerard *career officer*
Foulk, David Wingerd *retired military civilian executive*
Gerner, Andre Anthony *air force officer*
Harrigan, Nicholas Paul *military officer*
King, Charlotte Elaine *retired administrative officer*
King, Rosemary Ann *air force officer*
Kojac, Jeffrey Stanley *military officer*
Lee, James Gordon *air force officer*
Maddox, David Daniel *military officer*
Marlow, Edward A. *career officer*
Ninos, Nicholas Peter *retired miliatry officer, physician*
Ryan, Mary Gene *military officer, occupational health nurse*
Schrader, Harry Christian, Jr. *retired naval officer*
Smith, Charles Lewis *retired naval officer and association executive*
Spitze, Steven Clyde *army officer*
Todaro, Michael Joseph, Jr. *military officer*
Walden, Joseph Lawrence *army officer*
Washington-Knight, Barbara J. *military officer, nurse*
Watts, Van *retired career navy officer*

RELIGION

UNITED STATES

ALASKA

Anchorage
Dobler, David Lee *pastor*
Hurley, Francis T. *archbishop*
Parsons, Donald D. *bishop*
Williams, Charles D. *bishop*

Cordova
Harding, Richard Evans *pastor*

Fairbanks
Kaniecki, Michael Joseph *bishop*

ARIZONA

Coolidge
Shih, Marie *metaphysical healer*

Duncan
Ouzts, Eugene Thomas *minister, secondary education educator*

Mesa
Enniss, Leonard Franklin *religious educator*
Simpson, John Berchman, Jr. *clergy member, chaplain, retired law enforcement officer*

Oro Valley
Tinker, Robert Eugene *minister, educational consultant*

Paradise Valley
Sapp, Donald Gene *minister*

Phoenix
Darby, Wesley Andrew *minister, educator*
Dew, William Waldo, Jr. *bishop*
Kuzma, George Martin *bishop*
O'Brien, Thomas Joseph *bishop*

Safford
MacDonald, Robbin Rieck *clergyman*

Sierra Vista
Puckle, Donne Erving *priest*

Sun City
Lapsley, James Norvell, Jr. *minister, pastoral theology educator*

Sun City West
Schmitz, Charles Edison *evangelist*

Tucson
Moreno, Manuel D. *bishop*

CALIFORNIA

Altadena
Arzube, Juan Alfredo *bishop*

Anaheim
Nguyen, Tai Anh *minister*
Oaks, M(argaret) Marlene *minister*

Bakersfield
Aycock, Dale *minister*

Barstow
Jones, Nathaniel *bishop*

Berkeley
Lee, Young Ho (Jinwol) *Buddhist monk, educator*
Oliver, Mary Anne McPherson *religion educator*

Beverly Hills
Clemons, Barbara June *minister, cosmetology educator*

Camarillo
Oncken, Ellen Lorraine *minister, speaker*
Specht, Carl Frederick *chaplain*

Camp Pendleton
Pusateri, Richard Anthony *minister, naval chaplain*

Canoga Park
Dickey, Gary Alan *minister*

Carmichael
Probasco, Calvin Henry Charles *clergyman, college administrator*

Claremont
Kim, Chan-Hie *educator, clergyman*
Mata, Michael Anthony *religion educator*

Compton
Johnson, William R., Jr. *minister*

Costa Mesa
Stout, James Tilman *minister*
Williams, William Corey *theology educator, consultant*

Cupertino
Winslow, David Allen *chaplain, naval officer*

Danville
Davis, Ron Lee *clergyman, author*

Davis
Brown, Arthur Carl, Jr. *retired minister*

Downey
Wright, Jeff *minister, non-profit religious administrator*

Duarte
Driskill, James Lawrence *minister*

El Segundo
Baird, Albert Washington, III *minister*

Elk Grove
Talbert, Melvin George *bishop*

Escondido
Shanor, Clarence Richard *clergyman*

Fountain Valley
Einstein, Stephen Jan *rabbi*

Fresno
Armey, Douglas Richard *minister*
Lawless, John Howard *minister*
Steinbock, John Thomas *bishop*

Fullerton
Conway, Sally *writer, lecturer, counselor*

Glendora
Richey, Everett Eldon *religion educator*

Hume
Phillips, Robert East *religious camps administrator*

Jamul
Dobyns, Zipporah Pottenger *minister, educator, writer*

La Jolla
Freedman, David Noel *religion educator*
Wyle, Ewart Herbert *clergyman*

La Mirada
McIntosh, Gary Lynn *theology educator, consultant, writer*

Laguna Hills
Wheatley, Melvin Ernest, Jr. *retired bishop*

Lancaster
Runner, George Cyril, Jr. *minister, educational administrator*

Lindsay
Sanchez, Ruben Dario *minister, family counselor, parochial school educator, writer*

Los Angeles
Blaire, Stephen E. *bishop*
Borsch, Frederick Houk *bishop*
Boyd, Malcolm *minister, religious author*
Breuer, Stephen Ernest *temple executive*
Chedid, John G. *bishop*
Fitzgerald, Tikhon (Lee R. H. Fitzgerald) *bishop*
Kratzer, Cindy Carson *religious organization administrator*
Mahony, Roger M. Cardinal *archbishop*
Mc Pherson, Rolf Kennedy *clergyman, church official*
Ochoa, Armando *bishop*
O'Connor, Kevin Thomas *archdiocese development official*
Ward, John J. *bishop*
Wolf, Alfred *rabbi*

Malibu
Wilson, John Francis *educational administrator*

Menlo Park
Fuller, Glenn Straith *minister*

Mill Valley
Crews, William Odell, Jr. *seminary administrator*
DuBose, Francis Marquis *clergyman*

Monrovia
Huffey, Vinton Earl *clergyman*

Monterey
Ryan, Sylvester D. *bishop*
Shimpfky, Richard Lester *bishop*

Oakland
Crompton, Arnold *minister, educator*
Cummins, John Stephen *bishop*
Ice, Richard Eugene *retired minister, retirement housing company executive*
Langguth, Earl Leonard *clergyman, writer, poet*
Patten, Bebe Harrison *minister, chancellor*
Rosenbaum, Lawrence Alan *evangelist*
Schomer, Howard *retired clergyman, educator, social policy consultant*
Yamaoka, Seigen Haruo *bishop*

Orange
Driscoll, Michael P. *bishop*
Mc Farland, Norman Francis *bishop*

Oxnard
Oestmann, Irma Emma *minister*

Palm Desert
Hunt, Barnabas John *priest, religious order administrator*

Palo Cedro
Kroeker, Joanne Elizabeth *missionary, writer*

Pasadena
Dyrness, William Arthur *religion educator, dean*
Robeck, Cecil Melvin, Jr. *religious studies educator*
Sand, Faith Annette *writer, publisher religious material*
Sano, Roy I. *bishop*
Scholer, David Milton *religion educator*
White, Lyla Lee *religious organization administrator*

Pittsburg
Schmalenberger, Jerry Lew *pastor, seminary educator*

Pomona
Lewis, Tony Lloyd *pastor*

Redlands
Benney, Ghislaine Françoise *religious organization executive*
Langer, Richard Charles *minister*

Reedley
Dick, Henry Henry *minister*

Riverside
Andersen, Frances Elizabeth Gold *religious leadership educator*

Sacramento
Quinn, Francis A. *bishop*
Venema, Jon Roger *educator, pastor*
Weigand, William Keith *bishop*

Salinas
Kadden, Bruce Jay *rabbi*

San Anselmo
White, Ronald Cedric, Jr. *religion educator*

San Bernardino
Barnes, Gerald R. *bishop*

San Diego
Brom, Robert H. *bishop*
Chavez, Gilbert Espinoza *bishop*
Downing, David Charles *minister*
Hughes, Gethin B. *bishop*
Kraft, William Armstrong *retired priest*
Montali, Lawrence Richard, Jr. *religious newspaper editor*
Peck, Paul Lachlan *minister*
Savitripriya, Swami *religious leader, author*
Vogel, Walter Paul *priest, college counselor*

San Francisco
Hurley, Mark Joseph *bishop*
Kendall, Robert Daniel *priest, theology educator*
Levada, William Joseph *archbishop*
McGrath, Patrick Joseph *bishop*
Quinn, John R. *archbishop*
Rosen, Moishe *religious organization administrator*
Sevilla, Carlos A. *bishop*
Swing, William Edwin *bishop*
Turley-Moore, Susan Gwen *minister*

San Gabriel
Evangelista, Allan *clergy member, medical researcher*

San Jose
Soos, Richard Anthony *pastor*

Santa Barbara
Campbell, Robert Charles *clergyman, religious organization administrator*
Capps, Walter Holden *religion educator*
Gillquist, Peter Edward *church organization executive*

Santa Clara
DuMaine, R. Pierre *bishop*

Santa Cruz
Zerah, Aaron *minister, author*

Santa Monica
Hearn, Charles Virgil *minister*

Santa Rosa
Nash, Reford Brooks *minister*
Ziemann, G. Patrick *bishop*

Simi Valley
O'Berg, Robert Myron *minister*

Sonora
Patterson, Paul Edward *minister*

Stockton
Ivey-Smith, Janice Ross *clergy, author*
Montrose, Donald W. *bishop*

Sun Valley
Brewer, Ronald Ray *religious organization administrator*

Thousand Oaks
Reimnitz, Elroi *minister*

Vallejo
McGowan, Thomas Randolph *religious organization executive*

Vista
Rader, Paul Alexander *minister, administrator*

West Hollywood
Eger, Denise Leese *rabbi*

Woodland Hills
Skelly, John Joshua *clergyman, fundraiser*

COLORADO

Aurora
Stifel, Frederick Benton *pastor, biochemist, nutritionist*

Canon City
Hein, Kenneth Charles Lawrence *priest, educator*

Colorado Springs
Coriell, Bruce Richard *clergy*
Hanifen, Richard Charles *bishop*
Perkins, Floyd Jerry *theology educator*

Denver
Burrell, Calvin Archie *minister*
Morgan, David Forbes *minister*
Richards, Kent Harold *religion educator*
Sallquist, Gary Ardin *minister, planned giving administrator*
Sun, Charles Changkyun *minister, college president*
Swenson, Mary Ann *bishop*

Englewood
O'Connell, Robert Houston *religious educator, writer, editor*
Pounds, Elton William *pastoral care educator*
Weissenbuehler, Wayne *former bishop, pastor*

Fort Collins
Pape, Arnis Weston *minister*
Rolston, Holmes, III *theologian, educator, philosopher*

Fort Morgan
Long, Connie Sue *church youth worker*

Littleton
Hepler, Ovid Mansfield *minister*

Pueblo
Tafoya, Arthur N. *bishop*

Westcliffe
Jones, Daniel Edwin, Jr. *bishop*

CONNECTICUT

Hartford
Hart, Donald Purple *bishop*

HAWAII

Honolulu
DiLorenzo, Francis X. *bishop*
Gau, Wayne Watson *church abbot, educational consultant*

Kaneohe
Chappell, David Wellington *religion educator*

Ocean View
Gilliam, Jackson Earle *bishop*

Wahiawa
Crisp, George Robert *pastor*

IDAHO

Boise
Brown, Tod David *bishop*
Caufield, Marie Celine *religious organization administrator*
Thornton, John S., IV *bishop*

Inkom
Houston, James Russell *retired minister*

Lewiston
Greenawalt, Shirley Pomerinke *church youth director*

Moscow
Tate, Stan Davis *priest, clinical bioethicist*

ILLINOIS

Chicago
George, Francis *bishop*

INDIANA

Indianapolis
Page, Curtis Matthewson *minister*

MONTANA

Froid
Clark, Ruth Ann *lay worker, educator*

Great Falls
Milone, Anthony M. *bishop*

Helena
Brunett, Alexander J. *bishop*
Jones, Charles Irving *bishop*

NEBRASKA

Omaha
Curtiss, Elden F. *bishop*

NEVADA

Las Vegas
Flammang, Susann *author, publisher*
Walsh, Daniel Francis *bishop*

Reno
Chrystal, William George *minister*
Shamlian, Barbara Sue *religion educator, biblical researcher*
Straling, Phillip Francis *bishop*
Walrath, Harry Rienzi *minister*

NEW MEXICO

Albuquerque
Dunn, Mary Price *religious foundation executive*
Griffin, W. C. *bishop*
Sheehan, Michael Jarboe *archbishop*
Thompson, Kenneth Randall *evangelist*

Farmington
Plummer, Steven Tsosie *bishop*

Las Cruces
Ramirez, Ricardo *bishop*

Portales
Overton, Edwin Dean *campus minister, educator*

Roswell
Skariah, Matthew *religious organization administrator*

Santa Fe
Arnold, Talitha Jane *minister*

OKLAHOMA

Oklahoma City
Taylor-Grigsby, Queenie Delores *minister, consultant*

OREGON

Bend
Connolly, Thomas Joseph *bishop*

Corvallis
Goman, Jon Gifford *university chaplain, educator*
Steiner, Kenneth Donald *bishop*

Hillsboro
Morgan, Gwendolyn Jean *minister, writer*
Rice, Richard Lee, Jr. *minister, office manager*

Lake Oswego
Ladehoff, Robert Louis *bishop*

Portland
Carver, Loyce Cleo *clergyman*
Richards, Herbert East *minister emeritus, commentator*
Schwanz, Judith Ann *seminary educator*

Salem
Muntz, J(ohn) Richard *clergyman*

West Linn
Bohrer, Richard William *religious writer, editor, educator*

UTAH

Bountiful
Carter, Richard Bert *retired church official, retired government official*

Ogden
Harrington, Mary Evelina Paulson (Polly Harrington) *religious journalist, writer, educator*

Provo
Thorstenson, Clark T. *religious studies educator, administrator*

Salt Lake City
Hinckley, Gordon B. *church official*
Masters, Lorraine Susanne *religious organization administrator*
Monson, Thomas Spencer *church official, publishing company executive*
Niederauer, George H. *bishop*
Smith, Eldred Gee *church leader*

WASHINGTON

Belfair
Walker, E. Jerry *retired clergyman*

Bothell
Foster, David William *minister*

East Wenatchee
Edwards, Charles Garland *minister, counselor, health educator*

Edmonds
Dunbar, R. Allan *college administrator, clergyman*

Everett
Flora, Mary Ellen *bishop*

Fort Lewis
Tille, James Eugene *army chaplain*

Greenbank
Tuell, Jack Marvin *retired bishop*

Hoquiam
Maier, Anthony Alvin *pastor, counselor*

Kirkland
Beyerl, Paul Vincent *priest, educator*

Port Angeles
Jones, Douglas Michael *pastor*

Prosser
Cooper, Lynn Dale *retired minister, retired navy chaplain*

Quilcene
Ross, Lanson Clifford, Jr. *religion educator, humanitarian, author*

Redmond
White, Tim Dale *minister*

Renton
Warren, Larry Michael *clergyman*

Seattle
Galvin, Elias *bishop*
Leed, Jean Ann *religious organization administrator*
Mackenzie, Donald Matthew, Jr. *minister*
Murphy, Thomas Joseph *archbishop*
Warner, Vincent W. *bishop*

Spanaway
Westbrook, T. L. *bishop*

Spokane
Keller, Robert M. *bishop*
Lee, Richard Francis James *evangelical clergyman, media consultant*
Polley, Harvey Lee *retired missionary and educator*
Skylstad, William S. *bishop*
Terry, Frank Jeffrey *bishop*

Sunnyside
Capener, Regner Alvin *minister, electronics engineer, author, inventor*

Tacoma
Wold, David C. *bishop*

Vancouver
Congdon, Roger Douglass *theology educator, minister*

WYOMING

Cheyenne
Hart, Joseph H. *bishop*

TERRITORIES OF THE UNITED STATES

AMERICAN SAMOA

Pago Pago
Weitzel, John Quinn *bishop*

GUAM

Agana
Apuron, Anthony Sablan *archbishop*

CANADA

ALBERTA

Calgary
Curtis, John Barry *archbishop*
O'Byrne, Paul J. *bishop*

Camrose
Campbell, John D. *religious organization administrator*

Edmonton
Doyle, Wilfred Emmett *retired bishop*
Mac Neil, Joseph Neil *archbishop*

McLennan
Légaré, Henri Francis *archbishop*

Saint Paul
Roy, Raymond *bishop*

BRITISH COLUMBIA

Abbotsford
Holdcroft, Leslie Thomas *clergyman, educator*

Kamloops
Sabatini, Lawrence *bishop*

Prince George
Kerr, Nancy Karolyn *pastor, mental health consultant*

Richmond
Plomp, Teunis (Tony Plomp) *minister*

Vancouver
Exner, Adam *archbishop*

Victoria
De Roo, Remi Joseph *bishop*

SASKATCHEWAN

Prince Albert
Morand, Blaise E. *bishop*

Regina
Bays, Eric *retired bishop*
Mallon, Peter *archbishop*

Saltcoats
Farquharson, Walter Henry *minister, church official*

Saskatoon
Jacobson, Sverre Theodore *retired minister*

YUKON TERRITORY

Whitehorse
Lobsinger, Thomas *bishop*

HONG KONG

Hong Kong
Chiang, Samuel Edward *theological educator, humanities educator*

ADDRESS UNPUBLISHED

Bauer, Judy Marie *minister*
Charleston, Steve *bishop*
Cory, Angelica Jo *spiritual consultant, author*
Crabtree, Davida Foy *minister*
Derickson, Stanley Lewis *minister, writer*
Dornette, Ralph Meredith *church organization executive, educator, minister*
Emerson, R. Clark *priest, business administrator*
Finley, Mitchel Brent *writer*
Frame, John Timothy *retired bishop*
Frank, Donald Herbert *minister*
Greenbaum, Alan Howard *rabbi*
Greiner Makenna, Carrie Ann *religious science practitioner*
Harrisville, Roy Alvin, III *pastor, educator*
Hoops, William James *clergyman*
Johnson, Alice Elaine *retired academic administrator*
Lotz, Albert Frank, III (Trey Lotz) *religious organization auditor*
Lotz, Linda Ann *religious organizer*
Mangini, Richard Alan *religious organization executive*
McBean, Sharon Elizabeth *church administrator*
McConnell, Calvin Dale *clergyman*
Naghi, Ladislau-George *priest*
Parsons, Elmer Earl *retired clergyman*
Pelotte, Donald Edmond *bishop*
Russell, Patrick James *priest*
Setchko, Edward Stephen *minister, theology educator, psychologist*
Swanson, Paul Rubert *minister*
Williams, John Christopher Richard *bishop*

SCIENCE: LIFE SCIENCE

UNITED STATES

ALASKA

Anchorage
Davies, Garry *biology educator*
Kudenov, Jerry David *zoology educator*

Fairbanks
White, Robert Gordon *research director, biology educator*

Juneau
Wilbur, Robert L. *biologist, science editor*

ARIZONA

Bisbee
Johnson, Heidi Smith *science educator*
Milton, John P. *ecologist, educator, author, photographer*

Flagstaff
Grim, J(ohn) Norman *biology educator, electron microscopy consultant*
Phillips, Arthur Morton, II *botanist, consultant*

Glendale
Devlin, David Stuart *biology educator*

Kingman
McNichols, Robert Ray *forester*

Litchfield Park
Ollson, Mickey Louis *zoo owner*

Phoenix
Bolin, Vernon Spencer *microbiologist, consultant*
Erickson, Robert Porter *geneticist educator*
Idouraine, Ahmed *nutritionist, food chemist*
Papp, Henry *science association administrator*

Tempe
Severe, Salvatore Francis *school psychologist*

Tucson
Cogut, Theodore Louis *environmental specialist, meteorologist*
Cortner, Hanna Joan *science administrator, research scientist, educator*
D'Silva, Aecio Moura *aquaculture scientist*
Gerba, Charles Peter *microbiologist, educator*
Grissino-Mayer, Henri Dee *research scientist*
Kline, Natasha Cale *biologist*
Lai, LiWen *molecular geneticist, educator*
McCormick, Floyd Guy, Jr. *agricultural educator, college administrator*
Mebrahtu, Yemane Berhan *medical microbiologist, entomologist, researcher*
Norem, Margaret Alice *agronomist, editor*
Racowsky, Catherine *reproductive physiologist, researcher*
Shannon, Robert Rennie *optical sciences center administrator, educator*
Spizizen, John *microbiologist*

Window Rock
Hathaway, Loline *zoo and botanic park curator*

CALIFORNIA

Alameda
Koenig, Gina Lee *microbiologist*

Angwin
Ness, Bryan Douglas *biologist, educator*

Arcadia
Morse, Judy *science foundation administrator*

Arcata
Botzler, Richard George *wildlife educator*
Ogan, Chester Vance *wildlife biologist*

Atherton
Goodman, Christopher Bettencourt *cytogeneticist*

Bakersfield
Anderson, Cliffton *science educator*

Berkeley
Barrett, Reginald Haughton *biology educator, wildlife management educator*
Bern, Howard Alan *science educator, research biologist*
Burnside, Mary Beth *biology educator, researcher*
Dahlsten, Donald Lee *entomology educator, university dean*
Gold, Lois Swirsky *research scientist*
Markell, Edward Kingsmill *medical parasitologist, educator*
Robertson, Jacqueline Lee *entomologist*
Sensabaugh, George Frank, Jr. *forensic sciences educator*
Wake, David Burton *biology educator*
Willhite, Calvin Campbell *toxicologist*
Wohletz, Leonard Ralph *soil scientist, consultant*

Bonsall
Alling, Abigail Kingsley *scientist, expedition director*

Chico
Stern, Kingsley Rowland *botanist, educator*
Vaught, Tony Steven *aquaculturist*

Chino
Pfuntner, Allan Robert *entomologist*

Chula Vista
Neudecker, Stephen K. *marine ecologist, museum professional*
Thomas, Teresa Ann *microbiologist, educator*

Claremont
Taylor, Roy Lewis *botanist, educator*

Concord
Ivy, Edward Everett *entomologist, consultant*

Costa Mesa
Visco, Kim Kelly *biologist, educator*

Cupertino
Cheeseman, Douglas Taylor, Jr. *wildlife tour executive, photographer, educator*

Daly City
Dowlin, Janice Marie *science administrator*

Davis
Amirkhanian, John David *geneticist, researcher, educator*
Armstrong, Peter Brownell *biologist*
Bernoco, Domenico *immunogeneticist, educator*
Bradford, G. Eric *animal science educator emeritus*
Butler, Edward Eugene *plant pathology educator*
Gasser, James Scott *biologist, educator*
Gifford, Ernest Milton *biologist, educator*
Hirsh, Dwight Charles, III *microbiologist*
Jones, James Henry *physiology educator, researcher*
Kunkee, Ralph Edward *viticulture and enology educator*
Laidlaw, Harry Hyde, Jr. *entomology educator*
Nielsen, Donald Rodney *soil and water science educator*
Stewart, James Ian *agricultural water scientist, cropping system developer, consultant*
Williams, William Arnold *agronomy educator*

Duarte
Davagnino, Juan V. *scientist*
Lundblad, Roger Lauren *research director*
Natarajan, Rama *research scientist*
Smith, Steven Sidney *molecular biologist*

El Centro
Flock, Robert Ashby *retired entomologist*

El Sobrante
Gilbert, William Marshall *retired biologist, educator*

Fairfield
Link, Julia Anne *urban horticulture educator*

Fountain Valley
Phipps, Donald William, Jr. *microbiologist*

Fresno
Sidhu, Gurmel Singh *geneticist, research scientist*

Gilroy
McGrogan, Michael Patrick *molecular and cell biologist*

Granada Hills
Lorbeer, George Coe *retired science educator*

Irvine
Campbell, Diane Rita *biologist, educator*
Dandashi, Fayad Alexander *operations research scientist*
Demetrescu, Mihai Constantin *research scientist, educator, computer company executive*
Erickson, Richard Alan *biologist*
Larson, Kirk David *pomologist and extension specialist*

Lawton, Michael James *entomologist, pest management specialist*

La Jolla
Dulbecco, Renato *biologist, educator*
Fishman, William Harold *cancer research foundation executive, biochemist*
Guillemin, Roger C. L. *physiologist*
Lewin, Ralph Arnold *biologist*
McRee, Duncan Everett *molecular biologist, researcher*
Subramani, Suresh *biology educator*

Laguna Niguel
Coleman, Roger Dixon *bacteriologist*

Lake Arrowhead
Asher, James Edward *forestry consultant, engineer, arborist, forensic expert*

Lewiston
McColm, George Lester *international agricultural consultant, journalist*

Loma Linda
Longo, Lawrence Daniel *physiologist, obstetrician-gynecologist*
Zuccarelli, Anthony Joseph *molecular biology and biochemistry educator*

Los Altos
Zoltan, Elizabeth *psychology educator, consultant*

Los Angeles
Arbib, Michael Anthony *neuroscientist, educator, cybernetician*
Bakus, Gerald Joseph *biology educator*
Buth, Donald George *biology educator*
Collias, Nicholas Elias *zoology educator, ornithologist*
Davies, Kelvin James Anthony *research scientist, educator, consultant, author*
Fain, Gordon Lee *physiology educator*
Gallup, Marc Richmond *biology educator, paleontologist*
Haglund, Thomas Roy *research biologist, consultant, educator*
Kadner, Carl George *biology educator emeritus*
Korge, Paavo *cell physiologist*
McClure, William Owen *biologist*
Mockary, Peter Ernest *clinical laboratory scientist, researcher*
Mohr, John Luther *biologist, environmental consultant*
Rotter, Jerome Israel *medical geneticist*
Schopf, James William *paleobiologist*
Shi, Wenyuan *microbiologist*
Smulders, Anthony Peter *biology educator*
Szego, Clara Marian *cell biologist, educator*
Taylor, Charles Ellett *biologist*
Valentine, Jane Lee *environmental health sciences educator*

Los Banos
Castellano, Valen Edward *biologist*

Los Gatos
Krozel, Jimmy Alan *research scientist, artist*

Manteca
Rainey, Barbara Ann *sensory evaluation consultant*

Martinez
Gerlach, William Edward *agricultural marketing executive*

Menlo Park
Rebert, Charles Sidney *research neuroscientist, educator*

Merced
Olsen, David Magnor *chemistry and astronomy educator*

Mill Valley
Faber, Phyllis Mavis *biologist, consultant*

Moffett Field
Fletcher, Douglas Gerald *research scientist*
Ross, Muriel Dorothy *research scientist*
Strawa, Anthony Walter *research scientist*

Monterey
Parsons, Christina Marie *science writer, education consultant*

Mountain View
Babcock, Rosemary Ann Douglas *animal behavior researcher, naturalist, biomedical librarian, multimedia writer, editor, producer*
Li, Shengqiang *virologist*

Muir Beach
Bowyer, Jane Baker *science educator*

Napa
Jones, Wayne Ross *agronomist*

Oakland
Cherry, Lee Otis *scientific institute director*
Parrott, Joel *zoo director*
Whitsel, Richard Harry *biologist, entomologist*

Orange
Dumars, Kenneth W. *medical geneticist educator, pediatrician*

Palo Alto
Bodnar, Jackie Sue *molecular biologist, geneticist*
Garland, Harry Thomas *research administrator*
Hess, Frederick Dana *science administrator, educator*
Lipsick, Joseph Steven *research scientist, medical educator*
Scoledes, Aristotle Georgius Michale *retired science and technology educator, research consultant*
Suermondt, Henri Jacques *research scientist*

Parlier
Stapleton, James Jay *agricultural scientist, consultant*

Pasadena
Lewis, Edward B. *biology educator*
Medina-Puerta, Antonio *scientist*
Meyerowitz, Elliot Martin *biologist, educator*
Randolph, Linda Marie *geneticist*
Tappan, Janice Ruth Vogel *animal behavior researcher*

Pomona
Stiffler, Daniel Francis *biology educator*

Prather
Warren, Barbara Kathleen (Sue Warren) *wildlife biologist*

Richmond
Rudin, Norah *forensic genetic consultant, science writer*

Riverside
Eastmond, David Albert *environmental toxicology educator*
Embleton, Tom William *horticultural science educator*
Erwin, Donald Carroll *plant pathology educator*
Hamilton, Solomon Maximy *physiologist, educator*
Martins-Green, Manuela *cell biologist*
Miller, Thomas Albert *entomology educator*
Scora, Rainer Walter *botanist*

Roseville
Sydor, Richard Paul *social science educator*

Sacramento
Baker, Maria *zoological park administrator*
Booze, Thomas Franklin *toxicologist*
Hackney, Robert Ward *plant pathologist, nematologist, parasitologist, molecular genetecist*
Host, Lawrence A. *conservation biologist*
Loewy, Erich Hans *bioethicist, educator*
Rosenberg, Dan Yale *retired plant pathologist*

San Bernardino
Mian, Lal Shah *entomologist*

San Diego
Ballard, Rex Kevin *science administrator*
Boyce, Ker *electrophysiologist, cardiologist*
Burkhart, Brad John *horticulturist, landscape architect*
Callaway, John Charles *wetland ecologist*
Crick, Francis Harry Compton *science educator, researcher*
Gulliver, Edward Quentin *marine consultant, writer*
McGraw, Donald Jesse *biologist, historian of science, writer*
Myers, Douglas George *zoological society administrator*
Panetta, Joseph Daniel *biotechnology executive*
Risser, Arthur Crane, Jr. *zoo administrator*
Stowell, Larry Joseph *agricultural consultant*
Weinrich, James Donald *psychobiologist, educator*
Wu, Ellen Yung-hua *pharmacology research scientist*

San Fernando
McCraven, Eva Stewart Mapes *health service administrator*

San Francisco
Anderson, David E. *zoological park administrator*
Borson, Daniel Benjamin *physiology educator, inventor, researcher, lawyer*
Brown, Walter Creighton *biologist*
Handler, Evelyn *science administrator*
Vyas, Girish Narmadashankar *virologist, immunohematologist*

San Jose
Taylor, Kendrick Jay *microbiologist*

San Luis Obispo
Piirto, Douglas Donald *forester, educator*

San Marcos
Liggins, George Lawson *microbiologist, diagnostic company executive*

San Marino
Hanson, George Peter *retired research botanist, real estate investor*

San Simeon
Jennings, Mark Russell *biologist*

Santa Ana
Glazier, Ron *zoological park administrator*

Santa Barbara
Botkin, Daniel Benjamin *biologist, environmental scientist*
Hatherill, John Robert *toxicologist, educator*
Lambrecht, Frank Laurent *medical entomologist, parasitology researcher*
Manclark, Charles Robert *microbiologist, researcher*
Samuel, Charles E. *virologist, educator*
Schneider, Edward Lee *botanic garden administrator*

Santa Clara
Li, Cindy *scientist*

Santa Cruz
Brown, George Stephen *physics educator*

Santa Monica
Li, Shuguang *research scientist*
Lin, Hun-Chi *molecular biologist*

Santee
Hardy, Ben(son B.) *orchid nursery executive*

Sebastopol
Walton, James Stephen *research scientist*

Sonoma
Shultz, Fred Townsend *geneticist, biologist*

South San Francisco
Biroc, Sandra Lyn *bilogical scientist*
Bussiere, Jeanine Louise *toxicologist*
Ruppert, Siegfried *scientist*

Stanford
Francke, Uta *medical geneticist, genetics researcher, educator*
Hoffman, Neil Eugene *cell biologist*
Matin, A. *microbiology educator, consultant*
Sanders, William John *research scientist*

Stockton
Magness, Rhonda Ann *microbiologist*

Sun Valley
Dergrigorian, Ronald *water microbiologist*

Sunnyvale
Drmanac, Radoje *molecular biologist*
Mansfield, Elaine Schultz *molecular geneticist, automation specialist*
Zheng, Qiang *research scientist*

Terra Bella
Gletne, Jeffrey Scott *forester*

Thousand Oaks
Chen, Mary Yun-Chun *research engineer*
Yan, Qiao *neurobiologist*

Vallejo
Demetrios, Michael B. *wildlife theme park director*

Vandenberg AFB
Ehrsam, Eldon Edward *operations research analyst, real estate broker*

Ventura
Arita, George Shiro *biology educator*
Huszczuk vel Huszcza, Andrew Richard *physiologist*
Parigian, Michael John *forensic scientist*

Visalia
Day, Kevin Ross *pomologist, researcher, consultant, farmer*

Vista
Winslow, Philip Charles *agriculturist, marketing consultant*

Walnut
Smith, Harry Mendell, Jr. *science educator*

West Hills
Centorino, James Rocco *science educator*

Westwood
Brydon, Harold Wesley *entomologist, writer*

Woodland
Hauptmann, Randal Mark *biotechnologist*

Woodland Hills
Fox, Stuart Ira *physiologist*

Yosemite National Park
Mitchell, Jerry Michael *biologist*

COLORADO

Arvada
Reynolds-Sakowski, Dana Renee *science educator*

Boulder
Armstrong, David Michael *biology educator*
Johnson, Thomas Eugene *biology educator*
Staehelin, Lucas Andrew *cell biology educator*

Buena Vista
Moore, Judith Lynn *animal scientist*

Colorado Springs
Clifford, Walter Jess *microbiologist, immunologist*
Comes, Robert George *research scientist*
Schwebach, Gerhard Hermann *microbiologist*
Zimkas, Charles Patrick, Jr. *space foundation director*

Crested Butte
Willey, Robert Bruce *biology educator*

Denver
Ehret, Josephine Mary *microbiologist, researcher*
Freiheit, Clayton Fredric *zoo director*
Heifets, Leonid *microbiologist, researcher*
Jones, Stephanie Lee *biologist, ornithologist, botanist*
Puck, Theodore Thomas *geneticist, biophysicist, educator*
Rose, Gregory Mancel *neurobiologist*
Salmon, Merlyn Leigh *laboratory executive*
Schanfield, Moses Samuel *geneticist, educator*

Englewood
Brierley, James Alan *research administrator*
Matsumura, Masazumi *research scientist, biochemist*

Estes Park
Jones, A. Durand *park administrator*

Fort Collins
Burns, Denver P. *forestry research administrator*
Fausch, Kurt Daniel *fisheries ecology educator*
Harold, Ruth Laura *research biologist*
Lamb, Berton Lee, II *policy analyst, researcher*
Lameiro, Gerard Francis *research institute director*
Mitchell, Carl Jack *medical entomologist, research scientist*
Mortvedt, John Jacob *soil scientist*
Reddy, A. S. N. *plant molecular biology educator*
Seidel, George Elias, Jr. *animal scientist, educator*
Smith, Gary Chester *meat scientist, researcher*
Smith, Ralph Earl *virologist*
Sofos, John Nikolaos *food science and microbiology educator*
Williamson, Samuel Chris *research ecologist*

Grand Junction
Taylor, Hal Richard *agricultural journalist*

Lake City
Richard, Camille Elizabeth *ecologist, consultant*

Littleton
Sincoff, Steven Lawrence *science administrator, scientist*

Longmont
Christopher, Perry Lee *laboratory technician*
Ulrich, John August *microbiology educator*

Thornton
Pennak, Robert William *biologist, educator*

Westminster
Dotson, Gerald Richard *biology educator*
Wilson, Vincent Lee *geneticist, toxicologist, educator*

HAWAII

Aiea
Coller, Beth-Ann Griswold *molecular biologist, research scientist*

Haleiwa
Woolliams, Keith Richard *arboretum and botanical garden director*

Honolulu
Donlon, Timothy A. *cytogeneticist*
Fok, Agnes Kwan *cell biologist, educator*
Hertlein, Fred, III *industrial hygiene laboratory executive*
Kristiansen, Michael Sigurd *botanical gardens director*
Lamoureux, Charles Harrington *botanist, arboretum administrator*
Smith, Dean Orren *physiology educator*
Teramura, Alan Hiroshi *science educator*
Zaleski, Halina Maria *animal scientist*

Kamuela
Young, Ernest *park administrator*

Kula
Wilson, Peter Trimble *fisheries development consultant*

Pearl City
Kanenaka, Rebecca Yae *microbiologist*

Tripler Army
Uyehara, Catherine Fay Takako (Yamauchi) *physiologist, educator, pharmacologist*

IDAHO

Aberdeen
Sparks, Walter Chappel *horticulturist, educator*

Boise
Brownfield, Shelby Harold *soil scientist*
Burton, Lawrence DeVere *agriculturist, educator*

Coeur D Alene
Adams, Elinor Ruth *retired laboratory technician*

Hayden Lake
Lehrer, William Peter, Jr. *animal scientist*

Idaho Falls
Reno, Harley Wayne *environmental scientist*

Mc Call
Greer, Jerry Dean *forester*

Moscow
Larsen, Michael John *research mycologist*
Ulliman, Joseph James *forester, educator*

Nampa
Redfield, David Allen *chemistry educator*

Pocatello
Connelly, John William *wildlife research biologist*

Post Falls
Brede, Andrew Douglas *research director, plant breeder*

LOUISIANA

Baton Rouge
Pillay, Michael *botanist, researcher*

MASSACHUSETTS

Boston
Stahl, Gregory Lee *physiologist, researcher*

MISSOURI

Lees Summit
Louderback, Truman Eugene *environmental project manager*

MONTANA

Bozeman
Costerton, John William Fisher *microbiologist*
Gough, Robert Edward *horticulturist, editor, educator, writer*
Lavin, Matthew T. *horticultural educator*

Butte
Mitman, Grant Gregory *biology educator*
Peoples, Donald R. *research scientist*

Great Falls
Paulson-Ehrhardt, Patricia Helen *laboratory administrator*

Hamilton
Dorward, David William *microbiologist, consultant*

Havre
Clouse, Vickie Rae *biology and paleontology educator*

Helena
Johnson, John Philip *geneticist, researcher*

Miles City
Bellows, Robert Alvin *research physiologist*

Missoula
Salwasser, Hal *forest ecologist*

Sidney
Cochran, Verlan Leyerl *soil scientist*
Spencer, Neal Raymond *entomologist*

NEVADA

Boulder City
Shrader, Thomas Henry *biologist*

Fallon
Isidoro, Edith Annette *horticulturist*

Henderson
Fletcher, Donald Warren *microbiologist, educator*

Reno
Gray, Elizabeth Marie *biologist*
Johnson, Arthur William, Jr. *planetarium executive*
Von Bartheld, Christopher Stephen *neurobiologist*
Wehrli, John Erich *biotechnology executive*

NEW MEXICO

Albuquerque
Kluger, Matthew Jay *physiologist, educator*
Lapham, Sandra C. *research scientist, physician*
Nikula, Kristen Jan *veterinary and experimental pathologist*
Partridge, L(loyd) Donald *science educator*
Perez-Castro, Ana Veronica *developmental biology researcher*
Root, Robert Alan *ecologist, project manager*
Rypka, Eugene Weston *microbiologist*
Wilcox, Michael John *vision systems researcher, medical educator*

Carlsbad
Deckert, Frank *park administrator*
Goldstein, Barry Bruce *biologist, food company executive, lawyer*

Clayton
Malcolm-Callis, Kathryn Janette *animal scientist*

Las Cruces
Briggs, Dinus Marshall *agriculturist*
McCarthy, Charlotte Marie *microbiologist, educator*
Richman, David Bruce *entomologist, educator*

Rio Rancho
Bartels, Aloysia de Bessierés *mariculturist, seafood producer*

OREGON

Ashland
Christianson, Roger Gordon *biology educator*
MacMillen, Richard Edward *biological sciences educator, researcher*

Astoria
An, Haejung *food technology educator*

Bend
Lutzky, Frank Joseph, Jr. *science educator, project management consultant*

Clackamas
Wall, Brian Raymond *forest economist, policy analyst, business consultant, telemarketing salesexecutive*

Corvallis
Blus, Lawrence John *biologist*
Castellano, Michael Angelo *research forester*
Ho, Iwan *research plant pathologist*
Liegel, Leon Herman *soil scientist, research forester*
Radovsky, Frank Jay *zoologist, museum administrator*
Ream, Lloyd Walter, Jr. *molecular biology educator*
Rygiewicz, Paul Thaddeus *plant ecologist*
Stormshak, Fredrick *physiology educator*
Young, J. Lowell *soil chemist, biologist*

Gresham
Arney, James Douglas *forestry biometrics consultant*

Lake Oswego
Ellington, Will Boyd *forester, consultant*

Newport
Weber, Lavern John *marine science administrator, educator*

Portland
Gillette, Richard Gareth *neurophysiology educator, researcher*
Grimsbo, Raymond Allen *forensic scientist*
Hagenstein, William David *forester, consultant*
Han, Zhong-Sheng *neurobiologist, researcher*
Jarrell, Wesley Michael *soil and ecosystem science educator, researcher, consultant*
Marshall, David Brownell *biologist, consultant*
Reiness, C(ecil) Gary *biology educator*
Richardson, Kathleen *microbiologist, educator*

Prineville
Demmer, Richard James *biologist*

Salem
Bellman, Michael Stanley *forester, freelance writer*
Tallman, John Gary *biology educator*

The Dalles
Gladwell, Marilyn Meilan *microbiologist*

TEXAS

Dallas
McKnight, Steven Lanier *molecular biologist*

UTAH

Ephraim
Gardner, Paul Allen *biology educator*

Logan
Barnard, Dale Lynn *microbiologist*
Bissonette, John Alfred *research scientist*
Healey, Mark Calvin *biologist, educator*
Yang, Shiguang *parasitologist, educator*

Provo
Cox, Paul Alan *biologist, educator*
Heckmann, Richard Anderson *zoology educator*
McArthur, Eldon Durant *geneticist, researcher*
Smith, H(oward) Duane *zoology educator*
Tolman, Richard Robins *zoology educator*
White, Clayton M. *science educator, environmental consultant*

Salt Lake City
Carlquist, John Frederick *microbiologist, immunologist*
Creel, Donnell Joseph *research scientist, educator*
Opitz, John Marius *clinical geneticist, pediatrician*
Parks, Thomas Norville *neurobiologist*

Tooele
Burton, Frederick Glenn *laboratory director*

West Valley City
Rosvall, Patricia Lynn *biology educator*

WASHINGTON

Bellevue
Robins, Robert Edward *research scientist*

Carnation
Beshur, Jacqueline E. *pet training consultant, writer*

Centralia
Kyte, Lydiane *botanist*

Des Moines
Ross, Geraldine Yvonne *biologist, educator*

Federal Way
Duggan, Edward Martin *science and mathematics educator*

Friday Harbor
Brookbank, John W(arren) *retired microbiology educator*

Hansville
Blalock, Ann Bonar *policy analyst, evaluation researcher*

Kent
Schneider, Eugene Saul *microbiologist, laboratory administrator*

Nespelem
Paris, Richard Wayne *forester*

Oak Harbor
Skud, Bernard Einar *marine biologist*

Olympia
Curtis, Robert Orin *research forester*
Raphael, Martin George *research wildlife biologist*

Port Ludlow
Yunker, Conrad Erhardt *biologist*

Poulsbo
Tozer, William Evans *entomologist, educator*

Pullman
Blatner, Keith Allan *forest economics educator, consultant*
Calza, Roger Ernest *animal science genetics and cell biology educator*
Edwards, Gerald Elmo *botany educator*
Fellman, John Keegan *physiology educator, biochemist*
Sarkar, Dipak Kumar *physiologist, educator*

Redmond
Kelman, Bruce Jerry *toxicologist, consultant*

Richland
Anderson, James Arthur *research laboratory administrator*
Bian, Randy Xindi *research scientist*
Chikalla, Thomas David *retired science facility administrator*

Seattle
Binder, Marc David *neuroscientist, educator*
Boersma, P. Dee *zoology educator*
Byers, Breck Edward *geneticist, educator*
Campbell, Lee Ann *microbiology educator*
Disteche, Christine M. *geneticist*
Edmonds, Robert Leslie *forestry educator*
Iwasaki, Kouichi *molecular geneticist*
Lee, Qwihee Park *plant physiologist*
Leung, David Wai-Hung *molecular biologist*
McLaughlin, Peter Donald *research scientist*
Miller, Robert Carmi, Jr. *microbiology educator, university administrator*
Miller, Robert Victor *scientific research administrator*
Motulsky, Arno Gunther *geneticist, physician, educator*
Ning, Xue-Han (Hsueh-Han Ning) *physiologist, researcher*
Rasco, Barbara A. *food chemistry educator*
Sherwood, Anne Lesley *molecular biologist*
Stoeck, Jennifer Elizabeth *scientific institute administrator*
Tukey, Harold Bradford, Jr. *horticulture educator*
Wott, John Arthur *arboretum and botanical garden executive, horticulture educator*
Yao, Meng-Chao *molecular geneticist*

Spokane
Richard, Gerald Lawrence *soil scientist*

Sumner
Jackson, Edward Milton *toxicologist, researcher, business executive*

Tacoma
Champ, Stanley Gordon *scientific company executive*
Otten, Thomas *zoological park director*

Taholah
Workman, Larry Joe *natural resources interpreter, photographer-writer*

Walla Walla
Gary, Walter J(oseph) *entomologist, educator*

Wenatchee
Raese, John Thomas *physiologist*
Schrader, Lawrence Edwin *plant physiologist, educator*

WYOMING

Elk Mountain
Hall, Alan Herman *toxicologist, educator*

Green River
Weber, Marian Frances *laboratory administrator, educator*

Jackson
Davis, Randy L. *soil scientist*

Lander
Kesselheim, A. Donn *environmental education educator*

Laramie
Field, Ray Arvid *animal science educator*
Legg, David E. *entomologist, educator*
Reiners, William Arnold *botany educator*

Sheridan
Klaus, Marion *biologist, educator*

CANADA

ALBERTA

Calgary
Yoon, Ji-Won *virology, immunology and diabetes educator, research administrator*

BRITISH COLUMBIA

Vancouver
Newman, Murray Arthur *aquarium administrator*
Suzuki, David Takayoshi *geneticist, science broadcaster*

Victoria
Finlay, Audrey Joy *environmental educator, consultant, naturalist*
Loring, Thomas Joseph *forest ecologist*

SASKATCHEWAN

Saskatoon
Khachatourians, George Gharadaghi *microbiology educator*
Oelck, Michael M. *plant geneticist, researcher*

ADDRESS UNPUBLISHED

Allen, Lew, Jr. *laboratory executive, former air force officer*
Baker, Joseph Roderick, III *aviculturist*
Baldwin, C. Andrew, Jr. *retired science educator*
Barabino, William Albert *science and technology researcher, inventor*
Barter Bowlus, Nadine Christena *biology educator*
Bautista, Anthony Hernandez *biomedical company executive*
Bhat, Bal Krishen *geneticist, plant breeder*
Burisch, Danny B. Catselas *microbiologist*
Christenson, Daniel Paul *biologist, conservationist, educator*
Diamond, Rochelle Anne *biologist*
Dubesa, Elaine J. *biotechnology company executive*
Fraker, Mark Arnott *environmental scientist*
Gennaro, Antonio L. *biology educator*
Gore, James Franklin *wildlife biologist*
Hampton, Richard Owen *research plant pathologist and virologist, educator*
Herz, Michael Joseph *marine environmental scientist*
Hildebrand, Milton *zoology educator, retired*
Honour, Lynda Charmaine *research scientist, educator, psychotherapist*
Janigro, Damir *physiologist, educator*
Jarvik, Gail Pairitz *medical geneticist*
Krassa, Kathy Boltrek *molecular biologist*
Langer, Glenn Arthur *cellular physiologist, educator*
Latham, James Richard *research scientist*
Maslansky, Carol Jeanne *toxicologist*
Meador, James Parnell *toxicologist*
Olson, Phillip David LeRoy *agriculturist, chemist*
Palade, George Emil *biologist, educator*
Pyle, Robert Michael *naturalist, writer*
Riley, Erin Lee *biology educator, forensic scientist*
Scott, David Clinton *research scientist*
Soulé, Michael Ellman *biologist*
Starr, Robert Irving *plant physiologist, chemist*
Todsen, Thomas Kamp *botanist*
Weinstock, Ronald Jay *research and development company executive*
Werner, Richard Allen *retired entomologist*

SCIENCE: MATHEMATICS AND COMPUTER SCIENCE

UNITED STATES

ALASKA

Anchorage
Murray, Robert Henry *technical manager*

Fairbanks
Morris, Deanna Ruth *mathematics tutor*

Tununak
Bond, Ward Charles *mathematics and computer educator*

ARIZONA

Avondale
SantaVicca, Edmund Frank *information scientist*

Chandler
Rudibaugh, Melinda Campbell *mathematics educator*

Fort Huachuca
Clark, Brian Thomas *mathematical statistician, operations research analyst*

Gilbert
Stith, Joseph *computer infosystems specialist, author*

Phoenix
Doto, Irene Louise *statistician*

Prescott
Anderson, Arthur George *laboratory director, former computer company executive, consultant*

Scottsdale
Loch, Patricia Ann *software company executive, consultant*

Sierra Vista
Sizemore, Nicky Lee *computer scientist*

Tempe
Bristol, Stanley David *mathematics educator*
Downs, Floyd L. *mathematics educator*

Tucson
Gregg, Kenneth Stephen *computer scientist*
Re Velle, Jack B(oyer) *statistician, consultant*
Smarandache, Florentin *mathematics researcher, writer*
Trueblood, Mark *systems engineer*

CALIFORNIA

Antioch
Neimann, Albert Alexander *mathematician, business owner*

Berkeley
Anderson, Thomas E. *computer scientist, educator*
Bertram, Christopher D. *artificial intelligence researcher*
Bickel, Peter John *statistician, educator*
Fateman, Richard J. *computer science educator, researcher*
Henzinger, Thomas Anton *computer science educator*
Marks, Gregory Todd *mathematics educator*
McKusick, Marshall Kirk *computer scientist*
Pinney, Edmund *educator, mathematician*

Burbank
Mesrobian, Edmond *computer scientist, computer architect*

Calabasas
Ross, David Edward *software engineer*

Camarillo
Vannix, C(ecil) Robert *programmer, systems analyst*

Carlsbad
Fairhurst, Jeffrey Thomas *software consultant*

Carmichael
Givant, Philip Joachim *mathematics educator, real estate investment executive*

Carson
Kowalski, Kazimierz *computer science educator, researcher*
Suchenek, Marek Andrzej *computer science educator*
Yoshida, Kosaku *quantitative methods educator*

Castroville
Guglielmo, Eugene Joseph *software engineer*

IDAHO

Rexburg
Terry, Steven Spencer *mathematics educator, consultant*

MASSACHUSETTS

Burlington
Knutson, Stanley *software professional*

MONTANA

Bozeman
Cimikowski, Robert John *computer scientist*

NEVADA

Carson City
Yoder, Marianne Eloise *software developer, consultant*

Gardnerville
Woodside, George Robert *computer software developer*

Incline Village
Welsch, Suzanne Carol *mathematics educator*

Las Vegas
Dalpatadu, Rohan Jayantha *mathematician, educator*
Kunz, Charles Alan *computer consultant*
Snyder, John Henry *computer science educator, consultant*

Minden
McCullough, William Edward *metrologist*

NEW JERSEY

Princeton
Lehmann, Erich Leo *statistics educator*

NEW MEXICO

Albuquerque
Ehrhorn, Thomas Frederick *software quality assurance engineer*
Lee, Elizabeth Tan *mathematics educator*
Sciame, Donald Richard *computer systems analyst, dentist, magician, locksmith*
Smith, David Alan *systems programmer*
Sobolewski, John Stephen *computer information scientist, consultant*
Stone, Alexander Paul *mathematics educator*

Carlsbad
Swenson, David Aaron *computer scientist, educator*

Farmington
Hagan, Richard Francies *computer system educator*

Jemez Springs
Sigler, Marjorie Diane *computer programming executive, analyst*

Las Cruces
Kilmer, Neal Harold *software engineer*
Reinfelds, Juris *computer science educator*

Los Alamos
Kellner, Richard George *mathematician, computer scientist*
Tingley, Walter Watson *computer systems manager*

Santa Fe
Buchser, John Robert *computer scientist*
Price, Thomas Munro *computer consultant*

NORTH CAROLINA

Charlotte
Nelson, Barbara Secrest *educational developer*

OREGON

Albany
Yu, Kitson Szewai *computer science educator*

Beaverton
Tsujio, Hirokazu *computer consultant*

Corvallis
Parks, Harold Raymond *mathematician, educator*
Stalley, Robert Delmer *retired mathematics educator*
Wechsler, Susan Linda *software design engineer*

Eugene
Truax, Donald Robert *mathematics educator*

Hillsboro
Bhagwan, Sudhir *computer industry and research executive, consultant*
Glew, Andrew Forsyth *computer architect, inventor*
Spangler, Lynice Sue *software engineer*

Portland
Hall, Howard Pickering *engineering and mathematics educator*
Phillips, David Spencer *statistician, educator*
Reid, Christopher Ervin *mathematician, software engineer*

Wilsonville
Bruggere, Thomas H. *computer science company executive*

UTAH

Draper
Averett, Robert Lee *educator, information system professional*

Logan
Cheng, Heng-Da *computer scientist*
Miller, Ruth Elsie *mathematics educator, industrial designer*

Ogden
Gregson, Garry Evan *statistical engineer, information consultant*

Provo
Garner, Lynn Evan *mathematics educator*
Hansen, James Vernon *computer science, information systems educator*
Lang, William Edward *mathematics educator*

Salt Lake City
Guldahl, Martin Granville *software engineer*
Thomas, Linda Marri Gandy *programmer, analyst*
Williamson, David Henry *data processing professional*

WASHINGTON

Bainbridge Island
Ulin, Samuel Alexander *computer systems developer*

Bothell
Jaundalderis, Julia Lee *software engineer*

Everett
Duernberger, Paul M. *computer services director, computer and electrical engineering educator*
Labayen, Louie Anthony Lopez *information analyst, consultant*

Federal Way
Cunningham, John Randolph *systems analyst*

Lacey
Wells, Roger Stanley *software engineer*

Lynnwood
Vierheller, Todd *software engineering consultant*

Pullman
Gupta, Barbara Mackay *mathematics educator*
Hildebrandt, Darlene Myers *information scientist*

Redmond
Applegate, Arthur David *computer software developer, consultant*
Houseworth, Derek Eugene *software test engineer*
Huang, Xuedong David *senior reseacher*
Kimmich, Jon Bradford *computer science program executive*
Lomet, David Bruce *computer scientist*
MacKenzie, Peter Sean *instructional designer*

Richland
Cowley, Paula Jean *computer scientist, consultant*

Seattle
Bridwell, C. Joseph *computer systems analyst*
Burkhart, Richard Henry *mathematician*
Criminale, William Oliver, Jr. *applied mathematics educator*
Dieli, Mary Adelaide *software engineer consultant*
Eldenburg, Mary Jo Corliss *mathematics educator*
Gates, Theodore Allan, Jr. *software engineer*
Gillispie, Steven Brian *systems analyst, researcher*
Michael, Ernest Arthur *mathematics educator*
Nelson, Walter William *computer programmer, consultant*
Nijenhuis, Albert *mathematician, educator*
Smith, Gregory Laurence *computer scientist, consultant*
Wegelin, Jacob Andreas *statistician*
Whitman, Scott Randy *computer scientist*
Whitney, Lisa VanderSluis *technology professional*
Zabinsky, Zelda Barbara *operations researcher, industrial engineering educator*

Shoreline
Reddecliffe, Karin Linnae Ellis *educator*

Spokane
Mayer, Herbert Carleton, Jr. *computer consultant*

WYOMING

Cheyenne
Southworth, Rod Brand *computer science educator*

Laramie
Davis, Frank Grodavent Foy *database manager*
Porter, A. Duane *mathematics educator*

CANADA

ALBERTA

Calgary
Pinter, Joseph Kalman *mathematician*

BRITISH COLUMBIA

Burnaby
Han, Jiawei *computer scientist, educator*

Vancouver
Zhu, Jun *mathematics educator*

SASKATCHEWAN

Regina
Koh, Eusebio Legarda *mathematics educator*

ADDRESS UNPUBLISHED

Aaron, Bud *systems analyst*
Abu-Mostafa, Ayman Said *computer consultant*
Allison, Robert Clyde *business and computers consultant*
Barrett, Christine Khan *engineering project management coordinator*
Basch, Reva *information services company executive*
Campione, Mary Ellen *software engineer, consultant, writer*
Davenport, William Harold *mathematics educator*
Denny, John Leighton, Jr. *mathematics educator*
Frishberg, Nancy Jo *computer company executive, linguist*
Gabrielian, Armen *computer scientist, researcher, consultant*
Glassman, Arthur Joseph *software engineer*
Graham, Kirsten R. *computer science educator*
Greever, Margaret Quarles *retired mathematics educator*
Grober, Michael *computer industry professional*
Haley, Richard Edward, Jr. *computer scientist*
Holland, Michael James *computer services administrator*
Idury, Ramana Murthy *computer scientist*
Jensen, John Michael *mathematics educator, consultant*
Klementiev, Alexandre Alexandrovich *computer scientist, consultant, educator*
Leader, Jeffery James *mathematics educator*
Lundgren, Susan Elizabeth *information technology consultant, musician*
Merilan, Jean Elizabeth *statistics educator*
Mints, Grigori Efroim *specialist in mathematical logic*
Monroe, Mary-Lynne *computer consultant, special education educator*
Newman, Richard D. *computer resources professional, software developer*
Norman, E. Gladys *business computer educator, consultant*
Pendleton, Joan Marie *microprocessor designer*
Purdy, Teddy George, Jr. *programmer, analyst, researcher, consultant*
Redfield, John Duncan *computer programmer, artist*
Schmidt, Christopher Van Alst *systems programmer*
Shillington, Keith Allan *principal, consultant*
Stilman, Boris *computer science educator, researcher*
Suppes, Patrick *statistics, education, philosophy and psychology educator*
Tu, Samson W. *computer science researcher*
Tuul, Johannes *mathematician, educator*
Vu, Dung Quoc *systems analyst*
Winter, Donald Christopher *computer systems architect*
Wong, Rebecca Kimmae *mathematics educator, consultant*
Wu, Hung-Hsi *mathematician, educator*

SCIENCE: PHYSICAL SCIENCE

UNITED STATES

ALASKA

Anchorage
Ennis, William Lee *physics educator*
Mabry, Monte Del *geophysicist*
Myers, Mark D. *petroleum geologist, researcher*
O'Brien, David Keran *marine geologist, environmental scientist*
Patrick, Leslie Dayle *hydrologist*

Fairbanks
Duffy, Lawrence Kevin *biochemist, educator*
Fathauer, Theodore Frederick *meteorologist*
Fischer, Robert Edward *meteorologist*
Helfferich, Merritt Randolph *technology transfer administrator*
Hopkins, David Moody *geologist*
Lingle, Craig Stanley *glaciologist, educator*
McNutt, Stephen Russell *volcanologist, geophysical scientist*

ARIZONA

Flagstaff
Chen, Jian Hua *medical physicist*
Eastman, Michael Paul *chemistry educator*
Shoemaker, Eugene Merle *geologist*
Sinton, William Merz *astronomer, educator*
Zoellner, Robert William *chemistry educator*

Fort Defiance
Moore, Derrith Rachelle *environmental engineer*

Glendale
Pearson, Keith Laurence *retired environmental scientist*

Mesa
Kokanovich, Jon Douglas *crime laboratory director, forensic chemist*
Ramaswamy, Padmanabhan *materials scientist*

Page
Leus McFarlen, Patricia Cheryl *water chemist*

Phoenix
Bolin, Vladimir Dustin *chemist*
Depies, Lisa J. *physicist*
Lichtenberg, Larry Ray *chemist, consultant, researcher*

Scottsdale
Hockmuth, Joseph Frank *physicist, psychotherapist*

Sedona
Otto, Klaus *physicist, physical chemist*

Tempe
Black, Kristine Mary *physicist*
Harris, Joseph *retired biochemistry educator*
Juvet, Richard Spalding, Jr. *chemistry educator*
Lovvik, Daryl Vaughn *geologist, consultant*
Moore, Carleton Bryant *geochemistry educator*
Pettit, George Robert *chemistry educator, cancer researcher*
Wyman, Max McDonald *real estate broker, spatial technologies scientist*

Tucson
Baker, Victor Richard *geology and hydrology researcher, educator, planetary sciences researcher*
Barrett, Bruce Richard *physics educator*
Broderick, Jon Palmer *geologist, mining company executive*
Buras, Nathan *hydrology and water resources educator*
Darling, Mary Elizabeth *environmental affairs consultant*
Dickinson, Robert Earl *atmospheric scientist, educator*
Fernandez, Clemente Guajardo *environmental specialist*
Fink, James Brewster *geophysicist, consultant*
Glass, Richard Steven *chemistry educator*
Hallick, Richard Bruce *biochemistry educator*
Hunten, Donald Mount *planetary scientist, educator*
Kamilli, Robert Joseph *geologist*
Kiersch, George Alfred *geological consultant, retired educator*
Lamb, Willis Eugene, Jr. *physicist, educator*
Lunine, Jonathan Irving *planetary scientist, educator*
Mead, Kathryn Nadia *astrophysicist, educator*
Salzman, William Ronald *chemistry educator*
Schultz, Thomas Robert *hydrogeologist*
Sewell, Charles Robertson *geologist, exploration company executive, investor*
White, Raymond Edwin, Jr. *astronomer, educator, researcher*
Willis, Clifford Leon *geologist*

CALIFORNIA

Anaheim
Brigham, Gerald Allen *research physicist, consultant*

Arcadia
Bars, Itzhak *physics educator, researcher, consultant*
Slover, Archy F. *chemist*

Arcata
Cranston, Frederick Pitkin *physics educator*

Berkeley
Calvin, Melvin *chemist, educator*
Chamberlain, Owen *nuclear physicist*
Glaser, Donald Arthur *physicist*
Haller, Eugene Ernest *materials scientist, educator*
Hartman, Hyman *biochemist*
Hearst, John Eugene *chemistry educator, pharmaceutical executive*
Kurtzman, Ralph Harold *retired biochemist, researcher, consultant*
Perry, Dale Lynn *chemist*
Phillips, John Gardner *educator, astrophysicist*
Roitman, James Nathaniel *chemist*
Seaborg, Glenn Theodore *chemistry educator*
Steiner, Herbert Max *physics educator*
Townes, Charles Hard *physics educator*
Weber, Eicke Richard *physicist*
Yuan Tseh Lee *chemistry educator*

Bonita
Wood, Fergus James *geophysicist, consultant*

Burbank
Ingersoll, John Gregory *physicist, energy specialist, educator*

Burlingame
Friend, David Robert *chemist*
Hotz, Henry Palmer *physicist*

Calabasas
Haile, Marcus Alfred *retired chemistry educator*

Camarillo
Leerabhandh, Marjorie Bravo *chemist, educator*

Canyon Lake
Schilling, Frederick Augustus, Jr. *geologist, consultant*

Carmel
Vagnini, Livio Lee *chemist, forensic consultant*

China Lake
Chapman, Robert Dale *research chemist*
Erickson, Eric Douglas *chemist*

Claremont
White, Kathleen Merritt *geologist*

Compton
Wang, Charles Ping *scientist*

Costa Mesa
Berdjis, Fazlollah *physicist*
Lattanzio, Stephen Paul *astronomy educator*
Lorance, Elmer Donald *organic chemistry educator*

Davis
Hsieh, You-Lo *fiber and polymer scientist, educator*
Hullar, Theodore Lee *environmental educator*
Kelly, Peter Bernard *chemistry educator, researcher*
Mazelis, Mendel *plant biochemist, educator, reseacher*
Shelton, Robert Neal *physics educator, researcher*
Stumpf, Paul Karl *biochemistry educator emeritus*
Wooten, Frederick (Oliver) *applied science educator*

Downey
Kostoulas, Ioannis Georgiou *physicist*

Boulder
Baker, Daniel Neil *physicist*
Bartlett, Albert Allen *retired physics educator*
Bond, Wendell Anson *petroleum geologist, oil company executive*
Cech, Thomas Robert *chemistry and biochemistry educator*
Garstang, Roy Henry *astrophysicist, educator*
Gossard, Earl Everett *physicist*
Irwin, Charles Dennis, Jr. *geological consultant*
Little, Charles Gordon *geophysicist*
Miller, Harold William *nuclear geochemist*
Randel, William John *physicist*
Spangler, Timothy Chester *meteorologist, program director*
Tatarskii, Valerian Il'Ich *physics researcher*
Todd, Paul Wilson *biophysicist, educator*
Toon, Owen Brian *earth scientist*
Trenberth, Kevin Edward *atmospheric scientist*
Whiteside, Lowell Stanley *seismologist*

Canon City
Fair, Annie May *geological computer specialist*

Colorado Springs
Rogers, Steven Ray *physicist*

Commerce City
Hanson, Edward Alvin *chemist*

Denver
Barker, Fred *research geologist, scientific editor*
Brown, Mark Steven *medical physicist*
Carrara, Paul Edward *geologist, researcher*
Clark, Aaron Lee *environmental consulting executive*
Dean, Walter Edward, Jr. *research geologist*
Eaton, Gareth Richard *chemistry educator, university dean*
Friedman, Jules Daniel *geologist*
Johnson, Walter Earl *geophysicist*
Klipping, Robert Samuel *geophysicist*
Kranak, Peter Val *geologist*
Massaro, Anthony Scott *environmental consultant*
McDermott, Dirk Wade *geophysicist*
Morse, Helvise Glessner *physical and life sciences educator*
Peregrine, David Seymour *astronomer, consultant*
Pratt, Walden Penfield *research geologist*
Price, Leigh Charles *petroleum geologist and geochemist*
Ross, Sherman Edward *biochemist*
Snee, Lawrence Warren *geologist*
Starkey, Harry Charles *geologist*
Weihaupt, John George *geosciences educator, scientist, university administrator*
Zinke, Sally Griffiths *geophysicist, consultant*

Durango
Campbell, John Arthur *geology educator, researcher*

Englewood
Rosich, Rayner Karl *physicist*

Evergreen
Cumella, Stephen Paul *geologist*
Haun, John Daniel *petroleum geologist, educator*
Heyl, Allen Van, Jr. *geologist*

Fort Collins
Ethridge, Frank Gulde *geology educator, consultant*
Harold, Franklin Marcel *research scientist*
Saysette, Janice Elaine *vertebrate paleontologist, zoo archaeologist*

Golden
Freeman, Val LeRoy *geologist*
Furtak, Thomas Elton *physicist, educator, author, consultant*
Gibson, Richard Ingram *geophysicist*
Hodgden, Hugh Jerry *geological consulting executive*
Morrison, Roger Barron *geologist*
Nyarady, Stefan Alan *analytical chemist*
Sims, Paul Kibler *geologist*
Slatt, Roger Malcolm *petroleum geologist*
Tilton, John Elvin *mineral economics educator*
Witters, Robert Dale *chemist, educator*

Grand Junction
Chenoweth, William Lyman *consulting geologist*
Duray, John R. *physicist*

Greeley
Jones, Loretta Lucek *chemistry educator, writer*

Lakewood
Higley, Debra Kay *geologist*
Hughes, Travis Hubert *geologist*
Mauter, Warren Eugene *chemist, business development manager*
Parker, John Marchbank *consulting geologist*
Rakowski, John Michael *geologist*

Littleton
Lowell, James Diller *geologist*
Sjolander, Gary Walfred *physicist*

Monument
Henrickson, Eiler Leonard *retired geologist, educator*

Vail
McDaniel, Gary Allan *geologist*

HAWAII

Camp Smith
Surface, Stephen Walter *water treatment chemist, environmental protection specialist*

Hanalei
Chuan, Raymond Lu-Po *scientific researcher, consultant*

Hawaii National Park
Keszthelyi, Laszlo P. *volcanologist, geologist*
Swanson, Donald Alan *geologist*

Hilo
Schnell, Russell Clifford *atmospheric scientist, researcher*

Honolulu
Chambers, Kenneth Carter *astronomer*
Franke, Adrian Amadeus Harald *natural products chemist, researcher*
Hawke, Bernard Ray *planetary scientist*
Kong, Laura S. L. *geophysicist*
McCord, Thomas B. *geophysicist, educator*
Raleigh, Cecil Baring *geophysicist*
Rubin, Kenneth Howard *geochemistry educator, artist*
Scheuer, Paul Josef *chemistry educator*
Seff, Karl *chemistry educator*
Yount, David Eugene *physicist, educator*

Manoa
Rosendal, Hans Erik *meteorologist*

Pukalani
Fredericksen, Walter Mailand *behavioral and ocean sciences educator emeritus*

IDAHO

Idaho Falls
Cox, Jim *petroleum geologist, technical writer*
Gehrke, Robert James *physicist*
McAtee, Richard Everett *retired chemist, consultant*
Zohner, Steven K. *environmental scientist*

Moscow
Goszczynski, Stefan *chemistry educator*
Miller, Maynard Malcolm *geologist, educator, research institute director, explorer, state legislator*
Shreeve, Jean'ne Marie *chemist, educator*
Stumpf, Bernhard Josef *physicist*

Pocatello
Hazen, Dean Scott *meteorologist*
Parker, Barry Richard *physics educator*

Post Falls
Emigh, Roger Alan *materials scientist*

MONTANA

Billings
Darrow, George F. *natural resources company owner, consultant*

Bozeman
Anacker, Edward William *retired chemistry educator*
Montagne, John *geology educator*

Columbia Falls
Spade, George Lawrence *scientist*

Great Falls
Oard, Michael John *meteorologist*

Kalispell
Namen, Anthony Eugene *biochemist, immunologist*

Missoula
Field, Richard Jeffrey *chemistry educator*
Houpis, Harry Louis Francis *research physicist*

Rollins
Zelezny, William Francis *retired physical chemist*

NEVADA

Henderson
Bentley, Kenton Earl *aerospace scientist, researcher*
Holloway, Robert Wester *radiochemist*

Las Vegas
Hemmers, Oliver Andreas *physicist*
Kenny, Ray *geology and geochemistry educator, researcher*
Kielhorn, Richard Werner *chemist*
Lepp, Stephen Henry *physicist, educator*
Nacht, Steve Jerry *geologist*
Peck, Gaillard Ray, Jr. *aerospace and business consultant, business owner*
Phillips, William Grant *health physicist, nuclear emergency consultant*

Mercury
Soeder, Daniel John *geologist, hydrologist*

Reno
Garside, Larry Joe *research geologist*
Granger, Arthur Earle *geologist*
Noble, Donald Charles *geologist, educator*
Reitz, Ronald Charles *biochemist, educator*
Taranik, James Vladimir *geologist, educator*

Wellington
Drew, Charles Milton *chemist*

NEW MEXICO

Albuquerque
Barsis, Edwin Howard *physicist*
Chronister, Richard Davis *physicist*
Cramer, James Dale *physicist*
Dasgupta, Amitava *chemist, educator*
Derr, John Sebring *geophysicist, seismologist*
Doak, Robert A., Jr. *geologist*
Elston, Wolfgang Eugene *geology educator, researcher*
Finley, James Daniel *physics educator*
Harrison, Charles Wagner, Jr. *applied physicist*
Hylko, James Mark *health physicist*
Klein, Cornelis *geology educator*
Passman, Stephen Lee *theoretical mechanics scientist*
Payton, Daniel Nelson, III *physicist*
Picraux, Samuel Thomas *applied physics researcher*
Robinson, Charles Paul *nuclear physicist, diplomat, business executive*
Sasaki, Darryl Yoshio *research chemist*
Vianco, Paul Thomas *metallurgist*

Kirtland AFB
Degnan, James Henry *physicist*
Garth, John Campbell *physicist, researcher*

Las Cruces
Lease, Jane Etta *environmental science consultant*
Okrasinski, Richard Joseph *meteorologist*
Rayson, Gary Donn *chemistry educator*

Las Vegas
Cheavens, Thomas Henry *chemistry educator*

Los Alamos
Clinard, Frank Welch, Jr. *materials scientist, researcher*
Cucchiara, Alfred Louis *health physicist*
Garvey, Doris Burmester *environmental administrator*
Grilly, Edward Rogers *physicist*
Gula, William Peter *physicist*
Hakkila, Eero Arnold *retired nuclear safeguards technology chemist*
Hanson, Kenneth Merrill *physicist*
Hill, Roger Eugene *physicist*
Hirt, Cyril William *physicist*
Jagnow, David Henry *petroleum geologist*
Johnson, James Daniel *theoretical physicist*
Loge, Gary Wayne *scientist*
McNally, James Henry *physicist, defense consultant*
Michaudon, André Francisque *physicist*
O'Brien, Harold Aloysius, Jr. *nuclear chemist, physics researcher, consultant*
Pack, Russell T. *theoretical chemist*
Ramsay, John Barada *research chemist, educator*
Rofer, Cheryl Kathrine *chemist*
Schoenborn, Benno P. *biophysicist, educator*
Simon-Gillo, Jehanne E. *physicist*
Snell, Charles Murrell *physicist, astrophysicist*

Santa Fe
Cowan, George Arthur *chemist, bank executive, director*
Fisher, Philip Chapin *physicist*
Garland, Kathleen Anne *geologist*
Gell-Mann, Murray *theoretical physicist, educator*

Socorro
Broadhead, Ronald Frigon *petroleum geologist*
Kottlowski, Frank Edward *geologist*
Sanford, Allan Robert *research seismologist, educator*

White Sands Missile Range
Sallee, Wesley W(illiam) *nuclear chemist*

OREGON

Ashland
Abrahams, Sidney Cyril *physicist, crystallographer*
Grover, James Robb *chemist, editor*

Beaverton
Bates, Kenneth Norris *scientist*

Corvallis
Dalrymple, Gary Brent *research geologist*
Denison, William Clark *mycologist, educator*
Koch, William Frederick *paleontologist*
Loveland, Walter David *chemist, chemistry educator*
Moore, George W(illiam) *geologist*
Simoneit, Bernd Rolf Tatsuo *geochemistry educator*

Eugene
Baldwin, Ewart Merlin *geologist, educator*
Girardeau, Marvin Denham *physics educator*
Hansen, Carl Frederick *chemistry educator*
He, Xianguo *chemist, consultant*
Page, Catherine Jo *chemistry educator*
Peticolas, Warner Leland *physical chemistry educator*
Youngquist, Walter Lewellyn *consulting geologist*

Mcminnville
Hamby, Drannan Carson *chemist, educator*
Johns, David M. *conservationist*

Monmouth
White, Donald Harvey *physics educator emeritus*

Otter Rock
Kassner, Michael Ernest *materials science educator, researcher*

Portland
Abel, William Edward *applied physicist, consultant*
Grout, Marilyn Ann *geologist, researcher, consultant*
Leung, Pui-Tak (Peter Leung) *physicist, educator, researcher*
Lincoln, Sandra Eleanor *chemistry educator*
Marsh, John Harrison *environmental planner, lawyer*
Seierstad, Alberta June *chemist*
Weeks, Wilford Frank *retired geophysics educator, glaciologist*

Tigard
Goldman, Sergey Yuri *programmer, physicist*

White City
Kreil, Curtis Lee *research chemist*

TEXAS

Dallas
Timmer, Robert Scott *geologist*

San Angelo
Ruggles, James Austin *biochemist*

UTAH

Garrison
Beeston, Joseph Mack *metallurgist*

Logan
Dennison, John Robert *physicist, educator*
Emert, George Henry *biochemist, academic administrator*
Powers, Linda Sue *biophysicist, educator*

Provo
Benson, Alvin K. *geophysicist, consultant, educator*
Robins, Morris Joseph *chemistry educator*
Smith, Marvin Artell *biochemistry educator*

Salt Lake City
Armentrout, Peter Bruce *chemistry educator*
Baczuk, Robert Joseph *analytical chemist, consultant*
Dworzanski, Jacek Pawel *analytical biochemist, researcher*
Ekdale, Allan Anton *geology educator, paleontology researcher*
Facelli, Julio Cesar *physics researcher, university administrator*
Gladysz, John Andrew *chemistry educator*
Kenison, Lynn T. *chemist*
Liou, Kuo-Nan *atmospheric science educator, researcher*
Ludlow, James Alden *physicist*
Morse, Michael David *chemistry educator, researcher*
O'Halloran, Thomas Alphonsus, Jr. *physicist, educator*
Rashba, Emmanuel Iosif *physicist, educator*
Tuddenham, W(illiam) Marvin *chemist, metallurgist, consultant*
Wall, Lloyd L. *geological engineer*

Sandy
Henderson, LaVell Merl *retired biochemistry educator*

VIRGINIA

Hampton
Turner, Robert Elwood *physicist*

WASHINGTON

Bellevue
Chen, Ching-Hong *medical biochemist, biotechnology company executive*
Delisi, Donald Paul *fluid mechanician, geophysicist*
Fremouw, Edward Joseph *physicist*
Miller, Hillard Craig *physicist*
Rossi, Amadeo Joseph *chemist*
Russell, James T. *physicist and inventor*
Sturtevant, David Charles *environmental management consultant*

Bothell
Alvi, Khisal Ahmed *chemist*
Garr, Cheryl Denise *research chemist*

Ellensburg
Rosell, Sharon Lynn *physics and chemistry educator, researcher*
Yu, Roger Hong *physics educator*

Manchester
Fearon, Lee Charles *chemist*

Olympia
Bloomquist, Rodney Gordon *geologist*
Icenogle, Ronald Dean *physical chemist, plastics engineer, writer, educator*
Walsh, Timothy John *geologist*
Yake, William Ellsworth *environmental scientist, poet*

Pasco
Weed, Ronald Leaming *radiation safety consultant, educator*

Port Ludlow
Dunning, Kenneth Laverne *research physicist*

Pullman
Banas, Emil Mike *physicist, educator*
Collins, Gary Scott *physicist, researcher*
Hamilton, Charles Howard *metallurgy educator*
Hinman, George Wheeler *physics educator*
Ryan, Clarence Augustine, Jr. *biochemistry educator*

Redmond
Malik, Sohail *chemistry educator, researcher, consultant*

Renton
Hu, John Chih-An *retired chemist, research engineer*

Richland
Ballou, Nathan Elmer *chemist*
Fruchter, Jonathan Sewell *research scientist, geochemist*
Huang, Fan-H Frank *materials scientist, researcher*
Onishi, Yasuo *environmental researcher*
Ramesh, Kalahasti Subrahmanyam *materials scientist*
Stenner, Robert David *environmental and health research engineer, toxicologist*
Stockton, Roderick Alan *chemist*
Vargo, George James, Jr. *health physicist*
Xantheas, Sotiris Stavros *chemist, researcher*

Seattle
Battisti, David Stephen *atmospheric sciences educator*
Brown, Craig William *physical chemist*
Champoux, James Joseph *biochemist, educator*
Daggett, Valerie D. *biophysicist, educator*
Dehmelt, Hans Georg *physicist*
Erdmann, Joachim Christian *physicist*
Evans, Bernard William *geologist, educator*
Felton, Samuel Page *biochemist*
Fischer, Edmond Henri *biochemistry educator*
Fischer, Fred Walter *physicist, engineer, educator*
Floss, Heinz G. *chemistry educator, scientist*
Hayes, Cecil Edward *physicist*
Henley, Ernest Mark *physics educator, university dean emeritus*
Kiehn, Arthur John *chemist, educator*
Krebs, Edwin Gerhard *biochemistry educator*
Loud, Oliver Schule *physical sciences educator, retired*

PROFESSIONAL INDEX 895 SOCIAL SCIENCE

Malins, Donald Clive *biochemistry, researcher*
McKnight, Gary Lee *biochemist, researcher*
McPhaden, Michael James *oceanographer, educator*
Pearsall, Thomas Perine *physics and electronics educator*
Rehr, John Jacob *physicist, educator*
Reinhardt, William Parker *chemical physicist, educator*
Soreide, David Christien *physicist*
Teng, Shengyi *science researcher*
Walsh, Kenneth Andrew *biochemist*

Spokane
Benson, Allen B. *chemist, educator, consultant*
Campbell, Harry Woodson *geologist, mining engineer*
Willardson, Robert Kent *physicist, manufacturing technology executive*

Tacoma
Harding, Karen Elaine *chemistry educator and department chair*
Tobiason, Frederick Lee *chemistry educator*

Vancouver
Schramm, Willfried *biochemist*

Walla Walla
Wade, Leroy Grover, Jr. *chemistry educator*

WYOMING

Casper
Doelger, Nancy Micklich *geologist, minerals environmental specialist*
Ptasynski, Harry *geologist, oil producer*

Laramie
Branthaver, Jan Franklin *research chemist*
Dana, George Frederick (Pete Dana) *consulting geologist*
Frost, Carol D. *geology educator*
Hausel, William Dan *economic geologist*
Meyer, Edmond Gerald *energy and natural resources educator, resources scientist, entrepreneur, former chemistry educator, university administrator*

Pinedale
Gregory, Joel Patrick *geologist, consultant*

Wapiti
Sowerwine, Elbert Orla, Jr. *chemist, chemical engineer*

CANADA

ALBERTA

Calgary
Kwok, Sun *astronomer*
Milone, Eugene Frank *astronomer, educator*

Edmonton
Page, Don Nelson *theoretical gravitational physics educator*

BRITISH COLUMBIA

Vancouver
Smith, Michael *biochemistry educator*
Zakarauskas, Pierre *physicist, educator*

JAPAN

Hokkaido
Carté, George Wayne *geophysicist*

ADDRESS UNPUBLISHED

Ball, Lawrence *retired physical scientist*
Betlach, Mary Carolyn *biochemist, molecular biologist*
Black, Carolyn Bicknell *science and education educator*
Borges, William, III *environmental scientist*
Brandt, Alan Erwin *insect biotechnology company executive, consultant*
Cahn, Robert Nathan *physicist*
Crespi, Vincent Henry *physicist*
Curtis, Bruce Franklin *geologist, consultant*
Davies, John Tudor *physicist*
Feng, Joseph Shao-Ying *physicist, electrical engineer*
Flor, Loy Lorenz *chemist, corrosion engineer, consultant*
Frauenfelder, Hans *physicist, educator*
Goeringer, Kabrena Eileen *chemist*
Hatcher, Herbert John *biochemist, microbiologist*
Hill, Carol Ann *geologist, writer, researcher*
Hirschler, Marcelo Miguel *fire science consultant*
Holub, Robert Frantisek *nuclear chemist, physicist*
Hook, Vivian Yuan-Wen Ho *biochemist, neuroscientist*
Hubbard, Gregory Scott *physicist*
Inlow, Rush Osborne *chemist*
Johnson, LeRoy F. *chemist*
Jones, Thornton Keith *research chemist*
Levy, Ezra Cesar *aerospace scientist, real estate broker*
Lillegraven, Jason Arthur *paleontologist, educator*
Lloyd, Joseph Wesley *physicist, researcher*
Lo, Shui-yin *physicist*
Matossian, Jesse Nerses *physicist*
Mauzy, Michael Philip *environmental consultant, chemical engineer*
McKinstry, Lydia *chemistry educator*
Monson, Janet Marlene *biochemist*
Murphy, David Hazlett *geologist*
Olsen, Clifford Wayne *consultant, retired physical chemist*
Pall-Pallant, Teri *paleontologist, inventor, behavioral scientist, design engineer, advertising agency executive*
Peersen, Olve Breien *biochemist*
Petersen, Arne Joaquin *chemist*
Posin, Daniel Q. *physics educator, television lecturer*
Poskanzer, Arthur M. *nuclear physicist and chemist*
Price, Clifford Warren *retired metallurgist, researcher*
Price, Paul Buford *physicist, educator*
Procunier, Richard Werner *environmental scientist, administrator*
Pyper, James William *chemist*
Rosenkilde, Carl Edward *physicist*
Ross, Timothy Michael *geologist*
Schelar, Virginia Mae *chemistry consultant*
Shariff, Asghar J. *geologist*
Sharon, Timothy Michael *physicist*
Stanley, George Dabney, Jr. *geology educator*
Steinert, Leon Albert *mathematical physicist*
Steinlicht, Steven *astrologer, minister, educator*
Steinmetz, John Charles *geologist, paleontologist*
Tedford, Charles Franklin *biophysicist*
Timmons, Clara Elizabeth *chemist, educator*
Tsvankin, Ilya Daniel *geophysics educator*
Umezawa, Ado *physicist*
Van Riper, Kenneth Alan *astrophysicist and researcher*
Victor, Andrew Crost *physicist, consultant, small business owner*
West, Jack Henry *petroleum geologist*
Winterlin, Wray LaVern *environmental chemist emeritus, educator*
Young, Lih-Jiuan Shiau (Lily Young) *environmental and utility industries consultant*
Zaffaroni, Alejandro C. *biochemist, medical research company executive*

SOCIAL SCIENCE

UNITED STATES

ALASKA

Anchorage
Kernodle, Una Mae *home economics curriculum specialist, retired secondary education educator*
Mobley, Charles Murray *archaeologist*
Suddock, Frances Suter Thorson *grief educator, writer*

Fairbanks
Herrmann, Mark Leonard *economics educator, consultant*
McBeath, Gerald Alan *political science educator*

Willow
Snyder, Jo Anna W. *cartographer, computer graphics designer*

ARIZONA

Casa Grande
Davies, Harriett Marie (Lolly Davies) *educator*

Chino Valley
Hale, James LeRoy (John Hale) *forensic document analyst, consultant*

Flagstaff
Lew, Alan August *geography and urban planning educator, consultant*
Smith, Zachary Alden *political science and public administration educator*
Van Otten, George Arnold *geography and public planning educator*

Mesa
Ness, James Joseph *law enforcement educator*
Riggs, Robert Edwon *law and political science educator*

Phoenix
Bostwick, Todd William *city archaeologist*
Breternitz, Cory Dale *archaeological company executive, consultant*
Doyel, David Elmond *archaeologist, museum director*
Ennis, Kent Taylor *economist*

Prescott
Christenson, Andrew Lewis *archaeologist*

Sacaton
Stephenson, Larry Kirk *strategic planner, management and geography educator*

Scottsdale
Farris, Martin Theodore *economist, educator*

Sedona
Eggert, Robert John, Sr. *economist*

Sun City West
Wyckoff, J. B. *international economic development consultant*

Tempe
Alisky, Marvin Howard *political science educator*
Arreola, Daniel David *geography educator*
Balling, Robert C., Jr. *geography educator*
Farber, Bernard *sociologist, educator*
Gordon, Leonard *sociology educator*
Lounsbury, John Frederick *geographer, educator*
Metcalf, Virgil Alonzo *economics educator*
Miller, Warren Edward *political scientist*
Montero, Darrel Martin *sociologist, social worker, educator*
Palumbo, Dennis James *political scientist, educator*
Schneller, Eugene S. *sociology educator*
Simon, Sheldon Weiss *political science educator*
Weigend, Guido Gustav *geographer, educator*

Thatcher
Jernigan, Earl Wesley *archaeologist, museum director*

Tucson
Badertscher, Vera Marie *political consultant and freelance writer*
Billings, Richard Bruce *economics educator, consultant*
Birkby, Walter Hudson *forensic anthropologist, consultant*
Block, Michael Kent *economics and law educator, public policy association executive, former government official, consultant*
Brewer, David L. *sociologist*
Denton, Michael John *research economist, electric utility expert, consultant*
Fishback, Price Vanmeter *economics educator*
Fontana, Bernard Lee *retired anthropologist, writer, consultant*
Marshall, Robert Herman *economics educator*
Nugent, Daniel Frederick *social anthropologist, educator*
Parezo, Nancy Jean *anthropologist, curator*
Rodeffer, Stephanie Lynn Holschlag *archaeologist, government official*
Smith, Vernon Lomax *economist, researcher*
Snyder, Richard Gerald *research scientist, administrator, educator, consultant*
Soren, David *archaeology educator, administrator*
Stubblefield, Thomas Mason *agricultural economist, educator*
Wahlke, John Charles *political science educator*

Yuma
Norton, Dunbar Sutton *economic developer*

CALIFORNIA

Arcata
Emenhiser, JeDon Allen *political science educator, academic administrator*

Atascadero
Cotter, Cornelius Philip *political scientist, educator*

Bakersfield
Glynn, James A. *sociology educator, author*
Mann, Everett Edward *retired social sciences educator*
Oswald, Donald James *economics educator*

Berkeley
Adelman, Irma Glicman *economics educator*
Alhadeff, David Albert *economics educator*
Bellah, Robert Neelly *sociologist, educator*
Brandes, Stanley Howard *anthropology educator, writer*
Breslauer, George William *political science educator*
Chodorow, Nancy Julia *sociology educator*
Collier, David *political science educator*
Curry, Landon *political science educator*
Debreu, Gerard *economics and mathematics educator*
Deck, Richard Allen *political scientist, consultant, writer*
Foster, Mary Frazer (Mary Frazer LeCron) *anthropologist*
Hall, Bronwyn Hughes *economics educator*
Hu, Teh-wei *economics educator*
Johanson, Donald Carl *physical anthropologist*
Joyce, Rosemary Alexandria *anthropology educator*
Judge, George Garrett *economics educator*
Kirch, Patrick Vinton *anthropology educator*
Laguerre, Michel Saturnin *anthropology educator*
Lane, Sylvia *economist, educator*
Leonard, David King *political science educator*
Luker, Kristin *sociology educator*
Mayer, Thomas *economics educator*
Norgaard, Richard Bruce *economist, educator, consultant*
Obstfeld, Maurice *economics educator, consultant*
Quigley, John Michael *economist, educator*
Sarich, Vincent M. *anthropologist, educator*
Thorne, Barrie *sociologist, educator*
Waltz, Kenneth Neal *political science educator*
Wilensky, Harold L. *political science and industrial relations educator*

Beverly Hills
Berton, Peter Alexander Menquez *emeritus international relations educator, lecturer*

Burlingame
Schwantes, Robert Sidney *international relations executive*

Calistoga
Spindler, George Dearborn *anthropologist, educator, author, editor*

Chico
Chiñas, Beverly Newbold *anthropologist, retired educator*
Cottrell, Robert Charles *history educator*
Farrer, Claire Anne Rafferty *anthropologist, folklorist, educator*
Marvin, Grace Maria *sociology, educator*
McNall, Scott Grant *sociology educator*
Rodrigue, Christine M(ary) *geography educator, business consultant*
Thatcher, Carol Jean *sociology and psychology educator, writer*

Claremont
Borcherding, Thomas Earl *economist*
Kingshill, Konrad *social sciences educator*
Likens, James Dean *economics educator*
Mc Donald, Lee Cameron *political science educator*
Palmer, Hans Christian *economics educator*
Pitney, John Joseph, Jr. *political science educator*
Schneider, Tammi Joy *archaeology educator*

Compton
Drew, Sharon Lee *sociologist*

Corona
Farr, John Kevin *social sciences educator*

Davis
Cook, Roberta Lynn *agricultural economist, educator*
Crowley, Daniel John *anthropologist*
Goldstone, Jack Andrew *sociologist*
Jarvis, Lovell Stuber *economist, educator*
Lofland, John Franklin *sociologist, educator*
McCann, Richard James *economist, consultant*
Musolf, Lloyd Daryl *political science educator, institute administrator*
Wegge, Leon Louis François *economics educator*

El Cajon
Harmon, Warren Wayne *geography educator*

El Cerrito
Keith, Bruce Edgar *political analyst, geneologist*

Fair Oaks
Parker, Brian Prescott *forensic scientist*

Fallbrook
Bryant, Don Estes *economist, scientist*

Fort Bragg
Gallagher, Patrick Francis *anthropologist*

Fresno
Dackawich, S. John *sociology educator*
Kus, James Stedry *geography educator, archaeologist*

Fullerton
Boyum, Keith Orel *political scientist, consultant*
Parman, Susan Morrissett *anthropologist, writer*
Peretz, Paul *political economist, educator*
Sheeran, Lori Kay *anthropology educator*

Hayward
Basu, Asoke Ariel *sociologist, educator*
Jun, Jong Sup *public administration educator*

Irvine
Mason, Roger Deen *archaeologist*
McGuire, Martin Cyril *economics educator*
Morgan, Patrick Michael *political science educator*
Solingen, Etel *social sciences educator*
Solinger, Dorothy Jane *political scientist, educator*

La Jolla
Cowhey, Peter Francis *international relations educator, government official, consultant*
Erie, Steven Philip *political science educator*
Krause, Lawrence Berle *economics educator*
Luhrmann, Tania Marie *social anthropologist*
Palinkas, Lawrence Albert *anthropologist, educator*

Laguna Hills
Barbera, Henry Raymond *sociology educator*
Wolfson, Murray *economics educator*

Lake Forest
Smoot, Skipi Lundquist *psychologist*

Long Beach
Campbell, Carole Ann *sociology educator*

Los Angeles
Aberbach, Joel David *political science educator, author*
Alexander, Jeffrey Charles *sociology educator*
Anawalt, Patricia Rieff *anthropologist*
Anderson, Austin Gilman *economics research company consultant*
Blakely, Edward James *economics educator*
Brubaker, William Rogers *sociology educator*
Campbell, David Charles *economist*
Castaneda, Carlos *anthropologist, author*
Champagne, Duane Willard *sociology educator*
Clark, Burton Robert *sociologist, educator*
Darby, Michael Rucker *economist, educator*
Dawson, Adam *private investigator, former newspaper editor*
Dreier, Peter *politics and public policy educator, journalist*
Friedheim, Robert Lyle *political scientist, educator*
Goldberg, Edward Morris *political science educator*
Goldstein, Michael Saul *sociologist*
Graddy, Elizabeth Ann *economics educator*
Hirsch, Werner Zvi *economist, educator*
Kamrany, Nake Mohammad *economics and law educator, lawyer*
Koletty, Stephen Ronald *geographer, educator*
La Force, James Clayburn, Jr. *economist, educator*
Leibowitz, Arleen A. *economist*
Light, Ivan Hubert *sociology educator*
Mack, Brenda Lee *sociologist, public relations consulting company executive*
Nixon, John Harmon *economist*
Renteln, Alison Dundes *political science educator*
Roy, William Glenn *sociology educator*
Siler, Michael Joe *social sciences educator*
Sklar, Richard Lawrence *political science educator*
Studenmund, Arnold Harwood *economist, educator*
Tull, Tanya *social scientist*
Wilson, David Allen *political science educator, economic development consultant*
Wong, James Bok *economist, engineer, technologist*

Los Osos
Lee, Georgia *archaeologist, editor, publisher*

Malibu
Caldwell, Dan Edward *political science educator*
Monsma, Stephen Vos *political scientist, educator*

Menlo Park
Vane, Sylvia Brakke *anthropologist, cultural resource management company executive*

Modesto
Brereton, Alyn Robert *behavioral primatologist, researcher*

Moffett Field
Ambrosia, Vincent Gerard *geographer and researcher*

Monterey
Boger, Dan Calvin *economics educator, statistical and economic consultant*
Eitelberg, Mark Jan *public administration educator, consultant*
McGrath, Erika Weis *economics educator, management consultant*

Moraga
Chaffee, Wilber Albert *political science educator*
Chase, Kristine Louise *economics educator, academic administrator*
Longo, Patrizia *political science educator*

Northridge
Harwick, Betty Corinne Burns *sociology educator*
Soto, Shirlene Ann *history educator, consultant*

Oakland
Anderson, Robert T. *anthropologist, researcher, physician*

Oceanside
Blow, John Needham *social services educator*
Hertweck, Alma Louise *sociology and child development educator*
Stewart, Kenneth Malcolm *retired anthropologist, researcher*

Pasadena
Balswick, Jack Orville *social science educator*
Oliver, Robert Warner *economics educator*

Pebble Beach
Noorzoy, Mohammad Siddieq *economist, educator*

Pico Rivera
Harwick, Wayne Thomas *economist*

Placentia
Gobar, Alfred Julian *economic consultant, educator*

Porterville
Dale, Daniel R. *criminology educator, college dean*

Redlands
Baty, Roger Mendenhall *anthropology educator*

Redondo Beach
McWilliams, Margaret Ann *home economics educator, author*
Naples, Caesar Joseph *public policy educator, lawyer, consultant*

Riverside
Seeber, James J. *sociology educator*
Taylor, R. Ervin, Jr. *archaeologist*

Rohnert Park
Byrne, Noel Thomas *sociologist, educator*
Parker, Sue Taylor *anthropologist, educator*
Phillips, Peter Martin *sociologist, educator, media researcher*

Rolling Hills Estates
Castor, Wilbur Wright *futurist, author, consultant*

Sacramento
Bruce, Thomas Edward *psychology educator, thanatologist*
Garth-Lewis, Kimberley Anne *political science consultant*
Kando, Thomas Matthew *sociology educator, author*
Reinhard, Raymond Miller *public policy analyst, consultant*
Romero, Philip Joseph *economic and policy advisor*
Sitilides, John *government relations executive*
Tashjian, Gregory Kimball Thaddeus *political consultant, writer*
Wender, Deborah Elizabeth *policy consultant, social worker*
Zeman, Valerie Denise *home economics educator*

San Diego
Aitken, Stuart Campbell *geography educator*
Andrain, Charles Franklin *political science educator*
Case, Charles Calvin *anthropology educator*
Emerick, Robert Earl *sociologist, educator*
Gazell, James Albert *public administration educator*
Getis, Arthur *geography educator*
Hamilton, James Douglas *economics educator*
Huston, Mark Louis *economics educator*
Price, Bonnie Burns *political science educator*
Storer, Norman William *sociology educator*
Wagener, Robert John *bioethicist, mediator*
Williams, Michael Wayne *public policy analyst, researcher*
Wood, James Leslie *sociology educator*

San Francisco
Beebe, John Howard (Jack Beebe) *economist, banker*
Brown, H. William *urban economist, private banker*
Gruen, Claude *economist, consultant*
Hada, John Juji *East Asian international affairs educator*
Handwerker, Lisa *medical anthropologist, public health consultant*
Marston, Michael *urban economist, asset management executive*
Mayer, Neil Stephen *economist, consultant*
McCormick, Frank Edward *economist*
Meister, Gerry *social studies educator*
Murray, Stephen O. *sociologist consultant*
Smith, Robert Charles *political science educator, researcher*
Soh, Chunghee Sarah *anthropology educator*
Warner, Rollin Miles, Jr. *economics educator, real estate broker*
Wong, Bernard P. *anthropologist*

San Jose
Guenter, Scot Michael *social sciences educator*
McDowell, Jennifer *sociologist, composer, playwright, publisher*
Voth, Alden H. *political science educator*

San Luis Obispo
Lutrin, Carl Edward *political science educator*

San Marcos
Baker, Therese Louise *sociology educator*

San Ramon
Tilden, Kevin Archer *political consultant*

Santa Barbara
Bimber, Bruce Allen *political science educator*
Comanor, William S. *economist, educator*
Frech, Harry Edward, III *economics educator, consultant*
Hatch, Elvin James *anthropology educator*
Kolstad, Charles Durgin *economics and environmental studies educator*

Santa Clara
Hom, Gloria Sun *social science educator*
Sault, Nicole Landry *anthropologist and educator*
Shefrin, Harold Marvin (Hersh Shefrin) *economist, educator, consultant*

Santa Cruz
Grieson, Ronald Edward *economist*
Laird, John Scott *government analyst*
Markovits, Andrei Steven *political science educator*

Santa Monica
Wolf, Charles, Jr. *economist, educator*

Simi Valley
Whitley, David Scott *archaeologist*

Stanford
Abramovitz, Moses *economist, educator*
Arrow, Kenneth Joseph *economist, educator*
Boskin, Michael Jay *economist, government official, university educator, consultant*
Friedman, Milton *economist, educator emeritus, author*
Fuchs, Victor Robert *economics educator*
George, Alexander Lawrence *political scientist, educator*
Granovetter, Mark *sociology educator*
Huntington, Hillard Griswold *economist*
Kreps, David Marc *economist, educator*
Lewis, John Wilson *political science educator*
March, James Gardner *social scientist, educator*
Paul, Benjamin David *anthropologist, educator*
Ricardo-Campbell, Rita *economist, educator*
Rothwell, Geoffrey Scott *economics educator*
Smelser, Neil Joseph *sociologist*
Solomon, Ezra *economist, educator*
Triska, Jan Francis *retired political science educator*

Stockton
Werner, Roger Harry *archaeologist*

Sun City
Fisher, Weston Joseph *economist*

Sylmar
Yguado, Alex Rocco *economics educator*

Torrance
Talmo, Regina Marie *social studies educator*

Van Nuys
Krueger, Kurt Arnold *sports psychologist, institute administrator*

Ventura
Khanjian, Ara *economics educator*

West Hills
Wlodarski, Robert James *archaeologist*

Whittier
McKenna, Jeanette Ann *archaeologist*

Woodland Hills
Nierenberg, Norman *urban land economist, retired state official*

Yorba Linda
Kiley, Robert Ralph *governmental affairs consultant*

COLORADO

Boulder
Beer, Francis Anthony *political science educator*
Glahe, Fred Rufus *economics educator*
Kaempfer, William Hutchison *economics educator*
Maskus, Keith Eugene *economist*
Regoli, Robert Michael *sociologist, researcher*
Walker, Deward Edgar, Jr. *anthropologist, educator*

Colorado Springs
Adams, Tucker Hart *economic research company executive*
Hendrickson, David Calvin *political science educator*

Denver
Adler, Peter *sociologist, educator*
Birkhead, John Andrew *political science educator*
Drury, Doris Marie *economics educator, consultant, researcher*
McEwan, Gordon Francis *archaeologist, museum curator*
Miller, Robert Reuben *political science educator*
Muth, John William *economics educator*
Penn, Meade Love Thomas *social sciences researcher, library assistant*
Struever, Stuart McKee *archaeologist*
Thomas, Stephen Cecil *Chinese politics educator, university official*

Englewood
Hendrick, Hal Wilmans *human factors educator*

Estes Park
Moore, Omar Khayyam *experimental sociologist*

Fort Carson
Chomko, Stephen Alexander *archaeologist*

Fort Collins
Berry, Kenneth J. *sociology educator*
Hodgdon, Linwood L. *sociology educator*
Maloney, Thomas J. *anthropologist, educator, writer*
Revier, Charles Franklin *economics educator*
Standing Bear, Zugguelgeres Galafach *criminologist, forensic scientist, educator*

Golden
Andrist, Chris G. *crime lab supervisor/forensic scientist*

Greeley
Kelsey, Michael Loyal *geography educator*
McDaniel, Bruce Alan *economist, educator*
Reichel, Philip Lee *sociology educator*

Lakewood
Baenziger, Marsha Sims *archaeologist*
Thomson, Marjorie Belle *sociology educator, consultant*

Littleton
Chapman, Richard LeRoy *public policy researcher*
James, Franklin Joseph, Jr. *public policy educator*
Lohman, Loretta Cecelia *social scientist, consultant*
Milliken, John Gordon *research economist*

Nederland
Greenawald, Glenn Dale *social studies trainer, curriculum developer, researcher*

Pueblo
Wright, Edward N. *political science educator*

DISTRICT OF COLUMBIA

Washington
Cobble, Steven Bruce *political consultant, strategist*

HAWAII

Hilo
Castberg, Anthony Didrick *political science educator, researcher*

Honolulu
Brennan, Jerry Michael *economics educator, statistician, researcher, clinical psychologist*
Cho, Lee-Jay *social scientist, demographer*
Dove, Michael Roger *anthropology researcher*
Gaydos, Gregory George *political scientist, educator*
Kassebaum, Gene Girard *sociology educator*
Klieger, Paul Christiaan *anthropologist, researcher*
Laney, Leroy Olan *economist, banker*
Lee, Oliver Minseem *political science educator*
Morse, Richard *social scientist*
Rambo, A. Terry *anthropologist, research program director*
Retherford, Robert Dennis *demographer*
Riggs, Fred Warren *political science educator*
Smyth, Thomas Jenner *economist, state official*
Solheim, Wilhelm Gerhard, II *anthropologist, educator*
Sponsel, Leslie Elmer *anthropologist, ecologist*
Steinhoff, Patricia Gayle *sociology educator*
White, Geoffrey Miles *anthropologist*

Kaneohe
Boggs, Stephen Taylor *cultural anthropologist, researcher, consultant*

Pearl City
Castillo, Richard Joseph *psychiatric anthropologist, educator*

IDAHO

Boise
Overgaard, Willard Michele *retired political scientist, jurisprudent*
Raymond, Gregory Alan *political science educator*
Yohe, Robert Michael *archaeologist, researcher*

Caldwell
Lonergan, Wallace Gunn *economics educator, management consultant*

Moscow
Ghazanfar, Shaikh Mohammed *economics educator, researcher*
Martin, Boyd Archer *political science educator emeritus*

Sandpoint
Glock, Charles Young *sociologist*

MASSACHUSETTS

Waltham
Bittner, Egon *sociology educator*

MONTANA

Billings
Heicksen, Martin Henry *retired archaeology and biblical literature educator*

Birney
Valentine, Christine Spicer Jones *human services counselor*

Bozeman
Spencer, Robert C. *political science educator*
Stroup, Richard Lyndell *economics educator, writer*

Helena
Schleicher, Robert Earl *economist*

NEVADA

Carson City
Anderson, Bernard Joseph *social studies educator*

Incline Village
Jones, Robert Alonzo *economist*

Las Vegas
Beck, Colleen Marguerite *archaeologist*
Rich, Ray *human behavior educator*

Reno
Chu, Shih-Fan (George Chu) *economics educator*
Davis, Paul Bryan *political science educator*
Eadington, William Richard *economist, educator*
Siegel, Richard Lewis *political science educator*
Wendel, Jeanne Lauretta *economics educator*

NEW MEXICO

Albuquerque
Condie, Carol Joy *anthropologist, research facility administrator*
Hamilton, David Boyce *economist, economics educator*
Heady, Ferrel *retired political science educator*
Lamphere, Louise *anthropology and women's studies educator*
May, Philip Alan *sociology educator*
Schwerin, Karl Henry *anthropology educator, researcher*
Straus, Lawrence Guy *anthropology educator, editor-in-chief*
Stuart, David Edward *anthropologist, author, educator*

Aztec
Moore, Roger Albert, Jr. *archaeologist*

Las Cruces
Givens, Steven Wendell *economic development planner*
Kirkpatrick, David Teal *archaelogist*
Lease, Richard Jay *police science educator, former police officer*

Las Vegas
Riley, Carroll Lavern *anthropology educator*

Mesilla
Alexander, Andrew Dallas, Jr. *archaeologist, petroglyph researcher*
Brown, Timothy Charles *social science professional*
Mather, E. Cotton *geography educator*

Santa Fe
Kingman, Elizabeth Yelm *anthropologist*
Schaafsma, Polly Dix *archaeologist, researcher*
Williams, Stephen *anthropologist, educator*

Taos
Young, Jon Nathan *archaeologist*

OREGON

Ashland
Houston, John Albert *political science educator*

Bend
Early, Daniel Keefe *anthropologist, sociologist, educator*

Corvallis
Castle, Emery Neal *agricultural and resource economist, educator*
Harter, Lafayette George, Jr. *economics educator emeritus*

Eugene
Aikens, C(lyde) Melvin *anthropology educator, archaeologist*
Burris, Vallon Leon, Jr. *sociologist, educator*
Gwartney, Patricia Anne *sociology educator*
Simonds, Paul Emery *anthropologist*

Mcminnville
Blodgett, Forrest Clinton *economics educator*

Monmouth
Shay, Roshani Cari *political science educator*

Neotsu
Archer, Stephen Hunt *economist, educator*

Oregon City
DeWolfe, Fred Stanley *social science educator, consultant*

Portland
Broughton, Ray Monroe *economic consultant*
Clucas, Richard Allen *political science educator*
Davis, James Allan *gerontologist, educator*
Mandel, Robert Michael *social sciences educator*
Mitchell, John William *economist*
Vatter, Harold Goodhue *economics educator*

Salem
Ackerson, Duane Wright, Jr. *economist*
Thompson, George Frederick, Jr. *public management educator*

Tualatin
Kuga, Mark Wayne *economist*

Woodburn
Miles, Donald Geoffrey *economist*

UTAH

Ephraim
Poulson, Lynn Hansen *home and family studies educator, writer*

Logan
Batabyal, Amitrajeet Amarnath *economics educator*

Ogden
Bailey, Charles Richard *political consultant*
Holt, Ronald Lawrence *anthropologist, educator*

Provo
Bahr, Howard Miner *sociologist, educator*
Daynes, Byron Wilford *political science educator*
Kunz, Phillip Ray *sociologist, educator*

Salt Lake City
Girton, Lance *economics educator*
Gochnour, Natalie *economist*
Rock, James Martin *economics educator, administrator*
Summer, Lyle C. *state agency economist, economics educator*

West Jordan
Rowley, Maxine Lewis *home economics educator, writer*

VIRGINIA

Arlington
Fuchs, Roland John *geography educator, university science official*

WASHINGTON

Bellingham
Hoover, Kenneth R. *political science educator, writer*

Des Moines
Ortmeyer, Carl Edward *retired demographer*

Ellensburg
Jacobs, Robert Cooper *political scientist, consultant*

Issaquah
Pearson, Belinda Kemp *economist, consultant*

Kirkland
Edelhertz, Herbert *criminologist, policy analyst*

Lynnwood
Shin, Suk-han *geography educator, director Korean-American affairs*

Pullman
Ackerman, Robert Edwin *anthropology educator*
Dunlap, Riley Eugene *sociologist*

Rosa, Eugene Anthony *sociologist, environmental scientist, educator*
Short, James Franklin, Jr. *sociology educator, researcher*

Richland
Roop, Joseph McLeod *economist*
Serot, David Elliot *economist, consultant*

Seattle
Barth, Ernest A.T. *sociologist, educator*
Beyers, William Bjorn *geography educator*
Chirot, Daniel *sociology and international studies educator*
Djao, Angela Wei *sociology educator*
Downing, Douglas Allan *economics educator, writer*
Ellings, Richard James *political and economic research institution executive*
Gamache, Adrien Edmond *economist, valuation consultant*
Hadley, Eleanor Martha *economist*
Lang, Kurt *sociologist, educator, writer*
Startz, Richard *economist*
Wolfle, Dael Lee *public affairs educator*
Woods, Ronald Earl *foreign policy educator*
Zerbe, Richard Olis, Jr. *public affairs educator*

Tacoma
Hands, D(ouglas) Wade *economics educator*

Vancouver
Craven, James Michael *economist, educator*

Walla Walla
Kenworthy, Eldon Gordon (Bud Kenworthy) *political science educator*

WYOMING

Laramie
Chai, Winberg *political science educator, foundation chair*
Gill, George Wilhelm *anthropologist*
Harkin, Michael Eugene *anthropologist, educator, writer*
Marston, Richard Alan *geography educator, consultant*

CANADA

ALBERTA

Calgary
Forbis, Richard George *archaeologist*

Edmonton
Krotki, Karol Jozef *sociology educator, demographer*

BRITISH COLUMBIA

Vancouver
Aberle, David Friend *anthropologist, educator*
Feaver, George A. *political science educator*
Nemetz, Peter Newman *policy analysis educator, economics researcher*
Pearson, Richard Joseph *archaeologist, educator*

Victoria
Barber, Clarence Lyle *economics educator*

ADDRESS UNPUBLISHED

Anderson, Louise Stout *crime analyst*
Baerwald, Hans H. *political science educator*
Bardhan, Pranab *economics educator*
Batson, Raymond Milner *retired cartographer*
Beckman, James Wallace Bim *economist, marketing executive*
Bonnell, Victoria Eileen *sociologist*
Bracey, Earnest Norton *political science educator*
Chance, Edward Wayne *administration and leadership studies educator*
Chauvin, Yves *cognitive scientist*

Collier, Ruth Berins *political science educator*
Crampton, Esther Larson *sociology and political science educator*
Farah, Tawfic Elias *political scientist, educator*
Fott, David Samuel *political science educator*
Fox, Richard Lorain *political science educator*
Garcia, Arleen Elena *archaeologist, researcher*
Glick, Reuven *economist*
Gobalet, Jeanne Gallatin *demographer*
Gogerty, David Calvin *economist*
Haberlin, William Earl *economist, consultant*
Hirsch, Walter *economist, researcher*
Holmes, Paul Luther *political scientist, educational consultant*
Horan, Adel Edward *sociology and psychology educator*
Hosek, James Robert *economist*
Isely, Barbara J. *sociologist, consultant*
Kealiinohomoku, Joann Wheeler *anthropologist, dance ethnologist, educator*
Kechichian, Joseph Albert *political scientist, educator*
Kohan, Dennis Lynn *international trade educator, consultant*
Lonergan, Thomas Francis, III *criminal justice consultant*
Markovich, Patricia *economist, art consultant*
Martin, Catherine Elizabeth *anthropology educator*
Martin, Sally S. Kees *family studies educator*
Rocca, James Victor *political science educator*
Sharpe, William Forsyth *economics educator*
Steinhauser, Sheldon Eli *sociology and gerontology educator, consultant*
Stiglitz, Joseph Eugene *economist*
Textor, Robert Bayard *cultural anthropology writer, consultant, educator*
Tonello-Stuart, Enrica Maria *political economist*
Trinkl, Frank Herman *economist, educator*
Ward, Albert Eugene *research center executive, archaeologist, ethnohistorian*
Wonders, William Clare *geography educator*
Zeitlin, Maurice *sociology educator, author*